HANDWÖRTERBUCH
DEUTSCH-ENGLISCH
ENGLISCH-DEUTSCH
GERMAN-ENGLISH
ENGLISH-GERMAN
DICTIONARY

KLETT
HANDWÖRTERBUCH
DEUTSCH-ENGLISCH
ENGLISCH-DEUTSCH

Collins

London • Glasgow • Toronto

Klett

Stuttgart

Webster's New World German Dictionary

Concise Edition

Prentice Hall
New York • London • Toronto • Sydney • Tokyo • Singapore

FIRST PAPERBACK EDITION, 1992

EDITORS/REDAKTEURE
Peter Terrell & Horst Kopleck

ASSISTANT EDITORS/MITARBEITER
Jimmy Burnett
Andrea Ender
Philip Ladd
Reinhold Trott

COPY EDITOR/REDAKTIONSASSISTENTIN
Daphne Trotter

Prentice Hall General Reference
15 Columbus Circle
New York, NY 10023

A Webster's New World Book™

Webster's New World™, Prentice HalL, and colophons are
registered trademarks of Simon & Schuster, Inc.

Dictionary Editorial Offices: New World Dictionaries,
850 Euclid Avenue, Clevelend, Ohio 44114

Originally published in Great Britain
Published by arrangement with William Collins Sons & Co. Ltd.

Manufactured in the United States of America

1 2 3 4 5 6 7 8 9 10

ISBN 0-13-953621-3

INTRODUCTION

This dictionary provides the user wishing to learn, read and understand German with a detailed and clearly structured analysis of the German and English languages and of the correspondence between them. Emphasis is placed on current usage–from the colloquial to the more formal–and there is extensive treatment of all areas relevant to the modern world.

To facilitate communication and self-expression in the foreign language, the basic, most frequently used words in the language are treated in depth, so that the user may express himself correctly and idiomatically–both orally and in writing. A unique guiding system of indicating words helps the user to pinpoint meaning and identify the correct translation from among all the possible translations given.

Compiled by a team of experienced German and English linguists and lexicographers, this reference book combines comprehensive coverage with outstanding clarity, simplicity and economy, making it an efficient and ideal working tool for school, self-study and professional life.

EINLEITUNG

Dieses Wörterbuch bietet dem Benutzer für das Lernen, Lesen und Verstehen des Englischen eine detaillierte und klar strukturierte Analyse der englischen und der deutschen Sprache und der Wechselbeziehungen zwischen beiden. Das Hauptgewicht liegt auf dem modernen Sprachgebrauch–von der Umgangssprache bis zur förmlicheren Ausdrucksweise–und alle für die heutige Zeit relevanten Bereiche werden eingehend behandelt.

Um die Verständigung und Ausdrucksfähigkeit in der Fremdsprache zu erleichtern, werden die grundlegenden und am häufigsten gebrauchten Wörter ausführlich behandelt, so daß dem Benutzer eine mündlich wie schriftlich korrekte und idiomatisch richtige Verwendung der Sprache ermöglicht wird. Ein einzigartiges Kennzeichnungssystem hilft dem Benutzer, Bedeutungsunterschiede zu erkennen und die jeweils richtige Übersetzung unter allen angegebenen Übersetzungsmöglichkeiten herauszufinden.

Dieses Nachschlagewerk wurde von einem Team erfahrener englischer und deutscher Linguisten und Lexikographen zusammengestellt und verbindet Ausführlichkeit mit außerordentlicher Klarheit, Einfachheit und Prägnanz. Hierdurch wird es zu einem leistungsstarken und vorzüglichen Arbeitsmittel für die Schule, zum Selbststudium und im Beruf.

CONTENTS

INHALT

How to use the dictionary

Layout and order

1.1 Alphabetical order is followed throughout. Where a letter occurs in brackets in a headword, this letter is counted for the alphabetical order, eg **Beamte(r)** will be found in the place of **Beamter**, **vierte(r, s)** in the place of **vierter**.

1.2 Abbreviations, acronyms and proper nouns will be found in their alphabetical place in the word list.

1.3 Superior numbers are used to differentiate between words of like spelling.

Benutzungshinweise

Aufbau und Anordnung der Einträge

1.1 Die alphabetische Anordnung der Einträge ist durchweg gewahrt. In Klammern stehende Buchstaben in einem Stichwort unterliegen ebenfalls der Alphabetisierung, so findet man z.B. **Beamte(r)** an der Stelle von **Beamter, vierte(r, s)** unter **vierter**.

1.2 Abkürzungen, Akronyme und Eigennamen sind in alphabetischer Ordnung im Wörterverzeichnis zu finden.

1.3 Hochgestellte Ziffern werden verwendet, um zwischen Wörtern gleicher Schreibung zu unterscheiden.

rowing[1], rowing[2]; durchsetzen[1], durchsetzen[2].

1.4 Compounds will be found in their alphabetical place in the word list. The term "compound" is taken to cover not only solid and hyphenated compounds (**eg Bettwäsche, large-scale**) but also attributive uses of English nouns (**eg defence mechanism**) and other set collocations (**eg long jump**). Where the alphabetical order permits, compounds are run on in blocks with the first element printed in boldface type at the beginning of each block. Where possible a general translation has been given for the compound element.

1.4 Zusammengesetzte Wörter stehen an ihrer Stelle im Alphabet. Der Begriff „zusammengesetzte Wörter" bezeichnet nicht nur zusammengeschriebene oder durch Bindestrich verbundene Komposita (z.B. **Bettwäsche, large-scale**) sondern auch die attributive Verwendung englischer Substantive (z.B. **defence mechanism**) und andere feste Verbindungen (z.B. **long jump**). Wo die alphabetische Ordnung es gestattet, werden die Zusammensetzungen in Blöcken angeordnet, wobei der erste Bestandteil am Kopf jedes Blocks in Fettdruck erscheint. Wo immer möglich, ist für das erste Element eine allgemeine Übersetzung angegeben.

Silber- *in cpds* silver.

From this the user can derive the translation for compounds not given in the word list.

Daraus kann der Benutzer die Übersetzung hier nicht angegebener Zusammensetzungen erschließen.

1.5 Phrasal verbs (marked ♦) will be found immediately after the main headword entry.

1.5 *Phrasal verbs* (durch ♦ gekennzeichnet) folgen unmittelbar auf das Hauptstichwort.

1.6 Idioms and set phrases will normally be found under the first meaningful element or the first word in the phrase which remains constant despite minor variations in the phrase itself. Thus 'to throw out the baby with the bathwater' is included under '**baby**' whereas 'to lend sb a hand' is treated under '**hand**' because it is equally possible to say 'to give sb a hand'.
Certain very common verbs such as be, get, have, make, put, bringen, haben, geben, machen, tun, which form the basis of a great many phrases, eg to make sense, to make a mistake, etw in Ordnung bringen, etw in Gang bringen, have been considered as having a diminished meaning and in such cases the set phrase will be found under the most significant element in the phrase.

1.6 Redensarten und feste Wendungen sind im allgemeinen unter dem ersten bedeutungstragenden Element oder dem ersten Wort der Wendung, das trotz leichter Abwandlungen in der Wendung selbst unverändert bleibt, zu finden. So ist 'to throw out the baby with the bathwater' unter '**baby**' aufgenommen, 'to lend sb a hand' dagegen wird unter '**hand**' abgehandelt, weil es ebenfalls möglich ist, 'to give sb a hand' zu sagen.
Bei als Funktionsverben gebrauchten Verben wie be, get, have, make, put, bringen, haben, geben, machen und tun, werden die meisten festen Wendungen, wie z.B. to make sense, to make a mistake, etw in Ordnung bringen, etw in Gang bringen, unter dem bedeutungstragenden Bestandteil der Wendung behandelt.

Indicating material

General indicating material in the dictionary is printed in italics and takes the following forms:

2.1 Indicators in parentheses:

2.1.1 synonyms and partial definitions

gefühlvoll *adj (empfindsam)* sensitive; *(ausdrucksvoll)* expressive; *(liebevoll)* loving.

2.1.2 within verb entries, typical subjects of the headword

peel 3 *vi (wallpaper)* sich lösen; *(paint)* abblättern; *(skin, person)* sich schälen *or* pellen *(col)*.

2.1.3 within noun entries, typical noun complements of the headword

Schar *f* **-en** crowd, throng *(liter)*; *(von Vögeln)* flock; *(von Insekten etc)* swarm.

2.2 Collocators, not in parentheses:

2.2.1 within transitive verb entries, typical objects of the headword

dent 2 *vt car* eindellen, verbeulen; *(col) pride* anknacksen *(col)*.

2.2.2 within adjective entries, typical nouns modified by the headword

neu *adj* new; *Kräfte, Hoffnung auch* fresh; *Wäsche* clean; *Wein* young.

2.2.3 within adverb entries, typical verbs or adjectives modified by the headword

vaguely *adv* vage; *remember also* dunkel; *speak also* unbestimmt; *understand* ungefähr, in etwa.

2.3 Field labels are used:

2.3.1 to differentiate various meanings of the headword

Jungfrau *f* virgin; *(Astrol)* Virgo.

2.3.2 when the meaning in the source language is clear but may be ambiguous in the target language.

Virgo *n (Astrol)* Jungfrau *f*.

A full list of labels is given on pages xviii–xix.

2.4 Style labels are used to mark all words and phrases which are not neutral in style level or which are no longer current in the language. This labelling is given for both source and target languages and serves primarily as an aid to the non-native speaker.
When a style label is given at the beginning of an entry or category it covers all meanings and phrases in that entry or category.

(col)   denotes colloquial language typically used in an informal conversational context or a chatty letter, but which would be inappropriate in more formal speech or writing.

(col!)   denotes words which are potentially offensive.

(col!!)   denotes words which are highly offensive.

(sl)   combined with a field label eg *(Mil sl)*, *(Sch sl)* it denotes that the expression belongs to the jargon of that group.

Erklärende Zusätze

Allgemeine erklärende Zusätze im Wörterbuch sind kursiv gedruckt und erscheinen in folgender Form:

2.1 Indikatoren, in Klammern stehend:

2.1.1 Synonyme und Teildefinitionen

2.1.2 typische Substantiv-Ergänzungen in Verb-Einträgen

2.1.3 typische Substantiv-Ergänzungen des Stichworts in Substantiv-Einträgen

2.2 Kollokatoren, ohne Klammern stehend:

2.2.1 typische Objekte des Stichworts bei transitiven Verb-Einträgen

2.2.2 typische, durch das Stichwort näher bestimmte Substantive in Adjektiv-Einträgen

2.2.3 typische, durch das Stichwort näher bestimmte Verben oder Adjektive bei Adverb-Einträgen

2.3 Sachbereichsangaben werden verwendet:

2.3.1 um die verschiedenen Bedeutungen des Stichworts zu unterscheiden

2.3.2 wenn die Bedeutung in der Ausgangssprache klar ist, jedoch in der Zielsprache mehrdeutig sein könnte.

Eine vollständige Liste dieser Sachbereichsangaben befindet sich auf den Seiten xviii und xix.

2.4 Stilangaben werden verwendet zur Kennzeichnung aller Wörter und Wendungen, die keiner neutralen Stilebene oder nicht mehr dem modernen Sprachgebrauch angehören. Die Angaben erfolgen sowohl in der Ausgangs- als auch in der Zielsprache und sollen in erster Linie dem Nicht-Muttersprachler helfen.
Stilangaben zu Beginn eines Eintrages oder einer Kategorie beziehen sich auf alle Bedeutungen und Wendungen innerhalb dieses Eintrages oder dieser Kategorie.

(col)   bezeichnet umgangssprachlichen Gebrauch, wie er für eine formlose Unterhaltung oder einen zwanglosen Brief typisch ist, in förmlicherer Rede oder förmlicherem Schriftverkehr jedoch unangebracht wäre.

(col!)   bezeichnet Wörter, an denen unter Umständen Anstoß genommen wird.

(col!!)   bezeichnet Wörter, die allgemein als anstößig gelten.

(sl)   weist in Verbindung mit einer Sachbereichsangabe, z.B. *(Mil sl)*, *(Sch sl)*, auf die Zugehörigkeit des Ausdrucks zum Jargon dieser Gruppe hin.

(geh)	denotes elevated style of spoken or written German such as might be used by an educated speaker choosing his words with care.	*(geh)*	bezeichnet einen gehobenen Stil sowohl im gesprochenen wie geschriebenen Deutsch, wie er von gebildeten, sich gewählt ausdrückenden Sprechern verwendet werden kann.
(form)	denotes formal language such as that used on official forms, for official communications and in formal speeches.	*(form)*	bezeichnet förmlichen Sprachgebrauch, wie er uns auf Formularen, im amtlichen Schriftverkehr oder in förmlichen Ansprachen begegnet.
(spec)	indicates that the expression is a technical term restricted to the vocabulary of specialists.	*(spec)*	gibt an, daß es sich um einen Fachausdruck handelt, der dem Wortschatz von Fachleuten angehört.
(dated)	indicates that the word or phrase, while still occasionally being used especially by older speakers, now sounds somewhat old-fashioned.	*(dated)*	weist darauf hin, daß solche Wörter bzw. Wendungen heute recht altmodisch klingen, obwohl sie besonders von älteren Sprechern noch gelegentlich benutzt werden.
(old)	denotes language no longer in current use but which the user will find in reading.	*(old)*	bezeichnet nicht mehr geläufiges Wortgut, das dem Benutzer jedoch noch beim Lesen begegnet.
(obs)	denotes obsolete words which the user will normally only find in classical literature.	*(obs)*	bezeichnet veraltete Wörter, die der Benutzer im allgemeinen nur in der klassischen Literatur antreffen wird.
(liter)	denotes language of a literary style level. It should not be confused with the field label *(Liter)* which indicates that the expression belongs to the field of literary studies, or with the abbreviation *(lit)* which indicates the literal as opposed to the figurative meaning of a word.	*(liter)*	bezeichnet literarischen Sprachgebrauch. Es sollte nicht mit der Sachbereichsangabe *(Liter)* verwechselt werden, die angibt, daß der betreffende Ausdruck dem Gebiet der Literaturwissenschaft angehört, und ebensowenig mit der Abkürzung *(lit)*, die die wörtliche im Gegensatz zur übertragenen Bedeutung eines Wortes bezeichnet.

Grammatical Information

Gender

3.1 All German nouns are marked for gender in both sections of the dictionary.

3.2 Where more than one German noun of the same gender are given consecutively as interchangeable translations, the gender is given only after the last translation.

3.3 Where a German translation consists of an adjective plus a noun, the adjective is given in the indefinite form which shows gender and therefore no gender is given for the noun.

Grammatische Angaben

Geschlecht

3.1 Alle deutschen Substantive sind in beiden Teilen des Wörterbuches mit der Geschlechtsangabe versehen.

3.2 Wo mehrere deutsche Substantive gleichen Geschlechts als austauschbare Übersetzungen hintereinander stehen, wird das Geschlecht nur nach der letzten Übersetzung angegeben.

computer *n* Computer, Rechner *m*.

3.3 Wenn eine deutsche Übersetzung aus einem Adjektiv und einem Substantiv besteht, wird das Adjektiv in der unbestimmten Form angegeben, die das Geschlecht erkennen läßt. Für das Substantiv erfolgt daher keine Geschlechtsangabe.

große Pause; zweites Frühstück.

3.4 Nouns of the form **Reisende(r)** *mf decl as adj* can be either masculine or feminine and take the same declensional ending as adjectives.

3.4 Substantive nach dem Muster **Reisende(r)** *mf decl as adj* können sowohl männlich wie weiblich sein und haben die gleichen Deklinationsendungen wie Adjektive.

m **der Reisende, ein Reisender, die Reisenden** *pl*
f **die Reisende, eine Reisende, die Reisenden** *pl*

3.5 Nouns of the form **Beamte(r)** *m decl as adj* take the same declensional endings as adjectives.

3.5 Substantive nach dem Muster **Beamte(r)** *m decl as adj* haben die gleichen Deklinationsendungen wie Adjektive.

der Beamte, ein Beamter, die Beamten *pl*

3.6 Adjectives of the form **letzte(r, s)** do not exist in an undeclined form and are only used attributively.

3.6 Adjektive nach dem Muster **letzte(r, s)** haben keine unflektierte Form und werden nur attributiv verwendet.

der letzte Mann, ein letzter Mann
die letzte Frau, eine letzte Frau
das letzte Kind, ein letztes Kind

3.7 Nouns of the form **Schüler(in** *f)* *m* are only used in the bracketed form in the feminine.

3.7 Substantive nach dem Muster **Schüler(in** *f)* *m* werden nur im Femininum in der eingeklammerten Form benutzt.

der/ein Schüler
die/eine Schülerin

3.8 The feminine forms are shown, where relevant, for all German noun headwords; unless otherwise indicated, the English translation will be the same as for the masculine form.
Where there is no distinction between the translations given for the masculine and feminine forms and yet the context calls for a distinction, the user should prefix the translation with 'male/female *or* woman *or* lady ...'

3.8 Für alle deutschen Substantive, die ein natürliches Geschlecht haben, wird die weibliche neben der männlichen Form angegeben. Wenn nicht anders angegeben, lautet die englische Form für beide gleich.
Wo die für die männliche und die für die weibliche Form angegebene Übersetzung dieselbe ist, im entsprechenden Zusammenhang aber betont werden soll, daß es sich um einen Mann bzw. eine Frau handelt, sollte der Benutzer der Übersetzung 'male/female *or* woman *or* lady' voranstellen.

male teacher, female *or* woman *or* lady teacher

Nouns

Substantive

4.1 Nouns marked *no pl* are not normally used in the plural or with an indefinite article or with numerals.

4.1 Substantive mit der Angabe *no pl* werden im allgemeinen nicht im Plural, mit dem unbestimmten Artikel oder mit Zahlwörtern verwendet.

4.2 Nouns marked *no art* are not normally used with either a definite or an indefinite article except when followed by a relative clause.

4.2 Mit *no art* bezeichnete Substantive stehen im allgemeinen weder mit dem unbestimmten noch mit dem bestimmten Artikel, außer wenn ein Relativsatz von ihnen abhängig ist.

4.3 The plural endings are given for all German noun headwords except for certain regular noun endings. A complete list of these is given on page xvi.
The plural endings of German compound nouns are only given where the final element does not exist as a headword in its own right.

4.3 Bei allen deutschen Substantiv-Stichwörtern ist der Plural angegeben, mit Ausnahme bestimmter regelmäßiger Endungen. Diese sind in einer vollständigen Liste auf Seite xvi erfaßt.
Der Plural ist bei zusammengesetzten Substantiven nur dann angegeben, wenn das letzte Element der Zusammensetzung nicht als Einzelwort vorkommt.

4.4 Irregular plural forms of English nouns are given on the English-German side.

4.4 Unregelmäßige Pluralformen englischer Substantive sind im englisch-deutschen Teil angegeben.

4.4.1 Most English nouns take *-s* in the plural.

4.4.1 Die meisten englischen Substantive bilden den Plural durch Anhängen von *-s*.

bed -s, site -s, key -s, roof -s

4.4.2 Nouns ending in -s, -z, -x, -sh, -ch take -es.

4.4.2 Substantive, die auf -s, -z, -x, -sh, -ch enden, erhalten die Endung -es.

gas -es, box -es, patch -es

4.4.3 Nouns ending in -y preceded by a consonant change the -y to ie and add -s in the plural, except in the case of proper nouns.

4.4.3 Substantive, die auf Konsonant + -y enden, verwandeln im Plural das auslautende -y in -ie, auf das die Pluralendung -s folgt. Ausnahmen bilden Eigennamen.

lady – ladies, berry – berries
Germany – the two Germanys

Adjectives and adverbs

Adjektive und Adverbien

5.1 As a general rule, adjective translations consisting of more than one word should be used after not before the noun.

5.1 Grundsätzlich sollten Übersetzungen von Adjektiven, die aus mehreren Wörtern bestehen, nur nachgestellt oder adverbial gebraucht und nicht dem Substantiv vorangestellt werden.

ordnungsgemäß *adj* in accordance with the rules

5.2 On the German-English side of the dictionary adverbs have only been treated as separate grammatical entries distinct from adjective entries:

5.2 Im deutsch-englischen Teil des Wörterbuches sind Adverbien als selbständige grammatische Einträge von Adjektiven nur dann unterschieden worden,

(a) when their use is purely adverbial

(a) wenn es sich um echte Adverbien handelt

höchst, wohl, sehr

(b) when the adverbial use is as common as the adjective use

(b) wenn der adverbiale Gebrauch genauso häufig ist wie der adjektivische

schön

(c) when the English translation of the adverbial use cannot be derived from the adjectival translations by the rules of adverb formation.

(c) wenn die englische Übersetzung eines adverbial verwendeten Adjektivs nicht mit Hilfe der Regeln erschlossen werden kann, nach denen im Englischen Adverbien aus Adjektiven gebildet werden.

gut

Where no separate entry is given for the adverbial use of a German adjective, the user should form the English adverb from the translations given according to the rules given on page xv.

Wo für den adverbialen Gebrauch eines deutschen Adjektivs kein gesonderter Eintrag vorliegt, ist es dem Benutzer selbst überlassen, aus den angegebenen Übersetzungen die englischen Adverbien nach den auf Seite xv angeführten Regeln zu bilden.

5.3 On the English-German side of the dictionary adverbs have only been entered when separate translations are necessary, which differ from those of the related adjective. Normally the German translation of an English adverb takes the same form as the translation of the related adjective. For example:

5.3 Im englisch-deutschen Teil des Wörterbuchs sind Adverbien nur dann als gesonderte Einträge aufgenommen worden, wenn eine eigenständige Übersetzung erforderlich ist. Normalerweise ist die deutsche Übersetzung eines englischen Adverbs gleichlautend mit der des entsprechenden Adjektivs. Zum Beispiel:

he is astute er ist scharfsinnig
..., he remarked astutely ..., bemerkte er scharfsinnig

Verbs

Verben

6.1 All German verbs which form the past participle without ge- are marked with an asterisk in the text.

6.1 Alle Verben im Deutschen, die das 2. Partizip ohne ge- bilden, sind im Text durch Sternchen gekennzeichnet.

umarmen* *vt insep ptp* **umarmt**
manövrieren* *vti ptp* **manövriert**

6.2 All German verbs beginning with a prefix which can allow separability are marked *sep* or *insep* as appropriate.

6.2 Alle deutschen Verben, die mit einer oft trennbaren Vorsilbe beginnen, werden durch *sep* oder *insep* (= trennbar/untrennbar) bezeichnet.

unterliegen *vi insep* es unterliegt keinem Zweifel, daß ...
umschalten *vti sep* wir schalten jetzt um nach Hamburg

Verbs beginning with the prefixes be-, er-, ver-, zer- are always inseparable.

Verben mit den Vorsilben be-, er-, ver-, zer- sind immer untrennbar.

6.3 All German verbs which take 'sein' as the auxiliary are marked *aux sein*.

6.3 Alle deutschen Verben, die die zusammengesetzten Zeiten mit „sein" bilden, sind durch *aux sein* gekennzeichnet.

gehen *pret* **ging,** *ptp* **gegangen** *aux sein*

Where the auxiliary is not stated, 'haben' is used.

Erfolgt keine Angabe, ist „haben" zu verwenden.

6.4 German irregular verbs composed of prefix and verb are marked *irreg*, and the forms can be found under the simple verb. For example, the irregular forms of 'eingehen' will be found under 'gehen'.

6.4 Zusammengesetzte unregelmäßige Verben im Deutschen sind durch *irreg* bezeichnet, ihre Stammformen sind beim Simplex angegeben. So sind beispielsweise die Stammformen von „eingehen" unter „gehen" zu finden.

6.5 If the present or past participle of a verb has adjectival value it is treated as a separate headword in its alphabetical place.

6.5 Wenn 1. oder 2. Partizip eines Verbs den Status eines Adjektivs haben, werden sie als eigenständige Stichwörter in alphabetischer Reihenfolge aufgeführt.

gereift *adj (fig)* mature.
growing *adj (lit, fig)* wachsend; *child* heranwachsend.

Phrasal verbs

Phrasal verbs

7.1 Phrasal verbs are covered in separate entries marked ♦ following the main headword.

7.1 *Phrasal verbs* sind in eigenen Einträgen abgehandelt. Sie sind durch ♦ gekennzeichnet und folgen dem Stichworteintrag für das Simplex.

7.2 Phrasal verbs are treated in four grammatical categories:

7.2 *Phrasal verbs* werden unter vier grammatischen Kategorien abgehandelt:

7.2.1 *vi*

7.2.1 *vi*

♦ **grow apart** *vi (fig)* sich auseinanderentwickeln.

7.2.2 *vi +prep obj*
This indicates that the verbal element is intransitive but that the particle requires an object.

7.2.2 *vi + prep obj*
Hiermit soll gezeigt werden, daß das Verbelement intransitiv ist, daß aber die Partikel ein Objekt erfordert.

♦ **hold with** *vi + prep obj (col)* **I don't** ~ ~ **that** ich bin gegen so was *(col)*.

7.2.3 *vt*
This indicates that the verbal element is transitive. In most cases the object can be placed either before or after the particle; these cases are marked *sep*.

7.2.3 *vt*
Dies gibt an, daß das Verbelement transitiv ist. In den meisten Fällen kann das Objekt vor oder hinter der Partikel stehen; diese Fälle sind mit *sep* bezeichnet.

♦ **hand in** *vt sep* abgeben; *forms, resignation* einreichen.

In some cases the object must precede the particle; these cases are marked *always separate*.

In einigen Fällen muß das Objekt der Partikel vorangehen; solche Fälle sind durch *always separate* bezeichnet.

♦ **get over with** *vt always separate* hinter sich *(acc)* bringen.
let's ~ **it** ~ (~) bringen wir's hinter uns.

Occasionally the object must come after the particle; these cases are marked *insep*.

Gelegentlich muß das Objekt der Partikel nachgestellt werden; solche Fälle sind durch *insep* bezeichnet.

♦ **strike up** *vt insep* **(a)** *(band) tune* anstimmen.
(b) *friendship* schließen; *conversation* anfangen.

7.2.4 *vt + prep obj*
This indicates that both the verbal element and the particle require an object.

7.2.4 *vt +prep obj*
Hiermit wird gezeigt, daß sowohl das Verbelement wie die Partikel ein Objekt verlangen.

♦ **take upon** *vt +prep obj* **he has taken it** ~ **himself to ...**
er hat die Verantwortung auf sich genommen, zu ...

In cases where a prepositional object is optional its translation is covered under *vi* or *vt*.

In Fällen, wo ein Präpositionalobjekt möglich, aber nicht nötig ist, findet man die entsprechende Übersetzung unter *vi* oder *vt*.

♦ **get off** *vi (from bus, train etc)* aussteigen *(prep obj* aus*)*; *(from bicycle, horse)* absteigen *(prep obj* von*)*.
♦ **go down** *vi* hinuntergehen *(prep obj acc)*.

For example:

Zum Beispiel:

he got off er stieg aus/ab
he got off the bus er stieg aus dem Bus aus
he got off his bicycle er stieg von seinem Fahrrad ab
she went down sie ging hinunter
she went down the street sie ging die Straße hinunter

8.1 Punctuation and Symbols

8.1 Satzeichen und Symbole

,	between translations indicates that the translations are interchangeable; between source language phrases indicates that the phrases have the same meaning.	,	zwischen Übersetzungen zeigt an, daß die Übersetzungen gleichwertig sind; zwischen Wendungen in der Ausgangssprache zeigt an, daß die Wendungen die gleiche Bedeutung haben.
;	between translations indicates a difference in meaning which is clarified by indicating material unless: **(a)** the distinction has already been made within the same entry; **(b)** the distinction is self-evident.	;	zwischen Übersetzungen zeigt einen Bedeutungsunterschied an, der durch erklärende Zusätze erläutert ist, außer: **(a)** wenn die Unterscheidung innerhalb desselben Eintrags schon gemacht worden ist; **(b)** wenn die Unterscheidung offensichtlich ist.
:	between a headword and a phrase indicates that the headword is normally only used in that phrase.	:	zwischen Stichwort und Wendung gibt an, daß das Stichwort im allgemeinen nur in der aufgeführten Wendung vorkommt.
~	is used within an entry to represent the headword whenever it occurs in an unchanged form. In German headwords of the form **Reisende(r)** *mf decl as adj*, and **höchste(r, s)** *adj* it only replaces the element outside the bracket. In German compound blocks it represents the compound element exactly as given at the beginning of the block. If it is given with a capital, any occurrence in a compound or phrase where it requires a small letter is clearly shown eg **Wochen-**: ...; **w~lang** *adj, adv* ...	~	wird innerhalb von Einträgen verwendet, um das unveränderte Stichwort zu ersetzen. Bei deutschen Stichwörtern des Typs **Reisende(r)** *mf decl as adj* und **höchste(r, s)** *adj* ersetzt der Strich den außerhalb der Klammer stehenden Teil des Wortes. In deutschen Komposita-Blöcken ersetzt der Strich den Bestandteil der Zusammensetzung genau, wie er am Kopf des Blocks erscheint. Soll von Großschreibung auf Kleinschreibung übergegangen werden, ist dies angegeben, z.B. **Wochen-**: ...; **w~lang** *adj, adv* ...
—	separates two speakers.	—	unterscheidet zwischen zwei Sprechern.
≃	indicates that the translation is the cultural equivalent of the term and may not be exactly the same in every detail.	≃	weist darauf hin, daß die Übersetzung eine Entsprechung ist, die auf Grund kultureller Unterschiede nicht in allen Aspekten deckungsgleich ist.
*	after a German verb indicates that the past participle is formed without *ge-*.	*	nach einem deutschen Verb gibt an, daß das 2. Partizip ohne *ge-* gebildet wird.
also, auch	used after indicating material denotes that the translation(s) following it can be used in addition to the first translation given in the respective entry, category or phrase.	**also, auch**	nach erklärenden Zusätzen gibt an, daß die folgende(n) Übersetzung(en) zusätzlich zu der ersten Übersetzung, die in dem Eintrag oder der Kategorie angegeben ist, benutzt werden kann/können.

Phonetic Symbols / Zeichen der Lautschrift

Vowels/Vokale

matt	[a]	
Fahne	[aː]	
Vater	[ɐ]	
	[ɑː]	calm, part
	[æ]	sat
	[ɒ]	cot
Chanson	[ã]	
Chance	[ãː]	
	[ɑ̃ː]	double *entendre*
Etage	[e]	egg
Seele, Mehl	[eː]	
Wäsche, Bett	[ɛ]	
zählen	[ɛː]	
Teint	[ɛ̃ː]	
mache	[ə]	above
	[ɜː]	burn, earn
Kiste	[ɪ]	pit, awfully
Vitamin	[i]	
Ziel	[iː]	peat
Oase	[o]	
oben	[oː]	
Fondue	[õ]	
Chanson	[õː]	
Most	[ɔ]	
	[ɔː]	born
ökonomisch	[ø]	
blöd	[øː]	
Götter	[œ]	
Parfum	[œ̃ː]	
zuletzt	[u]	
Mut	[uː]	pool
Mutter	[ʊ]	put
Typ	[y]	
Kübel	[yː]	
Sünde	[ʏ]	

Diphthongs/Diphthonge

weit	[ai]	
	[aɪ]	buy, die, my
Haus	[au]	
	[aʊ]	house, now
	[eɪ]	pay, mate
	[ɛə]	pair, mare
	[əʊ]	no, boat
	[ɪə]	mere, shear
Heu, Häuser	[ɔy]	
	[ɔɪ]	boy, coin
	[ʊə]	tour, poor

Consonants/Konsonanten

Ball	[b]	ball
mich	[ç]	
denn	[d]	den
fern	[f]	field
gern	[g]	good
Hand	[h]	hand
ja, Million	[j]	yet, million
Kind	[k]	kind
links, Pult	[l]	left, little
matt	[m]	mat
Nest	[n]	nest
lang	[ŋ]	long
Paar	[p]	put
rennen	[r]	run
fassen	[s]	sit
Stein, Schlag	[ʃ]	shall
Tafel	[t]	tab
	[θ]	thing
	[ð]	this
wer	[v]	very
	[w]	wet
Loch	[x]	loch
singen	[z]	pods, zip
genieren	[ʒ]	measure

Other signs/Andere Zeichen

|	glottal stop/Knacklaut
[ʳ]	[r] pronounced before a vowel/vor Vokal ausgesprochenes [r]
[ˈ]	main stress/Hauptton
[ˌ]	secondary stress/Nebenton

The Pronunciation of German

German pronunciation is largely regular, and a knowledge of the basic patterns is assumed.
A list of the symbols used is given on page xiii.

Stress
1. The stress and the length of the stressed vowel are shown for every German headword.
2. The stressed vowel is usually marked in the headword, either with a dot if it is a short vowel
  eg **sofǫrt, Mạtte**
or a dash if it is a long vowel or diphthong
  eg **hōchmütig, kaufen**

Glottal Stop
1. A glottal stop (*Knacklaut*) occurs at the beginning of any word starting with a vowel.
2. A glottal stop always occurs in compounds between the first and second elements when the second element begins with a vowel.
3. When a glottal stop occurs elsewhere it is marked by a hairline before the vowel
  eg **Be|ạmte(r)**

Vowel length
1. Where phonetics are given for the headword a long vowel is indicated in the transcription by the length mark after it
  eg **Chemie** [çe'mi:]
2. Where no phonetics are given a short stressed vowel is marked with a dot in the headword
  eg **Mụtter**
and a long stressed vowel is marked with a dash
  eg **Vāter**
3. Unstressed vowels are usually short; if not, phonetics are given for that vowel
  eg **Ạlmosen** [-o:-]

Diphthongs and double vowels
1. Where phonetics are not given, vowel combinations which represent a stressed diphthong or a stressed long vowel are marked with an unbroken dash in the headword
  eg **beiderlei, Haar, sieben**
2. *ie*
Stressed *ie* pronounced [i:] is marked by an unbroken line
  eg **sieben**
When the plural ending -*n* is added, the pronunciation changes to [-i:ən]
  eg **Allegorie,** *pl* **Allegorien** [-i:ən]
When *ie* occurs in an unstressed syllable the pronunciation of that syllable is given
  eg **Hortensie** [-iə]
3. *ee* is pronounced [e:]
When the plural ending -*n* is added, the change in pronunciation is shown
  eg **Allee** *f* -**n** [-e:ən]

Consonants
Where a consonant is capable of more than one pronunciation the following rules have been assumed:
1. *v*
  (i) *v* is generally pronounced [f]
    eg **Vater** ['fa:tɐ]

Where this is not the case phonetics are given
  eg **Sklave** [skla:və]
  (ii) Words ending in -*iv* are pronounced [i:f] when undeclined, but when an ending is added the   pronunciation changes to [i:v]
  eg **aktiv** [ak'ti:f]
    aktive (as in 'der aktive **Sportler**') [ak'ti:və]
2. *ng*
  (i) *ng* is generally pronounced [ŋ]
    eg **Finger** ['fɪŋɐ]
Where this is not the case phonetics are given
  eg **Angora** [aŋ'go:ra]
  (ii) In compound words where the first element ends in -*n* and the second element begins with *g*- the two sounds are pronounced individually
    eg **Eingang** ['aingaŋ]
    ungeheuer ['ʊngəhɔyɐ]
3. *tion* is always pronounced [-tsio:n] at the end of a word and [-tsion-] in the middle of a word
  eg **Nation** [na'tsio:n]
    national [natsio'na:l]
4. *st, sp*
  (i) Where *st* or *sp* occurs in the middle or at the end of a word the pronunciation is [st], [sp]
    eg **Fest** [fɛst], **Wespe** ['vɛspə]
  (ii) At the beginning of a word or at the beginning of the second element of a compound word the standard pronunciation is [ʃt] [ʃp].
    eg **Stand** [ʃtant], **sperren** ['ʃpɛrən]
    Abstand ['ap-ʃtant], **absperren** ['ap-ʃpɛrən]
5. *ch*
  (i) *ch* is pronounced [ç] after *ä-, e-, i-, ö-, ü-, y-, ai-, ei-, äu, eu-* and after consonants
    eg **ich** [ɪç], **Milch** [mɪlç]
  (ii) *ch* is pronounced [x] after *a-, o-, u-, au-*
    eg **doch** [dɔx], **Bauch** [baux]
Phonetics are given for all words beginning with *ch*.
6. *ig* is pronounced [ɪç] at the end of a word.
  eg **König** ['kø:nɪç]
When an ending beginning with a vowel is added, it is pronounced [ɪg]
  eg **Könige** ['kø:nɪgə]
7. *h* is pronounced [h]
  (i) at the beginning of a word
  (ii) between vowels in interjections
    eg **oho** [o'ho:]
  (iii) in words such as **Ahorn** ['a:hɔrn] and **Uhu** ['u:hu].
It is mute in the middle and at the end of non-foreign words
  eg **leihen** ['laiən], **weh** [ve:]
Where *h* is pronounced in words of foreign origin, this is shown in the text.
8. *th* is pronounced [t].
9. *qu* is pronounced [kv].
10. *z* is pronounced [ts].
Phonetics are given where these rules do not apply and for foreign words which do not follow the German pronunciation patterns.

Adjectives and Adverbs

Declension of German adjectives

Adjectives ending in *-abel, -ibel, -el* drop the *-e-* when declined.

miserabel	ein miserabler Stil
	eine miserable Handschrift
	ein miserables Leben
heikel	ein heikler Fall
	eine heikle Frage
	ein heikles Problem

Adjectives ending in *-er, -en* usually keep the *-e-* when declined, except:

(a) in language of an elevated style level

    finster   seine finstren Züge

(b) in adjectives of foreign origin

    makaber   eine makabre Geschichte
    integer   ein integrer Beamter

Adjectives ending in *-auer, -euer* usually drop the *-e-* when declined.

    teuer   ein teures Geschenk
    sauer   saure Gurken

Comparison of German adjectives and adverbs

Irregular comparative and superlative forms are given in the text, including those of adjectives and adverbs with the vowels *-a-, -o-, -u-* which take an umlaut.

    hoch *adj comp* **höher**, *superl* **höchste(r, s)** or
    (adv) **am höchsten**

Where no forms are given in the text, the comparative and superlative are formed according to the following rules:

(a) Both adjectives and adverbs add *-er* for the comparative before the declensional endings.

    schön – schöner
    eine schöne Frau – eine schönere Frau

(b) Most adjectives add *-ste(r, s)* for the superlative.

    schön – schönste(r, s)
    ein schöner Tag – der schönste Tag

(c) Most adverbs form the superlative according to the following pattern.

    schön – am schönsten
    schnell – am schnellsten

(d) Adjectives and adverbs of one syllable or with the stress on the final syllable add *-e* before the superlative ending:

    (i) always if they end in *-s, -ß, -st, -tz, -x, -z*
    (ii) usually if they end in *-d, -t, -sch*
    spitz *adj* **spitzeste(r, s)**
    adv **am spitzesten**
    gerecht *adj* **gerechteste(r, s)**
    adv **am gerechtesten**

The same applies if they are used with a prefix or in compounds, regardless of where the stress falls.

    unsanft *adj* **unsanfteste(r, s)**
    adv **am unsanftesten**

Adjektive und Adverbien

Adverbialbildung im Englischen

(a) Die meisten Adjektive bilden das Adverb durch Anhängen von *-ly*:

    strange -ly, odd -ly, beautiful -ly

(b) Adjektive, die auf Konsonant +*y* enden, wandeln das auslautende *-y* in *-i* um und erhalten dann die Endung *-ly*:

    happy – happily
    merry – merrily

(c) Adjektive, die auf *-ic* enden, bilden normalerweise das Adverb durch Anhängen von *-ally*:

    scenic -ally
    linguistic -ally

Steigerung der englischen Adjektive und Adverbien

Adjektive und Adverbien, deren Komparativ und Superlativ im allgemeinen durch Flexionsendungen gebildet werden, sind im Text durch *(+er)* bezeichnet, z.B.

    young *adj (+er)*

Komparativ und Superlativ aller nicht durch *(+er)* bezeichneten Adjektive und Adverbien sind mit *more* und *most* zu bilden. Das gilt auch für alle auf *-ly* endenden Adverbien, z.B.

    grateful more grateful most grateful
    fully more fully most fully

Unregelmäßige Formen des Komparativs und Superlativs sind im Text angegeben, z.B.

    bad *adj comp* **worse**, *superl* **worst**
    well *adv comp* **better**, *superl* **best**

Die flektierten Formen des Komparativs und Superlativs werden nach folgenden Regeln gebildet:

(a) Die meisten Adjektive und Adverbien fügen *-er* zur Bildung des Komparativs und *-est* zur Bildung des Superlativs an:

    small smaller smallest

(b) Bei auf Konsonant +*y* endenden Adjektiven und Adverbien wird das auslautende *-y* in *-i* umgewandelt, bevor die Endung *-er* bzw. *-est* angefügt wird:

    happy happier happiest

(c) Mehrsilbige Adjektive auf *-ey* wandeln diese Endsilbe in *-ier, -iest* um:

    homey homier homiest

(d) Bei Adjektiven und Adverbien, die auf stummes *-e* enden, entfällt dieser Auslaut:

    brave braver bravest

(e) Bei Adjektiven und Adverbien, die auf *-ee* enden, entfällt das zweite *-e*:

    free freer freest

(f) Adjektive und Adverbien, die auf einen Konsonanten nach einfachem betontem Vokal enden, verdoppeln den Konsonanten im Auslaut:

    sad sadder saddest

Nach Doppelvokal wird der auslautende Konsonant nicht verdoppelt:

    loud louder loudest

Regular German Noun Endings

The genitive and plural of a large number of German nouns is formed according to regular patterns. These patterns are:

nom		gen	pl
-ade	*f*	-ade	-aden
-ant	*m (wk)*	-anten	-anten
-anz	*f*	-anz	-anzen
-ar	*m*	-ars	-are
-är	*m*	-ärs	-äre
-at	*nt*	-at(e)s	-ate
-atte	*f*	-atte	-atten
-chen	*nt*	-chens	-chen
-ei	*f*	-ei	-eien
-elle	*f*	-elle	-ellen
-ent	*m (wk)*	-enten	-enten
-enz	*f*	-enz	-enzen
-esse	*f*	-esse	-essen
-ette	*f*	-ette	-etten
-eur	*m*	-eurs	-eure
-eurin	*f*	-eurin	-eurinnen
-euse	*f*	-euse	-eusen
-graph	*m (wk)*	-graphen	-graphen
-heit	*f*	-heit	-heiten
-ie	*f*	-ie	-ien
-ik	*f*	-ik	-iken
-in	*f*	-in	-innen
-ine	*f*	-ine	-inen
-ion	*f*	-ion	-ionen
-ist	*m (wk)*	-isten	-isten
-ium	*nt*	-iums	-ien
-ius	*m*	-ius	-iusse
-ive	*f*	-ive	-iven
-ivum	*nt*	-ivums	-iva
-keit	*f*	-keit	-keiten
-lein	*nt*	-leins	-lein
-ling	*m*	-lings	-linge
-ment	*nt*	-ments	-mente
-mus	*m*	-mus	-men
-nis	*f*	-nis	-nisse
-nis	*nt*	-nisses	-nisse
-nom	*m (wk)*	-nomen	-nomen
-oge	*m (wk)*	-ogen	-ogen
-or	*m*	-ors	-oren
-rich	*m*	-richs	-riche
-schaft	*f*	-schaft	-schaften
-sel	*nt*	-sels	-sel
-tät	*f*	-tät	-täten
-tiv	*nt, m*	-tivs	-tive
-tum	*nt*	-tums	-tümer
-ung	*f*	-ung	-ungen
-ur	*f*	-ur	-uren

On the German-English side of the dictionary we have not shown plural endings where these regular patterns apply. All other plural endings are shown in the entry

> **Fang** *m* ⁻e
> **Norm** *f* -en

Genitive endings are formed

for masculine and neuter nouns by adding *-s* or *-es*

> **der Mann:** *(gen)* **des Mann(e)s**
> **das Rad:** *(gen)* **des Rad(e)s**

for feminine nouns: no change

> **die Frau:** *(gen)* **der Frau**

Masculine or neuter nouns ending in *-s*, *-ß*, *-x* and *-z* always take the full form of *-es* for the genitive

> **das Glas:** *(gen)* **des Glases**
> **das Maß:** *(gen)* **des Maßes**
> **der Komplex:** *(gen)* **des Komplexes**
> **der Geiz:** *(gen)* **des Geizes**

Masculine or neuter nouns ending in *-sch* or *-st* normally take the full form of *-es*, as do those ending in a double consonant

> **der Wunsch:** *(gen)* **des Wunsches**
> **der Gast:** *(gen)* **des Gastes**
> **das Feld:** *(gen)* **des Feldes**
> **der Kampf:** *(gen)* **des Kampfes**

Masculine or neuter nouns ending in *-en*, *-em*, *-el*, *-er* and *-ling* always take the short form of *-s*

> **der Regen:** *(gen)* **des Regens**
> **der Atem:** *(gen)* **des Atems**
> **der Mantel:** *(gen)* **des Mantels**
> **der Sänger:** *(gen)* **des Sängers**
> **der Flüchtling:** *(gen)* **des Flüchtlings**

Masculine or neuter nouns ending in *-ß* preceded by a short vowel will change the *ß* to *ss*

> **der Fluß:** *(gen)* **des Flusses**

If the genitive is not formed according to these patterns it will be shown in the entry after the gender and before the plural ending

> **Herz** *nt* -ens, en
> **Klerus** *m* -, *no pl*

If only one ending is given this will be the plural, unless otherwise indicated.

Weak nouns

Weak nouns (marked as *wk*) have the same *-en* ending in the accusative, genitive and dative cases in both singular and plural forms

> **der Mensch:** *(acc)* **den Menschen**
> *(gen)* **des Menschen**
> *(dat)* **dem Menschen**

Abbreviations

Abkürzung	abbr	abbreviation
Akkusativ	acc	accusative
Adjektiv	adj	adjective
Verwaltung	Admin	administration
Adverb	adv	adverb
Landwirtschaft	Agr	agriculture
Anatomie	Anat	anatomy
Archäologie	Archeol	arch(a)eology
Architektur	Archit	architecture
Artikel	art	article
Kunst	Art	art
Astrologie	Astrol	astrology
Astronomie	Astron	astronomy
attributiv	attr	attributive
österreichisch	Aus	Austrian
australisch	Austral	Australian
Kraftfahr-zeugwesen	Aut	automo-biles
Hilfsverb	aux	auxiliary
Luftfahrt	Aviat	aviation
Kindersprache	baby-talk	
biblisch	Bibl	biblical
Biologie	Biol	biology
Botanik	Bot	botany
Bundesrepu-blik Deutsch-land	BRD	Federal Re-public of Germany
britisch	Brit	British
Hoch- und Tiefbau	Build	building
Kartenspiel	Cards	
Chemie	Chem	chemistry
Schach	Chess	
umgangs-sprachlich	col	colloquial
derb	col!	potentially offensive
anstößig	col!!	highly offensive
Handel	Comm	commerce
Komparativ	comp	comparative
Computer	Comp	computers
Konjunktion	conj	conjunction
Zusammen-ziehung	contr	contraction
Kochen	Cook	cooking
Kompositum	cpd	compound
Dativ	dat	dative
altmodisch	dated	
Deutsche De-mokratische Republik	DDR	German Democratic Republic
dekliniert	decl	declined
bestimmt	def	definite
demonstrativ	dem	demonstrative
Dialekt	dial	dialect
Verkleinerung	dim	diminutive
Akkusativ-objekt	dir obj	direct ob-ject
kirchlich	Eccl	ecclesiastical
Volkswirtschaft	Econ	economics
Elektrizität	Elec	electricity
betont	emph	emphatic
besonders	esp	especially

Abkürzungen

etwas	etw	something
Euphemismus	euph	euphemism
Femininum	f	feminine
Mode	Fashion	
übertragen	fig	figurative
Finanzen	Fin	finance
Fischerei	Fishing	
Forstwesen	Forest	forestry
förmlich	form	formal
Fußball	Ftbl	football
gehoben	geh	elevated
Genitiv	gen	genitive
Geographie	Geog	geography
Geologie	Geol	geology
Grammatik	Gram	grammar
Heraldik	Her	heraldry
Geschichte	Hist	history
Gartenbau	Hort	horticulture
scherzhaft	hum	humorous
Jagd	Hunt	hunting
Imperativ	imper	imperative
unpersönlich	impers	impersonal
Industrie	Ind	industry
unbestimmt	indef	indefinite
Dativobjekt	indir obj	indirect ob-ject
Infinitiv	infin	infinitive
untrennbar	insep	inseparable
Versiche-rungswesen	Insur	insurance
Interjektion	interj	interjection
interrogativ	interrog	interrogative
unveränderlich	inv	invariable
irisch	Ir	Irish
ironisch	iro	ironical
unregelmäßig	irreg	irregular
jemand, jeman-des, jemandem, jemanden	jd, jds jdm, jdn	somebody, somebody's
Rechtswesen	Jur	law
Sprachwissen-schaft	Ling	linguistics
wörtlich	lit	literal
literarisch	liter	literary
Literatur	Liter	literature
Maskulinum	m	masculine
Mathematik	Math	mathematics
Maß	Measure	
Mechanik	Mech	mechanics
Medizin	Med	medicine
Meteorologie	Met	meteorology
Metallurgie	Metal	metallurgy
militärisch	Mil	military
Bergbau	Min	mining
Mineralogie	Miner	mineralogy
Straßenver-kehr	Mot	motoring and transport
Musik	Mus	music
Mythologie	Myth	mythology
Substantiv	n	noun
nautisch	Naut	nautical
verneint	neg	negative
nordenglisch	N Engl	Northern English

norddeutsch	*N Ger*	North German	schottisch	*Scot*	Scottish
Nationalsozia-lismus	NS	Nazism	Bildhauerei	*Sculpt*	sculpture
			trennbar, ver-änderbare	sep	separable
Neutrum	*nt*	neuter	Folge		
Zahlwort	*num*	numeral	Handarbeiten	*Sew*	sewing
Objekt	*obj*	object	süddeutsch	*S Ger*	South Ger-man
obsolet	*obs*	obsolete			
veraltet	*old*		Singular	*sing*	singular
Optik	*Opt*	optics	Skisport	*Ski*	skiing
Vogelkunde	*Orn*	ornithology	Slang, Jargon	*sl*	slang
Parlament	*Parl*	parliament	Sozialwissen-schaften	*Sociol*	social sciences
Passiv	*pass*	passive			
pejorativ	*pej*	pejorative	Raumfahrt	*Space*	space flight
persönlich/Person	*pers*	personal/person	Fachausdruck	*spec*	specialist term
Pharmazie	*Pharm*	pharmacy	Börse	*St Ex*	Stock Ex-change
Philosophie	*Philos*	philosophy			
Phonetik	*Phon*	phonetics	etwas	*sth*	something
Fotografie	*Phot*	photography	Konjunktiv	*subjunc*	subjunctive
Physik	*Phys*	physics	Nachsilbe	*suf*	suffix
Physiologie	*Physiol*	physiology	Superlativ	*superl*	superlative
Plural	*pl*	plural	Landvermes-sung	*Surv*	surveying
poetisch	*poet*	poetic			
Dichtung	*Poet*	poetry	schweizerisch	*Sw*	Swiss
Politik	*Pol*	politics	Technik	*Tech*	technology
Possessiv-	*poss*	possessive	Nachrichten-technik	*Telec*	telecommuni-cations
prädikativ	*pred*	predicative			
Vorsilbe	*pref*	prefix	Textilien	*Tex*	textiles
Präposition	*prep*	preposition	Theater	*Theat*	theatre, theater
Präsens	*pres*	present			
Presse	*Press*		Fernsehen	*TV*	television
Präteritum, Imperfekt	*pret*	preterite, imperfect	Typographie, Buchdruck	*Typ*	typography and printing
Pronomen	*pron*	pronoun	Hochschule	*Univ*	university
sprichwörtlich	*prov*	proverbial	(nord)ameri-kanisch	*US*	(North) American
Sprichwort	*Prov*	proverb			
Partizip Prä-sens	*prp*	present par-ticiple	gewöhnlich	*usu*	usually
Psychologie	*Psych*	psychology	Verb	*vb*	verb
Partizip Per-fekt	*ptp*	past parti-ciple	Tiermedizin	*Vet*	veterinary medicine
Warenzeichen	®	trademark	intransitives Verb	*vi*	intransitive verb
Rundfunk	*Rad*	radio			
Eisenbahn	*Rail*	railways	reflexives Verb	*vr*	reflexive verb
selten	*rare*		transitives Verb	*vt*	transitive verb
regelmäßig	*reg*	regular			
Relativ-	*rel*	relative	schwache Deklination	*wk*	weak declension
Religion	*Rel*	religion			
jemand(em, -en)	*sb*	somebody	Zoologie	*Zool*	zoology
Schulwesen	*Sch*	school	ptp ohne ge-	*	ptp without ge-
Naturwissen-schaften	*Sci*	science			

A

A, a [aː] *nt* -, - **A, a.** **das A und O** the be-all and end-all; *(eines Wissensgebietes)* the basics *pl;* **von A bis Z** *(fig col)* from beginning to end; **wer A sagt, muß auch B sagen** *(prov)* in for a penny, in for a pound *(prov).*

à [a] *prep (esp Comm)* at.

Aal *m* **-e** eel. **sich winden wie ein** ~ to wriggle like an eel.

aalen *vr (col)* to stretch out. **sich in der Sonne** ~ to bask in the sun.

aalglatt *adj (pej)* slippery (as an eel), slick.

Aas *nt* **-e (a)** *(Tierleiche)* carrion, rotting carcass. **(b)** *pl* **Äser** *(col: Luder)* bugger *(col!).* **kein** ~ not a single bloody person *(col).*

aasen *vi (col)* to be wasteful. **mit etw** ~ to waste sth.

Aasgeier *m (lit, fig)* vulture.

ab [ap] **1** *prep* +*dat (räumlich)* from; *(zeitlich auch)* as of. **Kinder** ~ **14 Jahren** children from (the age of) 14; **Soldaten** ~ **Gefreitem** soldiers from private up; ~ **Werk** *(Comm)* ex works; ~ **sofort** as of now/then. **2** *adv* **of. die nächste Straße rechts** ~ the next street off to the right; **München** ~ **12²⁰ Uhr** *(Rail)* leaving Munich 12.20; ~ **wann?** from when?, as of when?; ~ **nach Hause** off you go home; ~ **ins Bett mit euch!** off to bed with you; **Tell** ~ *(Theat)* exit Tell; **N und M** ~ *(Theat)* exeunt N and M; ~ **durch die Mitte!** *(col)* beat it! *(col),* hop it! *(col);* ~ **und zu** from time to time, now and then.

ab|ändern *vt sep* to alter *(in* +*acc* to); *Gesetzentwurf* to amend *(in*+*acc* to); *Strafe, Urteil* to revise *(in*+*acc* to).

Ab|änderung *f siehe vt* alteration *(gen* to); *(Parl, Jur)* amendment; revision.

Ab|änderungsantrag *m (Parl)* proposed amendment. **einen** ~ **einbringen** to submit an amendment.

ab|arbeiten *sep* **1** *vt Schuld* to work off. **2** *vr* to slave (away).

Ab|art *f* variety *(auch Biol); (Variation)* variation *(gen* on).

ab|artig *adj* abnormal, deviant.

Abbau *m no pl* **(a)** *(von Personal, Produktion etc)* reduction *(gen* in, of), cutback *(gen* in). **(b)** *(von Kohlen etc)* mining. **(c)** *(Chem)* decomposition. **(d)** *(lit, fig: Demontage)* dismantling.

abbauen *sep* **1** *vt* **(a)** *(demontieren) Gerüst, System* to dismantle; *Gerüst auch, Zelt* to take down; *Lager* to break, to strike. **(b)** *(verringern) Produktion, Personal, Bürokratie* to cut back, to reduce. *Arbeitsplätze* ~ to make job cuts. **(c)** *Kohle etc* to mine. **(d)** *(Chem)* to break down, to decompose. **2** *vi (col: erlahmen)* to flag, to wilt.

abbeißen *sep irreg* **1** *vt* to bite off. **2** *vi* to take a bite.

abbekommen* *vt sep irreg* to get. **etwas** ~ to get some (of it); *(beschädigt werden)* to get damaged; *(verletzt werden)* to get hurt; **das Auto/er hat dabei ganz schön was** ~ *(col)* the car/he really copped it *(col);* **nichts** ~ not to get any (of it); *(nicht beschädigt werden)* not to get damaged; *(nicht verletzt werden)* to come off unscathed; **sein(en) Teil** ~ *(lit, fig)* to get one's fair share.

abberufen* *vt sep irreg Diplomaten etc* to recall.

Abberufung *f* recall.

abbestellen* *vt sep* to cancel; *jdn* to put off.

Abbestellung *f* cancellation.

abbezahlen* *vt sep Raten, Auto etc* to pay off.

abbiegen *sep irreg* **1** *vt* **(a)** to bend; *(abbrechen)* to bend off. **(b)** *(col: verhindern) Frage, Thema* to head off, to avoid. **das Gespräch** ~ to change the subject; **zum Glück konnte ich das** ~ luckily I managed to stop that. **2** *vi aux sein* to turn off *(in* +*acc* into); *(Straße)* to bend. **nach rechts** ~ to turn (off to the) right.

Abbild *nt (Kopie)* copy, reproduction; *(Spiegelbild)* reflection; *(Wiedergabe)* picture, portrayal. **er ist das genaue** ~ **seines Vaters** he's the spitting image of his father.

abbilden *vt sep (lit, fig)* to depict, to portray; *(wiedergeben)* to reproduce.

Abbildung *f* **(a)** *(Illustration)* illustration; *(Schaubild)* diagram. **(b)** *(Wiedergabe)* reproduction.

abbinden *vt sep irreg* **(a)** *(losbinden)* to undo, to untie. **(b)** *(Med) Arm, Bein etc* to ligature.

Abbitte *f* apology. **(bei jdm wegen etw)** ~ **tun** to make *or* offer one's apologies (to sb for sth).

abblasen *vt sep irreg* **(a)** **eine Hauswand mit Sandstrahl** ~ to sandblast a house wall. **(b)** *(col) Veranstaltung, Feier, Streik* to call off.

abblättern *vi sep aux sein (Putz, Farbe)* to flake (off).

abblenden *vt sep Lampe* to shade, to screen; *Scheinwerfer* to dip *(Brit),* to dim *(US).*

Abblendlicht *nt (Aut)* dipped *(Brit)* or dimmed *(US)* headlights *pl.*

abblitzen *vi sep aux sein (col)* to be sent packing *(bei by) (col).* **jdn** ~ **lassen** to send sb packing.

abblocken *vt sep (Sport, fig)* to block.

abbrausen *vt sep* to give a shower. **sich** ~ to have *or* take a shower.

abbrechen *sep irreg* **1** *vt* **(a)** to break off. **etw von etw** ~ to break sth off sth; *sich (dat)* **einen** ~ *(col) (Umstände machen)* to make heavy weather of it *(col); (sich sehr anstrengen)* to bust a gut *(col).* **(b)** *Zelt* to take down; *Lager* to strike; *(niederreißen)* to demolish, to pull down. **(c)** *(beenden)* to break off; *Streik* to call off. **2** *vi* **(a)** *aux sein* to break off; *(Bleistift, Fingernagel)* to break. **(b)** *(aufhören)* to break off, to stop.

abbremsen *vt sep Motor* to brake; *(fig)* to curb.

abbrennen *sep irreg* **1** *vt Gehöft, Dorf* to burn down; *Feuerwerk, Rakete* to let off; *Kerze etc* to burn. **ein Feuerwerk** ~ to have a fireworks display. **2** *vi aux sein* to burn down.

abbringen *vt sep irreg* **jdn davon** ~, **etw zu tun** to stop sb doing sth; *(abraten auch)* to persuade sb not to do sth; **jdn von etw** ~ to make sb change his/her mind about sth; **jdn vom Rauchen** ~ to get sb to stop smoking.

abbröckeln *vi sep aux sein* to crumble away; *(fig)* to fall off. **der Ruf der Firma ist am A**~ the firm's reputation is gradually declining.

Abbruch *m no pl* **(a)** *(das Niederreißen)* demolition. **(b)** *(Beendigung)* breaking off; *(von Veranstaltung etc)* stopping. **es kam zum** ~ **des Kampfes** the fight had to be stopped. **(c)** *(Schaden)* harm, damage. **einer Sache** *(dat)* ~ **tun** to do (some) harm *or* damage to sth.

Abbruch-: ~**arbeiten** *pl* demolition work; **a**~**reif** *adj* only fit for demolition; ~**unternehmer** *m* demolition contractor.

abbrühen *vt sep* to scald; *siehe* **abgebrüht**.

abbuchen *vt sep (im Einzelfall)* to debit *(von to, against)*; *(durch Dauerauftrag)* to pay by standing order *(von from)*.

Abbuchung *f siehe vt* debit; (payment by) standing order.

abbürsten *vt sep Staub* to brush off *(von etw sth)*; *Schuhe* to brush.

abbüßen *vt sep Strafe* to serve.

Abc [aːbeːˈtseː] *nt -, -* (*lit, fig*) ABC. **Namen nach dem ~ ordnen** to put names in alphabetical order.

abchecken [ˈaptʃɛkn] *vt sep* to check.

Abc-Schütze *m (hum)* school-beginner.

ABC-Waffen *pl* atomic, biological and chemical weapons.

Abdampf *m* exhaust steam.

abdampfen *vi sep aux sein (fig col: losgehen, -fahren)* to hit the road (col).

abdanken *vi sep* to resign; *(König etc)* to abdicate.

Abdankung *f (Thronverzicht)* abdication; *(Rücktritt)* resignation.

abdecken *vt sep* **(a)** *(freilegen) Tisch* to clear; *Bett* to turn down; *Haus* to tear the roof off. **(b)** *(zudecken) Grab, Loch* to cover (over). **(c)** *(ausgleichen, einschließen)* to cover.

Abdeckung *f* cover.

abdichten *vt sep (isolieren)* to insulate; *Loch, Leck, Rohr* to seal (up); *Ritzen* to stop up. **gegen Luft/ Wasser ~** to make airtight/watertight.

Abdichtung *f (Isolierung)* insulation; *(Verschluß, Dichtung)* seal.

abdienen *vt sep (Mil: ableisten)* to serve.

abdrängen *vt sep* to push away *(von from)*. **einen Spieler vom Ball ~** to push a player off the ball.

abdrehen *sep* **1** *vt* **(a)** *Gas, Wasser, Hahn* to turn off; *Licht, Radio auch* to switch off. **(b)** *Film* to shoot, to film. **(c)** *Hals* to wring. **jdm den Hals ~** to wring sb's neck *(col; col: ruinieren)* to bankrupt sb. **2** *vi aux sein or haben (Richtung ändern)* to change course. **nach Osten ~** to turn east.

abdriften *vi sep aux sein* to drift (away).

abdrosseln *vt sep Motor* to throttle down; *(fig) Produktion* to cut down (on).

Abdruck[1] *m, pl* **Abdrücke** imprint, impression; *(Stempel~)* stamp; *(Finger~, Fuß~)* print. **einen ~ machen** to take or make an impression.

Abdruck[2] *m -e (Kopie)* copy; *(Nachdruck)* reprint.

abdrucken *vt sep* to print. **wieder ~** to reprint.

abdrücken *sep* **1** *vt* **(a)** *Gewehr* to fire. **(b)** *Vene* to constrict. **jdm die Luft ~** *(col) (lit)* to squeeze all the breath out of sb; *(fig)* to force sb into bankruptcy, to squeeze the lifeblood out of sb. **2** *vi* to pull or squeeze the trigger.

abdunkeln *vt sep Lampe* to dim; *Zimmer auch* to darken.

abduschen *vt sep siehe* **abbrausen**.

ab|ebben *vi sep aux sein* to die or fade away.

Abend *m -e* evening. **am ~** in the evening; *(jeden ~)* in the evening(s); **am ~ des 4. April** on the evening or night of April 4th; **gegen ~** towards (the) evening; **~ für ~** every evening or night, night after night; **eines ~s** one evening; **den ganzen ~ (über)** the whole evening; **guten ~** good evening; **letzten ~** yesterday evening, last night; **zu ~ essen** *(geh)* to have supper or dinner, to dine *(form)*; **je später der ~, desto schöner or netter die Gäste** *(prov)* the best guests always come late; **man soll den Tag nicht vor dem ~ loben** *(Prov)* don't count your chickens before they're hatched *(Prov)*.

abend *adv* **gestern/morgen/Mittwoch ~** yesterday/tomorrow/Wednesday evening, last/ tomorrow/Wednesday night.

Abend- **~andacht** *f* evening service; **~anzug** *m* dinner jacket, DJ *(col)*, tuxedo *(US)*; **~brot** *nt* supper; **~brot essen** to have (one's) supper;

~dämmerung *f* dusk, twilight; **~essen** *nt* supper, evening meal, dinner; **mit dem ~essen auf jdn warten** to wait supper or dinner for sb; **a~füllend** *adj* taking up the whole evening; *Film, Stück* full-length; **~gymnasium** *nt* night school; **~kasse** *f (Theat)* box office; **~kleid** *nt* evening dress or gown; **~kleidung** *f* evening dress no pl; **~kurs(us)** *m* evening classes *pl (für in)*; **~land** *nt* no pl *(geh)* West, western world; **a~ländisch** *(geh) adj* western, occidental *(liter)*.

abendlich *adj no pred* evening *attr*. **die ~e Stille** the quiet of the evening; **es war schon um drei Uhr ~ kühl** at three it was already as cool as in the evening.

Abend-: **~mahl** *nt (Eccl)* (Holy) Communion; **~mahlzeit** *f* evening meal; **~programm** *nt (Rad, TV)* evening('s) programmes *(Brit)* or programs *(US) pl*; **~rot** *nt* sunset.

abends *adv* in the evening; *(jeden Abend)* in the evening(s). **spät ~** late in the evening; **~ um neun** at nine in the evening.

Abend-: **~schule** *f* night school; **~schüler** *m* night-school student; **~stern** *m* evening star; **~stunde** *f* evening (hour); **sich bis in die ~stunden hinziehen** to go on (late) into the evening; **~vorstellung** *f* evening performance; **~zeitung** *f* evening paper.

Abenteuer *nt -* adventure; *(Liebes~ auch)* affair. **ein militärisches ~** a military venture; **auf ~ aussein** to be looking for adventure.

abenteuerlich *adj* **(a)** adventurous; *(erlebnishungrig auch)* adventuresome. **(b)** *(phantastisch)* bizarre; *Erzählung auch* fantastic.

Abenteuer-: **~lust** *f* thirst for adventure; **~roman** *m* adventure story; **~spielplatz** *m* adventure playground.

Abenteurer *m -* adventurer *(auch pej)*.

Abenteu(r)erin *f* adventuress.

aber **1** *conj* **(a)** but. **~ dennoch** or **trotzdem** but still; **schönes Wetter heute, was? — ja, ~ etwas kalt** nice weather, eh? — yes, a bit cold though; **da er ~ nicht wußte ...** however, since he didn't know ...; **oder ~** or else. **(b)** *(zur Verstärkung)* **~ ja!** oh, yes!; *(sicher)* but of course; **~ selbstverständlich!** but of course; **~ nein!** oh, no!; *(selbstverständlich nicht)* of course not!; **~ Renate!** but Renate!; **~, ~!** tut, tut!; **das ist ~ schrecklich!** but that's awful!; **das mach' ich ~ nicht!** I will not do that!; **das ist ~ heiß/schön!** that's really hot/nice; **du hast ~ einen schönen Ball** you've got a nice ball, haven't you?; **bist du ~ braun!** aren't you brown!; **das geht ~ zu weit!** that's really going too far!

2 *adv (liter)* **tausend und ~ tausend** thousands upon thousands.

Aber *nt -* or *(col)* **-s** but. **kein ~!** no buts (about it); **die Sache hat ein ~** there's just one snag.

Aberglaube(n) *m* superstition; *(fig auch)* myth.

abergläubisch *adj* superstitious.

Aberhunderte *pl* hundreds upon hundreds *pl*.

ab|erkennen* *vt sep or (rare) insep irreg* **jdm etw ~** to strip sb of sth.

Ab|erkennung *f* deprivation, stripping.

aber-: **~malig** *adj attr* repeated; **~mals** *adv* once more.

ab|ernten *vti sep* to harvest.

Abertausende *pl* thousands upon thousands *pl*.

aberwitzig *adj (liter) siehe* **wahnwitzig**.

abfackeln *vt Erdgas* to burn off.

abfahrbereit *adj* ready to leave.

abfahren *sep irreg aux sein* **1** *vi* **(a)** to leave, to depart *(von from)*; *(Schiff auch)* to sail. **der Zug fährt um 8⁰⁰ von Bremen ab** the train leaves Bremen at 8 o'clock; **der Zug ist abgefahren** *(lit)* the train has left; *(fig)* we've/you've *etc* missed the boat. **(b)** *(col: abgewiesen werden)* **jdn ~ lassen** to tell sb to get lost (col).

2 *vt* **(a)** *Stück von Mauer etc* to knock off. **der**

Trecker hat ihm ein Bein abgefahren the tractor severed his leg. **(b)** *aux sein or haben Strecke (bereisen)* to cover; *(Polizei etc)* to patrol. **wir mußten die ganze Strecke noch einmal ~, um ... zu suchen** we had to go over the whole stretch again to look for ... **(c)** *(abnutzen)* to wear out; *Reifen auch* to wear down; *(benutzen) Fahrkarte* to use. **abgefahrene Reifen/Schienen** worn tyres/rails. **(d)** *(Film, TV) Kamera* to roll; *Film* to start. **bitte ~!** roll 'em!
3 *vr (Reifen etc)* to wear down.

Abfahrt *f* **(a)** *(von Zug, Bus etc)* departure. **bis zur ~ sind es noch fünf Minuten** there's still five minutes before the train/bus goes; **Vorsicht bei der ~ des Zuges!** stand clear, the train is about to leave! **(b)** *(Ski) (Talfahrt)* descent; *(~sstrecke)* (ski-)run. **(c)** *(Autobahn~)* exit. **die ~ nach Gießen** the exit for Gießen.

Abfahrts-: ~**lauf** *m (Ski)* downhill; ~**zeit** *f* departure time.

Abfall *m, pl* **Abfälle (a)** waste; *(Haus~)* rubbish, garbage *(esp US)*; *(Straßen~)* litter *(Brit)*, trash *(US)*. **(b)** *no pl (Lossagung)* break *(von with)*. **(c)** *no pl (Rückgang)* drop *(gen in)*, fall *(gen in)*; *(Verschlechterung auch)* deterioration.

Abfall-: ~**beseitigung** *f* refuse *or* garbage *(US)* disposal; ~**eimer** *m* rubbish bin, trashcan *(US)*.

abfallen *vi sep irreg aux sein* **(a)** *(herunterfallen)* to fall *or* drop off; *(Blätter, Blüten etc)* to fall. **(b)** *(col: herausspringen)* **wieviel fällt bei dem Geschäft für mich ab?** how much do I get out of the deal? **(c)** *(fig: übrigbleiben)* to be left (over). **(d)** *(schlechter werden)* to go downhill; *(Sport: zurückbleiben)* to drop back. **(e) alle Unsicherheit/ Furcht fiel von ihm ab** all his uncertainty/fear left him. **(f)** *(Fraktion: von Partei etc)* to break away *(von from)*. **vom Glauben ~** to leave the faith. **(g)** *(sich senken: Gelände)* to fall away; *(sich vermindern: Druck, Temperatur)* to fall.

abfällig *adj Bemerkung, Kritik* disparaging; *Lächeln* derisive; *Urteil* adverse. **über jdn ~ reden/ sprechen** to be disparaging about sb.

Abfall-: ~**produkt** *nt (lit, fig)* waste-product; ~**verwertung** *f* waste utilization.

abfälschen *vti sep (Sport)* to deflect.

abfangen *vt sep irreg* **(a)** *Flugzeug, Funkspruch, Brief, Ball* to intercept; *Menschen auch* to catch *(col)*; *Schlag* to block; *(col: anlocken) Kunden* to lure away. **(b)** *(bremsen) Fahrzeug* to bring under control; *Flugzeug auch* to pull out; *Aufprall* to absorb; *Trend* to check.

Abfangjäger *m (Mil)* interceptor.

abfärben *vi sep* **(a)** *(Wäsche)* to run. **paß auf, die Wand färbt ab!** be careful, the paint comes off the wall. **(b)** *(fig)* **auf jdn ~** to rub off on sb.

abfassen *vt sep (verfassen)* to write; *Entwurf* to draft.

abfaulen *vi sep aux sein* to rot away *or* off.

abfeiern *vt sep (col)* **Überstunden ~** to take time off in lieu of overtime pay.

abfertigen *sep* **1** *vt* **(a)** *(versandfertig machen) Pakete, Waren* to prepare for dispatch, to process; *Gepäck* to check (in); *(be- und entladen) Flugzeug* to make ready for take-off. **(b)** *(bedienen) Kunden etc* to attend to; *(col: Sport) Gegner* to deal with. **jdn kurz ~** *(col)* to snub sb. **2** *vti (kontrollieren) Waren, Reisende* to clear.

Abfertigung *f* **(a)** *siehe vt (a)* making ready for dispatch, processing *(form)*; checking; making ready for take-off. **(b)** *(~sstelle)* dispatch office. **(c)** *(Bedienung) (von Kunden)* service; *(von Antragstellern)* dealing with. **(d)** *(von Waren, Reisenden)* clearance. **die ~ an der Grenze** customs clearance.

abfeuern *vt sep* to fire.

abfinden *sep irreg* **1** *vt* to pay off; *Gläubiger auch* to settle with; *(entschädigen)* to compensate. **er wurde von der Versicherung mit 20.000 DM**

abgefunden he was paid DM 20,000 (in) compensation by the insurance company; **jdn mit leeren Versprechungen ~** to fob sb off with empty promises. **2** *vr* **sich mit jdm/etw ~** to come to terms with sb/sth; **er konnte sich nie damit ~, daß ...** he could never accept the fact that ...

Abfindung *f (von Gläubigern)* paying off; *(Entschädigung)* compensation.

abflachen *sep* **1** *vt* to level (off), to flatten (out). **2** *vr (Land)* to flatten out. **3** *vi (fig: sinken)* to decline.

abflauen *vi sep aux sein* **(a)** *(Wind)* to die down. **nach (dem) A~ des Windes** when the wind had died down. **(b)** *(fig) (Erregung)* to die away; *(Interesse auch)* to wane; *(Börsenkurse)* to drop; *(Geschäfte, Konjunktur)* to fall off.

abfliegen *sep irreg* **1** *vi aux sein (Aviat)* to take off *(nach for)*; *(Zugvögel)* to migrate. **sie sind gestern nach München abgeflogen** they flew to Munich yesterday. **2** *vt aux sein (fig)* to fly over.

abfließen *vi sep irreg aux sein (wegfließen)* to drain *or* flow away; *(durch ein Leck)* to leak away. **ins Ausland ~** *(Geld)* to flow out of the country.

Abflug *m* take-off; *(von Zugvögeln)* migration.

abflugbereit *adj* ready for take-off.

Abfluß *m* **(a)** *(Abfließen)* draining away; *(durch ein Leck)* leakage. **dem ~ von Kapital ins Ausland Schranken setzen** to impose limits on the (out)flow of capital out of the country. **(b)** *(~stelle)* drain; *(von Teich etc)* outlet; *(~rohr)* drainpipe; *(von sanitären Anlagen)* wastepipe.

Abfluß-: ~**rinne** *f* gutter; ~**rohr** *nt* outlet; *(im Gebäude)* wastepipe; *(außen am Gebäude)* drainpipe; *(unterirdisch)* drain.

Abfolge *f (geh)* sequence, succession.

abfordern *vt sep* **jdm etw ~** to demand sth from sb.

abfragen *vt sep* **(a)** *(esp Sch)* **jdn etw ~** to question sb on sth; *(Lehrer)* to test sb orally on sth. **(b)** *(Comp)* to call up; *Datei* to interrogate.

abfrieren *sep irreg* **1** *vi aux sein* **ihm sind die Füße abgefroren** his feet got frostbite; **abgefroren sein** *(Körperteil)* to be frostbitten. **2** *vt* **sich** *(dat)* **einen ~** *(col)* to freeze to death *(col)*.

Abfuhr *f* **-en (a)** *no pl (Abtransport)* removal. **(b)** *(col: Zurückweisung)* snub, rebuff. **jdm eine ~ erteilen** to snub *or* rebuff sb; *(Sport)* to thrash sb *(col)*; **sich** *(dat)* **eine ~ holen** to meet with a snub.

abführen *sep* **1** *vt* **(a)** *(wegführen)* to lead away; *(ableiten) Gase etc* to draw off. **~!** away with him/her etc! **(b)** *(abgeben) Betrag* to pay *(an+acc* to*)*. **2** *vi* **(a)** *(wegführen)* **der Weg führt hier (von der Straße) ab** the path leaves the road here; **das würde vom Thema ~** that would take us off the subject. **(b)** *(den Darm anregen)* to have a laxative effect.

abführend *adj* laxative *no adv*. **~ wirken** to have a laxative effect.

Abführmittel *nt* laxative.

Abfüll-: ~**anlage** *f* bottling plant; ~**betrieb** *m* bottling factory.

abfüllen *vt sep* **(a)** *(in Flaschen)* to bottle; *Flasche* to fill. **Wein in Flaschen ~** to bottle wine. **(b)** **jdn ~** *(col)* to get sb pickled *(col) or* sloshed *(col)*.

Abgabe *f* **(a)** *no pl (Abliefern)* handing in; *(von Gepäck auch)* depositing; *(Übergabe: von Brief etc)* delivery. **zur ~ von etw aufgefordert werden** to be told to hand sth in. **(b)** *no pl (Verkauf)* sale. **(c)** *no pl (von Wärme etc)* giving off; *(von Schuß, Salve)* firing; *(von Erklärung etc)* giving; *(von Stimme)* casting. **(d)** *(Sport: Abspiel)* pass. **(e)** *(Steuer)* tax; *(auf Tabak etc auch)* duty; *(soziale ~)* contribution.

Abgabetermin *m* closing date; *(für Dissertation etc)* submission date.

Abgang *m no pl* **(a)** *(Absendung)* dispatch. **vor ~ der Post** before the post goes. **(b)** *(Abfahrt)* departure. **(c)** *(aus einem Amt)* departure; *(Schul~)* leaving. **seit seinem ~ vom Gymna-**

sium since he left the grammar school. **(d)** *(Theat, fig)* exit.

Abgangszeugnis *nt* leaving certificate.

Abgas *nt* exhaust *no pl*, exhaust fumes, waste gas *(esp Tech)*.

Abgas-: a~**frei** *adj Motor, Fahrzeug* exhaust-free; a~**frei verbrennen** to burn without producing exhaust; ~**wolke** *f* cloud of exhaust.

abge|arbeitet *adj (verbraucht)* workworn; *(erschöpft)* exhausted.

abgeben *sep irreg* **1** *vt* **(a)** *(abliefern)* to hand in; *Gepäck* to deposit; *(übergeben)* to deliver; *(weggeben)* to give away; *(gegen Gebühr)* to sell; *(an einen anderen Inhaber)* to hand over; *(überlassen) Auftrag* to pass on *(an+acc to)*; *(abtreten) Posten* to hand over *(an+acc to)*. **Kinderwagen abzugeben** pram for sale; **jdm etw von seinem Kuchen** ~ to give sb some of one's cake. **(b)** *(Sport) Punkte, Rang* to concede; *(abspielen)* to pass. **(c)** *Schuß, Salve* to fire; *Erklärung* to give; *Stimmen* to cast. **(d)** *Rahmen, Hintergrund, Stoff, Material etc* to provide; *(verkörpern)* to make. **den Vermittler** ~ *(col)* to act as mediator. **2** *vr* **sich mit jdm/etw** ~ *(sich beschäftigen)* to bother oneself with sb/sth; *(sich einlassen)* to associate with sb/sth. **3** *vi (Sport)* to pass.

abgebrannt *adj pred (col)* broke *(col)*.

abgebrochen *adj (nicht beendet) Studium* uncompleted. **er ist ~er Mediziner** *(col)* he broke off his medical studies.

abgebrüht *adj (col: skrupellos)* hard-boiled *(col)*, hardened.

abgedroschen *adj (col)* hackneyed, well-worn; *Witz auch* corny *(col)*. **eine ~e Phrase** a cliché.

abgefeimt *adj* cunning, wily.

abgegriffen *adj Buch* (well-)worn; *(fig) Phrasen etc* hackneyed.

abgehackt *adj* clipped. ~ **sprechen** to clip one's words.

abgehangen *adj (gut)* ~ well-hung.

abgehärtet *adj* tough, hardy; *(fig)* hardened. **gegen Erkältungen** ~ **sein** to be immune to colds.

abgehen *sep irreg aux sein* **1** *vi* **(a)** *(abfahren)* to leave, to depart *(form) (nach for)*. **(b)** *(Theat: abtreten)* to exit. **(c)** *(ausscheiden)* to leave. **von der Schule** ~ to leave school. **(d)** *(sich lösen) Knopf etc* to come off; *(herausgehen: Farbe etc auch)* to come out. **(e)** *(abgesandt werden)* to be sent or dispatched; *(Funkspruch)* to be sent. **etw ~ lassen** to dispatch sth. **(f)** *(col: fehlen)* **jdm geht Verständnis/Taktgefühl ab** sb lacks understanding/tact. **(g)** *(abgezogen werden)* **(von etw)** ~ *(von Preis)* to be taken off (sth); *(von Verdienst auch)* to be deducted (from sth); **davon gehen 5% ab 5%** is taken off that. **(h)** *(abzweigen)* to branch off; *(bei Gabelung auch)* to fork off. **(i)** *(abweichen) von einem Plan/einer Forderung* ~ to give up a plan/demand; **von seiner Meinung** ~ to change one's opinion. **(j)** *(verlaufen)* to go. **es ging nicht ohne Streit ab** there was an argument.
 2 *vt (entlanggehen)* to walk along; *(Mil) Gelände* to patrol.

abgehetzt *adj* out of breath.

abgekämpft *adj* exhausted.

abgeklärt *adj* serene, tranquil.

abgelagert *adj Wein* mature; *Holz, Tabak* seasoned.

abgelegen *adj (entfernt) Dorf, Land* remote; *(einsam)* isolated.

abgeleiert *adj (pej)* banal, trite.

abgelten *vt sep irreg Ansprüche* to satisfy.

abgemacht 1 *interj* OK, that's settled; *(bei Kauf)* it's a deal. **2** *adj* **eine ~e Sache** a fix *(col)*.

abgemagert *adj (sehr dünn)* thin; *(ausgemergelt)* emaciated.

abgemergelt *adj* emaciated.

abgemessen *adj Schritt, Worte* measured, deliberate.

abgeneigt *adj* adverse *pred (dat to)*. **ich wäre gar nicht** ~ *(col)* actually I wouldn't mind.

abgenutzt *adj* worn, shabby; *Besen* worn-out; *Reifen* worn-down; *(fig) Klischees* well-worn.

Abge|ordnete(r) *mf decl as adj* (elected) representative; *(von Parliament)* member of parliament.

abgeraten *vi sep irreg aux sein (geh)* **vom Weg** ~ to lose one's way.

abgerissen *adj Kleidung* tattered; *Worte, Gedanken* disjointed.

Abgesandte(r) *mf decl as adj* envoy.

abgeschieden *adj (geh: einsam)* secluded. ~ **leben/wohnen** to live in seclusion.

Abgeschiedenheit *f* seclusion.

abgeschlagen *adj (a) (besiegt)* defeated. **er landete** ~ **auf dem 8. Platz** he finished up way down in 8th place. **(b)** *(erschöpft)* shattered *(col)*.

abgeschlossen *adj (einsam)* isolated; *(attr: geschlossen) Wohnung* self-contained.

Abgeschlossenheit *f* isolation.

abgeschmackt *adj* fatuous; *Witz auch* corny; *Preise* outrageous.

abgesehen 1 *ptp of* **absehen**. **es auf jdn** ~ **haben** to have it in for sb *(col)*; *(interessiert sein)* to have one's eye on sb; **du hast es nur darauf** ~**, mich zu ärgern** you're only trying to annoy me. **2** *adv:* ~ **von jdm/etw** apart from sb/sth; ~ **davon, daß ...** apart from the fact that ...

abgespannt *adj* weary, tired.

abgespielt *adj Schallplatte* worn.

abgestanden *adj Luft, Wasser* stale; *Bier, Limonade etc* flat.

abgestorben *adj Glieder* numb; *Pflanze, Ast, Gewebe* dead.

abgestumpft *adj (gefühllos) Person* insensitive; *Gefühle, Gewissen* dulled.

abgetakelt *adj (pej col)* worn out, shagged out *(col!)*.

abgetan *adj pred* finished with. **damit ist die Sache** ~ that settles the matter.

abgetragen *adj* worn. ~**e Kleider** old clothes.

abgewinnen *vt sep irreg* **(a)** *(lit)* **jdm etw** ~ to win sth from sb. **(b)** *(fig)* **jdm ein Lächeln** ~ to persuade sb to smile; **dem Meer Land** ~ to reclaim land from the sea; **einer Sache keinen Reiz** ~ **können** to be unable to see anything attractive in sth.

abgewogen *adj Urteil, Worte* balanced.

abgewöhnen *vt sep* **jdm etw** ~ to cure sb of sth; *das Rauchen, Trinken* to get sb to give up sth; **sich (dat) das Trinken** ~ to give up drinking; **noch einen zum A~** *(hum)* one last one; *(von Alkohol auch)* one for the road; **das/die ist ja zum A~** *(col)* that/she is enough to put anyone off.

abgewrackt *adj (abgetakelt) Mensch* worn-out.

abgezehrt *adj* emaciated.

abgießen *vt sep irreg* **(a)** *Flüssigkeit* to pour off; *Kartoffeln* to strain. **(b)** *(Art, Metal)* to cast.

Abglanz *m* reflection *(auch fig)*. **nur ein schwacher** *or* **matter** ~ *(fig)* a pale reflection.

abgleiten *vi sep irreg aux sein (geh: abrutschen)* to slip; *(Gedanken)* to wander; *(Fin: Kurs)* to drop, to fall. **von etw** ~ to slip off sth.

Abgott *m*, **Abgöttin** *f* idol. **jdn zum** ~ **machen** to idolize sb.

abgöttisch *adj* idolatrous. **jdn** ~ **lieben** to idolize sb; **jdm** ~ **lauschen** to listen adoringly to sb.

abgrasen *vt sep Feld* to graze; *(fig col) Geschäfte* to scour, to comb; *Thema* to do to death *(col)*.

abgrenzen *sep* **1** *vt Gelände* to fence off; *(fig) Rechte, Befugnisse, Begriff* to delimit *(gegen, von from)*. **etw durch einen Zaun/eine Mauer/Hecke** ~ to fence/wall/hedge sth off. **2** *vr* to dis(as)sociate oneself *(gegen from)*.

Abgrenzung *f* **(a)** *no pl siehe vt* fencing/walling/hedging off; *(fig)* delimitation. **(b)** *siehe vr* dis-

(as)sociation *(gegen* from). **(c)** *(Zaun)* fencing *no pl.*

Abgrund *m* precipice; *(Schlucht, fig)* abyss, chasm. **sich am Rande eines ~es befinden** *(lit, fig)* to be on the edge of a precipice; **in einen ~ von Verrat blicken** *(fig)* to stare into a bottomless pit of treason.

abgründig *adj Humor, Ironie* cryptic.

abgrundtief *adj Haß, Verachtung* profound.

abgucken *vti sep* to copy. **jdm etw ~ to copy sth from sb; bei jdm (etw) ~** *(Sch)* to copy (sth) from *or* off *(col)* sb.

Abguß *m* **(a)** *(Art, Metal) (Vorgang)* casting; *(Form)* cast. **(b)** *(dial: Ausguß)* sink.

abhaben *vt sep irreg (col)* **(a)** *Brille, Hut* to have off; *(abgemacht haben)* to have got off. **(b)** *(abbekommen)* to have. **willst du ein Stück ~?** do you want a bit?

abhacken *vt sep* to chop off, to hack off; *siehe* **abgehackt.**

abhaken *vt sep (markieren)* to tick *or (esp US)* check off; *(fig)* to cross off.

abhalten *vt sep irreg* **(a)** *Kälte, Hitze, Fliegen* to keep off. **(b)** *(hindern)* to stop, to prevent. **jdn von etw/von der Arbeit ~** to keep sb from sth/ from working; **jdn davon ~, etw zu tun** to prevent sb from doing sth; **laß dich nicht ~!** don't let me/us *etc* stop you. **(c)** *(veranstalten)* to hold.

Abhaltung *f no pl (Durchführung)* holding.

abhandeln *vt sep* **(a)** *Thema* to treat, to deal with. **(b)** *(abkaufen)* **jdm etw ~** to do a deal with sb for sth. **(c) jdm 8 Mark ~** to beat sb down 8 marks.

abhanden *adv:* **~ kommen** to get lost; **jdm ist etw ~ gekommen** sb has lost sth.

Abhang *m* slope, incline.

abhängen *sep* **1** *vt* **(a)** *Bild* to take down; *(Rail) Wagen* to uncouple; *Anhänger* to unhitch. **(b)** *(col: hinter sich lassen)* jdn to shake off *(col).* **2** *vi* **(a)** *irreg (Fleisch etc)* to hang; *siehe* **abgehangen. (b)** *irreg* **von etw ~** to depend on sth, to be dependent on sth; **das hängt ganz davon ab** it all depends. **(c)** *(Telec col)* **er hat abgehängt** he hung up (on me *etc).*

abhängig *adj* dependent *(auch euph: süchtig); Satz auch* subordinate; *Rede* indirect. **von etw ~ sein** to be dependent on sth; *(Gram)* to be governed by sth; **voneinander ~ sein** to be dependent on each other.

Abhängigkeit *f* **(a)** *no pl (Bedingtheit)* dependency *no pl (von* on); *(Gram: von Sätzen)* subordination *(von* to). **(b)** *(Angewiesensein, euph: Sucht)* dependence *(von* on). **gegenseitige ~** interdependence.

abhärten *sep* **1** *vt* to toughen up. **2** *vi* **das härtet ab** that toughens you up. **3** *vr* to toughen oneself up. **sich gegen etw ~** to toughen oneself against sth; *(fig)* to harden oneself to sth; *siehe* **abgehärtet.**

Abhärtung *f siehe vb* toughening up; hardening.

abhauen *sep irreg* **1** *vi aux sein (col)* to clear out; *(verschwinden auch)* to push off. **hau ab!** beat it *(col).* **2** *vt Kopf* to chop off; *Baum* to chop down; *Verputz, Schicht* to knock off.

abheben *sep irreg* **1** *vti* **(a)** *(anheben)* to lift (up), to raise; *(abnehmen)* Karte to take off; *Telefonhörer* to pick up, to lift; *Telefon* to answer; *(Sew)* Masche to slip. **(b)** *Geld* to withdraw. **wenn Sie ~ wollen** if you wish to make a withdrawal. **2** *vi* **(a)** *(Flugzeug)* to take off; *(Rakete)* to lift off. **(b)** *(Cards: vor Spielbeginn etc)* to cut. **3** *vr* **sich von jdm/etw or gegen jdn/etw ~** to stand out from/against sb/sth; **sich wohltuend gegen etw ~** to contrast pleasantly with sth.

abheften *vt sep* **(a)** *Rechnungen etc* to file away. **(b)** *(Sew)* to tack, to baste.

abhelfen *vi sep irreg +dat* to remedy; *einem Fehler auch* to rectify.

abhetzen *sep* **1** *vt Tiere* to exhaust, to tire out. **hetz' mich nicht so ab!** *(col)* stop hustling me like

that! *(col).* **2** *vt* to wear *or* tire oneself out; *siehe* **abgehetzt.**

abheuern *sep (Naut)* **1** *vi* to be paid off. **2** *vt* to pay off.

Abhilfe *f no pl* remedy, cure. **~ schaffen** to take remedial action.

abholen *vt sep* to collect *(bei* from); *Bestelltes auch* to call for *(bei* at); *Fundsache* to claim *(bei* from); *jdn* to call for; *(mit dem Wagen auch)* to pick up. **jdn am Bahnhof/Flughafen ~** to meet sb at the station/airport; *(mit dem Wagen auch)* to pick sb up from the station/airport; **etw ~ lassen** to have sth collected; **„Geldbörse gefunden, abzuholen bei ...“** "purse found, claim by ...".

Abholung *f* collection.

abholzen *vt sep Wald* to clear, to deforest.

Abhör|anlage *f* bugging system.

abhorchen *vt sep* to sound, to listen to. **einen Patienten ~** to listen to a patient's chest.

abhören *vt sep* **(a)** *(auch vi: überwachen) Gespräch* to bug; *(mithören)* to listen in on; *Telefon* to tap. **abgehört werden** *(col)* to be bugged. **(b)** *(zuhören) Schallplatte etc* to listen to. **(c)** *(Med)* to sound, to listen to. **einen Patienten ~** to listen to a patient's chest. **(d)** *(Sch: abfragen)* **einem Schüler etw ~** to test a pupil orally on sth.

Abhörgerät *nt* bugging device.

abhungern *vr sep* **er mußte sich** *(dat)* **sein Studium ~** he had to starve his way through college *etc;* **sich** *(dat)* **10 Kilo ~** to lose 10 kilos by going on a starvation diet.

Abi *nt* **-s** *(Sch col)* = **Abitur.**

ab|irren *vi sep aux sein (geh)* to lose one's way; *(fig: Gedanken)* to wander. **vom Weg(e) ~** to wander off the path. **vom Thema ~** to digress.

Abitur *nt* **-e** *school-leaving exam and university entrance qualification,* ≈ A-levels *pl (Brit).* **(das) ~ machen** to take (one's) school-leaving exam *or* A-levels *(Brit).*

Abiturient(in *f) m person who is doing/has done the Abitur.*

Abiturzeugnis *nt certificate of having passed the Abitur,* ≈ A-level certificate *(Brit).*

abjagen *vt sep* **jdm etw ~** to get sth off sb.

abkämmen *vt sep (fig)* to comb, to scour.

abkämpfen *vr sep* to fight hard; *siehe* **abgekämpft.**

abkanzeln *vt sep (col)* **jdn ~** to give sb a dressing-down.

abkapseln *vr sep (fig)* to cut oneself off.

abkarten *vt sep* to rig *(col),* to fix. **die Sache war von vornherein abgekartet** the whole thing was a put-up job *(col).*

abkassieren* *vti sep (col)* to cash up *(col).* **bei jdm ~** to get sb to pay; **darf ich (bei Ihnen) ~?** could I ask you to pay now?

abkauen *vt sep Fingernägel* to bite; *Bleistift* to chew.

abkaufen *vt sep* **jdm etw ~** to buy sth from sb; *(col: glauben)* to buy sth *(col).*

Abkehr *f no pl* turning away *(von* from); *(von Glauben etc)* renunciation *(von* of).

abkehren *sep* **1** *vt (geh) Blick, Gesicht* to avert, to turn away. **2** *vr (fig)* to turn away *(von* from).

abklappern *vt sep (col) Läden, Straße* to scour, to comb *(nach* for); *Kunden* to call on.

abklären *sep* **1** *vt (klarstellen)* to clear up, to clarify. **2** *vr* **(a)** *(sich setzen)* to clarify. **(b)** *(sich beruhigen)* to calm down; *siehe* **abgeklärt.**

Abklatsch *m* **-e** *(Art)* cast, casting; *(fig pej)* poor imitation *or* copy.

abklemmen *vt sep Nabelschnur, Leitung* to clamp.

abklingen *vi sep irreg aux sein* **(a)** *(leiser werden)* to die *or* fade away. **(b)** *(nachlassen)* to wear off, to abate; *(Erregung, Fieber auch)* to subside.

abklopfen *vt sep* **(a)** *Staub etc* to brush off; *Teppich, Polstermöbel* to beat. **(b)** *(beklopfen)* to tap; *(Med)* to sound, to percuss *(form).*

ạbknabbern vt sep (col) to nibble off; Knochen to gnaw at.

ạbknallen vt sep (col) to shoot down (col).

ạbknappen, ạbknapsen vt sep (col) sich (dat) jeden Pfennig ~ müssen to have to scrimp and save; **er hat mir 20 Mark abgeknapst** he got 20 marks off me.

ạbknicken sep 1 vt (abbrechen) to break or snap off; (einknicken) to break. 2 vi aux sein (abzweigen) to fork or branch off.

ạbknöpfen vt sep (a) (lit) to unbutton. (b) (col: ablisten) jdm etw ~ to get sth off sb.

ạbkochen vt sep (keimfrei machen) to sterilize (by boiling).

ạbkommandieren* vt sep (Mil) (zu Einheit) to post; (zu bestimmtem Dienst) to detail (zu for).

ạbkommen vi sep irreg aux sein (a) von etw ~ (abirren) to wander off sth; **vom Kurs** ~ to deviate from one's course; (vom Thema) ~ to get off the subject, to digress. (b) (aufgeben) von etw ~ to drop sth; (von Angewohnheit) to give sth up; (von Idee, Plan) to abandon sth; **von einer Meinung** ~ to revise one's opinion.

Ạbkommen nt - agreement (auch Pol).

ạbkömmlich adj available. nicht ~ sein to be unavailable.

Ạbkömmling m (Nachkomme) descendant; (fig) adherent.

ạbkönnen vt sep irreg (col) (a) (trinken) er kann nicht viel ab he can't take much (drink). (b) (mögen) das kann ich nicht ab I can't stand it.

ạbkoppeln vt sep (Rail) to uncouple; Anhänger to unhitch; (Space) to separate; Pferd to untie.

ạbkratzen sep 1 vt Schmutz etc to scratch off; (mit einem Werkzeug) to scrape off. 2 vi aux sein (col: sterben) to kick the bucket (col).

ạbkriegen vt sep (col) siehe abbekommen.

ạbkühlen sep 1 vt to cool; Speise auch to cool down. 2 vi aux sein to cool down. 3 vr to cool down; (Beziehungen) to become cool(er).

Ạbkühlung f cooling.

Ạbkunft f no pl (liter) descent, origin; (Nationalität auch) extraction.

ạbkürzen sep 1 vt (a) (abschneiden) **den Weg** ~ to take a short cut. (b) (verkürzen) to cut short; Verfahren to shorten; Aufenthalt, Urlaub auch to curtail. (c) Namen to abbreviate. 2 vi (verkürzt schreiben) to use abbreviations.

Ạbkürzung f (a) (Weg) short cut. (b) (von Wort) abbreviation.

ạbladen vti sep irreg Last, Wagen to unload; Schutt to dump; (esp Comm) Passagiere, Ware to offload; (fig col) Ärger auch to vent (bei jdm on sb).

Ạblage f -n place to keep/put sth. wir brauchen eine ~ für die Akten we need somewhere for our files; etw als ~ benutzen (für Akten, Bücher etc) to use sth for storage.

ạblagern sep 1 vt (deponieren) to leave, to store. 2 vi aux sein or haben (ausreifen) to mature; (Holz auch) to season. ~ lassen to allow to mature; Holz auch to (allow to) season. 3 vr to be deposited.

Ạblagerung f (abgelagerter Stoff) deposit.

ạblassen sep irreg 1 vt (a) (herauslaufen lassen) Wasser, Luft to let off; Motoröl auch to drain off; Dampf to let off. (b) (ermäßigen) to knock off (col). er hat mir 20 Mark abgelassen he knocked 20 marks off for me (col). 2 vi (liter) (a) (mit etw aufhören) to desist. von einem Vorhaben etc ~ to abandon a plan etc. (b) (jdn in Ruhe lassen) von jdm ~ to leave sb alone.

Ạblauf m (a) (Abfluß) drain; (Rinne) drainage channel. (b) (Verlauf) course; (von Verbrechen) sequence of events (gen in); (von Handlung in Buch etc) development. der ~ der Ereignisse the course of events; **es gab keinerlei Störungen im** ~ **des Programms** the programme went off without any disturbances. (c) (von Zeitraum, Frist etc) expiry. nach ~ von 4 Stunden after 4 hours (have/had passed or gone by); **nach** ~ **des Jahres/dieser Zeit** at the end of the year/this time.

ạblaufen sep irreg 1 vt (a) (abnutzen) Schuhsohlen, Schuhe to wear out; Absätze to wear down. sich (dat) **die Beine** or **Hacken nach etw** ~ (col) to walk one's legs off looking for sth. (b) aux sein or haben (entlanglaufen) Strecke to go or walk over; Stadt, Straßen, Geschäfte to comb, to scour. 2 vi aux sein (a) (abfließen: Flüssigkeit) to drain or run away or off; (trocken werden: Geschirr) to dry off. (b) (vonstatten gehen) to go off. (c) ~ **lassen** (abspulen, abspielen) Platte, Tonband to play; Film to run. (d) (ungültig werden: Paß etc) to expire, to run out; (enden: Frist, Vertrag etc auch) to run out, to be up. (e) (Zeitraum) to pass, to go by.

Ạbleben nt no pl (form) demise (form).

ạblecken vt sep to lick; Teller to lick (clean).

ạblegen sep 1 vt (a) (niederlegen) to put down; Last, Waffen auch to lay down; (Zool) Eier to lay. (b) Schriftwechsel to file (away). (c) (ausziehen) Kleider to take off, to remove. (d) (nicht mehr tragen) Anzug, Kleid to discard, to cast off. **abgelegte Kleider** cast-off clothes. (e) (aufgeben) Mißtrauen, Scheu, Stolz to lose, to shed; Namen to give up. (f) Schwur, Eid to swear; Gelübde auch to make; Zeugnis to give; Bekenntnis, Beichte to make; Prüfung to take, to sit; (erfolgreich) to pass. 2 vi (a) (Schiff) to cast off; (Space auch) to separate. (b) (Garderobe ~) to take one's things off.

Ạbleger m - (Bot) layer; (fig: Zweigunternehmen) branch, subsidiary.

ạblehnen vt sep (a) auch vi (zurückweisen, nein sagen) to decline; Antrag, Vorschlag, Bewerber to reject; (Parl) Gesetzentwurf to throw out. **eine** ~**de Antwort** a negative answer; **ein** ~**der Bescheid** a rejection; **dankend** ~ to decline with thanks. (b) (mißbilligen) to disapprove of.

Ạblehnung f (a) (Zurückweisung) refusal; (von Antrag etc) rejection. (b) (Mißbilligung) disapproval. auf ~ stoßen to meet with disapproval.

ạbleiern vt sep (col) Gedicht etc to reel off.

ạbleisten vt sep (form) Zeit to serve; Wehrdienst to do.

ạbleiten sep vt (a) (herleiten) to derive; (logisch folgern auch) to deduce (aus from). (b) (umleiten) Fluß to divert; (herausleiten) Rauch, Flüssigkeit to draw off or out; (ablenken) Blitz to conduct.

Ạbleitung f (a) siehe vt derivation; deduction; diversion; drawing off or out; conduction. (b) (Wort, Math) derivative.

ạblenken sep 1 vt (a) (ab-, wegleiten) to deflect (auch Phys), to turn aside. (b) er ließ sich durch nichts ~ he wouldn't let anything distract him; **das lenkt mich ab** (zerstreut mich) it takes my mind off things; **jdn von seinem Schmerz/seinen Sorgen** ~ to take sb's mind off his pain/worries. (c) (abbringen) to divert; Verdacht to avert. 2 vi (a) (vom Thema) ~ to change the subject. (b) **das lenkt ab** (zerstreut) it takes your mind off things; (stört) it's distracting. 3 vr to take one's mind off things.

Ạblenkung f (a) (Ab-, Wegleitung) deflection (auch Phys). (b) (Zerstreuung) diversion, distraction. ~ **brauchen** to need something to take one's mind off things.

Ạblenkungsmanöver nt diversionary tactic; (um von Thema abzulenken auch) red herring.

ạblesen vt sep irreg (a) (auch vi: vom Blatt) to read. **er muß (alles/seine Rede)** ~ he has to read everything/his speech (from notes etc); (jdm) **etw von den Lippen** ~ to lip-read sth (that sb says). (b) (auch vi: registrieren) Meßgeräte, Barometer, Strom to read. **nächste Woche wird abgelesen** the meter(s) will be read next week. (c) (herausfinden, erkennen, folgern) to see. **jdm etw vom Gesicht** ~ to read sth in sb's face; **das**

konnte man ihr vom Gesicht ~ it was written all over her face; **jdm jeden Wunsch von den Augen** ~ to anticipate sb's every wish.

ableugnen *vt sep* Schuld, Tat to deny.

Ableugnung *f* denial.

ablichten *vt sep (form)* to photocopy; *(fotografieren)* to photograph.

Ablichtung *f (form) siehe vt* photocopy; photograph.

abliefern *vt sep* to hand in *(bei* to); *(liefern)* to deliver *(bei* to); *(col)* Kinder to deposit *(col) (bei* with).

Ablieferung *f (von Waren)* delivery.

abliegen *vi sep irreg (entfernt sein)* **das Haus liegt weit ab** the house is quite a distance away; *siehe* **abgelegen**.

ablisten *vt sep* **jdm etw** ~ to trick sb out of sth.

ablocken *vt sep* **jdm etw** ~ to get sth out of sb.

ablöschen *vt sep* **(a)** *(mit dem Löschblatt)* to blot. **(b)** *(Cook)* to add water to.

ablösen *sep* **1** *vt* **(a)** *(abmachen)* to take off, to remove; Etikett etc auch to detach. **(b)** *(Fin)* Schuld, Hypothek to pay off, to redeem. **(c)** *(ersetzen)* Wache to relieve; Amtsinhaber to replace. **(d)** *(fig: an Stelle treten von)* to take the place of; *(Methode, System)* to supersede. **2** *vr* **(a)** *(abgehen)* to come off; *(Lack etc auch)* to peel off. **(b)** *(auch* **einander** ~*)* to take turns; *(Fahrer, Kollegen auch, Wachen)* to relieve each other.

Ablösesumme *f (Sport)* transfer fee.

Ablösung *f* **(a)** *(von Hypothek, Schuld)* paying off, redemption. **(b)** *(Wache)* relief; *(Entlassung)* replacement. **bei dieser Arbeit braucht man alle zwei Stunden eine** ~ you need relieving every two hours in this work.

abluchsen *vt sep (col)* **jdm etw** ~ to get *or* wangle *(col)* sth out of sb.

Abluft *f no pl (Tech)* used air.

ablutschen *vt sep* to lick.

abmachen *vt sep (col)* **(a)** *(entfernen)* to take off. **(b)** *(vereinbaren)* Termin etc to agree (on). **(c)** *(besprechen)* to settle. **etw mit sich allein** ~ to sort sth out for oneself.

Abmachung *f* agreement.

abmagern *vi sep aux sein* to get thinner, to lose weight.

Abmagerung *f no pl* emaciation.

Abmagerungskur *f* diet. **eine** ~ **machen** to be on a diet, to be dieting; *(anfangen)* to go on a diet.

abmalen *vt sep (abzeichnen)* to paint.

Abmarsch *m* departure; *(von Soldaten auch)* march-off. **beim** ~ when marching off; **zum** ~ **antreten** *(Mil)* to fall in for the march-off.

abmarschbereit *adj* ready to move off.

abmarschieren* *vi sep aux sein* to move off.

abmelden *sep* **1** *vt* **(a)** Telefon to have disconnected; *(bei Verein)* jdn to cancel the membership of. **sein Auto** ~ to take one's car off the road; **ein Kind von einer Schule** ~ to take a child away from a school. **(b)** *(col)* **er/sie ist bei mir abgemeldet** I don't want anything to do with him/her. **2** *vr* to ask for permission to be absent; *(im Hotel)* to check out. **sich bei jdm** ~ to tell sb that one is leaving; **sich polizeilich** ~ to notify the police that one is moving away.

Abmeldung *f (von Telefon)* disconnection; *(bei der Polizei)* cancellation of one's registration. **seit der** ~ **meines Autos** since I took my car off the road.

abmergeln *vr sep* to slave away.

abmessen *vt sep irreg (a)* to measure; *(fig)* Worte to weigh. **(b)** *(abteilen)* to measure off.

Abmessung *f usu pl* measurement; *(Ausmaß)* dimension.

abmildern *vt sep* Geschmack, Worte to tone down; Aufprall to cushion, to soften; Schock to lessen.

abmontieren* *vt sep* Räder, Teile to remove *(von etw* from sth*)*; Maschine to dismantle.

abmühen *vr sep* to struggle (away).

abmustern *sep (Naut)* **1** *vt* Besatzung to pay off. **2** *vi* to sign off, to leave the ship.

abnagen *vt sep* to gnaw off; Knochen to gnaw.

Abnahme *f* **-n (a)** *(Wegnahme)* removal; *(Amputation)* amputation. **(b)** *(Verringerung)* decrease *(gen* in*)*; *(bei Anzahl, Menge auch)* drop *(gen* in*)*; *(von Kräften, Energie, Interesse, Nachfrage)* decline *(gen* in*)*. **(c)** *(von Prüfung)* holding; *(von Neubau, Fahrzeug etc)* inspection. **(d)** *(Comm)* purchase. **bei** ~ **von 50 Exemplaren** if you/we etc purchase or take 50 copies; **keine/gute** ~ **finden** not to sell/to sell well.

abnehmbar *adj* removable, detachable.

abnehmen *sep irreg* **1** *vt* **(a)** *(herunternehmen)* to take off, to remove; Hörer to lift, to pick up; Obst to pick; *(lüften)* Hut to raise; Vorhang, Bild, Wäsche to take down; Maschen to decrease; *(amputieren)* to amputate.

(b) *(an sich nehmen)* **jdm etw** ~ to take sth from sb; *(fig)* Arbeit, Sorgen to relieve sb of sth; **darf ich Ihnen den Mantel** ~? can I take your coat?; **kann ich dir etwas** ~? *(tragen)* can I take something for you?; *(helfen)* can I do anything for you?; **jdm die Beichte** ~ to hear confession from sb; **jdm ein Versprechen** ~ to make sb promise sth.

(c) *(wegnehmen)* to take away *(jdm* from sb*)*; *(rauben, abgewinnen)* to take *(jdm* off sb*)*.

(d) *(begutachten)* Gebäude, Auto to inspect; *(abhalten)* Prüfung to hold.

(e) *(abkaufen)* to take *(dat* off*)*, to buy *(dat* from, off*)*.

(f) *(fig col: glauben)* to buy *(col)*. **dieses Märchen nimmt dir keiner ab!** nobody'll buy that!

(g) Fingerabdrücke to take.

2 *vi* **(a)** *(sich verringern)* to decrease; *(Niveau, Kräfte)* to decline; *(Fieber)* to go down; *(Mond)* to wane; *(beim Stricken)* to decrease. **(an Gewicht)** ~ to lose weight. **(b)** *(Telec)* to answer.

Abnehmer *m* - *(Comm)* buyer, customer. **viele/wenige** ~ **finden** to sell well/badly.

Abneigung *f* dislike *(gegen* of*)*; *(Widerstreben)* aversion *(gegen* to*)*.

abnorm, abnormal *adj* abnormal.

Abnormität *f* abnormality.

abnötigen *vt sep (geh)* **jdm etw** ~ to force sth from sb; **jdm Respekt** ~ to gain sb's respect.

abnutzen *vtr sep* to wear out.

Abnutzung *f* wear (and tear).

Abonnement [abɔnə'mãː] *nt* **-s** *or* **-e (a)** *(Zeitungs~)* subscription. **eine Zeitung im** ~ **beziehen** to subscribe to a newspaper. **(b)** *(Theater~)* season ticket.

Abonnent(in *f)* *m (Zeitungs~)* subscriber; *(Theater~)* season-ticket holder.

abonnieren* *vt* Zeitung to subscribe to; Konzertreihe etc to have a season ticket to.

abordnen *vt sep* to delegate.

Ab|ordnung *f* delegation.

Abort[1] *m* **-e** *(dated)* lavatory, toilet.

Abort[2] *m* **-e** *(Fehlgeburt)* miscarriage; *(Abtreibung)* abortion.

abpacken *vt sep* to pack. **ein abgepacktes Brot** a wrapped loaf.

abpassen *vt sep* **(a)** *(abwarten)* Gelegenheit to wait for. **den richtigen Zeitpunkt** ~ to wait for the right time; **etw gut** ~ to time sth well. **(b)** *(auf jdn warten)* to catch; *(jdm auflauern)* to way-lay.

abpausen *vt sep* to make a tracing of.

abpfeifen *sep irreg (Sport)* **1** *vi (Schiedsrichter)* to blow one's whistle. **2** *vt* **das Spiel/die erste Halbzeit** ~ to blow the whistle for the end of the game/for half-time.

Abpfiff *m (Sport)* final whistle.

abpflücken *vt sep* to pick.

abplagen *vr sep* to struggle (away).

abprallen *vi sep aux sein* von *or* an etw *(dat)* ~ *(Ball)* to bounce *or (Kugel)* to ricochet off sth; **an jdm** ~ *(fig)* to make no impression on sb.

Abpraller *m - (Sport)* rebound.

abputzen *sep vt* to clean; *Schmutz* to clean off. **sich** *(dat)* **die Nase/den Hintern** ~ to wipe one's nose/bottom; **putz dir die Schuhe ab!** wipe your feet!

abquälen *sep* **1** *vr* to struggle (away). **2** *vt* **sich** *(dat)* **ein Lächeln** ~ to force a smile.

abqualifizieren* *vt sep* to dismiss, to write off.

abquetschen *vt sep* to crush. **sich** *(dat)* **den Arm** ~ to get one's arm crushed.

abrackern *vr sep (col)* to slave away. **sich mit etw** ~ to struggle with sth.

abrasieren* *vt sep* to shave off; *(col) Gebäude* to flatten.

abraten *vti sep irreg* **jdm (von) etw** ~ to advise sb against sth.

abräumen *vti sep* to clear up *or* away. **den Tisch** ~ to clear the table.

abreagieren* *sep* **1** *vt Spannung, Wut* to work off, to get rid of. **seinen Ärger an anderen** ~ to take it out on others. **2** *vr* to work it off. **er war ganz wütend, aber jetzt hat er sich abreagiert** he was furious, but he's simmered down now.

abrechnen *sep* **1** *vi* **(a)** *(Kasse machen)* to cash up. **darf ich** ~**?** would you like your bill *(Brit) or* check *(US)* now? **(b)** **mit jdm** ~ to settle up with sb; *(fig)* to get even with sb. **2** *vt (abziehen)* to deduct.

Abrechnung *f* **(a)** *(Aufstellung)* statement *(über* +*acc* for); *(Rechnung)* bill, invoice; *(Bilanz)* balancing; *(fig: Rache)* revenge. **der Tag der** ~ *(fig)* the day of reckoning. **(b)** *(Abzug)* deduction. **nach** ~ **von** after (the deduction of); **in** ~ **stellen** *(form)* to deduct.

Abrede *f* **etw in** ~ **stellen** to deny *or* dispute sth.

abregen *vr sep (col)* to calm *or* cool down. **reg dich ab!** relax!, cool it! *(col)*.

abreiben *vt sep irreg Schmutz, Rost* to clean *or* rub off; *(trocknen)* to rub down.

Abreibung *f (col: Prügel)* hiding, thrashing.

Abreise *f* departure *(nach* for). **bei meiner** ~ on my departure.

abreisen *vi sep aux sein* to leave *(nach* for).

abreißen *sep irreg* **1** *vt* **(a)** *(abtrennen)* to tear off; *Tapete, Blätter auch* to strip (off). **er hat sich** *(dat)* **den Knopf abgerissen** he's torn his button off; **er wird dir nicht (gleich) den Kopf** ~ *(col)* he won't bite your head off *(col)*. **(b)** *(niederreißen) Gebäude* to pull down. **2** *vi aux sein (sich lösen)* to come off; *(fig: unterbrochen werden)* to break off. **das reißt nicht ab** *(fig)* there is no end to it; **den Kontakt** *etc* **nicht** ~ **lassen** to stay in touch.

Abreißkalender *m* tear-off calendar.

abrichten *vt sep* to train. **der Hund ist auf Einbrecher abgerichtet** the dog is trained to go for burglars.

Abrichtung *f* training.

abriegeln *vt sep (verschließen) Tür* to bolt; *(absperren) Straßen, Gebiet* to cordon off.

abringen *vt sep irreg* **jdm etw** ~ to wring *or* force sth out of sb; **sich** *(dat)* **ein Lächeln** ~ to force a smile; **dem Meer Land** ~ *(liter)* to wrest land away from the sea *(liter)*.

Abriß *m* **(a)** *(Abbruch)* demolition. **(b)** *(Übersicht)* outline, summary. **(c)** *(von Eintrittskarte etc)* tear-off part.

abrollen *sep* **1** *vt (abwickeln)* to unwind; *Stoff* to unroll. **2** *vi aux sein* **(a)** *(abfahren: Züge, Waggons)* to roll off *or* away. **(b)** *(col: vonstatten gehen) (Programm)* to run; *(Veranstaltung)* to go off; *(Ereignisse)* to unfold. **mein ganzes Leben rollte noch einmal vor meinen Augen ab** my whole life passed before me again.

abrücken *sep* **1** *vt (wegschieben)* to move away. **2**

vi *aux sein* **(a)** *(fig: sich distanzieren)* to dissociate oneself *(von* from). **(b)** *(Mil etc)* to move out.

Abruf *m* **(a)** **sich auf** ~ **bereit halten** to be ready to be called (for); **auf** ~ **zur Verfügung stehen** to be available on call. **(b)** *(Comm)* **etw auf** ~ **bestellen/kaufen** to order/buy sth (to be delivered) on call. **(c)** *(Comp)* retrieval.

abruf-: ~**bar** *adj Daten* retrievable; ~**bereit** *adj* **(a)** *Arzt etc* on call; *(abholbereit)* ready to be called for; **(b)** *(Comm, Fin)* ready on call.

abrufen *vt sep irreg* **(a)** *(wegrufen)* to call away. **(b)** *(Comm)* to request delivery of; *(Fin: abheben)* to withdraw. **(c)** *(Comp)* Daten to retrieve.

abrunden *vt sep (lit, fig)* to round off. **eine Zahl nach oben/unten** ~ to round a number up/down.

Abrundung *f (lit, fig)* rounding off. **zur** ~ **von etw** to round sth off.

abrupt *adj* abrupt.

abrüsten *vi (Mil, Pol)* to disarm.

Abrüstung *f no pl (Mil, Pol)* disarmament.

abrutschen *vi sep aux sein (abgleiten)* to slip; *(fig) (Leistungen)* to go downhill; *(moralisch)* to let oneself go.

absäbeln *vt sep (col)* to hack *or* chop off.

absacken *vi sep aux sein (sinken)* to sink; *(Boden, Gebäude auch)* to subside; *(fig col: nachlassen)* to fall off; *(verkommen)* to go to pot *(col)*.

Absage *f* -**n** refusal; *(auf Einladung auch)* negative reply. **das ist eine** ~ **an die Demokratie** that's a denial of democracy; **jdm/einer Sache** ~ **erteilen** to reject sb/sth.

absagen *sep* **1** *vt (rückgängig machen) Veranstaltung, Besuch* to cancel, to call off; *(ablehnen) Einladung* to decline. **2** *vi* to decline. **jdm** ~ to tell sb that one can't come; **in letzter Minute** ~ to cry off at the last minute.

absägen *vt sep* **(a)** *(abtrennen)* to saw off. **(b)** *(fig col)* to chuck *or* bring out *(col)*.

absahnen *sep (fig col)* **1** *vt Geld* to rake in; *(sich verschaffen)* to cream off. **2** *vi* to make a killing *(col)*.

absatteln *vti sep* to unsaddle.

Absatz *m, pl* **Absätze (a)** *(Abschnitt)* paragraph; *(Jur)* section. **einen** ~ **machen** to start a new paragraph. **(b)** *(Treppen~)* half-landing. **(c)** *(Schuh~)* heel. **spitze Absätze** stiletto heels; **auf dem** ~ **kehrtmachen** to turn on one's heel. **(d)** *(Verkauf)* sales *pl*. **guten** ~ **finden** to sell well.

Absatz-: ~**fähig** *adj* marketable, saleable; ~**gebiet** *nt* sales area; ~**schwierigkeiten** *pl* sales problems *pl*; ~**steigerung** *f* increase in sales.

absaufen *vi sep irreg aux sein (col) (ertrinken)* to drown; *(Motor)* to flood; *(Schiff etc)* to go down.

absaugen *vt sep Flüssigkeit* to suck out *or* off; *Teppich, Sofa* to hoover ®, to vacuum.

abschaben *vt sep* to scrape off.

abschaffen *sep vt* **(a)** to abolish, to do away with. **(b)** *(nicht länger halten)* to get rid of.

Abschaffung *f* abolition.

abschälen *vtr sep* to peel off.

abschalten **1** *vti sep (lit, fig col)* to switch off. **2** *vr* to switch itself off.

abschätzen *vt sep* to estimate; *Menschen, Fähigkeiten* to assess. **seine Lage** ~ to take stock of one's position; **ein** ~**der Blick** an appraising look.

abschätzig *adj* disparaging. **sich** ~ **über jdn äußern** to make disparaging remarks about sb.

Abschätzung *f* siehe **Schätzung**.

Abschaum *m no pl* scum. **der** ~ **der Menschheit** the scum of the earth.

abscheiden *vt sep irreg (ausscheiden)* to give off, to produce; *(Biol auch)* to secrete.

Abscheu *m or f no pl* repulsion, abhorrence *(vor* +*dat* at). **vor jdm/etw** ~ **haben** *or* **empfinden** to loathe sb/sth; **jdm** ~ **einflößen** to fill sb with loathing.

abscheuern *vt sep* **(a)** *Schmutz* to scrub off. **(b)**

abscheulich *(abschürfen) Haut* to rub *or* scrape off. **(c)** *Kleidung* to wear thin.
abscheulich *adj* abominable, loathsome; *Verbrechen auch* heinous; *Anblick auch* repulsive. **wie** ~**!** how awful!; ~ **kalt** hideously cold.
Abscheulichkeit *f (Untat)* atrocity, abomination; *(no pl: Widerwärtigkeit)* loathsomeness; *(von Verbrechen auch)* heinousness; *(von Geschmack, Anblick)* repulsiveness.
abschicken *vt sep* to send; *Paket, Brief* to send off, to dispatch.
abschieben *sep irreg 1 vt* **(a)** *(wegschieben)* to push away *(von* from); *(fig) Verantwortung, Schuld* to shift *(auf+acc* onto). **(b)** *(ausweisen) Ausländer* to deport. **(c)** *(col: loswerden)* to get rid of. **jdn in eine andere Abteilung** ~ to shunt sb off to another department *(col)*. **2** *vi aux sein (col)* to clear off *(col)*.
Abschiebung *f (Ausweisung)* deportation.
Abschied *m* -**e (a)** *(Trennung)* farewell, parting. **von jdm/etw** ~ **nehmen** to say goodbye to sb/sth, to take one's leave of sb/sth; **ein** ... **zum** ~ **a farewell** ...; **es war ein** ~ **für immer** it was goodbye for ever; **beim** ~ **meinte er,** ... as he was leaving he said ...; **ihr** ~ **von der Bühne/vom Film** her farewell from the stage/from film; *(letzte Vorstellung)* her farewell performance; **der** ~ **von der Vergangenheit** the break with the past. **(b)** *(von Beamten)* resignation; *(von Offizieren)* discharge. **seinen** ~ **nehmen** to hand in one's resignation/to apply for a discharge.
Abschieds-: ~**besuch** *m* farewell visit; ~**brief** *m* farewell letter; ~**feier** *f* farewell party; ~**schmerz** *m* pain of parting; ~**stunde** *f* hour of parting; ~**szene** *f* farewell scene.
abschießen *vt sep irreg (auf+acc* at) **(a)** *Geschoß, Gewehr* to fire; *Pfeil* to shoot; *Rakete* to launch; *(auf ein Ziel)* to fire. **(b)** *(außer Gefecht setzen) Flugzeug* to shoot down. **(c)** *(totschießen) Wild* to shoot. **(d)** *(fig col: abschieben)* to get rid of.
abschirmen *sep 1 vt* **(a)** to shield; *(vor Licht auch)* to screen. **2** *vr* to shield oneself *(gegen* from); *(sich schützen)* to protect oneself *(gegen* from *or* against); *(sich isolieren)* to cut oneself off *(gegen* from).
Abschirmung *f no pl* **(a)** *(Schutz)* protection. **(b)** *(fig: Isolierung)* isolation.
abschlachten *vt sep* to slaughter.
Abschlachtung *f* slaughter.
abschlaffen *vi sep aux sein (col)* to flag.
Abschlag *m* **(a)** *(Preisnachlaß)* reduction. **(b)** *(Zahlung)* part payment *(auf+acc* of).
abschlagen *vt sep irreg* **(a)** *(mit Hammer etc)* to knock off; *(mit Beil etc)* to chop off; *Baum* to chop down; *(herunterschlagen)* to knock down. **etw vom Preis** ~ to knock sth off the price. **(b)** *(ablehnen)* to refuse; *Einladung, Bitte auch, Antrag* to turn down. **jdm etw** ~ to refuse sb sth. **(c)** *(zurückschlagen) Angriff, Feind* to drive off. **(d)** *siehe* **abgeschlagen**.
abschlägig *adj* negative. **jdn/etw** ~ **bescheiden** *(form)* to turn sb/sth down.
Abschlag(s)zahlung *f* part payment.
abschleifen *sep irreg 1 vt Unebenheiten* to grind down; *Holzboden* to sand (down). **2** *vr (fig) (Angewohnheit etc)* to wear off; *(Mensch)* to have the rough edges taken off. **das schleift sich (noch) ab** *(fig)* that'll wear off.
Abschleppdienst *m* breakdown service *(Brit)*, (vehicle) recovery service.
abschleppen *sep 1 vt* **(a)** *Fahrzeug, Schiff* to tow, to take in tow; *(bei widerrechtlichem Parken)* to tow away. **(b)** *(col) Menschen* to drag along; *(aufgabeln)* to pick up *(col)*. **2** *vr* **sich mit etw** ~ *(col)* to struggle with sth.
Abschlepp-: ~**fahrzeug** *nt* breakdown *(Brit)* or recovery vehicle, wrecker *(US)*; ~**seil** *nt* tow-rope.

abschließbar *adj* lockable.
abschließen *sep irreg 1 vt* **(a)** *(zuschließen)* to lock. **(b)** *(beenden) Sitzung, Vortrag etc* to conclude, to bring to a close. **sein Studium** ~ to graduate; **mit abgeschlossenem Studium** with a degree. **(c)** *(vereinbaren) Geschäft* to transact; *Versicherung* to take out; *Wette* to place. **einen Vertrag** ~ *(Pol)* to conclude a treaty; *(Jur, Comm)* to conclude a contract. **2** *vr (sich isolieren)* to cut oneself off. **sich von der Außenwelt** ~ to shut oneself off from the outside world; *siehe* **abgeschlossen**. **3** *vi* **(a)** *(zuschließen)* to lock up. **sieh mal nach, ob auch abgeschlossen ist** will you see if everything's locked? **(b)** *(enden)* to come to a close. **(c)** *(Comm: Vertrag schließen)* to conclude the deal. **(d)** *(Schluß machen)* to finish, to end. **mit der Vergangenheit** ~ to break with the past.
abschließend 1 *adj* concluding. **2** *adv* in conclusion, finally.
Abschluß *m* **(a)** *(Beendigung)* end; *(col:* ~*prüfung)* final examination; *(Univ)* degree. **zum** ~ **möchte ich** ... finally *or* to conclude I would like ...; **zum** ~ **kommen** to come to an end; **etw zum** ~ **bringen** to finish sth. **(b)** *no pl (Vereinbarung)* conclusion. **bei** ~ **des Vertrages** on completion of the contract. **(c)** *(Rand etc)* border.
Abschluß-: ~**feier** *f (Sch)* speech *or* prizegiving day; ~**prüfung** *f (Sch)* final examination; *(Univ auch)* finals *pl*; ~**zeugnis** *nt (Sch)* leaving certificate, diploma *(US)*.
abschmecken *vt sep (kosten)* to taste; *(würzen)* to season.
abschmettern *vt sep (col) (Sport)* to smash; *(fig: zurückweisen)* to throw out.
abschmieren *vt sep (Tech) Auto* to grease.
abschminken *vt sep* **(a)** *Gesicht, Haut* to remove the make-up from. **sich** ~ to remove one's make-up. **(b)** *(col: aufgeben)* **sich** *(dat)* **etw** ~ to get sth out of one's head.
abschmirgeln *vt sep* to sand down.
abschnallen *sep 1 vt* to unfasten, to undo. **2** *vr* to unfasten one's seat belt. **3** *vi (col)* **(a)** *(nicht mehr folgen können)* to give up. **(b)** *(fassungslos sein)* to be staggered *(col)*.
abschneiden *sep irreg 1 vt (lit, fig)* to cut off; *Blumen, Fingernägel, Haar* to cut. **jdm das Wort** ~ to cut sb short. **2** *vi bei etw gut/schlecht** ~ *(col)* to come off well/badly in sth.
Abschnitt *m* **(a)** section; *(Math)* segment; *(Mil)* sector, zone; *(Geschichts*~*, Zeit*~*)* period. **(b)** *(Kontroll*~*) (von Scheck etc)* counterfoil; *(von Karte)* section; *(von Papier)* slip.
abschnitt(s)weise *adv* in sections.
abschnüren *vt sep* to cut off *(von* from). **jdm das Blut** ~ to cut off sb's circulation; **jdm die Luft** ~ *(lit)* to stop sb breathing; *(fig)* to ruin sb.
abschöpfen *vt sep Fett* to skim off; *(fig) Ruhm* to reap. **den Gewinn** ~ to siphon off the profits.
abschotten *vr sep* **sich gegen etw** ~ *(fig)* to cut oneself off from sth.
abschrägen *vt sep* to slope; *Holz, Brett* to bevel. **ein abgeschrägtes Dach** a sloping roof.
abschrauben *vt sep* to unscrew.
abschrecken *sep 1 vt* **(a)** *(fernhalten)* to deter, to put off; *(verjagen: Hund, Vogelscheuche)* to scare off. **ich lasse mich dadurch nicht** ~ I won't be deterred by that. **(b)** *(abkühlen) Stahl* to quench; *(Cook)* to rinse with cold water. **2** *vi (Strafe)* to act as a deterrent.
abschreckend *adj (warnend)* deterrent. **ein** ~**es Beispiel** a warning; **eine** ~**e Wirkung haben,** ~ **wirken** to act as a deterrent.
Abschreckung *f* deterrent.
Abschreckungs-: ~**mittel** *nt* deterrent; ~**waffe** *f* deterrent (weapon).
abschreiben *sep irreg 1 vt* **(a)** to copy *(bei, von* from); *(kopieren)* to copy out. **(b)** *(Comm: absetzen, abziehen)* to deduct. **(c)** *(verlorengeben)* to

write off. **er ist bei mir abgeschrieben** I'm finished with him. **2** *vi* **(a)** *(Sch)* to copy, to crib *(col)*. **(b) jdm ~** to write to sb to tell him/her that one cannot come *etc*.

Abschreibung *f (Comm)* deduction.

abschreiten *vt sep irreg (entlanggehen) Gelände* to patrol; *(inspizieren)* Front to inspect.

Abschrift *f* copy.

abschrubben *vt sep (col) Schmutz* to scrub off; *Rücken, Fußboden* to scrub (down).

abschuften *vr sep (col)* to slog one's guts out *(col)*.

abschürfen *vt sep* to graze.

Abschürfung *f (Wunde)* graze.

Abschuß *m* **(a)** *(das Abfeuern)* firing, shooting; *(von Rakete)* launch(ing). **(b)** *(das Außer-Gefecht-Setzen)* shooting down; *(von Panzer)* knocking out. **die Luftwaffe erzielte zwölf Abschüsse** the air force shot down twelve planes. **(c)** *(von Wild)* shooting. **Fasanen sind jetzt zum ~ freigegeben** pheasant-shooting is now permitted; **zum ~ freigegeben sein** *(fig)* to be fair game.

abschüssig *adj* sloping. **eine sehr ~e Straße** a steep road.

Abschuß-: ~liste *f* **er steht auf der ~liste** *(col)* his days are numbered; **~rampe** *f* launch(ing) pad.

abschütteln *vt sep (lit, fig)* to shake off.

abschütten *vt sep* Flüssigkeit *etc* to pour off; *(Cook)* to drain off; Kartoffeln *etc* to drain.

abschwächen *sep* **1** *vt* to weaken; Formulierung to tone down. **2** *vr* to fall off, to diminish; *(Lärm)* to decrease; *(Preisauftrieb, Andrang)* to ease off.

Abschwächung *f siehe vb* weakening; toning down; decrease; easing off.

abschweifen *vi sep aux sein (lit, fig) (von* from*)* to stray, to wander (off); *(Redner auch)* to digress.

Abschweifung *f* digression.

abschwellen *vi sep irreg aux sein (Entzündung, Fluß)* to go down; *(Lärm)* to die away.

abschwenken *sep* **1** *vi aux sein* to turn away; *(Kamera)* to pan. **er ist nach links abgeschwenkt** *(lit)* he turned off to the left; *(fig)* he swung (over) to the left; **(nach rechts) ~** *(Mil)* to wheel (right). **2** *vt* **(a)** *(abschütteln)* Tropfen to shake off. **(b)** *(Cook)* to drain (off).

abschwindeln *vt sep* **jdm etw ~** to swindle sb out of sth.

abschwirren *vi sep aux sein* to whirr off; *(fig col: weggehen)* to buzz off *(col)*.

abschwören *vi sep irreg (old, liter)* to renounce *(dat* sth*)*. **dem Glauben/Teufel ~** to renounce one's faith/the devil; **dem Alkohol ~** *(col)* to give up drinking.

Abschwung *m (Sport)* dismount; *(Econ)* downward trend, recession.

absegnen *vt sep (col)* to give one's blessing to.

absehbar *adj* foreseeable. **in ~er/auf ~e Zeit** in/for the forseeable future; **die Folgen sind noch gar nicht ~** there's no telling what the consequences will be.

absehen *sep irreg* **1** *vt* **(a)** *(abgucken)* **(bei) jdm etw ~** to pick sth up from sb. **(b)** *(voraussehen)* to foresee. **es ist ganz klar abzusehen, daß** ... it's easy to see that ...; **das Ende läßt sich noch nicht ~** the end is not yet in sight; *siehe* **abgesehen 1. 2** *vi* **von etw ~** *(verzichten)* to refrain from sth; *(nicht berücksichtigen)* to disregard sth; **davon ~, etw zu tun** to dispense with doing sth; *siehe* **abgesehen 2.**

abseifen *vt sep* to soap down.

abseilen *sep* **1** *vt* to lower down on a rope. **2** *vr (Bergsteiger)* to abseil (down).

absein *vi sep irreg aux sein (col)* **(a)** *(weg sein)* to be off. **die Farbe/der Knopf ist ab** the paint/button has come off. **(b)** *(abgelegen sein)* to be far away.

abseitig *adj* **(a)** *(ausgefallen)* esoteric. **(b)** *(pervers)* perverse.

abseits *adv (abgelegen)* out of the way, remote; *(Sport)* offside. **~ vom Wege** off the beaten

track; **~ stehen** *(fig)* to be on the outside; *(Sport)* to be offside; **~ bleiben, sich ~ halten** *(fig)* to keep to oneself.

Abseits *nt* - *(Sport)* offside. **im ~ stehen** to be offside; **im ~ leben** *(fig)* to live in the shadows.

Abseits-: ~position, ~stellung *f* offside position; **~tor** *nt* offside goal.

absenden *vt sep* to send; *(mit der Post auch)* to post *(Brit)*, to mail *(esp US)*.

Absender(in *f)* *m* - sender; *(Adresse)* (sender's) address.

abservieren* *sep* **1** *vi* to clear the table. **2** *vt* **(a)** Geschirr, Tisch to clear. **(b)** *(col: entlassen, kaltstellen)* **jdn ~** to push sb out, to get rid of sb. **(c)** *(col: umbringen)* to do in *(col)*. **(d)** *(Sport col: besiegen)* to thrash *(col)*.

absetzbar *adj* Ware saleable; Betrag deductible.

absetzen *sep* **1** *vt* **(a)** *(abnehmen)* Hut, Brille to take off; *(hinstellen)* Gepäck, Glas to set or put down. **(b)** *(aussteigen lassen)* Fahrgast to drop. **(c)** Theaterstück to take off; Fußballspiel, Versammlung, Termin to cancel; Punkt von der Tagesordnung to delete. **(d)** *(entlassen)* to dismiss; König to depose. **(e)** *(Med)* Medikament to stop taking; Behandlung to discontinue. **(f)** *(Comm)* Waren to sell. **sich gut ~ lassen** to sell well. **(g)** *(abziehen)* Betrag to deduct. **das kann man ~** that is tax-deductible.

2 *vr* **(a)** *(Chem, Geol)* to be deposited; *(Feuchtigkeit, Staub etc)* to collect. **(b)** *(col: weggehen)* to get or clear out *(aus of) (col)*; *(Sport: Abstand vergrößern)* to pull ahead. **sich nach Brasilien ~** to clear off to Brazil.

3 *vi* **er trank das Glas aus, ohne abzusetzen** he emptied his glass in one.

4 *vt impers* **es setzt etwas ab** *(col)* there'll be trouble.

Absetzung *f* **(a)** *(Entlassung) (von Beamten)* dismissal; *(von König)* deposing, deposition. **(b)** *(von Theaterstück etc)* withdrawal; *(von Fußballspiel, Termin etc)* cancellation; *(von Punkt auf der Tagesordnung)* deletion.

absichern *sep* **1** *vt* to safeguard; *(garantieren)* to cover; Bauplatz, Gefahrenstelle to make safe. **2** *vr (sich schützen)* to protect oneself; *(sich versichern)* to cover oneself.

Absicht *f* **-en** *(Vorsatz)* intention; *(Zweck)* purpose; *(Jur)* intent. **in der besten ~** with the best of intentions; **die ~ haben, etw zu tun** to intend to do sth; **eine ~ mit etw verfolgen** to have something in mind with sth; **ernste ~en haben** *(col)* to have serious intentions; **das war nicht meine ~** I didn't intend that; **etw mit/ohne ~ tun** to do/not to do sth deliberately *or* on purpose.

absichtlich *adj* deliberate, intentional. **etw ~ tun** to do sth on purpose *or* deliberately.

absinken *vi sep irreg aux sein (Schiff)* to sink; *(Boden auch)* to subside; *(Interesse, Leistungen)* to fall *or* drop off; *(fig: moralisch ~)* to go downhill.

absitzen *sep irreg* **1** *vt* **(a)** *(verbringen)* Zeit to sit out; *(verbüßen)* Strafe to serve. **(b)** *(abnutzen)* Hose *etc* to wear thin. **2** *vi aux sein* **(vom Pferd) ~** to dismount (from a horse).

absolut *adj* absolute; *(völlig auch)* complete, total. **~ nicht/nichts** absolutely not/nothing; **das ist ~ unmöglich** that's quite *or* absolutely impossible.

Absolutheits|anspruch *m* claim to absolute right. **einen ~ vertreten** to claim absoluteness.

Absolution *f (Eccl)* absolution. **jdm die ~ erteilen** to grant *or* give sb absolution.

Absolvent(in *f)* [apzɔl'vɛnt(m)] *m (Univ)* graduate. **die ~en eines Lehrgangs** the students who have completed a course.

absolvieren* [apzɔl'viːrən] *vt insep* Studium, Probezeit to complete; Schule to finish, to graduate from *(US)*; Prüfung to pass.

absonderlich *adj* peculiar, strange.

absondern *sep* **1** *vt* **(a)** *(trennen)* to separate;

(isolieren) to isolate. **(b)** *(ausscheiden)* to secrete. **2** *vr (Mensch)* to cut oneself off. **sie sondert sich immer seh~ ab** she always keeps herself very much to ~ self.

Absonder *.ng f* **(a)** *siehe vt* separation; isolation; secretion. **(b)** *(abgeschiedener Stoff)* secretion.

absorbiere~ *vt insep (lit, fig)* to absorb.

Absorption *f* absorption.

abspalten *vtr sep* to split off; *(Chem)* to separate *(off)*.

abspannen *sep* **1** *vt Pferd, Wagen* to unhitch. **2** *vi (fig: entspannen)* to relax; *siehe* **abgespannt.**

absparen *vt sep* **sich** *(dat)* **ein Auto vom Lohn ~** to save up for a car from one's wages; **sich** *(dat)* **etw vom Munde ~** to scrimp and save for sth.

abspecken *sep (col)* **1** *vt* to shed. **2** *vi* to lose weight.

abspeisen *vt sep (fig: abfertigen)* **jdn mit etw ~** to fob sb off with sth.

abspenstig *adj* **jdm jdn/etw ~ machen** to lure sb/sth away from sb; **jdm die Freundin ~ machen** to pinch sb's girlfriend *(col).*

absperren *sep* **1** *vt* **(a)** *(versperren)* to block off. **(b)** *Strom etc* to turn *or* shut off. **(c)** *(zuschließen)* to lock. **2** *vi* to lock up.

Absperrung *f* **(a)** *(Abriegelung)* blocking *or* closing off. **(b)** *(Sperre)* barrier.

Abspiel *nt (Sport)* pass.

abspielen *sep* **1** *vt* **(a)** *Tonband etc* to play; *(vom Blatt)* *Musik* to sight-read; *siehe* **abgespielt. (b)** *(Sport)* *Ball* to pass. **2** *vr (sich ereignen)* to happen.

absplittern *vti sep (vi: aux sein)* to chip off; *Holz auch* to splinter off.

Absprache *f* arrangement. **ohne vorherige ~** without prior consultation.

absprechen *sep irreg* **1** *vt* **(a)** **jdm etw ~** *(verweigern)* **Recht** to deny sb sth; *(in Abrede stellen)* **Begabung** to dispute sb's sth; **er ist wirklich sehr klug, das kann man ihm nicht ~** there's no denying that he's very clever. **(b)** *(verabreden)* *Termin* to arrange. **2** *vr* **sich mit jdm ~** to make an arrangement with sb; **die beiden hatten sich vorher abgesprochen** they had agreed on what to do/say *etc* in advance.

abspringen *vi sep irreg aux sein* **(a)** *(herunterspringen)* to jump down *(von* from*); (herausspringen)* to jump out *(von* of*); (Aviat)* to jump *(von* from*); (bei Gefahr)* to bale out. **(b)** *(sich lösen)* to come off; *(Farbe, Lack auch)* to flake or peel off. **(c)** *(fig col: sich zurückziehen)* to get out; *(von Partei, Kurs etc)* to back out.

abspritzen *vt sep* **etw/jdn ~** to spray sth/sb down; *Schmutz* to spray off *(von etw* sth*).*

Absprung *m* jump *(auch Aviat)*, leap; *(Sport)* take-off. **den ~ schaffen** *(fig)* to make the break *(col);* **er hat den ~ gewagt** *(fig)* he took the leap.

abspulen *vt sep Kabel, Garn* to unwind.

abspülen *sep* **1** *vt Hände, Geschirr* to rinse; *Fett etc* to rinse off. **2** *vi* to wash up.

abstammen *vi sep no ptp* to be descended *(von* from*).*

Abstammung *f* descent; *(Abkunft auch)* origin. **ehelicher/unehelicher ~** *(Jur)* of legitimate/ illegitimate birth; **französischer ~** of French extraction or descent.

Abstand *m* **(a)** *(Zwischenraum)* distance; *(kürzer)* gap, space; *(Zeit~)* interval; *(fig: Distanz)* distance. **mit ~** by far, far and away; **~ von etw gewinnen** *(fig)* to distance oneself from sth; **in Abständen von 10 Minuten** at 10 minute intervals; **~ halten** to keep one's distance; **mit großem ~ führen** to lead by a wide margin. **(b)** *(form: Verzicht)* **davon ~ nehmen, etw zu tun** to refrain from doing sth.

Abstandssumme *f (form)* indemnity.

abstatten *vt sep (form)* **jdm einen Besuch ~** to pay sb a visit; **jdm seinen Dank ~** to give thanks to sb.

abstauben *vti sep* **(a)** *Möbel etc* to dust. **(b)** *(col) (wegnehmen)* to nick *(col); (schnorren)* to cadge *(von, bei, dat* off, from*).*

Abstauber *m* - *(Ftbl col)* **(a)** *(auch ~tor)* easy goal. **(b)** *(Spieler)* goal-hanger *(col).*

Abstecher *m* - *(Ausflug)* trip; *(Umweg)* detour, side-trip.

abstecken *vt sep* **(a)** *(lit, fig)* **Gelände, Verhandlungsposition** to mark out. **(b)** **Kleid, Naht** to pin.

abstehen *sep irreg* **1** *vi (entfernt stehen)* to stand away; *(nicht anliegen)* to stick out. **~de Ohren** ears that stick out; *siehe* **abgestanden. 2** *vt (col)* **sich** *(dat)* **die Beine ~** to stand for hours.

Absteige *f* **-n** cheap hotel.

absteigen *vi sep irreg aux sein* **(a)** *(heruntersteigen)* to get off *(von etw* sth*).* **(b)** *(abwärts gehen)* to make one's way down; *(Bergsteiger auch)* to climb down. **in ~der Linie** in the line of descent; **auf dem ~den Ast sein** *(col)* to be going downhill, to be on the decline; **gesellschaftlich ~** to go down in society. **(c)** *(einkehren)* to stay; *(im Hotel auch)* to put up *(in* + *dat* at*).* **(d)** *(Sport: Mannschaft)* **aus der ersten Liga ~** to be relegated from the first division.

Absteiger *m* - *(Sport)* relegated team.

abstellen *vt sep* **(a)** *(hinstellen)* to put down. **(b)** *(unterbringen)* to put; *(Aut: parken auch)* to park. **(c)** *(abrücken, entfernt stellen)* to put away from. **(d)** *(abkommandieren)* to order off, to detail; *Offizier auch* to second. **(e)** *(abdrehen)* to turn off. **(f)** *(sich abgewöhnen)* to give up, to stop. **(g)** *(unterbinden)* *Mangel, Unsitte etc* to bring to an end. **das läßt sich nicht/läßt sich ~** nothing/something can be done about it.

Abstell-: ~gleis *nt* siding; **jdn aufs ~gleis schieben** *(fig)* to cast sb aside; **~raum** *m* storeroom.

abstempeln *vt sep* to stamp; *Post* to postmark; *(fig)* to brand *(zu, als* as*).*

absterben *vi sep irreg aux sein (eingehen, Med, fig)* to die; *(gefühllos werden: Glieder)* to go or grow numb; *siehe* **abgestorben.**

Abstieg *m* **-e** *(das Absteigen)* way down, descent; *(Niedergang)* decline; *(Sport)* relegation.

abstimmen *sep* **1** *vi* to take a vote. **über etw** *(acc)* **~** to vote on sth; **über etw** *(acc)* **~ lassen** to put sth to the vote; **geheim ~** to have a secret ballot. **2** *vt Instrumente* to tune *(auf* +*acc* to*); Farben, Kleidung* to match *(auf* +*acc* with*); Termine* to coordinate *(auf* +*acc* with*); (anpassen)* to suit *(auf* +*acc* to*).* **gut auf etw** *(acc)/***aufeinander abgestimmt sein** *(Instrumente)* to be in tune with sth/ with each other; *(Farben, Speisen etc)* to go well with each other; *(Termine)* to fit in well with sth/with each other; *(einander angepaßt sein)* to be well-suited to sth/(to each other); **etw miteinander ~** *(vereinbaren)* to settle sth amongst ourselves/themselves *etc.* **3** *vr* **sich ~ (mit jdm/miteinander)** to come to an agreement (with sb/amongst ourselves/themselves *etc).*

Abstimmung *f (Stimmabgabe)* vote; *(geheime ~)* ballot. **eine ~ durchführen** to take a vote.

Abstimmungs|ergebnis *nt* result of the vote.

abstinent *adj* teetotal.

Abstinenz *f no pl* teetotalism, abstinence.

Abstinenzler(in *f)* *m* - teetotaller *(Brit),* teetotaler *(US).*

abstoppen *vti sep (auch Sport)* to stop; *(mit Stoppuhr)* to time.

Abstoß *m (Ftbl)* goal kick; *(nach Fangen des Balls)* clearance.

abstoßen *sep irreg* **1** *vt* **(a)** *(wegstoßen)* *Boot* to push off or out; *(abschlagen)* *Ecken* to knock off. **(b)** *(zurückstoßen)* to repel; *(Comm)* *Ware, Aktien* to sell off; *(fig: anwidern)* to repel. **dieser Stoff stößt Wasser ab** this material is water-repellent; **gleiche Pole stoßen sich ab** like poles repel (each other). (c) (*Ftbl*) den Ball ~ to take the goal kick; (*nach Fangen*) to clear (the ball). 2 *vr* (*esp Sport: Mensch*) sich mit den Füßen vom Boden ~ to push oneself off. 3 *vi* (*anwidern*) to be repulsive. sich von etw abgestoßen fühlen to find sth repulsive.

abstoßend *adj Aussehen, Äußeres* repulsive.

Abstoßung *f* (*Phys*) repulsion.

abstottern *vt sep* (*col*) to pay off.

abstrahieren* [apstra'hiːrən] *vti insep* to abstract (*aus* from).

abstrahlen *vt sep Wärme etc* to emit.

abstrakt [ap'strakt] *adj* abstract.

abstrampeln *vr sep* (*fig col*) to sweat (away) (*col*).

abstreichen *vt sep irreg* (*wegstreichen*) to wipe off.

abstreifen *vt sep* (a) (*abtreten*) *Schuhe, Füße* to wipe. (b) (*abziehen*) *Kleidung, Schmuck* to take off, to slip off; (*entfernen*) *Haut* to shed; (*fig*) *Gewohnheit, Fehler* to get rid of.

abstreiten *vt sep irreg* (*leugnen*) to deny. das kann man ihm nicht ~ you can't deny it.

Abstrich *m* (a) (*Kürzung*) cutback. ~e machen to cut back (*an+dat* on); (*weniger erwarten etc*) to lower one's sights. (b) (*Med*) swab; (*Gebärmutter*~) smear. einen ~ machen to take a swab/smear.

abstrus [ap'struːs] *adj* (*geh*) abstruse.

abstufen *vt sep Gelände* to terrace; *Farben* to shade; *Gehälter, Steuern, Preise* to grade.

Abstufung *f* (*Nuance*) shade; (*Stufe*) grade.

abstumpfen *sep* 1 *vt Mensch* to dull; *siehe* **abgestumpft**. 2 *vi aux sein* (*fig: Geschmack etc*) to become dulled. diese Arbeit stumpft ab this work dulls the mind.

Absturz *m siehe vi* crash; fall. ein Flugzeug zum ~ bringen to bring a plane down.

abstürzen *vi sep aux sein* (*Flugzeug*) to crash; (*Bergsteiger*) to fall.

abstützen *sep* 1 *vt* to support (*auch fig*); *Haus, Mauer auch* to shore up. 2 *vr* to support oneself.

absuchen *vt sep* to search; *Gegend auch* to comb, to scour; *Himmel* to scan; (*Scheinwerfer*) to sweep.

absurd *adj* absurd. ~es Drama *or* Theater theatre of the absurd.

Absurdität *f* absurdity (*auch Philos*).

Abszeß *m* -sse abscess.

Abt *m* ⁻e abbot.

abtakeln *vt sep Schiff* to unrig; *siehe* **abgetakelt**.

abtasten *vt sep* to feel; (*Elec*) to scan; (*bei Durchsuchung*) to frisk (*auf+acc* for).

abtauen *sep* 1 *vt* to thaw out; *Kühlschrank* to defrost. 2 *vi aux sein* to thaw.

Abtei *f* abbey.

Abteil *nt* -e compartment.

abteilen *vt sep* (*abtrennen*) to divide off.

Abteilung *f* (*in Firma, Kaufhaus*) department; (*in Krankenhaus, Jur*) section; (*Mil*) unit, section.

Abteilungsleiter *m* head of department.

abtelefonieren* *vi sep* to telephone to say one can't make it.

abtippen *vt sep* (*col*) to type out.

Äbtissin *f* abbess.

abtönen *vt sep Farbe* to tone down.

Abtönung *f* (*Farbton*) tone, shade.

abtöten *vt sep* (*lit, fig*) to destroy, to kill (off); *Nerv* to deaden.

abtragen *vt sep irreg* (a) (*abbauen*) *Gebäude, Mauer* to take down; (*Fluß*) *Ufer* to erode. (b) (*abbezahlen*) *Schulden* to pay off. (c) (*abnutzen*) *Kleider* to wear out; *siehe* **abgetragen**.

abträglich *adj* detrimental (*dat* to, for); *Kritik etc* adverse.

Abtragung *f* (*Geol*) erosion.

Abtransport *m* transportation; (*aus Katastrophengebiet*) evacuation. beim ~ der Gefangenen when the prisoners were being taken away.

abtransportieren* *vt sep* to transport; (*aus Katastrophengebiet*) to evacuate.

abtreiben *sep irreg* 1 *vt* (a) vom Kurs ~ to carry off course. (b) *Kind* to abort. sie hat das Kind abgetrieben *or* ~ lassen she had an abortion. 2 *vi* (a) *aux sein* (vom Kurs) ~ to be carried off course. (b) (*Abort vornehmen*) to carry out an abortion; (*Abort vornehmen lassen*) to have an abortion.

Abtreibung *f* abortion. eine ~ vornehmen lassen to have an abortion.

abtrennen *vt sep* (a) (*lostrennen*) to detach; *Knöpfe, Besatz etc* to remove; *Bein, Finger etc* (*durch Unfall*) to sever, to cut off. „hier ~" "detach here". (b) (*abteilen*) to separate off; (*mit Zwischenwand etc auch*) to partition off.

abtreten *sep irreg* 1 *vt* (a) *Teppich* to wear (out); *Schnee, Schmutz* to stamp off. sich (*dat*) die Füße ~ to wipe one's feet. (b) (*überlassen*) (*jdm or an jdn* to sb) to hand over; *Gebiet, Land auch* to cede; *Ansprüche* to transfer. 2 *vi aux sein* (*Theat*) to go off (stage); (*Mil*) to dismiss; (*col: zurücktreten*) (*Politiker*) to resign; (*Monarch*) to abdicate. ~! (*Mil*) dismiss!

Abtreter *m* - (*Fuß*~) doormat.

Abtretung *f* (*an+acc* to) transfer; (*von Ansprüchen auch, von Gebiet*) ceding, cession.

Abtritt *m* (*Theat*) exit; (*Rücktritt*) (*von Minister*) resignation; (*von Monarch*) abdication.

abtrocknen *sep* 1 *vt* to dry. 2 *vi* to dry up, to do the drying-up.

abtropfen *vi sep aux sein* to drip; (*Geschirr*) to drain. etw ~ lassen to let sth drain.

abtrotzen *vt sep jdm etw* ~ (*geh*) to wring sth out of sb.

abtrünnig *adj* renegade, (*rebellisch*) rebel. **jdm/ einer Gruppe** ~ **werden** to desert sb/a group.

abtun *vt sep irreg* (*fig: beiseite schieben*) to dismiss. etw mit einem Achselzucken/einem Lachen ~ to shrug/laugh sth off; etw kurz ~ to brush sth aside; *siehe* **abgetan**.

abtupfen *vt sep Tränen* to dab away; *Gesicht, Wunde* to dab.

ab|urteilen *vt sep* to pass sentence *or* judgement on.

abverlangen* *vt sep siehe* **abfordern**.

abwägen *vt sep irreg* to weigh up; *Worte* to weigh. er wog beide Möglichkeiten gegeneinander ab he weighed up the two possibilities; *siehe* **abgewogen**.

Abwahl *f* voting out. es kam zur ~ des gesamten Vorstands the whole committee was voted out.

abwählen *vt sep* to vote out (of office); (*Sch*) *Fach* to give up.

abwälzen *vt sep Schuld, Verantwortung* to shift (*auf+acc* onto); *Arbeit* to unload (*auf+acc* onto); *Kosten* to pass on (*auf+acc* to). die Schuld von sich ~ to shift the blame onto somebody else.

abwandeln *vt sep Melodie* to adapt; *Thema auch* to modify.

abwandern *vi sep aux sein* to move (away) (*aus* from); (*Kapital*) to be transferred (*aus* out of). viele Spieler/Abonnenten *etc* wandern ab a lot of players/subscribers *etc* are transferring.

Abwandlung *f* adaptation, variation; (*von Thema etc auch*) modification.

Abwärme *f* waste heat.

abwarten *sep* 1 *vt* to wait for. das Gewitter ~ to wait till the storm is over; er kann es nicht mehr ~ he can't wait any longer; das bleibt abzuwarten that remains to be seen. 2 *vi* to wait. warten Sie ab! just wait a bit!; ~ und Tee trinken (*col*) to wait and see; eine ~de Haltung einnehmen to play a waiting game.

abwärts *adv* down; (*nach unten auch*) downwards. „~!" (*im Fahrstuhl*) "going down!".

abwärtsgehen *vi impers aux sein* (*fig*) mit ihm/dem Land geht es abwärts he/the country is going downhill.

Abwärtstrend *m* downwards *or* downhill trend.

Abwasch *m no pl* washing-up *(Brit)*. **den ~ machen** to do the washing-up *(Brit)*, to wash the dishes; **dann kannst du das auch machen, das ist (dann) ein ~** *(col)* then you could do that as well and kill two birds with one stone *(prov)*.

abwaschbar *adj Tapete* washable.

abwaschen *sep irreg* 1 *vt Gesicht* to wash; *Geschirr* to wash; *Schmutz* to wash off; *Auto* to wash down. **den Schmutz (vom Gesicht) ~** to wash the dirt off (one's face). 2 *vi* to wash up *(Brit)*, to do the washing-up *(Brit)*, to wash the dishes.

Abwaschwasser *nt* washing-up water *(Brit)*, dishwater; *(fig col)* dishwater *(col)*.

Abwasser *nt* sewage *no pl*.

Abwasserkanal *m* sewer.

abwechseln *vir sep* to alternate. **sich** *or* **einander ~** to alternate; *(Menschen auch)* to take turns; **sich mit jdm ~** to take turns with sb.

abwechselnd *adv* alternately. **er war ~ fröhlich und traurig** he alternated between being happy and sad.

Abwechslung *f* change; *(Zerstreuung)* diversion. **eine angenehme/schöne ~** a pleasant/nice change; **zur ~** for a change; **für ~ sorgen** to provide entertainment; **hier haben wir wenig ~** there's not much variety in life here.

abwechslungs-: **~halber** *adv* for a change; **~los** *adj* monotonous; **~reich** *adj* varied.

Abweg ['apveːk] *m* **jdn auf ~e führen** to lead sb astray *(auch moralisch)*; **auf ~e geraten** *or* **kommen** to go astray; *(moralisch auch)* to stray from the straight and narrow.

abwegig ['apveːgɪç] *adj (geh)* erroneous; *(bizarr)* eccentric; *Verdacht* groundless.

Abwehr *f no pl* **(a)** defence *(Brit)*, defense *(US)* *(gen against)*; *(~truppen)* defence *(Brit)* *or* defense *(US)* troops; *(Spionage~)* counter-intelligence *(service)*; *(Schutz)* protection *(gen against)*. **der ~ von etw dienen** to provide *or* give protection against sth. **(b)** *(Zurückweisung)* repulse; *(Abweisung)* rejection. **die ~ des Feindes** repelling the enemy; **auf ~ stoßen** to be repulsed.

abwehrbereit *adj (Mil)* ready for defence *(Brit)* *or* defense *(US)*.

abwehren *sep* 1 *vt* **(a)** *Gegner* to fend *or* ward off; *Ball* to clear; *Schlag* to parry, to ward off. **(b)** *(fernhalten)* to keep away; *Krankheitserreger* to protect against; *Gefahr, üble Folgen* to avert. **(c)** *(abweisen)* Anschuldigung to dismiss. **eine ~de Geste** a dismissive wave of the hand. 2 *vi (Sport)* to clear; *(Torwart auch)* to make a save. **mit dem Kopf ~** to head clear; **zur Ecke ~** to clear and concede a corner.

Abwehr-: **~kampf** *m (Mil, Sport)* defence *(Brit)*, defense *(US)*; **~reaktion** *f (Psych)* defence *(Brit)* *or* defense *(US)* reaction; **~spieler** *m* defender.

abweichen *vi sep irreg aux sein (sich entfernen)* to deviate; *(sich unterscheiden)* to differ. **voneinander ~** *(Theorien)* to diverge, to differ; **vom Kurs ~** to deviate *or* depart from one's course; **vom Thema ~** to digress; **vom rechten Weg ~** *(fig)* to wander off the straight and narrow; **ich weiche erheblich von seiner Meinung ab** I hold quite a different view from him; **~des Verhalten** *(Psych, Sociol)* deviant behaviour.

Abweichler(in *f)* *m* - *(Pol)* deviant.

abweichlerisch *adj (Pol)* deviant.

Abweichung *f siehe* abweichen deviation; difference; *(von Theorien)* divergence. **zulässige ~** *(Tech)* tolerance; *(zeitlich, zahlenmäßig)* allowance.

abweisen *vt sep irreg* to turn down; *(wegschicken)* to turn away; *(Jur) Klage* to dismiss. **er läßt sich nicht ~** he won't take no for an answer.

abweisend *adj Ton, Blick* cold, chilly.

abwenden *sep reg or irreg* 1 *vt* **(a)** *(zur Seite wen-*

den) to turn away; *Blick* to avert; *Kopf* to turn. **(b)** *(verhindern)* Unheil to avert. 2 *vr* to turn away.

abwerben *vt sep irreg* to woo away *(dat from)*.

abwerfen *sep irreg* 1 *vt* to throw off; *Reiter* to throw; *Bomben, Flugblätter etc* to drop; *Ballast* to jettison; *Blätter, Nadeln* to shed; *(Cards)* to discard; *(Comm) Gewinn* to yield. 2 *vti (Sport) Ball* to throw out; *Latte* to knock off *or* down.

abwerten *vt sep* **(a)** *auch vi (Fin)* to devalue. **(b)** *(fig) Ideale* to debase, to cheapen.

abwertend *adj* pejorative.

Abwertung *f (Fin)* devaluation.

abwesend *adj (form)* absent; *(iro: zerstreut auch)* far away. **die A~en** the absentees.

Abwesenheit *f* absence. **in ~** *(+gen)* in the absence of; **durch ~ glänzen** *(iro)* to be conspicuous by one's absence.

abwickeln *sep* 1 *vt* **(a)** *(abspulen)* to unwind; *Verband auch* to remove. **(b)** *(fig: erledigen)* to deal with, to handle; *(abschließen)* to conclude. 2 *vr* to unwind; *(vonstatten gehen)* to go *or* pass off.

Abwicklung *f (Erledigung)* handling; *(Abschluß)* completion, conclusion. **die Polizei sorgte für eine reibungslose ~ der Veranstaltung** the police made sure that the event went *or* passed off smoothly.

abwiegeln *sep* 1 *vt* to appease. 2 *vi* to calm things down.

abwiegen *vt sep irreg* to weigh out.

abwimmeln *vt sep (col) jdn* to get rid of; *Auftrag* to get out of. **die Sekretärin hat mich abgewimmelt** his secretary turned me away; **laß dich nicht ~** don't let them get rid of you.

abwinken *sep* 1 *vi (col) (abwehrend)* to wave it/him *etc* aside; *(fig: ablehnen)* to say no. **als er merkte, wovon ich reden wollte, winkte er gleich ab** when he realised what I wanted to talk about he immediately put me off. 2 *vti ein Rennen ~* to wave the chequered *(Brit)* *or* checkered *(US)* flag.

abwirtschaften *vi sep (col)* to go downhill. **endgültig abgewirtschaftet haben** to have eventually reached rock bottom.

abwischen *vt sep Staub, Schmutz etc* to wipe off *or* away; *Augen, Tränen* to dry.

abwracken *vt sep Schiff, Auto* to break (up); *siehe* abgewrackt.

Abwurf *m* throwing off; *(von Reiter)* throw; *(von Bomben etc)* dropping; *(von Ballast)* jettisoning; *(Sport: von Speer etc)* throwing. **ein ~ vom Tor** a goal-throw, a throw-out.

abwürgen *vt sep (col)* to scotch; *Motor* to stall. **etw von vornherein ~** to nip sth in the bud.

abzahlen *vt sep* to pay off.

abzählen *vt sep* to count. **das läßt sich an den (fünf) Fingern ~** *(fig)* any fool can see that *(col)*; **abgezähltes Geld** exact money; *(Fahrgeld)* exact fare.

Abzählreim *m* counting rhyme *(such as "eeny meeny miney mo", for choosing a person)*.

Abzahlung *f (a) (Rückzahlung)* repayment, paying off. **(b)** *(Ratenzahlung)* hire purchase *(Brit)*, HP *(Brit)*, installment plan *(US)*; *(Rate)* (re)payment, instalment *(Brit)*, installment *(US)*. **etw auf ~ kaufen** to buy sth on HP *(Brit)* *or* on hire purchase *(Brit)* *or* on the installment plan *(US)*.

abzapfen *vt sep jdm Blut ~** to take blood from sb; **jdm Geld ~** to get some money out of sb.

Abzeichen *nt* badge; *(Mil)* insignia *pl*.

abzeichnen *sep* 1 *vt* **(a)** to draw. **(b)** *(signieren)* to initial. 2 *vr* to stand out; *(fig) (deutlich werden)* to emerge, to become apparent; *(drohend bevorstehen)* to loom (on the horizon).

Abziehbild *nt* transfer, decal *(US)*.

abziehen *sep irreg* 1 *vt* **(a)** to skin; *Fell, Haut* to remove; to strip off. **(b)** *Bett* to strip. **(c)** *Ring etc* to take off. **(d)** *Schlüssel* to take out, to remove. **(e)** *(zurückziehen) Kapital* to withdraw; *Truppen auch* to pull out; *(subtrahieren) Zahlen* to take away, to subtract; *Steuern* to deduct. **DM 20 vom Preis** ~ to take DM 20 off the price. **(f)** *(Typ: vervielfältigen)* to run off; *(Phot) Bilder* to make prints of. **etw zwanzigmal** ~ to run off twenty copies of sth. **(g)** *(schleifen)* to sharpen; *Parkett* to sand (down). **2** *vi* **(a)** *aux sein (sich verflüchtigen: Rauch)* to escape, to go away. **(b)** *aux sein (Soldaten)* to pull out *(aus of)*, to withdraw *(aus* from); *(col: weggehen)* to go off *or* away. **zieh ab!** *(col)* clear off! *(col)*. **(c)** *(abdrücken)* to pull the trigger, to fire.

abzielen *vi sep auf etw (acc)* ~ *(Mensch)* to aim at sth; *(in Rede)* to get at sth; *(Bemerkung, Maßnahme etc)* to be aimed *or* directed at sth.

Abzug ['aptsuːk] *m* **(a)** *no pl (von Truppen, Kapital etc)* withdrawal. **jdm freien** ~ **gewähren** to give *or* grant sb a safe conduct. **(b)** *(usu pl: vom Lohn etc)* deduction; *(Rabatt)* discount. **(c)** *(Typ)* copy; *(Korrekturfahne)* proof; *(Phot)* print. **(d)** *(Öffnung für Rauch, Gas)* flue. **(e)** *(am Gewehr)* trigger.

abzüglich *prep+gen (Comm)* minus, less.

Abzweig *m* junction.

abzweigen *sep* **1** *vi aux sein* to branch off. **2** *vt (col)* to set *or* put on one side.

Abzweigung *f* junction, turn-off; *(Gabelung)* fork.

abzwingen *vt sep irreg* **jdm Respekt etc** ~ to gain sb's respect *etc*; **er zwang sich** *(dat)* **ein Lächeln ab** he forced a smile.

ach [ax] *interj* oh. ~ **nein!** oh no!; *(überrascht)* no!, really!; *(ablehnend)* no, no!; ~ **so!** I see!; ~ **was** *or* **wo!** of course not; ~ **was** *or* **wo, das ist doch nicht so schlimm!** come on now, it's not that bad; ~ **wirklich?** oh really?

Ach *nt:* **mit** ~ **und Krach** *(col)* by the skin of one's teeth *(col)*.

Achat *m* **-e** agate.

Achillesferse *f* Achilles heel.

Achse ['aksə] *f* **-n (a)** axis. **(b)** *(Tech)* axle. **auf** ~ **sein** *(col)* to be out and about.

Achsel ['aksl] *f* **-n (a)** shoulder. **die** ~**n** *or* **mit den** ~**n zucken** to shrug (one's shoulders). **(b)** *(~höhle)* armpit.

Achsel-: ~**haare** *pl* underarm hair; ~**höhle** *f* armpit; ~**klappe** *f*, ~**stück** *nt* epaulette; ~**zucken** *nt* shrug; **mit einem** ~**zucken with a shrug (of one's shoulders); a~zuckend** *adj* **er stand a~zuckend da** he stood there shrugging his shoulders; **er nahm es a~zuckend zur Kenntnis** he acknowledged it with a shrug of his shoulders.

Achsen-: ~**bruch** *m* broken axle; ~**kreuz** *nt* coordinate system; ~**mächte** *pl (Hist)* Axis powers *pl.*

Achs-: ~**lager** *nt* axle bearing; ~**last** *f* axle weight.

acht[1] *num* eight. **für** *or* **auf** ~ **Tage** for a week; **heute/morgen in** ~ **Tagen** a week today/tomorrow, today/tomorrow week; **heute vor** ~ **Tagen** war ich ... a week ago today I was ...; *siehe* **vier.**

acht[2]**: sich in** ~ **nehmen** to take care, to look out; **etw außer** ~ **lassen** to disregard sth.

Acht[1] *f* **-en** eight; *(beim Eislaufen etc)* figure (of) eight; *siehe* **Vier.**

Acht[2] *f no pl (Hist)* outlawry, proscription.

achtbar *adj (geh)* worthy.

Acht|eck *nt* octagon.

acht|eckig *adj* octagonal, eight-sided.

achtel *adj* eighth; *siehe* **viertel.**

Achtel *nt* - eighth.

Achtelnote *f* quaver, eighth note *(US)*.

achten **1** *vt* to respect. **2** *vi* **auf etw** *(acc)* ~ to pay attention to sth; **auf die Kinder** ~ to keep an eye on the children; **darauf** ~, **daß** ... to see that ..., to take care that ...

ächten *vt (Hist)* to outlaw, to proscribe; *(fig)* to ostracize.

achtenswert *adj Person* worthy; *Bemühungen, Handlung auch* commendable.

achte(r, s) *adj* eighth; *siehe* **vierte(r, s).**

Achte(r) *mf decl as adj* eighth; *siehe* **Vierte(r).**

Achter *m* - *(Rudern)* eight.

Achter-: ~**bahn** *f* big dipper *(Brit)*, roller coaster; ~**deck** *nt (Naut)* afterdeck.

achtfach *adj* eightfold; *siehe* **vierfach.**

achtgeben *vi sep irreg* to take care, to be careful *(auf+acc* of); *(aufmerksam sein)* to pay attention *(auf+acc* to). **auf jdn/etw** ~ *(beaufsichtigen)* to keep an eye on sb/sth, to look after sb/sth.

acht-: ~**hundert** *num* eight hundred; ~**kantig** *adj* **jdn** ~**kantig rausschmeißen** *(col)* to fling sb out on his/her ear *(col)*.

achtlos *adj* careless, thoughtless. **viele gehen** ~ **daran vorbei** many people just pass by without noticing.

Achtlosigkeit *f* carelessness, thoughtlessness.

achtmal *adv* eight times.

achtsam *adj (sorgfältig)* careful. **mit etw** ~ **umgehen** to be careful with sth.

Acht-: ~**stundentag** *m* eight hour day; **a~tägig** *adj* lasting a week, week-long.

Achtung *f no pl* **(a)** ~! watch out!, look out!; *(Mil: Befehl)* attention!; ~, ~! *(your)* attention please!; ~ **Hochspannung!" "danger, high voltage"**; „~ **Stufe!" "mind the step"**; ~, **fertig, los!** ready, steady, go! **(b)** *(Wertschätzung)* respect *(vor+dat* for). **die** ~ **vor sich selbst** one's self-respect; **bei aller** ~ **vor jdm/etw** with all due respect to sb/sth; **jdm** ~ **einflößen** to command *or* gain sb's respect; **sich** *(dat)* ~ **verschaffen** to make oneself respected; **alle** ~! good for you/him *etc!*

Achtung *f no pl (fig: gesellschaftlich)* ostracism.

Achtungserfolg *m* reasonable success.

achtzehn *num* eighteen; *siehe* **vierzehn.**

achtzig *num* eighty. **jdn auf** ~ **bringen** *(col)* to make sb's blood boil *(col)*; **auf** ~ **sein** *(col)* to be livid, to be hopping mad *(col)*; *siehe* **vierzig.**

ächzen *vi* to groan *(vor+dat* with). ~ **und stöhnen** to moan and groan.

Acker *m* ⁼ *(Feld)* field. **den** ~/**die** ~ **bestellen** to till the soil/plough the fields.

Acker-: ~**bau** *m* agriculture, farming; ~**bau betreiben** to farm the land; ~**bau und Viehzucht** farming; ~**furche** *f* furrow; ~**gaul** *m (pej)* farm horse, old nag *(pej)*; ~**gerät** *nt* agricultural implement; ~**krume** *f* topsoil; ~**land** *nt* arable land.

ackern *vi (col)* to slog away *(col)*.

a conto *adv (Comm)* on account.

Action ['ækʃən] *f no pl* action.

ad absurdum *adv* ~ **führen** *Argument etc* to reduce to absurdity.

ad acta *adv:* **etw** ~ **legen** *(fig)* to consider sth finished; *Frage, Problem* to consider sth closed.

Adam *m* **seit** ~**s Zeiten** *(col)* since the year dot *(col)*; **bei** ~ **und Eva anfangen** *(col)* to start right from scratch *(col)* *or* from square one *(col)*.

Adams-: ~**apfel** *m (col)* Adam's apple; ~**kostüm** *nt (col)* **im** ~**kostüm** in one's birthday suit *(col)*.

Adapter *m* - adapter, adaptor.

adäquat *adj (geh) Belohnung, Übersetzung* adequate; *Stellung, Verhalten* suitable; *Kritik* valid. **einer Sache** *(dat)* ~ **sein** to be adequate to sth.

addieren* *vti* to add (up).

Addition *f* addition.

Adel *m no pl (Geschlecht, Stand)* nobility; *(Brit auch)* peerage; *(hoher auch)* aristocracy. **von** ~ **sein** to be a member of the nobility; **er stammt aus altem** ~ he comes from an old aristocratic family; ~ **verpflichtet** noblesse oblige.

adeln *vt (lit, fig)* to ennoble; *(den Titel "Sir" verleihen)* to knight; *(niedrigen Adel verleihen)* to give a title to.

Adels-: ~prädikat *nt* mark of nobility *(in a name)*; ~stand *m* nobility; *(Brit auch)* peerage; *(hoher auch)* aristocracy; in den ~stand erheben siehe **adeln**; ~titel *m* title.

Ader *f* -n vein; *(fig: Veranlagung)* bent. **eine ~ für etw haben** to have feeling for sth; **eine poetische/musikalische ~ haben** to have a feeling for poetry/music, to have a poetic/musical bent; **jdn zur ~ lassen** *(old, fig col)* to bleed sb.

Adhäsion *f (Phys)* adhesion.

Adhäsionsverschluß *m* adhesive seal.

ad hoc *adv (geh)* ad hoc.

Adjektiv *nt* adjective.

Adjutant *m* adjutant; *(von General)* aide(-de-camp).

Adler *m* - eagle.

Adler-: ~auge *nt (fig)* ~augen haben to have eyes like a hawk, to be eagle-eyed; ~blick *m (fig)* eagle eye; ~horst *m* eyrie.

adlig *adj (lit, fig)* noble. ~ **sein** to belong to the aristocracy.

Adlige(r) *mf decl as adj* member of the nobility, nobleman/woman; *(Brit auch)* peer/peeress; *(hoher auch)* aristocrat.

Administration *f* administration.

administrativ *adj* administrative.

Admiral *m, pl* -e *or* **Admiräle (a)** admiral. **(b)** *(Zool)* red admiral.

Admiralität *f* **(a)** *(die Admirale)* admirals *pl.* **(b)** *(Marineleitung)* admiralty.

adoptieren* *vt* to adopt.

Adoption *f* adoption.

Adoptiv-: ~eltern *pl* adoptive parents *pl;* ~kind *nt* adopted child.

Adrenalin *nt no pl* adrenalin.

Adreßbuch *nt* directory; *(privat)* address book.

Adresse *f* -n *(Anschrift, Comp)* address. **eine Warnung an jds ~ (acc) richten** *(fig)* to address a warning to sb; **dieser Vorwurf geht an Ihre ~** this reproach is directed at *or* addressed to you (personally); **an der falschen ~ sein** *(col)* to have gone/come to the wrong person.

adressieren* *vt* to address *(an +acc* to).

adrett *adj (dated)* neat.

Adria *f* Adriatic (Sea).

Adriatisches Meer *nt (form)* Adriatic Sea.

Advent [at'vɛnt] *m* -e Advent. **erster/vierter ~** first/fourth Sunday in Advent.

Advents-: ~kalender *m* Advent calendar; ~kranz *m* Advent wreath; ~sonntag *m* Sunday in Advent; ~zeit *f* Advent.

Adverb [at'vɛrp] *nt* -(i)en adverb.

Advokat [atvo'kaːt] *m (wk)* -en, -en *(old Jur, fig)* advocate.

Aerobic *nt* aerobics sing.

Aero-: ~dynamik *f* aerodynamics; a~dynamisch *adj* aerodynamic.

Affäre *f* -n **(a)** *(Angelegenheit)* affair, business *no pl; (Liebesabenteuer)* affair. **in eine ~ verwickelt sein** to be mixed up in *or* involved in an affair; **sich aus der ~ ziehen** *(col)* to get (oneself) out of it. **(b)** *(Zwischenfall)* incident, episode.

Affe *m (wk)* -n, -n **(a)** *(Menschen~)* ape. **der Mensch stammt vom ~n ab** man is descended from the apes; **klettern wie ein ~ to** climb like a monkey; **einen ~n haben** *(col)* to have had one over the eight *(col).* **(b)** *(col: Kerl)* clown, berk *(Brit col).*

Affekt *m* -e emotion, affect *(form).* **im ~ handeln** to act in the heat of the moment.

Affekthandlung *f* act committed under emotional stress.

affektiert *adj (pej)* affected. **sich ~ benehmen** to be affected, to behave affectedly.

Affektiertheit *f* affectation, affectedness.

Affen-: a~artig *adj* like a monkey; *(wie ein Menschenaffe)* apelike; **mit a~artiger Geschwindigkeit** *(col)* like greased lightning *(col)*, in a flash

(col); ~haus *nt* ape house; ~hitze *f (col)* sweltering heat; ~käfig *m* monkey's/ape's cage; ~liebe *f* blind adoration *(zu* of); ~schande *f (col)* crying shame *(col);* ~tempo *nt (col)* in *or* mit einem ~tempo at breakneck speed *(col); (laufen auch)* like the clappers *(col);* ~theater *nt (col)* carry-on *(col),* fuss; **ein ~theater aufführen** to make a fuss; ~zahn *m (col)* siehe ~tempo.

affig *adj (col) (eitel)* stuck-up *(col),* conceited; *(geziert)* affected; *(lächerlich)* ridiculous, ludicrous.

Äffin *f* female monkey/ape.

Affront [a'frõː] *m* -s *(geh)* affront, insult *(gegen* to).

Afghane *m (wk)* -n, -n, **Afghanin** *f* Afghan.

afghanisch *adj* Afghan. ~er Windhund Afghan (hound).

Afghanistan *nt* Afghanistan.

Afrika *nt* Africa.

Afrikaans *nt* Afrikaans.

Afrikaner(in *f)* *m* - African.

afrikanisch *adj* African.

Afro-: ~-Amerikaner *m* Afro-American; ~-Asiat *m* Afro-Asian; ~-Look *m* Afro-look.

After *m -* *(form)* anus.

AG [aː'geː] *f* -s = **Aktiengesellschaft** (public) limited company, plc *(Brit),* corporation, inc. *(US).*

Ägäis [ɛ'gɛːɪs] *f* Aegean (Sea).

ägäisch [ɛ'gɛːɪʃ] *adj* Ä~es Meer Aegean Sea.

Agent *m* agent.

Agenten-: ~ring *m* spy ring; ~tätigkeit *f* espionage; **ihre ~tätigkeit** her activity as an agent.

Agentur *f* agency.

Agenturbericht *m* (news) agency report.

Aggregat *nt (Geol)* aggregate; *(Tech)* unit, set of machines.

Aggregatzustand *m* state.

Aggression *f* aggression *(gegen* towards). ~en gegen jdn empfinden to feel aggressive *or* aggression towards sb.

Aggressions-: a~geladen *adj* charged with aggression; ~trieb *m (Psych)* aggressive impulse.

aggressiv *adj* aggressive.

Aggressivität *f* aggression, aggressiveness.

Aggressor *m* aggressor.

agieren* *vi* to operate, to act; *(Theat)* to act. **als jd ~** *(Theat)* to act or play the part of sb.

agil *adj (körperlich)* agile, nimble. **(geistig) ~** sharp, mentally agile.

Agitation *f (Pol)* agitation. ~ **treiben** to agitate.

Agitator *(in f)* [-'toːrɪn] *m (Pol)* agitator.

agitatorisch *adj (Pol)* Rede inflammatory, agitating *attr.*

agitieren* *vi* to agitate.

agnostisch *adj* agnostic.

Agonie *f (lit, fig geh)* death throes *pl.* **in (der) ~ liegen** to be in the throes of death.

Agrar-: ~land *nt* agrarian country; ~politik *f* agricultural policy.

Ägypten *nt* Egypt.

Ägypter(in *f)* *m -* Egyptian.

ägyptisch *adj* Egyptian.

ah [aː] ah, oh.

äh [ɛ] *interj (beim Sprechen)* er, um; *(Ausdruck des Ekels)* ugh.

aha *interj* aha; *(verstehend auch)* I see.

Aha-Erlebnis *nt* sudden insight.

Ahn *m (wk)* -en, -en *(geh)* ancestor, for(e)father *(liter).*

ahnden *vt (geh)* Freveltat, Verbrechen to avenge; Übertretung, Verstoß to punish.

Ahndung *f siehe* vt avenging; punishment.

Ahne *f* -n *(geh: weiblicher Vorfahr)* ancestress.

ähneln *vi* +*dat* to resemble. **sich** *or* **einander** *(geh)* ~ to resemble one another; **in diesem Punkt ähnelt sie sehr ihrem Vater** she's very like her father in this respect.

ahnen vt (voraussehen) to foresee, to know; Gefahr, Tod etc to have a presentiment or premonition of; (vermuten) to suspect; (erraten) to guess. **das kann ich doch nicht ~!** how am I expected to know that!; **nichts Böses ~** to be unsuspecting; **nichts Böses ~d** unsuspectingly; **ohne es zu ~** without suspecting; **davon habe ich nichts geahnt** I didn't have the slightest inkling of it.

Ahnen-: ~**forschung** f genealogy; ~**galerie** f ancestral portrait gallery; ~**reihe** f ancestral line.

Ahn-: ~**frau** f (liter) ancestress; ~**herr** m (liter) ancestor.

ähnlich adj similar (+dat to). **ein dem Rokoko ~er Stil** a style similar to rococo, a similar style to rococo; **~ wie er/sie** like him/her; **sie sind sich ~** they are similar or alike; **ein ~ aussehender Gegenstand** a similar-looking object; **ich denke ~** I think likewise; **jdm ~ sehen** to be like sb, to resemble sb; **das sieht ihm (ganz) ~!** (col) that's just like him!, that's him all over! (col); **(etwas) Ä~es** something similar, something like it/that. **A~es** something similar, something like it/that.

Ähnlichkeit f similarity (mit to). **mit jdm/etw ~ haben** to resemble sb/sth, to be like sb/sth.

Ahnung f (a) (Vorgefühl) hunch, presentiment; (düster) foreboding, premonition. (b) (Vorstellung, Wissen) idea; (Vermutung) suspicion. **keine ~!** (col) no idea! (col), I haven't a clue! (col); **er hat keine blasse** or **nicht die geringste ~** he hasn't the faintest idea (col); **ich hatte keine ~, daß ...** I had no idea that ...; **hast du eine ~, wo er sein könnte?** have you any idea where he could be?; **du hast keine ~, wie schwierig das ist** you have no idea how difficult it is; **hast du eine ~!** (iro col) a (fat) lot you know (about it)! (col).

Ahnungs-: **a~los** adj (nichtsahnend) unsuspecting; (unwissend) clueless (col); ~**losigkeit** f (Unwissenheit) ignorance; **a~voll** adj (geh) full of presentiment or (Böses ahnend) foreboding.

ahoi [a'hɔy] interj (Naut) **Schiff ~!** ship ahoy!

Ahorn m -e maple.

Ahornblatt nt maple leaf.

Ähre f -n ear; (allgemeiner, Gras~) head.

Aids [eɪts, eɪdz] nt -, no pl AIDS.

Airbus ['ɛːrbʊs] m (Aviat) airbus.

ais, Ais ['aɪs] nt - A sharp.

Akademie f academy; (Fachschule) college.

Akademiker(in f) m - person with a university education; (Student) (university) student; (Hochschulabsolvent) (university) graduate; (Universitätslehrkraft) academic.

akademisch adj (lit, fig) academic. **das ~e Proletariat** (the) jobless graduates pl; **~ gebildet sein** to have (had) a university education.

Akazie [-iə] f acacia.

Akelei f columbine.

Akklamation f (form) **Wahl per** or **durch ~** election by acclamation.

akklimatisieren vr (lit, fig) to become acclimatized (in+dat to).

Akkord m -e (a) (Mus) chord. (b) (Stücklohn) piece rate. **im ~ arbeiten** to do piecework.

Akkord-: ~**arbeit** f piecework; ~**arbeiter** m piece-worker.

Akkordeon [-ɔn] nt -s accordion.

Akkord-: ~**lohn** m piece wages pl, piece rate; ~**zuschlag** m piece rate bonus.

akkreditieren vt (Pol) to accredit (bei to, at).

Akkreditierung f (Pol) accrediting, accreditation (bei to, at).

Akku ['aku] m -s (col) = Akkumulator.

Akkumulation f accumulation.

Akkumulator m accumulator.

akkumulieren vtir to accumulate.

akkurat adj precise; (sorgfältig auch) meticulous.

Akkusativ m accusative.

Akkusativ|objekt nt accusative or direct object.

Akne f -n acne.

Akontozahlung f payment on account.

Akquisition [akvizitsi'oːn] f (old) acquisition; (Comm) canvassing.

Akribie f no pl (geh) meticulousness.

akribisch adj (geh) meticulous, precise.

Akrobat(in f) m (wk) -en, -en acrobat.

Akrobatik f no pl acrobatics pl.

akrobatisch adj acrobatic.

Akt m -e (a) (Tat) act; (Zeremonie) ceremony. (b) (Theat, Zirkus~) act. (c) (Art: ~bild) nude. (d) (Geschlechts~) sexual act, coitus no art (form).

Akt|aufnahme n nude (photograph).

Akte f -n file, record. **die ~ Schmidt** the Schmidt file; **das kommt in die ~n** this goes on file or record; **etw zu den ~n legen** to put sth on file.

Akten-: ~**deckel** m folder; ~**koffer** m attaché case; **a~kundig** adj on record; ~**mappe** f (a) (Umschlag) folder, file; (b) siehe ~**tasche**; ~**notiz** f memo(randum); ~**ordner** m file; ~**schrank** m filing cabinet; ~**tasche** f briefcase, portfolio; ~**zeichen** nt reference.

Aktfoto nt nude (photograph).

Aktie ['aktsjə] f share; (~nschein) share certificate. ~**n** shares, stock sing; **die ~n fallen/steigen** share prices are falling/rising; **die ~n stehen gut** shares are buoyant; **wie stehen die ~n?** (hum col) how are things?

Aktien-: ~**besitz** m shareholdings pl; ~**gesellschaft** f joint-stock company; ~**kapital** nt share capital; ~**kurs** m share price; ~**markt** m stock market.

Aktion f (Handlung) action (auch Mil); (Kampagne) campaign; (geplantes Unternehmen, Einsatz) operation (auch Mil). **in ~** in action.

Aktionär(in f) m shareholder, stockholder (esp US).

Aktionärsversammlung f shareholders' meeting.

Aktions-: ~**einheit** f (Pol) working unity; **a~fähig** adj capable of action; ~**radius** m (Aviat, Naut) range; (fig: Wirkungsbereich) scope.

aktiv adj active; (Econ) Bilanz positive; (Mil) Soldat etc on active service. **sich ~ an etw** (dat) **beteiligen** to take an active part in sth.

Aktiv nt (Gram) active.

Aktiva pl assets. ~ **und Passiva** assets and liabilities.

Aktive(r) mf decl as adj (Sport) active participant.

aktivieren [akti'viːrən] vt to activate; (fig) Arbeit, Kampagne to step up; Mitarbeiter to get moving.

Aktivist(in f) m activist.

Aktivität f activity.

Aktiv-: ~**posten** m (lit, fig) asset; ~**seite** f assets side.

Aktmodell nt nude model.

aktualisieren vt to make topical.

Aktualität f relevance (to the current situation), topicality. ~**en** pl (geh: neueste Ereignisse) current events.

aktuell adj relevant (to the current situation), Frage auch topical; Buch, Film auch of topical interest; Problem, Theorie current; (Fashion: modern) Mode latest attr, current. **von ~em Interesse** of topical interest/~**er Bedeutung** of topical interest/of relevance to the present situation; **dieses Problem ist nicht mehr ~** this is no longer a problem; **eine ~e Sendung** (Rad, TV) a current-affairs programme.

Aktzeichnung f nude (drawing).

Akupunktur f acupuncture.

Akustik f no pl acoustics pl.

akustisch adj acoustic. **ich habe dich rein ~ nicht verstanden** I simply didn't catch what you said (properly).

akut adj (Med, fig) acute; Frage auch pressing.

Akzent m -e accent; (Betonung) stress. **den ~ auf etw** (acc) **legen** (lit) to stress sth. ~**e setzen** (fig) to bring out or emphasize the main points.

akzentfrei adj without an accent.
akzentuieren* vt to articulate, to enunciate; *(betonen)* to stress; *(fig: hervorheben)* to accentuate.
Akzentverschiebung f *(fig)* shift of emphasis.
akzeptabel adj acceptable.
akzeptieren* vt to accept.
Akzeptierung f acceptance.
à la [a la] adv à la.
Alabaster m - alabaster.
Alarm m -e *(Warnung)* alarm; *(Flieger~)* air-raid warning; *(Zustand)* alert. **~! fire!** etc; **~ schlagen** to give or raise the alarm.
Alarm-: **~anlage** f alarm system; **a~bereit** adj on the alert; **~bereitschaft** f alert; **in ~bereitschaft sein** or **stehen** to be on the alert; **in ~bereitschaft versetzen** to put on the alert, to alert; **~glocke** f alarm bell.
alarmieren* vt Polizei etc to alert; *(fig: beunruhigen)* to alarm. **~d** *(fig)* alarming.
Alarm-: **~ruf** m warning cry; **~signal** nt alarm signal; **~stufe** f alert stage; **~übung** f practice exercise or drill; **~zustand** m alert; **im ~zustand sein** to be on the alert.
Alaska nt Alaska.
Albaner(in f) m - Albanian.
Albanien [-iən] nt Albania.
albanisch adj Albanian.
Alben pl of **Album**.
albern adj silly. **sich ~ benehmen** to act silly; **~es Zeug** (silly) nonsense.
Albernheit f **(a)** no pl silliness, foolishness. **(b)** *(Tat)* silly prank; *(Bemerkung)* inanity.
Album nt, pl **Alben** album.
alert adj *(geh)* vivacious, lively.
Alge f -n alga.
Algebra f no pl algebra.
Algerien [-iən] nt Algeria.
Algerier(in f) [-iɐ, -iərin] m - Algerian.
algerisch adj Algerian.
alias adv alias, also or otherwise known as.
Alibi nt -s *(Jur, fig)* alibi.
Alimente pl maintenance sing.
Alkohol ['alkoho:l, alko'ho:l] m -e alcohol; *(Getränke auch)* drink. **seinen Kummer im ~ ertränken** to drown one's sorrows; **unter ~ stehen** to be under the influence (of alcohol or drink).
Alkohol-: **a~arm** adj low in alcohol; **~ausschank** m sale of alcohol; **~einfluß** m **unter ~einfluß** under the influence of alcohol or drink; **a~frei** adj non-alcoholic; *Getränk auch* soft; **~gehalt** m alcohol(ic) content; **~genuß** m consumption of alcohol; **a~haltig** adj alcoholic.
Alkoholiker(in f) m - alcoholic.
alkoholisch adj alcoholic.
Alkoholismus m alcoholism.
Alkohol-: **~konsum** m consumption of alcohol; **~spiegel** m jds **~spiegel** the level of alcohol in sb's blood; **~steuer** f duty or tax on alcohol; **~sünder** m *(col)* drunk(en) driver; **~verbot** nt ban on alcohol; **der Arzt hat ihm ~verbot verordnet** the doctor told him not to touch alcohol; **~vergiftung** f alcohol(ic) poisoning.
all indef pron **all mein/sein Geld** all my/his money.
All nt no pl *(Sci, Space)* space no art; *(außerhalb unseres Sternsystems)* outer space no art; *(liter, geh)* universe. **Spaziergang im ~** space walk.
alle 1 pron siehe **alle(r, s)**. 2 adv *(col)* all gone. **die Milch ist ~** the milk's all gone, there's no milk left; **etw ~ machen** to finish sth off.
alledem pron **bei/trotz** etc **~** with/in spite of etc all that; **von ~ stimmt kein Wort** there's not a word of truth in any of it; **zu ~** moreover.
Allee f -n [-eːən] avenue.
Allegorie f allegory.
allegorisch adj allegorical.
allein 1 adj pred alone; *Gegenstand, Wort auch* by itself, on its own; *(ohne Begleitung, Hilfe auch)* by oneself, on one's own; *(einsam)* lonely. **von ~**

by oneself/itself; **ganz ~** *(einsam)* all alone; *(ohne Begleitung, Hilfe)* all by oneself, all on one's own. 2 adv *(nur)* alone. **das ist ~ seine Verantwortung** that is his responsibility alone; **~ schon der Gedanke** the very or mere thought ...; **der Gedanke ~** the thought alone ...; **das Porto ~ kostet ...** the postage alone costs ..., just the postage is ...
Allein-: **~erbe** m sole or only heir; **~gang** m *(col)* *(Sport)* solo run; *(von Bergsteiger)* solo climb; *(fig: Tat)* solo effort; **etw im ~gang machen** *(fig)* to do sth on one's own; **~herrscher** m autocrat, absolute dictator.
alleinig adj attr sole, only.
Allein-: **~sein** nt being on one's own no def art, solitude; *(Einsamkeit)* loneliness; **a~stehend** adj living alone; **~stehende(r)** mf decl as adj single person; **~unterhalter** m solo entertainer; **~vertretung** f *(Comm)* sole agency.
allemal adv *(ohne Schwierigkeit)* without any problem or trouble. **was er kann, kann ich noch ~** anything he can do I can do too; **ein für ~** once and for all.
allenfalls adv *(nötigenfalls)* if need be; *(höchstens)* at most; *(bestenfalls)* at best.
alle(r, s) 1 indef pron **(a)** attr all; *(bestimmte Menge, Anzahl)* all the. **~ Kinder unter 10 Jahren** all children under 10; **im Geschäft war ~s Brot ausverkauft** all the bread in the shop was sold out; **wir haben ~n Haß vergessen** we have forgotten all (our or the) hatred; **~ Anwesenden** all those present; **mit ~m Nachdruck** with every emphasis; **trotz ~r Mühe** in spite of every effort; **ohne ~n Grund** without any reason, with no reason at all; **mit ~r Deutlichkeit** quite distinctly; **in ~r Unschuld** in all innocence; **ohne ~n Zweifel** without any doubt.
(b) *(substantivisch)* **~s** sing everything; **~** pl all; *(alle Menschen)* all, everybody, everyone; **~s, was ...** all or everything that/everybody or everyone who ...; **das ~s** all that; **~s Schöne** everything beautiful; **~s Gute** all the best; **~s und jedes** anything and everything; **in ~m** *(in jeder Beziehung)* in everything; **~s in ~m** all in all; **trotz ~m** in spite of everything; **vor ~m** above all; **das ist ~s, das wäre ~s** that's all, that's it *(col)*; **das ist ~s andere als ...** that's anything but ...; **das geht dich doch ~s nichts an!** none of (all) that has anything to do with you!; **es hat ~s keinen Sinn mehr** nothing makes sense any more; **was habt ihr ~s gemacht?** what did you get up to?; **wer war ~s da?** who was there?; **was er (nicht) ~s weiß!** the things he knows!; **die haben mir ~ nicht gefallen** I didn't like any of them; **~ beide/drei** both of them/all three of them; **~ diejenigen, die ...** all (those) who ...; **diese ~** all (of) these; **der Kampf ~r gegen ~** the free-for-all; **~ für einen und einer für ~** all for one and one for all; **sie kamen ~** they all came, all of them came; **sie haben ~ kein Geld mehr** none of them has any money left.
(c) *(mit Zeit-, Maßangaben)* usu pl every. **~ fünf Minuten/fünf Meter** every five minutes/ five metres; **~ Jahre wieder** year after year. 2 adv siehe **alle**.
aller-: **~beste(r, s)** adj very best, best ... of all; **ich wünsche Dir das A~beste** (I wish you) all the best; **der/die/das A~beste** the very best/the best of all; **~dings** adv **(a)** *(einschränkend)* though, mind you; **das ist ~dings wahr, aber ...** that may be true, but ...; **(b)** *(bekräftigend)* certainly; **~erste(r, s)** adj very first; **~frühestens** adv at the very earliest.
Allergie f *(Med, fig)* allergy. **eine ~ gegen etw haben** to be allergic to sth *(auch fig hum)*; *(fig auch)* to have an aversion to sth.
allergisch adj *(Med, fig)* allergic *(gegen* to). **auf etw** *(acc)* **~ reagieren** to be allergic to sth.
Aller-: **a~hand** adj inv *(substantivisch)* *(allerlei)* all

kinds of things; *(ziemlich viel)* rather a lot; *(attributiv)* all kinds *or* sorts of; rather a lot of; **das ist ja a~hand!** *(zustimmend)* that's quite something!, not bad at all! *(col); (empört)* that's too much! **~heiligen** *nt* All Saints' Day; **a~höchste(r, s)** *adj* **von a~höchster Stelle** from the very highest authority; **es wird a~höchste Zeit, daß ...** it's really high time that ...; **a~höchstens** *adv* at the very most; **a~lei** *adj inv (substantivisch)* all sorts *or* kinds of things; *(attributiv)* all sorts *or* kinds of; **a~letzte(r, s)** *adj* very last; *(a~neueste)* very latest; *(col: unmöglich)* most awful *attr (col)*; **der/das ist das ~letzte** *(col)* he's/it's the absolute end! *(col)*; **~liebste(r, s)** *adj* **es wäre mir das a~liebste** *or* **am a~liebsten, wenn ...** I would much prefer it if ...; **a~meiste(r, s)** *adj* most ... of all; **die ~meisten** the vast majority; **a~nächste(r, s)** *adj (in Folge)* very next; *(räumlich)* nearest; *Verwandte* very closest; **in a~nächster Zeit** in the very near future; **a~neu(e)ste(r, s)** *adj* very latest; **a~seits** *adv* on all sides, on every side; **guten Abend a~seits!** good evening everybody; **a~spätestens** *adv* at the very latest.

Allerwelts- in *cpds (Durchschnitts-)* common; *(nichtssagend)* commonplace; **~kerl** *m* Jack of all trades.

Aller-: **a~wenigstens** *adv* at the very least; **a~wenigste(r, s)** *adj* least ... of all; *(pl)* fewest ... of all; *(äußerst wenig)* very little; *(pl)* very few; **die a~wenigsten Menschen wissen das** very few people know that; **das ist doch das ~wenigste, was man erwarten könnte** but that's the very least one could expect; **das am a~wenigsten!** least of all that!; **~werteste(r)** *m decl as adj (hum)* posterior *(hum)*.

alles *indef pron siehe* **alle(r, s)**.

allesamt *adv* all (of them/us *etc*). **ihr seid ~ Betrüger!** you're all cheats!

Alles-: **~fresser** *m* omnivore; **~kleber** *m* all-purpose adhesive; **~wisser** *m* - *(iro)* know-all *(col)*, know-it-all *(US col)*.

allgegenwärtig *adj* omnipresent, ubiquitous.

allgemein 1 *adj* general; *Feiertag* public; *Wahlrecht* universal; *Wehrpflicht* compulsory. **im ~en** in general, generally; **im ~en Interesse** in the common interest; **auf ~en Wunsch** by popular request; **die ~e Meinung** the general opinion; **zur ~en Überraschung** to everyone's surprise. **2** *adv* generally; *(ausnahmslos von allen)* universally; *(nicht spezifisch)* in general terms. **es ist ~ bekannt** it's common knowledge; **es ist ~ üblich** it's the general rule; **~ verbreitet** widespread; **~ zugänglich** open to all.

Allgemein-: **~bildung** *f* general *or* all-round education; **a~gültig** *adj attr* general, universal; **~heit** *f (no pl: Öffentlichkeit)* general public; *(alle)* everyone, everybody; **~medizin** *f* general medicine; **Arzt für ~medizin** general practitioner, GP; **a~verständlich** *adj no pred* generally intelligible; **~wohl** *nt* public good *or* welfare.

Allheilmittel *nt* cure-all, panacea *(esp fig)*.

Allianz *f* alliance.

Alliierte(r) *mf decl as adj* ally. **die ~n** *(im 2. Weltkrieg)* the Allies.

Alliteration *f (Poet)* alliteration.

All-: **a~jährlich** *adj* annual, yearly; **~macht** *f (esp von Gott)* omnipotence; **a~mächtig** *adj* all-powerful, omnipotent; **~mächtige(r)** *m decl as adj (Gott)* **der ~mächtige** Almighty God, the Almighty; **~mächtiger! good Lord!**

allmählich 1 *adj attr* gradual. **2** *adv* gradually; *(col: endlich)* at last. **es wird ~ Zeit** *(col)* it's about time; **ich werde (ganz) ~ müde** *(col)* I'm beginning to get tired; **hoffentlich kommst du ~!** *(col)* are you coming at last?; **wir sollten ~ gehen** *(col)* shall we think about going?

allmonatlich *adj* monthly.

Allotria *nt no pl (col) (Unfug)* monkey business *(col) no indef art; (Lärm)* racket *(col)*, din.

Allrad|antrieb *m* all-wheel drive.

allseitig *adj (allgemein)* general; *(ausnahmslos)* universal; *(vielseitig)* all-round *attr.* **~ begabt sein** to be an all-rounder; **zur ~en Zufriedenheit** to the satisfaction of all *or* everyone.

allseits *adv (überall)* everywhere, on all sides; *(in jeder Beziehung)* in every respect.

Alltag *m (fig)* everyday life. **der ~ der Ehe** the mundane *or* day-to-day side of married life.

alltäglich *adj* **(a)** *(tagtäglich)* daily. **(b)** *(üblich)* everyday *attr*, ordinary; *Gesicht, Mensch* ordinary; **es ist ganz ~** it's nothing unusual.

all|umfassend *adj* all-embracing, global.

Allüren *pl* odd behaviour *(Brit) or* behavior *(US)*; *(geziertes Verhalten)* affectations *pl*; *(eines Stars etc)* airs and graces *pl*.

all-: **~wissend** *adj* omniscient; **A~wissenheit** *f* omniscience; **~wöchentlich** *adj* weekly; **~zeit** *adv (geh)* always.

allzu *adv* all too; *(+neg)* too. **~ viele Fehler** far too many mistakes.

allzu-: **~gern** *adv* **mögen** only too much; *(bereitwillig)* only too willingly; **nicht ~gern** not all that much/willingly, not too much/willingly; **er ißt Muscheln nur ~gern** he's only too fond of mussels; **~sehr** *adv* too much; **mögen** all too much; **sich freuen** only too; **versuchen** too hard; **sich ärgern, enttäuscht sein** *or:* **nicht ~sehr mögen/enttäuscht sein** not to like too much/not to be too disappointed; **~viel** *adv* too much; **~viel ist ungesund** *(Prov)* you can have too much of a good thing *(prov)*.

Allzweck- in *cpds* all-purpose.

Alm *f* **-en** alpine pasture.

Almosen [-o:-] *nt* - *(geh: Spende)* alms *pl (old)*. **~** *pl (fig)* charity.

Alpdruck *m (lit, fig)* nightmare. **wie ein ~druck auf jdm lasten** to weigh sb down, to oppress sb.

Alpen *pl* **die ~** the Alps *pl*.

Alpen-: **~glühen** *nt* - alpenglow; **~paß** *m* alpine pass; **~rose** *f* Alpine rose; **~veilchen** *nt* cyclamen; **~vorland** *nt* foothills *pl* of the Alps.

Alphabet *nt* **-e** alphabet. **nach dem ~** alphabetically, in alphabetical order.

alphabetisch *adj* alphabetical. **~ geordnet** arranged in alphabetical order.

alphabetisieren* *vt* to make literate.

Alphastrahlen *pl* alpha rays *pl*.

Alphorn *nt* alp(en)horn.

alpin *adj* alpine.

Alpinist(in) *f) m* alpinist.

Alptraum *m (lit, fig)* nightmare.

als *conj* **(a)** *(nach comp)* than. **ich kam später ~ er** I came later than he (did) *or* him.

(b) *(bei Vergleichen)* so viel/soweit **~** möglich as much/far as possible; **nichts/niemand/nirgend anders ~** nothing/nobody/nowhere but; **eher** *or* **lieber ... ~** rather ... than; **anders sein ~** to be different from; **das machen wir anders ~ ihr** we do it differently from you; **alles andere ~** anything but.

(c) **es sieht aus, ~ würde es bald schneien** it looks as if *or* though it will snow soon; **~ ob ich das nicht wüßte!** as if I didn't know!

(d) **sie ist zu alt, ~ daß sie das noch verstehen könnte** she is too old to understand; **die Zeit war zu knapp, ~ daß wir ...** the time was too short for us to ...

(e) *(in Temporalsätzen)* when; *(gleichzeitig)* as. **damals, ~** (in the days) when; **gerade, ~** just as.

(f) *(in der Eigenschaft)* as. **~ Beweis** as proof; **~ Antwort/Warnung** as an answer/a warning; **sich ~ wahr/falsch erweisen** to prove to be true/false; **~ Kind/Mädchen** *etc* as a child/girl *etc*.

also 1 *conj (folglich)* so, therefore. **2** *adv* so; *(nach*

Unterbrechung anknüpfend) well; (zusammen-fassend, erklärend) that is. ~ **doch** so ... after all; **du machst es** ~? so you'll do it then?; ~ **wie ich schon sagte** well (then), as I said before. **3** interj well. **na** ~! there you are!, you see?; ~ gut or schön well all right then; ~ so was/so **eine Frechheit!** well (I never)/what a cheek!

alt adj, comp ⁼er, superl ⁼este(r, s) or (adv) am ⁼esten (a) old; (sehr ~) Sage, Aberglaube auch, Griechen, Geschichte ancient; Sprachen classical. **das ~e Rom** ancient Rome; **das A~e Testament** the Old Testament; **die A~ Welt** the Old World; ~ **und jung** (everybody) old and young; **ein drei Jahre ~es Kind** a three-year-old child; **wie ~ bist du?** how old are you? etw ~ **kaufen** to buy sth second-hand; **ich werde heute nicht ~ (wer-den)** (col) I won't last long today/tonight etc (col); ~**e Liebe rostet nicht** (Prov) true love never dies (prov). **(b)** (dieselbe, gewohnt) same old. **sie ist ganz die ~e (Ingrid)** she's the same old Ingrid; **er ist nicht mehr der ~e** he's not what he was or the man he was; **alles beim ~en las-sen** to leave everything as it was.

Alt m -e (Mus) alto; (von Frau auch) contralto.
Altar m, pl Altäre altar.
Alt-: a~**backen** adj (fig) Mensch, Ansichten old-fashioned; ~**bau** m old building; ~**bauwohnung** f old flat; a~**bekannt** adj well-known; a~**bewährt** adj Methode etc well-tried; Tradition etc long-standing; ~**bier** nt top-fermented German dark beer; ~**bundeskanzler** m former German/ Austrian Chancellor; a~**deutsch** adj old Ger-man; Möbel, Stil German Renaissance.
Alte siehe **Alte(r), Alte(s).**
Alt-: a~**ehrwürdig** adj venerable; Bräuche time-honoured (Brit), time-honored (US); a~**ein-gesessen** adj old-established; ~**eisen** nt scrap metal.
Alten-: ~**heim** nt old people's home; ~**pfleger** m old people's nurse; ~**tagesstätte** f old people's day home; ~**teil** nt sich aufs ~**teil setzen** or **zurückziehen** (fig) to retire from public life.
Alte(r) mf decl as adj (alter Mann, col: Ehemann, Vater) old man; (alte Frau, col: Ehefrau, Mutter) old woman; (col: Vorgesetzter) boss. **die ~n** (Eltern) the folk(s) pl (col); (Tiereltern) the parents pl; (ältere Generation) the old people pl or folk pl.
Alter nt - age; (letzter Lebensabschnitt) old age. **im** ~ in one's old age; **in deinem** ~ at your age; **er ist in deinem** ~ he's your age; **im** ~ **von 18 Jahren** at the age of 18; **45, das ist doch kein** ~ (col) 45, that's no age at all.
älter adj (a) comp of **alt** older; Bruder, Tochter etc auch elder. **werden Frauen ~ als Männer?** do women live longer than men?; **Holbein der A~e** Holbein the Elder. **(b)** attr (nicht ganz jung) elderly.
altern vi aux sein to age; (Mensch auch) to get older; (Wein) to mature.
alternativ adj (geh) alternative.
Alternativ- in cpds alternative.
Alternative f alternative (etw zu tun of doing sth).
alternierend adj alternate; Strom, Verse alternating.
alt|erprobt adj well-tried.
alters adv (geh): **von** or **seit** ~ (her) from time immemorial.
Alters-: a~**bedingt** adj related to a particular age; related to or caused by old age; ~**erschei-nung** f age or old age; ~**forschung** f gerontol-ogy; ~**fürsorge** f care of the elderly; ~**genosse** m contemporary; ~**grenze** f age limit; (Renten-alter) retirement age; ~**gründe** pl aus ~**grün-den** for reasons of age pl; ~**gruppe** f age-group; ~**heim** nt old people's home; ~**klasse** f (Sport) age-group; ~**präsident** m president by seniority; ~**prozeß** m ageing process; ~**rente** f old age pension; ~**ruhegeld** nt retirement ben-

efit; **a~s** chwach adj Mensch old and infirm; Au-to, Möbel decrepit; ~**schwäche** f siehe adj infir-mity; decrepitude; ~**sitz** m sein ~**sitz war Mün-chen** he spent his retirement in Munich; ~**stufe** f age group; (Lebensabschnitt) age; ~**werk** nt later works pl.
Altertum nt no pl antiquity no art.
Altertümer pl antiquities pl.
altertümlich adj (aus dem Altertum) ancient; (altehrwürdig) old-world; (altmodisch) old-fashioned no adv; (veraltet) antiquated.
Altertums-: ~**forscher** m archeologist; ~**for-schung** f archeology; ~**wert** m: **das hat schon** ~**wert** (hum) it has antique value (hum).
Alte(s) nt decl as adj das ~ (das Gewohnte, Tradi-tionelle) the old; (alte Dinge) old things pl; **er hängt sehr am** ~**n** he clings to the past.
Älteste(r) mf decl as adj oldest; (Sohn, Tochter auch) eldest.
älteste(r, s) adj superl of **alt** oldest; Bruder etc auch eldest.
Alt-: ~**griechisch(e)** nt classical Greek; a~**hergebracht** adj traditional; ~**herrenmann-schaft** f (Sport) team of players over thirty; ~**hoch-deutsch(e)** nt Old High German.
Altist(in f) m (Mus) alto.
alt-: ~**jüngferlich** adj old-maidish; ~**klug** adj pre-cocious; A~**klugheit** f precociousness.
ältlich adj oldish.
Alt-: ~**material** nt scrap; ~**meister** m doyen; (Sport) ex-champion; ~**metall** nt scrap metal; a~**modisch** adj old-fashioned; (rückständig) out-moded; ~**papier** nt wastepaper; ~**philologie** f classical philology; a~**rosa** adj old rose; ~**schlüssel** m (Mus) alto clef; ~**schnee** m old snow; ~**stadt** f old town; **die Ulmer** ~**stadt** the old part of Ulm; ~**steinzeit** f Palaeolithic Age, Old Stone Age; ~**stimme** f (Mus) alto (von Frau auch) contralto; a~**testamentarisch** adj Old Tes-tament attr; a~**väterlich** adj Bräuche ancestral; (altmodisch) old-fashioned no adv; Erscheinung etc patriarchal; ~**waren** pl second-hand goods pl; ~**warenhändler** m second-hand dealer.
Altweiber-: ~**geschwätz** nt old woman's talk; ~**sommer** m (Nachsommer) Indian summer.
Alufolie f tin foil.
Aluminium nt no pl aluminium, aluminum (US).
Aluminiumfolie f tin foil.
am prep **= an dem (a)** (zur Bildung des Superlativs) **er war** ~ **tapfersten** he was (the) bravest; **er hat** ~ **tapfersten gekämpft** he fought (the) most bravely; **sie war** ~ **schönsten** she was (the) most beautiful; ~ **besten machen wir das morgen** it would be best to do it tomorrow; ~ **seltsamsten war ...** the strangest thing was ... **(b)** (als Zeit-angabe) on. ~ **letzten Sonntag** last Sunday; ~ **8. Mai** on the eighth of May, on May (the Brit) eighth; (geschrieben) on May 8th; ~ **Morgen/ Abend** in the morning/evening. **(c)** (als Orts-angabe) on the; (bei Gebirgen) at the foot of the. **(d)** (col: als Verlaufsform) **ich war gerade** ~ **Schlafen** I was just sleeping.
Amateur [-'tø:ɐ] m amateur.
amateurhaft [ama'tø:ɐ-] adj amateurish.
Amber m -(n) ambergris.
Ambition f (geh) ambition. ~**en auf etw** (acc) **haben** to have ambitions of getting sth.
ambivalent [-va'lɛnt] adj ambivalent.
Ambivalenz [-va'lɛnts] f ambivalence.
Amboß m -sse anvil.
ambulant adj (Med) Versorgung, Behandlung out-patient attr. ~**e Patienten** out-patients.
Ambulanz f (Klinikstation) out-patient depart-ment, out-patients sing.
Ambulanzwagen m ambulance.
Ameise f -n ant.
Ameisen-: ~**bär** m anteater; ~**haufen** m anthill; ~**säure** f formic acid; ~**staat** m ant colony.

amen *interj* amen.
Amen *nt* - amen. **sein** ~ **zu etw geben** to give one's blessing to sth; **das ist so sicher wie das** ~ **in der Kirche** *(col)* you can bet your bottom dollar on that *(col)*.
Amerika *nt* America.
Amerikaner(in *f)* *m* - **(a)** American. **(b)** *(Gebäck) flat iced cake.*
amerikanisch *adj* American.
amerikanisieren* *vt* to Americanize.
Amerikanisierung *f* Americanization.
Amerikanistik *f* American studies *pl.*
Ami *m* -s *(col)* Yank *(col)*; *(Soldat)* GI *(col)*.
Amme *f* -n *(old)* foster-mother; *(Nährmutter)* wet nurse.
Ammenmärchen *nt* fairy tale *or* story.
Ammoniak *nt no pl* ammonia.
Amnesie *f (Med)* amnesia.
Amnestie *f* amnesty.
amnestieren* *vt* to grant an amnesty to.
Amöbe *f* -n *(Biol)* amoeba.
Amok *m:* ~ **laufen** to run amok *or* amuck.
Amok-: ~**fahrer** *m* mad *or* lunatic driver; ~**läufer** *m* madman; ~**schütze** *m* crazed gunman.
Amor *m* - Cupid.
Amortisation *f (Econ)* amortization.
amortisieren* *vr* to pay for itself.
amourös [amu'rø:s] *adj (geh)* amorous.
Ampel *f* -n **(a)** *(Verkehrs~)* (traffic) lights *pl (Brit)*, (traffic) light *(US)*. **(b)** *(geh: Hängeblumentopf)* hanging flowerpot.
Ampelphase *f* traffic light sequence. **die langen** ~**n an dieser Kreuzung** the length of time the lights take to change at this junction.
Ampere [am'pɛːɐ] *nt* - amp.
Amperemeter [am'pɛːɐ-] *nt* ammeter.
Amphibie [-iə] *f (Zool)* amphibian.
Amphibienfahrzeug *nt* amphibious vehicle.
amphibisch *adj* amphibious.
Amphitheater *nt* amphitheatre *(Brit)*, amphitheater *(US)*.
Ampulle *f* -n *(Behälter)* ampoule.
Amputation *f* amputation.
amputieren* *vt* to amputate. **jdm den Arm** ~ to amputate sb's arm.
Amsel *f* -n blackbird.
Amt *nt* ⁼er **(a)** *(Stellung)* office; *(Posten)* post. **im** ~ **sein** to be in office; **jdm aus einem** ~ **entfernen** to remove sb from office. **(b)** *(Aufgabe)* duty, task. **seines** ~**es walten** *(geh)* to carry out *or* discharge *(form)* one's duties. **(c)** *(Behörde) (Einwohnermelde~, Finanz~)* registration/tax office; *(Stadtverwaltung)* council offices *pl.* **zum zuständigen** ~ **gehen** to go to the relevant authority; **von** ~**s wegen** *(auf behördliche Anordnung hin)* officially. **(d)** *(Telefon~)* operator; *(Zentrale)* exchange. **geben Sie mir bitte ein** ~ could you give me a line please. **(e)** *(Eccl: Messe)* High Mass.
amtieren* *vi* **(a)** *(Amt innehaben)* to be in office. ~**d** incumbent; **als Außenminister** ~ to hold the post of foreign minister. **(b)** *(fungieren)* **als** ... ~ to act as ...
amtlich *adj* official; *(wichtig)* Miene, Gebaren officious; ~**es Kennzeichen** registration (number), license number *(US)*.
Amtmann *m, pl* -**männer** *or* -**leute, Amtmännin** *f (Admin)* senior civil servant.
Amts-: ~**anmaßung** *f* unauthorized assumption of authority; ~**arzt** *m* medical officer; **a**~**ärztlich** *adj* Zeugnis from the medical officer; **a**~**ärztlich untersucht werden** to have an official medical examination; ~**bereich** *m* area of competence; ~**dauer** *f* term of office; ~**deutsch(e)** *nt* officialese; ~**eid** *m* oath of office; **den** ~**eid ablegen** to be sworn in, to take the oath of office; ~**einsetzung** *f* inauguration;

~**enthebung** *f* dismissal from office; ~**geheimnis** *nt* **(a)** *(geheime Sache)* official secret; **(b)** *(Schweigepflicht)* official secrecy; ~**gericht** *nt* county *(Brit)* or district *(US)* court; ~**geschäfte** *pl* official duties *pl*; ~**handlung** *f* official duty; ~**hilfe** *f* cooperation between authorities; ~**leitung** *f (Telec)* exchange line; ~**mißbrauch** *m* abuse of one's position; ~**periode** *f* term of office; ~**richter** *m* ≈ county *(Brit)* or district *(US)* court judge; ~**schimmel** *m (hum)* officialdom; **der** ~**schimmel wiehert** officialdom rears its ugly head; ~**sprache** *f* official language; ~**vorstand,** ~**vorsteher** *m* head *or* chief of a/the department *etc*; ~**weg** *m* **auf dem** ~**weg** through official channels; ~**zeichen** *nt (Telec)* dialling tone *(Brit)*, dial tone *(US)*; ~**zeit** *f* period of office; ~**zimmer** *nt* office.
Amulett *nt* -e amulet, charm.
amüsant *adj* amusing.
amüsieren* **1** *vt* to amuse. **amüsiert zuschauen** to look on with amusement. **2** *vr (sich vergnügen)* to have a good time, to have fun. **sich über etw** *(acc)* ~ to find sth funny; *(unfreundlich)* to make fun of sth.
Amüsierviertel *nt* nightclub district.
an 1 *prep+dat* **(a)** *(räumlich: wo?)* at; *(~ etw dran)* on. **am Haus/Bahnhof** at the house/station; **am Fenster sitzen** to sit at *or* by the window; **am Tatort** at the scene of the crime; ~ **der Tür/ Wand** on the door/wall; ~ **der Donau/Autobahn/ am Ufer** by *or* (direkt ~ gelegen) on the Danube/ motorway/bank; **zu nahe** ~ **etw stehen** to be too near to sth; ~ **der gleichen Stelle** at *or* on the same spot; **jdn** ~ **der Hand nehmen** to take sb by the hand; **unten am Fluß** down by the river; **sie wohnen Tür** ~ **Tür** they live next door to one another; **sich** *(dat)* **die Hand am Tuch abwischen** to wipe one's hand on the cloth.
(b) *(zeitlich)* on. ~ **diesem Abend** (on) that evening; ~ **dem Abend, als ich ...** the evening I ...; **siehe am.**
(c) *(jung* ~ **Jahren sein** to be young in years; **fünf** ~ **der Zahl** five in number; ~ **etw arbeiten/ schreiben/kauen** to be working on/writing/ chewing sth; ~ **etw sterben** to die of sth; **arm** ~ **Fett/reich** ~ **Kalorien** low in fat/high in calories; **was haben Sie** ~ **Weinen da?** what wines do you have?; ~ **der ganzen Sache ist nichts** there is nothing in it; **es** ~ **der Leber etc haben** *(col)* to have liver *etc* trouble; **das gefällt mir nicht** ~ **ihm** that's what I don't like about him; **sie hat etwas** ~ **sich, das ...** there is something about her that ...; **es ist** ~ **ihm, etwas zu tun** *(geh)* it's up to him to do something.
2 *prep+acc* **(a)** *(räumlich: wohin?)* to; *(gegen)* on, against. **etw** ~ **die Wand/Tafel schreiben** to write sth on the wall/blackboard; **etw** ~ **etw hängen** to hang sth on sth; **A**~ **den Vorsitzenden ...** *(bei Anschrift)* The Chairman ... **(b)** *(zeitlich: woran?)* ~ **die Zukunft/Vergangenheit denken** to think of the future/past; **bis** ~ **mein Lebensende** to the end of my days. **(c)** ~ **die Arbeit gehen** to get down to work; **ich habe eine Bitte/Frage** ~ **Sie** I have a request to make of you/question to ask you; **ein Gruß/eine Frage** ~ **jdn** greetings/a question to sb; ~ **(und für) sich** actually; **dagegen ist** ~ **(und für) sich nichts einzuwenden** there are really no objections to that.
3 *adv* **(a)** *(ungefähr)* about. ~ **(die) hundert** about a hundred. **(b)** *(Ankunftszeit)* **Frankfurt** ~! **18.30** *(Rail)* arriving Frankfurt 18.30. **(c) von diesem Ort** ~ from here onwards; **von diesem Tag/heute** ~ from this day/today on(wards). **(d)** *(col: angeschaltet, angezogen)* on. **Licht** ~! lights on!; **ohne etwas** ~ with nothing on.
Anachronismus [-kr-] *m (geh)* anachronism.
anachronistisch [-kr-] *adj (geh)* anachronistic.
Anagramm *nt (Liter)* anagram.

analog *adj* **(a)** analogous *(+dat, zu* to). **(b)** *(Comp)* analogue *attr.*
Analogie *f* analogy.
Analogrechner *m* analogue computer.
Analphabet(in *f)* *m (wk)* **-en, en** illiterate (person).
Analyse *f* **-n** analysis *(auch Psych).*
analysieren* *vt* to analyze.
Analytiker(in *f)* *m* - analyst.
analytisch *adj* analytical.
Anämie *f* anaemia *(Brit),* anemia *(US).*
Ananas *f* - *or* **-se** pineapple.
Anarchie *f* anarchy.
Anarchismus *m* anarchism.
Anarchist(in *f)* *m* anarchist.
anarchistisch *adj* anarchistic.
Anästhesie *f* anaesthesia *(Brit),* anesthesia *(US).*
Anästhesist(in *f)* *m* anaesthetist *(Brit),* anesthesiologist *(US).*
Anatomie *f* **(a)** anatomy. **(b)** *(Institut)* anatomical institute.
anatomisch *adj* anatomical.
anbahnen *sep* **1** *vt* to initiate. **2** *vr (sich andeuten)* to be in the offing; *(Unangenehmes)* to be looming; *(Möglichkeiten, Zukunft etc)* to be opening up. **zwischen den beiden bahnt sich etwas an** *(Liebesverhältnis)* there is something going on between those two.
Anbahnung *f* initiation *(von, gen* of).
Anbau¹ *m* *no pl (Anpflanzung)* cultivation, growing.
Anbau² *m* **-ten** *(Nebengebäude)* extension; *(freistehend)* annexe.
anbauen *sep* **1** *vt* **(a)** to grow. **(b)** *(Build)* to add, to build on. **etw ans Haus** ~ to build sth onto the house. **2** *vi* to build an extension.
Anbau-: ~**fläche** *f* (area of) cultivable land; ~**gebiet** *nt* **ein gutes** ~**gebiet für etw** a good area for growing sth; ~**möbel** *pl* unit furniture.
anbehalten* *vt* *sep irreg* to keep on.
anbei *adv (form)* enclosed. ~ **schicken wir Ihnen** ... please find enclosed ...
anbeißen *sep irreg* **1** *vi (Fisch)* to bite; *(fig auch)* to take the bait. **2** *vt Apfel etc* to bite into. **ein angebissener Apfel** a half-eaten apple; **sie sieht zum A** ~ **aus** *(col)* she looks nice enough to eat.
anbelangen* *vt* *sep* to concern. **was das/mich anbelangt** ... as far as that is/I am concerned ...
anbellen *vt* *sep* to bark at.
anbeten *vt* *sep* to worship.
Anbetracht *m:* **in** ~ *(+gen)* in consideration *or* view of; **in** ~ **dessen, daß** ... in consideration *or* view of the fact that ...
anbetreffen* *vt* *sep irreg siehe* **anbelangen.**
anbetteln *vt* *sep* **jdn** ~ to beg from sb; **jdn um etw** ~ to beg sth from sb.
anbiedern *vr* *sep (pej)* **sich (bei jdm)** ~ to get pally (with sb) *(col).*
anbieten *sep irreg* **1** *vt* to offer *(jdm etw* sb sth*).* **2** *vr* **(a)** *(Mensch)* **sich (als etw)** ~ to offer one's services (as sth); **du darfst dich den Männern nicht so** ~ you shouldn't make yourself so available; **der Ort bietet sich für die Konferenz an** that is the obvious place for the conference. **(b)** *(in Betracht kommen: Gelegenheit)* to present itself. **das bietet sich als Lösung an** that would provide a solution.
Anbieter *m* - supplier.
anbinden *vt* *sep irreg (an+acc or dat* to) to tie (up); *Pferd auch* to tether; *siehe* **angebunden.**
Anblick *m* sight. **beim ersten** ~ at first sight; **du bist ein** ~ **für die Götter** you really look a sight.
anblicken *vt* *sep* to look at. **jdn lange/feindselig** ~ to gaze/glare at sb.
anblinzeln *vt* *sep* **(a)** *(blinzelnd ansehen)* to squint at. **(b)** *(zublinzeln)* to wink at.
anbraten *vt* *sep irreg* to brown.
anbrechen *sep irreg* **1** *vt Packung, Flasche etc* to

open; *Vorrat, Ersparnisse, Geldsumme* to break into; *siehe* **angebrochen. 2** *vi aux sein (Epoche etc)* to dawn; *(Tag auch)* to break; *(Nacht)* to fall; *(Jahreszeit)* to begin; *(Winter)* to close in.
anbrennen *vi sep irreg aux sein* to catch fire; *(Holz, Kohle etc)* to catch light; *(Essen)* to burn; *(Stoff)* to get scorched. **mir ist das Essen angebrannt** I burnt the food; *siehe* **angebrannt.**
anbringen *vt* *sep irreg* **(a)** *(befestigen)* to fix, to fasten *(an+dat* (on)to); *(aufstellen, aufhängen)* to put up; *Telefon, Feuermelder etc* to put in, to install. **(b)** *(äußern) Bemerkung, Beschwerde* to make *(bei* to*); Kenntnisse, Wissen* to display; *Argument* to use. **er konnte seine Kritik/seinen Antrag nicht mehr** ~ he couldn't get his criticism/motion in; *siehe* **angebracht. (c)** *(col: loswerden) Ware* to get rid of.
Anbruch *m* *no pl (geh: Anfang)* beginning; *(von Zeitalter, Epoche)* dawn(ing). **bei** ~ **des Tages/ Morgens** at daybreak, at break of day; **bei** ~ **der Nacht/Dunkelheit** at nightfall.
anbrüllen *vt* *sep (Löwe etc)* to roar at; *(col: Mensch)* to shout *or* bellow at.
Anchovis [an'ɕoːvɪs, an'ʃoːvɪs] *f* - anchovy.
Andacht *f* **-en** **(a)** *no pl (das Beten)* (silent) prayer *or* worship. **(b)** *(Gottesdienst)* prayers *pl.* **(c)** *(Versenkung)* rapt interest; *(Ehrfurcht)* reverence. **in tiefe(r)** ~ **versunken sein** to be completely absorbed.
andächtig *adj* **(a)** *(im Gebet)* in prayer. **(b)** *(versunken)* rapt; *(ehrfürchtig)* reverent.
andauern *vi sep* to continue; *(anhalten)* to last. **das dauert noch an** that is still going on; **der Regen dauert noch an** the rain hasn't stopped.
andauernd *adj* *(ständig)* continuous; *(anhaltend)* continual. **wenn du mich** ~ **unterbrichst** ... if you keep on interrupting me ...
Anden *pl* **die** ~ the Andes.
Andenken *nt* *no pl* **(a)** memory. **zum** ~ **an jdn/ etw** *(an Verstorbenen etc)* in memory *or* remembrance of sb/sth; *(an Freunde/Urlaub etc)* to remind you/us *etc* of sb/sth. **(b)** *(Reise~)* souvenir *(an +acc* of*); (Erinnerungsstück)* memento, keepsake *(an+acc* from*).*
ander(e)nfalls *adv* otherwise.
andere(r, s) *indef pron* **1** *(adjektivisch)* different; *(weiterer)* other. **ein** ~**r Mann/ein** ~**s Auto/eine** ~ **Frau** a different man/car/woman; *(ein weiterer etc)* another man/car/woman; **jede** ~ **Frau hätte** ... any other woman would have ...; **das machen wir ein** ~**s Mal** we'll do that another time; **er ist ein** ~**r Mensch geworden** he is a changed man.
2 *(substantivisch)* **(a)** *(Ding)* **ein** ~**r** a different one; *(noch einer)* another one; **etwas** ~**s** something *or (in Fragen)* anything else; **alle** ~**n** all the others; **das ist etwas ganz** ~**s** that's something quite different; **hast du etwas** ~**s gedacht?** did you think otherwise?; **ich habe** ~**s zu tun** I've other things to do; **nichts** ~**s** nothing else; **nichts** ~**s als** ... nothing but ...; **es blieb mir nichts** ~**s übrig, als selbst hinzugehen** I had no alternative but to go myself; **alles** ~ **als zufrieden** anything but pleased, far from pleased; **unter** ~**m** among other things; **es kam eins zum** ~**n** one thing led to another; **sie hat sich eines** ~**n besonnen** she changed her mind; **von einem Tag zum** ~**n** overnight.
(b) *(Person)* **ein** ~**r/eine** ~ a different person; *(noch einer)* another person; **jeder** ~/**kein** ~**r** anyone/no-one else; **niemand** ~**s** no-one else; **das haben mir** ~ **auch schon gesagt** other people *or* others have told me that too; **die** ~**n** the others; **alle** ~**n** all the others, everyone else; **jemand** ~**s** somebody *or (in Fragen)* anybody else; **sie hat einen** ~**n** she has someone else; **der eine oder der** ~ **von unseren Kollegen** one *or* other of our colleagues; **einer nach dem** ~**n** one after the other; **eine schöner als die** ~ each one

more beautiful than the next.
and(e)rserseits adv on the other hand.
andermal adv: ein ~ some other time.
ändern 1 vt to change, to alter; Kleidungsstück to alter. **ich kann es nicht** ~ I can't do anything about it; **das ändert nichts an der Tatsache, daß** ... that doesn't alter the fact that ... **2** vr **(a)** to change, to alter. **(b)** (Mensch) to change; (sich bessern) to change for the better. **wenn sich das nicht ändert** ... if things don't improve ...
andernfalls adv otherwise.
anders adv **(a)** (sonst) else. **jemand/niemand** ~ somebody or anybody/nobody else; **wer/wo** ~? who/where else?; **irgendwo** ~ somewhere else. **(b)** (verschieden) differently; (andersartig) sein, aussehen, klingen, schmecken different (als to). **als jd denken/reagieren/aussehen** to think/react differently/look different from sb; ~ **als jd** (geh: im Gegensatz zu) unlike sb; ~ **ausgedrückt** to put it another way; **das machen wir so und nicht** ~ we'll do it this way and no other way; **wie nicht** ~ **zu erwarten** was to be expected; **sie ist** ~ **geworden** she has changed; **wie könnte es** ~ **sein?** how could it be otherwise?; **es geht nicht** ~ there's no other way; **ich kann nicht** ~ (kann es nicht lassen) I can't help it; (muß leider) I have no choice.
Anders-: **a~artig** adj no comp different; **~denkende(r)** mf decl as adj dissident, dissenter; **a~farbig** adj of a different colour (Brit) or color (US); **a~(he)rum** adv the other way around; **a~lautend** adj attr (form) contrary; **a~lautende Berichte** reports to the contrary; **a~wo** adv elsewhere; **a~woher** adv from elsewhere; **a~wohin** adv elsewhere.
anderthalb num one and a half. ~ **Pfund Kaffee** a pound and a half of coffee.
Änderung f change, alteration (an +dat, gen in, to); (an Kleid, Gebäude) alteration (an+dat to).
Änderungs-: **~antrag** m (Parl) amendment; **~schneider** m tailor (who does alterations); **~vorschlag** m suggested change or alteration; **einen ~vorschlag machen** to suggest a change or an alteration.
anderweitig 1 adj attr (andere, weitere) other. **2** adv (anders) otherwise; (an anderer Stelle) elsewhere. ~ **vergeben/besetzt werden** to be given to/filled by someone else; **etw** ~ **verwenden** to use sth for a different purpose.
andeuten sep **1** vt (zu verstehen geben) to hint, to intimate (jdm etw sth to sb); (kurz erwähnen) Problem to mention briefly; (erkennen lassen) to indicate. **2** vr to be indicated; (Gewitter) to be in the offing.
Andeutung f (Anspielung, Anzeichen) hint; (flüchtiger Hinweis) brief mention; (Spur) sign, trace. **eine ~ machen** to hint (über+acc at), to drop a hint (über+acc about).
andeutungsweise adv (als Anspielung, Anzeichen) by way of a hint; (flüchtiger Hinweis) in passing. **jdm** ~ **zu verstehen geben, daß** ... to hint to sb that ....
andichten vt sep jdm etw ~ (col) Fähigkeiten to credit sb with sth.
Andrang m no pl (Zustrom, Gedränge) crowd, crush.
andrehen vt sep **(a)** (anstellen) to turn on. **(b)** jdm etw ~ (col) to palm sth off on sb.
androhen vt sep to threaten (jdm etw sb with sth).
Androhung f threat. **unter** ~ **von Gewalt** with the threat of violence; **unter** ~ **(Jur)** under penalty (von, gen of).
Andruck m (Typ) proof.
andünsten vti sep (Cook) to braise lightly.
an|ecken vi sep aux sein (col) **(bei jdm/allen)** ~ to rub sb/everyone up the wrong way.
an|eignen vr sep sich (dat) etw ~ (etw erwerben) to acquire sth; (etw wegnehmen) to appropriate sth;

(sich mit etw vertraut machen) to learn sth.
An|eignung f siehe vr acquisition; appropriation; learning.
an|einander adv ~ **denken** to think of each other; **sich** ~ **gewöhnen** to get used to each other; ~ **vorüber-/vorbeigehen** to go past each other; ~ **befestigen** to stick together; **zu dicht** ~ too close together.
an|einander- in cpds together; **~geraten*** vi sep irreg to come to blows (mit with); (streiten) to have words (mit with); **~grenzen** vi sep to border on each other; **~hängen** vi sep irreg **(a)** (zusammenhängen) to be linked (together); **(b)** (fig: Menschen) to be attached to each other; **~kleben** sep **1** vt to stick together; **2** vi to be stuck together; (col: unzertrennlich sein) to be glued together (col); **~reihen** vt sep to string together.
Anekdote f -n anecdote.
an|ekeln vt sep (anwidern) to disgust, to nauseate.
Anemone f -n anemone.
an|erkannt adj recognized; Tatsache auch established; Werk standard; Experte acknowledged.
an|erkennen* vt sep or insep irreg Staat, König, Rekord to recognize; Forderung auch to accept; Vaterschaft to accept, to acknowledge; (würdigen) Leistung, Bemühung to appreciate. ..., **das muß man** ~ (zugeben) ... you can't argue with that; (würdigen) ... one has to appreciate that; **als gleichwertiger Partner anerkannt sein** to be accepted as an equal partner.
an|erkennenswert adj commendable.
An|erkennung f siehe vt recognition; acceptance; acknowledgement; appreciation.
an|erziehen* vt insep irreg: jdm etw ~ (Kindern) to instil sth into sb.
an|erzogen adj acquired. **das ist alles** ~ she etc has just been trained to be like that.
anfahren sep irreg **1** vi aux sein (losfahren) to start (up). **angefahren kommen** (Wagen, Fahrer) to drive up; (Zug) to pull up; **beim A~** when starting (up); **das A~ am Berg üben** to practice a hill start. **2** vt (a) (liefern) Kohlen, Kartoffeln to deliver. **(b)** (ansteuern) Ort to stop or call at; Hafen auch to put in at. **(c)** (anstoßen) Passanten, Baum etc to run into, to hit.
Anfahrt f (~sweg, ~szeit) journey; (Zufahrt) approach.
Anfall m **(a)** attack; (Wut~, epileptisch) fit. **einen** ~ **haben/bekommen** (lit) to have an attack/fit; (fig col) to have or throw a fit (col); **in einem** ~ **von** (fig) in a fit of. **(b)** (Ertrag, Nebenprodukte) yield (an+dat of); (von Zinsen auch) accrual. **(c)** (von Reparaturen, Kosten) amount (an+dat of); (form: Anhäufung) accumulation. **bei** ~ **von Reparaturen** if repairs are necessary.
anfallen sep irreg **1** vt (überfallen) to attack; (Sittenstrolch etc) to assault. **2** vi aux sein (Zinsen) to accrue; (Nebenprodukte) to be obtained; (sich anhäufen) to accumulate. **die ~den Kosten/Reparaturen** the costs/repairs incurred; **die ~de Arbeit** the work which comes up.
anfällig adj (nicht widerstandsfähig) delicate; Motor, Maschine temperamental. **für etw/eine Krankheit** ~ **sein** to be susceptible to sth/prone to an illness.
Anfälligkeit f siehe adj delicateness; temperamental nature; susceptibility; proneness.
Anfang m, pl **Anfänge** (Beginn) beginning, start; (Ursprung) beginnings pl, origin. **zu** or **am** ~ to start with; (anfänglich) at first; ~ **Fünfzig** in one's early fifties; ~ **Juni/1978** etc at the beginning of June/1978 etc; **von** ~ **an** (right) from the beginning or start; **von** ~ **bis Ende** from start to finish; **den** ~ **machen** to start or begin; (den ersten Schritt tun) to make the first move; **einen neuen** ~ **machen** to make a new start; **aller** ~ **ist schwer** (Prov) the first step is always the most difficult; **das ist der** ~ **vom Ende** it's the

beginning of the end.
anfangen sep irreg **1** vt **(a)** (beginnen) to start, to begin; Streit to start. **(b)** (anstellen, machen) to do. **das mußt du anders ~** you'll have to go about it differently; **nichts mit sich/jdm anzufangen wissen** not to know what to do with oneself/sb; **damit kann ich nichts ~** (nützt mir nichts) that's no good to me; (verstehe ich nicht) it doesn't mean a thing to me; **mit dir ist heute (aber) gar nichts anzufangen!** you're no fun at all today! **2** vi to begin, to start. **du hast angefangen!** (bei Streit) you started it!; **es fing zu regnen an** or **an zu regnen** it started raining or to rain; **das fängt ja schön an!** (iro) that's a good start!; **jetzt fängt das Leben erst an** life is only just beginning; **mit etw ~** to start sth; **bei einer Firma ~** to start working for a firm.

Anfänger(in f) m - beginner; (Neuling) novice; (Aut) learner; (col: Nichtskönner) amateur (pej).
Anfängerkurs(us) m beginners' course.
anfänglich 1 adj attr initial. **2** adv at first, initially.
anfangs 1 adv at first, initially. **wie ich schon ~ erwähnte** as I mentioned at the beginning. **2** prep +gen **~ der zwanziger Jahre/des Monats** in the early twenties/at the beginning of the month.
Anfangs-: ~buchstabe m first letter; **kleine/große ~buchstaben** small/capital initials; **~gehalt** nt starting salary; **~stadium** nt initial stage; **meine Versuche sind schon im ~stadium steckengeblieben** my attempts never really got off the ground.
anfassen sep **1** vt **(a)** (berühren) to touch. **(b)** (bei der Hand nehmen) **jdn ~** to take sb's hand or sb by the hand; **sich ~** to take each other by the hand. **(c)** (fig: anpacken) Problem to tackle, to go about. **2** vi **(a)** (berühren) to feel. **nicht ~!** don't touch! **(b)** (mithelfen) **mit ~** to give a hand.
anfauchen vt sep (Katze) to spit at; (fig col) to snap at.
anfechtbar adj contestable.
anfechten vt sep irreg (nicht anerkennen) to contest; Aussage auch to challenge; Urteil to appeal against; Vertrag to dispute.
Anfechtung f **(a)** siehe vt (a) contesting; challenging; appeal (gen against); disputing. **(b)** (Versuchung) temptation.
anfeinden vt sep to treat with hostility.
Anfeindung f hostility. **trotz aller ~en** in spite of all the hostility.
anfertigen vt sep to make; Schriftstück to draw up; Hausaufgaben to do; Protokoll to take down. **sich** (dat) **einen Anzug** etc **~ lassen** to have a suit etc made.
Anfertigung f siehe vt making; drawing up; taking down.
anfeuchten vt sep to moisten.
anfeuern vt sep (fig: ermutigen) to spur on.
Anfeuerung f (fig) spurring on.
Anfeuerungsruf m cheer.
anflehen vt sep to beseech, to implore (um for). **ich flehe dich an, tu das nicht!** I beg you, don't!
anfliegen sep irreg **1** vi aux sein (auch angeflogen kommen) (Flugzeug) to come in to land; (Vogel, Geschoß) to come flying up. **2** vt (Flugzeug) Flughafen, (Mil) Stellung to approach; (landen) to land (in/auf in/on). **diese Fluggesellschaft fliegt Bali an** this airline flies to Bali.
Anflug m **(a)** (Flugweg) flight; (das Heranfliegen) approach. **wir befinden uns im ~ auf Paris** we are now approaching Paris. **(b)** (Spur) trace.
anfordern vt sep to request; Waren to order.
Anforderung f **(a)** no pl (das Anfordern) request (gen, von for). **bei der ~ von Ersatzteilen** when ordering spare parts. **(b)** (Anspruch) requirement; (Belastung) demand. **große ~en an jdn/etw stellen** to make great demands on sb/sth.
Anfrage f inquiry; (Parl) question.

anfragen vi sep to inquire (bei jdm of sb), to ask (bei jdm sb).
anfressen vt sep irreg **(a)** (Maus) to nibble at; (Vogel) to peck (at). **(b)** (zersetzen) to eat away.
anfreunden vr sep to make or become friends. **sich mit etw ~** (fig) to get to like sth.
anfügen vt sep to add.
anfühlen sep **1** vt to feel. **2** vr to feel. **sich glatt/weich** etc **~** to feel smooth/soft etc.
Anfuhr f -en transport(ation).
anführen vt sep **(a)** (vorangehen, befehligen) to lead. **(b)** (zitieren) to quote, to cite; Tatsachen, Beispiel auch to give; Grund, Beweis to give, to offer; (benennen) jdn to name, to cite. **(c)** jdn ~ (col) to have sb on (col), to take sb for a ride (col).
Anführer m leader; (pej: Anstifter) ringleader.
Anführung f **(a)** leadership; (Befehligung auch) command. **unter ~ von ...** under the leadership of ... **(b)** (Zitat) quotation.
Anführungs-: ~zeichen nt quotation mark, inverted comma; **~zeichen unten/oben** quote/unquote.
anfüllen vt sep to fill (up). **mit etw angefüllt sein** to be full of sth, to be filled with sth.
Angabe ['anga-] f **-n (a)** usu pl (Aussage) statement; (Zahl, Detail) detail. **~n über etw** (acc) **machen** to give details about sth; **laut ~n** (+gen) according to; **~n zur Person** (form) personal details or particulars. **(b)** (Nennung) giving. **wir bitten um ~ der Einzelheiten/Preise** please give or quote details/prices; **ohne ~ von Gründen** without giving any reasons. **(c)** no pl (col: Prahlerei) showing off; (Reden auch) boasting.
angeben ['ange-] sep irreg **1** vt **(a)** (nennen) to give; (als Zeugen) to name, to cite; (erklären) to explain; (beim Zoll) to declare; (anzeigen) Temperatur etc to indicate; (aussagen) to state; (behaupten) to maintain. **(b)** (bestimmen) Tempo, Kurs to set; (Mus) Tempo, Note to give. **den Takt ~** (klopfen) to beat time. **2** vi (prahlen) to show off; (durch Reden auch) to boast, to brag (mit about).
Angeber ['ange-] m (Prahler) show-off, poser (col).
Angeberei [ange-] f no pl (Prahlerei) showing-off, posing (col) (mit about); (verbal auch) boasting, bragging (mit about).
angeberisch ['ange-] adj Reden boastful; Benehmen, Tonfall pretentious, showy.
angeblich ['ange-] **1** adj attr so-called, alleged. **2** adv supposedly, allegedly. **er ist ~ Musiker** he's supposed to be a musician.
angeboren ['ange-] adj innate, inherent; (Med, fig col) congenital (bei with).
Angebot ['ange-] nt **(a)** offer; (bei Auktion) bid; (Comm: Offerte auch) tender (über +acc, für for). **(b)** no pl (Comm, Fin) supply (an+dat, von of); (Auswahl) selection (an + dat of). **~ und Nachfrage** supply and demand; **im ~** (col) on special offer.
angebracht ['ange-] adj appropriate; (sinnvoll) reasonable.
angebrannt ['ange-] adj burnt. **es riecht hier so ~** there's a smell of burning here.
angebrochen ['ange-] adj Packung, Flasche open(ed). **was sollen wir mit dem ~en Abend machen?** what shall we do with the rest of the evening?; **das Parken kostet für jede ~e Stunde eine Mark** parking costs one mark for every hour or part of an hour.
angebunden ['ange-] adj kurz ~ sein (col) to be abrupt or curt.
angegossen ['ange-] adj wie ~ sitzen or passen to fit like a glove.
angegraut ['ange-] adj grey; Haar auch greying.
angegriffen ['ange-] adj Gesundheit weakened; Mensch, Aussehen frail; (nervlich) strained.
angehalten ['ange-] adj ~ sein, etw zu tun to be required or obliged to do sth.

angehaucht ['angə-] *adj* **links/rechts** ~ **sein** to have left-/right-wing tendencies *or* leanings.

angeheiratet ['angə-] *adj* related by marriage. **ein** ~**er Cousin** a cousin by marriage.

angeheitert ['angə-] *adj (col)* merry *(col)*, tipsy.

angehen ['angeː-] *sep irreg* **1** *vi* **(a)** *(col: beginnen) (Feuer)* to start burning, to catch; *(Licht)* to come on, to go on. **(b)** *(entgegentreten)* **gegen jdn/etw** ~ to fight sb/sth; **gegen Mißstände, Zustände** to take measures against sth. **2** *vt* **(a)** *(anpacken) Aufgabe* to tackle. **(b)** *(bitten)* to ask *(jdm um etw sb for sth)*. **(c)** *(betreffen)* to concern. **was mich angeht** as far as I'm concerned; **das geht ihn gar nichts an** that's none of his business. **3** *vi impers* **das geht nicht/keinesfalls an** that's quite out of the question.

angehend ['angeː-] *adj Musiker, Künstler* budding; *Lehrer, Ehemann, Vater* prospective.

angehören* ['angə-] *vi sep+dat* to belong to; *(einer Partei, einer Familie auch)* to be a member of.

Angehörige(r) ['angə-] *mf decl as adj* **(a)** *(Mitglied)* member. **(b)** *(Familien~)* relative, relation. **der nächste** ~ the next of kin.

Angeklagte(r) ['angə-] *mf decl as adj* accused, defendant.

angeknackst ['angə-] *adj (col) Mensch* uptight *(col)*; *Selbstbewußtsein* weakened. **er/seine Gesundheit ist** ~ he is in bad shape.

angekratzt ['angə-] *adj (col)* seedy *(col)*.

Angel *f* **-n** **(a)** *(Tür~, Fenster~)* hinge. **die Welt aus den** ~**n heben** *(fig)* to turn the world upside down. **(b)** *(Fischfanggerät)* fishing rod, fishing pole *(US)*. **die** ~ **auswerfen** to cast (the line).

Angelegenheit ['angə-] *f* matter; *(politisch, persönlich)* affair; *(Aufgabe)* concern. **das ist nicht meine** ~ that's not my concern *or* business.

angelegt ['angə-] *adj* calculated *(auf+acc* for*)*.

angelernt ['angə-] *adj Arbeiter* semi-skilled.

Angel-: ~**gerät** *nt* fishing tackle *no pl*; ~**haken** *m* fish-hook.

angeln **1** *vi* **(a)** to fish. ~ **gehen** to go angling *or* fishing. **(b)** *(zu greifen versuchen, hervorziehen)* to fish. **nach etw** ~ to fish (around) for sth. **2** *vt* *Fisch* to fish for; *(fangen)* to catch. **sich** *(dat)* **einen Mann** ~ *(col)* to catch (oneself) a man.

Angel-: ~**punkt** *m* crucial *or* central point; *(Frage)* key *or* central issue; ~**rute** *f* fishing rod, fishing pole *(US)*.

Angelsachse *m decl as adj* Anglo-Saxon.

angelsächsisch *adj* Anglo-Saxon.

Angel-: ~**schein** *m* fishing permit; ~**schnur** *f* fishing line.

angemessen ['angə-] *adj (passend)* appropriate *(dat* to, for*)*; *(adäquat)* adequate *(dat for)*; *Preis* reasonable, fair. **eine der Leistung** ~**e Bezahlung** payment commensurate with input.

angenehm ['angə-] *adj* pleasant, agreeable. **das wäre mir sehr** ~ I should be very grateful; **es ist mir gar nicht** ~, **daß er mich besuchen will** I don't like the idea of him wanting to visit me; **wenn Ihnen das** ~**er ist** if you prefer; **(sehr)** ~**!** *(form)* delighted (to meet you); **das A~e mit dem Nützlichen verbinden** to combine business with pleasure.

angenommen ['angə-] **1** *adj* assumed; *Kind* adopted. **2** *conj* assuming.

angepaßt ['angə-] *adj* conformist.

Angepaßtheit ['angə-] *f* conformism.

angeregt ['angə-] *adj* lively, animated. ~ **diskutieren** to have a lively *or* an animated discussion.

angereichert ['angə-] *adj* enriched.

angeschlagen ['angə-] *adj (col) Mensch, Aussehen, Nerven* shattered *(col)*; *Gesundheit* poor.

angeschlossen ['angə-] *adj* affiliated *(dat* to *or* with*)*, associated *(dat* with*)*.

angeschmiert ['angə-] *adj pred (col)* in trouble. **der/die A~e sein** to have been had *(col)*.

angeschrieben ['angə-] *adj (col)* **bei jdm gut/**

schlecht ~ **sein** to be in sb's good/bad books.

angesehen ['angə-] *adj* respected.

Angesicht ['angə-] *nt* **-er** *(geh)* face. **von** ~ **zu** ~ face to face; **im** ~ **+gen** *(fig)* in the face of.

angesichts ['angə-] *prep+gen* in the face of; *(im Hinblick auf)* in view of.

angespannt ['angə-] *adj Nerven, Lage* tense, strained; *Aufmerksamkeit* close, keen; *(Comm) Markt, Lage* tight, overstretched.

angestammt ['angə-] *adj (überkommen)* traditional; *(ererbt) Rechte* hereditary; *Besitz* inherited.

angestellt ['angə-] *adj pred* ~ **sein** to be an employee *or* on the staff *(bei* of*)*; **fest** ~ **sein** to be a permanent employee.

Angestellte(r) ['angə-] *mf decl as adj* (salaried) employee; *(Büro~)* office-worker, white-collar worker.

Angestellten- ['angə-]: ~**gewerkschaft** *f* white-collar union; ~**versicherung** *f* (salaried) employee's insurance.

angestrengt ['angə-] *adj Gesicht* strained; ~ **arbeiten/denken** to work/think hard; ~ **diskutieren** to have an intense discussion.

angetan ['angətan] *adj pred* **(a)** **von jdm/etw** ~ **sein** to be taken with sb/sth; **das Mädchen hat es ihm** ~ he has fallen for that girl. **(b)** **dazu** ~ **sein, etw zu tun** *(geh)* to be suitable for doing sth; *(Atmosphäre, Benehmen etc)* to be apt to do sth.

angetrunken ['angə-] *adj* inebriated.

angewandt ['angə-] *adj attr Wissenschaft etc* applied.

angewidert ['angə-] *adj* nauseated, disgusted. **vom Leben** ~ sick of life.

angewiesen ['angə-] *adj* **auf jdn/etw** ~ **sein** to have to rely on sb/sth, to be dependent on sb/sth; **auf sich selbst** ~ **sein** to be left to one's own devices; **darauf bin ich nicht** ~ I don't need it.

angewöhnen ['angə-] *vt sep* **jdm etw** ~ to get sb used to sth, to accustom sb to sth; **sich** *(dat)* **etw** ~**/es sich** *(dat)* ~, **etw zu tun** to get into the habit of sth/of doing sth.

Angewohnheit ['angə-] *f* habit.

angewurzelt *adj* **wie** ~ **dastehen** to be rooted to the spot.

angiften ['angɪ-] *vt sep (pej inf)* to snap at.

Angina [aŋ'giːna] *f, pl* **Anginen** *(Med)* angina. ~ **pectoris** angina (pectoris).

angleichen ['angl-] *sep irreg* **1** *vt* to bring into line, to align *(dat, an+acc* with*)*. **2** *vr (gegenseitig: Kulturen, Geschlechter, Methoden)* to grow closer together. **sich jdm/einer Sache** ~ *(einseitig)* to become like sb/sth.

Angleichung *f* alignment *(an +acc* with*)*.

Angler(in *f)* *m* - angler.

angliedern ['angl-] *vt sep (dat, an+acc* to*)* *(Verein, Partei)* to affiliate; *Land* to annex.

Angliederung *f* siehe **vt** affiliation; annexation.

anglikanisch [aŋgli-] *adj* Anglican. **die A~e Kirche** the Anglican Church, the Church of England.

Anglist(in *f)* [aŋ'glɪ-] *m* English specialist, Anglicist; *(Student)* English student; *(Professor etc)* English lecturer/professor.

Anglistik [aŋ'glɪ-] *f* English (language and literature).

Angora- [aŋ'goːra]: ~**katze** *f* Angora cat; ~**wolle** *f* Angora (wool).

angreifbar ['angr-] *adj* open to attack.

angreifen ['angr-] *sep irreg* **1** *vt* **(a)** to attack. **(b)** *(schwächen) Organismus, Nerven* to weaken; *Gesundheit, Pflanzen* to affect. **2** *vi* to attack.

Angreifer ['angr-] *m* - attacker *(auch Sport, fig)*.

angrenzen ['angr-] *vi sep* **an etw** *(acc)* ~ to border on sth, to adjoin sth.

angrenzend *adj attr* adjacent *(an +acc* to*)*, adjoining *(an etw (acc)* sth*)*.

Angriff ['angr-] *m (Mil, Sport, fig)* attack *(gegen, auf*

+*acc* on); *(Luft~)* (air) raid. ~ **ist die beste Verteidigung** *(prov)* attack is the best means of defence; **etw in** ~ **nehmen** to tackle sth.

Angriffs-: ~**fläche** *f* target; **jdm/einer Sache eine** ~**fläche bieten** *(lit, fig)* to provide sb/sth with a target; ~**krieg** *m* war of aggression; ~**lust** *f* aggressiveness, aggression; **a~lustig** *adj* aggressive; ~**spiel** *nt (Sport)* aggressive *or* attacking game; ~**spieler** *m (Ftbl)* forward.

angrinsen ['angr-] *vt sep* to grin at.

Angst *f* ⁼e *(innere Unruhe, Psych)* anxiety *(um* about); *(Sorge)* worry *(um* about); *(Befürchtung)* fear *(um* for, *vor+dat* of); *(Existenz~)* angst. **(vor etw dat)** ~ **haben** to be afraid *or* scared (of sth); ~ **um jdn/etw haben** to be anxious *or* worried about sb/sth; ~ **bekommen** *or* **kriegen** to become afraid *or* scared; **aus** ~, **etw zu tun** for fear of doing sth; **keine** ~! don't worry; **jdm** ~ **einflößen** *or* **einjagen** to frighten sb.

angst *adj pred* **ihr wurde** ~ **(und bange)** she became worried *or* anxious.

Angsthase *m (col)* scaredy-cat *(col).*

ängstigen **1** *vt* to frighten; *(unruhig machen)* to worry. **2** *vr* to be afraid; *(sich sorgen)* to worry. **sich vor etw** *(dat)* ~ to be afraid of sth; **sich wegen etw** ~ to worry about sth.

ängstlich *adj (verängstigt)* anxious, apprehensive; *(schüchtern)* timid, timorous.

Ängstlichkeit *f siehe adj* anxiety, apprehension; timidity, timorousness.

Angst-: ~**macher** *m (col)* scaremonger; ~**schrei** *m* cry of fear; ~**schweiß** *m* cold sweat; **mir brach der** ~**schweiß aus** I broke out in a cold sweat; **a~voll** *adj* apprehensive, fearful; ~**zustand** *m* state of panic; ~**zustände bekommen** to get into a state of panic.

angucken ['angu-] *vt sep* to look at.

angurten ['angu-] *vtr sep siehe* **anschnallen.**

anhaben *vt sep irreg* **(a)** *(angezogen haben)* to have on, to wear. **sie hatte ein schwarzes Kleid an** she was wearing a black dress, she had on a black dress. **(b)** *(zuleide tun)* to do harm. **die Kälte kann mir nichts** ~ the cold doesn't worry *or* bother me. **(c)** *(am Zeuge flicken)* **Sie können/die Polizei kann mir nichts** ~! *(col)* you/the police can't touch me.

anhaften *vi sep* **(a)** *(lit)* to stick *(an+dat* to). **(b)** *(fig)+dat* to stick to, to stay with.

anhalten *sep irreg* **1** *vi* **(a)** *(stehenbleiben)* to stop. **(b)** *(fortdauern)* to last. **(c)** *(werben)* **um die Hand eines Mädchens** ~ to ask for a girl's hand in marriage. **2** *vt* **(a)** *(stoppen)* to stop. **(b)** *(anleiten)* to urge, to encourage; *siehe* **angehalten.**

anhaltend *adj* continuous, incessant.

Anhalter(in *f)* *m* - hitch-hiker. **per** ~ **fahren** to hitch-hike, to hitch *(col).*

Anhaltspunkt *m (Vermutung)* clue *(für* about); *(für Verdacht)* grounds *pl*. **ich habe keinerlei** ~**e I** have no idea.

anhand, an Hand *prep+gen siehe* **Hand (d).**

Anhang *m, pl* **Anhänge (a)** *(Nachtrag)* appendix. **(b)** *no pl (Gefolgschaft)* following; *(Angehörige)* family.

anhängen *sep* **1** *vt* **(a)** *(an+acc* to) *(ankuppeln)* to attach; *(Rail auch)* to couple on; *Anhänger* to hitch up; *(fig: anfügen)* to add *(dat, an +acc* to). **(b)** *(col)* **jdm etw** ~ *(nachsagen, anlasten)* to blame sb for sth, to blame sth on sb; *schlechten Ruf, Spitznamen* to give sb sth; *Verdacht, Schuld* to pin sth on sb. **2** *vi irreg (fig)* **(a)** *(anhaften)* **jdm** ~ to stay with sb; *(schlechter Ruf, Gefängnisstrafe auch)* to stick with sb. **(b)** *(sich zugehörig fühlen)+dat* to adhere to, to subscribe to.

Anhänger(in *f)* *m* - **(a)** supporter; *(von Sportart auch)* fan; *(von Partei auch)* follower. **(b)** *(Wagen)* trailer. **(c)** *(Schmuckstück)* pendant. **(d)** *(Koffer~ etc)* tag, label.

Anhängerschaft *f siehe* **Anhänger (a)** support-

ers *pl*; fans *pl*; followers *pl.*

anhänglich *adj Kind, Freundin* clinging; *Haustier* devoted.

Anhänglichkeit *f siehe adj* tendency to cling to one; devotion.

Anhängsel *nt* **(a)** *(Überflüssiges, Mensch)* appendage *(an+dat* to). **(b)** *(Schildchen)* tag; *(an Kette)* pendant.

anhauchen *vt sep* to breathe on; *siehe* **angehaucht.**

anhauen *vt sep (col: ansprechen)* to accost *(um* for). **jdn um etw** ~ to (try to) touch sb for sth *(col).*

anhäufen *sep* **1** *vt* to accumulate, to amass; *Vorräte, Geld* to hoard. **2** *vr* to pile up, to accumulate; *(Zinsen)* to accumulate, to accrue.

Anhäufung *f siehe vt* accumulation, amassing; hoarding.

anheben *vt sep irreg* **(a)** *(hochheben)* to lift (up); *Glas* to raise. **(b)** *(erhöhen)* to raise.

Anhebung *f* increase *(gen, von* in).

anheften *vt sep* to fasten (on) *(an +acc or dat* to).

anheimelnd *adj (geh)* homely; *Klänge* familiar.

anheimfallen *vi sep irreg aux sein+dat (liter)* to pass *or* fall to; *einem Betrug* to fall victim to.

anheizen *vt sep* **(a)** *Ofen* to light. **(b)** *(fig col) Wirtschaft* to stimulate; *(verschlimmern) Krise* to aggravate.

anheuern *vti sep (Naut, fig)* to sign on *or* up.

Anhieb *m: auf* ~ *(col)* straight *or* right away, first go *(col);* **das kann ich nicht auf** ~ **sagen** I can't say offhand.

anhimmeln *vt sep (col)* to idolize, to worship.

Anhöhe *f* hill.

anhören *sep* **1** *vt* **(a)** to hear; *Schallplatten, Konzert* to listen to. **(b)** *(zufällig mithören)* to overhear. **ich kann das nicht mehr mit** ~ I can't listen to that any longer. **(c)** *(anmerken)* **man konnte ihr/ihrer Stimme die Verzweiflung** ~ one could hear the despair in her voice. **2** *vr* **(a) sich** *(dat)* **etw** ~ to listen to sth; **das höre ich mir nicht mehr länger mit an** I'm not going to listen to that any longer. **(b)** *(klingen)* to sound. **das hört sich ja gut an** *(col)* that sounds good.

Anhörung *f* hearing.

animalisch *adj* animal; *(pej auch)* bestial, brutish.

Animierdame *f* nightclub *or* bar hostess.

animieren* *vt* **(a)** *(anregen)* to encourage. **jdn zu einem Streich** ~ to put sb up to a trick; **durch das schöne Wetter animiert** prompted by the good weather. **(b)** *(Film)* to animate.

Animier-: ~**lokal** *nt* hostess bar, clipjoint *(pej);* ~**mädchen** *nt* nightclub *or* bar hostess.

Animosität *f (geh: Feindseligkeit)* animosity, hostility *(gegen* towards).

Anis [a'niːs] *m* -e *(Gewürz)* aniseed; *(Pflanze)* anise.

Anisett *m* -s *m* anisette, aniseed liqueur.

ankämpfen *vi sep* **gegen etw** ~ to fight (against) sth; *gegen Wind, Strömung* to battle against sth.

ankarren *vt sep (col)* to cart along.

Ankauf *m* purchase. **An- und Verkauf von ...** we buy and sell ...

ankaufen *vti sep* to purchase, to buy.

Anker *m* - *(Naut, Archit, fig)* anchor. **vor** ~ **gehen** to drop anchor; **vor** ~ **liegen** to lie *or* ride at anchor; **den/die** ~ **lichten** to weigh anchor.

ankern *vi (Anker werfen)* to anchor; *(vor Anker liegen)* to be anchored.

Anker-: ~**platz** *m* anchorage; ~**winde** *f* capstan.

anketten *vt sep* to chain up *(an +acc or dat* to). **angekettet sein** *(fig)* to be tied up.

ankläffen *vt sep (pej)* to bark at; *(kleiner Hund)* to yap at.

Anklage *f* **(a)** *(Jur)* charge; *(~vertretung)* prosecution. **gegen jdn** ~ **erheben** to bring *or* prefer charges against sb; **(wegen etw) unter** ~ **stehen** to have been charged (with sth). **(b)** *(fig) (Beschuldigung)* accusation; *(Anprangerung)* indictment *(an+acc* of).

Anklagebank f dock. **auf der ~ (sitzen)** *(lit, fig)* (to be) in the dock.

anklagen *vt sep (Jur)* to charge, to accuse. **jdn einer Sache** *(gen) or* **wegen etw ~** to charge sb with sth, to accuse sb of sth.

anklagend *adj Ton* accusing; *Blick* reproachful.

Anklagepunkt m charge.

Ankläger m - *(Jur)* prosecutor.

Anklage-: **~schrift** f indictment; **~vertreter** m (public) prosecutor, counsel for the prosecution.

anklammern *sep* 1 *vt (mit Büroklammer)* to clip *(an+acc or dat* (on)to); *(mit Heftmaschine)* to staple *(an+acc or dat* on(to), to). 2 *vr* **sich an jdn/etw** *(acc or dat)* ~ to cling to sb/sth.

Anklang m (a) *no pl (Beifall)* approval. ~ **(bei jdm) finden** to meet with (sb's) approval; **großen/wenig/keinen ~ finden** to be very well/ poorly/badly received. **(b)** *(Reminiszenz)* **Anklänge an etw** *(acc)* **enthalten** to be reminiscent of sth.

ankleben *vt sep* to stick up *(an +acc or dat* on). **Plakate ~ verboten** stick no bills.

Ankleidekabine f changing cubicle.

ankleiden *vtr sep (geh)* to dress.

Ankleideraum m dressing-room; *(im Schwimmbad, Geschäft)* changing room.

anklingen *vi sep aux sein (erinnern)* to be reminiscent *(an+acc* of); *(angeschnitten werden)* to be touched (up)on.

anklopfen *vi sep* to knock *(an +acc or dat* at, on).

anknabbern *vt sep (col) (annagen)* to gnaw or nibble (at). **zum A~ (aussehen)** *(fig)* (to look) good enough to eat.

anknacksen *vt sep (col) Knochen* to crack; *Fuß, Gelenk etc* to crack a bone in.

anknipsen *vt sep* to switch on; *Schalter* to flick.

anknüpfen *sep* 1 *vt Beziehungen* to establish; *Gespräch* to start up. 2 *vi* **an etw** *(acc)* ~ to take sth up.

Anknüpfung f *(fig)* siehe vt establishing; starting up. **in ~ an etw** *(acc)* following on from sth.

Anknüpfungspunkt m link.

ankommen *sep irreg aux sein* 1 *vi* (a) to arrive. **bist du gut angekommen?** did you arrive safely or get there all right?; **bei etw angekommen sein** to have reached sth, to have got to sth; **das Kind soll in 6 Wochen ~** the baby is due (to arrive) in 6 weeks. **(b)** *(sich nähern)* to approach. **(c)** *(Anklang, Anregung finden) (bei* with) to go down well; *(Mode, Neuerungen)* to catch on. **damit kommst du bei ihm nicht an!** you won't get anywhere with him like that; **es ist erstaunlich, wie er bei Mädchen ankommt** it's amazing what a success he is with the girls. **(d)** *(sich durchsetzen)* **gegen etw ~** *gegen Gewohnheit, Sucht etc* to be able to fight sth; **er ist zu stark, ich komme gegen ihn nicht an** he's too strong, I'm no match for him.

2 *vi impers* (a) *(wichtig sein)* **es kommt auf etw** *(acc)* **an** sth matters; **es kommt darauf an, daß wir ...** what matters is that we ...; **darauf soll es mir/uns** *etc* **nicht ~** that doesn't matter. **(b)** *(abhängig sein)* to depend *(auf +acc* on). **es kommt darauf an** it (all) depends; **es käme auf einen Versuch an** we'd have to give it a try. **(c)** *(col)* **es darauf ~ lassen** to chance it; **laß es nicht drauf ~!** don't push your luck! *(col);* **er ließ es auf einen Streit/einen Versuch ~** he was prepared to argue about it/to give it a try.

ankoppeln *vt sep (Rail)* to couple up *(an+acc* to); *(Space)* to link up *(an +acc* with, to).

ankotzen *vt sep (col: anwidern)* to make sick *(col)*.

ankratzen *vt sep (fig)* jds *Ruf etc* to damage; *siehe* **angekratzt.**

ankreiden *vt sep (fig)* **jdm etw** *(dick or* übel) ~ to hold sth against sb.

ankreuzen *vt sep* to mark with a cross.

ankündigen *sep* 1 *vt* (a) *(ansagen, anmelden)* to announce; *(auf Plakat, in Zeitung etc)* to advertise. **(b)** *(auf etw hindeuten)* to be a sign of. 2 *vr (fig)* to be heralded *(durch* by). **der Frühling kündigt sich an** spring is in the air.

Ankündigung f announcement; *(vorherige Benachrichtigung)* advance notice.

Ankunft f, pl **Ankünfte** arrival.

Ankunftszeit f time of arrival.

ankuppeln *vt sep siehe* **ankoppeln.**

ankurbeln *vt sep Maschine* to wind up; *(fig) Wirtschaft, Konjunktur* to boost, to reflate.

Ankurbelung f *(fig)* reflation.

anlächeln *vt sep* to smile at.

anlachen *vt sep* to smile at. **sich** *(dat)* **jdn ~** *(col)* to pick sb up *(col)*.

Anlage f **-n** (a) *(Fabrik~)* plant. **(b)** *(Grün~, Park~)* (public) park; *(um ein Gebäude herum)* grounds *pl*. **(c)** *(Einrichtung) (Mil, Elec)* installation(s); *(Sport~ etc)* facilities *pl*. **(d)** *(col: Stereo~)* (stereo) system *or* equipment. **(e)** *(usu pl: Veranlagung)* aptitude, gift *(zu* for); *(Neigung)* predisposition, tendency *(zu* to). **(f)** *(Kapital~)* investment. **(g)** *(Beilage zu einem Schreiben)* enclosure. **als ~ or in der ~ erhalten Sie ...** please find enclosed ...

Anlageberater m investment consultant.

anlangen *sep* 1 *vi aux sein (an einem Ort)* to arrive. **am Gipfel angelangt sein** to have reached the summit. 2 *vt (betreffen)* to concern. **was mich anlangt** as far as I am concerned.

Anlaß m, pl **Anlässe** (a) *(Veranlassung)* (immediate) cause *(zu* for). **welchen ~ hatte er, das zu tun?** what prompted him to do that?; **es besteht kein ~ ...** there is no reason ...; **etw zum ~ nehmen, zu ...** to use sth as an opportunity to ...; **beim geringsten/bei jedem ~** for the slightest reason/at every opportunity; **das gibt ~ zur Sorge** this gives cause for concern. **(b)** *(Gelegenheit)* occasion. **aus diesem ~** on this occasion.

anlassen *vt sep irreg* 1 *vt* (a) *Motor* to start (up). **(b)** *(col) Mantel* to keep on; *Wasserhahn, Motor, Licht, Radio* to leave on. 2 *vr* **sich gut/schlecht ~** to get off to a good/bad start.

Anlasser m - *(Aut)* starter.

anläßlich *prep +gen* on the occasion of.

anlasten *vt sep* **jdm etw ~** to blame sb for sth; **jdm etw als Schwäche ~** to regard *or* see sth as a weakness on sb's part.

Anlauf m, pl **Anläufe** (a) *(Sport)* run-up. **mit/ ohne ~** with a run-up/from standing; **~ nehmen** to take a run-up. **(b)** *(fig: Versuch)* attempt, try. **beim ersten/zweiten ~** at the first/second attempt.

anlaufen *sep irreg* 1 *vi aux sein* (a) *(beginnen)* to begin, to start; *(Saison auch, Film)* to open; *(Motor)* to start. **(b)** *rot/blau ~* to turn *or* go red/blue. **(c)** *(Sport: Anlauf nehmen)* to take a run-up. 2 *vt (Naut) Hafen etc* to put into, to call at.

Anlaufzeit f *(fig)* time to get going or started.

Anlegebrücke f landing stage, jetty.

anlegen *sep* 1 *vt* (a) *Leiter* to put up *(an+acc* against); *Brett, Karte* to lay (down) *(an+acc* next to, beside); *Lineal* to position, to set. **das Gewehr ~** to raise the gun to one's shoulder; **strengere Maßstäbe ~** to lay down or to impose stricter standards *(bei* in). **(b)** *Kartei, Akte* to start; *Vorräte* to lay in; *Garten etc* to lay out. **(c)** *(investieren) Geld* to invest; *(ausgeben)* to spend *(für* on). **(d)** *es darauf ~, daß ...* to be determined that ...; *siehe* **angelegt.** 2 *vi* (a) *(Naut)* to berth. **(b)** *(Gewehr ~)* to aim *(auf+acc* at). 3 *vr* **sich mit jdm ~** to pick an argument with sb.

Anlegeplatz m berth.

Anleger m - *(Fin)* investor.

anlehnen *sep* 1 *vt* to lean or rest *(an+acc* against). **angelehnt sein** *(Tür)* to be ajar; *(Fenster)* to be slightly open. 2 *vr (lit)* to lean *(an+acc* against);

sich an etw *(acc)* ~ *(fig)* to follow sth.
Anlehnung *f* **(a)** *(Anschluß)* dependence *(an+acc on)*. ~ **an jdn suchen** to seek sb's support. **(b)** *(Imitation)* **in** ~ **an jdn/etw** following sb/sth.
Anlehnungs-: ~**bedürfnis** *nt* need of loving care; **a**~**bedürftig** *adj* needing loving care.
Anleihe *f* **-n** *(Fin)* loan; *(Wertpapier)* bond. **eine** ~ **aufnehmen** to take out a loan; **bei jdm eine** ~ **machen** to borrow (money) from sb.
anleinen *vt sep (festmachen)* to tie up. **den Hund** ~ **to put the dog's lead on.**
anleiten *vt sep* **(a)** *(unterweisen)* to teach, to instruct. **(b)** *(erziehen)* **jdn zu etw** ~ to teach sb sth.
Anleitung *f (Erklärung, Hilfe)* instructions *pl.* **unter der** ~ **seines Vaters** under his father's guidance or direction.
anlernen *vt sep (ausbilden)* to train; *siehe* **angelernt.**
anlesen *vt sep irreg (aneignen)* **sich** *(dat)* **etw** ~ to learn sth by reading.
anliefern *vt sep* to deliver.
Anlieferung *f* delivery.
Anliegen *nt* - **(a)** *(Bitte)* request. **(b)** *(wichtige Angelegenheit)* matter of concern.
anliegen *vi sep irreg* **(a)** *(anstehen, vorliegen)* to be on. **(b)** *(Kleidung)* to fit closely or tightly *(an etw (dat)* sth); *(Haar)* to lie flat *(an+dat* against, on).
anliegend *adj* **(a)** *Ohren* flat. **(eng)** ~ *Kleidung* tight- or close-fitting. **(b)** *(in Briefen)* enclosed. **(c)** *Grundstück* adjacent.
Anlieger *m* - neighbour *(Brit)*, neighbor *(US)*; *(Anwohner)* (local) resident. ~ **frei** no thoroughfare — residents only.
Anlieger-: ~**staat** *m* **die** ~**staaten des Schwarzen Meers** the countries bordering (on) the Black Sea; ~**verkehr** *m* (local) residents' vehicles.
anlocken *vt sep* to attract; *Tiere* auch to lure.
Anlockung *f* attraction.
anlügen *vt sep irreg* to lie to, to tell lies to.
anmachen *vt sep* **(a)** *(col: befestigen)* to put up *(an +acc or dat* on). **(b)** *(zubereiten)* to mix; *Salat* to dress. **(c)** *(anstellen)* Radio, Licht, Heizung *etc* to put or turn on; *Feuer* to light. **(d)** *(col: ansprechen)* **er versuchte ständig, sie anzumachen** he kept trying to chat her up *(col)*.
anmahnen *vt sep* to send a reminder about.
anmalen *sep* **1** *vt* to paint. **2** *vr (pej: schminken)* to paint one's face or oneself.
Anmarsch *m no pl (Mil)* advance. **im** ~ **sein** to be advancing *(auf+acc* on); *(hum)* to be on the way.
anmarschieren* *vi sep aux sein (Mil)* to advance.
anmaßen *vr sep* **sich** *(dat)* **etw** ~ *Befugnis, Recht* to claim sth (for oneself); *Titel, Macht, Autorität* to assume sth; **sich** *(dat)* **ein Urteil über etw** *(acc)* ~ to presume to pass judgement on sth.
anmaßend *adj* presumptuous.
Anmaßung *f* presumption, presumptuousness. **es ist eine** ~ **zu meinen, ...** it is presumptuous to maintain that ...
Anmeldeformular *nt* application form.
anmelden *sep* **1** *vt* **(a)** *(ankündigen)* Besuch to announce. **(b)** *(bei Schule, Kurs etc)* to enrol *(bei at, zu* for). **(c)** *(eintragen lassen)* Patent to apply for; *neuen Wohnsitz, Auto* to register *(bei* at); *Fernseher* to get a licence *(Brit)* or license *(US)* for. Konkurs ~ to declare oneself bankrupt. **(d)** *(Telec)* **ein Gespräch nach Deutschland** ~ to book a call to Germany. **(e)** *(geltend machen)* Recht, Ansprüche, *(zu Steuerzwecken)* to declare. **ich melde starke Bedenken an** I have serious doubts about that. **2** *vr* **(a)** *(ankündigen: Besucher)* to announce one's arrival. **(b)** *(an Schule, zu Kurs etc)* to enrol (oneself) *(an+dat, zu* for). **sich polizeilich** ~ to register with the police. **(c)** *(sich einen Termin geben lassen)* to make an appointment.
Anmeldung *f (an Schule, zu Kurs etc)* enrolment

(an+dat at, *zu* for); *(bei Polizei)* registration. **nur nach vorheriger** ~ by appointment only.
anmerken *vt sep (sagen)* to say; *(als Fußnote)* to note. **jdm seine Verlegenheit** *etc* ~ to notice sb's embarrassment *etc*; **sich** *(dat)* **etw** ~ **lassen** to let sth show.
Anmerkung *f* note.
anmieten *vt sep* to rent.
anmustern *vti (Naut)* to sign on.
Anmut *f no pl* grace; *(Grazie auch)* gracefulness; *(Schönheit)* beauty, loveliness.
anmuten *sep* **1** *vt (geh)* to appear, to seem *(jdn* to sb). **2** *vi* **eine eigenartig** ~**de Geschichte** a story that strikes one as odd.
anmutig *adj (geh) (geschmeidig)* Bewegung graceful; *(hübsch anzusehen)* lovely, charming.
annageln *vt sep* to nail on *(an +acc* or *dat* -to). **er stand wie angenagelt da** he stood there rooted to the spot.
annagen *vt sep* to gnaw (at).
annähen *vt sep* to sew on *(an +acc or dat* -to); *Saum* to sew up.
annähern *sep* **1** *vt* to bring closer *(dat, an+acc* to). **2** *vr* **(a)** *(lit, fig: sich nähern)* to approach *(einer Sache (dat)* sth). **(b)** *(sich angleichen, näherkommen)* to come closer *(dat, an+acc* to).
annähernd **1** *adj (ungefähr)* approximate, rough. **2** *adv (etwa)* roughly; *(fast)* almost. **nicht** ~ **soviel** not nearly as much.
Annäherung *f (lit, fig)* approach *(an+acc* towards); *(von Standpunkten)* convergence *(dat, an +acc* with). **die** ~ **zwischen Ost und West** the rapprochement of East and West.
Annäherungsversuch *m* overtures *pl*.
Annahme *f* **-n** **(a)** *(Vermutung, Voraussetzung)* assumption. **in der** ~**, daß ...** on the assumption that ...; **von einer** ~ **ausgehen** to work on an assumption. **(b)** *siehe* **annehmen (a)** acceptance; taking; approval; passing; adoption. ~ **an Kindes Statt** *(child)* adoption.
Annahme-: ~**frist** *f* ~**frist bis zum 17. Juli** closing date 17th July; **die** ~**frist einhalten** to meet the deadline; ~**stelle** *f (für Pakete, Telegramme)* counter; *(für Lotto etc)* (national lottery etc) agency; *(für Reparaturen)* reception; *(für Material)* delivery point; ~**verweigerung** *f* refusal.
Annalen *pl* annals *pl.* **in die** ~ **eingehen** *(fig)* to go down in the annals or in history.
annehmbar *adj* acceptable; *(nicht schlecht)* reasonable, not bad.
annehmen *sep irreg* **1** *vt* **(a)** to accept; *einen Rat* to take; *(billigen)* to approve; *Gesetz* to pass; *Resolution* to adopt. **(b)** *(vermuten, voraussetzen)* to assume. **von jdm etw** ~ *(erwarten)* to expect sth of sb; *(glauben)* to believe sth of sb; **was nehmen Sie denn von mir an!** what do you take me for?; *siehe* **angenommen. (c)** *(sich aneignen)* to adopt; Gewohnheit *etc* auch to pick up; *Staatsangehörigkeit* auch to take on; *Gestalt, Namen* to assume, to take on. **jdn an Kindes Statt** ~ to adopt sb. **2** *vr* **sich jds/einer Sache** ~ to look after a person/a matter.
Annehmlichkeit *f (Bequemlichkeit)* convenience. ~**en** *pl* comforts *pl.*
annektieren* *vt* to annex.
Annexion *f* annexation.
anno *adj* in the year. **von** ~ **dazumal** *(col)* or **Tobak** *(col)* from the year dot *(col)*; **ein Überbleibsel von** ~ **dazumal** *(col)* a hangover from the olden days.
Anno Domini *adv* in the year of Our Lord.
Annonce [a'nõːsə] *f* **-n** advertisement, advert *(Brit col)*, ad *(col)*.
annoncieren* [anõ'siːrən] *vti* to advertise.
annullieren* *vt (Jur)* to annul.
Anode *f* **-n** anode.
an|öden *vt sep (col: langweilen)* to bore stiff.

anomal adj (regelwidrig) unusual, abnormal; (nicht normal) strange, odd.

Anomalie f anomaly.

anonym adj anonymous.

Anonymität f anonymity.

Anorak m -s anorak (Brit), parka.

an|ordnen vt sep (a) (befehlen, festsetzen) to order. (b) (nach Plan ordnen, aufstellen) to arrange; (systematisch) to order.

An|ordnung f (a) (Befehl) order. **laut (polizeilicher)** ~ by order (of the police); **auf** ~ **des Arztes** on doctor's orders; ~**en treffen** to give orders. (b) (Aufstellung) arrangement; (systematische ~) order; (Formation) formation.

an|organisch adj (Chem) inorganic.

anormal adj (col) = **anomal**.

anpacken sep (col) 1 vt (a) (anfassen) to take hold of, to grab. (b) (handhaben, beginnen) to tackle, to set about. (c) (umgehen mit) jdn to treat. 2 vi (helfen: auch **mit** ~) to lend a hand.

anpassen sep 1 vt (a) Kleidung to fit (dat on). (b) (abstimmen) **etw einer Sache** (dat) ~ to suit sth to sth. (c) (angleichen) **etw einer Sache** (dat) ~ to bring sth into line with sth. 2 vr to adapt (oneself) (dat to); (einer Situation etc) to adjust (dat to); (gesellschaftlich) to conform. **wir mußten uns (ihren Wünschen)** ~ we had to fit in with their wishes or them; siehe **angepaßt**.

Anpassung f (an+acc to) adaptation; (an Gesellschaft, Normen etc) adjustment.

Anpassungs-: **a**~**fähig** adj adaptable; ~**fähigkeit** f adaptability; ~**schwierigkeiten** pl difficulties pl in adapting.

anpeilen vt sep (mit Radar, Funk etc) to take a bearing on. **etw** ~ (fig inf) to have one's sights on sth.

anpeitschen vt sep to force.

anpfeifen vt sep irreg (Sport) 1 vi to blow the whistle. 2 vt **das Spiel** ~ to start the game (by blowing one's whistle).

Anpfiff m (Sport) (starting) whistle; (Spielbeginn) kick-off.

anpflanzen vt sep (bepflanzen) to plant; (anbauen) to grow.

Anpflanzung f (a) siehe vt planting; growing. (b) (Fläche) cultivated area.

anpirschen vr sep to creep up (an +acc on).

anpöbeln vt sep (col) to pester.

Anprall m impact. **beim** ~ **gegen** on impact with.

anprangern vt sep to denounce.

anpreisen sep vt sep irreg to extol (jdm etw sth to sb). **sich (als etw)** ~ to sell oneself as sth.

Anprobe f fitting.

anprobieren* vt sep to try on.

anpumpen vt sep (col) to borrow from. **jdn um 50 Mark** ~ to touch sb for 50 marks (col).

anquatschen vt sep (col) to speak to; **Mädchen** to chat up (col).

Anrainer m - neighbour (Brit), neighbor (US). **die** ~ **der Nordsee** the countries bordering (on) the North Sea.

anraten vt sep irreg jdm etw ~ to recommend sth to sb; **auf A**~ **des Arztes** etc on the doctor's etc advice or recommendation.

anrechnen vt sep (a) (in Rechnung stellen) to charge for (jdm sb). (b) (gutschreiben) to count, to take into account (jdm sb). **das alte Auto rechnen wir (Ihnen) mit DM 500 an** we'll allow (you) DM 500 for the old car. (c) (bewerten) jdm **etw hoch** ~ to think highly of sb for sth; **jdm etw als Fehler** ~ (Lehrer) to count sth as a mistake; (fig) to consider sth as a fault on sb's part; **ich rechne es ihm als Verdienst an, daß ...** I think it is greatly to his credit that ...

Anrecht nt (Anspruch) right, entitlement (auf +acc to). **ein** ~ **auf etw** (acc) **haben** to be entitled to sth, to have a right to sth.

Anrede f form of address; (Brief~ auch)

salutation (form).

anreden vt sep to address. **jdn mit „du"** ~ to address sb as "du"; **jdn mit seinem Titel** ~ to address sb by his title.

anregen vt sep (a) (ermuntern) to prompt (zu to). **jdn zum Denken** ~ to make sb think. (b) (geh: vorschlagen) Verbesserung to propose, to suggest. (c) (beleben) to stimulate; Appetit auch to whet, to sharpen. **Kaffee regt an** coffee has a stimulating effect; siehe **angeregt**.

anregend adj stimulating.

Anregung f (a) (Antrieb, Impuls) stimulus. (b) (Vorschlag) idea. **auf** ~ **von** or +gen at or on the suggestion of. (c) (Belebung) stimulation.

Anregungsmittel nt stimulant.

anreichen vt sep to pass, to hand.

anreichern vt sep (gehaltvoller machen) to enrich.

Anreise f (Anfahrt) journey there/here. **die** ~ **zu diesem abgelegenen Ort ist sehr mühsam** it is very difficult to get to this remote place.

anreisen vi sep aux sein (a) (ein Ziel anfahren) to make a/the journey or trip (there/here). (b) (eintreffen) (auch angereist kommen) to come.

anreißen vt sep irreg (a) (kurz zur Sprache bringen) to touch on. (b) (pej col) Kunden to attract.

Anreiz m incentive. **ein** ~ **zum Lernen** a learning incentive.

anreizen sep 1 vt (anspornen) to encourage. 2 vi to act as an incentive (zu to).

anrempeln vt sep (anstoßen) to bump into; (absichtlich) Menschen to jostle.

anrennen vi sep irreg aux sein **gegen etw** ~ **gegen** Wind etc to run against sth; (Mil) to storm sth.

Anrichte f -n (Schrank) dresser; (Büfett) sideboard.

anrichten vt sep (a) Speisen to prepare. **es ist angerichtet** (form) dinner etc is served (form). (b) (fig) Unheil etc to cause, to bring about. **da hast du aber etwas angerichtet!** (col) (verursacht) you've started something there all right; (angestellt) you've really made a mess there.

anrosten vi sep aux sein to get (a bit) rusty.

anrüchig adj (von üblem Ruf) of ill repute; Lokal etc notorious.

anrücken vi sep aux sein (Truppen) to advance; (Polizei etc) to move in.

Anruf m call; (Mil: eines Wachtpostens) challenge. **etw auf** ~ **tun** to do sth when called.

Anrufbeantworter m (telephone) answering machine, answerphone.

anrufen sep irreg 1 vt (a) (zurufen) to shout to; (Telec) to call, to phone, to ring (Brit); (Mil: Posten) to challenge. **darf ich dich** ~? can I give you a ring? (Brit), can I call you? (b) (fig: appellieren an) to appeal to (um for). 2 vi (col: telefonieren) to phone, to make a (phone) call. **bei jdm** ~ to phone sb; **kann man Sie** ~? are you on the phone?

Anrufer m caller.

Anrufung f (Gottes, der Heiligen etc) invocation; (Jur) appeal (gen to).

anrühren vt sep (a) (berühren, sich befassen) to touch; (fig) Thema to touch on. **er rührt kein Fleisch/keinen Alkohol an** he doesn't touch meat/alcohol. (b) (mischen) Farben to mix; Sauce to blend; (verrühren) to stir.

ans = **an das**.

Ansage f -n announcement; (Cards) bid.

ansagen sep 1 vt (a) to announce. **jdm den Kampf** ~ to declare war on sb. (b) (Cards) to bid; (Skat) to declare. 2 vr (Besuch ankündigen) to say that one is coming.

Ansager(in f) m - (Rad etc) announcer.

ansammeln sep 1 vt (a) (anhäufen) to accumulate. (b) (zusammenkommen lassen) to gather together; Truppen to concentrate. 2 vr (a) (sich versammeln) to gather, to collect. (b) (aufhäufen) to accumulate; (Staub, Wasser auch) to collect; (Druck, fig: Wut) to build up; (Zinsen) to build up.

Ansammlung f (a) (Anhäufung) accumulation; (Sammlung) collection; (von Druck, Wut) build-up; (Haufen) pile. (b) (Auflauf) gathering, crowd; (von Truppen) concentration.

ansässig adj (form) resident. **alle in diesem Ort A~en** all local residents.

Ansatz m (a) (von Hals, Arm, Henkel etc) base. (b) (Tech) (Zusatzstück) attachment; (zur Verlängerung) extension; (Naht) join. (c) (erstes Anzeichen, Beginn) first sign(s pl), beginning(s pl); (Ausgangspunkt) starting-point.

Ansatz-: ~**punkt** m starting-point; ~**stück** nt (Tech) attachment; (zur Verlängerung) extension.

ansaugen vt sep to suck or draw in.

anschaffen sep 1 vt (sich dat) etw ~ to get oneself sth; (kaufen) to buy sth; **sich** (dat) **Kinder** ~ (col) to have children. 2 vi (col: durch Prostitution) ~ **gehen** to be on the game (col).

Anschaffung f acquisition. **ich habe mich zur** ~ **eines Autos entschlossen** I have decided to buy a new car. ~**en machen** to acquire things; (kaufen) to make purchases.

Anschaffungs-: ~**kosten** pl cost sing of purchase; ~**preis** m purchase price.

anschalten vt sep to switch on.

anschauen vt sep to look at; (prüfend) to examine. **sich** (dat) **etw** ~ to have a look at sth.

anschaulich adj clear; (lebendig, bildhaft) vivid; Beschreibung graphic; Beispiel concrete. **etw** ~ **machen** to illustrate sth.

Anschauung f (Ansicht, Auffassung) view; (Meinung) opinion. **nach neuerer** ~ according to the current way of thinking.

Anschauungsmaterial nt illustrative material, visual aids pl.

Anschein m appearance; (Eindruck) impression. **allem** ~ **nach** to all appearances, apparently; **den** ~ **erwecken, als ...** to give the impression that ...; **es hat den** ~**, als ob ...** it appears that or seems as if ...

anscheinend adv apparently.

anschicken vr sep **sich** ~**, etw zu tun** (geh: im Begriff sein) to be about to do sth.

anschieben vt sep irreg Fahrzeug to push.

anschießen sep irreg 1 vt (a) (verletzen) to shoot (and wound); Vogel (in Flügel) to wing; siehe **angeschossen**. (b) (col: kritiseren) to hit out at (col). 2 vi aux sein (col) (heranrasen) to shoot up. **angeschossen kommen** to come shooting along or (auf einen zu) up.

anschimmeln vi sep aux sein to (start to) go mouldy.

Anschiß m -sse (col) bollocking (col!).

Anschlag m (a) (Plakat) poster; (Bekanntmachung) notice. **einen** ~ **machen** to put up a poster/notice. (b) (Überfall) attack (auf+acc on); (Attentat) attempt on sb's life. **einen** ~ **zum Opfer fallen** to be assassinated. (c) (von Klavier(spieler), Schreibmaschine) touch. **200 Anschläge in der Minute** = 40 words per minute. (d) (bei Hebel, Knopf etc) stop. **etw bis zum** ~ **durchdrücken** to push sth right down. (e) (Mil) **ein Gewehr im** ~ **haben** to have a rifle at the ready.

Anschlagbrett nt notice-board (Brit), bulletin board (US).

anschlagen sep irreg 1 vt (a) (befestigen) to fix on (an+acc -to); (mit Nägeln) to nail on (an+acc -to); (aushängen) Plakat to put up, to post (an+acc on). (b) Taste, Akkord to strike. **eine schnellere Gangart** ~ (fig) to speed up; **einen anderen Ton** ~ (fig) to change one's tune. (c) (beschädigen, verletzen) Geschirr to chip. 2 vi (a) (Welle) to beat (an+acc auf). (b) (Laut geben) (Hund) to give a bark; (Vogel) to give a screech. (c) (wirken: Arznei etc) to work, to take effect.

anschleichen sep irreg 1 vi aux sein to creep along or (auf einen zu) up. **angeschlichen kommen** (col) to come creeping along/up. 2 vr **sich an jdn/etw**

~ **to creep up on sb/sth**; (sich anpirschen) to stalk sth.

anschleppen vt sep (a) Auto to tow-start. (b) (col: unerwünscht mitbringen) to bring along; (nach Hause) to bring home; Freund etc auch to drag along (col).

anschließen sep irreg 1 vt (a) (an+acc to) (Tech, Elec, Telec etc: verbinden) to connect; (in Steckdose) to plug in. (b) (fig: hinzufügen) to add; siehe **angeschlossen**. 2 vr **sich jdm** or **an jdn** ~ (folgen) to follow sb; (zugesellen) to join sb; (beipflichten) to side with sb; **sich einer Sache** (dat) or **an etw** (acc) ~ (folgen) to follow sth; (beitreten, sich beteiligen) to join sth; (beipflichten) to endorse sth; (angrenzen) to adjoin sth; **sich an ein Datennetz** ~ to link up with a data network. 3 vi **an etw** (acc) ~ to follow sth.

anschließend 1 adv afterwards. 2 adj following. **Essen mit** ~**em Tanz** dinner with a dance afterwards.

Anschluß m (a) (Verbindung) connection; (Beitritt) entry (an+acc into); (an Klub) joining (an +acc of). ~ **haben nach** (Rail) to have a connection to; **den** ~ **verpassen** (Rail etc) to miss one's connection; (fig) to miss the boat (col). **ihm gelang der** ~ **an die Spitze** (Sport) he managed to catch up with the leaders. (b) (Telec) connection; (weiterer Apparat) extension. ~ **bekommen** to get through; **kein** ~ **unter dieser Nummer** number unobtainable. (c) **im** ~ **an** (+acc) (nach) subsequent to, following. (d) (fig: Kontakt) contact (an+acc with); ~ **finden** to make friends (an +acc with); **er sucht** ~ he wants to make friends.

Anschlußzug m (Rail) connecting train, connection.

anschmiegen vr sep **sich an jdn/etw** ~ (Kind, Hund) to snuggle or nestle up to or against sb/sth; (Kleidung) to cling to sb/sth.

anschmiegsam adj Wesen affectionate; Material smooth.

anschmieren vt sep (a) (bemalen) to smear. (b) (col) (betrügen) to con (col); (Streiche spielen) to play tricks on; siehe **angeschmiert**.

anschnallen sep 1 vt Rucksack to strap on; Skier to clip on. 2 vr (Aviat, Aut) to fasten one's seat belt. **bitte** ~! fasten your seat belts, please!

Anschnallpflicht f in Taxis **ist jetzt** ~ you now have to wear a seat belt in taxis.

anschnauzen vt sep (col) to yell at.

anschneiden vt sep irreg (a) Brot etc to (start to) cut. (b) (fig) Frage, Thema to touch on. (c) (Aut) Kurve, (Sport) Ball to cut.

Anschovis [an'ʃoːvɪs] f - anchovy.

anschrauben vt sep to screw on (an +acc -to).

anschreiben sep irreg 1 vt (a) (aufschreiben) to write up (an+acc on). **etw mit Kreide** ~ to chalk sth up; siehe **angeschrieben**. (b) (col: in Rechnung stellen) to chalk up. (c) Behörde, Versandhaus etc to write to. 2 vi (col) **sie läßt immer** ~ she always buys on tick (col).

anschreien vt sep irreg to shout or yell at.

Anschrift f address.

anschuldigen vt sep to accuse (gen of).

Anschuldigung f accusation.

anschwärzen vt sep (fig col) **jdn** ~ to blacken sb's name (bei with).

anschweißen vt sep to weld on (an +acc -to).

anschwellen vi sep irreg aux sein to swell (up); (Lärm) to rise. **dick angeschwollen** very swollen.

anschwemmen vt sep to wash up or ashore.

anschwimmen vt sep irreg 1 vi to swim towards. 2 vi aux sein **gegen etw** ~ to swim against sth.

anschwindeln vt sep (col) **jdn** ~ to tell sb fibs (col).

ansehen vt sep irreg (a) (betrachten) to look at. **er sah mich ganz böse an** he gave me an angry look; **hübsch** etc **anzusehen** pretty etc to look at; **das sehe sich einer an!** just look at that!

(b) *(fig)* to regard, to look upon *(als, für as)*. **ich sehe es als meine Pflicht an** I consider it to be my duty; *siehe* **angesehen.**

(c) (sich *dat)* **etw ~ to** (have a) look at sth; *Fernsehsendung* to watch sth; *Film, Stück, Veranstaltung* to see sth; **sich** *(dat)* **jdn/etw gründlich ~** *(lit,fig)* to take a close look at sb/sth.

(d) das sieht man ihm an/nicht an he looks it/doesn't look it; **man kann ihm die Strapazen der letzten Woche ~** he's showing the strain of the past week; **man sieht ihm sein Alter nicht an** he doesn't look his age; **jdm etw an den Augen** *or* **an der Nasenspitze** *(hum)* **~** to tell *or* guess sth by looking at sb.

(e) etw (mit) ~ to watch sth, to see sth happening; **ich kann das nicht länger mit ~** I can't stand it any more.

Ansehen *nt no pl* **(a)** *(Aussehen)* appearance. **jdn vom ~ kennen** to know sb by sight. **(b)** *(guter Ruf)* good reputation, standing. **großes ~ genießen** to enjoy a good reputation; **an ~ verlieren** to lose credit *or* standing. **(c)** *(Jur)* **ohne ~ der Person** without respect of person.

ansehnlich *adj (beträchtlich)* considerable; *Leistung* impressive.

anseilen *vt sep* **jdn/sich ~** to rope sb/oneself up.

ansein *vi sep irreg aux sein (col)* to be on.

ansetzen *sep* **1** *vt* **(a)** *(in Stellung bringen)* to place in position. **das Glas ~** to raise the glass to one's lips; **an welcher Stelle muß man den Wagenheber ~?** where should the jack be put *or* placed? **(b)** *(festlegen) Kosten, Termin* to fix *(mit at, auf+acc for)*. **(c)** *(einsetzen)* **jdn auf jdn/etw ~** to put sb on(to) sb/sth. **(d)** *(entstehen lassen)* **Fett ~** to put on weight; **Rost ~** to get rusty. **(e)** *(Cook) (vorbereiten)* to prepare; *(auf den Herd setzen)* to put on. **2** *vr (Rost)* to form; *(Kalk etc)* to be deposited. **3** *vi* **(a)** *(beginnen)* to start, to begin. **zur Landung ~** *(Aviat)* to come in to land; **zum Sprung/Spurt ~** to get ready to jump/to start one's spurt. **(b)** *(Cook: sich festsetzen)* to stick.

Ansicht *f* **-en (a)** view. **~ von hinten/vorn** rear/front view; **~ von oben/unten** view from above/below, top/bottom view *(Tech)*. **(b)** *(das Betrachten, Prüfen)* inspection. **zur ~** *(Comm)* for (your/our *etc)* inspection; **jdm Waren zur ~ schicken** *(Comm)* to send sb goods on approval. **(c)** *(Meinung)* opinion, view. **nach ~ +gen** in the opinion of; **meiner ~ nach** in my opinion *or* view; **anderer/der gleichen ~ sein** to be of a different/the same opinion, to disagree/agree; **ich bin ganz Ihrer ~** I entirely agree with you; **die ~en sind geteilt** opinions differ, opinion is divided.

Ansichts-: **~karte** *f* picture postcard; **~sache** *f* **das ist ~sache** that is a matter of opinion.

ansiedeln *sep* **1** *vt* to settle; *Tierart* to introduce. **2** *vr* to settle; *(Industrie etc)* to set up.

Ansiedlung *f* settlement.

Ansinnen *nt (dated, geh: Vorschlag)* suggestion.

ansonsten *adv* otherwise.

anspannen *vt sep* **(a)** *(straffen)* to tauten, to tighten; *Muskeln* to tense. **(b)** *(anstrengen)* to strain, to tax; *Geduld, Mittel auch* to stretch. **alle seine Kräfte ~** to strain every nerve; *siehe* **angespannt. (c)** *Wagen, Pferd* to hitch up.

Anspannung *f (fig)* strain; *(körperliche Anstrengung auch)* effort.

Anspiel *nt (Sport)* start of play. **das ~ haben** to start play; *(Ftbl)* to kick off.

anspielen *sep* **1** *vt (Sport)* to play the ball *etc* to; *Spieler* to pass to. **2** *vi* **auf jdn/etw ~** to allude to sb/sth; **worauf wollen Sie ~?** what are you driving at?, what are you insinuating?

Anspielung *f* allusion *(auf +acc to)*; *(böse)* insinuation, innuendo *(auf +acc regarding)*.

anspitzen *vt sep Bleistift etc* to sharpen.

Ansporn *m no pl* incentive.

anspornen *vt sep (fig)* to spur on, to encourage *(zu to)*.

Ansprache *f (Rede)* address, speech. **eine ~ halten** to make a speech.

ansprechbar *adj* **(a) er ist beschäftigt/wütend und zur Zeit nicht ~** he's so busy/angry that you can't talk to him just now. **(b)** *Patient* responsive.

ansprechen *sep irreg* **1** *vt* **(a)** *(anreden)* to speak to; *(belästigend)* to accost. **jdn auf etw** *(acc)* **~** to ask *or* approach sb about sth; **damit sind Sie alle angesprochen** this is directed at all of you. **(b)** *(gefallen)* to appeal to; *(Eindruck machen auf)* to make an impression on. **2** *vi (auf +acc to) (reagieren)* *(Patient, Gaspedal etc)* to respond; *(Meßgerät auch)* to react. **diese Tabletten sprechen bei ihr nicht an** these tablets don't have any effect on her.

ansprechend *adj (reizvoll) Äußeres, Verpackung etc* attractive, appealing.

anspringen *sep irreg* **1** *vt (anfallen)* to jump; *(Raubtier)* to pounce on; *(Hund: hochspringen)* to jump up at. **2** *vi aux sein (Motor)* to start. **das Auto springt nicht an** the car won't start.

Anspruch *m, pl* **Ansprüche (a)** *(esp Jur)* claim; *(Recht)* right *(auf+acc to)*. **~ auf Schadenersatz erheben/haben** to make a claim for damages/to be entitled to damages. **(b)** *(Anforderung)* demand; *(Standard)* standard, requirement. **große** *or* **hohe Ansprüche stellen** to be very demanding; *(hohes Niveau verlangen)* to demand high standards; **den Ansprüchen gerecht werden** to meet the requirements. **(c)** *(Behauptung)* claim. **diese Theorie erhebt keinen ~ auf Unwiderlegbarkeit** this theory does not claim to be irrefutable. **(d) etw in ~ nehmen** *Recht* to claim sth; *jds Hilfe* to enlist sth; *Möglichkeiten, Kantine etc* to take advantage of sth; *Zeit, Kräfte* to take up sth; **darf ich Ihre Aufmerksamkeit in ~ nehmen?** may I have your attention?; **das nimmt mich sehr in ~** it keeps me very busy.

anspruchslos *adj (bescheiden)* modest, unassuming; *(wenig Pflege etc erfordernd)* undemanding; *Literatur, Musik* low-brow.

anspruchsvoll *adj (viel verlangend)* demanding; *(übertrieben ~)* hard to please, fastidious; *(hohe Ansprüche stellend)* Stil, Buch ambitious; *(kultiviert)* sophisticated.

anspucken *vt sep* to spit at *or* on.

anspülen *vt sep* to wash up *or* ashore.

anstacheln *vt sep* to spur (on); *(antreiben)* to drive *or* goad on.

Anstalt *f* **-en (a)** institution *(auch euph)*; *(Institut)* institute. **(b) ~en** *pl (Maßnahmen)* measures *pl*; *(Vorbereitungen)* preparations *pl*; **~en/keine ~en machen, etw zu tun** to make a/no move to do sth.

Anstand *m no pl (Schicklichkeit)* decency, propriety; *(Manieren)* (good) manners *pl*. **keinen ~ haben** to have no sense of decency/no manners.

anständig **1** *adj* decent; *Witz auch* clean; *(ehrbar)* respectable; *(col: beträchtlich)* sizeable, large. **das war nicht ~ von ihm** that was pretty bad of him; **eine ~e Tracht Prügel** *(col)* a good hiding. **2** *adv* decently. **sich ~ benehmen** to behave oneself; **sich ~ hinsetzen** to sit properly.

Anständigkeit *f* decency; *(Ehrbarkeit)* respectability.

Anstands-: **~formen** *pl* manners *pl*; **a~halber** *adv* out of politeness; **a~los** *adv* without difficulty.

anstarren *vt sep* to stare at.

anstatt **1** *prep+gen* instead of. **2** *conj* **~ zu arbeiten** instead of working.

anstauen *vr sep* to accumulate; *(Blut in Adern etc)* to congest; *(fig auch: Gefühle)* to build up. **angestaute Wut** pent-up rage.

anstechen *vt sep irreg* to make a hole in, to pierce;

Kartoffeln, Fleisch to prick; *Reifen* to puncture; *Faß* to tap, to broach.
anstecken *sep* 1 *vt* **(a)** *(befestigen)* to pin on; *Ring* to put *or* slip on. **(b)** *(anzünden)* to light; *(in Brand stecken)* to set fire to. **(c)** *(Med,fig)* to infect. 2 *vr* **sich (mit etw)** ~ to catch sth *(bei* from). 3 *vi (Med, fig)* to be infectious *or* catching; *(durch Berührung,fig)* to be contagious.
ansteckend *adj (Med, fig)* infectious, catching *pred (col); (durch Berührung,fig)* contagious.
Anstecknadel *f* pin, badge.
Ansteckung *f (Med)* infection; *(durch Berührung)* contagion.
Ansteckungsgefahr *f* danger of infection.
anstehen *vi sep irreg* **(a)** *(in Schlange)* to queue (up) *(Brit),* to stand in line *(nach* for). **(b)** *(Verhandlungspunkt)* to be on the agenda. **anstehende Probleme** problems facing us/them *etc.*
ansteigen *vi sep irreg aux sein* to rise; *(Temperatur, Preis, Zahl auch)* to go up, to increase.
anstelle *prep+gen* instead of, in place of.
anstellen *sep* 1 *vt* **(a)** to place; *(anlehnen)* to lean *(an+acc* against). **(b)** *(beschäftigen)* to employ, to take on; *siehe* **angestellt. (c)** *(anmachen, andrehen)* to turn on; *(in Gang setzen auch)* to start. **(d)** *Betrachtung, Vermutung etc* to make; *Vergleich auch* to draw. **(e)** *(machen, unternehmen)* to do; *(fertigbringen)* to manage. **(f)** *(col: Unfug treiben)* to get up to. **etwas** ~ to get up to mischief; **was hast du da wieder angestellt!** what have you done now?, what have you been up to now? 2 *vr* **(a)** *(Schlange stehen)* to queue (up) *(Brit),* to stand in line. **(b)** *(col: sich verhalten)* to act, to behave. **sich dumm/ungeschickt** ~ to act stupid/clumsily, to be stupid/clumsy. **(c)** *(col: sich zieren)* to make a fuss, to act up *(col).* **stell dich nicht so an!** don't make such a fuss!
Anstellung *f* employment.
ansteuern *vt sep* to make *or* steer *or* head *(auch hum)* for.
Anstich *m (von Faß)* tapping, broaching.
Anstieg *m* **-e (a)** *(Aufstieg)* climb, ascent; *(Weg)* ascent. **(b)** *(von Temperatur, Kosten, Preisen etc)* rise, increase *(gen* in).
anstiften *vt sep (anzetteln)* to instigate; *(verursachen)* to cause. **jdn zu etw** ~ to incite sb to (do) sth, to put sb up to sth *(col).*
Anstifter *m* instigator *(+gen, zu* of).
Anstiftung *f (von Mensch)* incitement *(zu* to); *(von Tat)* instigation.
anstimmen *vt sep* **(a)** *(singen)* to begin singing; *(Chorleiter) Grundton* to give; *(Kapelle)* to strike up, to start playing. **(b)** *(fig)* **ein Geschrei/ Proteste** *etc* ~ to start crying/protesting *etc.*
Anstoß *m* **(a)** impetus, impulse. **den (ersten)** ~ **zu etw geben** to initiate sth, to get sth going; **den** ~ **zu etw bekommen** to be prompted *or* encouraged to do sth; **es bedurfte eines neuen** ~**es** new impetus was needed. **(b)** *(Ftbl)* kick-off. **(c)** *(Ärgernis)* annoyance *(für* to). ~ **erregen** to cause offence *(bei* to); **ein Stein des** ~**es** *(umstrittene Sache)* a bone of contention.
anstoßen *sep irreg* 1 *vi* **(a)** *aux sein* **(an etw** *acc)* ~ to bump into sth. **(b)** *(mit den Gläsern)* ~ to clink glasses; **auf jdn/etw** ~ to drink to sb/sth. **(c)** *(Ftbl)* to kick off. **(d)** *(angrenzen)* **an etw** *(acc)* ~ to adjoin sth; *(Land auch)* to border on sth. 2 *vt* **jdn** to knock (into); *(mit dem Fuß)* to kick; *(in Bewegung setzen)* to give a push.
anstößig *adj (Verhalten; Kleidung* indecent.
anstrahlen *vt sep* to floodlight; *(im Theater)* to spotlight; *(strahlend ansehen)* to beam at.
anstreben *vt sep* to strive for.
anstreichen *vt sep irreg* **(a)** *(mit Farbe etc)* to paint. **(b)** *(markieren)* to mark. **(jdm) etw als Fehler** ~ to mark sth wrong.
Anstreicher *m* - (house) painter.
anstrengen *sep* 1 *vt* **(a)** to strain; *Muskel, Geist* to

exert; *(strapazieren) jdn* to tire out; *esp Patienten* to fatigue. **das viele Lesen strengt meine Augen/ mich an** all this reading puts a strain on my eyes/is a strain (for me); *siehe* **angestrengt. (b)** *(Jur)* **eine Klage** ~ to initiate *or* institute proceedings *(gegen* against). 2 *vr* to make an effort; *(körperlich auch)* to exert oneself. **sich mehr** ~ to make more of an effort.
anstrengend *adj (körperlich)* strenuous; *(geistig)* demanding; *(erschöpfend)* exhausting, tiring. **das ist** ~ **für die Augen** it's a strain on the eyes.
Anstrengung *f* effort; *(Strapaze)* strain. **große** ~**en machen** to make every effort.
Anstrich *m (das Anmalen, Tünchen)* painting; *(Farbüberzug)* paint; *(fig: Anflug)* touch. **ein zweiter** ~ a second coat of paint.
Ansturm *m* onslaught; *(auf Kaufhaus etc)* rush; *(auf Bank)* run; *(Menschenmenge)* crowd.
anstürmen *vi sep aux sein* **gegen etw** ~ *(Mil)* to attack *or* storm sth; *(Wellen, Wind)* to pound sth; *(fig: ankämpfen)* to attack sth.
Antagonismus *m* antagonism.
antanzen *vi sep aux sein (col)* to turn *or* show up *(col).*
Antarktis *f no pl* Antarctic.
antarktisch *adj* antarctic.
antasten *vt sep* **(a)** *Ehre, Würde* to offend; *Rechte* to infringe. **(b)** *(berühren)* to touch.
Anteil *m* **-e (a)** share. **(b)** *(Beteiligung)* ~ **an etw** *(dat)* **haben** *(beitragen)* to contribute to sth; *(teilnehmen)* to take part in sth. **(c)** *(Teilnahme: an Leid etc)* sympathy *(an+dat* with). **an etw** *(dat)* ~ **nehmen** an Leid etc to be deeply sympathetic over sth; *an Freude etc* to share in sth. **(d)** *(Interesse)* interest *(an+dat* in), concern *(an+dat* about). **regen** ~ **an etw** *(dat)* **nehmen** to take a lively interest in sth.
anteilig *adj* proportionate, proportional.
Anteilnahme *f no pl (Beileid)* sympathy *(an+dat* with).
antelefonieren* *vti sep (col)* to phone. **bei jdm** ~ to phone sb up.
Antenne *f* **-n** *(Rad, TV)* aerial, antenna *(US); (Zool)* feeler, antenna. **eine/keine** ~ **für etw haben** *(fig inf)* to have a/no feeling for sth.
Anthologie *f* anthology.
Anthrazit *m* **-e** anthracite.
anthrazit(farben) *adj* charcoal-grey, charcoal.
Anthropologe *m,* **Anthropologin** *f* anthropologist.
Anthropologie *f* anthropology.
anthropologisch *adj* anthropological.
Anti- *pref* anti; ~**alkoholiker** *m* teetotaller *(Brit),* teetotaler *(US);* **a~autoritär** *adj* anti-authoritarian; ~**babypille** *f (col)* (contraceptive) pill; ~**biotikum** *nt, pl* ~**biotika** antibiotic; **a~demokratisch** *adj* antidemocratic; ~**faschismus** *m* antifascism; ~**faschist** *m* antifascist; **a~faschistisch** *adj* antifascist; ~**held** *m* antihero; ~**heldin** *f* antiheroine.
antik *adj (Hist)* ancient; *(Comm, col)* antique.
Antike *f no pl* antiquity. **die Kunst der** ~ the art of the ancient world.
Anti-: ~**kommunismus** *m* anticommunism; ~**kommunist** *m* anticommunist; **a~kommunistisch** *adj* anticommunist; ~**körper** *m (Med)* antibody.
Antilope *f* **-n** antelope.
Anti-: ~**pathie** *f* antipathy *(gegen* to); ~**pode** *m* *(wk)* **-n, -n** antipodean; **die Engländer sind die** ~**poden Australiens** the English live on the opposite side of the world from Australia.
antippen *vt sep* to tap; *Pedal, Bremse* to touch; *(fig) Thema* to touch on.
Antiquar(in *f)* *m* antiquarian *or (von moderneren Büchern)* second-hand bookseller.
Antiquariat *nt* antiquarian *or (modernerer Bücher)* second-hand bookshop *(Brit)* or bookstore

(US). **modernes** ~ remainder bookshop.

antiquarisch *adj* antiquarian; *(von moderneren Büchern)* second-hand. **ein Buch** ~ **kaufen** to buy a book second-hand.

antiquiert *adj (pej)* antiquated.

Antiquität *f usu pl* antique.

Antiquitäten-: ~**geschäft** *nt* antique shop *(Brit)* or store *(US)*; ~**handel** *m* antique business *or* trade; ~**händler** *m* antique dealer.

Anti-: ~**semit** *m* antisemite; **a**~**semitisch** *adj* antisemitic; **a**~**septisch** *adj* antiseptic; **a**~**statisch** *adj* antistatic; ~**teilchen** *nt (Phys)* antiparticle; ~**these** *f* antithesis.

Antlitz *nt* **-e** *(poet)* countenance *(liter)*, face.

Antrag *m, pl* **Anträge** (a) *(auf+acc for)* application; *(Gesuch auch)* request; *(Formular)* application form. **einen** ~ **auf etw** *(acc)* **stellen** to make an application for sth. (b) *(Jur)* petition; *(bei Gericht)* claim. **einen** ~ **auf etw** *(acc)* **stellen** to file a petition/claim for sth. (c) *(Parl)* motion.

Antragsformular *nt* application form.

Antragsteller(in *f)* *m* - claimant; *(für Kredit etc)* applicant.

antreffen *vt sep irreg* to find; *Situation auch* to meet. **er ist schwer anzutreffen** it's difficult to catch him in; **ich habe ihn in guter Laune angetroffen** I found him in a good mood.

antreiben *vt* (a) *(vorwärtstreiben) Tiere, Gefangene* to drive; *(fig)* to urge. **jdn zur Eile/Arbeit** ~ to urge sb to hurry up/to work; **ich lasse mich nicht** ~ I won't be pushed. (b) *(bewegen) Rad etc* to drive; *(mit Motor auch)* to power.

Antreiber *m (pej)* slave-driver *(pej)*.

antreten *sep irreg* **1** *vt Reise, Strafe* to begin; *Stellung, Amt* to take up; *Erbe, Erbschaft* to come into. **den Beweis** ~, **daß** ... to prove that ...; **seine Lehrzeit** ~ to start one's apprenticeship. **2** *vi aux sein* (a) *(sich aufstellen)* to line up; *(Mil)* to fall in. (b) *(erscheinen)* to assemble; *(bei einer Stellung)* to start; *(zum Dienst)* to report. (c) *(zum Wettkampf)* to compete.

Antrieb *m* (a) impetus *no pl; (innerer)* drive. **aus eigenem** ~ on one's own initiative, off one's own bat *(col)*. (b) *(Triebkraft)* drive. **Auto mit elektrischem** ~ electrically driven *or* powered car.

Antriebs-: ~**kraft** *f (Tech)* power; ~**rad** *nt* drive wheel.

antrinken *vt sep irreg (col)* to start drinking. **sich** *(dat)* **einen (Rausch/Schwips)** ~ to get (oneself) drunk/tipsy; **sich** *(dat)* **Mut** ~ to give oneself Dutch courage; **eine angetrunkene Flasche** an opened bottle; *siehe* **angetrunken.**

Antritt *m no pl (Beginn)* beginning. **bei** ~ **der Reise** when beginning one's journey; **nach** ~ **der Stellung** after taking up the post.

antun *vt sep irreg* (a) *(erweisen)* **jdm (große) Ehre** ~ to pay (great) tribute to sb. (b) *(zufügen)* **jdm etw** ~ to do sth to sb. **sich** *(dat)* **ein Leid** ~ to injure oneself; **jdm Schaden/Unrecht** ~ to do sb an injury/injustice. (c) *(Sympathie erregen)* **es jdm** ~ to appeal to sb; *siehe* **angetan.**

anturnen ['antœrnən] *sep (col)* **1** *vt (Drogen, Musik)* to turn on *(col).* **2** *vi* to turn you on *(col).*

Antwort *f* **-en** (a) answer, reply; *(Lösung, bei Examen)* answer. **sie gab mir keine** ~ **auf die Frage** she didn't reply to *or* answer my question; **in** ~ **auf etw** *(acc) (form)* in reply to sth; **um umgehende** ~ **wird gebeten** please reply by return. (b) *(Reaktion)* response. **als** ~ **auf etw** *(acc)* in response to sth.

antworten *vti* (a) to answer, to reply. **jdm** ~ to answer sb, to reply to sb; **was soll ich ihm** ~? what should I tell him?; **mit Ja/Nein** ~ to answer yes/no. (b) *(reagieren)* to respond *(auf+acc to, mit with).*

anvertrauen* *sep* **1** *vt* **jdm etw** ~ *(übergeben)* to entrust sth to sb *or* sb with sth; *(vertraulich erzählen)* to confide sth to sb. **2** *vr* **sich jdm** ~

(sich mitteilen) to confide in sb.

Anverwandte(r) *mf decl as adj (geh)* relative, relation.

anvisieren* ['anvi-] *vt sep (fig)* to set one's sights on.

anwachsen *vi sep irreg aux sein* (a) *(festwachsen)* to grow on; *(Pflanze etc)* to take root; *siehe* **angewachsen.** (b) *(zunehmen) (auf+acc to)* to increase, to grow.

Anwachsen *nt* increase, growth. **im** ~ **sein** to be on the increase, to be growing.

Anwalt *m, pl* **Anwälte** (a) *siehe* **Rechtsanwalt.** (b) *(fig: Fürsprecher)* advocate.

Anwaltsbüro *nt* (a) lawyer's office. (b) *(Firma)* firm of lawyers *or* solicitors *(Brit).*

Anwalts-: ~**kammer** *f professional association of lawyers* ≈ Law Society *(Brit);* ~**kosten** *pl* legal expenses *pl;* ~**praxis** *f* legal practice; *(Räume)* lawyer's office.

Anwandlung *f (Laune)* mood; *(Drang)* impulse. **aus einer** ~ **heraus** on (an) impulse.

anwärmen *vt sep* to warm up.

Anwärter(in *f)* *m (Kandidat)* candidate *(auf+acc for); (Sport)* contender *(auf +acc for); (Thron~)* heir *(auf+acc to).*

anwehen *vt sep Sand* to blow; *Schnee* to drift.

anweisen *vt sep irreg* (a) *(anleiten) Schüler* to instruct; *(befehlen auch)* to order. (b) *(zuweisen) (jdm etw sb sth)* to allocate; *Zimmer auch* to give. **jdm einen Platz** ~ to show sb to a seat. (c) *Geld* to transfer. (d) *siehe* **angewiesen.**

Anweisung *f* (a) *(Fin)* payment; *(auf Konto etc)* transfer. (b) *(Anordnung)* instruction, order. (c) *(Zuweisung)* allocation. (d) *(Anleitung)* instructions *pl.*

anwendbar *adj Theorie, Regel* applicable *(auf +acc to).* **das ist in der Praxis nicht** ~ that is not practicable.

anwenden *vt sep auch irreg* (a) *(gebrauchen)* to use *(auf+acc on).* (b) *Theorie, Prinzipien* to apply *(auf+acc to); Erfahrung, Einfluß* to use, to bring to bear *(auf+acc on).* **sich auf etw** *(acc)* ~ **lassen** to be applicable to sth; *siehe* **angewandt.**

Anwender *m (esp Comp)* user.

Anwendung *f siehe vt* use; application. **etw zur** ~ **bringen** *(form)* to use/apply sth.

anwerben *vt sep irreg* to recruit *(für to).*

Anwerbung *f* recruitment.

anwerfen *vt sep irreg (Tech)* to start up.

anwesend *adj (form)* present. **ich war nicht ganz** ~ *(hum col)* my thoughts were elsewhere.

Anwesende(r) *mf decl as adj* person present. **die** ~**n** those present.

Anwesenheit *f* presence. **in** ~ +*gen or* **von** in the presence of.

Anwesenheitsliste *f* attendance list.

anwidern *vt sep* **jdn** ~ *(Essen, Anblick)* to make sb feel sick; **es/er widert mich an** I can't stand it/him; *siehe* **angewidert.**

Anwohner *m* - resident. **die** ~ **des Rheins** the people who live along *or* on the Rhine.

Anzahl *f no pl* number. **eine ganze** ~ quite a number.

anzahlen *vt sep Ware* to pay a deposit on, to make a down payment on. **100 DM** ~ to pay DM 100 down *or* DM 100 as a deposit.

Anzahlung *f* deposit, down payment *(für, auf +acc on); (erste Rate)* first instalment *(Brit)* or installment *(US).* **eine** ~ **machen** *or* **leisten** *(form)* to pay a deposit.

anzapfen *vt sep Faß* to broach; *Telefon, elektrische Leitung* to tap. **jdn (um Geld)** ~ *(col)* to touch sb (for money); **jdn** ~ *(col: Telec)* to tap sb's phone.

Anzeichen *nt* sign; *(Med auch)* symptom. **alle** ~ **deuten darauf hin, daß** ... all the signs are that ...

Anzeige *f* (a) *(bei Behörde)* report *(wegen of); (bei Gericht)* legal proceedings *pl.* **jdn/etw zur** ~ **bringen** *(form) (bei Polizei)* to report sb/sth to the

police; *(bei Gericht)* to take sb/bring sth to court.
(b) *(Bekanntgabe) (Karte, Brief)* announcement;
(in Zeitung auch) notice; *(Inserat, Reklame)* advertisement. **(c)** *(~tafel etc)* display.
anzeigen *vt sep* **(a)** *(bei der Polizei)* to report
sb (to the police); *(bei Gericht)* to institute legal
proceedings against sb. **(b)** *(bekanntgeben)*
Heirat etc to announce. **(c)** *(angeben) Temperatur,*
Zeit, Geschwindigkeit to show, to indicate.
Anzeige-: ~**blatt** *nt* advertiser; ~**teil** *m* advertisement section.
anzeigepflichtig *adj* notifiable.
Anzeiger *m (Tech)* indicator.
Anzeigetafel *f* indicator board.
anzetteln *vt sep* to instigate.
anziehen *sep irreg* **1** *vt* **(a)** *Kleidung* to put on. **sich**
(dat) **etw** ~ to put sth on. **(b)** *(straffen)* to pull
(tight); *Bremse (betätigen)* to apply, to put on;
Zügel to pull; *Schraube* to tighten. **(c)** *(Magnet,*
fig) to attract; *Geruch, Feuchtigkeit* to absorb. **sich**
von etw angezogen fühlen to feel attracted to
sth. **2** *vi* **(a)** *(beschleunigen)* to accelerate. **(b)**
(Chess etc) to make the first move. **(c)** *(Fin:*
Preise) to rise. **3** *vr* **(a)** *(sich kleiden)* to get
dressed. **(b)** *(fig: Gegensätze)* to attract each
other.
anziehend *adj (ansprechend)* attractive.
Anziehung *f* attraction.
Anziehungskraft *f (Phys)* force of attraction;
(fig) attraction, appeal. **eine große** ~ **auf jdn**
ausüben to attract sb strongly.
Anzug *m, pl* **Anzüge (a)** *(Herren~)* suit. **(b)** *(das*
Heranrücken) approach. **im** ~ **sein** to be coming;
(Gewitter, Gefahr) to be in the offing; *(Krankheit)*
to be coming on. **(c)** *(Chess etc)* opening move.
Weiß ist als erster im ~ white has first move.
anzüglich *adj* lewd, suggestive. ~ **werden** to get
personal.
Anzüglichkeit *f* lewdness, suggestiveness. ~**en**
lewd *or* suggestive remarks.
anzünden *vt sep Feuer* to light. **das Haus** ~ to set
fire to the house, to set the house on fire.
Anzünder *m* lighter.
anzweifeln *vt sep* to question, to doubt.
apart *adj* distinctive, unusual; *Mensch, Aussehen,*
Kleidungsstück auch striking.
Apartheid [a'pa:ethait] *f no pl* apartheid.
Apartment [a'partmənt] *nt* -s flat *(Brit)*, apartment *(esp US)*.
Apathie *f* apathy; *(von Patienten)* listlessness.
apathisch *adj* apathetic; *Patient* listless.
Aperitif *m* -s *or* -e aperitif.
Apfel *m* ⁻ apple. **in den sauren** ~ **beißen** *(fig col)* to
swallow the bitter pill; **etw für einen** ~ **und ein**
Ei kaufen *(col)* to buy sth dirt cheap *(col) or* for a
song *(col)*; **der** ~ **fällt nicht weit vom Stamm**
(Prov) it's in the blood.
Apfel-: ~**baum** *m* apple tree; ~**blüte** *f* **(a)** apple
blossom; **(b)** *(das Blühen)* blossoming of the apple trees; ~**kompott** *nt* stewed apples; ~**kuchen**
m apple cake; ~**mus** *nt* apple purée *or (als Beilage)* sauce; ~**saft** *m* apple juice; ~**schimmel** *m*
dapple-grey (horse).
Apfelsine *f* orange.
Apfel-: ~**strudel** *m* apfelstrudel; ~**tasche** *f* apple
turnover; ~**wein** *m* cider.
Apokalypse *f* -n apocalypse.
apokalyptisch *adj* apocalyptic.
apolitisch *adj* non-political, apolitical.
Apostel *m* - apostle.
Apostel-: ~**brief** *m* epistle; ~**geschichte** *f* Acts of
the Apostles *pl*.
Apostroph *m* -e apostrophe.
Apotheke *f* -n chemist's *(Brit)*, pharmacy *(US)*.
apothekenpflichtig *adj* available only at a
chemist's *(Brit) or* pharmacy *(US)*.
Apotheker(in *f) m* - pharmacist, (dispensing)
chemist *(Brit)*.

Apparat *m* -e **(a)** apparatus *no pl*, appliance;
(kleineres, technisches, mechanisches Gerät auch)
device, gadget; *(Röntgen~ etc)* machine. **(b)**
(Radio) radio; *(Fernseher)* set. **(c)** *(Telefon)*
(tele)phone; *(Anschluß)* extension. **am** ~ on the
phone; *(als Antwort)* speaking; **wer war am** ~?
who did you speak to?; **bleiben Sie am** ~! hold
the line. **(d)** *(Personen und Hilfsmittel)* set-up;
(Verwaltungs~, Partei~) machinery, apparatus;
(technischer etc) equipment, apparatus.
Apparatur *f* equipment *no pl*, apparatus *no pl*.
Appartement [apartə'mã:] *nt* -s **(a)** *siehe*
Apartment. (b) *(Zimmerflucht)* suite.
Appell *m* -e **(a)** *(Aufruf)* appeal *(an+acc* to, *zu*
for*)*. **einen** ~ **an jdn richten** to (make an) appeal
to sb. **(b)** *(Mil)* roll call. **zum** ~ **antreten** to line up
for roll call.
appellieren* *vi* to appeal *(an +acc* to*)*.
Appetit *m no pl (lit, fig)* appetite. ~ **auf etw** *(acc)*
haben to feel like sth; **guten** ~! enjoy your meal;
jdm den ~ **verderben** to spoil sb's appetite.
Appetit-: **a~anregend** *adj Speise etc* appetizing;
a~lich *adj (lit, fig)* appetizing; ~**losigkeit** *f* lack
of appetite; ~**zügler** *m* - appetite suppressant.
applaudieren* *vti* to applaud.
Applaus *m no pl* applause.
apportieren* *vti* to retrieve, to fetch.
Appretur *f (Mittel)* finish; *(Tex)* starch; *(Wasserundurchlässigkeit)* waterproofing.
approbiert *adj Arzt* registered, certified.
Après-Ski [apre'ʃi:] *nt* -s **après-ski.**
Aprikose *f* -n apricot.
Aprikosenmarmelade *f* apricot jam.
April *m no pl* April. ~, ~! April fool!; **der erste** ~
April Fool's Day; **jdn in den** ~ **schicken** to make
an April fool of sb; *siehe* **März.**
April-: ~**scherz** *m* April fool's trick; **das ist doch**
wohl ein ~**scherz** *(fig)* it's got to be a joke;
~**wetter** *nt* April weather.
apropos [apro'po:] *adv* by the way, that reminds
me. ~ **Afrika** talking about Africa.
Aqua-: ~**marin** *nt* -e aquamarine; ~**planing** *nt no*
pl (Aut) aquaplaning.
Aquarell *nt* -e watercolour *(Brit)*, watercolor
(US).
Aquarell-: ~**farbe** *f* watercolour *(Brit)*; watercolor *(US)*; ~**maler** *m* watercolourist *(Brit)*, watercolorist *(US)*; ~**malerei** *f* watercolour *(Brit)*
or watercolor *(US)* painting.
Aquarium *nt* aquarium.
Äquator *m no pl* equator.
Aquavit [akva'vi:t] *m* -e aquavit.
äquivalent [-va'lɛnt] *nt* -e equivalent; *(Ausgleich)*
compensation.
Äquivalenz [-va'lɛnts] *f* equivalence.
Ar *nt or* -e *(Measure)* are *(100 m²)*.
Ära *f* **Ären** era. **die** ~ **Adenauer** the Adenauer
era.
Araber *m* - *(auch Pferd)*, **Araberin** *f* Arab.
Arabien [-iən] *nt* Arabia.
arabisch *adj* Arab; *Ziffer, Sprache etc* Arabic.
Arbeit *f* **(a)** work; *(~stelle, Aufgabe)* job; *(Pol,*
Econ, Lohn für ~) labour *(Brit)*, labor *(US)*. ~ **und**
Kapital capital and labour; **Tag der** ~ Labour
Day; **die** ~ **en an der Autobahn** the work on the
motorway; **viel** ~ **machen** to be a lot of work
(jdm for sb*)*; **das ist/kostet viel** ~ it's a lot of work
or a big job; **an** *or* **bei der** ~ **sein** to be working;
sich an die ~ **machen, an die** ~ **gehen** to get
down to work, to start working; **an die** ~! to
work!; **etw ist in** ~ work on sth is in progress;
erst die ~, **dann das Vergnügen** *(prov)* business
before pleasure *(prov)*; **ganze** *or* **gründliche** ~
leisten *(lit, fig iro)* to do a good job.
(b) *no pl (Mühe)* trouble, bother. **jdm** ~ **machen** to put sb to trouble; **machen Sie sich keine**
~! don't go to any trouble *or* bother; **einer (geregelten)** ~ **nachgehen** to have a (steady) job;

ohne ~ sein to be out of work; **zur ~ gehen/von der ~ kommen** to go to/come back from work; **seine ~ besteht darin, zu ... his** job is to ... **(c)** *(Produkt)* work; *(handwerkliche)* piece of work; *(Prüfungs~)* *(examination)* paper; *(wissenschaftliche)* paper; *(Sch)* test. **~en korrigieren** to mark test papers; **eine ~ schreiben/ schreiben lassen** to do/set a test.

arbeiten 1 *vi* to work *(an +dat* on). **die Zeit arbeitet für/gegen uns** time is on our side/against us; **er arbeitet für zwei** *(col)* he does the work of two; **die Anlage arbeitet elektrisch/mit Kohle** the plant runs on electricity/coal; **bei einer Firma/Zeitung ~** to work for a firm/newspaper; **die ~de Bevölkerung** the working population. **2** *vr* **(a) sich zu Tode ~** to work oneself to death. **(b)** *(sich fortbewegen)* to work oneself *(in + acc* into, *durch* through, *zu* to). **sich nach oben/an die Spitze ~** *(fig)* to work one's way up/to the top. **(c)** *impers* **es arbeitet sich gut/schlecht** you can/can't work well.

Arbeiter(in *f)* *m* - worker; *(im Gegensatz zum Angestellten)* blue-collar worker; *(auf Bau, Bauernhof)* labourer *(Brit),* laborer *(US); (bei Straßenbau, im Haus)* workman. **~ und ~innen** male and female workers.

Arbeiter-: ~bewegung *f* labour *(Brit) or* labor *(US)* movement; **~familie** *f* working-class family; **~führer** *m (Pol)* leader of the working classes; **~gewerkschaft** *f* blue-collar (trade) union, labor union *(US);* **~jugend** *f* young workers *pl;* **~kind** *nt* child from a working-class family; **~klasse** *f* working class(es *pl);* **~lied** *nt* workers' song; **~partei** *f* workers' party; **~schaft** *f* work force; **~und-Bauern-Staat** *m (DDR)* workers' and peasants' state; **~viertel** *nt* working-class area; **~wohlfahrt** *f* workers' welfare association.

Arbeitgeber *m* employer.
Arbeitgeber-: ~anteil *m* employer's contribution; **~verband** *m* employers' federation.
Arbeitnehmer *m* employee.
Arbeitnehmer-: ~anteil *m* employee's contribution; **~schaft** *f* employees *pl.*
Arbeitsablauf *m* work routine; *(von Fabrik)* production *no art.*
arbeitsam *adj* industrious, hard-working.
Arbeitsamkeit *f* industriousness.
Arbeits-: ~amt *nt* employment exchange, job centre *(Brit);* **~anzug** *m* working suit; **~atmosphäre** *f* work(ing) atmosphere, work climate; **~auffassung** *f* attitude to work; **~aufwand** *m* expenditure of energy; *(Ind)* use of labour *(Brit) or* labor *(US);* **mit geringem/großem ~aufwand** with little/a lot of work; **~ausfall** *m* loss of working hours; **~bedingungen** *pl* working conditions *pl;* **~beginn** *m* start of work; **~beschaffung** *f (Arbeitsplatzbeschaffung)* job creation; **~besuch** *m* working visit; **~eifer** *m* enthusiasm for one's work; **~erlaubnis** *f* work permit; **~erleichterung** *f* **das bedeutet eine große ~erleichterung** that makes the work much easier; **~essen** *nt (esp Pol)* working lunch/dinner; **a~fähig** *adj Person* able to work; *(gesund)* fit to work; **~friede(n)** *m* peaceful labour *(Brit) or* labor *(US)* relations *pl, no art;* **~gang** *m (Abschnitt)* operation; **~gebiet** *nt* field of work; **~gemeinschaft** *f* team; *(Sch, Univ)* study-group; **~genehmigung** *f* work permit; **~gericht** *nt* industrial tribunal; **~gruppe** *f* team; **a~intensiv** *adj* labour-intensive *(Brit),* labor-intensive *(US);* **~kampf** *m* industrial action; **~kleidung** *f* working clothes *pl;* **~klima** *nt* work climate, work(ing) atmosphere; **~kollege** *m (bei Angestellten etc)* colleague; *(bei Arbeitern)* fellow worker, workmate; **~kosten** *pl* labor *(Brit) or* labour *(US)* costs *pl;* **~kraft** *f* **(a)** *no pl* capacity for work; **seine ~kraft verkaufen** to sell one's labour *(Brit) or* labor *(US);* **(b)** *(Ar-*

beiter) worker; **~lager** labour *(Brit) or* labor *(US)* camp; **~leistung** *f (quantitativ)* output; *(qualitativ)* performance; **~lohn** *m* wages *pl.*
arbeitslos *adj* unemployed, out of work. **~ werden** to be made redundant *(Brit),* to lose one's job.
Arbeitslosen-: ~geld *nt* unemployment benefit; **~hilfe** *f* supplementary benefit; **~unterstützung** *f* unemployment benefit, dole money *(Brit col);* **~versicherung** *f* ≈ National Insurance *(Brit),* social insurance *(US);* **~zahlen** *pl,* **~ziffer** *f* unemployment figures *pl.*
Arbeitslose(r) *mf decl as adj* employed person/ man/woman *etc.* **die ~n** the umemployed; **die Zahl der ~n** the number of unemployed *or* of people out of work.
Arbeits-: ~mangel *m* lack of work; **~markt** *m* labour *(Brit) or* labor *(US)* market; **~material** *nt* material for one's work; *(Sch)* teaching aids *pl;* **~methode** *f* method of working; **~minister** *m* Employment Secretary *(Brit),* Labor Secretary *(US);* **~mittel** *nt siehe* **~material;** **~moral** *f* attitude to work; *(in Betrieb)* work climate; **~niederlegung** *f* walkout; **~papiere**, *pl* cards, employment papers *(form) pl.*
arbeitsparend *adj* labour-saving *(Brit),* labor-saving *(US).*
Arbeits-: ~platz *m* **(a)** *(~stätte)* place of work; *(im Großraumbüro)* work station; **am ~platz** at work; **(b)** *(Stelle)* job; **freie ~plätze** vacancies **~platzcomputer** *m* business computer; **~probe** *f* sample of one's work; **~prozeß** *m* work process; **~raum** *m* workroom; *(für geistige Arbeit)* study; **~recht** *nt* industrial law; **~rhythmus** *m* work rhythm; **a~scheu** *adj* work-shy; **~schluß** *m* end of work; **nach ~schluß** after work; **a~sparend** *adj* = **arbeitsparend;** **~stätte** *f* place of work; **~stelle** *f* **(a)** place of work; **(b)** *(Stellung)* job; **~stil** *m* work-style, style of working; **~suche** *f* search for work *or* a job; **auf ~suche sein** to be looking for a job, to be job-hunting; **~tag** *m* workday; **~takt** *m (Tech)* **(a)** *(von Motor)* power stroke; **(b)** *(bei Fließbandarbeit)* time for an/the operation, phase time; **~tätigkeit** *f* work; **~technik** *f* technique of working; **~teilung** *f* division of labour *(Brit) or* labor *(US);* **~tempo** *f* rate of work; **~tier** *nt (fig)* glutton for work; *(Geistesarbeiter auch)* workaholic *(col);* **~tisch** *m* work-table; *(für geistige Arbeit)* desk; *(für handwerkliche Arbeit)* workbench; **~überlastung** *f (von Mensch)* overworking.
Arbeit-: ~suche *f* = **Arbeitssuche; ~suchende(r)** *mf decl as adj* person *etc* looking for a job.
Arbeits-: a~unfähig *adj* unable to work; *(krank)* unfit for work; **~unfähigkeit** *f siehe adj* inability to work; unfitness for work; **~unfall** *m* industrial accident; **a~unwillig** *adj* reluctant *or* unwilling to work; **~verhältnis** *nt* employee-employer relationship; **ein ~verhältnis eingehen** to enter into employment; **~verhältnisse** *pl* working conditions *pl;* **~vermittlung** *f (Amt)* employment exchange; *(privat)* employment agency; **~vertrag** *m* contract of employment; **~weise** *f (Praxis)* way *or* method of working; *(von Maschine)* mode of operation; **die ~weise dieser Maschine** the way this machine works; **~welt** *f* working world; **die industrielle ~welt** the world of industry; **~wut** *f* work mania; **a~wütig** *adj* **~wütig sein** to be a workaholic *(col);* **~zeit** *f* working hours *pl;* **während der ~zeit** in *or* during working hours; **~zeitverkürzung** *f* reduction in working hours; **~zeugnis** *nt* reference from one's employer; **~zimmer** *nt* study.
archaisch *adj* archaic.
Archäologe *m,* **Archäologin** *f* archaeologist *(Brit),* archeologist *(US).*
Archäologie *f* archaeology *(Brit),* archeology *(US).*

archäologisch *adj* archaeological *(Brit)*, archeological *(US)*.

Arche *f* **-n** die ~ **Noah** Noah's Ark.

Archipel *m* **-e** archipelago.

Architekt(in *f)* *m (wk)* **-en, -en** *(lit,fig)* architect.

architektonisch *adj* architectural.

Architektur *f* architecture.

Archiv *nt* archives *pl.*

Archivar(in *f)* [-'vaɪɐ, -'vaːrɪn] *m* archivist.

archivieren* [-'viːrən] *vt* to put into the archives.

Areal *nt* **-e** area.

Arena *f, pl* **Arenen** *(lit,fig)* arena; *(Zirkus~, Stierkampf~)* ring.

arg *comp* **⁼er,** *superl* **⁼ste(r, s)** *or (adv)* **am ⁼sten 1** *adj (esp S Ger) (schlimm)* bad; *Wetter auch, Gestank, Katastrophe, Verlust, Blamage, Verlegenheit, Schicksal* terrible; *Enttäuschung* bitter. **sein ~ster Feind** his worst enemy; **etw liegt im ~en** sth is at sixes and sevens. **2** *adv* **(a)** *(schlimm)* badly. **er hat sich ~ vertan** *(col)* he's made a bad mistake; **es zu ~ treiben** to go too far. **(b)** *(col: sehr)* very.

Argentinien [-iən] *nt* Argentina, the Argentine.

Argentinier(in *f)* [-iə, iərɪn] *m* Argentinean.

argentinisch *adj* Argentine, Argentinean.

Ärger *m no pl* **(a)** *annoyance; (stärker)* anger. **wenn ihn der ~ packt** when he gets annoyed/angry. **(b)** *(Unannehmlichkeiten)* trouble; *(Erlebnisse auch)* bother. **jdm ~ machen** *or* **bereiten** to cause sb a lot of trouble *or* bother; **~ bekommen** *or* **kriegen** *(col)* to get into trouble; **mach keinen ~!** *(col)* don't cause any trouble!; **so ein ~!** *(col)* what a nuisance!; **es gibt ~** *(col)* there'll be trouble.

ärgerlich *adj* **(a)** *(verärgert)* annoyed, cross. **~ über** *or auf* **jdn/über etw** *(acc)* **sein** to be annoyed with sb/about sth. **(b)** *(unangenehm)* annoying; *(stärker)* maddening, infuriating.

ärgern 1 *vt* to annoy, to irritate; *(stärker)* to make angry. **jdn krank/zu Tode ~** to drive sb mad. **2** *vr (ärgerlich sein/werden)* to be/get annoyed; *(stärker)* to be/get angry *(über jdn/etw* with sb/about sth). **über so etwas könnte ich mich krank/zu Tode ~** that sort of thing drives me mad.

Ärgernis *nt* **(a)** *no pl (Anstoß)* offence, outrage. **wegen Erregung öffentlichen ~ses angeklagt werden** to be charged with offending public decency. **(b)** *(etwas Anstößiges)* outrage; *(etwas Ärgerliches)* terrible nuisance.

Arglist *f no pl (Hinterlist)* cunning, craftiness; *(Boshaftigkeit)* malice; *(Jur)* fraud.

arglistig *adj* cunning, crafty; *(böswillig)* malicious. **~e Täuschung** fraud.

arglos *adj* innocent.

Arglosigkeit *f* innocence.

Argument *nt* argument.

argumentieren* *vi* to argue.

Argus|auge *nt (geh)* eagle eye. **mit ~ eagle-eyed.**

Argwohn *m no pl* suspicion. **jds ~ erregen** to arouse sb's suspicions; **~ gegen jdn hegen** to be suspicious of sb; **mit** *or* **voller ~** suspiciously.

argwöhnisch *adj* suspicious.

Arie [-iə] *f (Mus)* aria.

Aristokrat(in *f)* *m (wk)* **-en, -en** aristocrat.

Aristokratie *f* aristocracy.

aristokratisch *adj* aristocratic.

Arithmetik *f no pl* arithmetic.

arithmetisch *adj* arithmetic(al).

Arkade *f (Bogen)* arch(way). **~n** *pl (Bogengang)* arcade.

Arktis *f no pl* Arctic.

arktisch *adj* arctic.

arm *adj, comp* **⁼er,** *superl* **⁼ste(r, s)** *or (adv)* **am ⁼sten** *(lit, fig)* poor. **die A~en** the poor *pl;* **du machst mich noch mal ~** *(col)* you'll be the ruin of me; **~ an etw** *(dat)* **sein** to be somewhat lacking in sth; **der Boden ist ~ an Nährstoffen** the

soil is poor in nutrients; **~ an Vitaminen** low in vitamins; **um jdn/etw ~er werden/sein** to lose/ have lost sb/sth; **um 55 Mark ~er sein** to be 55 marks worse off *or* poorer; **ach, du/Sie A~er!** *(iro)* you poor thing!; **~ dran sein** *(col)* to have a hard time of it.

Arm *m* **-e** *(Anat, Tech, fig)* arm; *(Fluß~ auch)* branch; *(Ärmel)* sleeve. **~ in ~** arm in arm; **jdn im ~ or in den ~en halten** to hold sb in one's arms; **jdn in die ~e nehmen** to take sb in one's arms; **sich in den ~en liegen** to lie in each other's arms; **jdn auf den ~ nehmen** *(fig col)* to pull sb's leg *(col);* **jdm unter die ~e greifen** *(fig)* to help sb out; **jdn mit offenen ~en empfangen** *(fig)* to welcome sb with open arms; **der ~ des Gesetzes** the long arm of the law; **einen langen/ den längeren ~ haben** *(fig)* to have a lot of/more pull *(col) or* influence.

Armaturenbrett *nt* instrument panel; *(Aut)* dashboard.

Arm-: **~band** *nt* bracelet; *(von Uhr)* (watch)strap; **~banduhr** *f* wristwatch; **~beuge** *f* **(a)** inside of one's elbow; **(b)** *(Sport)* arm bend; **~binde** *f* armband; *(Med)* sling; **~bruch** *m (Med)* broken arm; **~brust** *f* crossbow.

Armee *f* **-n** [-eːən] *(Mil, fig)* army; *(Gesamtheit der Streitkräfte)* (armed) forces *pl.*

Ärmel *m* **-** sleeve. **sich** *(dat)* **die ~ hochkrempeln** *(lit, fig)* to roll up one's sleeves; **etw aus dem ~ schütteln** to produce sth just like that.

Ärmelkanal *m* (English) Channel.

ärmellos *adj* sleeveless.

Armen-: **~haus** *nt (old)* poorhouse; **~recht** *nt (Jur)* legal aid; **~viertel** *nt* poor district *or* quarter.

Arm-: **~gelenk** *nt* elbow joint; **a~lang** *adj* arm-length; **~lehne** *f* armrest; **~leuchter** *m (pej col: Dummkopf)* twit *(Brit col),* fool; *(euph: Arschloch)* bastard *(col!).*

ärmlich *adj (lit,fig)* poor; *Kleidung, Wohnung* shabby; *Verhältnisse* humble. **einen ~en Eindruck machen** to look poor/shabby; **aus ~en Verhältnissen** from a poor family.

armselig *adj (dürftig)* miserable; *(mitleiderregend)* pathetic, pitiful; *Summe, Ausrede* paltry.

Armut *f no pl (lit,fig)* poverty. **~ an etw** *(dat)* lack of sth; **charakterliche ~** lack of character; **geistige ~** *(von Mensch)* lack of intellect.

Armutszeugnis *nt (fig)* **jdm/sich ein ~ ausstellen** to show sb's/one's shortcomings; **das ist ein ~ für ihn** that shows him up.

Aroma *nt, pl* **Aromen** *or* **-s (a)** *(Geruch)* aroma. **(b)** *(Geschmack)* flavour *(Brit),* flavor *(US).* **(c)** *no pl* flavouring *(Brit),* flavoring *(US).*

aromatisch *adj* aromatic; *(wohlschmeckend)* savoury *(Brit),* savory *(US).*

Arrangement* [arãʒə'mãː] *nt* **-s** arrangement.

arrangieren* [arãˈʒiːrən] **1** *vti* to arrange *(jdm* for sb). **2** *vr* **sich mit jdm ~** to come to an arrangement with sb; **sich mit etw ~** to come to terms with sth.

Arrest *m* **-s** *(Mil, Jur)* detention.

Arrestzelle *f* detention cell.

arretieren* *vt (Tech)* to lock (in place).

Arretierung *f* **(a)** locking. **(b)** *(Vorrichtung)* locking mechanism.

arriviert [-'viːɐt] *adj* successful; *(pej)* upstart.

arrogant *adj* arrogant.

Arroganz *f no pl* arrogance.

Arsch *m* **⁼e** *(col!)* arse *(col!),* ass *(US col!).* **auf den ~ fallen** *(fig: scheitern)* to fall flat on one's face; **leck mich am ~!** *(laß mich in Ruhe)* get stuffed! *(col),* fuck off! *(col!!);* *(verdammt)* bugger! *(col!),* fuck! *(col!!);* **jdm in den ~ kriechen** to lick sb's arse *(col!);* **am ~ der Welt** *(col)* in the back of beyond; **jem or am ~ sein** to be screwed up *(col).*

Arsch-: **~backe** *f (col!)* buttock, cheek; **~kriecher** *m (col!)* arse-licker *(col!);* **~loch** *nt (col!)*

Arsen *(Mensch)* bastard *(col!)*; *(Dummkopf)* stupid bastard *(col!)*.

Arsen *nt no pl* arsenic.

Arsenal *nt* -e *(lit, fig)* arsenal.

Art *f* -en **(a)** kind, sort, type; *(von Pflanze, Insekt etc auch)* variety; *(Biol)* species. **diese ~ Leute/ Buch** that kind *or* sort of person/book; **ein Heuchler schlimmster~** the worst type *or* kind of hypocrite; **einzig in seiner ~ sein** to be the only one of its kind, to be unique; **aus der ~ schlagen** not to take after anyone in the family; *(pej)* to be the black sheep of the family. **(b)** *(Methode)* way; *(Stil)* style. **die einfachste ~, etw zu tun** the simplest way to do sth *or* of doing sth; **auf diese ~ und Weise** in this way; **es entspricht nicht meiner ~** it's not my nature; **das ist eigentlich nicht seine ~** it's not like him; **Schnitzel nach ~ des Hauses** schnitzel à la maison. **(c)** *(Benehmen)* behaviour *(Brit)*, behavior *(US)*. **das ist doch keine ~!** that's no way to behave!

Arterie [-iə] *f* artery.

arteriell *adj* arterial.

Arteriosklerose *f* arteriosclerosis.

Art-: **~genosse** *m* animal/plant of the same species; *(Mensch)* person of the same type; **a~gleich** *adj* of the same species; *Mensch* of the same type.

Arthritis *f, pl* **Arthritiden** arthritis.

arthritisch *adj* arthritic.

artig *adj* Kind, Hund *etc* good, well-behaved *no adv*. **sei schön ~** be a good boy/dog *etc!*, be good!

Artikel *m* - *(auch Gram)* article; *(Comm auch)* item.

artikulieren* *vti* to articulate.

Artillerie *f* artillery.

Artillerist *m* artilleryman.

Artischocke *f* -n (globe) artichoke.

Artist(in *f) m* (circus/variety) artiste *or* performer.

Artistik *f* artistry; *(Zirkus-, Varietékunst)* circus/ variety performing.

artistisch *adj* **(a)** sein **~es Können** his ability as a performer; **eine ~e Glanzleistung** a feat of circus *etc* artistry. **(b)** *(geschickt)* masterly *no adv*. **(c)** *(formalkünstlerisch)* artistic.

Arznei *f (lit, fig)* medicine.

Arzneimittel *nt* drug.

Arzt *m* ⁼e doctor. **praktischer ~** general practitioner, GP *abbr*.

Ärzte-: **~kammer** ≃ General Medical Council *(Brit)*, State Medical Board of Registration *(US)*; **~schaft** *f* medical profession.

Arzthelferin *f* (doctor's) receptionist; nurse.

Ärztin *f* woman doctor; *siehe* Arzt.

ärztlich *adj* medical. **er ließ sich ~ behandeln** he got medical treatment.

Arzt-: **~praxis** *f* doctor's practice; **~rechnung** *f* doctor's bill.

As¹ *nt* -se *(lit, fig)* ace.

As² *nt (Mus)* A flat.

Asbest *nt no pl* asbestos.

aschblond *adj* ashblonde.

Asche *f no pl* ash(es *pl*); *(von Zigarette, Vulkan)* ash; *(sterbliche Überreste)* ashes *pl*. **zu ~ werden** to turn to dust.

Aschen-: **~bahn** *f* cinder track; **~becher** *m* ashtray; **~brödel, ~puttel** *nt* - *(Liter, fig)* Cinderella.

Aschermittwoch *m* Ash Wednesday.

asch-: **~fahl** *adj* ashen; **~grau** *adj* ash-grey.

äsen *(Hunt) vir* to graze, to browse.

Asiat(in *f) m (wk)* **-en, -en** Asian.

asiatisch *adj* Asian, Asiatic.

Asien [-iən] *nt* Asia.

Asket *m (wk)* **-en, -en** ascetic.

asketisch *adj* ascetic.

asozial *adj* antisocial.

Asoziale(r) *mf decl as adj (pej)* antisocial man/ woman *etc*. **~ pl** antisocial elements.

Aspekt *m* -e aspect. **unter diesem ~ betrachtet** looking at it from this aspect; **einen neuen ~ bekommen** to take on a different complexion.

Asphalt *m* -e asphalt.

Asphaltdecke *f* asphalt surface.

asphaltieren* *vt* to asphalt.

asphaltiert *adj* asphalt.

Aspik *m* -e aspic.

Aspirant(in *f) m (geh)* candidate *(auf+acc* for).

aß *pret of* **essen**.

Assel *f* -n woodlouse.

Assessor(in *f) m graduate* civil servant who has completed his/her traineeship.

Assistent(in *f) m* assistant.

Assistenz *f* assistance.

Assistenz|arzt *m* houseman *(Brit)*, intern *(US)*.

assistieren* *vi* to assist *(jdm sb)*.

Assoziation *f* association.

assoziieren* *vt (geh)* to associate. **mit Grün assoziiere ich Ruhe** I associate green with peace.

Ast *m* ⁼e **(a)** branch. **den ~ absägen, auf dem man sitzt** *(fig)* to dig one's own grave. **(b)** *(im Holz)* knot. **(c)** *(col)* **sich *(dat)* einen ~ lachen** to double up (with laughter).

Aster *f* -n aster, Michaelmas daisy.

Astgabel *f* fork (in a branch).

Ästhet *(in f) m (wk)* **-en, -en** aesthete *(Brit)*, esthete *(US)*.

Ästhetik *f* aesthetics *(Brit)*, esthetics *(US)* sing; *(eines Bildes)* aesthetics *pl*; *(Schönheitssinn)* aesthetic sense.

ästhetisch *adj* aesthetic *(Brit)*, esthetic *(US)*.

Asthma *nt no pl* asthma.

Asthmatiker(in *f) m* - asthmatic.

Astloch *nt* knothole.

astral *adj* astral.

astrein *adj (col)* **(a)** *(fig col: moralisch einwandfrei)* straight *(col)*, on the level *(col)*. **(b)** *(fig: echt)* genuine. **(c)** *(prima)* fantastic.

Astro-: **~loge** *m*, **~login** *f* astrologer; **~logie** *f* astrology; **a~logisch** *adj* astrological; **~naut(in** *f) m (wk)* **-en, -en** astronaut; **~nom(in** *f) m* astronomer; **~nomie** *f* astronomy; **a~nomisch** *adj (lit)* astronomical; *(fig auch)* astronomic; **~physik** *f* astrophysics *sing*; **~physiker(in** *f) m* astrophysicist.

Asyl *nt* -e *(politisch)* (political) asylum *no art*; *(geh: Schutz)* sanctuary *no art*. **um ~ bitten** to ask for (political) asylum.

Asylant(in *f) m* person seeking (political) asylum.

Asylrecht *nt (Pol)* right of (political) asylum.

asymmetrisch *adj* asymmetric(al).

Atelier [-'lie:] *nt* -s studio.

Atelierwohnung *f* studio apartment.

Atem *m no pl* **(a)** *(das Atmen)* breathing. **den ~ anhalten** *(lit, fig)* to hold one's breath; **mit angehaltenem ~** *(lit)* holding one's breath; **wieder zu ~ kommen** to get one's breath back; **den längeren ~ haben** *(fig)* to have more staying power; **jdn in ~ halten** to keep sb in suspense *or* on tenterhooks; **das verschlug mir den ~** it took my breath away. **(b)** *(lit, fig: ~luft)* breath. **~ holen** *or* **schöpfen** *(lit)* to take a breath; *(fig)* to get one's breath back.

Atem-: **a~beraubend** *adj* breathtaking; **~beschwerden** *pl* trouble in breathing; **a~los** *adj (lit, fig)* breathless; **~losigkeit** *f* breathlessness; **~not** *f* difficulty in breathing; **~pause** *f (fig)* breathing space; **eine ~pause einlegen/brauchen** to take/need a breather; **~wege** *pl (Anat)* respiratory tracts *pl*; **~zug** *m* breath; **in einem/ im selben ~zug** *(fig)* in one/the same breath.

Atheismus *m* atheism.

Atheist(in *f) m* atheist.

atheistisch *adj* atheist(ic).

Athen *nt* Athens.

Athener(in *f) m* Athenian.

Äther m no pl (a) ether. (b) (Rad) air.
Ätherwellen pl (Rad) radio waves pl.
Äthiopien [ɛ'tioːpiən] nt Ethiopia.
Äthiopier(in f) m [-piə, -iərin] - Ethiopian.
Athlet(in f) m (wk) -en, -en athlete.
athletisch adj athletic.
Atlantik m Atlantic.
atlantisch adj Atlantic. der A~e Ozean the Atlantic Ocean.
Atlas m, pl **Atlanten** or -se atlas.
atmen vi to breathe. **frei** ~ (fig) to breathe freely.
Atmosphäre f -n (Phys, fig) atmosphere.
atmosphärisch adj atmospheric. ~e **Störungen** atmospherics pl.
Atmung f no pl breathing; (Med) respiration.
Atmungs|organe pl respiratory organs pl.
Atoll nt -e atoll.
Atom nt -e atom.
Atom-: ~**angriff** m nuclear attack; ~**antrieb** m nuclear propulsion; **ein U-Boot mit** ~**antrieb** a nuclear-powered submarine.
atomar adj atomic, nuclear; Struktur atomic; Drohung nuclear.
Atom-: ~**bombe** f atomic or atom bomb; **a**~**bombensicher** adj atomic or nuclear blast-proof; ~**bombenversuch** m atomic or nuclear test; ~**bunker** m atomic or nuclear blast-proof bunker; ~**energie** f nuclear energy; **a**~**getrieben** adj nuclear-powered; ~**kern** m atomic nucleus; ~**kraft** f nuclear power; ~**kraftwerk** nt atomic or nuclear power station; ~**krieg** m atomic or nuclear war; ~**macht** f nuclear power; ~**meiler** m nuclear reactor; ~**müll** m nuclear or radioactive waste; ~**physik** f nuclear physics sing; ~**physiker** m nuclear physicist; ~**pilz** m mushroom cloud; ~**rakete** f nuclear-powered rocket; (Waffe) nuclear missile; ~**reaktor** m atomic or nuclear reactor; ~**rüstung** f nuclear armament; ~**spaltung** f nuclear fission; **die erste** ~**spaltung** the first splitting of the atom; ~**sprengkopf** m atomic or nuclear warhead; ~**strahlung** f nuclear radiation; ~**streitmacht** f nuclear capability; ~**strom** m (col) electricity generated by nuclear power; ~**test** m nuclear test; ~**waffe** f nuclear or atomic weapon; **a**~**waffenfrei** adj nuclear-free; ~**waffensperrvertrag** m nuclear or atomic weapons non-proliferation treaty; ~**zeitalter** nt atomic or nuclear age.
ätsch interj (col) ha-ha.
Attacke f -n (Angriff) attack. **eine** ~ **gegen jdn/ etw reiten** (fig) to attack sb/sth.
attackieren* vt (angreifen) to attack.
Attentat [-taːt] nt -e assassination; (~sversuch) assassination attempt. **ein** ~ **auf jdn verüben** to assassinate sb; to make an attempt on sb's life.
Attentäter(in f) m - assassin; (bei gescheitertem Versuch) would-be assassin.
Attest nt -e certificate.
attestieren* vt (form) to certify.
Attraktion f attraction.
attraktiv adj attractive.
Attraktivität f attractiveness.
Attrappe f -n dummy; (fig: Schein) sham. **bei ihr ist alles** ~ everything about her is false.
Attribut nt -e (geh, Gram) attribute.
atypisch adj (geh) atypical.
ätzen vti (a) to etch. (b) (Säure) to corrode.
ätzend adj (a) (lit) Säure corrosive. (b) Geruch pungent; Spott caustic.
au, aua interj ow, ouch.
Aubergine [obɛr'ʒiːnə] f aubergine, eggplant.
auch adv (a) (zusätzlich, gleichfalls) also, too, as well. ~ **nicht** not ... either; **das ist** ~ **nicht richtig** that's not right either; **er kommt** — **ich** ~ he's coming — so am I, me too; **ich mag das nicht** — **ich** ~ **nicht** I don't like that — nor or neither do I; **nicht nur ..., sondern** ~ not only ... but also ...; ~ **das noch!** that's all I needed!

(b) (tatsächlich) too, as well. **du siehst müde aus** — **das bin ich** ~ you look tired — (so) I am; **das müßt ihr aber** ~ **tun** but you have to do it; **so ist es** ~ (so) it is.
(c) (sogar) even. ~ **wenn du Vorfahrt hast** even if you (do) have right of way; **ohne** ~ **nur zu fragen** without even asking.
(d) (emph) **so was Ärgerliches aber** ~! it's really too annoying!; **wozu** ~? whatever for?
(e) (~ immer) **wie dem** ~ **sei** be that as it may; **was er** ~ **sagen mag** whatever he might say; **so schnell er** ~ **laufen mag** however fast he runs or may run, no matter how fast he runs.
Audienz f (bei Papst, König etc) audience.
Audimax nt no pl (Univ col) main lecture hall.
audiovisuell adj audiovisual.
Auditorium nt (a) (Hörsaal) lecture hall. (b) (geh: Zuhörerschaft) audience.
Auerhahn m capercaillie.
Auer|ochse m aurochs.
Auf nt inv: **das** ~ **und Ab** the up and down; (fig) the ups and downs.
auf 1 prep (a)+dat on. ~ (der Insel) Skye on the island of Skye; ~ **See** at sea; ~ **meinem Zimmer** in my room; ~ **der Bank/Post/Party** at the bank/ post office/party; **mein Geld ist** ~ **der Bank** my money is in the bank; ~ **der Straße** on or in the street; **etw** ~ **der Geige spielen** to play sth on the violin; ~ **einem Ohr taub/einem Auge kurzsichtig sein** to be deaf in one ear/short-sighted in one eye; **was fast es damit** ~ **sich?** what does it mean?; ~ **der Fahrt/dem Weg** etc on the journey/ way etc.
(b)+acc on, onto. **etw** ~ **etw stellen** to put sth on(to) sth or on top of sth; **sich** ~ **etw setzen/ legen** to sit/lie (down) on sth; **er fiel** ~ **den Rücken** he fell on(to) his back; **etw** ~ **einen Zettel schreiben** to write sth on a piece of paper; **er ist** ~ **die Orkney-Inseln gefahren** he has gone to the Orkney Islands; **geh mal** ~ **die Seite** go to the side; ~ **sein Zimmer/die Post/eine Party** etc **gehen** to go to one's room/the post office/a party etc; ~**s Gymnasium gehen** to go to (the) grammar school; **die Uhr** ~ **10 stellen** to put the clock to 10; **die Sitzung** ~ **morgen verschieben** to postpone the meeting until tomorrow.
(c)+acc ~ **10 km/drei Tage für 10 km/three days;** ~ **eine Tasse Kaffee/eine Zigarette(nlänge)** for a cup of coffee/a smoke; **ein Manuskript** ~ **Fehler prüfen** to check a manuscript for errors; ~ **seinen Vorschlag (hin)** at his suggestion; ~ **meinen Brief hin** because of or on account of my letter.
(d) **es geht** ~ **Weihnachten zu** Christmas is approaching; **er kam** ~ **mich zu und sagte** ... he came up to me and said ...; **die Nacht (von Montag)** ~ **Dienstag** Monday night; ~ **einen Polizisten kommen** 1.000 **Bürger** there is one policeman to every 1,000 citizens; ~ **den Millimeter/die Sekunde genau** to within one millimetre/second; ~ **ein glückliches Gelingen** etc! here's to a great success etc!; **die Dauer** ~ **ein Jahr reduzieren** to reduce the duration to one year.
2 adv (a) (offen) open. **Mund/Fenster** ~! open your mouth/the window. (b) (hinauf) up. ~ **und ab** or **nieder** (geh) up and down. (c) **Helm** ~! helmets on; **ich war die halbe Nacht** ~ I've been up half the night; ~ **nach Chicago!** let's go to Chicago; ~ **geht's!** let's go!; ~ **und davon** up and away; ~, **an die Arbeit!** come on, let's get on with it; **siehe aufsein.**
3 conj (old, liter) ~ **daß** that (old, liter).
auf|arbeiten vt sep (a) (erneuern) to refurbish, to do up; **Möbel** etc **auch** to recondition. (b) (erledigen) Korrespondenz etc to catch up with.
Auf|arbeitung f siehe vt refurbishing; reconditioning; catching up.
auf|atmen vi sep (lit, fig) to breathe or heave a sigh

of relief. **ein A~** a sigh of relief.

aufbacken *vt sep* to warm *or* crisp up.

aufbahren *vt sep Sarg* to lay on the bier; *Leiche* to lay out. **einen Toten feierlich ~** to put a person's body to lie in state.

Aufbau *m* (a) *no pl (das Aufbauen)* construction, building; *(das Wiederaufbauen)* reconstruction. **der wirtschaftliche ~** the building up of the economy. (b) *no pl (Struktur)* structure.

aufbauen *sep* 1 *vt* (a) *(errichten)* to put up; *(hinstellen) Ausstellungsstücke, Brettspiel etc* to set *or* lay out. (b) *(fig: gestalten) Organisation, Angriff, Spannung* to build up; *Zerstörtes* to rebuild; *Theorie* to construct. **sich** *(dat)* **eine (neue) Existenz ~** to build a new life for oneself. (c) *(fig: fördern) Gesundheit* to build up; *Star etc auch* to promote. (d) *(fig: gründen)* **etw auf etw** *(dat or acc)* **~** to base sth on sth. (e) *(strukturieren)* to construct; *Aufsatz, Rede auch, Komposition* to structure. 2 *vi (sich gründen)* to be based *(auf+dat or acc on)*. 3 *vr* (a) *(inf: sich postieren)* to take up position. **sich vor jdm ~** to draw oneself up to one's full height in front of sb. (b) *(sich bilden)* to build up. (c) *(sich gründen)* **sich auf etw** *(dat or acc)* **~** to be based on sth.

aufbäumen *vr sep (Tier)* to rear. **sich gegen jdn/ etw ~** *(fig)* to rebel *or* revolt against sb/sth.

aufbauschen *vt sep (fig)* to blow up, to exaggerate.

aufbegehren* *vi sep (geh)* to rebel *(gegen against)*.

aufbekommen* *vt sep irreg (col)* (a) *(öffnen)* to get open. (b) *Aufgabe* to get as homework.

aufbereiten* *vt sep* to process; *Trinkwasser auch* to purify; *Text etc* to work up.

aufbessern *vt sep* to improve; *Gehalt etc auch* to increase.

Aufbesserung *f siehe vt* improvement; increase.

aufbewahren* *vt sep* to keep; *(in Lager)* to store; *(behalten) alte Zeitungen etc auch* to save. **kann ich hier mein Gepäck ~ lassen?** can I leave my luggage here?

Aufbewahrung *f siehe vt* keeping; storage; saving. **jdm etw zur ~ anvertrauen** to entrust sth to sb's safekeeping.

aufbieten *vt sep irreg Menschen, Mittel* to muster; *Kräfte auch* to summon (up); *Polizei* to call in.

Aufbietung *f unter ~ aller Kräfte* ... summoning (up) all his/her *etc* strength ...

aufbinden *vt sep irreg* (a) *Schuh etc* to undo, to untie. (b) **laß dir doch so etwas nicht ~** *(fig)* don't fall for that.

aufblähen *sep* 1 *vt* to blow out; *(fig)* to inflate. 2 *vr* to blow out; *(Segel auch)* to billow out; *(Med)* to become swollen; *(fig pej)* to puff oneself up.

aufblasbar *adj* inflatable.

aufblasen *vt sep irreg* to blow up; *siehe* **aufgeblasen**.

aufbleiben *vi sep irreg aux sein* (a) to stay up. (b) *(geöffnet bleiben)* to stay open.

aufblenden *vi sep (Phot)* to increase the aperture; *(Aut)* to turn the headlights on full (beam).

aufblicken *vi sep* to look up. **zu jdm/etw ~** *(lit, fig)* to look up to sb/sth.

aufblitzen *vi sep (Licht)* to flash.

aufblühen *vi sep aux sein (lit, fig)* to blossom out; *(Blume auch)* to bloom; *(Kultur etc auch)* to (begin to) flourish.

aufbocken *vt sep Auto* to jack up.

aufbrauchen *vt sep* to use up.

aufbrausen *vi sep aux sein* (a) *(Brandung etc)* to surge; *(fig: Beifall, Jubel)* to break out. (b) *(fig: Mensch)* to flare up, to fly off the handle *(col)*.

aufbrausend *adj Temperament* irascible; *Mensch auch* quick-tempered, liable to flare up.

aufbrechen *sep irreg* 1 *vt* to break *or* force open; *Tresor auch, Auto* to break into; *Boden, Oberfläche* to break up. 2 *vi aux sein* (a) *(sich öffnen)* to open;

(Straßenbelag etc) to break up. (b) *(fig: Konflikte etc)* to break out. (c) *(sich auf den Weg machen)* to start *or* set out *or* off.

aufbringen *vt sep irreg* (a) *(beschaffen)* to find; *Geld auch* to raise; *Kraft, Mut auch* to summon up. (b) *(erzürnen)* to make angry. **jdn gegen jdn/etw ~** to set sb against sb/sth; *siehe* **aufgebracht**. (c) *(Naut) Schiff* to seize.

Aufbruch *m no pl (Abreise, das Losgehen)* departure. **das Zeichen zum ~ geben** to give the signal to set out *or* off.

aufbrummen *vt sep (col)* **jdm die Kosten ~** to land sb with the costs *(col)*; **eine Haftstrafe aufgebrummt bekommen** to get a sentence.

aufbügeln *vt sep* (a) *Kleidungsstück* to iron out. (b) *Flicken, Bild etc* to iron on.

aufbürden *vt sep (geh)* **jdm etw ~** *(fig)* to encumber sb with sth; **jdm die Schuld für etw ~** to put the blame for sth on sb.

aufdecken *vt sep* (a) *jdn* to uncover; *Bett(decke)* to turn down; *Spielkarten* to show. (b) *(fig) Wahrheit etc* to uncover; *Verbrechen auch* to expose; *Schwäche* to lay bare; *Geheimnis* to solve.

Aufdeckung *f siehe vt* (b) uncovering; exposure; laying bare; solving.

aufdrängen *sep irreg* 1 *vt* **jdm etw ~** to impose *or* force sth on sb. 2 *vr* to impose. **sich jdm ~** *(Mensch)* to impose oneself on sb; *(fig: Erinnerung)* to come involuntarily to sb's mind; **dieser Gedanke/Verdacht drängte sich mir auf** I couldn't help thinking/suspecting that.

aufdrehen *sep* 1 *vt* (a) *Wasserhahn* to turn on; *Ventil* to open; *Schraubverschluß* to unscrew; *Radio etc* to turn up. (b) *Haar* to put in rollers. 2 *vi (col: beschleunigen)* to open up; *siehe* **aufgedreht**.

aufdringlich *adj Benehmen, Tapete* obtrusive; *Geruch, Parfüm* powerful; *Farbe auch* loud; *Mensch* insistent, pushy *(col)*.

Aufdringlichkeit *f siehe adj* obtrusiveness; powerfulness; loudness; insistence, pushiness.

Aufdruck *m (Aufgedrucktes)* imprint.

aufdrucken *vt sep* **etw auf etw** *(acc)* **~** to print sth on sth.

aufdrücken *vt sep* (a) **etw auf etw** *(acc)* **~** to press *or* (mit Stempel etc) stamp sth on sth. (b) *(öffnen) Tür etc* to push open.

auf|einander *adv* (a) on (top of) each other *or* one another. (b) **sich ~ verlassen können** to be able to rely on each other *or* one another; **~ zufahren** to drive towards each other.

auf|einander-: **~folgen** *vi sep aux sein* to follow each other; **~folgend** *adj* successive; **drei schnell ~folgende Tore** three goals in quick succession; **~prallen** *vi sep aux sein (Autos etc)* to collide; *(Truppen, Meinungen)* to clash; **~stellen** *vt sep* to put on top of each other; **~stoßen** *vi sep irreg aux sein* to bump into each other, to collide; **~treffen** *vi sep irreg aux sein (Mannschaften, Gruppen etc)* to meet; *(Meinungen)* to clash; *(Kugeln, Gegenstände etc)* to hit each other.

Aufenthalt *m* **~e** (a) stay; *(das Wohnen)* residence. (b) *(esp Rail)* stop; *(bei Anschluß)* wait. **wie lange haben wir ~?** how long do we stop for?

Aufenthalts-: **~erlaubnis** *f* residence permit; **~ort** *m* whereabouts *sing or pl*; *(Jur)* residence; **~raum** *m* day room; *(in Betrieb)* recreation room.

auf|erlegen* *vt sep or insep (geh)* to impose *(jdm etw sth on sb)*.

auf|erstehen* *vi sep or insep irreg aux sein* to rise from the dead. **Christus ist auferstanden** Christ is (a)risen.

Auf|erstehung *f* resurrection.

auffädeln *vt sep* to thread *or* string (together).

auffahren *sep irreg* 1 *vi aux sein* (a) *(aufprallen)* **auf jdn/etw ~** to run *or* drive into sb/sth; **auf eine Sandbank ~** to run aground on a sandbank. (b) (*näher heranfahren*) to drive up. **zu dicht** ~ to drive too close behind (the car in front). (**c**) (*auf Autobahn*) to enter. (**d**) (*aufschrecken*) to start. **aus dem Schlaf** ~ to awake with a start. (**e**) (*aufbrausen*) to flare up, to fly into a rage. **2** *vt* (*herbeischaffen*) *Truppen etc* to bring up; (*col*) *Speisen etc* to serve up.

Auffahrt *f* approach road; (*Autobahn*~ *auch*) slip road; (*bei Haus etc*) drive.

Auffahr|unfall *m* collision.

auffallen *vi sep irreg aux sein* (**a**) (*sich abheben*) to stand out; (*unangenehm* ~) to attract attention; (*sich hervortun*) to be remarkable (*durch for*). **er ist schon früher als Extremist aufgefallen** he has already got a reputation for being an extremist; **angenehm/unangenehm** ~ to make a good/bad impression; **nur nicht** ~! just keep a low profile. (**b**) (*bemerkt werden*) **jdm fällt etw auf sb** notices sth, sth strikes sb; **was fällt dir an dem Satz auf?** what do you notice *or* what strikes you about this sentence?; **das muß dir doch aufgefallen sein!** surely you must have noticed (it).

auffallend *adj* conspicuous, noticeable; *Schönheit, Ähnlichkeit, Farbe, Kleider* striking. **er ist** ~ **intelligent** he is remarkably intelligent; **stimmt** ~! (*hum*) too true!, how right you are!

auffällig *adj* conspicuous; *Farbe, Kleidung* loud.

auffangen *vt sep irreg* (**a**) *Ball, Gesprächsfetzen* to catch; (*Telec*) *Nachricht* to pick up. (**b**) (*abfangen*) *Aufprall etc* to cushion, to absorb; *Faustschlag* to block; (*fig*) *Preissteigerung etc* to offset. (**c**) (*sammeln*) *Regenwasser etc* to collect, to catch; (*fig*) *Flüchtlinge etc* to assemble.

auffassen *vt sep* to interpret, to understand. **etw als etw** (*acc*) ~ to take sth as sth; **etw falsch/richtig** ~ to take sth the wrong way/in the right way.

Auffassung *f* view. **nach meiner/christlicher** ~ in my view/according to Christian belief.

Auffassungs-: ~**gabe** *f* intelligence, grasp; ~**sache** *f* (*col*) question of interpretation; (*Ansichtssache*) matter of opinion.

auffegen *vt sep* to sweep up.

auffindbar *adj* **es ist nicht** ~ it can't be found.

auffinden *vt sep irreg* to find, to discover.

auffischen *vt sep* to fish up; (*col*) *Schiffbrüchige* to fish out.

aufflammen *vi sep aux sein* (*lit, fig: Feuer, Unruhen etc*) to flare up.

auffliegen *vi sep irreg aux sein* (**a**) (*hochfliegen*) to fly up. (**b**) (*fig col*) (*Konferenz etc*) to break up; (*Rauschgiftring etc*) to be busted (*col*). **einen Schmuggelring/eine Konferenz** ~ **lassen** to bust a ring of smugglers (*col*)/to break up a meeting.

auffordern *vt sep* (**a**) to ask. **wir fordern Sie auf, ... you** are required to ... (**b**) (*bitten*) to ask, to invite; (*zum Wettkampf etc*) to challenge. (**c**) (*zum Tanz bitten*) to ask to dance.

Aufforderung *f* request; (*nachdrücklicher*) demand.

aufforsten *vt sep Gebiet* to reafforest; *Wald* to restock.

Aufforstung *f siehe vt* reafforestation; restocking.

auffressen *vt sep irreg* (*lit, fig*) to eat up. **er wird dich deswegen nicht gleich** ~ (*col*) he's not going to eat you (*col*).

auffrischen *vt sep* **1** *vt* to freshen (up); *Anstrich auch* to brighten up; (*ergänzen*) *Vorräte* to replenish; (*fig*) *Erinnerungen* to refresh; *Kenntnisse* to brush up; *persönliche Beziehungen* to renew; *Impfung* to boost. **2** *vi aux sein or haben* (*Wind*) to freshen. **3** *vi impers aux sein* to get fresher.

Auffrischung *f siehe vt* freshening (up); brightening up; replenishment; refreshing; brushing up; renewal; boosting.

aufführen *vt sep* **1** *vt* (**a**) to put on; *Drama, Oper auch* to stage, to perform. (**b**) (*auflisten*) to list; (*nen-*

nen) *Zeugen* to cite; *Beispiel* to give. **einzeln** ~ to itemize. **2** *vr* to behave.

Aufführung *f* performance.

auffüllen *vt sep* (**a**) (*vollständig füllen*) to fill up; (*nachfüllen*) to top up. (**b**) (*ergänzen*) *Flüssigkeit* to dilute; *Vorräte* to replenish; *Öl* to top up.

Aufgabe *f* (**a**) (*Arbeit, Pflicht*) job, task. **es ist nicht** ~ **der Regierung, ...** it is not the job *or* task of the government to ...; **sich** (*dat*) **etw zur** ~ **machen** to make sth one's job *or* business. (**b**) (*Zweck, Funktion*) purpose, job. (**c**) (*esp Sch*) (*Problem*) question; (*Math auch*) problem; (*zur Übung*) exercise; (*usu pl: Haus*~) homework *no pl*. (**d**) (*von Koffer, Postsendung*) handing in. (**e**) (*Verzicht auf weiteren Kampf etc*) (*Sport*) retirement; (*Mil etc*) surrender. **die Polizei forderte die Geiselnehmer zur** ~ **auf** the police appealed to the kidnappers to give themselves up *or* to surrender. (**f**) (*von Gewohnheit, Geschäft*) giving up; (*von Plänen, Forderungen auch*) dropping; (*von Hoffnung, Studium*) abandoning.

aufgabeln *vt sep* (*fig col*) *jdn* to pick up (*col*); *Sache* to get hold of.

Aufgabenbereich *m* area of responsibility.

Aufgang *m* (**a**) (*von Sonne, Mond*) rising; (*von Stern auch*) ascent. (**b**) (*Treppen*~) staircase.

aufgeben *vt sep irreg* **1** *vt* (**a**) *Hausaufgaben* to give; *Problem* to pose (*jdm for sb*). **jdm viel/nichts** ~ (*Sch*) to give sb a lot of/no homework. (**b**) *Koffer, Gepäck* to hand in; *Brief* to post (*esp Brit*), to mail; *Anzeige, Bestellung* to place. (**c**) *Kampf, Hoffnung, Arbeitsstelle, Patienten etc* to give up. **gib's auf!** why don't you give up? **2** *vi* (*sich geschlagen geben*) to give up *or* in.

aufgeblasen *adj* (*fig*) puffed up, self-important.

Aufgebot *nt* (**a**) (*zur Eheschließung*) **das** ~ **bestellen** to give notice of one's intended marriage; (*Eccl*) to put up the banns. (**b**) (*Ansammlung*) (*von Menschen*) contingent; (*von Material etc*) array.

aufgebracht *adj* outraged, incensed.

aufgedonnert *adj* (*pej col*) tarted up (*pej col*).

aufgedreht *adj* (*col*) in high spirits.

aufgedunsen *adj* swollen, bloated; *Gesicht auch* puffy.

aufgehen *vi sep irreg aux sein* (**a**) (*Sonne, Mond, Sterne*) to come up, to rise. (**b**) (*sich öffnen*) to open; (*Theat: Vorhang*) to go up; (*Knopf, Knoten etc*) to come undone. (**c**) (*aufkeimen*) to come up. (**d**) (*Cook*) to rise. (**e**) (*klarwerden*) **jdm geht etw auf** sb realizes sth, sth dawns on sb. (**f**) (*Math, fig*) to work out. **20 durch 6 geht nicht auf** 20 divided by 6 doesn't go. (**g**) **in etw** (*dat*) ~ (*fig*) to be wrapped up in sth, to be taken up with sth; **in Flammen** ~ to go up in flames.

aufgehoben *adj*: (**bei jdm**) **gut/schlecht** ~ **sein** to be/not to be safe (with sb).

aufgekratzt *adj* (*col*) in high spirits, full of beans (*col*).

aufgelegt *adj* **gut/schlecht** ~ in a good/bad mood.

aufgelöst *adj* (**a**) (*außer sich*) beside oneself (*vor +dat* with), distraught; (*bestürzt*) upset. **in Tränen** ~ in tears. (**b**) (*erschöpft*) exhausted.

aufgeräumt *adj* (*geh: gutgelaunt*) light-hearted.

aufgeregt *adj* (*erregt*) excited; (*nervös*) nervous; (*durcheinander*) flustered.

Aufgeregtheit *f no pl siehe adj* excitement; nervousness; flustered state.

aufgeschlossen *adj* (*nicht engstirnig*) open-minded (*für, gegenüber* about, as regards); (*empfänglich*) receptive, open (*für, gegenüber* to).

Aufgeschlossenheit *f no pl siehe adj* open-mindedness; receptiveness, openness.

aufgeschmissen *adj pred* (*col*) in a fix, snookered.

aufgeschwemmt *adj* bloated, swollen.

aufgetakelt *adj* (*pej*) dressed up to the nines (*col*).

aufgeweckt *adj* bright, quick, sharp.

aufgewühlt *adj* (*geh*) agitated, in a turmoil *pred*;

Gefühle auch, Meer turbulent.

aufgießen *vt sep irreg* **(a) etw (auf etw** *acc***)** ~ to pour sth on (sth). **(b)** *Kaffee, Tee* to make.

aufgliedern *sep* 1 *vt (in+acc* into) to split up, to (sub)divide; *(in Kategorien auch)* to break up. 2 *vr (in+acc* into) to (sub)divide, to break down.

aufgreifen *vt sep irreg* **(a)** *(festnehmen)* to pick up, to apprehend. **(b)** *Thema* to take up.

aufgrund *prep+gen,* **auf Grund** *siehe* **Grund.**

Aufguß *m* brew, infusion; *(fig pej)* rehash.

Aufgußbeutel *m* sachet (containing coffee/ herbs *etc)* for brewing; *(Teebeutel)* tea bag.

aufhaben *sep irreg* 1 *vt* **(a)** *Hut, Brille* to have on. **(b)** *Tür, Augen* to have open. **(c)** *(Sch: als Hausaufgabe)* **ich habe heute viel auf** I've got a lot of homework today. 2 *vi (Laden etc)* to be open.

aufhalsen *vt sep (col)* **jdm/sich etw** ~ to saddle *or* land sb/oneself with sth *(col).*

aufhalten *sep irreg* 1 *vt* **(a)** *Fahrzeug, Entwicklung* to stop, to halt; *(verlangsamen)* to hold up, to delay; *(abhalten, stören) (bei* from*)* to hold back, to keep back. **ich will dich nicht länger** ~ I don't want to keep *or* hold you back any longer. **(b)** *(col: offenhalten)* to keep open. **die Hand** ~ to hold one's hand out. 2 *vr* **(a)** *(an einem Ort bleiben)* to stay. **(b)** *(sich befassen)* **sich bei etw** ~ to dwell on sth.

aufhängen *sep* 1 *vt* **(a)** to hang up; *(Aut)* Rad to suspend. **(b)** *(töten)* to hang *(an+dat* from*).* 2 *vr (sich töten)* to hang oneself *(an +dat* from*).*

Aufhänger *m* tag, loop. **ein** ~ **(für etw)** *(fig col)* a peg to hang sth on.

Aufhängung *f (Tech)* suspension.

aufhäufen *vtr sep* to pile up, to accumulate.

aufheben *sep irreg* 1 *vt* **(a)** *(vom Boden)* to pick up; *größeren Gegenstand auch* to lift up. **(b)** *(nicht wegwerfen)* to keep. **jdm etw** ~ to keep sth for sb; *siehe* **aufgehoben. (c)** *(ungültig machen)* to abolish, to do away with; *Urteil* to reverse, to quash. **(d)** *(beenden) Blockade, Belagerung* to raise, to lift; *Beschränkung* to remove, to lift. **(e)** *(ausgleichen)* to offset, to make up for; *Schwerkraft* to neutralize, to cancel out. 2 *vr (sich ausgleichen)* to cancel each other out *(auch Math)*, to offset each other.

Aufheben *nt no pl* fuss. **viel** ~(**s**) **(von etw) machen** to make a lot of fuss (about *or* over sth).

Aufhebung *f* **(a)** *siehe vt (c)* abolition; reversal, quashing. **(b)** *siehe vt (d)* raising, lifting; removal, lifting.

aufheitern *sep* 1 *vt jdn* to cheer up; *Rede, Leben* to brighten up *(jdm* for sb*).* 2 *vr (Himmel, Wetter)* to clear up, to brighten up.

Aufheiterung *f (Met)* brighter period.

aufheizen *sep* 1 *vt* to heat (up). **die Stimmung** ~ to stir up feelings. 2 *vr* to heat up; *(fig)* to hot up *(col)*, to intensify.

aufhelfen *vi sep irreg (lit: beim Aufstehen)* to help up *(jdm* sb*).*

aufhellen *sep* 1 *vt* to brighten (up); *Haare* to lighten; *(fig: klären)* to throw *or* shed light upon. 2 *vr (Himmel, Wetter, fig: Miene)* to brighten (up).

aufhetzen *vt sep* to stir up, to incite. **jdn gegen jdn/etw** ~ to stir up sb *or* incite sb against sb/sth; **jdn zu etw** ~ to incite sb to (do) sth.

Aufhetzung *f* incitement, agitation.

aufheulen *vi sep* to howl *(vor* with*); (Sirene)* to (start to) wail; *(Motor)* to (give a) roar.

aufholen *sep* 1 *vt Zeit, Vorsprung* to make up; *Lernstoff* to catch up on. 2 *vi (Mannschaft, Schüler, Arbeiter)* to catch up.

aufhorchen *vi sep* to prick up one's ears, to sit up (and take notice).

aufhören *vi sep* to stop; *(bei Firma)* to finish; *(Musik, Lärm auch, Freundschaft)* to (come to an) end. **hör doch endlich auf!** (will you) stop it!; **mit etw** ~ to stop sth; **da hört sich doch alles auf!** *(col)* that's the (absolute) limit!

aufjagen *vt sep* to disturb.

aufjauchzen *vi sep* **vor Freude** ~ to give a shout of joy.

aufkaufen *vt sep* to buy up.

Aufkäufer *m* buyer.

aufkeimen *vi sep aux sein* to germinate, to sprout; *(fig) (Hoffnung, Liebe)* to burgeon (liter), to form; *(Zweifel)* to (begin to) take root.

aufklappbar *adj Verdeck* fold-back.

aufklappen *vt sep* to open up; *Klappe* to let down; *Verdeck* to fold back; *Messer* to unclasp; *Fenster, Buch* to open; *(hochschlagen) Kragen* to turn up.

aufklaren *vi sep (Met)* to clear (up).

aufklären *sep* 1 *vt* **(a)** *Mißverständnis, Irrtum* to clear up; *Verbrechen* to solve; *Ereignis, Vorgang* to throw light upon. **(b)** *jdn* to enlighten. **Kinder** ~ *(sexuell)* to tell children the facts of life; *(in der Schule)* to give children sex education; **jdn über etw** *(acc)* ~ to inform sb about sth. 2 *vr (Irrtum, Geheimnis)* to be cleared up; *(Himmel)* to clear up; *(fig: Gesicht)* to brighten (up).

Aufklärung *f* **(a)** *(Philos)* **die** ~ the Enlightenment. **(b)** *siehe vt (a)* clearing up; solution; *(von Vorgang)* elucidation. **(c)** *(Information)* enlightenment. **(d)** *(sexuelle)* ~ *(in Schulen)* sex education. **die** ~ **von Kindern** explaining the facts of life to children. **(e)** *(Mil)* reconnaissance.

Aufklärungs-: ~**arbeit** *f* educational work; ~**film** *m* sex education film; ~**flugzeug** *nt* reconnaissance plane; ~**kampagne** *f* information campaign; ~**schiff** *nt (Mil)* reconnaissance ship.

aufkleben *vt sep (auf+acc* to*)* to stick on; *(mit Leim, Klebstoff auch)* to glue on.

Aufkleber *m* sticker.

aufknacken *vt sep Nüsse etc, (col) Tresor* to crack; *Auto* to break into.

aufknöpfen *vt sep (öffnen)* to unbutton, to undo.

aufknoten *vt sep* to untie, to undo.

aufknüpfen *vt sep* **(a)** to hang *(an+dat* from*),* to string up *(col) (an+dat* on*).* **(b)** *(aufknoten)* untie, to undo.

aufkochen *vt sep* to bring to the boil.

aufkommen *vi sep irreg aux sein* **(a)** *(lit, fig: entstehen)* to arise; *(Nebel)* to come down; *(Wind)* to spring *or* get up; *(auftreten: Mode etc auch)* to appear (on the scene). **etw** ~ **lassen** *(fig) Zweifel, Kritik* to give rise to sth; **endlich kam Stimmung auf** at last things livened up. **(b)** ~ **für** *(Kosten tragen)* to bear the costs of, to pay for; *(Haftung tragen)* to be liable for. **für die Kinder** ~ *(finanziell)* to pay for the children's upkeep; **für die Kosten** ~ to bear the costs; **für den Schaden** ~ to pay for the damage.

Aufkommen *nt* **(a)** *no pl (das Auftreten)* appearance; *(von Methode, Mode etc auch)* advent, emergence. **(b)** *(Fin) (Summe, Menge)* amount; *(von Steuern)* revenue *(aus* from*).*

aufkreischen *vi sep (Mensch)* to scream, to shriek; *(Bremsen, Maschine)* to screech.

aufkrempeln *vi sep (sich)* **die Ärmel/Hose** ~ to roll up one's sleeves/trousers.

aufkreuzen *vi sep aux sein (col: erscheinen)* to turn *or* show up.

aufkriegen *vt sep (col) siehe* **aufbekommen.**

aufkündigen *vt sep Vertrag etc* to terminate.

auflachen *vi sep* to (give a) laugh.

aufladen *sep irreg* 1 *vt* **(a) etw (auf etw** *acc***)** ~ to load sth on(to) sth. **jdm/sich etw** ~ *(fig)* to saddle sb/oneself with sth. **(b)** *(elektrisch)* to charge; *(neu* ~*)* to recharge. **emotional aufgeladen** *(fig)* emotionally charged. 2 *vr (Batterie etc)* to be charged; *(neu* ~*)* to be recharged.

Auflage *f* **(a)** *(Ausgabe)* edition; *(Druck)* impression; *(*~*höhe)* number of copies; *(von Zeitung)* circulation. **(b)** *(Bedingung)* condition. **jdm etw zur** ~ **machen** to impose sth on sb as a condition; **jdm zur** ~ **machen, etw zu tun** to make it a

condition for sb to do sth; **die ~ haben, etw zu
tun** to be obliged to do sth. **(c)** *(Überzug)* plating
no pl, coating.

Auflage(n)-: ~**höhe** *f (von Buch)* number of
copies published; *(von Zeitung)* circulation;
~**ziffer** *f* circulation (figures *pl*); *(von Buch)*
number of copies published.

auflassen *vt sep irreg (col) (offenlassen)* to leave
open; *(aufbehalten)* Hut to keep *or* leave on. **die
Kinder länger ~** to let the children stay up
(longer).

auflauern *vi sep+dat* to lie in wait for.

Auflauf *m* **(a)** *(Menschen~)* crowd. **(b)** *(Cook)*
(baked) pudding *(sweet or savoury).*

auflaufen *vi sep irreg aux sein* **(a)** *(auf Grund
laufen: Schiff)* to run aground *(auf+acc or dat on).*
(b) *(aufprallen)* **auf jdn/etw ~** to run into sb/sth,
to collide with sb/sth; **jdn ~ lassen** *(Ftbl)* to
bodycheck sb.

Auflaufform *f (Cook)* ovenproof dish.

aufleben *vi sep aux sein* to revive; *(munter, lebendig werden)* to liven up, to come to life again;
(neuen Lebensmut bekommen) to find a new lease
of life. **Erinnerungen wieder ~ lassen** to revive
memories.

auflecken *vt sep* to lick up.

auflegen *sep* 1 *vt* **(a)** to put on; *Gedeck* to lay;
Hörer to put down, to replace. **(b)** *(herausgeben)
Buch* to publish, to print. **ein Buch neu ~** to
reprint a book; *(neu bearbeitet)* to bring out a new
edition of a book. 2 *vi (Telec)* to hang up.

auflehnen *vr sep* **sich gegen jdn/etw ~** to revolt
or rebel against sb/sth.

Auflehnung *f* revolt, rebellion.

auflesen *vt sep irreg (lit, fig col)* to pick up. **jdn/etw
von der Straße ~** to pick sb/sth up off the street.

aufleuchten *vi sep aux sein or haben (lit, fig)* to
light up.

auflisten *vt sep* to list.

Auflistung *f* listing; *(Liste auch)* list.

auflockern *sep* 1 *vt* **(a)** *Boden* to break up, to
loosen (up). **(b)** *Unterricht, Stoff, Vortrag* to make
less monotonous, to give relief to *(durch with).*
(c) *(entspannen)* to make relaxed; *Atmosphäre
auch* to ease. **in aufgelockerter Stimmung** in a
relaxed mood. 2 *vr* **(a)** *(Sport)* to limber *or*
loosen up. **(b)** *(Bewölkung)* to break up.

Auflockerung *f* **(a)** *(von Boden)* breaking up,
loosening (up). **ihm gelang die ~ einer ge-
spannten Atmosphäre** he succeeded in easing a
tense atmosphere. **(b)** *(von Bewölkung)* breaking
up.

auflodern *vi sep aux sein (Flammen, fig)* to flare
up; *(lodernd brennen)* to blaze.

auflösen *sep* 1 *vt* **(a)** *(in Flüssigkeit)* to dissolve;
(in Bestandteile zerlegen) to break down *(in+acc
into); (Math)* Gleichung to (re)solve; *siehe* **aufgelöst.** **(b)** *(aufklären)* Widerspruch etc to clear up,
to resolve; *Rätsel* to solve. **(c)** *(zerstreuen)* Wolken, Versammlung to disperse, to break up. **(d)**
(aufheben) to dissolve *(auch Parl); Einheit, Gruppe*
to disband; *Verlobung* to break off; *Vertrag* to
cancel; *Konto* to close; *Haushalt* to break up. 2 *vr*
(a) *(in Flüssigkeit)* to dissolve; *(Zweifel, Probleme)* to disappear. **(b)** *(sich zerstreuen)* to disperse; *(Wolken auch)* to break up; *(Nebel auch)* to
lift. **(c)** *(auseinandergehen) (Verband)* to disband;
(formell: esp Parl) to dissolve.

Auflösung *f siehe vt* **(a)** dissolving; breaking
down; (re)solving. **(b)** clearing up, resolving;
solving; *(fertige Lösung: von Rätsel etc)* solution.
(c) dispersal. **(d)** dissolving; disbanding; breaking off; cancellation; closing; breaking up; *(von
Parlament)* dissolution. **(e)** *(von Bildschirm)* resolution.

aufmachen *sep* 1 *vt* **(a)** *(öffnen)* to open; *(lösen,
aufknöpfen etc)* to undo. **(b)** *(eröffnen, gründen)
Geschäft, Unternehmen* to open (up). **(c)** *(gestal-*

ten) Buch, Zeitung to make up; *(in Presse) Ereignis,
Prozeß etc* to feature. 2 *vi (Tür öffnen)* to open the
door; *(Geschäft) (er)öffnen)* to open (up). 3 *vr* **(a)**
(sich zurechtmachen) to get oneself up. **(b)** *(sich
anschicken)* to get ready, to make preparations;
(aufbrechen) to set out.

Aufmacher *m (Press)* lead.

Aufmachung *f (a) (Kleidung)* turn-out. **in großer
~ erscheinen** to turn up dressed up to the nines.
(b) *(Gestaltung)* presentation, style; *(von Buch)*
presentation, make-up; *(Press etc)* layout.

aufmalen *vt sep* to paint on *(auf etw (acc) sth).*

Aufmarsch *m (Mil)* marching; *(Parade)*
marchpast; *(in Stellung, Kampflinie)* deployment.

aufmarschieren* *vi sep aux sein (heranmar-
schieren)* to march up; *(Mil: in Stellung gehen)* to
deploy; *(vorbeimarschieren)* to march past.

aufmerksam *adj* **(a)** *Zuhörer, Beobachter, Schüler*
attentive; *Blicke auch, Augen* keen; *(scharf beob-
achtend)* observant. **jdn auf etw (acc) ~ machen**
to draw sb's attention to sth; **auf etw (acc) ~
werden** to become aware of sth. **(b)** *(zuvorkommend)* attentive. **(das ist) sehr ~ von Ihnen**
(that's) most kind of you.

Aufmerksamkeit *f* **(a)** *no pl* attention, attentiveness. **das ist meiner ~ entgangen** it escaped
my attention. **(b)** *no pl (Zuvorkommenheit)* attentiveness. **(c)** *(Geschenk)* token (gift).

aufmöbeln *vt sep (col) Gegenstand* to do up *(col);
jdn (beleben)* to buck up *(col),* to pep up *(col).*

aufmucken *vt sep (col)* to protest *(gegen at,
against).*

aufmuntern *vt sep (aufheitern)* to cheer up; *(beleben)* to liven up.

Aufmunterung *f siehe vt* cheering up; livening
up.

aufmüpfig *adj (col)* rebellious.

aufnähen *vt sep* to sew on *(auf+acc to).*

Aufnahme *f-n* **(a)** *(Empfang, fig: Reaktion)* reception. **bei jdm freundliche ~ finden** *(lit, fig)* to
meet with a warm reception from sb; **die ~ in
ein Krankenhaus** admission (in)to hospital; **wie
war die ~ beim Publikum?** how did the audience
receive it or react? **(b)** *(in Verein)* admission *(in
+acc to).* **(c)** *no pl (lit, fig: Absorption)* absorption.
(d) *no pl (von Kapital etc)* raising. **(e)** *no pl (Beginn: von Gespräch etc)* start, commencement.
(f) *(Foto)* photo(graph); shot *(col); (Film~)* take.
(g) *(auf Tonband etc)* recording.

Aufnahme-: ~**antrag** *m* application for membership *or* admission; **a**~**bereit** *adj Kamera* ready to
shoot; *(fig)* receptive, open *(für to);* ~**bereitschaft** *f (fig)* receptiveness; **a**~**fähig** *adj Ohr* etw
a~**fähig sein** to be able to take sth in; ~**gebühr** *f*
enrolment fee; *(in Verein)* admission fee; ~**leiter**
m (Film) production manager; *(Rad, TV)* producer; ~**prüfung** *f* entrance examination; ~**studio** *nt* (film/recording) studio.

aufnehmen *vt sep irreg* **(a)** *(vom Boden)* to pick
up. **(b)** *(lit: empfangen, fig: reagieren auf)* to receive. **(c)** *(unterbringen)* to take (in); *(fassen)* to
take, to hold; *Einwanderer* to absorb. **(d)** *(in Verein)* to admit *(in+acc to); (Schule auch)* to take on.
(e) *(absorbieren)* to absorb, to take up; *(fig: eindringen lassen)* Eindrücke to take in; *(begreifen
auch)* to grasp. **(f)** *(mit einbeziehen)* to include, to
incorporate; *(aufgreifen)* Thema to take up. **(g)**
(esp Ftbl) Ball to take, to receive. **(h)** *(beginnen)*
Beziehung to establish; *Tätigkeit, Studium* to begin, to take up. **den Kampf ~** to commence battle; *(fig auch)* to take up the struggle. **(i)** *Hypothek
etc* to raise; *Kredit auch* to take up. **(j)** *(niederschreiben)* Protokoll, Diktat, *to take down; Persona-
lien* to take (down); *Telegramm* to take. **(k)** *(fotografieren)* to take (a photograph of), to photograph; *(filmen)* to film, to shoot *(col).* **(l)** *(auf
Tonband)* to record, to tape. **(m)** *(beim Stricken)
Maschen* to increase, to make. **(n)** **es mit jdm/etw**

~ können to be a match for sb/sth.
aufnötigen *vt sep* **jdm etw ~** to force sth on sb.
auf|oktroyieren* *vt sep* **jdm etw ~** *(geh)* to impose *or* force sth on sb.
auf|opfern *vr sep* to sacrifice oneself.
auf|opfernd *adj* self-sacrificing.
Auf|opferung *f* **(a)** *(Aufgabe)* sacrifice. **(b)** *(Selbst~)* self-sacrifice.
aufpassen *vi sep* **(a)** *(beaufsichtigen)* **auf jdn/etw ~** to keep an eye on sb/sth. **(b)** *(aufmerksam sein, achtgeben)* to pay attention. **paß auf!**, **aufgepaßt!** look, watch; *(sei aufmerksam)* pay attention; *(Vorsicht)* look out, watch out, mind (out).
Aufpasser(in *f)* *m* - *(pej: Aufseher, Spitzel)* spy *(pej)*, watchdog *(col)*; *(Beobachter)* supervisor; *(Wächter)* guard.
aufpeitschen *vt sep Meer, Wellen* to whip up; *(fig) Sinne* to inflame, to fire; *Menschen* to work up; *(stärker)* to whip up into a frenzy.
aufpflanzen *sep* **1** *vt (Mil) Bajonett* to fix. **2** *vr* **sich vor jdm ~** to plant oneself in front of sb.
aufpicken *vt sep (Vogel)* to peck up.
aufplatzen *vi sep aux sein* to burst open.
aufplustern *sep* **1** *vt Federn* to ruffle up. **2** *vr (Vogel)* to ruffle (up) its feathers; *(Mensch)* to puff oneself up.
aufpolieren* *vt sep (lit, fig)* to polish up.
aufprägen *vt sep* **jdm/einer Sache seinen Stempel ~** *(fig)* to leave one's mark on sb/sth.
Aufprall *m* **-e** impact.
aufprallen *vi sep aux sein* **auf etw** *(acc)* **~** to strike *or* hit sth; *(Fahrzeug auch)* to collide with sth.
Aufpreis *m* extra *or* additional charge. **gegen ~** for an extra *or* additional charge.
aufpumpen *vt sep* to pump up, to inflate; *Fahrrad* to pump up the tyres *(Brit) or* tires *(US)* of.
aufputschen *sep* **1** *vt* **(a)** *(aufwiegeln)* to rouse; *Gefühle, öffentliche Meinung* to stir up. **(b)** *(durch Reizmittel)* to stimulate. **~de Mittel** stimulants. **2** *vr* to pep oneself up *(col)*, to dope oneself *(Sport col)*.
Aufputschmittel *nt* stimulant.
aufquellen *vi sep irreg aux sein (anschwellen)* to swell (up). **aufgequollen** swollen; **etw ~ lassen** to soak sth (to allow it to swell up).
aufraffen *sep* **1** *vr* to force oneself to do sth. **sich zu einer Entscheidung ~** to force oneself to make a decision. **2** *vt Papiere, Eigentum* to gather up; *(schnell aufheben)* to snatch up.
aufragen *vi sep aux sein or haben (in die Höhe ~)* to rise; *(sehr hoch, groß auch)* to tower (up) *(über +dat* above, over). **die hoch ~den Türme** the soaring towers.
aufrappeln *vr sep (col)* **(a)** *siehe* **aufraffen 1**. **(b)** *(wieder zu Kräften kommen)* to recover, to get over it.
aufrauchen *vt sep (zu Ende rauchen)* to finish (smoking).
aufrauhen *vt sep* to roughen; *(Tex) Stoff* to nap.
aufräumen *sep* **1** *vt* to tidy *or* clear up; *(wegräumen auch)* to clear *or* put away. **2** *vi* **mit etw ~** to do away with sth; *siehe* **aufgeräumt.**
Aufräumungs|arbeiten *pl* clearing-up operations *pl*.
aufrechnen *vt sep* **etw gegen etw ~** to offset sth against sth.
aufrecht *adj (lit, fig)* upright; *Körperhaltung, Gangart auch* erect.
aufrecht|erhalten* *vt sep irreg* to maintain; *Kontakt, Bräuche auch* to keep up; *Behauptung auch* to stick to; *(moralisch)* to keep going.
Aufrecht|erhaltung *f siehe vt* maintenance, maintaining; keeping up; sticking *(gen* to).
aufregen *sep* **1** *vt (ärgerlich machen)* to irritate, to annoy; *(nervös machen)* to make nervous; *(beunruhigen)* to agitate; *(bestürzen)* to upset; *(erregen)* to excite. **du regst mich auf!** you're getting on my nerves. **2** *vr* to get worked up *(col)* or ex-

cited *(über+acc* about); *siehe* **aufgeregt.**
aufregend *adj* exciting.
Aufregung *f* excitement *no pl*; *(Beunruhigung)* agitation *no pl*. **nur keine ~!** don't get excited, don't get worked up *(col)*; **jdn in ~ versetzen** to get sb in a state *(col)*.
aufreiben *vt sep irreg* **(a)** *Haut etc* to chafe, to rub sore. **(b)** *(fig: zermürben)* to wear down. **(c)** *(Mil: völlig vernichten)* to wipe out, to annihilate.
aufreibend *adj (fig)* wearing, trying; *(stärker)* stressful.
aufreihen *sep* **1** *vt (in Linie)* to line up; *Perlen* to string. **2** *vr* to line up.
aufreißen* *sep irreg* **1** *vt* **(a)** *(aufbrechen)* to tear *or* rip open; *Straße* to tear *or* rip up. **(b)** *Tür, Fenster* to fling open; *Augen, Mund* to open wide. **(c)** *(col) Mädchen* to pick up *(col)*. **2** *vi aux sein (Naht)* to split, to burst; *(Hose)* to tear, to rip; *(Wunde)* to tear open; *(Wolkendecke)* to break up.
aufreizen *vt sep (herausfordern)* to provoke; *(aufwiegeln)* to incite.
aufreizend *adj* provocative.
aufrichten *sep* **1** *vt* **(a)** *Gegenstand* to put upright; *jdn* to help up; *Oberkörper* to straighten (up). **(b)** *(fig: moralisch)* to put new heart into. **2** *vr (gerade stehen)* to stand up (straight); *(gerade sitzen)* to sit up (straight); *(aus gebückter Haltung)* to straighten up. **sich im Bett ~** to sit up in bed.
aufrichtig *adj* sincere *(zu, gegen* towards); *(ehrlich auch)* honest.
Aufrichtigkeit *f siehe adj* sincerity; honesty.
aufrollen *vt sep* **(a)** *(zusammenrollen)* to roll up; *Kabel* to coil *or* wind up. **(b)** *(entrollen)* to unroll; *Fahne* to unfurl; *Kabel* to uncoil, to unwind. **(c)** *(fig) Problem* to go into. **einen Fall/Prozeß wieder ~** to reopen a case/trial.
aufrücken *vi sep aux sein (lit, fig)* to move up. **zum Geschäftsleiter ~** to be promoted to manager.
Aufruf *m (a)* appeal *(an +acc* to). **(b)** *(von Namen)* **nach ~** when called.
aufrufen *sep irreg* **1** *vt* **(a)** *Namen* to call. **Sie werden aufgerufen** your name *or* you will be called; **einen Schüler ~** to ask a pupil (to answer) a question. **(b) jdn zu etw ~** *(zu Mithilfe, Unterstützung etc)* to appeal to *or* call upon sb for sth. **(c)** *(Jur) Zeugen* to summon. **(d)** *(Comp)* to call up. **2** *vi* **zum Streik etc ~** to call for a strike etc.
Aufruhr *m* **-e** *(a)* *(Auflehnung)* revolt, rebellion, uprising. **(b)** *(Bewegtheit, fig: Erregung)* tumult, turmoil. **in ~ sein** to be in a turmoil; **jdn in ~ versetzen** to throw sb into a turmoil.
aufrühren *vt sep (lit, fig)* to stir up.
Aufrührer(in *f)* *m* - rabble-rouser.
aufrührerisch *adj* **(a)** *Rede, Pamphlet* rabble-rousing, inflammatory. **(b)** *attr (in Aufruhr)* rebellious; *(meuternd)* mutinous.
aufrunden *vt sep Zahl* to round up *(auf +acc* to).
aufrüsten *vti sep* to arm.
Aufrüstung *f* armament. **atomare ~** nuclear armament.
aufrütteln *vt sep* to rouse *(aus* from). **jdn/jds Gewissen ~** to stir sb/sb's conscience.
aufs = auf das.
aufsagen *vt sep Gedicht etc* to recite, to say.
aufsammeln *vt sep (lit, fig)* to pick up.
aufsässig *adj* rebellious.
Aufsässigkeit *f* rebelliousness.
Aufsatz *m* **(a)** *(Abhandlung)* essay; *(Schul~ auch)* composition. **(b)** *(oberer Teil)* top *or* upper part.
aufsaugen *vt sep irreg Flüssigkeit* to soak up; *(fig)* to absorb. **etw mit dem Staubsauger ~** to vacuum sth up.
aufscheuchen *vt sep* to startle.
aufscheuern *vt sep* to rub sore, to chafe.
aufschichten *vt sep* to stack, to pile up; *Stapel* to build up.
aufschieben *vt sep irreg Fenster, Tür* to slide open;

---

cited *(über+acc* about); *siehe* **aufgeregt.**

Riegel to push *or* slide back; *(fig: verschieben)* to put off, to postpone. **aufgeschoben ist nicht aufgehoben** *(prov)* putting something off does not mean it's cancelled.

Aufschlag *m* **(a)** *(das Aufschlagen)* impact. **(b)** *(Tennis etc)* service, serve. **sie hat ~ it's** her service *or* serve. **(c)** *(Preis~)* surcharge, extra charge. **(d)** *(Ärmel~)* cuff; *(Hosen~)* turn-up *(Brit)*, cuff *(US)*; *(Mantel~ etc)* lapel.

aufschlagen *sep irreg* **1** *vi* **(a)** *aux sein (auftreffen)* **auf etw** *(dat)* ~ to hit sth; **mit dem Kopf** *etc* **auf etw** *(acc or dat)* ~ to hit one's head *etc* on sth. **(b)** *aux haben or sein (Waren, Preise)* to rise, to go up *(um by)*. **(c)** *(Tennis etc)* to serve. **2** *vt* **(a)** *(durch Schlagen öffnen)* to crack. **jdm/sich den Kopf** ~ to crack sb's/one's head open. **(b)** *(aufklappen)* to open. **schlagt Seite 111 auf** open your books at page 111. **(c)** *Augen* to open. **(d)** *(aufbauen) Bett, Liegestuhl* to put up; *Zelt auch* to pitch; *Lager* to set up, to pitch. **(e)** *(Comm) Preise* to put up.

aufschließen *sep irreg* **1** *vt (öffnen)* to unlock. **jdm die Tür** *etc* ~ to unlock the door *etc* for sb; *siehe* **aufgeschlossen. 2** *vi* **(a)** *(öffnen)* **(jdm)** ~ to unlock the door (for sb). **(b)** *(heranrücken)* to close up; *(Sport)* to catch up *(zu* with).

aufschlitzen *vt sep* to rip open; *(mit Messer auch)* to slit open.

Aufschluß *m* *(Aufklärung)* information *no pl*. **(jdm)** ~ **über etw** *(acc)* **geben** to give (sb) information about sth.

aufschlüsseln *vt sep* to break down *(nach* into); *(klassifizieren)* to classify *(nach* according to).

aufschlußreich *adj* informative, instructive.

aufschnappen *vt sep* to catch; *(col) Wort etc* to pick up.

aufschneiden *sep irreg* **1** *vt* **(a)** to cut open; *Braten* to carve. **(b)** *(in Scheiben schneiden)* to slice. **2** *vi (col: prahlen)* to brag, to boast.

Aufschneider *m (col)* boaster, show-off *(col)*.

Aufschnitt *m no pl* (assorted) sliced cold meats, cold cuts.

aufschnüren *vt sep (lösen)* to untie, to undo; *Schuh auch* to unlace.

aufschrauben *vt sep Schraube etc* to unscrew; *Flasche etc* to take the top off.

aufschrecken *sep* **1** *vt* to startle; *(aus Gleichgültigkeit)* to jolt *(aus* out of). **2** *vi aux sein* to start (up), to be startled. **aus dem Schlaf** ~ to wake up with a start.

Aufschrei *m* yell; *(schrill)* scream, shriek. **ein ~ der Empörung** *(fig)* an outcry.

aufschreiben *vt sep irreg* **(a)** *(niederschreiben)* **etw** ~ to write *or* note sth down. **(b)** *(notieren)* **sich** *(dat)* **etw** ~ to make a note of sth.

aufschreien *vi sep irreg* to yell out; *(schrill)* to scream *or* shriek out.

Aufschrift *f* inscription; *(Etikett)* label.

Aufschub *m (Verzögerung)* delay; *(Vertagung)* postponement. **die Sache duldet keinen ~** *(geh)* the matter must not be delayed; **jdm ~ gewähren** to grant sb an extension.

aufschürfen *vt sep* **sich** *(dat)* **die Haut/das Knie** ~ to graze *or* scrape oneself/one's knee.

aufschütteln *vt sep Kissen* to shake *or* plump up.

aufschütten *vt sep* **(a)** *Flüssigkeit* to pour on. *Kaffee* ~ to make coffee. **(b)** *Kohle* to put on (the fire). **(c)** *Damm, Deich* to throw up.

aufschwatzen *vt sep (col)* **jdm etw** ~ to talk sb into taking sth.

aufschwingen *vr sep irreg* to swing oneself up; *(Vogel)* to soar (up). **sich zu etw** ~ *(sich aufraffen)* to bring oneself to do sth.

Aufschwung *m* **(a)** *(Antrieb)* lift; *(der Wirtschaft etc)* upturn, upswing *(gen* in). **durch diese Erfindung hat die Firma einen ~ genommen** this invention gave the firm a boost. **(b)** *(Turnen)* swing-up.

aufsehen *vi sep irreg* = **aufblicken.**

Aufsehen *nt no pl* sensation. **großes ~ erregen** to cause a sensation *or* stir; **ich möchte jedes ~ vermeiden** I want to avoid any fuss.

aufsehen|erregend *adj* sensational.

Aufseher(in *f) m (allgemein)* supervisor; *(Gefängnis~)* warder *(Brit)*, guard *(US)*; *(Park~, Museums~ etc)* attendant.

aufsein *vi sep irreg aux sein* **(a)** *(aufgestanden sein)* to be up. **(b)** *(geöffnet sein)* to be open.

aufsetzen *sep* **1** *vt* **(a)** *Brille etc, Miene etc* to put on; *Fuß* to put down. **(b)** *(verfassen)* to draft. **2** *vr* to sit up. **3** *vi (Flugzeug)* to touch down, to land.

Aufsetzer *m* - *(Sport)* bouncing ball.

aufseufzen *vi sep (tief)* ~ to heave a (deep) sigh.

Aufsicht *f no pl (Überwachung)* supervision *(über +acc* of); *(Obhut)* charge. **unter jds ~** *(dat)* under the supervision of sb; **bei einer Prüfung ~ führen** to invigilate an exam; **jdn ohne ~ lassen** to leave sb unsupervised.

Aufsichts-: **~beamte(r)** *m (in Museum, Zoo etc)* attendant; **~rat** *m* board (of directors).

aufsitzen *vi sep irreg* **(a)** *(aufgerichtet sitzen)* to sit up. **(b)** *aux sein (auf Reittier)* to mount; *(auf Fahrzeug)* to get on. **(c)** *aux sein (col: hereinfallen)* **jdm/einer Sache** ~ to be taken in by sb/sth.

aufspalten *vtr sep* to split; *(fig auch)* to split up.

aufspannen *vt sep* **(a)** *Netz, Sprungtuch* to stretch *or* spread out; *Schirm* to put up, to open. **(b)** *(aufziehen) Leinwand* to stretch *(auf +acc* onto); *Saite* to put on *(auf etw (acc)* sth).

aufsparen *vt sep* to save (up), to keep.

aufsperren *vt sep Tür, Schnabel* to open wide. **die Ohren ~** to prick up one's ears.

aufspielen *sep* **1** *vi (dated)* to play; *(anfangen)* to strike up. **2** *vr (col)* **(a)** *(sich wichtig tun)* to give oneself airs. **(b)** **sich als etw** ~ to set oneself up as sth; **sich als Boß** ~ to play the boss.

aufspießen *vt sep* to spear; *(durchbohren)* to run through; *(mit Hörnern)* to gore; *Fleisch (mit Spieß)* to skewer.

aufsplittern *vti sep (vi: aux sein) (Holz)* to splinter; *(Gruppe)* to split (up).

aufspringen *vi sep irreg aux sein* **(a)** *(hochspringen)* to jump up. **auf etw** *(acc)* ~ to jump onto sth. **(b)** *(auftreffen)* to bounce. **(c)** *(sich öffnen) (Tür)* to burst open; *(platzen)* to burst; *(Haut, Lippen etc)* to crack, to chap.

aufspüren *vt sep (lit, fig)* to track down.

aufstampfen *vi sep* to stamp. **mit dem Fuß ~** to stamp one's foot.

Aufstand *m* rebellion, revolt.

aufständisch *adj* rebellious, insurgent.

Aufständische(r) *mf decl as adj* rebel, insurgent.

aufstauen *sep* **1** *vt Wasser* to dam. **etw in sich** *(dat)* ~ to bottle sth up inside (oneself). **2** *vr* to collect; *(fig: Ärger)* to be bottled up.

aufstecken *sep* **1** *vt* **(a)** *(auf etw stecken)* to put on *(auf+acc* -to). **(b)** *(mit Nadeln)* to pin up; *Haar auch* to put up. **2** *vi (col: aufgeben)* to pack it in *(col)*; *(bei Rennen etc)* to drop out.

aufstehen *vi sep irreg aux sein* **(a)** *(sich erheben)* to get *or* stand up; *(morgens aus dem Bett)* to get up. **~ dürfen (Kranker)** to be allowed (to get) up; **da mußt du früher *or* eher ~!** *(fig col)* you'll have to do better than that! **(b)** *(col: offen sein)* to be open. **(c)** *(sich auflehnen)* to rise (in arms).

aufsteigen *vi sep irreg aux sein* **(a)** *(auf Berg, Leiter)* to climb (up); *(Flugzeug)* to climb; *(Nebel, Gefühl)* to rise; *(Gewitter, Wolken)* to gather. **einen Ballon ~ lassen** to release a balloon; **an die Oberfläche ~** to rise to the surface; **in jdm ~** *(Haß, Verdacht, Erinnerung etc)* to well up in sb. **(b)** *(auf Fahrrad etc)* to get on *(auf etw (acc)* (-to) sth). **(c)** *(fig: im Rang etc)* to rise *(zu* to); *(beruflich, Sport)* to be promoted *(in +acc* to).

Aufsteiger *m* **(a)** *(Sport)* promoted team. **(b)** *(sozialer)* ~social climber.

aufstellen *sep* **1** *vt* **(a)** *(aufrichten)* to put up *(auf*

+*dat* on); *Maschine* to install; *Falle* to set; *(Mil)* to deploy; *(postieren) Wachposten* to post. **(b)** *Truppe* to raise; *Spieler, Mannschaft* to select; *Kandidaten* to nominate. **(c)** *(erzielen) Rekord* to set (up). **(d)** *Forderung, Behauptung* to put forward; *System* to establish; *Programm, Rechnung, Liste* to draw up. **(e)** *Essen etc (auf Herd)* to put on. **2** *vr (sich postieren)* to stand; *(hintereinander)* to line up; *(Soldaten)* to fall into line. **sich im Karree/Kreis** etc ~ to form a square/circle etc.

Aufstellung f siehe vt **(a)** putting up; installation; setting; deployment; posting. **(b)** raising; selecting; nomination; *(Mannschaft)* line-up *(col)*, team. **(c)** setting. **(d)** putting forward; establishing; drawing up; *(Liste)* list; *(Tabelle)* table.

aufstemmen vt sep to force open.

Aufstieg m -e **(a)** no pl *(auf Berg)* climb, ascent; *(von Flugzeug, Rakete)* climb; *(von Ballon)* ascent. **(b)** *(fig)* rise; *(Sport, beruflich)* promotion *(in* +*acc* to*)*. **den** ~ **ins Management schaffen** to work one's way up into the management. **(c)** *(Weg)* way up *(auf etw (acc)* sth*)*, ascent *(auf*+*acc* of*)*.

Aufstiegs:- ~**chance,** ~**möglichkeit** f prospect of promotion.

aufstöbern vt sep *Wild* to start, to flush; *(col: entdecken)* to run to earth.

aufstocken vt sep *Vorräte* to build up.

aufstöhnen vi sep to give a loud groan.

aufstoßen sep irreg **1** vt *(öffnen)* to push open; *(mit dem Fuß)* to kick open. **2** vi aux sein **(a)** **auf etw** *(acc)* ~ to hit (on or against) sth. **(b)** *(rülpsen)* to burp.

Aufstoßen nt no pl burping, flatulence.

aufstrebend adj *(fig) Land, Volk* striving for progress; *junger Mann* ambitious.

Aufstrich m *(auf Brot)* spread.

aufstützen sep **1** vt *Kranken etc* to prop up; *Arme* to rest *(auf* +*acc* or *dat* on*)*. **2** vr to support oneself; *(im Bett, beim Essen)* to prop oneself up.

aufsuchen vt sep *Bekannten* to call on; *Arzt, Ort, Toilette* to go to.

auftakeln vt sep *(Naut)* to rig up. **sich** ~ *(pej col)* to tart oneself up *(col)*; siehe **aufgetakelt.**

Auftakt m **(a)** *(Beginn)* start. **den** ~ **zu etw bilden** to mark the beginning of sth. **(b)** *(Mus)* upbeat.

auftanken sep **1** vi to fill up; *(Aviat)* to refuel. **2** vt *10 Liter* to put in.

auftauchen vi sep aux sein **(a)** *(aus dem Wasser)* to surface; *(Taucher etc auch)* to come up. **(b)** *(fig) (sichtbar werden)* to appear; *(aus Nebel etc auch)* to emerge. **(c)** *(gefunden werden, kommen)* to turn up. **(d)** *(sich ergeben)* to arise.

auftauen sep **1** vi aux sein to thaw; *(fig auch)* to unbend. **2** vt to thaw; *Tiefkühlkost* to thaw (out).

aufteilen vt sep **(a)** *(aufgliedern)* to divide or split up *(in*+*acc* into*)*. **(b)** *(verteilen)* to share out *(an* +*acc* between*)*.

Aufteilung f siehe vt division; sharing out.

auftischen vt sep to serve up; *(fig col)* to come up with.

Auftrag m, pl **Aufträge (a)** no pl *(Anweisung)* orders pl, instructions pl; *(zugeteilte Arbeit)* job, task; *(Jur)* brief. **einen** ~ **ausführen** to carry out an order; **ich habe den** ~**,** **Ihnen mitzuteilen** ... I have been instructed to tell you ...; **in jds** ~ *(dat) (für jdn)* on sb's behalf; *(auf jds Anweisung)* on sb's instructions; **im** ~ or **i.A.: J. Burnett** pp *J. Burnett.* **(b)** *(über*+*acc* for*)* *(Comm)* order; *(bei Künstlern etc)* commission. **etw in** ~ **geben** to order/commission sth *(bei* from*)*.

auftragen sep irreg **1** vt **(a)** *(servieren)* to serve. **(b)** *Farbe, Salbe* to apply, to put on. **etw auf** *(acc)* ~ to apply sth to sth. **(c)** *jdm etw* ~ *(form)* to instruct sb to do sth. **(d)** *Kleider* to wear out. **2** vi *(übertreiben)* **dick** ~ *(col)* to lay it on thick *(col)*.

Auftraggeber(in f) m client, customer.

Auftrags:- ~**bestätigung** f confirmation of

order; **a**~**gemäß** adj, adv as instructed; *(Comm)* as per order; ~**rückgang** m drop in orders.

auftreffen vi sep irreg aux sein **auf etw** *(dat or acc)* ~ to hit or strike sth.

auftreiben vt sep irreg *(col: ausfindig machen)* to find, to get hold of *(col)*.

auftrennen vt sep to undo.

auftreten sep irreg **1** vi aux sein **(a)** *(lit)* to tread. **(b)** *(erscheinen, Theat)* to appear. **als Zeuge** ~ to appear as a witness; **gegen jdn/etw** ~ to stand up or speak out against sb/sth; **geschlossen** ~ to put up a united front. **(c)** *(fig: eintreten)* to occur; *(Schwierigkeiten etc)* to arise. **(d)** *(sich benehmen)* to behave. **als Vermittler** etc ~ to act as intermediary etc. **2** vt *Tür* etc to kick open.

Auftreten nt entrance; *(Theat: Szene)* scene. **(b)** *(Benehmen)* manner. **(c)** *(Vorkommen)* occurrence.

Auftrieb m no pl **(a)** *(Phys)* buoyancy; *(Aviat)* lift. **(b)** *(fig)* impetus; *(Preis*~*)* upward trend *(gen* in*)*; *(Ermunterung)* lift. **das wird ihm** ~ **geben** that will give him a lift.

auftrumpfen vi sep *(seine Leistungsstärke zeigen)* to show how good one is.

auftun sep irreg **1** vt *(col: ausfindig machen)* to find. **2** vr *(sich öffnen)* to open (up).

auftürmen sep **1** vt to pile up. **2** vr *(Gebirge etc)* to tower up; *(Schwierigkeiten)* to pile up.

aufwachen vi sep aux sein *(lit, fig)* to wake up. **aus einer Narkose** ~ to come out of an anaesthetic.

aufwachsen vi sep irreg aux sein to grow up.

Aufwand m no pl **(a)** *(von Geld)* expenditure *(an* +*dat* of*)*. **das erfordert einen großen** ~ **an Zeit/ Energie/Geld** that requires a lot of time/energy/ money. **(b)** *(Luxus, Prunk)* extravagance. **(großen)** ~ **treiben** to be (very) extravagant.

Aufwands|entschädigung f expense allowance.

aufwärmen sep **1** vt to heat or warm up; *(col: wieder erwähnen)* to bring up. **2** vr to warm up.

aufwarten vi sep *(zu bieten haben)* **mit etw** ~ to offer sth.

aufwärts adv up, upward(s); *(bergauf)* uphill. **den Fluß** ~ upstream.

Aufwärts:- ~**entwicklung** f upward trend *(gen* in*)*; **a**~**gehen** vi impers sep irreg aux sein **mit dem Staat/der Firma geht es a**~ things are improving for the country/firm; ~**haken** m *(Boxen)* uppercut; ~**trend** m upward trend.

aufwecken vt sep to wake (up); *(fig)* to rouse; siehe **aufgeweckt.**

aufweichen sep **1** vt to soften; *Brot* to soak. **2** vi aux sein to become soft.

aufweisen vt sep irreg to show. **das Buch weist einige Fehler auf** the book has some mistakes in it; **etw aufzuweisen haben** to have sth to show for oneself.

aufwenden vt sep irreg to use; *Energie* to expend; *Geld, Zeit* to spend. **viel Mühe/Zeit** ~**, etw zu tun** to take a lot of trouble/spend a lot of time doing sth.

aufwendig adj costly; *(üppig)* lavish.

Aufwendungen pl expenditure.

aufwerfen vt sep irreg **(a)** *(aufhäufen)* to pile up. **(b)** *Frage, Probleme* to raise, to bring up.

aufwerten vt sep **(a)** *(auch vi) Währung* to revalue. **(b)** *(fig)* to increase the value of.

Aufwertung f *(von Währung)* revaluation; *(fig)* increase in value.

aufwickeln vt sep **(a)** *(aufrollen)* to roll up; *(col) Haar* to put in curlers. **(b)** *(lösen)* to untie; *Windeln, Verband* to take off.

aufwiegeln vt sep to stir up. **jdn zum Streik/ Widerstand** ~ to incite sb to strike/resist.

aufwiegen vt sep irreg *(fig)* to offset. **das ist nicht mit Geld aufzuwiegen** that can't be measured in terms of money.

Aufwiegler(in *f) m* - agitator; *(Anstifter)* instigator.

aufwieglerisch *adj* seditious; *Rede, Artikel auch* inflammatory.

Aufwind *m (Aviat)* upcurrent. **neuen ~ bekommen** *(fig)* to get new impetus.

aufwirbeln *vti sep (vi: aux sein)* to swirl *or* whirl up. **(viel) Staub ~** *(fig)* to cause a (big) stir.

aufwischen *vti sep* to mop up.

aufwühlen *vt sep* **(a)** *(lit) Erde, Meer* to churn (up). **(b)** *(geh) Gefühle* to stir; *siehe* **aufgewühlt.**

aufzählen *vt sep* to list.

aufzeichnen *vt sep* **(a)** *Plan etc* to draw, to sketch. **(b)** *(notieren, Rad, TV)* to record.

Aufzeichnung *f* **(a)** *usu pl (Notiz)* note; *(Niederschrift auch)* record. **(b)** *(Tonband~, Film~)* recording.

aufzeigen *vt sep* to show.

aufziehen *sep irreg* **1** *vt* **(a)** *(hochziehen)* to pull *or* draw up; *Flagge, Segel* to hoist. **(b)** *(öffnen) Reißverschluß* to undo; *Schublade* to (pull) open; *Gardinen* to draw (back). **(c)** *(aufspannen) Saite, Reifen* to put on. **(d)** *(spannen) Feder, Uhr etc* to wind up. **(e)** *(großziehen)* to raise; *Kind auch* to bring up; *Tier auch* to rear. **(f)** *(col: veranstalten)* to set up; *Fest* to arrange. **(g)** *(verspotten)* **jdn ~** *(col)* to tease sb *(mit about)*. **2** *vi aux sein (dunkle Wolke)* to come up; *(Gewitter, Wolken auch)* to gather; *(aufmarschieren)* to march up.

Aufzucht *f no pl (das Großziehen)* rearing, raising.

Aufzug *m* **(a)** *(Fahrstuhl)* lift *(Brit)*, elevator *(US)*; *(Güter~)* hoist. **(b)** *(von Gewitter etc)* gathering. **(c)** *(Theat)* act. **(d)** *no pl (pej col: Kleidung)* get-up *(col)*.

aufzwingen *sep irreg* **1** *vt* **jdm etw/seinen Willen ~** to force sth on sb/impose one's will on sb. **2** *vr* **das zwingt sich einem doch förmlich auf** it's the only possible conclusion.

Aug|apfel *m* eyeball. **jdn/etw wie seinen ~ hüten** to cherish sb/sth like life itself.

Auge *nt* -n **(a)** eye. **gute/schlechte ~n haben** to have good/bad eyesight *or* eyes; **mit den ~n zwinkern/blinzeln** to wink/blink; **jdn mit** *or* **aus großen ~n ansehen** to look at sb wide-eyed; **mit bloßem** *or* **nacktem ~** with the naked eye; **mit verbundenen ~n** *(lit, fig)* blindfold; **etw im ~ haben** *(fig)* to have one's eye on sth; **ein sicheres ~ für etw haben** to have a good eye for sth; **ich kann doch meine ~n nicht überall haben** I can't see everything at once; **er machte große ~n** his eyes popped out of his head *(col)*; **ich konnte kaum aus den ~n sehen** I could hardly see straight; **geh mir aus den ~n!** get out of my sight!; **unter jds ~n** *(dat) (fig)* before sb's very eyes; **vor aller ~n** in front of everybody, for all to see; **jdn/etw mit anderen ~n (an)sehen** to see sb/sth in a different light; **seine ~n waren größer als sein Magen** *(col)* his eyes were bigger than his stomach; **aus den ~n, aus dem Sinn** *(Prov)* out of sight, out of mind *(Prov)*; **das ~ des Gesetzes** the law; **soweit das ~ reicht** as far as the eye can see; **er hatte nur ~n für sie** he only had eyes for her; **ich habe kein ~ zugetan** I didn't sleep a wink; **da blieb kein ~ trocken** *(hum)* there wasn't a dry eye in the place; **ein ~ auf jdn/etw geworfen haben** to have one's eye on sb/sth; **ein ~/beide ~n zudrücken** *(col)* to turn a blind eye; **etw im ~ behalten** to keep *or* bear sth in mind; **sie ließen ihn nicht aus den ~n** they didn't let him out of their sight; **jdn/etw aus den ~n verlieren** to lose sight of sb/sth; *(fig)* to lose touch with sb/sth; **das springt einem gleich ins ~** it hits you right in the face *(col)*; **jdm etw vor ~n führen** *(fig)* to make sb aware of sth; **etw ins ~ fassen** to contemplate sth; **etw noch genau** *or* **lebhaft vor ~n haben** to remember sth clearly *or* vividly; **jdm die ~n öffnen** *(fig)* to open sb's eyes; **ein ~ riskieren** *(hum)* to have a peep *(col)*;

das kann leicht ins ~ gehen *(fig col)* it might easily go wrong; **in meinen ~n** in my opinion *or* view; **mit einem lachenden und einem weinenden ~** with mixed feelings; **~ in ~ face to face; ~ um ~, Zahn um Zahn** *(Bibl)* an eye for an eye and a tooth for a tooth; **dem Tod ins ~ sehen** to look death in the face. **(b)** *(bei Kartoffel)* eye. **(c)** *(Punkt bei Spielen)* point.

Augen-: **~arzt** *m* eye specialist, ophthalmologist; **~aufschlag** *m* look.

Augenblick *m* moment. **jeden ~** any time *or* moment; **einen ~, bitte** one moment please!; **~mal!** *(col)* just a minute *or* second! *(col)*; **im ~ at** the moment; **im ersten ~** for a moment.

augenblicklich **1** *adj (sofortig)* immediate; *(gegenwärtig)* present, current. **2** *adv (sofort)* immediately; *(zur Zeit)* at the moment.

Augen-: **~braue** *f* eyebrow; **~entzündung** *f* inflammation of the eyes; **~farbe** *f* colour *(Brit) or* color *(US)* of eyes; **ihre ~farbe** the colour of her eyes; **~höhe** *f:* **in ~höhe** at eye level; **~höhle** *f* eye socket; **~klappe** *f* **(a)** eye patch; **(b)** *(für Pferde)* blinker, blinder *(US);* **~krankheit** *f* eye disease; **~licht** *nt no pl* (eye)sight; **~lid** *nt* eyelid; **~maß** *nt* eye; *(für Entfernungen)* eye for distance(s); *(fig)* perceptiveness; **nach ~maß** by eye; **ein gutes/schlechtes ~maß haben** to have a good eye/no eye for distance(s); **~merk** *nt no pl (Aufmerksamkeit)* attention; **jds/sein ~merk auf etw** *(acc)* **lenken** to direct sb's/one's attention to sth; **~operation** *f* eye operation; **~optiker** *m* optician; **~paar** *nt* pair of eyes; **~ränder** *pl* rims of the/one's eyes; **~schein** *m no pl* **(a)** *(Anschein)* appearance; **dem ~schein nach** by all appearances; **(b)** **jdn/etw in ~schein nehmen** to have a close look at sb/sth; **a~scheinlich** *adj* obvious, evident; **~tropfen** *pl* eyedrops *pl*; **~weide** *f* feast *or* treat for the eyes; **~wimper** *f* eyelash; **~winkel** *m* corner of the/one's eye; **~wischerei** *f (fig)* eyewash; **~zeuge** *m* eyewitness *(bei* to); **~zeugenbericht** *m* eyewitness account; **~zwinkern** *nt no pl* winking; **a~zwinkernd** *adj* winking *attr; (fig)* sly.

August *m* -e August; *siehe* **März.**

Auktion *f* auction.

Auktionator(in *f)* [-'to:rɪn] *m* auctioneer.

Aula *f, pl* **Aulen** *(Sch, Univ)* (assembly) hall.

Au-pair- [o'pɛːɐ]: **~Mädchen** *nt* au-pair (girl); **~-Stelle** *f* au-pair job.

aus **1** *prep+dat* **(a)** *(räumlich)* from; *(aus dem Inneren von)* out of. **~ dem Fenster/der Tür** out of the window/door; **~ unserer Mitte** from our midst.

(b) *(Herkunft, Quelle bezeichnend)* from. **~ dem Deutschen** from (the) German; **~ guter Familie** from a good family; **er ist ~ Köln** he's from Cologne; **~ der Goethezeit** from the time of Goethe.

(c) *(auf Ursache deutend)* out of. **~ Haß/Mitleid** out of hatred/sympathy; **~ Erfahrung** from experience; **~ Furcht vor/Liebe zu** for fear/love of; **~ dem Grunde, daß ...** for the reason that ...; **~ Spaß** for fun; **~ Versehen** by mistake; **~ sich heraus** of one's own accord.

(d) *(beschaffen ~)* (made out) of. **ein Herz ~ Stein** a heart of stone.

(e) **einen anständigen Menschen ~ jdm machen** to make sb into a decent person; **was ist ~ ihm/dieser Sache geworden?** what has become of him/this?; **~ ihm wird einmal ein guter Arzt** he'll make a good doctor one day.

(f) **~ dem Gleichgewicht** out of balance; **~ der Mode** out of fashion.

2 *adv siehe auch* **aussein (a)** *(col: vorbei, zu Ende)* over. **~ und vorbei** over and done with. **(b)** *(gelöscht)* out; *(an Geräten)* off. **Licht ~!** lights out! **(c)** *(Sport)* out, out of play. **(d)** *(in Verbin-*

dung mit von) **von München** ~ from Munich; **von sich** *(dat)* ~ of one's own accord; **von ihm** ~ as far as he's concerned; **ok, von mir** ~ OK, if you like.

Aus *nt no pl (Sport)* touch *no art.*

aus|arbeiten *vt sep* to work out; *(vorbereiten)* to prepare.

Aus|arbeitung *f siehe vt* working out; preparation.

aus|arten *vi sep aux sein (Party etc)* to get out of control. ~ **in** *(+acc) or* **zu** to degenerate into.

aus|atmen *vti sep* to breathe out, to exhale.

ausbaden *vt sep (col)* to carry the can for *(col)*.

Ausbau *m* **-ten** *siehe vt* removal; extension *(zu into)*; conversion *(zu* (in)*to)*; building up.

ausbauen *vt sep* **(a)** *(herausmontieren)* to remove *(aus* from). **(b)** *(lit, fig: erweitern)* to extend *(zu into)*; *(umbauen)* to convert *(zu* (in)*to)*; *Freundschaft* to build up.

ausbaufähig *adj Position* with good prospects; *Produktion, Markt* that can be extended; *Beziehungen* that can be built up.

ausbeißen *vt sep irreg sich (dat)* **an etw** *(dat)* **die Zähne** ~ *(fig)* to have a tough time of it with sth.

ausbessern *vt sep* to repair; *Wäsche etc auch* to mend.

Ausbesserung *f siehe vt* repair; mending.

Ausbesserungs-: ~**arbeiten** *pl* repair work *sing;* **a~bedürftig** *adj* in need of repair *etc.*

ausbeulen *vt sep Auto* to knock the dent(s) out of; *Kleidung* to make baggy; *siehe* **ausgebeult.**

Ausbeute *f (Gewinn)* profit, gain; *(Ertrag einer Grube etc)* yield *(an+dat in); (fig)* result(s); *(Einnahmen)* proceeds *pl.*

ausbeuten *vt sep (lit, fig)* to exploit.

Ausbeuter(in *f) m* - exploiter.

Ausbeutung *f* exploitation.

ausbezahlen* *vt sep Geld* to pay out.

ausbilden *vt sep* to train; *(unterrichten auch)* to instruct; *(akademisch)* to educate; *Fähigkeiten* to develop. **sich in etw** *(dat)*/**als** *or* **zu etw** ~ **lassen** *(esp Arbeiter, Lehrling)* to train in sth/as sth; **ein ausgebildeter Übersetzer** a qualified translator.

Ausbilder(in *f) m* - instructor, instructress.

Ausbildung *f siehe vt* training; instruction; education; development. **er ist noch in der** ~ he's still a trainee; **he hasn't finished his education.**

Ausbildungs-: ~**beihilfe,** ~**förderung** *f* grant; ~**platz** *m (Stelle)* training vacancy; ~**stand** *m* level of training; ~**zeit** *f* training period.

ausbitten *vr sep irreg* **sich** *(dat)* **(von jdm) etw** ~ **(geh)** to request sth (from sb) *(form);* **ich bitte mir Ruhe aus!** I will have silence!

ausblasen *vt sep irreg* to blow out; *Ei* to blow.

ausbleiben *vi sep irreg aux sein (fortbleiben)* to stay out; *(nicht erscheinen: Gäste)* to fail to appear; *(nicht eintreten: Erwartung etc)* to fail to materialize; *(aufhören: Puls, Atmung etc)* to stop. **es konnte nicht** ~**, daß** … it was inevitable that …

ausblenden *vti sep (TV etc)* to fade out; *(plötzlich)* to cut out.

Ausblick *m* **(a)** view *(auf+acc of)*. **(b)** *(fig)* prospect, outlook *(auf+acc for)*.

ausblicken *vi sep (geh)* **nach jdm** ~ to look for sb.

ausbooten *vt sep (col) jdn* to kick or boot out *(col)*.

ausbrechen *sep irreg* **1** *vt (herausbrechen) Steine* to break off *(aus* from). **2** *vi aux sein* **(a)** *(lit, fig: sich befreien)* to break out *(aus* auch *(auch Mil))* to escape *(aus* from). **(b)** *(Richtung ändern: Pferd, Wagen)* to swerve. **(c)** *(Krieg, Feuer, Schweiß etc)* to break out; *(Jubel, Zorn etc)* to erupt, to explode; *(Vulkan)* to erupt. **in Gelächter/Tränen/Jubel** ~ to burst out laughing/crying/cheering.

Ausbrecher(in *f) m* - *col: Gefangener)* escaped prisoner, escapee.

ausbreiten *sep* **1** *vt* to spread (out); *Arme* to stretch out; *(ausstellen, fig: zeigen)* to display; *Licht, Wärme* to spread. **2** *vr* **(a)** *(sich verbreiten)*

to spread. **(b)** *(col: sich breitmachen)* to spread oneself out. **(c)** **sich über etw** *(acc)* ~ *(fig)* to dwell on sth.

Ausbreitung *f* spread, spreading.

ausbrennen *sep irreg* **1** *vi aux sein* **(a)** *(zu Ende brennen)* to burn out. **(b)** *(völlig verbrennen)* to be burnt out, to be gutted. **er ist ausgebrannt** *(fig)* he's burnt out. **2** *vt (Med)* to cauterize.

Ausbruch *m* **(a)** *(aus* from) *(aus Gefängnis)* breakout *(auch Mil)*, escape *(auch fig)*. **(b)** *(Beginn)* outbreak; *(von Vulkan)* eruption. **zum** ~ **kommen** to break out. **(c)** *(fig: Gefühls~)* outburst.

ausbrüten *vt sep* to hatch; *(esp in Brutkasten)* to incubate; *(fig col) Plan etc* to cook up *(col)*.

Ausbuchtung *f* bulge; *(von Strand)* (small) cove.

ausbügeln *vt sep* to iron out; *(col) Fehler, Verlust* to make good.

Ausbund *m no pl:* **ein** ~ **an** *or* **von Tugend/Sparsamkeit** a paragon of virtue/a model of thrift.

ausbürgern *vt sep jdn* ~ to expatriate sb.

Ausbürgerung *f* expatriation.

Ausdauer *f no pl* staying power, stamina; *(Beharrlichkeit)* perseverance.

ausdauernd *adj (Mensch)* with staying power, with stamina; *(im Ertragen)* with endurance; *(beharrlich)* persevering; *Bemühungen etc* untiring.

ausdehnbar *adj* expandable; *(fig)* extendable *(auf+acc to)*.

ausdehnen *sep* **1** *vt* **(a)** *(vergrößern)* to expand. **(b)** *(fig)* to extend; *(zeitlich auch)* to prolong *(auf +acc to)*. **2** *vr* **(a)** *(größer werden)* to expand; *(sich erstrecken)* to extend, to stretch *(bis* as far as). **der Krieg dehnte sich über das ganze Land aus** the war spread over the whole country. **(b)** *(fig)* to extend *(über+acc* over, *bis* as far as, to); *(zeitlich)* to go on *(bis* until); *siehe* **ausgedehnt.**

Ausdehnung *f* **(a)** *siehe vt* expansion; extension; prolongation. **(b)** *(Umfang)* expanse.

ausdenken *vt sep irreg* **sich** *(dat)* **etw** ~ *(erfinden)* to think sth up; *(in Einzelheiten)* to think sth out; *Wunsch* to think of sth; *Überraschung* to plan sth; *(sich vorstellen)* to imagine sth; **eine ausgedachte Geschichte** a made-up story; **das ist nicht auszudenken** *(unvorstellbar)* it's inconceivable.

ausdienen *vi sep* **ausgedient haben** *(fig col)* to have had its day.

ausdiskutieren* *vt sep Thema* to discuss fully.

ausdrehen *vt sep (ausschalten)* to turn or switch off; *Licht auch* to turn out.

Ausdruck[1] *m, pl* **Ausdrücke** **(a)** *no pl* expression. **als** ~ **meiner Dankbarkeit** as an expression of my gratitude; **mit dem** ~ **des Bedauerns** *(form)* expressing regret; **etw zum** ~ **bringen** to express sth, to give expression to sth. **(b)** *(Wort)* expression; *(Fach~ auch)* term. **sich im** ~ **vergreifen** to use the wrong word.

Ausdruck[2] *m* **-e** *(Comp)* printout.

ausdrucken *vt sep (Comp)* to print out.

ausdrücken *sep* **1** *vt* **(a)** to press out, to squeeze out; *Pickel* to squeeze; *Zigarette* to stub out. **(b)** *(zum Ausdruck bringen)* to express *(jdm* to sb). **anders ausgedrückt** in other words; **einfach ausgedrückt** put simply. **2** *vr (Mensch)* to express oneself. **in ihrem Gesicht/Verhalten drückte sich Verzweiflung aus** her face/behaviour showed her despair.

ausdrücklich 1 *adj attr Wunsch* express, explicit. **2** *adv* explicitly; *(besonders)* particularly.

Ausdrucks-: **a~fähig** *adj* expressive; *(gewandt)* articulate; ~**fähigkeit** *f siehe adj* expressiveness; articulateness; **a~los** *adj* inexpressive; *Gesicht, Blick auch* expressionless; ~**losigkeit** *f siehe adj* inexpressiveness; lack of expression; ~**mittel** *nt* means of expression; **a~voll** *adj* expressive; ~**weise** *f* way of expressing oneself.

ausdünsten *vt sep Geruch* to give off.

Ausdünstung *f (Dampf)* vapour *(Brit)*, vapor

(US); (Geruch) smell.

aus|einander *adv (getrennt)* apart. **weit** ~ **far**
apart; *Meinungen* very different; **etw** ~ **schrei-**
ben to write sth as two words; **die beiden sind**
(im Alter) ein Jahr ~ there is a year between the
two of them; ~ **sein** *(col: Paar)* to have split up.

aus|einander-: ~**brechen** *sep irreg* 1 *vt* to break
in two; 2 *vi aux sein (lit, fig)* to break up; ~**fallen** *vi*
sep irreg aux sein (zerfallen) to fall apart; *(fig auch)*
to collapse; ~ **gehen** *vi sep irreg aux sein* **(a)** *(lit,*
fig: sich trennen) (Menschen) to part, to separate;
(Menge) to disperse; *(Versammlung, Ehe etc)* to
break up; **(b)** *(sich verzweigen: Weg etc)* to divide;
(zwei Wege) to diverge; *(fig: Ansichten etc)* to
differ; ~**halten** *vt sep irreg* to keep apart; *(unter-*
scheiden) Begriffe to distinguish between; *esp*
Zwillinge etc to tell apart; ~**klaffen** *vi sep aux sein*
to gape open; *(fig: Meinungen)* to be far apart, to
diverge (wildly); ~**laufen** *vi sep irreg aux sein* **(a)**
(zerlaufen) to melt; *(Farbe)* to run; **(b)** *(col: sich*
trennen) to break up; *(Menge)* to disperse;
~**leben** *vr sep* to drift apart; ~**nehmen** *vt sep*
irreg to take apart; *Maschine etc auch* to dismantle; *(kritisch)* to tear apart *or* to pieces; ~**set-**
zen *sep* 1 *vt (fig) (jdm* to sb) to explain; *(schriftlich*
auch) to set out; 2 *vr* **sich mit etw** ~**setzen** *(sich*
befassen) to work on; **sich kritisch mit etw** ~**set-**
zen to have a critical look at sth; **sich mit jdm**
~**setzen** to talk *or (sich streiten)* to argue with sb.

Aus|einandersetzung *f* **(a)** *(Diskussion)* dis-
cussion, debate *(über+acc* about, on*); (Streit)*
argument; *(feindlicher Zusammenstoß)* clash
(wegen over). **(b)** *(das Befassen)* examination
(mit of*); (kritisch)* analysis *(mit* of).

aus|erkoren *adj (liter)* chosen, selected.

aus|erlesen *adj (ausgesucht)* select; *Speisen,*
Weine auch choice *attr.*

aus|ersehen* *vt sep irreg (geh)* dazu ~ **sein**, **etw**
zu tun to be chosen to do sth.

Aus|erwählte(r) *mf decl as adj (geh)* chosen one.

ausfahrbar *adj* extendable; *Antenne, Fahrgestell*
retractable.

ausfahren *sep irreg* 1 *vi aux sein* **(a)** *(spazierenfah-*
ren) to go for a ride *or (im Auto auch)* drive. **(b)**
(abfahren) (Zug) to pull out *(aus* of*)*, to leave; **aus**
dem Hafen ~ *(Schiff)* to leave harbour. 2 **(a)**
(ausliefern) Waren to deliver. **(b)** **ein Auto** *etc*
(voll) ~ to drive a car *etc* flat out. **(c)** *(Tech)* to
extend; *Fahrgestell etc auch* to lower.

Ausfahrt *f* **(a)** *(auch Autobahn*~*)* exit. ~ **Güters-**
loh Gütersloh exit. **(b)** *no pl (Abfahrt)* departure. **der Zug hat keine** ~ the train has not been
cleared for departure. **(c)** *(Spazierfahrt)* drive,
ride.

Ausfall *m* **(a)** *(Verlust)* loss; *(das Versagen) (Tech,*
Med) failure; *(von Motor)* breakdown; *(Produk-*
tionsstörung) stoppage. **(b)** *no pl (von Sitzung, Un-*
terricht etc) cancellation. **(c)** *no pl (das*
Ausscheiden) dropping out.

ausfallen *vi sep irreg aux sein* **(a)** *(herausfallen)* to
fall out. **mir fallen die Haare aus** my hair is
falling out. **(b)** *(nicht stattfinden)* to be cancelled.
etw ~ **lassen** to cancel sth; **die Schule fällt mor-**
gen aus there's no school tomorrow. **(c)** *(nicht*
funktionieren) to fail; *(Motor)* to break down. **(d)**
(wegfallen: Verdienst) to be lost. **(e)** *(ausscheiden)*
to drop out. **(f)** **gut/schlecht** *etc* ~ to turn out
well/badly *etc*; **die Bluse fällt zu eng aus** the
blouse is too tight. **(g)** *siehe* **ausgefallen.**

ausfallend *adj* abusive.

Ausfälligkeit *f* abusiveness; *(Bemerkung)* abusive remark.

Ausfallstraße *f* arterial road.

ausfechten *vt sep irreg (fig)* to fight (out).

ausfegen *vt sep Zimmer* to sweep out.

ausfeilen *vt sep* to file (out); *siehe* **ausgefeilt.**

ausfertigen *vt sep (form) Dokument* to draw up;
Rechnung etc to make out; *Paß* to issue.

Ausfertigung *f (form)* **(a)** *no pl siehe vt* drawing
up; making out; issuing. **(b)** *(Abschrift)* copy. **in**
doppelter/dreifacher ~ in duplicate/triplicate.

ausfetten *vt sep* to grease.

ausfindig *adj:* ~ **machen** to find; *(Aufenthaltsort*
feststellen) to trace.

ausfliegen *sep irreg* 1 *vi aux sein* **ausgeflogen sein**
(fig col) to have gone out; **der Vogel ist ausge-**
flogen *(fig col)* the bird has flown. 2 *vt (Aviat)*
Verwundete etc to fly out *(aus* from*)*.

ausfließen *vi sep irreg aux sein (herausfließen)* to
flow out *(aus* of*); (auslaufen: Öl etc)* to leak *(aus*
out of*); (Eiter etc)* to be discharged.

ausflippen *vi sep aux sein (col)* to freak out *(col);*
siehe **ausgeflippt.**

Ausflucht *f, pl* **Ausflüchte** excuse. **Ausflüchte**
machen to make excuses.

Ausflug *m* trip, outing; *(esp mit Reisebüro)* excursion; *(Betriebs*~*, Schul*~*)* outing; *(Wanderung)*
walk, hike. **einen** ~ **machen** to go on a trip *etc.*

Ausflügler(in *f) m* - tripper.

Ausflugs-: ~**dampfer** *m* pleasure steamer; ~**lo-**
kal *nt* tourist café; *(am Meer)* seaside café; ~**ver-**
kehr *m (an Feiertagen)* holiday traffic; *(am*
Wochenende) weekend holiday traffic; ~**ziel** *nt*
destination (of one's outing).

Ausfluß *m* **(a)** *(das Herausfließen)* outflow. **(b)**
(~*stelle)* outlet. **(c)** *(Med)* discharge.

ausforschen *vt sep* **(a)** *Sache* to find out; *(erfor-*
schen) to investigate. **(b)** *jdn* to question.

ausfragen *vt sep* to question, to quiz *(col) (nach*
about*); (strenger)* to interrogate.

ausfransen *vi sep aux sein* to fray.

ausfressen *vt sep irreg (col: anstellen)* **etwas** ~ to
do something wrong; **was hat er denn wieder**
ausgefressen? what's he done now? *(col).*

Ausfuhr *f* **-en** *no pl (das Ausführen)* export;
(~*handel)* exports *pl.*

Ausfuhr- *in cpds* export; *siehe auch* **Export-.**

ausführbar *adj Plan* feasible, practicable.
schwer ~ difficult to carry out.

ausführen *vt sep* **(a)** *jdn* to take out; *Hund auch* to
take for a walk. **(b)** *(durchführen)* to carry out;
Gesetz to implement; *(Sport) Freistoß* to take. **die**
~**de Gewalt** *(Pol)* the executive. **(c)** *(erklären)* to
explain; *(darlegen)* to set out; *(argumentierend)* to
argue. **(d)** *(Comm) Waren* to export.

Ausfuhr-: ~**güter** *pl* export goods *pl*, exports *pl;*
~**hafen** *m* port of exportation.

ausführlich 1 *adj* detailed, full. 2 *adv* in detail, in
full. **sehr** ~ in great detail.

Ausführlichkeit *f* detail, fullness.

Ausführung *f (a) no pl siehe vt* **(b)** carrying out;
implementation; taking. **zur** ~ **gelangen** to be
carried out. **(b)** *(Erklärung)* explanation; *(von*
Thema etc) exposition. **(c)** *(von Waren)* design;
(Tech: äußere ~*)* finish; *(Qualität)* quality;
(Modell) model.

Ausfuhrzoll *m* export duty.

ausfüllen *vt sep* to fill; *Platz* to take up; *Formular*
to fill out. **jdn (ganz)** ~ *(Zeit in Anspruch nehmen)*
to take (all) sb's time; **ein ausgefülltes Leben** a
full life.

Ausgabe *f* **-n** **(a)** *no pl (Austeilung) (von Proviant*
etc) distribution, giving out; *(von Befehl, Fahrkar-*
ten etc) issuing; *(von Essen)* serving. **(b)** *(Schal-*
ter) counter. **(c)** *(von Buch etc)* edition; *(von*
Zeitschrift auch, von Aktien) issue. **(d)** *(Ausfüh-*
rung) version. **(e)** *(Geldaufwand)* expense, expenditure *no pl.* ~**en** *pl (Geldverbrauch)*
expenditure *sing (für* on*); (Kosten)* expenses *pl,*
costs *pl.* **(f)** *(Comp)* printout.

Ausgang *m* **(a)** *(Auslaß, Weg nach draußen)* exit,
way out *(gen, von* from*)*. **(b)** *(Erlaubnis zum Aus-*
gehen) permission to go out; *(Mil)* pass. ~ **haben**
to have the day off *or (am Abend)* the evening off;
(Mil) to have a pass. **(c)** *no pl (Ende)* end; *(von*
Epoche auch) close; *(von Roman, Film auch)* end-

ing; *(Ergebnis)* outcome, result. **ein Unfall mit tödlichem** ~ a fatal accident. **(d)** *no pl (Ausgangspunkt)* starting point; *(Anfang)* beginning.

Ausgangs-: ~**basis** *f* basis, starting point; ~**position** *f* initial *or* starting position; ~**punkt** *m* starting point; ~**sperre** *f* ban on going out; *(esp bei Belagerungszustand)* curfew; *(für Soldaten)* confinement to barracks; ~**sperre haben** to be forbidden to go out; *(Mil)* to be confined to barracks; ~**stellung** *f (Sport)* starting position; *(Mil)* initial position.

ausgeben *vt sep irreg* **(a)** *(austeilen) Proviant etc* to distribute, to give out; *(aushändigen) Dokumente, Fahrkarten, Aktien etc* to issue; *Befehl* to issue, to give; *Essen* to serve; *(Cards)* to deal; *(ausdrucken) Text* to print out. **(b)** *Geld* to spend *(für on)*. **eine Runde** ~ to stand a round; **ich gebe heute abend einen aus** *(col)* it's my treat this evening; **darf ich dir einen Whisky** ~? would you like a whisky? **(c)** **jdn/etw als** *or* **für jdn/etw** ~ to pass sb/sth off as sb/sth; **sich als jd/etw** ~ to pose as sb/sth.

ausgebeult *adj Kleidung* baggy; *Hut* battered.

ausgebucht *adj Reise etc* booked up.

Ausgeburt *f (pej) (der Phantasie etc)* monstrous product; **eine** ~ **der Hölle** a fiendish monster.

ausgedehnt *adj (breit, groß, fig: weitreichend)* extensive; *(zeitlich)* lengthy; *Spaziergang* long.

ausgedörrt *adj* dried up; *Boden, Kehle* parched; *Pflanzen* shrivelled; *Land, Gebiet* arid.

ausgefallen *adj (ungewöhnlich)* unusual; *(übertrieben)* extravagant.

ausgefeilt *adj (fig)* polished.

ausgeflippt *adj (col)* freaky *(col)*, freaked-out *(col)*. ~**er Typ** *(Hippie etc)* drop-out *(col)*.

ausgefuchst *adj (col)* clever; *(listig)* crafty *(col)*.

ausgeglichen *adj* balanced; *Spiel, Klima* even; *Torverhältnis* equal.

Ausgeglichenheit *f siehe adj* balance; evenness.

ausgehen *vi sep irreg aux sein* **(a)** *(weggehen)* to go out; *(spazierengehen auch)* to go (out) for a walk. **(b)** *(ausfallen: Haare, Federn, Zähne)* to fall out. **(c)** *(seinen Ausgang nehmen)* to start *(von at)*; *(herrühren: Idee etc)* to come *(von from)*. **(d)** *(abgeschickt werden: Post)* to be sent off. **die** ~**de Post** the outgoing mail. **(e)** *(zugrunde legen)* to start out *(von from)*. **gehen wir einmal davon aus, daß** ... let us assume that ... **(f) auf etw** *(acc)* ~ to be intent on sth. **(g)** *(enden)* to end. **gut/schlecht** ~ to turn out well/badly; *(Film etc)* to have a happy/sad ending; *(Abend, Spiel)* to end well/badly; **leer** ~ *(col)* to come away empty-handed. **(h)** *(zu Ende sein: Vorräte etc)* to run out. **ihm ist die Luft** *or* **der Atem ausgegangen** *(lit)* he ran out of breath; *(fig col)* he ran out of steam *(col)*. **(i)** *(aufhören zu brennen)* to go out.

Ausgeh|erlaubnis *f* permission to go out; *(Mil)* pass.

ausgehungert *adj* starved; *(abgezehrt) Mensch etc* emaciated.

Ausgeh-: ~**uniform** *f* walking-out uniform; ~**verbot** *nt siehe* **Ausgangssperre.**

ausgeklügelt *adj (col)* ingenious.

ausgekocht *adj (pej col: durchtrieben)* cunning.

ausgelassen *adj (heiter)* lively; *Stimmung* happy; *(wild) Kinder, Stimmung, Party* wild.

Ausgelassenheit *f siehe adj* liveliness; happiness; wildness.

ausgelastet *adj Mensch* fully occupied; *Maschine, Anlage* working to capacity.

ausgeleiert *adj Gummiband etc* worn.

ausgemacht *adj* **(a)** *(abgemacht)* agreed. **es ist eine** ~**e Sache, daß** ... it is agreed that ... **(b)** *attr (col: vollkommen)* complete, utter.

ausgemergelt *adj Gesicht* emaciated, gaunt.

ausgenommen *conj* except, apart from, aside from *(esp US)*. **alle, du** *or* **dich** ~ everyone except (for) *or* apart from you; **Anwesende** ~ present company excepted.

ausgeprägt *adj Gesicht* distinctive; *Eigenschaft* distinct; *Interesse* marked, pronounced.

ausgerechnet *adv* ~ **du/er** *etc* you/he *etc* of all people; ~ **heute/gestern** today/yesterday of all days; ~ **jetzt kommt er** he would have to come just now.

ausgereift *adj* mature.

ausgeruht *adj* (well) rested.

ausgeschlossen *adj pred (unmöglich)* impossible; *(nicht in Frage kommend)* out of the question. **es ist nicht** ~, **daß** ... it's just possible that ...; **jeder Irrtum ist** ~ there is no possibility of a mistake.

ausgeschnitten *adj Bluse, Kleid* low-cut. **ein tief** ~**es Kleid** a dress with a plunging neckline.

ausgesorgt *adj siehe* **aussorgen.**

ausgesprochen 1 *adj Schönheit* outstanding; *Vorliebe* definite; *Begabung* particular; *Ähnlichkeit auch* marked. ~**es Pech haben** to be really unlucky. **2** *adv* really.

ausgestorben *adj Tierart* extinct; *(fig)* deserted. **der Park war wie** ~ the park was deserted.

Ausgestoßene(r) *mf decl as adj* outcast.

ausgesucht *(erlesen) Wein* choice, select; *Gesellschaft* select; *Worte* well-chosen.

ausgetreten *adj Schuhe, Stufe* well-worn; *Pfad auch* well-trodden.

ausgewachsen *adj* fully-grown; *(col) Skandal* full-blown.

ausgewählt *adj* select; *Satz etc* well-chosen; *Werke* selected.

ausgewogen *adj* balanced; *Maß* equal. **ein** ~**es Kräfteverhältnis** an equal balance of powers.

Ausgewogenheit *f* balance.

ausgezeichnet *adj* excellent. **es geht mir** ~ I'm feeling marvellous.

ausgiebig **1** *adj Mahlzeit etc* substantial, large; *Mittagsschlaf* long; *Gebrauch* extensive. **2** *adv* ~ **frühstücken** to have a substantial breakfast; ~ **schlafen** to have a good (long) sleep; **etw** ~ **gebrauchen** to use sth extensively.

ausgießen *vt sep irreg (aus einem Behälter)* to pour out; *(weggießen)* to pour away; *Behälter* to empty.

Ausgleich *m* **-e** **(a)** *(Gleichgewicht)* balance; *(von Konto)* balancing; *(von Schulden)* settling; *(von Verlust, Fehler)* compensation; *(von Unterschieden)* balancing out; *(von Konflikten etc)* reconciliation. **zum/als** ~ **für etw** in order to compensate for sth; **er treibt zum** ~ **Sport** he does sport for exercise. **(b)** *no pl (Ballspiele)* equalizer; *(Tennis)* deuce.

ausgleichen *sep irreg* **1** *vt Unterschiede* to even out; *Unebenheit* to level out; *Konto* to balance; *Schulden* to settle; *Fehler* to make good; *Verlust, Mangel* to offset, to compensate for; *Konflikte etc* to reconcile. ~**de Gerechtigkeit** poetic justice; *siehe* **ausgeglichen. 2** *vi (Sport)* to equalize. **zum 1:1** ~ to equalize to make it 1 all. **3** *vr* to balance out; *(Einnahmen und Ausgaben)* to balance.

Ausgleichs-: ~**sport** *m* keep-fit activity; **als** ~**sport** to keep fit; ~**tor** *nt*, ~**treffer** *m* equalizer.

ausgraben *vt sep irreg (lit, fig)* to dig up; *Grube* to dig out; *Altertümer auch* to excavate; *(hervorholen)* to dig out; *alte Geschichten* to bring up.

Ausgrabung *f* excavation, dig; *(Fund)* find.

Ausguck *m* **-e** lookout.

Ausguß *m (Becken)* sink; *(Abfluß)* drain.

aushaben *sep irreg (col)* **1** *vt (fertig sein mit) Buch etc* to have finished; *(ausgezogen haben)* to have taken off. **2** *vi (Schule etc beendet haben)* to finish.

aushalten *vt sep irreg* **(a)** to bear, to stand. **es läßt sich** ~ it's bearable; **das ist nicht auszuhalten** *or* **zum A**~ it's unbearable; **ich halte es vor Hitze/zu Hause nicht mehr aus** I can't stand the heat/being at home any longer; **wie kann man es bei der Firma bloß** ~? how can anyone stand working for that firm?; **er hält viel/nicht viel aus** he can take a lot/can't take much. **(b)** *Ton* to hold. **(c)** *(col: unterhalten)* to keep. **sich von jdm**

lassen to be kept by sb.
aushandeln vt sep to negotiate.
aushändigen vt sep jdm etw/einen Preis ~ to hand sth over to sb/give sb a prize.
Aushändigung f handing over.
Aushang m, pl **Aushänge** notice, announcement; (das Aushängen) posting. **etw durch** ~ **bekanntgeben** to put up a notice about sth.
aushängen sep 1 vt (a) (bekanntmachen) Nachricht etc to put up. (b) (herausheben) Tür to unhinge. 2 vi irreg **am Schwarzen Brett** ~ to be on the noticeboard (Brit) or bulletin board (US).
ausharren vi sep (geh) to wait. **auf seinem Posten** ~ to stand by one's post.
ausheben vt sep irreg (a) Tür etc to take off its hinges. (b) Erde to dig out; Graben to dig. (c) (fig) Diebesnest to raid; Bande to make a raid on.
aushecken vt sep (col) Plan to cook up (col).
ausheilen sep 1 vt Krankheit to cure; Organ, Wunde to heal. 2 vi aux sein (Krankheit) to be cured; (Organ, Wunde) to heal.
aushelfen vi sep irreg to help out (jdm sb).
Aushilfe f (a) help, aid. **jdn zur** ~ **haben** to have sb to help out. (b) (Mensch) temporary worker; (esp im Büro auch) temp (col). **als** ~ **arbeiten** to help out; (im Büro auch) to temp (col).
Aushilfs-: ~**kraft** f temporary worker; (esp im Büro auch) temp (col); ~**lehrer** m supply teacher; ~**personal** nt temporary staff.
aushöhlen vt sep to hollow out; (fig: untergraben) to undermine.
Aushöhlung f (a) (ausgehöhlte Stelle) hollow. (b) no pl siehe vt hollowing out; undermining.
ausholen vi sep (zum Schlag) to raise one's hand/ arm etc; (zum Wurf) to reach back. **weit** ~ (zum Schlag, beim Tennis) to take a big swing; (fig: Redner) to go far afield; **zum Gegenschlag** ~ (lit, fig) to prepare for a counter-attack.
aushorchen vt sep (col) jdn to sound out.
aushungern vt sep to starve out; siehe **ausgehungert.**
auskennen vr sep irreg (an einem Ort) to know one's way around; (auf einem Gebiet) to know a lot (auf or in+dat about). **man kennt sich bei ihm nie aus** you never know where you are with him.
auskippen vt sep (col) to empty (out).
ausklammern vt sep Problem to ignore.
Ausklang m (geh) conclusion, end.
ausklappbar adj folding. **dieser Tisch ist** ~ this table can be opened out.
auskleiden vt sep (beziehen) to line.
ausklingen vi sep irreg aux sein (Feier etc) to end.
ausklopfen vt sep Teppich to beat; Pfeife to knock out.
ausknobeln vt sep (col) Plan to figure out (col).
auskochen vt sep (fig col: sich ausdenken) to cook up (col); siehe **ausgekocht.**
auskommen vi sep irreg aux sein (a) (genügend haben, zurechtkommen) to get by (mit on), to manage (mit on, with). **ohne jdn/etw** ~ to manage or do without sb/sth. (b) **mit jdm (gut)** ~ to get on or along well with sb.
Auskommen nt no pl (Einkommen) livelihood. **sein** ~ **haben/finden** to get by; **mit ihr ist kein** ~ she's impossible to get on with.
auskosten vt sep (genießen) to make the most of; Leben to enjoy to the full.
auskramen vt sep (col) to dig out, to unearth; (fig) alte Geschichten etc to bring up.
auskratzen vt sep (auch Med) to scrape out. **jdm die Augen** ~ to scratch sb's eyes out.
auskugeln vr sep sich (dat) **den Arm/die Schulter** ~ to dislocate one's arm/shoulder.
auskühlen sep 1 vt to cool down. 2 vi aux sein (abkühlen) to cool down; (Körper, Menschen) to chill through. **etw** ~ **lassen** to leave sth to cool.
auskundschaften vt sep to find out; Versteck to spy out; (esp Mil) to reconnoitre.

Auskunft f, pl **Auskünfte** (a) (Mitteilung) information no pl (über+acc about). **nähere** ~ further details; **eine detaillierte** ~ a detailed piece of information; **jdm eine** ~ **erteilen** or **geben** to give sb some information. (b) (Schalter) information office/desk; (am Bahnhof auch) enquiry office/desk; (Telec) directory enquiries no art (Brit), directory assistance no art (US).
Auskunfts-: ~**beamte(r)** m information officer; (am Bahnhof) information clerk; ~**person** f informer; (Beamter) information clerk; ~**schalter** m information desk.
auskuppeln vi sep to disengage the clutch.
auskurieren* vt sep (col) to cure; Krankheit auch to get rid of (col).
auslachen vt sep jdn to laugh at.
ausladen vt sep irreg (a) Ware, Ladung to unload. (b) (col) jdn ~ to tell sb not to come.
ausladend adj Gebärden, Bewegung sweeping.
Auslage f (a) (von Waren) display; (Schaufenster) window; (Schaukasten) showcase. (b) usu pl expense. **seine** ~**n für Essen** his outlay for food.
Ausland nt no pl foreign countries pl; (fig: die Ausländer) foreigners pl. **ins/im** ~ abroad; **aus dem** or **vom** ~ from abroad; **wie hat das** ~ **darauf reagiert?** what was the reaction abroad?; **Handel mit dem** ~ foreign trade.
Ausländer(in f) m - foreigner; (Admin, Jur) alien.
ausländerfeindlich adj hostile to foreigners.
Ausländerfeindlichkeit f hostility to foreigners, xenophobia.
ausländisch adj attr foreign; Erzeugnisse, Freunde etc auch from abroad.
Auslands-: ~**aufenthalt** m stay abroad; ~**deutsche(r)** mf expatriate German; ~**gespräch** nt international call; ~**investition** f foreign investment; ~**korrespondent** m foreign correspondent; ~**reise** f journey or trip abroad; ~**schutzbrief** m international motoring cover; ~**vertretung** f agency abroad; (von Firma) foreign branch.
auslassen sep irreg 1 vt (a) (weglassen, übergehen) to leave or miss out; (versäumen) Chance to miss. (b) (abreagieren) to vent (an+dat on). **seine Gefühle** ~ to let off steam (col). (c) Butter, Fett to melt. (d) Kleider etc to let out; Saum to let down. (e) siehe **ausgelassen.** 2 vr to talk (über+acc about). **sich über jdn/etw** ~ (pej) to go on about sb/sth (pej).
Auslassung f (a) (Weglassen) omission. (b) ~**en** pl (pej: Äußerungen) remarks pl.
auslasten vt sep (a) Fahrzeug to make full use of; Maschine auch to use to capacity. (b) jdn to occupy fully; siehe **ausgelastet.**
Auslauf m, pl **Ausläufe** (a) no pl (für Kinder, Tiere) room to run about. (b) no pl (das Auslaufen) discharge; (das Lecken) leakage.
auslaufen vi sep irreg aux sein (a) (Flüssigkeit) to run out (aus of); (Behälter) to empty; (undicht sein) to leak. (b) (Naut: Schiff) to sail. (c) (enden) (Modell, Serie) to be discontinued; (Vertrag etc) to run out. (d) (zum Stillstand kommen: Motor etc) to come to a stop. (e) (Farbe) to run.
Ausläufer m (a) (Met) (von Hoch) ridge; (von Tief) trough. (b) (Vorberge) foothill usu pl.
auslaugen vt sep (lit, fig) to exhaust.
auslecken vt sep to lick out.
ausleeren vt sep Gefäß to empty.
auslegen vt sep (a) (ausbreiten) to lay out; Waren etc auch to display; Köder to put down. (b) (bedecken) to cover; (auskleiden) to line. **den Boden/das Zimmer (mit Teppichen)** ~ to carpet the floor/room. (c) (deuten) to interpret. **etw falsch** ~ to misinterpret sth. (d) Geld to lend (jdm etw sb sth). **sie hat die 5 Mark für mich ausgelegt** she paid the 5 marks for me.
Ausleger m - (a) (von Kran etc) jib, boom. (b) (Deuter) interpreter.

Auslegung f (Deutung) interpretation. **falsche** ~ misinterpretation.

ausleiern vti sep (col) to wear out; siehe **ausgeleiert**.

Ausleihe f (Schalter) issue desk. **eine** ~ **ist nicht möglich** it is not possible to lend out anything.

ausleihen vt sep irreg (verleihen) to lend (jdm, an jdn to sb); (von jdm leihen) to borrow.

auslernen vi sep (Lehrling) to finish one's apprenticeship. **man lernt nie aus** (prov) you live and learn (prov).

Auslese f -n (a) no pl (Auswahl) selection. **natürliche** ~ natural selection; **eine** ~ **treffen** or **vornehmen** to make a selection. (b) (Wein) high-quality wine made from selected grapes.

auslesen vti sep irreg (col) Buch to finish reading.

ausliefern vt sep (a) Waren to deliver. (b) jdn to hand over (an+acc to); (an anderen Staat) to extradite (an+acc to); (fig: preisgeben) to leave (jdm in the hands of). **jdm/einer Sache ausgeliefert sein** to be at sb's mercy/the mercy of sth.

Auslieferung f siehe vt (a) delivery. (b) handing over; extradition.

Auslieferungs|abkommen nt extradition treaty.

ausliegen vi sep irreg (zur Ansicht) to be displayed; (Zeitschriften etc) to be available (to the public); (Liste) to be up.

auslöffeln vt sep ~ **müssen, was man sich eingebrockt hat** (col) to have to take the consequences.

auslöschen vt sep (a) Feuer etc to put out, to extinguish. (b) (auswischen) Spuren, Erinnerung to wipe out; Schrift to erase (an +dat from).

auslosen vt sep to draw lots for; Preis, Gewinner to draw.

auslösen vt sep Mechanismus, Alarm to trigger off; Kameraverschluß to release; (fig) Wirkung to produce; Begeisterung etc to arouse.

Auslöser m - (a) (trigger; (für Bombe) release button; (Phot) shutter release. (b) (Anlaß) cause.

Auslosung f draw.

Auslösung f siehe vt (a) triggering off; release; producing; arousing.

ausloten vt sep (Naut) Tiefe to sound; (fig geh) to plumb.

ausmachen vt sep (a) Feuer, Kerze, Zigarette to put out; elektrisches Licht auch, Radio, Gas to turn off. (b) (ermitteln, sichten) to make out. (c) (vereinbaren) to agree. **etw mit sich selbst** ~ **(müssen)** to (have to) sort sth out for oneself; siehe **ausgemacht.** (d) (bewirken, darstellen) (to go) to make up. **all der Luxus, der ein angenehmes Leben ausmacht** all the luxuries which go to make up a pleasant life. (e) (bedeuten) **viel/wenig** or **nicht viel** ~ to make a big/not much difference; **das macht nichts aus** that doesn't matter. (f) (stören) to matter (jdm to). **macht es Ihnen etwas aus, wenn ...?** would you mind if ...?

ausmalen vt sep sich (dat) etw ~ to imagine sth.

ausmanövrieren* vt sep to outmanoeuvre (Brit), to outmaneuver (US).

Ausmaß nt (Größe: von Gegenstand, Fläche) size; (Umfang: von Katastrophe) extent. **ein Verlust in diesem** ~ a loss on this scale.

ausmerzen vt sep Unkraut, Fehler to eradicate.

ausmessen vt sep irreg to measure (out).

ausmisten vt sep Stall to muck out; (fig col) Schrank etc to tidy out; Zimmer to clean out.

ausmustern vt sep Maschine, Fahrzeug etc to take out of service; (Mil: entlassen) to invalid out.

Ausnahme f -n exception. **mit** ~ **von Horst** with the exception of Horst; ~**n bestätigen die Regel** (prov) the exception proves the rule (prov).

Ausnahme-: ~**erscheinung** f exception; ~**fall** m exception, exceptional case; ~**zustand** m (Pol) state of emergency; **den** ~**zustand verhängen** to

declare a state of emergency.

ausnahmslos 1 adv without exception. 2 adj Bewilligung, Zustimmung unanimous.

ausnahmsweise adv **darf ich das machen?** — ~ **may I do that?** — just this once; **er darf heute** ~ **früher von der Arbeit weggehen** as an exception he may leave work earlier today.

ausnehmen sep irreg 1 vt (a) Fisch, Kaninchen to gut; Geflügel to draw. (b) (ausschließen) jdn to make an exception of. (c) (col) jdn to fleece; (beim Kartenspiel) to clean out. 2 vr (geh: wirken) **sich schön** or **gut/schlecht** ~ to look good/bad.

ausnehmend adj (geh) exceptional. **das gefällt mir** ~ **gut** I like that very much indeed.

ausnüchtern vti sep to sober up.

Ausnüchterung f sobering up.

Ausnüchterungszelle f drying-out cell.

ausnutzen vt sep to make use of; (ausbeuten) to exploit; Gelegenheit to make the most of; jds Gutmütigkeit etc to take advantage of.

Ausnutzung f use; (Ausbeutung) exploitation.

auspacken sep 1 vti Koffer to unpack; Geschenk to unwrap. 2 vi (col: alles sagen) to talk (col).

auspeitschen vt sep to whip.

auspfeifen vt sep irreg to boo.

ausplaudern vt sep to let out.

ausposaunen* vt sep (col) to tell the world about (col).

ausprägen vr sep (Begabung, Charaktereigenschaft etc) to reveal or show itself; siehe **ausgeprägt.**

Ausprägung f no pl (von Charakter) shaping.

auspressen vt sep Saft, Schwamm etc to squeeze out; Zitrone etc to squeeze.

ausprobieren* vt sep to try out.

Auspuff m -e exhaust.

Auspuff-: ~**gase** pl exhaust fumes pl; ~**rohr** nt exhaust; ~**topf** m silencer (Brit), muffler (US).

auspumpen vt sep to pump out.

ausputzen vi sep (Ftbl) to clear (the ball); (Ausputzer sein) to play sweeper.

Ausputzer m - (Ftbl) sweeper.

ausquartieren* vt sep to move out.

ausquetschen vt sep Zitrone etc to squeeze; (col: ausfragen) to grill (col); (aus Neugier) to pump (col).

ausradiern* vt sep to rub out, to erase; (fig: vernichten) to wipe out.

ausrangieren* vt sep Kleider to throw out; Maschine, Auto to scrap. **ein altes ausrangiertes Auto** an old disused car.

ausrauben vt sep to rob.

ausraufen vt sep **ich könnte mir die Haare** ~ I could kick myself.

ausräumen vt sep to clear out; (fig) Mißverständnisse, Konflikt to clear up; Vorurteile, Bedenken to dispel; (col: ausrauben) to clean out (col).

ausrechnen vt sep to work out; (ermitteln) Gewicht, Länge auch to calculate. **sich** (dat) **große Chancen** ~ to reckon that one has a good chance; siehe **ausgerechnet.**

Ausrede f excuse.

ausreden sep 1 vi to finish speaking. **er hat mich nicht mal** ~ **lassen** he didn't even let me finish (speaking). 2 vt jdm etw ~ to talk sb out of sth.

ausreichen vi sep to be sufficient or enough. **die Zeit reicht nicht aus** there is not sufficient time.

ausreichend 1 adj adequate; (Sch) satisfactory. 2 adv adequately.

Ausreise f **bei der** ~ on leaving the country; (Grenzübertritt) on crossing the border; **jdm die** ~ **verweigern** to prohibit sb from leaving the country.

Ausreise|erlaubnis f exit permit.

ausreisen vi sep aux sein to leave (the country).

Ausreisevisum nt exit visa.

ausreißen sep irreg 1 vt Haare, Blatt to tear out; Zahn to pull out; Blumen to pull up. **er hat sich** (dat) **kein Bein ausgerissen** (col) he didn't exactly overstrain himself. **2** *vi aux sein* (+*dat from*) (*col: davonlaufen*) to run away; (*Sport*) to break away.

Ausreißer(in) *f*) *m* - (*col*) runaway; (*Sport*) runner/cyclist who breaks away.

ausreiten *vi sep irreg aux sein* to go riding.

ausrenken *vt sep* to dislocate. **sich (fast) den Hals ~** (*col*) to crane one's neck.

ausrichten *vt sep* (**a**) (*aufstellen*) to line up. *jdn/ etw auf etw (acc)* ~ (*abstellen*) to gear sb/sth to sth. (**b**) (*veranstalten*) to organize. (**c**) (*erreichen*) to achieve. **ich konnte bei ihr nichts ~** I couldn't get anywhere with her. (**d**) (*übermitteln*) to tell; *Nachricht* to pass on. **kann ich etwas ~?** can I take a message?; **bitte richten Sie ihm einen Gruß aus** please give him my regards.

Ausrichtung *f siehe vt* (**a**) lining up. (**b**) organization. (**c**) (*fig*) (*auf Ideologie etc*) orientation (*auf +acc* towards); (*auf Bedürfnisse etc*) gearing (*auf +acc* to).

Ausritt *m* ride (out).

ausrollen *vt sep Teig, Teppich* to roll out.

ausrotten *vt sep* to wipe out; *Volk auch, Ungeziefer* to exterminate; *Religion, Ideen auch* to stamp out.

Ausrottung *f siehe vt* wiping out; extermination; stamping out.

ausrücken *vi sep aux sein* (**a**) (*Mil*) to move out; (*Polizei, Feuerwehr*) to turn out. (**b**) (*col: ausreißen*) to make off; (*von zu Hause*) to run away.

Ausruf *m* (*Ruf*) cry, shout.

ausrufen *vt sep irreg* to exclaim; *Schlagzeilen* to shout out; (*verkünden*) to call out; *Haltestellen, Streik* to call. **jdn zum König ~** to proclaim sb king; **jdn ~** (*lassen*) (*über Lautsprecher etc*) to page sb.

Ausrufezeichen *nt* exclamation mark (*Brit*) or point (*US*).

Ausrufung *f* proclamation. **die ~ eines Streiks** a strike call.

ausruhen *vtir sep* to rest; (*Mensch auch*) to have a rest; *siehe* **ausgeruht**.

ausrüsten *vt sep* (*lit,fig*) to equip. **ein Fahrzeug mit etw ~** to fit a car with sth.

Ausrüstung *f* (~*sgegenstände*) equipment; (*esp Kleidung*) outfit.

Ausrüstungsgegenstand *m* piece of equipment.

ausrutschen *vi sep aux sein* to slip; (*Fahrzeug*) to skid. **das Messer/die Hand ist mir ausgerutscht** my knife/my hand slipped.

Ausrutscher *m* - (*col: lit,fig*) slip.

Aussaat *f no pl* (*das Säen*) sowing.

aussäen *vt sep* (*lit,fig*) to sow.

Aussage *f* -**n** statement; (*Behauptung*) opinion; (*Bericht*) report; (*Jur*) (*eines Angeklagten*) statement; (*Zeugen~*) evidence *no pl*. **eine eidliche/ schriftliche ~** a sworn/written statement; **der Zeuge verweigerte die ~** the witness refused to give evidence; **eine ~ machen** to make a statement.

aussagen *sep* **1** *vt* to say (*über+acc* about); (*behaupten*) to state; (*unter Eid*) to testify. **2** *vi* (*Jur*) (*Zeuge*) to give evidence; (*Angeklagter*) to make a statement; (*unter Eid auch*) to testify. **für/gegen jdn ~** to give evidence for/against sb.

Aussatz *m no pl* (*Med*) leprosy.

Aussätzige(r) *mf decl as adj* (*lit,fig*) leper.

aussaugen *vt sep Saft etc* to suck out; *Wunde* to suck the poison out of; (*fig: ausbeuten*) to drain dry. **jdn bis aufs Blut ~** to bleed sb white.

ausschachten *vt sep* to dig, to excavate.

Ausschachtung *f* excavation.

ausschalten *vt sep* (**a**) (*abstellen*) to switch or turn off. (**b**) (*fig*) to eliminate.

Ausschaltung *f siehe vt* switching off; elimination.

Ausschank *m, pl* **Ausschänke** bar; (*no pl: Getränkeausgabe*) sale of drinks.

Ausschank|erlaubnis *f* licence (*Brit*), license (*US*).

Ausschau *f no pl:* **~ halten** to look out (*nach* for).

ausschauen *vi sep* (*geh*) to be on the look-out (*nach* for).

ausscheiden *sep irreg* **1** *vt* (*aussondern*) to take out; (*Physiol*) to excrete. **2** *vi aux sein* (**a**) (*aus einem Amt*) to retire (*aus* from); (*aus Firma*) to leave (*aus etw* sth); (*Sport*) to be eliminated; (*wegen Verletzung etc*) to drop out. (**b**) (*nicht in Betracht kommen: Möglichkeit etc*) to be ruled out. **das/er scheidet aus** that/he has to be ruled out.

Ausscheidung *f* (**a**) *no pl* (*das Aussondern*) removal; (*Physiol*) excretion. (**b**) (*Sport*) elimination; (*Vorkampf*) qualifying contest.

Ausscheidungs-: ~**kampf** *m* qualifying contest; (*Leichtathletik, Schwimmen*) heat; ~**spiel** *nt* qualifying match or game.

ausschenken *vti sep* to pour (out).

ausscheren *vi sep aux sein* (*Fahrzeug*) to leave the line or convoy; (*zum Überholen*) to pull out.

ausschicken *vt sep* to send out.

ausschiffen *vt sep* to disembark; *Ladung, Waren* to unload.

Ausschiffung *f siehe vt* disembarkation; unloading.

ausschildern *vt sep* to signpost.

ausschimpfen *vt sep* to tell off.

ausschlachten *vt sep* (**a**) to gut, to dress. (**b**) (*fig*) *Fahrzeuge, Maschinen etc* to cannibalize. (**c**) (*fig col: ausnutzen*) *Skandal, Ereignis* to exploit.

ausschlafen *sep irreg* **1** *vt Rausch etc* to sleep off. **2** *vir* to have a good sleep.

Ausschlag *m* (**a**) (*Med*) rash. (**b**) (*von Zeiger etc*) swing; (*von Kompaßnadel*) deflection. (**c**) (*fig*) **den ~ geben** (*fig*) to be the decisive factor; **die Stimme des Vorsitzenden gibt den ~** the chairman has the casting vote.

ausschlagen *sep irreg* **1** *vt* (**a**) (*herausschlagen*) to knock out. (**b**) *Feuer* to beat out. (**c**) (*auskleiden*) to line. (**d**) (*ablehnen*) to turn down. **jdm etw ~** to refuse sb sth. **2** *vi* (**a**) *aux sein or haben* (*Baum, Strauch*) to start to bud. (**b**) (*Pferd*) to kick. (**c**) *aux sein or haben* (*Zeiger etc*) to swing; (*Kompaßnadel*) to be deflected.

ausschlaggebend *adj* decisive; *Stimme auch* deciding. **das ist von ~er Bedeutung** that is of prime importance.

ausschließen *vt sep irreg* (**a**) (*aussperren*) to lock out. (**b**) (*ausnehmen*) to exclude; (*aus Gemeinschaft*) to expel; (*vorübergehend*) to suspend; (*Sport*) to disqualify; *Fehler, Möglichkeit etc* to rule out. **das eine schließt das andere nicht aus** the one does not exclude the other; **die Öffentlichkeit ~** (*Jur*) to exclude the public; *siehe* **ausgeschlossen**.

ausschließlich *adj attr* exclusive.

ausschlüpfen *vi sep aux sein* to slip out; (*aus Ei, Puppe*) to hatch out.

Ausschluß *m siehe* **ausschließen** (**b**) exclusion; expulsion; suspension; disqualification. **unter ~ der Öffentlichkeit stattfinden** to be closed to the public.

ausschmücken *vt sep* to decorate; (*fig*) *Erzählung* to embellish.

Ausschmückung *f siehe vt* decoration; embellishment.

ausschneiden *vt sep irreg* (*herauschneiden*) to cut out; *siehe* **ausgeschnitten**.

Ausschnitt *m* (**a**) (*Zeitungs~*) cutting, clipping. (**b**) (*Kleid~*) neck. **ein tiefer ~** a low neckline. (**c**) (*fig: Teil*) part; (*aus Film*) clip.

ausschöpfen *vt sep* (**a**) *Wasser etc* to ladle out (*aus etw* of). (**b**) (*leeren*) to empty; (*fig*) to exhaust.

ausschreiben *vt sep irreg* (**a**) to write out; (*ungekürzt schreiben*) to write (out) in full. (**b**) *Rechnung etc* to make out. (**c**) (*bekanntmachen*) to announce; *Wahlen* to call; *Stelle* to advertise.

Ausschreibung f (Bekanntmachung) (von Wahlen) calling; (von Stelle) advertising.

Ausschreitung f usu pl (Aufruhr) rioting no pl.

Ausschuß m (a) (Komitee) committee. (b) no pl (Comm) rejects pl; (fig col) trash.

ausschütten vt sep (a) (auskippen) to tip out; Eimer, Glas to empty. **jdm sein Herz** ~ (fig) to pour out one's heart to sb. (b) (Fin) Dividende etc to distribute.

Ausschüttung f (Fin) distribution.

ausschwärmen vi sep aux sein (Bienen, Menschen) to swarm out; (Mil) to fan out.

ausschweifend adj Leben dissipated; Phantasie wild.

Ausschweifung f (Maßlosigkeit) excess; (in Lebensweise) dissipation.

ausschweigen vr sep irreg to remain silent (über +acc, zu about).

ausschwenken vi sep aux sein (a) (Mil) to wheel. (b) (Kran etc) to swing out.

ausschwitzen vt sep to sweat out.

aussehen vi sep irreg to look. **gut** ~ to look good; (hübsch) to be good-looking; (gesund) to look well; **gesund/elend** ~ to look healthy/wretched; **es sieht nach Regen aus** it looks like rain; **wie jd/etw** ~ to look like sb/sth; **wie sieht's aus?** (col: wie steht's) how's things? (col); **es soll nach etwas** ~ it's got to look good; **es sieht danach** or **so aus, als ob** ... it looks as if ...; **so siehst du aus!** (col) that's what you think!; **es sieht nicht gut mit ihm aus** things don't look good for him.

Aussehen nt no pl appearance. **dem** ~ **nach** by the looks of it; **etw dem** ~ **nach beurteilen** to judge sth by appearances.

aussein sep irreg aux sein. **1** vi (col) (a) (zu Ende sein) (Schule) to finish; (Krieg, Stück) to have ended; (nicht ansein) (Feuer, Ofen) to be out; (Radio, Fernseher etc) to be off. **die Schule ist aus** school has finished or is out. (b) **auf etw** (acc) ~ to be (only) interested in sth; **auf jdn** ~ to be after sb (col). **2** vi impers **es ist aus (und vorbei) zwischen uns** it's (all) over between us; **es ist aus mit ihm** he is finished, he has had it (col).

außen adv ~ **bemalt** painted on the outside; ~ **an der Windschutzscheibe** on the outside of the windscreen; **von** ~ **sieht es gut aus** on the outside it looks good; **das Fenster geht nach** ~ **auf** the window opens outwards.

Außen-: ~**antenne** f outdoor aerial (Brit) or antenna (US); ~**arbeiten** pl work on the exterior; ~**aufnahme** f outdoor shot; ~**bahn** f outside lane; ~**bezirk** m outlying district; ~**bordmotor** m outboard motor.

aussenden vtr sep irreg to send out.

Außen-: ~**dienst** m external duty; **im** ~**dienst sein** to work outside the office; ~**handel** m foreign trade; ~**minister** m foreign minister, foreign secretary (Brit), secretary of state (US); ~**ministerium** nt foreign ministry, foreign office (Brit), state department (US); ~**politik** f (Gebiet) foreign politics sing; (bestimmte) foreign policy/policies; ~**politiker** m foreign affairs politician; **a**~**politisch** adj foreign policy attr; Sprecher on foreign affairs; ~**seite** f outside.

Außenseiter(in f) m - (Sport, fig) outsider.

Außenseiterrolle f role as an outsider. **eine** ~ **spielen** to play the role of an outsider.

Außen-: ~**spiegel** m (Aut) outside mirror; ~**stände** pl (esp Comm) outstanding debts pl, arrears pl; ~**stehende(r)** mf decl as adj outsider; ~**stelle** f branch; ~**stürmer** m (Ftbl) wing; ~**temperatur** f outside temperature; ~**wand** f outer wall; ~**welt** f outside world.

außer prep+dat or (rare) gen (a) (räumlich) out of. ~ **Sicht** out of sight; ~ **sich** (acc) **geraten** to go wild; ~ **sich** (dat) **sein** to be beside oneself; ~ **Haus sein/essen** to be/eat out; ~ **Atem** out of breath. (b) (ausgenommen) except (for); (ab-

gesehen von) apart from, aside from. **alle** ~ **mir** everyone except (for) me. (c) (zusätzlich zu) in addition to. **2** conj except. ~ **daß** ... except that ...; ~ **wenn** ... unless ...

außerdem adv besides; (dazu) in addition, as well; (überdies) anyway.

außerdienstlich adj (nicht dienstlich) Angelegenheit private; (außerhalb der Arbeitszeit) social.

außer|ehelich 1 adj extramarital; Kind illegitimate. **2** adv outside marriage.

äußere(r, s) adj (außerhalb gelegen, Geog) outer; Verletzung external; Schein, Eindruck outward.

Äußere(s) nt decl as adj exterior; (fig: Aussehen auch) outward appearance.

außer-: ~**europäisch** adj attr non-European; ~**gewöhnlich 1** adj unusual, out of the ordinary; (sehr) extremely.

außerhalb 1 prep+gen outside. ~ **der Stadt** outside the town, out of town. **2** adv (außen) outside; (~ der Stadt) out of town. ~ **stehen** (fig) to be on the outside.

außer|irdisch adj extraterrestrial.

äußerlich adj (a) external. (b) (fig) (oberflächlich) superficial; (scheinbar) outward. „**nur zur** ~**en Anwendung!**" for external use only; **rein** ~ **betrachtet** on the face of it.

Äußerlichkeit f (fig) triviality; (Oberflächlichkeit) superficiality; (Formalität) formality. ~**en** (outward) appearances.

äußern 1 vt (sagen) to say; Wunsch etc to express; Worte to utter; Kritik to voice. **seine Meinung** ~ to give one's views. **2** vr (Mensch) to speak; (Krankheit, Symptom) to show itself.

außer-: ~**ordentlich 1** adj extraordinary; (ungewöhnlich auch) exceptional; (bemerkenswert auch) remarkable; **2** adv (sehr) exceptionally, extremely; ~**parlamentarisch** adj extraparliamentary; ~**planmäßig** adj Besuch, Treffen unscheduled; ~**sinnlich** adj ~**sinnliche Wahrnehmung** extrasensory perception.

äußerst adv extremely, exceedingly.

außerstande adv (unfähig) incapable; (nicht in der Lage) unable. ~ **sein, etw zu tun** to be incapable of doing sth.

äußerstenfalls adv at most.

äußerste(r, s) adj (räumlich) furthest; Schicht outermost; Norden etc extreme; (zeitlich) latest possible; (fig) utmost. **mein** ~**s Angebot** my final offer; **im** ~**n Falle** if the worst comes to the worst; **mit** ~**r Kraft** with all one's strength.

Äußerste(s) nt decl as adj **bis zum** ~**n gehen** to go to extremes; **er hat sein** ~**s gegeben** he gave his all.

Äußerung f (Bemerkung) remark, comment; (Behauptung) statement; (Zeichen) expression.

aussetzen sep **1** vt (a) Kind, Haustier to abandon; Pflanzen to plant out; (Naut) Passagiere to maroon. (b) **jdn/etw einer Sache** (dat) ~ to expose sb/sth to sth; **jdm/einer Sache ausgesetzt sein** (ausgeliefert) to be at the mercy of sb/sth. (c) Belohnung, Preis to offer. (d) (unterbrechen) to interrupt; Debatte, Prozeß to adjourn. (e) (vertagen) Verfahren to suspend. (f) **an jdm/einer Sache etwas auszusetzen haben** to find fault with sb/sth; **daran ist nichts auszusetzen** there is nothing wrong with it; **was haben Sie daran auszusetzen?** what's your objection to it?

2 vi (aufhören) to stop; (bei Spiel) to sit out; (Herz) to stop (beating); (Motor auch) to fail. **mit der Pille/Behandlung** ~ to stop taking the pill/to interrupt the treatment; **ohne auszusetzen** without a break.

Aussetzung f (a) siehe vt (a) abandonment; planting out; marooning. (b) (Jur: von Verfahren) suspension.

Aussicht f (a) (Blick) view (auf+acc of). **mit** ~ **auf den Park** overlooking the park. (b) (fig) prospect (auf+acc of). **die** ~, **daß etw geschieht**

the chances of sth happening; **unser Plan hat große ~en auf Erfolg** our plan has every chance of succeeding; **etw in ~ haben** to have good prospects of sth; **jdm etw in ~ stellen** to promise sb sth; **das sind ja schöne ~en!** *(iro col)* what a prospect!

Aussichts-: **a~los** *adj* hopeless; *(zwecklos)* pointless; *(völlig hoffnungslos)* desperate; **~losigkeit** *f siehe adj* hoplessness; pointlessness; desperateness; **a~reich** *adj* promising; *Stellung* with good prospects; **~turm** *m* lookout tower.

aussiedeln *vt sep* to resettle.

Aussiedler *m (Auswanderer)* emigrant.

Aussiedlung *f* resettlement.

aussöhnen *sep* 1 *vt* **jdn mit jdm/etw ~** to reconcile sb with sb/to sth. 2 *vr* **sich mit jdm/etw ~** to become reconciled with sb/to sth; **wir haben uns wieder ausgesöhnt** we have made it up again.

Aussöhnung *f* reconciliation *(mit jdm* with sb, *mit etw* to sth).

aussondern *vt sep* to select; *Schlechtes* to separate out.

aussorgen *vi sep:* **ausgesorgt haben** to have no more money worries.

aussortieren* *vt sep* to sort out.

ausspannen *sep* 1 *vt* **(a)** *Tuch, Netz* to spread out; *Schnur, Leine* to put up. **(b)** *Pferde* to unhitch; *(aus Schreibmaschine) Bogen* to take out. **(c)** *(fig col)* **jdm die Freundin** *etc* **~** to pinch sb's girlfriend *etc (col)*. 2 *vi (sich erholen)* to have a break.

aussparen *vt sep (fig)* to omit.

Aussparung *f (Lücke)* gap.

aussperren *vt sep* to lock out.

Aussperrung *f (Ind)* lockout.

ausspielen *sep* 1 *vti* **(a)** *Karte* to play. **(b)** *(fig)* **jdn/etw gegen jdn/etw ~** to play sb/sth off against sb/sth. **(c)** *Gewinne* to give as a prize/as prizes. 2 *vi (Cards)* to lead. **wer spielt aus?** whose lead is it?

Ausspielung *f (im Lotto)* draw.

ausspionieren* *vt sep* *Pläne etc* to spy out; *Person* to spy on.

Aussprache *f* **(a)** pronunciation; *(Akzent)* accent. **(b)** *(Meinungsaustausch)* discussion, talks *pl*.

aussprechen *sep irreg* 1 *vt* *Wörter, Urteil etc* to pronounce; *Scheidung* to grant; *(äußern)* to express *(jdm* to sb); *Verdächtigung* to voice; *Warnung* to give. **der Regierung das Vertrauen ~** to pass a vote of confidence in the government. 2 *vr (Partner)* to talk things out; *(sein Herz ausschütten)* to say what's on one's mind. **sich für/gegen etw ~** to come out in favour of/against sth. 3 *vi (zu Ende sprechen)* to finish (speaking); *siehe* **ausgesprochen.**

Ausspruch *m* remark; *(geflügeltes Wort)* saying.

ausspucken *sep* 1 *vt* to spit out. 2 *vi* to spit.

ausspülen *vt sep* to rinse (out).

ausstaffieren* *vt sep (col)* to rig out; *(herausputzen)* to dress up.

Ausstand *m* **(a)** *(Streik)* strike. **in den ~ treten** to (go on) strike. **(b)** **seinen ~ geben** to hold a leaving party.

ausstatten *vt sep* to equip; *(versorgen)* to provide; *(möblieren)* to furnish. **mit Humor** *etc* **ausgestattet sein** to be endowed with a sense of humour *etc.*

Ausstattung *f* **(a)** *siehe vt* equipping; provision. **(b)** *(Ausrüstung)* equipment; *(Tech auch)* fittings *pl*; *(von Zimmer etc)* furnishings *pl*; *(Theat)* décor and costumes.

ausstechen *vt sep irreg* **(a)** *Torf, Plätzchen etc* to cut out. **(b)** *Augen* to gouge out. **(c)** *(fig) jdn (verdrängen)* to push out; *(übertreffen)* to outdo.

ausstehen *sep irreg* 1 *vt (ertragen)* to endure; *Sorge, Angst* to go through, to suffer. **ich kann ihn/so etwas nicht ~** I can't stand him/anything like that. 2 *vi* **(a)** to be due; *(Antwort)* to be still to come; *(Entscheidung)* to be still to be taken. **(b)**

(Schulden) to be outstanding.

aussteigen *vi sep irreg* **(a)** *aux sein* to get out *(aus* of); *(aus Bus, Zug etc auch)* to get off *(aus etw* sth). **alles ~!** everybody out!; *(von Schaffner)* all change! **(b)** *(col) (aus Geschäft etc)* to get out *(aus* of); *(aus Gesellschaft)* to drop out *(aus* of).

Aussteiger(in *f) m* - *(col)* drop-out.

ausstellen *vt sep* **(a)** *(zur Schau stellen)* to display; *(auf Messe, in Museum etc)* to exhibit. **(b)** *(ausschreiben)* to make out *(jdm* to sb). **einen Scheck auf jdn ~** to make out a cheque to sb. **(c)** *(ausschalten) Gerät* to turn off.

Aussteller(in *f) m* - **(a)** *(auf Messe)* exhibitor. **(b)** *(von Scheck)* drawer.

Ausstellung *f* **(a)** *(Kunst~, Messe)* exhibition. **(b)** *no pl (von Scheck etc)* making out; *(behördlich)* issuing.

Ausstellungs-: **~datum** *nt* date of issue; **~gelände** *nt* exhibition site; **~stück** *nt (in Ausstellung)* exhibit; *(in Schaufenster etc)* display item.

Aussterben *nt no pl* extinction. **vom ~ bedroht sein** to be threatened by extinction.

aussterben *vi sep irreg aux sein* to die out; *(esp Spezies, Geschlecht auch)* to become extinct; *siehe* **ausgestorben.**

Aussteuer *f* -**n** dowry.

aussteuern *vt sep Verstärker* to adjust.

Ausstieg *m* -**e** **(a)** *(Ausgang)* exit. **(b)** *(fig)* dropping out *(aus* of).

ausstopfen *vt sep Kissen etc, Tiere* to stuff.

Ausstoß *m* **(a)** *(esp Phys, Tech: das Ausstoßen)* expulsion, discharge. **(b)** *(Produktion)* output.

ausstoßen *vt sep irreg* **(a)** *(herausstoßen)* to discharge; *Atem* to expel; *(herstellen) Teile, Stückzahl* to turn out, to produce. **(b)** *(ausschließen) (aus Verein, Armee etc)* to expel *(aus from)*; *(verbannen)* to banish *(aus* from). **(c)** *(äußern)* to utter; *Schrei* to give.

ausstrahlen *sep* 1 *vt* to radiate *(auch fig)*; *esp Licht, Wärme auch* to give off; *(Rad, TV)* to transmit, to broadcast. 2 *vi* to radiate; *(Schmerz)* to spread *(bis in+acc* as far as).

Ausstrahlung *f* radiation; *(Rad, TV)* transmission, broadcast(ing); *(fig: von Mensch, Ort)* aura.

ausstrecken *sep* 1 *vt* to extend *(nach* towards); *Fühler auch* to put out; *Hand auch, Beine etc* to stretch out. 2 *vr* to stretch (oneself) out.

ausstreuen *vt sep* to scatter; *(fig) Gerücht* to spread.

ausströmen *sep* 1 *vi aux sein* **(a)** *(herausfließen)* to stream out *(aus* of); *(entweichen)* to escape *(aus* from). **(b)** *(ausstrahlen)* **etw strömt von jdm/etw aus** *(fig)* sb/sth radiates sth. 2 *vt Duft, Gas* to give off; *Wärme, Ruhe etc* to radiate.

aussuchen *vt sep (auswählen)* to choose; *(esp iro)* to pick; *siehe* **ausgesucht.**

Austausch *m* exchange; *(von Gedanken etc auch)* interchange; *(Ersatz)* replacement; *(Sport)* substitution. **im ~ für** *or* **gegen** in exchange for.

austauschbar *adj* (ex)changeable; *(untereinander ~)* interchangeable; *(ersetzbar)* replaceable.

Austausch-: **~motor** *m* replacement engine; **~student** *m* exchange student.

austeilen *vt sep* to distribute *(an +acc* among); *(aushändigen auch)* to hand out *(an +acc* to); *Spielkarten* to deal *(an +acc* to); *Essen* to serve; *Befehle* to give, to issue.

Austeilung *f* distribution; *(Aushändigung auch)* handing out; *(von Essen etc)* serving.

Auster *f* -**n** oyster.

austoben *vr sep (Mensch)* to let off steam; *(sich müde machen)* to tire oneself out. **ein Garten, wo sich die Kinder ~ können** a garden where the children can romp about.

austragen *sep irreg vt* **(a)** *Waren, Post etc* to deliver. **(b)** *Duell, Wettkampf etc* to hold. **einen Streit mit jdm ~** to have it out with sb. **(c)** **ein**

Kind ~ *(nicht abtreiben)* to have a child. **(d)** *(löschen) Zahlen, Daten* to take out. jdn ~ *(aus Liste)* to cancel sb's name. 2 *vr* to sign out; *(in Hotel)* to check out.

Austragung *f (Sport)* holding.

Austragungs|ort *m (Sport)* venue.

Australien [-iən] *nt* Australia.

Australier(in *f)* [-iɐ, -iərɪn] *m* - Australian.

australisch *adj* Australian.

austräumen *vt sep* **sein Traum von Reichtümern ist ausgeträumt** his dreams of riches are over.

austreiben *sep irreg* **1** *vt (vertreiben)* to drive out; *Teufel etc auch* to exorcize, to cast out *(esp old, liter).* jdm etw ~ to cure sb of sth; *(esp durch Schläge)* to knock sth out of sb. **2** *vi (sprießen)* to sprout.

austreten *sep irreg* **1** *vi aux sein* **(a)** *(herauskommen)* to come out *(aus of)*; *(Gas etc)* to escape *(aus from, through).* **(b)** *(col: zur Toilette gehen)* to go to the loo *or* john *(US) (col)*; *(Sch auch)* to be excused *(euph).* **(c)** *(ausscheiden)* to leave *(aus etw sth).* **2** *vt Pfad, Feuer etc* to tread out; *Schuhe* to wear out; *siehe* **ausgetreten.**

austricksen *vt sep (col: Sport, fig)* to trick.

austrinken *vti sep irreg* to finish. **trink (deine Milch) aus!** drink (your milk) up.

Austritt *m* **(a)** *no pl (von Flüssigkeit)* outflow; *(das Entweichen)* escape; *(von Blut)* issue. **(b)** *(das Ausscheiden)* leaving *aus nt (aus etw sth).*

austrocknen *sep* **1** *vi aux sein* to dry out; *(Fluß etc)* to dry up; *(Kehle)* to become parched. **2** *vt* to dry out; *(trockenlegen) Sumpf auch* to drain.

austüfteln *vt sep (col)* to work out; *(ersinnen)* to think up.

aus|üben *vt sep* **(a)** *Beruf, Kunst* to practise *(Brit),* to practice *(US); Gewerbe auch* to carry on; *Aufgabe, Funktion* to perform; *(innehaben) Amt* to hold. **(b)** *Druck, Einfluß* to exert *(auf+acc on); Macht, Recht* to exercise; *Wirkung* to have *(auf +acc on).*

Aus|übung *f siehe vt* **(a)** practice; performance. **in** ~ **seines Dienstes/seiner Pflicht** *(form)* in the execution of his duty. **(b)** exertion; exercise.

aus|ufern *vi sep aux sein (fig)* to get out of hand; *(Konflikt etc)* to escalate *(zu into).*

Ausverkauf *m* (clearance) sale; *(wegen Schließung)* closing-down sale; *(fig: Verrat)* sell-out.

ausverkauft *adj* sold out. **vor** ~**em Haus spielen** to play to a full house.

auswachsen *sep irreg* **1** *vi aux sein* **das ist (ja) zum A** ~ *(col)* it's enough to drive you mad *(col); siehe* **ausgewachsen.** **2** *vr* **sich zu etw** ~ *(fig: Streit etc)* to turn into sth.

Auswahl *f no pl* selection *(an +dat of); (Angebot auch)* range; *(Wahl)* choice; *(die Besten)* pick. **viele Sachen zur** ~ **haben** to have many things to choose from; **eine** ~ **treffen** to make a choice; *(mehrere auswählen)* to make a selection.

auswählen *vt sep* to select, to choose *(unter+dat from among); siehe* **ausgewählt.**

Auswahl-: ~**mannschaft** *f* representative team; ~**möglichkeit** *f* choice.

Auswanderer *m,* **Auswanderin** *f* emigrant.

auswandern *vi sep aux sein* to emigrate *(nach, in +acc to); (Volk)* to migrate.

Auswanderung *f* emigration; *(Massen~)* migration.

auswärtig *adj attr* **(a)** *(nicht ansässig)* non-local; *Schüler, Mitglied* from out of town. **(b)** *(Pol)* foreign. **das A~e Amt** the Foreign Office *(Brit),* the State Department *(US).*

auswärts *adv (außerhalb der Stadt)* out of town; *(Sport)* away. ~ **essen** to eat out.

Auswärtsspiel *nt (Sport)* away (game).

auswaschen *vt sep irreg* to wash out; *(spülen)* to rinse (out).

auswechselbar *adj* (ex)changeable; *(untereinander)* interchangeable; *(ersetzbar)* replaceable.

auswechseln *vt sep* to change; *(esp gegenseitig)* to exchange; *(ersetzen)* to replace; *(Sport)* to substitute *(gegen for).* **er ist wie ausgewechselt** *(fig)* he's a changed *or* different person.

Auswechselspieler(in *f) m* substitute.

Ausweg *m* way out; *(fig: Lösung auch)* solution. **der letzte** ~ the last resort.

Ausweg-: **a**~**los** *adj (fig)* hopeless; ~**losigkeit** *f (fig)* hopelessness.

ausweichen *vi sep irreg aux sein* to get out of the way *(+dat of); (fig)* to evade the point/issue *etc.* **jdm/einer Begegnung** ~ to avoid sb/a meeting; **eine** ~**de Antwort** an evasive answer.

Ausweich-: ~**manöver** *nt* evasive action; ~**möglichkeit** *f (lit)* possibility of getting out of the way; *(fig)* alternative.

ausweinen *vr sep* **sich bei jdm** ~ to have a cry on sb's shoulder; **sich** *(dat)* **die Augen** ~ to cry one's eyes out *(nach over).*

Ausweis *m* **-e** *(Mitglieds~/Leser~/Studenten~ etc)* (membership/library/student *etc)* card; *(Personal~)* identity card; *(Berechtigungsnachweis)* pass. ~, **bitte** your papers please.

ausweisen *sep irreg* **1** *vt (aus Land)* to expel, to deport. **2** *vr* to identify oneself. **können Sie sich** ~? do you have any means of identification?

Ausweis-: ~**kontrolle** *f* identity check; ~**papiere** *pl* identity papers *pl.*

Ausweisung *f* expulsion, deportation.

ausweiten *sep* **1** *vt* to widen; *(fig)* to expand *(zu into).* **2** *vr* to widen; *(esp Dehnbares)* to stretch; *(fig) (Thema, Bewegung)* to expand *(zu into); (sich verbreiten)* to spread.

Ausweitung *f* widening; *(Ausdehnung)* stretching; *(fig)* expansion; *(Verbreitung)* spreading.

auswendig *adv* by heart, from memory. **etw** ~ **können/lernen** to know/learn sth (off) by heart.

auswerfen *vt sep irreg* **(a)** *Anker, Netz* to cast. **(b)** *(hinausschleudern) Lava, Asche* to throw out.

auswerten *vt sep (bewerten)* to evaluate; *(analysieren)* to analyse.

Auswertung *f siehe vt* evaluation; analysis.

auswickeln *vt sep Paket, Bonbon etc* to unwrap.

auswiegen *vt sep irreg* to weigh (out); *siehe* **ausgewogen.**

auswirken *vr sep* ~ to have an effect *(auf+acc on).* **sich negativ** ~ to have a negative effect.

Auswirkung *f (Folge)* consequence; *(Wirkung)* effect; *(Rückwirkung)* repercussion.

auswischen *vt sep* to wipe out. **jdm eins** ~ *(col)* to get one over on sb *(col); (aus Rache)* to get one's own back on sb.

auswringen *vt sep irreg* to wring out.

Auswuchs *m* **(a)** *(out)growth; (Mißbildung)* deformity. **(b)** *(fig) (Erzeugnis)* product; *(Mißstand, Übersteigerung)* excess.

auswuchten *vt sep Räder* to balance.

auszahlen *sep* **1** *vt Geld etc* to pay out; *Arbeiter, Gläubiger* to pay off. **2** *vr (sich lohnen)* to pay (off).

auszählen *sep* **1** *vt Stimmen* to count (up); *(Boxen)* to count out. **2** *vi (bei Kinderspielen)* to count out.

Auszählung *f (von Stimmen etc)* counting (up), count.

auszeichnen *sep* **1** *vt* **(a)** *(mit Preisschild versehen)* to price. **(b)** *(ehren)* to honour *(Brit),* to honor *(US).* **jdn mit einem Orden** ~ to decorate sb (with a medal); **jdn mit einem Preis/Titel** ~ to award a prize/title to sb. **(c)** *(hervorheben)* to distinguish (from all others); *(kennzeichnen)* to be a feature of. **2** *vr* to stand out *(durch due to).* **der Wagen zeichnet sich durch ... aus** one of the car's main features is ...; *siehe* **ausgezeichnet.**

Auszeichnung *f* **(a)** *no pl (das Auszeichnen) (von Waren)* pricing; *(mit Orden)* decoration. **(b)** *(Markierung: an Ware)* ticket. **(c)** *(Ehrung)* honour *(Brit),* honor *(US),* distinction; *(Orden)* decoration; *(Preis)* award, prize. **mit** ~ **bestehen** to pass with distinction.

ausziehbar adj extendible; Antenne telescopic.
ein ~er Tisch a pull-out table.
ausziehen sep irreg **1** vt **(a)** (herausziehen) to pull out; (verlängern auch) to extend. **(b)** Kleider to take off; jdn to undress. **2** vr (sich entkleiden) to undress, to take off one's clothes. **3** vi aux sein (aufbrechen, abreisen) to set out; (aus einer Wohnung) to move (aus out of).

Auszubildende(r) mf decl as adj trainee; (als Handwerker auch) apprentice.

Auszug m **(a)** (das Weggehen) departure; (aus der Wohnung) move. **(b)** (Ausschnitt) excerpt; (aus Buch auch) extract; (Konto~) statement.

autark adj self-sufficient (auch fig), autarkical (Econ).

authentisch adj authentic.

Auto nt **-s** car, automobile (esp US, dated). **~ fahren** (selbst) to drive (a car); (als Mitfahrer) to go by car; **mit dem ~ fahren** to go by car.

Autobahn f motorway (Brit), highway (US).

Autobahn-: **~ausfahrt** f motorway (Brit) or highway (US) exit; **~dreieck** nt motorway (Brit) or highway (US) junction; **~kreuz** nt motorway (Brit) or highway (US) intersection; **~raststätte** f motorway (Brit) or highway (US) services pl.

Auto-: **~batterie** f car battery; **~biographie** f autobiography; **~bus** m bus; (Reiseomnibus) coach (Brit), bus; **~diebstahl** m car theft; **~fähre** f car ferry; **~fahren** nt driving (a car); (als Mitfahrer) going by car; **~fahrer** m (car)driver; **~fahrt** f drive; **~friedhof** m (col) car dump.

autogen adj autogenous. **~es Training** (Psych) relaxation through self-hypnosis.

Autogramm nt **-e** autograph.

Autogramm-: **~jäger** m autograph hunter; **~stunde** f autograph(ing) session.

Auto-: **~industrie** f car or automobile industry; **~karte** f road map; **~kino** nt drive-in cinema; **~knacker** m (col) car thief; **~krat** m (wk) **-en, -en** autocrat; **~marke** f make (of car).

Automat m (wk) **-en, -en** (auch fig: Mensch) machine; (Verkaufs~) vending machine; (Spiel~) slot-machine.

Automatic, Automatik[1] m **-s** (Aut) automatic.

Automatik[2] f automatic mechanism (auch fig); (Gesamtanlage) automatic system.

automatisch adj automatic.

Automatisierung f automation.

Automechaniker m motor mechanic.

Automobil-: **~ausstellung** f motor (Brit) or auto (US) show; **~club** m automobile association.

Auto-: **a~nom** adj autonomous (auch fig); **~nomie** f autonomy (auch fig); **~nummer** f (car) number.

Autopsie f (Med) autopsy.

Autor m author.

Auto-: **~radio** nt car radio; **~reifen** m car tyre (Brit) or tire (US); **~reisezug** m ≃ motorail train; **~rennbahn** f motor-racing circuit; **~rennen** nt (motor) race.

Autorin f authoress.

autorisieren* vt to authorize.

autoritär adj authoritarian.

Autorität f authority.

Auto-: **~schlange** f queue (Brit) or line of cars; **~schlosser** m panel beater; **~schlosserei** f body shop; **~stop(p)** m (esp S Ger) hitch-hiking; **per ~stop(p) fahren** to hitch(-hike); **~unfall** m car accident; **~ verkehr** m motor traffic; **~verleih** m, **~vermietung** f car hire (Brit) or rental; (Firma) car hire (Brit) or rental firm; **~werkstatt** f garage, car repair shop (US); **~zoom** [-'zu:m] nt (Phot) automatic zoom (lens); **~zubehör** nt motor accessories pl.

avancieren* [avã'si:rən] vi aux sein (dated, geh) to advance (zu to).

Avant- [avã]: **~garde** f (geh) (Art) avant-garde; (Pol) vanguard; **a~gardistisch** adj avant-garde.

Avocado, Avocato [avo'ka:do, -to] f **-s** avocado.

Axiom nt **-e** axiom.

Axt f **-e** axe (Brit), ax (US). **die ~ im Haus erspart den Zimmermann** (Prov) self-help is the best help; **die ~ an etw/an die Wurzel einer Sache legen** (fig) to strike at the very roots of sth.

Azalee [-'le:ə] f **-n** (Bot) azalea.

Azoren pl (Geog) Azores pl.

Azteke m (wk) **-n, -n, Aztekin** f Aztec.

Azubi m **-s** (col) = **Auszubildende(r).**

azurblau adj azure.

B

B, b [beː] -, - B, b. **B-dur/b-Moll** (the key of) B flat major/minor.
Baby ['beːbi] *nt* -s baby.
Baby-: b~sitten *vi insep* to babysit; **~sitter(in** *f)* *m* - babysitter; **~speck** *m (col)* puppy fat.
Bach *m* ¨e *(lit, fig)* stream.
Bachstelze *f* -n wagtail.
Backblech *nt* baking tray.
Backbord *nt no pl (Naut)* port (side).
backbord(s) *adv (Naut)* on the port side.
Backe *f* -n **(a)** cheek. **mit vollen ~n kauen** to eat away heartily. **(b)** *(col: Hinter~)* buttock, cheek.
backen *vt* to bake; *Brot, Kuchen auch* to make; *(braten) Fisch, Eier etc* to fry. **frisch/knusprig gebackenes Brot** fresh/crusty bread; **gebackener Fisch** fried fish; *(im Ofen)* baked fish.
Backen-: ~bart *m* sideboards *pl*, sideburns *pl;* **~knochen** *m* cheekbone; **~zahn** *m* molar.
Bäcker *m* - baker.
Bäckerei *f* baker's *(Brit)*, baker *(US); (Backstube)* bakery.
Bäcker-: ~junge *m (Lehrling)* baker's apprentice; **~laden** *m* baker's *(Brit)*, baker *(US);* **~meister** *m* master baker.
Back-: b~fertig *adj* oven-ready; **~fett** *nt* cooking fat; **~fisch** *m* **(a)** fried fish; **(b)** *(dated)* teenager; **~form** *f* baking tin; **~obst** *nt* dried fruit; **~ofen** *m* oven *(auch fig);* **~pflaume** *f* prune; **~pulver** *nt* baking powder.
Backstein *m* brick.
Back-: ~stube *f* bakery; **~waren** *pl* bread, cakes and pastries *pl.*
Bad *nt* ¨er **(a)** *(Wannen~, Phot)* bath; *(das Baden)* bathing. **ein ~ nehmen** to have *or* take a bath. **(b)** *(im Meer)* bathe, swim; *(das Baden)* bathing, swimming. **(c)** *(Badezimmer)* bathroom. **Zimmer mit ~** room with (private) bath. **(d)** *(Schwimm~)* (swimming) pool *or* baths. **die städtischen ~er** the public baths. **(e)** *(Heil~)* spa; *(See~)* (seaside) resort.
Bade-: ~anstalt *f* (public) swimming baths *pl;* **~anzug** *m* swimming costume; **~gast** *m* **(a)** *(im Kurort)* spa visitor; **(b)** *(im Schwimmbad)* bather, swimmer; **~(hand)tuch** *nt* bath towel; **~hose** *f* swimming trunks *pl;* **~kappe** *f* swimming cap; **~mantel** *m* bathrobe, dressing gown *(Brit);* **~matte** *f* bathmat; **~meister** *m (im Schwimmbad)* (pool) attendant; *(am Strand)* lifeguard.
baden 1 *vi* **(a)** to have a bath. **(b)** *(im Meer, Schwimmbad etc)* to swim, to bathe. **~ gehen** to go swimming. **(c)** *(col)* **~ gehen** to come a cropper *(col);* **wenn das passiert, gehe ich ~** I'll be for it if that happens *(col).* **2** *vt* **(a)** *Kind etc* to bath. **(b)** *Augen, Wunde etc* to bathe.
Bade-: ~sachen *pl* swimming things *pl;* **~saison** *f* swimming season; *(in Kurort)* spa season; **~salz** *nt* bath salts *pl;* **~strand** *m* (bathing) beach; **~wanne** *f* bath(tub); **~wasser** *nt* bath water; **~zimmer** *nt* bathroom.
Bagage [ba'gaːʒə] *f no pl (dated col: Gesindel)* crowd *(col).*
Bagatelle *f* trifle, bagatelle.
Bagatellsache *f (Jur)* minor case.
Bagger *m* - excavator; *(für Schlamm)* dredger.
baggern *vti Graben* to excavate; *Fahrrinne* to dredge.

Baggersee *m artificial lake in gravel pit etc.*
Bahn *f* -en **(a)** *(lit, fig)* path; *(von Fluß)* course; *(Astron auch)* orbit. **jdm/einer Sache die ~ frei machen** *(fig)* to clear the way for sb/sth; **die ~ ist frei** *(fig)* the way is clear; **sich** *(dat)* **~ brechen** *(fig)* to make headway; *(Mensch)* to forge ahead; **in gewohnten ~en verlaufen** *(fig)* to continue as before; **von der rechten ~ abkommen** *(geh)* to stray from the straight and narrow; **jdn auf die rechte ~ bringen** *(fig)* to put sb on the straight and narrow; **jdn aus der ~ werfen** *(fig)* to shatter sb.
(b) *(Eisen~)* railway *(Brit)*, railroad *(US); (Straßen~)* tram, streetcar *(US); (Zug)* train; *(Verkehrsnetz, Verwaltung)* railway *(Brit) usu pl*, railroad *(US).* **mit der ~** by train *or* rail/tram; **frei ~** *(Comm)* carriage free to station of destination.
(c) *(Sport)* track; *(für Pferderennen auch)* course; *(in Schwimmbecken)* pool; *(für einzelne Teilnehmer)* lane.
(d) *(Stoff~, Tapeten~)* length, strip.
Bahn-: ~arbeiter *m* railwayman, railroad *(US);* **~beamte(r)** *m* railway *(Brit) or* railroad *(US)* official; **b~brechend** *adj* pioneering; **~brechendes leisten** to pioneer new developments; **~bus** *m* railway *(Brit) or* railroad *(US)* bus.
Bahndamm *m* (railway *(Brit) or* railroad *US)* embankment.
bahnen *vt* **jdm/einer Sache den/einen Weg ~** *(fig)* to pave the way for sb/sth; **sich** *(dat)* **einen Weg ~** to fight one's way through.
Bahn-: ~fahrt *f* rail journey; **~fracht** *f* rail freight.
Bahnhof *m* station. **am** *or* **auf dem ~** at the station; **~ Schöneberg** Schöneberg station; **ich verstehe nur ~** *(hum col)* it's all Greek to me *(col);* **er wurde mit großem ~ empfangen** he was given the red carpet treatment.
Bahnhofs- *in cpds* station; **~gaststätte** *f* station restaurant; **~halle** *f* (station) concourse; **~mission** *f* charitable organization for helping rail travellers in difficulties.
Bahn-: b~lagernd *adj (Comm)* to be collected from the station; **~linie** *f* railway *(Brit) or* railroad *(US)* line *or* track; **~polizei** *f* railway *(Brit) or* railroad *(US)* police; **~schranke** *f* level *(Brit) or* grade *(US)* crossing barrier; **~steig** *m* platform; **~steigkarte** *f* platform ticket; **~übergang** *m* level *(Brit) or* grade *(US)* crossing; **beschrankter/unbeschrankter ~übergang** crossing with gates/unguarded level crossing; **~wärter** *m* gatekeeper.
Bahre *f* -n *(Kranken~)* stretcher; *(Toten~)* bier.
Baiser [bɛ'zeː] *nt* -s meringue.
Baisse ['bɛːs(ə)] *f* -n *(St Ex)* fall; *(plötzliche)* slump.
Bajonett *nt* -e bayonet.
Bajuware *m (wk)* -n, -n, **Bajuwarin** *f (old, hum)* Bavarian.
Bake *f* -n *(Verkehrszeichen)* distance warning signal; *(an Autobahn auch)* countdown marker.
Bakterie [-riə] *f* -n *usu pl* germ. **~n** germs *pl*, bacteria *pl.*
bakteriell *adj* bacterial, bacteria *attr.*
Bakteriologe *m*, **Bakteriologin** *f* bacteriologist.

bakteriologisch *adj* bacteriological; *Krieg* biological.

Balance [ba'lã:s(ə)] *f* **-n** balance, equilibrium. **die** ~ **halten/verlieren** to keep/lose one's balance.

Balance|akt [ba'lã:s(ə)-] *m* (*lit,fig*) balancing act.

balancieren* [balã'si:rən] **1** *vi aux sein* to balance. **über etw** (*acc*) ~ to balance one's way across sth. **2** *vt* to balance.

bald 1 *adv, comp* **eher,** *superl* **am ehesten (a)** soon. **er kommt** ~ **he'll** be coming soon; ~ **darauf** soon afterwards; **nicht so** ~ not in the near future; **bis** ~! see you soon. **(b)** (*fast*) almost, nearly. **sie platzt** ~ **vor** Neugier she's just about dying with curiosity. **2** *conj* (*geh*) ~ **hier,** ~ **da** now here, now there; ~ **so,** ~ **so** now this way, now that.

baldig *adj attr, no comp* quick, speedy; *Antwort, Wiedersehen* early.

baldmöglichst *adv* as soon as possible.

Baldrian *m* **-e** valerian.

Baldriantropfen *pl* valerian (drops *pl*).

Balearen *pl* **die** ~ the Balearics *pl*.

Balg¹ *m* **=e (a)** (*Tierhaut*) pelt, skin. **(b)** (*Blase*~) bellows *pl*.

Balg² *m or nt* **=er** (*pej col: Kind*) brat (*pej col*).

balgen *vr* to scrap (*um* over).

Balgerei *f* scrap, tussle.

Balkan *m* (~*länder*) **der** ~ the Balkans *pl*; **auf dem** ~ in the Balkans.

Balken *m* **- (a)** (*Holz*~, *Schwebe*~) beam; (*Stütz*~) prop; (*Quer*~) joist, crossbeam. **lügen, daß sich die** ~ **biegen** (*col*) to tell a pack of lies. **(b)** (*Strich*) bar; (*Uniformstreifen*) stripe. **(c)** (*an Waage*) beam.

Balkon [bal'kɔŋ, bal'ko:n] *m* **-s** *or* **-e** balcony; (*Theat*) (dress) circle.

Balkon-: ~**möbel** *pl* garden furniture *sing;* ~**tür** *f* French window(s).

Ball¹ *m* **=e** ball. ~ **spielen** to play ball; **am** ~ **sein** (*lit*) to have the ball; **immer am** ~ **sein** (*fig*) to be on the ball; **am** ~ **bleiben** (*lit*) to keep (possession of) the ball; (*fig*) to stay on the ball; **bei jdm am** ~ **bleiben** (*fig*) to keep in with sb; **jdm den** ~ **zuspielen** (*lit*) to pass (the ball) to sb; **jdm/sich gegenseitig die** ~**e zuspielen** (*fig*) to feed sb/ each other lines.

Ball² *m* **=e** (*Tanzfest*) ball. **auf dem** ~ at the ball.

Ballade *f* ballad.

Ballast [*auch* -'-] *m* (*rare*) **-e** (*Naut, Aviat*) ballast; (*fig*) burden, encumbrance. ~ **abwerfen** (*lit*) to discharge ballast; (*fig*) to get rid of a burden.

Ballaststoffe *pl* (*Med*) roughage *sing.*

Ballen *m* **- (a)** bale; (*Kaffee*~) sack. **in** ~ **verpacken** to bale. **(b)** (*Anat: an Daumen, Zehen*) ball; (*an Pfote*) pad.

ballen *vt Faust* to clench; *siehe* **geballt.**

Ballerina *f, pl* **Ballerinen** ballerina.

ballern *vi* (*col*) to shoot, to fire.

Ballett *nt* **-e** ballet. **beim** ~ **sein** (*col*) to be a ballet dancer.

Ballettänzer(in *f*) *m* ballet dancer.

Ballführung *f* (*Sport*) ball control.

Ballistik *f no pl* ballistics *sing.*

ballistisch *adj* ballistic.

Ball-: ~**junge** *m* (*Tennis*) ball boy; ~**kleid** *nt* ball gown.

Ballon [ba'lɔŋ, ba'loːn] *m* **-s** *or* **-e** balloon.

Ball-: ~**saal** *m* ballroom; ~**spiel** *nt* ball game.

Ballung *f* concentration; (*von Truppen auch*) massing.

Ballungs-: ~**gebiet** *nt*, ~**raum** *m* conurbation; ~**zentrum** *nt* centre (*Brit*) *or* center (*US*) (of population, industry *etc*).

Balsam *m* **-e** balsam; (*fig*) balm.

balsamieren* *vt* = **einbalsamieren.**

Balte *m* (*wk*) **-n,** **-n, Baltin** *f* er/sie ist ~ he/she comes from the Baltic.

Baltikum *nt* **das** ~ the Baltic States *pl.*

baltisch *adj* Baltic *attr.*

Balz *f* **-en (a)** (*Paarungsspiel*) courtship display. **(b)** (*Paarungszeit*) mating season.

Balz-: ~**ruf** *m* mating call; ~**zeit** *f* mating season.

Bambus *m* **-ses** *or* **-, -se** bamboo.

Bambus-: ~**rohr** *nt* bamboo cane; ~**sprossen** *pl* bamboo shoots *pl.*

Bammel *m no pl* (*col*) **(einen)** ~ **vor jdm/etw haben** to be scared of sb/sth.

banal *adj* banal, trite.

banalisieren* *vt* to trivialize.

Banalität *f* banality.

Banane *f* **-n** banana.

Bananen-: ~**dampfer** *m* banana boat; ~**republik** *f* (*Pol pej*) banana republic; ~**schale** *f* banana skin; ~**stecker** *m* jack plug.

Banause *m* (*wk*) **-n, -n** (*pej*) peasant (*col*); (*Kultur*~ *auch*) philistine.

band *pret of* **binden.**

Band¹ *nt* **=er (a)** (*Seiden*~ *etc*) ribbon; (*Isolier*~, *Maß*~, *Ziel*~) tape; (*Haar*~, *Hut*~) band; (*Schürzen*~) string. **(b)** (*Ton*~) tape. **etw auf** ~ **aufnehmen** to tape *or* record sth. **(c)** (*Fließ*~) conveyor belt; (*als Einrichtung*) production line; (*Montage*~) assembly line. **am** ~ **arbeiten** to work on the production line; **am laufenden** ~ (*fig*) non-stop, continuously. **(d)** (*Rad*) **auf dem 44m-**~ on the 44m band. **(e)** (*Anat*) *usu pl* ligament.

Band² *nt* **-e** (*liter*) **das** ~ **der Freundschaft/Liebe** *etc* the bonds *or* ties of friendship/love *etc.*

Band³ *m* **=e** (*Buch*~) volume. **darüber könnte man** ~**e schreiben/erzählen** you could write a book about it; **das spricht** ~**e** that speaks volumes.

Band⁴ [bɛnt] *f* **-s** (*Mus*) band.

Bandage [-'daːʒə] *f* **-n** bandage. **mit harten** ~**n** (*fig col*) with no holds barred.

bandagieren* [-'ʒiːrən] *vt* to bandage (up).

Band-: ~**aufnahme** *f* tape-recording; ~**breite** *f* (*von Meinungen etc*) range.

Bande¹ *f* **-n** gang; (*col: Gruppe*) bunch (*col*).

Bande² *f* **-n** (*Sport*) (*von Eisbahn*) barrier; (*Billiard*) cushion.

Banden-: ~**chef** *m* (*col*), ~**führer** *m* gang-leader; ~**diebstahl** *m* (*Jur*) gang robbery.

Banderole *f* **-n** tax *or* revenue seal.

bändigen *vt* to control; (*zähmen*) to tame.

Bändigung *f no pl siehe vt* controlling; taming.

Bandit *m* (*wk*) **-en, -en** bandit; (*fig pej*) brigand.

Band-: ~**maß** *nt* tape measure; ~**nudeln** *pl* ribbon noodles *pl*; ~**scheibe** *f* (*Anat*) disc; ~**scheibenschaden** *m* slipped disc; ~**wurm** *m* tapeworm.

bang(e) *adj* (~*er*) (*ängstlich*) scared, frightened; **mir ist** ~**e vor ihm** I'm scared *or* frightened of him. **(b)** (*geh: beklommen*) uneasy (*um* about). **es wurde ihr** ~ **ums Herz** her heart sank.

Bange *f no pl* (*esp N Ger*) **nur keine** ~! (*col*) don't worry.

bangen *vi* (*geh*) **um jds Leben** *etc* ~ to fear for sb's life *etc.*

Banjo ['bɛndʒo, 'bandʒo] *nt* **-s** banjo.

Bank¹ *f* **=e (a)** bench; (*Kirchen*~) pew; (*Anklage*~) dock. **auf** *or* **in der ersten/letzten** ~ on the front/ back bench *etc*; (*alle*) **durch die** ~ (*col*) every single one; **etw auf die lange** ~ **schieben** (*col*) to put sth off. **(b)** (*Arbeitstisch*) (work) bench.

Bank² *f* **-en (a)** (*Comm*) bank. **Geld auf der** ~ **liegen haben** to have money in the bank; **bei der** ~ at the bank. **(b)** (*bei Glücksspielen*) bank. **(die)** ~ **halten** (*col*) to be banker; **die** ~ **sprengen** to break the bank.

Bank-: ~**angestellte(r)** *mf* bank employee; ~**anweisung** *f* banker's order; ~**direktor** *m* director of a/the bank; ~**einbruch** *m* bank raid.

Bankelsänger *m* ballad-singer, minstrel.

Bankett¹ *nt* **-e** (*an Straßen*) shoulder.

Bankett² *nt* **-e** (*Festessen*) banquet.

Bank-: ~**fach** *nt* (*Beruf*) banking **(b)** (*Schließ-*

fach) safe-deposit box; ~**geheimnis** *nt* confidentiality in banking; ~**geschäft** *nt no pl* (~*wesen*) banking world; ~**guthaben** *nt* bank balance; ~**halter** *m (bei Glücksspielen)* banker.
Bankier [-'kie:] *m* -**s** banker.
Bank-: ~**kaufmann** *m* (qualified) bank clerk; ~**konto** *nt* bank account; ~**leitzahl** *f* bank code number; ~**note** *f* banknote, bill *(US)*; ~**raub** *m* bank robbery; ~**räuber** *m* bank robber.
bankrott *adj (lit, fig)* bankrupt. ~ **gehen** to go bankrupt; **jdn** ~ **machen** to bankrupt sb.
Bankrott *m* -**e** *(lit, fig)* bankruptcy. ~ **machen** to go bankrupt; **den** ~ **anmelden** *or* **erklären** to declare oneself bankrupt.
Bankrott|erklärung *f* declaration of bankruptcy; *(fig)* sellout *(col)*.
Bank|überfall *m* bank raid.
Bann *m* -**e** **(a)** *no pl (geh)* spell. **im** ~ **eines Menschen/einer Sache stehen** *or* **sein** to be under sb's spell/the spell of sth; **sie zog** *or* **zwang ihn in ihren** ~ she cast her spell over him. **(b)** *(Hist: Kirchen~)* excommunication.
bannen *vt* **(a)** *(geh: bezaubern)* to bewitch, to entrance. **(wie) gebannt** fascinated; *(stärker)* spellbound. **(b)** *Geister* to exorcize; *Gefahr* to ward off.
Banner *nt* - *(geh)* banner.
Bannmeile *f* inviolable precincts *pl (of city, Parliament etc)*.
Bantamgewicht *nt* bantamweight.
Baptist(in *f) m* Baptist.
bar *adj no comp* **(a)** cash. ~**es Geld** cash; **eine Summe in** ~ a sum in cash; **(in)** ~ **bezahlen** to pay (in) cash; ~ **auf die Hand** cash on the nail; **etw für** ~**e Münze nehmen** *(fig)* to take sth at face value. **(b)** *attr Unsinn* absolute. **(c)** *pred+gen (liter)* ~ **aller Hoffnung** devoid of hope, completely without hope. **(d)** *(liter: bloß)* bare. ~**en Hauptes** bareheaded.
Bar *f* -**s** bar.
Bär *m (wk)* -**en, -en** bear. **stark wie ein** ~ *(col)* (as) strong as an ox; **der Große/Kleine** ~ *(Astron)* the Great/Little Bear, Ursa Major/Minor; **jdm einen** ~**en aufbinden** *(col)* to have sb on *(col)*.
Baracke *f* -**n** hut, shack; *(pej: kleines Haus)* hovel.
Barbar *(in f) m (wk)* -**en, -en** *(pej)* barbarian.
Barbarei *f (pej)* barbarity; *(no pl: Kulturlosigkeit)* barbarism.
barbarisch *adj* **(a)** *(pej)* barbaric, barbarous. **(b)** *(col: fürchterlich)* terrible.
bärbeißig *adj (col)* grouchy *(col)*, grumpy.
Bardame *f* barmaid.
Barde *m (wk)* -**n, -n** *(Liter)* bard; *(iro)* minstrel.
Bären-: ~**dienst** *m* **jdm einen** ~**dienst erweisen** to do sb a disservice; ~**hunger** *m (col)* **einen** ~**hunger haben** to be famished *(col)*; ~**jagd** *f* bear hunt/hunting; ~**kräfte** *pl* the strength of an ox; **b**~**stark** *adj* strapping, strong as an ox.
Barett *nt* -**e** *or* -**s** cap; *(für Richter etc)* biretta.
barfuß *adj pred* barefoot(ed). ~ **gehen** to go/walk barefoot(ed).
barfüßig *adj* barefooted.
barg *pret of* **bergen.**
Bar-: ~**geld** *nt* cash; **b**~**geldlos 1** *adj* cashless; **b**~**geldloser Zahlungsverkehr** non-cash *or* credit transactions *pl*; **2** *adv* without using cash; ~**hocker** *m* (bar) stool.
Bärin *f* (she-)bear.
Bariton [-tɔn] *m* -**e** [-'to:nə] baritone.
Barkasse *f* -**n** launch; *(Beiboot auch)* longboat.
Barkauf *m* cash purchase.
Barke *f* -**n** *(Naut)* skiff; *(liter)* barque *(liter)*.
Barkeeper ['ba:rki:pə] *m* - barman, bartender.
Barkredit *m* cash loan.
barmherzig *adj (liter, Rel)* merciful; *(mitfühlend)* compassionate.
Barmherzigkeit *f (liter, Rel)* mercy, mercifulness; *(Mitgefühl)* compassion.

barock *adj* baroque.
Barock *nt or m no pl* baroque.
Barock- *in cpds* baroque; ~**zeit** *f* baroque period.
Barometer *nt* - *(lit, fig)* barometer. **das** ~ **steht auf Sturm** *(fig)* things look stormy.
Baron(in *f) m* -**e** baron/baroness.
Barren *m* - **(a)** *(Metall~)* bar; *(esp Gold~)* ingot. **(b)** *(Sport)* parallel bars *pl*.
Barriere *f* -**n** *(lit, fig)* barrier.
Barrikade *f* barricade. **auf die** ~**n gehen** *(lit, fig)* to go to the barricades.
Barsch *m* -**e** perch.
barsch *adj* brusque, curt; *Befehl auch* peremptory. **jdn** ~ **anfahren** to snap at sb.
Barschaft *f no pl* **meine ganze** ~ **bestand aus 10 Mark** all I had on me was 10 marks.
Barscheck *m* uncrossed cheque *(Brit)* or check *(US)*.
barst *pret of* **bersten.**
Bart *m* -**e (a)** beard; *(Schnurr~)* moustache *(Brit)*, mustache *(US)*; *(von Katze, Robbe etc)* whiskers *pl*. **(b)** *(fig col)* **(sich dat) etw in den** ~ **murmeln** to mutter sth in one's beard *(col)*; **jdm um den** ~ **gehen** to butter sb up *(col)*; **der Witz hat einen** ~ that's a real oldie *(col)*. **(c)** *(Schlüssel~)* bit.
Barthaar *nt* facial hair; *(Bart auch)* beard.
bärtig *adj* bearded.
Bart-: **b**~**los** *adj* beardless; *(glattrasiert)* cleanshaven; ~**stoppeln** *pl* stubble *sing*; ~**wuchs** *m* beard; *(esp weiblicher)* facial hair *no indef art*; **er hat starken** ~**wuchs** he has a heavy growth of beard.
Bar-: ~**verkauf** *m* cash sales *pl*; ~**vermögen** *nt* liquid assets *pl*; ~**zahlung** *f* cash payment; **(Verkauf) nur gegen** ~**zahlung** cash (sales) only.
Basar *m* -**e** bazaar.
Base¹ *f* -**n** *(old, dial)* cousin.
Base² *f* -**n** *(Chem)* base.
Baseball ['be:sbɔ:l] *m no pl* baseball.
basieren* *vi* to be based *(auf +dat on)*.
Basilikum *nt no pl* basil.
Basis *f, pl* **Basen (a)** *(Archit, Mil, Math)* base. **(b)** *(fig)* basis. **auf breiter** ~ on a broad basis. **(c)** *(Pol, Sociol)* ~ **und Überbau** foundation and superstructure; **die** ~ *(col)* the grass roots.
Basis|arbeit *f (Pol)* groundwork.
Basisgruppe *f* action group.
Baske *m (wk)* -**n, -n, Baskin** *f* Basque.
Basken-: ~**land** *nt* Basque region; ~**mütze** *f* beret.
Basketball *m no pl* basketball.
baskisch *adj* Basque.
Baß *m* -**sse (a)** bass. **(b)** *(Instrument)* double bass.
Baßbariton *m* bass baritone.
Baßgeige *f (col)* (double) bass.
Bassin [ba'sɛ:] *nt* -**s** *(Schwimm~)* pool.
Bassist(in *f) m* **(a)** *(Sänger)* bass. **(b)** *(im Orchester etc)* (double) bass player.
Baß-: ~**schlüssel** *m* bass clef; ~**stimme** *f* bass (voice); *(Partie)* bass (part).
Bast *m (rare)* -**e** *(zum Binden, Flechten)* raffia.
basta *interj* **(und damit)** ~! (and) that's that.
Bastard *m* -**e (a)** *(pej)* bastard. **(b)** *(Tier)* cross.
Bastelei *f (col)* handicraft; *(pej)* botched job *(col)*.
basteln 1 *vi* **(a)** *(als Hobby)* to make things with one's hands. **sie kann gut** ~ she is good with her hands. **(b) an etw** *dat* ~ to make sth, to work on sth; *(an etw herumbasteln)* to tinker with sth; **mit Holz** *etc* ~ to make things out of wood *etc*. **2** *vt* to make; *Geräte etc auch* to build.
Bastion *f (lit, fig)* bastion.
Bastler(in *f) m* - *(von Modellen etc)* modeller; *(von Möbeln auch)* do-it-yourself enthusiast. **ein guter** ~ **sein** to be clever with one's hands.
bat *pret of* **bitten.**
Bataillon [batal'joːn] *nt* -**e** *(Mil, fig)* battalion.
Batik *f or m* -**en** batik.
Batist *m* -**e** batiste, cambric.

Batterie f (Elec, Mil) battery; (Reihe von Flaschen etc auch) row.

Batteriegerät nt battery-powered radio etc.

Batzen m - (col) ein ~ Geld a tidy sum (col).

Bau n (a) no pl (das Bauen) building, construction. im ~ under construction; der ~ des Hauses dauerte ein Jahr it took a year to build the house. (b) no pl (Auf~) structure; (von Satz, Apparat auch) construction; (Körper~) build. von kräftigem ~ sein to be powerfully built. (c) no pl (~stelle) building site. auf dem ~ arbeiten to work on a building site. (d) pl -ten (Gebäude) building. (e) pl -e (Erdhöhle) burrow, hole; (Biber~) lodge; (Fuchs~) den; (Dachs~) set(t). (f) no pl (Mil sl) guardhouse. 4 Tage ~ 4 days in the guardhouse.

Bau-: ~arbeiten pl building or construction work sing; (Straßen~) roadworks pl (Brit), roadwork sing (US); ~arbeiter m building or construction worker.

Bauch m, pl Bäuche (a) (von Mensch) stomach, belly (col); (Anat) abdomen; (Fett~) paunch. ihm tat der ~ weh he had stomach-ache; sich (dat) den ~ vollschlagen (col) to stuff oneself (col); sich (dat) (vor Lachen) den ~ halten (col) to split one's sides (laughing); einen ~ ansetzen or kriegen to get a paunch; mit etw auf den ~ fallen (col) to come a cropper with sth (col). (b) (Hohlraum: von Schiff etc) belly, bowels pl.

Bauch-: ~ansatz m beginning of a paunch; ~höhle f abdomen.

bauchig adj Gefäß bulbous.

Bauch-: ~laden m tray; ~landung f (col) (Aviat) belly landing; (bei Sprung ins Wasser) belly-flop; ~muskel m stomach muscle; ~nabel m navel, belly-button (col); ~redner m ventriloquist; ~schmerzen pl stomach-ache; ~speck m (Cook) belly of pork; ~speicheldrüse f pancreas; ~tanz m belly-dance/dancing; ~tänzerin f belly-dancer; ~weh nt stomach-ache.

bauen 1 vt (a) to build, to construct; (anfertigen auch) to make; Höhle to dig. seine Hoffnung auf jdn/etw ~ to build up one's hopes on sb/sth; die Betten ~ (esp Mil) to make the beds; siehe gebaut. (b) (col: verursachen) Unfall to cause. da hast du Mist gebaut (col) you really messed that up (col). (c) (col: machen, ablegen) Prüfung etc to pass. seinen Doktor ~ to get one's doctorate. 2 vi (a) to build. wir haben neu gebaut we built a new house; hier wird viel gebaut there is a lot of building going on around here. (b) (vertrauen) auf jdn/etw ~ to rely or count on sb/sth.

Bauer m (wk) -n, -n (a) (Landwirt) farmer; (als Vertreter einer Klasse) peasant; (pej) country bumpkin, yokel. die dümmsten ~n haben die dicksten Kartoffeln (prov col) fortune favours fools (prov). (b) (Chess) pawn; (Cards) jack.

Bäuerchen nt (baby-talk) burp. (ein) ~ machen to burp.

Bäuerin f farmer's wife; (Landwirtin) farmer; (als Vertreterin einer Klasse) peasant (woman).

bäuerlich adj rural; (ländlich) Fest, Sitten rustic, country affair.

Bauern-: ~brot nt coarse rye bread; ~dorf nt farming or country village; ~fängerei f (col) con (col); ~frühstück nt bacon and potato omelette (Brit) or omelet (US); ~haus nt farmhouse; ~hof m farm; ~kriege pl (Hist) Peasant War(s); ~regel f country saying; ~schläue f native cunning.

Bauersfrau f farmer's wife.

Bau-: b~fällig adj dilapidated; Decke, Gewölbe unsafe; ~firma f building contractor; ~genehmigung f planning and building permission; ~gerüst nt scaffolding; ~grube f excavation; ~handwerk nt building trade; ~handwerker m (trained) building worker; ~herr m client (for whom sth is being built); ~holz nt building timber; ~ingenieur m civil engineer.

Bauj. = Baujahr.

Bau-: ~jahr nt year of construction; (von Auto) year of manufacture; mein Auto ist ~jahr 80 my car is a 1980 model; ~kasten m construction kit; (mit Holzklötzen) box of bricks; ~klotz m, ~klötzchen nt (building) block; ~klötze(r) staunen (col) to gape (in astonishment); ~kolonne f gang of building workers or (bei Straßenbau) navvies; ~kosten pl building or construction costs pl; ~land nt building land; (für Stadtplanung) development area; b~lich adj structural; in gutem b~lichem Zustand structurally sound.

Baum m, pl Bäume tree. auf dem ~ in the tree; heute könnte ich ~e ausreißen I feel full of energy today.

Baum-: ~grenze f tree line; ~krone f treetop; b~lang adj ein b~langer Kerl (col) a beanpole (col); ~rinde f tree bark; ~schule f tree nursery; ~stamm m tree-trunk; ~stumpf m tree stump.

Baumwolle f cotton. ein Hemd aus ~ a cotton shirt.

Bau-: ~platz m site (for building); ~polizei f building control department; ~ruine f (col) unfinished building; ~satz m construction kit.

Bausch m, pl Bäusche or -e (Papier~, Wolle~) ball. in ~ und Bogen lock, stock and barrel.

bauschen 1 vr (Segel) to billow (out); (Bluse etc) to bunch (up). 2 vt Segel, Vorhänge to fill.

Bausparer m saver with a building society (Brit) or savings and loan association (US).

Bauspar-: ~kasse f building society (Brit), savings and loan association (US); ~vertrag m savings contract with a building society (Brit) or savings and loan association (US).

Bau-: ~stein m stone (for building); (fig: Bestandteil) constituent; ~stelle f building or construction site; (bei Straßenbau) roadworks pl (Brit), roadwork sing (US); (bei Gleisbau) railway (Brit) or railroad (US) construction site; ~stil m architectural style; ~stoff m building material; ~unternehmen nt (Firma) building contractor; ~unternehmer m building contractor, builder; ~weise f type of construction; (Stil) style; ~werk nt construction; (Gebäude auch) edifice, building; ~zaun m hoarding, fence; ~zeit f time taken for building or construction; die ~zeit betrug drei Jahre it took three years to build.

Bayer(in f) ['baiɐ, -ərɪn] m (wk) -n, -n Bavarian.

bay(e)risch ['bai(ə)rɪʃ] adj Bavarian.

Bayern ['baiɐn] nt Bavaria.

Bazillus m, pl Bazillen (a) bacillus, microbe; (Krankheitserreger auch) germ. (b) (fig) cancer, growth.

Bd., Bde = Band, Bände.

be|absichtigen* vti to intend. eine Reise ~ (form) to intend to go on a journey; das hatte ich nicht beabsichtigt I didn't intend that to happen; wie beabsichtigt as planned or intended.

be|achten* vt (a) (befolgen) to observe; Gebrauchsanweisung to follow. (b) (berücksichtigen) etw nicht ~ to take into consideration. (c) (Aufmerksamkeit schenken) jdn to notice, to pay attention to. jdn nicht ~ to ignore sb, to take no notice of sb.

be|achtenswert adj noteworthy, remarkable.

be|achtlich adj (beträchtlich) considerable; Erfolg notable. (b) (bedeutend) Ereignis significant; Leistung considerable, excellent. er hat im Leben/Beruf B~es geleistet he has achieved a considerable amount in life/his job.

Be|achtung f siehe vt (a) observance; following. unter ~ der Vorschriften in accordance with the rules. (b) consideration. (c) notice, attention (gen to). ~ finden to receive attention; jdm keine ~ schenken to take no notice of sb.

Be|amten-: ~apparat m bureaucracy; ~laufbahn f career in the civil service; die ~laufbahn einschlagen to enter the civil service; ~tum nt no pl civil service; ~verhältnis nt im ~verhält-

nis stehen to be a civil servant.
Be|amte(r) m decl as adj official; (Staats~) civil
servant; (Zoll~ auch, Polizei~) officer; (dated:
Büro~, Schalter~) clerk. **er ist ein typischer ~r**
he is a typical bureaucrat.
be|amtet adj (form) appointed on a permanent
basis (by the state).
Be|amtin f siehe **Beamte(r)**.
be|ängstigend adj alarming. **sein Zustand ist ~**
his condition is giving cause for concern.
be|anspruchen* vt (a) (fordern) to claim. **etw ~**
können to be entitled to sth. **(b)** (erfordern) to
take; Zeit, Platz auch to take up. **(c)** (ausnützen) to
use; jds Geduld to demand; jds Hilfe to ask for. **(d)**
(strapazieren) Maschine etc to use; jdn to keep
busy. **etw stark ~** to put sth under a lot of stress.
Be|anspruchung f **(a)** (Forderung) claim (gen to).
(b) (Ausnutzung: von jds Geduld etc) demand (gen
on). **(c)** (Belastung) use; (von Beruf) demands pl.
be|anstanden* vt to object to; Rechnung to
query; Ware to complain about. **er hat an allem
etwas zu ~** he complains about everything.
Be|anstandung f complaint (gen about).
be|antragen* vt to apply for (bei to); (Jur) Strafe
to demand, to ask for; (vorschlagen: in Debatte
etc) to move, to propose. **er beantragte, versetzt
zu werden** he applied for a transfer.
Be|antragung f siehe vt application (gen for);
demand (gen for); proposal.
be|antworten* vt to answer; Anfrage, Brief auch
to reply to; Gruß, Beleidigung auch to respond to.
Be|antwortung f siehe vt (gen to) answer; reply;
response.
be|arbeiten* vt **(a)** (behandeln) to work on; Stein,
Holz to work, to dress. **(b)** (sich befassen mit) to
deal with; Fall auch to handle; Bestellungen etc to
process. **(c)** (redigieren) to edit; (neu ~) to
revise; (umändern) Roman etc to adapt; Musik to
arrange. **(d)** (col: einreden auf) jdn to work on. **(e)**
Land to cultivate.
Be|arbeiter(in f) m siehe vt (c) editor; reviser;
adapter; arranger.
Be|arbeitung f siehe vt (c) working (on); dress-
ing. **(b)** dealing with; handling; processing. **die
~ meines Antrags hat lange gedauert** it took a
long time to deal with my claim. **(c)** editing;
revising; adapting; arranging; (bearbeitete Ausgabe etc) edition; revision; adaptation; arrangement. **neue ~** (von Film etc) new version; **die
deutsche ~** the German version. **(d)** (von Land)
cultivation.
Be|arbeitungsgebühr f handling fee.
be|argwöhnen* vt to be suspicious of.
Beat [bi:t] m no pl **(a)** (Musik) beat or pop music.
(b) (Rhythmus) beat.
be|atmen* vt to give artificial respiration to. **jdn
künstlich ~** to keep sb breathing artificially.
Be|atmung f künstliche **~** artificial respiration.
Beatmusik ['bi:t-] f beat or pop music.
be|aufsichtigen* vt to supervise; Kind to mind;
Prüfung to invigilate at.
Be|aufsichtigung f siehe vt supervision; mind-
ing; invigilation.
be|auftragen* vt **(a)** (heranziehen) **jdm mit etw
~** to give sb the job of doing sth; (geschäftlich) to
commission sb to do sth. **(b)** (anweisen) Unter-
gebenen etc to instruct.
Be|auftragte(r) mf decl as adj representative.
be|äugen* vt (col) to gaze or look at.
bebauen* vt **(a)** Grundstück to build on, to develop. **(b)** (Agr) to cultivate; Land to farm.
Bebauung f no pl **(a)** (Vorgang) building (gen on);
(von Gelände) development. **(b)** (Agr) cultivation; (von Land) farming.
beben vi to tremble.
Beben nt - trembling; (Erd~) earthquake.
bebildern* vt Buch, Vortrag to illustrate.
Becher m - cup; (esp Porzellan~, Ton~ auch)

mug; (Plastik~ auch) beaker.
bechern vi (hum col) to have a few (col).
Becken nt - **(a)** (Wasch~, Geol) basin;
(Abwasch~) sink; (Toiletten~) bowl, pan;
(Schwimm~) pool. **(b)** (Anat) pelvis. **ein breites
~** broad hips. **(c)** (Mus) cymbal.
Becken- (Anat, Med): ~**bruch** m fractured pelvis;
~**knochen** m hip-bone.
bedacht adj **(a)** (überlegt) cautious. **(b) darauf ~
sein, etw zu tun** to be concerned about doing sth.
Bedacht m no pl (geh) **mit ~** (vorsichtig) prudent-
ly, carefully; (absichtlich) deliberately; **ohne ~**
without thinking.
bedächtig adj Schritt, Sprache measured no adv,
deliberate; (besonnen) thoughtful.
bedanken* vr to say thank-you. **sich bei jdm (für
etw) ~** to thank sb (for sth); **ich bedanke mich
herzlich** thank you very much; **dafür können Sie
sich bei Herrn Weitz ~** (iro col) you can thank Mr
Weitz for that (iro); **dafür wird er sich ~** (iro)
he'll just love that (iro).
Bedarf m no pl **(a)** (Bedürfnis) need (an+dat for);
(~smenge) requirements pl. **bei ~** as required;
Dinge des täglichen ~s basic or everyday
necessities; **alles für den häuslichen ~** all
household requirements; **seinen ~ an Wein/
Lebensmitteln etc einkaufen** to buy the wine/
food etc one needs; **an etw** (dat) **~ haben** to need
sth, to be in need of sth. **(b)** (Comm: Nachfrage)
demand (an+dat for). **(je) nach ~** according to
demand; **den ~ übersteigen** to exceed demand;
über ~ in excess of demand.
Bedarfs-: ~**deckung** f satisfaction of the/sb's
needs; ~**fall** m (form) **im ~fall** if necessary;
(wenn gebraucht) as necessary or required; ~**haltestelle** f request stop (Brit), flag stop (US).
bedauerlich adj regrettable, unfortunate.
bedauerlicherweise adv regrettably, unfortunately.
bedauern* vt **(a)** etw to regret. **wir ~, Ihnen
mitteilen zu müssen, ...** we regret to have to
inform you ...; **(ich) bedau(e)re!** I'm sorry. **(b)**
(bemitleiden) jdn to feel sorry for. **er ist zu ~** he is
to be pitied.
Bedauern nt no pl regret. **(sehr) zu meinem ~**
(much) to my regret.
bedauernswert adj Mensch pitiful; Zustand deplorable.
bedecken* 1 vt to cover. 2 vr (Himmel) to become
overcast, to cloud over.
bedeckt adj **(a)** covered. **(b)** (bewölkt) overcast,
cloudy. **bei ~em Himmel** when the sky is overcast or cloudy.
bedenken* vt irreg **(a)** (überlegen) to consider, to
think about. **wenn man es recht bedenkt, ...** if
you think about it properly ... **(b)** (in Betracht
ziehen) Umstand, Folgen etc to consider. **das hättest du vorher ~ sollen** you should have thought
about that before; **ich gebe zu ~, daß ...** (geh) I
would ask you to consider that ... **(c)** (geh: beschenken) **jdn mit einem Geschenk ~** to give sb a
present; **jdn reich ~** to be generous to sb; **mit
etw bedacht werden** to receive sth.
Bedenken nt - (a) usu pl (Zweifel, Einwand) doubt,
reservation, misgiving. **moralische ~** moral
scruples; **~ haben** to have one's doubts (bei
about); **ihm kommen ~** he is having second
thoughts. **(b)** no pl (das Überlegen) consideration
(gen of). **nach langem ~** after much thought.
bedenkenlos adj **(a)** (ohne Zögern) unhesitating.
(b) (skrupellos) thoughtless.
Bedenkenlosigkeit f no pl **(a)** (Bereitwilligkeit)
readiness, promptness. **(b)** (Skrupellosigkeit) unscrupulousness.
bedenkenswert adj worth considering.
bedenklich adj **(a)** (zweifelhaft) dubious, questionable. **(b)** (besorgniserregend) serious. **(c)** (besorgt) apprehensive, anxious. **jdn ~ stimmen** to

make sb apprehensive.

Bedenkzeit f um ~ **bitten** to ask for time to think about it.

bedeuten* vt **(a)** to mean. **das hat nichts zu ~ it** doesn't mean anything; *(macht nichts aus)* it doesn't matter; **das bedeutet nichts Gutes** that means trouble; **Geld bedeutet mir nichts** money means nothing to me. **(b)** *(geh: einen Hinweis geben)* to indicate. **man bedeutete mir, daß ...** I was given to understand that ...

bedeutend 1 adj **(a)** *(wichtig) Persönlichkeit* important, eminent; *Leistung, Rolle* major. **(b)** *(groß) Summe, Erfolg* considerable. **2** adv *(beträchtlich)* considerably.

bedeutsam adj significant; *(vielsagend auch)* meaningful.

Bedeutsamkeit f siehe adj significance; meaningfulness.

Bedeutung f **(a)** *(Sinn, Wortsinn)* meaning. **(b)** *(Wichtigkeit)* importance, significance. **von ~ sein** to be of significance.

Bedeutungs-: ~**lehre** f *(Ling)* semantics **sing** **b~los** adj **(a)** *(unwichtig)* insignificant, unimportant; **(b)** *(nichts besagend)* meaningless; ~**losigkeit** f insignificance, unimportance; **zur** ~**losigkeit verurteilt sein** to be condemned to insignificance; **b~voll** adj = **bedeutsam.**

bedienen* **1** vt **(a)** to serve; *(Kellner auch)* to wait on. **werden Sie schon bedient?** are you being served?; **hier wird man gut bedient** the service is good here; **er läßt sich gern ~** he likes to be waited on; **damit sind Sie sehr gut bedient** that should serve you very well; **ich bin bedient!** *(col)* I've had enough. **(b)** *(handhaben) Maschine etc* to operate. **(c)** *(Cards)* **eine Farbe/Karo ~** to follow suit/to follow suit in diamonds. **2** vi **(a)** to serve. **(b)** *(Cards)* **du mußt ~** you must follow suit; **falsch ~** to fail to follow suit. **3** vr **(a) bitte ~ Sie sich** please help or serve yourself. **(b)** *(geh: gebrauchen)* **sich jds/einer Sache ~** to use sb/sth.

Bedienstete(r) mf decl as adj public employee.

Bedienung f **(a)** no pl *(in Restaurant etc)* service; *(von Maschinen)* operation. **die ~ der Kunden** serving the customers. **(b)** *(~sgeld)* service (charge). **(c)** *(~spersonal)* staff; *(Kellner etc)* waiter/waitress.

Bedienungs-: ~**anleitung** f operating instructions pl; ~**zuschlag** m service charge.

bedingen vt **(a)** *(bewirken)* to cause; *(notwendig machen)* to necessitate; *(bestimmen: auch Psych, Physiol)* to condition. **sich gegenseitig ~** to be mutually dependent. **(b)** *(voraussetzen, verlangen)* to call for, to demand.

bedingt adj **(a)** *(eingeschränkt)* limited; *Lob auch* qualified. **(nur)** ~ **gelten** to be (only) partially valid; ~ **tauglich** *(Mil)* fit for limited duties. **(b)** *(an Bedingung geknüpft) Straferlaß* conditional.

Bedingung f condition; *(Erfordernis)* requirement. **mit** or **unter der ~, daß ...** on condition that ...; **unter keiner ~** on no condition; **es zur ~ machen, daß ...** to make it a condition that ...; **zu günstigen ~en** *(Comm)* on favourable terms.

bedingungslos adj *Kapitulation* unconditional; *Hingabe, Gehorsam* unquestioning.

bedrängen* vt *Feind* to attack; *gegnerische Mannschaft, Schuldner* to put pressure on; *(belästigen)* to plague. **sich in einer bedrängten Lage befinden** to be in dire straits.

Bedrängnis f *(geh: seelisch)* distress, torment. **in ~ geraten** to get into difficulties.

bedrohen* vt to threaten; *Gesundheit* to endanger. **vom Tode/von Überschwemmung bedroht** in mortal danger/in danger of being flooded.

bedrohlich adj *(gefährlich)* dangerous, alarming; *(unheilverkündend)* ominous, menacing.

Bedrohung f threat *(gen* to). **in ständiger ~ leben** to live under a constant threat.

bedrucken* vt to print on. **bedruckter Stoff** print, printed fabric.

bedrücken* vt to depress. **was bedrückt dich?** what's getting you down?

bedrückend adj depressing.

bedrückt adj *(niedergeschlagen)* depressed, dejected; *Schweigen* oppressive.

Beduine m *(wk)* **-n, -n, Beduinin** f Bedouin.

bedürfen vi irreg+gen *(geh)* to need, to require. **es bedarf einiger Mühe** it needs or requires some effort; **ohne daß es eines Hinweises bedurft hätte, ...** without having to be asked ...

Bedürfnis nt need; *(no pl: form: Anliegen)* wish. **die ~se des täglichen Lebens** everyday needs; **ich hatte das dringende ~, das zu tun** I felt an urgent need to do it; **das ~ nach Schlaf haben** to be in need of sleep.

Bedürfnis-: ~**anstalt** f *(dated form, hum)* public convenience *(Brit)*, comfort station *(US)*; ~**befriedigung** f satisfaction of one's/sb's needs; **b~los** adj *Mensch etc* undemanding, modest in one's needs.

bedürftig adj *(hilfs~)* needy, in need. **die B~en** the needy pl.

Bedürftigkeit f no pl need.

Beefsteak ['bi:fste:k] nt steak. **deutsches ~** hamburger.

belehren* vt *(iro, geh)* to honour *(Brit)*, to honor *(US)*.

beleiden* vt *(beschwören) Aussage* to swear to.

beleilen* vr to hurry (up), to get a move on *(col)*.

Beleilung interj *(col)* get a move on *(col)*.

beleindrucken* vt to impress. **davon lasse ich mich nicht ~** I won't be impressed by that.

beleindruckend adj impressive.

beleinflußbar adj impressionable, suggestible. **er ist nur schwer ~** he is hard to influence.

beleinflussen* vt jdn to influence. **er ist leicht/schwer zu ~** he is easily influenced/hard to influence.

Beleinflussung f *(das Beeinflussen)* influencing; *(Einfluß)* influence *(durch* of).

beleinträchtigen* vt *(stören)* to spoil; *Konzentration auch* to disturb; *Rundfunkempfang* to interfere with; *(vermindern) Sehvermögen, Reaktionen, Leistung* to impair. **jdn in seiner Freiheit ~** to restrict sb's freedom.

Beleinträchtigung f siehe vt spoiling; disturbance; interference *(gen* with); impairment.

belenden* vt to end; *Arbeit, Studium etc* to finish, to complete. **eine vorzeitig ~** to cut sth short.

Belend(ig)ung f no pl ending; *(Ende)* end; *(Fertigstellung)* completion; *(Schluß)* conclusion.

belengen* vt *(fig)* to stifle, to inhibit. ~**de Kleidung** restricting clothing.

belengt adj cramped; *(fig)* stifled. ~ **wohnen** to live in cramped conditions.

Belengtheit f *(von Räumen)* cramped conditions pl.

belerben* vt jdn ~ to be sb's heir.

belerdigen* vt to bury.

Belerdigung f burial; *(~sfeier)* funeral. **auf der falschen ~ sein** *(hum)* to have come to the wrong place.

Belerdigungs- in cpds siehe auch **Bestattungs-** funeral; ~**feier** f funeral service.

Beere f -n berry; *(Wein~)* grape. ~**n sammeln** to go berry-picking.

Beeren-: ~**auslese** f wine made from specially selected grapes; ~**obst** nt soft fruit.

Beet nt -e *(Blumen~)* bed; *(Gemüse~)* patch.

befähigen* vt jdn zu etw sb to do sth) to enable; *(Ausbildung)* to qualify, to equip.

befähigt adj **(a)** *(durch Ausbildung)* qualified. **(b)** **zu etw ~ sein** to be capable of doing sth.

Befähigung f no pl **(a)** **die ~ zum Richteramt** the qualifications to become a judge. **(b)** *(Können, Eignung)* capability, ability *(zu etw* to do sth).

befahl *pret of* **befehlen.**

befahrbar *adj Straße* passable; *Seeweg, Fluß* navigable. ~ **sein** *(Straße)* to be open to traffic; **nicht** ~ **sein** *(Straße, Weg)* to be closed (to traffic); *(wegen Schnee etc auch)* to be impassable.

befahren[1]* *vt irreg* **(a)** *Straße, Weg* to use. **der Paß kann nur im Sommer** ~ **werden** the pass is only open to traffic in summer; **diese Straße wird stark/wenig** ~ this road is used a lot/isn't used much. **(b)** *(Schiff, Seemann)* to sail.

befahren[2] *adj* **eine viel** *or* **stark/wenig** ~**e Straße** a much/little used road.

Befahren *nt no pl* use *(gen of).*

Befall *m no pl* attack; *(mit Schädlingen)* infestation.

befallen[1]* *vt irreg* **(a)** *(geh: überkommen)* to overcome; *(Angst auch)* to grip; *(Fieber, Krankheit)* to strike. **(b)** *(angreifen, infizieren)* to affect; *(Schädlinge, Ungeziefer)* to infest.

befallen[2] *adj* affected *(von* by*)*; *(von Schädlingen)* infested *(von* with*).*

befangen *adj* **(a)** *Lächeln* bashful; *Schweigen* awkward. **(b)** *Richter* prejudiced, bias(s)ed.

Befangenheit *f no pl siehe adj* **(a)** bashfulness, awkwardness. **(b)** bias, prejudice; *(Jur)* interest.

befassen* **1** *vr* **sich** ~ **mit** to deal with; *mit Forschungsbereich* to work on; **sie hat keine Zeit, sich mit ihren Kindern zu** ~ she has no time for her children. **2** *vt (form)* **mit etw befaßt sein** to be dealing with sth.

Befehl *m* **-e (a)** *(Anordnung)* order, command *(an +acc* to, *von* from*)*; *(Comp)* command. **wir hatten den** ~, ...we had orders *or* were ordered to...; **auf seinen** ~ **(hin)** on his orders; **auf** ~ **handeln** to act under orders; **auf höheren** ~ on orders from above; **zu** ~, **Herr Hauptmann** *(Mil)* yes, sir; ~ **ausgeführt!** mission accomplished; ~ **ist** ~ orders are orders; **dein Wunsch ist mir** ~ *(hum)* your wish is my command. **(b)** *(Befehlsgewalt)* command. **den** ~ **haben** *or* **führen** to be in command *(über+acc of).*

befehlen *pret* **befahl,** *ptp* **befohlen 1** *vi* to order; *(Befehle erteilen)* to give orders; *(den Befehl haben)* to be in command *(über+acc of).* **er befahl, den Mann zu erschießen** he ordered the man to be shot. **2** *vt* to order. **du hast mir gar nichts zu** ~ I won't take orders from you; **wie Sie** ~ as you wish.

befehligen* *vt (Mil)* to command.

Befehls-: ~**empfänger** *m* ~**empfänger sein** to follow orders *(gen* from*)*; ~**form** *f (Gram)* imperative; **b**~**gemäß** *adj* as ordered; ~**gewalt** *f (Mil)* command; ~**gewalt haben** to be in command *(über+acc* over*)*; ~**haber** *m* - commander; ~**notstand** *m (Jur)* obligation to obey orders; ~**ton** *m* peremptory tone; ~**verweigerung** *f (Mil)* refusal to obey orders.

befestigen* *vt* **(a)** *(an+dat* to*) (anbringen)* to fasten; *Boot* to tie up. **etw durch Nähen/Kleben** *etc* ~ to sew/glue *etc* sth. **(b)** *(fest, haltbar machen) Böschung, Deich* to reinforce; *Fahrbahn, Straße* to make up. **(c)** *(Mil)* to fortify.

Befestigung *f* **(a)** *(das Befestigen)* fastening; *(das Festmachen auch)* securing; *(von Boot)* tying up. **(b)** *(das Haltbarmachen)* reinforcement. **(c)** *(Mil)* fortification.

Befestigungs|**anlage** *f* fortification.

befeuchten* *vt* to moisten; *Wäsche* to dampen.

befeuern* *vt* **(a)** *(beheizen)* to fuel. **(b)** *(lit, fig: mit Geschossen)* to bombard.

befinden* *irreg* **1** *vr* **(a)** *(sein)* to be; *(liegen auch)* to be situated; *(esp in Maschine, Körper etc auch)* to be located. **unter ihnen befanden sich einige, die** ... there were some amongst them who ... **(b)** *(form: sich fühlen)* to feel. **2** *vt (form: erachten)* to deem *(form)*, to find. **etw für nötig/gut** ~ to deem *or* find sth (to be) necessary/good; **jdn für schuldig** ~ to find sb guilty. **3** *vi (geh: entscheiden)* to

decide *(über+acc* about*).* **darüber hat der Arzt zu** ~ that is for the doctor to decide.

Befinden *nt no pl* **(a)** *(form: Gesundheitszustand)* (state of) health; *(eines Kranken)* condition. **(b)** *(geh: Meinung)* **nach meinem** ~ in my view.

befindlich *adj usu attr (form) Gebäude, Park* situated, located; *(in Behälter)* contained. **der an der Tür** ~**e Haken** the hook on the door; **das im Umbau** ~**e Hotel** the hotel which is being renovated.

beflaggen* *vt Häuser* to decorate with flags; *Schiff* to dress.

beflecken* *vt* **(a)** *(lit)* to stain. **er hat sich mit Blut befleckt** *(fig)* he has blood on his hands. **(b)** *(fig auch) Ruf, Ehre* to besmirch.

befleißigen* *vr (geh)* **sich einer Sache** *(gen)* ~ to cultivate sth; **sich** ~, **etw zu tun** to make a great effort to do sth.

beflissen *adj (geh) (bemüht)* zealous, keen; *(pej: unterwürfig)* obsequious.

Beflissenheit *f siehe adj* zeal, keenness; obsequiousness.

beflügeln* *vt (geh)* to inspire.

befohlen *ptp of* **befehlen.**

befolgen* *vt* to follow; *Vorschrift auch* to comply with.

Befolgung *f siehe vt* following *(gen* sth*)*; compliance *(gen* with*).*

befördern* *vt* **(a)** *Waren* to transport, to carry; *Personen* to carry. **etw mit der Post/per Bahn** ~ to send sth by post/rail. **(b)** **er wurde zum Major befördert** he was promoted to major.

Beförderung *f siehe vt* **(a)** transportation; carriage. **die** ~ **eines Briefes dauert 3 Tage** a letter takes 3 days (to arrive). **(b)** promotion.

Beförderungs-: ~**bedingungen** *pl* conditions *pl* of carriage; ~**mittel** *nt* means of transport.

befrachten* *vt (lit, fig)* to load.

befragen* *vt* **(a)** *(über+acc, zu* about*)* to question; *Zeugen auch* to examine. **auf B**~ when questioned. **(b)** *(um Stellungnahme bitten)* to consult *(über+acc, nach* about*).*

Befragte(r) *mf decl as adj* person asked; *(in Umfrage auch)* interviewee. **alle** ~**n** all those asked.

Befragung *f siehe vt* **(a)** questioning; examining. **(b)** consultation *(gen* with *or* of*).* **(c)** *(Umfrage)* survey.

befreien* **1** *vt* **(a)** *(frei machen)* to free, to set free. **jdn aus einer schwierigen Lage** ~ to rescue sb from a tricky situation. **(b)** *(freistellen) (von* from*)* to excuse; *(von Militärdienst, Steuern)* to exempt. **(c)** *(reinigen) (von* of*) (von Ungeziefer etc)* to rid; *(von Schnee, Eis)* to free. **2** *vr* **(a)** *(Volk, Land)* to free oneself; *(entkommen)* to escape *(von, aus* from*).* **(b)** *(erleichtern)* to rid oneself *(von* of*)*, to free oneself *(von* from*).*

Befreier(in *f)* *m* - liberator.

befreit *adj (erleichtert)* relieved.

Befreiung *f siehe vt* **(a)** freeing, setting free. **(b)** *(von etw)* excusing; exemption. **um** ~ **von etw bitten** to ask to be excused/exempted from sth. **(c)** ridding; freeing. **(d)** *(Erleichterung)* relief.

Befreiungs-: ~**bewegung** *f* liberation movement; ~**front** *f* liberation front; ~**kampf** *m* struggle for liberation; ~**krieg** *m* war of liberation; ~**versuch** *m* escape attempt.

befremden* *vt* to amaze. **es befremdete mich zu hören,** ... I was taken aback to hear ...

Befremden *nt no pl* amazement.

befremdet *adj* taken aback.

befreunden* *vr* to make *or* become friends *(fig: mit einem Gedanken etc)* to get used to.

befreundet *adj* **wir sind schon lange (miteinander)** ~ we have been friends for a long time; **gut** *or* **eng** ~ **sein** to be good *or* close friends; **ein** ~**er Staat** a friendly nation.

befriedigen* **1** *vt* to satisfy; *Gelüste auch* to gratify. **2** *vi* to be satisfactory. **3** *vr* **sich (selbst)**

~ to masturbate.

befriedigend adj satisfactory; Verhältnisse, Leistung, Antwort auch adequate; Gefühl satisfying.

Befriedigung f siehe vt satisfaction; gratification. **sexuelle** ~ sexual satisfaction.

befristen* vt to limit, to restrict (auf +acc to).

befristet adj Genehmigung, Visum restricted; Arbeitsverhältnis, Anstellung temporary. ~ **sein/auf zwei Jahre** ~ **sein** (Paß etc) to be valid for a limited period/for two years.

befruchten* vt (lit) Eizelle to fertilize; Blüte to pollinate; (fig: geistig anregen) to stimulate.

Befruchtung f siehe vt fertilization; pollination; stimulation. **künstliche** ~ artificial insemination.

Befugnis f (form) authority. **eine** ~ **erhalten/ erteilen** to receive/give authority.

befugt adj (form) ~ **sein(, etw zu tun)** to have the authority (to do sth).

Befund m -e results pl, findings pl. **ohne** ~ (Med) (results) negative.

befürchten* vt to fear. **es ist zu** ~, **daß** ... it is (to be) feared that ...; **das ist nicht zu** ~ there is no fear of that.

Befürchtung f fear usu pl. **die schlimmsten** ~**en haben** to fear the worst.

befürworten* vt to approve.

Befürworter(in f) m - supporter; (von Idee auch) advocate.

Befürwortung f approval.

begabt adj talented; (esp geistig, musisch auch) gifted. **für etw** ~ **sein** to be talented at sth.

Begabung f (Anlage) talent; (esp geistig, musisch auch) gift. **er hat** ~ **zum Lehrer** he has a gift for teaching; **mangelnde** ~ a lack of talent.

begann pret of **beginnen**.

begatten* (esp Zool) 1 vt to mate with. 2 vr to mate; (geh, hum) to copulate.

Begattung f (esp Zool) mating; (geh, hum) copulation.

begeben vr irreg (a) (geh) to go. **sich nach Hause** ~ to make one's way home; **sich auf eine Reise** ~ to go on a journey; **sich zu Bett/zur Ruhe** ~ to retire; **sich in ärztliche Behandlung** ~ to undergo medical treatment; **sich an die Arbeit** ~ to commence work; **sich in Gefahr** ~ to expose oneself to danger. **(b)** (old liter: geschehen) to come to pass (old liter).

Begebenheit f (geh) occurrence, event.

begegnen* vi aux sein+dat (a) (treffen) to meet. **sich** or **einander** (geh) ~ to meet. **(b)** (stoßen auf) to encounter. **(c)** (widerfahren) **es war mir schon einmal begegnet, daß** ... it had happened to me once already that ... **(d)** (geh: entgegentreten) einer Krankheit, der Not to combat; Angriff to resist; einer Gefahr, Schwierigkeiten to meet, to face. **man begegnete mir nur mit Spott** I only met with derision.

Begegnung f encounter; (Treffen auch) meeting; (Sport auch) match.

begehen* vt (a) (verüben) Verbrechen, Ehebruch to commit; Fehler to make. **einen Mord an jdm** ~ to murder sb; **eine Dummheit/Unvorsichtigkeit** ~ to do something stupid/careless; **an jdm ein Unrecht** ~ to wrong sb; **Verrat an jdm/etw** ~ to betray sb/sth. **(b)** (entlanggehen) Weg to use. **(c)** (geh: feiern) to celebrate.

begehren* vt (geh, old) to desire.

Begehren nt - (a) (geh: Verlangen) desire (nach for). **(b)** (old: Wunsch, Forderung) wish.

begehrenswert adj desirable.

begehrlich adj (geh) covetous.

begehrt adj much sought-after; Partner etc auch, Ferienziel popular; Posten auch desirable.

Begehung f (form: eines Verbrechens) committing.

begeistern* 1 vt to fill with enthusiasm. **er ist für nichts zu** ~ he's not interested in doing anything.

2 vr to get enthusiastic (an +dat, für about).

begeisternd adj inspiring; Rede auch stirring.

begeistert adj enthusiastic (von about).

Begeisterung f no pl enthusiasm (über +acc about, für for). **in** ~ **geraten** to become enthusiastic.

Begeisterungs-: b~fähig adj Publikum etc quick to show one's enthusiasm; **~fähigkeit** f capacity for enthusiasm; **~sturm** m storm of enthusiasm.

Begierde f -n (geh) desire (nach for); (Sehnsucht) longing, yearning. **vor** ~ **brennen, etw zu tun** to be longing to do sth.

begierig adj (voll Verlangen) hungry, greedy; (gespannt) eager, keen.

begießen* vt irreg (a) (mit Wasser) to pour water on; Blumen, Beet to water; (mit Fett) Braten etc to baste; siehe **begossen**. **(b)** (fig col) freudiges Ereignis etc to celebrate. **das muß begossen werden!** that calls for a drink!

Beginn m no pl beginning, start. **zu** ~ **at the** beginning.

beginnen pret **begann**, ptp **begonnen** vti to start, to begin. **mit der Arbeit** ~ to start or begin work; **es beginnt zu regnen** it's starting to rain; **eine** ~**de Erkältung** the beginnings of a cold.

beglaubigen* vt (a) Testament, Unterschrift to witness; Abschrift to authenticate; Echtheit, Übersetzung to certify. **(b)** Botschafter to accredit (bei to).

Beglaubigung f siehe vt (a) witnessing, authentication; certification. **(b)** accrediting.

begleichen* vt irreg (lit, fig) to settle. **mit Ihnen habe ich noch eine Rechnung zu** ~ (fig) I've a score to settle with you.

Begleichung f settlement.

Begleitbrief m covering letter.

begleiten* vt to accompany (auch Mus).

Begleiter(in f) m - (a) companion; (zum Schutz) escort. **(b)** (Mus) accompanist.

Begleit-: ~erscheinung f side-effect; **das ist eine ~erscheinung des Alters** it's a symptom of old age; **~musik** f accompaniment; (in Film etc) incidental music; **~papiere** pl (Comm) accompanying documents pl; **~schein** m dispatch note; **~schreiben** nt covering letter; (für Waren auch) advice note; **~umstände** pl attendant circumstances pl.

Begleitung f (a) no pl company. **in** ~ **seines Vaters** accompanied by his father; **ich bin in** ~ hier I'm with someone. **(b)** (Begleiter) companion; (zum Schutz) escort. **ohne** ~ unaccompanied. **(c)** (Mus: Begleitmusik) accompaniment.

beglücken* vt jdn ~ to make sb happy; **er hat uns gestern mit seinem Besuch beglückt** (iro) he honoured (Brit) or honored (US) us with a visit yesterday; **ein** ~**des Gefühl** a cheering feeling.

beglückwünschen* vt to congratulate.

begnadet adj gifted.

begnadigen* vt to pardon.

Begnadigung f pardon.

begnügen* vr sich damit ~, etw zu tun to be content or satisfied to do sth.

Begonie [-niə] f begonia.

begonnen ptp of **beginnen**.

begossen adj **er stand da wie ein** ~**er Pudel** (col) he looked so sheepish.

begraben* vt irreg (a, g) to bury. **dort möchte ich nicht** ~ **sein** (col) I wouldn't like to be stuck in that hole (col); **damit kannst du dich** ~ **lassen** (col) you can stuff that (col!). **(b)** (aufgeben) Hoffnung to abandon; (beenden) Streit etc to end.

Begräbnis nt burial; (~feier) funeral.

begradigen* vt to straighten.

Begradigung f straightening.

begreifbar adj conceivable.

begreifen* irreg 1 vti to understand. ~, **daß** ... (einsehen) to realize that ...; **es ist kaum zu** ~ it's quite incomprehensible; **schnell/langsam** ~ to be quick/slow on the uptake; *siehe* **begriffen. 2** *vr* to be understandable. **es begreift sich, daß …** it is understood that …

begreiflich *adj* understandable. **ich kann mich ihm nicht ~ machen** I can't make myself clear to him.

begreiflicherweise *adv* understandably.

begrenzen* *vt* **(a)** *(Grenze sein von)* to mark the boundary of; *Straße etc* to line. **(b)** *(beschränken)* to restrict, to limit *(auf+acc* to).

begrenzt *adj (beschränkt)* restricted, limited.

Begrenztheit *f no pl (von Möglichkeiten, Talent)* limited nature; *(von Menschen)* limitations *pl.*

Begrenzung *f* **(a)** *(das Begrenzen) (von Gebiet, Straße etc)* demarcation; *(von Geschwindigkeit, Redezeit)* restriction. **(b)** *(Grenze)* boundary.

Begriff *m* **-e (a)** concept; *(Terminus)* term. **etw in ~e fassen** to put sth into words; **sein Name ist mir ein/kein ~** his name means something/ doesn't mean anything to me. **(b)** *(Vorstellung, Eindruck)* idea. **sich** *(dat)* **einen ~ von etw machen** to imagine sth; **du machst dir keinen ~ (davon)** *(col)* you've no idea *(col);* **für meine ~e** in my opinion. **(c) im ~ sein, etw zu tun** to be on the point of doing sth, to be about to do sth. **(d) schwer von ~ sein** *(col)* to be slow on the uptake.

begriffen *adj* **ein noch in der Entwicklung ~er Plan** a plan still in the process of being developed.

begrifflich *adj* conceptual.

Begriffs-: ~bestimmung *f* definition; **b~stutzig** *adj (col)* dense *(col).*

begründen* *vt* **(a)** *(Gründe anführen für)* to give reasons for; *(rechtfertigend) Forderung, Ansicht* to justify; *Verhalten* to account for; *Verdacht, Behauptung* to substantiate. **etw näher ~** to give specific reasons for sth; *siehe* **begründet. (b)** *(beginnen, gründen)* to establish; *Geschäft etc auch* to found.

Begründer *m* founder.

begründet *adj* well-founded; *(berechtigt)* justified. **es besteht ~e Hoffnung, daß …** there is reason to hope that …; **sachlich ~** founded on fact.

Begründung *f* **(a)** grounds *pl (für, gen* for*).* **etwas zur** *or* **als ~ sagen** to say something in explanation. **(b)** *(Gründung)* establishment; *(von Geschäft etc auch)* foundation.

begrüßen* *vt* **(a)** to greet; *(als Gastgeber auch)* to welcome. **(b)** *Kritik, Entschluß etc* to welcome.

begrüßenswert *adj* welcome.

Begrüßung *f* greeting; *(der Gäste)* welcoming; *(Zeremonie)* welcome.

Begrüßungs- *in cpds* welcoming.

begucken* *vt (col)* to (have a) look at.

begünstigen* *vt (Brit),* to favor *(US); Wachstum, Handel* to encourage; *Pläne, Beziehungen* to further; *(Jur)* to aid and abet. **durch die Dunkelheit begünstigt** assisted by the darkness.

Begünstigung *f* **(a)** *(Jur)* aiding and abetting. **(b)** *(Bevorzugung)* preferential treatment. **(c)** *(Förderung)* favouring *(Brit),* favoring *(US); (von Wachstum, Handel)* encouragement; *(von Plänen, Beziehungen)* furthering.

begut|achten* *vt* to give expert advice about; *Kunstwerk* to examine; *Projekte, Leistung* to judge; *(col: ansehen)* to have a look at.

Begut|achtung *f* (expert) assessment.

begütert *adj (reich)* wealthy, affluent.

begütigend *adj Worte etc* soothing. **~ auf jdn einreden** to calm sb down.

behaart *adj* hairy. **dicht ~** (thickly) covered with hair.

Behaarung *f* hairs *pl (+gen, an+dat* on*).*

behäbig *adj Mensch* portly; *(phlegmatisch, geruhsam)* stolid; *(fig) Leben* comfortable; *Sprache, Ton* complacent.

behaftet *adj:* **mit etw ~ sein** *mit Krankheit etc* to

be afflicted with sth; *mit Fehlern* to be full of sth; *mit Makel* to be tainted with sth.

Behagen *nt no pl* contentment. **mit ~ essen** to eat with relish.

behagen* *vi* **etw behagt jdm** sth pleases sb.

behaglich *adj* cosy; *(bequem)* comfortable. **es sich** *(dat)* **~ machen** to make oneself comfortable.

Behaglichkeit *f no pl siehe adj* cosiness; comfortableness.

behalten *vt irreg* to keep; *(nicht vergessen)* to remember. **~ Sie (doch) Platz!** please don't get up!; **den Hut auf dem Kopf ~** to keep one's hat on; **im Gedächtnis/im Kopf ~** to remember; **ich habe seine Adresse nicht ~** I've forgotten his address; **etw für sich ~** to keep sth to oneself.

Behälter *m* - container.

behämmert *adj (col)* screwy *(col).*

behandeln* *vt* to treat; *Thema, Frage etc* to deal with; *(umgehen mit)* to handle. **er weiß, wie man Kinder/die Maschine ~ muß** he knows how to handle children/the machine; **der ~de Arzt** the doctor in attendance.

Behandlung *f* treatment. **wir sind jetzt bei der ~ dieses Themas** we are now dealing with this theme; **die schlechte ~ seiner Frau und Kinder** the maltreatment of his wife and children; **bei wem sind Sie in ~?** who's treating you?

Behandlungs-: b~bedürftig *adj* in need of treatment; **~kosten** *pl* cost *sing* of treatment; **~methode** *f* (method of) treatment; **~raum** *m* treatment room; **~weise** *f* treatment.

Behang *m* -̈e *(Vorhang)* curtain; *(Wand~)* hanging; *(Schmuck)* decorations *pl.*

behängen* *vt* to decorate; *Wände auch* to hang.

beharren *vi (hartnäckig sein)* to insist *(auf+dat* on*); (nicht aufgeben)* to persist *(bei, auf+dat* in*).*

Beharren *nt no pl siehe vi* insistence *(auf* on*);* persistence *(bei, auf* in*).*

beharrlich *adj (hartnäckig)* insistent; *(ausdauernd)* persistent. **~ fortfahren, etw zu tun** to persist in doing sth.

Beharrlichkeit *f siehe adj* insistence; persistence.

behauen* *vt Holz* to hew; *Stein* to cut; *(mit dem Meißel)* to carve.

behaupten* **1** *vt* **(a)** to claim, to maintain. **von jdm ~, daß …** to say (of sb) that … **(b)** *Stellung, Recht* to maintain. **2** *vr* to assert oneself; *(bei Diskussion)* to hold one's own *(gegenüber, gegen* against*).* **sich auf dem Markt ~** to establish itself/oneself on the market.

Behauptung *f* **(a)** claim; *(esp unerwiesene ~)* assertion. **(b)** *(Aufrechterhaltung)* assertion; *(von Stellung)* successful defence *(Brit)* or defense *(US).*

Behausung *f (geh, hum: Wohnung)* dwelling.

beheben* *vt irreg (beseitigen)* to remove; *Mißstände* to remedy; *Schaden* to repair; *Störung* to clear.

Behebung *f no pl siehe vt* removal; remedying; repairing; clearing.

beheimatet *adj (Mensch)* resident *(in+dat* in*); (Pflanzen, Tiere)* native *(in +dat* to*).*

beheizbar *adj* heatable; *Heckscheibe* heated.

beheizen* *vt* to heat.

Behelf *m* substitute; *(Notlösung)* makeshift.

behelfen* *vr irreg* to manage.

Behelfsheim *nt* temporary home.

behelfsmäßig *adj* makeshift.

behelligen* *vt* to bother.

behend(e) *adj (geh) (flink)* swift, quick; *(gewandt)* nimble, agile.

beherbergen* *vt (lit, fig)* to house; *Gäste* to accommodate; *Flüchtlinge* to give shelter to.

beherrschen* **1** *vt (a) (herrschen über)* to rule, to govern; *(fig: dominieren)* to dominate. **(b)** *(zügeln)* to control. **(c)** *Handwerk, Tricks* to master; *Fahrzeug, Situation* to have control of. **er**

beherrscht drei Sprachen/das Klavier he has a command of three languages/he's a skilled pianist. 2 *vr* to control oneself. **ich kann mich ~!** *(iro col)* not likely! *(col)*.

beherrscht *adj (fig)* self-controlled.

Beherrschung *f no pl* control; *(Selbst~)* self-control; *(des Markts)* domination; *(eines Fachs)* mastery. **die ~ verlieren** to lose one's temper.

beherzigen* *vt* to take to heart, to heed.

beherzt *adj (geh)* courageous, brave.

Beherztheit *f no pl (geh)* courage, bravery.

behilflich *adj* helpful. **jdm (bei etw) ~ sein** to help sb (with sth).

behindern* *vt* to hinder; *Sicht* to impede; *(bei Sport, im Verkehr)* to obstruct.

Behinderte(r) *mf decl as adj* handicapped person. **die ~n** the handicapped *pl*.

Behinderung *f* hindrance; *(im Sport, Verkehr)* obstruction; *(körperlich, Nachteil)* handicap.

Behörde *f* -n authority *usu pl*; *(Amtsgebäude)* office *usu pl*.

behördlich *adj* official. **~ genehmigt** officially approved.

behüten* *vt* to look after. **jdn vor etw** *(dat)* **~** to save *or* protect sb from sth; **(Gott) behüte!** *(col)* God forbid!; **behütet** *(Jugend etc)* sheltered.

behutsam *adj* cautious, careful; *(zart auch)* gentle. **man muß es ihr ~ beibringen** it will have to be broken to her gently.

Behutsamkeit *f no pl* care(fulness), cautiousness; *(Zartheit auch)* gentleness.

bei *prep+dat* **(a)** *(in der Nähe von)* near; *(zum Aufenthalt)* at, with; *(Tätigkeitsbereich angebend, in Institutionen)* at; *(in Werken)* in; *(jdn betreffend)* with; *(Teilnahme bezeichnend)* at; *(unter, zwischen Menge)* among. **die Schlacht ~ Leipzig** the battle of Leipzig; **dicht ~ dem Ort, wo ...** very near the place where ...; **der Wert liegt ~ tausend Mark** the value is around a thousand marks; **~ seinen Eltern wohnen** to live with one's parents; **ich war ~ meiner Tante** I was at my aunt's; **~ Müller** *(auf Briefen)* c/o Müller; **sie sind ~ uns eingeladen** they're invited to our house; **er ist** *or* **arbeitet ~ der Post** he works for the post office; **~m Militär** in the army; **~m Fleischer** at the butcher's *(Brit)*, at the butcher; **~ Collins erschienen** published by Collins; **das war ~ ihm der Fall** that was the case with him; **~ einer Hochzeit sein** to be at a wedding; **ich habe kein Geld ~ mir** I have no money on me.

(b) *(Zeitspanne: während)* during; *(Zeitpunkt)* (up)on, at. **~m letzten Gewitter** during the last storm; **~ meiner Ankunft** on my arrival; **~m Erscheinen der Königin** as the queen appeared ...; **ich habe ihm ~ der Arbeit geholfen** I helped him with the work; **~ der Arbeit when** I'm *etc* working; **~ dem Zugunglück** in the train crash; **er verliert ~m Kartenspiel immer** he always loses at cards.

(c) *(Zustand, Umstand bezeichnend)* in. **~ Kerzenlicht** by candlelight; **etw ~ einer Flasche Wein bereden** to discuss sth over a bottle of wine; **~ guter Gesundheit sein** to be in good health; **~ zehn Grad unter Null** when it's ten degrees below zero; **~ offenem Fenster schlafen** to sleep with the window open; **~ Feuer Scheibe einschlagen** in case of fire break glass; **~ Nebel und Glatteis** when there is fog and ice; **~ solcher Hitze/solchem Wind** in such heat/such a wind; **~ seinem Talent** with his talent; **~ aller Vorsicht** in spite of all one's caution; **~ Gott** by God.

beibehalten* *vt sep irreg* to keep; *Bräuche, Regelung auch* to retain; *Leitsatz, Richtung* to keep to; *Gewohnheit* to keep up.

Beibehaltung *f no pl siehe vt* keeping; retention; keeping to; keeping up.

Beiboot *nt (Naut)* dinghy.

beibringen *vt sep irreg* **(a)** *(unterweisen in)* to teach *(jdm etw sb sth)*. **(b)jdm etw ~** *(mitteilen)* to break sth to sb; *(zu verstehen geben)* to get sth across to sb. **(c)** *(zufügen) Wunde, Niederlage* to inflict *(jdm etw sth on sb)*. **(d)** *(herbeischaffen)* to produce; *Beweis, Geld etc* to furnish, to supply.

Beichte *f* -n confession. **zur ~ gehen** to go to confession.

beichten *vti (lit, fig)* to confess *(jdm etw sth to sb)*.

Beicht-: **~geheimnis** *nt* seal of the confessional; **~stuhl** *m* confessional; **~vater** *m* father confessor.

beide *pron* **(a)** *(adjektivisch) (ohne Artikel)* both; *(mit Artikel)* two. **alle ~n Teller** both plates; **seine ~n Brüder** both his brothers, his two brothers; **ihr ~(n)/euch ~** you two; **euch ~n herzlichen Dank** many thanks to both of you. **(b)** *(substantivisch) (ohne Artikel)* both (of them); *(mit Artikel)* two (of them). **alle ~** both (of them); **keiner/keines** *etc* **von ~n** neither of them; **ich habe ~ nicht gesehen** I haven't seen either of them. **(c)** **~s** both; **(alles) ~s ist erlaubt** both are permitted.

beidemal *adv* both times.

beider-: **~lei** *adj attr inv* both; **~lei Geschlechts** of both sexes; **~seitig** *adj (auf beiden Seiten)* on both sides; *(gegenseitig) Vertrag etc* bilateral; *Einverständnis etc* mutual; **~seits 1** *adv* on both sides; **2** *prep+gen* on both sides of.

beidhändig *adj* ambidextrous.

beidrehen *vi sep (Naut)* to heave to.

beidseitig *adj (auf beiden Seiten)* on both sides; *(gegenseitig)* mutual.

bei|einander *adv* together. **du hast sie nicht alle ~** *(col)* you can't be all there *(col)*.

bei|einander-: **~halten** *vt sep irreg* to keep together; **~sein** *vi sep irreg aux sein (col) (gesundheitlich)* to be in good shape *(col)*; *(geistig)* to be all there *(col)*.

Beifahrer *m (Aut)* (front-seat) passenger; *(beim Motorrad)* pillion passenger; *(berufsmäßiger Mitfahrer, Sport)* co-driver.

Beifahrersitz *m* passenger seat; *(auf Motorrad)* pillion.

Beifall *m no pl (Zustimmung)* approval; *(Händeklatschen)* applause; *(Zuruf)* cheering, cheers *pl*. **~ finden** to meet with approval; **~ spenden/klatschen** to applaud.

beifällig *adj* approving. **~e Worte** words of approval.

Beifalls-: **~ruf** *m* cheer; **~sturm** *m* storm of applause.

Beifilm *m* short.

beifügen *vt sep (mitschicken)* to enclose *(dat* with*)*.

Beigabe *f* addition. **unter ~ eines Löffels Senf** adding a spoonful of mustard.

beige [beːʃ, ˈbɛːʒə] *adj* beige.

beigeben *sep irreg* **1** *vt (zufügen)* to add *(dat* to*)*; *(mitgeben)* jdn to assign *(jdm* to sb*)*. **2** *vi:* **klein ~** *(col)* to give in.

Beigeschmack *m* taste; *(fig: von Worten)* flavour *(Brit)*, flavor *(US)*.

Beiheft *nt* supplement.

beiheften *vt sep* to append, to attach.

Beihilfe *f* **(a)** *(finanziell)* financial assistance *no indef art; (Zuschuß)* allowance; *(Studien~)* grant; *(Subvention)* subsidy. **(b) wegen ~ zum Mord** *(Jur)* because of being an accessory to the murder.

Beiklang *m (fig)* overtone *usu pl*.

beikommen *vi sep irreg aux sein* **jdm ~** *(zu fassen bekommen)* to get hold of sb; *(fertig werden mit)* to get the better of sb; **einer Sache** *(dat)* **~** *(bewältigen)* to deal with sth.

Beil *nt* -e axe *(Brit)*, ax *(US)*; *(kleiner)* hatchet; *(Fleischer~)* cleaver; *(Fall~)* blade (of a/the guillotine).

Beilage f -n (a) (Gedrucktes) insert; (Beiheft) supplement. (b) (das Beilegen) enclosure; (in Buch) insertion. (c) (Cook) side-dish.

beiläufig adj casual; Bemerkung auch passing attr. etw ~ erwähnen to mention sth in passing.

Beiläufigkeit f (von Bemerkung etc) casualness; (Nebensächlichkeit) triviality. ~en trivia pl.

beilegen vt sep (a) (hinzulegen) to insert (dat in); (einem Brief) to enclose (dat with, in). (b) (schlichten) to settle. (c) = **beimessen**.

Beilegung f siehe vt (a) insertion; enclosure. (b) settlement.

beileibe adv: das darf ~ nicht passieren that mustn't happen under any circumstances; ~ kein ... by no means a ..., certainly no ...

Beileid nt no pl condolences pl. jdm sein ~ aussprechen to offer sb one's condolences.

Beileids- in cpds of condolence; ~karte f sympathy or condolence card.

beiliegend adj enclosed. ~ senden wir Ihnen ... please find enclosed ...

beim = **bei dem**.

beimessen vt sep irreg jdm/einer Sache Bedeutung ~ to attach importance to sb/sth.

beimischen vt sep to add (dat to).

Bein nt -e leg. sich kaum auf den ~en halten können to be hardly able to stay on one's feet; er ist noch gut auf den ~en he's still sprightly; jdm ein ~ stellen (lit, fig) to trip sb up; jdm wieder auf die ~e helfen (lit, fig) to help sb back on his feet; auf den ~en sein (nicht krank) to be on one's feet; wir sollten uns auf die ~e machen (col) we ought to be making tracks (col); jdm ~e machen (col) (antreiben) to make sb get a move on (col); (wegjagen) to make sb clear off (col); die ~e in die Hand nehmen (col) to take to one's heels; sich (dat) die ~e in den Bauch stehen (col) to stand about until one is fit to drop; mit beiden ~en auf der Erde stehen (fig) to have both feet firmly on the ground; mit einem ~ im Grab/im Gefängnis stehen (fig) to have one foot in the grave/to be likely to end up in jail; auf eigenen ~en stehen (fig) to be able to stand on one's own two feet; auf einem ~ kann man nicht stehen! (fig col) you can't stop at one!; etw auf die ~e stellen (fig) to get sth off the ground.

beinah(e) adv almost, nearly.

Beiname m epithet; (Spitzname) nickname.

Beinbruch m fracture of the leg. das ist kein ~ (fig col) it could be worse (col).

be|inhalten vt to contain.

Bein-: ~kleid nt usu pl breeches pl (old, hum); ~schiene f (Sport) shin pad; (Med) splint.

beipflichten vi sep jdm/einer Sache (in etw dat) ~ to agree with sb/sth (on sth).

Beiprogramm nt supporting programme (Brit) or program (US).

Beirat m advisory council or committee.

be|irren* vt to disconcert. sich nicht in etw (dat) ~ lassen not to let oneself be shaken in sth; er läßt sich nicht ~ he won't be put off.

beisammen adv together.

beisammen-: pref together; ~haben vt sep irreg (col) Geld, Leute to have got together; seinen Verstand ~haben to have all one's wits about one; er hat (sie) nicht alle ~ he's not all there; ~sein vi sep irreg aux sein (fig) (körperlich) to be in good shape; (geistig) to be all there; B~sein nt get-together.

Beischlaf m (Jur) sexual intercourse.

Beisein nt presence. in/ohne jds ~ in sb's presence/without sb being present.

beiseite adv aside (auch Theat). Spaß ~! joking apart!; jdn/etw ~ schaffen to get rid of sb/sth.

beisetzen vt sep (beerdigen) to bury; Urne to install (in its resting place).

Beisetzung f funeral; (von Urne) installing in its resting place.

Beisitzer(in f) m - (Jur) assessor; (bei Prüfung) observer.

Beispiel nt -e example. zum ~ for example or instance; wie zum ~ such as; sich (dat) ein ~ an jdm/etw nehmen to take a leaf out of sb's book/to take sth as an example; mit gutem ~ vorangehen to set a good example.

beispiel-: ~haft adj exemplary; ~los adj unprecedented; (unerhört) outrageous.

beispielsweise adv for example or instance.

beißen pret biß, ptp gebissen 1 vti to bite; (brennen: Geschmack, Schmerzen) to sting. in den Apfel ~ to take a bite out of the apple; der Hund hat mich ins Bein gebissen the dog has bitten my leg or me in the leg; der Rauch beißt in den Augen the smoke makes your eyes sting; etwas/nichts zu ~ (col: essen) something/nothing to eat; an etw (dat) zu ~ haben (fig) to have sth to chew over. 2 vr (Farben) to clash.

beißend adj (lit, fig) biting; Bemerkung cutting; Geschmack, Geruch pungent, sharp; Schmerz gnawing; Ironie, Spott bitter.

Beißzange f (pair of) pincers or pliers.

Beistand m -e (a) no pl help, assistance; (moralisch) support; (von Priester) presence. jdm ~ leisten to give sb assistance/give sb one's support. (b) (Jur) legal adviser.

Beistands-: ~pakt, ~vertrag m mutual assistance agreement.

beistehen vi sep irreg jdm ~ to stand by sb.

Beistell- in cpds side; ~tisch m occasional table.

beisteuern vt sep to contribute.

beistimmen vi sep = **zustimmen**.

Beitrag m -e (a) (Anteil) contribution; (Aufsatz auch) article. einen ~ zu etw leisten to make a contribution to sth. (b) (Betrag) contribution; (Versicherungs~) premium; (Mitglieds~) fee.

beitragen vti sep irreg to contribute (zu to).

Beitrags-: b~frei adj non-contributory; b~pflichtig adj contributory; b~pflichtig sein (Mensch) to have to pay contributions; ~satz m membership rate.

beitreten vi sep irreg aux sein+dat to join; einem Pakt to enter into; einem Vertrag to accede to.

Beitritt m siehe **beitreten** joining (zu etw sth); entering into (zu etw sth); accession (zu to). seinen ~ erklären to become a member.

Beitritts|erklärung f confirmation of membership.

Beiwerk nt additions pl; (modisch) accessories pl.

beiwohnen vi sep +dat (geh: dabeisein) to be present at.

Beize f -n (Beizmittel) corrosive fluid; (Metall~) pickling solution; (Holz~) stain.

beizeiten adv in good time.

beizen vt to steep in corrosive fluid; (Metal) to pickle; Holz to stain.

Beizmittel nt = **Beize**.

bejahen* vti to answer in the affirmative; (gutheißen) to approve of.

bejahend adj positive; Antwort affirmative.

bejahrt adj elderly, advanced in years.

bejammern* vt to lament.

bejammernswert adj deplorable, lamentable; Mensch, Schicksal pitiable.

bejubeln* vt to cheer; Ereignis to rejoice at.

bekämpfen* vt to fight; (fig auch) to combat; Ungeziefer to control.

Bekämpfung f fight, battle (von, gen against); (von Ungeziefer) controlling. zur ~ der Terroristen to fight or combat the terrorists.

bekannt adj (a) well-known (wegen for); Mensch auch famous. ~eren Spieler the better-known players; sie ist mir ~ I know her; es ist allgemein ~, daß... it is common knowledge that ... (b) (nicht fremd) familiar. jdn mit etw ~ machen to familiarize sb with sth; jdn (mit jdm) ~ machen to introduce sb (to sb); wir sind mit-

einander ~ we already know each other.
Bekanntenkreis m circle of acquaintances.
Bekannte(r) mf decl as adj friend; (entfernter ~) acquaintance.
Bekanntgabe f announcement.
bekanntgeben vt sep irreg to announce.
Bekanntheit f **wegen seiner** ~ because of his being well-known.
Bekanntheitsgrad m degree of fame.
bekanntlich adv ~ **gibt es …** it is known that there are …; **er hat** ~ **eine Schwäche für Frauen** he is known to have a weakness for women.
bekanntmachen vt sep to announce; (der Allgemeinheit mitteilen) to publicize; siehe **bekannt** (b).
Bekanntmachung f (a) siehe vt announcement; publicizing. (b) (Anschlag etc) announcement.
Bekanntschaft f acquaintance; (mit Materie, Gebiet) knowledge (mit of). **jds** ~ **machen** to make sb's aquaintance; **mit etw** ~ **machen** to come into contact with sth; **meine ganze** ~ (col) all my friends.
bekanntwerden vi sep irreg aux sein to become known; (Geheimnis) to leak out.
bekehren* vt to convert (zu to).
Bekehrung f conversion.
bekennen irreg 1 vt to confess, to admit; Sünde to confess. 2 vr **sich (für) schuldig** ~ to admit or confess one's guilt; **sich als …** ~ to declare oneself to be a …; **sich zu einem Glauben** ~ to profess a faith; **sich zu jdm/etw** ~ to declare one's support for sb/sth.
Bekenntnis nt (a) confession (zu of). **sein** ~ **zum Sozialismus** his declared belief in socialism; **ein** ~ **zur Demokratie ablegen** to declare one's belief in democracy. (b) (Rel: Konfession) denomination.
Bekenntnis-: ~**freiheit** f freedom of religious belief; ~**schule** f denominational school.
beklagen* 1 vt to lament; Tod, Verlust to mourn. **Menschenleben sind nicht zu** ~ there are no casualties. 2 vr to complain (über +acc, wegen about). **sich bei jdm** ~ to complain to sb; **ich kann mich nicht** ~ I can't complain.
beklagenswert adj Mensch pitiful; Zustand lamentable, deplorable; Unfall terrible.
Beklagte(r) mf decl as adj (Jur) defendant.
beklatschen* vt (applaudieren) to clap.
bekleben* vt **etw mit Papier/Plakaten** etc ~ to stick paper/posters etc on sth.
bekleckern* (col) 1 vt to stain. 2 vr **sich mit Saft** etc ~ to spill juice etc all over oneself; **er hat sich nicht gerade mit Ruhm bekleckert** (iro) he didn't exactly cover himself with glory.
bekleiden* vt (geh) (a) (anziehen) to dress (mit in). (b) Amt etc to occupy, to hold.
Bekleidung f (a) clothes pl, clothing; (Aufmachung) dress. (b) (form: eines Amtes) tenure.
beklemmend adj oppressive.
Beklemmung f usu pl feeling of oppressiveness; (Gefühl der Angst) feeling of apprehension.
beklommen adj apprehensive, anxious.
bekloppt adj (col) crazy (col).
beknackt adj (col) lousy (col).
beknien* vt (col) jdn to beg.
bekommen irreg 1 vt (a) to get; Geschenk, Brief, Lob, Belohnung auch to receive; Zug, Krankheit auch to catch; gutes Essen, Schlaganfall, ein Kind, Besuch to have; Spritze, Tadel auch to be given. **wir** ~ **anderes Wetter** the weather is changing; **wir** ~ **Regen/Schnee** we're going to have or get rain/snow; **einen Stein/Ball an den Kopf** ~ to be hit on the head by a stone/ball; **kann ich das schriftlich** ~? can I have that in writing?; **ich bekomme bitte ein Glas Wein** I'll have a glass of wine, please; **was** ~ **Sie dafür/von mir**? how much is that/how much do I owe you?; **er bekam es einfach nicht über sich, …** he just could not

bring himself to …
(b) **Flecken/Risse** ~ to get or become spotty/cracked, to develop spots/cracks; **Heimweh** ~ to get or become homesick; **graue Haare/eine Glatze** ~ to go grey/bald; **Hunger/Durst/Angst** ~ to get or become hungry/thirsty/afraid.
(c) **etw zu sehen** ~ to get to see sth; **das bekommt man hier nicht zu kaufen** you can't buy that here; **es mit jdm zu tun** ~ to get into trouble with sb; **wenn ich ihn zu fassen bekomme …** if I get my hands on him …; **etw gemacht** ~ to get or have sth done; **seine Arbeit fertig** ~ to get one's work finished.
2 vi aux sein+dat (zuträglich sein) **jdm (gut)** ~ to do sb good; **das Essen ist mir gut** ~ I enjoyed the meal; **jdm nicht or schlecht** ~ not to do sb any good; (Essen) not to agree with sb; **wie bekommt ihm die Ehe**? how is he enjoying married life?; **wohl bekomm's!** your health!
bekömmlich adj Mahlzeit, Speisen (easily) digestible; Klima beneficial. **schwer** ~ **sein** to be difficult to digest.
beköstigen* vt to cater for.
Beköstigung f catering (gen for); (Kost) food.
bekräftigen* vt to confirm; Vorschlag to back up. **etw nochmals** ~ to reaffirm sth.
Bekräftigung f confirmation. **zur** ~ **seiner Worte** to reinforce his words.
bekreuzigen* vr to cross oneself.
bekritteln* vt to find fault with.
bekümmern* vt to worry.
bekümmert adj worried (über +acc about).
bekunden* vt to show, to express. ~, **daß …** (Jur) to testify that …
Bekundung f expression, manifestation; (Jur) testimony.
belächeln* vt to smile at.
belachen* vt to laugh at.
beladen* irreg 1 vt to load; (fig: mit Sorgen etc) to burden. 2 vr (mit Gepäck etc) to load oneself up. **sich mit Verantwortung** ~ to take on responsibilities. 3 adj loaded; (fig: Mensch) burdened.
Belag m ̈-e coating; (Schicht) layer; (auf Pizza, Brot) topping; (auf Tortenboden, zwischen Brotscheiben) filling; (auf Zahn) plaque; (Zungen~) fur; (Fußboden~) covering; (Straßen~) surface.
Belagerer m - besieger.
belagern* vt (Mil, fig) to besiege.
Belagerung f siege.
Belagerungszustand m state of siege.
Belang m -e (a) (no pl: Wichtigkeit) **von/ohne** ~ (für jdn/etw) sein to be of importance/of no importance (to sb/sth). (b) ~e pl interests.
belangen* vt (Jur) to prosecute (wegen for); (wegen Beleidigung, Verleumdung) to sue.
belanglos adj inconsequential, trivial. **das ist für das Ergebnis** ~ that is irrelevant to the result.
Belanglosigkeit f (a) no pl inconsequentiality, triviality. (b) (Bemerkung) triviality.
belassen* vt irreg to leave. **wir wollen es dabei** ~ let's leave it at that.
belastbar adj (a) **bis zu 500 kg** ~ **sein** to have a maximum load of 500 kg. (b) (fig) Mensch resilient. (c) **wie hoch ist mein Konto** ~? what is the limit on my account?; **der Etat ist nicht unbegrenzt** ~ the budget is not unlimited.
Belastbarkeit f (a) (von Brücke, Aufzug) load-bearing capacity. (b) (von Menschen, Nerven) ability to take stress. (c) (von Stromnetz etc) maximum capacity; (von Menschen, Organ) maximum resilience.
belasten* 1 vt (a) (lit) **etw mit 50 Tonnen** ~ to put a 50 ton load on sth; **die Brücke/das Fahrzeug zu sehr** ~ to put too great a load on the bridge/to overload the vehicle. (b) (fig) **jdn mit etw** ~ **mit Arbeit** to load sb with sth; **mit Verantwortung, Sorgen** to burden sb with sth; **von Sorgen belastet** weighed down with cares. (c) (beanspruchen)

Stromnetz, Leitung to put a load on; *Atmosphäre* to pollute; *(Med) Körper, Menschen* to put a strain on, to strain. **jdn/etw zu sehr** *or* **stark** ~ to overstrain sb/sth. **(d)** *(Jur) Angeklagten* to incriminate. **(e)** *(Fin) Konto* to debit. **steuerlich belastet** taxed; **etw (mit einer Hypothek)** ~ to mortgage sth; **jdn mit den Kosten** ~ to charge the costs to sb. **2** *vr* **(a) sich mit etw** ~ to take sth on; *mit Sorgen* to burden oneself with sth. **(b)** *(Jur)* to incriminate oneself.

belästigen* *vt* to bother; *(zudringlich werden)* to pester; *(körperlich)* to molest.

Belästigung *f* annoyance; *(durch Lärm etc)* irritation; *(Zudringlichkeit auch)* pestering; *(körperlich)* molesting. **etw als eine ~ empfinden** to find sth annoying.

Belastung *f* **(a)** *(Last)* weight; *(von Fahrzeug etc)* load; *(fig: Bürde)* burden. **(b)** *(von Nerven, Körper)* strain *(gen* on*)*; *(von Umwelt)* pollution *(gen* of*)*; *(von Stromnetz)* load *(gen* on*)*. **(c)** *(Jur)* incrimination. **(d)** *(Fin) (von Etat, steuerlich)* burden *(gen* on*)*; *(mit Hypothek)* mortgage *(gen* on*)*.

Belastungs-: ~**material** *nt (Jur)* incriminating evidence; ~**probe** *f* endurance test; ~**zeuge** *m (Jur)* witness for the prosecution.

belaubt *adj* **dicht** ~ **sein** to have thick foliage.

belaufen* *vr irreg* **sich auf etw** *(acc)* ~ to amount to sth.

belauschen* *vt* to eavesdrop on.

beleben* **1** *vt* **(a)** *(anregen)* to liven up; *(neu* ~*)* to revive; *Konjunktur, jds Hoffnungen* to stimulate. **(b)** *(zum Leben erwecken)* to bring to life. **2** *vr* *(Konjunktur)* to be stimulated; *(Augen, Gesicht)* to light up; *(Natur, Stadt)* to come to life. **3** *vi* **das belebt** it livens you up.

belebend *adj* invigorating.

belebt *adj* **Straße** *etc* busy.

Belebung *f* revival; *(der Konjunktur)* stimulation.

Beleg *m* **-e (a)** *(Beweis)* piece of evidence; *(Quellennachweis)* reference. **(b)** *(Quittung)* receipt.

belegbar *adj* verifiable.

belegen* *vt* **(a)** *(bedecken)* to cover; *Brote, Tortenboden* to fill. **etw mit Fliesen/Teppich** ~ to tile/carpet sth; *siehe* **belegt. (b)** *(besetzen) Wohnung, Hotelbett* to occupy; *(reservieren)* to reserve; *(Univ) Fach* to take; *Vorlesung* to enrol for. **den fünften Platz** ~ to come fifth. **(c)** *(beweisen)* to verify. **mit Beispielen** ~ to illustrate.

Belegschaft *f (Beschäftigte)* staff; *(esp in Fabriken etc)* workforce.

belegt *adj* **Zunge** furred; *Stimme* hoarse; *Zimmer* occupied. **~e Brote** open sandwiches.

belehren* *vt (unterweisen)* to teach, to instruct; *(aufklären)* to inform *(über +acc* of*)*. **jdn eines anderen/Besseren** ~ to teach sb otherwise; **er ist nicht zu** ~ he won't be told; **ich bin belehrt!** I've learned my lesson.

Belehrung *f* explanation, lecture *(col)*; *(Anweisung)* instruction *(über+acc* about*)*; *(von Zeugen, Angeklagten)* caution.

beleibt *adj* stout, portly.

beleidigen* *vt jdn* to insult; *(Verhalten, Anblick)* to offend; *(Jur) (mündlich)* to slander; *(schriftlich)* to libel.

beleidigt *adj* insulted; *(gekränkt)* offended. ~ **wegkehen** to go in a huff *(col)*; **die** ~**e Leberwurst spielen** *(col)* to be in a huff *(col)*; **bist du jetzt** ~**?** have I offended you?

Beleidigung *f* insult; *(Jur) (mündliche)* slander; *(schriftliche)* libel. **etw als** ~ **auffassen** to take offence at sth.

beleihen* *vt irreg (Comm)* to lend money on.

belemmert *adj (col) (betreten)* sheepish; *(niedergeschlagen)* miserable; *(scheußlich)* lousy *(col)*.

belesen *adj* well-read.

Belesenheit *f* wide reading.

beleuchten* *vt* to light up, to illuminate; *Straße, Bühne etc* to light.

Beleuchter(in *f)* *m* - lighting technician.

Beleuchtung *f* **(a)** lighting; *(fig)* examination. **(b)** *(Licht)* light; *(Lichter)* lights *pl*.

beleumdet, beleumundet *adj* **gut/schlecht** ~ **sein** to have a good/bad reputation.

Belgien [-iən] *nt* Belgium.

Belgier(in *f)* [-iɐ, -iərɪn] *m* - Belgian.

belgisch *adj* Belgian.

belichten* *vt (Phot)* to expose.

Belichtung *f (Phot)* exposure.

Belichtungs-: ~**messer** *m* light meter; ~**zeit** *f* exposure (time).

belieben *nt no pl* **nach** ~ just as you/they *etc* like.

belieben* **1** *vi impers (geh)* **wie es Ihnen beliebt** as you wish. **2** *vt* **er beliebt zu scherzen** *(iro)* he must be joking.

beliebig **1** *adj* any. **eine/jede** ~**e Farbe** any colour at all, any colour you like; **in** ~**er Reihenfolge** in any order whatever; **die Auswahl ist** ~ the choice is free. **2** *adv* as you *etc* like. **Sie können** ~ **lange bleiben** you can stay as long as you like.

beliebt *adj* popular *(bei* with*)*.

Beliebtheit *f* popularity.

bellen *vi* to bark.

bellend *adj* **Husten** hacking; *Stimme* gruff.

Belletristik *f* fiction and poetry.

belobigen* *vt (form)* to commend.

belohnen* *vt* to reward.

Belohnung *f* reward; *(das Belohnen)* rewarding. **zur** *or* **als** ~ **(für)** as a reward (for).

belüften* *vt* to ventilate.

Belüftung *f* ventilation.

belügen* *vt* to lie to. **sich selbst** ~ to deceive oneself.

belustigen* **1** *vt* to amuse. **2** *vr (geh)* **sich über jdn/etw** ~ to make fun of sb/sth.

belustigt **1** *adj* amused. **2** *adv* in amusement.

bemächtigen* *vr (geh)* **sich eines Menschen** ~ to seize hold of sb; *(Gefühl, Gedanke)* to come over sb.

bemalen* **1** *vt* to paint. **2** *vr (pej: schminken)* to put on one's war paint *(col)*.

Bemalung *f* painting.

bemängeln* *vt* to find fault with, to fault.

bemannen* *vt U-Boot, Raumschiff* to man.

Bemannung *f* manning; *(Mannschaft)* crew.

bemerkbar *adj* noticeable, perceptible. **sich** ~ **machen** *(sich zeigen)* to make itself felt, to become noticeable; *(auf sich aufmerksam machen)* to draw attention to oneself.

bemerken* *vt* **(a)** *(wahrnehmen)* to notice. **(b)** *(äußern)* to remark, to comment. **nebenbei bemerkt** by the way.

bemerkenswert *adj* remarkable.

Bemerkung *f* remark, comment.

bemessen* *irreg* **1** *vt (zuteilen)* to allocate; *(einteilen)* to calculate. **meine Zeit ist knapp** ~ my time is limited. **2** *vr (form)* to be proportionate *(nach* to*)*.

bemitleiden* *vt* to pity, to feel sorry for. **er ist zu** ~ he is to be pitied; **sich selbst** ~ to feel sorry for oneself.

bemitleidenswert *adj* pitiable, pitiful.

bemittelt *adj* well-to-do, well-off.

bemogeln* *vt (col)* to cheat.

Bemühen *nt no pl (geh)* endeavours *pl (Brit)*, endeavors *pl (US) (um* for*)*.

bemühen* **1** *vt* to trouble, to bother; *Rechtsanwalt etc* to engage. **jdn zu sich** ~ to call in sb. **2** *vr* **(a)** to try hard, to endeavour *(Brit)*, to endeavor *(US)*. **sich um eine Stelle** ~ to try to get a job; **sich um jdn** ~ to look after sb; *(um jds Gunst)* to court sb; **bitte** ~ **Sie sich nicht** please don't trouble yourself. **(b)** *(geh: gehen)* **sich zu jdm** ~ to go to sb.

bemüht *adj* **(darum)** ~ **sein, etw zu tun** to

endeavour *(Brit)* or endeavor *(US)* or be at pains to do sth.

Bemühung f effort.

bemüßigt *adj* sich ~ fühlen/sehen *(geh, usu iro)* to feel called upon.

bemuttern* *vt* to mother.

benachbart *adj* neighbouring *(Brit)*, neighboring *(US)*; *Haus, Familie auch* next door.

benachrichtigen* *vt* to inform *(von* of); *(amtlich auch)* to notify *(von* of).

Benachrichtigung f notification; *(Comm)* advice note.

benachteiligen* *vt* to put at a disadvantage; *(wegen Geschlecht, Rasse, Glauben etc)* to discriminate against; *(körperliches Leiden auch)* to handicap. **benachteiligt sein** to be at a disadvantage/discriminated against/handicapped.

Benachteiligung f *siehe vt (das Benachteiligen)* disadvantaging; discrimination *(gen* against); *(Zustand)* disadvantage; discrimination *no pl.*

benebeln* *vt (col)* jds Sinne ~ to make sb's head swim; **benebelt sein** to be feeling dazed *or (von Alkohol auch)* muzzy *(col).*

Benediktiner m - *(Eccl auch ~in* f) Benedictine.

Benefiz-: ~konzert, ~spiel *nt* benefit.

Benehmen *nt no pl* behaviour *(Brit)*, behavior *(US).* **kein** ~ **haben** not to know how to behave.

benehmen* *vr irreg* to behave. **benimm dich!** behave yourself!; **sich gut** ~ to behave oneself, to behave well; **sich schlecht** ~ to behave (oneself) badly, to misbehave; *siehe* **benommen.**

beneiden* *vt* to envy. **jdn um etw** ~ to envy sb sth; **er ist nicht zu** ~ I don't envy him.

beneidenswert *adj* enviable.

Benelux-: ~länder, ~staaten *pl* Benelux countries *pl.*

benennen* *vt irreg* to name. **jdn/etw nach jdm** ~ to name sb/sth after *or* for *(US)* sb.

Benennung f *(das Benennen)* naming; *(Bezeichnung)* name, designation *(form).*

Bengel m -(s) boy, lad; *(frecher Junge)* rascal.

Benimm m *no pl (col)* manners *pl.*

benommen *adj* dazed.

benoten* *vt* to mark.

benötigen* *vt* to need, to require. **das benötigte Geld** the necessary money, the money needed.

Benotung f mark; *(das Benoten)* marking.

benutzbar *adj* usable; *Weg* passable.

benutzen* *vt* to use.

Benutzer m - user; *(von Leihbücherei)* borrower.

benutzerfreundlich *adj* user-friendly.

Benutzung f use. **jdm etw zur** ~ **überlassen** to put sth at sb's disposal.

Benzin *nt* -e petrol *(Brit)*, gas(oline) *(US)*; *(Reinigungs~)* benzine; *(Feuerzeug~)* lighter fuel.

Benzin-: ~feuerzeug *nt* petrol *(Brit)* or gasoline *(US)* lighter; ~gutschein m petrol *(Brit)* or gasoline coupon *(US)*; ~kanister m petrol *(Brit)* or gasoline *(US)* can; ~motor m petrol *(Brit)* or gasoline *(US)* engine; ~pumpe f fuel pump; ~uhr f fuel gauge; ~verbrauch m fuel consumption.

be|obachten* *vt* to observe; *(bemerken auch)* to notice, to see; *(genau verfolgen, betrachten auch)* to watch. **etw an jdm** ~ to notice sth in sb; **jdn** ~ **lassen** *(Polizei etc)* to put sb under surveillance.

Be|obachter(in f) m - observer.

Be|obachtung f observation; *(polizeilich)* surveillance. **die** ~ **habe ich oft gemacht** I've often noticed that.

Be|obachtungs-: ~gabe f er hat eine gute ~gabe he has a very observant eye; ~station f **(a)** *(Med)* observation ward; **(b)** *(Met)* weather station.

be|ordern* *vt* to order. **jdn zu sich** ~ to send for sb.

bepacken* *vt* to load (up).

bepflanzen* *vt* to plant.

Bepflanzung f **(a)** *(das Bepflanzen)* planting. **(b)** *(die Pflanzen)* plants *pl (gen* in).

bepinkeln* *(col)* **1** *vt* to pee on *(col).* **2** *vr* to wet oneself.

bequatschen* *vt (col)* **(a)** etw to talk over. **(b)** *(überreden)* to persuade.

bequem *adj* comfortable; *Weg, Methode* easy; *Ausrede* convenient; *(träge) Mensch* idle. **es sich** *(dat)* ~ **machen** to make oneself comfortable.

bequemen* *vr* sich (dazu) ~, etw zu tun to bring oneself to do sth.

Bequemlichkeit f *no pl (Behaglichkeit)* comfort; *(Trägheit)* idleness.

berappen* *vti (col)* **er mußte schwer** ~ he had to fork out a lot *(col).*

beraten* *irreg* **1** *vt* **(a)** jdn ~ to advise sb; **gut/schlecht** ~ **sein** to be well-/ill-advised; **sich von jdm** ~ **lassen(, wie…)** to ask sb's advice (on how …), to consult sb (about how…). **(b)** *(besprechen)* to discuss. **2** *vir* to discuss. **sich mit jdm** ~ to consult (with) sb *(über+acc* about).

beratend *adj* advisory, consultative. **jdm** ~ **zur Seite stehen** to act in an advisory capacity to sb.

Berater(in f) m - adviser, consultant.

Beratervertrag m consultancy contract.

beratschlagen* *vti insep* to discuss.

Beratung f **(a)** *(das Beraten)* advice; *(geschäftlich: bei Rechtsanwalt, Arzt etc)* consultation. **(b)** *(Besprechung)* discussion.

berauben* *vt* to rob. **jdn einer Sache (gen)** ~ to rob sb of sth; *seines Rechtes* to deprive sb of sth.

Beraubung f robbery; *(fig)* deprivation.

berauschen* **1** *vt (lit, fig)* to intoxicate; *(Droge auch)* to make euphoric. **2** *vr* **sich an etw** *(dat)* ~ *(lit, fig)* to become intoxicated with sth.

berauschend *adj* intoxicating. **das war nicht sehr** ~ *(iro)* that wasn't very exciting.

Berberteppich m Berber carpet.

berechenbar *adj Kosten* calculable; *Verhalten* predictable.

Berechenbarkeit f *siehe adj* calculability; predictability.

berechnen* *vt* **(a)** *(ausrechnen)* to calculate. **(b)** *(in Rechnung stellen)* to charge. **jdm zu viel** ~ to overcharge sb. **(c)** *(vorsehen)* to intend, to mean.

berechnend *adj (pej) Mensch* calculating.

Berechnung f *siehe vt* **(a)** calculation. **meiner** ~ **nach, nach meiner** ~ according to my calculations; **aus** ~ **handeln** to act in a calculating manner. **(b)** charge. **ohne** ~ without any charge.

berechtigen* *vti* to entitle. **(jdn) zu etw** ~ to entitle sb to sth; **das berechtigt zu der Annahme, daß …** this justifies the assumption that …

berechtigt *adj* justifiable; *Frage, Hoffnung, Anspruch* legitimate; *Forderung, Einwand auch* justified. ~ **sein, etw zu tun** to be entitled to do sth.

berechtigterweise *adv* legitimately, justifiably.

Berechtigung f **(a)** *(Befugnis)* entitlement; *(Recht)* right. **die** ~/**keine** ~ **haben, etw zu tun** to be entitled/not to be entitled to do sth. **(b)** *(Rechtmäßigkeit)* legitimacy, justifiability.

bereden* *vt* **(a)** *(auch vr: besprechen)* to discuss, to talk over. **(b)** *(überreden)* jdn zu etw ~ to talk sb into sth.

beredsam *adj (liter)* eloquent; *(iro: redefreudig)* talkative.

Beredsamkeit f *(liter)* eloquence; *(iro)* talkativeness.

beredt *adj (geh)* eloquent.

Beredtheit f *(geh)* eloquence.

Bereich m -e **(a)** area. **im** ~ **der Innenstadt** in the town centre area. **(b)** *(Einfluß~, Aufgaben~)* sphere; *(Sach~)* area, field; *(Sektor)* sector. **im** ~ **des Möglichen liegen** to be within the bounds of possibility.

bereichern* **1** *vt (lit, fig)* to enrich; *Sammlung etc* to enlarge. **2** *vr* to make a lot of money *(an+dat* out of). **sich auf Kosten anderer** ~ to feather one's nest at the expense of other people.

Bereicherung f **(a)** *(das Bereichern)* enrichment; *(von Sammlung)* enlargement. **(b)** *(Gewinn)* boon. **eine wertvolle** ~ a valuable addition.

bereifen* vt *(Aut)* to put tyres *(Brit)* or tires *(US)* on.

Bereifung f *(Aut)* set of tyres *(Brit)* or tires *(US)*. **die** ~ **bei diesem Auto** the tyres on this car.

bereinigen* vt to clear up.

Bereinigung f clearing up.

bereisen* vt **ein Land** to travel around; *(Comm)* **Gebiet** to travel, to cover.

bereit adj usu pred **(a)** *(fertig)* ready; *(vorbereitet auch)* prepared. **sich** ~ **machen** to get ready. **(b)** *(willens)* willing, prepared. **sich** ~ **erklären, etw zu tun** to agree to do sth.

bereiten vt **(a)** *(zu~)* to prepare *(dat for)*. **(b)** *(verursachen)* to cause; *Überraschung, Empfang, Freude, Kopfschmerzen* to give. **einer Sache** *(dat)* **ein Ende** ~ to put an end to sth.

bereit-: ~**halten** sep 1 vt irreg *Fahrkarten etc* to have ready; *(für den Notfall)* to keep ready; *(Überraschung* to have in store; 2 vr to stand by; ~**legen** vt sep to lay out ready; ~**liegen** vi sep irreg to be ready; ~**machen** vtr sep to get ready.

bereits adv already. ~ **vor drei Wochen** even three weeks ago; **das haben wir** ~ **gestern gemacht** we did that yesterday; ~ **am nächsten Tage** on the very next day.

Bereitschaft f **(a)** no pl readiness; *(Bereitwilligkeit auch)* willingness. **in** ~ **sein,** ~ **haben** *(Polizei, Soldaten etc)* to be on stand-by; *(Arzt)* to be on call. **(b)** *(Mannschaft)* squad.

Bereitschafts-: ~**arzt** m doctor on call; *(im Krankenhaus)* duty doctor; ~**dienst** m emergency service; ~**dienst haben siehe Bereitschaft.**

Bereit-: **b**~**stehen** vi sep irreg to be ready; *(Flugzeug auch, Truppen)* to stand by; **Ihr Wagen steht b**~ your car is waiting; **b**~**stellen** vt sep to provide, to supply; ~**stellung** f provision, supply.

Bereitung f preparation.

Bereit-: **b**~**willig** adj willing; ~**willigkeit** f willingness.

bereuen* vt to regret; *Schuld, Sünden* to repent of. ~**, etw getan zu haben** to regret having done sth; **das wirst du noch** ~! you'll regret it!

Berg m **-e** **(a)** mountain; *(esp kleiner auch)* hill. ~**e versetzen (können)** to (be able to) move mountains; **mit etw hinterm** ~ **halten** *(fig)* to keep quiet about sth; **in die** ~**e fahren** to go to the mountains; **über den** ~ **sein** *(col)* to be out of the woods; **über alle** ~**e sein** *(col)* to be miles away *(col)*; **da stehen einem ja die Haare zu** ~**e** it's enough to make your hair stand on end. **(b)** *(große Menge)* heap, pile; *(von Sorgen)* mass.

Berg-: in cpds mountain; *(Bergbau-)* mining; **b**~**ab** adv downhill; **es geht mit ihm b**~**ab** *(fig)* he is going downhill; ~**arbeiter** m miner; **b**~**auf** adv uphill; **es geht wieder b**~**auf** *(fig)* things are getting better or looking up; ~**bau** m mining.

bergen pret **barg,** ptp **geborgen** vt **(a)** *(retten)* *Menschen* to save, to rescue; *Leichen* to recover; *Ladung, Fahrzeug* to salvage. **aus dem Wasser tot/lebend geborgen werden** to be brought out of the water dead/alive. **(b)** *(geh: enthalten)* to hold. **diese Möglichkeit birgt die Gefahr in sich, daß** ... this possibility involves the danger that ... **(c)** *siehe* **geborgen.**

Berg-: ~**führer** m mountain guide; ~**gipfel** m mountain top or peak; ~**hang** m mountain slope; **b**~**hoch** adj *Wellen* mountainous; ~**hütte** f mountain hut.

bergig adj mountainous.

Berg-: ~**kamm** m mountain ridge; ~**kette** f mountain range; ~**kristall** m rock crystal; ~**kuppe** f (round) mountain top; ~**land** nt mountainous region; **das schottische** ~**land** the

Scottish mountains or hills.

Bergmann m, pl **-leute** miner.

Berg-: ~**not** f **in** ~**not sein/geraten** to be in/get into difficulties while climbing; ~**predigt** f *(Bibl)* Sermon on the Mount; ~**rettungsdienst** m mountain rescue service; ~**rücken** m mountain ridge; ~**rutsch** m landslide *(auch fig)*, landslip; ~**spitze** f mountain peak; **b**~**steigen** vi sep irreg aux sein or haben to go mountain climbing or mountaineering; **(das)** ~**steigen** mountaineering; ~**steiger** m mountaineer; ~**steigerei** f *(col)* mountaineering; ~**-und-Tal-Bahn** f big dipper, roller-coaster; ~**-und-Tal-Fahrt** f ride on the big dipper.

Bergung f no pl siehe **bergen (a)** saving, rescue; recovery; salvage, salvaging.

Bergungs-: ~**mannschaft** f, ~**trupp** m rescue team.

Berg-: ~**wacht** f mountain rescue service; ~**wand** f mountain face; ~**wanderung** f walk or hike in the mountains; ~**werk** nt mine; **im** ~**werk arbeiten** to work down the mines.

Bericht m **-e** report *(über +acc* about, on, *von* on); *(Erzählung auch)* account; *(Zeitungs~ auch)* story. **jdm über etw** *(acc)* ~ **erstatten** to give sb a report (on sth).

berichten* vti to report; *(erzählen)* to tell. **jdm über etw** *(acc)* ~ to report to sb about sth; to tell sb about sth; **mir ist (darüber) berichtet worden, daß** ... I have received reports that ...; **er berichtete von der Reise** he told us etc about his journey.

Bericht-: ~**erstatter** m reporter; *(Korrespondent)* correspondent; ~**erstattung** f reporting; **die** ~**erstattung über diese Vorgänge in der Presse** press coverage of these events; **zur** ~**erstattung zurückgerufen werden** to be called back to make a report.

berichtigen* vt to correct; *Fehler auch, (Jur)* to rectify.

Berichtigung f siehe vt correction; rectification.

berieseln* vt **(a)** to spray with water etc; *(durch Sprinkleranlage)* to sprinkle. **(b)** *(fig col)* **von etw berieselt werden** *(fig)* to be exposed to a constant stream of sth.

Berieselung f watering. **die** ~ **mit** or **durch etw** *(fig)* the constant stream of sth.

Berieselungs|anlage f sprinkler (system).

beritten adj mounted, on horseback.

Berlin nt Berlin.

Berliner[1] adj attr Berlin.

Berliner[2] m - *(Cook)* jam doughnut.

Berliner(in f) m - Berliner.

berlinerisch adj *(col)* Dialekt Berlin attr.

Bermudas pl **auf den** ~ in Bermuda.

Bernhardiner m - Saint Bernard (dog).

Bernstein m no pl amber.

Berserker m - **wie ein** ~ **arbeiten/kämpfen** to work/fight like mad or fury.

bersten pret **barst,** ptp **geborsten** vi aux sein *(geh)* to crack; *(auf~, zerbrechen)* to break; *(zerplatzen)* to burst. **vor Neugier/Zorn etc** ~ to be bursting with curiosity/anger etc.

berüchtigt adj notorious, infamous.

berückend adj charming, enchanting.

berücksichtigen* vt *(beachten, bedenken)* to take into account or consideration; *(in Betracht ziehen)* Antrag, Bewerber to consider. **das ist zu** ~ that must be taken into account or consideration.

Berücksichtigung f consideration. **in** or **unter** ~ **der Tatsache, daß** ... in view of the fact that ...

Beruf m **-e** occupation; *(akademischer auch)* profession; *(handwerklicher auch)* trade; *(Stellung)* job. **was sind Sie von** ~? what is your occupation etc?, what do you do for a living?; **von** ~ **Arzt/Bäcker/Hausfrau sein** to be a doctor by profession/baker by trade/housewife by occupation; **seinen** ~ **verfehlt haben** to have missed

berufen one's vocation; **von ~s wegen** on account of one's job.

berufen* *irreg* **1** *vt* **(a)** *(ernennen, einsetzen)* to appoint. **zum Minister/auf einen Lehrstuhl ~ werden** to be appointed minister/to a chair. **(b)** = **beschreien. 2** *vr* **sich auf jdn/etw ~** to refer to sb/sth. **3** *adj (ausersehen)* **zu etw ~ sein** to have a vocation for sth; *(esp Rel)* to be called to sth.

beruflich *adj (esp auf akademische Berufe bezüglich)* professional. **~e Aussichten** job prospects; **verschiedene ~e Tätigkeiten** different jobs; **~ ist sie sehr erfolgreich** she is very successful in her career; **er ist ~ viel unterwegs** he is away a lot on business.

Berufs-: **~aussichten** *pl* job prospects *pl;* **b~bedingt** *adj* occupational; **~berater** *m* careers adviser; **~beratung** *f* careers guidance; **~bezeichnung** *f* job title; **~boxen** *nt* professional boxing; **~erfahrung** *f* (professional) experience; **~feuerwehr** *f* fire service; **~fußball** *m* professional football; **~geheimnis** *nt* professional secret; *(Schweigepflicht)* professional secrecy, confidentiality; **~heer** *nt* professional *or* regular army; **~kleidung** *f* working clothes *pl;* **~krankheit** *f* occupational disease; **~leben** *nt* working *or* professional life; **im ~leben stehen** to be working *or* in employment; **b~mäßig** *adj* professional; **etw b~mäßig betreiben** to do sth on a professional basis; **~risiko** *nt* occupational hazard; **~schule** *f* vocational school, ≈ technical college *(Brit);* **~schüler** *m* student at vocational school *etc;* **~sport** *m* professional sport; **~sportler** *m* professional sportsman; **b~tätig** *adj* working; **b~tätig sein** to be working, to work; **~tätige(r)** *mf decl as adj* working person; **b~unfähig** *adj* unable to work; **~unfähigkeit** *f* inability to work; **~verband** *m* professional/trade organization; **~verbot** *nt* exclusion from a profession; **jdm ~verbot erteilen** to ban sb from his/her profession; *einem Arzt, Anwalt* to strike sb off; **~verkehr** *m* rush-hour traffic; **~wahl** *f* choice of occupation; **~wechsel** *m* change of occupation.

Berufung *f* **(a)** *(Jur)* appeal. **in die ~ gehen/~ einlegen** to appeal *(bei* to). *(in ein Amt etc)* appointment *(auf or an+acc* to). **(c)** *(innerer Auftrag)* vocation; *(Rel auch)* calling. **(d)** *(form)* **unter ~ auf etw** *(acc)* with reference to sth.

Berufungs-: **~frist** *f* period in which an appeal must be lodged; **~gericht** *nt* appeal court, court of appeal; **~klage** *f* appeal.

beruhen* *vi* to be based *or* founded *(auf+ dat* on). **das beruht auf Gegenseitigkeit** *(col)* the feeling is mutual; **etw auf sich ~ lassen** to let sth rest.

beruhigen* **1** *vt* to calm (down); *Baby* to quieten; *(trösten)* to comfort; *(versichern)* to reassure; *Magen* to settle; *Nerven auch* to soothe; *Gewissen* to appease. **na, dann bin ich ja beruhigt** well I must say I'm quite relieved; **~d** soothing; *(tröstlich)* reassuring. **2** *vr* to calm down; *(Krise auch)* to ease off; *(Verkehr, Kämpfe)* to subside; *(Börse, Magen)* to settle down; *(Sturm)* to die down, to abate.

Beruhigung *f no pl* **(a)** *siehe vt* calming (down); quietening; comforting; reassuring; settling; soothing; appeasement. **zu Ihrer ~ kann ich sagen …** you'll be reassured to know that … **(b)** *siehe vr* calming down, easing off; subsiding; settling down.

Beruhigungs-: **~mittel** *nt* sedative, tranquillizer; **~spritze** *f* sedative (injection).

berühmt *adj* famous. **das war nicht ~** *(col)* it was nothing to write home about *(col).*

berühmt-berüchtigt *adj* infamous, notorious.

Berühmtheit *f* **(a)** fame. **~ erlangen** to become famous. **(b)** *(Mensch)* celebrity.

berühren* **1** *vt* **(a)** to touch; *(erwähnen) Thema,*

Punkt to touch on. **B~ verboten** do not touch. **(b)** *(seelisch bewegen)* to move; *(auf jdn wirken)* to affect; *(betreffen)* to affect, to concern. **das berührt mich gar nicht!** that's nothing to do with me; **von etw peinlich berührt sein** to be embarrassed by sth. **2** *vr* to touch.

Berührung *f* touch; *(von Drähten etc, menschlich)* contact; *(Erwähnung)* mention. **mit jdm/etw in ~ kommen** to come into contact with sb/sth.

Berührungspunkt *m* point of contact.

besagen* *vt* to say; *(bedeuten)* to mean, to imply.

besagt *adj attr (form)* said *(form).*

besaiten* *vt* to string. **etw neu ~** to restring sth.

besamen* *vt* to fertilize; *(künstlich)* to inseminate.

Besamung *f siehe vt* fertilization; insemination.

besänftigen* *vt* to soothe; *Menge auch* to pacify.

Besänftigung *f siehe vt* soothing; pacifying.

besät *adj* covered; *(mit Blättern etc)* strewn.

Besatz *m* -̈e edging, trimming.

Besatzer *m* - *(pej col)* occupying forces *pl.*

Besatzung *f* **(a)** *(Mannschaft)* crew; *(Verteidigungstruppe)* garrison. **(b)** *(~sarmee)* occupying forces *pl.*

Besatzungs-: **~armee** *f* army of occupation; **~macht** *f* occupying power; **~truppen** *pl* occupying forces *pl;* **~zone** *f* occupied zone.

besaufen* *vr irreg (col)* to get plastered *(col).*

Besäufnis *nt (col)* booze-up *(col).*

beschädigen* *vt* to damage. **beschädigt** damaged.

Beschädigung *f* damage *(von* to).

beschaffen* **1** *vt* to get (hold of), to obtain *(jdm etw* sth for sb). **2** *adj (form)* **so ~ sein wie …** to be the same as …; **das ist so ~, daß …** that is such that …; **sie ist nun mal so ~** that is the way she is.

Beschaffenheit *f no pl* composition; *(körperlich)* constitution; *(Art, seelisch)* nature, qualities *pl.* **je nach ~ der Lage** according to the situation.

Beschaffung *f no pl* obtaining.

beschäftigen* **1** *vr* **sich mit etw ~** to occupy oneself with sth; *(sich befassen, abhandeln)* to deal with sth; **sich mit Literatur ~** to study literature; **sich mit jdm ~** to devote one's attention to sb. **2** *vt* **(a)** *(innerlich)* jdn ~ to be on sb's mind. **(b)** *(anstellen)* to employ. **(c)** *(eine Tätigkeit geben)* to keep occupied.

beschäftigt *adj* **(a)** busy. **mit Nähen/jdm ~ sein** to be busy sewing/with sb; **mit sich selbst ~ sein** to be preoccupied with oneself. **(b)** *(angestellt)* employed *(bei* by).

Beschäftigte(r) *mf decl as adj* employee.

Beschäftigung *f* **(a)** work *no indef art,* job; *(Anstellung, Angestelltsein)* employment. **einer ~ nachgehen** *(form)* to be employed. **(b)** *(Tätigkeit)* activity, occupation. **jdm eine ~ geben** to give sb something to do. **(c)** *(geistige ~)* preoccupation; *(mit Frage)* consideration *(mit* of).

Beschäftigungs-: **b~los** *adj* unoccupied; *(arbeitslos)* unemployed; **~therapie** *f* occupational therapy.

beschämen* *vt* to put to shame. **es beschämt mich, zu sagen …** I feel ashamed to have to say …

beschämend *adj* shaming; *(schändlich)* shameful.

beschämt *adj* ashamed.

beschatten* *vt* **(a)** *(überwachen)* to shadow, to tail. **(b)** *(Sport)* to mark closely. **(c)** *(geh: Schatten geben)* to shade.

Beschatter *m* - *(Polizist etc)* tail; *(Sport)* marker.

Beschattung *f siehe vt* **(a)** tailing. **(b)** marking.

Beschauer *m* - *(Betrachter)* spectator.

beschaulich *adj* Leben, Abend quiet, tranquil; *Charakter, Mensch* pensive, contemplative.

Beschaulichkeit *f siehe adj* quietness, tranquillity; pensiveness.

Bescheid *m* -e **(a)** *(Auskunft)* information; *(Nachricht)* notification; *(Entscheidung auf Antrag etc)* decision. **jdm (über etw** *acc or* **von etw)** ~ **sagen/geben** to let sb know (about sth), to tell sb (about sth); **jdm ordentlich** ~ **sagen** *(col)* to tell sb where to go *(col)*. **(b) (über etw** *(acc) or* **in etw** *dat)* ~ **wissen** to know (about sth); **er weiß schon** ~ he knows all about it.

bescheiden[1]* *irreg* 1 *vt* **(a)** *(form: entscheiden)* to decide upon. **etw abschlägig** ~ to turn sth down. **(b)** *(geh)* **es war ihr nicht beschieden, ...** it was not to be her lot to ... 2 *vr (geh)* to be content.

bescheiden[2] *adj* modest. **darf ich mal** ~ **fragen, ob ...** may I venture to ask whether ...; **eine** ~**e Frage** one small question.

Bescheidenheit *f* modesty. **nur keine falsche** ~ no false modesty now.

bescheinen* *vt irreg* to shine on. **vom Mond/von der Sonne beschienen** moonlit/sunlit.

bescheinigen* *vt* to certify; *Empfang* to confirm, to acknowledge; *(durch Quittung)* to give a receipt for. **hiermit wird bescheinigt, daß ...** this is to certify that ...; **jdm äußerste Kompetenz** ~ to confirm sb's extreme competence.

Bescheinigung *f siehe vt (das Bescheinigen)* certification; confirmation; *(Schriftstück)* certificate; written confirmation; *(Quittung)* receipt.

bescheißen* *vt irreg (col!) jdn* to cheat *(um* out of*)*.

beschenken* *vt jdn* to give presents/a present to. **jdn mit etw** ~ to give sb sth (as a present).

bescheren* *vti* **jdn** ~ to give sb a Christmas present/Christmas presents; **jdm eine Überraschung** ~ to give sb a nice surprise; **ihnen waren fünf Kinder beschert** they were blessed with five children.

Bescherung *f* **(a)** giving out of Christmas presents. **(b)** *(iro col)* **das ist ja eine schöne** ~! this is a nice mess; **da haben wir die** ~! what did I tell you!

bescheuert *adj (col)* stupid.

beschichten* *vt (Tech)* to coat, to cover.

beschicken* *vt* **(a) eine Ausstellung mit jdm/etw** ~ to send sb/sth to an exhibition. **(b)** *Hochofen* to charge.

beschießen* *vt irreg* to shoot *or* fire at; *(mit Geschützen, Phys)* to bombard.

Beschießung *f siehe vt* shooting *(gen at)*, firing *(gen on,* at*)*; bombardment *(gen* of*)*.

beschildern* *vt* to put a sign/signs on; *(mit Verkehrsschildern)* to signpost.

Beschilderung *f siehe vt* putting a sign *(von* on*)*; signposting; *(Schilder)* signs *pl*; signposts *pl*.

beschimpfen *vt jdn* to swear at.

Beschimpfung *f* **(a)** swearing *(gen* at*)*. **(b)** *(Schimpfwort)* insult.

beschirmen* *vt (geh: beschützen)* to shield.

Beschiß *m no pl (col!)* swindle, rip-off *(col)*.

beschissen *adj (col!)* bloody awful *(Brit col)*, lousy *(col)*.

Beschlag *m* ⁼**e** **(a)** *(an Koffer, Truhe)* fitting; *(an Tür, Möbelstück)* mounting; *(von Pferd)* shoes *pl*. **(b)** *(auf Glas, Spiegel etc)* condensation. **(c)** *jdn/ etw* **in** ~ **nehmen** to monopolize sb/sth; **mit** ~ **belegt sein** to be occupied.

beschlagen* *irreg* 1 *vt* **(a)** *Möbel, Türen* to put (metal) fittings on; *Huftiere* to shoe; *Schuhe* to put metal tips on. **(b)** *(anlaufen lassen: Dampf)* to steam up. 2 *vir (vi: aux sein)* *(Brille, Glas, Fenster)* to steam up, to mist up; *(Wand)* to get covered in condensation. 3 *adj (erfahren)* **in etw** *(dat)* **(gut)** ~ **sein** to be (well-)versed in sth.

Beschlagenheit *f no pl* sound knowledge *or* grasp *(in+dat* of*)*.

Beschlagnahme *f* **-n** confiscation, seizure.

beschlagnahmen* *vt insep* **(a)** to confiscate, to seize. **(b)** *(col: in Anspruch nehmen) (Mensch)* to monopolize, to hog *(col)*; *(Arbeit)* Zeit to take up.

beschleunigen* 1 *vt* to accelerate, to speed up; *Tempo auch* to increase; *Verfall* to hasten, to accelerate. 2 *vi (Fahrzeug, Fahrer)* to accelerate.

Beschleunigung *f* acceleration *(auch Aut, Phys)*, speeding up; *(von Tempo auch)* increase; *(von Verfall etc)* hastening.

beschließen* *irreg* 1 *vt* **(a)** to decide on; *Gesetz* to pass. ~, **etw zu tun** to decide to do sth. **(b)** *(beenden)* to end. 2 *vi* **über etw** *(acc)* ~ to decide on sth.

beschlossen *adj (entschieden)* decided, agreed. **das ist** ~**e Sache** that's been settled.

Beschluß *m* ⁼**sse** decision, resolution. **einen** ~ **fassen** to pass a resolution; **auf** ~ **des Gerichts** by order of the court.

Beschluß-: **b**~**fähig** *adj* **b**~**fähig sein** to have a quorum; ~**fähigkeit** *f no pl* quorum; ~**fassung** *f* (passing of a) resolution; **b**~**unfähig** *adj* **b**~**unfähig sein** not to have a quorum.

beschmeißen* *vt irreg (col: lit, fig)* to bombard.

beschmieren* 1 *vt Kleidung* to smear; *Wand* to bedaub; *Tafel* to scribble *or* scrawl all over. 2 *vr* to get (all) dirty.

beschmutzen* 1 *vt* to (make *or* get) dirty, to soil; *(fig) Ruf, Namen* to besmirch. 2 *vr* to make *or* get oneself dirty.

beschneiden* *vt irreg* **(a)** *(stutzen)* to trim; *Sträucher etc* to prune. **(b)** *(Med, Rel)* to circumcise. **(c)** *(fig: beschränken)* to cut back, to curtail.

Beschneidung *f no pl siehe vt* **(a)** trimming; pruning. **(b)** circumcision. **(c)** *(von Unterstützung etc)* cut-back; *(von Rechten)* curtailing.

beschneit *adj* snow-covered; *Berge auch* snow-capped.

beschnuppern* 1 *vt* to sniff at; *(fig col)* to sniff out; *jdn* to size up. 2 *vr (Hunde)* to sniff each other; *(fig col)* to size each other up.

beschönigen* *vt* to gloss over. ~**der Ausdruck** euphemism.

beschränken* 1 *vt (auf+acc* to*)* to limit, to restrict. 2 *vr (auf+acc* to*)* to be limited *or* restricted; *(esp Jur, Rede, Aufsatz etc auch)* to confine oneself; *(sich einschränken)* to restrict oneself.

beschrankt *adj Bahnübergang* with gates.

beschränkt *adj* **(a)** *(eingeschränkt, knapp)* limited; *Gebrauch auch* restricted. **wir sind zeitlich/finanziell** ~ we have only a limited amount of time/money; **Gesellschaft mit** ~**er Haftung** limited company *(Brit)*, corporation *(US)*. **(b)** *(pej) (geistig) Mensch* dim; *Intelligenz* limited; *(engstirnig auch)* narrow-minded.

Beschränktheit *f siehe adj* **(a)** limited nature. **(b)** limited intelligence; narrow-mindedness.

Beschränkung *f* limitation, restriction. **jdm** ~**en auferlegen** to impose restrictions on sb.

beschreiben* *vt irreg* **(a)** *(auch Kreis)* to describe. **sein Glück/Schmerz war nicht zu** ~ his happiness/pain was indescribable. **(b)** *(vollschreiben)* to write on. **ein eng beschriebenes Blatt** a closely written sheet.

Beschreibung *f* **(a)** description. **(b)** *(Gebrauchsanweisung)* instructions *pl*.

beschreien* *vt irreg (col)* **ich will es nicht** ~, **aber ...** I don't want to tempt fate, but ...

beschreiten* *vt irreg (lit geh, fig)* to follow.

beschriften* *vt* to write on; *(mit Aufschrift)* to label.

Beschriftung *f* **(a)** *(das Beschriften)* labelling. **(b)** *(Aufschrift)* writing; *(Etikett)* label.

beschuldigen* *vt* to accuse; *(esp Jur auch, liter)* to charge. **jdn einer Sache** *(gen)* ~ to accuse sb of sth; to charge sb with sth.

Beschuldigte(r) *mf decl as adj* accused.

Beschuldigung *f* accusation; *(esp Jur auch, liter)* charge.

beschummeln* *vt (col)* to cheat. **jdn um etw** ~ to cheat *or* diddle *(col)* sb out of sth.

Beschuß *m no pl (Mil)* fire; *(Phys)* bombarding. **jdn/etw unter** ~ **nehmen** *(Mil)* to (start to) bombard *or* shell sb/sth; *Stellung auch* to fire on sth; *(fig)* to attack sb/sth.

beschützen* vt to protect (vor +dat from).
Beschützer(in f) m - protector/protectress.
beschwatzen* vt (col) (a) (überreden) to talk over. (b) (bereden) to chat about.
Beschwerde f -n (a) (Mühe) hardship. (b) ~n pl (Leiden) trouble; **das macht mir immer noch ~n** it's still giving me trouble. (c) (Klage) complaint; (Jur) appeal. ~ **einlegen** (form) to lodge a complaint.
Beschwerde-: b~frei adj fit and healthy; ~frist f (Jur) period of time during which an appeal may be lodged.
beschweren* 1 vt (mit Gewicht) to weigh(t) down; (fig) (Kummer) to weigh on; (Mensch) to burden. 2 vr (sich beklagen) to complain.
beschwerlich adj arduous.
Beschwerlichkeit f difficulty; (von Reise, Aufgabe auch) arduousness no pl.
beschwichtigen* vt jdn to appease, to pacify; Kinder, jds Zorn, Gewissen to soothe.
Beschwichtigung f siehe vt appeasement, pacification; soothing.
beschwindeln* (col) (a) (belügen) jdn ~ to tell sb a lie or a fib (col). (b) (betrügen) to swindle.
beschwingt adj lively.
Beschwingtheit f liveliness.
beschwipst adj (col) tipsy.
beschwören* vt irreg (a) (beeiden) to swear to; (Jur auch) to swear on oath. (b) (anflehen) to implore, to beseech. (c) (Geister, Erinnerung) to conjure up; Schlangen to charm.
Beschwörung f (a) (das Flehen) entreaty. (b) siehe vt (c) conjuring up; charming.
beseelen* vt (erfüllen) neuer Mut beseelte ihn he was filled with fresh courage.
besehen* vt irreg to (take a) look at.
beseitigen* vt (a) (entfernen) to remove, to get rid of; Schwierigkeiten auch to sort out; Fehler auch to eliminate; Mißstände to get rid of, to do away with. (b) (euph: umbringen) to get rid of.
Beseitigung f no pl siehe vt (a) removal, getting rid of; sorting out; elimination; getting rid of, doing away with. (b) getting rid of.
Besen m - (a) broom. **ich fresse einen ~, wenn das stimmt** (col) if that's right, I'll eat my hat (col); **neue ~ kehren gut** (Prov) a new broom sweeps clean (Prov). (b) (pej col: Frau) old bag (col).
Besen-: ~**kammer** f, ~**schrank** m broom cupboard; ~**stiel** m broom-stick.
besessen adj (von bösen Geistern) possessed (von by); (von einer Idee etc) obsessed (von with). **wie ~** like one possessed.
Besessene(r) mf decl as adj one possessed no art. **die ~n** the possessed.
Besessenheit f no pl siehe adj possession; obsession.
besetzen* vt (a) (dekorieren) to trim; (mit Edelsteinen) to stud. (b) (belegen) to occupy; (reservieren) to reserve; (füllen) Plätze, Stühle to fill. **ist dieser Platz besetzt?** is this place taken?; siehe besetzt. (c) (esp Mil) to occupy. (d) Stelle to fill; (Theat) Rolle to cast. **eine Stelle neu ~ to find a** new person for a job.
besetzt adj (belegt) Leitung engaged (Brit), busy; WC occupied, engaged (Brit); Abteil, Tisch full (up); (vorgebucht) booked; Abteil etc taken.
Besetztzeichen nt (Telec) engaged (Brit) or busy tone.
Besetzung f (a) (von Stelle) filling; (von Rolle) casting; (Theat: Schauspieler) cast; (Sport: Mannschaft) team. **die Nationalelf in der neuen ~** the new line-up for the international side; **zweite ~** (Theat) understudy. (b) (esp Mil) occupation.
besichtigen* vt (ansehen) Stadt, Kirche to have a look at, to visit; Betrieb to tour; (zur Prüfung) Haus to view; Ware, Truppen to inspect.

Besichtigung f (von Sehenswürdigkeiten) sightseeing tour; (von Museum etc) tour; (zur Prüfung) (von Haus) viewing; (von Truppen) inspection.
besiedeln* vt (ansiedeln) to populate, to settle (mit with); (kolonisieren) to colonize. **dicht/dünn besiedelt** densely/thinly populated.
Besied(e)lung f no pl siehe vt settlement; colonization. **dichte/dünne ~** dense/thin population.
besiegeln* vt to seal.
besiegen* vt (schlagen) to defeat, to beat; (überwinden) to overcome.
besingen* vt irreg (a) Schallplatte to record. (b) (rühmen) jdn/etw ~ to sing the praises of sb/sth.
besinnen* vr irreg (überlegen) to reflect, to think; (erinnern) to remember (auf jdn/etw sb/sth); (es sich anders überlegen) to have second thoughts. **sich anders ~** to change one's mind; **ohne sich zu ~** without a moment's thought or hesitation.
besinnlich adj thoughtful, contemplative.
Besinnlichkeit f no pl thoughtfulness, contemplativeness.
Besinnung f no pl (a) consciousness. **bei/ohne ~ sein** to be conscious/unconscious; **die ~ verlieren** to lose consciousness; (fig) to lose one's head; **wieder zur ~ kommen** to regain consciousness; (fig) to come to one's senses; **jdn zur ~ bringen** (fig) to bring sb to his senses. (b) (das Sich-Besinnen) contemplation (auf+acc of).
Besinnungs-: b~los adj unconscious; (fig) blind; ~losigkeit f no pl (lit) unconsciousness.
Besitz m no pl (a) possession. **im ~ von etw sein** to be in possession of sth; **etw in ~ nehmen** to take possession of sth; **von etw ~ ergreifen** to seize possession of sth; **in privatem ~** in private ownership. (b) (Eigentum) property; (Landgut) estate.
Besitz-: ~**anspruch** m claim of ownership; (Jur) title; **seine ~ansprüche (auf etw acc) anmelden** to lay claim to sth; b~**anzeigend** adj (Gram) possessive.
besitzen* vt to possess, to own; Narbe, grüne Augen to have; Fähigkeiten to have, to possess. **die ~den Klassen** the propertied classes.
Besitzer(in f) m - owner; (von Wertpapieren auch, von Führerschein etc) holder; (Laden- etc auch) proprietor. **den ~ wechseln** to change hands.
Besitz-: ~**ergreifung** f seizure; b~**los** adj having no possessions; ~**nahme** f no pl seizure; ~**tum** nt (Eigentum) property no pl; (Grundbesitz) estate(s pl), property.
besoffen adj (col) (betrunken) pissed (Brit col), smashed (col); (verrückt) crazy.
Besoffene(r) mf decl as adj (col) drunk.
besohlen* vt to sole; (neu ~) to resole.
Besolden* vt to pay.
Besoldung f pay.
besondere(r, s) adj special; (bestimmt) particular; (hervorragend) Qualität, Schönheit etc exceptional. **eine ganz ~ Anstrengung** a quite exceptional effort; **unser ~s Interesse gilt ... we** are particularly or (e)specially interested in ...; **ohne ~ Begeisterung** without any particular enthusiasm; **im ~n** (im einzelnen) in particular cases; (vor allem) in particular.
Besonderheit f special feature; (besondere Eigenschaft) peculiarity.
besonders adv particularly, (e)specially. **nicht ~ viel Geld** not a particularly large amount of money; **das Essen/der Film war nicht ~** (col) the food/film was nothing special or nothing to write home about (col); **wie geht's dir? — nicht ~** (col) how are you? — not too hot (col).
besonnen adj considered, level-headed. **ihre ruhige, ~e Art** her calm and collected way.
Besonnenheit f no pl level-headedness.
besonnt adj sunny.
besorgen* vt (a) (kaufen, beschaffen etc) to get; (euph col: stehlen) to acquire (euph col). **jdm/sich**

etw ~ to get sth for sb/oneself. **(b)** *(erledigen)* to attend *or* see to. **(c)** *(versorgen)* to take care of, to look after. **(d)** *(col)* **es jdm ~** to sort sb out *(col)*, to fix sb *(col)*. **(e)** *(col!)* **es jdm ~** *(Mann: mit jdm schlafen)* to have it off with sb *(col)*.

Besorgnis *f* anxiety, worry.

besorgnis|erregend *adj* alarming, worrying.

besorgt *adj* **(a)** *(voller Sorge)* anxious, worried *(wegen* about). **(b)** **um jdn/etw ~ sein** to be concerned about sb/sth.

Besorgtheit *f no pl* concern.

Besorgung *f* **(a)** *(das Kaufen)* purchase. **(b)** **die ~ des Haushaltes** looking after the house. **(c)** *(Einkauf)* **~en machen** to do some shopping.

bespannen* *vt* **(a)** *(mit Material)* to cover; *(mit Saiten, Fäden)* to string. **(b)** *Wagen* to harness up.

Bespannung *f* **(a)** *no pl* covering; *(mit Saiten etc)* stringing; *(mit Pferden)* harnessing. **(b)** *(Material)* covering; *(Saiten, Fäden etc)* strings *pl*.

bespielbar *adj Rasen etc* playable.

bespielen* *vt* **(a)** *Tonband* to record on. **das Band ist mit klassischer Musik bespielt** the tape has a recording of classical music on it. **(b)** *(Sport)* to play on.

bespitzeln* *vt* to spy on.

Bespitz(e)lung *f* spying.

besprechen* *irreg* **1** *vt* **(a)** to discuss, to talk about. **wie besprochen** as arranged. **(b)** *(rezensieren)* to review. **(c)** *Tonband* to make a recording on. **2** *vr* **sich mit jdm ~** to confer with sb *(über* +*acc* about).

Besprechung *f* **(a)** discussion, talk; *(Konferenz)* meeting. **er ist bei einer ~, er hat eine ~** he's in a meeting. **(b)** *(Rezension)* review, notice.

besprengen* *vt* to sprinkle.

bespringen* *vt irreg (Tier)* to mount, to cover.

bespritzen* *vt* to spray; *(beschmutzen)* to spatter.

besprühen* *vt* to spray.

bespucken* *vt* to spit at.

besser *adj, adv, comp of* **gut** better. **~e Leute** a better class of people; **er hat ~e Tage gesehen** *(iro)* he has seen better days; **du willst wohl etwas B~es sein!** *(col)* I suppose you think you're better than other people; **~ ist ~** (it is) better to be on the safe side; **um so ~!** *(col)* so much the better!; **~ (gesagt)** or rather; **sie will immer alles ~ wissen** she always thinks she knows better; **das ist auch ~ so** it's better that way; **B~es zu tun haben** to have better things to do; **das solltest du ~ nicht tun** you had better not do that; **dann geh ich ~** then I'd better go; **das Essen war nur ein ~er Imbiß** the meal was just a glorified snack.

bessergehen *vi impers sep irreg aux sein* **es geht jdm besser** sb is feeling better; **jetzt geht's der Firma wieder besser** the firm is doing better again now.

bessern **1** *vt* to improve, to make better; *Verbrecher etc* to reform. **2** *vr (moralisch, im Benehmen)* to mend one's ways.

besser-: **~stehen** *vr sep irreg (col)* to be better off; **~stellen** *vt sep* **jdn ~stellen** to improve sb's financial position.

Besserung *f no pl* improvement; *(von Verbrecher etc)* reformation; *(Genesung)* recovery. **gute ~!** I hope you get better soon; **auf dem Wege der ~ sein** to be getting better, to be improving; *(Patient auch)* to be on the road to recovery.

Besser-: **~wisser** *m* - *(col)* know-all, know-it-all *(US)*; **b~wisserisch** *adj (col)* know-all *etc attr*.

Bestand *m* **-e** **(a)** *(Fortdauer)* continued existence, continuance. **von ~ sein/~ haben** to be permanent, to endure. **(b)** *(vorhandene Menge, Tiere)* stock *(an*+*dat* of). **~ aufnehmen** to take stock.

bestanden *adj* **nach ~er Prüfung** after passing the/an exam; **bei nicht ~er Prüfung** if you *etc* don't pass the exam.

beständig *adj* **(a)** *no pred (dauernd)* constant, continual. **(b)** *(gleichbleibend)* constant; *Mitarbeiter* steady; *Wetter* settled. **(c)** *no adv (widerstandsfähig)* resistant *(gegen* to); *(dauerhaft)* Freundschaft lasting.

Beständigkeit *f no pl siehe adj* **(a)** continual nature. **(b)** constancy; steadiness; settledness. **(c)** resistance; lastingness.

Bestands|aufnahme *f* stock-taking.

Bestandteil *m* component, part; *(fig)* integral part. **sich in seine ~e auflösen** to fall to pieces.

bestärken* *vt* to confirm. **jdn in seinem Vorsatz/Wunsch ~** to confirm sb in his intention/desire.

Bestärkung *f* confirmation.

bestätigen* **1** *vt* **(a)** to confirm; *(beurkunden auch)* to certify; *(Jur) Urteil* to uphold. **sich in etw** *(dat)* **bestätigt finden** to be confirmed in sth; ... **sagte er ~d** ... he said in confirmation; **jdn (im Amt) ~** to confirm sb's appointment. **(b)** *(Comm) Empfang, Brief* to acknowledge (receipt of). **2** *vr* to be confirmed, to be proved true.

Bestätigung *f siehe vt* **(a)** confirmation; upholding. **(b)** acknowledgement (of receipt).

bestatten* *vt* to bury. **wo liegt er bestattet?** where is he buried?

Bestatter *m* - undertaker, mortician *(US)*.

Bestattung *f* burial; *(Feuer~)* cremation; *(Feier auch)* funeral.

Bestattungs-: **~institut, ~unternehmen** *nt* undertaker's, mortician *(US)*; **~unternehmer** *m* undertaker, mortician *(US)*.

bestäuben* *vt* to dust; *(Bot)* to pollinate.

bestaunen* *vt* to marvel at, to gaze at in wonder.

beste *siehe* **beste(r, s)**.

bestechen *irreg* **1** *vt* **(a)** to bribe. **ich lasse mich nicht ~** I'm not open to bribery. **(b)** *(beeindrucken)* to captivate. **2** *vi (Eindruck machen)* to be impressive *(durch* because of).

bestechend *adj Schönheit, Eindruck* captivating; *Angebot* tempting.

bestechlich *adj* bribable, corruptible.

Bestechlichkeit *f no pl* corruptibility.

Bestechung *f* bribery; *(von Beamten etc auch)* corruption.

Bestechungs-: **~geld** *nt usu pl*, **~summe** *f* bribe; **~versuch** *m* attempted bribery.

Besteck *nt* **-e** **(a)** *(Eß~)* knives and forks *pl*, cutlery *sing*; *(Set, für ein Gedeck)* set of cutlery. **(b)** *(Instrumentensatz)* set of instruments. **chirurgisches ~** (set of) surgical instruments.

Besteckkasten *m* cutlery canteen.

bestehen *irreg* **1** *vt* **(a)** *Examen, Probe* to pass; *siehe* **bestanden**. **(b)** *Schicksalsschläge* to withstand; *Gefahr* to overcome; *Kampf* to win.

2 *vi* **(a)** *(existieren)* to exist. **die Universität besteht seit hundert Jahren** the university has been in existence *or* has existed for a hundred years; **es besteht die Hoffnung/der Verdacht, daß ...** there is a hope/a suspicion that ... **(b)** *(Bestand haben)* to continue to exist; *(Zweifel, Problem etc auch)* to persist. **(c)** *(sich zusammensetzen)* to consist *(aus* of). **in etw** *(dat)* **~** to consist in sth; *(Aufgabe)* to involve sth; **seine einzige Chance besteht darin, ...** his only chance is to ...; **die Schwierigkeit/das Problem besteht darin, daß ...** the difficulty/problem lies in the fact that ..., the difficulty/problem is that ... **(d)** *(standhalten, sich bewähren)* to hold one's own *(in* +*dat* in). **vor etw** *(dat)* **~** to stand up against sth. **(e)** *(bei Prüfung etc)* to pass. **(f)** **auf etw** *(dat)* **~** to insist on sth.

Bestehen *nt no pl* **(a)** existence. **seit ~ der Firma** ever since the firm came into existence *or* has existed. **(b)** *(Beharren)* insistence *(auf*+*dat* von). **(c)** *(von Prüfung etc)* passing.

bestehenbleiben* *vi sep irreg aux sein* to last, to endure; *(Frage, Hoffnung)* to remain.

bestehend *adj* existing; *Gesetze auch, Preise*

present, current.
bestehlen* *vt irreg* to rob *(um etw of sth).*
besteigen* *vt irreg* Berg, Leiter to climb; Fahrrad, Pferd to mount, to get or climb on(to); Bus, Flugzeug to get on; Auto to get into; Thron to ascend.
bestellen* 1 *vt* (a) *(anfordern, in Restaurant)* to order. **sich** *(dat)* **etw ~** to order sth; **das Material ist bestellt** the material has been ordered or is on order; **wie bestellt und nicht abgeholt** *(hum col)* like orphan Annie *(col).* (b) *(reservieren)* to book, to reserve. (c) *(ausrichten)* **bestell ihm (von mir), daß ...** tell him (from me) that ...; **soll ich irgend etwas ~?** can I take a message?; **er hat hier nicht viel/nichts zu ~** he doesn't have much/any say here. (d) *(kommen lassen) jdn* to send for, to summon. **ich bin für 10 Uhr bestellt** I have an appointment for or at 10 o'clock. (e) *(einsetzen, ernennen)* to nominate, to appoint. (f) *(bearbeiten) Land* to till. (g) *(fig)* **es ist schlecht um ihn bestellt** he is in a bad way. 2 *vi (in Restaurant)* to order.
Besteller *m* - customer.
Bestell-: **~nummer** *f* order number; **~schein** *m* order form.
Bestellung *f* (a) *(Anforderung, das Angeforderte)* order; *(das Bestellen)* ordering. (b) *(Reservierung)* booking, reservation. (c) *(Ernennung)* nomination, appointment. (d) *(von Land)* tilling.
besten *adv:* **am ~** *siehe* **beste(r, s) 2.**
bestenfalls *adv* at best.
bestens *adv (sehr gut)* very well.
beste(r, s) 1 *adj, superl of* **gut** (a) *attr* best. **im ~n Fall** at (the) best; **in ~n Händen** in the best of hands. (b) **das ~ wäre, wir ...** the best thing would be for us to...; **es steht nicht zum ~n** it does not look too promising or good; **jdn zum ~n halten** to pull sb's leg, to have sb on *(col)*; **etw zum ~n geben** *(erzählen)* to tell sth. (c) **der/die/das B~** the best; **ich will nur dein B~s** I've your best interests at heart; **sein B~s geben** to give of one's best. 2 *adv* **am ~n** best; **am ~n gehe ich jetzt** I'd or I had best be going now.
Beste(s) *nt siehe* **beste(r, s) 1** (c).
besteuern* *vt* to tax.
Besteuerung *f* taxation; *(Steuersatz)* tax.
Bestform *f (esp Sport)* top or best form.
bestialisch *adj* bestial; *(col)* awful, beastly *(col).*
besticken* *vt* to embroider.
Bestie [-tiə] *f* beast; *(fig)* animal.
bestimmen* 1 *vt* (a) to determine; Zeitpunkt etc auch to fix, to set; *(entscheiden auch)* to decide; Landschaft etc to characterize; Pflanze, Funde to classify. (b) *(vorsehen)* to intend, to mean *(für for).* **er ist zu Höherem bestimmt** he is destined for higher things; **wir waren füreinander bestimmt** we were meant for each other. 2 *vi* to decide *(über+acc on).* **du hast hier nicht zu ~** you don't make the decisions here; **er kann über sein Geld allein ~** it is up to him what he does with his money.
bestimmend *adj* Faktor, Einfluß determining, decisive. **für etw ~ sein** to be characteristic of sth; *(entscheidend)* to have a determining influence on sth.
bestimmt 1 *adj* (a) *(definite; (gewiß)* certain; *(festgesetzt)* Preis, Tag set, fixed. **suchen Sie etwas B~es?** are you looking for anything in particular? (b) *(entschieden)* Auftreten, Ton firm, decisive. 2 *adv* (a) *(sicher)* definitely, certainly. **ich weiß ganz ~, daß ...** I know for sure or for certain that ...; **ich komme ganz ~** I'll very definitely come. (b) *(wahrscheinlich)* no doubt. **das hat er ~ verloren** he's bound to have lost it.
Bestimmtheit *f* (a) *(Sicherheit)* certainty. **ich weiß aber mit ~, daß ...** but I know for sure or for certain that ... (b) *(Entschiedenheit)* firmness. **in** or **mit aller ~** quite categorically.
Bestimmung *f* (a) *(Vorschrift)* regulation. (b) *no*

pl (Zweck) purpose. **eine Anlage ihrer ~ übergeben** to officially open a new plant. (c) *(Schicksal)* destiny. (d) *(das Bestimmen)* determining; *(von Zeit etc)* fixing, setting; *(von Pflanze, Funden)* classification.
Bestimmungs-: **b~gemäß** *adj* as agreed; **~hafen** *m* (port of) destination; **~ort** *m* destination.
Best-: **~leistung** *f (esp Sport)* best performance; **seine persönliche ~leistung** *f* his personal best; **b~möglich** *adj no pred* best possible.
bestrafen* *vt* to punish; *(Jur) jdn* to sentence *(mit to); (Sport) Spieler, Foul* to penalize.
Bestrafung *f siehe vt* punishment, sentencing; penalization.
bestrahlen* *vt* to shine on; *(beleuchten)* Gebäude, Bühne to light up, to illuminate; *(Med)* to give radiotherapy to.
Bestrahlung *f* illumination; *(Med)* radiotherapy.
Bestreben *nt no pl* endeavour *(Brit)*, endeavor *(US).*
bestrebt *adj* **~ sein, etw zu tun** to endeavour *(Brit)* or endeavor *(US)* to do sth.
bestreichen* *vt irreg* to spread; *(mit Farbe)* to paint. **etw mit Butter/Fett/Öl ~** to butter/grease/oil sth.
bestreiken* *vt* to black. **bestreikt** strikebound; **die Fabrik wird zur Zeit bestreikt** there's a strike on in the factory at the moment.
bestreiten* *vt irreg* (a) *(abstreiten)* to dispute, to challenge; *(leugnen)* to deny. **jdm das Recht auf ... ~** to dispute etc sb's right to ...; **das will ich nicht ~** I'm not disputing or denying it. (b) *(finanzieren)* to pay for, to finance; Kosten to carry. (c) **er hat das ganze Gespräch allein bestritten** he did all the talking; **die Mannschaft hat fünf Spiele in zwei Wochen bestritten** the team has played five games in two weeks.
bestreuen* *vt* to cover *(mit with); (Cook)* to sprinkle.
Bestseller ['best-] *m* - best-seller.
Bestseller-: **~autor** *m* best-selling author; **~liste** *f* best-seller list.
bestücken* *vt* to fit, to equip; *(Mil)* to arm; Lager to stock.
bestürmen* *vt* to storm; *(mit Fragen, Bitten)* to bombard; *(mit Briefen, Anrufen)* to inundate.
bestürzen* *vt* to shake.
bestürzend *adj* alarming. **er sah mich bestürzt an** he looked at me in consternation.
Bestürzung *f* consternation.
Bestzeit *f (esp Sport)* best time.
Besuch *m* **-e** (a) visit *(gen* to); *(von Schule, Veranstaltung)* attendance *(gen* at). **bei jdm zu ~ sein** to be visiting sb; **(von jdm) ~ erhalten** to have or get a visit (from sb). (b) *(Besucher)* visitor; visitors *pl.* **er hat ~** he has visitors/a visitor.
besuchen* *vt jdn* to visit. Vortrag, Schule, Kino etc to go to.
Besucher(in *f)* *m* - visitor; *(pl: Publikum)* audience. **etwa 1.000 ~ waren zu der Veranstaltung gekommen** about 1,000 people went to the function.
Besuchs-: **~erlaubnis** *f (für Land)* visa; **~erlaubnis haben** to be allowed to receive visitors; **~zeit** *f* visiting time.
besucht *adj* **gut/schlecht ~ sein** to be well/badly attended.
besudeln* *vt (geh)* Wände to smear; Kleidung, Hände to soil; *(fig)* Namen, Ehre to sully.
betagt *adj (geh)* aged, well advanced in years.
betanken* *vt* Fahrzeug to fill up; Flugzeug to refuel.
betasten* *vt* to feel.
Betastrahlen *pl* beta rays *pl.*
betätigen* 1 *vt* (a) to operate; Muskeln, Gehirn to activate; Bremse auch to apply. 2 *vr* to busy oneself; *(körperlich)* to get some exercise. **sich**

politisch ~ to be active in politics; **sich literarisch/künstlerisch** ~ to do some writing/painting; **wenn er sich als Kindermädchen betätiging** when he acts as nanny.
Betätigung f **(a)** (*Tätigkeit*) activity. **(b)** *siehe vt* (*a*) operation; activation; application.
betäuben* vt (*unempfindlich machen*) to deaden; (*durch Narkose*) to anaesthetize (*Brit*), to anesthetize (*US*); (*fig*) *Kummer etc* to ease; (*fig: benommen machen*) to stun. ~**der Lärm** deafening noise; **ein** ~**der Duft** an overpowering smell.
Betäubung f (*Narkose*) anaesthetic (*Brit*), anesthetic (*US*). **örtliche** ~ local anaesthetic.
Betäubungsmittel nt anaesthetic (*Brit*), anesthetic (*US*).
Bete f **-n** beet. **rote** ~ beetroot.
beteiligen* **1** vt **jdn an etw** (*dat*) ~ to involve sb in sth; (*finanziell*) to give sb a share in sth. **2** vr to take part, to participate (*an+dat* in); (*finanziell*) to have a share (*an+dat* in). **sich an den Unkosten** ~ to contribute to the expenses.
beteiligt adj **an etw** (*dat*) ~**sein/werden** to be involved in sth, to have a part in sth; (*finanziell*) to have a share in sth.
Beteiligte(r) mf decl as adj person involved; (*an Diskussion auch*) participant; (*Teilhaber*) partner; (*Jur*) party.
Beteiligung f no pl (*Teilnahme*) (*an+dat* in) participation; (*finanziell*) share; (*an Unfall*) involvement.
beten **1** vi to pray (*um, für* for, *zu* to), to say one's prayers; (*bei Tisch*) to say grace. **2** vt to say.
beteuern* vt to declare; *Unschuld auch* to protest.
Beteuerung f siehe vt declaration; protestation.
betiteln* vt to entitle; (*anreden*) to address as.
Beton [be'tɔŋ, be'tõː] m **-s** concrete.
betonen* vt to emphasize; (*Gewicht legen auf auch*) to stress; *siehe* **betont**.
betonieren* vti to concrete. **betoniert** concrete.
Beton-: ~**klotz** m concrete block; ~**mischmaschine** f concrete-mixer.
betont adj *Höflichkeit* emphatic, deliberate; *Kühle, Sachlichkeit* pointed. **sich** ~ **einfach kleiden** to dress with pronounced simplicity.
Betonung f **(a)** no pl siehe vt emphasis; stressing. **(b)** (*Akzent, fig: Gewicht*) emphasis, stress.
betören* vt to bewitch, to beguile.
Betr. = **Betreff** re, ref.
betr. = **betreffend** regarding
Betracht m no pl **etw außer** ~ **lassen** to leave sth out of consideration, to disregard sth; **in** ~ **kommen** to be considered; **nicht in** ~ **kommen** to be out of the question; **jdn/etw in** ~ **ziehen** to take sb/sth into consideration.
betrachten* vt **(a)** (*sehen, beurteilen*) to look at. **bei näherem B** ~ on closer examination. **(b) als jdn/etw** ~ to regard or look upon or consider as sb/sth.
Betrachter m - observer.
beträchtlich adj considerable.
Betrachtung f **(a)** (*das Betrachten*) contemplation. **bei näherer** ~ on closer examination. **(b)** (*Überlegung*) reflection. **über etw** (*acc*) ~**en anstellen** to reflect on or contemplate sth.
Betrachtungsweise f **er hat eine andere** ~ he has a different way of looking at things.
Betrag m **-̈e** amount, sum.
betragen irreg **1** vi to be; (*Kosten, Rechnung auch*) to come to, to amount to. **der Unterschied beträgt 100 DM** the difference is or amounts to DM 100. **2** vr to behave.
Betragen nt no pl behaviour (*Brit*), behavior (*US*); (*esp im Zeugnis*) conduct.
betrauen* vt **jdn mit etw** ~ to entrust sb with sth.
betrauern* vt to mourn.
beträufeln* vt **den Fisch mit Zitrone** ~ to sprinkle lemon juice on the fish.
Betreff m **-e** (*form*) ~**: Ihr Schreiben vom ... re** or

reference your letter of ...
betreffen* vt irreg (*angehen*) to concern. **von dieser Regelung werde ich nicht betroffen** this rule does not concern or affect me; **was mich betrifft ...** as far as I'm concerned ...; **betrifft:** re; siehe **betroffen**.
betreffend adj attr (*erwähnt*) in question; (*zuständig, für etw relevant*) relevant. **das** ~**e Wort richtig einsetzen** to insert the appropriate word in the right place.
betreiben* vt irreg **(a)** (*vorantreiben*) to push ahead. **auf jds B** ~ (*acc*) **hin** at sb's instigation. **(b)** *Gewerbe, Handwerk* to carry on; *Handel auch* to do; *Politik* to pursue. **(c)** (*Tech*) to operate.
betreten¹* vt irreg to enter, to go/come into; *Spielfeld, Bühne, Brücke* to step onto; (*fig*) *Zeitalter etc* to enter. „**B**~ (**des Rasens**) **verboten!**“ "keep off (the grass)".
betreten² adj embarrassed.
Betretenheit f embarrassment.
betreuen* vt to look after.
Betreuer(in) f) m (*Kinder~*) child-minder; (*von Alten, Kranken*) nurse. **wir suchen noch** ~ **für ...** we are still looking for people to look after ...
Betreuung f looking after; (*von Patienten, Tieren etc*) care. **er wurde mit der** ~ **der Gruppe beauftragt** he was put in charge of the group.
Betrieb m **-e (a)** (*Firma*) business, concern; (*Fabrik*) factory, works *sing or pl.* **(b)** (*Tätigkeit*) work; (*von Maschine, Fabrik*) working, operation. **er hält den ganzen** ~ **auf** he's holding everything up; **außer** ~ out of order; **die Maschinen sind in** ~ the machines are running; **eine Maschine in/außer** ~ **setzen** to start a machine up/to stop a machine; **eine Maschine/Fabrik in** ~ **nehmen** to put a machine/factory into operation. **(c)** (*Betriebsamkeit*) bustle. **in den Geschäften herrscht großer** ~ the shops are very busy.
betrieblich adj attr company attr. **eine Sache** ~ **regeln** to settle a matter within the company.
Betriebs- in cpds (*Fabrik-*) factory, works; (*Firmen-*) company.
betriebsam adj busy, bustling no adv.
Betriebsamkeit f bustle; (*von Mensch*) active nature.
Betriebs-: ~**angehörige(r)** mf employee; ~**anleitung** f operating instructions no pl; **b**~**bereit** adj operational; ~**blindheit** f organizational blindness; **b**~**eigen** adj company attr; ~**ferien** pl (annual) holiday or vacation (*US*); ~**führung** f management; ~**geheimnis** nt trade secret; **b**~**intern** adj internal company attr; **etw b**~**intern regeln** to settle sth within the company; ~**klima** nt working atmosphere; ~**kosten** pl (*von Firma etc*) overheads pl; (*von Maschine*) running costs pl; ~**leiter** m (works or factory) manager; ~**leitung** f management; ~**prüfung** f (government) audit; ~**rat** m **(a)** (*Gremium*) works committee; **(b)** (*col: Person*) works committee member; ~**schluß** m (*von Firma*) end of business hours; (*von Fabrik*) end of factory hours; **nach** ~**schluß** after business/factory hours; **b**~**sicher** adj safe to operate; ~**störung** f breakdown; ~**system** nt (*Comp*) operating system; ~**unfall** m industrial accident; (*hum col*) accident; ~**wirt** m management expert; ~**wirtschaft** f business management.
betrinken* vr irreg to get drunk; siehe **betrunken**.
betroffen adj **(a)** affected (*von* by). **(b)** (*bestürzt*) taken aback; *Schweigen* awkward.
Betroffene(r) mf decl as adj person affected.
Betroffenheit f consternation.
betrüben* vt to sadden, to distress.
betrüblich adj sad, distressing; *Zustände* deplorable.
Betrug m no pl deceit, deception; (*Jur*) fraud. **das ist ja (alles)** ~ it's (all) a cheat or fraud.
betrügen vt irreg to deceive; (*geschäftlich auch*) to

cheat; *Freund(in)*, *Ehepartner auch* to be unfaithful to; *(Jur)* to defraud. **jdn um etw ~** to cheat sb out of sth; *(Jur)* to defraud sb of sth; **ich fühle mich betrogen** I feel betrayed; **sich um etw betrogen sehen** to feel deprived of sth.

Betrüger(in *f) m* - *(beim Spiel)* cheat; *(geschäftlich)* swindler; *(Jur)* defrauder.

Betrügerei *f* deceit; *(geschäftlich)* cheating *no pl*, swindling *no pl*; *(von Ehepartner)* deceiving *no pl*; *(Jur)* fraud.

betrügerisch *adj* deceitful; *(Jur)* fraudulent. **in ~er Absicht** with intent to defraud.

betrunken *adj* drunk *no adv*, drunken *attr*. **Fahren in ~em Zustand** drunken driving.

Betrunkene(r) *mf decl as adj* drunk.

Bett *nt* **-en** bed. **an jds ~** *(dat)* **sitzen** to sit at sb's bedside *or* by sb's bed; **im ~ in bed; jdn ins** *or* **zu ~ bringen** to put sb to bed; **ins ~ gehen** to go to bed; **mit jdm das ~ teilen** to share sb's bed; **er hat sich ins gemachte ~ gelegt** *(fig)* he had everything handed to him on a plate.

Bett-: **~bezug** *m* quilt cover; **~couch** *f* bed settee; **~decke** *f* blanket; *(gesteppt)* (continental) quilt, duvet.

Bettel-: **b~arm** *adj* destitute; **~brief** *m* begging letter.

Bettelei *f* begging.

Bettelmönch *m* mendicant *or* begging monk.

betteln *vi* to beg. **(bei jdm) um etw ~** to beg (sb) for sth.

Bettelstab *m*: **jdn an den ~ bringen** to reduce sb to beggary.

betten *vt (legen)* to make a bed for, to bed down; *Kopf* to lay. **wie man sich bettet, so liegt man** *(Prov)* as you make your bed so you must lie on it *(Prov)*; **er hat sich weich gebettet** *(fig)* he's done very nicely for himself.

Bett-: **~feder** *f* bedspring; **~federn** *pl (Daunen)* bed feathers; **~genosse** *m (dated, iro)* bedfellow; **~gestell** *nt* bedstead; **~hupferl** *nt* - *(S Ger)* bedtime sweet; **~kante** *f* edge of the bed; **~kasten** *m* linen drawer; **b~lägerig** *adj* bedridden, confined to bed; **~laken** *nt* sheet; **~lektüre** *f* bedtime reading.

Bettler(in *f) m* - beggar.

Bett-: **~nässen** *nt no pl* bed-wetting; **~nässer** *m* - bed-wetter; **~pfanne** *f* bedpan; **~pfosten** *m* bedpost; **~rand** *m* edge of the bed; **~ruhe** *f* bed rest; **~schwere** *f (col)* **die nötige ~schwere haben/bekommen** to be/get tired enough to sleep.

Bettuch *nt* sheet.

Bett-: **~vorleger** *m* bedside rug; **~wäsche** *f* bed linen; **~zeug** *nt* bedding.

betucht *adj (col)* well-to-do.

betulich *adj (übertrieben besorgt)* fussing *attr*; *Redeweise* twee.

betupfen* *vt* to dab; *(Med)* to swab.

Beuge *f* **-n** bend; *(Rumpf~)* forward bend; *(seitlich)* sideways bend; *(Knie~)* knee-bend.

Beugehaft *f (Jur)* coercive detention.

beugen 1 *vt* **(a)** to bend; *(Phys) Wellen* to diffract; *Strahlen, Licht* to deflect; *(fig) Stolz, Starrsinn* to break. **das Recht ~** to pervert the course of justice; **vom Alter gebeugt** bent *or* bowed by age; **von Kummer/Gram gebeugt** bowed down with grief/sorrow; *siehe* **gebeugt. (b)** *(Gram)* to decline; *Verb* to conjugate. **2** *vr* to bend; *(fig)* to submit, to bow *(dat to)*. **sich aus dem Fenster ~** to lean out of the window; **er beugte sich zu mir herüber** he leant across to me.

Beugung *f siehe vt* **(a)** bending, diffraction; deflection; breaking. **(b)** declension; conjugation.

Beule *f* **-n** *(von Stoß etc)* bump; *(Delle)* dent.

be|unruhigen* 1 *vt* to worry. **über etw** *(acc)* **beunruhigt sein** to be worried about sth. **2** *vr* to worry (oneself) *(über+acc, wegen* about*)*.

Be|unruhigung *f* concern.

be|urkunden* *vt* to certify; *Vertrag* to record;

Geschäft to document.

Be|urkundung *f* **(a)** *siehe vt* certification; recording; documentation. **(b)** *(Dokument)* documentation.

be|urlauben* *vt* to give leave; *(von Pflichten)* to excuse *(von* from*)*. **beurlaubt sein** to be on leave; *(suspendiert sein)* to have been relieved of one's duties; **sich ~ lassen** to take leave.

Be|urlaubung *f* granting of leave *(gen to)*; *(Beurlaubtsein)* leave.

be|urteilen* *vt* to judge *(nach* by, *from)*; *Leistung, Wert* to assess. **etw richtig/falsch ~** to judge sth correctly/to misjudge sth.

Be|urteilung *f siehe vt* judgement; assessment.

Beute *f no pl* **(a)** *(Kriegs~, fig hum)* spoils *pl*; *(Diebes~)* haul, loot; *(von Raubtieren etc)* prey; *(Jagd~)* bag. **~ machen** *(Dieb)* to make a haul. **(b)** *(liter: Opfer)* prey. **eine ~ einer Sache** *(gen)* **sein/werden** to have fallen prey/to fall prey to sth.

Beutel *m* - **(a)** bag; *(Tabaks~, Zool)* pouch. **(b)** *(col: Geld~)* *(von Frau)* purse; *(von Mann)* wallet *(Brit)*, billfold *(US)*.

Beute-: **~stück** *nt* booty; **~zug** *m* raid *(auch fig)*.

bevölkern* 1 *vt* **(a)** *(bewohnen)* to inhabit; *(beleben)* to crowd, to fill. **schwach/stark bevölkert** sparsely/densely populated. **(b)** *(besiedeln)* to populate. **2** *vr* to become inhabited; *(fig)* to fill up.

Bevölkerung *f (die Bewohner)* population.

Bevölkerungs-: **~dichte** *f* population density; **~explosion** *f* population explosion; **~schicht** *f* social stratum; **~zahl** *f* (total) population.

bevollmächtigen* *vt* to authorize *(zu etw* to do sth*)*.

Bevollmächtigte(r) *mf decl as adj* authorized representative.

Bevollmächtigung *f* authorization *(durch* from*)*.

bevor *conj* before. **~ Sie (nicht) die Rechnung bezahlt haben** until you pay the bill.

bevormunden* *vt* to treat like a child. **jdn ~ to** make sb's decisions (for him/her).

Bevormundung *f* **unsere ~ durch den Staat** the State's making up our minds for us.

bevorstehen *vi sep irreg* to be imminent; *(Winter etc)* to approach. **jdm ~** to be in store for sb; **das Schlimmste steht uns noch bevor** the worst is still to come.

bevorstehend *adj* forthcoming; *Gefahr, Krise* imminent; *Winter* approaching.

bevorzugen* *vt* to prefer; *(begünstigen)* to favour *(Brit)*, to favor *(US)*, to give preferential treatment to.

bevorzugt 1 *adj* preferred; *Behandlung* preferential; *(privilegiert)* privileged. **2** *adv* **jdn ~ bedienen** *etc* to give sb preferential treatment; **etw ~ abfertigen** *etc* to give sth priority.

Bevorzugung *f* preference *(gen* for*)*; *(vorrangige Behandlung)* preferential treatment *(bei* in*)*.

bewachen* *vt* to guard; *(Sport) Spieler* to mark.

Bewacher *m* - guard; *(Sport: von Spieler)* marker.

bewachsen *adj* overgrown *(mit* with*)*.

Bewachung *f* guarding; *(Wachmannschaft)* guard; *(Sport)* marking.

bewaffnen* 1 *vt* to arm. **2** *vr (lit, fig)* to arm oneself.

bewaffnet *adj* armed. **bis an die Zähne ~** armed to the teeth.

Bewaffnung *f* arming; *(Waffen)* weapons *pl*.

bewahren* *vt* **(a)** *(beschützen)* to protect *(vor +dat* from*)*. **(Gott) bewahre!** *(col)* heaven *or* God forbid! **(b)** *(beibehalten)* to keep, to retain.

bewähren* *vr* to prove oneself/itself; *(Methode, Sparsamkeit, Fleiß)* to pay off; *(Auto, Gerät etc)* to prove a good investment. **sich im Leben~** to make something of one's life; **es bewährt sich immer, das zu tun** it's always worth doing that; **ihre Freundschaft hat sich bewährt** their friend-

ship stood the test of time; *siehe* **bewährt**.
bewahrheiten* *vr* to prove (to be) well-founded; *(Prophezeiung)* to come true.
bewährt *adj* proven, tried and tested.
Bewahrung *f siehe vt* protection; retention.
Bewährung *f* (a) bei ~ der Methode if the method proves (to be) workable *or* valid. (b) *(Jur)* probation. eine Strafe zur ~ aussetzen to impose a suspended sentence; ein Jahr Gefängnis mit ~ a suspended sentence of one year with probation.
Bewährungs-: ~frist *f (Jur)* probation(ary) period; ~helfer *m* probation officer; ~probe *f* test; etw einer ~probe *(dat)* unterziehen to put sth to the test; ~zeit *f* time spent on probation.
bewaldet *adj* wooded.
bewältigen* *vt Schwierigkeiten* to cope with; *Arbeit, Aufgabe auch, Strecke* to manage; *Erlebnis etc* to get over; *(erledigen, beenden)* to deal with.
Bewältigung *f* die ~ der Schwierigkeiten/der Arbeit/eines Erlebnisses coping with the difficulties/managing the work/getting over an experience.
bewandert *adj* well-versed.
Bewandtnis *f* damit hat es eine andere ~ there's another reason *or* explanation for that; damit hat es folgende ~ the fact of the matter is this.
bewässern* *vt* to irrigate; *(mit Sprühanlage)* to water.
Bewässerung *f siehe vt* irrigation; watering.
Bewässerungs- *in cpds* irrigation.
bewegen[1]* *vt* to move. dieser Gedanke bewegt mich seit langem this has been on my mind a long time; *siehe* **bewegt**. 2 *vr* (a) to move. (b) *(Bewegung haben: Mensch)* to get some exercise. (c) *(fig: schwanken)* to vary, to range *(zwischen* between). der Preis bewegt sich um die 50 Mark the price is about 50 marks.
bewegen[2] *pret* **bewog**, *ptp* **bewogen** *vt* jdn zu etw ~ to induce *or* persuade sb to do sth; sich dazu ~ lassen, etw zu tun to let oneself be persuaded to do sth.
Beweggrund *m* motive.
beweglich *adj* (a) *(bewegbar)* movable; *Truppe* mobile. (b) *(wendig)* agile; *Fahrzeug* manoeuvrable *(Brit)*, maneuverable *(US)*. mit einem Kleinwagen ist man in der Stadt ~er you're more mobile in town with a small car.
Beweglichkeit *f no pl siehe adj* (a) movability; mobility. (b) agility; manoeuvrability *(Brit)*, maneuverability *(US)*.
bewegt *adj* (a) *Wasser, See* choppy; *Zeiten, Leben* eventful. (b) *Stimme, Worte* emotional.
Bewegung *f* (a) movement; *(Hand~ auch)* gesture; *(Sci, Tech auch)* motion. keine ~! don't move!; in ~ sein *(Fahrzeug)* to be moving, to be in motion; *(Menge)* to mill around; sich in ~ setzen to start moving; etw in ~ setzen to set sth in motion. (b) *(körperliche ~)* exercise. sich *(dat)* ~ verschaffen to get some exercise. (c) *(Ergriffenheit)* emotion. (d) *(Pol, Art etc)* movement.
Bewegungs-: ~freiheit *f* freedom of movement; *(fig)* freedom of action; b~los *adj* motionless, immobile; ~losigkeit *f* motionlessness, immobility; b~unfähig *adj* unable to move; *(gehunfähig)* unable to get about.
beweinen* *vt* to mourn (for), to weep for.
Beweis *m* -e *proof (für* of); *(Zeugnis)* evidence *no pl.* als *or* zum ~ as proof *or* evidence; ein eindeutiger ~ clear evidence; den ~ antreten *or* führen to offer evidence *or* proof; den ~ für etw erbringen to produce evidence *or* proof of sth.
Beweis-: ~aufnahme *f (Jur)* taking *or* hearing of evidence; b~bar *adj* provable, demonstrable.
beweisen *vt irreg* to prove. was zu ~ war QED; was noch zu ~ wäre that remains to be seen.
Beweis-: ~führung *f (Jur)* presentation of one's case; *(Math)* proof; *(Argumentation)* argu-

mentation, reasoning; ~grund *m* argument; ~kraft *f* value as evidence; ~last *f (Jur)* onus, burden of proof; ~material *nt* (body of) evidence; ~not *f (Jur)* lack of evidence; ~pflicht *f (Jur)* onus, burden of proof; ~stück *nt* exhibit.
bewenden *vt impers:* wir wollen es dabei ~ lassen let's leave it at that.
bewerben* *vr irreg (um* for) to apply *(als* for the post/job of); *(bei Wahl)* to stand; *(Comm:* um Auftrag) to quote.
Bewerber(in *f)* *m* - applicant; *(Pol)* candidate; *(Sport)* contender.
Bewerbung *f* application; *(Pol)* candidacy.
Bewerbungs-: ~bogen *m* application form; ~schreiben *nt* (letter of) application; ~unterlagen *pl* application documents *pl.*
bewerfen* *vt irreg* jdn/etw mit etw ~ to throw sth at sb/sth.
bewerkstelligen* *vt* to manage; *Geschäft* to bring off. es ~, daß jd etw tut to manage *or* contrive to get sb to do sth.
bewerten* *vt* jdn to judge; *Gegenstand* to put a value on; *Leistung auch, Schularbeit* to assess. etw mit der Note 5 ~ to give sth a mark of 5.
Bewertung *f siehe vt* judgement; valuation; assessment.
bewilligen* *vt* to allow; *Etat etc* to approve; *Geld etc auch* to grant; *Stipendium* to award.
Bewilligung *f siehe vt* allowing; approval; granting; awarding. die ~ für einen Kredit bekommen to be allowed *or* granted credit.
bewirken* *vt* (a) *(verursachen)* to cause, to bring about. ~, daß etw passiert to cause sth to happen. (b) *(erreichen)* to achieve.
bewirten* *vt* jdn ~ to wine and dine sb; jdn mit Kaffee und Kuchen ~ to entertain sb to coffee and cakes.
bewirtschaften* *vt Land* to farm, to cultivate.
Bewirtschaftung *f (von Land)* farming, cultivation.
Bewirtung *f (das Bewirten)* hospitality; *(im Hotel)* (food and) service. die ~ so vieler Gäste catering for so many guests.
bewog *pret* of **bewegen**[2].
bewogen *ptp* of **bewegen**[2].
bewohnbar *adj* habitable.
Bewohnbarkeit *f* habitability.
bewohnen* *vt* to live in; *Haus, Bau, Nest auch* to occupy; *(Volk)* to inhabit; *siehe* **bewohnt**.
Bewohner(in *f)* *m* - *(von Land, Gebiet)* inhabitant; *(von Haus etc)* occupier.
bewohnt *adj* inhabited; *Haus etc auch* occupied.
bewölken* *vr (lit, fig)* to cloud over.
bewölkt *adj* cloudy.
Bewölkung *f* clouding over; *(Wolken)* cloud.
Bewölkungs-: ~auflockerung *f* break-up of the cloud; ~zunahme *f* increase in cloud.
Bewuchs *m no pl* vegetation.
Bewund(e)rer(in *f)* *m* - admirer.
bewundern* *vt* to admire *(wegen* for).
bewundernswert *adj* admirable.
Bewunderung *f* admiration.
bewußt 1 *adj* (a) conscious. sich *(dat)* einer Sache *(gen)* ~ sein/werden to be/become aware *or* conscious of sth, to realize sth; es wurde ihm allmählich ~, daß ... he gradually realized (that) ... (b) *(willentlich)* deliberate, intentional; *Lüge* deliberate. (c) *(bekannt, besagt)* die ~e Kreuzung the crossroads in question. 2 *adv* (a) consciously. (b) *(willentlich)* deliberately, intentionally.
Bewußt-: b~los *adj* unconscious; b~los werden to become unconscious; ~lose(r) *mf decl as adj* unconscious man/woman/person *etc*; ~losigkeit *f* unconsciousness; bis zur ~losigkeit *(col) ad* nauseam; b~machen *vt sep* jdm etw b~machen to make sb conscious of sth, to make sb realize sth; sich *(dat)* etw b~machen to realize sth.

Bewußtsein nt no pl (a) (Wissen) awareness, consciousness. **etw kommt jdm zu(m) ~** sb becomes aware or conscious of sth; **jdm etw zu ~ bringen/ins ~ rufen** to make sb conscious or aware of sth; **im ~, daß** ... in the knowledge that ...; **er tat es mit (vollem) ~** he was (fully) aware of what he was doing. **(b)** (Philos, Psych, Med) consciousness. **das ~ verlieren/wiedererlangen** to lose/regain consciousness; **bei ~ sein** to be conscious; **bei vollem ~** fully conscious.

Bewußtseins-: **~bildung** f (Pol) shaping of political ideas; **b~erweiternd** adj **b~erweiternde Drogen** mind-expanding drugs; **~erweiterung** f consciousness raising; **~veränderung** f change in outlook.

bezahlbar adj affordable.

bezahlen* 1 vt **(a)** to pay. **(b)** Sache, Leistung to pay for. **etw bezahlt bekommen/für etw nichts bezahlt bekommen** to get/not to get paid for sth; **er hat seinen Fehler mit seinem Leben bezahlt** he paid for his mistake with his life. 2 vi to pay. **bezahlt** adj paid. **sich ~ machen** to pay off.

Bezahlung f **(a)** siehe vt payment; paying for (einer Sache (gen) sth). **(b)** (Lohn, Gehalt) pay; (für Dienste) payment. **ohne/gegen** or **für ~ without/** for payment.

bezähmen* 1 vt (fig geh) Begierden etc to control, to curb. 2 vr to control or restrain oneself.

bezaubern* vt (fig) to charm, to captivate.

bezaubernd adj enchanting, charming.

bezeichnen* vt **(a)** (kennzeichnen) to mark; Takt, Tonart to indicate. **(b)** (genau beschreiben) to describe. **(c)** (benennen) to call, to describe. **ich weiß nicht, wie man das bezeichnet** I don't know what it's called. **(d)** (bedeuten) to mean, to denote.

bezeichnend adj (für of) characteristic, typical.

bezeichnenderweise adv typically (enough).

Bezeichnung f **(a)** siehe vt (a, b) marking; indication; description. **(b)** (Ausdruck) expression, term.

bezeugen* vt to attest, to testify to. **~, daß** ... to attest the fact that ..., to testify that ...

bezichtigen* vt to accuse (einer Sache (gen) of sth).

beziehbar adj **(a)** Wohnung etc ready to move into. **(b)** Waren etc obtainable.

beziehen irreg 1 vt **(a)** (überziehen) Polster to cover. **die Betten frisch ~** to change the beds. **(b)** (einziehen in) Wohnung to move into. **(c)** Stellung, Standpunkt to take up. **(d)** (erhalten) to get. **(e)** (in Beziehung setzen) **etw auf jdn/etw ~** to apply sth to sb/sth; siehe **bezogen.** 2 vr **(a)** (Himmel) to cloud over. **(b)** **sich auf jdn/etw ~** to refer to sb/sth.

Bezieher(in f) m - (Abonnent) subscriber; (von Waren) purchaser; (von Einkommen) drawer.

Beziehung f **(a)** (Verhältnis) relationship. **(b)** usu pl (Kontakt) relations pl. **diplomatische ~en** diplomatic relations. **(c)** (Zusammenhang) connection (zu with), relation. **etw zu etw in ~ setzen** to relate sth to sth; **etw hat keine ~ zu etw** sth has no bearing on sth or no relationship to sth. **(d)** usu pl (Verbindung) connections pl (zu with). **seine ~en spielen lassen** to pull strings. **(e)** (Sympathie) feeling, affinity (zu for). **er hat überhaupt keine ~ zu seinen Kindern** he just doesn't relate to his children. **(f)** **in einer/keiner ~** in one/no respect or way; **in jeder ~** in every respect.

beziehungslos adj unrelated, unconnected.

beziehungsweise conj **(a)** (oder aber) or. **(b)** (im anderen Fall) and ... respectively. **zwei Briefmarken, die 50 ~ 70 Pfennig kosten** two stamps costing 50 and 70 Pfennig respectively. **(c)** (genauer gesagt) or rather, or that is to say.

beziffern* 1 vt (angeben) to estimate (auf+acc, mit at). 2 vr **sich ~ auf** (+acc) to amount to.

Bezirk m -e **(a)** (Gebiet) district. **(b)** (Admin) (Stadt) ≃ district; (von Land) ≃ region.

Bezirks-: **~klasse, ~liga** f (Sport) regional league; **~regierung** f regional administration; **~stadt** f ≃ county town.

bezirzen* vt (col) to bewitch.

bezogen adj **auf jdn/etw ~** referring to sb/sth.

Bezogene(r) mf decl as adj (Fin) (von Scheck) drawee; (von Wechsel) acceptor.

bezug siehe **Bezug (g).**

Bezug m -̈e **(a)** (für Kissen, Polster etc) cover; (für Kopfkissen) pillow-case, pillow-slip. **(b)** (Erwerb) buying, purchase; (von Zeitung) taking. **beim regelmäßigen ~ der Zeitung** ... if you take the newspaper on a regular basis ... **(c)** (von Einkommen, Rente etc) income, earnings pl. **(e)** (Zusammenhang) **= Beziehung (c).** **(f)** (form: Berufung) reference. **~ nehmen auf** (+acc) to refer to; **mit** or **unter ~ auf** (+acc) with reference to. **(g)** **in b~ auf** (+acc) regarding, with regard to, concerning.

bezüglich prep+gen (form) regarding, with regard to, re (Comm).

Bezugnahme f -n (form) reference. **unter ~ auf** (+acc) with reference to.

Bezugs-: **b~bereit, b~fertig** adj Haus etc ready to move into; **~person** f die wichtigste **~person des Kleinkindes** the person to whom the child relates most closely; **~punkt** m (lit, fig) point of reference; **~quelle** f source of supply; **~schein** m (ration) coupon.

bezuschussen* vt to subsidize.

Bezuschussung f subsidizing; (Betrag) subsidy.

bezwecken* vt to aim at. **etw mit etw ~** (Mensch) to intend sth by sth.

bezweifeln* vt to doubt. **das ist nicht zu ~** there's no doubt about it.

bezwingen* vt irreg to conquer; Feind auch to defeat, to overcome; (Sport) to beat, to defeat.

Bezwinger(in f) m - (von Berg, Feind) conqueror; (Sport) winner (gen over).

BGB ['be:ge:'be:] nt -, no pl = **Bürgerliches Gesetzbuch.**

BH [be:'ha:] m -(s) = **Büstenhalter** bra.

bibbern vi (col) (vor Angst) to tremble, to shake; (vor Kälte) to shiver.

Bibel f -n (lit) Bible; (fig) bible.

Bibel-: **b~fest** adj well versed in the Bible; **~spruch** m quotation from the Bible; **~wort** nt, pl **~worte** biblical saying.

Biber m - beaver.

Biber-: **~bettuch** nt flannelette; **~pelz** m beaver (fur).

Bibliographie f bibliography.

Bibliothek f -en library.

Bibliothekar(in f) m librarian.

biblisch adj biblical. **ein ~es Alter** a great age, a ripe old age.

Bidet [bi'de:] nt -s bidet.

bieder adj **(a)** (rechtschaffen) honest; Mensch, Leben auch upright. **(b)** (pej) conventional.

Bieder-: **~mann** m, pl **~männer** (pej geh) petty bourgeois; **b~männisch** adj (pej geh) petty bourgeois; Geschmack, Gesinnung auch philistine.

biegen pret **bog,** ptp **gebogen** 1 vt to bend; (fig: manipulieren) to wangle (col). **auf B~ oder Brechen** (col) by hook or by crook (col). 2 vi aux sein (Mensch, Wagen) to turn; (Weg, Straße auch) to curve. 3 vr to bend; (Holz, Plastik) to warp (Metall) to buckle. **sich vor Lachen ~** (fig) to double up with laughter.

biegsam adj flexible; Holz auch pliable; Metall auch malleable; Glieder, Körper supple.

Biegsamkeit f siehe adj flexibility; pliability; malleability; suppleness.

Biegung f **der Fluß/die Straße macht eine ~** the river/road curves or bends.

Biene f -n **(a)** bee. **(b)** (dated col: Mädchen) bird

(Brit col), chick *(esp US col)*.

Bienen-: b~fleißig *adj* industrious; **~honig** *m* real *or* natural honey; **~königin** *f* queen bee; **~korb** *m* (bee)hive; **~schwarm** *m* swarm (of bees); **~stich** *m (Cook)* cake coated with sugar and almonds filled with custard or cream; **~stock** *m* (bee)hive; **~wachs** *nt* beeswax; **~zucht** *f* beekeeping **~züchter** *m* beekeeper.

Bier *nt* **-e** beer. **zwei ~, bitte!** two beers, please; **das ist mein ~** *(fig col)* that's my business.

Bier- in cpds beer; **~bauch** *m (col)* beer gut *(col)*; **~brauerei** *f* (beer-)brewing; *(Betrieb)* brewery; **~deckel** *m* beer mat; **~dose** *f* beer can; **~ernst** *m (col)* deadly seriousness; **~faß** keg; **~flasche** *m* beer bottle; **~kasten** beer crate; **~keller** *m* beer cellar; **~krug** *m* tankard, beer mug; *(aus Steingut)* (beer) stein; **~leiche** *f (col)* drunk; **~ruhe** *f (col)* cool *(col)*; **~schinken** *m*, **~wurst** *f* ham sausage; **b~selig** *adj* Mensch boozed up *(col)*; **~zelt** *nt* beer tent.

Biest *nt* **-er** *(pej col)* **(a)** *(Tier)* creature; *(Insekt auch)* bug. **(b)** *(Mensch)* (little) wretch; *(Frau)* bitch *(col)*.

bieten *pret* **bot**, *ptp* **geboten 1** *vt* **(a)** to offer *(jdm etw sb sth, sth to sb)*; *(bei Auktion)* to bid *(auf+acc for)*; *Gelegenheit auch* to give. **jdm die Hand ~** to offer sb one's hand; **wer bietet mehr?** *(bei Auktion)* any more bids?; **diese Stadt hat nichts zu ~** this town has nothing to offer. **(b)** *(haben, aufweisen)* to have; *Problem, Schwierigkeit* to present. **das Hochhaus bietet fünfzig Familien Wohnung** the tower block provides accommodation for fifty families. **(c)** *(zeigen, darbieten)* Anblick, Bild to present; *Film* to show; *Leistung* to give. **die Mannschaft bot ein hervorragendes Spiel** the team played an excellent game. **(d)** *(zumuten)* **so etwas könnte man mir nicht ~** I wouldn't stand for that sort of thing; *siehe* **geboten. 2** *vi (Cards)* to bid. **3** *vr (Gelegenheit, Anblick etc)* to present itself *(jdm to sb)*.

Bieter(in *f)* *m* - bidder.

Bigamie *f* bigamy.

Bigamist(in *f)* *m* bigamist.

bigott *adj* overly pious; *(scheinheilig)* hypocritical.

Bikini *m* **-s** bikini.

Bilanz *f* **(a)** balance; *(Abrechnung)* balance sheet. **eine ~ aufstellen** to draw up a balance sheet. **(b)** *(fig: Ergebnis)* end result. **(die) ~ ziehen** to take stock *(aus of)*.

Bilanzprüfer *m* auditor.

bilateral *adj* bilateral.

Bild *nt* **-er (a)** *(lit,fig)* picture; *(Film)* frame. **ein ~ machen** to take a photo *or* picture; **ein ~ des Elends** a picture of misery. **(b)** *(Abbild)* image; *(Spiegel~ auch)* reflection. **sie ist ganz das ~ ihrer Mutter** she is the image of her mother. **(c)** *(Anblick, Ansicht)* sight. **das äußere ~ der Stadt** the appearance of the town. **(d)** *(Theat: Szene)* scene. **(e)** *(Metapher)* metaphor, image. **im ~ bleiben** to use the same metaphor. **(f)** *(Erscheinungs~)* character. **sie gehören zum ~ dieser Stadt** they are part of the scene in this town. **(g)** *(fig: Vorstellung)* image, picture. **im ~e sein** to be in the picture *(über+acc* about); **jdn ins ~ setzen** to put sb in the picture; **sich** *(dat)* **von jdm/etw ein ~ machen** to get an idea of sb/sth; **das ~ des Deutschen** the image of the German.

Bild-: ~ausfall *m (TV)* loss of vision; **~band** *m* illustrated book; **~beschreibung** *f (Sch)* description of a picture.

bilden 1 *vt* **(a)** to form; *(fig)* Charakter auch to shape, to mould; *Vermögen* to acquire; *(ausmachen)* Höhepunkt, Ausnahme, Gefahr etc to constitute. **sich** *(dat)* **eine Meinung ~** to form an opinion. **(b)** *(erziehen)* to educate. **2** *vr* **(a)** *(entstehen)* to form, to develop. **(b)** *(lernen)* to educate oneself; *(durch Lesen etc)* to improve one's

mind; *(durch Reisen etc)* to broaden one's mind. **3** *vi siehe vr* **(b)** to be educational; to improve the mind; to broaden the mind.

bildend *adj* **die ~e Kunst** art; **~er Künstler** artist.

Bilderbogen *m* illustrated broadsheet. **ein musikalischer ~** a musical medley.

Bilderbuch *nt* picture book.

Bilderbuch- *in cpds (fig)* perfect; **~landung** *f* **eine ~landung** a textbook landing.

Bilder-: ~geschichte *f* picture story; *(in Comic, Zeitung)* strip cartoon; **~rahmen** *m* pictureframe; **~rätsel** *nt* picture-puzzle; **b~reich** *adj* Buch etc full of pictures; *(fig)* Sprache rich in imagery.

Bild-: ~fläche *f* **(a)** *(Leinwand)* projection surface; **(b)** *(fig col)* **auf der ~fläche erscheinen** to appear on the scene; **von der ~fläche verschwinden** to disappear (from the scene); **b~haft** *adj* pictorial; *Beschreibung, Sprache* vivid; **~hauer** *m* sculptor; **~hauerei** *f* sculpture; **~hauerin** *f* sculptress; **b~hübsch** *adj* Mädchen (as) pretty as a picture; *Kleid, Garten* really lovely.

bildlich *adj* pictorial; *Ausdruck etc* figurative. **sich** *(dat)* **etw ~ vorstellen** to picture sth in one's mind's eye.

Bildnis *nt (liter)* portrait.

Bild-: ~platte *f* video disc; **~plattenspieler** *m* video disc player; **~punkt** *m (Comp)* pixel; **~qualität** *f (TV, Film)* picture quality; *(Phot)* print quality; **~reporter** *m* photojournalist; **~röhre** *f (TV)* cathode ray tube; **~schärfe** *f* definition *no indef art*; **~schirm** *m (TV, Comp)* screen; **~schirmgerät** *nt* visual display unit, VDU, monitor; **~schirmtext** *m* viewdata; **b~schön** *adj* beautiful; **~text** *m* caption.

Bildung *f* **(a)** *(Erziehung)* education; *(Kultur)* culture. **~ haben** to be cultured. **(b)** *no pl (das Formen)* formation, forming; *(fig: von Charakter etc auch)* shaping; *(von Vermögen)* acquisition. **zur ~ des Passivs** to form the passive.

Bildungs-: ~chancen *pl* educational opportunities *pl*; **~einrichtung** *f* educational institution; *(Kulturstätte)* cultural institution; **~gang** *m* school (and university/college) career; **~grad** *m* level of education; **~lücke** *f* gap in one's education; **~politik** *f* education policy; **~reise** *f* educational trip; **~roman** *m (Liter)* Bildungsroman, novel concerned with the intellectual or spiritual development of the main character; **~stand** *m*, **~stufe** *f* level of education; **~urlaub** *m* educational holiday; **~weg** *m* jds **~weg** the course of sb's education; **auf dem zweiten ~weg** through night school/the Open University etc; **~wesen** *nt* education system.

Bild-: ~unterschrift *f* caption; **~werfer** *m* projector; **~zuschrift** *f* reply enclosing photograph.

Billard ['bɪljart] *nt (Spiel)* billiards *sing*.

Billard-: ~kugel *f* billiard ball; **~stock** *m* billiard cue; **~tisch** *m* billiard table.

Billett [bɪl'jɛt] *nt* **-e** *or* **-s** *(dated)* ticket.

billig *adj* **(a)** cheap. **~ abzugeben** going cheap; **~ davonkommen** to get off lightly. **(b)** *(pej: primitiv)* cheap; *Ausrede* feeble.

billigen *vt* to approve. **etw stillschweigend ~** to condone sth; **~, daß jd etw tut** to approve of sb's doing sth.

Billigpreis *m* low price.

Billigung *f* approval. **jds ~ finden** to meet with sb's approval.

Billion *f* billion *(Brit)*, trillion *(US)*.

Bimmel *f* **-n** *(col)* bell.

bimmeln *vi (col)* to ring.

Bimsstein *m* pumice stone.

bin 1. pers sing pres of *sein*.

Binde *f* **-n (a)** *(Med)* bandage. **(b)** *(Arm~)* armband; *(Augen~)* blindfold. **(c)** *(Monats~)* (sanitary) towel *or* napkin *(US)*. **(d)** *(dated: Krawatte)* tie. **sich** (dat) **einen hinter die ~ gießen** or **kippen** (col) to put a few drinks away.

Binde-: **~gewebe** nt (Anat) connective tissue; **~glied** nt (fig) link; **~hautentzündung** f conjunctivitis; **~mittel** nt binder.

binden pret **band,** ptp **gebunden 1** vt (a) (zusammen~) to tie; (fest~) to bind; (fig geh) to bind, to unite. (b) (Buch etc) to bind; Strauß, Kranz to make up; Knoten, Schal to tie; Krawatte to knot. **sich** (dat) **die Schuhe ~** to tie (up) one's shoelaces. (c) (fesseln, befestigen) (an+acc to) to tie (up); Menschen auch to bind; (fig) (an einen Ort) to tie; (Versprechen, Vertrag, Eid etc) to bind. **jdm die Hände auf den Rücken ~** to tie sb's hands behind his back; **mir sind die Hände gebunden** (fig) my hands are tied; **nichts bindet mich an Glasgow** I have no special ties in Glasgow. (d) (festhalten) Staub, Erdreich to bind; (Chem) (aufnehmen) to absorb; (sich vebinden mit) to combine with; (Cook) Soße to bind. **2** vr (sich verpflichten) to commit oneself (an+acc to).

bindend adj binding (für on); Zusage definite.

Binder m - (Krawatte) tie, necktie (US).

Bindestrich m hyphen.

Bindfaden m string. **es regnet ~** (col) it's sheeting down (col).

Bindung f (a) tie (an +acc with); (Beziehung zu einem Partner) relationship (an+acc with); (Verpflichtung: an Beruf etc, durch Vertrag) commitment (an+acc to). (b) (Ski~) binding.

binnen prep+dat or (geh) gen (form) within.

Binnen-: **~gewässer** nt inland water; **~hafen** m river port; **~handel** m domestic trade; **~land** nt (Landesinneres) interior; **b~ländisch** adj inland; **~markt** m home market; **~meer** nt inland sea; **~schiffahrt** f inland navigation; **~staat** m landlocked country or state.

Binse f **-n** usu pl rush. **in die ~n gehen** (fig col) (mißlingen) to be a wash-out (col); (verlorengehen) to go west (col); (kaputtgehen) to give out (col).

Binsen-: **~wahrheit,** **~weisheit** f truism.

Bio- in cpds bio-; **~chemie** f biochemistry; **b~dynamisch** adj biodynamic.

Biograph(in f) m biographer.

Biographie f biography.

Bioladen m (col) health food shop (Brit) or store (US).

Biologe m, **Biologin** f biologist.

Biologie f biology.

biologisch adj biological.

Biophysik f biophysics sing.

Birke f **-n** birch.

Birma nt Burma.

Birnbaum m (Baum) pear tree; (Holz) pear-wood.

Birne f **-n** (a) pear. (b) (Glühlampe) (light) bulb. (c) (col: Kopf) nut (col).

birnenförmig adj pear-shaped.

bis 1 prep+acc (a) (zeitlich) until, till; (bis spätestens, nicht späte als) by. **~ Ende Mai bin ich noch in London** I'll be in London up to or until the end of May; **~ Ende Mai bin ich damit fertig** I'll have finished it by the end of May; **~ dahin ist er längst weg** he will have gone long before then; **~ wann gilt der Fahrplan/ist das fertig?** when is the timetable valid till/will that be finished by?; **~ wann?** till/by when?; **~ wann bleibt ihr hier?** when are you staying here till?; **~ dann!** see you then!; **von ... ~ (einschließlich)** ... from ... to or till or through (US) ... **(b)** (räumlich) to; (in Buch, Film etc auch) up to. **ich fahre nur ~ München** I'm only going to or as far as Munich; **~ dorthin sind es nur 5 km** it's only 5 km there; **~ hierher und nicht weiter** (lit, fig) this far and no further; **~ mindestens Carlisle** at least as far as Carlisle.

(c) (bei Zahlen) ~ up to; (bis zu einer unteren Grenze von) (down) to. **Kinder ~ sechs Jahre** children up to the age of six.

2 adv **(a)** (zeitlich) until, till; (bis spätestens) by. **~ zu diesem Zeitpunkt** up to this time; **das sollte ~ zum nächsten Sommer fertig sein** that should be finished by next summer; **~ auf weiteres** until further notice.

(b) (räumlich) to; durch, über, unter right. **~ an unser Grundstück** (right or up) to our plot; **es sind noch 10 km ~ nach Schlüchtern** it's another 10 km to Schlüchtern; **~ ins letzte/kleinste** (right) down to the last/smallest detail.

(c) (bei Zahlen) ~ **zu** up to; (bis zu einer unteren Grenze von) (down) to; **Gefängnis ~ zu 8 Jahren** a maximum of 8 years' imprisonment.

(d) ~ **auf** (+acc) (außer) except (for); (einschließlich) (right) down to.

3 conj **(a)** (beiordnend) to. **zehn ~ zwanzig Stück** ten to twenty; **bewölkt ~ bedeckt** cloudy or overcast. **(b)** (unterordnend: zeitlich) until, till; (nicht später als) by the time. **ich warte noch, ~ es dunkel wird** I'll wait until or till it gets dark; **~ es dunkel wird, möchte ich zu Hause sein** I want to get home by the time it's dark.

Bisam m or **-s** (Pelz) musquash.

Bisamratte f muskrat (beaver).

Bischof m -e bishop.

bischöflich adj episcopal.

bisexuell adj bisexual.

bisher adv until or till now; (und immer noch) up to now; **~ nicht** not until or till now, not before; (und immer noch nicht) not as yet; **~ habe ich es ihm nicht gesagt** I haven't told him as yet; **ein ~ unbekannter Stern** a hitherto unknown star.

bisherig adj attr (vorherig) previous; (momentan) present, up to now. **in meiner ~en Karriere** in my career up to now.

Biskuit [bɪs'kviːt] nt or m -s or -e sponge.

Biskuit-: **~gebäck** nt sponge cake/cakes; **~teig** m sponge mixture.

bislang adv = **bisher.**

Bison m -s bison.

biß pret of **beißen.**

Biß m -sse bite.

bißchen 1 adj inv **ein ~ Geld/Liebe/Wärme** a bit of or a little money/love/warmth; **das ~ Geld, das wir haben** what little money we have; **ich habe kein ~ Hunger** I'm not a bit hungry. **2** adv **ein ~ a bit, a little; ein ~ wenig** not very much; **ein ~ mehr/viel/teuer** etc a bit more/much/expensive etc; **ein ~ zu wenig** not quite enough.

Bissen m - (häppchen) (Imbiß) bite (to eat). **er will keinen ~ anrühren** he won't eat a thing; **sich** (dat) **jeden ~ vom** or **am Munde absparen** to watch every penny one spends.

bissig adj **(a)** vicious; Bemerkung caustic. **~ sein** to bite; **„Vorsicht, ~er Hund"** "beware of the dog". **(b)** (übellaunig) snappy.

Bißwunde f bite.

bist 2. pers sing pres of **sein.**

Bistum ['bɪstuːm] nt diocese, bishopric.

bisweilen adv (geh) from time to time.

Bit nt -s (Comp) bit.

Bittbrief m petition.

Bitte f **-n** request; (inständig) plea. **ich habe eine große ~ an dich** I have a big request to make of you; **er kann ihr keine ~ abschlagen** he can't refuse her anything.

bitte interj **(a)** (bittend, auffordernd) please. **~ schön/sehr;** bitte ~ nicht! no, please!, please don't; **ja ~!** yes please. **(b)** (bei höflicher Frage etc) ~ **schön?** (in Geschäft) can I help you?; (in Gaststätte) what would you like?; **~ (, Sie wünschen)?** what can I do for you?; **ja ~?** yes?; **~ (, nehmen Sie doch Platz)!** (form) please or do sit down; **aber ~!** sure (col); **na ~!** there you are! **(c)** (sarkastisch: nun gut) all right. **~, wie du willst** (all right) just as you like. **(d)** (Dank erwidernd) ~ **(sehr** or **schön)** you're welcome, not at all; **aber ~!** there's no need to thank me. **(e)** (nachfragend)

(wie) ~? (I beg your) pardon? *(auch iro)*, pardon me *(US)*, sorry?

bitten *pret* **bat**, *ptp* **gebeten** 1 *vt* (a) to ask; *(inständig)* to beg. **jdn um etw** ~ to ask/beg sb for sth; **jdn (darum)** ~, **etw zu tun** to ask *etc* sb to do sth; **darf ich Sie um Ihren Namen** ~? might I ask your name?; **er läßt sich nicht (lange)** ~ you don't have to ask him twice; **aber ich bitte dich!** not at all; **wenn** ~ **ich darf** *(form)* if you please, if you wouldn't mind; **ich bitte darum** *(form)* if you wouldn't mind; **ich muß doch (sehr)** ~! well I must say! (b) *(einladen)* to ask, to invite. **jdn auf ein Glas Wein** ~ to invite sb to have a glass of wine. (c) *(bestellen)* **jdn zu sich** ~ to ask sb to come and see one. 2 *vi* (a) to ask; *(inständig)* to plead, to beg. **um etw** ~ to ask (for) *or* request sth; to plead *or* beg for sth; **bei jdm um etw** ~ to ask sb for sth. (b) *(einladen)* **ich lasse** ~ would you ask him/her to come in now?; **darf ich (um den nächsten Tanz)** ~? may I have the pleasure (of the next dance)?

bittend *adj* pleading.

bitter *adj* bitter; *Schokolade* plain; *(fig) Geschmack* nasty; *Wahrheit, Lehre, Verlust* hard, painful; *Zeit, Schicksal* hard; *Ernst* deadly; *Hohn, Spott* cruel; *Not, Notwendigkeit* dire; *Leid, Unrecht* grievous. **bis zum** ~**en Ende** to the bitter end; **jdn** ~ **machen** to embitter sb, to make sb bitter; **etw** ~ **nötig haben** to be in dire need of sth; **solche Fehler rächen sich** ~ one pays dearly for mistakes like that.

Bitter-: **b**~**böse** *adj* furious; **damit ist es mir b**~**ernst** I am deadly serious *or* in deadly earnest; **b**~**kalt** *adj attr* bitterly cold; ~**keit** *f (lit, fig)* bitterness; **b**~**lich** *adv* bitterly; **b**~**süß** *adj (lit, fig)* bitter-sweet.

Bitt-: ~**gesuch** *nt,* ~**schrift** *f* petition; ~**steller(in** *f)* *m* - petitioner.

Biwak *nt -s or -e* bivouac.

bizarr *adj* bizarre.

Bizeps *m -e* biceps.

Bj. = **Baujahr.**

Blabla *nt no pl (col)* waffle (col).

Blag *nt -en,* **Blage** *f -n (pej col)* brat.

blähen 1 *vt* to swell; *Anorak, Gardine* to fill; *Nüstern* to flare. 2 *vr* to swell; *(Segel auch, Anorak, Gardine)* to billow; *(Nüstern)* to flare. 3 *vi (Speisen)* to cause flatulence *or* wind.

blähend *adj (Med)* flatulent.

Blähung *f usu pl (Med)* wind *no pl,* flatulence *no pl.*

blamabel *adj* shameful.

Blamage [bla'maːʒə] *f -n* disgrace.

blamieren* 1 *vt* to disgrace. 2 *vr* to make a fool of oneself.

blank *adj* (a) shiny, shining. **etw** ~ **polieren** to polish sth till it shines. (b) *(nackt)* bare; *Schwert* naked; *(col: ohne Geld)* broke; *(Cards: einzeln)* single. **eine Karte** ~ **haben** to have only one card of a suit. (c) *(rein)* pure, sheer; *Hohn* utter.

Blanko- *in cpds* blank; ~**scheck** *m* blank cheque *(Brit)* or check *(US)*; ~**vollmacht** *f* carte blanche.

Bläschen ['blɛːsçən] *nt (Med)* small blister.

Blase *f -n* (a) *(Seifen* ~*, Luft* ~*)* bubble. (b) *(Med)* blister. **sich. (dat)** ~**n laufen** *etc* to get blisters from walking *etc.* (c) *(Anat)* bladder. (d) *(pej col: Clique)* gang *(col)*, mob *(col)*.

Blasebalg *m (pair of)* bellows.

blasen *pret* **blies**, *ptp* **geblasen** 1 *vi* to blow. **zum Rückzug** ~ *(lit, fig)* to sound the retreat; **zum Aufbruch** ~ *(fig)* to say it's time to go; **es bläst** *(col)* it's blowy *(col) or* windy. 2 *vt* (a) to blow. (b) *Posaune etc* to play. (c) *(col)* **dir/ihm werd ich was** ~! I'll give you/him a piece of my mind.

Blasen-: ~**entzündung** *f* cystitis; ~**leiden** *nt* bladder trouble *no art.*

Bläser(in *f)* *m -* *(Mus)* wind player. **die** ~ **the wind** (section).

blasiert *adj (pej geh)* blasé.

Blasiertheit *f (pej geh)* blasé character; *(von Mensch)* blasé attitude.

Blas-: ~**instrument** *nt* wind instrument; ~**musik** *f* brass band music.

Blasphemie *f* blasphemy.

blasphemisch *adj* blasphemous.

blaß *adj* (a) *Haut, Farbe, Licht* pale. ~ **werden** to grow *or* go pale, to pale; *(vor Schreck auch)* to blanch; ~ **vor Neid werden** to go green with envy. (b) *(fig) Ahnung, Vorstellung* faint, vague; *Ausdruck* weak, insipid.

blaß- *in cpds* pale.

Blässe *f -n* paleness, pallor.

Blatt *nt* ⁻er (a) *(Bot)* leaf. **kein** ~ **vor den Mund nehmen** not to mince one's words. (b) *(Papier etc)* sheet. **ein** ~ **Papier** a sheet of paper; *(noch)* **ein unbeschriebenes** ~ **sein** *(unerfahren)* to be inexperienced; *(ohne Image)* to be an unknown quantity; **vom** ~ **singen/spielen** to sight-read. (c) *(Seite)* page. **das steht auf einem anderen** ~ *(fig)* that's another story. (d) *(Zeitung)* paper. (e) *(von Säge, Ruder)* blade. (f) *(Cards)* hand; *(Einzelkarte)* card. **das** ~ **hat sich gewendet** *(fig)* the tide has turned.

blätt(e)rig *adj Teig* flaky; *Farbe etc* flaking.

blättern 1 *vi* in einem *Buch* ~ to leaf through a book. 2 *vt Geldscheine, Spielkarten* to put down one by one.

Blätterteig *m* puff pastry.

Blatt-: ~**feder** *f (Tech)* leaf spring; ~**gemüse** *nt* greens *pl*; **ein** ~**gemüse** a leaf vegetable; ~**gold** *nt* gold leaf; ~**grün** *nt* chlorophyll; ~**laus** *f* greenfly, aphid; **b**~**los** *adj* leafless; ~**schuß** *m (Hunt)* shot through the shoulder to the heart; ~**silber** *nt* silver leaf; ~**werk** *nt no pl* foliage.

blau *adj* (a) blue. **Forelle** *etc* ~ *(Cook)* trout *etc* au bleu; **ein** ~**es Auge** *(col)* a black eye; **mit einem** ~**en Auge davonkommen** *(fig)* to get off lightly; ~**es Blut** blue blood; **ein** ~**er Brief** *(Sch)* letter informing parents that their child is likely to have to repeat a year; **ein** ~**er Fleck** a bruise; **er wird sein** ~**es Wunder erleben** *(col)* he won't know what's hit him *(col)*. (b) *usu pred (col: betrunken)* drunk, tight *(col)*.

Blau *nt - or (col) -s* blue.

Blau-: **b**~**äugig** *adj* blue-eyed; *(fig)* naïve; ~**äugigkeit** *f (fig)* naïvety; ~**beere** *f =* **Heidelbeere;** **b**~**blütig** *adj* blue-blooded.

Blaue *nt no pl* (a) **das** ~ **vom Himmel (herunter) lügen** *(col)* to tell a pack of lies; **jdm das** ~ **vom Himmel (herunter) versprechen** *(col)* to promise sb the moon. **ins** *(col, ohne Ziel)* **ins** ~ **hinein** *(col)* at random; **eine Fahrt ins** ~ a mystery tour.

Bläue *f no pl* blueness; *(des Himmels auch)* blue.

blau-: ~**grau** *adj* blue-grey; ~**grün** *adj* blue-green.

bläulich *adj* bluish, bluey.

Blau-: ~**licht** *nt (von Polizei etc)* flashing blue light; *(Lampe)* blue light; **mit** ~**licht** with its blue light flashing; **b**~**machen** *sep (col)* 1 *vi* to skip work; 2 *vt* **den Freitag/zwei Tage b**~**machen** to skip work on Friday/for two days; ~**mann** *m, pl* ~**männer** *(col)* boilersuit; ~**meise** *f* bluetit; ~**pause** *f* blueprint; ~**säure** *f* prussic acid; ~**tanne** *f* colorado spruce; ~**wal** *m* blue whale.

Blech *nt -e* (a) *no pl (sheet)* metal. (b) *(Blechstück)* metal plate. (c) *(Backblech)* baking tray. (d) *no pl (col: Blechinstrumente)* brass. (e) *no pl (col: Unsinn)* rubbish *no art (col)*.

Blech-: ~**bläser** the brass (section); ~**blasinstrument** *nt* brass instrument; ~**büchse,** ~**dose** *f* tin *(Brit)*, can.

blechen *vti (col)* to cough up *(col)*.

blechern *adj* (a) *attr* metal. (b) *Geräusch* tinny.

Blech-: ~**instrument** *nt* brass instrument; ~**kanister** *m* metal can; ~**kiste** *f (pej col)* (old) crate *(col)*; ~**lawine** *f (pej col)* vast column of cars; ~**napf** *m* metal bowl; ~**schaden** *m* damage

to the bodywork; ~**schere** ƒ (pair of) metal shears; ~**trommel** ƒ tin drum.
blecken vt **die Zähne** ~ to bare one's teeth.
Blei nt -e **(a)** no pl (Metall) lead. **jdm wie** ~ **in den Gliedern** or **Knochen liegen** (Schreck) to paralyze sb; (Depression) to weigh sb down. **(b)** (Lot) plumb, (plumb-)bob.
Bleibe ƒ -**n** place to stay.
bleiben pret **blieb**, ptp **geblieben** vi aux sein **(a)** to stay, to remain. **unbeachtet** ~ to go unnoticed; **unbeantwortet** ~ to be left or to remain unanswered; **in Übung/Form** ~ to keep in practice/form; **wach** ~ to stay or keep awake; **wenn das Wetter so bleibt** if the weather stays or keeps like this; **sitzen/stehen** ~ to remain seated/ standing; **bitte,** ~ **Sie doch sitzen** please don't get up; **von etw** ~ to stay or keep away from sth; **wo bleibst du so lange?** (col) what's keeping you?; **wo sind denn all die alten Häuser geblieben?** what happened to all the old houses?
  (b) (fig) **bei etw** ~ to keep or stick (col) to sth; **das bleibt unter uns** that's (just) between ourselves; **wir möchten unter uns** ~ we want to keep ourselves to ourselves.
  (c) (übrigbleiben) to be left, to remain. **es blieb keine andere Wahl** there was no other choice; **es bleibt abzuwarten** it remains to be seen; **es bleibt zu hoffen, daß ...** I/we can only hope that ...
  (d) (col: versorgt werden) **und wo bleibe ich?** and what about me?; **sieh zu, wo du bleibst!** that's your problem!
bleibend adj Wert, Erinnerung etc lasting; Schaden, Zähne permanent.
bleibenlassen vt sep irreg (col) **(a)** (unterlassen) **etw** ~ to give sth a miss (col); **das wirst du ganz schön** ~ you'll do nothing of the sort! **(b)** (aufgeben) to give up.
bleich adj pale. ~ **wie der Tod** deathly pale.
bleichen vt to bleach.
Bleich-: ~**gesicht** nt **(a)** (col: blasser Mensch) pasty-face (col); **(b)** (Weißer) paleface; ~**mittel** nt bleach.
bleiern adj **(a)** attr (aus Blei) lead. **wie eine** ~**e Ente schwimmen** (hum) to swim like a brick. **(b)** (fig) leaden; Verantwortung onerous. **es lag ihr** ~ **. in den Gliedern** her limbs were like lead.
Blei-: b~frei adj lead-free; ~**gehalt** m lead content; ~**gießen** nt New Year's Eve custom of telling fortunes by the shapes made by molten lead dropped into cold water; ~**haltig** adj **b~haltig sein** to contain lead; ~**kristall** nt lead crystal; ~**satz** m (Typ) hot-metal setting; ~**soldat** m ≈ tin soldier.
Bleistift m pencil; (zum Malen) crayon.
Bleistift-: ~**absatz** m stiletto heel; ~**spitzer** m pencil sharpener.
Bleivergiftung ƒ lead poisoning.
Blende ƒ -**n (a)** (Lichtschutz) shade, screen; (an Fenster) blind. **(b)** (Phot) (Öffnung) aperture; (Einstellungsposition) f-stop; (Vorrichtung) diaphragm. ~ **4 einstellen** to set the aperture to f/4. **(c)** (Film, TV) fade. **(d)** (Sew) trim.
blenden 1 vt **(a)** (lit, fig: bezaubern) to dazzle. **(b)** (blind machen) to blind. **2** vi to dazzle.
blendend adj splendid; Pianist, Schüler etc brilliant; Stimmung sparkling. **es geht mir** ~ I feel wonderful.
Blesse ƒ -**n** (Fleck) blaze.
bleu [blø:] adj inv (Fashion) light blue.
Blick m -**e (a)** (col: (flüchtiger ~) glance. **auf den ersten** ~ at first glance; Liebe **auf den ersten** ~ love at first sight; **auf den zweiten** ~ when one looks again; **mit einem** ~ at a glance; **jds** ~ (dat) **ausweichen** to avoid sb's eye; **jds** ~ **erwidern** to return sb's gaze; **jdn mit seinen** ~**en verschlingen** to devour sb with one's eyes; **sie zog alle** ~**e auf sich** everybody's eyes were drawn to her; **einen** ~ **auf etw** (acc) **werfen** to throw a

glance at sth; **jdm keinen** ~ **schenken** not to spare sb a glance; **er hat keinen** ~ **für sie** he takes no notice of her; **wenn** ~**e töten könnten!** if looks could kill!; **mein** ~ **fiel auf sein leeres Glas** my eyes fell on his empty glass; **den** ~ **heben** to look up; **den** ~ **senken** to look down.
  (b) (Augenausdruck) look in one's eyes. **den bösen** ~ **haben** to have the evil eye.
  (c) (Ausblick) view. **ein Zimmer mit** ~ **auf den Park** a room overlooking the park.
  (d) (Verständnis) **seinen** ~ **für etw schärfen** to increase one's awareness of sth; **einen (guten)** ~ **für etw haben** to have an eye for sth.
blicken vi (auf+acc at) to look; (flüchtig ~) to glance. **sich** ~ **lassen** to put in an appearance; **laß dich hier ja nicht mehr** ~**!** don't show your face here again!; **laß dich doch mal wieder** ~**!** why don't you drop in some time?; **das läßt tief** ~ that's very revealing.
Blick-: ~**fang** m eye-catcher; **als** ~**fang to catch the eye;** ~**feld** nt field of vision; **ins** ~**feld (der Öffentlichkeit) treten** to become the focus of (public) attention; ~**kontakt** m visual contact; ~**punkt** m **(a) im** ~**punkt der Öffentlichkeit stehen** to be in the public eye; **(b)** (fig: Standpunkt) point of view; ~**richtung** ƒ line of vision; (fig) outlook; ~**winkel** m (fig) viewpoint.
blieb pret of **bleiben**.
blies pret of **blasen**.
blind adj **(a)** (lit, fig) blind (für to); Zufall pure; Alarm false. **jdm** ~ **gehorchen** to obey sb blindly; **ein** ~**es Huhn findet auch mal ein Korn** (Prov) anyone can be lucky now and again; ~**er Fleck** (Physiol) blind spot; ~**e Gewalt** brute force; ~**er Eifer schadet nur** (Prov) it's not a good thing to be over-enthusiastic; **etw** ~ **herausgreifen** to pick sth at random. **(b)** (getrübt) dull; Spiegel etc clouded. **(c)** (Archit) false; Fenster blind, false. **(d)** ein ~**er Passagier** a stowaway.
Blinddarm m (Anat) appendix.
Blinddarm-: ~**entzündung** ƒ appendicitis; ~**operation** ƒ appendectomy.
Blindekuh ƒ no art ~ **spielen** to play blind man's buff.
Blinden-: ~**hund** m guide-dog; ~**schrift** ƒ braille.
Blinde(r) mf decl as adj blind person/man/woman etc. **die** ~**n** the blind; **das sieht doch ein** ~**r** (col) any fool can see that.
Blind-: ~**flug** m blind flight; ~**gänger** m (Mil, fig) dud; ~**heit** ƒ (lit, fig) blindness; **mit** ~**heit geschlagen** (fig) blind; **b~lings** adv blindly; ~**schleiche** ƒ slow-worm; **b~schreiben** vti sep irreg to touch-type; **b~wütig** adj in a blind rage.
blinken 1 vi **(a)** (funkeln) to gleam. **(b)** (Leuchtturm) to flash; (Aut) to indicate. **2** vt Signal to flash. **rechts/links** ~ to indicate right/left.
Blinker m - (Aut) indicator.
Blinklicht nt flashing light.
blinzeln vi to blink; (zwinkern) to wink; (geblendet) to squint.
Blitz m -**e (a)** (das Blitzen) lightning no pl, no indef art; (~strahl) flash of lightning; (Lichtstrahl) flash (of light). **vom** ~ **getroffen/erschlagen werden** to be struck by lightning; **wie vom** ~ **getroffen** (fig) thunderstruck; **einschlagen wie ein** ~ (fig) to come as a bombshell; **wie ein** ~ **aus heiterem Himmel** (fig) like a bolt from the blue; **wie der** ~ (col) like lightning. **(b)** (Phot col) flash; (Blitzlichtgerät auch) flashgun.
Blitz-: ~**ableiter** m lightning conductor; ~**aktion** ƒ lightning operation; ~**angriff** m (Mil) lightning attack; **b~artig** = **b~schnell; b~(e)blank** adj (col) spick and span.
blitzen 1 vi impers **es blitzt** there's lightning; **es blitzt und donnert** there's thunder and lightning; **es fing an zu** ~ lightning began. **2** vi **(a)** (strahlen) to flash, to sparkle. **vor Sauberkeit** ~ to be sparkling clean. **(b)** (Phot col) to use a flash.

Blitz-: ~**gerät** nt (Phot) flash(gun); ~**karriere** f eine ~**karriere machen** to have a meteoric rise; ~**krieg** m blitzkrieg; ~**licht** nt (Phot) flash(light); **b**~**sauber** adj spick and span; ~**schlag** m flash of lightning; **vom** ~**schlag getroffen** struck by lightning; **b**~**schnell 1** adj lightning attr; **2** adv like lightning; (plötzlich) verschwinden in a flash; ~**strahl** m flash of lightning; ~**umfrage** f quick poll; ~**würfel** m (Phot) flashcube.

Block m ⁻e **(a)** block (von, aus of) etw im ~ **kaufen** to buy sth in bulk. **(b)** pl auch -s (Häuser~) block. **(c)** pl -s (Rail) block. **(d)** (Pol) (Staaten~) bloc; (Fraktion) faction.

Blockade f (Absperrung) blockade.

Block-: ~**bildung** f (Pol) formation of blocs/ factions; ~**buchstabe** m block letter or capital.

blocken vti (Rail, Sport) to block.

Block-: ~**flöte** f recorder; **b**~**frei** adj nonaligned; ~**freiheit** f non-alignment; ~**haus** nt, ~**hütte** f log cabin.

blockieren* 1 vt **(a)** to block. **(b)** (mit Blockade) to blockade. **2** vi to jam.

Blockierung f siehe vt blocking; blockade.

Block-: ~**politik** f joint policy; ~**schokolade** f no pl cooking chocolate; ~**schrift** f block capitals pl or letters pl; ~**stunde** f (Sch) double period.

blöd(e) adj (col) silly, stupid; (ärgerlich) Sache, Situation stupid; Gefühl funny.

blödeln vi (col) to fool around; (Witze machen) to make jokes.

Blödhammel m (pej col) idiot (col).

Blödheit f **(a)** (Dummheit) stupidity. **(b)** (blödes Verhalten) stupid thing; (alberne Bemerkung) silly or stupid remark. **(c)** (Med) imbecility.

Blödian m -e (col), **Blödmann** m, pl -männer (col) idiot.

Blödsinn m no pl nonsense. **das ist doch** ~ that's nonsense; ~ **machen** to fool about.

blödsinnig adj stupid, idiotic.

blöken vi (Schaf) to bleat.

blond adj (blondhaarig) fair(-haired); (bei Frauen auch) blonde; (bei Männern auch) blond. ~**es Gift** (hum col) blonde bombshell (col).

blond-: ~**gefärbt** adj dyed blonde/blond; ~**haarig** adj fair-haired, blonde/blond.

blondieren* vt to bleach.

Blondine f blonde.

bloß 1 adj **(a)** (unbedeckt) bare. **etw auf der** ~**en Haut tragen** to wear sth next to the skin; **mit** ~**en Füßen** barefooted, barefoot; **mit der** ~**en Hand** with one's bare hand; **mit** ~**em Auge** with the naked eye. **(b)** attr (alleinig) mere; Neid, Dummheit sheer; Gedanke, Anblick very. **er kam mit dem** ~**en Schrecken davon** he got off with no more than a fright. **2** adv only. **wie kann so etwas** ~ **geschehen?** how on earth can something like that happen?; **tu das** ~ **nicht wieder!** don't you dare do that again; **geh mir** ~ **aus dem Weg** just get out of my way.

Blöße f -n (geh) bareness; (Nacktheit) nakedness. **sich** (dat) **eine** ~ **geben** (fig) to reveal a weak spot.

Bloß-: **b**~**legen** vt sep to uncover; (ausgraben auch, Med) to expose; (fig) Geheimnis to reveal; Hintergründe to bring to light; **b**~**liegen** vi sep irreg aux sein to be uncovered; (Ausgegrabenes auch, Med) to be exposed; **b**~**stellen** vt jdn to show up; Lügner, Betrüger to unmask, to expose; **2** vr to show oneself up; **sich als Lügner b**~**stellen** to show oneself to be a liar; ~**stellung** f siehe vt showing up; unmasking, exposing.

Blouson [blu'zõ:] m or nt -s blouson, bomber jacket.

Blücher m: **er geht ran wie** ~ (col) he doesn't hang about (col).

Bluff m -s bluff.

bluffen vti to bluff.

blühen vi **(a)** (Blume) to flower, to bloom; (Bäume) to be in bloom, to blossom. **(b)** (col: bevorstehen) to be in store (jdm for sb). ... **dann blüht dir aber was** ... then you'll be in for it (col).

blühend adj Baum blossoming; Aussehen radiant; Pflanze blooming; Garten full of flowers; (fig) Geschäft etc flourishing, thriving; Unsinn absolute; Phantasie vivid, lively. **wie das** ~**e Leben aussehen** to look the very picture of health.

Blume f -n **(a)** flower; (Topfblume) pot plant. **jdm etw durch die** ~ **sagen** to say sth in a roundabout way to sb. **(b)** (von Wein) bouquet; (von Bier) head.

Blumen- in cpds flower; ~**bank** f (am Fenster) windowsill; (~ständer) flower stand; ~**beet** nt flowerbed; ~**erde** f potting compost; ~**geschäft** nt florist; ~**kasten** m window box; ~**kohl** m no pl cauliflower; ~**meer** nt sea of flowers; ~**muster** nt floral pattern; **b**~**reich** adj full of flowers; (fig) Sprache etc flowery; ~**strauß** m bouquet, bunch of flowers; ~**topf** m flowerpot; **damit ist kein** ~**topf zu gewinnen** (col) that's nothing to write home about (col); ~**zucht** f flower growing; ~**zwiebel** f bulb.

blumig adj (lit, fig) flowery.

Bluse f -n blouse.

Blut nt no pl (lit, fig) blood. **er lag in seinem** ~ he lay in a pool of blood; **es ist viel** ~ **geflossen** there was a lot of bloodshed; **er kann kein** ~ **sehen** he can't stand the sight of blood; ~ **geleckt haben** (fig) to have tasted blood; **böses** ~ **machen** or **schaffen** to cause bad blood; **jdm steigt das** ~ **in den Kopf** the blood rushes to sb's head; **ihnen gefror** or **erstarrte das** ~ **in den Adern** their blood froze; **heißes** or **feuriges** ~ **haben** to be hot-blooded; **kaltes** ~ **bewahren** to remain unmoved; **(nur) ruhig** ~ keep your shirt on (col); **jdn/sich bis aufs** ~ **bekämpfen** to fight sb/fight bitterly; **frisches** ~ (fig) new blood; ~ **und Wasser schwitzen** (col) to sweat blood; **das liegt mir/ihm im** ~ it's in my/his blood.

Blut-: ~**ader** f vein; ~**alkohol(gehalt)** m blood alcohol level; ~**apfelsine** f blood orange; **b**~**arm** adj (Med, fig) anaemic (Brit), anemic (US); ~**armut** f (Med) anaemia (Brit), anemia (US); ~**austausch** m (Med) exchange transfusion; ~**bad** nt bloodbath; ~**bahn** f bloodstream; ~**bank** f blood bank; **b**~**befleckt** adj bloodstained; **b**~**beschmiert** adj smeared with blood; ~**bild** nt blood count; **b**~**buche** f copper beech; ~**druck** m blood pressure.

Blüte f -n **(a)** flower, bloom; (von Baum) blossom. **eine** ~ **seiner Phantasie** a figment of his imagination. **(b)** (das Blühen, Blütezeit) in (voller) ~ **stehen** to be in (full) flower/blossom; (Kultur, Geschäft) to be flourishing; **sich zur vollen** ~ **entfalten** to come into full flower; (Mädchen, Kultur) to blossom; **seine** ~ **erleben** (Kultur etc) to reach its peak; **in der** ~ **seiner Jahre** in the prime of his life. **(c)** (col: Falschgeld) dud (col).

Blut|egel m leech.

bluten vi to bleed (an+dat, aus from). **mir blutet das Herz** my heart bleeds.

Blüten-: ~**blatt** nt petal; ~**honig** m honey (made from flowers); ~**kelch** m calyx; ~**staub** m pollen.

Blut|entnahme f taking a blood sample.

Bluter m - (Med) haemophiliac (Brit), hemophiliac (US).

Blut|erguß m haemorrhage (Brit), hemorrhage (US); (blauer Fleck) bruise.

Bluterkrankheit f haemophilia (Brit), hemophilia (US).

Blütezeit f **(a)** **während der** ~ **der Kirschbäume** while the cherries were in blossom. **(b)** (fig) heyday; (von Mensch) prime.

Blut-: ~**farbstoff** m haemoglobin (Brit), hemoglobin (US); ~**fleck** m bloodstain; ~**gefäß** nt blood vessel; ~**gerinnsel** nt blood clot; ~**gruppe**

f blood group; ~**hund** *m (lit, fig)* bloodhound.
blutig *adj* **(a)** *(lit, fig)* bloody. **er hat ihn ~ ge-schlagen** he hit him and made him bleed. **(b)** *(col) Anfänger* absolute; *Ernst* deadly.
Blut-: **b~jung** *adj* very young; ~**konserve** *f* unit or pint of stored blood; ~**körperchen** *nt* blood corpuscle; ~**kreislauf** *m* blood circulation; ~**lache** *f* pool of blood; **b~leer** *adj* bloodless; ~**leere** *f no pl* lack of blood; **b~los** *adj* bloodless; *(fig)* anaemic *(Brit)*, anemic *(US)*; ~**orange** *f* blood orange; ~**probe** *f* blood test; ~**rache** *f* blood feud; ~**rausch** *m* frenzy; **b~rot** *adj (liter)* blood-red; **b~rünstig** *adj* bloodthirsty; ~**sauger** *m (lit, fig)* bloodsucker; *(Vampir)* vampire.
Blutsbruder *m* blood brother.
Blut-: ~**schande** *f* incest; ~**senkung** *f (Med)* sedimentation of the blood; **eine ~senkung machen** to test the sedimentation rate of the blood; ~**spender** *m* blood donor; ~**spur** *f* trail of blood; **b~stillend** *adj* styptic.
Blutstropfen ['bluːts-] *m* drop of blood.
Blutsturz *m* haemorrhage *(Brit)*, hemorrhage *(US)*.
Bluts-: **b~verwandt** *adj* related by blood; ~**verwandtschaft** *f* blood relationship.
Blut-: ~**tat** *f* bloody deed; ~**transfusion** *f* blood transfusion; **b~überströmt** *adj* streaming with blood; ~**übertragung** *f* blood transfusion.
Blutung *f* bleeding *no pl*; *(monatliche)* period.
Blut-: **b~unterlaufen** *adj* suffused with blood; *Augen* bloodshot; ~**untersuchung** *f* blood test; ~**vergießen** *nt no pl* bloodshed *no indef art*; ~**vergiftung** *f* blood-poisoning *no indef art*; ~**verlust** *m* loss of blood; ~**wurst** *f* blood pudding *(US)*, black pudding *(Brit)*; ~**zuckerspiegel** *m* blood sugar level; ~**zufuhr** *f* blood supply.
Bö-**en** gust (of wind); *(stärker, mit Regen)* squall.
Boa *f* -**s** *(Schlange, Schal)* boa.
Bob *m* -**s** bob(sleigh).
Bob-: ~**bahn** *f* bob(sleigh) run; ~**fahrer** *m* bobber.
Boccia ['bɔtʃa] *nt or f no pl* bowls *sing*.
Bock *m* -̈**e** **(a)** *(Reh~, Kaninchen~)* buck; *(Schafs~)* ram; *(Ziegen~)* he-goat, billy-goat. **alter ~** *(col)* old goat *(col)*; **sturer/geiler ~** *(col)* stubborn old devil *(col)*/randy *(Brit)* or horny old goat *(col)*; **den ~ zum Gärtner machen** *(fig)* to choose the worst possible person for the job; **einen ~ schießen** *(fig col)* to boob *(Brit col)*, to goof *(US col)*. **(b)** *(Gestell)* stand; *(Stützgerät)* support; *(für Auto)* ramp; *(aus Holzbalken, mit Beinen)* trestle; *(Säge~)* sawhorse. **(c)** *(Sport)* buck. **(d)** *(col: Lust)* ~̈**e** or **einen ~ haben, etw zu tun** to fancy doing sth.
Bockbier *nt* bock (beer) *(type of strong beer)*.
bocken *vi* **(a)** *(Zugtier etc)* to refuse to move; *(nicht springen wollen: Pferd)* to refuse. **vor einer Hürde ~** to refuse to jump. **(b)** *(col: Auto, Mensch)* to play up.
bockig *adj (col)* contrary, awkward.
Bockmist *m (col: dummes Gerede)* bullshit *(col!)*. **~ machen** to make a balls-up *(col!)*.
Bockshorn *nt:* **sich von jdm ins ~ jagen lassen** to let sb upset one.
Bock-: ~**springen** *nt* leapfrog; *(Sport)* vaulting; ~**sprung** *m* leapfrog; *(Sport)* vault; ~**wurst** *f* bockwurst *(large frankfurter)*.
Boden *m* -̈ **(a)** ground; *(Erdreich auch)* soil; *(Fuß~)* floor; *(no pl: Terrain)* soil. **auf spanischem ~** on Spanish soil; **zu ~ fallen** to fall to the ground; **festen ~ unter den Füßen haben** to be on firm ground, to be on terra firma; **den ~ unter den Füßen verlieren** *(lit)* to lose one's footing; *(fig: in Diskussion)* to get out of one's depth; **ihm wurde der ~ (unter den Füßen) zu heiß** *(fig)* things were getting too hot for him; **ich hätte (vor Scham) im ~ versinken können** *(fig)* I was so ashamed that I wished the

ground would swallow me up; **am ~ zerstört sein** *(col)* to be shattered *(col)*; **(an)** ~ **verlieren** *(fig)* to gain/lose ground; **~ gutmachen** *(fig)* to make up ground; **etw aus dem ~ stampfen** *(fig)* to conjure sth up out of nothing; *Häuser* to build overnight; **auf fruchtbaren ~ fallen** *(fig)* to fall on fertile ground; **jdm/einer Sache den ~ bereiten** *(fig)* to prepare the ground for sb/sth.
(b) *(unterste Fläche)* bottom; *(Torten~)* base.
(c) *(Dach~, Heu~)* loft.
(d) *(fig: Grundlage)* **auf dem ~ der Tatsachen stehen** to base oneself on fact; **auf dem ~ der Tatsachen bleiben** to stick to the facts; **sich auf unsicherem ~ bewegen** to be on shaky ground; **einer Sache** *(dat)* **den ~ entziehen** to knock the bottom out of sth.
Boden-: ~**belag** *m* floor covering; ~**ertrag** *m (Agr)* crop yield; ~**fläche** *f (Agr)* area of land; *(von Zimmer)* floor space or area; ~**frost** *m* ground frost; ~**haftung** *f (Aut)* road holding *no indef art*; ~**heizung** *f* underfloor heating; ~**kammer** *f* attic; ~**kontrolle** *f (Space)* ground control; **b~los** *adj* bottomless; *(col: unerhört)* indescribable, incredible; ~**personal** *nt (Aviat)* ground personnel *pl*; ~**satz** *m* sediment; *(von Kaffee auch)* grounds *pl*; ~**schätze** *pl* mineral resources *pl*; ~**schicht** *f* layer of soil; *(Geol)* stratum; ~**see** *m*: **der ~** *see* Lake Constance; ~**spekulation** *f* land speculation; ~**station** *f (Space)* ground station; ~**turnen** *nt* floor exercises *pl*.
bog *pret of* **biegen.**
Bogen *m* - or -̈ **(a)** curve, bend; *(Math)* arc; *(Mus)* tie; *(bei verschiedenen Noten)* slur; *(Ski)* turn. **einen ~ fahren** *(Ski)* to do a turn; **den ~ heraushaben** *(col)* to have got the hang of it *(col)*; **einen ~ machen** *(Fluß etc)* to curve; **einen großen ~ um jdn/etw machen** *(meiden)* to give sb/sth a wide berth; **jdn in hohem ~ hinauswerfen** *(col)* to fling sb out. **(b)** *(Archit)* arch. **(c)** *(Waffe, Mus: Geigen~ etc)* bow. **den ~ überspannen** *(fig)* to go too far. **(d)** *(Papier~)* sheet (of paper).
Bogen-: **b~förmig** *adj* arched; ~**gang** *m (Archit)* arcade; ~**schießen** *nt* archery; ~**schütze** *m* archer, bowman.
Bohle *f* -**n** (thick) board.
böhmisch *adj* Bohemian. **das sind für mich ~e Dörfer** *(col)* that's all Greek to me *(col)*.
Bohne *f* -**n** bean. **dicke/grüne/weiße ~n** broad/green or French or runner/haricot beans; **blaue ~** *(col)* bullet; **nicht die ~** *(col)* not one little bit; **du hast wohl ~n in den Ohren** *(col)* are you deaf or something?
Bohnen-: ~**eintopf** *m* bean stew; ~**kaffee** *m* real coffee; **gemahlener ~kaffee** ground coffee; ~**kraut** *nt* savory; ~**stange** *f (fig col)* beanpole *(col)*; ~**stroh** *nt:* **dumm wie ~stroh** *(col)* (as) thick as two (short) planks *(col)*; ~**suppe** *f* bean soup.
bohnern *vti* to polish.
Bohnerwachs *nt* floor polish or wax.
bohren 1 *vt* to bore; *(mit Bohrer auch)* to drill; *(hineindrücken) Pfahl, Schwert etc* to sink *(in + acc* into). **2** *vi* **(a)** to bore *(in + acc* into); to drill *(nach* for). **in einem Zahn ~** to drill a tooth; **in der Nase ~** to pick one's nose. **(b)** *(fig) (drängen)* to keep on; *(peinigen: Schmerz, Zweifel etc)* to gnaw. **3** *vr* **sich in/durch etw** *(acc)* **~** to bore its way into/through sth.
bohrend *adj (fig) Blick* piercing; *Schmerz, Zweifel* gnawing; *Frage* probing.
Bohrer *m* - *(elektrisch)* drill; *(Hand~)* gimlet.
Bohr-: ~**insel** *f* drilling rig; *(für Öl auch)* oilrig; ~**loch** *nt* borehole; *(in Holz, Metall etc)* drill-hole; ~**maschine** *f* drill; ~**turm** *m* derrick.
Bohrung *f* **(a)** *siehe vt* boring; drilling; sinking. **(b)** *(Loch)* bore(-hole); *(in Metall etc)* drill-hole.

böig adj siehe **Bö** gusty; squally.
Boiler ['bɔylɐ] m - hot-water heater.
Boje f -n buoy.
Bolivien [-iən] nt Bolivia.
Böller m - (small) cannon (for ceremonial use).
Bollwerk nt (lit, fig) bulwark.
Bolschewismus m Bolshevism.
Bolzen m - (a) (Tech) pin; (esp mit Gewinde) bolt.
(b) (Geschoß) bolt.
bolzen (col) 1 vi to kick about. 2 vt Ball to slam.
Bombardement [bɔmbardə'mãː] nt -s bombardment; (mit Bomben) bombing. **ein ~ von** (fig) a deluge of.
bombardieren* vt (lit) to bomb; (fig) to bombard.
Bombardierung f bombing; (fig) bombardment.
bombastisch adj bombastic.
Bombe f -n bomb; (Sport col: Schuß) cracker (col).
wie eine ~ einschlagen to come as a (real) bombshell; **eine ~ platzen lassen** (fig) to drop a bombshell.
Bomben- in cpds (Mil) bomb; (col: hervorragend) fantastic (col), great (col); **~angriff**, **~anschlag** m bomb attack; **~erfolg** m (col) smash hit (col); **b~fest** adj (col) Klebestelle absolutely secure; **es steht b~fest, daß** ... it's absolutely certain or a dead cert (col) that ...; **~geschäft** nt (col) ein **~geschäft sein** to be a gold mine; **ein ~geschäft machen** to do a roaring trade (col) (**mit** in); **~hitze** f (col) sweltering heat no indef art; **~leger(in** f) m bomber; **~Krater** m bomb crater; **b~sicher** adj (a) (Mil) bombproof; (b) (col) dead certain (col); **~splitter** m bomb fragment; **~teppich** m einen **~teppich legen** to blanket-bomb an/the area; **~trichter** m bomb crater.
Bomber m - bomber.
Bon [bɔŋ] m -s voucher; (Kassenzettel) receipt.
Bonbon [bɔŋ'bɔŋ] nt or m -s sweet (Brit), candy (US).
Bonbonniere [bɔŋbo'niɛːrə] f -n box of chocolates.
Bongo [bɔŋgo] nt or f -s bongo (drum).
Bonus m - or -se bonus; (Univ, Sport: Punktvorteil) bonus points pl.
Bonze m -n big shot (col).
Boot nt -e boat. **~ fahren** to go out in a boat; **wir sitzen alle in einem ~** (fig) we're all in the same boat.
Boots-: **~fahrt** f boat trip; **~haus** nt boathouse; **~mann** m, pl **~leute** (Naut) bo'sun, boatswain; (Dienstgrad) petty officer.
Bord[1] m no pl **an ~** (eines Schiffes) aboard or on board (a ship); **alle Mann an ~!** all aboard!; **an ~ gehen** to go aboard; **Mann über ~!** man overboard!; **über ~ gehen** to go overboard; (fig) to go by the board; **über ~ werfen** (lit, fig) to throw overboard, to jettison; **von ~ gehen** to leave the ship/the plane; (esp Passagiere am Ziel) to disembark.
Bord[2] nt -e (Wandbrett) shelf.
Bord-: **~buch** nt log(book); **~computer** m (Space) on-board computer.
Bordell nt -e brothel.
Bord-: **~funk** m (Naut) (ship's) radio; (Aviat) (aircraft) radio equipment; **~funker** m (Naut, Aviat) radio operator; **~stein(kante** f) m kerb (Brit), curb (US).
borgen vti (a) (erhalten) to borrow (von from). (b) (geben) to lend, to loan (jdm etw sb sth, sth to sb).
Borke f -n bark.
borniert adj bigoted, narrow-minded.
Börse f -n (a) (Geld~) purse; (für Männer) wallet (Brit), billfold (US). (b) (Fin) stock market, stock exchange.
Börsen-: **~bericht** m stock market report; **~geschäft** nt (Wertpapierhandel) stockbroking; (Transaktion) stock market transaction; **~kurs** m stock market price; **~makler** m stockbroker; **~notierung** f quotation (on the stock exchange);

~spekulation f speculation on the stock market; **~tendenz** f stock market trend.
Borste f -n bristle.
Borstenvieh nt pigs pl, swine pl.
borstig adj (lit, fig) bristly.
Borte f -n braid trimming.
bös|artig adj malicious, nasty; Tier vicious; (Med) malignant.
Bös|artigkeit f siehe adj maliciousness, nastiness; viciousness; malignancy.
Böschung f embankment; (von Straße auch) bank.
böse adj (a) bad; (stärker) evil, wicked; (col: unartig auch) naughty; Überraschung, Geschichte, Wunde nasty. **ein ~r** Geist an evil spirit; **das war keine ~ Absicht** there was no harm intended; **das war nicht ~ gemeint** I/he etc didn't mean it nastily; **~ Folgen** dire consequences; **~ Zeiten** bad times; **das/es sieht ~ aus** things look/it looks bad. (b) (verärgert) angry (+dat, auf+acc, mit with). **im ~n auseinandergehen** to part on bad terms.
Böse(s) nt decl as adj evil; (Schaden, Leid) harm. **jdm ~s antun** to do sb harm; **ich will dir doch nichts ~s** I don't mean you any harm; **ich dachte an or ahnte gar nichts ~s, als** ... I was quite unsuspecting when ...
Bösewicht m -e or -er (old, hum) villain.
Bos-: **b~haft** adj malicious; **~haftigkeit** f maliciousness; **~heit** f malice; (Bemerkung, Handlung) malicious remark/thing to do.
Boß m -sse (col) boss (col).
böswillig adj malicious; (Jur auch) wilful. **in ~er Absicht** with malicious intent.
Böswilligkeit f malice, maliciousness.
bot pret of **bieten.**
Botanik f botany.
Botaniker(in f) m - botanist.
botanisch adj botanic.
Bote m (wk) -n, -n (a) messenger; (Kurier) courier; (Post~) postman (Brit), mailman (US). (b) (fig: Anzeichen) herald.
Botengang m errand. **einen ~gang machen** to run an errand.
Botin f siehe **Bote** (a) messenger; courier; postwoman (Brit), mailwoman (US).
Botschaft f (a) (Mitteilung) message; (esp amtlich) communication. **eine freudige ~** good news; **die Frohe ~** the Gospel. (b) (Pol: Vertretung) embassy.
Botschafter(in f) m - ambassador.
Bottich m -e tub.
Bouillon [buljɔn, bul'jɔː] f -s stock; (auf Speisekarte) bouillon, consommé.
Bouillonwürfel m stock cube.
Boulevard- [bulə'vaːr-]: **~blatt** nt (col) tabloid; **~presse** f (col) popular press; **~stück** nt light play/comedy; **~theater** nt light theatre (Brit) or theater (US); **~zeitung** f tabloid.
Bouquet [bu'keː] nt -s = **Bukett.**
Bourgeoisie [burʒoa'ziː] f (geh) bourgeoisie.
Boutique [bu'tiːk] -n boutique.
Bowle ['boːlə] f -n (Getränk) punch.
Bowling ['boːlɪŋ] nt -s (tenpin) bowling. **~ spielen** gehen to go bowling.
Bowlingbahn f bowling alley.
Box f (a) (Behälter) box. (b) (für Pferde) Box; (in Großgarage) parking place; (für Rennwagen) pit. (c) (Lautsprecher~) speaker.
Boxen nt no pl (Sport) boxing.
boxen 1 vi to box; (zur Übung) to spar; (mit Fäusten zuschlagen) to hit out, to punch. **gegen jdn ~** to fight sb. 2 vt jdn to punch, to hit. 3 vr (a) (col: sich schlagen) to have a punch-up (col) or a fight. (b) (sich einen Weg bahnen) to fight one's way.
Boxer m - (Sportler, Hund) boxer.
Boxer-: **~motor** m (Tech) opposed cylinder engine; **~nase** f boxer's nose, broken nose.
Box-: **~handschuh** m boxing glove; **~kalf** nt no pl

box calf; ~**kampf** m fight, (boxing) match; ~**ring** m boxing ring; ~**sport** m boxing.
Boykott [bɔy'kɔt] m -e or -s boycott.
boykottieren* [bɔykɔ'tiːrən] vt to boycott.
brabbeln vi (col) to mumble, to mutter.
brach pret of **brechen.**
brachial adj **mit** ~**er Gewalt** with brute force.
Brach-: ~**land** nt fallow (land); **b**~**liegen** vi sep irreg (lit, fig) to lie fallow.
brachte pret of **bringen.**
Branche ['brãːʃə] f -n (Gewerbe) trade; (Wirtschaftszweig) industry. **in welcher** ~ **sind Sie tätig?** what line (of business) are you in?
Branchen-: ~**kenntnis** f knowledge of the trade/industry; **b**~**üblich** adj usual in the trade/industry; ~**verzeichnis** nt yellow pages.
Brand m ̈-e (a) (Feuer) fire; (lodernd auch) blaze. **in** ~ **geraten** to catch fire; **in** ~ **stehen** to be on fire; **etw in** ~ **stecken** to set fire to sth. (b) (von Porzellan etc) firing. (c) (fig col: großer Durst) raging thirst. (d) (Pflanzenkrankheit) blight.
Brand-: **b**~**aktuell** adj (col) Thema, Frage red-hot (col); Buch hot from the presses; ~**bekämpfung** f firefighting; ~**blase** f (burn) blister; ~**bombe** f incendiary bomb; **b**~**eilig** adj (col) extremely urgent; ~**gefahr** f danger of fire; ~**geruch** m smell of burning; ~**herd** m source of the fire; (fig) source; ~**katastrophe** f fire disaster; ~**mal** nt -e brand; (fig auch) stigma; **b**~ **marken** vt insep (fig) jdn als etw **b**~**marken** (fig) to brand sb (as) sth; ~**meister** m fire chief; **b**~**neu** adj (col) brand-new; ~**opfer** nt (a) (Rel) burnt offering; (b) (Mensch) fire victim; ~**salbe** f ointment for burns; ~**satz** m incendiary device; ~**schaden** m fire damage; ~**schutz** m fire protection; ~**stelle** f fire, blaze; (verbrannte Stelle) burnt patch; ~**stifter** m arsonist; ~**stiftung** f arson.
Brandung f surf, breakers pl.
Brand-: ~**ursache** f cause of a/the fire; ~**wunde** f burn; ~**zeichen** nt brand.
brannte pret of **brennen.**
Branntwein m spirits pl. **Whisky ist ein** ~ whisky is a (type of) spirit.
Branntwein-: ~**brenner** m distiller; ~**brennerei** f distillery; ~**steuer** f tax on spirits.
Brasil f -(s) Brazil cigar.
Brasilianer(in f) m - Brazilian.
brasilianisch adj Brazilian.
Brasilien [-iən] nt Brazil.
Bratapfel m baked apple.
braten pret **briet,** ptp **gebraten** 1 vti to roast; (ohne Fett) to bake; (in der Pfanne) to fry. 2 vi (col: in der Sonne) to roast.
Braten m - roast. **kalter** ~ cold meat; **ein fetter** ~ (fig) a prize catch; **den** ~ **riechen** (col) to smell a rat (col).
Braten-: ~**fleisch** nt meat for roasting/frying; ~**soße** f gravy; ~**wender** m - fishslice.
Brat-: **b**~**fertig** adj oven-ready; ~**fett** nt fat for frying/roasting; ~**fisch** m fried fish; ~**hähnchen, ~hendl** -(n) (Aus, SGer) nt roast chicken; ~**hering** m fried herring; ~**huhn** nt roast chicken; (zum Braten) roasting chicken; ~**kartoffeln** pl fried potatoes; ~**ofen** m oven; ~**pfanne** f frying pan, skillet (US); ~**röhre** f oven; ~**rost** m grill.
Bratsche f -n viola.
Bratwurst f (fried) sausage.
Brauch m, pl **Bräuche** custom, tradition. **das ist bei uns so** ~ (col) that's traditional with us.
brauchbar adj (a) (benutzbar) useable; Plan workable; (nützlich) useful. (b) (ordentlich) Mensch, Idee reasonable.
Brauchbarkeit f usefulness; (von Plan) workability.
brauchen 1 vt (a) (nötig haben) to need (für, zu for). **es braucht alles seine Zeit** everything takes time; **wie lange braucht man, um** ...? how long

does it take to ...? (b) (benutzen) to use. **wir können das/ihn nicht** ~ (col) we've no use for that/him. (c) (col: verbrauchen) to use (up). **2 aux** to need. **du brauchst es ihm nicht (zu) sagen** you needn't tell or don't need to tell him that; **du hättest das nicht (zu) tun** ~ you needn't have done that, you didn't need to do that; **du brauchst nur an(zu)rufen** you only have or need to call; **es braucht nicht gleich zu sein** it doesn't need to be done immediately; **es hätte nicht zu sein** ~ there was no need for that; (hätte nicht geschehen müssen) that needn't have happened.
Brauchtum nt customs pl, traditions pl.
Braue f -n (eye)brow.
brauen vti Bier to brew; (col) Tee to brew up; Kaffee to make.
Brauer m - brewer.
Brauerei f brewery.
braun adj brown; (col: ~haarig) brown-haired; (pej) Nazi. ~ **werden** (Mensch) to get a (sun-)tan, to go or get brown.
Braun nt - brown.
Braun-: **b**~**äugig** adj brown-eyed; ~**bär** m brown bear.
Bräune f no pl brown(ness); (von Sonne) (sun-)tan.
bräunen 1 vt (Cook) to brown; (Sonne etc) to tan. **2** vi (Cook) to go or turn brown; (Mensch) to tan, to go brown; (Sonne) to tan. **sich in der Sonne** ~ **lassen** to get a (sun-)tan.
Braun-: **b**~**gebrannt** adj attr (sun-)tanned, brown; **b**~**haarig** adj brown-haired; Frau auch brunette; ~**kohle** f brown coal.
bräunlich adj brownish, browny.
Braunschweig nt Brunswick.
Bräunung f browning; (von Haut) bronzing. **eine tiefe** ~ **der Haut** a deep (sun-)tan.
Brause f -n (a) shower. **sich unter die** ~ **stellen** to have a shower. (b) (~aufsatz) shower attachment; (an Schlauch, Gießkanne) rose, sprinkler. (c) (Getränk) pop; (Limonade) (fizzy) lemonade; (~pulver) lemonade powder.
brausen 1 vi (a) (tosen) to roar; (sprudeln: Wasser, Brandung) to foam. ~**der Beifall** thunderous applause. (b) aux sein (rasen, rennen) to race. (c) auch vr (duschen) to (have a) shower. **2** vt Körperteil, Kinder to put under the shower.
Brause-: ~**pulver** nt lemonade powder; ~**tablette** f lemonade tablet.
Braut f, pl **Bräute** bride; (dated: Verlobte) fiancée.
Brautführer m person who gives away the bride.
Bräutigam m -e (bride)groom; (dated: Verlobter) fiancé.
Braut-: ~**jungfer** f bridesmaid; ~**kleid** nt wedding dress; ~**leute** pl, ~**paar** nt bridal couple; (dated: Verlobte) engaged couple; ~**schau** f: **auf** ~**schau sein** to be looking for a wife; ~**schleier** m wedding or bridal veil.
brav adj (a) Kind good, well-behaved. **sei schön** ~! be a good boy/girl. (b) (rechtschaffen) worthy (auch iro); (bieder) Frisur, Kleid plain. ~ **seine Pflicht tun** to do one's duty worthily. (c) (dated:

bravo ['braːvo] interj well done; (für Künstler) bravo.
Bravoruf m cheer.
Bravour [bra'vuːr] f no pl (geh) bravura.
bravourös [bravu'røːs] adj (meisterhaft) brilliant.
BRD [beːʔerˈdeː] f = **Bundesrepublik Deutschland** FRG.
Brech-: **b**~**bar** adj breakable; ~**bohne** f French bean; ~**eisen** nt crowbar; (von Dieb) jemmy, jimmy (US).
brechen pret **brach,** ptp **gebrochen 1** vt (a) to break; (geh: pflücken) Blumen to pluck. **sich/jdm den Arm** ~ to break one's/sb's arm; **das wird ihm den Hals** ~ (fig) that will be his downfall. (b) (erbrechen) to bring up. **2** vi (a) aux sein to break.

mir bricht das Herz it breaks my heart; **mit jdm/etw ~** to break with sb/sth; **~d voll sein to** be full to bursting. **(b)** *(sich erbrechen)* to be sick, to throw up. **3** *vr (Wellen)* to break; *(Lichtstrahl)* to be refracted; *(Schall)* to rebound *(an +dat off).*

Brecher *m -* *(Welle)* breaker; *(Tech)* crusher.

Brech-: **~mittel** *nt* emetic; **er/das ist das reinste ~mittel** he/it makes me feel ill; **~reiz** *m* nausea; **~stange** *f* crowbar.

Brechung *f (der Wellen)* breaking; *(des Lichts)* refraction; *(des Schalls)* rebounding.

Brei *m -e* mush, paste; *(für Kinder, Kranke)* mash; *(Hafer~)* porridge; *(Grieß~)* semolina; *(Reis~)* rice pudding; *(Papier~)* pulp. **jdn zu ~ schlagen** *(col)* to beat sb to a pulp *(col)*; **um den heißen ~ herumreden** *(col)* to beat about the bush *(col).*

breiig *adj* mushy.

breit 1 *adj* broad; *(esp bei Maßangabe)* wide; *Bekanntenkreis, Publikum, Interessen auch* wide; *Schrift* broadly spaced. **etw ~er machen** to broaden or widen sth; **die ~e Masse** the masses *pl.* **2** *adv* **~ gebaut** sturdily built; **sich ~ hinsetzen** to sit down squarely.

breitbeinig *adj* with one's legs apart.

Breite *f -n* **(a)** breadth; *(von Dialekt, Aussprache)* broadness; *(esp bei Maßangabe)* width. **der ~ nach** widthways; **etw in aller ~ erklären** to explain sth in great detail; **in die ~ gehen** *(col: dick werden)* to put it on a bit *(col)*. **(b)** *(Geog)* latitude; *(Gebiet)* part of the world. **es liegt 20° nördlicher ~** it lies 20° north.

breiten *vtr* to spread.

Breiten-: **~grad** *m* (degree of) latitude; **~kreis** *m* parallel; **~sport** *m* popular sport; **~wirkung** *f* widespread impact.

Breit-: **b~gefächert** *adj* ein **b~gefächertes Angebot** a wide range; **b~machen** *vr sep (col)* **mach dich doch nicht so b~!** don't take up so much room; **sie hat sich im Zimmer b~gemacht** she spread her things all over the room; **b~schlagen** *vt sep irreg (col)* **sich b~schlagen lassen** to let oneself be talked round; *Thema, Witz* to flog to death *(col)*; **~wandfilm** *m* film for the wide screen.

Bremsbelag *m* brake lining.

Bremse[1] *f -n* brake. **auf die ~(n) treten/steigen** *(col)* to put on or apply/slam on the brake(s).

Bremse[2] *f -n (Insekt)* horsefly.

bremsen 1 *vi* to brake. **der Wind bremst the wind** slows you *etc* down; **mit etw ~** *(col)* to cut down (on) sth. **2** *vt* **(a)** *Fahrzeug* to brake. **(b)** *(fig)* to restrict, to limit; *Entwicklung* to slow down. **er ist nicht zu ~** *(col)* there's no stopping him. **3** *vr (col)* **ich kann mich ~** not likely!

Brems-: **~flüssigkeit** *f* brake fluid; **~klotz** *m* brake block; **~kraft** *f* braking power; **~leistung** *f* braking efficiency; **~licht** *nt* brake light; **~pedal** *nt* brake pedal; **~spur** *f* skid mark *usu pl.*

Bremsung *f* braking.

Bremsweg *m* braking distance.

brennbar *adj* combustible, inflammable. **leicht ~** highly inflammable.

brennen *pret* **brannte,** *ptp* **gebrannt 1** *vi* to burn; *(Haus, Wald auch)* to be on fire; *(Glühbirne etc)* to be on; *(Zigarette)* to be alight; *(Stich)* to sting; *(Füße)* to hurt, to be sore. **das Streichholz brennt nicht** the match won't light; **auf der Haut ~** to burn the skin; **das Licht ~ lassen** to leave the light on; **es brennt!** fire!, fire!; *(fig)* it's urgent; **wo brennt's denn?** *(col)* what's the panic?; **darauf ~,** etw zu tun to be dying to do sth. **2** *vt* burn; *Branntwein* to distil; *Porzellan, Ziegel* to fire, to bake; *Tier* to brand; *siehe* **gebrannt.**

brennend *adj (lit, fig)* burning; *Zigarette* lighted; *Durst* raging; *Haß* consuming. **das interessiert**

mich ~ *(col)* I would be incredibly interested.

Brenner *m -* **(a)** *(Tech)* burner. **(b)** *(Branntwein~)* distiller.

Brennerei *f* distillery.

Brennessel *f* stinging nettle.

Brenn-: **~holz** *nt* firewood; **~ofen** *m* kiln; **~punkt** *m (Math, Opt)* focus; **im ~punkt des Interesses stehen** to be the focus of attention; **~schere** *f* curling tongs *pl*; **~spiritus** *m* methylated spirits *sing or pl*; **~stab** *m* fuel rod; **~stoff** *m* fuel.

brenzlig *adj (col) Situation etc* precarious. **die Lage wurde ihm zu ~** things got too hot for him.

Bresche *f -n* breach, gap. **in die ~ springen** *(fig)* to step into the breach; **für jdn/etw eine ~ schlagen** *(fig)* to stand up for sb/sth.

Bretagne [bre'tanjə] *f* **die ~** Brittany.

Brett *nt -er* **(a)** board; *(länger und dicker)* plank; *(Regal)* shelf. **hier ist die Welt mit ~ern vernagelt** this is a parochial little place; **er hat ein ~ vor dem Kopf** *(col)* he's really thick. **(b)** **~er** *pl (fig) (Bühne)* boards *pl*; *(Boden des Boxrings)* floor, canvas; *(Skier)* planks *pl (col)*; **die ~er, die die Welt bedeuten** the stage.

Bretter-: **~bude** *f* booth; *(pej)* shack; **~zaun** *m* wooden fence; *(an Baustellen auch)* hoarding.

Brettspiel *nt* board game.

Brezel *f -n* pretzel.

Brief *m -e* **(a)** letter; *(Bibl)* epistle. **etw als ~ schicken** to send sth (by) letter post; **jdm ~ und Siegel auf etw (acc) geben** to give sb one's word. **(b)** *(St Ex:* **~kurs)** selling rate.

Brief- *in cpds* letter; **~beschwerer** *m -* paperweight; **~bombe** *f* letter bomb.

Briefchen *nt* ein **~ Streichhölzer** a book of matches; **ein ~ Nadeln** a packet of needles/pins.

Brief-: **~drucksache** *f* circular; **~fach** *nt* pigeonhole; **~freund(in** *f)* *m* penfriend, pen-pal; **~freundschaft** *f* eine **~freundschaft mit jdm haben** to be penfriends with sb; **~geheimnis** *nt* privacy of the post; **~ kasten** *m* letter box, mail box *(US)*; **~kopf** *m* letterhead; **~kurs** *m (St Ex)* selling rate; **~lich** *adj* by letter; **mit jdm ~lich verkehren** to correspond with sb.

Briefmarke *f* stamp.

Briefmarken- *in cpds* stamp; **~automat** *m* stamp machine; **~kunde** *f* philately; **~sammler** *m* stamp collector, philatelist; **~sammlung** *f* stamp collection.

Brief-: **~öffner** *m* letter opener, paper knife; **~papier** *nt* letter paper, notepaper; **~porto** *nt (Gebühr)* letter rate; **~sendung** *f* letter, item sent by letter post; **~tasche** *f* wallet *(Brit)*, billfold *(US)*; **~taube** *f* carrier pigeon; **~träger(in** *f)* *m* postman/-woman, mailman/-woman *(US)*; **~umschlag** *m* envelope; **~verkehr** *m* correspondence; **~wahl** *f* postal vote; **~wähler** *m* postal voter; **~wechsel** *m* correspondence.

briet *pret of* **braten.**

Brigade *f* **(a)** *(Mil)* brigade. **(b)** *(DDR)* (work) team or group.

Brikett *nt -s* briquette.

Brikettzange *f* fire tongs *pl.*

brillant [brɪl'jant] *adj* brilliant.

Brillant [brɪl'jant] *m* diamond.

Brillantschmuck *m* diamonds *pl.*

Brille *f -n* **(a)** glasses *pl*, spectacles *pl*; *(Schutz~)* goggles *pl.* **eine ~** a pair of glasses or spectacles; **eine ~ tragen** to wear glasses. **(b)** *(Klosett~)* (toilet) seat.

Brillen-: **~etui** *nt* glasses or spectacle case; **~schlange** *f (hum)* four-eyes *(hum)*, woman who wears glasses; **~träger(in** *f)* *m* er ist **~träger** he wears glasses.

Brimborium *nt (col)* fuss.

bringen *pret* **brachte,** *ptp* **gebracht** *vt* **(a)** *(her~)* to bring; *(holen auch)* to get *(jdm* for *sb)*; *(weg~)* to take. **der Besuch hat mir Blumen**

gebracht my visitors brought me flowers; **wir haben der Gastgeberin Blumen gebracht** we took our hostess flowers; **jdn zum Bahnhof/nach Hause** ~ to take sb to the station/home; **das Essen auf den Tisch** ~ to serve the food; **er bringt es nicht übers Herz** *or* **über sich he can't bring himself to do it; etw an sich** *(acc)* ~ to acquire sth; **etw mit sich** ~ to involve sth; **etw hinter sich** *(acc)* ~ to get sth over and done with.
  (b) *(ein~) Gewinn* to bring in; *(Boden etc)* to produce; *Ärger* to cause; *Freude, Vorteile* to give. **das bringt nichts** *(fig col)* it's pointless.
  (c) *(lenken, bewirken)* to bring. **das bringt dich vors Gericht/ins Gefängnis** you'll end up in court/prison if you do that; **das Gespräch auf etw** *(acc)* ~ to bring the conversation around to sth; **jdn in Gefahr** ~ to put sb in danger; **jdn zum Lachen/Weinen** ~ to make sb laugh/cry; **jdn zur Verzweiflung** ~ to drive sb to despair; **jdn zur Vernunft** ~ to bring sb to his senses; **jdn dazu** ~, **etw zu tun** to get sb to do sth; **jdn um etw** ~ to make sb lose sth, to do sb out of sth; **jdn ums Leben** ~ to kill sb.
  (d) *(leisten, erreichen)* **es auf 80 Jahre** ~ to reach the age of 80; **das Auto bringt 180 km/h** *(col)* the car can do 180 km/h; **es zu etwas/nichts** ~ to get somewhere/nowhere; **es weit** ~ to do very well, to get far; **er hat es bis zum Direktor gebracht** he made it to director.
  (e) *(senden) Bericht etc* to broadcast; *(im Fernsehen auch)* to show. **was bringt das Fernsehen/Radio heute abend?** what's on television/the radio tonight?
  (f) *(veröffentlichen)* to print, to publish. **alle Zeitungen brachten es auf der ersten Seite** all the papers had it on the front page.
  (g) *(aufführen) Stück* to do.
  (h) *(col: schaffen, können)* **das bringt er nicht** he's not up to it; **er bringt's** he's got what it takes; **das bringt's doch nicht!** that's no damn use! *(col).*
brisant *adj (fig)* controversial.
Brisanz *f (fig)* controversial nature.
Brise *f* **-n** breeze.
Brite *m (wk)* **-n, -n, Britin** *f* Briton, Britisher *(US).* **er ist** ~ he is British; **die** ~**n** the British.
britisch *adj* British. **die B**~**en Inseln** the British Isles.
bröckelig *adj* crumbly; *Mauer* crumbling.
bröckeln *vti* to crumble.
Brocken *m* - lump, chunk; *(fig: Bruchstück)* scrap; *(col: Person)* lump *(col).* **ein paar** ~ **Spanisch** a smattering of Spanish; **ein harter** ~ a tough nut to crack.
brocken *vt Brot* to break.
brodeln *vi (Wasser, Suppe)* to bubble. **es brodelt** *(fig)* there is seething unrest.
Brokat *m* **-e** brocade.
Brokkoli *pl* broccoli *sing.*
Brom *nt no pl* bromine.
Brombeere *f* blackberry, bramble.
Bronchie [-iə] *f usu pl* bronchial tube.
Bronchitis *f, pl* **Bronchitiden** bronchitis.
Bronze ['brɔ̃:sə] *f* **-n** bronze.
Bronzemedaille *f* bronze medal.
Brosche *f* **-n** brooch.
Broschüre *f* **-n** brochure; *(Heft)* booklet.
Brot *nt* **-e** bread; *(Laib)* loaf (of bread); *(Scheibe)* slice (of bread); *(Sandwich)* sandwich; *(fig: Unterhalt)* daily bread *(hum),* living. **ein** ~ **mit Käse** a slice of bread and cheese; **das ist ein hartes** ~ *(fig)* that's a hard way to earn one's living.
Brot-: ~**aufstrich** *m* spread *(for bread);* ~**belag** *m* topping *(for bread).*
Brötchen *nt* roll. **kleine** ~ **backen** *(col)* to set one's sights lower.
Brötchengeber *m (hum)* employer, provider *(hum).*
Brot-: ~**erwerb** *m* (way of earning one's) living;

~**kasten** *m* bread bin; ~**korb** *m* bread basket; **jdm den** ~**korb höher hängen** *(fig)* to keep sb short; ~**krume** *f* breadcrumb; ~**kruste** *f* crust; ~**rinde** *f* crust; ~**schnitte** *f* sandwich; ~**zeit** *f* *(S Ger: Pause)* tea break; ~**zeit machen** to have a tea break.
Bruch *m* ⁼**e (a)** *(~stelle)* break; *(in Porzellan etc auch)* crack; *(das Brechen)* breaking. **zu** ~ **gehen** to get broken; ~ **machen** *(col)* to smash *(mit etw* sth). **(b)** *(fig) (mit Vergangenheit, Partei, im Stil etc)* break; *(von Gesetz)* breaking, infringement; *(von Vertrag)* breach. **in die** ⁼**e gehen** *(Ehe, Freundschaft)* to break up; **es kam zum** ~ **zwischen ihnen** they broke up. **(c)** *(zerbrochene Ware)* broken biscuits/chocolate *etc; (Porzellan)* breakage. **(d)** *(Knochen~)* fracture, break; *(Eingeweide~)* hernia, rupture. **sich** *(dat)* **einen** ~ **heben** to rupture oneself. **(e)** *(Math)* fraction.
(f) *(col: Einbruch)* break-in.
Bruch-: ~**band** *nt* truss; ~**bude** *f (pej)* hovel; **b**~**fest** *adj* unbreakable.
brüchig *adj* brittle, fragile; *Gestein, Ehe, Moral* crumbling; *Leder,* *(fig) Stimme* cracked. ~ **werden** *(Gestein, Macht etc)* to (begin to) crumble; *(Ehe, Verhältnisse auch)* to (begin to) break up; *(Leder)* to crack or split.
Bruch-: ~**landung** *f* crashlanding; ~**rechnung** *f* fractions *sing or pl; (Aufgabe)* sum with fractions; ~**stelle** *f* break; *(von Knochen auch)* fracture; ~**strich** *m (Math)* line (of a fraction); ~**stück** *nt* fragment; *(von Lied, Rede etc auch)* snatch; **b**~**stückhaft** *adj* fragmentary; ~**teil** *m* fraction; **im** ~**teil einer Sekunde** in a fraction of a second; ~**zahl** *f (Math)* fraction.
Brücke *f* **-n (a)** *(lit, fig, Naut, Zahn~)* bridge. **alle** ~**n hinter sich** *(dat)* **abbrechen** *(fig)* to burn one's bridges behind one; **jdm goldene** ~**n bauen** to make things easy for sb; ~**n schlagen** *(fig)* to forge links. **(b)** *(Turnen)* crab; *(Teppich)* rug.
Brücken-: ~**kopf** *m (Mil, fig)* bridgehead; ~**schlag** *m (fig)* das war der erste ~**schlag** that forged the first link.
Bruder *m* ⁼ **(a)** brother. **unter** ⁼**n** *(col)* between friends. **(b)** *(Mönch)* friar, brother. **(c)** *(col: Mann)* guy *(col).* **ein warmer** ~ *(dated)* a pansy *(col);* **euch** ~ **kenn' ich** *(pej)* I know you lot.
Bruder-: ~**krieg** *m* war between brothers; ~**kuß** *m (fig)* fraternal kiss.
brüderlich *adj* fraternal, brotherly *no adv.* ~ **teilen** to share and share alike.
Brüderlichkeit *f no pl* brotherliness.
Bruder-: ~**mord** *m* fratricide; ~**mörder** *m* fratricide; ~**schaft** *f (Eccl)* brotherhood; **mit jdm** ~**schaft trinken** to agree to use the familiar *du (over a drink).*
Brühe *f* **-n** *(Suppe)* (clear) soup; *(als Suppengrundlage)* stock; *(pej) (schmutzige Flüssigkeit)* sludge; *(Getränk)* dishwater *(col),* muck *(col).*
Brüh-: **b**~**heiß** *adj* scalding (hot); **b**~**warm** *adj (col)* hot from the press *(col);* **er hat das sofort b**~**warm weitererzählt** he promptly spread it around; ~**würfel** *m* stock cube; ~**wurst** *f* sausage *(to be heated in water).*
brüllen *vti* to shout, to roar; *(pej: laut weinen)* to yell, to bawl; *(Stier)* to bellow; *(Elefant)* to trumpet. **das ist zum B**~ *(col)* it's a scream *(col).*
Brummbär *m (col)* crosspatch *(col).*
brummen *vti* **(a)** *(Insekt)* to buzz; *(Bär)* to growl; *(Motor, singen)* to drone; *(Kreisel etc)* to hum. **mir brummt der Kopf** my head is throbbing. **(b)** *(murren)* to grumble. **(c)** *(col: in Haft sein)* to be locked up *(col).*
Brummer *m* - *(col)* fly; wasp; bee. **(b)** *(Lastwagen)* juggernaut.
brummig *adj* grumpy.
Brumm-: ~**kreisel** *m (col)* humming-top; ~**schädel** *m (col)* thick head *(col).*
brünett *adj* dark(-haired). **sie ist** ~ she is a

brunette.
Brünette f brunette.
Brunft f ‑e (*Hunt*) = **Brunst.**
Brunnen m - (**a**) well; (*fig liter*) fountain. (**b**) (*Spring~*) fountain. (**c**) (*Heilquelle*) spring.
Brunnen-: ~**kresse** f watercress; ~**schacht** m well shaft; ~**vergifter(in** f) m - (*fig pej*) (political) trouble-maker; ~**wasser** nt well water.
Brunst f (*von männlichen Tieren*) rut; (*von weiblichen Tieren*) heat; (*~zeit*) rutting season.
Brunst-: ~**schrei** m mating call; ~**zeit** f rutting season.
brüsk adj brusque, curt.
brüskieren* vt to snub.
Brüskierung f snub.
Brüssel nt Brussels.
Brust f ‑e (**a**) chest; (*fig: Inneres, Cook*) breast.
einen zur ~ nehmen (*col*) to have a quickie (*col*); sich in die ~ werfen (*fig*) to puff oneself up; mit geschwellter ~ (*fig*) as proud as a peacock; schwach auf der ~ sein (*col*) to have a weak chest; (*hum: an Geldmangel leiden*) to be a bit short (*col*). (**b**) (*weibliche ~*) breast. einem Kind die ~ geben to breastfeed a baby. (**c**) (*~schwimmen*) breast-stroke.
Brust-: ~**bein** nt breastbone, sternum; ~**bild** nt half-length portrait.
brüsten vr to boast, to brag (*mit about*).
Brust-: ~**höhe** f: in ~**höhe** chest high; ~**kasten** (*col*), ~**korb** m thorax; ~**krebs** m breast cancer, cancer of the breast; ~**schwimmen** nt breast-stroke; b~**schwimmen** vi infin only to swim or do the breast-stroke; ~**stimme** f chest-voice; ~**stück** nt (*Cook*) breast; ~**tasche** f breast pocket; (*Innentasche*) inside (breast) pocket; ~**ton** m im ~**ton der Überzeugung** in a tone of utter conviction; ~**umfang** m chest measurement; (*von Frau*) bust measurement.
Brüstung f parapet; (*Balkon~ etc auch*) balustrade; (*Fenster~*) breast.
Brust-: ~**warze** f nipple; ~**weite** f = ~**umfang.**
Brut f ‑en (**a**) no pl (*das Brüten*) incubating. (**b**) (*die Jungen*) brood; (*pej*) lot, mob (*col*).
brutal adj brutal; (*gewalttätig auch*) violent.
Brutalität f (**a**) no pl siehe adj brutality; violence. (**b**) (*Gewalttat*) act of violence or brutality.
brüten 1 vi to incubate; (*fig*) to ponder (*über+dat* over). ~**de Hitze** oppressive or stifling heat. 2 vt (*künstlich*) to incubate; (*Tech*) to breed.
Brüter m - (*Tech*) breeder (reactor). **schneller** ~ fast-breeder (reactor).
Brut-: ~**kasten** m (*Med*) incubator; ~**reaktor** m breeder (reactor); ~**stätte** f (*lit, fig*) breeding ground (gen for).
brutto adv gross.
Brutto- in cpds gross; ~**einkommen** nt gross income; ~**registertonne** f register ton; ~**sozialprodukt** nt gross national product, GNP.
Brutzeit f incubation (period).
brutzeln (*col*) 1 vi to sizzle (away). 2 vt to fry (up).
Bub m (*wk*) -en, -en (*S Ger, Aus, Sw*) boy, lad.
Bube m (*wk*) -n, -n (*Cards*) jack, knave.
Bubikopf m bobbed hair no pl, bob.
Buch nt ‑er (**a**) book; (*Band*) volume; (*Dreh~*) script. er redet wie ein ~ (*col*) he never stops talking; ein Gentleman, wie er im ~e steht a perfect example of a gentleman; ein Tor, wie es im ~e steht a textbook goal; ein ~ mit sieben Siegeln (*fig*) a closed book. (**b**) usu pl (*Comm: Geschäfts~*) books pl, accounts pl. über etw (*acc*) ~ führen to keep a record of sth. zu ~(**e**) schlagen to make a (significant) difference.
Buch-: ~**binder(in** f) m bookbinder; ~**druck** m no pl letterpress (printing); ~**drucker** m printer; ~**druckerei** f (*Betrieb*) printery.
Buche f -n beech (tree).
Buch|ecker f -n beechnut.
buchen vt (**a**) (*Comm*) to enter; (*Kasse, fig: regi-*

strieren) to register. **etw als Erfolg** ~ to put sth down as a success. (**b**) (*vorbestellen*) to book.
Buchen-: ~**holz** nt beech wood; ~**wald** m beech wood.
Bücher-: ~**bord**, ~**brett** nt bookshelf.
Bücherei f (lending) library.
Bücher-: ~**freund** m book-lover, ~**gestell** nt bookcase; ~**narr** m book-freak (*col*); ~**regal** nt bookshelf; ~**schrank** m bookcase; ~**verzeichnis** nt bibliography; ~**wand** f wall of bookshelves; ~**wurm** m (*lit, fig hum*) bookworm.
Buchfink m chaffinch.
Buch-: ~**führung** f book-keeping, accounting; ~**halter(in** f) m book-keeper; ~**haltung** f (**a**) = ~**führung**; (**b**) (*Abteilung*) accounts department; ~**handel** m book trade; **im** ~**handel erhältlich** available in bookshops (*Brit*) or bookstores (*US*); ~**händler** m bookseller; ~**handlung** f bookshop (*Brit*), bookstore (*US*); ~**laden** m bookshop (*Brit*), bookstore (*US*); ~**macher** m bookmaker, bookie (*col*); ~**prüfer** m auditor; ~**prüfung** f audit; ~**rücken** m spine.
Buchse ['buksə] f -n (*Elec*) socket; (*Tech*) (*von Zylinder*) liner; (*von Lager*) bush.
Büchse ['byksə] f -n (**a**) tin; (*Konserven~*) can, tin (*Brit*); (*Sammel~*) collecting box. (**b**) (*Gewehr*) rifle, (shot)gun.
Büchsen-: ~**fleisch** nt canned or tinned (*Brit*) meat; ~**milch** f tinned (*Brit*) or evaporated milk; ~**öffner** m can or tin (*Brit*) opener.
Buchstabe m -n letter; (*esp Druck~*) character. **kleiner** ~ small letter; **großer** ~ capital (letter); **dem** ~**n nach** (*fig*) literally; **auf den** ~**n genau** (*fig*) to the letter; **nach dem** ~**n des Gesetzes** according to the letter of the law.
buchstabieren* vt to spell.
buchstäblich adj literally.
Buchstütze f bookend.
Bucht f -en bay.
Buchung f (*Comm*) entry; (*Reservierung*) booking.
Buckel m - (**a**) hump(back), hunchback; (*col: Rücken*) back. **einen** ~ **machen** (*Katze*) to arch its back; **er kann mir den** ~ **(he)runterrutschen** (*col*) he can (go and) take a running jump (*col*); **80 Jahre auf dem** ~ **haben** (*col*) to be 80 (years old). (**b**) (*col: Auswölbung*) bulge, hump.
buck(e)lig adj hunchbacked; (*col*) Straße bumpy.
buckeln vi (*pej*) to bow and scrape.
bücken vr sich nach etw ~ to bend down or to stoop to pick sth up; siehe gebückt.
Bückling m (**a**) (*Cook*) smoked herring. (**b**) (*hum col:* Verbeugung) bow.
buddeln vti (*col*) to dig.
Buddhismus m Buddhism.
Buddhist(in f) m Buddhist.
buddhistisch adj Buddhist(ic).
Bude f -n (**a**) hut; (*Markt~, Verkaufs~*) stall, booth; (*Zeitungs~*) kiosk. (**b**) (*pej col: Laden, Lokal etc*) dump (*col*). (**c**) (*col*) (*Zimmer*) room; (*von Untermieter auch*) digs pl (*col*); (*Wohnung*) pad (*col*). **Leben in die** ~ **bringen** to liven the place up; **jdm die** ~ **einrennen** to pester sb; **jdm auf die** ~ **rücken** to come around.
Budget [by'dʒeː] nt -s budget.
Büfett nt -s or -s (**a**) (*Geschirrschrank*) sideboard. (**b**) (*Schanktisch*) bar; (*Verkaufstisch*) counter. (**c**) kaltes ~ cold buffet.
Büffel m - buffalo.
Büffelei f (*col*) swotting (*col*), cramming (*col*).
büffeln (*col*) 1 vi to swot (*col*), to cram (*col*). 2 vt Lernstoff to swot up (*col*).
Bug m ‑e or -e (*Schiffs~*) bow; (*Flugzeug~*) nose.
Bügel m - (**a**) (*Kleider~*) (coat-)hanger. (**b**) (*Steig~*) stirrup. (**c**) (*Brillen~*) side or ear-piece.
Bügel-: ~**brett** nt ironing board; ~**eisen** nt iron; ~**falte** f crease in one's trousers; b~**fertig** adj ready for ironing; b~**frei** adj non-iron.
bügeln 1 vt to iron; Hose to press. 2 vi to iron.

bugsieren* vt (a) (Naut) to tow. (b) (col) Möbelstück etc to edge. **jdn aus dem Zimmer ~** to steer or hustle sb out of the room.

buh interj boo.

buhen vi (col) to boo.

buhlen vi (pej: werben) **um jds Gunst ~** to woo or court sb's favour.

Buhmann m, pl **-männer** (col) bogeyman (col).

Bühne f **-n** (a) (lit, fig) stage; (von Aula etc auch) platform. **über die ~ gehen** (col) to go (off); **etw über die ~ bringen** (col) to stage sth; **hinter der ~** (lit, fig) behind the scenes; **von der ~ abtreten** to make one's exit. (b) (Theater) theatre (Brit), theater (US); (als Beruf) stage. **zur ~ gehen** to go on the stage.

Bühnen-: ~**anweisung** f stage direction; ~**arbeiter** m stagehand; ~**ausstattung** f props pl; ~**autor** m playwright, dramatist; ~**bearbeitung** f stage adaptation; ~**bild** nt (stage) set; ~**bildner** m set-designer; ~**erfolg** m success; (Stück auch) (stage) hit; ~**personal** nt theatre (Brit) or theater (US) staff; ~**stück** nt (stage) play; ~**techniker** m stage technician.

Buhruf m boo, catcall.

Bukett nt **-s** or **-e** (geh: Blumen~, von Wein) bouquet.

Bulgare m (wk) **-n, -n, Bulgarin** f Bulgarian.

Bulgarien [-iən] nt Bulgaria.

bulgarisch adj Bulgarian.

Bull|auge nt (Naut) porthole.

Bulldogge f bulldog.

Bulldozer ['buldo:zɐ] m - bulldozer.

Bulle m (wk) **-n, -n** (a) bull. (b) (col: starker Mann) great ox of a man. (c) (pej: Polizist) cop (col). **die ~n** the fuzz (pej), the cops (col).

Bullenhitze f (col) sweltering heat.

bullern vi (col) (Wasser) to bubble; (Ofen) to roar.

bullig adj (col) (a) brawny, beefy (col). (b) Hitze sweltering, boiling (col).

bum interj bang; (tiefer) boom.

Bumerang m **-s** or **-e** (lit, fig) boomerang.

Bummel m - stroll; (Lokal ~) pub-crawl. **einen ~ durch die Stadt machen** to go for a stroll around (the) town.

Bummelant(in f) m (wk) (col) (a) (Trödler) slowcoach (Brit col), slowpoke (US col). (b) (Faulenzer) loafer (col), idler.

Bummelei f (col) (Trödelei) dawdling; (Faulenzerei) loafing about (col), idling.

bummeln vi (a) aux sein (spazierengehen) to stroll; (ausgehen) to go out on the town. (b) (trödeln) to dawdle. (c) (faulenzen) to laze around.

Bummel-: ~**streik** m go-slow (Brit), slowdown (US); ~**zug** m (col) slow or stopping train.

Bums m **-e** (col: Schlag) bang, thump.

bumsen 1 vi impers (col: dröhnen) **es bumste, als ...** there was a thump or thud when ...; **es hat gebumst** (von Fahrzeugen) there's been a crash. **2** vi (a) (schlagen) to thump. (b) aux sein (prallen, stoßen) to bump, to bang. (c) (col: koitieren) to have it off (col), to have sex. **3** vt (col) **jdn ~** to lay sb (col), to have sex with sb; **gebumst werden** to get laid (col).

Bumslokal nt (pej col) (low) dive.

Bund[1] m ̈**e** (a) (Bündnis) alliance; (Organisation) association. **den ~ fürs Leben schließen** to take the marriage vows. (b) (Pol: Bundesstaat) Federal Government. (c) (BRD col: Bundeswehr) **der ~** the army. (d) (an Kleidern) waist-band.

Bund[2] nt **-e** (von Stroh, Reisig etc) bundle; (von Radieschen, Spargel etc) bunch.

Bündel nt - bundle, sheaf; (Stroh~) sheaf; (von Radieschen etc) bunch; (fig: von Problemen etc) cluster. **sein ~ schnüren** to pack one's bags.

bündeln vt Zeitungen to bundle up; Stroh to sheave; Karotten etc to tie into bunches/a bunch.

bündelweise adv by the bundle, in bundles.

Bundes- in cpds federal; ~**bahn** f (BRD, Aus, Sw)

Federal Railway(s pl); ~**bank** f Federal bank; ~**behörde** f Federal authority; ~**bürger** m West German citizen; ~**deutsche(r)** mf West German; ~**gebiet** nt (BRD) federal territory; ~**genosse** m ally, confederate; ~**gerichtshof** m (BRD) Federal Supreme Court; ~**grenzschutz** m (BRD) Federal Border Guard; ~**kabinett** nt Federal cabinet; ~**kanzler** m (BRD, Aus) West German/Austrian Chancellor; ~**land** nt state; ~**liga** f (BRD Sport) national league; ~**minister** m (BRD, Aus) Federal Minister; ~**mittel** pl Federal funds pl; ~**nachrichtendienst** m (BRD) Federal Intelligence Service; ~**post** f: **die (Deutsche)** ~**post** the (German) Federal Post (Office); ~**präsident** m (BRD, Aus) (Federal) President; ~**rat** m Bundesrat (upper house of the West German Parliament); ~**regierung** f (BRD, Aus) Federal Government; ~**republik** f Federal Republic; ~**republik Deutschland** Federal Republic of Germany; ~**staat** m federal state; ~**straße** f trunk road (Brit), main highway (US).

Bundestag m Bundestag (lower house of the West German Parliament).

Bundestags- (BRD): ~**abgeordnete(r)** m German member of Parliament, member of the Bundestag; ~**fraktion** f group or faction in the Bundestag; ~**präsident** m President of the Bundestag or West German Parliament; ~**wahl** f (federal) parliamentary elections pl.

Bundes-: ~**trainer** m (BRD Sport) national coach; ~**verfassungsgericht** nt (BRD) Federal Constitutional Court; ~**wehr** f (BRD) army, (West German) armed forces pl; **b~weit** adj nationwide.

Bundhose f knee breeches pl.

bündig adj (a) (schlüssig) conclusive; (kurz, bestimmt) concise, succinct. (b) (in gleicher Ebene) flush pred, level.

Bündnis nt alliance.

Bundweite f waist measurement.

Bungalow ['bungalo] m **-s** bungalow.

Bunker m - (a) bunker; (Luftschutz~) air-raid shelter. (b) (Sammelbehälter) bin; (Kohlen~) bunker; (c) (Mil sl: Gefängnis) guardhouse.

Bunsenbrenner m Bunsen burner.

bunt adj (a) (farbig) coloured (Brit), colored (US); (mehrfarbig) colourful (Brit), colorful (US); (vielfarbig) multi-coloured (Brit), multi-colored (US); (gefleckt) mottled, spotted. ~ **gestreift** brightly striped; ~**e Farben** bright colours; ~**es Glas** stained glass; **etw ~ anstreichen** to paint sth colourfully (Brit) or colorfully (US); ~ **fotografieren** (col) to photograph in colour. (b) (fig: abwechslungsreich) varied. **eine ~e Menge** a motley crowd; **ein ~es Bild** a colourful picture. (c) **jetzt wird's mir aber zu ~!** (col) that's going too far!

Bunt-: **b~bemalt** adj attr brightly painted; ~**film** m (col) colour (Brit) or color (US) film; **b~gemischt** adj attr Programm varied; **b~gestreift** adj attr brightly striped; ~**papier** nt coloured (Brit) or colored (US) paper; ~**specht** m spotted woodpecker; ~**stift** m coloured (Brit) or colored (US) pencil; ~**wäsche** f coloreds pl (Brit), coloreds pl (US).

Bürde f m (lit, fig) burden.

Burg f **-en** castle.

Bürge m (wk) **-n, -n** guarantor; (fig) guarantee (für of). **für jdn ~ sein** to be sb's guarantor.

bürgen vi **für etw ~** to guarantee sth; **für jdn ~** (Fin) to stand surety for sb; (fig) to vouch for sb.

Bürger m - citizen; (Sociol, pej) bourgeois.

Bürger-: ~**initiative** f action group; ~**krieg** m civil war.

bürgerlich adj (a) civil; Pflicht civic. **B~es Gesetzbuch** Civil Code. (b) (dem Bürgerstand angehörend) middle-class (auch pej), bourgeois (esp pej); (Hist) bourgeois. ~**es Essen/Küche** good plain food/cooking; ~**es Trauerspiel** (Liter)

domestic tragedy.
Bürgerliche(r) *mf decl as adj* commoner.
Bürger-: ~**meister(in** *f*) *m* mayor; ~**pflicht** *f* civic duty; ~**recht** *nt usu pl* civil rights *pl*; ~**rechtler** *m* - civil rights campaigner; ~**rechtsbewegung** *f* civil rights movement; ~**schaft** *f* citizens *pl*; *(Vertretung)* City Parliament; ~**schreck** *m* bogey of the middle classes; ~**steig** *m* pavement *(Brit)*, sidewalk *(US)*; ~**tum** *nt no pl (Hist)* bourgeoisie *(Hist)*.
Burgfriede(n) *m (fig)* truce.
Bürgin *f siehe* **Bürge.**
Bürgschaft *f (Jur) (gegenüber Gläubigern)* security, surety; *(Haftungssumme)* penalty.
Burgunder *m - (auch:* ~**wein)** burgundy.
Büro *nt* -s office.
Büro- *in cpds* office; ~**angestellte(r)** *mf* office worker; ~**bedarf** *m* office supplies *pl*; ~**kaufmann** *m* administrative assistant; ~**klammer** *f* paper clip; ~**kraft** *f* (office) clerk.
Bürokrat *m (wk)* -en, -en bureaucrat.
Bürokratie *f* bureaucracy.
Büro-: ~**schluß** *m* office closing time; **nach** ~**schluß** after office hours; ~**stunden** *pl* office hours *pl*; ~**tätigkeit** *f* office work.
Bursche *m (wk)* -n, -n **(a)** *(col: Kerl)* fellow, guy *(col)*. **ein übler** ~ a bad lot. **(b)** *(Lauf*~*)* boy.
Burschen-: ~**schaft** *f* student fraternity; ~**schaft(l)er** *m* - member of a student fraternity.
burschikos *adj* **(a)** *(jungenhaft)* (tom)boyish. **(b)** *(unbekümmert)* casual.
Bürste *f* -n brush.
bürsten *vt* to brush.
Bürsten(haar)schnitt *m* crew cut.
Bus *m* -ses, -se bus; *(Reise*~ *auch)* coach *(Brit)*.
Busbahnhof *m* bus/coach *(Brit)* station.
Busch *m* ⁻e bush. **etwas ist im** ~ *(col)* there's something up; **mit etw hinter dem** ~ **halten** *(col)* to keep sth quiet; **bei jdm auf den** ~ **klopfen** *(col)* to sound sb out; **sich in die** ⁻**e schlagen** *(col)* to slip away.
Büschel *nt* - *(von Gras, Haaren)* tuft; *(von Heu, Stroh)* bundle.
buschig *adj* bushy.
Busch-: ~**messer** *nt* machete; ~**werk** *nt* bushes *pl*.
Busen *m* - *(von Frau)* bust, bosom.
Busen-: **b**~**frei** *adj* topless; ~**freund** *m (iro)* bosom friend.
Bus-: ~**fahrer(in** *f*) *m* bus/coach *(Brit)* driver;

~**fahrt** *f* bus/coach *(Brit)* ride; ~**haltestelle** *f* bus-stop; ~**linie** *f* bus route. **welche** ~**linie fährt zum Bahnhof?** which bus goes to the station?
Bussard *m* -e buzzard.
Buße *f* -n **(a)** *(Rel)* repentance, penitence; *(Auflage)* penance; *(tätige* ~*)* atonement. ~ **tun** to do penance. **(b)** *(Jur: Geldstrafe)* fine.
büßen 1 *vt* to pay for. **das sollst du mir** ~ I'll make you pay for that. **2** *vi* **für etw** ~ *(auch Rel)* to atone for sth; *für Leichtsinn etc* to pay for sth.
Büßer(in *f*) *m* - penitent.
Bußgeld *nt* fine.
Bußgeldbescheid *m* notice of payment due *(for traffic offence etc)*.
Buß-: ~**tag,** ~- **und Bettag** *m* day of prayer and repentance.
Büste *f* -n bust; *(Schneider*~*)* tailor's dummy.
Büstenhalter *m* bra.
Butan *nt* -e, **Butangas** *nt* butane (gas).
Bütten(papier) *nt no pl* handmade paper *(with deckle edge)*.
Büttenrede *f* carnival speech.
Butter *f no pl* butter. **alles (ist) in** ~ *(col)* everything is fine or hunky-dory *(col)*; **jdm die** ~ **auf dem Brot nicht gönnen** *(fig col)* to begrudge sb the very air he breathes; **wir lassen uns nicht die** ~ **vom Brot nehmen** *(col)* we're going to stick up for our rights.
Butter- *in cpds* butter; ~**berg** *m (col)* butter mountain; ~**blume** *f* buttercup; ~**brot** *nt* piece of bread and butter; *(Sandwich)* sandwich; **für ein** ~**brot** *(col)* for next to nothing; **das mußt du mir nicht ständig aufs** ~**brot schmieren** there's no need to keep rubbing it in; ~**brotpapier** *nt* greaseproof paper *(Brit)*, oil paper *(US)*; ~**creme** *f* butter cream; ~**cremetorte** *f* cream cake; ~**dose** *f* butter dish.
Butter-: ~**keks** *m* ≈ morning coffee biscuit; ~**milch** *f* buttermilk.
buttern *vt* **(a)** *Brot* to butter. **(b)** *(col: investieren)* to put *(in+acc* into).
Butter-: ~**seite** *f* **auf die** ~**seite fallen** *(fig col)* to fall on one's feet *(col)*; **die** ~**seite des Lebens** the pleasant side of life; **b**~**weich** *adj* beautifully soft; *(Sport sl) Aufschlag* gentle.
Buxtehude *nt* **aus/nach** ~ *(col)* from/to the back of beyond *(col)*.
Byte [bait] *nt* -s *(Comp)* byte.
bzgl. = **bezüglich.**
bzw. = **beziehungsweise.**

C

C, c [tseː] *nt* -, - C, c. **C-Schlüssel** *m* alto *or* C clef.
C = **Celsius**.
ca. = **circa** approx.
Cabriolet [-'leː] *nt* -s *(Aut)* convertible.
Café [ka'feː] *nt* -s café.
Cafeteria *f* -s cafeteria.
Calais [ka'leː] *nt* **die Straße von** ~ the Straits of Dover.
Callgirl ['koːlgøːʁl] *nt* -s callgirl.
Calvados [kalva'doːs] *m* -, - calvados.
Calypso *m* -s calypso.
Camembert ['kaməmbeːʁ] *m* -s Camembert.
Camp [kɛmp] *nt* -s camp.
campen ['kɛmpn] *vi* to camp.
Camper(in *f)* ['kɛmpɐ, -ərɪn] *m* - camper.
Camping ['kɛmpɪŋ] *nt no pl* camping *no art.* **zum** ~ **fahren** to go camping.
Camping- *in cpds* camping; ~**artikel** *m* piece of camping equipment; *pl* camping equipment sing; ~**platz** *m* camping site.
Campus *m* -, *no pl (Univ)* campus.
Cannabis *m* -, *no pl* cannabis.
Cape [keːp] *nt* -s cape.
Caravan [ka(ː)ravan] *m* -s **(a)** *(Kombiwagen)* estate car *(Brit)*, station wagon. **(b)** *(Wohnwagen)* caravan *(Brit)*, trailer *(US)*.
Casanova [kaza'noːva] *m* -s *(fig)* Casanova.
Cashewnuß ['kɛʃu-] *f* cashew (nut).
catchen ['kɛtʃn] *vi* to do catch-wrestling, to do all-in wrestling.
Catcher(in *f)* ['kɛtʃɐ, -ərɪn] *m* - all-in wrestler, catch wrestler.
Cayennepfeffer [ka'jɛn-] *m* cayenne (pepper).
CB ['tseː'beː] = **Citizen-Band** Citizen Band.
cbm = **Kubikmeter** cubic metre.
ccm = **Kubikzentimeter** cc.
CDU ['tseːdeː'uː] *f* = **Christlich-Demokratische Union**.
Cellist(in *f)* [tʃɛ'lɪst(ɪn)] *m (wk)* cellist.
Cello ['tʃɛlo] *nt* -s *or* **Celli** cello.
Cellophan ® [tsɛlo'faːn] *nt no pl* cellophane.
Celsius ['tsɛlzius] *no art, inv* Celsius.
Celsiusskala *f* Celsius scale.
Cembalo ['tʃɛmbalo] *nt* -s cembalo, harpsichord.
ces, Ces [tsɛs] *nt, gen* - *(Mus)* C flat.
Ceylon ['tsailon] *nt* Ceylon.
Chamäleon [ka'mɛːleɔn] *nt* -s *(lit, fig)* chameleon.
Champagner [ʃam'panjɐ] *m* - champagne.
Champignon ['ʃampɪnjɔŋ] *m* -s mushroom.
Chance ['ʃãːsə] *f* -n chance; *(bei Wetten)* odds *pl*. **keine** ~ **haben** not to have *or* stand a chance; **im Beruf** ~**n haben** to have good career prospects.
Chancengleichheit ['ʃãːsən-] *f* equality of opportunity.
Chanson [ʃã'sõː] *nt* -s (satirical) song.
Chaos ['kaːos] *nt* -, *no pl* chaos.
Chaot(in *f)* [ka'oːt(ɪn)] *m (wk)* -en, -en **(a)** *(Pol pej)* anarchist *(pej)*. **(b)** *(col)* **du bist vielleicht ein** ~ you're so chaotic.
chaotisch [ka'oːtɪʃ] *adj* chaotic. ~**e Zustände** a state of (utter) chaos.
Charakter [ka'raktɐ] *m* -e [-'teːrə] character. **ein Mann von** ~ a man of character; **der vertrauliche** ~ **dieses Gespräches** the confidential nature of this conversation.
Charakter-: ~**darsteller** *m* character actor;

~**eigenschaft** *f* character trait; **c**~**fest** *adj* of strong character; ~**festigkeit** *f* strength of character.
charakterisieren* [ka-] *vt* to characterize.
Charakterisierung *f* characterization.
Charakteristik [ka-] *f* description; *(typische Eigenschaften)* characteristics *pl*.
Charakteristikum [ka-] *nt, pl* **Charakteristika** *(geh)* characteristic.
charakteristisch [ka-] *adj* characteristic *(für* of).
Charakter-: **c**~**lich 1** *adj* (of) character, personal; **c**~**liche Stärke/Mängel** strength of character/character defects; **2** *adv* in character; **jdn c**~**lich stark prägen** to have a strong influence on sb's character; **c**~**los** *adj* **(a)** *(niederträchtig)* unprincipled; **c**~**los handeln** to act in an unprincipled way; **(b)** *(ohne Prägung)* characterless; *Spiel, Vortrag* insipid; ~**losigkeit** *f (Niederträchtigkeit)* lack of principle; *(Handlung)* unprincipled behaviour *(Brit)* or behavior *(US) no pl*; ~**merkmal** *nt* characteristic; ~**rolle** *f* character part; ~**schwäche** *f* weakness of character; ~**stärke** *f* strength of character; **c**~**voll** *adj (ausgeprägt)* full of character; ~**zug** *m* characteristic.
Charge ['ʃarʒə] *f* -n **(a)** *(Mil, fig)* rank. **(b)** *(Theat)* bit part.
charmant [ʃar'mant] *adj* charming.
Charme [ʃarm] *m no pl* charm.
Charter- ['tʃartɐ]: ~**flug** *m* charter flight; ~**(flug)gesellschaft** *f* charter(flight) company; ~**maschine** *f* charter plane.
chartern ['tʃartɐn] *vt Schiff, Flugzeug* to charter.
Chassis [ʃa'siː] *nt* -, - [-iːs] chassis.
Chauffeur [ʃɔ'føːʁ] *m* chauffeur.
Chaussee [ʃo'seː] *f* -n [-eːon] *(dated)* high road.
Chauvi ['ʃoːvi] *m* -s *(col)* male chauvinist pig, MCP.
Chauvinismus [ʃovi-] *m* chauvinism.
Chauvinist(in *f)* *m* chauvinist.
chauvinistisch [ʃovi-] *adj* chauvinist(ic).
checken ['tʃɛkn] **1** *vt* **(a)** *(überprüfen)* to check. **(b)** *(col: verstehen)* to get *(col)*. **2** *vti (Eishockey)* to block; *(anrempeln)* to barge.
Check- ['tʃɛk-]: ~**liste** *f* checklist; ~**point** [-pɔynt] *m* -s checkpoint.
Chef(in *f)* [ʃef] *m* -s boss; *(von Bande, Delegation etc)* leader; *(von Organisation, col: Schuldirektor)* head; *(der Polizei)* chief; *(Mil: von Kompanie)* commander. **er ist der** ~ **vom ganzen** he's the boss here.
Chef-: ~**arzt** *m* senior consultant; ~**etage** *f* executive floor; ~**koch** *m* chef, head cook; ~**redakteur** *m* editor-in-chief; ~**redaktion** *f* **(a)** *(Aufgabe)* (chief) editorship; **(b)** *(Büro)* main editorial office; ~**sekretärin** *f* personal assistant/ secretary; ~**visite** *f (Med)* consultant's round.
Chemie [çe'miː] *f no pl (lit, fig)* chemistry; *(col: Chemikalien)* chemicals *pl*.
Chemie-: ~**arbeiter** *m* chemical worker; ~**faser** *f* synthetic fibre *(Brit)* or fiber *(US)*.
Chemikalie [çemi'kaːliə] *f* -n *usu pl* chemical.
Chemiker(in *f)* ['çe:-] *m* - chemist.
chemisch ['çe:-] *adj* chemical.
Chemotechniker [çemo-] chemical engineer.
chic [ʃɪk] *adj* = **schick**.

Chicorée ['ʃikore:] *f or m no pl* chicory.
Chiffon ['ʃifõ(:)] *m* -s chiffon.
Chiffre ['ʃifrə] *f* -n (a) cipher. (b) *(in Zeitung)* box number.
chiffrieren* [ʃif-] *vti* to encipher, to code. **chiffriert** coded.
Chile ['tʃi:le] *nt* Chile.
Chilene [tʃi'le:nə] *m (wk)* -n, -n, **Chilenin** *f* Chilean.
chilenisch [tʃi-] *adj* Chilean.
Chili ['tʃi:li] *m no pl* chil(l)i.
China ['çi:na] *nt* China.
Chinakohl *m* Chinese cabbage.
Chinese [çi-] *m (wk)* -n, -n Chinaman; *(heutig auch)* Chinese.
Chinesin [çi-] *f* Chinese woman; *(heutig auch)* Chinese.
chinesisch [çi-] *adj* Chinese. **die C~e Mauer** the Great Wall of China.
Chinesisch(e) [çi-] *nt decl as adj* Chinese.
Chinin [çi'ni:n] *nt no pl* quinine.
Chip [tʃɪp] *m* -s (a) *(Spiel~, Comp)* chip. (b) *usu pl (Kartoffel~)* (potato) crisp *(Brit)*, potato chip *(US)*.
Chirurg(in *f)* [çi'rʊrg(ɪn)] *m (wk)* -en, -en surgeon.
Chirurgie [çɪrʊr'gi:] *f* surgery.
chirurgisch [çi-] *adj* surgical. **ein ~er Eingriff** surgery *no indef art.*
Chlor [klo:ɐ] *nt no pl* chlorine.
Chloro- [kloro-]: **~form** *nt no pl* chloroform; **~phyll** *nt no pl* chlorophyll.
Choke [tʃo:k] *m* -s choke.
Cholera ['ko:lera] *f no pl* cholera.
Choleriker(in *f)* [ko-] *m* - hot-tempered person.
cholerisch [ko-] *adj* choleric.
Cholesterin [ko-] *nt no pl* cholesterol.
Cholesterinspiegel *m* cholesterol level.
Chor [ko:ɐ] *m* -e (a) choir; *(Theat)* chorus. **im ~ sprechen/rufen** to speak/shout in chorus. (b) *(Archit: Altarraum)* chancel, choir.
Choral [ko'ra:l] *m, pl* **Choräle** *(Kirchenlied)* hymn.
Choreo- [koreo-]: **~graph(in** *f)* *m* choreographer; **~graphie** *f* choreography.
Chor- [‘ko:ɐ]: **~gesang** *m (Lied)* choral music; *(das Singen)* choral singing; **~gestühl** *nt* choir stalls *pl.*
Chorist(in *f)* [ko-] *m* = **Chorsänger(in).**
Chor- ['ko:ɐ]: **~knabe** *m* choirboy; **~leiter** *m* choirmaster; **~sänger(in** *f)* *m* member of a choir; *(im Kirchenchor)* chorister.
Chose ['ʃo:zə] *f* -n *(col: Angelegenheit)* thing.
Chr. = **Christus.**
Christ [krɪst] *m (wk)* -en, -en Christian.
Christbaum *m* Christmas tree.
Christbaum-: **~kugel** *f* Christmas tree ball; **~schmuck** *m* Christmas tree decorations *pl.*
Christ- ['krɪst-]: **~demokrat** *m* Christian Democrat; **c~demokratisch** *adj* Christian Democratic.
Christen- ['krɪsten-]: **~heit** *f* Christendom; **~pflicht** *f* (one's) Christian duty; **~tum** *nt no pl* Christianity.
Christi *gen of* **Christus.**
Christianisierung [krɪ-] *f* conversion to Christianity.
Christin [‘krɪstɪn] *f* Christian.
Christkind ['krɪst-] *nt no pl* infant Jesus, Christ Child; *(das Geschenke bringt)* Father Christmas.
christlich ['krɪ-] **1** *adj* Christian. **C~er Verein Junger Männer** Young Men's Christian Association. **2** *adv* as a Christian.
Christus ['krɪstus] *m, gen* **Christi** Christ; *(~figur auch)* figure of Christ. **vor Christi Geburt, vor ~** before Christ, BC; **nach Christi Geburt, nach ~** AD, Anno Domini; **Christi Himmelfahrt** Ascension Day.
Chrom [kro:m] *nt no pl* chrome.
Chromosom [kro-] *nt* -en chromosome.

Chronik ['kro:-] *f* chronicle.
chronisch ['kro:-] *adj (Med, fig)* chronic.
Chronist(in *f)* [kro-] *m* chronicler.
Chronologie [kronolo'gi:] *f* chronology.
chronologisch [kro-] *adj* chronological.
Chrysantheme [kryzan'te:mə] *f* **-n** chrysanthemum.
Chuzpe ['xʊtspə] *f no pl (col)* chutzpa(h) *(col)*.
Cineast(in *f)* [sine'ast(ɪn)] *m (wk)* -en, -en cineast(e).
circa ['tsɪrka] *adv* = **zirka**.
Circulus vitiosus ['tsɪrkulus vi'tsio:zʊs] *m, pl* **Circuli vitiosi** *(geh: Teufelskreis)* vicious circle.
cis, Cis [tsɪs] *nt, gen - (Mus)* C sharp.
City ['sɪti] *f* -s city centre.
Clan [kla:n] *m* -s *(lit, fig)* clan.
clean [kli:n] *adj pred (Drogen sl)* off drugs.
Clearing ['kli:rɪŋ] *nt* -s *(Econ)* clearing.
clever ['klɛvɐ] *adj* clever; *(gerissen)* crafty.
Clinch [klɪntʃ] *m no pl (Boxen, fig)* clinch. **jdn in den ~ nehmen** *(lit)* to go into a clinch with sb; *(fig)* to get stuck into sb *(col)*.
Clip *m* -s clip; *(Ohr~)* (clip-on) earring.
Clique ['klɪkə] *f* -n group; *(pej)* clique.
Cliquen-: **~bildung** *f* forming of cliques; **~wirtschaft** *f (pej inf)* cliquey set-up *(inf)*.
Clochard [klo'ʃa:r] *m* -s tramp.
Clou [klu:] *m* -s *(von Geschichte)* (whole) point; *(von Show)* highlight, high spot. **das ist doch gerade der ~** but that's just it, but that's the whole point.
Clown [klaun] *m* -s *(lit, fig)* clown. **den ~ spielen** to clown around, to play the fool; **sich/jdn zum ~ machen** to make a clown of oneself/sb.
Clownerie [klaunə'ri:] *f* clowning (around) *no pl.*
Club *m* -s = **Klub.**
cm = **Zentimeter** cm.
Co. = **Kompanie** Co.
Coach [ko:tʃ] *m* -s *(Sport)* coach.
Cockpit *nt* -s cockpit.
Cocktail ['kɔkte:l] *m* -s (a) cocktail. (b) *(~party)* cocktail party.
Cocktail-: **~kleid** *nt* cocktail dress; **~party** *f* cocktail party.
Code [ko:t] *m* -s = **Kode.**
Cognac ® ['kɔnjak] *m* -s cognac.
Coiffeur [koa'fø:ɐ] *m*, **Coiffeuse** [koa'fø:zə] *f (geh)* hair stylist.
Cola *f* -s *(col)* Coke ® *(col)*.
Collage [kɔ'la:ʒə] *f* -n *(Art, fig)* collage.
Collie *m* -s collie.
Comeback [kam'bɛk] *nt* -(s), -s comeback.
Compact-disc *f* compact disk.
Computer [kɔm'pju:tɐ] *m* - computer.
Computer- *in cpds* computer-; **~generation** *f* computer generation; **c~gerecht** *adj* (ready) for the computer; **c~gesteuert** *adj* computer-controlled.
computerisieren* [kɔmpjutəri'zi:rən] *vti* to computerize.
Conférencier [kõferã'sie:] *m* -s compère, MC.
Container [kɔn'te:nɐ] *m* - container; *(für Schutt etc)* skip.
Container- *in cpds* container; **~bahnhof** *m* container depot; **~terminal** *m or nt* container terminal; **~verkehr** *m* container traffic.
Contergankind *nt (col)* thalidomide child.
cool ['ku:l] *adj (col: gefaßt)* cool.
Copyright ['kɔpirait] *nt* -s copyright.
Cord *m* -e or -s *(Tex)* cord, corduroy.
Cord- *in cpds* cord, corduroy; **~jeans** *pl* cords *pl.*
Cordon bleu [kɔrdõ'blø] *nt* -, -s -s *(Cook)* veal cordon bleu.
Cornichon [kɔrni'ʃõ:] *nt* -s gherkin.
Corpus delicti *nt, pl* **Corpora** - corpus delicti; *(hum)* culprit *(col)*.
Couch [kautʃ] *f* -(e)s or *(col)* -en couch.
Couch-: **~garnitur** *f* three-piece suite; **~tisch** *m*

coffee table.
Couleur [ku'løːɐ] f -s (geh) kind, sort.
Coup [kuː] m -s coup. einen ~ (gegen jdn/etw) landen to bring off a coup (against sb/sth).
Coupé [ku'peː] nt -s coupé.
Coupon [ku'põː] m -s coupon, voucher.
Courage [ku'raːʒə] f no pl (geh) courage.
couragiert [kura'ʒiːɐt] adj (geh) courageous.
Courtage [kʊr'taːʒə] -n (Fin) commission.
Cousin [ku'zɛ̃ː] m -s, **Cousine** [ku'ziːnə] f cousin.
Cover ['kavɐ] nt -s cover.
Cracker ['krɛkɐ] m -(s) (a) cracker. (b) (Feuerwerkskörper) banger (Brit), fire-cracker (US).
Creme [kreːm] f -s (Haut~, Cook, fig) cream. die ~ der Gesellschaft the cream of society.
cremefarben adj cream.
cremig adj creamy.

Crew [kruː] f -s crew.
Croupier [kru'pieː] m -s croupier.
Crux f no pl (Schwierigkeit) trouble, problem.
CSU [tseː|ɛs'|uː] f = **Christlich-Soziale Union.**
cum laude adv (Univ) cum laude (form), with distinction.
Cup [kap] m -s (Sport) cup.
Curling ['køːɐlɪŋ] nt no pl curling.
Curriculum nt, pl **Curricula** (geh) curriculum.
Curry ['kari] m or nt no pl curry.
Currywurst f curried sausage.
Cursor [auch:'køːɐsɐ] m -s (Comp) cursor.
Cut [kœt] m -s (dated) cutaway.
Cutter(in f) ['katɐ, -ərin] m - (Film, Rad, TV) editor.
C.V.J.M. [tseːfaujɔt'|ɛm] m = **Christlicher Verein Junger Männer** YMCA.

D

D, d [de:] *nt* -, - D, d.

da 1 *adv* **(a)** *(örtlich) (dort)* there; *(hier)* here. ~ draußen out there; hier und ~, ~ und dort here and there; he, Sie ~! hey, you there!; ~ bin ich/sind wir here I am/we are; ~ bist du ja! there you are!; ~ kommt er ja here he comes; ~, wo ... where ...; ach, ~ war der Brief! so that's where the letter was; ~ hast du dein Geld! (here you are,) there's your money; ~ siehst du, was du angerichtet hast now see what you've done.
(b) *(zeitlich: dann, damals)* then. ich ging gerade aus dem Haus, ~ schlug es zwei I was just going out of the house when the clock struck two; ~ kommen Sie mal gleich mit *(col)* you just come along with me.
(c) *(daraufhin)* sagen to that; *lachen* at that. sie weinte, ~ ließ er sich erweichen when she started to cry he softened.
(d) *(folglich)* so. es war niemand im Zimmer, ~ habe ich ... there was nobody in the room, so I ...
(e) *(col)* there. ~ haben wir aber Glück gehabt! we were lucky there!; was gibt's denn ~ zu lachen/fragen? what's so funny about that?/what is there to ask?; ~ kann man nichts machen nothing can be done about it; ~ kann man nur lachen/sich nur wundern you can't help laughing/being amazed.
2 *conj* **(a)** *(weil)* as, since, seeing that. **(b)** *(liter: als)* when.

dabehalten* *vt sep irreg* to keep (here/there); *Schüler* to keep behind.

dabei *adv* **(a)** *(örtlich)* with it; *(bei Gruppe von Menschen, Dingen)* there.
(b) *(gleichzeitig)* at the same time; *(währenddessen, dadurch)* in the course of this. warum arbeiten Sie im Stehen? Sie können doch auch ~ sitzen why are you working standing up? you can sit down while you're doing it; ... orkanartige Winde; ~ kam es zu schweren Schäden ... gale-force winds, which have resulted in serious damage.
(c) *(außerdem)* sie ist schön und ~ auch noch klug she's pretty, and clever as well.
(d) *(wenn, während man etw tut)* in the process; *ertappen, erwischen* at it. hast du ~ etwas gelernt? did you learn anything from it?; ~ darf man nicht vergessen, daß ... it shouldn't be forgotten that ...; die ~ entstehenden Kosten the expenses arising from this/that; wir haben ihn ~ ertappt, wie er über den Zaun stieg we caught him in the act of climbing over the fence.
(e) *(in dieser Angelegenheit)* das Schwierigste ~ the most difficult part of it; mir ist nicht ganz wohl ~ I don't really feel happy about it; er hat ~ einen Fehler gemacht he's made a mistake; es kommt doch nichts ~ heraus nothing will come of it.
(f) *(einräumend: obwohl)* (and) yet. er hat mich geschlagen, ~ hatte ich gar nichts gemacht he hit me and I hadn't even done anything.
(g) es bleibt ~, daß ihr morgen alle mitkommt we'll stick to that, you're all coming tomorrow; ich bleibe ~ I'm not changing my mind; lassen wir es ~ let's leave it at that!;

was ist schon ~? so what? *(col)*, what of it? *(col)*; was ist schon ~, wenn man das tut? what harm is there in doing that?; ich finde gar nichts ~ I don't see any harm in it; was hast du dir denn ~ gedacht? what were you thinking of?

dabeibleiben *vi sep irreg aux sein* to stay or stick *(col)* with it; *(bei Firma)* to stay on; *siehe* dabei **(g)**.

dabeihaben *vt sep irreg (col)* to have with one.

dabeisein *vi sep irreg aux sein* **(a)** to be there *(bei* at); *(mitmachen)* to be involved *(bei* in). ich bin dabei! count me in!; er will überall ~ he wants to be in on everything. **(b)** *(im Begriff sein)* ~, etw zu tun to be just doing sth; ich bin (gerade) dabei I'm just doing it.

dabeisitzen *vi sep irreg* to sit there. bei einer Besprechung ~ to sit in on a discussion.

dabeistehen *vi sep irreg* to stand there.

dableiben *vi sep irreg aux sein* to stay (on); (jetzt wird) dageblieben! (you just) stay right there!

Dach *nt* ⁻er **(a)** roof. mit jdm unter einem ~ wohnen to live under the same roof as sb; unter'm ~ wohnen *(col)* to live in an attic; *(im obersten Stock)* to live right on the top floor; unter ~ und Fach sein *(abgeschlossen)* to be in the bag *(col)*; *(Vertrag, Geschäft auch)* to be signed and sealed; *(in Sicherheit)* to be safe; *(Ernte)* to be safely in. **(b)** *(fig col)* jdm eins aufs ~ geben *(schlagen)* to smash sb on the head *(col)*; *(ausschimpfen)* to give sb a (good) talking to; jdm aufs ~ steigen *(col)* to get onto sb *(col)*.

Dach- *in cpds* roof; ~boden *m* attic; ~decker *m* - roofer; *(mit Ziegeln)* tiler; ~fenster *nt* skylight; *(ausgestellt)* dormer window; ~first *m* ridge of the roof; ~garten *m* roof garden; ~gepäckträger *m (Aut)* roof rack; ~geschoß *nt* attic storey; *(oberster Stock)* top floor or storey; ~giebel *m* gable; ~kammer *f* attic room; ~luke *f* skylight; ~organisation *f* umbrella or *(Comm)* parent organization; ~rinne *f* gutter.

Dachs *m* -e **(a)** badger. **(b)** ein junger ~ *(col)* a young whippersnapper.

Dachsbau *m* badger's sett.

Dach-: ~schaden *m* (a) *(lit)* damage to the roof; **(b)** *(col)* einen ~schaden haben to have a screw loose *(col)*; ~stube *f* attic (room).

dachte *pret of* denken.

Dach-: ~terrasse *f* roof terrace; ~verband *m* umbrella organization; ~wohnung *f* attic flat *(Brit)* or apartment; ~ziegel *m* roofing tile; ~zimmer *nt* attic (room).

Dackel *m* - dachshund.

dadurch *adv (emph* dadurch**) (a)** *(örtlich)* through there; *(wenn Bezugsobjekt vorher erwähnt)* through it. **(b)** *(kausal)* thereby *(form)*; *(aus diesem Grund auch)* because of this/that; *(auf diese Weise)* in this/that way. was willst du ~ gewinnen? what do you hope to gain by that?; meinst du, ~ wird alles wieder gut? do you think that will make everything all right again?; ~, daß er das tat, hat er ... by doing that he ...

dafür *adv (emph* dafür**) (a)** *(für das, diese Tat etc)* for that/it. ~ war er nicht zu haben it wasn't his scene *(col)*; *(erlaubte es nicht)* he wouldn't have it; ~ ist er immer zu haben he never says no to that; ich bin nicht ~ verantwortlich, was mein Bruder macht I'm not responsible for what my

96

brother does; ~ **bin ich ja hier** that's what I'm here for; **er ist** ~ **bestraft worden, daß er frech zum Lehrer war** he was punished for being cheeky to the teacher.

(b) *(Zustimmung)* for that/it, in favour (of that/it). **ich bin (ganz)** ~**, daß wir das machen** I'm (all) for doing that.

(c) *(als Ersatz)* instead, in its place; *(bei Tausch)* in exchange; *(als Gegenleistung)* in return.

(d) *(zum Ausgleich)*. **in Mathematik ist er schlecht,** ~ **kann er gut Fußball spielen** he's very bad at maths but he makes up for it at football.

(e) *(im Hinblick darauf)* ~**, daß er erst drei Jahre ist, ist er sehr klug** seeing *or* considering that he's only three he's very clever.

dafür-: ~**halten** *vi sep irreg (geh)* to be of the opinion; **nach meinem D~halten** in my opinion; ~**können** *vt sep irreg* **er kann nichts** ~ he can't help it; **er kann nichts** ~**, daß er dumm ist** he can't help being stupid.

dagegen 1 *adv (emph* **dagegen) (a)** *(örtlich)* against it. **(b)** *(als Einwand, Ablehnung)* against that/it. ~ **sein** to be against it; **etwas/nichts** ~ **haben** to object/not to object; **was hat er** ~**, daß wir früher anfangen?** what has he got against us starting earlier?; **haben Sie was** ~**, wenn ich rauche?** do you mind if I smoke?; **sollen wir ins Kino gehen? — ich hätte nichts** ~ (einzuwenden) shall we go to the cinema? — that's okay by me *(col)*. **(c)** *(als Gegenmaßnahme)* unternehmen about it; *(Medikamente einnehmen etc)* for it. ~ **läßt sich nichts machen** nothing can be done about it. **(d)** *(verglichen damit)* in comparison. **(e)** *(als Ersatz)* eintauschen for that/it/them. **2** *conj (im Gegensatz dazu)* on the other hand, however.

dagegen-: ~**halten** *vt sep irreg* **(a)** *(vergleichen)* to compare it/them with; **(b)** *(fig: einwenden)* to object; ~**sprechen** *vi sep irreg* to be against it; **was spricht** ~**, daß wir es so machen?** what is there against us doing it that way?; **es spricht nichts** ~**, es so zu machen** there's no reason not to do it that way.

dagewesen *adj siehe* **dasein.**

dahaben *vt sep irreg* to have here/there; *(in Geschäft etc)* to have in stock.

daheim *adv* at home; *(nach prep)* home. **bei uns** ~ back home; ~ **sein** *(lit, fig)* to be at home; *(nach Reise)* to be home; **wo bist du** ~**?** where's your home?

Daheim *nt no pl* home.

daher 1 *adv (auch* **daher) (a)** *(von dort)* from there. **(b)** *(durch diesen Umstand)* that is why. ~ **weiß ich das** that's how *or* why I know that; ~ **die große Eile** hence all the hurry; ~ **kommt es, daß** ... that is (the reason) why ...; **das kommt** ~**, daß** ... that is because ... **2** *conj (deshalb)* that is why.

daher-: ~**gelaufen** *adj* **jeder** ~**gelaufene Kerl** any Tom, Dick or Harry; ~**kommen** *vi sep irreg aux sein* to come along; ~**reden** *sep* **1** *vi* to talk away; **red doch nicht so** (dumm) ~**!** I don't talk such rubbish!; **2** *vt* to say without thinking; **was er alles** ~**redet** the things he comes out with! *(col)*; **das war nur so** ~**geredet** I/he *etc* just said that.

dahin 1 *adv (emph* **dahin) (a)** *(räumlich)* there; *(hierhin)* here. **kommst du auch** ~**?** are you coming too?; **bis** ~ as far as there, up to that point; **ist es noch weit bis** ~**?** is it far still? **(b)** *(fig: so weit)* ~ **kommen** to reach such a state; **du wirst es** ~ **bringen, daß** ... you'll bring things to such a state that ... **(c)** *(in dem Sinne)* **er äußerte sich** ~ **gehend, daß** ... he said something to the effect that ...; **eine** ~ **gehende Aussage** a statement to that effect; **er hat den Bericht** ~ **(gehend)** interpretiert, daß ... he interpreted the

report as saying ...; **wir haben uns** ~ **geeinigt, daß** ... we have agreed that ...; **seine Meinung geht** ~**, daß** ... he tends to the opinion that ... **2** *adj pred* ~ **sein** to have gone; **das Auto ist** ~ *(hum col)* the car has had it *(col)*.

dahingegen *adv* on the other hand.

dahingehen *vi sep irreg aux sein (geh: Zeit etc)* to pass.

dahingehend *adv siehe* **dahin 1 (c).**

dahin-: ~**gestellt** *adj* ~**gestellt sein lassen, ob** ... to leave it open whether ...; **es sei** ~**gestellt, ob** ... it is an open question whether ...; ~**leben** *vi sep* to exist, to vegetate *(pej)*; ~**sagen** *vt sep* to say without (really) thinking; ~**schleppen** *vr sep (lit: sich fortbewegen)* to drag oneself along; *(fig: Verhandlungen, Zeit)* to drag on; ~**schwinden** *vi sep irreg aux sein (geh) (Geld, Kraft)* to dwindle (away); *(vergehen: Zeit)* to go past; ~**stehen** *vi sep irreg* to be debatable.

dahinten *adv (emph* **dahinten)** over there.

dahinter *adv (emph* **dahinter)** behind (it/that/ him *etc)*. **(da ist) nichts** ~ *(fig)* there's nothing behind it.

dahinter-: ~**klemmen, ~knien** *vr sep (col)* to put one's back into it; ~**kommen** *vi sep irreg aux sein (col)* to find out; ~**stecken** *vi sep (col)* to be behind it/that; ~**stehen** *vi sep irreg (unterstützen)* to back it/that, to be behind it/that.

Dahlie [-iə] *f* **-n** dahlia.

Dakapo *nt* **-s** encore.

da-: ~**lassen** *vt sep irreg* to leave (here/there); ~**liegen** *vi sep irreg* to lie there.

dalli *adv (col)* ~**,** ~**!** on the double! *(col)*; **mach ein bißchen** ~**!** get a move on! *(col)*.

Dalmatiner *m* **-** *(Hund)* dalmatian.

damalig *adj attr* at that time; **Sitten auch** in those days. **der** ~**e Kanzler** the then Chancellor.

damals *adv* at that time, then. **seit** ~ since then; **von** ~ of that time; ~**, als** ... at the time when ...

Dame *f* **-n (a)** lady. **meine** ~ **n und Herren!** ladies and gentlemen!; **Hundert-Meter-Staffel der** ~**n** women's *or* ladies' hundred metre relay. **(b)** *(Spiel)* draughts *sing (Brit)*, checkers *sing (US)*; *(Doppelstein)* king; *(Cards, chess)* queen.

Damebrett *nt* draught(s)board, checkerboard *(US)*.

Dämel *m* **-** *(col)* jerk *(col!)*.

Damen- *in cpds* ladies'; ~**bart** *m* facial hair; ~**begleitung** *f*: **in** ~**begleitung** in the company of a lady; ~**bekanntschaft** *f* female acquaintance *(col)*; **eine** ~**bekanntschaft machen** to make the acquaintance of a lady/young lady; ~**besuch** *m* lady visitor/visitors; ~**binde** *f* sanitary towel *or* napkin *(US)*; ~**gesellschaft** *f* hen party *(col)*; *(gesellige Runde)* ladies' gathering; **d~haft** *adj* ladylike *no adv*; **sich d~haft benehmen** to behave in a ladylike way; ~**oberbekleidung** *f* ladies' wear; ~**sattel** *m* **im** ~**sattel reiten** to ride side-saddle; ~**toilette** *f (WC)* ladies' toilet *or* restroom *(US)*; ~**wahl** *f* ladies' excuse-me.

Damhirsch *m* fallow deer.

damit 1 *adv (emph auch* **damit) (a)** with it/that/ them. **was soll ich** ~**?** what am I meant to do with that?; **ist Ihre Frage** ~ **beantwortet?** does that answer your question?; **meint er mich** ~**?** does he mean me?; **was ist** ~**?** what about it?; **wie wäre es** ~**?** how about it?; **wie sieht es** ~ **aus?** what's happening about it?; **muß er denn immer wieder** ~ **ankommen?** must he keep on about it?; ~ **ist nichts** *(col)* it's no go *(col)*; **hör auf** ~**!** *(col)* lay off! *(col)*; ~ **hat es noch Zeit** there's no hurry for that; **was willst du** ~ **sagen?** what's that supposed to mean?; ~ **will ich nicht sagen, daß** ... I don't mean to say that ...; ~ **fing der Streit an** that's how the argument started; **der Streit fing** ~ **an, daß er behauptete** ... the argument started when he said ...

(b) *(bei Befehlen)* with it. **weg** ~**!** away with it;

her ~! give it here! (col).

(c) (begründend) because of that. ~ ist es klar, daß er es war from that it's clear that it was him.

2 conj so that. ~ er nicht fällt so that he does not fall.

dämlich adj (col) stupid.

Dämlichkeit f stupidity.

Damm m -e (a) (Deich) dyke; (Stau~) dam; (Hafen~) wall; (Ufer~, Straßen~) embankment; (fig) barrier. (b) (fig col) wieder auf dem ~ sein to be back to normal; nicht recht auf dem ~ sein to be a bit under the weather (col).

Dammbruch m breach in a/the dyke etc.

dämmen vt (a) (geh) (lit) to dam; (fig) to check. (b) (Tech) Wärme to keep in; Schall to absorb.

dämm(e)rig adj Licht dim, faint; Stunden twilight attr. es wird ~ (abends) dusk is falling; (morgens) dawn is breaking.

Dämmerlicht nt twilight; (abends auch) dusk; (Halbdunkel) half-light.

dämmern 1 vi (a) (Tag, Morgen) to dawn; (Abend) to fall. als der Tag or Morgen/Abend dämmerte ... as dawn was breaking/dusk was falling; es dämmerte ihm, daß ... (col) it dawned on him that ... (b) (im Halbschlaf sein) to doze. vor sich hin ~ (Kranker) to be semi-conscious. 2 vi impers es dämmert (morgens) dawn is breaking; (abends) dusk is falling; jetzt dämmert's (bei) mir! (col) now it's dawning (on me)!

Dämmer-: ~schein m (liter) glow; ~schoppen m early evening drink; ~stunde f twilight, dusk.

Dämmerung f twilight; (Abend~ auch) dusk; (Morgen~ auch) dawn; (Halbdunkel) half-light. in der ~ at dusk/dawn.

Dämmerzustand m (Halbschlaf) dozy state; (Bewußtseinstrübung) semi-conscious state.

Dämmung f insulation.

Dämon m, pl **Dämonen** demon.

Dampf m -e (a) steam. ~ ablassen (lit, fig) to let off steam. (b) (col: Wucht, Schwung) force. jdm ~ machen (col) to make sb get a move on (col); ~ dahinter machen to get a move on (col); mit ~ (col) at full tilt.

Dampf- in cpds steam; ~antrieb m steam drive; ~bügeleisen nt steam iron.

dampfen vi (a) to steam. ein ~des Bad a steaming hot bath. (b) aux sein (Zug, Schiff) to steam.

dämpfen vt (a) (abschwächen) to muffle; Geräusch, Schall auch to deaden; Farbe to mute; Licht, Stimme to lower; Wut to calm; Freude, Stimmung to dampen; Aufprall to deaden; siehe gedämpft. (b) (Cook) to steam.

Dampfer m - steamer, steamship. auf dem falschen ~ sein (fig col) to have got the wrong idea.

Dämpfer m - (Mus) (bei Klavier) damper; (bei Geige, Trompete) mute. dadurch hat er einen ~ bekommen that dampened his spirits.

Dampf-: ~kessel m (Tech) steam-boiler; ~kochtopf m pressure cooker; ~lokomotive, ~lok (col) f steam engine or locomotive; ~maschine f steam(-driven) engine; ~schiff nt steamship, steamer; ~walze f steamroller.

Damwild nt fallow deer.

danach adv (emph auch danach) (a) (zeitlich) after that/it; (nachher auch) afterwards. zehn Minuten ~ war sie schon wieder da ten minutes later she was back.

(b) (in der Reihenfolge) (örtlich) behind (that/it/him etc); (zeitlich) after that/it/him etc.

(c) (dementsprechend) accordingly; (laut diesem) according to that. ~ sein (Wetter, Stimmung etc) to be right; die Torte hat nur 2 Mark gekostet — ~ ist sie auch the gateau only cost 2 marks — it tastes like it too; sie sieht nicht ~ aus she doesn't look (like) it; (als ob sie so was gern hätte) she doesn't look the type; ~ zu urteilen judging by that; mir war nicht ~ (col) or ~

zumute I didn't feel like it.

(d) (in bestimmte Richtung) towards it. er griff schnell ~ he grabbed at it.

(e) sie sehnte sich ~, ihren Sohn wiederzusehen she longed to see her son again; ~ kann man nicht gehen you can't go by that; wenn es ~ ginge, was mir Spaß macht, dann ... if it were a matter of what I enjoy then ...

Dandy ['dɛndi] m -s dandy.

Däne m (wk) -n, -n Dane, Danish man/boy.

daneben adv (emph auch daneben) (a) (räumlich) next to him/her/that/it etc; links/rechts ~ to the left/right of sb/sth; wir wohnen im Haus ~ we live in the house next door. (b) (verglichen damit) in comparison. (c) (außerdem) as well (as that); (gleichzeitig) at the same time.

daneben-: ~benehmen* vr sep irreg (col) to make an exhibition of oneself; ~gehen vi sep irreg aux sein (a) (verfehlen: Schuß etc) to miss; (b) (col: scheitern) to go wrong; ~geraten* vi sep irreg aux sein to go wrong; (Übersetzung) not to hit the mark; ~greifen vi sep irreg to miss; (fig col: mit Schätzung etc) to be wide of the mark; im Ton ~greifen to strike the wrong note; ~hauen vi sep irreg (a) (beim Schlagen) to miss; (b) (col: sich irren) to be wide of the mark; ~liegen vi sep irreg (col: sich irren) to be way out (col); ~raten vi sep irreg (col) to guess wrong; ~sein vi sep irreg aux sein (col) (verwirrt sein) to be completely confused; (sich nicht wohl fühlen) to be feeling out of sorts.

Dänemark nt Denmark.

Dänin f Dane, Danish woman/girl.

dänisch adj Danish.

Dänisch(e) nt decl as adj Danish.

Dank m no pl thanks pl. herzlichen or vielen ~ many thanks, thank you very much, thanks a lot (col); vielen herzlichen/tausend ~! many/very many thanks!, thanks a million! (col); jdm für etw ~ sagen (liter) to express one's or give (esp Eccl) thanks to sb for sth; jdm zu ~ verpflichtet sein (form) to owe sb a debt of gratitude; mit bestem ~ zurück! many thanks for the loan; (iro: Retourkutsche) thank you — the same to you!; das ist der ~ dafür that's all the thanks you get; zum ~ (dafür) as a way of saying thank you.

dank prep+gen or dat thanks to.

dankbar adj (a) (dankerfüllt) grateful; (erleichtert, froh) thankful; Publikum, Zuhörer appreciative. jdm ~ sein to be grateful to sb (für for); sich ~ erweisen to show one's gratitude (gegenüber to). (b) (lohnend) Aufgabe, Rolle rewarding; (haltbar) hard-wearing.

Dankbarkeit f gratitude (gegen, gegenüber to).

danke interj thank you, thanks (col), ta (Brit col); (ablehnend) no thank you. ~ ja, ja, ~ yes please, yes, thank you; ~ nein, nein, ~ no thank you; ~ schön or sehr thank you or thanks (col) very much; ~ vielmals many thanks.

danken 1 vi (a) to express one's thanks. jdm ~ to thank sb (für for); danke! yes please!; (ablehnend) no thank you, no thanks (col); man dankt (col) thanks (col), ta (Brit col); jdm ~ lassen to send sb one's thanks; nichts zu ~ don't mention it; na, ich danke (iro) no thank you; ~d erhalten/ablehnen to receive/decline with thanks. (b) (ablehnen) to decline. 2 vt (a) (geh: verdanken) ihm danke ich es, daß ... I owe it to him that ... (b) jdm etw ~ to thank sb for sth; man hat es mir schlecht gedankt, daß ich das getan habe I got small thanks for doing it.

dankenswert adj Bemühung commendable; Hilfe kind; (lohnenswert) Aufgabe, Arbeit rewarding.

Dankeschön nt no pl thank-you.

Dankesworte pl words pl of thanks; (von Redner) vote sing of thanks.

Dank-: ~gottesdienst m service of thanksgiving; ~sagung f (Brief) note of thanks; ~schreiben nt

letter of thanks.
dann adv (a) then. ~ **und** ~ about then; ~ **und wann** now and then; **gerade** ~, **wenn** ... just when ... **(b)** (unter diesen Umständen) then. **wenn** ..., ~ if ..., (then); **nein, selbst** ~ **nicht** no, not even then; **selbst** ~/**selbst** ~ **nicht, wenn** ... even/not even if ...; **erst** ~, **wenn** ... only when ...; **ja,** ~! (oh) well then!; **wenn er seine Gedichte selbst nicht versteht, wer** ~? if he can't understand his own poems, who can?; ~ **eben nicht** well, in that case (there's no more to be said); ~ **erst recht nicht!** in that case no way (col); ~ **will ich lieber gehen** well, I'd better be getting along (then); **also** ~ **bis morgen** see you tomorrow then. **(c)** (außerdem) ~ ... **noch** on top of that.
dannen adv: **von** ~ (liter: weg) away.
daran adv (auch **dran**) **(a)** (räumlich) **hängen** on it/that; **schieben, lehnen, stellen** against it/that; **legen** next to it/that; **kleben, machen** to it/that. **nahe** or **dicht** ~ right up against it; **nahe** ~ **sein, etw zu tun** to be on the point of doing sth; **zu nahe** ~ too close (to it); ~ **vorbei** past it; ~ **kommen** to touch it/that. **(b)** (zeitlich) **danach anschließend) im Anschluß** ~ following that/this. **(c)** (col) = **dran (b, c)**. **(d)** arbeiten on it/that; **sterben, erinnern, Bedarf, Mangel** of it/that; **sich beteiligen, arm, reich** in it/that; **sich klammern** to it/that. **wird sich etwas** ~ **ändern?** will that change at all?; **wir können nichts** ~ **machen** we can't do anything about it; ~ **sieht man, wie** ... there you (can) see how ...; **das Beste/Schönste etc** ~ the best/nicest etc thing about it; **es ist nichts** ~ (ist nicht fundiert) there's nothing in it; (ist nichts Besonderes) it's nothing special.
daran-: ~**gehen** vi sep irreg aux sein to set about it; ~**gehen, etw zu tun** to set about doing sth; ~**machen** vr sep (col) to set about it; **sich** ~**machen, etw zu tun** to set about doing sth; ~**setzen** sep 1 vt **seine ganzen Kräfte** ~**setzen, etw zu tun** to spare no effort to do sth; 2 vr (sich ~**machen**) to get down to it.
darauf adv (emph **darauf**) **(a)** (räumlich) on it/that/them etc; (in Richtung) towards it/that/them etc; **schießen, zielen, losfahren** at it/that/them etc; (fig) basieren, aufbauen on it/that; **zurückführen, beziehen** to it/that. **er schlug mit dem Hammer** ~ he hit it with the hammer; **seine Behauptungen stützen sich** ~, **daß** ... his claims are based on the supposition that ...
(b) (Reihenfolge) after that. **die Tage, die** ~ **folgten** the days which followed; ~ **folgte** ... that was followed by ..., after that came ...
(c) (als Reaktion) sagen, reagieren to that. ~ **antworten** to answer that; **eine Antwort** ~ **an** answer to that.
(d) bestehen, verlassen, wetten, Zeit/Mühe verschwenden, Einfluß on that/it; hoffen, warten, sich vorbereiten, gefaßt sein for that/it; trinken to that/it; **stolz sein** of that/it. **ich bin stolz** ~, **daß sie gewonnen hat** I'm proud that she won, I'm proud of her winning; **ich bestehe** ~, **daß du kommst** I insist that you come; **wir freuen uns schon** ~, **daß du bald kommst** we're looking forward to your or you coming; **wir kamen auch** ~ **zu sprechen** we talked about that too; **wie kommst du** ~? what makes you think that?; ~ **willst du hinaus!** that's what you're getting at!
dara003ffolgend adj attr after him/it/that etc; Tag etc following; Wagen etc behind pred.
daraufhin adv (emph **daraufhin**) (danach) after that, thereupon; (aus diesem Anlaß, deshalb) as a result of that/this); (im Hinblick darauf) with regard to that/this. **wir müssen es** ~ **prüfen, ob** ... we must test it to see whether ...
daraus adv (emph auch **daraus**) out of that/it/them; (aus dieser Angelegenheit) from that/it/them. ~ **ergibt sich, daß** ... it follows from this that ...

därben vi (geh: hungern) to starve.
darbieten sep irreg (geh) 1 vt **(a)** (vorführen) Tänze etc to perform; (vortragen) Lehrstoff to present. **(b)** (anbieten) to offer; Speisen to serve. 2 vr to present itself.
Darbietung f performance; (das Dargebotene) act.
darbringen vt sep irreg (geh) Opfer to offer.
darein adv (emph auch **darein**) (räumlich: hinein) in there; (wenn Bezugsobjekt vorher erwähnt) in it/them.
darein- pref siehe auch **drein-**; ~**finden** vr sep irreg (geh) to come to terms with it.
darin adv (emph auch **darin**) **(a)** (räumlich) in there; (wenn Bezugsobjekt vorher erwähnt) in it/them. **(b)** (in dieser Beziehung) in that respect. ~ **ist er ganz groß** (col) he's very good at that; **die beiden unterscheiden sich** ~, **daß** ... the two of them differ in that ...; **der Unterschied liegt** ~, **daß** ... the difference is that ...
darlegen vt sep to explain (jdm to sb); Theorie, Ansichten auch to expound (jdm to sb).
Darlegung f explanation.
Darleh(e)n nt - loan. **als** ~ as a loan.
Darm m -e intestine(s pl), bowel(s pl); (für Wurst) (sausage) skin; (für Saiten, Schläger etc) gut.
Darm- in cpds intestinal; ~**ausgang** m anus; ~**grippe** f gastric influenza; ~**krebs** m cancer of the intestine; ~**tätigkeit** f peristalsis no art; **die** ~**tätigkeit fördern** to stimulate the movement of the bowels; ~**trägheit** f under-activity of the intestines.
Darre f -n drying kiln or oven; (Hopfen~) oast.
darreichen vt sep (liter: anbieten) to offer (jdm etw sb sth, sth to sb).
darstellbar adj (in Literaturwerk etc) portrayable; (durch Diagramm etc) representable; (beschreibbar) describable. **schwer/leicht** ~ hard/easy to portray/show/describe.
darstellen sep 1 vt **(a)** to show; (ein Bild entwerfen von) to portray, to depict; (Theat) to play; (beschreiben) to describe. **etw kurz** ~ to give a short description of sth; **er stellt nichts dar** (fig) he's nothing special. **(b)** (bedeuten) to constitute, to represent. 2 vr (Eindruck vermitteln) to appear (jdm to sb); (sich erweisen) to show oneself.
Darsteller m - (Theat) actor. **der** ~ **des Hamlet** the actor playing Hamlet.
Darstellerin f (Theat) actress.
darstellerisch adj dramatic. **eine** ~**e Höchstleistung** a magnificent piece of acting.
Darstellung f portrayal; (in Buch, Bild auch) depiction; (durch Diagramm etc) representation; (Beschreibung) description; (Bericht) account. **eine falsche** ~ **der Fakten** a misrepresentation of the facts; **er gab eine großartige** ~ **des Hamlet** his performance as Hamlet was superb.
darüber adv (emph auch **darüber**) **(a)** (räumlich) over that/it/them; (höher als etw) above (there/it/them); (direkt auf etw) on top (of it/them). **geh** ~, **nicht hierüber!** go over there, not here!; ~ **hinweg sein** (fig) to have got over it. **(b)** (deswegen, in dieser Beziehung) about that/it. **sich** ~ **beschweren/beklagen, daß** ... to complain/moan that ... **(c)** (davon) about that/it. **sie führt eine Liste** ~ she keeps a list of it. **(d)** (mehr, höher) above or over that. **21 Jahre und** ~ 21 years and above or over; ~ **hinaus** over and above that.
darüber-: ~**fahren** vi sep irreg aux sein (fig) to run over it; **wenn du mit der Hand** ~**fährst,** ... if you run your hand over it ...; ~**liegen** vi sep irreg (fig) to be higher; ~**stehen** vi sep irreg (fig) to be above such things.
darum adv (emph **darum**) siehe auch **drum (a)** (räumlich) around that/it/him/her/them. ~ **herum** around about it/him/her/them). **(b)** (um diese Angelegenheit) **es geht** ~, **daß** ... the thing is that ...; ~ **geht es mir/geht es mir nicht** that's my

point/that's not the point for me; **es geht mir ~,
Ihnen das klarzumachen** I'm trying to make it
clear to you; **ich gäbe viel ~, die Wahrheit zu
erfahren** I would give a lot to learn the truth. (c)
(deshalb) that's why, because of that. **eben ~**
that is exactly why; **warum willst du nicht mitkommen? — ~!** *(col)* why don't you want to
come? — I just don't.

darunter *adv (emph auch* **darunter)** **(a)** *(räumlich)* under that/it/them. **~ hervorkommen** to
appear from underneath. **(b)** *(weniger)* under
that. **Leute im Alter von 35 Jahren und ~** people
aged 35 and under; **~ macht sie's nicht** *(col)* she
won't do it for less. **(c)** *(dabei)* among them. **~
waren viele Ausländer** there were a lot of
foreigners among them. **(d) was verstehen Sie
~?** what do you understand by that/it?; **~ kann
ich mir nichts vorstellen** that doesn't mean anything to me.

darunter-: **~fallen** *vi sep irreg aux sein (fig) (da-
zugerechnet werden)* to be included; *(davon betroffen werden)* to come under it/them; **~mischen**
sep **1** *vt Mehl* to mix in; **2** *vr (Mensch)* to mingle
with them; **~setzen** *vt sep Unterschrift* to put to it.

das *art etc siehe* **der**[2].

Dasein *nt no pl* existence; *(Anwesendsein)* presence.

dasein *vi sep irreg aux sein* to be there. **noch ~** to be
still there; *(übrig sein auch)* to be left; **wieder ~**
to be back; **ich bin gleich wieder da** I'll be right
back; **ist Post für mich da?** is there any mail for
me?; **war der Briefträger schon da?** has the
postman been yet?; **sie ist nur für ihren Mann da**
she lives for her husband; **ein Arzt, der immer
für seine Patienten da ist** a doctor who always
has time for his patients; **voll ~** *(col)* to be all
there *(col)*; **es ist alles schon mal dagewesen** it's
all been done before; **ein nie dagewesener
Erfolg** an unprecedented success.

Daseins-: **~berechtigung** *f* right to exist;
~kampf *m* struggle for survival.

dasitzen *vi sep irreg* to sit there. **ohne einen Pfennig ~** *(col)* to be left without a penny.

dasjenige *dem pron siehe* **derjenige.**

daß *conj* that. **ich bin überzeugt, ~ du das Richtige
getan hast** I'm sure (that) you have done the
right thing; **ich bin dagegen, ~ ihr alle kommt**
I'm against you all coming; **das liegt daran, ~ ...**
that is because ...; **~ du es mir nicht verlierst!**
see that you don't lose it!

dasselbe *dem pron siehe* **derselbe.**

dastehen *vi sep irreg aux haben or sein* **(a)** to stand
there. **steh nicht so dumm da!** don't just stand
there looking stupid. **(b)** *(fig)* **gut/schlecht ~** to
be in a good/bad position; **allein ~** to be on one's
own; **einzig ~** to be unique or unparalleled; **jetzt
stehe ich als Lügner da** now I'm left looking like
a liar; **wie stehe ich jetzt da!** *(Selbstlob)* just look
at me now!; *(Vorwurf)* I look a proper fool!

Datei *f* file.

Daten **(a)** *pl of* **Datum.** **(b)** *(Comp etc)* data *pl.*

Daten-: **~bank** *f* database; *(größer)* data bank;
~schutz *m* data protection *no art;* **~technik** *f*
computer science; **~träger** *m* data carrier; **~ty-
pist(in** *f)* *m* terminal operator; **~übertragung** *f*
data transmission; **~verarbeitung** *f* data processing; **~verarbeitungsanlage** *f* computer.

datieren* *vti* to date. **dieser Brief datiert vom 1.
Januar** this letter is dated January 1st.

Dativ *m (Gram)* dative (case).

Dativ|objekt *nt (Gram)* indirect object.

dato *adv:* **bis ~** *(Comm, col)* to date.

Dattel *f* **-n** date.

Datum *nt, pl* **Daten** **(a)** date. **was für ein ~ haben
wir heute?** what is the date today?; **das heutige
~** today's date; **ein Brief ohne ~** an undated
letter; **ein Nachschlagewerk neueren ~s** a recent reference work. **(b)** *usu pl (Statistik, Comp*

etc) piece of data.

Datums-: **~grenze** *f (Geog)* (international) date
line; **~stempel** *m* date stamp.

Dauer *f no pl (das Andauern)* duration; *(Zeitspanne)*
period, term; *(Länge: einer Sendung etc)* length.
während der ~ des Vertrages/Krieges for the
duration of the contract/war; **für die ~ eines
Monats** for a period of one month; **seine Begeisterung war nicht von ~** his enthusiasm was
short-lived; **von langer/kurzer ~ sein** to last a
long time/not to last long; **auf die ~** in the long
run; **das kann auf die ~ nicht so weitergehen** it
can't go on like that indefinitely; **auf ~** permanently.

Dauer- *in cpds* permanent; **~auftrag** *m (Fin)*
standing order; **~belastung** *f* continual pressure
no indef art; (von Maschine) constant load; **~bren-
ner** *m* **(a)** *(Ofen)* slow burning stove; **(b)** *(col:
Dauererfolg)* long runner; **~erfolg** *m* long-run-
ning success; **~gast** *m* permanent guest; *(häufiger Gast)* regular visitor, permanent fixture
(hum).

dauerhaft *adj Zustand, Farbe* permanent; *Frieden,
Beziehung* lasting; *Stoff* durable.

Dauerhaftigkeit *f* permanence; *(von Material)*
durability.

Dauer-: **~karte** *f* season ticket; **~lauf** *m (Sport)*
jog; *(das Laufen)* jogging; **im ~lauf** at a jog *or*
trot; **einen ~lauf machen** to go jogging; **~lut-
scher** *m* lollipop *(Brit)*, popsicle ® *(US).*

dauern *vi* **(a)** *(an~)* to last, to go on. **die Verhandlungen ~ schon drei Wochen** the negotiations have already been going on for three
weeks. **(b)** *(Zeit benötigen)* to take a while; *(lange)* to take a long time. **das dauert noch** *(col)* it'll
be some time yet; **es dauerte lange, bis er sich
befreit hatte** it took him a long time to get free;
das dauert mir zu lange it takes too long for me;
es dauert jetzt nicht mehr lange it won't take
much longer.

dauernd **1** *adj Regelung* lasting; *Wohnsitz* permanent; *(fortwährend) Unterbrechung* constant,
perpetual. **2** *adv etw ~ tun* to keep (on) doing sth.

Dauer-: **~obst** *nt* fruit suitable for storing; **~par-
ker** *m* - long-stay parker; **~redner** *m (pej)* interminable speaker; **~regen** *m* continuous rain;
~schlaf *m* prolonged sleep; **~stellung** *f* permanent position; **~ton** *m* continuous tone; **~wel-
le** *f* perm, permanent wave; **~wirkung** *f*
(long-)lasting effect; **~wurst** *f* salami; **~zustand**
m permanent state of affairs.

Däumchen *nt dim of* **Daumen.**

Daumen *m* - thumb. **jdm die Daumen drücken**
to keep one's fingers crossed for sb; **~ drehen**
to twiddle one's thumbs; **den ~ auf etw** *(acc)*
halten *(col)* to hold on to sth.

Daumen-: **~abdruck** *m* thumbprint; **~nagel** *m*
thumbnail; **~schraube** *f* jdm die **~schrauben
anlegen** *(fig, col)* to put the (thumb)screws on sb.

Daune *f* -n down feather. **~n** down *sing.*

Daunen-: **~bett** *nt,* **~decke** *f* (down-filled) duvet;
d~weich *adj* soft as down.

davon *adv (emph auch* **davon) (a)** *(räumlich)* from
there; *(wenn Bezugsobjekt vorher erwähnt)* from
it/them; *(mit Entfernungsangabe)* away (from
there/it/them). **weg ~!** *(col)* get away from
there/it/them.

(b) *(fig)* **ich bin weit ~ entfernt, Ihnen Vorwürfe machen** zu wollen the last thing I want to
do is reproach you; **wenn wir einmal ~ absehen,
daß ...** if for once we overlook the fact that ...;
und ~ kommt die rote Farbe and that's where
the red comes from; **das kommt ~!** that's what
you get!; **~ hat man nur Ärger** you get nothing
but trouble with it; **~ wird man müde** it makes
you tired; **was habe ich ~?** what do I get out of it?

(c) *(mit Passiv)* **~ betroffen werden** to be
affected by it/them. **~**

(d) *(Anteil)* of that/it/them. **nehmen Sie doch noch etwas ~!** do have some more!; **das Doppelte ~** twice that.

(e) *(darüber) hören, wissen, sprechen* about that/it/them; *verstehen, halten* of that/it/them. **genug ~!** enough of this!

davon-: ~**bleiben** *vi sep irreg aux sein (col)* to keep away; *(nicht anfassen)* to keep one's hands off; ~**fahren** *vi sep irreg aux sein* to drive away; *(auf Fahrrad etc)* to ride away; *(Zug)* to pull away; ~**fliegen** *vi sep irreg aux sein* to fly away; ~**gehen** *vi sep irreg aux sein (geh)* to walk away; ~**jagen** *vt sep* to chase off *or* away; ~**kommen** *vi sep irreg aux sein (entkommen)* to get away, to escape; *(nicht bestraft werden)* to get away with it; **mit dem Schrecken/dem Leben/einer Geldstrafe ~kommen** to escape with no more than a shock/ with one's life/to get off with a fine; ~**lassen** *vt sep irreg* **die Finger ~lassen** *(col)* to keep one's hands *or* fingers off (it/them); ~**laufen** *vi sep irreg aux sein* to run away *(jdm/vor jdm* from sb); *(verlassen)* to walk out *(jdm* on sb); **es ist zum D~laufen!** *(col)* it's all too much!; **die Preise sind den Löhnen ~gelaufen** prices have outstripped wages; ~**machen** *vr sep* to make off; ~**schleichen** *vir sep irreg (vi: aux sein)* to creep away *or* off; ~**tragen** *vt sep irreg* **(a)** *(wegtragen)* to carry away; *Preis* to carry off; *Sieg, Ruhm* to win; **(b)** *Schaden, Verletzung* to suffer; ~**ziehen** *vi sep irreg aux sein (liter)* to leave; *(Sport col)* to pull away *(jdm* from sb).

davor *adv (emph* **davor) (a)** *(räumlich)* in front (of that/it/them); *(wenn Bezugsobjekt vorher erwähnt)* in front of it/them. **(b)** *(zeitlich)* before that; *(bevor man etw tut)* beforehand. **(c)** *bewahren, schützen* from that/it; *warnen* about that/it; *Angst haben* of that/it; *sich ekeln* by that/it. **ich habe Angst ~, daß der Hund beißen könnte** I'm afraid that the dog might bite.

davor-: ~**stehen** *vi sep irreg aux haben or sein* to stand in front of it/them; ~**stellen** *sep* **1** *vt* to put in front of it/them; **2** *vr* to stand in front of it/them.

dazu *adv (emph* **dazu). (a)** *(dabei, damit)* with it; **er ist dumm und ~ auch noch faul** he's stupid and lazy with it *or* into the bargain *(col)*; ... **und ~ nicht unintelligent** ... and not unintelligent either; **noch ~** as well, too; ~ **serviert man am besten Reis** it's best to serve rice with it. **(b)** *(dahin)* to that/it. **das führt ~, daß weitere Forderungen gestellt werden** that will lead to further demands being made; **wie konnte es nur ~ kommen** how could that happen?; **wie komme ich ~?** *(empört)* why on earth should I?; ... **aber ich bin nicht ~ gekommen** ... but I didn't get around to it.

(c) *(dafür, zu diesem Zweck)* for that/it. **ich bin zu alt ~,** noch tanzen zu gehen I'm too old to go dancing; **ich habe ihm ~ geraten** I advised him to (do that); ~ **bereit sein, etw zu tun** to be prepared to do sth; ~ **ist er da** that's what he's there for; **das Recht ~** the right to do it.

(d) *(darüber, zum Thema)* about that/it. **was meinst du ~?** what do you think about that?

(e) *im Gegensatz/Vergleich ~* in contrast to/comparison with that.

dazu-: ~**geben** *vt sep irreg* to add; ~**gehören*** *vi sep* to belong (to it/us *etc*); *(als Ergänzung)* to go with it/them; *(eingeschlossen sein)* to be included (in it/them); **das gehört ~** *(versteht sich von selbst)* it's all part of it; **es gehört schon einiges ~, das zu tun** it takes a lot to do that; ~**gehörig** *adj attr* which goes/go with it/them; *Schlüssel etc* belonging to it/them; *Werkzeuge, Material* necessary; ~**kommen** *vi sep irreg aux sein* **(a)** *(ankommen)* to arrive (on the scene); **(b)** *(hinzugefügt werden)* to be added; **kommt noch etwas ~?** will there by anything else?; **es kommt noch**

~**, daß er faul ist** added to that he's lazy; ~**lernen** *vt sep* viel/nichts ~**lernen** to learn a lot more/ nothing new; **schon wieder was ~gelernt!** you learn something (new) every day!

dazumal *adv (old)* in those days.

dazu-: ~**rechnen** *vt sep Betrag* to add on; ~**schreiben** *vt sep irreg* to add; ~**setzen** *vr sep* to join him/us *etc*; ~**tun** *vt sep irreg (col)* to add; **er hat es ohne dein D~tun geschafft** he managed it without your doing/saying *etc* anything.

dazwischen *adv* in between; *(in der betreffenden Menge, Gruppe)* amongst them, in with them.

dazwischen-: ~**fahren** *vi sep irreg aux sein* **(a)** *(eingreifen)* to intervene; **(b)** *(unterbrechen)* to interrupt; ~**funken** *vi sep (col: eingreifen)* to put one's oar in *(col)*; ~**kommen** *vi sep irreg aux sein (störend erscheinen)* to get in the way; ... **wenn nichts ~kommt!** ... if all goes well; **mir ist leider etwas ~gekommen, ich kann nicht dabeisein** something has come *or* cropped up, I'm afraid I can't be there; ~**reden** *vi sep* to interrupt *(jdm* sb); ~**rufen** *vti sep irreg* to yell out; ~**stehen** *vi sep irreg aux haben or sein* **(a)** *(lit)* to be amongst *or (zwischen zweien)* between them; **(b)** *(zwischen den Parteien)* to be neutral; *(geh: hindernd)* to be in the way; ~**treten** *vi sep irreg aux sein* to intervene; *(störend)* to come between them.

DB [de:'be:] *f* = **Deutsche Bundesbahn.**

DDR [de:de:'|ɛr] *f* = **Deutsche Demokratische Republik** GDR, German Democratic Republic, East Germany.

DDR-Bürger *m* East German.

Dealer(in *f)* ['di:lɐ, -ərɪn] *m* - *(col)* pusher.

Debakel [de- *-* debacle. **ein ~ erleiden** *(Stück etc)* to be a debacle.

Debatte *f* -**n** debate. **etw zur ~ stellen** to put sth up for discussion *or (Parl)* debate; **das steht hier nicht zur ~** that's not the issue.

debattieren* *vti* to debate *(über etw* sth).

Debet *nt* -**s** *(Fin)* debits *pl.*

Debüt [de'by:] *nt* -**s** debut. **sein ~ als etw geben** to make one's debut as sth.

Debütant(in *f)* *m (wk)* person making his/her debut.

debütieren* *vi (Theat, fig)* to make one's debut.

Dechant *m (Eccl)* dean.

dechiffrieren* [deʃɪ'fri:rən] *vt* to decode, to decipher.

Deck *nt* -**s** deck; *(in Parkhaus)* level. **an ~ gehen** to go on deck; **alle Mann an ~!** all hands on deck!

Deck-: ~**adresse** *f* accommodation *or* cover *(US)* address; ~**anstrich** *m* top coat; ~**bett** *nt* feather quilt; ~**blatt** *nt (von Zigarre)* wrapper; *(Schutzblatt)* cover.

Decke *f* -**n** **(a)** *(lit, fig)* blanket; *(Tisch~)* cloth; *(Stepp~)* quilt. **sich nach der ~ strecken** *(fig)* to cut one's coat according to one's cloth; **mit jdm unter einer ~ stecken** *(fig)* to be hand in glove with sb. **(b)** *(Zimmer~)* ceiling; **an die ~ gehen** *(col)* to hit the roof *(col)*; **vor Freude an die ~ springen** *(col)* to jump for joy; **mir fällt die ~ auf den Kopf** *(fig col)* I feel really claustrophobic. **(c)** *(Schicht)* layer; *(Straßen~)* surface.

Deckel *m* - lid; *(von Schachtel auch, von Flasche)* top; *(Buch~)* cover. **du kriegst gleich eins auf den ~** *(col)* you're going to catch it *(col)*.

decken 1 *vt* **(a)** *(zu~, Fin, begatten)* to cover. *(Ftbl auch)* to mark; *Komplizen* to cover up for. **ein Dach mit Ziegeln ~** to roof a building with tiles; **mein Bedarf ist gedeckt** I have all I need; *(fig col)* I've had enough. **(b)** *Tisch, Tafel* to set, to lay *(Brit)*. **sich an einen gedeckten Tisch setzen** *(fig)* to be handed everything on a plate; **ein Tuch über etw** *(acc)* ~ to cover sth with a cloth. **2** *vi* to cover; *(Boxen)* to guard; *(Ftbl auch)* to mark. **3** *vr* **(a)** *(Interessen, Begriffe)* to coincide; *(Aussagen)* to correspond, to agree. **(b)** *(Boxer etc)* to cover oneself.

Deck-: ~**farbe** *f* opaque water colour; ~**hengst** *m* stud(horse), stallion; ~**mantel** *m* *(fig)* mask; **unter dem** ~**mantel von** ... under the guise of ...; ~**name** *m* assumed name; *(Mil)* code name; ~**offizier** *m* *(Naut)* ≃ warrant officer; ~**platte** *f* *(Build)* slab; ~**schicht** *f* surface layer; *(von Straße)* surface; *(Geol)* top layer.

Deckung *f* **(a)** *(Schutz)* cover; *(Ftbl, Chess)* defence; *(Boxen etc)* guard. **in** ~ **gehen** to take cover. **(b)** *(Verheimlichung)* **die** ~ **von etw** covering up for sth. **(c)** *(Comm, Fin)* *(von Scheck, Wechsel)* cover; *(das Decken)* covering; *(das Begleichen)* meeting. **zur** ~ **seiner Schulden** to meet his debts. **(d) eine** ~ **der Nachfrage ist unmöglich** demand cannot possibly be met. **(e)** *(Übereinstimmung)* **lassen sich diese Standpunkte zur** ~ **bringen?** can these points of view be reconciled?

Deckungs-: ~**fehler** *m* *(Ftbl)* defensive error; ~**feuer** *nt* *(Mil)* covering fire; **d**~**gleich** *adj (Math)* congruent; **d**~**gleich sein** *(fig)* to coincide; *(Aussagen)* to agree.

Decoder [deˈkoːdɐ, dɪˈkoʊdə] *m* - decoder.

decodieren* *vt* to decode.

Deduktion *f* deduction.

deduzieren* *vt* to deduce *(aus* from*)*.

de facto *adv* de facto.

Defätismus *m no pl* defeatism.

defätistisch *adj* defeatist *no adv.*

defekt *adj Gerät etc* faulty, defective.

Defekt *m* **-e** fault, defect; *(Med)* deficiency.

defensiv *adj* defensive.

Defensive [-ˈziːvə] *f no pl* defensive. **in der** ~ **on the defensive; jdn in die** ~ **drängen** to force sb onto the defensive.

defilieren* *vi aux haben or sein (Mil)* to march past; *(fig)* to parade past.

definierbar *adj* definable.

definieren* *vt* to define.

Definition *f* definition.

definitiv *adj* definite.

Defizit *nt* **-e** deficit; *(Mangel)* deficiency *(an+dat* of*)*.

defizitär *adj* in deficit. **eine** ~**e Haushaltspolitik führen** to follow an economic policy which can only lead to deficit.

Deflation *f (Econ)* deflation.

deflationär *adj* deflationary *no adv.*

deflorieren* *vt* to deflower.

Deformation *f* deformation, distortion; *(Mißbildung)* deformity; *(Entstellung)* disfigurement.

deformieren* *vt (lit, fig: mißbilden)* to deform; *(entstellen)* to disfigure. **eine deformierte Nase** a misshapen nose.

Defroster *m* - *(Aut)* heated windscreen; *(Sprühmittel)* de-icer.

deftig *adj* **(a)** *Witz, Humor* ribald. **(b)** *Lüge* whopping *(col)*, huge; *Mahlzeit* solid; *Wurst etc* substantial, good solid *attr; Ohrfeige* cracking *(col)*.

Degen *m* - *(Sportfechten)* épée.

degenerieren* *vi aux sein* to degenerate *(zu* into*)*.

degeneriert *adj* degenerate.

degradieren* *vt (Mil)* to demote *(zu* to*)*; *(fig: herabwürdigen)* to degrade. **jdn/etw zu etw** ~ *(fig)* to lower sb/sth to the level of sth.

Degradierung *f (Mil)* demotion *(zu* to*)*; *(fig)* degradation.

dehnbar *adj (lit, fig)* elastic.

Dehnbarkeit *f no pl* elasticity.

dehnen 1 *vt* to stretch; *(Med auch)* to dilate; *Laut, Silbe* to lengthen. **2** *vr (auch Ozean etc)* to stretch.

Dehnung *f siehe vt* stretching; dilation; lengthening.

Deich *m* **-e** dyke, dike *(esp US).*

Deichsel [-ks-] *f* **-n** shaft; *(Doppel*~*)* shafts *pl.*

deichseln [-ks-] *vt (col)* to wangle *(col)*. **das werden wir schon** ~ we'll wangle it somehow.

dein *poss pron (adjektivisch) (in Briefen:* **D**~*)* your.

herzliche Grüße, D~**e Elke** with best wishes, yours *or (herzlicher)* love Elke.

deiner *pers pron gen of* **du** *(geh)* of you.

deine(r, s) *poss pron (substantivisch)* yours. **der/ die/das** ~ *(geh)* yours; **die D**~**n** *(geh)* your family; **das D**~ *(geh: Besitz)* what is yours.

deinerseits *adv (auf deiner Seite)* for your part; *(von deiner Seite)* on your part.

deinesgleichen *pron inv* people like you.

deinet-: ~**wegen** *adv (wegen dir)* because of you, on account of you; *(dir zuliebe)* for your sake; *(um dich)* about you; *(für dich)* on your behalf; ~**willen** *adv* **um** ~**willen** for your sake.

deins *poss pron* yours.

de jure *adv* de jure.

Dekade *f (10 Tage)* ten days; *(10 Jahre)* decade.

dekadent *adj* decadent.

Dekadenz *f no pl* decadence.

Dekan *m* **-e** *(Univ, Eccl)* dean.

Dekanat *nt (Univ)* office of dean; *(Eccl)* deanery.

Deklamation *f* declamation. ~**en** *(pej)* (empty) rhetoric sing.

deklamieren* *vti* to declaim.

Deklaration *f* declaration.

deklarieren* *vt* to declare.

deklassieren* *vt* **(a)** *(Sociol, herabsetzen)* to downgrade. **(b)** *(Sport: übertreffen)* to outclass.

Deklination *f (Gram)* declension.

deklinieren* *vt (Gram)* to decline.

Dekolleté [dekɔlˈteː] *nt* **-s** low-cut *or* décolleté neckline.

dekolletiert [dekɔlˈtiːɐt] *adj Kleid* low-cut, décolleté.

Dekor *m or nt* **-s** *or* **-e** decoration; *(von Raum auch, Theat, Film etc)* décor.

Dekorateur(in *f)* [dekoraˈtøːɐ, -øːˈrɪn] *m* interior designer; *(Schaufenster*~*)* window-dresser.

Dekoration *f* **(a)** *no pl (das Ausschmücken)* decorating, decoration. **(b)** *(Einrichtung)* décor *no pl; (Fenster*~*)* window-dressing; *(Theat: Bühnenbild)* set. **zur** ~ **dienen** to be decorative. **(c)** *(Ordensverleihung)* decoration.

Dekorations-: ~**maler** *m* (interior) decorator; *(Theat)* scene-painter; ~**stoff** *m (Tex)* furnishing fabric; ~**stück** *nt* piece of the décor; **das ist nur ein** ~**stück** that's just for decoration.

dekorativ *adj* decorative.

dekorieren* *vt* to decorate; *Schaufenster* to dress.

Dekostoff *m (Tex)* furnishing fabric.

Dekret *nt* **-e** decree.

Delegation *f* delegation.

delegieren* *vt* to delegate *(an +acc* to*)*.

Delegierte(r) *mf decl as adj* delegate.

delikat *adj* **(a)** *(wohlschmeckend)* exquisite, delicious. **(b)** *(behutsam)* delicate. **(c)** *(heikel) Problem* delicate, sensitive; *(gewagt)* risqué.

Delikateß- *in cpds* top-quality, fine.

Delikatesse *f (Leckerbissen, fig)* delicacy.

Delikatessengeschäft *nt* delicatessen.

Delikt *nt* **-e** *(Jur)* offence; *(schwerer)* crime.

Delinquent [delɪŋˈkvɛnt] *m (geh)* offender.

Delirium *nt* delirium. **im** ~ **sein** to be delirious; *(col: betrunken)* to be paralytic *(col)*.

Delle *f* **-n** *(col: eingedrückte Stelle)* dent.

Delphin¹ *m* **-e** *(Zool)* dolphin.

Delphin² *no pl, Delphinschwimmen** *nt* butterfly.

Delta *nt, pl* **-s** *or* **Delten** *(Geog)* delta.

dem 1 *dat of def art* **der, das** **(a)** to the; *(mit Präposition)* the. **(b) wenn** ~ **so ist** if that is the way it is; **wie** ~ **auch sei** be that as it may. **2** *dat of dem pron* **der, das** **(a)** *attr* to that; *(mit Präposition)* that. **(b)** *(substantivisch)* to that one; that one; *(Menschen)* to him; him. **3** *dat of rel pron* **der, das** to whom, that *or* who(m) ... to; *(mit Präposition)* who(m); *(von Sachen)* to which, which *or*

that ... to; (mit Präposition) which.
Demagoge m demagogue.
demagogisch adj Rede etc demagogic.
Demarkationslinie f (Pol, Mil) demarcation line.
demaskieren* 1 vt to unmask, to expose. 2 vr to take off one's mask.
Dementi nt -s denial.
dementieren* 1 vt to deny. 2 vi to deny it.
dem|entsprechend 1 adv correspondingly; (demnach) accordingly. 2 adj appropriate.
dem-: ~**gegenüber** adv (wohingegen) on the other hand; (im Vergleich dazu) in contrast; ~**gemäß** adv, adj = ~**entsprechend.**
Demission f (Pol: Rücktritt) resignation.
dem-: ~**nach** adv therefore; (~entsprechend) accordingly; ~**nächst** adv soon.
Demo f -s (col) demo (col).
Demographie f demography.
demographisch adj demographic.
Demokrat(in f) m (wk) **-en, -en** democrat.
Demokratie f democracy.
Demokratieverständnis nt understanding of (the meaning of) democracy.
demokratisch adj democratic.
demokratisieren* vt to democratize, to make democratic.
Demokratisierung f democratization.
demolieren* vt to wreck, to smash up; (Rowdy auch) to vandalize.
Demonstrant(in f) m (wk) demonstrator.
Demonstration f demonstration.
Demonstrations-: ~**material** nt teaching material; ~**objekt** nt teaching aid; ~**recht** nt right to demonstrate; (Gesetz) law on demonstrations; ~**zug** m demonstration.
demonstrativ adj demonstrative (auch Gram); Beifall acclamatory; Protest, Fehlen pointed. **der Botschafter verließ** ~ **den Saal** the ambassador pointedly left the room.
demonstrieren* vti to demonstrate.
Demontage [-'ta:ʒə] f -n (lit, fig) dismantling.
demontieren* vt (lit, fig) to dismantle; Räder to take off.
demoralisieren* vt to demoralize.
Demoskop(in f) m (wk) **-en -en** (opinion) pollster.
Demoskopie f no pl (public) opinion research.
demoskopisch adj ~**es Institut** (public) opinion research institute; **alle** ~**en Voraussagen waren falsch** all the predictions in the opinion polls were wrong; **eine** ~**e Untersuchung** a (public) opinion poll.
demselben dat of **derselbe, dasselbe.**
Demut f no pl humility. **in** ~ with humility.
demütig adj Bitte, Blick humble.
demütigen 1 vt Besiegten, Volk to humiliate; stolzen Menschen etc to humble. 2 vr to humble oneself (vor+dat before).
Demütigung f humiliation.
demzufolge adv therefore.
den 1 (a) acc of def art **der** the. (b) dat pl of def art **der, die, das** the; to the. 2 acc of dem pron **der** (a) attr that. (b) (substantivisch) that one; (Menschen) him. 3 acc of rel pron that who(m), that; (von Sachen) which, that.
denen 1 dat pl of dem pron **der, die, das** to them; (mit Präposition) them. 2 dat pl of rel pron **der, die, das** to whom, that or who(m) ... to; (mit Präposition) whom; (von Sachen) to which, that or which ... to; which.
Denk-: ~**ansatz** m starting point; ~**anstoß** m jdm ~**anstöße geben** to give sb food for thought; ~**art** f way of thinking; d~**bar** 1 adj conceivable; **es ist durchaus d~bar, daß er kommt** it's quite likely that he'll come; 2 adv extremely; **der d~bar schlechteste Eindruck** the worst possible impression.
Denken nt no pl thinking.

denken pret **dachte,** ptp **gedacht** 1 vi (überlegen) to think (über+acc about, of). **bei sich** ~ to think to oneself; **wo** ~ **Sie hin!** what an idea!; **der Mensch denkt, Gott lenkt** (Prov) man proposes, God disposes (Prov); **das gibt mir/einem zu** ~ it makes you think; **wie** ~ **Sie darüber?** what do you think about it?; **kleinlich** ~ to be petty-minded; **alle, die damals liberal gedacht haben,** ... all those who were thinking along liberal lines ...; **an jdn/etw** ~ to think of sb/sth; **daran ist gar nicht zu** ~ that's (quite) out of the question; **ich denke nicht daran!** no way! (col), not on your life!; **ich denke nicht daran, das zu tun** there's no way I'm going to do that (col); **solange ich** ~ **kann** (for) as long as I can remember; **denk daran!** don't forget!; **an das Geld habe ich gar nicht mehr gedacht** I had forgotten all about the money; **die viele Arbeit, ich darf gar nicht daran** ~ all that work, it doesn't bear thinking about.
2 vt to think. **was denkst du jetzt?** what are you thinking?; **ich denke gar nichts** I'm not thinking about anything; **(nur) Schlechtes/ Gutes von jdm** ~ to think ill/well of sb; **wer hätte das (von ihr) gedacht!** who'd have thought it (of her)!; **was sollen bloß die Leute** ~! what will people think!; **ich denke schon** I think so; **ich denke nicht** I don't think so, I think not; **für jdn/etw gedacht sein** to be intended or meant for sb/sth; **so war das nicht gedacht** it wasn't meant that way.
3 vr **(a)** (vorstellen) **das kann ich mir** ~ I can imagine; **ich habe mir das so gedacht:** ... this is what I had in mind: ...; **das habe ich mir gedacht** I thought so; **dachte ich mir's doch!** I knew it! **(b)** (beabsichtigen) **sich** (dat) **etw bei etw** ~ to mean sth by sth; **ich habe mir nichts Böses dabei gedacht** I meant no harm (in it).
Denker(in f) m - thinker. **das Volk der Dichter und** ~ the nation of poets and philosophers.
Denkerstirn f (hum) lofty brow.
Denk-: d~**fähig** adj capable of thinking; **als d~fähiger Mensch** as an intelligent person; ~**fähigkeit** f ability to think; d~**faul** adj (mentally) lazy; ~**faulheit** f (mental) laziness; ~**fehler** m flaw in the/one's reasoning.
Denkmal [-ma:l] nt =**er** or (geh) **-e** (lit, fig) monument (für to); (Standbild) statue. **er hat sich** (dat) **ein** ~ **gesetzt** he has earned himself a place in history.
Denkmalschutz m protection of historical monuments. **etw unter** ~ **stellen** to classify sth as a historical monument.
Denk-: ~**pause** f eine ~**pause einlegen** to have a break to think things over; ~**prozeß** m thought-process; ~**schrift** f memorandum; ~**sport** m mental exercise; ~**sportaufgabe** f brain-teaser.
denkste interj (col) that's what you think.
Denk-: ~**vermögen** nt intellectual capacity; ~**weise** f way of thinking; d~**würdig** adj memorable, notable; ~**würdigkeit** f memorability, notability; ~**zettel** m (col) warning; **jdm einen** ~**zettel verpassen** to give sb a warning.
denn 1 conj **(a)** (kausal) because, for (esp liter). **(b)** (geh: vergleichend) than. **schöner** ~ **je** more beautiful than ever. **(c)** (konzessiv) **es sei** ~, **(daß)** unless. 2 adv (verstärkend) **wann/wie/wo** ~? when/how/where?; **warum** ~ **nicht?** why not?; **was soll das** ~? what's all this then?
dennoch adv nevertheless, nonetheless. **und** ~, **... und nur; ...**
denselben 1 acc of **derselbe.** 2 dat of **dieselben.**
dental adj (Med, Ling) dental.
Denunziant(in f) m (wk) (pej) informer.
Denunziation f (pej) informing no pl (von on, against); (Anzeige) denunciation (von of).
denunzieren* vt (pej) to inform on or against, to denounce (bei to).

Deodorant nt -s or -e deodorant.
Deospray nt or m deodorant spray.
Depesche f -n (dated) dispatch.
Deponie f dump, disposal site.
deponieren* vt (geh) to deposit.
deportieren* vt to deport.
Depot [de'po:] nt -s depot; (Aufbewahrungsort auch) depository; (in Bank) strong room.
Depp m -e(n) (dial pej) twit (col).
Depression f depression. ~en haben to suffer from depression.
depressiv adj depressive; (Econ) depressed.
deprimieren* vt to depress.
deprimiert adj depressed.
der[1] **1 (a)** gen of def art die sing, pl of the. **(b)** dat of def art die sing to the; (mit Präposition) the. **2** dat of dem pron die sing **(a)** (adjektivisch) to that; (mit Präposition) that. **(b)** (substantivisch) to her; her. **3** dat of rel pron die sing to whom, that or who(m) ... to; (mit Präposition) who(m); (von Sachen) to which, which ... to; which.
der[2], **die**, **das**, pl **die 1** def art the. die Engländer the English pl; **der** Hans (col)/**der** Faust Hans/Faust; **der** Rhein the Rhine; **der** Michigansee Lake Michigan; **die** „Bismarck" the "Bismarck"; **der** Lehrer/**die** Frau (im allgemeinen) teachers pl/women pl; **der** Tod/**die** Liebe/**das** Leben death/love/life; **das** Rauchen smoking; **das** Viktorianische England Victorian England; **in dem** England, das ich kannte in the England (that or which) I knew; er hat sich **den** Fuß verletzt he has hurt his foot; **10** Mark die Stunde 10 marks an or per hour; **der und der** Wissenschaftler such and such a scientist.
2 dem pron **(a)** (attr) (jener, dieser) that; pl those. **(b)** (substantivisch) he/she/it; pl those. **der**/ **die war es** it was him/her; **der mit der großen Nase** the one with or him (col) with the big nose; **der und schwimmen**? swimming?, (what) him?; **der und der/die und die** so-and-so; **das und das** such and such. **3** rel pron (Mensch) who, that; (Gegenstand, Tier) which, that.
der|art adv **(a)** (Art und Weise) in such a way. sein Benehmen war ~, daß ... his behaviour was so bad that ... **(b)** (Ausmaß) (vor adj) so; (vor vb) so much, to such an extent. ein ~ unzuverlässiger Mensch such an unreliable person, so unreliable a person.
der|artig 1 adj bei ~en Versuchen in such tests, in tests of that kind. **2** adv = derart.
derb adj **(a)** (kräftig) strong; Kost coarse. **(b)** (grob) coarse; Sprache, Humor auch earthy, crude (pej).
Derbheit f siehe adj **(a)** strength; coarseness. **(b)** coarseness; earthiness, crudeness.
Derby ['dɛrbɪ] nt -s derby.
der|einst adv (liter) **(a)** (in der Zukunft) one day. **(b)** (früher) at one time, once.
deren 1 gen pl of dem pron der, die, das their. **2 (a)** gen sing of rel pron die whose. **(b)** gen pl of rel pron der, die, das whose; of whom; (von Sachen) of which.
derent-: ~wegen adv (weswegen) because of whom, on whose account; (von Sachen) because of which, on account of which; ~willen adv um ~willen (rel) for whose sake; (von Sachen) for the sake of which.
dergestalt adv (geh) in such a way.
dergleichen dem pron inv **(a)** (adjektivisch) ~ Dinge things of that kind. **(b)** (substantivisch) that sort of thing. er tat nichts ~ he did nothing of the kind; und ~ **(mehr)** and suchlike.
Derivat [-'va:t] nt (Chem, Ling) derivative.
derjenige, diejenige, dasjenige, pl **diejenigen** dem pron **(a)** (substantivisch) the one; pl those. du warst also derjenige, welcher! (col) so you're the one! **(b)** (adjektivisch) the; pl those.
derlei dem pron inv = dergleichen.

Dermato-: ~loge m, ~login f dermatologist; ~logie f dermatology.
derselbe, dieselbe, dasselbe, pl **dieselben** dem pron the same; es sind immer dieselben it's always the same ones or the same people; **ein und derselbe Mensch** one and the same person.
derweil(en) adv in the meantime, meanwhile.
derzeit adv (jetzt) at present, at the moment.
derzeitig adj attr (jetzig) present, current.
des[1] gen of def art der[2], das of the.
des[2], **Des** nt no pl (Mus) D flat.
Desaster [de'zastɐ] nt - disaster.
Deserteur(in f) [-'tø:ɐ, -'tø:ərɪn] m (Mil, fig) deserter.
desertieren* vi aux sein or haben (Mil, fig) to desert.
Desertion f (Mil, fig) desertion.
desgleichen adv (ebenso) likewise, also.
deshalb adv, conj therefore; (aus diesem Grunde) because of that. ich bin ~ hergekommen, weil ich dich sprechen wollte the reason I came here was that I wanted to speak to you; ~ **muß er** nicht dumm sein that does not necessarily mean he is stupid; ~ **frage ich ja** that's exactly why I'm asking.
Design [di'zaɪn] nt -s design.
Designer(in f) [di'zaɪnɐ, -ərɪn] m - designer.
designiert [dezɪ'gni:ɐt] adj attr **der** ~e Vorsitzende/Nachkomme the chairman elect/ prospective successor.
des|illusionieren* vt to disillusion.
Des|infektionsmittel nt disinfectant.
des|infizieren* vt to disinfect.
Des|infizierung f disinfection.
Des|interesse nt lack of interest (an +dat in).
des|interessiert adj uninterested.
deskriptiv adj descriptive.
desolat adj (geh) desolate; Zustand, wirtschaftliche Lage desperate.
Des|organisation f disorganization; (Auflösung auch) disruption. **auf der Tagung herrschte eine** völlige ~ there was complete chaos at the conference.
des|organisieren* vt to disorganize.
des|orientieren* vt to disorient(ate).
Despot [dɛs'po:t] m (wk) -en, -en despot.
despotisch [dɛs'po:tɪʃ] adj despotic.
Despotismus [dɛspo-] m no pl despotism.
desselben gen of derselbe, dasselbe.
dessen 1 gen of dem pron der[2], das his; (von Sachen, Tieren) its. **2** gen of rel pron der[2], das whose; (von Sachen) of which, which ... of.
dessen|ungeachtet adv (geh) nevertheless.
Dessert [dɛ'se:ɐ] nt -s dessert.
Dessin [dɛ'sɛ̃:] nt -s (Tex) pattern, design.
Destillation [dɛstɪla'tsio:n] f -(a) (Chem) distillation. **(b)** (Branntweinbrennerei) distillery.
destillieren* [dɛstɪ'li:rən] vt to distil.
desto conj ~ **mehr/besser** all the more/better; ~ **wahrscheinlicher ist es, daß wir** ... that makes it all the more probable that we ...; siehe **je.**
destruktiv [dɛstruk'ti:f] adj destructive.
deswegen adv = deshalb.
Detail [de'tai] nt -s detail; (Filmeinstellung) big close-up. **ins ~ gehen** to go into detail(s); **im ~** in detail; **bis ins kleinste ~** (right) down to the smallest detail; **in allen ~s** in the greatest detail.
Detail-: ~frage f question of detail; ~kenntnis f usu pl detailed knowledge no pl.
detailliert [deta'ji:ɐt] adj detailed.
Detektei f (private) detective agency.
Detektiv(in f) m private detective.
Detektiv-: ~büro nt detective agency; ~roman m detective novel.
Detektor m (Tech) detector.
determinieren* vt to determine.
Detonation f explosion, blast. etw (acc) zur ~

bringen to detonate sth.

detonieren* *vi aux sein* to explode, to go off.

Deut *m* (um) keinen ~ not one iota *or* jot; **seine Ratschläge sind keinen ~ wert** his advice is not worth tuppence; **dafür gebe ich keinen ~** I don't give a hang for it *(col)*.

deutbar *adj* interpretable. **nicht/schwer ~** impossible/difficult to interpret.

deuteln *vi (geh)* to quibble, to cavil. **daran gibt es nichts zu ~!** there are no ifs and buts about it!

deuten 1 *vt (auslegen)* to interpret; **Zukunft** to read. **etw falsch ~** to misinterpret sth. **2** *vi* **(a)** **(mit dem Finger) auf etw** *(acc)* ~ to point (one's finger) at sth. **(b)** *(fig: hinweisen)* to indicate. **alles deutet darauf, daß ...** all the indications are that ...

deutlich *adj* clear. ~ **sichtbar** clearly visible; **ich fühle ~, daß ...** I have the distinct feeling ...; **jdm etw ~ vor Augen führen** *or* **zu verstehen geben** to make sth perfectly clear *or* plain to sb; **muß ich ~er werden?** have I not made myself clear *or* plain enough?

Deutlichkeit *f* clarity. **etw mit aller ~ sagen** to make sth perfectly clear *or* plain.

deutsch *adj* German. **~e Schrift** Gothic script; **~er Schäferhund** Alsatian *(Brit)*, German shepherd; **~e Gründlichkeit** *etc* German *or* Teutonic efficiency *etc*; **D~e Mark** deutschmark, German mark; **sich (auf)~ unterhalten** to speak (in) German; **auf ~ heißt das ...** in German it means ...; **mit jdm ~ reden** *(fig col: deutlich)* to speak bluntly with sb; **auf gut ~ (gesagt)** *(fig col)* in plain English.

Deutsch *nt no pl* German. **gut(es) ~ sprechen** to speak good German.

Deutsch-: **~amerikaner** *m* German American; **d~-amerikanisch** *adj* German-American.

Deutsch(e) *nt* **-n**, *no pl (Sprache)* German. **aus dem ~en/ins ~e übersetzt** translated from (the)/into German.

deutsch-|englisch *adj* **(a)** *(Pol)* Anglo-German. **(b)** *(Ling)* German-English.

Deutsche(r) *mf decl as adj* **er ist ~r** he is (a) German.

Deutsch-: **d~feindlich** *adj* anti-German, Germanophobic; **d~-französisch** *adj* **(a)** *(Pol)* Franco-German; **der D~-Französische Krieg** the Franco-Prussian war; **(b)** *(Ling)* German-French; **d~freundlich** *adj* pro-German, Germanophile.

Deutschland *nt* Germany.

Deutschland-: **~frage** *f (Pol)* German question; **~lied** *nt* West German national anthem; **~politik** *f* home *or* domestic policy; *(von fremdem Staat)* policy towards Germany.

Deutsch-: **~lehrer** *m* German teacher; **~schweizer** *m* German Swiss; **d~schweizerisch** *adj* German-Swiss; **d~sprachig** *adj* Bevölkerung, Gebiete German-speaking; Zeitung, Ausgabe German-language; Literatur German; **d~sprachlich** *adj* German(-language); **d~sprechend** *adj* German-speaking; **d~stämmig** *adj (of German origin)*; **~stunde** *f* German lesson; **~tümelei** *f (pej)* hyper-Germanness.

Deutung *f* interpretation. **eine falsche ~** a misinterpretation.

Devise [de'vi:zə] *f* **-n** **(a)** *(Wahlspruch)* motto. **(b)** *(Fin)* ~**n** *pl* foreign exchange *or* currency.

Devisen- in *cpds* foreign exchange; **~ausgleich** *m* foreign exchange offset; **~bestimmungen** *pl* foreign exchange control regulations *pl*; **~börse** *f* foreign exchange market; **~geschäft** *nt* foreign exchange dealing; **~handel** *m* foreign currency *or* exchange dealings *pl*; **~kurs** *m* exchange rate, rate of exchange.

devot [de'vo:t] *adj (pej geh: unterwürfig)* obsequious.

Dezember *m* - December; *siehe* **März.**

dezent *adj* discreet.

dezentral *adj* decentralized.

dezentralisieren* *vt* to decentralize.

Dezernat *nt (Admin)* department.

Dezernent(in *f)* *m (Admin)* head of department.

Dezibel ['de:tsibel, -'bel] *nt* - decibel.

dezidiert *adj (geh)* firm, determined.

Deziliter *m or nt* decilitre *(Brit)*, deciliter *(US)*.

dezimal *adj* decimal.

Dezimale *f* **-n** decimal.

Dezimal-: **~rechnung** *f* decimals *pl*; **~stelle** *f* auf zwei ~**stellen genau** correct to two decimal places; **~zahl** *f* decimal number.

dezimieren* *(fig)* **1** *vt* to decimate. **2** *vr* to be decimated.

Dezimierung *f (fig)* decimation.

DFB [de:|ɛf'be:] *m* = **Deutscher Fußball-Bund** German Football Association.

DGB [de:ge:'be:] *m* = **Deutscher Gewerkschaftsbund** Federation of German Trade Unions.

d.h. = **das heißt** i.e.

Dia *nt* **-s** *(Phot)* slide, transparency.

Diabetes [dia'be:tɛs] *m no pl* diabetes.

Diabetiker(in *f)* *m* - diabetic.

diabetisch *adj* diabetic.

Diadem *nt* **-e** diadem.

Diadochenkämpfe *pl (fig)* power struggle.

Diagnose *f* **-n** diagnosis. **eine ~ stellen** to make a diagnosis.

diagnostizieren* *vti (Med, fig)* to diagnose.

diagonal *adj* diagonal. **ein Buch ~ lesen** *(col)* to flick through a book.

Diagonale *f* **-n** diagonal.

Diagramm *nt* **-e** diagram.

Diakon *m* **-e(n)** *(Eccl)* deacon.

Diakonie *f (Eccl)* social welfare work.

Dialekt *m* **-e** dialect.

dialektfrei *adj* without an accent.

Dialektik *f (Philos)* dialectics *sing or pl*.

dialektisch *adj (Philos)* dialectical.

Dialog *m* **-e** dialogue.

Dialogregie *f (Film)* script supervision.

Diamant *m (wk)* **-en, -en** diamond.

diamanten *adj attr* diamond.

Diamant-: **~nadel** *f* **(a)** diamond brooch; **(b)** *(an Tonarm)* diamond (stylus); **~schleifer** *m* diamond polisher; **~schmuck** *m* diamonds *pl*.

diametral *adj* **~ entgegengesetzt** *(fig)* diametrically opposed.

Diaphragma [dia'fragma] *nt, pl* **Diaphragmen** diaphragm.

Dia- *(Phot):* **~positiv** *nt* slide, transparency; **~projektor** *m* slide projector.

diät *adv* kochen, essen according to a diet; **leben** on a special diet.

Diät *f* **-en** *(Med)* diet. ~ **halten** to keep to a strict diet; **nach einer ~ leben** to be on a diet *or* (wegen Krankheit) special diet; **jdn auf ~ setzen** *(col)* to put sb on a diet.

Diäten *pl (Parl)* parliamentary allowance.

Diät-: **~kost** *f* dietary foods; **~kost bekommen** to be on a special diet; **~kur** *f* dietary *or* dietetic treatment.

dich 1 *pers pron acc of* **du** you. **2** *refl pron* yourself. **wie fühlst du ~?** how do you feel?

dicht 1 *adj* **(a)** Gefieder, Haar, Hecke thick; Laub, Nebel *auch*, Wald, Gewühl dense; Verkehr *auch* heavy; Gewebe close; *(fig: konzentriert)* Programm full. **in ~er Folge** in quick succession. **(b)** *(undurchlässig)* watertight; airtight; Vorhänge thick, heavy. **nicht ~ sein** to leak; **er ist nicht ganz ~** *(col)* he's crackers *(col)*. **(c)** *(col: zu)* shut, closed. **2** *adv* **(a)** *(nahe)* closely. ~ **an** ~ **stehen** to stand close together; ~ **gefolgt von** closely followed by. **(b)** *(sehr stark)* bevölkert densely; ~ **behaart sein** to be very hairy. **(c)** *(mit Präpositionen)* ~ **an/bei** close to; ~ **dahinter/davor**

right behind/in front; ~ **hintereinander** right behind one another; ~ **beieinander** close together.

dicht-: ~**auf** adv closely; ~**auf folgen** to follow close behind; ~**behaart** adj attr (very) hairy; ~**bevölkert** adj attr densely populated.

Dichte f -n (a) no pl siehe adj (a) thickness; denseness; heaviness; closeness; fullness. (b) (Phys) density.

dichten[1] 1 vt to write. 2 vi to write poems.

dichten[2] vt (undurchlässig machen) to seal, to make watertight/airtight.

Dichter(in f) m - poet; (Schriftsteller) writer, author.

dichterisch adj poetic; (schriftstellerisch) literary. ~**e Freiheit** poetic licence (Brit) or license (US).

Dichter-: ~**kreis** m circle of poets; ~**lesung** f reading (by a poet/writer from his own works); ~**wort** nt -e (literary) quotation.

dicht-: ~**gedrängt** adj attr closely packed; ~**halten** vi sep irreg (col) to keep one's mouth shut (col).

Dichtkunst f art of poetry; (Schriftstellerei) creative writing.

dichtmachen vti sep (col) to shut up, to close. (**den Laden**) ~ to shut up shop.

Dichtung[1] f (a) no pl literature; (in Versform) poetry. ~ **und Wahrheit** (fig) fact and fantasy. (b) (Dichtwerk) poem, poetic work; literary work.

Dichtung[2] f (Tech) seal; (in Wasserhahn etc) washer; (Mech) gasket.

dick adj (a) thick; Mensch, Körperteil, Buch, Brieftasche fat; Baum, Stamm big, thick; (col) Gehalt, Rechnung, Gewinn big, fat; (col) Tränen, Geschäft, Fehler, Auto big; Zigarre big fat. **ein** ~**er Brocken** (col) a tough nut (to crack); ~ **machen** (Speisen) to be fattening; **er hat es** ~**(e)** (col) (satt) he's had enough of it; (viel) he's got enough and to spare; **das ist ein** ~**es Lob** that's high praise; **ach, du** ~**es Ei!** (col) bloody hell! (Brit col!); **das ist ein** ~**er Hund** (col) that's a bit much (col); **das** ~**e Ende kommt noch** (prov) the worst is yet to come; **eine** ~**e Suppe** (col: Nebel) a real peasouper (col); **durch** ~ **und dünn** through thick and thin. (b) (geschwollen) swollen; Beule big. (c) (col) Freundschaft, Freund close. **mit jdm** ~ **befreundet sein** to be thick with sb (col).

Dick-: **d**~**bauchig** adj Vase bulbous; **d**~**bäuchig** adj Mensch potbellied; ~**darm** m (Anat) colon.

Dicke f -n (a) thickness. (b) (von Menschen, Körperteilen) fatness.

Dicke(r) mf decl as adj (col) fatty (col), fatso (col).

dick-: ~**fellig** adj (col) thick-skinned; ~**flüssig** adj thick, viscous; ~**häutig** adj thick-skinned.

Dickicht nt -e thicket; (fig) jungle.

Dick-: ~**kopf** m (a) (Starrsinn) obstinacy, stubbornness; **einen** ~**kopf haben** to be obstinate or stubborn. (b) (Mensch) obstinate so-and-so (col); **d**~**köpfig** adj (fig) stubborn; **d**~**leibig** adj Buch massive; Mensch corpulent; **d**~**lich** adj plump; ~**milch** f (Cook) sour milk; ~**schädel** m (col) = ~**kopf**; ~**wanst** m (pej col) fatso (col).

Didaktik f teaching methods pl.

didaktisch adj didactic.

die art etc siehe **der**[2].

Dieb(in f) m -e thief. **haltet den** ~! stop thief!

Diebes-: ~**bande** f gang of thieves; ~**gut** nt stolen goods pl; **d**~**sicher** adj thief-proof.

diebisch adj (a) (lit) Gesindel etc thieving attr. (b) (col) Freude, Vergnügen impish.

Diebstahl ['di:p-ʃtaːl] m ⁼e theft. **einfacher/schwerer** ~ petty/grand larceny; **bewaffneter** ~ armed robbery; **geistiger** ~ plagiarism.

Diebstahl-: **d**~**sicher** adj theft-proof; ~**versicherung** f insurance against theft.

diejenige dem pron siehe **derjenige**.

Diele f -n (a) floorboard. (b) (Vorraum) hall.

Dielenbrett nt floorboard.

dienen vi (a) to serve (jdm sb, einer Sache (dat) sth); dem Fortschritt, der Erforschung to aid; dem Verständnis to promote; (nützlich sein) to be of use or service (jdm to sb). **es dient einer guten Sache** it is in a good cause; **womit kann ich Ihnen** ~? what can I do for you?; (im Geschäft auch) can I help you?; **damit ist mir wenig gedient** that's no use or good to me; **als/zu etw** ~ to serve as/for sth. (b) (Militärdienst leisten) to do (one's) military service.

Diener m - (a) servant. (b) (col: Verbeugung) bow.

Dienerin f maid.

dienern vi (fig pej) to bow and scrape (vor+dat to).

Dienerschaft f servants pl, domestic staff.

dienlich adj useful, helpful. **jdm/einer Sache** ~ **sein** to help sb/sth, to be of help to sb/sth.

Dienst m -e (a) service; (Arbeitsstelle) position. **in jds** ~**(en)** (dat) **stehen** to be in sb's service; **Oberst außer** ~ retired colonel; **im** ~**(e)** der **Menschheit** in the service of humanity; **jdm einen schlechten** ~ **erweisen** to do sb a disservice; **jdm gute** ~**e leisten** or **tun** to serve sb well; ~ **am Kunden** customer service; **etw in** ~ **stellen** to put sth into service; **jdm zu** ~**en stehen** to be at sb's disposal. (b) (Berufsausübung, Amtspflicht) duty; (Arbeit, Arbeitszeit) work. ~ **haben** (Arzt etc) to be on duty; (Apotheke) to be open; **im** ~ **sein** (Angestellter etc) to be working; **nach** ~ after work; ~ **tun** to serve (bei in, als as).

Dienstag m Tuesday. ~ **abend/morgen** (on) Tuesday evening/morning; ~ **abends/vormittags** on Tuesday evenings/mornings; **am** ~ on Tuesday; **hast du** ~ **Zeit?** have you time on Tuesday?; **alle** ~**e** every Tuesday; **eines** ~**s** one Tuesday; **die Nacht von** ~ **auf Mittwoch** the night of Tuesday to Wednesday; **den (ganzen)** ~ **über** all (day) Tuesday, the whole of Tuesday; ~ **in acht Tagen** or **in einer Woche** a week on Tuesday, Tuesday week; ~ **vor einer Woche** or **acht Tagen** a week (ago) last Tuesday.

dienstags adv on Tuesdays, on a Tuesday. ~ **abends** on Tuesday evenings.

Dienst-: ~**alter** nt length of service; ~**älteste(r)** mf (most) senior member of staff; ~**antritt** m assumption of one's duties; (jeden Tag) commencement of work; **d**~**anweisung** f instructions pl, regulations pl; **d**~**bar** adj **d**~**bare Geister** willing hands; **sich** (dat) **etw d**~**bar machen** to utilize sth; **d**~**beflissen** adj zealous; **d**~**bereit** adj (a) Apotheke open pred; Arzt on duty; (b) (hilfsbereit) obliging; ~**bezüge** pl salary sing; ~**bote** m servant; ~**boteneingang** m tradesmen's or service entrance; ~**eid** m oath of service; **d**~**eifer** m zeal; **d**~**eifrig** adj zealous, assiduous; **d**~**frei** adj free; **d**~**frei haben/bekommen** to have/be given a day etc off; ~**gebrauch** m (Mil, Admin) **nur für den** ~**gebrauch** for official use only; ~**geheimnis** nt official secret; ~**gespräch** nt business call; (von Beamten) official call; ~**grad** m (Mil: Rangstufe) rank; **d**~**habend** adj attr Arzt, Offizier duty attr, on duty; ~**herr** m employer; ~**jahr** nt usu pl (Mil, Admin) year of service; ~**leistung** f service; ~**leistungsbetrieb** m service industry; **d**~**lich** 1 adj Angelegenheiten business attr; Schreiben, Befehl official; **d**~**lich werden** (col) to become businesslike; 2 adv on business; **wir haben hier d**~**lich zu tun** we have business here; ~**mädchen** nt maid; ~**ordnung** f (Admin) official regulations pl; (Mil) service regulations pl; **d**~**pflichtig** adj (esp Mil) liable for compulsory service; ~**plan** m duty rota; ~**rang** m grade; (Mil) rank; ~**reise** f business trip; **auf** ~**reise on a business trip; ~**schluß** m end of work; **nach** ~**schluß** (von Arbeiter etc) after work; ~**stelle** f (Admin) department; ~**stunden** pl working hours pl; **d**~**tauglich** adj (Mil) fit for service; **d**~**tuend** adj Arzt duty attr, on duty; **d**~**unfähig**

adj unfit for work; *(Mil)* unfit for duty; **d~untauglich** *adj (Mil)* unfit for service; **~vergehen** *nt* breach of duty; **~wagen** *m* company car; *(von Beamten)* official car; **~weg** *m* **auf dem ~weg** through official channels; **~wohnung** *f* police/army *etc* house; **~zeit** *f* (a) period of service; **(b)** *(Arbeitszeit)* working hours *pl*; *(Mil)* hours *pl* of duty; **~zeugnis** *nt* testimonial.
dies *dem pron inv* this; *pl* these. **~ sind** these are; **siehe dieser.**
diesbezüglich *adj (form)* regarding this.
diese *dem pron siehe* **dieser.**
Diesel *m* - diesel.
dieselbe *dem pron siehe* **derselbe.**
Diesel-: **~motor** *m* diesel engine; **~öl** *nt* diesel oil.
dieser, diese, dies(es), *pl* **diese** *dem pron* this; *(~ dort, da)* that; *pl* these; *(~ dort, da)* those. **diese(r, s) hier** this (one); **diese(r, s) da** that (one); **dieser ..., jener ...** the latter ..., the former ...; **dies und das, dieses und jenes** this and that; **diese Nacht** tonight; **dies alles** all this/that.
diesig *adj* Wetter, Luft misty.
dies-: **~jährig** *adj attr* **die ~jährige Ernte** this year's harvest; **~mal** *adv* this time; **~malig** *adj attr* **der ~malige Preis** the price this time; **~seitig** *adj* Ufer *etc* near(side) *attr*, (on) this side; **~seits** *prep+gen* on this side of; **D~seits** *nt no pl* **das D~seits** this life.
Dietrich *m* -e skeleton key.
diffamieren* *vt* to defame.
diffamierend *adj* defamatory.
Diffamierung *f* defamation (of character); *(Bemerkung etc)* defamatory statement.
Diffamierungskampagne *f* smear campaign.
Differential [-'tsiaːl] *nt* -e *(Aut: auch* **~getriebe** *nt)* differential (gear).
Differential- *in cpds* (Tech, Math) differential; **~rechnung** *f (Math)* differential calculus.
Differenz *f* difference; *(Abweichung)* discrepancy.
Differenzbetrag *m* difference, balance.
differenzieren* *vti* to make distinctions/a distinction *(zwischen+dat* between, *bei* in); *(abändern)* to make changes/a change in, to modify; *(den Unterschied verstehen)* to differentiate *(zwischen+dat* between, *bei* in). **genau ~** to make a precise distinction.
differieren* *vi* to differ.
diffus *adj* Gedanken *etc* confused.
digital *adj* digital.
Digital- *in cpds* digital.
Diktat *nt* (a) dictation. **etw nach ~ schreiben** to write sth from dictation. **(b)** *(fig: Gebot)* dictate; *(Pol auch)* diktat.
Diktator *m* dictator.
diktatorisch *adj* dictatorial.
Diktatur *f* dictatorship.
diktieren* *vt* Brief, *(fig)* Bedingungen to dictate.
Diktiergerät *nt* dictating machine.
Diktion *f* style.
Dilemma *nt* -s dilemma.
Dilettant(in *f)* *m (wk)* amateur, dilettante *(pej)*.
dilettantisch *adj* amateurish.
Dill *m* -e *(Bot, Cook)* dill.
Dimension *f* dimension.
DIN ® [dɪn, diːn] *f no pl* = **Deutsche Industrie-Norm** German Industrial Standard. **~** A4 A4.
Diner [di'neː] *nt* -s *(form) (Mittagessen)* luncheon; *(Abendessen)* dinner.
Ding *nt* -e *or (col)* -er thing. **das ist ein ~ der Unmöglichkeit** that is totally impossible; **guter ~e sein** *(geh)* to be in good spirits; **jedes ~ hat zwei Seiten** *(Prov)* there are two sides to everything; **gut ~ will Weile haben** *(Prov)* it takes time to do a thing well; **vergangene/berufliche ~e** past events/professional matters; **so wie die ~e liegen, nach Lage der ~e** as things are; **über den**

~en stehen to be above things; **vor allen ~en** above all (things), first and foremost; **es müßte nicht mit rechten ~en zugehen, wenn ...** it would be more than a little strange if ...; **das ~(s) da** *(col)* that thing (over) there; **das ist ein ~!** now there's a thing! *(col)*; **da hast du dir aber ein ~ geleistet** that was quite something you got up to *(col)*; **was macht ihr bloß für ~er?** the things you do! *(col)*.
dingfest *adj* **jdn ~ machen** to arrest sb.
Dingi ['dɪŋgi] *nt* -s dinghy.
dinglich *adj* material.
Dings, Dingsbums, Dingsda *nt no pl (col)* thingummyjig *(col)*.
dinieren* *vi (geh)* to dine *(form)*.
Diode *f* -n diode.
Diözese *f* -n diocese.
Diphtherie [dɪfte'riː] *f* diphtheria.
Dipl. = **Diplom.**
Dipl. Ing. = **Diplomingenieur** academically qualified engineer.
Diplom *nt* -e diploma. **ein ~ machen** to take *or* do one's diploma.
Diplom- *in cpds* (vor Berufsbezeichnung) qualified; **~arbeit** *f* dissertation.
Diplomat *m (wk)* -en, -en diplomat.
Diplomatie *f (lit, fig)* diplomacy.
diplomatisch *adj (Pol, fig)* diplomatic.
diplomiert *adj* qualified.
dir *pers pron dat of* **du** to you; *(nach Präpositionen)* you.
direkt 1 *adj* direct; *Erledigung* immediate; *(genau)* Hinweis plain; Auskunft clear. **eine ~e Verbindung** a through train/direct flight. **2** *adv* **(a)** *(unmittelbar)* directly; *(geradewegs auch)* straight; *(übertragen)* live; telephonieren direct. **~ von/nach** straight *or* direct from/to; **~ an/unter** directly *or* right by/under; **(b)** *(unverblümt)* bluntly. **jdm etw ~ ins Gesicht sagen** to tell sb sth (straight) to his face; **~ fragen** to ask outright *or* straight out. **(c)** *(col: geradezu)* really.
Direktion *f* management; *(Direktionsbüro)* manager's office.
Direktive *f (geh)* directive.
Direktmandat *nt (Pol)* direct mandate.
Direktor *m,* **Direktorin** *f* director; *(von Gefängnis)* governor, warden *(US)*; *(von Hochschule)* principal; *(von Schule)* head (teacher), principal *(esp US)*.
Direktorat *nt* **(a)** *(Amt)* directorship; *(von Schule)* headship, principalship *(esp US)*. **(b)** *(Diensträume: von Schule)* head (teacher)'s *or* principal's *(esp US)* study *or* room.
Direktorium *nt* board of directors, directorate.
Direkt-: **~übertragung** *f (Rad, TV)* live transmission; **~verbindung** *f (Rail)* through train; *(Aviat)* direct flight.
Dirigent(in *f)* *m (wk)* (Mus) conductor.
dirigieren* *vt* **(a)** *(auch vi) (Mus)* to conduct; *(fig)* to lead. **(b)** Verkehr *etc* to direct.
Dirndl *nt* - *(auch* **~kleid)** dirndl.
Dirne *f* -n *(Prostituierte)* prostitute.
dis, Dis *nt* -, - *(Mus)* D sharp.
Disco *f* -s disco.
Disharmonie *f (lit, fig)* discord.
disharmonisch *adj (lit, fig)* discordant.
Diskette *f (Data)* diskette.
Diskettenlaufwerk *nt* disk drive.
Diskjockey ['dɪskdʒɔke] *m* -s disc jockey, DJ.
Diskont *m* -e *(Fin)* discount.
Diskontsatz *m (Fin)* discount rate.
Diskothek *f* -en discotheque.
diskreditieren* *vt (geh)* to discredit.
Diskrepanz *f* discrepancy.
diskret *adj* discreet; Gespräch confidential.
Diskretion *f* discretion; *(vertrauliche Behandlung)* confidentiality. **strengste ~ wahren** to preserve

the strictest confidence.
diskriminieren* vt to discriminate against.
diskriminierend adj discriminatory.
Diskriminierung f discrimination.
Diskus m, pl -se or **Disken** discus.
Diskussion f discussion. **zur ~ stehen** to be under discussion; **etw zur ~ stellen** to put sth up for discussion.
Diskussions-: **~beitrag** m contribution to the discussion; **~teilnehmer** m participant (in a discussion).
Diskus-: **~werfen** nt no pl throwing the discus; **~werfer(in** f) m discus-thrower.
diskutabel adj worth discussing.
diskutieren* vti to discuss. **über etw** (acc) **~ to** discuss sth; **darüber läßt sich ~** that sounds like something we could talk about.
dispensieren* [dɪspɛn'ziːrən] vt jdn to excuse (von from).
disponieren* [dɪsponiːrən] vi (geh) (a) (verfügen) **ich kann nicht über sie ~** I can't tell her what to do; **über etw** (acc) (frei) **~** to do as one wishes with sth. (b) (planen) to make arrangements.
disponiert [dɪspo'niːɐt] adj (geh) **gut/schlecht ~ sein** to be in good/bad form.
Disposition [dɪspozi'tsioːn] f (geh) (a) (Verfügung) **jdm zur** or **zu jds ~ stehen** to be at sb's disposal; **jdm etw zur ~ stellen** to place sth at sb's disposal. (b) (Anordnung) arrangement. **seine ~en treffen** to make (one's) arrangements.
Disput [dɪs'puːt] m -e (geh) dispute.
disqualifizieren* vt to disqualify.
Disqualifizierung f disqualification.
Dissertation f (Doktorarbeit) thesis.
Dissident(in f) m (wk) dissident.
dissonant adj dissonant.
Dissonanz f (Mus) dissonance; (fig) (note of) discord.
Distanz f distance (auch Sport); (fig) (Abstand, Entfernung) detachment; (Zurückhaltung) reserve. **~ halten** or **wahren** (lit, fig) to keep one's distance; **auf ~ gehen** (fig) to become distant.
distanzieren* **1** vr sich von jdm/etw **~** to dissociate oneself from sb/sth. **2** vt (Sport) to outdistance.
distanziert adj Verhalten distant.
Distel f -n thistle.
Distrikt m -e district.
Disziplin f -en discipline (auch Sport).
disziplinarisch adj disciplinary. **jdn ~ bestrafen** to take disciplinary action against sb.
Disziplinar-: **~strafe** f punishment; **eine ~strafe bekommen** to be disciplined; **~verfahren** nt disciplinary proceedings pl.
disziplinieren* vt to discipline.
Disziplin-: **d~los** **1** adj undisciplined; **2** adv in an undisciplined manner; **~losigkeit** f lack no pl of discipline.
dito adv (Comm, hum) ditto.
Diva ['diːva] f -s star; (Film) screen goddess.
divergieren* [diver'giːrən] vi to diverge.
divers [di'vɛrs] adj attr various. „**D~es**" miscellaneous".
Dividende [divi'dɛndə] f -n (Fin) dividend.
dividieren* [divi'diːrən] vti to divide (durch by).
Division [divi'zioːn] f (Math, Mil) division.
Diwan m -e divan.
DKP [deːkaː'peː] f = **Deutsche Kommunistische Partei**.
DM ['deː|ɛm] no art - = **Deutsche Mark**.
D-Mark ['deːmark] f - deutschmark, (West) German mark.
Dobermann m, pl **-männer** Doberman (pinscher).
doch 1 conj (aber, allein) but; (jedoch, trotzdem) but still, yet. **und ~ hat er es getan** but he still did it, but still he did it.
2 adv (a) (betont: dennoch) after all; (trotzdem,

sowieso) anyway. **jetzt ist er ~ nicht gekommen** now he hasn't come after all; **du weißt es ja ~** besser you know better than I do anyway; **und ~, ... and yet ...
(b)** (betont: tatsächlich) really. **also ~!** so it is/so he did! etc; **er hat es gestohlen — also ~!** he stole it — so it was him!; **es ist ~ so, wie ich** vermutet hatte so it (really) is as I thought; **das ist er ~!** (why,) that is him!
(c) (als bejahende Antwort) yes I do/it does etc. **hat es dir nicht gefallen? — (~,) ~!** didn't you like it? — (oh) yes I did!
(d) (auffordernd) nicht übersetzt aber emphatisches „to do" wird oft gebraucht. **komm ~ do** come; **seid ~ endlich still!** do keep quiet!, keep quiet, can't you?; **laß ihn ~!** just leave him!; **nicht ~!** don't (do that)!
(e) sie ist **~ noch so jung** but she's still so young; **das ist ~ wohl nicht wahr?** that's not true, is it?; **du hast ~ nicht etwa ...?** you haven't ..., have you?, surely you haven't ...(, have you?): **es war ~ ganz interessant** it was really or actually quite interesting; **Sie wissen ~, wie das so** ist (well,) you know how it is, don't you?; **wenn ~** if only.
Docht m -e wick.
Dock nt -s dock.
docken* vti to dock.
Docker m - docker.
Dogge f -n mastiff. **deutsche ~** great Dane.
Dogma nt, pl **Dogmen** dogma.
dogmatisch adj (Rel, fig) dogmatic.
Dohle f -n (Orn) jackdaw.
Doktor m (auch col: Arzt) doctor. **den ~ machen** (col) to do a doctorate or PhD.
Doktorand(in f) m (wk) **-en, -en** PhD student.
Doktor-: **~arbeit** f doctoral or PhD thesis; **~grad** m doctorate, PhD; **~hut** m (fig) doctorate.
Doktorin f doctor.
Doktor-: **~prüfung** f examination for a/one's doctorate; **~titel** m doctorate; **~vater** m supervisor; **~würde** f doctorate.
Doktrin f -en doctrine.
doktrinär adj doctrinal; (pej: stur) doctrinaire.
Dokument nt document; (fig: Zeugnis) record.
Dokumentar- in cpds documentary; **~film** m documentary (film).
Dokumentation f documentation.
dokumentieren* vt to document; (fig: zu erkennen geben) to reveal, to show.
Dolch m -e dagger; (col: Messer) knife.
Dolchstoß (esp fig) m stab (auch fig). **ein ~ (von** hinten) (fig) a stab in the back.
Dollar m -s dollar.
dolmetschen vti to interpret.
Dolmetscher(in f) m - interpreter.
Dolmetscherschule f school of interpreting.
Dolomiten pl (Geog) **die ~** the Dolomites pl.
Dom m -e cathedral.
Domäne f -n (fig) domain, province.
domestizieren* vt to domesticate.
dominant adj dominant (auch Biol), dominating.
Dominante f -n (a) (Mus) dominant. (b) (wichtigster Faktor) dominant or dominating feature.
Dominanz f (Biol, Psych) dominance.
dominieren* **1** vi (vorherrschen) to predominate; (Mensch) to dominate. **2** vt to dominate.
dominierend adj dominating, dominant.
Domizil nt -e (geh, hum) domicile (form).
Dompfaff m (Orn) bullfinch.
Dompteur [dɔmp'tøːɐ] m, **Dompteuse** [-'tøːzə] f trainer; (von Raubtieren) tamer.
Donau f die **~** the Danube.
Donner m (lit, fig) thunder no indef art, no pl; **(~schlag)** clap of thunder. **wie vom ~ gerührt** (fig col) thunderstruck.
donnern 1 vi impers to thunder. **es donnerte in der** Ferne there was (the sound of) thunder in the

distance. 2 *vi aux haben or (bei Bewegung) sein to* thunder. **gegen etw ~** *(schlagen)* to hammer on sth; *(schimpfen)* to thunder against sth. **3** *vt (col: schleudern, schlagen)* to slam, to crash.
donnernd *adj (fig)* Beifall thunderous.
Donnerschlag *m* clap of thunder, thunderclap. **die Nachricht traf mich wie ein ~** the news left me thunderstruck.
Donnerstag *m* Thursday; *siehe* **Dienstag.**
donnerstags *adv* on Thursdays.
Donner-: **~stimme** *f* thunderous voice; **~wetter** *nt (fig col: Schelte)* row; **~wetter!** *(col) (anerkennend)* my word!; *(zornig)* blast (it)! *(col).*
doof *adj (col)* stupid; *Mensch auch* thick *(col).*
dopen *(Sport)* **1** *vt* to dope. **2** *vir* to take drugs.
Doping *nt* **-s** *(Sport)* doping.
Dopingkontrolle *f (Sport)* dope check.
Doppel *nt* **- (a)** *(Duplikat)* duplicate (copy) *(gen, zu of).* **(b)** *(Tennis etc)* doubles *sing.*
Doppel- *in cpds* double; **~agent** *m* double agent; **~band** *m (von doppeltem Umfang)* double-sized volume; *(zwei Bände)* two volumes *pl*; **~belastung** *f* double burden *(gen* on*)*; **steuerliche ~belastung** double taxation; **~bett** *nt* double bed; *(zwei Betten)* twin beds *pl*; **d~bödig** *adj Koffer etc* double-bottomed, false-bottomed; *(d~deutig)* ambiguous; **~decker** *m* **- (a)** *(Aviat)* biplane; **(b)** *(Bus)* double-decker (bus); **d~deutig** *adj* ambiguous; **~deutigkeit** *f* ambiguity; **~fenster** *nt* double window; *(~verglasung)* double glazing; **~gänger(in** *f) m* **-** double, doppelgänger *(esp Liter)*; **~haus** *nt* semi-detached house, semi *(Brit col),* duplex (house) *(US)*; **er bewohnt eine Hälfte eines ~hauses** he lives in a semi-(detached house); **~kinn** *nt* double chin; **~korn** *m type of schnapps*; **d~läufig** *adj* double-barrelled; **~moral** *f* double standards *pl*; **~name** *m (Nachname)* double-barrelled name; **~paß** *m (Ftbl)* one-two; **~punkt** *m* colon; **d~seitig** *adj* double-sided; *Lungenentzündung* double; **d~seitige Anzeige** double page spread; **~sinn** *m* double meaning; **d~sinnig** *adj* ambiguous; **~spiel** *nt* **(a)** *(Tennis)* (game of) doubles *sing*; **(b)** *(fig)* double game; **~stecker** *m* two-way adaptor; **~stunde** *f (Sch)* double period.
doppelt 1 *adj* double; *(verstärkt) Enthusiasmus* redoubled; *(mit zwei identischen Teilen)* twin *attr*; *(zweimal soviel)* twice; *(Comm) Buchführung* double-entry; *Staatsbürgerschaft* dual. **die ~e Freude/Menge** double *or* twice the pleasure/amount; **~er Boden** false *or* double bottom; **~e Moral** double standards *pl*; **in ~er Hinsicht** in two respects; **ein ~es Spiel treiben** to play a double game. **2** *adv* **sehen, zählen** double; *(zweimal)* twice; *(direkt vor Adjektiv)* doubly. **~** *so schön/soviel etc* twice as nice/much *etc*; **sie ist ~ so alt wie ich** she is twice as old as me; **die Karte habe ich ~** I have two of these cards; **~ gemoppelt** *(col)* saying the same thing twice over; **sich ~ in acht nehmen** to be doubly careful; **~ genäht hält besser** *(prov)* better safe than sorry *(prov).*
Doppelte(r) *m decl as adj (col)* double.
Doppelte(s) *nt decl as adj* double. **das ~ bezahlen** to pay twice as much; **etw um das ~ erhöhen** to double sth.
Doppel-: **~verdiener** *m* **sie sind ~verdiener** they have two incomes; **~zentner** *m* 100 kilos; **~zimmer** *nt* double room; **d~züngig** *adj* two-faced; **d~züngig reden** to say one thing and mean another; **~züngigkeit** *f no pl* two-facedness.
Dorado *nt* **-s** *(fig)* eldorado.
Dorf *nt* **-̈er** *village*; *(fig)* backwater. **das Leben auf dem ~e** village life.
Dorf- *in cpds* village; **~bewohner** *m* villager; **~jugend** *f* young people *pl* of the village; **~krug** *m* village inn *or* pub *(Brit).*
dörflich *adj* village *attr*; *(ländlich)* rustic, rural.
Dorn *m* **-en (a)** *(Bot, fig)* thorn. **das ist mir ein ~**

im Auge *(fig)* it's a thorn in my flesh; *(Anblick)* I find it an eyesore. **(b)** *pl* **-e** *(Sporn)* spike; *(von Schnalle)* tongue; *(Tech: Werkzeug)* awl.
Dornbusch *m* briar, thornbush.
Dornen-: **~hecke** *f* thorn(y) hedge; **~krone** *f (Bibl)* crown of thorns; **d~reich** *adj* thorny.
dornig *adj* thorny.
Dorn-: **~röschen** *nt* Sleeping Beauty; **~röschenschlaf** *f (fig)* slumber; **aus seinem ~röschenschlaf erwachen** to awake from one's slumbers.
dörren 1 *vt* to dry. **2** *vi aux sein* to dry; *(austrocknen)* to dry up.
Dörr-: **~fleisch** *nt* dried meat; **~obst** *nt* dried fruit; **~pflaume** *f* prune.
Dorsch *m* **-e** *type of cod.*
dort *adv* there; *siehe* **da 1 (a).**
dort-: **~her** *adv* **von ~her** from there; **~hin** *adv* there; **bis ~hin** as far as there; **~hinauf** *adv* up there; **~hinaus** *adv* out there; **frech bis ~hinaus** *(col)* really cheeky; **das ärgert mich bis ~hinaus** *(col)* that really gets me *(col)*; **~hinein** *adv* in there; **~hinunter** *adv* down there.
dortig *adj* **die ~en Behörden** the authorities there.
Dose *f* **-n (a)** *(Blech~)* tin; *(Konserven~)* can, tin *(Brit)*; *(Bier~)* can; *(esp aus Holz)* box; *(mit Deckel)* jar; *(Pillen~, für Schmuck)* box; *(Zucker~)* bowl. **in ~n** *(Konserven)* canned, tinned *(Brit).* **(b)** *(Elec)* socket.
dösen *vi (col)* to doze.
Dosen- *in cpds* canned, tinned *(Brit)*; **~bier** *nt* canned beer; **~milch** *f* evaporated milk; **~öffner** *m* can-opener, tin-opener *(Brit).*
dosieren* *vt (lit, fig)* to measure out.
Dosierung *f (Dosis)* dosage, dose.
dosig *adj (col)* dozy *(col).*
Dosis *f, pl* **Dosen** *(lit, fig)* dose.
Dossier [dɔ'sie:] *nt* **-s** dossier.
dotieren* *vt Posten* to remunerate; *Preis* to endow.
Dotierung *f* endowment; *(von Posten)* remuneration.
Dotter *m or nt* **-** yolk.
doubeln ['duːbln] **1** *vt jdn* to stand in for; *Szene* to shoot with a stand-in. **ein Stuntman hat die Szene für ihn gedoubelt** a stuntman doubled for him in the scene. **2** *vi* to stand in; *(als Double arbeiten)* to work as a stand-in.
Double ['duːbl] *nt* **-s** *(Film etc)* stand-in.
down [daun] *adj pred (col)* **~ sein** to be down.
Dozent *(in* f) *m (wk)* lecturer *(für* in*)*, (assistant) professor *(US) (für* of*).*
Dozentur *f* lectureship *(für* in*)*, (assistant) professorship *(US) (für* of*).*
dozieren* *vi (Univ)* to lecture *(über+acc* on, an *+dat* at*)*; *(pej auch)* to pontificate *(über+acc* about*).*
dpa ['deːpeːˈʔaː] *f* **= Deutsche Presse-Agentur.**
Dr. ['dɔktɔr] **= Doktor. Dr.rer.nat./rer.pol./phil.** PhD; **Dr. theol./jur.** DD/LLD; **Dr. med.** M.D.
Drache *m (wk)* **-n, -n** *(Myth)* dragon.
Drachen *m* **- (a)** *(Papier~)* kite; *(Sport: Fluggerät)* hang-glider. **einen ~ steigen lassen** to fly a kite. **(b)** *(pej col: zänkisches Weib)* dragon *(col).*
Drachen-: **~fliegen** *nt (Sport)* hang-gliding; **~flieger** *m (Sport)* hang-glider.
Dragée [dra'ʒeː] *nt* **-s (a)** *(Bonbon)* sugar-coated chocolate sweet. **(b)** *(Pharm)* dragee, sugar-coated pill.
Draht *m* **-̈e** wire. **auf ~ sein** *(col)* to be on the ball *(col)*; **du bist wohl heute nicht ganz auf ~** *(col)* you're not quite with it today *(col).*
Draht- *in cpds* wire; **~bürste** *f* wire brush; **~esel** *m (hum)* trusty bicycle; **~gitter** *nt* wire netting; **~haardackel** *m* wire-haired dachshund; **d~haarig** *adj* wire-haired.
drahtig *adj Haar, Mensch* wiry.
Draht-: **d~los** *adj Telegrafie* wireless; **~schere** *f*

wire cutters pl.
Drahtseil nt wire cable. **Nerven wie ~e** (col) nerves of steel.
Drahtseil-: ~bahn f cable railway; **~künstler** m (Seiltänzer) tightrope walker.
Draht-: ~verhau m or nt wire entanglement; **~zaun** m wire fence; **~zieher(in** f) m (fig) wire-puller.
drakonisch adj draconian.
drall adj Mädchen, Arme strapping, sturdy.
Drall m -e (a) (von Kugel, Ball) spin; (Abweichung von Bahn) swerve; (col: von Auto) pull. **einen ~ nach links haben** (Auto) to pull to the left. (b) (fig: Hang) tendency.
Drama nt, pl **Dramen** (lit, fig) drama.
Dramatik f (lit, fig) drama.
Dramatiker(in f) m - dramatist.
dramatisch adj (lit, fig) dramatic.
dramatisieren* vt (lit, fig) to dramatize.
Dramaturg(in f) m (wk) -en, -en artistic director; (TV) drama producer.
dramaturgisch adj dramatic; Abteilung drama attr.
dran adv (col) (a) (an der Reihe) **jetzt bist du ~** it's your turn now; **(wenn er erwischt wird,) dann ist er ~** (if he gets caught) he'll be for it (col). (b) **schlecht ~ sein** to be in a bad way; **gut ~ sein** to be well-off; **früh/spät ~ sein** to be early/late. (c) **an ihm ist nichts ~** he doesn't have much going for him; **was ist an ihm ~, daß ...?** what is there about him that ...?; **da ist alles ~!** that's got everything; **da wird schon etwas (Wahres) ~ sein** there must be something in that; **ich weiß nicht, wie ich (bei ihm) ~ bin** I don't know where I stand (with him).
dranbleiben vi sep irreg aux sein (col) to stay close; (am Apparat) to hang on. **am Gegner ~** to stick to one's opponent.
Drang m -e (Antrieb) urge (auch Physiol); (Sehnsucht) yearning (nach for); (nach Wissen) thirst (nach for).
drang pret of **dringen**.
drangehen vi sep irreg aux sein (col) (a) (berühren etc) to touch (an etw (acc) sth). (b) (in Angriff nehmen) ~, **etw zu tun** to get down to doing sth.
Drängelei f (col) pushing, jostling.
drängeln (col) 1 vi to push, to jostle. **2** vr **sich nach vorne ~** to push one's way to the front.
drängen 1 vi (a) (in Menge) to push. (b) (fordern) to press (auf+acc for). **auf Antwort ~** to press for an answer; **er drängte zur Eile** he urged us/them etc to hurry. (c) **die Zeit drängt** time presses. **2** vt (a) (drücken, schieben) to push. (b) (auffordern) to press. **3** vr (Menge) to throng; (fig: Termine etc) to mount up. **sich nach vorn ~** to push or force one's way to the front; siehe **gedrängt**.
Drängen nt no pl urging; (Bitten) requests pl; (Bestehen) insistence.
drängend adj pressing, urgent.
drangsalieren* vt to pester, to plague.
dranhalten vr sep irreg (col: sich beeilen) to get a move on (col).
drankommen vi sep irreg aux sein (col: an die Reihe kommen) to have one's turn; (Sch: beim Melden) to be called; (Frage, Aufgabe etc) to come up. **jetzt kommst du dran** now it's your turn.
dranmachen sep (col) 1 vr = **daranmachen**. **2** vt **etw (an etw** acc) ~ to put sth on (sth).
drannehmen vt sep irreg (col) Schüler to ask.
dransetzen vtr sep (col) = **daransetzen**.
drapieren* vt to drape.
drastisch adj drastic; (deutlich) graphic.
drauf adv (col) siehe auch **darauf**. **~ und dran sein, etw zu tun** to be on the point of doing sth; **etw ~ haben** (col) (können) to be able to do sth just like that (col); **Kenntnisse** to be well up on sth (col); **Witze, Sprüche** to have sth off pat (col); **160**

Sachen ~ haben (col) to be doing 160.
Drauf-: ~gänger m go-getter; **d~gängerisch** adj go-getting; (negativ) reckless; **d~geben** vt irreg sep (a) **jdm eins d~geben** (col) to give sb a smack; (b) (dazugeben) noch etwas **d~geben** to add some extra (col); **d~gehen** vi sep irreg aux sein (col); (verbraucht werden) to be used up; (kaputtgehen) to be smashed up; (sterben) to bite the dust (col); **dabei gehen mindestens zwei Tage d~** that'll take at least two days; **d~halten** vi sep irreg (als Ziel) to aim for it; **d~kommen** vi sep irreg aux sein (col) (sich erinnern) to remember; (begreifen) to catch on, to get it (col); **jdm d~kommen** to get on to sb (col); **d~kriegen** vt sep (col) **etw (auf etw** acc) **d~kriegen** to get or fit sth on(to sth); **eins d~kriegen** to catch it (col); **d~legen** vti sep (col) **20 Mark d~legen** to lay out an extra 20 marks.
drauflos adv immer feste **~!** (just) keep at it!
drauflos-: ~arbeiten vi sep (col) to work away, to beaver away (col); **~gehen** vi sep irreg aux sein (col: auf ein Ziel) to make straight for it.
drauf-: ~machen vt sep (col) **einen ~machen** to make a night of it (col); **D~sicht** f (col) top view; **~stehen** vi sep irreg (col) **auf etw** (dat) **~stehen** to stand on sth; (Aufschrift) to be on sth; **~zahlen** sep (col) (a) vti = **~legen**; (b) vi (fig: Einbußen erleiden) to pay the price.
draus adv = **daraus**.
draußen adv outside; (im Freien auch) outdoors; (da ~, weit weg von hier) out there; **~ auf dem Lande/im Garten** out in the country/garden; **hier ~** out here; **nach ~** outside; **weit ~** far out.
drechseln vt to turn (on a wood lathe).
Drechsler(in f) m - (wood) turner.
Dreck m no pl (a) dirt; (Schlamm) mud; (Kot) muck; (fig: (Schund) rubbish; (Schmutz, Obszönes) dirt, filth. **~ machen** to make a mess; **mit ~ und Speck** (ungewaschen) unwashed; **im ~ sitzen** (col) to be in a mess or jam (col); **aus dem gröbsten ~ heraus sein** (col) to be past the worst; **jdn wie den letzten ~ behandeln** (col) to treat sb like dirt; **der letzte ~ sein** (pej col: Mensch) to be the lowest of the low; **~ am Stecken haben** (fig) to have a skeleton in the cupboard; **etw in den ~ ziehen** (fig) to drag sth through the mud. (b) (col) (Kram) business, stuff (col); (Kleinigkeit) little thing. **sich einen ~ um jdn/etw kümmern** not to give a damn about sb/sth (col); **mach deinen ~ alleine!** do it yourself; **das geht ihn einen ~ an** that's none of his business.
Dreck|arbeit f (col) (a) (lit, fig) dirty work. (b) (pej: niedere Arbeit) donkey work.
dreckig adj (lit, fig) dirty; (stärker) filthy. **~ lachen** to give a dirty laugh; **es geht mir ~** (col) I'm in a bad way.
Dreck-: ~loch nt (pej) hole (col); **~pfoten** pl (col) (lit, fig) dirty paws pl; **~sack** m (pej col) dirty thing (col); **~sau** f (col!) filthy swine (col!); **~schleuder** f (pej: Mensch) foul-mouthed person; **~schwein** nt (col!) dirty pig (col!).
Dreckskerl m (col!) (dirty) swine (col!).
Dreckspatz m (col: Kind) mucky pup (col).
Dreck(s)zeug nt (col) damn stuff (col). **das ist doch ein ~** damn this stuff (col).
Dreh m -s or -e (List) dodge; (Kunstgriff) trick. **den ~ herausbaben** to get the hang of it.
Dreh-: ~arbeiten pl (Film) shooting sing; **~bank** f lathe; **d~bar** adj rotating, revolving attr; **d~bar sein** to rotate or revolve; **~beginn** m (Film) start of shooting; **~brücke** f swing bridge; **~buch** nt (Film) screenplay, (film) script; **~buchautor** m scriptwriter, screenplay writer; **~bühne** f revolving stage.
drehen 1 vt to turn (auch Tech: auf Drehbank); (um eine Achse auch) to rotate, to revolve; Kreisel to spin; Zigaretten to roll; Film to shoot; (fig: verdrehen) to twist; (col: schaffen) to fix (col). **das**

Gas hoch/auf klein ~ to turn the gas up high/ down low; **Fleisch durch den Wolf** ~ to put meat through the mincer; **ein Ding** ~ *(col)* to play a prank; *(Verbrecher)* to pull a job *(col)*; **wie man es auch dreht und wendet** no matter how you look at it.

2 *vi* to turn; *(Wind)* to shift, to change; *(Film)* to shoot, to film; *(Zigaretten* ~*)* to roll one's own. **am Radio** ~ to turn a knob on the radio.

3 *vr* **(a)** *(lit)* to turn *(um about)*; *(um Achse auch)* to rotate, to revolve; *(Kreisel)* to spin; *(Wind)* to shift, to change. **sich um sich (selbst)** ~ to revolve on its own axis; **mir dreht sich alles im Kopf** my head is spinning; **sich** ~ **und winden** *(fig)* to twist and turn. **(b)** *(fig)* **sich um etw** ~ *(betreffen)* to concern sth, to be about sth; *(um zentrale Frage)* to centre *(Brit)* or center *(US)* on sth; **alles dreht sich um sie** she's the focus of attention; **es dreht sich darum, daß** ... the point is that ...

Dreher(in *f)* **m** - lathe operator.

Dreh-: ~**knopf** m knob; ~**kran** m slewing or rotary crane; ~**kreuz** nt turnstile; ~**moment** nt torque; ~**orgel** f barrel-organ; ~**orgelspieler** m organ-grinder; ~**ort** m *(Film)* location; ~**punkt** m pivot; ~**scheibe** *f*(a) *(Rail)* turntable; **(b)** *(Töpferscheibe)* potter's wheel; ~**stuhl** m swivel-chair; ~**tür** *f* revolving door.

Drehung f turn; *(um eigene Achse auch)* rotation, revolution. **eine** ~ **um 180°** a 180° turn; **80** ~**en pro Minute** 80 revs or revolutions per minute.

Drehwurm m *(col)*: **einen** ~ **kriegen/haben** to get/be giddy.

Drehzahl *f* number of revolutions or revs.

Drehzahlmesser m rev counter.

drei num three. **aller guten Dinge sind** ~**!** *(prov)* all good things/all disasters come in threes!; *(nach zwei mißglückten Versuchen)* third time lucky!; **sie sieht aus, als ob sie nicht bis** ~ **zählen könnte** *(col)* she looks pretty empty-headed; *siehe* **vier.**

Drei *f* **-en** three; *siehe* **Vier.**

Drei-D- [draɪˈdeː] *in cpds* 3-D.

dreidimensional *adj* three-dimensional.

Drei|eck nt **-e** triangle.

drei|eckig *adj* triangular.

Drei|ecks-: ~**tuch** nt triangular shawl; *(Med)* triangular bandage; ~**verhältnis** nt eternal triangle.

Drei|einigkeit *f* Trinity.

dreifach 1 *adj* triple. **die** ~**e Menge** three times or triple or treble the amount; **ein** ~**es Hoch!** three cheers! **2** *adv* three times. ~ **abgesichert** trebly secure; *siehe* **vierfach.**

Dreifache(s) *nt decl as adj* **das** ~ triple or treble the amount, three times as much; **etw um das** ~ **vermehren** to multiply sth by three.

Drei-: ~**fuß** m tripod; *(Schemel)* three-legged stool; ~**gangrad** nt three-speed bike; ~**gangschaltung** f three-speed gear; **d**~**hundert** num three hundred; ~**käsehoch** m **-s** *(col)* tiny tot *(col)*; ~**klang** m triad; ~**königstag** m feast of Epiphany; **d**~**mal** adv three times; *siehe* **viermal;** ~**meilenzone** f three-mile zone.

drein-: ~**blicken** vi sep traurig etc ~**blicken** to look sad etc; ~**reden** vi sep *(col)* *(dazwischenreden)* to interrupt; *(sich einmischen)* to interfere *(bei* in, with*)*; **ich lasse mir da von niemandem** ~**reden** I won't have anyone interfering (with this); ~**schauen** vi sep = ~**blicken.**

Drei-: **d**~**polig** *adj Kabel* three-core; *Steckdose, Stecker* three-pin; ~**rad** nt tricycle; ~**springer** m triple-jumper; ~**sprung** m triple jump, hop, step and jump.

dreißig num thirty; *siehe auch* **vierzig.**

dreißig- *in cpds siehe auch* **vierzig-;** ~**jährig** *adj* **der** ~ **jährige Krieg** the Thirty Years' War.

dreist *adj* bold, audacious.

Dreistigkeit *f* **(a)** *no pl* boldness, audacity. **(b)** *(Handlung)* bold or audacious act.

dreiteilig *adj Kostüm etc* three-piece *attr.*

dreiviertel [ˈdraɪˈfɪrtl] *siehe auch* **viertel 1** *adj* threequarter. **eine** ~ **Stunde** threequarters of an hour. **2** *adv* threequarters.

Dreiviertel-: **d**~**lang** *adj* threequarter-length; ~**literflasche** f three-quarter litre *(Brit)* or liter *(US)* bottle; ~**mehrheit** f threequarters majority; ~**stunde** f threequarters of an hour *no indef art;* ~**takt** m im ~ **takt** in three-four time.

Dreiweg- *in cpds (Elec)* three-way; ~**stecker** m three-way adapter.

drei-: ~**wöchentlich 1** *adj attr* three-weekly; **2** *adv* every three weeks; ~**wöchig** *adj attr* three-week; ~**zehn** *adj num* thirteen. **jetzt schlägt's aber** ~**zehn** *(col)* that's a bit much; *siehe* **vierzehn.**

Dresche *f no pl (col)* ~ **kriegen** to get a thrashing.

dreschen *pret* **drosch,** *ptp* **gedroschen 1** *vt* **(a)** *Korn* to thresh. **Skat** ~ *(col)* to play skat. **(b)** *(col: prügeln)* to thrash. **2** *vr (col: sich prügeln)* to have a fight.

Dresch-: ~**flegel** m flail; ~**maschine** f threshing machine.

Dreß m **-sse** *(Sport)* (sports) kit; *(für Fußball auch)* strip.

Dresseur [-ˈsøːɐ] m trainer.

dressieren *vt* **(a)** to train. **zu etw dressiert sein** to be trained *etc* to do sth. **(b)** *(Geflügel)* to dress.

Dressman [ˈdrɛsmən] m, pl **Dressmen** male model.

Dressur f training; *(für* ~*reiten)* dressage.

dribbeln vi to dribble. **mit dem Ball** ~ to dribble the ball.

Dribbling nt **-s** dribbling. **ein** ~ a piece of dribbling.

Drift *f* **-en** *(Naut)* drift.

driften vi *aux sein (Naut, fig)* to drift.

Drill m *no pl (Mil, fig)* drill; *(Sch auch)* drills *pl.*

drillen vti to drill. **auf etw** *(acc)* **gedrillt sein** *(fig col)* to be obsessed at doing sth.

Drilling m **(a)** triplet. **(b)** *(Jagdgewehr)* triple-barrelled shotgun.

drin *adv (col) siehe auch* **darin, drinnen** **(a)** in it. **er/es ist da** ~ he/it is in there; **in der Flasche ist noch etwas** ~ there's still something in the bottle. **(b)** *(col)* **bei ihm ist alles** ~ anything's possible with him; **bis jetzt ist noch alles** ~ everything is still quite open; **das ist doch nicht** ~ *(geht nicht)* that's not on *(col).*

dringen *pret* **drang,** *ptp* **gedrungen** vi **(a)** *aux sein (durch etw)* ~ to penetrate (sth); **an die Öffentlichkeit** ~ to leak or get out. **(b)** *(geh)* aux sein **in jdn** ~ to press or urge sb; **sich gedrungen fühlen, etw zu tun** to feel obliged to do sth. **(c)** **auf etw** *(acc)* ~ to insist on sth.

dringend *adj (eilig, wichtig)* urgent, pressing; *(nachdrücklich, zwingend)* strong; *Gründe* compelling. **ein** ~**er Fall** *(Med)* an emergency; ~ **verdächtig** strongly suspected; ~ **empfehlen** to recommend strongly.

dringlich *adj* urgent, pressing.

Dringlichkeit *f* urgency.

Dringlichkeits-: ~**antrag** m *(Parl)* emergency motion; ~**stufe** *f* priority; ~**stufe 1** top priority.

drinnen *adv* inside; *(im Haus auch)* indoors. **hier/dort** ~ in here/there; **ich gehe nach** ~ *(col)* I'm going in(side).

drinstecken vi sep *(col)* **da steckt eine Menge Geld/Arbeit etc drin** a lot of money/work etc has gone into it; **er steckt bis über die Ohren drin** he's up to his ears in it; **da steckt man nicht drin** you never can tell (what will happen).

dritt *adv* **wir kommen zu** ~ three of us are coming together.

dritt- *in cpds* third; ~**älteste(r, s)** *adj* third oldest.

Drittel nt - third; siehe **Viertel**[1].

drittens adv thirdly.

Dritte(r) mf decl as adj third person, third man/woman etc; (Unbeteiligter) third party. **in dieser Angelegenheit ist er der lachende ~** he comes off best from this; **im Beisein ~r** in the presence of a third party; siehe **Vierte(r)**.

dritte(r, s) adj third. **von ~r Seite** from a third party; siehe **vierte(r, s)**.

dritt-: ~**größte(r, s)** adj third-biggest; **d~klassig** adj third-rate (pej), third-class; **d~letzte(r, s)** adj third from last; **d~rangig** adj third-rate.

DRK ['deːˈɛrˈkaː] nt = Deutsches Rotes Kreuz.

droben adv (old, dial) up there.

Droge f -n drug.

Drogen-: **d~abhängig** adj addicted to drugs; ~**abhängige(r)** mf decl as adj drug addict; ~**abhängigkeit** f drug addiction no art; **d~süchtig** adj addicted to drugs; ~**süchtige(r)** mf decl as adj drug addict; ~**szene** f drug scene.

Drogerie f chemist's (Brit), drugstore (US).

Drogist(in f) m chemist (Brit), druggist (US).

Drohbrief m threatening letter.

drohen vi to threaten (jdm sb). **er droht mit Selbstmord** he threatens to commit suicide; **jdm droht etw** sb is being threatened by sth; **jdm droht Gefahr** sb is in danger; **es droht ein Streik** there is the threat of a strike; **das Schiff drohte zu sinken** the ship was in danger of sinking.

drohend adj threatening, menacing; (bevorstehend) Gefahr, Krieg imminent, impending.

Drohne f -n drone.

dröhnen vi to roar; (Donner) to rumble; (Musik, Stimme) to boom; (Raum etc) to resound, to echo. **mir dröhnt der Kopf** my head is ringing.

Drohung f threat.

drollig adj comical, droll; Kätzchen etc cute.

Dromedar [auch: 'droː-] nt -e dromedary.

Drops m or nt - fruit drop.

drosch pret of **dreschen**.

Droschke f -n (Pferde~) (hackney) cab, hackney-carriage; (dated: Taxi) (taxi-)cab.

Droschkenkutscher m cab driver.

Drossel f -n (Orn) thrush.

drosseln vt Motor etc to throttle; Heizung to turn down; Strom, Tempo, Produktion to cut down.

Drosselung f siehe vt throttling, turning down; cutting down.

drüben adv over there; (auf der anderen Seite, col: auf DDR/BRD bezogen) on the other side. **hier/dort** or **da ~** over here/there; **nach/von ~** over/from over there.

drüber adv (col) = **darüber**.

Druck[1] m -e (Phys, fig) pressure. **unter ~ stehen** (lit,fig) to be under pressure; **jdn unter ~ setzen** (fig) to put pressure on sb, to pressurize sb; **durch einen ~ auf den Knopf** by pressing the button.

Druck[2] m -e (a) (das Drucken) printing; (Art des Drucks, Schriftart) print; (Druckwerk) copy. **das Buch ist im ~** the book is being printed; **in ~ gehen** to go to press. (b) (Kunst~) print.

Druck-: ~**ausgleich** m pressure balance; ~**buchstabe** m printed character or letter; **in ~buchstaben schreiben** to print.

Drückeberger m - (pej col) shirker.

Drückebergerei f no pl (pej col) shirking.

druck|empfindlich adj sensitive (to pressure).

drucken vti (Typ, Tex) to print; siehe **gedruckt**.

drücken 1 vt (a) Hand, Hebel to press; Knopf auch to push. **jdm etw in die Hand ~** to press or slip sth into sb's hand; **jdn ~** to squeeze sb; (umarmen) to hug sb; **jdn zur Seite ~** to push sb aside. (b) (Schuhe, Korsett etc) to pinch, to nip. **mich drückt der Magen** my stomach feels heavy. (c) (verringern) Leistung, Niveau to lower. (d) (Gewichtheben) to press. **2** vi (a) to press; (Wetter, Hitze) to be oppressive; (Brille, Schuhe etc) to

pinch. auf die Stimmung ~ to dampen one's mood. (b) (drängeln, stoßen) to push. **3** vr (a) (sich quetschen) to squeeze. **sich aus dem Zimmer ~** to slip out of the room. (b) (col) (vor etw (dat) sth) to shirk; (vor Militärdienst) to dodge. **sich (um etw etw) ~** to get out of (doing) sth.

drückend adj Last, Steuern heavy; Sorgen serious; Armut grinding; Wetter, Hitze oppressive, close. **es ist ~ heiß** it's oppressively hot.

Drucker(in f) m - printer.

Drücker m - (Knopf) (push) button; (Türklinke) handle; (col: von Pistole etc) trigger. **am ~ sein** or **sitzen** (fig col) to be the key person; **auf den letzten ~** (fig col) at the last minute.

Druckerei f printing works pl, printery.

Drucker-: ~**presse** f printing press; ~**schwärze** f printer's ink.

Druck-: ~**fahne** f galley(-proof), proof; ~**fehler** m misprint; **d~fertig** adj ready to print; **d~fest** adj Werkstoff pressure-resistant; ~**knopf** m (Sew) press-stud (Brit), snap fastener (US); (Tech) push-button; ~**legung** f printing; ~**luft** f compressed air; ~**luftbremse** f air-brake; ~**mittel** nt (fig) form of pressure; ~**platte** f printing plate; ~**pumpe** f pressure pump; **d~reif** adj ready for printing, passed for press; (fig) polished; ~**sache** f printed matter; ~**schrift** f (a) (Schriftart) printing; **in ~schrift schreiben** to print; (b) (gedrucktes Werk) pamphlet.

drucksen vi (col) to hum and haw (col).

Druck-: ~**stelle** f (auf Obst, Haut) bruise; ~**taste** f pushbutton; ~**verband** m (Med) pressure bandage; ~**welle** f shock wave.

drum adv (col) siehe auch **darum** around. ~ (he)**rumreden** to beat about the bush; **da wirst du nicht ~ (he)rumkommen** there's no getting out of it; **sei's ~!** (geh) never mind; **das D~ und Dran** the paraphernalia; (Begleiterscheinungen) the fuss and bother; **mit allem D~ und Dran** with all the bits and pieces (col); (Mahlzeit) with all the trimmings.

Drumherum nt no pl trappings pl.

drunter adv siehe auch **darunter** under(neath). ~ **und drüber** upside down, topsyturvy.

Drüse f -n gland.

Drüsenfieber nt glandular fever.

Dschungel m - (lit, fig) jungle.

Dschungel-: ~**fieber** nt yellow fever; ~**krieg** m jungle war/warfare.

Dschunke f (Naut) -n junk.

dt. = deutsch.

du pers pron (familiar form of address) you. **D~** (in Briefen) you; **jdn mit ~ anreden** to say "du" (to sb); **mit jdm auf ~ und ~ stehen** to be pals with sb; **mit jdm per ~ sein** to be on familiar terms with sb; **~ bist es** it's you; **~, ich muß jetzt aber gehen** listen, I have to go now; **~, ~, ~!** (hum: drohend) naughty, naughty.

Du nt -(s) **jdm das ~ anbieten** to suggest that sb uses "du" or the familiar form of address.

Dualsystem nt (Math) binary system.

Dübel m - plug; (Holz~) dowel.

dübeln vti to plug.

dubios adj (geh) dubious.

Dublette f (a) duplicate. (b) (Boxen) one-two.

ducken 1 vt to duck; (fig pej) to cringe, to cower. **sich in eine Ecke ~** to duck or dodge into a corner; **sich geduckt.** **2** vi (fig pej) to cower.

Duckmäuser m - (pej) toady.

Duckmäusertum nt (pej) toadying.

dudeln vti (col) to tootle. **das Radio dudelt schon den ganzen Tag** the (damn) radio's been playing all day.

Dudelsack m bagpipes pl.

Dudelsack-: ~**pfeifer**, ~**spieler** m (bag)piper.

Duell nt -e (lit, fig) duel (um over).

Duellant [due'lant] m (wk) dueller, duellist.

duellieren* [due'liːrən] vr to (fight a) duel.

Duett *nt* -**e** (**a**) (*Mus, fig*) duet. **etw im** ~ **singen** to sing sth as a duet. (**b**) (*fig col: Paar*) duo (*col*).

Duft *m* ⁼**e** (pleasant) smell, scent; (*von Blumen, Parfüm auch*) fragrance; (*von Essen*) smell, aroma.

duftе *adj, adv* (*dated col*) great (*col*).

duften *vi* to smell (*nach of*). **das duftet** that smells nice.

duftend *adj attr* nice-smelling; *Parfüm, Blumen etc* fragrant.

duftig *adj Kleid, Stoff* light, gossamery.

Duft-: ~**marke** *f* scent mark; ~**note** *f* (*von Parfüm*) scent; ~**stoff** *m* scent; (*für Parfüm, Waschmittel etc*) fragrance; ~**wasser** *nt, pl* ~**wässer** toilet water; ~**wolke** *f* (*iro*) cloud of perfume.

dulden *vt* (**a**) (*zulassen*) to tolerate. **etw still-schweigend** ~ to connive at sth; **er ist hier nur geduldet** he's only here on sufferance. (**b**) (*geh: erdulden*) to suffer.

duldsam *adj* tolerant (*gegenüber of, jdm gegenüber towards sb*).

Duldsamkeit *f* tolerance.

Duldung *f* toleration. **mit stillschweigender** ~ **der Behörden** with the (tacit) connivance of the authorities.

dumm *adj comp* ⁼**er**, *superl* ⁼**ste(r, s)** *or* (*adv*) **am** ⁼**sten** (**a**) stupid dumb (*esp US*); *Mensch auch* thick (*col*); (*unklug, unvernünftig auch*) silly, foolish. **der** ~**e August** (*col*) the clown; ~**e Gans** silly goose; ~**es Zeug** (**reden**) (to talk) nonsense *or* rubbish; **ein** ~**es Gesicht machen**, ~ **gucken** to look stupid; **jdn wie einen** ~**en Jungen behandeln** (*col*) to treat sb like a child; **du willst mich wohl für** ~ **verkaufen** you must think I'm stupid; **ich lasse mich nicht für** ~ **verkaufen** I'm not so stupid (*col*); **sich** ~ **stellen** to act stupid; ~ **fragen** to ask a silly question/silly questions; ~ **dastehen** to look stupid; **der D**~ **sein** to be left to carry the can (*col*); **sich** ~ **und dämlich reden** (*col*) to talk till one is blue in the face (*col*); **sich** ~ **und dämlich verdienen** to earn the earth (*col*); **jetzt wird's mir zu** ~ I've had enough.

(**b**) (*ärgerlich*) annoying; *Gefühl* nasty; *Sache, Geschichte auch* silly. **es ist zu** ~, **daß er nicht kommen kann** it's too bad that he can't come; **so etwas D**~**es** how stupid; (*wie ärgerlich*) what a nuisance.

dummdreist *adj* insolent.

Dummejungenstreich *m* silly *or* childish prank.

dummerweise *adv* unfortunately.

Dummheit *f* (**a**) *no pl* stupidity; (*Unvernunft*) foolishness. (**b**) (*dumme Handlung*) stupid thing.

Dummkopf *m* (*col*) idiot, fool.

dümmlich *adj* silly, stupid.

dumpf *adj* (**a**) *Geräusch, Ton* muffled. ~ **aufprallen** to land with a thud. (**b**) *Geruch, Geschmack etc* musty; (*fig*) *Atmosphäre* stifling. (**c**) *Gefühl, Ahnung* vague; *Schmerz* dull.

Dumpingpreis ['dampɪŋ-] *m* give-away price.

Düne *f* -**n** (sand-)dune.

Dung *m no pl* dung, manure.

Düngemittel *nt* fertilizer.

düngen 1 *vt* to fertilize. 2 *vi* **im Garten** ~ to put fertilizer on the garden.

Dünger *m* - fertilizer.

dunkel *adj* (**a**) dark. **im D**~**n** in the dark; **im Zimmer** ~ **machen** (*col*) to darken the room; **sich** ~ **kleiden** to dress in dark colours. (**b**) (*tief*) *Stimme, Ton* deep. (**c**) (*unbestimmt, unklar*) vague. **in dunkler Vorzeit** in the dim and distant past; **im** ~**n tappen** (*fig*) to be in the dark. (**d**) (*pej: zwielichtig*) shady (*col*), dubious.

Dunkel *nt no pl* (*lig, fig*) darkness. **im** ~ **der Nacht** at dead of night.

Dünkel *m no pl* (*pej geh*) conceit, arrogance.

dunkel- *in cpds* dark; ~**blond** *adj* light brown; ~**haarig** *adj* dark-haired.

dünkelhaft *adj* (*pej geh*) arrogant, conceited.

Dunkel-: **d**~**häutig** *adj* dark-skinned; ~**heit** *f* (*lit, fig*) darkness; **bei Einbruch der** ~**heit** at nightfall; ~**kammer** *f* (*Phot*) darkroom; ~**mann** *m, pl* ~**männer** (*pej*) shady character.

dunkeln *vi impers* **es dunkelt** (*geh*) darkness is falling, it is growing dark.

Dunkel-: **d**~**rot** *adj* dark red, maroon; ~**ziffer** *f* estimated number of unreported/undetected cases.

dünken *vti impers* (*old, geh*) **das dünkt mir gut zu sein** it seems good to me.

dünn *adj* thin; *Kaffee, Tee* watery, weak; (*fein*) *Schleier, Strümpfe* fine; *Besiedlung auch* sparse. ~ **gesät** (*fig*) few and far between; **sich** ~ **machen** (*hum*) to breathe in; *siehe* **dünnmachen**.

Dünn-: **d**~**besiedelt** *adj attr* sparsely populated; ~**darm** *m* small intestine; **d**~**flüssig** *adj* thin; *Teig* runny; **d**~**gesät** *adj attr* sparse; **d**~**häutig** *adj* (*lit, fig*) thin-skinned; **d**~**machen** *vr sep* (*col*) to make oneself scarce; ~**pfiff** (*col*), ~**schiß** (*col*) *m* the runs (*col*).

Dunst *m* ⁼**e** mist, haze; (*Dampf*) steam; (*Smog*) smog; (*Zigaretten*) ~ fug; (*Geruch*) smell. **jdm blauen** ~ **vormachen** (*col*) to tell sb stories (*col*).

Dunst|abzugshaube *f* extractor hood.

dünsten *vt* (*Cook*) to steam; *Obst* to stew.

Dunstglocke *f* haze; pall of smog.

dunstig *adj* hazy, misty; (*verräuchert*) smoky.

Dunst-: ~**kreis** *m* atmosphere; (*von Mensch*) society; ~**schleier** *m* veil of mist; ~**wolke** *f* cloud of smog.

Dünung *f* (*Naut*) swell.

Duo *nt* -**s** duo.

Duplikat *nt* duplicate (copy).

Dur *nt no pl* (*Mus*) major. **in G-**~ in G major.

durch 1 *prep*+*acc* (**a**) through. ~ **den Fluß waten** to wade across the river; ~ **die ganze Welt reisen** to travel all over the world. (**b**) (*mittels*) through, by (means of); (*in Passivkonstruktion: von*) by. **Tod** ~ **den Strang** death by hanging; **Tod** ~ **Herzschlag** death from a heart attack; ~ **die Post** by post; **etw** ~ **die Zeitung bekanntgeben** to announce sth in the press; **er ist** ~ **das Fernsehen bekannt geworden** he became famous through television. (**c**) (*aufgrund, infolge von*) due to, owing to.

2 *adv* (**a**) (*hin*~) through. **die ganze Nacht** ~ all through the night, throughout the night; **es ist 4 Uhr** ~ it's past 4 o'clock; ~ **und** ~ **kennen** through and through; *verlogen, überzeugt* completely, utterly; ~ **und** ~ **naß** wet through; **das geht mir** ~ **und** ~ that goes right through me. (**b**) (*Cook col*) (**gut**) ~ well-done. **das Fleisch ist noch nicht** ~ the meat isn't done yet.

durch|ackern *sep* (*col*) *vtr* to plough through (*durch etw sth*).

durch|arbeiten *sep* 1 *vti* to work through. 2 *vr* **sich durch etw** ~ to work (one's way) through sth.

durch|atmen *vi sep* to breathe deeply.

durch|aus *adv* (*emph auch* **durch|aus**) (**a**) (*unbedingt*) **wenn du das** ~ **willst** if you insist, if you absolutely must; **das ist** ~ **nötig** that is absolutely necessary; **er will** ~ **recht haben** he (absolutely) insists that he is right. (**b**) (*bekräftigend*) quite; *verständlich, richtig, möglich auch* perfectly; *gefallen* really. **das läßt sich** ~ **machen** that sounds feasible; **ich bin** ~ **Ihrer Meinung** I quite *or* absolutely agree with you; **es ist** ~ **anzunehmen, daß sie kommt** it's highly likely that she'll be coming. (**c**) (*in verneinten Sätzen*) ~ **nicht** (*als Verstärkung*) by no means; (*als Antwort*) not at all; (*stärker*) absolutely not; **etw** ~ **nicht tun wollen** to refuse absolutely to do sth; **das ist** ~ **kein Witz** that's no joke at all; **er ist** ~ **kein schlechter Mensch** he is by no means a bad person.

durchbacken *vt sep Kuchen* to bake through.

durchbeißen *sep irreg* 1 *vt* to bite through. 2 *vr*

(col) to struggle through *(durch etw sth).*

durchblättern *vt sep Buch* to leaf through.

Durchblick *m* vista *(auf+acc* of*); (Ausblick)* view *(auf+acc* of*).* **den ~ haben** *(fig col)* to know what's what *(col).*

durchblicken *vi sep* **(a)** *(lit)* to look through *(durch etw sth).* **(b)** *(fig)* **etw ~ lassen** to hint at sth. **(c)** *(col: verstehen)* to understand. **blickst du da durch?** do you get it? *(col).*

Durchblutung *f* circulation (of blood) *(gen* to*).*

durchbohren[1]* *vt insep* to drill through; *(mit Schwert)* to run through; *(Kugel)* to go through. **jdn mit Blicken ~** *(fig)* to look piercingly at sb.

durchbohren[2] *sep* **1** *vt* **etw durch etw ~** *Loch, Tunnel* to drill sth through sth. **2** *vr* to bore (one's way) through *(durch etw sth).*

durchbohrend *adj* piercing.

durchboxen *vr sep (fig col)* to fight (one's way) through *(durch etw sth).*

durchbraten *vti sep irreg* to cook through. **durchgebraten** well done.

durchbrechen[1] *sep irreg* **1** *vt* to break (in two). **2** *vi aux sein* **(a)** *(in zwei Teile)* to break (in two). **(b)** *(Knospen)* to appear; *(Sonne auch)* to break through *(durch etw sth).*

durchbrechen[2]* *vt insep irreg* to break; *Mauer, Blockade etc* to break through.

durchbrennen *vi sep irreg aux sein (Sicherung etc)* to blow; *(col: davonlaufen)* to run away. **jdm ~** *(col)* to run away from sb.

durchbringen *vt sep irreg* **(a)** *(durch etw sth)* to get through; *(durch Krankheit)* to pull through; *(für Unterhalt sorgen)* to provide for. **(b)** *Geld* to get through.

Durchbruch *m* **(a)** *(Mil, fig)* breakthrough. **jdm/ etw zum ~ verhelfen** to help sb/sth on the road to success. **(b)** *(von Sonne)* breaking through *(durch etw sth); (von Charakter)* revelation. **zum ~ kommen** *(fig)* to show itself.

durchdenken* *vt irreg insep* to think out *or* through. **gut durchdacht** well thought out.

durchdrehen *sep* **1** *vt Fleisch etc* to mince. **2** *vi* **(a)** *(Aut: Räder)* to spin. **(b)** *(col)* to go mad; *(nervlich)* to crack up *(col).* **ganz durchgedreht sein** *(col)* to be really uptight *(col)* or *(verwirrt)* confused.

durchdringen[1] *vi sep irreg aux sein* **(a)** to penetrate *(durch etw sth); (Sonne)* to come through *(durch etw sth).* **bis zu jdm ~** *(fig)* to get as far as sb. **(b)** *(sich verständlich machen)* **zu jdm ~** to get through to sb.

durchdringen[2]* *vt insep irreg Materie, Dunkelheit etc* to penetrate; *siehe* **durchdrungen.**

durchdringend *adj* piercing; *Kälte, Wind auch* biting; *Geruch* pungent.

durchdrücken *vt sep* **(a)** *(durch Presse)* to press through; *Creme, Teig* to pipe. **(b)** *(fig) Gesetz, Reformen etc* to push through; *seinen Willen* to get. **(c)** *Knie, Kreuz etc* to straighten.

durchdrungen *adj pred ~* imbued *(von* with*).* **ganz von einer Idee ~ sein** to be taken with an idea.

durch|einander **1** *adv* muddled up, in a muddle. **alles ~ essen/trinken** to eat/drink indiscriminately. **2** *adj pred ~* **sein** *(col) (Mensch)* to be confused *or (aufgeregt)* in a state *(col); (Zimmer etc)* to be in a mess *or* muddle.

Durch|einander *nt no pl (Unordnung)* mess, muddle; *(Wirrwarr)* confusion.

durch|einander-: **~bringen** *vt sep irreg* to muddle *or* mix up; *(verwirren) jdn* to confuse; **~geraten***, **~kommen** *vi sep aux sein* to get mixed *or* muddled up; **~reden** *vi sep* to all talk at once; **~werfen** *vt sep irreg* to muddle up.

durchfahren[1] *vi sep irreg aux sein* **(a)** to go through *(durch etw sth).* **(b)** *(nicht anhalten/ umsteigen)* to go straight through. **er ist bei Rot durchgefahren** he jumped the lights; **die Nacht ~** to travel through the night.

durchfahren[2]* *vt insep irreg* to travel through;

(fig: Schreck etc) to shoot through. **ein Gedanke durchfuhr ihn blitzartig** a (sudden) thought flashed through his mind.

Durchfahrt *f* way through. **auf der ~ sein** to be passing through; **~ bitte freihalten!** please keep access free; **~verboten!** no through road.

Durchfahrts-: **~straße** *f* through road; **~verbot** *nt* **seit wann besteht hier ~verbot?** since when has this been a no through road?

Durchfall *m* **(a)** *(Med)* diarrhoea *no art (Brit),* diarrhea *no art (US).* **(b)** *(Mißerfolg)* failure.

durchfallen *vi sep irreg aux sein* **(a)** to fall through *(durch etw sth).* **(b)** *(col: nicht bestehen)* to fail; *(Theaterstück auch)* to flop; *(Wahlkandidat)* to be defeated. **jdn ~ lassen** to fail sb; **beim Publikum ~** to be a flop with the public.

durchfeiern *vi sep* to celebrate all night.

durchfinden *vir sep irreg (lit, fig)* to find one's way through *(durch etw sth).* **ich finde (mich) hier nicht mehr durch** *(fig)* I am simply lost.

durchfliegen[1] *vi sep irreg aux sein* **(a)** to fly through *(durch etw sth); (ohne Landung)* to fly non-stop *or* direct. **(b)** *(col: in Prüfung)* to fail *(durch etw, in etw (dat)* sth*).*

durchfliegen[2]* *vt insep irreg Luft, Wolken* to fly through; *Land* to fly over; *Strecke* to cover; *(flüchtig lesen)* to skim through.

durchfließen* *vt insep irreg (lit, fig)* to flow through.

Durchflug *m* flight through. **Passagiere auf dem ~** transit passengers.

durchfluten* *vt insep (geh: Fluß)* to flow through; *(fig: Licht, Sonne)* to flood.

durchforschen* *vt insep Gegend* to search; *Land, Fachgebiet* to explore; *Akten* to search through.

durchforsten* *vt insep (fig) Akten* to go through.

durchfragen *vr sep* to ask one's way.

durchfressen *vr sep irreg (durch etw sth) (Säure etc, Tier)* to eat (its way) through. **sich (bei jdm) ~** *(pej col)* to live off sb.

durchfroren *adj* frozen stiff.

Durchfuhr *f* transit.

durchführbar *adj* practicable, feasible.

Durchführbarkeit *f* feasibility, practicability.

durchführen *sep* **1** *vt* **(a)** *(durchleiten) (durch etw sth) jdn* to take through; *Leitung* to run through. **(b)** *(verwirklichen)* to carry out; *Gesetz* to implement; *(unternehmen) Expedition* to undertake; *Messung* to take; *Kursus* to run; *Wahl, Prüfung* to hold. **2** *vi* **zwischen/unter etw** *(dat)* **~** *(Straße etc)* to go between/under sth.

Durchführung *f siehe* **vt** **(a)** taking through; running through. **(b)** carrying out; implementation; undertaking; taking; running; holding.

durchfüttern *vt sep (col)* to feed. **sich von jdm ~ lassen** to live off sb.

Durchgabe *f* announcement; *(telefonisch)* message (over the telephone).

Durchgang *m* **(a)** passage. **(b)** *(das Durchgehen)* **~ verboten!** no right of way; **beim ~ durch das Tal** going through the valley. **(c)** *(von Wahl, Sport)* round; *(beim Rennen)* heat.

durchgängig *adj* universal, general.

Durchgangs-: **~lager** *nt* transit camp; **~stadium** *nt* transition stage; **~straße** *f* through road; **~verkehr** *m* through traffic; *(Transitverkehr)* transit traffic.

durchgeben *vt sep irreg (Rad, TV) Hinweis, Wetter* to give; *Nachricht, Lottozahlen* to announce. **jdm etw telefonisch ~** to telephone sth to sb; **es wurde im Radio durchgegeben** it was announced on the radio.

durchgefroren *adj Mensch* frozen stiff.

durchgehen *sep irreg aux sein* **1** *vi* **(a)** to go through *(durch etw sth).* **(b)** *(toleriert werden)* **jdm etw ~ lassen** to let sb get away with sth; **das lasse ich nochmal ~** I'll let it pass. **(c)** *(gehalten werden für)* **für etw ~** to pass for sth, to be taken for sth. **(d)** *(ohne Unterbrechung)* to go straight through; *(Flug, Zug)* to be direct. **(e)** *(Pferd)* to bolt. **seine Frau ist ihm durchgegangen** his wife has run off and left him; **mit etw ~** to run or make off with sth. **(f)** *(außer Kontrolle geraten)* **mit jdm ~** *(Nerven etc)* to get the better of sb. **2** *vt (durchsprechen etc)* to go or run through.

durchgehend 1 *adj Öffnungszeiten* round-the-clock *attr*, continuous; *Straße* straight; *Verkehrsverbindung* direct; *Zug, Fahrkarte* through *attr*. **2** *adv* throughout, right through. **~ geöffnet** open right through; open 24 hours.

durchgeschwitzt *adj* soaked in sweat.

durchgreifen *vi sep irreg* to reach through *(durch etw sth)*; *(fig)* to take (strong) action.

durchgucken *vi sep (Mensch)* to look through *(durch etw sth)*.

durchhaben *vt sep irreg (col)* **etw ~** to have got sth through *(durch etw sth)*; *(durchgelesen etc haben)* to have got through sth.

durchhalten *sep irreg* **1** *vt Zeit, Kampf etc* to survive; *Streik* to see through; *Belastung* to stand; *(Sport) Tempo* to keep up. **das Rennen ~** to stay the course. **2** *vi* to hold out.

Durchhalte-: **~parole** *f* rallying call; **~vermögen** *nt* staying power.

durchhängen *vi sep irreg (lit, fig)* to sag.

durchhauen *vt sep* to chop in two; *(spalten)* to split. **jdn ~** *(col)* to give sb a walloping *(col)*.

durchhelfen *vi sep irreg* **jdm (durch etw) ~** to help sb through *(sth)*.

durchhungern *vr sep* to scrape by.

durchkämmen *sep*, **durchkämmen*** *insep vt (absuchen)* to comb (through).

durchkämpfen *sep* **1** *vt* to push through. **2** *vr* to battle one's way through *(durch etw sth)*.

durchkauen *vt sep Essen* to chew (thoroughly); *(col: besprechen)* to go over or through.

durchklingen *vi sep irreg aux haben or sein (durch etw sth)* to sound through; *(fig)* to come through. **etw ~ lassen** to hint at sth.

durchkommen *vi sep irreg aux sein (durch etw sth)* to come through; *(durchgelangen, telefonisch, in Prüfung)* to get through; *(Patient)* to pull through; *(finanziell)* to get by; *(im Radio)* to be announced. **mit etw ~** *(mit Forderungen)* to succeed with sth; *(mit Betrug)* to get away with sth; **er kam mit seiner Stimme nicht durch** he couldn't make his voice heard; **damit kommt er bei mir nicht durch** he won't get away with that with me.

durchkreuzen* *vt insep* **(a)** *Wüste, Ozean* to cross. **(b)** *(fig) Pläne etc* to thwart.

durchladen *vi sep irreg Gewehr* to reload.

Durchlaß *m*, *pl* **Durchlässe** *(Durchgang)* passage, way through; *(für Wasser)* duct.

durchlassen *vt sep irreg (durch etw sth)* to let through; *(eindringen lassen)* to let in.

durchlässig *adj Material* permeable; *Zelt, Schuh* leaky; *Grenze* open. **eine ~e Stelle** *(lit, fig)* a leak.

Durchlaucht *f* **-en** **(Euer) ~** Your Highness.

Durchlauf *m* **(a)** *(das Durchlaufen)* flow. **(b)** *(Comp)* run. **(c)** *(Sport)* heat.

durchlaufen[1] *sep irreg* **1** *vt Schuhe* to go through, to wear out. **2** *vi aux sein (durch etw sth)* to go through; *(Flüssigkeit auch)* to run through.

durchlaufen[2]* *vt insep irreg Gebiet* to run through; *Strecke* to cover, to run; *(Astron) Bahn* to describe; *Schule, Phase* to go through.

Durchlauf-: **~erhitzer** *m* - continuous-flow water heater; **~zeit** *f (Comp)* length of a/the run.

durchleben* *vt insep* to experience; *Jugend* to have.

durchlesen *vt sep irreg* to read through. **sich** *(dat)* **etw ~** to read sth through.

durchleuchten* *vt insep* to X-ray; *(fig) Sache* to investigate. **sich ~ lassen** to have an X-ray.

Durchleuchtung *f (Med)* X-ray examination; *(fig: von Angelegenheit etc)* investigation.

durchlöchern* *vt insep* to make holes in; *(fig)* to undermine completely. **(mit Schüssen) ~** to riddle with bullets.

durchlüften *vti sep* to air thoroughly.

durchmachen *sep* **1** *vt (erdulden, durchlaufen)* to go through; *Krankheit* to have; *Lehre* to serve; *(fig) Entwicklung* to undergo. **er hat viel durchgemacht** he has been or gone through a lot; **eine ganze Nacht ~** *(col: durchfeiern)* to make a night of it. **2** *vi (col) (durcharbeiten)* to work right through; *(durchfeiern)* to keep going all night/day etc.

Durchmarsch *m* **der ~ durch die Stadt** the march through the town.

durchmarschieren* *vi sep aux sein* to march through *(durch etw sth)*.

Durchmesser *m* - diameter. **120 cm im ~** 120 cm in diameter.

durchmischen *vt sep* to mix thoroughly.

durchmüssen *vi sep irreg (col) (durch etw sth)* to have to get through; *(durch Unangenehmes)* to have to go through with.

durchnässen* *vt insep* to soak, to drench. **völlig durchnäßt** wet through, drenched.

durchnehmen *vt sep irreg (Sch)* to do.

durchnumerieren* *vt sep* to number consecutively.

durch|organisieren* *vt sep* to organize down to the last detail.

durchpauken *vt sep (col)* **(a)** *Lernstoff* to swot up *(col)*. **(b)** *Gesetz, Schüler* to push through.

durchpausen *vt sep* to trace.

durchpeitschen *vt sep* to flog; *(fig)* to rush through.

durchpressen *vt sep* to press through.

durchprügeln *vt sep* to thrash, to beat.

durchqueren* *vt insep* to cross.

durchrasen *vi sep aux sein*, **durchrasen*** *vt insep* to race or tear through.

durchrechnen *vt sep* to calculate.

durchregnen *vi sep impers* **es regnet durchs Dach** *durch* the rain is coming through the roof; **es hat die Nacht durchgeregnet** it rained all through the night.

Durchreiche *f* **-n** *(serving)* hatch *(Brit)*, pass-through *(US)*.

durchreichen *vt sep* to pass through *(durch etw sth)*.

Durchreise *f* journey through. **auf der ~ sein** to be passing through.

durchreisen *vi sep aux sein*, **durchreisen*** *vt insep* to travel through.

Durchreisende(r) *mf decl as adj* traveller (passing through), transient *(US)*.

Durchreisevisum *nt* transit visa.

durchreißen *vti sep irreg (vi: aux sein)* to tear in two.

durchringen *vr sep irreg* **sich dazu ~, etw zu tun** to bring or force oneself to do sth.

durchrosten *vi sep aux sein* to rust through.

durchrufen *vi sep irreg (col)* to ring *(bei jdm sb)*.

durchrutschen *vi sep aux sein (lit)* to slip through *(durch etw sth)*.

durchs = **durch das**.

Durchsage *f* announcement. **eine ~ der Polizei** a police announcement.

durchsagen *vt sep* = **durchgeben**.

durchsägen *vt sep* to saw through.

durchsausen *vi sep aux sein (col)* **(a)** to rush through. **(b)** *(col: nicht bestehen)* to fail, to flunk *(col) (durch etw, in etw (dat)* (in) sth).

durchschaubar *adj (fig) Plan, Ereignisse* clear; *Lüge* transparent. **eine leicht ~e Lüge** a lie that is easy to see through; **schwer ~er Charakter** inscrutable character.

durchschauen[1]* *vt insep (begreifen)* to understand. **du bist durchschaut!** you've been found out.

durchschauen² *vti sep* = **durchsehen**.
durchscheinen *vi sep irreg (durch etw* sth) *(lit, fig)* to shine through; *(Farbe)* to show through.
durchscheinend *adj* transparent.
durchscheuern *vt sep* to wear through. **sich** *(dat)* **die Haut** ~ to graze one's skin.
durchschieben *vt sep irreg* to push *or* shove *(col)* through *(durch etw* sth).
durchschießen¹ *vi sep irreg* **durch etw** ~ to shoot through sth.
durchschießen²* *vt insep irreg (lit, fig)* to shoot through. **ein Gedanke durchschoß mich** a thought flashed through my mind.
durchschimmern *vi sep (durch etw* sth) to shimmer through; *(Farbe, fig)* to show through.
durchschlafen *vi sep irreg* to sleep through.
Durchschlag *m* **(a)** *(Kopie)* carbon (copy). **(b)** *(Küchengerät)* sieve, strainer.
durchschlagen¹ *sep irreg* **1** *vt* **etw** ~ *(entzweischlagen)* to chop through sth; *(Cook)* to sieve sth. **2** *vi* **(a)** *aux sein (durchkommen) (durch etw* sth) to come through; *(fig: Charakter, Eigenschaft)* to show through. **bei ihm schlägt der Vater durch** you can see his father in him. **(b)** *aux sein (Wirkung haben)* to catch on. **auf etw** *(acc)* ~ to make one's/its mark on sth; **auf jdn** ~ to rub off on sb. **(c)** *aux sein (Sicherung)* to blow, to go. **3** *vr* to fight through; *(im Leben)* to struggle through *or* along.
durchschlagen²* *vt insep irreg* to blast a hole in.
durchschlagend *adj* Sieg sweeping; *Erfolg* tremendous; *Beweis* decisive, conclusive. **eine** ~**e Wirkung haben** to be totally effective.
Durchschlagpapier *nt* flimsy; *(Kohlepapier)* carbon paper.
Durchschlagskraft *f (von Geschoß)* penetration; *(fig: von Argument)* decisiveness.
durchschlängeln *vr sep (durch etw* sth) *(Fluß)* to wind (its way) through, to meander through; *(Mensch)* to thread one's way through; *(fig)* to manoeuvre *(Brit) or* maneuver *(US)* one's way through.
durchschleusen *vt sep* **(a)** ein Schiff ~ to pass a ship through a lock. **(b)** *(fig: durch schmale Stelle)* to guide through *(durch etw* sth).
durchschlüpfen *vi sep aux sein* to slip through *(durch etw* sth).
durchschmecken *vt sep* to taste. **man kann den Essig** ~ the taste of vinegar comes through.
durchschneiden¹ *vt sep irreg* to cut in two.
durchschneiden²* *vt insep irreg* to cut through; *(Schiff)* Wellen to plough through. **jdm die Kehle** ~ to cut *or* slit sb's throat.
Durchschnitt *m* average; *(in Statistik)* mean. **der** ~ *(normale Menschen)* the average person; *(die Mehrheit)* the majority; **im** ~ on average; **im** ~ **100 km/h fahren** to average 100 kmph; **über/unter dem** ~ above/below average; **guter** ~ **sein** to be a good average.
durchschnittlich 1 *adj* average; *Wert auch* mean *attr.* **2** *adv (im Durchschnitt)* verdienen, essen etc on average. ~ **begabt/groß** of average ability/height; **die Mannschaft hat sehr** ~ **gespielt** the team played a very average game.
Durchschnitts- *in cpds* average; ~**alter** *nt* average age; ~**gesicht** *nt* ordinary *or* nondescript *(pej)* face; ~**mensch** *m* average person; ~**wert** *m* average *or* mean *(Math)* value.
durchschreiben *vt sep irreg* to make a (carbon) copy of.
durchschreiten* *vt insep irreg (geh)* to stride through.
Durchschrift *f* (carbon) copy.
Durchschuß *m (Loch)* bullet hole. **ein** ~ **durch den Darm** a gunshot wound right through the intestine.
durchschütteln *vt sep Mischung* to shake thoroughly; *(in Auto, Bus etc)* jdn to shake about.
durchschwimmen *vi sep irreg aux sein,* **durch-**

schwimmen* *vt insep irreg* to swim through.
durchschwitzen *vt sep* to soak with sweat.
durchsegeln¹ *vi sep aux sein* **(a)** *(Schiff)* to sail through *(durch etw* sth). **(b)** *(col: nicht bestehen)* to fail, to flunk *(col) (durch etw, bei etw* sth).
durchsegeln²* *vt insep Meer* to sail across.
durchsehen *sep irreg* **1** *vi* **(a)** *(hindurchschauen)* to look through *(durch etw* sth). **ein Stoff, durch den man** ~ **kann** see-through material. **(b)** *(col: verstehen)* = **durchblicken (c)**. **2** *vt (überprüfen)* etw ~ to have a look through sth *(auf +acc for)*.
durchsein *vi sep irreg aux sein (col)* to be through *(durch etw* sth); *(vorbeigekommen sein)* to have gone; *(Cook: Steak, Gemüse)* to be done.
durchsetzen¹ *sep* **1** *vt Maßnahmen* to put through; *Forderung* to push through; *Vorschlag, Plan* to carry through; *Ziel* to achieve. **etw bei jdm** ~ to get sb to agree to sth; **seinen Willen (bei jdm)** ~ to get one's (own) way (with sb). **2** *vr* **(a)** *(Mensch)* to assert oneself *(bei jdm with* sb); *(Partei etc)* to be successful. **sich gegen etw** ~ to win through against sth; **sich mit etw** ~ to be successful with sth; **sich im Leben** ~ to make a success of one's life. **(b)** *(Idee, Neuheit)* to be accepted, to catch on.
durchsetzen²* *vt insep* **mit etw durchsetzt** interspersed with sth; **mit subversiven Elementen durchsetzt** infiltrated by subversive elements.
Durchsetzung *f siehe* **durchsetzen**¹ **1** putting through; pushing through; carrying through; achievement.
Durchsicht *f* examination, inspection. **jdm etw zur** ~ **geben** to give sb sth to check through; **bei** ~ **der Bücher** on checking the books.
durchsichtig *adj (lit, fig)* transparent.
Durchsichtigkeit *f no pl (lit, fig)* transparency.
durchsickern *vi sep aux sein (lit, fig)* to trickle through; *(fig: trotz Geheimhaltung)* to leak out. **Informationen** ~ **lassen** to leak information.
durchsieben¹ *vt sep* to sieve, to sift; *(fig) Bewerber etc* to sift through.
durchsieben²* *vt insep (col)* **von Kugeln durchsiebt** riddled with bullets.
durchsitzen *sep irreg vt Sessel etc* to wear out (the seat of).
durchspielen *vt sep* to go *or* run through.
durchsprechen *vt sep irreg* Problem, Möglichkeiten to talk over *or* through.
durchspülen *vt sep* to rinse (out) thoroughly.
durchstarten *vt sep (Aviat)* to overshoot; *(Aut)* to accelerate off again; *(beim Anfahren)* to rev up.
durchstechen¹ *sep irreg* **1** *vt Nadel, Spieß* to stick through *(durch etw* sth). **2** *vi* to pierce.
durchstechen²* *vt insep irreg* to pierce; *(mit Degen etc)* to run through; *(mit Nadel)* to prick.
durchstecken *vt sep* to put *or* stick *(col)* through *(durch etw* sth).
durchstehen *vt sep irreg Zeit, Prüfung, Situation* to get through; *Krankheit* to get over; *Tempo, Qualen* to stand; *Abenteuer* to have.
Durchstehvermögen *nt* staying power.
durchsteigen *vi sep irreg aux sein* **(a)** to climb through *(durch etw* sth). **(b)** *(col: verstehen)* = **durchblicken (c)**.
durchstellen *vt sep (Telec)* to put through. **ich stelle durch** I'll put you through.
durchstöbern* *insep,* **durchstöbern** *sep vt* to hunt *or* rummage through *(nach for)*; *(durchwühlen)* to ransack *(nach looking for)*.
Durchstoß *m* breakthrough.
durchstoßen¹* *vt insep irreg* to break through.
durchstoßen² *vti sep irreg (vi: aux sein)* to break through *(auch Mil)*. **etw (durch etw)** ~ to push sth through (sth).
durchstreichen *vt sep irreg* to cross out.
durchstreifen* *vt insep irreg* to roam through.
durchströmen* *vt insep (lit, fig)* to flow through.
durchsuchen* *vt insep (nach for)* to search

(through); jdn to search, to frisk.
Durchsuchung f search *(auf+dat* for*)*.
Durchsuchungsbefehl m search warrant.
durchtrainieren* vt sep *Sportler, Körper* to get fit. **(gut) durchtrainiert** in superb condition.
durchtränken* vt insep to soak, to saturate.
durchtrennen sep, **durchtrennen*** insep vt *(schneiden)* to cut *(through)*; *Nerv, Sehne* to sever.
durchtreten sep irreg 1 vt **(a)** *Pedal* to step on; *Starter* to kick. **(b)** *(abnutzen) Schuh, Sohle* to go or wear through. **2** vi aux sein *(durchsickern)* to come through *(durch etw sth)*. **bitte weiter ~** *(form: weitergehen)* pass along please.
durchtrieben adj cunning, sly.
Durchtriebenheit f no pl cunning, slyness.
durchwachen* vt insep **die Nacht ~** to stay awake all through the night.
durchwachsen adj **(a)** *(lit)* Speck streaky; *Fleisch, Schinken* with fat running through (it). **(b)** pred *(hum col: mittelmäßig)* so-so *(col)*.
Durchwahl f *(Telec)* direct dialling; *(bei Firma)* extension.
durchwählen vi sep *(Telec)* to dial direct. **nach London ~** to dial London direct.
durchwandern* vt insep *Gegend* to walk through; *(hum) Zimmer, Straßen etc* to wander through.
durchweben* vt insep irreg to interweave *(mit, von* with*)*.
durchweg adv without exception. **~ gut** good in every way.
durchweichen sep **1** vi aux sein to get wet through; *(weich werden: Karton, Boden)* to go soggy. **2** vt to soak; *Boden, Karton* to make soggy.
durchwinden vr sep irreg = **durchschlängeln.**
durchwühlen sep, **durchwühlen*** insep vt to rummage through *(nach* for*)*; *Zimmer auch* to ransack *(nach* looking for*)*.
durchwursteln vr sep *(col)* to muddle through.
durchzählen vt sep to count.
durchzechen¹ vi sep to carry on drinking.
durchzechen²* vt insep **die Nacht ~** to spend the night drinking; **eine durchzechte Nacht** a night of drinking.
durchziehen¹ sep irreg 1 vt **(a)** to pull through *(durch etw sth)*. **(b)** *(col: erledigen)* etw ~ to get sth through. **2** vi aux sein **(a)** *(durchkommen)* to pass through *(durch etw sth)*. **(b)** *(Cook)* to soak. **3** vr to run through *(durch etw sth)*.
durchziehen²* vt insep irreg *(durchwandern)* to pass through, to go/come through; *(Straße, Fluß, fig: Thema)* to run through; *(Geruch)* to fill, to pervade.
durchzucken* vt insep *(Blitz)* to flash across; *(fig: Gedanke)* to flash through.
Durchzug m **(a)** no pl *(Luftzug)* draught *(Brit)*, draft *(US)*. **(b)** *(durch ein Gebiet)* passage; *(von Truppen)* march through.
dürfen pret **durfte**, ptp **gedurft** or *(modal aux)* **dürfen** vi **(a)** *(Erlaubnis haben)* etw tun ~ to be allowed to do sth, to be permitted to do sth; **darf ich? — ja, Sie ~** may I? — yes, you may; **darf ich ins Kino?** may I go to the cinema?
(b) *(verneint)* **man darf etw nicht (tun)** *(sollte, muß nicht)* one must not or mustn't do sth; *(hat keine Erlaubnis)* one isn't allowed to do sth, one may not do sth; **er durfte das nicht** he wasn't allowed to; **hier darf man nicht rauchen** smoking is prohibited here; **du darfst ihm das nicht übelnehmen** you must not take offence at him; **das darf doch nicht wahr sein!** that can't be true!; **da darf er sich nicht wundern** that shouldn't surprise him.
(c) *(in Höflichkeitsformeln)* **Ruhe, wenn ich bitten darf!** quiet, (if you) please!; **darf ich Sie bitten, das zu tun?** may or could I ask you to do that?; **was darf es sein?** can I help you?; **dürfte ich bitte Ihren Paß sehen** may or might I see your passport, please.

(d) *(Veranlassung haben, können)* **wir freuen uns, Ihnen mitteilen zu ~** we are pleased to be able to tell you; **man darf doch wohl fragen** one can or may ask, surely?
(e) **das dürfte ...** *(als Annahme)* that must ...; *(sollte)* that should ..., that ought to ...; *(könnte)* that could ...; **das dürfte wohl das Beste sein** that is probably the best thing.
dürftig adj **(a)** *(ärmlich)* wretched, miserable; *Bekleidung* poor. **(b)** *(pej: unzureichend)* miserable, pathetic *(col)*; *Kenntnisse* scanty; *Ausrede* auch feeble; *Ersatz* poor attr.
dürr adj **(a)** dry; *Boden* arid, barren; *Ast, Strauch* withered. **(b)** *(pej: mager)* scrawny, scraggy.
Dürre f **-n** **(a)** *(Zeit der ~)* drought. **(b)** no pl *(Trockenheit)* dryness; *(von Boden)* aridity.
Dürre-: ~**jahr** nt year of drought; ~**katastrophe** f drought disaster; ~**periode** f drought.
Durst m no pl *(lit, fig)* thirst *(nach* for*)*. **~ haben** to be thirsty; **~ bekommen** to get thirsty; **den ~ löschen** to quench one's thirst; **einen über den ~ getrunken haben** *(col)* to have had one too many.
dursten vi *(geh)* to be thirsty, to thirst *(liter)*.
dürsten **1** vt impers *(liter)* **mich dürstet** I thirst *(liter)*; **es dürstet ihn nach Rache** he is thirsting for revenge. **2** vi *(fig)* to thirst *(nach* for*)*.
durstig adj thirsty. **diese Arbeit macht ~** this is thirsty work *(col)*, this work makes you thirsty.
Durst-: d~**löschend**, d~**stillend** adj thirst-quenching; ~**strecke** f hard times pl.
Durtonleiter f major scale.
Duschbad nt shower(-bath).
Dusche f **-n** shower. **unter der ~ sein** to be in the shower; **das war eine kalte ~** *(fig)* that really brought him/her etc down with a bump.
duschen vir to have or take a shower, to shower. **(sich) kalt ~** to have or take a cold shower.
Dusch-: ~**gelegenheit** f shower facilities pl; ~**kabine** f shower (cubicle); ~**raum** m shower room, showers pl; ~**vorhang** m shower curtain.
Düse f **-n** nozzle; *(Mech auch, von Flugzeug)* jet.
Dusel m no pl *(col)* **(a)** *(Glück)* luck. **da hat er (einen) ~ gehabt** he was lucky. **(b)** *(Trancezustand)* daze, dream; *(durch Alkohol)* fuddle.
duselig adj *(schlaftrunken)* drowsy; *(benommen)* dizzy; *(esp durch Alkohol)* befuddled.
Düsen-: ~**antrieb** m jet propulsion; ~**bomber** m jet bomber; ~**flugzeug** nt jet plane, jet; d~**getrieben** adj jet-propelled; ~**jäger** m *(Mil)* jet fighter; ~**triebwerk** nt jet power-unit.
Dussel m **-** *(col)* twit *(Brit col)*, twerp *(col)*.
dusselig, dußlig adj *(col)* stupid.
Dusseligkeit, Dußligkeit f *(col)* stupidity.
düster adj gloomy; *Bild, Gedanken* sombre *(Brit)*, somber *(US)*; dismal; *(unheimlich) Gestalten* sinister.
Düsterheit, Düsterkeit f gloominess; *(Dunkelheit)* gloom, dark(ness).
Dutzend nt **-e** dozen. **ein halbes ~** half-a-dozen, a half-dozen; **zwei/drei ~** two/three dozen; ~**e** pl *(col)* dozens pl.
Dutzend-: d~**mal** adv *(col)* **(ein)** d~**mal** dozens of times; ~**ware** f *(pej)* *(cheap)* mass-produced item; d~**weise** adv in dozens, by the dozen.
duzen vr wir ~ **uns** we use "du" or the "du"-form.
Duzfreund m good friend.
Dynamik f no pl **(a)** *(Phys)* dynamics. **(b)** *(fig)* dynamism.
dynamisch adj *(Phys, fig)* dynamic; *Renten* ≈ index-linked.
Dynamit nt no pl *(lit, fig)* dynamite.
Dynamo m **-s** dynamo.
Dynastie f dynasty.
D-Zug ['dɛtsuːk] m fast train; *(hält nur in großen Städten)* through train. **ein alter Mann ist doch kein ~** *(col)* I am going as fast as I can.
D-Zug-Tempo nt *(col)* fantastic speed *(col)*. **im ~** like greased lightning *(col)*.

E

E, e [e:] *nt* -, - E, e.

Ebbe *f* -n **(a)** ebb tide; *(Niedrigwasser)* low tide. ~ **und Flut** ebb and flow; **bei** ~ **baden** to swim when the tide is going out; *(bei Niedrigwasser)* to swim at low tide; **es ist** ~ the tide is going out; *(es ist Niedrigwasser)* it's low tide, the tide is out. **(b)** *(fig)* **in meinem Geldbeutel ist** ~ my finances are at a pretty low ebb at the moment.

eben 1 *adj (glatt)* smooth; *(gleichmäßig)* even; *(gleich hoch)* level; *(flach)* flat. **zu** ~**er Erde** at ground level. **2** *adv* **(a)** just. **mein Bleistift war doch** ~ **noch da** my pencil was there (just) a minute ago; **ich gehe** ~ **zur Bank** I'll just go to the bank; **das reicht so** *or* **nur** ~ **aus** it's only just enough. **(b) das ist** ~ **so** that's just the way it is; **dann bleibst du** ~ **zu Hause** then you'll just have to stay at home. **(c)** *(gerade or genau das)* exactly, precisely. **das ist es ja** ~! that's just *or* precisely it!; **nicht** ~ **billig** not exactly cheap.

Ebenbild *nt* image. **das genaue** ~ **seines Vaters** the spitting image of his father.

ebenbürtig *adj (gleichwertig)* equal; *Gegner* evenly matched. **jdm an Kraft** ~ **sein** to be sb's equal in strength.

eben-: ~**da** *adv (gerade dort)* ~**da will auch ich hin** that is exactly where I am going too; ~**darum** *adv* for that very reason; ~**der,** ~**die,** ~**das** *pron* he; she; it; ~**deshalb,** ~**deswegen** *adv* that is exactly why; ~**diese(r, s)** *adj* this very.

Ebene *f* -n plain; *(Hoch~)* plateau; *(Math, Phys)* plane; *(fig)* level. **auf höchster/der gleichen** ~ *(fig)* at the highest/the same level.

eben-: ~**erdig** *adj* at ground level; ~**falls** *adv* as well, likewise; **er hat** ~**falls nichts davon gewußt** he knew nothing about it either.

Ebenholz *nt* ebony.

Ebenmaß *nt (von Gestalt etc)* perfect proportions *pl; (von Versen)* even flow.

ebenso *adv (genauso)* just as; *(auch, ebenfalls)* as well. **das kann doch** ~ **eine Frau machen** a woman can do that just as well; **er hat ein** ~ **großes Zimmer wie wir** he has just as big a room as we have.

ebenso-: ~**gern** *adv* **ich mag sie** ~**gern** I like her just as much; **ich komme** ~**gern morgen** I'd just as soon come tomorrow; ~**gut** *adv* (just) as well; ~**lang(e)** *adv* just as long; ~**oft** *adv* just as often; ~**sehr** *adv* just as much; ~**viel** *adv* just as much; ~**wenig** *adv* just as little.

Eber *m* - boar.

Eber|esche *f* rowan, mountain ash.

ebnen *vt* to level (off), to make level. **jdm den Weg** ~ *(fig)* to smooth the way for sb.

Echo *nt* -s echo; *(fig)* response *(auf+ acc* to*)*. **ein lebhaftes** ~ **finden** *(fig)* to meet with a lively response *(bei* from*)*.

Echolot *nt (Naut)* echo-sounder, sonar; *(Aviat)* sonic altimeter.

Echse ['ɛksə] *f* -n *(Zool)* lizard.

echt 1 *adj, adv* **(a)** real, genuine; *Haar, Perlen, Gold* real; *Unterschrift, Geldschein, Gemälde* genuine. **(b)** *(typisch)* typical. **ein** ~**er Bayer** a real *or* typical Bavarian; ~ **englisch** typically English. **2** *adv (col)* really. **ich hab'** ~ **keine Zeit** I really don't have any time.

Echtheit *f* genuineness; *(von Unterschrift, Do-*

kument auch) authenticity.

Eck- *in cpds* corner; ~**ball** *m (Sport)* corner; ~**bank** *f* corner seat.

Ecke *f* -**n (a)** corner *(auch Sport); (Kante)* edge; *(von Kragen)* point. **Kantstraße** ~ **Goethestraße** at the corner of Kantstraße and Goethestraße; **gleich um die** ~ just around the corner; **jdn in die** ~ **drängen** *(fig)* to push sb into the background; **an allen** ~**n und Enden sparen** to pinch and scrape *(col)*; **jdn um die** ~ **bringen** *(col)* to bump sb off *(col)*; **mit jdm um ein paar** ~**n herum verwandt sein** *(col)* to be distantly related to sb, to be sb's second cousin twice removed *(hum col)*. **(b)** *(Käse~, Kuchen~)* wedge. **(c)** *(col: Gegend)* corner, area. **aus welcher** ~ **kommst du?** what part of the world are you from?

Eck-: ~**fahne** *f (Sport)* corner flag; ~**haus** *nt* corner house.

eckig *adj* angular; *Klammer* square; *(spitz)* sharp.

Eck-: ~**kneipe** *f (col)* pub on the corner *(Brit)*; ~**pfeiler** *m (fig)* cornerstone; ~**pfosten** corner post; ~**schrank** *m* corner cupboard; ~**stoß** *m (Ftbl)* corner kick; ~**zahn** *m* canine tooth.

edel *adj* noble; *(hochwertig)* precious; *Wein, Speisen* fine.

Edel-: ~**fäule** *f (bei Weintrauben)* noble rot; ~**frau** *f (Hist)* noblewoman; ~**gas** *nt* rare gas; ~**holz** *nt* precious wood; ~**mann** *m, pl* ~**leute** *(Hist)* noble(man); ~**metall** *nt* precious metal; ~**mut** *m (liter)* magnanimity; **e~mütig** *adj (liter)* magnanimous; ~**pilzkäse** *m* blue (vein) cheese; ~**rost** *m* patina; ~**stahl** *m* high-grade steel; ~**stein** *m* precious stone; *(geschliffener auch)* jewel, gem; ~**tanne** *f* noble fir; ~**weiß** *nt* edelweiss.

Eden *nt no pl* **der Garten** ~ *(Bibl)* the Garden of Eden.

Editor(in *f)* [-'to:rin] *m* editor.

EDV [e:de:'fau] *f* = **elektronische Datenverarbeitung.**

Efeu *m no pl* ivy.

Eff|eff *nt no pl (col)* **etw aus dem** ~ **können** to be able to do sth standing on one's head *(col)*; **etw aus dem** ~ **kennen** to know sth inside out.

Effekt *m* -e effect.

Effekten *pl (Fin)* stocks and bonds *pl.*

Effekten-: ~**börse** *f* stock exchange; ~**handel** *m* stock dealing.

Effekthascherei *f (col)* showmanship. **das ist reine** ~ it's just done for effect.

effektiv 1 *adj* **(a)** effective. **(b)** *(tatsächlich)* actual. **2** *adv* actually. ~ **kein** absolutely no.

Effektivität *f* effectiveness.

Effektivlohn *m* actual wage.

effektvoll *adj* effective.

Effet [e'fe:] *m* -s spin. **den Ball mit** ~ **schießen** to put spin on a ball.

effizient *adj* efficient.

EG [e:'ge:] *f* = **Europäische Gemeinschaft** EEC.

egal *adj, adv* **(a)** *pred* **das ist** ~ that doesn't matter, that doesn't make any difference; **das ist mir ganz** ~ it's all the same to me; ~ **wo/wie** it doesn't matter where/how, no matter where/how. **(b)** *(col: gleichartig)* the same, identical.

egalitär adj (geh) egalitarian.
Egge f -n (Agr) harrow.
Ego nt -s (Psych) ego.
Egoismus m ego(t)ism.
Egoist(in f) m (wk) ego(t)ist.
egoistisch adj ego(t)istical.
Ego-: ~**zentriker(in** f) m - egocentric; **e~zentrisch** adj egocentric.
eh 1 interj hey. **2** adv **(a)** seit ~ **und je** for ages, since the year dot (col); **wie** ~ **und je** just as before. **(b)** (col: sowieso) anyway. **ich komme** ~ **nicht dazu** I won't get around to it anyway.
ehe conj (bevor) before. ~ **(daß) ich mich auf andere verlasse, mache ich lieber alles selbst** rather than rely on others, I would prefer to do everything myself.
Ehe f -n marriage. **er versprach ihr die** ~ he promised to marry her; **die** ~ **eingehen** (form) to enter into matrimony (form); **eine unglückliche** ~ **führen** to have an unhappy marriage; **die** ~ **brechen** (form) to commit adultery; **sie hat drei Kinder aus erster** ~ she has three children from her first marriage.
Ehe-: **e~ähnlich** adj (form) **in einer e~ähnlichen Gemeinschaft leben** to cohabit (form); ~**anbahnungsinstitut** nt marriage bureau; ~**beratung** f marriage guidance; ~**bett** nt (fig) marital bed; ~**brecher** m - adulterer; ~**brecherin** f adulteress; **e~brecherisch** adj adulterous; ~**bruch** m adultery.
ehedem adv (old) formerly.
Ehe-: ~**frau** f wife; ~**gatte** m, ~**gattin** f (form) spouse (form); ~**gemeinschaft** f (form) wedlock (form), matrimony; ~**krach** m marital row; ~**leben** nt married life; ~**leute** pl (form) married couple; (in Briefadresse) Mr and Mrs.
ehelich adj marital; Pflichten, Rechte auch conjugal; Kind legitimate.
ehelichen vt (dated, hum) to wed (old).
ehelos adj unmarried, single.
Ehelosigkeit f no pl unmarried state; (Rel) celibacy.
ehemalig adj attr former. ~**er Häftling** ex-convict; **mein E~er/meine E~e** (hum col) my ex (col).
ehemals adv (form) formerly, previously.
Ehe-: ~**mann** m, pl ~**männer** married man; (Partner) husband; ~**paar** nt (married) couple; ~**partner(in** f) m husband, wife; **beide** ~**partner** both partners (in the marriage).
eher adv **(a)** (früher) earlier, sooner. **nicht** ~ **als** not before. **(b)** (lieber) rather, sooner; (wahrscheinlicher) more likely; (leichter) more easily. **um so** ~, **als** the more so because; **das ist** ~ **möglich** that is more likely or probable. **(c)** (vielmehr) more. **er ist** ~ **faul als dumm** he's more lazy than stupid, he's lazy rather than stupid.
Ehe-: ~**ring** m wedding ring; ~**scheidung** f divorce; ~**schließung** f marriage ceremony, wedding.
Ehestand m no pl matrimony, marriage. **in den** ~ **treten** (form) to enter into matrimony.
ehestens adv ~ **morgen** tomorrow at the earliest.
eheste(r, s) 1 adj **bei** ~**r Gelegenheit** at the earliest opportunity. **2** adv ~**n** (am liebsten) best of all; (am wahrscheinlichsten) most likely; (am leichtesten) the easiest; **am** ~**n würde ich mir ein Auto kaufen** what I'd like best (of all) would be to buy myself a car; **das geht wohl am** ~**n** that's probably the best way.
Ehe-: ~**streit** m marital argument; ~**vermittlung** f (Büro) marriage bureau; ~**versprechen** nt (Jur) promise to marry.
ehrbar adj (achtenswert) respectable; (ehrenhaft) honourable (Brit), honorable (US); Beruf auch reputable.
Ehre f -n honour (Brit), honor (US); (Ruhm) glory.

etw in ~**n halten** to treasure or cherish sth; **jdm** ~/**wenig** ~ **machen** to do sb credit/not do sb any credit; **auf** ~ **und Gewissen** on my/his etc honour; **etw um der** ~ **willen tun** to do sth for the honour of it; **seine Kenntnisse in allen** ~**n, aber** ... I don't doubt his knowledge, but ...; **sich** (dat) **etw zur** ~ **anrechnen** to count sth an honour; **das rechne ich ihm zur** ~ an I consider that a point in his honour; **mit wem habe ich die** ~? (iro, form) with whom do I have the honour of speaking? (form); **um der Wahrheit die** ~ **zu geben** ... (geh) to be perfectly honest ...; **wir geben uns die** ~, **Sie zu** ... **einzuladen** (form) we request the honour of your company at ... (form); **zu** ~**n** (+gen) in honour of; ~, **wem** ~ **gebührt** (prov) honour where honor is due (prov).
ehren vt to honour (Brit), to honor (US). **etw ehrt jdn** sth does sb credit or honour; **Ihr Vertrauen ehrt mich** I am honoured by your trust; **jdm ein** ~**des Andenken bewahren** to treasure sb's memory; siehe **geehrt**.
Ehren-: ~**amt** nt honorary office or post; **e~amtlich 1** adj honorary; **2** adv in an honorary capacity.
Ehrenbürger m freeman.
Ehrenbürgerrecht nt **die Stadt verlieh ihr das** ~ she was given the freedom of the city.
Ehren-: ~**doktor** m honorary doctor; ~**doktorwürde** f: **ihm wurde die** ~ **doktorwürde verliehen** he was made an honorary doctor or given an honorary doctorate; ~**garde** f guard of honour (Brit) or honor (US); ~**gast** m guest of honour (Brit) or honor (US); ~**gericht** nt tribunal; **e~haft** adj honourable (Brit), honorable (US); ~**haftigkeit** f honourableness (Brit), honorableness (US); **e~halber** adv **er wurde e~halber zum Vorsitzenden auf Lebenszeit ernannt** he was made honorary president for life; ~**legion** f legion of honour (Brit) or honor (US); ~**mitglied** nt honorary member; ~**mal** nt memorial; ~**mann** m, pl ~**männer** man of honour (Brit) or honor (US); ~**mitgliedschaft** f honorary membership; ~**platz** m (lit) place of honour (Brit) or honor (US); (fig) special place; ~**rechte** pl (Jur) civil rights pl; ~**rettung** f zu seiner ~**rettung sei gesagt, daß** ... in his favour (Brit) or favor (US) it must be said that ...; **e~rührig** adj defamatory; ~**runde** f (Sport) lap of honour (Brit) or honor (US); ~**sache** f matter of honour (Brit) or honor (US); ~**sache!** (col) you can count on me; ~**tag** m (Geburtstag) birthday; (großer Tag) big day; ~**titel** m honorary title; ~**tor** nt (Sport) consolation goal; ~**tribüne** f VIP rostrum; ~**urkunde** f certificate; **e~voll** adj honourable (Brit), honorable (US); ~**vorsitzende(r)** mf honorary chairman/chairwoman; ~**wache** f guard of honour (Brit) or honor (US); **e~wert** adj Mensch honourable (Brit), honorable (US); ~**wort** nt word of honour (Brit) or honor (US); ~**wort!** (col) cross my heart! (col); **Urlaub auf** ~**wort** parole; **e~wörtlich** adj Versprechen solemn, faithful.
Ehr-: **e~erbietig** adj respectful, deferential; ~**erbietung** f respect, deference.
Ehrfurcht f no pl deep respect (vor +dat for); (Scheu) reverence (vor +dat for).
ehrfurchtgebietend adj Stimme authoritative.
ehrfürchtig adj reverent.
Ehrgefühl nt sense of honour (Brit) or honor (US).
Ehrgeiz m no pl ambition.
ehrgeizig adj ambitious.
ehrlich 1 adj honest; Name good; Wunsch sincere. **eine** ~**e Haut** (col) an honest soul; **er hat** ~**e Absichten** (col) his intentions are honourable (Brit) or honorable (US); ~ **verdientes Geld** hard-earned money; ~ **gesagt** ... quite frankly or honestly ...; ~ **währt am längsten** (Prov) honesty is the best policy (Prov). **2** adv (wirklich) honestly. ~! honestly!, really!

Ehrlichkeit f no pl honesty; (von Gefühlen etc) sincerity.

Ehr-: e~los adj dishonourable (Brit), dishonorable (US); ~losigkeit f dishonourableness (Brit), dishonorableness (US); (Schlechtigkeit) infamy.

Ehrung f honour (Brit), honor (US); (Sieger~ etc) honouring (Brit), honoring (US).

ehrwürdig adj venerable.

Ei nt -er (a) egg; (Physiol auch) ovum. das ~ des Kolumbus finden to come up with just the thing; das ~ will klüger sein als die Henne you're trying to teach your grandmother to suck eggs (prov); jdn wie ein rohes ~ behandeln (fig) to handle sb with kid gloves; wie auf ~ern gehen (col) to step gingerly; wie aus dem ~ gepellt aussehen (col) to look spruce; sie gleichen sich wie ein ~ dem anderen they are as alike as two peas (in a pod); das sind ungelegte ~er! (col) we'll cross that bridge when we come to it. (b) ~er pl (col: Geld) marks; (in GB) quid (col); (in US) bucks (col). (c) ~er pl (col!: Hoden) balls pl (col!).

Eibe f -n (Bot) yew.

Eiche f -n oak.

Eichel f -n (a) (Bot) acorn. (b) (Anat) glans.

Eichelhäher m jay.

eichen vt to calibrate; (prüfen auch) to check against official specifications. darauf bin ich geeicht! (col) that's right up my street (col).

Eichenholz nt oak. ein Tisch aus ~holz an oak table.

Eichhörnchen nt squirrel.

Eich-: ~maß nt standard measure; (Gewicht) standard weight; ~strich m line measure.

Eid m -e oath. einen ~ leisten or schwören to take or swear an oath (auf etw (acc) on sth); ich nehme es auf meinen ~, daß ... I would be prepared to swear that ...; unter ~ under oath; eine Erklärung an ~es Statt abgeben (Jur) to make a solemn declaration .

Eidechse ['aidɛksə] f -n (Zool) lizard.

eidesstattlich adj solemn. eine ~e Erklärung abgeben to make a solemn declaration.

Eid-: ~genosse m, ~genossin f (Schweizer) Swiss citizen; ~genossenschaft f Schweizerische ~genossenschaft Swiss Confederation; e~genössisch adj (schweizerisch) Swiss.

Eidotter m or nt egg yolk.

Eier-: ~becher m eggcup; ~farbe f paint used for colouring eggs at Easter; ~handgranate f (Mil) (pineapple) hand grenade; ~kopf m (col) egghead (col); ~laufen nt egg and spoon race; ~likör m advocaat; ~löffel m eggspoon.

eiern vi (col) to wobble.

Eier-: ~schale f eggshell; e~schalenfarben adj cream, off-white; ~speise f egg dish; ~stock m (Anat) ovary; ~tanz m einen ~tanz aufführen (fig col) to go through all kinds of contortions; ~uhr f egg timer.

Eifer m no pl (Begeisterung) enthusiasm; (Eifrigkeit) eagerness, keenness. in ~ geraten to get agitated; mit großem ~ bei der Sache sein to put one's heart into it; im ~ des Gefechts (fig col) in the heat of the moment.

Eiferer m - (liter) fanatic; (Rel auch) zealot.

eifern vi (liter) (a) gegen jdn/etw ~ to inveigh against sb/sth. (b) (streben) nach etw ~ to strive for sth.

Eifersucht f jealousy (auf +acc of).

eifersüchtig adj jealous (auf +acc of).

Eifersuchtsszene f ihr Mann hat ihr eine ~ gemacht her husband's jealousy caused a scene.

eiförmig adj egg-shaped, oval.

eifrig adj eager; Leser, Sammler keen, avid; (begeistert) enthusiastic; (emsig) zealous. sie diskutierten ~ they were involved in an animated discussion.

Eigelb nt egg yolk.

eigen adj (a) own; (selbständig) separate. seine

~e Wohnung haben to have a flat of one's own, to have one's own flat; etw sein ~ nennen (geh) to have sth to call one's own; sich (dat) etw zu ~ machen to adopt sth; ich möchte kurz in ~er Sache sprechen I would like to say something on my own account. (b) (typisch) typical. das ist ihm ~ that is typical of him; der ihm ~e Zynismus his characteristic cynicism. (c) (seltsam) strange, peculiar. (d) (ordentlich) particular; (übergenau) fussy. in Gelddingen ist er sehr ~ he is very particular about money matters.

Eigen|art f (Besonderheit) peculiarity; (Eigenschaft) characteristic; (Eigentümlichkeit von Personen) idiosyncrasy.

eigen|artig adj peculiar; (sonderbar auch) strange.

Eigen-: ~bau m no pl er fährt ein Fahrrad Marke ~bau (hum col) he rides a home-made bike; ~bedarf m (von Mensch) personal use; (von Staat) domestic requirements pl; der Hausbesitzer machte ~bedarf geltend the landlord claimed that he needed the house/flat for himself; ~brötler(in f) m - (col) loner, lone wolf; (komischer Kauz) oddball (col); e~brötlerisch adj (col) solitary; (komisch) eccentric; ~dynamik f momentum; eine ~dynamik entwickeln to gather momentum; ~gewicht nt (Comm) net weight; (Sci) dead weight; e~händig adj Unterschrift etc in one's own hand, handwritten; Übergabe personal; eine Arbeit e~händig machen to do a job oneself; ~heim nt one's own home; ~heit f = ~art; ~initiative f initiative of one's own; ~kapital nt personal captial; (von Firma) company capital; ~leben nt no pl one's own life; (selbständige Existenz) independent existence; ein ~leben entwickeln to develop a life of its own; ~lob nt self-importance; ~lob stinkt! (prov) don't blow your own trumpet! (prov); e~mächtig 1 adj (selbstherrlich) high-handed; (e~verantwortlich) taken/done etc on one's own authority; (unbefugt) unauthorized; 2 adv high-handedly; (entirely) on one's own authority; without any authorization; ~mächtigkeit f (Selbstherrlichkeit) high-handedness no pl; (unbefugtes Handeln) unauthorized behaviour (Brit) or behavior (US) no pl; ~name m proper name; ~nutz m no pl self-interest; e~nützig adj selfish.

eigens adv specially.

Eigenschaft f (Attribut) quality; (Chem, Phys etc) property; (Merkmal) characteristic, feature; (Funktion) capacity.

Eigenschaftswort nt adjective.

Eigen-: ~sinn m no pl stubbornness, obstinacy; e~sinnig adj stubborn, obstinate; e~ständig adj independent; ~ständigkeit f independence.

eigentlich 1 adj real, actual. 2 adv actually; (überhaupt) anyway. was willst du ~ hier? what do you want here anyway?; wissen Sie ~, wer ich bin? do you know who I am?; ~ müßtest du das wissen you should really know that.

Eigentor nt (lit, fig) own goal.

Eigentum nt no pl property.

Eigentümer(in f) m - owner.

eigentümlich adj (a) curious, odd. (b) (geh: typisch) jdm/einer Sache ~ sein to be characteristic of sb/sth.

eigentümlicherweise adv oddly enough.

Eigentümlichkeit f (a) (Kennzeichen) characteristic. (b) (Eigenheit) peculiarity.

Eigentums-: ~delikt nt (Jur: Diebstahl) theft; ~recht nt right of ownership; ~wohnung f owner-occupied flat (Brit) or apartment; er kaufte sich (dat) eine ~wohnung he bought a flat (of his own).

Eigen-: e~verantwortlich 1 adj autonomous; 2 adv on one's own authority; e~willig adj with a mind of one's own; (e~sinnig) self-willed; (un-

konventionell) unconventional.

eignen *vr* to be suitable *(für, zu* for, *als* as). **er eignet sich nicht zum Lehrer** he's not suited to teaching; *siehe* **geeignet**.

Eigner(in *f) m* - *(form)* owner.

Eignung *f* suitability; *(Befähigung)* aptitude.

Eignungs-: ~**prüfung** *f,* ~**test** *m* aptitude test.

Eiland *nt* **-e** *(liter)* isle *(liter)*.

Eil-: ~**bote** *m* messenger; **per** *or* **durch** ~**boten** express; ~**brief** *m* express letter.

Eile *f no pl* hurry. **in** ~ **sein** to be in a hurry; **das hat keine** ~ there is no hurry, it's not urgent; **in der/meiner** ~ in the hurry/my haste; **nur keine** ~! don't rush!

Eileiter *m (Anat)* Fallopian tube.

eilen *vi* **(a)** *aux sein* to hurry. **er eilte dem Ertrinkenden zu Hilfe** he rushed to help the drowning man; **eile mit Weile** *(Prov)* more haste less speed *(Prov).* **(b) eilt!** *(auf Briefen etc)* urgent; **es eilt** it's urgent.

eilig *adj* **(a)** *(schnell)* quick, hurried. **es** ~ **haben** to be in a hurry *or* rush; **nur nicht so** ~! don't be in such a hurry *or* rush! **(b)** *(dringend)* urgent.

Eil-: ~**paket** *nt* express parcel; ~**tempo** *nt:* **etw im** ~**tempo machen** to do sth in a rush; ~**zug** *m* fast stopping train; ~**zustellung** *f* special delivery.

Eimer *m* - bucket; *(Müll~)* (rubbish) bin. **ein** ~ **(voll) Wasser** a bucket(ful) of water; **es gießt wie aus** ~**n** *(col)* it's bucketing down *(col);* **im** ~ **sein** *(col)* to be up the spout *(col)* or be ruined.

ein¹ *adv (an Geräten)* **E**~/**Aus** on/off; **er geht bei uns** ~ **und aus** he is always round at our place; **ich weiß nicht mehr** ~ **noch aus** I'm at my wits' end.

ein², **eine**, **ein** 1 *num* one. **er ist ihr** ~ **und alles** he means everything to her; *siehe* **eins.** 2 *indef art* a; *(vor Vokalen)* an. ~ **Europäer** a European; ~ **Hotel** a *or* an hotel; **der Sohn** ~**es Lehrers** the son of a teacher, a teacher's son; **was für** ~ **Wetter!** some weather.

Ein|akter *m* - *(Theat)* one-act play.

einander *pron* one another, each other.

ein|arbeiten *sep* 1 *vr* to settle in. 2 *vt jdn* to train.

Ein|arbeitungszeit *f* training period.

ein|armig *adj* one-armed.

ein|äschern *vt sep Leichnam* to cremate; *Stadt etc* to reduce to ashes.

Ein|äscherung *f (von Leichnam)* cremation.

ein|atmen *vti sep* to breathe in.

ein|äugig *adj* one-eyed.

Einbahnstraße *f* one-way street.

einbalsamieren* *vt sep* to embalm.

Einbalsamierung *f* embalming.

Einband *m* book cover.

einbändig *adj* one-volume *attr.*

Einbau *m* **-ten** installation.

einbauen *vt sep* to install, to put in.

Einbauküche *f* (fully-)fitted kitchen.

Einbaum *m* dug-out (canoe).

Einbaumöbel *pl* built-in *or* fitted furniture; *(Schränke)* fitted cupboards *pl.*

einbegriffen *adj* included.

einbehalten* *vt sep irreg* to keep back.

einbeinig *adj* one-legged.

einberechnen* *vt sep* to allow for (in one's calculations). ~**, daß** ... to allow for the fact that ...

einberufen* *vt sep irreg Parlament* to summon; *Versammlung* to convene, to call; *(Mil)* to call up, to draft (US).

Einberufung *f* **(a)** *(einer Versammlung)* calling; *(des Parlaments)* summoning. **(b)** *(Mil)* conscription; *(~sbescheid)* call-up.

Einberufungs-: ~**bescheid,** ~**befehl** *m (Mil)* call-up *or* draft (US) papers *pl.*

einbetten *vt sep* to embed *(in + acc* in); *Rohr, Kabel* to lay *(in + acc* in); *siehe* **eingebettet.**

Einbettzimmer *nt* single room.

einbeziehen* *vt sep irreg* to include *(in + acc* in).

Einbeziehung *f* inclusion. **unter** ~ **von etw** including sth.

einbiegen *vi sep irreg aux sein* to turn (off) *(in + acc* into). **links** ~ to turn (off to the) left.

einbilden *vr sep* **(a) sich** *(dat)* **etw** ~ to imagine sth; **er bildet sich** *(dat)* **ein, daß** ... he's got hold of the idea that ...; **das bildest du dir nur ein** that's just your imagination; **was bildest du dir eigentlich ein?** what's got into you? **(b)** *(stolz sein)* **sich** *(dat)* **viel auf etw** *(acc)* ~ to be conceited about sth; **darauf können Sie sich etwas** ~! that's something to be proud of!; **darauf brauchst du dir nichts einzubilden** that's nothing special; *siehe* **eingebildet.**

Einbildung *f* **(a)** *(Vorstellung)* imagination; *(irrige Vorstellung)* illusion. **das sind** ~**en** that's pure imagination. **(b)** *(Dünkel)* conceit.

Einbildungskraft *f* (powers *pl* of) imagination.

einbinden *vt sep irreg Buch* to bind.

einblenden *sep (Film, TV, Rad)* 1 *vt* to insert, to slot in; *(nachträglich) Musik etc* to dub on. 2 *vr* **sich in etw** *(acc)* ~ to link up with sth.

einbleuen *vt sep (col) jdm etw* ~ *(einschärfen)* to drum sth into sb.

Einblick *m (fig: Kenntnis)* insight. ~ **in etw** *(acc)* **gewinnen** to gain an insight into sth; ~ **in die Akten nehmen** to examine the files; **jdm** ~ **in etw** *(acc)* **gewähren** to allow sb to look at sth.

einbrechen *vi sep irreg aux sein* **(a)** *(einstürzen)* to fall or cave in. **er ist (auf dem Eis) eingebrochen** he fell through the ice. **(b)** *aux sein or haben (Einbruch verüben)* to break in. **bei mir ist eingebrochen worden** I've been burgled *or* burglarized (US); **in neue Absatzmärkte** *etc* ~ to break into new markets *etc.* **(c)** *(Dämmerung etc)* to fall; *Winter* to set in. **bei** ~**der Nacht** at nightfall.

Einbrecher(in *f) m* - burglar.

einbringen *sep irreg* 1 *vt Geld, Ernte, Schiff* to bring in; *Ruhm, Nachteil* to bring; *Zinsen* to earn; *(Parl)* to introduce. **das bringt nichts ein** *(fig)* it's not worth it; **etw in die Ehe** ~ to bring sth into the marriage. 2 *vr (col)* **sich (in einer Diskussion)** ~ to involve oneself (in a discussion).

einbrocken *vt sep (col) jdm/sich etwas* ~ to land sb/oneself in it *(col);* **da hast du dir etwas Schönes eingebrockt!** you've really let yourself in for it there.

Einbruch *m* **(a)** *(~diebstahl)* burglary, break-in *(in + acc* in); *(Mil: in Front)* breakthrough *(in + acc* of). **der** ~ **in die Bank** the break-in at the bank. **(b)** *(von Wasser)* penetration. **(c)** *(Einsturz, Fin)* collapse. **(d)** *(des Winters)* onset. **bei/vor** ~ **der Nacht/Dämmerung** at/before nightfall/dusk.

Einbruch(s)-: ~**diebstahl** *m (Jur)* burglary, breaking and entering *(form);* **e**~**sicher** *adj* burglar-proof.

Einbuchtung *f* indentation; *(Bucht)* inlet, bay.

einbürgern *sep* 1 *vt Person* to naturalize; *Fremdwort, Gewohnheit* to introduce. 2 *vr (Person)* to become *or* be naturalized; *(Brauch, Tier)* to become established; **das hat sich so eingebürgert** *(Brauch)* it's just the way we/they *etc* have come to do things.

Einbürgerung *f siehe vt* naturalization; introduction.

Einbuße *f* loss *(an + dat* in).

einbüßen *sep vt* to lose; *(durch eigene Schuld)* to forfeit.

eincremen *vt sep* to put cream on.

eindämmen *vt sep Fluß* to dam; *(fig)* to check, to contain.

Eindämmung *f* **(a)** *(Damm)* dam. **(b)** *siehe vt* damming; checking, containing.

eindecken *sep* 1 *vr* **sich (mit etw)** ~ to stock up (with sth). 2 *vt (col: überhäufen)* **mit Arbeit eingedeckt sein** to be inundated with work.

eindeutig *adj* clear; *(nicht zweideutig)* unambiguous; *Witz* explicit. **jdm etw** ~ **sagen** to tell sb sth quite plainly.

eindeutschen *vt sep Fremdwort* to Germanize.

eindimensional *adj* one-dimensional.

eindösen *vi sep aux sein (col)* to doze off.

eindrängen *vr sep* to crowd in *(in +acc -to)*; *(fig)* to intrude *(in+acc* upon).

eindrehen *vt sep* **(a)** to screw in *(in+acc -to)*. **(b)** *Haar* to put in rollers.

eindringen *vi sep irreg aux sein* **(a)** *(einbrechen)* in etw *(acc)* ~ to force one's way into sth; **in unsere Linien/das Land** ~ *(Mil)* to penetrate our lines/to enter the country. **(b) in etw** *(acc)* ~ *(Messer, Wasser)* to penetrate sth; *(Fremdwörter etc)* to find its way into sth. **(c)** *(bestürmen)* **auf jdn** ~ to go for sb, to attack sb *(mit* with); *(mit Fragen, Bitten etc)* to besiege sb.

eindringlich *adj (nachdrücklich)* insistent; *(dringend auch)* urgent; *Schilderung* vivid. **ich habe ihn** ~ **gebeten ...** I urged him ..

Eindringling *m* intruder.

Eindruck *m* -ë impression. **den** ~ **erwecken, als ob** *or* **daß** ... to give the impression that ...; **großen** ~ **auf jdn machen** to make a big impression on sb; **er will** ~ **(bei ihr) machen** *or* **schinden** *(col)* he's out to impress (her).

eindrücken *vt sep Fenster* to break; *Tür, Mauer* to push down; *(Sturm, Explosion)* to blow in/down; *(einbeulen)* to dent; *Brustkorb* to crush; *Nase* to flatten.

eindrucksvoll *adj* impressive.

eine *siehe* ein², **eine(r, s)**.

ein|ebnen *vt sep (lit)* to level (off); *(fig)* to level out.

Ein|ehe *f* monogamy.

ein|eiig *adj Zwillinge* identical.

ein|einhalb *num* one and a half; *siehe* **anderthalb**.

einen *vtr (geh)* to unite.

ein|engen *vt sep (lit)* to constrict; *(fig)* to restrict. **jdn in seiner Freiheit** ~ to restrict sb's freedom.

Ein|engung *f (lit)* constriction; *(fig)* restriction.

eine(r, s) *indef pron adj* **(a)** one; *(jemand, somebody, someone. der/die/das* ~ the one; **das** ~ **Gute war** ... the one good thing was ...; **er denkt immer nur an das** ~ he only thinks of one thing; **sein** ~**r Sohn** *(col)* one of his sons; **die** ~**n sagen so, die anderen** ... some (people) say one thing and others ...; ~**r für alle, alle für** ~**n** *(prov)* all for one and one for all *(prov)*; **du bist mir vielleicht** ~**(r)!** *(col)* you're a fine one *(col)*; **sieh mal** ~**r an!** *(iro)* well what do you know! *(col)*; **in** ~**m fort, in** ~**r Tour** *(col)* non-stop. **(b)** *(man)* one *(esp form)*, you. **wie kann** ~**r nur so dumm sein!** how could anybody be so stupid! **(c)** ~**s** *(auch* **eins)** one thing; ~**s sag' ich dir** I'll tell you one thing; **noch** ~**s, bevor ich's vergesse** (there's) one other thing before I forget; **es kam** ~**s zum anderen** it was (just) one thing after another. **(d)** *(col)* **sich** *(dat)* ~**n genehmigen** to have a quick one *(col)*; **jdm** ~ **kleben** to thump sb one *(col)*.

Einer *m* - **(a)** *(Math)* unit. **(b)** *(Ruderboot)* single scull.

einerlei *adj pred inv (gleichgültig)* **das ist mir ganz** ~ it's all the same to me; ~, **was/wer** ... no matter what/who ...

Einerlei *nt no pl* monotony.

einerseits *adv* ~ ... **andererseits** ... on the one hand ... on the other hand ...

einfach 1 *adj* **(a)** simple; *Mensch* ordinary; *Essen* plain. **(b)** *(nicht doppelt) Knoten* simple; *Fahrkarte* single *(Brit)*, one-way. 2 *adv* simply. ~ **gemein** downright mean; **das ist doch** ~ **dumm** that's (just) plain stupid.

Einfachheit *f siehe adj* simplicity; ordinariness; plainness. **der** ~ **halber** for the sake of simplicity.

einfädeln *sep* 1 *vt* **(a)** *Nadel, Faden* to thread *(in +acc* through). **(b)** *(col) Plan etc* to engineer. 2 *vr* **sich in eine Verkehrskolonne** ~ to filter into a

stream of traffic.

einfahren *sep irreg* 1 *vi aux sein (Zug, Schiff)* to come in *(in+acc -to)*. 2 *vt* **(a)** *(kaputtfahren) Mauer, Zaun* to knock down. **(b)** *Ernte* to bring in. **(c)** *Fahrgestell etc* to retract. **(d)** *Wagen* to run in *(Brit)*, to break in *(US)*; *siehe* **eingefahren**.

Einfahrt *f* **(a)** *no pl (das Einfahren)* entry *(in +acc* to); *(Min)* descent. **Vorsicht bei (der)** ~ **des Zuges!** stand well back, the train is arriving. **(b)** *(Eingang)* entrance; *(von Autobahn)* sliproad.

Einfall *m* **(a)** idea; *(Grille, Laune)* notion. **es war nur so ein** ~ it was just an idea; **er hat** ~**e wie ein altes Haus** *(hum)* he has some weird ideas. **(b)** *(Mil)* invasion *(in+acc* of).

einfallen *vi sep irreg aux sein* **(a)** to collapse; *siehe* **eingefallen**. **(b)** *(eindringen)* **in ein Land** ~ to invade a country. **(c)** *(Licht)* to fall; *(in ein Zimmer etc)* to come in *(in+acc -to)*. **(d)** *(mitsingen, mitreden)* to join in; *(dazwischenreden)* to break in *(in+acc* on). **(e)** *(Gedanke)* **jdm** ~ to occur to sb; **hast du dir etwas** ~ **lassen?** have you had any ideas?, have you thought of anything?; **da mußt du dir schon etwas Besseres** ~ **lassen!** you'll really have to think of something better; **was fällt Ihnen ein!** what are you thinking of!; **dabei fällt mir mein Onkel ein, der** ... that reminds me of my uncle, who ...; **es fällt mir jetzt nicht ein** I can't think of it *or* it won't come to me at the moment; **es wird Ihnen schon wieder** ~ it will come back to you.

Einfalls-: **e**~**los** *adj* unimaginative; **e**~**reich** *adj* imaginative; ~**reichtum** *m* imaginativeness.

Einfalt *f no pl* naivety.

einfältig *adj* naive.

Einfaltspinsel *m (col)* simpleton.

Einfamilienhaus *nt* family house.

einfangen *vt sep irreg (lit, fig)* to catch, to capture.

einfärben *vt sep Stoff, Haar* to dye.

einfarbig *adj* all one colour *(Brit)* or color *(US)*, plain; *Stoff* self-coloured *(Brit)*, self-colored *(US)*.

einfassen *vt sep Beet, Kleid* to edge; *Edelstein* to set. **ein Grundstück (mit einem Zaun)** ~ to put a fence around a plot of land.

Einfassung *f (von Beet)* border; *(von Edelstein)* setting.

einfetten *vt sep* to grease; *Leder, Schuhe* to dubbin; *Haut, Gesicht* to rub cream into.

einfinden *vr sep irreg* to come; *(eintreffen)* to arrive.

einflechten *vt sep irreg* to twine; *(fig: ins Gespräch etc)* to work in *(in+acc -to)*.

einfliegen *vt sep irreg Proviant, Truppen* to fly in *(in+acc -to)*.

einfließen *vi sep irreg aux sein* to flow in. **er ließ nebenbei** ~, **daß** ... he let it drop that ...

einflößen *vt sep jdm etw* ~ to pour sth down sb's throat; *Medizin auch* to give sb sth; *Ehrfurcht, Mut etc* to instil sth into sb.

Einfluß *m* **(a)** influence. **unter dem** ~ **von jdm/ etw stehen** to be under the influence of sb/sth; ~ **auf jdn haben/ausüben** to have/exert an influence on sb; ~ **nehmen** to bring an influence to bear. **(b)** *(von Luft)* influx.

Einfluß-: ~**bereich** *m* sphere of influence; ~**nahme** *f* exertion of influence *(gen* by); **e**~**reich** *adj* influential.

einflüstern *vt sep jdm etw* ~ to whisper sth to sb; *(fig)* to insinuate sth to sb.

einförmig *adj* uniform; *(eintönig)* monotonous.

Einförmigkeit *f siehe adj* uniformity; monotony.

einfrieren *sep irreg* 1 *vi aux sein* to freeze; *(Wasserleitung)* to freeze up. 2 *vt Nahrungsmittel, Löhne etc* to freeze; *(Pol) Beziehungen* to suspend.

einfügen *sep* 1 *vt Steine etc* to fit *(in+acc* into); *(nachtragen)* to insert *(in +acc* in), to add *(in +acc* to). 2 *vr* to fit in *(in+acc -to)*; *(sich anpassen)* to adapt *(in+acc* to).

Einfügung f insertion, addition.

einfühlen vr sep sich in jdn ~ to empathize with sb; **sich in etw** (acc) ~ in Situation, jds Probleme to understand sth, to sympathize with sth; in Gedicht, Rolle to feel one's way into sth.

einfühlsam adj sensitive; Mensch auch understanding.

Einfühlungsvermögen nt empathy. **mit großem** ~ with a great deal of sensitivity.

Einfuhr f -en import; (das Einführen auch) importing.

Einfuhr- in cpds import; ~**artikel** m import.

einführen vt sep **(a)** to introduce (in+acc into); Mode, Sitte to start; (hineinstecken auch) to insert. **jdn in sein Amt** ~ to install sb (in office). **(b)** (Comm) Waren to import.

Einfuhr-: ~**genehmigung** f import permit; ~**hafen** m port of entry; ~**land** nt importing country; ~**sperre** f, ~**stopp** m ban on imports.

Einführung f introduction (in +acc to); (Amts~) installation.

Einführungs- in cpds introductory.

Einfuhr-: ~**verbot** nt ban on imports; ~**zoll** m import duty.

einfüllen vt sep to pour in.

Einfüllstutzen m (Aut) filler pipe.

Eingabe f **(a)** (form: Gesuch) petition (an+acc to). **(b)** (Comp) input.

Eingang m **(a)** entrance (in+acc to); (Zutritt, Aufnahme) entry. „**kein** ~!" "no entrance"; **in etw** (acc) ~ **finden** to find one's way into sth. **(b)** (Comm: Waren~, Post~) delivery; (Erhalt) receipt. **wir bestätigen den** ~ **Ihres Schreibens vom ...** we acknowledge receipt of your letter of the ...; **den** ~ **or die** ~**e bearbeiten** to deal with the in-coming mail.

eingängig adj Melodie, Spruch catchy.

eingangs 1 adv at the beginning. **2** prep+gen (form) at the beginning of.

Eingangs-: ~**bestätigung** f (Comm) acknowledgement of receipt; ~**datum** nt date of receipt; ~**halle** f entrance hall; ~**stempel** m (Comm) receipt stamp; ~**tür** f entrance, door.

eingeben vt sep irreg **(a)** (verabreichen) to give. **(b)** (einspeichern) **dem Computer etw** ~ **to feed** or input sth into the computer.

eingebettet adj **in or zwischen Hügeln** ~ nestling among the hills.

eingebildet adj **(a)** (hochmütig) conceited. **(b)** (imaginär) imaginary. **ein** ~**er Kranker** a hypochondriac.

eingeboren adj (einheimisch) native; (angeboren) innate, inborn (dat in).

Eingeborene(r) mf decl as adj native (auch hum).

Eingebung f inspiration.

eingedenk (old, liter) prep +gen bearing in mind. ~ **dessen, daß ...** bearing in mind that ...

eingefahren adj Verhaltensweise well-worn. **die Diskussion bewegte sich in** ~**en Gleisen** the discussion covered the same old well-worn topics.

eingefallen adj Wangen hollow; Gesicht gaunt.

eingefleischt adj attr (überzeugt) confirmed; (unverbesserlich) dyed-in-the-wool. ~**er Junggeselle** (hum) confirmed bachelor.

eingehen sep irreg aux sein **1** vi **(a)** (Aufnahme finden: Wort, Sitte) to be adopted (in +acc in). **in die Geschichte** ~ to go down in history. **(b)** (ankommen: Briefe, Waren etc) to arrive. **eingegangene Post/Spenden** mail/donations received. **(c)** (sterben: Tiere, Pflanze) to die (an+dat of); (col: Firma etc) to fold. **bei dieser Hitze/Kälte geht man ja ein!** (col) this heat/cold is just too much (col). **(d)** (behandeln) **auf etw** (acc) ~ **auf Frage etc** to go into sth; **niemand ging auf meine Frage ein** nobody took any notice of my question; **auf jdn/etw** ~ to give (one's) time and attention to sb/sth. **(e)** (zustimmen) **auf einen**

Vorschlag/Plan ~ to go along with a suggestion/plan. **2** vt (abmachen, abschließen) to enter into; Risiko to take; Wette to make.

eingehend adj detailed, in-depth.

eingekeilt adj hemmed in; (fig) trapped.

Eingemachte(s) nt decl as adj bottled fruit/vegetables; (Marmelade) preserves pl.

eingemeinden* vt sep to incorporate (in+acc, nach into).

eingenommen adj **für jdn/etw** ~ **sein** to be taken with sb/sth; **gegen jdn/etw** ~ **sein** to be biased against sb/sth; **er ist sehr von sich** (dat) **selbst** ~ he really fancies himself.

eingeschnappt adj (col) cross. ~ **sein** to be in a huff.

eingeschossig ['aɪngəʃɔsɪç] adj Haus single-storey (Brit), single-story (US).

eingeschränkt adj (eingeengt) restricted, limited; (sparsam) careful.

eingeschrieben adj Mitglied, Brief registered.

eingeschworen adj confirmed; Gemeinschaft close. **auf etw** (acc) ~ **sein** to swear by sth; **auf eine Politik** ~ **sein** to be committed to a policy.

eingesessen adj Familie old-established.

eingespannt adj busy.

eingespielt adj Mannschaft, Team (well-)adjusted to playing/working together. **aufeinander** ~ **sein** to be used to one another.

Eingeständnis nt admission, confession.

eingestehen* vt sep irreg to admit, to confess.

eingestellt adj links/rechts ~ **sein** to have leanings to the left/right; **wer so** ~ **ist wie er** anyone who thinks as he does; **gegen jdn** ~ **sein** to be set against sb; **ich bin im Moment nicht auf Besuch** ~ I'm not prepared for visitors.

eingetragen adj Verein, Warenzeichen registered.

Eingeweide nt - usu pl entrails pl, innards pl.

Eingeweihte(r) mf decl as adj initiate. **ein paar** ~ a chosen few.

eingewöhnen* vr sep to settle down (in+dat in).

Eingewöhnung f settling down.

eingießen vt sep irreg (hineinschütten) to pour in (in+acc -to); (einschenken) to pour.

eingleisig adj single-track. **er denkt sehr** ~ (fig) he's completely single-minded.

eingliedern sep **1** vt to integrate (in+acc into). **2** vr to integrate oneself (in+acc into).

Eingliederung f integration.

eingraben sep irreg **1** vt to bury (in+acc in); Pflanze etc to dig in (in+acc -to). **2** vr to dig oneself in (auch Mil). **dieses Erlebnis hat sich seinem Gedächtnis eingegraben** this experience has engraved itself on his memory.

eingravieren* vt sep to engrave (in +acc in).

eingreifen vi sep irreg (einschreiten, Mil) to intervene. **in jds Rechte** (acc) ~ to intrude (up)on sb's rights.

Eingreifen nt no pl intervention.

eingrenzen vt sep to enclose; (fig) Problem to delimit.

Eingriff m **(a)** (Med) operation. **(b)** (Übergriff) intervention. **ein** ~ **in jds Rechte** an intrusion (up)on sb's rights.

einhaken sep **1** vt to hook in (in+acc -to). **2** vi (col: Punkt aufgreifen) to intervene; (in Unterhaltung auch) to break in. **3** vr sie hakte sich bei ihm ein she put or slipped her arm through his.

Einhalt m no pl jdm/einer Sache ~ gebieten to stop sb/sth.

einhalten vt sep irreg (beachten) to keep; Spielregeln to follow; Diät, Vertrag to keep; Verpflichtungen to carry out. **die Zeit** ~ to keep to time or schedule.

Einhaltung f siehe **einhalten** keeping; following; keeping to; carrying out.

einhämmern vt sep Nagel etc to hammer in (in +acc -to). **jdm etw** ~ (fig) to hammer sth into sb.

einhandeln vt sep **(a)** (gegen, für for) to trade. **(b)**

(bekommen) **sich** *(dat)* **etw** ~ *(col)* to get sth.

einhändig *adj* one-handed.

einhängen *sep* **1** *vt Tür* to hang; *Fenster* to put in; *(Telec) Hörer* to put down. **2** *vi (Telec)* to hang up.

einheften *vt sep* **(a)** *(Sew)* to tack in. **(b)** *Akten etc* to file.

einheimisch *adj* native, indigenous; *Produkt, Mannschaft* local.

Einheimische(r) *mf decl as adj* local.

einheimsen *vt sep (col)* to collect; *Erfolg, Ruhm auch* to walk off with; *Geld auch* to rake in *(col)*.

Einheirat *f* marriage *(in +acc into)*.

einheiraten *vi sep* **in einen Betrieb** ~ to marry into a business.

Einheit *f* **(a)** unity; *(das Ganze)* whole. **eine geschlossene** ~ **bilden** to form an integrated whole. **(b)** *(Mil, Sci)* unit.

einheitlich *adj (gleich)* the same, uniform; *(genormt)* standard(ized); *(in sich geschlossen)* unified. **wir müssen** ~ **vorgehen** we must act in a unified fashion.

Einheitlichkeit *f siehe adj* uniformity; standardization; unity.

Einheits-: ~**front** *f (Pol)* united front; *(Volksfront)* popular front; ~**gewerkschaft** *f* unified trade *(Brit) or* labor *(US)* union; ~**kleidung** *f* uniform; ~**liste** *f (Pol)* single *or* unified list of candidates; ~**preis** *m* standard price.

einheizen *sep* **1** *vi* to put the heating on. **jdm (tüchtig)** ~ *(col) (die Meinung sagen)* to haul sb over the coals; *(zu schaffen machen)* to make things hot for sb. **2** *vt Zimmer* to heat (up).

einhellig *adj* unanimous.

einhergehen *vi sep irreg aux sein* to walk.

einholen *vt sep* **(a)** *Boot, Netz* to pull in; *Fahne, Segel* to lower. **(b)** *Rat, Erlaubnis* to get. **(c)** *(erreichen) Laufenden* to catch up; *Vorsprung, Zeit* to make up. **(d)** *auch vi* = **einkaufen**.

Einholung *f* **(a)** *(von Fahne)* lowering. **(b)** *(von Rat etc)* obtaining.

Einhorn *nt* unicorn.

einhüllen *vt sep* to wrap (up) *(in +acc in)*. **in Wolken eingehüllt** shrouded in clouds.

einhundert *num siehe* **hundert**.

einig *adj* **(a)** *(geeint)* united. **(b)** *(einer Meinung)* agreed, in agreement *(über+acc on, about, in +dat on)*. **sich** *(dat)* **über etw** *(acc)* ~ **werden** to agree on sth; **wir sind uns** ~, **daß ...** we are agreed that ...; **wir werden schon miteinander** ~ **werden** we will manage to come to an agreement.

einige *indef pron siehe* **einige(r, s)**.

einigemal *adv* a few times.

einigen 1 *vt Volk etc* to unite; *Streitende* to reconcile. **2** *vr* to reach (an) agreement *(über+acc about)*. **sich auf einen Kompromiß** ~ to agree to a compromise.

einige(r, s) *indef pron* **(a)** *sing (etwas)* some; *(ziemlich viel)* (quite) some. **in** ~**r Entfernung** some distance away; **das wird** ~**s kosten** that will cost something; **dazu ist noch** ~**s zu sagen** there are still one or two things to say about that; **mit** ~**m guten Willen** *(mit Anstrengung)* with a bit of effort. **(b)** *pl* some; *(mehrere)* several; *(ein paar auch)* a few. **mit Ausnahme** ~**r weniger** with a few exceptions; ~ **hundert Menschen** a few hundred people; **in** ~**n Tagen** in a few days; **vor** ~**n Tagen** the other day, a few days ago.

einigermaßen *adv* rather, somewhat; *(vor adj)* fairly; *(ungefähr)* to some extent. ~ **Bescheid wissen** to have a fair idea; **wie geht's dir?** — ~ how are you? — all right, not too bad.

einiges *indef pron siehe* **einige(r, s)**.

Einigkeit *f no pl* unity; *(Übereinstimmung)* agreement.

Einigung *f* **(a)** *(Pol)* unification. **(b)** *(Übereinstimmung)* agreement. **über etw** *(acc)* ~ **erzielen** to come to *or* reach agreement on sth.

ein|impfen *vt sep* **jdm etw** ~ to din sth into sb.

einjagen *vt sep* **jdm Furcht/einen Schrecken** ~ to give sb a fright.

einjährig *adj Kind, Tier* one-year-old; *Pflanze* annual. **nach** ~**er Pause** after a break of one year.

einkalkulieren* *vt sep* to reckon on; *Kosten* to take into account.

einkassieren* *vt sep* **(a)** *Geld, Schulden* to collect. **(b)** *(col: wegnehmen)* to take; *Dieb* to nab *(col)*.

Einkauf *m* **(a)** *(das Einkaufen)* buying, purchase. **Einkäufe machen** to go shopping; **ich muß noch ein paar Einkäufe machen** I still have a few things to buy. **(b)** *(usu pl: Gekauftes)* purchase. **(c)** *no pl (Comm: Abteilung)* purchasing (department).

einkaufen *sep* **1** *vt* to buy. **2** *vi* to shop; *(Comm)* to buy. ~ **gehen** to go shopping.

Einkäufer *m (Comm)* buyer.

Einkaufs- *in cpds* shopping; ~**bummel** *m* einen ~**bummel machen** to go on a shopping spree; ~**leiter** *m (Comm)* chief buyer; ~**netz** *nt* string bag; ~**preis** *m* wholesale price; ~**tasche** *f* shopping bag; ~**wagen** *m* trolley *(Brit)*, cart *(US)*; ~**zettel** *m* shopping list.

einkehren *vi sep aux sein* **(a)** *(in Gasthof)* to (make a) stop *(in+dat at)*. **(b)** *(geh: Ruhe, Frühling)* to come.

einkellern *vt sep* to store in a cellar.

einkerben *vt sep* to cut a notch/notches in.

einkerkern *vt sep* to incarcerate.

einkesseln *vt sep* to encircle.

einklagen *vt sep Schulden* to sue for (the recovery of).

einklammern *vt sep* to put in brackets.

Einklang *m* **(a)** *(Mus)* unison. **(b)** *(geh: Übereinstimmung)* harmony. **in** ~ **bringen** to harmonize; **im** ~ **mit etw stehen** to be in accord with sth.

einkleben *vt sep* to stick in *(in +acc -to)*.

einkleiden *vt sep* to fit out. **jdn/sich völlig neu** ~ to buy sb/oneself a completely new wardrobe.

einklemmen *vt sep* **(a)** *(quetschen)* to jam. **er hat sich die Hand in der Tür eingeklemmt** he caught his hand in the door. **(b)** *(festdrücken)* to clamp.

einknicken *sep* **1** *vt Papier* to crease; *Streichholz, Äste* to snap. **2** *vi aux sein (Strohhalm)* to get bent; *(Äste)* to snap; *(Knie)* to give way, to buckle.

einkochen *vt sep Gemüse* to preserve; *Obst auch, Marmelade* to bottle.

einkommen *vi sep irreg aux sein* to come in.

Einkommen *nt* - income.

Einkommens-: ~**ausfall** *m* loss of income; **e**~**schwach** *adj* low-income *attr;* **e**~**stark** *adj* high-income *attr.*

Einkommen(s)steuer *f* income tax.

Einkommen(s)steuer-: ~**erklärung** *f* income tax return; **e**~**pflichtig** *adj* liable to income tax.

Einkommensverhältnisse *pl* (level of) income.

einkreisen *vt sep Feind, Wild* to surround; *(fig) Problem* to consider from all sides.

Einkreisung *f (von Feind etc)* surrounding; *(Pol)* isolation.

einkriegen *sep (col)* **1** *vt* to catch up. **2** *vr* **sie konnte sich gar nicht mehr darüber** ~, **daß ...** she couldn't get over the fact that ...; **krieg dich mal wieder ein!** control yourself!

Einkünfte *pl* income *sing; (einer Firma auch)* receipts.

einkuppeln *vi sep (Aut)* to let the clutch in.

einladen *vt sep irreg* **(a)** to invite. **jdn zu einer Party** ~ to ask sb to a party; **jdn auf ein Bier** ~ to invite sb for a beer; **laß mal, ich lade dich ein** let me treat you; **wir sind heute abend eingeladen** we've been invited out this evening. **(b)** *Waren* to load *(in +acc into)*.

einladend *adj* inviting; *Speisen* appetizing.

Einladung *f* invitation.

Einlage *f* **(a)** *(in Brief etc)* enclosure. **(b)**

(Schuh~) insole; *(zum Stützen)* (arch) support. **(c)** *(Sew)* padding; *(Versteifung)* interfacing. **(d)** *(Zahn~)* temporary filling. **(e)** *(Cook)* noodles, egg etc added to a clear soup. **(f)** *(Zwischenspiel)* interlude. **(g)** *(Fin: Kapital~)* investment; *(Spar~ auch)* deposit.

einlagern *vt sep* to store.

Einlagerung *f* storage.

Einlaß *m* **(a)** *no pl (Zutritt)* admission. **jdm ~ gewähren** to admit sb. **(b)** *(Tech)* inlet.

einlassen *sep irreg* **1** *vt* to let in *(in+acc* -to); **Person** *auch* to admit; **Wasser** to run *(in+acc into).*
2 *vr* **(a) sich auf etw** *(acc)* **~** to get involved in sth; *(sich zu etw verpflichten)* to let oneself in for sth; **sich auf einen Kompromiß ~** to agree to a compromise; **ich lasse mich auf keine Diskussion ein** I'm not having any discussion about it. **(b) sich mit jdm ~** *(pej: Umgang pflegen mit)* to get mixed up *or* involved with sb; **sie läßt sich mit jedem ein** she'll go with anyone.

Einlauf *m* **(a)** *no pl (Sport) (am Ziel)* finish; *(ins Stadion etc)* entry. **beim ~ in die Zielgerade ...** coming into the final straight ... **(b)** *(Med)* enema. **jdm einen ~ machen** to give sb an enema.

einlaufen *sep irreg* **1** *vi aux sein* **(a)** to come in *(in +acc* -to); *(ankommen auch)* to arrive *(in+acc* in); *(Wasser)* to run in *(in +acc* -to). **(b)** *(eingehen: Stoff)* to shrink. **2** *vt* **Schuhe** to wear in. **3** *vr (Motor, Maschine)* to be run in, to be broken in *(US).*

einläuten *vt sep neues Jahr* to ring in; *(Sport) Runde* to sound the bell for.

einleben *vr sep* to settle down *(in or an+dat* in).

einlegen *vt sep* **(a)** *(hineintun)* to insert *(in+acc* in), to put in *(in+acc* -to); *Film auch* to load *(in +acc* into). **(b)** *Sonderschicht, Spurt* to put on; *Pause* to have; *(Aut) Gang* to engage. **(c)** *(in Holz etc)* to inlay. **(d)** *(fig) Protest* to register. **ein gutes Wort für jdn ~** to put in a good word for sb *(bei* with); **ein Veto ~** to use one's veto. **(e)** *(Cook) Heringe etc* to pickle. **(f)** *Haare* to set, to put in rollers.

Einlegesohle *f* insole.

einleiten *vt sep* **(a)** *(in Gang setzen)* to initiate; **Maßnahmen** *auch, Schritte* to introduce, to take; **neues Zeitalter** to mark the start of, to inaugurate; *(Jur) Verfahren* to institute; *(Med) Geburt* to induce. **(b)** *(beginnen)* to start; *(eröffnen)* to open. **(c)** *Abwässer etc* to discharge *(in+acc* into).

einleitend *adj* introductory. **er sagte ~, daß ... he** said by way of introduction that ...

Einleitung *f* **(a)** *siehe vt* **(a)** initiation; introduction; inauguration; institution; induction. **(b)** *(Vorwort)* introduction; *(Mus)* prelude. **(c)** *(von Abwässern)* discharge *(in +acc into).*

einlenken *vi sep (fig)* to yield, to give way.

einlesen *sep irreg* **1** *vr* **sich in ein Gebiet ~** to get into a subject. **2** *vt* **Daten** to feed *(in+acc* into).

einleuchten *vi sep* to be clear *(jdm* to sb). **ja, das leuchtet mir ein!** yes, I see that.

einleuchtend *adj* reasonable, plausible.

einliefern *vt sep* **Waren** to deliver. **jdn ins Krankenhaus ~** to admit sb to hospital; **jdn ins Gefängnis ~** to put sb in prison.

Einlieferung *f (von Waren)* delivery; *(ins Krankenhaus)* admission *(in+acc* to); *(ins Gefängnis)* committal *(in+acc* to).

Einlieferungsschein *m* certificate of posting.

einlochen *vt sep (col: einsperren)* to lock up.

einlösen *vt sep Pfand* to redeem; *Scheck, Wechsel* to cash (in); *(fig) Wort, Versprechen* to keep.

Einlösung *f siehe vt* redemption; cashing (in); keeping.

einlullen *vt sep (fig col)* **jdn mit schönen Worten ~** to soft-talk sb.

einmachen *vt sep* to preserve; *(in Gläser auch)* to bottle.

Einmachglas *nt* bottling jar.

einmal *adv* **(a)** *(ein einziges Mal)* once; *(erstens)*

first of all, firstly. **~ sagt er dies, ~ das** sometimes he says one thing, sometimes another; **auf ~** *(plötzlich)* all at once; *(zugleich)* at once; **~ mehr** once again; **~ und nie wieder** once and never again; **noch ~** again; **wenn sie da ist, ist es noch ~ so schön** it's twice as nice when she's there; **~ ist keinmal** *(Prov)* once doesn't count. **(b)** *(früher, vorher)* once; *(später, in Zukunft)* one day. **waren Sie schon ~ in Rom?** have you ever been to Rome?; **es war ~ ...** once upon a time there was ...; **das war ~!** that was then. **(c) nicht ~** not even; **wieder ~** again; **sag ~, ist das wahr?** tell me, is it true?; **gib mir ~ das Buch** give me that book.

Einmal|eins *nt no pl* (multiplication) tables *pl; (fig)* ABC, basics *pl.* **das ~ lernen** to learn one's tables; **das kleine/große ~** (multiplication) tables up to ten/over ten.

einmalig *adj* unique; *Anschaffung, Zahlung* one-off; *(col: hervorragend)* fantastic, amazing.

Einmaligkeit *f* uniqueness.

Einmannbetrieb *m* **(a)** one-man business. **(b)** **etw auf ~ umstellen** to convert sth for one-man operation.

Einmarkstück *nt* one-mark piece.

Einmarsch *m* entry *(in +acc* into); *(in ein Land)* invasion *(in+acc* of).

einmarschieren* *vi sep aux sein* to march in *(in +acc* -to).

einmauern *vt sep (ummauern)* to wall in *(in+acc* in).

einmieten *vr sep* **sich bei jdm ~** to take lodgings with sb.

einmischen *vr sep* to interfere *(in +acc* in).

Einmischung *f* interference *(in +acc* in).

einmonatig *adj attr* one-month.

einmontieren* *vt sep* to fit in *(in +acc* -to).

einmotorig *adj Flugzeug* single-engine(d).

einmummen *vt sep* **Kleider** etc to put in mothballs.

einmünden *vi sep aux sein in etw (acc)* **~** *(Fluß)* to flow into sth; *(Straße)* to run *or* lead into sth.

Einmündung *f (von Fluß)* confluence; *(von Straße)* junction.

Einmütigkeit *f* unanimity.

einmütig *adj* unanimous.

einnähen *vt sep* to sew in *(in +acc* -to); *(enger machen)* to take in.

Einnahme *f* **-n (a)** *(Mil)* seizure, capture. **(b)** **~n** *pl* income *sing; (Geschäfts~)* takings *pl; (aus Einzelverkauf)* proceeds *pl; (eines Staates)* revenue *sing;* **~n und Ausgaben** income and expenditure.

Einnahmequelle *f* source of income; *(eines Staates)* source of revenue.

einnehmen *vt sep irreg* **(a)** to take; *(lit, fig) Platz etc* to take (up), to occupy; *Stelle (innehaben)* to have, to occupy; *Haltung, Standpunkt etc* to take up; *Steuern* to collect. **die eingenommenen Gelder** the takings. **(b) er nahm uns alle für sich ein** he won us all over; **jdn gegen sich ~** to set sb against oneself.

einnehmend *adj* likeable, charming. **er hat ein ~es Wesen** he's a likeable character; *(hum col)* he has taking ways of his own.

einnicken *vi sep aux sein (col)* to nod off.

einnisten *vr sep (lit)* to nest; *(Parasiten, Ei)* to lodge; *(fig)* to park oneself *(bei* on).

Ein|öde *f* wilderness.

ein|ölen *sep* **1** *vt* to oil. **2** *vr* to rub oneself with oil.

ein|ordnen *sep* **1** *vt* **(a)** *Bücher etc* to (put in) order; *Akten* to file. **(b)** *(klassifizieren)* to classify. **2** *vr* **(a)** *(in Gemeinschaft etc)* to fit in *(in+acc* -to). **(b)** *(Aut)* to get in(to) lane.

einpacken *sep* **1** *vt* **(a)** *(einwickeln)* to wrap up *(in +acc* in); *(auch fig)* to pack. **(b)** *(hineintun)* to pack *(in +acc* into). **2** *vi* to pack. **dann können wir ~** *(col)* in that case we may as well forget it.

einparken *vti sep* to park. **(in eine Parklücke) ~** to get into a parking space.

Einparteien- *in cpds* one-party.

einpassen *vt sep* to fit in *(in +acc -to)*.

einpauken *vt sep (col)* **jdm etw** ~ to drum sth into sb.

einpendeln *vr sep (fig)* to settle down; *(Preise etc)* to level off.

einpennen *vi sep aux sein (col)* to drop off *(col)*.

Einpfennigstück *nt* one-pfennig piece.

einpferchen *vt sep* Vieh to pen in *(in +acc -to)*; *(fig)* to coop up *(in +acc in)*.

einpflanzen *vt sep* to plant *(in +dat in)*; *(Med)* to implant *(jdm in(to) sb)*.

einplanen *vt sep* to plan (on), to include in one's plans; *Verzögerungen, Verluste* to allow for.

einpökeln *vt sep* Fisch, Fleisch to salt.

einprägen *sep* **1** *vt* Muster, Spuren to imprint, to impress; *Inschrift* to stamp. **sich** *(dat)* **etw** ~ to remember sth; *(auswendig lernen)* to memorize sth, to commit sth to memory. **2** *vr* **sich jdm** ~ to make an impression on sb.

einprägsam *adj* easily remembered; *Slogan, Melodie auch* catchy.

einprogrammieren* *vt sep* Daten to feed in.

einprügeln *sep (col)* **1** *vt* **jdm etw** ~ to din sth into sb *(col)*. **2** *vi* **auf jdn** ~ to lay into sb *(col)*.

einquartieren* *sep* **1** *vt* to quarter; *(Mil auch)* to billet. **Gäste bei Freunden** ~ to put visitors up with friends. **2** *vr* to be quartered *(bei with)*; *(Mil auch)* to be billeted *(bei on)*; *(Gäste)* to stop *(bei with)* *(col)*.

einquetschen *vt sep* = **einklemmen (a)**.

einrahmen *vt sep (lit, fig)* to frame.

einrasten *vti sep (vi: aux sein)* to engage.

einräumen *vt sep* **(a)** *Wäsche, Bücher etc* to put away; *Schrank, Regal etc* to fill. **(b)** *(zugestehen)* to concede, to admit; *Freiheiten etc* to allow; *Frist, Kredit* to grant, to allow. **die Presse räumte diesem Skandal viel Platz ein** the press devoted a lot of space to this scandal.

einrechnen *vt sep* to include. **ihn (mit) eingerechnet** including him.

einreden *sep* **1** *vt* **jdm/sich etw** ~ to talk sb/oneself into believing sth, to persuade sb/oneself of sth; **das redest du dir nur ein!** you're only imagining it. **2** *vi* **auf jdn** ~ to keep on and on at sb.

einreiben *vt sep irreg* **er rieb sich** *(dat)* **das Gesicht mit Creme ein** he rubbed cream into his face.

einreichen *vt sep* Antrag, Unterlagen to submit *(bei to)*; *(Jur)* Klage to file; *(bitten um)* Versetzung, Pensionierung to apply for, to request.

einreihen *sep* **1** *vt (einordnen, einfügen)* to put in *(in +acc -to)*; *(klassifizieren)* to classify. **2** *vr* **sich in etw** *(acc)* ~ to join sth.

Einreiher *m* - single-breasted suit/jacket/coat.

einreihig *adj* Anzug etc single-breasted.

Einreise *f* entry *(in +acc* into, to*)*. **bei der** ~ **in die DDR** when entering the GDR, on entry to the GDR.

Einreise|erlaubnis *f* entry permit.

einreisen *vi sep aux sein* to enter the country. **er reiste in die Schweiz ein** he entered Switzerland.

Einreise-: ~**verbot** *nt* refusal of entry; ~**verbot haben** to have been refused entry; ~**visum** *nt* entry visa.

einreißen *sep irreg* **1** *vt* **(a)** *Papier, Nagel* to tear. **(b)** *Zaun etc* to tear or pull down. **2** *vi aux sein (Papier)* to tear; *(fig col: Unsitte etc)* to catch on *(col)*, to get to be a habit *(col)*.

einrenken *sep* **1** *vt* Gelenk, Knie to put back in place; *(fig col)* to sort out. **2** *vr (fig col)* to sort itself out.

einrennen *vt sep irreg (col)* Tür to break down.

einrichten *sep* **1** *vt* **(a)** *(möblieren)* Wohnung to furnish; *(ausstatten)* Hobbyraum to fit out; *Praxis, Labor* to equip, to fit out. **eine Wohnung modern** ~ to furnish a flat in a modern style. **(b)**

(gründen, eröffnen) to set up; *Konto* to open. **(c)** *(fig: arrangieren)* to arrange, to fix. **ich werde es** ~**, daß wir um zwei Uhr da sind** I'll arrange for us to be there at two. **2** *vr* **(a)** *(sich möblieren)* to furnish one's house etc. **(b)** *(sich der Lage anpassen)* to get along or by, to manage; *(sparsam sein)* to cut down. **(c)** **sich auf etw** *(acc)* ~ to prepare oneself for sth; **auf Tourismus eingerichtet sein** to be geared to tourism.

Einrichtung *f* **(a)** *(das Einrichten; von Wohnung)* furnishing; *(von Hobbyraum)* fitting-out; *(von Labor, Praxis)* equipping. **(b)** *(Wohnungs~)* furnishings *pl; (Geschäfts~ etc)* fittings *pl; (Labor~ etc)* equipment *no pl*. **(c)** *(Gründung, Eröffnung)* setting-up; *(von Konto)* opening. **(d)** *(behördlich, wohltätig)* institution; *(öffentliche ~)* facility. **(e)** *(Gewohnheit)* **zur ständigen** ~ **werden** to become an institution.

Einrichtungsgegenstand *m* item of furniture.

einritzen *vt sep* to carve in *(in +acc -to)*.

einrollen *vt sep (einwickeln)* to roll up *(in+acc in)*. **sich** *(dat)* **die Haare** ~ to put one's hair in rollers.

einrosten *vi sep aux sein* to rust up; *(fig: Glieder)* to stiffen up; *(Kenntnisse etc)* to get rusty.

einrücken *sep* **1** *vi aux sein (Mil: in ein Land)* to move in *(in+acc -to)*. **2** *vt* Zeile to indent; *Anzeige (in Zeitung)* to insert.

einrühren *vt sep* to stir or mix in *(in+acc -to)*.

eins *num* one. **es ist** ~ it's one (o'clock); ~ **zu** ~ *(Sport)* one all; ~ **mit jdm sein** *(übereinstimmen)* to be in agreement with sb; **das ist doch alles** ~ *(col)* it's all one or all the same; **sehen und handeln waren** ~ when I/he etc saw it I/he etc had to do something; ~ **a** *(col)* first-rate *(col)*; **siehe eine(r, s) (c), vier**.

Eins *f* -**en** *one; (Sch auch)* A.

einsacken[1] *vt sep (col: erbeuten)* to grab *(col)*; *Geld, Gewinne* to rake in *(col)*.

einsacken[2] *vi sep aux sein (einsinken)* to sink; *(Boden auch)* to subside.

einsalzen *vt sep* Fisch, Fleisch to salt.

einsam *adj (a)* lonely; *(einzeln)* solitary. ~ **leben** to live a lonely/solitary life. **(b)** *(abgelegen)* Haus, Insel secluded; Dorf isolated; *(menschenleer)* empty. **(c)** *(col)* ~**e Klasse/Spitze** absolutely fantastic *(col)*.

Einsamkeit *f siehe adj* **(a)** loneliness; solitariness. **er liebt die** ~ he likes solitude. **(b)** seclusion; isolation; emptiness.

einsammeln *vt sep* to collect (in).

Einsatz *m* **(a)** *(~teil)* insert; *(Schubladen~, Koffer~)* tray; *(Topf~)* compartment. **(b)** *(Spiel~)* stake; *(Kapital~)* investment. **den** ~ **erhöhen** to raise the stakes. **(c)** *(Mus)* entry. **der Dirigent gab den** ~ the conductor raised his baton and brought in the orchestra. **(d)** *(Verwendung)* use; *(esp Mil)* deployment; *(von Arbeitskräften)* employment. **im** ~ in use; **die Ersatzspieler kamen nicht zum** ~ the reserves weren't used; **unter** ~ **aller Kräfte** by making a supreme effort. **(e)** *(Aktion) (Mil)* action; *(von Polizei)* intervention. **im** ~ in action; **zum** ~ **kommen** to go into action; **bei seinem ersten** ~ the first time he saw action; **sich zum** ~ **melden** to report for duty. **(f)** *(Hingabe)* commitment. **etw unter** ~ **seines Lebens tun** to risk one's life to do sth.

Einsatz-: ~**befehl** *m* order to go into action; **e~bereit** *adj* ready for use; *(Mil)* ready for action; **e~fähig** *adj* fit for use; *(Mil)* fit for action; Sportler fit; ~**kommando** *(Mil) nt* task force; ~**leiter** *m* head of operations; ~**wagen** *m (bei Straßenbahn, Bus)* extra tram/bus.

einschalten *sep* **1** *vt* **(a)** *(in Betrieb setzen)* to switch on; Sender to tune in to. **(b)** *(einfügen)* to interpolate. **(c)** jdn ~ to bring sb in. **2** *vr* **(a)** *(Heizung etc)* to switch itself on. **(b)** *(eingreifen)* to intervene.

Einschaltquote *f (TV)* viewing figures *pl*.

einschärfen *vt sep* **jdm etw** ~ to impress sth (up)on sb.

einschätzen *vt sep* to assess *(auch Fin)*, to evaluate. **falsch** ~ to misjudge; **wie ich die Lage einschätze** as I see the situation; **jdn hoch/ niedrig** ~ to have a high/low opinion of sb; **etw zu hoch/niedrig** ~ to overestimate/underestimate sth.

Einschätzung *f* assessment, evaluation. **falsche** ~ misjudgement; **nach meiner** ~ in my estimation.

einschenken *vt sep* to pour (out). **darf ich Ihnen noch Wein** ~? can I give you some more wine?

einscheren *vi sep aux sein* to get back (into lane).

einschicken *vt sep* to send in *(an +acc to)*.

einschieben *vt sep irreg* to put in *(in +acc -to)*. **eine Pause** ~ to have a break.

einschießen *sep irreg* **1** *vt Scheibe (mit Ball etc)* to smash (in). **2** *vi* **(a)** *(Sport)* to score. **er schoß zum 1:0 ein** he scored to make it 1-0. **(b) auf jdn** ~ to shoot at sb.

einschiffen *sep* **1** *vt* to ship. **2** *vr* to embark.

Einschiffung *f (von Personen)* boarding, embarkation; *(von Gütern)* loading.

einschl. = **einschließlich** incl.

einschlafen *vi sep irreg aux sein* to fall asleep, to go to sleep; *(Bein, Arm)* to go to sleep; *(fig: Freundschaft)* to peter out. **ich kann nicht** ~ I can't get to sleep; **vor dem E~ zu nehmen** *(Medizin)* to be taken before retiring.

einschläfern *vt sep (schläfrig machen)* to make sleepy; *Gewissen* to soothe; *(narkotisieren)* to give a soporific; *(töten) Tier* to put to sleep.

einschläfernd *adj* soporific; *(langweilig)* monotonous.

Einschlag *m* **(a)** *(von Geschoß)* impact. **der** ~ **der Granate war deutlich zu sehen** the place where the grenade had landed was clearly visible. **(b)** *(Aut: des Lenkrads)* lock. **(c)** *(Zusatz, Beimischung)* element.

einschlagen *sep irreg* **1** *vt* **(a)** *Nagel* to hammer or knock in; *Pfahl* to drive in. **(b)** *(zertrümmern)* to smash in; *Zähne* to knock out. **(c)** *(einwickeln) Ware* to wrap up. **(d)** *(Aut) Räder* to turn. **(e)** *(wählen) Weg* to take; *Kurs* to follow; *Laufbahn etc* to enter on. **das Schiff änderte den eingeschlagenen Kurs** the ship changed from its previous course. **2** *vi* **(a) (in etw** *acc)* ~ to hit (sth); **es muß irgendwo eingeschlagen haben** something must have been struck by lightning; **gut** ~ *(col)* to go down well, to be a big hit *(col)*. **(b) auf jdn/etw** ~ to hit out at sb/sth. **(c)** *(zur Bekräftigung)* to shake on it.

einschlägig *adj* appropriate; *Literatur, Paragraph auch* relevant. **er ist** ~ **vorbestraft** *(Jur)* he has a previous conviction for a similar offence.

einschleichen *vr sep irreg (lit, fig)* to creep in *(in +acc -to)*. **sich in jds Vertrauen** ~ *(fig)* to worm one's way into sb's confidence.

einschleppen *vt sep (fig) Krankheit etc* to bring in.

einschleusen *vt sep* to smuggle in *(in +acc -to)*.

einschließen *vt sep irreg* **(a)** to lock up *(in+acc in)*. **er schloß sich in seinem Zimmer ein** he locked himself (up) in his room. **(b)** *(umgeben)* to surround. **(c)** *(fig: beinhalten)* to include.

einschließlich **1** *prep+gen* including, inclusive of. **2** *adv* **bis S. 205** ~ up to and including p.205; **vom 1. bis** ~ **31. Oktober** from 1st to 31st October inclusive.

einschlummern *vi sep aux sein (geh)* to fall asleep.

Einschluß *m* **mit** *or* **unter** ~ **von** *(form)* including.

einschmeicheln *vr sep* **sich bei jdm** ~ to ingratiate oneself with sb; **~de Stimme** silky voice.

einschmieren *vt sep (mit Fett)* to grease; *(mit Öl)* to oil; *Gesicht (mit Creme)* to put cream on.

einschmuggeln *vt sep* to smuggle in *(in+acc -to)*. **er hat sich in den Saal eingeschmuggelt** he

sneaked into the hall.

einschnappen *vi sep aux sein* **(a)** *(Schloß, Tür)* to click shut. **(b)** *(col: beleidigt sein)* to take offence *(Brit)* or offense *(US)*, to get into a huff *(col)*.

einschneiden *vt sep irreg* to cut. **tief eingeschnittene Felsen** steep cliffs.

einschneidend *adj (fig)* drastic, radical.

einschneien *vi sep aux sein* to get snowed in. **eingeschneit sein** to be snowed in.

Einschnitt *m* cut; *(Med)* incision; *(im Tal, Gebirge)* cleft; *(im Leben)* decisive point.

einschnüren *vt sep* **(a)** *(einengen)* to cut into. **dieser Kragen schnürt mir den Hals ein** this collar is strangling me. **(b)** *Paket* to tie up.

einschränken *sep* **1** *vt* to cut back; *Bewegungsfreiheit, Recht* to limit, to restrict; *Wünsche* to moderate; *Behauptung* to qualify. **~d möchte ich sagen, daß ...** I'd like to qualify that by saying ...; **das Rauchen** ~ to cut down on smoking. **2** *vr (sparen)* to economize. **sich im Trinken** ~ to cut down on one's drinking; *siehe* **eingeschränkt.**

Einschränkung *f siehe vt* cutting back; limitation, restriction; moderation; qualification; *(Vorbehalt)* reservation.

einschrauben *vt sep* to screw in *(in +acc -to)*.

Einschreib(e)brief *m* registered letter.

einschreiben *sep irreg* **1** *vt (eintragen)* to enter; *siehe* **eingeschrieben.** **2** *vr (für Abendkurse etc)* to enrol; *(Univ)* to register.

Einschreiben *nt* registered letter/parcel. **einen Brief als** ~ **schicken** to send a letter by registered mail.

Einschreibung *f* enrolment; *(Univ)* registration.

einschreiten *vi sep irreg aux sein* to take action *(gegen against)*; *(dazwischentreten)* to intervene, to step in.

Einschreiten *nt no pl* intervention.

Einschub *m* insertion.

einschüchtern *vt sep* to intimidate.

Einschüchterung *f* intimidation.

einschulen *vt sep* to send to school. **eingeschult werden** *(Kind)* to start school.

Einschulung *f* first day at school. **die** ~ **findet im Alter von 6 Jahren statt** children start school at the age of 6.

Einschuß *m* **(a)** *(~stelle)* bullet hole; *(Med)* point of entry. **(b)** *(Ftbl)* (shot into) goal.

einschütten *vt sep* to tip in *(in +acc -to)*; *Flüssigkeiten* to pour in *(in+acc -to)*. **er hat sich** *(dat)* **noch etwas Kaffee eingeschüttet** he poured himself (out) some more coffee.

einschweißen *vt sep (Tech)* to weld in *(in+acc -to)*; *(in Plastik)* to shrink-wrap.

einschwenken *vi sep aux sein* to turn or swing in *(in+acc -to)*. **auf etw** *(acc)* ~ *(fig)* to go along with sth.

einsehen *vt sep irreg* to see; *(prüfen auch)* to inspect; *Fehler, Schuld auch* to recognize. **das sehe ich nicht ein** I don't see why.

Einsehen *nt*: **ein** ~ **haben** to have some understanding, *(mit, für* for*)*; *(Vernunft, Einsicht)* to see reason; **hab doch ein** ~! be reasonable!

einseifen *vt sep* to soap; *(col: betrügen)* to con *(col)*.

einseitig *adj* one-sided; *Ernährung* unbalanced; *(Jur, Pol) Erklärung, Kündigung* unilateral. **~e Lähmung** paralysis of one side of the body.

Einseitigkeit *f* one-sidedness; *(von Ernährung)* imbalance.

einsenden *vt sep irreg* to send in, to submit *(an +acc to)*.

Einsender(in *f)* *m* sender; *(bei Preisausschreiben)* competitor.

Einsendeschluß *m* closing date (for entries).

Einsendung *f* **(a)** *(bei Wettbewerb etc)* entry. **(b)** *no pl (das Einsenden)* sending in, submission.

einsetzen *sep* **1** *vt* **(a)** *(einfügen)* to put in *(in +acc -to)*; *Maschinenteil auch* to insert *(in +acc into)*, to fit in *(in+acc -to)*; *(schreiben auch)* to enter *(in +acc in)*. **jdm einen Goldzahn ~** to give sb a gold tooth. **(b)** *(ernennen)* to appoint; *Nachfolger* to name. **jdn in ein Amt ~** to appoint sb to an office. **(c)** *(verwenden)* to use; *Truppen, Polizei* to deploy; *Busse, Sonderzüge* to put on. **(d)** *(beim Glücksspiel)* to stake; *Leben* to risk. **2** *vi (beginnen)* to start, to begin; *(Mus)* to come in. **3** *vr* **sich (voll) ~** to show (complete) commitment *(in+dat* to*)*; **sich für jdn/etw ~** to support sb/sth; **ich werde mich dafür ~, daß ...** I will do what I can to see that ...

Einsetzung *f* appointment *(in +acc* to*)*.

Einsicht *f* **(a)** *(in Akten, Bücher)* inspection *(in +acc* of*)*. **~ in etw** *(acc)* **haben/verlangen** to look/ask to look at sth. **(b)** *(Vernunft)* sense, reason; *(Erkenntnis)* insight. **zur ~ kommen** to come to one's senses; **zu der ~ kommen, daß ...** to recognize that ...; **haben Sie doch ~!** have a heart!; *(seien Sie vernünftig)* be reasonable!

einsichtig *adj* **(a)** *(vernünftig)* reasonable; *(verständnisvoll)* understanding. **(b)** *(verständlich, begreiflich)* understandable. **jdm etw ~ machen** to make sb understand *or* see sth.

Einsichtnahme *f* **-n** *(form)* inspection. **er bat um ~ in die Akten** he asked to inspect *or* see the files; **„zur ~"** "for attention".

einsickern *vi sep aux sein* to seep in *(in+acc -to)*; *(fig)* to filter in *(in +acc -to)*.

Einsiedler(in *f)* *m* hermit; *(fig auch)* recluse.

einsilbig *adj* monosyllabic.

einsinken *vi sep irreg aux sein (im Morast, Schnee)* to sink in *(in+acc or dat -to)*; *(Boden etc)* to subside, to cave in. **eingesunkene Wangen** sunken *or* hollow cheeks.

einspannen *vt sep* **(a)** *(in Schraubstock)* to clamp in *(in+acc -to)*. **(b)** *(in Schreibmaschine)* to insert *(in+acc* in, into*)*. **(c)** *Pferde* to harness. **(d)** *(fig: arbeiten lassen)* to rope in *(für etw* to do sth*)*. **jdn für seine Zwecke ~** to use sb for one's own ends; *siehe* **eingespannt.**

einsparen *vt sep* to save, to economize on; *Kosten* to cut down on; *Posten* to eliminate.

Einsparung *f* **(a)** economy. **(b)** *siehe vt* saving; cutting down *(von* on*)*; elimination.

einspeichern *vt sep Daten* to feed in *(in+acc -to)*.

einsperren *vt sep* to lock up *(in +acc or dat* in*)*.

einspielen *sep* **1** *vr (Mus, Sport)* to warm up; *(Regelung, Arbeit)* to work out. **aber das spielt sich alles noch ein** but things should sort themselves out all right; **sich aufeinander ~** to become attuned to one another; *siehe* **eingespielt.** **2** *vt (Film etc)* to bring in, to gross; *Kosten* to recover.

einsprachig *adj* monolingual.

einspringen *vi sep irreg aux sein (col: aushelfen)* to stand in; *(mit Geld etc)* to help out.

Einspritz- *(Aut)*: **~düse** *f* injector; **~motor** *m* injection engine; **~pumpe** *f* injection pump.

einspritzen *vt sep (Aut, Med)* to inject. **er spritzte ihr Insulin ein** he gave her an insulin injection.

Einspruch *m* objection *(auch Jur)*. **~ einlegen** *(Admin)* to file an objection; **gegen etw ~ erheben** to raise an objection to sth.

Einspruchsfrist *f* *(Jur)* period for filing an objection.

einspurig *adj (Rail)* single-track; *(Aut)* single-lane. **die Straße ist nur ~ befahrbar** it's single-lane traffic only.

einst *adv (geh)* **(a)** *(früher)* once. **(b)** *(in ferner Zukunft)* one day.

einstampfen *vt sep Bücher* to pulp (down).

Einstand *m* **(a)** **er hat gestern seinen ~ gegeben** yesterday he celebrated starting his new job. **(b)** *(beim Tennis)* deuce.

einstanzen *vt sep* to stamp in *(in +acc -to)*.

einstechen *vt sep irreg* to pierce; *Nadel* to put *or* stick in *(in+acc -to)*; *(Cook)* to prick.

einstecken *vt sep* **(a)** *(in etw stecken)* to put *or* stick in *(in+acc -to)*; *Gerät* to plug in. **(b)** *(in die*

Tasche etc) **(sich** *dat)* **etw ~** to take sth; **hast du deinen Paß eingesteckt?** have you got your passport with you? **(c)** *(in den Briefkasten)* to post, to mail *(esp US)*. **(d)** *(col) Kritik etc* to take; *(verdienen) Geld, Profit* to pocket *(col)*. **der Boxer mußte viel ~** the boxer had to take a lot of punishment.

einstehen *vi sep irreg aux sein* **(a)** *(sich verbürgen)* **für jdn/etw ~** to vouch for sb/sth; **ich stehe dafür ein, daß ...** I will vouch that ... **(b)** *(Ersatz leisten)* **für etw ~** to make good sth.

einsteigen *vi sep irreg aux sein* **(a)** *(in ein Fahrzeug etc)* to get in *(in+acc -to)*; *(in Zug auch, in Bus)* to get on *(in+acc -to)*. **~!** *(Rail etc)* all aboard! **(b)** *(in ein Haus etc)* to climb *or* get in *(in+acc -to)*. **(c)** *(col)* **in die Politik/ins Verlagsgeschäft ~** to go into politics/publishing.

einstellbar *adj* adjustable.

einstellen *sep* **1** *vt* **(a)** *(hineinstellen)* to put in. **Bücher ins Regal ~** to put books away on the shelves. **(b)** *(anstellen) Arbeitskräfte* to take on. **(c)** *(beenden)* to stop; *(endgültig auch)* to discontinue; *Expedition, Suche* to call off; *(Mil) Feuer* to cease. **(d)** *(regulieren)* to adjust *(auf+acc* to*)*; *Fotoapparat (auf Entfernung)* to focus *(auf+acc* on*)*; *Wecker* to set *(auf +acc* for*)*; *Sender* to tune in to. **(e)** *(Sport) Rekord* to equal. **2** *vr* **(a) sich auf jdn/etw ~** *(sich richten nach)* to adapt oneself to sb/sth; *(sich vorbereiten auf)* to prepare oneself for sb/sth; *siehe* **eingestellt. (b)** *(erscheinen)* to appear; *(Fieber, Regen)* to set in; *(Wort, Gedanke)* to come to mind; *(Jahreszeiten)* to come, to arrive.

einstellig *adj Zahl* single-digit.

Einstellplatz *m* *(auf Hof)* carport; *(in Großgarage)* (covered) parking space.

Einstellung *f* **(a)** *(Anstellung)* employment. **(b)** *(Beendigung) siehe vt* **(c)** stopping; discontinuation; calling-off; cessation. **der Sturm zwang uns zur ~ der Suche** the storm forced us to call off the search. **(c)** *(Film: Szene)* take. **(d)** *(Gesinnung, Haltung)* attitude; *(politisch, religiös etc)* views *pl*.

Einstellungs-: **~gespräch** *nt* interview; **~stopp** *m* halt in recruitment; **~termin** *m* starting date.

Einstieg *m* **-e (a)** *no pl (das Einsteigen)* getting in; *(in Bus)* getting on; *(von Dieb: in Haus etc)* entry; *(fig: zu einem Thema etc)* lead-in *(zu* to*)*. **kein ~** no entrance. **(b)** *(von Bus, Bahn)* door.

einstig *adj attr* former.

einstimmen *sep* **1** *vi (in ein Lied etc)* to join in. **2** *vt (Mus) Instrument* to tune. **jdn/sich auf etw** *(acc)* **~** *(fig)* to get sb/oneself in the mood for sth.

einstimmig 1 *adv* singen, rufen in unison. **2** *adj* *(einmütig)* unanimous.

Einstimmigkeit *f* unanimity.

einstöckig *adj Haus* two-storey *(Brit)*, two-story *(US)*.

einstöpseln *vt sep (Elec)* to plug in *(in+acc -to)*.

einstreichen *vt sep irreg (col) Geld, Gewinn* to pocket *(col)*.

einstreuen *vt sep* to sprinkle in *(in+acc -to)*; *(fig) Bemerkung etc* to slip in *(in+acc -to)*.

einströmen *vi sep aux sein* to flood in *(in+acc -to)*; *(Licht, fig auch)* to stream in *(in +acc -to)*. **~de Kaltluft** a stream of cold air.

einstudieren* *vt sep Rolle* to study; *Theaterstück* to rehearse.

einstufen *vt sep* to classify. **in eine Kategorie etc ~** to put into a category etc.

Einstufung *f* classification. **nach seiner ~ in eine höhere Gehaltsklasse** after he was put on a higher salary grade.

einstündig *adj attr* one-hour.

einstürmen *vi sep aux sein* **auf jdn ~** *(Mil)* to storm sb; *(fig)* to assail sb.

Einsturz *m* collapse.

einstürzen *vi sep aux sein* to collapse. **auf jdn ~**

(fig) to overwhelm sb.

Einsturzgefahr *f* danger of collapse.

einstweilen *adv* in the meantime; *(vorläufig)* temporarily.

einstweilig *adj attr* temporary. **~e Verfügung** *(Jur)* temporary *or* interim injunction.

eintägig *adj attr* one-day.

Eintagsfliege *f (Zool)* mayfly; *(fig)* nine-day wonder.

eintauchen *sep* 1 *vt* to dip *(in+acc* in, into); *(völlig)* to immerse *(in +acc* in). 2 *vi aux sein (Schwimmer)* to dive in; *(U-Boot)* to dive.

Eintausch *m* exchange, swap *(col)*. **im ~ gegen** *or* **für etw** in exchange for sth.

eintauschen *vt sep* to exchange, to swap *(col)* *(gegen, für* for); *(umtauschen) Devisen* to change.

eintausend *num siehe* **tausend**.

einteilen *vt sep* **(a)** to divide (up) *(in+acc* into). **(b)** *(sinnvoll aufteilen) Zeit, Arbeit* to plan (out), to organize; *Geld* to budget. **(c)** *(dienstlich verpflichten)* to detail *(zu* for). **er ist als Aufseher eingeteilt** he has been assigned the job of supervisor.

einteilig *adj Badeanzug* one-piece *attr*.

Einteilung *f siehe vt* **(a)** division. **(b)** planning, organization; budgeting. **(c)** assignment.

eintönig *adj* monotonous.

Eintönigkeit *f* monotony.

Eintopf *m* stew.

Eintracht *f no pl* harmony, concord.

einträchtig *adj* peaceable.

Eintrag *m* -e *(schriftlich)* entry *(in+acc* in).

eintragen *sep irreg* 1 *vt* **(a)** *(in Liste etc)* to enter; *(amtlich)* to register; *siehe* **eingetragen. (b)** *jdm Gewinn ~* to bring sb profit; **das trägt nur Schaden ein** that will only do harm. 2 *vr* to sign; *(im Hotel)* to check in. **er trug sich in die Warteliste ein** he put his name down on the waiting list.

einträglich *adj* profitable.

Eintragung *f* entry *(in +acc* in).

eintreffen *vi sep irreg aux sein* **(a)** *(ankommen)* to arrive. **(b)** *(fig: wahr werden)* to come true.

eintreiben *vt sep irreg* **(a)** *Vieh* to drive in *(in+acc* -to). **(b)** *Geldbeträge* to collect.

eintreten *sep irreg* 1 *vi* **(a)** *aux sein* **in etw** *(acc)* **~** to enter sth; *(in Zimmer etc auch)* to go/come into sth; *(in Verein etc)* to join sth. **(b)** **auf jdn ~** to kick sb. **(c)** *aux sein (sich ereignen) (Tod)* to occur; *(Zeitpunkt)* to come; *(beginnen) (Dunkelheit, Nacht)* to fall; *(Tauwetter)* to set in. **(d)** *aux sein* **für jdn/etw ~** to stand up for sb/sth. 2 *vt (zertrümmern)* to kick in.

eintrichtern *vt sep (col)* **jdm etw ~** to drum sth into sb.

Eintritt *m* **(a)** *(das Eintreten)* entry *(in+acc* (in)to); *(ins Zimmer etc auch)* entrance; *(in Verein etc)* joining *(in+acc* of). **beim ~ ins Zimmer** on entering the room; **der ~ ins Geschäftsleben** getting into the business world. **(b)** *(~sgeld)* admission *(in+acc* to). **~ frei!** admission free; **„~ verboten“** "no admittance". **(c) bei ~ eines solchen Falles** in such an event; **der ~ des Todes** the moment when death occurs.

Eintritts-: **~geld** *nt* entrance money, admission charge; **~karte** *f* (entrance) ticket; **~preis** *m* admission charge.

eintrocknen *vi sep aux sein* to dry up.

eintrudeln *vi sep aux sein (col)* to drift in *(col)*.

eintunken *vt sep Brot* to dunk *(in +acc* in).

ein|üben *vt sep* to practise *(Brit)*, to practice *(US)*; *Theaterstück etc* to rehearse.

einverleiben* *vi sep and insep* **(a)** *Gebiet, Land* to annex *(dat* to). **(b)** *(hum col)* **sich** *(dat)* **etw ~** *(essen, trinken)* to put sth away *(col)*.

Einvernehmen *nt no pl (Eintracht)* harmony; *(Übereinstimmung)* agreement. **in gutem ~ leben** to live in perfect harmony; **im ~ mit jdm** in agreement with sb.

einvernehmlich *adj (form) Regelung* joint.

einverstanden *adj* **~! okay!, agreed!; ~ sein** to agree; **ich bin mit deinem Verhalten/mit dir gar nicht ~** I don't approve of your behaviour; **sich mit etw ~ erklären** to give one's agreement to sth.

Einverständnis *nt* agreement; *(Zustimmung)* consent. **wir haben uns in gegenseitigem ~ scheiden lassen** we were divorced by mutual consent; **im ~ mit jdm handeln** to act with sb's consent.

Einwaage *f no pl (Comm: Reingewicht)* weight of contents *of* can *or* jar excluding juice etc.

Einwand *m* -e objection. **einen ~ erheben** to raise an objection.

Einwanderer *m* immigrant.

einwandern *vi sep aux sein* to immigrate *(nach,* in *+acc* to).

Einwanderung *f* immigration *(nach,* in*+acc* to).

Einwanderungs- *in cpds* immigration.

einwandfrei *adj* **(a)** *(ohne Fehler)* perfect; *Sprache, Arbeit auch* faultless; *Benehmen* impeccable. **er spricht ein ~es Spanisch** he speaks perfect Spanish. **(b)** *(unzweifelhaft)* indisputable; *Beweis auch* definite. **etw ~ beweisen** to prove sth beyond doubt.

einwechseln *vt sep Geld* to change *(in +acc, gegen* into).

einwecken *vt sep* to preserve; *Obst auch* to bottle.

Einweckglas *nt* preserving jar.

Einweg- ['ainveːk]: **~flasche** *f* non-returnable bottle; **~verpackung** *f* disposable wrapping.

einweichen *vt sep* to soak.

einweihen *vt sep* **(a)** *(feierlich eröffnen)* to open *(officially)*; *(fig)* to christen. **(b)** **jdn in etw** *(acc)* **~** to initiate sb into sth; **er ist eingeweiht** he knows all about it; *siehe* **Eingeweihte(r).**

Einweihung(sfeier) *f* (official) opening.

einweisen *vt sep irreg* **(a)** *(in Krankenhaus)* to admit *(in+acc* to). **(b)** *(in Arbeit unterweisen)* **jdn ~** to introduce sb to his job *or* work. **(c)** *(Aut)* to guide in *(in+acc* -to).

Einweisung *f siehe vt* **(a)** admission *(in+acc* to). **(b)** **die ~ der neuen Mitarbeiter übernehmen** to assume responsibility for introducing new employees to their jobs *or* work. **(c)** guiding in.

einwenden *vt sep irreg* **etwas/nichts gegen etw einzuwenden haben** to have an objection/no objection to sth, to object/not to object to sth; **er hat immer etwas einzuwenden** he always has some objection to make.

Einwendung *f* objection *(auch Jur)*.

einwerfen *sep irreg* 1 *vt* **(a)** *Fensterscheibe etc* to break, to smash. **(b)** *Brief* to post, to mail *(esp US)*; *Münze* to insert. **(c)** *(fig) Bemerkung* to throw in. 2 *vi (Sport)* to throw in, to take the throw-in.

einwickeln *vt sep* **(a)** to wrap (up). **(b)** *(col: überreden)* to take in. **da hat er sich schön ~ lassen** he's really been taken for a ride *(col)*.

einwilligen *vi sep (in+acc* to) to consent, to agree.

Einwilligung *f (in+acc* to) consent, agreement.

einwinken *vt sep* to guide *or* direct in.

einwirken *vi sep* **auf jdn/etw ~** to have an effect on sb/sth; *(beeinflussen)* to influence sb/sth.

Einwirkung *f* influence; *(einer Sache auch)* effect. **unter (der) ~ von Drogen etc** under the influence of drugs etc; **unter (der) ~ eines Schocks stehen** to be suffering from shock.

einwöchig *adj* one-week *attr*.

Einwohner(in *f)* *m* - inhabitant.

Einwohner-: **~meldeamt** *nt* residents' registration office; **sich beim ~meldeamt (an)melden** ≈ to register with the police; **~schaft** *f no pl* population, inhabitants *pl*; **~zahl** *f* population.

Einwurf *m* **(a)** *(von Münze)* insertion; *(von Brief)* posting, mailing *(esp US)*. **(b)** *(Sport)* throw-in.

(c) *(Schlitz)* slot; *(von Briefkasten)* slit. **(d)** *(fig)* interjection; *(Einwand)* objection.

Einzahl f singular.

einzahlen vt sep to pay in. **Geld auf ein Konto** ~ **to** pay money into an account.

Einzahlung f payment; *(auf Sparkonto auch)* deposit.

Einzahlungs- in cpds paying-in; ~**frist** f payment deadline.

einzäunen vt sep to fence in.

Einzäunung f fence, fencing; *(das Umzäunen)* fencing-in.

einzeichnen vt sep to draw in. **ist der Ort eingezeichnet?** is the place marked?

Einzel nt - *(Tennis)* singles sing.

Einzel-: ~**antrieb** m *(Tech)* independent drive; ~**ausgabe** f separate edition; ~**behandlung** f individual treatment; ~**blattzuführung** f sheet-feed; ~**erscheinung** f isolated occurrence; ~**fall** m individual case; *(Sonderfall)* isolated or one-off case; ~**gänger(in** f) m - loner; ~**haft** f solitary (confinement).

Einzelhandel m retail trade. **im** ~ **erhältlich** available retail.

Einzelhandels- in cpds retail.

Einzel-: ~**händler** m retailer; ~**heit** f detail, particular; **etw in allen** ~**heiten schildern** to describe sth right down to the last detail; ~**kind** nt only child.

Einzeller m - *(Biol)* single-celled organism.

einzeln adj **(a)** individual; *(getrennt)* separate; *(von Paar) Schuh etc* odd. **bitte** ~ **eintreten** please come in one (person) at a time; **die** ~**en Städte, die wir besucht haben** the individual cities which we visited; ~ **aufführen** to list separately or individually. **(b)** *(alleinstehend) Baum, Haus* single, solitary. **(c)** *(mit pl n: einige, vereinzelte)* some. ~**e Besucher kamen schon früher** one or two visitors came earlier. **(d)** *(substantivisch)* **der/die** ~**e** the individual; **ein** ~**er** an individual, a single person; *(ein einziger Mensch)* one single person; ~**e** some (people), a few (people); **jeder** ~**e** (each and) every one of you/them *etc*; ~**es** some; ~**es hat mir gefallen** I liked some of it; **das** ~**e** the particular; **jedes** ~**e** each one; **etw im** ~**en besprechen** to discuss sth in detail.

Einzel-: ~**person** f single person; ~**radaufhängung** f *(Aut)* independent suspension; ~**stück** nt **ein schönes** ~**stück** a beautiful piece; ~**stücke verkaufen wir nicht** we don't sell them singly; ~**teil** nt individual or separate part; *(Ersatzteil)* spare part; **etw in seine** ~**teile zerlegen** to take sth to pieces; ~**wesen** nt individual; ~**zelle** f single cell *(auch Biol)*; ~**zimmer** nt single room.

einzementieren* vt sep Stein to cement.

einziehen sep irreg 1 vt **(a)** *(einfügen)* Faden to thread; *(in einen Bezug etc)* to put in; *(Build: einbauen)* Wand etc to put in. **(b)** *(zurückziehen)* Krallen, Fahrgestell to retract, to draw in; Bauch, Netz to pull in; Flagge, Segel to lower, to take down. **den Kopf** ~ to duck (one's head). **der Hund zog den Schwanz ein** the dog put his tail between his legs. **(c)** *(Mil) (zu into) Personen* to call up, to draft *(esp US); Fahrzeuge etc* to requisition. **(d)** *(einfordern) Steuern* to collect; *Banknoten* to withdraw (from circulation); *Führerschein* to take away; *Vermögen* to confiscate; *(fig) Erkundigungen* to make *(über+acc* about). **2** vi aux sein **(a)** *(in Haus)* to move in. **(b)** *(auch Mil: einmarschieren)* to march in *(in+acc* -to). **(c)** *(einkehren)* to come *(in+dat* into). **wenn der Friede im Lande einzieht** when peace comes to our country. **(d)** *(eindringen)* to soak in *(in* +acc -to).

Einziehung f **(a)** *(Mil) (von Personen)* call-up, drafting *(esp US); (von Fahrzeugen)* requisitioning. **(b)** *(Einforderung) (von Vermögen)* con-

fiscation; *(von Banknoten, Führerschein etc)* withdrawal; *(von Steuern etc)* collection.

einzig 1 adj **(a)** attr only, sole. **ich sehe nur eine** ~**e Möglichkeit** I can see only one (single) possibility; **kein** ~**es Mal** not once, not one single time. **(b)** *(emph)* absolute. **dieses Fußballspiel war eine** ~**e Schlammschlacht** this football match was just one big mudbath. **(c)** pred *(~artig)* unique. **(d)** *(substantivisch)* **der/die** ~**e** the only one; **das** ~**e** the only thing; **kein** ~**er** nobody, not a single person. **2** adv *(allein)* only, solely. **die** ~ **mögliche Lösung** the only possible solution; ~**und allein** solely; **das** ~ **Wahre** the only thing; *(das beste)* the real McCoy.

einzig|**artig** adj unique.

Einzig|**artigkeit** f uniqueness.

Einzimmer- in cpds one-room.

Einzug m **(a)** *(in Haus etc)* move *(in+acc* into). **(b)** *(Einmarsch)* entry *(in* +acc into). **(c)** *(fig: von Stimmung, Winter etc)* advent. **der Frühling etc hält seinen** ~ spring etc is coming. **(d)** *(von Steuern)* collection; *(von Banknoten)* withdrawal.

Einzugs-: ~**bereich** m catchment area; ~**feier** f house-warming (party).

einzwängen vt sep *(lit)* to squeeze or jam in; *(fig)* jdn to constrict.

Eis nt - **(a)** no pl ice. **zu** ~ **gefrieren** to freeze, to turn to ice; **das** ~ **brechen** *(fig)* to break the ice; **etw auf** ~ **legen** *(fig col)* to put sth on ice or into cold storage. **(b)** *(Speise~)* ice(-cream). ~ **am Stiel** ice(d)-lolly *(Brit)*, popsicle ® *(US)*.

Eis-: ~**bahn** f ice-rink; ~**bär** m polar bear; ~**becher** m sundae; **e**~**bedeckt** adj ice-covered; ~**bein** nt *(Cook)* knuckle of pork; ~**berg** m iceberg; **die Spitze des** ~**bergs** *(fig)* the tip of the iceberg; ~**beutel** m ice pack; ~**block** m block of ice; ~**blume** f usu pl frost pattern; ~**brecher** m icebreaker.

Eischnee m *(Cook)* beaten white of egg.

Eis-: ~**creme** f ice(-cream); ~**decke** f sheet of ice; ~**diele** f ice-cream parlour *(Brit)* or parlor *(US)*.

Eisen nt - iron. **mehrere** ~ **im Feuer haben** *(fig)* to have more than one iron in the fire; **zum alten** ~ **gehören** *(fig)* to be on the scrap heap; **man muß das** ~ **schmieden, solange es heiß ist** *(Prov)* strike while the iron is hot *(Prov)*.

Eisenbahn f railway *(Brit)*, railroad *(US)*; *(~wesen)* railways *(Brit)* pl, railroad *(US); (col: Zug)* train; *(Spielzeug~)* train set. **es ist (aller) höchste** ~ *(col)* it's getting late.

Eisenbahn-: ~**abteil** nt compartment; ~**brücke** f railway *(Brit)* or railroad *(US)* bridge.

Eisenbahner(in f) m - railwayman *(Brit)*, railway employee *(Brit)*, railroader *(US)*.

Eisenbahn-: ~**fähre** f train ferry; ~**fahrkarte** f rail or train ticket; ~**fahrt** f train or rail ride; ~**netz** nt rail network; ~**schaffner** m (railway) guard *(Brit)*, (railroad) conductor *(US)*; ~**strecke** f railway line *(Brit)*, railroad *(US)*; ~**überführung** f footbridge; ~**wagen** m railway *(Brit)* or railroad *(US)* carriage; ~**waggon** m *(Güter~)* goods wagon.

Eisen-: ~**erz** nt iron ore; **e**~**haltig** adj Gestein iron-bearing; **das Wasser ist e**~**haltig** the water contains iron; ~**mangel** m iron deficiency; ~**oxyd** nt ferric oxide; ~**präparat** nt *(Med)* iron tonic/tablets pl; ~**stange** f iron bar; **e**~**verarbeitend** adj attr iron processing; ~**waren** pl ironmongery sing *(Brit)*, hardware sing *(US)*; ~**warenhandlung** f ironmonger's *(Brit)*, hardware store *(US)*; ~**zeit** f Iron Age.

eisern adj **(a)** attr *(aus Eisen)* iron. **der E**~**e Vorhang** the Iron Curtain; ~**e Lunge** *(Med)* iron lung. **(b)** Disziplin, Wille iron attr; Energie unflagging; Ruhe unshakeable. ~**e Gesundheit** iron constitution; **er schwieg** ~ he remained resolutely silent; **er ist** ~ **bei seinem Entschluß geblieben** he stuck firmly to his decision; **mit** ~**er**

Faust with an iron hand; **in etw** (dat) ~ **sein** to be adamant about sth; **mit ~em Besen kehren** to make a clean sweep; ~ **sparen** to save resolutely. (c) attr Reserve emergency; Ration auch iron.
Eiseskälte f icy cold.
Eis-: ~**fach** nt freezer compartment, ice-box; ~**fläche** f (surface of the) ice; e~**frei** adj free of ice pred; e~**gekühlt** adj chilled; ~**hockey** nt ice hockey, hockey (US).
eisig adj (lit, fig) icy.
Eis-: ~**kaffee** m iced coffee; e~**kalt** adj (a) icy-cold; (b) (fig) (abweisend) icy, cold; (kalt und berechnend) cold-blooded, cold and calculating; (dreist) cool; ~**kunstlauf** m figure skating; ~**kunstläufer** m figure skater; ~**lauf** m ice-skating; e~**laufen** vi sep irreg aux sein to ice-skate; ~**läufer** m ice-skater; ~**meer** nt polar sea; **Nördliches/Südliches** ~**meer** Arctic/Antarctic Ocean; ~**pickel** m ice axe (Brit) or ax (US), ice pick.
Eisprung m (Physiol) ovulation no art.
Eis-: ~**regen** m sleet; ~**revue** f ice revue, ice show; ~**schießen** nt curling; ~**schmelze** f thaw; ~**schnellauf** m speed skating; ~**schnelläufer** m speed skater; ~**scholle** f ice floe; ~**schrank** m refrigerator; ~**tanz** m ice-dancing; ~**torte** f ice-cream cake; ~**verkäufer** m ice-cream seller or man (col); ~**vogel** m (Orn) kingfisher; ~**würfel** m ice cube; ~**zapfen** m icicle; ~**zeit** f Ice Age.
eitel adj vain; (eingebildet auch) conceited.
Eitelkeit f vanity.
Eiter m no pl pus.
eit(e)rig adj Ausfluß purulent; Wunde festering.
eitern vi to discharge pus, to suppurate.
Eiweiß nt (egg-)white, white of egg; (Chem) protein.
Eiweiß-: ~**gehalt** m protein content; e~**haltig** adj Fleisch ist sehr e~**haltig** meat is high in protein or contains a lot of protein; ~**mangel** m protein deficiency; ~**präparat** nt protein preparation.
Eizelle f (Biol) egg cell.
Ejakulation f ejaculation.
Ekel[1] m no pl disgust, revulsion; (Übelkeit) nausea. **vor jdm/etw einen ~ haben** to loathe sb/sth; **dabei empfinde ich ~** it gives me a feeling of disgust etc; **er hat das Essen vor ~ ausgespuckt** he spat out the food in disgust; **er konnte es vor ~ nicht tun** he was too disgusted to do it.
Ekel[2] nt - (col) obnoxious person, horror (col).
ekel|erregend adj nauseating, revolting.
ekelhaft, ek(e)lig adj disgusting, revolting; (col) Problem, Chef nasty (col), horrible.
ekeln 1 vt to disgust, to revolt. 2 vt impers **es ekelt mich vor diesem Anblick** the sight of it fills me with disgust or revulsion. 3 vr to feel disgusted. **sich vor etw** (dat) ~ to find sth disgusting.
EKG [eːkaːˈɡeː] nt -s = **Elektrokardiogramm** ECG.
Eklat [eˈklaː(ː)] m -s (geh: Aufsehen) sensation.
eklatant adj Fall sensational; Beispiel striking; Verletzung flagrant.
eklig adj = ek(e)lig.
Eklipse f -n eclipse.
Ekstase f -n ecstasy. **in ~ geraten** to go into ecstasies; **jdn in ~ versetzen** to send sb into ecstasies.
ekstatisch adj ecstatic.
Ekzem nt -e (Med) eczema.
Elan m no pl élan, zest.
elastisch adj elastic; Gang, Metall, Holz springy; (fig) Muskel, Mensch strong and supple; (flexibel) flexible, elastic.
Elastizität f siehe elastisch elasticity; springiness; flexibility. **die ~ seines Körpers** the supple strength of his body.
Elch m -e elk.
Elefant m elephant. **wie ein ~ im Porzellanladen**

(col) like a bull in a china shop (prov).
elegant adj elegant.
Eleganz f elegance.
Elegie f elegy.
elektrifizieren* vt to electrify.
Elektrifizierung f electrification.
Elektrik f (Anlagen) electrical equipment.
Elektriker(in f) m - electrician.
elektrisch adj electric; Entladung, Widerstand electrical. ~**e Geräte** electrical appliances; ~**er Schlag/Strom** electric shock/current; **der ~e Stuhl** the electric chair; **wir kochen/heizen ~ we** cook/heat by electricity.
Elektrische f -n (dated) tram, streetcar (US).
elektrisieren* 1 vt (lit, fig) to electrify. **ich habe mich elektrisiert** I got an electric shock; **wie elektrisiert** (as if) electrified. 2 vi to give an electric shock.
Elektrizität f electricity.
Elektrizitätswerk nt (electric) power station; (Gesellschaft) electric power company, Electricity (Generating) Board (Brit).
Elektro- [eˈlɛktro] in cpds electro- (auch Sci), electric; ~**artikel** m electrical appliance.
Elektrode f -n electrode.
Elektro-: ~**gerät** nt electrical appliance; ~**geschäft** nt electrical shop (Brit) or store (US); ~**herd** m electric cooker; ~**kardiogramm** nt (Med) electrocardiogram; ~**magnet** m electromagnet; ~**mechaniker** m electrician; e~**mechanisch** adj electromechanical; e~**motor** m electric motor.
Elektron nt -en [elɛkˈtroːnən] electron.
Elektronen-: ~**(ge)hirn** nt electronic brain; ~**rechner** m (electronic) computer.
Elektronik f electronics sing; (Teile) electronics pl.
elektronisch adj electronic.
Elektro-: ~**rasierer** m electric shaver or razor; ~**schock** m (Med) electric shock, electroshock; ~**technik** f electrical engineering; ~**techniker** m electrician; (Ingenieur) electrical engineer; e~**technisch** adj electrical.
Element nt element; (Elec) cell. **kriminelle ~e** (pej) criminal elements; **in seinem ~ sein** to be in one's element.
elementar adj (grundlegend) elementary; Gewalt, Trieb elemental.
Elementarteilchen nt (Phys) elementary particle.
elend adj (a) wretched, miserable; (krank) wretched, awful. **mir ist ganz ~** I feel really awful. (b) (col: furchtbar) Hunger, Wetter awful. **ich habe ~ gefroren** I was miserably cold.
Elend nt no pl (Unglück, Not) misery, distress; (Verwahrlosung) squalor; (Armut) poverty. **(wie) ein Häufchen ~** (col) (looking) a picture of misery; **da kann man das heulende ~ kriegen** (col) it's enough to make you scream (col).
elendig(lich) adv (geh) wretchedly. ~ **zugrunde gehen** to come to a wretched end.
Elendsviertel nt slums pl, slum area.
elf num eleven; siehe **vier.**
Elf f -en (Sport) team, eleven.
Elfe f -n elf.
Elfenbein nt ivory.
elfenbeine(r)n adj ivory.
Elfenbein-: ~**küste** f Ivory Coast; ~**turm** m (fig) ivory tower.
elfmal adv eleven times; siehe **viermal.**
Elfmeter m (Ftbl) penalty (kick) (für to, for). **einen ~ schießen** to take a penalty.
Elfmeter-: ~**punkt** m (Ftbl) penalty spot; ~**schießen** nt (Ftbl) sudden-death play-off; **durch ~schießen entschieden** decided on penalties; ~**schütze** m (Ftbl) penalty-taker.
Elftel nt - eleventh.
elfte(r, s) adj eleventh; siehe **vierte(r, s).**

eliminieren* *vt* to eliminate.
elitär 1 *adj* elitist. **2** *adv* in an elitist fashion.
Elite *f* -n elite.
Elitetruppe *f (Mil)* crack *or* elite troops *pl.*
Elixier *nt* -e elixir *(liter)*, tonic.
Elle *f* -n *(Anat)* ulna *(spec).* **alles mit der gleichen ~ messen** *(fig)* to measure everything by the same yardstick.
Ell(en)bogen *m* - elbow. **die ~ gebrauchen** *(fig)* to be pushy *(col)* or ruthless.
Ell(en)bogenfreiheit *f (fig)* elbow room.
ellenlang *adj (fig col)* incredibly long *(col)*; *Kerl* incredibly tall *(col).*
Ellipse *f* -n *(Math)* ellipse.
elliptisch *adj (Math)* elliptic(al).
Elsaß *nt, gen - or -sses das ~* Alsace.
Elsässer(in *f)* *m* - Alsatian, inhabitant of Alsace.
Elsässer, elsässisch *adj* Alsatian.
Elster *f* -n magpie. **eine diebische ~ sein** *(fig)* to be a thief.
elterlich *adj* parental.
Eltern *pl* parents *pl.* **nicht von schlechten ~ sein** *(col)* to be quite something *(col).*
Eltern-: **~abend** *m (Sch)* parents' evening; **~haus** *nt (lit, fig)* (parental) home; **e~los** *adj* orphaned; **~sprechtag** *m* open day (for parents); **~teil** *m* parent.
Email [eˈmai] *nt* -s, **Emaille** [eˈmaljə] *f* -n enamel.
emaillieren* [emaˈjiːrən] *vt* to enamel.
Emanze *f* -n *(usu pej)* women's libber *(col).*
Emanzipation *f* emancipation.
emanzipatorisch *adj* emancipatory.
emanzipieren* *vr* to emancipate oneself.
Embargo *nt* -s embargo.
Emblem *nt* -e emblem.
Embryo *m* -s *or* -nen [-yˈoːnən] embryo.
embryonal *adj attr (Biol, fig)* embryonic.
Emigrant(in *f)* *m* emigrant; *(politisch)* émigré.
Emigration *f* emigration. **in der ~ leben** to live in self-imposed exile.
emigrieren* *vi aux sein* to emigrate.
eminent *adj (geh) Person* eminent. **von ~er Bedeutung** of the utmost significance.
Eminenz *f (Eccl)* **(Seine) ~** *(His)* **Eminence.**
Emirat *nt* emirate.
Emission *f* **(a)** *(Fin)* issue. **(b)** *(Phys)* emission.
Emotion *f* emotion.
emotional *adj* emotional; *Ausdrucksweise* emotive.
emotions-: **~geladen** *adj* emotionally-charged; **~los** *adj* free of emotion, unemotional.
empfahl *pret of* **empfehlen.**
empfand *pret of* **empfinden.**
Empfang *m* -e reception *(auch Rad, TV)*; *(von Brief, Ware etc)* receipt. **etw in ~ nehmen** to receive sth; *(Comm)* to take delivery of sth; **(zahlbar) nach/bei ~** *(+gen)* (payable) on receipt (of).
empfangen *pret* **empfing,** *ptp ~* *vt* to receive *(auch Rad, TV)*; *(begrüßen)* to greet, to receive *(form)*; *(herzlich)* to welcome; *(abholen) Besuch* to meet.
Empfänger(in *f)* *m* - recipient, receiver *(auch Rad, TV)*; *(Adressat)* addressee; *(Waren~)* consignee. **~ unbekannt** *(auf Briefen)* not known at this address.
empfänglich *adj (aufnahmebereit)* receptive *(für* to); *(anfällig)* susceptible *(für* to).
Empfänglichkeit *f siehe adj* receptivity; susceptibility.
Empfängnis *f* conception.
Empfängnis-: **e~verhütend** *adj* contraceptive; **e~verhütende Mittel** *pl* contraceptives *pl*; **~verhütung** *f* contraception.
Empfangs-: **~bereich** *m (Rad, TV)* reception area; **~bestätigung** *f* (acknowledgment of) receipt; **~chef** *m (von Hotel)* head porter; **~dame** *f* receptionist; **~gerät** *nt* (radio/TV) set, receiver;

~störung *f (Rad, TV)* interference *no pl.*
empfehlen *pret* **empfahl,** *ptp* **empfohlen 1** *vt* **(jdm) etw/jdn ~** to recommend sth/sb (to sb); **jdm ~, etw zu tun** to recommend *or* advise sb to do sth; **ich würde dir Vorsicht/Geduld ~** I would recommend caution/patience. **2** *vr* **(a)** to recommend itself/oneself. **sich als Experte** *etc* **~** to offer one's services as an expert *etc*; **es empfiehlt sich, das zu tun** it is advisable to do that. **(b)** *(dated, hum: sich verabschieden)* to take one's leave. **ich empfehle mich!** I'll take my leave.
empfehlenswert *adj* to be recommended.
Empfehlung *f* recommendation; *(Referenz)* reference; *(form: Gruß)* regards *pl.* **auf ~ von** on the recommendation of; **mit freundlichen ~en** *(am Briefende)* with best regards.
Empfehlungsschreiben *nt* letter of recommendation, testimonial.
empfinden *pret* **empfand,** *ptp* **empfunden** *vt* to feel. **etw als Beleidigung ~** to find sth insulting; **jdn als Störenfried ~** to see sb as a troublemaker.
Empfinden *nt no pl* feeling. **meinem ~ nach** to my mind.
empfindlich *adj* **(a)** sensitive *(auch Phot, Tech)*; *Gesundheit, Stoff* delicate; *(leicht reizbar)* touchy *(col).* **~ reagieren** to be sensitive *(auf+acc* to); **~e Stelle** *(lit)* sensitive spot; *(fig auch)* sore point. **(b)** *Verlust, Kälte, Strafe* severe. **deine Kritik hat ihn ~ getroffen** your criticism cut him to the quick.
Empfindlichkeit *f siehe adj* **(a)** sensitivity *(auch Phot, Tech)*; delicateness; touchiness *(col).*
empfindsam *adj Mensch* sensitive.
Empfindung *f* feeling; *(Sinnes~ auch)* sensation.
empfing *pret of* **empfangen.**
empfohlen *ptp of* **empfehlen.**
empfunden *ptp of* **empfinden.**
empirisch *adj* empirical.
empor *adv (liter)* upwards, up.
empor-: **~arbeiten** *vr sep (geh)* to work one's way up; **~blicken** *vi sep (liter: lit, fig)* to look up *(zu* to).
Empore *f* -n *(Archit)* gallery.
empören* 1 *vt* to outrage; *siehe* **empört. 2** *vr* to be indignant *or* outraged *(über +acc* at).
empörend *adj* outrageous.
Empor-: **e~heben** *vr sep irreg (geh)* to raise; **e~kommen** *vi sep irreg aux sein (geh)* to rise (up); *(fig) (aufkommen)* to come to the fore; *(vorankommen)* to go up in the world; **~kömmling** *m (pej)* upstart; **e~ragen** *vi sep aux haben or sein (geh: lit, fig)* to tower *(über+acc* above); **e~steigen** *sep irreg aux sein (geh)* *vti* to climb (up); *(fig: Karriere machen)* to climb, to rise.
empört *adj* indignant, outraged *(über +acc* at).
Empörung *f no pl (Entrüstung)* indignation *(über +acc* at). **über etw in ~ geraten** to get indignant about sth.
emsig *adj* busy, industrious; *Treiben* bustling.
Emsigkeit *f siehe adj* industriousness; bustle.
Emu *m* -s emu.
End- *in cpds* final; **~abnehmer** *m* buyer; **~abrechnung** *f* final account; **~betrag** *m* final amount.
Ende *nt* -n end; *(Ergebnis)* outcome, result; *(Ausgang eines Films, Romans etc)* ending. **~ Mai/der Woche** at the end of May/the week; **er ist ~ vierzig** he is in his late forties; **er wohnt am ~ der Welt** *(col)* he lives at the back of beyond; **bis ans ~ der Welt** to the ends of the earth; **letzten ~s** in the end, at the end of the day; **einer Sache** *(dat)* **ein ~ machen** to put an end to sth; **damit muß es jetzt ein ~ haben** there has to be an end to this now, this must stop now; **ein ~ nehmen** to come to an end; **ein böses ~ nehmen** to come to a bad end; **... und kein ~ ...** with no end in sight, ... without end; **es ist noch ein gutes** *or* **ganzes ~** *(col)* there's still quite a way to go (yet); **am ~ at**

the end; *(schließlich)* in the end; *(col: möglicher-weise)* perhaps; **am** ~ **sein** *(fig)* to be at the end of one's tether; **ich bin mit meiner Weisheit am** ~ I'm at my wit's end; **meine Geduld ist am** ~ my patience is at an end; **zu** ~ finished, over; **etw zu** ~ **führen** to finish (off) sth; **ein Buch zu** ~ **lesen** to finish (reading) a book; **zu** ~ **gehen** to come to an end; *(Vorräte)* to run out; ~ **gut, alles gut** *(Prov)* all's well that ends well *(Prov)*.

End|effekt *m:* **im** ~ *(col)* in the final analysis, at the end of the day.

enden *vi* to end, to finish; *(Zug)* to terminate; *(sterben)* to meet one's end. **auf etw** *(acc)* ~ *(Wort)* to end with sth; **der Streit endete vor Gericht** the quarrel ended up in court; **wie wird das noch mit ihm** ~? what will become of him?; **das wird böse** ~! no good will come of it!

End|ergebnis *nt* final result.

endgültig *adj* final; **Antwort** definite; **Fassung** definitive.

Endivie [-viə] *f* endive.

End-: ~**lagerung** *f* permanent disposal; ~**lauf** *m* final.

endlich 1 *adv* finally, at last; *(am Ende)* eventually, in the end. **hör** ~ **damit auf!** will you stop that!; **komm doch** ~! come on! **2** *adj (Math, Philos)* finite.

endlos *adj* endless. **ich mußte** ~ **lange warten** I had to wait for an interminably long time.

Endlosigkeit *f* endlessness.

End-: ~**phase** *f* final stage(s *pl*); ~**produkt** *nt* end or final product; ~**punkt** *m (lit, fig)* end.

Endrunde *f (Sport)* finals *pl; (fig)* final round.

Endrunden-: ~**spiel** *nt* final (match); ~**teilnehmer** *m* finalist.

End-: ~**spiel** *nt (Sport)* final; *(Chess)* end game; ~**spurt** *m (Sport, fig)* final spurt; ~**station** *f (Rail etc)* terminus; *(fig)* end of the line; ~**stufe** *f* final stage; ~**summe** *f* (sum) total.

Endung *f (Gram)* ending.

End-: ~**verbraucher** *m* consumer, end-user; ~**ziel** *nt* ultimate goal; ~**zweck** *m* ultimate purpose.

Energie *f (Sci, fig)* energy. **mit ganzer** ~ with all one's energy.

Energie-: ~**bedarf** *m* energy requirement; ~**gewinnung** *f* generation of energy; ~**krise** *f* energy crisis; **e~los** *adj* lacking in energy; ~**politik** *f* energy policy/politics *sing* or *pl*; ~**träger** *m* source of energy; ~**verbrauch** *m* energy consumption; ~**versorgung** *f* supply of energy; ~**zufuhr** *f* energy supply.

energisch *adj (entschlossen, streng)* forceful, firm; **Protest** energetic, strong. ~ **durchgreifen** to take vigorous or firm action; **etw** ~ **verteidigen** to defend sth vigorously; **etw** ~ **dementieren** to deny sth strenuously.

eng *adj* **(a)** *(lit, fig)* narrow; **Raum** cramped; **Kleidung** tight, close-fitting. **ein Kleid** ~**er machen** to take a dress in; **im** ~**eren Sinne** in the narrow sense; **in die** ~**ere Wahl kommen** to be shortlisted. **(b)** *(nah, vertraut)* close. ~ **nebeneinander** close together; **eine Feier im** ~**sten Kreise** a small party for close friends; **mit jdm** ~ **befreundet sein** to be a close friend of sb.

Engagement [ãgaʒəˈmãː] *nt* **-s (a)** *no pl* commitment *(für* to). **(b)** *(Theat)* engagement.

engagieren* [ãgaˈʒiːrən] **1** *vt* to engage. **2** *vr* to be/become committed *(für* to); *(in einer Bekanntschaft)* to become involved. **er hat sich sehr dafür engagiert, daß ...** he completely committed himself to ...; **ein engagierter Film** a (socially/politically) committed film.

Enge *f* **-n (a)** *no pl (lit, fig)* narrowness; *(von Wohnung)* crampedness; *(Gedrängtheit)* crush; *(von Kleid)* tightness. **(b)** *(Engpaß)* pass, defile. **jdn in die** ~ **treiben** *(fig)* to drive sb into a corner.

Engel *m* **-** *(lit, fig)* angel. **ein guter** ~ *(fig)* a guard-

ian angel; **wir sind alle keine** ~ *(prov)* none of us is perfect.

Engelmacher(in *f)* *m (euph col)* backstreet abortionist.

Engels-: ~**geduld** *f* **sie hat eine** ~**geduld** she has the patience of a saint; ~**haar** *nt* angel's hair, *type of Christmas tree decoration*; ~**zungen** *pl:* **(wie) mit** ~**zungen reden** to use all one's powers of persuasion.

Eng-: **e~herzig** *adj* petty, hidebound; ~**herzigkeit** *f* pettiness.

England *nt* England.

Engländer *m* **- (a)** Englishman; English boy. **die** ~ *pl* the English, the Britishers *(US)*; **er ist** ~ he's English. **(b)** *(Tech)* adjustable spanner, monkey wrench.

Engländerin *f* Englishwoman; English girl.

englisch 1 *adj* English; *siehe* **deutsch**. **2** *adv (Cook)* rare.

Englisch(e) *nt decl as adj* English; *siehe* **Deutsch(e)**.

englisch-: ~**deutsch** *etc adj* Anglo-German *etc;* **Wörterbuch** English-German *etc;* ~**sprachig** *adj* **Gebiet** English-speaking.

Eng-: **e~maschig** *adj* close-meshed; ~**paß** *m (narrow)* pass, defile; *(Mot, fig)* bottleneck.

en gros [ãˈgro] *adv* wholesale.

engstirnig *adj* narrow-minded.

Enkel *m* **- (~kind)** grandchild; **(~sohn)** grandson; *(Nachfahr)* descendant.

Enkelin *f* granddaughter.

Enkel-: ~**kind** *nt* grandchild; ~**sohn** *m* grandson; ~**tochter** *f* granddaughter.

enorm *adj* enormous; *(col: herrlich, kolossal)* tremendous *(col)*. **er verdient** ~ **viel (Geld)** *(col)* he earns an enormous amount (of money).

en passant [ãpaˈsã] *adv* en passant, in passing.

Ensemble [ãˈsãbl] *nt* **-s** ensemble; *(Besetzung)* cast.

ent|arten* *vi aux sein* to degenerate *(zu* into).

ent|artet *adj* degenerate.

Ent|artung *f* degeneration.

entbehren* *vt (vermissen)* to miss; *(auch vi: verzichten)* to do without; *(zur Verfügung stellen)* to spare. **wir können ihn heute nicht** ~ we cannot spare him today.

entbehrlich *adj* dispensable.

Entbehrung *f* privation, deprivation. ~**en auf sich** *(acc)* **nehmen** to make sacrifices.

entbinden* *irreg* **1** *vt* **(a)** **Frau** to deliver. **(b)** *(von Amt etc)* to release *(von* from). **2** *vi (Frau)* to give birth.

Entbindung *f* delivery, birth; *(von Amt etc)* release.

Entbindungsstation *f* maternity ward.

entblößen* *vt (form)* to expose *(auch Mil)*; **Kopf** to bare; *(fig)* **sein Innenleben** to lay bare.

entblößt *adj* bare.

entbrennen* *vi irreg aux sein (liter) (Kampf, Streit)* to flare up; *(Liebe)* to be aroused.

entdecken* *vt* to discover; **Fehler** auch to detect; *(erspähen)* to spot.

Entdecker(in *f)* *m* **-** discoverer.

Entdeckung *f* discovery; *(von Fehler auch)* detection.

Ente *f* **-n (a)** duck. **(b)** *(col) (Falschmeldung)* hoax, false report; *(Aut)* Citroën 2CV, deux-chevaux.

ent|ehren* *vt* to dishonour *(Brit)*, to dishonor *(US)*.

ent|eignen* *vt* to dispossess; **Besitz** to expropriate.

Ent|eignung *f* *siehe vt* dispossession; expropriation.

ent|eisen* *vt* to de-ice; **Kühlschrank** to defrost.

Enten-: ~**braten** *m* roast duck; ~**ei** *nt* duck's egg.

ent|erben* *vt* to disinherit.

Enterhaken *m* grappling iron or hook.

Enterich *m* drake.

entern (Naut) vti Schiff to board.

entfachen* vt (geh) Feuer to kindle; Krieg, Streit to provoke.

entfahren* vi irreg aux sein jdm ~ to escape sb's lips.

entfallen* vi irreg aux sein+dat (a) der Name ist mir ~ the name has slipped my mind. (b) (nicht in Betracht kommen) not to apply; (wegfallen) to be dropped. (c) auf jdn/etw ~ (Geld, Kosten) to be allotted to sb/sth; auf jeden ~ 100 Mark each person will receive/pay 100 marks.

entfalten* 1 vt (a) (lit) to unfold. (b) (fig) (entwickeln) to develop; (darlegen) Plan to unfold; (zeigen) Pracht to display. 2 vr (Knospe, Blüte) to open, to unfold; (fig) to develop; (Schönheit) to blossom (out). hier kann ich mich nicht ~ I can't make full use of my abilities here.

Entfaltung f unfolding (auch von Plan); (Entwicklung) development; (von Schönheit) blossoming; (von Prunk, Tatkraft) display. zur ~ kommen to develop; (Schönheit) to blossom.

entfärben* vt to take the colour (Brit) or color (US) out of.

entfernen* 1 vt to remove (von, aus from). das entfernt uns (weit) vom Thema that takes us a long way from our subject. 2 vr sich (von or aus etw) ~ (weggehen) to go away (from sth), to leave (sth); sich unerlaubt von der Truppe ~ (Mil) to go absent without leave; sich zu weit ~ to go too far away; sich von jdm ~ (fig) to become estranged from sb.

entfernt 1 adj Ort, Verwandter distant; Ähnlichkeit remote. 10 km ~ von 10 km (away) from. 2 adv remotely, slightly. ~ verwandt distantly related; das hat nur ~ mit dieser Angelegenheit zu tun that is only vaguely related with this matter; nicht im ~esten! not in the slightest.

Entfernung f (a) distance. aus kurzer/großer ~ (schießen) (to fire) from close/long range; aus einiger ~ from a distance; in einiger ~ at a distance. (b) (das Entfernen) removal. unerlaubte ~ von der Truppe absence without leave.

Enfernungsmesser m - (Phot) rangefinder.

entfesseln* vt (fig) to unleash.

entfesselt adj unleashed; Trieb unbridled; Naturgewalten raging. vor Begeisterung ~ wild with enthusiasm.

entfetten* vt to de-grease.

Entfettungskur f weight-reducing course.

entflammbar adj inflammable.

entflammen* 1 vt (fig) to (a)rouse. 2 vi aux sein to burst into flames; (fig) (Streit) to flare up; (Leidenschaft) to be (a)roused or inflamed. in Liebe ~ to fall passionately in love.

entfliegen* vi irreg aux sein to fly away, to escape (dat or aus from).

entfliehen* vi irreg aux sein (geh) to escape, to flee (dat or aus from).

entfremden* 1 vt to alienate (auch Sociol, Philos), to estrange. jdn einer Person/Sache (dat) ~ to alienate or estrange sb from sb/sth. 2 vr to become alienated or estranged (dat from).

Entfremdung f alienation, estrangement.

entfrosten* vt to defrost.

Entfroster m - defroster.

entführen* vt jdn to abduct, to kidnap; Beute etc to carry off; Flugzeug to hijack; (hum col: wegnehmen) to make off with.

Entführer(in f) m abductor, kidnapper; (Flugzeug~ etc) hijacker.

Entführung f siehe vt abduction, kidnapping; hijack(ing).

entgegen 1 adv (liter) der Sonne/der Zukunft etc ~! on towards the sun/future etc! 2 prep+dat ~ meiner Bitte contrary to my request.

entgegenbringen vt sep irreg jdm etw ~ (fig) Achtung, Verständnis etc to show sth for sb.

entgegengehen vi sep irreg aux sein +dat to go

towards, to approach; (um jdn zu treffen) to go to meet; (fig) einer Gefahr, dem Tode, der Zukunft to face. dem Ende ~ (Leben, Krieg) to approach its end; Schwierigkeiten ~ to be heading for difficulties.

entgegengesetzt adj Richtung etc opposite. einander ~e Interessen/Meinungen opposing or conflicting interests/views; genau ~ denken/handeln to think/do exactly the opposite.

entgegenhalten vt sep irreg +dat (a) (lit) jdm etw ~ to hold sth out towards sb. (b) (fig) einer Sache ~, daß ... to object to sth that ...; dem hielt sie entgegen, daß ... she made the objection that ...

entgegenkommen vi sep irreg aux sein+dat to come towards, to approach; (fig) to accommodate. das kommt unseren Plänen sehr entgegen that fits in very well with our plans.

Entgegenkommen nt (Gefälligkeit) obligingness; (Zugeständnis) concession.

entgegenkommend adj (fig) obliging, accommodating.

Entgegennahme f no pl (form) (Empfang) receipt; (Annahme) acceptance.

entgegennehmen vt sep irreg (empfangen) to receive; (annehmen) to accept.

entgegensehen vi sep irreg (fig) einer Sache (dat) ~ to await sth; (freudig) to look forward to sth; einer Sache ~ müssen to have to expect sth.

entgegensetzen vt sep +dat etw einer Sache ~ to set sth against sth; wir können diesen Forderungen nichts ~ we have nothing to counter these claims with; dem habe ich entgegenzusetzen, daß ... against that I'd like to say that ...; jdm/einer Sache Widerstand ~ to put up resistance to sb/sth; siehe entgegengesetzt.

entgegenstehen vi sep irreg +dat (fig) to stand in the way of, to be an obstacle to. dem steht nichts entgegen there's no objection to that.

entgegenstellen sep +dat 1 vt = entgegensetzen. 2 vr sich jdm/einer Sache ~ to oppose sb/sth.

entgegentreten vi sep irreg aux sein +dat einer Politik to oppose; Behauptungen to counter; einer Gefahr, Unsitten to take steps against.

entgegenwirken vi sep +dat to counteract.

entgegnen vti to reply; (kurz, barsch) to retort (auf+acc to).

Entgegnung f reply; (kurz, barsch) retort.

entgehen* vi irreg aux sein +dat (a) (entkommen) to escape; Verfolgern, dem Feind to escape from. (b) (fig: nicht bemerkt werden) dieser Fehler ist mir entgangen I missed this mistake; ihr entgeht nichts she doesn't miss a thing; sich (dat) etw ~ lassen to miss sth.

entgeistert adj dumbfounded.

Entgelt nt no pl (form) remuneration (form). gegen ~ for a fee.

entgleisen* vi aux sein (a) (Rail) to be derailed. (b) (fig: Mensch) to misbehave.

Entgleisung f derailment; (fig) faux pas, clanger (col).

entgräten* vt Fisch to fillet, to bone.

enthaaren* vt to remove unwanted hair from.

enthalten* irreg 1 vt to contain. (mit) ~ sein in (+dat) to be included in. 2 vr (a) (geh) sich einer Sache (gen) ~ to abstain from sth; sich einer Bemerkung nicht ~ können to be unable to refrain from making a remark. (b) sich (der Stimme) ~ to abstain.

enthaltsam adj abstemious; (geschlechtlich) chaste.

Enthaltsamkeit f siehe adj abstemiousness; chastity.

Enthaltung f abstinence; (Stimm~) abstention.

enthärten* vt Wasser to soften; Metall to anneal.

enthaupten* vt to decapitate; (als Hinrichtung auch) to behead.

Enthauptung *f siehe vt* decapitation; beheading.

enthäuten* *vt* to skin.

entheben* *vt irreg* **jdn einer Sache** *(gen)* ~ to relieve sb of sth.

enthemmen* *vti* **jdn** ~ to make sb lose his inhibitions; **Alkohol wirkt ~d** alcohol has a disinhibiting effect.

enthüllen* *vt* to reveal; **Skandal, Lüge auch** to expose; **Denkmal** to unveil.

Enthüllung *f siehe vt* revealing; exposure; unveiling. **noch eine sensationelle** ~ another sensational revelation *or* disclosure.

Enthusiasmus *m* enthusiasm.

Enthusiast(in *f)* *m* enthusiast.

enthusiastisch *adj* enthusiastic.

entjungfern* *vt* to deflower.

entkalken* *vt* to decalcify.

entkernen* *vt Orangen etc* to remove the pips from; **Kernobst** to core; **Steinobst** to stone.

entkleiden* *vtr (geh)* to undress.

entkommen* *vi irreg aux sein* to escape, to get away *(+dat, aus* from*)*.

Entkommen *nt* escape.

entkorken* *vt Flasche* to uncork.

entkräften* *vt (schwächen)* to weaken; *(erschöpfen)* to exhaust; *(fig: widerlegen) Behauptung* to invalidate.

Entkräftung *f (Erschöpfung)* exhaustion; *(Widerlegung)* invalidation.

entkrampfen* *vt (fig)* to relax, to ease.

Entkrampfung *f (fig)* relaxation, easing.

entladen* *irreg* **1** *vt* to unload; *Batterie etc* to discharge. **2** *vr (Gewitter)* to break; *(elektrische Spannung, Batterie, Waffe)* to discharge; *(Sprengladung)* to explode; *(fig) (Emotion)* to vent itself; *(Spannung)* to release itself.

Entladung *f* **(a)** *(das Entladen)* unloading. **(b)** *siehe vr* breaking; discharge; explosion; venting; release.

entlang 1 *prep* along. ~ **dem Fluß, den Fluß** ~ along the river. **2** *adv* along. **hier** ~ this way.

entlang- *pref* along; **~gehen** *vti sep irreg aux sein* to walk along, to go along.

enlarven* *vt (fig)* to expose.

entlassen* *vt irreg (aus* from*) (kündigen)* to dismiss; *(nach Stellenabbau)* to make redundant; **Patienten, Soldaten** to discharge; *(aus dem Gefängnis, aus Verpflichtungen)* to release.

Entlassung *f siehe vt* dismissal; making redundant; discharge; release. **es gab 20 ~en** there were 20 redundancies.

Entlassungs-: **~gesuch** *nt* (letter of) resignation; **ein ~gesuch stellen** to tender one's resignation; **~zeugnis** *nt (Sch)* school leaving certificate.

entlasten* *vt* to relieve the strain on; *(Mil, Rail)* to relieve; **Gewissen, Verkehr** to ease; *(Arbeit abnehmen)* to take some of the load off; *(Jur) Angeklagten* to exonerate; *(Comm) Vorstand* to approve the activities of; *(von Verpflichtungen)* **jdn** to release.

Entlastung *f* relief *(auch Mil, Rail etc)*; *(von Achse etc, Herz)* relief of the strain *(+gen* on*)*; *(Jur)* exoneration; *(Comm: des Vorstands)* approval; *(von Verpflichtungen etc)* release. **zu seiner** ~ **führte der Angeklagte an, daß ...** in his defence *(Brit) or* defense *(US)* the defendant stated that ...

Entlastungs-: **~material** *nt (Jur)* evidence for the defence *(Brit) or* defense *(US)*; **~zeuge** *m (Jur)* defence *(Brit) or* defense *(US)* witness; **~zug** *m* relief *(Brit) or* extra train.

entlaufen* *vi irreg aux sein* to run away *(dat, von* from*)*. **ein ~es Kind** a runaway child; **ein ~er Sträfling** an escaped convict; **ein ~er Hund** a lost dog.

entledigen* *(form) vr* **sich einer Person/Sache** *(gen)* ~ to rid oneself of sb/sth; **sich seiner Kleidung** ~ to remove one's clothes.

entleeren* *vt* to empty; **Darm** to evacuate.

entlegen *adj* remote.

entleihen* *vt irreg* to borrow *(von, aus* from*)*.

Entleiher *m* - borrower.

Entlein *nt* duckling.

entloben* *vr* to break off one's engagement.

entlocken* *vt* **jdm/einer Sache etw** ~ to elicit sth from sb/sth.

entlohnen* *vt* to pay; *(fig)* to reward.

Entlohnung *f* pay(ment); *(fig)* reward.

entlüften* *vt* to ventilate, to air; **Bremsen** to bleed.

Entlüfter *m* - ventilator.

Entlüftung *f siehe vt* ventilation, airing; bleeding.

entmachten* *vt* to deprive of power; *(stürzen)* to topple.

entmannen* *vt* to castrate.

Entmannung *f* castration.

entmilitarisieren *vt* to demilitarize.

entmündigen* *vt (Jur)* to (legally) incapacitate, to declare incapable of managing one's own affairs; *(wegen Geisteskrankheit auch)* to certify.

Entmündigung *f siehe vt (Jur)* (legal) incapacitation; certification.

entmutigen* *vt* to discourage, to dishearten. **sich nicht** ~ **lassen** not to be discouraged.

Entmutigung *f* discouragement.

Entnahme *f -n (form)* removal; *(von Blut)* extraction; *(von Geld)* withdrawal.

entnehmen* *vt irreg (aus, dat)* to take (from); *(aus Kasse) Geld* to withdraw (from); *(fig: folgern)* to infer (from). **wie ich Ihren Worten entnehme, ...** I gather from what you say that ...

entnerven* *vt* to unnerve. **~d** nerve-racking.

entpuppen* *vr* **sich als Betrüger etc** ~ to turn out to be a cheat etc.

entrahmen* *vt Milch* to skim.

enträtseln* *vt* to solve; **Sinn, Schrift** to decipher.

entreißen* *vt irreg* **jdm etw** ~ *(lit, fig)* to snatch sth (away) from sb.

entrichten* *vt (form)* to pay.

Entrichtung *f (form)* payment.

entrinnen* *vi irreg aux sein (geh)* +*dat* to escape from; **dem Tod** to escape. **es gibt kein E~** there is no escape.

entrücken *adj (geh verzückt)* enraptured. **der Wirklichkeit** ~ **sein** to live in a world of one's own.

entrümpeln* *vt* to clear out.

Entrümp(e)lung *f* clear-out.

entrüsten* **1** *vt (empören)* to fill with indignation, to outrage. **2** *vr* **sich** ~ **über** *(+acc) (sich empören)* to be outraged at.

entrüstet *adj* indignant, outraged.

Entrüstung *f* indignation *(über +acc* at*)*.

Entsafter *m* - juice extractor.

entsagen* *vi* +*dat (geh)* **der Welt** ~ to renounce the world.

Entsagung *f (geh)* renunciation.

Entsatz *m no pl (Mil)* relief.

entschädigen* *vt (für* for*) (lit, fig)* to compensate, to recompense; *(Kosten erstatten)* to reimburse. **das Theaterstück entschädigte uns für das lange Warten** the play made up for the long wait.

Entschädigung *f siehe vt* compensation, recompense; reimbursement.

Entschädigungssumme *f* compensation.

entschärfen* *vt (lit, fig)* to defuse.

entscheiden* *irreg* **1** *vti* to decide. ~ **Sie, wie es gemacht werden soll!** you decide how it is to be done; **den Kampf (um etw) für sich** ~ to secure victory in the struggle (for sth); **über etw** *(acc)* ~ to decide (on) sth; **es ist noch nichts entschieden** nothing has been decided (as) yet; **darüber habe ich nicht zu** ~ that is not for me to decide. **2** *vr (Mensch)* to decide, to make up one's mind; *(Angelegenheit)* to be decided. **sich für jdn/etw** ~ to decide in favour of sb/sth.

entscheidend *adj* decisive; *Augenblick, Fehler auch* crucial. **die ~e Stimme** *(bei Wahlen etc)* the deciding *or* casting vote; **der alles ~e Augenblick** the all decisive moment; **das E~e** the decisive *or* deciding factor.

Entscheidung *f* decision. **eine ~ treffen** to make a decision; **wie ist die ~ ausgefallen?** which way did the decision go?; **es geht um die ~, ob** ... it's a question of deciding whether ...

Entscheidungs-: **~befugnis** *f* decision-making powers *pl*; **~freiheit** *f* freedom of decision-making; **e~freudig** *adj* able to make decisions, decisive; **~kampf** *m* show-down *(auch fig)*; *(Sport)* decider; **~schlacht** *f* decisive battle; *(fig)* show-down *(col)*; **~spiel** *nt* decider, play-off.

entschieden *adj* **(a)** *(entschlossen)* determined, resolute; *Befürworter* staunch. **etw ~ ablehnen** to reject sth firmly. **(b)** *no pred (eindeutig)* decided, distinct. **das geht ~ zu weit** that's definitely going too far.

Entschiedenheit *f (Entschlossenheit)* determination, resolution. **etw mit aller ~ dementieren** to deny sth categorically.

entschlacken* *vt (Med) Körper* to purify.

entschlafen* *vi irreg aux sein (geh)* to fall asleep.

entschleiern* *vt (lit, fig)* to unveil.

entschließen* *vr irreg* to decide *(für, zu* on*)*. **ich entschloß mich zum Kauf dieses Hauses** I decided to buy this house; **sich zu nichts ~ können** to be unable to make up one's mind; **ich bin fest entschlossen** I am absolutely determined; **zu allem entschlossen sein** to be ready for anything; **kurz entschlossen** straight away.

Entschließung *f* resolution.

entschlossen *adj* determined, resolute. **~ handeln** to act resolutely *or* with determination.

Entschlossenheit *f* determination, resolution.

entschlüpfen* *vi aux sein (dat* from*)* to escape, to slip away; *(fig: Wort etc)* to slip out.

Entschluß *m* decision; *(Vorsatz)* resolution, resolve. **aus eigenem ~ handeln** to act on one's own initiative; **es ist mein fester ~** ... it is my firm intention ...

entschlüsseln* *vt* to decipher; *Funkspruch auch* to decode.

Entschluß-: **e~freudig** *adj* decisive; **~kraft** *f* decisiveness; **e~los** *adj* indecisive.

entschuldbar *adj* excusable, pardonable.

entschuldigen* **1** *vt* to excuse. **etw mit etw ~** to excuse sth as due to sth; **das ist durch nichts zu ~!, das läßt sich nicht ~!** that is inexcusable!; **jdn bei jdm ~** to make sb's excuses *or* apologies to sb; **einen Schüler ~ (lassen)** to ask for a pupil to be excused; **ich bitte mich zu ~** I beg to be excused. **2** *vi* **~ Sie (bitte)!** excuse me; *(Verzeihung auch)* sorry; *(bei Frage etc)* sorry, pardon me *(esp US)*. **3** *vr* **sich (bei jdm) ~** to excuse oneself; *(um Verzeihung bitten)* to apologize (to sb) *(wegen etw (gen)* for sth*)*; **sich ~ lassen** to send one's apologies.

Entschuldigung *f (Grund)* excuse; *(Bitte um ~)* apology; *(Sch: Brief)* note. **~!** excuse me; *(Verzeihung auch)* sorry; *(jdn) (wegen einer Sache) um ~ bitten* to apologize (to sb) (for sth); **ich bitte vielmals um ~ (, daß ich mich verspätet habe)!** I do apologize (for being late)!

entschwefeln* *vt* to desulphurize.

Entschwef(e)lung *f* desulphurization.

entschwinden* *vi irreg aux sein (geh: lit, fig)* to vanish.

entsenden* *vt irreg or reg (geh)* to dispatch.

entsetzen* **1** *vt* **(a)** to horrify, to appal. **(b)** *(Mil)* to relieve. **2** *vr* **sich über jdn/etw ~** to be horrified *or* appalled at sb/sth; *siehe* **entsetzt.**

Entsetzen *nt no pl* horror; *(Erschrecken)* terror. **mit ~ sehen, daß** ... to be horrified/terrified to see that ...

entsetzlich *adj* dreadful, appalling.

entsetzen* *adj* horrified, appalled *(über +acc* at, by*)*. **ein ~er Schrei** a cry of horror.

entsichern* *vt* to release the safety catch of.

entsinnen* *vr irreg (einer Sache (gen), an etw (acc)* sth*)* to remember, to recall. **wenn ich mich recht entsinne** if my memory serves me correctly.

entsorgen* *vt* **eine Stadt ~** to dispose of a town's refuse and sewage.

Entsorgung *f* waste management.

Entsorgungspark *m* (nuclear) waste dump.

entspannen* **1** *vt Muskeln, Nerven etc* to relax; *(fig) Lage auch* to ease. **2** *vr* to relax *(auch fig)*; *(ausruhen)* to rest; *(nach der Arbeit etc)* to unwind; *(Lage etc)* to ease.

Entspannung *f* relaxation *(auch fig)*; *(Pol)* détente, easing of tension *(+gen* in*)*.

Entspannungs-: **~politik** *f* policy of détente; **~übungen** *pl (Med etc)* relaxation exercises.

entsprechen* *vi irreg +dat* to correspond to; *Vorschriften* to be in accordance with; *(genügen) Anforderungen* to meet; *Erwartungen* to come up to; *einer Beschreibung* to answer, to fit; *einer Bitte, einem Wunsch etc* to meet, to comply with. **sich ~** to correspond, to tally.

entsprechend **1** *adj* corresponding; *(zuständig)* relevant; *(angemessen)* appropriate. **2** *adv* accordingly; *(ähnlich, gleich)* correspondingly. **er wurde ~ bestraft** he was suitably *or* appropriately punished. **3** *prep+dat* in accordance with, according to; *(ähnlich, gleich)* corresponding to. **er wird seiner Leistung ~ bezahlt** he is paid according to output.

Entsprechung *f* equivalent; *(Analogie)* parallel; *(Übereinstimmung)* correspondence.

entspringen* *vi irreg aux sein* **(a)** *(Fluß)* to rise. **(b)** *+dat: sich herleiten von)* to spring from.

entstaatlichen* *vt* to denationalize.

entstammen* *vi aux sein +dat* to stem *or* come from.

entstehen* *vi irreg aux sein (ins Dasein treten)* to come into being; *(seinen Ursprung haben)* to originate; *(sich entwickeln)* to arise *(aus, durch* from*)*; *(hervorkommen)* to emerge *(aus, durch* from*)*; *(verursacht werden)* to result *(aus, durch* from*)*; *(Kunstwerk: geschrieben/gebaut etc werden)* to be written/built etc. **wir wollen nicht den Eindruck ~ lassen,** ... we don't want to give rise to the impression that ...; **für ~den** *or* **entstandenen Schaden** for damages incurred.

Entstehung *f (das Werden)* genesis, coming into being; *(das Hervorkommen)* emergence; *(Ursprung)* origin; *(Bildung)* formation.

Entstehungs-: **~geschichte** *f* genesis; **~ort** *m* place of origin.

entsteinen* *vt* to stone.

entstellen* *vt (lit, fig)* to distort; *(verunstalten) Gesicht* to disfigure. **etw entstellt wiedergeben** to distort *or* misrepresent sth.

Entstellung *f siehe vt* distortion; disfigurement.

entstören* *vt Radio, Telefon* to free from interference; *Staubsauger* to suppress.

enttarnen* *vt Spion* to blow the cover of *(col)*.

enttäuschen* **1** *vt* to disappoint; *Vertrauen* to betray. **enttäuscht sein über (+acc)/von** to be disappointed at/by. **2** *vi* **unsere Mannschaft hat sehr enttäuscht** our team were very disappointing.

Enttäuschung *f* disappointment. **jdm eine ~ bereiten** to disappoint sb.

entthronen* *vt (lit, fig)* to dethrone.

entvölkern* *vt* to depopulate.

entwachsen* *vi irreg aux sein +dat* **(a)** to outgrow, to grow out of. **(b)** *(geh: herauswachsen aus)* to spring from.

entwaffnen* *vt (lit, fig)* to disarm.

entwaffnend *adj (fig)* disarming.

Entwaffnung *f* disarming; *(eines Landes)* disarmament.

entwarnen* vi to sound the all-clear.

Entwarnung f all-clear.

entwässern* vt to drain.

Entwässerung f drainage.

entweder [auch: 'ɛntveːdə] conj ~ ... oder ... either ... or ...; ~ oder! yes or no.

entweichen* vi irreg aux sein to escape (+dat, aus from).

entwenden* vt (form) jdm etw ~ to steal or purloin (hum, form) sth from sb.

entwerfen* vt irreg Zeichnung to sketch; Muster, Modell to design; Gesetz, Schreiben etc to draft, to draw up; Plan to devise, to draw up; (fig) Bild to draw; (in Umrissen darstellen) to outline.

entwerten* vt (a) (im Wert mindern) to devalue. (b) (ungültig machen) to make invalid; Briefmarke, Fahrschein to cancel.

Entwerter m - (ticket-)cancelling machine.

Entwertung f siehe vt devaluation; invalidation; cancellation.

entwickeln* 1 vt to develop (auch Phot); Gas etc to produce, to generate; Mut, Energie to show, to display. etw zu etw ~ to develop sth into sth. 2 vr to develop (zu into); (Gase etc) to be produced or generated. das Projekt entwickelt sich gut the project is coming along or progressing nicely.

Entwicklung f development; (von Gasen etc) production, generation; (von Mut, Energie) show, display; (Phot) developing. in der ~ at the development stage; (Jugendliche etc) still developing.

Entwicklungs-: e~fähig adj capable of development; diese Stelle ist e~fähig this position has prospects; ~geschichte f evolution; ~helfer m VSO worker (Brit), Peace Corps worker (US); ~hilfe f foreign aid; ~jahre pl adolescent or formative (auch fig) years, adolescence; ~land nt developing or third-world country; ~stadium nt, ~stufe f stage of development; ~zeit f period of development; (Phot) developing time.

entwirren* vt (lit, fig) to disentangle, to unravel.

entwischen* vi aux sein (col) to escape, to get away (dat, aus from).

entwöhnen* vt jdn ~ to break sb of the habit (+dat, von of), to cure sb (+dat, von of); Säugling, Jungtier to wean.

Entwöhnung f siehe vt cure, curing; weaning.

entwürdigen* 1 vt to degrade. 2 vr to degrade oneself.

Entwürdigung f degradation.

Entwurf m ⸚e (a) (Skizze, Abriß) outline, sketch; (Design) design; (Archit, Tech) blueprint. (b) (Vertrags~, von Plan) draft; (Gesetz~) bill.

entwurzeln* vt (lit, fig) to uproot.

entzerren* vt to correct.

entziehen* irreg 1 vt (+dat from) to withdraw, to take away; Gunst etc to withdraw; Flüssigkeit, (Chem) to extract. jdm Alkohol/Nikotin ~ to deprive sb of alcohol/nicotine; jdm die Erlaubnis etc ~ to take sb's permit etc away; dem Redner das Wort ~ to ask the speaker to stop. 2 vr sich jdm/einer Sache ~ to evade or elude sb/sth; sich seiner Verantwortung ~ to shirk one's responsibilities; das entzieht sich meiner Kenntnis that is beyond my knowledge; sich jds Blicken ~ to be hidden from sight.

Entziehung f withdrawal; (Behandlung) treatment for drug addiction/alcoholism.

Entziehungskur f cure for drug addiction/alcoholism.

entzifferbar adj siehe vt decipherable; decodable.

entziffern* vt to decipher; Funkspruch auch to decode.

entzücken* vt to delight. von jdm/über etw (acc) entzückt sein to be delighted by sb/at sth.

Entzücken nt no pl delight, joy. in ~ geraten to go into raptures.

entzückend adj delightful, charming.

Entzug m no pl (einer Lizenz etc, Med) withdrawal.

Entzugs|erscheinung f withdrawal symptom.

entzündbar adj (lit, fig) inflammable. leicht ~ highly inflammable; (fig) easily roused.

entzünden* 1 vt Feuer to light; (fig) Streit etc to spark off; Haß to inflame. 2 vr (a) to catch fire; (fig) (Streit) to be sparked off; (Haß) to be inflamed. (b) (Med) to become inflamed. entzündet inflamed.

entzündlich adj Gase, Brennstoff inflammable; (Med) inflammatory.

Entzündung f (a) (Med) inflammation. (b) ignition (esp Sci, Tech). Funken führten zur ~ des Heus sparks led to the hay catching fire.

entzwei adj pred in two, in half; (kaputt) broken; (zerrissen) torn.

entzweien* vt to turn against each other.

entzweigehen* vi sep irreg aux sein to break (in two or half).

Enzian ['ɛntsiaːn] m -e gentian; (Branntwein) spirit distilled from the roots of gentian.

Enzyklika f, pl Enzykliken (Eccl) encyclical.

Enzyklopädie f encyclop(a)edia.

Enzym nt -e enzyme.

Epen pl of Epos.

Epidemie f (Med, fig) epidemic.

epidemisch adj (Med, fig) epidemic.

Epik f epic poetry.

Epilepsie f epilepsy.

Epileptiker(in f) m - epileptic.

epileptisch adj epileptic.

Epilog m -e epilogue.

episch adj (lit, fig) epic.

Episode f -n episode.

Epoche f -n epoch.

epochemachend adj epoch-making.

Epos nt, pl Epen epic (poem).

Equipe [e'kɪp] f -n team.

er pers he; (von Dingen) it; (von Hund etc) it, he. wenn ich ~ wäre if I were him or he (form); ~ ist es it's him, it is he (form); sie ist größer als ~ she is taller than he is or than him.

er|achten* vt (geh) jdn/etw für or als etw ~ to consider sb/sth (to be) sth.

Er|achten nt no pl: meines ~s in my opinion.

er|arbeiten* vt (a) Vermögen etc to work for; Wissen etc to acquire. (b) Entwurf etc to work out.

Erb-: ~anlage f usu pl hereditary factor(s pl); ~anspruch m claim to an/the inheritance.

erbarmen* 1 vr jdn ~ to arouse sb's pity; es kann einen ~ it's pitiable; er sieht zum E~ aus he's a pitiful sight. 2 vr (+gen) to take pity (on) (auch hum col). Herr, erbarme dich (unser)! Lord, have mercy (upon us)!

Erbarmen nt no pl (Mitleid) pity, compassion (mit on); (Gnade) mercy (mit on). aus ~ out of pity; ohne ~ pitiless(ly), merciless(ly); er kennt kein ~ he knows no mercy.

erbarmenswert adj pitiable, wretched, pitiful.

erbärmlich adj (erbarmenswert, pej: dürftig) pitiful, wretched; (gemein, schlecht) wretched, miserable.

Erbärmlichkeit f (Elend) wretchedness, misery; (fig: Dürftigkeit, Gemeinheit etc) wretchedness, miserableness.

Erbarmungs-: e~los adj (lit, fig) pitiless, merciless; ~losigkeit f (lit, fig) pitilessness, mercilessness; e~voll adj compassionate, full of pity.

erbauen* vt (a) (lit, fig: errichten) to build. (b) (fig: seelisch) to edify, to uplift. er ist von meinem Plan nicht besonders erbaut (col) he isn't particularly enthusiastic about my plan.

Erbauer(in f) m - builder; (fig auch) architect.

erbaulich adj edifying (auch iro), uplifting.

Erbauung f siehe vt building; edification.

Erb-: e~berechtigt adj entitled to inherit; e~biologisch adj (Jur) e~biologisches Gutachten blood test *(to establish paternity)*.

Erbe[1] *m (wk)* **-n**, **-n** *(lit, fig)* heir *(einer Person (gen)* of *or* to sb, *einer Sache (gen)* to sth)*. **jdn zum** *or* **als ~n einsetzen** to make sb one's/sb's heir.

Erbe[2] *nt no pl* inheritance; *(fig)* heritage; *(esp Unerwünschtes)* legacy.

erbeben* *vi aux sein (geh)* to shudder.

erben 1 *vt (lit, fig)* to inherit *(von* from)*; *(col: geschenkt bekommen)* to get, to be given. **bei ihm ist nichts zu ~** *(col)* you won't get anything out of him. **2** *vi* to inherit.

erbeuten* *vt (Tier) Opfer* to carry off; *(Dieb)* to get away with; *(im Krieg)* to capture.

Erb-: **~faktor** *m (Biol)* hereditary factor, gene; **~feind** *m* traditional *or* arch enemy; **~folge** *f* (line of) succession.

erbieten* *vr irreg (geh)* **sich ~, etw zu tun** to offer to do sth.

Erbin *f* heiress.

erbittern* *vt* to enrage, to incense.

erbittert *adj Widerstand, Gegner etc* bitter.

Erbitterung *f* rage.

Erbkrankheit *f* hereditary disease.

erblassen* *vi aux sein* to (go) pale, to blanch. **vor Neid ~** to go green with envy.

Erblasser(in *f)* *m* - *(Jur)* person who leaves an inheritance.

erblich *adj* hereditary. **er ist ~ (vor)belastet** it runs in the family.

erblicken* *vt (geh)* to see; *(erspähen)* to spot.

erblinden* *vi aux sein* to go blind.

Erblindung *f* loss of sight.

erblühen* *vi aux sein (geh)* to bloom, to blossom.

Erbmasse *f* estate; *(Biol)* genetic make-up.

erbosen* *(geh)* **1** *vt* to infuriate. **2** *vr* **sich ~ über** *(+acc)* to become infuriated at.

erbrechen* *vtir irreg (sich) ~ (Med)* to vomit, to be sick *(Brit) (nicht vt)*; **etw bis zum E~ tun** *(fig)* to do sth ad nauseam.

Erbrecht *nt* law of inheritance.

erbringen* *vt irreg* to produce, to furnish.

Erbschaft *f* inheritance. **eine ~ machen** to come into an inheritance.

Erbschaftssteuer *f* estate *or* death duties *pl*.

Erbschleicher(in *f)* *m* legacy-hunter.

Erbse *f* **-n** pea.

Erbsensuppe *f* pea soup.

Erb-: **~stück** *nt* heirloom; **~sünde** *f (Rel)* original sin; **~teil** *nt (Jur: auch m)* (share of an/the) inheritance.

Erd|achse *f* earth's axis.

erdacht *adj Geschichte* made-up.

Erdball *m (liter)* globe, world.

Erdbeben *nt* earthquake.

Erdbeere *f* strawberry.

Erdboden *m* ground, earth. **etw dem ~ gleichmachen** to level sth, to raze sth to the ground; **als hätte ihn der ~ verschluckt** as if the earth had swallowed him up.

Erde *f* **-n (a)** *(Welt)* earth, world. **auf der ganzen ~** all over the world. **(b)** *(Boden)* ground. **unter der ~** underground, below ground; **du wirst mich noch unter die ~ bringen** *(col)* you'll be the death of me yet *(col)*; **über der ~** above ground. **(c)** *(Erdreich, Bodenart)* soil, earth *(auch Chem)*. **(d)** *(Elec: Erdung)* earth *(Brit)*, ground *(US)*.

erden *vt (Elec)* to earth *(Brit)*, to ground *(US)*.

erdenklich *adj attr* conceivable, imaginable. **sich *(dat)* alle ~e Mühe geben** to take the greatest (possible) pains; **alles E~e tun** to do everything conceivable *or* imaginable.

Erd-: **~gas** *nt* natural gas; **~geschoß** *nt* ground floor, first floor *(US)*; **im ~geschoß** on the ground/first floor; **~innere(s)** *nt* interior *or* bowels *pl* of the earth; **~kruste** *f* earth's crust; **~kugel** *f* earth, globe; **~kunde** *f* geography; **~nußf** peanut, groundnut; **~oberfläche** *f* earth's surface; **~öl** *nt* (mineral) oil, petroleum.

erdolchen* *vt* to stab (to death). **jdn mit Blicken ~** to look daggers at sb.

Erdreich *nt* soil, earth.

erdreisten* *vr* **sich ~, etw zu tun** to have the audacity to do sth; **wie können Sie sich ~!** how dare you!

erdrosseln* *vt* to strangle, to throttle.

erdrücken* *vt* to crush (to death); *(fig: überwältigen)* to overwhelm. **~de Übermacht/~des Beweismaterial** overwhelming superiority/ evidence; **die Schuld erdrückte ihn** the sense of guilt oppressed him.

Erd-: **~rutsch** *m* landslide, landslip; **~schicht** *f* layer (of the earth), stratum; **~stoß** *m* (seismic) shock; **~teil** *m* continent.

erdulden* *vt* to endure, to suffer.

Erdung *f (Elec)* earth(ing), ground(ing) *(US)*.

er|eifern* *vr* to get worked up *(über* +*acc* over)*.

er|eignen* *vr* to occur, to happen.

Er|eignis *nt* event; *(Vorfall auch)* incident.

er|eignis-: **~los** *adj* uneventful; **~reich** *adj* eventful.

Erektion *f (Physiol)* erection.

Eremit *m (wk)* **-en**, **-en** hermit.

er|erben* *vt* to inherit.

erfahren* **1** *vt irreg* **(a)** *Nachricht etc* to learn, to find out; *(hören)* to hear *(von* about, of)*. **etw ~ to** find out about sth; **darf man Ihre Absichten ~?** might one inquire as to your intentions? **(b)** *(erleben)* to experience; *(empfangen) Verständnis* to receive. **2** *vi irreg* to hear *(von* about, of)*. **3** *adj* experienced.

Erfahrenheit *f* experience.

Erfahrung *f* experience. **aus (eigener) ~** from (one's own) experience; **nach meiner ~** in my experience; **~en sammeln** to gain experience; **die ~ hat gezeigt, daß ... experience has shown that ...; **etw in ~ bringen** to learn *or* find out sth; **eine ~ machen** to have an experience; **ich habe die ~ gemacht, daß ...** I have found that ...; **mit dieser neuen Mitarbeiterin haben wir nur gute ~en gemacht** we have found this new employee (to be) completely satisfactory; **ich habe mit der Ehe nur schlechte ~en gemacht** I've had a very bad experience of marriage.

Erfahrungs-: **~austausch** *m (Pol)* exchange of experiences; **e~gemäß** *adv* **e~gemäß ... as experience shows ...

erfaßbar *adj* ascertainable.

erfassen* *vt* **(a)** *(mitreißen: Auto, Strömung)* to catch. **(b)** *(Furcht, Verlangen etc)* to seize. *Angst* **erfaßte sie** she was seized by fear. **(c)** *(begreifen)* to grasp. **(d)** *(registrieren)* to record, to register. **alle Fälle werden statistisch erfaßt** statistics of all cases are being recorded.

Erfassung *f* registration, recording.

erfinden* *vt irreg* to invent. **das hat sie glatt erfunden** she made it all up; **frei erfunden** completely fictitious.

Erfinder(in *f)* *m* - inventor.

erfinderisch *adj* inventive; *(findig auch)* ingenious.

Erfindung *f* invention; *(Erdichtung, Lüge auch)* fabrication.

Erfolg *m* **-e** success; *(Ergebnis, Folge)* result, outcome. **mit/ohne ~** successfully/without success *or* unsuccessfully; **~/keinen ~ haben** to be successful/unsuccessful; **sie warnte mich mit dem ~, daß ... the result of her warning me was that ...; **viel ~!** good luck.

erfolgen* *vi aux sein (form) (vollzogen werden)* to be effected *(form) or* carried out; *(stattfinden)* to take place. **nach erfolgter Zahlung** when payment has been made; **es erfolgte keine Antwort** no answer was forthcoming.

Erfolg-: **e~los** *adj* unsuccessful, without success; **~losigkeit** *f* lack of success, unsuccessfulness; **e~reich** *adj* successful.

Erfolgs-: ~**erlebnis** nt feeling of success, sense of achievement; ~**leiter** f (fig) ladder to success; ~**mensch** m success, successful person.

erfolgversprechend adj promising.

erforderlich adj necessary, requisite. **unbedingt** ~ (absolutely) essential or imperative.

erfordern* vt to require, to call for.

Erfordernis nt requirement.

erforschen* vt Land to explore; Probleme auch to investigate; Meinung, Wahrheit to find out. **sein Gewissen** ~ to examine one's conscience.

Erforscher m (eines Landes) explorer; (in Wissenschaft) investigator.

Erforschung f siehe vt exploration; investigation (+gen into); finding out.

erfragen* vt Weg to ask; Einzelheiten etc to obtain.

erfreuen* 1 vt to please, to delight; Herz to gladden. **sehr erfreut!** (form) pleased to meet you!; **ja, sagte er erfreut** yes, he said delightedly. **2** vr **sich einer Sache** (gen) ~ (geh) to enjoy sth.

erfreulich adj pleasant; Neuerung, Besserung etc welcome; (befriedigend) gratifying. **es ist wenig** ~, **daß wir** ... it's not very satisfactory that we ...; **es wäre** ~, **wenn die Regierung** ... it would be good if the government ...; **sehr** ~! very nice!; **wir haben** ~ **viel geleistet** it's very encouraging how much we've done.

erfreulicherweise adv happily.

erfrieren* 1 vi irreg aux sein to freeze to death; (Pflanzen) to be killed by frost. **erfrorene Glieder** frostbitten limbs. **2** vt **sich** (dat) **die Füße** ~ to suffer frostbite in one's feet.

erfrischen* 1 vti to refresh. **2** vr to refresh oneself; (sich waschen) to freshen up.

erfrischend adj (lit, fig) refreshing.

Erfrischung f refreshment.

erfüllen* 1 vt (a) Raum etc to fill. **Haß/Liebe etc erfüllte ihn** he was filled with hate/love etc; **es erfüllt mich mit Genugtuung, daß** ... it gives me great satisfaction to see that ...; **ein erfülltes Leben** a full life. (b) (ausführen, einhalten) to fulfil (Brit), to fulfill (US); Bedingungen auch to meet, to comply with; Wunsch, Pflicht auch to carry out; Erwartungen auch to come up to; (Jur) Soll to achieve; Plan to carry through; Zweck to serve. **ihr Wunsch wurde erfüllt** their wish came true. **2** vr (Wunsch, Voraussagung) to be fulfilled, to come true.

Erfüllung f fulfilment (Brit), fulfillment (US); (einer Aufgabe auch) performance; (eines Solls) achievement; (eines Plans) execution. **in** ~ **gehen** to be fulfilled.

ergänzen* vt to supplement; (vervollständigen) to complete; Fehlendes to supply; Vorräte to replenish; Bericht auch to add (sth) to; Worte to add; Gesetz to amend. **sich** ~ to complement one another; ~d **hinzufügen** to add (zu to).

Ergänzung f (a) (das Ergänzen) supplementing; (Vervollständigung) completion; (von Fehlendem) supply(ing); (eines Berichts) addition (+gen to); (von Gesetz) amendment; (von Lager, Vorräten) replenishing. (b) (Zusatz, zu Buch etc) supplement; (Hinzugefügtes, Person) addition; (zu einem Gesetz) amendment.

ergattern* vt (col) to get hold of.

ergeben* irreg 1 vt to yield, to produce; (zum Ergebnis haben) to result in; Summe to amount to. **2** vr (a) (kapitulieren) (dat to) to surrender, to capitulate. **sich in etw** (acc) ~ to submit to sth. (b) (folgen) to result, to arise (aus from). **daraus können sich Nachteile** ~ this could turn out to be disadvantageous. (c) (sich herausstellen) to come to light. **es ergab sich, daß unsere Befürchtungen** ... it turned out that our fears ... **3** adj (hingeben, treu) devoted; (demütig) humble; (unterwürfig) submissive. **jdm treu** ~ **sein** to be loyally devoted to sb.

Ergebenheit f (Hingabe, Treue) devotion; (Demut)

humility; (Unterwürfigkeit) submissiveness.

Ergebnis nt result; (Sport auch) score; (Auswirkung auch) consequence, outcome. **die Verhandlungen führten zu keinem** ~ the negotiations were inconclusive; **zu einem** ~ **kommen** to come to or reach a conclusion.

ergebnislos adj unsuccessful, fruitless. ~ **bleiben/verlaufen** to come to nothing.

ergehen* irreg 1 vi aux sein (a) (form) to go out (an +acc to); (Gesetz) to be enacted. ~ **lassen** to issue, to send; to enact. (b) **sie ließ alles über sich** (acc) ~ she submitted to everything. **2** vi impers aux sein **es ist ihm schlecht/gut ergangen** he fared badly/well; **es wird ihm schlecht** ~ he will suffer. **3** vr (fig) **sich in etw** (dat) ~ to indulge in sth; **sich (in langen Reden) über ein Thema** ~ to hold forth at length on sth.

Ergehen nt no pl (geh) (state of) health.

ergiebig adj (lit, fig) productive; Geschäft profitable, lucrative; (fruchtbar) fertile; (sparsam im Verbrauch) economic.

ergießen* vr irreg (geh) to pour forth (liter) or out (auch fig).

ergo conj therefore, ergo (liter, hum).

ergötzen* (geh) 1 vt to delight. **2** vr **sich an etw** (dat) ~ to take delight in sth.

ergrauen* vi aux sein to go grey (Brit) or gray (US).

ergreifen* vt irreg (lit, fig) to seize; (fassen auch) to grasp, to grip; Beruf to take up; Maßnahmen to take; (innerlich bewegen) to move. **von Furcht etc ergriffen werden** to be seized with fear etc; **er ergriff das Wort** he began to speak; (Parl, bei Versammlung etc) he took the floor.

ergreifend adj (fig) moving.

ergriffen adj (fig) moved.

Ergriffenheit f emotion.

ergründen* vt Sinn etc to fathom; Ursache, Motiv to discover.

Ergründung f siehe vt fathoming; discovery.

Erguß m =sse effusion; (Samen~) ejaculation; (fig) outpouring.

erhaben adj (a) Gedanken, Stil lofty, elevated; Schönheit, Anblick sublime; Augenblick solemn. (b) (überlegen) superior. ~ **lächeln** to smile in a superior way; **über etw** (acc) ~ (sein) (to be) above sth; **über jeden Verdacht** ~ **sein** to be above suspicion.

Erhalt m no pl receipt. **bei/nach** ~ on receipt.

erhalten* irreg 1 vt (a) to get, to receive; Resultat, Genehmigung to obtain, to get. **das Wort** ~ to receive permission to speak. (b) (bewahren) to preserve; Gesundheit etc auch to maintain. **jdn am Leben** ~ to keep sb alive; **er hat sich** (dat) **seinen Optimismus** ~ he retained his optimism; **gut** ~ well preserved (auch hum col). **2** vr (Brauch etc) to last.

erhältlich adj obtainable, available. **schwer** ~ difficult to obtain, hard to come by.

Erhaltung f (Bewahrung) preservation.

erhängen* vt to hang. **Tod durch E~** death by hanging; **sich** ~ to hang oneself.

erhärten* 1 vt to harden; (fig) Behauptung etc to corroborate. **2** vr (fig: Verdacht) to harden.

erheben* irreg 1 vt (a) to raise. **jdn in den Adelsstand** ~ to raise or elevate sb to the peerage. (b) Gebühren to charge, to levy; Steuern (auferlegen) to impose. **2** vr (a) (aufstehen) to get up, to rise. (b) (sich auflehnen) to rise (up), to revolt. (c) (aufragen) to rise (über +dat above).

erhebend adj elevating, uplifting; (beeindruckend) impressive.

erheblich adj (beträchtlich) considerable; (Verletzung serious; (relevant) pertinent.

Erhebung f (a) (Boden~) elevation. (b) (Aufstand) uprising, revolt. (c) (von Gebühren) levying. (d) (Umfrage etc) investigation, inquiry.

erheitern* 1 vt to cheer (up); (belustigen) to amuse. **2** vr to be amused (über +acc by).

Erheiterung f amusement.

erhellen* 1 vt to illuminate; (fig: klären auch) to elucidate. **2** vr (lit, fig) to brighten; (plötzlich) to light up.

erhitzen* 1 vt to heat (auf +acc to). **die Gemüter ~ to** whip up feeling. **2** vr to get hot, to heat up; (fig: sich erregen) to become heated (an+dat over). **die Gemüter erhitzten sich** feelings were running high.

Erhitzung f heating up; (fig: Erregung) excitement.

erhoffen* vt to hope for. **was erhoffst du dir davon?** what do you hope to gain from it?

erhöhen* 1 vt to raise; Preise auch, Produktion, Wirkung, Spannung to increase. **jdn im Rang ~ to** promote sb; **erhöhte Temperatur haben** to have a temperature. **2** vr to rise, to increase.

Erhöhung f (a) raising; (von Produktion, Wirkung) increase; (von Spannung) heightening. **(b)** (Lohn~) rise (Brit), raise (US); (Preis~) increase. **(c)** (Hügel) hill, elevation.

Erhöhungszeichen nt (Mus) sharp (sign).

erholen* vr (von from) to recover; (sich entspannen auch) to relax, to have a rest; (fig: Preise, Aktien auch) to rally, to pick up. **du siehst sehr erholt aus** you look very rested.

erholsam adj restful, refreshing.

Erholung f siehe vr recovery (auch fig); relaxation, rest. **zur ~ in die Schweiz fahren** to go to Switzerland for a holiday (esp Brit) or a vacation (US) and a rest; **er braucht dringend ~** he badly needs a rest.

Erholungs-: **e~bedürftig** adj in need of a rest, run-down; **~heim** nt rest home; (Ferienheim) holiday home; **~kur** f rest cure; **~ort** m spa, health resort; **~pause** f break; **~reise** f holiday (Brit) or vacation (US) trip.

erhören* vt Gebet etc to hear; Bitte to yield to.

Erika f, pl **Eriken** (Bot) heather.

er|innern* 1 vt jdn an etw (acc) **~** to remind sb of sth; **jdn daran ~, daß** ... to remind sb that ... **2** vr sich an jdn/etw **~** to remember or recall sb/sth; **soweit ich mich ~ kann** as far as I remember; **wenn ich mich recht erinnere** if I remember rightly. **3** vi **~ an** (+acc) to be reminiscent of.

Er|innerung f (an +acc of) memory, recollection; (euph: Mahnung) reminder; (Andenken) memento. **~en** pl (Lebens~) reminiscences pl; (Liter) memoirs pl; **zur ~ an** (+acc) in memory of; (an Ereignis) in commemoration of; (als Andenken) as a memento of; **jdn/etw in guter ~ behalten** to have pleasant memories of sb/sth.

Er|innerungs-: **~schreiben** nt (Comm) reminder; **~stück** nt keepsake.

erkalten* vi aux sein (lit, fig) to cool (down).

erkälten* vr to catch (a) cold. **sich** (dat) **die Blase ~** to catch a chill in one's bladder.

erkältet adj **wir sind alle ~** we all have colds.

Erkältung f cold; (leicht) chill. **eine ~ bekommen** to catch a cold/chill.

erkämpfen* vt to win, to secure. **sich** (dat) **etw ~** to win sth; **er hat sich** (dat) **seine Position hart erkämpft** he fought hard for his position.

erkaufen* vt (fig) to buy. **etw teuer ~** to pay dearly for sth; **den Erfolg mit seiner Gesundheit ~** to achieve success at the price of one's health.

erkennbar adj (wieder~) recognizable; (sichtbar) visible; (ersichtlich) discernible.

erkennen* irreg **1** vt (wieder~, einsehen) to recognize (an+dat by); (wahrnehmen) to see, to make out; Unterschied to see. **er hat erkannt, daß das nicht stimmte** he realized that it wasn't right; **jdm zu ~ geben, daß** ... to give sb to understand that ...; **sich zu ~ geben** to reveal oneself (als to be); **~ lassen** to show, to reveal; **du bist erkannt!** I see what you're after, I know your game. **2** vi **~ auf** (+acc) (Jur) Freispruch to grant; Strafe to impose; (Sport) Freistoß to give,

to award.

erkenntlich adj **sich (für etw) ~ zeigen** to show one's gratitude or appreciation (for sth).

Erkenntnis f (Wissen) knowledge no pl; (das Erkennen) recognition, realization; (Entdeckung) discovery. **zu der ~ kommen, daß** ... to come to the realization that ..., to realize that ...

Erkennungs-: **~dienst** m police records department; **e~dienstlich** adv **jdn e~dienstlich behandeln** to fingerprint and photograph sb; **~marke** f identity disc; **~melodie** f signature tune; **~zeichen** nt identification; (Mil: Abzeichen) badge.

Erker m - bay; (kleiner Vorbau) oriel.

erklärbar adj explicable, explainable. **leicht ~** easily explained; **schwer ~** hard to explain.

erklären* 1 vt (a) (erläutern) to explain (jdm etw sth to sb). **ich kann mir nicht ~, warum** ... I can't understand why ... (b) (bekanntgeben) to declare (als to be); Rücktritt to announce; (Politiker, Pressesprecher etc) to say. **einem Staat den Krieg ~** to declare war on a country; **eine Ausstellung etc für eröffnet ~** to declare an exhibition etc open; **jdn für schuldig etc ~** to pronounce sb guilty etc. **2** vr (a) (Sache) to be explained. **das erklärt sich daraus, daß** ... it can be explained by the fact that ...; **das erklärt sich (von) selbst** that's self-explanatory. **(b)** (Mensch) to declare oneself. **er erklärte sich für gesund** he said that he was in good health.

erklärend adj explanatory. **einige ~e Worte a** few words of explanation.

erklärlich adj (a) = **erklärbar**. (b) (verständlich) understandable.

erklärt adj attr Gegner etc professed, avowed; Favorit, Liebling acknowledged.

Erklärung f (a) explanation. (b) (Bekanntgabe) declaration; (eines Politikers etc) statement.

erklingen* vi irreg (geh) aux sein to ring out. **ein Lied ~ lassen** to burst (forth) into song.

erkranken* vi aux sein to be taken ill (an +dat with); (Organ, Pflanze, Tier) to become diseased (an+dat with). **er ist am Magen erkrankt** he has contracted a stomach illness.

Erkrankung f illness; (von Organ, Pflanze, Tier) disease.

erkunden* vt (esp Mil) Gelände etc to reconnoitre; (feststellen) to find out.

erkundigen* vr **sich nach etw/jdm ~** to ask about sth/after sb; **ich werde mich ~** I'll find out.

Erkundigung f inquiry; (Nachforschung auch) investigation. **~en einholen** to make inquiries.

Erkundung f (Mil) reconnaissance.

erlahmen* vi aux sein (lit, fig) to flag.

erlangen* vt to attain, to achieve.

Erlaß m -sse (a) decree, enactment. (b) (Straf~ etc) remission.

erlassen* vt irreg (a) Verfügung to pass; Gesetz to enact. (b) Strafe etc to remit; Gebühren to waive. **jdm etw ~** Schulden etc to release sb from sth; Gebühren to waive sth for sb; **jdm die Strafarbeit ~** to let sb off a punishment.

erlauben* 1 vt to allow, to permit. **jdm etw ~** to allow or permit sb (to do) sth; **es ist mir nicht erlaubt, das zu tun** I am not allowed or permitted to do that; **~ Sie?** may I?; **~ Sie, daß ich das Fenster öffne?** do you mind if I open the window?; **~ Sie, daß ich mich vorstelle** allow me or permit me to introduce myself; **~ Sie mal!** do you mind!; **soweit es meine Zeit erlaubt** (form) time permitting. **2** vr **sich** (dat) **etw ~** (gestatten, sich gönnen) to allow or permit oneself sth; (wagen) Bemerkung to venture sth; (sich leisten) **sich** (dat) **etw zu tun ~** to afford sth; **sich** (dat) **...etw zu tun** (sofrei sein) to take the liberty of doing sth; (sich leisten) **etw ~** to afford to do sth; **was ~ Sie sich (eigentlich)!** how dare you!

Erlaubnis f permission; (Schriftstück) permit. **(jdn) um ~ bitten** to ask (sb) (for) permission.

erläutern* vt to explain, to elucidate; *Text* to comment on. ~**d** explanatory; ~**d fügte er hinzu** he added in explanation.

Erläuterung f *siehe* vt explanation, elucidation; commentary. **zur** ~ in explanation.

Erle f **-n** alder.

erleben* vt to experience; *(noch lebend erreichen)* to live to see; *(durchmachen) schwere Zeiten* to go through; *Abenteuer, Enttäuschung, Erfolg* to have; *Jahrhundertwende* to see. **im Urlaub habe ich viel erlebt** I had an eventful time on holiday; **was haben Sie im Ausland erlebt?** what sort of experiences did you have abroad?; **er hat schon viel Schlimmes erlebt** he's had a lot of bad times *or* experiences; **ich habe es oft erlebt** I've often seen it happen; **so wütend habe ich ihn noch nie erlebt** I've never seen *or* known him so furious; **das werde ich nicht mehr** ~ I shan't live to see that; **er möchte mal etwas** ~ he wants to have a good time; **das muß man erlebt haben** you've got to have experienced it for yourself; **na, der kann was** ~**!** *(col)* he's going to be for it! *(col)*.

Erlebnis *nt (Abenteuer)* adventure.

erledigen* **1** vt **(a)** to deal with; *Akte etc* to process; *(ausführen) Auftrag* to carry out; *Sache* to settle. **Einkäufe** ~ to do the shopping; **ich habe noch einiges in der Stadt zu** ~ I've still got a few things to do in town; **das ist erledigt** that's taken care of, that's been done. **(b)** *(col) (ermüden)* to wear out; *(ruinieren)* to finish, to ruin; *(töten)* to do in *(col); (k.o. schlagen)* to finish off. **2** vr **das hat sich erledigt** that's all settled; **sich von selbst** ~ to take care of itself.

erledigt adj *(col) (erschöpft)* shattered *(col)*, done in *pred (col); (ruiniert)* finished, ruined.

Erledigung f *(Ausführung)* execution, carrying out; *(Durchführung, Beendung)* completion; *(einer Sache)* settlement. **die** ~ **meiner Korrespondenz** dealing with my correspondence; **einige** ~**en in der Stadt** a few things to do in town; **in** ~ **Ihrer Anfrage** *(form)* further to your inquiry *(form)*.

erlegen* vt *Wild* to shoot, to bag *(Hunt)*.

erleichtern* vt *(einfacher machen)* to make easier; *(fig) Last, Los* to lighten; *(lindern) Not, Schmerz etc* to relieve. **sein Herz/Gewissen** ~ to unburden one's heart/conscience; **jdn um etw** ~ *(hum)* to relieve sb of sth; **erleichtert aufatmen** to breathe a sigh of relief.

Erleichterung f *(von Last etc)* lightening; *(Linderung)* relief. **das trägt zur** ~ **meiner Aufgabe bei** it makes my work easier.

erleiden* vt *irreg* to suffer.

erlernen* vt to learn.

erlesen adj exquisite. **ein** ~**er Kreis** a select circle.

erleuchten* vt to light (up), to illuminate.

Erleuchtung f *(Eingebung)* inspiration.

erliegen* vi *irreg aux sein+dat (lit, fig)* to succumb to; *einem Irrtum* to be the victim of. **zum E**~ **kommen** to come to a standstill.

erlogen adj made-up.

Erlös m **-e** proceeds pl *(+gen* from).

erlöschen* vi *irreg aux sein (Feuer)* to go out; *(Gefühle, Interesse)* to die; *(Anspruch etc)* to expire, to lapse; *(Firma)* to be dissolved. **ein erloschener Vulkan** an extinct volcano.

erlösen* vt *(retten)* to save, to rescue *(aus, von* from); *(Rel)* to redeem, to save; *(von Sünden, Qualen)* to deliver *(esp Bibl)*, to release.

erlösend adj relieving, liberating. **sie sprach das** ~**e Wort** she spoke the word he/she/everybody *etc* was waiting for.

Erlöser(in f) m - *(Rel)* Redeemer; *(Befreier)* saviour.

Erlösung f release, deliverance; *(Erleichterung)* relief; *(Rel)* redemption.

ermächtigen* vt to authorize, to empower *(zu etw* to do sth).

Ermächtigung f authorization.

ermahnen* vt to exhort, to urge; *(warnend)* to warn; *(Jur)* to caution. **jdn zur Aufmerksamkeit** ~ to urge sb to be attentive; **jdn im Guten** ~ to give sb a friendly warning.

Ermahnung f exhortation, urging; *(warnend)* warning; *(Jur)* caution.

Ermang(e)lung f: **in** ~ +gen because of the lack of.

ermäßigen **1** vt to reduce. **2** vr to be reduced.

Ermäßigung f reduction; *(Steuer~)* relief.

ermattet adj *(geh)* exhausted, weary.

ermessen* vt irreg *(einschätzen) Größe, Wert* to estimate; *(begreifen können)* to appreciate.

Ermessen nt no pl *(Urteil)* judgement; *(Gutdünken)* discretion. **nach meinem** ~ in my judgement; **nach menschlichem** ~ as far as anyone can judge; **nach eigenem** ~ **handeln** to act on one's own discretion; **in jds** ~ *(dat)* **liegen** to be at sb's discretion.

Ermessens-: ~**entscheidung** f *(Jur)* discretionary decision; ~**frage** f matter of discretion.

ermitteln* **1** vt to determine *(auch Chem, Math)*, to ascertain; *Person* to trace; *Tatsache* to establish. **2** vi to investigate. **gegen jdn** ~ to investigate sb.

Ermittlung f **(a)** *no pl siehe* vt determination, ascertaining; tracing; establishing. **(b)** *(esp Jur: Erkundigung)* investigation, inquiry. ~**en anstellen** to make inquiries *(über+acc* about).

Ermittlungs-: ~**ausschuß** m committee of inquiry; ~**richter** m *(Jur)* examining magistrate; ~**verfahren** nt *(Jur)* preliminary proceedings pl.

ermöglichen* vt to facilitate, to make possible. **jdm das Studium** ~ to make it possible for sb to study.

ermorden* vt to murder; *(Pol)* to assassinate.

Ermordung f murder; *(Pol)* assassination.

ermüden* **1** vt to tire. **2** vi *aux sein* to tire, to become tired; *(Tech)* to fatigue.

Ermüdung f fatigue *(auch Tech)*, tiredness.

Ermüdungs|erscheinung f sign of fatigue.

ermuntern* vt *(ermutigen)* to encourage *(jdn zu etw* sb to do sth); *(aufmuntern)* to cheer up.

ermutigen* vt *(ermuntern)* to encourage; *(Mut geben)* to give courage.

Ermutigung f encouragement.

ernähren* **1** vt to feed; *(unterhalten)* to support, to keep. **schlecht/gut ernährt** undernourished/well-fed. **2** vr to eat. **sich von etw** ~ to live on sth; **sich von Übersetzungen** ~ to earn one's living by doing translations.

Ernährer(in f) m - breadwinner, provider.

Ernährung f feeding; *(Nahrung)* food, nourishment, nutrition *(esp Med)*. **die** ~ **einer großen Familie** feeding a big family; **falsche/richtige/pflanzliche** ~ the wrong/a proper/a vegetarian diet.

Ernährungs-: ~**gewohnheiten** pl eating habits pl; ~**weise** f diet.

ernennen* vt irreg to appoint *(jdn zu etw* sb sth).

Ernennung f appointment *(zu* as).

erneuern* vt to renew; *(renovieren)* to renovate; *(restaurieren)* to restore; *(auswechseln) Maschinenteile* to replace; *(wiederbeleben)* to revive.

Erneuerung f *siehe* vt renewal; renovation; restoration; replacement; revival.

erneut **1** adj *attr* renewed. **2** adv *(once)* again.

erniedrigen* **1** vt *(demütigen)* to humiliate; *(herabsetzen)* to degrade. **2** vr *(pej)* to humble oneself; to lower oneself.

Erniedrigung f *siehe* vt humiliation; degradation.

Erniedrigungszeichen nt *(Mus)* flat (sign).

Ernst m no pl seriousness. **im** ~ seriously; **allen** ~**es** in all seriousness, quite seriously; **ist das Ihr** ~**?** are you (really) serious?; **das kann doch nicht dein** ~ **sein!** you can't be serious!; **es ist**

mir ~ damit I'm serious about it, I'm in earnest; mit einer Drohung ~ machen to carry out a threat; der ~ des Lebens the serious side of life; mit ~ bei der Sache sein to do sth seriously.

ernst adj serious. es (mit jdm/etw) ~ meinen to be serious (about sb/sth); jdn/etw ~ nehmen to take sb/sth seriously; es steht ~ um ihn things don't look too good for him.

Ernst-: ~fall m emergency; im ~fall in case of emergency; e~gemeint adj attr serious; e~haft adj serious; (eindringlich, eifrig) earnest; ~haftigkeit f siehe adj seriousness; earnestness; e~lich adj serious.

Ernte f -n (a) harvest (an+dat of); (von Äpfeln, fig) crop. die ~ seines Fleißes the fruits of his labour. (b) (das Ernten) (von Getreide) harvest(ing); (von Kartoffeln) digging; (von Äpfeln etc) picking.

Ernte-: ~arbeiter m harvester; (von Kartoffeln, Obst) picker; ~(dank)fest nt harvest festival.

ernten vt Getreide to harvest, to reap; Kartoffeln to get in; Äpfel, Erbsen to pick; (fig) Früchte, Unfrieden to reap; (Un)dank, Spott to get.

ernüchtern* vt to sober up; (fig) to bring down to earth. ~d sobering; ich war sehr ernüchtert my illusions were shattered.

Ernüchterung f sobering-up; (fig) disillusionment.

Er|oberer m -, **Er|oberin** f conqueror.

er|obern* vt to conquer; Festung, Stadt to capture; (fig) Sympathie etc to win; (col: ergattern) to get hold of.

Er|oberung f (lit, fig) conquest; (einer Festung, Stadt) capture.

er|öffnen* 1 vt to open; Konkursverfahren to institute. jdm etw ~ (hum, geh) to disclose or reveal sth to sb. 2 vr (Aussichten etc) to open up.

Er|öffnung f siehe vt opening; institution; disclosure, revelation.

Er|öffnungs-: ~ansprache f inaugural or opening address; ~kurs m opening price.

erogen adj erogenous.

er|örtern* vt to discuss (in detail).

Er|örterung f discussion.

Erosion f (Geol, Med) erosion.

Erotik f eroticism.

erotisch adj erotic.

Erpel m - drake.

erpicht adj auf etw (acc) ~ sein to be keen on sth.

erpressen* vt to blackmail; Geld etc to extort.

Erpresser(in f) m - blackmailer; (bei Entführung) kidnapper.

erpresserisch adj Methode blackmailing attr.

Erpressung f blackmail; (von Geld etc) extortion.

erproben* vt (lit, fig) to test. erprobt tried and tested.

erraten* vt irreg to guess.

errechnen* vt to calculate, to work out.

erregbar adj excitable; (sexuell) easily aroused; (empfindlich) sensitive.

Erregbarkeit f siehe adj excitability; ability to be aroused; sensitivity.

erregen* 1 vt (a) (aufregen) jdn, Nerven etc to excite; (erzürnen) to infuriate. er war vor Wut ganz erregt he was in a rage; erregte Diskussionen heated discussions; freudig erregt excited. (b) (erzeugen) to arouse; Aufsehen, Heiterkeit to cause, to create; Aufmerksamkeit to attract. 2 vr to get worked up or excited (über +acc about, over); (sich ärgern) to get annoyed (über+acc at).

Erreger m - (Med) cause.

Erregung f excitement; (sexuell auch) arousal; (Beunruhigung) agitation; (Wut) rage. in ~ geraten to get excited/aroused/agitated/into a rage.

erreichbar adj reachable; (nicht weit) within reach; Ziel attainable. leicht ~ easily reached/within easy reach/easily attainable; schwer ~

sein (Ort) not to be very accessible; (Mensch) to be difficult to get hold of; der Direktor ist nie ~ the director is never available.

erreichen* vt to reach; Zug to catch; Zweck to achieve; (einholen) to catch up with. ein hohes Alter ~ to live to a great age; vom Bahnhof leicht zu ~ within easy reach of the station; wann kann ich Sie morgen ~? when can I get in touch with you tomorrow?; wir haben nichts erreicht we achieved nothing.

errichten* vt to erect, to put up; (fig: gründen) to set up.

Errichtung f no pl erection, construction; (fig: Gründung) setting-up.

erringen* vt irreg to gain.

erröten* vi aux sein to blush.

Errungenschaft f achievement; (col: Anschaffung) acquisition.

Ersatz m no pl substitute (auch Sport); (für Altes, Mitarbeiter) replacement; (Mil: ~truppen) replacements pl; (das Ersetzen) replacement, substitution; (von Kosten) reimbursement. als or zum ~ as a substitute/replacement; als ~ für jdn einspringen to stand in for sb; für etw ~ leisten (Jur) to pay compensation for sth.

Ersatz-: ~dienst m (Mil) alternative service; ~kasse f private health insurance; ~mann m, pl ~männer or ~leute replacement; (Sport) substitute; ~spieler m (Sport) substitute; ~teil nt spare (part); e~weise adv as an alternative.

ersaufen* vi irreg aux sein (col) to drown; (Aut) to flood.

erschaffen vt irreg to create.

Erschaffung f creation.

erscheinen* vi irreg aux sein to appear; (Buch auch) to come out. es erscheint (mir) wünschenswert it seems or appears desirable (to me).

Erscheinen nt no pl appearance; (von Buch auch) publication. um rechtzeitiges ~ wird gebeten you are kindly requested to attend punctually.

Erscheinung f (a) no pl (das Erscheinen) appearance. in ~ treten (Merkmale) to appear; (Gefühle) to show themselves. (b) (äußere ~) appearance; (Natur~, Vorkommnis) phenomenon; (Krankheits~, Alters~) symptom; (Zeichen) sign. (c) (Gestalt) figure. (d) (Geister~) apparition; (Traumbild) vision.

Erscheinungs-: ~form f manifestation; ~jahr nt (von Buch) year of publication.

erschießen* irreg 1 vt to shoot (dead). 2 vr to shoot oneself; siehe erschossen.

Erschießung f shooting; (als Todesstrafe) execution.

erschlaffen* vi aux sein (ermüden) to tire; (schlaff werden) to go limp; (Interesse) to flag.

Erschlaffung f siehe vi tiredness; limpness; flagging.

erschlagen* 1 vt irreg to kill. 2 adj (col: todmüde) worn out, dead beat (col).

erschleichen* vt irreg (sich dat) etw ~ to obtain sth by devious means; sich (dat) jds Vertrauen ~ to worm oneself into sb's confidence.

erschließen* irreg 1 vt Gebiet, Absatzmarkt to develop, to open up; Bodenschätze to tap. 2 vr sich jdm ~ (verständlich werden) to disclose itself to sb.

erschlossen adj Gebiet developed.

erschöpfen* 1 vt to exhaust. 2 vr (a) (körperlich) to exhaust oneself. (b) (fig) sich in etw (dat) ~ to amount to nothing more than sth.

erschöpfend adj (a) (ermüdend) exhausting. (b) (ausführlich) exhaustive.

Erschöpfung f exhaustion. bis zur ~ arbeiten to work to the point of exhaustion.

erschossen adj (col) (völlig) ~ sein to be whacked (col), to be dead (beat) (col).

erschrecken* 1 vt to frighten, to scare;

(bestürzen) to startle. **2** pret auch **erschrak,** ptp auch **erschrocken** vir (vi: aux sein) to be frightened (vor+dat by); (bestürzt sein) to be startled. **sie erschrak beim Gedanken, daß ...** the thought that ... gave her a start or a scare; **sie erschrak bei dem Knall** the bang made her jump; siehe **erschrocken.**

erschreckend adj alarming, frightening. **~ wenig Leute** alarmingly few people.

erschrocken adj frightened, scared; (bestürzt) startled.

erschüttern* vt to shake; Glaubwürdigkeit to cast doubt on; Gesundheit to upset. **erschüttert sein** to be shaken or shattered by sth; **ihn kann nichts ~** he always keeps his cool (col).

erschütternd adj shattering.

Erschütterung f (des Bodens etc) tremor, vibration; (seelische Ergriffenheit) emotion, shock. **die Krise kann zu einer ~ des Staates führen** this crisis could rock the state.

erschweren* vt to make more difficult. **~de Umstände** (Jur) aggravating circumstances; **es kommt noch ~d hinzu, daß ...** to compound matters ...

Erschwerung f obstruction (gen to). **das bedeutet eine ~ meiner Arbeit** that will make my job more difficult.

erschwindeln* vt to obtain by fraud.

erschwinglich adj Preise affordable.

ersehen* vt irreg **etw aus etw ~** to see sth from sth.

ersehnt adj longed-for.

ersetzen* vt to replace.

Ersetzung f no pl replacing; (von Unkosten) reimbursement.

ersichtlich adj obvious, clear.

ersinnen* vt irreg to devise, to think up.

ersparen* vt Vermögen, Zeit, Kummer to save. **jdm/sich etw ~** to spare or save sb/oneself sth; **ich kann mir jeglichen Kommentar ~** I don't think I need to comment; **ihr blieb auch nichts erspart** she was spared nothing; **das Ersparte** the savings pl.

Ersparnis f (a) no pl (an Zeit etc) saving (an+dat of). (b) usu pl savings pl.

erst adv (a) first. **mach ~ (ein)mal die Arbeit fertig** finish your work first; **wenn du das ~ einmal hinter dir hast** once you've got that behind you. (b) (nicht früher als, nicht mehr als, bloß) only; (nicht früher als auch) not until. **gerade ~** just; **~ gestern** only yesterday; **~ jetzt verstehe ich** I have only just understood; **~ morgen** not until tomorrow; **wir fahren ~ später** we're not going until later; **~ als** only when, not until. (c) **da ging's ~ richtig los** then it really got going; **da fange ich ~ gar nicht an** I simply won't bother to begin; **jetzt ~ recht!/recht nicht!** just for that I will/won't do it; **wäre er doch ~ zurück!** if only he were back!; **diese Gerüchte darf man gar nicht ~ aufkommen lassen** these rumours mustn't even be allowed to start.

erstarren* vi aux sein (Finger) to grow stiff; (Flüssigkeit) to solidify; (Gips, Zement etc) to set; (fig: Blut) to freeze, to run cold; (Lächeln) to freeze; (vor Entsetzen) to be paralyzed (vor +dat with).

erstatten* vt (a) Unkosten to refund. (b) (form) (Straf)anzeige gegen jdn ~ to report sb.

Erstattung f no pl (von Unkosten) reimbursement.

erstaunen* vti to astonish, to amaze; siehe **erstaunt.**

Erstaunen nt no pl astonishment, amazement. **jdn in ~ (ver)setzen** to astonish or amaze sb.

erstaunlich adj astonishing, amazing.

erstaunt adj astonished, amazed (über +acc about). **er sah mich ~ an** he looked at me in astonishment or amazement.

Erst-: **~ausgabe** f first edition; **e~beste(r, s)** adj attr siehe **erste(r, s) (b).**

erstechen* vt irreg to stab to death.

erstehen* irreg **1** vt (col) to get. **2** vi aux sein (form) to arise.

ersteigen* vt irreg to climb.

ersteigern* vt to buy at an auction.

Ersteigung f ascent.

erstellen* vt (a) (bauen) to construct. (b) Liste etc to draw up.

erstens adv first(ly), in the first place.

erste(r, s) adj (a) first; Seite der Zeitung front. **~ Etage** first floor (Brit), second floor (US); **der ~ Rang** (Theat) the dress-circle, the (first) balcony (US); **~ Qualität** top quality; **E~ Hilfe** first aid; **der E~ in der Klasse** top of the class; **als ~s** first of all; **fürs ~** for the time being; **in ~r Linie** first and foremost; **zum ~n, zum zweiten, zum dritten** (bei Auktionen) going, going, gone!; siehe **vierte(r, s).** (b) **er hat den ~ n besten Kühlschrank gekauft** he bought the first fridge he saw, he bought any old fridge (col).

erstere(r, s) adj the former.

erstgenannt adj attr first-mentioned.

ersticken* **1** vt jdn to suffocate, to smother; Feuer to smother; (fig) Aufruhr to suppress. **mit erstickter Stimme** in a choked voice. **2** vi aux sein to suffocate; (Feuer) to go out. **an etw (dat) ~** to be suffocated by sth; **an einer Gräte ~** to choke (to death) on a bone; **vor Lachen ~** to choke with laughter; **in der Arbeit ~** (col) to be snowed under with work.

Erstickung f suffocation, asphyxiation.

Erstickungs-: **~gefahr** f danger of suffocation; **~tod** m death by suffocation, asphyxia.

Erst-: **e~klassig** adj first-class, first-rate; **~kommunion** f first communion.

Erstling m first (child); (Werk) first work.

erst-: **~malig** **1** adj first; **2** adv for the first time; **~mals** adv for the first time.

erstrangig ['eːɐstraŋɪç] adj first-rate.

erstreben* vt to strive for.

erstrebenswert adj worthwhile; Beruf desirable.

erstrecken* vr to extend (auf, über+acc over); (räumlich auch) to stretch (auf, über+acc over); (zeitlich auch) to last (auf, über+acc for).

Erststimme f first vote.

erstunken adj: **das ist ~ und erlogen** (col) that's a pack of lies.

Erstwähler m first-time voter.

ersuchen* vt (form) to request (jdn um etw sth of sb).

Ersuchen nt - (form) request.

ertappen* vt to catch. **ich habe ihn dabei ertappt** I caught him at it.

erteilen* vt to give; Lizenz to issue; Auftrag auch to place (jdm with sb). **jdm einen Verweis ~** to reproach sb.

Erteilung f siehe vt giving; issue; placing.

ertönen* vi aux sein (geh) to sound, to ring out. **~ lassen** to sound.

Ertrag m -ë (von Acker) yield; (Einnahmen) return.

ertragen* vt irreg to bear; (esp in Frage auch) to stand. **wie erträgst du nur seine Launen?** how do you stand his moods?

erträglich adj bearable, endurable; (leidlich) tolerable.

ertragreich adj Geschäft profitable, lucrative.

ertränken* **1** vt to drown. **2** vr to drown oneself.

erträumen* vt to dream of, to imagine.

ertrinken* vi irreg aux sein to drown, to be drowned.

Ertrinken nt no pl drowning.

Ertüchtigung f (geh) getting in trim. **körperliche ~** physical training.

er|übrigen* **1** vt Zeit, Geld to spare. **2** vr to be unnecessary or superfluous.

erwachen* vi aux sein to awake, to wake (up);

(aus Ohnmacht etc) to come around *(aus from)*; *(fig: Verdacht)* to be aroused. **ein böses E~** *(fig)* a rude awakening.

erwachsen* 1 *vi irreg aux sein (geh)* to arise, to develop; *(Vorteil, Kosten etc)* to result. **daraus erwuchsen ihm Unannehmlichkeiten** that caused him some trouble. 2 *adj* grown-up, adult. **~ sein** *(Mensch)* to be grown-up *or* an adult.

Erwachsenenbildung *f* adult education.

Erwachsene(r) *mf decl as adj* adult, grown-up.

erwägen* *vt irreg* to consider.

Erwägung *f* consideration. **etw in ~ ziehen** to take sth into consideration.

erwähnen* *vt* to mention, to refer to.

erwähnenswert *adj* worth mentioning.

Erwähnung *f* mention *(gen* of), reference *(gen* to).

erwärmen* 1 *vt* to warm. 2 *vr* to warm up. **sich für jdn/etw ~** *(fig)* to take to sb/sth; **ich kann mich für Goethe nicht ~** Goethe leaves me cold.

erwarten* *vt* to expect. **etw von jdm ~** to expect sth from *or* of sb; **ein Kind ~** to be expecting (a baby); **das war zu ~** that was to be expected; **er erwartet, daß wir sofort gehorchen** he expects us to obey immediately; **sie kann den Sommer kaum noch ~** she's really looking forward to the summer; **was mich da wohl erwartet?** I wonder what awaits me there.

Erwartung *f* expectation; *(Spannung, Ungeduld)* anticipation. **in ~ Ihrer baldigen Antwort** *(form)* in anticipation of your early reply.

erwartungs-: ~gemäß *adv* as expected; **~voll** *adj* expectant.

erwecken* *vt* **(a)** *(liter: aus Schlaf etc)* to rouse. **etw zu neuem Leben ~** to resurrect sth. **(b)** *(fig)* *Begeisterung etc* to arouse; *Hoffnungen, Zweifel* to raise; *Erinnerungen* to bring back.

erwehren* *vr (+gen) (geh)* to ward off. **er konnte sich kaum der Tränen ~** he could hardly hold back his tears.

erweichen* *vt* to soften; *(fig: überreden auch)* to move. **sich nicht ~ lassen** to be unmoved.

erweisen* *irreg* 1 *vt* **(a)** *(nachweisen)* to prove. **eine erwiesene Tatsache** a proven fact. **(b)** *(zuteil werden lassen)* to show. **jdm einen Dienst ~** to do sb a service. 2 *vr* **sich als etw ~** to prove to be sth, to turn out to be sth; **sich jdm gegenüber dankbar ~** to show one's gratitude to sb.

erweitern* *vtr* to widen, to enlarge; *Geschäft* to expand; *Kleid* to let out; *(Med)* to dilate; *(fig) Kenntnisse* to broaden; *Macht* to extend.

Erweiterung *f siehe vtr* widening, enlargement; expansion; letting out; dilation; broadening; extension.

Erwerb *m no pl* acquisition; *(Kauf)* purchase. **beim ~ eines Autos** when buying a car.

erwerben* *vt irreg* to acquire; *Ehre, Vertrauen, (Sport) Titel* to win, to gain; *(käuflich)* to purchase. **sich** *(dat)* **etw ~** to acquire *etc* sth; **er hat sich** *(dat)* **große Verdienste um die Firma erworben** he has done great service for the firm.

Erwerbs-: e~bar *adj (form)* capable of gainful employment; **~fähigkeit** *f (form)* fitness for work; **e~los** *adj* **= arbeitslos**; **e~tätig** *adj* (gainfully) employed; **~tätigkeit** *f* gainful employment; **e~unfähig** *adj* unable to work; **~unfähigkeit** *f* inability to work.

Erwerbung *f* acquisition.

erwidern* *vt* **(a)** to reply *(auf +acc* to). **(b)** *Besuch, Grüße, Blick, (Mil) Feuer* to return; *Gefühle* to reciprocate.

Erwiderung *f (Antwort)* reply, answer. **in ~ Ihres Schreibens vom ... *(form)*** in reply to your letter of the ...

erwirtschaften* *vt Gewinn etc* to make by good management.

erwischen* *vt (col)* to catch. **jdn beim Stehlen ~** to catch sb stealing; **du darfst dich nicht ~ lassen** you mustn't get caught; **ihn hat's erwischt!** *(verliebt)* he's got it bad *(col)*; *(krank)* he's got it; *(gestorben)* he's had it *(col)*.

erwünscht *adj Wirkung etc* desired; *Eigenschaft, Kenntnisse* desirable; *(willkommen)* welcome.

erwürgen* *vt* to strangle, to throttle.

Erz *nt* -e ore.

erzählen* *vti* **(a)** to tell. **er hat den Vorfall erzählt** he told (us *etc)* about the incident; **jdm etw ~** to tell sth to sb; **man erzählt sich, daß ... people say that ...; wem ~ Sie das!** *(col)* you're telling me!; **das kannst du einem anderen ~** *(col)* pull the other one *(col)*; **mir kannst du nichts ~** *(col)* don't give *or* tell me that! *(col)*; **dem werd' ich was ~!** *(col)* I'll have something to say to him; **er kann gut ~** he's a good story-teller. **(b)** *(Liter)* to narrate. **~de Dichtung** narrative fiction.

Erzähler(in *f)* *m* - narrator *(auch Liter)*; *(Geschichten~)* story-teller; *(Schriftsteller)* narrative writer.

erzählerisch *adj* narrative.

Erzählung *f (Liter)* story, tale; *(das Erzählen)* narration; *(Bericht)* account.

Erz-: ~bischof *m* archbishop; **~bistum** *nt* archbishopric; **~engel** *m* archangel.

erzeugen* *vt* to produce; *Strom auch* to generate; *(fig: bewirken)* to give rise to, to create.

Erzeuger(in *f) m* - *(Comm)* producer.

Erzeugerpreis *m* manufacturer's price.

Erzeugnis *nt* product; *(Agr)* produce *no indef art, no pl.*

Erzeugung *f no pl* production; *(von Strom auch)* generation; *(geistige, künstlerische)* creation.

Erz-: ~feind *m* arch-enemy; **~grube** *f* ore mine; **~hütte** *f* smelting works *sing or pl.*

erziehbar *adj Kind* educable; *Tier* trainable. **ein Heim für schwer ~e Kinder** a home for difficult children.

erziehen* *vt irreg Kind* to bring up; *Tier, Körper* to train; *(ausbilden)* to educate. **ein Kind zur Sauberkeit ~** to bring a child up to be clean; **gut/schlecht erzogen** well/badly brought-up.

Erzieher(in *f) m* - educator.

erzieherisch *adj* educational.

Erziehung *f no pl* upbringing; *(Ausbildung)* education; *(das Erziehen)* bringing up; *(von Tieren, Körper)* training.

Erziehungs-: ~anstalt *f* approved school, borstal *(Brit)*, reformatory *(US)*; **e~berechtigt** *adj* having parental authority; **~berechtigte(r)** *mf* parent *or* (legal) guardian.

erzielen* *vt Erfolg, Ergebnis* to achieve; *Kompromiß, Geschwindigkeit* to reach; *Gewinn* to make, to realize; *(Gegenstand) Preis* to fetch; *(Sport) Tor, Punkte* to score; *Rekord* to set.

erzittern* *vi aux sein (liter)* to tremble.

erzkonservativ *adj* ultraconservative.

erzürnen* *vt (geh)* to anger, to incense.

erzwingen* *vt irreg* to force. **etw von jdm ~** to force sth out of sb.

es *pers pron* it; *(auf männliches Wesen bezogen) (nom)* he; *(acc)* him; *(auf weibliches Wesen bezogen) (nom)* she; *(acc)* her. **wer ist da? — ich bin ~** who's there? — it's me; **sie ist klug, er ist ~ auch** she is clever, so is he; **wer ist die Dame? — ~ ist meine Frau** who's the lady? — it's *or* she's my wife; **alle dachten, daß das unrecht war, aber niemand sagte ~** everyone thought it was unjust, but nobody said so; **ich hoffe ~** I hope so; **~ sitzt sich bequem hier** it's comfortable sitting here; **~ wurde getanzt** there was dancing; **~ kamen viele Leute** a lot of people came; **~ lebe der König!** long live the king! **Es** *nt* - *(Mus: Dur)* E flat.

Esche *f* -n ash-tree.

Esel *m* - donkey; *(col: Dummkopf)* (silly) ass. **ich ~!** silly me!; **störrisch wie ein ~** as

stubborn as a mule.
Eselin *f* she-ass.
Esels-: ~**brücke** *f* (*Gedächtnishilfe*) mnemonic, aide-mémoire; ~**ohr** *nt* (*fig*) dog-ear; **ein Buch mit** ~**ohren** a dog-eared book.
Eskalation *f* escalation.
eskalieren* *vti* (*vi: aux sein*) to escalate.
Eskapade *f* (*fig*) escapade.
Eskimo *m* -s Eskimo.
Eskorte *f* -n (*Mil*) escort.
eskortieren* *vt* to escort.
esoterisch *adj* esoteric.
Espe *f* -n aspen.
Espenlaub *nt* aspen leaves *pl*. **zittern wie** ~ to shake like a leaf.
Espresso *m* -s espresso.
Esprit [ɛs'priː] *m no pl* wit.
Eß-: **e**~**bar** *adj* edible, eatable; *Pilz* edible; **habt ihr irgend etwas** ~**bares im Haus?** have you got anything to eat in the house?; **nicht e**~**bar** inedible, uneatable; ~**besteck** *nt* set of cutlery.
essen *pret* **aß**, *ptp* **gegessen** *vti* to eat. **gut/ schlecht** ~ (*Appetit haben*) to have a good/poor appetite; **in dem Restaurant kann man gut** ~ that's a good restaurant; **warm/kalt** ~ to have a hot/cold meal; **etw zum Frühstück** ~ to have *or* eat sth for breakfast; ~ **Sie gern Äpfel?** do you like apples?; **beim E**~ **sein** to be in the middle of a meal; ~ **gehen** (*auswärts*) to eat out; **nach dem Kino gingen wir noch** ~ after the cinema we went for a meal.
Essen *nt* - (*Mahlzeit*) meal; (*Nahrung*) food; (*Küche*) cooking. **bleib doch zum** ~ stay for lunch/ supper, stay for a meal; **das** ~ **kochen** *or* **machen** (*col*) to get the meal; **jdn zum** ~ **einladen** to invite sb for a meal.
Essen(s)-: ~**ausgabe** *f* serving of meals; (*Stelle*) serving counter; ~ **marke** *f* meal voucher; ~**zeit** *f* mealtime; **bei uns ist um 12** ~**zeit** we have lunch at 12.
essentiell [ɛsɛn'tsiɛl] *adj* (*geh*) essential.
Essenz *f* essence.
Esser *m* - **ein guter/schlechter** ~ a good/poor eater.
Eßgeschirr *nt* dinner service.
Essig *m* -e vinegar. **damit ist es** ~ (*col*) it's all off.
Essig-: ~**essenz** *f* vinegar concentrate; ~**gurke** *f* (pickled) gherkin; ~**säure** *f* acetic acid.
Eß-: ~**kastanie** *f* sweet chestnut; ~**löffel** *m* soup/ dessert spoon; (*in Rezept*) tablespoon; ~**tisch** *m* dining table; ~**zimmer** *nt* dining room.
Estragon *m no pl* tarragon.
Estrich *m* -e stone/clay *etc* floor.
etablieren* **1** *vt* (*dated*) to establish. **2** *vr* to establish oneself; (*Comm*) to set up.
etabliert *adj* established. **die** ~**e Oberschicht** the upper echelons of the establishment.
Etablissement [etablɪsə'mãː] *nt* -s establishment.
Etage [e'taːʒə] *f* -n floor. **in** *or* **auf der 2.** ~ on the 2nd (*Brit*) *or* 3rd (*US*) floor.
Etagen-: ~**bett** *nt* bunk bed; ~**heizung** *f* heating system which covers one floor of a building.
Etappe *f* -n (**a**) stage; (*einer Strecke auch*) leg. (**b**) (*Mil*) communications zone.
Etappen-: ~**sieg** *m* (*Sport*) stage-win; **e**~**weise** *adv* step by step, stage by stage.
Etat [e'taː] *m* -s budget.
Etat-: ~**jahr** *nt* financial year; ~**posten** *m* item in the budget.
etc. = **et cetera** [ɛt'tseːtera] etc.
etepetete [eːtəpe'teːtə] *adj pred* (*col*) fussy, pernickety (*col*).
Ethik *f* ethics *pl* (*als Fach sing*).
ethisch *adj* ethical.
ethnisch *adj* ethnic.
Etikett *nt* -e (*lit,fig*) label.
Etikette *f* etiquette.
etikettieren* *vt* (*lit, fig*) to label.

etliche(r, s) *indef pron* (**a**) *sing attr* quite a lot of. (**b**) **etliche** *pl* (*substantivisch*) quite a few, several people/things; (*attr*) several, quite a few. (**c**) ~**s** *sing* (*substantivisch*) quite a lot.
Etüde *f* -n (*Mus*) étude.
Etui [ɛt'viː, e'tyiː] *nt* -s case.
etwa *adv* (**a**) (*ungefähr, annähernd*) about, approximately. **so** ~, ~ **so** more or less like this. (**b**) (*zum Beispiel*) for instance. (**c**) (*entrüstet, erstaunt*) **hast du** ~ **schon wieder kein Geld dabei?** don't tell me you haven't got any money again!; **willst du** ~ **schon gehen?** (surely) you don't want to go already! (**d**) (*zur Bestätigung*) **Sie kommen doch, oder** ~ **nicht?** you are coming, aren't you?; **sind Sie** ~ **nicht einverstanden?** do you mean to say that you don't agree?; **ist das** ~ **wahr?** (surely) it's not true! (**e**) (*in Gegenüberstellung, einschränkend*) **nicht** ~, **daß ...** (it's) not that ...; **ich wollte dich nicht** ~ **beleidigen** I didn't intend to insult you.
etwaig ['ɛtvaːɪç] *adj attr* possible. ~**e Unkosten** any costs which might arise.
etwas *indef pron* (**a**) (*substantivisch*) something; (*fragend, bedingend auch, verneinend*) anything; (*unbestimmter Teil einer Menge*) some; any. **kannst du mir** ~ (*davon*) **leihen?** can you lend me some (of it)?; **ohne** ~ **zu erwähnen** without saying anything; ~ **sein** (*col*) to be somebody (*col*); **aus ihm wird nie** ~ (*col*) he'll never become anything; **er kann** ~ he's good; **sein Wort gilt** ~ beim Chef what he says counts for something with the boss; **das ist sicher, wie nur** ~ (*col*) that's as sure as (sure) can be (*col*); ~ **Kaltes** something cold. (**b**) (*adjektivisch*) some; (*fragend, bedingend auch*) any. ~ **Salz?** some salt? (**c**) (*adverbial*) ~ **besser** somewhat better, a little better.
Etwas *nt no pl* **das gewisse** ~ that certain something.
Etymologie *f* etymology.
euch *pers pron dat, acc of* **ihr** (*in Briefen: E*~) you; (*dat auch*) to/for you; (*refl*) yourselves. **ein Freund von** ~ a friend of yours; **wascht** ~**!** wash yourselves; **setzt** ~**!** sit down!
euer **1** *poss pron* (*in Briefen: E*~) your. **E**~ (*Briefschluß*) yours. **2** *pers pron gen of* **ihr.** ~ **aller heimlicher Wunsch** the secret wish of all of you.
Eukalyptus *m, pl* **Eukalypten** eucalyptus *pl*.
Eule *f* -n owl. ~**n nach Athen tragen** (*prov*) to carry coals to Newcastle (*prov*).
Euphemismus *m* euphemism.
Euphorie *f* euphoria.
euphorisch *adj* euphoric.
eure(r, s) *poss pron* yours. **der/die/das** ~ (*geh*) yours.
eurerseits *adv* (*von eurer Seite*) on your part.
euresgleichen *pron inv* people like you.
euretwegen *adv* (*wegen euch*) because of you, on your account; (*euch zuliebe auch*) for your sake.
Euro- *in cpds* Euro-; ~**cheque** *m* Eurocheque.
Europa *nt* Europe.
Europäer(in *f*) *m* - European.
europäisch *adj* European. **das E**~**e Parlament** the European Parliament; **E**~**e (Wirtschafts)gemeinschaft** European (Economic) Community, Common Market.
Europa-: ~**meister** *m* European champion; (*Team, Land*) European champions *pl*; ~**meisterschaft** *f* European championship; ~**pokal** *m* (*Sport*) European cup; ~**rat** *m* Council of Europe; ~**straße** *f* Euroroute.
Euro-: ~**scheck** *m* Eurocheque; ~**vision** *f* Eurovision.
Euter *nt* - udder.
Euthanasie *f* euthanasia.
ev. = **evangelisch**.
e.V. = **eingetragener Verein**.
evakuieren* [evaku'iːrən] *vt* to evacuate.

Evakuierung [evaku'i:rʊŋ] *f* evacuation.
evangelisch [evaŋ'ge:lɪʃ] *adj* Protestant.
Evangelist [evaŋe'lɪst] *m* evangelist.
Evangelium [evaŋ'ge:liʊm] *nt* Gospel; (*fig*) gospel.
Eva(s)kostüm *nt* (*dated hum*) **im ~** in her birthday suit (*hum*).
eventuell [evɛntu'ɛl] **1** *adj attr* possible. **2** *adv* possibly, perhaps. **~ rufe ich Sie später an** I may possibly call you later.
Evolution [evolu'tsio:n] *f* evolution.
Evolutionstheorie *f* theory of evolution.
evtl. = **eventuell.**
EWG [e:ve:'ge:] *f* = **Europäische Wirtschaftsgemeinschaft** EEC.
ewig 1 *adj* eternal; *Eis, Schnee* perpetual; (*col*) *Nörgelei etc auch* never-ending. **2** *adv* for ever, eternally. **auf ~** for ever; **das dauert ja ~, bis ...** it'll take ages until ...; **~ dankbar** eternally grateful; **ich habe Sie ~ lange nicht gesehen** (*col*) I haven't seen you for ages.
Ewigkeit *f* eternity; (*col*) ages. **in die ~ eingehen** to go to eternal rest; **bis in alle ~** for ever; **eine ~ dauern** (*col*) to take ages.
ex *adv* (*col*) **etw ~ trinken** to drink sth down in one.
Ex- in *cpds* ex.
exakt *adj* exact. **~ arbeiten** to work accurately.
exaltiert *adj* exaggerated, effusive.
Examen *nt, pl* - *or* **Examina** exam, examination; (*Univ*) finals *pl.* **~ machen** to do *or* take one's exams *or* finals.
Examens-: **~angst** *f* exam nerves *pl;* **~arbeit** *f* dissertation; **~kandidat** *m* candidate (for an examination).
examinieren* *vt* (*geh*) to examine.
exekutieren* *vt* (*form*) to execute.
Exekution *f* execution.
Exekutionskommando *nt* firing squad.
Exekutive [-'ti:və] *f* executive.
Exempel *nt* **die Probe aufs ~ machen** to put it to the test.
Exemplar *nt* **-e** specimen; (*Buch~*) copy.
exemplarisch *adj* exemplary. **jdn ~ bestrafen** to punish sb as an example (to others).
exerzieren* *vti* to drill; (*fig*) to practise (*Brit*), to practice (*US*).
Exerzierplatz *m* (*Mil*) parade ground.
Exhibitionismus [ɛkshibɪtsio'nɪsmʊs] *m* exhibitionism.
Exhibitionist(in *f*) [ɛkshibɪtsio'nɪst(ɪn)] *m* exhibitionist.
exhumieren* *vt* to exhume.
Exil *nt* **-e** exile. **im (amerikanischen) ~ leben** to live in exile (in America); **ins ~ gehen** to go into exile.
Exilregierung *f* government in exile.
existent *adj* (*geh*) existing, existent.
Existentialismus [ɛksɪstɛntsia'lɪsmʊs] *m* existentialism.
existentialistisch [-tsia'lɪstɪʃ] *adj* existential(ist).
existentiell [ɛksɪstɛn'tsiɛl] *adj* (*geh*) existential. **von ~er Bedeutung** of vital significance.
Existenz *f* existence; (*Lebensgrundlage*) livelihood; (*pej col: Person*) character, customer (*col*). **eine gescheiterte ~** (*col*) a failure; **sich eine ~ aufbauen** to make a life for oneself.
Existenz-: **~berechtigung** *f* right to exist. **e~fähig** *adj* able to exist; *Firma* viable; **~grundlage** *f* basis of one's livelihood; **~kampf** *m* struggle for survival; **~minimum** *nt* subsistence level; (*Lohn*) minimal living wage; **das Gehalt liegt noch unter dem ~minimum** that is not even a living wage.
existieren* [ɛksɪs'ti:rən] *vi* to exist.
exklusiv *adj* exclusive.
Exklusivbericht *m* (*Press*) exclusive (report).
exklusive [-'zi:və] *prep+gen* exclusive of, excluding.
Exklusivität [-zivi'tɛ:t] *f* exclusiveness.

Exkommunikation *f* (*Eccl*) excommunication.
Exkrement *nt usu pl* (*geh*) excrement *no pl*, ex- creta *pl.*
Exkursion *f* (*study*) trip.
Exmatrikulation *f* (*Univ*) being taken off the university register. **bei seiner ~** when he left university.
exmatrikulieren* *vt* (*Univ*) to take off the university register.
Exorzismus *m* exorcism.
Exot(e) *m* (*wk*) **-en, -en, Exotin** *f* exotic *or* tropical animal/plant *etc;* (*Mensch*) exotic foreigner.
exotisch *adj* exotic.
Expander *m* - (*Sport*) chest-expander.
expandieren* *vt* to expand.
Expansion *f* (*Phys, Pol*) expansion.
expansiv *adj* expansionist; *Wirtschaftszweige* expanding.
Expedition *f* (*Forschungs~, Mil*) expedition.
Experiment *nt* experiment.
experimentell *adj* experimental.
experimentieren* *vi* to experiment.
Experte *m* (*wk*) **-n, -n, Expertin** *f* expert (*für* in).
explizit *adj* explicit.
explodieren* *vi aux sein* (*lit, fig*) to explode.
Explosion *f* explosion. **etw zur ~ bringen** to detonate *or* explode sth.
Explosionsgefahr *f* danger of explosion.
explosiv *adj* (*lit, fig*) explosive.
Exponent *m* (*Math, fig*) exponent.
exponieren* *vt* (*herausheben*) to expose. **an exponierter Stelle stehen** to be in an exposed position.
Export *m* **-e** export (*an +dat* of); (*~waren*) exports *pl.*
Export- in *cpds* export; **~abteilung** *f* export department; **~artikel** *m* export; **~geschäft** *nt* export trade.
exportieren* *vti* to export.
Exportkaufmann *m* exporter.
Exposé [ɛkspo'ze:] *nt* **-s** (*für Film etc*) outline.
Expreß-: **~brief** *m* express letter; **~gut** *nt* express goods *pl.*
Expressionismus *m* expressionism.
Expressionist(in *f*) *m* expressionist.
expressionistisch *adj* expressionist *no adv.*
exquisit *adj* exquisite.
extensiv *adj* extensive.
extra *adv* (*besonders*) extra, (*e*)specially; (*eigens, ausschließlich*) (*e*)specially, just; (*gesondert*) separately; (*zusätzlich*) extra, in addition; (*col: absichtlich*) on purpose. **jetzt tu ich's ~!** (*col*) just for that I will do it!
Extra-: **~ausgabe** *f*, **~blatt** *nt* special edition; **~tour** *f* (*fig col*) **sich** (*dat*) **~touren leisten** to do one's own thing (*col*).
extravagant [-va'gant] *adj* extravagant; *Kleidung auch* flamboyant.
Extravaganz [-va'gants] *f siehe adj* extravagance; flamboyance.
Extrawurst *f* (*col: Sonderwunsch*) special favour (*Brit*) *or* favor (*US*). **er will immer eine ~ (gebraten haben)** he always wants something different.
extrem *adj* extreme; *Belastung* excessive. **~ schlecht/gut** extremely badly/well; **die Lage hat sich ~ verschlechtert** the situation has deteriorated enormously; **ich habe mich ~ beeilt** I hurried as much as I could.
Extrem *nt* **-e** extreme. **von einem ~ ins andere fallen** to go from one extreme to the other.
Extremfall *m* extreme (case).
Extremist(in *f*) *m* extremist.
extremistisch *adj* extremist.
extrovertiert [-ver'ti:ɐt] *adj* extrovert.
Exzellenz *f* Excellency.
exzentrisch *adj* (*Math, fig*) eccentric.
Exzeß *m* **-sse** excess. **bis zum ~** to excess.

F

F, f [ɛf] *nt* -, - F, f. **nach Schema F** *(col)* in the usual old way.
Fa. = **Firma.**
Fabel *f* -n **(a)** fable. **(b)** *(col)* fantastic story.
Fabel-: **f~haft** *adj* splendid, magnificent; **~tier,** **~wesen** *nt* mythical creature.
Fabrik *f* -en factory.
Fabrik|anlage *f* plant; *(~gelände)* factory site.
Fabrikant(in *f) m* **(a)** industrialist. **(b)** *(Hersteller)* manufacturer.
Fabrikat *nt* **(a)** *(Marke)* make; *(von Nahrungs- und Genußmitteln)* brand. **(b)** *(Produkt)* product; *(Ausführung)* model.
Fabrikation *f* manufacture, production.
Fabrik- *in cpds* factory; **~direktor** *m* managing director (of a factory); **~gelände** *nt* factory site.
fabrizieren* *vt* **(a)** *(dated: industriell)* to produce. **(b)** *(col) Möbelstück etc* to make; *geistiges Produkt* to produce; *Geschichte* to concoct, to fabricate.
fabulieren* *vi* *(geh)* **(a)** *(pej: schwätzen)* to romance. **(b)** *(erzählen)* to spin a yarn.
Facette [fa'sɛtə] *f* facet.
Fach *nt* -̈er **(a)** compartment; *(in Handtasche etc auch)* pocket; *(in Schrank, Regal etc)* shelf; *(für Briefe etc)* pigeonhole. **(b)** *(Wissens-, Sachgebiet)* subject; *(Gebiet)* field; *(Handwerk)* trade. **ein Mann vom ~** an expert; **sein ~ verstehen** to know one's stuff *(col) or* one's subject/trade.
Fach-: **~arbeiter** *m* skilled worker; **~arzt** *m* specialist *(für in)*; **~ausdruck** *m* technical *or* specialist term; **~bereich** *m* **(a)** (special) field; **(b)** *(Univ)* school, faculty; **~buch** *nt* reference book; **wasserbautechnische ~bücher** specialist books on hydraulic engineering.
fächeln *(geh) vt* to fan.
Fächer *m* - fan; *(fig)* range, array.
fächer-: **~artig,** **~förmig 1** *adj* fan-shaped; **2** *adv* like a fan.
Fach-: **~gebiet** *nt* (special) field; **f~gemäß,** **f~gerecht** *adj* expert; *Ausbildung* specialist *attr*; **~geschäft** *nt* specialist shop *(Brit) or* store *(US)*; **~geschäft für Lederwaren** leather shop; **~handel** *m* specialist shops *pl (Brit) or* stores *pl (US)*; **~hochschule** *f* technical/art college; **~idiot** *m (col)* narrow-minded specialist; **~jargon** *m* technical jargon; **~kenntnisse** *pl* specialized knowledge; **~kreise** *pl*: **in ~kreisen** among experts; **f~kundig** *adj* informed *no adv*; *(erfahren)* with a knowledge of the subject; *(fachmännisch)* proficient; **jdn f~kundig beraten** to give sb informed advice; **~lehrer** *m* specialist subject teacher.
fachlich *adj* technical; *Ausbildung* specialist *attr*; *(beruflich)* professional. **~ hochqualifiziert** highly qualified in one's field.
Fach-: **~literatur** *f* specialist literature; **~mann** *m, pl* **~leute** expert; **f~männisch** *adj* expert; **f~männisch ausgeführt** professionally done; **~personal** *nt* specialist staff; **~richtung** *f* subject area; **~schule** *f* technical college; **~simpelei** *f (col)* shop-talk; **f~simpeln** *vi insep (col)* to talk shop; **f~spezifisch** *adj* technical, subject-specific; **~sprache** *f* technical terminology; **f~sprachlich 1** *adj* technical; **2** *adv* in technical terminology; **~welt** *f* profession; **~werk** *nt no pl* half-timbering; **~werkhaus** *nt* half-timbered

house; **~wissen** *nt* (specialized) knowledge of the/one's subject; **~wörterbuch** *nt* specialist dictionary; *(technisches auch)* technical dictionary; **~zeitschrift** *f* specialist journal; *(für Berufe)* trade journal.
Fackel *f* -n *(lit, fig)* torch.
fackeln *vi (col)* **da wird nicht lange gefackelt** there won't be any shilly-shallying.
Fackel-: **~schein** *m* torchlight; **~zug** *m* torchlight procession.
fad(e) *adj* **(a)** *Geschmack* insipid; *Essen auch* tasteless. **(b)** *(fig: langweilig)* dull.
Faden[1] *m* -̈ *(lit, fig)* thread; *(Bohnen~, an Marionetten)* string; *(Med)* stitch. **der rote ~** *(fig)* the central theme; **den ~ verlieren** *(fig)* to lose the thread; **alle ~ laufen hier zusammen** this is the nerve centre *(Brit) or* center *(US)* of the whole business; **er hält alle ~ in der Hand** he holds the reins; **sein Leben hing an einem ~** his life was hanging by a thread.
Faden[2] *m* - *(Naut)* fathom.
Faden-: **~kreuz** *nt* crosshair; **~nudeln** *pl* vermicelli *pl*; **f~scheinig** *adj (fig)* flimsy; *Argument auch, Moral* threadbare *no adv*.
Fagott *nt* -e bassoon.
fähig *adj* capable, competent, able. **sie ist ein ~er Kopf** she has an able mind; **(dazu) ~ sein, etw zu tun** to be capable of doing sth; **zu allem ~ sein** to be capable of anything.
Fähigkeit *f* ability; *(praktisches Können)* skill. **die ~ haben, etw zu tun** to be capable of doing sth; **bei deinen ~en ...** with your talents ...
fahl *adj* pale.
fahnden *vi* to search *(nach for)*.
Fahndung *f* search.
Fahndungs-: **~aktion** *f* search; **~buch** *nt,* **~liste** *f* wanted (persons) list.
Fahne *f* -n **(a)** flag; *(von Verein etc auch)* banner; *(Mil auch)* colours *pl (Brit)*, colors *pl (US)*. **die ~ hochhalten** *(fig)* to keep the flag flying; **etw auf seine ~ schreiben** *(fig)* to take up the cause of sth; **mit fliegenden ~n zu jdm/etw überlaufen** to go over to sb/sth. **(b)** *(col)* **eine ~ haben** to reek of alcohol. **(c)** *(Typ)* galley (proof).
Fahnen-: **~eid** *m* oath of allegiance; **~flucht** *f (Mil, fig)* desertion; **f~flüchtig** *adj* **f~flüchtig sein** *(Mil, fig)* to be a deserter; **~flüchtige(r)** *mf (Mil, fig)* deserter; **~mast** *m,* **~stange** *f* flagpole.
Fähnrich *m (Mil)* officer cadet; *(Hist)* ensign. **~ zur See** midshipman.
Fahr-: **~ausweis** *m (form)* ticket; **~bahn** road; *(Fahrspur)* lane; **f~bar** *adj* on castors; *Kran* mobile; **f~barer Untersatz** *(hum)* wheels *pl (hum)*; **f~bereit** *adj* in running order.
Fähre *f* -n ferry.
fahren *pret* **fuhr,** *ptp* **gefahren 1** *vi aux sein* **(a)** *(Fahrzeug, Fahrgast)* to go; *(reisen)* to travel; *(Fahrer)* to drive; *(Schiff)* to sail; *(Kran, Rolltreppe etc)* to move. **mit dem Zug/Motorrad/Taxi ~** to go by train/motorbike/taxi; **mit dem Aufzug ~** to take the lift, to ride the elevator *(US)*; **wollen wir ~ oder zu Fuß gehen?** shall we go by car/bus *etc* or walk?; **links/rechts ~** to drive on the left/ right; **wie lange fährt man von hier nach Basel?** how long does it take to get to Basle from here?; **gegen einen Baum ~** to drive *or* go into a tree.

(b) *(losfahren)* to go, to leave.

(c) *(verkehren)* es ~ **täglich zwei Fähren** there are two ferries a day; **die U-Bahn fährt alle fünf Minuten** the underground goes *or* runs every five minutes.

(d) blitzartig fuhr es ihm durch den Kopf, daß ... the thought suddenly flashed through his mind that ...; **was ist (denn) in dich gefahren?** what's got *(Brit) or* gotten *(US)* into you?; **in seine Kleider** ~ to fling on one's clothes; **der Blitz fuhr in die Eiche** the lightning struck the oak; **sich** *(dat)* **mit der Hand über die Stirn** ~ to pass one's hand over one's brow; **einen** ~ **lassen** *(col)* to fart *(col)*.

(e) *(zurechtkommen)* **(mit jdm/etw) gut/ schlecht** ~ to get on all right/not very well (with sb/sth); **(bei etw) gut/schlecht** ~ to do well/badly (with sth).

2 *vt* **(a)** *(lenken)* **Auto, Bus** etc to drive; **Fahrrad, Motorrad** to ride. **(b)** *aux sein* **Straße, Strecke, Buslinie** etc to take. **welche Strecke fährt der 59er?** which way does the 59 go?; **ich fahre lieber Autobahn als Landstraße** I prefer (driving on) motorways to ordinary roads. **(c)** *(benutzen)* **Kraftstoff** etc to use. **(d)** *(befördern)* to take; *(hier- her~)* to bring; *(Lastwagen, Taxi: gewerbsmäßig)* to carry. **ich fahre dich nach Hause** I'll take *or* drive you home, I'll give you a lift home. **(e)** *aux sein* **Geschwindigkeit** to do. **(f)** *aux haben or sein (Sport)* **Rennen** to take part in; **Runde** etc to do; **Zeit, Rekord** etc to clock up. **(g)** *(Tech) (steuern, betreiben)* to run; *(durchführen)* **Sonder- schicht** to put on.

3 *vr* **der neue Wagen fährt sich gut** the new car is nice to drive.

fahrend *adj* itinerant. ~**es Volk** travelling peo- ple; **ein** ~**er Sänger** a wandering minstrel.

fahrenlassen* *vt sep irreg* **Hoffnung** to abandon.

Fahrer(in *f)* *m* - **(a)** driver. **(b)** *(Sport col)* **(Rad~)** cyclist; **(Motorrad~)** motorcyclist.

Fahrerflucht *f* hit-and-run driving. ~**begehen** to be involved in a hit-and-run.

Fahr-: ~**erlaubnis** *f (form)* driving licence *(Brit)*, driver's license *(US)*; ~**gast** *m* passenger; ~**ge- legenheit** *f* transport *no indef art*; ~**geschwin- digkeit** *f (form)* speed; ~**gestell** *nt (Aut)* chassis.

Fährhafen *m* ferry terminal.

fahrig *adj* nervous; *(unkonzentriert)* distracted.

Fahrkarte *f* ticket; *(fig)* passport *(nach to)*.

Fahrkarten-: ~**ausgabe** *f* ticket office; ~**auto- mat** *m* ticket machine; ~**kontrolle** *f* ticket in- spection; ~**schalter** *m* ticket office.

Fahr-: **f**~**lässig** *adj* negligent *(auch Jur)*; **f**~**lässig handeln** to be guilty of negligence; ~**lässigkeit** *f* negligence *(auch Jur)*; ~**lehrer** *m* driving in- structor.

Fährmann *m, pl* -**männer** *or* -**leute** ferryman.

Fahr-: ~**plan** *m* timetable, schedule *(US)*; *(fig)* schedule; **f**~**planmäßig 1** *adj* scheduled; **2** *adv* on schedule; *verlaufen* according to schedule; ~**praxis** *f no pl* driving experience *no indef art*; ~**preis** *m* fare; ~**prüfung** *f* driving test.

Fahrrad *nt* bicycle, bike *(col)*.

Fahrrad-: ~**fahrer** *m* cyclist; ~**händler** *m* bicy- cle dealer; *(Geschäft)* cycle shop *(Brit) or* store *(US)*; ~**weg** *m* cycle path.

Fahr-: ~**rinne** *f (Naut)* shipping channel, fairway; ~**schein** *m* ticket; ~**schule** *f* driving school; ~**schüler** *m* learner driver *(Brit)*, student driver *(US)*; ~**spur** *f* lane; ~**stil** *m* style of driving/rid- ing/skiing *etc*; ~**streifen** *m* lane; ~**stuhl** *m* lift *(Brit)*, elevator *(US)*; ~**stunde** *f* driving lesson.

Fahrt *f* -**en** journey; *(Aut auch)* drive; *(Ausflug)* trip; *(Naut)* voyage; *(Über~)* crossing. **nach zwei Stunden** ~ after travelling for two hours; **was kostet eine** ~ **nach London?** how much is it to London?; **gute** ~! safe journey!; **volle** ~ **voraus!** *(Naut)* full speed ahead!; **jdn in** ~ **bringen** *(col)*

to get sb going; **in** ~ **sein** *(col)* to have got going; *(wütend)* to be mad *(col)*.

Fahr-: **f**~**tauglich** *adj* fit to drive; ~**tauglichkeit** *f* fitness to drive.

Fährte *f* -**n** tracks *pl*; *(Witterung)* scent; *(Spuren)* trail. **auf der richtigen/falschen** ~ **sein** *(fig)* to be on the right/wrong track; **jdn auf eine falsche** ~ **locken** *(fig)* to put sb off the scent.

Fahrtechnik *f* driving technique.

Fahrten-: ~**buch** *nt* driver's log; ~**messer** *nt* sheath knife; ~**schreiber** *m* tachograph.

Fahrtest *m* road test.

Fahrt-: ~**kosten** *pl* travelling *(Brit) or* traveling *(US)* expenses *pl*; ~**richtung** *f* direction of travel; *(im Verkehr)* direction of the traffic; **entgegen der/in** ~**richtung** *(im Zug)* with one's back to the engine/facing the engine; *(im Bus etc)* facing backwards/the front; **die Autobahn ist in** ~**rich- tung Norden gesperrt** the northbound section of the motorway is closed; ~**richtungsanzei- ger** *m (Aut)* indicator.

Fahr-: **f**~**tüchtig** *adj* fit to drive; **Wagen** etc road- worthy; ~**tüchtigkeit** *f* driving ability; road- worthiness.

Fahrtwind *m* airstream.

Fahr-: **f**~**untauglich** *adj* unfit to drive; **Wagen** etc unroadworthy; ~**verbot** *nt* driving ban; **jdn mit** ~**verbot belegen** to ban sb from driving; ~**ver- halten** *nt (von Fahrer)* behaviour *(Brit) or* behav- ior *(US)* behind the wheel; *(von Wagen)* road performance; ~**wasser** *nt* **(a)** *(Naut)* = ~**rin- ne; (b)** *(fig)* **in jds** ~**wasser geraten** to get in with sb; **in ein gefährliches** ~**wasser geraten** to get on to dangerous ground; ~**weise** *f* seine ~**weise** his driving; ~**werk** *nt* **(a)** *(Aviat)* undercarriage, landing gear; **(b)** *(Aut)* chassis; ~**zeit** *f* time for the journey; **bei einer** ~**zeit von fünf Stunden** on a five-hour journey.

Fahrzeug *nt* vehicle; *(Luft~)* aircraft; *(Wasser~)* vessel.

Fahrzeug-: ~**führer** *m (form)* driver of a vehicle; ~**halter** *m* vehicle owner; ~**papiere** *pl* vehicle documents *pl*.

Faible ['fɛːbl] *nt* -**s** *(geh)* liking; *(Schwäche auch)* weakness; *(Vorliebe auch)* penchant.

fair [fɛːɐ] **1** *adj* fair *(gegen* to). **2** *adv* fairly. ~ **spielen** *(Sport)* to play fairly; *(fig)* to play fair.

Fäkalien [-ɪən] *pl* faeces *pl*.

Faksimile [fak'ziːmile] *nt* -**s** facsimile.

Faktor *m* factor *(auch Math)*.

Faktum *nt, pl* **Fakten** fact.

fakturieren* *vt (Comm)* to invoice.

Fakultät *f (Univ)* faculty.

Falke *m* -**n** falcon; *(fig)* hawk.

Falkner(in *f)* *m* - falconer.

Fall *m* ⁼**e (a)** *(Sturz)* fall; *(fig: von Menschen, Regie- rung auch)* downfall. **zu** ~ **kommen** *(lit, geh)* to fall; **über die Affäre ist er zu** ~ **gekommen** *(fig)* the affair was his downfall; **zu** ~ **bringen** *(lit geh)* to trip up; *(fig) Menschen, Regierung* to cause the downfall of; *Gesetz, Plan etc* to thwart.

(b) *(Umstand, Jur, Med, Gram)* case. **gesetzt den** ~ **assuming (that); für den** ~, **daß ich** ... **in case I** ...; **für alle** ~**e** just in case; **auf jeden/ keinen** ~ at any rate/on no account; **das mache ich auf keinen** ~ there's no way I'm going to do that; **im** ~**(e)** +*gen* in the event of; **auf alle** ~**e** in any case, anyway; **für solche** ~**e** for such occasions; **im äußersten** ~**(e)** if the worst comes to the worst; **im günstigsten/schlimmsten** ~**(e)** at best/worst; **in diesem** ~ in this case *or* in- stance; **jds** ~ **sein** *(col)* to be sb's cup of tea *(col)*; **klarer** ~! *(col)* you bet! *(col)*, you bet! *(col)*; **der erste/zweite/dritte/vierte** ~ *(Gram)* the nominative/genitive/dative/accusative case.

Fallbeil *nt* guillotine.

Falle *f* -**n (a)** *(lit, fig)* trap. **in eine** ~ **geraten** *or* **gehen** *(lit)* to get caught in a trap; *(fig)* to fall into a trap; **jdm in die** ~ **gehen** to walk or fall into sb's trap; **in der** ~ **sitzen** to be trapped; **jdm eine** ~ **stellen** (fig) to set a trap for sb. **(b)** (col: Bett) bed. **in die** ~ **gehen** to hit the hay (col).

fallen pret **fiel**, ptp **gefallen** vi aux sein **(a)** to fall. **etw** ~ **lassen** to drop sth; **über etw** (acc) ~ to fall over sth; **durch eine Prüfung** ~ to fail an exam.

(b) (abfallen, sinken) to drop, to fall; (Aktien, Barometer) to fall; (Nachfrage, Ansehen) to fall off. **im Preis/Wert** ~ to drop or fall in price/ value.

(c) (im Krieg) to fall, to be killed. **mein Mann ist gefallen** my husband was killed in the war.

(d) (erobert werden: Festung, Stadt etc) to fall.

(e) (sich ereignen: Datum etc) to fall (auf+acc on); (gehören) to come (unter+acc under, in+acc within, under). **in eine Zeit** ~ to belong to an era.

(f) (zufallen: Erbschaft etc) to go (an+acc to). **das Elsaß fiel an Frankreich** Alsace fell or (nach Verhandlungen) went to France.

(g) (gemacht werden) (Entscheidung) to be made; (Urteil) to be passed; (Schuß) to be fired; (Sport: Tor) to be scored; (Wort) to be uttered or spoken; (Name) to be mentioned; (Bemerkung) to be made.

fällen vt **(a)** Baum to fell. **(b)** (fig) Entscheidung to make; Urteil to pass.

fallenlassen* vt sep irreg to drop.

Fallensteller m - (Hunt) trapper.

fällig adj due pred; Rechnung, Betrag auch payable; Wechsel mature(d). **längst** ~ long overdue; **die** ~**en Zinsen** the interest due; ~ **werden** to become or fall due; (Wechsel) to mature.

Fälligkeit f (Fin) settlement date; (von Wechseln) maturity.

Fall|obst nt windfalls pl.

Fallout [fɔ:'laut] m -s fall-out.

Fallrückzieher m (Ftbl) overhead kick, bicycle kick.

falls conj (wenn) if; (für den Fall, daß) in case.

Fallschirm m parachute. **mit dem** ~ **abspringen** to parachute; **etw mit dem** ~ **abwerfen** to drop sth by parachute.

Fallschirm-: ~**absprung** m parachute jump; ~**jäger** m (Mil) paratrooper; ~**springer** m parachutist; ~**truppe** f (Mil) paratroops, paras pl.

Fall-: ~**strick** m (fig) trap, snare; ~**studie** f case study; ~**tür** f trapdoor.

Fällung f no pl **(a)** (von Bäumen) felling. **(b)** (Jur: eines Urteils) passing; (einer Entscheidung) reaching.

fallweise adv from case to case.

falsch adj **(a)** wrong. **richtig/wahr oder** ~ right or wrong/true or false; **alles** ~ **machen** to do everything wrong; **wie man's macht, ist es** ~ (col) whatever I/you etc do it's bound to be wrong; ~**er Alarm** (lit, fig) false alarm; **etw** ~ **verstehen** to misunderstand sth, to get sth wrong; **etw** ~ **schreiben/aussprechen** to spell/pronounce sth wrongly, to misspell/mispronounce sth; **die Uhr geht** ~ the clock is wrong; ~ **spielen** (Mus) to play the wrong note/notes; (unrein) to play off key or out of tune; (Cards) to cheat; ~ **singen** to sing out of tune or off key; **Sie sind hier** ~ you're in the wrong place; **da sind Sie bei mir an den F**~**en geraten** you've picked the wrong person (in me); ~ **liegen** (col) to be wrong (bei, in+dat about, mit in).

(b) (unecht) Zähne etc false; Geld forged; Paß fake.

(c) (unaufrichtig) Gefühl, Freund etc false. **ein** ~**es Spiel (mit jdm) treiben** to play (sb) false.

fälschen vt to forge, to fake; Tatsachen to falsify; siehe **gefälscht**.

Fälscher(in f) m - forger.

Falsch-: ~**fahrer** m person/car driving in the wrong direction/on the wrong side of the road etc; ~**geld** nt counterfeit or forged money.

fälschlich 1 adj false. **2** adv wrongly, falsely; (versehentlich) by mistake.

fälschlicherweise adv wrongly, falsely.

Falsch-: ~**meldung** f (Press) false report; ~**münzer(in** f) m - forger, counterfeiter; ~**münzerei** f forgery, counterfeiting; **f**~**spielen** vi sep (Cards) to cheat; ~**spieler** m (Cards) cheat.

Fälschung f forgery.

fälschungssicher adj forgery-proof.

Falsett nt -e falsetto.

Falt-: ~**blatt** nt leaflet; (in Zeitschrift etc) insert; ~**boot** nt collapsible boat.

Falte f -n fold; (Knitter~) crease; (in Haut) wrinkle. **die Stirn in** ~**n legen** to knit one's brow.

falten vtr to fold. **die Stirn** ~ to knit one's brow.

Falten-: f~**los** adj Haut unlined; **f**~**reich** adj Haut wrinkled; ~**rock** m pleated skirt.

Falter m - (Tag~) butterfly; (Nacht~) moth.

faltig adj (zerknittert) creased; (in Falten gelegt) hanging in folds; Gesicht, Haut wrinkled.

Falz m -e (Kniff, Faltlinie) fold.

falzen vt Papierbogen to fold.

Fam. = **Familie**.

familiär adj **(a)** family attr. **(b)** (zwanglos) informal; (pej: plump-vertraulich) familiar. **mit jdm** ~ **verkehren** to be on familiar terms with sb.

Familie [fa'mi:liə] f family. ~ **Müller** the Müller family; ~ **Otto Francke** (als Anschrift) Mr. & Mrs. Otto Francke and family; ~ **haben** (col) to have a family; **aus guter** ~ **sein** to come from a good family; **es liegt in der** ~ it runs in the family; **zur** ~ **gehören** to be one of the family; **es bleibt in der** ~ it'll stay in the family; **das kommt in den besten** ~**n vor** (hum) that can happen in the best of families.

Familien- [-iən-] in cpds family; ~**angehörige(r)** mf dependant; ~**anschluß** m: **Unterkunft mit** ~**anschluß** accommodation where one is treated as one of the family; ~**anzeigen** pl personal announcements pl; ~**kreis** m family circle; ~**mitglied** nt member of the family; ~**name** m surname, family name (US); ~**oberhaupt** nt head of the family; ~**packung** f family(-size) pack; ~**planung** f family planning; ~**stand** m marital status; ~**vater** m father of a family; ~**verhältnisse** pl family circumstances; ~**vorstand** m (form) head of the family.

famos adj (dated col) capital (dated col), splendid.

Fan [fɛn] m -s fan.

Fanal nt -e (liter) signal (gen for).

Fanatiker(in f) m - fanatic.

fanatisch adj fanatical.

Fanatismus m fanaticism.

fand pret of **finden**.

Fanfare f -n (Mus) fanfare.

Fang m ⁻e **(a)** no pl (das Fangen) hunting; (Fischen) fishing. **(b)** no pl (Beute) (lit, fig) catch; (fig: von Gegenständen) haul. **(c)** usu pl (Hunt: Kralle) talon. **in den** ~**en** +gen (fig) in the clutches of.

fangen pret **fing**, ptp **gefangen 1** vti to catch; Verbrecher, Soldat etc auch to capture; siehe **gefangen. 2** vr **(a)** (in einer Falle etc) to get caught. **(b)** (das Gleichgewicht wiederfinden) to steady oneself; (beim Reden etc) to compose oneself; (seelisch) to get on an even keel again.

Fänger m - (Tier~) hunter; (Sport) catcher.

Fang-: ~**frage** f catch or trick question; ~**schiff** nt fishing boat; (mit Netzen) trawler.

Farb- in cpds colour (Brit), color (US); ~**aufnahme** f colour (Brit) or color (US) photo(graph); ~**bad** nt dye-bath; ~**band** nt (von Schreibmaschine) (typewriter) ribbon.

Farbe f -n **(a)** colour (Brit), color (US). ~ **bekommen** to get a bit of colour; ~ **verlieren** to go pale. **(b)** (Maler~) paint; (für Farbbad) dye; (Druck~) ink. **(c)** (Cards) suit. ~ **bekennen** (fig) to nail one's colours to the mast.

farb|echt adj colourfast (Brit), colorfast (US).

Färbemittel nt dye.

farb|empfindlich adj (Phot) colour-sensitive (Brit), color-sensitive (US).

färben 1 vt to colour (Brit), to color (US); Stoff, Haar to dye; siehe **gefärbt. 2** vi (ab~) to run. **3** vr to change colour. **sich grün/blau** ~ to turn green/blue.

Farben- in cpds colour (Brit), color (US); **f~blind** adj colour-blind (Brit), color-blind (US); **f~froh** adj colourful (Brit), colorful (US); **f~prächtig** adj gloriously colourful (Brit) or colorful (US); **~reichtum** m wealth of colours (Brit) or colors (US); **~sinn** m sense of colour (Brit) or color (US) (auch Biol).

Farb-: **~fernsehen** nt colour (Brit) or color (US) television; **~film** m colour (Brit) or color (US) film; **~gebung** f colouring (Brit), coloring (US).

farbig adj coloured (Brit), colored (US); (fig) Schilderung vivid, colourful (Brit), colorful (US).

Farbige(r) mf decl as adj coloured (Brit) or colored (US) man/woman/person etc. **die** ~n coloured people pl.

Farb-: **~kasten** m paintbox; **f~los** adj (lit, fig) colourless (Brit), colorless (US); **~losigkeit** f (lit, fig) colourlessness (Brit), colorlessness (US); **~stift** m coloured (Brit) or colored (US) pen; (Buntstift) crayon; **~stoff** m (Lebensmittel~) (artificial) colouring (Brit) or coloring (US); (Haut~) pigment; **~ton** m shade; (Tönung) tint.

Färbung f colouring (Brit), coloring (US); (Tönung) tinge; (fig) slant, bias.

Farce ['farsə] f **-n** (Theat, fig) farce.

Farm f **-en** farm.

Farmer m **-** farmer.

Farn m **-e, Farnkraut** nt fern.

Färöer pl Faeroes pl, Faeroe Islands pl.

Fasan m **-e** or **-en** pheasant.

Fasching m **-e** or **-s** Shrovetide carnival.

Faschismus m fascism.

Faschist(in f) m fascist.

faschistisch adj fascist.

faseln (pej) **1** vi to drivel (col). **2** vt **Blödsinn** ~ to talk drivel.

Faser f **-n** fibre (Brit), fiber (US).

fas(e)rig adj fibrous; Fleisch, Spargel stringy (pej); (zerfasert) frayed.

Faser-: **~pflanze** f fibre (Brit) or fiber (US) plant; **~platte** f fibreboard (Brit), fiberboard (US).

Faß nt, pl **Fässer** barrel; (kleines Bier~) keg; (zum Gären, Einlegen) vat; (zum Buttern) churn; (für Öl, Benzin etc) drum. **vom** ~ on tap; Bier on draught (Brit) or draft (US); **Bier vom** ~ draught beer; **ein** ~ **ohne Boden** (fig) a bottomless pit; **das schlägt dem** ~ **den Boden aus** (col) that's too much!

Fassade f (lit, fig) façade.

Faß-: **f~bar** adj comprehensible; **das ist doch nicht f~bar!** that's incomprehensible!; **~bier** nt draught (Brit) or draft (US) beer.

Fäßchen nt dim of **Faß**.

fassen 1 vt **(a)** (ergreifen) to take hold of; (hastig, kräftig) to grab, to seize; (festnehmen) Einbrecher etc to apprehend, to seize. **jdn am Arm** ~ to take/grab sb by the arm; **faß!** seize! **(b)** (fig) Entschluß to make, to take; Mut to take. **den Gedanken** ~, **etw zu tun** to form the idea of doing sth. **(c)** (begreifen) to grasp. **es ist nicht zu** ~ it's unbelievable. **(d)** (enthalten) to hold. **(e)** (fig: ausdrücken) to express. **in Verse/Worte** ~ to put into verse/words; **etw weit/eng** ~ to interpret sth broadly/narrowly. **2** vi (greifen) **an/in etw** (acc) ~ to feel sth; (berühren) to touch sth; **faß mal unter den Tisch** feel under the table. **3** vr (sich beherrschen) to compose onself. **sich in Geduld** ~ to possess one's soul in patience; **sich kurz** ~ to be brief; siehe **gefaßt**.

Fasson [fa'sõ:] f **-s** style; (Art und Weise) way. **aus der** ~ **geraten** (lit) to lose its shape.

Fassonschnitt [fa'sõ:-] m (für Herren) short back and sides.

Fassung f **(a)** (von Juwelen) setting; (von Bild) frame; (Elec) holder. **(b)** (Bearbeitung) version. **ein Film in deutscher** ~ a film with German dubbing. **(c)** no pl (Ruhe, Besonnenheit) composure. **etw mit** ~ **tragen** to take sth calmly; **völlig außer** ~ **geraten** to lose all self-control; **jdn aus der** ~ **bringen** to disconcert or throw (col) sb.

Fassungs-: **f~los** adj aghast, stunned; **~losigkeit** f complete bewilderment; **~vermögen** nt capacity; **das übersteigt mein ~vermögen** that is beyond me.

fast adv almost, nearly. ~ **nie** hardly ever.

fasten vi to fast.

Fastenzeit f (Eccl) Lent.

Fastnacht f no pl Shrovetide carnival.

Fastnachtszeit f carnival period.

Faszination f fascination.

faszinieren* vti to fascinate (an +dat about). **~d** fascinating.

fatal adj (geh) (verhängnisvoll) fatal, fateful; (peinlich) embarrassing, awkward.

Fata Morgana f **- -s** (lit, fig) Fata Morgana (liter), mirage.

Fatzke m **-s** (col) stuck-up twit (col).

fauchen vti to hiss.

faul adj **(a)** (verfault) bad; Eier, Obst auch, Holz rotten; Geschmack, Geruch auch, Wasser foul; Laub rotting. **(b)** (träge) lazy, idle. **(c)** (verdächtig) fishy (col), suspicious; Ausrede feeble; Kompromiß uneasy; (dumm) Witz bad. **hier ist etwas** ~ (col) there's something fishy here (col).

faulen vi aux sein or haben to rot; (Zahn) to decay; (Lebensmittel) to go bad.

faulenzen vi to laze or loaf (esp pej col) about.

Faulenzer m **-** layabout.

Faulenzerei f lazing or loafing (esp pej col) about.

Faulheit f laziness, idleness.

faulig adj going bad; Geruch, Geschmack foul.

Fäulnis f no pl rot; (von Zahn) decay. **in** ~ **übergehen** to go rotten.

Faul-: **~pelz** m (col) lazybones sing (col); **~tier** nt sloth; (col: Mensch) lazybones sing (col).

Fauna f, pl **Faunen** fauna.

Faust f, pl **Fäuste** fist. **jdm mit der** ~ **ins Gesicht schlagen** to punch sb in the face; **mit der** ~ **auf den Tisch schlagen** (lit) to thump the table (with one's fist); (fig) to take a hard line; **die** ~ **in der Tasche ballen** (fig) to choke back one's anger; **das paßt wie die** ~ **aufs Auge** (paßt nicht) it's all wrong; (Farbe) it clashes horribly; (paßt gut) it's just the job (col); **auf eigene** ~ (fig) on one's own initiative, off one's own bat (col); reisen, fahren under one's own steam.

Faustball m form of volleyball.

Fäustchen nt: **sich** (dat) **ins** ~ **lachen** to laugh up one's sleeve.

faustdick adj (col) **eine ~e Lüge** a whopper (col), a whopping (great) lie (col); **er hat es** ~ **hinter den Ohren** he's a crafty one (col).

fausten vt Ball to punch.

Faust-: **f~groß** adj as big as a fist; **~handschuh** m mitt(en).

Faustkampf m fist-fight.

Faust-: **~pfand** nt security; **~recht** nt no pl law of the jungle; **~regel** f rule of thumb; **~schlag** m punch.

Favorit(in f) [favo'ri:t(ɪn)] m (wk) **-en, -en** favourite (Brit), favorite (US).

Faxen pl ~ machen to fool around.

Fazit nt **-s** or **-e das** ~ **der Untersuchungen war** ... on balance the result of the investigations was ...; **wenn wir aus diesen vier Jahren das** ~ **ziehen** if we take stock of these four years.

FDP [efde:'pe:] f = **Freie Demokratische Partei**.

Feature ['fi:tʃe] nt **-s** (Rad, TV, Press) feature.

Februar m -e February; *siehe* **März.**
fechten *pret* **focht,** *ptp* **gefochten** *vi (Sport)* to fence; *(geh: kämpfen)* to fight. **das F~** fencing.
Fechter(in f) m - fencer.
Fecht-: ~**hieb** m (fencing) cut; ~**sport** m fencing.
Feder f **-n (a)** *(Vogel~)* feather. ~**n lassen müssen** *(col)* not to escape unscathed; **in den ~n liegen** *(col)* to be/stay in one's bed *or* pit *(col).* **(b)** *(Schreib~)* quill; *(an ~halter)* nib. **ich greife zur** ~ ... I take up my pen ... **(c)** *(Tech)* spring.
Feder-: ~**ball** m *(Spiel)* badminton; ~**besen** m feather duster; ~**bett** nt continental quilt *(Brit),* comforter *(US);* **f~führend** adj **(a)** *Behörde* in overall charge *(für of);* **(b)** **diese Firma ist bei Computern f~führend** this firm are the market-leaders in computers; ~**führung** f **unter der ~führung** +gen under the overall control of; **die ~führung haben** to be in overall charge; ~**gewicht** nt *(Sport)* featherweight; ~**halter** m (dip) pen; *(Füll~)* (fountain) pen; ~**kernmatratze** f interior sprung mattress; ~**kiel** m quill; ~**kissen** nt feather cushion; *(in Bett)* feather pillow; ~**krieg** m *(fig)* war of words; **f~leicht** adj light as a feather; ~**lesen** nt: **nicht viel ~lesens mit jdm/etw machen** to make short work of sb/sth; **ohne langes ~lesen** without any further ado; ~**mäppchen** nt pencil case.
federn vi **(a)** (als Eigenschaft) to be springy. **(b)** *(zurück~ etc)* to spring back; *siehe* **gefedert.**
federnd adj *(Tech)* sprung. **einen ~en Gang haben** to have a springy step.
Federstrich m **mit einem ~** with a single stroke of the pen.
Federung f springs pl; *(Aut)* suspension.
Feder-: ~**vieh** nt *(col)* poultry; ~**waage** f spring balance; ~**weiße(r)** m decl als adj (dial) new wine; ~**zeichnung** f pen-and-ink drawing.
Fee f **-n** ['feːən] fairy.
Fegefeuer nt das ~ purgatory.
fegen 1 vt to sweep; *(auf~)* to sweep up. **2** vi **(a)** to sweep (up). **(b)** aux sein *(col: jagen)* to sweep.
Fehde f **-n** *(Hist)* feud. **mit jdm eine ~ ausfechten** to feud or carry on a feud with sb.
fehl adj: ~ **am Platz(e)** out of place.
Fehl-: ~**anzeige** f *(col)* dead loss *(col);* ~**anzeige!** no go *(col);* **f~bar** adj fallible; ~**besetzung** f miscasting; ~**betrag** m deficit; ~**diagnose** f wrong diagnosis; ~**einschätzung** f false estimation.
fehlen 1 vi **(a)** *(mangeln)* to be lacking; *(nicht vorhanden sein)* to be missing; *(in der Schule etc)* to be away or absent *(in+dat* from). **jdm fehlt etw** sb lacks sth, sb doesn't have sth; *(wird schmerzlich vermißt)* sb misses sth; **mir fehlt Geld** I'm missing some money; **mir ~ 20 Pfennig am Fahrgeld** I'm 20 pfennigs short for my fare; **mir ~ die Worte** words fail me; **du fehlst mir sehr** I miss you a lot; **der/das hat mir gerade noch gefehlt!** *(col)* he/that was all I needed *(iro).* **(b) was fehlt dir?** what's the matter (with you)?; **mir fehlt nichts** there's nothing the matter (with me); **weit gefehlt!** *(fig)* you're way out! *(col);* (ganz im Gegenteil) far from it!
2 vi impers **es fehlt an etw** *(dat)* there is a lack of sth; *(völlig)* there is no sth, sth is missing; **es ~ drei Messer** there are three knives missing; **es fehlt jdm an etw** *(dat)* sb lacks sth; **wo fehlt es?** what's the trouble? what's up? *(col);* **es fehlte nicht viel, und ich hätte ihn verprügelt** I almost hit him.
Fehl|entscheidung f wrong decision.
Fehler m - **(a)** *(Irrtum)* mistake, error; *(Sport)* fault. **ihr ist ein ~ unterlaufen** she made a mistake. **(b)** *(Mangel)* fault, defect. **einen ~ aufweisen** to prove faulty; **einen ~ an sich** *(dat)* **haben** to have a fault; **in den ~ verfallen, etw zu tun** to make the mistake of doing sth.
Fehler-: **f~frei** adj perfect; *Arbeit, Aussprache etc auch* faultless, flawless; *Messung, Rechnung* cor-

rect; **f~freier Lauf/Sprung** *(Sport)* clear round/ jump; ~**grenze** f margin of error; **f~haft** adj *(Tech)* faulty, defective; *Ware* substandard, imperfect; *Messung, Rechnung* incorrect; *Arbeit, Aussprache* poor; **f~los** adj = **f~frei.**
Fehl-: ~**farbe** f *(Cards)* missing suit; *(Nicht-Trumpf)* plain or side suit; ~**geburt** f miscarriage; **f~gehen** vi sep irreg aux sein *(geh: sich irren)* to be wrong or mistaken; ~**griff** m mistake; ~**information** f incorrect information no pl; ~**leistung** f slip, mistake; **Freudsche ~leistung** Freudian slip; ~**paß** m *(Ftbl)* bad pass; ~**schlag** m *(fig)* failure; **f~schlagen** vi sep irreg aux sein to go wrong; *(Hoffnung)* to come to nothing; ~**schluß** m false conclusion; ~**start** m false start; *(Space)* faulty launch; ~**tritt** m *(geh)* false step; *(fig)* *(Vergehen)* slip, lapse; *(Affäre)* ~**urteil** nt miscarriage of justice; ~**verhalten** nt *(Psych)* abnormal behaviour *(Brit)* or behavior *(US);* ~**versuch** m unsuccessful attempt; ~**zündung** f misfiring no pl; **eine ~zündung** a backfire.
Feier f **-n** celebration; *(Party)* party; *(Zeremonie)* ceremony. **zur ~ von etw** to celebrate sth.
Feier|abend m *(Arbeitsschluß)* end of work; *(Geschäftsschluß)* closing time. ~ **machen** to finish work, to knock off *(col); (Geschäfte)* to close; **ich mache jetzt ~** I think I'll call it a day *(col);* **nach** ~ after work; **jetzt ist aber** ~! *(fig col)* enough is enough; **schönen** ~! have a nice evening!
feierlich adj *(ernsthaft, würdig)* solemn; *(festlich)* festive; *(förmlich)* ceremonial. **das ist ja nicht mehr ~** *(col)* that's beyond a joke *(col).*
Feierlichkeit f **(a)** *usu pl* solemnity; festiveness; ceremony. **(b)** usu pl celebrations pl.
feiern 1 vt **(a)** to celebrate; *Party, Orgie* to hold. **das muß gefeiert werden!** that calls for a celebration. **(b)** *(umjubeln)* to fête. **2** vi to celebrate.
Feier-: ~**schicht** f cancelled shift; ~**stunde** f ceremony; ~**tag** m holiday.
feig(e) 1 adj cowardly. **2** adv in a cowardly way. **er zog sich ~ zurück** he retreated like a coward.
Feige f **-n** fig.
Feigen-: ~**blatt** nt fig leaf; **ein ~blatt für etw** *(fig)* a front to hide sth; **als demokratisches ~blatt** *(fig)* to give a veneer of democracy.
Feigheit f cowardice.
Feigling m coward.
feilbieten vt sep irreg *(old)* to offer for sale.
Feile f **-n** file.
feilen vti to file. **an etw** *(dat)* ~ *(fig)* to perfect sth.
feilschen vi *(pej)* to haggle *(um over).*
fein adj **(a)** fine; *Humor, Ironie* delicate. **(b)** *(erlesen)* excellent, choice; *Geruch, Geschmack* delicate; *(prima)* great *(col),* fine. **ein ~er Kerl** a great guy *(col);* **das ist etwas F~es** that's really something *(col);* ~ **(he)raussein** to be sitting pretty. **(c)** *Gehör etc* sensitive, keen. **(d)** *(vornehm)* refined, fine *(esp iro),* posh *(col).* **nicht ~ genug sein** not to be good enough; **sich ~ machen** to get all dressed up.
Feind(in f) m **-e** enemy. **jdn zum ~ haben** to have sb as an enemy; **sich** *(dat)* **jdn zum ~ machen** to make an enemy of sb.
Feind- *in cpds* enemy; ~**berührung** f contact with the enemy; ~**bild** nt concept of an/the enemy.
feindlich adj *(Mil)* enemy; *(feindselig)* hostile. **jdm/etw ~ gegenüberstehen** to be hostile to sb/sth.
Feindschaft f hostility. **sich** *(dat)* **jds ~ zuziehen** to make an enemy of sb.
feindselig adj hostile.
Feindseligkeit f hostility.
Fein-: **f~fühlig** adj sensitive; ~**gefühl** nt no pl sensitivity; ~**gold** nt refined gold.
Feinheit f *siehe* **fein adj (a)** fineness; delicacy. **(b)** excellence; delicateness. **(c)** keenness.
Fein-: ~**kost** f „~kost" "Delicatessen"; ~**kost-**

handlung f delicatessen; ~**mechaniker** m precision engineer; ~**schmecker** m - gourmet; (fig) connoisseur; ~**schnitt** m (Tabak) fine cut; ~**silber** nt refined silver; f~**sinnig** adj sensitive; ~**wäsche** f delicates pl; ~**waschmittel** nt mild(-action) detergent.

feist adj fat; Mensch auch obese.

feixen vi (col) to smirk.

Feld nt -er field; (Sport: Spiel~ auch) pitch; (auf Spielbrett) square; (offenes Gelände) open country. **auf freiem** ~ in the open country; **gegen jdn/etw zu** ~**e ziehen** (fig) to crusade against sb/sth; **Argumente ins** ~ **führen** to bring arguments to bear; **das** ~ **räumen** (fig) to bow out; **jdm das** ~ **überlassen** to give way to sb; (freiwillig) to hand over to sb.

Feld- in cpds field; ~**arbeit** f (Agr) work in the fields; (Sci, Sociol) fieldwork; ~**arbeiter** m fieldworker; ~**besteck** nt eating irons pl; ~**bett** nt campbed; ~**blume** f wild flower; ~**flasche** f canteen (Mil), water bottle; ~**herr** m (old) commander; ~**jäger** m (Mil) military policeman; **die** ~**jäger** the military police; ~**marschall** m (old) field marshal; ~**maus** f field mouse; ~**salat** m lamb's lettuce; ~**spieler** m (Sport) player; ~**stecher** m - (pair of) binoculars or field glasses; ~**verweis** m sending-off.

Feld-Wald-und-Wiesen- in cpds (col) common-or-garden.

Feld-: ~**webel** m sergeant; ~**weg** m track across the fields; ~**zug** m (Mil, fig) campaign.

Felge f -n (Tech) (wheel) rim.

Fell nt -e fur; (von Schaf) fleece; (von toten Tieren) skin, fell. **einem Tier das** ~ **abziehen** to skin an animal; **ihm sind die** ~**e weggeschwommen** (fig) all his hopes were dashed; **ein dickes** ~ **haben** to be thickskinned, to have a thick skin; **jdm das** ~ **über die Ohren ziehen** to pull the wool over sb's eyes.

Fels-: ~**block** m, ~**brocken** m boulder.

felsenfest adj firm. ~ **überzeugt sein** to be firmly convinced; **sich** ~ **auf jdn verlassen** to put one's complete trust in sb.

felsig adj rocky.

Fels-: ~**massiv** nt rock massif; ~**spalte** f crevice; ~**vorsprung** m ledge; ~**wand** f rock face.

feminin adj feminine; (pej) effeminate.

Femininum nt, pl **Feminina** (Gram) feminine noun.

Feminismus m feminism.

Feminist(in f) m (wk) -en,-en feminist.

feministisch adj feminist.

Fenchel m no pl fennel.

Fenster nt - window. **weg vom** ~ (col) out of the game (col), finished; **Geld zum** ~ **hinauswerfen** (col) to chuck money down the drain.

Fenster- in cpds window; ~**bank** f, ~**brett** nt windowsill, window ledge; ~**flügel** m side of a casement window; ~**glas** nt window glass; (in Brille) plain glass; ~**kreuz** nt mullion and transom; ~**laden** m shutter; ~**leder** nt chamois, shammy (leather); ~**platz** m window seat; ~**putzer** m window cleaner; ~**rahmen** m window frame; ~**scheibe** f window pane; ~**sims** m window ledge, windowsill.

Ferien ['feːrɪən] pl holidays pl (Brit), vacation sing (US, Univ); (Parlaments~, Jur) recess sing. **die großen** ~ the summer holidays (Brit), the long vacation (US, Univ); ~ **machen** to take a holiday; **in die** ~ **fahren** to go on holiday.

Ferien- in cpds holiday (Brit), vacation (US); ~**gast** m holidaymaker (Brit), vacationist (US); (Besuch) person staying on holiday (Brit) or vacation (US); ~**ort** m holiday (Brit) or vacation (US) resort; ~**reise** f holiday (Brit), vacation (US).

Ferkel nt - piglet; (fig) pig.

Ferment nt -e enzyme.

fern adj (a) (räumlich) distant, faraway. ~ **von**

hier a long way (away) from here; **von** ~(e) betrachtet seen from a distance; **der F**~**e Osten** the Far East; **von** ~(e) **kennen** (fig) to know (only) slightly. (b) (zeitlich) far-off. **in nicht zu** ~**er Zeit** in the not-too-distant future; **der Tag ist nicht mehr** ~, **wo ...** the day is not far off when ...

Fern-: f~**ab** adv far away; ~**amt** nt (telephone) exchange; ~**bedienung** f remote control; f~**bleiben** vi sep irreg aux sein to stay away (dat, von from); ~**bleiben** nt absence.

Ferne f -n (a) (räumlich) distance. **aus der** ~ from a distance. (b) (zeitlich) **in weiter** ~ **liegen** to be in the distant future.

ferner adj, adv further. **für die** ~**e Zukunft** for the long term; **unter** ~ **liefen rangieren** (col) to be an also-ran.

Fern-: ~**fahrer** m long-distance lorry (Brit) or truck driver; f~**gelenkt** adj = f~**gesteuert**; ~**gespräch** nt long-distance call; f~**gesteuert** adj remote-controlled; Rakete guided; (fig) manipulated (von by); ~**glas** nt (pair of) binoculars; f~**halten** vtr sep irreg to keep away; ~**heizung** f district heating; ~**kurs(us)** m correspondence course; ~**lastverkehr** m long-distance goods traffic; ~**lenkung** f remote control; ~**licht** nt (Aut) full or high beam; **mit** ~**licht fahren** to drive on full beam; f~**liegen** vi sep irreg (fig) (jdm) f~**liegen** to be far from sb's thoughts or mind; **es liegt mir f**~, **das zu tun** far be it from me to do that; **nichts liegt mir f**~**er** nothing could be further from my mind.

Fernmelde- in cpds telecommunications, (Mil) signals.

Fernmelder m (Mil col) signaller (Brit), signaler (US).

Fernmelde-: ~**satellit** m communications satellite; ~**technik** f telecommunications sing; ~**wesen** nt telecommunications sing.

Fern-: f~**mündlich** 1 adj telephone attr; 2 adv by telephone; ~**ost** no art aus/in ~**ost** from/in the Far East; ~**östlich** adj Far Eastern attr; ~**rohr** nt telescope; ~**ruf** m (form) telephone number; ~**schreiben** nt telex; ~**schreiber** m teleprinter; (Comm) telex; f~**schriftlich** adj by telex.

Fernseh- in cpds television, TV; ~**apparat** m television or TV (set).

fernsehen vi sep irreg to watch television or TV.

Fernsehen nt no pl television, TV. **vom** ~ **übertragen werden** to be televised; **im** ~ on television or TV.

Fernseher m - (col) (Gerät) television, TV, telly (Brit col); (Zuschauer) (television) viewer.

Fernseh-: ~**gebühr** f television licence (Brit) or license (US) fee; ~**gerät** nt television or TV set; ~**programm** nt (a) (Kanal) channel, station (US); (b) (Sendung) programme (Brit), program (US); (Sendefolge) programmes pl (Brit), programs pl (US); (c) (~zeitschrift) (television) programme (Brit) or program (US) guide; ~**schirm** m television or TV screen; ~**sendung** f television programme (Brit) or program (US); ~**spiel** nt television play; ~**teilnehmer** m (form) television viewer; ~**turm** m television tower; ~**zuschauer** m (television) viewer.

Fernsicht f (eine) **gute** ~ **haben** to be able to see a long way.

Fernsprech- in cpds (form) siehe auch **Telefon-** telephone; ~**apparat** m telephone; ~**buch** nt telephone directory.

Fernsprecher m - (form) (public) telephone.

Fernsprech-: ~**gebühr** f telephone charges pl; ~**zelle** f (tele)phone box or booth (US), callbox.

Fern-: f~**stehen** vi sep irreg (jdm) **jdm/etw f**~**stehen** to have no connection with sb/sth; **ich stehe ihm ziemlich f**~ I'm not on very close terms with him; f~**steuern** vt sep to operate by remote control; siehe f~**gesteuert**; ~**steuerung** f remote control; ~**straße** f major road, highway (US);

~**studium** nt multi-media course, ≈ Open University course (Brit); ~**universität** f ≈ Open University (Brit); ~**unterricht** m = ~**studium**; ~**verkehr** m long-distance traffic; ~**wärme** f district heating; ~**weh** nt wanderlust; ~**ziel** nt long-term goal.
Ferse f -**n** heel. **jdm (dicht) auf den** ~**n bleiben** to stay hard on sb's heels.
Fersengeld nt: ~ **geben** to take to one's heels.
fertig adj **(a)** (zu Ende, vollendet) finished; (ausgebildet) qualified; (reif) Mensch, Charakter mature. **etw** ~ **kaufen** to buy sth ready-made; Essen to buy sth ready-cooked; ~ **ausgebildet** fully qualified; **mit etw** ~ **sein** to have finished sth; ~ **essen/lesen** to finish eating/reading; **mit jdm** ~ **sein** (fig) to be finished with sb; **mit jdm/etw** ~ **werden** to cope with sb/sth; **ich werde damit nicht** ~ I can't cope with it. **(b)** (bereit) ready. ~ **zur Abfahrt** ready to leave. **(c)** (col) shattered (col); (ruiniert) finished. **mit den Nerven** ~ **sein** to be at the end of one's tether.
Fertig- in cpds finished; (Build) prefabricated; ~**bau** m -**ten** prefabricated building; **f**~**bringen** vt sep irreg **(a)** (vollenden) to get done; **(b)** (imstande sein) to manage; (iro) to be capable of; **ich brachte es nicht f**~, **ihr die Wahrheit zu sagen** I couldn't bring myself to tell her the truth; **er bringt das f**~ (iro) I wouldn't put it past him.
Fertig-: ~**gericht** nt ready-to-serve meal; ~**haus** nt prefabricated house, prefab.
Fertigkeit f skill.
Fertig-: **f**~**machen** vt sep **(a)** (vollenden) to finish; **(b)** (bereit machen) to get ready; **sich f**~**machen** to get ready; **(c)** (col) **jdn f**~**machen** (erledigen) to do for sb; (ermüden) to take it out of sb; (deprimieren) to get sb down; (abkanzeln) to lay into sb (col); **f**~**stellen** vt sep to complete; ~**stellung** f completion.
Fertigung f production.
Fertigungs- in cpds production; ~**straße** f production line.
Fertigware f finished product.
Fes, fes nt - (Mus) F flat.
fesch adj (col) (modisch) smart; (hübsch) attractive.
Fessel f -**n (a)** (lit,fig) bond, fetter; (Kette) chain. **jdm** ~**n anlegen** to fetter sb. **(b)** (Anat) (von Huftieren) pastern; (von Menschen) ankle.
fesseln vt **(a)** to tie (up), to bind; (mit Handschellen) to handcuff; (mit Ketten) to chain (up). **ans Bett gefesselt** (fig) confined to bed; **jdn an sich** ~ (fig) to bind sb to oneself. **(b)** (faszinieren) to grip.
fesselnd adj gripping.
fest adj **(a)** (hart) solid. ~**e Nahrung** solid food, solids pl. **(b)** (stabil) solid; Gewebe, Schuhe strong, sturdy; (Comm, Fin) stable. **(c)** (sicher, entschlossen) firm. ~ **versprechen** to promise faithfully; **eine** ~**e Meinung von etw haben** to have definite views on sth; **etw ist** ~ sth is definite; ~ **entschlossen sein** to be absolutely determined. **(d)** (kräftig) firm; Schlag hard. ~ **zuschlagen** to hit hard. **(e)** (nicht locker) tight; Griff firm; (fig) Schlaf sound. ~ **packen** to grip firmly; **die Tür** ~ **schließen** to shut the door tight; ~ **schlafen** to sleep soundly. **(f)** (ständig) regular; Freund(in) steady; Stellung, Mitarbeiter permanent; Kosten, Einkommen fixed. ~ **befreundet sein** to be good friends; (Freund und Freundin) to be going steady.
Fest nt -**e (a)** (Feier) celebration; (Party) party. **man soll die** ~**e feiern, wie sie fallen** (prov) make hay while the sun shines (Prov). **(b)** (Weihnachts~) Christmas.
Fest-: ~**akt** m ceremony; **f**~**angestellt** adj employed on a permanent basis; **f**~**beißen** vr sep irreg (Hund etc) to get a firm grip (an+dat on); (fig: nicht weiterkommen) to get bogged down (an

+dat in); ~**beleuchtung** f festive lights pl; (col: im Haus) blazing lights pl; **f**~**binden** vt sep irreg to tie up (an+dat to); ~**essen** nt banquet; **f**~**fahren** vr sep irreg (lit,fig) to get bogged down; ~**geld** nt (Fin) time deposit; ~**halle** f festival hall.
festhalten sep irreg **1** vt **(a)** to keep hold of, to hold on to. **(b)** (inhaftieren) to hold, to detain. **(c)** (speichern) to record; Atmosphäre etc to capture. **etw schriftlich** ~ to record sth. **2** vi **an etw** (dat) ~ to hold or stick (col) to sth. **3** vr to hold on (an +dat to). **halt dich fest!** (lit) hold tight!; **halt dich fest, und hör dir das an!** (col) brace yourself and listen to this!
festigen 1 vt to strengthen. **2** vr to become stronger.
Festiger m - (Haar~) setting lotion.
Festigkeit f no pl strength; (fig) steadfastness.
Festigung f strengthening.
Festival ['fɛstivəl, 'fɛstival] nt -**s** festival.
Fest-: **f**~**kleben** vti sep (vi: aux sein) to stick (firmly) (an+dat on)to); ~**kleid** nt formal dress; **f**~**klemmen** sep **1** vt to wedge fast; (mit Klammer) to clip; **2** vir (vi: aux sein) to jam; ~**komma** nt (Comp) fixed point; **f**~**krallen** vr sep (Tier) to dig one's claws in (an+dat-to); (Mensch) to dig one's nails in (an+dat -to); (fig) to cling (an +dat to).
Festland nt mainland; (nicht Meer) dry land.
festlegen sep **1** vt **(a)** (festsetzen) Termin etc to fix; Regelung, Arbeitszeiten to lay down. **etw schriftlich** ~ to put sth down in writing. **(b)** **jdn auf etw** (acc) ~ (festnageln) to tie sb (down) to sth; (verpflichten) to commit sb to sth. **(c)** Geld to tie up. **2** vr **sich darauf** ~, **etw zu tun** to commit oneself to doing sth.
Festlegung f siehe vt (a, b) **(a)** fixing; laying-down. **(b)** tying-down; commitment.
festlich adj festive; (feierlich) solemn; (prächtig) magnificent. **etw** ~ **begehen** to celebrate sth.
Fest-: **f**~**liegen** vi sep irreg **(a)** (f~gesetzt sein) to have been fixed or definitely decided; **(b)** (Fin: Geld) to be tied up; **(c)** (nicht weiterkönnen) to be stuck; (Naut) to be aground; **f**~**machen** sep **1** vt **(a)** (befestigen) to fix on (an+dat -to), to fasten (an +dat (on)to); (Naut) to moor; **(b)** (vereinbaren) to arrange; **ein Geschäft f**~**machen** to clinch a deal; **2** vi (Naut) to moor; ~**mahl** nt (geh) banquet, feast; **f**~**nageln** vt sep (lit) to nail (down/up/ on); (fig col) jdn to nail down (auf+acc to); ~**nahme** f -**n** arrest; **f**~**nehmen** vt sep irreg to arrest; **vorläufig f**~**nehmen** to take into custody; ~**platte** f (Comp) hard disk; ~**preis** m (Comm) fixed price; ~**rede** f speech; **die** ~**rede halten** to give the main speech; ~**saal** m hall; (Tanzsaal) ballroom; **f**~**schrauben** vt sep to screw (on) tight; **f**~**schreiben** vt sep irreg (fig) to establish.
festsetzen sep **1** vt **(a)** to fix (bei, auf+acc at); Ort, Termin auch to arrange (auf+acc, bei for). **(b)** (inhaftieren) to detain. **2** vr (Staub, Schmutz) to collect; (fig: Gedanke) to take root.
Festsetzung f **(a)** siehe vt (a) fixing; arrangement. **(b)** (Inhaftierung) detention.
festsitzen vi sep irreg to be stuck; (Schmutz) to cling.
Festspiele pl festival sing.
fest-: ~**stecken** sep **1** vt to pin (an+dat (on)to, in +dat in); Haare to pin up; **2** vi aux sein (steckenbleiben) to be stuck; ~**stehen** vi sep irreg (sicher sein) to be certain; (beschlossen sein) to have been settled or fixed; ~**stehend** adj **(a)** (Mech) fixed; **(b)** attr (bestimmt) definite; Redewendung set; ~**stellbar** adj (herauszufinden) ascertainable.
feststellen vt sep **(a)** (Mech) to lock (fast). **(b)** (ermitteln) to ascertain, to find out; Personalien, Ursache auch to establish; Schaden to assess; Krankheit to diagnose. **der Arzt konnte nur noch seinen Tod** ~ the doctor found him to be dead.

(c) *(erkennen)* to tell *(an+dat* from*)*; *Fehler* to find, to detect; *(bemerken)* to discover; *(einsehen)* to realize. **ich mußte entsetzt/überrascht ~, daß ...** I was horrified/surprised to find that ... **(d)** *(aussprechen)* to stress, to emphasize.

Feststellung *f* **(a)** *siehe vt* **(b)** ascertainment; establishment; assessment; diagnosis. **(b)** *(Erkenntnis)* conclusion. **(c)** *(Wahrnehmung)* observation. **die ~ machen, daß ...** to realize that ...; **ist das eine Frage oder eine ~?** is that a question or a statement (of fact)? **(d)** *(Bemerkung)* remark, observation. **die ~ machen, daß ...** to remark *or* observe that ...

Festtag *m* **(a)** *(Ehrentag)* special day. **(b)** *(Feiertag)* holiday, feast(day) *(Eccl.)*.

fest-: **~treten** *sep irreg* **1** *vt* to tread down; *(in Teppich etc)* to tread in *(in+acc* -to*)*; **2** *vr* to get trodden down/in; **~umrissen** *adj attr* clear-cut.

Festung *f* fortress; *(Burgfeste)* castle.

Fest-: **f~verwurzelt** *adj attr* deep-rooted; **f~verzinslich** *adj* fixed-interest *attr*; **~vortrag** *m* lecture, talk; **~woche** *f* festival week; **die ~wochen** the festival *sing.*

Fete, Fête ['fɛːtə, 'fɛːtə] *f* **-n** party.

Fetischist *m (wk)* fetishist.

fett *adj* **(a)** *(~haltig) Speisen* fatty. **~ essen** to eat fatty food; **ein ~er Brocken** *(fig)* a lucrative deal. **(b)** *(dick)* fat; *(Typ)* bold. **(c)** *(üppig) Boden, Weide)* rich; *Beute, Gewinn* fat; *Geschäft* lucrative. **~e Jahre** fat years.

Fett *nt* **-e** fat; *(zum Schmieren)* grease. **~ ansetzen** to put on weight; *(Tiere)* to fatten up; **sein ~ bekommen** *(col)* to get one's come-uppance *(col)*.

Fett-: **f~arm** *adj* low-fat; **f~arm essen** to eat low-fat foods; **~auge** *nt* globule of fat; **~creme** *f* skin cream with oil; **~druck** *m (Typ)* bold type.

fetten *vt* to grease.

Fett-: **~fleck(en)** *m* grease spot, greasy mark; **f~frei** *adj* fat-free; *Milch* low-fat; *Kost* non-fatty; *Creme* non-greasy; **f~gedruckt** *adj attr (Typ)* bold; **~gehalt** *m* fat content; **f~haltig** *adj* fatty.

Fettigkeit *f* siehe *adj* greasiness; oiliness.

Fett-: **~kloß** *m (pej)* fatty *(col)*; **f~leibig** *adj (geh)* obese, corpulent; **~leibigkeit** *f (geh)* obesity, corpulence; **f~los** *adj* fat-free; **~näpfchen** *nt (col)*: **ins ~näpfchen treten** to put one's foot in it *(bei jdm* with sb*)*; **~polster** *nt (hum col)* flab *no pl*; **~polster haben** to be well-padded; **f~reich** *adj* high-fat; **f~reich essen** to eat foods with a high fat content; **~sack** *m (pej) fatso (col)*; **~schicht** *f* layer of fat; **~stift** *m* lip salve; **~sucht** *f no pl (Med)* obesity; **f~süchtig** *adj (Med)* obese; **~wanst** *m (pej)* potbelly; *(Mensch)* fatso *(col)*.

Fetzen *m* - shred; *(Papier~, Gesprächs~)* scrap; *(Kleidung)* rag. **das Kleid ist in ~ gegangen** the dress has fallen to pieces; **etw in ~/in tausend ~ (zer)reißen** to tear sth to shreds/into a thousand pieces; ..., **daß die ~ fliegen** *(col)* ... like mad *(col)*.

fetzen *vi aux sein (col: rasen)* to tear.

fetzig *adj (col)* lively.

feucht *adj* damp; *Lippen* moist; *(feuchtheiß) Klima* humid; *Hände* sweaty; *Tinte, Farbe* wet. **sie hatte ~e Augen** her eyes were moist; **ein ~er Abend** *(hum)* a boozy night; **eine ~e Aussprache haben** *(hum col)* to splutter when one speaks; **das geht dich einen ~en Kehricht** *or* **Dreck an** *(col!)* it's none of your damn business *(col)*.

feucht-: **~fröhlich** *adj (hum)* boozy; **~heiß** *adj* muggy.

Feuchtigkeit *f no pl* **(a)** *siehe adj* dampness; moistness; humidity; sweatiness; wetness. **(b)** *(Flüssigkeit)* moisture; *(Luft~)* humidity.

Feuchtigkeits-: **~creme** *f* moisturizer; **~gehalt**, **~grad** *m* moisture content.

feuchtwarm *adj* muggy, humid.

feudal *adj (Pol, Hist)* feudal; *(col)* plush *(col)*.

Feudal- *in cpds* feudal; **~herrschaft** *f* feudalism.

Feudalismus *m* feudalism.

Feuer *nt* - **(a)** *(Flamme, Kamin~)* fire. **am ~** by the fire; **~ machen** to light a/the fire; **~ hinter etw** *(acc)* **machen** *(fig)* to chase sth up; **jdm ~ unter dem Hintern machen** *(col)* to put a bomb under sb *(col)*; **du spielst mit dem ~** *(fig)* you're playing with fire; **sie sind wie ~ und Wasser** they're as different as chalk and cheese; **~ legen** to start a fire; **~ fangen** to catch fire; **für jdn durchs ~ gehen** to go through fire and water for sb; **haben Sie ~?** do you have a light?; **jdm ~ geben** to give sb a light. **(b)** *(Naut, Funk~)* beacon; *(von Leuchtturm)* light. **(c)** **das/sie hat bei ihm ~ gefangen** he was really taken with it/her; **~ und Flamme sein** *(col)* to be dead keen *(col) (für* on*)*. **(d)** *(Schießen)* fire. **~! fire!; ~ frei!** open fire!; **das ~ eröffnen** to open fire; **das ~ einstellen** to cease fire; **etw unter ~ *(acc)* nehmen** to open fire on sth.

Feuer- *in cpds* fire; **~alarm** *m* fire alarm; **~anzünder** *m* firelighter; **~befehl** *m (Mil)* order to fire; **~bekämpfung** *f* fire-fighting; **f~beständig** *adj* fire-resistant; **~bestattung** *f* cremation; **~eifer** *m* zeal; **~einstellung** *f* cessation of fire; *(Waffenstillstand)* cease-fire; **f~fest** *adj* fire-proof; *Geschirr* heat-resistant; **~gefahr** *f* fire hazard *or* risk; **bei ~gefahr** in the event of fire; **f~gefährlich** *adj* inflammable; **~haken** *m* poker; **~leiter** *f (am Haus)* fire escape; **~löscher** *m* - fire extinguisher; **~meer** *nt (liter)* sea of flames; **~melder** *m* - fire alarm.

feuern **1** *vi* **(a)** *(heizen)* mit Öl/Holz ~ to have oil heating/use wood for one's heating. **(b)** *(Mil)* to fire. **2** *vt* **(a)** *Ofen* to light. **(b)** *(col) (werfen)* to fling; *(Ftbl) Ball* to slam; *(ins Tor)* to slam in. **(c)** *(col: entlassen)* to fire *(col)*.

Feuer-: **~pause** *f* break in the firing; *(vereinbart)* ceasefire; **f~polizeilich** *adj Bestimmungen* laid down by the fire authorities; **~probe** *f* **die ~probe bestehen** *(fig)* to pass the (acid) test; **f~rot** *adj* fiery red.

Feuersbrunst *f (geh)* conflagration.

Feuer-: **~schein** *m* glow of the fire; **~schiff** *nt* lightship; **~schlucker** *m* - fire-eater; **~schutz** *m* **(a)** *(Vorbeugung)* fire prevention; **(b)** *(Mil: Deckung)* covering fire; **f~speiend** *adj attr Drache* fire-breathing; *Berg* belching flames; **~stein** *m* flint; **~stelle** *f* campfire site; *(Herd)* fireplace; **~taufe** *f* **die ~taufe bestehen/erhalten** to go through/have a baptism of fire; **~treppe** *f* fire escape; **~tür** *f* fire door.

Feuerung *f* heating; *(Brennstoff)* fuel.

Feuer-: **~versicherung** *f* fire insurance; **~wache** *f* fire station; **~waffe** *f* firearm; **~wechsel** *m* exchange of fire.

Feuerwehr *f* fire brigade *(Brit)* or department *(US)*. **fahren wie die ~** *(col)* to drive like the clappers *(Brit col)*, to drive flat out.

Feuerwehr-: **~auto** *nt* fire engine; **~mann** *m* fireman.

Feuer-: **~werk** *nt* fireworks *pl*; *(fig)* cavalcade; **~werkskörper** *m* firework; **~zangenbowle** *f* red wine punch containing rum which has been flamed *off*; **~zeug** *nt* (cigarette) lighter.

Feuilleton [fœjɛ'tõ, 'fœjətõ] *nt* **-s** *(Press)* feature section; *(Artikel)* feature (article).

feurig *adj* fiery.

Fez *m no pl (dated col: Spaß)* larking about *(col)*.

Fiaker *m* - *(Aus) (Kutsche)* (hackney) cab; *(Kutscher)* cab driver, cabby *(col)*.

Fiasko *nt* **-s** *(col)* fiasco.

Fibel *f* **-n** *(Sch)* primer.

Fiber *f* **-n** fibre *(Brit)*, fiber *(US)*.

Fiche [fiːʃ] *m or nt* **-s** *(micro)*fiche.

Fichte *f* **-n** *(Bot)* spruce.

Fichten- *in cpds* spruce; **~zapfen** *m* spruce cone.

ficken *vti (col!!)* to fuck *(col!!)*.

fidel adj (dated col) jolly, merry.
Fidel f -n fiddle.
Fidschi|inseln pl Fiji Islands.
Fieber nt - temperature; (Krankheit) fever. ~
  haben to have a temperature; to be feverish; **40°**
  ~ **haben** to have a temperature of 40; (jdm) das
  ~ **messen** to take sb's temperature; **im** ~ **seiner**
  Leidenschaft in a fever of passion.
Fieber- in cpds feverish; **f~haft** adj (lit, fig)
  feverish.
fieb(e)rig adj feverish.
Fieberkurve f temperature curve.
fiebern vi to have a temperature; (schwer) to
  be feverish. **vor Ungeduld** (dat) ~ (fig) to be
  in a fever of impatience.
Fieberthermometer nt thermometer.
Fiedel f -n (old, pej: Geige) fiddle.
fiedeln vti (hum, pej) to fiddle.
fiel pret of **fallen**.
fies adj (col) nasty, horrible.
Figur f figure; (Roman~, Film~ etc) character;
  (von Männern) physique. **auf seine** ~ **achten** to
  watch one's figure; **eine gute/schlechte/traurige**
  ~ **abgeben** to cut a good/poor/sorry figure; **eine**
  komische ~ (col) a strange character.
Fiktion f fiction.
fiktiv adj fictitious.
Filet [fi'le:] nt -s (Cook) fillet; (Rinder~) fillet
  steak; (zum Braten) piece of sirloin or tenderloin
  (US).
filetieren* vt to fillet.
Filet- [fi'le:-]: ~**steak** nt fillet steak; ~**stück** nt
  piece of sirloin or tenderloin (US).
Filiale f -n branch.
Filialleiter m branch manager.
Filius m -se (hum) son, offspring (hum).
Film m -e (a) film; (Spiel~ auch) movie (esp US).
  in einen ~ **gehen** to go and see a film (Brit) or
  movie (US); **da ist bei mir der** ~ **gerissen** (col) I
  had a mental blackout (col). **(b)** (~branche)
  films pl, the movies pl (esp US). **zum** ~ **gehen** to
  go into films.
Film- in cpds film, movie (esp US); ~**atelier** nt film
  studio; ~**bewertungsstelle** f ≃ board of film
  classification; ~**diva** f (dated) screen goddess.
Filmemacher(in f) m film-maker.
Film-: ~**festspiele** pl film festival; ~**geschäft** nt
  film or movie (esp US) industry; ~**geschichte** f
  history of the cinema; ~**geschichte machen** to
  make cinema history; ~**gesellschaft** f film company; ~**größe** f great star of the screen; ~**held** m
  screen or movie (esp US) hero; ~**hochschule** f
  film school.
filmisch adj cinematic.
Film-: ~**kamera** f film or movie (esp US) camera;
  (Schmalfilmkamera) cine-camera (Brit); ~**kritik** f
  film criticism; (Artikel) film review; (Kritiker)
  film critics pl; ~**musik** f film music; **die origi-
  nale** ~**musik** the original soundtrack; ~**preis** m
  film or movie (esp US) award; ~**produzent** m
  film or movie (esp US) producer; ~**regie** f direction of a/the film; ~**regisseur** m film or movie
  (esp US) director; ~**riß** m (lit) tear in a film; (col)
  mental blackout (col); ~**rolle** f (Spule) spool of
  film; (für Fotoapparat) roll of film; (Part) film
  part; ~**schaffende(r)** mf decl as adj film-maker;
  ~**schauspieler(in** f) m film or movie (esp US)
  actor/actress; ~**star** m filmstar, movie star (esp
  US); ~**sternchen** nt starlet; ~**theater** nt (form)
  cinema (Brit), movie theater (US); ~**trick** m film
  stunt; ~**verleih** m film distributors pl; ~**vorstellung** f film show.
Filou [fi'lu:] m -s (dated col) devil (col).
Filter m or (esp Tech) nt - filter. **eine Zigarette**
  mit/ohne ~ a filter-tipped/plain cigarette.
Filterkaffee m filter or drip (US) coffee.
filtern vti to filter.
Filter-: ~**papier** nt filter paper; ~**tüte** f filter bag.

Filterung f filtering.
Filterzigarette f filter-tipped cigarette.
filtrieren* vt to filter.
Filz m -e (Tex) felt.
filzen vt (col) (durchsuchen) jdn to frisk, to search;
  Gepäck etc to search; (berauben) to do over (col).
Filzhut m felt hat.
Filzokratie f (hum) nepotism.
Filz-: ~**pantoffel** m (carpet) slipper; ~**schreiber**,
  ~**stift** m felt-tip (pen).
Fimmel m - (col) obsession (mit about). **du hast**
  wohl einen ~! you're crazy (col).
Finale nt -s or - (Mus) finale; (Sport) final.
Finalist m finalist.
Finanz- in cpds financial; ~**amt** nt tax office;
  ~**beamte(r)** mf tax official; ~**behörde** f tax authority.
Finanzen pl finances pl. **das übersteigt meine** ~
  that's beyond my means.
finanziell adj financial.
finanzieren* vt to finance. **frei** ~ **to finance**
  privately; **ich kann meinen Urlaub nicht** ~ I
  can't afford a holiday.
Finanzierung f financing. **zur** ~ **von etw** to
  finance sth.
Finanz-: ~**jahr** nt financial year; **f~kräftig** adj
  financially strong; ~**minister** m minister of
  finance; ~**politik** f financial policy; **f~schwach**
  adj financially weak; **f~stark** adj financially
  strong; ~**wesen** nt financial system.
Findelkind nt (old) foundling (old).
finden pret **fand**, ptp **gefunden 1** vt **(a)** to find;
  Anklang, Zustimmung auch, Beifall to meet with;
  Berücksichtigung, Beachtung to receive. **ich finde**
  es nicht I can't find it; **es war nicht/nirgends**
  zu ~ it was not/nowhere to be found; **es ließ**
  sich niemand ~ we/they etc couldn't find anybody; **etwas an jdm** ~ to see something in sb;
  nichts dabei ~ to think nothing of it. **(b)** (ansehen, betrachten) to think. **es kalt/warm/ganz erträglich** ~ to find it cold/warm/quite tolerable;
  etw gut/zu teuer/eine Frechheit ~ to think (that)
  sth is good/too expensive/a cheek; **jdn blöd/nett**
  ~ to think (that) sb is stupid/nice; **wie findest du**
  das? what do you think?; ~ **Sie?** do you think so?;
  ich finde, wir sollten ... I think we should ...;
  ich fände es besser, wenn ... I think it would
  be better if ...
  2 vi (lit, fig: den Weg ~) to find one's way. **er**
  findet nicht nach Hause he can't find his way
  home; **ich finde schon allein hinaus** I can see
  myself out; **zu sich selbst** ~ to sort oneself out.
  3 vr **(a)** (zum Vorschein kommen) to be found;
  (wiederauftauchen auch) to turn up; (sich befinden
  auch) to be. **(b)** (in Ordnung kommen: Angelegenheit etc) to sort itself out; (Mensch: zu sich ~) to
  sort oneself out. **(c)** (sich fügen) **sich in etw** (acc)
  ~ to reconcile oneself to sth. **(d)** (sich treffen)
  (lit, fig) to find each other.
Finder(in f) m - finder.
Finderlohn m reward for the finder.
findig adj resourceful.
Findigkeit f resourcefulness.
Finesse f **(a)** (Feinheit) refinement; (Kunstfertigkeit) finesse no pl. **mit allen** ~**n** with all the
  refinements. **(b)** (Trick) trick.
fing pret of **fangen**.
Finger m - finger. **mit** ~**n auf jdn zeigen** (fig) to
  look askance at sb; **jdm mit dem** ~ **drohen** to
  wag one's finger at sb; **jdm auf die** ~ **hauen**
  (lit)/**klopfen** (fig) to give sb a rap on the knuckles;
  sich (dat) **nicht die** ~ **schmutzig machen** (lit, fig)
  not to get one's hands dirty; **das kann sich jeder**
  an den (**fünf**) ~**n abzählen** (col) it sticks out a
  mile (col); **das läßt er nicht mehr aus den** ~**n** he
  won't let it out of his hands; **jdn/etw in die** ~
  bekommen to get one's hands on sb/sth; **er hat**
  überall seine ~ **drin** (col) he has a finger in every

pie *(col)*; **wenn man ihm den kleinen ~ gibt, nimmt er (gleich) die ganze Hand** *(prov)* give him an inch and he'll take a mile *(col)*; **lange ~ machen** *(hum col)* to be light-fingered; **jdm in die ~ geraten** to fall into sb's hands *or* clutches; **die ~ von etw lassen** *(col)* to keep away from sth; **jdm (scharf) auf die ~ sehen** to keep an eye on sb; **sich** *(dat)* **etw aus den ~n saugen** to conjure sth up; **sich** *(dat)* **die ~ nach etw lecken** *(col)* to be dying for sth; **keinen ~ krumm machen** *(col)* not to lift a finger *(col)*; **mir juckt es in den ~n(, etw zu tun)** *(col)* I'm itching to (do sth); **jdn um den kleinen ~ wickeln** to twist sb around one's little finger; **etw im kleinen ~ haben** to have a natural feel for sth.

Finger-: **~abdruck** *m* fingerprint; **f~breit** *adj* the width of a finger; **~farbe** *f* finger paint; **f~fertig** *adj* nimble-fingered, dexterous; **~fertigkeit** *f* dexterity; **~hakeln** *nt* finger-wrestling; **~handschuh** *m* glove; **~hut** *m* **(a)** *(Sew)* thimble; **(b)** *(Bot)* foxglove; **~knöchel** *m* knucklebone; **~kuppe** *f* fingertip; **~ling** *m* fingerstall.

fingern *vi* **an etw** *(dat)* **~** to fiddle with sth; **nach etw ~** to fumble (around) for sth.

Finger-: **~nagel** *m* fingernail; **~spitze** *f* fingertip; **das muß man in den ~spitzen haben** you have to have a feel for it; **~spitzengefühl** *nt* *no pl* sensitivity; **~zeig** *m* **-e** hint.

fingieren* [fɪŋ'giːrən] *vt* *(vortäuschen)* to fake; *(erdichten)* to fabricate. **fingiert** *(vorgetäuscht)* bogus; *(erfunden)* fictitious.

Finish ['fɪnɪʃ] *nt* **-s (a)** *(Endverarbeitung)* finish. **(b)** *(Sport: Endspurt)* final spurt.

Fink *m* *(wk)* **-en, -en** finch.

Finne *m* *(wk)* **-n, -n, Finnin** *f* Finn.

finnisch *adj* Finnish; *siehe* **deutsch.**

Finnisch(e) *nt* **-n** Finnish; *siehe* **Deutsch(e).**

Finnland *nt* Finland.

finster *adj* **(a)** *(lit, fig)* dark; *Zimmer, Wald, Nacht* dark (and gloomy). **im F~n** in the dark; **es sieht ~ aus** *(fig)* things look bleak. **(b)** *(dubios)* shady. **(c)** *(mürrisch, düster)* grim; *Wolken* dark, black. **~ entschlossen sein** to be grimly determined; **jdn ~ ansehen** to give sb a black look. **(d)** *(unheimlich)* *Gestalt, Blick, Gedanken* sinister.

Finsternis *f* **(a)** darkness. **(b)** *(Astron)* eclipse.

Finte *f* **-n (a)** *(Sport)* feint. **(b)** *(List)* ruse.

Firlefanz *m* *no pl* *(col)* **(a)** *(Kram)* frippery. **(b)** *(Albernheit)* **~ machen** to clown around.

firm *adj* *pred* **in etw** *(dat)* **~ sein** to have a sound knowledge of sth.

Firma *f*, *pl* **Firmen** company, firm. **die ~ Wahlster/Lexus** Wahlster(s)/Lexus; **die ~ dankt** *(hum)* much obliged (to you).

Firmament *nt* *no pl* *(poet)* firmament *(liter).*

Firmen-: **~inhaber** *m* owner of a/the company; **~name** *m* company name; **~register** *nt* register of companies; **~schild** *nt* company sign; **~verzeichnis** *nt* trade directory; **~wagen** *m* company car; **~zeichen** *nt* trademark.

firmieren* *vi*: **als ... ~** *(Comm, fig)* to trade under the name of ...

Firmung *f* *(Rel)* confirmation. **jdm die ~ erteilen** to confirm sb.

First *m* **-e** *(Dach~)* (roof) ridge.

Fis *nt* **-** *(Mus)* F sharp. **in ~/f~** in F sharp major/minor.

Fisch *m* **-e (a)** fish. **~e/drei ~e fangen** to catch fish/three fish(es); **das sind kleine ~e** *(fig col)* that's child's play *(col)*; **ein großer ~** *(fig col)* a big fish; **ein kleiner ~** one of the small fry; **sich wohl fühlen wie ein ~ im Wasser** to be in one's element; **stumm wie ein ~ sein** to be as silent as a post; **weder ~ noch Fleisch** neither fish nor fowl. **(b)** **~e** *pl* *(Astrol)* Pisces.

Fisch- *in cpds* fish; **~becken** *nt* fishpond; **~bestand** *m* fish population; **~dampfer** *m* trawler.

fischen *vti* *(lit, fig)* to fish. **mit (dem) Netz ~ to** trawl; **Heringe ~** to fish for herring.

Fischer *m* **-** fisherman.

Fischer-: **~boot** *nt* fishing boat; **~dorf** *nt* fishing village.

Fischerei *f* **(a)** fishing. **(b)** *(~gewerbe)* fishing industry, fisheries *pl.*

Fischerei- *in cpds* fishing; **~grenze** *f* fishing limit.

Fischernetz *nt* fishing net.

Fischfang *m* *no pl* **vom ~ leben** to live by fishing; **zum ~ auslaufen** to set off for the fishing grounds.

Fischfanggebiet *nt* fishing grounds *pl.*

Fisch-: **~filet** *nt* fish fillet; **~frikadelle** *f* fishcake; **~geruch** *m* smell of fish, fishy smell; **~geschäft** *nt* fishmonger; **~gräte** *f* fish bone; **~grätenmuster** *nt* herringbone (pattern); **~gründe** *pl* fishing grounds *pl*, fisheries *pl*; **~händler** *m* fishmonger; *(Großhändler)* fish merchant; **~konserve** *f* canned fish; **~kutter** *m* fishing cutter; **~laden** *m* fishmonger; **~markt** *m* fish market; **~mehl** *nt* fish meal; **~otter** *m* otter; **~schuppe** *f* (fish) scale; **~schwarm** *m* shoal of fish; **~stäbchen** *nt* fish finger *(Brit)*, fish stick *(US)*; **~sterben** *nt* death of fish; **~zucht** *f* fish-farming; **~zug** *m* *(fig: Beutezug)* raid, foray.

Fisimatenten *pl* *(col)* *(Ausflüchte)* excuses *pl*; *(Umstände)* fuss; *(Albernheiten)* nonsense.

Fiskus *m* *no pl* *(fig: Staatskasse)* Treasury.

Fistelstimme *f* falsetto.

fit *adj* *pred* fit. **sich ~ halten** to keep fit.

Fitness, Fitneß *f* *no pl* physical fitness.

Fittich *m* **-e** *(liter)* wing. **jdn unter seine ~e nehmen** *(hum)* to take sb under one's wing.

Fitzelchen *nt* *(col)* little bit.

fix *adj* **(a)** *(col: flink)* quick. **mach ~!** look lively! **(b)** *(col)* **~ und fertig sein** to be all finished; *(bereit)* to be all ready; *(erschöpft, emotional)* to be shattered *(col)*; **jdn ~ und fertig machen** *(nervös machen)* to drive sb mad; *(erschöpfen, emotional)* to shatter sb *(col)*. **(c)** **~e Idee** obsession.

fixen *vi* *(col: Drogen spritzen)* to fix *(col).*

Fixer(in *f)* *m* **-** *(col)* fixer *(col).*

Fixierbad *nt* *(Phot)* fixer.

fixieren* *vt* **(a)** *(anstarren)* **jdn/etw ~** to stare at sb/sth. **(b)** *(festlegen)* to specify; *(schriftlich niederlegen)* to record. **er ist zu stark auf seine Mutter fixiert** *(Psych)* he has a mother fixation. **(c)** *(Phot)* to fix.

Fixierung *f* *(Festlegung)* *siehe* *vt* **(b)** specification; recording; *(Psych)* fixation.

Fix-: **~kosten** *pl* fixed costs *pl*; **~stern** *m* fixed star.

Fixum *nt*, *pl* **Fixa** basic salary.

FKK [efka:'ka:] *no art* = **Freikörperkultur.**

FKK-: **~Anhänger** *m* **~-Anhänger sein** to be a nudist; **~-Strand** *m* nudist beach.

flach *adj* **(a)** flat; *Gebäude* low; *Abhang* gentle; *Gewässer* shallow. **~ liegen** to lie flat; **die ~e Hand** the flat of one's hand; **eine ~e Brust** a hollow chest; *(Busen)* a flat chest; **auf dem ~en Land** in the middle of the country. **(b)** *(fig)* flat; *Geschmack* insipid; *(oberflächlich)* shallow. **~ atmen** to take shallow breaths.

Flachdach *nt* flat roof.

Fläche *f* **-n** *(auch Math)* area; *(Ober~)* surface; *(Gelände, Land~, Wasser~)* expanse.

Flächen-: **~brand** *m* extensive fire; **sich zu einem ~brand ausweiten** *(fig)* to spread to epidemic proportions; **~inhalt** *m* area; **~maß** *nt* square measure.

Flach-: **f~fallen** *vi* *sep* *irreg* *aux* *sein* *(col)* not to come off; *(Regelung)* to end; **~land** *nt* lowland; **f~liegen** *vi* *sep* *irreg* *(col)* to be laid up; **~mann** *m*, *pl* **~männer** *(col)* hipflask.

Flachs [flaks] *m* *no pl* **(a)** *(Bot, Tex)* flax. **(b)** *(col: Neckerei, Witzelei)* kidding *(col).*

flachsen ['flaksn] vi (col) to kid around (col).
Flachzange f flat-nosed pliers pl.
flackern vi (lit, fig) to flicker.
Fladen m - (a) (Cook) round flat dough-cake. (b) (col: Kuh~) cowpat.
Fladenbrot nt round flat loaf.
Flagge f -n flag. die ~ streichen (fig) to capitulate; ~ zeigen to nail one's colours (Brit) or colors (US) to the mast.
flaggen vi geflaggt haben to fly flags/a flag.
Flaggenmast m flagpole.
Flagg-: ~offizier m flag officer; ~schiff nt (lit, fig) flagship.
flagrant adj flagrant; siehe in flagranti.
Flair [flɛː] nt no pl (geh) atmosphere; (Nimbus) aura.
Flak f - or -s = Flug(zeug)abwehrkanone anti-aircraft gun; (Einheit) anti-aircraft unit.
Flakon [fla'kõː] nt or m -s bottle, flacon.
flambieren* vt (Cook) to flambé.
Flame m (wk) -n, -n, **Flämin** f Fleming.
Flamingo [fla'mɪŋgo] m -s flamingo.
flämisch adj Flemish.
Flämisch(e) nt Flemish; siehe Deutsch(e).
Flamme f -n (lit, fig) flame. in ~n stehen/ aufgehen to be in flames/go up in flames.
flammend adj fiery. mit ~em Gesicht blazing.
flammendrot adj (geh) flame red, blazing red.
Flammen-: ~meer nt sea of flames; ~werfer m flame-thrower.
Flandern nt Flanders sing.
Flanell m -e flannel.
flanieren* vi to stroll, to saunter.
Flanke f -n (Anat, Mil) flank; (Sport) (Turnen) flank-vault; (Ftbl) cross; (Spielfeldseite) wing.
flanken vi (Ftbl) to centre (Brit), to center (US).
Flanken-: ~angriff m (Mil) flank attack; ~ball m (Ftbl) cross; ~deckung f (Mil) flank defence (Brit) or defense (US).
flankieren* vt (Mil, fig) to flank. ~de Maßnahmen supporting measures.
Flansch m -e flange.
Flasche f -n (a) bottle. mit der ~ aufziehen to bottle-feed; eine ~ Wein/Bier a bottle of wine/ beer; zur ~ greifen (fig) to hit the bottle. (b) (col: Versager) dead loss (col).
Flaschen-: ~bier nt bottled beer; f~grün adj bottle-green; ~hals m neck of a bottle; (fig) bottleneck; ~kind nt bottle-fed baby; ~milch f bottled milk; ~öffner m bottle-opener; ~pfand nt deposit on a/the bottle; ~post f message in a/the bottle; per ~post in a bottle; ~zug m block and tackle.
Flatter-: f~haft adj fickle; ~haftigkeit f fickleness.
flatt(e)rig adj fluttery; Puls fluttering.
flattern vi (lit, fig) to flutter; (mit den Flügeln schlagen) to flap its wings; (Fahne, Segel) to flap; (Haar) to fly; (col: Mensch) to be in a flap (col). ein Brief flatterte mir auf den Schreibtisch a letter arrived on my desk.
flau adj (a) Brise, Wind slack. (b) Stimmung flat. (c) (übel) queasy; (vor Hunger) faint. mir ist ~ (im Magen) I feel queasy. (d) (Comm) slack. in meiner Kasse sieht es ~ aus (col) my finances aren't too healthy (col).
Flaum m no pl fluff, down.
Flaum-: ~bart m downy beard, bum-fluff (col) no indef art; ~feder f down feather.
flaumig adj downy.
flauschig adj fleecy; (weich) soft.
Flausen pl (col) (a) (Unsinn) nonsense; (Illusionen) fancy ideas pl (col). ~ im Kopf haben to have fancy ideas. (b) (Ausflüchte) excuses pl.
Flaute f -n (a) (Naut) calm. das Schiff geriet in eine ~ the ship was becalmed. (b) (fig) slack period.
fläzen vr (col) to sprawl (in+acc in).

Flechte f -n (Bot, Med) lichen.
flechten pret flocht, ptp geflochten vt Haar to plait; Kranz, Korb to weave.
Flechtwerk nt = Geflecht.
Fleck m -e or -en (a) (Schmutz~) mark. dieses Zeug macht ~en this stuff stains (in/auf etw (acc) sth); einen ~ auf der Weste haben (fig) to have blotted one's copybook. (b) (Farb~) patch. (c) (Stelle) spot, place. auf demselben ~ in the same place; sich nicht vom ~ rühren not to budge; nicht vom ~ kommen not to get any further; vom ~ weg on the spot.
Fleckchen nt ein schönes ~ (Erde) a lovely little spot.
Flecken m - (a) (old: Markt~) small town. (b) = Fleck (a, b).
fleckenlos adj (lit, fig) spotless.
Fleckenwasser nt stain-remover.
Fleckfieber nt typhus fever.
fleckig adj marked; Obst blemished; Tierfell speckled; Gesichtshaut blotchy.
Fledermaus f bat.
Flegel m - (Lümmel) lout, yob (col); (Kind) brat (col).
Flegel|alter nt awkward adolescent phase.
Flegelei f uncouthness no pl.
Flegel-: f~haft adj uncouth; ~haftigkeit f uncouthness; ~jahre pl = ~alter.
flegeln vr to loll, to sprawl.
flehen vi (geh) to plead (um+acc for, zu with).
flehentlich adj imploring, pleading. jdn ~ bitten to plead with sb.
Fleisch nt no pl (a) flesh. vom ~ fallen (col) to lose (a lot of) weight; sich (dat or acc) ins eigene ~ schneiden to cut off one's nose to spite one's face (prov); sein eigen ~ und Blut (liter) his own flesh and blood; jdm in ~ und Blut übergehen to become second nature to sb. (b) (Nahrungsmittel) meat; (Frucht~) flesh.
Fleisch- in cpds (Cook) meat; (Anat) flesh; ~beschau f (a) meat inspection; (b) (hum col) cattle market (col); ~beschauer(in f) m meat inspector; ~brocken m lump of meat; ~brühe f meat stock; (Gericht) bouillon.
Fleischer m - butcher.
Fleischerei f butcher.
Fleischer-: ~haken m meat hook; ~handwerk nt butcher's trade; ~hund m (lit) butcher's dog; (fig) brute of a dog; ein Gemüt wie ein ~hund haben (col) to be a callous brute; ~laden m butcher's (shop); ~messer nt butcher's knife.
Fleisch-: f~farben, f~farbig adj flesh-coloured (Brit), flesh-colored (US); f~fressend adj carnivorous; ~fresser m (Zool) carnivore.
fleischig adj fleshy.
Fleisch-: ~käse m meat loaf; ~klopfer m steak hammer; ~kloß m, ~klößchen nt (a) meat ball; (b) (pej col) mountain of flesh; f~lich adj attr Kost meat; (old liter: Begierden) carnal; f~los adj (a) (ohne Fleisch) meatless; Kost, Ernährung vegetarian; f~los essen/kochen to eat no meat/to cook without meat; (b) (fig: mager) thin, lean; ~saft m meat juices pl; ~salat m diced meat salad with mayonnaise; f~verarbeitend adj attr meat-processing; ~vergiftung f food poisoning (from meat); ~waren pl meat products pl; ~wolf m mincer, meat grinder (esp US); ~wunde f flesh wound; ~wurst f pork sausage.
Fleiß m no pl industriousness. ~ aufwenden to apply oneself; mit ~ kann es jeder zu etwas bringen anybody can succeed if he works hard; mit ~ bei der Sache sein to work hard; ohne ~ kein Preis (Prov) success never comes easily.
fleißig adj hard-working no adv, industrious; Sammler keen. ~ studieren/arbeiten to study/ work hard; ~ wie die Bienen sein to work like beavers; ein ~er Arbeiter a hard worker.
flennen vi (pej col) to blubb(er).

fletschen *vti:* **die Zähne ~** to bare one's teeth.

flexibel *adj (lit, fig)* flexible.

Flexibilität *f* flexibility.

flicken *vt* to mend; *(mit Flicken)* to patch.

Flicken *m* - patch. **eine Jacke mit ~** a patched jacket.

Flick-: ~schuster *m (old)* cobbler; *(fig pej)* bungler *(col);* **~schusterei** *f* **das ist ~schusterei** *(fig pej)* that's a patch-up job; **~werk** *nt* **die Reform war reinstes ~werk** the reform had been carried out piecemeal; **~zeug** *nt (Nähzeug)* sewing kit; *(für Reifen)* (puncture) repair outfit.

Flieder *m* - lilac.

flieder-: ~farben, ~farbig *adj* lilac.

Fliege *f* **-n (a)** fly. **sie fielen um wie die ~n** they were dropping like flies; **sie starben wie die ~n** they fell like flies; **er tut keiner ~ etwas zuleide** *(fig)* he wouldn't hurt a fly; **zwei ~n mit einer Klappe schlagen** *(prov)* to kill two birds with one stone *(prov);* **ihn stört die ~ an der Wand** every little thing irritates him; **die** *or* **'ne ~ machen** *(col)* to beat it *(col).* **(b)** *(Schlips)* bow tie.

fliegen *pret* **flog,** *ptp* **geflogen 1** *vi aux sein* to fly. **nach Köln fliegt man zwei Stunden** it's a two-hour flight to Cologne; **ich kann doch nicht ~!** I haven't got wings *(col);* **auf jdn/etw ~** *(col)* to be mad about sb/sth *(col);* **von der Leiter ~** *(col)* to fall off the ladder; **durchs Examen ~** *(col)* to fail one's exam; **aus der Firma ~** *(col)* to get the sack *(col);* **~der Puls** racing pulse; **geflogen kommen** to come flying; **in den Papierkorb ~** to go into the wastepaper basket; **ein Schuh flog ihm an den Kopf** he had a shoe flung at him; **aus der Kurve ~** to skid off the bend. **2** *vt* to fly.

fliegend *adj attr* Fische, Untertasse, Start flying. **in ~er Eile** in a tremendous hurry; **~e Hitze** hot flushes *pl.*

Fliegen-: ~draht *m* wire mesh; **~fänger** *m (Klebestreifen)* fly-paper; **~fenster** *nt* wire-mesh window; **~gewicht** *nt (Sport, fig)* flyweight; **~gewichtler** *m* - *(Sport)* flyweight; **~gitter** *nt* fly screen; **~klatsche** *f* fly-swat; **~pilz** *m* fly agaric.

Flieger *m* - airman; *(col: Flugzeug)* plane.

Flieger- (Mil): ~alarm *m* air-raid warning; **~angriff** *m* air-raid; **~horst** *m (Mil)* military airfield.

fliehen *pret* **floh,** *ptp* **geflohen** *vi* to flee; *(entkommen)* to escape *(aus* from*).* **vor jdm/der Polizei ~** to flee from sb/the police; **aus dem Lande ~** to flee the country.

fliehend *adj* Kinn receding; *Stirn* sloping.

Fliehkraft *f* centrifugal force.

Fliese *f* **-n** tile. **etw mit ~n auslegen** to tile sth.

Fließ-: ~arbeit *f* *no pl* production-line work; **~band** *nt* conveyor-belt; **am ~band arbeiten** to work on the assembly *or* production line.

fließen *pret* **floß,** *ptp* **geflossen** *vi* to flow; *(Fluß auch, Tränen)* to run. **es ist genug Blut geflossen** enough blood has been shed.

fließend *adj* flowing; Leitungswasser running; Verkehr moving; Übergang fluid. **sie spricht ~ Französisch** she speaks fluent French.

Fließ-: ~heck *nt* fastback; **~komma** *nt (Comp)* floating point.

Flimmer-: ~kasten *m,* **~kiste** *f (col)* box *(col).*

flimmern *vi* to shimmer; *(TV)* to flicker. **es flimmert mir vor den Augen** everything is swimming in front of my eyes.

flink *adj (geschickt)* nimble; *Zunge* quick. **ein bißchen ~** *(col)* get a move on!; **mit etw ~ bei der Hand sein** to be quick *(off the mark)* with sth.

Flinkheit *f siehe adj* nimbleness; quickness.

Flinte *f* **-n** *(Schrot~)* shotgun. **die ~ ins Korn werfen** *(fig)* to throw in the sponge.

Flipper *m* -, **Flipperautomat** *m* pinball machine.

flippern *vi* to play pinball.

Flirt [flœrt] *m* **-s** *(Flirten)* flirtation.

flirten ['flœrtn] *vi* to flirt.

Flittchen *nt* - *(pej col)* slut.

Flitter *m* - **(a)** *(~schmuck)* sequins *pl.* **(b)** *no pl (pej: Tand)* trumpery.

flittern *vi* to glitter, to sparkle.

Flitterwochen *pl* honeymoon *sing.* **in den ~ sein** to be on honeymoon.

flitzen *vi aux sein (col)* to whizz *(col),* to dash.

Flitzer *m* - *(col) (Fahrzeug)* sporty little job *(col); (Schnelläufer)* streak of lightning *(col).*

floaten ['flo:tn] *vti (Fin)* to float. **~ (lassen)** to float.

Flocke *f* **-n (a)** flake; *(Schaum~)* blob (of foam). **(b) ~n** *pl (col: Geld)* dough *(col).*

flockig *adj* fluffy.

flog *pret of* **fliegen.**

floh *pret of* **fliehen.**

Floh *m* **=e (a)** *(Zool)* flea. **es ist leichter, einen Sack ~e zu hüten, als ...** ... is absolutely impossible; **jdm einen ~ ins Ohr setzen** *(col)* to put an idea into sb's head. **(b)** *(col: Geld)* **~e** *pl* dough *(col).*

Flohmarkt *m* flea market.

Flor *m* **-e (a)** *(dünnes Gewebe)* gauze; *(Trauer~)* crêpe. **(b)** *(Teppich~)* pile.

Flora *f pl* **Floren** flora.

Florett *nt* **-e** *(Waffe)* foil.

florieren* *vi* to flourish, to bloom.

Florist(in *f)* *m (wk)* **-en, -en** florist.

Floskel *f* **-n** set phrase. **eine abgedroschene ~** a hackneyed phrase.

floskelhaft *adj* cliché-ridden, stereotyped.

floß *pret of* **fließen.**

Floß *nt* **-e** raft.

Flosse *f* **-n** *(Fisch~, Aviat)* fin; *(Wal~, Robben~, Taucher~)* flipper; *(col: Hand)* paw *(col).*

Flöte *f* **-n (a)** pipe; *(Quer~)* flute; *(Block~)* recorder; *(Pikkolo~)* piccolo. **(b)** *(Kelchglas)* flute glass. **(c)** *(Cards)* flush.

flöten *vti (Vogel, hum)* to warble.

Flöten-: ~gehen *vi sep aux sein (col)* to go for a burton *(col);* **~spieler** *m* piper; flautist; **~ton** *m* sound of flutes/a flute; **jdm die ~töne beibringen** *(col)* to teach sb what's what *(col).*

Flötist(in *f)* *m (wk)* **-en, -en** flautist; piccolo player.

flott *adj* **(a)** *(zügig)* Fahrt quick; Tempo brisk; Bedienung speedy *(col);* Tänzer good; *(flüssig)* Stil, Artikel racy *(col); (schwungvoll)* Musik lively; Auto sporty. **aber ein bißchen ~!** and look lively! **(b)** *(schick)* smart. **(c)** *(lebenslustig)* fun-loving, fast-living. **ein ~es Leben führen** to be a fast liver. **(d)** *pred* **wieder ~ werden** *(Schiff)* to be refloated; *(fig col) (Auto etc)* to get back on the road; *(Unternehmen)* to get back on its feet.

Flotte *f* **-n** *(Naut)* fleet.

Flotten-: ~basis *f,* **~stützpunkt** *m* naval base.

Fluch *m* **=e** curse. **ein ~ lastet auf diesem Haus** there is a curse on this house.

fluchen *vi* to curse *(auf* or *über jdn/etw (acc)* sb/sth*).*

Flucht *f* **-en (a)** *(Fliehen)* flight; *(geglückt auch)* escape. **die ~ ergreifen** to take flight; **ihm glückte die ~** he succeeded in escaping; **auf der ~ sein** to be fleeing; *(Dieb)* to be on the run; **jdn/etw in die ~ schlagen** to put sb/sth to flight; **die ~ nach vorn antreten** to take the bull by the horns. **(b)** *(Häuser~)* row. **(c)** *(Zimmer~)* suite.

flucht|artig *adj* hasty. **in ~er Eile** in great haste.

flüchten *vi* **(a)** *aux sein (davonlaufen)* to flee; *(erfolgreich auch)* to escape. **vor der Wirklichkeit ~** to escape reality. **(b)** *auch vr (vi: aux sein) (Schutz suchen)* to take refuge.

Flucht-: ~fahrzeug *nt* escape vehicle; *(von Dieb)* getaway vehicle; **~gefahr** *f* risk of escape; **~hilfe** *f* **~hilfe leisten** to aid an escape.

flüchtig *adj* **(a)** *(geflüchtet)* **~ sein** to be at large. **(b)** *(kurz)* fleeting. **(c)** *(oberflächlich)* cursory. **etw ~ lesen** to skim through sth; **jdn ~ kennen**

to have met sb briefly. **(d)** *(Chem)* volatile.
Flüchtigkeit *f* **(a)** *(Kürze)* briefness. **(b)** *(Oberflächlichkeit)* cursoriness. **(c)** *(Chem)* volatility.
Flüchtigkeitsfehler *m* careless mistake.
Flüchtling *m* refugee.
Flüchtlings- in *cpds* refugee; ~**hilfe** *f* aid to refugees; ~**lager** *nt* refugee camp.
Flucht-: ~**linie** *f* alignment; ~**punkt** *m* vanishing point; ~**verdacht** *m* **bei** ~**verdacht** if an attempt to abscond is thought likely; ~**versuch** *m* escape attempt; ~**weg** *m* escape route.
Flug *m* **-e** flight; *(Ski~)* jump. **im** ~**(e)** in the air; **einen** ~ **antreten** to take off *(nach for)*; **wie im** ~**(e)** *(fig)* in a flash; **die letzte Woche verging wie im** ~**(e)** last week flew past.
Flug-: ~**bahn** *f* flight path; *(von Rakete auch)* trajectory; *(Kreisbahn)* orbit; ~**begleiter(in** *f)* *m* steward/stewardess; **f**~**bereit** *adj* ready for take-off; ~**blatt** *nt* leaflet; ~**dauer** *f* flying time.
Flügel *m* **- (a)** wing; *(von Hubschrauber)* blade; *(Windmühlen~)* sail, vane; *(Altar~)* sidepiece; *(Fenster~)* casement; *(Mil)* flank. **einem Vogel/jdm die** ~ **stutzen** to clip a bird's/sb's wings. **(b)** *(Konzert~)* grand piano.
Flügel-: ~**schraube** *f* wing bolt; ~**stürmer** *m* *(Sport)* wing forward; ~**tür** *f* double door.
Flug-: **f**~**fähig** *adj* able to fly; *Flugzeug (in Ordnung)* airworthy; ~**gast** *m* (airline) passenger.
flügge *adj* fully-fledged; *(fig) Jugendlicher* independent. ~ **werden** *(lit)* to be able to fly; *(fig)* to leave the nest.
Flug-: ~**gelände** *nt* airfield; ~**gesellschaft** *f* airline; ~**hafen** *m* airport; ~**höhe** *f* flying height, altitude; **unsere** ~**höhe beträgt 10.000 Meter** we are flying at an altitude of 10,000 metres; ~**kapitän** *m* captain; ~**karte** *f* (Ticket) plane ticket; ~**körper** *m* projectile; ~**leitung** *f* air-traffic *or* flight control; ~**linie** *f* (a) *(Strecke)* air route; **(b)** *(~gesellschaft)* airline; ~**lotse** *m* air-traffic *or* flightcontroller; ~**minute** *f* 30~**minuten von hier** 30 minutes by air from here; ~**netz** *nt* network of air routes; ~**objekt** *nt:* **ein unbekanntes** ~**objekt** an unidentified flying object, a UFO; ~**personal** *nt* flight personnel *pl*; ~**plan** *m* flight schedule; ~**platz** *m* airfield; *(größer)* airport; ~**preis** *m* air fare; ~**reise** *f* (flight); **eine** ~**reise machen** to travel by air; ~**reisende(r)** *mf* (airline) passenger; ~**route** *f* air-route.
flugs [fluːks] *adv* *(dated)* without delay, speedily.
Flug-: ~**sand** *m* drifting sand; ~**schanze** *f* (Sport) ski-jump; ~**schein** *m* **(a)** pilot's licence *(Brit)* or license *(US)*; **(b)** *(~karte)* air ticket; ~**schreiber** *m* flight recorder; ~**schrift** *f* pamphlet; ~**sicherung** *f* air traffic control; ~**steig** *m* gate; ~**stunde** *f* (a) flying hour; **zehn** ~**stunden entfernt** ten hours away by air; **(b)** *(Unterricht)* flying lesson; **f**~**technisch** *adj* aeronautical; *Erfahrung, Fehler* flying *attr*; **f**~**tüchtig** *adj* airworthy; ~**verbindung** *f* air connection; ~**wesen** *nt no pl* aviation *no art*; ~**zeit** *f* flying time.
Flugzeug *nt* **-e** plane, aircraft, aeroplane *(Brit)*, airplane *(US)*.
Flugzeug- in *cpds* aircraft; ~**absturz** *m* plane or air crash; ~**besatzung** *f* aircrew; ~**entführer** *m* hijacker; ~**entführung** *f* hijacking; ~**führer** *m* (aircraft) pilot; ~**halle** *f* (aircraft) hangar; ~**katastrophe** *f* air disaster; ~**träger** *m* aircraft carrier; ~**unglück** *nt* plane *or* air crash.
fluktuieren* *vi* to fluctuate.
Flunder *f* **-n** flounder.
Flunkerei *f* *(col)* **(a)** *(no pl: Flunkern)* story-telling. **(b)** *(kleine Lüge)* story.
flunkern *(col)* **1** *vi* to tell stories. **2** *vt* to make up.
Flunsch *m* **-e** *(col)* pout. **einen** ~ **ziehen** to pout.
Fluor *nt no pl (Chem)* fluorine; *(~verbindung)* fluoride.
Flur¹ *m* **-e** corridor; *(in Privathaus)* hall; *(oben in Privathaus)* landing.

Flur² *f* **-en** *(geh)* open fields *pl*. **durch Wald/Feld und** ~ through woods/fields and meadows; **allein auf weiter** ~ **stehen** *(fig)* to be out on a limb.
Fluß *m* **¨sse (a)** river. **unten am** ~ down by the river(side). **(b)** *(von Verkehr, Rede, Strom)* flow. **etw in** ~ *(acc)* **bringen** to get sth moving; **im** ~ **sein** *(sich verändern)* to be in a state of flux; *(im Gange sein)* to be in progress.
Fluß- in *cpds* river; **f**~**ab(wärts)** *adv* downstream, downriver; **f**~**aufwärts** *adv* upstream, upriver; ~**diagramm** *nt* flow chart.
flüssig *adj* **(a)** liquid; *Honig, Lack* runny; *Glas, Metall auch* molten. **(b)** *Stil, Spiel* flowing, fluid. ~ **lesen** to read fluently; **den Verkehr** ~ **halten** to keep the traffic flowing. **(c)** *Geld* available. ~**es Vermögen** liquid assets *pl*; **Wertpapiere** ~ **machen** to realize securities; **ich bin im Moment nicht** ~ *(col)* I'm out of funds at the moment.
Flüssigkeit *f* (a) liquid; *(esp Anat)* fluid. **(b)** *no pl (von Metall)* liquidity; *(von Geldern)* availability; *(von Stil)* fluidity.
flüssigmachen *vt sep* to realize.
Fluß-: ~**lauf** *m* course of a/the river; ~**mündung** *f* estuary; ~**pferd** *nt* hippopotamus.
flüstern *vti* to whisper. **das kann ich dir** ~ *(col)* take it from me *(col)*; **dem werde ich was** ~ *(col)* I'll tell him a thing or two *(col)*.
Flüster-: ~**propaganda** *f* underground rumours *pl (Brit)* or rumors *pl (US)*; ~**stimme** *f* whisper; ~**ton** *m* whisper; **sich im** ~**ton unterhalten** to talk in whispers.
Flut *f* **-en (a)** incoming *or* flood tide; *(Zustand)* high tide. **die** ~ **kommt** the tide's coming in; **die** ~ **geht zurück** the tide has started to go out. **(b)** *usu pl (Wassermasse)* waters *pl*. **(c)** *(fig: Menge)* flood. **eine** ~ **von Tränen** floods of tears.
fluten *vi aux sein (geh: lit, fig)* to flood.
Flut-: ~**licht** *nt* floodlight; ~**mündung** *f* estuary.
flutschen *vi (col)* **(a)** *aux sein (rutschen)* to slide. **(b)** *(funktionieren)* to go well.
Flutwelle *f* tidal wave.
Föderation *f* federation.
föderativ *adj* federal.
Fohlen *nt* **- foal; *(männlich auch)* colt; *(weiblich auch)* filly.
Föhn *m* **-e** *warm dry Alpine wind*, foehn.
Föhre *f* **-n** Scots pine (tree).
Folge *f* **-n (a)** sequence; *(Cards auch)* run; *(Fortsetzung)* instalment *(Brit)*, installment *(US)*; *(TV, Rad)* episode. **in rascher** ~ in quick succession; **in der** *or* **für die** ~ *(form)* in future. **(b)** *(Ergebnis)* consequence. **dies hatte seine Entlassung zur** ~ this resulted in his dismissal; **die** ~**n werden nicht ausbleiben** there will be repercussions. **(c)** *(form)* **einem Befehl/einer Einladung** ~ **leisten** to obey an order/to accept an invitation.
Folge|erscheinung *f* result, consequence.
folgen *vi* **(a)** *aux sein* to follow *(jdm/einer Sache sb/sth)*. **auf jdn (im Rang)** ~ to come after sb; ~ **Sie mir (bitte)!** come with me please; **wie folgt** as follows; **daraus folgt, daß ...** it follows from this that ...; **können Sie mir** ~? do you follow (me)? **(b)** *(gehorchen)* to obey.
folgend *adj* following. ~**es** the following; **im** ~**en** in the following; *(schriftlich auch)* below.
folgendermaßen *adv* like this, as follows.
folgen-: ~**los** *adj* without consequences; **das konnte nicht** ~**los bleiben** that was bound to have serious consequences; ~**schwer** *adj* serious; **die Maßnahme erwies sich als** ~**schwer** the measure had serious consequences.
Folge-: **f**~**richtig** *adj* (logically) consistent; ~**richtigkeit** *f* logical consistency.
folgern *vti* to conclude. **daraus läßt sich** ~, **daß ...** we can conclude from this that ...
Folgerung *f* conclusion.
Folgezeit *f* following period.

folglich adv, conj consequently, therefore.
folgsam adj obedient.
Folgsamkeit f obedience.
Folie ['fo:liə] f (Plastik~) film; (Metall~) foil.
Folklore f no pl folklore; (Volksmusik) folk music.
folkloristisch adj folkloric; Kleidung ethnic.
Folter f -n (lit,fig) torture. jdn auf die ~ spannen (fig) to keep sb on tenterhooks.
Folterbank f rack.
Folterer m - torturer.
foltern 1 vt to torture; (quälen auch) to torment. **2** vi to use torture.
Folterung f torture.
Fön ® m -e hair-dryer.
Fond [fõ:] m -s (a) (geh: Wagen~) back. (b) (Hintergrund) background. (c) (Cook: Fleischsaft) meat juices pl.
Fonds [fõ:] m - (a) (lit,fig) fund. (b) (Fin: Schuldverschreibung) government bond.
fönen vt to dry (with a hair-dryer).
Fontäne f -n jet (of water).
foppen vt (col) jdn ~ (necken) to pull sb's leg (col).
forcieren* [fɔr'si:rən] vt to push; Tempo to force; Konsum, Produktion to push or force up.
forciert [fɔr'si:ɐt] adj forced.
Förder-: ~anlage f conveyor; ~band nt conveyor belt.
Förderer m -, **Förderin** f sponsor; (Gönner) patron.
Förder-: ~korb m (Min) cage; ~leistung f (Min) output.
förderlich adj beneficial (dat to). guten Beziehungen ~ sein to be conducive to good relations.
fordern 1 vt (a) (verlangen) to demand; Preis to ask; (in Aufrufen) to call for; (Anspruch erheben auf) to claim. viel von jdm ~ to ask or demand a lot of sb. (b) (fig: kosten) Opfer to claim. (c) (fig: herausfordern) to challenge. (d) (Sport) to make demands on. **2** vi to make demands.
fördern vt (a) (unterstützen) to support; (propagieren) to promote; (finanziell) bestimmtes Projekt to sponsor; jds Talent, Neigung to encourage, to foster; Verdauung to aid; Appetit to stimulate; Untersuchung, Wahrheitsfindung, Wachstum to further; Verbrauch to boost. jdn beruflich ~ to help sb in his career. (b) Bodenschätze to extract.
Förderturm m (Min) winding tower; (auf Bohrstelle) derrick.
Forderung f (a) (Verlangen) demand (nach for); (Lohn~ etc) claim; (in Aufrufen etc) call. eine ~ nach etw erheben to call for sth; jds ~ erfüllen to meet sb's demands/claim. (b) (Comm: Anspruch) claim (an+acc on). (c) (Herausforderung) challenge.
Förderung f (a) siehe fördern (a) support; promotion; sponsorship; encouragement; fostering; aid; stimulation; furtherance; boosting. (b) (Gewinnung) extraction.
Forelle f trout.
Form f -en (a) form; (Gestalt, Umriß) shape. in ~ von Dragees in the form of pills; seine ~ verlieren/aus der ~ geraten to lose its shape; einer Sache (dat) ~ ~ (und Gestalt) geben (lit,fig) to give sth shape; feste ~ annehmen (fig) to take shape; gewalttätige ~en annehmen (fig) to become violent. (b) (Umgangs~en) ~en pl manners pl; die ~ wahren to observe the proprieties; der ~ wegen for the sake of form; in aller ~ formally. (c) (Kondition) form. in ~ bleiben/kommen to keep/get (oneself) in shape; groß in ~ in great form. (d) (Gieß~) mould; (Kuchen~) baking tin (Brit) or pan (US); (Hut~, Schuh~) block.
formal adj formal; Besitzer, Grund technical.
Form|aldehyd m no pl formaldehyde.
Formalität f formality. alle ~en erledigen to go through all the formalities.
Format nt -e (a) format. (b) (Persönlichkeit)

stature. (c) (fig: Niveau) class (col), quality.
Formation f formation; (Gruppe) group.
Form-: f~bar adj (lit,fig) malleable; f~beständig adj f~beständig sein to hold its shape; ~blatt nt form.
Formel f -n formula; (von Eid etc) wording; (Floskel) set phrase. etw auf eine ~ bringen to reduce sth to a formula.
formelhaft adj Sprache, Stil stereotyped. ~ reden to talk in set phrases.
formell adj formal.
formen vt to form, to shape; Eisen to mould; Wörter to articulate.
formenreich adj with a great variety of forms.
Form-: ~fehler m irregularity; (gesellschaftlich) breach of etiquette; ~gebung f (geh) design.
formieren* 1 vt Truppen to draw up; Kolonne, Zug to form (into); (bilden) to form. **2** vr to form up.
Formierung f formation; (von Truppen) drawing-up.
förmlich adj (a) (formell) formal. (b) (regelrecht) positive.
Förmlichkeit f formality. bitte keine ~en! please don't stand on ceremony.
formlos adj (a) shapeless. (b) (zwanglos) informal, casual. (c) (Admin) Antrag unaccompanied by a form/any forms.
Form-: ~sache f formality; f~schön adj elegantly proportioned; ~schönheit f elegant proportions pl; ~tief nt loss of form; sich in einem ~tief befinden to be badly off form.
Formular nt -e form.
formulieren* vt to word, to phrase. ... wenn ich es mal so ~ darf ... if I might put it like that.
Formulierung f wording. eine bestimmte ~ a particular phrase.
Formung f (a) no pl (das Formen) forming, shaping; (von Eisen) moulding; (von Wörtern) articulation. (b) (Form) shape.
formvollendet adj perfect; Vase etc perfectly formed.
forsch adj dynamic.
forschen vi to search (nach for); (Forschung betreiben) to research (über+acc on or into).
forschend adj inquiring; (musternd) searching.
Forscher(in f) m - (a) researcher; (in Naturwissenschaften) research scientist. (b) (Forschungsreisender) explorer.
Forschung f research no pl. verschiedene ~en various studies; ~ und Lehre research and teaching.
Forschungs- in cpds research; ~auftrag m research assignment; ~reise f expedition; ~reisende(r) mf decl as adj explorer.
Forst m -e(n) forest.
Forst|amt nt forestry office.
Förster(in f) m - forest warden or ranger (US).
Forstwirtschaft f forestry.
Fort [fo:ɐ] nt -s fort.
fort adv (a) (weg) away; (verschwunden) gone. ~ mit ihm/damit! away with him/it!; er ist ~ he has left or gone; weit ~ far away. (b) (weiter) on. und so ~ and so on; in einem ~ incessantly.
fort- pref in cpds (weg) away; siehe weg-.
Fort-: f~begeben* vr sep irreg (geh) to depart; ~bestand m no pl continued existence; f~bestehen* vi sep irreg to continue to exist; f~bewegen* vtr sep to move; ~bewegung f no pl locomotion; f~bilden vt sep jdn/sich f~bilden to continue sb's/one's education; ~bildung f no pl further education; berufliche ~bildung further vocational training; f~bleiben vi sep irreg to stay away; ~bleiben nt no pl absence; f~bringen vt sep irreg to take away; (zur Reparatur, Reinigung etc) to take in; Brief, Paket etc to post; ~dauer f continuance, continuation; f~dauern vi sep to continue; f~dauernd **1** adj continuing; (in der Vergangenheit) continued; **2** adv constantly, con-

tinuously; **f~entwickeln*** *vtr sep* to develop; **~entwicklung** *f no pl* development; **f~fahren** *sep* 1 *vi aux sein* (a) *(wegfahren)* to go away; *(Fahrer)* to drive off; *(abfahren)* to leave, to go; *(einen Ausflug machen)* to go out; (b) *(weitermachen)* to continue; **f~fahren**, **etw zu tun** to continue doing sth *or* to do sth; 2 *vt Wagen* to drive away; **~fall** *m* discontinuance; **f~fallen** *vi sep irreg aux sein (ausgelassen werden)* to be omitted; *(Bedenken etc)* to vanish; *(Zuschuß etc)* to be discontinued; **f~führen** *vt sep* (a) *(fortsetzen)* to continue, to carry on; (b) *(wegführen)* to take away; **~führung** *f* continuation; **~gang** *m no pl* (a) *(Weggang)* departure *(aus* from*);* (b) *(Verlauf)* progress; **f~gehen** *vi sep aux sein* to go away, to leave; **f~geschritten** *adj* advanced; **er kam zu f~geschrittener Stunde** he came at a late hour; **~geschrittenenkurs(us)** *m* advanced course; **f~gesetzt** *adj* constant; **f~jagen** *sep* 1 *vt* to chase out *(aus, von* of*);* 2 *vi aux sein* to race off; **~kommen** *nt* (a) *(lit, fig)* progress; (b) *(Auskommen)* **sein ~kommen finden** to find a means of earning one's living; **f~lassen** *vt sep* (a) *(weggehen lassen)* **jdn f~lassen** to let sb go; (b) *(auslassen)* to leave out, to omit; **f~laufen** *vi sep irreg aux sein* to run away; **f~laufend** *adj Handlung* ongoing *no adv; Zahlungen* regular; *(andauernd)* continual; **f~laufend numeriert** consecutively numbered; **f~machen** *vr sep (col)* to clear out *(col);* **f~nehmen** *vt sep irreg* to take away *(jdm* from sb*);* **f~pflanzen** *vr sep (Mensch)* to reproduce; *(Schall, Licht)* to travel; **~pflanzung** *f no pl* reproduction; **f~räumen** *vt sep* to clear away; **f~reißen** *vt sep irreg* to tear away; *(Menge, Flut, Strom)* to sweep *or* carry away; *(fig)* to carry away; **jdn/etw mit sich f~reißen** *(lit)* to carry *or* sweep sb/sth along; *(fig)* to carry sb/sth away; **f~schaffen** *vt sep* to remove; **f~schenken** *vr sep (col)* to clear off *(aus* out of*) (col);* **f~schreiten** *vi sep irreg aux sein* to progress, to advance; *(Zeit)* to march on; *siehe* **f~geschritten; f~schreitend** *adj* progressive; *Alter, Wissenschaft* advancing.

Fortschritt *m* advance, progress *no pl.* **gute ~e machen** to make good progress; **dem ~ dienen** to further progress.

fortschrittlich *adj* progressive *(auch Pol); Mensch, Ideen auch* forward-looking.

Fort-: **f~setzen** *sep* 1 *vt* to continue; *(nach Unterbrechung auch)* to resume; 2 *vr (zeitlich)* to continue; *(räumlich)* to extend; **~setzung** *f* (a) continuation; *(nach Unterbrechung auch)* resumption; (b) *(Rad, TV)* episode; *(eines Romans)* instalment *(Brit),* installment *(US);* **„~setzung folgt"** "to be continued"; **~setzungsroman** *m* serialized novel; **f~stehlen** *vr sep irreg (geh)* to steal away; **f~währen** *vi sep (geh)* to continue, to persist; **f~während** *adj no pred* constant, continual; **f~wirken** *vi sep* to continue to have an effect; **f~ziehen** *sep irreg* 1 *vt* to pull away, to drag away; 2 *vi aux sein* to move on; (b) *(von einem Ort)* to move away *(aus* from*).*

Forum *nt, pl* **Foren** forum.

Forumsdiskussion *f* forum (discussion).

Fossil *nt* **-ien** *(pl)* fossil.

Foto *nt* **-s** photo(graph), snap(shot) *(col).* **ein ~ machen** to take a photo(graph).

Foto- *in cpds* photo; **~album** *nt* photograph album; **~amateur** *m* amateur photographer; **~apparat** *m* camera; **~atelier** *nt* (photographic) studio.

fotogen *adj* photogenic.

Fotograf *m* photographer.

Fotografie *f* (a) photography. (b) *(Bild)* photo(graph).

fotografieren* 1 *vt* to photograph, to take a photo(graph) of. **sich ~ lassen** to have one's photo(graph) taken. 2 *vi* to take photo(graph)s.

Fotografin *f* photographer.

fotografisch *adj* photographic.

Foto-: **~kopie** *f* photocopy; **~kopierer** *(col) m,* **~kopiergerät** *nt* photocopier; **f~kopieren*** *vt insep* to photocopy; **~labor** *nt* darkroom; **~modell** *nt* photographic model; **~reporter** *m* press photographer.

Foul [faul] *nt* **-s** *(Sport)* foul.

Foul|elfmeter ['faul-] *m (Ftbl)* penalty (kick).

foulen ['faulən] *vti (Sport)* to foul.

Foulspiel ['faul-] *nt (Sport)* foul play.

Fox *m* **-e** (a) fox-terrier. (b) *(auch* **~trott)** foxtrot.

Foyer [foa'je:] *nt* **-s** foyer; *(in Hotel auch)* lobby.

Fr. = **Frau** Mrs, Ms; *(unverheiratet)* Miss, Ms.

Fracht *f* **-en** freight *no pl; (von Flugzeug, Schiff auch)* cargo; *(~preis auch)* freightage *no pl.*

Frachtbrief *m* consignment note, waybill.

Frachter *m* - freighter.

Fracht-: **f~frei** *adj* carriage paid *or* free; **~gut** *nt* freight *no pl;* **~kosten** *pl* freight charges *pl;* **~raum** *m* hold; *(Ladefähigkeit)* cargo space; **~schiff** *nt* cargo ship, freighter.

Frack *m* **-e** tails *pl,* tail coat. **im ~** in tails.

Frack-: **~hemd** *nt* dress shirt; **~sausen** *nt:* **~sausen haben** *(col)* to be in a funk *(col);* **~weste** *f* waistcoat *(Brit) or* vest *(US) worn with tails;* **~zwang** *m* requirement to wear tails; **„~zwang"** "tails".

Frage *f* **-n** question. **eine ~ zu etw** a question on sth; **jdm eine ~ stellen** to ask sb a question; **auf eine dumme ~ bekommt man eine dumme Antwort** *(prov)* ask a silly question (get a silly answer) *(prov);* **das ist (doch sehr) die ~** that's (just) the question; **das ist die große ~** that's the sixty-four thousand dollar question *(col);* **das ist gar keine ~, das steht außer ~** there's no question about it; **ohne ~** without question *or* doubt; **in ~ kommen** to be possible; **sollte er für diese Stelle in ~ kommen, ...** if he should be considered for this post ...; **für jdn/etw nicht in ~ kommen** to be out of the question for sb/sth; **in ~ kommend** possible; *Bewerber* worth considering.

Fragebogen *m* questionnaire; *(Formular)* form.

fragen 1 *vti* to ask. **nach** *or* **wegen** *(col)* **jdm ~** to ask for sb; *(nach jds Befinden)* to ask after sb; **ich fragte sie nach den Kindern** I asked her how the children were doing; **nach Arbeit/Post ~** to ask whether there is/was any work/mail; **nach den Ursachen ~** to inquire as to the causes; **nach den Folgen ~** to care about the consequences; **wegen etw ~** to ask about sth; **das frage ich dich!** I could ask you the same; **da fragst du noch?** you still have to ask?; **frag nicht so dumm!** don't ask silly questions; **da fragst du mich zuviel** *(col)* I really couldn't say; **man wird ja wohl noch ~ dürfen** *(col)* I only asked *(col);* **wenn ich (mal) ~ darf?** if I might ask?; **ohne lange zu ~** without asking a lot of questions.

2 *vr* to wonder. **das/da frage ich mich** I wonder; **das frage ich mich auch** that's just what I was wondering; **es/man fragt sich, ob ...** it's questionable/one wonders whether ...; **da muß man sich ~, ob ...** you can't help wondering if ...

fragend *adj* questioning, inquiring.

Frager(in *f) m* - questioner.

Fragerei *f* questions *pl.*

Frage-: **~steller(in** *f) m* - questioner; *(Interviewer)* interviewer; **~stellung** *f* (a) formulation of a/the question; (b) *(Frage)* question; **~stunde** *f* *(Parl)* question time; **~zeichen** *nt* question mark *(auch fig);* **dastehen/dasitzen wie ein ~zeichen** *(col)* to slouch.

fraglich *adj* (a) doubtful, questionable. (b) *attr (betreffend)* in question.

fraglos *adv* undoubtedly, unquestionably.

Fragment *nt* fragment.

fragmentarisch adj fragmentary.
fragwürdig adj dubious.
Fragwürdigkeit f dubiousness.
Fraktion f (a) (Pol) = parliamentary or congressional (US) party; (Sondergruppe) group, faction. (b) (Chem) fraction.
Fraktions- in cpds (Pol) party; **f~los** adj independent; **~mitglied** nt member of a parliamentary etc party; **~sitzung** f party meeting; **~vorsitzende(r)** mf party whip; **~zwang** m requirement to follow the party whip.
Fraktur f (a) (Typ) Gothic print. **~ reden** (col) to be blunt. (b) (Med) fracture.
frank adv: **~ und frei** frankly, openly.
Franken¹ nt Franconia.
Franken² m - (Schweizer) **~** (Swiss) franc.
frankieren* vt to stamp; (mit Maschine) to frank.
Frankierung f franking.
franko adj inv (Comm) carriage paid; (von Postsendungen) post-free, postpaid.
Frankreich nt France.
Franse f -n (loose) thread; (von Haar) strand of hair. **~n** (als Besatz) fringe; (Pony) fringe (Brit), bangs pl (US).
Franzbranntwein m alcoholic liniment.
Franzose m -n Frenchman; French boy.
Französin f Frenchwoman; French girl.
französisch adj French. **die ~e** Schweiz French-speaking Switzerland; **~es** Bett divan bed; **sich (auf) ~ empfehlen** (col) to leave without saying good-bye/paying; siehe **deutsch**.
Französisch(e) nt decl as adj French; siehe **Deutsch(e)**.
frappant adj striking.
frappieren* vt (verblüffen) to astound.
Fräse f -n (Werkzeug) milling cutter; (für Holz) moulding cutter; (Boden~) rotary hoe.
fräsen vt to mill; Holz to mould.
fraß pret of **fressen**.
Fraß m -e (a) etw einem Tier zum **~ vorwerfen** to feed sth to an animal; **jdn den Kritikern zum ~ vorwerfen** to throw sb to the critics. (b) (pej col: Essen) muck (col) no indef art. (c) (Abfressen) **vom ~ befallen** eaten away.
Fratze f -n (Grimasse) grimace; (col: Gesicht) mug (col); (fig: Zerrbild) caricature. **jdm eine ~ schneiden** to pull or make a face at sb.
Frau f -en (a) woman; (Ehe~) wife. **jdn zur ~ haben** to be married to sb. (b) (Anrede, mit Namen) Mrs, Ms; (für eine unverheiratete ~) Miss, Ms. **~ Doktor** doctor.
Frauchen nt dim of **Frau** (col) (a) (Ehefrau) little woman. (b) (Herrin von Hund) mistress.
Frauen- in cpds women's; (einer bestimmten Frau) woman's; (Sport auch) ladies'; **~arbeit** f female labour (Brit) or labor (US); **~arzt** m gynaecologist (Brit), gynecologist (US); **~beruf** m career for women; **~bewegung** f feminist movement; **f~feindlich** adj anti-women pred; Mensch, Verhalten auch misogynous; **~heilkunde** f gynaecology (Brit), gynecology (US); **~held** m lady-killer; **~klinik** f gynaecological (Brit) or gynecological (US) clinic; **~kloster** nt convent; **~rechtlerin** f feminist; **f~rechtlerisch** adj feminist; **sich f~rechtlerisch betätigen** to be involved in women's rights or (in der heutigen Zeit auch) Women's Lib; **~zimmer** nt (old) woman; (hum, pej) female (col), broad (US col).
Fräulein nt - or -s (a) young lady. **ein altes** or **älteres ~** an elderly spinster. (b) (Anrede) Miss. (c) (Verkäuferin) assistant (Brit), sales clerk (US); (Kellnerin) waitress. **„~!" "Miss!";** das **~ vom Amt** (dated) the switchboard girl.
fraulich adj feminine; (reif) womanly no adv.
frech adj cheeky (esp Brit), fresh (esp US); Lüge bare-faced no adv. **~ wie Oskar sein** (col) to be a little monkey (col).
Frechdachs m (col) cheeky monkey (col).

Frechheit f (a) no pl impudence, cheek (esp Brit). **die ~ besitzen, zu ...** to have the impudence to ... (b) (Äußerung, Handlung) piece of cheek (esp Brit) or impudence. **sich** (dat) **einige ~en erlauben** to be a bit cheeky (esp Brit) or fresh (esp US).
Fregatte f frigate.
frei adj (a) free; Blick clear. **~e Hand haben** to have a free hand; **aus der ~en Hand zeichnen** to draw freehand; **jdm zur ~en Verfügung stehen** to be completely at sb's disposal; **aus ~en Stücken** or **~em Willen** of one's own free will; **~ nach ...** based on ...; **~ nach Goethe** (Zitat) to adapt a phrase of Goethe's; **ich bin so ~** (form) may I?; **von Kiel nach Hamburg hatten wir ~e Fahrt** we had a clear run from Kiel to Hamburg; **für etw ~e Fahrt geben** (fig) to give sth the go-ahead; **der Film ist ~ ab 16 (Jahren)** the film may be seen by people over (the age of) 16; **sich von etw ~ machen** to free onself from sth.
(b) Schriftsteller etc freelance; (nicht staatlich) private. **~er Beruf** independent profession; **als ~er Mitarbeiter arbeiten** to work freelance; **~er Markt** open market; **~e Marktwirtschaft** free market economy; **die ~e Wirtschaft** private enterprise.
(c) (ohne Hilfsmittel) Rede extemporary. **~ schwimmen** to swim unaided or on one's own; **~ in der Luft schweben** to hang in mid-air; **ein Vortrag in ~er Rede** a talk given without notes; **~ sprechen** to extemporize.
(d) (verfügbar) Mittel, Geld available; Zeit, Mensch free. **morgen/Mittwoch ist ~** tomorrow/Wednesday is a holiday; **einen Tag ~ nehmen/haben** to take/have a day off; **ist hier** or **ist dieser Platz noch ~?** is this seat free?; **„Zimmer ~"** "vacancies"; **eine Stelle wird ~** a position is becoming vacant; **einen Platz ~ machen** (aufstehen) to vacate a seat; **einen Platz für jdn ~ lassen** to leave a seat for sb.
(e) (offen) open. **unter ~em Himmel** in the open (air); **im ~en Raum** (Astron) in (outer) space; **eine Frage im ~en Raum stehenlassen** to leave a question hanging; **auf ~er Strecke** (Rail) between stations; (Aut) on the road.
(f) (unbekleidet) bare. **sich ~ machen** (beim Arzt) to take one's clothes off, to strip; **~ lassen** to leave bare.
Frei-: **f~bad** nt open-air swimming pool, lido; **f~bekommen*** vt sep irreg (a) jdn **f~bekommen** to get sb freed or released; (b) **einen Tag f~bekommen** to get a day off; **~berufler(in** f) m - self-employed person; **f~beruflich** adj self-employed; **~betrag** m tax allowance; **~brief** m (fig) licence (Brit), license (US).
Freie nt -n, no pl **im ~n** in the open (air).
Freier m - (a) (dated, hum) suitor. (b) (col: von Dirne) (prostitute's) client, john (US col).
Frei-: **~exemplar** nt free copy; **~flug** m free flight; **~frau** f baroness (by marriage); **~gabe** f siehe **~geben** release; lifting of controls (gen on); opening; passing; **f~geben** sep irreg 1 vt to release (an+acc to); Preise to lift controls on; Straße, Strecke to open; Film to pass; **etw zum Verkauf f~geben** to allow sth to be sold on the open market; **jdm den Weg f~geben** to let sb past; **2** vi jdm **f~geben** to give sb a holiday; **f~gebig** adj generous; **~gebigkeit** f generosity; **~gehege** nt open-air enclosure; **f~haben** vi sep irreg to have a free period; **~hafen** m free port; **eine Stunde f~haben** (Sch) to have a free period; **~hafen** m free port; **f~halten** sep irreg 1 vt (a) (nicht besetzen) to keep free or clear; (b) (reservieren) to keep, to save; (c) (bezahlen) to pay for; **sich von jdm f~halten lassen** to let sb pay for one; **2** vr **sich von etw f~halten** to avoid sth; von Verpflichtungen to keep oneself free of sth; **~handel** m free trade; **~handelszone** f free trade area; **f~händig** adj Zeichnung freehand; **f~händig radfahren** to ride

with no hands; f~**hängend** adj attr suspended.

Freiheit f freedom; (Pol auch) liberty; **in** ~ (dat) **sein** to be free; **jdn in** ~ **setzen** to set sb free; **jdm die** ~ **schenken** to give sb his/her etc freedom; **dichterische** ~ poetic licence (Brit) or license (US); **alle** ~**en haben**, to have all the freedom possible; **die** ~ **haben, etw zu tun** to be free or at liberty to do sth; **sich** (dat) **die** ~ **nehmen, etw zu tun** to take the liberty of doing sth.

freiheitlich adj liberal; Verfassung based on the principle of liberty; Demokratie free.

Freiheits-: ~**beraubung** f (Jur) wrongful deprivation of personal liberty; ~**bewegung** f liberation movement; ~**entzug** m imprisonment; ~**kampf** m fight for freedom; ~**kämpfer** m freedom-fighter; ~**rechte** pl civil rights and liberties pl; ~**statue** f Statue of Liberty; ~**strafe** f prison sentence.

Frei-: f~**heraus** adv candidly, frankly; ~**herr** m baron; ~**karte** f free or complimentary ticket; f~**kaufen** vt jdn/sich f~**kaufen** to buy sb's/one's freedom; f~**kommen** vi sep irreg aux sein (entkommen) to get out (aus of); (befreit werden) to be released or freed (aus, von from); ~**körper-kultur** f no pl nudism; f~**lassen** vt sep irreg to set free, to free; (aus Haft auch) to release; Hund to let off the lead; ~**lassung** f release; (von Sklaven) setting free; ~**lauf** m (Aut) neutral; (bei Fahrrad) freewheel; f~**laufen** vr sep irreg (Sport) to get free; f~**lebend** adj living free; f~**legen** vt sep to expose; Ruinen, Trümmer to uncover; ~**legung** f siehe vt exposure; uncovering.

freilich adv (a) (allerdings) admittedly. (b) (esp S Ger: natürlich) of course.

Freilicht- in cpds open-air; ~**bühne** f open-air theatre (Brit) or theater (US).

Frei-: f~**machen** sep 1 vt to stamp; (mit Frankiermaschine) to frank; 2 vi to take time off; **ich habe eine Woche f~gemacht** I took a week off; **3** vr to take time off; ~**maurer** m Mason, Freemason.

freimütig adj frank, honest.

Freimütigkeit f frankness, honesty.

Frei-: ~**raum** m (fig) freedom no art (zu for); **die Universität ist kein gesellschaftlicher** ~**raum** university isn't a social vacuum; f~**schaffend** adj attr freelance; ~**schaffende(r)** mf decl as adj freelance; ~**schärler** m - guerrilla; f~**setzen** vt sep to release; (euph) Arbeitskräfte to make redundant; (vorübergehend) to lay off; ~**setzung** f release; (euph) dismissal; (vorübergehend) laying off; f~**sprechen** vt sep irreg to acquit; **jdn von einem Verdacht f~sprechen** to clear sb of suspicion; ~**spruch** m acquittal; **es ergeht** ~**spruch** the verdict is "not guilty"; f~**stehen** vi sep irreg (a) **es steht jdm f~, etw zu tun** sb is free to do sth; **das steht Ihnen völlig f~** that is completely up to you; (b) (leerstehen) to stand empty; f~**stellen** vt sep (a) (anheimstellen) **jdm etw f~stellen** to leave sth (up) to sb; (b) (befreien) to exempt.

Freistil- in cpds freestyle.

Frei-: ~**stoß** m (Ftbl) free kick; ~**stunde** f free hour; (Sch) free period.

Freitag m Friday; for cpds siehe **Dienstag**.

freitags adv on Fridays.

Frei-: ~**tod** m suicide; f~**tragend** adj self-supporting; Brücke cantilever; ~**übung** f exercise; ~**umschlag** m stamped addressed envelope.

freiweg ['frai'vek] adv openly; (freiheraus) straight out, frankly.

Frei-: ~**wild** nt (fig) fair game; f~**willig** adj voluntary; Versicherung, Unterricht optional; **sich f~willig melden** to volunteer (zu, für for); ~**willige(r)** mf decl as adj volunteer; ~**zeichen** nt (Telec) ringing tone.

Freizeit f (a) free or leisure time. (b) (Zusammenkunft) weekend/holiday course.

Freizeit-: ~**gestaltung** f organization of one's leisure time; ~**kleidung** f casual clothes pl;

(Warengattung) leisurewear no pl.

Frei-: f~**zügig** adj (a) (reichlich) Gebrauch liberal; (b) (moralisch) permissive; ~**zügigkeit** f siehe adj (a) liberalness; (b) permissiveness; (c) (Orts-ungebundenheit) freedom of movement.

fremd adj (a) (unbekannt) strange; (ausländisch) foreign; Planeten other; Welt different. **jdm** ~ **sein** to be foreign or alien to sb; **es ist mir** ~, **wie** ... I don't understand how ...; **ich bin hier** ~ I'm a stranger here; **sich** (dat) ~ **werden** to become strangers; **sich** ~ **fühlen** to feel like a stranger. (b) (andern gehörig) someone else's; Bank, Firma different; (Comm, Pol) outside attr. **unter** ~**em Namen** under an assumed name; **in** ~**e Hände übergehen** to come under outside control.

Fremde f no pl (liter) **die** ~ foreign parts pl; **in die** ~ **gehen** to go to foreign parts.

Fremden-: ~**führer** m (tourist) guide; (Buch) guide(book); ~**legion** f Foreign Legion; ~**verkehr** m tourism no def art; ~**zimmer** nt guest room; „~**zimmer**" "rooms to let" (Brit), "rooms for rent" (US).

Fremde(r) mf decl as adj stranger; (Ausländer) foreigner; (Admin, Pol) alien; (Tourist) visitor.

Fremd-: f~**gehen** vi sep irreg aux sein (col) to be unfaithful; ~**körper** m foreign body; (fig) alien element; f~**ländisch** adj foreign no adv; (exotisch) exotic.

Fremdsprache f foreign language.

Fremdsprachen-: ~**korrespondentin** f bilingual secretary; ~**unterricht** m language teaching.

Fremd-: f~**sprachig** adj in a foreign language; f~**sprachlich** adj f~**sprachlicher Unterricht** (foreign) language teaching; ~**wort** nt foreign word; **Rücksichtnahme ist für ihn ein** ~**wort** (fig) he's never heard of the word consideration.

frenetisch adj frenetic, frenzied.

Frequenz f frequency; (Stärke) numbers pl.

Fressalien [-ion] pl (col) grub sing (col).

Fresse f -n (col!) (Mund) gob (col!); (Gesicht) mug (col). **die** ~ **halten** to shut one's face (col!).

fressen pret **fraß**, ptp **gefressen** 1 vi (a) to feed, to eat; (col!: Menschen) to eat; (gierig) to guzzle. **jdm aus der Hand** ~ (fig col) to eat out of sb's hand. (b) (zerstören) to eat away (an etw (dat) sth).

2 vt (Tier, col!: Mensch) to eat; (sich ernähren von) to feed on; (col!: gierig essen) to guzzle, to scoff; (col: verbrauchen) Benzin, Ersparnisse to eat up. **Kilometer** ~ f no pl (col) (übermäßiges Essen) guzzling; (Gefräßigkeit) gluttony. **ein Loch in den Geldbeutel** ~ to make a big hole in one's pocket; **ich habe dich zum F**~ **gern** (col) you're good enough to eat (col); **sie sah mich an, als ob sie mich** ~ **wollte** (col) she gave me a murderous look; **jdn/etw gefressen haben** (col) to have had one's fill of sb/sth; **jetzt hat er es endlich gefressen** (col) he's got it at last (col); **einen Narren an jdm/etw gefressen haben** to dote on sb/sth.

3 vr (a) (sich bohren) to eat one's way (in+acc into). (b) **sich voll/satt** ~ to gorge oneself.

Fressen nt - (a) no pl food; (col!) grub (col). (b) (Gelage) blow-out (col).

Fresser m - (Tier) eater; (col!: gieriger Mensch) pig (col), greedyguts (col).

Fresserei f no pl (col) (übermäßiges Essen) guzzling; (Gefräßigkeit) gluttony.

Freß-: ~**gier** f voraciousness; (pej: von Menschen) gluttony; ~**napf** m feeding bowl; ~**paket** nt (col) food parcel; ~**sucht** f (col) gluttony; (krankhaft) craving for food.

Frettchen nt ferret.

Freude f -n pleasure; (innig) joy (über+acc at). ~ **an etw** (dat) **haben** to get or derive pleasure from sth; ~ **am Leben haben** to enjoy life; **es ist mir eine** ~, **zu ...** it's a real pleasure for me to ...; **es macht ihnen keine/wenig** ~ they don't enjoy it (at all)/much; **jdm eine** ~ **machen** or **bereiten** to make sb happy; **zu meiner großen** ~ to my great delight; **aus Spaß an der** ~ *(col)* for the fun *or* hell *(col)* of it; **mit** ~**n** with pleasure.

Freuden-: ~**feuer** *nt* bonfire; ~**haus** *nt (dated, hum)* house of ill repute; ~**mädchen** *nt (dated, hum)* lady of easy virtue *(euph)*, prostitute; ~**tanz** *m* **einen** ~**tanz aufführen** to dance with joy; ~**taumel** *m* ecstasy.

freudestrahlend *adj no pred* beaming with delight.

freudig *adj* joyful; *(begeistert)* enthusiastic. **jdn** ~ **stimmen** to raise sb's spirits; **etw** ~ **erwarten** to look forward to sth with great pleasure; ~ **überrascht sein** to have a delightful surprise.

Freud-: **f**~**los** *adj* joyless, cheerless; ~**losigkeit** *f no pl* joylessness, cheerlessness.

freuen 1 *vr* **(a)** to be glad *or* pleased *(über +acc* about). **sich über ein Geschenk** ~ to be pleased with a present; **er freut sich sehr an seinen Kindern** his children give him a lot of pleasure; **sich mit jdm** ~ to share sb's happiness; **sich seines Lebens** ~ to enjoy life. **(b) sich auf jdn/ etw** ~ to look forward to seeing sb/to sth; **sich zu früh** ~ to get one's hopes up too soon. 2 *vt impers* to please. **es freut mich/ihn, daß ...** I'm/he's pleased *or* glad that ...; **es freut mich sehr, Ihre Bekanntschaft zu machen** *(form)* (I'm) pleased to meet you.

Freund *m* -**e** friend; *(Liebhaber)* boyfriend. **ein** ~ **der Kunst** an art-lover; **er ist kein** ~ **vieler Worte** he's a man of few words; **ich bin kein** ~ **von so etwas** I'm not one for that sort of thing.

Freundchen *nt (col)* my friend *(iro)*. ~! ~! watch it, my friend!

Freundeskreis *m* circle of friends.

Freundin *f* friend; *(Liebhaberin)* girlfriend.

freundlich *adj* **(a)** friendly *no adv; Wetter etc* pleasant; *Zimmer, Farben* cheerful; *(Fin, Comm: günstig)* favourable *(Brit)*, favorable *(US)*. **jdn** ~ **behandeln** to be friendly towards sb; **bitte recht** ~! smile please! **(b)** *(liebenswürdig)* kind *(zu* to). **würden Sie bitte so** ~ **sein und das tun?** would you be so kind as to do that?

freundlicherweise *adv* kindly.

Freundlichkeit *f* **(a)** *no pl siehe adj* friendliness; pleasantness; cheerfulness; favourableness. *(Brit)*, favorableness *(US)*. **würden Sie (wohl) die** ~ **haben, das zu tun?** would you be kind enough to do that? **(b)** *(Handlung, Gefälligkeit)* kindness. **jdm ein paar** ~**en sagen** to say a few kind words to sb.

Freundschaft *f* friendship. **in aller** ~ in all friendliness; **da hört die** ~ **auf** *(col)* friendship doesn't go that far.

freundschaftlich *adj* friendly *no adv.* **jdm** ~ **gesinnt sein** to feel friendly towards sb; **jdm** ~ **auf die Schulter klopfen** to give sb a friendly slap on the back.

Freundschafts-: ~**besuch** *m (Pol)* goodwill visit; ~**preis** *m* (special) price for a friend; ~**spiel** *nt (Sport)* friendly match, friendly; ~**vertrag** *m (Pol)* treaty of friendship.

Frevel *m* - *(geh)* sin *(gegen* against*)*; *(fig)* crime *(an+dat* against).

frevelhaft *adj (geh)* sinful; *Leichtsinn* wanton.

Frevler(in *f)* *m* - *(liter)* sinner.

Frieden *m* - peace. **im** ~ in peacetime; **im** ~ **leben** to live in peace; ~ **schließen** to make one's peace; *(Pol)* to make peace; ~ **stiften** to make peace; **jdn in** ~ **lassen** to leave sb in peace; **um des lieben** ~**s willen** *(col)* for the sake of peace and quiet; **ich traue dem** ~ **nicht** *(col)* something (fishy) is going on *(col)*.

Friedens- *in cpds* peace; ~**bemühung** *f usu pl* effort to achieve peace; ~**bewegung** *f* peace movement; ~**kämpfer** *m* peace campaigner; ~**nobelpreis** *m* Nobel peace prize; ~**pfeife** *f* peace-pipe; ~**politik** *f* policy of peace; ~**richter**

m justice of the peace, JP; ~**schluß** *m* peace agreement; ~**sicherung** *f* maintenance of peace; **Maßnahmen zur** ~ **sicherung** peacekeeping measures; ~**stifter** *m* peacemaker; ~**taube** *f* dove of peace; ~**truppen** *pl* peacekeeping forces *pl;* ~**vertrag** *m* peace treaty.

friedfertig *adj* peaceable.

Friedfertigkeit *f* peaceableness.

Friedhof *m* cemetery; *(Kirchhof)* graveyard.

friedlich *adj* peaceful; *(friedfertig) Mensch* peaceable; *Charakter, Art* placid. **etw auf** ~**em Wege lösen** to solve sth by peaceful means; **damit er endlich** ~ **ist** *(col)* to keep him happy; **nun sei doch endlich** ~! *(col)* give it a rest! *(col)*.

friedliebend *adj* peace-loving.

frieren *pret* **fror,** *ptp* **gefroren** 1 *vi* **(a)** *auch vt impers (sich kalt fühlen)* to be/get cold. **ich friere, es friert mich** I'm cold; **ich friere an den Zehen** my toes are/get cold. **(b)** *aux sein (gefrieren)* to freeze. 2 *vi impers* to freeze. **heute nacht hat es gefroren** it was below freezing last night.

Friese *m (wk)* -**n, -n, Friesin** *f* Fri(e)sian.

frigid(e) *adj* frigid.

Frikadelle *f (Cook)* rissole.

Frikassee *nt* -**s** *(Cook)* fricassee.

frisch *adj* **(a)** fresh; *(feucht) Farbe, Fleck* wet. ~**e** Eier new-laid eggs; ~ **gestrichen** newly painted; *(auf Schild)* wet paint; ~ **gewaschen** clean; **das Bett** ~ **beziehen** to change the bed; **sich** ~ **machen** to freshen up; **mit** ~**en Kräften** with renewed strength; **das ist mir noch** ~ **in Erinnerung** that is still fresh in my memory; **jdn auf** ~**er Tat ertappen** to catch sb red-handed *or* in the act. **(b)** *(munter) Wesen, Art* bright, cheery; *(gesund) Aussehen* fresh. ~ **und munter sein** *(col)* to be bright and cheery; ~ **gewagt ist halb gewonnen** *(Prov)* a good start is half the battle. **(c)** *(kühl)* cool, chilly; *Luft, Wind auch* fresh.

Frische *f no pl* **(a)** freshness. **in alter** ~ *(col)* as always. **(b)** *(Kühle)* coolness, chilliness; *(von Luft, Wind auch)* freshness.

Frisch-: **f**~**gebacken** *(col) Ehepaar* newly wed; ~**haltebeutel** *m* airtight bag; ~**luft** *f* fresh air; ~**milch** *f* fresh milk; ~**wasser** *nt* fresh water; **f**~**weg** *adv (munter)* straight out *(col)*.

Friseur *[fri'zøːɐ] m* hairdresser.

Friseursalon *m* hairdresser's *(Brit)*, hairdressing salon.

Friseuse *[fri'zøːzə] f* hairdresser.

Frisiercreme *f* haircream.

frisieren* 1 *vt* **(a)** **jdn** ~, **jdm das Haar** ~ to do sb's hair; **sie ist stets gut frisiert** her hair is always beautifully done. **(b)** *(col) Abrechnung* to fiddle; *Bericht* to doctor *(col)*. **die Bilanzen** ~ to cook the books *(col)*. **(c)** *Auto* to soup up *(col)*. 2 *vr* to do one's hair.

Frisier-: ~**spiegel** *m* dressing (table) mirror; ~**tisch** *m* dressing table.

Frisör *m* -**e, Frisöse** *f* -**n** hairdresser.

Frist *f* -**en** *(Zeitraum)* period; *(Zeitpunkt)* deadline *(zu* for*)*; *(bei Rechnung)* last date for payment. **eine** ~ **einhalten/verstreichen lassen** to meet a deadline/to let a deadline pass; *(bei Rechnung)* to pay/not to pay within the period stipulated; **innerhalb kürzester** ~ without delay; **jdm eine** ~ **von vier Tagen geben** to give sb four days grace.

fristen *vt* **ein kümmerliches Dasein** ~ to eke out a miserable existence; *(Partei, Institution)* to exist on the fringes.

Frist-: **f**~**gerecht** *adj* within the period stipulated; **f**~**los** *adj* without notice; **jdn f**~**los entlassen** to dismiss sb without notice; ~**verlängerung** *f* extension.

Frisur *f* hairstyle.

Friteuse *[fri'tøːzə] f* chip pan *(Brit)*, deep fat fryer.

fritieren* *vt* to (deep-)fry.

frivol *[fri'voːl] adj* frivolous; *(anzüglich) Witz, Bemerkung* risqué.

Frivolität [frivoli'tɛ:t] *f nɔ pl* frivolity; *(von Witz etc)* suggestiveness.

Frl. = **Fräulein** Miss, Ms.

froh *adj* happy; *(dankbar auch)* glad; *(erfreut auch)* glad, pleased. **über etw** *(ɔcc)* ~ **sein** to be pleased with sth; **um etw** ~ **sein** to be grateful for sth; **seines Lebens nicht (mehr)** ~ **werden** not to enjoy life any more.

frohgestimmt *adj (geh)* happy, joyful *(liter)*.

fröhlich 1 *adj* cheerful, merry. **2** *adv (unbekümmert)* blithely, gaily.

Fröhlichkeit *f no pl* happiness; *(gesellige Stimmung)* merriment, gaiety.

Froh-: f~locken* *vi (geh)* to rejoice *(über +acc over, at)*; ~**sinn** *m no pl* cheerfulness; **f~sinnig** *adj* cheerful.

fromm *adj* **(a)** *(gläubig)* religious; Christ, Leben devout, pious; *(scheinfeilig)* sanctimonious. **(b)** *(old: gehorsam)* docile. ~ **wie ein Lamm sein** to be as gentle as a lamb.

Frömmelei *f (pej)* false piety.

Frömmigkeit *f siehe* **fromm (a)** religiousness; devoutness, piousness; sanctimoniousness.

frönen *vi+dat (geh)* to indulge in.

Fronleichnam *no art ro pl* Corpus Christi.

Front *f* **-en** front. **die hintere/rückwärtige** ~ the back/the rear; **auf breiter** ~ along a wide front; **an der** ~ at the front; **klare** ~**en schaffen** *(fig)* to clarify the position; ~ **gegen jdn/etw machen** to make a stand against sb/sth; **in** ~ **liegen/gehen** *(Sport)* to be in/take the lead.

frontal 1 *adj no pred* frontal; Zusammenstoß head-on. **2** *adv* frontally; zusammenstoßen head-on.

Front-: ~**antrieb** *m (Aut)* front-wheel drive; ~**motor** *m* front-mounted engine.

fror *pret of* **frieren**.

Frosch *m* **-e** frog. **einen** ~ **im Hals haben** *(col)* to have a frog in one's throat; **sei kein** ~! *(col)* be a sport!

Frosch-: ~**hüpfen** *ni* leapfrog; ~**mann** *m* frogman; ~**maul** *nt (fig col)* pout; ~**perspektive** *f etw* **aus der** ~**perspektive sehen** to get a worm's-eye view of sth; ~**schenkel** *m* frog's leg.

Frost *m* **-e (a)** frost. **bei eisigem** ~ in heavy frost; ~ **(ab)bekommen** *(Hände, Ohren)* to get frostbitten. **(b)** *(Med: Schüttel~)* fit of shivering.

Frost-: **f~beständig** *adj* frost-resistant; ~**beule** *f* chilblain.

frösteln 1 *vi* to shiver. **2** *vt impers* **es fröstelte mich** I shivered.

Fröster *m* - freezer

frostig *adj (lit, fig)* frosty.

Frost-: ~**schutz** *m* protection against frost; ~**schutzmittel** *nt (Aut)* antifreeze.

Frottee [frɔ'te:] *nt or m* **-s** terry towelling.

Frottee-: ~**(hand)tuch** *nt* (terry) towel; ~**kleid** *nt* towelling dress.

frottieren* *vt Haut* to rub; jdn, sich to rub down.

Frottier(hand)tuch *nt* (terry) towel.

Frotzelei *f (col)* teasing.

frotzeln *vti (col)* to tease. **über jdn** ~ to make fun of sb.

Frucht *f* **-e** *(Bot, fig)* fruit; *(Embryo)* foetus; *(no pl: Getreide)* crops *pl.* ~**e** *(Obst)* fruit *sing;* ~**e tragen** *(lit, fig)* to bear fruit.

fruchtbar *adj (lit, fig)* fruitful; Boden fertile. **etw für jdn** ~ **machen** to use sth to benefit sb.

Fruchtbarkeit *f siehe adj* fruitfulness; fertility.

Fruchtbarmachung *f (von Wüste)* reclamation.

Frucht-: ~**becher** *m* fruit sundae; ~**bonbon** *m or nt* fruit drop; **f~bringend** *adj (geh)* fruitful.

Früchtchen *nt (col) (Tunichtgut)* good-for-nothing; *(Kind)* rascal *(col)*. **du bist mir ein sauberes** *or* **nettes** ~ *(iro)* you're a right one *(col)*.

fruchten *vi* to bear fruit. **nichts** ~ to be fruitless.

Fruchtfleisch *nt* flesh *(of a fruit)*.

fruchtig *adj* fruity.

Frucht-: **f~los** *adj (fig)* fruitless; ~**losigkeit** *f*

---

fruitlessness; ~**saft** *m* fruit juice.

früh 1 *adj* early. **am** ~**en Morgen** in the early morning; **ein Werk des** ~**en Picasso** an early work by Picasso. **2** *adv* **(a)** early; *(in jungen Jahren)* at an early age; *(in Entwicklung)* early on. **es ist noch** ~ **am Tag** it is still early in the day; **von** ~ **bis spät** from morning till night. **(b) morgen** ~ tomorrow morning; **heute** ~ this morning.

Früh- *in cpds* early; **f~auf** *adv* **von f~auf** from an early age; ~**aufsteher** *m* - early riser, early bird *(col)*; ~**dienst** *m* early shift; ~**dienst haben** to be on early shift.

Frühe *f no pl (Morgen)* **in der** ~ early in the morning; **in aller** ~ at the crack of dawn.

früher *comp of* **früh 1** *adj* **(a)** earlier. **in** ~**en Jahren/Zeiten** in the past; **in** ~**em Alter** when he/she etc was younger. **(b)** *(ehemalig)* former, previous. **der Kontakt zu seinen** ~**en Freunden ist abgebrochen** he lost contact with his old friends.

2 *adv* **(a)** earlier. ~ **geht's nicht** that's the soonest possible; **das hättest du** ~ **sagen müssen** you should have said that before *or* sooner; ~ **oder später** sooner or later. **(b)** *(in vergangenen Zeiten)* **Herr X,** ~ **Direktor eines ... Herr X,** formerly director of a ...; **ich habe ihn** ~ **mal gekannt** I used to know him; ~ **habe ich so etwas nie gemacht** I never used to do that kind of thing; ~ **stand hier eine Kirche** there used to be a church here; **Erzählungen von/Erinnerungen an** ~ stories/memories of times gone by; **ich kannte/kenne ihn von** ~ I knew him before/I've known him some time.

frühestens *adv* at the earliest. **wann kann das** ~ **fertig sein?** when's the earliest it can be ready?

frühestmöglich *adj attr* earliest possible.

Frühgeburt *f* premature birth; *(Kind)* premature baby.

Frühjahr *nt* spring.

Frühjahrs-: ~**müdigkeit** *f* springtime lethargy; ~**putz** *m* spring-cleaning.

Frühling *m* spring. **es wird** ~, **der** ~ **kommt** spring is coming; **im** ~ in spring; **einem neuen** ~ **entgegengehen** *(fig)* to start to flourish again; **seinen zweiten** ~ **erleben** to go through one's second adolescence.

Frühlings- *in cpds* spring; ~**anfang** *m* first day of spring; **f~haft** *adj* springlike.

Früh-: ~**messe** *f* early mass; **f~morgens** *adv* early in the morning; ~**nebel** *m* early morning mist; **f~reif** *adj* precocious; *(körperlich)* mature at an early age; ~**rentner** *m* person who has retired early; ~**schicht** *f* early shift; ~**schoppen** *m* morning/lunchtime drink; ~**sport** *m* early morning exercise.

Frühstück *nt* **-e** breakfast; *(~spause)* morning *or* coffee break. **zweites** ~ = elevenses *(Brit col)*, midmorning snack.

frühstücken *insep* **1** *vi* to have breakfast. **2** *vt etw* ~ to have sth for breakfast.

Frühstücks-: ~**fleisch** *nt* luncheon meat; ~**pause** *f* morning *or* coffee break.

Früh-: ~**warnsystem** *nt* early warning system; ~**werk** *nt* early work; ~**zeit** *f* early days *pl;* **f~zeitig 1** *adj* early; *(vorzeitig auch)* premature; **2** *adv* early; *(vorzeitig)* prematurely; *(ziemlich am Anfang)* early on.

Frust *m no pl (col)* frustration.

Frustration *f* frustration.

frustrieren* *vt* to frustrate; *(col: enttäuschen)* to upset.

Fuchs [fʊks] *m* **-e** *(a) (Tier, Fell, fig)* fox. **er ist ein schlauer** ~ *(col)* he's a cunning old devil *(col) or* fox *(col)*; **wo sich die** ~**e** *or* **wo sich Hase und** ~ **gute Nacht sagen** *(hum)* in the back of beyond. **(b)** *(Pferd)* chestnut; *(mit hellerem Schwanz und Mähne)* sorrel; *(col: Mensch)* redhead.

fuchsen ['fʊksn] *vt (col)* to annoy.

fuchsig ['fʊksɪç] *adj (col: wütend)* mad *(col)*.

Füchsin ['fʏksɪn] *f* vixen.

Fuchs-: ~ **jagd** *f* fox-hunt/-hunting; **f~rot** *adj* Fell red; *Pferd* chestnut; *Haar* ginger; ~**schwanz** *m* **(a)** fox's tail; **(b)** *(Säge)* handsaw; **f~teufelswild** *adj (col)* hopping mad *(col)*.

Fuchtel *f* **-n** *(fig col)* **unter jds** ~ under sb's control *or* thumb.

fuchteln *vi (col)* **(mit den Händen)** ~ to wave one's hands about *(col)*.

Fug *m:* **mit** ~ **und Recht** *(geh)* with complete justification.

Fuge *f* **-n (a)** joint; *(Ritze)* gap, crack. **in allen** ~**n krachen** to creak at the joints; **aus den** ~**n gehen** to come apart at the seams. **(b)** *(Mus)* fugue.

fügen 1 *vt* **(a)** *(setzen)* to put, to place; *(geh) Worte, Satz* to formulate. **(b)** *(geh: bewirken)* to ordain. **2** *vr* to obey. **sich jdm/einer Sache** *(geh)* ~ to bow to sb/sth; *einem Befehl etc* to comply with sth; **es fügte sich, daß ...** *(geh)* it so happened that ...

fügsam *adj Mensch* obedient.

Fügsamkeit *f* obedience.

Fügung *f* **eine glückliche** ~ a stroke of good fortune; **göttliche** ~ divine providence; **eine** ~ **des Schicksals** an act of fate.

fühlbar *adj (spürbar)* perceptible.

fühlen *vtir* to feel. **sich krank/verantwortlich** ~ to feel ill/responsible; **wie** ~ **Sie sich?** how do you feel?; **da hat er sich aber gefühlt** *(col)* he felt really great *(col)*.

Fühler *m* - *(Zool)* feeler; *(von Schnecke)* horn. **seine** ~ **ausstrecken** *(col)* to put out feelers.

Fühlung *f* contact. **mit jdm in** ~ **bleiben/stehen** to stay/be in contact *or* touch with sb.

fuhr *pret of* **fahren**.

Fuhre *f* **-n** *(Ladung)* load.

führen 1 *vt* **(a)** *(hin~, herum~)* to take. **eine alte Dame über die Straße** ~ to help an old lady over the road; ~ **Sie mich zum Geschäftsführer!** take me to the manager!; **eine Klasse zum Abitur** ~ to see a class through to A-levels; **der Hinweis führte die Polizei auf die Spur des Diebes** that tip put the police on the trail of the thief; **was führt Sie zu mir?** *(form)* what brings you to me?; **ein Land ins Chaos** ~ to reduce a country to chaos.

(b) *(an~)* to lead; *Firma etc* to run; *Armee etc* to command.

(c) *(handhaben) Pinsel, Kamera etc* to wield. **das Glas an die Lippen** ~ to raise one's glass to one's lips.

(d) *(haben, mit~)* to carry; *Autokennzeichen, Namen* to have, to bear. **Geld/seine Papiere bei sich** ~ *(form)* to carry money/one's papers on one's person; **der Fluß führt Hochwasser** the river is running high.

(e) *(Laden: im Angebot haben)* to stock.

2 *vi* **(a)** *(in Führung liegen)* to lead. **die Mannschaft führt mit 10 Punkten Vorsprung** the team has a lead of 10 points. **(b)** *(verlaufen) (Straße)* to go; *(Kabel, Pipeline etc)* to run; *(Spur)* to lead. **die Brücke führt über die Elbe** the bridge crosses the Elbe. **(c)** *(als Ergebnis haben)* **zu etw** ~ to lead to sth; **das führt zu nichts** that will come to nothing; **es führte zu dem Ergebnis, daß er entlassen wurde** it resulted in *or* led to his being dismissed; **wohin soll das alles nur** ~? where is it all leading (us)?

3 *vr (form: sich benehmen)* to conduct oneself.

führend *adj* leading *attr; Rolle, Persönlichkeit auch* prominent. **diese Firma ist im Stahlbau** ~ that is one of the leading firms in steel construction; **die Sowjets sind im Schach** ~ the Soviets lead the world in chess.

Führer(in *f)* *m* - **(a)** *(Leiter)* leader; *(Oberhaupt)* head. **(b)** *(Fremden~, Berg~)* guide. **(c)** *(form: Lenker)* driver; *(von Flugzeug)* pilot; *(von Kran, Fahrstuhl)* operator. **(d)** *(Buch)* guide.

Führer-: ~**haus** *nt* cab; **f~los** *adj* leaderless *no adv; Wagen* driverless *no adv;* ~**schaft** *f* leadership; *(Oberhäupter)* heads *pl;* ~**schein** *m (für Auto)* driving licence *(Brit)*, driver's license *(US)*; **den** ~**schein machen** *(Aut)* to learn to drive; *(die Prüfung ablegen)* to take one's (driving) test; **ihm wurde der** ~**schein entzogen** he lost his licence; ~**scheinentzug** *m* disqualification from driving.

Führung *f* **(a)** *no pl* direction; *(von Partei, Expedition etc)* leadership; *(Mil)* command; *(eines Unternehmens etc)* management. **(b)** *no pl (die Führer)* leaders *pl,* leadership *sing;* *(Mil)* commanders *pl;* *(eines Unternehmens etc)* directors *pl.* **(c)** *(Besichtigung)* guided tour *(durch of).* **(d)** *no pl (Vorsprung)* lead. **in** ~ **gehen/liegen** to go into/be in the lead. **(e)** *no pl (Betragen)* conduct. **(f)** *(form: Lenken)* **zur** ~ **eines Kraftfahrzeugs berechtigt sein** to be licensed to drive a motor vehicle. **(g)** *no pl (Betreuung)* running. **die** ~ **der Akten/Bücher** keeping the files/books.

Führungs-: ~**anspruch** *m* claim to leadership; **seinen** ~**anspruch anmelden** to make a bid for the leadership; ~**kraft** *f* executive; ~**schicht** *f* ruling classes *pl;* ~**spitze** *f* highest echelon of the leadership; *(eines Unternehmens)* top management; ~**stab** *m (Mil)* command *no pl;* *(Comm)* top management.

Fuhr-: ~**unternehmen** *nt* haulage business; ~**unternehmer** *m* haulier, haulage contractor; ~**werk** *nt* wag(g)on; *(mit Pferden)* horse and cart; **f~werken** *vi insep (col)* **in der Küche f~werken** to bustle around in the kitchen.

Fülle *f* *no pl* **(a)** *(Körpermasse)* corpulence, portliness. **(b)** *(Stärke)* fullness. **(c)** *(Menge)* wealth.

füllen 1 *vt* to fill; *(Cook)* to stuff. **etw in Flaschen** ~ to bottle sth; **etw in Säcke** ~ to put sth into sacks. **2** *vr (Theater, Badewanne)* to fill up.

Füllen *nt* - foal.

Füller *m* -, **Füllfederhalter** *m* fountain pen.

Füllgewicht *nt (Comm)* weight at time of packing; *(auf Dosen)* net weight.

füllig *adj Mensch* corpulent, portly; *Figur* ample.

Füllung *f* filling; *(Fleisch~, Polster~)* stuffing; *(Tür~)* panel; *(von Pralinen)* centre *(Brit)*, center *(US)*.

Fummel *m* - *(col)* rag.

Fummelei *f (col)* fidgeting, fiddling; *(col: Petting)* petting, groping *(col)*.

fummeln *vi (col)* to fiddle; *(hantieren)* to fumble; *(bei Petting)* to pet, to grope *(col)*.

Fund *m* **-e** find; *(das Entdecken)* discovery, finding.

Fundament *nt (lit, fig)* foundation *(usu pl).* **das** ~ **zu etw legen** to lay the foundations for sth.

fundamental *adj* fundamental.

Fund-: ~**büro** *nt* lost property office *(Brit)*, lost and found *(US)*; ~**grube** *f (fig)* treasure trove.

fundieren* *vt (fig)* to back up.

fundiert *adj* sound. **schlecht** ~ unsound.

fündig *adj (Min)* rich. ~ **werden** to make a strike; *(fig)* to strike it lucky.

Fund-: ~**ort** *m* **der** ~**ort von etw** (the place) where sth is/was found; ~**sachen** *pl* lost property *sing;* ~**stätte** *f,* ~**ort**.

fünf *num* five. **seine** ~ **Sinne beisammen haben** to have all one's wits about one; ~**(e) gerade sein lassen** *(col)* to turn a blind eye; *siehe* **vier**.

Fünf- *in cpds* five; ~**eck** *nt* pentagon; **f~eckig** *adj* pentagonal, five-cornered.

Fünfer *m* - *(col)* five-pfennig piece; five-marks.

Fünf-: **f~fach** *adj* fivefold; ~**jahr(es)plan** *m* five-year plan; **f~jährig** *adj* Frist, Plan five-year; *Kind* five-year-old; ~**kampf** *m (Sport)* pentathlon; ~**ling** *m* quintuplet; **f~mal** *adv* five times; ~**prozentklausel** *f* clause debarring parties with less than 5% of the vote from Parliament; **f~tägig** *adj* five-day *attr;* **f~tausend** *num* five thousand.

Fünftel nt - fifth.

fünfte(r, s) adj fifth; siehe **vierte(r, s)**.

fünfzehn num fifteen.

fünfzig num fifty.

Fünfziger m - (col) (Mensch) fifty-year-old; (Geld) fifty.

fungieren* [fuŋ'giːrən] vi to function (als as a).

Funk m no pl radio, wireless. **über** ~ by radio.

Funk-: ~**amateur** m radio ham; ~**ausstellung** f radio and television exhibition.

Funke m -ns, -n, **Funken** m - (a) (lit, fig) spark. ~**n sprühen** to spark; **arbeiten, daß die** ~**n fliegen** (col) to work like mad (col); **zwischen den beiden sprang der** ~ **über** (col) something clicked between them (col). **(b)** (ein bißchen) scrap; (von Hoffnung auch) glimmer; (von Anstand auch) spark.

funkeln vi to sparkle; (Sterne) to twinkle; (Augen) (vor Freude) to gleam; (vor Zorn) to flash; (Edelmetall) to gleam.

funkelnagelneu adj (col) brand-new.

funken 1 vti to radio. **SOS** ~ to send out or radio an SOS. **2** vi impers **endlich hat es bei ihm gefunkt** (col) the light finally dawned (on him).

Funker m - radio or wireless operator.

Funk- in cpds radio; ~**gerät** nt **(a)** no pl radio equipment; **(b)** (Sprechfunkgerät) radio set, walkie-talkie; ~**haus** nt broadcasting studios pl; ~**kolleg** nt educational radio broadcasts pl; ~**meßgerät** nt radar (equipment) no pl; ~**sprechverkehr** m radiotelephony; ~**spruch** m radio signal; (Mitteilung) radio message; ~**stille** f radio silence; ~**streife** f police radio patrol.

Funktion f (Zweck, Math) function; (no pl: Tätigkeit) functioning; (Amt) office; (Stellung) position. **in** ~ **treten/sein** to come into/be in operation; **etw außer** ~ **setzen** to stop sth functioning.

Funktionär(in f) m functionary, official.

funktionell adj functional.

funktionieren* vi to work; (Maschine etc auch) to function, to operate.

funktionsfähig adj able to function; Maschine working pred.

Funzel f -n (col) dim light, gloom.

Für nt: **das** ~ **und Wider** the pros and cons pl.

für prep+acc for. ~ **was ist denn dieses Werkzeug?** (col) what is this tool for?; ~ **zwei arbeiten** (fig) to do the work of two people; ~**s erste** for the moment; ~**s nächstemal** next time; **sich** ~ **etw entscheiden** to decide in favour (Brit) or in favor (US) of sth; **was Sie da sagen, hat etwas** ~ **sich** there's something in what you're saying; **er hat was** ~ **sich** he's not a bad person; **Tag** ~ **Tag** day after day; **Schritt** ~ **Schritt** step by step.

Fürbitte f (Eccl, fig) intercession.

Furche f -n furrow; (Wagenspur) rut.

furchen vt to furrow. **eine gefurchte Stirn** a furrowed brow.

Furcht f no pl fear. **aus** ~ **vor jdm/etw** for fear of sb/sth; ~ **vor jdm/etw haben** to be afraid of sb/sth; **jdn in** ~ **versetzen, jdm** ~ **einflößen** to frighten or scare sb.

furchtbar adj terrible, awful. **ich habe einen** ~**en Hunger** I'm ever so hungry (col).

furcht|einflößend adj terrifying, fearful.

fürchten 1 vt **jdn/etw** ~ to be afraid of sb/sth, to fear sb/sth; **es war schlimmer, als ich gefürchtet hatte** it was worse than I had feared. **2** vr to be afraid (vor+dat of). **3** vi **für** or **um etw** ~ to fear for sth; **zum F**~ **aussehen** to look frightening; **da kannst du das F**~ **lernen** it will scare you stiff.

fürchterlich adj terrible, awful.

Furcht-: **f**~**erregend** adj terrifying, fearful. **f**~**los** adj fearless; ~**losigkeit** f fearlessness; **f**~**sam** adj timorous; ~**samkeit** f timorousness.

für|einander adv for each other, for one another.

Furie ['fuːriə] f (Myth) fury; (fig) hellcat.

Furnier nt -e veneer.

furnieren* vt to veneer.

Furore f or nt no pl sensation. ~ **machen** (col) to cause a sensation.

Fürsorge f no pl **(a)** (Betreuung) care; (Sozial~) welfare. **(b)** (col: Sozialamt) welfare (col). **der** ~ **zur Last fallen** to be a burden on the state. **(c)** (col: Sozialunterstützung) social security (Brit), welfare (US). **von der** ~ **leben** to live on social security (Brit) or the welfare (US).

fürsorgend adj caring. **jdn** ~ **betreuen** to care for sb.

Fürsorger(in f) m - (church) welfare worker.

fürsorglich adj caring. **jdn sehr** ~ **behandeln** to lavish care on sb.

Fürsprache f recommendation. **für jdn** ~ **einlegen** to put in a word of recommendation for sb (bei with).

Fürsprecher(in f) m advocate.

Fürst m (wk) -en, -en prince; (Herrscher) ruler. **wie ein** ~ **leben** to live like a lord.

Fürsten-: ~**haus** nt royal house; ~**tum** nt principality.

Fürstin f princess; (Herrscherin) ruler.

fürstlich adj (lit, fig) princely no adv. **jdn** ~ **bewirten** to entertain sb right royally; ~ **leben** to live like a lord.

Furunkel nt or m - boil.

Fürwort nt -̈er (Gram) pronoun.

Furz m -̈e (col!) fart (col).

furzen vi (col!) to fart (col).

Fusel m - (pej) rotgut (col), hooch (US col).

Fusion f amalgamation; (von Unternehmen) merger; (von Atomkernen, Zellen) fusion.

fusionieren* vti to amalgamate; (Unternehmen) to merge.

Fuß m -̈e **(a)** foot. **zu** ~ on foot; **er ist gut/schlecht zu** ~ he's good/not so good on his feet; **sich jdm zu** ~**en werfen** to prostrate oneself before sb; **jdm zu** ~**en fallen/liegen** to fall/lie at sb's feet; **das Publikum lag ihm zu** ~**en** he had the audience at his feet; **den** ~ **in die Tür stellen** to get one's foot in the door; **kalte** ~**e bekommen** (lit, fig) to get cold feet; **bei** ~**! heel!**; **jdm etw vor die** ~**e werfen** (lit) to throw sth at sb; (fig) to tell sb to keep sth; **jdn/etw mit** ~**en treten** (lit) to kick sb/sth about; (fig) to trample all over sb/sth; **(festen)** ~ **fassen** (lit, fig) to gain a foothold; (sich niederlassen) to settle down; **auf eigenen** ~**en stehen** (fig) to be able to stand on one's own two feet; **auf großem** ~ **leben** to live the high life; **mit jdm auf gutem** ~ **stehen** to be on good terms with sb.

(b) (von Gegenstand) base; (Tisch-, Stuhlbein) leg; (von Schrank, Gebirge) foot. **auf schwachen/tönernen** ~**en stehen** to be built on sand.

(c) pl - (Längenmaß) foot.

Fuß-: ~**abdruck** m footprint; ~**angel** f (lit) mantrap; (fig) catch, trap; ~**bad** nt foot bath.

Fußball m football; (Sportart auch) soccer.

Fußballer m - (col) footballer.

Fußball-: ~**mannschaft** f football team; ~**platz** m football or soccer pitch; ~**spiel** nt football or soccer match; (Sportart) football; ~**spieler** m football or soccer player; ~**toto** m or nt football pools pl; ~**verein** m football club.

Fuß-: ~**bank** f footstool; ~**boden** m floor; ~**bodenbelag** m floor covering; ~**bremse** f footbrake; ~**eisen** nt mantrap.

Fussel f -n fluff no pl. **eine** ~ a bit of fluff.

fusselig adj fluffy. **sich** (dat) **den Mund** ~ **reden** (col) to talk till one is blue in the face.

fusseln vi (Stoff, Kleid etc) to go bobbly (col).

fußen vi to rest, to be based (auf +dat on).

Fuß|ende nt (von Bett) foot.

Fußgänger(in f) m - pedestrian.

Fußgänger-: ~**brücke** f footbridge; ~**überweg** m pedestrian crossing (Brit), crosswalk (US);

(auch ~**überführung)** pedestrian bridge; ~**unterführung** *f* pedestrian subway; ~**zone** *f* pedestrian precinct.
Fuß-: ~**gelenk** *nt* ankle; ~**leiste** *f* skirting board *(Brit),* baseboard *(US).*
fußlig *adj* = **fusselig.**
Fuß-: ~**marsch** *m* walk; *(Mil)* march; ~**matte** *f* doormat; ~**note** *f* footnote; ~**pflege** *f* chiropody, podiatry *(US);* ~**pfleger** *m* chiropodist, podiatrist *(US);* ~**pilz** *m (Med)* athlete's foot *no art;* ~**sohle** *f* sole of the foot; ~**spitze** *f* toes *pl;* **sich auf die** ~**spitzen stellen** to stand on tiptoe; ~**stapfen** *m* footprint; **in jds** ~**stapfen treten** *(fig)* to follow in sb's footsteps; ~**stütze** *f* footrest; ~**tritt** *m (Stoß)* kick; **jdm einen** ~**tritt geben** to kick sb, to give sb a kick; **einen** ~**tritt bekommen** *(fig)* to be kicked out; ~**volk** *nt* **(a)** *(Mil old)* footmen *pl;* **(b)** *(fig)* **das** ~**volk** the rank and file; ~**wanderung** *f* walk; ~**weg** *m* **(a)** footpath; **(b) es sind nur 15 Minuten** ~**weg**

it's only 15 minutes walk.
futsch *adj pred (col: weg)* gone, vanished.
Futter *nt* - **(a)** *no pl* food, feed; *(für Kühe, Pferde etc auch)* fodder. **gut im** ~ **sein** to be well-fed. **(b)** *(Kleider~, Briefumschlag~)* lining.
Futteral *nt* -e case.
Futter-: ~**häuschen** *nt* bird box; ~**krippe** *f* manger; **an der** ~**krippe sitzen** *(col)* to be well-placed.
futtern *(hum col)* **1** *vi* to stuff oneself *(col).* **2** *vt* to scoff.
füttern *vt* **(a)** to feed. „**F**~ **verboten"** "do not feed the animals". **(b)** *Kleidungsstück* to line.
Futter-: ~**napf** *m* bowl; ~**neid** *m (fig)* material envy; ~**pflanze** *f* forage plant; ~**stoff** *m* lining *(material);* ~**trog** *m* feeding trough.
Fütterung *f* feeding.
Futur *nt* -e *(Gram)* **(erstes)** ~ future (tense); **zweites** ~ future perfect.
futuristisch *adj* futuristic.

G

G, g [geː] nt -, - G, g.

g = Gramm.

gab pret of **geben.**

Gabe f -n **(a)** (dated: Geschenk) gift, present (gen of, from). **(b)** (Begabung) gift. **die ~ haben, etw zu tun** to have a gift for doing sth.

Gabel f -n fork; (Heu~, Mist~) pitchfork; (Telec) rest, cradle.

Gabel-: g~förmig adj forked no adv; ~frühstück nt buffet lunch.

gabeln vtr to fork.

Gabelstapler m - fork-lift truck.

Gabelung f fork.

Gabentisch m table for Christmas or birthday presents.

gackern vi (lit, fig) to cackle.

gaffen vi to gape, to stare (nach at).

Gaffer(in f) m - **die neugierigen ~ bei einem Unfall** the nosy people standing gaping at an accident.

Gag [gɛk] m -s (Film~) gag; (Werbe~) gimmick.

Gage ['gaːʒə] f -n (esp Theat) fee.

gähnen vi (lit, fig) to yawn. **~de Leere** total emptiness; **ein ~der Abgrund** a yawning abyss; **ein G~** a yawn; **das G~ unterdrücken** to stop oneself (from) yawning.

Gala f no pl formal dress. **sich in ~ werfen** to get all dressed up.

Gala- in cpds formal; (Mil) full ceremonial; (Theat) gala; **~anzug** m formal dress; (Mil) full dress.

galaktisch adj galactic.

galant adj (dated) gallant.

Gala-: ~uniform f (Mil) (full) dress uniform; ~vorstellung f (Theat) gala performance.

Galeere f -n galley.

Galerie f gallery. **auf der ~** in the gallery.

Galgen m - gallows pl; (Film) boom. **jdn an den ~ bringen** to bring sb to the gallows.

Galgen-: ~frist f (col) reprieve; **jdm eine ~frist geben** to give sb a reprieve, to reprieve sb; ~humor m gallows humour (Brit) or humor (US); ~strick, ~vogel m (col) gallows bird (col).

Galionsfigur f figurehead.

gälisch adj Gaelic.

Galle f -n gall; (Organ) gallbladder; (Flüssigkeit auch) bile. **seine ~ verspritzen** (fig) to pour out one's venom; **jdm kommt die ~ hoch** sb's blood begins to boil; **die ~ läuft ihm über** (col) he's livid.

galle(n)bitter adj bitter; Bemerkung caustic.

Gallen- in cpds gall; ~blase f gall-bladder; ~stein m gallstone.

gallig adj bitter; (fig) caustic.

gallisch adj Gallic.

Galopp m -s or -e gallop. **im ~** (lit) at a gallop; (fig) at top speed; **langsamer ~** canter.

galoppieren* vi aux haben or sein to gallop.

galt pret of **gelten.**

Gamasche f -n gaiter.

Gammastrahlen pl gamma rays pl.

Gammel m no pl (col) junk (col), rubbish.

gamm(e)lig adj (col) Lebensmittel old, ancient; Kleidung tatty (col).

Gammler(in f) m - drop-out.

gang adj: **~ und gäbe sein** to be the usual thing.

Gang¹ m ~e **(a)** (no pl: ~art) walk, way of

---

walking, gait; (eines Pferdes) gait. **einen leichten/ schnellen ~ haben** to be light on one's feet/to be a fast walker; **seinen ~ verlangsamen/beschleunigen** to slow down/to speed up.
(b) (Besorgung) errand; (Spazier~) walk. **einen ~ machen** to go on an errand/to go for a walk; **einen ~ zum Anwalt machen** to pay a visit to one's lawyer; **einen schweren ~ tun** to do something difficult; **das war für ihn immer ein schwerer ~** it was always hard for him; **den ~ nach Canossa antreten** (fig) to eat humble pie.
(c) (Ablauf) course; (eines Dramas) development. **der Motor hat einen leisen ~** the engine runs quietly; **seinen gewohnten ~ gehen** (fig) to run its usual course; **etw in ~ bringen** or **setzen** to get sth going; **etw in ~ halten** (lit, fig) to keep sth going; **in ~ kommen** to get going; **in ~ sein** to be going; (fig) to be off the ground; **in vollem ~** in full swing; **es ist etwas im ~(e)** (col) something's up (col).
(d) (Arbeits~) operation; (Speisenfolge) course. **ein Essen mit vier ~en** a four-course meal.
(e) (Verbindungs~) passage(way); (Rail, in Gebäuden) corridor; (Hausflur) (offen) passage(way); (hinter Eingangstür) hallway; (im oberen Stock) landing; (Theat, Aviat, in Kirche) aisle; (Aviat, in Stadion) gangway; (in einem Bergwerk) tunnel, gallery; (Anat) duct; (Min: Erz~) vein; (Tech: eines Gewindes) thread.
(f) (Mech) gear. **den ersten ~ einlegen** to engage first (gear); **auf** or **in den dritten ~ schalten** to change or shift (US) into third (gear).

Gang² [gɛŋ] f -s gang.

Gang|art f walk, way of walking, gait; (von Pferd) gait. **eine schnellere ~ vorlegen** to walk faster.

gangbar adj (lit) Weg, Brücke passable; (fig) practicable. **nicht ~** impassable/impracticable.

Gängelband nt: **jdn am ~ führen** (fig) (Lehrer etc) to spoon-feed sb; (Mutter) to keep sb tied to one's apron strings.

gängeln vt (fig) **jdn ~** to treat sb like a child; (Mutter) to keep sb tied to one's apron strings.

gängig adj **(a)** (üblich) common; (aktuell) current; (vertretbar) possible. **(b)** (gut gehend) Waren popular. **die ~ste Ausführung** the best-selling model.

Gangschaltung f gears pl.

Gangster ['gɛŋstɐ] m - gangster.

Gangster-: ~boß m gang boss; ~braut f (gang) moll (col); ~methoden pl strong-arm tactics pl.

Gangway ['gɛŋweɪ] f -s (Naut) gangway; (Aviat) steps pl.

Ganove [ga'noːvə] m -n (col) crook.

Ganoven-: ~ehre f honour (Brit) or honor (US) among(st) thieves; ~sprache f underworld slang.

Gans f ¨-e goose.

Gänse- in cpds goose; ~blümchen nt daisy; ~braten m roast goose; ~füßchen pl (col) inverted commas pl; ~haut f (fig) goose-pimples pl, goose-flesh; ~marsch m: **im ~marsch** in single or Indian file.

Gänserich m -e gander.

ganz 1 adj **(a)** whole, entire; (vollständig) complete; Wahrheit whole. **eine ~e Zahl** a whole

169

number; **eine** ~**e Note** (Mus) a semi-breve (Brit), a whole note (US); ~ **England/London** the whole of England/London, all England/London; **die** ~**e Zeit** all the time, the whole time; **sein** ~**es Geld/ Vermögen** all his money/fortune, his entire or whole fortune; **seine** ~**e Kraft** all his strength; **ein** ~**er Mann** a real or proper man; **etw im** ~**en kaufen** to buy sth as a whole; **im (großen und)** ~**en (genommen)** on the whole, all in all. (**b**) (col: unbeschädigt) intact. **etw wieder** ~ **machen** to mend sth; **wieder** ~ **sein** to be mended. (**c**) (col: nicht mehr als) ~**e 200 Mark im Monat** all of 200 marks a month.

2 adv (völlig, ziemlich) quite; (ausnahmslos) completely; (sehr) really; (genau) exactly, just. ~ **hinten/vorn** right at the back/front; **nicht** ~ not quite; ~ **gewiß!** absolutely; **ein** ~ **gutes Buch** (ziemlich) quite a good book; (sehr gut) a very or really good book; **ein** ~ **billiger Trick** a really cheap trick; **er hat** ~ **recht** he's quite or absolutely right; ~ **allein** all alone; **du bist ja** ~ **naß** you're all wet; ~ **Aufmerksamkeit** etc **sein** to be all attention etc; **eine Zeitschrift** ~ **lesen** to read a magazine right through or from cover to cover; ~ **und gar** completely, utterly; ~ **und gar nicht** not at all, not in the least; **noch nicht** ~ **zwei Uhr** not quite two o'clock yet; **ein** ~ **klein wenig** just a tiny bit; **das mag ich** ~ **besonders gerne** I'm particularly fond of that; **sie ist** ~ **die Mutter** she's just or exactly like her mother; **etw** ~ **oder gar nicht machen** to do sth properly or not at all.

Gänze f no pl (form) entirety.

Ganze(s) nt decl as adj **das** ~ the whole; (alle Sachen zusammen) the (whole) lot; (ganzer Satz, ganze Ausrüstung) the complete set. **etw als** ~**s sehen** to see sth as a whole; **das** ~ **kostet ...** altogether it costs ...; **das** ~ **gefällt mir gar nicht** I don't like it at all; **aufs** ~ **gehen** (col) to go all out; **es geht ums** ~ everything's at stake.

Ganzheit f (Einheit) unity; (Vollständigkeit) entirety. **in seiner** ~ in its entirety.

ganzheitlich adj integral.

Ganzheitsmethode f look-and-say method.

ganzjährig adj all-year attr.

gänzlich adv completely, totally.

ganztägig adj all-day attr.

ganztags adv arbeiten full-time.

Ganztags-: ~**beschäftigung** f full-time occupation; ~**schule** f all-day schooling no pl or schools pl; ~**stelle** f full-time job.

Ganzton m (Mus) (whole) tone.

gar 1 adv (**a**) (überhaupt) at all; (ganz) quite. ~ **keines** not a single one, none whatsoever or at all; ~ **kein Grund** no reason whatsoever or at all; ~ **nichts** nothing at all; ~ **nicht schlecht** not bad at all, not at all bad. (**b**) **er wäre** ~ **zu gern noch länger geblieben** he would really have liked to stay longer; **ein** ~ **feiner Mensch** (old) a really splendid person. (**c**) (sogar) even. **wie alt ist er?** — **70, wenn nicht** ~ **80** how old is he? — 70, if not 80. **2** adj Speise done pred, cooked.

Garage [ga'ra:ʒə] f -n garage; (Hoch~, Tief~) car-park (Brit), parking garage (US).

Garantie f (lit, fig) guarantee. **die Uhr hat ein Jahr** ~ the watch is guaranteed for a year or has a year's guarantee; **das fällt noch unter die** ~ that's covered by the guarantee.

Garantie-: ~**frist** f guarantee period; ~**lohn** m guaranteed minimum wage.

garantieren* 1 vt to guarantee (jdm etw sb sth). **er konnte mir nicht** ~, **daß ...** he couldn't guarantee that ... **2** vi to give a guarantee. **für etw** ~ to guarantee sth.

garantiert adv guaranteed; (col) I bet (col). **er kommt garantiert nicht** I bet he won't come (col), he's bound not to come.

Garantieschein m guarantee.

Garaus m: (col) **jdm den** ~ **machen** to do sb in

(col), to bump sb off (col).

Garbe f -n (Korn~) sheaf; (Mil: Schuß~) burst of fire. **zu** ~**n binden** to bind into sheaves.

Garde f -n guard. **bei der** ~ in the Guards; **die alte** ~ (fig) the old guard.

Gardemaß nt: ~ **haben** (hum) to be as tall as a tree.

Garderobe f -n (**a**) (Kleiderbestand) wardrobe. (**b**) (Kleiderablage) hall-stand; (im Theater, Kino etc) cloakroom (Brit), checkroom (US). (**c**) (Theat: Umkleideraum) dressing-room.

Garderoben-: ~**frau** f cloakroom (Brit) or checkroom (US) attendant; ~**haken** m coat hook; ~**marke** f cloakroom (Brit) or checkroom (US) number; ~**schein** m cloakroom (Brit) or checkroom (US) ticket; ~**ständer** m hat-stand.

Gardine f curtain, drape (US); (Scheiben~) net curtain.

Gardinen-: ~**predigt** f (col) jdm eine ~**predigt halten** to give sb a talking-to; ~**stange** f curtain rail; (zum Ziehen) curtain rod.

garen (Cook) vti to cook.

gären 1 vi aux haben or sein to ferment; (fig: Gefühle etc) to seethe. **die Wut gärte in ihm** he was seething with anger. **2** vt to ferment.

Garn nt -e thread; (Baumwoll~ auch) cotton; (Häkel~, fig: Seemanns~) yarn. **ein** ~ **spinnen** (fig) to spin a yarn.

Garnele f -n (Zool) prawn, shrimp.

garnieren* vt Kuchen, Kleid to decorate; Gericht, (fig) Reden etc to garnish.

Garnierung f siehe vt decoration; garnishing.

Garnison f (Mil) garrison.

Garnison(s)- in cpds garrison.

Garnitur f (Satz) set; (Unterwäsche) set of underwear. **die erste** ~ (fig) the pick of the bunch; **erste/zweite** ~ **sein** to be first-rate/second-rate.

Garnrolle f spool; (von Baumwolle, Nähgarn) cotton reel.

Garten m ⸚ garden; (Obst~) orchard. **botanischer/zoologischer** ~ botanic/zoological gardens pl; **im** ~ **arbeiten** to do some gardening; **das ist nicht in seinem** ~ **gewachsen** (fig col: Ideen) he didn't think of that himself.

Garten- in cpds garden; ~**arbeit** f gardening no pl; ~**bau** m horticulture; ~**gerät** nt gardening tool; ~**haus** nt summer house; ~**laube** f (~häuschen) summer house; ~**lokal** nt beer garden; (Restaurant) garden café; ~**möbel** pl garden furniture; ~**schere** f secateurs pl (Brit), pruning-shears pl; ~**schlauch** m garden hose; ~**zwerg** m garden gnome; (pej col) squirt (col).

Gärtner(in f) m gardener.

Gärtnerei f (Baumschule, für Setzlinge) nursery; (für Obst, Gemüse, Schnittblumen) market-garden (Brit), truck farm (US).

gärtnerisch adj attr gardening. **wenn man sich** ~ **betätigt** if you do some gardening.

gärtnern vi to do gardening.

Gärung f fermentation; (fig) ferment, turmoil.

Gas nt -e gas; (Aut: ~pedal) accelerator, gas pedal (esp US). ~ **geben** (Aut) to accelerate, to step on the gas (col); ~ **wegnehmen** (Aut) to decelerate.

Gas- in cpds gas; **g~beheizt** adj gas-heated; ~**flasche** f bottle of gas, gas canister; **g~förmig** adj gaseous; ~**geruch** m smell of gas; ~**hahn** m gastap; ~**heizung** f gas central heating; ~**herd** m gas cooker; ~**kammer** f gas chamber; ~**kocher** m camping stove; ~**laterne** f gas (street) lamp; ~**leitung** f (Rohr) gas pipe; ~**licht** nt gaslight; (Beleuchtung) gaslighting; ~**maske** f gasmask; ~**ofen** m (Heizofen) gas fire or heater; ~**pedal** nt (Aut) accelerator (pedal), gas pedal (esp US).

Gasse f -n lane; (Durchgang) alley(way); (S Ger, Aus: Straße) street.

Gassen-: ~**hauer** m (old, col) popular melody; ~**junge** m (pej) street urchin or arab.

Gassi adv (col) **mit einem Hund ~ gehen** to take a dog for walkies (col).

Gast m ‑e guest; (Besucher auch, Tourist) visitor; (in einer ~stätte) customer; (Theat) guest (star); **vor geladenen ~en** before an invited audience; **wir haben heute abend ~e** we're having people around this evening; **bei jdm zu ~ sein** to be sb's guest(s); **in einem anderen Ort zu ~ sein** to visit another place.

Gast|arbeiter m immigrant or foreign worker.

Gäste-: **~bett** nt spare or guest bed; **~buch** nt visitors' book; **~haus** nt guest house; **~zimmer** nt guest room.

Gast-: **g~freundlich** adj hospitable; **~freundlichkeit, ~freundschaft** f hospitality; **~geber** m host; **~geberin** f hostess; **~haus** nt, **~hof** m inn; **~hörer(in** f) m (Univ) observer, auditor (US); **~land** nt host country; **g~lich** adj hospitable; **~lichkeit** f hospitality.

Gastritis f, pl **Gastritiden** gastritis.

Gastrolle f (Theat) **eine ~ spielen** (lit) to make a guest appearance; (fig) to put in a fleeting appearance.

Gastronomie f (Kochkunst) gastronomy; (form: Gaststättengewerbe) catering trade.

Gast-: **~spiel** nt (Theat) guest performance; **ein ~spiel geben** (lit) to give a guest performance; (fig col) to put in a brief appearance; **~stätte** f (Speise~) restaurant; (Trinklokal) pub (Brit), bar; **~wirt(in** f) m (Besitzer) restaurant owner; (Pächter) restaurant manager(ess f); (von Trinklokal) landlord/landlady; **~wirtschaft** f inn.

Gas-: **~uhr** f gas meter; **~verbrauch** m gas consumption; **~vergiftung** f gas poisoning; **~versorgung** f (System) gas supply (gen to); **~werk** nt gasworks sing or pl; (Verwaltung) gas board; **~zähler** m gas meter; **~zentralheizung** f gas central heating.

Gatte m ‑n (form) husband, spouse (form).

Gatter nt ‑ (Tür) gate; (Zaun) fence; (Rost) grating, grid.

Gattin f (form) wife, spouse (form).

Gattung f (Biol) genus; (Liter, Mus, Art) genre, form; (fig: Sorte) type, kind.

Gattungsbegriff m generic concept.

GAU = größter anzunehmender Unfall maximum credible accident, MCA.

Gaudi nt or (S Ger, Aus) f no pl (col) fun.

Gaukler m ‑ (liter) travelling (Brit) or (US) entertainer.

Gaul m, pl **Gäule** (pej) nag, hack.

Gaumen m ‑ palate (auch fig), roof of the/one's mouth. **die Zunge klebte ihm vor Durst am ~** his tongue was hanging out (with thirst).

Gauner m ‑ rogue, rascal; (Betrüger) crook; (hum col: Schelm auch) scamp.

Gaunerbande f bunch of rogues/crooks.

Gaunerei f swindling no pl, cheating no pl.

gaunerhaft adj rascally no adv.

gaunern vi (col) (betrügen) to swindle, to cheat; (stehlen) to thieve. **er hat sich durchs Leben gegaunert** he cheated his way through life.

Gaunersprache f underworld jargon.

Gaze ['gaːzə] f ‑n gauze.

Gazelle f gazelle.

ge|artet adj **gutmütig/freundlich ~ sein** to be good-natured/have a friendly nature; **sie ist ganz anders ~** she has a completely different nature.

Ge|äst nt no pl branches pl.

geb. = geboren.

Gebäck nt ‑e (Kekse) biscuits pl (Brit), cookies pl (US); (Teilchen) pastries pl.

gebacken ptp of **backen**.

Gebälk nt ‑e timberwork no pl, timbers pl.

geballt adj (fig: konzentriert) concentrated.

gebannt adj spellbound. **wie ~** as if spellbound.

gebar pret of **gebären**.

Gebärde f ‑n gesture; (lebhafte auch) gesticulation.

gebärden* vr to behave, to conduct oneself (form).

Gebärdenspiel nt no pl gestures pl, gesticulation(s).

Gebaren nt no pl behaviour (Brit), behavior (US); (Geschäfts~) conduct.

gebären pret **gebar**, ptp **geboren 1** vt to give birth to; (fig liter: erzeugen) to breed. **geboren werden** to be born; **wo sind Sie geboren?** where were you born?; **aus der Not geborene Ideen** ideas springing from necessity; siehe **geboren. 2** vi to give birth.

Gebärmutter f (Anat) womb, uterus.

Gebäude nt ‑ building; (fig: Gefüge) structure.

Gebäude-: **~komplex** m (building) complex; **~reinigung** f (das Reinigen) commercial cleaning; (Firma) cleaning contractors pl.

gebaut adj built. **gut/stark ~ sein** to be well-built/ sturdily built.

gebefreudig adj generous, open-handed.

Gebeine pl (geh) bones pl, mortal remains pl (liter).

Gebell nt no pl barking.

geben pret **gab**, ptp **gegeben 1** vt (a) (auch vi) to give. **wer hat dir das gegeben?** who gave you that?; **gib's mir!** give it to me!, give me it!; **sich** (dat) **(von jdm) etw ~ lassen** to ask sb for sth; **was darf ich Ihnen ~?** what can I get you?; **~ Sie mir bitte zwei Flaschen Bier** I'd like two bottles of beer, please; **ich gebe dir das Auto für 100 Mark** I'll give you the car for 100 marks; **ein gutes Beispiel ~** to set a good example; **jdn/etw verloren ~** to give sb/sth up as lost; **~ Sie mir bitte Herrn Braun** (Telec) can I speak to Mr Braun please?; **Gott gebe, daß ...** God grant that ...; **es war ihm nicht gegeben, seine Eltern lebend wiederzusehen** he was not to see his parents alive again; **in die Post ~** to post; **ein Auto in Reparatur ~** to have a car repaired; **ein Kind in Pflege ~** to put or place a child in care; **2 + 2 gibt 4** 2 + 2 makes 4; **das gibt keinen Sinn** that doesn't make sense; **Rotwein gibt Flecken** red wine leaves stains; **was wird heute im Theater gegeben?** what's on at the theatre today?; **er gibt Englisch** he teaches English.

(b) **viel/nicht viel auf etw** (acc) **~** to set great store/not much store by sth; **ich gebe nicht viel auf seinen Rat** I don't think much of his advice; **etw von sich ~** Laut, Worte, Flüche to utter sth.

2 vi (auch vr) (Cards) to deal; (Tennis: Aufschlag haben) to serve. **wer gibt?** whose deal/serve is it?

3 vt impers **es gibt** (+acc) there is/are; **was gibt's?** what's the matter?, what's up?; **was gibt's zum Mittagessen?** what's for lunch?; **freitags gibt es bei uns immer Fisch** we always have fish on Fridays; **heute gibt's noch Regen** it's going to rain today; **dafür gibt es 10% Rabatt** you get 10% discount for it; **das gibt's doch nicht!** I don't believe it!; **da gibt's nichts** (col) there's no two ways about it (col); **gleich gibt's was!** (col) there'll be trouble in a minute!

4 vr **(a)** (nachlassen) to ease off, to let up; (sich erledigen) to sort itself out; (aufhören) to stop. **sich gefangen/verloren ~** to give oneself up/to give oneself up for lost; **das wird sich schon ~** it'll all work out. (b) (sich benehmen) to behave.

Geber m ‑ giver; (Cards) dealer.

Gebet nt ‑e prayer. **sein ~ verrichten** to say one's prayers; **jdn ins ~ nehmen** (fig) to take sb to task.

Gebetbuch nt prayer-book.

gebeten ptp of **bitten**.

gebeugt adj Haltung stooped; Kopf bowed; Schultern sloping. **~ sitzen/stehen** to sit/stand hunched up.

Gebiet nt ‑e area, region; (Fläche) area; (Staats~)

gebieten

territory; *(fig: Fach)* field; *(Teil~)* branch. **auf diesem ~** in this field.
gebieten* *irreg* **1** *vti (verlangen)* to demand; *(befehlen)* to command. **jdm etw ~** to command sb to do sth. **2** *vi (liter: herrschen)* to have command *(über +acc* over). **über ein Land/Volk ~** to have dominion over a country/nation.
Gebieter *m* - *(liter)* master.
Gebieterin *f (liter, old)* mistress.
gebieterisch *adj (geh)* imperious; *(herrisch)* domineering; *Ton* peremptory.
Gebiets-: **~anspruch** *m* territorial claim; **~hoheit** *f* territorial sovereignty.
Gebilde *nt* - thing, construction.
gebildet *adj* educated; *(gelehrt)* learned, erudite; *(kultiviert)* cultured.
Gebirge *nt* - mountains *pl*, mountain range. **im/ins ~** in/into the mountains.
gebirgig *adj* mountainous.
Gebirgs- *in cpds* mountain; **~bahn** *f* mountain railway *crossing a mountain range;* **~rücken** *m* mountain ridge; **~straße** *f* mountain road; **~zug** *m* mountain range.
Gebiß *nt* **-sse** *(die Zähne)* (set of) teeth; *(künstliches ~)* dentures *pl*.
gebissen *ptp of* **beißen.**
Gebläse *nt* - blower.
geblasen *ptp of* **blasen.**
geblichen *ptp of* **bleichen.**
geblieben *ptp of* **bleiben.**
geblümt *adj* flowered.
Geblüt *nt no pl (geh: Abstammung)* descent, lineage. **von edlem ~** of noble blood.
gebogen **1** *ptp of* **biegen. 2** *adj Nase* Roman.
geboren **1** *ptp of* **gebären. 2** *adj* born. **blind ~ sein** to have been born blind; **er ist blind ~** he was born blind; **~er Engländer sein** to be English by birth; **Hanna Schmidt ~e** *or* **geb.** Müller. Hanna Schmidt, née Müller.
geborgen **1** *ptp of* **bergen. 2** *adj* **sich ~ fühlen/~ sein** to feel/be secure or safe.
Geborgenheit *f* security.
geborsten *ptp of* **bersten.**
Gebot *nt* **-e (a)** *(Gesetz)* law; *(Regel, Vorschrift)* rule; *(Bibl)* commandment; *(moralisch)* precept; *(geh: Erfordernis)* requirement. **das ~ der Stunde** the needs of the moment; **das ~ der Vernunft** the dictates of reason. **(b)** *(Verfügung)* command. **jdm zu ~e stehen** to be at sb's command *or (Geld etc)* disposal. **(c)** *(Comm: bei Auktionen)* bid.
geboten **1** *ptp of* **bieten, gebieten. 2** *adj (geh) (ratsam)* advisable; *(notwendig)* necessary; *(dringend ~)* imperative. **bei aller ~en Achtung** with all due respect.
Gebr. = **Gebrüder** Bros.
gebracht *ptp of* **bringen.**
gebrannt **1** *ptp of* **brennen. 2** *adj* **ein ~es Kind scheut das Feuer** *(Prov)* once bitten twice shy *(Prov)*.
gebraten *ptp of* **braten.**
Gebrauch *m, pl* **Gebräuche** *(Benutzung)* use; *(eines Wortes auch)* usage; *(Anwendung)* application; *(Brauch)* custom. **falscher ~** misuse; **mis-application; von etw ~ machen** to make use of sth; **etw in ~** *(dat)* **haben** to use sth; **allgemein in ~** *(dat)* in general use; **zum äußerlichen/innerlichen ~** to be taken externally/internally; **vor ~ (gut) schütteln** shake (well) before use.
gebrauchen* *vt (benutzen)* to use; *(anwenden)* to apply. **sich zu etw ~ lassen** to be useful for sth; *(ausnutzen)* to be used as sth; **nicht mehr zu ~ sein** to be no longer any use; **er/das ist zu nichts zu ~** he's/that's (of) no use to anybody; **das kann ich gut ~** I can really use that; **ich könnte ein neues Kleid ~** I could use a new dress, I could do with a new dress.
gebräuchlich *adj (verbreitet)* common; *(gewöhn-*

lich) usual, customary. **nicht mehr ~** *(Ausdruck etc)* no longer used.
Gebrauchs-: **~anweisung** *f (für Arznei)* directions *pl; (für Geräte etc)* instructions *pl*; **etw g~fähig machen** to put sth into working order; **g~fertig** *adj* ready for use; *Nahrungsmittel* instant; **~gegenstand** *m* basic commodity.
gebraucht *adj* second-hand, used. **etw ~ kaufen** to buy sth second-hand.
Gebrauchtwagen *m* used *or* second-hand car.
gebräunt *adj (braungebrannt)* (sun-)tanned.
Gebrechen *nt - (geh)* affliction.
gebrechlich *adj* frail.
gebrochen **1** *ptp of* **brechen. 2** *adj* broken. **~en Herzens** broken-hearted; **~ Deutsch sprechen** to speak broken German.
Gebrüder *pl (Comm)* ~ **Müller** Müller Brothers.
gebückt *adj* **eine ~e Haltung** a stoop; **~ gehen** to stoop.
Gebühr *f* **-en (a)** charge; *(Post~)* postage *no pl; (Honorar)* fee; *(Studien~)* fees *pl; (Vermittlungs~)* commission; *(Rad, TV)* licence *(Brit)*, license *(US)*. **~en erheben** to make a charge, to charge postage/a fee *etc;* **zu ermäßigter ~** at a reduced rate; **~ (be)zahlt Empfänger** postage to be paid by addressee. **(b)** *(Angemessenheit)* **nach ~** suitably, properly; **über ~** excessively.
gebühren* *(geh)* **1** *vi* to be due *(dat* to). **ihm gebührt Anerkennung** he deserves *or* is due recognition. **2** *vr* to be proper *or* fitting. **wie es sich gebührt** as is proper.
gebührend *adj (verdient)* due; *(angemessen)* suitable; *(geziemend)* proper.
Gebühren-: **~erhöhung** *f* increase in charges/fees; **g~frei** *adj* free of charge; *Brief, Paket* postfree; **g~pflichtig** *adj* chargeable; **g~pflichtige Verwarnung** *(Jur)* fine; **jdn g~pflichtig verwarnen** to fine sb.
gebunden **1** *ptp of* **binden. 2** *adj* tied *(an+acc* to sth); *Kapital* tied up; *Preise* controlled; *(Ling, Phys, Buch)* bound; *Wärme* latent; *(Mus)* legato. **vertraglich ~ sein** to be bound by contract; **anderweitig ~ sein** to be otherwise engaged.
Geburt *f* **-en** *(lit, fig)* birth. **von ~ by birth; von ~ an** from birth; **das war eine schwere ~!** *(fig col)* that took some doing *(col)*.
Geburten-: **~kontrolle,** **~regelung** *f* birth control; **~rückgang** *m* drop in the birth rate; **g~schwach** *adj Jahrgang* with a low birth rate; **g~stark** *adj* with a high birth rate.
gebürtig *adj* **~er Londoner sein** to have been born in London, to be a native Londoner.
Geburts-: **~anzeige** *f* birth announcement; **~datum** *nt* date of birth; **~fehler** *m* congenital defect; **~helfer(in** *f)* **~m** *(Arzt)* obstetrician; **~hilfe** *f (als Fach)* obstetrics *sing; (von Hebamme auch)* midwifery; **~jahr** *nt* year of birth; **~land** *nt* native country; **~ort** *m* birth place.
Geburtstag *m* birthday. **herzlichen Glückwunsch zum ~!** happy birthday!, many happy returns (of the day)!; **jdm zum ~ gratulieren** to wish sb (a) happy birthday *or* many happy returns (of the day); **heute habe ich ~** it's my birthday today; **~ feiern** to celebrate one's/sb's birthday; **jdm etw zum ~ schenken** to give sb sth for his/her birthday.
Geburtstags- *in cpds* birthday.
Geburts-: **~urkunde** *f* birth certificate; **~wehen** *pl* labour *(Brit)* or labor *(US)* pains *pl*.
Gebüsch *nt* **-e** bushes *pl; (Unterholz)* undergrowth.
gedacht **1** *ptp of* **denken, gedenken. 2** *adj Linie, Fall* imaginary.
Gedächtnis *nt* memory; *(Andenken auch)* remembrance. **etw aus dem ~ hersagen** to recite sth from memory; **wenn mich mein ~ nicht trügt** if my memory serves me right; **zum ~ an die Toten** in memory *or* remembrance of the dead.

Gedächtnis-: ~feier f commemoration; ~hilfe f memory aid, mnemonic; ~lücke f gap in one's memory; ~schwund m amnesia, loss of memory; ~verlust m loss of memory.

gedämpft adj Geräusch muffled; Farben, Instrument, Stimmung muted; Licht, Freude subdued. **mit ~er Stimme** in a low voice.

Gedanke m -n thought (über +acc on, about); (Idee, Plan, Einfall) idea; (Konzept) concept; (Betrachtung) reflection (über+acc on). **der bloße ~ an ...** the mere thought of ...; **da kam mir ein ~** then I had an idea; **in ~n vertieft/verloren sein** to be deep/lost in thought; **jdn auf andere ~n bringen** to take sb's mind off things; **sich (dat) über etw (acc) ~n machen** to think about sth; **(sich sorgen)** to worry about sth; **etw ganz in ~n (dat) tun** to do sth without thinking; **jds ~n lesen** to read sb's mind or thoughts; **auf einen ~n kommen** to have or get an idea; **auf dumme ~n kommen (col)** to get up to mischief; **jdn auf den ~n bringen, etw zu tun** to give sb the idea of doing sth.

Gedanken-: ~freiheit f freedom of thought; ~lesen nt mind-reading; **g~los** adj (unüberlegt) unthinking; (zerstreut) absent-minded; (rücksichtslos) thoughtless; **etw g~los tun** to do sth without thinking; ~losigkeit f siehe adj lack of thought; absentmindedness; thoughtlessness; ~sprung m mental leap; ~strich m dash; ~übertragung f telepathy (auch fig), thought transference; **g~verloren** adj lost in thought.

gedanklich adj intellectual; (vorgestellt) imaginary.

Gedärme pl intestines pl.

Gedeck nt -e (Tisch~) cover; (Menü) set meal, table d'hôte; (in Lokal) cover charge; **set drink served with cover charge. ein ~ auflegen** to set a place.

gedeckt adj Farben muted; Gang covered.

Gedeih m: **auf ~ und Verderb** for better or (for) worse.

gedeihen pret **gedieh**, ptp **gediehen** vi aux sein to thrive, to flourish; (geh: sich entwickeln) to develop; (fig: vorankommen) to make progress. **die Sache ist so weit gediehen, daß ...** the matter has reached the point or stage where ...

Gedeihen nt no pl (Gelingen) success.

Gedenken nt no pl memory. **zum ~ an jdn** in memory or remembrance of sb.

gedenken* vi irreg +gen (geh: denken an) to remember, to think of; (feierlich) to commemorate. ~, **etw zu tun** to propose to do sth.

Gedenk-: ~feier f commemoration; ~minute f minute's silence; ~stätte f memorial; ~stein m memorial stone; ~stunde f hour of commemoration; ~tag m commemoration day.

Gedicht nt -e poem. **die ~ Enzensbergers** Enzensberger's poetry or poems; **dieses Kleid ist ein ~** (fig col) this dress is sheer poetry.

gediegen adj (a) Metall pure. (b) (von Qualität) high-quality; (geschmackvoll) tasteful; (rechtschaffen) upright; Verarbeitung solid; Kenntnisse sound.

gedieh pret of **gedeihen.**

gediehen ptp of **gedeihen.**

Gedränge nt no pl (Menschenmenge) crowd, crush; (Drängeln) jostling.

gedrängt adj packed; (fig) Stil terse. ~ **voll** packed full, jam-packed (col).

gedroschen ptp of **dreschen.**

gedruckt adj lügen wie ~ (col) to lie through one's teeth.

gedrückt adj depressed, dejected. ~**er Stimmung sein** to be in low spirits, to feel depressed.

gedrungen 1 ptp of **dringen.** 2 adj Gestalt sturdy, stocky.

geduckt adj Haltung, Mensch crouching; Kopf lowered.

Geduld f no pl patience. **mit jdm/etw ~ haben** to be patient or have patience with sb/sth; **mir reißt die ~, ich verliere die ~** my patience is wearing thin, I'm losing my patience.

gedulden* vr to be patient.

geduldig adj patient. ~ **wie ein Lamm** meek as a lamb.

Gedulds-: ~faden m jetzt reißt mir aber der ~faden! (col) I'm just about losing patience; ~probe f trial of (one's) patience; ~spiel nt puzzle.

gedungen adj (pej geh) Mörder hired.

gedurft ptp of **dürfen.**

ge|ehrt adj honoured (Brit), honored (US). **Sehr ~e Damen und Herren!** Ladies and Gentlemen!; (in Briefen) Dear Sirs; Dear Sir or Madam; **Sehr ~er Herr Kurz!** Dear Mr Kurz.

ge|eignet adj (passend) suitable; (richtig) right. **sie ist für diesen Posten nicht ~** she's not the right person for this job; **im ~en Augenblick** at the right moment; **er wäre zum Lehrer gut/schlecht ~** he would/wouldn't make a good teacher.

Gefahr f -en (a) danger (für to, for); (Bedrohung) threat (für to, for). **die ~en des Verkehrs/dieses Berufs** the dangers or perils or hazards of the traffic/this job; **in ~ sein/schweben** to be in danger or jeopardy; **außer ~ (nicht gefährdet)** not in danger; (nicht mehr gefährdet) out of danger; (Patient) off the danger list; **sich einer ~ aussetzen** to put oneself in danger; **es besteht die ~, daß ...** there's a risk or the danger that ... (b) (Wagnis, Risiko) risk (für to, for). **auf eigene ~** at one's own risk or (stärker) peril; ~ **laufen, etw zu tun** to run the risk of doing sth.

gefährden* vt to endanger; Chancen etc auch to jeopardize; (bedrohen) to threaten.

Gefährdung f no pl (a) siehe vt endangering; jeopardizing. (b) (Gefahr) danger (gen to).

gefahren ptp of **fahren.**

Gefahren-: ~stelle f danger spot; ~zulage f danger money.

gefährlich adj dangerous; (gewagt auch) risky.

Gefährlichkeit f siehe adj dangerousness; riskiness.

Gefahr-: **g~los** adj safe; ~losigkeit f safety. **Gefährte** m (wk) -n, -n, **Gefährtin** f (geh: lit, fig) companion.

Gefälle nt - (Neigung) (von Fluß) drop, fall; (von Land, Straße) slope; (Neigungsgrad) gradient; (fig: Unterschied) difference. **das Gelände hat ein starkes ~** the land slopes down steeply; **starkes ~!** steep hill.

gefallen[1]* vi irreg to please (jdm sb). **es gefällt mir (gut)** I like it (very much or a lot); **es gefällt ihm, wie sie spricht** he likes the way she talks; **das gefällt mir gar nicht** I don't like it at all; **sich (dat) etw ~ lassen** (dulden) to put up with sth.

gefallen[2] 1 ptp of **fallen, gefallen[1].** 2 adj (Mil) killed in action.

Gefallen[1] nt no pl (geh) pleasure. **an etw (dat) ~ finden** to derive pleasure from sth; **an jdm ~ finden** to take to sb.

Gefallen[2] m - favour (Brit), favor (US). **jdn um einen ~ bitten** to ask a favour of sb; **tun Sie mir den ~ und schweigen Sie** would you do me a favour and be quiet; **ihm zu ~** to please him.

Gefallene(r) mf decl as adj soldier killed in action.

gefällig adj (a) (hilfsbereit) helpful, obliging. (b) (ansprechend) pleasing; (freundlich) pleasant. (c) **sonst noch etwas ~?** (iro) will there be anything else?

Gefälligkeit f (a) (Gefallen) favour (Brit), favor (US). **jdm eine ~ erweisen** to do sb a favour. (b) no pl (gefälliges Wesen) pleasantness. **etw aus ~ tun** to do sth out of the kindness of one's heart.

gefälligst adv (col) kindly. **sei ~ still!** will you

kindly keep your mouth shut! *(col)*.

gefangen 1 *ptp of* **fangen. 2** *adj (~genommen)* captured; *(fig)* captivated. **sich ~ geben** to give oneself up, to surrender.

Gefangenen-: **~austausch** *m* exchange of prisoners; **~lager** *nt* prison camp; **~wärter** *m* prison officer, (prison) warder.

Gefangene(r) *mf decl as adj* prisoner. **500 ~ machen** *(Mil)* to take 500 prisoners.

Gefangen-: **g~halten** *vt sep irreg* to hold prisoner; *Tiere* to keep in captivity; *(fig)* to captivate; **~nahme** *f* **-n** capture; *(Verhaftung)* arrest; **g~nehmen** *vt sep irreg Mensch* to take captive *or* prisoner; *(verhaften)* to arrest; *(fig)* to captivate; **~schaft** *f* captivity; **in ~schaft geraten** to be taken prisoner.

Gefängnis *nt* prison, jail; *(~strafe)* imprisonment. **im ~ sitzen** *(col)* to be in prison; **ins ~ kommen** to be sent to prison; **zwei Jahre ~ bekommen** to get two years' imprisonment.

Gefängnis- *in cpds* prison; **~aufseher** *m* warder *(Brit)*, guard *(US)*, prison officer; **~direktor** *m* prison governor, prison warden *(esp US)*; **~insasse** *m* inmate; **~strafe** *f* prison sentence; **er wurde zu einer ~strafe verurteilt** he was sent to prison, he was given a prison sentence; **~wärter** *m siehe* **~aufseher**; **~zelle** *f* prison cell.

gefärbt *adj* coloured *(Brit)*, colored *(US)*; *Haar, Stoff* dyed; *Lebensmittel* artificially coloured *(Brit)* or colored *(US)*; *(fig)* Bericht biased.

Gefasel *nt no pl (pej)* drivel *(col)*.

Gefäß *nt* **-e** vessel *(auch Anat, Bot)*; *(Behälter)* receptacle.

gefaßt *adj (ruhig)* composed, calm. **auf etw** *(acc)* **~ sein** to be prepared *or* ready for sth; **er kann sich auf etwas ~ machen** *(col)* I'll give him something to think about *(col)*.

Gefecht *nt* **-e** *(lit, fig)* battle; *(Mil)* engagement; *(Scharmützel)* skirmish. **ein hartes ~** fierce fighting; **jdn/etw außer ~ setzen** *(lit, fig)* to put sb/sth out of action; **Argumente ins ~ führen** to advance arguments; **im Eifer des ~s** *(fig)* in the heat of the moment.

gefechtsbereit *adj* ready for action; *(einsatzfähig)* (fully) operational.

gefedert *adj (Matratze)* sprung.

gefeiert *adj* celebrated.

gefeit *adj* **gegen etw ~ sein** to be immune to sth.

gefestigt *adj* Tradition established; *Charakter* steadfast.

Gefieder *nt* **-** plumage, feathers *pl*.

gefiedert *adj* feathered.

Geflecht *nt* **-e** *(lit, fig)* network; *(Gewebe)* weave; *(Rohr~)* wickerwork.

gefleckt *adj* spotted; *Blume, Vogel* speckled; *Haut* blotchy.

Geflimmer *nt no pl* shimmering; *(Film, TV)* flicker(ing); *(heiße Luft)* heat-haze.

geflissentlich *adj (geh)* deliberate.

geflochten *ptp of* **flechten**.

geflogen *ptp of* **fliegen**.

geflohen *ptp of* **fliehen**.

geflossen *ptp of* **fließen**.

Geflügel *nt no pl (Zool, Cook)* poultry *no pl*.

Geflügel- *in cpds* poultry; **~händler** *m* poulterer, poultry dealer; **~schere** *f* poultry shears *pl*.

geflügelt *adj* winged. **~e Worte** familiar quotations.

Geflüster *nt no pl* whispering.

gefochten *ptp of* **fechten**.

Gefolge *nt* **-** retinue; *(Trauer~)* cortège. **im ~ in** the wake (+gen of); **etw im ~ haben** *(fig)* to bring sth in its wake.

Gefolgschaft *f (die Anhänger)* following; *(Hist: Gefolge)* retinue.

gefragt *adj* in demand *pred*.

gefräßig *adj* gluttonous; *(fig geh)* voracious.

Gefräßigkeit *f* gluttony.

Gefreite(r) *mf decl as adj (Mil)* lance corporal *(Brit)*, private first class *(US)*.

gefressen *ptp of* **fressen**. **jdn ~ haben** *(col)* to be sick of sb *(col)*.

gefrieren *vi irreg aux sein (lit, fig)* to freeze.

Gefrier-: **~fach** *nt* freezer compartment; **g~getrocknet** *adj* freeze-dried; **~punkt** *m* freezing point; **~truhe** *f* freezer, deep freeze.

gefroren *ptp of* **frieren, gefrieren**.

Gefüge *nt* - *(lit, fig)* structure.

gefügig *adj* submissive; *(gehorsam)* obedient. **jdn ~ machen** to make sb bend to one's will.

Gefühl *nt* **-e** feeling; *(~sregung auch)* emotion. **etw im ~ haben** to have a feel for sth; **ich habe ein ~, als ob ...** I feel as though ..; **ein ~ für Zahlen/Musik** a feeling for figures/music; **ein ~ für Gerechtigkeit/Anstand** a sense of justice/decency.

gefühllos *adj* insensitive, unfeeling; *Bein* numb.

Gefühllosigkeit *f siehe adj* insensitivity; numbness.

Gefühls-: **~ausbruch** *m* emotional outburst; **g~betont** *adj* emotional; *Rede, Äußerung auch* emotive; **~duselei** *f (pej)* mawkishness; **g~ kalt** *adj* cold; **~kälte** *f* coldness; **~leben** *nt* emotional life; **g~mäßig** *adj* instinctive; **~mensch** *m* emotional person; **~regung** *f* stir of emotion; *(seelische Empfindung)* feeling.

gefühlvoll *adj (empfindsam)* sensitive; *(ausdrucksvoll)* expressive; *(liebevoll)* loving.

gefüllt *adj (Cook)* stuffed; *Pralinen* with soft centres *(Brit)* or centers *(US)*; *Brieftasche* full.

gefunden 1 *ptp of* **finden. 2** *adj* **das war ein ~es Fressen für ihn** that was handing it to him on a plate.

gefürchtet *adj* dreaded *usu attr*.

Gegacker *nt no pl (lit, fig)* cackle, cackling.

gegangen *ptp of* **gehen**.

gegeben 1 *ptp of* **geben. 2** *adj* given; *(Philos: real)* factual. **unter den ~en Umständen** given the circumstances; **bei den ~en Tatsachen** given these facts; **etw als ~ voraussetzen** to assume sth; **zu ~er Zeit** in due course.

gegebenenfalls *adv* should the situation arise.

Gegebenheit *f usu pl* (actual) fact; *(Zustand)* condition.

gegen *prep+acc* **(a)** *(wider)* against. **X ~ Y** *(Sport, Jur)* X versus Y; **~ seinen Befehl** contrary to *or* against his orders; **haben Sie ein Mittel ~ Schnupfen?** do you have anything for colds?; **nichts ~ jdn/etw haben** to have nothing against sb/sth. **(b)** *(in Richtung auf)* towards, toward; *(nach)* to; *(an)* against. **~ einen Baum fahren** to drive into a tree; **etw ~ das Licht halten** to hold sth to *or* against the light; **~ Osten fahren** to travel to(wards) the east; **es wird ~ Abend kühler** it grows cooler towards evening. **(c)** *(ungefähr)* round about, around. **ich komme ~ Abend vorbei** I'll come around early this evening. **(d)** *(gegenüber)* towards, toward, to. **gerecht ~ alle** fair to all. **(e)** *(im Austausch für)* for. **~ bar** for cash; **~ Quittung** against a receipt; **~ Bezahlung** in exchange for payment. **(f)** *(verglichen mit)* compared with.

Gegen-: **~angriff** *m (Mil, fig)* counterattack; **~argument** *nt* counterargument; **~beispiel** *nt* counterexample; **~besuch** *m* return visit; **jdm einen ~besuch machen** to return sb's visit; **~beweis** *m* **den ~beweis zu etw erbringen** to produce evidence against sth.

Gegend *f* **-en** area; *(geographisches Gebiet, Körper~)* region. **die ~ von London** the London area; **hier in der ~** around here; **die ganze ~ spricht davon** the whole neighbourhood *(Brit)* or neighborhood *(US)* is talking about it.

Gegendarstellung *f (Press)* reply.

gegen|einander *adv* against each other; *(im Austausch)* for each other; *(zueinander)* to(wards)

each other.
gegen|einander-: ~**halten** *vt sep irreg (lit)* to hold together; *(fig)* to compare; ~**stehen** *vi sep irreg (fig)* to be on opposite sides; *(Aussagen)* to conflict; ~**stoßen** *vi sep irreg aux sein* to bump into each other; *(kollidieren)* to collide.

Gegen-: ~**erklärung** *f* counterstatement; *(Dementi)* denial, disclaimer; ~**fahrbahn** *f* oncoming lane; ~**frage** *f* counterquestion; **jdm eine** ~**frage stellen** to ask sb a question in reply (to his); ~**gerade** *f (Sport)* back straight; ~**gewicht** *nt* counterbalance *(auch fig)*, counterweight; ~**gift** *nt* antidote *(gegen* to); ~**kandidat** *m* rival candidate; ~**kurs** *m (lit, fig)* opposite course; **einen** ~**kurs steuern** to take an opposing course of action; ~**leistung** *f* service in return; **als** ~**leistung für etw** in return for sth; ~**licht** *nt* etw **bei** *or* **im** ~ **aufnehmen** *(Phot)* to take a contrejour photo(graph) of sth; ~**liebe** *f* requited love; *(fig: Zustimmung)* approval; **der Vorschlag stieß auf wenig** ~**liebe** the suggestion was hardly welcomed with open arms; ~**maßnahme** *f* countermeasure; ~**maßnahmen zur Bekämpfung der Inflation** measures to counter inflation; ~**meinung** *f* opposite opinion; ~**mittel** *nt (Med)* antidote *(gegen* to); ~**partei** *f* other side; *(Sport)* opposing side; *(Jur)* opposing party; ~**probe** *f* crosscheck; ~**reaktion** *f* counter-reaction; ~**rede** *f (Antwort)* reply; *(Widerrede)* contradiction; ~**richtung** *f* opposite direction.

Gegensatz *m* **-e** opposite; *(Kontrast)* contrast; *(Unvereinbarkeit)* conflict; *(Unterschied)* difference. **im** ~ **zu** unlike, in contrast to; **einen krassen** ~ **zu etw bilden** to contrast sharply with sth; ~**e ausgleichen** to even out differences.
gegensätzlich *adj (konträr)* contrasting; *(widersprüchlich)* opposing; *(unterschiedlich)* different; *(unvereinbar)* conflicting. **eine** ~**e Meinung** a conflicting view.

Gegen-: ~**schlag** *m (Mil)* reprisal; *(fig)* retaliation *no pl*; **zum** ~**schlag ausholen** to prepare to retaliate; ~**seite** *f (lit, fig)* other side; **g**~**seitig** *adj* mutual; **sie beschuldigten sich g**~**seitig** they (each) accused one another; **sich g**~**seitig ausschließen** to be mutually exclusive; **in g**~**seitigem Einverständnis** by mutual agreement; ~**seitigkeit** *f* mutuality; **ein Vertrag auf** ~**seitigkeit** a reciprocal treaty; ~**sinn** *m* **im** ~**sinn** in the opposite direction; ~**spieler** *m* opponent; *(bei Mannschaftsspielen auch)* opposite number; ~**sprechanlage** *f* (two-way) intercom.
Gegenstand *m* **-e** *(Ding)* object, thing; *(Thema)* subject; *(der Neugier etc, Philos)* object. ~ **des Gespötts** laughing stock.
gegenständlich *adj* concrete; *(Philos)* objective; *(Art)* representational.
gegenstandslos *adj (grundlos)* groundless; *(hinfällig)* irrelevant.
Gegen-: ~**stimme** *f (Parl)* vote against; ~**stoß** *m (Mil, Sport)* counterattack; ~**stück** *nt* opposite; *(passendes* ~**stück)** counterpart.
Gegenteil *nt* opposite *(von* of); *(Umkehrung)* reverse *(von* of). **im** ~! on the contrary!; **ganz im** ~ quite the reverse; **das** ~ **bewirken** to have the opposite effect; *(Mensch)* to achieve the exact opposite; **ins** ~ **umschlagen** to swing to the other extreme.
gegenteilig *adj Ansicht, Wirkung* opposite, contrary. **eine** ~**e Meinung** a different opinion; **ich habe nichts G**~**es gehört** I've heard nothing to the contrary.
Gegentor *nt (esp Ftbl)* **ein** ~ **hinnehmen müssen** to concede a goal; **ein** ~ **erzielen** to score.
gegen|über 1 *prep+dat* **(a)** *(örtlich)* opposite. **er wohnt mir** ~ he lives opposite me; **er saß mir schräg** ~ he sat diagonally across from me. **(b)** *(zu)* to; *(in bezug auf)* with regard to, toward(s); *(angesichts, vor)* in the face of; *(im Vergleich*

zu) in comparison with. **mir** ~ **hat er das nicht geäußert** he didn't say that to me; **er ist allem Neuen** ~ **wenig aufgeschlossen** he's not very open-minded about anything new. **2** *adv* opposite. **der Park** ~ the park opposite; **die Leute von** ~ *(col)* the people opposite.
Gegen|über *nt* - *(bei Kampf)* opponent; *(bei Diskussion)* opposite number. **mein** ~ **im Zug** the person opposite me in the train.
gegen|über-: ~**liegen** *sep irreg* **1** *vi+dat* to be opposite, to face; **2** *vr* **sich** *(dat)* ~**liegen** to face each other; ~**liegend** *adj attr* opposite; ~**sehen** *vr sep irreg+dat* **sich einer Aufgabe** ~**sehen** to be faced *or* confronted with a task; ~**sitzen** *vi sep irreg* to sit opposite *or* facing; ~**stehen** *vi sep irreg* +*dat* to be opposite, to face; **jdm feindlich/freundlich** ~**stehen** to have a hostile/friendly attitude towards sb; **einer Gefahr** ~**stehen** to be faced with a danger; ~**stellen** *vt sep (konfrontieren mit)* to confront *(dat* with); *(fig: vergleichen)* to compare *(dat* with); **G**~**stellung** *f* confrontation; *(fig: Vergleich)* comparison; ~**treten** *vi sep irreg aux sein* **jdm** ~**treten** to face sb.
Gegen-: ~**verkehr** *m* oncoming traffic; ~**vorschlag** *m* counter-proposal.
Gegenwart *f no pl* **(a)** present; *(Gram)* present (tense). **die Musik der** ~ contemporary music; **die Probleme der** ~ the problems of today. **(b)** *(Anwesenheit)* presence. **in** ~ **von** in the presence of.
gegenwärtig 1 *adj attr (jetzig)* present; *(heutig auch)* current, present-day. **(b)** *(geh: anwesend)* present *pred*. **2** *adv (augenblicklich)* at present; *(heutzutage auch)* currently.
gegenwartsbezogen *adj Roman etc* relevant to present times.
Gegen-: ~**wehr** *f* resistance; ~**wert** *m* equivalent; ~**wind** *m* headwind; **g**~**zeichnen** *vt sep* to countersign; ~**zeuge** *m* witness for the other side; ~**zug** *m* **im** ~**zug zu etw** as a countermove to sth.
gegessen *ptp of* **essen.**
geglichen *ptp of* **gleichen.**
gegliedert *adj* jointed; *(fig)* structured.
geglitten *ptp of* **gleiten.**
geglommen *ptp of* **glimmen.**
geglückt *adj Feier* successful; *Überraschung* real.
Gegner(in *f)* *m* - opponent *(auch Sport)*, adversary; *(Rivale)* rival; *(Feind)* enemy.
gegnerisch *adj attr* opposing; *(Mil: feindlich)* enemy attr, hostile; *Übermacht* of the enemy.
Gegnerschaft *f* opposition.
gegolten *ptp of* **gelten.**
gegoren *ptp of* **gären.**
gegossen *ptp of* **gießen.**
gegr. = gegründet established, est.
gegraben *ptp of* **graben.**
gegriffen *ptp of* **greifen.**
Gehabe *nt no pl (col)* affected behaviour *(Brit)* or behavior *(US).*
gehabt *ptp of* **haben.**
Gehackte(s) *nt decl as adj* mince *(Brit)*, minced *or* ground *(US)* meat.
Gehalt[1] *m* **-e** content. **der** ~ **an Eiweiß** the protein content.
Gehalt[2] *nt* **-er** salary.
gehalten 1 *ptp of* **halten. 2** *adj:* ~ **sein, etw zu tun** *(form)* to be required to do sth.
gehaltlos *adj Nahrung* unnutritious; *(fig)* empty.
Gehalts-: ~**abrechnung** *f* salary statement; ~**anspruch** *m* salary claim; ~**empfänger** *m* ~**empfänger sein** to receive a salary, to be salaried; ~**erhöhung** *f* salary increase; *(regelmäßig)* increment; ~**klasse** *f* salary bracket; ~**konto** *nt* current *(Brit)* or checking *(US)* account; ~**kürzung** *f* cut in salary; ~**wunsch** *m* salary requirement; ~**zulage** *f (*~**erhöhung)** salary increase; *(regelmäßig)* increment; *(Extrazulage)* bonus.

gehaltvoll adj Speise nutritious, nourishing; (fig) rich in content.

gehandikapt [gə'hɛndikɛpt] adj handicapped.

Gehänge nt - garland; (Ohr~) drop, pendant.

gehangen ptp of **hängen**.

geharnischt adj (fig) Antwort etc sharp, strong.

gehässig adj spiteful.

Gehässigkeit f spite, spitefulness.

gehäuft adj Löffel heaped.

Gehäuse nt - (a) case, casing; (Lautsprecher~) box. (b) (Schnecken~) shell. (c) (Obst~) core.

gehbehindert adj disabled.

Gehege nt - reserve; (im Zoo) enclosure, compound; (Wild~) preserve. **jdm ins ~ kommen** (fig col) to get under sb's feet (col); (ein Recht streitig machen) to poach on sb's preserves.

geheiligt adj Brauch, Recht sacred.

geheim adj secret. **seine ~sten Gefühle/Wünsche** his innermost or most private feelings/wishes; **streng ~** top secret.

Geheim-: ~**bund** m secret society; ~**dienst** m secret service; ~**fach** nt secret compartment; **g~halten** vt sep irreg **etw (vor jdm) g~halten** to keep sth a secret (from sb).

Geheimhaltung f secrecy. **zur ~ von etw verpflichtet sein** to be sworn to secrecy about sth.

Geheimnis nt secret; (rätselhaftes ~) mystery. **das ~ der Schönheit/des Erfolgs** the secret of beauty/success; **aus etw ein/kein ~ machen** to make a big secret about sth/no secret of sth.

Geheimnis-: ~**krämer** m (col) mystery-monger (col); **g~voll** adj mysterious; **g~voll tun** to be mysterious.

Geheim-: ~**polizei** f secret police; ~**rat** m privy councillor; ~**ratsecken** pl (col) **er hat ~ratsecken** he is going bald at the temples; ~**rezept** nt secret recipe; ~**tip** m (personal) tip; ~**waffe** f secret weapon.

Geheiß nt no pl (geh) **auf jds ~** (acc) at sb's behest.

geheißen ptp of **heißen**.

gehemmt adj Mensch inhibited.

gehen pret **ging**, ptp **gegangen** aux sein 1 vi (a) to go; (zu Fuß) to walk; (abfahren, ausscheiden auch) to leave; (blicken: Fenster) to look out (auf +acc, nach onto). **über die Straße ~** to cross the road; **auf die andere Seite ~** to cross (over) to the other side; **zu jdm ~** to go to see sb; **er ging im Zimmer auf und ab** he walked or paced up and down the room; **wie lange geht man bis zum Bus?** how long a walk is it to the bus?; **wie geht man dorthin?** how do you get there?; **das Kind lernt ~** the baby is learning to walk; **wo er geht und steht** wherever he goes or is; **schwimmen/schlafen ~** to go swimming/to bed; **mit jdm ~** (befreundet sein) to go out with sb, to be with sb; **mit der Zeit/Mode ~** to move with the times/follow the fashion; **in sich** (acc) **~** to think things over; **nach einer Regel ~** to follow a or go by a rule; **das geht gegen meine Überzeugung** that goes or runs against my convictions; **er ging so weit, zu behaupten ...** (fig) he went so far as to claim ...; **das geht zu weit** (fig) that's going too far; **wie geht das Lied/Gedicht?** how does the song/poem go?; **heute geht ein scharfer Wind** there's a biting wind today; **die See geht hoch** there's a high sea, the sea is running high; **die Reise geht über Dresden** we/they etc are going via Dresden; **~ wir!** let's go; **das Schiff geht nach Harwich** the boat is going to or is bound for Harwich; **jdm aus dem Weg ~** to get or move out of sb's way.

(b) (funktionieren) to work; (Auto, Uhr) to go. **die Uhr geht falsch/richtig** the clock is wrong/right.

(c) (dauern) to go on. **wie lange geht das denn noch?** how much longer is it going to go on?

(d) (reichen) to go. **der Rock geht ihr bis zum Knie** her skirt goes down to her knees; **in die**

Tausende ~ to run into (the) thousands.

(e) (Teig) to rise; (vor dem Backen auch) to prove.

(f) (urteilen) **nach etw ~** to go by sth.

(g) (sich kleiden) **in etw** (dat) **~** to wear sth.

(h) (ertönen: Klingel) to go, to ring.

(i) **wie ~ die Geschäfte?** how's business?; **wieviele Leute ~ in deinen Wagen?** how many people can you get in your car?; **in diese Schachtel ~ 20 Stück** this packet holds 20; **das Buch ging um ...** the book was about ...; **mein Vorschlag geht dahin, daß ...** my suggestion is that ...; **diese Schublade geht schwer** this drawer is very stiff; **nichts geht über** (+acc) **...** there's nothing to beat ...; **there's nothing better than ...; in die Politik ~** to go into politics; **in die Gewerkschaft/Partei ~** to join the union/party; **unter die Künstler/Säufer ~** (usu hum) to join the ranks of artists/alcoholics; **das geht doch nicht** (ist nicht möglich) that's not or.; **Dienstag geht auch nicht** (col) Tuesday is no good either; **was geht hier vor sich?** what's going on here?

2 vi impers (a) (gesundheitlich) **wie geht es Ihnen?** how are you?; (zu Patient) how are you feeling?; (danke,) **es geht** (col) all right or not too bad(, thanks) (col); **es geht ihm gut/schlecht** he's quite well/not at all well; **sonst geht's dir gut?** (iro) are you sure you're feeling quite all right? (iro).

(b) (ergehen) **wie geht's?** how are things?; (bei Arbeit etc) how's it going?; **es geht not too bad, so-so; mir ist es genauso gegangen** (ich habe dasselbe erlebt) it was just the same with me; (ich habe dasselbe empfunden) I felt the same way; **laß es dir gut ~** look after yourself, take care of yourself.

(c) **es geht** (läßt sich machen) it's all right or OK (col); **solange es geht** as long as possible; **geht es?** (ohne Hilfe) can you manage?; **es geht nicht** (ist nicht möglich) it can't be done, it's impossible; (kommt nicht in Frage) it's not on; **so geht das, das geht so** that/this is how it's done; **so geht es or das** (eben) (so ist das Leben) that's how it goes; **morgen geht es nicht** tomorrow's no good.

(d) (betreffen) **ich weiß nicht, worum es geht** I don't know what this is about; **es geht um seinen Vertrag** it's about or it concerns his contract; **es geht um meine Ehre** my honour is at stake; **es geht ihm nur um eins** he's only interested in one thing; **darum geht es mir nicht** that's not the point; (spielt keine Rolle) that's not important to me; **wenn es nach mir ginge ...** if it were or was up to me ..., if I had my way ...

(e) (führen) **dann geht es immer geradeaus** (Straßenrichtung) then it's just straight on.

3 vt **er ging einen Kilometer** he walked a kilometre; **ich gehe immer diese Straße** I always walk or go along this road.

Gehen nt no pl (Zu-Fuß-~, Sport) walking; (Abschied) leaving.

gehenlassen* sep irreg 1 vt (col: in Ruhe lassen) to leave alone. 2 vr (a) to lose one's self-control. (b) (nachlässig sein) to let oneself go.

Geher(in f) m - (Sport) walker.

gehetzt adj harassed.

geheuer adj **nicht ~** (beängstigend) scary (col); (spukhaft) creepy (col); (verdächtig) fishy; (unwohl) uneasy; **es ist mir nicht ganz ~** it's scary (col); it gives me the creeps (col); it seems a bit fishy to me; I feel uneasy about it.

Gehilfe m (wk) **-n, -n**, **Gehilfin** f (kaufmännischer ~) trainee; (Jur) accomplice.

Gehirn nt **-e** brain; (Geist) mind.

Gehirn-: ~**chirurg** m brain surgeon; ~**erschütterung** f concussion; ~**schlag** m stroke; ~**wäsche** f brainwashing no pl; **jdm einer ~wäsche unterziehen** to brainwash sb.

gehoben 1 ptp of **heben. 2** adj Ausdrucksweise elevated, lofty; (anspruchsvoll) sophisticated; Stellung senior; Stimmung elated. ~er Dienst professional and executive levels of the civil service. **Gehöft** nt -e farm.

geholfen ptp of **helfen.**

Gehölz nt -e (geh) copse; (Dickicht) undergrowth.

Gehör nt -e hearing; (Mus) ear. kein musikalisches ~ haben to have no ear for music; ein schlechtes ~ haben to be hard of hearing; nach dem ~ spielen to play by ear; absolutes ~ perfect pitch; das ~ verlieren to go deaf; ~ finden to gain a hearing; er fand kein ~ he was not given a hearing; jdm ~/kein ~ schenken to listen/not to listen to sb; sich (dat) ~ verschaffen to gain attention; (bei Behörde) to obtain a hearing.

gehorchen* vi to obey (jdm sb); (Wagen, Maschine etc) to respond (jdm/einer Sache to sb/sth). seine Stimme gehorchte ihm nicht mehr he lost control over his voice.

gehören* **1** vi **(a)** jdm ~ to belong to sb, to be sb's. **(b)** (den richtigen Platz haben) to belong; (Gegenstand auch) to go. das gehört nicht hierher (Vorschlag) that is irrelevant here; das gehört nicht zur Sache that's irrelevant; er gehört ins Bett he should be in bed. **(c)** ~ zu (zählen zu) to be one of; (Bestandteil sein von) to be part of; (Mitglied sein von) to belong to; es gehört zu seinen Pflichten it's one of his duties; zur Familie ~ to be one of the family; dazu gehört Mut that takes courage; dazu gehört (schon) einiges or etwas that takes some doing (col). **2** vr to be (right and) proper. das gehört sich einfach nicht that's just not done.

gehörig adj **(a)** (geh) nicht zur Sache ~ irrelevant. **(b)** attr, adv (gebührend) proper. mit dem ~en Respekt with proper respect. **(c)** (col: beträchtlich, groß) good attr, well and truly adv. eine ~e Achtung vor jdm haben to have a healthy respect for sb.

gehörlos adj (form) deaf.

Gehörlose(r) mf decl as adj (form) deaf person.

gehorsam adj obedient.

Gehorsam m no pl obedience. jdm den ~ verweigern to refuse to obey sb.

Gehorsamkeit f obedience.

Gehörsinn m sense of hearing.

Gehsteig m pavement (Brit), sidewalk (US).

Gehweg m footpath.

Geier m - (lit, fig) vulture. weiß der ~ (col) God knows (col).

Geifer m no pl slaver; (fig pej) venom.

geifern vi to slaver; (Schaum vor dem Mund haben) to foam at the mouth. gegen jdn/etw ~ to revile sb/sth.

Geige f -n violin. die erste/zweite ~ spielen (lit) to play first/second violin; (fig) to call the tune/play second fiddle.

geigen 1 vi to play the violin. **2** vt Lied to play on the violin.

Geigen-: ~bogen m violin bow; ~kasten m violin-case.

Geiger(in f) m - violinist.

Geigerzähler m Geiger counter.

geil adj randy, horny; (pej: lüstern) lecherous.

Geilheit f siehe adj randiness, horniness; lecherousness.

Geisel f -n hostage. jdn als ~ nehmen to take sb hostage.

Geisel-: ~nahme f -n taking of hostages no pl; ~nehmer(in** f) m hostage-taker.

Geiß f -en (Ziege) (nanny-)goat.

Geißbock m billy-goat.

Geißel f -n (lit, fig) scourge; (dial: Peitsche) whip.

geißeln vt (anprangern) to castigate.

Geist m -er (a) no pl (Denken, Vernunft) mind. ~ und Materie mind and matter; etw im ~(e) vor sich sehen to see sth in one's mind's eye; sich im

~(e) als etw/an einem Ort sehen to picture oneself as sth/in a place. **(b)** (Rel: Seele, außerirdisches Wesen) spirit; (Gespenst) ghost. ~ und Körper mind and body; seinen ~ aufgeben to give up the ghost; der Heilige ~ the Holy Ghost or Spirit; der ~ Gottes the Spirit of God; von allen guten ~ern verlassen sein (col) to have taken leave of one's senses (col). **(c)** (no pl: Intellekt) intellect, mind; (fig: Denker, Genie) mind. ~ haben to have a good mind or intellect; (Witz) to be witty; hier scheiden sich die ~er this is the parting of the ways; sie sind verwandte ~er they are kindred spirits. **(d)** no pl (Wesen, Gesinnung) spirit. in jds ~ handeln to act in the spirit of sb.

Geister-: ~bahn f ghost train; ~fahrer m (col) ghost-driver (US col), person driving in the wrong direction; ~hand f: wie von ~hand as if by magic.

geistern vi aux sein to wander like a ghost. der Gedanke geisterte durch sein Hirn the thought haunted him.

Geister-: ~stadt f ghost town; ~stimme f ghostly voice; ~stunde f witching hour.

Geistes-: g~abwesend adj absent-minded; ~abwesenheit f absent-mindedness; ~arbeiter m brain-worker (col); ~armut f intellectual poverty; g~blitz m brainwave; ~gabe f intellectual gift; ~gegenwart f presence of mind; g~gegenwärtig adj quick-witted; g~gegenwärtig duckte er sich unter das Steuer with great presence of mind he ducked below the steering wheel; g~gestört adj mentally disturbed or (stärker) deranged; ~größe f (a) no pl (Genialität) greatness of mind; **(b)** (genialer Mensch) great mind, genius; ~haltung f mental attitude; g~krank adj mentally ill; ~kranke(r) mf mentally ill person; die ~kranken the mentally ill; ~krankheit f mental illness; (Wahnsinn) insanity; ~verfassung f frame of mind; g~verwandt adj die beiden sind g~verwandt they are kindred spirits; ~wissenschaft f arts subject; die ~wissenschaften the arts; (als Studium) the humanities; ~wissenschaftler m arts scholar; (Student) arts student; g~wissenschaftlich adj Fach arts attr; ~zustand m mental condition; jdn auf seinen ~zustand untersuchen to give sb a psychiatric examination.

geistig adj **(a)** (unkörperlich) spiritual. ~-seelisch mental and spiritual. **(b)** (intellektuell) intellectual; (Psych) mental. ~e Arbeit intellectual work; ~ anspruchsvoll/anspruchslos intellectually demanding/undemanding, highbrow/lowbrow; ~er Diebstahl plagiarism; ~es Eigentum intellectual property; ~ behindert/zurückgeblieben mentally handicapped/retarded; etw vor seinem ~en Auge sehen to see sth in one's mind's eye. **(c)** attr (alkoholisch) spirituous.

geistlich adj spiritual; (religiös) religious. ~es Amt/~er Orden religious office/order; ~es Recht canon law; der ~e Stand the clergy.

Geistliche f (wk) -n, -n woman priest; (von Freikirchen) woman minister.

Geistliche(r) m decl as adj clergyman; (Priester) priest; (von Freikirchen) minister; (Gefängnis~, Militär~ etc) chaplain.

Geistlichkeit f siehe **Geistliche(r)** clergy; priesthood; ministry.

Geist-: g~los adj stupid; (langweilig) dull; (einfallslos) unimaginative; ~losigkeit f (a) no pl siehe adj stupidity; dullness; unimaginativeness; **(b)** (Äußerung) stupid remark; g~reich adj (witzig) witty; (klug) intelligent; (einfallsreich) ingenious; Beschäftigung, Gespräch intellectually stimulating; g~tötend adj soul-destroying; g~voll adj Mensch, Äußerung wise; Buch, Beschäftigung intellectual.

Geiz m no pl meanness.

geizen *vi* to be mean; *(mit Worten, Zeit)* to be sparing.

Geizhals *m* miser.

geizig *adj* mean.

Geizkragen *m (col)* skinflint *(col)*.

gekannt *ptp of* **kennen**.

Gekicher *nt no pl* giggling.

Gekläff *nt no pl* yapping.

gekleidet *adj* dressed. **weiß** ~ dressed in white.

Geklimper *nt no pl (col) (Klavier~)* tinkling; *(stümperhaft)* plonking *(col)*; *(von Geld)* jingling.

Geklirr(e) *nt no pl* clinking; *(von Fensterscheiben)* rattling; *(von Ketten etc)* clanking; *(von Waffen)* clashing.

geklungen *ptp of* **klingen**.

Geknatter *nt no pl (von Motorrad)* roaring.

geknickt *adj (col)* glum, dejected.

gekniffen *ptp of* **kneifen**.

gekommen *ptp of* **kommen**.

gekonnt 1 *ptp of* **können**. 2 *adj* neat; *(meisterhaft)* masterly.

Gekrakel *nt no pl (col)* scrawl.

gekräuselt *adj* ruffled.

Gekreisch(e) *nt no pl* screeching.

Gekritzel *nt no pl (Gekritzeltes)* scribble.

gekrochen *ptp of* **kriechen**.

gekühlt *adj* chilled.

gekünstelt *adj* artificial; *Sprache, Benehmen auch* affected.

Gel *nt* **-e** gel.

Gelächter *nt* - laughter. **in** ~ **ausbrechen** to burst out laughing; **jdn dem** ~ **preisgeben** *(geh)* to make sb a laughing stock.

gelackmeiert *adj (col)* conned *(col)*.

geladen 1 *ptp of* **laden**. 2 *adj* loaded; *(Phys)* charged; *(col: wütend)* hopping mad *(col)*.

Gelage *nt* - feast, banquet.

gelagert *adj* **in anders/ähnlich** ~**en Fällen** in different/similar cases.

gelähmt *adj* paralyzed.

Gelände *nt* - (a) *(Land)* open country; *(Mil: Terrain)* ground. **offenes** ~ open country; **schwieriges** ~ difficult terrain *or* country. (b) *(Gebiet)* area. (c) *(Grundstück)* grounds *pl; (Bau~)* site.

Gelände-: ~**fahrt** *f* cross-country drive; ~**fahrzeug** *nt* cross-country vehicle; **g**~**gängig** *adj Fahrzeug* suitable for cross-country work.

Geländer *nt* - railing(s *pl);* *(Treppen~)* bannister(s *pl).*

gelang *pret of* **gelingen**.

gelangen* *vi aux sein* **an/auf etw** *(acc)*/**zu etw** ~ *(lit, fig)* to reach sth; *(fig: mit Mühe)* to attain sth; *(erwerben)* to acquire sth; **zum Ziel** ~ to reach one's goal; **in jds Besitz** ~ to come into sb's possession; **in die richtigen/falschen Hände** ~ to fall into the right/wrong hands; **zu Ruhm** ~ to achieve fame; **zu einer Überzeugung** ~ to become convinced; **an die Macht** ~ to come to power.

gelangweilt *adj* bored *no adv*.

gelassen 1 *ptp of* **lassen**. 2 *adj* calm. **etw** ~ **hinnehmen** to take sth calmly.

Gelassenheit *f* calmness.

Gelatine [ʒelaˈtiːnə] *f no pl* gelatine.

gelaufen *ptp of* **laufen**.

geläufig *adj* common; *(vertraut)* familiar. **das ist mir nicht** ~ I'm not familiar with that.

gelaunt *adj pred* **gut/schlecht** ~ good-/bad-tempered; *(vorübergehend)* in a good/bad mood.

gelb *adj* yellow; *(bei Verkehrsampel)* amber *(Brit)*.

Gelb *nt* - *or* *(col)* **-s** yellow; *(von Verkehrsampel)* amber *(Brit)*.

Gelbe(s) *nt decl as adj (vom Ei)* yolk. **das war nicht gerade das** ~ **vom Ei** *(col)* that wasn't exactly brilliant.

gelbgrün *adj* yellowish-green.

gelblich *adj* yellowish; *Gesichtsfarbe* sallow.

Gelb-: ~**sucht** *f* jaundice; **g**~**süchtig** *adj* jaundiced.

Geld *nt* **-er** (a) money. **bares/großes/kleines** ~ cash/notes *pl (Brit)*, bills *pl (US)*/change; ~ **und Gut** wealth and possessions; ~ **aufnehmen** to raise money; **zu** ~ **machen** to sell off; *(mit etw)* ~ **machen** *(col)* to make money *(from sth)*; **etw für teures** ~ **kaufen** to pay a lot for sth; **er hat** ~ **wie Heu** *(col)* he's stinking rich *(col)*; **mit** ~ **um sich werfen** to chuck one's money around *(col)*; **jdm das** ~ **aus der Tasche ziehen** to squeeze money out of sb; **am** ~ **hängen** *or* **kleben** to be tight with money; **hinterm** ~ **hersein** *(col)* to be out for money; **das ist nicht für** ~ **zu haben** *(col)* that can't be bought; **sie/das ist nicht mit** ~ **zu bezahlen** *(col)* she/that is priceless; **nicht für** ~ **und gute Worte** *(col)* not for love nor money; ~ **oder Leben!** your money or your life!; ~ **stinkt nicht** *(Prov)* there's nothing wrong with money; ~ **regiert die Welt** *(Prov)* money makes the world go round *(prov)*.

(b) *(~summen)* ~**er** *pl* money, monies *pl;* **staatliche** ~**er** state funds *pl or* money.

(c) *(St Ex:* ~*kurs)* buying rate.

Geld-: ~**angelegenheit** *f* financial matter; **jds** ~**angelegenheiten** sb's financial affairs; ~**anlage** *f* (financial) investment; ~**automat** *m* cash dispenser; ~**beutel** *m,* ~**börse** *f* purse; **tief in den** ~**beutel greifen** *(col)* to dig deep (into one's pocket) *(col)*; ~**dinge** *pl* financial *or* money matters *pl;* ~**einwurf** *m* slot; **beim** ~**einwurf** when inserting the money; ~**geber(in** *f) m* financial backer; *(esp Rad, TV)* sponsor; *(hum: Arbeitgeber)* employer; ~**geschäft** *nt* financial transaction; ~**gier** *f* avarice; **g**~**gierig** *adj* avaricious; ~**knappheit** *f* shortage of money; ~**kurs** *m (St Ex)* buying rate.

geldlich *adj* financial.

Geld-: ~**mangel** *m* lack of money; ~**markt** *m* money market; ~**menge** *f* money supply; ~**mittel** *pl* funds *pl;* ~**quelle** *f* source of income; ~**schein** *m* banknote *(Brit)*, bill *(US)*; ~**schrank** *m* safe; ~**schwierigkeiten** *pl* financial difficulties *pl;* ~**sorgen** *pl* **in** ~**sorgen sein** to have financial worries; ~**spende** *f* donation, gift of money; ~**strafe** *f* fine; **jdn zu einer** ~**strafe verurteilen** to fine sb; ~**stück** *nt* coin; ~**umlauf** *m* circulation of money; ~**verkehr** *m* transactions *pl;* ~**verleiher** *m* moneylender; ~**verschwendung** *f* waste of money; ~**wechsel** *m* exchange of money; „~**wechsel**" "bureau de change"; ~**wert** *m* cash value; *(Fin: Kaufkraft)* currency value.

geleckt *adj* **wie** ~ **aussehen** to be neat and tidy.

Gelee [ʒeˈleː] *m or nt* **-s** jelly.

gelegen 1 *ptp of* **liegen**. 2 *adj* (a) *(befindlich) Haus* situated. (b) *(passend)* **zu** ~**er Zeit** at a convenient time; **das kommt mir sehr** ~ that's most convenient. (c) *pred (wichtig)* **mir ist viel/nichts daran** ~ it matters a great deal/doesn't matter to me.

Gelegenheit *f* (a) *(günstiger Umstand)* opportunity. **bei** ~ some time (or other); **bei passender/der ersten (besten)** ~ when I get the opportunity/at the first opportunity. (b) *(Anlaß)* occasion. **bei dieser** ~ on this occasion. (c) *(~skauf)* bargain.

Gelegenheits-: ~**arbeit** *f* (a) casual work *no pl;* (b) *(eines Autors)* minor work; ~**arbeiter** *m* casual labourer *(Brit) or* laborer *(US)*; ~**kauf** *m* bargain; ~**raucher** *m* occasional smoker; ~**trinker** *m* occasional drinker.

gelegentlich 1 *adj attr* occasional. 2 *adv (manchmal)* occasionally, now and again; *(bei Gelegenheit)* some time (or other). **lassen Sie** ~ **etwas von sich hören!** keep in touch.

gelehrig *adj* quick to learn. **sich bei etw** ~ **anstellen** to be quick to grasp sth.

Gelehrsamkeit f (geh) learning, erudition.

gelehrt adj learned, erudite; (wissenschaftlich) scholarly.

Gelehrte(r) mf decl as adj scholar.

Geleit nt -e (Hist: Gefolge) retinue; (Begleitung, Mil) escort; (Leichenzug) cortège. **freies** or **sicheres** ~ safe conduct; **jdm das** ~ **geben** to escort or accompany sb.

geleiten* vt (geh) to escort.

Geleitschutz m escort. **jdm** ~ **gewähren** or **geben** to give sb an escort; (persönlich) to escort sb.

Gelenk nt -e joint; (Hand~) wrist; (Fuß~) ankle; (Ketten~) link; (Scharnier~) hinge.

gelenkig adj supple.

Gelenkigkeit f suppleness.

gelernt adj trained; Arbeiter skilled.

gelesen ptp of **lesen**.

geliebt adj dear, beloved (liter, Eccl).

Geliebte f decl as adj sweetheart; (Mätresse) mistress, lover.

Geliebte(r) m decl as adj sweetheart; (Liebhaber) lover.

geliefert adj ~ **sein** (col) to have had it (col).

geliehen ptp of **leihen**.

gelind(e) adj (geh) gentle; (mild) Urteil, Schmerz, Ausdruck mild. ~ **gesagt** to put it mildly.

gelingen pret **gelang**, ptp **gelungen** vi aux sein to succeed, to be successful. **es gelang ihm, das zu tun** he succeeded in doing it; **es gelang ihm nicht, das zu tun** he failed to do it, he didn't succeed in doing it; **dein Plan wird dir nicht** ~ you won't succeed with your plan; **es will mir nicht** ~ I can't seem to manage it.

Gelingen nt no pl (geh) (Glück) success; (erfolgreiches Ergebnis) successful outcome. **gutes** ~ **für Ihren Plan!** good luck with your plan!; **auf gutes** ~! to success!

gelitten ptp of **leiden**.

gellen vi to shrill; (von lauten Tönen erfüllt sein) to ring. **der Lärm gellt mir in den Ohren** the noise makes my ears ring.

gellend adj shrill, piercing.

geloben* vt (geh) to vow, to swear. **das Gelobte Land** (Bibl) the Promised Land.

Gelöbnis nt (geh) vow.

gelockt adj Haar curly; Mensch curly-haired.

gelogen ptp of **lügen**.

gelöst adj relaxed.

gelt interj (S Ger) right.

gelten pret **galt**, ptp **gegolten** 1 vi (a) (gültig sein) to be valid; (Gesetz) to be in force; (Preise) to be effective; (zählen) to count. **die Wette gilt!** it's a bet!; **das gilt nicht!** that doesn't count!; (nicht erlaubt) that's not allowed!; **das Gesetz gilt für alle** the law applies to everyone. (b) +dat (bestimmt sein für) to be meant for or aimed at. (c) (zutreffen) **für jdn/etw** ~ to hold (good) for sb/sth, to go for sb/sth; **das gleiche gilt auch für ihn** the same goes for him too. (d) ~ **als** to be regarded as; **es gilt als sicher, daß** ... it seems certain that ... (e) ~ **lassen** to accept; **das lasse ich** ~! I'll agree to that!, I accept that!; **für diesmal lasse ich es** ~ I'll let it go this time.

2 vti impers (geh) **es gilt, ... zu** ... it is necessary to ...; **jetzt gilt es, zusammenzuhalten** it is now a question of sticking together.

3 vt (wert sein) to be worth. **was gilt die Wette?** what do you bet?

geltend adj attr Preise current; Gesetz in force; Meinung etc prevailing. ~ **machen** (form) to assert; **einen Einwand** ~ **machen** to raise an objection.

Geltung f (Gültigkeit) validity; (Ansehen) prestige. ~ **haben** to be valid; (Gesetz) to be in force; (Preise) to be effective; (Einfluß haben) to carry weight; (angesehen sein) to be recognized; **an** ~ **verlieren** to lose prestige; **einer Sache** (dat) ~

verschaffen to enforce sth; **sich** (dat) ~ **verschaffen** to establish one's position; **etw zur** ~ **bringen** to show sth off to advantage; (durch Kontrast) to set sth off; **zur** ~ **kommen** to show to advantage; (durch Kontrast) to be set off.

Geltungs-: ~**bedürfnis** nt no pl need for admiration; **g**~**bedürftig** adj needing admiration; ~**dauer** f no pl period of validity; ~**drang** m no pl need for admiration; ~**sucht** f no pl craving for admiration; **g**~**süchtig** adj craving admiration.

Gelübde nt - (Rel, geh) vow. **ein/das** ~ **ablegen** to take a vow.

gelungen 1 ptp of **gelingen**. 2 adj attr (a) (geglückt) successful. **eine nicht so recht** ~**e Überraschung** a surprise that didn't quite come off. (b) (col: drollig) funny, priceless.

Gelüst nt -e (geh) desire.

gelüsten* vt impers (liter, iro) **mich gelüstet nach** ... I have a craving for ...

Gemach nt -er (geh) chamber (old, form).

gemächlich adj leisurely no adv; Mensch unhurried. **ein** ~ **fließender Strom** a gently flowing river.

gemacht adj (a) **für etw** ~ **sein** to be made for sth; **das ist für ihn wie** ~ it's made for him; **ein** ~**er Mann sein** to be made. (b) (gewollt, gekünstelt) false, contrived.

Gemahl m -e (geh, form) spouse (old, form), husband; (Prinz~) consort.

Gemahlin f (geh, form) spouse (old, form), wife; (von König auch) consort.

Gemälde nt - painting; (fig: Schilderung) portrayal.

Gemäldegalerie f picture gallery.

gemasert adj Holz grained.

gemäß 1 prep+dat in accordance with. 2 adj appropriate (dat to). **eine ihren Fähigkeiten** ~**e Arbeit** a job suited to her abilities.

gemäßigt adj moderate; Klima, Zone temperate; Optimismus etc qualified.

Gemäuer nt - (geh) masonry, walls pl.

Gemecker nt no pl (von Ziegen) bleating; (col: Nörgelei) moaning.

gemein adj (a) (niederträchtig) mean; (roh, unverschämt auch) nasty; Verräter, Lüge contemptible. **ein** ~**er Streich** a dirty or rotten trick. (b) (ordinär) vulgar; Bemerkung, Witz auch dirty, coarse. (c) (col: unangenehm) horrible, awful. **die Prüfung war** ~ **schwer** the exam was horribly difficult. (d) **etw** ~ **mit jdm/etw haben** to have sth in common with sb/sth; **das ist beiden** ~ it is common to both of them. (e) **das** ~**e Volk** the common people; **der** ~**e Mann** the ordinary man.

Gemeinbesitz m common property.

Gemeinde f -n (a) (Kommune) municipality; (~bewohner auch) community. (b) (Pfarr~) parish; (beim Gottesdienst) congregation.

Gemeinde-: ~**abgaben** pl rates pl (Brit), local taxes pl (US); ~**amt** nt local authority; (Gebäude) local administrative office; ~**beamte(r)** m local government officer; ~**ordnung** f bylaws pl, ordinances pl (US); ~**rat** m district council; (Mitglied) district councillor (Brit), councilman (US); ~**schwester** f district nurse; ~**steuer** f rates pl (Brit), local taxes pl (US); ~**wahl** f local election.

Gemeineigentum nt common property.

Gemein-: **g**~**gefährlich** adj Verbrecher dangerous; **er/das ist g**~**gefährlich** he/it is a public menace; ~**gefährlichkeit** f danger to the public; ~**gut** nt (lit, fig) common property.

Gemeinheit f (a) no pl (Niedertracht) meanness. (b) (Tat) mean or dirty trick; (Worte) mean thing. **das war eine** ~ that was a mean thing to do/say.

Gemein-: **g**~**hin** adv generally; ~**kosten** pl overheads pl (Brit), overhead (US); **g**~**nützig** adj of benefit to the public; (wohltätig) charitable; ~**nützigkeit** f die ~**nützige einer Organisation** the charitable status of an organization;

~**platz** m platitude, commonplace.
gemeinsam 1 adj common; Freund mutual; Konto, Aktion, Ausflug joint. **ihnen ist vieles** ~ they have a great deal in common; **die Firma ist** ~**es Eigentum der beiden Brüder** the two brothers are joint owners of the firm; **unser** ~**es Leben** our life together; **der G**~**e Markt** the Common Market; **mit jdm** ~**e Sache machen** (pej) to gang up with sb. **2** adv together. **etw** ~ **haben** to have sth in common; **es gehört den beiden** ~ it belongs jointly to the two of them.
Gemeinsamkeit f (gemeinsame Interessen, Eigenschaft etc) common ground no pl. **die** ~**en zwischen ihnen sind sehr groß** they have a great deal in common.
Gemeinschaft f community; (Gruppe) group; (Zusammensein) company. **in** ~ **mit** jointly with; **die** ~ **mit jdm** sb's companionship; **eheliche** ~ (Jur) matrimony.
Gemeinschafts-: ~**antenne** f party aerial (Brit) or antenna (US); ~**arbeit** f teamwork; ~**aufgabe** f joint task; ~**küche** f communal kitchen; (Kantine) canteen; ~**kunde** f social studies pl; ~**leistung** f collective achievement; ~**raum** m common room; **g**~**schädigend** adj Verhalten antisocial; ~**schule** f interdenominational school; ~**wohnung** f shared house/apartment etc.
Gemein-: ~**sinn** m public spirit; **g**~**verständlich** adj generally comprehensible no adv; **sich g**~**verständlich ausdrücken** to make oneself generally understood; ~**wesen** nt community; ~**wohl** nt public welfare; **das dient dem** ~**wohl** it is in the public interest.
Gemenge nt - (a) (Mischung) mixture (aus of); (Durcheinander) jumble (aus of). (b) (Gewühl) bustle; (Hand~) scuffle.
gemessen 1 ptp of **messen**. **2** adj (würdevoll) measured.
Gemetzel nt - bloodbath.
gemieden ptp of **meiden**.
Gemisch nt -e (a) (auch Aut) mixture (aus of). (b) no pl (Durcheinander) jumble (aus of).
gemischt adj mixed; (col: nicht sehr gut auch) patchy. **mit** ~**en Gefühlen** with mixed feelings.
Gemischt-: **g**~**rassig** adj of mixed race; (mit mehreren Rassen) multi-racial; ~**warenhandlung** f (dated) general store.
gemocht ptp of **mögen**.
gemolken ptp of **melken**.
Gemse f -n chamois.
Gemurmel nt no pl murmuring.
Gemüse nt - vegetables pl. **frisches** ~ fresh vegetables; **ein** ~ a vegetable; **junges** ~ (hum col) youngsters pl.
Gemüse-: ~**beilage** f vegetables pl; ~**eintopf** m vegetable stew; ~**händler** m greengrocer; ~**handlung** f, ~**laden** m greengrocer's (Brit), greengrocer; ~**markt** m vegetable market; ~**platte** f (Cook) eine ~**platte** assorted vegetables pl; ~**suppe** f vegetable soup.
gemußt ptp of **müssen**.
gemustert adj patterned.
Gemüt nt -er (a) (Geist) mind; (Charakter) nature, disposition; (Seele) soul; (Gefühl) feeling. **viel** ~ **haben** to be very warm-hearted; **etwas fürs** ~ (hum) something for the soul; (Film, Buch etc) something sentimental; **sich** (dat) **etw zu** ~**e führen** (beherzigen) to take sth to heart; (hum col) Speise, Buch etc to indulge in sth. (b) (fig: Mensch) person; (pl) people. **die** ~**er erregen** to cause a stir; **wir müssen warten, bis sich die** ~**er beruhigt haben** we must wait until feelings have cooled down.
gemütlich adj (a) (behaglich) comfortable; (freundlich) friendly no adv; (zwanglos) informal; (klein und intim) cosy (Brit), cozy (US). **wir verbrachten einen** ~**en Abend** we spent a very pleasant evening; **es sich** (dat) ~ **machen** to

make oneself comfortable; **langsam wurde es** ~ gradually the atmosphere became more relaxed. (b) Mensch good-natured, pleasant; (gelassen) easy-going no adv, relaxed no adv. **in** ~**em Tempo** at a leisurely speed
Gemütlichkeit f siehe adj (a) comfortableness; friendliness; informality; cosiness. (b) good-naturedness, pleasantness; easy-going nature. **da hört doch die** ~ **auf!** (col) that's going too far; **in aller** ~ (gemächlich) at one's leisure.
Gemüts-: ~**art** f disposition, nature; ~**bewegung** f emotion; **g**~**krank** adj emotionally disturbed; ~**krankheit** f emotional disorder; ~**lage** f mood; ~**mensch** m good-natured, phlegmatic person; ~**ruhe** f calmness; (Kaltblütigkeit) composure; (Phlegma) placidness; **in aller** ~**ruhe** (col) (as) cool as a cucumber (col); (gemächlich) at a leisurely pace; ~**zustand** m frame of mind.
gemütvoll adj sentimental; (warmherzig) warmhearted.
gen prep+acc (old, liter) toward.
Gen nt -e gene.
genannt ptp of **nennen**.
genas pret of **genesen**.
genau 1 adj exact, precise. **haben Sie die** ~**e Zeit?** have you got the right time?; **G**~**eres further** details pl; **man weiß nichts G**~**es über ihn** no-one knows anything definite about him. **2** adv ~! (col) exactly!, precisely!, quite! ~ **das Gegenteil** just or exactly the opposite; ~ **in der Mitte** right in the middle; **ich kenne ihn** ~ I know just what he's like; **etw** ~ **wissen** to know sth for certain; **er nimmt es sehr** ~ he's very particular (mit etw about sth); **einen Entschluß** ~ **überlegen** to think a decision over very carefully; **meine Uhr geht** ~ my watch keeps accurate time; ~ **auf die Minute** exactly on time; **so** ~ **wollte ich es gar nicht wissen!** (iro) you can spare me the details.
genaugenommen adv strictly speaking.
Genauigkeit f exactness, precision.
genauso adv (vor Adjektiv) just as; (alleinstehend) just or exactly the same.
genauso- = **ebenso-**.
genehmigen* vt Baupläne etc to approve; (erlauben) to sanction; (Lizenz erteilen) to license; Aufenthalt to authorize; (zugestehen) to grant. **sich** (dat) **einen** ~ (hum col) to have a little drink.
Genehmigung f siehe vt approval; sanction; licence (Brit), license (US); authorization; (Schein) permit. **mit freundlicher** ~ **von** by kind permission of.
genehmigungspflichtig adj (form) requiring official approval; (mit Visum, Stempel) requiring official authorization.
geneigt adj (geh) Aufmerksamkeit kind. ~ **sein, etw zu tun** to be inclined to do sth.
General m -e or =e (Mil) general. **Herr** ~ General.
General-: ~**angriff** m (Mil, fig) general attack; ~**direktor** m chairman (Brit), president (US); ~**intendant** m (Theat, Mus) director; ~**konsulat** nt consulate general; ~**major** m major general; ~**probe** f (Theat, fig) dress rehearsal; ~**sekretär** m secretary general; ~**stab** m general staff; ~**streik** m general strike; **g**~**überholen*** vt infin and ptp only **etw g**~**überholen** to give sth a complete overhaul; ~**überholung** f complete overhaul; ~**versammlung** f general meeting; ~**vertretung** f sole agency.
Generation f generation.
Generationskonflikt m generation gap.
Generator m generator.
generell adj general.
genesen pret **genas**, ptp ~ vi aux sein (geh) to convalesce; (fig) to recuperate.
Genesende(r) mf decl as adj convalescent.
Genesung f convalescence, recovery (auch fig). **auf dem Wege der** ~ on the road to recovery.
Genesungs-: ~**prozeß** m convalescence;

~**urlaub** m convalescent leave.
Genetik f genetics sing.
genetisch adj genetic.
Genf nt Geneva.
Genfer adj attr der ~ See Lake Geneva; ~ **Konvention** f Geneva Convention.
genial adj Entdeckung, Mensch brilliant; Künstler, Stil auch inspired; (erfinderisch) ingenious. **ein** ~**er Mensch** a genius; **ein** ~**es Werk** a work of genius.
Genialität f genius; (Erfindungsreichtum) ingenuity.
Genick nt -e neck. **sich** (dat) **das** ~ **brechen** to break one's neck; **jdm/einer Sache das** ~ **brechen** (fig) to finish sb/sth.
Genick-: ~**schuß** m shot in the neck; ~**starre** f stiffness of the neck; (Med) (cerebral) meningitis; ~**starre haben** (col) to have a stiff neck.
Genie [ʒe'niː] nt -s genius.
genieren* [ʒe'niːrən] vr to be embarrassed. **sich vor Fremden** ~ to be shy with strangers; **ich geniere mich, das zu sagen** I don't like to say it; **er genierte sich (gar) nicht, das zu tun** it didn't bother him (at all) to do that.
genießbar adj (eßbar) edible; (trinkbar) drinkable. **er ist heute nicht** ~ (fig col) he is unbearable today.
genießen pret **genoß**, ptp **genossen** vt (a) (lit, fig) to enjoy. **den Wein muß man** ~ **you must savour** (Brit) or savor (US) the wine; **er ist heute nicht zu** ~ (col) he is unbearable today. **(b)** (essen) to eat; (trinken) to drink. **das Essen ist kaum zu** ~ the meal is scarcely edible.
Genießer(in f) m - connoisseur; (des Lebens) pleasure-lover; (Feinschmecker) gourmet.
genießerisch adj appreciative. ~ **zog er an seiner Zigarre** he puffed at his cigar with relish.
Geniestreich [ʒe'niː-] m stroke of genius.
Genitalien [-iən] pl genitals pl.
Genitiv m genitive.
Genius m, pl **Genien** ['geːniən] genius.
genommen ptp of **nehmen**.
genoß pret of **genießen**.
Genosse m (wk) -n, -n comrade; (pej: Kumpan) mate (Brit col), buddy (US col).
genossen ptp of **genießen**.
Genossen-: ~**schaft** f co-operative; **g**~**schaftlich** co-operative; **g**~**schaftlich organisiert** organized as a co-operative.
Genossenschafts-: ~**bank** f co-operative bank; ~**betrieb** m co-operative.
Genossin f siehe **Genosse**.
genötigt adj ~ **sein, etw zu tun** to be obliged to do sth; **sich** ~ **sehen, etw zu tun** to feel obliged to do sth.
Genre ['ʒãːrə] nt -s genre.
genug adj enough. **das ist wenig** ~ that's precious little; **und damit noch nicht** ~ and that's not/that wasn't all; **sie sind jetzt** ~, **um** ... there are enough of them now to ...; **jetzt ist('s) aber** ~! that's enough!; (von etw) ~ **haben** to have enough (of sth); (überdrüssig sein) to have had enough (of sth).
Genüge f no pl **zur** ~ enough; **etw zur** ~ **kennen** to know sth well enough; (abwertend) to know sth only too well; **jdm** ~ **tun** (geh) to satisfy sb.
genügen* vi **(a)** (ausreichen) to be enough or sufficient (dat for). **das genügt (mir)** that's enough (for me). **(b)** Anforderungen to satisfy; Erwartungen to fulfil (Brit), to fulfill (US).
genügend 1 adj (a) inv (ausreichend) enough, sufficient. (b) (befriedigend) satisfactory. 2 adv (reichlich) enough, sufficiently.
genügsam adj (anspruchslos) Tier, Pflanze undemanding; Mensch auch modest. **ein** ~**es Leben führen** to live modestly.
Genügsamkeit f simple needs pl.
Genugtuung f satisfaction (über +acc at). **ich**

---

hörte mit ~, **daß** ... it gave me great satisfaction to hear that ....
Genus nt, pl **Genera** (Gram) gender.
Genuß m =sse **(a)** no pl (das Zusichnehmen) consumption; (von Drogen) taking, use; (von Tabak) smoking. **nach dem** ~ **der Pilze** after eating the mushrooms. **(b)** (Vergnügen) pleasure. **etw mit** ~ **essen** to eat sth with relish. **(c)** no pl (Nutznießung) **in den** ~ **von etw kommen** (von Vergünstigungen) to enjoy sth; (von Rente, Prämie etc) to be in receipt of sth.
genüßlich adj pleasurable. **er schmatzte** ~ **he** smacked his lips with relish.
Genuß-: ~**mittel** nt semi-luxury foods and tobacco; **g**~**reich** adj enjoyable; **g**~**süchtig** adj hedonistic.
Geograph(in f) m geographer.
Geographie f geography.
geographisch adj no pred geographic(al).
Geologe m, **Geologin** f geologist.
Geologie f geology.
geologisch adj no pred geological.
Geometrie f geometry.
geometrisch adj geometric.
ge|ordnet adj Leben, Zustände well-ordered. **in** ~**en Verhältnissen leben** to live a well-ordered life; ~**e Verhältnisse schaffen** to put things on an orderly basis.
Gepäck nt no pl luggage no pl, baggage no pl; (Mil: Marsch~) baggage; (von Soldat, Pfadfinder etc) kit; (von Bergsteiger) pack. **mit leichtem** ~ **reisen** to travel light.
Gepäck-: ~**abfertigung** f (Stelle) (am Bahnhof) luggage or baggage office; (am Flughafen) baggage check-in; ~**ablage** f luggage or baggage rack; ~**annahme** f (am Bahnhof) (zur Beförderung) (in-counter of the) luggage or baggage office; (zur Aufbewahrung) (in-counter of the) left-luggage office (Brit) or checkroom (US); (am Flughafen) luggage or baggage check-in; ~**aufbewahrung** f left-luggage office (Brit), baggage checkroom (US); ~**kontrolle** f luggage or baggage control or check; ~**netz** nt luggage or baggage rack; ~**schein** m luggage or baggage ticket; ~**schließfach** nt luggage or baggage locker; ~**stück** nt piece of luggage or baggage; ~**träger** m (a) (Person) porter (Brit), baggage handler; (b) (am Fahrrad) carrier; ~**wagen** m luggage van (Brit), baggage car (US).
Gepard m -e cheetah.
gepfeffert adj (col) Preise steep; Fragen, Prüfung tough; Kritik biting.
gepfiffen ptp of **pfeifen**.
gepflegt 1 adj **(a)** (nicht vernachlässigt) well looked after; Mensch, Hund, Aussehen well-groomed. **(b)** (col: kultiviert) civilized; Atmosphäre sophisticated; Ausdrucksweise cultured; Sprache cultured, refined. **(c)** (erstklassig) Speisen excellent. 2 adv (kultiviert) **sich** ~ **unterhalten** to have a civilized conversation; **sich** ~ **ausdrücken** to have a cultured way of speaking; **sehr** ~ **wohnen** to live in style.
Gepflogenheit f (geh) (Gewohnheit) habit; (Verfahrensweise) practice; (Brauch) custom, tradition.
Geplänkel nt - skirmish; (fig) squabble.
Geplapper nt no pl babbling; (fig: Geschwätz auch) chatter(ing).
Geplärr(e) nt no pl bawling; (von Radio) blaring.
geplättet adj pred (col) flabbergasted (col).
Geplauder nt no pl (geh) chatting.
Gepolter nt no pl (Krach) din; (an Tür etc) banging.
Gepräge nt no pl (fig: Eigentümlichkeit) character; (Aura) aura. **das hat den 60er Jahren ihr** ~ **gegeben** it left its mark or stamp on the sixties.
gepriesen ptp of **preisen**.
gepunktet adj Linie dotted; Stoff, Kleid spotted.
gequält adj Lächeln forced; Miene, Ausdruck

pained; *Gesang, Stimme* strained.
Gequatsche *nt no pl (pej col)* gabbing *(col)*; *(Blöd-sinn)* twaddle *(col)*.
gequollen *ptp of* **quellen.**
gerade, **grade** *(col)* **1** *adj* straight; *Zahl* even; *(aufrecht) Haltung* upright. ~ **gewachsen sein** *(Mensch)* to be clean-limbed; *(Baum)* to be straight; **das** ~ **Gegenteil** the very opposite, just the opposite; ~**sitzen/stehen** to sit up/stand up straight.
2 *adv* **(a)** *(im Augenblick, soeben)* just. **wenn Sie** ~ **Zeit haben** if you have time just now; **wo Sie** ~ **da sind** while you're here; **er wollte** ~ **aufstehen** he was just about to get up; ~ **erst** only just; **da wir** ~ **von Geld sprechen,** ... talking of money ...
(b) *(knapp)* just. ~ **so viel, daß er davon leben kann** just enough for him to live on; ~ **noch** only just; **das hat** ~ **noch gefehlt!** *(iro)* that's all we wanted!
(c) *(genau)* just; *(direkt)* right. ~ **zur rechten Zeit** at exactly the right time, just at the right time; ~ **deshalb** that's just *or* exactly why; **das ist es ja**~! that's just it!
(d) *(speziell, besonders)* especially. ~, **weil** ... just because ...; ~ **du solltest dafür Verständnis haben** you especially should understand; **sie ist nicht** ~ **eine Schönheit** she's not exactly a beauty; **warum** ~ **das?** why that of all things?; **warum** ~ **heute/ich?** why today of all days/me of all people?; **warum hat er es** ~ **so gemacht?** why on earth did he do it like that?
(e) *(col: erst recht)* **nun** ~! you try and stop me now! *(col)*; **jetzt** ~ **nicht!** I'll be damned if I will! *(col)*.
Gerade *f (wk)* -**n**, -**n** *(a) (Math)* straight line. **(b)** *(Sport) (von Renn-, Laufbahn)* straight; *(beim Boxen)* straight left/right.
gerade-: ~**aus** *adv* straight ahead; *gehen, fahren auch* straight on; ~**biegen** *vt sep irreg (lit, fig)* to straighten out; ~**halten** *sep irreg* **1** *vt* to hold straight; **2** *vr* to hold oneself (up) straight; ~**heraus** *(col)* **1** *adj pred* forthright, frank; **2** *adv* frankly; ~**heraus gesagt** quite frankly.
gerädert *adj (col)* **wie** ~ **sein, sich wie** ~ **fühlen** to be *or* feel (absolutely) whacked *(col)*.
gerade-: ~**sogut** *adv* (just) as well; ~**soviel** *adv* just as much; ~**stehen** *vi sep irreg aux haben or sein* **(a)** *(aufrecht stehen)* to stand up straight; **(b)** **für jdn/etw** ~**stehen** *(fig)* to be answerable for sb/sth; ~**wegs** *adv* straight; ~**zu** *adv (beinahe)* virtually, almost; **das ist doch** ~**zu Selbstmord** that's nothing short of suicide; **das ist ja** ~**zu lächerlich!** that is absolutely ridiculous!
geradlinig *adj* straight; *Abstammung* direct; *Entwicklung etc* linear; *(fig: aufrichtig)* straight.
gerammelt *adv:* ~ **voll** *(col)* (jam-)packed *(col)*.
Gerangel *nt no pl (Balgerei)* scrapping; *(fig: zäher Kampf)* wrangling.
Geranie [-ɪə] *f* geranium.
gerannt *ptp of* **rennen.**
Geraschel *nt no pl* rustle, rustling.
Gerät *nt* -**e** **(a)** *(Stück)* piece of equipment; *(Apparat)* gadget; *(elektrisches* ~*)* appliance; *(Radio*~, *Fernseh*~*)* set; *(Meß*~*)* instrument; *(Werkzeug, Garten*~*)* tool. **(b)** *no pl (Ausrüstung)* equipment *no pl; (von Handwerker)* tools *pl.*
geraten[1] **1** *vi irreg aux sein* **(a)** *(zufällig gelangen)* to get *(in+acc* into). **an jdn** ~ *(jdn kennenlernen)* to come across sb; **an etw** *(acc)* ~ to get sth, to come by sth; **an den Richtigen/Falschen** ~ to come to the right/wrong person; **das Schiff ist in einen Sturm** ~ the boat got caught in a storm; **unter schlechten Einfluß** ~ to come under a bad influence. **(b)** *(sich entwickeln, ausfallen)* to turn out. **ihm gerät einfach alles** everything he does is a success. **2** *adj (geh: ratsam)* advisable.
geraten[2] *ptp of* **raten, geraten**[1].

Geräte-: ~**schuppen** *m* toolshed; ~**turnen** *nt* apparatus gymnastics *no pl.*
Geratewohl *nt:* **aufs** ~ on the off-chance; *auswählen etc* at random.
Gerätschaften *pl (Ausrüstung)* equipment *sing; (Werkzeug)* tools *pl.*
Geratter *nt no pl* clatter(ing); *(von Maschinengewehr)* chatter(ing).
geraum *adj attr* **vor** ~**er Zeit** some time ago; **seit** ~**er Zeit** for some time.
geräumig *adj* spacious, roomy.
Geräumigkeit *f no pl* spaciousness, roominess.
Geräusch *nt* -**e** sound; *(esp unangenehm)* noise.
Geräusch-: **g**~**arm** *adj* quiet; ~**kulisse** *f* background noise; *(Film, Rad, TV)* sound effects *pl;* **g**~**los** *adj* silent; ~**losigkeit** *f no pl* silence; ~**pegel** *m* sound level; **g**~**voll** *adj (laut)* loud; *(lärmend)* noisy.
gerben *vt* to tan.
Gerber *m* - tanner.
gerecht *adj* just; *(unparteiisch auch)* fair; *(recht-schaffen)* upright. ~ **gegen jdn sein** to be fair *or* just to sb; ~**er Lohn für alle Arbeiter!** fair wages for all workers!; **den Schlaf des G**~**en schlafen** *(usu hum)* to sleep the sleep of the just; ~**er Zorn** righteous anger; **jdm/einer Sache** ~ **werden** to do justice to sb/sth; **den Bedingungen** ~ **werden** to fulfil *(Brit) or* fulfill *(US)* the conditions.
gerechtfertigt *adj* justified.
Gerechtigkeit *f* justice; *(das Gerechtsein)* justness; *(Unparteilichkeit)* fairness; *(Rechtschaffenheit)* righteousness. **jdm** ~ **widerfahren lassen** to be just to sb; *(fig)* to do justice to sb
Gerechtigkeits-: ~**gefühl** *nt,* ~**sinn** *m* sense of justice.
Gerede *nt no pl* talk; *(Klatsch)* gossip(ing). **jdn ins** ~ **bringen** to get sb talked about.
geregelt *adj Arbeit, Mahlzeiten* regular; *Leben* well-ordered.
gereichen* *vi (geh)* **jdm zur Ehre** ~ to redound to sb's honour *(form);* **zum Vorteil** ~ to be an advantage to sb.
gereift *adj (fig)* mature.
gereizt *adj (verärgert)* irritated; *(reizbar)* irritable, touchy; *(nervös)* edgy. **im Zimmer herrschte** ~**e Stimmung** there was a strained atmosphere in the room.
Gereiztheit *f siehe adj* irritation; irritability; edginess; strainedness.
Gericht[1] *nt* -**e** *(Speise)* dish.
Gericht[2] *nt* -**e** *(Behörde)* court (of justice); *(Gebäude)* court(house), law courts *pl; (die Richter)* court, bench. **vor** ~ **erscheinen/aussagen** to appear/testify in court; **vor** ~ **stehen** to stand trial; **jdn/einen Fall vor** ~ **bringen** to take sb/sth to court; **das Jüngste** ~ the Last Judgement; **über jdn zu** ~ **sitzen** *(fig)* to sit in judgement on sb; **mit jdm *(scharf)* ins** ~ **gehen** *(fig)* to judge sb harshly.
gerichtlich *adj* judicial; *Entscheidung etc* court; *Medizin* forensic; *Verhandlung* legal. **laut** ~**em Beschluß** according to the decision of a/the court; **ein** ~**es Nachspiel haben** to finish up in court; ~ **gegen jdn vorgehen** to take legal proceedings against sb; **eine Sache** ~ **klären** to settle a matter in court.
Gerichts-: ~**akten** *pl* court records *pl;* ~**arzt** *m* court doctor; ~**barkeit** *f* jurisdiction; ~**beschluß** *m* court decision; ~**diener** *m (old)* court usher; ~**entscheid** *m,* ~**entscheidung** *f* court decision; ~**ferien** *pl* court vacation, recess; ~**hof** *m* court (of justice), law court; **Oberster** ~**hof** Supreme Court (of Justice); ~**kosten** *pl* court costs *pl;* ~**medizin** *f* forensic medicine; ~**mediziner** *m* forensic doctor; **g**~**medizinisch** *adj* forensic medical *attr;* ~**reporter** *m* legal correspondent; ~**saal** *m* courtroom; ~**schreiber** *m* clerk of the court; ~**termin** *m* date of a/the

trial; *(für Zivilsachen)* date of a/the hearing; ~**verfahren** nt court or legal proceedings pl; **ein** ~**verfahren gegen jdn einleiten** to institute legal proceedings against sb; ~**verhandlung** f trial; *(zivil)* hearing; ~**vollzieher** m bailiff; ~**weg** m **auf dem** ~**weg** through the courts.

gerieben 1 ptp of **reiben. 2** adj *(fig col)* smart, sharp; *(verschlagen auch)* sly, fly *(col).* **der ist verdammt** ~ there are no flies on him *(col).*

geriet pret of **geraten**[1].

gering adj **(a)** *(niedrig)* low; *Menge* small; *Wert* little attr; *(kurz)* Zeit, Entfernung short. **Berge von** ~**er Höhe** low hills; **seine Leistung erhielt eine zu** ~**e Bewertung** his performance wasn't rated highly enough. **(b)** *(unbedeutend, unerheblich)* slight; *Chance auch* small, slim; *Bedeutung, Rolle* minor. **das ist meine** ~**ste Sorge** that's the least of my worries; **die Kosten sind nicht** ~ the costs are not inconsiderable; **nicht im** ~**sten** not in the least or slightest; **nichts G**~**eres als** ... nothing less than; **kein G**~**erer als Freud** ... no less a person than Freud. **(c)** *(unzulänglich)* Qualität, Kenntnisse poor; *(abschätzig)* Meinung low, poor. **geringelt** adj Muster ringed; Socken hooped.

Gering-: g~**fügig** adj *(unwichtig)* insignificant; Unterschied slight; Vergehen, Verletzung minor; Betrag small; **sein Zustand hat sich g**~**fügig gebessert** his condition is marginally improved; ~**fügigkeit** f **(a)** insignificance; slightness; **ein Verfahren wegen** ~**fügigkeit einstellen** *(Jur)* to dismiss a case because of the trifling nature of the offence; **(b)** *(Kleinigkeit)* small thing, trifle; g~**schätzen** vt sep *(verachten)* Menschen, Leistung to have a low opinion of; *(mißachten)* Gefahr, Folgen to disregard; g~**schätzig** adj contemptuous; ~**schätzung** f no pl *(Ablehnung)* disdain; *(schlechte Meinung)* low opinion *(für, gen* of*); (für menschliches Leben)* low regard *(für, gen* for*).*

gerinnen* vi irreg aux sein to coagulate; *(Blut auch)* to clot; *(Milch auch)* to curdle. **mir gerann das Blut in den Adern** *(fig)* my blood ran cold.

Gerinnsel nt *(Blut*~*)* clot.

Gerinnung f siehe vi coagulation; clotting; curdling.

Gerippe nt - skeleton; *(von Schirm, Gebäude)* frame; *(fig: Grundplan)* framework. **er ist nur noch ein** ~ he's nothing but skin and bones.

gerippt adj ribbed no adv.

gerissen 1 ptp of **reißen. 2** adj crafty, cunning.

Gerissenheit f cunning.

geritten ptp of **reiten.**

geritzt adj pred *(col)* **die Sache ist** ~ everything's fixed up or settled.

Germane n *(wk)* -n, -n, **Germanin** f Teuton.

germanisch adj Germanic.

Germanist(in f*)* m Germanist; *(Student auch)* German student; *(Wissenschaftler auch)* German specialist.

Germanistik f German (studies pl). ~ **studieren** to study German.

gern(e) adv, comp **lieber**, superl **am liebsten (a)** *(freudig)* with pleasure; *(bereitwillig auch)* willingly, readily. **(aber)** ~! of course!; **kommst du mit?** — **ja,** ~ are you coming too? — oh yes, I'd like to; ~ **geschehen!** you're welcome!, not at all!; **von mir aus kann er ja** ~ **älter sein** I don't mind if he's older; **etw** ~ **tun** to like doing sth or to do sth *(esp US);* **etw** ~ **essen/trinken** to like sth; **sie ißt am liebsten Spargel** asparagus is her favourite *(Brit)* or favorite *(US)* food; **er sieht** or **hat es nicht** ~, **wenn wir zu spät kommen** he doesn't like us coming too late; **ein** ~ **gesehener Gast** a welcome visitor; **das glaube ich** ~ I can quite or well believe it; **jdn/etw** ~ **haben** or **mögen** to like sb/sth, to be fond of sb/sth; **jdn/etw am liebsten haben** or **mögen** to like sb/sth best or most; **ich hätte** or **möchte** ~ ... I would like ...; **du kannst mich mal** ~ **haben!**

(col) (you can) go to hell! *(col);* siehe **lieber.**

  (b) *(gewöhnlich, oft)* **etw** ~ **tun** to tend to do sth; **morgens läßt er sich** ~ **viel Zeit** he likes to leave himself a lot of time in the mornings.

Gernegroß m -, -e *(hum)* **er war schon immer ein kleiner** ~ he always did like to act big *(col).*

gerochen ptp of **riechen.**

Geröll nt -e detritus no pl; *(größer)* boulders pl.

geronnen ptp of **rinnen, gerinnen.**

Gerste f -n barley.

Gersten-: ~**korn** nt **(a)** barleycorn; **(b)** *(Med)* stye; ~**saft** m *(hum)* John Barleycorn *(hum),* beer.

Gerte f -n switch; *(Reit*~ *auch)* crop.

gertenschlank adj slim and willowy.

Geruch m ⁼e **(a)** smell *(nach* of*); (Duft auch)* fragrance *(nach* of*); (von Speise etc auch)* aroma *(nach* of*).* **(b)** no pl *(~ssinn)* sense of smell. **(c)** no pl *(fig: Ruf)* reputation. **in den** ~ **von etw kommen** to get a reputation for sth.

geruchlos adj odourless *(Brit),* odorless *(US); (duftlos)* scentless.

Geruch(s)-: ~**organ** nt organ of smell, olfactory organ; ~**sinn** m sense of smell.

Gerücht nt -e rumour *(Brit),* rumor *(US).* **das halte ich für ein** ~ *(col)* I have my doubts about that.

gerüchteweise adv **etw** ~ **hören** to hear sth rumoured *(Brit)* or rumored *(US);* ~ **ist bekanntgeworden, daß** ... rumour *(Brit)* or rumor *(US)* has it that ...

gerufen ptp of **rufen.**

geruhsam adj peaceful; *Spaziergang etc* leisurely no adv. ~ **essen** to eat in peace (and quiet).

Gerümpel nt no pl junk.

Gerundium nt gerund.

gerungen ptp of **ringen.**

Gerüst nt -e scaffolding no pl; *(Gestell)* trestle; *(fig: Gerippe)* framework *(zu* of*).*

ges, Ges nt - *(Mus)* G flat.

gesalzen adj *(fig col)* Preis, Rechnung steep, stiff.

gesammelt adj Aufmerksamkeit, Kraft collective; Werke collected.

gesamt adj attr whole, entire. **die** ~**e Familie** the whole family; **die** ~**en Kosten** the total costs.

Gesamt-: ~**auflage** f *(von Zeitung etc)* total circulation; *(von Buch)* total edition; ~**ausgabe** f complete edition; ~**betrag** m total (amount); g~**deutsch** adj all-German; ~**eindruck** m general impression; ~**fläche** f total area; ~**gewicht** nt total weight.

Gesamtheit f totality. **die** ~ **der** ... all the ...; *(die Summe)* the totality of ...; **die** ~ **(der Bevölkerung)** the population (as a whole); **in seiner** ~ in its entirety; **das Volk in seiner** ~ the nation as a whole.

Gesamt-: ~**hochschule** f polytechnic; ~**kosten** pl total costs pl; ~**lage** f general situation; ~**masse** f *(Comm)* total assets pl; ~**note** f *(Sch)* overall mark; ~**schaden** m total damage; **ein** ~**schaden von 5.000 Mark** damage totalling *(Brit)* or totaling *(US)* 5,000 marks; ~**schule** f comprehensive school; ~**sieger** m *(Sport)* overall winner; ~**summe** f total (amount); ~**übersicht** f general survey *(über+acc* of*);* ~**umsatz** m total turnover; ~**werk** nt complete works pl; ~**wert** m total value; **im** ~**wert von** ... totalling *(Brit)* or totaling *(US)* ... in value; ~**wertung** f *(Sport)* overall placings pl; **er liegt in der** ~**wertung vorn** he has the overall lead; ~**zahl** f total number; ~**zusammenhang** m general view.

gesandt ptp of **senden**[1].

Gesandte(r) m decl as adj *(Pol)* envoy; *(col: Botschafter)* ambassador.

Gesandtschaft f legation; *(col: Botschaft)* embassy.

Gesang m ⁼e **(a)** *(Lied, Vogel*~*)* song. **geistliche** ~**e** religious hymns and chants. **(b)** no pl *(das*

Singen) singing.

Gesang-: ~**buch** nt (Eccl) hymnbook; ~**lehrer** m singing teacher.

gesanglich adj vocal; Begabung for singing.

Gesangverein m choral society.

Gesäß nt -e seat, bottom, posterior (hum).

Gesäßtasche f back pocket.

gesättigt adj (Chem) saturated.

Geschädigte(r) mf decl as adj victim.

Geschäft nt -e (a) (Gewerbe, Handel) business no pl; (~sabschluß) (business) deal or transaction. **wie geht das** ~? how's business?; **mit jdm ins** ~ **kommen** to do business with sb; **im** ~ **sein** to be in business; **ein** ~ **tätigen** to carry out a transaction; **ein gutes/schlechtes** ~ **machen** to make a good/bad deal; **dabei hat er ein** ~ **gemacht** he made a profit out of it; **das war für mich ein/kein** ~ that was a good/bad bit of business for me; ~**e mit etw machen** to make money out of sth. **(b)** (Aufgabe) duty. **seinen** ~**en nachgehen** to go about one's business. **(c)** (Firma) business; (Laden) shop (Brit), store (US). **im** ~ **at work**; (im Laden) in the shop. **(d)** (baby-talk: Notdurft) **ein** ~ **machen** to do a job (baby-talk); **sein** ~ **verrichten** to do one's business (euph).

Geschäfte-: g~**halber** adv verreist on business; verhindert because of business; ~**macher** m (pej) profiteer.

geschäftig adj (betriebsam) busy. ~**es Treiben** hustle and bustle.

Geschäftigkeit f (geschäftiges Treiben) hustle and bustle.

geschäftlich 1 adj (das Geschäft betreffend) business attr; (sachlich) Ton businesslike. **2** adv verreist on business; verhindert because of business. ~ **unterwegs** away on business; **ich habe mit ihm etwas G~es zu besprechen** I have some business to discuss with him.

Geschäfts-: ~**abschluß** business deal or transaction; ~**aufgabe**, ~**auflösung** f closure of a/the business; ~**bank** f commercial bank; ~**bedingungen** pl terms of business pl; ~**bereich** m (Parl) responsibilities pl; **Minister ohne** ~**bereich** minister without portfolio; ~**beziehungen** pl business connections pl (zu with); ~**brief** m business letter; ~**bücher** pl books pl, accounts pl; ~**frau** f businesswoman; g~**führend** adj attr executive; (stellvertretend) acting; Regierung caretaker; ~**führer** m (von Laden) manager; (von GmbH) managing director; (von Verein) secretary; (von Partei) whip; ~**führung** f management; ~**haus** nt (a) (Gebäude) business premises pl; (von Büros) office block; **(b)** (Firma) house, firm; ~**inhaber(in** f) m owner; ~ **jahr** nt financial year; ~**kapital** nt working capital; ~**kosten** pl business expenses pl; **das geht alles auf** ~**kosten** it's all on expenses; ~**leitung** f management; ~**mann** m, pl ~**leute** businessman; g~**mäßig** adj businesslike no adv; ~**ordnung** f standing orders pl; **eine Frage zur** ~**ordnung** a question on a point of order; ~**partner** m business partner; ~**räume** pl (business) premises pl; (Büroräume) offices pl; ~**reise** f business trip; **auf** ~**reise sein** to be on a business trip; g~**schädigend** adj bad for business; g~**schädigendes Verhalten** conduct no art injurious to the interests of the company (form); ~**schluß** m close of business; (von Läden) closing-time; **nach** ~**schluß** after working hours/closing-time; ~**stelle** f offices pl; ~**straße** f shopping street; ~**tätigkeit** f business activity; g~**tüchtig** adj business-minded; ~**welt** f business world; ~**zimmer** nt office.

geschah pret of geschehen.

gescheckt adj spotted; Pferd skewbald, pinto (US).

geschehen pret **geschah**, ptp ~ vi aux sein to happen (jdm to sb); (ausgeführt werden) to be done; (Verbrechen) to be committed. **es ist nun**

einmal ~ what's done is done; **es wird ihm nichts** ~ nothing will happen to him; **das geschieht ihm (ganz) recht** it serves him (jolly well col) right; **was soll mit ihm/damit** ~? what is to be done with him/it?; **als er sie sah, war es um ihn** ~ he was lost the moment he set eyes on her; **da war es um meine Seelenruhe** ~ that was an end to my peace of mind.

Geschehen nt - events pl, happenings pl.

gescheit adj clever; Mensch, Idee auch bright; (vernünftig) sensible. **du bist wohl nicht recht** ~? you must be out of your mind or off your head; **sei** ~! be sensible.

Geschenk nt -e present, gift; (Schenkung) gift. **jdm ein** ~ **machen** to give sb a present; **das war ein** ~ **des Himmels** it was a godsend

Geschenk- in cpds gift; ~**artikel** m gift; ~**packung** f gift pack or box; (von Pralinen) gift box; ~**papier** nt gift-wrapping paper; ~**sendung** f gift parcel.

Geschichte f -n (a) no pl (Historie) history. **Alte/ Neuere** ~ ancient/modern history; ~ **machen** to make history; **das ist längst** ~ that's ancient history. **(b)** (Erzählung, Lügen~) story; (Märchen, Fabel etc auch) tale; (Kurz~) short story. ~**n erzählen** to tell stories. **(c)** (col: Angelegenheit, Sache) affair, business no pl. **das sind alte** ~**n** that's old hat (col); **alte** ~**n wieder aufwärmen** to rake up the past; **eine schöne** ~! (iro) a fine how-do-you-do! (col); **die** ~ **mit seinem Magen** the business with his stomach; **mach keine** ~**n!** don't be silly! (col); (Dummheiten) don't get up to anything silly!

Geschichten|erzähler m (lit, fig) storyteller.

geschichtlich adj (historisch) historical; (bedeutungsvoll) historic. ~ **belegt** or nachgewiesen sein to be a historical fact.

Geschichts-: ~**buch** nt history book; ~**fälschung** f falsification of history; ~**forscher** m historian; ~**forschung** f historical research; ~**kenntnis** f historical knowledge no pl; ~**lehrer** m history teacher; ~**schreiber** m historian; ~**schreibung** f historiography.

Geschick[1] nt -e (geh) (Schicksal) fate; 'usu pl: politische etc Entwicklung) fortune. **ein gütiges** ~ good fortune, providence.

Geschick[2] nt no pl (~lichkeit) skill.

Geschicklichkeit f siehe geschickt skill; cleverness; agility. **für etw** ~ **haben** to be clever at sth.

Geschicklichkeitsspiel nt game of skill.

geschickt adj skilful (Brit), skillful (US); (taktisch auch) clever; (beweglich) agile.

Geschicktheit f = Geschicklichkeit.

geschieden ptp of scheiden.

Geschiedene(r) mf decl as adj divorcee.

geschienen ptp of scheinen.

Geschirr nt -e (a) no pl (Teller etc) crockery (Brit), tableware; (Küchen~) pots and pans pl, kitchenware; (Porzellan) china. **(das)** ~ **spülen** to wash or do the dishes, to wash up (Brit); **feuerfestes** ~ ovenware. **(b)** (Service) (dinner/tea etc) service; (Gläser) set of glasses; (feuerfestes ~) set of ovenware. **(c)** (von Zugtieren) harness.

Geschirr-: ~**schrank** m china cupboard; ~**spülen** nt washing-up; ~**spülmaschine** f dishwasher; ~**tuch** nt tea towel (Brit), dishtowel (US).

geschissen ptp of scheißen.

geschlafen ptp of schlafen.

geschlagen ptp of schlagen.

Geschlecht nt -er (a) sex; (Gram) gender. **Jugendliche beiderlei** ~**s** young people of both sexes; **das andere** ~ the opposite sex. **(b)** no pl (geh: Geschlechtsteil) sex (liter). **(c)** (liter) (Gattung) race; (Sippe) house; (Abstammung) lineage. **das menschliche** ~ the human race.

geschlechtlich adj sexual. ~**e Erziehung** sex education; **mit jdm** ~ **verkehren** to have sexual intercourse with sb.

Geschlechtlichkeit f sexuality.

Geschlechts-: ~**akt** m sex act; ~**erziehung** f sex education; **g**~**krank** adj suffering from VD; **g**~**krank sein** to have VD; ~**krankheit** f venereal disease; ~**leben** nt sex life; **g**~**los** adj asexual (auch Biol), sexless; ~**losigkeit** f asexuality (auch Biol), sexlessness; ~**merkmal** nt sex(ual) characteristic; ~**organ** nt sex organ; **g**~**reif** adj sexually mature; ~**reife** f sexual maturity; **g**~**spezifisch** adj (Sociol) sex-specific; ~**teil** nt genitals pl; ~**trieb** m sex drive; ~**umwandlung** f sex change; ~**verkehr** m sexual intercourse.

geschlichen ptp of **schleichen.**

geschliffen 1 ptp of **schleifen²**. **2** adj Manieren polished, refined; Sätze polished.

geschlossen 1 ptp of **schließen. 2** adj closed; (vereint) unified. **in sich** (dat) ~ self-contained; Mensch, Charakter well-rounded; Handlung wellknit; **ein** ~**es Ganzes** a unified whole; ~**e Gesellschaft** (Fest) private function; ~**e Ortschaft** built-up area. **3** adv ~ **für etw sein/stimmen** to be/vote unanimously in favour of sth; ~ **hinter jdm stehen** to stand solidly behind sb.

Geschlossenheit f unity.

geschlungen ptp of **schlingen.**

Geschmack m ⁻e or (hum, col) ⁻er (lit, fig) taste; (Aroma) flavour (Brit), flavor (US); (no pl: ~ssinn) sense of taste. **je nach** ~ to one's own taste; **Salz (je) nach** ~ **hinzufügen** add salt to taste; **an etw** (dat) ~ **finden** to acquire a taste for sth; **auf den** ~ **kommen** to acquire a taste for it; **er hat einen guten** ~ (fig) he has good taste; **das ist nicht nach meinem** ~ that's not to my taste; **die** ⁻**er sind verschieden** tastes differ; **über** ~ **läßt sich (nicht) streiten** (Prov) there's no accounting for taste(s) (prov).

geschmacklich adj (lit, fig) as regards taste.

geschmacklos adj (lit, fig) tasteless.

Geschmacklosigkeit f **(a)** (lit, fig) tastelessness, lack of taste; (Taktlosigkeit auch) bad taste. **(b)** (Beispiel der ~) example of bad taste; (Bemerkung) remark in bad taste.

Geschmacks-: ~**frage** f question of (good) taste; ~**richtung** f taste; (von Speisen etc) flavour (Brit), flavor (US); ~**sache** f matter of taste; **das ist** ~**sache** it's (all) a matter of taste; ~**sinn** m sense of taste; ~**verirrung** f unter ~**verirrung leiden** (iro) to have no taste.

geschmackvoll adj tasteful.

geschmeidig adj **(a)** Haar, Leder, Haut supple; Fell sleek; (weich) Handtuch, Haar soft; Teig workable. **(b)** (fig) (anpassungfähig) flexible; (wendig) adroit.

Geschmeidigkeit f no pl siehe adj **(a)** suppleness; sleekness; softness. **(b)** flexibility, adroitness.

Geschmier(e) nt no pl (col) mess; (Geschriebenes) scribble, scrawl.

geschmissen ptp of **schmeißen.**

geschmolzen ptp of **schmelzen.**

Geschmorte(s) nt decl as adj (Cook) braised meat.

Geschnatter nt no pl (lit) cackling; (fig) jabbering.

Geschnetzelte(s) nt decl as adj (Cook) meat cut into strips stewed to produce a thick sauce.

geschniegelt adj (pej) flashy.

geschnitten ptp of **schneiden.**

geschoben ptp of **schieben.**

gescholten ptp of **schelten.**

Geschöpf nt ⁻e (Geschaffenes) creation; (Lebewesen) creature.

geschoren ptp of **scheren¹.**

Geschoß¹ nt ⁻sse projectile (form); (Wurf~, Rakete etc auch) missile; (Kugel auch) bullet.

Geschoß² nt ⁻sse (Stockwerk) floor, storey (Brit), story (US).

Geschoßbahn f trajectory.

geschossen ptp of **schießen.**

geschraubt adj (pej) Stil, Redeweise pretentious.

Geschrei nt no pl shouts pl, shouting; (von Verletzten, Babys, Popfans) screams pl, screaming; (fig: Aufhebens) fuss, to-do (col). **viel** ~ **um etw machen** to make a big fuss about sth.

geschrieben ptp of **schreiben.**

geschrie(e)n ptp of **schreien.**

geschritten ptp of **schreiten.**

geschunden ptp of **schinden.**

Geschütz nt ⁻e gun. **schweres** ~ heavy artillery; **schweres** ~ **auffahren** (fig) to bring up one's big guns.

Geschütz-: ~**feuer** nt shell fire; ~**rohr** nt gun barrel.

geschützt adj Winkel, Ecke sheltered; Pflanze, Tier protected.

Geschwader nt - squadron.

Geschwafel nt no pl (pej col) waffle (col).

Geschwätz nt no pl (pej) prattle; (Klatsch) tittletattle (col), gossip.

geschwätzig adj talkative; (klatschsüchtig) gossipy.

Geschwätzigkeit f no pl siehe adj talkativeness; gossipy nature.

geschweift adj (a) curved. (b) Stern with a tail.

geschweige conj ~ (denn) let alone.

geschwiegen ptp of **schweigen.**

geschwind adj quick, fast no adv.

Geschwindigkeit f speed; (Phys: von Masse) velocity. **mit einer** ~ **von** ... at a speed of ...; **mit höchster** ~ at top speed.

Geschwindigkeits-: ~**begrenzung,** ~**beschränkung** f speed limit; **gegen die** ~**begrenzung verstoßen** to exceed the speed limit; ~**kontrolle** f speed check; ~**messer** m tachometer; (Aut auch) speedometer; ~**überschreitung** f exceeding the speed limit no art, speeding no art.

Geschwister pl brothers and sisters pl. **haben Sie noch** ~? do you have any brothers or sisters?

Geschwister-: ~**liebe** f brotherly/sisterly love; (gegenseitig) love between a brother and a sister; ~**paar** nt brother and sister pl.

geschwollen 1 ptp of **schwellen. 2** adj (pej) turgid.

geschwommen ptp of **schwimmen.**

geschworen ptp of **schwören.**

Geschworene(r) mf decl as adj juror. **die** ~**n** the jury sing or pl.

Geschwulst f ⁻e growth; (Hirn~, Krebs~ etc auch) tumour (Brit), tumor (US).

geschwunden ptp of **schwinden.**

geschwungen 1 ptp of **schwingen. 2** adj curved.

Geschwür nt -e ulcer; (Furunkel) boil; (fig) ulcer.

gesegnet adj (geh) **mit etw** ~ **sein** to be blessed with sth; ~**es Neues Jahr!** Happy New Year; **einen** ~**en Schlaf haben** to be a sound sleeper.

gesehen ptp of **sehen.**

Geselle m (wk) -n, -n (a) (Handwerks~) journeyman. (b) (dated col: Bursche) fellow.

gesellen* vr sich zu jdm ~ to join sb.

Gesellen-: ~**brief** m articles pl; ~**prüfung** f examination to become a journeyman.

gesellig adj sociable, convivial; Tier gregarious; Verkehr social. ~**es Beisammensein** social gathering.

Geselligkeit f (a) no pl sociability; (geselliges Leben) social intercourse. **die** ~ **lieben** to be sociable. (b) (Veranstaltung) social gathering.

Gesellschaft f (a) (Sociol, Vereinigung) society; (Comm) company. **die** ~ **verändern** to change society. (b) (Abend~) reception, party; (Gäste) guests pl, party. **geschlossene** ~ private party. (c) (Umgang, Begleitung) company. **in schlechte** ~ **geraten** to get into bad company; **jdm** ~

leisten to keep sb company; **darf ich Ihnen ~ leisten?** may I join you? **(d)** *(Kreis von Menschen)* group of people; *(pej)* crowd *(col)*. **wir waren eine bunte ~** we were a mixed bunch.

Gesellschafter(in *f*) *m* - **(a)** *(Unterhalter)* companion; *(euph: Prostituierte)* escort. **ein guter ~ sein** to be good company. **(b)** *(Comm) (Teilhaber)* shareholder; *(Partner)* partner. **stiller ~** sleeping *(Brit)* or silent *(US)* partner.

gesellschaftlich *adj* social. **er ist ~ erledigt** he's ruined socially.

Gesellschafts-: **~anzug** *m* formal dress; **g~fähig** *adj Verhalten* socially acceptable; *Mensch, Aussehen auch* presentable; **~form** *f* social system; **~kapital** *nt (Comm)* authorized capital; **~klasse** *f (Sociol)* social class; **~klatsch** *m* society gossip; **~kleidung** *f* formal dress; **~kritik** *f* social criticism; **g~kritisch** *adj* critical of society; **g~kritisch denken** to have a critical attitude towards society; **~ordnung** *f* social system; **~reise** *f* group tour; **~roman** *m* social novel; **~schicht** *f* social stratum; **~spiel** *nt* party game; **~stück** *nt (Theat)* comedy of manners; *(Art)* genre painting; **~system** *nt* social system; **~tanz** *m* ballroom dance.

Gesenk *nt* **-e** *(Tech)* die.

gesessen *ptp of* **sitzen**.

Gesetz *nt* **-e** *(Jur, Natur~, Prinzip)* law; *(~buch)* statute book; *(Parl)* act; *(Vorlage)* bill; *(Satzung, Regel)* rule. **das Copyright~** the Copyright Act; **nach dem ~** under the law *(über+acc* on); **vor dem ~** in (the eyes of the) law; **im Sinne des ~es** within the meaning of the act; **steht etwas davon im ~?** is there any law about it?; **das ~ der Schwerkraft** the law of gravity; **das oberste ~** **(der Wirtschaft** *etc*) the golden rule (of industry *etc*); **ein ungeschriebenes ~** an unwritten rule.

Gesetz-: **~blatt** *nt* law gazette; **~entwurf** *m* (draft) bill.

Gesetzes-: **~brecher(in** *f*) *m* - law-breaker; **~hüter** *m (iro)* guardian of the law; **~novelle** *f* amendment; **~text** *m* wording of a/the law; **g~treu** *adj* law-abiding; **~treue** *f* law abidingness; **~übertretung** *f* infringement of a/the law.

Gesetz-: **g~gebend** *adj attr* legislative, lawmaking; **die g~gebende Gewalt** the legislature; **~geber** *m* legislator, lawmaker; **~gebung** *f* legislation *no pl*.

gesetzlich 1 *adj Bestimmungen, Vertreter, Zahlungsmittel* legal; *Feiertag, Reglungen* statutory; *(rechtmäßig)* lawful, legitimate. 2 *adv* legally; *(durch Gesetze auch)* by law; *(rechtmäßig)* lawfully, legitimately.

Gesetzlichkeit *f no pl (Gesetzmäßigkeit)* legality.

Gesetz-: **g~los** *adj* lawless; **~losigkeit** *f* lawlessness; **g~mäßig** *adj (gesetzlich)* legal; *(rechtmäßig)* lawful, legitimate; **~mäßigkeit** *f siehe adj* legality; lawfulness, legitimacy.

gesetzt 1 *adj (reif)* sedate, sober. **ein Herr im ~en Alter** a man of mature years. 2 *conj* **~ den Fall, ...** assuming (that) ...

Gesetz-: **g~widrig** *adj* illegal; *(unrechtmäßig)* unlawful; **~widrigkeit** *f siehe adj* illegality; unlawfulness *no pl*.

ges. gesch. = gesetzlich geschützt reg'd.

Gesicht *nt* **-er** **(a)** face. **ein trauriges/böses/wütendes ~ machen** to look sad/cross/angry; **ein langes ~ machen** to pull a long face; **was machst du denn heute für ein ~?** what's up with you today?; **jdm ins ~ sehen** to look sb in the face; **den Tatsachen ins ~ sehen** to face facts; **jdm etw ins ~ sagen** to tell sb sth to his face; **mir schien die Sonne ins ~** the sun was (shining) in my eyes; **es stand ihm im ~ geschrieben** it was written all over his face; **jdm ins ~ springen** *(fig col)* to go for sb; **sein wahres ~ zeigen** to show (oneself in) one's true colours *(Brit)* or colors *(US)*; **jdm wie aus dem ~ geschnitten sein** to be

the spitting image of sb; **das/sein ~ verlieren** to lose face; **das ~ wahren** to save face. **(b)** *(fig) (Aussehen)* look, appearance; *(geh: Charakter)* character. **die Sache bekommt ein anderes ~** the matter takes on a different complexion.

(c) *no pl* **das Zweite ~** second sight; **etw aus dem ~ verlieren** *(lit, fig)* to lose sight of sth; **jdn/etw zu ~ bekommen** to set eyes on sb/sth.

Gesichts-: **~ausdruck** *m* (facial) expression; *(Mienenspiel auch)* face; **einen ängstlichen ~ausdruck haben** to look scared; **~creme** *f* face cream; **~farbe** *f* complexion; **~haut** *f* facial skin; **~kreis** *m* **(a)** *(dated: Umkreis)* field of vision; **jdn aus dem/seinem ~kreis verlieren** to lose sight of sb; **(b)** *(fig)* horizons *pl*, outlook; **g~los** *adj (fig)* faceless; **~packung** *f* face pack; **~pflege** *f* facial care; **~punkt** *m (Betrachtungsweise)* point of view; *(Einzelheit)* point; **unter diesem ~punkt betrachtet** looked at from this standpoint; **~verlust** *m* loss of face; **~wasser** *nt* face lotion; **~winkel** *m* visual angle; *(fig)* angle; **aus** or **unter diesem ~winkel betrachtet** looked at from this angle; **~züge** *pl* features *pl*.

Gesindel *nt no pl (pej)* riff-raff *pl*.

gesinnt *adj usu pred* **jdm gut/übel ~ sein** to be well/ill disposed to(wards) sb; **jdm freundlich/feindlich ~ sein** to be friendly/hostile to sb; **sozial ~ sein** to be socially minded; **er ist anders ~ als wir** his views are different from ours.

Gesinnung *f (Charakter)* cast of mind; *(Ansichten)* views *pl*, basic convictions *pl*; *(Einstellung)* fundamental attitude; *(Denkart)* way of thinking; *(einer Gruppe)* ethos. **seine wahre ~ zeigen** to show (oneself in) one's true colours *(Brit)* or colors *(US)*.

Gesinnungs-: **~genosse** *m* like-minded person; **g~los** *adj (pej)* unprincipled; **sich g~los verhalten** to show a total lack of character; **~losigkeit** *f* lack of principle; **~schnüffelei** *f (pej)* **~schnüffelei betreiben** to pry into people's political convictions; **~täter** *m* person motivated by political/moral convictions; **g~treu** *adj* true to one's convictions; **~wandel** *m* conversion.

gesittet *adj* **(a)** *(wohlerzogen)* well-mannered, well-behaved. **(b)** *(zivilisiert)* civilized.

Gesocks *nt no pl (pej)* riff-raff *pl*.

Gesöff *nt* **-e** *(pej)* muck *(col)*; *(Bier)* piss *(col!)*.

gesoffen *ptp of* **saufen**.

gesogen *ptp of* **saugen**.

gesondert *adj* separate.

gesonnen 1 *ptp of* **sinnen**. 2 *adj* **~ sein, etw zu tun** to be of a mind to do sth.

gespalten *adj Bewußtsein* split; *Lippe* cleft.

Gespann *nt* **-e** *(Pferde~)* horse and cart; *(zur Personenbeförderung)* horse and carriage; *(fig col: Paar)* pair. **ein gutes ~ abgeben** to make a good team.

gespannt *adj* **(a)** *Seil, Schnur* taut. **(b)** *(fig)* tense; *Beziehungen auch* strained. **seine Nerven waren aufs äußerste ~** his nerves were at breaking point. **(c)** *(neugierig)* curious; *(begierig)* eager; *Aufmerksamkeit* rapt. **in ~er Erwartung** in eager anticipation; **ich bin ~, wie er darauf reagiert** I wonder how he'll react to that; **ich bin auf seine Reaktion sehr ~** I'm dying to see how he'll react to that; **ich bin ~ wie ein Flitz(e)bogen** *(hum col)* I'm on tenterhooks; **da bin ich aber ~!** I'm looking forward to that; *(iro)* that I'd like to see!

Gespanntheit *f no pl siehe adj* **(a)** tension. **(b)** tension; strain. **(c)** curiosity; eagerness.

Gespenst *nt* **-er** ghost; *(fig: Gefahr)* spectre *(Brit)*, specter *(US)*. **~er sehen** *(fig col)* to imagine things.

Gespenster-: **~geschichte** *f* ghost story; **g~haft** *adj* ghostly *no adv*; *(fig)* eerie, eery; **das Licht flackerte g~haft** the light flickered eerily; **~stunde** *f* witching hour.

gespenstisch adj = **gespensterhaft.**
gespie(e)n ptp of **speien.**
gespielt adj feigned. **mit** ~**em Interesse** with a pretence (Brit) or pretense (US) of being interested.
Gespinst nt -e (fig geh) web; (der Phantasie) product, fabrication.
gesponnen ptp of **spinnen.**
Gespött nt no pl mockery; (Gegenstand des Spotts) laughing stock. **sich zum** ~ **der Leute machen** to make oneself a laughing stock.
Gespräch nt -e (a) (Unterhaltung) conversation; (Diskussion) discussion; (Dialog) dialogue. ~e (Pol) talks; **ein** ~ **unter vier Augen** a confidential or private talk; **im** ~ **sein** to be under discussion; **mit jdm ins** ~ **kommen** to get into conversation with sb; (fig) to establish a dialogue with sb. **(b)** (~sstoff) **das** ~ **des Tages** the topic of the hour; **das** ~ **der Stadt** the talk of the town; **zum** ~ **werden** to become a talking-point. **(c)** (Telec: Anruf) (telephone) call.
gesprächig adj talkative; (mitteilsam) communicative.
Gesprächs-: ~**einheit** f (Telec) unit; ~**gegenstand** m topic; ~**partner** m ~**partner bei der Diskussion sind die Herren X, Y und Z** taking part in the discussion are Mr X, Mr Y and Mr Z; **mein** ~**partner bei den Verhandlungen** my opposite number at the talks; **wer war dein** ~**partner?** who did you talk with?; ~**stoff** m topics pl; (Diskussionsstoff) topics to discuss; ~**thema** nt topic.
gespreizt adj (fig) affected, unnatural.
gesprenkelt adj speckled.
gesprochen ptp of **sprechen.**
gesprossen ptp of **sprießen.**
gesprungen ptp of **springen.**
Gespür nt no pl feel(ing).
gest. = **gestorben.**
Gestalt f -en **(a)** (lit, fig) form; (Umriß auch) shape. **in** ~ **von** (fig) in the form of; (feste) ~ **annehmen** to take shape; **einer Sache** (dat) ~ **geben** to shape sth; **sich in seiner wahren** ~ **zeigen** (fig) to show (oneself in) one's true colours (Brit) or colors (US). **(b)** (Wuchs) build. **(c)** (Persönlichkeit, Traum~) figure; (Liter auch, pej: Mensch) character.
gestalten* **1** vt to shape, to form (zu into); Wohnung to lay out; Programm, Abend to arrange; Schaufenster to dress; Freizeit to structure. **ich gestalte mein Leben so, wie ich will** I organize my life the way I want to; **etw interessanter** etc ~ to make sth more interesting etc; **schöpferisches G**~ creative expression. **2** vr (sich entwickeln) to develop (zu into).
Gestalter(in f**)** m - creator.
gestalterisch adj formal, creative.
Gestaltung f siehe vt shaping, forming (zu into); lay-out; arrangement; dressing; structuring.
gestanden **1** ptp of **stehen, gestehen. 2** adj attr **ein** ~**er Mann** a mature and experienced man.
geständig adj ~ **sein** to have confessed.
Geständnis nt confession. **jdm ein** ~ **machen** to make a confession to sb.
Gestänge nt - (von Gerüst) bars pl, struts pl; (von Zelt) frame; (von Maschine) linkage.
Gestank m no pl stink, stench.
gestatten* vti to allow, to permit; (einwilligen in) to agree or consent to. **jdm** ~**, etw zu tun** to allow or permit sb to do sth; ~ **Sie, daß ich ...?** may I ...?; **wenn Sie** ~ ... with your permission ...; **sich** (dat) **etw** ~ to permit or allow oneself sth; **wenn ich mir eine Bemerkung** ~ **darf** (geh) if I might be permitted a comment.
Geste ['gɛstə, 'geːstə] f -**n** (lit, fig) gesture.
Gesteck nt -e flower arrangement.
gestehen vti irreg to confess (jdm etw sth to sb). **offen gestanden** quite frankly.

Gestein nt -e rock(s); (Schicht) rock stratum.
Gesteins-: ~**brocken** m rock; ~**masse** f mass of rock.
Gestell nt -e **(a)** stand; (Regal) shelf; (Ablage) rack; (Bett~, Brillen~) frame; (Fahr~) chassis. **(b)** (fig col: Beine) pins (col) pl. **langes** ~ beanpole (col).
gestellt adj (unecht) posed.
gestelzt adj stilted.
gestern adv yesterday. ~ **abend** (früh) yesterday evening; (spät) last night; **die Zeitung von** ~ yesterday's paper; **Ansichten von** ~ outdated views; **er ist nicht von** ~ (col) he wasn't born yesterday.
gestiefelt adj **der G**~**e Kater** Puss-in-Boots; ~ **und gespornt** (fig col) ready and waiting.
gestiegen ptp of **steigen.**
Gestik ['gɛstɪk] f no pl gestures pl.
gestikulieren* [gɛstiku'liːrən] vi to gesticulate.
gestimmt adj **froh/düster** ~ in a cheerful/sombre mood.
Gestirn nt -e star, heavenly body.
gestoben ptp of **stieben.**
Gestöber nt - (Schnee~) snowstorm.
gestochen **1** ptp of **stechen. 2** adj Handschrift clear, neat. ~ **scharfe Fotos** needle-sharp photographs.
gestohlen **1** ptp of **stehlen. 2** adj **der/das kann mir** ~ **bleiben** (col) he/it can go hang (col).
gestorben ptp of **sterben.**
gestört adj disturbed; Rundfunkempfang poor, with a lot of interference. ~**er Kreislauf** circulation problems; **Kinder aus** ~**en Familien** children from problem families.
gestoßen ptp of **stoßen.**
Gestotter nt no pl stuttering, stammering.
gestreift adj striped. **eine rot-grün** ~**e Bluse** a red and green striped blouse.
gestrichen **1** ptp of **streichen. 2** adj **(a)** frisch ~**!** wet paint. **(b)** (genau voll) ~ **voll** level; (sehr voll) full to the brim; **ein** ~**er Teelöffel voll** a level teaspoon(ful); **er hat die Hosen** ~ **voll** (col) he's shitting himself (col!); **ich habe die Nase** ~ **voll** (col) I'm fed up to the back teeth with it (col).
gestrig adj attr yesterday's. **unser** ~**es Schreiben** our letter of yesterday; **die ewig G**~**en** the stick-in-the-muds.
gestritten ptp of **streiten.**
Gestrüpp nt -e undergrowth, brushwood; (fig) jungle.
gestunken ptp of **stinken.**
Gestüt nt -e stud; (Anlage auch) stud farm.
Gesuch nt -e petition (auf, um+acc for); (Antrag) application (auf, um+acc for). **ein** ~ **einreichen** to lodge a petition/an application.
gesucht adj (begehrt) sought after. **sehr** ~ (very) much sought after.
gesund adj, comp ⁻**er** superl ⁻**este(r, s)** or adv **am** ⁻**esten** healthy; (leistungsfähig) fit; Unternehmen, Politik auch sound. ~ **und munter** hale and hearty; **ich fühle mich nicht ganz** ~ I don't feel too well; ~ **leben** to live a healthy life; **jdn** ~ **schreiben** to certify sb (as) fit; **sonst bist du** ~**?** (iro col) are you feeling all right? (iro); **wieder** ~ **werden** to recover.
gesunden* vi aux sein (geh) to recover (auch fig), to regain one's health.
Gesundheit f no pl siehe adj health; fitness; soundness; (von Klima, Lebensweise etc) healthiness. **bei guter** ~ in good health; ~**!** bless you; **auf Ihre** ~**!** your (very good) health.
gesundheitlich adj ~ **geht es mir nicht besonders** my health is not particularly good; **aus** ~**en Gründen** for health reasons.
Gesundheits-: ~**amt** nt public health department; ~**apostel** m (iro) health freak (col); ~**behörde** f health authorities pl; **g**~**fördernd** adj healthy, good for the health; ~**fürsorge** f health

care; ~pflege f hygiene; öffentliche ~pflege public health (care); ~schaden m health defect; ~schäden damage to one's health; g~schädlich adj unhealthy, damaging to (one's) health; ~wesen nt health service; ~zeugnis nt health certificate; ~zustand m no pl state of health.

gesund-: ~schrumpfen sep 1 vt (fig) to trim down; 2 vr to streamline; ~stoßen vr sep irreg (col) to line one's pockets (col).

Gesundung f no pl (lit, fig) recovery; (Genesung) convalescence, recuperation.

gesungen ptp of singen.

gesunken ptp of sinken.

getan ptp of tun. nach ~er Arbeit when the day's work is done.

Getier nt no pl (a) (Tiere, esp Insekten) creatures pl. (b) (einzelnes) creature.

getigert adj (mit Streifen) striped; (mit Flecken) piebald.

Getöse nt no pl din, racket; (von Auto, Beifall etc) roar. mit ~ with a din.

getragen adj (a) Kleidung secondhand. (b) (fig) Melodie, Tempo etc stately no adv.

Getränk nt -e drink, beverage (form).

Getränke-: ~automat m drinks machine or dispenser; ~karte f (in Café) list of beverages; (in Restaurant) wine list; ~steuer f alcohol tax.

getrauen* vr to dare. getraust du dich das? do you dare do that?

Getreide nt - grain, cereal.

Getreide-: ~(an)bau m cultivation of grain or cereals; ~ernte f grain harvest; ~feld nt grain field, cornfield (Brit); ~pflanze f cereal (plant); ~speicher m silo.

getrennt adj separate. ~ leben to be separated, to live apart; ~ schlafen not to sleep together.

getreten ptp of treten.

getreu adj (a) (genau, entsprechend) faithful, true no adv. (b) pred+dat true to.

Getriebe nt - (a) (Tech) gears pl; (~kasten) gearbox; (Antrieb) drive; (von Uhr) movement, works pl. (b) (lebhaftes Treiben) bustle, hurly-burly.

getrieben ptp of treiben.

Getriebeschaden m gearbox trouble no indef art.

getroffen ptp of treffen.

getrogen ptp of trügen.

getrost adv du kannst dich ~ auf ihn verlassen you need have no fears about relying on him; die Firma könnte ~ etwas mehr zahlen the company could easily pay a little more.

getrunken ptp of trinken.

Getto nt -s ghetto.

Getue [gə'tuːə] nt no pl (pej) to-do (col), fuss. ein ~ machen to make a to-do (col) or fuss.

Getümmel nt no pl turmoil. sich ins ~ stürzen to plunge into the tumult or hurly-burly.

Getuschel nt no pl whispering.

ge|übt adj Auge, Ohr, Griff practised (Brit), practiced (US); Fahrer, Segler etc proficient. im Reden ~ sein to be a proficient talker.

Gewächs nt -e (a) (Pflanze) plant. (b) (Med) growth.

gewachsen 1 ptp of wachsen¹. 2 adj (a) (von allein entstanden) evolved. (b) einer Sache (dat) ~ sein to be up to sth; er ist seinem Bruder (an Stärke/Intelligenz) durchaus ~ he is his brother's equal in strength/intelligence.

Gewächshaus nt greenhouse; (Treibhaus) hothouse.

gewagt adj (a) (kühn) daring; (gefährlich) risky. (b) (moralisch bedenklich) risqué.

gewählt adj Sprache refined no adv, elegant.

gewahr adj pred eine(r) Sache ~ werden to become aware of sth.

Gewähr f no pl guarantee. dadurch ist die ~ gegeben, daß ... that guarantees that ...; die Angabe erfolgt ohne ~ we accept no liability for the accuracy of this information.

gewähren* vt to grant; Rabatt, Vorteile to give; Sicherheit, Schutz to afford, to give. jdm Unterstützung ~ to provide sb with support; jdn ~ lassen (geh) not to stop sb.

gewährleisten* vt insep to ensure (jdm etw sb sth); (garantieren) to guarantee (jdm etw sb sth).

Gewährleistung f guarantee. zur ~ der Sicherheit to ensure safety.

Gewahrsam m no pl (a) (Verwahrung) safekeeping. etw in ~ nehmen to take sth into safekeeping. (b) (Haft) custody. jdn in ~ nehmen to take sb into custody.

Gewährsmann m, pl -männer or -leute source.

Gewährung f no pl siehe vt granting; giving; affording.

Gewalt f -en (a) (Macht, Herrschaft) power. die ausübende/gesetzgebende/richterliche ~ the executive/legislature/judiciary; elterliche ~ parental authority; jdn/etw in seine ~ bringen to gain control of sb/sth; unter jds ~ (dat) stehen to be under sb's control. (b) no pl (Zwang) force; (~tätigkeit) violence. ~ anwenden to use force; höhere ~ acts/an act of God; nackte ~ brute force; mit ~ by force; etw mit aller ~ wollen (col) to want sth desperately; jdm/einer Sache ~ antun to do violence to sb/sth; einer Frau ~ antun to violate a woman. (c) no pl (Heftigkeit, Wucht) force; (elementare Kraft auch) power.

Gewalt-: ~akt m act of violence; ~anwendung f use of force or violence.

Gewaltenteilung f separation of powers.

Gewalt-: ~herrschaft f no pl tyranny; ~herrscher m tyrant.

gewaltig adj (a) (heftig) Sturm etc violent. (b) (groß, riesig) colossal, immense; Anblick tremendous; Stimme powerful; (col: sehr groß) Unterschied, Hitze etc tremendous, colossal (col). sich ~ irren to be very much mistaken.

Gewalt-: g~los 1 adj non-violent; 2 adv without force/violence; ~losigkeit f no pl non-violence; ~marsch m forced march; (fig) marathon; ~maßnahme f (fig) drastic measure; g~sam 1 adj forcible; Tod violent; 2 adv forcibly, by force; ~tat f act of violence; g~tätig adj violent; ~tätigkeit f (no pl: Brutalität) violence; (Handlung) act of violence; ~verbrechen nt crime of violence; ~verbrecher m violent criminal; ~verzicht m non-aggression.

Gewand nt -̈er (geh: Kleidungsstück) garment; (weites, langes) robe, gown; (Eccl) vestment, robe; (fig: Äußeres) look; (fig: Maske) guise.

gewandt 1 ptp of wenden. 2 adj skilful (Brit), skillful (US); (körperlich) nimble; Auftreten, Stil elegant.

Gewandtheit f no pl siehe adj skilfulness; nimbleness; elegance.

gewann pret of gewinnen.

Gewäsch nt no pl (pej col) twaddle (col).

gewaschen ptp of waschen.

Gewässer nt - stretch of water. ~ pl inshore waters pl, lakes, rivers and canals pl; ein fließendes/stehendes ~ a stretch of running/ standing water.

Gewässerschutz m prevention of water pollution.

Gewebe nt - (Stoff) fabric, material; (~art) weave; (Biol) tissue; (fig) web.

Gewehr nt -e (Flinte) rifle; (Schrotbüchse) shotgun. ~ ab! (Mil) order arms!; das ~ über! (Mil) shoulder arms!; präsentiert das ~! (Mil) present arms!; ~ bei Fuß stehen (Mil) to stand at order arms; (fig col) to be at the ready; ran an die ~e! (dated col) let's get started.

Gewehr-: ~kolben m rifle butt/butt of a shotgun; ~kugel f rifle bullet; ~lauf m rifle barrel/barrel of a shotgun.

Geweih nt -e (set of sing) antlers pl.

Gewerbe nt - trade. das älteste ~ der Welt (hum)

the oldest profession in the world *(hum)*; **ein** ~ **(be)treiben** to carry on a trade.

Gewerbe-: ~**aufsichtsamt** *nt* ≃ factory inspectorate; ~**betrieb** *m* commercial enterprise; ~**ordnung** *f* trading regulations *pl*; ~**schein** *m* trading licence *(Brit)* or license *(US)*; ~**steuer** *f* trade tax; ~**treibende(r)** *mf decl as adj* trader.

gewerblich *adj* commercial; *(industriell)* industrial. **die** ~**e Wirtschaft** industry; **diese Räume dürfen nicht** ~ **genutzt werden** these rooms are not to be used for commercial purposes.

gewerbsmäßig 1 *adj* professional. ~**e Unzucht** *(form)* prostitution. **2** *adv* professionally, for gain.

Gewerkschaft *f* (trade *or* labor *US*) union.

Gewerkschaft(l)er(in *f***)** *m* - trade *or* labor *(US)* unionist.

gewerkschaftlich *adj* (trade *or* labor *US*) union *attr.* **wir haben uns** ~ **organisiert** we organized ourselves into a union.

Gewerkschafts- *in cpds* (trade *or* labor *US*) union; ~**bewegung** *f* (trade *or* labor *US*) union movement; ~**bund** *m* federation of trade *or* labor *(US)* unions, ≃ Trades Union Congress *(Brit)*, ≃ Federation of Labor *(US)*; ~**mitglied** *nt* member of a/the (trade *or* labor *US*) union.

gewesen 1 *ptp of* **sein**[1]. **2** *adj attr* former.

gewichen *ptp of* **weichen.**

gewichst [gə'vɪkst] *adj (col)* fly *(col)*, crafty.

Gewicht *nt* -**e** *no pl (lit, fig)* weight. **dieser Stein hat ein** ~ **von 100 kg** this rock weighs 100 kg; **spezifisches** ~ specific gravity; ~ **haben** *(lit)* to be heavy; *(fig)* to carry weight; **ins** ~ **fallen** to be crucial; **nicht ins** ~ **fallen** to be of no consequence; **einer Sache** *(dat)* ~ **beimessen** to set (great) store by sth.

Gewicht-: ~**heben** *nt no pl (Sport)* weight-lifting; ~**heber** *m* - weight-lifter.

gewichtig *adj (fig) (wichtig)* weighty; *(einflußreich)* influential.

Gewichts-: ~**klasse** *f (Sport)* weight (category); ~**kontrolle** *f* weight check; **g**~**los** *adj* weightless; *(fig)* lacking substance; ~**verlust** *m* weight loss; ~**zunahme** *f* increase in weight.

gewieft *adj (col)* fly *(col)*, crafty *(in+dat* at*)*.

gewiesen *ptp of* **weisen.**

gewillt *adj* ~ **sein, etw zu tun** to be willing to do sth; *(entschlossen)* to be determined to do sth.

Gewimmel *nt no pl* swarm; *(Menge)* crush, throng.

Gewinde *nt* - *(Tech)* thread.

Gewinde- *(Tech)*: ~**bohrer** *m* (screw) tap; ~**bolzen** *m* threaded bolt.

Gewinn *m* -**e** **(a)** *(Ertrag)* profit. ~ **abwerfen** to make a profit; **aus etw** ~ **schlagen** *(col)* to make a profit out of sth; **etw mit** ~ **verkaufen** to sell sth at a profit. **(b)** *(Preis, Treffer)* prize; *(bei Glücksspiel)* winnings *pl*. **jedes Los ist ein** ~ every ticket a winner. **(c)** *no pl (fig: Vorteil)* gain. **das ist ein großer** ~ **(für mich)** that is of great benefit (to me).

Gewinn-: ~**anteil** *m* **(a)** *(Comm)* dividend; **(b)** *(beim Wetten etc)* share; ~**ausschüttung** *f* prize draw; ~**beteiligung** *f* *(Ind)* profit-sharing; **g**~**bringend** *adj (lit, fig)* profitable; ~**chance** *f* chance of winning; ~**chancen** *(beim Wetten)* odds.

gewinnen *pret* **gewann,** *ptp* **gewonnen 1** *vt* **(a)** to win. **jdn (für etw)** ~ to win sb over (to sth); **jdn für sich** ~ to win sb over (to one's side); **jdn zum Freund** ~ to win sb as a friend; **den Eindruck** ~, **daß** ... to gain the impression that ...; **Zeit** ~ to gain time; **was ist damit gewonnen?** what good is that?; **wie gewonnen, so zerronnen** *(prov)* easy come easy go *(prov)*. **(b)** *(als Profit)* to make (a profit of). **(c)** *(erzeugen)* to produce, to obtain; *Erze etc* to mine, to extract; *(aus Altmaterial)* to reclaim. **2** *vi* **(a)** to win *(bei, in+dat* at*)*. **(b)**

(profitieren) to gain. **an Bedeutung** ~ to gain (in) importance; **an Geschwindigkeit** ~ to gain speed.

gewinnend *adj (fig)* winning, winsome.

Gewinner(in *f***)** *m* - winner.

Gewinn-: ~**spanne** *f* profit margin; ~**streben** *nt* pursuit of profit; ~**sucht** *f* profit-seeking; **g**~**süchtig** *adj* profit-seeking *attr*; **g**~**trächtig** *adj* profitable.

Gewinnung *f no pl (von Kohle)* mining; *(von Zucker etc)* extraction.

Gewirr *nt no pl* tangle; *(fig: Durcheinander)* jumble; *(von Paragraphen, Straßen)* maze; *(von Stimmen)* confusion, babble.

gewiß 1 *adj* **(a)** *(sicher)* certain, sure *(+gen* of*)*. **(ja)** ~! certainly, sure *(esp US)*; **ich bin dessen** ~ *(geh)* I'm certain *or* sure of it. **(b)** *attr* certain. **ein gewisser Herr Müller** a certain Herr Müller; **in gewissem Maße** to a certain extent. **2** *adv (geh)* certainly. **ich weiß es ganz** ~ I'm certain of it.

Gewissen *nt no pl* conscience. **ein schlechtes** ~ a guilty *or* bad conscience; **jdn/etw auf dem** ~ **haben** to have sb/sth on one's conscience; **jdm ins** ~ **reden** to have a serious talk with sb; **das mußt du vor deinem** ~ **verantworten** you'll have to answer to your own conscience for that.

Gewissen-: **g**~**haft** *adj* conscientious; ~**haftigkeit** *f no pl* conscientiousness; **g**~**los** *adj* unprincipled; ~**losigkeit** *f* lack of principle.

Gewissens-: ~**bisse** *pl* pangs of conscience *pl*; **mach dir deswegen keine** ~**bisse!** there's nothing for you to feel guilty about; ~**bisse bekommen** to get a guilty conscience; ~**entscheidung,** ~**frage** *f* matter of conscience; ~**gründe** *pl* conscientious reasons *pl*; ~**konflikt** *m* moral conflict; ~**not** *f* moral dilemma.

gewissermaßen *adv (sozusagen)* so to speak, as it were; *(auf gewisse Weise)* in a way, to an extent.

Gewißheit *f* certainty. **mit** ~ with certainty; **wissen for certain** *or* sure; **sich** *(dat)* ~ **verschaffen** to find out for certain.

Gewitter *nt* - thunderstorm; *(fig)* storm.

Gewitterluft *f* thundery atmosphere.

gewittern* *vi impers* **es gewittert** it's thundering.

Gewitter-: ~**regen,** ~**schauer** *m* thundery shower; ~**wolke** *f* thundercloud; *(fig col)* storm-cloud.

gewittrig *adj* thundery.

gewitzt *adj* crafty, cunning.

gewoben *ptp of* **weben.**

gewogen 1 *ptp of* **wiegen**[2]. **2** *adj (geh)* well-disposed *(+dat* towards*)*.

gewöhnen* **1** *vt* **jdn an etw** *(acc)* ~ to accustom sb to sth; **jdn an Höflichkeit** ~ to teach sb to be polite; **jdn/etw gewöhnt sein** *(col)* to be used to sb/sth. **2** *vr* **sich an jdn/etw** ~ to get used to sb/sth; **sich daran** ~, **etw zu tun** to get used *or* accustomed to doing sth.

Gewohnheit *f* habit. **aus** *(lauter)* ~ from *(sheer)* force of habit; **die** ~ **haben, etw zu tun** to have a habit of doing sth; **sich** *(dat)* **etw zur** ~ **machen** to make a habit of sth.

Gewohnheits-: **g**~**mäßig 1** *adj* habitual; **2** *adv (ohne nachzudenken)* automatically; ~**mensch** *m* creature of habit; ~**recht** *nt (Jur)* common law; ~**trinker** *m* habitual drinker; ~**verbrecher** *m* habitual criminal.

gewöhnlich 1 *adj* **(a)** *attr (allgemein, üblich)* usual; *(normal)* normal; *(alltäglich)* everyday. **ein** ~**er Sterblicher** an ordinary mortal. **(b)** *(pej: ordinär)* common. **2** *adv* normally, usually. **wie** ~ as usual.

Gewöhnlichkeit *f (pej)* commonness.

gewohnt *adj* usual. **etw** *(acc)* ~ **sein** to be used to sth.

gewohntermaßen *adv* usually.

Gewöhnung *f no pl (das Sich-Gewöhnen)* habituation *(an+acc* to*)*; *(das Angewöhnen)* training *(an +acc* in*)*; *(Sucht)* habit, addiction.

Gewölbe nt - (Decken~) vault; (Keller~ auch) vaults pl.

gewölbt adj Stirn domed; Himmel, Decke vaulted.

gewollt adj forced, artificial.

gewonnen ptp of **gewinnen**.

geworben ptp of **werben**.

geworden ptp of **werden**.

geworfen ptp of **werfen**.

gewrungen ptp of **wringen**.

Gewühl nt no pl (Gedränge) crowd, throng; (Verkehrs~) chaos, snarl-up (col).

gewunden 1 ptp of **winden**. 2 adj Weg, Fluß etc winding; Erklärung roundabout no adv, tortuous.

gewunken (dial) ptp of **winken**.

gewürfelt adj check(ed).

Gewürz nt -e spice; (Kräutersorte) herb; (Pfeffer, Salz) seasoning.

Gewürz-: ~bord nt spice rack; ~gurke f pickled gherkin; ~nelke f clove; ~ständer m spice rack.

gewußt ptp of **wissen**.

Geysir ['gaizır] m -e geyser.

gez. = **gezeichnet**.

gezackt adj Fels jagged; Blatt serrated.

gezähnt adj serrated; (Tech) cogged; Briefmarke perforated.

gezeichnet adj marked; (als Straffälliger auch) branded. **vom Tode ~ sein** to have the mark of death on one.

Gezeiten pl tides pl.

Gezeiten-: ~kraftwerk nt tidal power station; ~wechsel m turn of the tide.

Gezeter nt no pl (col: Schimpfen) nagging.

gezielt adj purposeful; Schuß well-aimed; Frage, Maßnahme etc specific; Hilfe well-directed. **~ schießen** to shoot to kill.

geziert adj affected.

Geziertheit f affectedness.

gezogen ptp of **ziehen**.

Gezwitscher nt no pl chirruping, twitter(ing).

gezwungen 1 ptp of **zwingen**. 2 adj (nicht entspannt) forced; Atmosphäre strained; Stil, Benehmen stiff.

gezwungenermaßen adv of necessity. **etw ~ tun** to be forced to do sth, to do sth of necessity.

ggf. = **gegebenenfalls**.

Gicht f no pl (nach Med) gout.

Giebel m - gable; (Tür~, Fenster~) pediment.

Giebel-: ~dach nt gabled roof; ~fenster nt gable window; ~haus nt gabled house; ~wand f gable end or wall.

Gier f no pl (nach for) greed; (Lüsternheit) lust.

gierig adj greedy; (nach Geld) avaricious; (lüstern) lustful. **~ nach etw sein** to be greedy for sth; (nach Macht auch, sexuell) to lust for sth.

gießen pret **goß**, ptp **gegossen** 1 vt (a) to pour; (verschütten) to spill; Pflanzen to water. (b) Metall to cast (zu into). 2 vi impers to pour. **es gießt in Strömen** it's pouring down.

Gießer m - (Metall) caster, founder.

Gießerei f (Werkstatt) foundry.

Gieß-: ~kanne f watering can; ~kannenprinzip nt no pl (col) principle of indiscriminate all-round distribution.

Gift nt -e (lit, fig) poison; (Schlangen~, fig: Bosheit) venom. **~ nehmen** to poison oneself; **das ist ~ für ihn** (col) that is very bad for him; **darauf kannst du ~ nehmen** (col) you can bet your life on it (col); **~ und Galle spucken** (col) to be fuming.

giften vi (col) to be vitriolic (gegen about).

Gift-: g~frei adj non-toxic; ~gas nt poison gas; g~grün adj bilious green; g~haltig adj poisonous, toxic.

giftig adj (a) (Gift enthaltend) poisonous; Chemikalien etc auch toxic. (b) (fig) (boshaft) venomous; (zornig) vitriolic. (c) (grell) bilious.

Gift-: ~mischer(in f) m - preparer of poison; (fig) trouble-maker; ~müll m toxic waste; ~pfeil m

poisoned arrow; ~pilz m poisonous toadstool; ~schlange f poisonous snake; ~zahn m fang; ~zwerg m (col) spiteful little devil (col).

Gigant m giant.

gigantisch adj gigantic, colossal.

Gilde f -n guild.

Gin [dʒɪn] m -s gin. **~ tonic** gin and tonic.

ging pret of **gehen**.

Ginster m - (Bot) broom; (Stech~) gorse.

Gipfel m - (a) (Berg~) summit; (Spitze) peak. (b) (fig: Höhepunkt) height; (des Ruhms, der Karriere auch) peak. **das ist der ~!** (col) that's the limit. (c) (~konferenz) summit.

Gipfel-: ~konferenz f (Pol) summit conference; ~leistung f crowning achievement.

gipfeln vi to culminate (in +dat in).

Gipfel-: ~punkt m (lit) zenith; (fig) high point; ~stürmer m (liter) conqueror of a/the peak; ~treffen nt (Pol) summit (meeting).

Gips m -e plaster. **einen Arm in ~ legen** to put an arm in plaster.

Gips- in cpds plaster; ~abdruck m plaster cast; ~bein nt (col) leg in plaster.

gipsen vt to plaster; Arm, Bein to put in plaster.

Gipser m - plasterer.

Gips-: ~figur f figure (of Paris) figure; ~verband m (Med) plaster cast.

Giraffe f -n giraffe.

Girlande f -n garland (aus of).

Giro ['ʒiːro] nt -s (Fin) (bank) giro; (Indossament) endorsement. **durch ~** by giro.

Giro-: ~bank f giro bank; ~konto nt current (Brit) or checking (US) account; ~verkehr m giro system; (~geschäft) giro transfer (business).

girren vi (lit, fig) to coo.

Gis nt - (Mus) G sharp.

Gischt m -e or f -en spray.

Gitarre f -n guitar.

Gitarrespieler(in f) m, **Gitarrist(in** f) m guitarist, guitar-player.

Gitter nt - bars pl; (vor Schaufenstern etc) grille; (in Fußboden, Straßendecke) grid, grating; (feines Draht~) (wire-)mesh.

Gitter-: ~fenster nt barred window; ~stab m bar; ~zaun m paling; (mit gekreuzten Stäben) lattice fence.

Glacéhandschuh [gla'seː-] m kid glove. **jdn mit ~en anfassen** to handle sb with kid gloves.

Gladiator m gladiator.

Gladiole f -n (Bot) gladiolus.

Glanz m no pl gleam; (von Oberfläche auch) shine; (Funkeln, von Augen) sparkle; (von Haaren, Seide) sheen; (von Farbe) gloss; (blendend: von Sonne) glare; (fig) (der Schönheit, Jugend) radiance; (von Ruhm) glory; (Pracht) splendour (Brit), splendor (US). **mit ~ und Gloria** (iro col) in grand style; **eine Prüfung mit ~ bestehen** (col) to pass an exam with flying colours (Brit) or colors (US).

Glanz|abzug m (Phot) glossy or gloss print.

glänzen vi (lit, fig) to shine; (glitzern) to glisten; (funkeln) to sparkle; (blenden) to glare; (Nase) to be shiny. **vor jdm ~ wollen** to want to shine in front of sb.

glänzend adj shining; (strahlend) radiant; (blendend) dazzling; (glitzernd) glistening; (funkelnd) sparkling; Papier glossy, shiny; Stoff, Nase shiny; (fig) brilliant; Aussehen, Fest dazzling; (erstklassig) splendid. **~ in Form** (col) in splendid form; **wir haben uns ~ amüsiert** we had a wonderful time; **mir geht es ~** I'm just fine.

Glanz-: ~lack m gloss (paint); ~leistung f brilliant achievement; g~los adj (lit, fig) dull; Lack, Oberfläche matt; ~nummer f big number, pièce de résistance; ~papier nt glossy paper; ~punkt m (fig) highlight, high spot; ~stück nt pièce de résistance; g~voll adj (fig) brilliant; (prachtvoll) glittering; ~zeit f heyday.

Glas nt -er or (als Maßangabe) - (a) (Stoff, Gefäß)

glass; *(Konserven~)* jar. **ein ~ Milch** a glass of milk; **ein ~ Marmelade** a jar of jam; **zwei ~ Wein** two glasses of wine; **zu tief ins ~ schauen** *(col)* to have one too many. **(b)** *(Brillen~)* lens *sing*; *(Fern~)* binoculars *pl*.

Glas- *in cpds* glass; **~bläser** *m* glassblower; **~bruch** *m* broken glass.

Gläschen ['glɛːsçən] *nt dim of* **Glas** *(Getränk)* little drink.

Glaser *m* - glazier.

Glaserei *f* **(a)** *no pl (Handwerk)* glasswork. **(b)** *(Werkstatt)* glazier's workshop.

Gläsertuch *nt* glasscloth.

Glas-: **~faser** *f* fibreglass *(Brit)*, fiberglass *(US)*; **~fenster** *nt* glass window; **~fiberstab** *m (Sport)* fibreglass *(Brit)* or fiberglass *(US)* pole; **~form** *f* glass mould; *(Cook)* glass or Pyrex ® dish; **~geschirr** *nt* glassware; **~haus** *nt* greenhouse; *(in botanischen Gärten etc)* glasshouse; **wer (selbst) im ~haus sitzt, soll nicht mit Steinen werfen** *(Prov)* people who live in glass houses shouldn't throw stones *(Prov)*.

glasieren* *vt* to glaze; *Kuchen* to ice, to frost *(US)*.

glasig *adj Blick* glassy; *(Cook) Kartoffeln* waxy; *Speck, Zwiebeln* transparent.

Glas-: **~kasten** *m* glass case; *(in Fabrik, Büro)* glass box; **g~klar** *adj (lit)* clear as glass; *(fig)* crystal-clear; **~kugel** *f* glass ball; *(Murmel)* marble; **~perle** *f* glass bead; **~platte** *f* glass top; **~scheibe** *f* sheet of glass; *(Fenster~)* pane of glass; **~scherbe** *f* piece of broken glass; **~scherben** broken glass; **~schneider** *m* glass cutter; **~schrank** *m* glass-fronted cupboard; **~splitter** *m* splinter of glass.

Glasur *f* glaze; *(Metall)* enamel; *(Zuckerguß)* icing, frosting *(US)*.

Glas-: **~waren** *pl* glassware *sing*; **~watte**, **~wolle** *f* glass wool.

glatt *comp* **-er** *or* **⁼er**, *superl* **-este(r, s)** *or* **⁼este(r, s)** *or (adv)* **am -esten** *or* **⁼esten 1** *adj* **(a)** *(eben)* smooth; *Haar* straight; *(Med) Bruch* clean; *(faltenlos) Stoff* uncreased. **(b)** *(schlüpfrig)* slippery. **(c)** *(fig) Landung, Ablauf* smooth. **(d)** *attr (col: klar, eindeutig)* outright; *Lüge, Unsinn etc auch* downright. **(e)** *(pej: allzu gewandt)* smooth, slick. **2** *adv* **(a)** smoothly. **er hat sich ~ aus der Affäre gezogen** he wriggled neatly out of the whole affair. **(b)** *(ganz, völlig)* completely; *leugnen, ablehnen* flatly. **die Rechnung ist ~ aufgegangen** the sum works out exactly.

Glätte *f no pl* smoothness *(auch fig)*; *(von Haar)* sleekness; *(Schlüpfrigkeit)* slipperiness.

Glatt|eis *nt* ice. „**Vorsicht ~!**" "danger, black ice"; **sich auf ~ begeben** *(fig)* to be skating on thin ice; **jdn aufs ~ führen** *(fig)* to take sb for a ride *(col)*.

glätten 1 *vt (glattmachen)* to smooth out; *(glattstreichen)* Haar, Tuch to smooth. **2** *vr* to smooth out; *(Wellen, fig)* to subside.

Glatt-: **g~gehen** *vi sep irreg aux sein* to go smoothly; **g~hobeln** *vt sep* to plane smooth; **g~kämmen** *vt sep* to comb straight; **g~rasiert** *adj Mann, Kinn* clean-shaven; *Beine* shaved; **g~schleifen** *vt sep irreg* to rub smooth; *Diamanten etc* to grind smooth; **g~schneiden** *vt sep irreg* to cut straight; **g~streichen** *vt sep irreg* to smooth out; *Haare* to smooth (down); **g~weg** ['glatvɛk] *adv (col)* simply, just; **das ist g~weg erlogen** that's a blatant lie.

Glatze *f* - *m* bald head. **eine ~ bekommen/haben** to go/be bald.

Glatz-: **~kopf** *m* bald head; *(col: Mann mit Glatze)* baldie *(col)*; **g~köpfig** *adj* bald(-headed).

Glaube(n) *m no pl (Vertrauen, Rel)* faith *(an+acc* in*)*; *(Überzeugung)* belief *(an+acc* in*)*. **in gutem ~n** in good faith; **(bei jdm) ~n finden** to be believed (by sb); **den ~n an jdn/etw verlieren** to lose faith in sb/sth; **jdm ~n schenken** to give

credence to sb.

glauben *vti* to believe *(an +acc* in*)*; *(meinen, vermuten)* to think. **jdm ~** to believe sb; **das glaube ich dir nicht** I don't believe you; **glaube es mir** believe me; **jdm (etw) aufs Wort ~** to take sb's word (for sth); **d(a)ran ~ müssen** *(col)* to cop it *(col)*; *(sterben auch)* to buy it *(col)*; **das glaubst du doch selbst nicht!** you can't be serious; **ob du es glaubst oder nicht, ...** believe it or not ...; **wer's glaubt, wird selig** *(iro)* a likely story *(iro)*; **wer hätte das je geglaubt!** who would have thought it?; **er glaubte sich unbeobachtet** he thought nobody was watching him; **es ist nicht zu ~** it's incredible *or* unbelievable; **ich glaube, ja** I think so; **ich glaube, nein** I don't think so.

Glaubens-: **~bekenntnis** *nt* creed; **~eifer** *m* religious zeal; **~frage** *f* question of faith; **~freiheit** *f* religious freedom; **~gemeinschaft** *f* religious sect; *(christliche auch)* denomination; **~kampf** *m* religious battle; **~satz** *m* dogma, doctrine; **~streit** *m* religious controversy.

glaubhaft *adj* credible, believable; *(einleuchtend)* plausible. **(jdm) etw ~ machen** to satisfy sb of sth.

Glaubhaftigkeit *f no pl* credibility; *(Evidenz)* plausibility.

gläubig *adj* religious; *(vertrauensvoll)* trusting.

Gläubige(r) *mf decl as adj* believer. **die ~n** the faithful.

Gläubiger(in *f) m* - *(Comm)* creditor.

glaublich *adj*: **kaum ~** scarcely credible.

glaubwürdig *adj* credible. **~e Quellen** reliable sources.

Glaubwürdigkeit *f no pl* credibility.

gleich 1 *adj (identisch, ähnlich)* same; *(~wertig, ~berechtigt, Math)* equal. **die/das ~e ... wie** the same ... as; **in ~em Abstand** at an equal distance; **zu ~en Teilen** in equal parts; **in ~er Weise** in the same way; **mit ~er Post** with the same post; **das ~e, aber nicht dasselbe Auto** the same (type of) car, but not the identical one; **wir wollten alle das ~e** we all wanted the same thing; **es waren die ~en, die ...** it was the same ones who/which ...; **zwei mal zwei (ist) ~ vier** two times two equals *or* is four; **jdm (an etw dat) ~ sein** to be sb's equal in sth; **ihr Männer seid doch alle ~!** you men are all the same!; **es ist mir (alles *or* ganz) ~** it's all the same to me; **ganz ~ wer/was** *etc* no matter who/what *etc*; **G~es mit G~em vergelten** to pay like with like; **~ und ~ gesellt sich gern** *(Prov)* birds of a feather flock together *(Prov)*.

2 *adv* **(a)** *(ebenso)* equally; *(auf ~e Weise)* alike, the same. **sie sind ~ groß/alt** they are the same size/age.

(b) *(räumlich)* immediately, just. **~ hinter dem Haus** just behind the house.

(c) *(sofort)* immediately, right away; *(bald)* in a minute. **~ am Anfang** at the very beginning; **~ danach** right after(wards); **ich komme ~** I'm just coming; **es ist ~ drei Uhr** it's very nearly three o'clock; **das habe ich mir ~ gedacht** I thought that straight away; **warum nicht ~ so?** why didn't you say/do that in the first place?; **wann machst du das? — ~!** when are you going to do it? — in just a moment; **so wirkt das Bild ~ ganz anders** suddenly, the picture has changed completely; **er ging ~ in die Küche** he went straight to the kitchen; **bis ~!** see you in a while.

(d) *(in Fragesätzen)* again. **wie war doch ~ Ihr Name?** what was your name again?

Gleich-: **g~altrig** *adj* (of) the same age; **g~artig 1** *adj* of the same kind *(+dat* as*)*; *(ähnlich)* similar *(+dat* to*)*; **2** *adv* in the same way; similarly; **~artigkeit** *f* similarity; **g~auf** *adj (esp Sport)* equal; **g~auf liegen** to be lying equal; **g~bedeutend** *adj* synonymous *(mit* with*)*; *(so gut wie)* tantamount *(mit* to*)*; **~behandlung** *f* equal

treatment; g~**berechtigt** adj with equal rights;
g~**berechtigt sein** to have equal rights; ~**be-**
rechtigung f equal rights sing or pl, equality
(+gen, von for); g~**bleiben** sep irreg aux sein **1**
vi to remain the same; **2** vr **sich** (dat) g~**bleiben**
(Mensch) to remain the same; **das bleibt sich**
g~ it doesn't matter; g~**bleibend** adj constant,
steady; **bei** g~**bleibendem Gehalt** when one's
salary stays the same.

gleichen pret **glich,** ptp **geglichen** vi jdm/einer
Sache ~ to be like sb/sth; **sich** ~ to be alike; **jdm**
an Schönheit ~ to be sb's equal in beauty.

Gleich-: g~**falls** adv (ebenfalls) likewise; (auch)
also; **danke** g~**falls!** thank you, (and) the same
to you; g~**farbig** adj (of) the same colour (Brit) or
color (US); g~**förmig** adj (einheitlich, fig: eintönig) uniform (auch Phys); ~**förmigkeit** f uniformity; g~**geschlechtig** adj (Biol, Zool) of the same
sex, same-sex attr; g~**geschlechtlich** adj (a)
homosexual; **(b)** = g~**geschlechtig**; g~**gesinnt**
adj like-minded; g~**gestellt** adj equal (+dat to,
with), on a par (+dat with); **rechtlich** g~**gestellt**
equal in law.

Gleichgewicht nt no pl (lit, fig) balance, equilibrium; **das** ~ **verlieren** to lose one's balance;
(fig) to be thrown off balance; **das** ~ **(be)halten**
(lit) to keep one's balance; (fig) to retain one's
equilibrium; **jdn aus dem** ~ **bringen** to throw sb
off balance.

gleichgewichtig adj balanced.

Gleichgewichts-: ~**sinn** m sense of balance;
~**störung** f impaired balance.

gleichgültig adj indifferent (gegenüber to, towards); (uninteressiert) apathetic (gegenüber towards); (unwesentlich) trivial. **Politik ist ihm** ~
he doesn't care about politics; ~, **was er tut no**
matter what he does; **bin ich dir gänzlich** ~
geworden? have I become a matter of complete
indifference to you?

Gleichgültigkeit f indifference (gegenüber to,
towards); (Desinteresse) apathy (gegenüber towards).

Gleichheit f **(a)** no pl (gleiche Stellung) equality;
(Identität) identity; (Übereinstimmung) uniformity; (Ind) parity. **(b)** (Ähnlichkeit) similarity.

Gleichheits-: ~**prinzip** nt principle of equality;
~**zeichen** nt (Math) equals sign.

Gleich-: ~**klang** m (fig) harmony, accord;
g~**kommen** vi sep irreg aux sein+dat **(a) niemand**
kommt ihm an Dummheit g~ no-one can equal
him for stupidity; **(b)** (g~bedeutend sein mit) to
be tantamount or equivalent to; ~**lauf** m no pl
(Tech) synchronization; g~**laufend** adj parallel
(mit to); (Tech) synchronized; g~**lautend** adj
identical; ~**macherei** f (pej) levelling down (pej),
egalitarianism; ~**maß** nt no pl **(a)** (Ebenmaß)
evenness; (von Proportionen) symmetry; **(b)** (Eintönigkeit) monotony (pej), regularity; g~**mäßig**
adj even, regular; (Puls auch steady; Abstände
regular; etw g~**mäßig verteilen** to distribute
sth equally; **die Farbe** g~**mäßig auftragen** to
apply the paint evenly; ~**mäßigkeit** f siehe adj
evenness, regularity; ~**steadiness; regularity;
~**mut** m equanimity, serenity.

Gleichnis nt **(a)** (Liter) simile. **(b)** (Allegorie)
allegory; (Bibl) parable.

Gleich-: g~**rangig** adj Beamte etc equal in rank
(mit to), at the same level (mit as); **Probleme etc**
equally important; g~**richten** vt sep (Elec) to
rectify.

gleichsam adv (geh) as it were. ~, **als ob** just as if.

Gleich-: g~**schalten** vt sep (pej) to bring into line;
~**schaltung** f (pej) bringing into line; g~**schen-**
k(e)lig adj Dreieck isosceles; ~**schritt** m no pl
(Mil) marching in step; **im** ~**schritt** (lit, fig) in
step; **im** ~**schritt, marsch!** forward march!;
g~**seitig** adj Dreieck equilateral; g~**setzen** vt sep
(als dasselbe ansehen) to equate (mit with); (als

gleichwertig ansehen) to treat as equivalent (mit
to); ~**stand** m no pl **(a)** (Sport) **den** ~**stand erzie-**
len to draw level; **das Spiel wurde beim** ~**stand**
von 4:4 beendet the game ended in a 4-all draw;
(b) (Pol) equal stage of development; g~**stellen**
vt sep **(a)** (rechtlich etc) to treat as equal; siehe
gleichgestellt; (b) = g~**setzen**; ~**strom** m
(Elec) direct current, DC; g~**tun** vt impers sep
irreg **es jdm** g~**tun** to equal or match sb.

Gleichung f equation.

Gleich-: g~**viel** adv (geh) nonetheless; g~**viel ob**
no matter whether; g~**wertig** adj of the same
value; (gleich zu bewerten) Leistung, Qualität
equal (+dat to); Gegner evenly matched; g~**wohl**
(geh) adv nevertheless, nonetheless; g~**zeitig**
adj simultaneous; **ihr sollt nicht alle** g~**zeitig**
reden you mustn't all speak at the same time;
~**zeitigkeit** f simultaneity; g~**ziehen** vi sep irreg
(col) to catch up (mit with).

Gleis nt -e (Rail) line, track; (einzelne Schiene)
rail; (Bahnsteig) platform; (fig) rut. ~ **6** platform
or track (US) 6; **aus dem** ~ **springen** to jump the
rails; **aus dem** ~ **kommen** (fig) to go off the rails
(col); **wieder ins richtige** ~ **kommen** (fig) to get
back on the rails (col).

Gleis-: ~**arbeiten** pl work on the line; ~**bau** m no
pl railway (Brit) or railroad (US) construction;
~**kettenfahrzeug** nt caterpillar vehicle; ~**kör-**
per m railway (Brit) or railroad (US) track.

gleißen vi (liter) to gleam, to glisten.

gleiten pret **glitt,** ptp **geglitten** vi aux sein **(a)** to
glide; (Blick) to pass; (Hand auch) to slide. **ein**
Lächeln glitt über ihr Gesicht a smile flickered
across her face. **(b)** (rutschen) to slide; (Auto) to
skid; (ent~: Gegenstand) to slip. **ins G**~ **kom-**
men to start to slide or slip.

gleitend adj ~**e Löhne** sliding wage scale; ~**e**
Arbeitszeit flexible working hours pl,
flex(i)time.

Gleit-: ~**flug** m glide; **im** ~**flug niedergehen** to
glide down; ~**klausel** f (Comm) escalator clause;
~**komma** nt floating point; ~**zeit** f flex(i)time.

Gletscher m - glacier.

Gletscher-: ~**bach** m glacial stream; ~**spalte** f
crevasse; ~**wasser** nt glacier water.

glich pret of **gleichen.**

Glied nt -er **(a)** (Körperteil) limb; (Finger~,
Zehen~) joint. **seine** ~**er recken** to stretch
(oneself); **das steckt ihr noch in den** ~**ern** she
still hasn't got over it. **(b)** (Penis) penis. **(c)**
(Ketten~, fig) link. **(d)** (Teil) section, part. **(e)**
(Mil) rank. **ins** ~ **zurücktreten** to step back into
the ranks.

gliedern 1 vt **(a)** (ordnen) to order, to organize.
(b) (unterteilen) to (sub)divide (in+acc into). **2** vr
sich ~ **in** (+acc) to (sub)divide into.

Glieder-: ~**puppe** f jointed doll; (Marionette)
(string) puppet, marionette; ~**reißen** nt,
~**schmerz** m rheumatic pains pl.

Gliederung f (das Gliedern) organization; (das
Unterteilen) subdivision. **(b)** (Aufbau) structure.

Glied-: ~**maßen** pl limbs pl; ~**staat** m member
state.

glimmen pret **glomm** ptp **geglommen** vi to
glow.

Glimmstengel m (hum col) fag (Brit col), cigarette, butt (US col).

glimpflich adj (mild) mild, light. ~ **davonkom-**
men to get off lightly; ~ **ablaufen** or **verlaufen** to
pass off without serious consequences.

glitschen vi aux sein (col) to slip (aus out of).

glitschig adj (col) slippery, slippy (col).

glitt pret of **gleiten.**

glitzern vi to glitter; (Stern auch) to twinkle.

global adj **(a)** (weltweit) global, worldwide. **(b)**
(ungefähr, pauschal) general.

Globetrotter m - globetrotter.

Globus m, pl **Globen** or **-se** globe; (col: Kopf) nut

(col), bonze *(Brit col)*.
Glöckchen *nt* (little) bell.
Glocke *f* **-n** *(auch Blüte)* bell; *(Käse~ etc)* cover; *(Taucher~)* (diving) bell. **etw an die große ~ hängen** *(col)* to shout sth from the rooftops.
Glocken-: **~blume** *f* bellflower, campanula; **g~förmig** *adj* bell-shaped; **~geläut(e)** *nt* (peal of) bells; **~klöppel** *m* clapper; **~läuten** *nt* (peal of) bells; **~schlag** *m* stroke (of a/the bell); *(von Uhr auch)* chime; **~spiel** *nt (in Turm)* carillon; *(automatisch auch)* chimes *pl*; *(Instrument)* glockenspiel; **~strang** *m* bell rope; **~stuhl** *m* bell cage; **~ton** *m* sound of a/the bell; **~turm** *m* belfry.
Glöckner *m* - bellringer.
glomm *pret of* **glimmen**.
glorifizieren* *vt* to glorify.
Glorifizierung *f* glorification.
glorreich *adj* glorious. **seine Laufbahn ~ beenden** to bring one's career to a glorious conclusion.
Glossar *nt* **-e** glossary.
Glosse *f* **-n** *(Press, Rad etc)* satirical commentary. **(b)** *(col)* **seine ~n über jdn/etw machen** *(col)* to make snide comments about sb/sth *(col)*.
glossieren* *vt (Press, Rad etc)* to do a satirical commentary on.
Glotzauge *nt (col)* **~n machen** to stare (goggle-eyed), to gawp.
Glotze *f* **-n** *(col)* goggle-box *(col)*.
glotzen *vi (pej col)* to gape *(auf, in+acc* at).
Glück *nt no pl* **(a)** luck. **ein ~!** how lucky!, what a stroke of luck!; **~/kein ~ haben** to be lucky/unlucky; **er hat das ~ gehabt, zu ...** he was lucky enough to ...; **auf gut ~** *(aufs Geratewohl)* on the off-chance; *(unvorbereitet)* trusting to luck; *(wahllos)* at random; **du hast ~ im Unglück gehabt** it could have been a great deal worse (for you); **viel ~ (bei...)!** good luck *or* the best of luck (with ...)!; **~ bei Frauen haben** to be successful with women; **jdm zum Geburtstag ~ wünschen** to wish sb (a) happy birthday; **zum ~** luckily, fortunately; **das ist dein ~!** that's lucky for you!; **mehr ~ als Verstand haben** to have more luck than brains; **sie weiß noch nichts von ihrem ~** *(iro)* she doesn't know anything about it yet; **damit wirst du bei ihr kein ~ haben** you won't have any joy with her (with that) *(col)*; **sein ~ machen** to make one's fortune; **sein ~ probieren** to try one's luck; **er kann von ~ sagen, daß ...** he can count himself lucky that ...; **das hat mir gerade noch zu meinem ~ gefehlt!** *(iro)* that was all I wanted; **man kann niemanden zu seinem ~ zwingen** *(prov)* you can lead a horse to water but you can't make him drink *(prov)*.
(b) *(Freude)* happiness. **eheliches ~** wedded *or* marital bliss; **er ist ihr ganzes ~** he is her whole life.
Glück-: **~auf** *nt no pl* (cry of) "good luck"; **g~bringend** *adj* lucky, propitious *(form)*.
Glucke *f* **-n** *(Bruthenne)* broody hen; *(mit Jungen)* mother hen.
glucken *vi (brüten)* to brood; *(fig col)* to sit around.
glücken *vi aux sein* to be successful. **nicht ~** to be a failure; **es ist ihm geglückt zu fliehen** he succeeded in escaping; **es wollte nicht ~** it wouldn't go right.
gluckern *vi* to glug.
glücklich 1 *adj* **(a)** *(froh)* happy. **ein ~es Ende** a happy ending; **~ machen** to bring happiness. **(b)** *(erfolgreich, vom Glück begünstigt)* lucky, fortunate; *(vorteilhaft, erfreulich)* happy. **~e Reise!** have a pleasant journey! **2** *adv* **(a)** *(froh, selig)* happily. **(b)** *(mit Glück)* by luck; *(vorteilhaft, erfreulich)* happily. **(c)** *(col: endlich, zu guter Letzt)* finally, eventually.
glücklicherweise *adv* luckily, fortunately.
glücklos *adj* hapless, luckless.

Glücks-: **~bote** *m* bearer of (the) glad tidings; **~bringer** *m* - *(Talisman)* lucky charm.
glückselig *adj* blissful.
Glückseligkeit *f* bliss, rapture.
glucksen *vi* **(a)** *(Kleinkind)* to gurgle; *(Erwachsener)* to chortle. **(b)** *(gluckern)* to glug.
Glücks-: **~fall** *m* stroke of luck; **durch einen ~fall** by a lucky chance; **~gefühl** *nt* feeling of happiness; **~kind** *nt* child of Fortune; **~klee** *m* four-leaf(ed) clover; **~pilz** *m* lucky beggar *(col)*; **~rad** *nt* wheel of fortune; **~ritter** *m* adventurer; **~sache** *f* das ist ~sache it's a matter of luck; **das war reine ~sache** it was pure luck *or* a pure fluke *(col)*; **~spiel** *nt* game of chance; **~spieler** *m* gambler; **~strähne** *f* lucky streak; **~tag** *m* lucky day; **~treffer** *m* stroke of luck; *(beim Schießen, Ftbl)* lucky shot, fluke *(col)*; **~zahl** *f* lucky number.
Glückwunsch *m* **-e** congratulations *pl (zu* on). **herzlichen ~** congratulations; **herzlichen ~ zum Geburtstag!** happy birthday, many happy returns (of the day).
Glüh- *(Elec)*: **~birne** *f* (electric) light bulb; **~draht** *m* filament.
glühen *vi* to glow. **vor Fieber ~** to be flushed with fever; **der Haß glühte in ihm** he was burning with hatred. **2** *vt* to heat until red-hot.
glühend *adj* glowing; *(heiß)* **~/Metall** red-hot; **Hitze** blazing; *(fig: leidenschaftlich)* ardent; **Haß** burning; **Wangen** flushed, burning.
Glüh-: **~faden** *m (Elec)* filament; **~lampe** *f (form)* electric light bulb; **~wein** *m* glühwein, mulled wine, glogg *(US)*; **~würmchen** *nt* glow-worm; *(fliegend)* firefly.
Glut *f* **-en (a)** *(glühende Masse, Kohle)* embers *pl*; *(Tabaks~)* burning ash; *(Hitze)* heat. **(b)** *(fig liter)* *(glühende Farbe, Hitze)* glow; *(Leidenschaft)* ardour *(Brit)*, ardor *(US)*.
Glut-: **~hitze** *f* sweltering heat; **g~rot** *adj (liter)* fiery red.
Glyzerin *nt no pl (Chem)* glycerin(e).
GmbH [ge:|ɛmbeː'ha:] *f* **-s** = **Gesellschaft mit beschränkter Haftung** limited company, Ltd *(Brit)*, Inc *(US)*.
Gnade *f* **-n** *(Barmherzigkeit)* mercy; *(Rel)* grace; *(Gunst)* favour *(Brit)*, favor *(US)*; *(Verzeihung)* pardon. **um ~ bitten** to ask for mercy; **bei jdm ~ finden** to find favour with sb; **~ vor Recht ergehen lassen** to temper justice with mercy; **ohne ~** without mercy; **~! mercy!; Euer ~n!** *(Hist)* Your Grace; **die ~ haben, etw zu tun** *(iro)* to graciously consent to do sth.
gnaden *vi:* **(dann) gnade dir Gott!** (then) God help you *or* heaven have mercy on you.
Gnaden-: **~akt** *m* act of mercy; **~brot** *nt no pl* **jdm/einem Tier das ~brot geben** to keep sb/an animal in his/her/its old age; **einem Pferd das ~brot geben** to put a horse out to grass; **~frist** *f* (temporary) reprieve; **eine ~frist von 24 Stunden** 24 hours' grace; **~gesuch** *nt* plea for clemency; **g~los** *adj* merciless; **~losigkeit** *f* mercilessness; **~schuß** *m* **einem Tier den ~schuß geben** to put an animal out of its misery; **~stoß** *m* coup de grâce *(with sword etc, fig)*; **~tod** *m (geh)* mercy killing, euthanasia.
gnädig *adj (barmherzig)* merciful; *(herablassend)* gracious; **Strafe** lenient; *(freundlich)* kind. **~es Fräulein** *(form)* madam; *(jüngere Dame)* miss; **~e Frau** *(form)* madam, ma'am; **~er Gott!** *(col)* merciful heavens! *(col)*; **Gott sei uns ~!** *(geh)* Lord preserve us; **sei doch so ~, und mach mal Platz!** *(iro)* would you be so good as to make some room?; **es ~ machen** to show leniency.
Gnom *m (wk)* **-en, -en** gnome.
Gnu *nt* **-s** *(Zool)* gnu.
Gobelin [gobə'lɛ̃:] *m* **-s** tapestry, Gobelin.
Gockel *m* - *(esp S Ger)* cock; *(fig)* old goat *(col)*.
Go-Kart *m* **-s** kart, go-cart.

Gold *nt no pl (lit,fig)* gold. **nicht mit ~ zu bezahlen** *or* **aufzuwiegen sein** to be worth one's weight in gold; **ein Herz aus ~** a heart of gold; **er hat ~ in der Kehle** he has a golden voice; **es ist nicht alles ~, was glänzt** *(Prov)* all that glitters is not gold *(Prov)*.

Gold- *in cpds* gold; *(von Farbe)* golden; **~ader** *f* vein of gold; **~barren** *m* gold ingot; **~barsch** *m* *(Rotbarsch)* redfish; **g~blond** golden blond.

golden *adj attr (lit, fig)* golden; *(aus Gold)* gold, golden *(liter)*. **~e Schallplatte** gold disc; **~er Humor** irrepressible sense of humour; **~e Worte** words of wisdom; **ein ~es Herz haben** to have a heart of gold; **die ~e Mitte wählen** to strike a happy medium; **~e Hochzeit** golden wedding (anniversary); **das G~e Zeitalter** *(Myth, fig)* the golden age; **der Tanz ums G~e Kalb** *(fig)* the worship of Mammon.

Gold-: **g~farben**, **g~farbig** *adj* golden, gold-coloured *(Brit)*, gold-colored *(US)*; **~fisch** *m* goldfish; **~gräber** *m* gold-digger; **~grube** *f (lit, fig)* goldmine; **~hamster** *m* (golden) hamster.

goldig *adj (fig col)* allerliebst) sweet, cute *(col)*. **du bist vielleicht ~!** *(iro)* the ideas you get!

Gold-: **~junge** *m (col)* golden boy *(col)*; **~klumpen** *m* gold nugget.

Goldmedaille *f* gold medal.

Goldmedaillengewinner *m* gold medallist *(Brit)* or medalist *(US)*.

Gold-: **~mine** *f* gold mine; **~rausch** *m* gold fever; **~regen** *m (Bot)* laburnum; *(Feuerwerkskörper)* Roman candle; *(fig)* riches *pl*; **~reserve** *f (Fin)* gold reserves *pl*; **g~richtig** *adj (col)* absolutely *or* dead *(col)* right; **Mensch** all right *(col)*; **~schatz** *m* golden treasure; *(von Geld)* hoard of gold; **~schmied** *m* goldsmith; **~schnitt** *m no pl* gilt edging; **~stück** *nt* piece of gold; *(fig col)* treasure; **~sucher** *m* gold-hunter; **~waage** *f* gold *or* bullion balance; **jedes Wort auf die ~waage legen** *(sich vorsichtig ausdrücken)* to weigh one's words; *(überempfindlich sein)* to be hypersensitive; **~währung** *f* gold standard; **~zahn** *m* gold tooth.

Golf¹ *m -e (Meerbusen)* gulf.

Golf² *nt no pl (Sport)* golf.

Golfer(in *f)* *m - (col)* golfer.

Golf- *in cpds (Sport)* golf; **~platz** *m* golf course; **~schläger** *m* golf club; **~spieler** *m* golfer; **~staaten** *pl* **die ~staaten** the Gulf States *pl*; **~strom** *m (Geog)* Gulf Stream.

Gondel *f -n* gondola.

gondeln *vi aux sein (col) (reisen)* to travel around; *(herumfahren)* to drive around. **durch die Welt ~** to go globetrotting *(col)*.

Gong *m -s* gong; *(bei Boxkampf etc)* bell.

Gongschlag *m* stroke of the gong.

gönnen *vt* **jdm etw ~** not to grudge sb sth; *(zuteil werden lassen)* to allow sb sth; **jdm etw nicht ~** to grudge sb sth; not to allow sb sth; **sich** *(dat)* **etw ~** to allow oneself sth; **er gönnte mir keinen Blick** he didn't spare me a single glance; **ich gönne ihm diesen Erfolg von ganzem Herzen** I'm delighted for him that he's had this success; **das sei ihm gegönnt** I don't grudge him that.

Gönner(in *f)* *m -* patron.

Gönner-: **g~haft** *adj (pej)* patronizing; **g~haft tun** to play the big benefactor; **~miene** *f (pej)* patronizing air.

gor *pret of* **gären**.

Gör *nt -en (N Ger col)* **(a)** *(kleines Kind)* brat *(pej col)*, kid *(col)*. **(b)** *(auch* **Göre:** *Mädchen)* (cheeky *or* saucy) little miss.

Gorilla *m -s* gorilla; *(col: Leibwächter)* heavy *(col)*.

Gosche *f -n (esp S Ger pej)* gob *(col)*, mouth. **halt die ~!** shut your mouth *or* gob *(col)*.

goß *pret of* **gießen**.

Gosse *f -n (Rinnstein, fig)* gutter. **in der ~ enden** *or* **landen** to end up in the gutter.

Gossensprache *f* gutter language.

Gote *m (wk) -n, -n, Gotin** *f* Goth.

Gotik *f no pl (Art)* Gothic (style); *(Epoche)* Gothic period.

gotisch *adj* Gothic.

Gott *m -̈er* **(a)** god; *(als Name)* God. **~ der Herr** the Lord God; **~ der Allmächtige** Almighty God; **der liebe ~** the dear Lord; **er ist ihr ~** she worships him like a god; **bei ~ schwören** to swear by Almighty God.

(b) **dein Schicksal liegt in ~es Hand** your fate is in God's hands; **dem lieben ~ den Tag stehlen** to laze the day(s) away; **den lieben ~ einen guten Mann sein lassen** *(col)* to take things as they come; **wie ~ ihn geschaffen hat** *(hum col)* as naked as the day he was born; **ein Bild für die ~er** *(hum col)* a sight for sore eyes; **das wissen die ~er** *(col)* God (only) knows; **ich bin weiß ~ nicht prüde, aber ...** God knows I'm no prude but ...; **so ~ will** *(geh)* God willing, D.V.; **~ und die Welt** *(fig)* everybody; **über ~ und die Welt reden** *(fig)* to talk about everything under the sun; **leider ~es** alas; **wie ~ in Frankreich leben** *(col)* to be in clover.

(c) **grüß ~!** *(esp SGer, Aus)* hello, good morning/afternoon/evening; **~ hab' ihn selig!** God have mercy on his soul; **in ~es Namen!** for heaven's sake!; **ach (du lieber) ~!** *(col)* oh Lord! *(col)*; **großer ~!** good God!; **bei ~!** by God!; **~ behüte** *or* **bewahre!, da sei ~ vor!** God *or* Heaven forbid!; **um ~es willen!** for heaven's *or* God's sake!; **~ sei Dank!** thank God!

Gott|erbarmen *nt* **zum ~** *(col)* pitiful(ly), pathetic(ally) *(col)*.

Götter-: **g~gleich** *adj* godlike; **~speise** *f (Cook)* jelly *(Brit)*, jello *(US)*.

Gottes-: **~anbeterin** *f (Zool)* praying mantis; **~beweis** *m* proof of the existence of God; **~dienst** *m* service; **zum ~dienst gehen** to go to church; **g~fürchtig** *adj* godfearing; **~gabe** *f* gift from God; **~haus** *nt* place of worship; **~lästerer** *m* blasphemer; **~lästerung** *f* blasphemy; **~lohn** *m no pl* **etw für einen ~lohn tun** to do sth for love; **~mutter** *f* Mother of God; **~sohn** *m* Son of God; **~urteil** *nt* trial by ordeal.

gott-: **~gegeben** *adj* god-given; **~gewollt** *adj* willed by God.

Gottheit *f (Göttergestalt)* deity. **jdn wie eine ~ verehren** to worship sb like a god.

Göttin *f* goddess.

göttlich *adj (lit, fig)* divine.

Gott-: **g~lob** *interj* thank heavens; **g~los** *adj* godless; *(verwerflich)* ungodly; **~losigkeit** *f no pl* godlessness; **~vater** *m no pl* God the Father; **g~verdammt** *adj attr (col!)* goddamn(ed) *(col!)*, damn(ed) *(col!)*; **g~verlassen** *adj* godforsaken; **~vertrauen** *nt* trust in God.

Götze *m (wk) -n, -n (lit, fig)* idol.

Götzen-: **~bild** *nt* idol, graven image *(Bibl)*; **~dienst** *m*, **~verehrung** *f* idolatry.

Gourmet [gʊrˈmeː] *m -s* gourmet.

Gouvernante [guvɛrˈnantə] *f -n (dated)* governess.

Gouverneur [guvɛrˈnøːɐ] *m* governor.

Grab *nt -̈er* grave; *(Gruft)* tomb; *(fig: Untergang)* end, ruination. **jdn zu ~e tragen** to bear sb to his grave; **ein Geheimnis mit ins ~ nehmen** to take a secret with one to the grave; **verschwiegen wie ein ~** (as) silent as the grave; **er würde sich im ~e umdrehen, wenn ...** he would turn in his grave if ...; **du bringst mich noch ins ~!** you'll send me to an early grave!; **sich** *(dat)* **sein eigenes ~ schaufeln** *(fig)* to dig one's own grave; **seine Hoffnungen** *etc* **zu ~e tragen** *(geh)* to abandon one's hopes *etc*.

graben *pret* **grub**, *ptp* **gegraben 1** *vti* to dig. **nach Gold/Erz ~** to dig for gold/ore. **2** *vr* **sich in etw** *(acc)* **~** *(Zähnen, Krallen)* to sink into sth;

das hat sich mir tief ins Gedächtnis gegraben *(geh)* it has imprinted itself firmly on my memory.

Graben *m* ⁼ ditch; *(trockener ~, Mil)* trench; *(Sport)* ditch; *(Sport: Wasser~)* water-jump. **im ~ liegen** *(Mil)* to be in the trenches.

Grabenkrieg *m (Mil)* trench warfare.

Gräber *pl of* **Grab.**

Gräberfeld *nt* cemetery, burial ground.

Grabes- *(liter):* **~stille** *f* deathly hush; **~stimme** *f* sepulchral voice.

Grab-: **~inschrift** *f* epitaph, inscription *(on gravestone etc)*; **~kammer** *f* burial chamber; **~legung** *f* burial; **~mal** *nt, pl* **-mäler** *or (geh)* **-e** monument; *(~stein)* gravestone; **~platte** *f* memorial slab; **~rede** *f* funeral oration; **~schänder(in** *f) m* - defiler of the grave(s)/of graves; **~schändung** *f* defilement of graves; **~stätte** *f* grave; *(Gruft)* tomb; **~stein** *m* gravestone, tombstone; **~stelle** *f* (burial) plot.

Gracht *f* -en canal.

Grad *m* -e *(Sci, Univ, fig)* degree; *(Mil)* rank. **ein Winkel von 45 ~** an angle of 45 degrees; **auf dem 32. ~ nördlicher Breite** latitude 32 degrees north; **null ~** zero; **es kocht bei 100 ~** boiling occurs at 100 degrees; **ein Verwandter zweiten/ dritten ~es** a relative once/twice removed; **Verbrennungen ersten ~es** *(Med)* first-degree burns; **bis zu einem gewissen ~e** to a certain degree; **in hohem ~(e)** to a large extent; **im höchsten ~(e)** extremely.

Grad-, grad- = Gerad-, gerade-.

grad(e) *adj (col)* = **gerade.**

Grad-: **~einteilung** *f* calibration, graduation; **~messer** *m (fig)* gauge *(gen, für of)*; **~netz** *nt (Geog)* latitude and longitude grid.

graduell *adj (allmählich)* gradual; *(gering)* slight.

graduieren* **1** *vi (Univ)* to graduate. **2** *vt (in Grade einteilen)* to calibrate, to graduate.

Graduierte(r) *mf decl as adj* graduate.

Graf *m (wk)* -en, -en count; *(als Titel)* Count; *(britischer ~)* earl; *(als Titel)* Earl.

Grafengeschlecht *nt* family of counts/earls.

Grafik = Graphik.

Gräfin *f* countess.

gräflich *adj* count's/earl's.

Grafschaft *f* land of a count; earldom; *(Admin)* county.

Grahambrot *nt* (type of) wholemeal *(Brit) or* wholewheat *(US)* bread.

Gralshüter *m (fig)* guardian.

Gram *m no pl (geh)* grief, sorrow. **vom ~ gebeugt** bowed down with grief or sorrow.

grämen **1** *vr* **sich über jdn/etw ~** to grieve over sb/sth; **sich zu Tode ~** to die of grief *or* sorrow. **2** *vt* to grieve.

grämlich *adj* morose.

Gramm *nt* -e *or (nach Zahlenangabe)* - gram. **100 ~ Mehl** 100 grams of flour.

Grammatik *f* grammar.

grammatikalisch *adj* grammatical.

grammatisch *adj* grammatical.

Grammophon ® [gramoˈfoːn] *nt* -e gramophone.

Granatapfel pomegranate.

Granate *f* -n *(Mil) (Geschoß)* shell; *(Hand~)* grenade; *(Ftbl sl: Schuß aufs Tor)* cannonball *(col)*.

Granat-: **~feuer** *nt* shelling, shellfire; **~splitter** *m* shell/grenade splinter; **~trichter** *m* shell crater; **~werfer** *m* mortar.

grandios *adj* magnificent, superb.

Granit *m* -e granite. **auf ~ beißen (bei ...)** to bang one's head against a brick wall (with ...).

grantig *adj (col)* grumpy.

Grapefruit [ˈɡreːpfruːt] *f* -s grapefruit.

Graphik *f* **(a)** *no pl (Art)* graphic arts *pl; (Technik, Comp)* graphics. **(b)** *(Art: Darstellung)* graphic; *(Druck)* print; *(Schaubild)* illustration; *(technisches Schaubild)* diagram.

Graphiker(in *f) m* - graphic artist; *(Illustrator)* illustrator.

graphisch *adj* graphic; *(schematisch)* diagrammatic, schematic.

Grapho-: **~loge** *m,* **~login** *f* graphologist; **~logie** *f* graphology.

grapschen *(col)* **1** *vt* **(sich** *dat)* **etw ~** to grab sth. **2** *vi* **nach etw ~** to make a grab at sth.

Gras *nt* ⁼er **(a)** grass. **ins ~ beißen** *(col)* to bite the dust *(col)*; **das ~ wachsen hören** *(zuviel hineindeuten)* to read too much into things; **über etw** *(acc)* **~ wachsen lassen** *(fig)* to let the dust settle on sth; **wo er zuschlägt, wächst kein ~ mehr** *(col)* he really packs a punch. **(b)** *gen* -, *no pl (Drogen sl: Marihuana)* grass.

Gras- *in cpds* grass; **g~bewachsen** *adj* grassy, grass-covered; **~büschel** *nt* tuft of grass.

grasen *vi* to graze.

Gras-: **~fläche** *f* grassland; *(Rasen)* patch of grass; **g~grün** *adj* grass-green; **~halm** *m* blade of grass; **~hüpfer** *m - (col)* grasshopper; **~land** *nt no pl* grassland; **~mücke** *f (Orn)* warbler; **~narbe** *f* turf; **~samen** *m* grass seed.

grassieren* *vi* to be rife.

gräßlich *adj* **(a)** hideous. **(b)** *(intensiv, unangenehm)* dreadful; *Mensch* horrible.

Gräßlichkeit *f* **(a)** hideousness. **(b)** *(gräßliche Tat etc)* atrocity.

Grat *m* -e *(Berg~)* ridge; *(Archit)* hip *(of roof); (fig) (dividing)* line, border.

Gräte *f* -n *(fish-)bone.* **ich brech' dir alle ~n einzeln!** *(col)* I'll break every bone in your body.

Gratifikation *f* bonus.

gratis *adv* free; *(Comm)* free (of charge).

Gratis- *in cpds* free; **~probe** *f* free sample.

Grätsche *f* -n *(Sport)* straddle.

grätschen **1** *vi aux sein* to do a straddle (vault). **2** *vt Beine* to straddle, to put apart.

Gratulant(in *f) m* well-wisher.

Gratulation *f* congratulations *pl.*

Gratulationscour [-kuːɐ] *f* congratulatory reception.

gratulieren* *vi* **jdm (zu einer Sache) ~** to congratulate sb (on sth); **jdm zum Geburtstag ~** to wish sb many happy returns (of the day); **(ich) gratuliere!** congratulations!

Gratwanderung *f (fig)* tightrope walk.

grau *adj* grey *(Brit),* gray *(US); (trostlos)* bleak. **~e Haare bekommen, ~ werden** *(col)* to go grey; **er malte die Lage ~ in ~** *(fig)* he painted a bleak picture of the situation; **~e Eminenz** éminence grise; **die (kleinen) ~n Zellen** *(hum)* the little grey cells; **der ~e Alltag** drab reality; **in ~er Vorzeit** *(fig)* in the dim and distant past; **das ist bloß ~e Theorie** that's all very well in theory.

Grau *nt* -(s) grey *(Brit),* gray *(US); (fig)* dullness, drabness.

Grau-: **g~äugig** *adj* grey-eyed *(Brit),* gray-eyed *(US);* **g~blau** *adj* grey-blue *(Brit),* gray-blue *(US);* **g~braun** *adj* greyish *(Brit) or* grayish *(US)* brown; **~brot** *nt siehe* **Mischbrot.**

grauen *vi impers* **mir graut vor etw** *(dat)* I dread sth; **mir graut vor ihm** I'm terrified of him.

Grauen *nt no pl* **(a)** horror *(vor of).* **(b)** *(grauenhaftes Ereignis)* horror.

grauen-: **~haft,** **~voll** *adj* terrible, atrocious.

Grau-: **~gans** *f* grey(lag) *(Brit) or* gray(lag) *(US)* goose; **g~grün** *adj* grey-green *(Brit),* gray-green *(US);* **g~haarig** *adj* grey-haired *(Brit),* gray-haired *(US);* **g~meliert** *adj attr* greying *(Brit),* graying *(US).*

Graupe *f* -n *usu pl* grain of pearl barley. **~n** pearl barley *sing.*

Graupel *f* -n (small) hailstone. **~n** soft hail *sing.*

Graupel-: **~regen** *m,* **~schauer** *m* sleet.

Graupensuppe *f* barley broth *or* soup.

Graus *m no pl (old)* horror. **es war ein ~ zu sehen, wie ...** it was terrible to see how ...

grausam *adj (gefühllos, roh)* cruel *(gegen, zu* to).
sich ~ für etw rächen to take (a) cruel revenge
for sth.
Grausamkeit *f* **(a)** *no pl* cruelty.· **(b)** *(grausame
Tat)* (act of) cruelty; *(stärker)* atrocity.
Grauschimmel *m (Pferd)* grey *(Brit)* or gray *(US)*
(horse).
grausen *vi impers siehe* **grauen.**
Grausen *nt no pl* horror *(vor* of). **da kann man das
kalte ~ kriegen** *(col)* it's enough to give you the
creeps *(col).*
grausig *adj* terrible, atrocious.
Grau-: ~**ton** *m* grey colour *(Brit)*, gray color *(US)*;
~**zone** *f (fig)* grey *(Brit)* or gray *(US)* area.
Graveur(in *f)* [gra'vøːɐ, -øːrɪn] *m* engraver.
gravieren* [gra'viːrən] *vt* to engrave.
gravierend [gra'viːrənt] *adj* serious, grave.
Gravitation [gravita'tsioːn] *f* gravitation.
gravitätisch [gravi'tɛːtɪʃ] *adj* grave, solemn.
Gravur [gra'vuːɐ] *f* engraving.
Grazie [-iə] *f no pl (Liebreiz)* grace(fulness).
grazil *adj* (delicately) slender, gracile *(liter).* ~
gebaut sein to have a delicate figure.
graziös *adj* graceful; *(lieblich)* charming.
greifbar *adj (konkret)* tangible, concrete;
(erreichbar) available; *Ware* available, in stock
pred. **in g~barer Nähe** within reach.
greifen *pret* **griff,** *ptp* **gegriffen 1** *vt (nehmen,
packen)* to take hold of, to grasp; *(grapschen)* to
seize, to grab; *(fangen)* to catch; *Akkord* to strike.
diese Zahl ist zu niedrig gegriffen *(fig)* this
figure is too low; **zum G~ nahe sein** *(Sieg)* to be
within reach; **die Gipfel waren zum G~ nahe**
you could almost touch the peaks; **aus dem
Leben gegriffen** taken from life.
2 *vi* **(a) um sich ~** *(fig)* to spread, to gain
ground; **unter etw** *(acc)* ~ to reach under sth;
nach einer Sache ~ to reach for sth; *(um zu
halten)* to clutch or *(hastig)* grab at sth; **an etw**
(acc) ~ *(fassen)* to grasp sth; *(berühren)* to touch
sth; **zu etw** ~ to reach for sth; *zu Methoden,
Mitteln* to resort to sth; **sich** *(dat)* **an den Kopf** or
an die Stirn ~ *(fig)* to shake one's head in disbelief; **in die Saiten/Tasten** ~ to strike up a tune; **zu
den Waffen** ~ to take up arms; **zum Äußersten** ~
to resort to extremes; **nach der Macht** ~ to try to
seize power. **(b)** *(nicht rutschen, einrasten)* to
grip; *(fig: wirksam werden)* to be effective.
Greifer *m - (Tech)* grab.
Greifvogel *m* bird of prey.
Greis *m -e* old man.
greis *adj* aged; *(ehrwürdig)* venerable; *(altersgrau)*
grey *(Brit)*, gray *(US)*, hoary *(liter, hum).* **sein ~es
Haupt schütteln** *(usu iro)* to shake one's wise old
head.
Greisen-: ~**alter** *nt* extreme old age; **g~haft** *adj*
very old, aged *attr; (von jüngerem Menschen)* like
an old man/woman.
Greisin *f* old lady.
grell *adj Stimme, Ton* shrill, piercing; *Licht* glaring; *Farbe* garish, loud; *Gegensatz* sharp; *(stärker)* glaring.
Gremium *nt* body; *(Ausschuß)* committee.
Grenadier *m -e (Mil: Infanterist)* infantryman.
Grenz- *in cpds* border, frontier; ~**bereich** *m*
frontier or border zone or area; *(fig)* limits *pl;* **im
~bereich liegen** *(fig)* to lie at the limits.
Grenze *f -n* border; *(Landes~ auch)* frontier;
(Stadt~, zwischen Grundstücken) boundary;
(fig: zwischen Begriffen) dividing line, boundary;
(fig: äußerstes Maß) limits *pl,* bounds *pl.* **die ~
zwischen Spanien und Frankreich** the Spanish-
French border or frontier; **die ~ zu Österreich**
the Austrian border; **über die ~ gehen/fahren** to
cross the border; **einer Sache** *(dat)* ~**n setzen** to
set a limit or limits to sth; **keine ~n kennen** *(fig)*
to know no bounds; **seine ~n kennen** to know
one's limitations; **seiner Großzügigkeit sind**

keine ~n gesetzt there is no limit to his generosity; **hart an der ~ des Erlaubten** bordering on
the limits of what is permitted; **sich in ~n halten**
(fig) to be limited; **die oberste/unterste ~** *(fig)*
the upper/lower limit; **alles hat seine ~n** there
are limits to everything.
grenzen *vi* **an etw** *(acc)* ~ *(lit)* to border (on) sth;
(fig) to border or verge on sth.
Grenzen-: **g~los 1** *adj (lit, fig)* boundless; **2** *adv*
boundlessly; *(fig)* immensely; ~**losigkeit** *f*
boundlessness; *(fig)* immensity.
Grenzer *m - (col) (Zöllner)* customs man; *(Grenz-
soldat)* border or frontier guard.
Grenz- *in cpds* border, frontier; ~**fall** *m* borderline case; ~**gänger** *m - (Arbeiter)* international
commuter *(across a local border)*; ~**gebiet** *nt (lit,
fig)* border area; ~**konflikt** *m* border or frontier
dispute; ~**kontrolle** *f* frontier control; ~**linie** *f*
border; *(Sport)* line; ~**situation** *f* borderline situation; ~**stadt** *f* border town; ~**streitigkeit** *f*
boundary dispute; *(Pol)* border or frontier dispute; ~**übergang** *m* **(a)** border or frontier
crossing(-point); **(b)** = ~**übertritt;** ~**übertritt** *m*
crossing of the border; ~**verkehr** *m* border or
frontier traffic; ~**verlauf** *m* boundary line *(between countries)*; ~**zwischenfall** *m* border incident.
Gretchenfrage *f (fig)* crunch question *(col)*,
sixty-four-thousand-dollar-question *(col).*
Greuel *m - (no pl: Abscheu)* horror; *(~tat)* atrocity. ~ **vor etw haben** to have a horror of sth; **er/es
ist mir ein ~** I loathe or detest him/it; **die Prüfung ist mir ein ~** I'm really dreading the exam.
Greuel-: ~**märchen** *nt* horror story; ~**propaganda** *f* atrocity propaganda; ~**tat** *f* atrocity.
greulich *adj siehe* **gräßlich.**
Griebe *f -n* *usu pl* ≈ crackling *no indef art, no pl.*
Grieche *m (wk)* **-n, -n, Griechin** *f* Greek.
Griechenland *nt* Greece.
griechisch *adj* Greek; *Architektur, Vase, Stil auch*
Grecian. **die ~e Tragödie** Greek tragedy; **das
G~e** Greek; **~-römisch** Graeco-Roman.
Griesgram *m -e* grouch *(col)*, misery.
griesgrämig *adj* grumpy, grouchy *(col).*
Grieß *m -e (Cook)* semolina.
Grieß-: ~**brei** *m* semolina; ~**pudding** *m* semolina
pudding.
Griff *m -e* **(a)** *(das Greifen)* **der ~ nach etw** reach-
ing for sth; **einen tiefen ~ in den Geldbeutel tun**
(fig) to dig deep in one's pocket; **der ~ nach der
Flasche** taking to the bottle; **der ~ nach der
Macht** the bid for power. **(b)** *(Handgriff)* grip,
grasp; *(beim Ringen etc)* hold. **mit festem ~**
firmly; **jdn/etw in den ~ bekommen** *(fig)* to gain
control of sb/sth; *(geistig)* to get a grasp of sth;
(mit jdm/etw) einen guten or **glücklichen ~ tun**
to make a wise choice (with sb/sth). **(c)** *(Stiel,
Knauf)* handle; *(Pistolen~)* butt; *(Schwert~)* hilt;
(an Saiteninstrumenten) neck. **(d)** *usu pl (Hunt:
Kralle)* talon.
griff *pret of* **greifen.**
griffbereit *adj* ready to hand, handy.
Griffel *m - (Schreibstift)* slate pencil.
griffig *adj Fahrbahn etc* that has a good grip; *(fig)*
Ausdruck useful, handy.
Grill *m -s* grill; *(Aut: Kühler~)* grille.
Grille *f -n* **(a)** *(Zool)* cricket. **(b)** *(dated col: Laune)*
silly notion or idea.
grillen 1 *vt* to grill. **2** *vt* **sich (in der Sonne)** ~
(lassen) *(col)* to soak up the sun.
Grimasse *f -n* grimace. ~**n schneiden** to make
faces.
grimmig *adj* **(a)** *(zornig)* furious. ~ **lächeln** to
smile grimly; **~er Humor** grim humour. **(b)**
(sehr groß, heftig) Kälte etc severe.
Grind *m -e (Schorf)* scab.
grinsen *vi* to grin; *(höhnisch auch)* to smirk.
Grinsen *nt no pl siehe vi* **grin;** smirk.

Grippe f -n 'flu, influenza; (Erkältung) cold.
Grippe- in cpds 'flu, influenza; ~**welle** f wave of 'flu or influenza.
Grips m -e (col) nous (Brit col), sense.
grob adj comp ⁼**er**, superl ⁼**ste(r, s)** or (adv) am ⁼**sten (a)** (nicht fein) coarse; Arbeit dirty attr. **(b)** (ungefähr) rough. ~ **geschätzt** at a rough estimate. **(c)** (schlimm) gross (auch Jur). den ⁼**sten Schmutz habe ich schon weggeputzt** I have already cleaned off the worst of the dirt; **ein** ~**er Fehler** a bad mistake; **wir sind aus dem G**~**sten heraus** we're out of the woods (now). **(d)** (brutal, derb) rough; (fig: derb) coarse; (unhöflich) ill-mannered. ~ **gegen jdn werden** to become offensive (towards sb).
Grob- in cpds coarse; **g**~**gemahlen** adj attr coarseground; ~**heit** f **(a)** no pl (lit, fig) coarseness; (Brutalität) roughness; (fig: Unhöflichkeit) ill-manneredness; **(b)** (Beschimpfung) foul language no indef art.
Grobian m -e boor, lout.
grobkörnig adj coarse-grained.
gröblich adj (geh) gross. **jdn** ~ **beleidigen** to insult sb grossly; **jdn** ~ **beschimpfen** to call sb rude names.
Grob-: **g**~**maschig** adj large-meshed; (~**ge**strickt) loose-knit attr; **g**~**schlächtig** adj coarse; Mensch heavily built; ~**schnitt** m (Tabak) coarse cut.
Grog m -s grog.
groggy ['grɔgi] adj pred (Boxen) groggy; (col: erschöpft) all-in (col).
grölen vti (pej) to bawl. ~**de Menge** raucous crowd.
Groll m no pl (geh: Zorn) anger, wrath (liter); (Erbitterung) resentment. **einen** ~ **gegen jdn hegen** to harbour (Brit) or harbor (US) a grudge against sb.
grollen vi (geh) **(a)** (Donner etc) to rumble, to roll. **(b)** (jdm) ~ (old) to be filled with wrath (against sb) (liter).
Grönland nt Greenland.
Grönländer(in f) m - Greenlander.
Gros [groː] nt - [groːs] greater part, bulk.
Groschen m (col) 10-pfennig piece; (Aus) groschen; (fig) penny, cent (US). **der** ~ **ist gefallen** (hum col) the penny has dropped (col).
Groschen-: ~**grab** nt (hum) (Spielautomat) one-armed bandit; **diese Parkuhr ist ein richtiges** ~**grab** this parking meter just swallows up your money; ~**heft** nt (pej) pulp magazine; (Krimi auch) penny dreadful (dated); ~**roman** m (pej) cheap or dime (US) novel.
groß comp ⁼**er**, superl ⁼**te(r, s)** or (adv) am ⁼**ten 1** adj big; Fläche, Haus, Summe auch, Dose, Packung etc large; Erfolg, Interesse, Schreck, Hoffnung auch, Freude, Leid, Höhe, Breite great; Buchstabe auch capital; Pause, Rede auch long; (hoch, hochgewachsen) tall; (bedeutend) Werk, Persönlichkeit etc great; Lärm a lot of; Geschwindigkeit high. **wie** ~ **bist du?** how tall are you?; **du bist** ~ **geworden** you've grown; **ein ganz** ~**es Haus/Bau** a great big house/book; **die Wiese ist 10.000 m²** ~ the field is 100 metres square; **die** ~**e Masse** (fig) the vast majority; **ich habe nur** ~**es Geld** I haven't any change on me; **im** ~**en und ganzen (gesehen)** (taken) by and large; **die** ~**en Ferien** the long holidays; **die G**~**en** (Erwachsene) the grown-ups; **mit etw** ~ **geworden den sein** to have grown up with sth; ~ **und klein** young and old (alike); ~**e Worte machen** to use big words; ~**en Hunger haben** to be very hungry; **eine der** ⁼**eren Firmen** one of the major companies; **ich habe** ~**e Lust zu etw** I would really like sth; **ich habe keine** ~**e Lust** I don't particularly want to; ~**e Mode sein** to be all the fashion; **er ist kein** ~**er Esser** (col) he's not a big eater; **ich bin kein** ~**er Redner** (col) I'm no great speaker; **jds** ~**e Stunde** sb's big moment;

einen ~**en Namen haben** to be a big name; **er hat G**~**es geleistet** he has achieved great things; **Friedrich der G**~**e** Frederick the Great; **G**~-Paris Greater Paris; **der G**~**e Ozean** the Pacific. **2** adv jdn ~ **anblicken** to give sb a hard stare; **was soll man da schon** ~ **machen/sagen?** (col) you can't really do/say anything, can you?; ~ **daherreden** (col) to talk big (col); ~ **und breit** (fig col) at great or enormous length; ~ **machen** (baby-talk) to do number two (baby-talk); **ein Wort** ~ **schreiben** to write a word with a capital; **ganz** ~ **rauskommen** (col) to make the big time (col).
Groß- pref Great; (vor Städtenamen) Greater.
Groß-: ~**abnehmer** m (Comm) bulk buyer; ~**aktionär** m major or principal shareholder; ~**alarm** m red alert; **g**~**angelegt** adj attr large-scale, on a large scale; ~**angriff** m large-scale attack; **g**~**artig** adj tremendous; (prächtig) Bauwerk etc magnificent; **er hat** ~**artiges** geleistet he has achieved great things; ~**artigkeit** f (Pracht) magnificence; ~**aufnahme** f (Phot, Film) close-up; ~**bank** f big bank; ~**betrieb** m large concern; (Agr) big farm; ~**brand** m major fire; ~**britannien** nt (Great) Britain; ~**buchstabe** m capital (letter), upper case letter (Typ).
Größe f -n **(a)** size. **nach der** ~ **according to size.** **(b)** no pl (Höhe, Körper~) height; (Flächeninhalt) area; (Maße) dimensions pl; (Math, Phys) quantity. **eine unbekannte** ~ (lit, fig) an unknown quantity. **(c)** no pl (Ausmaß) extent; (Bedeutsamkeit) significance. **(d)** no pl (Erhabenheit) greatness. **(e)** (bedeutender Mensch) important figure.
Groß-: ~**einkauf** m bulk purchase; ~**einsatz** m ~**einsatz der Polizei** etc large-scale operation by the police etc; ~**eltern** pl grandparents pl; ~**enkel** m great-grandchild; (Junge) great-grandson; ~**enkelin** f great-granddaughter.
Größen-: ~**klasse** f (Comm) (size) class; ~**ordnung** f scale; (Größe) magnitude; (Math) order (of magnitude).
großenteils adv for the most part.
Größen-: ~**unterschied** m (im Format) difference in size; (in der Höhe) difference in height; ~**verhältnis** nt proportions pl (gen between); (Maßstab) scale; **im** ~**verhältnis 1:100** on the scale 1:100; ~**wahn(sinn)** m megalomania, delusions pl of grandeur; **g**~**wahnsinnig** adj megalomaniac; **g**~**wahnsinnig sein** to be a megalomaniac.
größer comp of **groß**.
Groß-: ~**fahndung** f large-scale manhunt; ~**familie** f extended family; ~**feuer** nt major fire; ~**format** nt large size; (bei Büchern, Fotos auch) large format; **g**~**formatig** adj large-size; Bücher, Fotos auch large-format; ~**grundbesitzer** m big landowner.
Großhandel m wholesale trade no art. **etw im** ~ **kaufen** to buy sth wholesale.
Großhandels- in cpds wholesale.
Groß-: ~**händler** m wholesaler; ~**handlung** f wholesale business; **g**~**herzig** adj generous, magnanimous; ~**herzigkeit** f generosity, magnanimity; ~**hirn** nt cerebrum; ~**industrielle(r)** mf major industrialist.
Grossist m wholesaler.
Groß-: ~**jährig** adj (dated) of age; **g**~**jährig werden** to come of age; ~**kapital** nt das ~**kapital** big business; ~**kapitalist** m big capitalist; ~**konzern** m large combine; **g**~**kotzig** adj (pej col) swanky (col); ~**küche** f canteen kitchen; ~**kundgebung** f mass rally.
Großmacht f (Pol) big or great power.
Großmachtpolitik f power politics.
Groß-: ~**mannssucht** f no pl (pej) craving for status; ~**markt** m central market; **g**~**maschig** adj = **grobmaschig**; ~**maul** nt (pej col) big-mouth (col); **g**~**mäulig** adj (pej col) big-mouthed attr

(col); ~**mut** *f* magnanimity; **g**~**mütig** *adj* magnanimous; ~**mutter** *f* grandmother; **das kannst du deiner** ~**mutter erzählen!** *(col)* who do you think you're kidding? *(col)*; **g**~**mütterlich** *adj attr* **(a)** *(von der ~ mutter)* of one's grandmother; **im g**~**mütterlichen Haus wohnen** to live in one's grandmother's house; **(b)** *(in der Art einer ~mutter)* grandmotherly; ~**offensive** *f (Mil)* major offensive; ~**onkel** *m* great-uncle; ~**produktion** *f* large-scale production.

Großraum *m (einer Stadt)* **der ~ München** the Munich area *or* conurbation, Greater Munich.

Großraumbüro *nt* open-plan office.

Groß-: g~**räumig** *adj* **(a)** *(geräumig)* roomy, spacious; **(b)** *(über g*~*Flächen)* extensive; **(c)** *(im g*~*en Umkreis)* **g**~**räumiges Umfahren eines Gebietes** making a large detour around an area; ~**razzia** *f* large-scale raid; ~**rechner** *m (Comp)* mainframe; ~**reinemachen** *nt* thorough cleaning, ≈ spring-cleaning; **g**~**schnäuzig** *adj (pej col)* big-mouthed *attr (col)*; **g**~**schreiben** *vt sep irreg* **g**~**geschrieben werden** *(fig col)* to be stressed; ~**schreibung** *f* capitalization; **g**~**sprecherisch** *adj (pej)* boastful; **g**~**spurig** *adj (pej)* flashy *(col)*.

Großstadt *f* city.

Großstädter *m* city-dweller.

großstädtisch *adj* big-city *attr.*

Großstadt- *in cpds* city; ~**mensch** *m* citydweller.

Groß-: ~**tante** *f* great-aunt; ~**tat** *f* great feat; ~**teil** *m* large part; **zum** ~**teil** for the most part.

größtenteils *adv* in the main, for the most part.

größte(r, s) *superl of* **groß.**

Größt-: ~**maß** *nt* maximum amount *(an+dat of)*; **g**~**möglich** *adj attr* greatest possible.

groß-: ~**tuerisch** [-tuːərɪʃ] *adj (pej)* boastful, bragging; ~**tun** *sep irreg (pej) vi* to boast, to show off.

Großvater *m* grandfather.

großväterlich *adj* **(a)** *(vom Großvater)* of one's grandfather. **das** ~**e Erbe** one's inheritance from one's grandfather. **(b)** *(in der Art eines Großvaters)* grandfatherly.

Groß-: ~**veranstaltung** *f* big event; *(~kundgebung)* mass rally; ~**verdiener** *m* big earner.

Großwild *nt* big game.

Großwild-: ~**jagd** *f* big-game hunting; **eine** ~**jagd** a big-game hunt; ~**jäger** *m* big-game hunter.

Groß-: **g**~**ziehen** *vt sep irreg* to raise; *Tier* to rear; **g**~**zügig** *adj* generous; *(weiträumig)* spacious; *Plan* large-scale, ambitious; ~**zügigkeit** *f siehe adj* generosity; spaciousness; (large) scale, ambitiousness.

grotesk *adj* grotesque.

Groteske *f* **-n** grotesque; grotesque play/novel.

Grotte *f* **-n** grotto.

grub *pret of* **graben.**

Grübchen *nt* dimple.

Grube *f* **-n** *(auch Min)* pit; *(kleine)* hole, hollow. **wer andern eine ~ gräbt(, fällt selbst hinein)** *(Prov)* you can easily fall into your own trap.

Grübelei *f* brooding *no pl.*

grübeln *vi* to brood *(über +acc* about, over*).*

Grübler(in *f) m* - brooder, brooding type.

grüblerisch *adj* pensive, brooding.

Gruft *f* **¨e** tomb, vault; *(in Kirchen)* crypt.

grün *adj* green; *(Pol auch)* ecologist. ~**e Heringe** fresh herrings; ~**er Salat** lettuce; **die G**~**e Insel** the Emerald Isle; **ein** ~**er Junge** *(col)* a greenhorn *(col)*; ~**es Licht (für etw) geben** *(fig)* to give the green light (for sth); **vom** ~**en Tisch aus** from a bureaucratic ivory tower; ~**e Minna** *(col)* Black Maria *(Brit col)*, paddy wagon *(US col)*; **sich ~ und blau** *or* **gelb ärgern** *(col)* to be furious; **jdn ~ und blau schlagen** *(col)* to beat sb black and blue; ~**e Welle** phased traffic lights; ~**e Welle bei 60 km/h** traffic lights phased for 60

kmph; auf keinen ~en Zweig kommen *(fig col)* to get nowhere; **die beiden sind sich gar nicht ~** *(col)* there's no love lost between them; **das ist dasselbe in G~** *(col)* it's the same thing.

Grün- *in cpds* green; ~**anlage** *f* green space *or* area; **g**~**äugig** *adj* green-eyed; **g**~**blau** *adj* greenish blue, greeny blue.

Grund *m* **¨e (a)** *no pl (Erdboden, ~fläche)* ground. **~ und Boden** land; **in ~ und Boden** *(fig) sich blamieren, schämen* utterly; *verdammen* outright; **bis auf den ~ zerstören** to raze to the ground. **(b)** *no pl (von Gefäßen, Becken etc)* bottom. **auf ~ laufen** *(Naut)* to run aground; **das Glas bis auf den ~ leeren** to drain the glass. **(c)** *no pl (lit, fig: Fundament)* foundation(s *pl*); *(das Innerste)* depths *pl.* **von ~ auf** entirely, completely; **von ~ auf neu gebaut** rebuilt from scratch; **einer Sache** *(dat)* **auf den ~ gehen** *(fig)* to get to the bottom of sth; **im'~e (genommen)** basically, fundamentally. **(d)** *(Ursache)* reason; *(Beweg~ auch)* grounds *pl.* **aus gesundheitlichen** *etc* ~**en** for health *etc* reasons; **ohne ~** without reason; **auf ~ von** on the basis of; **auf ~ von Zeugenaussagen** on the strength of the witnesses' testimonies; **auf ~ einer Verwechslung** owing to a mistake; **ich habe ~ zu der Annahme, daß ... I** have reason to believe that ...; **einen ~ zum Feiern haben** to have good cause for (a) celebration; **du hast keinen ~ zum Klagen** you have no cause for complaint; **ich habe berechtigten ~ zu glauben, daß ... I** have good reason to believe that ...; **aus diesem ~** for this reason; **mit gutem ~** with good reason; **aus '~en** (*+gen)* for reasons (of).

Grund- *in cpds* basic; ~**anstrich** *m* first coat; ~**besitz** *m* land, property; *(das Besitzen)* ownership of land *or* property; ~**besitzer** *m* landowner; ~**buch** *nt* land register; **g**~**ehrlich** *adj* thoroughly honest; ~**eigentum** *nt* = ~**besitz.**

gründen 1 *vt* to found; *Argument etc* to base *(auf +acc* on*)*; *Geschäft* to set up. **2** *vt* **sich auf etw** *(acc)* **~** to be based *or* founded *(in+dat* on*).* **3** *vt* **sich auf etw** *(acc)* **~** to be based *or* founded on sth.

Gründer(in *f) m* - founder.

Grund-: **g**~**falsch** *adj* utterly wrong; ~**farbe** *f* primary colour *(Brit) or* color *(US)*; *(Grundierfarbe)* ground colour *(Brit) or* color *(US)*; ~**festen** *pl (fig)* foundations *pl*; **etw bis in die ~festen erschüttern** to shake sth to its very foundations; ~**fläche** *f (Math)* base; ~**form** *f* basic form; *(Gram)* infinitive; ~**gebühr** *f* basic charge.

Grundgesetz *nt (BRD Pol)* **das ~** the Constitution.

grundgesetzwidrig *adj* contrary to the Constitution, unconstitutional.

Grundhaltung *f* basic position.

grundieren* *vt* to undercoat.

Grundierung *f* **(a)** *no pl (das Grundieren)* undercoating. **(b)** *(Farbe, Fläche)* undercoat.

Grund-: ~**kurs** *m* basic course; ~**lage** *f* basis; **als** ~**lage für etw dienen** to serve as a basis for sth; **auf der ~ lage** *+gen or* **von** on the basis of; **die** ~**lagen einer Wissenschaft** the fundamental principles of a science; **jeder** ~**lage entbehren** to be completely unfounded; **g**~**legend** *adj* fundamental, basic *(für* to*)*; *Werk* standard.

gründlich 1 *adj* thorough; *Arbeit auch* painstaking. **2** *adv* thoroughly. **jdm ~ die Meinung sagen** to give sb a piece of one's mind; **da haben Sie sich ~ getäuscht** you're completely mistaken there.

Gründlichkeit *f no pl* thoroughness.

Grund-: ~**linie** *f (Math, Sport)* baseline; **g**~**los** **1** *adj* **(a)** *Tiefe etc* bottomless; **(b)** *(fig: unbegründet)* groundless, unfounded; **2** *adv (fig)* without reason; ~**losigkeit** *f (fig)* groundlessness; ~**mauer** *f* foundation wall; **bis auf die ~mauern niederbrennen** to be gutted; ~**nahrungsmittel**

nt basic food(stuff).

Gründonnerstag [gry:n-] *m* Maundy Thursday.

Grund-: ~**ordnung** *f* basic order; ~**pfeiler** *m* (*Archit*) supporting pier; (*fig*) cornerstone, keystone; ~**rechenart** *f* basic arithmetical operation; ~**recht** *nt* basic *or* constitutional right; ~**riß** *m* (*von Gebäude*) ground plan; (*Abriß*) outline, sketch.

Grundsatz *m* principle. **aus** ~ on principle; **ein Mann mit Grundsätzen** a man of principle.

grundsätzlich 1 *adj* fundamental; *Frage* of principle. **2** *adv* (*allgemein, im Prinzip*) in principle; (*aus Prinzip*) on principle; (*immer*) always. **ihre Meinungen sind** ~ **verschieden** their views are fundamentally different; **das ist** ~ **verboten** it is absolutely forbidden.

Grundsatz|urteil *nt* judgement that establishes a principle.

Grund-: ~**schuld** *f* mortgage; ~**schule** *f* primary (*Brit*) *or* elementary school; ~**schüler** *m* primary (*Brit*) *or* elementary(-school) pupil; ~**schullehrer** *m* primary (*Brit*) *or* elementary(-school) teacher; ~**stein** *m* (*lit, fig*) foundation stone; **den** ~**stein zu etw legen** (*lit*) to lay the foundation stone of sth; (*fig*) to lay the foundations for sth; ~**stellung** *f* (*Turnen, Chess*) starting position; ~**steuer** *f* (*local*) property tax, ≃ rates *pl* (*Brit*); ~**stimmung** *f* prevailing mood; ~**stock** *m* basis, foundation; ~**stoff** *m* (*Rohstoff*) raw material; (*Chem*) element.

Grundstück *nt* plot (of land); (*Anwesen*) estate; (*Bau*~ *auch*) site; (*bebaut*) property.

Grundstücksmakler *m* estate agent (*Brit*), realtor (*US*).

Grund-: ~**studium** *nt* (*Univ*) basic course; ~**stufe** *f* first stage; (*Sch*) ≃ junior (*Brit*) *or* grade (*US*) school; ~**ton** *m* (*Mus*) (*eines Akkords*) root; (*einer Tonleiter*) tonic keynote; (~*farbe*) ground colour (*Brit*) *or* color (*US*).

Gründung *f* founding, foundation; (*von Heim, Geschäft*) setting up. **die** ~ **einer Familie** getting married (and having a family).

Grund-: **g**~**verkehrt** *adj* completely wrong; **g**~**verschieden** *adj* totally *or* entirely different; ~**wasser** *nt* ground water; ~**wasserspiegel** *m* water table, ground-water level; ~**wehrdienst** *m* national (*Brit*) *or* selective (*US*) service; ~**zug** *m* essential feature *or* trait; **etw in seinen** ~**zügen darstellen** to outline (the essentials of) sth.

grünen *vi* (*geh*) to turn green; (*fig: Liebe, Hoffnung*) to blossom (forth).

Grüne(r) *m decl as adj* (**a**) (*Pol*) Ecologist, Green. **die** ~**n** (*als Partei*) the Greens. (**b**) (*dated col: Polizist*) cop (*col*).

Grüne(s) *nt decl as adj* (*Gemüse*) greens *pl*, green vegetables *pl*. **ins** ~ **fahren** to go to the country.

Grün-: ~**fläche** *f* green space *or* area; ~**futter** *nt* green fodder, greenstuff; **g**~**gelb** *adj* greenish yellow, greeny-yellow; ~**gürtel** *m* green belt; ~**kohl** *m* (curly) kale; **g**~**lich** *adj* greenish; ~**schnabel** *m* (*col*) (little) whippersnapper (*col*); (*Neuling*) greenhorn (*col*); ~**span** *m no pl* verdigris; ~**streifen** *m* central reservation (*Brit*), median (strip) (*US*); (*am Straßenrand*) grass verge.

grunzen *vti* to grunt.

Gruppe *f* -**n** group; (*von Mitarbeitern auch*) team; (*Mil*) ≃ squad; (*Klasse, Kategorie auch*) class.

Gruppen- *in cpds* group; ~**arbeit** *f* teamwork; ~**bild** *nt* group portrait; ~**führer** *m* group leader; (*Mil*) squad leader; ~**reise** *f* group travel *no pl*; ~**sex** *m* group sex; ~**sieg** *m* (*Sport*) **den** ~**sieg erringen** to win in one's group; ~**sieger** *m* (*Sport*) group winnner; **g**~**spezifisch** *adj* group specific; ~**therapie** *f* group therapy; **g**~**weise** *adv* in groups; (*Ind, Comm, Sport auch*) in teams; (*Mil*) in squads.

gruppieren* *vtr* to group.

Gruppierung *f* grouping; (*Gruppe*) group; (*Pol auch*) faction.

Gruselfilm *m* horror film.

grus(e)lig *adj* horrifying, gruesome.

gruseln 1 *vti impers* **mich** *or* **mir gruselt auf Friedhöfen** cemeteries give me the creeps. **2** *vr* **hier würde ich mich** ~ a place like this would give me the creeps.

Gruß *m* -̈e (**a**) greeting; (~*geste, Mil*) salute. **er ging ohne** ~ **an mir vorbei** he walked past me without saying hello; **viele** ~̈**e** best wishes (*an* +*acc to*); **sag ihm einen schönen** ~ say hello to him (from me); **einen (schönen)** ~ **an Ihre Gattin!** my regards to your wife. (**b**) (*als Briefformel*) **mit bestem** ~ *or* **besten** ~̈**en** yours; (*bei Anrede Mr/Mrs/Miss/Ms X*) yours sincerely, Yours truly (*esp US*); (*bei Anrede Sir(s)/Madam*) Yours faithfully, Yours truly (*esp US*).

Gruß-: ~**adresse**, ~**botschaft** *f* message of greeting.

grüßen 1 *vt* (**a**) to greet; (*Mil*) to salute. **grüß dich!** (*col*) hello there!, hi! (*col*). (**b**) (*Grüße übermitteln*) **Otto läßt dich (schön)** ~ Otto sends his regards. **2** *vi* to say hello; (*Mil*) to salute. **Otto läßt** ~ Otto sends his regards.

Gruß-: ~**formel** *f* form of greeting; (*am Briefanfang*) salutation; (*am Briefende*) complimentary close, ending; ~**telegramm** *nt* greetings telegram; (*Pol*) goodwill telegram; ~**wort** *nt* greeting.

Grütze *f* -**n** (**a**) groats *pl*; (*Brei*) gruel. **rote** ~ (type of) red fruit jelly. (**b**) *no pl* (*col: Verstand*) brains (*col*).

gucken ['gʊkn, (*N Ger*) 'kʊkn] **1** *vi* (*sehen*) to look (*zu at*); (*heimlich auch*) to peep, to peek; (*hervorschauen*) to peep (*aus out of*). **laß mal** ~! let's have a look. **2** *vt* (*col*) **Fernsehen** ~ to watch television *or* telly (*Brit col*).

Gucker *m* - (*col*) (**a**) (*Fernglas*) telescope; (*Opernglas*) opera glass(es). (**b**) *pl* (*Augen*) peepers (*col*).

Guck-: ~**kasten** *m* (*col: Fernseher*) telly (*Brit col*) tube (*US col*); ~**loch** *nt* peephole.

Guerilla[1] [ge'rɪlja] *f* -**s** (**a**) (~*krieg*) guerilla warfare. (**b**) (~*einheit*) guerilla unit.

Guerilla[2] [ge'rɪlja] *m* -**s** (~*kämpfer*) guerilla.

Gulasch *nt or m* -**e** *or* -**s** goulash.

Gulasch-: ~**kanone** *f* (*Mil sl*) field kitchen; ~**suppe** *f* goulash soup.

Gulden *m* - (*niederländisch*) g(u)ilder, gulden.

Gully ['gʊli] *m or nt* -**s** drain.

gültig *adj* valid. **nach den** ~**en Bestimmungen** according to current regulations; **ab wann ist der Fahrplan** ~? when does the timetable come into force?; ~ **werden** to become valid; (*Gesetz, Vertrag*) to come into effect; (*Münze*) to become legal tender.

Gültigkeit *f no pl* validity; (*von Gesetz*) legal force. **das Fünfmarkstück verliert im Herbst seine** ~ the five-mark piece ceases to be legal tender in the autumn.

Gummi *nt or m* -**s** (*Material*) rubber; (*Radier*~) rubber (*Brit*), eraser; (~*band*) rubber *or* elastic (*Brit*) band; (*in Kleidung etc*) elastic; (*col: Kondom*) rubber (*col*), Durex ®.

Gummi- *in cpds* rubber; ~**artig 1** *adj* rubbery; **2** *adv* like rubber; ~**band** *nt* rubber *or* elastic (*Brit*) band; (*in Kleidung*) elastic; ~**bärchen** *nt* jelly baby; ~**baum** *m* rubber plant; ~**boot** *nt* rubber dinghy.

gummieren* *vt* to gum.

Gummierung *f* (*gummierte Fläche*) gum.

Gummi-: ~**knüppel** *m* rubber truncheon (*Brit*) *or* billy (*US*); ~**paragraph** *m* (*col*) ambiguous clause; ~**reifen** *m* rubber tyre; ~**schlauch** *m* rubber hose; (*bei Fahrrad etc*) inner tube; ~**stiefel** *m* rubber boot, wellington (boot) (*Brit*); ~**zelle** *f* padded cell.

Gunst f no pl favour (Brit), favor (US); (Wohlwollen auch) goodwill; (des Schicksals etc) benevolence. **zu meinen/deinen** ~en in my/your favour; **jdm eine ~ erweisen** (geh) to do sb a kindness; **in jds ~** (dat) **stehen** to be in favour with sb.

günstig adj favourable (Brit), favorable (US); (zeitlich, bei Reisen etc) convenient; Angebot, Preis etc reasonable, good. **jdm/einer Sache ~ gesinnt sein** (geh) to be favourably disposed towards sb/sth; **bei ~er Witterung** weather permitting; **die Stadt liegt ~ (für)** the town is well situated (for); **wie komme ich am ~sten nach ...?** what's the best or easiest way to get to ...?; **im ~sten Fall(e)** with luck; **etw ~ kaufen/ verkaufen** to buy/sell sth for a good price; **DM 30?, das war aber ~ 30 marks?**, that's a bargain.

Günstling m (pej) favourite (Brit), favorite (US).

Gurgel f -n throat; (Schlund) gullet. **jdm die ~ zudrücken** or **abschnüren** (lit, fig) to strangle sb; **dann springt sie mir an die ~!** (col) she'll kill me (col).

gurgeln vi (a) (den Rachen spülen) to gargle. (b) (Wasser, Laut) to gurgle.

Gurke f -n (a) cucumber; (Essig~) gherkin. **saure ~n** pickled gherkins. (b) (hum col: Nase) hooter (col).

Gurken-: ~**hobel** m slicer; ~**salat** m cucumber salad.

gurren vi (lit, fig) to coo.

Gurt m -e (Gürtel, Patronen~) belt; (Sicherheits~) safety belt; (Riemen) strap.

Gürtel m - belt. **den ~ enger schnallen** (lit, fig) to tighten one's belt.

Gürtel-: ~**linie** f waist; **ein Schlag unter die ~linie** (lit) a punch/blow etc below the belt; **das war ein Schlag unter die ~linie** (fig) that really was below the belt; ~**reifen** m radial (tyre (Brit) or tire US); ~**rose** f (Med) shingles sing or pl.

Guru m -s guru.

Guß m, pl **Güsse** (a) (Metal) (no pl: das Gießen) casting, founding; (~stück) cast. **(wie) aus einem ~** (fig) a unified whole. (b) (Strahl) stream, gush; (col: Regen~) cloudburst, downpour. (c) (Zucker~) icing, frosting (US); (durchsichtig) glaze.

Guß-: ~**eisen** nt cast iron; **g~eisern** adj cast-iron; ~**form** f mould (Brit), mold (US).

gut comp **besser**, superl **beste(r, s)** or (adv) **am besten** 1 adj good. **probieren Sie unsere ~en Weine/Speisen!** try our fine wines/food; **er ist in der Schule/in Spanisch sehr ~** he's very good at school/Spanish; **das ist ~ gegen** or **für** (col) **Husten** it's good for coughs; **wozu ist das ~?** (col) what's that for?; **sei so ~ (und) gib mir das** would you mind giving me that; **dafür ist er sich zu ~** he wouldn't stoop to that sort of thing; **sind die Bilder ~ geworden?** did the pictures turn out all right?; **es wird alles wieder ~!** everything will be all right; **wie ~, daß ...** how fortunate that ...; **~, daß du das endlich einsiehst** it's a good thing you realize it at last; **ich will es damit ~ sein lassen** I'll leave it at that; **laß mal ~ sein!** that'll do; **jetzt ist aber ~!** (col) that's enough; **das ist ja alles ~ und schön, aber ...** that's all very well but ...; **ein ~es Pfund Reis** a good pound of rice; **~!** good; (in Ordnung) (all) right, OK; **also ~!** all right or OK then; **du bist ~!** (col) you're a fine one!

2 adv well. **~ schmecken/riechen** to taste/ smell good; **sie spricht ~ Schwedisch** she speaks good Swedish; **er hat es in seiner Jugend nicht ~ gehabt** he had a hard time (of it) when he was young; **er hatte es immer ~ bei seinen Eltern** his parents were always good to him; **du hast es ~!** you've got it made; **das kann ~ sein** that may well be; **so ~ wie nichts** next to nothing; **so ~ wie nicht** hardly, scarcely; **so ~ wie verloren** as good as lost; **so ~ ich kann** as well as

I can; **es dauert ~ drei Stunden** it lasts a good three hours; **~ und gern** easily; **paß ~ auf!** be very careful; **ich kann ihn jetzt nicht ~ im Stich lassen** I can't very well let him down now.

Gut nt -er (a) (Eigentum) property; (lit, fig: Besitztum) possession. **irdische ~er** worldly goods. (b) no pl (das Gute) good, Good. **~ und Böse** good and evil. (c) (Ware, Fracht~) item. **~er** goods; (Fracht~) freight sing, goods (esp Brit). (d) (Land~) estate.

Gut-: ~**achten** nt - report; ~**achter(in** f) m - expert; (Schätzer auch) valuator; (Jur: Prozeß) expert witness; **g~artig** adj Kind, Hund etc goodnatured; Geschwür benign; **g~aussehend** adj good-looking; **g~bezahlt** adj attr highly-paid; **g~bürgerlich** adj solid middle-class; Küche homely, good plain; ~**dünken** nt no pl discretion; **nach (eigenem) ~dünken** at one's own discretion.

Güte f no pl (a) (Herzens~, Freundlichkeit) goodness, kindness. **würden Sie die ~ haben, zu ...** (form, iro) would you have the goodness or kindness to ...; **ein Vorschlag zur ~** a conciliatory proposal; **ach du liebe** or **meine ~!** (col) goodness me! (b) (einer Ware) quality.

Güteklasse f (Comm) grade.

Gute(r) mf decl as adj **der/die ~** the dear kind soul; (mitleidig) the poor soul; **die ~n und die Bösen** the good and the bad; (col: in Filmen etc) the goodies and the baddies (col).

Güter-: ~**abfertigung** f (a) no pl dispatch of freight or goods (esp Brit); (b) (Abfertigungsstelle) freight or goods (esp Brit) office; ~**fernverkehr** m long-distance haulage; ~**trennung** f (Jur) separation of property; **in ~trennung leben** to have separation of property; ~**verkehr** m freight or goods (esp Brit) traffic; ~**wagen** m (Rail) freight car (US), goods truck (Brit); ~**zug** m freight or goods (esp Brit) train.

Gute(s) nt decl as adj ~**s tun** to do good; **alles ~e!** all the best!; **das führt zu nichts ~m** it'll lead to no good; **das ist des ~n zuviel** that is too much of a good thing; **das ~ daran** the good thing about it; **das ~ im Menschen** the good in man; **ich sage es dir im g~n** I want to give you a friendly piece of advice.

Güte-: ~**siegel** nt (Comm) stamp of quality; ~**zeichen** nt mark of quality; (fig auch) hallmark.

Gut-: **g~gehen** sep irreg aux sein 1 vi impers **es geht ihm g~** he is doing well or nicely; (er ist gesund) he is well; **sonst geht's dir g~!** (iro) are you in your right mind?; 2 vi to go (off) well; **das ist noch einmal g~gegangen** it turned out all right; **g~gehend** adj attr thriving; **g~gelaunt** adj cheerful, in a good mood; **g~gemeint** adj attr well-meant; **g~gläubig** adj trusting; (vertrauensselig auch) credulous; **g~gläubigkeit** f siehe adj trusting nature; credulity; **g~haben** vt sep irreg etw **g~haben** to have sth coming (to one) (col) (bei from); ~**haben** nt - (Fin, Bank~) credit; **auf meinem Konto ist ein ~haben von DM 500** my account is DM 500 in credit; **g~heißen** vt sep irreg to approve of; (genehmigen) to approve; **g~herzig** adj kind-hearted; ~**herzigkeit** f kind-heartedness.

gütig adj kind; (edelmütig) gracious.

gütlich adj amicable. **sich an etw** (dat) **~ tun** to make free with sth.

Gut-: **g~machen** vt sep (a) (in Ordnung bringen) Fehler to put right, to correct; Schaden to make good; (b) (gewinnen) to make (bei out of, on); **g~mütig** adj good-natured; ~**mütigkeit** f goodnaturedness; **g~nachbarlich** 1 adj neighbourly (Brit), neighborly (US); **2** adv as good neighbours (Brit) or neighbors (US).

Gutsbesitzer(in f) m lord of the manor; (als Klasse) landowner.

Gut-: ~**schein** m voucher, coupon; (für Umtausch)

credit note; **g~schreiben** *vt sep irreg* to credit *(dat* to); **~schrift** *f (Bescheinigung)* credit note; *(Betrag)* credit (item). **Guts-:** **~haus** *nt* manor (house); **~hof** *m* estate. **gut-:** **~situiert** *adj attr* well-off; **~tun** *vi sep irreg* **jdm ~tun** to do sb good; **das tut ~** that's good; **~unterrichtet** *adj attr* well-informed; **~verdienend** *adj attr* with a good salary, high-income; **~willig** *adj* willing; *(nicht böswillig)* well-meaning. **Gymnasiallehrer** ≃ grammar school teacher *(Brit)*, high school teacher *(US)*. **Gymnasiast(in** *f) m (wk)* **-en, -en** ≃ grammar

school pupil *(Brit)*, high school student *(US)*. **Gymnasium** *nt (Sch)* ≃ grammar school *(Brit)*, high school *(US)*. **Gymnastik** *f* keep-fit exercises *pl*; *(Turnen)* gymnastics *sing*. **~ machen** to do keep-fit (exercises)/gymnastics. **gymnastisch** *adj* gymnastic. **Gynäkologe** *m*, **Gynäkologin** *f* gynaecologist *(Brit)*, gynecologist *(US)*. **Gynäkologie** *f* gynaecology *(Brit)*, gynecology *(US)*. **gynäkologisch** *adj* gynaecological *(Brit)*, gynecological *(US)*.

H

H, h [haː] *nt* -, - H, h; *(Mus)* B.
ha = **Hektar** hectare.
Haag *m:* **Den ~** The Hague.
Haar *nt* **-e** hair. **sie hat schönes ~** *or* **schöne ~e** she has nice hair; **~e auf den Zähnen haben** to be a tough customer; **~e lassen (müssen)** to come off badly; **jdm kein ~ krümmen** not to harm a hair of sb's head; **darüber laß dir keine grauen ~e wachsen** don't lose any sleep over it; **jdm aufs ~ gleichen** to be the spitting image of sb; **das ist an den ~en herbeigezogen** that's rather far-fetched; **an jdm kein gutes ~ lassen** to pull sb to pieces; **sich** *(dat)* **in die ~e kriegen** *(col)* to quarrel; **sich** *(dat)* **in den ~en liegen** to be at loggerheads; **jdm die ~e vom Kopf fressen** *(col)* to eat sb out of house and home.
Haar-: **~ansatz** *m* hairline; **~ausfall** *m* hair loss; **~breit** *nt:* **um kein ~breit** not an inch; **~bürste** *f* hairbrush.
haaren *vi (auch vr: Tier)* to moult *(Brit)*, to molt *(US); (Pelz, Teppich)* to shed.
Haarersatz *m (form)* hairpiece; *(Perücke)* wig.
Haaresbreite *f inv* **um ~** almost, very nearly; *verfehlen* by a hair's breadth; **er wich nicht um ~ von seiner Meinung ab** he did not change his opinion one iota.
Haar-: **~festiger** *m* - (hair) setting lotion; **h~genau** *adj* exact; **jdm etw h~genau erklären** to explain sth to sb in great detail; **das trifft h~genau zu** that's absolutely right.
haarig *adj* hairy; *(col) (heikel, gefährlich)* hairy *(col); (schwierig)* nasty.
Haar-: **~klammer** *f* hairgrip *(Brit)*, barrette *(US);* **h~klein** *adv* in minute detail; **~nadel** *f* hairpin; **~nadelkurve** *f* hairpin bend; **~netz** *nt* hairnet; **~pflege** *f* hair care; **h~scharf** *adj* Beschreibung exact; **das hat ihn h~scharf verfehlt** it only missed him by a hair's breadth; **~schleife** *f* hair ribbon; **~schnitt** *m* haircut; **~schopf** *m* mop *or* shock of hair; **~sieb** *nt* fine sieve; **~spalter(in)** *f* m - pedant, hairsplitter; **~spalterei** *f* splitting hairs *no indef art, no pl;* **h~spalterisch** *adj* hairsplitting; **~spange** *f* hair slide, barrette *(US);* **~spitze** *f* end (of a hair); **~strähne** *f* strand *or (dünner)* wisp of hair; **h~sträubend** *adj* hair-raising; *(unglaublich)* Frechheit incredible; **~töner** *m* - hair-tinting lotion; **~trockner** *m* - hair dryer; **~waschmittel** *nt* shampoo; **~ wasser** *nt* hair lotion; **~wuchs** *m* growth of hair; **einen kräftigen ~wuchs haben** to have a thick head of hair; **~wuchsmittel** *nt* hair restorer.
Hab *nt:* **~ und Gut** *sing vb* possessions, belongings, worldly goods *all pl.*
Habe *f no pl (geh)* possessions *pl*, belongings *pl.*
haben *pret* **hatte,** *ptp* **gehabt 1** *vt* to have, to have got *(esp Brit).* **ich habe eine Idee** I have *or* got *(esp Brit)* an idea; **ein Meter hat 100 cm** there are 100 cm in a metre; **da hast du 10 Mark** there's 10 Marks; **die ~'s (ja)** *(col)* they can afford it; **wie hätten Sie es gern?** how would you like it?; **ich kann das nicht ~** *(col)* I can't stand it; **Ferien ~** to be on holiday; **er wollte sie zur Frau ~** he wanted to make her his wife; **Hunger/Angst/Sorgen ~** to be hungry/afraid/worried; **was hat er denn?** what's the matter with him?; **hast du**

was? are you all right?, is (there) something the matter with you?; **was ~ wir heute für ein Wetter?** what's the weather like today?; **heute ~ wir 10°** it's 10° today; **es gut/schön ~** to have it good/nice; **sie hat es warm in ihrem Zimmer** it's warm in her room; **er hat es nicht leicht mit ihr** he has a hard time (of it) with her; **es am Herzen ~** *(col)* to have heart trouble; **es in den Beinen ~** *(col)* to have trouble with one's legs; **er hat es mit dem Malen** *(col)* he has a thing about painting *(col);* **du hast zu gehorchen** *(müssen)* you must obey, you have to obey, you have got to obey *(esp Brit);* **ich habe zu tun** I'm busy; **etw auf dem Boden liegen ~** to have sth lying on the floor; **etw ist zu ~** *(erhältlich)* sth is to be had; **jd ist zu ~** *(col) (nicht verheiratet)* sb is single; *(sexuell)* sb is available; **für etw zu ~ sein** to be keen on sth; **für ein gutes Essen ist er immer zu ~** he's always willing to have a good meal; **ich hab's** *(col)* I've got it, I know; **du kannst mich gern ~!** *(col)* get lost! *(col);* **da hast du's/~ wir's!** *(col)* there you/we are; **woher hast du denn das?** where did you get that from?; **wie gehabt!** some things don't change; **jd hat eine nette Art an sich** *(dat)* there is something nice about sb; **sie werden schon merken, was sie an ihm ~** they'll see how valuable he is; **etwas mit jdm ~** *(col)* to have a thing with sb *(col);* **etwas von etw ~** *(col)* to get something out of sth; **das hast du jetzt davon** now see what's happened; **nichts von etw ~** *(col)* to get nothing out of sth; **die blonden Haare hat sie von ihrem Vater** she gets her blond hair from her father; **er hat etwas von einem Erpresser (an sich dat)** he's a bit of a blackmailer; **dieses Werk von Braque hat viel von Picasso** this work by Braque owes much to Picasso.
2 *vr (col: sich anstellen)* to make a fuss. **was hast du dich denn so?** what are you making such a fuss about?
3 *vr impers (col)* **und damit hat es sich** and that's that; **die Sache hat sich** *(ist erledigt)* that's done.
4 *aux* **ich habe/hatte gerufen** I have/had called, I've/I'd called; **ich habe gestern angerufen** I called yesterday; **du hättest den Brief früher schreiben können** you could have written the letter earlier; **etw getan ~** to have done sth.
Haben *nt no pl* credit. **im ~ stehen** to be on the credit side.
Habenichts *m* **-e** *(pej)* have-not.
Haben-: **~seite** *f* credit side; **~zinsen** *pl* interest on credit *sing.*
Hab-: **~gier** *f* greed, acquisitiveness; **h~gierig** *adj* greedy, acquisitive; **h~haft** *adj (geh)* jds/einer Sache **h~haft werden** to get hold of sb/sth.
Habicht *m* **-e** hawk.
Habilitation *f (Lehrberechtigung)* postdoctoral lecturing qualification.
habilitieren* *vr* to qualify as a university lecturer.
Hab-: **~schaft** *f*, **~seligkeiten** *pl* belongings *pl;* **~sucht** *f* greed, acquisitiveness; **h~süchtig** *adj* greedy, acquisitive.
Hack-: **~beil** *nt* chopper, cleaver; **~block** *m* chopping block; **~braten** *m* meat loaf; **~brett**

(a) chopping board; **(b)** *(Mus)* dulcimer.
Hacke[1] *f* **-n** *(Ferse, Absatz)* heel.
Hacke[2] *f* **-n** *(Pickel)* pickaxe *(Brit)*, pickax *(US); (Garten~)* hoe.
hacken 1 *vt (zerkleinern)* to chop; *(im Fleischwolf)* to mince *(Brit)*, to grind *(US); Garten* to hoe; *Loch* to hack; *(Vogel)* to peck. **2** *vi (nach at)* to hack; *(Vogel)* to peck *(nach at); (im Garten)* to hoe.
Hacker *m* - *(Comp)* hacker.
Hack-: ~**fleisch** *nt* mince *(Brit)*, minced *(Brit)* or ground *(US)* meat; **aus jdm** ~**fleisch machen** *(col)* to make mincemeat of sb *(col);* ~**klotz** *m* chopping block; ~**ordnung** *f (lit, fig)* pecking order.
Häcksel *nt* or *m* no *pl* chaff.
hadern *vi (dated geh) (streiten)* to quarrel; *(unzufrieden sein)* to be at odds.
Hafen *m* ⁼ **(a)** harbour *(Brit)*, harbor *(US); (Handels~)* port; *(~anlagen)* docks *pl.* **in den** ~**einlaufen** to put into harbour/port. **(b)** *(fig)* haven. **in den** ~ **der Ehe einlaufen** to enter the state of matrimony.
Hafen- in *cpds* harbour *(Brit)*, harbor *(US);* port; ~**anlagen** *pl* docks *pl;* ~**arbeiter** *m* dockworker, docker; ~**polizei** *f* harbour *(Brit)* or harbor *(US)* police; ~**rundfahrt** *f* (boat-)trip round the harbour *(Brit)* or harbor *(US);* ~**stadt** *f* port; *(am Meer auch)* seaport; ~**viertel** *nt* dock area.
Hafer *m* - oats *pl.* **ihn sticht der** ~ *(col)* he's feeling his oats *(col).*
Hafer-: ~ **brei** *m* porridge; ~**flocken** *pl* rolled oats *pl;* ~**korn** *nt* (oat) grain; ~**mehl** *nt* oatmeal; ~**schleim** *m* gruel.
Haff *nt* **-s** or **-e** lagoon.
Haft *f* no *pl (vor dem Prozeß)* custody; *(~strafe)* imprisonment; *(~zeit)* prison sentence; *(politisch)* detention. **sich in** ~ **befinden** to be in custody/prison/detention; **eine schwere** ~ **verhängen** to impose a long term of imprisonment; **in** ~ **nehmen** to take into custody, to detain.
Haft-: ~**anstalt** *f* detention centre *(Brit)* or center *(US);* **h~bar** *adj (für jdn)* legally responsible; *(für etw)* (legally) liable; ~**befehl** *m* warrant; **einen** ~**befehl gegen jdn austellen** to issue a warrant for sb's arrest; ~**dauer** *f* term of imprisonment.
haften[1] *vi (für) für jdn* ~ to be (legally) responsible for sb; **für etw** ~ to be (legally) liable for sth; **die Versicherung hat für den Schaden nicht gehaftet** the insurance company did not accept liability (for the damage); **für Garderobe kann nicht gehaftet werden** all articles are left at owner's risk.
haften[2] *vi (lit, fig)* to stick *(an* +*dat* to); *(Reifen, Phys)* to adhere; *(Rauch, Geruch)* to cling *(an* +*dat* to); *(Blick)* to become fixed.
haftenbleiben *vi sep irreg aux sein (lit, fig)* to stick *(an or auf* +*dat* to); *(Geruch)* to cling; *(Phys)* to adhere.
Häftling *m* prisoner; *(politisch auch)* detainee.
Haft-: ~**pflicht** *f (Schadensersatzpflicht)* (legal) liability; **h~pflichtig** *adj* liable; **h~pflichtversichert** *adj* **h~pflichtversichert sein** to have personal liability insurance; *(Aut)* ≈ to have third-party insurance; ~**pflichtversicherung** *f* personal or public *(US)* liability insurance *no indef art; (Aut)* ≈ third-party insurance; ~**richter** *m* magistrate; ~**schalen** *pl* contact lenses *pl;* ~**strafe** *f* prison sentence.
Haftung *f* **(a)** *(Jur)* (legal) liability; *(für Personen)* (legal) responsibility. **(b)** *(Tech, Phys, von Reifen)* adhesion.
Hage-: ~**butte** *f* **-n** rose hip; ~**dorn** *m* hawthorn.
Hagel *m* no *pl (lit, fig)* hail.
Hagelkorn *nt* **(a)** hailstone. **(b)** *(Med)* eye cyst.
hageln 1 *vi impers* **es hagelt** it's hailing. **2** *vi* **etw hagelt auf jdn** *(lit, fig)* sth hails down on sb. **3** *vt impers (lit)* to hail (down). **es hagelte etw** *(fig)* sth hailed down.

Hagel-: ~**schauer** *m* (short) hailstorm; ~**schlag** *m (Met)* hail; ~**sturm** *m* hailstorm.
hager *adj* gaunt, thin.
Häher *m* - jay.
Hahn *m* ⁼**e (a)** *(männlicher Vogel)* cock; *(jünger)* cockerel. ~ **im Korb sein** *(col)* to be cock of the walk; **danach kräht kein** ~ **mehr** *(col)* no one cares two hoots about that any more *(col).* **(b)** *pl* **auch -en** *(Tech)* tap, faucet *(US).* **(c)** *(Abzug)* trigger.
Hähnchen *nt (Cook)* chicken.
Hahnenschrei *m* cockcrow. **beim ersten** ~ *(fig)* at cockcrow.
Hai(fisch) *m* **-e** *(lit, fig)* shark.
Häkchen *nt* **(a)** *(Sew)* (small) hook. **(b)** *(Zeichen)* tick, check *(US).*
häkeln *vti* to crochet.
Häkelnadel *f* crochet hook.
haken 1 *vi (klemmen)* to stick. **es hakt** *(fig col)* there's some delay; **es hakt (bei jdm)** *(col: nicht verstehen)* sb is stuck. **2** *vt (befestigen)* to hook *(an* +*acc* to).
Haken *m* - **(a)** hook *(auch Boxen).* **die Sache hat einen** ~ *(col)* there's a snag or a catch; **einen** ~ **schlagen** to dart sideways. **(b)** *(Zeichen)* tick, check *(US).*
Haken-: ~**kreuz** *nt* swastika; ~**nase** *f* hooked nose, hooknose.
halb 1 *adj* half. **ein** ~**er Meter** *etc* half a metre *etc;* **der** ~**e Tag** *etc* half the day *etc;* **eine** ~**e Stunde** half an hour; **alle** ~**e Stunde** every half hour; **ein** ~**es Jahr** six months *pl;* **auf** ~**em Wege** or ~**er Strecke** halfway; **zum** ~**en Preis** (at) half price; **Kleid mit** ~**em Arm** dress with half-length sleeves; **eine** ~**e Note** a minim *(Brit)*, a half-note *(US);* **ein** ~**er Ton** a semitone; ~**e Pause** minim/half-note rest; ~ **zehn** half past nine, half nine *(col);* **fünf (Minuten) vor/nach** ~ **zwei** twenty-five (minutes) past one/to two; ~**e Arbeit leisten** to do a bad job; **die** ~**e Wahrheit** half of the truth; **nichts H~es und nichts Ganzes** neither one thing nor the other; **mit** ~**em Ohr** with half an ear; **sich nur wie ein** ~**er Mensch fühlen** to feel only half a person; **keine** ~**en Sachen** not to do things by halves; **die** ~**e Stadt/Welt** half the town/world; **sie ist schon eine** ~**e Schottin** she is already half Scottish; **(noch) ein** ~**es Kind sein** to be scarcely more than a child.
2 *adv* half; *(beinahe)* almost. **die Zeit ist** ~ **vorbei** half the time has already gone; ~ **so gut** half as good; **etw nur** ~ **verstehen** to only half understand something; **ich hörte nur** ~ **zu** I was only half listening; **das ist** ~ **so schlimm** it's not as bad as all that; *(Zukünftiges)* that won't be too bad; **etw nur** ~ **machen** to only half-do sth *(col);* **wir haben uns** ~ **totgelacht** we almost died laughing; **mit jdm** ~ **und** ~ or ~**e-~e machen** *(col)* to go halves with sb; **gefällt es dir?** — ~ **und** ~ do you like it? — sort of *(col).*
Halb- in *cpds* half; **h~amtlich** *adj* semi-official; ~**bildung** *f* smattering of knowledge *(pej);* **h~bitter** *adj Schokolade* semi-sweet; ~**blut** *nt no pl (Mensch)* half-breed; *(Tier)* crossbreed; ~**bruder** *m* half-brother; ~**dunkel** *nt* semi-darkness; *(Dämmerung)* dusk; ~**edelstein** *m* semi-precious stone.
Halbe(r) *m* or *f decl as adj (col)* half a litre *(Brit)* or liter *(US)* (of beer).
Halb-: **h~fertig** *adj attr* half-finished; *(fig)* immature; **h~fest** *adj Zustand, Materie* semi-solid; *Gelee* half-set; ~**finale** *nt* semi-final; **h~gar** *adj attr* half-cooked; **h~gott** *m (Myth, fig)* demigod; ~**götter in Weiß** *(iro)* doctors; ~**heit** *f (pej)* half-measure; **er ist nicht für** ~**heiten** he is not one for half-measures; **h~herzig** *adj* half-hearted.
halbieren* *vt* to halve; *(schneiden)* to cut in half.
Halbierung *f* halving.
Halb-: ~**insel** *f* peninsula; ~**jahr** *nt* half-year

(auch Comm), six months; **h~jährig** *adj attr Kind* six-month-old; *Lehrgang etc* six-month; **h~jähr-lich 1** *adj* half-yearly *(auch Comm),* six-monthly; **2** *adv* every six months, twice yearly; **~kreis** *m* semicircle; **~kugel** *f* hemisphere; **nördliche/ südliche ~kugel** northern/southern hemisphere; **h~lang** *adj Rock* mid-calf length; *Haar* chin-length; **(nun) mach mal h~lang!** *(col)* now wait a minute!; **h~laut 1** *adj* low; **2** *adv* in a low voice; **h~leinen** *adj attr Stoff* fifty per cent linen; **~leiter** *m (Phys)* semiconductor; **h~links** *adv (Sport)* spielen (at) inside left; **h~links abbiegen** to fork left; **das Auto kam von h~links** the car approached from the left; **h~mast** *adv* at half-mast; **h~matt** *adj Stoff* semimatt; **~messer** *m* radius; **~metall** *nt* semi-metal; **~mond** *m* half-moon; *(Symbol)* crescent; **wir haben ~mond** there's a half-moon; **h~nackt** *adj attr* half-naked; **h~offen** *adj attr* half-open; **~pension** *f* half-board *(Brit),* European plan *(US);* **h~rechts** *adv (Sport)* spielen (at) inside right; **h~rechts abbiegen** to fork right; **das Auto kam von h~rechts** the car approached from the right; **h~reif** *adj attr* half-ripe; **h~rund** *adj attr* semicircular; **~rund** *nt* semicircle, half circle; **im ~rund** in a semicircle; **~schatten** *m* half shadow; **~schlaf** *m* light sleep, doze; **im ~schlaf sein** to be half asleep; **~schuh** *m* shoe; **~schwergewichtler** *m* light-heavyweight; **~schwester** *f* half-sister; **~seide** *f* fifty per cent silk; **h~seiden** *adj (lit)* fifty per cent silk; *(fig) Dame* fast; *(homosexuell)* gay; **h~seidenes Milieu** the demimonde; **h~seitig** *adj Anzeige* half-page; **h~seitig gelähmt** hemiplegic; **~starke(r)** *m decl as adj* hooligan, rowdy; **h~tags** *adv* in the mornings/afternoons; **h~tags arbeiten** to work part-time.

Halbtags-: **~arbeit,** **~beschäftigung** *f* part-time job; **~kraft** *f* part-time employee.

Halb-: **~ton** *m* half-tone; *(Mus)* semitone; **h~voll** *adj attr* half-filled; **h~wach** *adj attr* half awake; **in h~wachem Zustand** half awake; **~wahrheit** *f* half truth; **~waise** *f* child/person who has lost one parent; **h~wegs** *adv* partly; *gut* reasonably; *annehmbar* halfway; **wenn es dir wieder h~wegs besser geht** when you're feeling a bit better; **~welt** *f* demimonde; **~wertzeit** *f* half-life; **~wissen** *nt (pej)* superficial knowledge; **h~wüchsig** *adj* adolescent; **~wüchsige(r)** *mf decl as adj* adolescent; **~zeit** *f (Sport) (Hälfte)* half; *(Pause)* half-time.

Halde *f* **-n (a)** *(Abfall~)* mound, heap; *(Min: Abbau~)* slagheap. **(b)** *(geh: Abhang)* slope.

half *pret of* **helfen.**

Hälfte *f* **-n** half. **die ~ der Kinder war abwesend** half the children were absent; **die ~ von etw** half (of) sth; **die ~ ist gelogen** half of it is lies; **Rentner zahlen die ~** pensioners pay half price; **um die ~ steigen** to increase by half; **es ist zur ~ fertig** it is half finished; **das werde ich zur ~ bezahlen** I will pay half (of it); **meine bessere ~** *(hum col)* my better half *(hum col);* **auf der ~ des Weges** halfway.

Halfter¹ *m or nt - (für Tiere)* halter.

Halfter² *f* **-n** *or nt - (Pistolen~)* holster.

Hall *m* **-e** echo.

Halle *f* **-n** hall; *(Hotel~)* lobby; *(Fabrik~)* shed; *(Sport~)* (sports) hall, gym(nasium). **Fußball in der ~** indoor football.

hallen *vi* to reverberate, to echo *(auch fig).*

Hallen- *in cpds (Sport)* indoor; **~(schwimm)bad** *nt* indoor swimming pool.

hallo ['halo, ha'lo:] *interj* hello.

Halluzination *f* hallucination.

Halm *m* **-e** stalk, stem; *(Gras~)* blade of grass; *(Stroh~, zum Trinken)* straw.

Halogenscheinwerfer *m* halogen headlamp.

Hals *m* **-e (a)** neck. **sich** *(dat)* **nach jdm/etw den ~**

verrenken *(col)* to crane one's neck to see sb/sth; **jdm um den ~ fallen** to fling one's arms around sb's neck; **sich jdm an den ~ werfen** *(fig col)* to throw oneself at sb; **das wird ihm noch den ~ brechen** *(col)* it'll ruin him; **~ über Kopf abreisen** to leave in a rush; **ihm steht das Wasser bis zum ~** *(fig)* he is up to his neck in it *(col);* **jdn auf dem** *or* **am ~ haben** *(col)* to be lumbered *or* saddled with sb *(col);* **jdn jdm auf den ~ hetzen** *(col)* to put sb onto sb; **jdm mit etw vom ~(e) bleiben** *(col)* not to bother sb with sth *(col);* **sich jdn/etw vom ~e schaffen** *(col)* to get sb/sth off one's back *(col).*

(b) *(Kehle, Rachen)* throat. **sie hat es im ~** *(col)* she has a sore throat; **aus vollem ~(e)** at the top of one's voice; **es hängt mir zum ~ heraus** *(col)* I'm sick and tired of it; **sie hat es in den falschen ~ bekommen** *(col) (sich verschlucken)* it went down the wrong way; *(falsch verstehen)* she took it wrongly; **etw bleibt jdm im ~ stecken** *(lit, fig)* sth sticks in sb's throat; **er kann den ~ nicht voll (genug) kriegen** *(fig col)* he is never satisfied.

Hals-: **~abschneider** *m* - *(pej col)* shark *(col);* **h~abschneiderisch** *adj (pej col) Preise* extortionate; *Mensch* cutthroat *(col);* **~ausschnitt** *m* neck(line); **~band** *nt (Hunde~)* collar; **h~brecherisch** *adj* dangerous; *Tempo* breakneck; *Fahrt* hair-raising; **~entzündung** *f* sore throat; **~kette** *f (Schmuck)* necklace; **~krause** *f* ruff.

Hals-Nasen-Ohren-Arzt *m* ear, nose and throat specialist.

Hals-: **~schlagader** *f* carotid (artery); **~schmerzen** *pl* sore throat *sing;* **h~starrig** *adj* stubborn; **~starrigkeit** *f* stubbornness; **~tuch** *nt* scarf; **~- und Beinbruch** *interj* good luck; **~weh** *nt* sore throat; **~wirbel** *m* cervical vertebra.

Halt *m* **-e (a)** *(für Füße, Hände)* hold; *(lit, fig: Stütze)* support; *(fig: innerer ~)* security *no art.* **~ haben** *(Ding)* to hold; **keinen ~ haben** to have no hold/support; **to be insecure;** **ohne inneren ~** insecure. **(b)** *(geh: Anhalten)* stop.

halt¹ *interj* stop.

halt² *adv (dial) siehe* **eben 2 (b).**

haltbar *adj* **(a)** **~ sein** to keep (well); **~e Lebensmittel** food which keeps (well); **etw ~ machen** to preserve sth; **~ bis 6.11.** to keep by 6 Nov. **(b)** *(widerstandsfähig)* durable; *Stoff, Kleider* hard-wearing. **(c)** *Theorie* tenable.

Haltbarkeit *f* **(a)** *(von Lebensmitteln)* **eine längere ~ haben** to keep longer; **Lebensmittel von kurzer ~** perishable food. **(b)** *siehe adj (b)* durability; hard-wearingness.

Haltbarkeitsdatum *nt* best-before date.

Haltegriff *m* handle; *(in Bus)* strap; *(an Badewanne)* handrail.

halten *pret* **hielt,** *ptp* **gehalten 1** *vt* **(a)** *(festhalten)* to hold; *(zurückhalten)* to stop; *(behalten, besitzen)* Haustier, Vorsprung, Versprechen to keep; *Rekord, Kurs, Position* to hold; *Auto* to run; *(beibehalten)* Temperatur, Tempo to keep up. **den Mund ~** *(col)* to keep one's mouth shut *(col);* **ich konnte ihn es gerade noch ~** I just managed to grab hold of him/it; **sie ist nicht zu ~** *(fig)* there's no holding her; **es hält mich hier nichts mehr** there's nothing to keep me here any more; **hält dich niemand** nobody's stopping you; **die Wärme ~** to retain heat; **sich** *(dat)* **jdn/etw ~** to keep sb/sth; **den Ton ~** to stay in tune; **die These läßt sich nicht länger ~** this thesis is no longer tenable; **(mit jdm) Verbindung ~** to keep in touch (with sb).

(b) *(abhalten)* Vorlesung to give; *Rede auch* to make; *Gottesdienst* to hold; *Wache* keep. **Mittagsschlaf ~** to have an afternoon nap.

(c) *(Sport) Ball* to save.

(d) einen Fuß ins Wasser ~ to put one's foot into the water; **er hält seine Kinder sehr streng**

he's very strict with his children; **es mit etw so/anders** ~ to handle sth like this/differently; **das kannst du** ~ **wie du willst** that's completely up to you; **etw einfach** ~ to keep sth simple; **der Film hält nicht, was er verspricht** the film doesn't live up to expectations; **jdn/etw für jdn/ etw** ~ to take sb/sth for sb/sth; **jdn für ehrlich** ~ to think or consider sb is honest; **wofür** ~ **Sie mich?** what do you take me for?; **etw von jdm/ etw** ~ to think sth of sb/sth; **ich halte nichts davon, das zu tun** I don't think much of doing that; **nicht viel vom Sparen** ~ not to be a great one for saving (col).

2 vi (a) (festhalten, zusammenhalten) to hold. **kannst du mal 'n Moment** ~? can you just hold that (for) a moment? (b) (bestehen bleiben, haltbar sein) to last; (Stoff) to wear well. (c) (stehenbleiben, anhalten) to stop. **zum H~ bringen** to bring to a stop or standstill. (d) (Sport) to make a save. (e) Sport **hält jung** sport keeps you young; **auf etw** (acc) ~ (zielen) to aim at sth; (steuern) to head for sth; **etwas mehr nach links** ~ to keep more to the left; (zielen) to aim more to the left; **zu jdm** ~ to stand or stick by sb; (sehr) **auf etw** (acc) ~ (Wert legen) to attach (a lot of) importance to sth; **auf sich** (acc) ~ (auf Äußeres achten) to take a pride in oneself.

3 vr (a) (sich festhalten) to hold on (an+dat -to). (b) (sich nicht verändern) to keep; (Wetter) to last; (Preise) to hold; (nicht verschwinden) to last; (Geruch etc) to stay; (seine Position behaupten) to hold on. **er hat sich gut gehalten** (col) he's well-preserved; **sich auf den Beinen** ~ to stay on one's feet; **sich gut** ~ (in Prüfung, Spiel etc) to make a good showing, to do well; **er hält sich sehr aufrecht** he holds or carries himself very erect; **der Autofahrer hielt sich ganz rechts** the driver kept to the right; **sich an ein Versprechen** ~ to keep a promise; **sich an den Text** ~ to keep or stick to the text; **sich an jdn** ~ (sich wenden an) to ask sb; (sich richten nach) to follow sb; **sich nicht** ~ **können** to be unable to control oneself. (c) **er hält sich für besonders klug** he thinks he's very clever.

Halter m - (a) (Halterung) holder. (b) (Jur: Kraftfahrzeug~, Tier~) owner.

Halterung f mounting; (für Regal etc) support.

Halte-: ~**schild** nt stop or halt sign; ~**signal** nt (Rail) stop signal; ~**stelle** f stop; ~**verbot** nt (absolutes) ~**verbot** no stopping; (Bereich) no stopping zone; **eingeschränktes** ~**verbot** no waiting; (Bereich) no waiting zone.

Halt-: **h~los** adj (schwach) insecure; (hemmungslos) unrestrained; (unbegründet) groundless; ~**losigkeit** f siehe adj lack of security; uninhibitedness; groundlessness; **h~machen** vi sep to stop; **vor nichts h~machen** (fig) to stop at nothing; **vor niemandem h~machen** (fig) to spare no-one.

Haltung f (a) (Körper~) posture; (Stellung) position. ~ **annehmen** (esp Mil) to stand to attention. (b) (fig) (Auftreten) manner; (Einstellung) attitude. (c) no pl (Beherrschtheit) composure. ~ **bewahren** to keep one's composure. (d) no pl (von Tieren, Fahrzeugen) owning.

Halunke m (wk) -n, -n scoundrel.

Hamburger(in f) m - native of Hamburg.

hämisch adj malicious, spiteful. **er hat sich** ~ **gefreut** he gloated.

Hammel m: ~**beine** pl: **jdm die** ~**beine langziehen** (hum col) to give sb a dressing-down; ~**fleisch** nt mutton; ~**keule** f (Cook) leg of mutton; ~**sprung** m (Parl) division.

Hammer m – hammer. **das ist ein** ~! (col) (unerhört) that's absurd!; (prima) that's fantastic! (col).

hämmern 1 vi (lit, fig) to hammer; (col: beim Klavierspielen etc) to pound. 2 vt to hammer; Metall-

gefäße, Schmuck etc to beat. **jdm etw ins Bewußtsein** ~ (col) to hammer sth into sb's head (col).

Hammerwerfen nt no pl hammer(-throwing).

Hammond|orgel ['hæmənd-] f electric organ.

Hämorrhoiden [hɛmɔrɔ'iːdən] pl piles pl, haemorrhoids (Brit) pl, hemorrhoids (US) pl.

Hampelmann m, pl -**männer** (a) jumping jack. (b) (col: willenloser Mensch) **er ist nur ein** ~ he just lets people walk all over him.

hampeln vi to jump about; (zappeln) to fidget.

Hamster m - hamster.

Hamsterer(in f) m - (col) squirrel (col).

Hamsterkauf m panic-buying no pl. **Hamsterkäufe machen** to buy in order to hoard; (bei Knappheit) to panic-buy.

hamstern vti (speichern) to hoard; (Hamsterkäufe machen) to panic-buy.

Hand f ~e (a) hand. **jdm die** ~ **geben** to give sb one's hand; **jdn an die** or **bei der** ~ **nehmen** to take sb by the hand; **jdm etw aus der** ~ **nehmen** to take sth off sb (auch fig); **mit der** ~, **von** ~ by hand; **von** ~ **geschrieben/genäht** handwritten/ handsewn.

(b) no pl (Sport: ~spiel) hand-ball.

(c) (Besitz, Obhut) possession, hands. **aus privater** ~ privately; **etw aus der** ~ **geben** to let sth out of one's sight; **etw geht in jds** ~**e über** sth passes into sb's hands; **zu** ~**en von jdm** for the attention of sb.

(d) ~**e hoch!** hands up!; ~**e weg!** hands off!; ~ **aufs Herz** cross your heart; **eine** ~ **wäscht die andere** (Prov) if you scratch my back I'll scratch yours; **ich wasche meine** ~**e in Unschuld** (geh) I wash my hands of it; **bei etw die** or **seine** ~ **im Spiel haben** to have a hand in sth; **er hat überall seine** ~ **im Spiel** he has a finger in every pie; **etw hat weder** ~ **noch Fuß** sth doesn't make sense; **sich mit** ~**en und Füßen gegen etw wehren** to fight sth tooth and nail; **rechter/linker** ~ on the right-/left-hand side; **eine ruhige/sichere** ~ **a** steady hand; **eine lockere** ~ **haben** (hum col) to let fly at the slightest provocation; **bei etw eine glückliche** ~ **haben** to have a lucky touch with sth; **in festen** ~**en sein** to be spoken for; **mit leeren/vollen** ~**en** empty-handed/open-handedly; **alle** ~**e voll zu tun haben** to have one's hands full; **sich die** ~ **fürs Leben reichen** (geh) to tie the knot; **die** ~ **für jdn ins Feuer legen** to vouch for sb; **jdn auf** ~**en tragen** to cherish sb; (bei etw) **mit** ~ **anlegen** to lend a hand (with sth); ~ **an jdn legen** (geh) to lay a hand on sb; **die** ~ **auf etw** (dat) **halten** to keep a tight rein on sth; **das liegt auf der** ~ (col) that's obvious; **an** ~ **eines Beispiels** by means of an example; **an** ~ **dieses Berichts** from this report; **aus erster/zweiter** ~ first/ second hand; **zur** ~ **haben** to have sth to hand; **Ausrede, Erklärung** to have sth ready; **mit etw schnell bei der** ~ **sein** (col) to be ready with sth; **jdm in die** ~ **arbeiten** to play into sb's hands; **jdm in die** ~**e fallen** or **geraten** to fall into sb's hands; **jdn/etw in die** ~**e kriegen** or **bekommen** to get one's hands on sb/sth; **jdn (fest) in der** ~ **haben** to have sb (well) in hand; **von der** ~ **in den Mund leben** to live from hand to mouth; **ich habe diese Entscheidung nicht in der** ~ it's not in my hands; **etw gegen jdn in der** ~ **haben** to have some hold on sb; **in jds** ~ **sein** to be in sb's hands; **etw in die** ~ **nehmen** to pick sth up; (fig) to take sth in hand; **jdm etw in die** ~**e spielen** to pass sth on to sb; **hinter vorgehaltener** ~ on the quiet; **etw geht jdm flott/leicht von der** ~ sb does sth quickly/finds sth easy; **es ist nicht von der** ~ **zu weisen** it cannot be denied; **zur** ~ **sein** to be at hand; **jdm zur** ~ **gehen** to lend sb a helping hand.

Hand|arbeit f work done by hand; (Gegenstand) handmade article; (körperliche Arbeit) manual work; (Nähen, Sticken etc, als Schulfach) needlework *no pl*; *(Stricken)* knitting *no pl*; *(Häkeln)* crochet(ing) *no pl*. **etw in ~ herstellen** to make sth by hand; **diese Tischdecke ist ~** this table-cloth is handmade.

Hand|arbeitsgeschäft *nt* needlework and wool shop *(Brit)* or store *(US)*.

Hand-: **~auflegen** *nt no pl* laying on of hands; **~ausgabe** *f (Buch)* concise edition; **~ball** *m or (col) nt (Spiel)* handball; **~bedienung** *f*, **~betrieb** *m* manual operation; **mit ~betrieb** hand-operated; **~bewegung** *f (Geste, Zeichen)* gesture; **~bibliothek** *f* reference library *(with open shelves)*; **~bohrer** *m* gimlet; **~bohrmaschine** *f* (hand) drill; **~breit** *f* - ≈ six inches; **~bremse** *f* brake; *(Aut)* handbrake *(Brit)*, parking brake *(US)*; **~buch** *nt* handbook, reference book; *(technisch)* manual; **~creme** *f* hand cream.

Händedruck *m* handshake.

Handel *m no pl (das Handeln)* trade; *(esp illegal)* traffic; *(Wirtschaftszweig auch)* commerce; *(Warenmarkt)* market; *(Abmachung)* deal. **~ mit etw** trade in sth; **im ~ sein** to be on the market; **etw in den ~ bringen/aus dem ~ ziehen** to put sth on/take sth off the market; **(mit jdm) ~ treiben** to trade (with sb).

handeln 1 *vi* **(a)** to trade. **er handelt mit Gemüse** he trades *or* deals in vegetables; **er handelt mit Drogen** he traffics in drugs. **(b)** *(feilschen)* to bargain, to haggle *(um* about, over*)*; **ich lasse mit mir ~** I'm open to persuasion; *(in bezug auf Preis)* I'm open to offers. **(c)** *(tätig werden)* to act. **(d) von etw ~** to deal with sth. **2** *vr impers* **es handelt sich dabei um ein Versehen** this is an error; **sich um etw ~** to be about sth, to concern sth; **es handelt sich nur ums Überleben** it's simply a question of survival.

Handeln *nt no pl* **(a)** *(Feilschen)* bargaining, haggling. **(b)** *(das Handeltreiben)* trading. **(c)** *(Verhalten)* behaviour *(Brit)*, behavior *(US)*. **(d)** *(das Tätigwerden)* action.

handelnd *adj* **die ~en Personen in einem Drama** the characters in a drama.

Handels-: **~abkommen** *nt* trade agreement; **~bank** *f* merchant bank *(Brit)*, commercial bank; **~beziehungen** *pl* trade relations *pl*; **~bilanz** *f* balance of trade; **aktive/passive ~bilanz** balance of trade surplus/deficit; **~brauch** *m* commercial practice; **~defizit** *nt* trade deficit; **h~einig** *adj pred* **h~einig werden** to agree terms; **~gesellschaft** *f* commercial company; **~gesetz** *nt* commercial law; **~gewerbe** *nt* commerce *no art*; **~gut** *nt* commodity; **~kammer** *f* chamber of commerce; **~klasse** *f* grade; **~marine** *f* merchant navy; **~marke** *f* trade name; **~minister** *m* ≈ Trade Secretary *(Brit)*, Secretary of Commerce *(US)*; **~organisation** *f* trading organization; **~politik** *f* trade *or* commercial policy; **~recht** *nt* commercial law *no def art*; **h~rechtlich** **1** *adj* of/about commercial law; **2** *adv* according to commercial law; **~register** *nt* register of companies; **~reisende(r)** *mf decl as adj* commercial traveller *(Brit)* or traveler *(US)*; **~schiffahrt** *f* merchant shipping *no def art*; **~schranke** *f usu pl* trade barrier; **~schule** *f* commercial college; **~spanne** *f* profit margin; **~sperre** *f* trade embargo *(gegen* on*)*; **h~üblich** *adj* customary; **~unternehmen** *nt* commercial enterprise; **~verkehr** *m* trade; **~vertrag** *m* trade agreement; **~vertreter** *m* commercial traveller *(Brit)* or traveler *(US)*; **~vertretung** *f* trade mission; **~ware** *f* commodity; **~waren** *pl* commodities *pl*, merchandise *sing*; **~wert** *m* market value; **~zweig** *m* branch.

Hände-: **h~ringend** *adv* wringing one's hands; *(fig)* imploringly; **~trockner** *m* hand drier.

Hand-: **~feger** *m* hand brush; **~fertigkeit** *f* dexterity; **h~fest** *adj* **(a)** *(kräftig) Mensch* sturdy, robust; *Essen* substantial; **(b)** *(fig) Schlägerei* vio-

lent; *Skandal* huge; *Beweis* solid, tangible; *Lüge, Betrug* flagrant, blatant; **~fläche** *f* palm *or* flat (of the/one's hand); **h~gearbeitet**, **h~gefertigt** *adj* handmade; *Stickerei etc* handworked; **~gelenk** *nt* wrist; **aus dem ~gelenk** *(col) (ohne Mühe)* effortlessly; *(improvisiert)* off the cuff; **h~gemacht** *adj* handmade; **h~gemalt** *adj* hand-painted; **~gemenge** *nt* scuffle, fight; **h~genäht** *adj* handsewn; **~gepäck** *nt* hand baggage *no pl*; **h~geschrieben** *adj* handwritten; **h~gesteuert** *adj (Tech)* hand-operated; **~granate** *f* hand grenade; **h~greiflich** *adj Streit* violent; **h~greiflich werden** to become violent; **~greiflichkeit** *f usu pl* violence *no pl*; **~griff** *m* **(a)** *(Bewegung)* movement; *(im Haushalt)* chore; **mit einem ~griff öffnen** with one flick of the wrist; *(schnell)* in no time; **(b)** *(an Gegenstand)* handle; **~habe** *f (fig)* **ich habe gegen ihn keine ~habe** I have no hold on him; **etw als ~habe (gegen jdn) benutzen** to use sth as a lever (against sb); **h~haben*** *vt insep* to handle; *Maschine auch* to operate; *Gesetz* to implement; **~habung** *f* siehe *vt* handling; operation; implementation.

Handikap ['hɛndikɛp] *nt* **-s** *(Sport, fig)* handicap.

Hand-: **~kante** *f* side of the/one's hand; **~kantenschlag** *m* karate chop; **~käse** *m* strong-smelling round German cheese; **~koffer** *m* (small) suitcase; **~kuß** *m* kiss on the hand; **mit ~kuß** *(fig col)* with pleasure; **~langer** *m* - odd-job man, handyman; *(fig Untergeordneter)* dogsbody *(col)*; *(fig pej: Gehilfe)* henchman; **~langerarbeit** *f (pej)* donkey work *no pl*.

Händler(in *f)* *m* - trader, dealer; *(Ladenbesitzer)* shopkeeper, store owner *(US)*. **fliegender ~** street trader.

handlich *adj Gerät, Form* handy; *Gepäckstück* manageable.

Handlichkeit *f no pl* handiness; manageability.

Handlung *f* action; *(Tat)* act; *(von Drama)* plot. **der Ort der ~** the scene of the action.

Handlungs-: **~ablauf** *m* plot; **h~fähig** *adj Regierung* able to act; *(Jur)* empowered to act; **eine h~fähige Mehrheit** a working majority; **~fähigkeit** *f (von Regierung)* ability to act; *(Jur)* power to act; **~freiheit** *f* freedom of action; **h~unfähig** *adj Regierung* unable to act; *(Jur)* without power to act; **~unfähigkeit** *f (von Regierung)* inability to act; *(Jur)* lack of power to act; **~vollmacht** *f* proxy; **~weise** *f* way of behaving; **eine selbstlose ~weise** unselfish behaviour *(Brit)* or behavior *(US)*.

Hand-: **~pflege** *f* care of one's hands; **~puppe** *f* glove puppet; **~puppenspiel** *nt (Stück)* glove puppet show; **~rücken** *m* back of the/one's hand; **~schelle** *f usu pl* handcuff; **jdm ~schellen anlegen** to handcuff sb; **~schlag** *m* **(a)** *(Händedruck)* handshake; **ein Geschäft durch ~schlag abschließen** to shake on a deal; **(b) keinen ~schlag tun** not to do a stroke (of work); **~schrift** *f* **(a)** handwriting; *(fig)* (trade)mark; **etw trägt/verrät jds ~schrift** *(fig)* sth bears *or* has sb's (trade)mark; **(b)** *(Hist: Text)* manuscript; **h~schriftlich** **1** *adj* handwritten; **2** *adv* korrigieren, einfügen by hand.

Handschuh *m (Finger~)* glove; *(Faust~)* mitten.

Handschuhfach *nt (Aut)* glove compartment.

Hand-: **h~signiert** *adj* signed; **~spiel** *nt no pl (Sport)* handball; **~stand** *m (Sport)* handstand; **~steuerung** *f* manual control; **~streich** *m* **im ~streich** in a surprise coup; **~tasche** *f* handbag, purse *(US)*; **~tuch** *nt* towel; **das ~tuch werfen** *(fig)* to throw in the towel; **~umdrehen** *nt (fig)*: **im ~umdrehen** in the twinkling of an eye; **~voll** *f* - *(lit, fig)* handful; **~wäsche** *f* washing by hand; *(Wäschestücke)* hand wash.

Handwerk *nt* trade; *(Kunst~)* craft; *(fig: Tätigkeit)* business. **sein ~ verstehen** *(fig)* to know one's job; **jdm ins ~ pfuschen** *(fig)* to interfere in sb's job; **jdm das ~ legen** (*fig*) to put a stop to sb's game (*col*).

Handwerker(in *f*) *m* - (skilled) manual worker; (*Kunst~*) craftsman; craftswoman. **wir haben seit Wochen die ~ im Haus** we've had workmen in the house for weeks.

handwerklich *adj Ausbildung* as a manual worker/craftsman; (*fig*) technical. **~er Beruf** skilled trade; **~es Können** craftsmanship; **~e Fähigkeiten** manual skills.

Handwerks-: **~beruf** *m* skilled trade; **~betrieb** *m* workshop; **~kammer** *f* trade corporation; **~zeug** *nt no pl* tools *pl*; (*fig*) tools of the trade *pl*.

Hand-: **~wörterbuch** *nt* concise dictionary; **~zeichen** *nt* signal; (*Geste auch*) sign; (*bei Abstimmung*) show of hands; **durch ~zeichen** by a show of hands; **~zettel** *m* leaflet, handbill.

hanebüchen *adj* (*dated, geh*) outrageous.

Hanf *m no pl* (*Pflanze, Faser*) hemp.

Hang *m* ⁻**e** (a) (*Abhang*) slope. (b) *no pl* (*Neigung*) tendency.

Hangar ['haŋgaːɐ] *m* -s hangar.

Hänge-: **~bauch** *m* drooping belly (*col*); **~brücke** *f* suspension bridge; **~gleiter** *m* (*Sport*) hang-glider; **~lampe** *f* drop-light.

hangeln *vir* **er hangelte (sich) an einem Tau über den Fluß** he moved hand over hand along a rope over the river.

Hängematte *f* hammock.

Hängen *nt* **mit ~ und Würgen** (*col*) by the skin of one's teeth.

hängen 1 *vi pret* **hing**, *ptp* **gehangen** (a) to hang; (*sich festhalten*) to hang on (*an* +*dat* to); (*angeschlossen sein*) to be connected (up) (*an* +*dat* to); (*kleben*) to be stuck (*an* +*dat* on). **die Gardinen ~ schon** the curtains are already up; **mit ~den Schultern** with drooping shoulders; **die Blumen ließen die Köpfe ~** the flowers hung their heads; **den Kopf ~ lassen** (*fig*) to be downcast; **das Kleid hing ihr am Leib** (*col*) the dress hung on her; **das Bild hängt an der Wand** the picture is hanging on the wall; **sie hing ihm am Hals** she hung around his neck; **der Patient hängt an der künstlichen Niere/am Tropf** the patient is on the kidney machine/on the drip; **ihre Blicke hingen an dem Sänger** her eyes were fixed on the singer; **sie hängt dauernd am Telefon** (*col*) she's always on the phone; **er hängt den ganzen Tag vorm Fernseher** (*col*) he spends all day in front of the telly.

(b) (*lieben*) **an jdm/etw ~** to be very attached to sb/sth; **er hängt am Leben** he clings to life.

(c) **daran hängt viel Arbeit** there's a lot of work involved in that; **der Schrank hängt voller Kleider** the cupboard is full of clothes; **der Baum hängt voller Früchte** the tree is laden with fruit; **die ganze Sache hängt an ihm** it all depends on him.

2 *vt pret* **hängte**, *ptp* **gehängt** (*aufhängen, henken*) to hang; (*anschließen*) to connect (*an* +*acc* to); (*befestigen*) *Wohnwagen etc* to hitch up. **er hängte den Telefonhörer in die Gabel** he hung up.

3 *vr pret* **hängte**, *ptp* **gehängt sich an etw** (*acc*) **~** to hang on to sth; **er hängte sich ans Telefon** he got on the phone; **sich an jdn ~** (*sich anschließen*) to latch on to sb (*col*); (*gefühlsmäßig binden*) to become attached to sb; (*verfolgen*) to set off in (hot) pursuit of sb.

hängenbleiben *vi sep irreg aux sein* **(a)** to get caught (*an* +*dat* on). **(b)** (*Sport*) (*zurückbleiben*) to get left behind; (*nicht durch-, weiterkommen*) not to get through. **(c)** (*Sch col: nicht versetzt werden*) to stay down. **(d)** (*sich aufhalten*) to stay on. **bei einer Nebensächlichkeit ~** to get bogged down with a side issue. **(e)** (*haftenbleiben*) to get stuck or caught (*in, an* +*dat* on). **es bleibt ja doch alles an mir hängen** (*fig col*) in the end it's all down to

me anyhow (*col*); **der Verdacht ist an ihm hängengeblieben** suspicion rested on him; **vom Lateinunterricht ist bei ihm nicht viel hängengeblieben** (*fig col*) not much of his Latin stuck (*col*).

hängend *adj* hanging. **mit ~er Zunge kam er angelaufen** (*fig*) he came running up panting.

hängenlassen *sep irreg, ptp* **hängen(ge)lassen 1** *vt* **(a)** (*vergessen*) to leave behind. **(b)** (*col: im Stich lassen*) to let down. **2** *vr* to let oneself go.

Hänge-: **~pflanze** *f* trailing plant; **~schloß** *nt* padlock; **~schrank** *m* wall-cupboard.

Hanglage *f* sloping site. **in ~** situated on a slope.

Hannover [ha'noːfɐ] *nt* Hanover.

Hannoveraner(in *f*) *m* - Hanoverian.

Hansdampf *m* **-e** Jack-of-all-trades (and master of none). **er ist ein ~ in allen Gassen** he knows everybody and everything.

Hänselei *f* teasing *no pl*.

hänseln *vt* to tease.

Hansestadt *f* Hanseatic *or* Hanse town.

Hanswurst *m* **-e** *or* (*hum*) ⁻**e** clown.

Hantel *f* **-n** (*Sport*) dumb-bell.

hantieren* *vi* **(a)** (*arbeiten*) to be busy. **(b)** (*umgehen mit*) **mit etw ~** to handle sth. **(c)** (*herum~*) to tinker about (*an* +*dat* with, on).

hapern *vi impers* (*col*) **es hapert an etw** (*dat*) (*fehlt*) there is a lack of sth; **es hapert bei jdm mit etw** (*fehlt*) sb is short of sth; **mit der Grammatik hapert es bei ihm** he's poor at grammar.

Häppchen *nt dim of* **Happen** morsel; (*Appetithappen*) titbit.

häppchenweise *adv* (*col: lit, fig*) bit by bit.

Happen *m* - (*col*) mouthful, morsel; (*kleine Mahlzeit*) bite. **ein fetter ~** (*fig*) a good catch; **ich habe heute noch keinen ~ gegessen** I haven't had a bite to eat all day.

happig *adj* (*col*) steep (*col*).

Hardware ['haːdwɛə] *f* (*Comp*) hardware.

Harem *m* -s (*auch hum col*) harem.

Harfe *f* -n harp.

Harke *f* -n (*esp N Ger*) rake. **jdm zeigen, was eine ~ ist** (*fig col*) to show sb what's what (*col*).

harmlos *adj* (a) (*ungefährlich*) harmless; *Berg, Piste* easy; *Schnupfen, Entzündung etc* slight. **(b)** (*arglos*) innocent; (*friedlich*) harmless. **er ist ein ~er Mensch** he's harmless (enough).

Harmlosigkeit *f no pl siehe adj* **(a)** harmlessness; easiness; slightness. **(b)** innocence; harmlessness. **in aller ~** in all innocence.

Harmonie *f* (*Mus, fig*) harmony.

harmonieren* *vi* (*Mus, fig*) to harmonize; (*farblich auch*) to match.

Harmonika *f* -s *or* **Harmoniken** harmonica; (*Mund~ auch*) mouth organ; (*Zieh~*) accordion.

harmonisch *adj* harmonious; (*Mus, Math*) harmonic.

harmonisieren* *vt* (*Mus*) to harmonize; (*fig*) to coordinate.

Harn *m* -e urine. **~ lassen** to pass water.

Harnblase *f* bladder.

Harnisch *m* -e armour (*Brit*), armor (*US*). **jdn in ~ bringen** (*fig*) to get sb up in arms; **wenn sie das sieht, gerät sie in ~** it gets her hackles up when she sees that.

Harpune *f* -n harpoon.

harpunieren* *vti* to harpoon.

harren *vi* (*geh*) **jds/einer Sache ~, auf jdn/etw ~** to await sb/sth, to wait for sb/sth.

Harsch *m no pl* frozen snow.

harsch *adj* (a) harsh. **(b)** *Schnee* frozen.

hart *comp* ⁻**er**, *superl* ⁻**este(r, s)** *or* (*adv*) **am** ⁻**esten 1** *adj* **(a)** hard; *Winter auch, Strafe* severe; *Gesetze, Kurs* tough; *Auseinandersetzung* violent; *Wind* strong; *Ei* hard-boiled; (*stabil*) *Währung* stable; (*fig*) *Getränk, Droge* hard; *Verlust* cruel; *Wirklichkeit* harsh. **~ werden** to get hard, to harden; **Eier ~ kochen** to hard-boil eggs; **er hat einen ~en**

Schädel *or* **Kopf** *(fig)* he's obstinate; **ein** ~**es Herz haben** *(fig)* to have a hard heart, to be hard-hearted; ~ **en Dollars in hard dollars;** ~ **bleiben** to stand firm; ~ **mit jdm sein** to be hard on sb; **es geht** ~ **auf** ~ it's a tough fight. **(b)** *(rauh)* **Spiel, Gegner** rough; *(robust)* tough. **kalte Duschen machen** ~ cold showers make you tough; **er ist** ~ **im Nehmen** he's tough. **(c)** *(scharf)* **Konturen,** *(Phot)* **Negativ** sharp; **Klang, Akzent** harsh; **Gesichtszüge** hard.

2 *adv* **(a)** hard; *(scharf)* **konstrastiert** sharply; *(heftig, rauh)* roughly. ~ **klingen** to sound harsh; ~ **aneinandergeraten** to get into a fierce argument; **jdn** ~ **anfahren** to bite sb's head off *(col)*; **jdm** ~ **zusetzen** to press sb hard; **etw trifft jdn** ~ *(lit, fig)* sth hits sb hard; ~ **spielen** *(Sport)* to play rough; ~ **durchgreifen** to take tough *or* rigorous action; **jdn** ~ **anfassen** to be hard on sb. **(b)** *(nahe)* **close** *(an+dat* to*)*. **das ist** ~ **an der Grenze** that's almost going too far; **wir fuhren** ~ **am Abgrund vorbei** *(fig)* we were on the brink of disaster.

Härte *f* **-n** *siehe adj* **(a)** hardness; severity; toughness; violence; strength; stability; cruelty; harshness. **soziale** ~**n** social hardships. **(b)** roughness; toughness. **(c)** sharpness; harshness; hardness.

Härte-: ~**fall** *m* case of hardship; *(col:* Mensch*)* hardship case; ~**grad** *m* degree of hardness; ~**klausel** *f* hardship clause.

härten *vtir* to harden.

Hart-: ~**faserplatte** *f* hardboard, fiberboard *(US)*; **h**~**gefroren** *adj attr* frozen hard *pred*; **h**~**gekocht** *adj attr* hard-boiled; ~**geld** *nt* hard cash; **h**~**gesotten** *adj (fig)* hard-boiled; **h**~**herzig** *adj* hard-hearted; ~**herzigkeit** *f* hard-heartedness; ~**holz** *nt* hardwood; ~**käse** *m* hard cheese; **h**~-**näckig** *adj* stubborn; ~**näckigkeit** *f* stubbornness.

Härtung *f (Tech)* hardening.

Harz¹ *nt* **-e** resin; *(Mus)* rosin.

Harz² *m (Geog)* Harz Mountains *pl*.

Haschee *nt* **-s** *(Cook)* hash.

haschen *(dated, geh)* **1** *vt* to catch. **2** *vi* **nach Beifall/Lob** *etc* ~ to fish for applause/praise *etc*.

Häschen ['hɛsçən] *nt dim of* **Hase** young hare, leveret; *(col:* Kaninchen*)* bunny *(col)*.

Haschisch *nt* or *m no pl* hashish.

Hase *m (wk)* **-n, -n** hare; *(dial:* Kaninchen, Oster~, *in Märchen)* rabbit. **falscher** ~ *(Cook)* meat loaf; **wissen, wie der** ~ **läuft** *(fig col)* to know which way the wind blows; **alter** ~ *(fig col)* old hand; **da liegt der** ~ **im Pfeffer** *(col)* that's the crux of the matter; **mein Name ist** ~*(, ich weiß von nichts)* I don't know anything about anything.

Hasel-: ~**maus** *f* dormouse; ~**nuß** *f* hazelnut; ~**strauch** *m* hazel-bush.

Hasen-: **h**~**füßig** *adj (dated col)* chicken-hearted *(col)*; ~**pfeffer** *m (Cook)* ≈ jugged hare; ~**scharte** *f (Med)* hare-lip.

Haß *m no pl (auf+acc,* gegen *of)*. **(b)** *(col:* Wut*)* **einen** ~ **(auf jdn) haben** *(col)* to be really mad (with sb) *(col)*.

hassen *vti* to hate. **etw** ~ **wie die Pest** *(col)* to detest sth.

hassenswert *adj* hateful, odious.

haßerfüllt *adj* full of hate *or* hatred.

häßlich *adj* **(a)** *(auch* Vorfall *etc)* ugly. ~ **wie die Nacht** (as) ugly as sin. **(b)** *(gemein)* nasty, mean. ~ **über jdn sprechen** to be nasty *or* mean about sb.

Häßlichkeit *f siehe adj* **(a)** ugliness *no pl*. **(b)** nastiness *no pl*, meanness *no pl*; *(Bemerkung)* nasty remark.

Haßliebe *f* love-hate relationship *(für* with*)*.

Hast *f no pl* haste. **ohne** ~ without haste, without rushing; **mit einer solchen** ~ in such a hurry *or* rush.

haste *(col)* = **hast du.** ~ **was, biste was** *(prov)* money brings status.

hasten *vi aux sein (geh)* to hasten *(form)*, to hurry.

hastig *adj* hasty; **Essen** *auch,* **Worte** hurried. **nicht so** ~! not so fast!

hätscheln *vt (liebkosen)* to pet, to fondle; *(zu weich behandeln)* to mollycoddle; *(bevorzugen)* to pamper.

hatschi *interj* atishoo.

hatte *pret of* **haben.**

Haube *f* **-n (a)** bonnet; *(von Krankenschwester etc)* cap. **jdn unter die** ~ **bringen** *(hum)* to marry sb off; **unter der** ~ **sein/unter die** ~ **kommen** *(hum)* to be/get married. **(b)** *(bei* Vögeln*)* crest. **(c)** *(Bedeckung)* cover; *(Trocken~)* (hair) dryer, drying hood *(US)*; *(für* Kaffee-, Teekanne*)* cosy; *(Motor~)* bonnet *(Brit)*, hood *(US)*.

Hauch *m* **-e (a)** *(geh,* poet*)* *(Atem)* breath. **(b)** *(Luftzug)* breath of air, breeze. **(c)** *(Duft)* smell. **(d)** *(Andeutung)* hint, touch.

hauchdünn *adj* extremely thin; **Scheiben** wafer-thin; *(fig)* **Mehrheit** extremely narrow.

hauchen *vti* to breathe. **jdm etw** *(acc)* **ins Ohr** ~ *(liter)* to whisper sth in sb's ear.

hauch-: ~**fein** *adj* extremely fine; ~**zart** *adj* very delicate.

Haudegen *m (fig)* old campaigner.

Haue *f no pl (col:* Prügel*)* (good) hiding *(col)*.

hauen *pret* **haute,** *ptp* **gehauen 1** *vt* **(a)** *(col)* *(schlagen)* to hit, to clout *(col)*; *(verprügeln)* to hit, to thump *(col)*. **hau(t) ihn!** let him have it! *(col)*. **(b)** *(meißeln)* **Figur** to carve; **Stufen, Loch** to cut. **(c)** *(col:* stoßen*)* **jdn, Gegenstand** to shove *(col)*; **Körperteil** to bang, to knock *(an +acc* on, against*)*. **das haut einen vom Stuhl** it really knocks you sideways *(col)*. **(d)** *(col:* werfen*)* to chuck *(col)*, to fling. **(e)** *(dial)* **Baum** to chop (down); **Holz, Fleisch** to chop (up). **2** *vi (col:* schlagen*)* to hit. **jdm auf die Schulter** ~ to slap sb on the shoulder. **3** *vr* **(a)** *(sich prügeln)* to scrap, to fight. **(b)** *(sich setzen, legen)* to fling oneself.

Hauer *m* **- (a)** *(Min)* face-worker. **(b)** *(Zool)* tusk; *(hum:* großer Zahn*)* fang.

Häufchen *nt dim of* **Haufen** small pile. **ein** ~ **Unglück** *or* **Elend** a picture of misery.

Haufen *m* **- (a)** heap, pile. **jdn über den** ~ **rennen/fahren** *etc (col)* to knock sb down; **etw** *(acc)* **über den** ~ **werfen** *(col)* *(verwerfen)* to chuck sth out *(col)*; *(durchkreuzen)* to mess sth up *(col)*; **soviel Geld habe ich noch nie auf einem** ~ **gesehen** *(col)* I've never seen so much money altogether before. **(b)** *(col)* **ein** ~ **Arbeit/Geld** a load *or* heap of work/money, piles *or* loads of work/money *(all col)*; **ein** ~ **Unsinn** a load of nonsense *(col)*; **er hat einen ganzen** ~ **Freunde** he has loads of friends *(col)*. **(c)** *(Schar)* crowd. **dem** ~ **folgen** *(pej)* to follow the crowd; **der große** ~ *(pej)* the common herd.

häufen 1 *vt* to pile up, to heap up. **ein gehäufter Teelöffel Salz** a heaped teaspoonful of salt. **2** *vr* *(lit, fig:* sich ansammeln*)* to mount up; *(zahlreicher werden:* Unfälle, Fehler *etc)* to occur increasingly often. **das kann schon mal vorkommen, es darf sich nur nicht** ~ these things happen, just as long as they don't happen too often.

haufenweise *adv (col)* **etw** ~ **haben** to have piles *or* heaps *or* loads of sth *(all col)*.

häufig 1 *adj* frequent. **2** *adv* often, frequently.

Häufigkeit *f* frequency.

Häufung *f* **(a)** *(fig:* das Anhäufen*)* accumulation. **(b)** *(das* Sich-Häufen*)* increasing number.

Haupt *nt, pl* **Häupter (a)** *(geh:* Kopf*)* head. **entblößten** ~**es** bareheaded; **gesenkten/erhobenen** ~**es** with one's head bowed/raised. **(b)** *(zentrale* Figur*)* head.

Haupt- *in cpds* main, principal, chief; ~**akteur** *m (lit, fig)* leading light; *(pej)* main figure; ~**akzent** *m (fig)* **auf etw** *(acc)* **den** ~**akzent legen** to put the main emphasis on sth; ~**anteil** *m* main part; ~**bahnhof** *m* main or central station; ~**beruf** *m* main occupation; **h**~**beruflich 1** *adj Lehrer, Gärtner etc* full-time; **2** *adv* full-time; **h**~**beruflich tätig sein** to be in full-time employment; ~**beschäftigung** *f* main occupation; ~**betrieb** *m* **(a)** headquarters *sing or pl*; **(b)** *(geschäftigste Zeit)* peak period; ~**darsteller(in** *f)* *m* principal actor/actress, leading man/lady; ~**fach** *nt (Sch, Univ)* main subject, major *(US)*; **etw im** ~**fach studieren** to study sth as one's main subject, to major in sth *(US)*; ~**figur** *f (Liter)* central character; *(fig)* central figure; ~**film** *m* main film; ~**gericht** *nt* main course.

Hauptgeschäft *nt* **(a)** *(Zentrale)* head office, headquarters *sing or pl.* **(b)** *(Hauptverdienst)* major part of one's business.

Hauptgeschäfts-: ~**stelle** *f* head office, headquarters *sing or pl*; ~**straße** *f* main shopping street; ~**zeit** *f* peak (shopping) period.

Haupt-: ~**gewicht** *nt (fig)* main emphasis; ~**gewinn** *m* first prize; ~**grund** *m* main reason; ~**hahn** *m* mains cock; ~**last** *f* main load; *(fig)* main burden; ~**leitung** *f* mains *pl.*

Häuptling *m* chief(tain); *(esp von Dorf)* headman.

Haupt-: ~**mahlzeit** *f* main meal; ~**mann** *m, pl* -**leute** *(Mil)* captain; ~**merkmal** *nt* main feature; ~**motiv** *nt* **(a)** *(Beweggrund)* primary or main motive; **(b)** *(Art, Liter, Mus)* main or principal motif; ~**nahrungsmittel** *nt* staple food; ~**niederlassung** *f* head office, headquarters *sing or pl*; ~**person** *f (lit, fig)* central figure; ~**post** *f (col),* ~**postamt** *nt* main post office; ~**quartier** *nt (Mil, fig)* headquarters *sing or pl*; ~**reisezeit** *f* peak travelling *(Brit)* or traveling *(US)* time(s *pl)*; ~**rolle** *f* main role, lead; **die** ~**rolle spielen** *(fig)* to be all-important; *(wichtigste Person sein)* to play the main role; ~**sache** *f* main thing; *(in Brief, Rede etc)* main point; **in der** ~**sache** in the main, mainly; **h**~**sächlich 1** *adv* mainly, principally; **2** *adj* main, principal; ~**saison** *f* peak or high season; ~**satz** *m (Gram)* main clause; ~**schalter** *m (Elec)* master switch; ~**schlagader** *f* aorta; ~**schlüssel** *m* master key; ~**schuld** *f* main blame, main guilt *(esp Jur)*; ~**schuldige(r)** *mf* person mainly to blame, main offender *(esp Jur)*; ~**schule** *f* ≈ secondary modern (school) *(Brit)*, junior high (school) *(US)*; ~**sitz** *m* head office, headquarters *sing or pl*; ~**stadt** *f* capital (city); ~**straße** *f* main or major road; *(im Stadtzentrum etc)* main street; ~**teil** *m* main part; *(größter Teil auch)* major part; ~**thema** *nt* main topic; *(Mus, Liter)* main theme; ~**tribüne** *f* main stand; *(Sport auch)* grandstand.

Hauptverkehrs-: ~**straße** *f (in Stadt)* main street; *(Durchgangsstraße)* main thoroughfare; *(zwischen Städten)* main highway, trunk road *(Brit)*; ~**zeit** *f* peak traffic times *pl*; *(in Stadt, bei Pendlern auch)* rush hour.

Haupt-: ~**wohnsitz** *m* main place of residence; ~**wort** *nt (Gram)* noun.

hau ruck *interj* heave-ho.

Haus *nt, pl* **Häuser (a)** *(Wohn~)* house; *(Firmengebäude)* building. **ins/im** ~ indoors; **mit jdm** ~ **an** ~ **wohnen** to live next door to sb; **von** ~ **zu** ~ **gehen** to go from door to door or from house to house; **vor vollem** ~ **spielen** to play to a full house.

(b) *(Zuhause, Heim)* home. ~ **und Hof** *(fig)* house and home; **etw ins/frei** ~ **liefern** *(Comm)* to deliver sth to the door/to deliver sth carriage paid; **wir liefern frei** ~ we offer free delivery; **jdm das** ~ **verbieten** not to allow sb in the house; **aus dem** ~ **sein** to be away from home; **außer** ~ **essen** to eat out; **ins** ~ **stehen** *(fig)* to be coming up, to be forthcoming; **jdm steht etw ins** ~ *(fig)* sb is facing sth; **nach** ~**e** *(lit, fig)* home; **zu** ~**e at**

home *(auch Sport)*; **bei jdm zu** ~**e** at sb's (place), **in** sb's house or home; **bei uns zu** ~**e** at home; **für niemanden zu** ~**e sein** to be at home to nobody; **irgendwo zu** ~**e sein** *(Mensch, Tier)* to live somewhere; *(sich heimisch fühlen)* to be at home somewhere; **sich wie zu** ~**e fühlen** to feel at home; **fühl dich wie zu** ~**e!** make yourself at home!

(c) *(Bewohnerschaft eines* ~*es)* household. **ein Freund des** ~**es** a friend of the family; **der Herr des** ~**es** *(form)* the master of the house.

(d) *(geh: Herkunft)* **aus gutem/bürgerlichem** ~**(e)** from a good/middle-class family; **von** ~**e aus** *(ursprünglich)* originally; *(von Natur aus)* naturally.

(e) **das** ~ **Windsor/Siemens** the House of Windsor/Siemens; **das erste** ~ **am Platze** the best hotel in town; *(Kaufhaus)* the best store in town; **Hohes** ~! *(form)* ≈ honourable members (of the House)!; **dieses hohe** ~ the or this House.

(f) *(von Schnecke)* shell, house *(col).*

(g) **grüß dich, altes** ~! *(col)* hallo, old chap *(col).*

Haus-: ~**angestellte(r)** *mf* domestic servant; ~**anzug** *m* leisure suit; ~**apotheke** *f* medicine chest; ~**arbeit** *f* **(a)** housework *no pl*; **(b)** *(Sch)* homework *no indef art, no pl*; ~**arrest** *m (im Internat)* detention; *(Jur)* house arrest; ~**arzt** *m* family doctor, GP; ~**aufgaben** *pl* homework *no indef art, no pl*; **h**~**backen** *adj (fig)* drab, homely *(US)*; ~**bau** *m* house building; *(das Bauen)* building of a/the house; ~**besetzer** *m* squatter; ~**besetzung** *f* squat; ~**besitzer(in** *f)* *m* home-owner; *(Hauswirt)* landlord/landlady; ~**besuch** *m* home visit; ~**bewohner** *m* (house) occupant or occupier.

Häuschen ['hɔʏsçən] *nt* **(a)** *dim of* **Haus. (b)** *(fig col)* **ganz aus dem** ~ **sein** to be out of one's mind (with excitement/fear etc) *(col).*

Haus-: **h**~**eigen** *adj* belonging to a/the hotel/firm etc; ~**eigentümer** *m* home-owner; *(Hauswirt)* landlord/landlady.

hausen *vi* **(a)** *(pej: wohnen)* to live. **(b)** *(wüten)* **(übel or schlimm)** ~ to wreak or create havoc; **wie die Wandalen** ~ to act like vandals.

Häuser-: ~**block** *m* block (of houses); ~**front** *f* front of a row of houses; ~**makler** *m* estate agent *(Brit)*, realtor *(US)*; ~**reihe**, ~**zeile** *f* row of houses; *(aneinandergebaut)* terrace.

Hausfrau *f* housewife.

Hausfrauenart *f* **Wurst** etc **nach** ~ home-made-style sausage etc.

Haus-: ~**friede(n)** *m* domestic peace; ~**friedensbruch** *m (Jur)* trespass *(in sb's house)*; ~**gebrauch** *m* **für den** ~**gebrauch** *(Gerät)* for domestic or household use; **sein Französisch reicht für den** ~**gebrauch** *(col)* his French is good enough to get by; ~**gehilfin** *f* home help; **h**~**gemacht** *adj* home-made; ~**gemeinschaft** *f* household.

Haushalt *m* -**e (a)** household; *(* ~*sführung)* housekeeping. **den** ~ **führen** to run the household; **jdm den** ~ **führen** to keep house for sb. **(b)** *(fig: Biol etc)* balance. **(c)** *(Etat)* budget.

haushalten *vi sep irreg* **(a)** **mit etw** ~ to be economical with sth. **(b)** *(den Haushalt führen)* to keep house.

Haushälter(in *f)* *m* - housekeeper.

Haushalts- *in cpds* household; *(Pol)* budget; ~**artikel** *m* household article; ~**buch** *nt* housekeeping book; ~**debatte** *f (Parl)* budget debate; ~**führung** *f* housekeeping; ~**gerät** *nt* household appliance; ~**hilfe** *f* domestic help; ~**jahr** *nt (Pol, Econ)* financial or fiscal year; ~**kasse** *f* household budget; ~**mittel** *pl (Pol)* budgetary funds *pl*; ~**plan** *m (Pol)* budget; ~**politik** *f (Pol)* budgetary policy; **h**~**politisch** *adj* concerning budgetary policy.

Haus-: ~**haltung** *f (das Haushaltführen)* housekeeping; ~**herr** *m* **(a)** head of the household; *(Gastgeber)* host; **(b)** *(Jur)* householder; ~**her-**

rin *f* lady of the house; *(Gastgeberin)* hostess; h~**hoch 1** *adj* (as) high as a house/houses; *(fig) Sieg* crushing; **der h~hohe Favorit** the hot favourite *(col)*; **2** *adv* high (in the sky); h~**hoch gewinnen** to win hands down *or* by miles *(col)*; **jdm** h~**hoch überlegen sein** to be head and shoulders above sb; h~**hohe(r, s)** *adj siehe* h~**hoch**.

hausieren* *vi* to hawk, to peddle *(mit etw sth)*. **mit etw ~ gehen** *(fig) mit Plänen* to hawk sth about.

Hausierer(in *f)* *m* - hawker, peddler.

Haus-: h~**intern** *adj* internal company *attr*; ~**kleid** *nt* hostess gown; ~**lehrer(in** *f)* *m* (private) tutor.

häuslich *adj* domestic; *Mensch* domesticated; *(das Zuhause liebend)* home-loving. **der ~e Herd** the family home; **sich irgendwo ~ einrichten** *or* **niederlassen** to settle in somewhere.

Häuslichkeit *f* domesticity.

Hausmacherart *f* **Wurst** *etc* **nach ~** home-made-style sausage *etc*.

Haus-: ~**mann** *m*, *pl* ~**männer** *(den Haushalt versorgender Mann)* man undertaking the role of housewife, house-husband *(hum)*; ~**mannskost** *f* plain cooking; ~**marke** *f (eigene Marke)* own brand; *(bevorzugte Marke)* favourite *(Brit)* or favorite *(US)* brand; ~**meister** *m* caretaker, janitor; ~**mitteilung** *f* internal memo; ~**mittel** *nt* household remedy; ~**ordnung** *f* house rules *pl*; ~**rat** *m no pl* household equipment; ~**ratsversicherung** *f* (household) contents insurance; ~**recht** *nt* right(s *pl*) as a householder *(to forbid sb entrance)*; ~**sammlung** *f* house-to-house *or* door-to-door collection; ~**schlüssel** *m* front-door key, house key; ~**schuh** *m* slipper; ~**schwamm** *m* dry rot.

Hausse ['hoːs(ə)] *f* -**n** *(Econ)* boom *(an+dat* in); *(St Ex)* bull market.

Haus-: ~**segen** *m* **bei ihnen hängt der ~segen schief** *(hum)* they're a bit short on domestic bliss *(col)*; ~**stand** *m* household, home; **einen ~stand gründen** to set up house *or* home; ~**suchung** *f* house search; ~**suchungsbefehl** *m* search-warrant; ~**tier** *nt* domestic animal; *(aus Liebhaberei gehalten)* pet; ~**tür** *f* front door; **gleich vor der ~tür** *(fig col)* right on one's doorstep; ~**verbot** *nt* **jdm ~verbot erteilen** to ban sb from the house; **in einem Lokal ~ verbot haben** to be barred *or* banned from a bar; ~**verwalter** *m* (house) supervisor; ~**verwaltung** *f* property management; ~**wirt** *m* landlord; ~**wirtin** *f* landlady.

Hauswirtschaft *f* **(a)** housekeeping. **(b)** *(Sch)* home economics *sing*.

hauswirtschaftlich *adj* domestic.

Haut *f*, *pl* **Häute** skin; *(dick, esp von größerem Tier)* hide. **naß bis auf die ~** soaked to the skin; **nur ~ und Knochen sein** to be nothing but skin and bones; **mit ~ und Haar(en)** *(col)* completely; **das geht unter die ~** *(col)* that gets under your skin; **in seiner ~ möchte ich nicht stecken** *(col)* I wouldn't like to be in his shoes; **ihm ist nicht wohl in seiner ~** *(col) (unzufrieden)* he's (feeling) rather unsettled; *(unbehaglich)* he feels uneasy; **er kann nicht aus seiner ~ heraus** *(col)* he can't change the way he is, a leopard can't change its spots *(prov)*; **aus der ~ fahren** *(col)* to go through the roof *(col)*; **sich auf die faule ~ legen** *(col)* to sit back and do nothing; **seine ~ zu Markte tragen** *(col)* to risk one's neck; **seine eigene ~ retten** *(col)* to save one's own skin; **sich seiner ~ wehren** *(col)* to defend oneself.

Haut- *in cpds* skin; ~**abschürfung** *f* graze; ~**arzt** *m* skin specialist, dermatologist; ~**ausschlag** *m* (skin) rash.

Häutchen *nt* - *dim of* **Haut** *(auf Flüssigkeit)* skin; *(Anat, Bot)* membrane.

häuten 1 *vt Tiere* to skin. **2** *vr (Tier)* to shed its skin; *(hum: Mensch)* to peel.

Haut-: h~**eng** *adj* skintight; ~**farbe** *f* skin colour *(Brit)* or color *(US)*; *(Teint)* complexion; h~**farben** *adj* flesh-coloured *(Brit)*, flesh-colored *(US)*; h~**nah** *adj* (very) close; *Schilderung, Szene* vivid, graphic; ~**pflege** *f* skin care; ~**wunde** *f* skin wound.

Havarie [hava'riː] *f (Naut, Aviat)* accident; *(Schaden)* damage *no indef art, no pl*.

Haxe *f* -**n** *(Cook)* leg (joint); *(S Ger col) (Fuß)* foot; *(Bein)* leg.

Hbf = **Hauptbahnhof.**

h.c. [haː'tseː] = **honoris causa. Dr. ~** honorary doctor.

Hebamme *f* -**n** midwife.

Hebe-: ~**balken** *m* lever; ~**bühne** *f* hydraulic ramp.

Hebel *m* - lever. **den ~ ansetzen** to position the lever; *(fig col)* to tackle it; **alle ~ in Bewegung setzen** *(col)* to move heaven and earth; **am längeren ~ sitzen** *(col)* to have the whip hand.

Hebel-: ~**kraft** *f* leverage; ~**wirkung** *f* leverage.

heben *pret* **hob**, *ptp* **gehoben 1** *vt* **(a)** to lift; *Arm, Fernglas auch, Augenbraue, Wrack* to raise; *Schatz* to dig up. **die Stimme ~** to raise one's voice; **einen ~ gehen** *(col)* to go for a drink; **er hebt gern einen** *(col)* he likes a drink; **heb deine Füße!** pick your feet up!; *siehe* **gehoben. (b)** *(steigern)* to increase; *Stimmung, Wohlstand* to improve; *Geschmack, jds Ansehen* to enhance. **das hebt den Mut** it's good for morale. **2** *vr* **(a)** to rise; *(Nebel, Deckel)* to lift. **(b)** *(verbessern, steigern)* to improve. **da hob sich seine Stimmung** that cheered him up. **3** *vi (Sport)* to do weight-lifting.

Hebräer(in *f)* *m* - Hebrew.

hebräisch *adj* Hebrew.

Hebung *f* **(a)** *(von Schatz, Wrack etc)* recovery, raising. **(b)** *(fig: Verbesserung)* improvement; *(von Effekt, Selbstbewußtsein)* heightening; *(von Lebensstandard, Niveau)* rise.

hecheln *vi* **(a)** *(col: lästern)* to gossip. **(b)** *(keuchen)* to pant.

Hecht *m* -**e** *(Zool)* pike; *(col: Bursche)* guy *(col)*. **er ist (wie) ein ~ im Karpfenteich** *(fig)* he certainly shakes people up.

hechten *vi aux sein (col)* to dive.

Hechtsprung *m (beim Schwimmen)* racing dive; *(beim Turnen)* forward dive; *(Ftbl col)* dive.

Heck *nt* -**e** *or* -**s** *(Naut)* stern; *(Aviat)* tail, rear; *(Aut)* rear, back.

Heck|antrieb *m (Aut)* rear-wheel drive.

Hecke *f* -**n** hedge; *(am Wegrand)* hedgerow.

Hecken-: ~**rose** *f* dogrose, wild rose; ~**schere** *f* hedge-clippers *pl*; ~**schütze** *m* sniper.

Heck-: ~**fenster** *nt (Aut)* rear window; ~**klappe** *f (Aut)* hatchback *(Brit)*, tailgate *(US)*.

Heckmeck *m no pl (col) (dummes Gerede)* nonsense, rubbish; *(Umstände)* fuss, palaver *(col)*.

Heck-: ~**motor** *m (Aut)* rear engine; ~**scheibe** *f (Aut)* rear window; ~**tür** *f (Aut)* hatchback *(Brit)*, tailgate *(US)*; ~**türmodell** *nt* hatchback.

Heer *nt* -**e** *(lit, fig)* army. **beim ~** in the army.

Heeresleitung *f* command.

Hefe *f* -**n** yeast.

Hefe-: ~**gebäck** *nt* yeast-risen pastry; ~**pilz** *m* yeast plant; ~**teig** *m* yeast dough.

Heft¹ *nt* -**e** *(von Werkzeug, Messer)* handle; *(von Dolch, Schwert)* hilt. **das ~ in der Hand haben** *(fig)* to hold the reins; **jdm das ~ aus der Hand nehmen** *(fig)* to seize control/power from sb.

Heft² *nt* -**e** *(Schreib~)* exercise book; *(Zeitschrift)* magazine; *(Comic~)* comic; *(Nummer)* number, issue; *(geheftetes Büchlein)* booklet.

Heftchen *nt* **(a)** *dim of* **Heft².** **(b)** *(pej) (billiger Roman)* rubbishy or pulp novel *(pej)*; *(Comic~)* rag *(pej col)*. **(c)** *(Fahrkarten~, Briefmarken~)* book of tickets/stamps.

heften 1 *vt* **(a)** *(nähen) Saum* to tack (up); *Buch* to sew, to stitch; *(klammern)* to clip *(an+acc to)*; *(mit Heftmaschine auch)* to staple *(an +acc to)*. **(b)** *(befestigen)* to pin, to fix. **den Blick auf jdn/ etw ~** to stare at sb/sth. **2** *vr* **sich an jds Fersen** *or* **Sohlen ~** *(fig)* to dog sb's heels.

Hefter *m* - (loose-leaf) file.

heftig *adj* violent; *Schmerz, Liebe* intense; *Erkältung, Fieber* severe; *Weinen* bitter; *Kampf, Wind, Widerstand* fierce; *Regen, Frost* heavy. **ein ~er Regenguß** a downpour; **er hat sich ~ in sie verliebt** he has fallen violently in love with her; **~ nicken/rühren** to nod/stir vigorously.

Heftigkeit *f no pl siehe adj* violence; intensity; severity; bitterness; ferocity; heaviness.

Heft-: **~klammer** *f* staple; **~maschine** *f* stapler; **~pflaster** *nt* (sticking) plaster, adhesive tape *(US)*; **~zwecke** *f* drawing-pin *(Brit)*, thumb-tack *(US)*.

hegen *vt* **(a)** *Wild, Pflanzen* to care for, to tend. **jdn ~ und pflegen** to lavish care and attention on sb. **(b)** *Groll, Verdacht* to harbour *(Brit)*, to harbor *(US)*; *Mißtrauen, Abneigung* to feel; *Zweifel* to entertain; *Hoffnung, Wunsch* to cherish. **ich hege den starken Verdacht, daß ...** I have a strong suspicion that ...

Hehl *nt or m*: **kein** *or* **keinen ~ aus etw machen** to make no secret of sth.

Hehler(in *f)* *m* - receiver (of stolen goods), fence *(col)*.

Hehlerei *f no pl* receiving (stolen goods).

Heia *f no pl (baby-talk)* **ab in die ~** off to bye-byes *(baby-talk)*.

Heide[1] *m (wk)* **-n, -n, Heidin** *f* heathen, pagan.

Heide[2] *f* **-n** moor, heath.

Heide-: **~kraut** *nt* heather; **~land** *nt* moorland, heathland.

Heidelbeere *f* bilberry, blueberry *(esp US)*.

Heiden- *(col)*: **~angst** *f*: **eine ~angst vor etw** *(dat)* **haben** to be scared stiff of sth *(col)*; **~arbeit** *f* real slog *(col)*; **~geld** *nt* packet *(col)*; **~krach, ~lärm** *m* unholy din *(col)*; **~respekt** *m* healthy respect; **~spaß** *m* terrific fun; **einen ~spaß haben** to have a whale of a time *(col)*; **~spektakel** *m* awful row; *(Schimpfen)* awful fuss.

Heidentum *nt no pl* paganism.

Heidin *f siehe* **Heide**[1].

heidnisch *adj* heathen, pagan.

heikel *adj* **(a)** *Situation, Thema* tricky, delicate. **(b)** *(dial) Mensch* particular, pernickety *(col)* *(in bezug auf +acc* about*)*.

heil *adj* **(a)** *(unverletzt) Mensch* unhurt; *Glieder* unbroken; *Haut* undamaged. **wieder ~ sein/ werden** *(wieder gesund)* to be/get better again; *(Wunde)* to have healed/to heal up; **~ nach Hause kommen** to get home safe and sound; **etw ~ überstehen** *Unfall* to come through sth without a scratch; *Prüfung* to get through sth; **mit ~er Haut davonkommen** to escape unscathed. **(b)** *(col: ganz)* intact; *Kleidungsstück* decent *(col)*. **die ~e Welt** an ideal world *(without problems etc)*.

Heil **1** *nt no pl* **(a)** *(Wohlergehen)* well-being, good. **(b)** *(Eccl, fig)* salvation. **sein ~ in der Flucht suchen** to flee for one's life. **2** *interj* Ski/Petri **~!** good skiing/fishing!

Heiland *m* **-e** *(Rel)* Saviour, Redeemer.

Heil-: **~anstalt** *f* nursing home; *(für Sucht- oder Geisteskranke)* home; **~bad** *nt (Bad)* medicinal bath; *(Ort)* spa; **h~bar** *adj* curable; **h~bringend** *adj (Rel)* redeeming; *Wirkung* beneficial; *Kräuter* medicinal.

Heilbutt *m* **-e** halibut.

heilen **1** *vi aux sein* to heal (up). **2** *vt* to cure; *Wunde, (Rel)* to heal. **als geheilt entlassen werden** to be discharged with a clean bill of health; **jdn von etw ~** *(lit,fig)* to cure sb of sth; **von jdm/etw geheilt sein** *(fig)* to have got over sb/sth.

heilend *adj* healing.

heilfroh *adj pred (col)* jolly glad *(col)*.

heilig *adj* **(a)** holy; *(bei Namen von Heiligen)* Saint; **jdm ~ sein** *(lit, fig)* to be sacred to sb; **H~er Abend** Christmas Eve; **H~e Maria** Holy Mary; **der H~e Geist/Stuhl** the Holy Spirit *or* Ghost/ See; **die H~en Drei Könige** the Three Wise Men; **die H~e Schrift** the Holy Scriptures *pl*. **(b)** *Pflicht* sacred; *Zorn* righteous; *Stille, Schauer* awed. **es ist mein ~er Ernst** I am deadly serious. **(c)** *(col: groß)* incredible *(col)*; *Respekt auch* healthy.

Heilig|abend *m* Christmas Eve.

heiligen *vt* to hallow; *Sonntag etc* to keep holy. **der Zweck heiligt die Mittel** the end justifies the means.

Heiligen-: **~bild** *nt* holy picture; **~schein** *m* halo; **jdn mit einem ~schein umgeben** *(fig)* to put sb on a pedestal.

Heilige(r) *mf decl as adj (lit,fig)* saint. **ein sonderbarer ~r** *(col)* a queer fish *(col)*.

Heilig-: **~keit** *f* holiness; **Seine ~keit** his Holiness; **h~sprechen** *vt sep irreg* to canonize; **~sprechung** *f* canonization; **~tum** *nt (Stätte)* shrine; *(Gegenstand)* (holy) relic; **jds ~tum sein** *(col) (Zimmer)* to be sb's sanctum; *(Gegenstand etc)* to be sacrosanct (to sb).

Heil-: **~kraft** *f* healing power; **h~kräftig** *adj Pflanze, Tee* medicinal; **~kraut** *nt usu pl* medicinal herb; **~kunde** *f* medicine; **~kundige(r)** *mf decl as adj* healer; **h~los** *adj* unholy *(col)*; *Schreck* terrible; **~methode** *f* cure; **~mittel** *nt (lit, fig)* remedy, cure; *(Medikament)* medicine; **~pflanze** *f* medicinal plant; **~praktiker** *m* non-medical practitioner; **~quelle** *f* medicinal spring; **h~sam** *adj Erfahrung, Strafe* salutary; *Wirkung* beneficial; *(dated: heilend)* healing.

Heils|armee *f* Salvation Army.

Heilung *f (von Wunde)* healing; *(von Krankheit, Kranken)* curing.

Heilungsprozeß *m* healing process.

heim *adv* home.

Heim *nt* **-e** home; *(Studentenwohn~)* hall of residence, hostel.

Heim- *in cpds* home; **~arbeit** *f (Ind)* homework, outwork *both no indef art*; **~arbeiter** *m (Ind)* homeworker.

Heimat *f* **-en** home. **die ~ verlassen** to leave one's home.

Heimat- *in cpds* home; **~dichter** *m* regional writer; **~film** *m* sentimental film in idealized regional setting; **~kunde** *f (Sch)* local history; **~land** *nt* native country; **h~lich** *adj* native; *Bräuche, Dialekt* local; *Gefühle* nostalgic; *Klänge* of home; **h~los** *adj* homeless; **~lose(r)** *mf decl as adj* homeless person; **~museum** *nt* local history museum; **~ort** *m* home town/village; **~vertriebene(r)** *mf decl as adj* displaced person.

heim-: **~begeben*** *vr sep irreg* to make one's way home; **~bringen** *vt sep irreg (nach Hause bringen)* to take home; *(~begleiten)* to take home.

Heimchen *nt* **~ (am Herd)** *(pej: Frau)* housewife.

heimelig *adj* cosy, homely.

Heim-: **h~fahren** *vti sep irreg (vi: aux sein)* to drive home; **~fahrt** *f* journey home; *(Naut)* return voyage; **h~finden** *vi sep irreg* to find one's way home; **h~gehen** *vi sep irreg aux sein* to go home; **h~holen** *vt sep* to fetch home; **Gott hat ihn h~geholt** he has been called to his Maker.

heimisch *adj* **(a)** *(einheimisch)* indigenous, native *(in+dat* to*)*; *(national)* home; *(ortsansässig)* local; *(regional)* regional. **(b)** *(vertraut)* familiar. **sich ~ fühlen** to feel at home; **~ werden** to become acclimatized *(an, in+dat* to*)*.

Heim-: **~kehr** *f no pl* homecoming; **h~kehren** *vi sep aux sein* to return home *(aus* from*)*; **~kehrer(in** *f)* *m* homecomer; **~kind** *nt* child brought up in a home; **h~kommen** *vi sep irreg aux sein* to come home; **~leiter** *m* warden of a/the home/

hostel; **h~leuchten** *vi sep (fig col)* **jdm h~leuchten** to give sb a piece of one's mind.
heimlich 1 *adj* secret. **2** *adv* secretly; *lachen* inwardly. **er blickte sie ~ an** he stole a glance at her; **sich ~ entfernen** to sneak away; **~, still und leise** *(col)* quietly, on the quiet.
Heimlichkeit *f* secrecy; *(Geheimnis)* secret. **in aller ~** secretly, in secret.
Heimlich-: **~tuer(in** *f)* *m* - secretive person; **~tuerei** *f* secrecy; **h~tun** *vi irreg* to be secretive *(mit* about).
Heim-: **~reise** *f* homeward journey; *(Naut)* homeward voyage; **h~reisen** *vi sep aux sein* to travel home; **h~schicken** *vt sep* to send home; **~spiel** *nt (Sport)* home match; **~statt** *f* home.
heimsuchen *vt sep* to strike; *(für längere Zeit)* to plague; *(Gespenst)* to haunt; *(Krankheit, Alpträume)* to afflict; *(col: besuchen)* to descend on *(col)*. **von Dürre/Krieg heimgesucht** drought-stricken/war-torn.
heimtückisch *adj* insidious; *(boshaft)* malicious; *Glatteis, Maschine* treacherous.
Heim-: **h~wärts** *adv* homewards; **~weg** *m* way home; **sich auf den ~weg machen** to head for home; **~weh** *nt* homesickness *no art;* **~weh haben** to be homesick *(nach* for); **~werker** *m* handyman; **h~zahlen** *vt sep* **jdm etw h~zahlen** to pay sb back for sth.
Heini *m* -s *(pej col)* guy *(col)*. **blöder ~** silly idiot.
Heinzelmännchen *nt* **die ~** the little people.
Heirat *f* -en marriage.
heiraten 1 *vt* to marry. **2** *vi* to get married, to marry. **in eine reiche Familie ~** to marry into a rich family.
Heirats-: **~antrag** *m* proposal (of marriage); **jdm einen ~antrag machen** to propose to sb; **~anzeige** *(Annonce)* advertisement for a marriage partner; **h~fähig** *adj* marriageable; **~schwindler** *m* person who makes a marriage proposal in order to obtain money; **~vermittler** *m* marriage broker; **~vermittlung** *f* matchmaking *no pl; (Büro)* marriage bureau.
heiser *adj* hoarse.
Heiserkeit *f* hoarseness.
heiß *adj (lit, fig)* hot; *Zone* torrid; *Thema* hotly disputed; *Diskussion, Kampf* heated, fierce; *Begierde, Liebe, Wunsch* burning. **jdm wird ~** sb is getting hot; **sie hat einen ~en Kopf** she has a burning forehead; **etw ~ machen** to heat sth up; **es wird nichts so ~ gegessen wie es gekocht wird** *(prov)* things are never as bad as they seem; **es ging ~ her** things got heated; **die Stadt ist ~ umkämpft** the town is being fiercely fought over; **jdn/etw ~ und innig lieben** to love sb/sth madly; **~e Tränen weinen** to cry one's heart out; **sich die Köpfe ~ reden** to talk till one is blue in the face; **jdn ~ machen** *(col)* to turn sb on *(col)*; **ein ~es Eisen** a hot potato; **ein ~es Eisen anfassen** *(col)* to grasp the nettle; **~er Draht** hot line; **~e Spur** hot trail.
heißblütig *adj* hot-blooded.
heißen *pret* **hieß**, *ptp* **geheißen 1** *vi* **(a)** to be called *(Brit)* or named. **wie ~ Sie/heißt die Straße?** what's your name/the name of the street?; **ich heiße Müller** I'm called *or* my name is Müller; **sie heißt jetzt anders** she has changed her name; **eigentlich heißt es richtig X** actually the correct word is X; **... und wie sie alle ~ ... and the rest of them. (b)** *(bestimmte Bedeutung haben)* to mean. **was heißt „gut" auf englisch?** what is the English for "gut"?; **was soll das ~?** what does that mean?; **das will schon etwas ~** that's quite something. **(c)** **das heißt** that is; *(in anderen Worten)* that is to say.
2 *vt (geh)* **(a)** *(nennen)* to call. **(b)** *(auffordern)* to tell. **jdn willkommen ~** to bid sb welcome.
3 *vi impers* **es heißt, daß ... they say that ...; in der Bibel/in seinem Brief heißt es, daß ... the**

Bible/his letter says that ...; **es heißt hier ... it says here ...; nun heißt es handeln** now we must do something.
Heiß-: **h~ersehnt** *adj attr* much longed for; **h~geliebt** *adj* dearly beloved; **~hunger** *m* voracious appetite; **etw mit ~hunger verschlingen** *(lit, fig)* to devour sth; **h~hungrig** *adj* ravenous, voracious; **h~laufen** *vi sep irreg aux sein (Motor)* to overheat; **~luft** *f* hot air; **~mangel** *f (Gerät)* rotary iron; *(Geschäft)* laundry specializing in ironing sheets *etc;* **h~umstritten** *adj attr* hotly debated; **~wasserbereiter** *m* water-heater.
heiter *adj (fröhlich)* cheerful; *(ausgeglichen)* serene; *(amüsant)* Geschichte amusing; *(hell, klar)* Farbe, Himmel, Tag bright; Wetter fine; *(Met)* fair. **~ werden** to become cheerful; *(Wetter)* to clear up; **das kann ja ~ werden!** *(iro)* that sounds great *(iro)*; **aus ~em Himmel** *(fig)* out of the blue.
Heiterkeit *f no pl siehe adj* cheerfulness; serenity; amusingness; brightness, fineness; *(heitere Stimmung)* merriment.
Heiz-: **h~bar** *adj* heated; **schwer h~bar** difficult to heat; **~(bett)decke** *f* electric blanket.
heizen 1 *vi* to have the heating on. **der Ofen heizt gut** the stove gives off a good heat; **mit Holz/Strom ~** to use wood/electricity for heating. **2** *vt (warm machen)* to heat; *(verbrennen)* to burn.
Heizer *m* - *(von Hochofen)* boilerman.
Heiz-: **~gerät** *nt* heater; **~kissen** *nt* electric heat pad; **~körper** *m (Gerät)* heater; *(von Zentralheizung)* radiator; **~lüfter** *m* fan heater; **~material** *nt* (heating) fuel; **~sonne** *f* electric fire.
Heizung *f* heating; *(Heizkörper)* heater.
Heizungs-: **~anlage** *f* heating system; **~monteur** *m* heating engineer; **~rohr** *nt* heating pipe.
Hektar *nt or m* -e hectare.
Hektik *f no pl* hectic rush; *(von Leben etc)* hectic pace. **sie arbeitet mit einer solchen ~** she works at such a hectic pace; **nur keine ~** take it easy.
hektisch *adj* hectic.
Hektoliter *m or nt* hectolitre *(Brit)*, hectoliter *(US)*.
Held *m (wk)* -en, -en hero. **der ~ des Tages** the hero of the hour; **kein ~ in etw** *(dat)* **sein** not to be very brave about sth; *(in Schulfach etc)* to be no great shakes at sth *(col)*; **du bist mir ein schöner ~!** *(iro)* some hero you are!
Helden-: **~dichtung** *f* heroic poetry; **h~haft**, **h~mütig** *adj* heroic; **~tat** *f* heroic deed; **~tum** *nt no pl* heroism.
Heldin *f* heroine.
helfen *pret* **half**, *ptp* **geholfen** *vi* to help *(jdm* sb). **jdm bei etw ~** to help sb with sth, to lend sb a hand with sth; **ihm ist nicht zu ~** *(fig)* he is beyond help; **ich kann mir nicht ~, ich muß es tun** I can't help doing it; **ich werd' ihm (schon) ~!** I'll give him what for *(col)*; **ich werde dir ~, die Tapeten zu beschmieren** I'll teach you to mess up the wallpaper; **man muß sich** *(dat)* **nur zu ~ wissen** *(prov)* you just have to use your head; **er weiß sich** *(dat)* **nicht mehr zu ~** he's at his wits' end; **diese Arznei hilft gegen** *or* **bei Kopfweh** this medicine is good for headaches; **es hilft nichts** it's no use *or* no good; **da hilft alles nichts ...** there's nothing for it ...; **was hilft's?** what's the use?
Helfer(in *f)* *m* - helper; *(Mitarbeiter)* assistant; *(von Verbrecher)* accomplice. **ein ~ in der Not** a friend in need.
Helfershelfer *m* accomplice.
hell *adj (a) (optisch)* light; *Licht, Himmel* bright; *Haar, Haut* fair. **es wird ~** it's getting light; **~ bleiben** to stay light; **am ~en Tage** in broad daylight; **in ~en Flammen** in flames, ablaze; **~es Bier** ≈ lager. **(b)** *Ton etc* high(-pitched). **(c)** *(col: klug)* bright; *Augenblicke* lucid. **er ist ein ~er Kopf** he has brains. **(d)** *attr (stark, groß)* great; *Verzweiflung, Unsinn* sheer, utter; *Neid* pure. **von etw ~ begeistert sein** to be very

enthusiastic about sth; **in ~en Scharen** in great numbers.

hell- in cpds (esp auf Farben bezüglich) light; **~auf** adv completely, utterly; **~blond** adj very fair, blonde.

hẹlle adj pred (col) bright, clever.

Hẹller m - **darauf geb ich keinen (roten) ~** I wouldn't give you tuppence (Brit) or a red cent (US) for it; **auf ~ und Pfennig** to the last penny.

Hẹlle(s) nt decl as adj = lager.

hẹll-: **~haarig** adj fair-haired; **~häutig** adj fair-skinned; **~hörig** adj (Archit) poorly sound-proofed; **~hörig sein** (fig: Mensch) to have sharp ears; **jdn ~hörig machen** to make sb prick up their ears.

hẹllicht adj: **am ~en Tage** in broad daylight.

Hẹlligkeit f no pl siehe hell (a) lightness; brightness; fairness; (helles Licht) light; (Phys, Astron) luminosity.

hẹll-: **~sehen** vi infin only **~sehen können** to be clairvoyant; **H~seher(in** f) m (lit, fig) clairvoyant; **~seherisch** adj attr clairvoyant; **~wach** adj (lit, fig) wide-awake; **H~werden** nt no pl daybreak.

Hẹlm m **-e** helmet.

Hẹmd nt **-en** shirt; (Unter~) vest (Brit), undershirt (US). **etw wie sein ~ wechseln** (fig) to change sth with monotonous regularity; **für dich gebe ich mein letztes ~ her** (col) I'd give you the shirt off my back (col); **naß bis aufs ~** wet through; **jdn bis aufs ~ ausziehen** (fig col) to have the shirt off sb's back (col).

Hẹmdbluse f shirt(-blouse), shirtwaist (US).

Hẹmds-: **~ärmel** m in **~ärmeln** in one's shirt sleeves; **h~ärmelig** adj shirt-sleeved; (fig col: salopp) pally (col); Ausdrucksweise casual.

Hemisphäre f **-n** hemisphere.

hẹmmen vt Entwicklung to hinder; Lauf der Dinge, Maschine to check; (verlangsamen) to slow down; Wasserlauf to stem; (Psych) to inhibit.

Hẹmmung f **(a)** (Psych) inhibition; (Bedenken) scruple. **da habe ich ~en** I've got scruples about that; **keine ~en kennen** to have no inhibitions; **nur keine ~en** don't feel inhibited. **(b)** siehe vt hindering; check (gen to); slowing down; stemming.

Hẹmmungs-: **h~los** adj (rückhaltlos) unrestrained; (skrupellos) unscrupulous; **~losigkeit** f siehe adj lack of restraint; unscrupulousness.

Hẹngst m **-e** stallion; (Kamel~, Esel~) male.

Hẹngst-: **~fohlen,** **~füllen** nt (male) foal, colt.

Hẹnkel m - handle.

Hẹnkel- in cpds with a handle; **~mann** m, pl **~männer** (col) canteen.

hẹnken vt (dated) to hang.

Hẹnker m - hangman; (Scharfrichter) executioner. **was zum ~** (col) what the devil (col); **scher dich zum ~!** (col) go to the devil! (col).

Hẹnne f **-n** hen.

hẹr adv **(a)** **von Frankreich/dem Meer ~** from France/the sea; **~ zu mir!** (col) come here (to me); **um mich ~** (all) around me; **von weit ~** from a long way off; **~ damit!** (col) give me that; **immer ~ damit!** (col) let's have it/them (then). **(b)** **von der Idee/Form ~** as far as the idea/form goes; **vom finanziellen Standpunkt ~** from the financial point of view. **(c)** (zeitlich) **ich kenne ihn von früher ~** I know him from before; **von der Schule/meiner Kindheit ~** since school/my childhood; siehe hersein (a).

herạb adv down. **die Treppe ~** down the stairs; **von oben ~** from above.

herạb- pref down; **~blicken** vi sep (lit, fig) to look down (auf +acc on); **~hängen** vi sep irreg to hang down; **~lassen** sep irreg 1 vt to let down, to lower; 2 vr (lit, fig) to lower oneself; **sich zu etw ~ lassen** to condescend or deign to do sth; **~lassend** adj condescending; **~mindern** vt sep (schlechtma-

chen) Leistung etc to belittle; (reduzieren) Geschwindigkeit, Niveau to reduce; **~sehen** vi sep irreg (lit, fig) to look down (auf +acc on); **~setzen** vt sep Ware, Preise to reduce; Niveau to lower; (schlechtmachen) Leistungen, jdn to belittle; **zu stark ~gesetzten Preisen** at greatly reduced prices; **~sinken** vi sep irreg aux sein to sink (down); (Wasserstand) to drop, to fall; **~stürzen** sep 1 vt to push off (von etw sth); 2 vi aux sein to fall off (von etw sth); (Felsbrocken) to fall down (von from); 3 vr to jump off (von etw sth); **~würdigen** sep 1 vt to disparage; 2 vr to lower oneself.

herạn adv bis an etw (acc) ~ right beside sth; (mit Bewegungsverb) right up to sth.

herạn-: **~bilden** vt sep to train (up); (in der Schule) to educate; **~bringen** vt sep irreg (herbringen) to bring over; **die Schüler an diese Probleme ~bringen** to introduce the pupils to these problems; **~eilen** vi sep aux sein to hurry over; **~führen** sep 1 vt jdn to lead up; **jdn an etw** (acc) **~führen** to introduce sb to sth; 2 vi an etw (acc) **~führen** (lit, fig) to lead to sth; **~gehen** vi sep irreg aux sein to go up (an +acc to); **ich würde nicht näher ~gehen** I wouldn't go any nearer; **an etw ~gehen** an Problem, Aufgabe to tackle sth; **~kommen** vi sep irreg aux sein (a) to draw near (an +acc to), to approach (an etw (acc) sth); **auf 1:3 ~kommen** to pull back to 1-3; **er läßt alle Probleme an sich ~kommen** he always adopts a wait-and-see attitude; **an den Chef/Motor kommt man nicht ~** you can't get hold of the boss/get at the engine; **(b)** (sich messen können) an jdn/etw **~kommen** to be up to the standard of sb/sth; **~lassen** vt sep irreg **jdn an etw** (acc) **~lassen** to let sb near sth; **er läßt keinen an sich ~** he won't let anyone near him; **~machen** vr sep (col) **sich an etw** (acc) **~machen** to get down to sth; **sich an jdn ~machen** to approach sb; an Frau to chat sb up (col); **~nahen** vi sep aux sein (geh) to approach; **~reichen** vi sep an jdn/etw **~reichen** (lit) to reach sb/sth; (fig: sich messen können) to come near sb/sth; **~reifen** vi sep aux sein (geh) to ripen; (fig) to mature; **~rücken** sep 1 vi aux sein (sich nähern) to approach (an etw (acc) sth); (dicht aufrücken) to come/go nearer (an +acc to); 2 vt to pull/push up (an +acc to); **~tragen** vt sep irreg to bring (over); **etw an jdn ~tragen** (fig) to take/bring sth to sb; **~treten** vi sep irreg aux sein (lit) to come/go up (an +acc to); **näher ~treten** to come/go nearer; **mit etw an jdn ~treten** (sich wenden an) to approach sb with sth; **~wachsen** vi sep irreg aux sein (geh) to grow; (Kind) to grow up; **die ~wachsende Generation** the rising generation; **H~wachsende(r)** mf decl as adj adolescent; **~wagen** vr sep to venture near; **sich an etw** (acc) **~wagen** to venture to tackle sth; **~ziehen** vt sep irreg (a) to draw near (an +acc to); (b) (zu Hilfe holen) to call in; Literatur to consult; etw zum Vergleich **~ziehen** to use sth by way of comparison; (c) Arbeitskräfte, Kapital to bring in.

herạuf adv up. **vom Tal ~** up from the valley; **von unten ~** up from below. 2 prep +acc up. **den Berg/die Treppe ~** up the mountain/stairs.

herạuf- pref up; **~arbeiten** vt sep (lit, fig) to work one's way up; **~beschwören*** vt sep irreg Vergangenheit to evoke; Unglück, Krise to cause; **~bringen** vt sep irreg to bring up; **~führen** sep 1 vt Pferd etc to lead up; jdn to show up; 2 vi (Weg etc) to lead up; **~kommen** vi sep irreg aux sein to come up; **~setzen** vt sep Preise etc to increase; **~steigen** vi sep irreg aux sein to climb up; (Rauch) to rise; (Erinnerungen) to well up (in jdm in sb); **~ziehen** sep irreg 1 vt to pull up; 2 vi aux sein (Gewitter, Unheil etc) to approach.

herạus adv out. **~ damit!** (col: gib her) hand it over!; **~ mit der Sprache** out with it! (col); **zum Fenster ~** out of the window; **nach vorn ~**

wohnen to live at the front; **aus dem Wunsch ~ ... out of the desire to ...**

heraus- *pref* out; ~**arbeiten** *vt sep (aus Stein, Holz)* to carve *(aus* out *of)*; *(fig)* to bring out; ~**bekommen** *vt sep irreg* **(a)** *Fleck, Nagel etc* to get out *(aus* of*)*; **(b)** *(ermitteln) Täter, Geheimnis* to find out *(aus jdm* from sb*)*; *Lösung, Aufgabe* to work out; **(c)** *Wechselgeld* to get back; ~**boxen** *vt sep (aus* of*) Ball* to punch out; *(col) jdn* to bail out *(col)*; ~**bringen** *vt sep irreg* **(a)** to bring out *(aus* of*)*; **(b)** *siehe* ~**bekommen (a, b)**; **(c)** *(auf den Markt bringen)* to bring out; **jdn/etw ganz groß** ~**bringen** *(col)* to give sb/sth a big build-up; **(d)** *(col: hervorbringen) Worte* to say; **aus ihm war kein Wort** ~**zubringen** they couldn't get a single word out of him; ~**drücken** *vt sep* to squeeze out *(aus* of*)*; ~**fahren** *sep irreg* **1** *vi aux sein* to come out *(aus* of*)*; **2** *vt* **(a)** *Auto* to drive out *(aus* of*)*; **(b)** *(Sport)* **eine gute Zeit** ~**fahren** to make good time; ~**finden** *sep irreg* **1** *vt Fehler, Täter etc* to find out; *(~lesen) Gesuchtes* to pick out *(aus* from*)*; **2** *vir* to find one's way out *(aus* of*)*.

Herausforderer *m* - challenger.

herausfordern *sep* **1** *vt* to challenge *(zu* to*)*; *(provozieren)* to provoke *(zu etw* to do sth*)*; *Kritik, Protest* to invite; *Gefahr, Unglück* to court. **das Schicksal** ~ to tempt providence. **2** *vi zu etw* ~ *(provozieren)* to invite sth.

herausfordernd *adj* provocative; *(Auseinandersetzung suchend)* Haltung, Blick challenging.

Herausforderung *f* challenge; *(Provokation)* provocation.

Herausgabe *f* **(a)** return; *(von Personen)* handing over. **(b)** *(von Buch etc)* publication.

herausgeben *sep irreg* **1** *vt* **(a)** *(zurückgeben)* to return, to give back; *Gefangene etc* to hand over. **(b)** *(veröffentlichen)* to issue; *Buch, Zeitung* to publish; *(bearbeiten)* to edit. **(c)** *(Wechselgeld geben) Betrag* to give as change. **wieviel hat er dir herausgegeben?** how much change did he give you? **(d)** *(herausreichen)* to hand out *(aus* of*)*. **2** *vi (Wechselgeld geben)* to give change *(auf* +acc for*)*. **können Sie (mir)** ~? can you give me change?; **falsch** ~ to give the wrong change.

Herausgeber(in *f)* *m (Verleger)* publisher; *(Redakteur)* editor.

heraus-: ~**gehen** *vi sep irreg aux sein (aus* of*)* to go out; *(Fleck, Korken etc)* to come out; **aus sich** ~ **gehen** *(fig)* to come out of one's shell; ~**greifen** *vt sep irreg* to pick out *(aus* of*)*; *Beispiel* to take; ~**haben** *vt sep irreg (col)* **(a) ich will ihn aus der Firma** ~**haben** I want him out of the firm; **(b)** *Rätsel, Aufgabe* to have solved; *Geheimnis* to have found out; ~**halten** *sep irreg* **1** *vt* **(a)** *Hand, Gegenstand* to put out *(aus* of*)*; **(b)** *(fernhalten) Tiere, Eindringlinge* to keep out *(aus* of*)*; **2** *vr* to keep out of it; ~**holen** *vt sep* **(a)** *(aus* of*)* to get out; *(~bringen)* to bring out; **(b)** *(fig col)* Antwort, Geheimnis to get out *(aus* of*)*; *Vorteil, Sieg* to gain *(aus* from*)*; *Zeit* to make up; *Ergebnis* to get; ~**hören** *vt sep (wahrnehmen)* to hear; *(fühlen)* to detect *(aus* in*)*; ~**kehren** *vt sep (lit)* to sweep out *(aus* of*)*; *(fig: betonen)* to parade; **den Vorgesetzten** ~**kehren** to act the boss.

herauskommen *vi sep irreg aux sein* **(a)** *(lit, fig)* to come out *(aus* of*)*; *(Schwindel etc)* to come to light. **er ist nie aus seinem Dorf herausgekommen** he has never been out of his village; **aus sich** ~ to come out of one's shell; **er kam aus dem Staunen nicht heraus** he couldn't get over his astonishment; **aus einer schwierigen Lage** ~ to get out of a difficult situation; **aus seinen Schwierigkeiten** ~ to get over one's difficulties. **(b)** *(Resultat haben)* **bei etw** ~ to come of sth; **und was soll dabei** ~? and what is that supposed to achieve?, and where is that supposed to get us?; **es kommt auf dasselbe heraus** it comes (down) to the same thing. **(c)** *(Cards)* to lead.

heraus-: ~**kriegen** *vt sep (col) siehe* ~**bekommen;** ~**lesen** *vt sep irreg* **(a)** *(erkennen)* to gather *(aus* from*)*; **(b)** *(aussondern)* to pick out *(aus* from*)*; ~**locken** *vt sep* to entice out *(aus* of*)*; **etw aus jdm** ~**locken** *(ablisten)* to get sth out of sb; ~**machen** *sep (col)* **1** *vt (aus* of*)* to take out; *Fleck* to get out; **2** *vr (sich gut entwickeln)* to come on (well); *(nach Krankheit)* to pick up; ~**nehmbar** *adj* removable; ~**nehmen** *vt sep irreg* **(a)** to take out *(aus* of*)*; *Kind (aus der Schule etc)* to take away *(aus* from*)*; **sich** *(dat)* **die Mandeln** ~**nehmen lassen** to have one's tonsils out; **den Gang** ~**nehmen** *(Aut)* to put the car into neutral; **(b)** *(col: sich erlauben)* **sich** *(dat)* **Freiheiten** ~**nehmen** to take liberties; **Sie nehmen sich zuviel** ~ you're going too far; ~**platzen** *vi sep aux sein (col) (spontan sagen)* to blurt it out; *(lachen)* to burst out laughing; ~**putzen** *vt sep jdn* to dress up; *Stadt, Wohnung etc* to deck out; **sich** ~**putzen** to get dressed up; ~**ragen** *vi sep siehe* **hervorragen;** ~**reden** *vr sep* to talk one's way out of it *(col)*; ~**reißen** *vt sep irreg* **(a)** *(lit) (aus* of*)* to tear out; *Zahn, Baum* to pull out; **(b) jdn aus etw** ~**reißen** *(aus Umgebung)* to tear sb away from sth; *(aus Schlaf)* to startle sb out of sth; *(col: aus Schwierigkeiten)* to get sb out of sth *(col)*; ~**rücken** *sep* **1** *vt* to push out *(aus* of*)*; *(col: hergeben) Geld* to cough up *(col)*; *Beute, Gegenstand* to hand over; **2** *vi aux sein* **(a)** *(lit)* to move out; **(b)** *(col: hergeben)* **mit etw** ~**rücken** *(mit Geld)* to cough sth up *(col)*; *(mit Beute)* to hand sth over; *(col: aussprechen)* to come out with sth; ~**rutschen** *vi sep aux sein (lit, fig)* to slip out *(aus* of*)*; **das ist mir nur so** ~**gerutscht** it just slipped out somehow; ~**schauen** *vi sep (dial)* **(a)** *(Mensch)* to look out *(aus* of*)*; **(b)** *(zu sehen sein)* to show; **(c) was schaut dabei (für mich)** ~? what's in it for me? *(col)*; ~**schlagen** *sep irreg* **1** *vt* **(a)** *(lit)* to knock out *(aus* of*)*; **(b)** *(col) Geld* to make; *Gewinn, Vorteil* to get; *Zeit* to gain; **2** *vi aux sein (Flammen)* to shoot out; ~**schleudern** *vt sep (werfen)* to hurl out *(aus* of*)*; *(fig) Fragen, Vorwürfe* to burst out with; ~**schmecken** *vt sep* to taste; ~**schmeißen** *vt sep irreg (col: lit, fig)* to chuck out *(aus* of*)*.

heraussein *vi sep irreg aux sein (col)* to be out; *(bekannt sein)* to be known; *(entschieden sein)* to have been settled; *(Gesetz)* to be in force. **aus dem Gröbsten** ~ to be over the worst.

heraus-: ~**springen** *vi sep irreg aux sein (col)* **(a)** *(lit)* to jump or leap out; **(b)** *(sich lösen)* to come out; **(c)** *(col) siehe* ~**schauen (c);** ~**stellen** *sep* **1** *vt* **(a)** *(lit)* to put outside; **(b)** *(fig: hervorheben)* to emphasize, to underline; *jdn* to give prominence to; **2** *vr (Wahrheit)* to come to light; **sich als falsch/richtig** ~**stellen** to prove to be wrong/correct; **es stellte sich** ~, **daß** ... it turned out or emerged that ...; **das muß sich erst** ~**stellen** that remains to be seen; ~**strecken** *vt sep* to stick out *(zu, aus* of*)*; ~**streichen** *vt sep irreg* **(a)** *Fehler etc* to cross out, to delete *(aus* in*)*; **(b)** *(betonen) Verdienste etc* to stress; ~**stürzen** *vi sep aux sein (eilen)* to rush out *(aus* of*)*; ~**suchen** *vt sep* to pick out; ~**treten** *vi sep irreg aux sein* to come out *(aus* of*)*, to emerge *(aus* from*)*; *(Adern etc)* to stand out; ~**winden** *vr sep irreg (fig)* **sich aus etw** ~**winden** to wriggle out of sth; ~**wollen** *vi sep* to want to get out *(aus* of*)*; **nicht mit etw** ~**wollen** *(col: sagen wollen)* not to want to come out with sth *(col)*; ~**ziehen** *vt sep irreg* to pull out *(aus* of*)*; *(~schleppen)* to drag out *(aus* of*)*.

herb *adj Geruch* sharp; *Parfüm* tangy; *Wein* dry; *Enttäuschung, Verlust* bitter; *Worte, Kritik* harsh.

herbei-: ~**eilen** *vi sep aux sein* to hurry or rush over; ~**führen** *vt sep* to bring about; ~**holen** *vt sep* to bring; *Arzt, Polizisten* to fetch; ~**laufen** *vi sep irreg aux sein* to come running up; ~**rufen** *vt sep irreg* to call over; *Verstärkung* to call in; *Arzt, Polizei* to call; ~**schaffen** *vt sep* to bring; *Geld* to get hold of; *Beweise* to produce; ~**sehnen** *vt sep* to long for; ~**strömen** vi sep aux sein to come flocking.

Herberge f -n no pl lodging no indef art; (Jugend~) (youth) hostel.

Herbergs-: ~**mutter** f/~**vater** m (youth hostel) warden.

her-: ~**bestellen*** vt sep (col) to send for; ~**bitten** vt sep irreg to ask to come; ~**bringen** vt sep irreg to bring (here).

Herbst m -e autumn, fall (US). **im** ~ in autumn, in the fall (US).

Herbst- in cpds autumn, fall (US); ~**anfang** m beginning of autumn or fall (US); ~**ferien** pl autumn or fall (US) holiday(s); (Sch) half-term holiday(s); **h**~**lich** adj autumn attr, fall attr (US); **das Wetter ist h**~**lich kühl** the cooler days of autumn or fall (US) are upon us.

Herd m -e **(a)** (Küchen~) cooker, stove; (Kohle~) range. **(b)** (Krankheits~) focus; (von Erdbeben) epicentre (Brit), epicenter (US); (fig: von Rebellion etc) seat.

Herde f -n (lit) herd; (von Schafen) flock. **der** ~ **folgen** (pej) to follow the herd.

Herdentrieb m (lit, fig pej) herd instinct.

Herdplatte f (von Elektroherd) hotplate.

herein adv in. ~! come in!; **hier** ~! in here!; **von (dr)außen** ~ from outside.

herein- pref in; ~**bekommen** vt sep irreg (col) Waren to get in; Radiosender to get; Unkosten etc to recover; ~**bitten** vt sep irreg to ask (to come) in; ~**brechen** vi sep irreg aux sein (Wasser, Flut) to gush in; **das Unglück brach über ihn** ~ misfortune overtook him; ~**bringen** vt sep irreg **(a)** to bring in; **(b)** (col) Geldverlust to make good; Zeit-, Produktionsverlust to make up for; ~**drängen** vir sep to push one's way in; ~**dringen** vi sep irreg aux sein (Licht, Wasser) to come in (in+acc -to); **ein Geräusch drang ins Zimmer** ~ a sound was heard in the room; ~**fallen** vi sep irreg aux sein **(a)** to fall in (in+acc -to); **(b)** (col) to fall for it (col); (betrogen werden) to be had (col); **auf jdn/etw** ~**fallen** to be taken in by sb/sth; **mit jdm/etw** ~**fallen** to have a bad deal with sb/sth; ~**führen** vt sep to show in; ~**holen** vt sep to bring in (in +acc -to); ~**kommen** vi sep irreg aux sein to come in (in+acc -to); **wie ist er** ~**gekommen?** how did he get in?; ~**lassen** vt sep irreg to let in (in+acc -to); ~**legen** vt sep (col) jdn ~**legen** to take sb for a ride (col); ~**platzen** vi sep aux sein (col) to burst in (in+acc -to); **bei jdm** ~**platzen** to burst in on sb; ~**regnen** vi impers sep **es regnet** ~ the rain is coming in; ~**schauen** vi sep (dial) to look in (in +acc -to); **(bei jdm)** ~**schauen** (col) to look sb up; ~**schneien** sep 1 vi impers **es schneit** ~ the snow's coming in; 2 vi aux sein (col) to drop in (col); ~**spazieren*** vi sep aux sein to breeze in (in +acc -to); ~**spaziert!** come right in!; ~**strömen** vi sep aux sein (in+acc -to) to stream in; ~**stürmen** vi sep aux sein to storm in (in +acc -to); ~**stürzen** vi sep aux sein to rush in (in+acc -to).

Her-: **h**~**fahren** sep irreg 1 vi aux sein to come here; **hinter jdm h**~**fahren** to drive along behind sb; 2 vt to drive here; ~**fahrt** f journey here; **h**~**fallen** vi sep irreg aux sein **über jdn h**~**fallen** to attack sb; (kritisieren) to pull sb to pieces; **über etw** (acc) **h**~**fallen** to descend upon sth; **über Eßbares** etc to pounce upon sth; **h**~**finden** vi sep irreg (col) to find one's way here.

Hergang m no pl (von Schlacht) course. **der** ~ **des Unfalls** the way the accident happened.

her-: ~**geben** sep irreg 1 vt (weggeben) to give away; (aushändigen) to hand over; (zurückgeben) to give back; **gib das** ~! give me that; **viel/wenig** ~**geben** (col: erbringen) to be a lot of use/not to be much use; **das Thema gibt viel/nichts** ~ there's a lot/nothing to this topic; **was seine Beine** ~**gaben** as fast as his legs would carry him; **seinen Namen für etw** ~**geben** to lend one's

name to sth; 2 vr **sich zu etw** ~**geben** to be a party to sth; ~**gebracht** adj **in** ~**gebrachter Weise** in the traditional way; ~**gehen** sep irreg aux sein 1 vi **(a) hinter/neben jdm** ~**gehen** to walk along behind/beside sb; **(b)** ~**gehen und etw tun** (einfach tun) just to go and do sth; 2 vi impers (col: zugehen) **es ging heiß** ~ things got heated; **hier geht es hoch** ~ there's plenty going on here; ~**gehören*** vi sep to belong here; ~**gelaufen** adj attr (pej) siehe **dahergelaufen;** ~**haben** vt sep irreg (col) **wo hat er das** ~? where did he get that from?; ~**halten** vi sep irreg **für etw** ~**halten** to pay for sth; **als Entschuldigung für etw** ~**halten** to be used as an excuse for sth; ~**holen** vt sep (col) to fetch; ~**holen lassen** to send for; **weit** ~**geholt sein** (fig) to be far-fetched; ~**hören** vi sep (col) to listen; **alle mal** ~**hören!** everybody listen.

Hering m -e **(a)** herring; (col: Schwächling) weakling. **wie die** ~**e zusammengedrängt** packed in like sardines. **(b)** (Zeltpflock) (tent) peg (Brit) or stake (US).

her-: ~**kommen** vi sep irreg aux sein to come here; (sich nähern) to come, to approach; (~stammen) to come from; ~**kömmlich** adj conventional.

Herkunft f no pl origin; (soziale) background. **er ist britischer** (gen) ~ he is of British origin.

Herkunftsland nt (Comm) country of origin.

her-: ~**laufen** vi sep irreg aux sein to come running; **hinter jdm** ~**laufen** (lit, fig) to run after sb; ~**leiten** sep 1 vt (folgern) to derive (aus from); 2 vr sich von etw ~**leiten** to be derived from sth; ~**locken** vt sep to entice, to lure; ~**machen** sep (col) 1 vr **sich über etw** (acc) ~**machen** (in Angriff nehmen) Arbeit, Essen to get stuck into sth (col); (Besitz ergreifen) to pounce (up)on sth; **sich über jdn** ~**machen** to lay into sb (col); 2 vt **viel** ~**machen** to look impressive.

Hermelin m -e (Pelz) ermine.

hermetisch adj hermetic. ~ **abgeriegelt** completely sealed off.

her-: ~**müssen** vi sep irreg (col) **(a) das muß** ~ I/we have to have it; **(b)** (kommen müssen) to have to come (here); **hinter jdm** ~**müssen** to have to go after sb; ~**nehmen** vt sep irreg (beschaffen) to get, to find. **wo soll ich das** ~**nehmen?** where am I supposed to get that from?

Heroin [hero'iːn] nt no pl heroin.

heroisch [he'roːɪʃ] adj (geh) heroic.

Herr m (wk) -(e)n, -en **(a)** (Gebieter) lord, master; (Herrscher) ruler (über +acc of); (von Hund) master. **die** ~**en der Schöpfung** (hum: Männer) the gentlemen; **sein eigener** ~ **sein** to be one's own master or boss; ~ **der Lage bleiben** to remain master of the situation; **über jdn/etw** ~ **werden** to master sb/sth; **niemand kann zwei** ~**en dienen** (prov) no man can serve two masters (prov).
(b) (Gott, Christus) Lord. **Gott, der** ~ the Lord God.
(c) (feiner ~, Mann) gentleman. „~**en"** (Toilette) "gentlemen" (Brit), "men's room" (US).
(d) (vor Eigennamen) Mr. **mein** ~! sir!; **der** ~ **wünscht?** what can I do for you, sir?; **ja,** ~ **Doktor/Professor** yes, Doctor/Professor; ~ **Präsident/Vorsitzender** Mr President/Chairman; **der** ~ **Präsident/Vorsitzende** the President/Chairman; **lieber** ~ **A, sehr geehrter** ~ **A** (in Brief) Dear Mr A; **sehr geehrte** ~**en** (in Brief) Dear Sirs.

Herrchen nt (col: von Hund) master.

Herren- in cpds men's; (auf einzelnes Exemplar bezüglich) man's; ~**abend** m stag night; ~**ausstatter** m - men's outfitter; ~**begleitung** f in ~**begleitung** in the company of a gentleman; ~**bekleidung** f menswear; ~**besuch** m gentleman visitor/visitors; ~**friseur** m men's hairdresser, barber; ~**haus** nt manor house; **h**~**los** adj abandoned; Hund etc stray; ~**toilette** f men's room (US), gents sing (Brit).

Herrgott m (dated col) (Anrede) God, Lord. **der ~ the Lord** (God); **~ noch mal!** (col) damn it all! (col).

Herrgottsfrühe f: **in aller ~** (col) at the crack of dawn.

herrichten sep 1 vt (a) (vorbereiten) to get ready (dat, für for); Bett to make; Tisch to set. (b) (instand setzen) to do up (col).2 vr (dial) to get dressed up.

Herrin f (Hist) female ruler; (von Hund) mistress.

herrisch adj overbearing, imperious.

herrje, herrjemine interj goodness gracious.

herrlich adj marvellous (Brit), marvelous (US); Kleid gorgeous, lovely. **wir haben uns ~ amüsiert** we had marvellous fun.

Herrlichkeit f (a) no pl (Pracht) magnificence, splendour (Brit), splendor (US). **die ~ Gottes** the glory of God. (b) usu pl (Gegenstand) treasure.

Herrschaft f (a) (Macht) power; (Staatsgewalt) rule; (Kontrolle) control. **sich der ~ bemächtigen** to seize power; **unter der ~** under the rule (gen, von of); **er verlor die ~ über sich** he lost his self-control; **er verlor die ~ über sein Auto** he lost control of his car. (b) **die ~en** (Damen und Herren) the ladies and gentlemen; **(meine) ~en!** ladies and gentlemen.

herrschaftlich adj (vornehm) grand.

Herrschafts-: ~anspruch m claim to power; **~bereich** m territory.

herrschen 1 vi (a) (über etw (acc) sth) to rule; (König) to reign; (fig: Mensch) to dominate. (b) (vor~) (Angst, Ungewißheit) to prevail; (Krankheit) to be rampant. **überall herrschte Freude** there was joy everywhere; **im Zimmer herrschte bedrückende Stille** it was oppressively quiet in the room; **hier ~ ja Zustände!** things are in a pretty state around here! 2 vi impers **es herrscht schlechtes Wetter** we're having bad weather; **es herrscht Ungewißheit darüber, ob** ... there is uncertainty about whether ...

herrschend adj Partei, Klasse ruling; König reigning; Verhältnisse, Meinungen prevailing; Mode current.

Herrscher(in f) m - ruler (über+acc of).

Herrscher-: ~geschlecht nt ruling dynasty; **~haus** nt ruling house.

Herrschsucht f domineeringness.

herrschsüchtig adj domineering.

her-: ~rufen vt sep irreg to call (over); **~rühren** vi sep von etw **~rühren** to be due to sth, to stem from sth; **~sagen** vt sep to recite; **~sehen** vi sep irreg (a) to look this way; (b) **hinter jdm/etw ~sehen** to follow sb with one's eyes; **~sein** vi sep irreg aux sein (a) **das ist schon 5 Jahre ~** that was 5 years ago; **wie lange ist es ~?** how long ago was it?; (b) (~stammen) to come from; **mit jdm/etw ist es nicht weit ~** (col) sb/sth is not up to much (col); (c) **hinter jdm/etw ~sein** to be after sb/sth; **~stammen** vi sep (a) **wo stammst du ~?** where do you come from?; (b) (~rühren) **von etw ~stammen** to stem from sth.

herstellen vt sep (a) (erzeugen) to produce; (industriell auch) to manufacture. **in Deutschland hergestellt** made in Germany. (b) (zustande bringen) to establish; (Telec) Verbindung to make; Stromkreis to complete. (c) (gesundheitlich) jdn to restore to health. **er ist wieder ganz hergestellt** he has quite recovered.

Hersteller(in f) m - (Produzent) manufacturer.

Herstellung f no pl siehe vt (a) production; manufacture. (b) establishment; making; completion.

Herstellungs-: ~kosten pl manufacturing or production costs pl; **~land** nt country of manufacture.

hertragen vt sep irreg (col) (an bestimmten Ort) to carry here. **etw hinter jdm ~** to carry sth

behind sb.

herüber adv (hierher) over here; (über Straße, Grenze) across.

herüber- pref over; (über Straße, Grenze) across; **~fahren** sep irreg 1 vi aux sein **er ist gestern ~gefahren** he came or (mit Auto) drove across yesterday; 2 vt Fahrgast, Güter to take over/ across; **~holen** vt sep to fetch; **~kommen** vi sep irreg aux sein to come over/across (über etw (acc) sth); (col: zu Nachbarn) to pop round (col); **~reichen** sep 1 vt to pass (über+acc over); 2 vi to reach across (über etw (acc) sth); **~retten** vt sep etw **in die Gegenwart ~retten** to preserve sth; **~wechseln** vi sep aux sein or haben **in unsere Partei ~wechseln** to swap over to our party; **~ziehen** sep irreg (über etw (acc) sth) 1 vt to pull over/across; (fig) to win over; 2 vi aux sein (Truppen, Wolken) to move over/across.

herum adv um Ulm **~** around Ulm; **um 50 ~** around 50; **links/rechts ~** around to the left/ right; **hier/dort ~** around here/there; **oben ~** (über Gegenstand, Berg) over the top; (in bezug auf Körper) around the top; **unten ~** (unter Gegenstand) underneath; (um Berg, in bezug auf Körper) around the bottom.

herum- pref around; siehe auch umher-; **~ärgern** vr sep (col) **sich mit jdm/etw ~ärgern** to keep struggling with sb/sth; **~basteln** vi sep (col) to tinker about (an+dat with); **~bekommen** vt sep irreg (col) jdn to talk round; **~blättern** vi sep (in einem Buch) **~blättern** to browse through a book; **~bummeln** vi sep (col) (a) (trödeln) to mess about (col); (b) aux sein (spazieren) to stroll around (in etw/dat) sth); **~doktern** vi sep (col) an jdm/einer Krankheit **~doktern** to try to cure sb/an illness; **~drehen** sep 1 vt to turn; jdm das Wort im Mund **~drehen** to twist sb's words; 2 vr to turn around; (im Liegen) to turn over; 3 vi (col) **an etw** (dat) **~drehen** to fiddle about with sth; **~drücken** vr sep (a) (sich aufhalten) to hang around (col) (um etw sth); (b) (vermeiden) **sich um etw ~drücken** to dodge sth; **~erzählen** vt sep **erzähl das nicht ~** don't spread it around; **~fahren** sep irreg 1 vi aux sein (a) to travel or (mit Auto) drive around; (b) (sich rasch umdrehen) to spin around; 2 vt to drive around; **~fragen** vi sep (col) to ask around (bei among); **~fuchteln** vi sep (col) (mit den Händen) **~fuchteln** to wave one's hands around; **~führen** sep 1 vt to lead around (um etw sth); (bei Besichtigung) to take or show around; 2 vi **um etw ~führen** to go around sth; **~fuhrwerken** vi sep (col) to bustle about; **~fummeln** vi sep (col) (an+dat with) to fiddle about; (basteln) to tinker (about); **~gammeln** vi sep (col) to bum around (col); **~gehen** vi sep irreg aux sein (col) (a) to go around (um etw sth); (b) (ziellos) to wander around (in etw (dat) sth); **es ging ihm im Kopf ~** it went round and round in his head; (c) (~gereicht werden) to be passed around; etw **~gehen lassen** to circulate sth; (d) Zeit to pass; **~geistern** vi sep aux sein (col) (Gespenster etc) to haunt (in etw (dat) sth); (Mensch) to wander around; **~hacken** vi sep (col) **auf jdm ~hacken** to pick on sb (col); **~hängen** vi sep irreg (col) (a) to hang around; (b) (sich lümmeln) to loll about; (c) (ständig zu finden sein) to hang out (col); **~kommen** vi sep irreg aux sein (col) (a) (um eine Ecke etc) to come around (um etw sth); (b) (~gehen können) to get around (um etw sth); (c) (vermeiden können) **um etw ~kommen** to get out of sth; (d) **er ist viel ~gekommen** he has been around a lot; **~kriegen** vt sep (col) jdn to talk around; **~laufen** vi sep irreg aux sein (col) to run or (gehen) walk around (um etw sth); **~lungern** vi sep (col) to hang around; **~machen** sep (col) 1 vi **an etw** (dat) **~machen** (sich beschäftigen) to fuss about sth; (~fingern) to pick at sth; 2 vt to put around (um etw sth); **~nörgeln** vi sep **an jdm/etw**

~**nörgeln** to find fault with sb/sth; ~**quälen** *vr sep (col)* to struggle; **sich mit Rheuma** ~**quälen** to be plagued by rheumatism; ~**reden** *vi sep (col)* to chat away; **um etw** ~**reden** *(ausweichend)* to talk around sth; ~**reißen** *vt sep irreg* to swing around (hard); **das Steuer** ~**reißen** *(fig)* to change course; ~**reiten** *vi sep irreg (fig col)* **auf jdm/etw** ~**reiten** to keep on at sb/about sth; ~**schlagen** *sep irreg* 1 *vt Papier, Tuch* to wrap around *(um etw* sth); 2 *vr (col)* **sich mit jdm/etw** ~**schlagen** *(fig)* to struggle with sb/sth; ~**schleppen** *vt sep (col) Sachen* to lug around *(col)*; **jdn** to drag around; **etw mit sich** ~**schleppen** *Sorge, Problem* to be troubled by sth; *Krankheit* to have sth; ~**schnüffeln** *vi sep (col)* to sniff around *(in etw (dat)* sth); *(fig)* to snoop around *(in+dat* in); ~**schreien** *vi sep irreg (col)* to shout out loud; ~**sein** *vi sep irreg aux sein (col)* **(a)** *(vorüber sein)* to be past *or* over; **(b)** *(in jds Nähe sein)* **um jdn** ~**sein** to be around sb; ~**sprechen** *vr sep irreg* to get about; ~**stehen** *vi sep irreg aux sein (Sachen)* to be lying around; *(Menschen)* to stand around *(um jdn/etw* sb/sth); ~**stochern** *vi sep (col)* to poke about; **im Essen** ~**stochern** to pick at one's food; ~**streiten** *vr sep irreg (col)* to squabble; ~**tragen** *vt sep irreg (col)* **(a)** to carry about; **Sorgen mit sich** ~**tragen** to have worries; **(b)** *(weitererzählen)* to spread around; ~**treiben** *vr sep irreg (col) (sich aufhalten)* to hang around *(in +dat* in) *(col)*; *(liederlich leben)* to hang around in bad places/ company.

Herumtreiber(in *f) m - (pej)* tramp.

herum-: ~**wälzen** *vr sep* to roll around; **sich (schlaflos) im Bett** ~**wälzen** to toss and turn; ~**werfen** *sep irreg* 1 *vt* **(a)** *(col)* to throw around *(in etw (dat)* sth); **(b)** *Kopf* to turn (quickly); *Steuer* to throw around; 2 *vr* **sich (im Bett)** ~**werfen** to toss and turn (in bed); ~**wursteln** *vi sep (col)* to fiddle around *(an +dat* with) *(col)*; ~**ziehen** *sep irreg* 1 *vi aux sein* to move around; **in der Welt** ~**ziehen** to roam the world; 2 *vt* **etw mit sich** ~**ziehen** to take sth around with one.

herunter 1 *adv* down. ~! get down!; ~ **mit ihm** get him down; ~ **damit** get it down; *(in bezug auf Kleider)* get it off. 2 *prep +acc* **den Berg** ~ down the mountain.

herunter- *pref* down; *siehe auch herab-;* ~**bekommen** *vt sep irreg siehe* ~**kriegen;** ~**bringen** *vt sep irreg* **(a)** to bring down; **(b)** *(col) siehe* ~**kriegen;** ~**drücken** *vt sep* to press down; *Preise* to force down; *Niveau* to lower; ~**fallen** *vi sep irreg aux sein* to fall down; **von etw** ~**fallen** to fall off sth; ~**gehen** *vi sep irreg aux sein* to go down; *(Temperatur, Preise auch)* to drop; **mit den Preisen** ~**gehen** to lower one's prices; ~**gekommen** *adj Haus* dilapidated; *Stadt* run-down; *Mensch* down-at-heel; ~**handeln** *vt sep (col) Preis* to beat down; **etw um 20 Mark** ~**handeln** to get 20 marks knocked off sth; ~**hauen** *vt sep irreg (col)* **jdm eine** ~**hauen** to give sb a clip around the ear *(col)*; ~**holen** *vt sep* to fetch down; *(col) Vogel, Flugzeug* to bring down; ~**klappen** *vt sep Kragen* to turn down; *Sitz* to fold down; *Deckel* to close; ~**kommen** *vi sep irreg aux sein* **(a)** to come down; *(fig col: verfallen) Stadt, Firma)* to go downhill; *(gesundheitlich)* to become run-down; *siehe* ~**gekommen;** ~**können** *vi sep irreg* to be able to get down; ~**kriegen** *vt sep (col)* *(~holen, schlucken können)* to get down; *(abmachen können)* to get off; ~**lassen** *sep irreg vt Gegenstand* to let down; *Hose* to take down; ~**leiern** *vt sep (col)* to reel off; ~**machen** *vt sep (col)* **(a)** *(schlechtmachen)* to run down, to knock *(col)*; **(b)** *(zurechtweisen)* to tell off; **(c)** *(abmachen)* to take down; *Farbe, Dreck* to take off; ~**nehmen** *vt sep irreg* to take down; *(col: von Schule)* to take away; ~**putzen** *vt sep (col)* **jdn** ~**putzen** to tear sb off a strip *(col)*; ~**rasseln** *vt*

sep (col) to rattle off; ~**reißen** *vt sep irreg (col)* **(a)** to pull down; **(b)** *(abreißen)* to pull off; ~**schlucken** *vt sep* to swallow; ~**schrauben** *vt sep (lit) Deckel* to screw off; *(fig) Ansprüche, Niveau* to lower; ~**sehen** *vi sep irreg (lit, fig)* to look down *(auf +acc* on); ~**sein** *vi sep irreg aux sein (col)* **(a)** to be down; *(abgeschnitten sein)* to be (cut) off; **(b)** **mit den Nerven/der Gesundheit** ~**sein** to be at the end of one's tether/to be run-down; ~**setzen** *vt sep (col) siehe* **herabsetzen;** ~**spielen** *vt sep (col) Problem, Vorfall* to play down; ~**wirtschaften** *vt sep (col)* to bring to the brink of ruin; ~**wollen** *vi sep (col)* to want to get down; ~**ziehen** *vt sep irreg* to pull down.

hervor *adv aus etw* ~ out of sth; **hinter dem Tisch** ~ out from behind the table.

hervor-: ~**bringen** *vt sep irreg* **(a)** *Blüten* to produce; *Worte* to utter; **(b)** *(verursachen)* to create; ~**gehen** *vi sep irreg aux sein* **(a)** *(geh: entstammen)* to come *(aus* from); **(b)** **daraus geht** ~, **daß** ... from this it follows that ...; **(c)** **als Sieger** ~**gehen** to emerge victorious; ~**heben** *vt sep irreg* to emphasize; ~**ragen** *vi sep* to jut out, to project; *(fig: sich auszeichnen)* to stand out; ~**ragend** *adj (ausgezeichnet)* outstanding; **er hat H**~**ragendes geleistet** his achievement was outstanding; **das hat** ~**ragend geklappt** it worked beautifully; ~**rufen** *vt sep irreg* **(a)** **jdn** ~**rufen** to call sb out; *(Theat etc)* to call for sb; **(b)** *(bewirken) Bewunderung* to arouse; *Reaktion, Krankheit* to cause; ~**stechen** *vi sep irreg aux sein (lit, fig)* to stand out; ~**stechend** *adj* striking; ~**stoßen** *vt sep irreg Worte* to gasp (out); ~**treten** *vi sep irreg aux sein* **(a)** *(heraustreten)* to emerge *(hinter +dat* from behind); *(Backenknochen)* to protrude; *(Adern)* to bulge; **(b)** *(sichtbar werden)* to stand out; ~**tun** *vr sep irreg* to distinguish oneself; *(col: sich wichtig tun)* to show off *(mit etw* sth); ~**wagen** *vr sep* to dare to come out; ~**zaubern** *vt sep (lit, fig)* to conjure up; ~**ziehen** *vt sep irreg* to pull out *(unter +dat* from under).

Herweg *m* way here.

Herz *nt -ens, -en* **(a)** *(lit, fig)* heart. **mir schlug das** ~ **bis zum Hals** my heart was pounding; **die** ~**en höher schlagen lassen** to make people's hearts beat faster; **ein goldenes** ~ a heart of gold; **schweren** ~**ens** with a heavy heart; **es gab mir einen Stich ins** ~ it hurt me; **seinem** ~**en Luft machen** to give vent to one's feelings; **sich** *(dat)* **etw vom** ~**en reden** to get sth off one's chest; **du sprichst mir aus dem** ~**en** that's just what I feel; **jdm das** ~ **schwer machen** to sadden sb; **im Grund seines** ~**ens** in his heart of hearts; **aus tiefstem** ~**en** from the bottom of one's heart; **mit ganzem** ~**en** wholeheartedly; **ich weiß, wie es dir ums** ~ **ist** I know how you feel; **jdm sein** ~ **schenken** to give sb one's heart; **dieser alte Hund ist mir ans** ~ **gewachsen** I have grown fond of this old dog; **er hat sie in sein** ~ **geschlossen** he has grown fond of her; **sein** ~ **an jdn/etw hängen** to commit oneself heart and soul to sb/sth; **sich** *(dat)* **ein** ~ **fassen** to take heart; **ihm rutschte das** ~ **in die Hose** *(col)* his heart sank; **ein** ~ **und eine Seele sein** to be the best of friends; **alles, was das** ~ **begehrt** everything one's heart desires; **er hat das** ~ **auf dem rechten Fleck** his heart is in the right place; **es liegt mir am** ~ I am very concerned about it; **jdm etw ans** ~ **legen** to entrust sth to sb; **etw auf dem** ~**en haben** to have sth on one's mind; **jdm/etw auf** ~ **und Nieren prüfen** to examine sb/sth very thoroughly; **eine schwere Last fiel ihr vom** ~**en** a heavy load was lifted from her mind; **von** ~**en** with all one's heart; **etw von** ~**en gern tun** to love doing sth; **von** ~**en kommend** heartfelt; **sich** *(dat)* **etw zu** ~**en nehmen** to take sth to heart.

(b) *pl - (Cards) (no pl: Farbe)* hearts *pl; (Karte)* heart.

Herz- in cpds (Anat, Med) cardiac; ~**anfall** m heart attack; ~**beschwerden** pl heart trouble sing; **h~bewegend** adj heart-rending.

Herzchen nt (col: Kosewort) darling.

herzeigen vt sep to show. **zeig (mal) her!** let's see; **das kann man ~** that's worth showing off.

Herzens-: ~**bedürfnis** nt (dated) **es ist mir ein** ~**bedürfnis** it is a matter dear to my heart; ~**brecher** m - (fig col) heart-breaker; **h~gut** adj good-hearted; ~**lust** f **nach** ~**lust** to one's heart's content; ~**wunsch** m dearest wish.

Herz-: **h~erfrischend** adj refreshing; **h~ergreifend, h~erweichend** adj heart-rending; ~**fehler** m heart defect; **h~förmig** adj heart-shaped; **h~haft** adj (kräftig) hearty; Händedruck, Griff firm; Geschmack strong; **alle langten h~haft zu** everyone got stuck in (col); **das schmeckt h~haft** that's tasty.

herziehen sep irreg **1** vt to pull closer. **jdn/etw hinter sich** (dat) ~ to pull sb/sth (along) behind one. **2** vi aux sein **(a)** hinter jdm ~ to march along behind sb. **(b)** über jdn/etw ~ (col) to pull sb/sth to pieces (col).

Herz-: ~**infarkt** m heart attack; ~**kammer** f ventricle; ~**klappe** f (heart) valve; ~**klopfen** nt no pl **ich hatte/bekam** ~**klopfen** my heart was/started pounding; (durch Kaffee etc) I had/got palpitations; **mit** ~**klopfen** with a pounding heart; **h~krank** adj suffering from a heart condition; ~**kranzgefäß** nt usu pl coronary (blood) vessel; ~**leiden** nt heart condition.

herzlich 1 adj Empfang, Mensch warm; Lachen hearty; Bitte sincere. ~**e Grüße an ...** remember me to ...; **mit** ~**en Grüßen** kind regards; ~**en Dank!** thank you very much indeed; ~**es Beileid!** you have my deepest sympathy. **2** adv (sehr) ~ **gern!** with the greatest of pleasure!; ~ **schlecht** pretty awful; ~ **wenig** precious little; **ich habe es** ~ **satt** I'm sick and tired of it.

Herzlichkeit f siehe adj warmth; heartiness; sincerity.

Herz-: **h~los** adj heartless; ~**losigkeit** f heartlessness no pl; ~**mittel** nt cardiac drug.

Herzog ['hɛrtsoːk] m ‡e duke.

Herzogin ['hɛrtsoːgɪn] f duchess.

Herzogtum nt dukedom, duchy.

Herz-: ~**schlag** m (einzelner) heartbeat; (~tätigkeit) heart rate; (~stillstand) heart failure no indef art; ~**schrittmacher** m pacemaker; ~**schwäche** f an ~**schwäche leiden** to have a weak heart; **h~stärkend** adj **ein h~stärkendes Mittel** a cardiac stimulant; **h~zerreißend** adj heartbreaking.

Hessen nt Hesse.

hessisch adj Hessian.

hetero-: ~**gen** adj (geh) heterogeneous; ~**sexuell** adj heterosexual.

Hetze f no pl **(a)** (Hast) (mad) rush, hurry. **(b)** (pej: ~kampagne) smear campaign.

hetzen 1 vt **(a)** (lit, fig: jagen) to hound. **die Hunde auf jdn** ~ to set the dogs on sb. **(b)** (col: antreiben) to rush, to hurry. **2** vr to hurry oneself. **3** vi **(a)** auch aux sein to rush. **(b)** (pej: Haß schüren) to stir up hatred (gegen against); (col: lästern) to say malicious things. **bei jdm gegen jdn** ~ to try to set sb against sb.

Hetzer(in f) m - rabble-rouser, agitator.

Hetzerei f **(a)** no pl (Hast) (mad) rush. **(b)** (das Haßschüren) rabble-rousing, agitation.

Hetz-: ~**jagd** f (lit, fig) hounding (auf +acc of); ~**kampagne** f smear campaign.

Heu nt no pl hay. **Geld wie** ~ **haben** (col) to have pots of money (col).

Heuboden m hayloft.

Heuchelei f hypocrisy.

heucheln 1 vi to be a hypocrite. **2** vt Mitleid etc to feign.

Heuchler(in f) m - hypocrite.

heuchlerisch adj hypocritical.

heuer adv (S Ger, Aus, Sw) this year.

Heuer f -n (Naut) pay.

heuern vt to sign on, to hire.

Heu-: ~**fieber** nt hay fever; ~**gabel** f pitchfork, hayfork; ~**haufen** m haystack.

heulen vi to howl; (Motor) to roar; (Sirene) to wail. **ich hätte** ~ **können** I could have wept; **es ist einfach zum H~** it's enough to make you weep.

Heulen nt no pl siehe vi howling; roaring; wailing.

Heul-: (col) ~**peter** m, ~**suse** f cry-baby (col); ~**ton** m (von Sirene) wail.

Heu-: ~**schnupfen** m hay fever; ~**schrecke** f -n grasshopper; (in heißen Ländern) locust; ~**speicher** m barn.

heute adv today. ~ **morgen** this morning; ~ **abend** this evening, tonight; ~ **früh** this morning; ~ **nacht** tonight; **bis** ~ (bisher) to this day; ~ **in einer Woche** a week today, today week; **lieber** ~ **als morgen** the sooner the better; **von** ~ **auf morgen** (fig: plötzlich) overnight, from one day to the next; **der Mensch von** ~ modern man.

heutig adj attr today's; (gegenwärtig) modern, contemporary. **am** ~**en Abend** this evening; **unser** ~**es Schreiben** (Comm) our letter of today('s date); **bis zum** ~**en Tage** to this day.

heutzutage adv nowadays.

Hexe f -n witch; (col: altes Weib) old hag.

hexen vi to do witchcraft. **ich kann doch nicht** ~ (col) I'm not a magician.

Hexen-: ~**häuschen** nt gingerbread house; ~**jagd** f witch hunt; ~**kessel** m (fig) pandemonium no indef art; ~**meister** m sorcerer; ~**schuß** m (Med) lumbago.

Hexerei f witchcraft no pl; (Zaubertricks) magic no pl.

HG = Handelsgesellschaft.

hg. = herausgegeben von.

Hickhack m or nt -s (col) squabbling no pl.

Hieb m -e **(a)** (Schlag) stroke, blow; (Peitschen~) lash; (Fechten) cut. **(b)** (~wunde) gash, slash. **(c)** ~**e** pl (col: Prügel) ~**e bekommen** to get a hiding.

hieb- und stichfest adj (fig) watertight.

hielt pret of **halten.**

hier adv here. **dieser** ~ this one (here); ~ **draußen** out here; ~ **herum** hereabouts, around here; **er ist von** ~ he's a local (man); **Tag Klaus,** ~ (spricht) Hans (Telec) hello Klaus, it's Hans; ~ **spricht Dr. Müller** (Telec) this is Dr Müller (speaking); ~ **und da** (every) now and then.

hieran adv here. ~ **erkenne ich es** I recognize it by this.

Hierarchie f hierarchy.

hierarchisch adj hierarchical.

hier-: ~**auf** adv on this; (daraufhin) hereupon; ~**aufhin** adv hereupon; ~**aus** adv out of/from this, from here; ~**aus folgt daß ...** from this it follows that ...; ~**bei** adv (bei dieser Gelegenheit) on this occasion; (in diesem Zusammenhang) in this connection; ~**bleiben** vi sep irreg aux sein to stay here; ~**geblieben!** stop!; ~**durch** adv (lit) through here; (fig) through this; ~**durch teilen wir Ihnen mit, daß ...** we hereby inform you that ...; ~**für** adv for this; ~**her** adv here.

hierhergehören* vi sep to belong here; (fig: relevant sein) to be relevant. **nicht** ~**de Bemerkungen** irrelevant remarks.

hier-: ~**hin** adv here; **bis** ~**hin** up to here; ~**in** adv (lit, fig) in this; ~**mit** adv with this, herewith (form); ~**mit ist der Fall erledigt** this settles the matter; ~**mit erkläre ich ...** (form) I hereby declare ... (form); ~**nach** adv after this, afterwards; (daraus folgend) according to this; ~**sein** vi sep irreg aux sein to be here; **während meines H~seins** during my stay; ~**über** adv (fig) about this; ~**über ärgere ich mich** this makes me angry; ~**unter** adv (lit) under this or here; (fig) by this *or* that; *(in dieser Kategorie)* among these; ~unter fallen auch die Sonntage this includes Sundays; ~von *adv* from this; ~von habe ich nichts gewußt I knew nothing about this; ~von abgesehen apart from this; ~vor *adv* in front of this *or* here; ~vor ekele ich mich it revolts me; ~vor hat er großen Respekt he has a great respect for this; ~zu *adv (dafür)* for this; *(dazu)* with this; *(außerdem)* in addition to this, moreover; *(zu diesem Punkt)* about this; ~zu gehören auch die Katzen this also includes the cats; ~zulande *adv* in these parts.

hiesig *adj attr* local. meine ~en Verwandten my relatives here; er ist kein H~er he is not a local (man).

hieß *pret of* **heißen.**

Hi-Fi-Anlage ['haifi-] *f* hi-fi set *or* system.

Hilfe *f* -n (a) *no pl* help; *(für Notleidende)* aid, relief. (zu) ~! help!; jdm zu ~ kommen to come to sb's aid *or* assistance; jdm ~ leisten to help sb; bei jdm ~ suchen to seek sb's help *or* assistance; mit ~ with the help *or* aid *(gen of)*; etw zu ~ nehmen to use sth; ohne fremde ~ gehen to walk unaided. (b) *(Hilfsmittel)* aid. du bist mir eine schöne ~! *(iro)* a fine help you are!

Hilfe-: ~leistung *f* aid, assistance; unterlassene ~leistung *(Jur)* denial of assistance; ~ruf *m* call for help; ~stellung *f (Sport, fig)* support; h~suchend *adj* seeking help; *Blick* beseeching.

Hilf-: h~los *adj* helpless; ~losigkeit *f* helplessness; h~reich *adj* helpful.

Hilfs-: ~aktion *f* relief action; ~arbeiter *m* labourer *(Brit)*, laborer *(US)*; *(in Fabrik)* unskilled worker; h~bedürftig *adj* in need of help; *(notleidend)* needy, in need *pred*; h~bereit *adj* helpful, ready to help *pred*; ~bereitschaft *f* helpfulness, readiness to help; ~dienst *m* emergency service; *(bei Katastrophenfall)* (emergency) relief service; ~kraft *f* assistant; *(Aushilfe)* temporary worker; ~maßnahme *f* relief action *no pl*; *(zur Rettung)* rescue action *no pl*; ~mittel *nt* aid; ~organisation *f* relief organization; ~programm *nt* relief programme *(Brit)* or program *(US)*; ~schule *f (dated)* school for backward children; ~verb *nt* auxiliary (verb); ~werk *nt* relief organization.

Himalaja *m* der ~ the Himalayas *pl*.

Himbeere *f* raspberry.

Himmel *m* - (a) sky. am ~ in the sky; zwischen ~ und Erde in midair; jdn/etw in den ~ heben *or* loben to praise sb/sth to the skies; ihr hängt der ~ voller Geigen everything in the garden is lovely for her; so was fällt nicht einfach vom ~ things like that don't grow on trees. (b) *(Rel)* heaven. im ~ in heaven; in den ~ kommen to go to heaven; das schreit zum ~ it's a scandal; es stinkt zum ~ *(col)* it stinks to high heaven *(col)*; (ach) du lieber ~! *(col)* good Heavens! *(col)*; um ~s willen *(col)* for Heaven's sake *(col)*.

Himmel-: ~bett *nt* four-poster (bed); h~blau *adj* sky-blue.

Himmelfahrt *f* (a) **Christi** ~ the Ascension of Christ; **Mariä** ~ the Assumption of the Virgin Mary. (b) *(no art: Feiertag)* Ascension Day.

Himmelfahrts-: ~kommando *nt (Mil col)* suicide squad; *(Unternehmen)* suicide mission; ~tag *m* Ascension Day.

Himmel-: h~hoch 1 *adj* sky-high; 2 *adv* high into the sky; h~hoch jauchzend, zu Tode betrübt up one minute and down the next; ~reich *nt no pl (Rel)* Kingdom of Heaven; h~schreiend *adj* outrageous, appalling.

Himmels-: ~körper *m* heavenly *or* celestial body; ~richtung *f* direction; die vier ~richtungen the four points of the compass.

himmelweit *adj* ein ~er Unterschied a world of difference; wir sind noch ~ davon entfernt we're still nowhere near it.

himmlisch *adj (lit, fig)* heavenly; *Geduld* infinite. der ~e Vater our Heavenly Father.

hin *adv* (a) *(räumlich)* nach außen ~ *(fig)* outwardly; ~ fahre ich mit dem Zug, zurück ... on the way out I'll take the train, coming back ...; ~ und her *(räumlich)* to and fro, back and forth; etw ~ und her überlegen to think about sth a lot; das H~ und Her the comings and goings *pl*; nach langem H~und Her eventually; Feiertag ~, Feiertag her holiday or no holiday, whether it's a holiday or not; ~ und zurück there and back; einmal London ~ und zurück a return to London *(Brit)*, a roundtrip ticket to London *(US)*; ~ und wieder (every) now and again. (b) *(zeitlich)* es sind nur noch drei Tage ~ it's only three days from now; gegen Mittag ~ towards midday; über die Jahre ~ over the years.

(c) auf meine Bitte/meinen Vorschlag ~ at my request/suggestion; auf meinen Brief ~ on account of my letter; auf sein Versprechen/ seinen Rat ~ on the basis of his promise/his advice; etw auf etw *(acc)* ~ untersuchen to inspect sth for sth; nichts wie ~ *(col)* let's go then!; wo ist es/sie ~? where has it/she gone?

hinab *adv, pref siehe* **hinunter.**

hin|arbeiten *vi sep:* auf etw *(acc)* ~ auf Ziel to work towards sth.

hinauf *adv* up. den Berg ~ up the mountain.

hinauf- *pref* up; ~arbeiten *vr sep (lit, fig)* to work one's way up; ~führen *vti sep* to lead up; ~gehen *vi sep irreg aux sein* to go up; mit dem Preis ~gehen to put up the price; ~reichen *sep* 1 *vi* to reach up; 2 *vt* to pass up; ~ziehen *vt sep irreg* to pull up.

hinaus *adv* (a) *(räumlich)* ~ (mit dir)! (get) out!, out you go!; über *(+acc)* ~ beyond, over; hier/dort ~ this/that way out; hinten/vorn ~ at the back/front; zur Straße ~ facing the street. (b) *(zeitlich)* auf Jahre ~ for years to come; bis weit über die Siebzig ~ until well over seventy; über Mittwoch ~ until after Wednesday. (c) *(fig)* über *(+acc)* ... ~ over and above ...; darüber ~ over and above this.

hinaus-: ~befördern* *vt sep (col)* jdn to kick out *(col)* *(aus of)*; ~drängen *sep (aus of)* 1 *vt* to force out; *(eilig)* to hustle out; 2 *vi aux sein* to push one's way out; ~fahren *sep irreg* 1 *vi aux sein (a)* aus etw ~fahren to go out of sth, to leave sth; (b) *(reisen)* to go out; aufs Meer ~fahren to put out to sea; 2 *vt Wagen* to drive out *(aus of)*; ~finden *vi sep irreg* to find the way out *(aus of)*; ~fliegen *vi sep irreg aux sein* (a) to fly out *(aus of)*; (b) *(col:* ~geworfen werden) to get kicked out *(col)*; ~führen *sep* 1 *vi* (a) to lead out *(aus of)*; über etw *(acc)* ~führen *(lit, fig)* to go beyond sth; 2 *vt* to lead out *(aus of)*; *(Weg, Reise)* to take *(über +acc* beyond); ~gehen *sep irreg aux sein* 1 *vi* (a) to go out(side); (b) auf etw *(acc)* ~gehen *(Tür)* to open onto sth; *(Fenster auch)* to look onto sth; (c) *(fig: überschreiten)* über etw *(acc)* ~gehen to go beyond sth; das geht über meine Kräfte ~ it's too much for me; 2 *vi impers* wo geht es ~? where's the way out?; ~kommen *vi sep irreg aux sein* (a) to come out(side); (b) *(fig: ~laufen)* das kommt auf dasselbe ~ it boils down to or comes to the same thing; ~komplimentieren* *vt sep (hum)* to usher out *(aus of)*; ~laufen *vi sep irreg aux sein (aus of)* (a) *(lit)* to run out; (b) *(fig)* es läuft auf dasselbe ~ it amounts or comes to the same thing; ~lehnen *vr sep* to lean out *(aus of)*; ~nehmen *vt sep irreg* to take out *(aus of)*; ~ragen *vi sep aux sein* to jut out *(über +acc* beyond); über jdn/etw ~ragen *(fig)* to tower above sb/sth; ~schaffen *vt sep* to take out *(aus of)*; ~schieben *vt sep irreg* (a) *Gegenstand* to push out *(aus of)*; *(fig)* to put off, to postpone; ~schießen *vi sep irreg aux sein* (~rennen) to shoot out *(aus of)*;

über das Ziel ~schießen *(fig)* to overshoot the mark; **~schmeißen** *vt sep irreg (col)* to kick *or* chuck out *(col) (aus of)*; **~sehen** *vi sep irreg* to look out *(aus of)*; **~sein** *vi sep irreg aux sein* **über etw** *(acc)* **~sein** *über Kindereien, ein Alter* to be past sth; *über Enttäuschungen* to have got over sth; **~setzen** *vt sep* to put out(side); **jdn ~setzen** *(col)* to kick sb out *(col)*; **~stellen** *vt sep* to put out(side); *Sportler* to send off; **~strecken** *vt sep* to stick *or* put out *(aus of)*; **~stürzen** *vi sep aux sein (aus of)* **(a)** *(~fallen)* to fall out; **(b)** *(~eilen)* to rush out; **~tragen** *vt sep irreg* **(a)** to carry out *(aus of)*; **(b) etw in alle Welt ~tragen** to spread sth abroad; **~wachsen** *vi sep irreg aux sein* **über etw** *(acc)* **~wachsen** *(fig)* to outgrow sth; **er wuchs über sich selbst ~** he surpassed himself; **~weisen** *sep irreg* **1** *vt* **jdn ~weisen** to show sb the door; **2** *vi* to point out(wards); **~werfen** *vt sep irreg (aus of)* **(a)** to throw out; **einen Blick ~werfen** to take a look out(side); **(b)** *(col: entfernen)* to chuck *or* kick out *(col)*; **~wollen** *vi sep* to want to get out *(aus of)*; **worauf willst du ~?** *(fig)* what are you getting *or* driving at?; **hoch ~wollen** to aim high; **~ziehen** *sep irreg* **1** *vt* **(a)** *(nach draußen ziehen)* to pull out *(aus of)*; **(b)** *(fig) Verhandlungen etc* to protract, to drag out; *Urlaub etc* to prolong; **2** *vi aux sein* to go out *(aus of)*; **auf s Land ~ziehen** to move out into the country; **3** *vr (Verhandlungen etc)* to drag on; *(Abfahrt etc)* to be delayed; **~zögern** *sep* **1** *vt* to delay, to put off; **2** *vr* to be delayed, to be put off.

hin-: **~bekommen*** *vt sep irreg (col)* **das hast du gut ~bekommen** you've made a good job of it; **~blättern** *vt sep (col) Geld* to fork out *(col)*; **H~blick** *m*: **im** *or* **in H~blick auf** *(+acc) (angesichts)* in view of; *(mit Bezug auf)* with regard to; **~blicken** *vi sep* to look *(auf+acc, nach* at, towards*)*; **~bringen** *vt sep irreg* **(a)** to take there; **(b)** *(fig) Zeit* to spend; **(c)** *(fig col: zustande bringen)* to get done.

hinderlich *adj* **~ sein** to be in the way; **jds Karriere** *(dat)* **~ sein** to be a hindrance to sb's career; **jdm ~ sein** to get in sb's way.

hindern 1 *vt* **(a)** *Wachstum* to impede; **jdn** to hinder *(bei in)*. **(b)** *(abhalten von)* to prevent *(an +dat* from*)*, to stop. **ich will Sie nicht ~** I shan't stand in your way. **2** *vi* to be a hindrance *(bei* to*)*.

Hindernis *nt* **(a)** *(lit, fig)* obstacle; *(beim Sprechen)* impediment. **sie empfand das Kind als ~ für ihre Karriere** she saw the child as a hindrance to *or* an obstacle for her career. **(b)** *(beim ~ lauf)* jump.

Hindernis-: **~lauf** *m*, **~rennen** *nt* steeplechase.

Hinderungsgrund *m* obstacle.

hindeuten *vi sep* to point *(auf +acc, zu* at*)*. **es deutet alles darauf hin, daß ...** everything indicates that ...

hindrehen *vt sep (fig col)* to sort out.

hindurch *adv* through. **mitten ~** straight through; **das ganze Jahr ~** throughout the year; **die ganze Zeit ~** all the time; **Jahre ~** for years.

hindurchgehen *vi sep irreg aux sein (lit, fig)* to go through *(durch etw* sth*)*.

hindürfen *vi sep irreg* to be allowed to go *(zu* to*)*.

hinein *adv* in. **~ mit dir!** *(col)* in you go!; **in etw** *(acc)* **~** into sth; **bis tief in die Nacht ~** well into the night.

hinein- *pref in*; *siehe auch* **ein-, herein-;** **~bekommen*** *vt sep irreg (col)* to get in *(in+acc* to*)*; **~blicken** *vi sep* to look in *(in+acc -to)*; **~bringen** *vt sep irreg (~tragen)* to bring/take in *(in+acc -to)*; **~denken** *vr sep irreg* **sich in ein Problem ~denken** to think oneself into a problem; **sich in jdn ~denken** to put oneself in sb's position; **~fallen** *vi sep irreg aux sein* to fall in *(in+acc -to)*; **~finden** *vr sep irreg (fig) (sich vertraut machen)* to find one's feet; *(sich abfinden)* to come to terms with it; **~fressen** *vt sep irreg (col)* **etw in sich**

(acc) **~fressen** *(lit)* to wolf sth (down) *(col)*; *(fig) Kummer etc* to suppress sth; **~gehen** *vi sep irreg aux sein* **(a)** to go in; **in etw** *(acc)* **~gehen** to go into sth; **(b)** *(~passen)* to go in *(in+acc* to*)*; **~geraten*** *vi sep irreg aux sein* **in etw** *(acc)* **~geraten** to get involved in sth; **~knien** *vr sep (fig col)* **sich in etw** *(acc)* **~knien** to get into sth *(col)*; **~kommen** *vi sep irreg aux sein (in+acc -to)* **(a)** to come in; **(b)** *(lit, fig: ~gelangen können)* to get in; **~kriegen** *vt sep (col)* to get in *(in+acc -to)*; **~legen** *vt sep (lit, fig)* to put in *(in +acc -to)*; **~lesen** *vt sep irreg* **etw in etw** *(acc)* **~lesen** to read sth into sth; **~passen** *vi sep* **in etw** *(acc)* **~passen** to fit into sth; *(fig)* to fit in with sth; **~platzen** *vi sep aux sein (fig col)* to burst in *(in +acc -to)*; **~reden** *vi sep (lit: unterbrechen)* to interrupt *(jdm* sb*)*; **jdm ~reden** *(fig: sich einmischen)* to interfere in sb's affairs; **~schlagen** *vt sep irreg (in+acc -to) Nagel* to knock in; **~schlingen** *vt sep irreg* **etw (gierig) in sich ~schlingen** to devour sth (greedily); **~schütten** *vt sep* to pour in *(in+acc -to)*; **etw in sich ~schütten** *(col)* to knock sth back *(col)*; **~setzen** *sep* **1** *vt* to put in *(in+acc -to)*; **2** *vr (in Fahrzeug)* to get into *(in etw (acc)* sth*)*; *(in Sessel)* to sit (oneself) down *(in +acc* in(to)*)*; **~spielen** *vi sep (beeinflussen)* to have a part to play *(in+acc* in*)*; **~stecken** *vt sep (in+acc -to)* to put in; **Geld/Arbeit in etw** *(acc)* **~stecken** to put money/some work into sth; **~steigern** *vr sep* to get worked up; **sich in seinen Ärger ~steigern** to work oneself up into a temper; **sie hat sich in die Vorstellung ~gesteigert, daß ...** she has managed to convince herself that ...; **~stopfen** *vt sep* to stuff *or* cram in *(in+acc -to)*; **Essen in sich** *(acc)* **~stopfen** to stuff oneself with food; **~stürzen** *sep* **1** *vi aux sein* to plunge in *(in+acc -to)*; *(~eilen)* to rush in *(in+ acc -to)*; **2** *vt* to throw *or* hurl in *(in +acc -to)*; **3** *vr* to plunge in *(in+acc -to)*; **sich in die Arbeit ~stürzen** to throw oneself into one's work; **sich ins Vergnügen ~stürzen** to plunge in and start enjoying oneself, to let it all hang out *(col)*; **~tun** *vt sep irreg* to put in *(in+acc -to)*; **einen Blick in etw** *(acc)* **~tun** to take a look in sth; **ins Buch etc** to take a look at sth; **~versetzen*** *vr sep* **sich in jdn** *or* **in jds Lage ~versetzen** to put oneself in sb's position; **sich in eine Rolle ~versetzen** to empathize with a part; **~wachsen*** *vi sep irreg aux sein* **in etw** *(acc)* **~wachsen** *(lit, fig)* to grow into sth; **~wollen** *vi sep (col)* to want to get in *(in +acc -to)*; **~ziehen** *vt sep irreg* to pull *or* drag in *(in+acc -to)*; **jdn in eine Angelegenheit ~ziehen** to drag sb into an affair.

hin-: **~fahren** *sep irreg* **1** *vi aux sein* to go there; *(mit Fahrzeug auch)* to drive there; **2** *vt* to drive *or* take there; **H~fahrt** *f* outward journey; *(Naut)* voyage out; **~fallen** *vi sep irreg aux sein* to fall (down).

hinfällig *adj* **(a)** frail. **(b)** *(fig: ungültig)* invalid.

hin-: **~finden** *vir sep irreg (col)* to find one's way there; **~fliegen** *vi sep irreg aux sein* to fly there; *(col: ~fallen)* to fall over; **H~flug** *m* outward flight.

hinführen *vti sep* to lead there. **wo soll das ~?** *(fig)* where is this leading to?

hing *pret of* **hängen**.

Hingabe *f no pl (fig) (Begeisterung)* dedication; *(Selbstlosigkeit)* devotion. **mit ~ tanzen/singen** *etc* to dance/sing *etc* with abandon.

hingeben *sep irreg* **1** *vt* to give up. **2** *vr* **sich einer Sache** *(dat)* **~** *der Arbeit* to devote oneself to sth; *dem Laster, der Verzweiflung* to abandon oneself to sth; **sich Hoffnungen/einer Illusion ~** to cherish hopes/to labour *(Brit)* or labor *(US)* under an illusion; **sie gab sich ihm hin** she gave herself to him.

hingebungsvoll 1 *adj (selbstlos)* devoted. **2** *adv* devotedly; *(begeistert)* with abandon; *lauschen* raptly.

hingegen conj however.

hin-: ~**gehen** vi sep irreg aux sein (a) (dorthin gehen) to go (there); **gehst du auch** ~? are you going too?; **wo geht es hier** ~? where does this go?; (b) (fig: tragbar sein) **das geht gerade noch** ~ that will just about do; ~**gehören** vi sep to belong; ~**gelangen** vi sep aux sein to go there; ~**geraten** vi sep irreg aux sein **irgendwo** ~**geraten** to get somewhere; **wo bin ich denn hier** ~**geraten?** (col) what kind of place is this then?; ~**gerissen** adj enraptured; ~**gerissen lauschen** to listen with rapt attention; **ich bin ganz** ~- **und hergerissen** (iro) that's absolutely great (iro); ~**halten** vt sep irreg (a) lit to hold out (jdm to sb); (b) (fig) jdn to put off, to stall.

hinhauen sep irreg (col) **1** vt (a) (nachlässig machen) to knock off (col). (b) (hinwerfen) to slam down. **2** vi (a) (zuschlagen) to hit hard. (b) aux sein (fallen) to fall flat. (c) (gutgehen) **das wird schon** ~ it will be OK (col) or all right. (d) (klappen) to work. (e) (ausreichen) to do. **3** vr (col) (sich schlafen legen) to crash out (col).

hinhören vi sep to listen.

hinken vi (a) to limp. (b) (fig: Beispiel, Vergleich) to be inappropriate.

hin-: ~**kommen** vi sep irreg aux sein (a) (da) ~**kommen** to get there; **wie komme ich zu dir** ~? how do I get to your place?; (b) (gehören) to go; **wo ist das Buch** ~**gekommen?** where has the book got to?; **wo kämen wir denn** ~, **wenn** ... (col) where would we be if ...; (c) (col: auskommen) to manage; **wir kommen** (damit) ~ we'll manage; (d) (col: ausreichen, stimmen) to be right; ~**kriegen** vt sep (col) (a) (fertigbringen) to do, to manage; (b) (in Ordnung bringen) to mend, to fix; (gesundheitlich) to cure; ~**langen** vi sep (col) (zupacken) to grab him/her etc; (anfassen) to touch; (zuschlagen) to take a (good) swipe (col); ~**länglich** **1** adj adequate; **2** adv adequately; (zu Genüge) sufficiently; ~**laufen** vi sep irreg aux sein (a) to run there; (b) (col: nicht fahren) to walk; ~**legen** sep **1** vt (a) to put down; Zettel to leave (jdm for sb); Verletzten etc to lay down; (col: bezahlen müssen) to fork out (col); (b) (col: glänzend darbieten) to give; **2** vr to lie down; **sich der Länge nach** ~**legen** (col) to fall flat; ~**nehmen** vt sep irreg (ertragen) to take; ~**neigen** sep **1** vr (zu towards) (Mensch) to lean; (fig) to incline; **2** vi (fig) **zu etw** ~**neigen** to incline towards sth; ~**passen** vi sep to fit (in); (gut aussehen) to go (well); ~**reichen** vi sep (a) (ausreichen) to be enough; (b) (sich erstrecken) **bis zu etw** ~**reichen** to stretch to sth; ~**reichend** adj (ausreichend) adequate; (genug) sufficient; (reichlich) ample; **H**~**reise** f journey out, outward journey; (mit Schiff) outward voyage; ~**reißen** vt sep irreg (fig: begeistern) to thrill; **sich** ~**reißen lassen** to let oneself get carried away; siehe ~**gerissen**; ~**reißend** adj Landschaft, Anblick enchanting; Schönheit, Mensch captivating; ~**richten** vt sep to execute; **H**~**richtung** f execution; ~**sagen** vt sep to say without thinking; ~**schaffen** vt sep **etw zu jdm** ~**schaffen** to get sth to sb; ~**schauen** vi sep siehe ~**sehen**; ~**schicken** vt sep to send; ~**schleppen** sep **1** vt to carry, to lug (col); (col: mitnehmen) to drag along; **2** vr (Mensch) to drag oneself along; (fig) to drag on; ~**schmeißen** vt sep irreg (col) (hinwerfen) to fling down (col); (fig: aufgeben) Arbeit etc to chuck in (col), to pack in (Brit col); ~**schreiben** sep irreg **1** vt to write; (flüchtig) to scribble down (col); **2** vi (col) to write; ~**sehen** vi sep irreg to look; **ich kann** (gar) **nicht** ~**sehen** I can't bear to look; **bei genauerem H**~**sehen** on closer inspection.

hinsein vi sep irreg aux sein (col) (a) (kaputt sein) to have had it (col). (b) (verloren sein) to be lost; (Ruhe) to be gone; (ruiniert sein) to be in ruins. (c)

hinsetzen sep **1** vt to put or set down. **2** vr to sit down.

Hinsicht f no pl **in dieser** ~ in this respect; **in mancher** or **gewisser** ~ in some or many respects or ways; **in finanzieller/wirtschaftlicher** ~ financially/economically; **in beruflicher** ~ with regard to my/his job.

hinsichtlich prep+gen (bezüglich) with regard to; (in Anbetracht) in view of.

hin-: ~**sollen** vi sep (col) **wo soll ich/das Buch** ~? where do I/does the book go?; **H**~**spiel** nt (Sport) first leg; ~**stellen** sep **1** vt (a) to put down; (col) Gebäude to put up; (abstellen) Fahrzeug to put; (b) jdn/etw **als** jdn/etw ~**stellen** to make sb/sth out to be sb/sth; **2** vr to stand; (Fahrer) to park; ~**strecken** sep **1** vt Hand, Gegenstand to hold out; **2** vr to stretch out.

hint|an-: ~**setzen**, ~**stellen** vt sep (zurückstellen) to put last; (vernachlässigen) to neglect.

hinten adv (a) behind; (am rückwärtigen Ende) at the back. **ein Blick nach** ~ a look behind; **von weit** ~ from the very back; ~ **im Buch/auf der Liste** at the back of the book/at the end of the list; **sich** ~ **anstellen** to join the end of the queue (Brit) or line (US); ~ **im Bild** in the back of the picture; **etw** ~ **anfügen** to add sth at the end; **von** ~ from behind; ~ **im Auto** in the back of the car; **nach** ~ fallen, ziehen backwards; **ich sehe ihn am liebsten von** ~ (col) I'll be glad to see the back of him; **ein nach** ~ **gelegenes Zimmer** a room facing the back; **das Auto da** ~ the car back there; **sie waren ziemlich weit** ~ they were quite far back.

(b) (fig) ~ **und vorn** betrügen left, right and centre (Brit) or center (US); **bedienen hand and foot; das stimmt** ~ **und vorn nicht** that is absolutely untrue; **das reicht** ~ **und vorn nicht** that's nowhere near enough; **ich weiß nicht mehr, wo** ~ **und vorn ist** I don't know whether I'm coming or going.

hinten-: ~**dran** adv (col) at the back; ~**herum** adv (a) from the back; **kommen Sie** ~**herum** come around the back; (b) (fig col) (auf Umwegen) in a roundabout way; (illegal) under the counter; ~**über** adv **er fiel** ~**über** he fell over backwards.

hinter prep +dat or (mit Bewegungsverben) +acc (a) behind. ~ jdm/etw her behind sb/sth; ~ **die Wahrheit kommen** to get to the truth; **sich** ~ jdn **stellen** (fig) to support sb; ~**jdm/etw stehen** (lit, fig) to be behind sb/sth; ~ **der Tür hervor** (out) from behind the door; jdn **weit** ~ **sich** (dat) lassen to leave sb a long way behind; **vier Kilometer** ~ **der Grenze** four kilometres beyond the border. (b) **etw** ~ **sich** (dat) **haben** (zurückgelegt haben) to have got through sth; Strecke to have covered sth; (überstanden haben) to have got sth over with; **anstrengende Tage** to have had sth; Studium to have completed sth; **sie hat viel** ~ **sich** she has been through a lot; **etw** ~ **sich** (acc) **bringen** to get sth over with; Strecke to cover sth; Arbeit to get sth done.

Hinter-: ~**achse** f rear axle; ~**ausgang** m back or rear exit; ~**backe** f usu pl buttock; **sich auf die** ~**backen setzen** (fig col) to get down to it; ~**bänkler** m - (Pol pej) backbencher; ~**bein** nt **sich auf die** ~**beine stellen** or **setzen** (fig col: sich anstrengen) to pull one's socks up (col).

Hinterbliebene(r) mf decl as adj surviving dependent. **die** ~**n** the bereaved family.

hinter|einander adv one behind the other; (zeitlich gleichzeitig) one after the other. ~ **hereinkommen** to come in one by one; **zwei Tage** ~ two days running; **dreimal** ~ three times in a row.

hinter|einander-: ~her *adv* behind one another; ~schalten *vt sep (Elec)* to connect in series.

hintere(r, s) *adj* back; *(von Tier, Gebäude, Zug auch)* rear. **der/die/das H~** the one at the back.

Hinter-: h~fragen* *vt insep* to analyze; ~gedanke *m* ulterior motive; **h~gehen*** *vt insep irreg (betrügen)* to deceive; *(umgehen) Gesetze* to circumvent.

Hintergrund *m (von Bild, fig)* background; *(von Saal)* back; *(Theat: Kulisse)* backcloth. **im** ~ in the background; **im** ~ **der Bühne** at the back of the stage; **vor dem** ~ *(lit, fig)* against the background; **in den** ~ **treten** *(fig)* to retreat into the background.

Hinter-: h~gründig *adj* cryptic, enigmatic; ~halt *m* **(a)** ambush; **jdn aus dem** ~halt überfallen to ambush sb; **im** ~halt lauern to lie in wait; **(b)** *(col)* etw im ~halt haben to have sth in reserve; h~hältig *adj* underhand(ed), devious; ~hältigkeit *f* underhandedness, deviousness.

hinterher *adv* behind; *(zeitlich)* afterwards.

hinterher-: ~kommen *vi sep irreg aux sein* **(a)** *(räumlich)* to follow (behind); *(zeitlich)* to come after; **(b)** *(als letzter kommen)* to bring up the rear; ~laufen *vi sep irreg aux sein* to run behind *(jdm* sb*)*; **jdm** ~laufen *(fig col: sich bemühen um)* to run around after sb; ~sein *vi sep irreg aux sein (col)* to be after *(jdm* sb*)*; ~sein, daß ... *(fig)* to see to it that ...

Hinter-: ~hof *m* backyard; ~kopf *m* back of one's head; **etw im** ~kopf haben/behalten *(col)* to have/keep sth in the back of one's mind; ~land *nt* hinterland; h~lassen* *vt insep irreg* to leave; *(jdm etw* sb sth*)*; h~lassene Werke/Schriften posthumous works; ~lassenschaft *f* estate; *(literarisch, fig)* legacy; h~legen* *vt insep* to deposit; *(als Pfand)* to leave; ~legung *f* deposit.

Hinterlist *f no pl* **(a)** *siehe adj* craftiness, cunning; deceitfulness. **(b)** *(Trick, List)* ruse, trick.

hinterlistig *adj (tückisch)* crafty, cunning; *(betrügerisch)* deceitful.

Hintermann *m, pl* ~er **(a)** person/car behind (one). **mein** ~ the person/car behind me. **(b)** *(Gewährsmann)* contact. **die** ~er des Skandals the men behind the scandal.

Hintern *m - (col)* bottom, backside *(col)*. **jdm den** ~ versohlen to smack sb's bottom; **ein paar auf den** ~ bekommen to get one's bottom smacked; **sich auf den** ~ setzen *(eifrig arbeiten)* to buckle down to work; **jdm in den** ~ kriechen to suck up to sb.

Hinter-: ~rad *nt* rear *or* back wheel; h~rücks *adv* from behind; *(fig: heimtückisch)* behind sb's back; ~seite *f* back; h~sinnig *adj* cryptic.

hinterste(r, s) *adj superl* of **hintere(r, s)** very back; *(entlegenste)* remotest.

Hinter-: ~teil *nt* (a) *(col)* backside *(col); (von Tier)* hindquarters *pl*; **(b)** *auch* back *or* rear part; ~treffen *nt* **im** ~treffen sein to be at a disadvantage; **ins** ~treffen geraten to fall behind; h~treiben* *vt insep irreg (fig)* to foil, to thwart; *Gesetz* to block; ~treppe *f* back stairs *pl*; ~tür *f* back door *(fig col)* loophole; **durch die** ~tür through the back door; **sich** *(dat)* eine ~tür *or* ein ~türchen offenhalten *(fig)* to leave oneself a loophole *or* a way out; ~wäldler *m - (col)* backwoodsman, hillbilly *(esp US)*; ~wäldlerisch *adj (col)* backwoods *attr*; h~ziehen* *vt insep irreg Steuern* to evade; *Material* to appropriate; ~ziehung *f siehe vt* evasion; appropriation; ~zimmer *nt* back room.

hintun *vt sep irreg (col)* to put. **ich weiß nicht, wo ich ihn** ~ soll *(fig)* I can't (quite) place him.

hinüber *adv* over; *(über Straße auch)* across.

hinüber-: ~fahren *sep irreg* 1 *vt (über etw (acc)* sth*)* to take across; *Auto* to drive across; 2 *vi aux sein* to travel *or* go across; **über den Fluß** ~fahren to cross the river; ~führen *sep* 1 *vt jdn (über*

die Straße) ~führen to take sb across (the street); 2 *vi Straße, Brücke* to go across *(über etw (acc)* sth*)*; ~gehen *vi sep irreg aux sein* to go across *or* over; ~kommen *vi sep irreg aux sein (über etw (acc)* sth*)* to come across; *(über Hindernis, zu Besuch)* to come over; *(~können)* to get across/over; ~reichen *sep* 1 *vt* to pass across; *(über Zaun etc)* to pass over *(jdm* to sb, *über etw (acc)* sth*)*; 2 *vi* to reach across *(über etw (acc)* sth*); (fig)* to extend *(in +acc* into*)*; ~sein *vi sep irreg aux sein (col) (verdorben sein)* to be off *(Brit)* or bad; *(unbrauchbar, tot sein)* to have had it *(col)*; ~wechseln *vi sep aux haben or sein* to change over *(zu, in+acc* to*)*; ~ziehen *sep irreg* 1 *vt* to pull across *(über etw (acc)* sth*); (fig: umstimmen)* to win over *(auf+acc* to*)*; 2 *vi aux sein Wolken etc* to move across *(über etw (acc)* sth*)*.

hinunter *adv* down. **bis** ~ **zu** down to. 2 *prep* +acc **den Berg** ~ down the mountain.

hinunter- *pref* down; ~bringen *vt sep irreg* to take down; **das bringe ich nicht** ~ *(col) (trinken)* I can't drink that stuff; ~gehen *vi sep irreg aux sein* to go down; *(Flugzeug)* to descend *(auf+acc* to*)*; ~gießen *vt sep irreg, ~kippen *vt sep (col) Getränke* to knock back *(col)*; ~schlingen *vt sep irreg (col)* to gulp down; *Essen* to gobble down; ~schlucken *vt sep* to swallow (down); *(fig) Beleidigung* to swallow; *Kritik* to take; *Ärger, Tränen* to choke back; ~spülen *vt sep* **(a)** to flush away; **(b)** *Essen, Tablette* to wash down; *(fig) Ärger* to soothe; ~stürzen *sep* 1 *vi aux sein* **(a)** *(~fallen)* to tumble down; **(b)** *(eilig ~laufen)* to rush down; 2 *vt jdn* to throw *or* hurl down; *Getränk* to gulp down; 3 *vr* to throw *or* fling oneself down.

Hinweg *m* way there. **auf dem** ~ on the way there.

hinweg *adv* **(a)** *(old: fort)* away. **(b)** **über jdn** ~ *(fig)* over sb's head; **über eine Zeit/zwei Jahre** ~ over a period of time/over (a period of) two years.

hinweg- *pref* away; ~bringen *vt sep irreg (fig) jdn über etw (acc)* ~bringen to help sb to get over sth; ~gehen *vi sep irreg aux sein über etw (acc)* ~gehen *(fig)* to pass over sth; ~helfen *vi sep irreg (fig) jdm über etw (acc)* ~helfen to help sb get over sth; ~kommen *vi sep irreg aux sein (fig) über etw (acc)* ~kommen to get over sth; **ich komme nicht darüber** ~, **daß ...** *(col)* I can't get over the fact that ...; ~sehen *vi sep irreg (über jdn/etw* ~sehen to ignore sb/sth; **darüber** ~sehen, **daß ...** to overlook the fact that ...; ~setzen *vr sep (fig) sich über etw (acc)* ~setzen to disregard sth; ~täuschen *vt sep* **darüber** ~täuschen, **daß ...** to hide the fact that ...; **sich nicht darüber** ~täuschen lassen, **daß ...** not to blind oneself to the fact that ...; ~trösten *vt sep jdn über etw (acc)* ~trösten to console sb about sth.

Hinweis *m* -e **(a)** *(Rat)* tip, piece of advice; *(amtlich)* notice. **darf ich mir den** ~ erlauben, **daß ...?** may I point out that ...?; ~e **für den Benutzer** notes for the user. **(b)** *(Verweis)* reference. **unter** ~ **auf** *(+acc)* with reference to. **(c)** *(Anhaltspunkt)* indication. **sachdienliche** ~e relevant information.

hinweisen *sep irreg* 1 *vt* **jdn auf etw (acc)** ~ to point sth out to sb. 2 *vi* **auf jdn/etw** ~ to point to sb/sth; *(verweisen)* to refer to sb/sth; **darauf** ~, **daß ...** to point out that ...; *(nachdrücklich)* to stress that ...; *(anzeigen)* to indicate that ...

Hinweis-: ~schild *nt*, ~tafel *f* sign.

hin-: ~wenden *vtr sep irreg* to turn *(zu, nach* towards*)*; **H~wendung** *f (fig)* turn *(zu* toward*)*; ~werfen *sep irreg* 1 *vt* **(a)** to throw down; **jdm etw** ~werfen to throw sth to sb; **(b)** *Bemerkung* to drop casually; *Wort* to say casually; **eine** ~geworfene Bemerkung a casual remark; **(c)** *(col: aufgeben) Arbeit, Stelle* to chuck (in) *(col)*; 2 *vr* to

throw *or* fling oneself down; ~**wirken** *vi sep*
auf etw *(acc)* ~**wirken** to work towards sth.
Hinz *m:* ~ **und Kunz** *(col)* every Tom, Dick and
Harry *(col)*.

hin-: ~**ziehen** *sep irreg* **1** *vt* **(a)** *(zu sich ziehen)* to
draw *or* pull *(zu* towards); *(fig: anziehen)* to at-
tract *(zu* to); **(b)** *(fig: in die Länge ziehen)* to drag
out; **2** *vi aux sein* **(a)** to move *(über+acc* across, *zu*
towards); **(b)** *Wolken, Rauch* to drift, to move *(an*
+dat across); **3** *vr* **(a)** *(lange dauern)* to drag on;
(b) *(sich erstrecken)* to stretch, to extend; ~**zie-**
len *vi sep* **auf etw** *(acc)* ~**zielen** to aim at sth.
hinzu *adv (obendrein)* besides, in addition.
hinzu-: ~**fügen** *vt sep* to add *(dat* to); *(beilegen)* to
enclose; **H~fügung** *f* addition; **unter H~fügung**
von etw *(form)* by adding sth; ~**kommen** *vi sep*
irreg aux sein **(a) sie kam gerade ~, als ...** she
happened to come on the scene when ...; **es**
werden später noch mehrere ~**kommen** more
people will be joining us later; **(b)** *(zusätzlich*
eintreten) to ensue; *(beigefügt werden)* to be added; **es kommt noch ~, daß ...** there is also the
fact that ...; **kommt sonst noch etwas ~?** will
there be anything else?; ~**nehmen** *vt sep irreg* to
include; ~**treten** *vi sep irreg aux sein* **(a)** *(heran-*
treten) to come up; **zu den anderen** ~**treten** to
join the others; **(b)** *(zusätzlich)* siehe ~**kommen**
(b); ~**tun** *vt sep irreg (col)* to add; ~**zählen** *vt sep*
to add; ~**ziehen** *vt sep irreg* to consult.
Hiobsbotschaft *f* bad news *no pl.*
Hirn *nt* **-e (a)** *(Anat)* brain. **(b)** *(col) (Kopf)* head;
(Verstand) brains *pl,* mind. **sich** *(dat)* **das** ~
zermartern to rack one's brain(s); **streng einmal**
dein ~ **an** think hard. **(c)** *(Cook)* brains *pl.*
Hirn- *siehe auch* **Gehirn-;** ~**gespinst** *nt* fantasy;
~**hautentzündung** *f (Med)* meningitis; **h~rissig,**
h~verbrannt *adj* hare-brained.
Hirsch *m* **-e** deer; *(Rot~)* red deer; *(männlicher*
Rot~) stag; *(Cook)* venison.
Hirsch-: ~**käfer** *m* stag-beetle; ~**kuh** *f* hind;
~**leder** *nt* buckskin, deerskin.
Hirse *f* **-n** millet.
Hirt *m (wk)* **-en, -en** herdsman; *(Schaf~)* shep-
herd.
Hirte *m* **-n** *(Eccl)* shepherd. **der Gute** ~ the Good
Shepherd.
Hirtenhund *m* sheepdog.
hissen *vt* to hoist.
Historiker(in *f) m* - historian.
historisch *adj* historical; *(bedeutsam) Ereignis*
historic. **das ist** ~ **belegt** there is historical evidence for this.
Hit *m* **-s** *(Mus, fig col)* hit.
Hit-: ~**liste** *f* charts *pl;* ~**parade** *f* hit parade.
Hitze *f* **-n (a)** heat; *(~zeit, ~welle)* hot spell. **vor**
~ **umkommen** to be sweltering; **bei starker/**
mäßiger ~ **backen** *(Cook)* bake in a hot/moderate
oven. **(b)** *(fig)* passion. **in** ~/**leicht in** ~ **geraten**
to get heated/to get worked up easily; **sich in** ~
reden to get oneself all worked up; **in der** ~ **des**
Gefecht(e)s *(fig)* in the heat of the moment.
Hitze-: h~beständig *adj* heat-resistant; ~**bestän-**
digkeit *f* heat resistance; **h~empfindlich** *adj*
sensitive to heat; **h~frei** *adj* **h~frei haben** *to*
have time off from school on account of excessively
hot weather; ~**welle** *f* heat wave.
hitzig *adj* **(a)** *Mensch* hot-headed; *Streit, Debatte*
heated; *Temperament* passionate. ~ **werden**
(Mensch) to flare up; *(Debatte)* to grow heated;
nicht so ~! don't get excited! **(b)** *(Zool)* on heat.
Hitz-: ~**kopf** *m* hothead; **h~köpfig** *adj* hot-
headed; ~**schlag** *m (Med)* heat-stroke.
hl. = **heilig.**
Hl. = **Heilige(r)** St.
H-Milch ['haː-] *f* long-life milk.
HNO-Arzt [haːɛnˈoː-] *m* ENT specialist.
hob *pret of* **heben.**
Hobby *nt* **-s** hobby.

Hobel *m* - *(Tech)* plane; *(Cook)* slicer.
Hobel-: ~**bank** *f* carpenter's bench; ~**maschine** *f*
planer, planing machine.
hobeln *vt* **(a)** *auch vi (Tech)* to plane *(an etw (dat)*
sth*).* **wo gehobelt wird, da fallen Späne** *(Prov)*
you can't make an omelette *(Brit) or* omelet
(US) without breaking eggs *(Prov).* **(b)** *(Cook)*
to slice.
Hoch *nt* **-s (a)** ein ~ **dem Brautpaar** a toast to the
bride and groom. **(b)** *(Met, fig)* high.
hoch *attr* **hohe(r, s)** *comp* **höher,** *superl* **=ste(r,**
s) *or (adv)* **am =sten 1** *adj* high; *Baum, Leiter* tall;
Betrag large; *Strafe, Gewicht* heavy; *Profit, Verlust*
auch, *Lotteriegewinn* big; *Gut, Glück, Alter* great;
Schaden extensive; *Persönlichkeit* distinguished;
Besuch, Feiertag important; *Offizier* high-ranking. **das Hohe Haus** *(Parl)* the House; **ein hohes**
Tier *(col)* a big fish *(col);* **das Hohe C** top C; **ein**
hohes Alter erreichen to live to a ripe old age;
das ist mir zu ~ *(col)* that's above my head; **hohe**
Flut spring tide; **der hohe Norden** the far North.
 2 *adv* **(a)** *(nach oben)* up; *(in einiger Höhe)* high.
er sah zu uns ~ he looked up to us; ~ **empor-**
ragend towering (up); **die Nase** ~ **tragen** *(col)* to
go around with one's nose in the air *(col);* ~ **oben**
high up; **die Sonne steht** ~ the sun is high in the
sky; ~ **werfen/wachsen** to throw high/grow tall.
 (b) verehren, versichern, begabt highly; verlieren heavily; gewinnen handsomely; verschuldet
deeply; erfreut very. **das rechne ich ihm** ~ **an** (I
think) that is very much to his credit; ~ **hinaus-**
wollen to aim high, to be ambitious; **zehn Mann**
~ *(col)* ten of them; **wenn es** ~ **kommt** *(col)* at
(the) most, at the outside; ~ **setzen** *or* **spielen** *(im*
Spiel) to play for high stakes.
 (c) *(Math)* **7** ~ **3** 7 to the power of 3, 7 to the
3rd.
 (d) *(col)* **es ging** ~ **her** there were lively
goings-on *(col);* ~ **und heilig versprechen** to
promise faithfully; ~ **und heilig schwören** to
swear blind *(col).*
hoch- *pref (in Verbindung mit Bewegungsverb)* up;
versichert, begabt etc highly; zufrieden, erfreut,
elegant etc very; besteuert heavily; verschuldet
deeply.
Hoch-: ~**achtung** *f* deep respect; **bei aller** ~**ach-**
tung vor jdm/etw with (the greatest) respect for
sb/sth; **mit vorzüglicher** ~**achtung** *(form: Brief-*
schluß) yours faithfully; **h~achtungsvoll** *adv*
(Briefschluß) yours faithfully; ~**adel** *m* high
nobility; **h~aktuell** *adj* highly topical; ~**amt** *nt*
(Eccl) High Mass; **h~angesehen** *adj attr* highly
regarded; **h~arbeiten** *vr sep* to work one's way
up; ~**bau** *m no pl* structural engineering; **h~be-**
gabt *adj attr* highly talented; **h~betagt** *adj* aged
attr, advanced in years; ~**betrieb** *m* peak period;
(im Verkehr) rush hour; ~**betrieb haben** to be at
one's/its busiest; **h~bringen** *vt sep irreg (col)* **(a)**
to bring *or* take up; **(b)** *(col: h~heben können)* to
get up; **(c)** *(fig: leistungsfähig machen)* to get going; *Kranken* to get back on his etc feet; ~**burg** *f*
(fig) stronghold; **h~deutsch** *adj* High German;
h~dotiert *adj attr Arbeit* highly paid.
Hochdruck *m* **(a)** *(Met, Phys)* high pressure. **mit**
~ **arbeiten** to work at full stretch. **(b)** *(Med)* high
blood pressure. **(c)** *(Typ)* relief print.
Hoch-: ~**ebene** *f* plateau; **h~empfindlich** *adj*
(Tech) Material, Instrumente highly sensitive;
Film fast; *Stoff* very delicate; **h~entwickelt** *adj*
attr Kultur, Land highly developed; *Geräte,*
Methoden sophisticated; **h~fahren** *sep irreg* **1** *vi*
aux sein **(a)** to go up; *(in Auto auch)* to drive up; **(b)**
(erschreckt) to jump; **2** *vt* to take up; *(in Auto auch)*
to drive up; ~**finanz** *f* high finance; **h~fliegen** *vi*
sep irreg aux sein to fly up; *(hochgeschleudert*
werden) to be thrown up; **h~fliegend** *adj* ambitious; *(übertrieben)* high-flown; ~**form** *f* top
form; ~**frequenz** *f (Elec)* high frequency; ~**ge-**

birge nt high mountains pl; **~gefühl** nt elation; **h~gehen** vi sep irreg aux sein (a) to rise; (b) (col: hinaufgehen) to go up; (c) (col: explodieren) to blow up; (Bombe) to go off; **etw h~gehen lassen** to blow sth up; (d) (col: wütend werden) to go through the roof (col); (e) (col: gefaßt werden) to get caught; **jdn h~gehen lassen** to bust sb (col); **h~geistig** adj highly intellectual, highbrow no adv; **h~gelegen** adj attr ein **h~gelegener Ort** a place situated high up; **~genuß** m great or special treat; (großes Vergnügen) great pleasure; **h~geschätzt** adj attr Mensch highly esteemed; Sache greatly valued; **h~geschlossen** adj Kleid etc high-necked; **~gesteckt** adj (fig) Ziele ambitious; **h~gestellt** adj attr (fig) Persönlichkeit high-ranking; **h~gestochen** adj Reden high-faluting; Stil pompous; (eingebildet) stuck-up; **h~gewachsen** adj tall; **h~gezüchtet** adj Motor souped-up (col); Geräte fancy (col); Tiere, Pflanzen overbred.

Hochglanz m high polish; (Phot) gloss. **etw auf ~ polieren** or **bringen** to polish sth until it shines.

hochglänzend adj very shiny; Fotoabzug very glossy; Möbel highly polished.

Hochglanz-: **~papier** nt high gloss paper; **~politur** f mirror polish or finish; (Poliermittel) (furniture) polish.

Hoch-: **h~gradig** adj no pred extreme; **h~hackig** adj Schuhe high-heeled; **h~halten** vt sep irreg to hold up; (fig) to uphold; **~haus** nt high-rise or multi-storey building; **h~heben** vt sep irreg Hand to hold up; Last to lift up; **h~intelligent** adj highly intelligent; **h~interessant** adj very interesting; **h~jagen** vt sep (col) (a) (aufscheuchen) Menschen to get up; (b) (sprengen) to blow up; (c) Motor to rev up; **h~kant** adv (a) **h~kant stellen** to put on end; (b) (fig col) **jdn h~kant hinauswerfen** to chuck sb out on his/her ear (col); **h~klappen** vt sep Tisch to fold up; Sitz to tip up; Deckel to lift up; Kragen to turn up; **h~kommen** vi sep irreg aux sein (a) (col) to come up; (b) (col) das Essen ist **ihm h~gekommen** he threw up (his meal) (col); (c) (aufstehen können) to (manage to) get up; (fig: gesund werden) to get back on one's feet; (d) (col: gesellschaftlich) to come up in the world; **~konjunktur** f boom; **h~rempeln** vt sep to roll up; **~kultur** f (very) advanced civilization; **~land** nt highland; **das schottische ~land** the Scottish Highlands pl; **h~leben** vi sep **jdn h~leben lassen** to give three cheers for sb; **er lebe h~!** three cheers (for him)!

Hochleistungs-: **~motor** m high-performance engine; **~sport** m competitive sport.

Hoch-: **h~modern** adj very modern, ultramodern; **~mut** m arrogance; **h~mütig** adj arrogant; **h~näsig** adj (col) snooty (col); **~nebel** m (low) stratus; **h~nehmen** vt sep irreg (a) to lift; Kind to pick or lift up; (b) **jdn h~nehmen** (col) (necken) to pull sb's leg; (schröpfen) to fleece sb (col); (verhaften) to pick sb up; **~ofen** m blast furnace; **~parterre** nt raised ground floor; **h~prozentig** adj Getränke high-proof; Lösung highly concentrated; **~rad** nt penny-farthing; **h~rechnen** vt sep to project; **~rechnung** f projection; **h~rot** adj bright red; **mit h~rotem Gesicht** with one's face as red as a beetroot (Brit), with a bright red face; **~ruf** m cheer; **~saison** f high season; **h~schlagen** sep irreg 1 vt Kragen to turn up; 2 vi aux sein (Wellen) to surge up; (Flammen) to leap up; **h~schrauben** vt sep (fig) Preise to force up; Erwartungen to raise; Forderungen to increase.

Hochschul-: **~abschluß** m degree; **~absolvent** m graduate; **~(aus)bildung** f university education.

Hochschule f college; (Universität) university.

Hochschul-: **~lehrer** m college/university teacher, lecturer (Brit); **~reife** f er hat (die)

~reife ≃ he's got his A-levels (Brit), he's graduated from high school (US); **~studium** nt higher education.

hochschwanger adj pregnant, well advanced in pregnancy.

Hochsee-: **~fischerei** f deep-sea fishing; **~schiffahrt** f ocean-going shipping.

Hoch-: **~seil** nt high wire, tightrope; **~sitz** m (Hunt) (raised) hide; **~sommer** m height of the summer; **h~sommerlich** adj very summery.

Hochspannung f (Elec, fig) high tension.

Hochspannungs-: **~leitung** f high tension line, power line; **~mast** m pylon.

Hoch-: **h~spielen** vt sep (fig) to blow up; **~sprache** f standard language; **~sprung** m high jump.

höchst adv (überaus) highly, extremely.

Höchst- in cpds (obere Grenze angebend) (mit adj) maximum; (mit adj) siehe **Hoch-**; (mit adj: Intensität ausdrückend) extremely, most; **~alter** nt maximum age.

Hoch-: **~stapelei** f (Jur) fraud; (einzelner Fall) confidence trick; **~stapler** m - confidence trickster, con man (col); (fig) fraud.

Höchst-: **~betrag** m maximum amount; **~bietende(r)** mf decl as adj highest bidder.

hoch-: **~stecken** vt sep to pin up; Haare auch to put up; **~stehend** adj (gesellschaftlich) of high standing; (geistig) highly intellectual; (entwicklungsmäßig) superior; **~stellen** vt sep (a) Stühle etc to put up; (b) Heizung etc, Kragen to turn up.

hochstenfalls adv (at the) (most).

höchstens adv (a) at the most. (b) (außer) except.

höchste(r, s) 1 adj, superl of **hoch** highest; Wuchs, Baum tallest; Betrag, Summe largest; Strafe, Gewicht heaviest; Lotteriegewinn biggest; Schaden most expensive; (maximal) Verdienst, Temperatur, Geschwindigkeit etc maximum attr; Fest most important; Offizier highest-ranking; Genuß, Glück, Freude, Ehre, Gut greatest; Gefahr, Wichtigkeit utmost, greatest; Konzentration extreme. **zu meiner ~n Zufriedenheit** to my great satisfaction; **im ~n Fall(e)** at the most; **die ~ Instanz** (Jur) the supreme court of appeal; **~ Zeit** high time; **aufs ~ erfreut** etc extremely or highly pleased etc.

2 adv am **~n** highest; schätzen, versichern most; besteuert, verlieren (the) most heavily; verschuldet (the) most deeply; **in der Rangordnung am ~n stehen** to be the highest up in the hierarchy; am **~n stehen** (Kurse, Temperatur) to be at its highest.

Höchste(s) nt decl as adj (fig) highest good. **nach dem ~n streben** to aspire to perfection.

Höchst-: **~fall** m im **~fall** at the most; **~form** f (Sport) top form; **~geschwindigkeit** f top or maximum speed; **~grenze** f upper limit.

Hochstimmung f high spirits pl.

Höchst-: **~leistung** f best performance; (bei Produktion) maximum output; **~maß** nt maximum amount (an+dat of); **h~persönlich** adv personally; **es ist der Prinz h~persönlich** it's the prince in person; **~stand** m highest level; **h~wahrscheinlich** adv most probably.

Hoch-: **~tal** nt high-lying valley; **~tour** f auf **~touren laufen/arbeiten** to be working flat out (col); **h~tourig** adj Motor high-revving; **h~tourig laufen** to run at high revs; **h~trabend** adj (pej) pompous; **h~treiben** vt sep irreg to drive up; (fig) Preise to force up; **~- und Tiefbau** m structural and civil engineering; **h~verehrt** adj attr highly esteemed; **h~verehrter Herr Präsident!** Mr President, Sir!; **~verrat** m high treason; **~verräter** m traitor; **h~verschuldet** adj attr deep in debt; **~wald** m timber forest; **~wasser** nt high tide; (in Flüssen) high water; (Überschwemmung) flood; **~wasser haben** (Fluß) to be in flood; **h~wertig** adj high-quality; Nahrungsmittel highly nutritious; Stahl high-grade;

~würden m no pl (Eccl: Anrede) Reverend Father; **~zahl** f exponent.

Hochzeit f -en wedding. **~ feiern** to have a wedding; **man kann nicht auf zwei ~en tanzen** (prov) you can't have your cake and eat it (prov).

Hochzeits- in cpds wedding; **~fest** nt wedding celebration; **~reise** f honeymoon; **~tag** m wedding day; (Jahrestag) wedding anniversary.

hochziehen sep irreg 1 vt (a) to pull up; Fahne to run up; Augenbrauen to raise. **(b)** (bauen) Wand to put up (col). **2** vr to pull oneself up.

Hocke f -n squatting position; (Übung) squat; (beim Turnen) squat vault; (beim Skilaufen) crouch.

hocken 1 vi (a) to squat, to crouch. **(b)** (col: sitzen) to sit; (auf Hocker) to perch. **2** vr (a) to squat. **(b)** (col: sich setzen) to sit down.

Hocker m - (Stuhl) stool.

Höcker m - (von Kamel, col: Buckel) hump.

Hockey ['hɔkɛ] nt no pl hockey, field hockey (US).

Hoden m - testicle.

Hodensack m scrotum.

Hof m -e (a) (Platz) yard; (Innen~) courtyard. **(b)** (Bauern~) farm. **(c)** (Fürsten~) court. **bei ~e** at court; **am ~e Ludwigs XIV** at the court of Louis XIV. **(d)** einem Mädchen den **~ machen** (dated) to court a girl (dated). **(e)** (um Sonne, Mond) halo.

hoffen 1 vi to hope. **auf jdn ~** to set one's hopes on sb; **auf etw ~** (acc) to hope for sth; **da bleibt nur zu ~** one can only hope; **ich will nicht ~, daß er das macht** I hope he doesn't do that. **2** vt to hope for. **~ wir das Beste!** let's hope for the best!; **ich hoffe es** I hope so; **das will ich (doch wohl) ~** I should hope so; **ich will es nicht ~** I hope not.

hoffentlich adv hopefully. **~!** I hope so; **~ nicht** I/we hope not.

Hoffnung f hope; (auf Gott) trust (auf+acc in). **sich** (dat) **~en machen** to have hopes; **sich** (dat) **keine ~en machen** not to hold out any hopes; **er macht sich ~en bei ihr** (col) he fancies his chances with her (col); **mach dir keine ~(en)!** don't build up your hopes; **jdm ~en machen** to raise sb's hopes; **jdm auf etw** (acc) **~en machen** to lead sb to expect sth; **die ~aufgeben/verlieren** to abandon/lose hope; **sich falschen ~en hingeben** to delude oneself; **guter ~ sein** (euph: schwanger) to be expecting.

Hoffnungs-: **h~los** adj hopeless; **~losigkeit** f no pl hopelessness; (Verzweiflung) despair; **~schimmer** m glimmer of hope; **h~voll** 1 adj hopeful; (vielversprechend) promising; **2** adv full of hope.

hofieren* vt to court.

höflich adj polite.

Höflichkeit f (a) no pl politeness. **jdm etw mit aller ~ sagen** to tell sb sth very politely. **(b)** (höfliche Bemerkung) compliment.

Höflichkeits-: **~besuch** m courtesy visit; **~floskel** f polite phrase; **h~halber** adv out of courtesy.

hohe adj siehe hoch.

Höhe f -n (a) height; (Flug~, Berg~ auch) altitude; (von Schnee, Wasser) depth. **in die/der ~** (up) into/in the air; **in einer ~ von** at a height/an altitude of; **in die ~ gehen/treiben** (fig: Preise etc) to go up/force up; **er geht immer gleich in die Höhe** (col) he always flares up.

(b) (An~) hill; (Gipfel) top, summit; (fig: ~punkt, Blütezeit etc) height. **auf der ~ sein** (fig col) (leistungsfähig) to be at one's best; (gesund) to be fighting fit (col); **nicht auf der ~ sein** (fig col) to feel below par; **die ~n und Tiefen des Lebens** the ups and downs of life; **das ist doch die ~!** (fig col) that's the limit!

(c) (von Preisen, Temperatur, Geschwindigkeit, Strafe) level; (von Summe, Gewinn, Verlust, Geldstrafe) size; (von Wert, Druck) amount; (von Schaden) extent. **ein Betrag in ~ von** an amount of; **ein Scheck in ~ von** a cheque (Brit) or check

(US) for (the amount of); **Zinsen in ~ von** interest at the rate of; **bis zu einer ~ von** up to a maximum of.

(d) (Mus) pitch; (Rad: Ton~) treble no pl.

(e) (Naut, Geog: Breitenlage) latitude. **die beiden Schwimmer liegen auf gleicher ~** the two swimmers are level with each other.

Hoheit f (a) no pl (Staats~) sovereignty (über +acc over). **(b)** member of a/the royal family; (als Anrede) Highness.

Hoheits-: **~bereich** m (Rechtsbereich) jurisdiction; **~gebiet** nt sovereign territory; **~gewalt** f (national) jurisdiction; **~gewässer** pl territorial waters pl; **h~voll** adj majestic; **~zeichen** nt national emblem.

Höhen-: **~angst** f fear of heights; **~flug** m high-altitude flight; **geistiger ~flug** intellectual flight; **~lage** f altitude; **~luft** f mountain air; **~messer** m - (Aviat) altimeter; **~sonne** f mountain sun; (Lampe) sunray lamp; **~unterschied** m difference in altitude.

Hohepriester m (lit, fig) high priest.

Höhepunkt m height, peak; (des Tages, Lebens, einer Veranstaltung) high spot; (eines Stücks, Orgasmus) climax. **auf dem ~ ... at** the peak (gen of); **den ~ erreichen** to reach a climax; (Krankheit) to reach a crisis; **den ~ überschreiten** to pass the peak.

hohe(r, s) adj siehe hoch.

höher adj comp of hoch (lit, fig) higher; Macht superior; Klasse upper; Auflage bigger. **~e Schule** secondary school, high school (esp US); **~e Gewalt** an act of God; **in ~em Maße** to a greater extent; **sich ~ versichern** to increase one's insurance; **sich zu H~em berufen fühlen** to feel called to higher things.

höhergestellt adj attr higher, more senior.

hohl adj (lit, fig) hollow; Geschwätz etc empty, shallow; Blick empty, vacant. **ein ~es Kreuz** a hollow back; **in der ~en Hand** in the hollow of one's hand.

Höhle f -n cave; (in Baum) hole, hollow bit; (Tierbehausung) cave, den; (fig: schlechte Wohnung) hovel, hole (col).

Höhlen- in cpds cave; **~forschung**, **~kunde** f speleology; **~mensch** m caveman.

Hohl-: **~kopf** m (pej) numskull (col); **~körper** m hollow body; **~kreuz** nt (Med) hollow back; **~maß** nt measure of capacity; **~raum** m hollow space; (Build auch) cavity; **~spiegel** m concave mirror.

Höhlung f hollow.

Hohn m no pl scorn. **nur ~ und Spott ernten** to get nothing but scorn and derision; **das ist der reine ~** it's sheer mockery.

Hohngelächter nt scornful laughter.

höhnisch adj scornful.

Hokuspokus m no pl (Zauberformel) hey presto; (fig) (Täuschung) hocus-pocus (col), jiggery-pokery (col); (Drumherum) palaver (col), fuss.

hold adj (poet, dated) fair, sweet. **das Glück war ihm ~** fortune smiled upon him.

holen vt to get; (abholen) to fetch, to pick up; Sieg, Preis auch to win; Krankheit auch to catch. **gestern hat ihn die Polizei geholt** the police came to take him away yesterday; **jdn ~ lassen** to send for sb; **sich** (dat) **eine Erkältung ~** to catch a cold; **dabei ist nichts zu ~** (col) there's nothing in it; **bei ihm ist nichts zu ~** (col) you etc won't get anything out of him.

Holland nt Holland.

Holländer[1] m - Dutchman. **die ~** the Dutch (people).

Holländer[2] m no pl Dutch cheese.

Holländerin f Dutchwoman, Dutch girl.

holländisch adj Dutch.

Hölle f -n hell. **die ~ auf Erden** hell on earth; **in die ~ kommen** to go to hell; **ich werde ihm die ~**

heiß machen (col) I'll give him hell (col); **es war die (reinste)** ~ (col) it was (pure) hell (col).

Höllen- in cpds of hell, infernal; (col: groß) hellish (col), infernal (col); **~angst** f terrible fear; **eine ~angst haben** to be scared stiff (col); **~lärm** m infernal noise; **~qual** f (fig col) agony; **~qualen ausstehen** to suffer agony.

höllisch adj (a) attr infernal, of hell. (b) (col: groß) dreadful, hellish (col). **es tut** ~ **weh** it hurts like hell (col); **die Prüfung war** ~ **schwer** the exam was hellish(ly) difficult (col).

Holm m **-e (a)** (von Barren) bar; (von Geländer) rail; (von Leiter) side rail. (b) (Griff) shaft.

holp(e)rig adj Weg bumpy; Rede clumsy.

holpern vi to bump, to jolt.

holterdiepolter adv helter-skelter.

Holunder m - elder.

Holunder-: **~beere** f elderberry; **~busch, ~strauch** m elder bush.

Holz nt **-er (a)** wood; (zum Bauen, Schreinern auch) timber, lumber (US). **ein** ~ a piece of wood or timber; (~art) a wood; **aus** ~ made of wood, wooden; ~ **fällen** to fell trees; **aus einem anderen/demselben** ~ **geschnitzt sein** (fig) to be cast in a different/the same mould (Brit) or mold (US); **aus hartem** ~ **geschnitzt sein** (fig) to be made of sterner stuff. (b) (Kegel) skittle, ninepin. **gut** ~! have a good game!

Holz in cpds wood; (aus ~ auch) wooden; (Build, Comm etc) timber; **~apfel** m crab apple; **~bearbeitung** f woodworking; (im Sägewerk) timber processing; **~bestand** m stock of wood or timber; **~bläser** m woodwind player; **~blasinstrument** nt woodwind instrument; **~block** m block of wood; **~bündel** nt bundle of wood.

Hölzchen nt small piece of wood; (Streichholz) match.

holzen vi (esp Ftbl col) to hack.

hölzern adj (lit, fig) wooden.

Holz-: **~fällen** nt no pl tree-felling, lumbering; **~fäller** m - woodcutter, lumberjack; **~faserplatte** f (wood) fibreboard (Brit) or fiberboard (US); **h~frei** adj Papier wood-free; **~hacken** nt no pl chopping wood; **h~haltig** adj Papier woody; **~hammer** m mallet; **jdm etw mit dem ~hammer beibringen** to hammer sth into sb (col); **~hammermethode** f (col) sledgehammer method (col); **~haufen** m pile of wood; **~haus** nt wooden or timber house.

holzig adj woody; Spargel auch stringy, tough.

Holz-: **~klotz** m block of wood; (Spielzeug) wooden brick; **er saß da wie ein ~klotz** (col) he sat there like a block or lump of wood; **~kohle** f charcoal; **~kopf** m (fig col) blockhead (col); **~scheit** nt piece of (fire)wood, log; **~schuh** m wooden shoe, clog; **~span** m wood chip; **~stoß** m pile of wood; **~verarbeitung** f wood-processing; **~weg** m auf dem **~weg sein** (fig col) to be on the wrong track (col); **~wirtschaft** f timber industry; **~wolle** f wood-wool; **~wurm** m woodworm.

homo- in cpds homo; **~gen** adj homogeneous; **~genisieren*** vt to homogenize.

Homöopath m (wk) **-en, -en** homoeopath (Brit), homeopath (US).

Homo-: **~sexualität** f homosexuality; **h~sexuell** adj homosexual; **~sexuelle(r)** mf decl as adj homosexual.

Honig m no pl honey. **sie schmierte ihm** ~ **ums Maul** (col) she buttered him up (col).

Honig-: **~biene** f honey bee; **~kuchen** m honeycake; **~kuchenpferd** nt (col) **grinsen wie ein ~kuchenpferd** to grin like a Cheshire cat; **~lecken** nt (fig) **das ist kein ~lecken** it's no picnic; **~melone** f honeydew melon; **h~süß** adj as sweet as honey; (fig) Worte, Ton honeyed; Lächeln sickly sweet; **~wabe** f honeycomb.

Honorar nt **-e** fee; (Autoren~) royalty.

Honoratioren [honora'tsio:rən] pl dignitaries pl.

honorieren* vt (Comm) to honour (Brit), to honor (US), to meet; (fig: anerkennen) to reward. **meine Arbeit wird schlecht honoriert** my work is poorly remunerated.

Hopfen m - (Bot) hop; (beim Brauen) hops pl. **bei ihm ist** ~ **und Malz verloren** (col) he's a dead loss (col).

hoppeln vi aux sein (Hase) to lollop.

hoppla interj whoops. **~, jetzt komm' ich!** look out, here I come!

hops adj pred (col) ~ **gehen** (verlorengehen) to get lost; (entzweigehen) to get broken; (verhaftet werden) to get nabbed (col); (sterben) to kick the bucket (col); **jdn** ~ **nehmen** (verhaften) to nab sb (col); ~ **sein** (verloren) to be lost; (Geld) to be down the drain (col); (entzwei) to be kaputt (col).

hopsen vi aux sein (col) to hop, to skip.

Hopser m (col: kleiner Sprung) (little) jump.

hörbar adj audible. **sich** ~ **machen** to speak up.

horchen vi to listen (dat, auf+acc to); (heimlich) to eavesdrop.

Horde f **-n** (lit, fig) horde.

hören vti (a) to hear. **ich höre dich nicht** I can't hear you; **ich hörte ihn kommen** I heard him coming; **gut/schlecht** ~ to have good/bad hearing; **schwer** ~ to be hard of hearing; **du hörst wohl schlecht!** (col) you must be deaf!; **das läßt sich** ~ (fig) that doesn't sound bad; **ich habe es sagen** ~ I've heard it said; **er hört sich gern reden** he likes the sound of his own voice; **na hör mal!, na** ~ **Sie mal!** wait a minute!, look here!; **von etw** ~ to hear about or of sth; **von jdm gehört haben** to have heard of sb; **von jdm** ~ (Nachricht bekommen) to hear from sb; **Sie werden noch von mir** ~ (Drohung) you'll be hearing from me; **man hörte nie mehr etwas von ihm** he was never heard of again; **laß mal** ~! (col) tell us; **etwas/nichts von sich** ~ **lassen** to get/not to get in touch; **lassen Sie von sich** ~ keep in touch; **ich lasse von mir** ~ I'll be in touch; **er kommt, wie ich höre** I hear he's coming; **man höre und staune!** would you believe it!; **ich will davon nichts gehört haben** I don't want to know anything about it.

(b) (anhören) Vortrag, Radio to listen to; Berichte, Sänger to hear.

(c) **auf jdn/etw** ~ to listen to sb/sth; **er will nicht** ~ he won't listen; **der Hund hört auf den Namen Joe** the dog answers to the name of Joe.

Hören nt no pl hearing; (Radio~) listening. **das** ~ **von Musik** listening to music; **es verging ihm** ~ **und Sehen** he didn't know whether he was coming or going (col).

Hörensagen nt: **vom** ~ from hearsay.

hörenswert adj worth listening to.

Hörer(in f) m - (Rad) listener; (Univ) student/person (attending lectures); (Telec) receiver.

Hörerschaft f (Rad) listeners pl, audience.

Hör-: **~fehler** m (Med) hearing defect; **das war ein ~fehler** I/he etc misheard it; **~funk** m radio; **~gerät** nt hearing aid.

hörig adj enslaved; (Hist) in bondage. **sie ist ihm (sexuell)** ~ he has (sexual) power over her.

Horizont m **-e** (lit, fig) horizon. **am** ~ on the horizon; **das geht über meinen** ~ (fig) that is beyond me; **er hat einen beschränkten** ~ he has limited horizons.

horizontal adj horizontal.

Horizontale f **-(n)** (Math) horizontal (line).

Hormon nt **-e** hormone.

hormonell adj hormone attr, hormonal. **jdn** ~ **behandeln** to give sb hormone treatment.

Hörmuschel f **-n** (Telec) earpiece.

Horn nt **-er** (von Tieren, Mus) horn; (fig col: Beule) bump. **jdn mit den** ~**ern aufspießen** to gore sb; **sich** (dat) **die** ~**er abstoßen** (col) to sow one's wild oats; **den Stier bei den** ~**ern packen** (fig) to take the bull by the horns; **jdm ~er aufsetzen** *(col)* to cuckold sb; **ins gleiche/in jds ~ blasen** to chime in.

Hornbrille *f* horn-rimmed spectacles *pl.*

Hörnchen *nt* - **(a)** little horn. **(b)** *(Gebäck)* croissant. **(c)** *(Zool)* squirrel.

Hornhaut *f* callous; *(des Auges)* cornea.

Hornisse *f* -n hornet.

Hornist *m* horn player.

Hornochs(e) *m (fig col)* blockhead *(col)*, idiot.

Horoskop *nt* -e horoscope.

horrend *adj* horrendous.

Hörrohr *nt* ear trumpet; *(Med)* stethoscope.

Horror *m no pl* horror *(vor +dat of)*.

Horror- in *cpds* horror; **~film** *m* horror film.

Hör-: **~saal** *m (Univ)* lecture room *or* hall; **~spiel** *nt (Rad)* radio play.

Horst *m* -e *(Nest)* nest; *(Adler~)* eyrie.

Hort *m* -e **(a)** *(Kinder~)* day-home for schoolchildren in the afternoon. **(b)** *(old, poet: Schatz)* hoard, treasure. **(c)** *(geh: Zuflucht)* refuge, shelter.

horten *vt Geld, Vorräte etc* to hoard; *Rohstoffe etc* to stockpile.

Hortensie [-iə] *f* hydrangea.

Hörweite *f* **in/außer ~** within/out of hearing *or* earshot.

Hose *f* -n trousers *pl*, pants *pl; (Damen~ auch)* slacks *pl; (Bade~)* swimming trunks *pl; (Unter~)* underpants *pl*, pants *pl (Brit)*; **ich brauche eine neue ~** I need a new pair of trousers *or* pants, I need some new trousers *or* pants; **die ~n anhaben** *(fig col)* to wear the trousers *or* pants *(col)*; **die ~n voll haben** to be wetting oneself *(col)*; **in die ~ gehen** *(col)* to be a complete flop *(col)*.

Hosen-: **~anzug** *m* trouser suit *(Brit)*, pantsuit *(US)*; **~bein** *nt* trouser leg; **~boden** *m* seat (of trousers); **den ~boden vollkriegen** *(col)* to get a smacked bottom; **sich auf den ~boden setzen** *(col)* to get stuck in *(col)*; **~bund** *m* waistband; **~rock** *m* culottes *pl*, pantskirt; **~schlitz** *m* flies *pl*, fly; **~träger** *pl* (a pair of) braces *pl (Brit)* or suspenders *pl (US)*.

Hospital *nt* -e *or* **Hospitäler** *(dated: Krankenhaus)* hospital.

Hospiz *nt* -e hospice.

Hostess, Hosteß *f, pl* **Hostessen** hostess.

Hostie ['hɔstiə] *f (Eccl)* host.

Hotel *nt* -s hotel.

Hotel- in *cpds* hotel; **~fach** *nt* hotel management.

Hotel garni *nt* bed and breakfast hotel.

Hr. = **Herr** Mr.

Hrsg. = **Herausgeber** ed.

Hub *m* -e **(a)** *(Kolben~)* (piston) stroke. **(b)** *(bei Kränen: Leistung)* hoisting capacity.

Hub(b)el *m* - *(col)* bump.

hubb(e)lig *adj (col)* bumpy.

hüben *adv* over here, (on) this side. **~ und drüben** on both sides.

Hub-: **~kraft** *f* lifting *or* hoisting capacity; **~raum** *m (Aut)* cubic capacity.

hübsch *adj* pretty; *Geschenk, Wohnung* nice. **sich ~ machen** to make oneself look pretty; **er macht das schon ganz ~** he's doing it very nicely; **das war ~/nicht ~ von dir** that was nice/not nice of you; **na, ihr beiden H~en** *(col)* well, you two; **eine ~e Geschichte/Bescherung** *(iro)* a pretty kettle of fish; **das kann ja ~ werden** *(col)* that'll be just great; **das ist doch ganz ~ weit** it's pretty far, it's a fair old way *(col)*; **ganz ~ viel bezahlen** to pay quite a bit; **das wirst du ~ sein lassen** *(col)* you'll do nothing of the kind; **immer ~ langsam!** *(col)* nice and easy.

Hubschrauber *m* - helicopter.

Hucke *f* -n **jdm die ~ vollhauen** *(col)* to give sb a good hiding.

huckepack *adv* piggy-back, pick-a-back.

Huf *m* -e hoof. **einem Pferd die ~e beschlagen** to shoe a horse.

Huf-: **~eisen** *nt* horseshoe; **~schmied** *m* blacksmith.

Hüft: **~bein** *nt* hip-bone; **~bruch** *m* fractured hip.

Hüfte *f* -n hip; *(von Tieren)* haunch. **bis an die ~n reichen** to come up to the waist.

Hüft-: **~gelenk** *nt* hip joint; **~gürtel, ~halter** *m* girdle; **h~hoch** *adj Pflanzen etc* waist-high; *Wasser etc* waist-deep.

Huftier *nt* hoofed animal.

Hüft-: **~knochen** *m* hip-bone; **~schmerz** *m* pain in the hip.

Hügel *m* - hill; *(Erdhaufen)* mound.

hügelig *adj* hilly.

Hügel-: **~kette** *f* range *or* chain of hills; **~land** *nt* hilly country.

Huhn *nt* -er chicken *(auch Cook)*; *(Henne auch)* hen; *(Gattung)* fowl. **da lachen ja die ~er** *(col)* it's enough to make a cat laugh *(col)*; **sie sah aus wie ein gerupftes ~** *(col)* she looked as though she'd been dragged through a hedge backwards *(col)*; **ein verrücktes ~** a queer fish *(col)*; **ein dummes** *(col)* **~** a silly goose.

Hühnchen *nt* (young) chicken, pullet. **mit jdm ein ~ zu rupfen haben** *(col)* to have a bone to pick with sb *(col)*.

Hühner-: **~auge** *nt (Med)* corn; **~brühe** *f (clear)* chicken broth; **~ei** *nt* hen's egg; **~klein** *nt no pl (Cook)* chicken trimmings *pl*; **~stall** *m* henhouse, chicken-coop; **~stange** *f* perch, (chicken) roost.

huldigen *vi+dat (geh) einem Künstler* to pay homage to; *einer Ansicht* to subscribe to; *einem Glauben* to embrace; *einem Laster* to indulge in.

Hülle *f* -n cover; *(für Ausweiskarten etc auch)* holder; *(Cellophan~)* wrapping; *(liter, hum: Kleidung)* clothes *pl*, piece of clothing. **die ~ fallen lassen** to strip off; **die sterbliche ~** the mortal remains *pl*; **in ~ und Fülle** in abundance; **Whisky/Sorgen in ~ und Fülle** whisky/worries galore.

hüllen *vt (geh)* to wrap. **in Nebel gehüllt** shrouded in mist; **sich in seinen Mantel ~** to wrap oneself up in one's coat; **sich (über etw acc) in Schweigen ~** to remain silent (about sth).

hüllenlos *adj* unclothed.

Hülse *f* -n **(a)** *(Schale)* hull, husk; *(Schote)* pod. **(b)** *(Kapsel)* case; *(für Film)* cartridge.

Hülsenfrucht *f usu pl* pulse.

human *adj* humane; *(verständnisvoll auch)* considerate.

Humanist(in *f)* *m* humanist; *(Altsprachler)* classicist.

humanistisch *adj siehe n* humanist(ic); classical. **~ gebildet** educated in the classics *or* humanities; **~es Gymnasium** secondary school with bias on Latin and Greek; ≈ grammar school *(Brit)*.

humanitär *adj* humanitarian.

Humanität *f no pl* humaneness, humanity.

Humanmedizin *f* (human) medicine.

Humbug *m no pl (col)* humbug *(col)*.

Hummel *f* -n bumble-bee.

Hummer *m* - lobster.

Humor *m* - humour *(Brit)*, humor *(US)*; *(Sinn für ~)* sense of humour. **er hat keinen (Sinn für) ~** he has no sense of humour; **er nahm die Bemerkung mit ~ auf** he took the remark in good humour; **er hat einen eigenartigen ~** he has a strange sense of humour; **er verliert nie den ~** he never loses his sense of humour.

Humorist(in *f)* *m* humourist *(Brit)*, humorist *(US)*; *(Komiker)* comedian.

Humor-: **h~los** *adj* humourless *(Brit)*, humorless *(US)*; **h~voll** *adj* humourous *(Brit)*, humorous *(US)*, amusing; **er kann sehr h~voll erzählen** he is a very amusing talker.

humpeln *vi* **(a)** *aux sein* to hobble. **(b)** *(ständig* hinken) to have a limp.

Humpen *m* - tankard, mug; *(aus Ton)* stein.

Humus *m* -, *no pl* humus.

Hund *m* -e dog; *(Jagd~ auch)* hound; *(col!: Schurke)* bastard *(col!)*. **junger ~** puppy, pup; **~e, die bellen, beißen nicht** empty vessels make most noise *(Prov)*; **wie ~ und Katze leben** to live like cat and dog; **damit kann man keinen ~ hinterm Ofen hervorlocken** *(col)* that's not going to tempt anybody; **er ist bekannt wie ein bunter ~** *(col)* everybody knows him; **da liegt der ~ begraben** *(col)* that's the problem; **er ist ein armer ~** he's a poor devil *(col)*; **er ist völlig auf dem ~** *(col)* he's really gone to the dogs *(col)*; **auf den ~ kommen** *(col)* to go to the dogs *(col)*; **vor die ~e gehen** *(col)* to go to the dogs *(col)*.

Hunde-: **~arbeit** *f (fig col)* eine **~arbeit** an awful job; **h~elend** *adj (col)* **mir ist h~elend** I feel lousy *(col)*; **~futter** *nt* dog food; **~halsband** *nt* dog collar; **~halter(in** *f)* *m (form)* dog owner; **~hütte** *f (lit, fig)* (dog) kennel; **h~kalt** *adj (col)* freezing cold; **~kuchen** *m* dog-biscuit; **~leben** *nt (col)* dog's life *(col)*; **~leine** *f* dog lead *or* leash; **~marke** *f* dog licence disc *(Brit)*, dog tag *(US)*; **h~müde** *adj pred, adv (col)* dog-tired; **~narr** *m (col)* fanatical dog lover, dog freak *(col)*; **~rasse** *f* breed (of dog).

hundert *num* a *or* one hundred. **einige ~ Menschen** a few hundred people.

Hundert *nt* -e hundred. **es geht in die ~e** it runs into the hundreds; **einer unter ~en** one out of hundreds; **zu ~en** in (their) hundreds.

Hunderter *m* - hundred; *(col: Geldschein)* hundred.

Hundert-: **h~fach 1** *adj* hundredfold; **die h~fache Menge** a hundred times the amount; **2** *adv* a hundred times; **h~fünfzigprozentig** *adj (iro)* fanatical; **~jahrfeier** *f* centenary, centennial *(US)*; **h~jährig** *adj attr* (one-)hundred-year-old; **h~mal** *adv* a hundred times; **~meterlauf** *m (Sport)* **der/ein ~meterlauf** the/a 100 metres *(Brit)* *or* meters *(US)*; **h~prozentig** *adj* (a *or* one) hundred per cent; *Alkohol* pure; **ein h~prozentiger Konservativer** *etc* an out-and-out conservative *etc*; **Sie haben h~prozentig recht** you're absolutely right.

Hundertsel *nt* - hundredth.

hundertste(r, s) *adj* hundredth. **vom H~n ins Tausendste kommen** *(fig)* to get carried away.

hunderttausend *num* a *or* one hundred thousand. **H~e von Menschen** hundreds of thousands of people.

Hunde-: **~salon** *m* dog parlour *(Brit)* *or* parlor *(US)*; **~sohn** *m (pej liter)* cur; **~steuer** *f* dog licence *(Brit)* *or* license *(US)* fee; **~wetter** *nt (col)* filthy weather; **~zucht** *f* dog breeding.

Hündin *f* bitch.

Hunds-: **h~gemein** *adj (col)* mean; *(schwierig)* fiendishly difficult; **es tut h~gemein weh** it hurts like hell *(col)*; **h~miserabel** *adj (col)* lousy *(col)*; **~tage** *pl* dog days *pl*.

Hüne *m (wk)* -n, -n **ein ~ von Mensch** a giant of a man.

Hünen-: **~grab** *nt* megalithic grave; **h~haft** *adj* gigantic.

Hunger *m no pl (lit, fig)* hunger *(nach* for); *(Hungersnot auch)* famine; *(nach Sonne etc)* yearning. **~ bekommen/haben** to get/be hungry; **~ auf etw** *(acc)* **haben** to feel like (eating) sth; **ich habe ~ wie ein Wolf** *or* **Bär** *(col)* I could eat a horse *(col)*; **vor ~ sterben** to die of hunger *or* starvation, to starve to death; **ich sterbe vor ~** *(col)* I'm starving *(col)*.

Hunger-: **~gefühl** *nt* hungry feeling; **~künstler** *m* **ich bin doch kein ~künstler** I'm not on a starvation diet.

hungern 1 *vi* **(a)** to go hungry, to starve. **jdn ~ lassen** to let sb go hungry. **(b)** *(fasten)* to go

without food. **(c)** *(fig geh: verlangen)* to hunger *(nach* for). **2** *vr* **sich zu Tode ~** to starve oneself to death; **sich schlank ~** to go on a starvation diet.

hungernd *adj, no comp* hungry, starving.

Hungersnot *f* famine.

Hunger-: **~streik** *m* hunger strike; **~tuch** *nt* **am ~tuch nagen** *(fig)* to be starving.

hungrig *adj (lit, fig)* hungry *(nach* for). **~ nach** *or* **auf** *(acc)* **etw sein** to feel like (eating) sth.

Hupe *f* -n horn. **auf die ~ drücken** to press/sound the horn.

hupen *vi* to sound the horn, to hoot.

hüpfen *vi aux sein* to hop; *(Ball)* to bounce. **vor Freude ~** to jump for joy; **das ist gehüpft wie gesprungen** *(col)* it's six of one and half a dozen of the other *(col)*; **H~ spielen** to play hopscotch.

Hup-: **~konzert** *nt (col)* hooting (of car horns); **~signal, ~zeichen** *nt (Aut)* hoot.

Hürde *f* -n **(a)** *(Sport, fig)* hurdle. **eine ~ nehmen** to take a hurdle. **(b)** *(Viehzaun)* fold, pen.

Hürdenlauf *m (Sportart)* hurdling; *(Wettkampf)* hurdles *pl or sing*.

Hure *f* -n whore.

huren *vi (col)* to go whoring.

Hurensohn *m (pej)* bastard *(col!)*, son of a bitch *(US col!)*.

hurra [hʊˈraː, ˈhʊra] *interj* hurray, hurrah.

Hurra *nt* -s cheers *pl*.

Hurra-: **~geschrei** *nt* cheering; **~patriotismus** *m* jingoism, chauvinism; **~ruf** *m* cheer.

Hurrikan *m* -e *or* -s hurricane.

hurtig *adj* nimble; *(schnell)* quick.

husch *interj (aufscheuchend)* shoo; *(schnell)* quick, quickly now. **und ~, weg war er** and whoosh! he was gone.

huschen *vi aux sein* to dart; *(Mäuse etc auch)* to scurry; *(Lächeln)* to flash.

hüsteln *vi* to give a little cough.

husten 1 *vi* to cough. **auf etw** *(acc)* **~** *(col)* not to give a damn for sth *(col)*. **2** *vt* to cough (up). **denen werde ich was ~** *(col)* I'll tell them where they can get off *(col)*.

Husten *m no pl* cough. **~ haben** to have a cough.

Husten-: **~anfall** *m* coughing fit; **~bonbon** *m or nt* cough drop; **~mittel** *nt* cough medicine/drop; **~reiz** *m* irritation of the throat; **~saft** *m* cough mixture; **h~stillend** *adj* **das wirkt h~stillend** it relieves coughs; **~tropfen** *pl* cough drops *pl*.

Hut[1] *m* -e hat. **den ~ aufsetzen/abnehmen** *(geh)* to put on/take off one's hat; **vor jdm den ~ abnehmen** *(fig)* to take off one's hat to sb; **~ ab vor solcher Leistung!** I take my hat off to that; **das kannst du dir an den ~ stecken!** *(col)* you can keep it; **unter einen ~ bringen** *(col)* to reconcile; *Termine* to fit in; **da geht einem der ~ hoch** *(col)* it's enough to make you blow your top *(col)*; **seinen ~ nehmen (müssen)** *(col)* to (have to) go; **das ist doch ein alter ~!** *(col)* that's old hat! *(col)*.

Hut[2] *f no pl* **(a)** *(geh)* protection, keeping. **unter** *or* **in meiner ~** in my keeping; *(Kinder)* in my care. **(b)** **auf der ~ sein** to be on one's guard *(vor+dat* against).

hüten 1 *vt* to look after, to mind; *Geheimnisse* to keep. **das Bett/Haus ~** to stay in bed/indoors; **hüte deine Zunge!** *(geh)* watch your tongue! **2** *vr* to guard *(vor+dat* against), to beware *(vor+dat* of). **ich werde mich ~!** not likely!; **ich werde mich ~, ihm das zu erzählen** there's no chance of me telling him that; **sich ~, etw zu tun** to take care not to do sth.

Hüter(in *f)* *m* - guardian, keeper.

Hut-: **~krempe** *f* brim (of a hat); **~macher (in** *f)* *m* hatter; *(für Damen auch)* milliner; **~schachtel** *f* hatbox; **~schnur** *f* **das geht mir über die ~schnur** *(col)* that's going too far.

Hütte *f* -n **(a)** hut; *(schäbiges Häuschen auch)* shack; *(Holz~, Block~)* cabin. **(b)** *(Tech: Hüt-*

tenwerk) iron and steel works *pl or sing.*
Hütten-: ~**arbeiter** *m* worker in an iron and steel works; ~**industrie** *f* iron and steel industry; ~**käse** *m* cottage cheese; ~**werk** *nt siehe* **Hütte (b).**
hutz(e)lig *adj Obst* dried; *Mensch* wizened.
Hyäne *f* -**n** hyena; *(fig)* wildcat.
Hyazinthe [hya'tsɪntə] *f* -**n** hyacinth.
Hydrant *m* hydrant.
Hydraulik *f* hydraulics *sing; (Antrieb, Anlage)* hydraulics *pl.*
hydraulisch *adj* hydraulic.
Hygiene [hy'giːnə] *f no pl* hygiene.
hygienisch [hy'giːnɪʃ] *adj* hygienic.
Hymne ['hymnə] *f* -**n** hymn; *(National~)* (national) anthem.
hyper-: ~**modern** *adj (col)* ultramodern; ~**sen-**

sibel *adj* hypersensitive.
Hypnose *f* -**n** hypnosis. **jdn in** ~ **versetzen** to put sb under hypnosis.
Hypnotiseur [hypnoti'zøːɐ] *m* hynotist.
hypnotisieren* *vt* to hypnotize.
Hypothek *f* -**en** mortgage; *(fig: Belastung)* burden of guilt. **eine** ~ **aufnehmen** to raise a mortgage; **etw mit einer** ~ **belasten** to mortgage sth.
Hypotheken-: ~**bank** *f* bank specializing in mortgages; ~**brief** *m* mortgage certificate; ~**darlehen** *nt* mortgage (loan); **h**~**frei** *adj* unmortgaged.
Hypothese *f* -**n** hypothesis.
hypothetisch *adj* hypothetical.
Hysterie *f* hysteria.
hysterisch *adj* hysterical. **einen** ~**en Anfall bekommen** *(fig)* to have hysterics.

I

I, i [iː] *nt* -, - **I, i. das Tüpfelchen auf dem ~** *(fig)* the final touch.
i [iː] *interj (col)* ugh *(col)*.
i.A. = **im Auftrag** pp.
iberisch *adj* Iberian. **die I~e Halbinsel** the Iberian Peninsula.
IC [iːˈtseː] *m* **-s** = **Intercity-Zug.**
ich *pers pron* I. **immer ~!** it's always me!; **~ Idiot!** what an idiot I am!; **und ~ Idiot habe es gemacht** and idiot that I am, I did it; **~ nicht!** not me!; **~ selbst I myself; wer hat gerufen? — ~!** who called? — (it was) me, I did.
Ich *nt* **-(s)** self; *(Psych)* ego. **das eigene ~** one's (own) self/ego; **mein zweites ~** *(selbst)* my other self; *(andere Person)* my alter ego.
Ich-: **i~bezogen** *adj* egocentric; **~form** *f* first person; **~-Roman** *m* novel in the first person.
ideal *adj* ideal.
Ideal *nt* **-e** ideal. **sie ist mein ~ einer Frau** she's my ideal woman.
Ideal- *in cpds* ideal; **~fall** *m* ideal case; **im ~fall** ideally; **~gewicht** *nt* ideal weight.
idealisieren* *vt* to idealize.
Idealismus *m* idealism.
Idealist *m* idealist.
idealistisch *adj* idealistic.
Ideal-: ~typ(us) *m (Sociol)* ideal type; **~vorstellung** *f* ideal.
Idee *f* **-n** [iˈdeːən] **(a)** idea. **die ~ zu etw** the idea for sth; **wie kommst du denn auf die ~?** whatever gave you that idea?; **ich kam auf die ~, Andrea zu fragen** I hit on the idea of asking Andrea; **jdn auf die ~ bringen, etw zu tun** to give sb the idea of doing sth. **(b)** *(ein wenig)* shade, trifle. **eine ~ Salz** a touch of salt; **keine ~ besser** not a whit better.
ideell *adj, Wert, Ziele* non-material; *Bedürfnisse, Unterstützung* spiritual.
ideen- [iˈdeːən-]: **~arm** *adj* lacking in ideas; **~los** *adj* devoid of ideas; **~reich** *adj* full of ideas.
identifizieren* **1** *vt* to identify. **2** *vr* **sich ~ mit** to identify with.
Identifizierung *f* identification.
identisch *adj* identical *(mit* with).
Identität *f* identity.
Ideologe *m*, **Ideologin** *f* ideologist.
Ideologie *f* ideology.
ideologisch *adj* ideological.
Idiom *nt* **-e** idiom.
idiomatisch *adj* idiomatic.
Idiot *m (wk)* **-en, -en** idiot.
Idioten-: **~hügel** *m (hum col)* beginners' *or* nursery *(Brit)* slope; **i~sicher** *adj (col)* foolproof *no adv.*
Idiotie *f* idiocy.
Idiotin *f* idiot.
idiotisch *adj* idiotic.
Idol *nt* **-e** idol.
Idylle *f* **-n** idyll.
idyllisch *adj* idyllic.
IG [iːˈgeː] *f* **-s** = **Industriegewerkschaft.**
Igel *m* **-** *(Zool)* hedgehog.
igitt(igitt)! *interj* ugh! *(col).*
Iglu [ˈiːglu] *m or nt* **-s** igloo.
Ignorant *m* ignoramus.
Ignoranz *f* ignorance.

ignorieren* *vt* to ignore.
ihm *pers pron dat of* **er, es** *(bei Personen)* to him; *(bei Tieren und Dingen)* to it; *(nach Präpositionen)* him/it. **ich gab es ~ I** gave it (to) him/it; **es war ~, als ob er träumte** he felt as though he were dreaming; **es ist ~ nicht gut** he doesn't feel well; **sie schnitt ~ die Haare** she cut his hair (for him); **ein Freund von ~** a friend of his, one of his friends; **wir gingen zu ~ (nach Hause)** we went to his place; **sie hat ~ einen Pulli gestrickt** she knitted him a sweater.
ihn *pers pron acc of* **er** him; *(bei Tieren, Dingen)* it.
ihnen *pers pron dat of* **sie** *pl* to them; *(nach Präpositionen)* them; *siehe* **ihm.**
Ihnen *pers pron dat of* **Sie** to you; *(nach Präpositionen)* you; *siehe* **ihm.**
ihr 1 *pers pron* **(a)** *2. pers pl nom* you. **(b)** *dat of* **sie** *sing (bei Personen)* to her; *(bei Tieren und Dingen)* to it; *(nach Präpositionen)* her/it; *siehe* **ihm. 2** *poss pron* **(a)** *(einer Person)* her; *(eines Tiers, Dings)* its. **(b)** *(von mehreren)* their.
Ihr *poss pron your.* **~ Franz Müller** *(Briefschluß)* yours, Franz Müller.
ihrer *pers pron* **(a)** *gen of* **sie** *sing (bei Personen)* of her. **wir werden ~ gedenken** *(geh)* we will remember her. **(b)** *gen of* **sie** *pl* of them.
Ihrer *pers pron gen of* **Sie** of you.
ihre(r, s) *poss pron (substantivisch)* **(a)** *(einer Person)* hers; *(eines Tiers)* its. **I~ Majestät Her Majesty; sie und die I~n** *(geh: Familie)* she and her family. **(b)** *(von mehreren)* theirs. **sie taten das ~** *(geh)* they did their bit.
Ihre(r, s) *poss pron sing and pl (substantivisch)* yours. **tun Sie das ~** *(geh)* you do your bit.
ihrerseits *adv (bei einer Person)* for her part; *(bei mehreren)* for their part; *(von ihrer Seite)* on her/their part.
Ihrerseits *adv* for your part; *(von Ihrer Seite)* on your part.
ihresgleichen *pron inv (von einer Person)* people like her; *(von mehreren)* people like them; *(von Dingen)* others like it. **eine Frechheit, die ~ sucht!** an incredible cheek!
Ihresgleichen *pron inv* people like you.
ihret-: **~wegen, ~willen** *adv (bei Personen) (wegen ihr/ihnen) (sing)* because of her; *(pl)* because of them; *(für sie)* on her/their behalf; *(bei Dingen und Tieren) (sing)* because of it; *(pl)* because of them; **sie sagte, ~wegen könnten wir gehen** she said that, as far as she was concerned, we could go.
Ihret-: **~wegen, ~willen** *adv* because of you; *(für Sie)* on your behalf.
ihrige *poss pron (old, geh)* **der/die/das ~** *(von einer Person)* hers; *(von mehreren)* theirs.
Ihrige *poss pron* **der/die/das ~** yours.
i.J. = **im Jahre.**
Ikone *f* **-n** icon.
illegal *adj* illegal.
Illegalität *f* illegality.
illegitim *adj* illegitimate.
Illusion *f* illusion. **sich** *(dat)* **~en machen** to delude oneself; **darüber macht er sich keine ~en** he doesn't have any illusions about it.
illusionär *adj* illusionary.
illusorisch *adj* illusory. **es ist völlig ~, zu glau-**

Illustration 231 indiskutabel

ben ... it's a complete illusion to believe ...

Illustration f illustration. **zur ~ von etw** to illustrate sth.

illustrieren* vt to illustrate (jdm etw sth for sb).

Illustrierte f (wk) **-n, -n** magazine.

Iltis m **-se** polecat.

im prep **= in dem (a) in the. ~ zweiten Stock** on the second floor; **~ Kino/Theater** at the cinema/ theatre; **~ Bett** in bed; **~ „Faust"** in "Faust"; **~ Mai** in May; **~ Alter von 91 Jahren** at the age of 91; **~ nächsten Jahr** next year. **(b) nicht ~ geringsten** not in the slightest; **~ Kommen/ Gehen sein** to be coming/going; **etw ~ Liegen/ Stehen tun** to do sth lying down/standing up; **~ Trab/Laufschritt** at a trot/run.

Image ['ɪmɪtʃ] nt **-s** image.

Imagepflege f (col) image-building.

imaginär adj imaginary.

Imbiß m **-sse** snack.

Imbiß-: ~halle f snack bar; **~stube** f cafe.

Imitation f imitation.

Imitator m, **Imitatorin** f imitator; (von einem Bild) copyist.

imitieren* vt to imitate.

Imker m **-** beekeeper.

immanent adj inherent, intrinsic. **einer Sache** (dat) **~ sein** to be inherent in sth.

Immatrikulation f matriculation.

immatrikulieren* vr to matriculate.

immens adj immense.

immer adv (a) always. **schon ~** always; **für ~** for ever, for always; **~ diese Probleme!** all these problems!; **~, wenn ...** whenever ...; **~ mal** (col) from time to time; **~ geradeaus gehen** to keep going straight on; **~ und ewig** (liter) for ever and ever; **~ noch** still; **~ noch nicht** still not; **~ wieder** again and again; **etw ~ wieder tun** to keep on doing sth; **wie ~** as always.
(b) (+comp) **~ besser** better and better; **~ häufiger** more and more often; **~ größer werdende Schulden** constantly increasing debts.
(c) wer/wie/wann/wo/was (auch) **~** whoever/ however/whenever/wherever/whatever.
(d) (col: jeweils) **gib mir ~ drei Bücher auf einmal** give me three books at a time; **~ am dritten Tag** every third day.

immer-: ~fort adv the whole time; **~grün** adj attr (lit,fig) evergreen; **~hin** advanyhow, at any rate; (wenigstens) at least; (schließlich) after all; **~während** adj attr perpetual; **~zu** adv the whole time.

Immigrant(in f) m immigrant.

Immigration f immigration.

immigrieren* vi aux sein to immigrate.

Immobilien [-'bi:liən] pl real estate sing; (in Zeitungsannoncen) property sing.

Immobilienhändler m estate agent (Brit), realtor (US).

immun adj immune (gegen to).

Immunität f immunity.

Imperativ m (Gram) imperative.

Imperfekt nt **-e** (Gram) imperfect (tense).

Imperialismus m imperialism.

imperialistisch adj imperialistic.

impfen vt to vaccinate, to inoculate.

Impf-: ~paß m vaccination card; **~pistole** f vaccination gun; **~schein** m vaccination certificate; **~schutz** m protection given by vaccination; **~stoff** m vaccine, serum.

Impfung f vaccination, inoculation.

Impfzwang m compulsory vaccination.

implizieren* vt to imply.

implodieren* vi aux sein to implode.

imponieren* vi to impress (jdm sb). **das imponiert mir** it's impressive.

imponierend adj impressive.

Import m **-e** import. **der ~ sollte den Export nicht**

übersteigen imports should not exceed exports.

Importeur [ɪmpɔr'tøːɐ] m importer.

Import- in cpds import; **~geschäft** nt (Handel) import trade; (Firma) import business.

importieren* vt to import.

Importland nt importing country.

imposant adj imposing; Leistung impressive.

impotent adj impotent.

Impotenz f impotence.

imprägnieren* vt to impregnate; (wasserdicht machen) to waterproof.

Imprägnierung f impregnation; (von Geweben) waterproofing.

Impressionismus m impressionism.

Impressionist m impressionist.

impressionistisch adj impressionistic.

Impressum nt, pl **Impressen** imprint.

Improvisation [ɪmproviza'tsioːn] f improvization.

improvisieren* [-vi'ziːrən] vti to improvize.

Impuls m **-e** impulse. **etw aus einem ~ heraus tun** to do sth on impulse; **einer Sache** (dat) **neue ~e geben** to give sth new impetus.

impulsiv adj impulsive. **~ handeln** to act impulsively.

imstande adj pred **~ sein, etw zu tun** (fähig) to be capable of doing sth; (in der Lage) to be in a position to do sth; **er ist zu allem ~** he's capable of anything.

in 1 prep siehe auch **im, ins (a)** (räumlich) (wo? +dat) in; (wohin?+acc) in, into. **sind Sie schon ~ Deutschland gewesen?** have you ever been to Germany?; **~ die Schule gehen** to go to school; **er ist ~ der Schule** he's at or in school. **(b)** (zeitlich) (wann? +dat) in; (bis +acc) into. **~ diesem Jahr** (laufendes Jahr) this year; (jenes Jahr) in that year; **heute ~ zwei Wochen** two weeks today; **bis ~s 18. Jahrhundert** into or up to the 18th century. **(c) ~ Englisch steht er sehr schwach** he's very weak in or at English; **das ist ~ Englisch** it's in English; **~ die Hunderte gehen** to run into (the) hundreds; **es ~ sich haben** (col) (Text) to be tough; (Whisky) to have quite a kick; (Torte) to be heavy.
2 adj pred (col) **~ sein** to be in (col).

inaktiv adj inactive; Mitglied non-active.

In|angriffnahme f no pl (form) commencement.

In|anspruchnahme f no pl (form) (eines Kredits) taking out; (von Rechten) exertion. **im Falle einer ~ der Arbeitslosenunterstützung** where unemployment benefit has been sought.

Inbegriff m perfect example; (der Schönheit, des Bösen etc) epitome.

inbegriffen adj pred included.

Inbetriebnahme f **-n** (form) commissioning; (von Gebäude, U-Bahn etc) inauguration.

indem conj (a) (während) while; (in dem Augenblick) as. **(b)** (dadurch, daß) **~ man etw macht** by doing sth.

Inder(in f) m **-** Indian.

indessen adv (a) (inzwischen) meanwhile, (in the) meantime. **(b)** (jedoch) however.

Index m **-e** or **Indizes** ['ɪnditseːs] index. **auf dem ~ stehen** (fig) to be banned.

Indianer(in f) m **-** (Red or American) Indian.

indianisch adj (Red or American) Indian.

Indien ['ɪndiən] nt India.

indifferent adj (geh) indifferent (gegenüber to).

indigniert adj (geh) indignant.

Indikation f (Med) indication (Jur). **medizinische/ soziale ~** (Jur) medical/social grounds for the termination of pregnancy.

Indikativ m (Gram) indicative.

Indikator m indicator.

indirekt adj indirect.

indisch adj Indian.

indiskret adj indiscreet.

Indiskretion f indiscretion.

indiskutabel adj out of the question.

indisponiert adj (geh) indisposed.
Individualist [ɪndividua'lɪst] m individualist.
individualistisch [ɪndividua'lɪstɪʃ] adj individualistic.
Individualität [ɪndividuali'tɛːt] f no pl individuality.
individuell [ɪndivi'duɛl] adj individual. **etw ~ gestalten** to give sth a personal note; **es ist ~ verschieden** it differs from person to person.
Individuum [ɪndi'viːduʊm] nt, pl **Individuen** [ɪndi'viːduən] individual.
Indiz nt **-ien** [-iən] (a) (Jur) clue; (als Beweismittel) piece of circumstantial evidence. **alles beruht nur auf ~ien** everything rests only on circumstantial evidence. (b) (Anzeichen) sign, indication (für of).
Indizienbeweis m circumstantial evidence no pl; piece of circumstantial evidence.
indogermanisch adj Indo-Germanic.
indoktrinieren* vt to indoctrinate.
Indonesien [-iən] nt Indonesia.
indonesisch adj Indonesian.
Indossament nt (Comm) endorsement.
industrialisieren* vt to industrialize.
Industrialisierung f industrialization.
Industrie f industry. **in der ~ arbeiten** to be in industry.
Industrie- in cpds industrial; **~anlage** f industrial plant; **~betrieb** m industrial firm; **~erzeugnis** nt industrial product; **~gebiet** nt industrial area; **~gewerkschaft** f industrial trade union or labor union (US); **~kaufmann** m industrial manager.
industriell adj industrial.
Industrielle(r) mf decl as adj industrialist.
Industrie-: **~roboter** m industrial robot; **~staat** m industrial nation; **~- und Handelskammer** f chamber of industry and commerce; **~zweig** m branch of industry.
in|einander adv sein, liegen etc in each other; legen, hängen etc into each other. **~ übergehen** to merge (into each other); **sich ~ verlieben** to fall in love with each other.
in|einander-: **~fließen** vi sep irreg aux sein to merge; **~greifen** vi sep irreg (lit) to interlock; (Zahnräder) to mesh; (fig: Ereignisse etc) to overlap; **~passen** vi sep to fit into each other.
infam adj infamous.
Infanterie f infantry.
Infanterist m infantryman.
infantil adj infantile.
Infarkt m **-e** (Herz~) coronary.
Infektion f infection.
Infektions-: **~herd** m focus of infection; **~krankheit** f infectious disease.
Infiltration f infiltration.
Infinitiv m infinitive.
infizieren* 1 vt to infect. 2 vr to be infected (bei by).
in flagranti adv in the act, red-handed.
Inflation f inflation.
inflationär [ɪnflatsio'nɛːɐ] adj inflationary. **sich ~ entwickeln** to become inflated.
Inflations-: **i~hemmend** adj anti-inflationary; **~rate** f rate of inflation.
infolge prep +gen or von as a result of.
infolgedessen adv consequently.
Informatik f information science.
Informatiker(in f) m - information scientist.
Information f (a) information no pl (über +acc about, on). **eine ~** (a piece of) information; **zu Ihrer ~** for your information. (b) (~sstelle) information desk. (c) (~en nt pl (Comp) data.
informationell [ɪnfɔrmatsio'nɛl] adj informational.
Informations-: **~büro** n information bureau; **~fluß** m no pl flow of information; **~material** nt informative material; **~quelle** f source of infor-

mation; **~theorie** f information theory.
informativ adj informative.
informell adj informal.
informieren* 1 vt to inform (über +acc, von about). **da bist du falsch informiert** you've been misinformed. 2 vr to find out.
Infra-: **i~rot** adj infra-red; **~rotstrahler** m - infra-red lamp; **~struktur** f infrastructure.
Infusion f infusion.
Ing. = **Ingenieur**.
Ingenieur(in f) [ɪnʒe'niøːɐ, -iø:rɪn] m engineer.
Ingenieur-: **~büro** nt engineer's office; **~schule** f school of engineering.
Ingwer m no pl ginger.
Inh. = **Inhaber** prop.; **Inhalt**.
Inhaber(in f) m - (von Geschäft) owner; (von Konto, Lizenz, Rekord) holder; (von Scheck, Paß) bearer.
inhaftieren* vt insep to take into custody.
inhalieren* vti insep (Med, col) to inhale.
Inhalt m **-e** (a) contents pl; (von Buch, Begriff auch) content; (des Lebens) meaning. **was hatte das Gespräch zum ~?** what was the content of the discussion?; **ein Brief des ~s, daß ...** (form) a letter to the effect that ... (b) (Math) (Flächen~) area; (Raum~) volume.
inhaltlich adj as regards content.
Inhalts-: **~angabe** f summary, précis (esp Sch); **i~los** adj empty; Buch, Vortrag lacking in content; **i~reich** adj full; **~verzeichnis** nt list of contents.
inhuman adj (unmenschlich, brutal) inhuman.
Initiale [ini'tsiaːlə] f -n (geh) initial.
Initiative [initsia'tiːvə] f initiative. **aus eigener ~** on one's own initiative; **die ~ ergreifen** to take the initiative.
Initiator(in f) [ini'tsiaːtɔr, -'toːrɪn] m (geh) initiator.
Injektion f injection.
injizieren* [ɪnji'tsiːrən] vt (form) to inject (jdm etw sb with sth).
Inkaufnahme f no pl (form) acceptance. **unter ~ finanzieller Verluste** accepting the inevitable financial losses.
inkl. = **inklusive** incl.
inklusive [-ziːvə] 1 prep +gen inclusive of. 2 adv inclusive.
inkognito adv incognito.
inkompetent adj incompetent.
inkonsequent adj inconsistent.
Inkrafttreten nt no pl **bei ~ von etw** when sth comes/came into effect.
Inkubationszeit f incubation period.
Inland nt no pl (a) (als Staatsgebiet) home. **im ~ hergestellte Waren** home-produced goods; **im In- und Ausland** at home and abroad. (b) (Inneres eines Landes) inland. **im ~** inland.
Inland- in cpds (Comm) home, domestic; (Geog) inland; **~flug** m domestic or internal flight.
inländisch adj home attr, domestic; (Geog) inland.
Inlands-: **~gespräch** nt inland call; **~markt** m home or domestic market; **~porto** nt inland postage.
inmitten 1 prep +gen in the middle of. 2 adv **~ von** amongst, surrounded by.
innehaben vt sep irreg (form) Amt etc to hold.
innehalten vi sep irreg to pause, to stop. **in der Rede ~** to pause.
innen adv inside. **~ und außen** inside and out(side); **nach ~** inwards; **tief ~ tut es doch weh** deep down inside it really hurts; **das Band befördert die Kohle nach ~** the conveyor-belt carries the coal inside; **von ~** from the inside.
Innen-: **~antenne** f indoor aerial (Brit) or antenna (US); **~architekt** m interior designer; **~aufnahme** f indoor photo(graph); (Film) indoor shot; **~ausstattung** f interior décor no pl; (das Ausstat-

ten) interior decoration and furnishing; *(von Auto)* interior fittings *pl*; ~**bahn** *f (Sport)* inside lane; ~**dienst** *m* office duty; **im** ~**dienst sein to** work in the office; ~**einrichtung** *f* interior furnishing; ~**hof** *m* inner courtyard; ~**kurve** *f* inside bend; ~**leben** *nt no pl (col)* **(a)** *(seelisch)* emotional life; **(b)** *(körperlich)* insides *pl*; ~**minister** *m* minister of the interior; *(in GB)* Home Secretary; *(in den USA)* Secretary of the Interior; ~**ministerium** *nt* ministry of the interior; *(in GB)* Home Office; *(in den USA)* Department of the Interior; ~**politik** *f* domestic policy/ policies *pl*; **i**~**politisch** *adj* domestic, home *attr*; **auf i**~**politischem Gebiet** in the field of home affairs; ~**raum** *m* **(a)** inner room; **(b)** *no pl* room inside; *(von Wagen auch)* interior; *(von Stadion)* central area; **mit großem** ~**raum** with a lot of room inside; ~**seite** *f* inside; ~**stadt** *f* town/city centre *(Brit)* or center *(US)*; ~**tasche** *f* inside pocket; ~**temperatur** *f (in Gebäude)* indoor temperature; ~**welt** *f* inner world.

inner-: ~**betrieblich** *adj* internal company; **etw** ~**betrieblich regeln** to settle sth within the company; ~**deutsch** *adj* German domestic *attr*; ~**deutscher Handel** domestic trade in Germany.

Innereien *pl* innards *pl*.

innere(r, s) *adj* inner; *(im Körper befindlich, inländisch)* internal. **Facharzt für** ~ **Krankheiten** internist; **eine** ~ **Uhr** *(col)* an internal *or* a biological clock; **vor meinem** ~**n Auge** in my mind's eye; ~ **Führung** *(Mil)* moral leadership. **Innere(s)** *nt decl as adj* **(a)** inside; *(von Wagen, Schloß auch)* interior; *(Mitte)* middle. **das** ~ **nach außen kehren** to turn something inside out; **die Organe im** ~**n des Körpers** the organs inside the body. **(b)** *(fig: Gemüt, Geist)* heart. **ich wußte, was in seinem** ~**n vorging** I knew what was going on inside him.

innerhalb 1 *prep +gen* inside, within. ~ **dieser Regelung** within this ruling. **2** *adv* inside.

innerlich *adj* **(a)** *(körperlich)* internal. **dieses Medikament ist** ~ **anzuwenden** this medicine is to be taken internally. **(b)** *(geistig, seelisch)* inward, inner *no adv*; *Mensch* inward; *Hemmung* inner. **ein** ~ **gefestigter Mensch** a person of inner strength.

Innerlichkeit *f (liter)* inwardness.

inner-: ~**örtlich** *adj* in built-up areas; ~**parteilich** *adj* within the party; ~**parteiliche Demokratie** democracy (with)in the party structure.

innerste(r, s) *adj superl of* **innere(r, s)** innermost.

Innerste(s) *nt decl as adj (lit, fig)* heart. **bis ins** ~ **getroffen** hurt to the quick.

innewohnen *vi sep +dat* to be inherent in.

innig *adj Grüße, Beileid* heartfelt; *Vergnügen* deep; *Freundschaft* intimate. **mein** ~**ster Wunsch** my dearest wish; **jdn** ~ **lieben** to love sb deeply.

Innigkeit *f (von Empfindung)* depth; *(von Liebe)* intensity; *(von Freundschaft)* intimacy.

Innung *f (trade)* guild. **du blamierst die ganze** ~ *(hum col)* you're letting the whole side down.

in|offiziell *adj* unofficial.

Input ['input] *m or nt* **-s** input.

Inquisition *f* Inquisition.

ins = in das. ~ **Rollen kommen** to start rolling.

Insasse *m (wk)* **-n, -n, Insassin** *f (eines Fahrzeuges)* passenger; *(einer Anstalt)* inmate.

Insassenversicherung *f* passenger insurance.

insbesondere *adv* particularly.

Inschrift *f* inscription.

Insekt *nt* **-en** insect.

Insekten-: ~**bekämpfung** *f* insect control; ~**gift** *nt* insecticide; ~**plage** *f* plague of insects; ~**pulver** *nt* insect powder; ~**stich** *m* *(von Mücken, Flöhen)* insect bite; *(von Bienen, Wespen)* (insect) sting; ~**vertilgungsmittel** *nt* insecticide.

Insel *f* **-n** *(lit, fig)* island.

Insel-: ~**bewohner** *m* islander; ~**gruppe** *f* archipelago, group of islands; ~**staat** *m* island state; ~**volk** *nt* island race; ~**welt** *f* island world; **die** ~**welt Mittelamerikas** the world of the Central American islands.

Inserat *nt* advert *(Brit col)*, ad *(col)*, advertisement.

Inserent *m* advertiser.

inserieren* *vti* to advertise.

insgeheim *adv* secretly, in secret.

insgesamt *adv (alles zusammen)* altogether; *(im großen und ganzen)* all in all. **die Kosten belaufen sich auf** ~ **1.000 DM** the costs amount to a total of DM 1,000.

Insider ['insaidə] *m* - insider. **der Witz war nur für** ~ **verständlich** that was an in-joke.

insofern 1 *adv* in this respect. ~ ... **als** in so far as, inasmuch as. **2** [inzo'fɛrn] *conj (wenn)* if.

Insolvenz [inzolvɛnts] *f (Comm)* insolvency.

insoweit [in'zo:vait] *adv*, [inzo'vait] *conj siehe* **insofern.**

in spe [in'spe:] *adj (col)* **unser Schwiegersohn** ~ our son-in-law to be, our future son-in-law.

Inspekteur [inspɛk'tø:ɐ] *m (Mil)* Chief of Staff.

Inspektion *f* inspection; *(Aut)* service. **ich habe mein Auto zur** ~ **gebracht** I've taken my car in for a service.

Inspektionsreise *f* tour of inspection.

Inspektor(in *f)* [in'spɛktɔr, -'to:rin] *m* inspector.

Inspiration [inspira'tsio:n] *f* inspiration.

inspirieren* [inspi'ri:rən] *vt* to inspire. **sich von etw** ~ **lassen** to get one's inspiration from sth.

inspizieren* [inspi'tsi:rən] *vt* to inspect.

Installateur [instala'tø:ɐ] *m* plumber; *(Elektro~)* electrician; *(Gas~)* gas-fitter.

Installation [instala'tsio:n] *f* installation.

installieren* [insta'li:rən] *vt* to install *(auch fig)*.

instand *adj* **etw** ~ **halten** to keep sth in good condition; **etw** ~ **setzen** to get sth into condition.

Instandhaltung *f* maintenance.

inständig *adj* urgent. ~ **bitten** to beg; ~ **hoffen** to hope fervently.

Instandsetzung *f (von Gerät)* overhaul; *(von Gebäude)* restoration.

Instanz [in'stants] *f* **(a)** *(Behörde)* authority. **(b)** *(Jur)* court. **Verhandlung in erster/zweiter** ~ first/second court-case; **er ging von einer** ~ **zur anderen** he went through all the courts.

Instinkt [in'stiŋkt] *m* **-e** *(lit, fig)* instinct.

instinktiv [instiŋk'ti:f] *adj* instinctive.

Institut [insti'tu:t] *nt* **-e** institute.

Institution [institu'tsio:n] *f* institution.

instruieren* [instru'i:rən] *vt* to instruct; *(über Unternehmen, Plan etc)* to brief.

Instruktion [instruk'tsio:n] *f* instruction.

Instrument [instru'mɛnt] *nt* instrument.

instrumental [instrumɛn'ta:l] *adj (Mus)* instrumental.

Instrumental- *in cpds* instrumental.

Instrumentarium [instrumɛn'ta:riʊm] *nt* instruments *pl*; *(fig)* apparatus.

Insulaner(in *f)* *m* - *(usu hum)* islander.

Insulin *nt no pl* insulin.

inszenieren* *vt* **(a)** *(Theat)* to direct; *(TV)* to produce. **(b)** *(fig)* to stage-manage. **einen Streit** ~ to start an argument.

Inszenierung *f* production.

intakt *adj* intact.

integer *adj (geh)* **ein integrer Mensch** a person of integrity.

Integralrechnung *f* integral calculus.

Integration *f* integration.

integrieren* *vt* to integrate *(auch Math)*. **integrierte Gesamtschule** comprehensive (school) *(Brit)*.

Integrität *f* integrity.

Intellekt *m no pl* intellect.

intellektuell adj intellectual.
Intellektuelle(r) mf decl as adj intellectual.
intelligent adj intelligent.
Intelligenz f intelligence; (Personengruppe) intelligentsia pl.
Intelligenzbestie f (pej col) egghead (col).
Intelligenz-: ~quotient m IQ; ~test m intelligence test; einen ~test mit jdm machen to test sb's IQ.
Intendant m director; theatre-manager (Brit), theater-manager (US).
intendieren* vt (geh) to intend.
Intensität f intensity.
intensiv adj Arbeit, Forschung intensive; Farbe, Gefühl intense; Geruch powerful.
intensivieren* [-'vi:rən] vt to intensify.
Intensivierung f intensification.
Intensivstation f intensive care unit.
Intention f (geh) intention.
Inter- in cpds inter-; ~city-Zug m inter-city train.
interessant adj interesting. zu diesem Preis ist das nicht ~ für uns (Comm) we are not interested at that price; sich ~ machen to attract attention.
interessanterweise adv interestingly enough.
Interesse nt -n interest. ~ an jdm/etw or für jdn/etw haben to be interested in sb/sth; aus ~ out of interest; es liegt in Ihrem eigenen ~ it's in your own interest(s); sein ~ gilt ... his interest lies in ...; das ist für uns nicht von ~ that's of no interest to us.
Interesse-: i~halber adv out of interest; i~los adj indifferent; ~losigkeit f indifference.
Interessen-: ~gebiet nt field of interest; ~gegensatz m clash of interests.
Interessent(in f) m interested party. es haben sich mehrere ~en gemeldet several people have shown interest.
Interessenvertretung f representation of interests; (Personen) group representing one's interests.
interessieren* 1 vt to interest (für, an +dat in). das interessiert mich nicht! I'm not interested. 2 vr to be interested (für in).
interessiert adj interested (an +dat in). ~ zuhören to listen with interest; vielseitig ~ sein to have a wide range of interests; politisch ~ interested in politics.
Interims- in cpds interim; ~regierung f caretaker government.
Inter-: i~konfessionell adj interdenominational; ~kontinentalrakete f intercontinental missile.
Intermezzo [-'metso] nt -s or **Intermezzi** (Mus) intermezzo; (fig) interlude.
intern adj internal. diese Maßnahmen müssen ~ bleiben these measures must be kept private.
Internat nt boarding school.
international [ɪntɐnatsio'naːl] adj international.
Internationale [ɪntɐnatsio'naːlə] f -n Internationale.
Internatsschüler m boarder.
internieren* vt to intern.
Internierung f internment.
Internist(in f) m internist.
Interpol f Interpol.
Interpret m (wk) -en, -en interpreter (of music, art etc). Lieder verschiedener ~en songs by various singers.
Interpretation f interpretation.
interpretieren* vt to interpret. etw falsch ~ to misinterpret sth.
Interpretin f siehe **Interpret**.
Interpunktion f punctuation.
Intershop ['ɪntɐʃɔp] m -s (DDR) international shop.
Intervall [-'val] nt -e interval.
intervenieren* [-ve'niːrən] vi to intervene.
Intervention [-vɛn'tsioːn] f intervention.

Interview ['ɪntɐvjuː] nt -s interview.
interviewen* [-'vjuːən] vt to interview (jdn zu etw sb about sth).
Interviewer(in f) [-'vjuːɐ, -vjuːərɪn] m - interviewer.
intim adj intimate. ~e Beziehungen (euph: sexuell) intimate relations; ein ~er Kenner von etw sein to have an intimate knowledge of sth.
Intim-: ~bereich m (Anat) genital area; ~feind m best enemy; ~hygiene f personal hygiene.
Intimität f intimacy. zwischen den beiden kam es zu ~en they became intimate with each other.
Intim-: ~sphäre f private life; jds ~sphäre verletzen to invade sb's privacy; ~verkehr m intimacy; ~verkehr mit jdm haben to be intimate with sb.
intolerant adj intolerant (jdm/einer Sache gegenüber of sb/sth).
Intoleranz f intolerance.
Intonation f intonation.
intonieren* vt (a) einen Satz falsch ~ to give a sentence the wrong intonation. (b) (Mus) Melodie to sing; (Kapelle) to play; Ton to give.
intransitiv adj intransitive.
Intrigant(in f) m schemer, intriguer.
Intrige f -n intrigue.
intrigieren* vi to intrigue, to scheme.
introvertiert [-ver'tiːɐt] adj introverted. ~ sein to be an introvert.
Intuition [ɪntui'tsioːn] f intuition.
intuitiv [ɪntui'tiːf] adj intuitive.
intus adj (col) etw ~ haben (wissen) to have got sth into one's head (col); Essen, Alkohol to have sth down one (col).
Invalide [ɪnva'liːdə] m (wk) -n, -n disabled person, invalid.
Invalidenrente f disability pension.
Invalidität [ɪnvalidi'tɛːt] f disability.
Invasion [ɪnva:zioːn] f (lit, fig) invasion.
Inventar [ɪnvɛntaːɐ] nt -e (a) (Einrichtung) fittings pl; (Maschinen) equipment no pl, plant no pl. (b) (Verzeichnis) inventory; (Comm) assets and liabilities pl. er gehört schon zum ~ (hum) he's part of the furniture.
Inventur [ɪnvɛn'tuːɐ] f stocktaking. ~ machen to stocktake.
investieren* [ɪnvɛs'tiːrən] vti (Comm, fig) to invest. Gefühle in jdn ~ (col) to become emotionally involved with sb.
Investition [ɪnvɛst-] f investment.
Investment [ɪn'vɛstmənt] nt -s investment.
inwendig adj inside. jdn/etw in- und auswendig kennen (col) to know sb/sth inside out.
inwiefern, inwieweit adv to what extent. ~? in what way?
Inzest m -e incest no pl.
Inzucht f inbreeding.
inzwischen adv in the meantime, meanwhile. er ist ~ 18 geworden he's now 18.
Ion [ioːn] nt -en ion.
IOK [iːʔoː'kaː] nt = **Internationales Olympisches Komitee** IOC.
IQ = **Intelligenzquotient** IQ.
i.R. [iː'ɛr] = **im Ruhestand** retd.
Irak [i'raːk, 'iːrak] m (der) ~ Iraq.
Iraker(in f) m - Iraqi.
irakisch adj Iraqi.
Iran m (der) ~ Iran.
Iraner(in f) m - Iranian.
iranisch adj Iranian.
irden adj earthenware, earthen.
irdisch adj earthly no adv. den Weg alles I~en gehen to go the way of all flesh.
Ire m (wk) -n, -n Irishman; Irish boy. die ~n the Irish; er ist ~ he is Irish.
irgend 1 adv wenn ~ möglich if it's at all possible; wann du ~ kannst whenever you can; wer (es) ~ kann whoever can; so lange ich ~ kann as long

as I possibly can; **wo es ~ geht** wherever possible. **2** *mit indef pron* ~ **jemand** somebody; *(fragend, verneinend, bedingend)* anybody; **ich bin nicht** ~ **jemand** I'm not just anybody; ~ **etwas** something; *(fragend, verneinend, bedingend)* anything; **was zieh' ich an?** — ~ **etwas** what shall I wear? — anything, any old thing *(col)*; ~ **so ein Tier** some animal.

irgend|ein *indef pron* some; *(fragend, verneinend, bedingend)* any. **haben Sie noch ~en Wunsch?** is there anything else you would like?; **das kann ~ anderer machen** someone else can do it.

irgend|eine(r, s) *indef pron (nominal) (bei Personen)* somebody; *(bei Dingen)* something; *(fragend, verneinend, bedingend)* anybody/ anything. **welchen wollen Sie?** — ~**n** which one do you want? — any one, any old one *(col)*.

irgend|einmal *adv* sometime; *(fragend, bedingend)* ever.

irgendwann *adv* sometime. ~ **einmal** some time; *(fragend, bedingend)* ever.

irgendwas *indef pron (col) siehe* **irgend 2.**

irgendwelche(r, s) *indef pron* some; *(fragend, verneinend, bedingend, jede beliebige)* any.

irgendwer *indef pron (col) siehe* **irgend 2.**

irgendwie *adv* somehow (or other). **ist es ~ möglich?** is it at all possible?

irgendwo *adv* somewhere; *(fragend, verneinend, bedingend)* anywhere.

irgendwoher *adv* from somewhere; *(fragend, verneinend, bedingend)* from anywhere.

irgendwohin *adv* somewhere; *(fragend, verneinend, bedingend)* anywhere.

Irin *f* Irishwoman; Irish girl. **sie ist ~** she is Irish.

Iris *f* - iris.

irisch *adj* Irish.

Irland *nt* Ireland; *(Republik ~)* Eire.

Irländer(in *f)* *m* - *siehe* **Ire, Irin.**

Ironie *f* irony.

ironisch *adj* ironic, ironical.

ironisieren* *vt* to treat ironically.

irrational ['ɪratsɪoːaːl] *adj* irrational.

irr(e) **1** *adj* **(a)** *(geistesgestört)* crazy, insane. **das macht mich ganz ~** it's driving me crazy; **wie ~** *(fig col)* like crazy *(col)*. **(b)** *pred (verwirrt, unsicher)* confused. **(c)** *(col)* Party, Hut wild *(col)*, crazy *(col)*. **2** *adv (verrückt)* insanely; *(col: sehr)* incredibly *(col)*. ~ **gut** *(col)* way out *(col)*.

Irre *f* **jdn in die ~ führen** *(lit, fig)* to lead sb astray.

irreal *adj* unreal.

Irre-: **i~führen** *vt sep* to mislead; **sich i~führen lassen** to be misled; **i~führend** *adj* misleading; **~führung** *f* misleading.

irregulär *adj* irregular.

irrelevant ['ɪrelevant] *adj* irrelevant *(für* for, to).

irremachen *vt sep* to confuse, to muddle.

irren 1 *vi aux sein (umher~)* to wander. **2** *vir* to be mistaken *or* wrong. **I~ ist menschlich** *(Prov)* to err is human *(Prov)*; **jeder kann sich mal ~** anyone can make a mistake; **wenn ich mich**

nicht sehr irre ... unless I'm very much mistaken ...

Irren-: ~**anstalt** *f (dated)*, ~**haus** *nt (dated, pej)* lunatic asylum *(dated)*; **hier geht es zu wie im** ~**haus** *(col)* this place is an absolute madhouse.

irreparabel *adj* irreparable.

Irre(r) *mf decl as adj* lunatic; *(col auch)* madman. **ein armer ~r** *(hum col)* a poor fool.

Irr-: ~**fahrt** *f* wandering; ~**glaube(n)** *m (Rel, fig)* heresy; *(irrige Ansicht)* mistaken belief.

irrig *adj* incorrect, wrong.

irritieren* *vt (verwirren)* to confuse, to muddle; *(ärgern)* to irritate.

Irr-: ~**lehre** *f* heresy; ~**licht** *nt* will-o'-the-wisp.

Irrsinn *m no pl* madness, insanity. **so ein ~!** that's madness!

irrsinnig *adj* mad, crazy. **wie ein I~er** like a madman; **ein ~er Verkehr** *(col)* an incredible amount of traffic; ~ **komisch** incredibly funny.

Irrtum *m* mistake, error. **ein ~ von ihm** a mistake on his part; **im ~ sein** to be wrong *or* mistaken; ~**! wrong!**; ~ **vorbehalten** errors excepted.

irrtümlich **1** *adj attr* mistaken, erroneous. **2** *adv* mistakenly; *(aus Versehen)* by mistake.

irrtümlicherweise *adv* mistakenly; *(aus Versehen)* by mistake.

Irrweg *m (fig)* **auf dem ~ sein** to be on the wrong track; **zu studieren erwies sich für ihn als ~** going to university proved to be a mistake for him.

Ischias *m or nt no pl* sciatica.

Ischiasnerv *m* sciatic nerve.

Islam *m no pl* Islam.

islamisch *adj* Islamic.

Island *nt* Iceland.

Isländer(in *f)* *m* - Icelander.

isländisch *adj* Icelandic.

Isolation *f* **(a)** isolation; *(von Häftlingen)* solitary confinement. **(b)** *(Elec, gegen Lärm, Kälte etc)* insulation.

Isolierband *nt* insulating tape *(Brit)*, friction tape *(US)*.

isolieren* **1** *vt* **(a)** to isolate. **völlig isoliert leben** to live in complete isolation. **(b)** *elektrische Leitungen, Häuser, Fenster* to insulate. **2** *vr* to isolate oneself (from the world).

Isolier-: ~**haft** *f* solitary confinement; ~**station** *f* isolation ward.

Israel ['ɪsraɛl] *nt* Israel.

Israeli *m* -(s) Israeli.

israelisch *adj* Israeli.

iß *imper sing of* **essen.**

ist **3. pers sing pres of sein**[1].

Ist-: ~**-Bestand** *m (Geld)* cash in hand; *(Waren)* actual stock; ~**-Stärke** *f (Mil)* effective strength.

Italien [-ɪən] *nt* Italy.

Italiener(in *f)* [-'liɛnɐ, -ərɪn] *m* - Italian.

italienisch [-'liːnɪʃ] *adj* Italian. **die ~e Schweiz** Italian-speaking Switzerland.

i.V. = **in Vertretung** pp.

J

J, j [jɔt] *nt* -, - J, j.
ja *adv* **(a)** yes; *(bei Trauung)* I do. **kommst du morgen?** — ~ are you coming tomorrow? — **yes(, I am); haben Sie das gesehen?** — ~ did you see it? — yes(, I did); **ich glaube** ~ (yes) I think so; ~ **und amen zu allem sagen** *(col)* to accept everything without question.
(b) *(fragend, zweifelnd)* ~? really?; **ich habe gekündigt** — ~? I've quit — have you?
(c) aber ~! yes, of course; **das ist also abgemacht,** ~? that's agreed then, OK?; **ach** ~! oh yes; **nun** ~ oh well; ~ **doch** yes, of course; **sei** ~ **vorsichtig!** do be careful; **vergessen Sie es** *ja* **nicht!** don't forget, whatever you do!; **sie ist** ~ **erst fünf** (after all) she's only five; **das ist** ~ **richtig, aber ...** that's (certainly) right, but ...; **das ist gut,** ~ **sogar sehr gut** it's good, in fact it's (even) very good; **da haben wir's** ~ there you are (then); **da kommt er** ~ here he comes; **das sag' ich** ~! that's just what I'm saying; **das wissen wir** ~ **alle** we know that (anyway); **Sie wissen** ~, **daß ...** as you know ...; **Sie wissen** ~, **wie das so ist** you know how it is, (don't you?); **das ist** ~ **fürchterlich** that's (really) terrible.
Ja *nt* -(s) yes. **mit** ~ **antworten/stimmen** to answer/vote yes.
Jacht *f* -en yacht.
Jacke *f* -n jacket, coat *(esp US)*; *(Woll~)* cardigan. **das ist** ~ **wie Hose** *(col)* it's six of one and half a dozen of the other *(col)*.
Jacken-: ~**kleid** *nt (Kleid und Jacke)* two-piece; ~**tasche** *f* jacket *or* coat *(esp US)* pocket.
Jacketkrone ['dʒɛkɪt-] *f* jacket crown.
Jackett [ʒa'kɛt] *nt* -s jacket, coat *(esp US)*.
Jade *m or f no pl* jade.
Jagd *f* -en hunt; *(Ausführung der* ~) hunting; *(fig: Verfolgung)* hunt *(nach* for), chase *(nach* after); *(Wettlauf)* race. **die** ~ **auf Rotwild** deer-hunting; **auf die** ~ **(nach etw) gehen** *(lit, fig)* to go hunting (for sth); **auf jdn/etw** ~ **machen** *(lit, fig)* to hunt for sb/sth; **die** ~ **nach Geld** the pursuit of money.
Jagd-: j~**bar** *adj* ... **sind** j~**bar** ... may be hunted, ... are fair game; ~**beute** *f* bag; ~**bomber** *m (Mil)* fighter-bomber; ~**flieger** *m (Mil)* fighter pilot; ~**flugzeug** *nt (Mil)* fighter plane; ~**gebiet** *nt* hunting ground; ~**gesellschaft** *f* hunting party; ~**gewehr** *nt* hunting rifle; ~**hund** *m* hound; ~**revier** *nt* shoot; ~**schein** *m* hunting licence *(Brit) or* license *(US)*; **einen** ~**schein haben** *(hum col)* to be certified *(col)*; ~**wild** *nt* game; ~**wurst** *f* smoked sausage; ~**zeit** *f* hunting season.
jagen 1 *vt* to hunt; *(hetzen)* to chase, to drive. **jdn in die Flucht** ~ to put sb to flight; **ein Unglück jagte das andere** one misfortune followed on the other; **mit diesem Essen kannst du mich** ~ *(col)* I wouldn't touch that food with a barge pole *(Brit col) or* a ten foot pole *(US col)*. **2** *vi* **(a)** *(auf die Jagd gehen)* to hunt, to go hunting. **(b)** *aux sein (rasen)* to race. **nach etw** ~ to chase after sth.
Jäger *m* - **(a)** hunter, huntsman. **(b)** *(Mil: Flugzeug)* fighter (plane).
Jägerei *f no pl* hunting.
Jägerin *f* huntress, huntswoman.
Jäger-: ~**latein** *nt (col)* hunters' tales *pl*; ~**schnitzel** *nt (Cook)* cutlet served with mushroom sauce.

Jaguar *m* -e jaguar.
jäh *adj (geh)* **(a)** *(plötzlich)* sudden. **(b)** *(steil)* sheer. **der Abhang fällt** ~ **herab** the slope falls sharply.
Jahr *nt* -e year. **ein halbes** ~ six months *sing or pl*; **ein dreiviertel** ~ nine months *sing or pl*; **anderthalb** ~**e** one and a half years *sing*, eighteen months *sing or pl*; **zwei** ~**e Garantie** a two-year guarantee; **im** ~(e) **1066** in (the year) 1066; **die sechziger** ~**e** the sixties *sing or pl*; **alle zehn** ~**e** every ten years; **auf** ~**e hinaus** for years ahead; **auf** ~ **und Tag** to the very day; **einmal im** ~(e) once a year; **das Buch des** ~**es** the book of the year; **nach** ~ **und Tag** after (many) years; **mit den** ~**en** as the years go by; **zwischen den** ~**en** *(col)* between Christmas and New Year; **er ist zehn** ~**e (alt)** he is ten years old; **mit dreißig** ~**en** at the age of thirty; **in die** ~**e kommen** *(col)* to be getting on (in years); **in den besten** ~**en sein** to be in the prime of one's life.
jahr|aus *adv:* ~, **jahrein** year in, year out.
Jahrbuch *nt* yearbook; *(Kalender)* almanac.
jahrelang 1 *adj attr* lasting for years. ~**es Warten/**~**e Forschungen** years of waiting/ research. **2** *adv* for years. **und dann dauerte es noch** ~, **bevor ...** and then it took years until ...
jähren *vr* **heute jährt sich der Tag, an dem ...** it's a year ago today that ...
Jahres- *in cpds* annual, yearly; ~**abschluß** *m (Comm)* annual accounts *pl;* ~**beginn** *m* beginning of a/the new year; ~**beitrag** *m* annual subscription; ~**bericht** *m* annual report; ~**bestzeit** *f (Sport)* best time of the year; ~**bilanz** *f (Comm)* annual balance sheet; ~**einkommen** *nt* annual income; ~**ende** *nt* end of the year; ~**hauptversammlung** *f (Comm)* annual general meeting, AGM; ~**karte** *f* annual season ticket; ~**tag** *m* anniversary; ~**umsatz** *m (Comm)* yearly turnover; ~**urlaub** *m* annual holiday *or* leave; ~**wechsel** *m,* ~**wende** *f* new year; ~**zeit** *f* season.
Jahr-: ~**gang** *m* **(a)** *(Sch, Univ)* year; **er ist** ~**gang 1950** he was born in 1950; **(b)** *(einer Zeitschrift)* year's issues *pl;* **(c)** *(von Wein)* vintage, year; ~**hundert** *nt* -e century.
jahrhunderte-: ~**alt** *adj* centuries-old; ~**lang 1** *adj* lasting for centuries; **2** *adv* for centuries.
Jahrhundertwende *f* turn of the century.
jährlich 1 *adj* annual, yearly. **2** *adv* annually, yearly; *(Comm)* per annum. **zweimal** ~ twice a year.
Jahrmarkt *m* fair, funfair *(Brit)*.
Jahr-: ~**tausend** *nt* -e millennium, a thousand years; ~**tausende** thousands of years; ~**zehnt** *nt* -e decade; j~**zehntelang 1** *adj* lasting for decades; **2** *adv* for decades.
Jähzorn *m* violent temper.
jähzornig *adj* bad-tempered.
Jalousie [ʒalu'ziː] *f* venetian blind.
Jamaika *nt* Jamaica.
jamaikanisch *adj* Jamaican.
Jammer *m no pl (Elend)* misery, wretchedness; *(Klage)* wailing, lamentation. **es wäre ein** ~, **wenn ...** *(col)* it would be a crying shame if ... *(col)*.
Jammerlappen *m (pej col)* wet *(col)*.
jämmerlich 1 *adj* wretched; *Zustand auch* de-

plorable. **2** *adv (col: sehr)* terribly *(col)*.
jammern *vi* to wail *(über +acc* over); *(sich beklagen auch)* to moan.
jammerschade *adj* es ist ~ *(col)* it's a crying shame *(col)*.
Januar *m* **-e** January; *siehe* **März.**
Japan *nt* Japan.
Japaner(in *f)* *m* - Japanese.
japanisch *adj* Japanese; *siehe* **deutsch.**
Japanisch(e) *nt decl as adj* Japanese; *siehe* **Deutsch(e).**
Jargon [ʒar'gõː] *m* **-s** jargon.
Jasager *m* - *(pej)* yes-man.
Jasmin *m* **-e** jasmine.
Jastimme *f* vote in favour (of); *(Parl auch)* aye *(Brit)*, yea *(US)*.
jäten *vti* to weed. **Unkraut** ~ to weed.
Jauche *f* **-n** liquid manure; *(pej col) (Getränk)* piss *(col!)*; *(Abwasser)* sewage.
Jauchegrube *f* cesspool, cesspit.
jauchzen *vi (geh)* to rejoice *(liter)*; *(Publikum)* to cheer.
jaulen *vi (lit, fig)* to howl.
jawohl, jawoll *(hum col) adv* yes; *(Mil)* yes, sir; *(Naut)* aye, aye, sir.
Jawort *nt* **jdm das** ~ **geben** to consent to marry sb; *(bei Trauung)* to say "I do".
Jazz [dʒæz, jats] *m no pl* jazz.
Jazzkeller *m* jazz club.
je 1 *adv* **(a)** *(jemals)* ever. **(b)** *(jeweils)* every, each. **für** ~ **drei Stück zahlst du eine Mark** you pay one mark for (every) three; ~ **zwei Schüler aus jeder Klasse** two children from each class; **sie zahlten** ~ **eine Mark** they paid one mark each. **2** *prep +acc (pro)* per. ~ **Person zwei Stück** two per person. **3** *conj* **(a)** ~ **eher, desto** *or* **um so besser** the sooner the better; ~ **länger,** ~ **lieber** the longer the better. **(b)** ~ **nach** depending on; ~ **nachdem** it all depends; ~ **nachdem, wie/ob ...** depending on how/whether ...
Jeans [dʒiːnz] *pl* jeans.
Jeans-: ~**anzug** *m* denim suit; ~**stoff** *m* denim.
jedenfalls *adv* anyhow, in any case; *(zumindest)* at least, at any rate. **er ist nicht reif zum Studieren,** ~ **jetzt noch nicht** he's not mature enough to go to university, at least not yet.
jede(r, s) *indef pron* **(a)** *(adjektivisch) (einzeln)* each; *(von zweien auch)* either; *(~ von allen)* every; *(~r beliebige)* any. **ohne** ~ **Anstrengung** without any effort; **es kann** ~**n Augenblick passieren** it might happen any minute; **fern von** ~**r Kultur** far from all civilization. **(b)** *(substantivisch) (einzeln)* each (one); *(~ von allen)* everyone, everybody; *(~ beliebige)* anyone, anybody. ~**r von uns** each (one)/every one/any one of us; ~**r zweite** every other one; ~**r für sich** everyone for himself; **das kann nicht** ~**r** not everyone can do that; **er spricht nicht mit** ~**m** he doesn't speak to just anybody.
jedermann *indef pron* everyone, everybody; *(jeder beliebige auch)* anyone, anybody. **das ist nicht** ~**s Sache** it's not everyone's cup of tea *(col)*.
jederzeit *adv* at any time. **du kannst** ~ **kommen** you can come any time you like.
jedesmal *adv* every *or* each time. ~**, wenn sie ...** every time she ..., whenever she ...
jedoch *conj, adv* however. **er verlor** ~ **die Nerven** he lost his nerve however.
Jeep ® [dʒiːp] *m* **-s** jeep.
jegliche(r, s) *indef pron (adjektivisch)* any.
jeher ['jeːheːɐ] *adv:* **von** *or* **seit** ~ always; **das ist schon seit** ~ **so** it has always been like that.
jein *adv (hum)* yes and no.
jemals *adv* ever.
jemand *indef pron* somebody, someone; *(bei Fragen, bedingenden Sätzen auch, Negation)* anybody, anyone. **ist da** ~**?** is anybody *or* somebody

there?; **ohne** ~**en zu fragen** without asking anyone; ~ **anders/Neues** somebody else/new.
Jenaer Glas ® ['jeːnaɐ-] *nt* Pyrex ®, heatproof glass.
jene(r, s) *dem pron (geh)* **(a)** *(adjektivisch)* that; *pl* those; *(der Vorherige, die Vorherigen)* the former. **in** ~**r Zeit** at that time. **(b)** *(substantivisch)* that one; *pl* those (ones); *(der Vorherige, die Vorherigen)* the former; *siehe* **diese(r, s).**
jenseitig *adj attr Ufer* opposite. **das** ~**e Leben** the life after death.
jenseits 1 *prep +gen* on the other side of. **2 km** ~ **der Grenze** 2 kms beyond the border. **2** *adv* ~ **von** on the other side of; ~ **von Gut und Böse** beyond good and evil; *(hum col)* past it *(col)*.
Jenseits *nt no pl* hereafter. **jdn ins** ~ **befördern** *(col)* to send sb to kingdom come *(col)*.
Jesuit *m (wk)* **-en, -en** Jesuit.
Jesus *m gen* **Jesu** Jesus. ~ **Christus** Jesus Christ.
Jet [dʒɛt] *m* **-s** *(col)* jet.
Jeton [ʒəˈtõː] *m* **-s** chip.
jetzig *adj attr* present *attr*, current. **in der** ~**en Zeit** in our times.
jetzt *adv* now; *(heutzutage auch)* nowadays. **bis** ~ so far; **ich bin** ~ **(schon) fünf Tage hier** I have been here five days now; ~ **gleich** right now; ~ **schon?** already?
jeweilig *adj attr* respective; *(vorherrschend) Verhältnisse* prevailing. **die** ~**e Regierung** the government of the day.
jeweils *adv* at any one time; *(jedesmal)* each time; *(jeder einzelne)* each. ~ **am Monatsletzten** on the last day of each month; **die** ~ **größten aus einer Gruppe** the biggest from each group.
Jg. = **Jahrgang.**
Jh. = **Jahrhundert.**
jiddisch *adj* Yiddish.
Job [dʒɔp] *m* **-s** *(col)* job.
jobben ['dʒɔbn] *vi (col)* to work, to have a job.
Joch *nt* **-e** *(lit, fig)* yoke.
Jochbein *nt* cheek-bone.
Jockei ['jɔke], **Jockey** ['dʒɔki] *m* **-s** jockey.
Jod *nt no pl* iodine.
jodeln *vti* to yodel.
Jodler(in *f)* *m* - yodeller *(Brit)*, yodeler *(US)*.
Joga *m or nt no pl* yoga.
joggen ['dʒɔgn] *vi* to jog.
Jogger(in *f)* ['dʒɔgɐ, -ərɪn] *m* - jogger.
Jogging ['dʒɔgɪŋ] *nt no pl* jogging.
Joghurt *m or nt* **-s** *(col)* yog(h)urt.
Johannis-: ~**beere** *f* **rote/schwarze** ~**beere** redcurrant/blackcurrant; ~**nacht** *f* Midsummer's Eve.
johlen *vi* to howl.
Joint [dʒɔɪnt] *m* **-s** *(col)* joint *(col)*.
Jo-Jo *nt* **-s** yo-yo.
Joker ['joːkɐ, 'dʒoːkɐ] *m* - *(Cards)* joker.
Jolle *f* **-n** *(Naut)* jolly-boat, dinghy.
Jongleur [ʒõˈgløːɐ] *m* juggler.
jonglieren* [ʒõˈgliːrən] *vi (lit, fig)* to juggle.
Jordanien [-iən] *nt* Jordan.
Jordanier(in *f)* [-iɐ, -iərɪn] *m* - Jordanian.
Jota *nt* **-s** iota. **kein** ~ **not a jot** *or* one iota.
Journal [ʒʊrˈnaːl] *nt* **-e** journal; *(dated: Zeitschrift)* magazine.
Journalismus [ʒʊrnaˈlɪsmʊs] *m no pl* journalism.
Journalist(in *f)* [ʒʊrnaˈlɪst, -ɪstɪn] *m* journalist.
journalistisch [ʒʊrnaˈlɪstɪʃ] *adj* journalistic.
jovial [joˈviaːl] *adj* jovial.
jr. = **junior** jnr., jr.
Jubel *m no pl* jubilation; *(~rufe auch)* cheering. ~**, Trubel, Heiterkeit** laughter and merriment.
Jubeljahr *nt* **alle** ~**e (einmal)** *(col)* once in a blue moon *(col)*.
jubeln *vi* to cheer. **vor Freude** ~ to shout with joy.
Jubilar(in *f)* *m person celebrating an anniversary*.
Jubiläum *nt, pl* **Jubiläen** jubilee; *(Jahrestag)* anniversary.

Jubiläums- *in cpds* jubilee.
jucken 1 *vti* to itch. **der Rücken juckt mir** my back itches; **der Stoff juckt mich** this material makes me itch; **es juckt mich, das zu tun** *(col)* I'm itching to do it *(col)*; **das juckt mich doch nicht** *(col)* I don't care; **ihm juckt das Fell** *(col)* he's asking for a good hiding. **2** *vt (kratzen)* to scratch.
Juck-: ~**pulver** *nt* itching powder; ~**reiz** *m* itching.
Judas *m* -, -se *(fig liter)* Judas.
Judaslohn *m (liter)* blood money.
Jude *m (liter)* -n, -n Jew. **er ist** ~ he is a Jew.
Juden-: j~**feindlich** *adj* anti-Semitic; ~**stern** *m* star of David; ~**verfolgung** *f* persecution of the Jews.
Jüdin *f* Jew(ess).
jüdisch *adj* Jewish.
Judo *nt no pl* judo.
Jugend *f no pl* **(a)** (~*zeit*) youth. **frühe** ~ early youth, adolescence; **von** ~ **an** *or* **auf** from one's youth. **(b)** *(junge Menschen)* youth, young people *pl.* **die heutige** ~ the youth of today.
Jugend-: ~**alter** *nt* adolescence; ~**amt** *nt* youth welfare department; ~**arbeit** *f no pl* (~*fürsorge*) youth work; ~**bild** *nt* picture taken when one was young; ~**bilder Churchills** photographs of the young Churchill; ~**buch** *nt* book for the younger reader; ~**erinnerung** *f* youthful memory; **j~frei** *adj* suitable for young people; *Film* U(-certificate), G *(US)*; ~**freund** *m* friend of one's youth; ~**fürsorge** *f* youth welfare; **j~gefährdend** *adj* liable to corrupt the young; ~**gericht** *nt* juvenile court; ~**gruppe** *f* youth group; ~**herberge** *f* youth hostel; ~**jahre** *pl* days of one's youth *pl*; ~**kriminalität** *f* juvenile delinquency.
jugendlich *adj (jung)* young; *(jung wirkend)* youthful. **er kleidet sich immer sehr** ~ he always wears very youthful clothes; ~**e Banden** gangs of young youths; **ein** ~**er Täter** a young offender.
Jugendliche(r) *mf decl as adj* young person; *(männlicher* ~ *auch)* youth.
Jugendlichkeit *f* youthfulness.
Jugend-: ~**liebe** *f (Geliebter)* love of one's youth; ~**literatur** *f* literature for younger readers; ~**mannschaft** *f* youth team; ~**organisation** *f* youth organization; ~**pflege** *f* youth welfare; ~**pfleger** *m* youth (welfare) worker; ~**recht** *nt* law relating to young persons; ~**richter** *m (Jur)* magistrate *in a juvenile court;* ~**schutz** *m* protection of children and young people; ~**stil** *m (Art)* Art Nouveau; ~**strafe** *f* detention *no art* in a reform school *etc;* ~**sünde** *f* youthful misdeed; ~**traum** *m* youthful dream; ~**verband** *m* youth organization; ~**verbot** *nt* für einen Film ~**verbot aussprechen** to ban a film for young people; ~**zeit** *f* younger days *pl*; ~**zentrum** *nt* youth centre *(Brit)* or center *(US)*.
Jugoslawe *m (wk)* -n, -n, **Jugoslawin** *f* Yugoslav.
Jugoslawien [-iǝn] *nt* Yugoslavia.
jugoslawisch *adj* Yugoslav(ian).
Juli *m* -s July; *siehe* **März.**
jun. = **junior** jun.
jung *adj, comp* **-ёr,** *superl* **=ste(r, s)** *or (adv)* **am =sten** *(lit, fig)* young. ~ **und alt** (both) young and old; **von** ~ **auf** from one's youth; **sie ist 18 Jahre** ~ *(hum)* she's 18 years young *(hum)*; ~ **heiraten/ sterben** to marry/die young.
Junge *m (wk)* -n, -n *or (col)* **Jungs** boy; *(Cards col)* jack, knave. ~, ~! *(col)* boy oh boy *(col)*; **alter** ~ *(col)* my old pal *(col)*; **unsere Jungs haben gewonnen** our lads won.
Jungen-: j~**haft** *adj* boyish; **sie ist ein j~haftes Mädchen** she's a bit of a tomboy; ~**schule** *f* boys'

school.
jünger *adj* **(a)** *comp of* **jung** younger. **sie ist eine** ~**e Frau** she's a fairly young woman; **Holbein der J~e** the younger Holbein. **(b)** *Geschichte etc* recent.
Jünger *m* - *(Bibl, fig)* disciple.
Jüngerin *f* disciple.
Junge(s) *nt decl as adj (Zool)* young one; *(von Hund)* pup(py); *(von Katze)* kitten; *(von Wolf, Löwe, Bär)* cub; *(von Vogel)* young bird. **die** ~**n** the young.
Jungfer *f* -n *(old, hum: ledige Frau)* spinster. **eine alte** ~ an old maid.
Jungfern-: ~**fahrt** *f* maiden voyage; ~**flug** *m* maiden flight; ~**häutchen** *nt (Anat)* hymen, maidenhead; ~**rede** *f (Parl)* maiden speech.
Jungfrau *f* virgin; *(Astrol)* Virgo *no art.* **ich bin** ~ I am a virgin; I am (a) Virgo; **die** ~ **Maria** the Virgin Mary; **dazu bin ich gekommen wie die** ~ **zum Kind(e)** it just fell into my hands.
jungfräulich *adj* virgin; *(liter)* Seele pure.
Jungfräulichkeit *f siehe adj* virginity; purity.
Junggeselle *m* bachelor.
Junggesellen-: ~**wohnung** *f* bachelor flat *(Brit)* or apartment *(US)*; ~**zeit** *f* bachelor days *pl.*
Junggesellin *f* bachelor girl; *(älter)* single woman.
Junglehrer *m* student teacher.
Jüngling *m (liter, hum)* youth.
Jungsozialist *m (BRD Pol)* Young Socialist.
jüngst *adv (geh)* recently, lately.
jüngste(r, s) *adj* **(a)** *superl of* **jung** youngest. **(b)** *Werk, Ereignis* latest, (most) recent; *Zeit, Vergangenheit* recent. **in der** ~**n Zeit** recently; **das J~ Gericht** the Last Judgement; **der J~ Tag** Doomsday, the Day of Judgement; **sie ist auch nicht mehr die J~** she's no chicken *(col)*.
Jung-: ~**verheiratete(r)** *mf decl as adj* newly-wed; ~**wähler** *m* young voter.
Juni *m* -s June; *siehe* **März.**
junior *adj* Franz Schulz ~ Franz Schulz, Junior.
Junior *m* **(a)** *(usu hum: Sohn)* junior. **(b)** *(Comm: auch* ~**chef)** son of the chairman/boss. **(c)** *usu pl (Sport)* junior.
Junta ['xʊnta, 'jʊnta] *f, pl* **Junten** *(Pol)* junta.
Jupiter *m* Jupiter.
Jura *no art (Univ)* law.
Jurastudium *nt* study of law.
Jurist(in) *f)* *m* jurist, legal eagle *(hum col)*; *(Student)* law student.
Juristen-: ~**deutsch** *nt*, ~**sprache** *f no pl* legalese *(pej)*, legal jargon.
juristisch *adj* legal. **die J~e Fakultät** the Faculty of Law; **eine** ~ **e Person** a legal entity.
Juror(in *f)* ['juːror, -'roːrɪn] *m* juror; *(bei Wettbewerb)* judge.
Jury [ʒy'riː, 'ʒyːriː] *f* -s jury sing or pl; *(bei Wettbewerb auch)* judges pl.
Juso *m* -s *(BRD Pol)* = **Jungsozialist** Young Socialist.
justieren* *vt Waage* to adjust; *(Typ)* to justify.
Justiz [jʊs'tiːts] *f no pl (als Prinzip)* justice; *(als Institution)* judiciary; *(die Gerichte)* courts pl.
Justiz-: ~**beamte(r)** *m* judicial officer; ~**irrtum** *m* miscarriage of justice; ~**minister** *m* minister of justice ≃ Attorney General *(US)*, ≃ Lord (High) Chancellor *(Brit)*; ~**ministerium** *nt* ministry of justice, ≃ Department of Justice *(US)*; ~**mord** *m* judicial murder.
Jute *f no pl* jute.
Juwel [ju'veːl] *nt* -en *or (fig)* -e jewel, gem.
Juwelier *m* -e jeweller *(Brit)*, jeweler *(US)*.
Jux *m* -e *(col)* **etw aus** ~ **tun/sagen** to do/say sth in fun; **sich** *(dat)* **einen** ~ **aus etw machen** to make a joke (out) of sth.
jwd [jɔtveː'deː] *adv (hum)* in the back of beyond.

K

K, k [kaː] *nt* -, - K, k.
Kabarett *nt* -e *or* -s cabaret. **ein politisches** ~ **a** political satire.
Kabarettist(in *f)* *m* cabaret artist.
kabarettistisch *adj Darbietung* cabaret; *Stil* revue *attr*.
Kabbelei *f (col)* bickering, squabbling.
Kabel *nt* - cable; *(Draht)* wire; *(Telefon~)* flex, cord.
Kabelfernsehen *nt* cable television.
Kabeljau *m* -e *or* -s cod.
kabeln *vti* to cable.
Kabine *f* cabin; *(Umkleide~, Dusch~)* cubicle; *(Telec)* booth; *(Seilbahn~)* car.
Kabinett[1] *nt* -e *(Pol)* cabinet.
Kabinett[2] *m* -e *m high quality German white wine*.
Kabinetts-: ~**beschluß** *m* cabinet decision; ~**mitglied** *nt* cabinet member.
Kabinettstück *nt (old: einer Sammlung)* pièce de résistance; *(fig)* masterstroke; **sich** *(dat)* **ein** ~ **leisten** *(iro)* to goof *(col)*.
Kabrio *nt* -s *(col)*, **Kabriolett** [kabrio'lɛt, *(Aus, S Ger)* kabrio'leː] *nt* -s *(Aut)* convertible.
Kachel *f* -n (glazed) tile.
kacheln *vt* to tile.
Kachel|ofen *m* tiled stove.
Kacke *f no pl (col!)* crap *(col!)*.
kacken *vi (col!)* to crap *(col!)*.
Kadaver [ka'daːvɐ] *m* - carcass.
Kadavergehorsam *m (pej)* blind obedience.
Kadenz *f* cadence; *(Improvisation)* cadenza.
Kader *m* - *(Mil, Pol)* cadre; *(Sport)* squad; *(DDR, Sw: Fachleute)* group of specialists.
Kadett *m (wk)* -en, -en *(Mil)* cadet.
Kadettenanstalt *f* cadet school.
Kadi *m* -s *(col)* beak *(col)*. **jdn vor den** ~ **schleppen** to take sb to court.
Kadmium *nt* cadmium.
Käfer *m* - *(auch col: VW)* beetle.
Kaff *nt* -s *or* -e *(col)* dump *(col)*, hole *(col)*.
Kaffee [*or* ka'feː] *m* -s **(a)** coffee. **zwei** ~, **bitte!** two coffees please; ~ **mit Milch** white coffee *(Brit)*, coffee with milk; ~ **kochen** to make coffee; **das ist kalter** ~ *(col)* that's old hat *(col)*. **(b)** *no pl (Nachmittags~)* ≈ (afternoon) tea. ~ **und Kuchen** coffee and cakes, ≈ afternoon tea.
Kaffee-: ~**bohne** *f* coffee bean; ~-**Extrakt** *m* coffee essence; ~**filter** *m* coffee filter; *(col: Filterpapier)* filter (paper); ~**geschirr** *nt* coffee set; ~**haus** *nt* café; ~**kanne** *f* coffeepot; ~**klatsch** *(col) m no pl*, ~**kränzchen** *nt* coffee klatsch *(US)*, hen party *(col)*; ~**löffel** *m* coffee spoon; ~**maschine** *f* coffee machine; ~**mühle** *f* coffee grinder; ~**pause** *f* coffee break; ~**satz** *m* coffee grounds *pl*; **aus dem** ~**satz lesen** to read tea leaves; ~**service** *nt* coffee set; ~**strauch** *m* coffee tree; ~**tante** *f (hum)* coffee addict; *(in Café)* old biddy; ~**tasse** *f* coffee cup; ~**tisch** *m (Frühstückstisch)* breakfast table; *(nachmittags)* (afternoon) tea table; ~**wärmer** *m* - cosy (for coffee pot).
Käfig *m* -e cage.
kahl *adj Mensch, Kopf* bald; *(~geschoren)* shaved, shorn; *Wand, Raum, Baum* bare; *Landschaft* barren. **eine** ~**e Stelle** a bald patch; ~ **werden** *(Mensch)* to go bald; *(Baum)* to lose its leaves.

Kahl-: **k~geschoren** *adj Kopf* shaven; ~**heit** *f siehe adj* baldness; bareness; barrenness; ~**kopf** *m* bald head; *(Mensch)* bald person; **k~köpfig** *adj* bald(-headed); ~**schlag** *m (Forest)* clearing.
Kahn *m* -̧e **(a)** (small) boat. ~ **fahren** to go boating. **(b)** *(Lastschiff)* barge. **ein alter** ~ *(col)* an old tub *(col)*.
Kahnfahrt *f* row.
Kai *m* -e *or* -s quay; *(Uferdamm auch)* waterfront.
Kaianlage *f* quayside.
Kaimauer *f* quay wall.
Kairo *nt* Cairo.
Kaiser *m* - emperor. **sich um des** ~**s Bart streiten** *(fig)* to split hairs.
Kaiserin *f* empress.
kaiserlich *adj* imperial.
Kaiser-: ~**reich** *nt* empire; ~**schmarr(e)n** *m* - *(Cook)* sugared, cut-up pancake with raisins; ~**schnitt** *m* Caesarean (section).
Kajak *m or nt* -s kayak.
Kajüte *f* -n cabin; *(größer auch)* stateroom.
Kakadu *m* -s cockatoo.
Kakao [*auch* ka'kau] *m* -s cocoa. **jdn durch den** ~ **ziehen** *(col) (veralbern)* to make fun of sb; *(boshaft reden)* to run sb down.
Kakerlak *m* -en cockroach.
Kaktee *f* -n [-eːən], **Kaktus** *m* -, **Kakteen** [-eːən] *or (col)* -se cactus.
Kalauer *m* - corny joke; *(Wortspiel)* corny pun.
kalauern *vi (col)* to joke; to pun.
Kalb *nt* -̧er calf; *(von Rehwild auch)* fawn.
kalben *vi (Kuh)* to calve.
Kalbfleisch *nt* veal.
Kalbs-: ~**braten** *m* roast veal; ~**haxe** *f (Cook)* knuckle of veal; ~**leber** *f* calves' liver; ~**leder** *nt* calfskin; ~**schnitzel** *nt* veal cutlet.
Kaleidoskop *nt* -e kaleidoscope.
Kalender *m* - calendar; *(Taschen~)* diary.
Kalender-: ~**blatt** *nt* page of a/the calendar; ~**jahr** *nt* calendar year; ~**monat** *m* calendar month; ~**spruch** *m* calendar motto.
Kali *nt* -s potash.
Kaliber *nt* - *(lit, fig)* calibre *(Brit)*, caliber *(US)*.
Kalifornien [-iən] *nt* -s California.
Kalium *nt no pl* potassium.
Kalk *m* -e lime; *(zum Tünchen)* whitewash; *(Anat)* calcium. **gebrannter/gelöschter** ~ quicklime/slaked lime; **bei ihm rieselt schon der** ~ *(col)* he's going a bit gaga *(col)*.
kalken *vt (tünchen)* to whitewash; *(Agr)* to lime.
Kalk-: ~**grube** *f* lime pit; **k~haltig** *adj Boden* chalky; *Wasser* hard; ~**mangel** *m (Med)* calcium deficiency; *(von Boden)* lime deficiency; ~**ofen** *m* lime kiln; ~**stein** *m* limestone.
Kalkül *m or nt* -e *(geh)* calculation *usu pl*.
Kalkulation *f* calculation; *(Kostenrechnung)* costing.
kalkulieren* *vt* to calculate.
Kalorie *f* calorie.
Kalorien- [-iən]: **k~arm** *adj* low-calorie; ~**gehalt** *m* calorie content; **k~reich** *adj* high-calorie.
kalt *adj comp* -̈**er**, *superl* -̈**este(r, s)** *or (adv)* **am** -̈**esten** cold. **mir ist/wird** ~ I am/I'm getting cold; **im K~en** in the cold; ~**e Platte** cold meal; **abends essen wir** ~ we have a cold meal in the evening; **etw** ~ **stellen** to put sth to chill; **die**

239

Wohnung kostet ~ **480 DM** the flat costs 480 DM without heating; **jdm die** ~**e Schulter zeigen to** give sb the cold shoulder, to cold-shoulder sb; **da kann ich nur** ~ **lächeln** (col) that makes me laugh; **es überlief ihn** ~ cold shivers ran through him; **der** ~**e Krieg** the Cold War; **ein** ~**er Staatsstreich** a bloodless coup.

Kalt-: k~**bleiben** vi sep irreg aux sein (fig) to remain unmoved; ~**blüter** m - (Zool) cold-blooded animal; k~**blütig** adj (Zool, fig) cold-blooded; (gelassen) cool; ~**blütigkeit** f siehe adj cold-bloodedness; cool(ness).

Kälte f no pl coldness; (Wetter) cold; (~periode) cold spell. **fünf Grad** ~ five degrees below freezing; **vor** ~ **zittern** to shiver with cold; **bei dieser** ~ in this cold.

Kälte-: k~**beständig** adj cold-resistant; ~**einbruch** m cold spell; k~**empfindlich** adj sensitive to cold; ~**grad** m degree of frost; ~**technik** f refrigeration technology; ~**welle** f cold spell.

Kalt-: k~**lächelnd** adv (iro) cool as you please; k~**lassen** vt sep irreg (fig) **jdn** k~**lassen** to leave sb cold; ~**luft** f (Met) cold air; k~**machen** vt sep (col) to do in (col); ~**miete** f rent exclusive of heating; ~**schale** f (Cook) cold sweet soup; k~**schnäuzig** adj (col) (gefühllos) cold, callous; (unverschämt) insolent; k~**stellen** vt sep (col) jdn to put out of harm's way (col).

Kalzium nt no pl calcium.

kam pret of **kommen.**

Kamel nt -e (a) camel. (b) (col) clown (col). **ich** ~! silly me!

Kamel-: ~**haar** nt (Tex) camel hair; ~**treiber** m camel driver; (pej: Orientale) wog (pej).

Kamera f -s camera.

Kamerad m (wk) -en, -en (Mil etc) comrade; (Freund) friend.

Kameradschaft f comradeship, camaraderie.

kameradschaftlich adj comradely.

Kamera-: ~**führung** f camera work; ~**mann** m, pl ~**männer** cameraman.

Kamerun nt the Cameroons pl.

Kamille f -n camomile.

Kamillentee m camomile tea.

Kamin m -e (Schornstein) chimney; (Abzugsschacht) flue; (offene Feuerstelle) fireplace. **wir saßen am** ~ we sat in front of the fire.

Kamin-: ~**feger**, ~**kehrer** m - (dial) chimney sweep; ~**feuer** nt open fire; ~**sims** m or nt mantelpiece.

Kamm m ⁻e (a) comb. **alle/alles über einen** ~ **scheren** (fig) to lump everyone/everything together. (b) (von Vogel) comb. (c) (Cook) neck. (d) (Gebirgs~, Wellen~) crest.

kämmen 1 vt to comb. 2 vr to comb one's hair.

Kammer f -n (a) chamber; (Parl auch) house; (Ärzte~, Anwalts~) professional association; (Herz~) ventricle. (b) (Zimmer) small room.

Kammer-: ~**diener** m valet; ~**gericht** nt ≈ Supreme Court; ~**jäger** m (Schädlingsbekämpfer) pest controller; ~**konzert** nt chamber concert.

Kämmerlein nt chamber. **im stillen** ~ in private.

Kammer-: ~**musik** f chamber music; ~**orchester** nt chamber orchestra; ~**spiele** pl studio theatre (Brit) or theater (US); ~**ton** m concert pitch; ~**zofe** f chambermaid.

Kamm-: ~**garn** nt worsted; ~**stück** nt (Cook) shoulder.

Kampagne [kam'panjə] f -n campaign.

Kampf m ⁻e fight, struggle (um for); (Gefecht) battle; (Box~) fight, contest. **den** ~ **ansagen** (fig) to declare war on sb/sth; **es kam zum** ~ fighting broke out; **auf in den** ~! (hum) once more unto the breach! (hum); **er ist im** ~ **gefallen** he fell in action or battle; **der** ~ **ums Dasein** the struggle for existence; **der** ~ **um die Macht** the battle or struggle for power; **ein** ~ **auf Leben und Tod** a fight to the death; ~ **dem**

Atomtod! fight the nuclear menace!; **innere** ~**e** inner conflicts.

Kampf-: ~**ansage** f declaration of war; (Sport) announcement; ~**bahn** f sports stadium, arena; k~**bereit** adj ready for battle.

kämpfen 1 vi to fight, to struggle (um, für for). **gegen etw** ~ to fight (against) sth; **mit den Tränen** ~ to fight back one's tears; **ich habe lange mit mir** ~ **müssen, ehe ...** I had a long battle with myself before ... 2 vt (usu fig) Kampf to fight.

Kampfer m no pl camphor.

Kämpfer(in f) m - fighter.

kämpferisch adj aggressive.

Kampf-: k~**erprobt** adj battle-tried; k~**fähig** adj (Mil) fit for action; Boxer fit to fight; ~**flugzeug** nt fighter (plane); ~**geist** m fighting spirit; ~**handlung** f usu pl clash usu pl; ~**kraft** f fighting strength; k~**los** adj sich k~**los ergeben** to surrender without a fight; k~**lustig** adj belligerent, pugnacious; ~**platz** m battlefield; (Sport) arena, stadium; ~**richter** m (Sport) referee; ~**schrift** f broadsheet; ~**stärke** f (Mil) combat strength; ~**stoff** m weapon; k~**unfähig** adj (Mil) unfit for battle; (Sport) unfit; **ein Schiff** k~**unfähig machen** to put a ship out of action.

kampieren vi to camp (out). **im Wohnzimmer** ~ (col) to doss down in the sitting room (col).

Kanada nt Canada.

Kanadier [-iɐ] m - Canadian; (Sport) Canadian canoe.

Kanadierin [-iərɪn] f Canadian (woman/girl).

kanadisch adj Canadian.

Kanal m, pl **Kanäle** (a) (Schiffahrtsweg) canal; (Wasserlauf) channel; (zur Entwässerung) drain; (für Abwässer) sewer. **der** (**Ärmel**)~ the (English) Channel; **den** ~ **voll haben** (col) (betrunken sein) to be canned (col); (es satt haben) to have had a bellyful (col!). (b) (Radio, TV, fig: Weg) channel. **dunkle Kanäle** dubious channels.

Kanalisation f (Abwasserkanäle) sewerage system, sewers pl.

kanalisieren* 1 vt (fig) Energie etc to channel. 2 vti to lay sewers (in).

Kanaltunnel m channel tunnel.

Kanapee nt -s (old, hum) sofa, settee.

Kanarienvogel [-iən-] m canary.

Kandare f -n (curb) bit. **jdn an die** ~ **nehmen** (fig) to take sb in hand.

Kandidat(in f) m (wk) -en, -en candidate; (bei Bewerbung auch) applicant. **jdn als** ~**en aufstellen** to nominate sb.

Kandidatur f candidature, candidacy.

kandidieren* vi (Pol) to stand, to run (für for).

kandiert adj Frucht candied.

Kandis(zucker) m rock candy.

Känguruh ['kɛŋguru] m -s kangaroo.

Kaninchen nt rabbit.

Kaninchen-: ~**bau** m rabbit warren; ~**stall** m rabbit hutch.

Kanister m - can.

Kännchen nt pot; (für Milch) jug.

Kanne f -n can; (Tee~, Kaffee~) pot; (Milch~) churn; (Gieß~) watering can.

Kannibale m (wk) -n, -n, **Kannibalin** f cannibal.

kannibalisch adj cannibalistic; (brutal) brutal.

kannte pret of **kennen.**

Kanon m -s canon.

Kanonade f (Mil) barrage; (fig auch) tirade.

Kanone f -n (a) gun; (Hist) cannon; (col: Pistole) shooter (col). **mit** ~**n auf Spatzen schießen** (col) to take a sledgehammer to crack a nut. (b) (fig col: Könner) ace (col). (c) (col) **das ist unter aller** ~ that defies description.

Kanonen-: ~**boot** nt gunboat; ~**donner** m rumbling of guns; ~**futter** nt (col) cannon fodder; ~**kugel** f cannon ball; ~**rohr** nt gun barrel; **heiliges** ~**rohr!** (col) good grief (col).

Kantate f -n (Mus) cantata.

Kante *f* **-n** *(Ecke)* edge; *(Rand, Borte)* border; *(Web~)* selvedge. **Geld auf die hohe ~ legen** *(col)* to put money by.

kantig *adj Holz* edged; *Gesicht* angular.

Kantine *f* canteen.

Kanu *nt* **-s** canoe.

Kanzel *f* **-n (a)** pulpit. **(b)** *(Aviat)* cockpit.

Kanzlei *f (Dienststelle)* office; *(Büro eines Notars etc)* chambers *pl*.

Kanzler *m* - chancellor.

Kap *nt* **-s** cape.

Kapazität *f* capacity; *(fig: Experte)* expert, authority.

Kapelle *f* **(a)** *(Kirche)* chapel. **(b)** *(Mus)* band, orchestra.

Kapellmeister *m* director of music; *(Mil, von Tanzkapelle etc)* bandmaster, bandleader.

Kaper *f* **-n** *(Bot, Cook)* caper.

kapern *vt (Naut)* to seize; *(fig col)* to grab.

kapieren* *vti (col)* to get *(col)*, to understand. **kapiert? got it?** *(col)*; **er hat schnell kapiert** he caught on quick *(col)*.

Kapital *nt* **-e** *or* **-ien** [-iən] **(a)** *(Fin)* capital *no pl*; *(pl: angelegtes ~)* capital investments *pl*. **(b)** *(fig)* asset. **aus etw ~ schlagen** *(pej: lit, fig)* to make capital out of sth.

Kapital-: **~anlage** *f* capital investment; **~flucht** *f* flight of capital; **~gesellschaft** *f (Comm)* jointstock company; **k~intensiv** *adj* capital-intensive.

Kapitalismus *m* capitalism.

Kapitalist *m* capitalist.

kapitalistisch *adj* capitalist.

Kapital-: **~markt** *m* money market; **~verbrechen** *nt* serious crime; *(mit Todesstrafe)* capital crime.

Kapitän *m* **-e** captain. **~ zur See** captain.

Kapitel *nt* - **(a)** chapter; *(fig auch)* period; *(Angelegenheit)* chapter of events, story. **ein trauriges ~ a** sad story; **das ist ein anderes ~** that's another story. **(b)** *(Eccl: Dom~)* chapter.

Kapitulation *f* surrender, capitulation *(auch fig)* *(vor +dat* to).

kapitulieren* *vi* to capitulate; *(Mil also)* to surrender. **ich kapituliere, das ist zu schwierig** I give up, it's too difficult.

Kappe *f* **-n** cap; *(von Flasche etc)* top. **das nehme ich auf meine ~** *(fig col)* I'll take the responsibility for that.

kappen *vt (Naut)* Tau, Leine to cut.

Käppi *nt* **-s** cap.

Kapriole *f* **-n** *(fig)* caper. **~n machen** to cut capers.

kapriziös *adj (geh)* capricious.

Kapsel *f* **-n** capsule; *(Etui)* container; *(an Flasche)* cap, top.

kaputt *adj (col)* broken; *esp Maschine, Glühbirne etc* kaput *(col)*; *(erschöpft)* Mensch, Nerven shattered *(col)*; Beziehungen, Gesundheit ruined; Firma bust *pred (col)*. **irgend etwas muß an deinem Auto ~ sein** something must be wrong with your car; **der Fernseher ist ~** the TV's not working; **meine Hose ist ~** my trousers have had it *(col)*; **ein ~er Typ** *(col)* a bum *(col)*.

kaputt-: **~fahren** *vt sep irreg (col)* Auto to drive into the ground; *(durch Unfall)* to smash up; **~gehen** *vi sep irreg aux sein (col)* to break; *(esp Maschine)* to break down; *(Ehe)* to break up *(an +dat* because of); *(Beziehungen, Nerven)* to be ruined; *(Firma)* to go bust *(col)*; *(Kleidung)* to come to pieces; *(zerrissen werden)* to tear; *(Blumen)* to die off; **er ist am Alkohol ~gegangen** alcohol was his downfall; **~kriegen** *vt sep (col)* **das Auto ist nicht ~zukriegen** this car just goes on for ever; **wie hast du denn das ~gekriegt?** how did you manage to break it?; **~lachen** *vr sep (col)* to die laughing *(col)*; **~machen** *sep (col)* **1** *vt* to ruin; *Zerbrechliches* to break; *Brücke, Sandburg*

to knock down; *(erschöpfen)* jdn to wear out; **die Arbeit macht mich ~** this job will be the death of me *(col)*; **2** *vr (sich überanstrengen)* to wear oneself out; **~schlagen** *vt sep irreg (col)* to smash.

Kapuze *f* **-n** hood; *(Mönchs~)* cowl.

Kapuziner *m* - *(Bot)* nasturtium.

Karabiner *m* - *(Gewehr)* carbine.

Karacho *nt no pl*: **mit ~** *(col)* hell for leather *(col)*.

Karaffe *f* **-n** carafe; *(mit Stöpsel)* decanter.

Karambolage [karambo'la:ʒə] *f* **-n** *(Aut)* collision, crash; *(Billard)* cannon.

Karamel *m no pl* caramel *no pl*.

Karat *nt* **-e** *or (bei Zahlenangabe)* - carat.

Karate *nt no pl* karate. **~hieb** *m* karate chop.

Karawane *f* **-n** caravan.

Kardinal *m, pl* **Kardinäle** *(Eccl)* cardinal.

Kardinal-: **~fehler** *m* cardinal error; **~zahl** *f* cardinal (number).

Karenzzeit *f* waiting period.

Karfiol *m no pl (Aus)* cauliflower.

Karfreitag *m* Good Friday.

karg *adj* Vorrat, Gehalt meagre *(Brit)*, meager *(US)*. **etw ~ bemessen** to be mean with sth.

Kargheit *f* meagreness *(Brit)*, meagerness *(US)*.

kärglich *adj* meagre *(Brit)*, meager *(US)*; Mahl frugal.

Kargo *m* **-s** cargo.

Karibik *f* die ~ the Caribbean.

karibisch *adj* Caribbean. **das K~e Meer** the Caribbean Sea.

kariert *adj* Stoff, Muster checked, checkered *(esp US)*; Papier squared.

Karies ['ka:ries] *f no pl* caries.

Karikatur *f* caricature.

Karikaturist(in *f) m* cartoonist.

karikieren* *vt* to caricature.

Karitas *f no pl* charity.

karitativ *adj* charitable.

karmin(rot) *adj* carmine (red).

Karneval ['karnəval] *m* **-e** *or* **-s** carnival.

Karnevalszug *m* carnival procession.

Karnickel *nt* - *(col)* rabbit.

Karo *nt* **-s** *(Quadrat)* square; *(auf der Spitze stehend)* diamond, lozenge; *(Muster)* check; *(diagonal)* diamond; *(Cards)* *(Farbe)* diamonds *pl*; *(Karte)* diamond.

Karomuster *nt* checked *or* checkered *(esp US)* pattern.

Karosse *f* **-n** *(Prachtkutsche)* (state) coach.

Karosserie *f* bodywork.

Karosserie-: **~bauer** *m* coachbuilder; **~schaden** *m* damage to the bodywork.

Karotte *f* **-n** (small) carrot.

Karpaten *pl* Carpathians *pl*.

Karpfen *m* - carp.

Karre *f* **-n (a)** *siehe* **Karren**. **(b)** *(col: Auto)* (old) crate *(col)*.

Karree *nt* **-s** square; *(Häuserblock)* block. **einmal ums ~ gehen** to walk around the block.

Karren *m* - *(a)* *(Wagen)* cart; *(esp für Garten, Baustelle)* (wheel)barrow; *(für Gepäck etc)* trolley *(Brit)*, cart *(US)*. **(b)** *(fig col)* **jdm an den ~ fahren** to take sb to task; **jdn vor seinen ~ spannen** to use sb; **den ~ in den Dreck fahren** to get things in a mess; **den ~ aus dem Dreck ziehen** to get things sorted out.

Karriere *f* **-n** *(Laufbahn)* career. **~ machen** to make a career for oneself.

Karsamstag *m* Easter Saturday.

Karst *m* **-e** *(Geog, Geol)* karst, barren landscape.

Karte *f* **-n (a)** card. **jdm die ~ lesen** to tell sb's fortune from the cards; **mit offenen ~n spielen** *(fig)* to put one's cards on the table; **er spielt mit verdeckten ~n** *(fig)* he's playing his cards very close to his chest; **alle ~n in der Hand halten** *(fig)* to hold all the cards; **es ist unmöglich, ihm in die ~n zu sehen** *(fig)* it's impossible to know what he's up to; **alles auf eine ~ setzen** to put all

one's eggs in one basket (prov). **(b)** (Fahr~, Eintritts~) ticket; (Einladungs~) invitation (card). **die ~n, bitte!** tickets, please! **(c)** (Land~) map; (See~) chart. **(d)** (Speise~) menu; (Wein~) wine list.
Kartei f card index.
Kartei-: ~**karte** f file or record card; ~**kasten** m file-card box; ~**leiche** f (hum) non-active member; ~**schrank** m filing cabinet.
Kartell nt **-e** cartel.
Kartellamt nt monopolies commission.
Karten-: ~**haus** nt **(a)** house of cards; **wie ein ~haus (in sich) zusammenfallen** to collapse like a house of cards; **(b)** (Naut) chart room; ~**kunststück** nt card trick; ~**legen** nt fortune-telling (using cards); ~**spiel** nt **(a)** card-playing; (ein Spiel) card game; **beim ~spiel** when playing cards; **(b)** (Karten) pack or deck (of cards).
Kartoffel f **-n** potato. **rein in die ~n, raus aus den ~n** (col) first it's one thing, then it's another; **jdn fallenlassen wie eine heiße ~** (col) to drop sb like a hot brick (col).
Kartoffel- in cpds potato; ~**brei** m mashed potatoes pl; ~**chips** pl potato crisps pl (Brit), potato chips pl (US); ~**käfer** m Colorado beetle; ~**puffer** m potato fritter; ~**püree** nt mashed potatoes pl; ~**salat** m potato salad; ~**schalen** pl potato peel(ings); ~**schäler** m potato peeler.
Kartograph(in f) m cartographer.
Karton [kar'tõ, kar'toː] m **-s (a)** (Pappe) card, cardboard. **(b)** (Schachtel) cardboard box.
kartoniert adj Bücher hardback, cased.
Karussell nt **-s** or **-e** merry-go-round, roundabout (Brit).
Karwoche f (Eccl) Holy Week.
kaschieren* vt to conceal.
Kaschmir m **-e** (Tex) cashmere.
Käse m **- (a)** cheese. **(b)** (col: Unsinn) rubbish, twaddle (col).
Käse- in cpds cheese; ~**blatt** nt (col) rag (col); ~**brot** nt bread and cheese; ~**gebäck** nt cheese savouries (Brit) or savories (US) pl; ~**glocke** f cheese cover; ~**kuchen** m cheesecake.
Kaserne f **-n** barracks pl.
Kasernenhof m barrack square.
kasernieren* vt Truppen to quarter in barracks.
käsig adj **(a)** (fig col) Gesicht, Haut pasty, pale; (vor Schreck) white. **(b)** (lit) cheesy.
Kasino nt **-s (a)** (Spielbank) casino. **(b)** (Offiziers~) (officers') mess; (Speiseraum) dining room.
Kaskade f cascade.
Kaskoversicherung f (Aut) (Teil~) ≃ third party, fire and theft insurance; (Voll~) fully comprehensive insurance.
Kasper m - (im Puppenspiel) Punch; (col) clown (col).
Kasperl(e)-: ~**figur** f glove puppet; ~**theater** nt Punch and Judy (show).
Kaspisches Meer nt Caspian Sea.
Kassandraruf m gloomy prediction.
Kasse f **-n (a)** cashdesk, cash point; (in Supermarkt auch) checkout; (Zahlraum) cashier's office; (Theat etc) box office. **an der ~** (in Geschäft) at the desk. **(b)** (Geldkasten) cashbox; (in Läden) cash register, till; (bei Spielen) kitty; (in einer Spielbank) bank. **die ~n klingeln** the money is really rolling in; **unsere ~ ist leer** the coffers are empty. **(c)** (Bargeld) cash. **bei ~ sein** (col) to be flush (col); **wie bist du bei ~?** (col) how are you off for cash?; **knapp/gut/schlecht bei ~ sein** (col) to be short of cash/well-off/badly-off; **~ machen** to cash up; (col: gut verdienen) to make a bomb (col); **die ~ führen** to be in charge of the money; **die ~ stimmt!** (col) the money's OK (col); **zur ~ bitten** to ask for money; **jdn zur ~ bitten** to ask sb to pay up.
Kasseler nt - lightly smoked pork loin.

Kassen-: ~**arzt** m ≃ National Health doctor (Brit), panel doctor (US); ~**bericht** m financial report; ~**bestand** m cash in hand; ~**bon** m sales slip; ~**buch** nt cashbook; ~**erfolg** m (Theat etc) box-office hit; ~**magnet** m (Theat etc) big draw; ~**patient** m ≃ National Health patient (Brit); ~**preis** m cash price; ~**prüfung** f audit; ~**schlager** m (col) (Theat etc) box-office hit; (Ware) big seller; ~**stunden** pl hours of business; ~**sturz** m (Comm) cashing-up; ~**sturz machen** to check one's finances; (Comm) to cash up; ~**wart** m **-e** treasurer; ~**zettel** m sales slip.
Kasserolle f **-n** saucepan; (mit Henkeln) casserole.
Kassette f **(a)** cassette. **(b)** (Kästchen) case, box; (Geschenk~) gift set.
Kassetten-: ~**deck** nt cassette deck; ~**recorder** m cassette recorder.
Kassiber m - secret message.
kassieren* vt **(a)** Gelder etc to collect; (col) Abfindung, Finderlohn to pick up (col); Summe to make. **(b)** (col: wegnehmen) to take away, to confiscate. **2** vi **bei jdm ~** to collect the money from sb; **darf ich ~, bitte?** would you like to pay now?; **bei diesem Geschäft hat er ganz schön kassiert** he made a packet on the deal (col).
Kassierer(in f) m - cashier; (Bank~) clerk.
Kastagnette [kastan'jɛtə] f castanet.
Kastanie [-iə] f chestnut. **für jdn die ~n aus dem Feuer holen** (fig) to pull sb's chestnuts out of the fire.
Kastanien- [-iən]: ~**baum** m chestnut tree; **k~braun** adj maroon; Pferd, Haar chestnut.
Kästchen nt **(a)** small box; (für Schmuck) case, casket. **(b)** (auf kariertem Papier) square.
Kaste f **-n** caste.
Kasten m ⁻ **(a)** box (auch Sport); (Kiste) crate; (Brief~) postbox, letterbox; (Brot~) breadbin. **(b)** (col) (Gebäude) barn (col); (Auto) crate (col); (Schiff) tub (col); (Fernseher) box (Brit col), tube (US col); (Ftbl: Tor) goal. **er hat was auf dem ~** (col) he's brainy (col).
Kasten-: ~**form** f (Cook) (square) baking tin; ~**wagen** m (Aut) van, panel truck (US).
Kastrat m (wk) **-en, -en** eunuch; (Mus) castrato.
Kastration f castration.
kastrieren* vt (lit, fig) to castrate.
Katakombe f **-n** catacomb.
Katalog m **-e** catalogue.
katalogisieren* vt to catalogue.
Katalysator m (lit, fig) catalyst; (Aut) catalytic converter.
Katapult nt or m **-e** catapult.
katapultieren* **1** vt to catapult. **2** vt to catapult oneself; (Pilot) to eject.
Katapultsitz m ejector seat.
Katarrh m **-e** catarrh.
Kataster m or nt - land register.
Kataster|amt nt land registry.
katastrophal adj disastrous, catastrophic. **das sind ja ~e Zustände** it's a terrible state of affairs.
Katastrophe f **-n** disaster, catastrophe.
Katastrophen-: ~**alarm** m emergency alert; ~**dienst** m emergency service; ~**einsatz** m im ~**einsatz** on emergency duty; ~**gebiet** nt disaster area; ~**schutz** m disaster control; (im voraus) disaster prevention.
Katechismus m catechism.
Kategorie f category. **er gehört zur ~ derer, die ...** he's one of those who ...
kategorisch adj categorical, absolute; Ablehnung auch flat.
Kater m - **(a)** tom(cat). **wie ein verliebter ~** like an amorous tomcat. **(b)** (col: Katzenjammer) hangover.
Kater-: ~**frühstück** nt breakfast (of pickled herring etc) to cure a hangover; ~**stimmung** f depression,

the blues pl (col).
Kathedrale f -n cathedral.
Katheter m - (Med) catheter.
Kathode f -n (Phys) cathode.
Kathoden-: ~strahlen pl (Phys) cathode rays pl; ~strahlröhre f (TV etc) cathode ray tube.
Katholik(in f) m (wk) -en, -en (Roman) Catholic.
katholisch adj (Roman) Catholic. **sie ist streng ~** she's a strict Catholic.
Katholizismus m (Roman) Catholicism.
katzbuckeln vi (pej col) to bow and scrape.
Kätzchen nt (a) kitten. **(b)** (Bot) catkin.
Katze f -n cat. **sie ist eine falsche ~** she's two-faced; **meine Arbeit war für die Katz** (col) my work was a waste of time; **Katz und Maus mit jdm spielen** (col) to play cat and mouse with sb; **die ~ aus dem Sack lassen** (col) to let the cat out of the bag; **die ~ im Sack kaufen** to buy a pig in a poke (prov); **die ~ läßt das Mausen nicht** (Prov) the leopard cannot change its spots (prov); **bei Nacht sind alle ~n grau** all cats are grey at night.
Katzen-: ~auge nt (Rückstrahler) reflector; **k~haft** adj cat-like, feline; ~hai m dogfish; ~jammer m (col) (Kater) hangover; (jämmerliche Stimmung) depression, the blues pl (col); ~musik f (fig) caterwauling; ~sprung m (col) stone's throw; ~tisch m (hum) children's table; ~wäsche f (hum col) a lick and a promise (col).
Kauderwelsch nt no pl (pej) double dutch.
kauen vti to chew; Nägel to bite. **an etw** (dat) ~ to chew (on) sth; **an den Nägeln ~** to bite one's nails; **daran hatte ich lange zu ~** (fig) it took me a long time to get over it.
kauern vir (vi auch aux sein) to crouch (down); (ängstlich) to cower.
Kauf m, pl **Käufe** purchase. **das war ein günstiger ~** that was a good buy; **beim ~ eines Autos** when buying a car; **etw zum ~ anbieten** to offer sth for sale; **einen ~ tätigen** (form) to complete a purchase; **etw in ~ nehmen** (fig) to accept sth.
kaufen 1 vt (a) (auch sich (dat) ~) to buy, to purchase (esp form). **ich habe (mir) einen neuen Anzug gekauft** I bought (myself) a new suit; **etw für teures Geld ~** (col) to pay a lot (of money) for sth; **diese Zigaretten werden viel/nicht gekauft** a lot of people buy/nobody buys these cigarettes; **dafür kann ich mir nichts ~** (iro) what use is that to me! **(b)** (bestechen) jdn to bribe, to buy off; Stimmen to buy. **der Sieg war gekauft** it was fixed. **(c)** sich (dat) jdn ~ (col) to give sb a piece of one's mind (col); (tätlich) to fix sb (col). **2** vi to buy; (Einkäufe machen) to shop.
Käufer(in f) m - buyer, purchaser (esp form); (Kunde) customer, shopper.
Kauf-: ~haus nt department store; ~kraft f purchasing power.
käuflich adj (a) for sale. **Glück ist nicht ~** happiness cannot be bought; **etw ~ erwerben** (form) to purchase sth. **(b)** (fig) venal. ~ sein (Mensch) to be open to bribery; **ich bin nicht ~** you can't buy me!; ~e Liebe (geh) prostitution.
Käuflichkeit f (fig) corruptibility.
Kauf-: ~lust f desire to buy things; (StEx) buying; **k~lustig** adj in a buying mood; **in den Straßen drängten sich die ~lustigen** the streets were thronged with shoppers.
Kaufmann m, pl -leute **(a)** businessman; (Händler) trader. **(b)** (Einzelhandels~) small shopkeeper, grocer. **zum ~ gehen** to go to the grocer's (Brit) or grocer.
kaufmännisch adj commercial, business attr. ~er Angestellter office employee; ~e Lehre commercial training; **er wollte einen ~en Beruf ergreifen** he wanted to make a career in business; **er übt einen ~en Beruf aus** he is in business; ~ denken to think in business terms; **sie ist**

~ **veranlagt** she is commercially minded.
Kauf-: ~preis m purchase price; ~vertrag m bill of sale; ~wert m market value; ~zwang m obligation to buy; **kein/ohne ~zwang** no/without obligation.
Kaugummi m chewing gum.
Kaukasus m der ~ (the) Caucasus.
Kaulquappe f tadpole.
kaum 1 adv hardly, scarcely. ~ **jemand/jemals** hardly or scarcely anyone/ever; **wir hatten ~ noch Benzin** we had hardly any petrol left; **wohl** ~/**ich glaube ~** I hardly think so; **das wird wohl ~ stimmen** surely that can't be right/true; **das wird ~ passieren** that's hardly likely to happen; **das wird wohl ~ noch was werden** (col) that's hardly likely to come to anything. **2** conj hardly, scarcely. ~ **hatte er das gesagt, da ... hardly had he said that when ...**
Kaumuskel m jaw muscle.
kausal adj causal.
Kausalzusammenhang m causal connection.
Kautabak m chewing tobacco.
Kaution f (a) (Jur) bail. **er stellte 1000 Mark ~** he put up 1000 marks (as) bail; **gegen ~ on bail; jdn gegen ~ freibekommen** to bail sb out. **(b)** (Comm) security. **(c)** (für Miete) deposit.
Kautschuk m -e (india)rubber.
Kauz m, pl **Käuze (a)** screech owl. **(b)** (Sonderling) oddball (col). **ein komischer ~** an odd bird.
Käuzchen nt dim of Kauz (a).
kauzig adj odd, cranky.
Kavalier [kava'liːɐ] m -e gentleman. **er ist immer ~** he's always a gentleman.
Kavaliersdelikt nt trivial offence.
Kavallerie [kavalə'riː] f (Mil) cavalry.
Kaviar ['kaːviar] m -e caviar.
keck adj (dated) **(a)** (frech) cheeky, saucy. **(b)** (flott) pert, saucy. **(c)** (kühn) bold.
Kegel m - (a) (Spielfigur) skittle; (bei Bowling) pin. **(b)** (Geometrie) cone; (Berg~) peak. **(c)** (Licht~) beam (of light).
Kegel-: ~bahn f (bowling) lane; (Anlage) skittle-alley; (automatisch) bowling alley; ~bruder m (col) (eifriger Kegler) skittle-player; bowling fanatic; **k~förmig** adj conical.
kegeln vi to play skittles; (bei Bowling) to play bowls. ~ **gehen** to play skittles; to go bowling.
Kegler(in f) m - skittle-player; (bei Bowling) bowler.
Kehle f -n (Gurgel) throat. **er hat das in die falsche ~ bekommen** (lit) it went down the wrong way; (fig) he took it the wrong way; **eine trockene ~ haben** to be dry; **er hat Gold in der ~** (col) his voice is/could be a real gold-mine; **aus voller ~** at the top of one's voice.
Kehlkopf m larynx.
Kehlkopf|entzündung f laryngitis.
Kehllaut m guttural (sound).
Kehr-: ~aus m -, no pl last dance; (fig: Abschiedsfeier) farewell celebration; ~besen m broom; ~blech nt shovel.
Kehre f -n (sharp) bend.
kehren[1] vt to turn. **in sich** (acc) **gekehrt** (versunken) pensive; (verschlossen) introspective, introverted.
kehren[2] vti (fegen) to sweep. **jeder kehre vor seiner Tür!** (Prov) everyone should first put his own house in order.
Kehricht m or nt no pl (old, form) sweepings pl.
Kehr-: ~maschine f (Straßen~) road-sweeper; (Teppich~) carpet-sweeper; ~reim m chorus, refrain; ~schaufel f shovel; ~seite f (von Münze) reverse; (col: Rücken) back; (hum: Gesäß) backside (col); (fig: Nachteil) drawback; (fig: Schattenseite) other side; **die ~seite der Medaille** the other side of the coin.
kehrt interj (Mil) about turn!
Kehrt-: **k~machen** vi sep to do an about-turn;

(zurückgehen) to turn back; ~**wendung** *f* about-turn.

keifen *vi* to bicker.

Keil *m* **-e** *(lit,fig)* wedge.

Keile *pl (col)* thrashing, hiding.

Keil-: k~**förmig** *adj* wedge-shaped; ~**hosen** *pl* ski pants *pl*; ~**riemen** *m (Aut)* fan-belt.

Keim *m* **-e** shoot, sprout; *(Embryo, fig)* embryo; *(Krankheits~)* germ; *(fig: des Hasses etc)* seed *usu pl*. **etw im ~ ersticken** to nip sth in the bud; **den ~ zu etw legen** to sow the seeds of sth.

keimen *vi* to germinate; *(fig: Verdacht)* to be aroused.

Keim-: k~**frei** *adj* germ-free; *(Med auch,fig)* sterile; k~**frei machen** to sterilize; k~**tötend** *adj* germicidal; ~**zelle** *f* germ cell.

kein, keine, kein *indef pron* **(a)** *(adjektivisch)* no. **~ Mann/~e Häuser/~ Whisky** no man/houses/ whisky; **ich sehe da ~en Unterschied** I see no difference, I don't see any difference; **da sind ~e Häuser** there are no houses there, there aren't any houses there; **~e schlechte Idee** not a bad idea; **das ist ~e Antwort auf unsere Frage** that's not an answer to our question; **~ bißchen** not a bit; **ich habe ~ bißchen Lust** I've absolutely no desire to; **ich bin doch ~ Kind mehr!** I am not a child any longer; **in ~ster Weise** not in the least. **(b)** *(nicht einmal)* ~**e Stunde/ drei Monate** less than an hour/three months.

keine(r, s) *indef pron (niemand)* nobody, no-one; *(von Gegenstand)* not one, none. **es war ~r da** there was nobody there, there wasn't anybody there; *(Gegenstand)* there wasn't one there; **es waren ~ da** *(Gegenstände)* there weren't any there, there were none there; **ich habe ~s** I haven't got one; ~**r von uns/von uns (beiden)** none/neither of us; *(betont)* not one of us; ~**s der (beiden) Kinder** neither of the children; ~**s der sechs Kinder** none of the six children; *(betont)* not one of the six children; **ist Bier da? — nein, ich habe ~s gekauft** is there any beer? — no, I didn't buy any; **Tee haben wir, aber Kaffee haben wir ~n** we've got tea but no coffee; **hast du schon ein Glas? — nein, ich habe ~s** have you a glass? — no, I haven't got one.

keinerlei *adj attr inv* no ... whatever.

keinesfalls *adv* under no circumstances.

keineswegs *adv* not at all.

keinmal *adv* never once, not once.

keins = keines *siehe* **keine(r, s).**

Keks *m* **-e** biscuit *(Brit)*, cookie *(US)*.

Kelch *m* **-e (a)** goblet; *(liter)* cup. **(b)** *(Bot)* calyx.

Kelle *f* **-n** *(Suppen~ etc)* ladle; *(Schaumlöffel)* strainer; *(Maurer~)* trowel; *(Signalstab)* signalling disc.

Keller *m* **-** cellar; *(Geschoß)* basement.

Kellerei *f* wine cellars *pl*; *(Firma)* wine producer.

Keller-: ~**geschoß** *nt* basement; ~**gewölbe** *nt (Keller)* cellars *pl*; ~**lokal** *nt* cellar bar; ~**wohnung** *f* basement flat *(Brit)* or apartment.

Kellner *m* **-** waiter.

Kellnerin *f* waitress.

kellnern *vi (col)* to work as a waiter/waitress.

Kelte *m (wk)* **-n, -n, Keltin** *f* Celt.

Kelter *f* **-n** winepress; *(Obst~)* press.

keltern *vt* Trauben, Wein to press.

kennen *pret* **kannte,** *ptp* **gekannt** *vt* to know; *(geh: er~)* to recognize. **er kennt keine Müdigkeit** he doesn't know what tiredness is; **kein Erbarmen/Mitleid etc** ~ to know no mercy/pity *etc*; **so was ~ wir hier nicht!** we don't have that sort of thing here; **jdn als etw ~** to know sb to be sth; ~ **Sie sich schon?** do you know each other *(already)*?; ~ **Sie den (schon)?** *(Witz)* have you heard this one?; **kennst du mich noch?** do you remember me?; **wie ich ihn kenne ...** if I know him (at all) ...; **da kennst du mich aber schlecht** you don't know me.

kennenlernen *vt sep* to get to know; *(zum ersten Mal treffen)* to meet. **sich ~** to get to know each other; to meet each other; **ich freue mich, Sie kennenzulernen** *(form)* (I am) pleased to meet you *or* to make your acquaintance *(form)*; **der wird mich noch ~** *(col)* he'll have me to reckon with *(col)*; **bei näherem K~ erwies er sich als ...** on closer acquaintance he proved to be ...

Kenner(in *f)* *m* **-** expert *(von or gen* on*)*, authority *(von or gen* on*)*; *(Wein~ etc)* connoisseur.

kennerhaft *adj* **mit** ~**em Blick/Griff** with an expert eye/touch.

Kennermiene *f* connoisseur's expression. **mit** ~ **betrachtete er ...** he looked at ... like a connoisseur.

kenntlich *adj (zu erkennen)* recognizable *(an* +dat by*)*; *(deutlich)* clear. **etw** ~ **machen** to identify sth (clearly).

Kenntnis *f* **(a)** *(Wissen)* knowledge *no pl*. **über** ~**se von etw verfügen** to be knowledgeable about sth; **gute** ~**se in Mathematik haben** to have a good knowledge of mathematics. **(b)** *no pl (form)* **etw zur** ~ **nehmen** to take note of sth; **jdn von etw in** ~ **setzen** to inform or advise *(Comm, form)* sb about sth.

Kenn-: ~**wort** *nt, pl* ~**wörter** *(Chiffre)* code name; *(Losungswort)* password, code word; ~**zeichen** *nt* **(a)** *(Aut)* *(amtliches/polizeiliches)* ~**zeichen** number plate *(Brit)*, license plate *(US)*; **(b)** *(Markierung, Erkennungszeichen)* mark, sign; *(Eigenart)* characteristic *(für, gen* of*)*; *(für Qualität)* hallmark; **unveränderliche** ~**zeichen** distinguishing marks; k~**zeichnen** *vt insep* **(a)** to mark; *(durch Etikett auch)* to label; **(b)** *(charakterisieren)* to characterize; **jdn als etw** k~**zeichnen** to show sb to be sth; k~**zeichnend** *adj* typical, characteristic *(für* of*)*; ~**ziffer** *f* *(code)* number; *(Comm)* reference number.

kentern *vi aux sein (Schiff)* to capsize.

Keramik *f* **(a)** *no pl (Art)* ceramics *pl*; *(Gebrauchsgegenstände auch)* pottery. **(b)** *(Kunstgegenstand)* ceramic.

keramisch *adj* ceramic.

Kerbe *f* **-n** notch. **in die gleiche** ~ **hauen** *or* **schlagen** *(fig col)* to take the same line.

Kerbholz *nt:* **etwas auf dem** ~ **haben** *(col)* to have done something bad.

Kerker *m* **-** *(Hist, geh)* dungeon; *(Strafe)* imprisonment.

Kerl *m* **-e** *or* **-s** *(col)* fellow *(col)*, guy *(col)*; *(pej)* character. **du gemeiner** ~! you swine *(col)*; **ein ganzer** ~ a real man; **sie ist ein netter** ~ she's a nice girl.

Kern *m* **-e** *(von Obst)* pip, seed; *(von Steinobst)* stone; *(Nuß~)* kernel; *(Phys, Biol)* nucleus; *(von Reaktor)* core; *(fig)* crux, core; *(von Stadt)* centre *(Brit)*, center *(US)*.

Kern- *in cpds (Nuklear-)* nuclear; ~**fach** *nt (Sch)* core subject; ~**frage** central question; ~**gedanke** *m* central idea; ~**gehäuse** *nt* core; k~**gesund** *adj* as fit as a fiddle.

kernig *adj (fig) Ausspruch* pithy; *(urwüchsig)* earthy; *(kraftvoll)* robust, powerful.

Kern-: ~**kräfte** *pl* nuclear forces *pl*; ~**kraftwerk** *nt* nuclear power station; ~**land** *nt* heartland; k~**los** *adj* seedless, pipless; ~**obst** *nt* fruit with core and pips such as apples; ~**problem** *nt* central problem; ~**reaktor** *m* nuclear reactor; ~**satz** *m* key sentence, key phrase; ~**schmelze** *f* meltdown; ~**seife** *f* washing soap; ~**spaltung** *f* nuclear fission; **die erste** ~**spaltung** the first splitting of the atom; ~**stück** *nt (fig)* main item; *(von Theorie etc)* central part, core; ~**waffe** *f* nuclear weapon; k~**waffenfrei** *adj* nuclear-free; ~**zeit** *f* core time.

Kerze *f* **-n** *(Wachs~)* candle; *(Aut)* plug; *(Turnen)* shoulder-stand.

Kerzen-: k~**gerade** *adj* (as) straight as a die;

~**halter** m candlestick; ~**licht** nt, ~**schein** m candlelight; ~**schlüssel** m (spark) plug spanner.
Kescher m - fishing-net.
keß adj saucy.
Kessel m - **(a)** (Tee~) kettle; (für offenes Feuer) cauldron; (esp in Brauerei) vat; (Dampf~) boiler; (Behälter für Flüssigkeiten etc) tank. **(b)** (Mulde) basin.
Kessel-: ~**haus** nt boiler house; ~**pauke** f kettle drum; ~**stein** m scale, fur.
Ketchup ['kɛtʃap] m or nt -s ketchup.
Kette f -n (lit, fig) chain; (an Kettenfahrzeug) chain track; (von Truppen, Fahrzeugen) line; (Tex) warp. **eine** ~ **aus Perlen** etc a string of pearls etc; **einen Hund an die** ~ **legen** to chain up a dog; **seine** ~**s sprengen** (fig) to throw off one's chains.
ketten vt to chain (an +acc to). **jdn an sich** ~ (fig) to bind sb to oneself.
Ketten-: ~**antrieb** m chain drive; ~**fahrzeug** nt tracked vehicle; ~**glied** nt (chain-)link; ~**hund** m guard-dog; ~**karussell** nt merry-go-round (with gondolas suspended on chains); ~**rad** nt sprocket(-wheel); ~**raucher** m chainsmoker; ~**reaktion** f chain reaction; ~**schaltung** f derailleur gear; ~**schutz** m chain guard; ~**stich** m (Sew) chain stitch.
Ketzer(in f) m - (Eccl, fig) heretic.
keuchen vi to pant, to puff; (Asthmatiker etc) to wheeze.
Keuchhusten m whooping cough.
Keule f -n club; (Sport) (Indian) club; (Cook) leg.
Keulen-: ~**hieb**, ~**schlag** m blow with a club; **es traf ihn wie ein** ~**schlag** (fig) it hit him like a thunderbolt.
keusch adj (lit, fig) chaste.
Keuschheit f chastity.
kfm = **kaufmännisch**.
Kfz [kaǀɛfǀtsɛt] nt -(s) (form) = **Kraftfahrzeug** motor vehicle.
kg = **Kilogramm** kg.
KG [ka'geː] f -s = **Kommanditgesellschaft** limited partnership.
khaki adj pred khaki.
Kibbuz m, pl **Kibbuzim** or -e kibbutz.
kichern vi to giggle.
kicken (Ftbl) **1** vt to kick. **2** vi to play football; (den Ball ~) to kick.
Kicker m - (Ftbl sl) player.
kidnappen ['kɪtnɛpǝ] vt insep to kidnap.
Kidnapper(in f) ['kɪtnɛpɐ, -ǝrɪn] m - kidnapper.
Kidnapping ['kɪtnɛpɪŋ] nt -s kidnapping.
Kiebitz m -e (Orn) lapwing.
Kiefer¹ -n pine (tree); (Holz) pine(wood).
Kiefer² m - jaw; (~knochen) jawbone.
Kiefern-: ~**holz** nt pine(wood); ~**nadel** f pine needle; ~**zapfen** m pinecone.
Kieker m jdn auf dem ~ haben (col) to have it in for sb (col).
Kiel m -e (Schiffs~) keel; (Feder~) quill. **ein Schiff auf** ~ **legen** to lay down a ship.
Kielwasser nt wake, wash. **in jds** ~ **segeln** (fig) to follow in sb's wake.
Kieme f -n gill.
Kies m -e gravel; (am Strand) shingle.
Kiesel m, **Kieselstein** m pebble.
Kies-: ~**grube** f gravel pit; ~**weg** m gravel path.
Killer(in f) m - (col) killer, murderer; (gedungener) hit-man.
Kilo nt -(s) kilo.
Kilo- in cpds kilo-; ~**byte** [-'baɪt] nt (Comp) kilobyte; ~**gramm** nt kilogram(me); ~**hertz** nt kilohertz.
Kilometer m kilometre (Brit), kilometer (US); (col: Stundenkilometer) k (col).
Kilometer-: ~**geld** nt mileage (allowance); **k~lang 1** adj miles long; **ein k~langer Stau** a hold-up several miles/kilometres long; **2** adv for miles (miles), for miles on end; ~**stand** m

mileage; ~**stein** m milestone; **k~weit 1** adj miles long; **2** adv for miles (and miles); ~**zähler** m mileometer (Brit), odometer (US).
Kilo-: ~**watt** nt kilowatt; ~**wattstunde** f kilowatt hour.
Kimme f -n (von Gewehr) back sight.
Kind nt -er child, kid (col); (Kleinkind) baby; (esp Psych, Med) infant. **ein** ~ **erwarten/bekommen** to be expecting a baby/to have a baby or child; **von** ~ **auf** from childhood; **ein** ~ **seiner Zeit sein** to be a child of one's times; **sich freuen wie ein** ~ to be as pleased as Punch; **das weiß doch jedes** ~! any five-year-old would tell you that!; **das ist nichts für kleine** ~**er** (fig col) that's not for your ears/eyes; **mit** ~ **und Kegel** (hum col) with the whole family; **das** ~ **mit dem Bade ausschütten** to throw out the baby with the bathwater (prov); ~**er**, ~**er!** good heavens!
Kindbett nt im ~ in confinement.
Kinder-: ~**arbeit** f child labour (Brit) or labor (US); ~**arzt** m paediatrician (Brit), pediatrician (US); ~**bekleidung** f children's wear; ~**besteck** nt child's cutlery; ~**bett** nt child's bed; ~**buch** nt children's book.
Kinderei f childishness no pl.
Kinder-: ~**erziehung** f bringing up of children; (durch Schule) education of children; **k~feindlich** adj hostile to children, anti-children; Architektur, Planung not catering for children; ~**feindlichkeit** f anti-children attitude; (von Architektur) failure to cater for children; ~**freibetrag** m child allowance; **k~freundlich 1** adj Mensch fond of children; Gesellschaft child-orientated; Möbel, Architektur etc catering for children; **2** adv with children in mind; ~**funk** m children's radio; ~**garten** m kindergarten; ~**gärtner(in** f) m nursery-school teacher; ~**geld** nt child allowance; ~**heim** nt children's home; ~**hort** m day-nursery, crèche; ~**kleidung** f children's clothes pl; ~**klinik** f children's clinic; ~**krankenhaus** nt children's hospital; ~**krankheit** f children's disease; (fig) teething troubles pl; ~**krippe** f day-nursery, crèche; ~**laden** m (alternative) play-group; ~**lähmung** f poliomyelitis, polio; **k~leicht** adj childishly simple, dead easy (col); **es ist k~leicht** it's child's play; **k~lieb** adj fond of children; ~**lied** nt nursery rhyme; **k~los** adj childless; ~**losigkeit** f childlessness; ~**mädchen** f nanny; ~**narr** m er ist ein ~**narr** he adores children; ~**pflegerin** f children's nurse; **k~reich** adj with many children; Familie large; ~**reichtum** m an abundance of children; ~**reim** m nursery rhyme; ~**sachen** pl (Kleidung) children's clothes pl; (Spielsachen) toys pl; ~**schreck** m bog(e)yman; ~**schuh** m child's shoe; **etw steckt noch in den** ~**schuhen** (fig) sth is still in its infancy; **den** ~**schuhen entwachsen sein** (fig) (Mensch) to have grown up; (Technik etc) to be no longer in its infancy; ~**schutz** m protection of children; ~**sitz** m child's seat; ~**spiel** nt children's game; (fig) child's play no art; ~**spielplatz** m children's playground; ~**spielzeug** nt (children's) toys pl; ~**sprache** f children's language; (verniedlichend von Erwachsenen) baby talk no art; ~**sterblichkeit** f infant mortality; ~**stube** f (fig) upbringing; ~**stuhl** m child's chair; (Hochstuhl) high chair; ~**wagen** m pram (Brit), baby carriage (US); (Sportwagen) pushchair (Brit), babystroller (US); ~**zimmer** nt child's/children's room; (esp für Kleinkinder) nursery; ~**zulage** f, ~**zuschlag** m child allowance.
Kindes-: ~**alter** nt childhood; **seit frühestem** ~**alter** from infancy; ~**annahme** f adoption; ~**beine** pl: **von** ~**beinen an** from childhood; ~**entführung** f kidnapping (of a child/children); ~**mißhandlung** f child abuse.
Kind-: **k~gemäß** adj suitable for a child/children;

~**heit** f childhood; (früheste ~heit) infancy; ~**heitserinnerung** f childhood memory.
kindisch adj (pej) childish. **sich ~ über etw** (acc) **freuen** to be as pleased as Punch about sth.
kindlich 1 adj childlike; (pej) childish. **2** adv like a child.
Kinds- in cpds siehe **Kindes-**; ~**kopf** m (col) big kid (col).
Kinkerlitzchen pl (col) knicknacks pl (col); (dumme Streiche) tomfoolery sing (col).
Kinn nt -e chin.
Kinnhaken m hook to the chin.
Kino nt -s cinema (Brit), movie theater (US). **ins ~ gehen** to go to the cinema or pictures (Brit) or movies (esp US); **das ~ der zwanziger Jahre** the cinema (Brit) or movies (esp US) in the twenties.
Kino- in cpds cinema (Brit), movie (esp US); ~**besucher** m cinemagoer (Brit), movie-goer (US); ~**karte** f cinema (Brit) or movie-theater (US) ticket; ~**kasse** f cinema (Brit) or movie theater (US) box office.
Kintopp m or nt (dated) cinema (Brit), movie theater (US).
Kiosk m -e kiosk.
Kippe f -n **(a) auf der ~ stehen** (Gegenstand) to be balanced precariously; **sie steht auf der ~** (fig) it's touch and go with her. **(b)** (col: Zigarettenstummel) cigarette stub, dog-end (Brit col). **(c)** (Müll~, Min) tip.
kippen 1 vt **(a)** Behälter, Fenster to tilt; Ladefläche, Tisch to tip or tilt (up). „**bitte nicht ~**" "please do not tilt". **(b)** (schütten) to tip. **2** vi aux sein to tip over, to topple over. **aus den Latschen ~** (fig col) (überrascht sein) to fall through the floor (col); (ohnmächtig werden) to pass out.
Kipper m - (Aut) tipper, dump(er) truck.
Kipp-: ~**fenster** nt tilt window; ~**lore** f tipper wagon; ~**schalter** m rocker switch.
Kirche f -n church. **zur ~ gehen** to go to church.
Kirchen- in cpds church; ~**austritt** m leaving the Church no art; ~**bank** f pew; ~**besuch** m church-going; ~**buch** nt church register; ~**chor** m church choir; **k~feindlich** adj anticlerical; ~**fest** nt religious or church festival; ~**gemeinde** f parish; ~**jahr** nt church or ecclesiastical year; ~**licht** nt: **kein (großes)** ~**licht sein** (fig col) to be not very bright; ~**lied** nt hymn; ~**maus** f: **arm wie eine** ~**maus** poor as a church mouse; ~**recht** nt canon law; **k~rechtlich** adj canonical; ~**schiff** nt (Längsschiff) nave; (Querschiff) transept; ~**steuer** f church tax.
Kirch-: ~**gang** m going to church no art; ~**gänger(in** f) m - churchgoer; ~**hof** m churchyard; (Friedhof) graveyard.
kirchlich adj church attr; Zustimmung, Mißbilligung by the church; Gebot, Gericht ecclesiastical. **sich ~ trauen lassen** to have a church wedding; ~ **bestattet werden** to have a religious funeral.
Kirch-: ~**turm** m church steeple; ~**weih** f -en fair, kermis (US).
Kirmes f -sen (dial) fair, kermis (US).
Kirsch m - kirsch.
Kirsch- in cpds cherry; ~**baum** m cherry tree; (Holz) cherry (wood); ~**blüte** f cherry blossom.
Kirsche f -n cherry. **mit ihm ist nicht gut ~n essen** (col) it's best not to tangle with him.
Kirsch-: ~**kern** m cherry stone; ~**likör** m cherry brandy; ~**torte** f: **Schwarzwälder** ~**torte** Black Forest gateau; ~**wasser** nt kirsch.
Kissen nt - cushion; (Kopf~) pillow; (Stempel~, an Heftpflaster) pad.
Kissenbezug m cushion cover; (Kopf~) pillow case.
Kiste f -n **(a)** box; (für Wein etc) case; (Latten~) crate; (Truhe) chest; (col: Fernsehen) box (Brit col), tube (US col). **(b)** (col: Angelegenheit) affair.
kistenweise adv by the box/case etc.
Kitsch m no pl kitsch.

kitschig adj kitschy.
Kitt m -e (Fenster~) putty; (für Porzellan, Stein etc) cement; (fig) bond.
Kittel m - (Arbeits~) overall; (von Arzt, Laborant etc) (white) coat; (blusenartig) smock.
kitten vt to cement; Fenster to putty; (füllen) to fill; (fig) to patch up.
Kitz nt -e kid; (Reh~) fawn.
Kitzel m - tickle; (fig) thrill.
kitz(e)lig adj (lit, fig) ticklish.
kitzeln vti (lit, fig) to tickle.
Klacks m -e (col) (von Kartoffelbrei, Sahne etc) dollop (col); (von Senf, Farbe etc) blob (col). **das ist ein ~** that's nothing (col).
klacksen (col) vt Sahne etc to dollop (col); Farbe to splash.
Kladde f -n rough book; (Block) scribbling pad.
klaffen vi to gape. **da klafft eine Wunde** there is a gaping wound; **zwischen uns beiden klafft ein Abgrund** (fig) we are poles apart.
kläffen vi (pej, fig) to yap.
klaffend adj gaping; (fig) irreconcilable; Widerspruch blatant.
Kläffer m - (lit, fig: pej) yapper.
Klage f -n **(a)** (Beschwerde) complaint. **(bei jdm) über jdn/etw ~ führen** to lodge a complaint (with sb) about sb/sth; ~**n (über jdn/etw) vorbringen** to make complaints (about sb/sth); **Grund zur ~** reason for complaint. **(b)** (in Trauer) lament(ation) (um, über +acc for); (~laut) plaintive cry. **(c)** (Jur) action, suit; (Scheidungs~ auch) petition; (~schrift) charge. **eine ~ gegen jdn einreichen/erheben** to institute proceedings against sb.
Klage-: ~**erhebung** f (Jur) institution of proceedings; ~**frist** f (Jur) period for instituting proceedings; ~**laut** m plaintive cry; ~**lied** nt lament; **ein ~lied über jdn/etw anstimmen** (fig) to complain about sb/sth; ~**mauer** f **die ~mauer** The Wailing Wall.
klagen 1 vi **(a)** (jammern) to moan, to wail; (Tiere) to cry; (Trauer äußern) to lament (um jdn/etw sb/sth). **(b)** (sich beklagen) to complain (über +acc about). **über jdn nicht zu ~ haben** to have no complaints about sb. **(c)** (Jur) to sue (auf +acc for). **2** vt **jdm sein Leid/seine Not ~** to pour out one's sorrow/distress to sb.
klagend adj lamenting; Blick, Ton plaintive; Gesicht sorrowful; (jammernd) complaining.
Kläger(in f) m - (Jur) (im Zivilrecht) plaintiff; (in Scheidung) petitioner; (im Strafrecht auch) prosecuting party.
Klage-: ~**ruf** m plaintive cry; ~**schrift** f (Jur) charge; (bei Scheidung) petition; ~**weg** m (Jur) **auf dem ~weg(e)** by legal action; **den ~weg beschreiten** to take legal action.
kläglich 1 adj pitiful; Rest miserable; Niederlage, Verhalten despicable; (pej: dürftig) pathetic. **2** adv (in beschämender Weise) miserably.
klaglos adv uncomplainingly.
Klamauk m no pl (col) (Alberei) tomfoolery; (Theater) slapstick. ~ **machen** to fool about.
klamm adj (steif vor Kälte) numb; (naß und kalt) clammy.
Klammer f -n **(a)** (Wäsche~) peg (Brit), pin (US); (Hosen~, Med) clip; (Büro~) paperclip; (Heft~) staple; (Haar~) (hair)grip (Brit), barrette (US); (für Zähne) brace; (Bau~) clamp. **(b)** (in Text) bracket. ~ **auf/zu** open/close brackets; **in ~n** in brackets.
klammern 1 vt (an +acc to) Papier etc to staple; (Tech) to clamp; (Med) Wunde to clip; Zähne to brace. **2** vr **sich an jdn/etw ~** (lit, fig) to cling to sb/sth. **3** vi (Sport) to clinch.
klammheimlich (col) **1** adj secret. **2** adv on the quiet. ~ **aus dem Haus gehen** to sneak out of the house.
Klamotte f -n **(a)** ~**n** pl (col) (Kleider) clothes pl;

(Zeug) stuff *no pl.* **(b)** *(pej: Film etc)* rubbishy old film *etc.* **das sind doch alte ~n** *(col)* that's old hat *(col).*

klang *pret of* **klingen.**

Klang *m* ⁼e sound; *(Tonqualität)* tone. **~e** *(Musik)* sounds, tones.

Klang-: **~farbe** *f* tone colour *(Brit)* or color *(US)*; **k~lich 1** *adj* **k~liche Unterschiede** differences in sound; *(von Tonqualität)* tonal difference; **2** *adv* **k~lich gut sein** *(Musik, Stimme)* to sound good; *(Instrument, Gerät)* to have a good tone; **k~treu** *adj Wiedergabe* faithful; *Empfänger* high-fidelity; *Ton* true; **k~voll** *adj Stimme* sonorous; *(fig) Titel, Name* fine-sounding.

Klappbett *nt* folding bed.

Klappe *f* **-n** **(a)** flap; *(an Lastwagen)* tailgate; *(seitlich)* sidegate; *(an Kombiwagen)* back; *(von Tisch)* leaf; *(von Ofen)* shutter, flap; *(Klappdeckel)* (hinged) lid; *(an Oboe etc)* key; *(Falltür)* trapdoor; *(Film)* clapperboard; *(Herz~)* valve. **(b)** *(Schulter~)* strap; *(Hosen~, an Tasche)* flap; *(Augen~)* patch. **(c)** *(Fliegen~)* (fly) swat. **(d)** *(col: Mund)* **die ~ halten** to shut one's trap *(col)*; **eine große ~ haben** to have a big mouth *(col).*

klappen 1 *vt* **etw nach oben/unten ~** *Sitz, Bett* to fold sth up/down; *Kragen* to turn sth up/down; *Deckel* to lift sth/to lower sth; **etw nach vorn/hinten ~** *Sitz* to tip sth forward/back; *Deckel* to lift sth forward/back. **2** *vi* **(a)** to bang. **(b)** *(fig col)* to work; *(Aufführung, Abend)* to go smoothly. **hat es mit den Karten/dem Job geklappt?** did you get the tickets/job OK *(col)?*

Klapper *f* **-n** rattle.

klappern *vi* to clatter; *(Klapperschlange, Fenster)* to rattle. **er klapperte vor Kälte mit den Zähnen** his teeth were chattering with cold.

Klapper-: **~schlange** *f* *(Zool)* rattlesnake; **~storch** *m* er glaubt noch an den **~storch** he still thinks babies are found under the gooseberry bush.

Klapp(fahr)rad *nt* folding bicycle.

klapprig *adj* shaky.

Klapp-: **~sitz** *m* folding seat; **~stuhl** *m* folding chair; **~tisch** *m* folding table.

Klaps *m* **-e** *(Schlag)* smack, slap. **einen ~ haben** *(col)* to have a screw loose *(col).*

klar *adj* clear; *(fertig)* ready. **~ zum Gefecht** *(Mil)* ready for action; **~ Schiff machen** *(lit, fig)* to clear the decks; **~er Fall!** *(col)* sure thing *(col)*; **alles ~?** everything OK? *(col)*; **jetzt ist mir alles ~!** now I understand; **bei ~em Verstand sein** to be in full possession of one's faculties; **etw ~ und deutlich sagen** to spell sth out; **jdm etw ~ und deutlich sagen** to tell sb sth straight *(col)*; **etw ~ zum Ausdruck bringen** to make sth clear; **~ zutage treten** to become obvious; **sich** *(dat)* **über etw** *(acc)* **im ~en sein** to be aware of sth; **sich** *(dat)* **darüber im ~en sein, daß ... to realize that ...; **ins ~e kommen** to get things straight.

Klär|anlage *f* sewage plant; *(von Fabrik)* purification plant.

klären 1 *vt* to clear; *Wasser, Luft* to purify; *Abwasser* to treat; *Fall* to clarify, to clear up; *Frage* to settle. **2** *vi* *(Sport)* to clear (the ball). **3** *vr* *(Wasser, Himmel)* to clear; *(Wetter)* to clear up; *(Meinungen, Sachlage)* to become clear; *(Streitpunkte)* to be clarified; *(Frage)* to be settled.

Klare(r) *m decl as adj* *(col)* schnapps.

Klarheit *f* *(lit: Reinheit)* clearness; *(fig: Deutlichkeit)* clarity; *(geistige ~)* lucidity. **sich** *(dat)* **~ über etw** *(acc)* **verschaffen** to get clear about sth.

Klarinette *f* clarinet.

Klar-: **k~kommen** *vi sep irreg aux sein (col)* to manage, to get by; **mit jdm/etw k~kommen** to be able to cope with sb/sth; **k~kriegen** *vt sep (col)* to sort out; **k~legen** *vt sep* to make clear; **k~machen** *sep 1* *vt* to make clear; *Schiff* to make

ready; *Flugzeug* to clear; **jdm etw k~machen** to make sth clear to sb; **sich** *(dat)* **etw k~machen** to get clear about sth; **2** *vi* *(Naut)* to make ready; **zum Gefecht k~machen** to clear the decks for action; **k~sehen** *vi sep irreg* to see clearly; **in etw** *(dat)* **k~sehen** to have understood sth; **~sichtfolie** *f* transparent film; **~sichtpackung** *f* transparent pack; **k~stellen** *vt sep (klären)* to clear up, to clarify; **ich möchte k~stellen, daß ... I** want to make it clear that ...; **~text** *m* **im ~text** in clear; *(fig col)* in plain English.

Klärung *f* *(lit)* purification; *(fig)* clarification.

klarwerden *sep irreg aux sein 1* *vr* **sich** *(dat)* **(über etw** *acc)* **~** to get (sth) clear in one's mind. **2** *vi* **jetzt wird mir das klar** now it's clear, now I see.

klasse *adj inv (col)* great *(col).*

Klasse *f* **-n** class; *(Spiel~)* league; *(Steuer~ auch)* bracket; *(Güter~)* grade; *(Sch: ~nzimmer)* classroom. **ein Fahrschein erster/zweiter ~ a** first-/second-class ticket; **das ist (große) ~!** *(col)* that's great *(col).*

Klasse- *in cpds (col)* top-class; **~frau** *f* fantastic woman.

Klassen- *in cpds* class; **~arbeit** *f* (written) class test; **~beste(r)** *mf* **er ist ~beste(r)** he is top of the class; **~bewußtsein** *nt* class consciousness; **~buch** *nt* (class-)register; **~feind** *m* *(Pol)* class enemy; **~gegensatz** *m usu pl (Sociol)* class difference; **~gesellschaft** *f* class society; **~haß** *m* *(Sociol)* class hatred; **~justiz** *f* *(Pol)* legal system with class bias; **~kamerad** *m* classmate; **~kampf** *m* class struggle; **~krieg** *m* class warfare; **~lehrer, ~leiter** *m* class or form teacher; **k~los** *adj Gesellschaft* classless; *Krankenhaus* one-class; **~sprecher(in** *f)* *m* *(Sch)* class spokesperson; **~unterschied** *m* class difference; **~ziel** *nt* *(Sch)* **das ~ziel nicht erreichen** not to reach the required standard; *(fig)* not to make the grade; **~zimmer** *nt* classroom.

klassifizieren *vt* to classify.

Klassifizierung *f* classification.

Klassik *f no pl* classical period.

Klassiker(in *f)* *m* - classic. **ein ~ des Jazz** a jazz classic; **die antiken ~** the classics.

klassisch *adj* classical; *(typisch, zeitlos)* classic.

Klatsch *m* **-e** **(a)** splash; *(bei Schlag, Aufprall)* smack. **(b)** *(no pl col: Tratsch)* gossip.

Klatschbase *f* *(pej col)* gossip.

klatschen 1 *vi* **(a)** to clap. **in die Hände ~** to clap one's hands. **(b)** *(einen Klaps geben)* to slap. **jdm auf die Schenkel/sich** *(dat)* **gegen die Stirn ~** to slap sb's thighs/one's forehead. **(c)** *aux sein (aufschlagen) (harte Gegenstände)* to go smack; *(Flüssigkeiten)* to splash. **(d)** *(pej col: tratschen)* **über jdn/etw ~** to gossip about sb. **2** *vt* **(a)** to clap. **jdm Beifall ~** to applaud or clap sb. **(b)** *(knallen)* to smack, to slap; *(werfen)* to throw.

Klatschen *nt no pl (Beifall~)* applause; *(col: Tratschen)* gossiping.

Klatsch-: **~mohn** *m* (corn) poppy; **k~naß** *adj (col)* sopping wet *(col)*; **~spalte** *f* *(col)* gossip column; **~sucht** *f* passion for gossip; **k~süchtig** *adj* **ein k~süchtiger Mensch** a compulsive gossip; **~tante** *f* *(pej col)* gossip(monger).

Klaue *f* **-n** claw. **in den ~n der Verbrecher** *etc* in the clutches of the criminals *etc.*

klauen *(col)* **1** *vt* to pinch *(col)* **jdm etw** sth from sb). **2** *vi* to steal, to pinch things *(col).*

Klausel *f* **-n** clause; *(Vorbehalt)* proviso.

Klausur *f* **(a)** *(Univ)* exam, paper. **(b)** *no pl (Abgeschlossenheit)* seclusion. **eine Arbeit in ~ schreiben** to write an essay *etc* under examination conditions.

Klaviatur *f* [klavia'tu:rɛ] *f* keyboard.

Klavier [-'vi:ɐ] *nt* **-e** piano.

Klavier- *in cpds* piano; **~auszug** *m* piano score; **~begleitung** *f* piano accompaniment; **~stimmer** *m* piano-tuner.

Klebeband nt adhesive tape (Brit), sticky tape.
kleben 1 vi to stick. **an etw** (dat) ~ (lit) to stick to sth; **an seinen Händen klebt Blut** (fig) he has blood on his hands. **2** vt to stick; (mit Klebstoff auch) to glue; Film, Tonband to splice. **Marken** ~ (col: Insur) to pay stamps; **jdm eine** ~ (col) to belt sb one (col).
klebenbleiben vi sep irreg aux sein to stick (an +dat to); (fig col: nicht wegkommen) to get stuck.
Klebepflaster nt sticking plaster.
Kleber m - (im Mehl) gluten; (col: Klebstoff) glue.
Klebe-: ~**stelle** f join; (an Film) splice; ~**streifen** m adhesive tape; ~**zettel** m gummed label.
klebrig adj sticky; (klebfähig) adhesive.
Kleb-: ~**stoff** m adhesive; ~**streifen** m adhesive tape.
kleckern 1 vt to spill. **2** vi (a) to make a mess. (b) (tropfen) to spill.
Klecks m -e (Tinten~) (ink)blot; (Farb~) blob.
klecksen vi (mit Tinte) to make blots/a blob.
Klee m no pl clover. **jdn/etw über den grünen** ~ **loben** to praise sb/sth to the skies.
Kleeblatt nt cloverleaf; (fig: Menschen) three-some, trio. **vierblättriges** ~ four-leaf clover.
Kleid nt -er (a) (Damen~) dress. **ein zweiteiliges** ~ a two-piece (suit). (b) ~**er** pl (Kleidung) clothes pl. ~**er machen Leute** (Prov) fine feathers make fine birds (Prov). (c) (liter) (Fe-der~) plumage; (Pelz) coat; (fig: von Natur, Bäumen etc) mantle (liter).
kleiden 1 vr to dress. **2** vt (a) (lit,fig) to clothe. **etw in schöne Worte** ~ to dress sth up in fancy words. (b) **jdn** ~ (jdm stehen) to suit sb.
Kleider-: ~**bügel** m coathanger; ~**bürste** f clothes brush; ~**haken** m coat hook; ~**schrank** m wardrobe; ~**ständer** m coat-stand.
kleidsam adj flattering.
Kleidung f no pl clothes pl, clothing.
Kleidungsstück nt garment. ~**e** pl clothes pl.
Kleie f no pl bran.
klein adj (a) little, small; Finger little; Format, Gehalt, Zahl, (Hand)schrift, Buchstabe small; Pause, Vortrag short; (Mus) Terz minor. **der K~e Bär** the Little Bear, Ursa Minor; **haben Sie es nicht** ~**er?** haven't you got anything smaller?; **ein** ~ **bißchen** or **wenig** a little (bit); **ein** ~ **bißchen** or **wenig Salat** a little (bit of) salad; **ein** ~**es Bier, ein K~es** (col) ≈ half a pint, a half; **mein** ~**er Bruder** my little brother; **er ist** ~**er als sein Bruder** he's smaller than his brother; **er schreibt sehr** ~ his writing is very small; **sich** ~ **machen** to bend down low; to curl up tight; **macht euch ein bißchen** ~**er!** squeeze up closer; ~ **aber oho!** (col) good things come in small packages; **ein Wort** ~ **schreiben** to write a word with small initial letters; **im** ~**en** in miniature; **bis ins** ~**ste** in minute detail; **von** ~ **an** or **auf** (von Kindheit an) from his childhood; (von Anfang an) from the very beginning; ~**en Augenblick, bit-te!** just one moment, please; **einen Kopf** ~**er als jd sein** to be a head shorter than sb; **beim** ~**sten Schreck** at the slightest or smallest shock; **das** ~**ere Übel** the lesser evil; **ein paar** ~**ere Fehler** a few minor mistakes.
(b) (unbedeutend) petty (pej); Leute ordinary; (armselig) Verhältnisse humble. **er ist ein** ~**er Geist** he's small-minded; **der** ~**e Mann** the ordinary citizen, the man in the street; **ein** ~**er Ganove** a small-time crook; **sein Vater war (ein)** ~**er Beamter** his father was a minor civil ser-vant; ~ **anfangen** to start off in a small way.
Klein-: ~**anzeige** f small ad (Brit), classified ad; ~**arbeit** f detailed work; **in zäher/mühseliger** ~**arbeit** with rigorous/painstaking attention to detail; ~**asien** nt Asia Minor; ~**bauer** m small farmer, smallholder; ~**betrieb** m small business; ~**bildkamera** f 35mm camera; ~**bürger** m petty bourgeois; **k~bürgerlich**

adj lower middle-class, petty bourgeois (pej); ~**bürgertum** nt (Sociol) lower middle class, petty bourgeoisie.
Kleine(r) mf decl as adj (a) little one; little boy/girl; baby. **unser** ~**r** (Jüngster) our young-est (child); **die lieben** ~**n** (iro) the dear little things. (b) (col: auch ~**s**: Liebling) baby (col).
Klein-: ~**familie** f small family, nuclear family (Sociol); ~**format** nt small format; ~**garten** m allotment (Brit); ~**gärtner** m allotment holder (Brit); **k~gedruckt** adj attr in small print; ~**gedruckte(s)** nt small print; ~**geld** nt (small) change; **das nötige** ~ **geld haben** (col) to have the necessary wherewithal (col); **k~gemustert** adj small-patterned; **k~gewachsen** adj short, small; Baum small; **k~gläubig** adj (zweifle-risch) timid; **k~gläubig sein** to lack conviction; **k~hacken** vt sep to chop up small; ~**heit** f small-ness, small size; ~**holz** nt no pl firewood; **aus etw** ~**holz machen** (hum col) to smash sth to pieces; ~**holz aus jdm machen** (col) to make mince-meat out of sb (col).
Kleinigkeit f (a) little or small thing; (Bagatelle) trivial matter, trifle; (Einzelheit) minor detail. **ich habe noch ein paar** ~**en in der Stadt zu erledigen** I still have a few little things to attend to in town; **es war nur eine** ~ **zu reparieren** there was only something minor to be repaired; **die Reparatur/Prüfung war eine** ~ the repair job/exam was no trouble at all; **eine** ~ **essen** to have a bite to eat; **wegen** or **bei jeder** ~ for the slightest reason; **großen Wert auf** ~**en legen** to be a stickler for detail(s). (b) (ein bißchen) **eine** ~ **a little** (bit), a trifle; **eine** ~ **zu groß** a little (bit) etc too big.
Kleinigkeitskrämer m (pej) pedant.
Klein-: ~**kaliber** nt small bore; **k~kariert** adj (fig) small-time (col); **k~kariert denken** to think small; ~**kind** nt small child, infant (Psych); ~**kram** m (col) odds and ends pl; (Trivialitäten) trivia pl; ~**kredit** m personal loan; ~**krieg** m (fig) battle; **einen** ~**krieg mit jdm führen** to be fighting a running battle with sb.
kleinkriegen vt sep (a) (lit) Holz to chop (up); Nuß to break. (b) (col: kaputtmachen) to smash, to break. (c) (col) (gefügig machen) to bring into line (col); (unterkriegen) to get down; (körperlich) to tire out. **er ist einfach nicht kleinzukriegen** he just won't be beaten.
Klein-: ~**kunst** cabaret; **k~laut** adj subdued; **dann wurde er ganz k~laut** that made him shut up; **k~laut um Verzeihung bitten** to apologize rather sheepishly.
kleinlich adj petty; (knauserig) mean, stingy (col); (engstirnig) narrow-minded.
Kleinlichkeit f siehe adj pettiness; meanness, stinginess (col); narrow-mindedness.
kleinmachen vt sep (a) to chop or cut up. (b) (col) Geld to change.
Klein-: **k~mütig** adj fainthearted, timid; **k~schneiden** vt sep irreg to cut up small; **k~schreiben** vt sep irreg (fig) **k~geschrieben werden** to count for (very) little; ~**schreibung** f use of small initial letters; ~**stadt** f small town; **k~städtisch** adj provincial, small-town attr.
kleinste(r, s) superl of **klein**.
kleinstmöglich adj smallest possible.
Klein-: ~**tier** nt small animal; ~**vieh** nt: ~**vieh macht auch Mist** (prov) every little helps; ~**wa-gen** m small car.
Kleister m - (Klebstoff) paste.
kleistern vti (zusammenkleben) to paste.
Klemme f -n (a) (Haar~, für Papiere etc) clip; (Elec) crocodile clamp; (Med) clamp. (b) (fig col) **in der** ~ **sitzen** or **sein** to be in a fix (col); **jdm aus der** ~ **helfen** to help sb out of a fix (col).
klemmen 1 vt Draht etc to clamp, to clip; (in Spalt)

to wedge, to jam. **sich** *(dat)* **etw unter den Arm** ~ to tuck sth under one's arm. **2** *vr* to catch oneself *(in +dat* in). **sich hinter etw** *(acc)* ~ *(col)* to get stuck into sth *(col);* **sich hinter jdn** ~ *(col)* to get on to sb. **3** *vi (Tür, Schloß etc)* to stick, to jam.
Klempner *m* - plumber.
Klempnerei *f* (a) *no pl* plumbing. (b) *(Werkstatt)* plumber's workshop.
Klerus *m* -, *no pl* clergy.
Klette *f* **-n** *(Bot)* burdock; *(Blütenkopf)* bur(r); *(pej: lästiger Mensch)* nuisance. **sich wie eine** ~ **an jdn hängen** to cling to sb like a limpet.
Kletterer *m* - climber.
Klettergerüst *nt* climbing frame.
klettern *vi aux sein* to climb; *(mühsam)* to clamber. **auf Bäume** ~ to climb trees.
Kletterpflanze *f* climbing plant.
klicken *vi* to click.
Klient(in *f)* [kliˈɛnt(ɪn)] *m (wk)* **-en, -en** client.
Klima *nt* **-s** *or* **-te** [kliˈmaːtə] *(lit, fig)* climate.
Klima|anlage *f* air conditioning. **mit** ~ air-conditioned.
klimatisch *adj no pred* climatic.
Klimazone *f* (climatic) zone.
Klimbim *m no pl (col)* odds and ends *pl; (Umstände)* fuss.
Klimmzug *m (Sport)* pull-up.
klimpern *vi* to tinkle; *(stümperhaft)* to plonk away *(col); (auf Banjo)* to twang; *(Münzen)* to jingle.
Klinge *f* **-n** blade.
Klingel *f* **-n** bell.
Klingelknopf *m* bell push.
klingeln *vi* to ring *(nach* for); *(Motor)* to pink, to knock. **es hat schon geklingelt** *(in Schule)* the bell has already gone; **es hat geklingelt** *(an Tür)* somebody just rang the doorbell; **immer wenn es an der Tür klingelt** ... whenever the doorbell rings *or* goes ...
klingen *pret* **klang,** *ptp* **geklungen** *vi* to sound; *(Glocke, Ohr)* to ring; *(Glas)* to clink; *(Metall)* to clang. **nach etw** ~ to sound like sth.
Klinik *f* **-en** clinic; *(Universitäts*~) (university) hospital.
klinisch *adj* clinical. ~ **tot** clinically dead.
Klinke *f* **-n** *(Tür*~) (door) handle.
Klinker *m* - *(Ziegelstein)* clinker (brick).
klipp *adv:* ~ **und klar** clearly; *(offen)* frankly.
Klippe *f* **-n** *(Fels*~) cliff; *(im Meer)* rock; *(fig)* obstacle. ~**n umschiffen** *(lit, fig)* to negotiate obstacles.
klirren *vi* to clink; *(Fensterscheiben)* to rattle; *(Lautsprecher, Mikrofon)* to crackle; *(Eis)* to crunch. ~**de Kälte** *(liter)* crisp cold.
Klischee *nt* -s *(Typ)* plate; *(fig: Phrase)* cliché.
Klischeevorstellung *f* cliché, stereotype.
Klitoris *f* - clitoris.
Klo *nt* **-s** *(col)* loo *(Brit col),* john *(US col).*
Kloake *f* **-n** sewer.
klobig *adj* hefty *(col); Mensch* hulking great *(col).*
Klopapier *nt (col)* toilet *or* loo *(Brit col)* paper.
klopfen **1** *vt* to knock; *Fleisch, Teppich* to beat; *Steine* to knock down. **den Takt** ~ to beat time. **2** *vi* to knock; *(Herz)* to beat; *(vor Aufregung, Anstrengung auch)* to pound; *(Puls)* to throb; *(Motor)* to knock, to pink *(Brit).* **sie klopften wiederholt heftig an die Tür** they kept pounding away at the door; **es hat geklopft** there's someone knocking at the door; **jdm auf die Schulter/den Rücken** ~ to tap sb on the shoulder/to pat sb on the back; *(heftig)* to slap sb on the shoulder/back; **mit** ~**dem Herzen** with beating *or* pounding heart.
Klopfer *m* - *(Tür*~) (door) knocker; *(Fleisch*~) (meat) mallet; *(Teppich*~) carpet beater.
Klöppel *m* - *(Glocken*~) clapper; *(Spitzen*~) bobbin; *(Trommel*~) stick.
klöppeln *vi* to make (pillow) lace.
Klöppelspitze *f* pillow lace.
Klops *m* **-e** *(Cook)* meatball.

Klosett *nt* **-e** *or* **-s** lavatory.
Klosett-: ~**brille** *f* toilet seat. ~**bürste** *f* lavatory brush; ~**deckel** *m* lavatory seat lid; ~**frau** *f* lavatory attendant; ~**papier** *nt* toilet paper.
Kloß *m* -̈e dumpling; *(Fleisch*~) meatball; *(Bulette)* rissole. **einen** ~ **im Hals haben** *(fig)* to have a lump in one's throat.
Kloßbrühe *f:* **klar wie** ~ as clear as day; *(iro)* as clear as mud.
Kloster *nt* -̈ cloister; *(Mönchs*~ *auch)* monastery; *(Nonnen*~ *auch)* convent. **ins** ~ **gehen** to become a monk/nun.
Klosterschule *f* monastic/convent school.
Klotz *m* -̈e *(Holz*~) block (of wood); *(pej: Beton*~) concrete block; *(col: Person)* great lump *(col).* **jdm ein** ~ **am Bein sein** to be a hindrance to sb.
Klub *m* -s club.
Klub-: ~**abend** *m* club night; ~**garnitur** *f* (three-piece) suite; ~**jacke** *f* blazer; ~**sessel** *m* club chair.
Kluft *f* -̈e **(a)** *(Erdspalte)* cleft; *(in Bergen)* crevasse; *(Abgrund)* chasm. **(b)** *(fig)* gulf, gap. **in der Partei tat sich eine tiefe** ~ **auf** a deep rift opened up in the party. **(c)** *no pl (Uniform)* uniform; *(col: Kleidung)* gear *(col).*
klug *adj, comp* -̈**er,** *superl* -̈**ste(r, s)** clever, intelligent; *(vernünftig)* Entscheidung, Rat sound; *Überlegung* prudent; *Geschäftsmann* shrewd. **es wird am** ~**sten sein, wenn** ... it would be most sensible if ...; **es wäre politisch** ~ ... it would make good political sense ...; **ein** ~**er Kopf** a capable person; **in** ~**er Voraussicht** shrewdly; **ich werde daraus nicht** ~ I can't make head or tail of it; **aus ihm werde ich nicht** ~ I can't make him out; ~**e Reden halten** *(iro)* to make fine-sounding speeches; ~**e Bemerkungen/Ratschläge** *(iro)* clever *or* helpful remarks/advice *(iro);* **nun bin ich genau so** ~ **wir vorher** I am still none the wiser.
klugerweise *adv* (very) cleverly, (very) wisely.
Klugheit *f siehe adj* cleverness, intelligence; soundness; prudence; shrewdness. **aus** ~ (very) wisely; **menschliche** ~ human understanding.
Klug-: ~**redner** *m* know-all, know-it-all *(US);* ~**scheißer** *m* *(col!)* smart-ass *(col!).*
Klumpen *m* - lump; *(Gold*~) nugget; *(Blut*~) clot. ~ **bilden** *(Mehl etc)* to go lumpy.
Klumpfuß *m* club-foot.
klumpig *adj* lumpy.
km = Kilometer km.
km/h = Kilometer pro Stunde kph.
knabbern *vti* to nibble. **nichts zu** ~ **haben** *(col)* to have nothing to eat.
Knabe *m (wk)* -**n, -n** *(liter)* boy, lad.
Knaben-: ~**chor** *m* boys' choir; **k**~**haft** *adj* boyish.
Knäckebrot *nt* crispbread.
knacken **1** *vt (lit, fig)* to crack; *(col) Auto* to break into. **2** *vi (brechen)* to crack; *(Dielen, Stuhl)* to creak; *(knistern: Holz)* to crackle. **daran wird er zu** ~ **haben** *(col)* that'll give him something to think about.
Knacker *m* **(a)** type *of frankfurter.* **(b)** *(pej col)* **alter** ~ old fog(e)y *(col).*
knackig *adj* crisp; *(col) Mädchen* juicy *(col).*
Knacks *m* **-e** *(Sprung)* crack. **der Fernseher hat einen** ~ *(col)* there is something wrong with the television.
Knackwurst *f* type *of frankfurter.*
Knall *m* **-e** bang; *(mit Peitsche)* crack; *(von Korken)* pop; *(col: Krach)* trouble. ~ **auf Fall** *(col)* just like that *(col);* **einen** ~ **haben** *(col)* to be crazy *(col) or* crackers *(Brit col).*
knallen **1** *vi* **(a)** to bang, to explode; *(Schuß)* to ring out; *(Pfropfen)* to (go) pop; *(Peitsche)* to crack; *(Tür etc)* to bang, to slam; *(Auspuff)* to misfire; *(aux sein: auftreffen)* to bang. **mit der Tür** ~ to bang *or* slam the door; **draußen knallte es**

there was a shot/were shots outside; **nicht so frech, sonst knallt's** (col) don't be so cheeky, or there'll be trouble. (**b**) (col: Sonne) to blaze down. **2** vt to bang; Tür, Buch auch to slam; Schüsse to fire (off); Peitsche to crack. **den Hörer auf die Gabel ~** (col) to slam or bang down the receiver; **jdm eine ~** (col) to clout sb (col).

Knall-: ~frosch m jumping jack; **k~gelb** adj (col) bright yellow; **k~hart** adj (col) really hard; Film brutal; Porno hard-core; Job, Truppen, Mensch really tough; Schuß, Schlag really hard. **er sagte ihr k~hart ...** he said to her quite brutally ...

knallig adj (col) Farben loud, gaudy.

Knall-: ~körper m fire-cracker; **k~rot** adj (col) bright red.

knapp adj (**a**) (nicht ausreichend) scarce, in short supply; Gehalt low. **mein Geld ist ~** I'm short of money; **mein Geld wird ~** I am running short of money; **das Essen wird ~** we/they etc are running short of food; **mein Geld/meine Zeit ist ~ bemessen** I am short of money/time. (**b**) (gerade noch ausreichend) Zeit, Geld just enough; Mehrheit, Sieg narrow; Kleidungsstück etc (eng) tight; (kurz) short; Bikini scanty. **wir haben ~ verloren/gewonnen** we only just lost/won. (**c**) (nicht ganz) almost. **ein ~es Pfund Mehl** just under a pound of flour. (**d**) Stil, Worte concise; Geste terse; (lakonisch) Antwort pithy. (**e**) (gerade so eben) just. **mit ~er Not** only just.

Knappheit f shortage; (fig: des Ausdrucks) conciseness.

Knarre f -n (col: Gewehr) shooter (col).

knarren vi to creak. **eine ~de Stimme** a grating voice.

Knast m no pl (col) clink (col), can (US col).

Knatsch m no pl (col) trouble.

knattern vi (Motorrad) to roar; (Preßlufthammer) to hammer; (Maschinengewehr) to rattle; (Schüsse) to rattle out.

Knäuel m or nt - ball; (wirres) tangle; (von Menschen) group, knot.

Knauf m, pl **Knäufe** (Tür~) knob.

knauserig adj (col) mean, stingy (col).

knausern vi (col) to be mean or stingy (col) (mit with).

knautschen vti (col) to crumple (up).

Knautschzone f (Aut) crumple zone.

Knebel m - (Mund~) gag; (Paket~) (wooden) handle; (an Mänteln) toggle.

knebeln vt jdn, Presse to gag.

Kneb(e)lung f no pl (lit, fig) gagging.

Knecht m -e servant; (beim Bauern) (farm-) worker; (Stall~) stableboy; (fig: Sklave) slave (gen to).

knechten vt (geh) to subjugate, to oppress.

Knechtschaft f slavery.

kneifen pret **kniff**, ptp **gekniffen 1** vti to pinch. **jdn** or **jdm in den Arm ~** to pinch sb's arm. **2** vi (col: ausweichen) to back out (vor +dat of).

Kneifer m - (Brille) pince-nez.

Kneifzange f pliers pl; (kleine) pincers pl. **eine ~** (a pair of) pliers/(a pair of) pincers.

Kneipe f -n (col: Lokal) pub (Brit), bar.

Kneipenwirt m (col) publican (Brit), landlord (Brit), barkeeper (US).

Kneippkur f Kneipp cure, type of hydropathic treatment combined with diet, rest etc.

kneten vt to knead; Ton to work; Figuren to model.

Knet-: ~gummi m or nt plasticine ®; **~masse** f modelling (Brit) or modeling (US) clay.

Knick m -e or -s (Falte) crease; (Biegung) (sharp) bend; (bei Draht) kink. **einen ~ machen** to bend sharply.

knicken vti (vi: aux sein) to snap; Papier to fold. „**nicht ~!**" "do not bend".

knick(e)rig adj (col) stingy (col), mean.

Knicks m -e bob; (tiefer) curts(e)y. **einen ~ machen** to curts(e)y (vor +dat to).

knicksen vi to curts(e)y (vor +dat to).

Knie nt - (**a**) knee. **auf ~n** on bended knee; **auf die ~ fallen** to drop to one's knees; **jdm auf ~n danken** to go down on one's knees and thank sb; **in die ~ gehen** to kneel; (fig) to be brought to one's knees; **jdn in** or **auf die ~ zwingen** to force sb to his knees; **jdn übers ~ legen** (col) to put sb across one's knee; **etw übers ~ brechen** (fig) to rush (at) sth. (**b**) (Fluß~) sharp bend; (in Rohr) elbow.

Knie-: ~beuge f (Sport) knee bend; **~fall** m einen **~fall vor jdm machen** (lit, fig) to kneel before sb; **~gelenk** nt knee joint; **~hose** f knee breeches pl; **~kehle** f back of the knee; **k~lang** adj knee length.

knien [kni:n, 'kni:ən] **1** vi to kneel. **im K~** kneeling. **2** vr to kneel (down). **sich in die Arbeit ~** (fig) to get down to one's work.

Knie-: ~scheibe f kneecap; **~strumpf** m knee-length sock; **k~tief** adj knee-deep.

kniff pret of **kneifen**.

Kniff m -e (**a**) (col) trick. **den ~ bei etw heraushaben** to have the knack of sth (col). (**b**) (Falte) crease, fold.

kniff(e)lig adj (col) fiddly; (heikel) tricky.

knipsen 1 vt (**a**) (Phot col) to snap (col). (**b**) Fahrschein to punch, to clip. **2** vi (**a**) (Phot col) to take pictures. (**b**) **mit den Fingern ~** to snap one's fingers.

Knirps m -e (**a**) (Junge) whippersnapper. (**b**) ® telescopic umbrella.

knirschen vi (Sand, Schnee) to crunch; (Getriebe) to grind. **mit den Zähnen ~** to grind one's teeth.

knistern vi (Feuer) to crackle; (Papier, Seide) to rustle. **mit Papier etc ~** to rustle paper etc.

knitterfrei adj Stoff, Kleid crease-resistant.

knittern vti to crease, to crush.

knobeln vi (würfeln) to play dice; (um eine Entscheidung) to toss for it (col).

Knoblauch m no pl garlic.

Knoblauchzehe f clove of garlic.

Knöchel m - (**a**) (Fuß~) ankle. **bis über die ~ up** to the ankles. (**b**) (Finger~) knuckle.

knöcheltief adj ankle-deep.

Knochen m - bone. **Fleisch mit/ohne ~** meat on/off the bone; **er ist bis auf die ~ abgemagert** he is just skin and bones; **ihm steckt die Grippe/Angst in den ~** (col) he's got flu/he's scared stiff (col); **naß bis auf die ~** (col) soaked to the skin; **der Schreck fuhr ihm in die ~** he was paralyzed with shock; **sich bis auf die ~ blamieren** (col) to make a proper fool of oneself (col).

Knochen-: ~bau m bone structure; **~bruch** m fracture; **~gerüst** nt skeleton; **k~hart** adj (col) rock-hard; **~mark** nt bone marrow; **~mehl** nt bone meal; **~schinken** m ham on the bone; **k~trocken** adj (col) bone dry; (fig) Humor etc very dry.

knöchern adj (aus Knochen) bone.

knochig adj bony.

Knödel m - dumpling.

Knolle f -n (Bot) tubercule; (von Kartoffel) tuber.

knollig adj Wurzel tuberous; Auswuchs knobbly; Nase bulbous.

Knopf m -̈e (**a**) button. **etw an den ~en abzählen** to decide sth by tossing a coin. (**b**) (an Tür, Stock) knob; (Sattel~, Degen~) pommel. (**c**) (col) (Kind) little chap/little lass; (Kerl) chap, fellow.

knöpfen vt to button (up).

Knopfloch nt buttonhole.

Knorpel m - (Anat) cartilage; (Cook) gristle.

knorpelig adj (Anat) cartilaginous; Fleisch gristly.

knorrig adj Baum gnarled; Holz knotty; (fig) alter Mann rugged; (eigenwillig) Mensch surly, gruff.

Knospe f -n bud. **~n ansetzen** to bud.

knospen vi to bud. **~d** (lit, fig liter) budding.

Knoten m - knot (auch Naut); (Med: Geschwulst) lump; (Haar auch) bun.

knoten vt Seil etc to tie a knot in.

Knotenpunkt m (Mot) (road) junction (Brit), intersection; (Rail) junction; (fig) centre (Brit), center (US).

knotig adj knotted, full of knots; Äste, Finger gnarled.

knuffen vti (col) to poke (col); (mit Ellbogen) to nudge.

knüllen vti to crumple, to crease (up).

Knüller m - (col) sensation; (Press) scoop.

knüpfen 1 vt Knoten, Band to tie; Teppich to knot; Netz to mesh; Freundschaft to form. **jdn an den Galgen ~** (col) to string sb up (col); **große Erwartungen an etw** (acc) ~ to have great expectations of sth. 2 vr **sich an etw** (acc) ~ to be linked to sth.

Knüppel m - (a) stick; (Waffe) cudgel, club; (Polizei~) truncheon (Brit), night stick (US). **jdm ~ zwischen die Beine werfen** (fig) to put a spoke in sb's wheel. (b) (Aviat) joystick; (Aut) gear stick.

Knüppel-: k~dick (col) 1 adj Steak, Schicht very thick; 2 adv **wenn's kommt, kommt's immer gleich k~dick** it never rains but it pours (prov); **~schaltung** f (Aut) floor-mounted gear shift; **k~voll** adj (col) jam-packed.

knurren 1 vi (Hund etc) to growl; (Magen) to rumble; (bei Beklagten) to groan (über +acc about). 2 vti (mürrisch sagen) to growl.

Knurren nt no pl siehe vi growl(ing); rumbling; groaning.

knurrig adj grumpy; Angestellte etc disgruntled.

knusprig adj Braten crisp; Gebäck auch crunchy; (fig) Mädchen scrumptious (col).

Knute f -n **unter jds ~** (dat) **stehen** to be completely dominated by sb.

knutschen (col) 1 vt to neck with (col). 2 vir to neck (col).

k. o. [ka:'lo:] adj pred (Sport) knocked out; (fig col) whacked (col). **jdn ~ schlagen** to knock sb out.

koalieren* vi (esp Pol) to form a coalition.

Koalition f (esp Pol) coalition.

Koalitions- in cpds coalition; **~regierung** f coalition government.

Kobold m -e goblin, imp.

Koch m -̈e cook; (von Restaurant auch) chef. **viele ~e verderben den Brei** (Prov) too many cooks spoil the broth (Prov).

Koch-: ~apfel m cooking apple; **~buch** nt cookery book, cookbook; **k~echt** adj Farbe fast; Wäsche etc that may be boiled.

kochen 1 vi (a) (Flüssigkeit, Speise) to boil. **etw zum K~ bringen** to bring sth to the boil; **jdn zum K~ bringen** (fig col) to make sb's blood boil; **das Auto kocht** (col) the car is overheating; **er kochte vor Wut** (col) he was seething. **(b)** (Speisen zubereiten) to cook; (als Koch fungieren) to do the cooking. **er kocht gut** he's a good cook; **er kocht scharf/pikant** his cooking is highly seasoned/spiced. 2 vt **(a)** Nahrungsmittel, Wäsche to boil. **etw auf kleiner Flamme ~** to simmer sth over a low heat. **(b)** (zubereiten) Essen to cook; Kaffee, Tee to make. **etw gar/weich ~** to cook sth through/until (it is) soft; **Eier weich/hart ~** to soft-boil/hard-boil eggs.

kochend adj boiling. **~ heiß sein** to be boiling hot; (Suppe etc) to be piping hot.

kochendheiß adj attr boiling hot; Suppe etc piping hot.

Kocher m - (Herd) cooker, stove.

Koch-: k~fertig adj ready-to-cook; **~gelegenheit** f cooking facilities pl; **~herd** m cooker.

Köchin f cook; (von Restaurant auch) chef.

Koch-: ~kunst f cooking; **~löffel** m cooking spoon; **~platte** f (Herdplatte) hotplate; **~rezept** nt recipe; **~salz** nt cooking salt; **~topf** m (cooking) pot; (mit Stiel) saucepan; **~wäsche** f washing that can be boiled; **~zeit** f cooking time.

Kode [ko:t, 'ko:də] m -s code.

Köder m - bait; (fig auch) lure.

ködern vt (lit) to lure; (fig) to tempt. **jdn zu ~ versuchen** to woo sb; **jdn für etw ~** to rope sb into sth (col); **sich von jdm/etw nicht ~ lassen** not to be tempted by sb/sth.

Kodewort nt code word.

Koffein nt no pl caffeine.

koffeinfrei adj decaffeinated.

Koffer m - (suit)case, bag; (Schrank~) trunk; (Arzt~) bag; (für Schreibmaschine, Kosmetika etc) case. **die ~ pl** (Gepäck) the luggage or baggage or bags pl; **die ~ packen** (lit, fig) to pack one's bags.

Koffer-: ~gerät nt portable (set); **~kuli** m (luggage) trolley (Brit), cart (US); **~radio** nt portable radio; **~raum** m (Aut) boot (Brit), trunk (US); (Volumen) luggage space.

Kognak ['kɔnjak] m -s or -e brandy.

Kohl m -̈e (a) cabbage. **das macht den ~ auch nicht fett** (col) that's not much help. **(b)** (col: Unsinn) nonsense.

Kohldampf m no pl (col) **~ haben** to be famished.

Kohle f -n **(a)** coal; (Stück ~) (lump of) coal. **wir haben keine ~n mehr** we have no coal left; **zwei ~n** two lumps of coal; **(wie) auf glühenden** or **heißen ~n sitzen** to be like a cat on hot bricks. **(b)** (Verkohltes, Holz~, Art) charcoal. **(c)** (Tech) carbon. **(d)** (col: Geld) dough (col), cash (col). **die ~n stimmen** the money's right.

Kohle-: ~filter m charcoal filter; **~hydrat** nt carbohydrate.

Kohlen- in cpds coal; **~bergbau** m coal-mining; **~bergwerk** nt coalmine, pit, colliery; **~grube** f coalmine, pit; **~halde** f pile of coal; **~heizung** f coal heating; **~herd** m range; **~kasten** m coal-box; **~keller** m coal cellar; **~lager** nt (Vorrat) coal depot; (im Stollen, Berg) coal seam; **~monoxyd** nt carbon monoxide; **~ofen** m (coal-burning) stove; **~säure** f (Chem) carbonic acid; **ein Getränk ohne ~säure** a non-fizzy or still drink; **~schaufel** f coal shovel; **~stoff** m carbon; **~wasserstoff** m hydrocarbon.

Kohle-: ~papier nt carbon paper; **~tablette** f (Med) charcoal tablet; **~zeichnung** f charcoal drawing.

Kohl-: ~kopf m cabbage; **~meise** f great tit; **k~(pech)rabenschwarz** adj Haar jet black; Nacht pitch-black; **~rabi** m -(s) kohlrabi; **~rübe** f turnip; **k~schwarz** adj Haare, Augen jet black; Gesicht, Hände black as coal.

Koitus ['ko:itus] m -, - or -se coitus.

Koje f -n (esp Naut) bunk; (col: Bett) bed.

Kokain nt no pl cocaine.

kokett adj coquettish, flirtatious.

kokettieren* vi to flirt. **mit seinem Alter ~** to play on one's age; **mit einem Gedanken ~** to toy with an idea.

Kokos- in cpds coconut; **~milch** f coconut milk; **~nuß** f coconut; **~palme** f coconut palm.

Koks m -e coke.

Koksheizung f coke heating.

Kolben m - (Tech) piston; (Gewehr~) butt; (Chem: Destillier~) retort; (von Lötapparat) bit.

Kolben-: k~förmig adj club-shaped; **~ring** m piston ring.

Kolibri m -s humming bird.

Kollaborateur(in f) [-'tø:ɐ, -'tø:rɪn] m (Pol) collaborator.

Kollage [kɔ'la:ʒə] f -n (Art, fig) collage.

Kollaps m -e (Med) collapse.

Kolleg nt -s or -ien [-ən] (Univ: Vorlesung) lecture; (Vorlesungsreihe) (course of) lectures.

Kollege m (wk) -n, -n, **Kollegin** f colleague. **seine ~n vom Fach** his professional colleagues, his fellow doctors/teachers etc; **meine ~n** the people I work with; **Herr ~!** Mr X/Y.

kollegial adj cooperative. **sich ~ verhalten** to be cooperative.

Kollegialität f cooperativeness.

Kollegin *siehe* **Kollege.**
Kollegium *nt (Lehrer~ etc)* staff; *(Ausschuß)* working party.
Kollegmappe *f* document case.
Kollekte *f* -n *(Eccl)* collection.
Kollektion *f* collection; *(Sortiment)* range.
kollektiv *adj* collective.
Kollektiv *nt* collective.
Kollektiv-: ~**schuld** *f* collective guilt; ~**strafe** *f* collective punishment; ~**wirtschaft** *f (Econ)* collective economy.
Koller *m* - *(col) (Anfall)* funny mood; *(Wutanfall)* rage; *(Tropen~, Gefängnis~)* tropical/prison madness. **seinen ~ bekommen/haben** to get into/to be one of one's silly *or* funny moods; **einen ~ haben/bekommen** to be in/fly into a rage.
kollidieren* *vi (geh)* **(a)** *aux sein (Fahrzeuge)* to collide. **(b)** *aux sein or haben (fig)* to clash.
Kollier [kɔ'liːɐ] -s necklet, necklace.
Kollision *f (geh) (Zusammenstoß)* collision; *(Streit)* conflict, clash.
Kollisionskurs *m* **auf ~ gehen** *(fig)* to be heading for trouble.
Kolloquium *nt* colloquium.
Köln *nt* Cologne.
Kölner *adj attr* Cologne.
Kölnischwasser, Kölnisch Wasser *nt* eau de Cologne, cologne.
Kolonial-: ~**macht** *f* colonial power; ~**warenhändler** *m (dated)* grocer.
Kolonie *f* colony; *(Ferien~)* camp.
Kolonne *f* -n column; *(Autoschlange)* queue *(Brit)*, line; *(Arbeits~)* gang. „**Achtung** ~**!**" "convoy"; ~ **fahren** to drive in (a) convoy.
Koloß *m* -sse colossus.
kolossal 1 *adj* colossal, enormous. 2 *adv (col)* enormously.
Kolumbien [-iən] *nt* Colombia.
Kolumne *f* -n *(Typ, Press)* column.
Koma *nt* -s *or* -ta *(Med)* coma.
Kombi *m* -s *(Aut)* estate (car) *(Brit)*, station wagon *(esp US)*.
Kombination *f* **(a)** *(Verbindung, Zahlen~)* combination; *(Sport: Zusammenspiel)* (piece of) teamwork. **(b)** *(Schlußfolgerung)* deduction; *(Vermutung)* conjecture. **(c)** *(Kleidung)* suit, ensemble; *(Hemdhose)* combinations *pl*; *(Arbeitsanzug)* overalls *pl*, boilersuit; *(Flieger~)* flying suit.
Kombinationsschloß *nt* combination lock.
kombinieren* 1 *vt* to combine. 2 *vi (folgern)* to deduce; *(vermuten)* to suppose. **gut ~ können** to be good at deduction.
Kombi-: ~**wagen** *m* estate (car) *(Brit)*, station wagon *(esp US)*; ~**zange** *f* combination pliers *pl*.
Komet *m (wk)* -en, -en comet; *(fig)* meteor.
kometenhaft *adj (fig) Aufstieg* meteoric.
Komfort [kɔm'foːɐ] *m no pl (von Hotel etc)* luxury; *(von Möbel etc)* comfort; *(von Auto)* luxury features *pl*; *(von Gerät)* extras *pl*; *(von Wohnung)* amenities *pl*.
komfortabel *adj* luxurious, luxury *attr*; *(bequem) Sessel, Bett* comfortable.
Komik *f no pl (das Komische)* comic; *(komische Wirkung)* comic effect; *(lustiges Element: von Situation)* comic element.
Komiker *m - (lit, fig)* comedian, comic.
komisch *adj* **(a)** *(spaßig)* funny, comical; *(Theat)* comic. **(b)** *(seltsam)* funny, strange, odd. **das K~e daran ist ...** the funny *etc* thing about it is ...; **mir ist so ~** *(col)* I feel funny *or* strange *or* odd.
komischerweise *adv* funnily enough.
Komitee *nt* -s committee.
Komma *nt* -s *or* -ta comma; *(Math)* decimal point. **fünf ~ drei** five point three.
Kommandant *m (Mil)* commanding officer; *(Naut)* captain; *(von Stadt)* commandant.

kommandieren* 1 *vt* **(a)** *(befehligen)* to command, to be in command of. **(b)** *(befehlen) jdm etw ~* to command sb to do sth; **jdn an einen Ort ~** to order sb to a place. 2 *vi* **(a)** *(Befehlsgewalt haben)* to be in command. ~**der General** commanding general. **(b)** *(Befehle geben)* to give orders.
Kommando *nt* -s **(a)** *(Befehl)* command, order. **das ~ zum Schießen geben** to give the command *or* order to fire; **auf ~ schreit ihr alle ... on** the command (you) all shout ...; **ich kann doch nicht auf ~ lustig sein** I can't be cheerful to order; **wie auf ~ stehenbleiben** to stand still as if by command. **(b)** *(Befehlsgewalt)* command. **das ~ haben** to be in command *(über +acc* of). **(c)** *(Mil) (Behörde)* command; *(Abteilung)* commando.
Kommandobrücke *f (Naut)* bridge.
kommen *pret* **kam,** *ptp* **gekommen** *aux sein* 1 **(a)** to come; *(an~ auch)* to arrive; *(her~)* to come over; *(hervor~)* *(Blüten, Sonne)* to come out; *(Zähne auch)* to come through; *(sich entwickeln: Pflanzen)* to come on. **ich komme (schon)** I'm just coming; **er wird gleich ~** he'll be here right away; **der Nachtisch kommt gleich** dessert is coming straight away; **wann soll der Zug/das Baby ~?** when is the train/baby due?; **nach Hause ~** to come *or* get home; **der Wagen kommt in 16 sec. auf 100 km/h** the car does 0 to 100 km/h in 16 sec; **das Schlimmste kommt noch** the worst is yet to come; **ich komme zuerst an die Reihe** I'm first; **jetzt kommt's** here's your chance for it! *(col);* **bohren, bis Öl/Grundwasser kommt** to bore until one strikes oil/finds water; **jetzt muß bald die Grenze/Hannover ~** we should soon be at the border/in Hanover; **wie sie (gerade) ~** just as they come; **bitte kommen!** *(Telec)* come in please; **daher kommt es, daß... that's** why ...; **das kommt davon, daß ... that's because ...;** **das kommt daher, daß es soviel geregnet hat** that comes from all the rain we've had; **das kommt davon!** see what happens?
(b) *(stattfinden, sich zutragen)* to happen; *(TV, Rad, etc)* to be on. **ich glaube, es kommt ein Unwetter** I think there's some bad weather on the way; **was kommt diese Woche im Kino?** what's on at the cinema this week?; **egal, was kommt, ich bleibe fröhlich** whatever happens, I shall remain cheerful; **komme, was da wolle** come what may; **so mußte es ja ~** it had to happen; **das hätte nicht ~ dürfen** that should never have happened.
(c) *(kosten, sich belaufen)* **wie hoch kommt das?** what does that come to?; **das kommt zusammen auf 20 DM** that makes DM 20.
(d) *(gelangen)* **to get** out of the house; *(mit Hand etc erreichen können)* to reach. **wie komme ich nach London?** how do I get to London?; **ich komme zur Zeit nicht aus dem Haus** at the moment I never get out of this house; **durch den Zoll/die Prüfung ~** to get through customs/the exam; **zu einem Entschluß/einer Einigung ~** to come to a conclusion/an agreement; **in das Alter ~, wo ...** to reach the age when ...
(e) *(hingehören, gebracht werden)* to go. **das Buch kommt ins oberste Fach** the book goes on the top shelf; **in die Ecke kommt noch ein Schrank** another cupboard is to go in that corner; **ins Gefängnis ~** to go to prison; **in die Schule ~** to go to school; **ins Krankenhaus ~** to go into hospital.
(f) **komm, wir gehen** come along, we're going; **ach komm!** come on!; **komm, fang bloß nicht wieder damit an** come on, don't start that again; **wenn mir die Lust kommt** when I feel like it; **ihm kamen Zweifel** he started to have doubts; **jdm kamen die Tränen** tears come to sb's eyes; **ihm kam das Grausen** terror seized him; **mir kommt eine Idee** I just had an idea; **du kommst mir**

gerade recht *(iro)* you're just what I need; **das kommt mir gerade recht** that's just fine; **jdm frech/dumm** ~ to be cheeky to sb/to act stupid; **angelaufen** ~ to come running along *or (auf einen zu)* up; **kommt essen!** come and eat!; **jdn besuchen** ~ to come and visit sb; **neben jdm zu sitzen** ~ to end up sitting next to sb; **jdn** ~ **sehen** to see sb coming; **ich habe es** ~ **sehen** I saw it coming; **die Zeit für gekommen halten** to think the time has come; **jdn** ~ **lassen** *Arzt, Polizei, Schüler, Sekretärin* to send for sb; **etw** ~ **lassen** *Mahlzeit, Taxi* to order; *Kupplung* to let in; *Seil* to let come; *Motor* to start up; **in Bewegung** ~ to start moving; **ins Erzählen** ~ to get talking; **zum Blühen/ Wachsen** *etc* ~ to start flowering/growing; **zum Stehen/Stillsand** ~ to come to a halt/standstill; **kommt Zeit, kommt Rat** *(Prov)* things have a way of working themselves out; **wer zuerst kommt, mahlt zuerst** *(Prov)* first come first served.

(g) an etw *(acc)* ~ *(berühren)* to touch sth; *(sich verschaffen)* to get hold of sth; **auf etw** *(acc)* ~ *(sich erinnern)* to think of sth; *(sprechen über)* to get onto sth; **auf einen Gedanken** ~ to have a thought; **das kommt auf die Rechnung** that goes onto the bill; **auf ihn/darauf lasse ich nichts** ~ *(col)* I won't hear a word against him/it; **auf jeden** ~ **fünf Mark** there are five marks (for) each; **wie kommst du darauf?** what makes you think that?; **darauf bin ich nicht gekommen** I didn't think of that; **ich komme im Moment nicht auf seinen Namen** his name escapes me for the moment; **hinter etw** *(acc)* ~ *(herausfinden)* to find sth out; **mit einem Anliegen** ~ to have a request (to make); **um etw** ~ *(verlieren)* um *Besitz, Leben* to lose sth; **um** *Essen, Schlaf* zu (have to) go without sth; **zu etw** ~ *(Zeit finden für)* to get around to sth; *(erhalten)* to come by sth; *(erben)* to come into sth; **wie komme ich zu der Ehre?** to what do I owe this honour?; **hierzu kommt noch seine Kurzsichtigkeit** then there's his short-sightedness on top of that; **zu sich** ~ to come to; *(sich fassen)* to recover; *(sich finden)* to sort oneself out.

2 *vi impers* **es** ~ **jetzt die Nachrichten** and now the news; **es werden viele Leute** ~ a lot of people will come; **es kommt noch einmal so weit** *or* **dahin, daß** ... it will get to the point where ...; **so weit kommt es (noch)** that'll be the day *(col)*; **wie kommt es, daß du ...?** how is it that you ...?; **ich wußte, daß es so** ~ **würde** I knew that would happen; **dazu kam es gar nicht mehr** it didn't come to that; **es kamzum Streit** there was a quarrel; **es kam eins zum anderen** one thing led to another; **und so kam es, daß** ... and that is how it happened that ...; **es kam, wie es** ~ **mußte** the inevitable happened; **es kommt immer anders, als man denkt** *(prov)* things never turn out the way you expect; **es mag** ~, **wie es** ~ **will** whatever happens.

3 *vt (col: kosten)* to cost.

Kommen *nt no pl* coming. **ein einziges** ~ **und Gehen** a constant coming and going; **jd ist im** ~ sb is on his/her way up.

kommend *adj Jahr, Woche, Generation* coming; *Ereignisse, Mode* future. **der** ~ **Meister** the future champion; **(am)** ~**en Montag** next Monday.

Kommentar *m (Bemerkung, Stellungnahme)* comment; *(Press, Jur, Liter)* commentary. **kein** ~! no comment; **einen** ~ **(zu etw) (ab)geben** to comment on sth.

Kommentator *m* commentator.

kommentieren* *vt (Press etc)* to comment on; **kommentierte Ausgabe** annotated edition.

kommerzialisieren* *vt* to commercialize.

kommerziell *adj* commercial.

Kommilitone *m (wk)* **-n, -n, Kommilitonin** *f* fellow student.

Kommissar *m (Polizei~)* inspector; *(ranghöher)*

(police) superintendent.

Kommissariat *nt (Polizei) (Amt)* office of inspector; office of superintendent; *(Dienststelle)* superintendent's department.

kommissarisch **1** *adj* temporary. **2** *adv* on a temporary basis.

Kommission *f* **(a)** *(Ausschuß)* committee; *(zur Untersuchung)* commission. **(b)** *(Comm)* commission. **etw in** ~ **geben** to give (to a dealer) for sale on commission; **etw in** ~ **nehmen/haben** to take/ have sth on commission.

Kommode *f* **-n** chest of drawers; *(hohe)* tallboy *(Brit)*, highboy *(US)*.

kommunal *adj* local; *(von Stadt auch)* municipal.

Kommunal-: ~**abgaben** *pl* rates *pl (Brit)*, local taxes *pl (US)*; ~**verwaltung** *f* local government; ~**wahlen** *pl* local (government) elections *pl*.

Kommune *f* **-n (a)** *(Gemeinde)* community. **(b)** *(Wohngemeinschaft)* commune.

Kommunikation *f* communication.

Kommunion *f (Eccl)* (Holy) Communion.

Kommuniqué [kɔmyni'keː] *nt* **-s** communiqué.

Kommunismus *m* communism.

Kommunist(in *f)* *m* Communist.

kommunistisch *adj* communist.

kommunizieren* *vi* **(a)** to communicate. **(b)** *(Eccl)* to receive (Holy) Communion.

Komödie [-iə] *f* comedy; *(fig: heiteres Ereignis)* farce. ~ **spielen** *(fig)* to put on an act.

kompakt *adj* compact.

Kompakt|anlage *f (Rad)* audio system.

Kompanie *f (Mil)* company.

Komparativ *m (Gram)* comparative.

Komparse *m (wk)* **-n, -n, Komparsin** *f (Film)* extra; *(Theat)* supernumerary.

Kompaß *m* **-sse** compass. **nach dem** ~ by the compass.

Kompaßnadel *f* compass needle.

kompatibel *adj (Tech)* compatible.

Kompatibilität *f* compatibility.

Kompensation *f* compensation.

kompensieren* *vt* to compensate for, to offset.

kompetent *adj* competent; *(befugt)* authorized.

Kompetenz *f* (area of) authority *or* competence; *(eines Gerichts)* jurisdiction, competence. **da hat er ganz eindeutig seine** ~**en überschritten** he has clearly exceeded his authority here; **das fällt in die** ~ **dieses Amtes** that's the responsibility of this office; **seine mangelnde** ~ **in dieser Frage** his lack of competence in this issue.

Kompetenzstreitigkeiten *pl* dispute over respective areas of responsibility.

komplett **1** *adj* complete. **2** *adv* completely.

Komplex *m* **-e** complex.

komplex *adj* complex.

Komplikation *f* complication.

Kompliment *nt* compliment. **jdm** ~**e machen** to pay sb compliments *(wegen* on).

Komplize *m (wk)* **-n, -n, Komplizin** *f* accomplice.

komplizieren* *vt* to complicate.

kompliziert *adj* complicated; *(Med) Bruch* compound.

Komplott *nt* **-e** plot, conspiracy. **ein** ~ **schmieden** to hatch a plot.

Komponente *f* **-n** component.

komponieren* *vt* to compose.

Komponist(in *f)* *m* composer.

Komposition *f* composition.

Kompost *m* **-e** compost.

Komposthaufen *m* compost heap.

Kompott *nt* **-e** stewed fruit.

komprimieren* *vt* to compress; *(fig)* to condense.

Kompromiß *m* **-sse** compromise. **einen** ~ **schließen** to compromise.

Kompromiß-: **k~bereit** *adj* willing to compromise; ~**bereitschaft** *f* willingness to compro-

mise; k~los adj uncompromising; **~lösung** f compromise solution.

kompromittieren* **1** vt to compromise. **2** vr to compromise oneself.

Kondensation f (Chem, Phys) condensation.

Kondensator m (Aut, Chem) condenser; (Elec auch) capacitor.

kondensieren* vti (lit, fig) to condense; (fig auch) to distil (Brit), to distill (US).

Kondens-: **~milch** f evaporated milk; **~wasser** nt condensation.

Kondition f condition, shape; (Durchhaltevermögen) stamina. **wie ist seine ~?** what sort of condition is he in?; **~ haben, in ~ sein** to be in good condition; (fig: beim Tanzen, Trinken etc) to have stamina.

Konditionsschwäche f lack of fitness no pl.

Konditorei f cake shop; (mit Café) café.

Kondolenz- in cpds of condolence.

kondolieren* vi (jdm) ~ to offer one's condolences (to sb).

Kondom m or nt -e condom.

Konfekt nt -e confectionery.

Konfektion f (Herstellung) manufacture of ready-to-wear clothing; (Bekleidung) ready-to-wear clothes pl or clothing.

Konfektions- in cpds ready-to-wear.

Konferenz f conference; (Besprechung) meeting.

Konferenz- in cpds conference; **~schaltung** f (Telec) conference circuit; (Rad, TV) (television/radio) link-up.

Konfession f (religious) denomination.

Konfessions-: **k~los** adj non-denominational; **~schule** f denominational school.

Konfetti nt no pl confetti.

Konfirmation f (Eccl) confirmation.

konfiszieren* vt to confiscate.

Konfitüre f -n jam.

Konflikt m -e conflict. **bewaffneter ~** armed conflict; **er befindet sich in einem (inneren) ~** he is in a state of inner conflict.

Konflikt-: **~fall** m im **~fall** in case of conflict; **~herd** m (esp Pol) centre (Brit) or center (US) of conflict; **~situation** f conflict situation.

konform adj Ansichten etc concurring. **mit jdm ~ gehen** to be in agreement with sb (in + dat about).

Konformist(in f) m (pej) conformist.

konformistisch adj conformist, conforming.

Konfrontation f confrontation.

konfrontieren* vt to confront (mit with).

konfus adj confused, muddled.

Kongreß m -sse (Pol) congress; (US Pol) Congress; (fachlich) convention, conference.

Kongreß-: **~mitglied** nt (US Pol) congressman/-woman; **~teilnehmer** m person attending a congress/conference or convention.

kongruent adj (Math) congruent.

König m -e king.

Königin f (auch Zool) queen.

königlich **1** adj royal. **2** adv **sich ~ amüsieren** (col) to have the time of one's life (col).

Königreich nt kingdom, realm (poet).

Königs-: **k~blau** adj royal blue; **~krone** f royal crown; **k~treu** adj royalist.

Konjugation f conjugation.

konjugieren* vt to conjugate.

Konjunktion f (Astron, Gram) conjunction.

Konjunktiv m (Gram) subjunctive.

Konjunktur f economic situation; (Hoch~) boom. **steigende/fallende ~** upward/downward economic trend.

konjunkturell adj economic. **~ bedingt** caused by economic factors.

Konjunkturpolitik f policies aimed at preventing economic fluctuation.

konkav adj concave.

konkret adj concrete. **ich kann dir nichts K~es sagen** I can't tell you anything definite.

Konkurrent m rival; (Comm auch) competitor.

Konkurrenz f (Wettbewerb) rivalry; (~betrieb) competitors pl; (Gesamtheit der Konkurrenten) competition, competitors pl. **die ~ auf diesem Gebiet ist größer geworden** the competition in this field has increased; **jdm ~ machen** (Comm, fig) to compete with sb; (Comm) to be in/enter into competition with sb.

Konkurrenz-: **k~fähig** adj competitive; **~kampf** m competition; (zwischen zwei Menschen auch) rivalry; **ein ~kampf, bei dem wir uns durchgesetzt haben** a competitive situation in which we won out; **k~los** adj without competition.

konkurrieren* vi to compete.

Konkurs m -e bankruptcy. **in ~ gehen, ~ machen** (col) to go bankrupt.

Konkurs-: **~verfahren** nt bankruptcy proceedings pl; **~verwalter** m receiver; (von Gläubigern bevollmächtigt) trustee.

können pret **konnte**, ptp **gekonnt** or (bei modal aux) **~** vti, modal aux **(a)** (vermögen) to be able to. **ich kann es machen** I can do it, I am able to do it; **ich kann es nicht machen** I can't do it; **man konnte ihn retten** they managed to save him; **man konnte ihn nicht retten** they couldn't save him; **ich konnte es nicht verstehen** I couldn't or was unable to understand it; **ich habe es sehen ~** I could see it; **er hat es gekonnt** he was able to do it; **morgen kann ich nicht** I can't (manage) tomorrow; **das hättest du gleich sagen ~** you could or might have said that straight away; **ich kann das nicht mehr sehen** I can't stand the sight of it any more; **ich kann nicht mehr** I can't go on; (ertragen) I can't take any more; (essen) I can't eat any more; **so schnell er konnte** as fast as he could.

(b) (beherrschen) Sprache to know, to be able to speak; Schach to be able to play; Klavier spielen, lesen, schwimmen, Skilaufen etc to be able to; to know how to. **sie kann keine Mathematik** she can't do mathematics; **was ~ Sie?** what can you do?; **was du alles kannst!** the things you can do!; **er kann was** he's very capable; **er kann gut Englisch** he speaks English well.

(c) (dürfen) to be allowed to. **kann ich jetzt gehen?** can I go now?; **könnte ich ...?** could I ...?; **er kann sich nicht beklagen** he can't complain; **man kann wohl sagen, daß ...** one could well say that ...; **du kannst mich (mal)!** (col) get lost! (col); **kann ich mit?** (col) can I come with you?

(d) (möglich sein) Sie könnten recht haben you may be right; **er kann jeden Augenblick kommen** he might come any minute; **das kann nur er gewesen sein** it can only have been him; **wer könnte das gewesen sein?** who could it have been?; **das kann nicht sein** that can't be true; **es kann sein/es kann nicht sein, daß er dabei war** he may have been there/he couldn't have been there; **kann sein** maybe.

(e) für etw ~ to be responsible for sth; **ich kann nichts dafür** it's not my fault.

Können nt no pl ability, skill.

Könner m - expert.

konnte pret of **können**.

Konsens m -e agreement, consent.

konsequent adj consistent. **die Bestimmungen ~ einhalten** to observe the regulations strictly; **wir werden ~ durchgreifen** we will take rigorous action; **~e Weiterentwicklung eines Stils** logically consistent development of a style; **wenn du das ~ durchdenkst** if you follow it through to its logical conclusion; **ein Ziel ~ verfolgen** to pursue an objective single-mindedly.

Konsequenz f (a) (Schlußfolgerung) consequence. **die ~en tragen** to take the consequences; **(aus etw) die ~en ziehen** to take the appropriate step.

(b) *(Beharrlichkeit)* consistency; *(bei Maßnahmen)* rigorousness. **die ~, mit der er sein Ziel verfolgte** the single-mindedness with which he pursued his aim.

konservativ [-va-] *adj* conservative; *(Brit Pol)* Conservative, Tory.

Konservative(r) [-va-] *mf decl as adj* conservative; *(Brit Pol)* Conservative, Tory.

Konservatorium [-va-] *nt* conservatory.

Konserve [kɔn'zɛrvə] *f* **-n** preserved food; *(in Dosen)* tinned *(Brit)* or canned food; *(~ndose)* tin *(Brit)*, can; *(Med: Blut~ etc)* stored blood etc; blood bottle. **von ~n ernähren** to live out of cans.

Konserven-: **~büchse, ~dose** *f* tin *(Brit)*, can.

konservieren* [kɔnzɛr'viːrən] *vt* to preserve.

Konservierung *f* preservation.

Konsolidierung *f* consolidation.

Konsonant *m* consonant.

Konsorten *pl (pej col)* gang *(col)*, mob *(col)*. **X und ~ X** and his gang etc.

Konsortium [kɔn'zɔrtsiʊm] *nt* consortium.

Konspiration [kɔnspira'tsioːn] *f* conspiracy, plot.

konspirieren* [kɔnspi'riːrən] *vi* to conspire, to plot.

konstant [kɔn'stant] *adj* constant.

Konstante [kɔn'stantə] *f* **-n** constant.

konstatieren* [kɔnsta'tiːrən] *vt (geh)* to see, to notice; *(sagen)* to state.

Konstellation [kɔnstɛla'tsioːn] *f* constellation; *(fig)* line-up; *(von Faktoren etc)* combination.

Konstitution [kɔnstitu'tsioːn] *f (Pol, Med)* constitution.

konstruieren* [kɔnstru'iːrən] *vt* to construct; *(Gram auch)* to construe. **ein konstruierter Fall** a hypothetical case.

Konstruktion [kɔnstrʊk'sioːn] *f* construction; *(Entwurf, Bauart auch)* design.

Konstruktionsfehler *m (im Entwurf)* design fault; *(im Aufbau)* structural defect.

konstruktiv [kɔnstrʊk'tiːf] *adj* constructive.

Konsul *m* **-n** consul.

Konsulat *nt* consulate.

Konsultation *f (form)* consultation.

konsultieren* *vt (form)* to consult.

Konsum *m* **-s** **(a)** [kɔn'zuːm] *no pl (Verbrauch)* consumption. **(b)** ['kɔnzuːm, 'kɔnzʊm] *(Genossenschaft)* cooperative society; *(Laden)* cooperative store, co-op *(col)*.

Konsum|artikel *m* consumer item. **~** *pl* consumer goods *pl.*

Konsument *m* consumer.

Konsum-: **~gesellschaft** *f* consumer society; **~güter** *pl* consumer goods *pl.*

konsumieren* *vt* to consume.

Kontakt *m* **-e** contact; *(pl: Aut)* contact points *pl.* **mit jdm in ~ kommen** to come into contact with sb; **zu jdm ~ finden** to get to know sb; **mit jdm ~ aufnehmen/in ~ stehen** to get/be in touch with sb; **~ herstellen** to make contact; **den ~ unterbrechen** to break contact; **keinen ~ mehr haben, den ~ verloren haben** to be out of touch.

Kontakt-: **~anzeigen** *pl* personal column; **k~arm** *adj* **er ist k~arm** he finds it difficult to make friends; **k~freudig** *adj* sociable; **~linse** *f* contact lens; **~mann** *m, pl* **~männer** *(Agent)* contact; **~schale** *f* contact lens.

Konten *pl* of **Konto.**

kontern *vti* Schlag, Angriff to counter.

Kontinent *m* **-e** continent.

kontinental *adj* continental.

Kontingent [kɔntɪŋ'gɛnt] *nt* **-e** *(Comm)* quota, share; *(Zuteilung)* allocation.

kontinuierlich *adj* continuous.

Kontinuität *f* continuity.

Konto *nt, pl* **-s** or **Konten** account. **auf meinem/mein ~** in my/into my account. **das geht auf mein ~** *(col) (ich bin schuldig)* I am to blame for this; *(ich zahle)* this is on me *(col).*

Konto-: **~auszug** *m* (bank) statement; **~stand** *m* balance.

kontra *prep* +*acc* against; *(Jur)* versus.

Kontrabaß *m* double-bass.

Kontrahent [kɔntra'hɛnt] *m (bei Vertrag)* contracting party; *(Gegner)* opponent, adversary.

Kontrakt *m* **-e** contract.

konträr *adj (geh)* Meinungen contrary, opposite.

Kontrast *m* **-e** contrast.

Kontrastfarbe *f* contrasting colour *(Brit)* or color *(US).*

kontrastieren* *vi* to contrast.

Kontroll|abschnitt *m (Comm)* counterfoil *(Brit)*, stub.

Kontrollampe *f* pilot lamp; *(Aut: für Ölstand etc)* warning light.

Kontrollbeamte(r) *m* inspector; *(an der Grenze)* frontier guard; *(zur Paßkontrolle)* passport officer; *(zur Zollkontrolle)* customs officer; *(zur Überwachung)* security officer.

Kontrolle *f* **-n** *(Beherrschung, Regulierung)* control. **über jdn/etw die ~ verlieren** to lose control of sb/sth; **jdn/etw unter ~ haben/halten** to have/keep sb/sth under control. **(b)** *(Nachprüfung)* check *(gen* on); *(Aufsicht)* supervision; *(Paß~)* passport control; *(Zoll~)* customs examination. **zur ~ haben wir noch einmal alles nachgerechnet** we went over all the figures again to check; **die ~ von Lebensmitteln** the inspection of foodstuffs. **(c)** *(Stelle) (für Nach-/Überprüfung, Verkehr)* checkpoint; *(Paß~/Zoll~)* passport control/customs; *(vor Fabrik)* gatehouse; *(an der Grenze)* border post.

Kontrolleur [kɔntrɔ'løːɐ] *m* inspector.

kontrollieren* *vt* **(a)** *(regulieren, beherrschen)* to control. **(b)** *(nachprüfen, überwachen)* to check; *(Aufsicht haben über)* to supervise; Paß, Fahrkarte etc to inspect, to check. **die Qualität der Waren muß streng kontrolliert werden** a strict check must be kept on the quality of the goods; **jdn/etw nach etw ~** to haben/halten for sth.

Kontrolliste *f* check-list.

Kontroll-: **~kommission** *f* control commission; **~stelle** *f* checkpoint; **~turm** *m* control tower; **~uhr** *f* time clock; **~zentrum** *nt (Space)* control centre *(Brit)* or center *(US).*

kontrovers [kɔntro'vɛrs] *adj* controversial.

Kontroverse [kɔntro'vɛrzə] *f* **-n** controversy.

Kontur *f* **-en** outline, contour.

Konvention [kɔnvɛn'tsioːn] *f* convention. **sich über die ~en hinwegsetzen** to ignore conventions.

Konventionalstrafe [kɔnvɛntsio'naːl] *f* penalty or fine *(for* breach of contract).

konventionell [kɔnvɛntsio'nɛl] *adj* conventional.

Konversation [kɔnvɛrza'tsioːn] *f* conversation. **~ machen** to make conversation.

Konversationslexikon *nt* encyclopaedia *(Brit)*, encyclopedia *(US).*

konvex [kɔn'vɛks] *adj* convex.

Konvoi ['kɔnvɔy, -'-] *m* **-s** convoy. **im ~ fahren** to drive in convoy.

Konzentrat *nt* concentrate.

Konzentration *f* concentration *(auf* +*acc* on).

Konzentrations-: **~fähigkeit** *f* power of concentration *usu pl;* **~lager** *nt* concentration camp.

konzentrieren* **1** *vt* to concentrate *(auf* +*acc* on); Truppen *auch* to mass. **2** *vr* to concentrate *(auf* +*acc* on); *(Untersuchung, Arbeit etc)* to be concentrated *(auf* +*acc* on).

konzentriert *adj* **(a)** *(Chem)* concentrated. **(b)** **mit ~er Aufmerksamkeit** with all one's concentration; **~ arbeiten/zuhören** to work/listen with concentration; **~ nachdenken** to concentrate.

Konzept *nt* **-e** *(Rohentwurf)* draft, notes *pl;* *(Plan, Programm)* plan; *(Begriff, Vorstellung)* concept. **jdn aus dem ~ bringen** to break sb's train of

thought; (col: aus dem Gleichgewicht) to upset sb; **das paßt mir nicht ins ~** that doesn't fit in with my plans; (gefällt mir nicht) I don't like the idea.
Konzeption f (geh) conception.
konzeptionslos adj without a definite line.
Konzeptpapier nt rough paper.
Konzern m -e combine, group (of companies). **die ~e haben zuviel Macht** the big companies have too much power.
Konzert nt -e concert; (Komposition) concerto.
Konzert-: **~besucher** m concert-goer; **~flügel** m concert grand.
Konzertina f, pl **Konzertinen** concertina.
Konzert-: **~meister** m leader, concertmaster (US); **~pianist** m concert pianist; **~saal** m concert hall.
Konzession f (a) (Gewerbeerlaubnis) concession, licence (Brit), license (US). (b) (Zugeständnis) concession (an +acc to).
konzessionsbereit adj willing to make concessions.
Konzil nt -e or **-ien** [-iən] (Eccl, Univ) council.
konzipieren* vt to conceive; (entwerfen auch) to design.
Ko|operation f cooperation.
ko|operativ adj cooperative.
ko|operieren* vi to cooperate.
Ko|ordinate f **-en** (Math) coordinate.
Ko|ordination f coordination.
Ko|ordinator m, **Ko|ordinatorin** f coordinator.
ko|ordinieren* vt to coordinate.
Kopf m ⁻e (a) head. **mit bloßem ~** bareheaded; **~ an ~** shoulder to shoulder; (Pferderennen, Sport) neck and neck; **bis über den ~** (im Wasser) up to one's neck; (in Schulden) up to one's ears; **~ hoch!** chin up!; **auf dem ~ stehen** to stand on one's head; **jdm den ~ waschen** (col) to give sb a piece of one's mind (col); **den ~ oben behalten** to keep one's chin up; **jds ~ fordern** (lit, fig) to demand sb's head; **von ~ bis Fuß** from head to foot; **sich** (dat) **an den ~ fassen** (fig) to be speechless; **die ~e zusammenstecken** to put their heads together; (heimlich) to go into a huddle (col); **einen schweren ~ haben** to have a thick head; **Geld** etc **auf den ~ hauen** (col) to blow one's money etc (col); **jdm über den ~ wachsen** (lit) to outgrow sb; (fig: Sorgen etc) to be more than sb can cope with; **den ~ für jdn/etw hinhalten** (col) to take the blame for sb/sth; **etw auf den ~ stellen** (lit, fig: durchsuchen) to turn sth upside down; **Tatsachen auf den ~ stellen** to stand facts on their heads; **und wenn du dich auf den ~ stellst, ...** (col) no matter what you say/do ...; **jdn den ~ kosten** (lit) to cost sb his head; (fig) to cost sb his career or job; **~ und Kragen riskieren** (col) to risk one's neck; **auf jds ~ (acc) eine Belohnung aussetzen** to put a reward on sb's head; **er ist nicht auf den ~ gefallen** he's no fool; **jdm Beleidigungen an den ~ werfen** (col) to hurl insults at sb; **jdm etw auf den ~ zusagen** to say sth straight out to sb; **den ~ hängenlassen** (fig) to be downcast or despondent; **jdn vor den ~ stoßen** to antagonize sb; **jdm den ~ zurechtrücken** to bring sb to his/her senses; **mit dem ~ durch die Wand wollen** (col) to be determined to get one's own way regardless; **(jdm) zu ~(e) steigen** to go to sb's head; **ich war wie vor den ~ geschlagen** I was dumbfounded; **über jds ~ (acc) hinweg** over sb's head; **ein ~ Salat/Kohl** a head of lettuce/cabbage; **~ oder Zahl?** heads or tails?

(b) (Einzelperson) person. **pro ~** per person or head; **das Einkommen pro ~** per capita income.

(c) (fig) (Verstand) head; (Denker) thinker; (leitende Persönlichkeit) leader; (Bandenführer) brains sing. **sich** (dat) **über etw** (acc) **den ~ zerbrechen** to rack one's brains over sth; **er ist**

nicht ganz richtig im ~ (col) he is not quite right in the head; **ein kluger ~** an intelligent person; **er ist ein fähiger ~** he has a good head on his shoulders; **die besten ~e** the best brains or minds.

(d) (Sinn) head, mind. **sich** (dat) **etw durch den ~ gehen lassen** to think about sth; **nichts als Tanzen/Fußball im ~ haben** to think of nothing but dancing/football; **andere Dinge im ~ haben** to have other things on one's mind; **ich weiß kaum, wo mir der ~ steht** I scarcely know whether I'm coming or going; **den ~ verlieren** to lose one's head; **sich** (dat) **etw aus dem ~ schlagen** to put sth out of one's mind; **jdm den ~ verdrehen** to turn sb's head; **der Gedanke will mir nicht aus dem ~** I can't get the thought out of my head or mind; **das will mir nicht in den ~ hinein** I just can't understand it; **im ~** in one's head; **etw im ~ rechnen** to work sth out in one's head; **aus dem ~** from memory; **sie hat es sich** (dat) **in den ~ gesetzt, das zu tun** she has taken it into her head to do that; **seinen ~ durchsetzen** to get one's own way.
Kopf-: **~an-~-Rennen** nt neck-and-neck race; **~arbeit** f brain-work; **~bahnhof** m terminus (station); **~ball** m (Ftbl) header; **~bedeckung** f headgear; **ohne ~bedeckung** without a hat.
Köpfchen nt dim of **Kopf** little head; (fig hum) brains. **~ haben** to be brainy (col).
köpfen vti (a) jdn to behead; (hum) Flasche Wein to crack (open). (b) (Ftbl) to head. **ins Tor ~** to head the ball in.
Kopf-: **~ende** nt head; **~geld** nt head money; **~haut** f scalp; **~hörer** m headphone.
Kopf-: **~jäger** m head-hunter; **~kissen** nt pillow; **~kissenbezug** m pillow case; **~lage** f (Med) head presentation; **~länge** f **um eine ~länge** by a head; **k~lastig** adj (lit, fig) top-heavy; Flugzeug nose-heavy; **k~los** adj (fig) in a panic; (lit) headless; **k~los werden** to get into a flap (col); **~losigkeit** f (fig) panickiness; **~nicken** nt no pl nod (of the head); **~prämie** f reward; **~rechnen** nt mental arithmetic; **~salat** m lettuce; **k~scheu** adj jdn **k~scheu machen** to intimidate sb; **~schmerz** m usu pl headache; **~schmerzen haben** to have a headache; **sich** (dat) **wegen etw ~schmerzen machen** (fig) to worry about sth; **~schmerztablette** f aspirin, headache tablet; **~schuß** m shot in the head; **~schutz** m protection for the head; **~seite** f (von Münze) head, face side; **~sprung** m header, dive; **einen ~sprung machen** to dive (headfirst); **~stand** m headstand; **einen ~stand machen** to stand on one's head; **k~stehen** vi sep irreg aux sein (a) (lit) to stand on one's head; (b) (fig) (vor Ausgelassenheit) to go wild (with excitement); (durcheinander sein) to be all topsy-turvy (col); **~stein-pflaster** nt cobblestones pl; **eine Straße mit ~steinpflaster** a cobbled street; **~stütze** f headrest; **~tuch** nt (head)scarf; **k~über** adv (lit, fig) headfirst, headlong; **~verletzung** f head injury; **~wäsche** f shampoo, hair-wash; **~weh** nt siehe **~schmerz**; **~zerbrechen** nt sich (dat) **über etw** (acc) **~zerbrechen machen** to worry about sth.
Kopie f copy; (fig) carbon copy; (Durchschlag auch) carbon (copy); (Ablichtung) photocopy; (Phot) print.
kopieren* vti (lit, fig) to copy; (nachahmen) to imitate; (ablichten) to photocopy; (durchpausen) to trace; (Phot, Film) to print.
Kopierer m (photo)copier.
Kopier-: **~gerät** nt photocopier; **~papier** nt photocopy paper; **~stift** m indelible pencil.
Kopilot(in f) m co-pilot.
Koppel f **-n** (Weide) paddock, enclosure. **auf der ~** in the paddock etc.
koppeln vt (a) (zusammenbinden) to tie together. (b) (verbinden) to couple, to join (etw an etw (acc)

sth to sth); *zwei Dinge* to couple *or* join together; *(fig)* to link, to couple; *(als Bedingung)* to tie; *Ziele, Zwecke* to combine. **eine Dienstreise mit einem Urlaub ~** to combine a business trip with a holiday. **(c)** *(Elec)* to couple.

Kopp(e)lung *f no pl* **(a)** *(Elec)* coupling. **(b)** *(Verbindung)* *(lit)* coupling, joining; *(fig, von Raumschiffen)* link-up.

Koproduktion *f* co-production.

Koproduzent *m* co-producer.

Kopulation *f (Biol)* copulation, coupling.

kopulieren* *vi (koitieren)* to copulate.

Koralle *f* -n coral.

Korallen-: **~bank** *f* coral-reef; **~kette** *f* coral necklace.

Koran *m no pl* Koran.

Korb *m* ⁻e **(a)** basket; *(Fisch~ auch)* creel; *(Bienen~)* hive; *(Förder~)* cage. **ein ~ Äpfel** a basket of apples. **(b)** *(~geflecht)* wicker. **ein Sessel aus ~** a wicker(work) chair. **(c)** *(col: Abweisung)* refusal, rebuff. **einen ~ bekommen, sich** *(dat)* **einen ~ holen** to be turned down; **jdm einen ~ geben** to turn sb down.

Korbball *m* basket-ball.

Körbchen *nt* **(a)** *dim of* **Korb. ins ~!** *(baby-talk)* off to bye-byes *(baby-talk)*. **(b)** *(von Büstenhalter)* cup.

Korb-: **~geflecht** *nt* basketwork, wickerwork; **~sessel** *m* wicker(work) chair.

Kordel *f* -n cord.

Korea *nt* Korea.

Korinthe *f* -n currant.

Kork *m* -e cork.

Korken *m* - cork; *(aus Plastik)* stopper.

Korkenzieher *m* - corkscrew.

Korn¹ *nt* ⁻er **(a)** *(Samen~)* seed, grain; *(Pfeffer~)* corn; *(Salz~, Sand~, Phot)* grain; *(Hagel~)* stone. **(b)** *no pl (Getreide)* grain, corn *(Brit)*.

Korn² *m* - *or* -s *(Kornbranntwein)* corn schnapps.

Korn³ *nt* -e *(am Gewehr)* front sight, bead. **jdn/etw aufs ~ nehmen** *(fig col)* to start keeping tabs on sb/to hit out at sth.

Kornblume *f* cornflower.

Körnchen *nt* **ein ~ Wahrheit** a grain of truth.

körnig *adj* granular, grainy.

Körnung *f (Tech)* grain size; *(Phot)* granularity.

Körper *m* - body; *(Schiffs~)* hull. **~ und Geist** mind and body. **am ganzen ~ zittern/frieren** to tremble/to be cold all over.

Körper-: **~bau** *m* physique, build; **~beherrschung** *f* physical control; **k~behindert** *adj* physically handicapped, disabled; **~behinderte(r)** *mf* disabled person; **die ~behinderten** the disabled; **~geruch** *m* body odour *(Brit)* or odor *(US)*, BO *(col)*; **~gewicht** *nt* weight; **~größe** *f* height; **~kontakt** *m* physical contact; **~kraft** *f* physical strength.

körperlich *adj* physical; *(stofflich)* material, corporeal. **~e Arbeit** manual work; **~e Züchtigung** corporal punishment.

Körper-: **k~los** *adj* bodiless, incorporeal; **~maße** *pl* measurements *pl*; **~pflege** *f* personal hygiene; **~puder** *m* or *nt* body powder.

Körperschaft *f* corporation, (corporate) body. **gesetzgebende ~** legislative body; **~ des öffentlichen Rechts** public corporation *or* body.

Körper-: **~schwäche** *f* physical weakness; **~teil** *m* part of the body; **~temperatur** *f* body temperature; **~verletzung** *f (Jur)* physical injury; **fahrlässige ~verletzung** physical injury resulting from negligence; **schwere ~verletzung** grievous bodily harm; **~wärme** *f* body heat.

Korporal *m* -e *or* **Korporäle** corporal.

Korps [koːɐ] *nt* - [koːɐ(s)], - [koːɐs] *(Mil)* corps; *(Univ)* (duelling) corps.

korpulent *adj* corpulent.

korrekt *adj* correct.

Korrektur *f* correction; *(Typ)* *(Vorgang)* proof-

---

reading; *(Verbesserung)* proof correction; **~ lesen** to proof-read *(bei etw sth)*.

Korrespondent(in *f)* *m* correspondent.

Korrespondenz *f* correspondence. **mit jdm in ~ stehen** to be in correspondence with sb.

korrespondieren* *vi* to correspond.

Korridor *m* -e *(auch Luft~ etc)* corridor; *(Flur)* hall.

korrigieren* *vt (berichtigen)* to correct; *Aufsätze etc auch* to mark; *Meinung, Einstellung* to change.

Korrosion *f* corrosion.

Korrosionsschutz *m* corrosion prevention.

korrupt *adj* corrupt.

Korruption *f no pl* corruption.

Korsett *nt* -s *or* -e corset(s *pl*).

Korvette [kɔr'vɛtə] *f (Naut)* corvette.

Korvettenkapitän *m* lieutenant commander.

koscher *adj (Rel, fig col)* kosher.

Kose-: **~name** *m* pet name; **~wort** *nt* term of endearment.

K.-o.-Sieg [kaː'|oː-] *m* knock-out victory.

Kosmetik *f no pl* beauty culture; *(Kosmetika, fig)* cosmetics *pl*.

Kosmetiker(in *f)* *m* - beautician.

kosmetisch *adj* cosmetic. **ein ~es Mittel** a cosmetic.

kosmisch *adj* cosmic. **~ beeinflußt werden** to be influenced by the stars.

Kosmo-: **~naut(in** *f)* *m (wk)* -en, -en cosmonaut; **k~politisch** *adj* cosmopolitan.

Kosmos *m no pl* cosmos.

Kost *f no pl (Nahrung, Essen)* food, fare. **vegetarische/fleischlose ~** vegetarian/meatless diet; **geistige ~** *(fig)* intellectual fare; **leichte/schwere ~** *(fig)* easy/heavy going *(col)*; **~ und Logis** board and lodging.

kostbar *adj (wertvoll)* valuable, precious.

Kostbarkeit *f* **(a)** value, preciousness. **(b)** *(Gegenstand)* treasure, precious object; *(Leckerbissen)* delicacy.

Kosten *pl* cost(s); *(Jur)* costs *pl*; *(Un~)* expenses *pl*; *(Auslagen auch)* outlay. **die ~ tragen** to bear the cost(s); **auf ~ von** *or* +*gen (fig)* at the expense of; **auf meine ~** *(lit, fig)* at my expense; **auf seine ~ kommen** *(fig)* to get one's money's worth.

kosten¹ *vti (lit, fig)* to cost; *Zeit, Geduld etc* to take. **was kostet das?** how much does it cost?, how much is it?; **koste es, was es wolle** whatever the cost; **das lasse ich mich etwas ~** I don't mind spending a bit of money on it; **jdn sein Leben/den Sieg ~** to cost sb his life/the victory.

kosten² *vti (lit, fig: probieren)* to taste. **von etw ~** to taste sth.

Kosten-: **~ersparnis** *f* cost saving; **~erstattung** *f* reimbursement of expenses; **~frage** *f* question of cost(s); **k~los** *adj, adv* free (of charge); **k~pflichtig** *adj* **das ist k~pflichtig** there is a charge (on it); **ein Kfz k~pflichtig abschleppen** to tow away a car at the owner's expense; **~punkt** *m* cost question; **~punkt?** *(col)* what'll it cost? **~satz** *m* rate; **k~sparend** *adj* cost-saving; **~voranschlag** *m* (costs) estimate.

köstlich *adj (a) (Wein, Speise)* exquisite. **sich ~ amüsieren** to have a great time.

Köstlichkeit *f* **(a)** *no pl* exquisiteness. **(b)** *(Leckerbissen etc)* (culinary) delicacy.

Kost-: **~probe** *f (von Wein, Käse)* taste; *(fig)* sample; **k~spielig** *adj* expensive.

Kostüm *nt* -e **(a)** *(Theat: Tracht)* costume. **(b)** *(Schneider~)* costume *(dated)*, suit.

Kostüm-: **~bildner(in** *f)* *m* costume designer; **~fest** *nt* fancydress ball.

kostümieren* *vr* to dress up.

Kostüm-: **~probe** *f (Theat)* dress rehearsal; **~verleih** *m* (theatrical) costume agency.

kostümieren* *vr* to dress up.

Kotelett ['kɔtlɛt, kɔt'lɛt] *nt* -s chop, cutlet.

Kotelette f usu pl (side)whisker, sideburn (US).
Köter m - (pej) cur.
Kotflügel m (Aut) wing (Brit), fender (US).
kotzen vi (col!) to throw up (col), to puke (col!). **das ist zum K~** it makes you sick.
kotzübel adj (col!) **mir ist ~** I feel like throwing up (col).
KP [kaː'peː] f = **Kommunistische Partei.**
KPdSU [kaːpeːdeːɛsˈʔuː] f- = **Kommunistische Partei der Sowjetunion** Communist Party of the Soviet Union.
Krabbe f -n (Zool) (klein) shrimp; (größer) prawn.
krabbeln 1 vi aux sein to crawl. **2** vt (kitzeln) to tickle.
Krach m ⁻e **(a)** no pl (Lärm) noise, din (col); (Schlag) crash. **~ machen** to make a noise. **(b)** (col: Streit) row, quarrel. **mit jdm ~ haben** to (have a) row with sb; **mit jdm ~ kriegen** to get into trouble with sb; **~ schlagen** to make a fuss.
krachen vi **(a)** (Lärm machen) to crash, to bang; (Holz) to creak; (Schuß) to ring out; (Donner) to crash. **~d fallen** etc to fall etc with a crash; ..., **daß es nur so krachte** (lit) with a crash; (fig) with a vengeance. **(b)** aux sein (col: aufplatzen) to rip (open), to split.
Krächzen nt no pl croak(ing); (von Vogel) caw(ing).
krächzen vi to croak; (Vogel) to caw.
Kräcker m - (Cook) cracker.
Kraft f ⁻e **(a)** (körperlich, sittlich) strength no pl; (geistig, schöpferisch) powers pl; (von Prosa, Stimme) power, force; (Energie) energy, energies pl. **die ~e (mit jdm) messen** to pit one's strength (against sb); (fig) to pit oneself against sb; **seine ~e sammeln** to build up one's strength; **mit frischer ~** with renewed strength; **mit letzter ~** with one's last ounce of strength; **die ~ aufbringen, etw zu tun** to find the strength to do sth; **mit vereinten ~en werden wir ... if** we combine our efforts we will ...; **mit seinen ~en haushalten** to conserve one's energy; **das geht über meine ~e** it's more than I can take; **mit aller** or **voller ~** with all one's might; **er will mit aller ~ durchsetzen, daß ...** he will do his utmost to ensure that ...; **aus eigener ~** by himself/myself etc; **nach (besten) ~en** to the best of one's ability; **er tat, was in seinen ~en stand** he did everything (with)in his power; **nicht/wieder bei ~en sein** not to be in very good shape/to have (got) one's strength back; **wieder zu ~en kommen** to regain one's strength.
(b) (Macht, der Sonne) power; (Phys) force. **die treibende ~** (fig) the driving force; **das Gleichgewicht der ~e** (Pol) the balance of power; **halbe/volle ~ voraus!** half/full speed ahead.
(c) (usu pl: in Wirtschaft, Politik etc) force.
(d) no pl (Jur: Geltung) force. **in ~ sein/treten** to be in/come into force; **außer ~ sein** to be no longer in force; **außer ~ treten** to cease to be in force; **außer ~ setzen** to annul.
(e) (Arbeits~) employee, worker. **~e staff,** personnel no pl.
kraft prep +gen (form) by virtue of; (mittels) by use of. **~ meines Amtes** by virtue of my office.
Kraft-: **~aufwand** m effort; **~ausdruck** m swearword; **~brühe** f beef tea.
Kräfteverhältnis nt (Pol) balance of power; (von Mannschaften etc) relative strength.
Kraftfahrer(in f) m (form) motorist, driver; (als Beruf) driver.
Kraftfahrzeug nt motor vehicle.
Kraftfahrzeug-: **~brief** m (vehicle) registration document, logbook (Brit); **~mechaniker** m motor mechanic; **~schein** m (vehicle) registration document; **~steuer** f motor vehicle tax, road tax (Brit).
kräftig 1 adj strong; Muskel, Stimme auch powerful; Ausdrucksweise auch forceful; Haarwuchs,

Pflanze auch healthy; Schlag hard, powerful, hefty (col); Händedruck firm; Fluch violent; Suppe, Essen nourishing; (groß) Portion, Preiserhöhung huge; Beifall loud. **einen ~en Schluck nehmen** to take a good swig.
2 adv gebaut powerfully; zuschlagen, treten, pressen hard; klatschen loudly; lachen, mitsingen heartily; fluchen, niesen violently. **etw ~ schütteln** to give sth a good shake; **jdn ~ verprügeln** to give sb a good beating; **er hat sich ~ dagegen gewehrt** he objected most strongly; (körperlich) he put up a strong resistance; **es hat ~ geregnet/ geschneit** it rained/snowed heavily; **die Preise sind ~ gestiegen** prices have gone up a lot; **jdn ~ ausschimpfen** to give sb a good bawling out (col).
kräftigen vt (geh) jdn ~ to build up sb's strength; (Luft, Bad etc) to invigorate sb; (Essen, Mittel etc) to fortify sb; **ein ~des Mittel** a tonic.
kraftlos adj (schwach) feeble, weak; (schlaff) limp; (machtlos) powerless; (Jur) invalid.
Kraft-: **~probe** f test of strength; (zwischen zwei Gruppen etc) trial of strength; **~rad** nt motorcycle, motorbike; **~stoff** m fuel; **k~strotzend** adj exuding vitality; Pflanze healthy-looking; (muskulös) with bulging muscles; **~übertragung** f power transmission; **k~voll** adj Stimme powerful; **~wagen** m motor vehicle; **~werk** nt power station.
Kragen m - collar. **jdn am** or **beim ~ packen** to grab sb by the collar; (fig col) to collar sb; **mir platzte der ~** (col) I blew my top (col); **jetzt platzt mir aber der ~!** this is the last straw!; **jdn** or **jdm den ~ kosten** (fig) to be sb's downfall; (umbringen) to be the end of sb; **es geht ihm jetzt an den ~** (col) he's in for it now (col).
Kragenweite f (lit) collar size. **das ist nicht meine ~** (fig col) that's not my cup of tea (col).
Krähe f -n crow. **eine ~ hackt der anderen kein Auge aus** (Prov) birds of a feather stick together (Prov).
krähen vi to crow.
Krake m (wk) -n, -n octopus.
krakeelen* vi (col) to make a row or racket (col).
krakelig adj scrawly.
krakeln vti to scrawl, to scribble.
Kralle f -n claw; (von Raubvogel auch) talon; (pej: Fingernagel) claw. **jdn/etw in seinen ~n haben** (fig col) to have sb/sth in one's clutches.
krallen 1 vr sich an jdn/etw ~ (lit, fig) to cling to sb/sth; (Katze) to dig its claws into sb/sth; **sich in etw** (acc) ~ to sink its claws into sth; (mit Fingern) to dig one's fingers into sth; **sich jdn/ etw ~** (col) to get a hold of sb/to pinch sth. **2** vt **die Finger in etw** (acc)/um etw ~ to dig one's fingers into sth. **3** vi to claw (an +dat at).
Kram m no pl (col) (Gerümpel) junk; (Zeug) things pl, stuff (col); (Angelegenheit) business. **den ~ hinschmeißen** to chuck the whole thing (col).
Kramladen m (pej col) tatty little shop (col).
Krampf m ⁻e **(a)** (Zustand) cramp; (Verkrampfung) spasm; (wiederholt) convulsion(s pl). **(b)** no pl (col) (Getue) palaver (col); (Unsinn) rubbish.
Krampf-: **~ader** f varicose vein; **k~artig** adj convulsive.
krampfen 1 vt Finger, Hand to clench (um etw around sth). **2** vr sich um etw ~ to clench sth.
krampfhaft adj Zuckung convulsive; (col: angestrengt, verzweifelt) frantic, desperate; Lachen forced no adv; **sich ~ an etw** (dat) **festhalten** (lit, fig col) to cling desperately to sth.
Kran m ⁻e **(a)** crane. **(b)** (Hahn) tap, faucet (US).
Kranführer m crane driver.
Kranich m -e (Orn) crane.
krank adj comp ⁻er, superl ⁻ste(r, s) or (adv) am ⁻sten ill usu pred, sick (auch fig), not well; (leidend) invalid; Pflanze, Organ diseased; Zahn, Bein bad; Wirtschaft ailing. **~ werden** to fall ill;

schwer ~ seriously ill; **vor Aufregung/Angst** ~ sick with excitement/fear; **sich** ~ **melden** to let one's boss *etc* know that one is ill; *(telefonisch)* to phone in sick; *(esp Mil)* to report sick; **jdn** ~ **schreiben** to give sb a medical certificate; *(esp Mil)* to put sb on the sick-list; **er ist schon seit einem halben Jahr** ~ **geschrieben** he's been off sick for six months; **sich** ~ **stellen** to pretend to be ill, to malinger; **das macht mich** ~! *(col)* it gets on my nerves! *(col)*, it drives me round the bend! *(Brit col)*.

kränkeln *vi* to be ailing *(auch Wirtschaft)*, to be sickly, to be in poor health.

kranken *vi* to suffer *(an +dat* from). **das krankt daran, daß** ... *(fig)* it suffers from the fact that ...

kränken *vt* **jdn** ~ to hurt sb('s feelings); **sie war sehr gekränkt** she was very hurt; **jdn in seiner Ehre** ~ to offend sb's pride; ~**d** hurtful.

Kranken-: ~**bericht** *m* medical report; ~**besuch** *m* visit (to a sick person); *(von Arzt)* (sick-)call; ~**bett** *nt* sick-bed; ~**geld** *nt* sickness benefit; *(von Firma)* sickpay; ~**geschichte** *f* medical history.

Krankenhaus *nt* hospital. **ins** ~ **gehen** *(als Patient)* to go into (the US) hospital; **im** ~ **liegen** to be in (the US) hospital.

Krankenhaus- *in cpds* hospital; ~**aufenthalt** *m* stay in hospital; ~**kosten** *pl* hospital charges *pl*.

Kranken-: ~**kasse** *f (Versicherung)* medical *or* health insurance; *(Gesellschaft)* medical *or* health insurance company; **er ist in keiner** ~**kasse** he has no medical insurance; ~**pflege** *f* nursing; ~**pfleger** *m* orderly; *(mit Schwesternausbildung)* male nurse; ~**pflegerin** *f* nurse; ~**schein** *m* medical insurance card; ~**schwester** *f* nurse; ~**versicherung** *f* medical *or* health insurance; **soziale/private** ~**versicherung** state *or* national/private health insurance; ~**wagen** *m* ambulance; ~**zimmer** *nt* sick-room; *(im Krankenhaus)* hospital room.

Kranke(r) *mf decl as adj* sick person, invalid; *(Patient)* patient. **die** ~**n** the sick.

krankfeiern *vi sep (col)* to be off sick; *(vortäuschend)* to skive *(Brit col)*.

krankhaft *adj* **(a)** *Stelle, Zelle* diseased; *Vergrößerung, Zustand* morbid; *Aussehen* sickly. ~**e Veränderung** affection. **(b)** *(seelisch)* pathological. **sein Geiz ist schon** ~ his meanness is almost pathological.

Krankheit *f (lit, fig)* illness, sickness; *(eine bestimmte* ~ *wie Krebs, Masern etc auch, von Pflanzen)* disease. **wegen** ~ due to illness; **sich** *(dat)* **eine** ~ **zuziehen** to contract an illness *(form)*; **nach langer schwerer** ~ after a long serious illness; **während meiner** ~ during my illness.

Krankheits|erreger *m* disease-causing agent.

kränklich *adj* sickly, in poor health.

Krankmeldung *f* notification of illness.

Kränkung *f* insult. **etw als** ~ **empfinden** to take offence *(Brit)* or offense *(US)* at sth; **das war eine** ~ **seiner Gefühle** that hurt his feelings.

Kranz *m* ⁻**e (a)** wreath; *(Sieger~, Braut~ auch)* garland; *(fig: von Geschichten etc)* cycle. **(b)** *(Tech: Rad~)* rim; *(von Glocke auch)* lip.

Kranzgefäß *nt (Anat)* coronary artery.

kraß *adj Gegensatz, Worte, Stil* stark; *Farben* garish; *Unterschied, Fall, Haltung* extreme; *Ungerechtigkeit, Lüge* blatant; *Materialist, Unkenntnis* crass; *Egoist* out-and-out; *Außenseiter* rank.

Krater *m* - crater.

Kratz-: ~**bürste** *f* wire brush; *(col)* prickly character; **k**~**bürstig** *adj (col)* prickly.

Krätze *f no pl (Med)* scabies.

kratzen 1 *vti* **(a)** to scratch; *(ab*~ *auch)* to scrape *(von* off). **der Rauch kratzt (mich) im Hals** the smoke irritates my throat. **(b)** *(col: stören)* to bother. **das kratzt mich nicht** *(col)* I couldn't care

less (about that). **2** *vr* to scratch oneself.

Kratzer *m* - *(Schramme)* scratch.

kratzig *adj (col)* scratchy *(col)*.

Kraul *nt no pl (Schwimmen)* crawl. **(im)** ~ **schwimmen** to do the crawl.

kraulen[1] *(Schwimmen) aux haben or sein* **1** *vi* to do the crawl. **2** *vt* **er hat** *or* **ist 100 m gekrault** he did a 100m's crawl.

kraulen[2] *vt* to fondle. **jdn am Kinn** ~ to chuck sb under the chin.

kraus *adj* crinkly; *Haar, Kopf* frizzy; *Stirn* furrowed; *(fig: verworren)* muddled, confused. **die Stirn** ~ **ziehen** to knit one's brow; *(mißbilligend)* to frown.

Krause *f* -**n (a)** *(Hals~)* ruff; *(an Ärmeln etc)* ruffle, frill. **(b)** *(col: Frisur)* frizzy hair.

kräuseln 1 *vt Haar* to make frizzy; *(Sew)* to gather *(in small folds)*; *(Tex)* to crimp; *Stirn* to knit; *Wasseroberfläche* to ripple. **2** *vr (Haare)* to go frizzy; *(Stoff)* to go crinkly; *(Stirn)* to wrinkle up; *(Wasser)* to ripple.

Kraus-: **k**~**haarig** *adj* frizzy-haired; ~**kopf** *m* *(Frisur)* frizzy hair; *(Mensch)* curly-head.

Kraut *nt, pl* **Kräuter (a)** herb. **dagegen ist kein** ~ **gewachsen** *(fig)* there's nothing anyone can do about that. **(b)** *no pl (grüne Teile von Pflanzen)* foliage, stems and leaves *pl*; *(von Gemüse)* tops *pl*. **wie** ~ **und Rüben durcheinanderliegen** *(col)* to lie (about) all over the place *(col)*; **ins** ~ **schießen** *(lit)* to run to seed; *(fig)* to get out of control. **(c)** *no pl (Rot~, Weiß~)* cabbage.

Kräuter-: ~**butter** *f* herb butter; ~**käse** *m* herb cheese; ~**likör** *m* herbal liqueur; ~**tee** *m* herb(al) tea.

Krautsalat *m* ≈ coleslaw.

Krawall *m* -**e (a)** *(Aufruhr)* riot; *(col: Lärm)* racket *(col)*, din *(col)*. ~ **machen** *(col)* to kick up a row; *(randalieren)* to go on the rampage; *(sich beschweren)* to kick up a fuss.

Krawallmacher *m (col)* hooligan.

Krawatte *f* -**n** tie, necktie *(esp US)*.

Krawattennadel *f* tie-pin.

kraxeln *vi aux sein (SGer)* to clamber (up).

Kreation *f (Fashion etc)* creation.

kreativ *adj* creative.

Kreativität [kreativi'tɛːt] *f* creativity.

Kreatur *f (a) (lit, fig, pej)* creature. **(b)** *no pl (alle Lebewesen)* creation. **die** ~ all creation.

Krebs *m* -**e (a)** crab; *(Fluß~)* crayfish, crawfish *(US)*. **rot wie ein** ~ red as a lobster. **(b)** *(Astrol)* Cancer. **(c)** *(Med)* cancer; *(Bot)* canker.

Krebs-: **k**~**erregend** *adj* carcinogenic; **k**~**erregend wirken** to cause cancer; ~**kranke(r)** *mf* cancer victim; *(Patient)* cancer patient; **k**~**rot** *adj* red as a lobster; ~**tiere** *pl* crustaceans *pl*.

Kredit *m* -**e** credit; *(Darlehen)* loan; *(fig auch)* standing. **auf** ~ on credit; **er hat bei der Bank** ~ his credit is good with the bank; ~ **haben** *(fig)* to have standing.

Kredit-: ~**anstalt** *f* credit institution; ~**aufnahme** *f* borrowing; ~**brief** *m* letter of credit; **k**~**fähig** *adj* credit-worthy; ~**hai** *m* *(col)* loanshark; ~**institut** *nt* credit institution; ~**karte** *f* credit card; **k**~**würdig** *adj* credit-worthy.

Kredo *nt* -**s** *(lit, fig)* creed.

Kreide *f* -**n** chalk. **eine** ~ a piece of chalk; **bei jdm (tief) in der** ~ **stehen** to be (deep) in debt to sb.

Kreide-: **k**~**bleich** *adj (as)* white as a sheet; ~**felsen** *m* chalk cliff; ~**zeichnung** *f* chalk drawing.

kreieren* [kre'iːrən] *vt* to create.

Kreis *m* -**e (a)** circle. **einen** ~ **ziehen** to describe a circle; **einen** ~ **um jdn bilden** to make a circle around sb; **im** ~ **(sitzen)** (to sit) in a circle; **(weite)** ~**e ziehen** *(fig)* to have (wide) repercussions; **sich im** ~ **drehen** *(lit)* to go around in a circle; *(fig)* to go around in circles; **der** ~ **schließt sich** *(fig)* the wheel turns full circle; **der** ~ **seiner Leser** his readers *pl*; **weite** ~**e der**

Bevölkerung wide sections of the population; **im ~e von Freunden** among friends; **eine Feier im kleinen ~e** a celebration for a few close friends and relatives; **das kommt auch in den besten ~en vor** that happens even in the best of circles. (**b**) (*Elec: Strom~*) circuit. (**c**) (*Bereich: von Interessen etc*) sphere. (**d**) (*Stadt~, Land~*) district. ~ **Bonn** Bonn District.

Kreis-: ~**abschnitt** *m* segment; ~**ausschnitt** *m* sector; ~**bahn** *f* (*Astron, Space*) orbit.

kreischen *vi* to screech; (*Mensch auch*) to shriek.

Kreisel *m* - (*Tech*) gyroscope; (*Spielzeug*) (spinning) top.

kreisen *vi aux sein or haben* to circle (*um* around, *über* +*dat* over); (*um eine Achse*) to revolve (*um* around); (*Satellit, Planet auch*) to orbit (*um etw* sth); (*fig: Gedanken, Gespräch*) to revolve (*um* around). **die Arme ~ lassen** to swing one's arms around (in a circle).

kreisförmig *adj* circular.

Kreislauf *m* (*Blut~, Öl~, von Geld*) circulation; (*der Natur, des Wassers*) cycle.

Kreislauf-: ~**mittel** *nt* cardiac stimulant; ~**störungen** *pl* circulation trouble *sing*.

Kreissäge *f* circular saw.

Kreißsaal *m* delivery room.

Kreis-: ~**stadt** *f* district town, ≈ county town (*Brit*); ~**tag** *m* district assembly, ≈ county council (*Brit*); ~**verkehr** *m* roundabout (*Brit*), traffic circle (*US*); ~**wehrersatzamt** *nt* district recruiting office.

Krem *f* -*s or m* -*e* cream.

Krematorium *nt* crematorium.

kremig *adj* creamy.

Kreml *m* der ~ the Kremlin.

Krempe *f* -*n* (*Hut~*) brim.

Krempel *m* no *pl* (*col*) (*Sachen*) stuff (*col*); (*wertloses Zeug*) junk.

krepieren* *vi aux sein* (**a**) (*Mil sl: Bombe etc*) to explode. (**b**) (*col!: sterben*) to snuff it (*col*); (*col: elend sterben*) to die a wretched death.

Krepp *m* -*e or m* -*s* crepe.

Kreppapier *nt* crepe paper.

Kreppsohle *f* crepe sole.

Kresse *f no pl* cress.

Kreta *nt* Crete.

Kreuz *nt* -*e* (**a**) cross; (*als Anhänger etc*) crucifix. **ein ~ schlagen** *or* **machen** to make the sign of the cross; (*sich bekreuzigen auch*) to cross oneself; **mit jdm über ~ sein** (*fig*) to be on bad terms with sb; **sein ~ geduldig tragen** (*geh*) to bear one's cross with patience; **es ist ein ~ mit ihm/damit** he's/it's an awful problem; **ich mache drei ~e, wenn er geht** (*col*) it'll be such a relief when he has gone; **zu ~e kriechen** (*fig*) to eat humble pie, to eat crow (*US*). (**b**) (*Anat*) small of the back; (*von Tier*) back. **ich hab's im ~** (*col*) I have back trouble; **aufs ~ fallen** to fall on one's back; (*fig col*) to be staggered (*col*); **jdn aufs ~ legen** to throw sb on his back; (*fig col*) to take sb for a ride (*col*). (**c**) (*Mus*) sharp. (**d**) (*Autobahn~*) intersection. (**e**) (*Cards*) (*Farbe*) clubs *pl*; (*Karte*) club. **die ~-Dame** the Queen of Clubs.

kreuz *adj*: ~ **und quer** all over; **sie lagen ~ und quer durcheinander** they were lying all over the place.

Kreuz-: ~**bein** *nt* (*Anat*) sacrum; **k~brav** *adj* Kind as good as gold.

kreuzen 1 *vt* to cross (*auch Biol*). **die Arme ~** to fold one's arms. **2** *vr* to cross; (*Meinungen etc*) to clash. **3** *vi aux haben or sein* (*Naut*) to cruise.

Kreuzer *m* - (*Naut*) cruiser.

Kreuz-: ~**fahrer** *m* (*Hist*) crusader; ~**fahrt** *f* (*Naut*) cruise; **eine ~fahrt machen** to go on a cruise; ~**feuer** *nt* (*Mil, fig*) crossfire; **ins ~feuer (der Kritik) geraten** (*fig*) to come under fire; **k~förmig** *adj* cross-shaped; ~**gang** *m* cloister.

kreuzigen *vt* to crucify.

Kreuzigung *f* crucifixion.

Kreuz-: ~**otter** *f* (*Zool*) adder, viper; ~**ritter** *m* (*Hist*) crusader; ~**schmerzen** *pl* backache *sing*; ~**spinne** *f* (*Zool*) garden *or* cross spider.

Kreuzung *f* (**a**) (*Straßen~*) crossroads *sing or pl*, intersection (*esp US*). (**b**) (*das Kreuzen*) crossing; (*von Tieren auch*) cross-breeding. (**c**) (*Rasse*) hybrid; (*Tiere auch*) cross(-breed).

Kreuz-: ~**unglücklich** *adj* absolutely miserable; ~**verhör** *nt* cross-examination; **jdn ins ~verhör nehmen** to cross-examine sb; ~**weg** *m* (*fig*) crossroads *sing*; **k~weise** *adv* crosswise; **du kannst mich k~weise!** (*col!*) get stuffed! (*col!*); ~**worträtsel** *nt* crossword puzzle; ~**zeichen** *nt* sign of the cross; ~**zug** *m* (*lit, fig*) crusade.

Krevette [krɛ'vɛtə] *f* shrimp.

kribb(e)lig *adj* (*col*) fidgety (*col*); (*kribbelnd*) tingly (*col*).

kribbeln *vi* (**a**) (*jucken*) to itch; (*prickeln*) to tingle. **auf der Haut ~** to cause a prickling sensation; (*angenehm*) to make the skin tingle; **es kribbelt mir im Fuß** (*lit*) I have pins and needles in my foot; **es kribbelt mir in den Fingern, etw zu tun** (*col*) I'm itching to do sth. (**b**) *aux sein* (*Insekten*) **es kribbelt von Ameisen** the place is crawling with ants.

kriechen *pret* **kroch**, *ptp* **gekrochen** *vi aux sein* to creep, to crawl (*auch Schlange*); (*fig: Zeit*) to creep by; (*fig: unterwürfig sein*) to grovel (*vor* +*dat* before).

Kriecher *m* - crawler (*col*).

kriecherisch *adj* grovelling (*Brit*), groveling (*US*), servile.

Kriech-: ~**spur** *f* crawler lane; ~**tier** *nt* (*Zool*) reptile.

Krieg *m* -*e* war; (*Art der Kriegsführung*) warfare. ~ **anfangen mit** to start a war with; **einer Partei etc den ~ erklären** (*fig*) to declare war on a party etc; ~ **führen (mit** *or* **gegen)** to wage war (on); **im ~ sein (mit)** to be at war (with); **im ~e fallen** to be killed in action; **in den ~ ziehen** to go to war.

kriegen *vt* (*col*) to get; Bus, Schnupfen, Dieb *auch* to catch; Schlaganfall, eine Spritze, Besuch *auch* to have; Junge, ein Kind to have. **sie kriegt ein Kind** she's going to have a baby; **graue Haare/eine Glatze ~** to go grey/bald; **sie** *or* **es ~** (*col: Prügel*) to get a hiding; **es mit der Angst/Wut ~** to get scared/angry; **es mit jdm zu tun ~** to be in trouble with sb; **sie ~ sich (in Kitschroman)** boy gets girl; **dann kriege ich zuviel** then it gets too much for me; **ich kriege ein Steak** I'll have a steak; **jdn dazu ~, etw zu tun** to get sb to do sth; **etw gemacht ~** to get sth done.

Krieger *m* - warrior.

Kriegerdenkmal *nt* war memorial.

kriegerisch *adj* warlike *no adv*; Haltung *auch* belligerent. ~**e Auseinandersetzung** military conflict.

Krieg-: **k~führend** *adj* warring; ~**führung** *f* warfare *no art*; (*eines Feldherrn*) conduct of the war.

Kriegs-: ~**ausbruch** *m* outbreak of war; **k~bedingt** *adj* caused by war; ~**beginn** *m* start of the war; ~**beil** *nt* tomahawk; **das ~beil begraben** (*fig*) to bury the hatchet; ~**bemalung** *f* (*lit, hum*) warpaint; **k~beschädigt** *adj* war-disabled; ~**beschädigte(r)** *mf decl as adj* war-disabled (*man*)/(*serviceman*); ~**dienst** *m* (*old, form*) military service; ~**dienstverweigerer** *m* - conscientious objector; ~**ende** *nt* end of the war; ~**erklärung** *f* declaration of war; ~**erlebnis** *nt* war-time experience; ~**fall** *m* **im ~fall** in the event of war; ~**folge** *f* consequence of (a/the) war; ~**fuß** *m* (*col*) **mit jdm auf ~fuß stehen** to be at loggerheads with sb; **er steht mit den englischen Sprache auf ~fuß** his English is terrible; ~**gebiet** *nt* war-zone; ~**gefahr** *f* danger of war; ~**gefangene(r)** *mf* prisoner of war, P.O.W.; ~**gefangenschaft** *f* captivity; **in ~gefangenschaft**

sein to be a prisoner of war; ~**gericht** *nt* court-martial; **jdn vor ein** ~**gericht stellen** to court-martial *sb*; ~**herr** *m* **oberster** ~**herr** commander-in-chief; ~**hetze** *f* war-mongering; ~**hetzer** *m* - *(pej)* war-monger; ~**jahr** *nt* year of war; **die** ~**jahre** the war years; **im** ~**jahr** 1945 (during the war) in 1945; ~**kamerad** *m* war-time comrade; ~**kosten** *pl* cost of the war *sing*; ~**list** *f* *(old, liter)* stratagem; ~**marine** *f* navy; **k**~**mäßig** *adj* for war; **k**~**müde** *adj* war-weary; ~**opfer** *nt* war victim; ~**pfad** *m* *(liter)*: **auf dem** ~**pfad** on the war-path; ~**rat** *m* council of war; ~**rat halten** *(fig)* to have a pow-wow *(col)*; ~**recht** *nt* *(Mil)* martial law; ~**schäden** *pl* war damage; ~**schauplatz** *m* theatre *(Brit)* or theater *(US)* of war; ~**schiff** *nt* warship; ~**spiel** *nt* war game; ~**teilnehmer** *m* combatant; *(ehemaliger Soldat)* ex-serviceman; ~**verbrechen** *nt* war crime; ~**verbrecher** *m* war criminal; ~**verletzung** *f* war wound; ~**zeit** *f* wartime; **in** ~**zeiten** in times of war; ~**zustand** *m* state of war; **im** ~**zustand** at war.

Krim *f* **die** ~ the Crimea.
Krimi *m* **-s** *(col)* **(a)** (crime) thriller; *(mit Detektiv als Held)* detective novel; *(rätselhaft)* murder mystery. **(b)** *(TV)* detective series.
Kriminal-: ~**beamte(r)** *m* CID officer; ~**film** *m* crime film or movie *(esp US)*.
kriminalisieren* *vt* to criminalize.
Kriminalistik *f* criminology.
Kriminalität *f* crime; *(Ziffer)* crime rate.
Kriminal-: ~**kommissar** *m* detective superintendent; ~**komödie** *f* comedy thriller; ~**polizei** *f* criminal investigation department; ~**polizist** *m* detective, CID officer; ~**roman** *m* siehe **Krimi (a)**.
kriminell *adj* *(lit, fig col)* criminal. ~ **werden** to turn to crime.
Kriminelle(r) *mf decl as adj* criminal.
Krimskrams *m no pl (col)* odds and ends *pl*.
Kringel *m* - *(der Schrift)* squiggle; *(Cook)* ring.
kringelig *adj* crinkly. **sich** ~ **lachen** *(col)* to kill oneself (laughing) *(col)*.
kringeln *vr* to go frizzy. **sich** ~ **vor Lachen** *(col)* to kill oneself (laughing) *(col)*.
Kripo *f* **-s** *(col)* = **Kriminalpolizei. die** ~ the cops *(col) pl*, the CID.
Kripo- *in cpds (col)* police.
Krippe *f* **-n (a)** *(Futter~)* (hay)box. **(b)** *(Weihnachts~)* crib; *(Bibl auch)* manger. **(c)** *(Kinderhort)* crèche.
Krippenspiel *nt* nativity play.
Krise *f* **-n** crisis.
kriseln *vi impers (col)* **es kriselt** there is trouble brewing.
Krisen-: **k**~**fest** *adj* stable; ~**gebiet** *nt* crisis area; ~**herd** *m* flash point; ~**stab** *m* action or crisis committee.
Kristall[1] *m* **-e** crystal.
Kristall[2] *nt no pl* crystal.
Kristallglas *nt* crystal glass.
Kristallisation *f* crystallization.
kristallisieren* *vir (lit, fig)* to crystallize.
Kristall-: **k**~**klar** *adj* crystal-clear; ~**zucker** *m* refined sugar (in) crystals.
Kriterium *nt (Merkmal)* criterion.
Kritik *f* **-en (a)** *no pl* criticism *(an +dat of)*. **an jdm/etw** ~ **üben** to criticize sb/sth; **unter aller** ~ **sein** *(col)* to be beneath contempt. **(b)** *(Rezensieren)* criticism; *(Rezension auch)* review. **eine gute** ~ **haben** to get good reviews. **(c)** *no pl (die Kritiker)* critics *pl*. **(d)** *no pl (Urteilsfähigkeit)* discrimination. **ohne jede** ~ uncritically.
kritiklos *adj* uncritical.
kritisch *adj* critical. **jdm/einer Sache** ~ **gegenüberstehen** to be critical of sb/sth.
kritisieren* *vti* to criticize.
kritteln *vi* to find fault *(an +dat, über +acc with)*.

Kritzelei *f* scribble; *(das Kritzeln)* scribbling; *(an Wänden)* graffiti.
kritzeln *vti* to scribble.
kroch *pret of* **kriechen.**
Krokant *m no pl (Cook)* cracknel.
Krokette *f (Cook)* croquette.
Krokodil *nt* **-e** crocodile.
Krokodilleder *nt* crocodile skin.
Krokodilstränen *pl* crocodile tears *pl.*
Krokus *m* - *or* **-se** crocus.
Krone *f* **-n (a)** crown. **die** ~ *(fig)* the Crown. **(b)** *(Mauer~)* coping; *(Schaum~)* crest; *(Zahn~)* crown; *(Baum~)* top. **die** ~ **der Schöpfung** the pride of creation; **das setzt der Dummheit die** ~ **auf** *(col)* that beats everything for stupidity; **einen in der** ~ **haben** *(col)* to be tipsy; **dabei fällt dir kein Stein or Zacken aus der** ~ *(col)* it won't hurt you. **(c)** *(Währungseinheit)* crown.
krönen *vt (lit, fig)* to crown. **jdn zum König** ~ to crown sb king; **von Erfolg gekrönt sein/werden** to be crowned with success; **der** ~**de Abschluß** the culmination.
Kronenkorken *m* crown cap.
Kron-: ~**kolonie** *f* crown colony; ~**leuchter** *m* chandelier; ~**prinz** *m* crown prince; *(in Großbritannien auch)* Prince of Wales; *(fig)* heir apparent; ~**prinzessin** *f* crown princess.
Krönung *f* coronation; *(fig)* culmination.
Kronzeuge *m (Jur)* person who turns King's/Queen's evidence *or (US)* State's evidence; *(Hauptzeuge)* principal witness. ~ **sein, als** ~ **auftreten** to turn King's/Queen's/State's evidence; to appear as principal witness
Kropf *m* **-e (a)** *(von Vogel)* crop. **(b)** *(Med)* goitre.
kroß *adj (N Ger)* crisp; *Brötchen auch* crusty.
Krösus *m* **-se ich bin doch kein** ~ *(col)* I'm not made of money *(col)*.
Kröte *f* **-n (a)** *(Zool)* toad. **eine freche (kleine)** ~ *(col)* a cheeky (little) minx *(col)*. **(b)** ~**n** *pl (col: Geld)* pennies *(col)*.
Krücke *f* - **n (a)** crutch; *(fig)* prop. **an** ~**n** *(dat)* **gehen** to walk on crutches. **(b)** *(Schirm~)* crook.
Krückstock *m* walking-stick.
Krug *m* **-e** jug; *(Bier~)* (beer-)mug.
Krume *f* **-n (geh) (a)** *(Brot~)* crumb. **(b)** *(liter: Acker~)* (top)soil.
Krümel *m* - **(a)** *(Brot~ etc)* crumb. **(b)** *(col: Kind)* tiny tot *(col)*.
krümeln *vti* to crumble; *(beim Essen)* to make crumbs.
krumm *adj* **(a)** crooked; *(verbogen auch)* bent; *(hakenförmig)* hooked; *Beine auch* bandy; *Rücken* hunched. ~**e Nase** hook(ed) nose; ~ **gewachsen** crooked; **etw** ~ **biegen** to bend sth; ~ **und schief** askew; **sich** ~ **und schief lachen** *(col)* to fall about laughing *(col)*; **keinen Finger** ~ **machen** *(col)* not to lift a finger; **steh/sitz nicht so** ~ **da!** stand/sit up straight. **(b)** *(col: unehrlich)* crooked *(col)*. ~**er Hund** *(pej)* crooked swine; **ein** ~**es Ding drehen** *(col)* to do something crooked; **etw auf die** ~**e Tour versuchen** to try to wangle sth *(col)*.
krümmen 1 *vt* to bend. **die Katze krümmte den Buckel** the cat arched its back. **2** *vr* to bend; *(Fluß)* to wind; *(Straße)* to curve; *(Wurm)* to writhe. **sich** ~ **und winden** *(fig)* to squirm; **sich vor Lachen** ~ to double up with laughter; **sich vor Schmerzen** *(dat)* ~ to writhe with pain.
krummnehmen *vt sep irreg (col)* **(jdm) etw** ~ to take sth amiss.
Krümmung *f (von Weg, Fluß)* curve; *(Math, Med, Opt)* curvature.
Krüppel *m* - cripple. **zum** ~ **werden** to be crippled; **jdn zum** ~ **schlagen** to cripple sb.
Kruste *f* **-n** crust; *(von Schweinebraten)* crackling; *(von Braten)* crisped outside.
krustig *adj* crusty.
Kruzifix *nt* **-e** crucifix.

Kuba nt Cuba.

Kubaner(in f) m - Cuban.

kubanisch adj Cuban.

Kübel m - bucket; (für Jauche etc) container; (für Bäume) tub. **es regnet (wie) aus ~n** it's bucketing down.

Kubik nt - (Aut col: Hubraum) cc.

Kubik-: ~**meter** m or nt cubic metre (Brit) or meter (US); ~**zentimeter** m or nt cubic centimetre (Brit) or centimeter (US), cc.

Kubismus m (Art) cubism.

Küche f -n (a) kitchen; (klein) kitchenette. (b) (Kochkunst) cooking, cuisine.

Kuchen m - cake; (Torte auch) gateau; (mit Obst gedeckt) (fruit) flan (Brit), tart.

Küchen|abfälle pl kitchen scraps pl.

Kuchenblech nt baking sheet or tin.

Küchenchef m chef.

Kuchen-: ~**form** f cake tin; ~**gabel** f pastry fork.

Küchen-: ~**gerät** nt kitchen utensil; (kollektiv) kitchen utensils pl; (elektrisch) kitchen appliance; ~**geschirr** nt kitchenware no pl; ~**herd** m (electric/gas) cooker; ~**meister** m chef; ~**messer** nt kitchen knife; ~**schabe** f (Zool) cockroach; ~**schrank** m (kitchen) cupboard.

Kuchenteig m cake mixture; (Hefeteig) dough.

Küchen-: ~**tisch** m kitchen table; ~**waage** f kitchen scales pl; ~**zettel** m menu.

Kuckuck m -e (a) cuckoo. (b) (col: Siegel des Gerichtsvollziehers) bailiff's seal (for distraint of goods). (c) (col) **zum ~ (noch mal)!** hell's bells! (col); **hol's der ~!** botheration! (col); **geh zum ~** go to blazes (col); **das weiß der ~** heaven (only) knows (col).

Kuckucks-: ~**ei** nt cuckoo's egg; **man hat uns ein ~ei untergeschoben** (col) we've been left holding the baby (col); ~**uhr** f cuckoo clock.

Kuddelmuddel m or nt no pl (col) mess.

Kufe f -n (von Schlitten etc) runner; (von Flugzeug) skid.

Kugel f -n ball; (geometrische Figur) sphere; (Erd~) sphere, globe; (Kegel~) bowl; (Gewehr~) bullet; (für Luftgewehr) pellet; (Kanonen~) (cannon)ball; (beim ~stoßen) shot; (Murmel) marble. **eine ruhige ~ schieben** (col) to have a cushy number (col); (aus Faulheit) to swing the lead (col); **rund wie eine ~** (col) like a barrel.

Kugel-: **k~blitz** m (Met) ball-lightning; **k~förmig** adj spherical; ~**gelenk** nt (Anat, Tech) ball-and-socket joint; ~**hagel** m hail of bullets; ~**kopf** m golf-ball; ~**kopfschreibmaschine** f golf-ball typewriter; ~**lager** nt ball-bearing.

kugeln 1 vi aux sein (rollen, fallen) to roll. **2** vr to roll (about). **sich (vor Lachen) ~** (col) to double up (laughing).

Kugel-: **k~rund** adj as round as a ball; (col) Mensch tubby (col); ~**schreiber** m ballpoint (pen), biro ®; **k~sicher** adj bullet-proof; ~**stoßen** nt no pl shot-putting; ~**stoßer(in** f) m - shot-putter; ~**wechsel** m exchange of shots.

Kuh f -e cow. **heilige ~** (lit, fig) sacred cow.

Kuh-: ~**dorf** nt (pej col) one-horse town (col); ~**fladen** m cow-pat; ~**glocke** f cowbell; ~**handel** m (pej col) horse-trading (col) no pl; ~**haut** f **das geht auf keine ~ haut** (col) that's absolutely incredible; ~**herde** f herd of cows.

kühl adj (lit, fig) cool; (abweisend) cold. **mir wird etwas ~** I'm getting rather chilly; **etw ~ lagern** to store sth in a cool place; **einen ~en Kopf bewahren** to keep a cool head, to keep one's cool (col).

Kühle f no pl (lit) cool(ness); (fig) coolness; (Abweisung) coldness.

kühlen 1 vt to cool; (auf Eis) to chill. **2** vi to have a cooling effect.

Kühler m - (Tech) cooler; (Aut) radiator; (col: ~haube) bonnet (Brit), hood (US); (Sekt~) ice bucket.

Kühler-: ~**figur** f (Aut) radiator mascot; ~**haube** f (Aut) bonnet (Brit), hood (US).

Kühl-: ~**fach** nt freezer compartment; ~**haus** nt cold-storage depot; ~**mittel** nt (Tech) coolant; ~**raum** m cold storage room; ~**schrank** m refrigerator, fridge (Brit); ~**tasche** f cold bag; ~**truhe** f (chest) freezer, deep freeze (Brit); ~**turm** m (Tech) cooling tower.

Kühlung f (das Kühlen) cooling; (Kühle) coolness. **zur ~ des Motors** to cool the engine.

Kühlwasser nt radiator water, coolant.

Kuh-: ~**milch** f cow's milk; ~**mist** m cow dung.

kühn adj (lit, fig) bold. **das übertrifft meine ~sten Erwartungen** it's beyond my wildest dreams.

Kühnheit f boldness.

Kuh-: ~**stall** m cow shed; ~**weide** f pasture.

Küken nt - (Huhn) chick; (col: Nesthäkchen) baby of the family (col).

kulant adj accommodating; Bedingungen generous.

Kulanz f no pl siehe adj accommodating attitude; generousness. **eine Reparatur auf ~** a free repair.

Kuli m -s (a) (Lastträger) coolie; (fig) slave. (b) (col: Kugelschreiber) ballpoint, biro ®.

kulinarisch adj culinary.

Kulisse f -n scenery no pl; (fig: Hintergrund) background, backdrop. **das ist alles nur ~** (fig) that is only a façade; **einen Blick hinter die ~n werfen** (fig) to have a glimpse behind the scenes.

Kulissenschieber(in f) m - stagehand.

Kulleraugen pl (col) wide eyes pl.

kullern vti (vi: aux sein) (col) to roll.

Kult m -e cult; (Verehrung) worship. **einen ~ mit jdm/etw treiben** to make a cult out of sb/sth.

Kult-: ~**figur** f cult figure; ~**film** m cult film; ~**handlung** f ritual(istic) act.

kultisch adj ritual(istic).

kultivieren* [kulti'vi:rən] vt (lit, fig) to cultivate.

kultiviert adj Mensch cultured, refined; Geschmack, Unterhaltung cultivated. **wenn Sie ~ reisen wollen** if you want to travel in style; **Kerzen beim Essen, das ist sehr ~** meals by candlelight, very civilized.

Kultivierung [kulti'vi:rʊŋ] f (lit, fig) cultivation.

Kultstätte f place of worship.

Kultur f (a) (no pl: Kunst und Wissenschaft) culture. **er hat keine ~** he is uncultured. (b) (Lebensform) civilization. **dort leben verschiedene ~en harmonisch zusammen** different cultures live harmoniously together there. (c) (Bakterien~, Pilz~ etc) culture; (Bestand angebauter Pflanzen) plantation.

Kultur-: ~**austausch** m cultural exchange; ~**banause** m (col) philistine; ~**beutel** m toilet bag (Brit), washbag.

kulturell adj cultural.

Kultur-: ~**film** m documentary film; ~**geschichte** f history of civilization; ~**kreis** m culture group; ~**leben** nt cultural life; **k~los** adj uncultured; ~**losigkeit** f lack of culture; ~**pessimismus** m despair of civilization; ~**politik** f cultural and educational policy; ~**revolution** f cultural revolution; ~**stätte** f place of cultural interest; ~**stufe** f level of civilization; ~**teil** m (von Zeitung) arts section; ~**volk** nt civilized nation.

Kultus-: ~**minister** m minister of education and the arts; ~**ministerium** nt ministry of education and the arts.

Kümmel m - (a) no pl (Gewürz) caraway (seed). (b) (col: Schnaps) kümmel.

Kummer m no pl (Betrübtheit) grief, sorrow; (Unannehmlichkeit) trouble. **hast du ~?** have you got problems?; **aus or vor ~ sterben** to die of grief; **vor ~ vergehen** to be pining away with sorrow; **er fand vor ~ keinen Schlaf mehr** he was so griefstricken that he could no longer sleep; **wir**

sind (an) ~ gewöhnt (col) we're used to that sort of thing.

kümmerlich adj (a) (karg, armselig) wretched, miserable; Lohn, Rente auch paltry; Mahlzeit auch meagre (Brit), meager (US). (b) (schwächlich) puny.

kümmern 1 vt to concern. **was kümmert Sie das?** what business is that of yours?; **was kümmert mich das?** what's that to me? **2** vr **sich um jdn/ etw** ~ to look after sb/sth; **sich darum** ~, **daß** ... to see to it that ...; **kümmere dich gefälligst um deine eigenen Angelegenheiten!** mind your own business!; **er kümmert sich nicht darum, was die Leute denken** he doesn't care what people think.

Kumpan(in f) m **-e** (dated col) mate (Brit col), buddy (esp US col).

Kumpel m **-** or (col) **-s (a)** (Min: Bergmann) miner. **(b)** (col: Kollege, Freund) mate (Brit col), buddy (esp US col).

kündbar adj Vertrag terminable; Anleihe redeemable. **Beamte sind nicht ohne weiteres** ~ civil servants cannot be dismissed without good cause.

Kündbarkeit f (von Vertrag) terminability; (von Anleihe) redeemability.

Kunde[1] f no pl (geh) news sing, tidings pl (old).

Kunde[2] m (wk) **-n, -n** (auch pej col) customer.

künden vi (geh) **von etw** ~ to tell of sth.

Kunden-: ~**dienst** m customer service; ~**fang** m (pej) **auf** ~**fang sein** to be touting for customers; **ein Vertreter auf** ~**fang** a salesman chasing up some business; ~**kreis** m customers pl, clientèle; ~**werbung** f publicity (aimed at attracting custom or customers).

kundgeben vt sep irreg (dated) **etw** ~ to announce sth (jdm to sb); Gefühle etc to express sth.

Kundgebung f (Versammlung) rally.

kundig adj (geh) knowledgeable; (sach~) expert. **einer Sache** (gen) ~ **sein** to have a knowledge of sth.

kündigen 1 vt Stellung to hand in one's notice for; Abonnement, Mitgliedschaft to cancel; Vertrag to terminate; Tarife to discontinue; (col) jdn to dismiss. **jdm die Wohnung** ~ to give sb notice to quit his flat; **ich habe meine Wohnung gekündigt** I've given in notice that I'm leaving my flat; **die Stellung** ~ to hand in one's notice; **jdm die Stellung** ~ to give sb his/her notice; **sie hat ihm die Freundschaft gekündigt** she has broken off their friendship. **2** vi (Arbeitnehmer) to give in one's notice; (Mieter) to give notice. **jdm** ~ (Arbeitgeber) to give sb his notice; (Vermieter) to give sb notice to quit; **zum 1. April** ~ to give one's notice for April 1st; (Mieter) to give notice for April 1st; (bei Mitgliedschaft) to cancel one's membership as of April 1st.

Kündigung f **(a)** (Mitteilung) (von Vermieter) notice to quit; (von Mieter, von Stellung) notice; (von Vertrag) termination. **(b)** (das Kündigen) (von Arbeitgeber) dismissal; (von Arbeitnehmer) giving in one's notice; (von Vertrag) termination; (von Mitgliedschaft, Abonnement) cancellation.

Kündigungs-: ~**frist** f period of notice; **vierteljährliche** ~**frist haben** to have (to give) three months' notice; ~**grund** m grounds pl for giving notice; (von Arbeitgeber auch) grounds pl for dismissal; ~**schutz** m protection against wrongful dismissal.

Kundin f customer.

Kundschaft f customers pl.

Kundschafter m **-** spy; (Mil) scout.

kundtun vt sep irreg (geh) to make known.

künftig 1 adj future. **2** adv in future.

Kunst f **-̈e (a)** art. **die schönen** ~**e** fine art sing, the fine arts. **(b)** (Können, Fertigkeit) art, skill; (Kunststück) trick. **mit seiner** ~ **am Ende sein** to be at one's wits' end; **ärztliche** ~ medical skill;

das ist keine ~! it's like taking candy from a baby (col); (ein Kinderspiel) it's a piece of cake (col); **das ist eine brotlose** ~ there's no money in that; **was macht die** ~? (col) how's tricks? (col).

Kunst- in cpds (Art) art; (künstlich) artificial; ~**akademie** f college of art; ~**ausstellung** f art exhibition; ~**banause** m (pej) philistine; ~**druck** m art print; ~**druckpapier** nt art paper; ~**dünger** m artificial fertilizer; ~**erzieher** m art teacher; ~**erziehung** f (Sch) art; ~**faser** f manmade fibre (Brit) or fiber (US); ~**fehler** m professional error; (weniger ernst) slip; k~**fertig** adj (geh) skilful (Brit), skillful (US); ~**fertigkeit** f skill; ~**flieger** m stunt flyer; ~**flug** m aerobatics sing; k~**gerecht** adj (fachmännisch) skilful (Brit), skillful (US); ~**geschichte** f history of art, art history; ~**gewerbe** nt arts and crafts pl; k~**gewerbler(in** f) m - craftsman/ -woman; k~**gewerblich** adj k~**gewerbliche Gegenstände** craft objects; ~**griff** m trick, dodge (col); ~**handel** m art trade; ~**händler** m art dealer; ~**hochschule** f art college; ~**ken er** m art connoisseur; ~**kritik** f no pl art criticism; (die Kritiker) art critics pl; (Rezension) art review; ~**kritiker** m art critic.

Künstler(in f) m - **(a)** artist; (Unterhaltungs~) artiste. **bildender** ~ visual artist. **(b)** (Könner) genius (im + dat art).

künstlerisch adj artistic.

Künstler-: ~**name** m pseudonym; (von Schriftsteller auch) pen name; (von Schauspieler auch) stage name; ~**pech** nt (col) hard luck.

künstlich adj artificial; Zähne, Wimpern, Fingernägel false; Faserstoffe synthetic; Diamanten imitation, fake (col). **jdn** ~ **ernähren** (Med) to feed sb artificially; **sich** ~ **aufregen** (col) to get all worked up about nothing (col); **sich** ~ **dumm stellen** to pretend to be stupid.

Kunst-: ~**los** adj unsophisticated; ~**maler** m artist, painter; ~**pause** f pause for effect; (iro) awkward pause; ~**sammlung** f art collection; ~**schätze** pl art treasures pl; ~**seide** f artificial silk; ~**springen** nt diving; ~**stoff** m man-made material; ~**stück** nt trick; ~**stück!** (iro) no wonder!; **das ist kein** ~**stück** (fig) there's nothing to it; ~**turnen** nt gymnastics sing; ~**verstand** m appreciation of art; k~**voll** adj artistic; ~**werk** nt work of art.

kunterbunt adj Sammlung, Gruppe etc motley attr; (vielfarbig auch) multi-coloured (Brit), multi-colored (US); Programm varied. ~ **durcheinander** higgledy-piggledy (col).

Kupfer nt no pl copper.

Kupfergeld nt coppers pl, copper coins pl.

kupfern adj copper.

Kupfer-: k~**rot** adj copper-coloured (Brit), copper-colored (US); ~**stecher** m - copper(plate) engraver; ~**stich** m copperplate (engraving or etching).

kupieren* vt Schwanz, Ohren to dock.

Kupon [ku'põ:] m **-s** coupon.

Kuppe f **-n** (Berg~) (rounded) hilltop; (Finger~) tip.

Kuppel f **-n** dome, cupola.

Kuppeldach nt dome-shaped roof.

Kuppelei f (Jur) procuring.

kuppeln 1 vt (Tech) to couple; (fig auch) to link. **2** vi (Aut) to operate the clutch.

Kuppler(in f) m - (Jur) procurer/procuress.

Kupplung f (Tech) coupling; (Aut etc) clutch. **die** ~ **(durch)treten** to disengage the clutch; **die** ~ **kommen lassen** (Aut) to let the clutch in.

Kupplungs- in cpds (Aut) clutch; ~**pedal** nt clutch pedal.

Kur f **-en** (in Badeort) (health) cure; (Haar~ etc) treatment no pl; (Schlankheits~, Diät~) diet. **eine** ~ **fahren** to go to a health resort; **eine** ~ **machen** to take a cure; (Schlankheits~) to diet; **jdn zur** ~

schicken to send sb to a health resort.
Kür f **-en (a)** (Sport) free section. **eine ~ laufen** to do the free skating. **(b)** (old: Wahl) election.
Kuratorium nt (Vereinigung) committee.
Kurbel f **-n** crank.
kurbeln vti to turn, to wind.
Kurbelwelle f crankshaft.
Kürbis m **-se** pumpkin; (col: Kopf) nut (col).
küren vt (old, geh) to choose, to elect (zu as).
Kurgast m patient at a health resort.
Kurier m **-e** courier, messenger.
kurieren* vt (lit, fig) to cure (von of). **von ihm bin ich kuriert** I've gone right off him.
kurios adj (merkwürdig) curious, strange, odd.
Kuriosität f **(a)** (Gegenstand) curio(sity). **(b)** (Eigenart) peculiarity.
Kurkonzert nt concert (at a health resort).
Kürlauf(en nt) m free skating.
Kur-: **~ort** m health resort, spa; **~pfuscher** m (pej col) quack (doctor); **~pfuscherei** f (pej col) quackery.
Kurs m **-e (a)** (Naut, Aviat, fig) course; (Pol, Richtung auch) line. **harter/weicher ~** (Pol) hard/soft line; **den ~ ändern/beibehalten** (lit, fig) to alter/ hold (one's) course; **~ nehmen auf** (+acc) to set course for; **~ haben auf** (+acc) to be heading for. **(b)** (Fin: Wechsel~) exchange rate; (Aktien~) (going) rate; (Marktpreis) market value. **zum ~ von** at the rate of; **hoch im ~ stehen** (Aktien) to be high; (fig) to be popular (bei with). **(c)** (Lehrgang) course (in +dat, für in). **einen ~ besuchen** or **mitmachen** to attend a class.
Kurs-: **~änderung** f (lit, fig) change of course; **~buch** nt (Rail) timetable (Brit), schedule (US).
Kürschner(in f) m - furrier.
kursieren* vi aux haben or sein to be in circulation; (fig) to circulate.
kursiv adj italic. **etw ~ drucken** to italicize sth.
Kursivschrift f italics pl.
Kurskorrektur f (lit, fig) course correction.
Kursus m, pl **Kurse** (geh: Lehrgang) course.
Kurs-: **~wagen** m (Rail) through car; **~wert** m (Fin) market value.
Kurve ['kʊrvə] f **-n** (Math, col: Körperrundung) curve; (Biegung, Straßen~ auch) bend; (an Kreuzung) corner; (statistisch, Fieber~ etc) graph. **die Straße macht eine ~** the road bends; **die ~ kratzen** (col: schnell weggehen) to make tracks (col); **die ~ nicht kriegen** (col) not to get around to it.
kurven ['kʊrvn] vi aux sein (col) (Aviat) to circle. **durch Italien ~** to drive around Italy.
kurvenreich adj Straße winding; (col) Frau curvaceous, shapely. **„~e Strecke"** "bends".
kurz comp **-er**, superl **-ste(r, s)** or (adv) **am -esten 1** adj short; Zeit, Aufenthalt, Bericht, Antwort etc auch brief; Blick, Folge quick; Gedächtnis auch short-lived. **etw ~er machen** to shorten sth; **mach's ~!** make it quick; **den ~eren ziehen** (fig col) to get the worst of it; **mit ein paar ~en Worten** in a few brief words; **ein ~erer Weg** a quicker way; **in ~ester Frist** before very long.
2 adv **(a)** **~ atmen** to take short breaths; **eine Sache ~ abtun** to dismiss sth out of hand; **zu ~ kommen** to get a raw deal (col); **~ entschlossen** without a moment's hesitation; **~ gesagt** in a word; **sich ~ fassen** to be brief; **~ und bündig** concisely; **~ und gut** in short; **~ und schmerzlos** (col) short and sweet; **jdn/etw ~ und klein schagen** to beat sb up/to smash sth to pieces. **(b)** (für eine ~e Zeit) briefly. **ich habe ihn nur ~ gesehen** I only saw him briefly; **ich bleibe nur ~** I'll only stay for a short while; **darf ich mal ~ stören?** could I just interrupt for a moment? **(c)** (zeitlich, räumlich: nicht lang) shortly, just. **~ vor Köln/Ostern** shortly or just before Cologne/Easter; **er hat den Wagen erst seit ~em** he's only had the car for a short while; **seit**

~em gibt es Bier in der Kantine since recently there's been beer in the canteen; **über ~ oder lang** sooner or later; **(bis) vor ~em** (until) recently; **~ nacheinander** shortly after each other.
Kurz-: **~arbeit** f short time; **k~arbeiten** vi sep to be on short time; **k~ärm(e)lig** adj short-sleeved; **k~atmig** adj (fig) feeble, lame; (Med) short-winded.
Kürze f no pl shortness; (von Besuch, Bericht etc auch) brevity; (fig: Bündigkeit) conciseness; **in ~** shortly; **in aller ~** very briefly; **in der ~ liegt die Würze** (Prov) brevity is the soul of wit (prov).
kürzen vt to shorten; (Math) Bruch to cancel (down); Gehalt etc to cut back. **jdm das Gehalt etc ~** to cut back sb's salary etc.
Kurze(r) m decl as adj (col) **(a)** (Schnaps) short. **(b)** (Kurzschluß) short(-circuit).
kurzerhand adv without further ado; entlassen on the spot.
Kurz-: **~fassung** f abridged version; **k~fristig 1** adj short-term; Wettervorhersage short-range; **2** adv (auf kurze Sicht) for the short term; (für kurze Zeit) for a short time; **k~fristig seine Pläne ändern** to change one's plans at short notice; **k~gefaßt** adj concise; **~geschichte** f short story; **k~haarig** adj short-haired; **k~halten** vt sep irreg **jdn k~halten** to keep sb short; **k~lebig** adj short-lived, ephemeral.
kürzlich adv recently, lately. **erst ~** just recently.
Kurz-: **~meldung** f news flash; **~nachrichten** pl news headlines pl; (in Zeitung auch) news in brief; **~schluß** m **(a)** short-circuit; **(b)** (fig: auch **~schlußhandlung**) rash action; **~schrift** f shorthand; **k~sichtig** adj (lit, fig) short-sighted; **~sichtigkeit** f (lit, fig) short-sightedness; **~streckenläufer** m (Sport) sprinter; **k~treten** vi sep irreg (fig col) to go easy; **k~um** adv in a word.
Kürzung f shortening; (eines Buchs) abridgement; (von Gehältern, Produktion) cut (gen in).
Kurz-: **~urlaub** m short holiday (Brit) or vacation (US); (Mil) short leave; **~waren** pl haberdashery (Brit), notions pl (US); **k~weilig** adj entertaining; **~welle** f (Rad) short wave.
kuschelig adj (col) cosy, snug.
kuscheln vr **sich an jdn ~** to snuggle up to sb; **sich in etw** (acc) **~** to snuggle up in sth.
kuschen vir (Hund etc) to get down; (fig) to knuckle under.
Kusine f (female) cousin.
Kuß m **-sse** kiss.
Küßchen nt peck (col). **gib ~** give us a kiss.
küssen 1 vti to kiss. **jdm die Hand ~** to kiss sb's hand. **2** vr to kiss (each other).
Kuß-: **~hand** f **jdm eine ~hand zuwerfen** to blow sb a kiss; **jdn/etw mit ~hand nehmen** (col) to be only too glad to take sb/sth.
Küste f **-n** coast; (Ufer) shore.
Küsten- in cpds coastal; **~fischerei** f inshore fishing; **~gebiet** nt coastal area; **~gewässer** pl coastal waters pl; **~schiffahrt** f coastal shipping; **~wacht** f coastguard.
Küster m - verger, sexton.
Kutsche f **-n** coach, carriage; (col: Auto) jalopy (col).
Kutscher m - coachman, driver.
kutschieren* 1 vi aux sein to drive, to ride. **durch die Gegend ~** (col) to drive around. **2** vt to drive.
Kutte f **-n** habit.
Kutter m - (Naut) cutter.
Kuvert [ku'veːɐ, ku'veːɐ] nt **-s** (Brief~) envelope.
Kuvertüre [kuvɛr'tyːrə] f **-n** (Cook) (chocolate) coating.
kW = Kilowatt.
Kybernetik f cybernetics sing.
kyrillisch adj Cyrillic.
KZ [kaː'tsɛt] nt **-s** concentration camp.

L

L, l [ɛl] *nt* -, - L, l.
l = Liter.
labb(e)rig *adj (col) Bier, Suppe* watery; *Kaffee, Tee auch* weak; *Essen* mushy.
laben *vr (liter)* to feast (oneself) *(an +dat* on); *(an Quelle etc)* to refresh oneself *(mit, an +dat* with).
labern *(col)* 1 *vi* to prattle (on) *(col).* 2 *vt* to talk. **was laberst du denn da?** what are you prattling on about? *(col).*
labil *adj (physisch) Gesundheit* delicate; *Kreislauf* poor; *Patient* frail; *(psychisch)* weak.
Labor *nt* -s *or* -e laboratory, lab *(col).*
Laborant(in *f) m* lab(oratory) technician.
Laboratorium *nt* laboratory.
laborieren* *vi* to labour *(Brit),* to labor *(US) (an +dat* at); *(leiden)* to be plagued *(an +dat* by).
Labyrinth *nt* -e labyrinth; *(fig auch)* maze.
Lach|anfall *m* laughing fit.
Lache[1] ['laxə, 'laːxə] *f* -n puddle; *(von Benzin, Blut auch)* pool.
Lache[2] *f* -n *(col)* laugh.
lächeln *vi* to smile. **verlegen/freundlich ~** to give an embarrassed/a friendly smile.
Lächeln *nt no pl* smile.
lachen 1 *vi* to laugh *(über +acc* at). **jdn zum L~ bringen** to make sb laugh; **zum L~ sein** *(lustig)* to be hilarious; *(lächerlich)* to be laughable; **mir ist nicht zum L~** *(zumute)* I'm in no laughing mood; **daß ich nicht lache!** *(col)* don't make me laugh! *(col);* **da kann ich doch nur ~** I can't help laughing (at that); **du hast gut ~!** it's all right for you to laugh!; **gezwungen/verlegen ~** to give a forced/an embarrassed laugh; **wer zuletzt lacht, lacht am besten** *(Prov)* he who laughs last, laughs longest *(Prov);* **die Sonne lacht** the sun is shining brightly; **ihm lachte das Glück** Fortune smiled on him.
2 *vt* **da gibt es gar nichts zu ~** that's nothing to laugh about; *(es ist etwas Ernstes auch)* that's not funny; **er hat bei seiner Frau nichts zu ~** *(col)* he has a hard time of it with his wife; **das wäre doch gelacht, wenn ...** it would be ridiculous if ...; **das wäre doch gelacht!** that's dead easy *(col);* **sich schief ~** *(col)* to split one's sides (laughing) *(col).*
Lachen *nt no pl* laughter, laughing; *(Art des* ~s) laugh. **dir wird das ~ schon noch vergehen!** you'll soon be laughing on the other side of your face.
Lacher *m* - **die ~ auf seine Seite haben** to have the last laugh; *(einen Lacherfolg verbuchen)* to get a laugh.
Lach|erfolg *m* **ein ~ sein, einen ~ erzielen** to make everybody laugh.
lächerlich *adj* **(a)** ridiculous, absurd. **jdn/etw ~ machen** to make sb/sth look silly *(vor jdm* in front of sb); **jdn/sich ~ machen** to make a fool of sb/oneself *(vor jdm* in front of sb); **etw ins L~e ziehen** to make fun of sth. **(b)** *(geringfügig) Anlaß* trivial, petty.
Lächerlichkeit *f* **(a)** *no pl* ridiculousness; *(von Argument etc auch)* absurdity. **jdn der ~ preisgeben** to make a laughing stock of sb. **(b)** *(Geringfügigkeit)* triviality.
Lach-: **~gas** *nt* laughing gas; **l~haft** *adj* ludicrous; *Argument auch* laughable; **~krampf** *m*

einen ~krampf bekommen to go into fits of laughter.
Lachs [laks] *m* -e salmon.
Lachsalve *f* burst *or* roar of laughter.
Lachs-: **l~farben** *adj* salmon pink; **~forelle** *f* salmon *or* sea trout; **~schinken** *m* smoked, rolled fillet of ham.
Lack *m* -e *(Holz~, Nagel~)* varnish; *(Auto~)* paint.
Lack-: **~affe** *m (pej col)* flash Harry *(col);* **~farbe** *f* gloss paint.
lackieren* *vt Holz* to varnish; *Fingernägel auch* to paint; *Auto* to spray.
Lackierung *f* **(a)** *(das Lackieren) (von Autos)* spraying; *(von Möbeln)* varnishing. **(b)** *(der Lack) (von Auto)* paintwork; *(Holz~)* varnish.
Lackmuspapier *nt* litmus paper.
Lack-: **~schaden** *m* damage to paintwork; **~schuh** *m* patent-leather shoe.
Lade *f* -n chest; *(col: Schub~)* drawer.
Lade-: **~bühne** *f* loading ramp; **~fläche** *f* load area; **~hemmung** *f* **das Gewehr hat ~hemmung** the gun is jammed.
laden[1] *pret* **lud**, *ptp* **geladen** *vti* to load; *(Phys)* to charge. **das Schiff hat Autos geladen** the ship has a cargo of cars; **der Lkw hat zuviel geladen** the lorry is overloaded; **Verantwortung/Schulden auf sich** *(acc)* **~** to saddle oneself with responsibility/debts; **eine schwere Schuld auf sich** *(acc)* **~** to place oneself under a heavy burden of guilt; **er hatte schon ganz schön geladen** *(col)* he was already pretty tanked up *(col);* **mit Spannung geladen** charged with tension; *siehe* **geladen.**
laden[2] *pret* **lud**, *ptp* **geladen** *vt (liter: einladen)* to invite; *(form: vor Gericht)* to summon. **nur für geladene Gäste** by invitation only.
Laden[1] *m* ⁼ shop *(esp Brit),* store *(US); (col: Betrieb)* outfit *(col).* **der ~ läuft** *(col)* business is good.
Laden[2] *m* ⁼ *or* - *(Fenster~)* shutter.
Laden-: **~besitzer** *m* shopowner *(esp Brit),* shopkeeper *(esp Brit),* storekeeper *(US);* **~dieb** *m* shoplifter; **~diebstahl** *m* shoplifting; **~hüter** *m* non-seller; **~kasse** *f* till; **~kette** *f* chain of shops *or* stores; **~preis** *m* shop price; **~schluß** *m* **nach/vor ~schluß** after/before the shops *(esp Brit)* or stores *(US)* shut; **um fünf Uhr ist ~schluß** the shops/stores shut at five o'clock; **~tisch** *m* shop counter; **über den/unter dem ~tisch** over/under the counter.
Lade-: **~rampe** *f* loading ramp; **~raum** *m* load room; *(Aviat, Naut)* hold.
lädieren* *vt* to damage. **lädiert sein** *(hum)/aussehen (hum)* to be/look the worse for wear.
Ladung *f* **(a)** load; *(von Sprengstoff)* charge. **eine geballte ~ Schnee/Dreck** *(col)* a whole lot of snow/mud; **eine geballte ~ von Schimpfwörtern** a whole torrent of abuse. **(b)** *(Vorladung)* summons *sing.*
Lafette *f (Mil)* (gun)carriage.
lag *pret of* **liegen.**
Lage *f* -n **(a)** *(geographische* ~*)* situation, location. **in günstiger ~** well-situated; **eine gute/ruhige ~ haben** to be in a good/peaceful location. **(b)** *(Art des Liegens)* position. **(c)** *(Situation)* situation. **dazu bin ich nicht in der ~** I'm not in a position to

do that; **in der glücklichen ~ sein, etw zu tun to** be in the happy position of doing sth; **Herr der ~ sein** to be in control of the situation; **die ~ der Dinge erfordert es, daß ...** the situation requires that ... **(d)** *(Schicht)* layer. **(e)** *(Mus) (Stimm~)* register; *(Ton~)* pitch. **(f)** *(Runde)* round. **eine ~ schmeißen** *(col)* to stand a round.

Lage-: ~**bericht** *m* report; *(Mil)* situation report; ~**plan** *m* ground plan.

Lager *nt* - **(a)** *(Unterkunft)* camp; *(liter: Schlafstätte)* bed. **(b)** *(fig: Partei)* camp; *(von Staaten)* bloc. **ins andere ~ überwechseln** to change camps. **(c)** *pl auch* ∓ *(Vorratsraum)* store(room); *(von Laden)* stockroom; *(~halle)* warehouse; *(Vorrat)* stock. **etw auf ~ haben** to have sth in stock; *(fig)* **Witz** *etc* **to have sth at the ready. (d)** *(Tech)* bearing. **(e)** *(Geol)* bed.

Lager-: ~**bestand** *m* stock; ~**feuer** *nt* campfire; ~**halle** *f*, ~**haus** *nt* warehouse.

Lagerist(in *f)* *m* storeman/storewoman.

lagern 1 *vt* **(a)** *(aufbewahren)* to store. **kühl ~! store in a cool place. (b)** *(hinlegen)* **jdn** to lay down; *Bein etc* to rest. **einen Kranken weich ~** to lay an invalid on something soft; **das Bein hoch ~** to one's leg up; *siehe* **gelagert. 2** *vi* **(a)** *(Lebensmittel etc)* to be stored. **(b)** *(liegen)* to lie. **(c)** *(von Truppen)* to camp, to be encamped.

Lager-: ~**raum** *m* storeroom; *(in Geschäft)* stockroom; ~**stätte** *f* **(a)** *(old liter)* bed, couch *(liter)*; **(b)** *(Geol)* deposit.

Lagerung *f* storage; *(das Lagern auch)* storing.

Lagune *f* -**n** lagoon.

lahm *adj* **(a)** *(gelähmt)* Bein, Mensch lame; *(col: steif)* stiff. **er hat ein ~es Bein** he is lame in one leg. **(b)** *(col: langsam, langweilig)* dreary, dull; Geschäftsgang slow, sluggish. **eine ~e Ente sein** *(col)* to have no zip *(col)*.

lähmen *vt* to paralyze; *(fig) Industrie auch* to cripple; *Verhandlungen, Verkehr* to hold up. **er ist an beiden Beinen gelähmt** he is paralyzed in both legs; **vor Angst wie gelähmt sein** to be petrified.

lahmlegen *vt sep Verkehr, Produktion* to bring to a standstill; *Industrie auch* to paralyze.

Lähmung *f (lit)* paralysis; *(fig)* immobilization.

Laib *m* -**e** loaf.

laichen *vi* to spawn.

Laie *m (wk)* -**n**, -**n** layman; *(fig also, Theat)* amateur. **die ~n** *(Eccl)* the laity.

Laien-: l~**haft** *adj Arbeit* amateurish; *Urteil, Meinung* lay *attr only*; ~**prediger** *m* lay preacher; ~**theater** *nt* amateur theatre *(Brit) or* theater *(US)*; *(Ensemble)* amateur theatre *(Brit) or* theater *(US)* group.

Lakai *m (wk)* -**en**, -**en** *(lit, fig)* lackey.

Lake *f* -**n** brine.

Laken *nt* - sheet.

lakonisch *adj* laconic.

Lakritz *m* -**e** *(dial)*, **Lakritze** *f* -**n** liquorice *(Brit)*, licorice *(US)*.

lala *adv (col):* **so ~** so-so *(col)*, not too bad *(col)*.

lallen *vti* to babble; *(Betrunkener)* to mumble.

Lama *nt* -**s** llama.

Lamelle *f* **(a)** *(Biol)* lamella. **(b)** *(von Jalousien)* slat; *(von Heizkörper)* rib.

lamentieren* *vi* to moan, to complain.

Lametta *nt no pl* lametta.

Lamm *nt* ∓**er** lamb.

Lamm-: ~**braten** *m* roast lamb; ~**fell** *nt* lambskin; ~**fleisch** *nt* lamb; l~**fromm** *adj Gesicht, Miene* innocent; l~**fromm sein** to be like a (little) lamb; ~**wolle** *f* lambswool.

Lampe *f* -**n** light; *(Öl~, Steh~, Tisch~)* lamp; *(Glüh~)* bulb.

Lampen-: ~**fieber** *nt* stage fright; ~**schirm** *m* lampshade.

Lampion [lam'piõ:, lam'piɔŋ] *m* -**s** Chinese lantern.

lancieren* [lã'si:rən] *vt Produkt, Künstler* to launch; *Nachricht* to put out.

Land *nt* ∓**er** **(a)** *(Gelände, Festland)* land. **ein Stück ~ a** plot of land; **~ bestellen/bebauen** to till the soil/to cultivate the land; **an ~ gehen/schwimmen** to go/swim ashore; **~ sehen** *(lit)* to sight land; **endlich sehe ich ~** *(fig)* at last I can see the light at the end of the tunnel; **etw an ~ ziehen** to pull sth ashore; **einen Auftrag an ~ ziehen** *(col)* to land an order; **~ in Sicht! land ahoy!; ~ unter!** land submerged!

(b) *(ländliches Gebiet)* country. **auf dem ~(e)** in the country.

(c) *(Staat)* country, land *(esp liter)*; *(Bundes~)* *(in BRD)* Land, state; *(in Österreich)* province. **das ~ Hessen/Tirol** the state of Hesse/the province of Tyrol; **außer ~es sein** to be out of the country; **~ und Leute kennenlernen** to get to know the country and its inhabitants; **aus aller Herren ~ er** from all over the world.

Land-: ~**adel** *m* landed gentry; ~**arbeit** *f* agricultural work; l~**auf adv:** l~**auf, l~ab** the length and breadth of the country; ~**besitzer** *m* landowner; ~**bevölkerung** *f* rural population.

Lande-: ~**bahn** *f* landing strip; ~**erlaubnis** *f* landing permission; ~**fähre** *f* *(Space)* landing module.

landeinwärts *adv* inland.

landen *vti (vi: aux sein)* to land. **weich ~** to make a soft landing; **im Gefängnis ~** to land (up) in prison; **mit deinen Komplimenten kannst du bei mir nicht ~** your compliments won't get you anywhere with me.

Ländereien *pl* estates *pl*.

Länderspiel *nt* international *(match)*.

Landes-: ~**grenze** *f* *(von Staat)* national boundary; *(von Bundesland)* state/provincial boundary; ~**hauptstadt** *f* capital of the Land/province; ~**innere(s)** *nt* interior; ~**kunde** *f* regional studies *pl*; l~**kundig** *adj* l~**kundiger Reiseleiter** courier who knows the country; l~**kundlich** *adj Themen, Aspekte* regional; ~**meister** *m* *(Sport)* regional champion; ~**regierung** *f* government of a Land/ provincial government; ~**sprache** *f* national language; **der ~sprache unkundig sein** to not know the language; ~**teil** *m* region, area; ~**tracht** *f* national dress or costume; l~**üblich** *adj* customary; **das ist dort l~üblich** that's the custom there; ~**verrat** *m* treason; ~**verteidigung** *f* national defence *(Brit) or* defense *(US)*.

Landeverbot *nt* refusal of landing permission; ~ **erhalten** to be refused landing permission.

Land-: ~**flucht** *f* emigration to the cities; ~**friedensbruch** *m* *(Jur)* breach of the peace; ~**funk** *m* farming (radio) programme *(Brit) or* program *(US)*; ~**gericht** *nt* district court; ~**gut** *nt* estate; ~**haus** *nt* country house; ~**heer** *nt* army; ~**jäger** *m* *(Wurst)* pressed smoked sausage; ~**karte** *f* map; ~**klima** *nt* continental climate; ~**kreis** *m* administrative district; ~**krieg** *m* land warfare; l~**läufig** *adj* popular, common; **entgegen der l~läufigen Meinung** contrary to popular opinion; ~**leben** *nt* country life.

ländlich *adj* rural; *Tracht* country *attr*; *Tanz* country *attr*, folk *attr*; *Idylle* pastoral.

Land-: ~**luft** *f* country air; ~**macht** *f* land power; ~**plage** *f* plague; *(fig col)* pest; ~**ratte** *f* *(hum)* landlubber; ~**regen** *m* steady rain.

Landschaft *f* scenery *no pl*; *(einer bestimmten Gegend auch)* landscape; *(ländliche Gegend)* countryside. **eine öde ~** a barren landscape; **die ~ um London** the countryside around London; **die ~en Italiens** the types of countryside in Italy; **wir sahen eine reizvolle ~** we saw some delightful scenery; **in der ~ herumstehen** *(col)* to stand around; **die politische ~** the political scene.

landschaftlich *adj Schönheiten etc* scenic; *Besonderheiten* regional. **diese Gegend ist ~ ausgesprochen reizvoll** the scenery in this area is

particularly delightful; **das ist ~ unterschiedlich** it differs from one part of the country to another.
Landsitz m country seat.
Lands-: ~mann m, **~männin** f, pl **~leute** fellow countryman/-woman.
Land-: ~straße f country road; *(Straße zweiter Ordnung)* secondary *or* B *(Brit)* road; **~streicher(in** f) m - *(pej)* tramp, hobo *(US)*; **~streitkräfte** pl land forces pl; **~strich** m area; **ein flacher ~strich** a flat belt of land; **~tag** m Landtag *(state parliament)*.
Landung f *(von Flugzeug, Truppen etc)* landing. **zur ~ gezwungen werden** to be forced down.
Landungs-: ~boot nt landing craft; **~brücke** f jetty, landing stage; **~steg** m landing stage *(Brit)*, jetty.
Land-: ~urlaub m shore leave; **~vermesser** m land surveyor; **~vermessung** f land surveying; **~wein** m table wine, vin ordinaire; **~wirt** m farmer.
Landwirtschaft f agriculture, farming; *(Betrieb)* farm. **~ betreiben** to farm.
landwirtschaftlich adj agricultural.
Landwirtschafts- in cpds agricultural; **~ministerium** nt ministry of agriculture.
Landzunge f spit (of land), promontory.
lang comp **-er**, superl **-ste(r, s)** *or (adv)* **am -sten 1** adj **(a)** long; *Film, Roman, Aufenthalt, Rede auch* lengthy. **das war seit ~em geplant** that was planned a long time ago; **ich habe seit ~em nichts von ihm gehört** I haven't heard from him for a long time; **vor ~er Zeit** a long time ago; **hier wird mir die Zeit nicht ~** I won't get bored here; **etw ~er machen** to lengthen sth; **er machte ein ~es Gesicht** his face fell; **man sah überall nur ~e Gesichter** you saw nothing but long faces; **etw von ~er Hand vorbereiten** to prepare sth carefully; **einen ~en Hals machen** *(col)* to crane one's neck. **(b)** *(col: groß) Mensch* tall.
2 adv **der ~ erwartete Regen** the long-awaited rain; **der ~ ersehnte Urlaub** the longed-for holiday; **~ anhaltender Beifall** prolonged applause; **zwei Stunden ~** for two hours; **mein ganzes Leben ~** my whole life; **mein ganzes Leben ~ werde ich das nicht vergessen** I'll never forget that as long as I live; **~ und breit** at great length. **(b)** *(Geog)* longitude. **der Ort liegt auf 20 Grad östlicher ~** the town has a longitude of 20 degrees east.
langen *(col)* **1** vi **(a)** *(sich erstrecken, greifen)* to reach *(nach* for, in +acc in, into). **(b)** *(ausreichen)*

to be enough; *(auskommen)* to get by, to manage. **jetzt langt's mir aber!** I've had just about enough! **2** vt *(reichen)* **jdm etw ~** to hand sb sth; **jdm eine ~** to give sb a clip on the ear *(col)*.
Längen-: ~grad m degree of longitude; **~maß** nt measure of length.
Langeweile f no pl boredom. **~ haben** to be bored.
Lang-: ~finger m *(hum)* pick-pocket; **l~fristig 1** adj long-term; **2** adv in the long term; *planen* for the long term; **l~haarig** adj long-haired; **l~jährig 1** adj *Freundschaft, Gewohnheit* long-standing; *Erfahrung, Verhandlungen* many years of; *Mitarbeiter* of many years' standing; **2** adv for many years; **~lauf** m *(Ski)* cross-country skiing; **~läufer** m *(Ski)* cross-country skier; **l~lebig** adj long-lasting; *Gerücht, Mensch, Tier* long-lived; **l~legen** vr sep to have a lie-down.
länglich adj long, elongated.
Lang-: ~mut f no pl patience, forbearance; **l~mütig** adj patient, forbearing.
längs 1 adv lengthways, lengthwise. **2** prep +gen along. **~ der Straße stehen Kastanien** chestnut trees line the road.
Längs|achse f longitudinal axis.
langsam 1 adj slow. **2** adv **(a)** slowly. **fahr/sprich ~er!** slow down!, drive/speak (a bit) more slowly!; **immer schön ~!** *(col)* easy does it!; **~ aber sicher** slowly but surely. **(b)** *(allmählich)* **es wird ~ Zeit, daß ...** it's getting about time that ...; **ich muß jetzt ~ gehen** I must be getting on my way; **~ (aber sicher) reicht es mir** I've just about had enough.
Langschläfer m late-riser.
Langspielplatte f long-playing record.
Längs-: ~schnitt m longitudinal section; **~seite** f long side; *(Naut)* broadside; **l~seit(s)** adv, prep +gen alongside.
längst adv **(a)** *(seit langem, schon lange)* for a long time. **das ist ~ nicht mehr so** it hasn't been like that for a long time; **als wir ankamen, war der Zug ~ weg** when we arrived the train had long since gone. **(b)** *siehe* **lange (b)**.
Langstrecken-: ~flugzeug nt long-range aircraft; **~lauf** m *(Disziplin)* long-distance running; *(Wettkampf)* long-distance race; **~läufer** m long-distance runner.
Languste [laŋˈgʊstə] f **-n** crayfish, crawfish *(US)*.
langweilen insep **1** vt to bore. **2** vi to be boring. **3** vr to be/get bored.
Langweiler m - bore.
langweilig adj **(a)** boring. **(b)** *(col: langsam)* slow.
Lang-: ~welle f long wave; **l~wierig** adj long, lengthy; *Verhandlungen, Krankheit auch* prolonged; **~wierigkeit** f lengthiness; **~zeitprogramm** nt long-term programme *(Brit)* or program *(US)*.
Lanze f **-n** lance; *(zum Werfen)* spear. **für jdn eine ~ brechen** *(fig)* to take up the cudgels for sb, to go to bat for sb *(esp US)*.
lapidar adj succinct.
Lappalie [-iə] f trifle, petty little matter.
Lappe m *(wk)* **-n**, **-n**, **Lappin** f Lapp, Lapplander.
Lappen m - **(a)** *(Stück Stoff)* cloth, *(Wasch~)* face cloth. **(b)** *(col: Geldschein)* note *(Brit)*, bill *(US)*. **(c)** *(col)* **jdm durch die ~ gehen** to slip through sb's fingers.
läppern vr impers *(col)* **es läppert sich** it (all) mounts up.
läppisch adj silly. **wegen ~en zwei Mark macht er so ein Theater** he makes such a fuss about a mere two marks.
Lappland nt Lapland.
Lapsus m -, - mistake, slip; *(gesellschaftlich, diplomatisch)* faux pas.
Lärche f -n larch.
Larifari nt no pl *(col)* nonsense.
Lärm m no pl noise; *(Geräuschbelästigung auch)* din, racket; *(Aufsehen)* fuss. **viel ~ um jdn/etw**

machen to make a big fuss about sb/sth.
Lärm-: ~**belästigung** f noise nuisance; **l~emp-findlich** adj sensitive to noise.
lärmen vi to make a noise. ~**d** noisy.
Larve ['larfə] f **-n** (Tier~) larva.
las pret of **lesen**.
lasch adj (col) **(a)** (schlaff) Bewegungen feeble. **(b)** Erziehung, Polizei lax.
Lasche f **-n** (Schlaufe) loop; (Schuh~) tongue; (als Verschluß) tab, flap; (Tech) splicing plate.
Laserstrahl ['le:zɐ-] m laser beam.
lasieren* vt Bild, Holz to varnish; Glas to glaze.
lassen pret **ließ**, ptp **gelassen 1** vt **(a)** (unter~) to stop; (momentan aufhören) to leave. **laß das (sein)!** don't (do it)!; (hör auf) stop it!; **laß diese Bemerkungen!** that's enough of that kind of remark!; ~ **wir das!** let's leave it or that!; **er kann das Trinken nicht** ~ he can't stop drinking; **er kann es nicht** ~! he will keep on doing it!; **dann** ~ **wir es eben** let's drop the whole idea; **wenn du nicht willst, dann laß es doch** if you don't want to, then don't; **tu, was du nicht** ~ **kannst!** if you must, you must!
(b) (zurück~, be~) to leave. **jdn allein** ~ to leave sb alone; **etw** ~, **wie es ist** to leave sth (just) as it is.
(c) (über~) **jdm etw** ~ to let sb have sth; (behalten ~) to let sb keep sth; **das muß man ihr** ~ (zugestehen) you've got to grant her that.
(d) (hinein~, hinaus~) to let (in +acc into, aus out of); (col: los~) to let go; (in Ruhe ~) to leave sb. **Wasser in die Badewanne (laufen)** ~ to run water into the bath.
2 modal aux ptp ~ **(a)** (veranlassen) **etw tun** ~ to have or get sth done; **sich** (dat) **etw schicken** ~ to have sth sent to one; **jdm ausrichten** ~, **daß** ... to leave a message for sb that ...; **jdn kommen** ~ to send for sb; **mein Vater wollte mich studieren** ~ my father wanted me to study.
(b) (zu~) **jdn etw wissen/sehen** ~ to let sb know/see sth; **sie hat mich nichts merken** ~ she didn't show it/anything; **sich** (dat) **einen Bart wachsen** ~ to grow a beard; **den Tee ziehen** ~ to let the tea draw; **das Licht brennen** ~ to leave the light on; **jdn warten** ~ to keep sb waiting; **er hat sich überreden** ~ he let himself be persuaded; **ich lasse mich nicht zwingen** I won't be coerced; **das Fenster läßt sich nicht öffnen** (grundsätzlich nicht) the window doesn't open; (momentan nicht) the window won't open; **das Wort läßt sich nicht übersetzen** the word is untranslatable; **das läßt sich machen** that can be done; **es ließ sich nicht ändern** it couldn't be changed; **daraus läßt sich schließen, daß** ... one can conclude from this that ...
(c) (als Imperativ) **laß uns gehen!** let's go!; **laß es dir gutgehen!** take care of yourself!; **laß dir das gesagt sein!** let me tell you this!
3 vi **(a)** laß mal, ich mache das schon leave it, I'll do it. **(b)** (ab~) **von jdm/etw** ~ to give sb/sth up.
lässig adj (ungezwungen) casual. **das hat er ganz** ~ **hingekriegt** (col) pretty cool, the way he did that (col).
Lässigkeit f casualness.
läßlich adj (Eccl) Sünde venial, pardonable.
Lasso m or nt **-s** lasso.
Last f **-en (a)** load; (Trag~ auch) burden; (lit, fig: Gewicht) weight. **(b)** (fig: Bürde) burden. **jdm zur** ~ **fallen/werden** to be/become a burden on sb; **die** ~ **der Verantwortung/des Amtes** the burden of responsibility/the weight of office; **jdm eine** ~ **abnehmen** to take a load off sb's shoulders; **jdm etw zur** ~ **legen** to accuse sb of sth. **(c)** ~**en** (Kosten) costs; (des Steuerzahlers) charges; **soziale** ~**en** welfare costs or charges; **zu jds** ~**en gehen** to be chargeable to sb.
lasten vi to weigh heavily (auf +dat on). **auf dem**

Haus lastet noch eine Hypothek the house is still encumbered (with a mortgage) (form); **auf ihm lastet die ganze Verantwortung** all the responsibility rests on him.
Lasten|aufzug m hoist, goods lift (Brit) or elevator (US).
Laster¹ m - (col) lorry (Brit), truck.
Laster² nt - vice.
Lästerei f (col) **(a)** no pl (das Lästern) running down (über +acc of). **(b)** (Lästerwort) nasty remark.
lasterhaft adj depraved.
Lasterhöhle f den of vice or iniquity.
lästerlich adj malicious; (gottes~) blasphemous.
lästern 1 vi **über jdn/etw** ~ to make nasty remarks about sb/sth. **2** vt Gott to blaspheme against.
lästig adj tiresome; (ärgerlich auch) irksome, aggravating; Husten etc troublesome. **wie** ~! what a nuisance!; **jdm** ~ **sein** to bother sb; **dieser Verband ist mir** ~ this bandage is bothering me; **jdm** ~ **werden** to become a nuisance (to sb); (zum Ärgernis werden) to get annoying (to sb).
Last-: ~**kahn** m barge; ~**kraftwagen** m (form) heavy goods vehicle; ~**schiff** nt cargo ship; ~**schrift** f debit; (Eintrag) debit entry; ~**wagen** m lorry (Brit), truck; ~**wagenfahrer** m lorry (Brit) or truck driver; ~**zug** m truck-trailer (US), juggernaut (Brit).
Lasur f (auf Holz, Bild) varnish; (auf Glas, Email) glaze.
Latein nt Latin. ~ **mit seinem** ~ **am Ende sein** (col) to be stumped (col).
Latein-: ~**amerika** nt Latin America; **l~amerikanisch** adj Latin-American.
lateinisch adj Latin.
latent adj latent; Selbstmörder, Gefahr potential. ~ **vorhanden sein** to be latent.
Laterne f **-n** lantern; (Straßen~) streetlamp.
Laternenpfahl m lamp post.
Latinum nt no pl **kleines/großes** ~ ≃ Latin O-/A-level (exam) (Brit).
Latrine f latrine.
Latschen m - (col) (Hausschuh) slipper; (pej: Schuh) worn-out shoe.
latschen vi aux sein (col) to wander; (durch die Stadt etc) to traipse; (schlurfend) to slouch along.
Latte f **-n (a)** (schmales Brett) slat. **nicht alle auf der** ~ **haben** (col) to have a screw loose (col). **(b)** (Sport) bar; (Ftbl) (cross)bar. **(c)** (col: Liste) **eine ganze** ~ **von Vorstrafen** a whole string of previous convictions.
Latten-: ~**kreuz** nt corner of the goalpost; ~**zaun** m wooden fence.
Latz m ⁻e (Lätzchen, bei Kleidung) bib; (Hosen~) (front) flap. **jdm eins vor den** ~ **knallen** (col) to sock sb one (col).
Lätzchen nt bib.
Latzhose f (pair of) dungarees pl.
lau adj **(a)** Wind, Abend mild. **(b)** Flüssigkeit tepid, lukewarm; (fig) Haltung lukewarm.
Laub nt no pl leaves pl; (an Bäumen etc auch) foliage.
Laubbaum m deciduous tree.
Laube f **-n (a)** (Gartenhäuschen) summerhouse. **(b)** (Gang) pergola; (Arkade) arcade.
Laub-: ~**frosch** m (European) tree-frog; ~**säge** f fretsaw; ~**wald** m deciduous forest.
Lauch m (esp S Ger: Porree) leek.
Lauer f no pl **auf der** ~ **sein** or **liegen** to lie in wait.
lauern vi (lit, fig) to lurk, to lie in wait (auf +acc for); (col) to wait (auf +acc for). **ein** ~**der Blick** a furtive glance.
Lauf m, pl **Läufe (a)** (schneller Schritt) run; (Wett~) race. **sein** ~ **wurde immer schneller** he ran faster and faster; **einen** ~ **machen** to go for a run. **(b)** (Verlauf) course. **im** ~**e der Jahre**

through the years; **im ~e des Gesprächs** in the course of the conversation; **sie ließ ihren Gefühlen freien ~** she gave way to her feelings; **den Dingen ihren ~ lassen** to let matters take their course. **(c)** *(Gang, Arbeit)* running, operation. **(d)** *(Fluß~, Astron)* course. **der obere/untere ~ der Donau** the upper/lower reaches of the Danube. **(e)** *(Gewehr~)* barrel. **(f)** *(Hunt: Bein)* leg.

Laufbahn *f* career. **eine ~ einschlagen** to embark on a career.

Laufbursche *m* errand-boy, messenger boy.

laufen *pret* **lief,** *ptp* **gelaufen 1** *vi aux sein* **(a)** to run. **die Erde läuft um die Sonne** the earth moves around the sun; **es lief mir eiskalt über den Rücken** a chill ran up my spine.
(b) *(col: gehen)* to go; *(zu Fuß gehen)* to walk. **das Kind läuft schon** the child is already walking; **das L~ lernen** to learn to walk; **es sind nur 10 Minuten zu ~** it's only 10 minutes' walk; **er läuft dauernd zur Polizei** he's always running to the police.
(c) *(fließen)* to run; *(schmelzen: Käse, Butter)* to melt; *(undicht sein) (Gefäß, Wasserhahn)* to leak; *(Nase, Wunde)* to run. **in Strömen ~** to stream *or* pour (in/out/down *etc*); **Wasser in die Badewanne ~ lassen** to run water into the bath; **ihm läuft die Nase** he's got a runny nose.
(d) *(in Betrieb sein)* to run, to go; *(Uhr)* to go; *(Elektrogerät) (eingeschaltet sein)* to be on; *(funktionieren)* to work.
(e) *(fig: im Gange sein)* *(Prozeß, Verhandlung)* to go on, to be in progress; *(Bewerbung, Antrag)* to be under consideration; *(gezeigt werden) (Film, Stück)* to be on. **der Film lief schon, als wir ankamen** the film had already started when we arrived; **der Film läuft über drei Stunden** the film goes on for three hours; **etw läuft gut/ schlecht** sth is going well/badly; **mal sehen, wie die Sache läuft** let's see how things go; **die Dinge ~ lassen** to let things slide; **die Sache ist gelaufen** *(col)* it's in the bag *(col)*; **es ist zu spät, die Sache ist schon gelaufen** *(col)* it's too late now, it's all finished with.
(f) **das Auto läuft auf meinen Namen** the car is in my name; **das läuft unter „Sonderausgaben"** that comes under "special expenses".
2 *vt aux sein* **(a)** *auch aux haben (Sport)* Rekordzeit to run; *Rekord* to set. **Ski/Schlittschuh/Rollschuh** *etc* ~ to ski/skate/rollerskate *etc*. **(b)** *(fahren: Auto etc)* Geschwindigkeit, Strecke to do. **(c)** *(zu Fuß gehen)* to walk; *(schnell)* to run.
3 *vr* **sich müde ~** to tire oneself out; **in den Schuhen läuft es sich gut** these shoes are good for walking/running in.

laufend 1 *adj attr* Arbeiten, Ausgaben regular; *Monat, Jahr* current. **10 DM das ~e Meter** DM 10 per metre; **~e Nummer** serial number; *(von Konto)* number; **auf dem ~en bleiben/sein** to keep (oneself)/be up-to-date; **jdn auf dem ~en halten** to keep sb up-to-date. **2** *adv* continually, constantly.

laufenlassen *vt sep irreg (col)* jdn ~ to let sb go.

Läufer *m* - **(a)** *(Sport)* runner; *(Hürden~)* hurdler; *(Ftbl)* halfback; *(Chess)* bishop. **rechter/ linker ~** *(Ftbl)* right/left half. **(b)** *(Teppich)* rug; *(Treppen~, Tisch~)* runner.

Lauferei *f (col)* running about *no pl.*

Läuferin *f (Sport)* runner; *(Hürden~)* hurdler.

Lauf-: ~**feuer** *nt:* **sich wie ein ~ feuer verbreiten** to spread like wildfire; ~**gitter** *nt* playpen.

läufig *adj* on heat.

Lauf-: ~**junge** *m* errand-boy; ~**kunde** *m* occasional customer; ~**masche** *f* ladder *(Brit)*, run; ~**paß** *m:* **jdm den ~paß geben** *(col)* to give sb his/her marching orders *(col)*; ~**schritt** *m* trot; *(Mil)* double-quick; **im ~schritt** *(Mil)* at the double; ~**stall** *m* playpen; ~**steg** *m* catwalk; ~**werk** *nt* *(Mech)* running gear; *(von Uhr)*

movement; *(Comp)* drive; ~**zeit** *f* **(a)** *(von Wechsel, Vertrag)* period of validity; **(b)** *(von Maschine)* life.

Lauge *f* -**n** *(Chem)* lye; *(Seifen~)* soapy water.

Laune *f* -**n** *(Stimmung)* mood. **(je) nach (Lust und) ~** just as the mood takes one; **gute/schlechte ~ haben** to be in a good/bad mood. **(b)** *(Einfall)* whim. **etw aus einer ~ heraus tun** to do sth on a whim.

launenhaft, launisch *adj* moody; *(unberechenbar)* capricious.

Laus *f, pl* **Läuse** louse. **ihm ist (wohl) eine ~ über die Leber gelaufen** *(col)* something's biting him *(col)*.

Lausbub *m (hum)* rascal, scamp.

Lausch|angriff *m* bugging operation *(gegen* on*)*.

lauschen *vi* **(a)** *(geh)* to listen *(dat, auf* +acc to*)*. **(b)** *(heimlich)* to eavesdrop.

Lauscher(in *f)* *m* - eavesdropper.

Lausejunge *m (col)* little devil *(col)*; *(wohlwollend)* rascal.

lausen *vt* to delouse. **ich denk', mich laust der Affe!** *(col)* well blow me down! *(col)*.

lausig *(col)* **1** *adj* lousy *(col)*; *Kälte* perishing. **2** *adv* awfully.

laut¹ *adj* **(a)** loud. **~er sprechen** to speak up; ~ **auflachen** to burst out laughing; **etw ~(er) stellen** to turn sth up (loud). **(b)** *(lärmend)* noisy; *(aufdringlich)* Mensch loudmouthed; *Farbe etc* loud. **(c)** *(hörbar)* aloud pred, adv. **etw ~ sagen** *(lit)* to say sth out loud; *(fig)* to shout sth from the rooftops; **das kannst du ~ sagen** you can say that again; ~ **werden** *(bekannt)* to become known.

laut² *prep* +gen *or* dat according to.

Laut *m* -**e** sound. **keinen ~ von sich (dat) geben** not to make a sound.

Laute *f* -**n** lute.

lauten *vi* to be; *(Rede)* to go; *(Schriftstück)* to read. **auf den Namen ... ~** *(Paß)* to be in the name of ...; *(Scheck)* to be made out to ...

läuten *vti* to ring. **es hat geläutet** the bell rang; **er hat davon (etwas) ~ hören** *(col)* he has heard something about it.

lauter 1 *adj* *(geh)* Absichten honourable *(Brit)*, honorable *(US)*; Wahrheit honest. **2** *adv (nur)* nothing/nobody but. **~ Unsinn** sheer nonsense; **vor ~ Rauch kann man nichts sehen** you can't see anything for all the smoke.

läutern *vt (liter)* to purify; *(fig)* to reform.

lauthals *adv* at the top of one's voice.

Laut-: ~**lehre** *f* phonetics *sing*; **l~lich** *adj* phonetic; **l~los** *adj* noiseless; *(wortlos)* silent; ~**losigkeit** *f siehe adj* noiselessness; silence; **l~malend** *adj* onomatopoeic; ~**malerei** *f* onomatopoeia; ~**schrift** *f* phonetics *pl*.

Lautsprecher *m* (loud)speaker.

Lautsprecher-: ~**anlage** *f* öffentliche ~**anlage** public address *or* PA system; ~**wagen** *m* loudspeaker car/van.

Laut-: **l~stark** *adj* loud; *(Rad, TV etc)* high-volume; *Protest* vociferous; ~**stärke** *f siehe adj* loudness; volume; vociferousness; **ein Radio in voller ~stärke spielen lassen** to have a radio on full volume.

lauwarm *adj (lit, fig)* lukewarm.

Lava [ˈlaːva] *f,* **Laven** [ˈlaːvn] lava.

Lavendel [laˈvɛndl] *m* - lavender.

lavieren* [laˈviːrən] *vi* **(a)** *(Naut)* to tack. **(b)** *(fig)* to manoeuvre *(Brit)*, to maneuver *(US)*.

Lawine *f (lit, fig)* avalanche.

Lawinen-: **l~artig** *adj* like an avalanche; **l~artig anwachsen** to snowball; ~**gefahr** *f* danger of avalanches.

Layout [ˈleːˌaʊt] *nt* -**s** layout.

Lazarett [latsaˈrɛt] *nt* -**e** *(Mil)* sick bay; *(Krankenhaus)* hospital.

leasen [ˈliːzn] *vt (Comm)* to lease.

Leasing [ˈliːzɪŋ] *nt* -**s** *(Comm)* leasing *no art, no pl.*

Leben nt - life. das ~ life; am ~ sein/bleiben to be/stay alive; solange ich am ~ bin as long as I live; jdm das ~ retten to save sb's life; ein glückliches etc ~ führen to live a happy etc life; mit dem ~ davonkommen to escape with one's life; sein ~ aufs Spiel setzen to take one's life in one's hands; mit dem ~ abschließen to prepare for death; etw ins ~ rufen to bring sth into being; seines ~s nicht mehr sicher sein to fear for one's life; ums ~ kommen to die; sein ~ lassen (müssen) to lose one's life; jdn am ~ lassen to spare sb's life; sich (dat) das ~ nehmen to take one's (own) life; jdn wieder ins ~ zurückrufen to bring sb back to life; Bewußtlosen to revive sb; der Mann/die Frau meines ~s my ideal man/woman; etw für sein ~ gern tun to love doing sth; jdn künstlich am ~ erhalten to keep sb alive artificially; er hat es nie leicht gehabt im ~ he has never had an easy life; ein ~ lang one's whole life (long); ich habe noch nie im ~ geraucht I have never smoked in all my life; nie im ~! never!; im ~ ist das ganz anders in real life it's very different; ein Film nach dem ~ a film from real life; so ist das ~ (eben) that's life; ~ in etw (acc) bringen (col) to liven sth up.

leben vi to live; (am Leben sein) to be alive; (weiter~) to live on. ich möchte nicht mehr ~ I don't want to go on living; er wird nicht mehr lange zu ~ haben he won't live much longer; von etw ~ to live on sth; lebst du noch? (hum col) are you still in the land of the living? (hum); zum L~ zu wenig, zum Sterben zuviel it's barely enough to keep body and soul together; einsam ~ to lead a lonely life; hier läßt es sich (gut) ~ it's a good life here.

lebend adj live attr, alive pred; Wesen, Beispiel, Sprache living. ein Tier ~ fangen to catch an animal alive; ~es Inventar livestock.

Lebend-: ~geburt f live-birth; ~gewicht nt live weight.

lebendig adj (a) (nicht tot) live attr, alive pred; Wesen living. jdn bei ~em Leibe verbrennen to burn sb alive. (b) (fig: lebhaft) lively no adv; Darstellung, Bild auch vivid; Glaube fervent.

Lebens-: ~abend m old age; ~abschnitt m phase in one's life; ~alter nt age; ein hohes ~alter erreichen to have a long life; ~angst f fear of life; ~anschauung f philosophy of life; ~art f no pl (a) way of life; (b) (Manieren) manners pl; (Stil) style; ~auffassung f attitude to life; ~bedingungen pl living conditions pl; l~bejahend adj eine l~bejahende Einstellung a positive approach to life; ~bereich m area of life; ~dauer f life(span); (von Maschine) life; l~echt adj true-to-life; ~elixier nt das ist sein ~elixier (fig) he thrives on it; ~ende nt end of sb's/(one's) life; ~erfahrung f experience of life; ~erwartung f life expectancy; l~fähig adj (lit, fig) viable; ~form f (Biol) life-form; (Form des Zusammenlebens) way of life; ~frage f vital matter; l~fremd adj out of touch with life; ~freude f joie de vivre; l~froh adj full of the joys of life; ~führung f life-style; ~gefahr f (mortal) danger; „~gefahr!" "danger"; er schwebt in ~gefahr his life is in danger; außer ~gefahr sein to be out of danger; etw unter ~gefahr (dat) tun to risk one's life doing sth; l~gefährlich adj highly dangerous; Verletzung critical; ~gefährte m, ~gefährtin f ihr ~gefährte the man she lives with; ~gemeinschaft f long-term relationship; (Biol, Zool) symbiosis; ~geschichte f life-story; ~gewohnheit f habit; l~groß adj lifesize; ~größe f eine Figur in ~größe a lifesize figure; ~haltungskosten pl cost of living sing; ~hilfe f counselling (Brit), counseling (US); l~hungrig adj thirsty for life; ~inhalt m purpose in life; etw zu seinem ~inhalt machen to devote oneself to sth; ~jahr nt year of (one's) life; nach

Vollendung des 18. ~jahres on attaining the age of 18; ~kraft f vitality; ~künstler m master in the art of living; ~lage f situation; l~lang adj lifelong; Haft life attr, for life; l~länglich adj Rente, Strafe for life; sie hat ~länglich bekommen (col) she got life (col); ~lauf m curriculum vitae, résumé (US); ~lust f zest for life; l~lustig adj in love with life.

Lebensmittel pl food sing, groceries pl.

Lebensmittel-: ~geschäft nt grocer's (shop) (Brit), grocer (US); ~gesetz nt food law; ~händler m grocer.

Lebens-: l~müde adj tired of life; ein ~müder a potential suicide; l~nah adj true-to-life; l~notwendig adj essential; Organ vital (for life); ~qualität f quality of life; ~raum m (Biol) biosphere; ~regel f rule (of life); ~retter m rescuer; ~standard m standard of living; ~stellung f job for life; ~stil m lifestyle; l~tüchtig adj able to cope with life; ~umstände pl circumstances pl; ~unterhalt m seinen ~unterhalt verdienen to earn one's living; für jds ~unterhalt sorgen to support sb; ~versicherung f life insurance; eine ~versicherung abschließen to take out a life insurance; ~wandel m way of life; einen einwandfreien ~wandel führen to lead an irreproachable life; ~weg m journey through life; alles Gute für den weiteren ~weg every good wish for the future; ~weise f way of life; ~weisheit f maxim; (~erfahrung) wisdom; ~werk nt life's work; l~wert adj worth living; l~wichtig adj vital; ~wille m will to live; ~zeichen nt sign of life; kein ~zeichen mehr von sich geben to show no sign(s) of life; ~zeit f life(time); auf ~zeit for life; Beamter auf ~zeit permanent civil servant; ~ziel nt aim in life.

Leber f -n liver. ich habe es an der ~ (col) I've got liver trouble; frei or frisch von der ~ weg reden (col) to speak frankly.

Leber-: ~entzündung f hepatitis; ~fleck m liver spot; ~käse m no pl ≈ meat loaf; ~knödel m liver dumpling; ~krebs m cancer of the liver; ~leiden nt liver disorder; ~pastete f liver pâté; ~tran m cod-liver oil; ~wurst f liver sausage.

Lebewesen nt living thing. kleinste ~ microorganisms.

Lebewohl nt no pl (liter) farewell (liter).

Leb-: l~haft adj lively no adv; Verkehr brisk; (deutlich) Erinnerung vivid. es geht l~haft zu things are lively; ich kann mir l~haft vorstellen, daß ... I can (very) well imagine that ...; etw in l~er Erinnerung haben to remember sth vividly; ~kuchen m gingerbread; l~los adj Körper lifeless; l~loser Gegenstand inanimate object; ~tag m (col) mein/dein etc ~tag my/your etc life; das werde ich mein ~tag nicht vergessen I'll never forget that as long as I live; ~zeiten pl zu jds ~zeiten (Leben) in sb's lifetime; (Zeit) in sb's day.

lechzen vi (geh) nach etw ~ to thirst for sth.

leck adj leaky. ~ sein to leak; ~ schlagen to hole.

Leck nt -s leak.

lecken¹ vi (undicht sein) to leak.

lecken² vti to lick. an jdm/etw ~ to lick sb/sth.

lecker adj Speisen delicious.

Leckerbissen m (Speise) delicacy; (fig) gem.

Leckerei f delicacy.

Leckermaul nt (col) sweet-toothed child/person etc. ein ~ sein to have a sweet tooth.

led. = ledig.

Leder nt - (a) leather; (Wild~) suede. in ~ gebunden leather-bound; zäh wie ~ as tough as old boots (col). (b) (col: Fußball) ball. am ~ bleiben to stick with the ball.

Leder- in cpds leather; ~hose f leather trousers pl; (von Tracht) leather shorts pl; ~jacke f leather jacket.

ledern adj leather; (zäh) Fleisch leathery.

Leder-: ~**waren** pl leather goods pl; ~**zeug** nt leather gear.
ledig adj **(a)** single; Mutter unmarried. **(b)** (geh: frei) free. **(los und)** ~ **sein** to be footloose and fancy free; **aller Pflichten** (gen) ~ **sein** to be free of all commitments.
lediglich adv merely, simply.
Lee f no pl (Naut) lee.
leer adj empty; Blick blank. **eine** ~**e Stelle an** empty space; **ins L**~**e greifen** toclutch at thin air; **mit** ~**en Händen** (fig) empty-handed; ~ **laufen** (Motor) to idle; **etw** ~ **machen** to empty sth; **den Teller** ~ **essen** to eat everything on the plate; ~ **stehen** to stand empty.
Leere f no pl (lit, fig) emptiness. **(eine) geistige** ~ **a** mental vacuum; **(eine) gähnende** ~ **a gaping void.**
leeren vt to empty.
Leer-: ~**gewicht** nt unladen weight; ~**gut** nt empties pl; ~**lauf** m **(a)** neutral; (von Fahrrad) freewheel; **im** ~**lauf fahren** to coast; **(b)** (fig) slack; l~**laufen** vi sep irreg aux sein (Faß etc) to run dry; l~**laufen lassen** to drain; l~**stehend** adj empty; ~**taste** f space-bar.
Leerung f emptying. **nächste** ~: **18 Uhr** (an Briefkasten) next collection: 6 p.m.
Lefze f **-n** usu pl chaps pl; (von Pferd) lip.
legal adj legal, lawful.
legalisieren* vt to legalize.
Legalität f legality. **(etwas) außerhalb der** ~ (euph) (slightly) outside the law.
Legasthenie f dyslexia.
Legastheniker(in f) m - dyslexic.
Leg(e)henne f nt layer, laying hen.
legen 1 vt **(a)** (hin~) to lay down; (mit adv) to lay; (mit Raumangabe) to put, to place; (Sport sl) to bring down. **etw an die Luft** ~ to put sth out to air; **etw in Essig** etc ~ to preserve sth in vinegar etc. **(b)** (verlegen) Fliesen, Leitungen, Schienen to lay, to put down. **sich** (dat) **die Haare** ~ **lassen** to have one's hair set. **(c)** auch vi Eier to lay. **2** vr **(a)** (hin~) to lie down (auf +acc on). **sich ins Bett** ~ to go to bed; **sich zu jdm** ~ to lie down beside sb; **sich in die Sonne** ~ to lie in the sun. **(b)** (mit Ortsangabe) (nieder~: Nebel, Rauch) to settle (auf+acc on). **sich auf die Seite** ~ to lie on one's side; (Boot) to heel over; **sich in die Kurve** ~ to lean into the corner. **(c)** (nachlassen) to die down; (Rauch, Nebel) to clear.
legendär adj legendary.
Legende f **-n** legend.
leger [leˈʒeːɐ] adj casual, informal.
Legierung f alloy.
Legion f legion.
legislativ adj legislative.
Legislative f legislature, legislative assembly.
Legislaturperiode f parliamentary term.
legitim adj legitimate.
Legitimation f identification; (Berechtigung) authorization; (eines Kindes) legitimation.
legitimieren* **1** vt to legitimize; (berechtigen) to entitle. **2** vr to show (proof of) authorization; (sich ausweisen) to identify oneself.
Legitimität f no pl legitimacy.
Lehm m -e clay; (Dachboden) loam.
Lehm-: ~**boden** m clay soil; ~**hütte** f mud hut.
lehmig adj loamy; (tonartig) clayey.
Lehm-: ~**packung** f mudpack; ~**ziegel** m clay brick.
Lehne f **-n** (Arm~) arm(-rest); (Rücken~) back(-rest).
lehnen 1 vtr to lean (an +acc against). **2** vi to be leaning (an +dat against).
Lehnstuhl m easy-chair.
Lehr-: ~**amt** nt das ~**amt** the teaching profession; ~**auftrag** m (als Sonderlehrer) special teaching post; **einen** ~**auftrag für etw haben** (Univ) to give lectures on sth; ~**beruf** m **(a)** (als Lehrer)

teaching profession; **den** ~**beruf ergreifen** to go into teaching; **(b)** (Beruf mit ~zeit) trade requiring an apprenticeship; ~**brief** m (Zeugnis) apprenticeship certificate; ~**buch** nt textbook.
Lehre f **-n (a)** training; (im Handwerk) apprenticeship. **bei jdm in die** ~ **gehen** to serve one's apprenticeship with sb. **(b)** (von Christus, Marx etc) teachings pl; (von Kant, Freud etc) theory; (von Schall, Leben etc) science. **die christliche** ~ Christian doctrine. **(c)** (Erfahrung) lesson; (einer Geschichte) moral. **seine** ~**(n) aus etw ziehen** to learn a lesson from sth; **laß dir das eine** ~ **sein!** let that be a lesson to you!
lehren vti to teach. **jdn lesen** etc ~ to teach sb to read etc.
Lehrer(in f) m - teacher; (Flug~, Fahr~ etc) instructor/instructress. **er ist** ~ he's a teacher; ~ **für Naturwissenschaften** science teacher.
Lehrer-: ~**ausbildung** f teacher training; ~**kollegium** nt staff; ~**zimmer** nt staff (esp Brit) or teachers' room.
Lehr-: ~**gang** m course (für in); ~**geld** nt ~**geld für etw zahlen müssen** (fig) to pay dearly for sth; **laß dir dein** ~**geld zurückgeben!** (hum col) go to the bottom of the class! (hum col); l~**haft** adj didactic; ~**herr** m master (of an apprentice); ~**jahr** nt year as an apprentice; ~**kraft** f (form) teacher.
Lehrling m trainee; (im Handwerk) apprentice.
Lehrlings|ausbildung f training of trainees/apprentices.
Lehr-: ~**meister** m master; ~**methode** f teaching method; ~**mittel** nt teaching aid; ~**plan** m curriculum; ~**probe** f demonstration lesson, crit (col); ~**programm** nt teaching programme (Brit) or program (US); l~**reich** adj (informativ) instructive; ~**satz** m (Math, Philos) theorem; (Eccl) dogma; ~**stelle** f place; **dort sind noch zwei** ~**stellen frei** there are two vacancies for trainees/apprentices; ~**stuhl** m (Univ) chair (für of); ~**werkstatt** nt training workshop; ~**zeit** f apprenticeship.
Leib m **-er** (Körper) body. **Gefahr für** ~ **und Leben** (geh) danger to life and limb; **mit** ~ **und Seele** heart and soul; **etw am eigenen** ~**(e) spüren** to experience sth for oneself; **kein Hemd mehr am** ~ **haben** to be completely destitute; **sich** (dat) **jdn/etw vom** ~**e halten** to keep sb/sth at bay; **halt ihn mir vom** ~ keep him away from me.
Leib|eigenschaft f serfdom; (fig) bondage.
leiben vi: **wie er leibt und lebt** to a T (col).
Leibes-: ~**erziehung** f physical education; ~**frucht** f (geh) unborn child; ~**kraft** f: **aus** ~**kräften schreien** etc to shout etc with all one's might; ~**übung** f (physical) exercise; ~**übungen** (Schulfach) physical education no pl; ~**visitation** f body check.
Leibgericht nt favourite (Brit) or favorite (US) meal.
leibhaftig adj personified. **die** ~**e Güte** etc goodness etc personified.
leiblich adj Mutter, Vater natural; Kind by birth; Bruder, Schwester full.
Leib-: ~**rente** f life annuity; ~**wächter** m bodyguard; ~**wäsche** f underwear.
Leiche f **-n** corpse. **eine wandelnde** ~ (col) a corpse; **wie eine lebende** ~ **aussehen** to look like death (warmed up col); **er geht über** ~**n** (col) he'd stick at nothing; **nur über meine** ~! (col) over my dead body!
Leichen-: ~**beschauer** m - doctor conducting a post-mortem; l~**blaß** adj deathly pale; ~**halle** f mortuary; ~**hemd** nt shroud; ~**rede** f funeral address; ~**schändung** f desecration of corpses; ~**schau** f post-mortem (examination); ~**schmaus** m funeral meal; ~**tuch** nt shroud; ~**verbrennung** f cremation; ~**wagen** m hearse; ~**zug** m funeral procession.

leicht 1 adj **(a)** light; (aus ~em Material) Kleidung lightweight; (schwach, gering) slight; (Jur) Diebstahl, Vergehen etc minor, petty. ~e Musik/ ~es Essen light music/food; ~ gewürzt lightly seasoned; er hat einen leichten Schlaf he's a light sleeper; ~ bekleidet sein to be scantily clad; ~es Mädchen tart (col); mir ist so ~ ums Herz my heart is so light; nimm das nicht zu ~ don't take it too lightly. **(b)** (ohne Schwierigkeiten, einfach) easy. mit dem werden wir (ein) ~es Spiel haben he'll be no problem; keinen ~en Stand haben to have an easy time (of it) (bei, mit with); nichts ~er als das! nothing (could be) simpler; die Aufgabe ist ~ zu lösen the exercise is easy to do; ~ begreifen to understand quickly; das ist ~er gesagt als getan that's easier said than done.

2 adv **(a)** (schnell, unversehens) easily. er wird ~ böse he gets angry easily; ~ zerbrechlich very fragile; man kann einen Fehler ~ übersehen it's easy to miss a mistake; das ist ~ möglich that's quite possible; das passiert mir so ~ nicht wieder I won't let that happen again in a hurry (col). **(b)** (etwas) das ist ~ übertrieben it's slightly exaggerated.

Leicht-: ~athlet m (track and field) athlete; ~athletik f (track and field) athletics; ~bau(weise f) m lightweight construction; l~bewaffnet adj attr lightly armed; l~fallen vi sep irreg aux sein to be easy (jdm for sb); Sprachen sind mir schon immer l~gefallen I've always found languages easy; l~fertig adj thoughtless; etw l~fertig aufs Spiel setzen to risk sth heedlessly; ~fertigkeit f thoughtlessness; ~gewicht nt (Sport, fig) lightweight; Weltmeister im ~gewicht world lightweight champion; l~gläubig adj credulous; (leicht zu täuschen) gullible; ~gläubigkeit f siehe adj credulity; gullibility.

Leichtigkeit f ease. mit ~ with no trouble.

Leicht-: ~industrie f light industry; l~lebig adj easygoing; l~machen vt sep jdm etw l~machen to make sth easy for sb; es sich (dat) l~machen (nicht gewissenhaft sein) to make things too easy for oneself; ~matrose m ordinary seaman; ~metall nt light metal.

Leichtsinn m thoughtlessness. sträflicher ~ criminal negligence.

leichtsinnig adj thoughtless. ~ mit etw umgehen to be careless with sth.

Leicht-: l~verdaulich adj attr easily digestible; l~verderblich adj attr perishable; l~verletzt adj attr slightly injured; ~verletzte(r) mf decl as adj slightly injured person; l~verständlich adj attr readily understandable.

leid adj pred **(a)** es tut mir ~, daß ich so spät gekommen bin I'm sorry for coming so late; tut mir ~! (I'm) sorry!; er/sie tut mir ~ I'm sorry for him/her; sie kann einem ~ tun you can't help feeling sorry; das wird dir noch ~ tun you'll regret it, you'll be sorry. **(b)** (überdrüssig) jdn/ etw ~ sein to be tired of sb/sth.

Leid nt no pl sorrow no indef art; (Unglück) misfortune; (Böses, Schaden) harm. es soll dir kein ~ geschehen you will come to no harm; jdm sein ~ klagen to tell sb one's troubles.

leiden pret litt, ptp gelitten **1** vt **(a)** Hunger, Schmerz etc to suffer. **(b)** ich kann or mag ihn/es (gut) ~ I like him/it (very much); ich kann ihn/es nicht (gut) ~ I don't like him/it very much; er kann es nicht ~, wenn man ihn kritisiert he can't stand being criticized. **2** vi to suffer (an +dat, unter +dat from).

Leiden nt - **(a)** suffering. **(b)** (Krankheit) complaint.

leidend adj ailing; (col) Miene long-suffering. ~ aussehen to look ill.

Leidenschaft f passion. ich koche mit großer ~

cooking is a great passion of mine.

leidenschaftlich adj passionate. etw ~ gern tun to absolutely love doing sth.

Leidens-: ~genosse m, ~genossin f fellow-sufferer; ~geschichte f tale of woe; die ~geschichte (Christi) (Bibl) Christ's Passion; ~miene f (hum col) (long-)suffering expression.

leider adv unfortunately.

leidig adj attr tiresome.

leidlich 1 adj fair. **2** adv reasonably. wie geht's — danke, ~! how are you? — not too bad, thanks.

Leidtragende(r) mf decl as adj (Benachteiligter) der/die ~ the sufferer.

Leidwesen nt: zu jds ~ (much) to sb's disappointment.

Leier f -n (Mus) lyre; (Dreh~) hurdy-gurdy. es ist immer die gleiche ~ (col) it's always the same old story.

Leierkasten m barrel-organ, hurdy-gurdy.

leiern vti (col) Gedicht to drone.

Leih-: ~bücherei f hire(d) (Brit) or rental (US) car; ~bücherei f lending library.

leihen pret lieh, ptp geliehen vt (ver~) to lend; (ent~) to borrow; (mieten, aus~) to hire (esp Brit), to rent.

Leih-: ~gabe f loan; ~gebühr f hire charge; (für Buch) lending charge; ~haus nt pawnshop; ~mutter f surrogate mother; ~wagen m hire(d) (Brit) or rental (US) car.

Leim m -e glue. jdm auf den ~ gehen to be taken in by sb; aus dem ~ gehen (col: Sache) to fall apart.

leimen vt to glue. jdn ~ (col) to take sb for a ride (col); der Geleimte the mug (col).

Leine f -n cord; (Tau, Zelt~) rope; (Schnur) string; (Angel~, Wäsche~) line; (Hunde~) leash. Hunde bitte an der ~ führen! dogs should be kept on a leash; den Hund an die ~ nehmen to put the dog on a lead; ~ ziehen (col) to clear out (col).

leinen adj siehe Leinen linen; canvas; cloth.

Leinen nt - linen; (grob, segeltuchartig) canvas; (als Bucheinband) cloth.

Leinen- in cpds linen; canvas; cloth; ~band m cloth(-bound) volume; ~tuch nt linen (cloth); (grob) canvas; ~zeug nt linen.

Lein-: ~öl nt linseed oil; ~samen m linseed.

Leinwand f no pl canvas; (Film, für Dias) screen.

leise 1 adj **(a)** quiet; Musik soft; Radio auch low. das Radio ~r stellen to turn the radio down; mit ~r Stimme in a low voice; sprich doch ~r! keep your voice down a bit. **(b)** (gering, schwach) slight, faint; Schlaf, Regen, Berührung light; Wind, Seegang gentle. nicht die ~ste Ahnung haben not to have the slightest (idea).

Leisetreter m - (pej col) pussyfoot(er) (pej col).

Leiste f -n **(a)** (Holz~ etc) strip (of wood/metal etc); (Zier~) trim; (Umrandung) border; (zur Bilderaufhängung) rail. **(b)** (Anat) groin.

leisten vt **(a)** to achieve; Überstunden to do; (Maschine) to manage. etwas ~ (arbeiten) to do something; (Motor etc) to be quite powerful; gute Arbeit ~ to do a good job. **(b)** sich (dat) etw ~ to allow oneself sth; (sich gönnen) to treat oneself to sth; sich (dat) etw ~ können to be able to afford sth; diese Frechheit würde er sich bei mir nicht ~ he wouldn't try that sort of cheek with me; er hat sich tolle Sachen geleistet he got up to the craziest things.

Leisten m - (Schuh~) last. er schlägt alles über einen ~ he doesn't make distinctions.

Leistenbruch m (Med) hernia, rupture.

Leistung f **(a)** performance; (großartige, gute, Sociol) achievement; (Ergebnis) result(s); (geleistete Arbeit) work no pl; (Produktion: von Fabrik) output. das ist eine ~! that's quite an achievement; das ist keine besondere ~ that's nothing special; nach ~ bezahlt werden to be paid on results; seine schulischen ~en haben nachge-

lassen his school work has deteriorated. **(b)** (~*sfähigkeit*) capacity; (*eines Motors*) power. **(c)** (*von Krankenkasse etc*) benefit; (*Zahlung*) payment.

Leistungs-: ~**abfall** m (*in bezug auf Qualität*) drop in performance; (*in bezug auf Quantität*) drop in productivity; ~**druck** m pressure (to do well); l~**fähig** adj efficient; *Motor* powerful; ~**fähigkeit** f efficiency; (*von Motor*) power; l~**fördernd** adj conducive to efficiency; (*in Schule, Universität etc*) conducive to learning; ~**gesellschaft** f meritocracy; ~**klasse** f (*Sport*) class; ~**kontrolle** f (*Sch, Univ*) assessment; (*in der Fabrik*) productivity check; ~**kraft** f power; ~**kurs** m (*Sch*) set; ~**kurve** f productivity curve; ~**prämie** f productivity bonus; ~**prinzip** nt achievement principle; ~**sport** m competitive sport; ~**zulage** f productivity bonus.

Leit-: ~**artikel** m leader; ~**bild** nt model.
leiten 1 vt **(a)** to lead; *Verkehr* to route; *Gas, Wasser, (Phys)* to conduct. **etw an die zuständige Stelle** ~ to pass sth on to the proper authority; **sich von jdm/etw** ~ **lassen** (*lit, fig*) to (let oneself) be guided by sb/sth. **(b)** (*verantwortlich sein für*) to be in charge of; *Orchester, Theatergruppe etc* to direct; *Expedition, Sitzung, Verhandlungen* to lead; (*als Vorsitzender*) to chair. **2** vi (*Phys*) to conduct. **gut** ~ to be a good conductor.
leitend adj leading; *Gedanke, Idee* dominant; *Stellung, Position* managerial; *Ingenieur, Beamter* in charge; (*Phys*) conductive. **nicht** ~ (*Phys*) nonconductive; ~**e(r) Angestellte(r)** executive.
Leiter f -n (*lit, fig*) ladder; (*Steh*~) stepladder.
Leiter(in f) m - **(a)** leader; (*von Hotel, Geschäft*) manager; (*Abteilungs*~) head; (*von Chor, Theatergruppe etc*) director. **kaufmännischer** ~ sales director. **(b)** (*Phys*) conductor.
Leit-: ~**faden** m (*Fachbuch*) introduction; ~**gedanke** m central idea; ~**hammel** m bellwether; (*fig col*) leader; ~**linie** f (*fig*) broad outline; (*Bestimmung*) guideline; ~**motiv** m (*Mus, Liter, fig*) leitmotif; ~**planke** f crash-barrier; ~**satz** m basic principle; ~**spruch** m motto; ~**stelle** f regional headquarters pl.
Leitung f **(a)** no pl siehe vt (a) leading; routing; conducting. **(b)** no pl (*von Organisationen etc*) running; (*von Orchester etc*) direction; (*von Expedition*) leadership. **die** ~ **einer Abteilung haben** to be in charge of a department; **die** ~ **des Gesprächs hat Horst Bauer** Horst Bauer is leading or (*als Vorsitzender*) chairing the discussion. **(c)** (*die Leitenden*) leaders pl; (*eines Betriebes etc*) management sing or pl; (*einer Schule*) head teachers pl. **(d)** (*für Gas, Wasser*) main; (*im Haus*) pipe; (*Elec*) wire; (*im Haus*) wire; (*dicker*) cable; (*Überlandleitung*) line; (*Telefon*~) (*Draht*) wire; (*Verbindung*) line. **da ist jemand in der** ~ (*col*) there's somebody else on the line; **eine lange** ~ **haben** (*hum col*) to be slow on the uptake.
Leitungs-: ~**draht** m wire; ~**mast** m (*Elec*) (electricity) pylon; ~**rohr** nt main; (*im Haus*) (supply) pipe; ~**wasser** nt tapwater.
Leit-: ~**werk** nt (*Aviat*) tail unit; ~**wort** nt motto.
Lektion f lesson. **jdm eine** ~ **erteilen** (*fig*) to teach sb a lesson.
Lektor m, **Lektorin** f (*Univ*) foreign language assistant; (*Verlags*~) editor.
Lektorat nt (*im Verlag*) editorial office.
Lektüre f -n (*no pl: das Lesen*) reading; (*Lesestoff*) reading matter. **das wird zur** ~ **empfohlen** that is recommended reading; **das ist eine gute** etc ~ it makes good etc reading.
Lemming m lemming.
Lende f -n (*Anat, Cook*) loin.
Lenden-: ~**schurz** m loincloth; ~**stück** nt piece of loin.
Leninismus m Leninism.
lenkbar adj (*Tech*) steerable; *Kind* tractable;

Rakete guided. **leicht/schwer** ~ **sein** to be easy/difficult to steer.
lenken vt **(a)** (*steuern*) to steer; (*führen, leiten*) to guide. **gelenkte Wirtschaft** planned economy. **(b)** (*fig*) *Schritte, Gedanken, Aufmerksamkeit, Blick* to direct (*auf* +acc to); *Verdacht* to throw (*auf* +acc onto); *Gespräch* to lead; *Schicksal* to guide.
Lenker m - **(a)** (*Fahrrad*~ etc) handlebars pl. **(b)** (*Tech, fig*) guide.
Lenk-: ~**rad** nt (steering) wheel; ~**stange** f (*von Fahrrad etc*) handlebars pl.
Lenkung f **(a)** siehe vt steering; guidance; (*fig*) direction. **(b)** (*Tech: Lenkeinrichtung*) steering.
Lenz m -e (*liter: Frühling*) spring(time). **einen** ~ **schieben** (*col*), **sich** (*dat*) **einen** (*faulen*) ~ **machen** (*col*) to laze about, to swing the lead (*col*).
Leopard m (*wk*) -en, -en leopard.
Lepra f no pl leprosy.
Lerche f -n lark.
Lern-: l~**bar** adj learnable; l~**behindert** adj educationally handicapped; ~**eifer** m eagerness to learn; l~**eifrig** adj eager to learn.
lernen 1 vt to learn; *Bäcker, Schlosser etc* to train as. **lesen** etc ~ to learn to read etc; **Schreibmaschine** ~ to learn typing; **etw von/bei jdm** ~ to learn sth from sb; **er lernt's nie** he never learns. **2** vi to learn; (*arbeiten*) to study; (*als Berufsausbildung*) to train. **lerne fleißig in der Schule** work hard at school; **von ihm kannst du noch** ~! you could learn a thing or two from him; **er lernt bei der Firma Braun** he's training at Braun's.
Lern-: ~**hilfe** f educational aid; ~**mittel** pl schoolbooks and equipment pl: ~**schwester** f student nurse.
Les-: ~**art** f (*lit, fig*) version; l~**bar** adj legible; *Buch* readable.
Lesbierin ['lesbiərɪn] f lesbian.
lesbisch adj lesbian.
Lese f -n (*Wein*~) vintage.
Lese-: ~**brille** f reading glasses pl; ~**buch** nt reader; ~**lampe** f reading lamp.
lesen[1] pret **las**, ptp **gelesen** 1 vti **(a)** to read; (*Eccl*) *Messe* to say. **(b)** (*deuten*) *Gedanken* to read. **jdm** (**sein Schicksal**) **aus der Hand** ~ to read sb's palm. **2** vi (*Univ*) to lecture (*über* +acc on).
lesen[2] pret **las**, ptp **gelesen** vt **(a)** (*sammeln*) *Trauben, Beeren* to pick. **(b)** (*ver*~) *Erbsen, Linsen etc* to sort; *Salat* to clean.
lesenswert adj worth reading.
Lese-: ~**probe** f **(a)** (*Theat*) reading; **(b)** (*Ausschnitt aus Buch*) excerpt; ~**pult** nt lectern.
Leser(in f) m - reader.
Leseratte f (*col*) bookworm (*col*).
Leser-: ~**brief** m (*reader's*) letter; „~**briefe**" "letters to the editor"; ~**kreis** m readership; l~**lich** adj legible; ~**schaft** f readership.
Lese-: ~**saal** m reading room; ~**stoff** m reading material; ~**zeichen** nt bookmark(er); ~**zirkel** m magazine subscription club.
Lesung f (*auch Parl*) reading.
Lethargie f (*Med, fig*) lethargy.
lethargisch adj (*Med, fig*) lethargic.
Lettland nt Latvia.
Letzt f: **zu guter** ~ finally, in the end.
letzte(r, s) adj **(a)** (*örtlich, zeitlich*) last; (*restlich*) last (remaining). ~(**r**) **werden** to be last; **als** ~(**r**) **(an)kommen** to be the last to arrive, to arrive last; **auf dem** ~**n Platz liegen** to be last; **den** ~**n beißen die Hunde** (*Prov*) (the) devil take the hindmost (*prov*); **er wäre der** ~, **den ich ... ein** would be the last person I'd ...; **mein** ~**s Geld** the last of my money; **in** ~**r Zeit** recently; **zum** ~**n Mittel greifen** to resort to drastic methods; **der** **L**~ **Wille** the last will and testament; **zum** ~**en Mal** for the last time; **bis ins** ~ (right) down to

the last detail; **bis zum ~n** to the utmost. **(b)** *(neueste) Mode, Nachricht, Neuigkeit etc* latest. **(c)** *(schlechtester)* most terrible. **das ist der ~ Dreck** that's absolute trash; **jdn wie den ~n Dreck behandeln** to treat sb like dirt.

Letzte(r) *mf decl as adj* last; *(dem Rang nach)* lowest. **der ~ des Monats** the last (day) of the month; **der/die ~ in der Klasse sein** to be bottom of the class.

letztere(r, s) *adj* the latter.

Letzte(s) *nt decl as adj* last thing. **sein ~s geben to** do one's utmost; **das ist ja das ~!** *(col)* that really is the limit.

letzt-: **~lich** *adv* in the end; **~möglich** *adj attr* last possible.

Leuchte *f* **-n** light; *(col: Mensch)* genius.

leuchten *vi* **(a)** to shine; *(Feuer, Zifferblatt)* to glow; *(auf~)* to flash. **(b)** *(Mensch)* **mit einer Lampe in/auf etw** *(acc)* **~** to shine a lamp into/onto sth; **leuchte mal hierher!** shine some light over here.

leuchtend *adj* *(lit, fig)* shining; *Farbe* bright. **etw in den ~sten Farben schildern** to paint sth in glowing colours *(Brit)* or colors *(US)*.

Leuchter *m* - *(Kerzen~)* candlestick; *(Kron~)* chandelier.

Leucht-: **~farbe** *f* fluorescent paint/ink *etc*; **~feuer** *nt* navigational light; **~gas** *nt* town gas; **~geschoß** *nt* flare; **~käfer** *m* glow-worm; **~patrone** *f* flare; **~pistole** *f* flare pistol; **~rakete** *f* signal rocket; **~reklame** *f* neon sign; **~röhre** *f* fluorescent tube; **~schrift** *f* neon writing; **eine ~schrift** a neon sign; **~turm** *m* lighthouse.

leugnen **1** *vt* to deny. **~, etw getan zu haben to** deny having done sth; **es ist nicht zu ~, daß ... it** cannot be denied that ... **2** *vi* to deny everything.

Leukämie *f* leukaemia *(Brit)*, leukemia *(US)*.

Leukoplast ® *nt* **-e** sticking plaster, elastoplast ® *(Brit)*, Bandaid ® *(US)*.

Leumund *m no pl* reputation, name.

Leute *pl* **(a)** people *pl*. **alle ~** everybody; **kleine ~** *(fig)* ordinary people; **es ist nicht wie bei armen ~n** *(hum col)* we're not on the breadline yet *(hum col)*; **etw unter die ~ bringen** *(col)* Gerücht *etc* to spread sth around; **unter die ~ kommen** *(col) (Mensch)* to meet people; *(Gerüchte etc)* to go around. **(b)** *(Mannschaft, Arbeiter etc)* **der Offizier ließ seine ~ antreten** the officer ordered his men to fall in; **dafür brauchen wir mehr ~** we need more people/staff *etc* for that.

Leutnant *m* **-s** *or* **-e** (second) lieutenant. **~ zur See** sublieutenant *(Brit)*, lieutenant junior grade *(US)*.

leutselig *adj* *(umgänglich)* affable.

Leutseligkeit *f* affability.

Leviten [le'vi:tən] *pl*: **jdm die ~ lesen** *(col)* to haul sb over the coals *(col)*.

Lexikon *nt*, *pl* **Lexika** encyclopedia; *(Wörterbuch)* dictionary.

Liane *f* **-n** liana.

Libanese *m (wk)* **-n, -n, Libanesin** *f* Lebanese.

Libanon *m* **-(s) der ~** *(Land)* the Lebanon.

Libelle *f* *(Zool)* dragonfly.

liberal *adj* liberal.

Liberale(r) *mf decl as adj (Pol)* Liberal.

liberalisieren* *vt* to liberalize.

Liberalisierung *f* liberalization.

Liberalismus *m* liberalism.

Libero *m* **-s** *(Ftbl)* sweeper.

Libretto *nt* **-s** *or* **Libretti** libretto.

Libyen ['ly:biən] *nt* **-s** Libya.

Libyer(in *f)* ['ly:biɐ, -ərɪn] *m* - Libyan.

libysch ['ly:bɪʃ] *adj* Libyan.

Licht *nt* **-er** **(a)** light. **~ machen** *(anschalten)* to turn on the lights; *(anzünden)* to light a candle *etc*; **etw gegen das ~ halten** to hold sth up to the light; **gegen das ~ photographieren** to take a photograph into the light; **bei ~e besehen** *(fig)* in

the cold light of day; **jdm im ~ stehen** *(lit)* to stand in sb's light; **das ~ der Welt erblicken** *(geh)* to see the light of day. **(b)** *(fig)* light; *(Könner)* genius. **~ in eine (dunkle) Sache bringen** to shed some light on a matter; **etw ans ~ bringen** to bring sth out into the open; **ans ~ kommen** to come to light; **jdn hinters ~ führen** to lead sb up the garden path; **mir geht ein ~ auf** it's dawned on me; **kein gutes ~ auf jdn/etw werfen** to show sb/sth in a bad light; **etw ins rechte ~ rücken** to show sth in its true light.

licht *adj* **(a)** *(hell)* light. **(b)** *Wald* sparse.

Licht-: **~anlage** *f* lights *pl*; **l~beständig** *adj* Farben, Stoff non-fade; **~bild** *nt* photograph; *(Dia)* slide; **~bildervortrag** *m* illustrated, talk; **~blick** *m* *(fig)* ray of hope; **l~durchlässig** *adj* pervious to light; *(durchsichtig)* transparent; *(durchscheinend)* translucent; **l~echt** *adj* non-fade; **l~empfindlich** *adj* sensitive to light; **~empfindlichkeit** *f* sensitivity to light.

lichten[1] **1** *vt* Wald to thin (out). **2** *vr (Reihen, Wald, Haare)* to thin (out); *(Nebel)* to clear.

lichten[2] *vt* Anker to weigh.

Lichter-: **l~loh** *adv* **l~loh brennen** *(lit)* to be ablaze; *(fig: Herz)* to be aflame; **~meer** *nt* *(liter)* sea of light.

Licht-: **~geschwindigkeit** *f* speed of light; **~hupe** *f* *(Aut)* flash (of the headlights); **die ~hupe benutzen** to flash one's lights; **~jahr** *nt* light year; **~kegel** *m* *(Phys)* cone of light; *(von Scheinwerfer)* beam (of light); **~leitung** *f* lighting wire; **l~los** *adj* dark; **~maschine** *f* dynamo; *(für Drehstrom)* alternator; **~mast** lamppost; **~pause** *f* photocopy; *(bei Blaupausverfahren)* blueprint; **~punkt** *m* point of light; **~quelle** *f* source of light; **~schacht** *m* air shaft; **~schalter** *m* light switch; **~schein** *m* gleam of light; **l~scheu** *adj* averse to light; *(fig)* Gesindel shady; **~schranke** *f* light barrier; **~signal** *nt* light signal; **~spielhaus** *nt* cinema; **~strahl** *m* beam of light; **l~undurch lässig** *adj* opaque.

Lichtung *f* clearing, glade.

Lichtverhältnisse *pl* lighting conditions *pl*.

Lid *nt* **-er** eyelid.

Lidschatten *m* eye-shadow.

lieb *adj* **(a)** kind; *(nett)* nice; *(artig)* Kind good; Gast pleasant. **(viele) ~e Grüße** Deine Silvia love Silvia; **sich ~ um jdn kümmern** to be very kind to sb; **würdest du (bitte) so ~ sein und das Fenster aufmachen** would you be so kind as to open the window; **sich bei jdm ~ Kind machen** *(pej)* to suck up to sb. **(b)** *(angenehm)* **es wäre mir ~, wenn ...** I'd be glad if ...; **es wäre ihm ~er he** would prefer it; **am ~sten hätte ich ... what I'd** like most would be (to have) ...; **am ~sten lese ich Kriminalromane** best of all I like detective novels; **am ~sten hätte ich ihm eine geklebt!** *(col)* I could have stuck one on him *(col)*. **(c)** *(in Anrede)* dear. **~ste (r, s)** favourite *(Brit)*, favorite *(US)*; **der ~e Gott** the Good Lord; **~er Gott** *(Anrede)* dear God; **L~e Anna, ~er Klaus! ...** Dear Anna and Klaus, ...; **den ~en langen Tag** *(col)* the whole livelong day; **(ach) du ~er Himmel/~er Gott/~e Zeit** good heavens *or* Lord!

Liebe *f no pl* love *(zu jdm, für jdn* for *or* of sb, zu etw of sth)*. **die große ~** the love of one's life; **aus ~ zu jdm/einer Sache** for the love of sb/sth; **etw mit viel ~ tun** to do sth with loving care; **in ~ with love; sie/er ist gut in der ~** *(col)* she/he is good at making love.

liebebedürftig *adj* **~ sein** to need a lot of affection.

Liebelei *f (col)* flirtation; affair.

lieben *vti* to love; *(als Liebesakt)* to make love *(jdn to sb)*. **etw nicht ~** not to like sth; **etw ~d gern tun** to love to do sth.

Liebende(r) *mf decl as adj* lover.

liebenswert *adj* lovable, endearing.

liebenswürdig *adj* kind. **würden Sie so ~ sein und die Tür schließen?** would you be so kind as to shut the door?

liebenswürdigerweise *adv* kindly.

Liebenswürdigkeit *f (Höflichkeit)* politeness; *(Freundlichkeit)* kindness.

lieber 1 *adj comp of* **lieb. 2** *adv comp of* **gern (a)** *(vorzugsweise)* rather. **das tue ich ~** *(im Augenblick)* I'd rather do that; *(grundsätzlich)* I prefer doing that; **das würde ich ~ tun** I would prefer to do that; **ich trinke ~ Wein als Bier** I prefer wine to beer; **(das möchte ich) ~ nicht!** I'd rather not. **(b)** *(besser)* better. **bleibe ~ im Bett** you'd better stay in bed; **ich hätte ~ nachgeben sollen** I'd have done better to have given in; **nichts ~ als das** there's nothing I'd rather do/have.

Liebes- *in cpds* love; **~abenteuer** *nt* amorous adventure; **~affäre** *f* (love-)affair; **~akt** *m* sex act; **~beziehung** *f* romantic attachment; (sexual) relationship; **~brief** *m* love letter; **~erklärung** *f* declaration of love; **~geschichte** *f* (a) *(Liter)* love story; **(b)** *(col: Liebschaft)* love-affair; **~heirat** *f* love-match; **~kummer** *m* lovesickness; **~kummer haben** to be lovesick; **~leben** *nt* love-life; **~lied** *nt* love song; **~müh(e)** *f:* **das ist vergebliche ~müh(e)** that is futile; **~paar** *nt* lovers *pl*; **~roman** *m* romantic novel; **~spiel** *nt* loveplay; **~szene** *f* love scene; **~verhältnis** *nt* (sexual) relationship.

liebevoll *adj* loving.

lieb-: **~gewinnen*** *vt sep irreg* to grow fond of; **~geworden** *adj attr* well-loved; *Brauch* favourite *(Brit)*, favorite *(US)*; **~haben*** *vt sep irreg* to love; *(weniger stark)* to be (very) fond of.

Liebhaber(in *f)* *m* **- (a)** lover. **(b)** *(Interessent)* enthusiast; *(Sammler)* collector.

Liebhaberei *f (fig)* hobby. **etw aus ~ tun** to do sth as a hobby.

Liebhaberpreis *m* collector's price.

lieblich *adj* delightful; *Duft, Wein* sweet.

Liebling *m* darling; *(bevorzugter Mensch)* favourite *(Brit)*, favorite *(US)*.

Lieblings- *in cpds* favourite *(Brit)*, favorite *(US)*.

Lieb-: **l~los** *adj* unloving; *Bemerkung* unkind; *Benehmen* inconsiderate; **~schaft** *f* affair.

Liebste(r) *mf decl as adj* sweetheart.

Lied *nt* **-er** song; *(Kirchen~)* hymn. **das Ende vom ~** *(fig col)* the outcome (of all this); **davon kann ich ein ~ singen** I could tell you a thing or two about that *(col)*.

liederlich *adj (schlampig)* slovenly *attr, pred; (unmoralisch)* Leben, Mann dissolute; *Frau, Mädchen* loose. **ein ~es Frauenzimmer** *(pej)* a slut.

lief *pret of* **laufen.**

Lieferant *m* supplier; *(Auslieferer)* deliveryman.

Lieferanten|eingang *m* tradesmen's entrance; *(von Warenhaus etc)* goods entrance.

Liefer-: **l~bar** *adj (vorrätig)* available; **die Ware ist sofort l~bar** the article can be delivered at once; **~firma** *f* supplier; *(Zusteller)* delivery firm; **~frist** *f* delivery period; **die ~frist einhalten** to meet the delivery date.

liefern *vti* to supply; *Beweise, Informationen auch* to furnish; *Ertrag* to yield; *(col: stellen)* to provide; *(zustellen)* to deliver (*in +acc* to). **jdm etw ~** to supply sb with sth/provide sb with sth/deliver sth to sb; **wir ~ nicht ins Ausland** we don't supply the foreign market; *siehe* **geliefert.**

Liefer-: **~schein** *m* delivery note; **~termin** *m* delivery date.

Lieferung *f* delivery; *(Versorgung)* supply. **bei ~ zu bezahlen** payable on delivery.

Liefer-: **~vertrag** *m* supply/delivery contract; **~wagen** *m* van, panel truck *(US); (offen)* pick-up; **~zeit** *f* delivery period; **~zettel** *m* delivery order.

Liege *f* **-n** couch; *(Camping~)* camp bed *(Brit)*, cot *(US)*.

liegen *pret* **lag,** *ptp* **gelegen** *vi* **(a)** to lie. **hart/ weich ~** to lie on a hard/soft bed *etc;* **unbequem ~** to lie uncomfortably; **auf den Knien ~** to be kneeling; **im Krankenhaus ~** to be in hospital; **der Kranke muß unbedingt ~** the patient must stay lying down; **der Schnee liegt 50 cm hoch** the snow is 50 cm deep; **der Schnee bleibt nicht ~** the snow isn't lying; **etw ~ lassen** to leave sth.

(b) *(sich befinden, sein)* to be; *(Haus, Stadt etc auch)* to be situated, to lie. **Paris liegt an der Seine** Paris is (situated) on the Seine; **nach Süden/ der Straße ~** to face south/the road; **verstreut ~** to lie scattered; **das Haus liegt ganz ruhig** the house is in a very quiet location; **das liegt doch auf dem Weg/ganz in der Nähe** it's on the way; **das Schiff liegt am Kai** the ship is (tied up) alongside the quay; **die Betonung liegt auf der zweiten Silbe** the stress is on the second syllable; **so, wie die Dinge jetzt ~** as things stand at the moment; **damit liegst du (gold)richtig** *(col)* you're right there; **an der Spitze ~** to be right out in front; **der zweite Läufer liegt weit hinter dem ersten** the second runner is lying a long way behind the first; **die Preise ~ zwischen 60 und 80 Mark** the prices are between 60 and 80 marks.

(c) *(wichtig sein)* **es liegt mir wenig daran** that isn't very important to me; **mir liegt an guten Beziehungen** I am concerned that there should be good relations.

(d) *(begründet sein)* **an jdm/etw ~** to be because of sb/sth; **woran liegt es?** why is that?; **das liegt daran, daß ...** that is because ...; **an mir soll es nicht ~, wenn die Sache schiefgeht** it won't be my fault if things go wrong; **das liegt ganz bei dir** that is entirely up to you; **die Entscheidung liegt bei Ihnen** the decision rests with you.

(e) *(geeignet sein, passen)* **jdm liegt etw nicht** sth doesn't suit sb; *(Mathematik etc)* sb has no aptitude for sth; **Krankenschwester liegt mir nicht** *(col)* nursing doesn't appeal to me.

liegenbleiben *vi sep irreg aux sein* **(a)** *(nicht aufstehen)* to remain lying down; **(im Bett) ~** to stay in bed; **bleib liegen!** don't get up! **(b)** *(vergessen werden)* to get left behind; *(nicht verkauft werden)* to be left unsold; *(nicht ausgeführt werden)* to be left (undone).

liegend *adj (Art)* reclining. **~ aufbewahren** to store flat.

liegenlassen *vt sep irreg, ptp ~ or* **liegengelassen** *(nicht erledigen)* to leave; *(vergessen)* to leave (behind); *(herum~)* to leave lying about.

Liege-: **~platz** *m* place to lie; *(Ankerplatz)* moorings *pl;* **~sitz** *m* reclining seat; *(auf Boot)* couchette; **~stuhl** *m* (mit Holzgestell) deck chair; *(mit Metallgestell)* lounger; **~stütz** *m (Sport)* press-up; **~wagen** *m (Rail)* couchette coach *or* car *(esp US);* **~wiese** *f* lawn *(for sunbathing)*.

lieh *pret of* **leihen.**

ließ *pret of* **lassen.**

Lift *m* **-e** *or* **-s** *(Personen~)* lift *(Brit)*, elevator *(esp US)*.

Liga *f*, *pl* **Ligen** league.

liieren* *vt* to bring *or* get together. **liiert sein** to have joined forces; *(Firmen etc)* to be working together; *(Pol)* to be allied; *(ein Verhältnis haben)* to have a relationship.

Likör *m* **-e** liqueur.

lila *adj inv* purple.

Lilie [-iə] *f* lily.

Liliputaner(in *f)* *m* **-** midget.

Limit *nt* **-s** limit; *(Fin)* ceiling.

limitieren* *vt (form)* to limit; *(Fin)* to put a ceiling on.

Limonade *f* lemonade.

Limone *f* **-n** lime.

Limousine [limu'ziːnə] *f* saloon *(Brit)*, sedan *(US)*.

Linde *f* **-n** linden *or* lime (tree).

Lindenblütentee *m* lime blossom tea.
lindern *vt* to ease, to relieve.
Linderung *f* easing, relief.
Lineal *nt* -e ruler.
linear *adj* linear.
Linguistik *f* linguistics *sing*.
linguistisch *adj* linguistic.
Linie [-iə] *f* (a) line. ein Schreibblock mit ~n a ruled notepad; in einer ~ stehen to be in a line; sich in einer ~ aufstellen to line up; einer Sache *(dat)* fehlt die klare ~ there's no clear line to sth; eine ~ ziehen zwischen ... *(+dat)* *(fig)* to draw a line between ...; auf der ganzen ~ *(fig)* all along the line; auf die ~ achten to watch one's figure; in erster ~ first and foremost. (b) *(Verkehrsverbindung)* route. fahren Sie mit der ~ 2 take a *or* the 2; die ~ Köln-Bonn the Cologne-Bonn line.
Linien- [-iən]: ~bus *m* regular bus; ~flug *m* scheduled flight; ~papier *nt* lined paper; ~richter *m (Sport)* linesman; ~schiff *nt* regular service ship; l~treu *adj* loyal to the party line; l~treu sein to toe the party line; ~verkehr *m* regular traffic; *(Aviat)* scheduled traffic; im ~verkehr fahren to operate on regular services.
linieren* *vt* to rule, to draw lines on. liniert lined.
Linke *f (wk)* -n, -n (a) *(Hand)* left hand; *(Seite)* left side; *(Boxen)* left. zu seiner ~n to his left. (b) *(Pol)* Left.
Linke(r) *mf decl as adj (Pol)* left-winger, leftist *(pej)*.
linke(r, s) *adj attr* (a) left. die ~ Seite the left(-hand) side; *(von Stoff)* the wrong side; das mache ich mit der ~n Hand *(col)* I can do that with my eyes shut *(col)*; er ist heute mit dem ~n Bein zuerst aufgestanden *(col)* he got out of bed on the wrong side this morning *(col)*; ein ganz ~r Hund *(pej col)* a nasty piece of work *(pej col)*; ein ganz ~s Ding drehen *(col)* to get up to a bit of no good *(col)*. (b) *(Pol)* left-wing; *Flügel* left.
linkisch *adj* clumsy, awkward.
links 1 *adv* (a) on the left; *schauen, abbiegen* left. nach ~ (to the) left; von ~ from the left; ~ von etw left of sth; sich ~ halten to keep to the left; weiter ~ further to the left; sich ~ einordnen to move into the left-hand lane; jdn ~ liegenlassen *(fig col)* to ignore sb; das mache ich mit ~ *(col)* I can do that with my eyes shut *(col)*. (b) *(Pol)* on the left. nach ~ to the left; ~ von jdm left of sb; ~ von der Mitte left of centre; ~ stehen *(col)* to be left-wing. (c) *(verkehrt)* bügeln on the reverse; *tragen* inside out; ~ stricken to purl. 2 *prep +gen* on *or* to the left of.
Links-: ~abbieger *m* motorist/vehicle turning left; ~außen *m - (Ftbl)* outside left; *(Pol)* extreme left-winger; ~drall *m (von Billardball)* spin to the left; *(von Auto, Pferd)* pull to the left; *(Pol col)* leaning to the left; ~extremist *m* left-wing extremist; l~gerichtet *adj (Pol)* left-wing *no adv*; ~händer(in *f)* *m* - left-hander; ~händer sein to be left-handed; l~herum *adv* (around) to the left; ~kurve *f (von Straße)* left-hand bend; l~lastig *adj* listing to the left; *(fig)* leftist *(pej)*, leaning to the left; l~lastig sein to list/lean to the left; l~radikal *adj (Pol)* radically left-wing; die ~radikalen the left-wing radicals; ~radikalismus *m (Pol)* left-wing radicalism; l~rheinisch *adj* to *or* on the left of the Rhine; ~rutsch *m (Pol)* swing to the left; l~seitig *adj* on the left(-hand) side; l~seitig gelähmt paralyzed in the left side; ~verkehr *m no pl* driving on the left *no def art*; in Großbritannien ist ~verkehr they drive on the left in Britain.
Linoleum [li'no:leʊm] *nt no pl* linoleum, lino *(Brit)*.
Linse *f* -n (a) *(Bot, Cook)* lentil. (b) *(Opt)* lens.
linsen *vi (col)* to peek *(col)*.
Lippe *f* -n lip. es soll kein Wort über meine ~n kommen not a word shall pass my lips; er brach-

te kein Wort über die ~n he couldn't say *or* utter a word.
Lippen-: ~bekenntnis *nt* lip-service; ~stift *m* lipstick.
Liquidation *f (form)* liquidation. in ~ treten to go into liquidation.
liquid(e) *adj (Econ)* Firma solvent.
liquidieren* *vt* (a) jdn to liquidate. (b) *Geschäft* to wind up.
Liquidität *f (Econ)* liquidity.
lispeln *vti* to lisp.
List *f* -en *(Täuschung)* cunning; *(Plan)* trick. mit ~ und Tücke *(col)* with a lot of coaxing.
Liste *f* -n *(Aufstellung)* list; *(Wähler~)* register. sich in eine ~ eintragen to put one's name on a list.
Listen-: ~platz *m (Pol)* place on the party list; ~preis *m* list price.
listig *adj* cunning, wily *no adv*.
Litanei *f (Eccl, fig)* litany. eine ~ von Klagen a long list of complaints.
Litauen *nt* -s Lithuania.
litauisch *adj* Lithuanian.
Liter *m or nt* - litre *(Brit)*, liter *(US)*.
literarisch *adj* literary.
Literatur *f* literature.
Literatur-: ~angabe *f* bibliographical reference; ~gattung *f* literary genre; ~geschichte *f* history of literature; ~kritiker *m* literary critic; ~verzeichnis *nt* bibliography; ~wissenschaft *f* literary studies *pl*.
literweise *adv (lit)* by the litre *(Brit)* or liter *(US)*; *(fig)* by the gallon.
Litfaßsäule *f* advertising column.
Litho-: ~graph *m* lithographer; ~graphie *f* (a) *(Verfahren)* lithography; (b) *(Druck)* lithograph.
litt *ptp of* **leiden**.
Liturgie *f* liturgy.
Litze *f* -n braid; *(Elec)* flex.
live [laif] *adj pred, adv (Rad, TV)* live.
Live-Sendung [laif-] *f* live broadcast.
Lizenz *f* licence *(Brit)*, license *(US)*. etw in ~ herstellen to manufacture sth under licence.
Lizenz-: ~ausgabe *f* licensed edition; ~geber *m* licenser; *(Behörde)* licensing authority; ~gebühr *f* licence fee *(Brit)*, license fee *(US)*; ~inhaber *m* licensee; er ist ~inhaber he has a licence *(Brit)* or license *(US)*; ~spieler *m (Ftbl)* professional player.
Lkw [ɛlka:'ve:] *m* -(s) = **Lastkraftwagen**.
Lob *nt no pl* praise. (viel) ~ für etw bekommen to come in for a (lot of) praise for sth; jdm ~ spenden *or* zollen to praise sb.
loben *vt* to praise. jdn/etw ~d erwähnen to commend sb/sth; das lob ich mir that's what I like (to see/hear *etc*).
lobenswert *adj* laudable.
Lob-: ~hudelei *f (pej)* gushing; ~lied *nt* song of praise; ein ~lied auf jdn/etw anstimmen *(fig)* to sing sb's praises; ~rede *f* eulogy; eine ~rede auf jdn halten *(lit)* to make a speech in sb's honour *(Brit)* or honor *(US)*; *(fig)* to eulogize sb.
Loch *nt* ~er hole; *(Luft~)* gap; *(fig col: elende Wohnung)* dump *(col)*, hole *(col)*. sich *(dat)* ein ~ in den Kopf schlagen to gash one's head; ~er in die Luft gucken to gaze into space; ein großes ~ in jds Geldbeutel *(acc)* reißen *(col)* to make a big hole in sb's pocket.
lochen *vt* to punch holes/a hole in; *Fahrkarte* to punch.
Locher *m* - (a) punch. (b) *(Mensch)* punch-card operator.
löcherig *adj* full of holes.
Loch-: ~karte *f* punch card; ~streifen *m* (punched) paper tape.
Lochung *f* punching; *(Stelle)* perforation.
Lochzange *f* punch.
Locke *f* -n *(Haar)* curl. ~n haben to have curly

hair.

locken[1] *vtr Haar* to curl. **gelocktes Haar** curly hair.

locken[2] *vt* to lure. **jdn in einen Hinterhalt** ~ to lure sb into a trap; **die Henne lockte ihre Küken** the hen called to its chicks.

lockend *adj* tempting.

Locken-: ~**kopf** *m* curly hairstyle; *(Mensch)* curlyhead; ~**wickler** *m* - (hair-)curler.

locker *adj (lit, fig)* loose; *Kuchen, Schaum* light; *(nicht gespannt)* slack; *Haltung, Sitzweise* relaxed; *(col)* cool *(col)*. ~ **werden** *(lit, fig)* to get loose; *(Muskeln, Mensch)* to loosen up; **etw** ~ **machen** to loosen sth/make sth light/slacken sth; **etw** ~ **lassen** to slacken sth off; *Bremse* to let sth off; ~ **sitzen** *(Ziegel, Schraube etc)* to be loose; **bei ihr sitzt die Hand ziemlich** ~ she's quick to lash out; **bei ihm sitzt der Revolver** ~ he's trigger-happy; **das mache ich ganz** ~ *(col)* I can do it just like that *(col)*.

locker-: ~**lassen** *vi sep irreg (col)* **nicht** ~**lassen** not to let up; ~**machen** *vt sep (col) Geld* to shell out *(col)*.

lockern 1 *vt* **(a)** *(locker machen)* to loosen; *Seil, (lit, fig) Zügel* to slacken. **(b)** *(entspannen) Muskeln* to loosen up; *(fig) Vorschriften* to relax. **2** *vr* to work itself loose; *(Sport)* to loosen up; *(Verkrampfung)* to ease off; *(Atmosphäre)* to get more relaxed.

Lockerungsübung *f* loosening up exercise; *(zum Warmwerden)* limbering-up exercise.

lockig *adj Haar* curly; *Mensch* curlyheaded.

Lock-: ~**mittel** *nt* lure; ~**ruf** *m* call.

Lockung *f* lure; *(Versuchung)* temptation.

Lockvogel *m (lit, fig)* decoy.

Lodenmantel *m* loden (coat).

lodern *vi (lit, fig)* to blaze.

Löffel *m* - spoon; *(als Maß)* spoonful; *(von Bagger)* bucket. **den** ~ **abgeben** *(col)* to kick the bucket *(col)*; **jdm ein paar hinter die** ~ **geben** to give sb a clout around the ear(s).

löffeln *vt* to spoon.

log *pret of* **lügen**.

Logarithmus *m* logarithm.

Logbuch *nt* log(book).

Loge ['lo:ʒə] *f* -**n (a)** *(Theat)* box; *(Pförtner~)* lodge. **(b)** *(Freimaurer~)* lodge.

Logenplatz ['lo:ʒən-] *m (Theat)* seat in a box.

Logik *f* logic.

Logiker(in *f)* *m* - logician.

Logis [lo'ʒiː] *nt* - **Kost und** ~ board and lodging.

logisch *adj* logical; *(col: selbstverständlich)* natural. **gehst du auch hin?** — ~ are you going too? — of course.

logischerweise *adv* logically.

Logistik *f* **(a)** *(Math)* logic. **(b)** *(Mil)* logistics *sing*.

logo *interj (col)* you bet *(col)*.

Logopäde *m (wk)* -**n**, -**n**, **Logopädin** *f* speech therapist.

Logopädie *f* speech therapy.

Lohn *m* ≔e **(a)** *(Arbeitsentgelt)* wage(s), pay *no pl, no indef art.* **bei jdm in** ~ **und Brot stehen** *(geh)* to be in sb's employ *(form)*. **(b)** *(fig: Belohnung)* reward; *(Strafe)* punishment. **zum** ~ **für ...** as a reward/punishment for ...; **das ist nun der** ~ **für meine Mühe!** *(iro)* that's what I get for my trouble.

Lohn-: **l~abhängig** *adj* on a payroll; ~**abhängige(r)** *mf* worker; ~**abrechnung** *f* wages slip; ~**arbeit** *f* labour *(Brit)*, labor *(US)*; ~**ausfall** *m* loss of earnings; ~**büro** *nt* wages office; ~**empfänger** *m* wage-earner.

lohnen 1 *vir* to be worth it. **es lohnt (sich), etw zu tun** it is worth doing sth; **die Mühe lohnt sich** it is worth the effort; **das lohnt sich nicht für mich** it's not worth my while. **2** *vt* **jdm etw** ~ to reward sb for sth; **er hat mir meine Mühe schlecht gelohnt** he gave me poor thanks for my efforts.

löhnen *vti (col: bezahlen)* to shell out *(col)*.

lohnend *adj* rewarding; *(nutzbringend)* worthwhile; *(einträglich)* profitable.

lohnenswert *adj* worthwhile.

Lohn-: ~**erhöhung** *f* pay rise; ~**forderung** *f* pay claim; ~**fortzahlung** *f* continued payment of wages; ~**gruppe** *f* wage group; ~**kürzung** *f* wage cut; ~**liste** *f* payroll; ~**politik** *f* pay policy; ~**skala** *f* pay scale; ~**steuer** *f* income tax.

Lohnsteuer-: ~**jahresausgleich** *m* income tax return; ~**karte** *f* (income) tax card.

Lohn-: ~**stopp** *m* pay freeze; ~**streifen** pay slip; ~**tarif** *m* wage rate; ~**tüte** *f* pay packet; ~**verhandlung** *f* pay negotiations *pl*; ~**zahlung** *f* payment of wages.

Lok *f* -**s** = **Lokomotive** engine.

lokal *adj (örtlich)* local.

Lokal *nt* -**e** *(Gaststätte)* pub *(esp Brit)*, bar; *(Restaurant)* restaurant.

Lokal- *in cpds* local; ~**anästhesie** *f (Med)* local anaesthetic *(Brit)* or anesthetic *(US)*.

lokalisieren* *vt* **(a)** *(Ort feststellen)* to locate. **(b)** *(Med)* to localize.

Lokalität *f* locality; *(innen)* premises *pl.*

Lokal-: ~**kolorit** *nt* local colour *(Brit)* or color *(US)*; ~**nachrichten** *pl* local news *sing*; ~**patriotismus** *m* local patriotism; ~**teil** *m* local section; ~**termin** *m (Jur)* visit to the scene of the crime; ~**zeitung** *f* local newspaper.

Lokomotive *f* locomotive, (railway) engine.

Lokomotivführer *m* engine driver, engineer *(US)*.

Looping ['luːpɪŋ] *m* or *nt* -**s** *(Aviat)* looping the loop. **einen** ~ **machen** to loop the loop.

Lorbeer *m* -**en** *(lit: Gewächs)* laurel; *(als Gewürz)* bayleaf; *(~kranz)* laurel wreath. **sich auf seinen** ~**en ausruhen** *(fig col)* to rest on one's laurels.

Lorbeer-: ~**baum** *m* laurel (tree); ~**blatt** *nt* bayleaf; ~**kranz** *m* laurel wreath.

Los *nt* -**e (a)** *(für Entscheidung)* lot; *(in der Lotterie)* ticket. **das Große** ~ **ziehen** *(lit, fig)* to hit the jackpot; **etw durch das** ~ **entscheiden** to decide sth by drawing lots; **jdn durch das** ~ **bestimmen** to pick sb by drawing lots; **das** ~ **fiel auf mich** it fell to my lot. **(b)** *no pl (Schicksal)* lot. **er hat ein hartes** ~ his is a hard lot.

los *adj pred* **(a)** *(nicht befestigt)* loose. **der Hund ist von der Leine** ~ the dog is off the lead. **(b)** *(frei)* **jdn/etw** ~ **sein** *(col)* to be rid of sb/sth; **ich bin mein ganzes Geld** ~ *(col)* I'm cleaned out *(col)*. **(c)** *(col)* **etwas** ~ **machen** *(col)* to make sth happen; **was ist denn hier** ~? what's going on here?; **was ist** ~? what's the matter?; **irgendwas ist mit ihm** ~ there's something wrong with him; **mit dem ist doch nichts mehr** ~ he isn't up to much any more; **da war was** ~ there was plenty of action; *(Schlägerei etc)* all hell was let loose; **ist hier abends nichts** ~? isn't there anything to do here in the evenings?

2 *adv* **(a)** *(Aufforderung)* ~! come on!; **nichts wie** ~! let's get going; **(na)** ~, **mach schon!** (come on,) get on with it; ~, **fahr doch endlich** come on, start driving; **auf die Plätze, fertig,** ~ on your marks, get set, go! **(b)** *(weg)* **wir wollen früh** ~ we want to be off early.

los-: ~**binden** *vt sep irreg* to untie *(von from)*; ~**brechen** *sep irreg* **1** *vt* to break off; **2** *vi aux sein (Gelächter etc)* to break out; *(Sturm, Gewitter)* to break.

Löschblatt *nt* sheet of blotting paper.

löschen *vt* **(a)** *Feuer, Kerze* to put out, to extinguish; *Durst* to quench; *Tonband* to erase; *Schuld* to pay off; *Eintragung, (Comp)* to delete; *Konto* to close; *(aufsaugen)* Tinte to blot. **(b)** *(Naut) Ladung* to unload.

Lösch-: ~**fahrzeug** *nt* fire engine; ~**mittel** *nt* (fire-)extinguishing agent; ~**papier** *nt* (piece of) blotting paper; ~**zug** *m* set of fire-fighting appliances.

lose adj (lit, fig) loose; (nicht gespannt) Seil slack. **etw ~ verkaufen** to sell sth loose.

Lösegeld nt ransom (money).

losen vi to draw lots (um for).

lösen 1 vt (a) (losmachen) to remove (von from); Boot to cast off (von from); (aufbinden) to undo; Hände to unclasp; Handbremse to release; Husten, Krampf to ease; Muskeln to loosen up; (lit, fig: lockern) to loosen; **siehe gelöst.** (b) (klären) to solve; Konflikt to resolve. (c) (annullieren) Vertrag to cancel; Verlobung to break off; Verbindung to sever; Ehe to dissolve. (d) (kaufen) Karte to buy, to get.

2 vr (a) (sich losmachen) to detach oneself (von from); (sich ab~) to come off (von etw sth); (Knoten, Haare) to come undone; (Schuß) to go off; (Husten, Krampf) to ease; (Muskeln) to loosen up; (lit, fig: sich lockern) to (be)come loose. **sich von jdm ~** to break away from sb; **sich von etw ~** von Vorurteilen etc to rid oneself of sth. (b) (sich aufklären) to be solved. **sich von selbst ~** (Mordfall) to solve itself. (c) (in Flüssigkeit) to dissolve (in+dat in).

los-: ~**fahren** vi sep irreg aux sein (abfahren) to set off; (Fahrzeug) to move off; (Auto) to drive off; ~**gehen** vi sep irreg aux sein (a) (weggehen) to set off; (Schuß etc) to go off; (mit dem Messer) auf jdn ~**gehen** to go for sb (with a knife); (b) (col: anfangen) to start; **gleich geht's ~** it's just about to start; **jetzt geht's ~!** here we go!; (Reise, Bewegung) we're/you're off!; (c) (col: abgehen) to come off; ~**heulen** vi sep (col: weinen) to burst out crying; ~**kommen** vi sep irreg aux sein (Mensch) to get away (von from); (sich befreien) to free oneself (von from); ~**kriegen** vt sep (col: ablösen) to get off; ~**lachen** vi sep to burst out laughing; ~**lassen** vt sep irreg (a) to let go of; **der Gedanke läßt mich nicht mehr ~** the thought haunts me; (b) (col: abfeuern) Feuerwerk to let off; (c) jdn (auf jdn) ~**lassen** (fig col) to let sb loose (on sb); **die Hunde auf jdn ~lassen** to set the dogs on(to) sb; ~**laufen** vi sep irreg aux sein to start to run; ~**legen** vi sep (col) to get going; **nun leg mal ~ und erzähle ...** now come on and tell me/us ...

löslich adj soluble. **leicht/schwer ~** readily/not readily soluble.

los-: ~**lösen** sep 1 vt to remove (von from); (ablösen auch) to take off (von etw sth); (lockern) to loosen; **2** vr to detach oneself (von from); (sich ablösen auch) to come off (von etw sth); (lockern) to become loose; **sich von jdm ~lösen** to break away from sb; ~**machen** sep 1 vt to free; (~binden) to untie; **2** vi (col: sich beeilen) to step on it (col); **3** vr to get away (von from).

Losnummer f ticket number.

los-: ~**reißen** sep irreg 1 vt to tear off (von etw sth); **2** vr sich (von etw) ~**reißen** (Hund etc) to break free (from sth); (fig) to tear oneself away (from sth); ~**rennen** vi sep irreg aux sein (col) to run off; (anfangen zu laufen) to start to run; ~**sagen** vr sep **sich von etw** ~**sagen** to renounce sth; ~**schicken** vt sep to send off; ~**schießen** vi sep irreg **schieß ~!** (fig col) fire away! (col); ~**schlagen** vi sep irreg to hit out; **auf jdn** ~**schlagen** to go for sb; ~**schnallen** vt sep to unbuckle; ~**schrauben** vt sep to unscrew; (lockern auch) to loosen; ~**stürzen** vi sep aux sein to rush off; **auf jdn/etw** ~**stürzen** to pounce on sb/sth.

Lostrommel f drum (for lottery draw).

Losung f (a) motto. (b) (Kennwort) password.

Lösung f (a) solution (gen to); (das Lösen) solution (gen of); (eines Konfliktes) resolving. (b) (Chem) solution.

Lösungsmittel nt solvent.

loswerden vt sep irreg aux sein to get rid of; Gedanken to get away from; Geld (ausgeben) to

spend.

losziehen vi sep irreg aux sein (aufbrechen) to set out (in+acc, nach for).

Lot nt -e (a) (Senkblei) plumbline. **im ~ sein** to be in plumb; **die Sache ist wieder im ~** things have been straightened out. (b) (Math) perpendicular. **das ~ fällen** to drop a perpendicular.

loten vt to plumb.

löten vti to solder.

Lothringen nt Lorraine.

lothringisch adj of Lorraine, Lorrainese.

Löt-: ~**kolben** m soldering iron; ~**lampe** f blowlamp; ~**metall** nt solder.

Lotosblume f lotus (flower).

lotrecht adj (Math) perpendicular.

Lotse m (wk) -n, -n (Naut) pilot; (Flug~) air-traffic controller.

lotsen vt to guide. **jdn irgendwohin ~** (col) to drag sb somewhere (col).

Lotterie f lottery; (Tombola) raffle.

Lotterielos nt lottery/raffle ticket.

lott(e)rig adj (col) slovenly no adv.

Lotterleben nt (col) dissolute life.

Lotto nt -s national lottery. **(im) ~ spielen** to do the national lottery; **du hast wohl im ~ gewonnen** you must have won the pools (Brit).

Lotto-: ~**geschäft** nt, ~**laden** m (col) Lotto agency; ~**gewinn** m (Geld) Lotto winnings pl; ~**schein** m Lotto coupon; ~**zahlen** pl winning Lotto numbers pl.

Löwe m (wk) -n, -n lion; (Astron, Astrol) Leo.

Löwen-: ~**anteil** m (col) lion's share; ~**bändiger** m lion-tamer; ~**jagd** f lion hunt; ~**zahn** m dandelion.

Löwin f lioness.

loyal [loa'jaːl] adj loyal (jdm gegenüber to sb).

Loyalität [loajaliˈtɛːt] f loyalty.

LP [ɛlˈpeː] f -s = **Langspielplatte** LP.

Luchs [luks] m -e lynx.

Luchs|augen pl (col) eagle eyes pl.

Lücke f -n (lit, fig) gap; (Gesetzes~) loophole; (in Versorgung) hole.

Lücken-: ~**büßer**, ~**füller** m stopgap; l~**haft** adj full of gaps; Versorgung deficient; Gesetz, Alibi full of holes; **sein Wissen ist sehr l~haft** there are great gaps in his knowledge; l~**los** adj complete; Kenntnisse perfect; Versorgung, Überlieferung unbroken; ~**test** m (Sch) completion test.

lud pret of **laden**[1], **laden**[2].

Luder nt - (col) minx.

Luft f (a) air no pl. **im Zimmer ist schlechte ~** the air is stuffy in the room; **dicke ~** (col) a bad atmosphere; **(frische) ~ schnappen** (col) to get some fresh air; **die ~ ist rein** (col) the coast is clear; **aus der ~** from the air; **jdn an die (frische) ~ setzen** (col) to show sb the door; **in die ~ fliegen** (col) to explode; **etw in die ~ jagen** (col) to blow sth up; **leicht in die ~ gehen** (fig) to be quick to blow one's top (col); **es liegt etwas in der ~** there's something in the air; **in die ~ gucken** to stare into space; **das kann sich doch nicht in ~ aufgelöst haben** it can't have vanished into thin air; **die Behauptung ist aus der ~ gegriffen** this statement is pure invention; **vor Freude in die ~ springen** to jump for joy; **von ~ und Liebe leben** to live on love; **er ist ~ für mich** I'm not speaking to him.

(b) (Atem~) breath. **der Kragen schnürt mir die ~** this collar is choking me; **nach ~ schnappen** to gasp for breath; **die ~ anhalten** (lit) to hold one's breath; **mir bleibt mal die ~ weg** (col) (rede nicht) hold your tongue!; (übertreibe nicht) come off it! (col); **keine ~ mehr kriegen** not to be able to breathe; ~ **holen** to catch one's breath; **tief ~ holen** (lit, fig) to take a deep breath; **mir blieb vor Schreck die ~ weg** the shock took my breath away; **wieder ~ bekommen** (nach Sport etc) to get one's breath back;

(fig) to get a chance to catch one's breath; **seinem Herzen ~ machen** to get everything off one's chest; **seinem Zorn** *etc* **~ machen** to give vent to one's anger *etc*.
(c) *(fig: Spielraum)* space, room.
Luft: ~abwehr *f (Mil)* anti-aircraft defence *(Brit)* or defense *(US)*; **~angriff** *m* air-raid *(auf +acc* on)*; **~aufnahme** *f* aerial photo; **~ballon** *m* balloon; **~blase** *f* air bubble; **~brücke** *f* airlift.
Lüftchen *nt* breeze.
Luft-: l~dicht *adj* airtight *no adv;* **die Ware ist l~dicht verpackt** the article is in airtight packaging; **~druck** *m* air pressure; **l~durchlässig** *adj* pervious to air.
lüften 1 *vt* **(a)** to air. **(b)** *Schleier* to raise. **2** *vi (Luft hereinlassen)* to let some air in.
Luft-: ~fahrt *f* aviation *no art;* **~fahrzeug** *nt* aircraft; **~feuchtigkeit** *f* humidity; **~fracht** *f* air freight; **l~gekühlt** *adj* air-cooled; **l~getrocknet** *adj* air-dried; **~gewehr** *nt* air-rifle, **~herrschaft** *f* air supremacy; **~hoheit** *f* air sovereignty.
luftig *adj Zimmer* airy; *Kleidung* light.
Luft-: ~kampf *m* air battle; *(Duell)* dogfight; **~kissen** *nt* air cushion; **~kissenboot** *nt* hovercraft; **~krieg** *m* aerial warfare; **~kühlung** *f* aircooling; **~kurort** *m* health resort; **~landetruppe** *f* airborne troops *pl;* **l~leer** *adj* **(völlig) l~leer sein** to be a vacuum; **l~leerer Raum** vacuum; **~linie** *f* 200 km **~linie** 200 km as the crow flies; **~matratze** *f* airbed; **~pirat** *m* hijacker; **~post** *f* airmail; **mit ~post** by airmail; **~pumpe** *f (für Fahrrad)* (bicycle) pump; **~raum** *m* airspace; **~röhre** *f (Anat)* windpipe; **~schacht** *m* ventilation shaft; **~schicht** *f (Met)* layer of air; **~schiff** *nt* airship; **~schiffahrt** *f* aeronautics *sing;* **~schlacht** *f* air battle; **~schlange** *f* (paper) streamer; **~schloß** *nt (fig)* castle in the air; **~schneise** *f* air lane.
Luftschutz *m* anti-aircraft defence *(Brit)* or defense *(US)*.
Luftschutz-: ~bunker, ~keller *m* air-raid shelter; **~übung** *f* air-raid drill.
Luft-: ~spiegelung *f* mirage; **~sprung** *m* jump in the air; **~straße** *f* air route; **~streitkräfte** *pl* air force *sing;* **~strom** *m* stream of air; **~strömung** *f* current of air; **~stützpunkt** *m* airbase; **~temperatur** *f* air temperature.
Lüftung *f* airing.
Luft-: ~veränderung *f* change of air; **~verkehr** *m* air traffic; **~verschmutzung** *f* air pollution; **~versorgung** *f* air supplies *pl;* **~verteidigung** *f* air defence *(Brit)* or defense *(US)*; **~waffe** *f (Mil)* air force; **~weg** *m* etw **auf dem ~weg befördern** to transport sth by air; **~widerstand** *m* air resistance; *(in Gebäude)* draught *(Brit)*, draft *(US)*.
Lug *m:* **~ und Trug** lies *pl* (and deception).
Lüge *f* **-n** lie. **das ist alles ~** that's all lies; **jdn/etw ~n strafen** to give the lie to sb/sth.
lügen *pret* **log,** *ptp* **gelogen** *vi* to lie. **ich müßte ~, wenn ...** I would be lying if ...; **das ist gelogen!** *(col)* that's a lie!
Lügen-: ~detektor *m* lie detector; **~geschichte** *f* pack of lies; **~märchen** *nt* tall story; **~maul** *nt (pej col)* liar; **~propaganda** *f* propagandist lies *pl.*
Lügner(in *f) m* - liar.
lügnerisch *adj Mensch* lying *attr,* untruthful.
Luke *f* **-n** hatch; *(Dach~)* skylight.
lukrativ *adj* lucrative.
Lümmel *m* **-** *(pej)* lout, oaf.
lümmelhaft *adj (pej)* ill-mannered.
lümmeln *vr (col)* to sprawl; *(sich hin~)* to flop down.
Lump *m (wk)* **-en, -en** *(pej)* rogue.
lumpen *vt (col)* **er ließ sich nicht ~** he was very generous.
Lumpen *m* - rag.
Lumpen-: ~gesindel, ~pack *nt (pej)* rabble *pl*

(pej); **~kerl** *m (col)* bastard *(col);* **~sammler** *m* **(a)** rag-and-bone man; **(b)** *(hum)* last bus/tram *etc.*
lumpig *adj* **(a)** *Gesinnung, Tat* shabby, mean. **(b)** **~e 10 Mark** a measly 10 marks *(col).*
Lunge *f* **-n** lung. **(auf) ~ rauchen** to inhale; **sich** *(dat)* **die ~ aus dem Hals schreien** *(col)* to yell till one is blue in the face *(col).*
Lungen-: ~entzündung *f* pneumonia; **~flügel** *m* lung; **l~krank** *adj* tubercular; **l~krank sein** to have a lung disease; **~kranke(r)** *mf decl as adj* TB case; **~krankheit** *f* lung disease; **~krebs** *m* lung cancer.
Lunte *f* **-n ~ riechen** *(Verdacht schöpfen)* to smell a rat *(col); (Gefahr wittern)* to sense danger.
Lupe *f* **-n** magnifying glass. **solche Leute kannst du mit der ~ suchen** people like that are few and far between; **jdn/etw unter die ~ nehmen** *(col)* to take a close look at sb/sth, to investigate sb/sth.
lupenrein *adj (lit) Edelstein* flawless; *(fig) Gentleman, Intellektueller* through and through *pred.*
Lurch *m* **-e** amphibian.
Lusche *f* **-n** *(Cards)* low card; *(fig col: Versager)* dead loss *(col).*
Lust *f* **-ë** **(a)** *no pl (Freude)* pleasure, joy. **er hat die ~ daran verloren** he has lost all interest in it; **da kann einem alle ~ vergehen** it puts you off; **jdm die ~ an etw** *(dat)* **nehmen** to take all the fun out of sth for sb. **(b)** *no pl (Neigung)* inclination. **zu etw ~ haben** to feel like sth; **ich habe keine ~ zu arbeiten** I don't feel like working; **ich habe jetzt keine ~** I'm not in the mood just now; **ich hätte ~ dazu** I'd like to; **hast du ~?** how about it?; **auf etw** *(acc)* **~ haben** to fancy sth; **er kann bleiben, so lange er ~ hat** he can stay as long as he likes. **(c)** *(sinnliche Begierde)* desire; *(sexuell auch)* lust *(auch fig).* **~ haben** to feel desire.
Lüster *m* **-** **(a)** *(Leuchter)* chandelier. **(b)** *(Stoff, Glanzüberzug)* lustre *(Brit)*, luster *(US).*
lüstern *adj* lecherous.
Lust-: ~gefühl *nt* feeling of pleasure; **~gewinn** *m* pleasure.
lustig *adj Leute, Abend* cheerful. **die Party war ganz ~** the party was great fun; **er ist ein ganz ~er Typ** he's great fun; **so lange du ~ bist** *(col)* as long as you like; **es wurde ~** things got quite merry; **das kann ja ~ werden!** *(iro)* that's going to be fun *(iro);* **sich über jdn/etw ~ machen** to make fun of sb/sth.
Lüstling *m* lecher.
Lust-: l~los *adj* unenthusiastic; *(Fin) Börse* slack; **~molch** *m (hum col)* sex maniac *(col);* **~mord** *m* sex murder; **~prinzip** *nt (Psych)* pleasure principle; **~schloß** *nt* summer residence; **~spiel** *nt* comedy; **l~voll 1** *adj* full of relish; **2** *adv* with relish.
Lutheraner(in *f) m* - Lutheran.
lutschen *vti* to suck *(an etw (dat)* sth).
Lutscher *m* - lollipop *(Brit)*, popsicle ® *(US).*
Luv [lu:f] *f no pl (Naut)* windward.
Luxemburg *nt* Luxembourg.
luxemburgisch *adj* Luxembourgian.
luxuriös *adj* luxurious. **ein ~es Leben** a life of luxury.
Luxus *m no pl* luxury; *(pej: Verschwendung)* extravagance. **im ~ leben** to live in luxury.
Luxus- *in cpds* luxury; **~ausführung** *f* de luxe model; **~dampfer** *m* luxury cruise ship; **~limousine** *f* limousine; **~restaurant** *nt* first-class restaurant.
Lymphe ['lʏmfə] *f* -n lymph.
Lymphknoten *m* lymph(atic) gland.
lynchen ['lʏnçn 'lɪnçn] *vt (lit)* to lynch; *(fig)* to kill.
Lynch-: ['lʏnç-]: **~justiz** *f* lynch-law; **~mord** *m* lynching.
Lyrik *f no pl* lyric poetry or verse.
Lyriker(in *f) m* - lyric poet, lyricist.
lyrisch *adj (lit, fig)* lyrical; *Dichtung, Dichter* lyric.

M

M, m [εm] *nt* -, - M, m.

m = **Meter.**

Maat *m* -e *or* -en *(Naut)* (ship's) mate.

Mach|art *f* make; *(Muster)* design; *(lit, fig: Stil)* style.

machbar *adj* feasible, possible.

Mache *f no pl (col)* **reine ~ sein** to be (a) sham; **etw in der ~ haben** *(col)* to be working on sth; **jdn in der ~ haben** *(col)* to be having a go at sb *(col)*; *(verprügeln)* to be working sb over *(col)*.

machen 1 *vt* **(a)** to do; *(herstellen, bilden, formen, zubereiten)* to make. **was ~ Sie (beruflich)?** what do you do for a living?; **was habe ich nur falsch gemacht?** what have I done wrong?; **gut, wird gemacht** right, I'll get that done; **das ist zu/nicht zu ~** that can/can't be done; **(da ist) nichts zu ~** *(geht nicht)* (there's) nothing to be done; *(kommt nicht in Frage)* nothing doing; **wie man's macht, ist's verkehrt** whatever you do is wrong; **was machst du da?** what are you doing (there)?; **was machst du denn hier?** what (on earth) are you doing here?; **ich muß noch so viel ~** I still have so much to do; **ich kann da auch nichts ~** I can't do anything about it either; **so etwas macht man nicht** that sort of thing just isn't done; **wie ~ Sie das nur?** how do you do it; **sich/jdm etw ~ lassen** to have sth made for oneself/sb; **Bilder** *or* **Fotos ~** to take photos; **er ist für den Beruf wie gemacht** he's made for the job; **Bier wird aus Gerste gemacht** beer is made from barley; **aus Holz gemacht** made of wood; **das Essen ~** to get the meal; *siehe* **gemacht.**

(b) *(verursachen)* Schwierigkeiten, Arbeit to make *(jdm* for sb); *Mühe, Schmerzen* to cause *(jdm* for sb). **jdm Angst/Freude ~** to make sb afraid/happy; **jdm Kopfschmerzen ~** to give sb a headache; **das macht Hunger** that makes you hungry.

(c) *(bewirken)* to do; *(+infin)* to make. **das macht die Kälte** it's the cold that does that; **jdn lachen/etw vergessen ~** to make sb laugh/forget sth; **die Kälte macht, daß das Wasser gefriert** the cold makes the water freeze; **(viel) von sich reden ~** to be much talked about; **mach, daß du hier verschwindest!** (you just) get out of here!

(d) *(veranstalten)* Party to have, to give; *(teilnehmen an)* Lehrgang to do.

(e) *(ausmachen, schaden)* to matter. **macht nichts!** (it) doesn't matter; **macht das was?** does that matter?; **das macht sehr viel** it matters a lot; **das macht mir doch nichts!** that doesn't matter to me; **die Kälte macht mir nichts** I don't mind the cold; **die Kälte macht dem Motor nichts** the cold doesn't hurt the engine.

(f) *(erzielen)* Punkte, Preis to get, to win; *Doktor, Diplom etc* to do; *Gewinn, Verlust* to make.

(g) *(col: ergeben)* to make; *(kosten, Math)* to be. **drei und fünf macht acht** three and five is *or* are eight; **100 cm ~ einen Meter** 100 cm make a metre; **wieviel macht das (alles zusammen)?** how much is that *or* what does that make altogether?

(h) **was macht die Arbeit?** how's the work going?; **was macht dein Bruder?** how is your brother doing?; **mach's kurz!** make it brief; **mach's gut!** take care, all the best; **er wird's nicht mehr lange ~** *(col)* he won't last long; **mit mir kann man's ja ~!** *(col)* the things I put up

with! *(col)*; **das läßt er nicht mit sich ~** he won't stand for that; **jdn unglücklich ~** to make sb unhappy; **etw sauber/schmutzig ~** to get sth clean/dirty; **jdn alt/jung ~** *(aussehen lassen)* to make sb look old/young; **mach es ihm nicht noch schwerer** don't make it harder for him; **er macht es sich** *(dat)* **nicht leicht** he doesn't make it easy for himself; **etw aus jdm/etw ~** *(darstellen, interpretieren als)* to make sth of sb/sth; *(verwandeln in)* to make sth (out) of sth, to make sb/sth into sth; **jdn zu etw** *(dat)* **~** *(verwandeln in)* to turn sb into sth; *(Rolle, Image, Status geben)* to make sb sth; **jdm etw zur Hölle/Qual etc ~** to make sth hell/a misery etc for sb; **jdn zu seiner Frau ~** to make sb one's wife; **Halt ~** to call a halt; **das Geschirr ~** to do the dishes; **eine Prüfung ~** to take an exam; **ein Spiel ~** to play a game; **das Auto/den Kühlschrank ~ lassen** to have the car/refrigerator seen to; **er macht mir die Haare/Zähne** *(col)* he does my hair/teeth; **das Bett ~** to make the bed; **jetzt macht er auf beleidigt** *(col)* now he's playing the injured innocent; **den Ghostwriter für jdn ~** *(col)* to act as sb's ghost writer; **groß/klein ~** *(col: Notdurft)* to do a big/little job *(baby-talk).*

2 *vi* **(a)** **mach schon/schneller!** *(col)* get a move on! *(col)*, hurry up; **ich mach ja schon!** *(col)* I am hurrying; **sie machten, daß sie nach Hause kamen** they hurried home; **er macht in Politik/Malerei** *(col)* he's in politics/doing some painting; **jetzt macht sie auf große Dame** *(col)* she's playing the lady now; **sie macht auf gebildet** *(col)* she's doing her cultured bit *(col)*; **er macht auf Schau** *(col)* he's out for effect *(col)*; **laß ihn nur ~** *(verlaß dich auf ihn)* just leave it to him; **laß mich mal ~** let me do it; *(ich bringe das in Ordnung)* let me see to that; **gut, mache ich** right, I'll do that; **das macht müde** that makes you tired; **das Kleid macht schlank** that dress makes you look slim.

(b) *(col: Notdurft verrichten)* to go to the toilet; *(Hund etc)* to do its business *(euph)*. **(sich** *dat)* **in die Hosen ~** *(lit, fig)* to wet oneself; **ins Bett ~** to wet the bed.

3 *vr* **wie macht sich der Garten?** how is the garden coming along?; **der Schal macht sich sehr hübsch zu dem Kleid** the scarf looks very pretty with that dress; **sich an etw** *(acc)* **~** to get down to sth/doing sth; **sich auf den Weg ~** to get going; **sich verständlich/wichtig ~** to make oneself understood/important; **sich bei jdm beliebt/verhaßt ~** to make oneself popular with/hated by sb; **sich** *(dat)* **viel aus jdm/etw ~** to like sb/sth; **sich** *(dat)* **wenig aus jdm/etw ~** not to be very keen on sb/sth; **mach dir nichts daraus** don't let it bother you; **sich** *(dat)* **einen schönen Abend ~** to have a nice evening; **sich** *(dat)* **jdn zum Freund ~** to make sb one's friend; **sich zum Fürsprecher ~** to make oneself spokesman.

Machenschaften *pl* wheelings and dealings *pl.*

Macher *m* - *(col)* doer, man of action.

Macht *f* ⁻e **(a)** *no pl* power; *(Stärke auch)* might. **die ~ der Gewohnheit/des Schicksals** the force of habit/destiny; **alles in unserer ~ Stehende** everything in our power; **mit aller ~** with all one's might; **die ~ ergreifen/erringen** to seize/

280

gain power; **an die ~ kommen** to come to power; **an der ~ sein** to be in power; **die ~ übernehmen** to assume power. **(b)** *(Staat)* power. **böse/himmlische ~e** evil forces/heavenly powers.

Macht-: **~befugnis** *f* power, authority *no pl*; **~bereich** *m* sphere of influence; **~ergreifung** *f* seizure of power; **~haber** *m* - ruler; *(pej)* dictator.

mächtig 1 *adj* **(a)** *(einflußreich)* powerful. **(b)** *(sehr groß)* mighty; *Felsen auch, Körper* massive; *Stimme, Schlag auch* powerful; *Essen* heavy; *(col: enorm) Hunger, Durst* terrific *(col)*, tremendous. **~e Angst haben** *(col)* to be scared stiff. **(c)** *(liter)* **einer Sprache** *(gen)* **~ sein** to have a good command of a language. **2** *adv (col: sehr)* terrifically *(col)*, tremendously; *schneien, sich beeilen* like mad *(col)*. **sich ~ anstrengen** to make a tremendous effort.

Mächtigkeit *f (Größe)* mightiness.

Macht-: **~kampf** power struggle; **m~los** *adj* powerless; *(hilflos)* helpless; **~losigkeit** *f no pl* powerlessness; helplessness; **~mißbrauch** *m* misuse of power; **~position** *f* position of power; **~probe** *f* trial of strength; **~übernahme** *f* takeover *(durch by)*; **m~voll** *adj* powerful; **~wort** *nt* **ein ~wort sprechen** to exercise one's authority.

Machwerk *nt (pej)* sorry effort. **ein elendes ~ a** pathetic attempt; **das ist ein ~ des Teufels** that is the work of the devil.

Macke *f* -n *(col)* **(a)** *(Tick, Knall)* quirk. **eine ~ haben** *(col)* to have a screw loose *(col)*. **(b)** *(Fehler, Schadstelle)* fault.

Macker *m* - *(col)* fellow *(col)*, guy *(col)*. **spiel hier nicht den ~** don't come the tough guy here *(col)*.

Mädchen *nt* girl; *(Tochter auch)* daughter. **ein ~ für alles** *(col)* a dogsbody; *(im Haushalt auch)* a maid-of-all-work.

Mädchen-: **m~haft** *adj* girlish; *aussehen, sich kleiden* like a girl; **~klasse** *f* girls' class; **~kleidung** *f* girls' clothing; **~name** *m* **(a)** girl's name; **(b)** *(von verheirateter Frau)* maiden name; **~schule** *f* girls' school.

Made *f* -n maggot. **wie die ~ im Speck leben** *(col)* to live in luxury.

Mädel *nt* -(s) *(dial)* lass *(dial)*, girl.

madig *adj* maggoty; *Obst auch* worm-eaten. **jdm etw ~ machen** *(col)* to put sb off sth.

Magazin *nt* -e **(a)** *(Lager)* storeroom; *(Bibliotheks~)* stockroom. **(b)** *(am Gewehr)* magazine. **(c)** *(Zeitschrift)* magazine, journal; *(TV, Rad)* magazine programme *(Brit)* or program *(US)*.

Magd *f* -e *(old)* maid; *(Landarbeiterin)* farm lass.

Magen *m* - or - stomach. **auf nüchternen ~** on an empty stomach; **(die) Liebe geht durch den ~** *(Prov)* the way to a man's heart is through his stomach *(prov)*; **etw liegt jdm im ~** *(col)* sth lies heavily on sb's stomach; *(fig)* sth preys on sb's mind; **jdm auf den ~ schlagen** *(col)* to upset sb's stomach; *(fig)* to upset sb; **sich** *(dat)* **den ~ verderben** to upset one's stomach; **dabei dreht sich mir der ~ um** *(col)* it turns my stomach.

Magen-: **~beschwerden** *pl* stomach trouble *sing*; **~bitter** *m* bitters *pl*; **~geschwür** *nt* stomach ulcer; **~knurren** *nt no pl* tummy rumbles *pl (col)*; **m~krank** *adj* **m~krank sein** to have stomach trouble; **~krebs** *m* cancer of the stomach; **~leiden** *nt* stomach disorder; **~schmerzen** *pl* stomach-ache *sing*, tummy-ache *sing (col)*; **~verstimmung** *f* stomach upset.

mager *adj* **(a)** *(fettarm) Fleisch* lean, low-fat. **(b)** *(dünn)* thin, skinny *(col)*; *(abgemagert)* emaciated. **(c)** *Boden, Felder* poor, infertile. **(d)** *(dürftig)* meagre *(Brit)*, meager *(US)*; *Ergebnis* poor. **die sieben ~en Jahre** the seven lean years.

Mager-: **~milch** *f* skimmed milk; **~quark** *m* low-fat curd cheese.

Magie *f no pl* magic.

Magier ['maːgiɐ] *m* - magician.

---

magisch *adj* magic(al); *Quadrat, (Tech) Auge* magic. **mit ~er Gewalt** with magical force; *(fig)* as if by magic.

Magister *m* - *(Univ)* M.A., Master of Arts.

Magistrat *m* -e municipal authorities *pl*.

Magnat *m (wk)* -en, en magnate *(auch Hist)*.

Magnet-: **~band** *nt* magnetic tape; **~feld** *nt* magnetic field.

magnetisch *adj (lit, fig)* magnetic.

Magnetismus *m no pl* magnetism.

Magnet-: **~nagel** *f* magnetic needle; **~zündung** *f (Aut)* magneto ignition.

Mahagoni *nt no pl* mahogany.

Mähdrescher *m* combine (harvester).

mähen **1** *vt Gras* to cut; *Getreide auch* to reap; *Rasen* to mow. **2** *vi* to reap; *(Rasen ~)* to mow.

mähen[2] *vi (Schaf)* to bleat.

Mahl *nt* -e *(geh)* meal, repast *(form)*; *(Gast~)* banquet.

mahlen *pret* **mahlte**, *ptp* **gemahlen** *vti* to grind.

Mahlzeit *f* meal. **~!** *(col)* greeting used around mealtimes; *(guten Appetit)* enjoy your meal; **(prost)** **~!** *(iro col)* that's just great *(col)* or swell *(esp US col)*.

Mähmaschine *f* mower; *(Getreide~)* reaper.

Mahnbrief *m* reminder.

Mähne *f* -n *(lit, fig)* mane.

mahnen **1** *vt* **(a)** *(erinnern)* to remind *(wegen of)*; *(warnend)* to admonish *(wegen on account of)*. **gemahnt werden** *(Schuldner)* to receive a reminder. **(b)** *(auffordern)* jdn zur Eile/Geduld etc **~** to urge sb to hurry/be patient etc. **2** *vi* **(a)** *(wegen Schulden etc)* to send a reminder. **(b)** zur Eile/Geduld **~** to urge haste/patience; **der Lehrer mahnte zur Ruhe** the teacher called for quiet.

Mahn-: **~mal** *nt* memorial; **~schreiben** *nt* reminder.

Mahnung *f* **(a)** *(Ermahnung)* exhortation; *(warnend)* admonition. **(b)** *(Mahnbrief)* reminder.

Mai *m* -e May. **der Erste ~** May Day; *siehe* **März**.

Mai- *in cpds* May; *(Pol)* May Day; **~baum** *m* maypole; **~bowle** *f* white wine punch *(flavoured with woodruff)*; **~feier** *f* May Day celebrations *pl*; **~feiertag** *m (form)* May Day *no art*; **~glöckchen** *nt* lily of the valley; **~käfer** *m* cockchafer.

Mailand *nt* Milan.

Mais *m no pl* maize, (Indian) corn *(esp US)*.

Mais-: **~kolben** *m* corn cob; *(Gericht)* corn on the cob; **~korn** *nt* grain of maize or corn *(esp US)*.

Majestät *f* **(a)** *(Titel)* Majesty. **Seine/Ihre/Eure ~** His/Her/Your Majesty. **(b)** *(liter)* majesty.

majestätisch *adj* majestic.

Majestätsbeleidigung *f* lèse-majesté.

Major *m* -e *(Mil)* major; *(in Luftwaffe)* squadron leader *(Brit)*, major *(US)*.

Majoran *m* -e marjoram.

majorisieren* *vt* to outvote.

Majorität *f* majority.

makaber *adj* macabre; *Witz, Geschichte* sick.

Makel *m* - **(a)** *(Schandfleck)* stigma. **ohne ~** without a stain on one's reputation; **mit einem ~ behaftet sein** *(liter)* to be stigmatized. **(b)** *(Fehler)* blemish; *(bei Waren)* defect. **ohne ~** flawless.

Mäkelei *f* carping *no pl*, fault-finding *no pl (an +dat, über +acc* about, over).

makellos *adj Reinheit, Frische* spotless; *Charakter* unimpeachable; *Figur, Haut* flawless; *Kleidung* immaculate; *Alibi* watertight.

Makellosigkeit *f (Reinheit)* spotlessness; *(von Haut)* flawlessness; *(von Kleidung)* immaculateness.

mäkeln *vi (col: nörgeln)* to carp *(an +dat* at).

Make-up [meːkˈʔap] *nt* -s make-up; *(flüssig)* foundation.

Makkaroni *pl* macaroni *sing*.

Makler *m* - broker; *(Grundstücks~)* estate agent *(Brit)*, realtor *(US)*.

Maklergebühr *f* broker's commission, brokerage.

Makrele *f* -n mackerel.

Makro- *in cpds* macro-; **~kosmos** *m* macrocosm.

Makrone *f* -n macaroon.

Mal[1] *nt* -e **(a)** *(lit, fig: Fleck)* mark. **(b)** *pl auch* ⁼er *(liter: Ehren~)* memorial, monument.

Mal[2] *nt* -e time. **(nur) dieses eine ~** (just) this once; **das eine oder andere ~** now and then *or* again; **kein einziges ~** not once; **wenn du bloß ein einziges ~ auf mich hören würdest** if you would only listen to me for once; **ein für alle ~e** once and for all; **das vorige ~** the time before; **ein letztes ~** *(liter)* one last time; **als ich das letzte ~ in London war** (the) last time I was in London; **beim ersten/letzten ~** the first/last time; **zum ersten/letzten ~** for the first/last time; **von ~ zu ~** each *or* every time; **für dieses ~** for the time being; **mit einem ~e** all of a sudden.

mal[1] *adv (Math)* times; *(bei Flächenangaben)* by.

mal[2] *adv (col) siehe* **einmal.**

Malaria *f no pl* malaria.

Malbuch *nt* colouring *(Brit) or* coloring *(US)* book.

malen *vti* to paint; *(col: zeichnen)* to draw. **sich ~ lassen** to have one's portrait painted; **etw rosig/schwarz** *etc* **~** *(fig)* to paint a rosy/black *etc* picture of sth.

Maler(in *f) m* - painter; *(Kunst~ auch)* artist.

Malerei *f (no pl: Malkunst)* art; *(Bild)* painting; *(Zeichnung)* drawing.

malerisch *adj* **(a)** picturesque; *Landschaft auch* scenic. **(b)** *(bildnerisch)* in painting; *Talent* as a painter.

Malermeister *m* (master) painter.

Malheur [ma'løːɐ] *nt* -s *or* -e mishap. **das ist doch kein ~!** it's not serious.

Malkasten *m* paintbox.

Mallorca *nt* Majorca, Mallorca.

malnehmen *vti sep irreg* to multiply *(mit* by).

Maloche *f no pl (col)* graft *(col)*. **du mußt zur ~** you've got to go to work.

malochen* *vi (col)* to graft *(col)*, to sweat away *(col)*.

Mal-: **~stift** *m* crayon; **~technik** *f* painting technique.

Malteserkreuz *nt* Maltese cross.

maltesisch *adj* Maltese.

malträtieren* *vt* to ill-treat, to maltreat.

Malve ['malvə] *f* -n *(Bot)* mallow.

Malz *nt no pl* malt.

Malz-: **~bier** *nt* malt beer; **~bonbon** *nt or m* malt lozenge; **~kaffee** *m coffee substitute made from barley malt.*

Mama, Mami *f* -s *(col)* mummy, mommy *(US)*.

Mammut- *in cpds (lit, fig)* mammoth; *(lange dauernd)* marathon; **~baum** *m* sequoia, giant redwood.

mampfen *vti (col)* to munch, to chomp *(col)*.

man *indef pron* **(a)** you, one; *(ich)* one; *(wir)* we. **~ kann nie wissen** you *or* one can never tell; **das tut ~ nicht** that's not done. **(b)** *(jemand)* somebody, someone. **~ hat mir gesagt ...** I was told ...; **~ hat festgestellt, daß ...** it has been established that ... **(c)** *(die Leute)* they *pl*, people *pl*. **früher glaubte ~** people used to believe; **~ will die alten Häuser niederreißen** they want to pull down the old houses. **(d)** **~ nehme ...** take ...

Management ['mɛnɪdʒmənt] *nt* -s management.

managen ['mɛnɪdʒn] *vt* to manage. **ich manage das schon!** *(col)* I'll fix it somehow!

Manager ['mɛnɪdʒɐ] *m* - manager.

manch *indef pron* **~ eine(r)** many a person; **~ einem kann man nie Vernunft beibringen** some people never learn; **~ anderer** many another; **~er, der ...** many a person who ...; **~es Schöne** quite a few beautiful things; **(so)** **~es** a good many things; **in ~em hat er recht** he's right about some things.

mancherlei *adj inv (adjektivisch mit pl n)* various; *(substantivisch)* various things *pl*. **~ Bier** various kinds of beer.

manchmal *adv* sometimes.

Mandant(in *f) m (Jur)* client.

Mandarine *f* mandarin (orange), tangerine.

Mandat *nt (Auftrag, Vollmacht)* mandate *(auch Pol)*, authorization *(gen* from); *(Parl: Abgeordnetensitz)* seat. **sein ~ niederlegen** *(Parl)* to resign one's seat.

Mandel *f* -n **(a)** almond. **(b)** *(Anat)* tonsil.

Mandel-: **m~äugig** *adj (poet)* almond-eyed; **~baum** *m* almond tree; **~entzündung** *f* tonsilitis.

Mandoline *f* mandolin.

Manege [ma'neːʒə] *f* -n ring, arena.

Mangel[1] *f* -n mangle; *(Heiß~)* rotary iron. **jdn durch die ~ drehen** *(fig col)* to put sb through it *(col)*; *Prüfling etc auch* to put sb through the mill.

Mangel[2] *nt* ⁼ **(a)** *(Fehler)* fault; *(bei Maschine auch)* defect; *(Charakter~)* flaw. **(b)** *no pl (das Fehlen)* lack *(an* +dat of); *(Knappheit auch)* shortage *(an* +dat of); *(Med auch)* deficiency *(an* +dat of). **aus ~ an** *(+dat)* for lack of; **wegen ~s an Beweisen** for lack of evidence; **es herrscht ~ an etw** *(dat)* there is a shortage of sth.

Mängelbericht *m* list of faults.

Mangel-: **~beruf** *m* understaffed profession; **~erscheinung** *f (Med)* deficiency symptom.

mangelhaft *adj (unzulänglich)* poor; *Ausrüstung auch* inadequate; *Informationen, Interesse* insufficient; *(fehlerhaft)* Ware faulty; *(Schulnote auch)* unsatisfactory.

mangeln *vi impers* **es mangelt an etw** *(dat)* there is a lack of sth; *(unzureichend vorhanden auch)* there is a shortage of sth; **es mangelt jdm an etw** *(dat)* sb lacks sth; **~des Verständnis** *etc* a lack of understanding *etc*; **wegen ~der Aufmerksamkeit** through not paying attention.

Mangelware *f* scarce commodity. **~ sein** *(fig)* to be a rare thing; *(Ärzte, gute Lehrer etc)* not to grow on trees *(col)*.

Manie *f (Med, fig)* mania; *(fig auch)* obsession.

Manier *f* -en **(a)** *no pl (Art und Weise)* manner; *(eines Künstlers etc)* style. **in überzeugender ~** in a most convincing manner. **(b)** **~en** *pl (Umgangsformen)* manners; **das sind doch keine ~en** *(col)* that's no way to behave.

maniriert *adj* affected; *Benehmen auch* mannered.

manierlich 1 *adj Kind* well-mannered; *Benehmen* good; *Aussehen* respectable. **2** *adv essen* politely; *sich benehmen* properly; *sich kleiden* respectably.

Manifest *nt* -e *(Pol)* manifesto.

Maniküre *f* -n **(a)** *(Handpflege)* manicure. **(b)** *(Handpflegerin)* manicurist.

Manipulation *f* manipulation; *(Trick)* manoeuvre *(Brit)*, maneuver *(US)*.

manipulierbar *adj* manipulable. **leicht/schwer ~** easily manipulated/difficult to manipulate.

manipulieren* *vt* to manipulate.

Manko *nt* -s *(a)* *(Comm: Fehlbetrag)* deficit. **~ machen** *(col: bei Verkauf)* to make a loss. **(b)** *(fig: Nachteil)* shortcoming.

Mann *m* ⁼er **(a)** *m* man. **ein feiner ~** a (perfect) gentleman; **ein ~ aus dem Volk(e)** a man of the people; **der ~ im Mond** the man in the moon; **ein ~ der Wissenschaft** a man of science; **ein ~ von Format** *etc* a man of stature *etc*; **er ist nicht der ~ dafür** he's not the man for that; *(nicht seine Art)* he's not the sort; **wie ein ~** as one man; **etw an den ~ bringen** *(col)* to get rid of sth; **seinen ~ stehen** to hold one's own; **einen kleinen ~ im Ohr haben** *(hum col)* to be crazy *(col)*; **und ein ~, ein Wort, er hat sich gemacht** and, as good as his word, he did it; **~ für ~** *(allesamt)* every single one; **~ gegen ~** man against man; **pro ~** per head; **ein Gespräch von ~ zu ~** a man-to-man talk. **(b)** *(Ehe~)* husband. **~ und Frau werden to** become man and wife. **(c)** *pl* **Leute** *(Besatzungsmitglied)* hand, man; *(Sport, Cards)* player, man. **20 ~ 20 hands** *or* men; **mit ~ und Maus untergehen** to go down with all hands; *(Passagierschiff)* to go down with no survivors. **(d)** *(col: als Interjektion)* (my) God *(col)*; *(bewundernd, erstaunt auch)* hey. **mach schnell, ~!** hurry up, man!; **~, oh ~!** oh boy! *(col)*.

Männchen *nt dim of* **Mann (a)** little man; *(Zwerg)* man(n)ikin. **~ malen** to draw (little) matchstick men, ≈ to doodle. **(b)** *(Biol)* male; *(Vogel~ auch)* cock. **(c) ~ machen** *(Hund)* to (sit up and) beg.

Mannequin ['manəkɛ̃] *nt* **-s** (fashion) model.

Männer *pl of* **Mann.**

Männer-: **~chor** *m* male-voice choir; **~fang** *m (hum)* **auf ~fang ausgehen** to go looking for a man/for men; **~gesangverein** *m* male choral society; **m~mordend** *adj (hum)* man-eating; **~sache** *f (Angelegenheit)* man's business; *(Arbeit)* man's job; **Fußball war früher ~sache** football used to be a male preserve; **~stimme** *f* man's voice; *(Mus)* male voice.

Mannes-: **~alter** *nt* manhood *no art;* **im besten ~alter sein** to be in the prime of (one's) life; **~kraft** *f (dated, hum)* virility.

mannhaft *adj* manly *no adv; (tapfer)* manful, valiant; *(entschlossen)* resolute; *Widerstand* stout.

mannigfach *adj attr* manifold, multifarious.

mannigfaltig *adj (geh)* diverse, varied.

Mannigfaltigkeit *f* diversity, variety.

männlich *adj* **(a)** male; *Wort* masculine. **(b)** *(fig: mannhaft)* Mut, Entschluß manly; *Frau* mannish.

Männlichkeit *f (fig)* manliness; *(von Frau)* mannishness.

Mannsbild *nt (dated pej)* fellow.

Mannschaft *f (Sport, fig)* team; *(Naut, Aviat)* crew. **~(en)** *(Mil)* men *pl.*

Mannschafts- *in cpds (Sport)* team; **~aufstellung** *f* team line-up; *(das Aufstellen)* selection of the team; **~geist** *m* team spirit; **~raum** *m (Sport)* team quarters *pl; (Naut)* crew's quarters *pl.*

manns-: **~hoch** *adj* as high as a man; **der Schnee liegt ~hoch** the snow is six feet deep; **~toll** *adj* man-mad *(col)*.

Mannweib *nt (pej)* mannish woman.

Manometer *nt (Tech)* pressure gauge. **~!** *(col)* wow! *(col)*.

Manöver [ma'nøːvɐ] *nt* - *(lit, fig)* manoeuvre *(Brit)*, maneuver *(US)*.

manövrieren [manø'vriːrən] *vti (lit, fig)* to manoeuvre *(Brit)*, to maneuver *(US)*.

Manövrier- [manø'vriːɐ]: **m~fähig** *adj* manoeuvrable *(Brit)*, maneuverable *(US)*; **~fähigkeit** *f* manoeuvrability *(Brit)*, maneuverability *(US)*; **m~unfähig** *adj* disabled.

Mansarde *f* **-n** garret; *(Boden)* attic.

Manschette *f (Ärmelaufschlag)* cuff. **~n haben** *(col)* to be scared silly *(col)*.

Manschettenknopf *m* cufflink.

Mantel *m* ⁼ **(a)** coat; *(fig)* cloak, mantle. **(b)** *(Tech)* casing; *(Rohr~)* jacket.

Mantel- *in cpds (Tex)* coat; **~stoff** *m* coat fabric; **~tarifvertrag** *m* general agreement on conditions of employment.

manuell *adj Arbeit* manual. **etw ~ bedienen** to operate sth manually.

Manuskript *nt* **-e** manuscript; *(Rad, Film, TV)* script.

maoistisch *adj* Maoist.

Mappe *f* **-n** *(Aktenhefter)* folder, file; *(Aktentasche)* briefcase; *(Schul~)* (school) bag; *(Feder~, Bleistift~)* pencil case.

Marathon- *in cpds* marathon; **~lauf** *m* marathon; **~läufer** *m* marathon runner.

Märchen *nt* - fairy story; *(col)* tall story.

Märchen- *in cpds* fairytale; **~buch** *nt* book of fairytales; **~erzähler** *m* teller of fairytales; *(fig)* storyteller; **m~haft** *adj* fairytale *attr; (fig)* fabulous; **~land** *nt* fairyland; **~prinz** *m* Prince Charming.

Marder *m* - marten.

Margarine *f* margarine.

Marge ['marʒə] *f* **-n** *(Comm)* margin.

Maria *f* - Mary. **die Mutter ~** the Virgin Mary.

Marien- [-iːən]: **~bild** *nt* picture of the Virgin Mary; **~käfer** *m* ladybird.

Marihuana [mari'huaːna] *nt no pl* marijuana.

Marinade *f (Cook)* marinade; *(Soße)* mayonnaise-based sauce.

Marine *f* navy.

Marine- *in cpds* naval; **m~blau** *adj* navy blue; **~soldat** *m* marine.

marinieren* *vt Fisch, Fleisch* to marinate.

Marionette *f* marionette, puppet; *(fig)* puppet.

Marionetten- *in cpds* puppet; **~spieler** *m* puppeteer; **~theater** *nt* puppet theatre *(Brit)* or theater *(US)*.

Mark¹ *nt no pl (Knochen~)* marrow; *(Bot: Gewebe~)* medulla, pith. **bis ins ~** *(fig)* to the core; **jdn bis ins ~ treffen** *(fig)* to cut sb to the quick; **es geht mir durch ~ und Bein** *(col)* it goes right through me; **kein ~ in den Knochen haben** *(fig)* to have no backbone.

Mark² *f* - *or (hum)* ⁼er mark. **Deutsche ~** German mark, deutschmark; **vier ~ zwanzig** four marks twenty (pfennigs); **mit jeder ~ rechnen müssen** to have to count every penny.

markant *adj (ausgeprägt)* clear-cut; *Schriftzüge* clearly defined.

Marke *f* **-n (a)** *(bei Lebens- und Genußmitteln)* brand; *(bei Industriegütern)* make. **du bist (vielleicht) eine ~!** *(col)* you're a fine one *(col)*. **(b)** *(Brief~)* stamp; *(Essen~)* voucher; *(Rabatt~)* (trading) stamp; *(Lebensmittel~)* coupon. **auf ~n** *(col)* on coupons. **(c)** *(Erkennungs~)* disc, tag; *(Garderoben~)* ticket, check *(US); (Polizei~)* badge; *(Spiel~)* chip; *(Pfand~ etc)* token.

Marken-: **~artikel** *m* proprietary article; **~butter** *f* best quality butter; **~erzeugnis, ~fabrikat** *nt* proprietary article; **~name** *m* brand name.

Marketing *nt no pl* marketing.

markieren* *vt (lit, fig, Sport)* to mark; *(col: vortäuschen)* to play. **den starken Mann ~** to come the strong man *(col)*.

Markierung *f* marking; *(Zeichen)* mark.

markig *adj (kraftvoll)* vigorous, pithy.

Markise *f* **-n** awning.

Mark-: **~knochen** *m (Cook)* marrowbone; **~stein** *m (lit, fig)* milestone; **~stück** *nt* (one-)mark piece.

Markt *m* ⁼e **(a)** market; *(~platz)* marketplace; *(Jahr~)* fair. **~ abhalten** to hold a market; **dienstags ist ~** there is a market every Tuesday. **(b)** *(Comm)* market; *(Warenverkehr)* trade. **auf dem ~** on the market; **auf den ~ bringen** to put on the market.

Markt- *in cpds* market; **~anteil** *m* share of the market; **m~beherrschend** *adj* **m~beherrschend sein** to dominate the market; **~bude** *f* market stall; **~flecken** *m* small market town; **~forschung** *f* market research; **~frau** *f* market woman; **m~gerecht** *adj* geared to market requirements; **~halle** *f* covered market; **~lage** *f* state of the market; **~lücke** *f* gap in the market; **~platz** *m* marketplace; **am/auf dem ~platz** on/in the marketplace; **~schreier** *m* market crier; **m~schreierisch** *adj* loud and vociferous; *(fig)* blatant; **~stand** *m* market stall; **~weib** *nt (pej)* market woman; *(fig)* fish-wife; **~wert** *m* market value; **~wirtschaft** *f* market economy; **m~wirtschaftlich** *adj attr* free enterprise.

Marmelade *f* jam; *(Orangen~)* marmalade.

Marmeladenglas *nt* jam-jar.

Marmor m -e marble.
Marmorkuchen m marble cake.
marokkanisch adj Moroccan.
Marokko nt Morocco.
Marone f -n (sweet or Spanish) chestnut.
Marotte f -n quirk.
Mars m no pl (Myth, Astron) Mars.
marsch interj (a) (Mil) march. **vorwärts** ~! forward march! (b) (col) off with you. ~ **ins Bett!** off to bed with you!
Marsch[1] m -e (a) (das Marschieren) march; (Wanderung) hike. **sich in** ~ **setzen** to move off. (b) (~musik) march. **jdm den** ~ **blasen** (col) to give sb a rocket (col).
Marsch[2] f -en marsh, fen.
Marschall m, pl **Marschälle** (field) marshal.
Marsch-: ~**befehl** m (Mil) (für Truppen) marching orders pl; (für einzelnen) travel orders pl; **m~bereit** adj ready to move; ~**flugkörper** m cruise missile; ~**gepäck** nt pack.
marschieren* vi aux sein to march; (fig) to march off.
Marsch-: ~**land** nt marsh(land), fen; ~**musik** f military marches pl; ~**ordnung** f marching order; ~**richtung** f (lit) route of march; (fig) line of approach; ~**verpflegung** f rations pl; (Mil) field rations pl.
Marsmensch m Martian.
Marter f -n (liter) torment.
martern (liter) vt to torture, to torment.
Marterpfahl m stake.
martialisch [mar'tsia:lɪʃ] adj (geh) martial, warlike.
Martinshorn nt siren (of police etc). **mit** ~ with its siren blaring or going.
Märtyrer(in f) m - (Eccl, fig) martyr.
Martyrium nt (fig) ordeal.
Marxismus m Marxism.
Marxist(in f) m Marxist.
marxistisch adj Marxist.
März m -e March. **im** ~ in March; **im Monat** ~ in the month of March; **heute ist der zweite** ~ today is the second of March or March second (US); (geschrieben) today is 2nd March; **am ersten** ~ **fahren wir nach** ... on the first of March we are going to ...; **in diesem** ~ this March; **im Laufe des** ~ during March; **der** ~ **war sehr warm** March was very warm; **Anfang/Ende/ Mitte** ~ at the beginning/end/in the middle of March; **den 4.** ~ 1987 4th March 1987.
Masche f -n (a) (Strick~, Häkel~) stitch; (von Netz) hole. **die** ~**n eines Netzes** the mesh of a net; **durch die** ~**n schlüpfen** to slip through the net. (b) (col: Trick) trick, dodge (col). **die** ~ **raushaben** to know how to do it; **das ist seine neueste** ~ that's his latest (fad).
Maschendraht m wire netting.
Maschine f machine; (Motor) engine; (col: Motorrad) bike; (Schreib~) typewriter; (Flugzeug) plane. **etw mit der** ~ **schreiben** to type sth.
maschinell 1 adj Herstellung mechanical, machine attr. 2 adv mechanically, by machine.
Maschinen-: ~**bau** m mechanical engineering; ~**bauingenieur** m mechanical engineer; ~**fabrik** f engineering works sing or pl; **m~geschrieben** adj typewritten; ~**gewehr** nt machine-gun; **mit** ~**gewehr(en) beschießen** to machine-gun; ~**haus** nt machine room; ~**öl** nt lubricating oil; ~**park** m plant; ~**pistole** f submachine gun; ~**raum** m plant room; (Naut) engine-room; ~**schaden** m mechanical fault; (Aviat etc) engine fault; ~**schlosser** m engine fitter; ~**schrift** f typescript, typing; (Schriftart) typeface; **m~schriftlich** adj typewritten no adv; ~**stürmer** m - machine wrecker; (Hist) Luddite; ~**teil** nt machine part.
Maschinerie f (fig) machinery.
maschineschreiben vi sep irreg to type. **sie**

schreibt Maschine she types.
Maschinist(in f) m machine operator; (Schiffs~) engineer.
Maser f -n (von Holz) vein.
Masern pl measles sing.
Maserung f grain.
Maske f -n (lit, fig) mask. **die** ~ **fallen lassen** (fig) to throw off one's mask; **jdm die** ~ **herunterreißen** (fig) to unmask sb; **ohne** ~ (fig) undisguised; **unter der** ~ **von etw** (fig) under the guise of sth; **das ist alles nur** ~ that's all just pretence (Brit) or pretense (US).
Masken-: ~**ball** m masked ball; ~**bildner(in** f) m make-up artist.
Maskerade f (Verkleidung) costume; (fig) masquerade.
maskieren* 1 vt (a) (verkleiden) to dress up; (unkenntlich machen) to disguise. (b) (verbergen) to mask. 2 vr to dress up; (sich unkenntlich machen) to disguise oneself.
maskiert adj masked.
Maskierung f (Verkleidung) fancy-dress costume; (von Spion etc) disguise; (Verhüllung) masking.
Maskottchen nt (lucky) mascot.
Maskulinum nt, pl **Maskulina** masculine noun.
Masochismus m no pl masochism.
Masochist(in f) m masochist.
maß pret of **messen**.
Maß[1] nt -e (a) (~einheit) measure (für of); (Zollstock) rule; (Bandmaß) tape measure. ~**e und Gewichte** weights and measures; **das** ~ **aller Dinge** (fig) the measure of all things; **mit zweierlei** ~ **messen** (fig) to operate a double standard; **das** ~ **ist voll** (fig) that's enough (of that); **in reichem** ~(**e**) abundantly; **über das übliche** ~ **hinausgehen** to overstep the mark; **weder** ~ **noch Ziel kennen** to know no bounds.
(b) (Meßgröße) measurement; (von Zimmer, Möbelstück auch) dimension. **sich** (dat) **etw nach** ~ **anfertigen lassen** to have sth made to measure or order (US); ~ **nehmen** to measure up; **bei jdm** ~ **nehmen** to take sb's measurements.
(c) (Ausmaß) extent, degree. **ein gewisses** ~ **an** ... a certain degree of ...; **in hohem** ~(**e**) to a high degree; **in solchem** ~(**e**), **daß** ... to such an extent that ...; **in großem** ~**e** to a great extent; **in vollem** ~**e** fully; **in besonderem** ~**e** especially; **in höchstem** ~**e** extremely; **über alle** ~**en** (liter) extremely, beyond measure.
Maß[2] f (S Ger, Aus) litre (Brit) or liter (US) of beer.
Massage [ma'sa:ʒə] f -n massage.
Massagesalon m (euph) massage parlour (Brit) or salon (US).
Massaker nt - massacre.
massakrieren* vt to massacre.
Maß-: ~**anzug** m made-to-measure or made-to-order (US) suit; ~**arbeit** f (col) **das war** ~**arbeit** that was a neat bit of work.
Masse f -n (a) (Stoff, Phys) mass; (Cook) mixture. (b) (große Menge) heaps pl (col); (von Besuchern etc) host. **die** (**breite**) ~ **der Bevölkerung** etc the bulk of the population etc; **eine ganze** ~ (col) a great deal; **die** ~ **muß es bringen** (Comm) the profit only comes with quantity. (c) (Menschenmenge) crowd. (d) (Bevölkerungs~) masses pl (auch pej). **die breite** ~ the masses pl.
Maßeinheit f unit of measurement.
Massel m no pl (col) ~ **haben** to be dead lucky (col).
Massen- in cpds mass; ~**artikel** m mass-produced article; ~**bedarfsgüter** pl basic consumer goods pl; ~**grab** nt mass grave; ~**güter** pl bulk goods pl; **m~haft** adj on a huge or massive scale; **m~haft Sekt** etc (col) masses of champagne etc (col); ~**medien** pl mass media pl; ~**mord** m mass murder; ~**mörder** m mass murderer; ~**produktion** f mass production;

~**psychose** f mass hysteria; ~**szene** f crowd scene; ~**ware** f mass-produced article; **m~weise** adj siehe **m~haft**.

Masseur [ma'søːɐ] m masseur.

Masseuse [-'søːzə] f masseuse.

maßgebend, maßgeblich adj (entscheidend) Einfluß decisive; Meinung definitive; Text definitive, authoritative; Fachmann authoritative; (wichtig) Persönlichkeit leading; Beteiligung substantial; (zuständig) competent. ~**e Kreise** influential circles; **das war für mich nicht** ~ that didn't weigh auth with me.

maßgeschneidert adj Anzug made-to-measure, made-to-order (US), custom attr (US).

maßhalten vi sep irreg to practise (Brit) or practice (US) moderation.

Maßhalteparole f appeal for moderation.

massieren[1]* vt to massage.

massieren[2]* vt Truppen to mass.

massig 1 adj massive, huge. **2** adv (col: sehr viel) ~ **Geld** etc stacks of money etc (col).

mäßig adj (a) moderate. ~ **essen** to eat with moderation; ~ **rauchen** to smoke in moderation; ~**, aber regelmäßig** in moderation but regularly. **(b)** (schwach) Leistung etc mediocre; Begabung, Beifall moderate.

mäßigen 1 vt (mildern) Anforderungen to moderate; Sprache auch to tone down; Zorn, Ungeduld to curb. **sein Tempo** ~ to slacken one's pace; siehe **gemäßigt. 2** vr (im Essen, Trinken, Temperament) to restrain oneself. ~ **Sie sich in Ihren Worten!** tone down your language!

Mäßigkeit f (beim Essen, Trinken) moderation; (von Forderungen etc) moderateness).

Mäßigung f restraint.

massiv adj (a) (pur, stabil) solid. **(b)** (heftig) Beleidigung gross; Drohung, Kritik heavy; Anschuldigung severe. ~ **werden** (col) to turn nasty.

Massiv nt -e (Geol) massif.

Maßkrug m litre (Brit) or liter (US) beer mug; (Steinkrug) stein.

maßlos 1 adj extreme; Forderungen auch excessive; Freude, Ehrgeiz auch boundless; Mensch (in Essen etc) immoderate. **er raucht/trinkt** ~ he smokes/drinks to excess. **2** adv (äußerst) extremely; übertreiben grossly, hugely.

Maßlosigkeit f siehe adj extremeness; excessiveness; boundlessness; lack of moderation.

Maßnahme f -n measure. ~**n treffen, um etw zu tun** to take steps to do sth.

maßregeln vt insep (zurechtweisen) to reprimand; (bestrafen) to discipline.

Maßreg(e)lung f (a) no pl siehe vt reprimanding; disciplining. **(b)** (Rüge) reprimand.

Maßstab m (a) (Karten~) scale. **im** ~ **1:1000** on a scale of 1:1000. **(b)** (fig: Richtlinie, Kriterium) standard. **einen strengen** ~ **anlegen** to apply a strict standard (an +acc to); **als** ~ **dienen** to serve as a model; **sich** (dat) **etw zum** ~ **nehmen** to take sth as a yardstick.

maßstab(s)getreu adj (true) to scale. **eine** ~**e Karte** an accurate scale map.

maßvoll adj moderate.

Mast[1] m -en or -e (Naut, Rad, TV) mast; (Stange) pole; (Elec) pylon.

Mast[2] f -en (das Mästen) fattening.

Mastdarm m rectum.

mästen 1 vt to fatten. **2** vr (col) to gorge oneself.

Mast- in cpds (zu mästen) feeder; (gemästet) fattened; ~**futter** nt (fattening) feed; (für Schweine) mast; ~**schwein** nt (zu mästen) porker; (gemästet) fattened pig.

Masturbation f masturbation.

masturbieren* vtir to masturbate.

Matador m -e (Stierkampf) matador; (fig) kingpin.

Matchball m (Tennis) match point.

Material nt -ien [-iən] material; (Bau~, Gerät) materials pl; (Beweis~) evidence.

Materialfehler m defect in the material.

Materialismus m materialism.

Materialist(in f) m materialist.

materialistisch adj materialist(ic); (pej) materialistic.

Materialkosten pl cost of materials sing.

Materie [-iə] f (a) no pl (Phys, Philos) matter no art. **(b)** (Stoff, Thema) subject-matter no indef art.

materiell adj (a) (Philos) material, physical. **(b)** (wirtschaftlich) financial; Vorteile auch material; (gewinnsüchtig) materialistic. ~ **eingestellt sein** to be materialistic.

Mathe f no pl (Sch col) maths sing (Brit col), math (US col).

Mathematik f mathematics sing no art.

Mathematiker(in f) m mathematician.

mathematisch adj mathematical.

Matinee f -n [-iən] matinée.

Matjeshering m (col) young herring.

Matratze f -n mattress.

Mätresse f (dated pej) mistress.

Matriarchat nt matriarchy.

Matrikel f -n (Univ) matriculation register.

Matrixdrucker m dot-matrix printer.

Matrize f -n (Typ) matrix, mould (Brit), mold (US); (für Schreibmaschine) stencil. **etw auf** ~ **schreiben** to stencil sth.

Matrose m (wk) -n, -n sailor; (als Rang) rating (Brit), ordinary seaman.

Matrosenanzug m sailor suit.

Matsch m no pl (col) (breiige Masse) mush; (Schlamm) mud; (Schnee~) slush.

matschig adj (col) (breiig) gooey (col), mushy; (schlammig) muddy; Schnee slushy.

matt adj (a) (schwach) Kranker weak. **sich** ~ **fühlen** to have no energy. **(b)** Augen, Farbe dull; Farbe, Papier mat(t); Licht dim; Glühbirne opal, pearl; Spiegel cloudy, dull. **(c)** (fig) Ausdruck, Rede lame, feeble. **(d)** (Chess) (check)mate. **jdn** ~ **setzen** to checkmate sb (auch fig).

Matt nt -s (Chess) (check)mate.

Matte f -n mat. **auf der** ~ **stehen** (col) to be on the doorstep (col); (am Arbeitsplatz etc) to be in.

Mattigkeit f weariness; (von Kranken) weakness.

Mattlack m mat(t) varnish.

Mattscheibe f (Phot) focus(s)ing screen; (col: Fernseher) telly (Brit col), tube (US col). **eine** ~ **haben** (col: dumm sein) to be soft in the head (col); (nicht klar denken können) to have a mental block.

Mätzchen nt (col) antic. ~ **machen** to fool around (col).

mau adj pred (col) poor, bad. **mir ist** ~ I feel poorly (col).

Mauer f -n (lit, fig) wall. **etw mit einer** ~ **umgeben** to wall sth in; **die** ~**n einreißen** (fig) to tear down the barriers.

Mauerblümchen nt (fig col) wallflower.

mauern 1 vi (a) to build, to lay bricks. **(b)** (Ftbl sl) to stonewall (Ftbl sl), to play defensively; (fig) to stonewall (esp Parl). **2** vt to build.

Mauer-: ~**schwalbe** f, ~**segler** m swift; ~**vorsprung** m projection on a/the wall; ~**werk** nt (a) (Steinmauer) stonework, masonry; (Ziegelmauer) brickwork; **(b)** (die Mauern) walls pl.

Maul nt Mäuler m (von Tier) mouth; (von Löwe etc) jaws pl; (pej: von Mensch) gob (col!). **ein loses** or **lockeres** ~ **haben** (col) (frech sein) to be an impudent so-and-so (col); (indiskret sein) to be a blabbermouth (col); **das** ~ **zu weit aufreißen** (col!) to be too cocksure (col); **ein großes** ~ **haben** (col!) to be a big-mouth (col); **darüber werden sich die Leute das** ~ **zerreißen** (col) that will start people's tongues wagging; **dem Volk** or **den Leuten aufs** ~ **schauen** (col) to listen to what people really say; **halt's** ~! (col!) shut your face (col!); **jdm das** ~ **stopfen** (col!) to shut sb up (col).

maulen vi (col) to moan.

Maul-: ~**esel** m mule; **m~faul** adj (col) uncommunicative; ~**held** m *(pej)* loud-mouth *(col)*; ~**korb** m *(lit, fig)* muzzle; ~**tier** nt mule; ~- **und Klauenseuche** f *(Vet)* foot-and-mouth disease; ~**werk** nt *(col) siehe* **Mundwerk.**

Maulwurf m, pl **Maulwürfe** mole.

Maulwurfs-: ~**haufen,** ~**hügel** m mole-hill.

Maurer m - bricklayer. **pünktlich wie die** ~ *(hum)* super-punctual.

Maurer-: ~**arbeit** f bricklaying (work) *no pl*; ~**kelle** f (bricklayer's) trowel; ~**meister** m master builder.

Maus f, pl **Mäuse (a)** *(auch Comp)* mouse. **weiße** ~ *(fig col)* traffic cop *(col)*; **weiße Mäuse sehen** *(fig col)* to see pink elephants *(col)*; **eine graue** ~ *(col)* a mouse *(col)*. **(b) Mäuse** pl *(col: Geld)* bread *(col)*, dough *(col)*.

Mauschelei f *(col: Korruption)* fiddle *(col)*.

mauscheln vti *(manipulieren)* to fiddle *(col)*.

Mäuschen ['mɔysçən] nt **(a)** little mouse. **da möchte ich mal** ~ **sein** *(col)* I'd like to be a fly on the wall. **(b)** *(fig)* sweetheart *(col)*.

mäuschenstill ['mɔysçən-] adj dead quiet; *(reglos)* stock-still.

Mause-: ~**falle** f mouse-trap; ~**loch** nt mousehole; **sich in ein** ~**loch verkriechen** *(fig)* to crawl into a hole in the ground.

mausen vt *(dated col)* to pinch *(col)*.

Mauser f no pl *(Orn)* moult *(Brit)*, molt *(US)*. **in der** ~ **sein** to be moulting *(Brit)* or molting *(US)*.

mausern vr *(Orn)* to moult *(Brit)*, to molt *(US)*.

mausetot adj *(col)* stone-dead.

mausgrau adj **(a)** *(~farben)* mouse-grey *(Brit)*, mouse-gray *(US)*. **(b)** *(unauffällig)* mousy.

mausig adj: **sich** ~ **machen** *(col)* to get uppish *(col)*.

Mausoleum [-'leːʊm] nt, pl **Mausoleen** [-'leːən] mausoleum.

max. = **maximal.**

Maxi- *in cpds* maxi-.

maximal 1 adj maximum. **2** adv *(höchstens)* at most. **bis zu** ~ **$100** up to a maximum of $100.

Maximal- *in cpds* maximum.

Maxime f -n *(liter, Philos)* maxim.

maximieren* vt *(Econ)* to maximize.

Maximierung f *(Econ)* maximization.

Maximum nt, pl **Maxima** maximum *(an + dat* of).

Maxi-Single [-'sɪŋgl] f twelve-inch single.

Mayonnaise [majɔ'nɛːzə] f -n mayonnaise.

Mäzen m -e patron.

MdB [ɛm'deː'beː] m -s = **Mitglied des Bundestages** Member of the "Bundestag", ≈ MP.

m.E. = **meines Erachtens** in my opinion.

Mechanik f **(a)** no pl *(Phys)* mechanics sing. **(b)** *(Mechanismus)* mechanism.

Mechaniker(in f) m - mechanic.

mechanisch adj mechanical.

Mechanismus m mechanism.

Meckerei f *(col)* grumbling.

Meckerer m - *(col)* grumbler.

meckern vi *(Ziege)* to bleat; *(col: Mensch)* to moan, to bitch *(col)*.

Meckerziege f *(pej col)* sourpuss *(col)*.

Medaille [me'daljə] f -n *(bei Wettbewerben)* medal.

Medaillengewinner [me'daljən-] m medallist *(Brit)*, medalist *(US)*.

Medaillon [medal'jõː] nt -s *(Bildchen)* medallion; *(Schmuckkapsel)* locket.

Medien ['meːdiən] pl media pl.

Medikament nt medicine.

Meditation f meditation.

meditieren* vi to meditate.

Medium nt medium.

Medizin f -en **(a)** no pl *(Heilkunde)* medicine. **(b)** *(col: Heilmittel)* medicine.

Medizinball m *(Sport)* medicine ball.

Mediziner(in f) m - doctor; *(Univ)* medic *(col)*.

medizinisch adj **(a)** *(ärztlich)* medical. **M~e Fakultät** school or faculty of medicine; ~**-techni-**

sche Assistentin medical assistant. **(b)** *(heilend) Bäder* medicinal; *Shampoo* medicated.

Medizin-: ~**mann** m, pl -**männer** medicine man; *(hum: Arzt)* quack *(col)*, medico *(US col)*; ~**studium** nt study of medicine.

Meer nt -e sea; *(Welt~)* ocean. **am** ~**(e)** by the sea; **übers** ~ **fahren** to travel (across) the seas; **ans** ~ **fahren** to go to the sea(side); **über dem** ~ above sea-level.

Meer-: ~**busen** m gulf, bay; ~**enge** f straits pl, strait.

Meeres-: ~**arm** m arm of the sea, inlet; ~**boden,** ~**grund** m seabed; ~**klima** nt maritime climate; ~**kunde** f oceanography; ~**oberfläche** f surface of the sea; ~**spiegel** m sea-level; **über/unter dem** ~**spiegel** above/below sea-level; ~**tier** nt marine creature.

Meer-: ~**gott** m *(Myth)* sea-god; ~**göttin** f seagoddess; ~**jungfrau** f mermaid; ~**rettich** m horseradish; ~**salz** nt sea salt; ~**schweinchen** nt guineapig; ~**wasser** nt sea water.

mega-, Mega- *in cpds* mega-.

Mega-: ~**phon** nt megaphone; ~**tonne** f megaton; ~**watt** nt megawatt.

Mehl nt -e flour; *(grober)* meal; *(Pulver)* powder.

mehlig adj *Äpfel, Kartoffeln* mealy.

Mehl-: ~**sack** m flour bag; ~**schwitze** f *(Cook)* roux.

mehr 1 *indef pron inv comp of* **viel, sehr** more. **was wollen Sie** ~? what more do you want?; ~ **will er nicht bezahlen** he doesn't want to pay (any) more; **ist das alles,** ~ **kostet das nicht?** is that all it costs?

2 adv **(a)** *(in höherem Maße)* more. **immer** ~ more and more; ~ **oder weniger** more or less; ~ **Geschäftsmann als Arzt** more (of) a businessman than a doctor; ~ **ein juristisches Problem** more (of) a legal problem. **(b)** *(+neg: sonst, länger)* **ich habe kein Geld** ~ I haven't any more money; **du bist doch kein Kind** ~! you're no longer a child!; **es besteht keine Hoffnung** ~ there's no hope left; **kein Wort** ~! not another word!; **es war niemand** ~ **da** there was no-one left; **wenn niemand** ~ **einsteigt, ...** if nobody else gets in ...; **das benutzt man nicht** ~ it's no longer used; **das darf nicht** ~ **vorkommen** that must not happen again; **nicht** ~ **lange** not much longer; **nichts** ~ nothing more; **nie** ~ never again, nevermore *(liter)*; **ich will dich nie** ~ **wiedersehen** I don't ever want to see you again.

Mehr nt no pl *(Zuwachs)* increase.

Mehr-: ~**arbeit** f extra time or work; ~**aufwand** m additional expenditure; ~**bedarf** m greater need *(an + dat* of, for); *(Comm)* increased demand *(an + dat* for); ~**belastung** f excess load; *(fig)* additional burden; **m~deutig** adj ambiguous; ~**einnahme** f additional revenue.

mehren 1 vt *(liter: vergrößern)* to augment. **2** vr *(geh: sich vermehren)* to multiply.

mehrere *indef pron* several; *(verschiedene auch)* various.

mehrfach 1 adj multiple; *(zahlreich)* numerous; *(wiederholt)* repeated. **ein** ~**er Millionär** a multimillionaire; **der** ~**e Meister im 100-m-Lauf** the man who has several times been the 100 metres champion; **die Unterlagen in** ~**er Ausfertigung einsenden** to send in several copies of the documents. **2** adv *(öfter)* many or several times; *(wiederholt)* repeatedly.

Mehr-: ~**familienhaus** nt multiple dwelling *(form)*; **m~farbig** adj multicoloured *(Brit)*, multicolored *(US)*.

Mehrheit f majority. **die** ~ **besitzen/erringen** to have/gain a majority; **die** ~ **verlieren** to lose one's majority; **mit zwei Stimmen** ~ with a majority of two.

Mehrheits-: ~**beschluß** m majority decision; ~**prinzip** nt principle of majority rule; ~**wahl-**

recht *nt* majority vote system.

Mehr-: m~jährig *adj attr* of several years; **m~jährige Klinikerfahrung** several years of clinical experience; **~kosten** *pl* additional costs *pl*; **m~malig** *adj attr* repeated; **m~mals** *adv* several times; **~parteiensystem** *nt* multi-party system; **m~sprachig** *adj* multilingual; **m~sprachig aufwachsen** to grow up multilingual; **m~stimmig** *adj* *(Mus)* for several voices; **m~stimmiger Gesang** part-singing; **m~stimmig singen** to sing in harmony; **m~stöckig** *adj* multistorey *(Brit)*, multilevel *(US)*; **m~stündig** *adj attr* lasting several hours; **mit m~stündiger Verspätung eintreffen** to arrive several hours late; **m~tägig** *adj attr Konferenz* lasting several days; **m~teilig** *adj* in several parts; **~wegflasche** *f* returnable bottle; **~wert** *m* *(Econ)* added value; **~wertsteuer** *f* value added tax, VAT; **~zahl** *f* *no pl* **(a)** *(Gram)* plural; **(b)** *(Mehrheit)* majority.

Mehrzweck- *in cpds* multipurpose.

meiden *pret* **mied,** *ptp* **gemieden** *vt* to avoid.

Meile *f* **-n** mile. **das riecht man drei ~n gegen den Wind** *(col)* you can smell that a mile off *(col)*.

Meilen-: ~stein *m* *(lit, fig)* milestone; **m~weit** *adv* for miles; **m~weit entfernt** *(lit, fig)* miles away.

Meiler *m* **- (Kohlen~)** charcoal kiln; *(Atom~)* (atomic) pile.

mein *poss pron* **(a)** *(adjektivisch)* my. **(b)** *(old: substantivisch)* mine.

Mein|eid *m* perjury *no indef art.* **einen ~ leisten** to commit perjury.

meinen 1 *vi* *(denken, glauben)* to think. **ich meine, ... I think ...; ~ Sie?** (do) you think so?; **wie Sie ~!** as you wish; *(drohend auch)* have it your own way; **wenn du meinst!** if you like; **man sollte ~** one would have thought. **2** *vt (der Ansicht sein)* to think; *(sagen wollen)* to mean; *(col: sagen)* to say. **was ~ Sie dazu?** what do you think *or* say?; **~ Sie das im Ernst?** are you serious about that?; **das will ich ~!** I quite agree!; **wie ~ Sie das?** how do you mean?; **damit bin ich gemeint** that refers to me; **sie meint es gut** she means well; **er meint es ehrlich mit dem Mädchen** his intentions towards the girl are honourable; **sie meint es nicht böse** she means no harm.

meiner *pers pron gen of* **ich** of me.

meine(r, s) *poss pron (substantivisch)* mine. **der/die/das ~** *(geh)* mine; **ich tue das M~** *(geh)* I'll do my bit.

meinerseits *adv* for my part. **Vorschläge ~** suggestions from me.

meines-: ~gleichen *pron inv (meiner Art)* people like myself; **~teils** *adv* for my part.

meinet-: ~halben *(dated),* **~wegen** *adv* **(a)** *(wegen mir)* on my account; **(b)** *(von mir aus)* as far as I'm concerned; **~wegen!** if you like; **~willen** *adv:* **um ~willen** for my sake.

meins *poss pron* mine.

Meinung *f* opinion; *(Anschauung auch)* view. **meiner ~ nach** in my opinion; **ich bin der ~, daß ... I** take the view that ...; **seine ~ ändern** to change one's opinion *or* mind; **einer ~ sein** to think the same; **das ist auch meine ~!** that's just what I think; **jdm die ~ sagen** *(col)* to give sb a piece of one's mind *(col)*.

Meinungs-: ~äußerung *f* (expression of) opinion; **~austausch** *m* exchange of views *(über + acc* on, about); **~forscher** *m* (opinion) pollster; **~forschung** *f* (public) opinion polling; **~forschungsinstitut** *nt* opinion research institute; **~freiheit** *f* freedom of opinion; **~macher** *m* *(col)* opinion-maker; **~umfrage** *f* opinion poll; **~umschwung** *m* swing of opinion; **~verschiedenheit** *f* difference of opinion.

Meise *f* **-n** titmouse. **eine ~ haben** *(col)* to be crackers *(Brit col)* or crazy.

Meißel *m* **-** chisel.

meißeln *vti* to chisel.

meist *adv siehe* **meistens.**

meistbietend *adj* highest bidding; **~ versteigern** to auction to the highest bidder.

meisten: am ~ *adv superl of* **viel, sehr** the most, most of all.

meistens *adv* mostly; *(zum größten Teil)* for the most part.

meistenteils *adv siehe* **meistens.**

Meister *m* **- (a)** *(Handwerks~)* master (craftsman); *(Sport)* champion; *(Mannschaft)* champions *pl*. **seinen ~ machen** to take one's master craftsman's diploma. **(b)** *(Lehr~, Künstler)* master *(auch fig)*. **er hat seinen ~ gefunden** *(fig)* he's met his match; **es ist noch kein ~ vom Himmel gefallen** *(Prov)* no-one is born an expert.

meiste(r, s) *indef pron superl of* **viel (a)** *(adjektivisch)* **die ~n Leute** most people; **die ~n Gläser gingen kaputt** most of the glasses were broken; **meine ~ Zeit** most of my time. **(b)** *(substantivisch)* **die ~n (von ihnen)** most (of them).

Meister- *in cpds* master; **~brief** *m* master craftsman's diploma; **m~haft 1** *adj* masterly; **2** *adv* in a masterly manner; **er versteht es m~haft, zu lügen** he is brilliant at lying; **~hand** *f:* **von ~hand** by a master hand.

Meisterin *f (Handwerks~)* master craftswoman; *(Sport)* champion.

Meisterleistung *f* masterly performance; *(iro)* brilliant achievement.

meistern *vt* to master; *Schwierigkeiten* to overcome. **sein Leben ~** to come to grips with one's life.

Meisterschaft *f* **(a)** *(Sport)* championship; *(Veranstaltung)* championships *pl*. **(b)** *no pl (Können)* mastery.

Meisterschaftsspiel *nt* *(Sport)* championship match.

Meister-: ~stück *nt (von Handwerker)* work done to qualify as master craftsman; *(fig)* masterpiece; *(geniale Tat)* master stroke; **~werk** *nt* masterpiece.

meist-: ~gekauft *adj attr* best-selling; **~genannt** *adj attr* most frequently mentioned.

Mekka *nt (Geog, fig)* Mecca.

Melancholie [melaŋko'liː] *f* melancholy.

melancholisch [melaŋ'koːlɪʃ] *adj* melancholy.

Melasse *f* **-n** molasses.

Melde-: ~amt *nt* registration office; **~behörde** *f* registration authorities *pl*.

melden 1 *vt* to report; *(registrieren)* to register; *(ankündigen)* to announce. **Änderungen der Behörde** *(dat)* **~** to notify the authorities of changes; **wie soeben gemeldet wird** *(Rad, TV)* according to reports just coming in; **nichts zu ~ haben** *(col)* to have no say; **wen darf ich ~?** who(m) shall I say (is here)?

2 *vr* **(a)** to report *(zu for).* **sich für etw ~** *(esp Mil)* to sign up for sth; *(für Lehrgang)* to enrol for sth; **sich krank/zum Dienst ~** to report sick/for work; **sich auf eine Anzeige ~** to answer an advertisement. **(b)** *(fig: sich ankündigen)* to announce one's presence; *(Sport, zur Prüfung)* to enter (one's name) *(zu for).* **(c)** *(esp Telec: antworten)* to answer. **es meldet sich niemand** there's no answer. **(d)** *(von sich hören lassen)* to get in touch *(bei* with). **seitdem hat er sich nicht mehr gemeldet** he hasn't been heard of since; **wenn du was brauchst, melde dich** if you need anything give a shout *(col)*.

Melde-: ~pflicht *f* obligation to register; **polizeiliche ~pflicht** obligation to register with the police; **m~pflichtig** *adj* **(a)** obliged to register; **(b)** *Krankheit* notifiable.

Meldung *f* **(a)** *(Mitteilung)* announcement; *(Press, Rad, TV)* report *(über + acc* on, about). **~en vom Sport** sports news *sing.* **(b)** *(dienstlich, bei der Polizei)* report. **(eine) ~ machen** to make a

report. (c) (Sport, Examens~) entry.
meliert adj Haar streaked with grey (Brit) or gray (US); Wolle flecked.
melken pret **melkte** ptp **gemolken** vti (a) to milk. **frisch gemolkene Milch** milk fresh from the cow. (b) (fig col) to milk (col), to fleece (col).
Melodie f melody; (Weise auch) tune.
melodiös adj (geh) melodious.
melodisch adj melodic, tuneful.
melodramatisch adj melodramatic (auch fig).
Melone f -n (a) melon. (b) (Hut) bowler (Brit), derby (US).
Membran f -en (a) (Anat) membrane. (b) (Phys, Tech) diaphragm.
Memme f -n (col) cissy (col), yellow-belly (col).
Memoiren [me'moa:rən] pl memoirs pl.
Memorandum nt, pl **Memoranden** or **Memoranda** (Pol) memorandum.
Menge f -n (a) (Quantum) amount, quantity. (b) (col) (große Anzahl) lot, load (col); (Haufen auch) pile (col), heap (col). **eine ~ Zeit/Häuser** lots (col) of time/houses; **jede ~ masses** pl (col), loads pl (col); **wir haben jede ~ getrunken** we drank a hell of a lot (col); **eine ganze ~** quite a lot. (c) (Menschen~) crowd; (geh: Masse) mass; (pej: Pöbel) mob.
mengen 1 vt (geh) to mix (unter +acc with). **2** vr to mingle (unter +acc with).
Mengen-: ~**lehre** f (Math) set theory; ~**rabatt** m bulk discount.
Meniskus m, pl **Menisken** (Anat, Phys) meniscus.
Mensa f, pl **Mensen** (Univ) refectory (Brit), commons (US).
Mensch m (wk) -en, -en (a) (Person) person, man/woman. **von ~ zu ~** man to man/woman to woman; **es war kein ~ da** there was not a soul there; **als ~** as a person; **das konnte kein ~ ahnen!** no-one could have foreseen that! (b) (als Gattung) der ~ man; die ~en man sing, human beings pl; **ein Tier, das keine ~en mag** an animal that doesn't like people; **ich bin auch nur ein ~!** I'm only human; ~ **und Tier** man and beast. (c) (die Menschheit) die ~en mankind, man; **alle** ~**en** everyone. (d) (col: als Interjektion) hey. ~, **das habe ich ganz vergessen** damn (col), I completely forgot.
Mensch ärgere dich nicht nt no pl (Spiel) ludo.
Menschen- in cpds human; ~**affe** m ape; ~**alter** nt (a) (30 Jahre) generation; (b) (Lebensdauer) lifetime; ~**ansammlung** f gathering (of people); ~**auflauf** m crowd (of people); ~**feind** m misanthropist; **m**~**feindlich** adj Mensch misanthropic; Landschaft hostile to man; ~**fleisch** nt human flesh; ~**fresser(in** f) m - col: Kannibale) cannibal; ~**freund** m philanthropist; **m**~**freundlich** adj Mensch philanthropic; Gegend hospitable; ~**führung** f leadership; ~**gedenken** nt der kälteste Winter seit ~**gedenken** the coldest winter in living memory; ~**hai** m man-eating shark; ~**hand** f human hand; **von** ~**hand geschaffen** fashioned by the hand of man; ~**handel** m slave trade; (Jur) trafficking in human beings; ~**händler** m slave trader; (Jur) trafficker in human beings; ~**kenner** m judge of character; ~**kenntnis** f no pl knowledge of human nature; ~**kenntnis haben** to know human nature; ~**leben** nt human life; **ein** ~**leben lang** a whole lifetime; ~**leben waren nicht zu beklagen** there was no loss of life; **das Unglück hat zwei** ~**leben gefordert** the accident claimed two lives; **m**~**leer** adj deserted; ~**masse,** ~ **menge** f crowd (of people); **m**~**möglich** adj humanly possible; **das m**~**mögliche tun** to do all that is humanly possible; ~**raub** m (Jur) kidnapping; ~**recht** nt human right; ~**rechtskonvention** f Human Rights Convention; ~**scheu** f fear of people; **m**~**scheu** adj afraid of people; ~**schlag**

m (col) kind of people; ~**seele** f human soul; **keine** ~**seele** (fig) not a soul.
Menschenskind interj good heavens.
Menschen-: **m**~**unwürdig** adj beneath human dignity; Behandlung inhumane; Behausung unfit for human habitation; ~**verstand** m gesunder ~**verstand** common sense; ~**würde** f human dignity no art; **m**~**würdig** adj Behandlung humane; Unterkunft fit for human habitation.
Menschheit f die ~ mankind, humanity.
menschlich adj (a) human. **das** ~**e Leben** human life; **der** ~**e Körper/Geist** the human body/mind; **die** ~**e Gemeinschaft** human society; **er ist mir** ~ **sympathisch** I like him as a person; **(einigermaßen)** ~ **aussehen** (col) to look more or less human. (b) (human) Behandlung etc humane.
Menschlichkeit f no pl humanity no art. **aus reiner** ~ on purely humanitarian grounds.
Menschwerdung f (Bibl) incarnation.
Mensen pl of **Mensa.**
Menstruation [menstrua'tsio:n] f menstruation.
Mensur f (Univ) (students') fencing bout.
Mentalität f mentality.
Menthol nt -e menthol.
Menü nt -s (auch Comp) menu.
Menuett nt -e (Tanz, Mus) minuet.
Merk-: **m**~**bar** adj (wahrnehmbar) noticeable; ~**blatt** nt leaflet; (mit Anweisungen auch) instructions pl.
merken 1 vt (entdecken) to notice; (spüren) to feel; (erkennen) to realize. **davon habe ich nichts gemerkt** I didn't notice anything; **jdn etw** ~ **lassen** to make sb feel sth; **woran hast du das gemerkt?** how could you tell that?; **du merkst auch alles!** (iro) nothing escapes you, does it?; **das merkt keiner!** no-one will notice!; **ich merke keinen Unterschied** I can't tell the difference. **2** vr sich (dat) **jdn/etw** ~ to remember sb/sth; **das werde ich mir** ~! I won't forget that; **merk dir das!** mark my words!; sich (dat) **eine Autonummer** ~ to make a (mental) note of a licence number; **diesen Schriftsteller wird man sich** (dat) ~ **müssen** this author is someone to take note of.
merklich adj noticeable. **kein** ~**er Unterschied** no noticeable difference.
Merkmal nt -e characteristic, feature.
Merksatz m mnemonic.
Merkur m no pl (Myth, Astron) Mercury.
Merk-: **m**~**würdig** adj strange, odd; **er hat sich ganz m**~**würdig verändert** he has undergone a curious change; **m**~**würdigerweise** adv strangely enough; **m**~**würdigkeit** f no pl strangeness, oddness.
meschugge adj (col) nuts (col).
Meß-: ~**band** nt tape measure; **m**~**bar** adj measurable; ~**becher** m (Cook) measuring jug; ~**diener** m (Eccl) server, acolyte (form).
Messe f -n (a) (Eccl, Mus) mass. **zur** ~ **gehen** to go to mass. (b) (Ausstellung) (trade) fair. **auf der** ~ at the fair. (c) (Naut, Mil) mess.
Messe- in cpds fair; ~**gelände** nt exhibition centre (Brit) or center (US); ~**halle** f fair pavilion.
messen pret **maß**, ptp **gemessen 1** vti to measure; (zeitlich) to time; (abschätzen) Entfernung etc to judge. **jds Blutdruck** ~ (Arzt etc) to take sb's blood pressure; **während ich lief, maß er die Zeit** I ran and he timed me; **seine Kräfte mit jdm** ~ to match one's strength against sb's; **etw an etw** (dat) ~ (ausprobieren) to try sth out on sth; (vergleichen) to compare sth with sth. **2** vr (geh: in Wettkampf etc) to compete (mit against). **sich mit jdm/etw nicht** ~ **können** to be no match for sb/sth.
Messer nt - knife; (Tech auch) cutter, blade; (Rasier~) (cutthroat) razor. **unter dem** ~ **sein** (Med col) to be under the knife; **jdm das** ~ **an die Kehle setzen** (lit, fig) to hold a knife to sb's

throat; **die ~ wetzen** (*fig*) to prepare for the kill; **damit würden wir ihn ans ~ liefern** (*fig*) that would be putting his head on the block; **ein Kampf bis aufs ~** (*fig*) a fight to the finish; **auf des ~s Schneide stehen** (*fig*) to hang in the balance.

Messer- *in cpds* knife; **m~scharf** *adj* (*lit, fig*) razor-sharp; **m~scharf schließen** (*iro*) to conclude with incredible logic (*iro*); **~spitze** *f* knife point; **eine ~spitze** (**voll**) (*Cook*) a pinch; **~stecher(in** *f*) *m* - knifer (*col*); **~stecherei** *f* knife fight; **~stich** *m* knife thrust; (*Wunde*) stab wound; **~werfer** *m* knife-thrower.

Messe-: **~stadt** *f* (town with an) exhibition centre (*Brit*) *or* center (*US*); **~stand** *m* stand (at a fair).

Meßgerät *nt* (*für Öl, Druck etc*) measuring instrument, gauge.

Messias *m, gen* - (*Rel, fig*) Messiah.

Messing *nt no pl* brass.

Meß-: **~instrument** *nt* gauge; **~stab** *m* (*Aut: Öl-meßstab etc*) dipstick.

Messung *f* (**a**) (*das Messen*) measuring; (*das Ablesen*) reading; (*von Blutdruck*) taking. (**b**) (*Meßergebnis*) measurement; (*Ableseergebnis*) reading.

Meßwert *m* measurement; (*Ableseergebnis*) reading.

Metall *nt* -**e** metal.

Metall- *in cpds* metal-; **~arbeiter** *m* metalworker; **m~haltig** *adj* containing metal.

metallisch *adj* metal; (*metallartig*), (*fig*) *Stimme, Klang* metallic. **~ glänzen** to gleam like metal.

Metallurgie *f* metallurgy.

Metall-: **m~verarbeitend** *adj* **die m~verarbeitende Industrie** the metal-processing industry; **~verarbeitung** *f* metal processing.

Metapher [me'tafe] *f* -**n** (*Liter, Poet*) metaphor.

metaphorisch *adj* (*Liter, Poet*) metaphoric(al).

Metaphysik *f* metaphysics *sing*.

metaphysisch *adj* metaphysical.

Meteor *m* -**e** meteor.

Meteorit *m* (*wk*) -**en**, -**en** meteorite.

Meteorologe *m*, **Meteorologin** *f* meteorologist; (*im Wetterdienst*) weather forecaster.

Meteorologie *f* meteorology.

meteorologisch *adj* meteorological.

Meter *m or nt* - metre (*Brit*), meter (*US*). **in 500 ~ Höhe** at a height of 500 metres; **nach ~n** by the metre.

Meter-: **m~hoch** *adj Wellen etc* enormous; **~maß** *nt* (**a**) (*Bandmaß*) measuring tape; (**b**) (*Stab*) (metre (*Brit*) *or* meter (*US*)) rule; **~ware** *f* (*Tex*) piece goods; **m~weise** *adv* by the metre (*Brit*) *or* meter (*US*).

Methode *f* -**n** (**a**) method. **etw mit ~ machen** to do sth methodically. (**b**) **~n** *pl* (*Sitten*) behaviour (*Brit*), behavior (*US*); **was sind denn das für ~n?** what sort of way is that to behave?

Methodik *f* methodology.

methodisch *adj* methodical.

Methusalem *m* **alt wie ~** old as Methuselah.

Metier [me'tieː] *nt* -**s** (*hum*) job, profession.

Metrik *f* (*Poet, Mus*) metrics *sing*.

metrisch *adj* (*Sci*) metric; (*Poet, Mus auch*) metrical.

Metronom *nt* -**e** (*Mus*) metronome.

Metropole *f* -**n** (**a**) (*größte Stadt*) metropolis. (**b**) (*Zentrum*) capital.

Mett *nt no pl* (*Cook*) minced (*Brit*) *or* ground (*US*) pork.

Mette *f* -**n** (*Eccl*) matins *sing*; (*Abend~*) vespers *sing*.

Mettwurst *f* (smoked) pork/beef sausage.

Metzger *m* - butcher.

Metzger- *siehe* **Fleischer-**.

Metzgerei *f* butcher's (shop) (*Brit*), butcher (*US*).

Meuchel-: **~mord** *m* (treacherous) murder; **~mörder** *m* (treacherous) assassin.

Meute *f* -**n** pack (of hounds); (*fig pej*) mob.

Meuterei *f* mutiny; (*fig auch*) rebellion.

meutern *vi* to mutiny; (*col auch*) to rebel. **die ~den Soldaten** the mutinous soldiers.

Mexikaner(in *f*) *m* - Mexican.

mexikanisch *adj* Mexican.

Mexiko *nt* Mexico.

MEZ = **mitteleuropäische Zeit** CET.

MG [em'geː] *nt* -(**s**) = **Maschinengewehr**.

miau *interj* miaow.

miauen* *vi* to miaow.

mich **1** *pers pron acc of* **ich** me. **2** *reflexive pron* myself. **ich fühle ~ wohl** I feel fine.

mick(e)rig *adj* (*col*) pathetic; *Betrag auch* paltry; *altes Männchen* puny.

mied *pret of* **meiden**.

Mieder *nt* - (*Leibchen*) bodice.

Miederwaren *pl* corsetry *sing*.

Mief *m no pl* (*col*) fug; (*muffig*) stale air; (*Gestank*) stink, pong (*Brit col*). **im Büro ist so ein ~** the air in the office is so stale.

miefen *vi* (*col*) to stink, to pong (*Brit col*). **hier mieft es** there's a pong in here.

Miene *f* -**n** (*Gesichtsausdruck*) expression. **eine finstere ~ machen** to look grim; **gute ~ zum bösen Spiel machen** to grin and bear it.

Mienenspiel *nt* facial expressions *pl*.

mies *adj* (*col*) rotten (*col*), lousy (*col*). **jdn/etw ~ machen** to run sb/sth down.

Miesepeter *m* - (*col*) misery-guts (*col*).

miesepet(e)rig *adj* (*col*) grouchy (*col*).

Miesmacher *m* (*col*) kill-joy.

Miet|auto *nt* hire(d) car (*Brit*), rental car (*US*).

Miete *f* -**n** (*für Wohnung*) rent; (*für Gegenstände*) rental. **zur ~ wohnen** to live in rented accommodation (*Brit*) *or* accommodations (*US*).

mieten *vt* to rent; *Boot, Auto auch* to hire (*Brit*).

Mieter(in *f*) *m* - tenant; (*Untermieter*) lodger.

Miet|erhöhung *f* rent increase.

Mieterschutz *m* rent control.

Mietrecht *nt* rent law.

Miets-: **~haus** *nt* block of (rented) flats (*Brit*), apartment house (*US*); **~kaserne** *f* (*pej*) tenement house.

Miet-: **~verhältnis** *nt* tenancy; **~vertrag** *m* lease; **~wagen** *m* hire car (*Brit*), rental car (*US*); **~wohnung** *f* rented flat (*Brit*) *or* apartment; **~wucher** *m* ist **strafbar** charging exorbitant rent(s) is a punishable offence.

Mieze *f* -**n** (*col*) (**a**) (*Katze*) pussy (*col*). (**b**) (*Mädchen*) chick (*col*), bird (*Brit col*).

Migräne *f no pl* migraine.

Mikado *nt* -**s** (*Spiel*) pick-a-stick.

Mikro- *in cpds* micro-.

Mikrofiche [-fiːʃ] *m or nt* -**s** microfiche.

Mikrofon *nt* -**e** microphone.

Mikrokosmos *m* microcosm.

Mikroprozessor *m* microprocessor.

Mikroskop *nt* -**e** microscope.

mikroskopisch *adj* microscopic. **etw ~ untersuchen** to examine sth under the microscope.

Milbe *f* -**n** mite.

Milch *f no pl* milk; (*Fischsamen*) milt, soft roe. **~ geben** (*Kuh*) to yield milk.

Milch- *in cpds* milk; **~bart** *m* (*col*) fluffy beard; (*fig pej: Jüngling*) milksop; **~drüse** *f* mammary gland; **~flasche** *f* milk bottle; **~frau** *f* (*col*) dairy-woman; **~gebiß** *nt* milk teeth *pl*; **~geschäft** *nt* dairy; **~gesicht** *nt* (*col*) baby face.

milchig *adj* milky.

Milch-: **~kaffee** *m* milky coffee; **~kanne** *f* milk can; (*größer*) (milk) churn; **~mädchenrechnung** *f* (*col*) naïve fallacy; **~mann** *m, pl* -**männer** milkman; **~pulver** *nt* dried milk; **~reis** *m* round-grain rice; (*gekocht*) rice pudding; **~straße** *f* Milky Way; **~tüte** *f* milk carton; plastic bag of milk; **~wirtschaft** *f* dairy farming; **~zahn** *m* milk tooth.

mild(e) *adj* mild; *Seife auch* gentle; *(nachsichtig) Behandlung, Richter, Urteil* lenient. **jdn ~ stimmen** to put sb in a good mood; **eine ~e Gabe** alms *pl*; **~ gesagt** to put it mildly.
Milde *f no pl siehe adj* **(a)** mildness. **(b)** leniency. **~ walten lassen** to be lenient.
mildern *vt (geh) Schmerz* to ease; *Furcht* to calm; *Urteil, Zorn, Worte* to moderate; *Gegensätze* to make less crass. **~de Umstände** *(Jur)* extenuating circumstances.
Milderung *f no pl (von Schmerz)* easing; *(von Ausdruck, Strafe, des Klimas)* moderation.
mildtätig *adj (geh)* charitable.
Milieu [mi'liø:] *nt* **-s** *(Umwelt)* environment, milieu.
militant *adj* militant.
Militär[1] *nt no pl* military, armed forces *pl*. **beim ~ sein** *(col)* to be in the forces; **zum ~ gehen** to join up.
Militär[2] *m* **-s** (army) officer.
Militär- *in cpds* military; **~dienst** *m* military service; **(seinen) ~dienst ableisten** to do one's military service; **~gericht** *nt* court martial.
militärisch *adj* military. **~ grüßen** to salute.
Militarismus *m no pl* militarism.
Militarist(in *f)* *m* militarist.
Miliz *f* **-en** militia.
Milliardär(in *f)* *m* multi-millionaire, billionaire.
Milliarde *f* **-n** thousand millions *(Brit)*, billion *(US)*.
Milli- *in cpds* milli-; **~bar** *nt* - millibar; **~gramm** *nt* milligramme *(Brit)*, milligram *(US)*; **~meter** *m or nt* millimetre *(Brit)*, millimeter *(US)*; **~meterpapier** *nt* graph paper.
Million *f* million. **zwei ~en Einwohner** two million inhabitants.
Millionär(in *f)* *m* millionaire(ss). **es zum ~ bringen** to make a million.
Millionen-: **~auflage** *f* million copies *pl*; millions of copies; **~erbe** *m*, **~erbin** *f* inheritor of millions; **m~fach** 1 *adj* millionfold; 2 *adv* a million times; **m~schwer** *adj (col)* worth a few million; **~stadt** *f* town with over a million inhabitants.
Millionstel *nt* millionth.
Milz *f* **-en** spleen.
Milzbrand *m (Med, Vet)* anthrax.
mimen *(old)* 1 *vt* to mime. **er mimt den Unschuldigen** *(col)* he's acting the innocent. 2 *vi* to play-act.
Mimik *f no pl* facial expression.
mimisch *adj* mimic.
Mimose *f* **-n** mimosa. **empfindlich wie eine ~ sein** to be oversensitive.
Min., min. = **Minute(n).**
minder *adv* less. **und das nicht ~** and no less so.
minder-: **~begabt** *adj* less gifted; **~bemittelt** *adj (dated)* less well-off; **geistig ~bemittelt** *(iro)* mentally less gifted.
mindere(r, s) *adj attr* lesser; *Qualität* inferior.
Minderheit *f* minority.
Minderheitsregierung *f* minority government.
Minder-: **m~jährig** *adj* who is (still) a minor; **jährige(r)** *mf decl as adj* minor; **~jährigkeit** *f* minority.
mindern 1 *vt (herabsetzen) Würde, Verdienste* to diminish; *(verringern) Wert, Qualität* to reduce. 2 *vr* to diminish.
Minderung *f siehe vb* diminishing *no indef art;* reduction *(gen in)*.
minderwertig *adj* inferior; *Waren, Material, Arbeit auch* poor-quality; *Qualität auch* low.
Minderwertigkeit *f* inferiority.
Minderwertigkeits-: **~gefühl** *nt* feeling of inferiority; **~komplex** *m* inferiority complex.
Minderzahl *f* minority. **in der ~** in the minority.
Mindest- *in cpds* minimum; **~alter** *nt* minimum age.
mindeste 1 *adj attr* least, slightest. **das ~** the

(very) least; **ich verstehe nicht das ~ von (der) Kunst** I don't know the slightest thing about art. 2 *adv* **zum ~n** at the very least; **(nicht) im ~n** (not) in the least.
mindestens *adv* at least.
Mindest-: **~größe** *f* minimum size; *(von Menschen)* minimum height; **~maß** *nt* minimum amount *(an +dat of)*; **~umtausch** *m* minimum obligatory exchange.
Mine *f* **-n (a)** *(Min)* mine. **(b)** *(Mil)* mine. **auf eine ~ laufen** to hit a mine. **(c)** *(Bleistift~)* lead; *(Kugelschreiber~, Filzstift~)* refill.
Minen-: **~feld** *nt (Mil)* minefield; **~leger** *m* - *(Mil, Naut)* mine-layer; **~suchboot** *nt* minesweeper.
Mineral *nt* **-e** *or* **-ien** [-iən] mineral.
Mineral-: **~öl** *nt (mineral)* oil; **~ölsteuer** *f* tax on oil; **~quelle** *f* mineral spring; **~wasser** *nt* mineral water.
Mini- *in cpds* mini-.
Miniatur *f (Art)* miniature.
Miniatur- *in cpds* miniature; **~ausgabe** *f* miniature version; *(Buch)* miniature edition.
Minigolf *nt* crazy golf.
minimal *adj* minimal. **mit ~er Anstrengung** with a minimum of effort.
Minimal- *in cpds* minimum.
Minimum *nt, pl* **Minima** minimum *(an +dat of)*.
Minirock *m* mini-skirt.
Minister(in *f)* *m* - *(Pol)* minister *(Brit)* (*für* of), secretary *(für* for).
Ministerialbeamte(r) *m* ministry official.
ministeriell *adj attr* ministerial.
Ministerium *nt* ministry *(Brit)*, department.
Ministerpräsident(in *f)* *m* prime minister; *(eines Bundeslandes)* chief minister of a Federal German state.
Minna *f no pl* **jdn zur ~ machen** *(col)* to give sb a piece of one's mind.
Minne-: **~sang** *m* minnesong; **~sänger** *m* minnesinger.
minus 1 *prep +gen* minus, less; *(Math)* minus. 2 *adv* minus; *(Elec)* negative. **10 Grad ~** 10 degrees below zero; **~ machen** *(col)* to make a loss.
Minus *nt* **-, -** *(Fehlbetrag)* deficit; *(auf Konto)* overdraft; *(fig: Nachteil)* bad point; *(in Beruf etc)* disadvantage.
Minus-: **~pol** *m* negative pole; **~punkt** *m* penalty point; *(fig)* minus point; **~zeichen** *nt* minus sign.
Minute *f* **-n** minute. **auf die ~ (genau/pünktlich)** (right) on the dot; **in letzter ~** at the last minute; **es vergeht keine ~, ohne daß** ... not a moment goes by without ...
Minuten-: **m~lang** 1 *adj attr* several minutes of; 2 *adv* for several minutes; **~zeiger** *m* minutehand.
minuziös *adj (geh)* meticulous.
Minze *f* **-n** *(Bot)* mint.
Mio. = **Million(en).**
mir *pers pron dat of* **ich** to me; *(nach Präpositionen)* me. **ein Freund von ~** a friend of mine; **von ~ aus!** *(col)* I don't mind; **~ nichts, dir nichts** *(col)* without so much as a by-your-leave; **es war ~ nichts, dir nichts weg** the next thing I knew it had gone; **wie du ~, so ich dir** *(prov)* tit for tat *(col)*; *(als Drohung)* I'll get my own back.
Mirabelle *f* mirabelle, small yellow plum.
Misch-: **~batterie** *f* mixer tap; **~brot** *nt* bread made from more than one kind of flour; **~ehe** *f* mixed marriage.
mischen 1 *vtr* to mix. **sich unter die Menge ~** to mix with the crowd; **sich in etw** *(acc)* **~** to meddle in sth; **sich in das Gespräch ~** to butt into the conversation. 2 *vi (Cards)* to shuffle.
Misch-: **~farbe** *f* mixed *or* blended colour *(Brit) or* color *(US)*; *(Phys)* secondary colour; **~form** *f* mixture; *(von zwei Elementen auch)* hybrid

(form); ~ling *m (Mensch)* half-caste; *(Zool)* half-breed; ~masch *m* -e *(col)* hotchpotch; *(Essen auch)* concoction; ~maschine *f* cement-mixer; ~pult *nt (Rad, TV)* mixing panel.

Mischung *f* **(a)** *(das Mischen)* mixing. **(b)** *(lit, fig: Gemischtes)* mixture; *(von Tee etc auch)* blend.

Mischwald *m* mixed (deciduous and coniferous) woodland.

miserabel *adj (col)* lousy *(col); Gesundheit* wretched; *Benehmen* dreadful.

Misere *f* -n *(von Leuten, Wirtschaft etc)* plight; *(von Hunger, Krieg etc)* misery, miseries *pl*. **in einer ~ stecken** to be in a dreadful state; *(Mensch)* to be in a mess.

miß|achten* *vt insep (ignorieren)* to disregard.

Miß|achtung *f* **(a)** disregard. **(b)** *(Geringschätzung)* disrespect *(gen* for*).*

Mißbehagen *nt (geh) (Unbehagen)* uneasiness; *(Mißfallen)* discontent(ment).

mißbilden *ptp* **mißgebildet** *vt insep* to deform.

Mißbildung *f* deformity, malformation.

mißbilligen* *vt insep* to disapprove of.

Mißbilligung *f* disapproval.

Mißbrauch *m* abuse; *(falsche Anwendung)* misuse; *(von Notbremse, Feuerlöscher etc)* improper use. **unter ~ seines Amtes** in abuse of his office.

mißbrauchen* *vt insep* to abuse; *(geh: vergewaltigen)* to assault. **jdn zu etw ~** to use sb for sth *or* to do sth.

mißbräuchlich *adj (form)* improper.

mißdeuten* *vt insep* to misinterpret.

Mißdeutung *f* misinterpretation.

missen *vt (geh)* to do without. **das möchte ich nicht ~** I wouldn't do without it (for the world).

Miß|erfolg *m* failure; *(Theat, Buch etc auch)* flop *(col).*

Miß|ernte *f* crop failure.

mißfallen* *vi insep irreg* +*dat* to displease. **es mißfällt mir, wie er** ... I dislike the way he ...

Mißfallen *nt no pl* displeasure *(über* +*acc* at*).* **jds ~ erregen** to incur sb's displeasure.

Mißfallens-: ~bekundung, ~kundgebung *f* demonstration of displeasure.

mißfällig *adj Bemerkung* deprecatory.

Mißgeburt *f* deformed person/animal; *(fig col)* failure.

Mißgeschick *nt* mishap; *(Pech, Unglück)* misfortune.

mißglücken* *vi insep aux sein* to be unsuccessful. **der Versuch ist (ihm) mißglückt** the/his attempt was a failure.

mißgönnen* *vt insep* **jdm etw ~** to (be)grudge sb sth.

Mißgriff *m* mistake.

Mißgunst *f* resentment (at).

mißgünstig *adj* resentful *(auf* +*acc* towards*).*

mißhandeln* *vt insep* to ill-treat, to maltreat.

Mißhandlung *f* ill-treatment, maltreatment.

Mission *f (Eccl, Pol, fig)* mission; *(diplomatische Vertretung)* legation, mission *(US); (Gruppe)* delegation.

Missionar(in *f)* *m* missionary.

missionarisch *adj* missionary.

Mißklang *m* discord *(auch Mus)*, dissonance; *(Mißton, fig)* discordant note.

Mißkredit *m no pl* discredit. **jdn/etw in ~ bringen** to bring sb/sth into discredit.

mißlang *pret* of **mißlingen.**

mißlich *adj (geh)* awkward, difficult.

mißliebig *adj* unpopular.

Mißlingen *nt no pl* failure.

mißlingen *pret* **mißlang,** *ptp* **mißlungen** *vi aux sein* to be unsuccessful. **ein mißlungener Versuch** an unsuccessful attempt.

Mißmut *m* sullenness; *(Unzufriedenheit)* displeasure.

mißmutig *adj* sullen; *(unzufrieden)* discontented; *Äußerung, Aussehen* disgruntled.

mißraten* 1 *vi insep irreg aux sein* to go wrong. **der Kuchen ist mir ~** my cake was a failure. 2 *adj Kind* wayward.

Mißstand *m* anomaly; *(allgemeiner Zustand)* deplorable state of affairs *no pl; (Ungerechtigkeit)* abuse; *(Mangel)* defect.

Mißstimmung *f* **(a)** *(Uneinigkeit)* discord. **eine ~** a note of discord. **(b)** *(schlechte Laune)* bad mood; *(Unzufriedenheit)* discontent *no pl.*

Mißton *m (Mus, fig)* discordant note. **~e (Klang)** discordant sound; *(fig)* discord.

mißtrauen* *vi insep* +*dat* to mistrust.

Mißtrauen *nt no pl* mistrust *(gegenüber* of*).* **~ gegen jdn/etw haben** to be suspicious of sb/sth.

Mißtrauensvotum *nt* vote of no confidence.

mißtrauisch *adj* distrustful; *(argwöhnisch)* suspicious.

Mißverhältnis *nt* discrepancy.

mißverständlich *adj* unclear.

Mißverständnis *nt* misunderstanding.

mißverstehen* *vt insep irreg* to misunderstand.

Mißwahl, Misswahl *f* beauty contest.

Mißwirtschaft *f* maladministration.

Mist *m no pl* **(a)** *(Tierkot)* droppings *pl; (Pferde~, Kuh~ etc)* dung; *(Dünger)* manure. **das ist nicht auf seinem ~ gewachsen** *(col)* he didn't think that up himself. **(b)** *(col) (Unsinn)* nonsense; *(Schund)* rubbish. **~!** blast! *(col);* **da hat er ~ gemacht** *or* **gebaut** he really messed that up *(col);* **mach keinen ~!** don't be a fool!

Mistel *f* -n mistletoe *no pl.*

Mist-: ~fink *m (col)* dirty-minded character; *(Journalist etc)* muck-raker *(col);* ~gabel *f* pitchfork *(used for shifting manure);* ~haufen *m* manure heap; ~käfer *m* dung beetle; ~stück *m*, ~vieh *nt (col!) (Mann)* bastard *(col!); (Frau auch)* bitch *(col!);* ~wetter *nt (col)* lousy weather *(col).*

mit 1 *prep* +*dat* with. **~ dem Hut in der Hand** (with) his hat in his hand; **ein Topf ~ Suppe** a pot of soup; **wie wär's ~ einem Bier?** *(col)* how about a beer?; **~ der Bahn/dem Bus/dem Auto** by train/bus/car; **~ Gewalt** by force; **~ Bleistift schreiben** to write in pencil; **~ dem nächsten Flugzeug/Bus kommen** to come on the next plane/bus; **~ einem Wort** in a word; **~ achtzehn Jahren** at (the age of) eighteen; **es wird ~ jedem Tag schlimmer** it's getting worse every day; **~ der Zeit** in time; **etw ~ DM 50.000 versichern** to insure sth for DM 50,000; **~ 80 km/h** at 80 km/h; **~ 4:2 gewinnen** to win 4-2; **~ mir waren es 5** there were 5 including me; **du ~ deinen dummen Ideen** *(col)* you and your stupid ideas; **~ lauter Stimme** in a loud voice; **~ Verlust** at a loss.

2 *adv* **er wollte ~** *(col)* he wanted to come too; **er war ~ dabei** he was there too; **er ist ~ der Beste der Gruppe** he is among the best in the group; **das gehört ~ dazu** that's part and parcel of it; **etw ~ in Betracht ziehen** to consider sth as well.

Mit|arbeit *f* collaboration; *(Hilfe auch)* assistance; *(Teilnahme)* participation *(auch Sch).* **unter ~ von** in collaboration with.

mit|arbeiten *vi sep* to collaborate. **er hat beim Bau des Hauses mitgearbeitet** he helped build the house; **beim Unterricht ~** to take an active part in lessons; **seine Frau arbeitet mit** *(col)* his wife works too.

Mit|arbeiter(in *f)* *m (Betriebsangehöriger)* employee; *(Kollege)* colleague; *(an Projekt etc)* collaborator. **freier ~** freelance.

mitbekommen* *vt sep irreg* **(a)** to get *or* be given sth. **(b)** *(col: verstehen)* to get *(col).*

Mitbesitzer *m* joint-owner.

mitbestimmen* *sep* 1 *vi* to have a say *(bei* in*);* to participate *(bei* in*).* **~d sein** to have an influence *(bei, für* on*).* 2 *vt* to have an influence on.

Mitbestimmung *f* participation *(bei* in*).* **~ am**

Arbeitsplatz worker participation.

Mitbewerber *m* (fellow) competitor. **meine** ~ *(für Stelle)* the other applicants.

mitbringen *vt sep irreg* **(a)** to bring; *Freund, Begleiter* to bring along. **jdm etw von der Stadt/vom Bäcker** ~ to bring sb sth back from town/fetch sb sth from the baker's; **was sollen wir der Gastgeberin** ~? what should we take to our hostess? **(b)** *Mitgift, Kinder* to bring with one. **etw in die Ehe** ~ to have sth when one gets married. **(c)** *(fig) Befähigung etc* to have, to possess.

Mitbringsel *nt (Geschenk)* small present; *(Andenken)* souvenir.

Mitbürger *m* fellow citizen.

mitdürfen *vi sep irreg* **wir durften nicht mit** we weren't allowed to go along.

Mit|eigentümer *m* joint-owner.

mit|einander *adv* with one another; *(gemeinsam)* together. **wir haben lange** ~ **geredet** we had a long talk.

mit|empfinden* *sep irreg* **1** *vt* to share. **2** *vi* **mit jdm** ~ to sympathize with sb.

mit|erleben* *vt sep Krieg* to live through; *(im Fernsehen)* to watch.

mit|essen *vt sep irreg Schale etc* to eat as well.

Mit|esser *m* - blackhead.

mitfahren *vi sep irreg aux sein* to go (with sb). **sie fährt mit** she is going too; **(mit jdm)** ~ to go with sb; *(auf Reise auch)* to travel with sb; **kann ich (mit Ihnen)** ~? can you give me a lift?

Mitfahrer *m* passenger.

Mitfahrerzentrale *f* agency for arranging lifts.

Mitfahrgelegenheit *f* lift.

mitfühlen *vi sep siehe* **mitempfinden**.

mitfühlend *adj* compassionate.

mitführen *vt sep Papiere, Ware etc* to carry (with one); *(Fluß)* to carry along.

mitgeben *vt sep irreg* **jdm etw** ~ to give sb sth to take with them; *Rat, Erziehung* to give sb sth.

Mitgefühl *nt* sympathy.

mitgehen *vi sep irreg aux sein* **(a)** to go too or along. **mit jdm** ~ to go with sb. **(b)** *(fig: Publikum etc)* to respond (favourably) *(mit* to). **(c)** *(col)* **etw** ~ **lassen** to pinch sth *(col)*.

Mitgift *f* -en dowry.

Mitgiftjäger *m (col)* dowry-hunter.

Mitglied *nt* member *(gen, bei, in +dat* of).

Mitglieds-: ~**ausweis** *m* membership card; ~**beitrag** *m* membership subscription.

Mitgliedschaft *f* membership.

Mitglied(s)staat *m* member state.

mithaben *vt sep irreg* **etw** ~ to have sth (with one); **hast du alles mit?** have you got everything?

mithalten *vi sep irreg (bei Tempo etc)* to keep pace *(mit* with). **bei einer Diskussion** ~ **können** to be able to hold one's own in a discussion.

mithelfen *vi sep irreg* to help. **beim Bau des Hauses** ~ to help build the house.

Mithilfe *f* assistance, aid.

mithören *sep* **1** *vt* to listen to (too); *Gespräch* to overhear; *(heimlich)* to listen in on. **ich habe alles mitgehört** I heard everything. **2** *vi* to listen in *(bei* on); *(zufällig)* to overhear.

Mit|inhaber *m* joint-owner.

mitklingen *vi sep irreg (Ton, Saite)* to sound, to resonate. **in ihrer Äußerung klang ein leichter Vorwurf mit** there was a slight note of reproach in her remark.

mitkommen *vi sep irreg aux sein* **(a)** to come along *(mit* with). **ich kann nicht** ~ I can't come; **komm doch mit!** why don't you come too? **(b)** *(col) (mithalten)* to keep up; *(verstehen)* to follow. **da komme ich nicht mit** that's beyond me; **sie kommt in der Schule gut mit** she is getting on well at school.

mitkriegen *vt sep (col)* = **mitbekommen**.

mitlaufen *vi sep irreg aux sein* to run *(mit* with).

Mitläufer *m (Pol, pej)* fellow traveller *(Brit)* or

traveler *(US)*.

Mitlaut *m* consonant.

Mitleid *nt no pl* pity, compassion *(mit* for); *(Mitgefühl)* sympathy *(mit* with, for).

Mitleidenschaft *f:* **jdn/etw in** ~ **ziehen** to affect sb/sth (detrimentally).

mitleidig *adj* pitying; *(mitfühlend)* sympathetic; *Mensch auch* compassionate. ~ **lächeln** to smile pityingly.

mitleid(s)-: ~**los** *adj* heartless; ~**voll** *adj* compassionate.

mitmachen *vti sep* **(a)** *(teilnehmen) Spiel, Singen etc* to join in; *Reise* to go on; *Kurs* to do; *Mode* to follow. **etw** *(acc)* or **bei etw** *(dat)* ~ to join in sth; **meine Beine machen nicht mehr mit** my legs are giving up. **(b)** *(col: einverstanden sein)* **da macht mein Chef nicht mit** my boss won't go along with that; **ich mache das nicht mehr lange mit** I won't take that much longer. **(c)** *(erleben)* to live through; *(erleiden)* to go through.

Mitmensch *m* fellow man.

mitmenschlich *adj Kontakte etc* human.

mitmischen *vi sep (col) (sich beteiligen)* to be involved *(in +dat, bei* in); *(sich einmischen)* to interfere *(in +dat, bei* in sth).

mitnehmen *vt sep irreg* **(a)** to take (with one); *(ausleihen)* to borrow; *(kaufen)* to take. **jdn (im Auto)** ~ to give sb a lift; **einen Hamburger zum M**~ a hamburger to take away *(Brit)* or to go *(US)*. **(b)** *(erschöpfen) jdn* to exhaust, to weaken; *(beschädigen)* to be bad for. **mitgenommen aussehen** to look the worse for wear. **(c)** *(stehlen)* to walk off with. **(d)** *(col) Sehenswürdigkeit etc* to take in.

mitrechnen *vt sep* to count; *Betrag* to count in.

mitreden *sep* **1** *vi (Meinung äußern)* to join in *(bei etw* sth); *(mitbestimmen)* to have a say *(bei* in). **da kann er nicht** ~ he wouldn't know anything about that. **2** *vt* **Sie haben hier nichts mitzureden** this is none of your concern.

mitreisen *vi sep aux sein* to go/travel too. **mit jdm** ~ to go/travel with sb.

Mitreisende(r) *mf* fellow traveller *(Brit)* or traveler *(US)*.

mitreißen *vt sep irreg (Fluß, Lawine)* to sweep away. **seine Rede hat alle mitgerissen** everyone was carried away by his speech.

mitreißend *adj Rhythmus* infectious; *Reden* rousing; *Film, Fußballspiel* thrilling, exciting.

mitsamt *prep +dat* together with.

mitschneiden *vt sep irreg* to record.

Mitschnitt *m* recording.

mitschreiben *sep irreg* **1** *vt* **etw** ~ to write or take sth down. **2** *vi* to take notes.

Mitschrift *f* record; *(von Vorlesung etc)* notes *pl*.

Mitschuld *f* share of the blame *(an +dat* for); *(an einem Verbrechen)* complicity *(an +dat* in).

mitschuldig *adj (an Verbrechen)* implicated *(an +dat* in); *(an Unfall)* partly responsible *(an +dat* for).

Mitschuldige(r) *mf* accomplice.

Mitschüler *m* school-friend; *(in derselben Klasse)* class-mate.

mitsingen *sep irreg* **1** *vt* to join in (singing). **2** *vi* to sing along. **in einem Chor** ~ to sing in a choir.

mitspielen *vi sep (a)* to play too; *(in Team etc)* to play *(bei* in). **in einem Film** ~ to be in a film. **(b)** *(Gründe, Motive)* to play a part *(bei* in). **(c)** *(Schaden zufügen)* **er hat ihr übel/hart mitgespielt** he has treated her badly.

Mitspieler *m (Sport)* player; *(Theat)* member of the cast.

Mitsprache *f* a say.

Mitspracherecht *nt* right to a say in a matter. **jdm ein** ~ **einräumen** to allow sb a say *(bei* in).

mitsprechen *sep irreg* **1** *vt Gebet* to join in (saying). **2** *vi (mitbestimmen)* to have a say in sth.

Mitstreiter *m (geh)* comrade-in-arms.

mittag adv **gestern/heute** ~ at midday yesterday/ today, yesterday/today lunchtime.

Mittag m **-e (a)** midday. **jeden** ~ every day at midday, every lunchtime; **zu** ~ **essen** to have lunch. **(b)** (col: ~spause) lunch-hour, lunch-break. ~ **machen** to take one's lunch-hour.

Mittag|essen nt midday meal. **er kam zum** ~ he came to lunch.

mittäglich adj attr midday, lunchtime.

mittags adv at lunchtime. ~ **um 12 Uhr** at 12 noon; **sonnabends** ~ Saturday lunchtime.

Mittags-: ~**hitze** f midday heat; ~**pause** f lunch-hour, lunch-break; ~**pause machen/haben** to take/have one's lunch-hour etc; (Geschäft etc) to close at lunchtime; ~**ruhe** f period of quiet (after lunch); (in Geschäft) midday-closing; ~**schlaf** m afternoon nap; ~**stunde** f midday; **um die** ~**stunde** around midday; ~**zeit** f lunch time; **während** or **in der** ~**zeit** at lunch time.

Mittäter m accomplice.

Mitte f **-n** middle; (fig auch, von Kreis, Kugel etc, Pol) centre (Brit), center (US). **das Reich der** ~ (liter) the Middle Kingdom; **die** ~ **des Weges haben wir hinter uns** we have come more than halfway; ~**August** in the middle of August, in mid August; **er ist** ~ **vierzig** he's in his mid-forties; **die goldene** ~ the golden mean; **in der** ~ in the middle; (zwischen zwei Menschen) in between (them/us etc); (zwischen Ortschaften) halfway, midway; **einer aus unserer** ~ one of our number; **in unserer** ~ in our midst.

mitteilen sep **1** vt jdm etw ~ to tell sb sth; (benachrichtigen) to inform sb about sth; (bekanntgeben) to announce sth to sb; (Comm, Admin) to notify sb of sth. **2** vr to communicate (jdm with sb). **er kann sich gut/schlecht** ~ he finds it easy/difficult to communicate.

mitteilsam adj communicative.

Mitteilung f (Bekanntgabe) announcement; (Benachrichtigung) notification; (Comm, Admin) communication; (an Mitarbeiter etc) memo. **jdm (eine)** ~ **(von etw) machen** (form) to inform sb (of sth); (bekanntgeben) to announce sth to sb; (benachrichtigen) to inform sb (of sth).

Mitteilungsbedürfnis nt need to talk to other people.

Mittel nt - **(a)** (~ zum Zweck) means sing; (Maßnahme, Methode) way, method. ~ **und Wege finden** to find ways and means; ~ **zum Zweck** a means to an end; **kein** ~ **unversucht lassen** to try everything; **als letztes** ~ as a last resort; **ihm ist jedes** ~ **recht** he will do anything (to achieve his ends); **etw mit allen** ~**n verhindern** to do one's utmost to prevent sth. **(b)** pl (Geld~) funds pl, means pl. **(c)** (Medikament, kosmetisch) preparation; (Medizin) medicine; (Putz~) cleaning agent; (Wasch~) detergent. **welches** ~ **nimmst du?** (Med: einnehmen) what do you take?; **das ist ein** ~ **gegen Schuppen** that is for dandruff; **sich (dat) ein** ~ **verschreiben lassen** to get the doctor to prescribe something; **das beste** ~ **gegen etw** the best cure for sth. **(d)** (Math: Durchschnitt) average. **arithmetisches** ~ arithmetical mean.

Mittel-: ~**alter** nt Middle Ages pl; **m**~**alterlich** adj medieval; ~**amerika** nt Central America (and the Caribbean); **m**~**amerikanisch** adj Central American; **m**~**bar** adj indirect (auch Jur); **m**~**deutsch** adj (Geog, Ling) Central German; (BRD Pol) East German; ~**deutschland** nt (BRD: als Land) East Germany; ~**ding** nt (Mischung) cross; **ein** ~**ding** (weder das eine noch das andere) something in between; ~**europa** nt Central Europe; ~**europäer** m Central European; **m**~**europäisch** adj Central European; ~**feld** nt (Sport) midfield; ~**finger** m middle finger; **m**~**fristig** adj Finanzplanung, Politik medium-term; ~**gebirge** nt low mountain range; ~**gewicht** nt middleweight; **m**~**groß** adj medium-sized; ~**hochdeutsch** nt Middle High German; ~**klasse** f (a) (Comm) middle of the market; **(b)** (Sociol) middle classes pl; ~**klassewagen** m middle-market car; ~**linie** f centre (Brit) or center (US) line; **m**~**los** adj without means; (arm) impoverished; ~**losigkeit** f lack of means; (Armut) impoverishment; ~**maß** nt mediocrity no art; **das (gesunde)** ~**maß** the happy medium; **m**~**mäßig 1** adj mediocre; Schriftsteller, Spieler etc auch indifferent; **2** adv indifferently; **wie gefällt es dir hier?** — **so m**~**mäßig** how do you like it here? — so-so; ~**mäßigkeit** f mediocrity.

Mittelmeer nt Mediterranean (Sea), Med (col).

Mittelmeer- in cpds Mediterranean.

Mittelmeerraum m Mediterranean (region).

Mittel-: **m**~**prächtig** adj (hum col) not bad pred, so-so pred (col); ~**punkt** m (Math, räumlich) centre (Brit), center (US); (fig: visuell) focal point; **er steht im** ~**punkt des Interesses** he is the centre of attention; ~**scheitel** m centre parting (Brit), center part (US); ~**schicht** f (Sociol) middle class.

Mittelsmann m, pl **-männer** or **-leute** intermediary.

Mittel-: ~**stand** m middle classes pl; **m**~**ständisch** adj middle-class.

Mittelstrecken-: ~**flugzeug** nt medium-haul aircraft; ~**lauf** m middle-distance race; ~**rakete** f medium-range missile.

Mittel-: ~**streifen** m central reservation (Brit), median (strip) (US); ~**stück** nt middle part; ~**stufe** f (Sch) middle school (Brit), junior high (US); ~**stürmer** m (Sport) centre-forward; ~**weg** m middle course; **der goldene** ~**weg** the happy medium, the golden mean; ~**welle** f (Rad) medium wave(band); ~**wert** m mean.

mitten adv ~ **in/auf etw** (right) in the middle of sth; ~ **aus etw** (right) from the middle of sth; ~ **durch etw** (right) through the middle of sth; ~ **im Urwald** in the depths of the jungle; ~ **ins Gesicht** right in the face; ~ **unter uns** (right) in our midst.

mitten-: ~**drin** adv (right) in the middle of it; ~**durch** adv (right) through the middle.

Mitternacht f midnight no art.

mitternächtlich adj attr midnight. **zu** ~**er Stunde** (geh) at the midnight hour.

mittlere(r, s) adj attr **(a)** (dazwischenliegend) middle. **der/die/das** ~ the middle one; **der M**~ **Osten** the Middle East. **(b)** (den Mittelwert bildend) medium; (mittelschwer) Kursus, Aufgabe intermediate; (durchschnittlich) average; (Math) mean. ~**n Alters** middle-aged.

mittlerweile adv in the meantime.

Mitt-: ~**woch** m -e Wednesday; siehe **Dienstag**; **m**~**wochs** adv on Wednesdays.

mit|unter adv now and again, once in a while.

mitverantwortlich adj jointly responsible pred.

Mitverantwortung f share of the responsibility.

mitverdienen* vi sep to (go out to) work as well.

Mitverfasser m co-author.

Mitverschulden nt **ihn trifft ein** ~ **an diesem Vorfall** he was partly to blame for this incident.

mitwirken vi sep (an +dat, bei in) to play a part; (beteiligt sein) to be involved; (Theat, in Diskussion) to take part; (in Film) to appear.

Mitwirkende(r) mf decl as adj participant (an +dat, bei in); (in Theat) the cast pl.

Mitwirkung f (Beteiligung) involvement (an +dat, bei in); (an Buch, Film) collaboration (an +dat, bei on); (Teilnahme) (an Diskussion, Projekt) participation (an +dat, bei in); (von Schauspieler) appearance (an +dat, bei in). **unter** ~ **von** with the help of.

Mitwisser(in f) m - (Jur) accessory (gen to). ~ **einer Sache (gen) sein** to know about sth.

mitzählen vti sep to count; Betrag to count in.

Mixbecher m (cocktail) shaker.

mixen vt Getränke, (Rad, TV) to mix.
Mixer m - (a) (Bar~) cocktail waiter. (b) (Kü-chen~) blender; (Rührmaschine) mixer. (c) (Film, Rad, TV) mixer.
Mixgetränk nt mixed drink; (alkoholisch) cocktail.
Mixtur f (Pharm, Mus, fig) mixture.
ml = **Milliliter** millilitre (Brit), milliliter (US).
mm = **Millimeter**.
Möbel nt - (~stück) piece of furniture. ~ pl furniture sing.
Möbel- in cpds furniture; ~lager nt furniture showroom; ~packer m removal man; ~spedition f removal firm; ~stoff m furnishing fabric; ~stück nt piece of furniture; ~wagen m removal van (Brit), moving van (US).
mobil adj (a) mobile. ~ machen (Mil) to mobilize. (b) (col: flink, munter) lively.
Mobile ['mo:bilə] nt -s mobile.
Mobiliar nt no pl furnishings pl.
mobilisieren* vt (Mil, fig) to mobilize.
Mobilmachung f (Mil) mobilization.
möblieren* vt to furnish. **ein möbliertes Zimmer** a furnished room; **möbliert wohnen** to live in furnished accommodation (Brit) or accommodations (US).
mochte pret of **mögen**.
Möchtegern- in cpds (iro) would-be.
Modalität f usu pl (von Plan, Vertrag etc) arrangement; (von Verfahren, Arbeit) procedure.
Mode f -n fashion; (Sitte) custom. ~ sein to be the fashion; (Sitte) to be the custom; in ~/aus der ~ kommen to come into/go out of fashion.
Mode-: ~artikel m fashion accessory; m~bewußt adj fashion-conscious; ~farbe f in-colour (Brit), in-color (US); ~geschäft nt fashion shop (Brit) or store (US); ~heft, ~journal nt fashion magazine.
Modell nt -e model. **zu etw ~ stehen** to be the model for sth.
Modell-: ~eisenbahn f model railway; (als Spielzeug) train set; ~flugzeug nt model aeroplane or airplane (US).
modellieren* vti to model.
Modell-: ~kleid nt model (dress); ~versuch m (esp Sch) experiment.
Modem m -s modem.
Modenschau f fashion show.
Moder m no pl mustiness; (Schimmel) mildew. **es riecht nach ~** it smells musty.
Moderation f (Rad, TV) presentation.
Moderator(in f) m presenter.
Modergeruch m musty smell.
moderieren* vti (Rad, TV) to present.
mod(e)rig adj Geruch musty.
modern¹ vi aux sein or haben to rot.
modern² adj modern no adv; (modisch) fashionable; Ansichten, Eltern, Lehrer progressive.
Moderne f no pl (geh) modern age.
modernisieren* vt Gebäude to modernize; Kleidung to make more fashionable.
Mode-: ~schmuck m costume jewellery (Brit) or jewelry (US); ~schöpfer(in f) m fashion designer; ~tanz m popular dance; ~wort nt trendy word; ~zeitschrift f fashion magazine.
Modifikation f modification.
modifizieren* vt to modify.
modisch adj stylish, fashionable.
Modistin f milliner.
Modul -n nt (Comp) module.
modulieren* vt to modulate.
Modus m -, **Modi** (a) way. (b) (Gram) mood.
Mofa nt -s small moped.
mogeln vi to cheat.
mögen pret **mochte**, ptp **gemocht 1** vt to like. ~ **Sie ihn?** do you like him?; **was möchten Sie, bitte?** what would you like?; (Verkäufer) what can I do for you?; **nein danke, ich möchte lieber**

Tee no thank you, I would rather have tea. **2** vi (etw tun ~) to like to. **ich mag nicht mehr** I've had enough; (bin am Ende) I can't take any more; **kommen Sie mit?** — **ich möchte gern, aber** ... **are you coming too?** — I'd like to, but ...; **ich möchte lieber in die Stadt** I would prefer to go into town.
3 ptp ~ modal aux (a) to like to +infin; (wollen) to want. **möchten Sie etwasessen?** would you like something to eat?; **hier möchte ich nicht wohnen** (würde nicht gern) I wouldn't like to live here; (will nicht) I don't want to live here; **ich hätte gern dabeisein** ~ I would like to have been there; **man möchte meinen, daß** ... you would think that ...; **sie mag nicht bleiben** she doesn't want to stay.
(b) **es mag wohl sein, daß er recht hat, aber** ... he may well be right, but ...; **wie dem auch sein mag** however that may be; **mag kommen was da will** come what may; **es mochten etwa fünf Stunden vergangen sein** about five hours must have passed; **wie alt mag sie sein?** how old is she, I wonder?; **was mag das wohl heißen?** what might that mean?
(c) (Aufforderung, indirekte Rede) (sagen Sie ihm,) **er möchte zu mir kommen** would you tell him to come and see me; **Sie möchten zu Hause anrufen** you should call home.
Mogler(in f) m - cheat.
möglich adj possible; (attr: eventuell auch) potential. **alles ~e** everything you can think of; **alles M~e tun** to do everything possible; **er hat allen ~en Blödsinn gemacht** he did all sorts of stupid things; **so viel/bald wie** ~ as much/soon as possible; **es war mir nicht** ~ **mitzukommen** I couldn't manage to come; **nicht** ~! never!; **er tat sein** ~**stes** he did his utmost.
möglicherweise adv possibly. ~ **kommt er morgen** he may (possibly) come tomorrow.
Möglichkeit f (a) possibility. **es besteht die** ~, **daß** ... there is a possibility that ...; **nach** ~ if possible; **ist denn das die** ~? (col) I don't believe it! (b) (Aussicht) chance; (Gelegenheit auch) opportunity. **er hatte keine andere** ~ he had no other choice.
möglichst adv ~ **schnell/oft** as quickly/often as possible; **in** ~ **kurzer Zeit** as quickly as possible.
Mohammedaner(in f) [mohame'da:nɐ, -ɔrɪn] m - Mohammedan.
mohammedanisch [mohame'da:nɪʃ] adj Mohammedan.
Mohikaner [mohi'ka:nɐ] m - **der letzte** ~ (hum col) the very last one.
Mohn m -e (a) poppy. (b) (~samen) poppy seed.
Mohn- in cpds poppy; (Cook) poppyseed; ~blume f poppy.
Möhre f -n carrot.
Mohrenkopf m small chocolate-covered cream cake.
Mohrrübe f carrot.
mokieren* vr to sneer (über +acc at).
Mokka m -s mocha, strong coffee.
Molch m -e salamander.
Mole f -n (Naut) mole.
Molekül nt -e molecule.
molekular adj molecular.
molk pret of **melken**.
Molke f no pl whey.
Molkerei f dairy.
Molkerei-: ~butter f blended butter; ~produkt nt dairy product.
Moll nt -, - (Mus) minor (key). **a-~** A minor.
mollig adj (col) (a) cosy (Brit), cozy (US). (b) (rundlich) plump.
Molltonleiter f minor scale.
Moment¹ m -e moment. **jeden** ~ any moment; ~ **mal!** just a minute!; **im** ~ at the moment; **im ersten** ~ for a moment.

Moment² *nt* **-e** (*Umstand*) fact; (*Faktor*) factor; (*Bestandteil*) element.

momentan 1 *adj* (*vorübergehend*) momentary; (*augenblicklich*) present *attr.* **2** *adv* (*vorübergehend*) momentarily; (*augenblicklich*) at present.

Monarch(in *f*) *m* (*wk*) **-en, -en** monarch.

Monarchie *f* monarchy.

Monarchist(in *f*) *m* monarchist.

Monat *m* **-e** month. **der ~ Mai** the month of May; **sie ist im sechsten ~ (schwanger)** she's five months pregnant; **was verdient er im ~?** how much does he earn a month; **am 12. dieses ~s** on the 12th (of this month).

monatelang 1 *adj attr Verhandlungen, Kämpfe* which go/went *etc* on for months. **nach ~em Warten** after months of waiting; **mit ~er Verspätung** months late. **2** *adv* for months.

monatlich *adj* monthly. **~ stattfinden** to take place every month.

Monats-: **~anfang** *m* beginning of the month; **~blutung** *f* menstrual period; **~ende** *nt* end of the month; **~erste(r)** *m decl as adj* first (day) of the month; **~gehalt** *nt* monthly salary; **ein ~gehalt** one month's salary; **~karte** *f* monthly season ticket; **~lohn** *m* monthly wage; **~lohn bekommen** to be paid monthly; **~rate** *f* monthly instalment (*Brit*) or installment (*US*).

Mönch *m* **-e** monk; (*Bettel~ auch*) friar.

Mond *m* **-e** moon. **auf** *or* **hinter dem ~ leben** (*col*) to be behind the times; **in den ~ gucken** (*col*) to go empty-handed; **deine Uhr geht nach dem ~** (*col*) your watch/clock is way out (*col*).

mondän *adj* chic.

Mond-: **~aufgang** *m* moonrise; **~bahn** *f* lunar orbit; **~finsternis** *f* lunar eclipse; **~gesicht** *nt* moonface; **~(lande)fähre** *f* (*Space*) lunar module; **~landschaft** *f* lunar landscape; **~landung** *f* lunar landing; **~licht** *nt* moonlight; **~nacht** *f* (*geh*) moonlit night; **~schein** *m* moonlight; **~sonde** *f* (*Space*) lunar probe; **m~süchtig** *adj* **m~süchtig sein** to sleepwalk; **~untergang** *m* moonset.

Monetarismus *m* (*Econ*) monetarism.

Moneten *pl* (*col*) bread (*col*), dough (*col*).

Mongole *m* (*wk*) **-n, -n, Mongolin** *f* Mongolian, Mongol.

Mongolei *f* **die ~** Mongolia.

Mongolismus *m* (*Med*) mongolism.

mongoloid *adj* (*Med*) mongoloid.

monieren* **1** *vt* to complain about. **2** *vi* to complain.

Monitor *m* (*TV, Phys*) monitor.

Mono-, mono- *in cpds* mono-.

Mono-: **m~chrom** [mono'kro:m] *adj* monochrome; **m~gam** *adj* monogamous; **~gamie** *f* monogamy; **~gramm** *nt* monogram.

Monokel *nt* **-** monocle.

Monolog *m* **-e** (*Liter, fig*) monologue; (*Selbstgespräch*) soliloquy. **einen ~ halten** (*fig*) to hold a monologue, to talk on and on.

Monopol *nt* **-e** monopoly (*auf +acc, für* on).

monopolisieren* *vt* (*lit, fig*) to monopolize.

Monopol-: **~kapital** *nt* (*Kapital*) monopoly capital; (*Kapitalisten*) monopoly capitalism; **~stellung** *f* monopoly.

monoton *adj* monotonous.

Monotonie *f* monotony.

Monster *nt* **-** (*col*) monster.

Monster- *in cpds* (*usu pej*) mammoth, monster; **~film** *m* mammoth (film) production.

Monstranz *f* (*Eccl*) monstrance.

monströs *adj* monstrous; (*riesig groß*) massive.

Monstrum *nt, pl* **Monstren** (*lit, fig*) monster.

Monsun *m* **-e** monsoon.

Montag *m* Monday; *siehe* **Dienstag.**

Montage [mɔn'ta:ʒə] *f* **-n (a)** (*Tech*) (*Aufstellung*) installation; (*von Gerüst*) erection; (*Zusammen-*

bau) assembly. **(b)** (*Art*) montage; (*Film*) editing.

Montagehalle *f* assembly shop.

montags *adv* on Mondays.

Montan|industrie *f* coal and steel industry.

Monteur(in *f*) [mɔn'tø:ɐ, -'tø:rɪn] *m* (*Tech*) fitter; (*Aut*) mechanic.

montieren* *vt* (*Tech*) to install; (*zusammenbauen*) to assemble; (*befestigen*) to fit (*auf* or *an* +acc to); (*aufstellen*) *Gerüst* to erect.

Montur *f* (*col: Spezialkleidung*) gear (*col*), rig-out (*col*).

Monument *nt* monument.

monumental *adj* monumental.

Moor *nt* **-e** bog; (*Hoch~*) moor.

Moor-: **~bad** *nt* mud-bath; **~huhn** *nt* grouse.

moorig *adj* boggy.

Moos *nt* **-e (a)** moss. **~ ansetzen** to become covered with moss. **(b)** *no pl* (*col: Geld*) bread (*col*), dough (*col*).

moosig *adj* mossy.

Mop *m* **-s** mop.

Moped *nt* **-s** moped.

Mopedfahrer *m* moped rider.

Mops *m* **-e (a)** (*Hund*) pug (dog). **(b)** (*Dickwanst*) roly-poly (*col*). **(c)** **~e** *pl* (*col: Geld*) bread *sing* (*col*), dough *sing* (*col*).

mopsen *vt* (*col: stehlen*) to pinch (*col*).

mopsig *adj* (*col: frech*) **sich ~ machen, ~ werden** to get cheeky (*esp Brit*) or fresh (*esp US*).

Moral *f no pl* (*a*) (*Sittlichkeit*) morals *pl*. **die ~ sinkt/steigt** moral standards are declining/rising; **die bürgerliche ~** bourgeois morality; **eine doppelte ~** double standards *pl*. **(b)** (*Lehre*) moral. **und die ~ von der Geschicht'** and the moral of this story. **(c)** (*Disziplin: von Volk, Soldaten*) morale. **die ~ sinkt** morale is getting low.

Moral- *in cpds* moral; **~apostel** *m* (*pej*) upholder of moral standards.

moralisch *adj* moral. **das war eine ~e Ohrfeige für die Regierung** that was one in the eye for the government (*col*); **einen M~en haben** (*col*) to have (a fit of) the blues (*col*).

Moralist(in *f*) *m* moralist.

Moralpredigt *f* homily, sermon. **~en halten** to moralize.

Morast *m* **-e** (*lit, fig*) mire; (*Sumpf auch*) morass.

morastig *adj* marshy; (*schlammig*) muddy.

Mord *m* **-e** murder, homicide (*US*) (*an +dat* of); (*an Politiker etc*) assassination (*an +dat* of). **wegen ~es** for murder or homicide (*US*); **politischer ~** political killing; **dann gibt es ~ und Totschlag** (*col*) there'll be hell to pay (*col*).

Mord-: **~anschlag** *m* assassination (*auf +acc* of); (*erfolglos*) assassination attempt (*auf +acc* on); **einen ~anschlag auf jdn verüben** to assassinate sb; **~drohung** *f* threat on one's life.

morden *vti* (*liter*) to murder, to slay (*liter*).

Mörder(in *f*) *m* **-** murderer (*auch Jur*), killer; (*Attentäter*) assassin.

Mörder-: **~bande** *f* gang of killers; **~grube** *f*: **aus seinem Herzen keine ~grube machen** to speak frankly.

mörderisch 1 *adj* (*fig*) (*schrecklich*) dreadful, terrible; *Preise* iniquitous; *Konkurrenzkampf* cutthroat. **2** *adv* (*col: entsetzlich*) dreadfully, terribly. **~ schreien** to scream blue murder (*col*).

Mord-: **~fall** *m* murder or homicide (*US*) (case); **~kommission** *f* murder squad, homicide squad or division (*US*); **~prozeß** *m* murder trial.

Mords- *in cpds* (*col*) terrible, awful; (*toll, prima*) hell of a (*col*); **~kerl** *m* (*col*) (*verwegen*) hell of a guy (*col*); (*stark*) enormous fellow (*col*); **m~mäßig** (*col*) **1** *adj* incredible; **2** *adv* (+*vb*) terribly, awfully.

Mord-: **~verdacht** *m* suspicion of murder; **unter ~verdacht** (*dat*) **stehen** to be suspected of murder; **~waffe** *f* murder weapon.

Morgen *m* **-** (*a*) (*Tagesanfang*) morning. **am ~ in**

the morning; **bis in den ~ (hinein)** into the early hours; **eines ~s** one morning; **es wird ~** day is breaking; **guten ~!** good morning; **~!** *(col)* morning. **(b)** *(Measure)* ≃ acre. **drei ~ Land** three acres of land.

morgen *adv* **(a)** tomorrow. **~ früh** tomorrow morning; **~ in acht Tagen** a week (from) tomorrow; **~ um diese Zeit** this time tomorrow; **bis ~!** see you tomorrow; **~ ist auch (noch) ein Tag!** *(Prov)* there's always tomorrow; **die Technik von ~** the technology of tomorrow. **(b) gestern ~** yesterday morning; **heute ~** this morning.

Morgen- *in cpds* morning.

morgendlich *adj* morning *attr*; *(früh~)* early morning *attr*.

Morgen-: **~grauen** *nt* - dawn, daybreak; **~gymnastik** *f* morning exercises *pl*; **~land** *nt (old, liter)* Orient; **~luft** *f* early morning air; **~luft wittern** *(fig col)* to see one's chance; **~mantel** *m* dressing-gown; **~muffel** *m (col)* **er ist ein schrecklicher ~muffel** he's terribly grumpy in the mornings *(col)*; **~rock** *m* housecoat; **~rot** *nt no pl* sunrise; *(fig)* dawn(ing).

morgens *adv* in the morning. **(um) drei Uhr ~** at three a.m.; **von ~ bis abends** from morning to night; **Freitag ~** on Friday morning.

Morgen-: **~stunde** *f* morning hour; **bis in die frühen ~stunden** into the early hours (of the morning); **~stund(e) hat Gold im Mund(e)** *(Prov)* the early bird catches the worm *(Prov)*.

morgig *adj attr* tomorrow's.

Mormone *m (wk)* **-n, -n, Mormonin** *f* Mormon.

morsch *adj (lit, fig)* rotten; *Knochen* brittle; *Gebäude* ramshackle.

Morse|alphabet *nt* Morse (code).

morsen 1 *vi* to send a message in Morse (code). **2** *vt* to send in Morse (code).

Mörser *m* - mortar *(auch Mil)*.

Morsezeichen *nt* Morse signal.

Mörtel *m* - *(zum Mauern)* mortar; *(Putz)* stucco.

Mosaik *nt* **-e(n)** *(lit, fig)* mosaic.

Moschee *f* **-n** [-'eːən] mosque.

Moschus *m no pl* musk.

Möse *f* **-n** *(col!!)* cunt *(col!!)*.

Mosel[1] *f (Geog)* Moselle.

Mosel[2] *m* -, **Moselwein** *m* Moselle (wine).

mosern *vi (col)* to gripe *(col)*, to belly-ache *(col)*.

Moskau *nt* Moscow.

Moskauer *adj attr* Moscow *attr*.

Moskito *m* **-s** mosquito.

Moslem *m* **-s** Moslem.

moslemisch *adj attr* Moslem.

Most *m no pl* **(a)** unfermented fruit juice; *(für Wein)* must. **(b)** *(SGer, Sw: Obstwein)* fruit wine; *(Apfel~)* cider.

Motel *nt* **-s** motel.

Motiv *nt* **-e (a)** *(Psych, Jur, fig)* motive. **das ~ einer Tat** the motive for a deed. **(b)** *(Art, Liter)* subject; *(Leit~, Mus)* motif.

Motivation [-va'tsioːn] *f* motivation.

motivieren* [moti'viːrən] *vt* **(a)** *(begründen)* **etw (jdm gegenüber) ~** to give (sb) reasons for sth. **(b)** *(anregen)* to motivate.

Motor *m* **-en** [mo'toːrən] motor; *(von Fahrzeug)* engine; *(fig)* driving force *(gen in)*.

Motor-: **~antrieb** *m* motor drive; **mit ~antrieb** motor-driven; **~boot** *nt* motorboat; **~haube** *f* bonnet *(Brit)*, hood *(US)*; *(Aviat)* engine cowling.

motorisch *adj (Physiol)* motor *attr*.

motorisiert* *adj* motorized.

Motor-: **~jacht** *f* motor yacht; **~leistung** *f* engine performance.

Motorrad *nt* motorbike, motorcycle.

Motorradfahrer *m* motorcyclist.

Motor-: **~raum** *m* engine compartment; **~säge** *f* power saw; **~schaden** *m* engine trouble *no pl*; **~sport** *m* motor sport.

Motte *f* **-n** moth. **von ~n zerfressen** moth-eaten;

du kriegst die ~n! *(col)* blow me! *(col)*.

Motten-: **~kiste** *f (fig)* **etw aus der ~kiste hervorholen** to dig sth out; **~kugel** *f* mothball.

Motto *nt* **-s** *(Wahlspruch)* motto.

motzen *vi (col)* to beef *(col)*, to grouse *(col)*.

Möwe *f* **-n** seagull, gull.

MP [ɛm'piː] = **Maschinenpistole.**

Mrd. = **Milliarde.**

Mücke *f* **-n** *(Insekt)* mosquito, midge. **aus einer ~ einen Elefanten machen** *(col)* to make a mountain out of a molehill.

Muckefuck *m no pl (col)* coffee substitute.

mucken 1 *vi (col)* to mutter. **ohne zu ~** without a murmur. **2** *vr* to make a sound.

Mucken *pl (col)* moods *pl*. **(seine) ~ haben** to be moody; *(Sache)* to be temperamental.

Mückenstich *m* mosquito or gnat bite.

Mucks *m* **-e** *(col)* sound. **keinen ~ sagen** not to make a sound; *(widersprechend)* not to say a word.

mucksen *vr (col)* **sich nicht ~** not to move (a muscle); *(sich nicht äußern)* not to make a sound.

mucksmäuschenstill [-'mɔysçən-] *adj (col)* **(as)** quiet as a mouse.

müde *adj* tired; *Haupt* weary. **sie wird nicht ~, das zu tun** she never wearies of doing that.

Müdigkeit *f (Schlafbedürfnis)* tiredness; *(Schläfrigkeit)* sleepiness. **vor ~** *(dat)* **umfallen** to drop from exhaustion; **nur keine ~ vorschützen!** *(col)* don't (you) tell me you're tired.

Muff[1] *m no pl (N Ger: Modergeruch)* musty smell.

Muff[2] *m* **-e** muff.

Muffel *m* - *(col: Murrkopf)* grouch, grouser.

muff(e)lig *adj (col)* grumpy.

Muffensausen *nt (col):* **~ kriegen/haben** to be/ get scared stiff *(col)*.

muffig *adj (dial)* Geruch musty.

muh *interj* moo.

Mühe *f* **-n** trouble; *(Anstrengung auch)* effort; *(Arbeitsaufwand auch)* bother. **ohne ~** without any bother; **nur mit ~** only just; **mit Müh und Not** *(col)* with great difficulty; **wenig/keine ~ haben** not to have much bother *(etw zu tun* doing sth); **es ist der** *(gen)* **~ wert** it's worth the trouble *(etw zu tun* of doing sth); **sich** *(dat)* **keine ~ geben** to take no trouble; **gib dir keine ~!** *(hör auf)* don't bother, save yourself the trouble; **sich** *(dat)* **die ~ machen,** etw zu tun to take the trouble to do sth; **jdm ~ machen** to give sb some bother; **verlorene ~** a waste of effort.

mühelos *adj* effortless; *Sieg, Aufstieg auch* easy.

Mühelosigkeit *f siehe* **mühelos** effortlessness; ease.

muhen *vi* to moo, to low.

mühevoll *adj* laborious, arduous; *Leben* arduous.

Mühle *f* **-n (a)** mill; *(Kaffee~)* grinder. **(b)** *(fig: Routine)* treadmill. **(c)** *(~spiel)* nine men's morris. **(d)** *(col)* *(Auto)* crate *(col)*, banger *(col)*, jalopy *(col)*; *(Fahrrad)* boneshaker *(col)*.

Mühsal ['myːzaːl] *f* **-e** *(geh)* tribulation; *(Strapaze)* toil.

mühsam ['myːzaːm] **1** *adj* arduous. **2** *adv* with difficulty. **~ verdientes Geld** hard-earned money.

mühselig ['myːzeːlɪç] *adj* arduous.

Mulatte *m (wk)* **-n, -n, Mulattin** *f* mulatto.

Mulde *f* **-n** *(Geländesenkung)* hollow.

Mull *m (Gewebe)* muslin; *(Med)* gauze.

Müll *m no pl (Haushalts~)* rubbish, garbage *(esp US)*, refuse *(form)*; *(Gerümpel)* rubbish; *(Industrie~)* waste.

Müllabfuhr *f* refuse *or* garbage *(US)* collection; *(Stadtreinigung)* refuse *etc* collection department.

Müllbinde *f* gauze bandage.

Müll-: **~deponie** *f* waste disposal site, sanitary (land)fill *(US form)*; **~eimer** *m* rubbish bin *(Brit)*, garbage can *(US)*; **~kippe** *f* rubbish *or* garbage *(US)* dump; **~mann** *m, pl* **~männer** *(col)* dustman *(Brit)*, trash collector *(US)*; ~**schlucker** *m* - refuse chute; ~**tonne** *f* dustbin *(Brit)*, trashcan *(US)*.

mulmig *adj* uncomfortable. **mir war** ~ **zumute** *(lit)* I felt queasy; *(fig)* I had butterflies *(col)*.

Multi *m* -s *(col)* multinational (organization).

Multi- *in cpds* multi-; **m~lateral** *adj* multilateral; ~**millionär** *m* multimillionaire.

multipel *adj* multiple. **multiple Sklerose** multiple sclerosis.

multiplizieren* **1** *vt (lit, fig)* to multiply *(mit* by). **2** *vr (fig)* to multiply.

Mumie ['muːmiə] *f* mummy.

mumifizieren* *vt* to mummify.

Mumm *m no pl (col: Mut)* spunk *(dated col)*, guts *pl (col)*.

mümmeln *vi (col)* to nibble.

Mumpitz *m no pl (col)* balderdash *(dated col)*.

Mumps *m or (col) f* -, *no pl* (the) mumps *sing*.

München *nt* Munich.

Mund *m* ⁼er mouth; *(col: Mundwerk)* tongue. **etw in den** ~ **nehmen** to put sth in one's mouth; **dieses Wort nehme ich nicht in den** ~ I never use that word; **den** ~ **aufmachen** *(fig: seine Meinung sagen)* to speak up; **einen großen** ~ **haben** *(fig) (aufschneiden)* to talk big *(col)*; *(frech sein)* to be cheeky *(esp Brit) or* fresh *(esp US)*; **jdm den** ~ **verbieten** to order sb to be quiet; **halt den** ~! shut up! *(col)*, hold your tongue!; **er kann den** ~ **einfach nicht halten** *(col)* he can't keep his big mouth shut *(col)*; **jdm über den** ~ **fahren** to cut sb short; **jdm den** ~ **stopfen** *(col)* to shut sb up *(col)*; **in aller** ~ **e sein** to be on everyone's lips; **Sie nehmen mir das Wort aus dem** ~ you've taken the (very) words out of my mouth; **jdm nach dem** ~ **reden** *(col)* to say what sb wants to hear; **sie ist nicht auf den** ~ **gefallen** *(col)* she's never at a loss for words; **den** ~ **(zu) voll nehmen** *(col)* to talk (too) big *(col)*.

Mund|art *f* dialect.

mund|artlich *adj* dialect(al).

Mündel *nt or (Jur) m* - ward.

munden *vi (liter)* **jdm köstlich** ~ to taste delicious to sb; **sich** *(dat)* **etw** ~ **lassen** to savour *(Brit) or* savor *(US)* sth.

münden *vi (aux sein or haben (Fluß)* to flow *(in +acc* into); *(Straße)* to lead *(in +acc, auf +acc* into).

Mund-: **m~faul** *adj (col)* uncommunicative; **sei doch nicht so m~faul!** make an effort and say something!; **m~gerecht** *adj* bite-sized; ~**geruch** *m* bad breath; ~**harmonika** *f* mouth organ.

mündig *adj* of age; *(fig)* mature.

Mündigkeit *f* majority; *(fig)* maturity.

mündlich *adj* verbal; *Prüfung, Leistung* oral. ~**e Verhandlung** *(Jur)* hearing; **das M~e** *(col: Sch, Univ)* the oral; **alles weitere** ~! let's talk about it more when I see you.

Mund-: ~**raub** *m (Jur)* theft of food for personal consumption; ~**stück** *nt (von Pfeife, Blasinstrument)* mouthpiece; *(von Zigarette)* (filter-)tip; **m~tot** *adj (col)* **jdn m~tot machen** to silence sb.

Mündung *f (von Fluß, Rohr etc)* mouth; *(Trichter~)* estuary; *(Gewehr~)* muzzle.

Mund-: ~**wasser** *nt* mouthwash; ~**werk** *nt (col)* **ein freches/großes** ~**werk haben** to be cheeky *(esp Brit) or* fresh *(esp US)*/talk big *(col)*; **ihr** ~**werk steht nie still** her tongue never stops wagging *(col)*; ~**winkel** *m* corner of one's mouth; ~**-zu-**~**-Beatmung** *f* mouth-to-mouth resuscitation.

Munition *f* ammunition.

Munitions-: ~**depot** *nt* munitions dump; ~**fabrik** *f* munitions factory.

munkeln *vti* **man munkelt, daß** ... there's a rumour *(Brit) or* rumor *(US)* that ...

Münster *nt* - minster, cathedral.

munter *adj* **(a)** *(lebhaft)* lively *no adv*; *(fröhlich)* cheerful, merry. ~ **und vergnügt** bright and cheery; ~ **drauflos reden** to prattle away merrily. **(b)** *(wach)* awake; *(aufgestanden)* up and about.

Munterkeit *f (Lebhaftigkeit)* liveliness; *(Fröhlichkeit)* cheerfulness, merriness.

Münz|automat *m* slot machine.

Münze *f* -n coin. **jdm etw mit gleicher** ~ **heimzahlen** *(fig)* to pay sb back in his own coin for sth.

münzen *vt* to mint, to coin. **das war auf ihn gemünzt** *(fig)* that was aimed at him.

Münz-: ~**fernsprecher** *m (form)* pay phone; ~**tank** *m* coin operated petrol *(Brit) or* gas(oline) *(US)* pump.

mürb(e) *adj* crumbly; *(zerbröckelnd)* crumbling; *Fleisch* tender; *Obst* soft. **jdn** ~ **machen/kriegen** *(fig: zermürbt)* to wear sb down/to break sb.

Mürbeteig *m* short(-crust) pastry.

Murks *m no pl (col)* ~ **machen** to bungle things *(col)*; **das ist** ~! that's a botch-up *(col)*.

Murmel *f* -n marble.

murmeln *vti* to murmur; *(undeutlich)* to mumble; *(brummeln)* to mutter. **etw vor sich** *(acc)* **hin** ~ to mutter sth to oneself.

Murmeltier *nt* marmot. **schlafen wie ein** ~ to sleep like a log.

murren *vi* to grumble *(über +acc* about).

mürrisch *adj (abweisend)* sullen, morose; *(schlechtgelaunt)* grumpy.

Mus *nt* -e mush. **jdn zu** ~ **schlagen** *(col)* to make mincemeat of sb.

Muschel *f* -n **(a)** mussel *(auch Cook)*, bivalve; *(Schale)* shell. **(b)** *(Ohr~)* external ear. **(c)** *(Telec) (Sprech~)* mouthpiece; *(Hör~)* earpiece.

Muse *f* -n *(Myth)* Muse. **die leichte** ~ *(fig)* light entertainment; **von der** ~ **geküßt werden** *(fig)* to be inspired.

Museum [mu'zeːʊm] *nt, pl* **Museen** [mu'zeːən] museum.

Museums-: ~**führer** *m* museum guide; **m~reif** *adj (hum)* antique; **m~reif sein** to be almost a museum piece; ~**stück** *nt* museum piece.

Musical ['mjuːzikl] *nt* -s musical.

Musik *f* -en music. **das ist** ~ **in meinen Ohren** *(fig)* that's music to my ears.

musikalisch *adj* musical.

Musikant(in *f)* *m* musician, minstrel *(old)*.

Musik-: ~**begleitung** *f* musical accompaniment; ~**box** *f* jukebox.

Musiker(in *f)* *m* - musician.

Musik-: ~**hochschule** *f* college of music; ~**instrument** *nt* musical instrument; ~**kapelle** *f* band; ~**korps** *nt* music corps *sing*; ~**lehrer** *m* music teacher; ~**liebhaber** *m* music-lover; ~**saal** *m* music room; ~**sendung** *f* music programme *(Brit) or* program *(US)*; ~**stück** *nt* piece of music; ~**stunde** *f* music lesson.

musisch *adj Fächer* (fine) arts *attr*; *Begabung* for the arts; *Veranlagung, Mensch* artistic.

musizieren* *vi* to play. **sie saßen auf dem Marktplatz und musizierten** they sat in the market place playing their instruments.

Muskat *m* -e, **Muskatnuß** *f* nutmeg.

Muskel *m* -n muscle. ~**n haben** to be muscular; **seine** ~**n spielen lassen** *(lit, fig)* to flex one's muscles.

Muskel-: ~**kater** *m* aching muscles *pl*; ~**kater haben** to be stiff; ~**kraft** *f* physical strength; ~**krampf** *m* muscle cramp *no indef art*; ~**paket** *nt*, ~**protz** *m (col)* muscleman *(col)*; ~**riß** *m* torn muscle; ~**schwund** *m* muscular atrophy *or* wasting; ~**zerrung** *f* pulled muscle.

Muskulatur *f* muscular system.

muskulös *adj* muscular. ~ **gebaut sein** to have a muscular build.

Müsli *nt* -s muesli.

Muß *nt no pl* es ist ein/kein ~ it's/it's not a must.

Muße *f no pl* leisure. **dafür fehlt mir die** ~ I don't have the leisure; **etw mit** ~ **tun** to do sth in a leisurely way.

müssen 1 *modal aux pret* **mußte**, *ptp* ~ **(a)** *(Zwang)* to have to; *(Notwendigkeit auch)* to need to. **ich muß** *(Zwang)* I have to, I must *nur pres*, I've got to *(esp Brit)*; *(Notwendigkeit auch)* I need to; **ich muß nicht** *(Zwang)* I don't have to, I haven't got to *(esp Brit)*; *(Notwendigkeit auch)* I don't need to, I needn't; **muß er?** must he?, **does he have to?**, has he got to? *(esp Brit)*; **mußtest du?** did you have to?; **das muß irendwann mal gemacht werden** it will have to be done some time; **er sagte, er müsse bald gehen** he said he would have to go soon; **man mußte lachen/weinen** *etc* you couldn't help laughing/crying *etc*; **wenn es (unbedingt) sein muß** if it's absolutely necessary; **das muß man sich** *(dat)* **mal vorstellen!** (just) imagine that!; **was habe ich da hören** ~? what's this I hear?

(b) *(sollen)* **das müßtest du eigentlich wissen** you ought to *or* you should know that; **das mußt du nicht tun!** you oughtn't to *or* shouldn't do that.

(c) es muß geregnet haben it must have rained; **es muß wahr sein** it must be true; **es muß nicht wahr sein** it needn't be true; **es müssen zehntausend Zuschauer im Stadion gewesen sein** there must have been ten thousand spectators in the stadium; **er müßte schon da sein** he should be there by now; **so muß es gewesen sein** that's how it must have been; **man müßte noch mal von vorn anfangen können!** if only one could begin again!

2 *vi pret* **mußte**, *ptp* **gemußt wann müßt ihr zur Schule?** when do you have to go to school?; **der Brief muß heute noch zur Post** the letter must be mailed today; **ich muß mal** *(col)* I need to go to the loo *(Brit col)* or bathroom *(esp US)*.

Mußestunde *f* hour of leisure.

Mußheirat *f (col)* shotgun wedding *(col)*. **es war eine** ~ they had to get married.

müßig *adj (untätig)* idle; *Leben, Stunden* of leisure; *(unnütz)* futile.

Müßig-: ~**gang** *m (liter)* idleness; ~**gang ist aller Laster Anfang** *(Prov)* the devil finds work for idle hands *(Prov)*; ~**gänger(in** *f)* *m* - idler.

mußte *pret of* **müssen**.

Muster *nt* - **(a)** *(Vorlage)* pattern; *(für Brief, Bewerbung etc)* specimen. **nach einem** ~ **stricken** *etc* to knit *etc* from a pattern. **(b)** *(Probestück)* sample; *(Buch etc)* specimen. ~ **ohne Wert** sample of no commercial value. **(c)** *(fig: Vorbild)* model *(an +dat of)*. **als** ~ **dienen** to serve as a model; **ein** ~ **an Tugend** a paragon of virtue.

Muster- *in cpds* model; ~**beispiel** *nt* classic example; **m**~**gültig, m**~**haft** *adj* exemplary; **er hat sich m**~**haft verhalten** his conduct was exemplary; ~**knabe** *m (iro)* paragon.

mustern *vt* **(a)** *(betrachten)* to scrutinize. **(b)** *(Mil: inspizieren)* to inspect, to review. **(c)** *(Mil: für Wehrdienst)* **jdn** ~ to give sb his/her medical. **(d)** *Stoff siehe* **gemustert**.

Muster-: ~**prozeß** *m* test case; ~**schüler** *m* model pupil; *(fig)* star pupil.

Musterung *f* **(a)** pattern. **(b)** *(Mil) (von Truppen)* inspection, review; *(von Rekruten)* medical (examination). **(c)** *(durch Blicke)* scrutiny.

Mut *m no pl* courage, pluck *(col)*; *(Zuversicht)* heart. ~ **fassen** to pluck up courage; **mit frischem** ~ with new heart; **nur** ~! cheer up!,

keep your pecker up! *(Brit col)*; **jdm den** ~ **nehmen** to discourage sb; **den** ~ **verlieren** to lose heart; **jdm** ~ **machen** to encourage sb; **das gab ihr wieder neuen** ~ that gave her new heart; **mit dem** ~ **der Verzweiflung** with the courage born of desperation; **frohen/ guten** ~**es sein** *(geh)* to be in good spirits.

Mütchen *nt:* **sein** ~ **an jdm kühlen** *(col)* to take it out on sb *(col)*.

Mütig *adj (tapfer)* courageous, brave.

Mut-: **m**~**los** *adj* disheartened *no adv*; *(bedrückt)* despondent; **jdn m**~**los machen** to make sb lose heart; ~**losigkeit** *f* despondency.

mutmaßen *vti insep* to conjecture.

mutmaßlich 1 *adj attr Vater, Täter* presumed. **2** *adv* ~ **soll er der Vater sein** he is presumed to be the father.

Mutmaßung *f* conjecture.

Mutprobe *f* test of courage.

Mutter[1] *f* - mother. **sie ist jetzt** ~ **she's a mother** now; **sie ist** ~ **von drei Kindern** she's a mother of three; ~ **Natur/Erde** *(liter)* Mother Nature/ Earth; **wie bei** ~**n** *(col)* just like (at) home; *(Essen)* just like mother makes/used to make.

Mutter[2] *f* -**n** *(Tech)* nut.

Mutterboden *m* topsoil.

Mütterchen *nt* **(a)** *dim of* **Mutter**[1] mummy *(col)*, mommy *(US col)*. **(b)** *(alte Frau)* grandma.

Mutter-: ~**erde** *f* topsoil; ~**freuden** *pl* the joys of motherhood *pl*; ~**gesellschaft** *f (Comm)* parent company; ~**instinkt** *m* maternal instinct; ~**kuchen** *m (Anat)* placenta; ~**land** *nt* mother country; ~**leib** *m* womb.

mütterlich *adj* **(a)** maternal. **die** ~**en Pflichten** one's duties as a mother. **(b)** *(liebevoll besorgt)* motherly *no adv*. **jdn** ~ **umsorgen** to mother sb.

mütterlicherseits *adv* on his/her *etc* mother's side. **sein Großvater** ~ his maternal grandfather.

Mütterlichkeit *f* motherliness.

Mutter-: ~**liebe** *f* motherly love; **m**~**los** *adj* motherless; ~**mal** *nt* birthmark; ~**milch** *f* mother's milk; ~**mord** *m* matricide; ~**mörder** *m* matricide; ~**mund** *m (Anat)* cervix.

Mutterschaft *f* motherhood.

Mutterschafts-: ~**geld** *nt* maternity grant; ~**urlaub** *m* maternity leave.

Mutter-: ~**schutz** *m* legal protection of expectant and nursing mothers; ~**seelenallein** *adj, adv* all on one's own; ~**söhnchen** *nt (pej)* mummy's boy; ~**sprache** *f* native language, mother tongue; ~**stelle** *f* **bei jdm** ~**stelle vertreten** to take the place of sb's mother; ~**tag** *m* Mother's Day; ~**tier** *nt* mother (animal); *(Zuchttier)* brood animal; ~**witz** *m (Schläue)* mother wit; *(Humor)* natural wit.

Mutti *f* -s *(col)* mummy, mum, mommy *(US)*.

Mutwille *m* -**ns**, *no pl (böse Absicht)* malice. **etw aus** ~**n tun** to do sth out of malice.

mutwillig 1 *adj (böswillig)* malicious; *Zerstörung auch* wilful. **2** *adv (absichtlich)* wilfully.

Mütze *f* -**n** cap.

MWSt. = **Mehrwertsteuer** VAT.

mysteriös *adj* mysterious.

Mysterium *nt* mystery.

Mystik *f* mysticism *no art.*

mystisch *adj* mystic(al); *(fig: geheimnisvoll)* mysterious.

mythisch *adj* mythical.

Mythologie *f* mythology.

mythologisch *adj* mythologic(al).

Mythos *m* -, **Mythen** *(lit, fig)* myth.

N

N, n [ɛn] *nt* -, - N, n. **n-te** nth.
N = **Norden**.
na *interj (col)* **(a)** well. ~, **kommst du mit?** are you coming then?; ~, **du?** well?; ~ **ja** well; ~ **gut,** ~ **schön** all right, OK *(col)*; ~ **also!,** ~ **eben!** (well,) there you are (then)!; ~ **und ob!** *(auf jeden Fall)* you bet! *(col)*; *(und wie)* and how! *(col)*. **(b)** *(Ermahnung)* now; *(Zurückweisung)* well. ~ **(~)!** now then!; ~ **warte!** just you wait!; ~ **so was!** well, I never!; ~ **und?** so what?
Nabe *f* **-n** hub.
Nabel *m* - *(Anat)* navel, umbilicus *(spec)*; *(Bot)* hilum. **der** ~ **der Welt** *(fig)* the hub of the universe.
Nabelschnur *f (Anat)* umbilical cord.
nach 1 *prep+dat* **(a)** *(örtlich)* to. **ich fuhr mit dem Zug** ~ **Mailand** I took the train to Milan; **er ist schon** ~ **London abgefahren** he has already left for London; ~ **Osten/Westen** eastward(s)/westward(s); ~ **links/rechts** (to the) left/right; ~ **hinten/vorn** to the back/front; ~ **Norden zu** *or* **hin** to *or* towards *(esp Brit)* or toward *(esp US)* the north.
　(b) *(zeitlich, Reihenfolge)* after. **fünf (Minuten)** ~ **drei** five (minutes) past *or* after *(US)* three; **sie kam** ~ **zehn Minuten** she came ten minutes later; ~ **Empfang** *or* **Erhalt** on receipt; **drei Tage** ~ **Empfang** three days after receipt; **eine(r, s)** ~ **dem/der anderen** one after another; **(bitte)** ~ **Ihnen!** after you!; ~ **„mit"** **steht der Dativ** "mit" takes the dative.
　(c) *(entsprechend)* according to; *(im Einklang mit)* in accordance with. ~ **dem Gesetz** according to the law; ~ **Artikel 142c** under article 142c; **etw** ~ **Gewicht kaufen** to buy sth by weight; ~ **Verfassern** in order of authors; **die Uhr** ~ **dem Radio stellen** to put a clock right by the radio; **ihrer Sprache** ~ **(zu urteilen)** judging by her language; ~ **dem, was er gesagt hat** according to what he's said; ~ **allem, was ich weiß** as far as I know; ~ **einem Gedicht von Schiller** after a poem by Schiller; **er wurde** ~ **seinem Großvater genannt** he was called after *or* for *(US)* his grandfather.
　2 *adv* **(a)** *(räumlich)* **mir** ~**!** *(liter, hum)* follow me! **(b)** *(zeitlich)* ~ **und** ~ little by little; ~ **wie vor** still.
nach|äffen *vt sep (pej)* **Moden, Ideen** to ape; **jdn** to mimic.
nach|ahmen *vt sep* to imitate; *(karikieren)* to mimic; *(kopieren)* to copy.
nach|ahmenswert *adj* exemplary.
Nach|ahmer(in *f)* *m* - imitator; *(pej: Art, Liter)* copyist.
Nach|ahmung *f siehe vt* **(a)** *(das Imitieren)* imitation; mimicking; copying. **etw zur** ~ **empfehlen** to recommend sth as an example. **(b)** *(die Imitation)* imitation; impression; copy.
nach|arbeiten *sep* **1** *vt* **(a)** *(aufholen)* to make up. **(b)** *(überarbeiten)* to work over. **(c)** *(nachbilden)* to copy, to reproduce. **2** *vi* **wir müssen morgen** ~ we'll have to make up the work tomorrow.
Nachbar(in *f)* *m (wk)* **-n,** **-n** neighbour *(Brit)*, neighbor *(US)*. **Herr X war beim Konzert mein** ~ Mr X sat next to me at the concert; ~**s Garten** the next-door garden.

Nachbarhaus *nt* house next door.
nachbarlich *adj (freundlich)* neighbourly *no adv* *(Brit)*, neighborly *no adv* *(US)*; *(benachbart)* neighbouring *no adv* *(Brit)*, neighboring *no adv* *(US)*.
Nachbarschaft *f (Gegend)* neighbourhood *(Brit)*, neighborhood *(US)*; *(Nachbarn)* neighbours *pl* *(Brit)*, neighbors *pl* *(US)*; *(Nähe)* vicinity.
nachbehandeln* *vt sep (Med)* **jdn/etw** ~ to give sb after-care.
Nachbehandlung *f (Med)* follow-up treatment.
nachbessern *sep* **1** *vt* to put the finishing touches to. **2** *vi* to add the finishing touches.
nachbestellen* *vt sep* to order some more; *(Comm)* to reorder.
Nachbestellung *f (gen* for) repeat order.
nachbeten *vt sep (pej col)* to repeat parrot-fashion.
nachbezahlen* *sep* **1** *vt* to pay; *(später)* to pay later. **Steuern** ~ to pay back-tax. **2** *vi* to pay the rest.
nachbilden *vt sep* to copy; *(exakt)* to reproduce.
Nachbildung *f* copy; *(exakt)* reproduction.
nachdatieren* *vt sep* to postdate.
nachdem *conj (zeitlich)* after.
nachdenken *vi sep irreg* to think *(über +acc* about). **darüber darf man gar nicht** ~ it doesn't bear thinking about; **denk doch mal nach!** think about it!
Nachdenken *nt* thought, reflection. **nach langem** ~ after (giving the matter) considerable thought; **gib mir ein bißchen Zeit zum** ~ give me a bit of time to think (about it).
nachdenklich *adj* **Mensch, Miene** thoughtful, pensive. **jdn** ~ **stimmen** to set sb thinking; ~ **gestimmt sein** to be in a thoughtful mood.
Nachdenklichkeit *f no pl* thoughtfulness, pensiveness.
Nachdichtung *f (Liter)* free rendering.
Nachdruck *m* **(a)** *no pl (Betonung)* stress, emphasis. **besondern** ~ **darauf legen, daß ...** to stress *or* emphasize particularly that ...; **etw mit** ~ **betreiben** to pursue sth energetically. **(b)** *(das Nachdrucken)* reprinting; *(das Nachgedruckte)* reprint.
nachdrucken *vt sep* to reprint.
nachdrücklich *adj* emphatic. ~ **auf etw** *(dat)* **bestehen** to insist firmly on sth; **jdm** ~ **raten, etw zu tun** to urge sb to do sth; **jdn** ~ **warnen** to give sb a firm warning.
nach|eifern *vi sep* **jdm/einer Sache** ~ to emulate sb/sth.
nach|einander *adv (räumlich)* one after the other; *(zeitlich auch)* in succession. **zweimal** ~ twice running; **kurz** ~ shortly after each other; **drei Tage** ~ three days running, three days on the trot *(col)*.
nach|empfinden *vt sep irreg* **(a)** **Stimmung** to feel. **das kann ich ihr** ~ I can understand her feelings. **(b)** *(nachgestalten)* to adapt *(dat* from).
nach|erzählen* *vt sep* to retell.
Nach|erzählung *f* retelling; *(Sch)* (story) reproduction.
Nachf. = **Nachfolger**.
Nachfahr *m* **-en** *(liter)* descendant.
nachfahren *vi sep irreg aux sein* to follow (on).

jdm ~ to follow sb.

nachfassen vi sep **(a)** (noch einmal zufassen) to regain one's grip. **(b)** (col: nachforschen) to probe a bit deeper.

nachfeiern vti sep (später feiern) to celebrate later.

Nachfolge f no pl succession. **jds/die ~ antreten** to succeed sb/to succeed.

nachfolgen vi sep aux sein (hinterherkommen) to follow (on). **jdm ~** to follow sb; **jdm im Amt ~** to succeed sb in office.

nachfolgend adj following. **das N~e** the following.

Nachfolger(in f) m - (im Amt etc) successor. **Friedrich Reißnagel ~ successors** to Friedrich Reißnagel.

nachforschen vi sep to try to find out; (polizeilich etc) to carry out an investigation (dat into); (amtlich etc) to make inquiries (dat into).

Nachforschung f inquiry; (polizeilich etc) investigation. **~en anstellen** to make inquiries.

Nachfrage f **(a)** (Comm) demand (nach, in +dat for). **danach besteht eine rege ~** there is a great demand for it. **(b)** (Erkundigung) inquiry. **danke der ~** (form) thank you for your concern; (col) nice of you to ask.

nachfragen vi sep to ask, to inquire.

nachfüllen vt sep leeres Glas etc to refill; halbleeres Glas, Batterie etc to top up.

nachgeben sep irreg **1** vi **(a)** to give way (dat to); (federn) to give; (fig: Mensch) to give in (dat to). **(b)** (Comm: Preise, Kurse) to drop, to fall. **2** vt (noch mehr geben) **darf ich Ihnen noch etwas Gemüse ~?** may I give you a few more vegetables?

Nachgebühr f excess (postage).

Nachgeburt f afterbirth; (Vorgang) expulsion of the afterbirth.

nachgehen vi sep irreg aux sein **(a)** +dat (hinterhergehen) to follow; **jdm** auch to go after. **(b)** (Uhr) to be slow. **deine Uhr geht fünf Minuten nach** your clock is five minutes slow. **(c)** +dat (ausüben) Beruf to practise (Brit), to practice (US); Studium, Vergnügungen etc to pursue; Geschäften to go about. **einer geregelten Arbeit ~** to have a steady job. **(d)** +dat (erforschen) to investigate, to look into.

nachgelassen adj Werke, Papiere posthumous.

nachgemacht adj Gold, Leder etc imitation; Geld counterfeit.

nachgerade adv (geradezu) practically, virtually.

Nachgeschmack m (lit, fig) aftertaste. **einen üblen ~ hinterlassen** (fig) to leave a bad taste in the mouth.

nachgiebig adj **(a)** Material pliable; Boden etc yielding, soft. **~ sein** to give. **(b)** (fig) Mensch, Haltung soft; (konziliant) compliant. **sie behandelt die Kinder zu ~** she's too soft with the children.

Nachgiebigkeit f siehe adj **(a)** pliability; softness. **(b)** softness; compliance.

nachgießen vti sep irreg Wasser, Milch to add. **darf ich Ihnen (noch etwas Wein) ~?** would you like some more (wine)?

nachgrübeln vi sep to think (über +acc about); (sich Gedanken machen) to ponder (über +acc on).

nachgucken vti sep siehe **nachsehen**.

nachhaken vi sep (col) to dig deeper.

Nachhall m reverberation; (fig) echo.

nachhallen vi sep to reverberate.

nachhaltig adj lasting no adv. **ihre Gesundheit hat sich ~ gebessert** there has been a lasting improvement in her health.

nachhängen vi sep irreg+dat to give oneself up to. **seinen Erinnerungen ~** to lose oneself in one's memories.

Nachhauseweg m way home.

nachhelfen vi sep irreg to help. **er hat dem Glück**

ein bißchen nachgeholfen he engineered himself a little luck.

nachher adv **(a)** (danach) afterwards; (später auch) later. **bis ~** see you later! **(b)** (col: womöglich) **~ stimmt das gar nicht** that might not be true at all.

Nachhilfe f (Sch) private tuition.

Nachhilfe-: **~lehrer** m private tutor; **~stunde** f private lesson; **~unterricht** m private tuition.

nachhinein adv: **im ~** afterwards; (rückblickend) in retrospect.

nachhinken vi sep aux sein (fig col) to lag behind.

Nachholbedarf m **einen ~ an etw** (dat) **haben** to have a lot of sth to catch up on.

nachholen vt sep **(a)** (aufholen) to make up (for). **(b)** (nachkommen lassen) to get sb to join one.

Nachhut f -en (Mil) rearguard. **bei der ~** in the rearguard.

Nach|impfung f booster.

nachjagen vi sep aux sein+dat to chase (after).

nachklingen vi sep irreg aux sein (Ton, Echo) to go on sounding; (Worte, Erinnerung) to linger on.

Nachkomme m (wk) -n, -n descendant.

nachkommen vi sep irreg aux sein **(a)** (später kommen) to follow later. **Sie können Ihr Gepäck ~ lassen** you can have your luggage sent on (after). **(b)** (Schritt halten) to keep up. **(c)**+dat (erfüllen) einer Pflicht to carry out; einer Forderung, einem Wunsch to comply with.

Nachkommenschaft f descendants pl.

Nachkriegs- in cpds post-war.

Nachlaß m -lasse or -lässe **(a)** (Preis~) discount (auf +acc on). **(b)** (Erbschaft) estate. **literarischer ~** unpublished works pl.

nachlassen sep irreg **1** vt **(a)** **die Hälfte des Preises ~** to take 50% off the price; **10% vom Preis ~** to give a 10% discount. **(b)** (locker lassen) Seil to slacken. **(c)** siehe **nachgelassen**. **2** vi to decrease, to diminish; (Interesse auch) to flag, to wane; (Regen, Nasenbluten) to ease off; (Leistung, Geschäfte) to fall off; (Preise) to fall. **er hat in letzter Zeit sehr nachgelassen** he hasn't been nearly as good recently.

nachlässig adj careless; (unachtsam) thoughtless.

Nachlässigkeit f siehe adj carelessness; thoughtlessness.

Nachlaßverwalter m executor.

nachlaufen vi sep irreg aux sein +dat **jdm/einer Sache ~** to run after sb/sth; **den Mädchen ~** to chase girls.

nachlegen vt sep noch Kohlen/Holz **~** to put some more coal/wood on (the fire).

Nachlese f second harvest; (Ertrag) gleanings pl.

nachlesen sep irreg **1** vt (in einem Buch) to read; (nachschlagen) to look up. **man kann das in der Bibel ~** it says so in the Bible. **2** vi to have a second harvest; (Ähren ~) to glean.

nachliefern vt sep (später liefern) to deliver at a later date; (zuzüglich liefern) to make a further delivery of.

nachlösen vi sep to pay on the train/when one gets off; (zur Weiterfahrt) to pay the extra.

nachmachen vt sep **(a)** to copy; (nachäffen) to mimic; (fälschen) to forge. **sie macht mir alles nach** she copies everything I do; **das soll erst mal einer ~!** I'd like to see anyone else do that!; siehe **nachgemacht**. **(b)** (col: nachholen) to make up.

nachmessen vti sep irreg (prüfend messen) to check.

Nachmieter m unser **~** the tenant after us; **wir müssen einen ~ finden** we have to find someone to take over the flat etc.

nachmittag adv gestern/heute **~** yesterday/this afternoon.

Nachmittag m afternoon. **am ~** in the afternoon; **am heutigen ~** this afternoon.

nachmittäglich *adj no pred* afternoon *attr.*
nachmittags *adv* in the afternoon. **dienstags ~** on Tuesday afternoons.
Nachmittags-: ~**schlaf** *m* ~**schlaf halten** to have a sleep after lunch; ~**vorstellung** *f* matinée (performance).
Nachnahme *f* **-n** cash *or* collect *(US)* on delivery, COD; *(col:* ~*sendung)* COD parcel. **etw per ~ schicken** to send sth COD.
Nachnahme-: ~**gebühr** *f* COD charge; ~**sendung** *f* COD parcel.
Nachname *m* surname, family *or* last name.
nachplappern *vt sep* to repeat parrot-fashion.
Nachporto *nt* excess (postage).
nachprüfbar *adj* verifiable.
Nachprüfbarkeit *f* verifiability.
nachprüfen *vti sep* to verify, to check.
Nachprüfung *f (von Aussagen etc)* check *(gen* on).
nachrechnen *vti sep* to check.
Nachrede *f* **(a)** *(Verunglimpfung)* üble ~ *(Jur)* defamation of character; üble ~**n über jdn verbreiten** to cast aspersions on sb's character. **(b)** *(Epilog)* epilogue.
nachreden *vt sep* **(a)** *(wiederholen)* to repeat. **(b) jdm (etwas) Schlechtes ~** to speak badly of sb.
nachreichen *vt sep* to hand in later.
nachreisen *vi sep aux sein* **jdm ~** to follow sb.
Nachricht *f* **-en** (piece of) news; *(Botschaft)* message. **eine ~** a piece of news; a message; **die ~en** the news *sing (auch Rad, TV)*; **schlechte ~en** bad news; ~ **erhalten, daß ...** to receive (the) news that ...; **wir geben Ihnen ~** we'll let you know.
Nachrichten-: ~**agentur** *f* news agency; ~**dienst** *m* **(a)** *(Rad, TV)* news service; **(b)** *(Pol, Mil)* intelligence (service); ~**magazin** *nt* news magazine; ~**satellit** *m* (tele)communications satellite; ~**sperre** *f* news blackout; ~**sprecher** *m* newsreader; ~**technik** *f* telecommunications *sing.*
nachrücken *vi sep aux sein* to move up; *(Mil)* to advance.
Nachruf *m* obituary.
Nachruhm *m* fame after death.
nachsagen *vt sep* **(a)** *(wiederholen)* to repeat. **(b) jdm etw ~** to accuse sb of sth; **jdm Schlechtes ~** to speak ill of sb; **ihm wird nachgesagt, daß ...** it's said that he ...; **das lasse ich mir nicht ~!** I'm not having that said of me!
Nachsaison *f* off-season.
nachschauen *vti sep siehe* **nachsehen 1, 2 (a).**
nachschenken *vti sep* **darf ich Ihnen (etwas) ~?** may I top up your glass?
nachschicken *vt sep* to send on, to forward.
Nachschlag *m (col)* second helping.
nachschlagen *sep irreg* **1** *vt Stelle, Zitat* to look up. **2** *vi (in Lexikon etc)* to look.
Nachschlagewerk *nt* reference book *or* work.
nachschleichen *vi sep irreg aux sein* + *dat* to creep after.
Nachschlüssel *m* duplicate key; *(Dietrich)* skeleton key.
nachschmeißen *vt sep irreg (col)* **jdm etw ~** to fling sth after sb; **das ist ja nachgeschmissen!** it's a real bargain.
nachschnüffeln *vi sep (col)* **jdm ~** to spy on sb.
Nachschub ['naːxʃuːp] *m* supplies *pl (an* + *dat* of).
Nachschub- *(Mil):* ~**linie** *f* supply line; ~**weg** *m* supply route.
nachsehen *sep irreg* **1** *vi* to have a look; *(prüfen)* to check. **jdm/einer Sache ~** *(hinterherschauen)* to gaze after sb/sth. **2** *vt* **(a)** *(prüfen)* to check; *Schulaufgaben etc* to mark; *(nachschlagen)* to look up. **(b)** *(verzeihen)* **jdm etw ~** to forgive sb (for) sth.
Nachsehen *nt:* **das ~ haben** to be left standing; *(nichts bekommen)* to be left empty-handed.
nachsenden *vt sep irreg* to forward.
nachsetzen *sep* **1** *vi* **jdm ~** to pursue sb. **2** *vt Fuß*

to drag.
Nachsicht *f no pl (Milde)* leniency; *(Geduld)* forbearance. **er kennt keine ~** he knows no mercy; ~ **haben** to be lenient.
nachsichtig *adj (milde)* lenient; *(geduldig)* forbearing *(gegen, mit* with).
Nachsilbe *f* suffix.
nachsinnen *vi sep irreg* to ponder *(über* + *acc* over, about).
nachsitzen *vi sep irreg (Sch)* ~ **(müssen)** to be kept in; **jdn ~ lassen** to keep sb in.
Nachsommer *m* Indian summer.
Nachspann *m* **-e** credits *pl.*
Nachspeise *f* dessert, sweet *(Brit).*
Nachspiel *nt (Theat)* epilogue; *(Mus)* closing section; *(fig)* sequel. **das geht nicht ohne ~ ab** there are bound to be repercussions; **ein gerichtliches ~ haben** to have legal repercussions.
nachspielen *sep* **1** *vt* to play. **2** *vi (Sport)* to play extra time *(Brit)* or overtime *(US).* **der Schiedsrichter ließ ~** the referee allowed extra time.
nachspionieren* *vi sep (col)* **jdm ~** to spy on sb.
nachsprechen *vt sep irreg* to repeat. **jdm etw ~** to repeat sth after sb.
nächstbeste *adj attr* **der/die/das ~ ...** the first ... I/you etc see; **der ~ Zug/Job** the first train/job that comes along.
nachstehen *vi sep irreg* **jdm ~** to take second place to sb; **jdm in nichts *(dat)* ~** to be sb's equal in every way.
nachstehend *adj attr* following. ~**es müssen Sie beachten** you must take note of the following.
nachsteigen *vi sep irreg aux sein* **jdm ~** *(fig col)* to run after sb.
nachstellen *sep* **1** *vt (Tech) (neu einstellen)* to adjust; *(zurückstellen)* to put back. **2** *vi* **jdm ~** to follow sb; *(aufdringlich umwerben)* to pester sb.
Nächstenliebe *f* brotherly love; *(Barmherzigkeit)* compassion.
nächstens *adv* **(a)** *(bald einmal)* some time soon. **(b)** *(col: am Ende)* next.
nächste(r, s) *adj superl* of **nah(e) (a)** *(räumlich)* nearest. **das ~ Telefon** the nearest telephone; **ist dies der ~ Weg zum Bahnhof?** is this the quickest way to the station?; **in ~r Nähe** in the immediate vicinity; **aus ~r Nähe** from close by; **betrachten** at close quarters; **schießen** at close range; **im ~n Haus** next door. **(b)** *(zeitlich)* next. ~**s Mal** next time; **Ende ~n Monats** at the end of next month; **am ~n Tag** (the) next day; **in den ~n Tagen** in the next few days; **bei ~r Gelegenheit** at the earliest opportunity; **in ~r Zeit** some time soon. **(c) die ~n Verwandten** the immediate family; **der ~ Angehörige** the next of kin; **fürs ~** for the time being.
Nächste(r) *mf decl as adj* **(a)** next one. **der n~, bitte** next please, first please *(US, Scot).* **(b)** *(Mitmensch)* neighbour *(Brit),* neighbor *(US).* **jeder ist sich selbst der ~** *(Prov)* it's every man for himself.
Nächste(s) *nt decl as adj* **das ~** the next thing; *(das erste)* the first thing; **als ~s** next/first.
nächst-: ~**folgend** *adj attr* next; ~**gelegen** *adj attr* nearest; ~**höher** *adj attr* one higher; **die ~höhere Klasse** one class higher; ~**jährig** *adj attr* next year's; ~**liegend** *adj attr (lit)* nearest; *(fig)* most obvious; **das N~liegende** the most obvious thing (to do).
nachsuchen *vi sep* **(a)** to look. **(b)** *(form: beantragen)* **um etw ~** to request sth *(bei jdm* of sb).
nacht *adv* **heute ~** tonight; *(letzte)* last night; **Dienstag ~** (on) Tuesday night.
Nacht *f* **-e** *(lit, fig)* night. **es wird/ist ~** it's getting/ it is dark; **in der ~** at night; **in der ~ vom 12. zum 13. April** during the night of April 12th to 13th; **in der ~ auf Dienstag** during Monday night; **diese ~** tonight; **des ~s** *(geh)* at night; **bis tief in die ~** to work far into the night; **über ~** *(lit,*

fig) overnight; **sich** (*dat*) **die ~ um die Ohren schlagen** (*col*) to stay up all night (working *etc*); (**mit Feiern**) to make a night of it; **die ~ zum Tage machen** to stay up all night (working *etc*); **gute ~!** good night!; **na, dann gute ~!** (*col*) what a prospect!; **bei ~ und Nebel** (*col*) at dead of night.

Nacht- *in cpds* night; **~arbeit** *f* night-work; **~ausgabe** *f* late final (edition); **~blindheit** *f* night blindness; **~dienst** *m* night duty; **~dienst haben** to be on nights.

Nachteil *m* -e disadvantage. **~e durch etw haben** to lose by sth; **im ~ sein** to be at a disadvantage (*jdm gegenüber* with sb); **der ~, allein zu leben** the disadvantage of living alone.

nachteilig *adj* (*ungünstig*) disadvantageous; (*schädlich*) detrimental. **er hat sich sehr ~ über mich geäußert** he spoke very unfavourably (*Brit*) *or* unfavorably (*US*) about me.

nächtelang *adv* for nights (on end).

Nacht-: **~eule** *f* (*fig col*) night owl; **~falter** *m* moth; **~gebet** *nt* evening prayer; **~hemd** *nt* (*für Damen*) nightdress (*Brit*), nightgown; (*für Herren*) nightshirt.

Nachtigall *f* -en nightingale.

nächtigen *vi* (*geh*) to spend the night.

Nachtisch *m* dessert, sweet (*Brit*), pudding.

nächtlich *adj attr* night. **die ~e Stadt** the town at night; **zu ~er Stunde** at a late hour.

Nacht-: **~lokal** *nt* night club; **~mensch** *m* night person; **~portier** *m* night porter; **~programm** *nt* late-night programme (*Brit*) *or* program (*US*).

Nachtrag *m*, *pl* **Nachträge** postscript; (*zu einem Buch*) supplement.

nachtragen *vt sep irreg* (**a**) **jdm etw ~** (*lit*) to go after sb with sth. (**b**) (*fig*) to bear sb a grudge for sth. (**c**) (*hinzufügen*) to add.

nachtragend *adj* unforgiving.

nachträglich *adj* (*später*) later; (*verspätet*) belated; (*nach dem Tod*) posthumous.

nachtrauern *vi sep+dat* to mourn.

Nachtruhe *f* night's rest; (*in Anstalten*) lights-out.

nachts *adv* at night. **dienstags ~** (on) Tuesday nights.

Nacht-: **~schicht** *f* night shift; **~schicht haben** to be on nights; **n~schlafend** *adj*: **zu n~schlafender Zeit** in the middle of the night; **~schwärmer** *m* (*fig hum*) night owl; **~schwester** *f* night nurse; **~speicherofen** *m* storage heater.

nachts|über *adv* by night.

Nacht-: **~tisch** *m* bedside table; **~tischlampe** *f* bedside lamp; **~topf** *m* chamber pot.

nachtun *vt sep irreg* **es jdm ~** to copy sb.

Nacht-: **~vorstellung** *f* late-night performance; **~wache** *f* night-watch; (*im Krankenhaus*) night duty; **~wache haben** to be on night duty; **~wächter** *m* (*in Betrieben etc*) night watchman; **~zeug** *nt* night things *pl*; **~zug** *m* night train; **~zuschlag** *m* night supplement.

Nach|untersuchung *f* (*weitere Untersuchung*) further examination; (*spätere Untersuchung*) check-up.

nachvollziehbar *adj* comprehensible.

nachvollziehen* *vt sep irreg* to understand, to comprehend.

Nachwahl *f* (*Pol*) ≈ by-election.

Nachwehen *pl* after-pains *pl*; (*fig*) painful aftermath *sing*.

nachweinen *vi sep+dat* to mourn. **dieser Sache weine ich keine Träne nach** I won't shed any tears over that.

Nachweis *m* -e (*Beweis*) proof (*gen, für, über+acc* of); (*Zeugnis*) certificate. **den ~ für etw erbringen** *or* **liefern** to furnish proof of sth.

nachweisbar *adj* (*beweisbar*) provable; *Fehler* demonstrable; (*Tech*) detectable.

nachweisen *vt sep irreg* (*beweisen*) to prove; (*Tech*) to detect. **dem Angeklagten konnte seine**

Schuld nicht nachgewiesen werden the accused's guilt could not be proved.

nachweislich *adj* provable; *Fehler* demonstrable. **er war ~ in London** it can be proved that he was in London.

Nachwelt *f* **die ~** posterity.

nachwerfen *vt sep irreg* **jdm etw ~** (*lit*) to throw sth after *or* at sb; **das ist nachgeworfen** (*col*) that's a gift.

Nachwirkung *f* after-effect; (*fig*) consequence.

Nachwort *nt* epilogue.

Nachwuchs *m* (**a**) (*fig: junge Kräfte*) young people *pl* (in the profession/sport *etc*). **der schauspielerische ~** the up and coming actors. (**b**) (*hum: Nachkommen*) offspring *pl*.

Nachwuchs-: **~kraft** *f* junior member of the staff; **~sorgen** *pl* recruitment problems *pl*; **~spieler** *m* (*Sport*) junior.

nachzahlen *vti sep* to pay extra; (*später zahlen*) to pay later.

nachzählen *vti sep* to check.

Nachzahlung *f* (*nachträglich*) back-payment; (*zusätzlich*) additional payment.

nachziehen *sep irreg* **1** *vt* (**a**) (*hinterherziehen*) **etw ~** to drag sth behind one; **das rechte Bein ~** to drag one's right leg. (**b**) *Linie* to go over; *Lippen* to paint; *Augenbrauen* to pencil in. (**c**) *Schraube, Seil* to tighten (up). **2** *vi* (**a**) *aux sein+dat* (*folgen*) to follow. (**b**) (*col: gleichtun*) to follow suit.

Nachzügler(in *f*) ['naːxtsyːklɐ, -ərin] *m* - latecomer (*auch fig*).

Nackedei *m* -e *or* -s (*hum col*) naked person; (*Kind*) little bare monkey (*hum col*).

Nacken *m* - (nape of the) neck. **jdm im ~ haben** (*col*) to have sb on one's tail; **jdm im ~ sitzen** (*col*) to breathe down sb's neck; **ihm sitzt die Furcht im ~** he's frightened out of his wits (*col*).

nackt *adj* (*lit, fig*) naked; *Haut, Wand, Tatsachen* bare; *Wirklichkeit* stark. **~ baden/schlafen** to bathe/sleep in the nude; **das ~e Leben retten** to escape with one's bare life.

Nackt-: **~baden** *nt* nude bathing; **~badestrand** *m* nudist beach; **~heit** *f* nakedness; (*von Mensch auch*) nudity; (*Kahlheit*) bareness; **~kultur** *f* nudism.

Nadel *m* -n needle; (*Steck~, Haar~*) pin; (*Häkel~*) hook.

Nadel-: **~baum** *m* conifer; **~hölzer** *pl* conifers *pl*; **~kissen** *nt* pin-cushion; **~kopf** *m* pin-head.

nadeln *vi* (*Baum*) to shed (its needles).

Nadel-: **~öhr** *nt* eye of a needle; **~stich** *m* prick; (*beim Nähen, Med*) stitch; **~streifen** *pl* pinstripes *pl*; **~streifenanzug** *m* pinstripe(d) suit; **~wald** *m* coniferous forest.

Nagel *m* ∸ nail (*auch Anat*); (*Zwecke*) tack; (*an Schuhen*) hobnail, stud; (*Med*) pin. **sich** (*dat*) **etw unter den ~ reißen** (*col*) to pinch sth (*col*); **etw an den ~ hängen** (*fig*) to chuck sth in (*col*); **den ~ auf den Kopf treffen** (*fig*) to hit the nail on the head; **~ mit Köpfen machen** (*col*) to do the job properly.

Nagel-: **~bett** *nt* (*Anat*) bed of the nail; (*von Fakir*) bed of nails; **~bürste** *f* nailbrush; **~feile** *f* nail-file; **~haut** *f* cuticle.

Nägelkauen *nt* nail-biting.

Nagel-: **~lack** *m* nail varnish (*Brit*) *or* polish; **~lackentferner** *m* nail varnish (*Brit*) *or* polish remover.

nageln *vt* to nail (*an+acc* to); (*Med*) to pin.

Nagel-: **n~neu** *adj* (*col*) brand-new; **~pflege** *f* nail care; **~probe** *f* (*fig*) acid test; **~schere** *f* (pair of) nail-scissors *pl*.

nagen 1 *vi* (*lit, fig*) to gnaw (*an +dat* at); (*knabbern*) to nibble (*an+dat* at); (*Rost*) to eat (*an+dat* into). **2** *vt* to gnaw.

nagend *adj Hunger* gnawing; *Zweifel etc* nagging.

Nager *m* -, **Nagetier** *nt* rodent.

Nah|aufnahme *f* (*Phot*) close-up.

nah(e) *comp* **näher,** *superl* **nächte(r, s)** *or (adv)* **am nächsten 1** *adj* **(a)** *(örtlich)* near *pred,* nearby. **der N~e Osten** the Middle East; **von ~em** at close quarters; **jdm ~ sein** to be near (to) sb. **(b)** *(zeitlich)* near *pred,* approaching. **(c)** *(eng)* *Freund etc* close. **2** *adv* **(a)** *(örtlich)* near. **~e an** near *or* close to; **~e bei** close by, near; **~ vor** right in front of; **von ~ und fern** from near and far; **jdm zu ~(e) treten** *(fig)* to offend sb. **(b)** *(zeitlich)* **~ bevorstehend** approaching; **sie ist ~ an (die) achtzig** she's nearing eighty. **(c)** *(eng)* closely. **mit jdm ~ verwandt sein** to be closely related to sb. **3** *prep+dat* near (to). **dem Wahnsinn ~e sein** to be on the verge of madness.

Nähe *f no pl* **(a)** *(örtlich)* *(Nahesein)* nearness, proximity; *(Nachbarschaft)* vicinity. **in meiner ~** near me; **aus der ~** from close to. **(b)** *(zeitlich)* closeness.

nahebei *adv* nearby.

nahebringen *vt sep irreg+dat (fig)* **jdm etw ~** to bring sth home to sb.

nahegehen *vi sep irreg aux sein+dat (fig)* to upset.

nahekommen *vi sep irreg aux sein+dat (fig)* **jdm ~** *(vertraut werden)* to get on close terms with sb. **das kommt der Wahrheit schon eher nahe** that is getting nearer the truth.

nahelegen *vt sep (fig)* **jdm etw ~** to suggest sth to sb; **jdm ~, etw zu tun** to advise sb to do sth.

naheliegen *vi sep irreg (fig: Idee, Frage, Lösung)* to suggest itself. **der Verdacht liegt nahe, daß ...** it seems reasonable to suspect that ...

naheliegend *adj Gedanke* which suggests itself; *Vermutung* natural. **aus ~en Gründen** for obvious reasons.

nahen *vir aux sein (liter)* to approach *(jdm/einer Sache* sb/sth), to draw near *or* nigh *(liter)* *(jdm/einer Sache* sb/sth).

nähen 1 *vt* to sew; *Kleid* to make; *Wunde* to stitch (up), to suture *(spec)*. **2** *vi* to sew.

näher *comp of* **nah(e) 1** *adj* **(a)** *(örtlich)* nearer. **dieser Weg ist ~** this road is quicker; **die ~e Umgebung** the immediate vicinity. **(b)** *(zeitlich)* closer, sooner *pred.* **(c)** *(genauer) Auskünfte* further *attr,* more detailed. **(d)** *(enger) Verwandter, Beziehungen* closer. **die ~e Verwandtschaft** the immediate family. **2** *adv* **(a)** *(örtlich, zeitlich)* nearer. **(b)** *(genauer)* more closely; *ausführen* in more detail. **jdn ~ kennenlernen** to get to know better; **ich kenne ihn nicht ~** I don't know him well.

näherbringen *vt sep irreg+dat* **jdm etw ~** to give sb an understanding of sth.

Nähere(s) *nt decl as adj* further details *pl.*

Näherin *f* seamstress.

näherkommen *vi sep irreg aux sein (fig)* **jdm ~** to get closer to sb.

näherliegen *vi sep irreg (fig)* to be more obvious.

nähern *vr sich* **(jdm/einer Sache) ~** to approach (sb/sth), to draw nearer (to sb/sth).

nahestehen *vi sep irreg+dat (fig)* to be close to; *(Pol)* to sympathize with. **sich ~** *(Menschen, Ideen)* to be close; **eine den Konservativen ~de Zeitung** a paper with Conservative sympathies.

nahezu *adv* nearly, almost, virtually.

Nahkampf *m (Mil)* hand-to-hand fighting.

Nähkästchen *nt* **aus dem ~ plaudern** *(col)* to give away private details.

nahm *pret of* **nehmen.**

Näh-: ~maschine *f* sewing machine; **~nadel** *f* needle.

Nahost *m* **in/aus ~** in/from the Middle East.

Nährboden *m (lit)* fertile soil; *(für Bakterien)* culture medium; *(fig)* breeding-ground.

nähren *vt (geh)* to feed; *(fig) (steigern)* to increase, to feed; *(haben) Hoffnungen* to nurse. **er sieht gut genährt aus** he looks well-fed.

nahrhaft *adj Kost* nourishing; *Boden* fertile.

Nähr-: ~mittel *pl* cereal products *pl;* **~stoff** *m*

usu pl nutrient.

Nahrung *f no pl* food. **flüssige/feste ~** liquids/solids *pl;* **geistige ~** intellectual stimulation; **einer Sache** *(dat)* **(neue) ~ geben** to reinforce sth.

Nahrungs-: ~aufnahme *f* ingestion (of food) *(form);* **die ~aufnahme verweigern** to refuse food; **~mittel** *nt* food(stuff); **~suche** *f* search for food.

Nährwert *m* nutritional value.

Naht *f* **≖e** seam; *(Med)* stitches *pl,* suture *(spec);* *(Anat)* suture. **aus allen ~en platzen** to be bursting at the seams.

nahtlos *adj (lit) Teil, Anzug* seamless; *(fig) Übergang* smooth.

Nahtstelle *f* **(a)** *(lit)* seam. **(b)** *(fig)* link.

Nahverkehr *m* local traffic. **der öffentliche ~** local public transport.

Nahverkehrszug *m* local train.

Nähzeug *nt* sewing kit, sewing things *pl.*

Nahziel *nt* immediate aim *or* objective.

naiv *adj* naive.

Naivität [naivi'tɛːt] *f* naivety.

Name *m* **-ns, -n** name; *(fig: Ruf auch)* reputation. **mit ~n** by the name of; **dem ~n nach** by name; **ich kenne das Stück nur dem ~n nach** I've heard of the play but that's all; **dem ~n nach müßte sie Jugoslawin sein** judging by her name she must be Yugoslavian; **auf jds ~n** *(acc)* in sb's name; **unter dem ~n** under the name of; **er nannte seinen ~n** he gave his name; **einen ~n haben** *(fig)* to have a name; **sich** *(dat)* **einen ~n machen** to make a name for oneself; **die Dinge beim ~n nennen** to call a spade a spade; **im ~n** (+gen) on *or* in *(US)* behalf of; **im ~n des Volkes** in the name of the people.

namenlos *adj* **(a)** nameless *(auch fig),* unnamed; *Helfer* anonymous. **(b)** *(geh: unsäglich)* unspeakable.

namens 1 *adv (mit Namen)* by the name of. **2** *prep* +gen *(form: im Auftrag)* in the name of.

Namen(s)- *in cpds* name; **~änderung** *f* change of name; **~schild** *nt* nameplate; **~tag** *m* name day, Saint's day; **~vetter** *m* namesake; **~zeichen** *nt* initials *pl;* **~zug** *m* signature.

namentlich 1 *adj* by name. **~e Abstimmung** roll call vote; **~er Aufruf** roll call. **2** *adv* in particular.

namhaft *adj* **(a)** *(bekannt)* famous. **~ machen** *(form)* to identify. **(b)** *(beträchtlich)* considerable.

nämlich *adv* **(a)** namely. **(b)** *(denn)* **wir haben uns verspätet, wir haben ~ einen Umweg machen müssen** we were late since we had to make a detour.

nannte *pret of* **nennen.**

nanu *interj* well I never. **~, wer ist das denn?** hello (hello), who's this?

Napalm *nt no pl* napalm.

Napf *m* **-ë** bowl.

Napfkuchen *m* ≈ ring-shaped poundcake.

Narbe *f* **-n (a)** *(lit, fig)* scar. **(b)** *(Bot)* stigma. **(c)** *(Gras~)* turf.

narbig *adj* scarred.

Narkose *f* **-n jdm eine ~ geben** to give sb an anaesthetic *(Brit)* or anesthetic *(US);* **aus der ~ aufwachen** to come to from an/the anaesthetic *(US).*

Narkose|arzt *m* anaesthetist *(Brit),* anesthetist *(US).*

Narkotikum *nt, pl* **Narkotika** *(Med)* narcotic.

narkotisch *adj* narcotic; *Düfte* overpowering.

Narr *m* **(wk) -en, -en** fool. **jdn zum ~ en halten** to make a fool of sb.

narren *vt (geh)* **jdn ~** *(zum besten haben)* to make a fool of sb; *(täuschen)* to dupe sb.

Narren-: ~freiheit *f* **sie hat bei ihm ~freiheit** he gives her (a) free rein; **~kappe** *f* jester's cap; **n~sicher** *adj* foolproof.

Narrheit f (a) no pl folly. (b) (Streich) prank.
Närrin f fool.
närrisch adj foolish; (verrückt) mad; (col: sehr) madly. **die ~en Tage** Fasching and the period leading up to it; **ganz ~ auf etw sein** (col) to be crazy about sth (col).
Narzisse f -n narcissus.
narzißtisch adj narcissistic.
Nasal m -e nasal.
nasal adj nasal. **~er Ton** nasal twang.
naschen 1 vi to eat sweet things; (heimlich kosten) to pinch a bit (col). **darf ich mal ~?** can I try a bit?; **die Kinder haben den ganzen Tag nur genascht** the children have been nibbling all day. **2** vt to nibble. **hast du was zum N~?** have you something for my sweet tooth?
Nascherei f no pl nibbling; (von Süßigkeiten) eating sweets (Brit) or candy (US).
Nasch-: ~haft adj fond of sweet things; **~katze** f (col) guzzler; **ich bin halt so eine alte ~katze** I've got such a sweet tooth.
Nase f -n (a) nose. **sich die ~ putzen** to wipe one's nose; (sich schnäuzen) to blow one's nose; **pro ~** (hum) per head; (immer) **der ~ nachgehen** (col) to follow one's nose; **die richtige ~ für etw haben** (col) to have a nose for sth; **faß dich an deine eigene ~!** (col) you can or can't talk!; **jdm etw unter die ~ reiben** (col) to rub sb's nose in sth (col); **jdm auf der ~ herumtanzen** (col) to play sb up (col); **seine ~ gefällt mir nicht** (col) I don't like his face; **es muß nicht immer nach deiner ~ gehen** (col) you can't always have it your way; **ich sah es ihm an der ~ an** (col) I could see it on his face (col); **auf der ~ liegen** (col) (krank sein) to be laid up; (hingefallen sein) to be flat on one's face (col); **steck deine ~ ins Buch!** (col) get on with your book; **auf die ~ fallen** (lit, fig) to fall flat on one's face; **jdm etw vor der ~ wegschnappen** (col) just to beat sb to sth; **jdm die Tür vor der ~ zuschlagen** (col) to slam the door in sb's face; **jdm etw unter die ~ halten** to shove sth right under sb's nose (col); **jdm eins auf die ~ geben** (lit) to punch sb on the nose; (fig) to put sb in his/her place; **die ~ voll haben** (col) to have had enough; **jdn an der ~ herumführen** (als Täuschung) to lead sb by the nose; (als Scherz) to pull sb's leg; **jdm etw auf die ~ binden** (col) to tell sb all about sth; **er steckt seine ~ in alles (hinein)** (col) he pokes his nose into everything. (b) (col: Farbtropfen) run.
naselang adv: **alle ~** all the time, again and again.
näseln vi to talk or speak through one's nose.
Nasen-: ~bein nt nose bone; **~bluten** nt a nosebleed; **ein Mittel gegen ~bluten** something for nosebleeds; **ich habe ~bluten** my nose is bleeding; **~flügel** m side of the nose; **~höhle** f nasal cavity; **~länge** f (fig) **mit einer** or **um eine ~länge gewinnen** to win by a nose; **jdm eine ~länge voraus sein** to be a hair's breadth ahead of sb; **~loch** nt nostril; **~rücken** m bridge of the nose; **~spitze** f tip of the/sb's nose; **ich seh es dir an der ~spitze** an I can tell by your face; **~stüber** m - bump on the nose; **jdm einen ~stüber versetzen** (lit) to bop sb on the nose; (fig) to tick or tell sb off.
Nase-: n~rümpfend adj **er sagte n~rümpfend** wrinkling his nose, he said; **n~weis** adj cheeky; (vorlaut) precocious; **~weis** m -e (Vorlauter) cheeky (esp Brit) or precocious brat (col); (Überschlauer) know-all (col), wiseguy (col).
Nashorn nt rhinoceros, rhino.
naß adj wet. **etw ~ machen** to make sth wet; (für bestimmten Zweck) to wet sth; **sich ~ machen** (col) to wet oneself; **mit nassen Augen** with moist eyes; **wie ein nasser Sack** (col) like a wet rag (col).
Nassauer m - (col) scrounger.
Nässe f no pl wetness, moisture. **„vor ~ schützen"**

"keep dry"; **vor ~ triefen** to be dripping wet.
nässen 1 vi (Wunde) to discharge. **2** vt Bett to wet.
Naß-: n~forsch adj (col) brash; **n~kalt** adj chilly and damp, raw; **~rasur** f **die ~rasur** wet shaving; **eine ~rasur** a wet shave.
Nation f nation.
national [natsio'na:l] adj national; (patriotisch) nationalist(ic).
National- in cpds national; **n~bewußt** adj nationally conscious; **~elf** f international (football) team; **~flagge** f national flag; **~garde** f National Guard; **~gefühl** nt national feeling; **~gericht** nt national dish; **~hymne** f national anthem.
Nationalismus m nationalism.
Nationalist(in f) m nationalist.
nationalistisch adj nationalist(ic).
Nationalität f nationality.
National-: ~mannschaft f international team; **er spielt in der schottischen ~mannschaft** he plays for Scotland; **~ökonomie** f economics sing; **~sozialismus** m National Socialism; **~sozialist** m National Socialist; **~spieler** m international (footballer etc).
Natrium nt no pl sodium.
Natron nt no pl sodium compound, esp bicarbonate of soda.
Natter f -n adder, viper; (fig) snake.
Natur f (a) no pl nature. **gegen die ~** against nature; **ich bin von ~ aus schüchtern** I am shy by nature; **sein Haar ist von ~ aus blond** his hair is naturally blond. (b) no pl (freies Land) countryside. (c) (Wesensart) nature; (Mensch) type. **es liegt in der ~ der Sache** it is in the nature of things; **das geht gegen meine ~** it goes against the grain; **eine Frage allgemeiner ~** a question of a general nature; **das ist ihm zur zweiten ~ geworden** it's become second nature to him.
Naturalien [-ian] pl natural produce sing. **in ~ bezahlen** to pay in kind.
Naturalismus m nauralism.
Naturalist(in f) m naturalist.
naturalistisch adj naturalistic.
Natur-: ~beschreibung f description of nature; **~bursche** m nature-boy (col).
Naturell nt -e temperament, disposition.
Natur-: ~ereignis nt, **~erscheinung** f natural phenomenon; **~forscher** m natural scientist; **~freund** m nature-lover; **n~gegeben** adj (lit, fig) natural; **n~gemäß** adj natural; **~geschichte** f natural history; **~gesetz** nt law of nature; **n~getreu** adj true to life; (in Lebensgröße) life-size; **~heilkunde** f nature healing; **~heilverfahren** nt natural cure; **~katastrophe** f natural disaster; **~kunde** f natural history.
natürlich 1 adj natural. **in seiner ~en Größe** life-size; **eines ~en Todes sterben** to die of natural causes. **2** adv naturally. **die Krankheit verlief ganz ~** the illness took its natural course. **~!** naturally!, of course!, sure! (esp US).
natürlicherweise adv naturally.
Natürlichkeit f naturalness.
Natur-: ~notwendigkeit f physical inevitability; **~produkt** nt natural product; **~produkte** natural produce sing; **n~rein** adj pure, unadulterated; **~schutz** m nature conservancy; **unter ~schutz stehen** to be legally protected; **~schutzgebiet** nt nature reserve; **~talent** nt natural prodigy; **~trieb** m (natural) instinct; **n~verbunden** adj nature-loving; **~wissenschaft** f natural sciences pl; (Zweig) natural science; **~wissenschaftler** m (natural) scientist; **n~wissenschaftlich** adj scientific; **~zustand** m natural state.
Nautik f no pl nautical science, navigation.
nautisch adj navigational. **~e Meile** nautical mile.
Navigation [naviga'tsio:n] f navigation.
Navigations-: ~fehler m navigational error; **~raum** m charthouse.

Nazi m **-s** (pej) Nazi.
Nazismus m (pej: Nationalsozialismus) Nazi(i)sm.
nazistisch adj (pej) Nazi.
Nazizeit f Nazi period.
n.Chr. = **nach Christus** AD.
NDR [ende:'|ɛr] m = **Norddeutscher Rundfunk.**
Neandertaler m - Neanderthal man.
Neapel nt Naples.
Nebel m - mist; (dichter) fog; (Mil: künstlich) smoke; (fig) mist, haze. **bei** ~ in mist/fog; **das fällt wegen** ~(**s**) **aus** (hum col) it's all off.
Nebel-: ~**bank** f fog bank; **n**~**haft** adj (fig) nebulous; ~**horn** nt (Naut) foghorn.
neb(e)lig adj misty; (bei dichterem Nebel) foggy.
Nebel-: ~**scheinwerfer** m (Aut) fog light; ~**schleier** m (geh) veil of mist; ~(**schluß)leuchte** f (Aut) rear fog-light; ~**wand** f wall of fog; (Mil) smokescreen.
neben prep (**a**) (örtlich: +dat/acc) beside, next to. (**b**) (außer:+dat) apart from, aside from (esp US). (**c**) (verglichen mit: +dat) compared with.
nebenamtlich adj Tätigkeit secondary, additional. **das macht er nur** ~ he does that just as a secondary occupation.
neben|an adv next door. **die Tür** ~ the next door.
Neben|anschluß m (Telec) extension.
nebenbei adv (**a**) (gleichzeitig) at the same time. **etw** ~ **machen** to do sth on the side. (**b**) (außerdem) additionally, in addition. (**c**) (beiläufig) incidentally. ~ **bemerkt** or **gesagt** by the way, incidentally.
Neben-: ~**beruf** m extra job; **er ist im** ~**beruf Nachtwächter** he has a second job as a night watchman; **n**~**beruflich 1** adj extra, supplementary; **2** adv as a second job, as a sideline (col); **er verdient n**~**beruflich mehr als hauptberuflich** he earns more from his second job than he does from his main job; ~**beschäftigung** f (Zweitberuf) extra job; ~**buhler(in** f) m rival; ~**darsteller(in** f) m supporting actor/actress.
neben|einander adv (**a**) (räumlich) side by side; (bei Rennen) neck and neck. (**b**) (zeitlich) at the same time.
neben|einanderher adv side by side. **sie leben nur noch** ~ (Ehepaar etc) they're just two people living in the same house.
neben|einander-: ~**legen** vt sep to lay side by side; ~**stellen** vt sep to place side by side; (fig: vergleichen) to compare.
Neben-: ~**eingang** m side entrance; ~**einkünfte**, ~**einnahmen** pl supplementary income; ~**fach** nt (Sch, Univ) subsidiary (subject), minor (US); ~**fluß** m tributary; ~**frage** f side issue; ~**gebäude** nt (**a**) (Zusatzgebäude) annex; (**b**) (Nachbargebäude) adjacent building; ~**gedanke** m ulterior motive; ~**geräusch** nt (Rad, Telec) interference; ~**handlung** f (Liter) subplot; ~**haus** nt house next door.
nebenher adv (**a**) (zusätzlich) in addition. (**b**) (gleichzeitig) at the same time.
nebenhin adv (beiläufig) in passing, casually.
Neben-: ~**höhle** f (Physiol) sinus (of the nose); ~**kläger** m (Jur) joint plaintiff; ~**kosten** pl additional costs pl; ~**mann** m, pl ~**männer Ihr** ~**mann** the person next to you; ~**produkt** nt by-product; (weniger wichtig) side product; ~**raum** m (benachbart) adjoining room; (weniger wichtig) side room; ~**rolle** f supporting role; (fig) minor role; **das spielt für mich nur eine** ~**rolle** that's only of minor concern to me; ~**sache** f trifle, triviality; **das ist** ~**sache** that's irrelevant; **n**~**sächlich** adj minor, peripheral; ~**sächlichkeit** f triviality; ~**satz** m (Gram) subordinate clause; **n**~**stehend** adj **n**~**stehende Erklärungen** explanations in the margin; **n**~**stehende Abbildung** illustration opposite; ~**stelle** f (Telec) extension; (Comm) branch; ~**straße** f (in der Stadt) side street;

(Landstraße) minor road; ~**strecke** f (Rail) branch or local line; ~**tisch** m adjacent table; **am** ~**tisch** at the next table; ~**verdienst** m secondary income; ~**wirkung** f side effect; ~**zimmer** nt adjoining room; ~**zweck** m secondary aim.
neblig adj = **neb(e)lig.**
Necessaire [nesɛ'sɛːɐ] nt -s (Kulturbeutel) vanity bag; (zur Nagelpflege) manicure case; (Nähzeug) sewing bag.
necken vt to tease.
Neckerei f teasing no pl.
neckisch adj (scherzhaft) merry, teasing; (col: kokett, keß) Kleid, Frisur saucy; Spielchen mischievous.
nee adv (col) no, nope (col).
Neffe m (wk) **-n**, **-n** nephew.
Negation f negation.
Negativ nt (Phot) negative.
negativ adj negative. **jdm auf eine Frage** ~ **antworten** to answer sb's question in the negative; **sich** ~ **zu etw äußern** to speak negatively about sth.
Neger m - negro.
Negerin f negress.
Negerkuß m chocolate marshmallow.
negieren* vt (bestreiten) Tatsache to deny.
Negligé [negli'ʒeː] nt -s negligee.
nehmen pret **nahm**, ptp **genommen** vti to take; (verwenden) to use. **etw an sich** (acc) ~ (aufbewahren) to take charge of sth; (sich aneignen) to take sth (for oneself); **jdm etw** ~ to take sth (away) from sb; **jdm die Hoffnung** ~ to deprive sb of his/her hope; **die Mauer nimmt einem die ganze Sicht** the wall blocks the whole view; **er ließ es sich** (dat) **nicht** ~, **mich persönlich hinauszubegleiten** he insisted on showing me out himself; **diesen Erfolg lasse ich mir nicht** ~ I won't be robbed of this success; **sie** ~ **sich** (dat) **nichts** (col) there's nothing to choose between them; **man nehme ...** (Cook) take ...; ~ **Sie sich doch bitte!** please help yourself; **jdn zu sich** ~ to take sb in; **etw** ~, **wie es kommt** to take sth as it comes; **jdn** ~, **wie er ist** to take sb as he is; **etw auf sich** (acc) ~ to take sth upon oneself; **etw zu sich** ~ to take sth, to partake of sth (liter); **wie man's nimmt** (col) depending on your point of view; **sie weiß ihn zu** ~ she knows how to take him.
Nehrung f spit (of land).
Neid m no pl envy. **aus** ~ out of envy; **grün (und gelb) vor** ~ (col) green with envy; **das muß ihm der** ~ **lassen** (col) give the devil his due.
neiden vt **jdm etw** ~ to envy sb (for) sth.
Neider m - envious person. **reiche Leute haben viele** ~ rich people are much envied.
Neidhammel m (col) envious person.
neidisch adj envious. **auf jdn/etw** ~ **sein** to be envious of sb/sth.
neidlos adj ungrudging, without envy.
Neige f -n (**a**) (liter) **das Glas bis zur** ~ **leeren** to drain the cup to the dregs. (**b**) no pl (geh: Ende) **zur** ~ **gehen** to draw to a close; **die Vorräte gehen zur** ~ the provisions are fast becoming exhausted.
neigen 1 vt Kopf, Körper to bend; Glas to tip. **2** vr (Ebene) to slope; (Mensch) to bend; (unter Last: Bäume etc) to bow; (Gebäude etc) to lean; (kippen) to tip (up), to tilt (up). **3** vi **zu etw** ~ to have a tendency to sth; (für etw anfällig sein) to be prone to sth; **zu der Ansicht** ~, **daß ...** to be inclined to take the view that ...; siehe **geneigt.**
Neigung f (**a**) (das Neigen) inclination; (Gefälle auch) incline, gradient (esp Rail). (**b**) (Tendenz) tendency; (Veranlagung) leaning usu pl; (Hang, Lust) inclination. **künstlerische/politische** ~**en** artistic/political leanings; **aus** ~ **tun** to do sth by inclination; **keine** ~ **verspüren**, **etw zu tun** to have no inclination to do sth.

Neigungs-: ~ehe *f* love match; ~winkel *m* angle of inclination.

nein *adv* no. **kommt er?** — ~ is he coming? — no, (he isn't); **ich sage nicht** ~ I wouldn't say no; **Hunderte,** ~ **Tausende** hundreds, no *or* nay *(liter)* thousands; ~, **so was!** well I never!

Nein *nt no pl* no. **bei seinem** ~ **bleiben** to stick to one's refusal.

Nein-: ~sager(in *f*) *m* - **er ist ein ewiger** ~sager he always says no; ~stimme *f (Pol)* no(-vote), nay *(US)*.

Nektar *m no pl (Myth, Bot)* nectar.

Nektarine *f* nectarine.

Nelke *f* -n **(a)** carnation. **(b)** *(Gewürz)* clove.

nennen *pret* **nannte,** *ptp* **genannt 1** *vt* **(a)** *(bezeichnen)* to call. **jdn nach jdm** ~ to name sb after *or* for *(US)* sb; **das nenne ich Mut!** that's what I call courage!; **das nennst du schön?** you call that beautiful? **(b)** *(angeben, aufzählen)* to name; *(erwähnen)* to mention. **die genannten Namen** the names mentioned; **können Sie mir einen guten Anwalt** ~? could you give me the name of a good lawyer?; **das genannte Schloß** the castle referred to. **2** *vr* to call oneself; *(heißen)* to be called *(Brit)* or named. **und so was nennt sich Liebe** *(col)* and they call that love.

nennenswert *adj* considerable. **nicht** ~ not worth mentioning; **nichts N~es** nothing worth mentioning.

Nenner *m - (Math)* denominator. **etw auf einen** ~ **bringen** *(lit, fig)* to reduce sth to a common denominator.

Nennung *f (das Nennen)* naming; *(Sport)* entry.

Nennwert *m (Fin)* nominal *or* par value; **zum** ~ at par.

neo-, Neo- *in cpds* neo-.

Neon *nt no pl* neon.

Neon-: ~licht *nt* neon light; ~reklame *f* neon sign; ~röhre *f* neon tube.

Nepp *m no pl (col)* **der reinste** ~ daylight robbery *(col)*, a rip-off *(col)*.

neppen *vt (col)* to fleece *(col)*, to rip off *(col)*.

Nepplokal *nt (col)* clipjoint *(col)*.

Neptun *m* Neptune.

Nerv [nɛrf] *m* -en nerve. **leicht die** ~en **verlieren** to scare easily; **die** ~en **sind mit ihm durchgegangen** he lost control, he snapped *(col)*; **der hat (vielleicht)** ~en! *(col)* he's got a nerve! *(col)*; **es geht mir auf die** ~en *(col)* it gets on my nerves.

nerven ['nɛrfn] *(col)* **1** *vt* **jdn** ~ to get on sb's nerves. **2** *vi* **das nervt** it gets on your nerves.

Nerven- ['nɛrfn-]: ~arzt *m* neurologist; **n~aufreibend** *adj* nerve-racking; ~belastung *f* strain on the nerves *(col)*; ~gas *nt (Mil)* nerve gas; ~gift *nt* neurotoxin; ~heilanstalt *f* mental hospital; ~heilkunde *f* neurology; ~kitzel *m (fig)* thrill; ~klinik *f* psychiatric clinic; ~kostüm *nt (hum)* **ein starkes/schwaches** ~kostüm **haben** to have strong/weak nerves; **n~krank** *adj* suffering from a nervous disease; ~krankheit *f* nervous disorder; ~krieg *m (fig)* war of nerves; ~leiden *nt* nervous complaint; ~probe *f* trial; ~sache *f (col)* question of nerves; ~säge *f (col)* pain (in the neck) *(col)*; ~system *nt* nervous system; ~zusammenbruch *m* nervous breakdown.

nervlich ['nɛrflɪç] *adj* **der** ~e **Zustand des Patienten** the state of the patient's nerves; ~ **bedingt** nervous.

nervös [nɛr'vøːs] *adj* nervous; *(aufgeregt auch)* jumpy *(col)*, on edge *pred*.

Nervosität [nɛrvozi'tɛːt] *f* nervousness.

nervtötend ['nɛrf-] *adj (col)* nerve-racking; *Arbeit* soul-destroying.

Nerz *m* -e mink.

Nerzmantel *m* mink coat.

Nessel[1] *f* -n *(Bot)* nettle. **sich in die** ~n **setzen** *(col)* to put oneself in a spot *(col)*.

Nessel[2] *m - (Tex)* (untreated) cotton.

Nessel-: ~fieber *nt* nettle-rash fever; ~sucht *f* nettle rash.

Nest *nt* -er **(a)** *(Brutstätte)* nest. **(b)** *(fig: Schlupfwinkel)* hideout, lair. **(c)** *(fig: Heim)* nest, home. **sein eigenes** ~ **beschmutzen** to foul one's own nest; **da hat er sich ins warme** ~ **gesetzt** *(col)* he's got it made *(col)*. **(d)** *(fig: Bett)* bed. **(e)** *(pej col: Ort)* hole *(col)*, one-horse town *(col)*.

Nest-: ~beschmutzer *m (pej)* runner-down *(col)*, denigrator *(of one's family or country)*; ~beschmutzung *f (pej)* running-down *(col)*, denigration *(of one's family or country)*.

nesteln *vi* **an etw** *(dat)* ~ to fumble with sth.

Nest-: ~häkchen *nt* baby of the family; ~wärme *f (fig)* happy home life.

nett *adj* nice; *(hübsch auch)* pretty, cute. **das kann ja** ~ **werden!** *(iro)* that'll be nice (I don't think!) *(col)*; **sei so** ~ **und räum' auf!** would you mind clearing up?; ~, **daß Sie gekommen sind!** nice of you to come.

netterweise *adv* kindly.

Nettigkeit *f* **(a)** *no pl (nette Art)* kindness, goodness. **(b)** *(nette Worte)* ~en kind words.

netto *adv (Comm)* net.

Netto- *in cpds* net.

Netz *nt* -e **(a)** net; *(Spinnen~, fig: von Lügen etc)* web; *(Haar~)* (hair)net; *(Einkaufs~)* net bag; *(Gepäck~)* (luggage) rack. **ins** ~ **gehen** *(Ftbl)* to go into the net; **jdm ins** ~ **gehen** *(fig)* to fall into sb's trap; **jdm durchs** ~ **gehen** *(fig)* to give sb the slip. **(b)** *(System)* network; *(Strom~)* mains *sing or pl.* **(c)** *(Math)* net; *(Kartengitter)* grid.

Netz-: ~anschluß *m (Elec)* mains connection; ~ball *m (Tennis etc)* netball; ~gerät *nt* mains receiver; ~haut *f* retina; ~hemd *nt* string vest *(Brit)* or undershirt *(US)*; ~karte *f (Rail)* unlimited travel ticket; ~spannung *f* mains voltage; ~teil *nt* mains adapter; ~werk *nt (Elec, fig)* network; *(aus Draht)* netting.

neu *adj* new; *Kräfte, Hoffnung auch* fresh; *(kürzlich entstanden auch)* recent; *Wäsche* clean; *Wein* young. **das N~e Testament** the New Testament; **die N~e Welt** the New World; **ein** ~**er Anfang** a new *or* fresh start; ~**eren Datums of** (more) recent date; **die** ~(**e)ste Mode** the latest fashion; **die** ~**esten Nachrichten** the latest news; **ein ganz** ~**er Wagen** a brand-new car; **das ist mir** ~! that's new(s) to me; **in** ~**erer Zeit** in modern times; **erst in** ~**erer Zeit** only recently; **die** ~**eren Sprachen** modern languages; **seit** ~(**e)stem gibt es** ... since recently there has been ...; **aufs** ~**e** *(geh)* afresh; **auf ein** ~**es!** *(Aufmunterung)* let's try again; **der/die N~e** the newcomer, the new guy *(col)*; **was ist das N~e an dem Buch?** what's new about the book?; **weißt du schon das N~(e)ste?** have you heard the latest?; **was gibt's N~es?** *(col)* what's the latest?; **von** ~**em** *(von vorn)* from the beginning; *(wieder)* again, ~ **beginnen** to make a fresh start, to start again; **er ist** ~ **hinzugekommen** he's joined (him/them) recently; **ein Zimmer** ~ **einrichten** to refurnish a room.

Neu-: ~ankömmling *m* newcomer; ~anschaffung *f* new acquisition; **n~artig** *adj* new; **ein** n~**artiges Wörterbuch** a new type of dictionary; ~auflage *f* reprint; ~ausgabe *f* new edition.

Neubau *m* new house/building.

Neubau-: ~siedlung *f* new housing estate *(Brit)* or development; ~wohnung *f* newly-built flat.

Neu-: ~bearbeitung *f* revised edition; *(von Oper etc)* new version; *(das* ~bearbeiten*)* revision; reworking; ~beginn *m* new beginning(s); ~druck *m* reprint; ~einstellung *f* new appointment; ~entdeckung *f* rediscovery; *(Mensch)* new discovery; **n~entwickelt** *adj attr* newly developed; ~entwicklung *f* new development.

neuerdings adv recently. ~ raucht er wieder now he's started smoking again.

Neuerer m - innovator.

Neu-: n~eröffnet adj attr newly-opened; (wieder-eröffnet) reopened; ~eröffnung f (Wiedereröffnung) reopening; die ~eröffnung der Fluglinie the opening of the new airline; ~erscheinung f (Buch) new publication; (Schallplatte) new release.

Neuerung f innovation; (Reform) reform.

Neu|erwerbung f new acquisition.

neu(e)stens adv lately, recently.

Neu-: ~fassung f revised version; ~fundland nt Newfoundland; ~fundländer m - (Hund) Newfoundland (dog); n~geboren adj newborn; sich wie n~geboren fühlen to feel (like) a new man/woman; ~geborene(s) nt decl as adj new-born child; n~gewählt adj attr newly elected.

Neugier(de) f no pl curiosity, inquisitiveness; (pej auch) nosiness (col). aus ~ out of curiosity.

neugierig adj inqisitive, curious (auf +acc about); (pej) nos(e)y (col); (gespannt) longing to know. ein N~er an inquisitive person; (pej auch) a nos(e)y parker (col); jdn ~ machen to arouse sb's curiosity; ich bin ~, ob I wonder if; da bin ich aber ~! I can hardly wait (col).

Neu-: n~griechisch adj modern Greek; das ~griechische modern Greek; ~gründung f (Wiederbegründung) re-establishment; die ~gründung von Universitäten the founding of new universities.

Neuheit f (a) no pl novelty. (b) new thing/idea.

Neuigkeit f piece of news. ~en news sing.

Neujahr nt New Year.

Neujahrs-: ~abend m New Year's Eve, Hogmanay (Scot); ~tag m New Year's Day.

Neuland nt no pl virgin land; (fig) new ground.

neulich adv recently, the other day. ~ abend(s) the other evening.

Neuling m newcomer.

neumodisch adj fashionable; (pej) new-fangled (pej).

Neumond m new moon. bei ~ at new moon; heute ist ~ there's a new moon today.

Neun f -en nine. ach du grüne ~e! (col) well I'm blowed! (col); siehe Vier.

neun num nine. alle ~e! (beim Kegeln) strike!; siehe vier.

Neun-: n~hundert num nine hundred; n~mal adv nine times; siehe viermal; n~malklug adj (iro) smart-aleck attr (col).

Neuntel nt - ninth; siehe Viertel[1].

neuntens adv ninth(ly), in the ninth place.

neunte(r, s) adj ninth; siehe vierte(r, s).

neunzehn num nineteen; siehe vierzehn.

neunzig num ninety; siehe vierzig.

Neu-: ~ordnung f reorganization; (Reform) reform; ~philologe m modern linguist.

Neuralgie f neuralgia.

Neu-: ~reg(e)lung f adjustment; n~reich adj (pej) nouveau riche; ~reiche(r) mf (pej) nouveau riche.

Neuro- in cpds neuro; ~loge m, ~login f neurologist; ~logie f neurology.

Neurose f -n neurosis.

Neurotiker(in f) m - neurotic.

neurotisch adj neurotic.

Neu-: ~schnee m fresh snow; ~seeland nt New Zealand; n~seeländisch adj New Zealand; ~silber nt German silver; n~sprachlich adj modern language; n~sprachliches Gymnasium ≈ grammar school (Brit), high school (esp US, Scot) stressing modern languages; ~stadt f new town.

neutral adj neutral.

neutralisieren* vt to neutralize.

Neutralität f neutrality.

Neutron nt -en [nɔy'troːnən] neutron.

Neutrum nt, pl **Neutra** (Gram, fig) neuter.

Neu-: ~wahl f (Pol) new election; ~wert m value when new; n~wertig adj as new; ~zeit f modern times pl; Literatur der ~zeit modern literature; n~zeitlich adj modern; ~zugang m new entry; ~zulassung f (Aut) ≈ registration of a new vehicle.

nicht adv (a) (Verneinung) not. er raucht ~ (augenblicklich) he isn't smoking; (gewöhnlich) he doesn't smoke; kommst du? — nein, ich komme ~ are you coming? — no, I'm not (coming); ich kann das ~ — ich auch ~ I can't do it — neither or nor can I; ~ mehr als no more than; ~ heute und ~ morgen neither today nor tomorrow; er ~! not him. (b) (Bitte, Verbot) ~ berühren! do not touch; (gesprochen) don't touch; ~! don't!, no!; tu's ~! don't do it!; ~ doch! stop it!; bitte ~! please don't. (c) (rhetorisch) er kommt, ~ (wahr)? he's coming, isn't he?; er kommt ~, ~ wahr? he isn't coming, is he?; das ist schön, ~ (wahr)? it's nice, isn't it?; jetzt wollen wir Schluß machen, ~? let's leave it now, OK?

Nicht-, nicht- pref non-.

Nicht-: ~achtung f (+gen for) disregard; n~amtlich adj unofficial; ~angriffspakt m non-aggression pact; ~beachtung f non-observance; n~christlich adj non-Christian.

Nichte f -n niece.

Nicht-: ~einhaltung f non-compliance (+gen with); ~einmischung f (Pol) non-intervention; ~erscheinen nt non-appearance; ~gefallen nt: bei ~gefallen if not satisfied.

nichtig adj (a) (Jur: ungültig) void. (b) (unbedeutend) trivial.

Nichtigkeit f (a) (Jur: Ungültigkeit) invalidity, nullity. (b) no pl (Bedeutungslosigkeit) vainness, emptiness. (c) usu pl (Kleinigkeit) triviality, trivia pl.

Nicht-: ~mitglied nt non-member; n~öffentlich adj attr not open to the public; n~öffentliche Sitzung meeting in camera (Jur) or behind closed doors; ~raucher m (auch Rail) non-smoker; ich bin ~raucher I don't smoke; ~raucherabteil nt no-smoking compartment; n~rostend adj attr rustproof.

Nichts nt (a) no pl (Philos) nothingness; (Leere) emptiness, void. etw aus dem ~ aufbauen to build sth up from nothing; vor dem ~ stehen to be left with nothing. (b) pl -e (Mensch) nonentity.

nichts indef pron inv nothing. ich weiß ~ I don't know anything, I know nothing; ~ als nothing but; ~ (anderes) als nothing but; ~ von Besserem/Neues etc nothing better/new etc; ~ da! (col) (weg da) no you don't!; (ausgeschlossen) nothing doing (col); das ist ~ für mich that's not my cup of tea (col); für ~ und wieder ~ (col) for nothing at all; (es war) ~ mehr zu machen there was nothing more that could be done; ich weiß ~ Genaues I don't know any details; ~ wie raus/hin etc (col) let's get out/over there etc (on the double).

nichts|ahnend adj unsuspecting.

Nicht-: ~schwimmer m non-swimmer; sie ist ~schwimmer she's a non-swimmer; ~schwimmerbecken nt pool for non-swimmers.

nichts-: ~destotrotz adv notwithstanding (form), nonetheless; ~destoweniger adv nevertheless.

Nichtseßhafte(r) mf decl as adj (form) person of no fixed abode (form).

Nichts-: ~könner m incompetent person; ~nutz m -e good-for-nothing; n~nutzig adj useless; (unartig) good-for-nothing; n~sagend adj Buch, Worte meaningless; Mensch insignificant; Gesichtsausdruck blank; ~tuer(in f) m - idler; ~tun nt idleness; (Muße) leisure; viel Zeit mit ~tun verbringen to spend a lot of time doing nothing.

Nicht-: ~**tänzer** m non-dancer; **ich bin** ~**tänzer** I don't dance; ~**trinker** m non-drinker; **er ist** ~**trinker** he doesn't drink; ~**vorhandensein** nt absence; ~**wissen** nt ignorance; ~**zutreffende(s)** nt decl as adj (etwas) ~**zutreffendes** something incorrect; **zutreffendes (bitte) streichen!** (please) delete as applicable.

Nickel nt no pl nickel.

Nickelbrille f metal-rimmed glasses pl.

nicken vi to nod. **mit dem Kopf** ~ to nod one's head.

Nickerchen nt (col) forty winks (col). **ein** ~ **machen** to have forty winks.

Nicki m -s velour pullover.

nie adv never. ~ **im Leben,** ~ **und nimmer** never ever; ~ **wieder** or **mehr** never again; **fast** ~ hardly ever.

nieder 1 adj attr low; (weniger bedeutend) Klasse, Stand lower; (geringer) Geburt, Herkunft lowly; Volk common; Arbeit menial. 2 adv down.

Nieder- pref (Geog) lower; **n**~**beugen** sep 1 vt (lit, fig) to bow down; 2 vr to bend down; **n**~**brennen** vti sep irreg (vi: aux sein) to burn down; **n**~**brüllen** vt sep Redner to shout down; **n**~**deutsch** adj (Ling) Low German; ~**druck** m (Tech) low pressure; **n**~**drücken** vt sep (lit) to press down; (fig: bedrücken) jdn **n**~**drücken** to depress sb, to get sb down (col); ~**gang** m (fig: Verfall) decline; **n**~**gehen** vi sep irreg aux sein to descend; (Regen) to fall; (Gewitter) to break (auch fig); (Boxer) to go down; **n**~**geschlagen** adj dejected, despondent; ~**geschlagenheit** f dejection, despondency; **n**~**halten** vt sep irreg to hold or keep down; Volk to oppress; (Mil) to pin down; **n**~**kämpfen** vt sep Feuer to fight down; Feind to overcome; Tränen to fight back; **n**~**knien** vi sep aux sein to kneel down; **n**~**kommen** vi sep irreg aux sein (old) to be delivered (old) (mit of); ~**kunft** f -̈e (old) delivery; ~**lage** f defeat; **jdm eine** ~**lage beibringen** to inflict a defeat on sb.

Niederlande pl **die** ~ the Netherlands sing or pl, the Low Countries pl.

Niederländer(in f) m - Dutchman/Dutchwoman. **die** ~ the Dutch.

niederländisch adj Dutch, Netherlands.

niederlassen vr sep irreg (a) (geh) to sit down; (Vögel) to alight. (b) (Praxis, Geschäft eröffnen) to establish oneself. **sich als Arzt/Rechtsanwalt** ~ to set up as a doctor/lawyer.

Niederlassung f (a) no pl (das Niederlassen) settlement; (eines Arztes etc) setting-up. (b) (Siedlung) settlement. (c) (Comm) registered office; (Zweigstelle) branch.

niederlegen sep 1 vt (a) to lay or put down; Waffen to lay down. (b) (aufgeben) Amt, Mandat to resign (from), to give up; Führung to renounce, to give up. **die Arbeit** ~ (aufhören, streiken) to stop work. (c) (schriftlich festlegen) to write down. 2 vr to lie down.

Niederlegung f (a) (von Kranz) laying. (b) (von Amt, Mandat) resignation (from). ~ **der Arbeit** industrial action. (c) (schriftlich) setting-out.

Nieder-: **n**~**machen,** **n**~**metzeln** vt sep to massacre, to butcher; **n**~**prasseln** vi sep aux sein (Regen etc) to beat down; (fig: Beschimpfungen) to rain down; **n**~**reißen** vt sep irreg to pull down; (fig) Schranken to tear down; ~**rhein** m Lower Rhine; **n**~**rheinisch** adj Lower Rhine; **n**~**rheinisch** adj Lower Rhine; ~**sachsen** nt Lower Saxony; **n**~**schießen** vt sep irreg to shoot down.

Niederschlag m (a) (Met) precipitation (form); (Chem) precipitate; (Bodensatz) sediment, dregs pl. **radioaktiver** ~ (radioactive) fallout; **für morgen sind heftige** ~**e gemeldet** tomorrow there will be heavy rain/hail/snow. (b) (Boxen) knockdown blow.

niederschlagen sep irreg 1 vt (a) jdn to knock down; Aufstand, Revolte to put down; Augen to

lower, to cast down (liter); siehe **niederge-schlagen. (b)** (Chem) to precipitate. 2 vr (Flüssigkeit) to condense; (Bodensatz) to settle; (Chem) to precipitate. **sich in etw** (dat) ~ (Erfahrungen etc) to find expression in sth.

Niederschlags-: **n**~**frei** adj dry, without precipitation (form); ~**menge** f rainfall/snowfall, precipitation (form).

Nieder-: ~**schlagung** f (eines Aufstands) suppression; **n**~**schmettern** vt sep to batter down; (fig) to shatter; **n**~**schmetternd** adj Nachricht, Ergebnis shattering; **n**~**schreiben** vt sep irreg to write down; ~**schrift** f (das ~schreiben) writing down, (~geschriebenes) notes pl; (Protokoll) (einer Sitzung) minutes pl; (Jur) record; **n**~**setzen** sep 1 vt Kind, Glas to put down; 2 vr to sit down; ~**spannung** f (Elec) low voltage or tension; **n**~**stimmen** vt sep to vote down; **n**~**strecken** vt sep (geh) to lay low; **n**~**stürzen** vi sep aux sein to crash down; **n**~**tourig** [-tuːrɪç] adj low-revving; **n**~**tourig fahren** to drive with low revs.

Niedertracht f = Niederträchtigkeit.

niederträchtig adj malicious, spiteful. **jdn** ~ **verraten** to betray sb in a despicable way.

Niederträchtigkeit f (a) no pl so viel ~ hätte ich ihm nicht zugetraut I would not have suspected him of such a despicable act. (b) (Tat) malicious behaviour no pl (Brit) or behavior no pl (US).

niedertreten vt sep irreg to trample down.

Niederung f (Senke) depression.

Nieder-: **n**~**werfen** sep irreg 1 vt to throw or cast (liter) down; Aufstand to suppress; Gegner (lit) to floor; (fig) to overcome; **er wurde von einer Krankheit** **n**~**geworfen** he was laid low by an illness; 2 vr to prostrate oneself; ~**werfung** f (von Aufstand) suppression.

niedlich adj sweet, cute, pretty little attr.

Niedlichkeit f sweetness, cuteness.

niedrig adj low. ~ **fliegen** to fly low; ~**ste Preise** rock-bottom prices; **ich schätze seine Chancen sehr** ~ **ein** I don't think much of his chances.

Niedrig-: **n**~**stehend** adj Volk, Kultur primitive; ~**wasser** nt (Naut) low water.

niemals adv never.

niemand indef pron nobody, no-one. **es war** ~ **zu Hause** there was nobody at home, there wasn't anyone at home; ~ **anders kam** nobody else came; **ich habe** ~ **anders gesehen** I didn't see anybody else; **sag das** ~**(em)!** don't tell anybody.

Niemand m no pl **er ist ein** ~ he's a nobody.

Niemandsland nt no man's land.

Niere f -n kidney. **künstliche** ~ kidney machine; **es geht mir an die** ~**n** (col) it gets me down.

Nieren- in cpds (Anat) renal; **n**~**förmig** adj kidney-shaped; ~**leiden** nt kidney disease; ~**stein** m kidney stone, renal calculus (spec); ~**tisch** m kidney-shaped table.

nieseln vi impers to drizzle.

Nieselregen m drizzle.

niesen vi to sneeze.

Niespulver nt sneezing powder.

Niet m -e (spec), **Niete**[1] f -n rivet; (auf Kleidung) stud.

Niete[2] f -n (Los) blank; (col: Mensch) dead loss (col).

nieten vt to rivet.

Nietenhose f (pair of) studded jeans pl.

niet- und nagelfest adj (col) nailed down.

Nihilismus f [nihi'lɪsmus] m nihilism.

Nihilist [nihi'lɪst] m nihilist.

nihilistisch [nihi'lɪstɪʃ] adj nihilistic.

Nikolaus m -, -e or (hum col) **Nikoläuse** St Nicholas; (~tag) St Nicholas' Day.

Nikotin nt no pl nicotine.

Nikotin-: **n**~**arm** adj low-nicotine; **n**~**frei** adj nicotine-free; **n**~**haltig** adj containing nicotine; ~**vergiftung** f nicotine poisoning.

Nil m Nile.

Nilpferd nt hippopotamus, hippo.

Nimbus m -, -se (Heiligenschein) halo; (fig) aura.

Nimmer-: n~mehr adv (liter) nevermore (liter), never again; n~müde adj attr tireless, untiring; ~satt m -e glutton; ein ~satt sein to be insatiable; n~satt adj insatiable; ~wiedersehen nt (col) auf ~wiedersehen! I never want to see you again; auf ~wiedersehen verschwinden to disappear never to be seen again.

nippen vti to nip (an+dat at). am Wein ~ to sip (at) the wine.

Nippes pl knick-knacks pl, bric-à-brac sing.

nirgends, nirgendwo adv nowhere, not ... anywhere. ihm gefällt es ~ he doesn't like it anywhere; überall und ~ here, there and everywhere.

nirgendwohin adv nowhere, not ... anywhere.

Nische f -n alcove; (Koch~ etc) corner.

nisten vi to nest.

Nist-: ~kasten m nest(ing) box; ~platz m nesting place; ~zeit f (the) nesting season.

Nitrat nt nitrate.

Nitroglyzerin nt nitroglycerine.

Niveau [ni'vo:] nt -s (lit, fig) level. auf gleichem ~ liegen to be on the same level; diese Schule hat ein hohes ~ this school has high standards; unter ~ below par; unter meinem ~ beneath me; ein Hotel mit ~ a hotel with class.

niveau- [ni'vo:]: ~los adj mediocre; ~voll adj high-class.

Nivellierung [nivɛ'li:rʊŋ] f (Ausgleichung) levelling out.

nix indef pron (col) = nichts.

Nixe f -n water-sprite; (mit Fischschwanz) mermaid.

Nizza nt Nice.

NO = **Nordosten** NE.

nobel adj (edelmütig) noble; (col) (großzügig) generous, (kostspielig) extravagant; (elegant) posh (col). sich ~ zeigen (col) to be generous.

Nobelpreis m Nobel prize.

Nobelpreisträger m Nobel prize winner.

noch 1 adv (a) (weiterhin, bis jetzt) still. ~ nicht still not, not yet; bist du fertig? — ~ nicht are you ready? — not yet; ~ immer still; ~ nie never; ich gehe kaum ~ aus I hardly go out any more; ich möchte gerne ~ bleiben I'd like to stay on longer.

(b) (irgendwann) some time. er wird sich (schon) ~ daran gewöhnen he'll get used to it (one day); das kann ~ passieren that might still happen; er wird ~ kommen he'll come (yet).

(c) (eben, nicht später als) ich habe ihn ~ vor zwei Tagen gesehen I saw him only two days ago; er ist ~ am selben Tag gestorben he died the very same day; ~ im 18. Jahrhundert as late as the 18th century; können Sie das heute ~ erledigen? can you do it (for) today?

(d) (einschränkend) (only) just. (gerade) ~ gut genug (only) just good enough.

(e) (außerdem, zusätzlich) wer war ~ da? who else was there?; ~ etwas Fleisch some more meat; ~ einer another (one); ~ einmal once more; und es regnete auch ~ and on top of that it was raining.

(f) (bei Vergleichen) even, still, yet. ~ größer even bigger; das ist ~ besser that's better still; seien sie auch ~ so klein however small they might be.

(g) (col) Geld ~ und ~ or (hum col) ~er heaps and heaps of money (col); sie hat ~ und ~ versucht, ... she tried again and again to ...

2 conj weder X ~ Y neither X nor Y.

nochmalig adj attr renewed. eine ~e Überprüfung a further check.

nochmals adv again.

NOK [ɛnoː'ka] nt = **Nationales Olympisches Komitee.**

Nomade m (wk) -n, -n (lit, fig) nomad.

Nomaden- in cpds nomadic; ~tum nt nomadism.

Nomadin f (lit, fig) nomad.

nominal adj nominal.

Nominal- in cpds (Gram, Fin) nominal; ~wert m (Fin) nominal or par value.

Nominativ m nominative.

nominell adj nominal.

nominieren* vt to nominate.

nonchalant [nõʃa'lã:] adj (geh) nonchalant.

Nonkonformist(in f) m nonconformist.

nonkonformistisch adj nonconformist.

Nonne f -n nun.

Nonnenkloster nt convent, nunnery (old, hum).

Nonplus|ultra nt no pl (geh) ultimate.

Nonsens m no pl nonsense.

nonstop [nɔn'ʃtɔp, nɔn'stɔp] adv non-stop.

Nonstop- in cpds non-stop.

Noppe f -n (Knoten) burl; (Schlinge) loop.

Nord no art no pl (Naut, Met, liter) north.

Nord- in cpds (Geog) North; ~amerika nt North America; n~deutsch adj North German; ~deutschland nt North(ern) Germany.

Norden m no pl north; (von Land) North. von ~ her from the north; nach ~ north(wards), to the north; der Balkon liegt nach ~ the balcony faces north(wards).

Nord-: ~england nt the North of England; ~irland nt Northern Ireland, Ulster.

nördisch adj Wälder northern; Völker, Sprache nordic. ~e Kombination (Ski) nordic combined.

Nord-: ~kap nt North Cape; ~küste f north(ern) coast; ~länder(in f) m - Scandinavian.

nördlich 1 adj northern; Wind, Richtung northerly. der ~e Polarkreis the Arctic Circle; N~es Eismeer Arctic Ocean; 52 Grad ~er Breite 52 degrees north. 2 adv (the) north. ~ von Köln (gelegen) north of Cologne. 3 prep +gen (to the) north of.

Nordlicht nt northern lights pl, aurora borealis.

Nordost m north-east. aus ~ from the north-east.

Nordosten m north-east; (von Land) North East.

nord|östlich 1 adj Gegend north-eastern; Wind north-east(erly). 2 adv (to the) north-east. 3 prep +gen (to the) north-east of.

Nord-Ostsee-Kanal m Kiel Canal.

Nordpol m North Pole.

Nordpolargebiet nt Arctic (Zone).

Nordrhein-Westfalen nt North Rhine-Westphalia.

Nordsee f North Sea.

Nord-: ~seite f north(ern) side; (von Berg) north(ern) face; ~stern m North Star, Polar Star.

Nordwest m north-west. aus ~ from the north-west.

Nordwesten m north-west; (von Land) North-West.

nordwestlich 1 adj Gegend north-western; Wind north-west(erly). 2 adv (to the) north-west. 3 prep+gen (to the) north-west of.

Nordwind m north wind.

Nörgelei f carping, niggling.

nörgeln vi (an+dat about) to carp, to niggle.

Nörgler(in f) m - carper, niggler.

Norm f -en (a) norm; (Größenvorschrift) standard (specification). die ~ sein to be (considered) normal. (b) (Leistungssoll) quota, norm. die ~ erreichen to achieve one's quota.

normal adj normal; Format, Maß, Gewicht standard. bist du noch ~? (col) have you gone mad?

Normal- in cpds (üblich) normal; (genormt) standard; ~benzin nt two-star (petrol) (Brit), regular (gas) (US).

normalerweise adv normally, usually.

Normal-: ~fall m normal case; im ~fall normally; ~gewicht nt normal weight; (genormt) standard weight.

normalisieren* 1 *vt* to normalize. 2 *vr* to return to normal.

Normalisierung *f* normalization.

Normalität *f* normality, normalcy.

Normal-: ~**maß** *nt* standard (measure); ~**verbraucher** *m* average consumer; **Otto** ~**verbraucher** *(col)* the average person *or* punter *(col)*, John Doe *(US)*.

Normandie *f* Normandy.

normen, normieren* *vt* to standardize.

Normierung, Normung *f* standardization.

Norwegen *nt* Norway.

Norweger(in *f) m* - Norwegian.

norwegisch *adj* Norwegian. **das** N~**e** Norwegian.

Nostalgie *f* nostalgia.

nostalgisch *adj* nostalgic.

Not *f* ~**e** **(a)** *no pl (Mangel, Elend)* need(iness), poverty. **eine Zeit der** ~ a time of need; **aus** ~ out of poverty; ~ **leiden** to suffer deprivation; **in** ~ **leben** to live in poverty; **wenn** ~ **am Mann ist** if you/they *etc* are short *(col)*; *(im Notfall)* in an emergency; ~ **macht erfinderisch** *(Prov)* necessity is the mother of invention *(Prov)*.

(b) *(Bedrängnis)* distress *no pl*; *(Problem)* problem. **in seiner** ~ in his hour of need; **in unserer** ~ **blieb uns nichts anderes übrig** in this emergency we had no choice; **jdm seine** ~ **klagen** to tell sb one's troubles; **in** ~ **sein** to be in distress; **in** ~ **geraten** to get into serious difficulties.

(c) *no pl (Sorge, Mühe)* difficulty, trouble. **er hat seine liebe** ~ **mit ihr/damit** he really has problems with her/it.

(d) *(Zwang, Notwendigkeit)* necessity. **etw ohne** ~ **tun** to do sth without having to; **zur** ~ if need(s) be; *(gerade noch)* at a pinch; **aus der** ~ **eine Tugend machen** to make a virtue (out) of necessity.

not *adj (geh)* ~ **tun** to be necessary.

Notar(in *f) m* notary.

Notariat *nt* notary's office.

notariell *adj* notarial. ~ **beglaubigt** attested by a notary.

Not-: ~**arzt** *m* emergency doctor; ~**ausgang** *m* emergency exit; ~**behelf** *m* stopgap (measure), makeshift; ~**bremse** *f* emergency brake, communication cord *(Brit)*; **die** ~**bremse ziehen** *(Ftbl sl: foulen)* to hack sb down, to commit a blatant foul; ~**bremsung** *f* emergency stop.

Notdurft *f no pl (euph geh)* call of nature *(euph)*. **seine** ~ **verrichten** to relieve oneself.

notdürftig *adj (kaum ausreichend)* meagre *(Brit)*, meager *(US)*; *Kleidung* scanty; *(behelfsmäßig)* makeshift **no** *adv*, rough and ready **no** *adv*. **damit Sie sich wenigstens** ~ **verständigen können** so that you can at least communicate to some extent; **nachdem wir den Reifen** ~ **geflickt hatten** when we had patched up the tyre in a rough-and-ready way.

Note *f* ~**n** **(a)** *(Mus)* note. ~**n** *pl* music; ~**n lesen** to read music; **nach** ~**n spielen** to play from music. **(b)** *(Sch)* mark. **(c)** *(Pol)* note. **(d)** *(Bank~)* (bank)note *(Brit)*, bill *(US)*. **(e)** *no pl (Eigenart)* *(in bezug auf Gespräch, Brief etc)* note; *(in bezug auf Atmosphäre)* tone, character. **einer Sache** *(dat)* **eine persönliche** ~ **verleihen** to give sth a personal touch.

Noten-: ~**bank** *f* issuing bank; ~**blatt** *nt* sheet of music; ~**papier** *nt* manuscript paper; ~**presse** *f* money press; ~**schlüssel** *m* clef; ~**schrift** *f* musical notation; ~**ständer** *m* music stand.

Notfall *m* emergency. **für den** ~ **nehme ich einen Schirm mit** I'll take an umbrella (just) in case; **im** ~ if need be; **bei einem** ~ in case of emergency.

notfalls *adv* if necessary, if need be.

notgedrungen *adv* of necessity. **ich muß mich** ~

dazu bereit erklären I've no choice but to agree.

Notgroschen *m* nest egg.

notieren* 1 *vt* **(a)** *(Notizen machen)* to make a note of; *(schnell)* to jot down. **(b)** *(vormerken)* *(Comm) Auftrag* to note, to book. **jdn** ~ to put sb's name down. **(c)** *(St Ex: festlegen)* to quote *(mit* at). 2 *vi (St Ex: wert sein)* to be quoted *(auf*+acc at).

Notierung *f (Comm)* note; *(St Ex)* quotation.

nötig 1 *adj* necessary. **es ist nicht** ~, **daß er kommt** it's not necessary for him to come, there's no need for him to come; **wenn** ~ if necessary, if need be; **etw** ~ **haben** to need sth; **er hat das natürlich nicht** ~ *(iro)* but, of course, he's different; **ich habe es nicht** ~, **mich von dir anschreien zu lassen** I don't have to let you shout at me; **du hast es gerade** ~, **so zu reden** *(col)* you're a fine one to talk *(col)*; **das habe ich nicht** ~! I can do without that; **das** N~**ste the** (bare) necessities. 2 *adv (dringend)* **etw** ~ **brauchen** to need something urgently.

nötigen *vt (geh: zwingen)* to compel; *(Jur)* to coerce; *(auffordern)* to urge. **sich** ~ **lassen** to need urging; **lassen Sie sich nicht (erst)** ~! don't wait to be asked; *siehe* **genötigt**.

nötigenfalls *adv (form)* if necessary.

Nötigung *f (Zwang)* compulsion; *(Jur)* coercion.

Notiz *f* -**en** **(a)** *(Vermerk)* note; *(Zeitungs~)* item. **sich** *(dat)* ~**en machen** to make notes. **(b)** ~ **nehmen von** to take notice of; **keine** ~ **nehmen von** to ignore.

Notiz-: ~**block** *m* notepad; ~**buch** *nt* notebook.

Notlage *f* crisis; *(Elend)* plight. **jds** ~ *(acc)* **ausnützen** to exploit sb's situation; **in eine** ~ **geraten** to get into serious difficulties.

notlanden *pret* **notlandete,** *ptp* **notgelandet** *vi aux sein* to make an emergency landing.

Notlandung *f* emergency landing.

notleidend *adj* needy. **die** N~**en** the needy.

Not-: ~**lösung** *f* compromise solution; *(provisorisch)* temporary solution; ~**lüge** *f* white lie.

notorisch *adj* notorious.

Not-: ~**ruf** *m (Telec) (Gespräch)* emergency call; *(Nummer)* emergency number; ~**rufsäule** *f* emergency telephone; ~**schlachten** *pret* **n**~**schlachtete,** *ptp* **n**~**geschlachtet** *vt* to destroy, to put down; ~**schlachtung** *f* putting down; ~**signal** *nt* distress signal; ~**situation** *f* emergency.

Notstand *m* crisis; *(Pol)* state of emergency; *(Jur)* emergency.

Notstands-: ~**gebiet** *nt (wirtschaftlich)* depressed area; *(bei Katastrophen)* disaster area; ~**gesetze** *pl (Pol)* emergency laws *pl*.

notwassern *pret* **notwasserte,** *ptp* **notgewassert** *vi* to ditch *(Aviat sl)*.

Notwehr *f no pl* self-defence *(Brit)*, self-defense *(US)*. **aus/in** ~ in self-defence.

notwendig *adj* necessary. ~ **brauchen** to need urgently; **das** N~**ste** the (bare) essentials.

notwendigerweise *adv* of necessity, inevitably.

Notwendigkeit *f* necessity. **die** ~, **etw zu tun** the necessity of doing sth.

Notzucht *f (Jur)* rape.

Nougat ['nuːgat] *m on nt* -**s** nougat.

Novelle [no'vɛlə] *f* **(a)** novella. **(b)** *(Pol)* amendment.

November [no'vɛmbɐ] *m* - November; *siehe* **März**.

Novize [no'viːtsə] *m (wk)* -**n,** -**n,** **Novizin** *f* novice.

Novum ['noːvʊm] *nt, pl* **Nova** ['noːva] novelty.

NPD [ɛnpeː'deː] *f* = **Nationaldemokratische Partei Deutschlands**.

Nr. = **Nummer** No.

NS- [ɛn'ɛs-] *in cpds* Nazi.

Nuance [ny'ãːsə] *f* -**n** nuance; *(Kleinigkeit)* shade. **um eine** ~ **zu laut** a shade too loud.

nüchtern *adj* **(a)** *(ohne Essen)* **eine Medizin** ~ **einnehmen** to take a medicine on an empty stomach; **mit** ~**em/auf** ~**en Magen** with/on an empty stomach. **(b)** *(nicht betrunken)* sober. **wieder ~ werden** to sober up. **(c)** *(schmucklos)* sober; *(sachlich)* down-to-earth *no adv*, rational; *Zahlen, Tatsachen* bare, plain.

Nüchternheit *f* **(a)** *(Unbetrunkenheit)* soberness, sobriety. **(b)** *(Schmucklosigkeit)* soberness; *(Sachlichkeit)* rationality.

nuckeln *vi (col) (Mensch)* to suck *(an +dat* at); *(Tier)* to suckle *(an +dat* from). **am Daumen ~** to suck one's thumb.

Nudel *f* **-n** *usu pl* **(a)** *(als Beilage)* pasta *no pl*; *(als Suppeneinlage)* noodle. **(b)** *(col: Mensch) (dick) (komisch)* character.

Nudel-: ~brett *nt* pastryboard; **~holz** *nt* rolling pin; **~suppe** *f* noodle soup.

Nudismus *m* nudism.

Nudist(in *f)* *m* nudist.

Nugat *m or nt* **-s** nougat.

nuklear *adj attr* nuclear.

Null *f* **-en (a)** *(Zahl)* nought, zero; *(Gefrierpunkt)* zero. **die ~** the figure nought, zero; **gleich ~ sein** to be absolutely nil; **in ~ Komma nichts** *(col)* in less than no time; **seine Stimmung sank auf ~** *(col)* his mood sank; **im Jahre ~** in the year nought; **die Stunde ~** the new starting point. **(b)** *(col: Mensch)* dead loss *(col)*.

Null *num* zero; *(Telec)* O [ʒʊ] *(Brit)*, zero *(US)*; *(Sport)* nil; *(Tennis)* love. **~ Komma eins** (nought) point one; **es ist ~ Uhr zehn** it's ten past midnight; **~ Grad** zero degrees; **~ Fehler** no *or* zero *(col)* mistakes; **es steht ~ zu ~** there's no score; **das Spiel wurde ~ zu ~** beendet the game was a goalless draw; **~ und nichtig** *(Jur)* null and void.

null|achtfünfzehn *(col)* **1** *adj pred* run-of-the-mill *(col)*. **2** *adv* in a run-of-the-mill way.

Null|achtfünfzehn- *in cpds (col)* run-of-the-mill.

Nullpunkt *m* zero. **die Stimmung sank unter den ~** the atmosphere froze; **auf dem ~ angekommen sein** *(fig)* to have reached rock-bottom.

Null-: ~stellung *f* zero position; **in der ~stellung sein** to be on zero; **~tarif** *m (für Verkehrsmittel)* free travel; **... gibt es nicht zum ~tarif** *(fig)* you can't have ... for nothing; **~wachstum** *nt (Econ)* zero growth.

numerieren* *vt* to number.

numerisch *adj* numeric(al).

Numerus *m, pl* **Numeri** *(Gram)* number. **~ clausus** *(Univ)* restricted entry.

Nummer *f* **-n** number; *(Größe)* size; *(col: Mensch)* character; *(col!: Koitus)* screw *(col!)*. **unser Haus hat die ~ 25** our house is number 25; **nur eine ~ unter vielen sein** *(fig)* to be a cog (in the machine); **auf ~ Sicher gehen** *(col)* to play (it) safe; **eine ~ abziehen** *(col)* to put on an act.

Nummern-: ~konto *nt* numbered bank account; **~schild** *nt (Aut)* number plate, registration plate *(Brit)*, license plate *(US)*.

nun *adv* **(a)** *(jetzt)* now. **von ~ an** from now on, from here on in *(US)*; **~ erst only now;** **~ endlich** (now) at last; **was ~?** what now?; **was ~ (schon wieder)?** what (is it) now? **(b)** **er will ~ mal nicht** he simply doesn't want to; **~, wenn's unbedingt sein muß** well, if I/you *etc* really must; **das ist ~ (ein)mal** so that's just the way things are; **~ ja, aber ...** OK *(col)*, but ...; **~ ja** well yes; **~ gut** (well) all right, (well) OK *(col)*; **~ erst recht!** just for that (I'll do it) **(c)** *(bei Fragen)* **~?** well?; **~, wird's bald?** *(col)* come on then.

nunmehr *adv (geh) (jetzt)* now, at this point; *(von jetzt an)* henceforth *(form)*, from now on.

nur *adv* **(a)** *(einschränkend)* only, just. **ich habe ~ ein Stück Brot gegessen** I've only eaten a piece of bread; **alle, ~ ich nicht** everyone but me; **~ schade, daß ...** it's just a pity that ...; **~ daß** it's just that, only; **~ noch zwei Minuten** just another two minutes; **nicht ~ ..., sondern auch** not only ... but also; **alles, ~ das nicht!** any-

thing but that!; **warum möchtest du das denn wissen? — ach, ~ so!** why do you want to know? — oh no special reason; **ich hab' das ~ so gesagt** I was just talking.

(b) *(mit Fragepronomen)* -ever. **warum sie ~ dahin geht?** why ever does she go there?; **wie kannst du ~ (so etwas sagen)?** how could you (say such a thing)?; **sie bekommt alles, was sie ~ will** she gets whatever she wants.

(c) wenn (...) ~ if only; **wenn er ~ (erst) käme** if only he would come; **es wird klappen, wenn er ~ nicht die Nerven verliert** it will be all right as long as he doesn't lose his nerve.

(d) sagen Sie das ~ nicht Ihrer Frau! don't tell your wife (whatever you do); **geh ~!** just go; **~ zu!** go on; **sieh ~** just look; **~ her damit!** *(col)* let's have it; **Sie brauchen es ~ zu sagen** just say (the word); **er soll ~ lachen!** let him laugh.

Nürnberg *nt* Nuremberg.

nuscheln *vti (col)* to mutter, to mumble.

Nuß *f, pl* **Nüsse (a)** nut. **(b)** *(col: Mensch)* **eine taube ~** a dead loss *(col)*; **eine doofe ~** a stupid twit *(Brit col)* or clown *(col)*.

Nuß-: ~baum *m (Baum)* walnut tree; *(Holz)* walnut; **~knacker** *m* nutcracker; **~schale** *f* nutshell; *(fig: Boot)* cockleshell.

Nüster *f* **-n** nostril.

Nut *f* **-en** *(spec)*, **Nute** *f* **-n** groove.

Nutte *f* **-n** *(pej, col!)* tart *(col)*, hooker *(esp US col)*.

nutzbar *adj* us(e)able; *Bodenschätze* exploitable. **~ machen** to make us(e)able; *Sonnenenergie* to harness; *Bodenschätze* to exploit.

Nutzbarmachung *f* utilization; *(von Bodenschätzen)* exploitation.

nutzbringend *adj* profitable. **etw ~ anwenden** to use sth to good effect, to put sth to good use.

nütze *adj pred* **zu etw/nichts ~ sein** to be useful for sth/to be no use for anything.

Nutzen *m* **-** *(spec)* use; *(Nützlichkeit)* usefulness. **zum ~ der Öffentlichkeit** for the benefit of the public; **jdm von ~ sein** to be of use to sb. **(b)** *(Vorteil)* advantage, benefit; *(Gewinn)* profit. **jdm ~ bringen** *(Vorteil)* to be of advantage to sb; *(Gewinn)* to bring sb profit; **von etw ~ haben** to profit by sth.

nutzen, nützen 1 *vi* to be of use *(jdm zu etw* to sb for sth). **die Ermahnungen haben genützt/nichts genützt** the warnings had the desired effect/didn't do any good; **da nützt alles nichts** there's nothing to be done; **das nützt (mir/dir) nichts** that won't help (me/you); **wozu soll das alles ~?** what's the point of that? **2** *vt* to make use of; *Gelegenheit* to take advantage of.

Nutz-: ~fahrzeug *nt* farm vehicle; military vehicle *etc*; *(Comm)* commercial vehicle; **~fläche** *f* us(e)able floor space; *(Agr)* (agriculturally) productive land; **~last** *f* maximum load.

nützlich *adj* useful; *Hinweis, Buch auch* helpful. **~ für die Gesundheit** beneficial for the health; **sich ~ machen** to make oneself useful.

Nützlichkeit *f* usefulness, utility *(form)*.

nutzlos *adj* **(a)** useless; *(vergeblich)* futile, vain *attr*, in vain *pred*. **es ist völlig ~, das zu tun** it's absolutely pointless doing that. **(b)** *(unnötig)* needless. **sein Leben ~ aufs Spiel setzen** to risk one's life needlessly *or* unnecessarily.

Nutzlosigkeit *f* uselessness; *(Vergeblichkeit)* futility.

Nutznießer(in *f)* *m* **-** beneficiary.

Nutzung *f (Gebrauch)* use; *(das Ausnutzen)* exploitation. **ich habe ihm meinen Garten zur ~ überlassen** I gave him the use of my garden.

NW = *Nordwesten* NW.

Nylon ® ['naɪlɔn] *nt no pl* nylon.

Nylonstrumpf *m* ['naɪlɔn-] *m* nylon (stocking).

Nymphe ['nʏmfə] *f* **-n** nymph.

Nymphomanin [nʏmfo-] *f* nymphomaniac, nympho *(col)*.

O

O, o [oː] *nt* -, - O, o.
O = **Osten.**
o *interj* oh.
O|ase *f* -n, -n oasis; *(fig)* haven, oasis.
ob *conj* **(a)** *(indirekte Frage)* if, whether. **Sie müssen kommen,** ~ **Sie (nun) wollen oder nicht** like it or not, you have to come; ~ **er (wohl) morgen kommt?** I wonder if he'll come tomorrow; ~ **wir jetzt Pause machen?** shall we have a break now?; ~ **ich nicht lieber gehe?** maybe I'd better go; ~ **Sie mir wohl mal helfen können?** I wonder if you could help me. **(b)** *(verstärkend)* **und** ~ *(col)* you bet *(col)*; **und** ~ **ich das gesehen habe!** you bet I saw it! *(col)* **(c)** *(vergleichend)* **als** ~ as if; **(so) tun als** ~ *(col)* to pretend; **tu nicht so als** ~**!** stop pretending!
OB [oːˈbeː] *m* -s = **Oberbürgermeister.**
o.B. = **ohne Befund.**
Obacht *f no pl (esp S Ger)* ~**!** watch out!, careful!; ~ **geben auf** *(+acc)* *(aufmerken)* to pay attention to; *(bewachen)* to keep an eye on.
Obdach *nt no pl (geh)* shelter. **jdm** ~ **gewähren** to offer sb shelter; **kein** ~ **haben** to be homeless.
Obdach-: **o**~**los** *adj* homeless; **o**~**los werden** to be made homeless; ~**lose(r)** *mf decl as adj* homeless person; **die** ~**losen** the homeless.
Obdachlosen-: ~**asyl,** ~**heim** *nt* hostel or shelter for the homeless; ~**siedlung** *f* settlement for the homeless.
Obdachlosigkeit *f* homelessness.
Obduktion *f* post-mortem, autopsy.
obduzieren* *vt* to do a post-mortem or autopsy on.
O-Beine *pl (col)* bow or bandy legs *pl*.
oben *adv* **(a)** *(am oberen Ende)* at the top; *(an der Oberfläche)* on the surface; *(im Hause)* upstairs; *(in der Höhe)* up. ~ **und unten (von etw) verwechseln** to get sth upside down; **wo ist** ~ **(bei dem Bild)?** which is the right way up (for the picture)?; **wir wohnen rechts** ~ or ~ **rechts** we live on the top floor to the right; **die Abbildung** ~ **links** or **links** ~ the illustration in the top left-hand corner; **der ist** ~ **nicht ganz richtig** *(col)* he's not quite right up top *(col)*; ~ **ohne gehen** or **tragen** *(col)* to be topless; **ganz** ~ right at the top; **hier/dort** ~ up here/there; **die ganze Sache steht mir bis hier** ~ *(col)* I'm fed up to the back teeth with the whole thing *(col)*; **bis** ~ **(hin)** to the top; **hoch** ~ high (up) above; **weiter** ~ nearer the top; ~ **auf dem Berg/der Leiter/dem Dach** on top of the mountain/ladder/roof; ~ **am Himmel/im Norden** up in the sky/north; **nach** ~ up, upwards; *(im Hause)* upstairs; **der Fahrstuhl fährt nach** ~ the lift is going up; **der Weg nach** ~ *(fig)* the road to the top; **endlich hat sie den Weg nach** ~ **geschafft** *(fig)* she finally made it (to the top); **nach** ~ **zu** or **hin** towards the top; **von** ~ **hat man eine schöne Aussicht** there's a nice view from the top; **von** ~ **bis unten** from top to bottom; *(von Mensch)* from top to toe; **jdn von** ~ **bis unten mustern** to look sb up and down; **jdn von** ~ **herab behandeln** to treat sb condescendingly; **weiter** ~ further up.
(b) *(col: die Vorgesetzten)* **die da** ~ the powers that be *(col)*; **das wird** ~ **entschieden** that's decided higher up; **etw nach** ~ **(weiter)melden** to report sth to a superior; **der Befehl kommt von** ~ it's orders from above. **(c)** *(vorher)* above. **siehe** ~ see above; **wie** ~ **erwähnt** as mentioned above; **der weiter** ~ **erwähnte Fall** the case referred to above.
oben-: ~**an** *adv* at the top or on (the) top; ~**auf** *adv* on (the) top; **gestern war er krank, aber heute ist er wieder** ~**auf** *(col)* he wasn't well yesterday, but he's back on form today; ~**drauf** *adv (col)* on top; ~**drein** *adv (col)* on top of everything *(col)*; ~**erwähnt,** ~**genannt** *adj attr* above-mentioned; ~**hin** *adv* nur so ~**hin sagen** to say sth in an offhand way.
Ober *m* - *(Kellner)* waiter. **Herr** ~**!** waiter!
Ober-: ~**arm** *m* upper arm; ~**arzt** *m* senior physician; ~**aufseher** *m* (head) supervisor; *(im Gefängnis)* head warden *(Brit)* or guard *(US)*; ~**aufsicht** *f* supervision; **die** ~**aufsicht haben** to have overall control *(über +acc* of*)*; ~**befehl** *m (Mil)* **den** ~**befehl haben** to be in supreme command *(über +acc* of*)*; ~**befehlshaber** *m (Mil)* commander-in-chief; ~**begriff** *m* generic term; ~**bekleidung** *f* outer clothing; ~**bett** *nt* quilt; ~**bürgermeister** *m* mayor; ~**deck** *nt* upper or top deck.
obere(r, s) *adj attr* Ende, Stockwerke, *(Schul)*klassen upper, top. **die O**~**n** *(col)* the bosses; **die** ~**en Zehntausend** *(col)* high society.
Oberfläche *f* surface; *(Tech, Math)* surface area. **an die** ~ **kommen** *(lit)* to surface; *(fig)* to emerge; **an der** ~ **bleiben** *(lit)* to remain on the surface; **sein Referat blieb völlig an der** ~ his paper only scratched the surface.
oberflächlich *adj* superficial. ~**e Verletzung** surface wound; **bei** ~**er Betrachtung** at a quick glance; **seine Kenntnisse sind nur** ~ his knowledge doesn't go beyond the surface; ~ **arbeiten** to work superficially; **etw** ~ **lesen** to skim through sth; **jdn (nur)** ~ **kennen** to know sb (only) slightly; **nach** ~**er Schätzung** at a rough guess.
Oberflächlichkeit *f* superficiality.
Ober-: **o**~**gärig** *adj* Bier top fermented; ~**geschoß** *nt* top floor; **im zweiten** ~**geschoß** on the second *(Brit)* or third *(US)* floor; **o**~**halb 1** *prep* +gen above; **2** *adv* above; **o**~**halb von Basel** above Basel; **weiter o**~**halb** further or higher up; ~**hand** *f (fig)* upper hand; **die** ~**hand gewinnen** to get the upper hand *(über +acc* over*)*; ~**haupt** *nt (Repräsentant)* head; *(Anführer)* leader; ~**haus** *nt (Pol)* upper house; *(in GB)* House of Lords; ~**hemd** *nt* shirt; ~**herrschaft,** ~**hoheit** *f* sovereignty.
Oberin *f* **(a)** *(im Krankenhaus)* = **Oberschwester.** **(b)** *(Eccl)* Mother Superior.
Ober-: **o**~**irdisch** *adj* above ground; ~**kellner** *m* head waiter; ~**kiefer** *m* upper jaw; ~**kommando** *nt (*~**befehl)** Supreme Command; *(Befehlsstab)* headquarters *pl*; ~**körper** *m* upper part of the body; **mit bloßem** or **nacktem** ~**körper** stripped to the waist; ~**lauf** *m* **am** ~**lauf des Rheins** in the upper reaches of the Rhine; ~**leder** *nt* (leather) uppers *pl*; ~**leitung** *f (Elec)* overhead cable; ~**leutnant** *m* lieutenant *(Brit)*, first lieutenant *(US)*; *(Luftwaffe)* flying officer *(Brit)*, first lieutenant *(US)*; ~**licht** *nt (hochgelegenes Fenster)*

small, high window; (*Lüftungsklappe, über einer Tür*) fanlight, transom (window); ~**liga** *f (Sport)* top *or* first league; ~**lippe** *f* upper lip; ~**schenkel** *m* thigh; ~**schicht** *f* top layer; *(Sociol)* upper strata (of society) *pl*; ~**schwester** *f* senior nursing officer; *(von Station)* sister; ~**seite** *f* top (side).

Oberst *m (wk)* -en, -e(n) (a) *(Heer)* colonel. (b) *(Luftwaffe)* group captain *(Brit)*, colonel *(US)*.

oberste(r, s) *adj* (a) *(ganz oben)* Stockwerk, Schicht uppermost, very top. (b) *Gesetz, Prinzip* supreme; *Dienstgrad* most senior. **O**~**er Gerichtshof** supreme court; *(in GB)* High Court (of Justice); *(in USA)* Supreme Court.

Ober-: ~**stübchen** *nt (col)*: **er ist nicht ganz richtig im** ~**stübchen** he's not quite right up top *(col)*; ~**studienrat** *m* senior teacher; ~**stufe** *f* upper school; *(Univ)* advanced level; ~**teil** *nt or m* upper part, top; ~**trottel** *m (col)* prize idiot; ~**verwaltungsgericht** *nt* Higher Administrative Court; ~**wasser** *nt (fig col)* **sobald sein älterer Bruder dabei ist, hat er** ~**wasser** as soon as his elder brother is there he opens up; ~**weite** *f* bust measurement.

obgleich *conj* although, (even) though.

Obhut *f no pl (geh)* care. **jdn/etw jds** ~ *(dat)* **anvertrauen** to place sb/sth in sb's care.

obige(r, s) *adj attr* above. **der O**~ *(form)* the above *(form)*.

Objekt *nt* -e *(auch Gram)* object. **das** ~ **der Untersuchung** the object under examination.

objektiv *adj* objective. ~ **über etw** *(acc)* **urteilen** to judge sth objectively.

Objektiv *nt* (object) lens, objective.

Objektivität *f* objectivity. **sich um größte** ~ **bemühen** to try to be as objective as possible.

Objektsatz *m* object clause.

Oblate *f* -n wafer; *(Eccl)* host.

Obligation *f (auch Fin)* obligation.

obligatorisch *adj* obligatory; *Fächer, Vorlesung* compulsory; *Qualifikationen* necessary.

Oboe [o'bo:ə] *f* -n oboe.

Oboist [obo'ɪst] *m (wk)* oboist, oboe player.

Obolus *m* -se contribution.

Obrigkeit *f* (a) *(als Begriff)* authority. (b) *(Behörden)* **die** ~ the authorities *pl*.

Obrigkeits-: ~**denken** *nt* acceptance of authority; ~**staat** *m* authoritarian state.

Obrist *m (wk)* colonel.

obschon *conj (liter)* although.

Observatorium [ɔpzɛrva'to:rium] *nt* observatory.

obskur *adj* obscure; *(fragwürdig)* suspect, dubious.

Obst *nt no pl* fruit.

Obst-: ~**(an)bau** *m* fruit-growing; ~**baum** *m* fruit-tree; ~**garten** *m* orchard; ~**händler** *m* fruit merchant; ~**kuchen** *m* fruit flan.

Obstruktion *f (Pol)* obstruction, filibuster. ~ **betreiben** to obstruct, to filibuster.

Obst-: ~**saft** *m* fruit juice; ~**torte** *f* fruit flan.

obszön *adj* obscene.

Obszönität *f* obscenity.

Obus *m* -se *(col)* trolley bus.

obwohl *conj* although, (even) though.

Ochse ['ɔksə] *m (wk)* -n, -n (a) ox, bullock. ~ **am Spieß** roast ox; **er stand da wie der** ~ **vorm Berg** *(col)* he stood there utterly bewildered. (b) *(col: Dummkopf)* twit *(Brit col)*, clown *(col)*.

ochsen ['ɔksn] *(Sch sl)* vti to mug up *(col)*.

Ochsen- [ɔksn-]: ~**schwanzsuppe** *f* oxtail soup; ~**tour** *f (col: Schinderei)* slog *(col)*.

Ocker *m or nt* - ochre *(Brit)*, ocher *(US)*.

ocker-: ~**braun**, ~**gelb** *adj* ochre *(Brit)*, ocher *(US)*.

od. = oder.

Ode *f* -n ode.

öd(e) *adj* (a) *(verlassen)* Stadt, Strand deserted, empty; *(unbewohnt)* desolate, bleak; *(unbebaut)* waste. **öd und leer** dreary and desolate. (b) *(fig:*

fade) dreary, tedious; *Dasein* barren.

Öde *f* -n *(liter)* (a) *(einsame Gegend)* waste(land). (b) *(Langeweile)* dreariness, monotony.

oder *conj* (a) or. ~ **aber** or else; ~ **auch** or even; **eins** ~ **das andere** one or the other; **entweder ...** ~ **either ...** or. (b) *(in Fragen)* **so war's doch,** ~ **nicht?** that was what happened, wasn't it?; **du kommst doch,** ~? you're coming, aren't you?; **lassen wir es so,** ~? let's leave it at that, OK?

Ödipuskomplex *m* Oedipus complex.

Odyssee *f* -n [-eːən] *(Liter)* Odyssey; *(fig)* odyssey.

Ofen *m* ⁻ (a) *(Heiz~)* heater; *(Elektro~, Gas~ auch)* fire; *(Kohle~)* stove. **hinter dem** ~ **hocken** to be a stay-at-home; **jetzt ist der** ~ **aus** *(col)* that does it *(col)*. (b) *(Herd)* oven, stove; *(Back~)* oven. (c) *(Tech)* furnace, oven; *(Brenn~)* kiln; *(Hoch~)* blast furnace.

Ofen-: **o**~**fertig** *adj Gericht* oven ready; **o**~**frisch** *adj Brot* oven fresh; ~**heizung** *f* stove heating; ~**rohr** *nt* stovepipe; ~**schirm** *m* firescreen.

offen *adj (lit, fig)* open; *Bein* ulcerated; *Flamme* naked; *Stelle* vacant; *Rechnung* outstanding. **ein** ~**er Brief** an open letter; **die Haare** ~ **tragen** to wear one's hair loose; **der Laden hat bis 7 Uhr** ~ the shop stays open until 7 o'clock; ~**er Wein** wine by the carafe/glass; *(vom Faß)* wine on draught *(Brit)* or draft *(US)*; **auf** ~**er Strecke** *(Straße)* on the open road; *(Rail)* between stations; **auf** ~**er Straße** in the middle of the street; *(Landstraße)* on the open road; **auf** ~**er See** on the open sea; **Beifall auf** ~**er Szene** an outburst of applause; **mit** ~**em Munde dastehen** *(fig)* to stand gaping; ~**e Türen einrennen** *(fig)* to kick at an open door; **Tag der** ~**en Tür** open day; **jdn mit** ~**en Armen empfangen** to welcome sb with open arms; **allem Neuen gegenüber** ~ **sein** to be receptive or open to (all) new ideas; ~**e Handelsgesellschaft** general partnership; ~**e Stellen** vacancies; **die Entscheidung ist noch** ~ nothing has been decided yet; ~ **gestanden** or **gesagt** quite honestly; **etw** ~ **zugeben** to admit sth frankly; **seine Meinung** ~ **sagen** to speak one's mind; ~ **mit jdm reden** to be frank with sb.

offenbar 1 *adj* obvious. **sein Zögern machte** ~, **daß ...** it was obvious from the way he hesitated that ...; ~ **werden** to become obvious. **2** *adv* *(vermutlich)* apparently. **er hat** ~ **den Zug verpaßt** he must have missed the train; **da haben Sie** ~ **geirrt** you seem to have made a mistake.

offenbaren* 1 *vt* to reveal. **2** *vr* to reveal itself/oneself. **sich als etw** ~ to show oneself to be sth; **sich jdm** ~ to reveal oneself to sb.

Offenbarung *f* revelation.

Offenbarungs|eid *m (Jur)* oath of disclosure, sworn statement in bankruptcy cases. **den** ~ **leisten** *(lit)* to swear an oath of disclosure.

offen-: ~**bleiben** *vi sep irreg aux sein* to remain open; **alle** ~**gebliebenen Probleme** all unsolved problems; ~**halten** *vt sep irreg* to keep open.

Offenheit *f* openness, frankness.

offen-: ~**herzig** *adj* open, frank; *(hum col)* Kleid revealing; **O**~**herzigkeit** *f* openness, frankness; ~**kundig** *adj* obvious; *Beweise* clear; ~**lassen** *vt sep irreg* to leave open; ~**sichtlich** *adj* obvious; *Irrtum, Lüge auch* blatant.

offensiv *adj* offensive.

Offensive *f* offensive. **in die** ~ **gehen** to take the offensive.

offenstehen *vi sep irreg* (a) *(Tür, Fenster)* to be open. (b) *(Comm: Rechnung, Betrag)* to be outstanding. (c) **jdm** ~ *(fig: zugänglich sein)* to be open to sb; **die (ganze) Welt steht ihm offen** he has the (whole) world at his feet; **es steht ihr offen, sich uns anzuschließen** she's free to join us.

öffentlich *adj* public. **etw** ~ **bekanntmachen** to make sth public; **eine Persönlichkeit des** ~**en Lebens** a person in public life; **jdn** ~ **beschul-**

digen to accuse sb publicly; **die ~e Meinung/ Moral** public opinion/morality; **die ~e Ordnung** law and order; **~es Recht** *(Jur)* public law; **Anstalt des ~en Rechts** public institution; **~e Schule** state school, public school *(US)*; **die ~e Hand** (central/local) government; **Ausgaben der ~en Hand** public spending.

Öffentlichkeit *f (Allgemeinheit)* the (general) public. **die ~ scheuen** to shun publicity; **in aller ~** in public; **unter Ausschluß der ~** in private; *(Jur)* in camera; **als er das erstemal vor die ~ trat** when he made his first public appearance; **etw vor die ~ bringen** to bring sth before the public; **an die ~ gelangen** to become known; **die ~ einer Versammlung herstellen** to make a meeting public.

Öffentlichkeits|arbeit *f* public relations work.

öffentlich-rechtlich *adj attr* (under) public law.

Offerte *f* **-n** *(Comm)* offer; *(für Auftrag)* tender.

offiziell *adj* official. **wie von ~er Seite verlautet** according to official sources.

Offizier *m* **-e** officer.

Offiziers-: **~anwärter** *m* officer cadet; **~kasino** *nt* officers' mess; **~korps** *nt* officer corps; **~messe** *f* officers' mess.

öffnen 1 *vti* to open. **jdm den Blick für etw ~** to open sb's eyes to sth; **es hat geklingelt, könnten Sie mal ~?** that was the doorbell, would you answer it? **2** *vr (Tür, Blume, Augen)* to open; *(weiter werden)* to open out. **das Tal öffnet sich nach Süden** the valley opens to the south.

Öffner *m* **-** opener.

Öffnung *f* opening. **die ~ nach links** *(Pol)* the swing to the left.

Öffnungszeiten *pl* opening hours *pl*; *(von Geschäft)* hours of business *pl*.

Offsetdruck ['ɔfset-] *m* offset (printing).

oft *adv comp* **ᵎer,** *superl* **am ᵎesten** *(häufig)* often, frequently. **schon so ~, ~ genug** often enough; **wie ~ fährt der Bus?** how often does the bus go?; **wie ~ warst du schon in Deutschland?** how many times have you been to Germany?; **des ~eren** quite frequently; **je ~er ... the more often ...**

öfter(s) *adv* (every) now and then. **~ mal was Neues** *(col)* variety is the spice of life *(prov)*.

oftmals *adv (geh)* often, oft *(poet)*.

oh *interj* oh.

OHG = **offene Handelsgesellschaft.**

ohne 1 *prep* +*acc* **(a)** without. **~ Auto** without a car; **~ (die) Vororte hat die Stadt 100.000 Einwohner** the city has 100,000 inhabitants not counting the suburbs; **~ mich!** count me out!; **die Sache ist (gar) nicht (so) ~** *(col) (interessant)* it's not bad; *(schwierig)* it's not that easy *(col)*.

    (b) **ich hätte das ~ weiteres getan** I'd have done it without a second thought; **ja, das kann man ~ weiteres sagen** yes, that's true enough; **ich würde ~ weiteres sagen, daß ...** I would not hesitate to say that ...; **das Darlehen ist ~ weiteres bewilligt worden** the loan was granted without any problem; **ihm können Sie ~ weiteres vertrauen** you can trust him implicitly; **das läßt sich ~ weiteres arrangieren** that can easily be arranged; **das kann man nicht ~ weiteres voraussetzen** you can't just assume that automatically.

    2 *conj* **~ zu zögern** without hesitating; **~ daß ich ihn darum gebeten hätte** without my or me asking him.

ohne-: **~dies** *adv siehe* **~hin;** **~einander** *adv* without each other; **~gleichen** *adj inv* unparalleled; **ein Erfolg ~gleichen** an unparalleled success; **diese Frechheit ist ~gleichen!** I've never known such a cheek!; **~hin** *adv* anyway; **wir sind ~hin zu viel Leute** there are too many of us as it is; **es ist ~hin schon spät** it's late enough already.

Ohnmacht *f* **-en** *(Med)* faint; *(Machtlosigkeit)* helplessness. **in ~ fallen** to faint.

ohmächtig *adj (bewußtlos)* unconscious; *(machtlos)* powerless, helpless. **~ werden** to faint, to pass out; **~e Wut, ~er Zorn** helpless rage; **einer Sache** *(dat)* **~ gegenüberstehen** to be helpless in the face of sth; **~ zusehen müssen** to look on helplessly.

Ohnmachts|anfall *m (lit, fig)* fainting fit. **als ich das hörte, habe ich fast einen ~ bekommen** *(col)* when I heard that I nearly passed out.

oho *interj* oho, hello.

Ohr *nt* **-en** ear. **seine ~en sind nicht mehr so gut** his hearing isn't too good any more; **auf einem ~ taub sein** to be deaf in one ear; **auf dem ~ bin ich taub** *(fig)* nothing doing *(col)*; **bei jdm ein offenes ~ finden** to find sb a sympathetic listener; **die ~en anlegen** *(Hund)* to put its ears back; *(fig col)* to brace oneself; **mach** *or* **sperr die ~en auf!** *(col)* clean your ears out *(col)*; **jdm die ~en voll jammern** *(col)* to keep moaning at sb; **ganz ~ sein** *(hum)* to be all ears; **sich aufs ~ legen** *or* **hauen** *(col)* to kip down *(col)*; **sitzt er auf seinen ~en?** *(col)* is he deaf or something?; **jdm die ~en langziehen** *(col)* to tweak sb's ear(s); **jdm etw um die ~en hauen** *(col)* to hit sb over the head with sth; **schreib es dir hinter die ~en** *(col)* will you (finally) get that into your (thick) head *(col)*; **noch nicht trocken hinter den ~en sein** to be still wet behind the ears; **die Melodie geht ins ~** the tune is very catchy; **du hast wohl Watte in den ~en!** *(col)* are you deaf or something?; **ich habe seine Worte noch deutlich im ~** I can still hear his words clearly; **jdm in den ~en liegen** to keep on at sb *(col)*; **jdm übers ~ hauen** to pull a fast one on sb *(col)*; **bis über die** *or* **beide ~en verliebt sein** to be head over heels in love; **viel um die ~en haben** *(col)* to have a lot on (one's plate) *(col)*; **es ist mir zu ~en gekommen** it has come to my ears *(form)*; **das geht zum einen ~ hinein und zum anderen wieder hinaus** *(col)* it goes in one ear and out the other *(col)*; **halt die ~en steif!** take care.

Ohr *nt* **-e** eye.

Ohren-: **~arzt** *m* ear specialist; **o~betäubend** *adj (fig)* earsplitting; **~sausen** *nt (Med)* buzzing in one's ears; **~schmalz** *nt* earwax; **~schmaus** *m* **das Konzert war ein richtiger ~schmaus** the concert was a feast for the ears; **~schmerzen** *pl* earache; **~schützer** *pl* earmuffs *pl*; **~sessel** *m* wing chair.

Ohrfeige *f* **-n** slap (on *or* around the face); *(als Strafe)* box on the ears. **jdm eine ~ geben** *or* **verabreichen** to slap sb's face; **eine ~ bekommen** to get a slap around the face.

ohrfeigen *vt insep* **jdn ~** to box sb's ears; **ich könnte mich selbst ~, daß ich das gemacht habe** I could kick myself for doing it.

Ohr-: **~läppchen** *nt* (ear) lobe; **~muschel** *f* (outer) ear; **~ring** *m* earring; **~wurm** *m* earwig; **die Platte ist ein richtiger ~wurm** *(col)* that's a really catchy record *(col)*.

oje, ojemine *interj* oh dear.

Okkultismus *m* occultism.

Okkupation *f* occupation.

okkupieren* *vt* to occupy.

Öko- *in cpds* eco; **~bauer** *m (col)* ecologically-minded farmer.

Ökologe *m*, **Ökologin** *f* ecologist.

Ökologie *f* ecology.

ökologisch *adj* ecological, environmental.

Ökonomie *f* economy; *(als Wissenschaft)* economics *sing.* **politische ~ studieren** to study political economy.

ökonomisch *adj* economic; *(sparsam)* economical.

Ökosystem *nt* ecosystem.

Oktanzahl *f* octane rating. **Benzin mit einer hohen ~** high octane petrol.

Oktave [ɔk'taːvə] f -n octave.
Oktett nt -e octet.
Oktober m - October; siehe **März**.
ökumenisch adj ecumenical.
Öl nt -e oil. **auf** ~ **stoßen** to strike oil; ~ **fördern** to extract oil; **in** ~ **malen** to paint in oils; ~ **ins Feuer gießen** (prov) to add fuel to the fire (prov).
Öl-: ~**baum** m olive tree; ~**bild** nt oil painting, oil; ~**bohrung** f oil drilling.
Oldtimer ['ɔuldtaɪmɐ] m - (Auto) veteran car.
ölen vt to oil. **wie geölt** (col) like clockwork (col); **wie ein geölter Blitz** (col) like greased lightning (col).
Öl-: ~**farbe** f oil-based paint; (Art) oil (paint); **mit** ~**farben malen** to paint in oils; ~**feld** nt oil field; ~**film** m film of oil; ~**gemälde** nt oil painting; ~**götze** m (col) **wie ein** ~**götze** like a tailor's dummy (col); ~**heizung** f oil-fired central heating.
ölig adj oily; (fig auch) greasy.
Oligarchie f oligarchy.
oliv adj pred olive(-green).
Olive [o'liːvə] f -n olive.
Oliven-: ~**baum** m olive tree; ~**öl** nt olive oil.
olivgrün adj olive-green.
Öl-: ~ **jacke** f oilskin jacket; ~**kännchen** nt, ~**kanne** f oil can.
oll adj (N Ger col) old. **das sind** ~**e Kamellen** (col) that's old hat (col).
Öl-: ~**malerei** f oil painting; ~**meßstab** m (Aut) dip stick; ~**ofen** m oil heater; ~**plattform** f oil-rig; **öl**~**reich** adj oil-rich; ~**sardine** f sardine; **wie die** ~**sardinen** (col) crammed in like sardines (col); ~**scheich** m oil sheik; ~**spur** f patch of oil; ~**stand** m oil level; ~**standsanzeiger** m oil pressure gauge; ~**teppich** m oil slick.
Ölung f oiling. **die Letzte** ~ (Eccl) extreme unction.
Öl-: ~**vorkommen** nt oil deposit; ~**wanne** f (Aut) sump (Brit), oil pan (US); ~**wechsel** m oil change; **den** ~**wechsel machen** to change the oil.
Olymp m (Berg) Mount Olympus.
Olympiade f (Olympische Spiele) Olympic Games pl, Olympics pl.
Olympia-: ~**medaille** f Olympic medal; ~**sieger** m Olympic gold-medallist (Brit) or gold-medalist (US); ~**stadion** nt Olympic stadium.
olympisch adj (die Olympiade betreffend) Olympic. **die O**~**en Spiele** the Olympic Games.
Öl-: ~**zeug** nt oilskins pl; ~**zweig** m (lit, fig) olive-branch.
Oma f -s (col) granny (col), grandma (col).
Omelett [ɔm(ə)'lɛt] nt -e or -s omelette (Brit), omelet (US).
Omen nt - omen.
ominös adj (geh) ominous, sinister.
Omnibus m bus.
Omnibuslinie f bus route.
Onanie f masturbation, onanism.
onanieren* vi to masturbate.
ondulieren* vtr to crimp.
Onkel m - uncle.
Onyx m -e onyx.
OP [oː'peː] m -s = **Operationssaal**.
Opa m -s (col) grandpa (col), grandad (col).
Opal m -e opal.
Oper f -n opera; (Ensemble) Opera; (Opernhaus) Opera, Opera House. **in die** ~ **gehen** to go to the opera; **zur** ~ **gehen** to become an opera singer.
Operation f operation.
Operations-: ~**saal** m operating theatre (Brit) or room (US); ~**schwester** f theatre sister (Brit), operating room nurse (US).
operativ adj (Med) surgical. **eine Geschwulst** ~ **entfernen** to remove a growth by surgery.
Operette f operetta.
operieren* 1 vt Patienten, Krebs, Magen to operate on. **jdn am Magen** ~ to operate on sb's

stomach. 2 vi to operate (an jdm/etw on sb/sth). **sich** ~ **lassen** to have an operation.
Opern-: ~**arie** f (operatic) aria; ~**ball** m opera ball; ~**glas** nt opera glasses pl; ~**haus** nt opera house; ~**sänger** m opera singer; ~**text** m libretto.
Opfer nt - (a) (~**gabe**) sacrifice (auch fig). **für ihre Kinder scheut sie keine** ~ she sacrifices everything for her children; **wir müssen alle** ~ **bringen** we must all make sacrifices. **(b)** (geschädigte Person) victim. **jdm/einer Sache zum** ~ **fallen** to be (the) victim of sb/sth; **ein** ~ **einer Sache** (gen) **werden** to be a victim of sth, to fall victim to sth; **das Erdbeben forderte viele** ~ the earthquake claimed many victims.
Opfer-: **o**~**bereit** adj willing to make sacrifices; ~**bereitschaft** f readiness to make sacrifices; ~**gabe** f (liter) sacrificial offering; (Eccl) offering; ~**lamm** nt (lit, fig) sacrificial lamb; ~**mut** m self-sacrifice.
opfern 1 vt (lit, fig) to sacrifice; Feldfrüchte etc to offer (up). **sein Leben** ~ to sacrifice one's life. 2 vr (a) (sein Leben hingeben) to sacrifice one's life. **(b)** (col: sich bereit erklären) to be a martyr (col). **wer opfert sich, die Reste aufzuessen?** who's going to volunteer to eat up the remains?
Opfer-: ~**stätte** f sacrificial altar; ~**stock** m offertory box; ~**tier** nt sacrificial animal.
Opferung f (das Opfern) sacrifice; (Eccl) offertory.
Opiat nt opiate.
Opium nt no pl opium.
opponieren* vi to oppose (gegen jdn/etw sb/sth), to offer opposition (gegen to).
opportun adj (geh) opportune.
Opportunismus m opportunism.
Opportunist(in f) m opportunist.
opportunistisch adj opportunistic, opportunist. ~ **handeln** to act in an opportunist fashion.
Opposition f opposition. **etw aus lauter** or **reiner** ~ **tun** to do sth out of sheer contrariness.
oppositionell adj Gruppen, Kräfte opposition.
Oppositionsführer m leader of the opposition.
optieren* vi (Pol form) ~ **für** to opt for.
Optik f (a) (Phys) optics. **(b)** (Phot) lens system. **du hast wohl einen Knick in der** ~**!** (col) can't you see straight? (col); **das ist eine Frage der** ~ (fig) it depends on your point of view; **das ist nur hier wegen der** ~ (fig) it's just here for visual effect.
Optiker(in f) m - optician.
optimal adj optimal, optimum attr.
Optimismus m optimism.
Optimist(in f) m (wk) optimist.
optimistisch adj optimistic.
Option [ɔp'tsioːn] f option.
optisch adj visual; Gesetze, Instrumente optical. ~**e Täuschung** optical illusion.
Orakel nt - oracle.
orakeln* vi (col) (a) (rätseln) **wir haben lange orakelt, was der Satz bedeuten sollte** we spent a long time trying to decipher the sentence. **(b)** (weissagen) to prognosticate (hum).
oral adj oral.
Orange[1] [o'rãːʒə] f -n (Frucht) orange.
Orange[2] [o'rãːʒə] nt -, - or (col) -s orange.
orange(n) [o'rãːʒə(n)] adj orange.
Orangeat [orã'ʒaːt] nt candied (orange) peel.
orange- [o'rãːʒə-]: ~**farben**, ~**farbig** adj orange.
Orangen- [o'rãːʒən-]: ~**marmelade** f orange marmalade; ~**saft** m orange juice; ~**schale** f orange peel.
Orang-Utan m -s orang-utan, orang-outang.
Oratorium nt (a) (Mus) oratorio. **(b)** (Betraum) oratory.
Orchester [ɔr'kɛstɐ] nt - orchestra.
Orchidee f -n [-'deːən] orchid.
Orden m - (a) (Ehrenzeichen) decoration; (Mil

auch) medal. ~ **tragen** to wear one's decorations; **jdm einen ~ (für etw) verleihen** to decorate sb (for sth). **(b)** *(Gemeinschaft)* (holy) order. **in einem ~ eintreten, einem ~ beitreten** to become a monk/nun.

Ordens-: ~bruder *m (Eccl)* monk; **~gemeinschaft** *f* religious order; **~schwester** *f* nursing sister *or* nun.

ordentlich *adj* **(a)** *Mensch, Zimmer* tidy, neat. **stell den Stuhl wieder ~ hin** put the chair back neatly; **~ arbeiten** to be a thorough and precise worker. **(b)** *(ordnungsgemäß)* **~es Gericht** law court; **~es Mitglied** full member; **~er Professor** (full) professor. **(c)** *(anständig)* respectable. **sich ~ benehmen** to behave properly. **(d)** *(col: tüchtig, richtig)* ~ **essen/trinken** to eat/drink (really) well; **ein ~es Frühstück** a proper breakfast; **wir haben ~ gearbeitet** we really got down to it; **jetzt hab' ich aber ~ Appetit** I'm really hungry now; **eine ~e Tracht Prügel** a proper hiding. **(e)** *(annehmbar, ganz gut) Preis, Leistung* reasonable.

Order *f* -s *or* -n **(a)** *(Comm: Auftrag)* order. **(b)** *(Anweisung)* order. **sich an eine ~ halten** to keep to one's orders.

ordinär *adj* **(a)** *(gemein, unfein)* vulgar, common. **(b)** *(alltäglich)* ordinary.

Ordinarius *m, pl* **Ordinarien** [-iən] *(Univ)* professor *(für of)*.

ordnen 1 *vt Gedanken, Material* to order, to organize; *Finanzen, Privatleben* to put in order, to straighten out; *siehe* **geordnet. 2** *vr* to get into order. **die Menge ordnete sich zu einem Festzug** the crowd formed itself into a procession.

Ordner *m* - **(a)** *(bei Demonstration auch)* steward; *(bei Demonstration auch)* marshal. **(b)** *(Akten~)* file.

Ordnung *f* **(a)** *(geordneter Zustand)* order. ~ **halten** to keep things tidy; ~ **schaffen, für ~ sorgen** to put things in order, to tidy things up; **Sie müssen für mehr ~ in Ihrer Klasse sorgen** you'll have to keep your class in better order; **etw in ~ halten** to keep sth tidy; **etw in ~ bringen** *(reparieren)* to fix sth; *(herrichten)* to put sth in order; *(bereinigen)* to sort sth out; **ich finde es (ganz) in ~, daß ...** I find it quite right that ...; **(das ist) in ~!** *(col)* (that's) OK *(col)* or all right!; **geht in ~** *(col)* that's all right *or* OK *(col)*; **Ihre Bestellung geht in ~** we'll put your order through; **der ist in ~** *(col)* he's OK *or* all right *(col)*; **mit ihm/der Maschine ist etwas nicht in ~** there's something the matter with him/the machine; **es ist alles in bester ~** things couldn't be better; **jdn zur ~ rufen** to call sb to order; **bei ihm muß alles seine ~ haben** *(räumlich)* he has to have everything in its proper place; *(zeitlich)* he does everything according to a fixed schedule; **das Kind braucht seine ~** the child needs a routine. **(b)** *(Vorschrift)* rules *pl*. **sich an eine ~ halten** to keep to the rules; **ich frage nur der ~ halber** it's only a routine question. **(c)** *(Rang, Biol)* order. **Straße erster ~** first-class road; **das war ein Fauxpas erster ~** *(col)* that was a faux-pas of the first order.

Ordnungs-: ~amt *nt ≈* town clerk's office; **~fanatiker** *m* fanatic for order; **o~gemäß** *adj* in accordance with the rules, proper; **o~halber** *adv* as a matter of form; **~hüter** *m (hum)* custodian of the law *(hum)*; **~liebe** *f* love of order; **o~liebend** *adj* tidy-minded, orderly; **~ruf** *m* call to order; **der Präsident mußte mehrere ~rufe erteilen** the chairman had to call the meeting to order several times; **~sinn** *m* sense of order; **~strafe** *f* fine; **jdn mit einer ~strafe belegen** to fine sb; **o~widrig** *adj* irregular; *Parken, Verhalten (im Straßenverkehr)* illegal; **o~widrig handeln** to infringe rules *or* regulations; **~widrigkeit** *f* infringement *(of law or rule)*.

Organ *nt* -s, -e **(a)** *(Med, Biol, fig)* organ. **(b)** *(col: Stimme)* voice.

Organisation *f* organization.

Organisationstalent *nt* talent for organization. **er ist ein ~** he has a talent for organization.

Organisator *m* organizer.

organisatorisch *adj* organizational. **eine ~e Höchstleistung** a masterpiece of organization.

organisch *adj Chemie, Verbindung, Salz* organic; *Erkrankung, Leiden* physical. **sich ~ einfügen** to merge, to blend *(in +acc* with, into).

organisieren* 1 *vti* **(a)** to organize. **er kann ausgezeichnet ~** he's excellent at organizing. **(b)** *(col: stehlen)* to lift *(col)*, to get hold of. **2** *vr* to get organized; *(gewerkschaftlich auch)* to organize.

Organismus *m* organism.

Organist(in *f)* *m (wk)* organist.

Organ-: ~spender *m* donor *(of an organ)*; **~spenderausweis** *m* donor's card; **~verpflanzung** *f* transplant(ation) *(of organs)*.

Orgasmus *m* orgasm.

Orgel *f* -n organ.

Orgel- *in cpds* organ; **~pfeife** *f* organ pipe; **die Kinder standen da wie die ~pfeifen** *(hum)* the children were standing in order of height.

Orgie [-iə] *f* orgy. **~n feiern** *(lit)* to have orgies/an orgy; *(fig)* to go wild.

Orient ['oːriɛnt, oˈriɛnt] *m no pl (liter)* Orient. **der Vordere ~** the Near East.

Orientale [oriɛnˈtaːlə] *m (wk)* **-n, -n, Orientalin** *f* Oriental. **er ist ~** he is an Oriental.

orientalisch [oriɛnˈtaːlɪʃ] *adj* oriental.

orientieren* [oriɛnˈtiːrən] **1** *vti* **(a)** *(unterrichten)* to put sb in the picture *(über +acc* about). **gut/falsch orientiert** well/wrongly informed. **(b)** *(ausrichten) (lit, fig)* to orientate *(nach, auf* to, towards). **links orientiert sein** to tend to the left; **links orientierte Gruppen** left-wing groups. **2** *vr* **(a)** *(sich unterrichten)* to inform oneself *(über +acc* about *or* on). **(b)** *(sich zurechtfinden)* to orientate oneself *(an +dat, nach* by), to get one's bearings. **in einer fremden Stadt kann ich mich gar nicht ~** I just can't find my way around in a strange city. **(c)** *(sich ausrichten)* to adapt *or* orientate (oneself) *(an +dat* to).

Orientierung [oriɛnˈtiːrʊŋ] *f* orientation; *(Unterrichtung)* information. **die ~ verlieren** to lose one's bearings; **zu Ihrer ~** for your information.

Orientierungs-: ~punkt *m* point of reference; **~sinn** *m* sense of direction.

Original *nt* -e **(a)** original. **(b)** *(Mensch)* character.

original *adj* original. ~ **Meißener Porzellan** genuine Meissen porcelain.

Original-: ~ausgabe *f* first edition; **~fassung** *f* original (version); **o~getreu** *adj* true to the original.

Originalität *f no pl* **(a)** *(Echtheit)* authenticity, genuineness. **(b)** *(Urtümlichkeit)* originality.

originell *adj (selbständig) Idee, Argumentation* original; *(neu)* novel; *(geistreich)* witty. **das finde ich ~** *(von ihm)* that's pretty original/witty.

Orkan *m* -e hurricane.

Orkan-: ~artig *adj Wind* gale-force; *Beifall* thunderous; **~stärke** *f* hurricane force.

Ornament *nt* decoration, ornament.

Ornat *m* -e regalia *pl*; *(Eccl)* vestments *pl*; *(Jur)* official robes *pl.* **in vollem ~** *(col)* dressed up to the nines *(col)*.

Ornithologe *m (wk)*, **Ornithologin** *f (form)* ornithologist.

Ort[1] *m* -e place. ~ **der Handlung** *(Theat)* scene of the action; **an den ~ der Tat** *or* **des Verbrechens zurückkehren** to return to the scene of the crime; **der Stuhl steht wieder an seinem** ~ the chair is back in (its) place again; **am angegebenen** ~ in the place quoted, loc cit *abbr*; **an ~ und Stelle** on the spot, there and then; **an ~**

und Stelle ankommen to arrive (at one's destination); **das ist höheren ~s entschieden worden** (hum, form) the decision came from above; **in einem kleinen ~ in Cornwall** in a little spot in Cornwall; **~e über 100.000 Einwohner** places with over 100,000 inhabitants; **am ~** in the place; **das beste Hotel am ~** the best hotel in town; **wir haben keinen Arzt am ~** we have no resident doctor; **am ~ wohnen** to live locally; **mitten im ~** in the centre (of the place/town); **der nächste ~** the next village/town etc; **von ~ zu ~** from place to place.

Ort² m **=er** (Min) coal face, (working) face. **vor ~** at the (coal) face; (fig) on the spot.

Örtchen nt (col) loo (Brit col), john (US col).

orten vt to locate, to get a fix on.

orthodox adj (lit,fig) orthodox.

Orthographie f orthography.

orthographisch adj orthographic(al). **ein ~er Fehler** a spelling mistake.

Orthopäde m (wk) **-n, -n, Orthopädin** f orthopaedic (Brit) or orthopedic (US) specialist.

orthopädisch adj orthopaedic (Brit), orthopedic (US).

örtlich adj local. **das ist ~ verschieden** it varies from place to place; **jdn/etw ~ betäuben** to give sb/sth a local anaesthetic.

Örtlichkeit f locality. **sich mit den ~en vertraut machen** to get to know the place; **die ~en** (euph) the cloakroom (Brit euph), the comfort station (US euph).

Orts-: ~angabe f (bei Anschriften) (name of the) town; **ohne ~angabe** (von Buch) no place of publication indicated; **o~ansässig** adj local; **die ~ansässigen** the local residents.

Ortschaft f **-en** village; town. **geschlossene ~** built-up area.

Orts-: o~fremd adj non-local; **ich bin hier o~fremd** I'm a stranger here; **~gespräch** nt (Telec) local call; **~gruppe** f local branch or group; **~kenntnis** f local knowledge; **(gute) ~kenntnisse haben** to know one's way around (well); **~krankenkasse** f **Allgemeine ~krankenkasse** compulsory medical insurance scheme; **o~kundig** adj **ein ~kundiger** somebody who knows the place; **~name** m place name; **~netz** nt (Telec) local (telephone) exchange area; (Elec) local grid; **~netzkennzahl** f (Telec form) dialling (Brit) or area code; **~schild** nt place name sign; **~sinn** m sense of direction; **~tarif** m (Telec) charge for local phone-calls; **o~üblich** adj local; **das ist hier o~üblich** it's a local custom here; **~verkehr** m local traffic; **Gebühren im ~verkehr** (Telec) charges for local (phone) calls; **~zeit** f local time; **~zuschlag** m (local) weighting allowance.

Öse f **-n** loop; (an Kleidung) eye.

Ost m no pl (liter) East.

Ost- in cpds East; (geographisch auch) Eastern, the East of ...; **~afrika** nt East Africa; **~asien** nt Eastern Asia; **~-Berlin** nt East Berlin; **~ber-**

liner adj attr East Berlin; **~berliner** m East Berliner; **~block** Eastern bloc; **~blockland** nt, **~blockstaat** m Eastern bloc country; **o~deutsch** adj East German; **~deutschland** nt (Pol) East Germany; (Geog) Eastern Germany.

Osten m no pl (auch Pol) East. **der Ferne ~** the Far East; **der Nahe ~** the Middle East, the Near East; **im ~** in the East; **in den ~** to the East; **von ~** from the East.

ostentativ adj (geh) pointed.

Oster-: ~ei nt Easter egg; **~fest** nt Easter; **~glocke** f daffodil; **~hase** m Easter bunny.

österlich adj Easter.

Oster-: ~marsch m Easter demonstration; **~montag** m Easter Monday.

Ostern nt - Easter. **frohe** or **fröhliche ~!** Happy Easter!; **zu ~** at Easter.

Österreich nt Austria.

Österreicher(in f) m - Austrian.

österreichisch adj Austrian. **das Ö~e** (Ling) Austrian.

Ostersonntag m Easter Sunday.

Ost-: ~europa nt East(ern) Europe; **o~europäisch** adj East European; **~friese** m East Friesian; **~geld** nt (col) East German money; **~küste** f East coast.

östlich **1** adj Richtung, Winde easterly; Gebiete eastern. **30° ~er Länge** 30° (longitude) east. **2** adv **~ von Hamburg/des Rheins** (to the) east of Hamburg/the Rhine. **3** prep +gen (to the) east of.

Ost-: ~mark f (col) East German Mark; **~politik** f Ostpolitik, foreign policy regarding the Eastern bloc.

Östrogen [œstro'ge:n] nt **-e** oestrogen (Brit), estrogen (US).

Ostsee f die ~ the Baltic (Sea).

Ost-: ~staaten pl (in USA) the Eastern or East coast states; **o~wärts** adv eastwards; **~-West-Verhandlungen** pl East-West negotiations; **~wind** m east or easterly wind.

Otter¹ m - otter.

Otter² f **-n** viper, adder.

Ottomotor m internal combustion engine, otto engine.

Ouvertüre [uver'ty:rə] f **-n** overture.

oval [o'va:l] adj oval.

Oval [o'va:l] nt **-e** oval.

Ovation [ova'tsio:n] f ovation. **jdm eine ~** or **~en darbringen** to give sb an ovation.

Overall ['ouvərɔ:] m **-s** (Schutzanzug) overalls pl.

Oxid, Oxyd nt **-e** oxide.

Oxidation, Oxydation f oxidation.

oxidieren*, oxydieren* vti aux sein or haben to oxidize.

Ozean m **-e** ocean.

Ozean-: ~dampfer m ocean steamer; **~riese** m (col) ocean liner.

ozeanisch adj Flora oceanic; Sprachen Oceanic.

Ozelot m **-e** ocelot.

Ozon m or (col) nt m no pl ozone.

Ozonschicht f ozone layer.

P

P p [peː] *nt* -, - P, p.
Paar *nt* -e pair; *(Mann und Frau auch)* couple. **zwei** ~ **Socken** two pairs of socks; **ein** ~ **Würstchen** a couple of *or* two sausages.
paar *adj inv* **ein** ~ a few; *(zwei oder drei auch)* a couple of; **alle** ~ **Minuten/Wochen** every few minutes/weeks.
paaren 1 *vt Tiere* to mate, to pair; *(Sport)* to match. **2** *vr (Tiere)* to mate; *(fig)* to be coupled.
Paar-: ~**hufer** *pl (Zool)* cloven-hoofed animals *pl*; ~**lauf** *m*, ~**laufen** *nt* pair-skating, pairs *pl*.
paarmal *adv* **ein** ~ a few times; *(zwei- oder dreimal auch)* a couple of times.
Paarung *f* **(a)** *(Sport,fig liter)* combination; *(Sport: Begegnung)* draw, match. **(b)** *(Kopulation)* mating; *(Kreuzung)* crossing.
Paarungszeit *f* mating season.
paarweise *adv* in pairs, in twos.
Pacht *f* -en lease; *(Entgelt)* rent. **etw in** ~ **geben** to lease sth (out); **etw in** ~ **haben** to have sth on lease.
Pachtbrief *m* lease.
pachten *vt* to lease. **du hast das Sofa doch nicht für dich gepachtet** *(col)* don't hog the sofa *(col)*.
Pächter(in *f)* *m* leaseholder.
Pacht-: ~**grundstück** *nt* leasehold property; ~**gut** *nt*, ~**hof** *m* smallholding; ~**vertrag** *m* lease; ~**zins** *m* rent.
Pack¹ *m (von Büchern, Wäsche)* pile; *(zusammengeschnürt)* bundle.
Pack² *nt no pl (pej)* rabble *pl (pej)*.
Päckchen *nt* package; *(Post)* small parcel; *(Packung)* packet, pack. **ein** ~ **Zigaretten** a packet *or* pack *(esp US)* of cigarettes; **jeder hat sein** ~ **zu tragen** *(fig col)* we all have our cross to bear.
Pack|eis *nt* pack ice.
packen 1 *vti* **(a)** *Koffer* to pack; *(verstauen)* to pack (away). **etw in Watte** ~ wrap sth (up) in cotton wool; **jdn ins Bett** ~ *(col)* to tuck sb up (in bed). **(b)** *(fassen)* to grab (hold of); *(Gefühle)* to grip. **jdn am** *or* **beim Kragen** ~ *(col)* to grab sb by the collar; **das Theaterstück hat mich gepackt** I was really gripped by the play. **(c)** *(col: schaffen)* to manage. **hast du die Prüfung gepackt?** did you (manage to) get through the exam? **(d)** *(col: aufhören)* **ich pack's jetzt!** I'm going to pack it in *(col)*. **(e)** *(col: gehen)* ~ **wir's!** let's go. **(f)** *(col: kapieren)* **er packt es nie** he'll never get it *(col)*. **2** *vr (col)* to clear off.
Packen *m* - pile; *(Bündel)* bundle.
Packer(in *f)* *m* - packer.
Pack-: ~**esel** *m (fig)* packhorse; ~**papier** *nt* wrapping paper.
Packung *f* **(a)** *(Schachtel)* packet, pack. **eine** ~ **Zigaretten** a packet *or* pack *(esp US)* of cigarettes. **(b)** *(Med)* pack; *(Kosmetik)* beauty pack. **(c)** *(col: Niederlage)* hammering *(col)*.
Packzettel *m* packing slip.
Pädagoge *m*, **Pädagogin** *f* educationalist.
Pädagogik *f* educational theory.
pädagogisch *adj* educational. **P~e Hochschule** college of education; **seine ~en Fähigkeiten** his teaching ability.
Paddel *nt* - paddle.
Paddelboot *nt* canoe.
paffen 1 *vi (col: rauchen)* to puff away; *(nicht*

inhalieren) to puff. **2** *vt* to puff (away) at.
Page ['paːʒə] *m (wk)* -n, -n *(Hotel~)* page(boy), bellhop *(US)*.
Pagen-: ~**frisur** *f*, ~**kopf** *m* page-boy (hairstyle).
Paket *nt* -e *(Post)* parcel; *(Packung)* packet; *(fig)* package.
Paket-: ~**adresse** *f* stick-on address label; ~**annahme/~ausgabe** *f* parcels office; ~**karte** *f* dispatch form; ~**schalter** *m* parcels counter.
Pakistan *nt* Pakistan.
Pakistaner(in *f)* *m* -, **Pakistani** *m* -(s) Pakistani.
Pakt *m* pact. **einem** ~ **beitreten** to enter into an agreement.
Palast *m*, *pl* **Paläste** *(lit, fig)* palace.
Palästina *nt* Palestine.
Palästinenser(in *f)* *m* - Palestinian.
Palaver [pa'laːvɐ] *nt* - *(col)* unending discussion.
palavern* [pa'laːvən] *vi (col)* to ramble on.
Palette *f* **(a)** *(Malerei)* palette; *(fig)* range. **(b)** *(Stapelplatte)* pallet.
Palisade *f* palisade.
Palisander(holz *nt)* *m* - jacaranda.
Palme *f* -n palm. **jdn auf die** ~ **bringen** *(col)* to make sb see red *(col)*.
Palm-: ~**sonntag** *m* Palm Sunday; ~**wedel** *m* palm leaf.
Pampe *f no pl (col)* mush *(col)*.
Pampelmuse *f* -n grapefruit.
Pamphlet *nt* -e lampoon.
pampig *adj (col)* **(a)** *(breiig)* gooey *(col)*. **(b)** *(frech)* stroppy *(col)*.
pan- *pref* pan-; ~**amerikanisch** pan-American.
Panama *nt* Panama.
Panamakanal *m* Panama Canal.
Paneel *nt* -e *(einzeln)* panel; *(Täfelung)* panelling *(Brit)*, paneling *(US)*, wainscoting.
Panflöte *f* panpipes *pl*, Pan's pipes *pl*.
panieren* *vt* to bread, to coat with breadcrumbs.
Paniermehl *nt* breadcrumbs *pl*.
Panik *f* -en panic. **in** ~ **ausbrechen** to panic; **von** ~ **ergriffen** panic-stricken; **nur keine** ~! don't panic!
Panikmache *f (col)* panicmongering.
panisch *adj no pred* panic-stricken. **er hatte eine ~e Angst zu ertrinken** he was terrified of drowning; **sich** ~ **fürchten (vor)** to be petrified (of); **sie rannten** ~ **durcheinander** they ran about in panic.
Panne *f* -n **(a)** *(Störung)* breakdown. **mein Auto hatte eine** ~ my car broke down. **(b)** *(fig col)* boob (Brit col), goof *(US col)*. **mit jdm/etw eine** ~ **erleben** to have (a bit of) trouble with sb/sth; **uns ist eine** ~ **passiert** we've boobed (Brit col) or goofed *(US col)*; **da ist eine** ~ **passiert mit dem Brief** something has gone wrong with the letter.
Pannen-: ~**dienst** *m*, ~**hilfe** *f* breakdown service *(Brit)*, emergency road service *(US)*.
Panorama *nt*, *pl* **Panoramen** panorama.
panschen 1 *vt* to adulterate; *(verdünnen)* to water down. **2** *vi (col)* to splash (about).
Pantoffel *m* -n slipper. **unterm** ~ **stehen** *(col)* to be henpecked.
Pantoffelheld *m (col)* henpecked husband.
Pantomime¹ *f* -n mime.
Pantomime² *m (wk)* -n, -n mime.

pantschen vti = **panschen**.

Panzer m - **(a)** (Mil) tank. **(b)** (Hist: Rüstung) armour (Brit), armor (US) no indef art, suit of armour (Brit) or armor (US). **(c)** (Panzerung) armour (Brit) or armor (US) plate. **(d)** (Zool) shell; (dicke Haut) armour (Brit), armor (US). **(e)** (fig) shield.

Panzer-: ~**abwehr** f anti-tank defence (Brit) or defense (US); (Truppe) anti-tank unit; ~**abwehrkanone** f anti-tank gun; ~**faust** f bazooka; ~**glas** nt bulletproof glass; ~**grenadier** m armoured (Brit) or armored (US) infantryman; ~**kampfwagen** m armoured (Brit) or armored (US) vehicle; ~**kette** f tank-track.

panzern 1 vt to armour-plate (Brit), to armorplate (US). **gepanzerte Fahrzeuge** armoured vehicles. **2** vr (fig) to arm oneself.

Panzer-: ~**schrank** m safe; ~**truppe** f tank division.

Panzerung f armour (Brit) or armor (US) plating; (fig) shield.

Panzerwagen m armoured (Brit) or armored (US) car.

Papa m -s (col) daddy (col), pa (US col).

Papagei m -en parrot. **er plappert alles wie ein** ~ **nach** he repeats everything parrot fashion.

Papi m -s (col) daddy (col).

Papier nt -e **(a)** no pl paper. **ein Blatt** ~ a sheet of paper; **das steht nur auf dem** ~ that's only in theory. **(b)** (Schriftstück) paper. ~**e** pl (identity) papers pl; (Urkunden) documents pl; **er hatte keine** ~**e bei sich** he had no means of identification with him; **seine** ~**e bekommen** (entlassen werden) to get one's cards. **(c)** (Fin, Wert~) security.

Papier-: ~**deutsch** nt officialese; ~**fabrik** f paper mill; ~**korb** m wastepaper basket; ~**kram** m (col) bumf (Brit col), official document; ~**krieg** m (col) **vor lauter** ~**krieg kommen wir nicht zur Forschung** there's so much paperwork we can't get on with our research; **erst nach einem langen** ~**krieg** after going through a lot of red tape; ~**taschentuch** nt tissue, paper handkerchief; ~**tiger** m (fig) paper tiger.

Pappdeckel m (thin) cardboard.

Pappe f -n (Pappdeckel) cardboard; (Dach~) roofing felt. **das ist nicht von** ~ (col) that is really something.

Pappel f -n poplar.

pappen (col) **1** vt to stick (an or auf +acc on). **2** vi (col) (klebrig sein) to be sticky; (Schnee) to pack.

Pappen-: ~**deckel** m (thin) cardboard; ~**heimer** pl: **ich kenne meine** ~**heimer** (col) I know you lot/that lot (inside out); ~**stiel** m (fig col): **5000 Mark sind kein** ~**stiel** 5000 marks isn't peanuts (col); **das ist keinen** ~**stiel wert** that's not worth a penny.

papperlapapp interj (col) (stuff and) nonsense.

pappig adj (col) sticky.

Papp-: ~**karton** m (Schachtel) cardboard box; (Material) cardboard; ~**maché** [-maʃeː] nt -s papier-mâché; ~**schnee** m wet snow.

Paprika m -(s) (no pl: Gewürz) paprika; (~schote) pepper.

Paprikaschote f pepper. **gefüllte** ~**n** stuffed peppers.

Papst m ⸚e pope; (fig) high priest.

päpstlich adj papal; (fig pej) pontifical. ~**er als der Papst sein** to be more Catholic than the Pope.

Parabel f -n **(a)** (Liter) parable. **(b)** (Math) parabola, parabolic curve.

Parabolspiegel m parabolic reflector.

Parade f (a) (Mil) review. **die** ~**abnehmen** to take the salute. **(b)** (Sport: Fechten, Boxen) parry; (Ballspiele) save; (Reiten) check. **jdm in die** ~ **fahren** (fig) to cut sb off short.

Parade-: ~**beispiel** nt prime example; ~**stück** nt (fig) showpiece; (Gegenstand auch) pièce de résistance.

Paradies nt -e (lit, fig) paradise. **das** ~ **auf Erden** heaven on earth.

paradiesisch adj (fig) heavenly. **hier ist es** ~ **schön** this is paradise; ~ **leere Strände** blissfully empty beaches.

Paradiesvogel m bird of paradise.

paradox adj paradoxical.

Paradox nt -e paradox.

paradoxerweise adv paradoxically.

Paraffin nt -e (Chem) (~öl) paraffin (Brit), kerosene (US); (~wachs) paraffin wax.

Paragraph m (Jur) section; (Abschnitt) paragraph.

Paragraphenreiter m (col) pedant.

parallel adj parallel. ~ **laufen** to run parallel; ~ **schalten** (Elec) to connect in parallel.

Parallele f -n parallel (line); (fig) parallel. **eine** ~ **zu etw ziehen** (fig) to draw a parallel to sth.

Parallelogramm nt -e parallelogram.

Parallelschaltung f parallel connection.

paranoid [parano'iːt] adj paranoid, paranoiac.

Paranuß f (Bot) Brazil nut.

Paraphierung f (Pol) initialling (Brit), initialing (US).

Paraphrase f paraphrase; (Mus) variation.

Parapsychologie f parapsychology.

Parasit m (wk) -en, -en (Biol, fig) parasite.

parasitär adj (Biol, fig) parasitic(al).

parat adj prepared; (Werkzeug etc) handy. **er hatte immer eine Ausrede** ~ he was always ready with an excuse.

Pärchen nt (courting) couple.

Parcours [par'kuːʁ] m -, - show-jumping course; (Sportart) show-jumping.

Pardon [par'dõː] m or nt no pl **(a)** (dated) pardon. **(b)** (col) ~! (Verzeihung) sorry; **kein** ~ **kennen** to be ruthless; **das Zeug räumst du auf, da gibt's kein** ~ you'll clear that stuff up and that's that! (col).

Parfum [par'fœː] nt -s, **Parfüm** nt -e or -s perfume, scent.

Parfümerie f perfumery.

parfümieren 1 vt to scent. **2** vr to put scent on.

parieren [1] vt **(a)** (Fechten, fig) to parry; (Ftbl) to deflect. **(b)** (Reiten) to rein in. **2** vi to obey. **aufs Wort** ~ to jump to it.

Pariser [1] m - **(a)** Parisian. **(b)** (col: Kondom) rubber (col).

Pariser [2] adj attr Parisian.

Pariserin f Parisienne.

Parität f parity.

paritätisch adj equal. ~**e Mitbestimmung** equal representation.

Park m -s park; (von Schloß) grounds pl.

Parka m -s parka.

Park|anlage f park.

parken vti to park.

Parkett nt -e **(a)** (Fußboden) parquet (flooring). **sich auf jedem** ~ **bewegen können** (fig) to be able to move in any society. **(b)** (Tanzfläche) (dance) floor. **eine tolle Nummer aufs** ~ **legen** (col) to put on a great show. **(c)** (Theat) stalls pl, parquet (US). **wir sitzen** ~ we sit in the stalls.

Parkett-: ~**platz**, ~**sitz** m (Theat) seat in the stalls or parquet (US).

Park-: ~**gebühr** f parking fee; ~**haus** nt multistorey car park (Brit), multilevel parking garage (US); ~**landschaft** f parkland; ~**lücke** f parking space; ~**platz** m car park (Brit), parking lot (US); (für Einzelwagen) (parking) space; ~**scheibe** f parking disc; ~**uhr** parking meter; ~**verbot** nt parking ban; **hier ist** ~**verbot** there's no parking here.

Parlament nt parliament.

Parlamentarier(in f) [-iɐ, -iərɪn] m - parliamentarian.

parlamentarisch adj parliamentary.

Parlaments-: ~**ausschuß** m parliamentary committee; ~**beschluß** m decision of parliament; ~**ferien** pl recess; ~**gebäude** nt parliamentary building(s); ~**mitglied** nt member of parliament, MP (Brit); (in USA) Congressman; ~**sitzung** f sitting (of parliament); ~**wahl** f usu pl parliamentary election(s).

Parodie f parody (auf +acc on, zu of).

parodieren* vt to parody.

Parodontose f -n shrinking gums.

Parole f -n (a) (Mil) password. (b) (fig: Wahlspruch) motto; (Pol) slogan.

Paroli nt: jdm ~ **bieten** (geh) to defy sb.

Partei f (a) (Pol, Jur) party. **die** ~ **wechseln** to change parties; **die streitenden** ~**en** (Jur) the disputing parties; **für jdn** ~ **ergreifen** to side with sb; **gegen jdn** ~ **ergreifen** to take sides against sb; **ein Richter sollte über den** ~**en stehen** a judge should be impartial. (b) (im Mietshaus) tenant, party (form).

Partei-: ~**anhänger** m party supporter; ~**buch** nt party membership book; ~**chef** m party leader; ~**führung** f leadership of a party; (Vorstand) party executive; ~**genosse** m party member; ~**intern** adj internal party; **etw p**~**intern lösen** to solve sth within the party.

parteiisch adj bias(s)ed, partial.

Parteilichkeit f bias, partiality.

Partei-: ~**linie** f party line; **auf die** ~**linie einschwenken** to toe the party line; **p**~**los** adj independent, non-party; ~**mitglied** nt party member; ~**nahme** f -n partisanship; ~**politik** f party politics pl; ~**politisch** adj party political; ~**programm** nt (party) manifesto; ~**tag** m party conference or convention; ~**versammlung** f party meeting; ~**vorsitzende(r)** mf party leader; ~**vorstand** m party executive; ~**zugehörigkeit** f party membership.

Parterre [par'ter(ə)] nt -s (von Gebäude) ground floor (Brit), first floor (US). **im** ~ **wohnen** to live on the ground floor.

Parterrewohnung f ground-floor flat (Brit), first-floor apartment (US).

Partie f (a) (Teil, Theat, Mus) part. (b) (Sport) game; (Fechten) round. **eine** ~ **Schach spielen** to play a game of chess. (c) (Comm) lot, batch. (d) (col) catch. **eine gute** ~ (**für jdn**) **sein** to be a good catch for sb; **eine gute** ~ (**mit jdm**) **machen** to marry (into) money. (e) **mit von der** ~ **sein** to be in on it; **da bin ich mit von der** ~ count me in.

partiell [par'tsiel] adj partial.

Partikel f -n (Gram, Phys) particle.

Partisan(in f) m -en partisan.

Partisanenkrieg m partisan war; (Art des Krieges) guerrilla warfare.

Partitur f (Mus) score.

Partizip nt -ien [-iən] (Gram) participle. ~ **Präsens/Perfekt** present/past participle.

Partner(in f) m - partner; (Film) co-star. **als jds** ~ **spielen** (in Film) to play opposite sb; (Sport) to be partnered by sb.

Partnerschaft f partnership.

partnerschaftlich adj ~**es Verhältnis** (relationship based on) partnership; ~**e Zusammenarbeit** working together as partners.

Partnertausch m (Tanz, Tennis) change of partners; (sexuell) partner-swopping.

partout [par'tu:] adv **er will** ~ **ins Kino gehen** he insists on going to the cinema; **sie will** ~ **nicht nach Hause gehen** she just doesn't want to go home.

Party ['pa:rti] f -s party. **eine** ~ **veranstalten** to have a party; **bei** or **auf einer** ~ at a party.

Pasch m -e or -e (beim Würfelspiel) doublets pl.

Pascha m - pasha. **wie ein** ~ **like Lord Muck** (col).

Paß m, pl **Pässe** (a) passport. (b) (im Gebirge etc) pass. (c) (Ballspiele) pass.

passabel adj passable, reasonable.

Passage [pa'sa:ʒə] f -n passage; (Ladenstraße) arcade.

Passagier [pasa'ʒi:ɐ] m passenger.

Passagier-: ~**flugzeug** nt air-liner; ~**gut** nt passenger baggage.

Passah(fest) nt (Feast of the) Passover.

Paß|amt nt passport office.

Passant(in f) m (wk) passer-by.

Passat(wind) m -e trade wind.

Paßbild nt passport photo(graph).

passé [pa'se:] adj pred **diese Mode ist längst** ~ this fashion went out long ago; **die Sache ist längst** ~ that's all in the past.

passen[1] vi (a) to fit. **die Schuhe** ~ (**mir**) **gut** the shoes fit (me) nicely or are a good fit (for me); **der Deckel paßt nicht** the lid won't fit (on).
(b) (harmonieren) **zu etw** ~ to go with sth; **zu etw im Ton** ~ to match sth; **zu jdm** ~ (Mensch) to suit sb; **zueinander** ~ to go together; (Menschen auch) to be well matched; **das paßt zu ihm, so etwas zu sagen** that's just like him to say that; **es paßt nicht zu dir, Bier zu trinken** you don't look right drinking beer; **das Rot paßt da nicht** the red is all wrong there; **er paßt nicht in dieses Team** he is out of place in this team.
(c) (genehm sein) to suit. **er paßt mir einfach nicht** I just don't like him; **Sonntag paßt uns nicht** Sunday is no good for us; **es paßt ihr gar nicht, daß sie jetzt schlafen gehen soll** she doesn't like the idea of having to go to bed now; **das könnte dir so** ~! (col) you'd like that, wouldn't you?

passen[2] vi (Cards) to pass. (**ich**) **passe!** (I) pass!; **bei dieser Frage muß ich** ~ (fig) I'll have to pass on this question.

passend adj (a) (in Größe, Form) **gut/schlecht** ~ well-/ill-fitting. (b) (in Farbe, Stil) matching. **etwas dazu P**~**es** something to match. (c) (genehm) **Zeit, Termin** convenient; (angemessen) **Bemerkung, Kleidung** suitable; **Wort** right. **er findet immer das** ~**e Wort** he always knows the right thing to say. (d) **Geld** exact. **haben Sie es** ~? have you got the right money?

Paß-: ~**form** f fit; **eine gute** ~**form haben** to be a good fit; ~**foto** nt passport photo(graph); ~**höhe** f top of the pass.

passierbar adj passable; **Fluß, Kanal** negotiable.

passieren* 1 vt (a) auch vi to pass. **die Grenze** ~ to cross the border; **die Zensur** ~ to be passed by the censor. (b) (Cook) to strain. 2 vi aux sein (sich ereignen) to happen (mit to). **ist ihm etwas passiert?** has anything happened to him?; **beim Sturz ist ihm nichts passiert** he wasn't hurt in the fall; **es ist ein Unfall passiert** there has been an accident; **das kann auch nur mir** ~! just my luck!

Passierschein m pass, permit.

Passion f passion; (religiös) Passion. **etw aus** ~ **tun** to have a passion for doing sth.

passioniert adj enthusiastic, passionate.

Passions-: ~**blume** f passionflower; ~**zeit** f Lent.

passiv adj passive. **sich** ~ **verhalten** to be passive; ~**es Mitglied** non-active member; ~**e Handelsbilanz** (Comm) adverse trade balance.

Passiv nt -e (Gram) passive (voice).

Passiva [pa'si:va] pl (Comm) liabilities pl.

Passivität [pasivi'tɛ:t] f passivity.

Passiv- (Comm): ~**posten** m debit entry; ~**saldo** m debit account; ~**seite** f debit side.

Paß-: ~**kontrolle** f passport control; ~**photo** nt passport photo; ~**straße** f (mountain) pass.

Paste f -n paste.

Pastell nt -e (Gram) pastel (drawing).

Pastell-: ~**farbe** f pastel (crayon); (Farbton) pastel; **p**~**farben** adj pastel; ~**ton** m pastel shade.

Pastete f -n (a) (Schüssel~) pie; (Pastetchen) vol-au-vent; (ungefüllt) vol-au-vent case. (b)

(Leber~ etc) pâté.

pasteurisieren* [pastøri'ziːrən] *vt* to pasteurize.

Pastille *f* -n pastille.

Pastor *m*, **Pastorin** *f* = **Pfarrer(in)**.

pastoral *adj* pastoral.

Pate *m* -n godfather, godparent. **bei einem Kind ~ stehen** to be a child's godparent; **bei etw ~ gestanden haben** *(fig)* to be the force behind sth.

Paten-: **~kind** *nt* godchild; godson; goddaughter; **~onkel** *m* godfather; **~schaft** *f* duties *pl* as a godparent; **die ~schaft für jdn übernehmen** *(fig)* to adopt sb; **~stadt** *f* twin(ned) town *(Brit)*.

patent *adj (col)* ingenious, clever. **ein ~er Kerl** a great guy/girl *(col)*.

Patent *nt* -e *(Erfindung, Urkunde)* patent. **etw als** *or* **zum ~ anmelden** to apply for a patent on sth.

Patent|amt *nt* Patent Office.

Patentante *f* godmother.

Patent|anwalt *m* patent agent *or* attorney.

patentieren* *vt* to patent. **sich** *(dat)* **etw ~ lassen** to have sth patented.

Patent-: **~lösung** *f (fig)* patent remedy; **~schrift** *f* patent specification.

Pater *m*, *pl* - *or* **Patres** *(Eccl)* Father.

Paternoster *m* - *(Aufzug)* paternoster.

pathetisch *adj* emotional; *Rede, Stil auch* emotive; *Gehabe auch* histrionic.

Pathologie *f* pathology.

pathologisch *adj* pathological.

Pathos *nt no pl* emotiveness, emotionalism.

Patience [pa'siãːs] *f* -n patience *no pl*. **~n legen** to play patience.

Patient(in *f)* [pa'tsiɛnt(in)] *m (wk)* -en, -en patient.

Patin *f* godmother, godparent.

Patriarch *m (wk)* -en, -en *(lit, fig)* patriarch.

patriarchalisch *adj (lit, fig)* patriarchal.

Patriot(in *f)* *m (wk)* -en, -en patriot.

patriotisch *adj* patriotic.

Patriotismus *m* patriotism.

Patron(in *f)* *m* -e *(Eccl)* patron saint.

Patrone *f* -n *(Film, Mil, von Füller)* cartridge.

Patrouille [pa'trʊljə] *f* -n patrol. **~ gehen** to patrol.

patrouillieren* [patrʊl'jiːrən] *vi* to patrol. **an der Grenze ~** to patrol the border.

patsch *interj* splash, splat.

Patsche *f* -n *(col)* (tight) spot *(col)*. **in der ~ sitzen** to be in a jam *(col)*; **jdm aus der ~ helfen** to get sb out of a jam *(col)*.

patschen *vi (im Wasser)* to splash. **die Kinder ~ mit den Händen** *(col)* the children clap their hands (together).

Patsch-: **~händchen** *nt (col)* paw *(col)*; **p~naß** *adj (col)* dripping wet.

Patt *nt* -s *(lit, fig)* stalemate.

patzen *vi (col)* to boob *(Brit col)*, to goof *(US col)*.

Patzer *m* - *(col: Fehler)* boob *(Brit col)*, goof *(US col)*.

patzig *adj (col)* snotty *(col)*, insolent.

Pauke *f* -n *(Mus)* timpani *pl*. **mit ~n und Trompeten durchfallen** *(col)* to fail dismally; **auf die ~ hauen** *(col) (angeben)* to brag; *(feiern)* to paint the town red *(col)*.

pauken 1 *vi (col: lernen)* to swot (col). **2** *vt* to swot up *(col)*.

Paukenschlag *m* drum beat. **wie ein ~schlag** *(fig)* like a thunderbolt.

Pauker *m* - *(Sch col: Lehrer)* teacher.

Paukerei *f (Sch col)* swotting *(col)*.

Pausbacken *pl* chubby cheeks *pl*.

pausbäckig *adj* chubby-cheeked.

pauschal *adj (einheitlich)* flat-rate *attr only*; *(inklusiv)* inclusive. **die Werkstatt berechnet ~ pro Inspektion 250 DM** the garage has a flat rate of DM 250 per service; **die Gebühren werden ~ bezahlt** the charges are paid in a lump sum; **die Reisekosten verstehen sich ~** the travelling costs are inclusive; **so ~ kann man das nicht sagen** *(fig)* that's much too sweeping a state-

ment.

Pauschale *f* -n *(Einheitspreis)* flat rate; *(vorläufig geschätzer Betrag)* estimated amount.

Pauschal-: **~gebühr** *f* flat rate (charge); **~preis** *m (Einheitspreis)* flat rate; *(Inklusivpreis)* all-in price; **~reise** *f* package tour; **~summe** *f* lump sum; **~urteil** *nt* sweeping statement; **~versicherung** *f* comprehensive insurance *no pl*.

Pauschbetrag *m* flat rate.

Pause *f* -n **(a)** break; *(das Innehalten)* pause; *(Theat)* interval, intermission; *(Sch)* break *(Brit)*, recess *(US)*. **(eine) ~ machen, eine ~ einlegen** *(sich entspannen)* to have a break; *(rasten)* to take a rest; *(innehalten)* to pause; **nach einer langen ~ sagte er ...** after a long silence he said ... **(b)** *(Mus)* rest. **(c)** *(Durchzeichnung)* tracing.

pausen *vt* to trace.

Pausen-: **~brot** *nt* sandwich, something to eat at break *(Brit)* or in the recess *(US)*; **~hof** *m* playground, schoolyard; **p~los** *adj no pred* continuous; **er arbeitet p~los** he works non-stop; **~zeichen** *nt (Mus)* rest; *(Rad)* call sign.

pausieren* *vi* to (take a) break.

Pauspapier *nt* tracing paper; *(Kohlepapier)* carbon paper.

Pavian ['paːviaːn] *m* -e baboon.

Pavillon ['pavɪl'jõː] *m* -s pavilion.

Pazifik *m* Pacific.

pazifisch *adj* Pacific. **der P~e Ozean** the Pacific (Ocean).

Pazifismus *m* pacifism.

Pazifist(in *f)* *m* pacifist.

Pech *nt* -e **(a)** *(Stoff)* pitch. **die beiden halten zusammen wie ~ und Schwefel** *(col)* the two are inseparable. **(b)** *no pl (col: Mißgeschick)* hard luck. **bei etw ~ haben** to have bad luck with sth; **~ gehabt!** tough! *(col)*; **so ein ~!** just my/our *etc* luck!

Pech-: **p~(raben)schwarz** *adj (col)* pitch-black; *Haar* jet-black; **~strähne** *f (col)* unlucky patch; **~vogel** *m (col)* unlucky person; *(Frau auch)* Calamity Jane.

Pedal *nt* -e pedal. **(fest) in die ~e treten** to pedal (hard).

Pedant *m (wk)* pedant.

pedantisch *adj* pedantic.

Peddigrohr *nt* cane.

Pediküre *f* -n **(a)** *no pl (Fußpflege)* pedicure. **(b)** *(Fußpflegerin)* chiropodist *(Brit)*, podiatrist *(US)*.

Peep-Show ['piːpʃoː] *f* peepshow.

Pegel *m* - water depth gauge; *(Elec)* level recorder.

Pegelstand *m* water level.

peilen *vt Wassertiefe* to sound; *Sender* to take the bearings of; *Richtung* to plot; *(entdecken)* to detect. **die Lage ~** *(col)* to see how the land lies; **über den Daumen ~** *(col)* to guess roughly; **über den Daumen gepeilt** *(col)* at a rough estimate.

Peilgerät *nt* direction finder.

Peilung *f (von Wassertiefe)* sounding; *(von Sender)* locating; *(von Richtung)* plotting.

Pein *f no pl (geh, liter)* agony, suffering.

peinigen *vt* to torture; *(fig)* to torment. **von Schmerzen/Zweifeln gepeinigt** tormented by pain/doubt.

peinlich *adj* **(a)** *(unangenehm)* (painfully) embarrassing; *Lage, Fragen auch* awkward. **es war ihm ~(, daß ...)** he felt embarrassed (because ...); **das ist mir ja so ~** I feel awful about it. **(b)** *(gewissenhaft)* painstaking. **in seinem Zimmer herrschte ~e Ordnung** his room was meticulously tidy; **der Koffer wurde ~ genau untersucht** the case was given a very thorough going-over *(col)*; **er vermied es ~st, davon zu sprechen** he was at pains not to talk about it.

Peinlichkeit *f (Unangenehmheit)* embarrassment.

Peitsche *f* -n whip.

peitschen vti to whip; (fig) to lash.
Peitschen-: ~**hieb** m lash; ~**knall** m crack of a whip.
Pekinese m (wk) -n, -n pekinese, peke (col).
Pelikan m -e pelican.
Pelle f -n (col) skin. **der Chef sitzt mir auf der ~** (col) I've got the boss on my back (col); **er geht mir nicht von der ~** (col) he won't stop pestering me.
pellen vtr (col) to peel.
Pellkartoffeln pl potatoes pl boiled in their jackets.
Pelz m -e fur; (nicht gegerbt auch) hide.
Pelz- in cpds fur; ~**besatz** m fur trimming; ~**händler** m furrier.
pelzig adj furry.
Pelz-: ~**mantel** m fur coat; ~**tier** nt animal prized for its fur; ~**waren** pl furs pl.
Pendant [pā'dā:] nt -s counterpart.
Pendel nt - pendulum.
pendeln vi (a) (schwingen) to swing (to and fro). (b) aux sein (Zug, Fähre etc) to shuttle; (Mensch) to commute; (fig) to fluctuate.
Pendel-: ~**tür** f swing door; ~**uhr** f pendulum clock; ~**verkehr** m shuttle service; (Berufsverkehr) commuter traffic.
Pendler(in f) m - commuter.
penetrant adj (a) Geruch penetrating. **das schmeckt ~ nach Knoblauch** it has a very strong taste of garlic. (b) (fig: aufdringlich) insistent; Selbstsicherheit overpowering.
peng interj bang.
penibel adj pernickety (col), precise.
Penis m -, -se or **Penes** penis.
Penizillin nt -e penicillin.
Pennbruder m (col) tramp, hobo (US).
Penne f -n (a) (Sch sl) school. (b) (col: Herberge) doss house (col).
pennen vi (col) to kip (col).
Penner(in f) m - (col) (a) tramp, hobo (US). (b) (verschlafener Mensch) sleepyhead (col).
Pension [auch pā'zio:n] f -en (a) (Fremdenheim) guest-house. (b) no pl (Verpflegung) board. **halbe/volle ~** half/full board (Brit), European/American plan (US). (c) (Ruhegehalt) pension. (d) no pl (Ruhestand) retirement. **in ~ gehen** to retire; **in ~ sein** to be retired.
Pensionär(in f) [auch pāzio'nɛ:ɐ, -ɛːrın] m (Pension beziehend) pensioner; (im Ruhestand befindlich) retired person.
pensionieren* [auch pāzio'ni:rən] vt to retire. **sich ~ lassen** to retire.
Pensionierung f (Zustand) retirement; (Vorgang) pensioning-off.
Pensions-: ~**alter** nt retiring age; ~**anspruch** m right to a pension; **p~berechtigt** adj entitled to a pension; ~**preis** m price for full board (Brit) or American plan (US); **p~reif** adj (col) ready for retirement.
Pensum nt, pl **Pensa** or **Pensen** workload; (Sch) curriculum. **tägliches ~** daily quota; **er hat sein ~ nicht geschafft** he didn't achieve his target.
Pep m no pl (col) pep (col), life.
Peperoni pl chillies pl.
per prep (a) (mittels) by. **mit jdm ~ du sein** (col) to be on first-name terms with sb; **~ pedes** (hum) on shanks's pony (hum). (b) (Comm) (bis) by; (pro) per. **~ Adresse** care of, c/o.
perfekt adj (a) (vollkommen) perfect. (b) pred (abgemacht) settled. **die Sache ~ machen** to clinch the deal; **der Vertrag ist ~** the contract is all settled.
Perfekt nt -e perfect (tense).
Perfektion f perfection.
perfektionieren* [pɛrfɛktsio'ni:rən] vt to perfect.
Perfektionist(in f) m perfectionist.
Perforation f perforation.
perforieren* vt to perforate.

Pergament nt parchment; (Kalbs~ auch) vellum.
Pergamentpapier nt greaseproof paper.
Pergola f, pl **Pergolen** bower.
Periode f -n period (auch Physiol); (von Wetter auch) spell; (Math) repetend; (Elec) cycle. **0,33 ~** 0.33 recurring.
periodisch adj periodic(al); (regelmäßig) regular; (Phys) periodic.
peripher adj peripheral.
Peripherie f periphery; (von Stadt) outskirts pl. **an der ~ Bonns** on the outskirts of Bonn.
Peripheriegerät nt (Comp) peripheral.
Perle f -n (a) (auch fig) pearl. ~**n vor die Säue werfen** (prov) to cast pearls before swine (prov). (b) (Glas~, Holz~, von Schweiß) bead; (Luftbläschen) bubble. (c) (dated col: Hausgehilfin) maid.
perlen vi (sprudeln) to bubble; (fallen, rollen) to trickle.
Perlen-: ~**kette** f, ~**kollier** nt pearl necklace.
Perl-: ~**huhn** nt guinea fowl; ~**muschel** f pearl oyster; ~**mutt** nt no pl mother-of-pearl.
Perlon ® nt, no pl ≈ nylon.
Perlwein m sparkling wine.
permanent adj permanent.
perplex adj dumbfounded, thunderstruck.
Perser(in f) m - (a) Persian. (b) (col: Teppich) Persian carpet.
Perserteppich m Persian carpet.
Persianer m - (a) (Pelz) Persian lamb. (b) (auch ~**mantel**) Persian lamb (coat).
Persien [-iən] nt Persia.
Persiflage [pɛrzi'fla:zə] f -n pastiche, satire (gen, auf +acc on, of).
persisch adj Persian.
Person f -en (a) (auch Gram) person. ~**en** people, persons (form); **eine aus 6 ~en bestehende Familie** a family of 6; **die eigene ~** oneself; **ich für meine ~ ...** I myself ...; **ich hatte den Chef in ~ vor mir** I was talking to the boss himself; **er ist Finanz- und Außenminister in einer ~** he's the Chancellor of the Exchequer and Foreign Secre tary rolled into one; **natürliche/juristische ~** (Jur) natural/legal person; **sie ist die Geduld in ~** she's patience personified; **lassen wir seine ~ aus dem Spiel** let's leave personalities out of it; **er ist klein von ~** he's small in stature, he's a small person. (b) (pej: Frau) female. (c) (Liter, Theat) character.
Personal nt no pl personnel, staff. **ungenügend mit ~ versehen sein** to be understaffed.
Personal-: ~**abbau** m staff cuts pl; ~**abteilung** f personnel (department); ~**akte** f personal file; ~**angaben** pl particulars pl; ~**ausweis** m identity card; ~**büro** nt personnel (department); ~**chef** m personnel manager.
Personalien [-iən] pl particulars pl.
Personal-: ~**kartei** f personnel index; ~**leiter** m personnel manager; ~**pronomen** nt personal pronoun; ~**union** f ... **in ~union** ... in one.
personell adj staff attr, personnel attr. **unsere Schwierigkeiten sind rein ~** our difficulties are simply to do with staffing.
Personen-: ~**aufzug** m (passenger) lift (Brit), elevator (US); ~**beschreibung** f (personal) description; ~**gedächtnis** nt memory for faces; ~**kraftwagen** m (form) (private) car, automobile (US); ~**kreis** m group of people; ~**kult** m personality cult; ~**schaden** m injury to persons; ~**stand** m marital status; ~**standsregister** nt register of births, marriages and deaths; ~**verkehr** m passenger services pl; ~**waage** f pair of scales; ~**wagen** m (Rail) carriage (Brit), car; (Aut) (private) car, automobile (US); ~**zug** m passenger train; (Gegensatz: Schnellzug) slow train.
Personifikation f personification.
personifizieren* vt to personify.

persönlich 1 *adj* personal; *Atmosphäre* friendly.
~ **werden** to get personal. **2** *adv* personally; *(auf Briefen)* private (and confidential). **etw** ~ **meinen/nehmen** to mean/take sth personally; **Sie müssen** ~ **erscheinen** you are required to appear in person; ~**haften** *(Comm)* to be personally liable.
Persönlichkeit *f* personality. **er besitzt wenig** ~ he hasn't got much personality; **er ist eine** ~ **he's** quite a personality; ~**en des öffentlichen Lebens** public figures.
Perspektive [-'tiːvə] *f (Art, Opt)* perspective; *(Blickpunkt)* angle; *(fig: Zukunftsausblick)* prospects *pl.* **das eröffnet ganz neue** ~**n für uns** that opens new horizons for us.
perspektivisch [-'tiːvɪʃ] *adj* perspective *attr*, in perspective. **die Zeichnung ist nicht** ~ the drawing is not in perspective.
Peru *nt* Peru.
Peruaner(in *f) m* - Peruvian.
Perücke *f* -**n** wig.
pervers [pɛr'vɛrs] *adj* perverted. **ein** ~**er Mensch** a pervert.
Perversion [pɛrvɛr'zioːn] *f* perversion.
Perversität [pɛrvɛrzi'tɛːt] *f* perversion.
pervertieren* [pɛrvɛr'tiːrən] **1** *vt* to pervert. **2** *vi aux sein* to become perverted.
Pessar *nt* -**e** pessary; *(zur Empfängnisverhütung)* cap, diaphragm.
Pessimismus *m* pessimism.
Pessimist(in *f) m* pessimist.
pessimistisch *adj* pessimistic.
Pest *f no pl (Hist, Med)* plague. **jdn/etw wie die** ~ **hassen** *(col)* to loathe sb/sth; **jdn wie die** ~ **meiden** *(col)* to avoid sb like the plague; **wie die** ~ **stinken** *(col)* to stink to high heaven *(col)*.
Petersilie [-iə] *f* parsley.
Petition *f* petition.
Petro(l)chemie *f* petrochemistry.
Petroleum [pe'troːleʊm] *nt no pl* paraffin (oil) *(Brit)*, kerosene *(US)*.
Petunie [-iə] *f* petunia.
Petze *f* -**n, Petzer** *m* - *(Sch sl)* sneak *(Sch sl)*.
petzen *(col)* **1** *vt* **der petzt alles** he always tells; **er hat's dem Lehrer gepetzt** he told sir *(Sch sl)*. **2** *vi* to tell (tales).
Pf = Pfennig.
Pfad *m* -**e** path, track.
Pfadfinder *m* - (boy) scout. **er ist bei den** ~**n he's** in the (Boy) Scouts.
Pfadfinderin *f* girl guide *(Brit)*, girl scout *(US)*.
Pfaffe *m* *(wk)* -**n, -n** *(pej)* cleric *(pej)*.
Pfahl *m* ⁻**e** post; *(Zaun~ auch, Marter~)* stake; *(Brücken~)* pile.
Pfahlbau *m* -**ten** **(a)** *no pl (Bauweise)* building on stilts. **(b)** *(Haus)* pile dwelling.
Pfalz *f (Geog)* Palatinate.
Pfälzer(in *f) m* - **(a)** person from the Palatinate. **(b)** *(Wein)* wine from the Rhineland Palatinate.
pfälzisch *adj* Palatine.
Pfand *nt* ⁻**er** security; *(beim Pfänderspiel)* forfeit; *(Flaschen~)* deposit; *(fig geh)* pledge. **etw als** ~ **geben** *(lit, fig)* to pledge sth; *(beim Pfänderspiel)* to pay sth as a forfeit; **auf der Flasche ist 10 Pf** ~ there's 10 Pf (back) on the bottle *(col)*; **ein** ~ **einlösen** to redeem a pledge; **etw als** ~ **behalten** to keep sth as (a) security.
Pfandbrief *m* bond, debenture.
pfänden *vt (Jur)* to impound. **man hat ihm die Möbel gepfändet** they took away his furniture; **jdn** ~ **lassen** to get the bailiffs onto sb.
Pfand-: ~haus *nt*, ~**leihe** *f* pawnshop; ~**leiher** *m* - pawnbroker; ~**schein** *m* pawn ticket.
Pfändung *f* seizure, distraint *(form)*.
Pfanne *f* -**n** *(Cook)* pan. **jdn in die** ~ **hauen** *(col)* to tear a strip off sb *(col)*.
Pfannkuchen *m* pancake. **Berliner** ~ *(jam)* doughnut.

Pfarr|amt *nt* priest's office.
Pfarrei *f (Gemeinde)* parish; *(Amtsräume)* priest's office.
Pfarrer(in *f) m* - vicar; *(katholisch)* priest; *(von Freikirchen)* minister; *(Gefängnis~, Militär~ etc)* chaplain, padre.
Pfau *m* -**en** peacock. **aufgedonnert wie ein** ~ *(col)* dressed up to the nines *(col)*.
Pfauen|auge *nt (Tag~)* peacock butterfly.
Pfeffer *m* - pepper. **er kann bleiben, wo der** ~ **wächst!** *(col)* he can take a running jump *(col)*.
pfeff(e)rig *adj* peppery.
Pfeffer-: ~korn *nt* peppercorn; ~**kuchen** *m* gingerbread.
Pfefferminz(bonbon) *nt* -(**e**) peppermint.
Pfefferminze *f no pl* peppermint.
Pfeffermühle *f* pepper-mill.
pfeffern *vt* **(a)** *(Cook)* to pepper; *siehe* **gepfeffert.** **(b)** *(col) (heftig werfen)* to fling; *(hinauswerfen)* to sling out *(col)*. **jdm eine** ~ to clout sb one *(col)*.
Pfeffernuß *f* gingerbread ball.
Pfeife *f* -**n** **(a)** whistle; *(Quer~)* fife *(esp Mil)*; *(Orgel~)* pipe. **nach jds** ~ **tanzen** to dance to sb's tune. **(b)** *(zum Rauchen)* pipe. ~ **rauchen** to smoke a pipe.
pfeifen *pret* **pfiff,** *ptp* **gepfiffen** *vti* to whistle *(dat* for); *(auf einer Trillerpfeife)* to blow one's whistle; *(Mus)* to pipe; *(col) Spiel* to ref *(col)*. **auf dem letzten Loch** ~ *(col) (erschöpft sein)* to be on one's last legs *(col)*; *(finanziell)* to be on one's beam ends *(col)*; **ich pfeife darauf!** *(col)* I don't give a damn *(col)*; **das** ~ **ja schon die Spatzen von den Dächern** it's all over town.
Pfeifen-: ~kopf *m* bowl (of a pipe); ~**stopfer** *m* tamper; ~**tabak** *m* pipe tobacco.
Pfeifer *m* - piper.
Pfeiferei *f (col)* whistling.
Pfeifkonzert *nt* catcalls *pl*.
Pfeil *m* -**e** arrow; *(Wurf~)* dart. ~ **und Bogen** bow and arrow; **er schoß wie ein** ~ **davon** he was off like a shot.
Pfeiler *m* - *(lit, fig)* pillar; *(Brücken~ auch)* pier; *(Stütz~)* buttress.
Pfeil-: p~gerade *adj Linie* dead straight; **sie kam p~gerade auf uns zu** she headed straight for us; **p~schnell** *adj* as swift as an arrow *(liter)*; ~**spitze** *f* arrowhead; ~**wurfspiel** *nt* darts *pl*.
Pfennig *m* -**e** *or (nach Zahlenangabe)* - pfennig *(one hundredth of a mark)*. **30** ~ **30 pfennigs; er hat keinen** ~ **Geld** he hasn't got a penny to his name *or* doesn't have a dime *(US)*; **nicht für fünf** ~ *(col)* not the slightest (bit of); **er hat nicht für fünf** ~ **Verstand** *(col)* he hasn't an ounce of intelligence; **mit jedem** ~ **rechnen müssen** *(fig)* to have to count every penny; **jeden** ~ **umdrehen** *(fig col)* to think twice about every penny one spends.
Pfennig-: ~absatz *m* stiletto heel; ~**fuchser** *m* - *(col)* skinflint *(col)*; ~**stück** *nt* pfennig (piece).
Pferch *m* -**e** fold, pen.
pferchen *vt* to cram, to pack.
Pferd *nt* -**e** *(Tier, Turngerät)* horse; *(beim Schachspiel)* knight, horse *(US col)*. **zu** ~**e** on horseback; **aufs falsche/richtige** ~ **setzen** *(lit, fig)* to back the wrong/right horse; **wie ein** ~ **arbeiten** *(col)* to work like a Trojan; **keine zehn** ~**e brächten mich dahin** *(col)* wild horses wouldn't drag me there; **mit ihm kann man** ~**e stehlen** *(col)* he's a great sport *(col)*; **er ist unser bestes** ~ **im Stall** he's our best man.
Pferde-: ~äpfel horse droppings *pl or* dung *no pl*; ~**fuhrwerk** *nt* horse and cart; ~**fuß** *m* **die Sache hat aber einen** ~**fuß** there's just one snag; ~**gebiß** *nt* horsey teeth; ~**haar** *nt* horsehair; ~**knecht** *m* groom; ~**koppel** *f* paddock; ~**rennbahn** *f* race course; ~**rennen** *nt (Sportart)* (horse-)racing; *(einzelnes Rennen)* (horse-)race; ~**schwanz** *m* horse's tail; *(Frisur)* pony-tail; ~**stall** *m* stable; ~**stärke** *f* horse power *no pl*,

hp *abbr;* ~**wagen** *m (für Personen)* trap, horse-buggy *(US); (für Lasten)* horse and cart; ~**zucht** *f* horse breeding; *(Gestüt)* stud-farm.

pfiff *pret of* **pfeifen.**

Pfiff *m* -e (a) whistle. (b) *(Reiz)* style. **der Soße fehlt noch der letzte** ~ the sauce still needs that extra something.

Pfifferling *m* chanterelle. **er kümmert sich keinen** ~ **darum** *(col)* he doesn't give a damn about it *(col);* **keinen** ~ **wert** *(col)* not worth a thing.

pfiffig *adj* smart, cute.

Pfingsten *nt* - Whitsun, Pentecost *(Eccl).*

Pfingst-: ~**montag** *m* Whit Monday; ~**ochse** *m:* **herausgeputzt wie ein** ~**ochse** *(col)* dressed up to the nines *(col);* ~**rose** *f* peony; ~**sonntag** *m* Whit Sunday, Pentecost *(Eccl);* ~**zeit** *f* Whitsun(tide).

Pfirsich *m* -e peach.

Pflanze *f* -n (a) *(Gewächs)* plant. (b) *(col: Mensch)* **sie ist eine seltsame** ~ she is an odd bird *(col).*

pflanzen 1 *vt* to plant. **2** *vr (col)* to plonk oneself *(col).*

Pflanzen-: ~**fett** *nt* vegetable fat; ~**fresser** *m* herbivore; ~**kunde,** ~**lehre** *f* botany; ~**öl** *nt* vegetable oil; ~**reich** *nt* vegetable kingdom; ~**schädling** *m* pest; ~**schutz** *m* protection of plants; *(gegen Ungeziefer)* pest control; ~**schutzmittel** *nt* pesticide; ~**welt** *f* **die** ~**welt des Mittelmeers** the flora of the Mediterranean.

pflanzlich *adj attr* vegetable.

Pflanzung *f (das Pflanzen)* planting; *(Plantage)* plantation.

Pflaster *nt* - (a) *(Heft~)* (sticking-)plaster. (b) *(Straßen~)* (road) surface; *(Kopfstein~)* cobbles *pl.* **ein teures** ~ *(col)* a pricey place *(col).*

pflastern *vt* Straße to surface; *(mit Kopfsteinpflaster)* to cobble; *(mit Steinplatten)* to pave.

Pflasterstein *m (Kopfstein)* cobble(stone); *(Steinplatte)* paving stone.

Pflaume *f* -n (a) plum. **getrocknete** ~ prune. (b) *(col: Mensch)* twit *(Brit col),* dope *(col).*

Pflaumen-: ~**kompott** *nt* stewed plums *pl;* ~**kuchen** *m* plum tart; ~**mus** *nt* plum jam.

Pflege *f* no pl care; *(von Kranken auch)* nursing; *(von Garten auch)* attention; *(von Beziehungen, Künsten)* cultivation; *(von Maschinen, Gebäuden)* upkeep. **jdn/etw in** ~ **nehmen** to look after sb/ sth; **ein Kind in** ~ **nehmen** *(dauernd)* to foster a child; **ein Kind in** ~ **geben** to have a child fostered; *(von Behörden)* to foster a child out *(zu jdm* with sb).

Pflege-: p~**bedürftig** *adj* in need of care; ~**eltern** *pl* foster parents *pl;* ~**fall** *m* case for nursing; ~**geld** *nt (für* ~**kinder)** boarding-out allowance; *(für Kranke)* attendance allowance; ~**heim** *nt* nursing home; ~**kind** *nt* foster child; p~**leicht** *adj* easy-care.

pflegen 1 *vt* to look after; *Kranke auch* to nurse; *Beziehungen, Kunst* to cultivate; *Maschinen, Gebäude* to maintain. **2** *vi (gewöhnlich tun)* to be in the habit *(zu of).* **sie pflegte zu sagen** she used to say.

Pfleger *m* - *(im Krankenhaus)* orderly; *(voll qualifiziert)* (male) nurse.

Pflegerin *f* nurse.

Pflege-: ~**satz** *m* hospital and nursing charges *pl;* ~**sohn** *m* foster son; ~**station** *f* nursing ward; ~**tochter** *f* foster daughter.

pfleglich *adj* careful.

Pflicht *f* -en (a) *(Verpflichtung)* duty. **als Abteilungsleiter hat er die** ~, ... it's his responsibility as head of department ...; **Rechte und** ~**en** rights and responsibilities; **ich sehe es als meine** ~ **an,** it's my duty to; **es ist seine** ~ **gegenüber** + *dat* it's his duty towards; **die** ~ **ruft** duty calls; **das/Schulbesuch ist** ~ it's/going to school is compulsory; **es ist seine** (**verdammte** *col*) ~ **und Schuldigkeit(, das zu tun)** he damn well ought to (do it) *(col).* (b) *(Sport)* compulsory section.

Pflicht-: p~**bewußt** *adj* conscientious; **er ist sehr** p~**bewußt** he takes his duties very seriously; ~**bewußtsein** *nt* sense of duty; ~**fach** *nt* compulsory subject; ~**gefühl** *nt* sense of duty; p~**gemäß** *adj* dutiful; ~**lektüre** *f* compulsory reading *(Sch auch)* set book(s); ~**übung** *f* compulsory exercise; p~**vergessen** *adj* irresponsible; ~**vergessenheit,** ~**versäumnis** *f* neglect of duty *no pl;* p~**versichert** *adj* compulsorily insured; ~**versicherung** *f* compulsory insurance.

Pflock *m* ¨-e peg; *(für Tiere)* stake.

pflücken *vt* to pick, to pluck.

Pflücker(in *f)* *m* - picker.

Pflug *m* ¨-e plough *(Brit),* plow *(US).*

Pflugschar *f* -en ploughshare *(Brit),* plowshare *(US).*

Pforte *f* -n *(Tor)* gate; *(Geog)* gap. **die** ~ **zum** Himalaja the gateway to the Himalayas.

Pförtner(in *f)* *m* - porter; *(von Fabrik)* gateman; *(von Wohnhaus, Behörde)* doorman; *(von Schloß)* gatekeeper.

Pförtnerloge [-lo:ʒə] *f* porter's office; *(in Fabrik)* gatehouse; *(in Wohnhaus, Büro)* doorman's office.

Pfosten *m* - *(auch Ftbl)* post; *(senkrechter Balken)* upright; *(Fenster~, Tür~)* jamb; *(Stütze)* prop.

Pfote *f* -n (a) *(lit, fig col)* paw. **sich** *(dat)* **die** ~**n verbrennen** *(col)* to burn one's fingers. (b) *(col: schlechte Handschrift)* scribble, scrawl.

Pfropf *m* -e *or* ¨-e, **Pfropfen** *m* - *(Stöpsel)* stopper; *(Kork, Sekt~)* cork; *(Watte~ etc)* plug; *(von Faß)* bung; *(Med: Blut~)* (blood) clot.

pfropfen *vt* (a) *Flasche* to put the stopper in. (b) *(col: hineinwängen)* to cram. **gepfropft voll** crammed full.

pfui *interj (Ekel)* ugh, yuck; *(Mißbilligung)* tut tut; *(zu Hunden)* oy, hey; *(Buhruf)* boo. ~ **Teufel!** *(col)* ugh, yuck; ~, **schäm dich!** shame on you!

Pfund *nt* -e *or (nach Zahlenangabe)* - (a) *(Gewicht) (metrisches System)* 500 grams, half a kilo(gram); *(britisches System)* pound. **drei** ~ **Äpfel** three pounds of apples. (b) *(Währungseinheit)* pound. **zwanzig** ~ **Sterling** twenty pounds sterling; **das** ~ **sinkt** sterling *or* the pound is falling.

pfundig *adj (col)* fantastic, swell *no adv (col).*

Pfundskerl *m (col)* great guy *(col).*

pfundweise *adv* by the pound.

Pfusch *m* no pl *(col)* = **Pfuscherei.**

pfuschen *vi* to bungle; *(einen Fehler machen)* to slip up.

Pfuscher(in *f)* *m* - *(col)* bungler.

Pfuscherei *f (das Pfuschen)* bungling *no pl;* *(gepfuschte Arbeit)* botched-up job.

Pfütze *f* -n puddle.

PH [peː'haː] *f* -s = **Pädagogische Hochschule.**

Phallussymbol *nt* phallic symbol.

Phänomen *nt* -e phenomenon.

phänomenal *adj* phenomenal.

Phantasie *f* (a) no pl *(Einbildung)* imagination. **in seiner** ~ in his mind. (b) *usu pl (Trugbild)* fantasy.

Phantasie-: p~**begabt** *adj* imaginative; ~**gebilde** *nt* (a) *(phantastische Form)* fantastic form; (b) *(Einbildung)* figment of the imagination; p~**los** *adj* unimaginative; ~**losigkeit** *f* lack of imagination.

phantasieren* 1 *vi* to fantasize *(von* about); *(von Schlimmem)* to have visions *(von* of); *(Med)* to be delirious; *(Mus)* to improvise. **er phantasiert von einem großen Haus auf dem Lande** he has fantasies about a big house in the country. **2** *vt Geschichte* to dream up. **was phantasiert du denn da?** *(col)* what are you (going) on about? *(col).*

Phantasie-: p~**voll** *adj* highly imaginative; ~**vorstellung** *f* figment of the imagination.

Phantast *m (wk)* -en, -en dreamer, visionary.

phantastisch *adj* fantastic.

Phantom *nt* -e *(Trugbild)* phantom. **einem** ~

nachjagen *(fig)* to tilt at windmills.
Pharmakologie *f* pharmacology.
Pharmazeut(in *f) m (wk)* **-en, -en** pharmacist, druggist *(US)*.
pharmazeutisch *adj* pharmaceutical.
Pharmazie *f* pharmacy, pharmaceutics *sing*.
Phase *f* **-n** phase.
Philanthropie *f* philanthropy.
Philatelie *f* philately.
Philharmonie *f (Orchester)* philharmonic (orchestra); *(Konzertsaal)* philharmonic hall.
Philharmoniker *m* - **die** ~ the philharmonic (orchestra).
Philippine *m (wk)* **-n, -n, Philippinin** *f* Filipino.
Philippinen *pl* Philippines *pl*.
Philologe *m,* **Philologin** *f* philologist.
Philologie *f* philology.
Philosoph(in *f) m (wk)* **-en, -en** philosopher.
Philosophie *f* philosophy.
philosophieren* *vi* to philosophize *(über +acc* about*)*.
philosophisch *adj* philosophical.
Phlegmatiker(in *f) m* - apathetic person.
phlegmatisch *adj* apathetic.
Phobie [fo'bi:] *f* phobia *(vor* about*)*.
Phonetik *f* phonetics *study*.
phonetisch *adj* phonetic.
Phonotypistin *f* audio-typist.
Phosphat [fɔs'faːt] *nt* phosphate.
Phosphor ['fɔsfɔr] *m no pl* phosphorus.
Photo *nt* **-s** = **Foto**.
Phrase *f* **-n** phrase; *(pej)* hollow phrase. **das sind alles nur** ~**n** that's just talk; ~**n dreschen** *(col)* to churn out one cliché after another.
Phrasen-: ~**drescher** *m (pej)* windbag; ~**drescherei** *f (pej)* phrase-mongering; *(Geschwafel)* hot air; **p**~**haft** *adj* empty.
Physik *f no pl* physics *sing*.
physikalisch *adj* physical; *Experimente* physics *attr*; **das ist** ~ **nicht erklärbar** that can't be explained by physics.
Physiker(in *f) m* - physicist.
Physikum *nt no pl (Univ)* preliminary examination in medicine.
Physiologe *m,* **Physiologin** *f* physiologist.
Physiologie *f* physiology.
physiologisch *adj* physiological.
physisch *adj* physical.
Pianist(in *f) m* pianist.
Pickel *m* - **(a)** spot, pimple. **(b)** *(Spitzhacke)* pick(axe *(Brit)* or ax *US)*; *(Eis~)* ice axe *(Brit)*, ice ax *(US)*.
pick(e)lig *adj* spotty, pimply.
picken *vti* to peck *(nach* at*)*.
Picknick *nt* **-s** *or* **-e** picnic. ~ **machen** to have a picnic.
picknicken *vi* to (have a) picnic.
piekfein *adj (col)* posh *(col)*.
pieksauber *adj (col)* spotless.
piep *interj* tweet(-tweet).
Piep *m* **-e** *(col)* **er sagt keinen** ~ he doesn't say a (single) word; **keinen** ~ **mehr machen** to have had it *(col)*.
piepe, piep|egal *adj pred* **das ist mir** ~**!** *(col)* it's all one to me *(col)*.
piepen, pie|psen *vi (Vogel)* to cheep; *(Kinderstimme)* to pipe; *(Maus)* to squeak; *(Funkgerät etc)* to bleep. **bei dir piept's wohl!** *(col)* are you off your head?; **es war zum P**~**!** *(col)* it was a scream *(col)*.
Piepmatz *m (col: kleiner Vogel)* birdie *(col)*.
piepsig *adj (col)* squeaky.
Piepsstimme *f* squeaky voice.
Pier *m* **-s** *or* **-e** *or f* **-s** jetty, pier.
piesacken *vt (col) (quälen)* to torment; *(belästigen)* to pester.
Pietät [pie'tɛːt] *f* reverence *no pl*; *(Achtung)* respect.
pietätlos [pie'tɛːt-] *adj* irreverent.

Pigment *nt* pigment.
Pigmentfleck *m* pigmentation mark.
Pik[1] *m (col)* **einen** ~ **auf jdn haben** to have a grudge against sb.
Pik[2] *nt* **-s** *(Cards) (Farbe)* spades *pl*; *(Karte)* spade. ~**-As** ace of spades.
pikant *adj* piquant; *Witz, Geschichte auch* racy.
Pikanterie *f* **(a)** *no pl siehe adj* piquancy; raciness. **(b)** *(Bemerkung)* racy remark.
Pike *f* **-n** pike. etw **von der** ~ **auf lernen** *(fig)* to learn sth starting from the bottom.
piken *vti (col)* to prick.
pikiert *adj (col)* peeved, piqued. **sie machte ein** ~**es Gesicht** she looked peeved.
Pikkolo *m* **-s (a)** *(Kellnerlehrling)* trainee waiter. **(b)** *(fig)* mini-version, baby; *(auch* ~**flasche)** *quarter bottle of champagne.* **(c)** *(Mus: auch* ~**flöte)** piccolo.
piksen *vti (col)* to prick.
Pilger(in *f) m* - pilgrim.
Pilgerfahrt *f* pilgrimage.
pilgern *vi aux sein* to make a pilgrimage; *(col: gehen)* to wend one's way.
Pille *f* **-n** pill. **sie nimmt die** ~ she's on the pill.
Pilot(in *f) m (wk)* **-en, -en** pilot.
Pilotstudie *f* pilot study.
Pils -, -, **Pils(e)ner** *nt* - Pils.
Pilz *m* **-e (a)** fungus; *(giftig)* toadstool; *(eßbar)* mushroom; *(Atom~)* mushroom cloud. **wie** ~**e aus dem Boden schießen** to mushroom. **(b)** *(Haut~)* ringworm; *(Fuß~ auch)* athlete's foot.
Pilz-: ~**krankheit** *f* fungal disease; ~**vergiftung** *f* fungus poisoning.
Pimmel *m* - *(col: Penis)* willie *(col)*.
pingelig *adj (col)* finicky *(col)*, fussy.
Pingpong *nt* **-s** *(col)* ping-pong.
Pinguin ['pɪnguiːn] *m* **-e** penguin.
Pinie ['piːniə] *f* pine (tree).
Pinkel *m* - *(col)* **ein feiner** *or* **vornehmer** ~ a swell, Lord Muck *(col)*.
pinkeln *vi (col)* to pee *(col)*, to piddle *(col)*.
Pinscher *m* - pinscher.
Pinsel *m* - **(a)** brush. **(b)** *(col)* **ein eingebildeter** ~ a self-opinionated twerp *(col)*.
pinseln *vti (col)* to paint; *(pej: malen)* to daub.
Pinte *f* **-n** *(col: Lokal)* boozer *(Brit col)*, bar.
Pinzette *f* (pair of) tweezers *pl*.
Pionier *m* **-e (a)** *(Mil)* sapper. **(b)** *(fig)* pioneer.
Pionier|arbeit *f* pioneering work.
Pipi *nt or m* **-s** *(baby-talk)* wee-wee *(baby-talk)*. ~**machen** to do a wee-wee.
Pirat *m (wk)* **-en, -en** pirate.
Piratensender *m* pirate radio station.
Piraterie *f (lit, fig)* piracy.
Pirsch *f no pl* stalk. **auf (die)** ~ **gehen** to go stalking.
pirschen *vi* to stalk, to go stalking.
Piß *m no pl,* **Pisse** *f no pl (col!)* piss *(col!)*.
pissen *vi (col!)* to (have a) piss *(col!)*; *(regnen)* to piss down *(col!)*.
Pistazie [pɪs'taːtsiə] *f* pistachio.
Piste *f* **-n** *(Ski)* piste, (ski-)run; *(Rennbahn)* track; *(Aviat)* runway; *(behelfsmäßig)* airstrip.
Pistole *f* **-n** pistol. **jdn mit vorgehaltener** ~ **zwingen** to force sb at gunpoint; **jdm die** ~ **auf die Brust setzen** *(fig)* to hold a pistol to sb's head; **wie aus der** ~ **geschossen** *(fig)* like a shot.
pitsch(e)naß *adj (col)* soaking (wet).
pittoresk *adj* picturesque.
Pkw ['peːkaːveː] *m* **-s** = **Personenkraftwagen**.
placken *vr (col)* to slave (away) *(col)*.
Plackerei *f (col)* grind *(col)*.
plädieren* *vi (Jur, fig)* to plead *(für, auf +acc* for*)*.
Plädoyer [plɛdoa'jeː] *nt* **-s** *(Jur)* summing up, summation *(US); (fig)* plea.
Plage *f* **-n** *(fig)* nuisance. **man hat schon seine** ~ **mit dir** you are a nuisance.
Plagegeist *m* nuisance, pest.

plagen 1 vt to torment; (mit Bitten und Fragen auch) to pester. **ein geplagter Mann** a harassed man. **2** vr (**a**) (leiden) to be bothered (mit by). (**b**) (arbeiten) to slave away (col).
Plagiat nt plagiarism.
Plakat nt **-e** poster; (aus Pappe) placard.
Plakatfarbe f poster paint.
plakatieren* vt to placard; (fig) to broadcast.
Plakette f (Abzeichen) badge; (Münze) commemorative coin; (an Wänden) plaque.
Plan[1] m **-e** (**a**) plan. **den ~ fassen, etw zu tun** to plan to do sth; **~e machen** or **schmieden** to make plans; **nach ~ verlaufen** to go according to plan. (**b**) (Stadt~) (street-)map; (Grundriß, Bau~) blueprint; (Zeittafel) timetable (Brit), schedule (US).
Plan[2] m **-e auf den ~ treten** (fig) to come on the scene; **jdn auf den ~ rufen** (fig) to bring sb into the arena.
Plane f **-n** tarpaulin; (von LKW) hood; (Schutzdach) awning.
planen vti to plan.
Planer(in f) m - planner.
Planet m (wk) **-en, -en** planet.
Planetarium nt planetarium.
Planetensystem nt planetary system.
plangemäß adj = **planmäßig**.
planieren* vt Boden to level (off).
Planierraupe f bulldozer.
Planke f **-n** plank, board; (Leit~) crash barrier.
planlos adj unsystematic; (ziellos) random.
Planlosigkeit f lack of planning.
planmäßig adj (wie geplant) as planned; (pünktlich) on schedule; (methodisch) methodical. **~e Ankunft/Abfahrt** scheduled time of arrival/departure.
Planschbecken nt paddling pool.
planschen vi to splash around.
Plan-: **~soll** nt output target; **~stelle** f post.
Plantage [plan'taːʒə] f **-n** plantation.
Planung f planning. **in der ~** at the planning stage.
Plan-: **~wagen** m covered wagon; **~wirtschaft** f planned economy.
Plappermaul nt (col) chatterbox (col); (Schwätzer) gossip (col).
plappern 1 vi to prattle; (Geheimnis verraten) to blab (col). **2** vt Blödsinn to talk.
plärren vti (col: weinen) to bawl; (Radio) to blare (out).
Plastik[1] nt **-s** (Kunststoff) plastic.
Plastik[2] f (**a**) (Bildhauerkunst) plastic art (form). (**b**) (Skulptur) sculpture.
plastisch adj (**a**) (knetbar) malleable. (**b**) (dreidimensional) three-dimensional, 3-D; (fig: anschaulich) vivid. **~e Sprache** vivid language; **das kann ich mir ~ vorstellen** I can just picture it. (**c**) (Art, Med) plastic. **~e Chirurgie** plastic surgery.
Plastizität f no pl (**a**) (Formbarkeit) malleability. (**b**) (fig: Anschaulichkeit) vividness.
Plateau [pla'toː] nt **-s** plateau.
Platin nt no pl platinum.
platonisch adj platonic.
platsch interj splash, splosh.
platschen vi (col) to splash; (regnen) to pour.
plätschern vi to splash; (Bach auch) to babble. **eine ~de Unterhaltung** light conversation.
platschnaß adj (col) soaking (wet).
platt adj (**a**) (flach) flat. **etw ~ drücken** to flatten sth; **einen P~en** (col) or **einen ~en Reifen haben** to have a flat (tyre (Brit) or tire US). (**b**) (fig: geistlos) dull. (**c**) (col: verblüfft) **~sein** to be flabbergasted (col).
Platt nt no pl (col) Low German, Plattdeutsch.
plattdeutsch adj Low German.
Platte f **-n** (**a**) (Holz~) board; (Glas~/Metall~/Plastik~) sheet of glass/metal/plastic; (Beton~, Stein~) slab; (zum Pflastern) flagstone; (Kachel,

Fliese) tile; (Herd~) hotplate; (Tisch~) (table-)top; (Phot) plate; (Gedenktafel) plaque. (**b**) (Fleisch) serving-dish; (Torten~) cake plate. **kalte ~** cold dish. (**c**) (Schall~) record, disc. **etw auf ~ aufnehmen** to record sth; **die ~ kenne ich schon** (col) I've heard all that before (col); **leg doch mal eine neue ~ auf!** (col) change the record, can't you! (**d**) (col: Glatze) bald head; (kahle Stelle) bald patch.
plätten vt (dial) to iron, to press; siehe **geplättet**.
Platten-: **~leger** m - paver; **~sammlung** f record collection; **~spieler** m record-player; **~teller** m turntable; **~wechsler** m - record changer.
Platt-: **~fisch** m flatfish; **~form** f platform; (fig: Grundlage) basis; **~fuß** m flat foot; **p~füßig** adj, adv flat-footed; **~heit** f (**a**) no pl (Geistlosigkeit) dullness; (**b**) usu pl (Redensart etc) platitude.
Platz m **-e** (**a**) (freier Raum) room, space. **~ für jdn/etw schaffen** to make room for sb/sth; **mehr als 10 Leute haben hier nicht ~** there's not room for more than 10 people here; **jdm den (ganzen) ~ wegnehmen** to take up all the room; **~ machen** to get out of the way (col); **mach mal ein bißchen ~** make a bit of room; **~ für jdn/etw bieten** to have room for sb/sth; **~ da!** (col) (get) out of the way there! (col).
(**b**) (Sitzplatz) seat. **~ nehmen** to take a seat; **behalten Sie doch bitte ~!** (form) please remain seated (form); **der Saal hat 2.000 ~e** the hall seats 2,000; **mit jdm den ~ tauschen** to change places with sb; **~!** (zum Hund) sit!
(**c**) (Stelle, Ort, Rang, Arbeits~) place. **etw (wieder) an seinen ~ stellen** to put sth (back) in (its) place; **fehl** or **nicht am ~ sein** to be out of place; **auf die ~e, fertig, los!** (Sport) on your marks, get set, go!; **seinen ~ behaupten** to stand one's ground; **das Buch hat einen festen ~ auf der Bestsellerliste** the book is firmly established on the bestseller list; **den ersten ~ einnehmen** (fig) to come first; **auf ~ zwei** in second place; **jdn auf die ~e verweisen** (fig) to beat sb; **auf ~ wetten** to make a place bet; **wir haben noch einen freien ~ im Büro** we've still got one vacancy in the office; **das erste Hotel am ~** the best hotel in town.
(**d**) (umbaute Fläche) square. **auf dem ~** in the square.
(**e**) (Sport~) playing field; (Ftbl, Hockey) pitch (Brit), field; (Handball~, Tennis~) court; (Golf~) (golf) course. **einen Spieler vom ~ stellen** or **verweisen** to send a player off.
Platz-: **~angst** f (col) claustrophobia; **~angst bekommen** to get claustrophobic; **~anweiser(in** f) m - usher(ette).
Plätzchen nt (Gebäck) biscuit (Brit), cookie (US).
platzen vi aux sein (**a**) (aufreißen) to burst; (Naht, Hose, Haut) to split; (explodieren) to explode; (einen Riß bekommen) to crack. **wir sind vor Lachen fast geplatzt** we split our sides laughing; **ins Zimmer ~** (col) to burst into the room; **jdm ins Haus ~** (col) to descend on sb; (vor Wut/Neid) **~** (col) to be bursting (with rage/envy) (**b**) (col: scheitern) (Geschäft) to fall through; (Freundschaft) to break up; (Theorie, Verschwörung) to collapse; (Wechsel) to bounce (col). **die Verlobung ist geplatzt** the engagement is (all) off; **etw ~ lassen** Plan) to make sth fall through; Theorie to explode; Spionagering to smash sth.
Platz-: **~hirsch** m (lit) stag; (fig col: Mann) macho type; **~karte** f (Rail) seat reservation (ticket); **~konzert** nt open-air concert; **~mangel** m lack of space; **~miete** f (Theat) season ticket; (Sport) ground rent; **~patrone** f blank (cartridge); **~regen** m cloudburst; **das ist nur ein ~regen** it's only a (passing) shower; **p~sparend** adj space-saving attr; **das ist p~sparender** that saves more space; **~verweis** m sending-off; **~wahl** f

toss-up; ~**wart** m (Sport) groundsman; ~**wechsel** m change of place; (Sport) change of position; ~**wette** f place bet; ~**wunde** f laceration.

Plauderei f chat, conversation.

Plauderer m -, **Plauderin** f conversationalist.

plaudern vi to chat (über +acc, von about); (verraten) to talk. **mit ihm läßt sich gut** ~ he's easy to talk to.

Plausch m -e (col) chat.

plauschen vi (col) to have a chat.

plausibel adj plausible. **jdm etw** ~ **machen** to explain sth to sb.

Playback ['pleɪbæk] nt -s (a) (Bandaufnahme) backing track. (b) no pl (Verfahren) (bei Schallplatte) double-tracking no pl; (TV) miming no pl.

plazieren* 1 vt (a) (Platz anweisen) to put; (Tennis) to seed. (b) (zielen) Ball to position; Schlag to land. **gut plazierte Aufschläge** well-positioned services. 2 vr (a) (col: sich setzen, stellen) to plant oneself (col). (b) (Sport) to be placed; (Tennis) to be seeded. **der Läufer konnte sich gut/nicht** ~ the runner was well-placed/wasn't even placed.

Plazierung f (Einlauf) order; (Tennis) seeding; (Platz) place. **welche** ~ **hatte er?** where did he come in?

pleite adj pred, adv (col) Mensch broke (col); Firma auch bust (col). ~ **gehen** to go bust.

Pleite f -n (col) bankruptcy; (fig) washout (col). ~ **machen** to go bust (col); **damit/mit ihm haben wir eine** ~ **erlebt** it/he was a disaster.

Pleitegeier m (col) (a) (drohende Pleite) threat of bankruptcy. (b) (Bankrotteur) bankrupt.

plemplem adj pred (col) nuts (col).

Plenar-: ~**saal** m assembly room; ~**sitzung** f plenary session.

Plenum nt plenum.

Pleuelstange f connecting rod.

Plissee-: ~**falte** f pleat; ~**rock** m pleated skirt.

Plombe f -n (a) (Siegel) lead seal. (b) (Zahn~) filling.

plombieren* vt (a) (versiegeln) to seal. (b) Zahn to fill. **er hat mir zwei Zähne plombiert** he did two fillings.

plötzlich 1 adj sudden. 2 adv all of a sudden. **aber etwas** ~! (col) look sharp! (col); **das kommt alles so** ~ (col) it all happens so suddenly.

Pluderhose f Turkish trousers pl.

Plumeau [ply'moː] nt -s eiderdown, quilt.

plump adj Figur, Form ungainly no adv; Ausdruck clumsy; Bemerkung crass; Mittel, Lüge crude. ~**e Annäherungsversuche** very obvious advances.

plumps interj bang; (lauter) crash.

Plumps m -e (col) (Fall) tumble; (Geräusch) thud. **einen** ~ **machen** (baby-talk) to fall; **mit einem** ~ **ins Wasser fallen** to fall into the water with a splash.

plumpsen vi aux sein (col) to tumble. **er plumpste ins Wasser** he fell into the water with a splash.

Plumpsklo(sett) nt (col) earth closet.

plump-vertraulich 1 adj hail-fellow-well-met. 2 adv in a hail-fellow-well-met sort of way.

Plunder m no pl junk, rubbish.

Plünd(e)rer m - looter, plunderer.

Plündergebäck nt flaky pastry.

plündern vti to loot; (ausrauben) to raid; Obstbaum to strip.

Plünderung f looting, pillage.

Plural m -e plural. **im** ~ **stehen** to be in (the) plural.

plus 1 prep +gen plus. 2 adv plus. **bei** ~ **5 Grad** at 5 degrees (above freezing or zero).

Plus nt - (a) (Phys col: ~pol) positive (pole). (b) (Comm) (Zuwachs) increase; (Gewinn) profit; (Überschuß) surplus. (c) (fig: Vorteil) plus, advantage. **das ist ein** ~ **für dich** that's a point in your favour (Brit) or favor (US).

Plüsch m -e plush.

Plüsch- in cpds plush; ~**tier** nt ≈ soft toy.

Plus-: ~**pol** m (Elec) positive pole; ~**punkt** m (Sport) point; (Sch) extra mark; (fig) plus point, advantage; ~**quamperfekt** nt pluperfect.

Plutonium nt no pl plutonium.

pneumatisch [pnɔy'maːtɪʃ] adj pneumatic.

Po m -s (col) = **Popo**.

Pöbel m no pl rabble, mob.

pöbelhaft adj uncouth, vulgar.

pochen vi to knock; (Herz, Blut) to pound. **auf etw** (acc) ~ (fig) to insist on sth.

pochieren* [pɔ'ʃiːrən] vt Ei to poach.

Pocken pl smallpox.

Pocken-: ~**narbe** f pockmark; ~**(schutz)impfung** f smallpox vaccination.

Podest nt or m -e (Sockel) pedestal (auch fig); (Podium) platform; (Treppenabsatz) landing.

Podium nt (lit, fig) platform; (des Dirigenten) podium; (bei Diskussion) panel.

Podiumsdiskussion f panel discussion.

Poesie [poe'ziː] f (lit, fig) poetry.

Poet m (wk) -en, -en (geh) poet.

poetisch adj poetic.

Pointe ['poɛ̃tə] f -n (eines Witzes) punch-line; (einer Geschichte) point.

pointiert [poɛ̃'tiːɐt] adj trenchant, pithy.

Pokal m -e (zum Trinken) goblet; (Sport) cup.

Pokal-: ~**endspiel** nt cup final; ~**sieger** m cup-winners pl; ~**spiel** nt cup-tie.

Pökelfleisch nt salt meat.

pökeln vt Fleisch, Fisch to salt, to pickle.

Poker nt no pl poker.

pokern vi to play poker. **um etw** ~ (fig) to haggle for sth.

Pol m -e pole. **der ruhende** ~ (fig) the calming influence.

polar adj polar. ~**e Kälte** arctic coldness; ~ **entgegengesetzt** diametrically opposed.

polarisieren* vtr to polarize.

Polarisierung f polarization.

Polar-: ~**kreis** m polar circle; **nördlicher/südlicher** ~**kreis** Arctic/Antarctic circle; ~**licht** nt polar lights pl; ~**stern** m pole Star.

Pole m (wk) -n, -n Pole.

Polemik f polemics sing; (Streitschrift) polemic.

polemisch adj polemic(al).

polemisieren* vi to polemicize. ~ **gegen** to inveigh against.

Polen nt Poland.

Polente f no pl (dated col) cops pl (col).

Police [po'liːsə] f -n (insurance) policy.

Polier m -e site foreman.

polieren* vt (lit, fig) to polish. **jdm die Fresse** or **Schnauze** ~ (col!) to smash sb's face in (col).

Polier-: ~**mittel** nt polish; ~**wachs** nt wax polish.

Poliklinik f (Krankenhaus) clinic (for outpatients only); (Abteilung) outpatients' department.

Polin f Pole, Polish woman.

Politesse f (woman) traffic warden (Brit).

Politik f (a) no pl politics sing; (politischer Standpunkt) politics pl. **welche** ~ **vertritt er?** what are his politics?; **in die** ~ **gehen** to go into politics. (b) (bestimmte ~) policy. **ihre gesamte** ~ all their policies.

Politiker(in f) m - politician.

politisch adj political.

politisieren* 1 vi to talk politics, to politicize. 2 vt to politicize; jdn to make politically aware.

Politisierung f politicization.

Politologe m (wk), **Politologin** f political scientist.

Politologie f political science, politics sing.

Politur f polish. **die** ~ **ist runter** (fig col) the glamour (Brit) or glamor (US) has gone.

Polizei f police pl; (Gebäude) police station. **auf die** or **zur** ~ **gehen** to go to the police; **er ist bei der** ~ he's in the police (force).

Polizei- in cpds police; ~**aufsicht** f **unter** ~ **aufsicht stehen** to be under police surveillance;

~**beamte(r)** m police official; *(Polizist)* police officer; ~**dienststelle** f *(form)* police station; ~**direktion** f police headquarters pl; ~**haft** f detention; ~**kommissar** m (police) inspector.

polizeilich adj no pred police attr. ~**es Führungszeugnis** certificate issued by the police, stating that the holder has no criminal record; **sich** ~ **melden** to register with the police.

Polizei-: ~**präsident** m chief constable, chief of police *(US)*; ~**präsidium** nt police headquarters pl; ~**revier** nt *(~wache)* police station; ~**staat** m police state; ~**streife** f police patrol; ~**stunde** f closing time; ~**wache** f police station.

Polizist(in f) m policeman/policewoman.

polnisch adj Polish.

Polnisch(e) nt decl as adj Polish; *siehe* **Deutsch(e).**

Polohemd nt sports shirt; *(für Frau)* casual blouse.

Polster nt - **(a)** cushion; *(Polsterung)* upholstery no pl; *(bei Kleidung)* pad, padding no pl. **(b)** *(fig) (Fett~)* flab no pl *(col)*; *(Bauch)* spare tyre *(Brit)* or tire *(US)*; *(Geldreserve)* reserves pl.

Polster-: ~**garnitur** f three-piece suite; ~**möbel** pl upholstered furniture.

polstern vt to upholster; *Kleidung, Tür* to pad. **etw neu** ~ to re-upholster sth; **sie ist gut gepolstert** *(col)* she's well-padded; *(finanziell)* she's not short of the odd penny.

Polsterung f upholstery.

Polter|abend m party on the eve of a wedding with smashing of crockery, ≈ shower *(US)*.

Poltergeist m poltergeist.

poltern vi **(a)** to crash about. **was hat da eben so gepoltert?** what was that crash?; **es poltert** there's a real din going on. **(b)** *aux sein (sich laut bewegen)* to crash, to bang. **(c)** *(col: schimpfen)* to rant (and rave).

Poly-: ~**ester** m - polyester; ~**gamie** f polygamy.

Polyp m *(wk)* -en, -en **(a)** *(Zool)* polyp. **(b)** *(Med)* ~**en** adenoids. **(c)** *(hum col: Polizist)* cop *(col)*.

Poly-: ~**technikum** nt polytechnic, poly *(col)*; **p~technisch** adj polytechnic.

Pomade f hair-cream.

Pommern nt Pomerania.

Pommes frites [pɔm'frit(s)] pl chips pl *(Brit)*, French fries pl.

Pomp m no pl pomp.

pompös adj grandiose.

Pontius ['pɔntsiʊs] m: **von** ~ **zu Pilatus** from pillar to post.

Pony¹ ['pɔni] nt -s pony.

Pony² ['pɔni] m -s fringe *(Brit)*, bangs pl *(US)*.

Ponyfrisur f sie hat eine ~ she has a fringe *(Brit)*, she has bangs *(US)*.

Pool(billard) ['puːl(bɪljart)] nt pool.

Pop m no pl *(Mus)* pop; *(Art)* pop-art.

Popanz m -e *(Schreckgespenst)* bogey.

pop(e)lig adj *(col)* **(a)** *(knauserig)* stingy *(col)*. **(b)** *(dürftig)* crummy *(col)*.

Popelin m -e, **Popeline** f - poplin.

popeln vi *(col)* **(in der Nase)** ~ to pick one's nose.

Pop-: ~**gruppe** f pop group; ~**konzert** nt pop concert; ~ **musik** f pop music.

Popo m -s *(col)* bottom, bum *(col)*.

poppig adj *(col) (Art, Mus)* pop no adv; *Kleidung* trendy.

Popper m *(col)* new romantic.

populär adj popular *(bei* with).

popularisieren* vt to popularize.

Popularität f popularity.

populärwissenschaftlich adj popular science.

Pore f -n pore.

Porno m -s *(col)* porn *(col)*, porno *(US col)*.

Pornographie f pornography.

pornographisch adj pornographic.

porös adj *(durchlässig)* porous; *(brüchig)* perished.

Porree ['pɔre] m -s leek.

Portal nt -e portal.

Portemonnaie [pɔrtmɔ'neː] nt -s purse.

Portier [pɔr'tieː] m -s porter.

Portion f **(a)** *(beim Essen)* portion, helping. **eine halbe** ~ *(fig col)* a half-pint *(col)*; **eine zweite** ~ a second helping. **(b)** *(fig col: Anteil)* amount. **er besitzt eine ganze** ~ **Frechheit** he's got a fair bit of cheek *(col)*.

Porto nt, pl -s or **Porti** postage no pl *(für* on, for*)*; *(für Kisten etc)* carriage. ~ **zahlt Empfänger** postage paid.

portofrei adj postage paid.

Porträt [*auch* pɔr'trεː] nt -s *(lit, fig)* portrait.

porträtieren* vt jdn ~ to paint sb's portrait; *(fig)* to portray sb.

Portugal nt Portugal.

Portugiese m *(wk)* -n, -n, **Portugiesin** f Portuguese.

portugiesisch adj Portuguese.

Portwein m port.

Porzellan nt -e *(Material)* porcelain; *(Geschirr)* china.

Porzellan- in cpds china; ~**erde** f china clay; ~**geschirr** nt china, crockery; ~**manufaktur** f china factory.

Posaune f -n trombone; *(fig)* trumpet.

posaunen* *(col)* **1** vi to play the trombone. **2** vti *(fig)* to bellow, to bawl. **etw in alle Welt** ~ to tell sth to the whole world.

Posaunenbläser m trombonist.

Pose f -n pose.

posieren* vi to pose.

Position f position; *(Comm: auf Liste)* item.

Positionslicht nt navigation light.

positiv adj positive. **eine** ~**e Antwort** an affirmative (answer); **etw** ~ **wissen** to know sth for a fact; ~ **zu etw stehen** to be in favour *(Brit)* or favor *(US)* of sth.

Positiv nt *(Phot)* positive.

Positur f posture. **sich in** ~ **setzen/stellen** to adopt a posture.

Posse f -n farce.

Possen m - *(dated)* prank, tomfoolery no pl. ~ **reißen** to clown around.

Possessivpronomen nt possessive pronoun.

possierlich adj comical, funny.

Post f -en post, mail; *(~amt, ~wesen)* post office. **war die** ~ **schon da?** has the post or mail come yet?; **ist** ~ **für mich da?** are there any letters for me?; **etw mit der** ~ **schicken** to send sth by post or mail; **etw auf die** ~ **geben** to post or mail sth; **auf die** or **zur** ~ **gehen** to go to the post office; **mit getrennter** ~ under separate cover.

postalisch adj postal.

Post-: ~**amt** nt post office; ~**anweisung** f ≈ postal *(Brit)* or money order; ~**auto** nt post-office van; ~**beamte(r)** m, ~**beamtin** f post office official; ~**bote** m postman *(Brit)*, mailman *(US)*.

Posten m - **(a)** *(Anstellung)* post, job. **(b)** *(Mil: Wachmann)* guard; *(Stelle)* post. ~ **stehen** to stand guard; ~ **beziehen** to take up one's post. **(c) auf dem** ~ **sein** *(aufpassen)* to be awake; *(gesund sein)* to be fit; **nicht ganz auf dem** ~ **sein** to be off-colour *(Brit)* or off-color *(US)*. **(d)** *(Streik~)* picket. **(e)** *(Comm: Warenmenge)* quantity, lot. **(f)** *(Comm: im Etat)* item, entry.

Postenjäger m *(col)* go-getter *(col)*.

Poster nt -(s) poster.

Postfach nt post-office or PO box.

posthum adj posthumous.

postieren* **1** vt to position. **2** vr to position oneself.

Post-: ~**karte** f postcard; ~**kasten** m pillar box *(Brit)*, mailbox *(US)*; ~**kutsche** f mail coach, stagecoach; **p~lagernd** 1 adj to be called for; **2** adv poste restante *(Brit)*, general delivery *(US)*; ~**leitzahl** f post(al) code, Zip code *(US)*; ~**minister** m ≈ postmaster general; ~**sache** f post office mail *no pl;* ~**scheck** *m* (Post Office *or* National) Giro cheque' *(Brit);* ~**scheckamt** *nt* National Giro office *(Brit);* ~**scheckkonto** *nt* National *or* Post Office Giro account *(Brit);* ~**sparkasse** *f* Post Office savings bank; ~**stempel** *m* postmark.

postulieren* *vt* to postulate.

Post-: p~**wendend** *adv* by return (of post) *(Brit),* by return mail; ~**wertzeichen** *nt (form)* postage stamp *(form);* ~**wurfsendung** *f* postal door to door delivery; ~**zustellung** *f* mail delivery.

potent *adj* potent; *(fig) Phantasie* powerful.

Potential [poten'tsia:l] *nt* **-e** potential.

potentiell [poten'tsiel] *adj* potential.

Potenz *f* **(a)** *(Med)* potency; *(fig)* ability. **(b)** *(Math)* power. **zweite/dritte** ~ square/cube.

potenzieren* *vt (Math)* to raise to the power of; *(col: steigern)* to multiply.

Potpourri ['potpuri] *nt* **-s** *(Mus)* medley *(aus* of); *(fig)* assortment.

Pott *m* ¨**e** *(col)* pot.

Pott-: ~**asche** *f* potash; ~**wal** *m* sperm whale.

poussieren [pu'si:rən] *vi (dated col: flirten)* to flirt.

prä-, prae- *pref* pre-.

Prä\|ambel *f* preamble *(gen* to).

Pracht *f no pl* splendour *(Brit),* splendor *(US).* **in seiner vollen** *or* **ganzen** ~ in all its splendour; **es ist eine wahre** ~ it's (really) superb.

Pracht-: ~**entfaltung** *f* magnificent display; ~**exemplar** *nt* beauty *(col); (fig: Mensch)* fine specimen.

prächtig *adj (prunkvoll, großartig)* splendid.

Pracht-: ~**kerl** *m (col)* great guy *(col);* (~**exemplar)** beauty *(col);* ~**stück** *nt* = ~**exemplar.**

prädestinieren* *vt* to predestine.

Prädikat *nt (Gram)* predicate; *(Bewertung)* rating; *(Rangbezeichnung)* title. **Wein mit** ~ special quality wine.

Prag *nt* Prague.

prägen *vt* **(a)** to stamp; *Münzen* to mint; *Leder, Papier* to emboss; *(erfinden) Begriffe, Wörter* to coin. **(b)** *(fig: formen) Charakter* to form; *(Erlebnis, Kummer) jdn* to leave its/their mark on. **(c)** *(kennzeichnen) Stadtbild* to characterize.

Prägestempel *m* die, stamp.

Pragmatiker(in *f) m* - pragmatist.

pragmatisch *adj* pragmatic.

prägnant *adj* concise, terse.

Prägnanz *f* conciseness, terseness.

Prägung *f* **(a)** *siehe vt (a, b)* stamping; minting; embossing; coining; forming. **(b)** *(auf Münzen)* imprint; *(auf Leder, Papier)* embossing; *(Eigenart)* character; *(von Charakter)* mould *(Brit),* mold *(US).*

prahlen *vi* to brag *(mit* about).

Prahlerei *f* bragging *no pl.*

prahlerisch *adj* boastful, bragging *attr.*

Prahlhans *m, pl* **-hänse** *(col)* show-off.

Praktik *f* procedure, method; *(usu pl: Kniff)* practice, trick *(col).*

praktikabel *adj* practicable, practical.

Praktikant(in *f) m* trainee.

Praktiker(in *f) m* - practical man/woman.

Praktikum *nt, pl* **Praktika** practical training.

praktisch 1 *adj* practical; *(nützlich auch)* handy. ~**er Arzt** general practitioner; ~**es Beispiel** concrete example. **2** *adv* practically; *(in der Praxis)* in practice.

praktizieren* 1 *vi* to practise *(Brit),* to practice *(US).* **2** *vt (ausführen)* to put into practice.

Praline *f* chocolate, chocolate candy *(US).*

prall *adj Sack, Brieftasche* bulging; *Arme, Schenkel* big strong *attr; Sonne* blazing. ~ **gefüllt** filled to bursting.

prallen *vi aux sein* **gegen etw** ~ to crash into sth; *(Ball)* to bounce off sth.

prallvoll *adj* full to bursting; *Brieftasche* bulging.

Prämie [-iə] *f* premium; *(Belohnung)* bonus; *(Preis)*

prize.

prämien- [-iən]: ~**begünstigt** *adj* with benefit of premiums; ~**sparen** *vi sep infin, ptp only* to save in a bonus scheme.

präm(i)ieren* *vt (auszeichnen)* to give an award; *(belohnen)* to give a bonus. **etw mit dem ersten Preis** ~ to award sth first prize.

Präm(i)ierung *f* **(a)** *(das Prämieren)* **für diesen Film kommt eine** ~ **nicht in Frage** we can't possibly give this film an award. **(b)** *(Veranstaltung)* presentation.

Pranger *m* - stocks *pl,* pillory. **jdn/etw an den** ~ **stellen** *(fig)* to pillory sb/sth.

Pranke *f* **-n** *(auch col)* paw.

Präparat *nt* preparation.

präparieren* *vt* **(a)** *(konservieren)* to preserve. **(b)** *(Med: zerlegen)* to dissect.

Präposition *f* preposition.

Prärie *f* prairie.

Präsens *nt, pl* **Präsenzien** [-iən] present (tense).

präsent *adj* present. **etw** ~ **haben** to have sth at hand.

präsentieren* 1 *vt* to present. **jdm etw** ~ to present sb with sth. **2** *vr* to present oneself.

Präsenzbibliothek *f* reference library.

Präservativ [prezɛrva'tiːf] *nt* contraceptive, condom.

Präsident(in *f) m* president.

Präsidentschaft *f* presidency.

Präsidentschaftswahl *f* presidential election.

präsidieren* *vi* to preside.

Präsidium *nt (Vorsitz)* presidency; *(Führungsgruppe)* committee; *(Polizei~)* headquarters *pl.*

prasseln *vi* **(a)** *aux sein* to clatter; *(Regen)* to drum; *(fig)* to hail down. **(b)** *(Feuer)* to crackle.

prassen *vi (schlemmen)* to feast; *(in Luxus leben)* to live the high life.

Prasserei *f (Schlemmerei)* feasting; *(Luxusleben)* high life.

Prasselbeere *f* cranberry.

Präteritum *nt, pl* **Präterita** preterite.

präventiv [prɛvɛn'tiːf] *adj* prevent(at)ive.

Praxis *f, pl* **Praxen (a)** *no pl* practice; *(Erfahrung)* experience. **in der** ~ in practice; **die** ~ **sieht anders aus** the facts are different; **ein Idee in die** ~ **umsetzen** to put an idea into practice; **ein Beispiel aus der** ~ an example from real life. **(b)** *(eines Arztes, Rechtsanwalts)* practice. **(c)** *(Behandlungsräume)* surgery *(Brit),* doctor's office *(US); (Anwaltsbüro)* office.

Präzedenzfall *m* precedent.

präzis(e) *adj* precise.

präzisieren* *vt* to state more precisely.

Präzision *f* precision.

Präzisions- *in cpds* precision; ~**arbeit** *f* precision work; ~**arbeit leisten** to work with precision.

predigen *vti* to preach. **jdm etw** ~ *(fig)* to lecture sb on sth.

Prediger(in *f) m* - preacher/woman preacher.

Predigt *f* **-en** *(lit, fig)* sermon. **jdm eine** ~ **über etw** *(acc)* **halten** *(fig)* to give sb a sermon about sth.

Preis *m* **-e (a)** price *(für* of). **zum halben** ~ half-price; **um jeden** ~ *(fig)* at all costs. **(b)** *(bei Wettbewerben)* prize; *(Auszeichnung)* award. **(c)** *(Belohnung)* reward. **(d)** *no pl (liter: Lob)* praise *(auf +acc* of).

Preis-: ~**angabe** *f* **hier fehlt die** ~**angabe** there's no price given; ~**anstieg** *m* rise in prices; ~**ausschreiben** *nt* competition; p~**bewußt** *adj* price-conscious; ~**bindung** *f* price fixing; ~**brecher** *m (Firma)* undercutter; ~**disziplin** *f* price restraint.

preisen *pret* **pries,** *ptp* **gepriesen** *vt (geh)* to praise. **sich glücklich** ~ to count oneself lucky.

Preis-: ~**entwicklung** *f* price trend; ~**erhöhung** *f* price increase; ~**frage** *f* **(a)** question of price; **(b)** *(beim* ~**ausschreiben)** prize question *(in a*

competition); ~**gabe** *f (geh) (Aufgabe)* abandoning; *(von Geheimnis)* divulgence.
preisgeben *vt sep irreg (geh)* **(a)** *(ausliefern)* to leave to the mercy of. **(b)** *(aufgeben)* to abandon. **(c)** *(verraten)* to betray.
Preis-: ~**gefälle** *nt* price gap; **p**~**gekrönt** *adj* award-winning; ~**gericht** *nt* jury; **p**~**günstig** *adj* inexpensive; *etw* **p**~**günstig bekommen** to get sth at a good price; ~**lage** *f* price range.
preislich *adj no pred* price *attr*, in price.
Preis-: ~**nachlaß** *m* discount; **10%** ~**nachlaß bei Barbezahlung** 10% off cash sales; ~**politik** *f* prices policy; ~**rätsel** *nt* prize competition; ~**schild** *nt* price-tag; ~**schlager** *m* (all-time) bargain; ~**senkung** *f* price cut; **p**~**stabil** *adj* stable in price; ~**stopp** *m* price freeze; ~**träger(in** *f)* *m* prize-winner; *(Kultur~)* award-winner; ~**treiberei** *f* forcing up of prices; *(Wucher)* profiteering; ~**verleihung** *f* presentation (of prizes/awards); **p**~**wert** *adj* good value *pred;* **ein p**~**wertes Kleid** a dress which is good value (for money).
prekär *adj (peinlich)* awkward; *(schwierig)* precarious.
Prellbock *m (Rail)* buffers *pl*, buffer-stop; *(fig col)* scapegoat *(col)*, fallguy *(esp US col)*.
prellen 1 *vt* **(a)** to bruise; *(anschlagen)* to hit. **(b)** *(fig col: betrügen)* to swindle. **jdn um etw** ~ to swindle sb out of sth; **die Zeche** ~ to avoid paying the bill. **2** *vr* to bruise oneself.
Prellung *f* bruise, contusion.
Premiere [prə'miɛːrə, pre-] *f* **-n** premiere.
Premierminister [prə'miɛː-, pre-] *m* prime minister.
Presse *f* **-n** *(Mech, Zeitungen)* press. **eine gute** ~ **haben** to get a good press.
Presse-: ~**agentur** *f* news agency; ~**amt** *nt* press office; ~**erklärung** *f* press release; ~**freiheit** *f* freedom of the press; ~**konferenz** *f* press conference; ~**meldung** *f* press report.
pressen *vt* to press; *Obst auch* to squeeze; *(fig: zwingen)* to force *(in +acc* into).
Presse-: ~**notiz** *f* paragraph in the press; ~**stelle** *f* press office.
pressieren* *vi (S Ger, Aus, Sw) (Sache)* to be urgent. **mir pressiert's** I am in a hurry.
Preß-: ~**luft** *f* compressed air; ~**lufthammer** *m* pneumatic hammer.
Prestige [pres'tiːʒə] *nt no pl* prestige.
Preuße *m (wk)* **-n, -n, Preußin** *f* Prussian.
Preußen *nt* Prussia.
preußisch *adj* Prussian.
prickeln *vi (kribbeln)* to tingle; *(kitzeln)* to tickle; *(Bläschen bilden)* to sparkle, to bubble.
prickelnd *adj siehe vi* tingling; tickling; sparkling, bubbling. **der** ~**e Reiz der Neuheit** the thrill of novelty.
pries *pret of* **preisen.**
Priester *m* - priest.
Priesterin *f* priestess.
priesterlich *adj* priestly *no adv*.
Priester-: ~**seminar** *nt* seminary; ~**weihe** *f* ordination (to the priesthood).
prima *adj inv* **(a)** *(col)* fantastic *(col)*. **das hast du** ~ **gemacht** you did that beautifully. **(b)** *(Comm)* top-quality.
Prima *f, pl* **Primen** *(Sch)* eighth and ninth year of German secondary school.
Primaner(in *f)* *m* - *(Sch)* ≈ sixth-former.
primär *adj* primary.
Primas *m* -, **-se** *(Eccl)* primate.
Primat *m (wk)* **-en, -en** *(Zool)* primate.
Primel *f* **-n** *(Wald~)* (wild) primrose; *(farbige Garten~)* primula.
primitiv *adj* primitive.
Primzahl *f* prime (number).
Prinz *m (wk)* **-en, -en** prince.
Prinzessin *f* princess.

Prinzip *nt* **-ien** [-iən] principle. **aus** ~ on principle; **im** ~ in principle; **das funktioniert nach einem einfachen** ~ it works on a simple principle; **ein Mann mit** ~**ien** a man of principle.
prinzipiell *adj (im Prinzip)* in principle; *(aus Prinzip)* on principle.
Priorität *f* priority. ~**en** *pl (Comm)* preference shares *pl*, preferred stock *(US)*; ~ **vor etw** *(dat)* **haben** to take precedence over sth; ~**en setzen** to establish one's priorities.
Prise *f* **-n** *(kleine Menge)* pinch.
Prisma *nt, pl* **Prismen** prism.
Pritsche *f* **-n** **(a)** *(Liegestatt)* plank bed. **(b)** *(von Lkw)* platform.
privat [pri'vaːt] *adj* private. ~ **ist er ganz anders** he's quite different socially; **jdn** ~ **sprechen** to speak to sb in private; **ich sagte es ihm ganz** ~ I told him in absolute confidence; **etw an P**~ **verkaufen** *(Comm)* to sell sth to the public.
Privat- *in cpds* private; ~**adresse** *f* home address; ~**dozent** *m* outside lecturer; ~**gespräch** *nt* private conversation; *(am Telefon)* private call.
privatisieren* [privati'ziːrən] *vt* to privatize.
Privat-: ~**leben** *nt* private life; ~**person** *f* private individual; ~**recht** *nt* private *or* civil law; ~**sache** *f* private matter; **das ist meine** ~**sache** that's a private matter; ~**unterricht** *m* private tuition; ~**vermögen** *nt* private fortune; ~**wirtschaft** *f* private industry.
Privileg [privi'leːk] *nt* **-ien** [-'leːgiən] privilege.
privilegieren* [privile'giːrən] *vt* to favour *(Brit)*, to favor *(US)*. **privilegiert** privileged.
pro *prep* per. ~ **Jahr** per annum *(form)*, a year; ~ **Kopf** per capita *(form)*; ~ **Stück** each, apiece.
Pro *nt (das)* ~ **und Kontra** the pros and cons *pl*.
Probe *f* **-n** **(a)** *(Prüfung)* test. **die** ~ **(auf eine Rechnung) machen** to check a calculation; **er ist auf** ~ **angestellt** he's employed for a probationary period; **jdn/etw auf** ~ **nehmen** to take sb/sth on trial; **jdn/etw auf die** ~ **stellen** to put sb/sth to the test; **zur** ~ to try out. **(b)** *(Theat)* rehearsal. **(c)** *(Teststück, Beispiel)* sample.
Probe-: ~**abzug** *m* proof; ~**angebot** *nt* trial offer; ~**bohrung** *f* test drill; ~**exemplar** *nt* specimen (copy); **p**~**fahren** *sep irreg infin, ptp only* **1** *vt* to test-drive; **2** *vi aux sein* to go for a test drive; ~**fahrt** *f* test drive; ~**lauf** *m* trial run; *(Sport)* practice run.
proben *vti* to rehearse.
Probe-: ~**stück** *nt* specimen; **p**~**weise** *adv* on a trial basis; ~**zeit** *f* trial period.
probieren* **1** *vt* to have a try at; *(kosten) Speisen, Getränke* to sample; *(prüfen)* to test. **laß es mich mal** ~! let me have a go! **2** *vi (versuchen, kosten)* to try. **P**~ **geht über Studieren** *(Prov)* the proof of the pudding is in the eating *(Prov)*.
Problem *nt* **-e** problem.
Problematik *f* difficulty *(gen* with); *(Problembereich)* problems *pl*.
problematisch *adj* problematic; *(fragwürdig)* questionable.
problemlos *adj* problem-free.
Produkt *nt* **-e** *(lit, fig)* product.
Produktion *f* production.
Produktions- *in cpds* production; ~**ausfall** *m* loss of production; ~**kosten** *pl* production costs *pl*; ~**menge** *f* output; ~**mittel** *pl* means of production *pl*; ~**rückgang** *m* drop in production.
produktiv *adj* productive.
Produktivität *f* productivity.
Produzent(in *f)* *m* producer.
produzieren* **1** *vt* **(a)** *auch vi* to produce. **(b)** *(col: hervorbringen) Lärm* to make; *Entschuldigung* to come up with *(col)*; *Romane* to churn out *(col)*. **2** *vr (pej)* to show off.
Prof. = **Professor.**
profan *adj (weltlich)* secular; *(gewöhnlich)* mundane.

professionell adj professional.
Professor m, **Professorin** f **(a)** (Hochschul~) professor. **(b)** (Aus: Gymnasiallehrer) grammar school teacher (Brit), high school teacher (US).
Professur f chair (für in, of).
Profi m -s (col) pro (col).
Profil nt -e **(a)** (von Gesicht) profile; (fig: Ansehen) image. **im** ~ in profile; **die Partei hat mehr** ~ **bekommen** the party has sharpened its image. **(b)** (von Reifen, Schuhsohle) tread. **(c)** (Querschnitt) cross-section; (Längsschnitt) vertical section; (fig: Skizze) profile.
profilieren* 1 vt (scharf umreißen) to define. 2 vr (sich ein Image geben) to create a distinctive personal image for oneself. **er will sich akademisch/politisch** ~ he wants to make his mark academically/in politics.
profiliert adj (scharf umrissen) clear-cut no adv; (hervorstechend) distinctive.
Profilsohle f sole with a tread.
Profit m -e profit. ~ **aus etw ziehen** (lit) to make a profit from sth; (fig) to reap the benefits from sth; **den/keinen** ~ **von etw haben** to profit/not to profit from sth; **ohne/mit** ~ **arbeiten** to work unprofitably/profitably.
Profit-: p~**bringend** adj profitable; ~**gier** f greed for profit.
profitieren* vti to profit; (fig auch) to gain. **und was profitierst du dabei** or **davon?** what do you stand to gain by it?
Profit-: ~**jäger**, ~**macher** m (col) profiteer; ~**macherei** f (col) profiteering.
pro forma adv as a matter of form.
Pro-forma-Rechnung f pro forma invoice.
Prognose f -n prognosis; (Wetter~) forecast.
Programm nt -e programme (Brit), program (US, Comp); (Tagesordnung) agenda; (TV: Sender) channel; (Sendefolge) programmes (Brit) pl, programs (US) pl; (gedrucktes Radio~, TV~) programme (Brit) or program (US) guide; (Verlags~) list; (Kollektion) range. **nach** ~ **as** planned; **auf dem** ~ **stehen** to be on the programme/agenda.
Programm-: ~**heft** nt programme (Brit), program (US); ~**hinweis** m (Rad, TV) programme (Brit) or program (US) announcement.
programmieren* vti to programme (Brit), to program (US, Comp); (fig auch) to condition. **auf etw** (acc) **programmiert sein** (fig) to be geared to sth.
Programmierer(in f) m - programmer.
Programmiersprache f programming language.
Programmierung f programming; (fig auch) conditioning.
Programm-: ~**vorschau** f preview (für of); (Film) trailer; ~**zeitschrift** f programme (Brit) or program (US) guide.
progressiv adj progressive.
Projekt nt -e project.
Projektion f projection.
Projektor m projector.
projizieren* vt to project.
proklamieren* vt to proclaim.
Pro-Kopf-Einkommen nt per capita income.
Prokura f, pl **Prokuren** (form) power of attorney.
Prokurist(in f) m attorney.
Prolet m (wk) -en, -en (pej) prole (pej), pleb (pej).
Proletariat nt proletariat.
Proletarier [-iɐ] m - proletarian.
proletarisch adj proletarian.
Prolog m -e prologue.
Promenaden-: ~**deck** nt promenade deck; ~**mischung** f (hum) mongrel.
Promille nt - thousandth (part); (col: Alkoholspiegel) alcohol level. **0,8** ~ **80 millilitres** (Brit) or milliliters (US) alcohol level.
Promillegrenze f legal (alcohol) limit.

prominent adj prominent.
Prominente(r) mf decl as adj VIP.
Prominenz f VIP's pl.
Promotion[1] f (Univ) doctorate, PhD. **während seiner** ~ while he was doing his PhD.
Promotion[2] [prə'mouʃən] f (Comm) promotion.
promovieren* [promo'viːrən] vi to do a PhD; (Doktorwürde erhalten) to receive a doctorate.
prompt 1 adj prompt. **2** adv promptly; (wie erwartet) of course.
Pronomen nt - pronoun.
Propaganda f no pl propaganda. ~ **mit etw machen** to make propaganda out of sth.
Propagandist(in f) m **(a)** propagandist. **(b)** (Comm) demonstrator.
propagieren* vt to propagate.
Propangas nt propane gas.
Propeller m - propeller.
Propeller-: ~**antrieb** m propeller-drive; ~**flugzeug** nt propeller-driven plane; ~**turbine** f turboprop.
proper adj (col) neat, tidy.
Prophet(in f) m (wk) -en, -en prophet.
prophetisch adj prophetic.
prophezeien* vt to prophesy.
Prophezeiung f prophecy.
prophylaktisch adj prophylactic (form), preventive.
Proportion f proportion.
proportional [proportsio'naːl] adj proportional.
Proporz m -e proportional representation no art.
proppe(n)voll adj (col) jam-packed (col).
Prosa f no pl prose.
prosaisch [pro'zaːɪʃ] adj **(a)** (nüchtern) prosaic. **(b)** (Liter) prose attr.
prosit interj your health. ~ **Neujahr!** happy New Year!
Prosit nt -s toast. **ein** ~ **der Köchin!** here's to the cook!
Prospekt [pro'spɛkt] m -e brochure; (Werbezettel) leaflet; (Verzeichnis) catalogue.
prost interj cheers, cheerio.
Prostata f no pl prostate gland.
Prostituierte [prostitu'iːɐtə] f (wk) -n, -n prostitute.
Prostitution [prostitu'tsioːn] f prostitution.
Protagonist m (lit, fig) protagonist.
protegieren* [prote'ʒiːrən] vt Schriftsteller, Projekt to sponsor; Land, Regime to support.
Protein nt -e protein.
Protektion f (Schutz) protection; (Begünstigung) patronage.
Protektorat nt (Schirmherrschaft) patronage; (Schutzgebiet) protectorate.
Protest m -e protest. (scharfen) ~ **gegen jdn/etw erheben** to make a (strong) protest against sb/sth; **aus** ~ in protest; **unter** ~ protesting; (gezwungen) under protest.
Protestant(in f) m Protestant.
protestantisch adj Protestant.
protestieren* vi to protest.
Protest-: ~**marsch** m protest march; ~**schreiben** nt letter of protest. ~**welle** f wave of protest.
Prothese f -n artificial limb, prosthesis (Med, form); (Gebiß) dentures pl.
Protokoll nt -e **(a)** (Niederschrift) record; (von Sitzung) minutes pl; (bei Polizei) statement; (bei Gericht) transcript. (das) ~ **führen** (bei Sitzung) to take the minutes; (bei Gericht) to make a transcript of the proceedings; **etw zu** ~ **geben** to have sth put on record; (bei Polizei) to say sth in one's statement. **(b)** (diplomatisch) protocol. **(c)** (Strafzettel) ticket.
protokollarisch adj **(a)** (protokolliert) on record; (in Sitzung) minuted. **(b)** (zeremoniell) ~**e Vorschriften** rules of protocol.
Protokollführer m secretary; (Jur) clerk (of the court).

protokollieren* 1 *vi (bei Sitzung)* to take the minutes (down); *(bei Polizei)* to take a/the statement down. 2 *vt* to take down; *Sitzung* to minute.

Proto-: ~pļasma *nt* protoplasm; ~typ *m* prototype.

protzen *vi (col)* to show off. **mit etw** ~ to show sth off.

protzig *adj (col)* swanky *(col)*, showy *(col)*.

Proviant [pro'viant] *m -e* provisions *pl*, supplies *pl (esp Mil); (Reise~)* food for the journey.

Provinz [pro'vɪnts] *f -en* province; *(im Gegensatz zur Stadt)* provinces *pl (auch pej)*, country. **das ist finsterste** ~ *(pej)* it's a cultural backwater.

provinziell [provɪn'tsiɛl] *adj* provincial *(auch pej)*.

Provision [provi'zioːn] *f* commission. **auf** ~ **on** commission.

provisorisch [provi'zoːrɪʃ] *adj* temporary. **Straßen mit** ~**em Belag** roads with a temporary surface; **ich habe den Stuhl** ~ **repariert** I've fixed the chair up for the time being.

Provokation [provoka'tsioːn] *f* provocation.

provokativ, provokatorisch [provoka-] *adj* provocative, provoking.

provozieren* [provo'tsiːrən] *vti* to provoke.

Prozedur *f* **(a)** *(Vorgang)* procedure. **(b)** *(pej)* carry-on *(col)*.

Prozent *nt -e or (nach Zahlenangaben)* - per cent *no pl.* **fünf** ~ five per cent; **wieviel** ~? what percentage?; **zu zehn** ~ at ten per cent; **zu hohen** ~**en** at a high percentage; **dieser Whisky hat 35** ~ this whisky contains 35 per cent alcohol; ~**e bekommen** *(col)* to get a discount.

Prozentsatz *m* percentage; *(Zins)* interest rate.

prozentual *adj* percentage *attr.* ~**er Anteil** percentage; **etw** ~ **ausdrücken** to express sth as a percentage; ~ **gut abschneiden** to get a good percentage.

Prozeß *m -sse* **(a)** *(Straf~)* trial; *(Rechtsfall)* (court) case. **einen** ~ **gewinnen/verlieren** to win/ lose a case; **gegen jdn einen** ~ **anstrengen** to bring an action against sb; **es zum** ~ **kommen lassen** to go to court; **jdm den** ~ **machen** *(col)* to take sb to court; **mit jdm/etw kurzen** ~ **machen** *(fig col)* to make short work of sb/sth *(col)*. **(b)** *(Vorgang)* process.

Prozeß-: **p**~**führend** *adj* **p**~**führende Partei** litigant; ~**führung** *f* handling of a/the case.

prozessieren* *vi* to go to court. **er prozessiert mit fünf Firmen** he's got cases going on against five firms.

Prozession *f* procession.

Prozeßkosten *pl* legal costs *pl.*

Prozessor *m (Comp)* processor.

Prozeßordnung *f* legal procedure.

prüde *adj* prudish.

prüfen *vt* **(a)** *(auch vi) (Sch, Univ) jdn* to examine. **schriftlich geprüft werden** to have a written examination. **(b)** *(überprüfen)* to check *(auf +acc for); (untersuchen)* to examine; *(durch Ausprobieren)* to test; *Geschäftsbücher* to audit, to examine; *Lebensmittel, Wein* to inspect, to test; *Beschwerde* to investigate, to look into. **(c)** *(erwägen)* to consider. **etw nochmals** ~ to review sth. **(d)** *(mustern)* to scrutinize. **ein** ~**der Blick** a searching look. **(e)** *(heimsuchen)* to afflict. **er ist im Leben schwer geprüft worden** he's been much afflicted in his life.

Prüfer(in *f) m* - examiner; *(Wirtschafts~)* auditor.

Prüf-: ~**stand** *m* test bed; ~**stein** *m (fig)* touchstone *(für of or for)*, measure *(für of)*.

Prüfung *f siehe vt* **(a)** exam, examination. **eine** ~ **machen** to take an exam. **(b)** check; examination; test; audit; inspection; investigation. **nach der** ~ **wird das Auto ...** after being tested the car is ...; **bei nochmaliger** ~ **der Rechnung** on re-checking the account. **(c)** consideration. **(d)** *(Heimsuchung)* test, trial.

Prüfungs-: ~**angst** *f* exam nerves *pl*; ~**arbeit** *f* dissertation; ~**ausschuß** *m* board of examiners; ~**kandidat** *m* (examination) candidate; ~**ordnung** *f* exam(ination) regulations *pl.*

Prügel *m -* **(a)** *(Stock)* club. **(b)** ~ *pl (col: Schläge)* thrashing; ~ **bekommen** to get a thrashing.

Prügelei *f (col)* fight, punch-up *(Brit col)*.

Prügelknabe *m (fig)* whipping boy.

prügeln 1 *vti* to beat. 2 *vr* to fight. **sich mit jdm** ~ to fight sb; **sich um etw** *(acc)* ~ to fight over sth.

Prügelstrafe *f* corporal punishment.

Prunk *m no pl (Pracht)* splendour *(Brit)*, splendor *(US)*. **großen** ~ **entfalten** to put on a show of great splendour.

Prunk-: ~**saal** *m* palatial room; ~**stück** *nt* showpiece; **p**~**voll** *adj* magnificent.

prusten *vi (col)* to snort. **vor Lachen** ~ to snort with laughter.

PS [peː'ɛs] *nt =* **Pferdestärke** hp.

P.S., PS [peː'ɛs] *nt -, -* Postskript(um) PS.

Psalm *m -en* psalm.

Pseudo-, pseudo- *in cpds* pseudo.

Pseudonym *nt -e* pseudonym.

Psychiater *m -* psychiatrist.

Psychiatrie *f* psychiatry.

psychiatrisch *adj* psychiatric.

psychisch *adj Belastung etc* emotional, psychological; *Phänomen* psychic. ~**e Erkrankung** mental illness; ~ **gestört** emotionally *or* psychologically disturbed; **er ist** ~ **völlig am Ende** his nerves can't take any more.

Psycho- *in cpds* psycho-; ~**analyse** *f* psychoanalysis; ~**analytiker(in** *f) m* psychoanalyst; **p**~**analytisch** *adj* psychoanalytic(al); ~**loge** *m*, ~**login** *f* psychologist; ~**logie** *f* psychology; **p**~**logisch** *adj* psychological; ~**therapeut(in** *f) m* psychotherapist; **p**~**therapeutisch** *adj* psychotherapeutic; ~**therapie** *f* psychotherapy.

pubertär *adj* of puberty, adolescent.

Pubertät *f* puberty.

Pubertäts-: ~**alter** *nt* age of puberty; ~**störungen** *pl* adolescent disturbances *pl*; ~**zeit** *f* puberty (period).

publik *adj pred* public. ~ **werden** to become public knowledge; **die Sache ist längst** ~ that's long been common knowledge.

Publikation *f* publication.

Publikum *nt no pl* public; *(Zuschauer, Zuhörer)* audience; *(Sport)* crowd. **in diesem Lokal verkehrt ein schlechtes** ~ this pub attracts a bad type of customer; **sein** ~ **finden** to find a public.

Publikums-: ~**erfolg** *m* popular success; ~**liebling** *m* darling of the public; ~**verkehr** *m* „heute kein ~**verkehr**" "closed today for public business"; **p**~**wirksam** *adj* **p**~**wirksam sein** to have public appeal.

publizieren *vti* to publish.

Publizist(in *f) m* publicist; *(Journalist)* journalist.

Publizistik *f* journalism.

Pudding *m -s* ≈ blancmange.

Puddingpulver *nt* custard powder.

Pudel *m* poodle. **das ist des** ~**s Kern** *(fig)* that's what it's really all about.

Pudel-: ~**mütze** *f* pom-pom hat *(col)*; **p**~**naß** *adj* dripping wet; **p**~**wohl** *adj (col)* **sich p**~**wohl fühlen** to feel on top of the world *(col)*.

Puder *m or (col) nt* - powder.

Puderdose *f* (powder) compact.

pudern *vt* to powder.

Puder-: ~**quaste** *f* powder puff; ~**zucker** *m* icing sugar.

Puff[1] *m* ~**e** *(Stoß)* blow; *(in die Seite)* dig.

Puff[2] *m or nt -s (col)* brothel, cathouse *(esp US col)*.

puffen 1 *vt* **(a)** *(schlagen)* to thump; *(in die Seite)* to prod. **(b)** *Rauch* to puff. 2 *vi (col: puff machen)* to go bang; *(Rauch, Abgase)* to puff.

Puffer *m -* **(a)** *(Rail, Comp)* buffer. **(b)** *(Cook)* potato fritter.

Pufferzone *f* buffer zone.

Puffreis *m* puffed rice.

puh *interj (Abscheu)* ugh; *(Erleichterung)* phew.

Pulk *m* -s (a) *(Mil)* group. (b) *(Menge) (von Menschen)* bunch; *(von Dingen)* pile.

Pulle *f* -n *(col)* bottle. **volle ~ fahren** *(col)* to drive flat out *(col)*.

Pulli *m* -s *(col)*, **Pullover** [pʊ'loːvɐ] *m* - jumper *(Brit)*, sweater.

Pullunder *m* - slipover.

Puls *m* -e *(lit, fig)* pulse. **sein ~ geht regelmäßig** his pulse is regular; **jdm den ~ fühlen** to feel or take sb's pulse.

Puls|ader *f* artery. **sich** *(dat)* **die ~(n) aufschneiden** to slash one's wrists.

pulsieren* *vi (lit, fig)* to pulsate, to throb.

Puls-: **~schlag** *m* pulse-beat; *(fig)* pulse; **den ~schlag der Zeit spüren** to feel life pulsing around one; **~wärmer** *m* - wrist warmer.

Pult *nt* -e desk.

Pulver ['pʊlfɐ, -lvɐ] *nt* - powder. **er hat das ~ nicht erfunden** *(fig)* he'll never set the Thames on fire *(prov)*; **sein ~ verschossen haben** *(fig)* to have shot one's bolt.

Pulver-: **~faß** *nt (fig)* powder keg; **(wie) auf einem ~faß sitzen** *(fig)* to be sitting on a volcano.

pulv(e)rig ['pʊlv(ə)rɪç] *adj* powdery *no adv*.

pulverisieren* [pʊlveri'ziːrən] *vt* to pulverize.

Pulver-: **~kaffee** *m (col)* instant coffee; **~schnee** *m* powder snow.

Puma *m* -s puma.

Pummelchen *nt (col)* roly-poly *(col)*.

pumm(e)lig *adj (col)* chubby, plump.

Pump *m no pl (col)* **auf ~ kaufen/leben** to buy/live on tick *(Brit col)* or credit.

Pumpe *f* -n (a) pump. (b) *(col) (Herz)* ticker *(col)*.

pumpen *vti* (a) to pump. (b) *(col) (entleihen)* to borrow; *(verleihen)* to loan.

Pumpernickel *m* - pumpernickel.

Pumphose *f* knickerbockers *pl*.

Pumps [pœmps] *m* -, - pump.

puncto *prep* +*gen*: **in ~ X** where X is concerned.

Punk [paŋk] *m* -s (a) *no pl* punk. (b) *(auch* **~er:** *Mensch)* punk.

Punkt *m* -e (a) *(Tupfen)* spot, dot. (b) *(Satzzeichen)* full stop, period *(esp US)*; *(Typ)* point; *(auf dem i, Mus, Auslassungszeichen, von ~linie)* dot. **nun mach aber mal einen ~!** *(col)* come off it! *(col)*; **ohne ~ und Komma reden** *(col)* to talk nineteen to the dozen *(col)*. (c) *(Stelle)* point. **~ 12 Uhr** at 12 o'clock on the dot; **wir sind auf** *or* **an dem ~ angelangt, wo ...** we have reached the point where ...; **in diesem ~** on this point. (d) *(Bewertungseinheit)* point, mark; *(bei Prüfung)* mark. **nach ~en führen** to lead on points.

Punkt-: **p~gleich** *adj (Sport)* level; **~gleichheit** *f (Sport)* level score; **bei ~gleichheit** if the scores are level.

punktieren* *vt* (a) *(Med)* to aspirate. (b) *(mit Punkten)* to dot. **punktierte Linie** dotted line.

pünktlich 1 *adj* punctual. **2** *adv* on time. **er kam ~ um 3 Uhr** he came at 3 o'clock sharp; **~ da sein** to be there on time.

Pünktlichkeit *f* punctuality.

Punkt-: **~richter** *m* judge; **~sieg** *m* points win; **~sieger** *m* winner on points.

punktuell *adj* dealing with certain points. **~e Verkehrskontrollen** spot checks on traffic.

Punkt-: **~wertung** *f* points system; **in der ~wertung liegt er vorne** he's leading on points; **~zahl** *f* score.

Punsch *m* -e (hot) punch.

Pupille *f* -n pupil.

Puppe *f* -n (a) *(Kinderspielzeug)* doll *(col)*; *(Marionette)* puppet; *(Schaufenster~, Mil: Übungs~)* dummy; *(col: Mädchen)* doll *(col)*, bird *(esp Brit col)*. **die ~n tanzen lassen** *(col)* to live it up *(col)*; **bis in die ~n schlafen** *(col)* to sleep to all hours.

(b) *(Zool)* pupa.

Puppen- *in cpds* doll's; **p~haft** *adj* doll-like; **~haus** *nt* doll's house, dollhouse *(US)*; **~spiel** *nt* puppet show; **~spieler** *m* puppeteer; **~stube** *f* doll's house, dollhouse *(US)*; **~theater** *nt* puppet theatre *(Brit)* or theater *(US)*; **~wagen** *m* doll's pram *(Brit)* or baby carriage *(US)*.

Pups *m* -e, **Pupser** *m* - *(col: Furz)* rude noise/ smell.

pupsen *vi (col)* to make a rude noise/smell.

pur *adj (rein)* pure; *(unverdünnt)* neat; *(völlig)* sheer. **~er Unsinn** absolute nonsense; **~er Zufall** sheer coincidence; **Whisky ~** neat whisky.

Püree *nt* -s puree; *(Kartoffel~)* creamed potatoes *pl*.

Purist(in *f)* *m* purist.

puritanisch *adj (Hist)* Puritan; *(pej)* puritanical.

Purpur *m no pl* crimson.

Purpur-: **p~farben** *adj* crimson; **~mantel** *m* crimson *or* purple robe; **p~rot** *adj* crimson (red).

Purzelbaum *m* somersault. **einen ~ machen** *or* **schlagen** to turn a somersault.

purzeln *vi aux sein* to tumble.

Puste *f no pl (col)* puff *(col)*, breath. **außer ~ sein** to be out of puff *(col)*.

Pusteblume *f (col)* dandelion.

Pustel *f* -n *(Pickel)* pimple; *(Med)* pustule.

pusten *(col)* **1** *vi (blasen)* to puff; *(keuchen)* to puff (and pant). **2** *vt (blasen)* to puff, to blow.

Pute *f* -n turkey (hen). **dumme ~** *(col)* silly goose *(col)*.

Puter *m* - turkey (cock).

puterrot *adj* scarlet.

Putsch *m* -e coup (d'état), revolt.

putschen *vi* to rebel, to revolt.

Putschist(in *f)* *m* rebel.

Putschversuch *m* attempted coup (d'état).

Pütt *m* -s *(dial)* pit, mine.

Putte *f* -n *(Art)* cherub.

Putz *m no pl* (a) *(Build)* plaster; *(Rauh~)* roughcast. **eine Mauer mit ~ verkleiden** to roughcast a wall; **unter ~** under the plaster. (b) **auf den ~ hauen** *(col) (angeben)* to show off; *(ausgelassen feiern)* to have a rave-up *(col)*; *(meckern)* to kick up a fuss *(col)*. (c) *(dated: Kleidung)* finery. **in vollem ~ erscheinen** to arrive all dressed up in one's Sunday best.

putzen 1 *vt* to clean; *(scheuern auch)* to scrub; *(polieren auch)* to polish; *(wischen auch)* to wipe. **die Schuhe ~** to clean *or* polish one's shoes; **Fenster ~** to clean the windows; **sich** *(dat)* **die Nase ~** to wipe one's nose; *(sich schneuzen)* to blow one's nose; **sich** *(dat)* **die Zähne ~** to brush one's teeth; **einem Baby den Hintern/die Nase ~** to wipe a baby's bottom/nose. **2** *vr* (a) *(sich säubern)* to wash oneself. (b) *(dated: sich schmücken)* to dress oneself up.

Putzfrau *f* cleaning lady, char(woman) *(Brit)*.

putzig *adj (col) (komisch)* comical; *(niedlich)* cute.

Putz-: **~lappen** *m* cloth, *(Staubtuch)* duster; **~mittel** *nt (zum Scheuern)* cleansing agent; *(zum Polieren)* polish; **~mittel** *pl* cleaning things *pl*; **p~munter** *adj (col)* full of beans *(col)*; **~teufel** *m (col: Frau)* maniac for housework; **~tuch** *nt (Staubtuch)* duster; *(Wischlappen)* cloth; **~zeug** *nt* cleaning things *pl*.

Puzzle(spiel) ['pazl-] *nt* -s jigsaw (puzzle).

Pygmäe [py'gmɛːə] *m (wk)* -n, -n pygmy.

Pyjama [py'dʒaːma] *m* -s pyjamas *pl (Brit)*, pajamas *pl (US)*. **im ~** in his pyjamas.

Pyjamahose *f* pyjama *(Brit)* or pajama *(US)* trousers *pl*.

Pyramide *f* -n pyramid.

Pyrenäen [pyre'nɛːən] *pl* **die ~** the Pyrenees *pl*.

Pyro-: **~mane** *m (wk)* -n, -n, **~manin** *f* pyromaniac; **~manie** *f* pyromania; **~technik** *f* pyrotechnics *sing*; **p~technisch** *adj* pyrotechnic.

Python(schlange *f)* ['pyːtɔn-] *m* -s python.

Q

Q, q [ku:] *nt* -, - Q, q.
qkm = **Quadratkilometer.**
qm = **Quadratmeter.**
quabbelig *adj Qualle* slimy; *Pudding* wobbly.
Quacksalber *m* - *(pej)* quack (doctor).
Quacksalberei *f* quack medicine.
Quaddel *f* -n hives *pl*, rash; *(durch Insekten)* bite.
Quader *m (Math)* rectangular solid; *(Archit)* ashlar, stone block.
Quadrat *nt* -e *(Fläche, Potenz)* square. **vier zum ~** four squared; **drei Meter im ~** three metres square.
Quadrat- *in cpds* square.
quadratisch *adj Form* square; *(Math) Gleichung* quadratic.
Quadrat-: **~latschen** *pl (hum) (Schuhe)* clodhoppers *(col)*; *(Füße)* plates of meat *(Brit col)*; **~meter** *m or nt* square metre *(Brit)* or meter *(US)*.
Quadratur *f* quadrature. **das käme der ~ des Kreises gleich** *(geh)* that's like trying to square the circle.
Quadrat-: **~wurzel** *f* square root; **~zahl** *f* square number.
quadrieren* *vt Zahl* to square.
quak *interj (von Frosch)* croak; *(von Ente)* quack.
quaken *vi (Frosch)* to croak; *(Ente)* to quack; *(col: Mensch)* to squawk *(col)*.
quäken *vti (col)* to screech, to squawk.
Quäker(in *f) m* - Quaker.
Qual *f* -en *(Schmerz) (körperlich)* pain, agony; *(seelisch)* anguish. **jds ~(en) lindern** to lessen sb's suffering; **unter großen ~en sterben** to die in agony; **sein Leben war eine einzige ~** his life was a living death; **es ist eine ~, das mit ansehen zu müssen** it is agonizing to watch; **jeder Schritt wurde ihm zur ~** every step was agony for him; **er machte ihr das Leben zur ~** he made her life a misery; **die ~en, die sie um ihn ausgestanden hat** the suffering she has gone through because of him.
quälen 1 *vt* to torment; *Tiere auch* to tease; *(mit Bitten etc)* to pester. **jdn zu Tode ~** to torture sb to death; **~de Ungewißheit** agonizing uncertainty; **~der Durst** excruciating thirst; *siehe* **gequält. 2** *vr* **(a)** *(seelisch)* to torment oneself *(leiden)* to be in agony. **(b)** *(sich abmühen)* to struggle. **er mußte sich ~, damit er das schaffte** it was a struggle for him to do it; **sich durch ein Buch ~** to struggle through a book.
Quälerei *f* **(a)** *(Grausamkeit)* torture; *(seelische, nervliche Belastung)* torment. **das ist doch eine ~ für das Tier** that is cruel to the animal. **(b)** *(mühsame Arbeit)* struggle.
Quälgeist *m (col)* pest *(col)*.
Qualifikation *f* qualification. **er hat die ~ zu diesem Amt** he has the qualifications for this office; **zur ~ fehlten ihr nur wenige Sekunden** she only needed a few more seconds to qualify.
Qualifikationsspiel *nt* qualifying game.
qualifizieren* *vtr* to qualify *(für, zu for)*.
qualifiziert *adj (a) Arbeiter, Nachwuchs* qualified; *Arbeit* professional. **(b)** *(Pol) Mehrheit* requisite.
Qualität *f* quality. **von ausgezeichneter ~** (of) top quality.
qualitativ *adj* qualitative.

Qualitäts- *in cpds* quality; **~arbeit** *f* quality work; **~kontrolle** *f* quality control; **~ware** *f* quality goods *pl.*
Qualle *f* -n jellyfish.
Qualm *m no pl* dense smoke; *(Tabaks~)* fug.
qualmen 1 *vi* **(a)** to smoke. **es qualmt aus dem Schornstein** clouds of smoke are coming from the chimney. **(b)** *(col: Mensch)* to smoke. **sie qualmt einem die ganze Bude voll** she fills the whole place with smoke. **2** *vt (col) Zigarette, Pfeife* to puff away at *(col).*
qualmig *adj* smoky.
qualvoll *adj* painful; *Schmerzen* excruciating; *Gedanke* agonizing; *Anblick* harrowing.
Quant *nt* -en quantum.
Quanten *pl* **(a)** *pl of* **Quant, Quantum. (b)** *(col: Füße)* feet, plates of meat *(Brit col).*
Quantentheorie *f* quantum theory.
Quantität *f* quantity.
quantitativ *adj* quantitative.
Quantum *nt, pl* **Quanten** *(Menge)* quantity; *(Anteil)* quota *(an+dat* of).
Quarantäne *f* -n quarantine. **unter ~ stellen** to put in quarantine; **über das Gebiet wurde ~ verhängt** the area was placed under quarantine.
Quarantänestation *f* isolation ward.
Quark *m no pl* **(a)** (soft) curd cheese. **(b)** *(col: Unsinn)* rubbish. **so ein ~!** stuff and nonsense!; **das geht ihn einen ~ an!** it's none of his business!
Quark-: **~kuchen** *m* cheesecake; **~tasche** *f*, **~teilchen** *nt* curd cheese turnover.
Quart¹ *f* -en **(a)** *(Mus: auch* **~e)** fourth. **(b)** *(Fechten)* quarte.
Quart² *nt no pl (Typ)* quarto *(format).*
Quarta *f, pl* **Quarten** *(Sch) third year of German secondary school.*
Quartal *nt* -e quarter (year). **Kündigung zum ~** quarterly notice date.
Quartal(s)-: **~abschluß** *m* end of the quarter; **~säufer** *m (col)* heavy drinker; **q~weise** *adj* quarterly.
Quartaner(in *f) m* - *(Sch)* pupil in third year of German secondary school.
Quarte *f* -n *(Mus)* fourth.
Quartett *nt* -e **(a)** *(Mus)* quartet. **(b)** *(Cards) (Spiel)* ≈ happy families; *(Karten)* set of four cards.
Quartier *nt* -e **(a)** *(Unterkunft)* accommodation (Brit), accommodations *(US).* **wir sollten uns ein ~ suchen** we should look for a place to stay; **wir hatten unser ~ in einem alten Bauernhof** we stayed in an old farmhouse. **(b)** *(Mil)* quarters *pl,* billet.
Quarz *m* -e quartz.
Quarz-: **~lampe** *f* quartz lamp; **~uhr** *f* quartz clock.
quasi 1 *adv* virtually. **2** *pref* quasi.
Quasselei *f (col)* gabbling *(col)*, blethering *(col)*.
quasseln *vti* to gabble *(col)*, to blether *(col)*.
Quaste *f* -n *(Troddel)* tassle; *(von Pinsel)* bristles *pl; (Schwanz~)* tuft.
Quästur *f (Univ)* bursary.
Quatsch *m no pl (col)* **(a)** *(Unsinn)* rubbish. **das ist der größte ~, den ich je gehört habe** that is the biggest load of rubbish I have ever heard; **red**

334

keinen ~! don't talk rubbish!; **so ein ~!** what rubbish. **(b)** *(Dummheiten)* nonsense. **hört doch endlich mit dem ~ auf!** stop being so stupid!; **laß den ~** cut it out! *(col);* **~ machen** to mess about *(col);* **mach keinen ~, sonst** ... don't try anything funny or ...

quatschen *(col)* **1** *vti (dummes Zeug reden)* to gab (away) *(col).* **2** *vi* **(a)** *(plaudern)* to chatter, to natter *(Brit col).* **ich hab' mit ihm am Telefon gequatscht** I had a good natter with him on the phone. **(b)** *(etw ausplaudern)* to squeal *(col),* to talk.

Quatscherei *f (col)* blathering *(col),* yacking *(col).*

Quatschkopf *m (pej col) (Schwätzer)* windbag *(col); (Dummkopf)* fool, twit *(Brit col).*

Quecksilber *nt* mercury.

Quecksilber- in cpds mercury; **q~haltig** *adj* mercurial.

Quell *m* **-e** *(poet)* spring, source.

Quelle *f* **-n (a)** spring; *(von Fluß auch)* source; *(Erdöl~, Gas~)* well. **(b)** *(fig, für Waren)* source. **die ~ allen Übels** the root of all evil; **eine ~ der Freude** a source of pleasure; **aus zuverlässiger ~** from a reliable source; **an der ~ sitzen** *(fig)* to be well-placed.

quellen *vi pret* **quoll,** *ptp* **gequollen** *aux sein* **(a)** *(herausfließen)* to pour, to stream. **(b)** *(Reis, Erbsen)* to swell. **lassen Sie die Bohnen über Nacht ~** leave the beans to soak overnight.

Quellen-: **~angabe** *f* reference; **~forschung** *f* source research.

Quell-: **~fluß** *m* source (river); **~wasser** *nt* spring water.

Quengelei *f (col)* whining.

qureng(e)lig *adj* whining. **die Kinder wurden ~** the children started to whine.

quengeln *vi (col)* to whine.

quer *adv (schräg)* crosswise; *(rechtwinklig)* at right angles. **er legte sich ~ aufs Bett** he lay down across the bed; **die Spur verläuft ~ zum Hang** the path runs across the slope; **die Straße/ Linie verläuft ~** the road/line runs at right angles; **der Wagen stand ~ zur Fahrbahn** the car was at right angles to the road; **~ durch etw gehen/laufen** *etc* to go through sth; **~ über etw** *(acc)* **gehen/laufen** to go across sth.

Quer-: **~balken** *m* crossbeam; *(von Türrahmen)* lintel; *(Sport)* crossbar; **q~beet** *adv (col) (wahllos)* at random; *(~feldein)* across country.

Quere *f no pl* **jdm in die ~ kommen** to cross sb's path; **der Lastwagen kam mir in die ~** the lorry got in my way.

Querele *f* **-n** *usu pl (geh)* dispute, quarrel.

querfeld|ein *adv* across country.

Querfeld|einrennen *nt* cross-country; *(Aut)* autocross; *(mit Motorrädern)* motocross; *(Radrennen)* cyclecross.

Quer-: **~flöte** *f* (transverse) flute; **~format** *nt* oblong format; **q~gestreift** *adj attr* horizontally striped; **~kopf** *m (col)* awkward customer *(col);* **q~köpfig** *adj* perverse; **~latte** *f* crossbar; **q~legen** *vr (fig col)* to be awkward; **~paß** *m* cross; **~schläger** *m* ricochet.

Querschnitt *m (lit, fig)* cross-section.

querschnittsgelähmt *adj* paraplegic. **seit dem**

Autounfall ist er ~ since the car accident he has been paralyzed from the waist down.

Quer-: **q~stellen** *vr sep (fig col)* to be awkward; **~straße** *f* **das ist eine ~straße zur Hauptstraße** it runs at right angles to the high street; **bei** *or* **an der zweiten ~straße fahren Sie links ab** turn left at the second junction *(Brit) or* crossroads; **die Kaiserallee hat viele ~ straßen** there are lots of streets (going) off the Kaiserallee; **~streifen** *m* horizontal stripe; **~strich** *m* (horizontal) stroke *or* line; **~summe** *f (Math)* sum of digits of a number; **~treiber** *m (col)* troublemaker.

Querulant(in *f) m* grumbler.

Quer-: **~verbindung** *f* conection, link; **~verweis** *m* cross-reference.

quetschen 1 *vt (drücken)* to squash, to crush; *(aus einer Tube)* to squeeze. **etw in etw** *(acc)* **~** to squeeze sth into sth; **sich den Finger ~** to squash one's finger. **2** *vr (sich klemmen)* to be caught; *(sich zwängen)* to squeeze (oneself).

Quetschkommode *f (hum col)* squeeze box *(col).*

Quetschung, Quetschwunde *f (Med)* bruise, contusion *(form).*

Queue [kø:] *nt* **-s** *(Billard)* cue.

quicklebendig *adj (col)* Kind lively, active; *ältere Person auch* spry.

quiek(s)en *vi* to squeal, to squeak.

quietschen *vi (Tür, Schloß)* to squeak; *(Reifen, Mensch)* to squeal.

quietschvergnügt *adj (col)* happy as a sandboy *(col).*

Quint *f* **-en (a)** *(Mus: auch* **~e)** fifth. **(b)** *(Fechten)* quinte.

Quinta *f, pl* **Quinten** *(Sch)* second year of German secondary school.

Quintaner(in *f) m* **-** *(Sch)* pupil in second year of German secondary school.

Quint|essenz *f (geh)* quintessence.

Quintett *nt* **-e** quintet.

Quirl *m* **-e (a)** *(Cook)* whisk, beater. **(b)** *(col: Mensch)* live wire *(col).*

quirlen *vt* to whisk, to beat.

quirlig *adj* lively.

quitt *adj* **~ sein (mit jdm)** to be quits (with sb); **jdn/etw ~ sein** to be rid of sb/sth.

Quitte *f* **-n** quince.

quittieren* 1 *vt* **(a)** *(bestätigen) Betrag, Empfang* to give a receipt for. **lassen Sie sich** *(dat)* **die Rechnung ~** get a receipt for the bill. **(b)** *(beantworten)* to meet. **(c)** *(verlassen) Dienst* to quit, to resign. **2** *vi (bestätigen)* to sign.

Quittung *f (a)* receipt. **gegen ~** on production of a receipt; **eine ~ über 500 Mark** a receipt for 500 marks. **(b)** *(fig)* **das ist die ~ für Ihre Unverschämtheit** that is what you get for being so insolent; **er hat seine ~ bekommen** he's paid the penalty or price.

Quiz [kvɪz] *nt* **-, -** quiz.

Quizmaster ['kvɪsmaːstɐ] *m* **-** quizmaster.

quoll *pret of* **quellen.**

Quorum *nt no pl* quorum.

Quote *f* **-n (a)** *(Statistik) (Anteilsziffer)* proportion; *(Rate)* rate. **(b)** *(Econ, Quantum)* quota.

Quotient [kvo'tsiɛnt] *m* quotient.

Quotierung *f (Comm)* quotation.

R

R, r [ɛr] *nt* -, - R, r.
Rabatt *m* -e discount. **mit 10%** ~ **at (a) 10%** discount.
Rabatte *f (Beet)* border.
Rabattmarke *f (Comm)* (trading) stamp.
Rabatz *m no pl (col)* row, din.
Rabauke *m (wk)* -n, -n *(col)* hooligan, lout *(col)*.
Rabbi *m* -s, **Rabbiner** *m* - rabbi.
Rabe *m (wk)* -n, -n raven. **wie ein** ~ **stehlen** *(col)* to thieve like a magpie.
Raben-: ~**eltern** *pl (col)* bad parents *pl*; ~**mutter** *f (col)* bad mother; **r**~**schwarz** *adj* pitch-black; **Haare** jet-black; ~**vater** *m (col)* bad father.
rabiat *adj* Kerl, Autofahrer, Umgangston aggressive; Geschäftsleute, Methoden ruthless.
Rache *f no pl* revenge, vengeance. **das ist die** ~ **für deine Untat** this is the retribution for your misdeed; **(an jdm)** ~ **nehmen** *or* **üben to take revenge (on sb); etw aus** ~ **tun** to do sth in revenge; ~ **ist süß** *(prov)* revenge is sweet *(prov)*.
Rache-: ~**akt** *m* act of revenge *or* vengeance; **r**~**durstig** *adj* thirsting for revenge; ~**engel** *m* avenging angel.
Rachen *m* - throat, pharynx *(spec)*; *(von großen Tieren, fig)* jaws *pl*. **jdm etw in den** ~ **werfen** *(col)* to shove sth down sb's throat *(col)*.
rächen 1 *vt* jdn, Untat to avenge *(etw an jdm* sth on sb)*. **2** *vr (Mensch)* to get one's revenge *(an jdm für etw* on sb for sth)*; *(Sünde)* to be avenged. **deine Faulheit wird sich** ~ you'll pay for being so lazy.
Rächer(in *f)* *m* - avenger.
Rachitis *f no pl* rickets.
rachitisch *adj* rickety.
Rach-: ~**sucht** *f* vindictiveness; **r**~**süchtig** *adj* vindictive.
Racker *m* - *(col: Kind)* rascal *(col)*, monkey *(col)*.
rackern *vir (col)* to slave (away) *(col)*.
Rad *nt* ⁻er **(a)** wheel; *(Rolle)* castor; *(Zahn~)* gearwheel. **ein** ~ **schlagen** *(Sport)* to do a cart-wheel; **der Pfau schlägt ein** ~ the peacock is fanning out its tail; **nur ein** ~ *or* **Rädchen im Getriebe sein** *(fig)* to be only a cog in the works; **unter die** ⁻**er kommen** *(col)* to fall into bad ways; **das fünfte** ~ **am Wagen sein** *(col)* to be in the way. **(b)** *(Fahr~)* bicycle, bike *(col)*. **mit dem** ~ **fahren** to go by bicycle.
Radar *m or nt no pl* radar.
Radar-: ~**anlage** *f* radar (equipment) *no indef art*; ~**falle** *f* speed trap; ~**kontrolle** *f* radar speed check; ~**schirm** *m* radar screen.
Radau *m no pl (col)* din, racket *(col)*. ~ **machen** to kick up a row; *(Unruhe stiften)* to cause trouble.
Rad|aufhängung *f (Aut)* (wheel) suspension.
Rädchen *nt dim of* Rad small wheel; *siehe* Rad.
Raddampfer *m* paddle-steamer.
radebrechen *vti insep* to speak broken English/ German *etc*.
radeln *vi aux sein (col)* to cycle.
Rädelsführer *m* ringleader.
rädern *vt (Hist)* to break on the wheel; *siehe* **gerädert**.
Räderwerk *nt (Mech)* works *pl*; *(fig)* machinery.
radfahren *vi sep irreg aux sein* **(a)** to cycle. **ich fahre Rad** I ride a bicycle; **kannst du** ~? can you ride a bike? **(b)** *(pej col: kriechen)* to crawl *(col)*.
Radfahrer *m* **(a)** cyclist. **(b)** *(pej col)* crawler

(col).
Radfahrweg *m* cycle track.
Radgabel *f* fork.
radial *adj* radial.
Radiator *m* radiator.
radieren* *vti* **(a)** to rub out. **(b)** *(Art)* to etch.
Radiergummi *m* rubber *(Brit)*, eraser *(esp US)*.
Radierung *f (Art)* etching.
Radieschen [ra'diːsçən] *nt* radish. **sich** *(dat)* **die** ~ **von unten ansehen** *(hum col)* to be pushing up the daisies *(col)*.
radikal *adj* radical; Entfernen total; Ablehnung flat. ~ **gegen etw vorgehen** to take radical steps against sth.
Radikale(r) *mf decl as adj* radical.
Radikalisierung *f* radicalization.
Radikalismus *m (Pol)* radicalism.
Radikalkur *f (col)* drastic remedy.
Radio *nt* -s radio, wireless *(esp Brit)*. ~ **hören** to listen to the radio; **im** ~ on the radio.
Radio- *in cpds* radio; **r**~**aktiv** *adj* radioactive; **r**~**aktiver Niederschlag** (radioactive) fall-out; ~**aktivität** *f* radioactivity; ~**apparat** *m* radio (set); ~**durchsage** *f* radio announcement; ~**gerät** *nt* radio (set); ~**loge** *m*, ~**login** *f (Med)* radiologist; ~**logie** *f (Med)* radiology; ~**sender** *m (Rundfunkanstalt)* radio station; *(Sendeeinrichtung)* radio transmitter; ~**sendung** *f* radio programme *(Brit)* *or* program *(US)*; ~**station** *f* radio station; ~**teleskop** *nt* radio telescope; ~**wecker** *m* radio alarm (clock).
Radium *nt* radium.
Radius *m, pl* **Radien** [-iən] radius.
Rad-: ~**kappe** *f* hub cap; ~**lager** *nt* wheel bearing.
Radler(in *f)* *m* - *(col)* cyclist.
Rad-: ~**mantel** *m (Bereifung)* bicycle tyre *(Brit)* or tire *(US)*; ~**nabe** *f* (wheel) hub; ~**rennbahn** *f* cycle (racing) track; ~**rennen** *nt* cycle race; *(Sportart)* cycle racing; ~**rennfahrer** *m* racing cyclist; ~**sport** *m* cycling; ~**sportler** *m* cyclist; ~**tour** *f* cycle tour; ~**wechsel** *m* wheel change; ~**weg** *m* cycle track.
raffen *vt* **(a)** *(anhäufen)* to pile, to heap. **(b)** Stoff, Gardine to gather; langes Kleid, Rock to gather up.
Raff-: ~**gier** *f* greed, avarice; **r**~**gierig** *adj* grasping.
Raffinade *f (Zucker)* refined sugar.
Raffinerie *f* refinery.
Raffinesse *f (a) (Feinheit)* refinement *no pl*. **(b)** *(Schlauheit)* cunning *no pl*.
raffiniert *adj* **(a)** Zucker, Öl refined. **(b)** *(col)* Apparat fancy *(col)*; Kleidung stylish. **(c)** *(schlau)* cunning; *(durchtrieben auch)* crafty.
Raffiniertheit *f siehe adj* fanciness *(col)*; stylishness; cunning; craftiness.
Rage ['raːʒə] *f no pl (Wut)* rage, fury. **jdn in** ~ **bringen** to infuriate sb.
ragen *vi* to tower, to loom; *(heraus~)* to jut.
Ragout [ra'guː] *nt* -s ragout.
Rahm *m no pl* cream.
rahmen *vt* to frame; Dias to mount.
Rahmen *m* - **(a)** frame. **(b)** *(fig)* framework; *(Atmosphäre)* setting; *(Größe)* scale. **im** ~ **within the framework** *(gen* of)*; **im** ~ **des Möglichen** within the bounds of possibility; **im** ~ **bleiben** not to go too far; **aus dem** ~ **fallen** to go too far;

336

mußt du den immer aus dem ~ fallen! do you always have to show yourself up?; **ein Geschenk, das aus dem ~ des Üblichen fällt** a present with a difference; **in den ~ von etw passen** to blend in with sth; **das würde den ~ sprengen** it would be beyond my/our *etc* scope; **einer Feier den richtigen ~ geben** to provide the appropriate setting for a celebration; **in größerem/kleinerem ~** on a large/small scale.

Rahmen-: **~handlung** *f (Liter)* background story; **~plan** *m* outline plan; **~programm** *nt* framework; *(von Veranstaltung etc)* supporting acts *pl*; **~richtlinien** *pl* guidelines *pl*.

rahmig *adj* creamy.

Rahmkäse *m* cream cheese.

räkeln *vr* = **rekeln.**

Rakete *f* **-n** rocket *(auch Space)*; *(Mil auch)* missile.

Raketen- in *cpds* rocket; *(Mil auch)* missile; **~abwehr** *f* antimissile defence *(Brit) or* defense *(US)*; **~satz** *m* set of missiles; **~stufe** *f* stage (of a rocket/missile); **~stützpunkt** *m* missile base; **~werfer** *m* rocket launcher.

Rallye ['rali, 'rɛli] *f* **-s** rally.

Rallyefahrer *m* rally-driver.

rammdösig *adj (col)* giddy, dizzy.

Ramme *f* **-n** ram; *(für Pfähle)* pile-driver.

Rammelei *f (col: Gedränge)* crush *(col)*.

rammeln 1 *vt siehe* **gerammelt. 2** *vi (Hunt)* to mate; *(col!)* to have it off *(col!)*.

rammen *vt* to ram.

Rampe *f* **-n (a)** ramp. **(b)** *(Theat)* apron.

Rampenlicht *nt (Theat)* footlights *pl*. **sie möchte im ~ stehen** *(fig)* she wants to be in the limelight.

ramponieren* *vt (col)* to ruin; *Möbel* to bash about *(col)*. **er sah ziemlich ramponiert aus** he looked the worse for wear *(col)*.

Ramsch *m no pl (col)* junk, rubbish.

Ramsch-: **~händler** *m (pej)* junk dealer; **~laden** *m (pej)* junk shop; **~ware** *f (pej)* trashy goods *pl*, rubbish.

Rand *m* **⁼er (a)** edge; *(von Brunnen, Tasse)* rim, brim; *(von Abgrund)* brink. **voll bis zum ~** full to the brim; **am ~e erwähnen** to mention in passing; *interessieren, beteiligt sein* marginally; **am ~e des Waldes** at the edge of the forest; **am ~e der Stadt** on the outskirts of the town; **am ~e des Wahnsinns** on the verge of madness; **am ~e eines Krieges** on the brink of war; **etw am ~e miterleben** to experience sth from the sidelines; **am ~e der Gesellschaft** on the fringes of society.

(b) *(Umrandung)* border; *(Teller~)* edge, side; *(Brillen~)* rim; *(von Hut)* brim; *(Buch~, Heft~)* margin. **etw an den ~ schreiben** to write sth in the margin.

(c) *(Schmutz~)* ring. **rote ⁓er um die Augen haben** to have red rims around one's eyes.

(d) *(fig)* **sie waren außer ~ und Band** they were going wild; **allein komme ich damit nicht zu ~e** I can't manage (it) by myself; **halt den ~!** *(col)* shut your face *(col!)*.

randalieren* *vi* to rampage (about). **~de Jugendliche** (young) hooligans; **~de Studenten** rioting students; **die Gefangenen fingen an zu ~** the prisoners started to get violent.

Randalierer *m* **-** hooligan, trouble-maker.

Rand-: **~bemerkung** *f* marginal note; *(fig)* (passing) comment; **~erscheinung** *f* matter of minor importance; *(Nebenwirkung)* side effect; **~figur** *f* minor figure; **~gebiet** *nt (Geog)* fringe; *(Pol)* border territory; *(fig)* subsidiary; **~gruppe** *f* fringe group; **r~los** *adj* Brille rimless; *Hut* brimless; **~zone** *f* peripheral zone; **in der ~zone** on the periphery.

rang *pret of* **ringen.**

Rang *m* **⁼e (a)** *(Mil)* rank; *(in Firma)* position; *(gesellschaftlich auch)* position. **im ~ eines Hauptmanns stehen** to have the rank of captain;

im ~ höher/tiefer stehen to have a higher/lower rank/position, to rank higher/lower; **ein Mann ohne ~ und Namen** a man without any standing; **jdm den ~ ablaufen** *(fig)* to outstrip sb. **(b)** *(Qualität)* quality, class. **ein Künstler von ~** an artist of standing; **von hohem ~** high-class; **ein Essen ersten ~es** a first-rate meal. **(c)** *(Theat)* circle. **erster/zweiter ~** dress/upper circle; **vor leeren ⁓en spielen** to play to an empty house. **(d)** **⁓e** *nt pl (Sport)* stands *pl*. **(e)** *(Gewinnklasse)* prize category.

Rangälteste(r) *m (Mil)* senior officer.

rangehen *vi sep irreg aux sein (col)* to get stuck in *(col)*. **geh ran!** go on!; *siehe* **herangehen.**

Rangelei *f (col) siehe* **Gerangel.**

rangeln *vi (col)* to scrap; *(um Posten)* to wrangle *(um for)*.

Rang-: **~folge** *f* order of rank *(esp Mil)*; **~höchste(r)** *mf* senior person; *(Mil)* highest-ranking officer.

Rangierbahnhof [rã'ʒi:ɐ-] *m* marshalling yard.

rangieren [rã'ʒi:rən] **1** *vt (Rail)* to shunt, to switch *(US)*. **2** *vi (Rang einnehmen)* to rank. **an erster/letzter Stelle ~** to come first/last.

Rangier- [rã'ʒi:ɐ-]: **~gleis** *nt* siding, sidetrack *(US)*; **~lok(omotive)** *f* shunter, switcher *(US)*.

Rang-: **~liste** *f (Mil)* active list; *(Sport)* **er steht auf der ~liste der weltbesten Boxer** he ranks among the world's top boxers; **r~mäßig** *adj* according to rank; **~ordnung** *f* hierarchy; *(Mil)* (order of) ranks; **~stufe** *f* rank; **~unterschied** *m* social distinction; *(Mil)* difference of rank.

ranhalten *vr sep irreg (col: sich beeilen)* to get a move on *(col)*.

rank *adj (liter)* **~ und schlank** slender and supple.

Ranke *f* **-n** tendril; *(von Weinrebe)* shoot.

Ränke *pl (liter)* intrigue, cabal *(liter)*. **~ schmieden** to intrigue, to cabal *(liter)*.

ranken 1 *vr* **sich um etw ~** *(lit, fig)* to have grown up around sth. **2** *vi aux haben or sein* **an etw** *(dat)* **~** to entwine itself around sth.

Ränkeschmied *m (liter)* intriguer.

ran-: **~kommen** = **herankommen**; **~lassen** *vt irreg (col)* **jdn ~lassen** to let sb have a go; **sie läßt keinen (an sich** *acc***) ran** *(col)* she won't let anybody near her.

rann *pret of* **rinnen.**

rannte *pret of* **rennen.**

Ranzen *m* **-** *(a) (Schul~)* satchel. **(b)** *(col: Bauch)* belly *(col)*, gut *(col)*.

ranzig *adj* rancid.

rapid(e) *adj* rapid.

Rapier *nt* **-e** rapier.

Rappe *m (wk)* **-n, -n** black horse.

Rappel *m* **-** *(col) (a) (Fimmel)* craze. **seinen ~ kriegen** to get one of one's crazy moods. **(b)** *(Wutanfall)* **einen ~ kriegen** to throw a fit.

rapp(e)lig *adj (col) (a) (verrückt)* crazy *(col)* **(b)** *(nervös, unruhig)* jumpy *(col)*.

rappeln *vi (col) (lärmen)* to rattle. **bei dir rappelt's wohl!** are you crazy?

Rappen *m* **-** *(Sw)* centime, rappen.

Rapport *m* **-e** report. **sich zum ~ melden** to report.

Raps *m* **-e** *(Bot)* rape.

Rapunzel *f* **-n** *(Bot)* corn salad, lamb's lettuce.

rar *adj* rare. **sich ~ machen** *(col)* to stay away; *(sich zurückziehen)* to make oneself scarce.

Rarität *f* rarity.

rasant *adj (col) (a)* Tempo, Spurt lightning *attr (col)*; *Auto, Fahrer* fast; *Karriere* meteoric; *Entwicklung* rapid. **(b)** *(imponierend)* Leistung terrific.

Rasanz *f no pl (col: Geschwindigkeit)* speed.

rasch *adj (a) (schnell)* quick; *Tempo* great. **(b)** *(übereilt)* hasty. **2** *adv* quickly.

rascheln *vi* to rustle. **es raschelt (im Laub)** there's something rustling (in the leaves); **mit**

etw ~ to rustle sth.
rasen vi (a) *(wüten, toben)* to rave; *(Sturm)* to rage.
er raste vor Schmerz/Wut he was going wild with pain/he was mad with rage. **(b)** *aux sein (sich schnell bewegen)* to race, to tear; *(Puls)* to race. **das Auto raste in den Fluß** the car crashed into the river; **ras doch nicht so!** *(col)* don't go so fast!; **die Zeit rast** time flies.
Rasen m - grass *no indef art, no pl; (Zier~ auch)* lawn; *(von Sportplatz)* turf, grass; *(Sportplatz)* field, pitch *(Brit)*.
rasend 1 adj (a) *(enorm)* terrific; *Eile auch* tearing; *Hunger, Durst auch* raging; *Beifall auch* wild, rapturous; *Eifersucht* burning. **(b)** *(wütend)* furious. **er macht mich noch ~** he'll drive me crazy. **2** adv *(col)* terrifically; *weh tun, sich beeilen* like mad *(col)* or crazy *(col)*; *verliebt, eifersüchtig sein* madly *(col)*. ~ **gern!** I'd simply love to!
Rasende(r) mf decl as adj maniac.
Rasen-: ~**fläche** f lawn; ~**mäher** m lawn-mower; ~**sprenger** m - (lawn) sprinkler.
Raser m - *(col)* speed merchant *(col)*.
Raserei f (a) *(Wut)* fury, frenzy. **(b)** *(col: schnelles Fahren, Gehen)* mad rush.
Rasier- in cpds shaving; ~**apparat** m razor; *(elektrisch auch)* shaver.
rasieren* vtr to shave. **sich naß/trocken ~** to have a wet shave/to use an electric shaver.
Rasier-: ~**klinge** f razor blade; ~**messer** nt (open) razor; ~**pinsel** m shaving brush; ~**wasser** nt aftershave/pre-shave (lotion).
Räson [rɛ'zoː] f no pl jdn zur ~ **bringen** to make sb see sense.
Raspel f -n (a) *(Holzfeile)* rasp. **(b)** *(Cook)* grater.
raspeln vt to grate; *Holz* to rasp.
Rasse f -n *(Menschen~)* race; *(Tier~)* breed. **das Pferd/der Hund hat ~** the horse/dog has spirit.
Rassehund m thoroughbred dog.
Rassel f -n rattle.
rasseln vi (a) to rattle. **mit etw** *(dat)* ~ to rattle sth. **(b)** *aux sein (col)* **durch eine Prüfung** ~ to flunk an exam *(col)*.
Rassen- in cpds racial; ~**diskriminierung** f racial discrimination; ~**haß** m race hatred; ~**krawall** m race riot; ~**trennung** f racial segregation.
Rassepferd nt thoroughbred horse.
rassig adj *Pferd, Auto* sleek; *Frau* vivacious; *Wein* spirited, lively.
rassisch adj racial. **jdn** ~ **verfolgen** to persecute sb because of his/her race.
Rassismus m racialism, racism.
rassistisch adj racialist, racist.
Rast f no pl rest, repose *(liter)*. ~ **machen** to stop (to eat); *(Mil)* to make a halt; **ohne** ~ **und Ruh** *(liter)* without respite.
Raste f -n notch.
rasten vi to rest; *(Mil)* to make a halt. **wer rastet, der rostet** *(Prov)* you have to keep active.
Raster m - *(Archit)* grid; *(Phot: Gitter)* screen; *(TV)* raster; *(fig)* framework.
rastern vt *(TV)* to scan.
Rast-: ~**haus** nt (travellers' *(Brit)* or travelers' *US)* inn; **r~los** adj *(unruhig)* restless; *(unermüdlich)* tireless; ~**losigkeit** f restlessness; ~**platz** m resting place; *(an Autostraßen)* picnic area; ~**stätte** f service area, services pl.
Rasur f *(Bart~)* shave; *(das Rasieren)* shaving.
Rat m (a) pl **Ratschläge** *(Empfehlung)* advice no pl. **ein** ~ a piece of advice; **jdm um** ~ **fragen** to ask sb's advice; **jdm mit** ~ **und Tat zur Seite stehen** to support sb in (both) word and deed; **da ist guter** ~ **teuer** it's hard to know what to do. **(b)** no pl **jdn/etw zu** ~**e ziehen** to consult sb/sth; ~ **(für etw) wissen** to know what to do (about sth); **sie wußte sich** *(dat)* **keinen** ~ **mehr** she was at her wits' end. **(c)** pl ~**e** *(Körperschaft)* council. **der** ~ **der Gemeinde/Stadt** ≃ the district council; **im** ~ **sitzen** to be on the council.

Rate f -n instalment *(Brit)*, installment *(US)*. **auf** ~**n kaufen** to buy on hire purchase *(Brit)* or on the installment plan *(US)*; **in** ~**n zahlen** to pay in instalments.
raten pret **riet**, ptp **geraten** vti (a) *(Ratschläge geben)* to advise. **jdm gut/schlecht** ~ to give sb good/bad advice; **jdm zu etw** ~ to recommend sth to sb; **jdm** ~, **etw nicht zu tun** to advise sb against doing sth; **das würde ich dir nicht** ~ I wouldn't advise it; **das möchte ich dir auch geraten haben!** you better had *(col)*; **was** or **wozu** ~ **Sie mir?** what do you advise? **(b)** *(erraten)* to guess; *Kreuzworträtsel etc* to solve, to do. **rate mal!** (have a) guess; **dreimal darfst du** ~ I'll give you three guesses *(auch iro)*; **das rätst du nie!** you'll never guess!; **(gut) geraten!** good guess!; **falsch geraten!** wrong!
Raten-: ~**kauf** m *(Kaufart)* hire purchase *(Brit)*, HP *(Brit col)*, the installment plan *(US)*; **r~weise** adv in instalments *(Brit)* or installments *(US)*; ~**zahlung** f *(Zahlung in Raten)* payment by instalments *(Brit)* or installments *(US)*.
Ratespiel nt guessing game; *(TV)* quiz; *(Beruferaten etc auch)* panel game.
Rat-: ~**geber** m adviser, counsellor *(form)*; ~**haus** nt town hall; *(einer Großstadt)* city hall.
ratifizieren* vt to ratify.
Ratifizierung f ratification.
Ration [ra'tsioːn] f ration.
rational [ratsio'naːl] adj rational.
rationalisieren* [ratsionali'ziːrən] vti to rationalize.
Rationalisierung [ratsionali'ziːruŋ] f rationalization.
rationell [ratsio'nɛl] adj efficient.
rationieren* [ratsio'niːrən] vt to ration.
Rationierung [ratsio'niːruŋ] f rationing.
ratlos adj helpless. **ich bin völlig ~(,** wie **ich tun soll)** I just don't know what to do; **sie machte ein** ~**es Gesicht** she looked helpless.
Ratlosigkeit f helplessness. **in meiner ~** ... being at a loss ...
ratsam adj advisable.
Ratschlag m piece of advice. **ein guter** ~ a good piece of advice; **Ratschläge** advice; **drei Ratschläge** three pieces of advice.
Rätsel nt - (a) riddle; *(Kreuzwort~)* crossword (puzzle); *(Silben~, Bilder~ etc)* puzzle. **jdm ein** ~ **aufgeben** to ask sb a riddle. **(b)** *(fig: Geheimnis)* mystery *(um of)*. **vor einem** ~ **stehen** to be baffled; **es ist mir ein** ~, **wie** ... it's a mystery to me how ...
Rätsel-: ~**ecke** f puzzle corner; **r~haft** adj mysterious; **es ist mir r~haft** it's a mystery to me; ~**heft** nt puzzle book.
rätseln vi to puzzle (over sth).
Rätselraten nt guessing game.
Rats-: ~**herr** m councillor *(esp Brit)*, councilman *(US)*; ~**sitzung** f council meeting.
ratsuchend adj seeking advice. **sich** ~ **an jdn wenden** to turn to sb for advice; **R~e** those seeking advice.
Ratte f -n rat.
Ratten-: ~**gift** nt rat poison; ~**schwanz** m (a) *(lit)* rat's tail; **(b)** *(fig col: Serie, Folge)* string.
rattern vi to clatter; *(Maschinengewehr)* to chatter.
Raub m no pl (a) *(das Rauben)* robbery. **(b)** *(Entführung)* abduction. **(c)** *(Beute)* booty, loot. **ein** ~ **der Flammen werden** *(liter)* to fall victim to the flames.
Raub-: ~**bau** m no pl overexploitation (of natural resources); ~**bau an etw** *(dat)* **treiben** to overexploit etc sth; **mit seiner Gesundheit** ~**bau treiben** to ruin one's health; ~**druck** m pirate(d) edition.
rauben 1 vt (a) *(wegnehmen)* to steal. **(b)** *(entführen)* to abduct, to carry off. **(c)** *(fig)* **jdm etw** ~ to

rob sb of sth; **das hat uns viel Zeit geraubt** it cost us a lot of time. **2** *vi* to plunder, to pillage.

Räuber *m* - robber. ~ **und Gendarm** cops and robbers.

Räuberbande *f (pej)* bunch of thieves.

räubern *vi (col)* to thieve. **in der Speisekammer** ~ to raid the larder.

Räuberpistole *f (col)* far-fetched story.

Raub-: ~**fisch** *m* predatory fish; ~**gier** *f (liter)* rapacity; **r**~**gierig** *adj (liter)* rapacious; ~**katze** *f* (predatory) big cat; ~**kopie** *f* pirate copy; ~**mord** *m* robbery with murder; ~**mörder** *m* robber and murderer; ~**tier** *nt* predator, beast of prey; ~**überfall** *m* robbery; *(auf Bank etc auch)* raid; **einen** ~**überfall auf jdn verüben** to hold sb up; ~**vogel** *m* bird of prey.

Rauch *m no pl* smoke; *(giftig auch)* fumes *pl*. **sich in** ~ **auflösen** *(lit, fig)* to go up in smoke.

Rauch-: ~**abzug** *m* smoke outlet; ~**bombe** *f* smoke bomb.

rauchen 1 *vi (Rauch abgeben)* to smoke. **sie sah, daß es in unserer Küche rauchte** she saw smoke coming from our kitchen; **mir raucht der Kopf** my head's spinning. **2** *vti* to smoke. **eine** ~ **to** have a smoke; **hast du was zu** ~? have you got a smoke?; „**R**~ **verboten**" "no smoking"; **sich** *(dat)* **das R**~ **an-/abgewöhnen** to take up/give up smoking; **stark** ~ to be a heavy smoker.

Raucher *m* - *(auch Rail)* smoker.

Räucher|aal *m* smoked eel.

Raucher|abteil *nt* smoking compartment.

Räucherhering *m* kipper.

Raucherhusten *m* smoker's cough.

Raucherin *f* smoker.

Räucher-: ~**kerze** *f* incense cone; ~**schinken** *m* smoked ham; ~**speck** *m* ≏ smoked bacon; ~**stäbchen** *nt* joss stick.

Rauch-: ~**fang** *m (~abzug)* chimney hood; ~**fleisch** *nt* smoked meat; **r**~**frei** *adj* smokeless; ~**glocke** *f* pall of smoke.

rauchig *adj* smoky.

Rauch-: ~**säule** *f* column of smoke; ~**schleier** *m* veil of smoke; ~**schwaden** *pl* drifts of smoke *pl*; ~**signal** *nt* smoke signal; ~**verbot** *nt* ban on smoking; **hier herrscht** ~**verbot** smoking is not allowed here; ~**vergiftung** *f* fume poisoning; ~**vorhang** *m*, ~**wand** *f* smokescreen; ~**waren**[1] *pl* tobacco (products *pl*); ~**waren**[2] *pl (Pelze)* furs *pl*; ~**wolke** *f* cloud of smoke.

Räude *f -n (Vet)* mange.

räudig *adj* mangy.

rauf *adv (col) siehe* **herauf, hinauf.**

Raufbold *m -e (dated)* ruffian.

raufen 1 *vt Unkraut* to pull up. **sich** *(dat)* **die Haare** ~ to tear (at) one's hair. **2** *vir* to scrap.

Rauferei *f* scrap, rough-house *(col)*.

Rauf-: ~**lust** *f* pugnacity; **r**~**lustig** *adj* ready for a fight.

rauh *adj* **(a)** rough; *Wind* raw; *Winter, Klima* harsh; *(unwirtlich) Gebiet* bleak; *(hart) Mann* tough. **im** ~**en Norden** in the rugged north; **(die)** ~**e Wirklichkeit** harsh reality, the hard facts *pl*; ~, **aber herzlich** bluff; *Begrüßung, Ton* rough but jovial. **(b)** *Hals, Kehle* sore; *Stimme* husky; *(heiser)* hoarse. **(c)** *(col)* **in** ~**en Mengen** by the ton *(col)*, galore *(col)*; **Geld in** ~**en Mengen** tons of money.

Rauh-: ~**bein** *nt (col)* rough diamond; **r**~**beinig** *adj (col)* rough-and-ready.

Rauheit *f no pl* roughness; *(von Klima etc)* harshness; *(von Hals)* soreness; *(von Stimme)* huskiness.

Rauh-: ~**fasertapete** *f* woodchip paper; ~**haardackel** *m* wire-haired dachshund; **r**~**haarig** *adj* coarse-haired; ~**reif** *m* hoarfrost; *(gefrorener Nebel)* rime.

Raum *m, pl* **Räume (a)** room; *(no pl: Platz auch)* space; *(Gebiet, Bereich)* area; *(fig)* sphere. **auf engstem** ~ **leben** to live in a very confined space; **ein Frage im** ~ **stehen lassen** to leave a question unresolved; **der** ~ **Frankfurt** the Frankfurt area; ~ **gewinnen** *(Mil, fig)* to gain ground. **(b)** *no pl (Phys, Space)* space *no art*. **der offene** *or* **leere** ~ the void.

Raum-: ~**anzug** *m* spacesuit; ~**ausstatter(in** *f)* *m* - interior decorator.

Räumboot *nt* minesweeper.

räumen *vt* **(a)** *(verlassen) Gebäude, Gebiet* to evacuate; *(Mil: Truppen)* to withdraw from; *Wohnung* to move out of; *Sitzplatz* to vacate. **(b)** *(leeren) Gebäude, Lager* to clear *(von of)*. **(c)** *(weg~)* to shift; *Schnee, Schutt auch* to clear (away); *Minen* to clear. **räum deine Sachen in den Schrank** put your things away in the cupboard.

Raum-: ~**fähre** *f* space shuttle; ~**fahrer** *m* astronaut; *(sowjetisch)* cosmonaut.

Raumfahrt *f* space travel *no art* or flight *no art*. **das Zeitalter der** ~ the space age.

Raumfahrt- *in cpds* space; ~**behörde** *f* space authority; ~**programm** *nt* space programme *(Brit)* or program *(US)*.

Raumfahrzeug *nt* spacecraft.

Räumfahrzeug *nt* bulldozer; *(für Schnee)* snow-clearer.

Raum-: ~**flug** *m* space flight; ~**gewinn** *m* extra space gained; ~**inhalt** *m* volume, (cubic) capacity; ~**kapsel** *f* space capsule.

räumlich *adj* **(a)** *(den Raum betreffend)* spatial. ~**e Verhältnisse** physical conditions; **wir wohnen** ~ **sehr beengt** we live in very cramped conditions; **rein** ~ **ist das unmöglich** (just) from the point of view of space it's impossible. **(b)** *(dreidimensional)* three-dimensional. **ich kann mir das nicht** ~ **vorstellen** I can't really picture it.

Räumlichkeit *f* **(a)** *no pl* three-dimensionality. **(b)** ~**en** *pl* premises *pl*.

Raum-: ~**mangel** *m* lack of space; ~**maß** *nt* unit of volume; ~**not** *f* shortage of space; ~**pflegerin** *f* cleaner, cleaning lady; ~**schiff** *nt* spaceship; ~**sonde** *f* space probe; ~**station** *f* space station.

Räumung *f* clearing; *(von Wohnhaus)* vacation; *(wegen Gefahr etc)* evacuation; *(unter Zwang)* eviction; *(von Lager, Geschäft)* clearance.

Räumungs-: ~**befehl** *m* eviction order; ~**frist** *f* (period of) notice; ~**klage** *f* action for eviction; ~**verkauf** *m* clearance sale.

raunen *vti (liter)* to whisper. **es ging ein R**~ **durch die Menge** a murmur went through the crowd.

Raupe *f -n* **(a)** caterpillar. **(b)** *(Planier~)* bulldozer.

Raupen-: ~**fahrzeug** *nt* caterpillar (vehicle); ~**kette** *f* caterpillar track; ~**schlepper** *m* caterpillar (tractor).

raus *adv (col)* ~! (get) out!; *siehe* **heraus, hinaus.**

Rausch *m, pl* **Räusche (a)** *(Trunkenheit)* intoxication; *(Drogen~)* high *(col)*. **einen** ~ **haben** to be drunk; **etw im** ~ **tun** to do sth while one is drunk; **seinen** ~ **ausschlafen** to sleep it off. **(b)** *(liter: Ekstase)* ecstasy, rapture; *(Blut~, Mord~ etc)* frenzy.

rauschen *vi* **(a)** *(Wasser, Meer, Brandung)* to roar; *(sanft, Wind)* to murmur; *(Baum, Wald)* to rustle; *(Seide)* to swish; *(Radio etc)* to hiss; *(Regen)* to pour down; *(Applaus)* to resound. ~**de Feste** glittering parties. **(b)** *aux sein (sich bewegen) (Bach)* to rush; *(Geschoß)* to whizz. **(c)** *aux sein (col: Mensch)* to sweep. **sie rauschte aus dem Zimmer** she swept out of the room.

Rauschen *nt no pl siehe vi* roaring; murmuring; rustling; swishing; hissing. **das** ~ **des Regens** the sound of rain.

Rauschgift *nt* drug; *(Drogen)* drugs *pl*, narcotics *pl*.

Rauschgift-: ~**handel** *m* drug traffic; ~**händler** *m* drug trafficker; ~**sucht** *f* drug addiction;

r~süchtig adj drug-addicted; **er ist r~süchtig** he's a drug addict; **~süchtige(r)** mf drug addict.

rausfliegen vi sep irreg aux sein (col) to be chucked out (col).

rauskriegen vt sep (col) to get out; (herausfinden) to find out.

räuspern vr to clear one's throat.

rausreißen vt sep irreg (col) **jdn ~** to save sb's bacon (col).

rausschmeißen vt sep irreg (col) to chuck out (col). **das ist rausgeschmissenes Geld** that's money down the drain (col).

Rausschmeißer(in f) m - (col) bouncer; (letzter Tanz) last dance.

Rausschmiß m -sse (col) booting out (col). **man drohte uns mit dem ~** they threatened us with the push (col).

Raute f -n (a) (Bot) rue. (b) (Math) rhombus.

rautenförmig adj rhomboid, diamond-shaped.

Razzia f, pl **Razzien** ['ratsiən] raid, swoop (col).

Reagenzglas nt (Chem) test-tube.

reagieren* vi to react (auf +acc to).

Reaktion f (a) reaction (auf +acc on). (b) (Pol pej) reactionary forces pl.

reaktionär [reaktsio'nɛːɐ] adj (Pol pej) reactionary.

Reaktionär(in f) m (pej) reactionary.

Reaktions-: **~fähigkeit** f reactions pl; **r~schnell** adj with fast reactions; **r~schnell sein** to have fast reactions; **~zeit** f reaction time.

reaktivieren* [reakti'viːrən] vt (Sci) to reactivate; (fig) to revive; **Kenntnisse** to polish up.

Reaktor m reactor.

real adj real; (wirklichkeitsbezogen) realistic.

Real|einkommen nt real income.

Realization f realization; (TV, Rad, Theat) production.

realisierbar adj practicable, feasible.

realisieren* vt (a) **Pläne, Programm** to carry out; (TV, Rad, Theat) to produce. (b) (Fin) to realize.

Realisierung f realization.

Realismus m realism.

Realist(in f) m realist.

realistisch adj realistic.

Realität f reality. **~en** pl (Gegebenheiten) facts pl.

Realitäts-: **r~fremd** adj out of touch with reality; **~sinn** m sense of realism.

Real-: **~lexikon** nt specialist dictionary; **~lohn** m real wages pl; **~politik** f political realism; **~politiker** m political realist; **~schule** f ≃ secondary modern school (Brit), high school (US); **~wert** m (Fin) real value.

Rebe f -n (Ranke) shoot; (Weinstock) vine.

Rebell(in f) m (wk) -en, -en rebel.

rebellieren* vi to rebel, to revolt.

Rebellion f rebellion, revolt.

rebellisch adj rebellious.

Rebhuhn nt (common) partridge.

Reb-: **~laus** f vine pest; **~stock** m vine.

Rebus m or nt -, -se picture puzzle.

Rechaud [re'ʃoː] m or nt -s tea/coffee etc warmer; (für Fondue) spirit burner.

Rechen m - (Harke) rake.

Rechen-: **~aufgabe** f (arithmetical) problem; **~fehler** m (arithmetical) error; **~heft** nt arithmetic book; **~maschine** f adding machine; **~operation** f calculation.

Rechenschaft f account. **jdm über etw** (acc) **~ ablegen** to account to sb for sth; **jdm ~ schulden** to be accountable to sb; **jdn (für etw) zur ~ ziehen** to call sb to account (for or over sth).

Rechenschaftsbericht m report.

Rechen-: **~schieber** m slide-rule; **~zentrum** nt computer centre (Brit) or center (US).

Recherche [re'ʃɛrʃə] f -n investigation.

recherchieren* [reʃɛr'ʃiːrən] vti to investigate.

rechnen 1 vt (a) (addieren etc) to calculate. **rund gerechnet** in round figures. (b) (einstufen) to

count. **jdn/etw zu etw ~** to count sb among sth. (c) (veranschlagen) to estimate, to reckon. **wir hatten nur drei Tage gerechnet** we were only reckoning on three days; **das ist zu hoch/niedrig gerechnet** that's too high/low (an estimate). (d) (einberechnen) to take into account. **alles in allem gerechnet** taking everything into account.

2 vi (a) **falsch/richtig ~** to go wrong (in one's calculations), to calculate correctly; **gut/schlecht ~ können** to be good/bad at sums (esp Sch) or with figures; **~ lernen** to learn arithmetic. (b) (eingestuft werden) to count. **er rechnet noch als Kind** he still counts as a child. (c) (sich verlassen) **auf jdn/etw ~** to count on sb/sth. (d) **mit jdm/etw ~** to reckon with sb/sth; **damit ~ müssen, daß ...** to have to expect that ...; **du mußt damit ~, daß es regnet** you must reckon with it raining; **mit dieser Partei wird man ~ müssen** this party will have to be reckoned with; **damit hatte ich nicht gerechnet** I wasn't expecting that; **er rechnet mit einem Sieg** he reckons he'll win.

Rechnen nt no pl arithmetic; (esp Sch) sums pl.

Rechner m - (a) **ein guter ~ sein** to be good at arithmetic. (b) (Elektronen~) computer; (Taschen~) calculator.

rechnerisch adj arithmetical. **ich bin rein ~ überzeugt, aber ...** I'm convinced as far as the figures go but ...

Rechnung f (a) (Berechnung) calculation; (als Aufgabe) sum. **die ~ geht nicht auf** (lit, fig) it won't work (out). (b) (Kostenforderung) bill, check (US); (von Firma auch) invoice. **das geht auf meine ~** I'm paying; **laut ~** as per invoice; **auf eigene ~** on one's own account; (jdm) **etw in ~ stellen** to charge (sb) for sth; **einer Sache** (dat) **~ tragen** to bear sth in mind.

Rechnungs-: **~betrag** m (total) amount of a bill or check (US)/invoice; **~hof** m ≃ Auditor-General's office (Brit), audit division (US); **~jahr** nt financial year; **~prüfer** m auditor; **~prüfung** f audit.

Recht nt -e (a) (Rechtsordnung, sittliche Norm) law; (Gerechtigkeit auch) justice. **~ sprechen** to administer justice; **nach englischem ~** under English law; **für das ~ kämpfen** to fight for justice; **von ~s wegen** as of right; (col: eigentlich) by rights (col). (b) (Anspruch, Berechtigung) right (auf +acc to). **sein ~ fordern** to demand one's rights; **sein ~ bekommen** to get one's rights; **zu seinem ~ kommen** (lit) to gain one's rights; (fig) to come into one's own; **gleiches ~ für alle!** equal rights for all!; **das ~ des Stärkeren** the law of the jungle; **mit** or **zu ~** rightly; **und (das) mit ~** and rightly so; **im ~ sein** to be in the right; **das ist mein gutes ~** it's my right; **mit welchem ~?** by what right?

recht 1 adj (a) (richtig) right. **es soll mir ~ sein** it's OK (col) by me; **ganz ~!** quite right; **ist schon ~!** (col) that's OK (col); **alles, was ~ ist** (empört) fair's fair; (anerkennend) you can't deny it; **ich habe keine ~e Lust** I don't particularly feel like it; **nichts R~es** no good; **aus dem Jungen kann nichts R~es werden** that boy will come to no good; **er hat nichts R~es gelernt** he didn't learn any real trade; **nach dem R~en sehen** to see that everything's OK (col); **es ist nicht mehr als ~ und billig** it's only right and proper. (b) **~ haben** to be right; **~ behalten** to be right; **er will immer ~ behalten** he always has to be right; **jdm ~ geben** to admit that sb is right.

2 adv (a) (richtig) properly; (wirklich) really. **verstehen Sie mich ~** don't get me wrong (col); **wenn ich Sie ~ verstehe** if I understand you rightly; **sehe/höre ich ~?** am I seeing/hearing things?; **das geschieht ihm ~** it serves him right; **du kommst gerade ~, um ...** you're just in time to

Rechte ...; **das ist mir** ~ that suits me fine; **gehe ich** ~ **in der Annahme, daß** ...? am I correct in assuming that ...?; **hat es dir gefallen?** — **nicht so** ~ did you like it? ~ — not really; **man kann ihm nichts** ~ **machen** you can't do anything right for him; **man kann es nicht allen** ~ **machen** you can't please all of the people all of the time. **(b)** *(ziemlich, ganz)* quite, fairly *(col)*. ~ **viel** quite a lot. **(c)** *(sehr)* very, right *(dial)*. ~ **herzlichen Dank** thank you very much indeed.

Rechte *f (wk)* **-n, -n (a)** *(Hand)* right hand; *(Seite)* right(-hand) side; *(Boxen)* right. **(b)** *(Pol)* Right.

Recht-: ~**eck** *nt* rectangle; **r**~**eckig** *adj* rectangular.

Rechtens *gen of* **Recht** *(form)* **die Sache war nicht** ~ the matter was not right *or (Jur)* legal.

rechte(r, s) *adj attr* **(a)** right, right-hand. **jds** ~ **Hand sein** to be sb's right-hand man. **(b) ein** ~**r Winkel** a right angle. **(c)** *(konservativ)* right-wing. **der** ~ **Flügel** the right wing.

rechtfertigen *insep* **1** *vt* to justify. **2** *vr* to justify oneself.

Rechtfertigung *f* justification. **zu meiner** ~ **in my defence** *(Brit)* or **defense** *(US)*.

Recht-: ~**haber** *m* - *(pej)* know-all *(col)*; **r**~**haberisch** *adj* know-all *attr (col)*, self-opinionated.

rechtlich *adj (gesetzlich)* legal. ~ **zulässig** permissible in law, legal; ~ **nicht zulässig** not permissible in law, illegal.

Recht-: **r**~**los** *adj* **(a)** without rights; **(b)** *Zustand* lawless; ~**losigkeit** *f* **(a)** *(von Mensch)* lack of rights; **(b)** *(in Land)* lawlessness; **r**~**mäßig** *adj (legitim)* legitimate; *Erben, Besitzer auch* rightful; *(dem Gesetz entsprechend)* legal; **für r**~**mäßig erklären** to declare legal; ~**mäßigkeit** *f (Legitimität)* legitimacy; *(Legalität)* legality.

rechts 1 *adv* on the right. **nach** ~ (to the) right; **von** ~ from the right; **sich** ~ **einordnen** to take the right-hand lane; **sich** ~ **halten** to keep (to the) right; ~ **stehen** *or* **sein** *(Pol)* to be rightwing; ~ **stricken** to knit (plain); **zwei** ~, **zwei links** *(beim Stricken)* knit two, purl two. **2** *prep* +*gen* ~ **des Rheins** on the right of the Rhine.

Rechts- *in cpds (Jur)* legal; ~**abbieger** *m* - motorist/cyclist/car *etc* turning right; **die Spur für** ~**abbieger** the right-hand turn-off lane; ~**anspruch** *m* legal right; **einen** ~**anspruch auf etw** *(acc)* **haben** to be legally entitled to sth; ~**anwalt** *m* lawyer, attorney *(US)*; *(als Berater auch)* solicitor *(Brit)*; *(vor Gericht auch)* barrister *(Brit)*; ~**ausleger** *m (Boxen)* southpaw; ~**außen** *m* -, - *(Ftbl)* outside-right; ~**beistand**, ~**berater** *m* legal adviser; ~**brecher** *m* - law-breaker.

rechtschaffen *adj (redlich)* honest, upright.

Rechtschaffenheit *f* honesty, uprightness.

Rechtschreibung *f* spelling.

Rechts-: ~**drall** *m (von Billardball)* spin to the right; *(von Auto, Pferd)* pull to the right; *(Pol col)* leaning to the right; **einen** ~**drall haben** to spin/pull/lean to the right; ~**drehung** *f* turn to the right; ~**empfinden** *nt* sense of justice; ~**extremist** *m* right-wing extremist; ~**fall** *m* court case; **r**~**gerichtet** *adj (Pol)* right-wing; ~**geschäft** *nt* legal transaction; ~**geschichte** *f* legal history; ~**grundsatz** *m* legal maxim; **r**~**gültig** *adj* legally valid; ~**gültigkeit** *f* legal validity; ~**händer(in** *f)* *m* - right-handed person, right-hander *(esp Sport)*; ~**händer sein** to be right-handed; **r**~**händig** *adj* right-handed; **r**~**herum** *adv* (around) to the right; **r**~**kundig** *adj* versed in the law; ~**kurve** *f* right-hand bend; ~**lage** *f* legal position; **r**~**lastig** *adj* listing to the right; *(fig)* leaning to the right; **r**~**lastig sein** to lean to the right; ~**ordnung** *f* **eine** ~**ordnung** a system of laws; **die** ~**ordnung** the law; ~**partei** *f* right-wing party; ~**pflege** *f* administration of justice; ~**pfleger** *m official with certain judicial powers*.

Rechtsprechung *f* **(a)** *(Gerichtsbarkeit)* jurisdic-

tion. **(b)** *(richterliche Tätigkeit)* dispensation of justice. **(c)** *(bisherige Urteile)* precedents *pl*.

Rechts-: **r**~**radikal** *adj* radical right-wing; **die** ~**radikalen** the right-wing radicals; ~**radikalismus** *m* right-wing radicalism; **r**~**rheinisch** *adj* on the right of the Rhine; ~**ruck**, ~**rutsch** *m (Pol)* swing to the right; **r**~**rum** *adv (col)* to the right; ~**sache** *f* legal matter; *(Fall)* case; ~**schutz** *m* legal protection; ~**schutzversicherung** *f* legal costs insurance; ~**seitig** *adj* on the right(-hand) side; **r**~**seitig gelähmt** paralyzed in the right side; ~**staat** *m* state under the rule of law; **r**~**staatlich** *adj* **r**~**staatliche Ordnung** law and order; **r**~**stehend** *adj attr* righthand, on the right; *(Pol)* right-wing; ~**steuerung** *f* right-hand drive; ~**streit** *m* law-suit; ~**ver-kehr** *m* driving on the right *no def art*; **in Deutschland ist** ~**verkehr in** Germany they drive on the right; ~**verletzung** *f* infringement of the law; ~**weg** *m* **den** ~**weg beschreiten** to go to law; **der** ~**weg ist ausgeschlossen** ≃ the judges' decision is final; **r**~**widrig** *adj* illegal.

recht-: ~**winklig** *adj* right-angled; ~**zeitig 1** *adj (früh genug)* timely; *(pünktlich)* punctual; **um** ~**zeitige Anmeldung wird gebeten** you are requested to apply in good time; **2** *adv (früh genug)* in (good) time; *(pünktlich)* on time.

Reck *nt* **-e** *(Sport)* horizontal bar.

recken 1 *vt (aus-, emporstrecken)* to stretch. **den Kopf/Hals** ~ to crane one's neck; **die Glieder** ~ to stretch (oneself). **2** *vt* to stretch (oneself).

Reck-: ~**stange** *f* horizontal bar; ~**turnen** *nt* bar exercises *pl*.

Redakteur(in *f)* [-'tøːɐ, -'tøːrɪn] *m* editor.

Redaktion *f* **(a)** *no pl (das Redigieren)* editing. **(b)** *(Personal)* editorial staff. **(c)** *(~sbüro)* editorial office(s).

redaktionell [redaktsio'nɛl] *adj* editorial. **etw** ~ **bearbeiten** to edit sth.

Redaktionsschluß *m* time of going to press; *(Einsendeschluß)* copy deadline.

Rede *f* **-n (a)** *(Ansprache)* speech; *(Ansprache)* speech. **eine** ~ **halten** to make a speech; **direkte/indirekte** ~ direct/indirect speech *or* discourse *(US)*; **in freier** ~ without (consulting) notes; **der langen** ~ **kurzer Sinn** *(prov)* the long and the short of it. **(b)** *(Äußerungen)* words *pl*, language *no pl*. **seine frechen** ~**n** his cheek; **große** ~**n führen** to talk big *(col)*; **das ist meine** ~! that's what I've always said; **das ist nicht der** ~ **wert** it's not worth mentioning. **(c)** *(Gespräch)* conversation, talk. **die** ~ **kam auf** *(+acc)* the conversation turned to; **es war von einer Gehaltserhöhung die** ~ there was talk of a salary increase; **von Ihnen war eben die** ~ we were just talking about you; **aber davon war doch nie die** ~ but no-one was ever talking about that; **davon kann keine** ~ **sein** it's out of the question. **(d) es gibt die** ~, **daß** rumour *(Brit) or* rumor *(US)* has it that; **(jdm) für etw** ~ **und Antwort stehen** to account (to sb) for sth; **jdn zur** ~ **stellen** to take sb to task.

Rede-: ~**duell** *nt* verbal exchange; ~**fluß** *m* **er stockte plötzlich in seinem** ~**fluß** his flow of words suddenly stopped; ~**freiheit** *f* freedom of speech; **r**~**gewandt** *adj* eloquent; ~**gewandtheit** *f* eloquence; ~**kunst** *f* die ~**kunst** rhetoric.

reden 1 *vi* to talk, to speak. **R** ~ **während des Unterrichts** talking in class; **mit jdm** ~ to talk to sb; **so lasse ich nicht mit mir** ~! I won't be spoken to like that!; **sie hat geredet und geredet** she talked and talked; **mit jdm über jdn/etw** ~ to talk to sb about sb/sth; ~ **Sie doch nicht!** *(col)* come off it! *(col)*; **(viel) von sich** ~ **machen** to become (very much) a talking point; **du hast gut** ~! it's all very well for you (to talk); **darüber läßt sich** ~ that's a possibility; *(über Preis, Be-*

dingungen) I think we could discuss that; **er läßt mit sich ~** he could be persuaded; *(in bezug auf Preis)* he's open to offers; *(gesprächsbereit)* he's open to discussion; **R~ ist Silber, Schweigen ist Gold** *(Prov)* (speech is silver but) silence is golden *(Prov)*; **in so einem Dorf wird natürlich viel geredet** in a village like that naturally people talk a lot; **er kann gut ~** he is a good talker *or (als Redner)* speaker; **jdn zum R~ bringen** to get sb to talk. **2** *vt* to talk; *Worte* to say. **kein Wort ~** not to say a word; **einer Sache das Wort ~** to speak in favour *(Brit)* or favor *(US)* of sth; **Schlechtes über jdn ~** to say bad things about sb. **3** *vr* **sich heiser/in Wut ~** to talk oneself hoarse/into a fury.

Redens|art *f (Redewendung)* expression, idiom; *(Sprichwort)* saying; *(Phrase)* cliché. **bloße ~en** empty talk.

Rederei *f (Geschwätz)* chatter *no pl,* talk *no pl;* *(Klatsch)* gossip *no pl.*

Rede-: **~schwall** *m* torrent of words; **~verbot** *nt* ban on speaking; **jdm ~verbot erteilen** to ban sb from speaking; **~weise** *f* manner (of speaking); **~wendung** *f* idiomatic expression.

redigieren* *vt* to edit.

redlich *adj* honest. **sich** *(dat)* **etw ~ verdient haben** to have really earned sth; **~ (mit jdm) teilen** to share (things) equally (with sb).

Redlichkeit *f* honesty.

Redner(in *f)* *m* - speaker.

rednerisch *adj* rhetorical, oratorical. **~ begabt sein** to be a gifted speaker.

Rednerpult *nt* lectern.

redselig *adj* talkative.

Redseligkeit *f* talkativeness.

reduzieren* **1** *vt* to reduce. **2** *vr* to decrease, to diminish.

Reduzierung *f* reduction.

Reeder *m* - ship owner.

Reederei *f* shipping company.

reell *adj* **(a)** *(ehrlich)* honest, straight; *(Comm) Geschäft* sound; *Preis* fair. **(b)** *(wirklich)* real.

Referat *nt* **(a)** *(Univ)* seminar paper. **ein ~ halten** to present a seminar paper. **(b)** *(Admin: Ressort)* department.

Referendar(in *f)* *m* trainee (in civil service); *(Studien~)* student teacher; *(Gerichts~)* articled clerk.

Referendarzeit *f* traineeship; *(Studien~)* teacher training.

Referendum *nt, pl* **Referenden** referendum.

Referent(in *f)* *m* *(Sachbearbeiter)* consultant, expert; *(Redner)* speaker; *(Univ: Gutachter)* examiner.

referieren* *vi* to (give a) report *(über +acc* on).

reflektieren* **1** *vt* to reflect. **2** *vi* **(a)** *(nachdenken)* to reflect, to ponder *(über +acc* (up)on). **(b) auf etw** *(acc)* **~** to be interested in sth.

Reflex *m* **-e** reflection; *(Physiol)* reflex.

Reflexbewegung *f* reflex action.

Reflexion *f (Phys, fig)* reflection.

Reflexionswinkel *m (Phys)* angle of reflection.

reflexiv *adj (Gram)* reflexive.

Reform *f* **-en** reform.

Reformation *f* Reformation.

reformbedürftig *adj* in need of reform.

Reformer *m* - reformer.

Reform-: **r~freudig** *adj* avid for reform; **~haus** *nt* health food shop *(Brit)* or store *(US)*.

reformieren* *vt* to reform.

Reformkost *f* health food.

Refrain [rə'frɛ̃:, re-] *m* **-s** *(Mus)* chorus, refrain.

Regal *nt* **-e** *(Bord)* shelves *pl.*

Regatta *f, pl* **Regatten** regatta.

rege *adj (betriebsam)* lively. **ein ~s Treiben** a busy to-and-fro; **noch sehr ~ sein** to be very active still; **~ Beteiligung** lively participation; *(zahl-*

reich) good attendance.

Regel *f* **-n** **(a)** *(Vorschrift, Norm)* rule; *(Verordnung)* regulation. **nach allen ~n der Kunst** *(fig)* thoroughly; **sie überredete ihn nach allen ~n der Kunst, ...** she used every trick in the book to persuade him ... **(b)** *(Gewohnheit)* habit, rule. **sich** *(dat)* **etw zur ~ machen** to make a habit of sth; **in der ~** as a rule. **(c)** *(Monatsblutung)* period; *(Menstruation)* menstruation *no art.* **die ~ bekommen** to get one's period.

Regel-: **r~bar** *adj (steuerbar)* adjustable; **~fall** *m* rule; **im ~fall** as a rule; **r~los** *adj (ungeregelt)* irregular; *(unordentlich)* haphazard; **~losigkeit** *f* *siehe adj* irregularity; haphazardness; **r~mäßig** *adj* regular; **r~mäßig spazierengehen** to take regular walks; **er kommt r~mäßig zu spät** he's always late; **~mäßigkeit** *f* regularity.

regeln 1 *vt* **(a)** *(regulieren)* to control; *siehe* **geregelt. (b)** *(erledigen)* to see to; *(endgültig)* to settle; *Problem etc* to sort out; *(in Ordnung bringen)* to settle, to resolve. **wir haben die Sache so geregelt ...** we have arranged things like this ...; **gesetzlich geregelt sein** to be laid down by law. **2** *vr* to resolve itself.

regelrecht 1 *adj* real, proper; *Betrug, Beleidigung* downright; **das Spiel artete in eine ~e Schlägerei aus** the match degenerated into a regular brawl. **2** *adv* really; *beleidigend* downright.

Regelung *f* **(a)** *(Regulierung)* regulation, control. **(b)** *(Erledigung)* settling; *(von Unstimmigkeiten)* resolution. **(c)** *(Abmachung)* arrangement; *(Bestimmung)* ruling.

Regel-: **r~widrig** *adj* against the rules; *(gegen Verordnungen verstoßend)* against the regulations; **~widrigkeit** *f* irregularity; *(Verstoß auch)* breach of the rules.

regen 1 *vt (bewegen)* to move. **2** *vr (Mensch, Glied, Baum etc)* to move, to stir; *(Gefühl, Wind etc)* to stir. **unter den Zuhörern regte sich Widerspruch** there were mutterings of disapproval from the audience.

Regen *m* - rain; *(fig: von Schimpfwörtern, Blumen etc)* shower. **in den ~ kommen** to be caught in the rain; **ein warmer ~** *(fig)* a windfall; **jdn im ~ stehenlassen** *(fig)* to leave sb out in the cold; **vom ~ in die Traufe kommen** *(prov)* to fall out of the frying-pan into the fire *(prov).*

regen|arm *adj* dry, rainless.

Regenbogen *m* rainbow.

Regenbogen-: **~farben** *pl* colours *(Brit)* or colors *(US)* pl of the rainbow; **r~farben** *adj* rainbow-coloured *(Brit),* rainbow-colored *(US);* **~haut** *f (Anat)* iris; **~presse** *f* trashy magazines *pl.*

Regeneration *f* regeneration; *(fig auch)* revitalization.

regenerieren* **1** *vr (Biol)* to regenerate; *(fig)* to revitalize *or* regenerate oneself/itself; *(nach Anstrengung, Schock etc)* to recover. **2** *vt (Biol)* to regenerate; *(fig auch)* to revitalize.

Regen-: **~fall** *m usu pl* (fall of) rain; **tropische ~fälle** tropical rains; **r~frei** *adj* rainless; **~guß** *m* downpour; **~mantel** *m* raincoat; **r~reich** *adj* rainy; **~rinne** *f* gutter; **~schauer** *m* shower (of rain); **~schirm** *m* umbrella.

Regent(in *f)* *m* sovereign, reigning monarch.

Regen-: **~tag** *m* rainy day; **~tonne** *f* rain barrel; **~tropfen** *m* raindrop.

Regentschaft *f* reign.

Regen-: **~wald** *m (Geog)* rain forest; **~wasser** *nt* rainwater; **~wetter** *nt* rainy weather; **er macht ein Gesicht wie drei** *or* **sieben Tage ~wetter** *(col)* he's got a face as long as a month of Sundays *(col);* **~wolke** *f* rain cloud; **~wurm** *m* earthworm; **~zeit** *f* rainy season.

Regie [re'ʒi:] *f* **(a)** *(künstlerische Leitung)* direction; *(Theat, Rad, TV auch)* production *(Brit).* **die ~ bei etw führen** to direct/produce sth; **unter der ~ von** directed/produced by. **(b)** *(Leitung,*

Verwaltung) management. **etw in eigener ~ tun** to do sth oneself.

Regie- [re'ʒiː-]: **~anweisung** *f* (stage) direction; **~assistent** *m* assistant producer/director.

regieren* 1 *vi (herrschen)* to rule; *(fig)* to reign. 2 *vt Staat* to rule (over), to govern; *Markt, Fahrzeug* to control; *(Gram)* to govern.

Regierung *f* government; *(von Monarch)* reign; *(Zeitabschnitt)* period of government. **die ~ Brandt** the Brandt government *or* administration; **an die ~ kommen** to come to power; *(durch Wahl auch)* to come into *or* take office; **die ~ antreten** to take power; *(nach Wahl auch)* to take office.

Regierungs-: **~antritt** *m* coming to power; **~bank** *f* government bench; **~bezirk** *m* ≈ region *(Brit),* ≈ county *(US);* **~bildung** *f* formation of a government; **~chef** *m* head of a/the government; **der belgische ~chef** the head of the Belgian government; **~erklärung** *f* inaugural speech; *(in GB)* King's/Queen's Speech; **r~feindlich** *adj* anti-government *no adv;* **~form** *f* form of government; **r~freundlich** *adj* pro-government *no adv;* **~kreise** *pl* government circles *pl;* **~krise** *f* government(al) crisis; **~rat** *m* senior civil servant; **~sitz** *m* seat of government; **~sprecher** *m* government spokesman; **~system** *nt* system of government; **r~treu** *adj* loyal to the government; **~umbildung** *f* cabinet reshuffle *or* shake-up *(US);* **~vorlage** *f* government bill; **~wechsel** *m* change of government.

Regime [re'ʒiːm] *nt* **-s** *(pej)* regime.

Regime-: **~gegner** *m* opponent of the regime; **~kritiker** *m* critic of the regime.

Regiment *nt* **-e** *or (Mil)* **-er** **(a)** *(Herrschaft)* rule. **das ~ führen** *(col)* to be the boss *(col);* **ein strenges ~ führen** *(col)* to be strict. **(b)** *(Mil)* regiment.

Regiments- *in cpds* regimental.

Region *f* region.

regional *adj* regional. **~ verschieden sein** to vary from one region to another.

Regisseur(in *f)* [reʒɪ'søːɐ, -'søːrɪn] *m* director; *(Theat, Rad, TV auch)* producer *(Brit).*

Register *nt* - *(Liste, Mus)* register; *(Stichwortverzeichnis)* index. **alle ~ ziehen** *(fig)* to pull out all the stops.

Registertonne *f (Naut)* register ton.

Registratur *f* registration; *(Büro)* records office; *(Aktenschrank)* filing cabinet.

registrieren* *vti* to register; *(col: zur Kenntnis nehmen)* to note.

Registrierkasse *f* cash register.

Registrierung *f* registration.

reglementieren* *vt* to regulate; *jdn* to regiment.

Reglementierung *f siehe vt* regulation; regimentation.

Regler *m* - regulator, control.

reglos *adj* motionless.

regnen *vti impers* to rain. **es regnet in Strömen** it's pouring (with rain); **es regnet Proteste** protests are pouring in; **es regnete Vorwürfe** reproaches hailed down.

regnerisch *adj* rainy.

Regreß *m* **-sse** *(Jur)* recourse, redress.

Regreß-: **~anspruch** *m (Jur)* claim for compensation; **r~pflichtig** *adj* liable for compensation.

regsam *adj* active, alert, lively.

Regsamkeit *f* alertness, liveliness.

regulär *adj* normal; *(vorschriftsmäßig)* proper, regular. **~e Truppen** regular troops.

regulierbar *adj* adjustable.

regulieren* 1 *vt* **(a)** to regulate; *(nachstellen auch)* to adjust. **(b)** *Rechnung, Forderung* to settle. 2 *vr* to become more regular. **sich von selbst ~** to be self-regulating.

Regulierung *f* regulation.

Regung *f (Bewegung)* movement; *(des Gefühls, von*

Mitleid) stirring. **ohne jede ~** without a flicker (of emotion).

regungslos *adj* motionless.

Regungslosigkeit *f* motionlessness.

Reh *nt* **-e** deer; *(weiblich)* roe deer. **~e** deer.

Rehabilitation *f* rehabilitation; *(von Ruf, Ehre)* vindication.

rehabilitieren* 1 *vt* to rehabilitate; *Ruf, Ehre* to vindicate. 2 *vr* to rehabilitate *(form) or* vindicate oneself.

Reh-: **~bock** *m* roebuck; **~braten** *m* roast venison; **r~braun** *adj* russet; *Augen* hazel; **~keule** *f (Cook)* haunch of venison; **~kitz** *nt* fawn; **~rücken** *m (Cook)* saddle of venison.

Reibach *m no pl (col)* killing *(col).* **einen ~ machen** *(col)* to make a killing *(col).*

Reibe *f* **-n** *(Cook)* grater.

Reibeisen *nt* rasp; *(Cook)* grater; *(fig: zänkisches Weib)* shrew. **rauh wie ein ~** *(col)* like sandpaper.

Reibekuchen *m (Cook)* ≈ potato waffle.

reiben *pret* **rieb,** *ptp* **gerieben** 1 *vti* **(a)** to rub. **etw blank ~** to rub sth till it shines; **jdm den Rücken ~** to rub sb's back. **(b)** *(zerkleinern)* to grate. 2 *vr* to rub oneself *(an +dat* on, against*); (sich verletzen)* to scrape oneself *(an +dat* on*).*

Reiberei *f usu pl (col)* friction *no pl.*

Reibung *f* **(a)** *(das Reiben)* rubbing; *(Phys)* friction. **(b)** *(fig)* friction *no pl.*

Reibungs-: **~fläche** *f (fig)* source of friction; **r~los** *adj* frictionless; *(fig col)* trouble-free; **r~los verlaufen** to go off smoothly; **~wärme** *f (Phys)* frictional heat.

Reich *nt* **-e** **(a)** *(Herrschaft(sgebiet), Imperium)* empire; *(König~)* kingdom. **das Deutsche ~** the German Reich; **das Dritte ~** the Third Reich; **das ~ Gottes** the Kingdom of God. **(b)** *(Bereich, Gebiet)* realm. **das ~ der Tiere/Pflanzen** the animal/vegetable kingdom; **das ~ der Natur** the realm of nature; **das ist mein ~** *(fig)* that is my domain.

reich *adj* rich; *(wohlhabend auch)* wealthy; *(groß, vielfältig)* large, copious; *Auswahl, Erfahrung, Kenntnisse* wide; *Mahl* sumptuous; *Vegetation* rich. **~ heiraten** *(col)* to marry (into) money; **~ geschmückt** richly decorated; *Mensch* richly adorned; **eine ~ ausgestattete Bibliothek** a well stocked library; **~ mit Vorräten ausgestattet** amply stocked up with supplies; **jdn ~ belohnen** to give sb a rich reward; **jdn ~ beschenken** to shower sb with presents; **eine mit Kindern ~ beschenkte Familie** a family blessed with many children; **~ an etw (dat)** *sein* to be rich in sth; **in ~em Maße vorhanden sein** to abound; **~ illustriert** richly illustrated.

reichen 1 *vi* **(a)** *(sich erstrecken)* to stretch, to extend *(bis zu* to); *(Stimme auch)* to carry *(bis zu* to). **das Wasser reicht mir bis zum Hals** the water comes up to my neck; **jdm bis zur Schulter ~** to come up to sb's shoulder; **so weit ~ meine Beziehungen/Fähigkeiten nicht** my connections are not that extensive/my skills are not that wide-ranging; **so weit das Auge reicht** as far as the eye can see.

(b) *(langen)* to be enough, to suffice *(form).* **der Saal reicht nicht für so viele Leute** the room isn't big enough for so many people; **reicht mein Geld noch bis zum Monatsende?** will my money last until the end of the month?; **reicht das Licht zum Lesen?** is there enough light to read by?; **dazu reicht meine Geduld nicht** I haven't got enough patience for that; **jetzt reicht's (mir aber)!** *(Schluß)* that's enough!

2 *vt (entgegenhalten, geben)* to hand; *(her-über~, hinüber~ auch)* to pass (over); *(anbieten)* to serve. **jdm etw ~** to hand/pass sb sth; **jdm die Hand ~** to hold out one's hand (to sb); **sich die Hände ~** to join hands; *(zur Begrüßung)* to shake hands.

Reiche(r) *mf decl as adj* rich *or* wealthy man/ woman *etc*. die ~n the rich *or* wealthy.

Reich-: r~geschmückt *adj attr* richly adorned; r~haltig *adj* extensive; *Essen* rich; *Informationen* comprehensive; *Programm* varied; ~haltigkeit *f* *siehe adj* extensiveness; comprehensiveness; variety.

reichlich 1 *adj* ample; *Zeit, Geld, Platz* ample, plenty of. **2** *adv* **(a)** *(sehr viel)* belohnen, sich eindecken amply; *verdienen* richly. ~ **Trinkgeld geben** to tip generously; ~ **Zeit/Geld haben** to have plenty of time/money; ~ **vorhanden sein** to abound; **mehr als** ~ **belohnt** more than amply rewarded; **das ist** ~ **gerechnet** that's a generous estimate; ~ **1.000 Mark** a good 1,000 marks. **(b)** *(col: ziemlich)* pretty.

Reichtum *m (lit, fig)* wealth *no pl; (Besitz)* riches *pl*. **zu** ~ **kommen** to become rich; ~**er erwerben** to gain riches; **damit kann man keine** ~**er gewinnen** you won't get rich that way; **der** ~ **an Fischen** the abundance of fish.

Reichweite *f (von Geschoß, Sender)* range; *(greifbare Nähe)* reach; *(fig: Einflußbereich)* scope. **in** ~ **within range/the reach** *(gen of)*; **jd ist in** ~ sb is nearby; **außer** ~ out of range/reach *(gen of)*.

Reif *m siehe* **Rauhreif**.

reif *adj* ripe; *Ei, Mensch, Arbeit* mature. **in** ~**(er)em Alter** in one's mature(r) years; **im** ~**en Alter von ...** at the ripe old age of ...; ~ **zur Veröffentlichung** ripe for publication; **die Zeit ist** ~ the time is ripe; **eine** ~**e Leistung** *(col)* a brilliant achievement; **für etw** ~ **sein** *(col)* to be ready for sth.

Reife *f no pl (das Reifen)* ripening; *(das Reifsein)* ripeness; *(von Ei, Mensch, Arbeit)* maturity. **zur** ~ **kommen** to ripen; **ihm fehlt die** ~ he lacks maturity; **mittlere** ~ *(Sch)* first public examination in secondary school, ≈ O-Levels *pl (Brit)*.

reifen 1 *vt Obst* to ripen; *jdn* to mature; *siehe* **gereift**. **2** *vi aux sein* **(a)** *(Obst)* to ripen; *(Ei, Mensch)* to mature. **er reifte zum Manne** he became a man. **(b)** *(fig: Plan etc)* to mature. **zur Gewißheit** ~ to harden into certainty.

Reifen *m* - tyre *(Brit)*, tire *(US); (Spiel~, von Faß)* hoop; *(Arm~)* bangle.

Reifen-: ~**druck** *m* tyre *(Brit) or* tire *(US)* pressure; ~**panne** *f* puncture, flat; ~**profil** *nt* tyre *(Brit) or* tire *(US)* tread; ~**wechsel** *m* tyre *(Brit) or* tire *(US)* change.

Reife-: ~**prüfung** *f (Sch) siehe* **Abitur**; ~**zeit** *f* ripening time; *(von Ei)* period of incubation; *(Pubertät)* puberty *no def art*.

reiflich *adj* thorough, careful. **sich** *(dat)* **etw** ~ **überlegen** to consider sth carefully.

Reifung *f* ripening; *(von Ei)* maturation.

Reigen *m* - round dance; *(fig)* round. **ein bunter** ~ **von Melodien** a varied selection of melodies.

Reihe *f* -**n** **(a)** *(geregelte Anordnung)* row, line; *(Sitz~, Sew)* row; *(Serie, Math, Mus, fig)* series *sing*. **in Reih und Glied antreten** to line up in formation; **aus der** ~ **tanzen** *(fig col)* to be different; *(gegen Konventionen verstoßen)* to step out of line; **die** ~**n schließen** *(Mil, fig)* to close ranks; **die** ~**n lichten sich** *(fig)* the ranks are thinning; **in den eigenen** ~**n** within our/their *etc* own ranks.

(b) *(Reihenfolge)* **er ist an der** ~ it's his turn; **warte, bis du an die** ~ **kommst** wait till it's your turn; **der** ~ **nach** in order, in turn; **sie sollen der** ~ **nach hereinkommen** they are to come in one by one; **außer der** ~ out of turn; *(ausnahmsweise)* out of the usual way of things; **er kommt immer außer der** ~ he always comes just when he pleases.

(c) *(unbestimmte Anzahl)* number. **ein ganze** ~ **(von)** a whole lot (of).

(d) *(col: Ordnung)* **wieder in die** ~ **kommen** to get one's equilibrium back; *(gesundheitlich)* to get back on form; **in die** ~ **bringen** to put

straight.

reihen 1 *vt* **(a) Perlen auf eine Schnur** ~ to string beads (on a thread). **(b)** *(Sew)* to tack. **2** *vr* **etw reiht sich an etw** *(acc)* sth follows (after) sth.

Reihenfolge *f* order; *(notwendige Aufeinanderfolge)* sequence. **der** ~ **nach** in sequence; **zeitliche** ~ chronological order.

Reihen-: ~**haus** *nt* terraced house; ~**schaltung** *j̃ (Elec)* series connection; **in** ~**schaltung** in series; ~**untersuchung** *f* mass screening; **r**~**weise** *adv* **(a)** *(in Reihen)* in rows; **(b)** *(fig: in großer Anzahl)* by the dozen.

Reiher *m* - heron.

reihern *vi (col)* to puke (up) *(col!)*.

reih|um *adv* around. **es geht** ~ everybody takes their turn; **etw** ~ **gehen lassen** to pass sth around.

Reim *m* -**e** rhyme. **ein** ~ **auf „Hut"** a rhyme for "hat"; ~**e bilden** to make rhymes; ~**e schmieden** *(hum)* to write verse; **sich** *(dat)* **einen** ~ **auf etw** *(acc)* **machen** *(col)* to make sense of sth; **ich kann mir keinen** ~ **darauf machen** *(col)* I can see no rhyme (in)/or reason in it.

reimen *vtr* to rhyme *(auf +acc, mit* with). **das reimt sich nicht** *(fig)* it doesn't make sense.

Reim-: **r**~**los** *adj* unrhymed, non-rhyming; ~**schema** *nt* rhyme scheme; ~**wort** *nt, pl* -**wörter** rhyme.

rein¹ *adv (col)* = **herein, hinein**.

rein² **1** *adj* pure; *Wahrheit* plain; *Gewinn* clear; *(sauber)* clean; *Haut auch, Gewissen* clear. **das ist die** ~**ste Freude/der** ~**ste Hohn** *etc* it's pure *or* sheer joy/mockery *etc*; **er ist der** ~**ste Künstler** he's a real artist; **die** ~**e Arbeit kostet ...** the work alone costs ...; **eine** ~**e Jungenklasse** an all boys' class; **eine** ~**e Industriestadt** a purely industrial town; ~**en Tisch machen** *(fig)* to get things straight; **etw ins** ~**e schreiben** to write out a fair copy of sth; **etw ins** ~**e bringen** to clear sth up; **mit sich selbst ins** ~**e kommen** to sort things out with oneself. **2** *adv* **(a)** *(ausschließlich)* purely. ~ **theoretisch gesprochen** speaking purely theoretically. **(b)** *(col: ganz, völlig)* absolutely. ~ **alles/unmöglich** absolutely everything/impossible.

Rein(e)machefrau *f* cleaner, cleaning lady.

Reinemachen *nt no pl (col)* cleaning.

Rein-: ~**erlös**, ~**ertrag** *m* net profit(s).

rein(e)weg *adv (col)* completely, absolutely. **das ist** ~ **erlogen** it's a downright lie.

Reinfall *m (col)* disaster *(col); (Pleite auch)* flop *(col)*.

reinfallen *vi sep irreg aux sein (col)* = **hereinfallen, hineinfallen**.

Rein-: ~**gewicht** *nt* net(t) weight; ~**gewinn** *m* net(t) profit; ~**haltung** *f* keeping clean; **die** ~**haltung des Spielplatzes** keeping the playground clean.

Reinheit *f* purity; *(Sauberkeit)* cleanness.

reinigen 1 *vt* to clean. **etw chemisch** ~ to dryclean sth; **ein** ~**des Gewitter** *(fig col)* a row which clears/cleared the air. **2** *vr* to clean itself; *(Mensch)* to cleanse oneself.

Reinigung *f* **(a)** cleaning. **(b)** *(chemische* ~*)* *(Vorgang)* dry cleaning; *(Anstalt)* (dry) cleaner's *(Brit) or* cleaner *(US)*.

Reinigungs-: ~**creme** *f* cleansing cream; ~**mittel** *nt* cleansing agent.

reinkriegen *vt sep (col)* = **hereinbekommen, hineinbekommen**.

Reinkultur *f (Biol)* cultivation of pure cultures. **Kitsch in** ~ *(col)* pure unadulterated rubbish.

reinlegen *vt sep (col)* = **hereinlegen, hineinlegen**.

reinlich *adj* cleanly; *(ordentlich)* neat, tidy; *(klar)* clear.

Reinlichkeit *f siehe adj* cleanliness; neatness, tidiness; clearness.

Rein-: **r~rassig** adj pure-blooded; *Tier* pure-bred, thoroughbred; **~rassigkeit** f racial purity; *(von Tier)* pure breeding; **r~reiten** vt sep irreg **jdn r~reiten** *(col)* to get sb into a mess *(col)*; **~schrift** f *(Geschriebenes)* fair copy; **r~seiden** adj pure silk; **~vermögen** nt net assets pl; **r~waschen** sep irreg **1** vt *(von of)* to clear; **2** vr *(fig)* to clear oneself; **r~weg** adv = **rein(e)weg**.

Reis m -e rice.

Reisbrei m ≈ creamed rice.

Reise f -n journey, trip; *(Schiffs~)* voyage; *(Geschäfts~)* trip. **seine ~n durch Europa** his travels through Europe; **eine ~ mit der Eisenbahn/dem Auto** a train/car journey; **eine ~ zu Schiff** a sea voyage; **eine ~ machen** to go on a journey; **auf ~n sein** to be away (travelling *(Brit)* or traveling *(US)*); **er ist viel auf ~n** he does a lot of travelling; **wann gehen Sie auf die ~?** when do you go (away) on your trip?; **wohin geht die ~?** where are you off to?; **gute ~!** bon voyage!, have a good journey!

Reise-: **~andenken** nt souvenir; **~apotheke** f first aid kit; **~begleiter** m travelling *(Brit)* or traveling *(US)* companion; *(~leiter)* courier; **~bericht** m account of one's journey; *(Buch)* travel story; *(Film)* travelogue; **~beschränkungen** pl travel restrictions pl; **~beschreibung** f description of one's travels; travel book or story; *(Film)* travelogue; **~büro** nt travel agency; **~erleichterungen** pl easing of travel restrictions; **r~fertig** adj ready to leave; **~fieber** nt **vom ~fieber gepackt** excited about going on a trip; **~führer** m *(Buch)* guidebook; *(Person)* courier; **~gefährte** m travelling *(Brit)* or traveling *(US)* companion; **~geld** nt fare; **~gepäck** nt luggage, baggage; **~gesellschaft** f (tourist) party; *(im Bus auch)* coach party *(Brit)*; *(Veranstalter)* travel company; **~koffer** m suitcase; **~leiter** m courier; **~leitung** f *(das Leiten)* organization of a/the tourist party; *(~leiter)* courier(s); **~lektüre** f reading matter (for a journey); **etw als ~lektüre mitnehmen** to take sth to read on the journey; **~lust** f wanderlust, travel bug *(col)*; **r~lustig** adj keen on travel.

reisen vi aux sein to travel. **in etw** *(dat)* **~** *(Comm)* to travel in sth.

Reisende(r) mf decl as adj traveller *(Brit)*, traveler *(US)*; *(Fahrgast)* passenger; *(Comm)* (commercial) traveller *(Brit)*, traveler *(US)*.

Reise-: **~paß** m passport; **~pläne** pl plans pl (for a/the journey); **~proviant** m food for the journey; **~route** f route, itinerary; **~scheck** m traveller's cheque *(Brit)*, traveler's check *(US)*; **~schreibmaschine** f portable typewriter; **~spesen** pl travelling *(Brit)* or traveling *(US)* expenses pl; **~tasche** f grip, travelling *(Brit)* or traveling *(US)* bag; **~verkehr** m holiday traffic; **~vorbereitungen** pl travel preparations pl; **~zeit** f time for travelling *(Brit)* or traveling *(US)*; **die beste ~zeit für Ägypten** the best time to go to Egypt; **~ziel** nt destination.

Reisfeld nt paddy-field.

Reisig nt no pl brushwood, twigs pl.

Reiskorn nt grain of rice.

Reiß|aus m: **~ nehmen** *(col)* to clear off *(col)*.

Reiß-: **~brett** nt drawing-board; **~brettstift** m drawing pin *(Brit)*, thumb tack *(US)*.

reißen pret **riß**, ptp **gerissen 1** vt **(a)** *(zer~)* to tear, to rip. **(b)** *(ab~, ent~)* to tear, to pull, to rip *(etw von etw sth off sth)*; *(mit~, zerren)* to pull, to drag. **jdn zu Boden ~** to drag sb to the ground; **der Fluß hat die Brücke mit sich gerissen** the river swept the bridge away; **jdn aus seinen Träumen ~** to wake sb from his dreams; **hin und her gerissen sein** *(fig)* to be torn. **(c)** **etw an sich** *(acc)* **~** to seize sth; *Unterhaltung* to monopolize sth. **(d)** *(Sport)* Latte, Hürde to knock off. **(e)** *(töten)* to take, to kill. **(f)** *(col: machen)* Witze to

crack *(col)*; Possen to play.

2 vi **(a)** aux sein *(zer~)* to tear, to rip; *(Seil)* to tear, to break, to snap; *(Risse bekommen)* to crack. **mir ist die Kette gerissen** my chain has broken or snapped; **wenn alle Stricke ~** *(fig col)* if the worst comes to the worst. **(b)** *(zerren)* *(an +dat an)* to tug; *(wütend)* to tear. **(c)** *(col)* *(Gewichtheben)* to snatch; *(Leichtathletik)* to knock the bar off.

3 vr **(a)** *(sich verletzen)* to cut oneself *(an +dat on)*. **(b)** *(sich los~)* to tear oneself/itself. **(c)** *(col)* **sich um jdn/etw ~** to scramble to get sb/sth.

Reißen nt no pl **(a)** *(Gewichtheben: Disziplin)* snatch. **(b)** *(col: Glieder~)* ache.

reißend adj Fluß torrential, raging; Schmerzen searing; Verkauf, Absatz massive. **~en Absatz finden** to sell like hot cakes *(col)*.

Reißer m - *(col)* *(Buch, Film)* thriller; *(Ware)* big seller.

reißerisch adj sensational.

Reiß-: **r~fest** adj tearproof; **~leine** f ripcord; **~verschluß** m zip(-fastener) *(Brit)*, zipper *(US)*; **~wolf** m shredder; **~zahn** m fang; **~zwecke** f drawing pin *(Brit)*, thumb tack *(US)*.

Reit-: **~anzug** m riding-habit; **~bahn** f arena.

reiten pret **ritt**, ptp **geritten 1** vi aux sein to ride. **auf etw** *(dat)* **~** to ride (on) sth; **im Schritt/Galopp ~** to ride at a walk/gallop. **2** vt to ride. **ein schnelles Tempo ~** to ride at a fast pace.

Reiter m - *(a)* rider, horseman; *(Mil)* cavalryman. **(b)** *(Kartei~)* index-tab.

Reiterin f rider, horsewoman.

Reiterregiment nt cavalry regiment.

Reit-: **~gerte** f riding crop; **~hose** f riding-breeches pl; *(Sport)* jodhpurs pl; **~peitsche** f riding whip; **~pferd** nt saddle-horse, mount; **~sport** m (horse-)riding, equestrian sport *(form)*; **~stall** m riding-stable; **~stiefel** m riding-boot; **~turnier** nt horse show; *(Geländereiten)* point-to-point; **~weg** m bridle-path.

Reiz m -e *(a)* *(Physiol)* stimulus. **einen ~ auf etw** *(acc)* **ausüben** to act as a stimulus on sth. **(b)** *(Verlockung)* attraction, appeal; *(Zauber)* charm. **der ~ der Neuheit/des Verbotenen** the appeal of novelty/forbidden fruits; **(auf jdn) einen ~ ausüben** to hold great attraction(s for sb); **den ~ verlieren** to lose all one's/its charm; **weibliche ~e** feminine charms.

Reiz-: **r~bar** adj *(empfindlich)* sensitive, touchy *(col)*; *(erregbar, Med)* irritable; **leicht r~bar sein** to be very sensitive/irritable; **~barkeit** f siehe adj sensitivity, touchiness *(col)*; irritability.

reizen 1 vt **(a)** *(Physiol)* to irritate; *(stimulieren)* to stimulate. **(b)** *(verlocken)* to appeal to. **es würde mich ja sehr ~, ...** I'd love to ...; **Ihr Angebot reizt mich sehr** I find your offer very tempting. **(c)** *(ärgern)* to annoy; *(herausfordern)* to provoke. **jds Zorn ~** to arouse sb's anger; **siehe gereizt. (d)** *(Cards)* to bid. **2** vi **(a)** *(Med)* to irritate; *(stimulieren)* to stimulate. **zum Widerspruch ~** to invite contradiction. **(b)** *(Cards)* to bid.

reizend adj charming. **das ist ja ~** *(iro)* (that's) charming.

Reizhusten m chesty cough.

Reiz-: **r~los** adj dull, uninspiring; **~mittel** nt *(Med)* stimulant; **~stoff** m irritant.

Reizung f **(a)** *(Med)* stimulation; *(krankhaft)* irritation. **(b)** *(Herausforderung)* provocation.

Reiz-: **r~voll** adj charming, delightful; Aufgabe, Beruf attractive; **die Aussicht ist nicht gerade r~voll** the prospect is not particularly appealing; **~wäsche** f *(col)* sexy underwear; **~wort** nt emotive word.

rekapitulieren* vt to recapitulate.

rekeln vr *(col: sich strecken)* to stretch. **er rekelte sich im behaglichen Sessel** he snuggled down in the comfy chair.

Reklamation f complaint.

Reklame *f* -n (a) advertising. ~ **für jdn/etw machen** to advertise sb/sth; **mit etw** ~ **machen** *(pej)* to show off about sth. (b) *(Anzeige)* advertisement, advert *(Brit col)*, ad *(col)*; *(TV, Rad auch)* commercial.

Reklame-: ~**schild** *nt* advertising sign; ~**sendung** *f* commercial break; ~**trommel** *f:* die ~**trommel für jdn/etw rühren** *(col)* to beat the (big) drum for sb/sth, to do a lot of promotion for sb/sth; ~**zettel** *m* (advertising) leaflet.

reklamieren* 1 *vi (Einspruch erheben)* to complain, to make a complaint. **bei jdm wegen etw** ~ to complain to sb about sth. 2 *vt* (a) *(bemängeln)* to complain about *(etw bei jdm* sth to sb); *(in Frage stellen) Rechnung* to query *(etw bei jdm* sth with sb). (b) *(beanspruchen)* **jdn/etw für sich** ~ to lay claim to sb/sth.

rekonstruieren* *vt* to reconstruct.

Rekonstruktion *f* reconstruction.

Rekord *m* -e record.

Rekord- *in cpds* record; ~**halter**, ~**inhaber** *m* record-holder; ~**lauf** *m* record(-breaking) run; ~**marke** *f (Sport, fig)* record; ~**versuch** *m* attempt on the/a record; ~**zeit** *f* record time.

Rekrut *m (wk)* -en, -en *(Mil)* recruit.

rekrutieren* 1 *vt (Mil, fig)* to recruit. 2 *vr (fig)* **sich** ~ **aus** to be drawn from.

Rekrutierung *f* recruitment, recruiting.

Rektor *m,* **Rektorin** *f (Sch)* headteacher, principal *(esp US); (Univ)* vice-chancellor, rector *(US); (von Fachhochschule)* principal.

Relais [rə'leː] *nt* - [rə'leː(s)], - [rə'leːs] *(Elec)* relay.

Relation *f* relation.

relativ 1 *adj* relative. ~**e Mehrheit** *(Parl)* simple majority. 2 *adv* relatively.

relativieren* [relati'viːrən] *vt (geh)* to qualify.

Relativität [relativi'tɛːt] *f* relativity.

Relativ-: ~**pronomen** *nt* relative pronoun; ~**satz** *m* relative clause.

relevant [rele'vant] *adj* relevant.

Relevanz [rele'vants] *f* relevance.

Relief [reli'ɛf] *nt* -s *or* -e relief.

Religion *f* religion; *(Schulfach)* religious instruction *or* education, RI *(col)*.

Religions-: ~**bekenntnis** *nt* denomination; ~**freiheit** *f* freedom of worship; ~**gemeinschaft** *f* religious community; ~**lehrer** *m* teacher of religious education, RI teacher *(col)*; **r~los** *adj* not religious; ~**stunde** *f* religious education *no indef art,* RI lesson *(col)*; ~**unterricht** *m* religious education.

religiös *adj* religious. ~ **erzogen werden** to receive a religious upbringing.

Religiosität *f* religiousness.

Relikt *nt* -e relic.

Reling *f* -s *or* -e *(Naut)* (deck) rail.

remis [rə'miː] *adj inv* drawn. ~ **spielen** to draw; **die Partie ist** ~ the game has ended in a draw.

Remis [rə'miː] *nt* - [rə'miː(s)], - [rə'miːs] *or* -en [rə'miːzn] *(Schach, Sport)* draw.

Remittende *f* -n *(Comm)* return.

Remittent *m (Fin)* payee.

remittieren* *vt (Comm) Waren* to return; *Geld* to remit.

Remmidemmi *nt no pl (col) (Krach)* row, rumpus *(col); (Trubel)* rave-up *(col)*.

Rempelei *f (col)* jostling; *(Sport: Foul)* pushing.

rempeln *vti (col)* to jostle; to elbow; *(im Sport)* to barge *(jdn* into sb); *(foulen)* to push.

Ren *nt* -e reindeer.

Renaissance [rənɛ'sãːs] *f* -en (a) *(Hist)* renaissance. (b) *(fig)* revival, rebirth.

Rendezvous [rãde'vuː] *nt* - [-'vuː(s)], - [-'vuːs] rendezvous *(liter, hum),* date.

Rendite *f* -n *(Fin)* yield, return on capital.

renitent *adj* awkward, refractory.

Renitenz *f* awkwardness, refractoriness.

Renn- *in cpds* race; ~**bahn** *f* (race)track.

rennen *pret* **rannte**, *ptp* **gerannt** 1 *vi aux sein* to run. **um die Wette** ~ to have a race; **ins Unglück** ~ to rush headlong into disaster; **er rennt zu jedem Fußballspiel** he goes to every football match; **gegen jdn/etw** ~ to run into sb/sth; **er rannte mit dem Kopf gegen ...** he bumped his head against ... 2 *vt* (a) *aux haben or sein (Sport)* to run. (b) **jdn zu Boden** *or* **über den Haufen** ~ to knock sb down. (c) *(stoßen) Messer etc* to run.

Rennen *nt* - running; *(Sport) (Vorgang)* racing; *(Veranstaltung)* race. **totes** ~ dead heat; **gut im** ~ **liegen** *(lit, fig)* to be well placed; **das** ~ **ist gelaufen** *(lit)* the race is over; *(fig)* it's all over; **das** ~ **machen** *(lit, fig)* to win (the race).

Renner *m* - *(col)* winner, worldbeater.

Rennerei *f (col) (lit, fig: das Herumrennen)* running around; *(Hetze)* mad chase *(col)*.

Renn-: ~**fahrer** *m (Rad~)* racing cyclist; *(Motorrad~)* racing motorcyclist; *(Auto~)* racing driver; ~**pferd** *nt* racehorse; ~**piste** *f* (race)track; ~**platz** *m* racecourse; ~**rad** *nt* racing bike *(col)*; ~**saison** *f* racing season; ~**schlitten** *m* bob(sleigh); ~**schuhe** *pl (Sport)* spikes *pl*; ~**sport** *m* racing; ~**stall** *m (Tiere, Zucht)* stable; ~**strecke** *f (~bahn)* (race)track; ~**tag** *m* day of the race; ~**wagen** *m* racing car.

Renommee *nt* -s reputation, name.

renommiert *adj* renowned, famous *(wegen* for).

renovieren* [reno'viːrən] *vt* to renovate; *(esp tapezieren etc)* to redecorate, to do up *(col)*.

Renovierung [reno'viːruŋ] *f* renovation.

rentabel *adj* profitable. **es ist nicht** ~, **das reparieren zu lassen** it is not worth(while) having it repaired; **das ist eine rentable Sache** it will pay *(off)*.

Rentabilität *f* profitability.

Rente *f* -n pension; *(aus Versicherung, Lebens~)* annuity; *(aus Vermögen)* income. **in** ~ **gehen** *(col)/**sein** *(col)* to start drawing one's pension/to be on a pension.

Renten-: ~**alter** *nt* retirement age; ~**anspruch** *m* right to a pension; ~**basis** *f* annuity basis; ~**empfänger** *m* pensioner; ~**erhöhung** *f* pension increase; ~**papier** *nt (Fin)* fixed-interest security; ~**versicherung** *f* pension scheme.

Rentier *nt (Zool)* reindeer.

rentieren* *vir* to be worthwhile; *(Geschäft etc auch, Maschine)* to pay. **das rentiert (sich) nicht** it's not worth it.

Rentner(in *f) m* - pensioner; *(Alters~ auch)* senior citizen, old age pensioner *(Brit)*.

re|organisieren* *vt* to reorganize.

reparabel *adj* repairable.

Reparationen *pl* reparations *pl*.

Reparatur *f* repair. ~**en am Auto** car repairs; ~**en am Haus vornehmen** to do some repairs to the house; **in** ~ being repaired; **etw in** ~ **geben** to have sth repaired.

Reparatur-: **r~anfällig** *adj* prone to break down; **r~bedürftig** *adj* in need of repair; ~**kosten** *pl* repair costs *pl*; ~**werkstatt** *f* workshop; *(Auto~)* garage.

reparieren* *vt* to mend; *Auto* to repair.

Repertoire [reper'toaːə] *nt* -s repertory, repertoire *(auch fig)*.

Replik *f* -en *(fig geh)* riposte, reply.

Report *m* -e report.

Reportage [repor'taːʒə] *f* -n report.

Reporter *m* - reporter.

Repräsentant(in *f) m* representative.

Repräsentantenhaus *nt (US Pol)* House of Representatives.

repräsentativ *adj (stellvertretend, typisch)* representative *(für* of); *Haus, Auto* prestigious. **zu** ~**en Zwecken** for purposes of prestige; **die** ~**en Pflichten eines Botschafters** the social duties of an ambassador.

repräsentieren* 1 *vt* to represent. 2 *vi* to per-

form official duties.
Repressalie [-iə] *f* reprisal.
Repression *f* repression.
repressiv *adj* repressive.
Reprise *f* -n *(Mus)* recapitulation; *(Film, Theat)* rerun; *(nach längerer Zeit)* revival.
Reproduktion *f* reproduction.
reproduktiv *adj* reproductive.
reproduzieren* *vt* to reproduce.
Reptil *nt* -ien [-iən] reptile.
Republik *f* -en republic.
Republikaner(in *f)* *m* - republican.
republikanisch *adj* republican.
Republik-: ~**flucht** *f (DDR)* illegal crossing of the border; ~**flüchtling** *m (DDR)* illegal emigrant.
Requiem ['reːkviɛm] *nt* -s requiem.
Requisit *nt* -en equipment *no pl,* requisite *(form).* ~**en** *(Theat)* props, properties *(form).*
Requisiteur [-'tøːɐ] *m (Theat)* props *or* property manager.
Reseda *f* -s *(Bot) (Gattung)* reseda; *(Garten~)* mignonette.
Reservat [rezɐ'vaːt] *nt* (a) *(Wildpark)* reserve. (b) *(für Volksstämme)* reservation.
Reserve [re'zɛrvə] *f* -n (a) *(Vorrat)* reserve(s) *(an* +*dat* of); *(Geld)* savings *pl; (Mil, Sport)* reserves *pl.* (b) *(Zurückhaltung)* reserve. **jdn aus der** ~ **locken** to bring sb out of his/her shell *(col).*
Reserve-: ~**kanister** *m* spare can; ~**rad** *nt* spare (wheel); ~**reifen** *m* spare (tyre); ~**tank** *m* reserve tank; ~**truppen** *pl* reserves *pl;* ~**übung** *f* (army) reserve training *no pl.*
reservieren* [rezɐ'viːrən] *vt* to reserve.
reserviert *adj* Platz, Mensch reserved.
Reserviertheit *f* reserve.
Reservierung *f* reservation.
Reservist [rezɐ'vɪst] *m* reservist.
Reservoir [rezɐ'voaːɐ] *nt* -e reservoir; *(fig auch)* pool.
Residenz *f (Wohnung)* residence.
residieren* *vi* to reside.
Resignation *f (geh)* resignation.
resignieren* *vi* to give up. **resigniert** resigned; ... **sagte er** ~**d** ... he said with resignation.
resolut *adj* determined.
Resolution *f (Pol) (Beschluß)* resolution; *(Bittschrift)* petition.
Resonanz *f* (a) *(Mus, Phys)* resonance. (b) *(fig)* response *(auf* +*acc* to). **keine/große** ~ **finden** to meet with no/a good response.
resozialisieren* *vt* to rehabilitate.
Resozialisierung *f* rehabilitation.
Respekt *m no pl* respect; *(Angst)* fear. **bei allem** ~ **(vor jdm/etw)** with all due respect (to sb/for sth); **vor jdm/etw** ~ **haben** to have respect for sb/sth; *(Angst)* to be afraid of sb/sth.
respektabel *adj* respectable.
respektieren* *vt* to respect; *Wechsel* to honour *(Brit),* to honor *(US).*
respektive [rɛspɛk'tiːvə] *adv (geh, Comm)* (a) *siehe* **beziehungsweise.** (b) *(anders ausgedrückt)* or rather; *(genauer gesagt)* (or) more precisely.
Respekt-: **r**~**los** *adj* disrespectful, irreverent; ~**losigkeit** *f* (a) *(no pl: Verhalten)* disrespect(fulness), irreverence; (b) *(Bemerkung)* disrespectful remark.
Respektsperson *f* person to be respected.
respektvoll *adj* respectful.
Ressentiment [rɛsãtiˈmãː, rə-] *nt* -s resentment *no pl (gegen* against*).*
Ressort [rɛ'soːɐ] *nt* -s department. **in das** ~ **von jdm fallen** *(lit, fig)* to be sb's department.
Rest *m* -e (a) rest; *(Stoff~)* remnant. **die** ~**e einer** Stadt/Kultur the remains of a city/civilization; **der letzte** ~ the last bit; **dieser kleine** ~ this little bit that's left (over); **jdm/einer Sache den** ~ **geben** *(col)* to finish sb/sth off. (b) ~**e** *pl*

(Essens~) left-overs *pl.*
Restaurant [rɛstoˈrãː] *nt* -s restaurant.
Restaurator *m* restorer.
restaurieren* *vt* to restore.
Restaurierung *f* restoration.
Rest- *in cpds* remaining; ~**bestand** *m* remaining stock; ~**betrag** *m* balance; **r**~**lich** *adj* remaining, rest of the ...; **die r**~**lichen** the rest; **r**~**los 1** *adj* complete, total; 2 *adv* completely, totally; *begeistert* wildly; ~**posten** *m (Comm)* remaining stock; **ein** ~**posten** remaining stock; ~**summe** *f* balance, amount remaining.
Resultat *nt* result.
resultieren* *vi (geh)* to result *(in* +*dat* in*).* **aus etw** ~ to result from sth; **die daraus** ~**den** ... the resulting ...
Resümee *nt* -s *(geh)* summary, résumé.
resümieren* *vti (geh)* to summarize, to sum up.
Retorte *f* -n *(Chem)* retort. **aus der** ~ *(col)* synthetic.
Retortenbaby *nt* test-tube baby.
retour [re'tuːɐ] *adv (old, dial)* back.
Retourkutsche [re'tuːɐ-] *f (col)* tit-for-tat answer.
retten 1 *vt* to save; *(befreien)* to rescue. **jdm das Leben** ~ to save sb's life; **jdn vor jdm/etw** ~ to save sb from sb/sth; **ein** ~**der Gedanke** a bright idea that saved the situation; **bist du noch zu** ~? *(col)* are you out of your mind? *(col).* **2** *vr* to escape. **sich aus etw** ~ to escape from sth; **sich vor jdm/etw** ~ to escape (from) sb/sth; **sich vor etw nicht mehr** ~ **können** *(fig)* to be swamped with sth; **rette sich, wer kann!** (it's) every man for himself!
Retter(in *f)* *m* - rescuer; *(Rel)* Saviour *(Brit),* Savior *(US).*
Rettich *m* -e radish.
Rettung *f* rescue, deliverance *(liter); (Rel)* salvation. **die** ~ **kam in letzter Minute** the situation was saved in the last minute; *(für Schiffbrüchige etc)* help came in the nick of time; **auf** ~ **hoffen** to hope to be saved; **für den Patienten gibt es keine** ~ **mehr** the patient is beyond saving; **das/er war meine** ~ that/he was my salvation; **das war meine letzte** ~ that was my last hope.
Rettungs-: ~**aktion** *f* recue operation; ~**anker** *m* sheet anchor; *(fig)* anchor; ~**boot** *nt* lifeboat; ~**dienst** *m* rescue service; ~**kommando** *nt* rescue squad; **r**~**los 1** *adj* beyond saving; *Lage* hopeless; 2 *adv* verloren irretrievably; ~**mannschaft** *f* rescue team; ~**ring** *m* lifebelt; ~**schwimmer** *m* lifesaver; *(am Strand)* lifeguard.
retuschieren* *vt (Phot)* to retouch, to touch up *(col, auch fig).*
Reue *f no pl* remorse *(über* +*acc* at, about), repentance *(auch Rel) (über* +*acc* of); *(Bedauern)* regret *(über* +*acc* at, about).
reuelos *adj* unrepentant.
reuen *vt (liter)* **etw reut jdn** sb regrets sth.
reuevoll, reuig *adj (liter) siehe* **reumütig.**
reumütig *adj* remorseful; *Sünder* contrite. ~ **gestand er** ... full of remorse he confessed ...
Reuse *f* -n fish trap.
Revanche [re'vãːʃ(ə)] *f* -n revenge; *(~partie)* return match. **du mußt mir** ~ **geben!** you'll have to give him a return match.
revanchieren* [revãˈʃiːrən] *vr* (a) to get one's own back *(bei jdm für etw* on sb for sth*).* (b) *(sich erkenntlich zeigen)* to reciprocate. **sich bei jdm für eine Einladung** ~ to return sb's invitation.
Revanchismus [revãˈʃɪsmɵs] *m* revanchism.
revanchistisch [revãˈʃɪstɪʃ] *adj* revanchist.
Reverenz [reveˈrɛnts] *f (old)* **jdm seine** ~ **erweisen** to show one's reverence for sb.
Revers [re'veːɐ] *nt or m* - [re'veːɐ(s)], - [reveːɐs] *(an Kleidung)* lapel, revers *(esp US).*
revidieren* [reviˈdiːrən] *vt* to revise; *(Comm)* to audit.

Revier [re'vi:ɐ] *nt* **-e** (a) *(Polizei~) (Dienststelle)* (police) station, station house *(US)*; *(Dienstbereich)* beat, precinct *(US)*, patch *(col)*. (b) *(Zool: Gebiet)* territory. **die Küche ist mein ~** the kitchen is my preserve. (c) *(Hunt: Jagd~)* hunting ground, shoot. (d) *(Min: Kohlen~)* (coal)mine. **im ~ an der Ruhr** in the mines of the Ruhr.

Revision [revi'zio:n] *f* (a) *(von Meinung, Politik etc)* revision. (b) *(Comm: Prüfung)* audit. (c) *(Jur: Urteilsanfechtung)* appeal *(an +acc* to).

Revisionismus [revizio'nismʊs] *m* *(Pol)* revisionism.

revisionistisch [revizio'nɪstɪʃ] *adj* *(Pol)* revisionist.

Revisions-: **~frist** *f* time for appeal; **~verhandlung** *f* appeal hearing.

Revisor [re'vi:zɔr] *m (Comm)* auditor.

Revolte [re'vɔltə] *f* **-n** revolt.

revoltieren* [revɔl'ti:rən] *vi* to revolt, to rebel.

Revolution [revolu'tsio:n] *f (lit, fig)* revolution.

revolutionär [revolutsio'nɛ:ɐ] *adj (lit, fig)* revolutionary.

Revolutionär(in *f)* [revolutsio'nɛ:ɐ, -'nɛ:ər(ɪn)] *m* revolutionary.

revolutionieren* [revolutsio'ni:rən] *vt* to revolutionize.

Revolutions- *in cpds* revolutionary.

Revoluzzer [revo'lʊtsɐ] *m* - *(pej)* would-be revolutionary.

Revolver [re'vɔlvɐ] *m* - revolver, gun.

Revolver-: **~blatt** *nt (pej)* scandal sheet; **~held** *m (pej)* gunslinger.

Revue [rə'vy:] *f* **-n** [-y:ən] *(Theat)* revue. **etw ~ passieren lassen** *(fig)* to pass sth in review.

Revuetänzerin* [rə'vy:-] *f* chorus-girl.

rezensieren* *vt* to review.

Rezension *f* review, write-up *(col)*.

Rezept *nt* **-e** (a) *(Med)* prescription; *(fig)* remedy *(für, gegen* for). **auf ~** on prescription. (b) *(Cook, fig)* recipe.

rezeptfrei *adj* available without prescription. **2** *adv* over the counter.

Rezeption *f (von Hotel: Empfang)* reception.

Rezept-: **~pflicht** *f* prescription requirement; **r~pflichtig** *adj* available only on prescription.

Rezession *f (Econ)* recession.

rezitieren* *vti* to recite.

R-Gespräch ['ɛr-] *nt* reverse charge call *(Brit)*, collect call.

Rhabarber *m no pl (auch Gemurmel)* rhubarb.

Rhapsodie *f* rhapsody.

Rhein *m* Rhine.

Rhein-: **r~ab(wärts)** *adv* down the Rhine; **r~auf(wärts)** *adv* up the Rhine; **~fall** *m* Rhine Falls *pl*.

rheinisch *adj attr* Rhenish, Rhineland.

Rhein-: **~länder(in** *f)* *m* - Rhinelander; **r~ländisch** *adj* Rhineland; **~land-Pfalz** *nt* Rhineland-Palatinate; **~wein** *m* Rhine wine; *(weißer auch)* hock *(Brit)*.

Rhesus-: **~affe** *m* rhesus monkey; **~faktor** *m (Med)* rhesus or Rh factor.

Rhetorik *f* rhetoric.

rhetorisch *adj* rhetorical. **~e Frage** rhetorical question.

Rheuma *nt no pl* rheumatism.

Rheumatiker(in *f) m* - rheumatism sufferer.

rheumatisch *adj* rheumatic.

Rheumatismus *m* rheumatism.

Rhinozeros *nt* **-(ses)**, **-se** rhinoceros, rhino *(col)*; *(col: Dummkopf)* fool.

Rhodesien [-iən] *nt* Rhodesia.

rhodesisch *adj* Rhodesian.

Rhododendron [rodo'dɛndrɔn] *m or nt, pl* **Rhododendren** rhododendron.

rhythmisch *adj* rhythmic(al).

Rhythmus *m (Mus, Poet, fig)* rhythm.

Richtantenne *f* directional aerial *(esp Brit)* or antenna.

richten **1** *vt* (a) *(lenken)* to direct *(auf +acc* towards), to point *(auf +acc* at, towards); *Augen, Aufmerksamkeit* to turn *(auf +acc* towards), to focus *(auf +acc* on). (b) *(aus~)* **etw nach jdm/ etw ~** to suit sth to sb/sth; *Verhalten* to adapt sth to sb/sth. (c) *(adressieren) Briefe, Anfragen* to address *(an +acc* to); *Bitten, Forderungen* to make *(an +acc* to); *Kritik, Vorwurf* to direct *(gegen* at, against). (d) *(esp S Ger) (zurechtmachen)* to prepare, to get ready; *(in Ordnung bringen)* to do, to fix; *(reparieren)* to fix; *Haare* to do; *Tisch* to lay *(Brit)*, to set; *Betten* to make, to do. (e) *(instellen)* to set.
2 *vr* (a) *(sich hinwenden)* to focus, to be focussed *(auf +acc* on), to be directed *(auf +acc* towards). (b) *(sich wenden)* to consult *(an jdn* sb); *(Maßnahme, Vorwurf etc)* to be aimed *(gegen* at). (c) *(sich anpassen)* to follow *(nach jdm/etw* sb/sth). **sich nach den Vorschriften/den Sternen ~** to go by the rules/the stars; **sich nach jds Wünschen ~** to comply with sb's wishes; **wir ~ uns ganz nach unseren Kunden** we are guided entirely by our customers' wishes; **und richte dich (gefälligst) danach!** *(col)* (kindly) do as you're told. (d) *(abhängen von)* to depend *(nach* on). (e) *(esp S Ger: sich zurechtmachen)* to get ready.
3 *vi (liter: urteilen)* to judge *(über jdn* sb), to pass judgement *(über +acc* on).

Richter(in *f) m* - judge. **jdn/etw vor den ~ bringen** to take sb/sth to court; **sich zum ~ machen** *(fig)* to set (oneself) up in judgement.

Richter-: **r~lich** *adj attr* judicial; **~schaft** *f* judiciary, Bench.

Richt-: **~fest** *nt* topping-out ceremony; **~geschwindigkeit** *f* recommended speed.

richtig **1** *adj* (a) right *no comp; (zutreffend auch)* correct. **eine ~e Erkenntnis** a correct realization; **ich halte es für ~/das ~ste,** ... I think it would be right/best ...; **bin ich hier ~ bei Müller?** *(col)* is this right for the Müllers? (b) *(wirklich, echt)* real, proper. **der ~e Vater/die ~e Mutter** the real father/mother; **ein ~er Idiot** *etc* a right idiot *etc (col)*.
2 *adv* (a) *(korrekt)* correctly, right. **die Uhr geht ~** the clock is right; **du kommst gerade ~!** you're just in time. (b) *(col: ganz und gar)* really, real *(esp US col)*. (c) *(wahrhaftig)* right, correct. **das ist doch Paul! — ach ja, ~** that's Paul — oh yes, so it is.

Richtige(r) *mf decl as adj* right person/man/ woman *etc*. **sechs ~ im Lotto** six right in the lottery.

Richtige(s) *nt decl as adj* right thing. **das ist genau das ~** that's just the job *(col)*; **ich habe nichts ~s gegessen/gelernt** I haven't had a proper meal/I didn't really learn anything; **ich habe endlich was ~s gefunden** at last I've found something suitable.

richtiggehend **1** *adj attr Uhr, Waage* accurate; *(col: regelrecht)* real. **2** *adv (col)* ~ **intelligent** really intelligent.

Richtigkeit *f* correctness, accuracy; *(von Verhalten, einer Entscheidung)* correctness. **an der ~ von etw zweifeln** to doubt whether sth is right; **das hat schon seine ~** it's right enough.

Richtig-: **r~stellen** *vt sep* to correct; **~stellung** *f* correction.

Richt-: **~kranz** *m wreath used in the topping-out ceremony;* **~linie** *f usu pl* guideline; **~mikrofon** *nt* directional microphone; **~platz** *m* place of execution; **~preis** *m* recommended price; **~schnur** *f (fig: Grundsatz)* guiding principle.

Richtung *f* (a) direction. **in ~ Hamburg** in the direction of Hamburg; **in nördliche ~** towards the north, in a northerly direction; **die Autobahn/der Zug ~ Hamburg** the Hamburg autobahn/train; **die ~ ändern** to change direction(s);

eine ~ **nehmen** or **einschlagen** to head in a direction; **seine Gedanken nahmen eine neue** ~ his thoughts took a new turn; **in jeder** ~ each way; *(fig: in jeder Hinsicht)* in every respect. **(b)** *(Tendenz)* trend; *(die Vertreter einer* ~*)* movement; *(Denk*~*, Lehrmeinung)* school of thought.

Richtungs-: ~**änderung** *f* change in direction; **r**~**los** *adj* lacking a sense of direction; ~**losigkeit** *f* lack of a sense of direction; ~**wechsel** *m* *(lit, fig)* change of direction.

richtungweisend *adj* pointing the way. ~ **sein** to point the way (ahead).

Richtzahl *f* approximate figure.

Ricke *f* **-n** doe.

rieb *pret of* **reiben.**

riechen *pret* **roch,** *ptp* **gerochen 1** *vti* to smell. **gut/schlecht** ~ to smell good/bad; **nach etw** ~ to smell of sth; **an jdm/etw** ~ to sniff (at) sb/sth; **ich rieche das Gewürz gern** I like the smell of this spice; **das riecht nach Betrug** *(fig col)* that smacks of deceit; **jdn nicht** ~ **können** *(col)* to hate sb's guts *(col)*; **das konnte ich doch nicht** ~! *(col)* how was I (supposed) to know? **2** *vi (Geruchssinn haben)* **nicht mehr** ~ **können** to have lost one's sense of smell. **3** *vi impers* to smell. **es riecht angebrannt** there's a smell of burning.

Riecher *m* - *(col)* **einen guten** or **den richtigen** ~ **(für etw) haben** *(col)* to have a nose (for sth) *(col)*.

Ried *nt* **-e** *(Schilf)* reeds *pl.*

Riedgras *nt* sedge.

rief *pret of* **rufen.**

Riege *f* **-n** *(Sport)* team, squad.

Riegel *m* - **(a)** *(Verschluß)* bolt. **einer Sache** *(dat)* **einen** ~ **vorschieben** *(fig)* to clamp down on sth. **(b)** *(Schokolade)* bar; *(Seife auch)* cake.

Riemen *m* - **(a)** *(Treib*~*, Gürtel)* belt; *(an Kleidung, Koffer*~*)* strap; *(Schnürsenkel)* shoelace. **den** ~ **enger schnallen** *(col)* to tighten one's belt; **sich am** ~ **reißen** *(fig col)* to get a grip on oneself. **(b)** *(Sport)* oar.

Riemenantrieb *m* belt-drive.

Riese[1]: **das macht nach Adam** ~ **DM 3,50** *(hum col)* the way I learned it at school that makes DM 3.50.

Riese[2] *m (wk)* **-n, -n** *(lit, fig)* giant; *(col: Tausendmarkschein)* 1000 mark note, big one *(esp US col)*.

rieseln *vi aux sein (Wasser, Sand)* to trickle; *(Regen)* to drizzle; *(Schnee)* to flutter down. **der Kalk rieselt von der Wand** lime is crumbling off the wall; **ein Schauder rieselte mir über den Rücken** a shiver went down my spine.

Riesen- *pref* gigantic; *(Zool, Bot etc auch)* giant; ~**chance** *f* tremendous chance; ~**erfolg** *m* gigantic success; *(Theat, Film)* smash hit; ~**gebirge** *nt (Geog)* Sudeten Mountains *pl*; **r**~**groß** *adj* gigantic; ~**hunger** *m (col)* enormous appetite; ~**rad** *nt* big or Ferris wheel; ~**schlange** *f* boa; ~**schritt** *m* giant stride; **sich mit** ~**schritten nähern** *(fig)* to be drawing on apace; ~**slalom** *m* giant slalom.

riesig *adj* gigantic. **2** *adv (col: sehr)* enormously.

riet *pret of* **raten.**

Riff *nt* **-e** *(Felsklippe)* reef.

rigoros *adj* rigorous.

Rille *f* **-n** groove; *(in Säule)* flute.

Rimesse *f (Fin)* remittance.

Rind *nt* **-er (a)** *(Tier)* cow. ~**er** cattle *pl*; **10** ~**er 10** head of cattle. **(b)** *(col: Rindfleisch)* beef. **vom** ~ beef.

Rinde *f* **-n** *(Baum*~*)* bark; *(Brot*~*)* crust; *(Käse*~*)* rind.

Rinder-: ~**braten** *m (roh)* joint of beef; *(gebraten)* roast beef *no indef art*; ~**filet** *nt* fillet of beef; ~**herde** *f* herd of cattle; ~**zucht** *f* cattle farming.

Rindfleisch *nt* beef.

Rindsleder *nt* leather.

Rindvieh *nt* **(a)** *no pl* cattle *pl*. **10 Stück** ~ **10 head**

of cattle. **(b)** *pl* -**viecher** *(col: Dummkopf)* ass *(col)*.

Ring *m* **-e (a)** ring; *(von Menschen auch)* circle; *(Ketten*~*)* link; *(Rettungs*~*)* lifebelt; *(~straße)* ring road. **die** ~**e tauschen** to exchange rings; ~**e** *(Turnen)* rings; ~ **frei!** *(Boxen)* seconds out! **(b)** *(Vereinigung)* circle, group; *(Bande)* ring. **(c)** *(liter: Kreislauf)* circle, cycle. **der** ~ **schließt sich** the wheel turns full circle.

Ringel-: ~**blume** *f* marigold; ~**locke** *f* ringlet.

ringeln 1 *vt (Pflanze)* to (en)twine; *Schwanz etc auch* to curl; *siehe* **geringelt. 2** *vr* to go curly, to curl; *(Rauch)* to curl up(wards). **die Schlange ringelte sich um den Baum** the snake coiled itself around the tree.

Ringel-: ~**natter** *f* grass snake; ~**reigen,** ~**reihen** ring-a-ring-o' roses; ~**taube** *f* wood-pigeon.

ringen *pret* **rang,** *ptp* **gerungen 1** *vt* **die Hände** ~ to wring one's hands; **er rang ihr das Messer aus der Hand** he wrested the knife from her hand. **2** *vi* **(a)** *(lit, fig: kämpfen)* to wrestle. **mit dem Tode** ~ to wrestle with death. **(b)** *(streben)* **nach** or **um etw** ~ to struggle for sth; **ums Überleben** ~ *(liter)* to struggle to survive.

Ringen *nt no pl (Sport)* wrestling; *(fig)* struggle.

Ringer *m* - wrestler.

Ring-: ~**finger** *m* ring finger; **r**~**förmig** *adj* ringlike; ~**kampf** *m* fight; *(Sport)* wrestling match; ~**kämpfer** *m* wrestler; ~**richter** *m* referee.

rings *adv* (all) around.

ringsherum *adv* all (the way) around.

Ringstraße *f* ring road.

ringsum *adv* (all) around.

Rinne *f* - *(Rille)* groove; *(Furche, Abfluß*~*, Fahr*~*)* channel; *(Dach*~*, col: Rinnstein)* gutter.

rinnen *pret* **rann,** *ptp* **geronnen** *vi* **(a)** *aux sein (fließen)* to run. **das Geld rinnt ihm durch die Finger** *(fig)* money slips through his fingers. **(b)** *(undicht sein)* to leak.

Rinn-: ~**sal** *nt* **-e** rivulet; ~**stein** *m (Gosse)* gutter.

Rippchen *nt (Cook)* slightly cured pork rib.

Rippe *f* **-n** rib; *(von Apfelsine)* segment. **er hat nichts auf den** ~**n** *(col)* he's just skin and bones; **... damit du was auf die** ~**n kriegst** *(col)* ... to put a bit of flesh on you; **ich kann es mir nicht aus den** ~**n schneiden** *(col)* I can't just produce it from nowhere.

Rippen-: ~**bruch** *m* broken rib; ~**fell** *nt* pleura; ~**fellentzündung** *f* pleurisy; ~**speer** *m* or *nt* *(Cook)* spare rib; **Kasseler** ~**speer** slightly cured pork spare rib; ~**stoß** *m* dig in the ribs.

Risiko *nt, pl* -**s** or **Risiken** risk. **auf eigenes** ~ at one's own risk; **etw ohne** ~ **tun** to do sth without taking a risk.

riskant *adj* risky, chancy *(col)*.

riskieren* *vt (aufs Spiel setzen)* to risk; *(wagen)* to venture. **etwas/nichts** ~ to take chances/no chances; **seine Stellung** ~ to put one's job at risk; **in Gegenwart seiner Frau riskiert er kein Wort** when his wife is present he dare not say a word.

Rispe *f* **-n** *(Bot)* panicle.

riß *pret of* **reißen.**

Riß *m, pl* **Risse (a)** *(in Stoff, Papier etc)* tear, rip; *(in Erde, Gestein)* crevice, fissure; *(in Wand, Behälter etc)* crack; *(Haut*~*)* chap; *(fig: Kluft)* rift, split. **die Freundschaft hat einen** ~ **bekommen** a rift has developed in their friendship. **(b)** *(Tech etc: Zeichnung)* sketch, sketch plan.

rissig *adj (Boden, Leder)* cracked; *Haut* chapped.

Rist *m* **-e** *(am Fuß)* instep.

Riten *pl of* **Ritus.**

ritt *pret of* **reiten.**

Ritt *m* **-e** ride. **einen** ~ **machen** to go for a ride; **in einem** ~ *(col)* at one go *(col)*.

Ritter *m* - knight; *(Kavalier)* cavalier. **jdn zum** ~ **schlagen** to knight sb; **arme** ~ *pl (Cook)* sweet French toast soaked in milk.

Ritter-: ~**burg** f knight's castle; ~**kreuz** nt (Mil) Knight's Cross; ~**kreuzträger** m holder of the Knight's Cross; **r**~**lich** adj (lit) knightly; (fig) chivalrous; ~**lichkeit** f chivalry; ~**orden** m order of knights.

Rittersmann m, pl -**leute** (poet) knight.

Ritter-: ~**sporn** m (Bot) larkspur, delphinium; ~**stand** m knighthood.

Rittmeister m (old Mil) cavalry captain.

Ritual nt -e or -**ien** [-iən] (lit, fig) ritual.

rituell adj ritual.

Ritus m -, **Riten** rite; (fig) ritual.

Ritze f -n (Riß) crack; (Fuge) gap.

Ritzel nt - (Tech) pinion.

ritzen 1 vt to scratch; (einritzen) Namen etc auch to carve. **die Sache ist geritzt** (col) it's all fixed up. **2** vr to scratch oneself.

Rivale [ri'vaːlə] m (wk) -n, -n, **Rivalin** [ri'vaːlɪn] f rival.

rivalisieren* [rivali'ziːrən] vi **mit jdm** ~ to compete with sb; **34** ~**de Parteien** 34 rival parties.

Rivalität [rivali'tɛːt] f rivalry.

Rizinus(öl nt) m -, - or -se castor oil.

Roastbeef ['roːstbiːf] nt -s (roh) beef; (gebraten) roast beef.

Robbe f -n seal.

robben vi aux sein (Mil) to crawl.

Robben-: ~**fang** m seal hunting; ~**fänger** m seal hunter.

Robe f -n **(a)** (Abendkleid) evening gown. **(b)** (Amtstracht) (official) robe or robes pl.

Roboter m - robot.

Robotertechnik f robotics sing.

robust adj Mensch, Gesundheit robust; Material tough.

Robustheit f siehe adj robustness; toughness.

roch pret of **riechen.**

Rochade [rɔ'xaːdə, rɔ'ʃaːdə] f (Chess) castling. **die kleine/große** ~ castling king's side/queen's side.

Röcheln nt no pl groan; (Todes~) death rattle.

röcheln vi to groan; (Sterbender) to give the death rattle.

Rochen m - ray.

Rock¹ m ⁼e **(a)** (Damen~) skirt; (Schotten~) kilt. **(b)** (Jackett) jacket.

Rock² m no pl (Mus) rock.

Rocker m - rocker.

Rock-: ~**falte** f (von Damenrock) inverted pleat; (von Jackett) vent; ~**futter** nt skirt lining.

Rockmusik f rock music.

Rock-: ~**saum** m hem of a/the skirt; ~**schoß** m coat-tail; **an jds** ~**schößen hängen** to cling to sb's coat-tails (col); ~**zipfel an Mutters** ~**zipfel hängen** (col) to cling to (one's) mother's apron-strings (col).

Rodel m - sledge, toboggan, sleigh.

Rodelbahn f toboggan-run.

rodeln vi aux sein or haben to toboggan (auch Sport), to sledge.

Rodelschlitten m toboggan, sledge.

roden vt Wald, Land to clear.

Rodung f (das Roden, Fläche) clearing.

Rogen m - roe.

Roggen m no pl rye.

Roggenbrot nt rye bread.

roh adj **(a)** (ungekocht) raw. **(b)** (unbearbeitet) rough; Eisen, Metall crude. **(c)** (brutal) rough. ~**e Gewalt** brute force.

Roh-: ~**bau** m (Bauabschnitt) shell (of a/the house); **das Haus ist im** ~**bau fertig(gestellt)** the house is structurally complete; ~**diamant** m rough or uncut diamond; ~**eisen** nt pig iron.

Roheit f (a) no pl (Eigenschaft) roughness; (Brutalität auch) brutality. **(b)** (Tat) brutality. **(c)** (ungekochter Zustand) rawness.

Roh-: ~**entwurf** m rough draft; ~**ertrag** m gross proceeds pl; ~**kost** f raw fruit and vegetables pl; ~**leder** nt rawhide; ~**ling** m **(a)** (Grobian) brute,

ruffian; **(b)** (Tech) blank; ~**material** nt raw material; ~**öl** nt crude oil; ~**produkt** nt raw material.

Rohr nt -e **(a)** (Tech, Mech) pipe; (Geschütz~) (gun) barrel. **(b)** (Schilf~) reed; (Zucker~) cane; (für Stühle etc) cane, wicker no pl.

Rohrbruch m burst pipe.

Röhrchen nt tube; (Chem) test tube; (col: zur Alkoholkontrolle) breathalyzer. **ins** ~ **blasen (müssen)** (col) to be breathalyzed.

Röhre f -n **(a)** (Hohlkörper) tube; (Neon~) (neon) tube or strip; (Elektronen~) valve (Brit), tube (US); (fig: Fernsehgerät) telly (Brit col), tube (US col). **(b)** (Ofen~) warming oven; (Back~) oven. **in die** ~ **gucken** (col) to be left out.

Röhren-: **r**~**förmig** adj tubular; ~**hose** f (col) drainpipe trousers pl.

Rohr-: **r**~**geflecht** nt wickerwork, basketwork; ~**krepierer** m - (Mil sl) barrel burst; **ein** ~**krepierer sein** (fig) to backfire; ~**leitung** f pipe, conduit; ~**post** f pneumatic dispatch system. ~**spatz** m **schimpfen wie ein** ~**spatz** (col) to curse and swear; ~**stock** m cane; ~**zange** f pipe wrench; ~**zucker** m cane sugar.

Roh-: ~**seide** f wild silk; ~**stoff** m raw material; (St Ex) commodity; ~**zucker** m unrefined sugar; ~**zustand** m unprocessed state; **das Manuskript ist noch im** ~**zustand** the manuscript is still in a fairly rough state.

Rokoko nt no pl Rococo period; (Stil) Rococo, rococo.

Rolladen m, pl **Rolläden** or - (an Fenster, Tür etc) shutters pl; (von Schreibtisch) roll top.

Roll-: ~**bahn** f runway; ~**brett** nt skateboard.

Röllchen nt little roll; (von Garn) reel.

Rolle f -n **(a)** (Zusammengerolltes) roll; (Garn~, Zwirn~) reel; (Urkunde) scroll. **eine** ~ **Bindfaden** a ball of string. **(b)** (walzenförmig) roller; (an Möbeln, Kisten) castor; (an Flaschenzug) pulley. **(c)** (Sport) forward roll; (Aviat) roll. **die** ~ **rückwärts** the backward roll. **(d)** (Theat, Film, fig) role, part; (Sociol) role. **eine Ehe mit streng verteilten** ~**n** a marriage with strict allocation of roles; **jds** ~ **bei etw** (fig) sb's part in sth; **bei** or **in etw** (dat) **eine** ~ **spielen** to play a part in sth; (Mensch auch) to play a role in sth; **etw spielt eine große** ~ (**bei jdm**) sth is very important (to sb); **es spielt keine** ~, **(ob)** ... it doesn't matter (whether) ...; **bei ihm spielt Geld keine** ~ with him money is no object; **aus der** ~ **fallen** (fig) to forget oneself; **mußt du ständig aus der** ~ **fallen!** must you always show yourself up!

rollen 1 vi aux sein to roll; (Flugzeug) to taxi. **etw/den Stein ins R**~ **bringen** (fig) to start sth/the ball rolling; **es werden einige Köpfe** ~ **heads will roll. (b) mit den Augen** ~ to roll one's eyes. **2** vt to roll; Teig to roll out; Teppich, Papier to roll up. **3** vr to curl up.

Rollen-: ~**besetzung** f (Theat, Film) casting; ~**erwartung** f (Sociol) role expectation; ~**fach** nt (Theat) character; **r**~**förmig** adj cylindrical; **r**~**spezifisch** adj role-specific; ~**tausch** m exchange of roles; (Sociol auch) role reversal.

Roller m - **(a)** scooter. **(b)** (Walze, Naut: Welle) roller.

Roll-: ~**feld** nt runway; ~**film** m roll film; ~**kommando** nt raiding party; ~**kragen** m roll or polo neck; ~**mops** m rollmops, rolled pickled herring.

Rollo nt -s (roller) blind.

Roll-: ~**schinken** m smoked ham; ~**schrank** m roll-fronted cupboard.

Rollschuh m roller-skate. ~ **laufen** to roller-skate.

Rollschuh-: ~**bahn** f roller-skating rink; ~**laufen** nt rollerskating; ~**läufer** m roller-skater.

Roll-: ~**splitt** m grit; „~**splitt**" "loose chippings";

~**stuhl** m wheel-chair; ~**treppe** f escalator.

Rom nt Rome. **viele Wege führen nach** ~ (Prov) all roads lead to Rome (Prov); **das sind Zustände wie im alten** ~ (col) (unmoralisch) it's disgraceful; (primitiv) it's medieval (col).

Roman m -e novel. (**jdm**) **einen ganzen** ~ **erzählen** (col) to give sb a long rigmarole (col).

Roman-: ~**autor** m novelist; **r~haft** adj like a novel; ~**heft** nt cheap pulp novel; ~**held** m hero of a/the novel.

Romanik f (Archit, Art) Romanesque period; (Stil) Romanesque (style).

romanisch adj Volk, Sprache Romance; (Art) Romanesque.

Romanist(in f) m (Univ) teacher/student/scholar of Romance languages and literature.

Romanistik f (Univ) Romance languages and literature.

Roman-: ~**leser** m novel reader; ~**schreiber** m (col) novelist; (pej) scribbler; ~**schriftsteller** m novelist.

Romantik f (**a**) (Liter, Art, Mus) Romanticism; (Epoche) Romantic period. (**b**) (fig) romance.

Romantiker(in f) m - (Liter, Art, Mus) Romantic; (fig) romantic.

romantisch adj romantic; (Liter etc) Romantic.

Romanze f -n (Liter, Mus, fig) romance.

Römer m - (Weinglas) type of wineglass.

Römer(in f) m - Roman. **die alten** ~ the (ancient) Romans.

Römer-: ~**reich** nt Roman Empire; ~**topf** ® m (Cook) ≈ (chicken) brick.

römisch adj Roman.

römisch-katholisch adj Roman Catholic.

Rommé [rɔ'meː, 'rɔme] nt no pl rummy.

Rondo nt -s (Mus) rondo.

röntgen vt to X-ray.

Röntgen nt no pl X-raying.

Röntgen-: ~**apparat** m X-ray equipment no indef art, no pl; ~**aufnahme** f X-ray (plate); ~**augen** pl (hum) X-ray eyes pl (hum).

Röntgenologe m, **Röntgenologin** f radiologist.

Röntgenologie f radiology.

Röntgen-: ~**strahlen** pl X-rays pl; ~**untersuchung** f X-ray examination.

rosa adj inv pink. **ein** ~ or ~**nes** (col) **Kleid** a pink dress; **die Welt durch eine** ~(**rote**) **Brille sehen** to see the world through rose-coloured (Brit) or rose-colored (US) glasses; **in** ~(**rotem**) **Licht** in a rosy light.

rosa-: ~**farben**, ~**farbig**, ~**rot** siehe rosa.

Röschen ['røːsçən] nt (little) rose.

Rose f -n (Blume) rose. **er ist nicht auf** ~**n gebettet** (fig) life isn't a bed of roses for him.

Rosé m -s (wine).

Rosen-: ~**farben**, **r~farbig** adj rose-coloured (Brit) or rose-colored (US); ~**holz** nt rosewood; ~**knospe** f rosebud; ~**kohl** m Brussel(s) sprouts pl; ~**kranz** m (Eccl) rosary; **den** ~**kranz beten** to say a rosary; ~**montag** m Monday preceding Ash Wednesday; ~**montagszug** m Carnival parade which takes place on the Monday preceding Ash Wednesday; ~**öl** nt attar of roses; ~**strauch** m rosebush.

Rosette f rosette.

Roséwein m rosé wine.

rosig adj (lit, fig) rosy.

Rosine f raisin. (**große**) ~**n im Kopf haben** (col) to have big ideas; **sich** (dat) **die (besten)** ~**n herauspicken** (col) to take the pick of the bunch.

Rosmarin m no pl rosemary.

Roß nt, pl **-sse** or **-̈sser** (liter) steed (liter), horse. **hoch zu** ~ on horseback; **auf dem hohen** ~**sitzen** (fig) to be on one's high horse; ~ **und Reiter nennen** (fig geh) to name names.

Roß-: ~**haar** nt horsehair; ~**kastanie** f horse chestnut; ~**kur** f (col) kill-or-cure remedy; ~**täuscher** m (fig) horse-trader.

Rost[1] m no pl (auch Bot) rust. ~ **ansetzen** to start to rust.

Rost[2] m -e (Ofen~) grill. (Gitter~) grating, grille. **auf dem** ~ **braten** (Cook) to barbecue, to grill on charcoal.

Rost-: **r~beständig** adj rust-resistant; ~**bildung** f rust formation; ~**braten** m (Cook) ≈ roast; ~**bratwurst** f grilled or barbecued sausage; **r~braun** adj russet; Haar auburn.

Röstbrot nt toast.

rosten vi aux sein or haben to get rusty (auch fig). **alte Liebe rostet nicht** (Prov) old love never dies.

rösten vt Kaffee to roast; Brot to toast. **sich in der Sonne** ~ **lassen** to lie in the sun and bake.

Rost-: **r~farben** adj siehe **r~braun**; ~**fleck** m patch of rust; **r~frei** adj (Stahl) stainless.

rostig adj (lit, fig) rusty.

Röstkartoffeln pl fried potatoes.

Rost-: ~**laube** f (hum) rust-heap (hum); **r~rot** adj rust-coloured (Brit), rust-colored (US), russet; ~**schutz** m anti-rust protection; ~**schutzmittel** nt rust-proofer.

rot adj red (auch Pol). ~**e Bete** beetroot; **das R~e Kreuz** the Red Cross; **der R~e Platz** Red Square; **das R~e Meer** the Red Sea; **die R~e Armee** the Red Army; **die R~en** (pej) the reds; **in den** ~**en Zahlen stecken** to be in the red; ~ **werden**, **einen** ~**en Kopf bekommen** to blush, to go red; **sich** (dat) **etw** ~ (**im Kalender**) **anstreichen** (col) to make sth a red-letter day.

Rot nt -s or - red; (Wangen~) rouge. **bei** ~ **at red; die Ampel stand auf** ~ the lights were (at) red.

Rot|armist m soldier in the Red Army.

Rotation f rotation.

Rotations-: ~**achse** f axis of rotation; ~**maschine**, ~**presse** f (Typ) rotary press.

Rot-: ~**barsch** m rosefish; **r~blond** adj Haar sandy; Mann sandy-haired; Frau strawberry blonde; **r~braun** adj reddish brown; ~**buche** f (common) beech; ~**dorn** m hawthorn.

Röte f no pl redness, red; (Erröten) blush. **die** ~ **stieg ihr ins Gesicht** her face reddened.

Röteln pl German measles sing.

röten 1 vt (geh) to redden, to make red; Himmel to turn red. **ein gerötetes Gesicht** a flushed face. **2** vr to turn red.

Rot-: ~**filter** nt or m (Phot) red filter; ~**fuchs** m red fox; (Pferd) sorrel or bay (horse); (fig col) carrot-top (col); ~**gardist** m Red Guard; **r~glühend** adj Metall red-hot; **r~haarig** adj red-haired; ~**haut** f (dated hum) redskin; ~**hirsch** m red deer.

rotieren* vi to rotate.

Rot-: ~**käppchen** nt (Liter) Little Red Ridinghood; ~**kehlchen** nt robin; ~**kohl** m, ~**kraut** nt red cabbage.

Rotkreuz- in cpds Red Cross.

rötlich adj reddish.

Rotlicht nt red light.

Rotor m rotor.

Rotorflügel m (Aviat) rotor blade.

Rot-: **r~sehen** vi sep irreg (col) to see red (col); ~**stift** m red pencil; **dem** ~**stift zum Opfer fallen** (fig) to be scrapped; ~**tanne** f Norway spruce.

Rotte f -, -n gang; (Mil Aviat, Mil Naut) pair (of planes/ships operating together); (von Hunden etc) pack; (Hist) band.

Rottweiler m - (Hund) Rottweiler.

Rötung f reddening.

Rot-: **r~wangig** adj rosy-cheeked; ~**wein** m red wine; ~**wild** nt red deer.

Rotz m no pl (**a**) (col) snot (col). ~ **und Wasser heulen** to blubber; **Graf** ~ Lord Muck (col); **der ganze** ~ the whole bloody (Brit) or goddam (US) show (col). (**b**) (Vet) glanders sing.

rotzfrech adj (col) cocky (col).

rotzig adj (col) snotty (col).

Rotz-: ~**nase** f (col) (a) snotty nose (col); (b) (Kind) snotty-nosed brat (col); **r~näsig** adj (col) (a) snotty-nosed (col); (b) (frech) snotty (col).

Rouge [ruːʒ] nt -s rouge.

Roulade [ruˈlaːdə] f (Cook) ≃ beef olive.

Roulett(e) [ruˈlɛt(ə)] nt - or -s roulette.

Route ['ruːtə] f -n route.

Routine [ruˈtiːnə] f (Erfahrung) experience; (Gewohnheit, Trott) routine.

Routine-: ~**angelegenheit** f routine matter; **r~mäßig** 1 adj routine; 2 adv **ich gehe r~mäßig zum Zahnarzt** I make a routine visit to the dentist; **das wird r~mäßig überprüft** it's checked as a matter of routine; ~**sache** f routine matter; ~**untersuchung** f routine examination.

Routinier [rutiˈnieː] m -s old hand.

routiniert [rutiˈniːɐt] adj experienced.

Rowdy ['raudi] m, pl -s or **Rowdies** hooligan; (zerstörerisch) vandal; (lärmend) rowdy (type).

Rowdytum ['raudituːm] nt no pl hooliganism.

rubbeln vti (col) to rub.

Rübe f -n (a) turnip. **rote** ~ beetroot (Brit), red beet (US); **weiße** ~ white turnip. (b) (col: Kopf) nut (col). **eins auf die** ~ **kriegen** to get a bash on the nut (col).

Rubel m - rouble. **der** ~ **rollt** (col) the money's rolling in (col).

Rüben-: ~**kraut** nt, ~**saft** m sugar beet syrup; ~**zucker** m beet sugar.

rüber- in cpds (col) = **herüber-, hinüber-.**

Rubin m -e ruby.

rubinrot adj ruby-red, ruby.

Rubrik f (a) (Kategorie) category. (b) (Zeitungs~) section, column.

ruch-: ~**bar** adj ~**bar werden** (geh) to become known; ~**los** adj (dated, geh) dastardly (liter).

Ruck m -e jerk, tug; (von Fahrzeug) jolt, jerk; (Pol) swing, shift. **er stand mit einem** ~ **auf** he sprang to his feet; **sich** (dat) **einen** ~ **geben** (col) to make an effort; **etw in einem** ~ **erledigen** to do sth at one fell swoop.

Rück-: ~**ansicht** f rear view; ~**antwort** f reply; **um** ~**antwort wird gebeten** please reply.

ruck|artig adj jerky. **er stand** ~ **auf** he shot to his feet.

Rück-: ~**besinnung** f recollection; ~**bildung** f (Biol) degeneration; ~**blende** f flashback; ~**blick** m look back (auf +acc at); **im** ~**blick auf etw** (acc) looking back on; **r~blickend** adj retrospective; **r~blickend läßt sich sagen, daß** ... in retrospect we can say that ...; ~**datieren*** vt sep infin, ptp only to backdate.

rucken vi (a) (Fahrzeug) to jerk, to jolt. (b) (Taube) to coo.

Rücken m - back; (Nasen~) ridge; (Fuß~) instep; (Hügel~, Berg~) crest; (Buch~) spine. **auf dem/den** ~ on one's back; **den Feind im** ~ **haben** to have the enemy in one's rear; **den Wind im** ~ **haben** to have a tail wind; **er hat doch die Firma des Vaters im** ~ but he's got his father's firm behind him; **mit dem** ~ **zur Wand** (lit, fig) with one's back to the wall; **der verlängerte** ~ (hum col) one's posterior (hum col); ~ **an** ~ back to back; **hinter jds** ~ (dat) (fig) behind sb's back; **jdm/einer Sache den** ~ **kehren** (lit, fig) or **zudrehen** (lit) to turn one's back on sb/sth; **jdm in den** ~ **fallen** (fig) to stab sb in the back; **sich** (dat) **den** ~ **freihalten** (col) to cover oneself; **jdm den** ~ **decken** (fig col) to back sb up (col); **jdm den** ~ **stärken** (fig) to give sb encouragement.

rücken vi aux sein to move; (Platz machen) to move up or (zur Seite auch) over; (weiter~: Zeiger) to move on (auf +acc to). **näher** ~ to move closer; (Zeit) to get closer; **ins Manöver/an die Front** ~ to go off on manoeuvres/to go up to the front; **an etw** (dat) ~ an Uhrzeiger to move sth; an Krawatte to pull sth (straight); (schieben) to push sth; (ziehen) to pull at sth; **an jds Stelle**

(acc) ~ to take sb's place; **jdm auf den Leib** or **Pelz** (col) or **die Pelle** (col) ~ (zu nahe kommen) to crowd sb; (sich jdn vorknöpfen) to get on at sb; (hum: besuchen) to move in on sb; **einer Sache** (dat) **zu Leibe** ~ to have a go at sth.

Rücken-: ~**deckung** f (fig) backing; **jdm** ~**deckung geben** to back sb; ~**lage** f supine position; **er schläft in** ~**lage** he sleeps on his back; ~**lehne** f back, back-rest; ~**mark** nt spinal cord; ~**schmerz(en** pl) m backache; ~**schwimmen** nt backstroke; ~**stärkung** f (fig) moral support.

Rück|entwicklung f fall-off (gen in); (Biol) degeneration.

Rückenwind m tailwind.

Rück-: **r~erstatten*** vt sep infin, ptp only to refund; ~**erstattung** f refund; ~**fahrkarte** f return ticket (Brit), round-trip ticket (US); ~**fahrscheinwerfer** m (Aut) reversing light; ~**fahrt** f return journey; ~**fall** m (Med, fig) relapse; (Jur, subsequent offence (Brit) or offense (US); **r~fällig** adj (Med, fig) relapsed; (Jur) recidivistic (form); **r~fällig werden** (Med, fig) to relapse; (Jur) to lapse back into crime; ~**flug** m return flight; ~**fluß** m reflux, flowing back; ~**forderung** f ~**forderung des Geldes** demand for the return of the money; ~**frage** f question; **nach** ~ **frage bei der Zentrale** ... after checking this with the exchange ...; ~**führung** f (a) (Deduktion) tracing back; **die** ~**führung der Probleme auf** (+acc) tracing the problems back to; (b) (von Menschen) repatriation, return; ~**gabe** f return; ~**gaberecht** nt right of return; ~**gang** m drop (gen in); **r~gängig** adj (a) (Comm: zurückgehend) dropping; (b) **r~gängigmachen** (widerrufen) to undo; Bestellung, Termin to cancel; Verlobung, Hochzeit to call off; ~**gewinnung** f recovery; (von Land, Gebiet) reclaiming; (aus verbrauchten Stoffen) recycling.

Rückgrat nt -e spine, backbone. **er ist ein Mensch ohne** ~ (fig) he's got no backbone; **jdm das** ~ **stärken** (col) to give sb enouragement; **jdm das** ~ **brechen** to ruin sb.

Rückgratverkrümmung f curvature of the spine.

Rück-: ~**halt** m (a) (Unterstützung) support, backing; (b) (Einschränkung) **ohne** ~**halt** without reservation; **r~haltlos** adj complete; Unterstützung auch unqualified; ~**hand** f (Sport) backhand; ~**kauf** m repurchase; ~**kehr** f no pl return; **bei seiner** ~**kehr** on his return; **jdn zur** ~**kehr bewegen** to persuade sb to return; ~**lage** f (Fin: Reserve) reserve, reserves pl; (Ersparnisse auch) savings pl; ~**lauf** m no pl reverse running; (von Maschinenteil) return travel; (beim Tonband) fast rewind; **r~läufig** adj dropping; Tendenz downward; **eine** ~**läufige Entwicklung** a decline; ~**licht** nt rear light; **r~lings** adv (von hinten) from behind; (auf dem Rücken) on one's back; ~**marsch** m (Mil) march back; (~zug) retreat; ~**meldung** f (Univ) re-registration; ~**nahme** f -n taking back; **ich bestehe auf der** ~**nahme des Gerätes** I must insist that you take this set back; ~**paß** m (Sport) return pass; ~**porto** nt return postage; ~**reise** f return journey; ~**ruf** m (am Telefon) **Herr X hat angerufen und bittet um** ~**ruf** Mr X called and asked you to call back.

Rucksack m rucksack.

Rück-: ~**schau** f reflection (auf +acc on); (in Medien) review (auf +acc of); ~**schau halten** to reminisce; **auf etw** (acc) ~**schau halten** to look back on sth; ~**schein** m ≃ recorded delivery slip; ~**schlag** m (von Ball) rebound; (fig) set-back; (bei Patient) relapse; ~**schluß** m conclusion; **den** ~**schluß ziehen, daß** ... to conclude that ...; ~**schritt** m (fig) retrograde step; **r~schrittlich** adj reactionary; Entwicklung retrograde; ~**seite** f back; (von Buchseite, Münze) reverse;

siehe ~**seite** see over(leaf); ~**sendung** f return.
Rücksicht f -en (Nachsicht) consideration. ~**en** pl (Gründe, Interessen) considerations pl; **aus** or **mit** ~ **auf jdn/etw** out of consideration for sb/sth; **ohne** ~ **auf jdn/etw** with no consideration for sb/sth; **ohne** ~ **auf Verluste** (col) regardless; **auf jdn/etw** ~ **nehmen** to show consideration for sb/sth; **er kennt keine** ~ he's ruthless.
Rücksichtnahme f no pl consideration.
Rücksichts-: r~**los** adj thoughtless; (im Verkehr) reckless; (unbarmherzig) ruthless; ~**losigkeit** f siehe adj thoughtlessness no pl; recklessness; ruthlessness; **r**~**voll** adj considerate (gegenüber, gegen towards).
Rück-: ~**sitz** m (von Motorrad) pillion; (von Auto) back seat; ~**spiegel** m (Aut) rear(-view) mirror; (außen) outside mirror; ~**spiel** nt (Sport) return match; ~**sprache** f consultation; ~**sprache mit jdm nehmen** to confer with sb.
Rückstand m (a) (Überrest) remains pl; (bei Verbrennung, Bodensatz) residue. (b) (Verzug) delay; (bei Aufträgen) backlog. **im** ~ **sein/in** ~ **geraten** to be/fall behind; **mit 0:2 Toren im** ~ **sein** to be 2 goals down. (c) usu pl (Außenstände) arrears pl. ~**e eintreiben** to collect arrears.
rückständig adj (a) (überfällig) Betrag overdue. (b) (zurückgeblieben) backward. ~ **denken** to have antiquated ideas.
Rückständigkeit f no pl backwardness.
Rück-: ~**stau** m (von Wasser) backwater; (von Autos) tailback (Brit), line of cars; ~**stoß** m repulsion; (bei Gewehr) recoil; (von Rakete) thrust; ~**strahler** m - reflector; ~**strom** m (von Menschen, Fahrzeugen) return; **der** ~**strom der Urlauber aus Italien** the stream of holiday makers returning from Italy; ~**taste** f (an Schreibmaschine) backspace key.
Rücktritt m (a) (Amtsniederlegung) resignation; (von König) abdication. (b) (Jur: von Vertrag) withdrawal (von from).
Rücktrittbremse f backpedal brake.
Rücktritts-: ~**drohung** f threat to resign/abdicate; ~**recht** nt right of withdrawal.
Rück-: ~**vergüten*** vt sep infin, ptp only to refund (jdm etw sb sth); ~**vergütung** f refund; **r**~**versichern*** sep **1** vti to reinsure; **2** vr to check (up or back); ~**versicherung** f reinsurance; ~**wand** f back wall; (von Möbelstück etc) back; **r**~**wärtig** adj back; Tür auch, (Mil) rear.
rückwärts adv (a) (zurück) backwards. ~ **einparken** to back into a parking space. (b) (esp S Ger, Aus: hinten) behind, at the back. **von** ~ from behind.
Rückwärts-: ~**drehung** f reverse turn; ~**gang** m reverse gear; **im** ~**gang fahren** to reverse.
Rückweg m way back. **sich auf den** ~ **machen** to head back.
ruckweise adv jerkily. **sich** ~ **bewegen** to move jerkily.
Rück-: r~**wirkend** adj (Jur) retrospective; Lohn-, Gehaltserhöhung backdated; **das Gesetz tritt r**~**wirkend vom 1. Januar in Kraft** the law is made retrospective to the 1st January; ~**wirkung** f repercussion; **eine Zahlung mit** ~**wirkung vom ...** a payment backdated to ...; **r**~**zahlbar** adj repayable; ~**zahlung** f repayment; ~**zieher** m - (a) (col) **einen** ~ **zieher machen** to back out (col); (b) (Ftbl) overhead kick.
ruck, zuck adv in a flash. ~! jump to it!; **das geht** ~ it won't take a second.
Rückzug m (Mil) retreat. **auf dem** ~ **in the retreat**; **den** ~ **antreten** (lit, fig) to retreat.
Rückzugsgefecht nt (Mil, fig) rearguard action.
Rüde m (wk) -n, -n (Männchen) dog, male; (Hetzhund) hound.
rüde adj impolite; Antwort curt, brusque.
Rudel nt - (von Hunden, Wölfen) pack; (von Wildschweinen, Hirschen) herd; (fig dated) horde.

rudelweise adv in packs/herds/hordes.
Ruder nt - (von ~boot etc) oar; (Naut, Aviat: Steuer~) rudder; (fig: Führung) helm. **das** ~ **fest in der Hand haben** (fig) to be in control of the situation; **am** ~ **sein** (lit, fig)/**ans** ~ **kommen** (fig) to be at/to take over (at) the helm; **das** ~ **herumwerfen** (fig) to change tack.
Ruder-: ~**bank** f rowing seat; ~**blatt** nt (oar) blade; ~**boot** nt rowing boat (Brit), rowboat (US).
Ruderer m - oarsman.
Ruderin f oarswoman.
rudern 1 vi (a) aux haben or sein to row. (b) (Schwimmvögel) to paddle. **mit den Armen** ~ (fig) to flail one's arms about. **2** vt to row.
Ruder-: ~**regatta** f rowing regatta; ~**sport** m rowing no def art.
Rudiment nt rudiment.
rudimentär adj rudimentary.
Ruf m -e (a) (Aus~, Vogel~, fig: Auf~) call; (lauter) shout; (Schrei) cry. **dem** ~ **des Herzens folgen** (fig) to obey the voice of one's heart; **der** ~ **nach Freiheit** (fig) the call for freedom; **der** ~ **zur Ordnung** (fig) the call to order. (b) (Ansehen, Leumund) reputation. **einen guten** ~ **haben** to have a good reputation; **eine Firma von** ~ a firm with a good name; **von üblem** or **zweifelhaftem** ~ **sein** to have a bad reputation; **jdn/etw in schlechten** ~ **bringen** to give sb/sth a bad name; **sie ist besser als ihr** ~ she is better than she is made out to be. (c) (Univ: Berufung) offer of a chair. (d) (~ **nummer**) „~: 27785" „Tel: 27785".
rufen pret **rief**, ptp **gerufen 1** vi to call (nach for); (Mensch: laut ~) to shout; (Glocke etc) to sound (zu for). **um Hilfe** ~ to call for help; **die Pflicht ruft** duty calls; **die Arbeit ruft** my/your etc work is waiting. **2** vt (a) to call; (aus~) to cry; (Mensch: laut ~) to shout. **bravo** ~ to shout hooray. (b) (kommen lassen) to send for; Arzt, Polizei auch, Taxi to call. ~ **Sie ihn bitte!** please send him to me; **jdn zu Hilfe** ~ to call on sb to help; **du kommst wie gerufen** you're just the man/woman I wanted; **das kommt mir wie gerufen** that's just what I needed; (kommt mir gelegen) that suits me fine (col).
Rüffel m - (col) telling-off, ticking-off (col).
Ruf-: ~**mord** m character assassination; ~**mordkampagne** f smear campaign; ~**name** m Christian name (by which one is generally known); ~**nummer** f telephone number; ~**säule** f (für Taxi) telephone; (an Autobahn) emergency telephone; ~**zeichen** nt (von Telefon) ringing tone.
Rugby ['ragbi] nt no pl rugby, rugger (col).
Rüge f -n (Verweis) reprimand, rebuke; (Kritik) criticism no indef art. **jdm eine** ~ **erteilen** to reprimand sb (für, wegen for).
rügen vt (form) jdn to reprimand (wegen, für for); etw to reprimand.
Ruhe f no pl (a) (Schweigen, Stille) quiet, silence. ~! quiet!, silence!; **gebt** ~! be quiet!; **sich** (dat) ~ **verschaffen** to get silence; **es herrscht** ~ all is silent; (fig: Disziplin, Frieden) all is quiet; ~ **halten** (lit, fig) to keep quiet; **die** ~ **vor dem Sturm** (fig) the calm before the storm.
(b) (Ungestörtheit, Frieden) peace, quiet. ~ **ausstrahlen** to radiate a sense of calm; ~ **und Frieden** peace and quiet; **in** ~ **und Frieden leben** to live a quiet life; ~ **und Ordnung** law and order; **ich brauche meine** ~ I need a bit of peace; **laß mich in** ~! leave me in peace; **vor jdm** ~ **haben wollen** to want a rest from sb; (endgültig) to want to be rid of sb; **jdm keine** ~ **lassen** (Mensch) not to give sb any peace; **das läßt ihm keine** ~ he can't stop thinking about it; **zur** ~ **kommen** to get some peace; (solide werden) to settle down; **jdn zur** ~ **kommen lassen** to give sb a chance to rest; **keine** ~ **finden (können)** (Mensch) to get no rest; **die letzte** ~ **finden** (liter) to be

laid to rest *(liter)*.
 (c) *(Erholung)* rest, repose *(liter)*; *(~stand)* retirement; *(Stillstand)* rest. **sich zur ~ begeben** *(form)* to retire (to bed) *(form)*; **angenehme ~!** sleep well!; **sich zur ~ setzen** to retire.
 (d) *(Gelassenheit)* calm(ness); *(Disziplin)* quiet, order. **die ~ weghaben** *(col)* to be unflappable *(col)*; **~ bewahren** to keep calm; **die ~ selbst sein** to be calmness itself; **jdn aus der ~ bringen** to throw sb *(col)*; **sich nicht aus der ~ bringen lassen** not to (let oneself) get worked up; **sich** *(dat)* **etw in ~ ansehen** to look at sth in one's own time; **immer mit der ~** *(col)* don't panic.
Ruhe-: **r~bedürftig** *adj* in need of rest; **~gehalt** *nt (form)* superannuation; **~geld** *nt (form)* pension; **~lage** *f (von Mensch)* reclining position; *(Med: bei Bruch)* immobile position; **r~los** *adj* restless; **eine r~lose Zeit** a time of unrest; **~losigkeit** *f* restlessness.
ruhen *vi* **(a)**, *geh: liegen)* to rest; *(liter: schlafen)* to sleep. **nicht (eher) ~ bis** ... *(fig)* not to rest until ... **(b)** *(stillstehen)* to stop; *(Maschinen)* to stand idle; *(Arbeit auch, Verkehr)* to cease; *(Waffen)* to be laid down. **(c)** *(begraben sein)* to lie, to be buried. „**hier ruht** ...“ “here lies ...”; „**ruhe sanft!**“ “rest eternal“.
Ruhe-: **~pause** *f* break; **eine ~pause einlegen** to take a break; **~punkt** *m* place of rest; **~stand** *m* retirement; **im ~stand sein/leben** to be retired; **er ist Bankdirektor im ~stand** he is a retired bank director; **in den ~stand treten** to retire; **jdn in den ~stand versetzen** to retire sb; **~ständler** *m* - retired person; **~stätte** *f* resting place; **letzte ~stätte** last *or* final resting-place; **~stellung** *f (von Körper)* resting position; *(von Gegenstand)* resting point; *(von Maschinen)* off position; **r~störend** *adj* **r~störender Lärm** *(Jur)* disturbance of the peace; **~störer** *m* disturber of the peace; **~störung** *f (Jur)* disturbance of the peace; **~tag** *m* day off; *(von Geschäft etc)* closing day; „**Mittwoch ~tag**“ “closed (on) Wednesdays“.
ruhig 1 *adj* **(a)** *(still, geruhsam)* quiet; *Wetter, Meer* calm; *Überfahrt, Verlauf* smooth. **seid ~!** be quiet!; **sitz doch ~!** sit still!; **gegen 6 Uhr wird es ~er** it quietens down around 6 o'clock; **alles geht seinen ~en Gang** everything is going smoothly. **(b)** *(gelassen)* calm; *Gewissen* easy; *(sicher)* *Hand, Blick* steady. **nur ~** *(Blut)* take it easy *(col)*; **bei ~er Überlegung** on (mature) consideration; **du kannst/Sie können ganz ~ sein** I can assure you; **etw ~ mitansehen** *(gleichgültig)* to stand by and watch sth. 2 *adv* **du kannst ~ hierbleiben** feel free to stay here; **ihr könnt ~ gehen, ich passe schon auf** you just go and I'll look after things; **man kann ~ behaupten, daß** ... *(mit Recht)* one may well assert that ...; **du könntest ~ mal etwas für mich tun!** it's about time you did something for me!
Ruhm *m no pl* glory; *(Berühmtheit)* fame. **sich in seinem ~ sonnen** to rest on one's laurels.
rühmen 1 *vt (preisen, empfehlen)* to praise *(jdn wegen etw* sb for sth). 2 *vr* **sich einer Sache** *(gen)* **~** *(prahlen)* to boast about sth; *(stolz sein)* to pride oneself on sth; **ohne mich zu ~** without wishing to boast.
Ruhmes-: **~blatt** *nt (fig)* glorious chapter; **~tat** *f* glorious deed.
rühmlich *adj* praiseworthy; *Ausnahme* notable.
ruhm-: **~los** *adj* inglorious; **r~reich** *adj (liter)*, **r~voll** *adj* glorious.
Ruhr *f no pl (Krankheit)* dysentery.
Rühr|ei *nt* scrambled eggs *pl*.
rühren 1 *vi* **(a)** *(um~)* to stir. **(b)** **an etw** *(acc)* **~** *(anfassen)* to touch sth; *(fig: erwähnen)* to touch on sth; **von etw ~** to stem from sth; **das rührt daher, daß** ... that is because ... 2 *vt* **(a)** *(um~)*

Teig, Farbe to stir; *(schlagen)* *Eier* to beat. **(b)** *(lit, fig: bewegen)* to move; *Herz* to stir. **er rührte keinen Finger, um mir zu helfen** *(col)* he didn't lift a finger to help me *(col)*; **das kann mich nicht ~!** that leaves me cold; **jdn zu Tränen ~** to move sb to tears. 3 *vr* **(a)** to move; *(Blatt etc)* to stir; *(aktiv sein)* to buck up *(col)*; *(sich beeilen)* to get a move on *(col)*. **rührt euch!** *(Mil)* at ease!; **kein Lüftchen rührte sich** the air was still; **nichts hat sich gerührt** nothing happened. **(b)** *(Gewissen etc)* to be awakened.
rührend *adj* touching. **das ist ~ von Ihnen** that is sweet of you.
Ruhrgebiet *nt* Ruhr (area).
rührig *adj* active.
Rühr-: **~löffel** *m* mixing spoon; **r~selig** *adj (pej)* tear-jerking *(pej col)*; **~seligkeit** *f no pl* sentimentality; **~stück** *nt (Theat)* melodrama; **~teig** *m* sponge mixture.
Rührung *f no pl* emotion. **vor ~ nicht sprechen können** to be choked with emotion.
Ruin *m no pl* ruin. **vor dem ~ stehen** to be on the verge of ruin; **du bist noch mein ~!** *(hum col)* you'll be the ruin of me.
Ruine *f* **-n** *(lit, fig)* ruin.
ruinieren* *vt* to ruin. **sich ~** to ruin oneself.
rülpsen *vi* to belch.
Rülpser *m* - *(col)* belch.
rum *adv (col)* = **herum.**
Rum *m* **-s** rum.
Rumäne *m (wk)* **-n, -n, Rumänin** *f* Romanian.
Rumänien [-iən] *nt* Romania.
rumänisch *adj* Romanian.
rumkriegen *vt sep (col)* **jdn ~** to talk sb around.
Rummel *m no pl* **(a)** *(col) (Betrieb)* (hustle and) bustle; *(Getöse)* racket *(col)*; *(Aufheben)* fuss *(col)*. **der ganze ~** the whole carry-on *(col)*. **(b)** *(Jahrmarkt)* fair.
Rummelplatz *m (col)* fairground.
rumoren* 1 *vi* to make a noise; *(Mensch)* to bang about; *(Bauch)* to rumble; *(Gewissen)* to play up. 2 *vi impers* **es rumort in meinem Bauch** my stomach's rumbling; **es rumort im Volk** *(fig)* there is growing unrest among the people.
Rumpelkammer *f (col)* junk room *(col)*.
rumpeln *vi aux sein (sich polternd bewegen)* to rumble; *(Mensch)* to clatter.
Rumpf *m* **-e** trunk; *(Sport)* body; *(Statue)* torso; *(von Schiff)* hull; *(von Flugzeug)* fuselage.
rümpfen *vt* **die Nase ~** to turn up one's nose *(über +acc* at).
Rumpsteak ['rʊmp-steːk] *nt* rump steak.
rums *interj* bang.
Rum-: **~topf** *m* soft fruit in rum; **~verschnitt** *m* blended rum.
rund 1 *adj* round; *Figur, Arme* plump; *Klang* full. **~e 50 Jahre/2000 Mark** a good 50 years/2,000 marks; **ein ~es Dutzend Leute** a dozen or more people; **Konferenz am ~en Tisch** round-table talks *pl*. 2 *adv* **(a)** *(herum)* a)round. **~ um die Uhr** right (a)round the clock. **(b)** *(ungefähr)* (round) about, roughly. **(c)** *(fig: glattweg)* ablehnen flatly. **jetzt geht's ~** *(col)* this is where the fun starts *(col)*; **wenn der das erfährt, geht's ~** *(col)* there'll be a to-do when he finds out *(col)*.
Rund-: **~blick** *m* panorama; **~brief** *m* circular.
Runde *f* **-n** **(a)** *(Gesellschaft)* company. **in der ~ herumgehen** to be passed around. **(b)** *(Rundgang)* walk, turn; *(von Wachmann)* rounds *pl*; *(von Briefträger etc)* round. **die ~ machen** to do the rounds; *(herumgegeben werden)* to be passed around; **eine ~ machen** to go for a walk; *(mit Fahrzeug)* to go for a ride *or* run. **(c)** *(Sport) (bei Rennen)* lap; *(Boxen etc, Gesprächs~)* round. **über die ~n kommen** *(Sport, fig)* to pull through. **(d)** *(von Getränken)* round. **eine ~ spendieren** *or* **schmeißen** *(col)* to stand a round.
runden 1 *vt Lippen* to round. 2 *vr (lit: rund werden)*

to become round; (*Lippen*) to grow round. **sich zu etw ~** (*fig*) to develop into sth.

Rund-: **r~erneuern*** *vt sep infin, ptp only* to remould (*Brit*), to remold (*US*); **~fahrt** *f* tour; **eine ~fahrt machen** to go on a tour; **~frage** *f* survey (*an +acc, unter +dat of*).

Rundfunk *m* broadcasting; (*besonders Hörfunk*) radio. **im ~ on the radio; ~ hören** to listen to the radio; **beim ~ arbeiten** to be in broadcasting.

Rundfunk- *in cpds* radio; **~anstalt** *f* broadcasting corporation; **~gebühr** *f* radio licence (*Brit*) or license (*US*) fee; **~gerät** *nt* radio set; **~gesellschaft** *f* broadcasting company; (*Sendeanstalt*) radio station; **~sendung** *f* radio programme (*Brit*) or program (*US*); **~techniker** *m* radio engineer; **~zeitschrift** *f* radio programme (*Brit*) or program (*US*) guide.

Rund-: **~gang** *m* (*Spaziergang*) walk; (*zur Besichtigung*) tour (*durch of*); (*von Wachmann*) rounds *pl*; (*von Briefträger etc*) round; **~heit** *f* roundness; **r~heraus** *adv* straight out; **r~heraus gesagt** frankly; **r~herum** *adv* all around; (*fig col: völlig*) totally; **r~lich** *adj* plump; **~reise** *f* tour (*durch of*); **~schreiben** *nt* circular; **r~um** *adv* all around; (*fig*) completely; **r~weg** *adv* straight out.

Runkelrübe *f* mangel-wurzel.

runter *adv* (*col*) = **herunter, hinunter. ~!** down!

runter- *pref* (*col*) down; *siehe* **herunter-, hinunter-;** **~holen** *vt sep* to get down; **sich einen ~holen** (*col!*) to jerk off (*col!*).

Runzel *f* **-n** wrinkle.

runz(e)lig *adj* wrinkled.

runzeln 1 *vt* **Stirn** to wrinkle, to crease. **2** *vr* to become wrinkled.

Rüpel *m* - lout, yob(bo) (*Brit col*).

rüpelhaft *adj* loutish.

rupfen *vt* **Gänse, Hühner** to pluck; **Gras, Unkraut** to pull up. **jdn ~** (*fig col*) to fleece sb (*col*), to take sb to the cleaners (*col*); **wie ein gerupftes Huhn aussehen** to look like a shorn sheep.

Rupie ['ruːpiə] *f* rupee.

ruppig *adj* (*grob*) rough; **Benehmen, Antwort** gruff; **Äußeres** scruffy.

Rüsche *f* **-n** ruche, frill.

Ruß *m no pl* soot; (*von Kerze*) smoke.

Russe *m* (*wk*) **-n, -n** Russian, Russian man/boy.

Rüssel *m* - snout (*auch col: Nase*); (*Elefanten~*) trunk; (*von Insekt*) proboscis.

rußen *vi* (*Öllampe, Kerze*) to smoke; (*Ofen*) to produce soot.

rußig *adj* sooty.

Russin *f* Russian, Russian woman/girl.

russisch *adj* Russian. **~es Roulett** Russian roulette; **~e Eier** (*Cook*) egg(s) mayonnaise; *siehe* **deutsch.**

Russisch(e) *nt decl as adj* Russian; *siehe* **Deutsch(e).**

Rußland *nt* Russia.

rüsten 1 *vi* (*Mil*) to arm. **zum Kampf ~** to arm for battle; **gut/schlecht gerüstet sein** to be well/badly armed. **2** *vr* to prepare (*zu* for); (*lit, fig: sich wappnen*) to arm oneself (*gegen* for).

rüstig *adj* sprightly.

rustikal *adj* rustic. **sich ~ einrichten** to furnish one's home in a rustic style.

Rüstung *f* (a) (*das Rüsten*) armament; (*Waffen*) arms *pl*, weapons *pl*. (b) (*Ritter~*) armour (*Brit*), armor (*US*).

Rüstungs- *in cpds* arms; **~beschränkung** *f* arms limitation; **~industrie** *f* armaments industry; **~kontrolle** *f* arms control; **~wettlauf** *m* arms race.

Rüstzeug *nt no pl* (*fig*) qualifications *pl*.

Rute *f* **-n** (a) (*Gerte*) switch; (*esp Stock zum Züchtigen*) cane, rod; (*Birken~*) birch (rod). (b) (*Angel~*) (fishing) rod. (c) (*Hunt: Schwanz*) tail.

Rutsch *m* **-e** slip, slide; (*Erd~*) landslide; (*von Steinen*) rockfall; (*fig Pol*) shift, swing; (*col: Ausflug*) trip, outing. **guten ~!** (*col*) have a good new year; **in einem ~** in one go.

Rutschbahn *f* (*Kinder~*) slide.

rutschen *vi* *aux sein* (a) (*gleiten*) to slide; (*aus~, entgleiten*) to slip; (*Aut*) to skid; (*fig: Preise, Kurse*) to slip. **auf dem Stuhl hin und her ~** to fidget around on one's chair. (b) (*col: rücken*) to move up. **zur Seite ~** to move over. (c) (*~d kriechen*) to crawl.

rutschfest *adj* non-slip.

rutschig *adj* slippery, slippy (*col*).

rütteln 1 *vt* to shake (about). **2** *vi* to shake; (*Fahrzeug*) to jolt. **an etw** (*dat*) **~** to shake at; (*Fahrzeug Pol*) shift, swing. **an etw** (*dat*) **~ an Tür, Fenster etc** to rattle (at) sth; (*fig*) **an Grundsätzen etc** to shake sth; **daran ist nicht zu ~** (*col*) there's no doubt about that.

S

S, s [ɛs] *nt*, -, - S, s.
S = Süden S; **Seite** p.
s. = siehe.
Saal *m*, *pl* **Säle** hall; *(für Sitzungen etc)* room; *(Tanz~)* ballroom; *(Theater~)* auditorium.
Saal|ordner *m* usher.
Saat *f* **-en (a)** *(das Säen)* sowing. **(b)** *(Samen, ~gut)* seed(s) *(auch fig)*. **wenn die ~ aufgeht** *(lit)* when the seed begins to grow; *(fig)* when the seeds bear fruit; **die ~ für etw legen** *(fig)* to sow the seed(s) of sth. **(c)** *(junges Getreide)* young crop(s), seedlings *pl*.
Saat-: **~gut** *nt no pl* seed(s); **~korn** *nt* seed corn; **~zeit** *f* sowing time.
Sabbat *m* **-e** Sabbath.
sabbeln *(dial)*, **sabbern** *(col)* **1** *vi* to slobber. **vor sich hin ~** *(fig)* to mutter away to oneself. **2** *vt* to blather *(col)*. **dummes Zeug ~** to talk drivel *(col)*.
Säbel *m* - sabre *(Brit)*, saber *(US)*. **mit dem ~ rasseln** *(fig)* to rattle the sabre.
Säbel-: **~fechten** *nt* sabre *(Brit)* or saber *(US)* fencing; **~hieb** *m* stroke of one's sabre *(Brit)* or saber *(US)*.
säbeln *(col)* **1** *vt* to saw away at. **2** *vi* to saw away *(an +dat at)*.
Säbel-: **~rasseln** *nt no pl* sabre-rattling, *(Brit)* saber rattling *(US)*; **s~rasselnd** *adj* sabre-rattling *(Brit)*, saber-rattling *(US)*.
Sabotage [zabo'taːʒə] *f* **-n** sabotage. **~ treiben** to perform acts of sabotage.
Sabotage|akt *m* act of sabotage.
Saboteur(in *f)* [-'tøːɐ, -'tøːrɪn] *m* saboteur.
sabotieren* *vt* to sabotage.
Sa(c)charin *nt no pl* saccharin.
Sach-: **~bearbeiter** *m* specialist; *(Beamter)* official in charge *(für of)*; **~bereich** *m* (specialist) area; **~beschädigung** *f* damage to property; **~buch** *nt* non-fiction book; **~dienlich** *adj* useful; **~dienliche Hinweise** helpful information.
Sache *f* **-n (a)** thing; *(Gegenstand auch)* object. **~n** *pl (col: Zeug)* things *pl*; *(Jur)* property; **das liegt in der Natur der ~** that's in the nature of things.
(b) *(Angelegenheit)* matter; *(Frage auch)* question; *(Thema)* subject; *(Jur)* case; *(Aufgabe)* job; *(Vorfall)* business, affair; *(no pl: Ideal)* cause. **eine ~ der Polizei** a matter for the police; **das ist eine ganz tolle ~** it's really fantastic; **ich habe mir die ~ anders vorgestellt** I had imagined things differently; **das ist eine andere ~** that's a different matter; **das ist meine/seine ~** that's my/his business; **in ~n A gegen B** *(Jur)* in the case (of) A versus B; **er versteht seine ~ gut** he knows what he's doing; **er macht seine ~ gut** he's doing very well; *(beruflich)* he's doing a good job; **diese Frage können wir nicht hier mitbesprechen, das ist eine ~ für sich** we can't discuss this question now, it's a separate issue; **das ist so eine ~** *(col)* it's a bit tricky; **solche ~n liegen mir nicht** I don't like things like that; **wann ist die ~ passiert?** when did it (all) happen?; **was hat die Polizei zu der ~ gesagt?** what did the police say about it?; **das ist (eine) beschlossene ~** it's (all) settled; **mach keine ~n!** *(col)* don't be daft! *(col)*; **eine ~ des Geschmacks** a question of taste; **zur ~!** let's get on with it; *(Parl, Jur etc)* come to the point!; **das tut nichts zur ~** that doesn't matter;

bei der ~ sein to be with it *(col)*; **bei der ~ bleiben** to keep one's mind on the job; *(bei Diskussion)* to keep to the point; **so steht die ~** so that's the way things are; **für eine gerechte ~ kämpfen** to fight for a just cause.
(c) *(Tempo)* **mit 60/100 ~n** *(col)* at 60/100.
Sachertorte *f* a rich chocolate cake, sachertorte.
Sach-: **~frage** *f* factual question; **~gebiet** *nt* area; **s~gemäß, s~gerecht** *adj* proper; **bei s~gemäßer Anwendung** if used properly; **~kenntnis** *f (in bezug auf Wissensgebiet)* knowledge of the/his etc subject; *(in bezug auf ~lage)* knowledge of the facts; **s~kundig** *adj* (well-)informed *no adv*; **s~kundig antworten** to give an informed answer; **~lage** *f* state of affairs.
sachlich *adj* **(a)** *(faktisch)* Irrtum, Angaben factual; Grund, Einwand practical; *(sachbezogen)* Frage, Wissen relevant. **rein ~ hast du recht** from a purely factual point of view you are right. **(b)** *(objektiv)* Kritik etc objective; *(unemotional)* matter-of-fact. **bleiben Sie mal ~** don't get carried away; *(nicht persönlich werden)* stay objective. **(c)** *(schmucklos)* functional, businesslike.
sächlich *adj (Gram)* neuter.
Sachlichkeit *f* **(a)** *siehe adj* **(b)** objectivity; matter-of-factness. **(b)** *(Schmucklosigkeit)* functionality.
Sach-: **~register** *nt* subject index; **~schaden** *m* damage (to property).
Sachse ['zaksə] *m (wk)* **-n, -n, Sächsin** ['zɛksɪn] *f* Saxon.
Sachsen ['zaksn] *nt* Saxony.
sächsisch ['zɛksɪʃ] *adj* Saxon.
sacht(e) *adj (leise)* soft; *(sanft)* gentle; *(vorsichtig)* cautious, careful; *(allmählich)* gentle, gradual. **~, ~!** *(col)* take it easy!
Sach-: **~verhalt** *m* **-e** facts *pl* (of the case); **~verständige(r)** *mf decl as adj* expert, specialist; *(Jur)* expert witness; **~wert** *m* real value; **~werte** *pl* material assets *pl*; **~wörterbuch** *nt* specialist dictionary.
Sack *m* **-e (a)** sack; *(aus Papier, Plastik)* bag. **drei ~ Kohlen** three bags of coal; **mit ~ und Pack** *(col)* with bag and baggage; **jdn in den ~ stecken** *(fig col)* to put sb in the shade. **(b)** *(Anat, Zool)* sac. **(c)** *(col!: Hoden)* balls *pl (col!)*. **(d)** *(col!: Kerl, Bursche)* bastard *(col!)*. **fauler ~** lazy bastard.
Sackbahnhof *m* terminus.
sacken *vi aux sein (lit, fig: sinken)* to sink. **in die Knie ~** to sag at the knees.
Sack-: **~gasse** *f* cul-de-sac *(esp Brit)*, dead end; *(fig)* dead end; **in eine ~gasse geraten** *(fig)* to finish up a blind alley; *(Verhandlungen)* to reach an impasse; **~hüpfen** *nt no pl* sack-race; **~karre** *f* hand-cart; **~leinen** *nt*, **~leinwand** *f* sacking, burlap *(US)*.
Sadismus *m no pl* sadism.
Sadist(in *f)* *m* sadist.
sadistisch *adj* sadistic.
säen *vti* to sow; *(fig)* to sow (the seeds of). **dünn gesät** *(fig)* thin on the ground, few and far between.
Safari *f* **-s** safari. **eine ~ machen** to go on safari.
Safe [zeːf] *m or nt* **-s** safe.
Saffian *m no pl*, **Saffianleder** *nt* morocco (leather).

Safran m -e saffron.

Saft ¬e (Obst~) (fruit) juice; (Pflanzen~) sap; (Fleisch~) juice; (Husten~ etc) syrup; (col: Strom, Benzin) juice (col). **ohne** ~ **und Kraft** (fig) wishy-washy (col), effete.

saftig adj (a) (voll Saft) Obst, Fleisch juicy; Wiese, Grün lush. (b) (col: kräftig) Witz juicy (col); Rechnung, Ohrfeige hefty (col); Brief, Antwort potent.

Saftigkeit f (von Obst, Witz) juiciness; (von Wiese etc) lushness.

Saft-: ~**laden** m (pej col) dump (pej col); **s**~**los** adj not juicy; ~**presse** f fruit-press; ~**sack** m (col!) stupid bastard (col!).

saft- und kraftlos adj wishy-washy (col), effete.

Sage f -n legend; (altnordische) saga. **es geht die** ~**, daß** ... legend has it that ...; (Gerücht) rumour (Brit) or rumor (US) has it that ...

Säge f -n (Werkzeug) saw.

Säge-: ~**blatt** nt saw blade; ~**maschine** f mechanical saw; ~**mehl** nt sawdust; ~**messer** nt serrated knife; ~**mühle** f sawmill.

sagen vt (a) to say. **jdm etw** ~ to say sth to sb; (mitteilen, ausrichten) to tell sb sth; **sich** (dat) **etw** ~ to say sth to oneself; **unter uns gesagt** between you and me (and the gatepost hum col); **genauer/deutlicher gesagt** to put it more precisely/clearly; **könnten Sie mir** ~ ...? could you tell me ...?; **ich sag's ihm** I'll tell him; **ich habe mir** ~ **lassen,** ... I've been told ...; **was ich mir von ihm nicht alles** ~ **lassen muß!** the things I have to take from him!; **das kann ich Ihnen nicht** ~ I couldn't say; **so was sagt man doch nicht!** you mustn't say things like that; (bei Schimpfen, Fluchen) (mind your) language!; **das sage ich nicht!** I'm not telling; **was ich noch** ~ **wollte,** ... (col) there's something else I wanted to say ...; **dann will ich nichts gesagt haben** in that case forget I said anything; **ich sage, wie es ist** I'm just telling you the way it is; **um nicht zu** ~ not to say; **jdm** ~**, er solle etw tun** to tell sb to do sth; **hat er im Betrieb etwas zu** ~? does he have a say in the firm?; **das S**~ **haben** to have the say; **laß dir das gesagt sein** take it from me; **er läßt sich** (dat) **nichts** ~ he won't be told; **das laß ich mir von dem nicht** ~ I won't take that from him; **sie ließen es sich** (dat) **nicht zweimal** ~ they didn't need to be told twice; **ich möchte fast** ~, ... I'd almost say ...; **wenn ich so** ~ **darf** if I may say so; **da soll noch einer** ~, ... never let it be said ...

(b) (bedeuten, meinen) to mean. **was will er damit** ~? what does he mean (by that)?; **ich will damit nicht** ~, **daß** ... I don't mean to imply that ...; **damit ist nicht gesagt, daß** ... that doesn't mean (to say) that ...; **das hat nichts zu** ~ that doesn't mean anything; **sagt dir der Name etwas?** does the name mean anything to you?

(c) ~ **Sie mal/sag mal,** ... tell me, ..., say, ...; **du, Veronika, sag mal, wollen wir** ... hey, Veronika, listen, shall we ...; **wem** ~ **Sie das!** you don't need to tell me that!; **sag bloß!** you don't say!; **was Sie nicht** ~! you don't say!; **das kann man wohl** ~ you can say that again!; **ich muß schon** ~ I must say; **das muß man** ~ you must admit that; **das ist nicht gesagt** that's by no means certain; **leichter gesagt als getan** easier said than done; **gesagt, getan** no sooner said than done; **wie (schon) gesagt** as I/you etc said; **ich bin,** ~ **wir, in einer Stunde da** I'll be there in, let's say, an hour; **sage und schreibe 100 Mark** 100 marks, would you believe it.

sägen 1 vti to saw. 2 vi (hum col: schnarchen) to snore, to saw wood (US col).

Sagen-: ~**dichtung** f sagas pl; **s**~**haft** adj (a) (nach Art einer Sage) legendary; (b) (col: hervorragend) fantastic (col), terrific (col); **s**~**haft schnell** incredibly fast (col); **s**~**umwoben** adj legendary; ~**welt** f mythology, legend.

Säge-: ~**späne** pl wood shavings pl; ~**werk** nt sawmill.

Sago m no pl sago.

sah pret of **sehen.**

Sahara [za'haːra, 'zaːhara] f Sahara (Desert).

Sahne f no pl cream.

Sahne-: ~**bonbon** m or nt toffee; ~**eis** nt ice-cream; ~**torte** f cream gateau.

sahnig adj creamy.

Saison [zɛ'zõ, zɛ'zɔŋ] f -s season. **außerhalb der** ~ in the off-season.

saisonal [zɛzo'naːl] adj seasonal.

Saison- [zɛ'zõː] in cpds seasonal; ~**arbeit** f seasonal work; ~**arbeiter** m seasonal worker; **s**~**bedingt** adj seasonal; ~**beginn** m start of the season; ~**betrieb** m (Hochsaison) high season; (~geschäft) seasonal business; ~**eröffnung** f opening of the season; ~**geschäft** nt seasonal business; ~**schluß** m end of the season; ~**zuschlag** m in-season supplement.

Saite f -n (a) (Mus, Sport) string. (b) (fig liter) **eine** ~ **in jdm berühren** to strike a chord in sb; **andere** ~**n aufziehen** (col) to get tough.

Saiten|instrument nt string(ed) instrument.

Sakko m or nt -s sports jacket (Brit), sport coat (US); (aus Samt etc) jacket.

sakral adj sacred, sacral.

Sakrament nt sacrament.

Sakrileg nt -e sacrilege.

Sakristei f sacristy.

Salamander m - salamander.

Salami f -s salami.

Salamitaktik f (col) policy of small steps.

Salat m -e (a) (Pflanze, Kopf~) lettuce. (b) (Gericht) salad. **da haben wir den** ~! (col) now we're in a fine mess.

Salat-: ~**besteck** nt salad servers pl; ~**gurke** f cucumber; ~**kopf** m (head of) lettuce; ~**öl** nt salad oil; ~**platte** f salad; ~**schüssel** f salad bowl; ~**soße** f salad dressing.

Salbe f -n ointment.

Salbei m or f no pl sage.

salben vt (liter) to anoint.

salbungsvoll adj (pej) unctuous (pej).

saldieren* vt (Comm) to balance.

Saldo m, pl -s or **Salden** (Fin) balance. **per** ~ (lit, fig) on balance.

Säle pl of **Saal.**

Salmiak m or nt no pl sal ammoniac, ammonium chloride.

Salmiak-: ~**geist** m (liquid) ammonia; ~**pastille** f bitter-tasting lozenge, liquorice imp.

Salmonelle f pl salmonellae.

salomonisch adj Urteil worthy of a Solomon.

Salon [za'lõː, za'lɔŋ] m -s (a) (Gesellschaftszimmer) drawing room. (b) (Friseur~, Mode~ etc) salon.

Salon- [za'lõː-]: **s**~**fähig** adj (iro) socially acceptable; Leute, Aussehen presentable; **ein nicht s**~**fähiger Witz** an objectionable joke; ~**löwe** m (pej col) social lion.

salopp adj (a) (nachlässig) sloppy, slovenly; Manieren slovenly; Sprache slangy. (b) (ungezwungen) casual.

Salpeter m no pl saltpetre (Brit), saltpeter (US).

Salpetersäure f nitric acid.

Salto m, pl -s or **Salti** somersault. **ein anderthalbfacher** ~ a one-and-a-half somersault or turn; ~ **mortale** triple somersault.

Salut m -e (Mil) salute. ~ **schießen** to fire a salute; **21 Schuß** ~ 21-gun salute.

salutieren* vti (Mil) to salute.

Salve ['zalvə] f -n salvo, volley; (Ehren~) salute; (fig: von Applaus) volley, burst.

Salz nt -e salt. **das ist das** ~ **in der Suppe** (fig) that's what gives it that extra something; **wie eine Suppe ohne** ~ (fig) like ham without eggs (hum).

Salz-: **s**~**arm** adj (Cook) low-salt; **s**~**arm essen** to eat low-salt food; ~**bergwerk** nt salt mine;

~**brezel** f pretzel.
salzen pret **salzte**, ptp **gesalzen** vt to salt; siehe **gesalzen**.
Salz-: s~**frei** adj salt-free; Diät auch no-salt attr; ~**gebäck** nt savoury biscuits pl (Brit), savory cookies pl (US); ~**gurke** f pickled gherkin; s~**haltig** adj salty, saline; ~**hering** m salted herring.
salzig adj salty, salt.
Salz-: ~**kartoffeln** pl boiled potatoes pl; ~**korn** nt grain of salt; s~**los** adj salt-free; s~**los essen** not to eat salt; ~**lösung** f saline solution; ~**säule** f: **zur** ~**säule erstarren** (fig) to stand as though rooted to the spot; ~**säure** f hydrochloric acid; ~**see** m salt lake; ~**stange** f pretzel stick; ~**streuer** m - salt shaker, salt cellar; ~**wasser** nt salt water; ~**wüste** f salt flat.
Samariter m (Bibl, fig) Samaritan. **der Barmherzige** ~ the good Samaritan.
Sambia nt Zambia.
sambisch adj Zambian.
Same m -ns, -n (liter), **Samen** m - (a) (Bot, fig) seed; (fig auch) seeds pl. (b) (Menschen~, Tier~) sperm.
Samen-: ~**bank** f sperm bank; ~**erguß** m ejaculation; ~**flüssigkeit** f seminal fluid; ~**handlung** f seed shop (Brit) or store (US); ~**kapsel** f seed capsule; ~**korn** nt seed; ~**leiter** m vas deferens, sperm duct; ~**zelle** f sperm cell.
sämig adj thick, creamy.
Sammel-: ~**album** nt (collector's) album; ~**anschluß** m (Telec) private (branch) exchange; (von Privathäusern) party line; ~**band** m anthology; ~**becken** nt collecting tank; (fig) melting pot (von for); ~**begriff** m collective term; ~**bestellung** f joint order; ~**büchse** f collecting box; ~**karte** f (für mehrere Fahrten) multi-journey ticket; (für mehrere Personen) group ticket; ~**mappe** f file.
sammeln 1 vt to collect; Holz, Material, Erfahrungen auch to gather; Blumen, Pilze etc to pick, to gather; Truppen, Anhänger to gather, to assemble. **neue Kräfte** ~ to build up one's energy again. 2 vr (a) to gather, to collect; (Wasser, Geld etc) to collect, to accumulate; (Lichtstrahlen) to converge, to meet. (b) (fig: sich konzentrieren) to collect one's thoughts; siehe **gesammelt**. 3 vi to collect (für for).
Sammel-: ~**name** m collective term; ~**nummer** f (Telec) private exchange number, switchboard number; ~**punkt** m (Treffpunkt) assembly point.
Sammelsurium nt conglomeration.
Sammler(in f) m - collector.
Sammlung f (a) collection. (b) (fig: Konzentration) composure.
Samowar m -e samovar.
Samstag m -e Saturday; siehe **Dienstag**.
samstags adj on Saturdays.
samt 1 prep +dat together with. **sie kam** ~ **Katze** (hum) she came complete with cat. 2 adv **sie waren** ~ **und sonders ...** the whole lot of them were ... (col).
Samt m -e velvet. **in** ~ **und Seide** (liter) in silks and satins.
Samt- in cpds velvet; ~**handschuh** m velvet glove; **jdn mit** ~**handschuhen anfassen** (col) to handle sb with kid gloves (col).
sämtlich adj (alle) all; (vollständig) complete. **Schillers** ~**e Werke** the complete works of Schiller; ~**e Anwesenden** all those present.
samtweich adj velvety.
Sanatorium nt sanatorium (Brit), sanitarium (US).
Sand m -e sand; (Scheuer~) scouring powder; (Streu~) grit. **mit** ~ **bestreuen** to sand; **das/die gibt's wie** ~ **am Meer** (col) there are heaps of them (col); **auf** ~ **laufen** to run aground; **auf** ~ **bauen** (fig) to build upon sandy ground; **jdm** ~ **in die Augen streuen** (fig) to throw dust in sb's

eyes; ~ **ins Getriebe streuen** to throw a spanner in the works (Brit), to cause problems; **im** ~**e verlaufen** (col) to peter out; **den Kopf in den** ~ **stecken** to bury one's head in the sand.
Sandale f -n sandal.
Sand- in cpds sand; ~**bank** f sandbank; ~**boden** m sandy soil.
Sandel-: ~**holz** nt sandalwood; ~**öl** nt sandalwood oil.
Sand-: s~**farben**, s~**farbig** adj sand-coloured (Brit), sand-colored (US); ~**haufen** m heap of sand.
sandig adj sandy.
Sand-: ~**kasten** m sandpit (esp Brit), sandbox (US); ~**kastenspiele** pl (Mil) sand-table exercises pl; (fig) tactical manoeuvrings (Brit) or maneuverings (US) pl; ~**korn** nt grain of sand; ~**kuchen** m (Cook) sand-cake (a Madeira-type cake); ~**mann** m, ~**männchen** nt (in Geschichten) sandman; ~**papier** nt sandpaper; ~**sack** m sandbag; (Boxen) punchbag; ~**stein** m sandstone; s~**strahlen** vti insep to sandblast; ~**strahlgebläse** nt sandblasting equipment no indef art, no pl; ~**strand** m sandy beach; ~**sturm** m sandstorm.
sandte pret of **senden**[1].
Sand-: ~**uhr** f hour-glass; (Eieruhr) egg-timer; ~**wüste** f sandy waste; (Geog) (sandy) desert.
sanft adj gentle; Haut soft; Schlaf, Tod peaceful. **sich** ~ **anfühlen** to feel soft; **mit** ~**er Gewalt** gently but firmly; **er ist** ~ **entschlafen** he passed away peacefully.
Sänfte f -n litter; (esp im 17., 18. Jh. Europas) sedan-chair.
Sanftheit f siehe adj gentleness; softness.
Sanftmut f no pl (liter) gentleness.
sanftmütig adj (liter) gentle.
sang pret of **singen**.
Sang m ¬e (old liter) (Gesang) song; (das Singen) singing. **mit** ~ **und Klang** (lit) with drums drumming and pipes piping; (fig iro) durchfallen etc disastrously, catastrophically.
Sänger(in f) m - singer; (esp Jazz~, Pop~ auch) vocalist.
sang- und klanglos adv (col) without any ado, quietly. **sie ist** ~ **verschwunden** she just simply disappeared.
sanieren* 1 vt (a) Stadtteil to redevelop; Haus to renovate; Fluß to clean up. (b) (Econ) Unternehmen, Wirtschaft to rehabilitate, to put (back) on its feet. 2 vr (a) (Unternehmen, Industrie) to get back in good shape. (b) (col: sich bereichern) to line one's own pocket (col).
Sanierung f (a) siehe vt (a) redevelopment; renovation; cleaning up. (b) (Econ) rehabilitation.
Sanierungs-: ~**gebiet** nt redevelopment area; ~**maßnahme** f (für Gebiete etc) redevelopment measure; (Econ) rehabilitation measure.
sanitär adj no pred sanitary. ~**e Anlagen** sanitary facilities.
Sanitäter m - first-aid attendant; (Mil) (medical) orderly; (in Krankenwagen) ambulance man.
Sanitäts-: ~**auto** nt ambulance; ~**dienst** m (Mil) medical duty; (Heeresabteilung) medical corps; ~**kasten** m first-aid kit; ~**korps** nt medical corps; ~**offizier** m (Mil) Medical Officer, MO; ~**truppe** f medical corps; ~**wagen** m ambulance.
sank pret of **sinken**.
Sankt adj inv Saint.
Sanktion f sanction.
sanktionieren* vt to sanction.
sann pret of **sinnen**.
Saphir m -e sapphire.
Sardelle f anchovy.
Sardine f sardine.
Sardinenbüchse f sardine-can. **wie in einer** ~ (fig col) like sardines (col).
Sardinien [-iən] nt Sardinia.

sardinisch, sardisch adj Sardinian.
Sarg m ⁼e coffin, casket (US).
Sarg-: ~**deckel** m coffin lid, casket lid (US); ~**nagel** m coffin nail; (fig col: Zigarette) cancerstick (col); ~**träger** m pall-bearer.
Sarkasmus m sarcasm.
sarkastisch adj sarcastic.
saß pret of **sitzen**.
Satan m -e (Bibl, fig) Satan.
satanisch adj satanic.
Satansbraten m (hum col) young devil.
Satellit m (wk) -en, -en satellite.
Satelliten- in cpds satellite; ~**bahn** f satellite orbit; ~**foto** nt satellite picture; ~**staat** m satellite state; ~**stadt** f satellite town; ~**station** f space station.
Satin [za'tɛ̃ː] m -s satin.
Satire f -n satire (auf +acc on).
Satiriker(in f) m - satirist.
satirisch adj satirical.
satt adj (a) (gesättigt) Mensch full (up) (col); Magen, Gefühl full. ~ **sein** to have had enough (to eat), to be full (up) (col); ~ **werden** to have enough to eat; **von so was kann man doch nicht ~ werden** it's not enough to satisfy you; **das macht ~** it's filling; **sich (an etw** dat) ~ **essen** to eat one's fill (of sth); **wie soll sie ihre Kinder ~ kriegen?** (col) how is she supposed to feed her children?; **er ist kaum ~ zu kriegen** (col: lit, fig) he's insatiable; **er konnte sich an ihr nicht ~ sehen** he could not see enough of her; **jdn/etw ~ haben** or **sein** to be fed up with sb/sth (col). (b) (blasiert, übersättigt) well-fed; (selbstgefällig) smug. (c) (kräftig, voll) Farben rich, full.
Sattel m ⁼ saddle. **ohne ~** bareback; **er ist in allen** ⁼**n gerecht** or **sicher** (fig) he can turn his hand to anything; **fest im ~ sitzen** (fig) to be firmly in the saddle.
Sattel-: ~**dach** nt saddle roof; ~**decke** f saddlecloth; **s~fest** adj **s~fest sein** (Reiter) to have a good seat; **in etw** (dat) **s~fest sein** (fig) to have a firm grasp of sth.
satteln vt Pferd to saddle (up). **für etw gesattelt sein** (fig) to be ready for sth.
Sattel-: ~**schlepper** m articulated lorry (Brit), semitrailer (US), semi (US col); ~**tasche** f saddlebag; (Gepäcktasche am Fahrrad) pannier.
Sattheit f (a) (Gefühl) feeling of being full. (b) (Selbstgefälligkeit) smugness, self-satisfaction. (c) (von Farben) richness, fullness.
sättigen 1 vt (a) Hunger, Neugier to satisfy, to satiate. **ich bin gesättigt** I am replete. (b) (Comm, Chem) to saturate. 2 vi to be filling. 3 vr **sich an etw** (dat) or **mit etw** ~ to eat one's fill of sth.
sättigend adj Essen filling.
Sättigung f (a) (geh: Sattsein) repletion. **die ~ der Hungrigen** the feeding of the hungry. (b) (Chem, Comm) saturation.
Sättigungs-: ~**grad** m degree of saturation; ~**punkt** m saturation point.
Sattler m - saddler; (Polsterer) upholsterer.
sattsam adv amply; bekannt sufficiently.
Saturn m (Astron) Saturn.
Satz m -es, ⁼e (a) sentence; (Teilsatz) clause; (Jur: Gesetzabschnitt) clause. **ich kann nur ein paar ⁼e Italienisch** I only know a few phrases of Italian. (b) (Lehr~, Philos) proposition; (Math) theorem. (c) (Typ) (das Setzen) setting; (das Gesetzte) type no pl. **das Buch ist im ~** the book is being set. (d) (Mus) movement. (e) (Boden~) dregs pl; (Kaffee~) grounds pl. (f) (Zusammengehöriges) set. (g) (Sport) set; (Tischtennis) game. (h) (Tarif~) charge; (Spesen~) allowance. (i) (Sprung) leap, jump. **einen ~ machen** to leap, to jump; **mit einem ~** in one leap or bound.
Satz-: ~**ball** m (Sport) set point; (Tischtennis) game point; ~**bau** m sentence construction;

~**teil** m part of a/the sentence.
Satzung f constitution, statutes pl; (Vereins~) rules pl.
satzungsgemäß adj according to the statutes/rules.
Satzzeichen nt punctuation mark.
Sau f, pl **Säue** or (Hunt) -**en** (a) sow; (col: Schwein) pig; (Hunt) wild boar. **die ~ rauslassen** (fig col) to let it all hang out (col); **wie eine gesengte ~** (col) like a maniac (col). (b) (pej col: Schmutzfink) dirty swine (col); (Frau auch) bitch (col). (c) (fig col) **jdn zur ~ machen** to bawl sb out (col); **unter aller ~** bloody (Brit col) or goddamn (col) awful.
sauber adj (a) (rein, reinlich) clean. ~ **sein** (Hund etc) to be house-trained; (Kind) to be (potty-)trained. (b) (ordentlich) neat, tidy; (exact) accurate. (c) (anständig) honest, upstanding. (d) (col: großartig) fantastic, great. **du bist mir ja ein** ~**er Freund!** (iro) a fine friend you are! (iro).
sauberhalten vt sep irreg to keep clean.
Sauberkeit f (a) cleanness; (Hygiene, Ordentlichkeit) cleanliness. (b) (Anständigkeit) honesty.
säuberlich adj neat and tidy. **fein** ~ neatly and tidily.
saubermachen vt sep to clean.
säubern vt (a) to clean. (b) (fig euph) Partei, Buch to purge (von of); Saal, (Mil) Gegend to clear (von of).
Säuberung f siehe vt (a) cleaning. (b) purging; clearing; (Pol: Aktion) purge.
Säuberungs|aktion f cleaning-up operation; (Pol) purge.
Sau-: **s~blöd** adj (col) bloody (Brit col) or damn (col) stupid; ~**bohne** f broad bean.
Sauce ['zoːsə] f -n sauce; (Braten~) gravy.
Sauciere [zo'sieːrə, -'sieːrə] f -n sauce boat.
Saudi-: ~**Arabien** nt Saudi Arabia; **s~arabisch** adj Saudi attr, Saudi-Arabian.
saudumm adj (col) damn stupid (col). **sich** ~ **benehmen** to behave like a stupid idiot (col).
sauer adj (a) (nicht süß) sour; Wein, Bonbons acid(ic), sharp. **saure Drops** acid drops. (b) (verdorben) off pred (Brit), spoiled (US). ~ **werden** (Milch, Sahne) to go sour, to turn. (c) Gurke, Hering pickled; Sahne soured. (d) (Chem) acid(ic). **Saurer Regen** acid rain. (e) (col: schlecht gelaunt) (auf +acc with) mad (col), cross. ~ **reagieren** to get annoyed. (f) **das habe ich mir** ~ **verdient** I got that the hard way; **jdm das Leben** ~ **machen** to make sb's life a misery; **gib ihm Saures!** (col) let him have it! (col).
Sauer-: ~**ampfer** m sorrel; ~**braten** m braised beef (marinated in vinegar), sauerbraten (US).
Sauerei f (col) (a) (Unflätigkeit) ~**en erzählen** to tell filthy stories. (b) **so eine** ~! it's a bloody (esp Brit col) or downright disgrace. (c) (Dreck) mess.
Sauer-: ~**kirsche** f sour cherry; ~**kraut** nt sauerkraut, pickled cabbage.
säuerlich adj (lit, fig) sour; Wein auch sharp.
Sauermilch f sour milk.
Sauerstoff m no pl oxygen.
Sauerstoff- in cpds oxygen; ~**flasche** f oxygen cylinder; ~**gerät** nt breathing apparatus; (Med) (für künstliche Beatmung) respirator; (für Erste Hilfe) resuscitator; **s~haltig** adj containing oxygen; ~**mangel** m lack of oxygen; (akut) oxygen deficiency; ~**zufuhr** f oxygen supply.
Sauer-: ~**teig** m sour dough; **s~töpfisch** adj (pej col) sour; Mensch auch sour-faced.
saufen pret **soff**, ptp **gesoffen** vti (a) (Tiere) to drink. (b) (col: Mensch) to booze (col), to drink. **das S~** boozing; **wie ein Loch** ~ to drink like a fish.
Säufer(in f) m - (col) boozer (col), drunkard.
Sauferei f (col) - (a) (Trinkgelage) booze-up (col). (b) no pl (Trunksucht) boozing (col).

Säuferleber *f (col)* gin-drinker's liver *(col)*.
Sauf-: ~**gelage** *nt (pej col)* drinking bout, booze-up *(col)*; ~**kumpan** *m (pej col)* drinking pal.
saugen *pret* **sog** *or* **saugte,** *ptp* **gesogen** *or* **gesaugt** *vti* to suck; *(col: mit Staubsauger)* to vacuum. **an etw** *(dat)* ~ to suck sth; **an Pfeife** to draw on sth.
säugen *vt* to suckle.
Sauger *m* - **(a)** *(auf Flasche)* teat *(Brit)*, nipple *(US)*. **(b)** *(col: Staub~)* vacuum (cleaner).
Säugetier *nt* mammal.
Saug-: **s~fähig** *adj* absorbent; ~**fähigkeit** *f* absorbency.
Säugling *m* baby, infant *(form)*.
Säuglings- *in cpds* baby, infant *(form)*; ~**alter** *nt* babyhood; **das Kind ist noch im** ~**alter** the child is still a baby; ~**heim** *nt* home for babies; ~**pflege** *f* babycare; ~**schwester** *f* infant nurse; ~**sterblichkeit** *f* infant mortality.
Saug-: ~**napf** *m* sucker; ~**rohr** *nt* pipette.
Sau-: ~**haufen** *m (col)* bunch of layabouts *(col)*; **s~kalt** *adj (col)* bloody *(esp Brit col) or* damn *(col)* cold; ~**klaue** *f (col)* scrawl *(col)*.
Säule *f* -**n** column; *(col: Pfeiler, fig: Stütze)* pillar.
Saum *m, pl* **Säume** hem; *(Naht)* seam.
saumäßig *(col)* **1** *adj* lousy *(col)*; *(zur Verstärkung)* hell of a *(col)*. **2** *adv siehe adj* lousily; like hell.
säumen *vt (Sew)* to hem; *(fig geh)* to line.
säumig *adj (geh)* **Schuldner** defaulting; **Zahlung** outstanding, overdue.
saumselig *adj (geh)* dilatory.
Sauna *f, pl* -**s** *or* **Saunen** sauna.
Säure *f* -**n** **(a)** *(Chem, Magen~)* acid. **(b)** *siehe* **sauer (a)** sourness; acidity.
Säure-: **s~arm** *adj* low in acid; **s~frei** *adj* acid-free; ~**gehalt** *m* acid content.
Sauregurkenzeit *f (hum col)* bad time *or* period; *(in den Medien)* silly season.
säurehaltig *adj* acidic.
Saurier [-iɐ] *m* - dinosaur, saurian *(spec)*.
Saus *m*: **in** ~ **und Braus leben** to live like a lord.
säuseln 1 *vi (Wind)* to murmur, to sigh; *(Blätter)* to rustle; *(Mensch)* to purr. **2** *vt* to murmur, to purr.
sausen *vi* **(a)** *(Ohren, Kopf)* to buzz; *(Wind)* to whistle; *(Sturm)* to roar. **(b)** *aux sein (Geschoß, Peitsche)* to whistle. **(c)** *aux sein (col: Mensch)* to tear *(col)*, to charge *(col)*; *(Fahrzeug)* to roar. **in den Graben** ~ to fly into the ditch; **durch eine Prüfung** ~ to fail *or* flunk *(col)* an exam.
sausenlassen *vt sep irreg (col)* **jdn/etw** ~ to drop sb/sth; **das Kino heute abend laß ich sausen** I'll not bother going to the cinema tonight.
Sau-: ~**stall** *m (col)* pigsty *(col)*; ~**wetter** *nt (col)* bloody *(Brit col) or* damn *(col)* awful weather; **s~wohl** *adj pred (col)* **ich fühle mich s~wohl** I feel bloody *(Brit col) or* really good.
Saxophon *nt* -**e** saxophone, sax *(col)*.
Saxophonist(in *f) m* saxophone player, saxophonist.
S-Bahn ['ɛs-] *f* = **Schnellbahn, Stadtbahn.**
S-Bahnhof ['ɛs-] *m* suburban line station.
Schabe *f* -**n** cockroach.
schaben *vt* to scrape; **Fleisch** to chop finely; **Leder, Fell** to shave.
Schaber *m* - scraper.
Schabernack *m* -**e** prank, practical joke. **mit jdm einen** ~ **treiben** to play a prank on sb.
schäbig *adj* **(a)** *(abgetragen)* shabby. **(b)** **Kerl** mean; **Behandlung, Bezahlung** shabby.
Schäbigkeit *f siehe adj* **(a)** shabbiness. **(b)** meanness, shabbiness.
Schablone *f* -**n (a)** stencil; *(Muster)* template. **(b)** *(fig pej) (bei Arbeit, Arbeitsweise)* routine, pattern; *(beim Reden)* cliché. **in** ~**n denken** to think in a stereotyped way; **etw geht nach** ~ **sth** follows the same routine.
Schach *nt no pl* chess; *(Stellung im Spiel)* check. ~ **(dem König)!** check; ~ **und matt** checkmate; **im**

~ **stehen** to be in check; **jdn in** ~ **halten** *(fig)* stall sb; *(mit Pistole etc)* to keep sb covered.
Schach-: ~**brett** *nt* chessboard; **s~brettartig** *adj* chequered *(Brit)*, checkered *(US)*; ~**brettmuster** *nt* chequered *(Brit) or* checkered *(US)* pattern.
schachern *vi (pej)* **um etw** ~ to haggle over sth.
Schach-: ~**feld** *nt* square (on a chessboard); ~**figur** *f* chess piece; *(fig)* pawn; **s~matt** *adj (lit,* (check)mated; *(fig: erschöpft)* exhausted; **s~matt!** (check)mate; **jdn s~matt setzen** *(lit)* to (check)mate sb; *(fig)* to snooker sb *(col)*; ~**partie** *f* game of chess; ~**spiel** *nt (Spiel)* game of chess; *(Spielart)* chess art; *(Brett und Figuren)* chess set; ~**spieler** *m* chess player.
Schacht *m* -**e** shaft; *(Brunnen~)* well.
Schachtel *f* -**n (a)** box; *(Zigaretten~)* packet, pack. **eine** ~ **Pralinen** a box of chocolates. **(b)** *(pej: Frau)* bag *(col)*.
Schachtelsatz *m* complicated *or* multi-clause sentence.
Schach-: ~**turnier** *nt* chess tournament; ~**zug** *m (fig)* move.
schade *adj pred* **(das ist aber)** ~**!** what a pity *or* shame; **es ist** ~ **um jdn/etw** it's a pity *or* shame about sb/sth; **um sie ist es nicht** ~ she's no great loss; **für etw zu** ~ **sein** to be too good for sth; **sich** *(dat)* **für etw zu** ~ **sein** to consider oneself too good for sth.
Schädel *m* - skull. **mir brummt der** ~ *(col)* my head is spinning; *(vor Kopfschmerzen)* my head is throbbing; **einen dicken** ~ **haben** *(fig col)* to be stubborn.
Schädel-: ~**bruch** *m* fractured skull; ~**decke** *f* top of the skull.
schaden *vi* +*dat* to damage, to harm; **einem Menschen** to harm, to hurt. **Rauchen schadet Ihnen** smoking is bad for you; **das schadet nichts** it does no harm; *(macht nichts)* that doesn't matter; **es kann nichts** ~**, wenn ...** it wouldn't do any harm if ...; **das schadet dir gar nichts** it serves you right.
Schaden *m* ∓ damage *no pl, no indef art (durch caused by)* *(Personen~)* injury; *(Verlust)* loss; *(Unheil, Leid)* harm. **einen** ~ **verursachen** to cause damage; **ich habe einen** ~ **am Auto** my car has been damaged; **~ an der Lunge** lung damage; **~ aufweisen** to be defective; *(Organ)* to be damaged; **es soll sein** ~ **nicht sein** it will not be to his disadvantage; **den** ~ **von etw haben** to suffer for sth; **zu** ~ **kommen** to suffer; *(physisch)* to be injured; **an etw** *(dat)* ~ **nehmen** *(geh)* to damage sth; **jdm** ~ **zufügen** to harm sb; ~ **von etw abwenden** *(liter)* to preserve sth from harm; **durch** ~ **wird man klug** *(Prov)* you learn by your mistakes.
Schadenersatz *m* compensation. ~ **leisten** to pay compensation.
Schadenersatz-: ~**anspruch** *m* claim for compensation; **s~pflichtig** *adj* liable for compensation.
Schaden-: ~**freude** *f* malicious glee, gloating; ... **sagt er mit** ~**freude** ... he gloated; **s~froh** *adj* gloating.
schadhaft *adj no adv* faulty, defective; *(beschädigt)* damaged; *(abgenutzt)* **Kleidung** worn; **Zähne** decayed; **Gebäude** dilapidated.
schädigen *vt* to damage; **jdn** to hurt, to harm.
Schädigung *f siehe vt (gen* done to*)* damage; hurt, harm.
schädlich *adj* harmful; **Wirkung, Einflüsse** detrimental, damaging. ~ **für etw sein** to be damaging to sth.
Schädlichkeit *f* harmfulness.
Schädling *m* pest.
Schädlings-: ~**bekämpfung** *f* pest control *no art*; ~**bekämpfungsmittel** *nt* pesticide.
schadlos *adj* **sich an jdm** ~ **halten** to claim com-

pensation from sb.
Schadstoff m harmful substance.
Schaf nt -e sheep; (col: Dummkopf) twit (Brit col), dope (col). **das schwarze ~ sein** to be the black sheep (in +dat, gen of).
Schafbock m ram.
Schäfchen nt lamb, little sheep. **~ pl** (hum col: Anvertraute) flock sing; **sein ~ ins trockene bringen** (prov) to see oneself all right (col).
Schäfer m - shepherd.
Schäferhund m alsatian (dog) (Brit), German shepherd (dog).
Schäferin f shepherdess.
Schäferstündchen nt (euph hum) bit of hanky-panky (hum col).
Schaffell nt sheepskin.
Schaffen nt no pl **die Freude am ~** the joy of creation; **sein künstlerisches ~** his artistic creations pl.
schaffen[1] pret **schuf**, ptp **geschaffen** vt to create; (herstellen) to make. **dafür ist er wie geschaffen** he's just made for it; **Platz ~** to make room; **Ruhe ~** to establish order.
schaffen[2] **1** vt (a) (bewältigen) to manage; Prüfung to pass. **schaffst du's noch?** (col) can you manage?; **so, das wäre geschafft!** there, that's done; **das ist nicht zu ~** that can't be done; **wir haben nicht viel geschafft** we haven't got much done. (b) (col: überwältigen) jdn to see off (col). **das hat mich geschafft** it took it out of me; (nervlich) it got on top of me; **geschafft sein** to be shattered (col). (c) (bringen) **wie sollen wir das auf den Berg ~?** how will we manage to get that up the mountain?; **einen Koffer zum Bahnhof ~** to take or get a case to the station. (d) (verursachen) Ärger, Unruhe to cause, to create.
2 vi (a) (tun) to do. **ich habe damit nichts zu ~** that has nothing to do with me; **was haben Sie dort zu ~?** what do you think you're doing (there)?; **sich** (dat) **an etw** (dat) **zu ~ machen** to fiddle about with sth. (b) (zusetzen) (jdm schwer) **zu ~ machen** to cause sb (a lot of) trouble; (bekümmern) to worry sb (a lot). (c) (S Ger: arbeiten) to work.
Schaffenskraft f creativity.
Schaffner(in f) m - (im Bus) conductor/conductress; (Rail) guard (Brit), conductor/conductress (US).
Schaf-: **~herde** f flock of sheep; **~hirt** m shepherd.
Schafott nt -e scaffold.
Schafs-: **~käse** m sheep's milk cheese; **~milch** f sheep's milk.
Schaft m -e shaft (auch Archit); (von Gewehr) stock; (von Stiefel) leg; (von Schlüssel) shank.
Schaftstiefel pl high boots pl; (Mil) jackboots pl.
Schaf-: **~wolle** f sheep's wool; **~zucht** f sheep breeding no art.
Schakal m -e jackal.
Schal m -s or -e scarf; (Umschlagtuch) shawl.
schal adj Getränk flat; Wasser, Geschmack stale; (fig: geistlos) Witz stale, weak.
Schale f -n (a) (Schüssel) bowl; (flach) dish; (von Waage) pan. (b) (von Obst, Gemüse) skin; (abgeschält) peel no pl; (von Nüssen, Eiern, Muscheln) shell; (von Getreide) husk. **sich in ~ werfen** (col) to get dressed up; **in seiner rauhen ~ steckt ein guter Kern** beneath that rough exterior (there) beats a heart of gold (prov).
schälen 1 vti to peel; Tomate, Mandel to skin; Erbsen, Eier, Nüsse to shell; Getreide to husk. **2** vr to peel. **sich aus den Kleidern ~** to peel off (one's clothes).
Schalk m -e or -e (dated) joker. **ihm sitzt der ~ im Nacken** he's in a devilish mood.
Schall m -e or -e sound. **Name ist ~ und Rauch** what's in a name?; **das ist alles ~ und Rauch** it's all hollow words.

Schall-: **s~dämmend** adj sound-deadening; **~dämpfer** m sound absorber; (von Auto) silencer (Brit), muffler (US); (von Gewehr etc) silencer; (Mus) mute; **~dämpfung** f sound absorption; (Abdichtung gegen Schall) soundproofing; **s~dicht** adj soundproof.
schallen vi to sound; (Stimme, Glocke, Beifall) to ring (out); (widerhallen) to resound, to echo.
schallend adj Beifall, Ohrfeige resounding; Gelächter ringing. **~ lachen** to roar with laughter.
Schall-: **~geschwindigkeit** f speed of sound; **~grenze, ~mauer** f sound barrier.
Schallplatte f record.
Schallplatten- in cpds record; **~album** nt record case.
schalt pret of **schelten.**
Schalt-: **~anlage** f switchgear; **~bild** nt circuit diagram; **~brett** nt switchboard.
schalten 1 vt to switch, to turn. **etw auf „2" ~** to switch sth to "2"; **in Reihe/parallel ~** (Elec) to connect in series/in parallel. **2** vi (a) (Gerät) to switch, to change or shift (US) (up/down) into 2. **Gang ~** to change or shift (US) (up/down) into 2nd gear. (b) **~ und walten** to bustle around; **frei ~ (und walten) können** to have a free hand. (c) (col: begreifen) to latch on (col), to get it (col); (reagieren) to react.
Schalter m - (a) (Elec etc) switch. (b) (in Post, Bank, Amt) counter; (im Bahnhof) ticket window.
Schalter-: **~beamte(r)** m counter clerk; (im Bahnhof) ticket clerk; **~halle** f (in Post) hall; (in Bank) (banking) hall; (im Bahnhof) booking hall; **~stunden** pl hours of business pl.
Schalt-: **~hebel** m switch lever; (Aut) gear lever (Brit), gearshift; **an den ~hebeln der Macht sitzen** to hold the reins of power; **~jahr** nt leap year; **~knüppel** m (Aut) gear lever (Brit), gearshift; (Aviat) joystick; **~kreis** m integrierter **~kreis** integrated circuit; **~plan** m circuit diagram; **~pult** nt control desk; **~stelle** f (fig) co-ordinating point; **~tag** m leap day.
Schaltung f switching; (Elec) wiring; (Aut) gear change, gearshift.
Scham f no pl (a) shame. **er wurde rot vor ~** he went red with shame; **er versteckte sich vor ~** he hid himself in shame; **nur keine falsche ~!** (col) no need to be embarrassed!; **ohne ~** unashamedly. (b) (geh: Genitalien) private parts pl; (von Frau) pudenda pl.
Schambein nt pubic bone.
schämen vr to be ashamed. **du solltest dich ~!** you ought to be ashamed of yourself!; **sich wegen jdn/etw ~** to be ashamed of sb/sth; **sich für jdn ~** to be ashamed for sb; **sich vor jdm ~** to feel ashamed in front of sb.
Scham-: **~gefühl** nt sense of shame; **~gegend** f pubic region; **~haar** nt pubic hair; **s~haft** adj modest; (verschämt) bashful, coy; **~lippen** pl labia pl, lips pl of the vulva; **s~los** adj shameless; (unanständig auch) indecent; Lüge brazen, bare-faced; **sich s~los kleiden** to dress indecently; **~losigkeit** f siehe adj shamelessness; indecency.
schamponieren* vt to shampoo.
Scham-: **s~rot** adj red (with shame); **~röte** f blush of shame; **die ~röte stieg ihr ins Gesicht** her face flushed with shame; **~teile** pl private parts pl, genitals pl.
Schande f no pl disgrace. **~ über jdn bringen** to disgrace sb; **jdm/einer Sache ~ machen** to be a disgrace to sb/sth; **zu meiner ~ muß ich gestehen, ...** to my shame I have to admit that ...
schänden vt to violate; Ansehen, Namen to dishonour (Brit), to dishonor (US), to discredit.
Schandfleck m blot (in +dat on). **er war der ~ der Familie** he was the disgrace of his family.
schändlich adj disgraceful, shameful.
Schändlichkeit f disgracefulness, shamefulness.

Schand-: ~**mal** nt brand, stigma; ~**tat** f disgraceful deed; (hum) escapade; **zu jeder** ~**tat bereit sein** (col) to be always ready for mischief (col).

Schändung f siehe vt violation; dishonouring, dishonoring.

Schank-: ~**betrieb** m bar service; ~**erlaubnis** f licence (of publican) (Brit), excise license (US); ~**tisch** m bar.

Schanze f -n (Mil) fieldwork, entrenchment; (Sport) (ski-)jump.

Schar f -en crowd, throng (liter); (von Vögeln) flock; (von Insekten etc) swarm. **die Menschen kamen in (hellen)** ~**en nach Lourdes** people flocked to Lourdes.

scharen 1 vt **Menschen um sich** ~ to gather people around one. 2 vr **sich um jdn** ~ to gather around sb.

scharenweise adv (in bezug auf Menschen) in droves. **die Heuschrecken fielen** ~ **über die Saat her** swarms of locusts descended on the seed-crop.

scharf adj comp ⁼**er,** superl ⁼**ste(r, s)** or (adv) **am** ⁼**sten (a)** sharp; Verstand, Augen auch, Beobachter keen; Kälte, Wind biting; Auseinandersetzung, Konkurrenz, Protest fierce; Ton piercing, shrill; Brille sharply focusing. **ein Messer** ~ **machen** to sharpen a knife; **etw aufs** ~**ste verurteilen** to condemn sth in the strongest possible terms; **etw** ~ **einstellen** Bild, Diaprojektor etc to bring sth into focus; Sender to tune sth in (properly); ~ **aufpassen/zuhören** to pay close attention/to listen closely; **jdn** ~ **ansehen** to give sb a scrutinizing look; (mißbilligend) to look sharply at sb; ~ **nachdenken** to have a good or long think, to think long and hard; ~ **kalkulieren** to calculate exactly; **mit** ~**em Blick** (fig) with penetrating insight; ~ **bremsen** to brake sharply or hard.

(b) (hart, streng) Maßnahmen severe; (col) Prüfung strict, tough; Lehrer, Polizist tough; Bewachung close, tight; Hund fierce. **jdn** ~ **bewachen** to guard sb closely.

(c) (stark gewürzt) hot; (mit Salz, Pfeffer) highly seasoned; Geruch, Geschmack pungent, acrid; Getränk (stark) strong; (brennend) fiery; Waschmittel, Lösung caustic. ~ **würzen** to season highly; **Fleisch** ~ **anbraten** to sear meat; ~**e Sachen** (col) hard stuff (col).

(d) (echt) Munition etc, Schuß live. **etw** ~ **machen** to arm sth; ~**e Schüsse abgeben** to fire live bullets; ~ **schießen** (lit) (mit ~**er** Munition) to shoot with live ammunition; (auf den Mann) to aim to hit.

(e) (col) (geil) randy (Brit col), horny (US); (aufreizend) sexy (col); Film sexy (col), blue attr; (aufregend) Auto, Film cool (col), great (col). **jdn** ~ **machen** to turn sb on (col); **auf jdn/etw** ~ **sein** to be keen on sb/sth (col), to fancy sb/sth (col).

Scharfblick m (fig) perspicacity, keen insight.

Schärfe f -n siehe adj **(a)** sharpness; keenness; bite; ferocity; shrillness; (an Kamera, Fernsehen) focus. **(b)** severity; toughness; closeness, tightness. **(c)** hotness; pungency.

Scharf|einstellung f focusing.

schärfen vt (lit, fig) to sharpen.

Scharf-: s~**machen** vt sep (col) to stir up; ~**macher** m (col) agitator; ~**richter** m executioner; ~**schütze** m marksman; s~**sichtig** adj sharpsighted; (fig) perspicacious; ~**sinn** m astuteness; s~**sinnig** adj astute.

Scharlach m (a) no pl scarlet. **(b)** (auch ~**fieber**) scarlet fever.

scharlachrot adj scarlet (red).

Scharlatan m -e charlatan; (Arzt auch) quack.

Scharnier -e, **Scharniergelenk** nt hinge.

Schärpe f -n sash.

scharren vti to scrape; (Pferd, Hund) to paw; (Huhn) to scratch.

Scharte f -n nick; (Schieß~) embrasure. **eine** ~ **auswetzen** (fig) to make amends.

Schaschlik nt -s (shish-)kebab.

schassen vt (col) to boot out (col).

Schatten m - (lit, fig) shadow; (schattige Stelle) shade. **im** ~ **sitzen** to sit in the shade; **40 Grad im** ~ 40 degrees in the shade; **einen** ~ **auf etw** (acc) **werfen** (lit, fig) to cast a shadow on sth; **große Ereignisse werfen ihre** ~ **voraus** great events are often foreshadowed; **in jds** ~ (dat) **stehen** (fig) to be in sb's shadow; **jdn/etw in den** ~ **stellen** (fig) to put sb/sth in the shade; **nur noch ein** ~ **(seiner selbst) sein** to be (only) a shadow of one's former self; ~ **unter den Augen** shadows under the eyes.

Schatten-: ~**dasein** nt shadowy existence; s~**haft** adj (lit, fig) shadowy; ~**kabinett** nt (Pol) shadow cabinet; s~**los** adj shadowless; ~**morelle** f morello cherry; ~**riß** m silhouette; ~**seite** f shady side; (fig: Nachteil) drawback; **die** ~**seite(n) des Lebens** the dark side of life.

Schattierung f (lit, fig) shade.

schattig adj shady.

Schatulle f -n casket; (Geld~) coffer.

Schatz m -⁼e (a) (lit, fig) treasure. ~**e** pl (Boden~) natural resources pl; (Reichtum) riches pl, wealth sing. **(b)** (Liebling) sweetheart.

schätzbar adj assessable. **schwer** ~ difficult to assess.

Schätzchen nt darling.

schätzen 1 vt **(a)** (veranschlagen) to estimate (auf +acc at); Gemälde etc to value; (col: annehmen) to reckon. **die Besucherzahl wurde auf 500.000 geschätzt** the number of visitors was estimated at 500,000; **ich hätte sie älter geschätzt** I'd have said she was older. **(b)** (würdigen) to regard highly. **jdn** ~ to think highly of sb; **etw zu** ~ **wissen** to appreciate sth; **sich glücklich** ~ to consider oneself lucky. 2 vi (veranschlagen, raten) to guess. **schätz mal** have a guess.

Schatz-: ~**gräber** m - treasure-hunter; ~**kammer** f treasure chamber or vault; ~**kanzler** m (Brit Pol) Chancellor of the Exchequer.

Schätzung f estimate; (das Schätzen) estimation; (von Wertgegenstand) valuation. **nach meiner** ~ ... I reckon that ...

schätzungsweise adv (so vermutet man) it is estimated; (ungefähr) roughly; (so schätze ich) I think. **wann wirst du** ~ **kommen?** when do you think you'll come?

Schätzwert m estimated value.

Schau f -en (a) (Vorführung) show; (Ausstellung auch) display, exhibition. **etw zur** ~ **stellen** (ausstellen) to put sth on show, to display sth; (fig) to make a show of sth; (protzen mit) to show off sth; **etw zur** ~ **tragen** to display sth. **(b)** (col) **eine** ~ **abziehen** to put on a show; **das ist nur** ~ it's only show; **jdm die** ~ **stehlen** to steal the show from sb.

Schaubild nt diagram; (Kurve) graph.

Schauder m - shudder; (vor Angst, Kälte auch) shiver.

schauderhaft adj (fig col) dreadful, awful.

schaudern vi (vor Grauen, Abscheu) to shudder; (vor Kälte, Angst auch) to shiver. **ihr schaudert vor ihm** he makes her shudder.

schauen 1 vi to look. **traurig** etc ~ to look sad (col); **um sich** ~ to look around (one); **nach jdm/etw** ~ (suchen) to look for sb/sth; (sich kümmern um) to look after sb/sth; **da schau her!** (S Ger) well, well!; **schau, daß du** ... see (that) you ... 2 vt (geh) to see, to behold (old, liter). **Gott** ~ to see God.

Schauer m - (a) (Regen~) shower. **(b)** (Schauder) shudder.

Schauergeschichte f (col) horror story.

schauerlich adj (a) horrific, horrible; (gruselig) eerie, creepy (col). **(b)** (col: fürchterlich) dreadful, awful.

Schauermärchen *nt (col)* horror story.

Schaufel *f* -n shovel; *(kleiner: für Zucker etc)* scoop; *(Kehricht~)* dustpan; *(von Bagger)* scoop; *(von Schaufelrad)* paddle; *(von Turbine)* vane.

schaufeln *vti* to shovel; *Grab, Grube* to dig.

Schaufenster *nt* shop *(Brit)* or store *(US)* window.

Schaufenster-: ~**auslage** *f* window display; ~**bummel** *m* **einen** ~**bummel machen** to go window-shopping; ~**dekorateur** *m* window-dresser; ~**gestaltung** *f* window-dressing; ~**puppe** *f* display dummy.

Schau-: ~**geschäft** *nt* show business; ~**kampf** *m* exhibition bout; ~**kasten** *m* showcase.

Schaukel *f* -n swing.

schaukeln 1 *vi* **(a)** *(mit Schaukel)* to swing; *(im Schaukelstuhl)* to rock. **(b)** *(Fahrzeug)* to bounce (up and down); *(Schiff)* to pitch and toss. **2** *vt* to rock. **wir werden das Kind** *or* **das schon** ~ *(col)* we'll manage it.

Schaukel-: ~**pferd** *nt* rocking horse; ~**stuhl** *m* rocking chair.

Schau-: **s~lustig** *adj* curious; ~**lustige** *pl decl as adj* (curious) onlookers *pl.*

Schaum *m*, *pl* **Schäume** foam, froth; *(Seifen~)* lather; *(auf Getränken)* froth; *(von Bier)* head. **etw zu** ~ **schlagen** *(Cook)* to beat sth until frothy; ~ **schlagen** *(fig col)* to talk a lot of hot air *(col).*

Schaumbad *nt* bubble bath.

schäumen *vi* to foam, to froth; *(Shampoo, Waschmittel)* to lather (up). **vor Wut** ~ to be foaming with rage.

Schaumgummi *nt or m* foam rubber.

schaumig *adj siehe* **Schaum** frothy; lathery. **etw** ~ **schlagen** *(Cook)* to beat sth until frothy.

Schaum-: ~**krone** *f* white crest; ~**löffel** *m* skimmer; ~**schläger** *m (fig col)* hot-air merchant *(col);* ~**schlägerei** *f (fig col)* hot air *(col);* ~**stoff** *m* foam material; ~**wein** *m* sparkling wine.

Schau-: ~**platz** *m* scene; **vom** ~**platz berichten** to give an on-the-spot report; ~**prozeß** *m* show trial.

schaurig *adj* gruesome; *(col: sehr schlecht)* abysmal *(col).*

schaurig-schön *adj* gruesomely beautiful.

Schauspiel *nt (Theat)* drama, play; *(fig)* spectacle.

Schauspieler *m* actor, player; *(fig)* (play-)actor.

Schauspielerei *f* acting.

Schauspielerin *f (lit, fig)* actress.

schauspielerisch 1 *adj* acting. **2** *adv* as regards acting.

schauspielern *vi insep* to act.

Schauspiel-: ~**haus** *nt* playhouse, theatre *(Brit)*, theater *(US);* ~**schule** *f* drama school; ~**unterricht** *m* drama classes *pl.*

Scheck *m* -s cheque *(Brit)*, check *(US).* **mit (einem)** *or* **per** ~ **bezahlen** to pay by cheque; **ein** ~ **über DM 200** a cheque for DM 200.

Scheck-: ~**betrug** *m* cheque *(Brit)* or check *(US)* fraud; ~**betrüger** *m* cheque *(Brit)* or check *(US)* fraud; ~**buch**, ~**heft** *nt* chequebook *(Brit)*, checkbook *(US).*

scheckig *adj* spotted; *Pferd* dappled; *(verfärbt)* blotchy, patchy.

Scheckkarte *f* cheque card *(Brit)*, banker's card.

scheel *adj* **jdn** ~ **ansehen** to give sb a dirty look; *(abschätzig)* ~ **to look askance at sb.**

scheffeln *vt Geld* to rake in *(col).*

Scheibe *f* -n **(a)** disc, disk; *(Schieß~)* target; *(Eishockey)* puck; *(Wähl~)* dial; *(Tech: Dichtungs~)* washer; *(Töpfer~)* wheel; *(col: Schallplatte)* disc *(col).* **(b)** *(abgeschnittene)* ~ slice. **etw in** ~**n schneiden** to cut sth (up) into slices; **von ihm könntest du dir eine** ~ **abschneiden** *(fig col)* you could take a leaf out of his book *(col).* **(c)** *(Glas~)* (window)pane.

Scheiben-: ~**bremse** *f* disc brake; ~**honig**,

~**kleister** *interj (euph col)* sugar! *(euph col);* ~**schießen** *nt* target shooting; ~**waschanlage** *f* windscreen *(Brit)* or windshield *(US)* washers *pl;* ~**wischer** *m* windscreen *(Brit)* or windshield *(US)* wiper.

Scheich *m* -e sheik(h).

Scheide *f* -n sheath; *(Vagina)* vagina.

scheiden *pret* **schied**, *ptp* **geschieden 1** *vt* **(a)** *(geh: trennen)* to separate. **(b)** *Ehe* to dissolve; *Eheleute* to divorce. **eine geschiedene Frau/ein geschiedener Mann** a divorcee; **sich** ~ **lassen** to get a divorce, to get divorced; **von dem Moment an waren wir (zwei) geschiedene Leute** *(col)* after that it was the parting of the ways for us *(col).* **2** *vi aux sein (liter) (sich trennen)* to part; *(weggehen)* to depart. **aus dem Amt** ~ to retire from one's office; **aus dem Leben** ~ to depart this life. **3** *vr (Wege)* to divide; *(Meinungen)* to diverge.

Scheideweg *m (fig)* crossroads *sing.* **am** ~ **weg stehen** to be at a crossroads.

Scheidung *f* **(a)** *(das Scheiden)* separation. **(b)** *(Ehe~)* divorce. **in** ~ **leben** to be getting a divorce; **die** ~ **einreichen** to file a petition for divorce.

Scheidungs-: ~**grund** *m* grounds *pl* for divorce; *(hum: Mensch)* reason for his/her *etc* divorce; ~**prozeß** *m* divorce proceedings *pl.*

Schein[1] *m no pl* **(a)** *(Licht)* light; *(matt)* glow. **(b)** *(An~)* appearances *pl; (Vortäuschung)* pretence *(Brit)*, pretense *(US)*, sham. ~ **und Sein** appearance and reality; **den** ~ **wahren** to keep up appearances; **etw nur zum** ~ **tun** only to pretend to do sth.

Schein[2] *m* -e *(Geld~)* note *(Brit)*, bill *(US); (Bescheinigung)* certificate; *(Fahr~)* ticket.

scheinbar *adj* apparent; *(vorgegeben)* ostensible. **er hörte s~bar interessiert zu** he seemed to be listening with interest.

scheinen *pre* **schien**, *ptp* **geschienen** *vi* **(a)** *(leuchten)* to shine. **(b)** *auch vi impers (den Anschein geben)* to seem, to appear. **mir scheint, (daß)** ... it seems to me that ...; **wie es scheint** apparently.

Schein-: ~**gefecht** *nt* mock fight; **s~heilig** *adj* hypocritical; *(Arglosigkeit vortäuschend)* innocent; **tu nicht so s~heilig!** don't pretend to be so innocent; ~**heilige(r)** *mf siehe adj* hypocrite; sham; ~**heiligkeit** *f siehe adj* hypocrisy; feigned innocence; ~**tod** *m* apparent death; ~**werfer** *m (zum Beleuchten)* floodlight; *(im Theater)* spotlight; *(Such~)* searchlight; *(Aut)* (head)light, headlamp.

Scheiß *m no pl (col!)* shit *(col!)*, crap *(col!).* **mach keinen** ~! don't be so damn *(col)* silly.

Scheiß- *in cpds (col!)* bloody *(Brit col)*, fucking *(col!).*

Scheißdreck *m (col!)* shit *(col!)*, crap *(col!); (unangenehme Sache)* effing thing *(col!)*, bloody thing *(Brit col!).* **das geht dich einen** ~ **an** it's got bugger-all to do with you *(col!);* **einen** ~ **werd' ich tun!** like hell I will!

Scheiße *f no pl (col!)* shit *(col!)*, crap *(col!).* ~ **sein** to be bloody awful *(Brit col)* or goddamn *(col)* awful; ~! bloody hell! *(Brit col)*, shit! *(col!)*, bugger *(col!);* **in der** ~ **sitzen** to be in the shit *(col!).*

scheiß|egal *adj (col!)* **das ist mir doch** ~! I don't give a shit *(col!).*

scheißen *pret* **schiß**, *ptp* **geschissen** *vi (col!)* to shit *(col!)*, to crap *(col!).* **auf etw** *(acc)* ~ *(fig)* not to give a shit about sth *(col!).*

Scheißer *m* - *(col!: Arschloch)* bugger *(col!).*

Scheiß-: **s~freundlich** *adj (pej col)* as nice as pie *(iro col);* ~**haus** *nt (col!)* shithouse *(col!);* ~**kerl** *m (col!)* bastard *(col!)*, son-of-a-bitch *(US col!).*

Scheit *m* -e log, piece of wood.

Scheitel *m* - **(a)** *(Haar~)* parting *(Brit)*, part *(US).* **vom** ~ **bis zur Sohle** from top to toe. **(b)** *(höch-*

ster Punkt) vertex.
scheiteln *vt* to part.
Scheitelpunkt *m* vertex.
Scheiterhaufen *m* (funeral) pyre; (*Hist: zur Hinrichtung)* stake.
scheitern *vi aux sein (an +dat* because of) *(Mensch, Plan)* to fail; *(Verhandlungen, Ehe)* to break down; *(Regierung)* to founder *(an +dat* on).
Scheitern *nt no pl siehe vi* failure; breakdown; foundering. **das war zum ~ verurteilt** that was doomed to failure.
Schelle *f* -n (a) bell. (b) *(Tech)* clamp.
schellen *vi* to ring *(nach jdm* for sb). **es hat geschellt** the bell has gone; *(an der Tür)* that was the doorbell.
Schellfisch *m* haddock.
Schelm *m* -e (dated: *Spaßvogel)* rogue.
Schelmen-: ~**roman** *m* picaresque novel; ~**streich** *m* (dated) roguish prank.
schelmisch *adj* mischievous.
Schelte *f* -n scolding.
schelten *pret* **schalt,** *ptp* **gescholten** *(geh)* **1** *vt* to scold. **jdn einen Dummkopf ~** to call sb a blockhead. **2** *vi (schimpfen)* to curse.
Schema *nt, pl* **Schemen** *or* -**ta** scheme; *(Darstellung)* diagram; *(Muster)* pattern.
schematisch *adj* schematic; *(pej)* mechanical.
Schemel *m* - stool.
schemenhaft 1 *adj* shadowy. **2** *adv* **etw ~ sehen/ zeichnen** to see the outlines of sth/to sketch sth in.
Schenke *f* -n tavern, inn.
Schenkel *m* - **(a)** *(Anat: Ober~)* thigh. **sich** *(dat)* **auf die ~ schlagen** to slap one's thighs. **(b)** *(Math: von Winkel)* side.
schenken 1 *vt* **(a) jdm etw ~** to give sb sth (as a present); **etw geschenkt bekommen** to get sth as a present; **etw zum Geburtstag geschenkt bekommen** to get sth for one's birthday; **ich möchte nichts geschenkt haben!** *(lit)* I don't want any presents!; *(fig: bevorzugt werden)* I don't want any special treatment!; **das ist geschenkt!** *(col: nicht der Rede wert)* that's no great shakes *(col)*; **das ist (fast) geschenkt!** *(col: billig)* that's dirt cheap *(col)*, that's just about giving it away; **einem Kind das Leben ~** *(geh)* to give birth to a child; **jdm seine Aufmerksamkeit ~** to give sb one's attention; **jdm Vertrauen ~** to put one's trust in sb; **einem geschenkten Gaul sieht man nicht ins Maul** *(Prov)* don't look a gift-horse in the mouth *(Prov).* **(b)** *(erlassen)* **jdm etw ~** to let sb off sth; **ihm ist nie etwas geschenkt worden** *(fig)* he never had it easy.
2 *vr* **sich** *(dat)* **etw ~** to skip sth *(col);* **deine Komplimente kannst du dir ~!** you can keep your compliments *(col);* **er hat sich** *(dat)* **nichts geschenkt** he spared no pains.
Schenkung *f (Jur)* gift.
scheppern *vi (col)* to clatter. **es hat gescheppert** *(Autounfall)* there was a bang.
Scherbe *f* -n fragment, (broken) piece; *(Glas~ etc)* broken piece of glass *etc.* **etw in ~n schlagen** to shatter sth; **in ~n gehen** to shatter; *(fig)* to fall to pieces; ~**n bringen Glück** *(Prov)* broken crockery brings you luck.
Schere *f* -n **(a)** *(klein)* scissors *pl;* *(groß)* shears *pl.* **eine ~** a pair of scissors/shears. **(b)** *(Zool)* pincer; *(von Hummer, Krebs etc auch)* claw. **(c)** *(Turnen, Ringen)* scissors *sing.*
scheren[1] *pret* **schor,** *ptp* **geschoren** *vt* to clip; *Schaf, (Tech)* to shear; *Haare* to crop; *Bart (rasieren)* to shave; *(stutzen)* to trim.
scheren[2] *vtr* **(a) sich nicht um jdn/etw ~** not to care about sb/sth. **(b)** *(col)* **scher dich (weg)!** beat it! *(col);* **scher dich ins Bett!** get to bed!
Scherenschnitt *m* silhouette.
Schererei *f usu pl (col)* trouble *no pl.*
Scherflein *nt* **sein ~ (zu etw) beitragen** *(Geld)* to

contribute one's mite (towards sth); *(fig)* to do one's bit (for sth).
Scher-: ~**kopf** *m* shaving head; ~**messer** *nt* shearing knife.
Scherz *m* -e joke. **zum/im ~** as a joke/in fun; **einen ~ machen** to make a joke; *(Streich)* to play a joke; **mach keine ~e!** *(col)* you're joking!; **(ganz) ohne ~!** *(col)* no kidding! *(col).*
Scherz|artikel *m usu pl* joke (article).
scherzen *vi (geh)* to joke; *(albern)* to banter. **mit etw ist nicht zu ~** one can't trifle with sth.
Scherz-: ~**frage** *f* riddle; **s~haft** *adj* jocular; *(spaßig) Einfall* playful; **etw s~haft sagen** to say sth as a joke *or* in fun.
scheu *adj* shy. **mach doch die Pferde nicht ~** *(fig col)* keep your hair on *(col).*
Scheu *f no pl* fear *(vor +dat* of); *(Schüchternheit)* shyness; *(Hemmung)* inhibition; *(Ehrfurcht)* awe. **seine ~ verlieren** to lose one's inhibitions.
scheuchen *vt* to shoo (away).
scheuen 1 *vt Kosten, Arbeit* to shy away from; *Menschen, Licht* to shun. **weder Mühe noch Kosten ~** to spare neither trouble nor expense. **2** *vr* **sich vor etw** *(dat)* **~** *(Angst haben)* to be afraid of sth; *(zurückschrecken)* to shy away from sth. **3** *vi (Pferd etc)* to shy *(vor +dat* at).
Scheuer *f* -n barn.
Scheuer-: ~**besen** *m* scrubbing broom; ~**bürste** *f* scrubbing brush; ~**lappen** *m* floorcloth.
scheuern 1 *vti* **(a)** *(putzen)* to scour; *(mit Bürste)* to scrub. **(b)** *(reiben)* to chafe. **(c) jdm eine ~** *(col)* to clout sb one *(col).* **2** *vt* **sich (an etw** *dat)* **~** to rub (against sth); **sich** *(acc)* **(wund) ~** to chafe oneself.
Scheuer-: ~**sand** *m* scouring powder; ~**tuch** *nt* floorcloth.
Scheuklappe *f* blinker. ~**n haben** *(lit, fig)* to be blinkered.
Scheune *f* -n barn.
Scheunen-: ~**drescher** *m:* **wie ein ~ drescher fressen** *(col)* to eat like a horse *(col);* ~**tor** *nt* barn door.
Scheusal *nt, pl* -e *or (col)* **Scheusäler** monster.
scheußlich *adj* dreadful; *(abstoßend häßlich)* hideous. **es hat ~ weh getan** *(col)* it was terribly painful.
Scheußlichkeit *f siehe adj* dreadfulness; hideousness.
Schi *m* -er *or* - = **Ski.**
Schicht *f* -en **(a)** *(Lage)* layer; *(dünne ~)* film; *(Farb~)* coat; *(der Gesellschaft)* level, stratum. **breite ~en der Bevölkerung** large sections of the population. **(b)** *(Ind)* shift. **er muß ~ arbeiten** he has to work shifts.
Schicht-: ~**arbeit** *f* shift-work; ~**arbeiter** *m* shift-worker.
schichten *vt* to layer; *Holz, Bücher etc* to stack.
Schichtung *f* layering; *(von Holz, Büchern etc)* stacking.
Schicht-: ~**wechsel** *m* change of shifts; **s~weise** *adv* in layers; *(Farbe, Lack)* in coats.
schick *adj* elegant, smart; *Frauenmode* chic; *Wohnung auch, Möbel* stylish; *Auto* smart.
schicken 1 *vti* to send. **jdn einkaufen ~** to send sb to do the shopping. **2** *vr, vr impers (sich ziemen)* to be fitting *or* proper. **3** *vr* (dated: *sich abfinden)* **sich in etw** *(acc)* **~** to resign *or* reconcile oneself to sth.
Schickeria *f no pl (iro)* in-people *pl.*
schicklich *adj Kleidung etc* proper, fitting; *Verhalten* seemly, becoming.
Schicksal *nt* -e fate, destiny; *(Pech)* fate. **das ~ wollte es, (daß)** ... as fate would have it, ...; **das sind (schwere) ~e** those are tragic cases; **er hat ein schweres ~ gehabt** fate has been unkind to him; **(das ist) ~** *(col)* that's life; **jdn seinem ~ überlassen** to leave sb to his fate.
schicksalhaft *adj* fateful.

Schicksals-: ~**frage** f fateful question; ~**schlag** m great misfortune, stroke of fate.

Schiebe-: ~**dach** nt (Aut) sunroof; ~**fenster** nt sliding window.

schieben pret **schob,** ptp **geschoben** 1 vt (a) to push, to shove; (stecken) to put. **etw von sich** (dat) ~ (fig) to put sth aside; Schuld, Verantwortung to reject sth; **etw vor sich** (dat) **her** ~ (fig) to put off sth; **etw auf jdn/etw** ~ to put the blame for sth onto sb/sth. **(b)** (col: handeln mit) to traffic in; Drogen to push (col). **(c)** (col) **Wache** ~ to do guard duty. 2 vi (a) to push, to shove. **(b)** (col) **mit etw/Drogen** ~ to traffic in sth/push (col) drugs. **(c)** (col: betrügen) to wangle (col). 3 vr (a) (mit Anstrengung) to push, to shove. **(b)** (sich bewegen) to move.

Schieber m - (a) slide; (am Ofen etc) damper. **(b)** (Schwarzhändler) black marketeer; (Waffen~) gun-runner; (Drogen~) pusher (col).

Schiebetür f sliding door.

Schiebung f (Betrug) string-pulling; (im Sport) rigging; (Schiebergeschäfte) shady deals pl. **das war doch** ~ that was rigged or a fix.

schied pret of **scheiden.**

Schieds-: ~**gericht** nt court of arbitration; ~**richter** m (Sport) referee; (Hockey, Tennis) umpire; (Preisrichter) judge; ~**spruch** m (arbitral) award.

schief adj crooked, not straight pred; (nach einer Seite geneigt) lopsided, tilted; Winkel oblique; Blick wry; Absätze worn(-down); (fig: unzutreffend) inappropriate; Bild distorted. ~**e Ebene** (Phys) inclined plane; **auf die** ~**e Bahn geraten** (fig) to leave the straight and narrow; **du siehst die Sache ganz** ~! (fig) you're looking at it all wrong!; **jdn** ~ **ansehen** (fig) to look askance at sb.

Schiefer m - (Gesteinsart) slate.

Schiefer-: ~**dach** nt slate roof; ~**tafel** f slate.

schief-: ~**gehen** vi sep irreg aux sein to go wrong; **es wird schon** ~**gehen!** (hum) it'll be OK (col); ~**lachen** vr sep (col) to kill oneself (laughing) (col); ~**laufen** vi sep irreg aux sein (col) to go wrong; ~**liegen** vi sep irreg (col) to be wrong.

schielen vi to squint, to be cross-eyed. **auf etw** (acc) ~ (col) to steal a glance at sth; **nach etw** ~ to have an eye on sth; **er schielte auf ihre Beine** (col) he was ogling her legs.

schien pret of **scheinen.**

Schienbein nt shin; (~**knochen**) shinbone.

Schiene f -n rail; (Med) splint. ~**n** (Rail) track sing, rails pl; **aus den** ~**n springen** to leave or jump the rails.

schienen vt Arm, Bein to splint.

Schienen-: ~**bus** m rail bus; ~**fahrzeug** nt track vehicle; ~**netz** nt (Rail) rail network; ~**strang** m (section of) track.

schier 1 adj pure; (fig) sheer. 2 adv (beinahe) nearly, almost.

Schieß-: ~**befehl** m order to fire or shoot; ~**bude** f shooting gallery; ~**budenfigur** f (fig col) clown; ~**eisen** nt (col) shooting iron (col).

schießen pret **schoß,** ptp **geschossen** 1 vt to shoot; Kugel, Rakete to fire; Tor auch to score. **jdn in den Kopf/Bauch** ~ to shoot sb in the head/stomach; **ein paar Bilder** ~ (Phot col) to take a few shots. 2 vi (a) to shoot. **auf jdn/etw** ~ to shoot at sb/sth; **aufs Tor** ~ to shoot at goal; **das ist zum S**~ (col) that's a scream (col). **(b)** aux sein to shoot; (in die Höhe ~) to shoot up. **aus dem Boden** ~ (lit, fig) to spring or sprout up; **er kam um die Ecke geschossen** he shot around the corner; **jdm durch den Kopf** ~ (fig: Gedanke) to flash through sb's mind; **das Blut schoß ihm ins Gesicht** blood rushed or shot to his face; **die Tränen schossen ihr in die Augen** tears flooded her eyes.

Schießerei f gun battle; (das Schießen) shooting.

Schieß-: ~**gewehr** nt (hum) gun; ~**hund** m: **wie ein** ~**hund aufpassen** (col) to watch like a hawk; ~**pulver** nt gunpowder; ~**scharte** f embrasure; ~**scheibe** f target.

Schiff nt -e (a) ship. **(b)** (Archit) (Mittel~) nave; (Seiten~) aisle; (Quer~) transept.

Schiffahrt f shipping; (~**skunde**) navigation.

Schiffahrts-: ~**gesellschaft** f shipping company; ~**linie** f (a) (Schiffsweg) shipping route; **(b)** (Unternehmen) shipping line; ~**straße** f, ~**weg** m (Kanal) waterway; (~**linie**) shipping lane.

Schiff-: s~**bar** adj navigable; ~**barkeit** f navigability; ~**bau** m shipbuilding; ~**bauer** m shipwright; ~**bruch** m shipwreck; ~**bruch erleiden** (lit) to be shipwrecked; (fig) to fail; (Unternehmen) to founder; s~**brüchig** adj shipwrecked; ~**brüchige(r)** mf decl as adj shipwrecked person.

Schiffchen nt (a) (zum Spielen) little boat. **(b)** (Mil, Fashion) forage cap. **(c)** (Tex, Sew) shuttle.

schiffen (col) 1 vi (urinieren) to piss (col!). 2 vi impers (regnen) to piss down (col!).

Schiffer m - boatman, sailor; (von Lastkahn) bargee; (Kapitän) skipper.

Schiffer-: ~**klavier** nt accordion; ~**knoten** m sailor's knot; ~**mütze** f yachting cap.

Schiffschaukel f swing boat.

Schiffs-: in cpds ship's; ~**eigner** m shipowner; ~**junge** m ship's boy; ~**ladung** f shipload; ~**mannschaft** f ship's crew; ~**rumpf** m hull; ~**schraube** f ship's propeller; ~**verkehr** m shipping; ~**werft** f shipyard.

Schikane f -n (a) harassment. **das hat er aus reiner** ~ **gemacht** he did it out of sheer bloody-mindedness. **(b)** **mit allen** ~**n** (col) with all the trimmings. **(c)** (Sport) chicane.

schikanieren* vt to harass; Ehepartner, Freundin etc to mess around; Mitschüler to bully.

schikanös adj Mensch bloody-minded; Maßnahme etc harassing.

Schild[1] m -e shield; (von ~**kröte**) shell. **etwas/nichts Gutes im** ~**e führen** (fig) to be up to something/to be up to no good.

Schild[2] nt -er (Aushang, Verkehrs~) sign; (Wegweiser) signpost; (Namens~) nameplate; (Aut) number plate (Brit), license plate (US); (Preis~) ticket; (Etikett) label; (Plakat) placard; (an Monument, Haus, Grab) plaque; (von Mütze) peak.

Schilddrüse f thyroid gland.

schildern vt to describe; (skizzieren) to outline; Menschen, Landschaften to portray. ~ **Sie den Verlauf des Unfalls** give an account of how the accident happened.

Schilderung f (Beschreibung) description; (Bericht) account; (literarische ~) portrayal.

Schild-: ~**kröte** f tortoise; (Wasser~) turtle; ~**krötensuppe** f turtle soup; ~**laus** f scale insect.

Schilf nt -e reed.

Schilf-: ~**dach** nt thatched roof; ~**gras** nt reed; ~**rohr** nt reed.

Schillerlocke f (a) (Gebäck) cream horn. **(b)** (Räucherfisch) strip of smoked rock-salmon.

schillern vi to shimmer.

schillernd adj shimmering; (in Regenbogenfarben) iridescent; (fig) Charakter enigmatic.

Schimmel[1] m - (Pferd) white horse, grey (Brit), gray (US).

Schimmel[2] m no pl mould (Brit), mold (US).

schimm(e)lig adj mouldy (Brit), moldy (US). ~ **werden** to go mouldy.

schimmeln vi aux sein or haben (Nahrungsmittel) to go mouldy (Brit) or moldy (US).

Schimmelpilz m mould (Brit), mold (US).

Schimmer m no pl shimmer, gleam; (von Perlen, Seide) shimmer; (im Haar) sheen. **beim** ~ **der Lampe** in the soft glow of the lamp; **keinen (blassen)** ~ **von etw haben** (col) not to have the slightest or faintest idea about sth.

schimmern vi to glimmer, to gleam; (Perlen,

Seide) to shimmer.

Schimpanse *m (wk)* -n, -n chimpanzee, chimp *(col)*.

Schimpf *m no pl* mit ~ **und Schande** in disgrace.

schimpfen 1 *vi* to get angry; *(sich beklagen)* to grumble; *(fluchen)* to swear, to curse. **mit jdm** ~ to tell sb off; **auf** *or* **über jdn/etw** ~ to bitch about sb/sth *(col)*, to curse (about *or* at) sb/sth. **2** *vt (pej: nennen)* to call. **3** *vr* **sich etw** ~ *(col)* to call oneself sth.

Schimpf-: ~**kanonade** *f* barrage of abuse; ~**name** *m* nickname; ~**wort** *nt* swearword.

Schindel *f* -n shingle.

schinden *pret* **schindete,** *ptp* **geschunden 1** *vt* **(a)** *Gefangene, Tiere* to maltreat. **(b)** *(col: herausschlagen) Zeilen* to pad (out); *Arbeitsstunden* to pile up. **Zeit** ~ to play for time; **Mitleid** ~ to get some sympathy. **2** *vr (hart arbeiten)* to struggle. **sich mit etw** ~ to slave away at sth.

Schinderei *f (Plackerei)* struggle; *(Arbeit)* slavery *no indef art.*

Schindluder *nt (col)* **mit jdm** ~ **treiben** to make sb suffer; **mit etw** ~ **treiben** to abuse sth.

Schinken *m* - **(a)** ham; *(gekocht und geräuchert auch)* gammon. **(b)** *(pej col)* hackneyed and clichéed play/book/film; *(großes Buch)* tome; *(großes Bild)* great daub *(pej col)*.

Schinken-: ~**speck** *m* bacon; ~**wurst** *f* ham sausage.

Schippe *f* -n *(esp N Ger: Schaufel)* shovel, spade. **jdn auf die** ~ **nehmen** *(fig col)* to pull sb's leg *(col)*.

schippen *vt* to shovel. **Schnee** ~ to clear the snow.

Schirm *m* -e *(Regen~)* umbrella; *(Sonnen~)* sunshade, parasol; *(Mützen~)* peak; *(Röntgen~, Wand~, Bild~)* screen; *(Lampen~)* shade.

Schirm-: ~**bild** *nt* x-ray (picture); ~**herr(in** *f)* *m* patron; *(Frau auch)* patroness; ~**herrschaft** *f* patronage; ~**mütze** *f* peaked cap; ~**ständer** *m* umbrella stand.

schiß *pret of* **scheißen.**

Schiß *m no pl (col)* **(fürchterlichen)** ~ **haben** to be terrified *(vor + dat or)*.

schizophren *adj* **(a)** *(Med)* schizophrenic. **(b)** *(pej: widersinnig)* contradictory.

Schizophrenie *f* **(a)** *(Med)* schizophrenia. **(b)** *(pej: Widersinn)* contradictoriness.

schlabbern *(col)* *vti* to slurp.

Schlacht *f* -en battle. **die** ~ **bei** *or* **um X** the battle of X; **jdm eine** ~ **liefern** to battle with sb.

schlachten 1 *vt* to slaughter; *(hum) Sparschwein* to break into. **2** *vi* **heute wird geschlachtet** we're/ they're *etc* slaughtering.

Schlachtenbummler *m (col: Sport)* visiting *or* away supporter *or* fan.

Schlachter(in *f)* *m* - *(esp N Ger)* butcher.

Schlächter *m* - *(dial, fig)* butcher.

Schlachterei *f (esp N Ger)* butcher's (shop) *(Brit)*, butcher.

Schlacht-: ~**feld** *nt* battle-field; ~**fest** *nt* a country feast to eat up meat from freshly slaughtered pigs; ~**hof** *m* slaughter-house, abattoir; ~**messer** *nt* butcher's knife; ~**opfer** *nt* sacrifice; *(Mensch)* human sacrifice; ~**ordnung** *f* battle formation; ~**plan** *m* battle plan; *(für Feldzug)* campaign plan; *(fig auch)* plan of action; **s**~**reif** *adj (lit, fig)* ready for the slaughter; ~**ruf** *m* battle cry; ~**schiff** *nt* battleship; *(col: Auto)* tank *(col)*.

Schlachtung *f* slaughter(ing).

Schlachtvieh *nt no pl* animals *pl* for slaughter.

Schlacke *f* -n clinker *no pl*; *(Aschenteile auch)* cinders *pl*; *(Metal, Geol)* slag *no pl*; *(Physiol)* waste products *pl*.

schlackern *vi (col)* to tremble, to shake; *(Kleidung)* to hang loosely, to be baggy. **mit den Ohren** ~ *(fig)* to be (left) speechless.

Schlaf *m no pl* sleep. **einen leichten/tiefen** ~ **haben** to be a light/deep sleeper; **keinen** ~ **finden** to be unable to sleep; **um seinen** ~ **kommen/gebracht werden** to lose sleep; *(überhaupt nicht schlafen)* not to get any sleep; **jdn um seinen** ~ **bringen** to keep sb awake; ~ **haben** to be sleepy; **in tiefstem** ~ **liegen** to be sound *or* fast asleep; **das macht** *or* **kann er im** ~ *(fig col)* he can do that in his sleep.

Schlaf|anzug *m* pyjamas *pl (Brit)*, pajamas *pl (US)*.

Schläfchen *nt* nap, snooze. **ein** ~ **machen** to have a nap *or* snooze.

Schläfe *f* -n temple. **graue** ~**n** greying *(Brit)* or graying *(US)* temples.

schlafen *pret* **schlief,** *ptp* **geschlafen** *vi* to sleep; *(col: nicht aufpassen) (bei bestimmter Gelegenheit)* to be asleep; *(immer)* not to pay attention. **er schläft immer noch** he's still asleep, he's still sleeping; ~ **gehen** to go to bed; **sich** ~ **legen** to go to sleep; **schläfst du schon?** are you asleep?; **lange** ~ to sleep for a long time; *(spät aufstehen)* to sleep late, to have a long lie (in); **schlaf gut** sleep well; **bei jdm** ~ to stay overnight with sb; **das läßt ihn nicht** ~ *(fig)* it preys on his mind; **darüber muß ich erst mal** ~ *(fig: überdenken)* I'll have to sleep on it; **mit jdm** ~ *(euph)* to sleep with sb.

Schlafengehen *nt* going to bed. **vor dem** ~ before going to bed.

Schlafenszeit *f* bedtime.

Schläfer(in *f)* *m* - sleeper; *(fig)* dozy person *(col)*.

schlaff *adj* limp; *(locker) Seil* slack; *Disziplin* lax; *Haut* loose; *Muskeln* flabby; *(erschöpft)* worn-out *(col)*, exhausted; *(energielos)* listless.

Schlaffheit *f siehe adj* limpness; slackness; laxity; looseness; flabbiness; exhaustion; listlessness.

Schlafgelegenheit *f* place to sleep.

Schlafittchen *nt:* **jdn am** *or* **beim** ~ **nehmen** *(col)* to take sb by the scruff of the neck; *(zurechtweisen)* to give sb a dressing down *(col)*.

Schlaf-: ~**krankheit** *f* sleeping sickness; ~**lied** *nt* lullaby; **s**~**los** *adj (lit, fig)* sleepless; ~**losigkeit** *f* sleeplessness, insomnia *(Med)*; ~**mittel** *nt* sleeping pill; *(fig iro)* soporific; ~**mütze** *f (col)* dope *(col)*; **s**~**mützig** *adj (col)* dozy *(col)*, dopey *(col)*; ~**raum** *m* dormitory *(Brit)*, dorm *(Brit col)*.

schläfrig *adj* sleepy; *Mensch auch* drowsy.

Schläfrigkeit *f siehe adj* sleepiness; drowsiness.

Schlaf-: ~**rock** *m* dressing-gown; **Äpfel im** ~ rock baked apples in puff pastry; ~**saal** *m* dormitory; ~**sack** *m* sleeping-bag; ~**stelle** *f* place to sleep; ~**tablette** *f* sleeping pill; **s**~**trunken** *adv* drowsily, half-asleep; ~**wagen** *m* sleeping-car, sleeper *(Brit)*; **s**~**wandeln** *vi insep aux sein or haben* to sleepwalk; ~**wandler(in** *f)* *m* - sleepwalker; **s**~**wandlerisch** *adj* **mit** ~**wandlerischer Sicherheit** intuitively, instinctively; ~**zimmer** *nt* bedroom.

Schlag *m* -e **(a)** *(lit, fig)* blow; *(Faust~ auch)* punch; *(mit der Handfläche)* smack, slap; *(Handkanten~, Judo etc)* chop *(col)*; *(Ohrfeige)* cuff, clout; *(Tritt)* kick; *(mit Rohrstock etc)* stroke; *(Peitschen~)* stroke, lash; *(Glocken~)* chime; *(~anfall, Ruder~, Schwimmen, Tennis)* stroke; *(Herz~, Wellen~)* beat; *(Blitz~)* bolt; *(Donner~)* clap; *(Strom~)* shock. ~**e kriegen** to get a hiding *or* beating; **zum entscheidenden** ~ **ausholen** *(fig)* to strike the decisive blow; ~ **auf** ~ *(fig)* in quick succession; ~ **acht Uhr** *(col)* on the stroke of eight; **ein** ~ **ins Gesicht** *(lit, fig)* a slap in the face; **ein** ~ **ins Wasser** *(col)* a washout *(col)*; **auf einen** ~ *(col)* all at once; **mit einem** ~ **berühmt werden** to become famous overnight; **die haben keinen** ~ **getan** *(col)* they haven't done a stroke (of work); **einen** ~ **weghaben** *(col: blöd sein)* to have a screw loose *(col)*; **ich dachte, mich trifft der** ~

(col) I was thunderstruck.
(b) *(col: Wesensart)* type *(of person etc).* **vom gleichen ~ sein** to be cast in the same mould *(Brit)* or mould *(US); (pej)* to be tarred with the same brush; **vom alten ~** of the old school. **(c)** *(col: Portion)* helping.

Schlag-: ~**abtausch** *m (Boxen)* exchange of blows; *(fig)* (verbal) exchange; ~**ader** *f* artery; ~**anfall** *m* stroke; **s~artig 1** *adj* sudden, abrupt; **2** *adv* suddenly; ~**ball** *m* rounders sing; *(Ball)* rounders ball; **s~bar** *adj* beatable; ~**baum** *m* barrier; ~**bohrer** *m* percussion drill.

schlagen *pret* **schlug,** *ptp* **geschlagen 1** *vti* **(a)** to hit; *(hauen)* to beat; *(mit der flachen Hand)* to slap, to smack; *(mit der Faust)* to punch; *(treten)* to kick. **jdn bewußtlos ~** to knock sb out *or* unconscious; **jdn wieder ~** to beat sb unconscious; **um sich ~** to lash out; **mit der Faust auf den Tisch ~** to thump on the table with one's fist; **jdm etw aus der Hand ~** to knock sth out of sb's hand; **ihm schlug das Gewissen** his conscience pricked him; **einer Sache** *(dat)* **ins Gesicht ~** *(fig)* to be a slap in the face for sth. **(b)** *Teig, Eier* to beat; *(mit Schneebesen)* to whisk; *Sahne* to whip. **ein Ei in die Pfanne ~** to crack an egg into the pan. **(c)** *(läuten)* to chime; *Stunde* to strike. **die Uhr hat 12 geschlagen** the clock has struck 12; **eine geschlagene Stunde** a full hour. **(d)** *(flattern)* **mit den Flügeln ~** to flap its wings.
2 *vt* **(a)** *Gegner, Rekord* to beat. **jdn in etw** *(dat)* **~** to beat sb at sth; **na ja, ehe ich mich ~ lasse!** *(hum col)* yes, I don't mind if I do; **sich geschlagen geben** to admit defeat. **(b)** **das Schicksal schlug sie hart** fate dealt her a hard blow; **mit Blindheit geschlagen sein** to be blind. **(c)** *(fällen)* to fell. **(d)** *(Hunt: töten)* to kill. **(e)** *(spielen) Trommel* to beat; *(liter) Harfe, Laute* to pluck, to play. **(f)** *Kreis, Bogen* to describe; *Purzelbaum* to do; *Alarm* to raise; *Krach* to make. **Profit aus etw ~** to make profit from sth; **ein Schlacht ~** to fight a battle; **den Kragen nach oben ~** to turn up one's collar. **(g)** *(wickeln)* to wrap.
3 *vi* **(a)** *(Herz, Puls)* to beat; *(heftig)* to pound, to throb. **(b)** *(Regen)* to beat; *(Wellen auch)* to pound; *(Blitz)* to strike *(in etw (acc) sth)*. **(c)** *(singen: Nachtigall, Fink)* to sing. **(d)** *(betreffen)* **in jds Fach** *(acc)* **~** to be in sb's field. **(e)** *aux sein or haben (Flammen)* to shoot out *(aus of); (Rauch)* to pour out *(aus of)*. **(f)** *aux sein* **mit dem Kopf auf etw** *(acc)* **~** to hit one's head on sth; **auf die Nieren etc ~** to affect the kidneys *etc;* **er schlägt sehr nach seinem Vater** he takes after his father a lot.
4 *vr* **(a)** *(sich prügeln)* to fight; *(sich duellieren)* to duel. **als Schuljunge habe ich mich oft geschlagen** I often had fights when I was a schoolboy; **sich um etw ~** *(lit, fig)* to fight over sth. **(b)** *(sich bewähren)* to do, to fare. **sich tapfer or gut ~** to make a good showing. **(c)** *(sich begeben)* **sich nach links/Norden ~** to strike out to the left/for the North; **sich auf jds Seite ~** to side with sb; *(die Fronten wechseln)* to go over to sb.

schlagend *adj* **(a)** *Bemerkung, Vergleich* apt, appropriate; *Beweis* striking, convincing. **etw ~ beweisen/widerlegen** to prove/refute sth convincingly. **(b)** *Verbindung (Univ)* duelling.

Schlager *m* - **(a)** *(Mus)* pop-song; *(erfolgreich)* hit-song, hit. **(b)** *(col) (Erfolg)* hit; *(Verkaufs~)* bestseller.

Schläger *m* - **(a)** *(Tennis~, Federball~)* racket; *(Hockey~, Eishockey~)* stick; *(Golf~)* club; *(Kricket~, Baseball~, Tischtennis~)* bat; *(Polo~)* mallet. **(b)** *(Spieler) (Kricket)* batsman; *(Baseball)* batter. **(c)** *(Raufbold)* thug, ruffian.

Schlägerei *f* fight, brawl.

Schlager-: ~**parade** *f* hit-parade; ~**sänger** *m* pop singer.

Schlägertyp *m (col)* thug.

Schlag-: **s~fertig** *adj* quick-witted; ~**fertigkeit** *f* quick-wittedness; ~**instrument** *nt* percussion instrument; ~**kraft** *f (lit, fig)* power; *(Boxen)* punch(ing power); *(Mil)* strike power; **s~kräftig** *adj* powerful; *Beweise* clear-cut; ~**licht** *nt* **ein ~licht auf etw** *(acc)* **werfen** *(fig)* to highlight *or* spotlight sth; ~**loch** *nt* pothole; ~**mann** *m, pl* ~**männer** *(Rudern)* stroke; *(Kricket)* batsman; *(Baseball)* batter; ~**sahne** *f* (whipping) cream; *(geschlagen)* whipped cream; ~**seite** *f (Naut)* list; ~**seite haben** *(Naut)* to have a list; *(hum col)* to be half-seas over *(col);* ~**stock** *m (form)* truncheon *(Brit),* nightstick *(US);* ~**wort** *nt* **(a)** *pl* ~**wörter** *(Stichwort)* headword; **(b)** *pl* ~**worte** *(Parole)* catchword, slogan; ~**zeile** *f* headline; ~**zeilen machen** *(col)* to hit the headlines; ~**zeug** *nt* drums *pl;* *(in Orchester)* percussion *no pl;* ~**zeuger(in** *f) m* - drummer.

schlaksig *(col)* **1** *adj* gangling, gawky. **2** *adv* gawkily.

Schlamassel *m or nt* - *(col) (Durcheinander)* mix-up; *(mißliche Lage)* mess. **der** *or* **das (ganze) ~** *(Zeug)* the whole caboodle *(col)*.

Schlamm *m* **-e** *or* **=e** mud; *(Schlick auch)* sludge.

Schlammbad *nt* mudbath.

schlammig *adj* muddy; *(schlickig auch)* sludgy.

Schlampe *f* **-n** *(pej col)* slut *(col)*.

schlampen *vi (col)* to be sloppy *(in one's work)*.

Schlamperei *f (col)* sloppiness; *(schlechte Arbeit)* sloppy work. **das ist eine ~!** that's a disgrace.

schlampig *adj (col)* sloppy, careless.

schlang *pret of* **schlingen**.

Schlange *f* **-n (a)** snake, serpent *(liter); (fig: Frau)* Jezebel. **eine falsche ~** a snake in the grass. **(b)** *(Menschen~, Auto~)* queue *(Brit),* line *(US).* **~ stehen** to queue (up) *(Brit),* to stand in line *(US)*.

schlängeln *vr (Weg)* to wind (its way), to snake; *(Fluß auch)* to meander; *(Schlange)* to wriggle. **eine geschlängelte Linie** a wavy line.

Schlangen-: ~**beschwörer** *m* - snake-charmer; ~**biß** *m* snakebite; ~**gift** *nt* snake venom *or* poison; ~**haut** *f* snake's skin; *(Leder)* snakeskin; ~**linie** *f* wavy line; **(in)** ~**linien fahren** to swerve about; ~**mensch** *m* contortionist.

Schlangestehen *nt* queuing *(Brit),* standing in line *(US)*.

schlank *adj* slim. **ihr Kleid macht sie ~** her dress makes her look slim.

Schlankheit *f* slimness.

Schlankheitskur *f* diet. **eine ~ anfangen/machen** to go/be on a diet.

schlankweg *adv (col) ablehnen, sagen* point-blank, flatly.

schlapp *adj (col) (kraftlos)* shattered *(col); (energielos)* listless; *(nach Krankheit etc)* run-down.

Schlappe *f* **-n** *(col)* set-back; *(esp Sport)* defeat. **jdm eine ~ beibringen** to defeat sb.

Schlappen *m* - *(col)* slipper.

Schlapp-: ~**hut** *m* floppy hat; **s~machen** *vi sep (col)* to wilt; *(zusammenbrechen)* to collapse; **die meisten Manager machen mit 40 s~** most managers are finished by the time they're 40; ~**schwanz** *m (pej col)* weakling, softy *(col)*.

Schlaraffenland *nt* land of milk and honey.

schlau *adj* clever, smart; *(gerissen)* cunning; *Sprüche* clever. **ich werde nicht ~ aus ihm** I don't know what to make of him.

Schlauberger *m* - *(col)* clever-dick *(col)*.

Schlauch *m, pl* **Schläuche (a)** hose; *(Fahrrad~, Auto~)* (inner) tube. **sein Zimmer war eine Art ~** *(col)* his room was a sort of long, narrow corridor. **(b)** *(col: Strapaze)* slog *(col),* grind.

Schlauchboot *nt* rubber dinghy.

schlauchen *(col)* **1** *vt (Arbeit etc)* jdn to wear out. **2** *vi* **diese Arbeit schlaucht** this job takes it out of you.

schlauchlos *adj Reifen* tubeless.

Schläue, Schlauheit *f no pl* cunning.

Schlaufe f -n loop; (Aufhänger) hanger.
Schlawiner m - (hum col) villain, rogue.
schlecht 1 adj (a) bad; Geschmack, Leistung auch, Gesundheitszustand poor. **das S~e in der Welt** the evil in the world; **nur S~es über jdn sagen** not to have a good word to say for sb; **jdm ist (es) ~ sb** feels sick or ill; **~ aussehen** (Mensch) to look bad or sick or ill; (Lage) to look bad. **(b)** pred (ungenießbar) bad, off (Brit). **die Milch ist ~** the milk has gone off or is off.
2 adv badly; lernen, begreifen with difficulty. **sich ~ vertragen** (Menschen) to get along badly; (Dinge, Farben etc) not to go well together; **~ über jdn sprechen/von jdm denken** to speak/ think ill of sb; **er kann ~ nein sagen** he finds it hard to say no, he can't say no; **heute geht es ~** today is not very convenient; **das läßt sich ~ machen** that's not really possible or on (col); **er ist ~ zu verstehen** he is hard to understand; **ich kann sie ~ sehen** I can't see her very well; **auf jdn ~ zu sprechen sein** not to have a good word to say for sb; **~ und recht, mehr ~ als recht** after a fashion; **er hat nicht ~ gestaunt** (col) he wasn't half surprised (col).
schlechtbezahlt adj attr low-paid, badly paid.
schlechterdings adv (völlig) absolutely; (nahezu) virtually.
schlecht-: ~gehen vi impers sep irreg aux sein **es geht jdm ~** sb is in a bad way; (finanziell) sb is doing badly; **~gelaunt** adj attr bad-tempered; **~hin** adv (vollkommen) quite, absolutely; **Studenten ~hin** students as such or per se.
Schlechtigkeit f (a) no pl badness. **(b)** (schlechte Tat) misdeed.
schlechtmachen vt sep to denigrate, to run down.
schlecken 1 vti to lick (an etw (dat)) sth). **2** vi (esp SGer: Süßigkeiten essen) to eat sweets (Brit) or candies (US).
Schleckermaul nt (hum col) **sie ist ein richtiges ~** she really has a sweet tooth.
Schlegel m - (a) stick. **(b)** (Min) miner's hammer.
Schlehe f -n sloe.
Schlei m -e tench.
schleichen pret **schlich**, ptp **geschlichen 1** vi aux sein to creep; (heimlich auch) to sneak; (Fahrzeug) to crawl. **2** vr to creep, to sneak.
schleichend adj attr creeping; Krankheit, Gift insidious; Fieber lingering.
Schleich-: ~handel m illicit trading (mit in); **~weg** m secret path; **auf ~wegen** (fig) on the quiet; **~werbung** f a plug.
Schleier m - (lit, fig) veil; (von Wolken, Nebel auch) haze. **einen ~ vor den Augen haben** to have a mist in front of one's eyes; **einen ~ über etw** (acc) **breiten** (fig) to draw a veil over sth.
Schleier-: ~eule f barn owl; **s~haft** adj (col) mysterious.
Schleife f -n (a) loop (auch Aviat); (Straßen~) twisty bend. **(b)** (von Band) bow; (Schuh~) bow(-knot); (Fliege) bow tie; (Kranz~) ribbon.
schleifen¹ 1 vt (lit, fig) to drag; (ziehen auch) to haul; (Mus) Töne, Noten to slur. **2** vi (a) aux sein or haben to trail, to drag. **(b)** (reiben) to rub. **die Kupplung ~ lassen** (Aut) to slip the clutch; **die Zügel ~ lassen** (lit, fig) to slacken the reins.
schleifen² pret **schliff**, ptp **geschliffen** vt Messer etc to sharpen, to whet; Parkett to sand; Edelstein, Glas to cut; siehe **geschliffen**.
Schleif-: ~lack m (coloured (Brit) or colored US) laquer or varnish; **~maschine** f grinding machine; **~papier** nt abrasive paper; **~stein** m grindstone; **er sitzt da wie ein Affe auf dem ~stein** (col) he looks a proper Charlie sitting there (col).
Schleim m -e (a) slime; (Med) mucus. **(b)** (Cook) gruel.
Schleimhaut f mucous membrane.

schleimig adj (a) slimy; (Med) mucous. **(b)** (pej: unterwürfig) slimy (col).
Schleim-: s~lösend adj expectorant; **~scheißer** m (col!) bootlicker (col), arse-licker (col!).
schlemmen 1 vi (üppig essen) to feast. **2** vt to feast on.
Schlemmer(in f) m - gourmet, bon vivant.
Schlemmerei f feasting; (Mahl) feast.
schlendern vi aux sein to stroll, to amble.
Schlendrian m no pl (col) casualness; (Trott) rut.
Schlenker m - swerve. **einen ~ machen** to swerve.
schlenkern vti to swing, to dangle.
schlenzen vi (Sport) to scoop.
Schlepp m (Naut, fig): **jdn/etw in ~ nehmen** to take sb/sth in tow.
Schleppe f -n (von Kleid) train.
schleppen 1 vt (tragen) Lasten to lug, to schlepp (US col); (zerren) to drag, to schlepp (US col); Auto, Schiff to tow; (fig) to drag. **2** vr to drag oneself; (Verhandlungen etc) to drag on.
schleppend adj Gang dragging, shuffling; Abfertigung, Nachfrage sluggish. **die Unterhaltung kam nur ~ in Gang** conversation was very slow to start.
Schlepper m - (a) (Aut) tractor. **(b)** (Naut) tug. **(c)** (col: Kundenfänger) tout.
Schlepp-: ~kahn m (canal) barge; **~netz** nt trawl (net); **~tau** nt (Naut) tow rope; **jdn ins ~tau nehmen** (col) to take sb in tow.
Schlesien [-iən] nt Silesia.
Schlesier(in f) [-iɐ, -iɐrɪn] m - Silesian.
schlesisch adj Silesian.
Schleuder f -n (a) (Waffe) sling; (Wurfmaschine) catapult. **(b)** (Zentrifuge) centrifuge; (Wäsche~) spin-drier (Brit), dryer (US).
Schleuderhonig m extracted honey.
schleudern 1 vti (a) (werfen) to sling, to fling. **(b)** (Tech) to centrifuge, to spin; Honig to extract; Wäsche to spin-dry. **2** vi aux sein or haben (Aut) to skid. **ins S~ kommen** or **geraten** to go into a skid; (fig col) to run into trouble.
Schleuder-: ~preis m throwaway price; **~sitz** m (Aviat) ejector seat; (fig) hot seat; **~ware** f cut-price goods pl.
schleunigst adv at once. **aber ~!** and be quick about it!
Schleuse f -n (für Schiffe) lock; (zur Regulierung des Wasserlaufs) sluice.
schleusen vt Schiffe to pass through a lock, to lock; Wasser to channel; Menschen to filter; (fig: heimlich) to smuggle.
Schleusentor nt (für Schiffe) lock gate.
schlich pret of **schleichen**.
Schliche pl **jdm auf die ~ kommen** to get wise to sb.
schlicht adj simple. **die ~e Wahrheit** the plain or simple truth; **~ und einfach** plain and simple; **das ist ~ und einfach nicht wahr** that's just simply not true; **er sagte ~ und ergreifend nein** (hum col) he said quite simply no.
schlichten vti Streit (vermitteln) to mediate, to arbitrate (esp Ind); (beilegen) to settle.
Schlichter(in f) m - mediator; (Ind) arbitrator.
Schlichtheit f simplicity.
Schlichtung f siehe vti arbitration; settlement.
Schlick m -e silt; (Öl~) slick.
schlief pret of **schlafen**.
Schließe f -n fastening, fastener.
schließen pret **schloß**, ptp **geschlossen 1** vt (a) (zumachen) to close, to shut; (verriegeln) to bolt; (Betrieb einstellen) to close or shut down; Stromkreis to close. **eine Lücke ~** (lit) to close a gap; (fig auch) to fill a gap. **(b)** (beenden) Versammlung to close, to wind up; Brief to close. **(c)** (eingehen) Vertrag, Bündnis to conclude; Frieden auch to make; Freundschaft to form. **die Ehe ~** to get married. **(d)** etw in sich (dat) **~** (beinhalten: lit,

fig) to include sth; *(indirekt)* to imply; **jdn in die Arme ~** to embrace sb; **jdn/etw in sein Herz ~** to take sb/sth to one's heart; **daran schloß er eine Bemerkung** he added a remark (to this). **2** *vr* to close, to shut. **sich um etw ~** to close around sth.

3 *vi* **(a)** to close, to shut; *(Betrieb einstellen)* to close *or* shut down. **„geschlossen" "closed". (b)** *(enden)* to close, to conclude; *(St Ex)* to close. **(c)** *(schlußfolgern)* to infer. **auf etw** *(acc)* **~ lassen** to suggest sth; **von sich auf andere ~** to judge others by one's own standards; *siehe* **geschlossen**.

Schließfach *nt* left-luggage *(Brit)* or baggage *(US)* locker; *(Bank~)* safe-deposit box.

schließlich *adv (endlich)* in the end; *(immerhin)* after all. **er kam ~ doch** he came after all.

Schließung *f* closing; *(von Vertrag)* conclusion; *(Betriebseinstellung)* closure.

Schliff *m* **-e** *(das Schleifen)* cutting; *(Ergebnis)* cut; *(fig: Umgangsformen)* refinement, polish. **einer Sache den letzten ~ geben** *(fig)* to put the finishing touch(es) to sth.

schliff *pret of* **schleifen**[2].

schlimm *adj* bad. **sich ~ verletzen** to hurt oneself badly; **das war ~** that was terrible; **mit der neuen Frisur siehst du ~ aus** you look awful with that new hairdo; **das finde ich nicht ~** I don't find that so bad; **das ist halb so ~**! that's not so bad!; **er ist ~ dran** *(col)* he's in a bad way; **es steht ~ (um ihn)** things aren't looking too good (for him); **wenn es nichts S~eres ist!** if that's all it is!; **es gibt S~eres** it *or* things could be worse; **um so ~er** all the worse; **im ~sten Fall** if the worst comes to the worst.

schlimmstenfalls *adv* at (the) worst. **~ müssen wir im Auto schlafen** if the worst comes to the worst we'll have to sleep in the car.

Schlinge *f* **-n** loop; *(an Galgen)* noose; *(Med: Armbinde)* sling; *(Falle)* snare. **den Kopf aus der ~ ziehen** *(fig)* to get out of a tight spot.

Schlingel *m* - rascal.

schlingen *pret* **schlang**, *ptp* **geschlungen 1** *vt (binden)* Knoten to tie; *(umbinden)* Schal to wrap. **2** *vr* **sich um etw ~** to coil (itself) around sth. **3** *vi (hastig essen)* to bolt one's food.

schlingern *vi (Schiff)* to roll.

Schlips *m* **-e** *(col)* tie, necktie *(US)*. **mit ~ und Kragen** wearing a collar and tie; **jdm auf den ~ treten** to tread on sb's toes; **sich auf den ~ getreten fühlen** to feel offended.

Schlitten *m* - **(a)** sledge, sled; *(Pferde~)* sleigh; *(Rodel~)* toboggan. **mit jdm ~ fahren** *(col)* to give sb a rough time. **(b)** *(col: Auto)* car, motor *(col)*.

Schlitten-: **~fahren** *nt* sledging; *(Rodeln)* tobogganing; **~fahrt** *f* sledge ride; *(mit Rodel)* toboggan ride.

schlittern *vi aux sein* to slide; *(Wagen)* to skid.

Schlittschuh *m* (ice-)skate. **~ laufen** to (ice-)skate.

Schlittschuh-: **~laufen** *nt* (ice-)skating; **~läufer(in** *f)* *m* (ice-)skater.

Schlitz *m* **-e** slit; *(Einwurf~)* slot; *(Hosen~)* fly, flies *pl*.

Schlitz-: **~auge** *nt* slant eye; *(pej: Chinese)* Chink *(pej)*; **s~äugig** *adj* slant-eyed; **~ohr** *nt (fig)* crafty character, sly fox; **s~ohrig** *adj (fig)* crafty; **~verschluß** *m (Phot)* focal-plane shutter.

schloß *pret of* **schließen**.

Schloß *nt* **-sser (a)** castle; *(Palast)* palace; *(großes Herrschaftshaus)* mansion. **(b)** *(Tür~ etc)* lock; *(Vorhänge~)* padlock; *(an Handtasche etc)* fastener. **ins ~ fallen** to lock (itself); **jdn hinter ~ und Riegel bringen** to put sb behind bars.

Schlosser *m* - fitter, metalworker; *(für Schlösser)* locksmith.

Schlosserei *f (~werkstatt)* metalworking shop.

Schloß-: **~herr** *m* owner of a castle *etc*; *(Adliger)* lord of the castle; **~hof** *m* courtyard; **~hund** *m* **heulen wie ein ~hund** *(col)* to howl one's head off *(col)*; **~park** *m* castle *etc* grounds *pl*, estate.

Schlot *m* **-e** *(Schornstein)* chimney (stack), smokestack; *(von Vulkan)* chimney. **rauchen wie ein ~** *(col)* to smoke like a chimney *(col)*.

schlottern *vi* **(a)** *(zittern)* to shiver; *(vor Angst)* to tremble. **er schlotterte mit den Knien** he was shaking at the knees. **(b)** *(Kleider)* to be baggy.

Schlucht *f* **-en** gorge, ravine.

schluchzen *vti (lit, fig)* to sob.

Schluck *m* **-e** drink; *(ein bißchen)* drop; *(das Schlucken)* swallow; *(großer)* gulp; *(kleiner)* sip. **etw ~ für ~ austrinken** to drink every drop; **einen (kräftigen) ~ nehmen** to take a (long) drink *or* swig *(col)*.

Schluck|auf *m no pl* hiccups *pl*. **einen ~ haben** to have (the) hiccups.

Schluckbeschwerden *pl* difficulties *pl* in swallowing.

Schlückchen *nt dim of* **Schluck** drop.

schlucken 1 *vt (lit, fig col)* to swallow; *(hastig)* to gulp down; *(col) Alkohol* to booze *(col)*; *(col: verschlingen)* to swallow up; *Benzin, Öl* to guzzle. **2** *vi* to swallow; *(hastig)* to gulp; *(col: Alkohol trinken)* to booze *(col)*.

Schlucker *m* - *(col):* **armer ~** poor devil.

Schluck-: **~impfung** *f* oral vaccination; **~specht** *m (col)* boozer *(col)*; **s~weise** *adv* in sips.

schlud(e)rig *adj (col) Arbeit* slipshod *no adv*. **~ arbeiten** to work in a slipshod way.

schludern *vi (col)* to do sloppy work, to work sloppily.

schlug *pret of* **schlagen**.

Schlummer *m no pl (liter)* (light) slumber *(liter)*.

Schlummerlied *nt (geh)* lullaby.

schlummern *vi (liter)* to slumber *(liter)*.

Schlummerrolle *f* bolster.

Schlund *m* **-e** *(Anat)* pharynx, gullet; *(fig liter)* maw *(liter)*.

schlüpfen *vi aux sein* to slip; *(Küken)* to hatch (out).

Schlüpfer *m* - panties *pl*, knickers *pl*.

Schlupfloch *nt* gap; *(Versteck)* hideout; *(fig)* loophole.

schlüpfrig *adj* **(a)** slippery. **(b)** *(fig) Bemerkung* risqué.

Schlupfwinkel *m* hiding place; *(fig)* quiet corner.

schlurfen *vi aux sein* to shuffle.

schlürfen *vti* to slurp.

Schluß *m* **-sse (a)** *no pl (Ende)* end. **~! that'll do!**, stop!; **~ für heute!** that'll do for today; **... und damit ~!** ... and that's that!; **~ jetzt!** that's enough now!; **dann ist ~** that'll be it; **~ folgt** to be concluded; **zum ~ sangen wir ...** at the end we sang ...; **zum ~ möchte ich noch darauf hinweisen, daß** ... in conclusion I would like to point out that ...; **~ machen** to call it a day; *(Selbstmord begehen)* to end it all; **mit der Arbeit ~ machen** to stop work; **mit jdm ~ machen** to break with sb. **(b)** *(Folgerung)* conclusion. **aus etw den ~ ziehen, daß** ... to draw the conclusion from sth that ...

Schluß|akt *m (lit, fig)* final act.

Schlüssel *m* - *(lit, fig)* key; *(Tech)* spanner *(Brit)*, wrench; *(Verteilungs~)* ratio (of distribution); *(Mus)* clef.

Schlüssel-: **~bein** *nt* collarbone, clavicle *(form)*; **~blume** *f* cowslip; **~brett** *nt* keyboard; **~bund** *m or nt* bunch of keys; **~erlebnis** *nt (Psych)* crucial experience; **s~fertig** *adj* Neubau ready for occupancy; **~figur** *f* key figure; **~industrie** *f* key industry; **~kind** *nt (col)* latchkey child *(col)*; **~loch** *nt* keyhole; **~position** *f* key position; **~ring** *m* key ring; **~stellung** *f* key position.

schlußfolgern* *vi insep* to conclude, to infer.

Schluß-: ~**folgerung** *f* conclusion, inference; ~**formel** *f* (*in Brief*) complimentary close; (*bei Vertrag*) final clause.

schlüssig *adj* conclusive. **sich** (*dat*) (**über etw** *acc*) ~ **sein** to have made up one's mind (about sth).

Schluß-: ~**kapitel** *nt* concluding *or* final chapter; ~**licht** *nt* tail lamp; (*col: bei Rennen etc*) back marker; ~**licht in der Klasse sein** to be bottom of the class; ~**pfiff** *m* final whistle; ~**phase** *f* final stages *pl*; ~**stand** *m* final result; (*von Spiel auch*) final score; ~**stein** *m* (*Archit,fig*) keystone; ~**strich** *m* (*fig*) final stroke; **einen** ~**strich unter etw** (*acc*) **ziehen** to consider sth finished; ~**verkauf** *m* (end-of-season) sale; ~**wort** *nt* closing words *pl*; (~**rede**) closing speech; (*Nachwort*) postscript.

Schmach *f no pl* (*geh*) ignominy *no indef art*.

schmachten *vi* (*geh: leiden*) to languish. **nach jdm/etw** ~ to pine for sb/sth; **jdn** ~ **lassen** to torment sb.

Schmachtfetzen *m* (*hum*) tear-jerker (*col*).

schmächtig *adj* frail, weedy (*pej*).

schmachvoll *adj* (*geh*) *Niederlage* ignominious.

schmackhaft *adj* (*wohlschmeckend*) tasty. **jdm etw** ~ **machen** (*fig*) to make sth palatable to sb.

schmähen *vti* (*geh*) to abuse, to vituperate against (*liter*).

schmählich *adj* (*geh*) ignominious; (*demütigend*) humiliating.

Schmäh-: ~**rede** *f* (*geh*) diatribe; ~**schrift** *f* defamatory piece of writing; (*Satire*) lampoon.

Schmähung *f* (*geh*) abuse, vituperation (*liter*).

schmal *adj comp* **-er** *or* ⁼**er**, *superl* **-ste(r, s)** *or* ⁼**ste(r, s)** *or* (*adv*) **am -sten** *or* ⁼**sten** (a) narrow; *Hüfte auch, Mensch, Buch* slim; *Lippen* thin. **er ist sehr** ~ **geworden** he has got very thin. **(b)** (*fig: karg*) meagre (*Brit*), meager (*US*), slender.

schmalbrüstig *adj* narrow-chested; (*fig*) limited.

schmälern *vt* to diminish.

Schmälerung *f* diminishing.

Schmal-: ~**film** *m* cine-film; ~**filmkamera** *f* cine-camera (*Brit*), movie camera (*US*); ~**seite** *f* narrow side; ~**spur** *f* (*Rail*) narrow gauge; ~**spur-** *in cpds* (*pej*) small-time; ~**spurig** *adj* (*Rail*) *Strecke* narrow-gauge.

Schmalz¹ *nt* **-e** fat; (*Schweine*~) lard; (*Braten*~) dripping.

Schmalz² *m no pl* (*pej col*) schmaltz (*col*).

schmalzig *adj* (*pej col*) schmaltzy (*col*), slushy (*col*).

schmarotzen* *vi* to sponge, to freeload (*esp US*) (*bei* on, off); (*Biol*) to be parasitic (*bei* on).

Schmarotzer(in *f*) *m* - (*Biol*) parasite; (*fig auch*) sponger, freeloader (*esp US*).

Schmarr(e)n *m* - (a) (*SGer, Aus*) (*Cook*) pancake *cut up into small pieces*. (b) (*col: Quatsch*) rubbish (*col*).

schmatzen *vi* to eat noisily. **schmatz nicht so!** don't make so much noise when you eat!

Schmaus *m, pl* **Schmäuse** (*dated*) feast.

schmausen (*geh*) **1** *vi* to feast. **2** *vt* to feast on.

schmecken **1** *vi* (*Geschmack haben*) to taste (*nach* of); (*gut* ~) to taste good. **ihm schmeckt es** (*gut finden*) he likes it; (*Appetit haben*) he likes his food; **das schmeckt ihm nicht** (*lit, fig*) he doesn't like it; **nach etw** ~ (*fig*) to smack of sth; **das schmeckt nach mehr!** (*col*) it tastes more-ish (*hum col*); **schmeckt es (Ihnen)?** is it good?; are you enjoying your food *or* meal? (*esp form*); **das hat geschmeckt** that was good; **das schmeckt nicht (gut)** it doesn't taste nice; **es sich** ~ **lassen** to tuck in. **2** *vt* to taste.

Schmeichelei *f* flattery.

schmeichelhaft *adj* flattering.

schmeicheln *vi* to flatter (*jdm* sb). **es schmei-**

chelt mir, daß ... it flatters me that ...

Schmeichler(in *f*) *m* - flatterer; (*Kriecher*) sycophant.

schmeichlerisch *adj* flattering.

schmeißen *pret* **schmiß**, *ptp* **geschmissen** (*col*) **1** *vt* (a) (*werfen*) to sling (*col*), to chuck (*col,*; *Tür* to slam. **sich jdm an den Hals** ~ (*fig*) to throw oneself at sb. **(b)** (*spendieren*) **eine Runde** *or* **Lage** ~ to stand a round. **(c)** (*managen*) **den Laden** ~ to run the (whole) show; **die Sache** ~ to handle it. **2** *vi* (*werfen*) to throw, to chuck (*col*). **mit Steinen** ~ to throw stones; **mit etw um sich** ~ to chuck sth around (*col*).

Schmeißfliege *f* bluebottle.

Schmelz *m* **-e** (*Glasur*) glaze; (*Zahn*~) enamel.

schmelzen *pret* **schmolz**, *ptp* **geschmolzen** **1** *vi aux sein* (*lit,fig*) to melt. **2** *vt Metall, Fett* to melt; *Erz* to smelt.

Schmelz-: ~**hütte** *f* smelting plant *or* works *sing or pl*; ~**käse** *m* cheese spread; (*in Scheiben*) processed cheese; ~**ofen** *m* melting furnace; (*für Erze*) smelting furnace; ~**punkt** *m* melting point; ~**tiegel** *m* (*lit,fig*) melting pot; ~**wasser** *nt* melted snow and ice; (*Geog, Phys*) meltwater.

Schmerbauch *m* (*col*) paunch, potbelly.

Schmerz *m* **-en** pain; (*Kummer auch*) grief *no pl*. **ihre** ~**en** her pain; **sie schrie vor** ~**en** she cried out in pain; ~**en haben** to be in pain; ~**en in den Ohren/im Hals haben** to have ear-ache/to have a sore throat; **jdm** ~**en bereiten** to cause sb pain; **jdn/etw mit** ~**en erwarten** to wait impatiently for sb/sth.

schmerz|empfindlich *adj Mensch* sensitive to pain; *Körperteil* tender.

schmerzen (*geh*) *vti* to hurt; (*Wunde etc*) to be sore; (*Kopf, Bauch auch*) to ache. **es schmerzt** (*lit, fig*) it hurts; **eine** ~**de Stelle** a painful spot *or* area.

Schmerzens-: ~**geld** *nt* (*Jur*) damages *pl*; ~**schrei** *m* scream of pain.

Schmerz-: **s**~**frei** *adj* free of pain; *Operation* painless; **s**~**haft** *adj* (*lit, fig*) painful; **s**~**lich** *adj* (*geh*) painful; **s**~**lindernd** *adj* pain-relieving; **s**~**los** *adj* (*lit, fig*) painless; ~**losigkeit** *f* (*lit, fig*) painlessness; ~**mittel** *nt* pain-killer; **s**~**stillend** *adj* pain-killing, analgesic (*Med*); **s**~**stillendes Mittel** pain-killing drug, analgesic (*Med*); ~**tablette** *f* pain-killer, ≈ aspirin (*col*); **s**~**voll** *adj* (*fig*) painful.

Schmetterling *m* (*auch Schwimmart*) butterfly.

Schmetterlings-: ~**netz** *nt* butterfly net; ~**stil** *m* butterfly stroke.

schmettern **1** *vt* (*schleudern*) to smash; *Tür* to slam; (*Sport*) *Ball* to smash. **2** *vi* (a) (*Sport*) to smash, to hit a smash. **(b)** (*Trompete etc*) to blare (out); (*Sänger*) to bellow; (*Vogel*) to sing, to warble.

Schmied *m* **-e** (black)smith.

Schmiede *f* **-n** smithy, forge.

Schmiede-: ~**arbeit** *f* (*das Schmieden*) forging; (*Gegenstand*) piece of wrought-iron work; ~**eisen** *nt* wrought iron; **s**~**eisern** *adj* wrought-iron; ~**hammer** *m* blacksmith's hammer.

schmieden *vt* to forge (*zu* into); (*ersinnen*) *Plan* to hatch, to concoct; (*hum*) *Verse* to concoct. **geschmiedet sein** (*Gartentür etc*) to be made of wrought-iron.

schmiegen *vr* **sich an jdn** ~ to cuddle *or* snuggle up to sb; **sich um etw** ~ to hang gracefully on sth.

schmiegsam *adj* supple; *Stoff* soft; (*fig: anpassungsfähig*) adaptable, flexible.

Schmiere *f* **-n** (a) (*col*) grease; (*Salbe*) ointment. **(b)** (*pej*) (*schlechtes Theater*) flea-pit. **(c)** (*col*) **stehen** to be the look-out.

schmieren **1** *vt* (a) (*streichen*) to smear; *Butter, Aufstrich* to spread; *Brot* to butter; *Salbe, Make-up* to rub in (*in* +*acc* -to); (*einfetten, ölen*) to grease.

es läuft wie geschmiert it's going like clockwork; **jdm eine ~ (col)** to clout sb one (col). **(b)** *(pej: schreiben)* to scrawl. **(c)** *(col: bestechen)* **jdn ~** to grease sb's palm *(col)*. **2** *vi* **(a)** *(pej) (schreiben)* to scrawl; *(malen)* to daub. **(b)** *(col: bestechen)* to give a bribe/bribes.

Schmieren-: **~komödiant** *m (pej)* ham (actor); **~theater** *nt (pej: schlechtes Theater)* flea-pit.

Schmiererei *f (pej col) (Geschriebenes)* scrawl, scribble; *(Parolen etc)* graffiti *pl*; *(Malerei)* daubing; *(Schriftstellerei)* scribbling; *(das Schmieren)* scrawling, scribbling.

Schmier-: **~fink** *m (pej)* **(a)** *(Autor, Journalist)* hack, scribbler; **(b)** *(Schüler)* messy writer; **~geld** *nt (col)* bribe-money; **~heft** *nt* jotter.

schmierig *adj* greasy; *(fig: unanständig)* dirty, filthy.

Schmier-: **~mittel** *nt* lubricant; **~seife** *f* soft soap.

Schmierung *f* lubrication.

Schminke *f* -n make-up.

schminken **1** *vt* to make up. **sich** *(dat)* **die Lippen ~** to put on lipstick. **2** *vr* to put on make-up.

Schmirgel *m no pl* emery.

schmirgeln **1** *vt* to sand, to rub down. **2** *vi* to sand.

Schmirgelpapier *nt* sandpaper.

Schmiß *m* **-sse** **(a)** *(Narbe)* duelling scar. **(b)** *(dated: Schwung)* dash, élan.

schmiß *pret of* **schmeißen.**

schmissig *adj (dated)* dashing; *Musik auch* spirited.

Schmock *m* -e *or* -s *(pej)* hack *(col)*.

Schmöker *m* - book *(usu of light literature)*; *(dick)* tome.

schmökern *(col)* **1** *vi* to bury oneself in a book; *(in Büchern blättern)* to browse. **2** *vt* to bury oneself in.

schmollen *vi* to pout; *(gekränkt sein)* to sulk.

Schmoll-: **~mund** *m* pout; **~winkel** *m (col)* im **~winkel sitzen** to have the sulks *(col)*.

schmolz *pret of* **schmelzen.**

Schmorbraten *m* pot-roast.

schmoren **1** *vt* to braise. **2** *vi (Cook)* to braise; *(col: schwitzen)* to roast, to swelter. **jdn ~ lassen** to leave sb to stew.

Schmu *m no pl (col)* cheating. **~ machen** to cheat.

schmuck *adj (dated)* Haus etc neat, tidy; *Bursche, Mädel* smart, spruce.

Schmuck *m* **(a)** *(~stücke)* jewellery *(Brit)* no pl, jewelry *(US)* no pl. **(b)** *(Verzierung)* decoration; *(fig)* embellishment.

schmücken **1** *vt* to decorate, to adorn; *Rede* to embellish. **~des Beiwerk** embellishment. **2** *vr (zum Fest etc) (Mensch)* to adorn oneself; *(Stadt)* to be decorated.

Schmuck-: **~kasten** *m* jewellery *(Brit)* or jewelry *(US)* box; **s~los** *adj* plain; *(fig) Stil, Prosa etc* simple; **~losigkeit** *f siehe adj* plainness; simplicity; **~sachen** *pl* jewellery *(Brit)* sing, jewelry *(US)* sing; **~stück** *nt (Ring etc)* piece of jewellery *(Brit)* or jewelry *(US)*; *(fig: Prachtstück)* gem.

schmudd(e)lig *adj* messy; *(schmutzig auch)* dirty; *(schmierig, unsauber)* filthy.

Schmuggel *m no pl* smuggling.

Schmuggelei *f* smuggling *no pl*.

schmuggeln *vti (lit, fig)* to smuggle.

Schmuggeln *nt no pl* smuggling.

Schmuggelware *f* contraband *no pl*.

Schmuggler(in *f)* *m* - smuggler.

schmunzeln *vi* to smile.

Schmunzeln *nt no pl* smile.

schmusen *vi (col: zärtlich sein)* to cuddle. **mit jdm ~** to cuddle sb, to canoodle with sb *(col)*.

Schmutz *m no pl* dirt; *(fig auch)* filth, smut. **jdn/ etw in den ~ ziehen** *(fig)* to drag sb/sth through the mud.

schmutzen *vi* to get dirty.

Schmutz-: **~fink** *m (col) (unsauberer Mensch)* dirty slob *(col)*; *(Kind)* mucky pup *(col)*; *(fig: Mann)* dirty old man; **~fleck** *m* dirty mark.

schmutzig *adj* dirty. **sich ~ machen** to get oneself dirty; **~e Wäsche waschen** to wash one's dirty linen in public.

Schmutzigkeit *f* dirtiness.

Schmutzwasser *nt* dirty water.

Schnabel *m* **-** **(a)** *(Vogel~)* beak, bill. **(b)** *(von Kanne)* spout. **(c)** *(col: Mund)* mouth. **halt den ~!** shut your mouth *(col)*; **reden, wie einem der ~ gewachsen ist** to say exactly what comes into one's head; *(unaffektiert)* to talk naturally.

Schnabeltasse *f* feeding cup.

Schnack *m* **-s** *(N Ger col) (Unterhaltung)* chat; *(pej: Geschwätz)* silly talk.

schnacken *vi (N Ger col)* to chat.

Schnake *f* **-n** **(a)** *(col: Stechmücke)* gnat, midge. **(b)** *(Weberknecht)* daddy-long-legs.

Schnalle *f* **-n** *(Schuh~, Gürtel~)* buckle; *(an Handtasche, Buch)* clasp.

schnallen *vt* **(a)** to strap; *Gürtel* to buckle, to fasten. **(b)** *(col: begreifen)* **hast du das immer noch nicht geschnallt?** have you still not got the message?

Schnallenschuh *m* buckled shoe.

schnalzen *vi* **mit den Fingern ~** to snap or click one's fingers; **mit der Zunge ~** to click one's tongue.

schnappen **1** *vi* **(a)** **nach jdm/etw ~** to snap at sb/sth; *(greifen)* to snatch at sb/sth. **(b)** *aux sein* **die Tür schnappt ins Schloß** the door clicks shut. **2** *vt (col)* **(a)** *(ergreifen)* to snatch, to grab. **(b)** *(fangen)* to nab *(col)*.

Schnapp-: **~schloß** *nt (an Tür)* springlock; *(an Schmuck)* spring clasp; **~schuß** *m (Foto)* snap(shot).

Schnaps *m* **-e** *(klarer ~)* schnapps; *(col: Branntwein)* spirits *pl*; *(col: Alkohol)* booze *(col)*, liquor *(esp US col)*.

Schnäpschen ['ʃnɛpsçən] *nt (col)* little drink, wee dram *(esp Scot)*.

Schnaps-: **~flasche** *f* bottle of booze *(col)* or liquor *(esp US col)*; **~glas** *nt* small glass for spirits; **~idee** *f (col)* crackpot idea *(col)*; **~leiche** *f (col)* drunk.

schnarchen *vi* to snore.

schnarren *vi (Wecker etc)* to buzz; *(Maschine, Klingel)* to clatter. **mit ~der Stimme** in a rasping or grating voice.

Schnatter-: **~gans** *f (col)*, **~maul** *nt (col)* chatterbox.

schnattern *vi (Gans)* to gabble; *(Ente)* to quack; *(col: schwatzen)* to natter *(col)*.

schnauben *vi* to snort. **vor Wut ~** to snort with rage.

schnaufen *vi* **(a)** *(schwer atmen)* to wheeze; *(keuchen)* to puff, to pant. **(b)** *aux sein (sich keuchend bewegen: Auto)* to struggle.

Schnaufer *m* - *(col)* breath. **den letzten ~ tun** to breathe one's last.

Schnauferl *nt* - *(hum: Oldtimer)* veteran car.

Schnauzbart *m* walrus moustache *(Brit)* or mustache *(US)*.

Schnauze *f* **-n** **(a)** *(von Tier)* muzzle. **mit einer Maus in der ~** with a mouse in its mouth. **(b)** *(col) (von Fahrzeugen)* front; *(von Flugzeug, Schiff)* nose. **(c)** *(col: Mund)* gob *(col)*, trap *(col)*. **~! shut your trap *(col!)*; **auf die ~ fallen** to fall flat on one's face; *(fig)* to come a cropper *(col)*; **die ~ (gestrichen) voll haben** to be fed up to the back teeth *(col) (von etw* with sth); **eine große ~ haben** to have a big mouth *(col)*; **die ~ halten** to hold one's tongue; **frei nach ~ machen** to do sth any old how *(col)*.

schnauzen *vi (col)* to shout; *(jdn anfahren)* to snap.

Schnauzer *m* - **(a)** *(Hund)* schnauzer. **(b)** *(col: Bart)* walrus moustache *(Brit)* or mustache *(US)*.

Schnecke *f* **-n** **(a)** *(Zool, fig)* snail; *(Nackt~)* slug;

(Cook auch) escargot. **jdn zur ~machen** *(col)* to give sb a real bawling-out *(col)*. **(b)** *(Cook: Gebäck)* ≃ Chelsea bun.

Schnecken-: **s~förmig** *adj* spiral; *(Archit)* ornament scroll-shaped; **~haus** *nt* snail-shell; **sich in sein ~haus zurückziehen** *(fig col)* to retreat into one's shell; **~tempo** *nt* *(col)* **im ~tempo** at a snail's pace.

Schnee *m no pl* **(a)** *(auch TV)* snow. **vom ~ eingeschlossen sein** to be snowbound. **(b)** *(Ei~)* whisked *(Brit)* or whipped *(US)* egg-white. **Eiweiß zu ~ schlagen** to whisk *(Brit)* or whip *(US)* the egg-white(s) till stiff.

Schnee-: **~ball** *m* snowball; **~ballschlacht** *f* snowball fight; **s~bedeckt** *adj* snow-covered; *Berg auch* snow-capped; **~besen** *m* *(Cook)* whisk; **s~blind** *adj* snowblind; **~decke** *f* blanket or covering of snow; **~fall** *m* snowfall, fall of snow; **~flocke** *f* snowflake; **s~frei** *adj* free of snow; **~gestöber** *nt* *(leicht)* snow flurry; *(stark)* snowstorm; **~glöckchen** *nt* snowdrop; **~grenze** *f* snow-line; **~kette** *f (Aut)* snow chain; **~könig** *m*: **sich freuen wie ein ~könig** to be as pleased as Punch; **~mann** *m*, *pl* **~männer** snowman; **~matsch** *m* slush; **~pflug** *m (Tech, Ski)* snowplough *(Brit)*, snowplow *(US)*; **~regen** *m* sleet; **~schaufel** *f* snow-shovel, snow-pusher *(US)*; **~schmelze** *f* thaw; **~schuh** *m* snow-shoe; **~sturm** *m* snowstorm; *(stärker)* blizzard; **~treiben** *nt* driving snow; **~verwehung, ~wehe** *f* snowdrift; **s~weiß** *adj* snow-white; as white as snow; *Haare* snowy-white; **~wittchen** *nt* Snow White.

Schneid *m no pl (col)* nerve, courage.

Schneidbrenner *m (Tech)* oxyacetylene cutter.

Schneide *f* **-n** *(sharp or cutting)* edge; *(von Messer, Schwert)* blade.

schneiden *pret* **geschnitten** **1** *vi* to cut. **der Wind schneidet** the wind is biting.

2 *vt* **(a)** *(auch fig: meiden)* to cut; *(in Scheiben)* to slice; *(klein~)* Gemüse etc to chop; *(Sport)* Ball to slice; *(schnitzen)* Namen, Figuren to carve; *(Weg)* to cross. **sein schön/scharf geschnittenes Gesicht** his clean-cut/sharp features; **die Luft ist zum S~** *(fig col)* the air is very bad; **die Atmosphäre ist zum S~** *(fig col)* you could cut the atmosphere with a knife; **jdn ~** *(beim Überholen)* to cut in on sb; **weit/eng geschnitten sein** *(Sew)* to be cut wide/narrow. **(b)** *Film, Tonband* to edit. **(c)** *(col: operieren)* to operate on.

3 *vr* **(a)** *(Mensch)* to cut oneself. **sich in den Finger** *etc* **~** to cut one's finger *etc*. **(b)** *(col: sich täuschen)* **da hat er sich aber geschnitten!** he's very mistaken. **(c)** *(Linien, Straßen etc)* to intersect.

schneidend *adj* biting; *Kälte auch* bitter; *Schmerz* sharp; *Stimme* piercing.

Schneider *m* **-** **(a)** *(Beruf)* tailor; *(Damen~)* dressmaker. **(b)** *(col)* **frieren wie ein ~** to be/get frozen to the marrow *(col)*; **aus dem ~ sein** *(fig)* to be out of the woods. **(c)** *(Gerät)* cutter; *(col: für Brot etc)* slicer. **(d)** *(Schnake)* daddy-long-legs.

Schneiderei *f* **(a)** *no pl (Handwerk)* tailoring; *(für Damen)* dressmaking. **(b)** *(Werkstatt)* tailor's/dressmaker's workshop.

Schneiderin *f* tailor; *(Damen~)* dressmaker.

Schneidermeister *m* master tailor/dressmaker.

schneidern 1 *vi (beruflich)* to be a tailor/dressmaker; *(als Hobby)* to do dressmaking. **2** *vt* to make, to sew; *Herrenanzug* to tailor, to make.

Schneider-: **~sitz** *m* **im ~sitz sitzen** to sit cross-legged; **~werkstatt** *f* tailor's/dressmaker's workshop.

Schneidezahn *m* incisor.

schneidig *adj* dashing; *Tempo* fast.

schneien 1 *vi impers* to snow. **2** *vt impers* **es schneite Konfetti** confetti rained down. **3** *vi aux sein (fig)* to rain down. **jdm ins Haus ~** *(col)*

(Besuch) to drop in on sb; *(Rechnung, Brief)* to arrive through one's letterbox or in the mail.

Schneise *f* **-n** *(Wald~)* firebreak; *(Flug~)* flight path.

schnell *adj* quick; *Bedienung, Tempo auch, Auto, Zug, Strecke* fast; *Abreise, Hilfe* speedy. **~ gehen/ fahren** to walk/drive quickly/fast; **sie wird ~ böse** she loses her temper quickly; **diese dünnen Gläser gehen ~ kaputt** these thin glasses break easily; **er ist sehr ~ mit seinem Urteil** he's very quick to judge; **nicht so ~!** not so fast!; **ich muß mir nur noch ~ die Haare kämmen** I must just give my hair a quick comb; **sein Puls ging ~** his pulse was very fast; **das geht ~** *(grundsätzlich)* it doesn't take long; **das ging ~** that was quick; **in unserem Büro muß alles ~ gehen** in our office things must be done quickly or fast; **das werden wir ~ erledigt haben** we'll soon have that finished.

Schnelläufer *m (Sport)* sprinter.

Schnell-: **~bahn** *f* high-speed railway *(Brit)* or railroad *(US)*; **~boot** *nt* speedboat; **~dienst** *m* express service.

Schnelle *f* **-n** **(a)** *no pl (Schnelligkeit)* quickness, speed. **(b)** *(Strom~)* rapids *pl*. **(c)** **etw auf die ~ machen** to do sth in a rush.

schnellebig *adj* Zeit fast-moving.

schnellen *vi aux sein (lit, fig)* to shoot. **in die Höhe ~** to shoot up.

Schnell-: **~feuer** *nt (Mil)* rapid fire; **~feuergewehr** *nt* automatic pistol; **~gaststätte** *f* cafeteria, fast-food restaurant *(US)*; **~gericht** *nt* **(a)** *(Jur)* summary court; **(b)** *(Cook)* instant meal, convenience food *(esp pej)*, TV dinner *(US col)*; **~hefter** *m* spring folder.

Schnelligkeit *f (von Auto, Verkehr)* speed; *(von Tempo auch)* quickness; *(von Schritten auch, von Puls)* rapidity; *(von Bote, Hilfe)* speediness.

Schnell-: **~imbiß** *m* **(a)** *(Essen)* (quick) snack; **(b)** *(Raum)* snack-bar; **~kochtopf** *m (Dampfkochtopf)* pressure cooker; **~kurs** *m* crash course; **~paket** *nt* express parcel.

schnellstens *adv* as quickly as possible.

Schnell-: **~straße** *f* expressway; **~zug** *m* fast train; *(Fern~zug)* express (train).

Schnepfe *f* **-n** *(Orn)* snipe.

schneuzen 1 *vr* to blow one's nose. **2** *vt* **einem Kind/sich die Nase ~** to blow a child's/one's nose.

Schnickschnack *m no pl (col: Unsinn)* twaddle *(col)* no *indef art*, poppycock *(col)* no *indef art*.

schniefen *vi (dial)* to sniffle.

schniegeln *vtr (col)* siehe **geschniegelt**.

Schnippchen *nt* **jdm ein ~ schlagen** *(col)* to play a trick on sb.

schnippeln *vti (col)* to snip *(an +dat* at); *(mit Messer)* to hack *(an +dat* at).

schnippen 1 *vi* **mit den Fingern ~** to snap one's fingers. **2** *vt* **etw von etw ~** to flick sth off or from sth.

schnippisch *adj* saucy, pert.

Schnipsel *m or nt* **-** *(col)* scrap; *(Papier~)* scrap of paper.

schnitt *pret of* **schneiden**.

Schnitt *m* **-e** **(a)** *(cut; (Haar~ auch)* haircut; *(von Gesicht, Augen)* shape; *(Sew: ~muster)* pattern. **(b)** *(Film)* editing no *pl*. **~: L. Schwarz** editor-L. Schwarz. **(c)** *(Math)* *(~punkt)* (point of) intersection; *(Längs~, Quer~)* section; *(col: Durch~)* average. **im ~** on average.

Schnitt-: **~blumen** *pl* cut flowers *pl*; **~bohnen** *pl* French or green beans *pl*.

Schnitte *f* **-n** slice; *(belegt)* open sandwich; *(zusammengeklappt)* sandwich.

Schnitt-: **s~fest** *adj* Tomaten firm; **~fläche** *f (Math)* section.

schnittig *adj* smart; *Auto, Formen auch* stylish; *Tempo auch* snappy *(col)*.

Schnitt-: ~**lauch** m no pl chives pl; ~**muster** nt (Sew) (paper) pattern; ~**punkt** m intersection; ~**stelle** f (Comp) interface; ~**wunde** f cut; (tief) gash.

Schnitzel[1] nt or m - (Papier~) scrap of paper; (Holz~) shaving; (Karotten~) shred.

Schnitzel[2] nt - (Cook) veal/port cutlet, schnitzel.

Schnitzeljagd f paper-chase.

schnitzen vti to carve.

Schnitzer m - (a) (col) wood carver. (b) (col) (in Benehmen) boob (Brit col), goof (US col); (Fehler) howler (col).

Schnitzerei f (wood-)carving.

schnodd(e)rig adj (col) offhand, brash.

Schnodd(e)rigkeit f (col) brashness.

schnöd(e) adj (niederträchtig) despicable; Behandlung, Antwort contemptuous. ~**r Mammon/** ~**s Geld** filthy lucre.

Schnorchel m - (von U-Boot, Taucher) snorkel.

Schnörkel m - flourish; (an Möbeln, Säulen) scroll; (fig: Unterschrift) squiggle (hum), signature.

schnörkelig adj ornate; Rede auch flowery.

schnorren vti (col) to cadge (col) (bei from).

Schnorrer m - (col) cadger (col).

Schnösel m - (col) snotty(-nosed) little upstart (col).

schnuckelig adj (col: gemütlich) snug.

Schnüffelei f (fig col: das Spionieren) snooping no pl (col).

schnüffeln vi (a) (schnuppern) to sniff. **an etw** (dat) ~ to sniff (at) sth. (b) (fig col: spionieren) to snoop around (col).

Schnüffler(in f) m - (col) (fig) snooper (col), Nosey Parker (col); (Detektiv) sleuth (col).

Schnuller m - (col) dummy (Brit), pacifier (US); (auf Flasche) teat (Brit), nipple (US).

Schnulze f -n (col) schmaltzy film/song (col).

schnupfen vti (Tabak) ~ to take snuff.

Schnupfen m - cold. **(einen)** ~ **bekommen** to catch (a) cold; **(einen)** ~ **haben** to have a cold.

Schnupftabak m snuff.

schnuppe adj pred (col) jdm ~ **sein** to be all the same to sb; **das Wohl seiner Angestellten ist ihm völlig** ~ he couldn't care less about the welfare of his employees.

schnuppern vti to sniff. **an etw** (dat) ~ to sniff (at) sth.

Schnur f ⁼e (Bindfaden) string; (Kordel) cord; (Kabel) flex, lead.

Schnürchen nt es läuft or klappt alles wie am ~ everything's going like clockwork.

schnüren 1 vt Paket etc to tie up; Mieder to lace (up). **Schuhe zum S~** lace-up shoes. **2** vi (col: eng sein) to be too tight.

schnurgerade adj (dead) straight.

Schnurrbart m moustache (Brit), mustache (US).

schnurren vi (Katze) to purr; (Spinnrad etc) to hum, to whirr.

Schnurrhaare pl whiskers pl.

Schnür-: ~**schuh** m laced shoe, lace-up; ~**senkel** m shoelace; (für Stiefel) bootlace.

schnurstracks adv straight, directly. ~ **auf jdn/ etw zugehen** to make a bee-line for sb/sth (col).

schnurz adj (col) = schnuppe.

schob pret of **schieben**.

Schober m - (Scheune) barn.

Schock m -s shock. **unter** ~ **stehen** to be in (a state of) shock.

Schockeinwirkung f state of shock; **unter** ~ **stehen** to be in (a state of) shock.

schocken vt (col) to shock.

schockieren* vti to shock; (stärker) to scandalize. **schockiert sein** to be shocked (über +acc at).

Schocktherapie f shock therapy.

Schöffe m (wk) -n, -n, **Schöffin** f ≈ juror.

Schöffengericht nt court (with jury).

Schokolade f chocolate.

Schokoladen- in cpds chocolate; s~**braun** adj chocolate-coloured (Brit), chocolate-colored (US).

Scholle[1] f -n (Fisch) plaice.

Scholle[2] f -n (Eis~) (ice) floe; (Erd~) clod (of earth).

Scholli m: **mein lieber** ~! (col) (drohend) now look here!; (erstaunt) my oh my!

schon adv (a) (bereits) already; (in Fragen: überhaupt ~) ever. **er ist** ~ **da** he's there already, he's already there; **ist er** ~ **da?** is he there yet?; **warst du** ~ **dort?** have you been there yet?; (je) have you ever been there?; **mußt du** ~ **gehen?** must you go already, must you go so soon?; **er wollte** ~ **die Hoffnung aufgeben, als ...** he was just about to give up hope when ...; **ich warte nun** ~ **seit drei Wochen** I've already been waiting (for) three weeks; ~ **damals** even then; ~ **vor 100 Jahren** as far back as 100 years ago; ~ **am nächsten Tag** the very next day; **der Briefträger kommt** ~ **um 6 Uhr** the postman comes as early as 6 o'clock; **ich habe das** ~ **mal gehört** I've heard that before; **das habe ich dir doch** ~ **hundertmal gesagt** I've told you that a hundred times (before); **das habe ich** ~ **oft gehört** I've heard that often; **ich bin** ~ **lange fertig** I've been ready for ages; **wartest du** ~ **lange?** have you been waiting (for) long?; **wie** ~ **so oft** as so often (before); ~ **immer** always; **was,** ~ **wieder?** what - again?

(b) (allein bloß) just; (ohnehin) anyway. **allein** ~ **das Gefühl** ... just the very feeling ...; ~ **die Tatsache, daß** ... the very fact that ...; **wenn ich das** ~ **sehe/höre!** I can't bear to see/hear it; ~ **weil** if only because.

(c) (bestimmt) all right. **du wirst** ~ **sehen** you'll see (all right); **das wirst du** ~ **noch lernen** you'll learn that one day.

(d) (tatsächlich, allerdings) really. **das ist** ~ **eine Frechheit!** that's a real cheek!; **da gehört** ~ **Mut** etc **dazu** that takes real courage etc; **das ist** ~ **möglich** that's quite possible; **das mußt du** ~ **machen!** you really ought to do that.

(e) (einschränkend) ja ~, **aber ...** (col) yes (well), but ...; **da haben Sie** ~ **recht, aber ...** yes, you're right (there), but ...

(f) hör ~ **auf damit!** will you stop that!; **so antworte** ~! come on, answer; **nun sag** ~! come on, tell me/us etc; **ich komme ja** ~! I'm just coming!; **was macht das** ~, **wenn ...** what does it matter if ...; **3 Seiten schreiben, was ist das** ~? write 3 pages? that's nothing; **und wenn** ~! (col) so what? (col); ~ **gut** (col) all right, okay (col); **ich verstehe** ~ I understand; **danke, es geht** ~ thank you, I/we etc will manage.

schön 1 adj (a) (hübsch anzusehen) beautiful, lovely; Mann handsome.

(b) (nett, angenehm) good; Stimme, Musik, Wetter auch lovely; Gelegenheit great, splendid. **die** ~**en Künste** the fine arts; **die** ~**e Literatur** belletristic literature; **eines** ~**en Tages** one fine day; **das S~e beim Skilaufen ist ...** the nice or beautiful thing about skiing is ...; ~**en Urlaub!** have a good or nice holiday; ~, **daß du gekommen bist** (how) nice of you to come; **ein** ~**er frischer Wind** a nice cool wind.

(c) (iro) Unordnung fine, nice; Überraschung lovely; Unsinn absolute. **da hast du etwas S~es angerichtet** you've made a fine or nice mess; **du bist mir ein** ~**er Freund/Held** etc a fine friend/ hero etc you are; **das wäre ja noch** ~**er** (col) that's (just) too much!

(d) **das war nicht** ~ **von dir** (col) that wasn't very nice of you; **zu** ~, **um wahr zu sein** (col) too good to be true; **(also)** ~, **na** ~ okay, all right; ~ **und gut, aber ...** that's all very well but ...; **ein** ~**es Stück weiterkommen** to make good progress; **eine ganz** ~**e Menge** quite a lot.

2 adv (a) (bei Verben) well; scheinen brightly; schreiben beautifully. sich ~ anziehen to get dressed up; es ~ haben to be well off; (im Urlaub etc) to have a good time (of it); schlaf ~ sleep well; erhole dich ~ have a good rest. (b) (col: sehr, ziemlich) really. ~ weich/warm nice and soft/warm; sich (dat) ~ weh tun to hurt oneself a lot; sich ~ ärgern to be very angry; ganz ~ teuer/kalt pretty expensive/cold; ganz ~ lange quite a while. (c) iß mal ~ deinen Teller leer eat it all up nicely (now); sei ~ still/ordentlich etc (als Aufforderung) be nice and quiet/tidy etc; fahr ~ langsam drive nice and slowly.

schonen 1 vt Gesundheit, Herz, Kleider to look after, to take care of; eigene Nerven, Bremsen to go easy on; jds Nerven to spare; Gegner, Kind to be easy on; Teppich, Füße to save; (schützen) to protect. ein Waschmittel, das die Wäsche schont a detergent that is kind to your washing; vernünftiges Schalten schont das Getriebe careful gearchanging saves the gears. 2 vr to look after or take care of oneself.

schonend adj gentle; (rücksichtsvoll) considerate. jdm etw ~ beibringen to break sth to sb gently; etw ~ behandeln to treat sth with care.

Schoner[1] m - (Naut) schooner.

Schoner[2] m - cover; (für Rückenlehnen) antimacassar, chairback.

Schön-: s~färben sep 1 vt (fig) to gloss over; 2 vi to gloss things over; ~färberei f (fig) glossing things over.

Schonfrist f period of grace.

schöngeistig adj aesthetic (Brit), esthetic (US).

Schönheit f beauty.

Schönheits-: ~chirurgie f cosmetic surgery; ~fehler m blemish; (von Gegenstand) flaw; ~ideal nt ideal of beauty; ~königin f beauty queen; ~operation f cosmetic operation; ~pflege f beauty care; ~wettbewerb m beauty contest.

Schonkost f light diet.

Schönling m (pej) pansy (col), pretty boy (col).

Schön-: s~machen sep 1 vt Kind to dress up; Wohnung to decorate; 2 vr to get dressed up; (sich schminken) to make (oneself) up; ~schrift f in ~schrift in one's best (hand)writing; s~tun vi sep irreg jdm s~tun (schmeicheln) to flatter or soft-soap (col) sb; (sich lieb Kind machen) to pay court to sb, to play up to sb.

Schonung f (a) (Forest) (protected) forest plantation area. (b) (das Schonen) (von Gefühlen) sparing; (von Teppich, Kleidern) saving; (das Schützen) protection. der Patient braucht noch ein paar Wochen ~ the patient still needs looking after for a few weeks; zur ~ meiner Gefühle to spare my feelings; zur ~ Ihrer Augen to look after your eyes; zur ~ des Getriebes to give your gears a longer life. (c) (Nachsicht, Milde) mercy.

Schonungs-: s~los adj ruthless; Wahrheit blunt; Kritik savage; ~losigkeit f ruthlessness; (von Kritik) savageness; s~voll adj gentle.

Schönwetterperiode f period of fine weather.

Schonzeit f close season; (fig) honeymoon period.

Schopf m -̈e (shock of) hair. eine Gelegenheit beim ~ ergreifen or fassen to seize or grasp an opportunity with both hands.

schöpfen vt (a) auch vi (aus from) Wasser to scoop; Suppe to ladle. (b) Atem to draw, to take; Mut, Kraft to summon up; Hoffnung to find.

Schöpfer(in f) m - (a) creator; (Gott) Creator. (b) (col: Schöpflöffel) ladle.

schöpferisch adj creative.

Schöpf-: ~kelle f, ~löffel m ladle.

Schöpfung f creation. die ~ (Rel) the Creation.

Schoppen m - (Glas Wein) glass of wine.

schor pret of **scheren**[1].

Schorf m -e crust, scaly skin; (Wund~) scab.

Schorle f -n wine and soda water mix.

Schornstein m chimney; (von Schiff) funnel; (smoke)stack.

Schornsteinfeger(in f) m - chimney-sweep.

schoß pret of **schießen**.

Schoß m -̈e (a) lap. die Hände in den ~ legen (fig) to sit back (and take it easy); das ist ihm nicht in den ~ gefallen (fig) it didn't just fall into his lap. (b) (liter: Mutterleib) womb. im ~e der Familie in the bosom of one's family. (c) (an Kleidungsstück) tail.

Schoßhund m lap-dog.

Schößling m (Bot) shoot.

Schote f -n (Bot) pod.

Schotte m (wk) -n, -n Scot, Scotsman.

Schotten-: ~muster nt tartan; ~rock m kilt; (für Frauen) tartan skirt.

Schotter m - gravel; (im Straßenbau) (road) metal; (Rail) ballast.

Schotter-: ~decke f gravel surface; ~straße f gravel road.

Schottin f Scot, Scotswoman.

schottisch adj Scottish, Scots.

Schottland nt Scotland.

schraffieren* vt to hatch.

Schraffierung f hatching.

schräg 1 adj (a) (geneigt) sloping; Augen slanted, slanting; Kante bevelled (Brit), beveled (US). (b) (nicht gerade, nicht parallel) oblique. (c) (col: verdächtig) suspicious, fishy (col). ein ~er Vogel a queer fish (col). 2 adv (a) (geneigt) at an angle; halten on the slant, slanting. ~ stehende Augen slanting or slanted eyes. (b) (nicht gerade, nicht parallel) obliquely; überqueren, gestreift diagonally; (Sew) on the bias. ~ gegenüber/hinter diagonally opposite/behind; ~ rechts/links diagonally to the right/left; die Straße biegt ~ ab the road forks off; ~ gedruckt in italics.

Schräge f -n (a) (schräge Fläche) slope, sloping surface; (schräge Kante) bevel. (b) (Schrägheit) slant, angle; (im Zimmer) sloping ceiling.

Schräg-: ~kante f bevelled (Brit) or beveled (US) edge; ~lage f angle, slant; (von Flugzeug) bank(ing); ~schrift f (Handschrift) slanting hand(writing) or writing; (Typ) italics pl; ~streifen m (a) (Muster) diagonal stripe; (Sew) bias binding; ~strich m oblique.

Schramme f -n scratch.

schrammen vt to scratch.

Schrank m -̈e cupboard, closet (US); (Kleider~) wardrobe.

Schränkchen nt dim of **Schrank** small cupboard; (Arznei~) cabinet.

Schranke f -n barrier; (Rail: Gatter) gate; (fig) (Grenze) limit; (Hindernis) barrier. meine Geduld hat ~n there are limits to my patience; keine ~n kennen to know no bounds; (Mensch) not to know when to stop; einer Sache (dat) (enge) ~n setzen to put a limit on sth; jdn in seine ~n (ver)weisen (fig) to put sb in his place.

Schranken-: s~los adj (fig) Weiten boundless, unlimited; Forderungen unrestrained; ~wärter m gatekeeper (at rail crossing).

Schrank-: ~fach nt shelf; ~koffer m wardrobe trunk; ~wand f wall unit.

Schraube f -n (a) screw; (ohne Spitze) bolt. bei ihr ist eine ~ locker (col) she's got a screw loose (col). (b) (Naut, Aviat) propeller, prop (col). (c) (Sport) twist. (d) alte ~ (col) old bag (col).

schrauben vti to screw. etw in die Höhe ~ (fig) Preise, Rekorde to push sth up; Ansprüche to raise; siehe **geschraubt**.

Schrauben-: ~schlüssel m spanner (Brit), wrench; ~zieher m - screwdriver.

Schraub-: ~stock m vice; ~verschluß m screw top or cap.

Schrebergarten m allotment (Brit).

Schreck m -e fright, scare. vor ~ in fright; zittern

with fright; **zu meinem großen** ~**(en)** to my great horror or dismay; **einen** ~**(en) bekommen** to get a fright or scare; **auf den** ~ **(hin)** to get over the fright; **sich vom ersten** ~ **erholen** to recover from the initial shock; **freudiger** ~ pleasant surprise; **ach du** ~ (col) (oh) crumbs! (col); **o** ~ **laß nach** (hum col) for goodness sake! (col).

schrecken 1 vt (ängstigen) to frighten, to scare; (stärker) to terrify. **jdn aus dem Schlaf** ~ to startle sb out of his sleep. **2** vi aux sein **aus dem Schlaf** ~ to be startled out of one's sleep.

Schrecken m - **(a)** = **Schreck. (b)** (Furcht, Entsetzen) terror, horror. **seinen** ~ **vor etw** (dat) **verlieren** to loose one's fear or terror of sth; **er war der** ~ **der ganzen Lehrerschaft** he was the terror of all the teachers.

schrecken|erregend adj terrifying, horrifying.

Schreckens-: **s~bleich** adj as white as a sheet or ghost; ~**herrschaft** f (reign of) terror; ~**kammer** f chamber of horrors; ~**nachricht** f terrible news no pl or piece of news.

Schreck-: ~**gespenst** nt nightmare; **das** ~**gespenst der Inflation** the bogey of inflation; **s~haft** adj easily startled.

schrecklich adj terrible, dreadful; (col: sehr, groß auch) awful. **sich** ~ **freuen** (col) to be terribly or awfully pleased; ~ **gerne!** (col) I'd absolutely love to.

Schrecklichkeit f terribleness, dreadfulness.

Schreck-: ~**schraube** f (pej col) (old) battle-axe (col); (in bezug auf Äußeres) dolled-up old bag (col); ~**schuß** m warning shot; ~**sekunde** f moment of shock.

Schrei m -e cry, shout; (gellend) scream; (kreischend) shriek; (von Eule etc) screech; (von Hahn) crow. **der** ~ **nach Freiheit/Rache** the call for freedom/revenge; **ein** ~ **der Entrüstung** an (indignant) outcry; **der letzte** ~ (col) the latest thing, all the rage (col).

Schreib-: ~**bedarf** m writing materials pl, stationery; ~**block** m (writing) pad.

schreiben pret **schrieb**, ptp **geschrieben 1** vt **(a)** to write; Scheck auch, Rechnung to make out, to write out; (mit Schreibmaschine) to type (out); Klassenarbeit, Übersetzung to do; (berichten: Zeitung etc) to say. **jdm einen Brief** ~ to write a letter to sb, to write sb a letter; **seinen Namen unter etw** (acc) ~ to put one's signature to sth, to sign sth; **wo steht das geschrieben?** where does it say that?; **es steht geschrieben** (Rel) it is written; **es steht Ihnen im Gesicht geschrieben** it's written all over your face. **(b)** (orthographisch) to spell. **ein Wort falsch** ~ to misspell a word, to spell a word wrong(ly). **(c)** (Datum) wir ~ **heute den 10. Mai** today is the 10th May; **man schrieb das Jahr 1939** the year was 1939, it was (in) 1939.

2 vi to write; (tippen) to type; (berichten) to say. **jdm** ~ to write to sb, to write sb (US); **ich schrieb ihm, daß ...** I wrote and told him that ...; **an einem Roman** etc ~ to be working on or writing a novel etc; **wieviel Silben schreibt sie pro Minute?** what is her (typing) speed?; **mit Bleistift** ~ to write in pencil.

3 vr **(a)** (korrespondieren) to write (to each other), to correspond. **(b)** (geschrieben werden) to be spelt. **wie schreibt sich das?** how is that spelt?

Schreiben nt - **(a)** no pl writing. **(b)** (Mitteilung) communication (form); (Comm: Brief) letter.

Schreiber(in f) m - writer, author; (Gerichts~) clerk; (pej: Schriftsteller) scribbler.

Schreiberei f (col) writing no indef art; (pej: von Schriftsteller) scribbling.

Schreiberling m (pej: Schriftsteller) scribbler.

Schreib-: **s~faul** adj lazy (about letter-writing); **er ist s~faul** he's a poor correspondent; ~**faulheit** f laziness (about letter-writing); ~**fehler** m

(spelling) mistake; (aus Flüchtigkeit) slip of the pen; (Tippfehler) (typing) mistake or error; ~**heft** nt exercise book; ~**kraft** f typist; ~**maschine** f typewriter; **mit der** ~**maschine schreiben** to type; **mit der** ~**maschine geschrieben** typewritten, typed; ~**maschinenpapier** nt typing paper; ~**stube** f (Mil) orderly room; ~**tisch** m desk; ~**tischtäter** m mastermind behind the scenes (of a/the crime); ~**übung** f writing exercise; ~**unterlage** f pad; (auf ~tisch) desk pad; ~**waren** pl stationery sing, writing materials pl; ~**warenhändler** m stationer; ~**weise** f (Stil) style; (Rechtschreibung) spelling.

schreien pret **schrie**, ptp **geschrie(e)n 1** vti to shout, to cry out; (gellend) to scream; (vor Angst, vor Schmerzen) to cry out/to scream; (kreischend) to shriek; (heulen: Kind) to howl; (jammern) to moan; (Eule etc) to screech; (Hahn) to crow. **es war zum S~** (col) it was a scream (col) or a hoot (col); **nach etw** ~ (fig) to cry out for sth; **jdm etw ins Gesicht** ~ to shout sth in sb's face. **2** vr sich **heiser** ~ to shout oneself hoarse; (Baby) to cry itself hoarse.

schreiend adj Farben loud, garish; Unrecht glaring, flagrant.

Schrei-: ~**hals** m (col) (Baby) bawler (col); (Unruhestifter) noisy troublemaker; ~**krampf** m screaming fit.

Schrein m -e (old) shrine.

Schreiner m - carpenter, joiner; (Möbel~) cabinet-maker.

schreiten pret **schritt**, ptp **geschritten** vi aux sein (geh) (schnell gehen) to stride; (feierlich gehen) to walk; (stolzieren) to strut. **zu etw** ~ (fig) to proceed with sth; **zum Äußersten** ~ to take extreme measures; **zur Abstimmung** ~ to go to a vote.

schrie pret of **schreien**.

schrieb pret of **schreiben**.

Schrieb m -e (col) missive (hum).

Schrift f -en **(a)** writing; (~system) script; (Typ) type, typeface. **gotische** ~ Gothic script; **er hat eine schlechte** ~ he has bad handwriting. **(b)** (~stück) document; (Broschüre) leaflet; (Buch) work; (kürzere Abhandlung) paper. **seine früheren** ~**en** his early writings.

Schrift-: ~**art** f (Hand~) (Typ) type, typeface; ~**bild** nt script; ~**deutsch** nt written German; ~**form** f (Jur) **dieser Vertrag erfordert die** ~**form** this contract must be drawn up in writing; ~**führer** m secretary; ~**gelehrte(r)** m (Bibl) scribe.

schriftlich 1 adj written. **in** ~**er Form** in writing; **die** ~**e Prüfung** the written exam. **2** adv in writing. **ich bin** ~ **eingeladen worden** I have had a written invitation; **das kann ich Ihnen** ~ **geben** (fig col) I can tell you that for free (col).

Schrift-: ~**probe** f (Hand~) specimen of one's handwriting; ~**satz** m (Jur) legal document; ~**setzer** m typesetter, compositor; ~**sprache** f written language.

Schriftsteller m - author, writer.

Schriftstellerin f author(ess), writer.

schriftstellerisch adj literary. **er ist** ~ **begabt** he has literary talent or talent as a writer.

Schrift-: ~**stück** nt paper; (Jur) document; ~**tum** nt no pl literature; ~**verkehr**, ~**wechsel** m correspondence; ~**zeichen** nt character; ~**zug** m usu pl stroke; (Handschrift) hand.

schrill adj shrill; (fig) Mißklang jarring.

schritt pret of **schreiten**.

Schritt m -e **(a)** (lit, fig) step; (hörbar) footstep. **einen** ~ **zurücktreten** to step back; **ein paar** ~**e spazierengehen** to go for or take a short walk or stroll; **einen** ~ **machen** to take a step; **kurze/große** ~**e machen** to take small steps/long strides; **den ersten** ~ **tun** (fig) to make the first move; (etw beginnen) to take the first step; ~**e**

gegen jdn/etw unternehmen to take steps against sb/sth; **auf ~ und Tritt** *(lit, fig)* wherever or everywhere one goes; **~ für ~** step by step. **(b)** *(Gang)* walk, gait; *(Tempo)* pace. **~ halten** *(lit, fig)* to keep pace; **mit der Zeit ~ halten** to keep abreast of the times; **langsamen ~es** *(geh)* with slow steps. **(c)** *(~geschwindigkeit)* walking pace. **"~fahren"** "dead slow". **(d)** *(Maßangabe)* **mit zehn ~en Abstand** at a distance of ten paces. **(e)** *(Hosen~)* crotch.

Schrittempo *nt* walking speed.

Schritt-: **~macher** *m (Sport, Med)* pacemaker; *(fig auch)* pacesetter; **s~weise 1** *adv* gradually, little by little; **2** *adj* gradual.

schroff *adj (rauh, barsch)* curt; *(kraß, abrupt)* abrupt; *(steil) Fels, Klippe* precipitous. **~e Gegensätze** stark *or* sharp contrasts.

Schroffheit *f siehe adj* curtness; abruptness; precipitousness; *(schroffes Wort)* curt remark.

schröpfen *vt jdn ~ (fig)* to fleece sb *(col)*.

Schrot *m or nt* **-e (a)** whole-corn/-rye *etc* meal; *(Weizen)* wholemeal *(Brit)*, wholewheat *(US)*. **ein Schotte von echtem ~ und Korn** a true Scot; **vom alten ~ und Korn** *(fig)* of the old school. **(b)** *(Hunt)* shot.

Schrot-: **~büchse,** **~flinte** *f* shotgun; **~kugel** *f* pellet; **~ladung** *f* round of shot.

Schrott *m no pl* scrap metal. **ein Auto zu ~ fahren** to write off a car.

Schrott-: **~händler** *m* scrap dealer *or* merchant; **~haufen** *m (lit)* scrap heap; **~platz** *m* scrap yard; **s~reif** *adj* ready for the scrap heap; **~wert** *m* scrap value.

schrubben *vti* to scrub.

Schrubber *m* - (long-handled) scrubbing brush.

Schrulle *f* **-n (a)** *(Marotte)* quirk. **(b)** *(pej: alte Frau)* old crone.

schrullig *adj* odd, cranky.

schrump(e)lig *adj (col)* wrinkled.

schrumpfen *vi aux sein (lit, fig)* to shrink; *(Leber, Niere)* to atrophy; *(runzlig werden)* to get wrinkled; *(Exporte, Interesse)* to dwindle.

Schrumpf-: **~kopf** *m* shrunken head; **~leber** *f* cirrhosis of the liver.

Schrumpfung *f* shrinking; *(Raumverlust)* shrinkage; *(Med)* atrophy(ing); *(von Exporten)* dwindling.

Schub *m* **-e (a)** *(Stoß)* push, shove. **(b)** *(Phys)* thrust. **(c)** *(Gruppe, Anzahl)* batch.

Schuber *m* - slipcase.

Schub-: **~fach** *nt* drawer; **~karre** *f,* **~karren** *m* wheelbarrow; **~kasten** *m* drawer; **~kraft** *f (Phys)* thrust; **~lade** *f* **-n** drawer.

Schubs *m* **-e** *(col)* shove, push; *(Aufmerksamkeit erregend)* nudge.

schubsen *vti (col)* to shove, to push; *(Aufmerksamkeit erregend)* to nudge.

schubweise *adv* in batches.

schüchtern *adj* shy.

Schüchternheit *f* shyness.

schuf *pret of* **schaffen**[1].

Schuft *m* **-e** heel *(col)*, cad *(dated col)*.

schuften *vi (col)* to graft (away) *(col)*, to slave away.

Schufterei *f (col)* graft *(col)*, hard work.

schuftig *adj* mean, shabby.

Schuh *m* **-e** shoe. **jdm etw in die ~e schieben** *(col)* to put the blame for sth on sb; **wissen, wo jdn der ~ drückt** to know what is troubling sb; **umgekehrt wird ein ~ draus!** *(col)* quite the reverse is true.

Schuh- in *cpds* shoe; **~anzieher** *m* shoehorn; **~creme** *f* shoe polish *or* cream; **~macher** *m* shoemaker; **~nummer** *f (col)* shoe size; **~plattler** *m* - *Bavarian folk dance;* **~putzer** *m* bootblack, shoe-shine boy *(US)*; **ich bin doch nicht dein ~putzer!** I'm not your slave!; **~riemen** *m* strap (of a/one's shoe); *(Schnürsenkel)* shoelace; **~soh-**

le *f* sole (of a/one's shoe); **~werk** *nt no pl* footwear; **~wichse** *f (col)* shoe polish.

Schuko- ®: **~steckdose** *f* safety socket *(Brit)* *or* outlet *(US)*; **~stecker** *m* safety plug.

Schul-: **~abgänger(in** *f)* *m* - school-leaver; **~anfang** *m* beginning of term; *(~eintritt)* first day at school; **~anfänger** *m* child just starting school; **~arbeit** *f usu pl* homework *no pl;* **~aufgaben** *pl* homework *sing;* **~bank** *f* school desk; **die ~bank drücken** *(col)* to go to school; **~beginn** *m (~jahrsbeginn)* beginning of the school year; *(nach Ferien)* beginning of term; **(der) ~beginn ist um neun** school starts at nine; **~behörde** *f* education authority; **~beispiel** *nt (fig)* classic example *(für of)*; **~besuch** *m* school attendance; **~bildung** *f* (school) education; **~buch** *nt* schoolbook, textbook; **~bus** *m* school bus.

schuld *adj pred* **~ sein** *or* **haben** to be to blame *(an +dat* for)*; **er war** *or* **hatte ~ an dem Streit** the argument was his fault, he was to blame for the argument; **du hast** *or* **bist selbst ~** that's your own fault.

Schuld *f* **-en (a)** *no pl (Ursache, Verantwortlichkeit)* **die ~ an etw** *(dat)* **haben** to be to blame for sth; **die ~ auf sich** *(acc)* **nehmen** to take the blame; **jdm die ~ geben** *or* **zuschieben** to blame sb; **die ~ auf jdn schieben** to put the blame on sb; **die ~ bei anderen suchen** to try to blame somebody else; **das ist meine eigene ~** it's my own fault, I've only myself to blame; **durch meine/deine ~** because of me/you.

(b) *no pl (~gefühl)* guilt; *(Unrecht)* wrong; *(Rel: Sünde)* sin. **ich bin mir keiner ~ bewußt** I'm not aware of having done anything wrong; **~ auf sich** *(acc)* **laden** to burden oneself with a deep sense of guilt; **für seine ~ büßen** to pay for one's sin/sins; **~ und Sühne** crime and punishment.

(c) *(Zahlungsverpflichtung)* debt. **~en machen** to run up debts; **~en haben** to be in debt; **DM 10.000 ~en haben** to have debts of DM 10,000; **ich stehe tief in seiner ~** *(fig)* I'm deeply indebted to him.

Schuld-: **~bekenntnis** *nt* confession; **s~beladen** *adj* burdened with guilt; **s~bewußt** *adj* Mensch feeling guilty; Miene guilty; **~bewußtsein** *nt* feelings of guilt *pl.*

schulden *vt* to owe. **das schulde ich ihm** I owe it to him; **jdm Dank ~** to owe sb a debt of gratitude.

Schulden-: **s~frei** *adj* free of debt(s); Grundstück *etc* unmortgaged; **~last** *f* debts *pl.*

Schuld-: **~forderung** *f* claim; **~frage** *f* question of guilt; **s~frei** *adj* blameless; **~gefühl** *nt* feeling of guilt; **s~haft** *adj (Jur)* culpable.

Schuldienst *m* (school-)teaching *no art;* **im ~ sein** to be a teacher.

schuldig *adj* **(a)** *(schuldhaft, straffällig)* guilty; *(verantwortlich)* to blame *pred (an +dat* for)*; *(Rel)* sinful. **einer Sache** *(gen)* **~ sein, sich einer Sache** *(gen)* **~ machen** to be guilty of sth; **jdn ~ sprechen** to find sb guilty; **sich ~ bekennen** to admit one's guilt; *(Jur)* to plead guilty; **~ geschieden sein** to be the guilty party in a/the divorce. **(b)** *(geh: gebührend)* due. **jdm den ~en Respekt zollen** to give sb the respect due to him/her. **(c)** *(verpflichtet)* **jdm etw** *(acc)* **~ sein** *(lit, fig)* to owe sb sth; **was bin ich Ihnen ~?** how much do I owe you?; **jdm Dank ~ sein** to owe sb a debt of gratitude; **sie blieb mir die Antwort ~** she didn't have an answer.

Schuldigkeit *f no pl* duty. **seine ~ tun** to do one's duty.

Schul-: **~direktor** *m* head teacher, headmaster *(esp Brit)*, principal; **~direktorin** *f* head teacher, headmistress *(esp Brit)*, principal.

Schuld-: **~komplex** *m* guilt complex; **s~los** *adj (an Verbrechen)* innocent *(an +dat* of)*; *(an Fehler, Unglück etc)* blameless, free from blame; **s~los**

geschieden sein to be the innocent party in a/the divorce; ~**losigkeit** f siehe adj innocence; blamelessness.

Schuldner(in f) m - debtor.

Schuld-: ~**prinzip** nt (Jur) principle of the guilty party; ~**schein** m IOU, promissory note; ~**spruch** m verdict of guilty.

Schule f -n school. **in die** ~ **kommen/gehen** to start school/go to school; **in der** ~ at school; **die** ~ **wechseln** to change schools; **von der** ~ **abgehen** to leave school; **durch eine harte** ~ **gegangen sein** (fig) to have learned in a hard school; ~ **machen** to become the accepted thing; **aus der** ~ **plaudern** to tell tales out of school (col).

schulen vt to train.

Schüler(in f) m - schoolboy/schoolgirl; (einer bestimmten Schule) pupil; (Jünger) follower, disciple. **als** ~ **habe ich ...** when I was at school I ...; **alle** ~ **und** ~**innen dieser Stadt** all the schoolchildren of this town.

Schüler-: ~**austausch** m school or student exchange; ~**ausweis** m (school) student card; ~**lotse** m pupil acting as a road-crossing warden; ~**mitverwaltung** f school or student council; ~**schaft** f pupils pl.

Schul-: ~**fach** nt school subject; ~**ferien** pl school holidays pl (Brit) or vacation; ~**fernsehen** nt schools' or educational television; ~**fest** nt school function; **s~frei** adj **die Kinder haben morgen s~frei** the children don't have to go to school tomorrow; ~**funk** m schools' broadcast; ~**gebäude** nt school building; ~**gelände** nt school grounds pl; ~**geld** nt school fees pl; ~**heft** nt exercise book; ~**hof** m school playground (Brit), schoolyard.

schulisch adj Leistungen, Probleme at school; Angelegenheiten school attr. **aus** ~**er Sicht** from the school angle.

Schul-: ~**jahr** nt school year; (Klasse) year; **ihre** ~**jahre** her schooldays; ~**junge** m schoolboy; ~**kamerad** m schoolmate, schoolfriend; ~**kenntnisse** pl knowledge sing acquired at school; ~**klasse** f (school) class; ~**leiter** m head teacher, headmaster (esp Brit), principal; ~**leiterin** f head teacher, headmistress (esp Brit), principal; ~**mädchen** nt schoolgirl; ~**medizin** f orthodox medicine; ~**meinung** f received opinion; ~**meister** m (old, hum, pej) schoolmaster; **s~meisterlich** adj (pej) schoolmasterish; **s~meistern** insep 1 vt to lecture (at or to); 2 vi to lecture; ~**ordnung** f school rules pl; ~**pflicht** f compulsory school attendance no art; **es besteht** ~**pflicht** school attendance is compulsory; **s~pflichtig** adj Kind required to attend school; ~**politik** f education policy; ~**reife** f **die** ~**reife haben** to be ready to go to school; ~**schiff** nt training ship; ~**schluß** m end of school; ~**schluß ist um 13¹⁰** school finishes at 13.10; ~**sprecher(in** f) m head boy/girl (Brit); ~**stunde** f (school) period or lesson; ~**tag** m schoolday; **der erste** ~**tag** the/one's first day at school.

Schulter f -n shoulder. **breite** ~**n haben** (lit) to be broad-shouldered, to have broad shoulders; (fig) to have a broad back; **er ließ die** ~**n hängen** he was slouching; (niedergeschlagen) he hung his head; **jdm auf die** ~ **klopfen** to give sb a slap on the back; (lobend) to pat sb on the back; **die** or **mit den** ~**n zucken** to shrug one's shoulders; **etw auf die leichte** ~ **nehmen** to take sth lightly.

Schulter-: ~**blatt** nt shoulder blade; ~**höhe** f shoulder height; **in** ~**höhe** at shoulder level or height; ~**klappe** f (Mil) epaulette; **s~lang** adj shoulder-length.

schultern vt to shoulder.

Schulter-: ~**riemen** m shoulder strap; ~**stück** nt (a) (Mil) epaulette; (b) (Cook) piece of shoulder.

Schultüte f large conical bag of sweets/candy given to children on their first day at school.

Schulung f (Ausbildung) training; (Pol) political instruction.

Schul-: ~**unterricht** m school lessons pl; ~**weg** m way to/from school; (Entfernung) distance to/from school; ~**weisheit** f (pej) booklearning; ~**wesen** nt school system; ~**zeit** f (~jahre) schooldays pl; **nach 13jähriger** ~**zeit** after 13 years at school; ~**zeugnis** nt school report.

schummeln vi (col) to cheat (bei etw at sth).

schumm(e)rig adj Beleuchtung dim; Raum dimly-lit. **bei** ~**em Licht** in the half-light.

Schund m no pl (pej) trash, rubbish.

Schundroman m trashy novel.

schunkeln vi to link arms and sway from side to side in time to the music.

Schupo m -s (dated col) = **Schutzpolizist** cop (col), copper (Brit col).

Schuppe f -n (a) (Bot, Zool) scale. **es fiel mir wie** ~**n von den Augen** my eyes were opened, all was clear. **(b)** (Kopf~) ~**n** pl dandruff sing.

Schuppen m - **(a)** shed. **(b)** (col) (Haus etc) hole (pej col); (übles Lokal) dive (col).

schuppen 1 vt Fische to scale. 2 vr to flake.

Schuppen-: **s~artig** adj scale-like; ~**flechte** f (Med) psoriasis (spec).

schuppig adj scaly; (abblätternd auch) flaking.

Schur f -en (das Scheren) shearing.

schüren vt **(a)** Feuer, Glut to rake, to poke. **(b)** (fig) to stir up; Zorn etc to fan the flames of.

schürfen 1 vi (Min) to prospect (nach for). **tief** ~ (fig) to dig deep. 2 vt Bodenschätze to mine. 3 vtr to graze oneself. **sich am Knie** ~ to graze one's knee.

Schürf-: ~**recht** nt mining rights pl; ~**wunde** f graze, abrasion.

Schürhaken m poker.

Schurke m (wk) -n, -n (dated) villain, scoundrel.

Schurwolle f virgin wool. „**reine** ~" "pure new wool".

Schurz m -e apron; (Lenden~) loincloth.

Schürze f -n apron.

Schürzen-: ~**jäger** m (col) philanderer, one for the girls (col); ~**zipfel** m apron-string; **er hängt der Mutter noch am** ~**zipfel** he's still tied to his mother's apron strings.

Schuß m ⁼sse (a) shot; (~ Munition) round. **sechs** ~ or **Schüsse** six shots/rounds; (lit) **ein** ~ **ins Schwarze** (lit, fig) a bull's-eye; **weit vom** ~ **sein** (fig col) to be miles from where the action is (col); **er ist keinen** ~ **Pulver wert** (fig) he is not worth tuppence (Brit col) or a red cent (US col); **das war ein** ~ **vor den Bug** (fig) that was a warning shot across the bows; **ein** ~ **in den Ofen** (col) a complete waste of time. **(b)** (Ftbl) kick; (zum Tor auch) shot. **(c)** (Spritzer) (von Wein, Essig etc) dash; (von Whisky) shot; (von Humor etc auch) touch. **2** (col) **(gut)** **in** ~ **sein** to be in good shape or nick (col); (Mensch) to be on form; **etw in** ~ **halten** to keep sth in good shape.

Schuß-: ~**bereich** m (firing) range; **im** ~ **bereich** within range; **s~bereit** adj ready to fire; Gewehr auch cocked.

Schussel m - (col) dolt (col); (zerstreut) scatterbrain (col).

Schüssel f -n bowl; (Servier~ auch) dish; (Wasch~) basin.

schusselig adj (col) daft; (zerstreut) scatterbrained (col), muddle-headed (col).

Schuß-: ~**fahrt** f (Ski) schuss; (das ~fahren) schussing; ~**feld** nt field of fire; (Übungsplatz) firing range; **s~fest** adj bulletproof; ~**linie** f line of fire; (fig auch) firing line; ~**verletzung** f bullet wound; ~**waffe** f firearm; ~**waffengebrauch** m (form) use of firearms; ~**wechsel** m exchange of shots or fire; ~**weite** f range (of fire); **in/außer** ~**weite** within/out of range; ~**wunde** f bullet wound.

Schuster m - shoemaker. **auf ~s Rappen** (hum) by Shanks's pony; **~, bleib bei deinem Leisten!** (Prov) cobbler, stick to your last (Prov).

Schutt m no pl (Trümmer, Bau~) rubble; (Geol) debris, detritus (spec). **„~abladen verboten"** "no tipping"; **in ~ und Asche liegen** to be in ruins.

Schutt|abladeplatz m tip, dump.

Schüttelfrost m (Med) shivering fit.

schütteln 1 vt to shake; (rütteln) to shake about, to jolt (about). **den** or **mit dem Kopf ~** to shake one's head; **von Fieber geschüttelt werden** to be racked with fever. **2** vr to shake oneself; (vor Kälte) to shiver (vor with); (vor Ekel) to shudder (vor with, in). **sich vor Lachen ~** to shake with laughter.

schütten 1 vt to tip; Flüssigkeiten to pour; (ver~) to spill. **2** vi impers (col) **es schüttet** it's pouring (with rain), it's bucketing (down) (col).

schütter adj Haar thin.

Schutt-: ~haufen m pile or heap of rubble; **~platz** m tip.

Schutz m no pl protection (vor +dat, gegen against, from); (Zuflucht auch) shelter, refuge (vor +dat, gegen from); (der Natur, Umwelt etc) conservation; (esp Mil: Deckung) cover. **bei jdm ~ suchen** to look to sb for protection; **to seek refuge with sb; im ~ der Dunkelheit** under cover of darkness; **zum ~ der Augen** to protect the eyes; **jdn in ~ nehmen** (fig) to take sb's part.

Schutz-: ~anstrich m protective coat; **~anzug** m protective clothing no indef art, no pl; **s~bedürftig** adj in need of protection; **~behauptung** f lie to cover oneself; **~blech** nt mudguard; **~brief** m (Insur) (international) motoring cover; **~brille** f protective goggles pl; **~dach** nt porch; (an Haltestelle) shelter.

Schütze m (wk) **-n, -n (a)** marksman; (Schießsportler) rifleman; (Bogen~) archer; (Ftbl: Tor~) scorer. **(b)** (Astrol) Sagittarius no art. **sie ist ~** she's Sagittarius or a Sagittarian.

schützen 1 vt to protect (vor +dat, gegen from, against); (esp Mil: Deckung geben) to cover. **gesetzlich geschützt/urheberrechtlich geschützt** registered/protected by copyright; **ein geschützter Platz** a sheltered spot or place; **vor Sonnenlicht ~!** keep away from sunlight; **vor Nässe ~!** keep dry. **2** vi to give or offer protection (vor +dat, gegen against, from); (esp Mil: Deckung geben) to give cover. **3** vr to protect oneself (vor +dat, gegen from, against).

schützend adj protective. **ein ~es Dach** (gegen Wetter) a shelter.

Schützenfest nt fair featuring shooting matches.

Schutz|engel m guardian angel.

Schützen-: ~graben m trench; **~hilfe** f (fig) support; **jdm ~hilfe geben** to back sb up; **~loch** nt (Mil) foxhole; **~panzer** m armoured (Brit) or armoured (US) personnel carrier; **~verein** m rifle or shooting club.

Schutz-: ~farbe f (Biol) protective or adaptive colouring (Brit) or coloring (US); **~gebiet** nt (Pol) protectorate; **~gebühr** f (token) fee; **~haft** f (Jur) protective custody; **~haut** f protective covering; **~heilige(r)** mf patron saint; **~helm** m safety helmet; **~herrschaft** f (Pol) protection, protectorate; **~hülle** f protective cover; (Buchumschlag) dust cover or jacket; **s~impfen** ptp **s~geimpft** vt to vaccinate, to inoculate; **~impfung** f vaccination, inoculation; **~kleidung** f protective clothing.

Schützling m protégé; (esp Kind) charge.

Schutz-: s~los adj (wehrlos) defenceless (Brit), defenseless (US); (gegen Kälte etc) unprotected; **~macht** f (Pol) protecting power, protector; **~mann**, m, pl **~leute** (dated) policeman, constable (Brit); **~marke** f trademark; **~maßnahme** f precautionary measure; (~vorbeugend) pre-

ventive measure; **~schicht** f protective layer; (Überzug) protective coating; **~schild** m shield; (an Geschützen) gun shield; **~schirm** m (Tech) protective screen; **s~suchend** adj seeking protection; (nach Obdach) seeking refuge or shelter; **~umschlag** m dust cover or jacket; **~verband** m (Med) protective bandage or dressing; **~zoll** m protective duty or tariff.

schwabbelig adj (col) Körperteil flabby; Gelee wobbly.

schwabbeln vi (col) to wobble (about).

Schwabe m (wk) **-n, -n, Schwäbin** f Swabian.

Schwaben nt Swabia.

schwäbisch adj Swabian.

schwach adj comp **-er**, superl **-ste(r, s)** or (adv) **am -sten** weak (auch Gram); Gesundheit, Beteiligung, Gedächtnis poor; Ton, Anzeichen, Hoffnung faint, slight; Gehör poor, dull; Licht poor, dim; Wind light; (Comm) Nachfrage, Geschäft slack, poor. **~e Augen** weak or poor (eye)sight; **das ist ein ~es Bild** (col) or **eine ~e Leistung** (col) that's a poor show (col); **trotz des ~en Erfolges des** Buchs in spite of the book's lack of success; **jds ~e Seite** sb's weak point; **ein ~er Trost** cold or small comfort; **mach mich nicht ~!** (col) don't say that! (col); **auf ~en Beinen** or **Füßen stehen** (fig) to be on shaky ground; (Theorie) to be shaky; **~er werden** to grow weaker, to weaken; (Augen) to fail, to grow worse; (Stimme) to grow fainter; (Licht) to (grow) dim; (Ton) to fade; (Nachfrage) to fall off, to slacken; **~ besiedelt** or **bevölkert** sparsely populated; **~ besucht** poorly attended; **die S~en** the weak.

Schwäche f **-n** weakness; (von Gesundheit) poorness; (von Licht) dimness; (von Nachfrage) slackness. **eine ~ überkam** sie a feeling of weakness came over her; **menschliche ~n** human failings or frailties; **eine ~ für etw haben** to have a weakness for sth.

schwächen vt (lit, fig) to weaken.

Schwachheit f no pl (fig) weakness, frailty.

Schwachkopf m (col) dimwit (col), idiot.

schwächlich adj weakly; (zart auch) puny.

Schwächling m weakling.

Schwach-: s~sichtig adj (Med) poor- or weaksighted; **~sichtigkeit** f (Med) dimness of vision; **~sinn** m (Med) mental deficiency; (fig col) (unsinnige Tat) idiocy no indef art; (Quatsch) rubbish (col); **s~sinnig** adj (Med) mentally deficient; (fig col) daft (col), idiotic; **~sinnige(r)** mf decl as adj mental defective; (fig col) moron (col), imbecile (col); **~stelle** f weak point; **~strom** m (Elec) low-voltage or weak current.

Schwachung f weakening.

Schwaden m - usu pl cloud.

Schwadron f **-en** (Mil Hist) squadron.

schwadronieren* vi to bluster.

Schwafelei f (pej col) drivel no pl (col), twaddle no pl (col).

schwafeln (pej col) **1** vi to drivel (on) (col); (in einer Prüfung) to waffle (col). **2** vt **dummes Zeug ~** to talk drivel (col).

Schwager m - brother-in-law.

Schwägerin f sister-in-law.

Schwalbe f **-n** swallow. **eine ~ macht noch keinen Sommer** (Prov) one swallow doesn't make a summer (Prov).

Schwall m **-e** flood, torrent.

schwamm pret of **schwimmen**.

Schwamm m **-e (a)** sponge. **etw mit dem ~ abwischen** to sponge sth (down); **~ drüber!** (col) (let's) forget it! **(b)** (Haus~) dry rot.

schwammig adj (a) (lit) spongy. **(b)** (fig) Gesicht puffy, bloated; (vage) Begriff woolly.

Schwan m **-e** swan. **mein lieber ~!** (col) (überrascht) my goodness!; (drohend) my lad/girl.

schwand pret of **schwinden**.

schwanen vi impers **ihm schwante etwas** he

sensed something might happen; **mir schwant nichts Gutes** I've a feeling something nasty is going to happen.

Schwanen-: ~**gesang** m (fig) swansong; ~**hals** m swan's neck; (fig) swanlike neck; (Tech) gooseneck, swan-neck.

schwang pret of **schwingen.**

schwanger adj pregnant.

Schwangere f decl as adj pregnant woman.

schwängern vt to make pregnant, to impregnate (form). **mit etw geschwängert sein** (fig) to be impregnated with sth.

Schwangerschaft f pregnancy.

Schwangerschaftsabbruch m termination of pregnancy, abortion.

Schwank m ⁼e (Liter) merry or comical tale; (Theat) farce.

schwanken vi (a) (wanken, sich wiegen) to sway; (Schiff) (auf und ab) to pitch; (seitwärts) to roll; (beben) to rock. (b) aux sein (gehen) to stagger, to totter. (c) (variieren) to vary; (Preise, Stimmung etc auch) to fluctuate; (Kompaßnadel etc) to swing. (d) (unschlüssig sein) to waver; (zögern) to hesitate. (e) **ins S**~ **kommen** (Baum, Gebäude etc) to start to sway; (Preise, Kurs etc) to start to fluctuate or vary; (Überzeugung etc) to begin to waver.

schwankend adj (a) siehe vi (a) swaying; pitching; rolling; rocking. (b) Mensch staggering; Gang rolling; Schritt unsteady. (c) siehe vi (c) varying; fluctuating esp attr; oscillating; Kurs, Gesundheit auch unstable. (d) (unschlüssig) uncertain, wavering attr; (zögernd) hesitant. ~ **werden** to waver.

Schwankung f (a) (hin und her) swaying no pl; (auf und ab) shaking no pl, rocking no pl. **um die** ~**en des Turms zu messen** to measure the extent to which the tower sways. (b) siehe vi (c) variation (gen in); fluctuation.

Schwanz m ⁼e (a) (lit, fig) tail. **den** ~ **hängen lassen** (lit) to let its tail droop; (fig col) to be down in the dumps (col); **kein** ~ (col) not a (blessed) soul (col). (b) (col!!: Penis) prick (col!!).

schwänzen (col) **1** vt Stunde, Vorlesung to skip (col), to cut (col); Schule to play truant or hooky (esp US col) from, to skive off (Brit col). **2** vi to play truant, to play hooky (esp US col), to skive (Brit col).

Schwanz-: ~**feder** f tail feather; ~**flosse** f (auch Aviat) tail fin; **s**~**los** adj tailless.

schwappen vi (a) (Wasser) to slosh around. (b) aux sein (über~) to splash, to slosh.

Schwarm m ⁼e (a) swarm; (Flugzeugformation) flight. (b) (col: Angebeteter) idol. **der neue Englischlehrer ist ihr** ~ she's got a crush on the new English teacher (col).

schwärmen vi (a) aux sein to swarm. (b) (begeistert reden) to enthuse (von about), to go into raptures (von about). **für jdn/etw** ~ to be mad or crazy about sb/sth (col); **ins S**~ **kommen** or **geraten** to go into raptures.

Schwärmer m - (Begeisterter) enthusiast, zealot; (Phantast) dreamer, visionary; (sentimentaler ~) sentimentalist.

Schwärmerei f (Begeisterung) enthusiasm; (in Worten ausgedrückt) effusion no pl; (Verzückung) rapture.

schwärmerisch adj (begeistert) enthusiastic; Worte, Übertreibung effusive; (verliebt) infatuated; (verzückt) enraptured.

Schwarte f -n (a) (Speck~) rind. (b) (col: Buch) old book, tome (hum).

Schwartenmagen m (Cook) brawn.

schwarz adj comp ⁼er, superl ⁼este(r, s) or (adv) **am** ⁼**esten** (a) (lit, fig) black. **das S**~**e Brett** the notice-board (Brit), the bulletin board (US); ~**er** Humor black humour (Brit) or humor (US); ~**er** Kaffee/Tee black coffee/tea; **die S**~**e Kunst**

(Buchdruckerkunst) (the art of) printing; (Magie) the Black Art; ~**e Liste** blacklist; **jdn auf die** ~**e Liste setzen** to blacklist sb, to put sb on the blacklist; **das S**~**e Meer** the Black Sea; **S**~**er** Peter (Cards) children's card game; **jdm den S**~**en** Peter **zuschieben** (fig: die Verantwortung abschieben) to pass the buck to sb (col); **ein** ~**er Tag** a black day; **etw** ~ **auf weiß haben** to have sth in black and white; ~ **wie die Nacht/wie** Ebenholz jet-black; **in den** ~**en Zahlen** in the black; **sich** ~ **ärgern** to get extremely annoyed; **er wurde** ~ **vor Ärger** his face went black; **mit wurde** ~ **vor den Augen** I blacked out; **da kannst du schreien, bis du** ~ **wirst** (col) you can shout until you're blue in the face (col); **ins S**~**e treffen** (lit, fig) to score a bull's-eye.

(b) (col: ungesetzlich) illicit. **der** ~**e Markt** the black market; **sich** (dat) **etw** ~ **besorgen** to get sth illicitly/on the black market; ~ **über die Grenze gehen** to cross the border illegally.

(c) (col: katholisch) Catholic, Papist (pej); (Pol col: konservativ) conservative. **dort wählen alle** ~ they all vote conservative there.

Schwarz-: ~**afrika** nt Black Africa; ~**arbeit** f illicit work; (nach Feierabend) moonlighting (col); **s**~**arbeiten** vi sep to do illicit work; to moonlight (col); ~**arbeiter** m person doing illicit work; moonlighter (col); **s**~**braun** adj dark brown; ~**brenner** m illicit distiller, moonshine distiller (col); ~**brennerei** f illicit still, moonshine still (col); ~**brot** nt (braun) brown rye bread; (Pumpernickel) black bread, pumpernickel; ~**drossel** f blackbird.

Schwarze f (wk) -n, -n (Negerin) black woman; (Schwarzhaarige) brunette.

Schwärze f no pl (Dunkelheit) blackness.

schwärzen vtr to blacken.

Schwarze(r) m decl as adj (Neger) black; (Schwarzhaariger) dark man/boy; (col: Katholik) Catholic, Papist (pej). **die** ~**n** (Pol col) the Conservatives.

Schwarz-: **s**~**fahren** vi sep irreg aux sein (ohne zu zahlen) to travel without paying, to dodge paying the fare (col); ~**fahrer** m fare-dodger (col); **s**~**haarig** adj black-haired; **eine** ~**haarige** a brunette; ~**handel** m no pl black market; (Tätigkeit) black-marketeering; **im** ~**handel** on the black market; ~**händler** m black marketeer; **s**~**hören** vi sep (Rad) to use a radio without having a licence (Brit) or license (US); ~**hörer** m (Rad) radio-owner without a licence (Brit) or license (US); **s**~**malen** sep **1** vi to be pessimistic; **2** vt to be pessimistic about; ~**maler** m pessimist; ~**malerei** f pessimism; ~**markt** m black-market; ~**marktpreis** m black-market price; **s**~**sehen** sep irreg **1** vt to be pessimistic about; **2** vi (a) to be pessimistic; **für jdn/etw s**~**sehen** to be pessimistic about sb/sth; (b) (TV) to watch TV without a licence (Brit) or license (US); ~**seher** m (a) pessimist; (b) (TV) (TV) licence-dodger (Brit) or license-dodger (US) (col); ~**seherei** f pessimism; ~**sender** m pirate (radio) station; ~**wald** m Black Forest; ~**wälder** adj attr Black Forest; ~**wälder** Kirschtorte Black Forest gateau.

schwarzweiß adj black and white.

Schwarzweiß-: ~**aufnahme** f black and white (shot); ~**fernseher** m black and white or monochrome television (set); ~**film** m black and white film; ~**foto** nt black and white (photo).

Schwarz-: ~**wild** nt wild boars pl; ~**wurzel** f (Cook) salsify.

Schwatz m -e (col) chat, chinwag (col). **auf einen** ~ **kommen** to come for a chat.

schwatzen, schwätzen vti to talk; (pej: unaufhörlich) to chatter; (über belanglose Dinge) to prattle; (Unsinn reden) to blather (col); (klatschen) to gossip. **dummes Zeug** ~ to talk a lot of rubbish (col).

Schwätzer(in *f) m* - *(pej)* chatterer; *(Kind, Schüler)* chatterbox; *(Schwafler)* wind-bag *(col); (Klatschmaul)* gossip.

Schwätzerei *f (pej) (Gerede, im Unterricht)* talk, chatter; *(über Belanglosigkeiten, kindisch)* prattle; *(Unsinn)* drivel *(col); (Klatsch)* gossip.

schwatzhaft *adj* talkative, garrulous; *(klatschsüchtig)* gossipy.

Schwebe *f no pl* **in der ~ sein** *(fig)* to be in the balance; *(Jur, Comm)* to be pending.

Schwebe-: ~**bahn** *f* suspension railway *(Brit)* or railroad *(US);* ~**balken** *m (Sport)* beam.

schweben *vi* **(a)** to hang; *(in der Luft auch)* to float; *(Vogel etc)* to hover. **ihr war, als ob sie schwebte** she felt as if she was walking or floating on air; **etw schwebt jdm vor Augen** *(fig)* sb has sth in mind; *(Bild)* sb sees sth in his mind's eye. **(b)** *aux sein (durch die Luft gleiten)* to float, to sail; *(sich leichtfüßig bewegen)* to glide, to float. **(c)** *(schwanken)* to hover, to waver; *(Angelegenheit)* to hang or be in the balance. ~**des Verfahren** *(Jur)* pending case.

Schwebezustand *m (fig)* state of suspense; *(zwischen zwei Stadien)* in-between state.

Schwede *m (wk)* **-n, -n, Schwedin** *f* Swede.

Schweden *nt* Sweden.

schwedisch *adj* Swedish. **hinter ~en Gardinen** *(col)* behind bars.

Schwedisch(e) *nt decl as adj* Swedish; *siehe* **Deutsch(e).**

Schwefel *m no pl* sulphur *(Brit)*, sulfur *(US).*

Schwefel- *in cpds* sulphur *(Brit)*, sulfur *(US);* **s~haltig** *adj* containing sulphur *(Brit)* or sulfur *(US);* ~**säure** *f* suphuric *(Brit)* or sulfuric *(US)* acid.

schweflig *adj* sulphurous *(Brit)*, sulfurous *(US).*

Schweif *m* **-e** *(auch Astron)* tail.

schweifen *vi aux sein (lit geh, fig)* to roam. **warum in die Ferne ~ ...?** why roam so far afield ...?

Schweige-: ~**geld** *nt* hush-money; ~**marsch** *m* silent march (of protest); ~**minute** *f* one minute('s) silence.

schweigen *pret* **schwieg,** *ptp* **geschwiegen** *vi* to be silent; *(still sein auch)* to keep quiet. **~ Sie!** be silent or quiet!; **kannst du ~?** can you keep a secret?; **seit gestern ~ die Waffen** yesterday the guns fell silent; **plötzlich schweig er** suddenly he fell or went silent; **zu etw ~** to make no reply to sth; **ganz zu ~ von ...** to say nothing of ...

Schweigen *nt no pl* silence. **jdn zum ~ bringen** to silence sb *(auch euph).*

schweigend *adj* silent. **die ~e Mehrheit** the silent majority; **~ über etw** *(acc)* **hinweggehen** to pass over sth in silence.

Schweigepflicht *f* pledge of secrecy; *(von Anwalt)* requirement of confidentiality. **die ärztliche ~** medical confidentiality or secrecy; **unter ~ stehen** to be bound to observe confidentiality.

schweigsam *adj* silent; *(als Charaktereigenschaft)* reticent; *(verschwiegen)* discreet.

Schweigsamkeit *f siehe adj* silence; reticence; discretion.

Schwein *nt* **-e (a)** pig, hog *(US).* **sich wie die ~e benehmen** *(col)* to behave like pigs *(col).* **(b)** *(col: Mensch)* pig *(col); (gemein)* swine *(col)*, bastard *(col!)*. **ein armes/faules ~** a poor/lazy sod *(col); **kein ~** nobody, not one single person. **(c)** *no pl (col: Glück)* ~ **haben** to be lucky.

Schweinchen *nt dim of* **Schwein** little pig; *(fig col: Schmutzfink)* mucky pup *(col).*

Schweine-: ~**bauch** *m (Cook)* belly of pork; ~**braten** *m* joint of pork; *(gekocht)* roast pork; ~**filet** *nt* fillet of pork; ~**fleisch** *nt* pork; ~**geld** *nt (col)* **ein ~geld** a packet *(col);* ~**hund** *m (pej col)* bastard *(col!)*, swine *(col);* **den inneren ~hund überwinden** *(col)* to conquer one's weaker self; ~**kotelett** *nt* pork chop.

Schweinerei *f (col)* **(a)** *no pl* mess. **es ist eine ~, wenn ...** it's disgusting if ...; **so eine ~!** how disgusting! **(b)** *(Gemeinheit)* dirty or mean trick *(col); (Zote)* smutty or dirty joke; *(unzüchtige Handlung)* indecent act. **~en machen** to do dirty or filthy things; **das Buch besteht nur aus ~en** the book is just a lot of dirt or filth.

Schweine-: ~**schmalz** *nt* dripping; *(als Kochfett)* lard; ~**schnitzel** *nt* pork cutlet; ~**stall** *m (lit, fig)* pigsty, pig pen *(esp US).*

Schwein|igel *m (col)* dirty pig *(col).*

schweinisch *adj (col) Benehmen* piggish *(col)*, swinish *(col); Witz* dirty.

Schweinkram *m (col)* dirt, filth.

Schweins-: ~**galopp** *m:* **im ~galopp davonlaufen** *(hum col)* to go galumphing off *(col);* ~**haxe** *f (Cook)* knuckle of pork; ~**leder** *nt* pigskin; **s~ledern** *adj* pigskin; ~**ohr** *nt* pig's ear; *(Gebäck)* *(kidney-shaped)* pastry.

Schweiß *m no pl* sweat; *(von Mensch auch)* perspiration. **in ~ geraten** or **kommen** to break into a sweat; **der ~ brach ihm aus** he broke out in a sweat; **das hat viel ~ gekostet** it was a sweat *(col);* **im ~e seines Angesichts** *(Bibl, liter)* in the sweat of his brow *(Bibl, liter).*

Schweiß-: ~**ausbruch** *m* sweating *no indef art, no pl;* ~**band** *nt* sweatband; **s~bedeckt** *adj* covered in sweat; ~**brenner** *m (Tech)* welding torch; ~**drüse** *f (Anat)* sweat gland.

schweißen *vti (Tech)* to weld.

Schweißer(in *f) m* - *(Tech)* welder.

Schweiß-: ~**fuß** *m* sweaty foot; **s~gebadet** *adj* bathed in sweat; ~**naht** *f (Tech)* weld, welded joint; **s~naß** *adj* sweaty; ~**perle** *f* bead of perspiration or sweat; ~**stelle** *f* weld; **s~triefend** *adj* dripping with perspiration or sweat; ~**tropfen** *m* drop of sweat or perspiration.

Schweiz *f* **die ~** Switzerland.

Schweizer *adj attr* Swiss.

Schweizer(in *f) m* - Swiss.

Schweizer-: ~**deutsch** *nt* Swiss German; ~**garde** *f* Swiss Guard.

schweizerisch *adj* Swiss.

Schwelbrand *m* smouldering *(Brit)* or smoldering *(US)* fire.

schwelen *vi* to smoulder *(Brit)*, to smolder *(US).*

schwelgen *vi* to indulge oneself *(in +dat in).* **wir schwelgten in Kaviar und Sekt** we feasted on caviar and champagne; **in Farben/Worten ~** to revel in colour/in the sound of words; **in Gefühlen ~** to revel in one's emotions; **in Erinnerungen ~** to indulge in reminiscences.

Schwelle *f* **-n** *(Tür~, fig, Psych)* threshold. **an der ~ einer neuen Zeit** on the threshold of a new era; **an der ~ des Todes** at death's door.

schwellen 1 *vi pret* **schwoll,** *ptp* **geschwollen** *aux sein* to swell. **der Wind schwoll zum Sturm** the wind grew into a storm; *siehe* **geschwollen. 2** *vt (geh) Segel, Brust* to swell.

Schwellen|angst *f (Psych)* fear of entering a place.

Schwemme *f* **-n (a)** *(für Tiere)* watering place. **(b)** *(Überfluß)* glut *(an +dat of).*

schwemmen *vt (treiben) Sand etc* to wash.

Schwengel *m* - *(Glocken~)* clapper; *(Pumpen~)* handle.

Schwenk *m* **-s** *(Drehung)* wheel; *(Film)* pan, panning shot. **einen ~ machen** *(Kolonne)* to swing or wheel around.

Schwenk-: ~**arm** *m* swivel arm; **s~bar** *adj* swivelling; *Geschütz* traversable.

schwenken 1 *vt (schwingen)* to wave; *Lampe etc* to swivel; *Kran, Geschütz* to swing; *Kamera* to pan; *Kartoffeln* to toss; *Tanzpartnerin* to swing around, to spin (around). **2** *vi aux sein* to swing; *(Kolonne)* to wheel; *(Kamera)* to pan; *(fig)* to swing over, to switch. **links schwenkt!** *(Mil)* left wheel!

Schwenker *m* - *(Kognak~)* balloon glass.

Schwenkung f swing; (Mil) wheel; (von Geschütz) traverse; (von Kamera) pan(ning).

schwer 1 adj (a) (lit, fig) heavy. **ein 10 kg ~er Sack** a sack weighing 10 kgs or 10kgs in weight; **~ beladen/bewaffnet sein** to be heavily laden/armed.

(b) (ernst) Sorge, Unrecht, Unfall, Verlust, Krankheit serious, grave; Fehler, Enttäuschung auch big; Strafe severe. **~ erkältet sein** to have a heavy cold; **~ geprüft sein** to be sorely tried; **~ verletzt/krank sein** to be seriously wounded/ill; **~ verunglücken** to have a serious accident; **~ betroffen sein** to be hard hit.

(c) (hart, anstrengend) Arbeit, Tag, Schicksal hard; Frage, Entscheidung auch difficult, tough. **es ~ haben** to have a hard time (of it); **~ schuften müssen** to have to work hard; **er lernt ~** he's a slow learner; **~ hören** to be hard of hearing; **~ zu sehen/sagen** hard or difficult to see/say; **sich ~ entschließen können** to find it hard or difficult to decide.

(d) (col) **~es Geld machen** to make a packet (col); **ein ~er Junge** a (big-time) crook.

2 adv (col: sehr) really; gekränkt, verletzt deeply. **da mußte ich ~ aufpassen** I really had to watch out; **~ betrunken** rolling drunk (col); **~ verdienen** to earn a packet (col); **~ im Irrtum sein** to be badly or seriously mistaken; **er ist ~ in Ordnung** he's a good bloke (Brit col) or guy (col).

Schwer-: ~**arbeit** f heavy labour (Brit) or labor (US); ~**arbeiter** m labourer (Brit), laborer (US); ~**athlet** m weight-lifter; boxer; wrestler; ~**athletik** f weight-lifting sports, boxing, wrestling etc; **s~beladen** adj attr heavily-laden; **s~bepackt** adj attr heavily-loaded or -laden; **s~beschädigt** adj attr (seriously) disabled; ~**beschädigte(r)** mf disabled person; **s~bewaffnet** adj attr heavily armed.

Schwere f no pl siehe adj (a) heaviness. (b) seriousness, gravity; severity. (c) hardness; difficulty.

Schwere-: **s~los** adj weightless; ~**losigkeit** f weightlessness.

schwer|erziehbar adj attr maladjusted.

schwerfallen vi sep irreg aux sein to be difficult or hard (jdm for sb).

schwerfällig adj Gang clumsy, awkward; Verstand slow; Stil ponderous.

Schwerfälligkeit f siehe adj clumsiness, awkwardness; slowness; ponderousness.

Schwer-: ~**gewicht** nt (a) (Sport, fig) heavyweight; (b) (Nachdruck) emphasis; **das ~gewicht auf etw (acc) legen** to put the emphasis on sth; **s~gewichtig** adj heavyweight; ~**gewichtler(in** f) m - (Sport) heavyweight; **s~hörig** adj hard of hearing; ~**hörigkeit** f hardness of hearing; ~**industrie** f heavy industry; ~**kraft** f gravity; **s~krank** adj attr seriously or critically ill; ~**kranke(r)** mf seriously or critically ill patient; **s~lich** adv hardly, scarcely; **s~machen** vt sep es jdm/jdm das Leben **s~machen** to make it/life difficult for sb; ~**metall** nt heavy metal; ~**mut** f no pl melancholy; **s~mütig** adj melancholy; **s~nehmen** vt sep irreg etw **s~nehmen** to take sth hard.

Schwerpunkt m (Phys) centre (Brit) or center (US) of gravity; (fig) (Zentrum) centre (Brit), center (US), main focus; (Hauptgewicht) main emphasis. **den ~ auf etw (acc) legen** to put the main emphasis or stress on sth.

Schwerpunkt-: ~**streik** m pinpoint strike; ~**verlagerung** f shift of emphasis.

schwerreich adj attr (col) stinking rich (col).

Schwert nt -er sword. **das ~ ziehen** to draw one's sword.

Schwert-: ~**fisch** m swordfish; ~**hieb** m sword stroke; ~**lilie** f (Bot) iris.

schwertun vr sep irreg (col) sich (dat) mit etw ~ to make heavy weather of sth (col).

Schwertwal m killer whale.

Schwer-: ~**verbrecher** m criminal, felon (esp Jur); **s~verdaulich** adj attr Speisen indigestible; (fig auch) difficult; **s~verdient** adj attr Geld hard-earned; **s~verletzt** adj attr seriously injured; ~**verletzte(r)** mf serious casualty; (bei Unfall etc auch) seriously injured person; **s~verständlich** adj attr difficult to understand, incomprehensible; **s~wiegend** adj (fig) serious.

Schwester f -n sister; (Kranken~) nurse; (Stations~) sister; (Ordens~) nun, sister; (Gemeinde~) district nurse.

Schwester- in cpds sister; ~**firma** f sister or associate(d) company; ~**lich** adj sisterly.

Schwestern-: ~**heim** nt nurses' home; ~**helferin** f nursing auxiliary (Brit) or assistant (US).

schwieg pret of schweigen.

Schwieger-: ~**eltern** pl parents-in-law pl; ~**mutter** f mother-in-law; ~**sohn** m son-in-law; ~**tochter** f daughter-in-law; ~**vater** m father-in-law.

Schwiele f -n callus; (Vernarbung) welt.

schwielig adj Hände callused.

schwierig adj difficult; (schwer zu lernen etc auch) hard.

Schwierigkeit f difficulty. **in ~en geraten** to get into difficulties or trouble; **jdm ~en machen** to make difficulties or trouble for sb; **es macht mir überhaupt keine ~en** it won't be at all difficult for me; **mach keine ~en!** (col) don't be difficult, don't make any trouble; **ohne ~en** without any difficulty.

Schwierigkeitsgrad m degree of difficulty.

Schwimm-: ~**bad** nt swimming pool; (Hallenbad auch) swimming baths pl (Brit); ~**becken** nt (swimming) pool.

schwimmen pret **schwamm**, ptp **geschwommen** aux sein/haben vi (a) auch aux haben to swim. **~ gehen** to go swimming or for a swim. (b) (auf dem Wasser treiben) to float. (c) (col: überschwemmt sein: Boden) to be swimming (col), to be awash. **in Fett (dat) ~** to be swimming in fat; **in seinem Blut ~** to be soaked in blood; **im Geld ~** to be rolling in money (col). (d) (fig: unsicher sein) to be at sea, to flounder. **ins S~ geraten** (fig) to begin to flounder. (e) **es schwimmt mir vor den Augen** I feel dizzy. **2** vt auch aux haben (Sport) to swim.

Schwimmer m - (a) swimmer. (b) (Tech) float.

Schwimmerbecken nt swimmers' pool.

Schwimmerin f swimmer.

Schwimm-: ~**flosse** f (von Taucher) flipper; ~**halle** f swimming bath(s pl) (Brit), (indoor) swimming pool; ~**haut** f (Orn) web; ~**lehrer** m swimming instructor; ~**stil** m stroke; (Technik) (swimming) style; ~**unterricht** m swimming lessons pl; ~**verein** m swimming club; ~**vogel** m waterfowl; ~**weste** f life jacket.

Schwindel m no pl (a) (Gleichgewichtsstörung) dizziness. (b) (Lüge) lie; (Betrug) swindle, fraud, con (col). **das ist alles ~, was er da sagt** what he says is all a pack of lies or a big con (col).

Schwindel|anfall m dizzy turn, attack of dizziness.

Schwindelei f (col) (leichte Lüge) fib (col); (leichter Betrug) swindle.

Schwindel-: **s~erregend** adj (a) in **s~erregender Höhe** at a dizzy height; (b) Preise astronomical; ~**firma** f bogus firm or company; **s~frei** adj **s~frei sein** to have no fear of heights; **Linsey ist nicht s~frei** Linsey can't stand heights, Linsey suffers from vertigo; ~**gefühl** nt feeling of dizziness.

schwind(e)lig adj dizzy. **mir ist ~** I feel dizzy.

schwindeln 1 vi (a) **mir schwindelt** I feel dizzy; **mir schwindelte der Kopf** my head was reeling; **in ~der Höhe** at a dizzy height. (b) (col: lügen) to fib (col), to tell fibs (col). **2** vt (col) **das ist alles**

geschwindelt it's all lies. **3** vr **sich durch die Kontrollen** ~ to con or wangle one's way through the checkpoint (col).

schwinden pret **schwand,** ptp **geschwunden** vi aux sein (abnehmen) to dwindle; (Schönheit) to fade, to wane; (Erinnerung, Angst, Zeit, Dunkelheit) to fade away; (Kräfte) to fade, to fail. **sein Mut schwand** his courage failed him; **ihm schwanden die Sinne** (liter) he grew faint.

Schwindler m - swindler; (Hochstapler) con-man (col); (Lügner) liar, fraud.

schwindlig adj = **schwind(e)lig.**

Schwindsucht f (dated) consumption.

schwindsüchtig adj (dated) consumptive.

Schwinge f -n (liter, Flügel) wing.

schwingen pret **schwang,** ptp **geschwungen 1** vt to swing; (drohend) Schwert, Stock etc to brandish; Hut, Fahne to wave; siehe **geschwungen. 2** vr **sich auf etw** (acc) ~ to leap or jump onto sth, to swing oneself onto sth; **sich in etw** (acc) ~ to vault into sth, to swing oneself into sth. **3** vi **(a)** to swing. **(b)** (vibrieren: Brücke, Saite) to vibrate.

Schwinger m - (Boxen) swing.

Schwing-: ~**flügel** m casement window; ~**tür** f swing door.

Schwingung f (Phys, fig) vibration; (von Wellen) oscillation. **etw in** ~**(en) versetzen** to start sth vibrating; to start sth oscillating.

Schwips m -e (col) **einen (kleinen)** ~ **haben** to be tiddly (Brit col) or (slightly) tipsy.

schwirren vi aux sein to whizz; (Bienen, Fliegen etc) to buzz. **Gerüchte** ~ **durch die Presse** the press is buzzing with rumours; **mir schwirrt der Kopf** my head is buzzing.

Schwitzbad nt Turkish bath; (Dampfbad) steam bath.

Schwitze f -n (Cook) roux.

schwitzen 1 vi (lit,fig) to sweat; (Fenster) to steam up. **2** vt (Cook) Mehl to brown in fat. **3** vr **sich naß** ~ to get drenched in sweat.

Schwitzkasten m (Ringen) headlock. **jdn in den** ~ **nehmen** to put a headlock on sb.

Schwof m -e (col) hop (col), dance.

schwofen vi (col) to dance.

schwoll pret of **schwellen.**

schwören pret **schwor,** ptp **geschworen** vti to swear. **ich kann darauf** ~**, daß** ... I could swear to it that ...; **jdm/sich etw** ~ to swear sth to sb/ oneself; **auf jdn/etw** ~ (fig) to swear by sb/sth.

schwul adj (col) gay, queer (pej col).

schwül adj (lit, fig) Tag, Stimmung sultry; Wetter auch close, muggy.

Schwüle f no pl siehe adj sultriness; closeness, mugginess.

Schwulen- (col): ~**bar** f, ~**lokal** nt gay bar.

Schwule(r) mf decl as adj (col) gay, queer (pej col), fag (US pej col).

Schwulität f usu pl (col) trouble no indef art, difficulty. **in** ~**en kommen** to get into a fix (col); **jdn in** ~**en bringen** to get sb into trouble or hot water (col).

Schwulst m no pl (pej) (in der Sprache) bombast, pompousness; (in der Kunst) ornateness.

schwülstig adj (pej) Stil, Redeweise bombastic, pompous.

Schwund m no pl **(a)** (Abnahme) decrease (gen in), decline (gen in), dwindling (gen of). **(b)** (von Material) shrinkage. **(c)** (Med) atrophy.

Schwung m ⸚e **(a)** swing. **jdm/etw einen** ~ **geben** to give sb/sth a push. **(b)** no pl (fig: Elan) verve, zest; (von Mensch auch) go (col); (lit: Antrieb) momentum. **in** ~ **kommen** (lit: Schlitten etc) to gather or gain momentum; (fig auch) to get going; **jdn/etw in** ~ **bringen** (lit, fig) to get sb/sth going; ~ **in die Sache bringen** (col) to liven things up; **in** ~ **sein** (lit: Schlitten etc) to be going full speed; (fig) to be in full swing; **voller/ohne** ~ full of/lacking verve or zest. **(c)** no pl (col: Menge)

(Sachen) stack, pile (col); (Leute) bunch (col).

Schwung-: **s**~**haft** adj Handel flourishing, roaring; **sich s**~**haft entwickeln** to grow hand over fist; ~**kraft** f centrifugal force; ~**rad** nt flywheel; ~**voll** adj Linie, Bewegung sweeping; Rede, Aufführung lively.

Schwur m -e (Eid) oath; (Gelübde) vow.

Schwurgericht nt court with a jury. **vor das** ~ **kommen** to be tried by jury.

sechs [zεks] num six; siehe **vier.**

Sechs- [zεks-]: ~**eck** nt hexagon; **s**~**eckig** adj hexagonal; **s**~**fach 1** adj sixfold; **2** adv sixfold, six times; siehe **vierfach; s**~**hundert** num six hundred; **s**~**mal** adv six times; ~**tagerennen** nt six-day (bicycle) race; **s**~**tägig** adj six-day.

Sechstel [ˈzεkstl] nt - sixth.

sechstens [ˈzεkstns] adv sixth(ly), in the sixth place.

sechste(r, s) [ˈzεkstə] adj sixth. **einen** ~**n Sinn für etw haben** to have a sixth sense (for sth); siehe **vierte(r, s).**

sechzehn [ˈzεçtseːn] num sixteen.

Sechzehntel(note f) nt - (Mus) semiquaver (Brit), sixteenth note (US).

sechzig [ˈzεçtsɪç] num sixty; siehe **vierzig.**

SED [εsˈeːˈdeː] f = **Sozialistische Einheitspartei Deutschlands.**

Sediment nt (Geol) sediment.

Sedimentgestein nt (Geol) sedimentary rock.

See¹ f -n [ˈzeːən] sea. **an der** ~ by the sea, at the seaside; **an die** ~ **fahren** to go to the sea(side); **auf hoher** ~ on the high seas; **auf** ~ at sea; **in** ~ **stechen** to put to sea.

See² m -n [ˈzeːən] lake; (in Schottland) loch.

See-: ~**aal** m **(a)** (Zool) conger (eel); **(b)** (Comm) dogfish; ~**bad** nt (Kurort) seaside resort; ~**bär** m **(a)** (hum col) seadog (col); **(b)** (Zool) fur seal; ~**beben** nt seaquake; **s**~**fahrend** adj attr Volk seafaring; ~**fahrer** m seafarer; ~**fahrt** f **(a)** (Fahrt) (sea) voyage; (Vergnügungs~) cruise; **(b)** (Schiffahrt) seafaring no art; **s**~**fest** adj **s**~**fest sein** to be a good sailor; ~**gang** m swell; **hoher** ~**gang** heavy seas or swell; ~**gras** nt (Bot) eelgrass, sea grass or hay; ~**hafen** m seaport; ~**handel** m maritime trade; ~**herrschaft** f naval or maritime supremacy; ~**höhe** f sea level; ~**hund** m seal; ~**jungfrau** f (Myth) mermaid; ~**karte** f sea or nautical chart; ~**klima** nt maritime climate; **s**~**krank** adj seasick; **Paul wird leicht s**~**krank** Paul is a bad sailor; ~**krankheit** f seasickness; ~**lachs** m (Cook) pollack.

Seele f -n (Rel, fig, Mensch) soul; (Herzstück, Mittelpunkt) life and soul. **in tiefster** ~ (geh) in one's heart of hearts; **mit ganzer** ~ with all one's soul; **jdm aus der** ~ **sprechen** to express exactly what sb feels; **das liegt mir auf der** ~ it weighs heavily on my mind; **sich** (dat) **etw von der** ~ **reden** to get sth off one's chest; **sich** (dat) **die** ~ **aus dem Leib reden** (col) to talk until one is blue in the face (col); **das tut mir in der** ~ **weh** I am deeply distressed; **zwei** ~**n und ein Gedanke** (prov) two minds with but a single thought; **dann/ nun hat die liebe** or **arme** ~ **Ruh** that'll put him/us etc out of his/our etc misery; **eine** ~ **von Mensch** an absolute dear.

Seelen-: ~**amt** nt (Eccl) requiem; ~**friede(n)** m (geh) peace of mind; ~**heil** nt salvation of one's soul; (fig) spiritual welfare; ~**leben** nt inner life; ~**ruhe** f calmness, coolness; **in aller** ~**ruhe** calmly; (kaltblütig) as cool as you please; **s**~**ruhig** adv calmly; (kaltblütig) as cool as you please, as cool as a cucumber (col); ~**tröster** m (hum: Schnaps) pick-me-up (col); **s**~**verwandt** adj congenial (liter); **sie waren s**~**verwandt** they were kindred spirits; ~**verwandtschaft** f affinity; ~**wanderung** f (Rel) transmigration of souls, metempsychosis; ~**zustand** m psychological or mental state.

See-: ~leute pl of ~mann; ~lilie f sea lily.
seelisch adj (Rel) spiritual; (geistig) mental,
psychological; Belastung emotional; Grausamkeit mental. ~ **bedingt sein** to be psychologically
conditioned.
Seelöwe m sea lion.
Seelsorge f no pl spiritual welfare.
Seelsorger(in f) m - pastor.
See-: ~luft f sea air; ~macht f sea or maritime
power.
Seemann m, pl -leute sailor, seaman.
seemännisch adj nautical.
Seemanns-: ~garn nt no pl (col) sailor's yarn;
~garn spinnen to spin a yarn; ~heim nt sailors'
home; ~lied nt sea shanty.
Seemeile f nautical or sea mile.
Seengebiet ['ze:ən-] nt lakeland district.
Seenot f no pl distress. in ~ geraten to get into
distress.
Seenot-: ~(rettungs)dienst m sea rescue service; ~zeichen nt nautical distress signal.
See-: ~otter m sea otter; ~pferd(chen) nt sea-
horse; ~räuber m pirate; ~räuberei f piracy;
~recht nt maritime law; ~reise f (sea) voyage;
(Kreuzfahrt) cruise; ~rose f waterlily; ~schaden
m damage at sea, average (spec); ~schiffahrt f
maritime or ocean shipping; ~schlacht f naval or
sea battle; ~stern m (Zool) starfish; ~streit-
kräfte pl naval forces pl, navy; ~tang m seaweed; s~tüchtig adj seaworthy; ~ufer nt
lakeside; ~vogel m sea bird; ~volk nt (Nation)
seafaring nation or people; ~weg m sea route;
auf dem ~weg reisen to go or travel by sea;
~zeichen nt navigational aid; ~zunge f sole.
Segel nt - sail. **mit vollen** ~n under full sail or
canvas; (fig) with gusto; **die** ~ **streichen** (Naut)
to strike sail; (fig) to give in.
Segel-: ~boot nt sailing boat (Brit), sailboat (US);
s~fliegen vi infin only to glide; ~fliegen nt gliding; ~flieger m glider pilot; ~flugzeug nt
glider; ~jacht f (sailing) yacht, sailboat (US);
~klub m sailing club.
segeln vti (a) aux haben or sein to sail. **eine Strecke**
~ to sail a course; ~ **gehen** to go for a sail. (b)
aux sein (col) **durch eine Prüfung** ~ to flop in an
exam (col), to fail (in) an exam.
Segeln nt no pl sailing.
Segel-: ~regatta f sailing or yachting regatta;
~schiff nt sailing ship or vessel; ~sport m sailing no art; ~tuch nt canvas.
Segen m - (a) (lit, fig) blessing. **es ist ein** ~, **daß** ...
it is a blessing that ...; **jdm den** ~ **erteilen** to give
sb one's blessing or benediction; **meinen** ~ **hat**
er he has my blessing. (b) (col) **der ganze** ~ the
whole lot.
segensreich adj beneficial; Tätigkeit beneficent.
Segler m - (a) (Segelsportler) yachtsman, sailor.
(b) (Schiff) sailing vessel. (c) (Orn) swift.
Seglerin f yachtswoman.
Segment nt segment.
segnen vt (Rel) to bless; siehe gesegnet.
Segnung f (Rel) blessing, benediction.
sehbehindert adj partially sighted.
sehen pret **sah**, ptp **gesehen** 1 vt (a) to see; (an~
auch) to look at; Fernsehsendung auch to watch.
sieht man das? does it show?; **das kann man** ~
you can tell that (just by looking); **siehst du**
irgendwo mein Buch? can you see my book anywhere?; **von ihm war nichts mehr zu** ~ he was no
longer to be seen; **darf ich das mal** ~? can I have
a look at that? **ich kann diesen Kerl nicht mehr** ~
I can't stand the sight of that guy any more; **jdn**
kommen ~ to see sb coming; **jdn/etw zu** ~
bekommen to get to see sb/sth; **den möchte ich**
~, **der** ... I'd like to meet the man who ...; **da sieht**
man es mal wieder! that's typical; **also, wir** ~
uns morgen right, I'll see you tomorrow; **das**
müssen wir erst mal ~ that remains to be seen;

das sehe ich noch nicht (col) I still don't see that
happening; **das wollen wir (doch) erst mal** ~!
we'll see about that!
(b) (beurteilen) to see; (deuten auch) to look at.
wie siehst du das? how do you see it?; **das darf**
man nicht so ~ that's not the way to look at it; **du**
siehst das nicht richtig you've got it wrong; **das**
sehe ich anders that's not how I see it; **rein**
menschlich gesehen from a purely personal
point of view; **so gesehen** looked at in this way;
du hast wohl keine Lust, oder wie sehe ich das?
(col) you don't feel like it, do you?
(c) **sich** ~ **lassen** to put in an appearance, to
appear; **er läßt sich kaum noch bei uns** ~ he
hardly comes to see us any more; **er kann sich in**
der Nachbarschaft nicht mehr ~ **lassen** he can't
show his face in the neighbourhood any more;
kann ich mich in diesem Anzug ~ **lassen?** do I
look all right in this suit?; **das neue Rathaus**
kann sich ~ **lassen** the new town hall is certainly something to be proud of.
2 vr sich betrogen/getäuscht ~ to see oneself
cheated/deceived; **sich gezwungen** ~, **zu** ... to
see or find oneself obliged to ...
3 vi to see. **siehe oben/unten** see above/below;
siehst du (wohl)!, siehste! (col) you see!; **sieh**
doch! look (here)!; ~ **Sie mal!** look!; **er sieht**
gut/schlecht he can/cannot see very well; **laß**
mal ~ let me see or look or have a look, give us a
look (col); **na siehst du** (there you are,) you see?;
wie ich sehe ... I (can) see ...; **ich sehe schon, du**
willst nicht I can see you don't want to; **da kann**
man mal ~ that just shows (you), that just goes
to show; **mal** ~, **ob** ... (col) let's see if ...; **mal**
~! (col) we'll see; **sieh, daß du** ... see (that)
you ...; **das Boot sah kaum aus dem Wasser** the
boat hardly showed above the water; **das**
Fenster sieht auf den Garten the window looks
onto the garden; **nach jdm** ~ (jdn betreuen) to
look after sb; (jdn besuchen) to go/come to see sb;
nach etw ~ to look after sth; **darauf** ~, **daß** ... to
make sure (that) ...
Sehen nt no pl seeing; (Sehkraft) sight, vision. **ich**
kenne ihn nur vom ~ I only know him by sight.
sehenswert adj worth seeing.
Sehenswürdigkeit f sight. **die Kneipe ist wirk-**
lich eine ~! that pub is really (a sight) worth
seeing!
seherisch ['ze:ərɪʃ] adj attr prophetic.
Seh-: ~fehler m visual or sight defect; ~kraft f
(eye)sight.
Sehne f -n (a) (Anat) tendon, sinew. (b) (Bogen~)
string.
sehnen vr sich nach jdm/etw ~ to long or yearn
(liter) for sb/sth.
Sehnenzerrung f pulled tendon.
Sehnerv m optic nerve.
sehnig adj Mensch sinewy, wiry; Fleisch stringy.
sehnlich adj ardent; Erwartung eager. **sein** ~ster
Wunsch his fondest or most ardent (liter) wish.
Sehnsucht f ~e longing, yearning (nach for). ~
haben to have a longing or yearning.
sehnsüchtig adj longing, yearning; Wunsch etc
ardent; Erwartung eager.
sehnsuchtsvoll adj longing, yearning; Blick,
Brief, Schilderung wistful.
sehr adv (a) (mit adj, adv) very. **er ist** ~ **dafür/**
dagegen he is all for it/he is very much against
it; ~ **zu meiner Überraschung** very much to my
surprise; **es geht ihm** ~ **viel besser** he is very
much better; **wir haben** ~ **viel Zeit** we have
plenty of time or lots of time; **wir haben nicht** ~
viel Zeit we don't have very much time.
(b) (mit vb) very much, a lot. **so** ~ so much;
jdn so ~ **schlagen, daß** ... to hit sb so hard that
...; **sich über etw** (acc) **so** ~ **ärgern/freuen, daß**
... to be so (very) annoyed/pleased about sth
that ...; **wie** ~ how much; **wie** ~ **er sich auch**

bemühte, ... however much he tried ...; **sich** *(dat)* **etw ~ überlegen** to consider sth very carefully; **sich ~ anstrengen** to try very hard; **hat sie ~ geweint?** did she cry very much or a lot?; **freust du dich darauf? — ja, ~** are you looking forward to it? — yes, very much; **tut es weh? — ja, ~** does it hurt? — yes, a lot; **zu ~** too much.
Seh-: **~schwäche** *f* poor eyesight; **~test** *m* eye test; **~vermögen** *nt* powers of vision *pl.*
sei *imper sing, 1. and 3. pers sing subjunc of* **sein** *(imper)* be; *(subjunc)* am; is.
seicht *adj (lit, fig)* shallow.
Seichtheit *f (lit, fig)* shallowness.
seid *2. pers pl pres, imper pl of* **sein** are; *(imper)* be.
Seide *f* -n silk.
Seidel *nt - (Gefäß)* stein, (beer) mug.
seiden *adj attr (aus Seide)* silk, silken *(liter).*
Seiden- *in cpds* silk; **~band** *nt* silk ribbon; **~gewebe** *nt* silk fabric; **~glanz** *m* silky *or* silken sheen; **~papier** *nt* tissue paper; **~raupe** *f* silkworm; **~stoff** *m* silk cloth *or* fabric.
seidig *adj (wie Seide)* silky, silken.
Seife *f* -n soap.
Seifen-: **~blase** *f* soap-bubble; *(fig)* bubble; **~blasen machen** to blow (soap-)bubbles; **~kistenrennen** *nt* soap-box derby; **~lauge** *f* (soap)suds *pl;* **~pulver** *nt* soap powder; **~schale** *f* soap dish; **~schaum** *m* lather.
seifig *adj* soapy.
Seihe *f* -n strainer, colander.
seihen *vt (Flüssigkeit abgießen von)* to strain.
Seil *nt* -e rope; *(Hoch~)* tightrope, highwire. **auf dem ~ tanzen** *(fig)* to be walking a tightrope.
Seil-: **~bahn** *f* cable railway; *(Berg~ auch)* funicular; **s~hüpfen** *vi sep aux* sein to skip; **~schaft** *f (Bergsteigen)* rope, roped party; **s~springen** *vi sep irreg aux* sein to skip; **~tanz** *m* tightrope *or* high-wire act; **s~tanzen** *vi sep* to walk the tightrope *or* high-wire; **~tänzer** *m* tightrope walker, high-wire performer.
Sein *nt no pl* being *no art.* **~ und Schein** appearance and reality; **~ oder Nichtsein** to be or not to be.
sein¹ *pret* **war,** *ptp* **gewesen** *aux* sein **1** *vi* **(a)** to be. **wir waren** we were; **wir sind gewesen** we have been, we've been; **seien Sie nicht böse, aber** ... don't be angry but ...; **sei so nett und ...** be so kind as to ...; **das wäre gut** that would *or* that'd be a good thing; **es wäre schön gewesen** it would *or* it'd have been nice; **er ist Lehrer/ ein Verwandter** he is a teacher/a relative; **was sind Sie (beruflich)?** what do you do?; **in der Küche sind noch viele** there's *or* there are still plenty in the kitchen; **wenn ich Sie wäre** if I were *or* was you; **er war es nicht** it wasn't him; **das bist natürlich wieder du gewesen** of course it was you again; **das kann schon ~** that may well be; **das wär's!** that's all, that's it; **wie war das noch?** what was that again?; **bist du's/ist er's?** is that you/him?; **morgen bin ich in Rom** I'll *or* I will *or* I shall be in Rome tomorrow; **waren Sie mal in Rom?** have you ever been to Rome?; **wir waren essen** we went out for a meal; **wo warst du so lange?** what kept you?
(b) *(mit infin +zu)* **du bist nicht zu sehen** you cannot be seen; **das war ja vorauszusehen** that was to be expected; **wie ist das zu verstehen?** how is that to be understood?; **er ist nicht zu ersetzen** he cannot be replaced; **mit ihr ist ja nicht zu sprechen** you can't talk to her.
(c) was ist? what's the matter?, what is it?; **ist was?** what is it?; *(paßt dir was nicht)* is something the matter?; **das kann nicht ~** that can't be (true); ..., **es sei denn, daß ... ...** unless ...; **wie dem auch sei** be that as it may; **wie wäre es mit ...?** how about ...?, what about ...?; **wie wäre es, wenn wir ihn besuchen würden?** what about *or* how about going to see him?; **wenn du nicht**

gewesen wärest ... if it hadn't been for you ...; **er ist nicht mehr** *(euph)* he is no more *(euph liter);* **mir ist kalt** I'm cold; **was ist Ihnen?** what's the matter with you?; **mir ist, als hätte ich ihn früher schon einmal gesehen** I have a feeling I've seen him before.
2 *aux* to have. **er war jahrelang krank gewesen** he had been *or* he'd been ill for years; **er ist verschwunden** he has *or* he's disappeared; **er ist gestern verschwunden** he disappeared yesterday; **er ist geschlagen worden** he has been beaten.
sein² *poss pron (adjektivisch) (bei Männern)* his; *(bei Dingen)* its; *(bei Mädchen)* her; *(bei Tieren)* its, his/her; *(bei Ländern, Städten)* its, her; *(auf „man" bezüglich)* one's *(Brit),* his *(US),* your. **wenn man ~ Leben betrachtet** when one looks at one's *or* his *(US)* life, when you look at your life; **jeder hat ~e Probleme** everybody has his *or* their *(coll* problems; **er ist gut ~e zwei Meter** *(col)* he's a good two metres.
seiner *pers pron gen of* **er, es** *(geh)* **gedenke ~** remember him; **er war ~ nicht mächtig** he was not in command of himself.
seine(r, s) *poss pron (substantivisch)* his. **der/die/ das ~** *(geh)* his; **er hat das S~ getan** *(geh)* he did his bit; **jedem das S~** to each his own; **die S~n** *(geh)* his family, his people; *(auf „man" bezüglich)* one's *(Brit)* or his *(US)* family *or* people.
seiner-: **~seits** *adv (von ihm)* on his part; *(er selbst)* for his part; **~zeit** *adv* at that time.
seines *poss pron siehe* **seine(r, s).**
seinesgleichen *pron inv (gleichartig)* his kind *pl; (auf „man" bezüglich)* of one's own kind; *(pej)* the likes of him *pl.* **jdn wie ~ behandeln** to treat sb as an equal *or* on equal terms; **das sucht ~** it is unparalleled.
seinet-: **~wegen** *adv* **(a)** *(wegen ihm)* because of him, on his account; *(um ihn)* about him; **(b)** *(von ihm aus)* as far as he is concerned; **~ willen** *adv:* **um ~willen** for his sake.
seinlassen *vt sep irreg* **etw ~** *(aufhören)* to stop sth/doing sth; *(nicht tun)* to drop sth, to leave sth; **laß es sein!** stop that!
seins *poss pron* his.
seit 1 *prep +dat (Zeitpunkt)* since; *(Zeitdauer)* for, in. **~ wann?** since when?; **~ Jahren** for years; **schon ~ zwei Jahren nicht mehr** not since two years ago; **~ etwa einer Woche** since about a week ago, for about a week. **2** *conj* since.
seitdem 1 *adv* since then. **2** *conj* since.
Seite *f* -n side; *(Buch~, Zeitungs~)* page. **die hintere/vordere ~** the back/front; **auf beiden ~n des Hauses** on both sides of the house; **~ an ~ side by side; an jds ~** *(dat)* **gehen** to walk at *or* by sb's side; **jdn von der ~ ansehen** to give sb a sidelong glance; **zur ~ treten** to step aside; **die ~n wechseln** *(Sport)* to change ends *or* over; *(fig)* to change sides; **die Hände in die ~n gestemmt** with arms akimbo, with one's hands on one's hips; **jdm zur ~ stehen** *(fig)* to stand by sb's side; **das Recht ist auf ihrer ~** she has right on her side; **sich jdm an die ~ stellen** *(fig)* to put *or* set oneself beside sb; **jdn zur ~ nehmen** to take sb aside *or* on one side; **auf der einen ~ ..., auf der anderen (~)** ... on the one hand ..., on the other (hand) ...; **jds starke ~** sb's forte, sb's strong point; **jds schwache ~** sb's weakness, sb's weak spot; **sich von seiner besten ~ zeigen** to show oneself at one's best; **von dieser ~ kenne ich ihn gar nicht** I didn't know that side of him; **einer Sache** *(dat)* **die beste ~ abgewinnen** to make the best *or* most of sth; **von allen ~n** *(lit, fig)* from all sides; **nach allen ~n auseinandergehen** to scatter in all directions; **das habe ich von einer anderen ~ erfahren** *(fig)* I heard it from another source; **von meiner ~ aus** *(fig)* on my part.
seiten *prep +gen* **auf/von ~** on the part of.

Seiten- in cpds side; (esp Tech, Sci etc) lateral; ~**angabe** f page reference; ~**ansicht** f side view; (Tech) side elevation; ~**blick** m sidelong glance; **mit einem ~blick auf** (+acc) (fig) with one eye on; ~**fläche** f (Tech) lateral face or surface; ~**hieb** m (Fechten) side cut; (fig) side-swipe; ~**lage** f side position; **in ~lage schlafen** to sleep on one's side; **s~lang** adj several pages long, going on for pages; ~**linie** f (Tennis) sideline; (Ftbl etc) touchline.
seitens prep +gen (form) on the part of.
Seiten-: ~**scheitel** m side parting (Brit), side part (US); ~**schiff** nt (Archit) (side) aisle; ~**sprung** m (fig) bit on the side (esp hum col) no pl, infidelity; ~**stechen** nt stitch; ~**stechen haben** to have a stitch; ~**straße** f side-street, side road; ~**streifen** m verge; (der Autobahn) hard shoulder, berm (US); „~**streifen nicht befahrbar"** "soft verges" (Brit), "soft shoulder"; **s~verkehrt** adj the wrong way around; ~**wechsel** m (Sport) changeover; ~**weg** m side road, byway; ~**wind** m crosswind; ~**zahl** f page number.
seither [zait'heːɐ] adv since then.
seitlich 1 adj lateral (esp Sci, Tech), side attr. **2** adv at the side; (von der Seite) from the side. ~ **von** at the side of; **die Kisten sind ~ grün bemalt** the sides of the boxes are painted green. **3** prep +gen to or at the side of.
seitwärts adv sideways.
Sek., sek. = **Sekunde** sec.
Sekretär m **(a)** secretary. **(b)** (Schreibschrank) bureau, secretaire.
Sekretariat nt office.
Sekretärin f secretary.
Sekretion f (Physiol) secretion.
Sekt m **-e** sparkling wine, champagne.
Sekte f **-n** sect.
Sektierer(in f) m - sectarian.
sektiererisch adj sectarian.
Sektion f **(a)** section. **(b)** (Obduktion) postmortem (examination), autopsy.
Sektor m sector; (Sachgebiet) field.
Sektorengrenze f sector boundary.
Sektschale f champagne glass.
Sekunda f, pl **Sekunden** (Sch) sixth and seventh year of German secondary school.
Sekundaner(in f) m - (Sch) pupil in sixth and seventh year of German secondary school.
Sekundant m second.
sekundär adj secondary.
Sekundärliteratur f secondary literature.
Sekunde f **-n** (auch Mus, Math) second. **eine ~, bitte!** just a second, please; **auf die ~ genau** to the second.
Sekunden-: ~**bruchteil** m split second, fraction of a second; ~**schnelle** f: **in ~schnelle** in a matter of seconds; ~**zeiger** m second hand.
sekundieren* vi +dat to second; (unterstützen auch) to back up.
selber dem pron siehe **selbst 1**.
Selbermachen nt do-it-yourself, DIY; (von Kleidern etc) making one's own. **Möbel zum ~** do-it-yourself furniture.
selbst 1 dem pron **(a) ich/er/das Haus ~** I myself/ he himself/the house itself; **wir/sie/die Häuser ~** we ourselves/they themselves/the houses themselves; **sie ist die Tugend ~** she's virtue itself; ~ **ist der Mann/die Frau!** self-reliance is the name of the game (col); **er braut sein Bier ~** he brews his own beer; **zu sich ~ kommen** to collect one's thoughts; **eine Sache um ihrer ~ willen tun** to do sth for its own sake; **wie geht's?** — **gut, und ~?** how are things? — fine, (and) yourself? **(b)** (ohne Hilfe) alone, on one's/his/ your etc own. **das muß er ~ wissen** it's up to him; **das funktioniert von ~** it works by itself or automatically; **er kam ganz von ~** he came of his own

accord. **2** adv even. ~ **Gott** even God (himself); ~ **wenn** even if.
Selbst nt no pl self.
Selbst|achtung f self-respect, self-esteem.
selbständig adj independent; (steuerlich) self-employed. ~ **denken** to think for oneself; ~ **arbeiten/handeln** to work/act independently or on one's own; **sich ~ machen** (beruflich) to set up on one's own, to start one's own business; (hum: verschwinden) to grow legs (hum).
Selbständige(r) mf decl as adj independent businessman/-woman; (steuerlich) self-employed person.
Selbständigkeit f independence.
Selbst- in cpds self; ~**anzeige** f ~**anzeige erstatten** to come forward oneself; ~**auslöser** m (Phot) delayed-action shutter release, delay timer; ~**bedienung** f self-service; ~**bedienungsladen** m self-service shop (Brit) or store (US); ~**befriedigung** f masturbation; (fig) self-gratification; ~**beherrschung** f self-control; **die ~beherrschung verlieren** to lose one's self-control or temper; ~**bekenntnis** nt confession; ~**bestätigung** f self-affirmation; **das empfand er als ~bestätigung** it boosted his ego; ~**bestimmung** f self-determination; ~**beteiligung** f (Insur) excess; ~**betrug** m self-deception.
selbstbewußt adj (s~sicher) self-assured, self-confident.
Selbstbewußtsein nt self-assurance, self-confidence.
Selbst-: ~**bildnis** nt self-portrait; ~**darstellung** f self-portrayal; ~**disziplin** f self-discipline; ~**einschätzung** f self-assessment; ~**erhaltung** f self-preservation, survival; ~**erhaltungstrieb** m survival instinct; ~**erkenntnis** f self-knowledge; **s~ernannt** adj self-appointed; (in bezug auf Titel) self-styled; ~**fahrer** m (Aut) Autovermietung für ~**fahrer** self-drive car hire (Brit) or rental; **s~gebacken** adj home-baked, homemade; **s~gebaut** adj home-made, self-made; **Haus** self-built; ~**gedrehte** f decl as adj roll-up (col); ~**gedrehte rauchen** to roll one's own; **s~gefällig** adj smug, complacent; ~**gefälligkeit** f smugness, complacency; **s~gemacht** adj Möbel etc home-made; **s~gerecht** adj self-righteous; ~**gerechtigkeit** f self-righteousness; ~**gespräch** nt ~**gespräche führen** to talk to oneself; **s~gestrickt** adj **(a)** Pulli hand-knitted; **ist das s~gestrickt?** (did you knit it yourself?); **(b)** (col) Methode homespun, amateurish; **s~herrlich** adj (pej) **(a)** (eigenwillig) high-handed; **(b)** (s~gerecht) self-satisfied; ~**hilfe** f self-help; **zur ~ hilfe greifen** to take matters into one's own hands; ~**justiz** f arbitrary law; ~**justiz üben** to take the law into one's own hands; **s~klebend** adj self-adhesive; ~**kosten** pl (Econ) prime costs pl; ~**kostenpreis** m cost price (Brit); **zum ~kostenpreis** at cost; ~**kritik** f self-criticism; **s~kritisch** adj self-critical; ~**laut** m vowel; **s~los** adj selfless; ~**losigkeit** f selflessness; ~**mord** m (lit, fig) suicide; ~**mörder** m suicide; **s~mörderisch** adj (lit, fig) suicidal; ~**mordversuch** m suicide attempt, attempted suicide; **s~sicher** adj self-assured; ~**sicherheit** f self-assurance; ~**studium** nt private study; **etw im ~studium lernen** to learn sth by studying on one's own; ~**sucht** f egoism; **s~süchtig** adj egoistic; **s~tätig** adj **(a)** (automatisch) automatic, self-acting; **(b)** (eigenständig) independent; ~**tor** nt (Sport, fig) own goal; ~**tötung** f suicide; ~**überwindung** f will-power; ~**verdient** adj **s~ver-dientes Geld** money one has earned oneself; **s~vergessen** adj absent-minded; Blick faraway; ~**vergessenheit** f absent-mindedness; ~**verleugnung** f self-denial; ~**verschulden** nt one's own fault; **wenn ~verschulden vorliegt ...** if you yourself etc are at fault ...; **s~verschuldet** adj

wenn der Unfall s~verschuldet ist if there is personal responsibility for the accident; **~versorger** *m* **~versorger sein** to be self-sufficient *or* self-reliant; **Urlaub für ~versorger** self-catering holiday.

selbstverständlich 1 *adj Freundlichkeit* natural; *Wahrheit* self-evident. **das ist doch ~!** that goes without saying; **kann ich mitkommen? — ~ can I** come too? — of course; **das ist keineswegs ~** it cannot be taken for granted; **etw für ~ halten, etw als ~ hinnehmen** to take sth for granted. **2** *adv* of course.

Selbstverständlichkeit *f* naturalness; *(Unbefangenheit)* casualness *no indef art; (von Wahrheit)* self-evidence; *(selbstverständliche Wahrheit etc)* self-evident truth *etc*. **etw für eine ~ halten** to take sth as a matter of course.

Selbst-: ~verständnis *nt* **nach seinem eigenen ~verständnis** as he sees himself; **~versuch** *m* experiment on oneself; **~verteidigung** *f* self-defence *(Brit)*, self-defense *(US)*; **~vertrauen** *nt* self-confidence; **~wählferndienst** *m (Telec)* automatic dialling *(Brit) or* dial *(US)* service, subscriber trunk dialling *(Brit)*, STD *(Brit)*; **~wertgefühl** *nt* feeling of one's own worth *or* value, self-esteem; **s~zufrieden** *adj* self-satisfied; **~zufriedenheit** *f* self-satisfaction; **~zweck** *m* end in itself; **als ~zweck** as an end in itself.

selektiv *adj* selective.

selig *adj* **(a)** *(Rel)* blessed; *(old: verstorben)* late. **bis an mein ~es Ende** *(old, hum)* until the day I die. **(b)** *(überglücklich)* overjoyed; *Stunden* blissful.

Seligkeit *f* **(a)** *(Rel)* salvation. **(b)** *(Glück)* (supreme) happiness, bliss.

Selig-: s~sprechen *vt sep irreg (Eccl)* to beatify; **~sprechung** *f (Eccl)* beatification.

Sellerie *m* **-(s)** celeriac; *(Stangen~)* celery.

selten 1 *adj* rare. **2** *adv (nicht oft)* rarely, seldom; *(besonders)* exceptionally. **~ so gelacht!** *(col)* what a laugh! *(col)*.

Seltenheit *f* rarity. **das ist keine ~ bei ihr** it's nothing unusual with her.

Seltenheitswert *m* rarity value.

Selters *nt* **-, -** *(col)*, **Selter(s)wasser** *nt* soda (water).

seltsam *adj* strange; *(komisch auch)* odd.

seltsamerweise *adv* strangely enough.

Seltsamkeit *f* **(a)** *no pl* strangeness, oddness. **(b)** *(seltsame Sache)* oddity.

Semester *nt* - *(Univ)* semester *(US)*, term *(of a half-year's duration)*. **im 7./8. ~ sein** to be in one's 4th year; **ein älteres ~** a senior student; *(hum)* an old boy/girl.

Semester- *(Univ)*: **~ferien** *pl* vacation *sing*; **~schluß** *m* end of term, end of the semester *(US)*.

Semi- *in cpds* semi-; **~finale** ['zɛːmi-] *nt (Sport)* semifinal(s); **~kolon** [zemi'koːlɔn] *nt, pl* **-s** *or* **~kola** semicolon.

Seminar *nt* **-e (a)** *(Univ)* department; *(~übung)* seminar. **(b)** *(Priester~)* seminary. **(c)** *(Lehrer~, Studien~)* teacher training college, college of education.

Semit(in *f)* *m (wk)* **-en, -en** Semite.

semitisch *adj* Semitic.

Semmel *f* **-n** *(dial)* roll. **sie gehen weg wie warme ~n** *(col)* they're selling like hot cakes *(col)*.

Semmel-: ~brösel(n) *pl* breadcrumbs *pl*; **~knödel** *(S Ger, Aus)* *m* bread dumpling.

sen. = **senior** sen.

Senat *m* **-e** *(Pol, Univ)* senate.

Senator *m*, **Senatorin** *f* senator.

Sende-: ~bereich *m* transmission range; **~gebiet** *nt* area; **~leiter** *m* producer.

senden[1] *pret* **sandte,** *ptp* **gesandt 1** *vt* to send *(an +acc* to). **jdm etw ~** to send sb sth, to send sth to sb. **2** *vi* **nach jdm ~** to send for sb.

senden[2] *vti (Rad, TV)* to broadcast; *Signal etc* to transmit.

Sendepause *f (Rad, TV)* interval.

Sender *m* - transmitter; *(~kanal) (Rad)* station; *(TV)* channel *(Brit)*, station *(esp US)*.

Sende-: ~raum *m* studio; **~reihe** *f* (radio/television) series; **~schluß** *m (Rad, TV)* closedown; **bis zum ~schluß** until we close down; **~turm** *m* radio tower; **~zeichen** *nt* call sign; **~zeit** *f* broadcasting time.

Sendung *f* **(a)** *no pl (das Senden)* sending. **(b)** *(Brief~)* letter; *(Päckchen)* packet; *(Paket)* parcel; *(Comm)* consignment. **(c)** *(Rad, TV)* programme *(Brit)*, program *(US)*; *(Rad auch,* broadcast; *(das Senden)* broadcasting.

Senf *m* **-e** mustard. **seinen ~ dazugeben** *(col)* to put one's oar in *(col)*.

Senf-: ~früchte *pl (Cook)* pickles *pl*; **~gas** *nt (Chem)* mustard gas; **~korn** *nt* mustard seed; **~packung** *f (Med)* mustard poultice.

sengen 1 *vt* to singe. **2** *vi* to scorch.

senil *adj (pej)* senile.

senior *adj* senior.

Senior *m* **(a)** *(auch ~chef)* boss. **kann ich mal den ~ sprechen?** can I speak to Mr X senior? **(b)** *(Sport)* senior player. **die ~en** the seniors. **(c)** **~en** *pl* senior citizens *pl; (hum)* old folk *pl*.

Senioren-: ~karte *f* senior citizen's ticket; **~mannschaft** *f* senior team; **~paß** *m* senior citizen's travel pass.

Senke *f* **-n** valley.

senken 1 *vt* to lower; *Lanze, Fahne* to dip; *Kopf* to bow; *(Tech) Schraube, Schacht* to sink. **2** *vr* to sink; *(Decke)* to sag; *(Stimme)* to drop.

Senk-: ~fuß *m (Med)* fallen arches *pl*; **~grube** *f* cesspit; **~lot** *nt* plumbline; *(Gewicht)* plummet.

senkrecht *adj* vertical; *(Math)* perpendicular.

Senkrechte *f decl as adj* vertical; *(Math)* perpendicular.

Senkrechtstarter *m (Aviat)* vertical take-off aircraft; *(fig col)* whizz kid *(col)*.

Senkung *f* **(a)** sinking; *(von Boden, Straße)* subsidence; *(von Wasserspiegel)* drop *(gen* in*)*; *(als Maßnahme)* lowering. **(b)** *(Vertiefung)* hollow, valley.

Senner(in *f)* *m* - (Alpine) dairyman/dairymaid.

Sennerei *f (Gebäude)* Alpine dairy.

Sensation *f* sensation.

sensationell [zɛnzatsio'nɛl] *adj* sensational.

Sensations-: ~blatt *nt* sensational paper; **~lust** *f* desire for sensation; **~nachricht** *f* scoop; **~presse** *f* yellow press.

Sense *f* **-n** scythe. **dann ist ~!** *(col)* that's the end!

sensibel *adj* sensitive.

sensibilisieren* *vt* to sensitize.

Sensibilisierung *f* sensitization.

Sensibilität *f* sensitivity.

sensitiv *adj (geh)* sensitive.

Sensitivität *f (geh)* sensitivity.

Sensor *m* sensor.

sentimental *adj* sentimental.

Sentimentalität *f* sentimentality.

separat *adj* separate; *Wohnung, Zimmer* self-contained.

Separatismus *m (Pol)* separatism.

separatistisch *adj (Pol)* separatist.

September *m* - September; *siehe* **März.**

Septime *f* **-n** *(Mus)* seventh.

septisch *adj* septic.

Sequenz *f* sequence.

Serbe *m (wk)* **-n, -n** Serbian.

Serbien ['zɛrbiən] *nt* Serbia.

Serbin *f* Serbian (woman/girl).

serbisch *adj* Serbian.

Serenade *f* serenade.

Serie ['zeːriə] *f* series *sing*. **in ~ gehen** to go into production; **in ~ hergestellt werden** to be mass-produced.

Serien- ['zeːriən-]: s~**mäßig 1** adj Ausstattung standard; Herstellung series attr; **2** adv herstellen in series; **das wird s~mäßig eingebaut** it's a standard fitting; ~**nummer** f serial number; ~**produktion** f mass production; s~**weise** adv produzieren etc in series; (col: in Mengen) wholesale.

seriös adj (anständig) respectable; Firma sound.

Seriosität f siehe adj respectability; soundness.

Sermon m -e (pej) sermon, lecture.

Serpentine f winding road; (Kurve) double bend. **die Straße führt in** ~**n den Berg hinauf** the road winds or snakes its way up the mountain.

Serum nt, pl **Seren** serum.

Service[1] [zɛr'viːs] nt - [zer'viːsə] (Geschirr) dinner/ coffee etc service; (Gläser~) set.

Service[2] ['sɜːvɪs] m or nt -s (Comm, Sport) service.

servieren* [zɛr'viːrən] vti to serve (jdm etw sb sth, sth to sb).

Serviererin [zɛr'viːrərɪn] f waitress.

Servier- [zɛr'viːɐ-]: ~**tisch** m serving table; ~**wagen** m trolley (Brit), tea cart (US).

Serviette [zɛr'viɛtə] f serviette.

Servo- ['zɛrvo-] (Tech): ~**bremse** f servo brake; ~**lenkung** f servo steering.

Servus ['zɛrvʊs] interj (Aus, SGer) (beim Treffen) hello; (beim Abschied) goodbye, so long (col).

Sesam m -s sesame. ~, **öffne dich!** open Sesame!

Sessel m - (easy) chair; (Polstersessel) armchair.

Sessel-: ~**lehne** f (chair) arm; ~**lift** m chairlift.

seßhaft adj settled; (ansässig) resident. ~ **werden** to settle down.

Seßhaftigkeit f no pl settled form of existence; (von Lebensweise) settledness.

Set m or nt -s **(a)** set. **(b)** (Deckchen) tablemat.

Setter m - setter.

setzen 1 vt **(a)** to put, to place; (bei Spielen) Stein, Figur to move; (bestimmen) Ziel, Grenze, Termin, Norm to set. **etw auf die Rechnung** ~ to put sth on the bill; **etw an den Mund** ~ to put sth to one's mouth; **jdn an Land** ~ to put sb ashore; **jdn über den Fluß** ~ to take sb across the river; **Geld auf ein Pferd** ~ to put money on a horse; **auf seinen Kopf sind 100.000 Dollar gesetzt** there's 100,000 dollars on his head; **jdm ein Denkmal** ~ to build a monument to sb; **seinen Namen unter etw** (acc) ~ to put one's signature to sth; **seine Hoffnung in jdn/etw setzen** to put or place one's hopes in sb/sth; **dann setzt es was** (col) there'll be trouble. **(b)** (Hort: pflanzen) to plant.

2 vr **(a)** (Platz nehmen) to sit down; (Vogel) to alight. **sich auf einen Stuhl** ~ to sit down on a chair; **sich ins Auto** ~ to get into the car; **sich zu jdm** ~ to sit with sb. **(b)** (Kaffee, Tee, Lösung) to settle.

3 vi **(a)** (bei Glücksspiel, Wetten) to bet. **auf ein Pferd** ~ to bet on a horse; **auf jdn/etw** ~ (lit, fig) to back sb/sth. **(b)** (Typ) to set. **(c)** (springen) (Pferd, Läufer) to jump. **über einen Fluß** ~ to cross a river.

Setzer m - (Typ) typesetter.

Setz-: ~**kasten** m (Typ) case; (an Wand) ornament shelf; ~**ling** m (Hort) seedling.

Seuche f -n epidemic; (fig pej) scourge.

Seuchen-: s~**artig** adj epidemic; **sich s~artig ausbreiten** to reach epidemic proportions, to spread like the plague; ~**bekämpfung** f epidemic control; ~**gebiet** nt epidemic area.

seufzen vti to sigh.

Seufzer m - sigh.

Sex m no pl sex.

Sex-: ~-**Appeal** [-ə'piːl] m no pl sex appeal; ~**bombe** f (col) sex bomb (col); ~**film** m sex film; ~**foto** nt sex photo.

Sexismus m sexism.

sexistisch adj sexist.

Sexta f, pl **Sexten** (Sch) first year in a German secondary school.

Sextaner(in f) m - pupil in the first year of a German secondary school.

Sextant m (Naut) sextant.

Sexte f -n (Mus) sixth.

Sextett nt -e (Mus) sextet(te).

Sexual|erziehung f sex education.

Sexualität f no pl sexuality.

Sexual-: ~**leben** nt sex life; ~**mörder** m sex murderer; ~**trieb** m sex(ual) drive; ~**wissenschaft** f sexology.

sexuell adj sexual.

sexy ['zɛksi] adj pred (col) sexy (col).

sezieren* vti (lit, fig) to dissect.

Shampoo(n) [ʃam'pu:(n)] nt -s shampoo.

Shorts [ʃɔrts] pl (pair of) shorts.

Show [ʃoː] f -s show. **eine** ~ **abziehen** (col) to put on a show (col).

Show-: ~**geschäft** nt show business; ~**master** ['ʃoʊmaːstə] m - compère, emcee (US).

siamesisch adj ~**e Zwillinge** Siamese twins.

Siamkatze f Siamese (cat).

Sibirien [zi'biːriən] nt Siberia.

sibirisch adj Siberian.

sich refl pron **(a)** (acc) (+infin, bei „man") oneself; (3. pers sing) himself; herself; itself; (Höflichkeitsform) yourself; yourselves; (3. pers pl) themselves. ~ **wiederholen** to repeat oneself/itself. **(b)** (dat) (+infin, bei „man") to oneself; (3. pers sing) to himself; to herself; to itself; (Höflichkeitsform) to yourself/yourselves; (3. pers pl) to themselves. ~ **die Haare waschen** to wash one's hair; **sie hat** ~ **einen Pullover gekauft** she bought herself a pullover. **(c)** acc, dat (mit prep) (+infin, bei „man") one; (3. pers sing) him; her; it; (Höflichkeitsform) you; (3. pers pl) them. **haben Sie Ihren Ausweis bei** ~? do you have your pass on you? **(d)** (einander) each other, one another. **(e)** (impers) **hier sitzt es** ~ **gut** it's good to sit here; **dieses Auto fährt** ~ **gut** this car drives well.

Sichel f -n sickle; (Mond~) crescent.

sicher 1 adj **(a)** (gewiß) certain, sure. **der** ~**e Tod** certain death; **(sich dat) einer Sache/jds** ~ **sein** to be sure of sth/sb; **soviel ist** ~ **that** much is certain. **(b)** (geschützt) safe; (geborgen) secure. **vor jdm/etw** ~ **sein** to be safe from sb/sth; ~ **leben** to lead a secure life; ~ **ist** ~ you can't be too sure. **(c)** (zuverlässig) reliable; (fest) Gefühl, Zusage definite; Hand, Job steady; Stellung secure. **(d)** (selbstbewußt) confident. ~ **wirken/ auftreten** to give an impression of confidence. **2** adv **(a)** fahren etc safely. **(b)** (natürlich) of course. **du hast dich** ~ **verrechnet** you must have counted wrongly; **das weiß ich ganz** ~ I know that for certain; **aber er kommt** ~ **noch** I'm sure he'll come.

sichergehen vi sep irreg aux sein to be sure.

Sicherheit f (a) no pl (Gewißheit) certainty. **das ist mit** ~ **richtig** that is definitely right. **(b)** no pl (Schutz, das Sichersein) safety; (als Aufgabe von Sicherheitsbeamten etc) security. ~ **und Ordnung** law and order; **die öffentliche** ~ public security; **jdn/etw in** ~ **bringen** to get sb/sth to safety; ~ **im Straßenverkehr** road safety; **zu Ihrer eigenen** ~ for your own safety; **in** ~ **sein** to be safe. **(c)** no pl (Zuverlässigkeit) reliability; (von Hand, Einkommen) steadiness; (von Stellung) security. **(d)** no pl (Selbstbewußtsein) (self-)confidence. **(e)** (Comm) security; (Pfand) surety. ~ **leisten** (Comm) to offer security.

Sicherheits-: ~**abstand** m safe distance; ~**beamte(r)** m security officer; ~**bestimmungen** pl safety regulations pl; (betrieblich, Pol etc) security controls pl; ~**gurt** m seat belt; s~**halber** adv to be on the safe side; ~**kontrolle** f security check; ~**maßnahme** f safety precaution; (betrieblich, Pol etc) security measure; ~**nadel** f safety pin; ~**risiko** nt security risk;

~**schloß** *nt* safety lock; ~**truppen** *pl* security troops *pl*; ~**verschluß** *m* safety catch; ~**vorkehrung** *f* safety precaution; *(betrieblich, Pol etc)* security precaution.

sichern 1 *vt* (a) *(gegen, vor +dat* against) to safeguard; *(absichern)* to protect; *(sicher machen) Tür, Fahrrad etc* to secure; *Bergsteiger etc* to belay. (b) **jdm/sich etw** ~ to secure sth for sb/oneself. **2** *vr* to protect oneself *(vor +dat, gegen* against).

sicherstellen *vt sep* (a) *Waffen, Heroin* to take possession of. (b) *(garantieren)* to guarantee.

Sicherung *f* (a) *siehe vt (a)* safeguarding; protection; securing; belaying. (b) *(Schutz)* safeguard. (c) *(Elec)* fuse; *(von Waffe)* safety catch. **da ist (bei) ihm die** ~ **durchgebrannt** *(fig col)* he blew a fuse *(col)*.

Sicht *f no pl* (a) *(Sehweite)* visibility. **eine** ~ **von 30 Metern** 30 metres' visibility; **in** ~ **sein/kommen** to be in/come into sight; **auf lange/kurze** ~ *(fig)* in the long/short term; *planen* for the long/short term. (b) *(Ausblick, Gesichtspunkt)* view. **aus meiner/seiner** ~ from my/his point of view. (c) *(Comm)* **auf** *or* **bei** ~ at sight.

sichtbar *adj (lit, fig)* visible. ~ **werden** *(fig)* to become apparent.

sichten *vt* (a) *(durchsehen)* to look through; *(ordnen)* to sift through. (b) *(erblicken)* to sight.

Sicht-: ~**gerät** *nt* monitor; *(Comp auch)* VDU, visual display unit; ~**grenze** *f* visibility limit.

sichtlich 1 *adj* obvious. 2 *adv* obviously, visibly.

Sicht-: ~**verhältnisse** *pl* visibility *sing;* ~**vermerk** *m* visa; ~**weite** *f* visibility *no art;* **außer** ~**weite** out of sight

Sickergrube *f* soakaway.

sickern *vi aux sein* to seep; *(in Tropfen)* to drip. **in die Presse** ~ to be leaked to the press.

sie *pers pron 3. pers* (a) *sing (von Frau, weiblichem Tier) (nom)* she; *(acc)* her; *(von Dingen)* it; *(acc)* them *pl.* ~ **ist es** it's her. (b) *pl (nom)* they; *(acc)* them. ~ **sind es** it's them.

Sie *pers pron 2. pers sing or pl* you. **jdn mit** ~ **anreden** to call sb "Sie".

Sieb *nt* -e sieve; *(Tee~)* strainer; *(Gemüse~)* colander.

sieben[1] 1 *vt* to pass through a sieve; *(Cook)* to sift, to sieve. 2 *vi (fig col)* **bei der Prüfung wird stark gesiebt** the exam will weed a lot of people out.

sieben[2] *num* seven.

Sieben- *1 or* -**en** seven; *siehe* **Vier.**

Sieben- *in cpds siehe auch* **Vier-**; **s~hundert** *num* seven hundred; **s~mal** *adv* seven times; ~**meter** *m (Sport)* penalty; ~**sachen** *pl (col)* belongings *pl;* ~**schläfer** *m (Zool)* dormouse; **s~tausend** *num* seven thousand.

Siebtel *nt -* seventh.

siebtens *adv* seventh(ly), in the seventh place.

siebte(r, s) *adj* seventh; *siehe* **vierte(r, s).**

siebzehn *num* seventeen.

siebzig *num* seventy; *siehe* **vierzig.**

siedeln *vi* to settle.

sieden 1 *vi (Wasser, Zucker etc)* to boil. 2 *vt Seife, Leim* to produce by boiling. ~**d heiß** boiling hot.

Siedepunkt *m (Phys, fig)* boiling-point.

Siedler *m -* settler; *(Bauer)* smallholder.

Siedlung *f* (a) *(Ansiedlung)* settlement. (b) *(Wohn~)* housing estate *(Brit)*, development.

Sieg *m* -e victory *(über +acc* over). **einen** ~ **erringen** to win a victory; **einer Sache** *(dat)* **zum** ~ **verhelfen** to help sth to triumph.

Siegel *nt -* seal.

Siegellack *m* sealing wax.

siegeln *vt Urkunde* to affix a/one's seal to; *(ver~) Brief* to seal.

Siegelring *m* signet ring.

siegen *vi (Mil)* to be victorious; *(in Wettkampf)* to win. **über jdn/etw** ~ *(fig)* to triumph over sb/sth; *(in Wettkampf)* to beat sb/sth.

Sieger(in *f) m -* victor; *(in Wettkampf)* winner. **zweiter** ~ runner-up; ~ **werden** to win.

Siegerehrung *f (Sport)* presentation ceremony.

Sieger-: ~**macht** *f usu pl (Pol)* victorious power; ~**urkunde** *f (Sport)* winner's certificate.

Sieges-: **s~bewußt** *adj* confident of victory; ~**denkmal** *nt* victory monument; ~**feier** *f* victory celebration; ~**preis** *m* winner's prize; *(Boxen)* winner's purse; **s~sicher** *adj* certain of victory; ~**zug** *m* triumphal march.

siegreich *adj* victorious, triumphant; *(in Wettkampf)* winning *attr.*

siehe *imper sing of* **sehen** see.

Siel *nt or m* -e *(Schleuse)* sluice; *(Abwasserkanal)* sewer.

siezen *vt* **sich** ~ to address each other as "Sie".

Signal *nt* -e signal. **(ein)** ~ **geben** to give a signal.

Signalanlage *f* signals *pl,* set of signals.

signalisieren *vt (lit, fig)* to signal.

Signal-: ~**lampe** *f* signal lamp; ~**mast** *m* signal mast.

Signatur *f* (a) *(Bibliotheks~)* shelf mark. (b) *(auf Landkarten)* symbol.

Silbe *f* -n syllable. **er hat es mit keiner** ~ **erwähnt** he didn't say a word about it.

Silber *nt no pl* silver. **aus** ~ made of silver.

Silber- *in cpds* silver; ~**arbeit** *f* silverwork *no pl;* ~**besteck** *nt* silver(ware); **s~farben** *adj* silver; ~**fischchen** *nt* silverfish; ~**folie** *f* silver foil; ~**fuchs** *m* silver fox; ~**geld** *nt* silver; ~**hochzeit** *f* silver wedding (anniversary); ~**löwe** *m* puma; ~**möwe** *f* herring gull.

silbern *adj* silver. ~**e Hochzeit** silver wedding (anniversary).

Silber-: ~**pappel** *f* white poplar; ~**schmied** *m* silversmith; ~**stickerei** *f (Kunst)* silver embroidery; ~**streif(en)** *m (fig)* **es zeichnete sich ein** ~**streif(en) am Horizont ab** there was light at the end of the tunnel; ~**stück** *nt* silver coin; ~**waren** *pl* silver *sing;* **s~weiß** *adj* silvery white.

silbrig *adj* silvery.

Silhouette [zi'luɛtə] *f* silhouette.

Silikon *nt* -e silicone.

Silikon-: ~**chip** *m,* ~**plättchen** *nt* silicon chip.

Silikose *f* -n *(Med)* silicosis.

Silizium *nt no pl* silicon.

Silo *m* -s silo.

Silvester [zɪl'vɛstɐ] *m or nt -* New Year's Eve.

simpel *adj* simple; *(vereinfacht)* simplistic.

Simpel *m - (col)* simpleton.

Sims *m or nt* -e *(Fenster~)* sill; *(Gesims)* ledge.

Simulant(in *f) m* malingerer.

Simulator *m (Sci)* simulator.

simulieren *1 vi* **er simuliert nur** he's shamming. **2** *vt* (a) *Krankheit* to feign. (b) *(Sci)* to simulate.

simultan *adj* simultaneous.

Simultandolmetscher *m* simultaneous interpreter.

sind *1., 3. pers pl, bei Sie sing/pl pres of* **sein** are.

Sinfonie *f* symphony.

Sinfonie-: ~**konzert** *nt* symphony concert; ~**orchester** *nt* symphony orchestra.

Sinfoniker(in *f) m* - member of a symphony orchestra. **die Münchner** ~ the Munich Symphony Orchestra.

sinfonisch *adj* symphonic.

Singapur ['zɪŋgapuːrə] *nt* Singapore.

singen *pret* **sang**, *ptp* **gesungen** 1 *vti* (a) *(lit, fig)* to sing; *(esp Eccl: eintönig, feierlich)* to chant. **zur Gitarre** ~ to sing to the guitar; **ein** ~**der Tonfall** a lilt; **jdn in den Schlaf** ~ to sing sb to sleep. (b) *(col: gestehen)* to squeal *(col).* 2 *vr* **sich heiser** ~ to sing oneself hoarse.

Single[1] ['sɪŋgl] *f* -**s** *(Schallplatte)* single.

Single[2] ['sɪŋgl] *m* -**s** *(Alleinlebender)* single.

Sing-: ~**sang** *m* -**s** *(Gesang)* monotonous singing; ~**stimme** *f* vocal part.

Singular *m* singular.

Sing-: ~**vogel** m song-bird; ~**weise** f way of singing.

sinken pret **sank,** ptp **gesunken** vi aux sein **(a)** to sink; (Ballon) to descend; (Nebel) to come down. **ins Bett** ~ to fall into bed; **in jds Meinung/ Achtung** (dat) ~ to go down in sb's estimation. **(b)** (Boden, Gebäude) to subside; (Fundament) to settle. **in Schutt und Asche** ~ (geh) to fall in ruins. **(c)** (niedriger, geringer werden: Temperatur, Preise etc) to drop; (Ansehen) to diminish; (Hoffnung, Stimmung) to sink. **den Mut/die Hoffnung** ~ **lassen** to lose courage/hope.

Sinn m -e **(a)** sense; (Bedeutung) meaning. **er war von** ~**en** he was out of his senses or mind; **im übertragenen** ~ in the figurative sense; **der Satz (er)gibt keinen** ~ the sentence doesn't make sense.

(b) (Gedanken, Denkweise) mind. **sich** (dat) **jdn/etw aus dem** ~ **schlagen** to put sb/sth out of one's mind; **es kam ihm gar nicht in den** ~, **ihr zu helfen** it did not occur to him to help her; **das will mir einfach nicht in den** ~ I just can't understand it; **das geht mir nicht aus dem** ~ I can't get it out of my mind; **etw im** ~ **haben** to have sth in mind.

(c) (Verständnis) feeling. ~ **für Humor haben** to have a sense of humour; **er hat keinen** ~ **für Kunst** he has no appreciation of art.

(d) (Geist) spirit. **im** ~**e des Gesetzes** according to the spirit of the law; **im** ~**e des Verstorbenen** in accordance with the wishes of the deceased.

(e) (Zweck) point. **das ist nicht der** ~ **der Sache** that is not the point; **der** ~ **des Lebens** the meaning of life; **ohne** ~ **und Verstand sein** to make no sense at all; **das hat keinen** ~ there is no point in that; **es hat keinen** ~, **jetzt noch loszugehen** there's no point (in) starting out now.

Sinn-: ~**bild** nt symbol; **s**~**bildlich** adj symbolic(al).

sinnen pret **sann,** ptp **gesonnen** vi (geh) to ponder, to muse; (grübeln) to brood. **über etw** (acc) ~ to reflect on/brood over sth; **auf Verrat/Rache** ~ to plot treason/revenge.

Sinnes-: ~**eindruck** m sensory impression; ~**nerv** m sensory nerve; ~**organ** nt sense organ; ~**reiz** m sensory stimulus; ~**täuschung** f hallucination; ~**wandel** m change of mind.

sinngemäß adj **(a)** (inhaltlich) etw ~ **wiedergeben** to give the gist of sth. **(b)** (esp Jur: analog) corresponding, analogous. **etw** ~ **anwenden** to apply sth by analogy.

sinnig adj apt; Vorrichtung practical; (iro: wenig sinnvoll) clever.

sinnlich adj **(a)** (vital, sinnenfroh) sensuous; (erotisch) sensual. ~**e Liebe** sensual love. **(b)** ~ **wahrnehmbar** perceptible by the senses.

Sinnlichkeit f (Vitalität) sensuousness; (Erotik) sensuality.

sinnlos adj **(a)** (unsinnig) Redensarten, Geschwätz meaningless; Verhalten, Töten senseless. **(b)** (zwecklos) pointless; Wut blind. ~ **betrunken** blind drunk.

Sinnlosigkeit f siehe adj meaninglessness; senselessness; pointlessness.

sinn-: ~**verwandt** adj synonymous; ~**voll** adj Satz meaningful; (fig) sensible; (nützlich) useful.

Sintflut f (Bibl) Flood. **nach uns die** ~ (col) it doesn't matter what happens after we've gone.

sintflutartig adj ~**e Regenfälle** torrential rain.

Sinus m - (Math) sine.

Siphon ['zi:fõ] m -s siphon.

Sippe f -n (extended) family; (col: Verwandtschaft) clan (col).

Sippschaft f (pej col) tribe (col).

Sirene f -n (Tech, fig) siren.

Sirup m -e syrup.

Sisal(hanf) m no pl sisal (hemp).

Sit-in [sɪt'ɪn] nt -s sit-in. **ein** ~ **machen** to stage a sit-in.

Sitte f -n **(a)** (Brauch) custom; (Mode) practice. ~ **sein** to be the custom/the practice. **(b)** usu pl (gutes Benehmen) manners pl; (Sittlichkeit) morals pl. **gegen die (guten)** ~**n verstoßen** to offend common decency; **was sind denn das für** ~**n?** what sort of a way is that to behave!

Sitten-: ~**gesetz** nt moral law; ~**kodex** m moral code; **s**~**los** adj immoral; ~**losigkeit** f immorality; ~**polizei** f vice squad; ~**richter** m judge of public morals; **s**~**streng** adj highly moral; ~**strolch** m (col) sex fiend (col); ~**verfall** m decline in moral standards; ~**wächter** m (iro) guardian of public morals; **s**~**widrig** adj (form) immoral.

Sittich m -e parakeet.

sittlich adj moral.

Sittlichkeit f no pl morality.

Sittlichkeits-: ~**delikt** nt sexual offence (Brit) or offense (US); ~**verbrechen** nt sex crime; ~**verbrecher** m sex offender.

sittsam adj demure.

Sittsamkeit f demureness.

Situation f situation.

situiert adj gut/schlecht ~ **sein** to be well/poorly situated financially.

Sitz m -e **(a)** (~platz, Parl) seat. **(b)** (von Regierung, Universität, fig) seat; (Wohn~) residence; (von Firma, Verwaltung) headquarters pl. **(c)** no pl (Tech, von Kleidungsstück) sit; (von der Größe her) fit. **einen guten/schlechten** ~ **haben** to sit/fit well/badly.

sitzen vi pret **saß,** ptp **gesessen** aux haben or (Aus, SGer, Sw) sein (a) to sit; (Vogel) to perch. **er saß bei uns am Tisch** he was sitting at our table; **bleiben Sie bitte** ~! please don't get up; ~ **Sie bequem?** are you comfortable?; **etw im S**~ **tun** to do sth sitting down; **an einer Aufgabe** ~ to sit over a task; **einen** ~ **haben** (col) to have had one too many. **(b)** (col: im Gefängnis ~) to be inside (col). **(c)** (sein) to be. **er sitzt im Kultusministerium** (col) he's in the ministry of culture. **(d)** (angebracht sein) to sit. **der Deckel sitzt fest** the lid is on tightly; **locker** ~ to be loose; **fest** ~ to be stuck tight(ly); **deine Krawatte sitzt nicht richtig** your tie isn't straight; **das hat gesessen!** (col) that hit home. **(e)** (im Gedächtnis ~) to have sunk in.

sitzenbleiben vi sep irreg aux sein (col) **(a)** (Sch) to stay down. **(b)** **auf einer Ware** ~ to be left with a product. **(c)** (unverheiratete Frau) to be left on the shelf (col).

sitzenlassen vt sep irreg ptp ~ or **sitzengelassen** (col) **(a)** (Sch: nicht versetzen) to keep down (a year). **(b)** **eine Beleidigung auf sich** (dat) ~ to take an insult. **(c)** jdn ~ (im Stich lassen) to leave sb in the lurch; Freund(in) to stand sb up; (nicht heiraten) to jilt.

Sitz-: ~**fleisch** nt (col) ~**fleisch haben** to be able to sit still; ~**gelegenheit** f seats pl; ~**kissen** nt (floor) cushion; ~**ordnung** f seating plan; ~**platz** m seat; ~**reihe** f row of seats; ~**streik** m = Sit-in.

Sitzung f meeting; (Jur) session; (Parlaments~) sitting.

Sitzungssaal m conference hall.

Sizilianer(in f) m - Sicilian.

sizilianisch adj Sicilian.

Sizilien [zi'tsi:lisn] nt Sicily.

Skai ® nt no pl imitation leather.

Skala f, pl **Skalen** scale; (fig) range.

Skalp m -e scalp.

Skalpell nt -e scalpel.

skalpieren* vt to scalp.

Skandal m -e scandal; (col: Krach) fuss. **einen** ~ **machen** to cause a scandal; to make a fuss.

Skandal-: ~**blatt** nt (pej) scandal sheet; ~**ge-**

schichte f (bit or piece of) scandal.
skandalös adj scandalous.
Skandalpresse f (pej) gutter press.
Skandinavien [skandi'naːviən] nt Scandinavia.
Skandinavier(in f) m - Scandinavian.
skandinavisch adj Scandinavian.
Skat m -e (Cards) skat.
Skelett nt -e (lit, fig) skeleton.
Skepsis f no pl scepticism. mit/voller ~ scep-
tically.
Skeptiker(in f) m - sceptic.
skeptisch adj sceptical.
Sketch [skɛtʃ] m -e(s) (Art, Theat) sketch.
Ski [ʃiː] m -er ['ʃiːə] ski. ~ laufen to ski.
Ski- in cpds ski; ~**fahrer(in** f) m skier; ~**gebiet** nt
ski(ing) area; ~**hütte** f ski hut or lodge (US);
~**kurs** m skiing course; ~**lauf** m skiing;
~**läufer(in** f) m skier; ~**lehrer** m ski instructor;
~**lift** m ski-lift; ~**piste** f ski-run; ~**sport** m skiing; ~**springen** nt ski jumping; ~**stock** m ski
stick.
Skizze ['skɪtsə] f -n sketch; (fig: Grundriß) plan.
Skizzen- ['skɪtsn-]: ~**buch** nt sketchbook; **s~haft**
1 adj Zeichnung etc roughly sketched; Beschreibung etc (given) in broad outline; 2 adv etw
s~haft zeichnen to sketch sth roughly.
skizzieren* [skɪ'tsiːrən] vt to sketch; (fig) Plan etc
to outline.
Sklave ['sklaːvə] m (wk) -n, -n slave. ~ einer Sache
(gen) sein (fig) to be a slave to sth.
Sklaven- ['sklaːvn]: ~**arbeit** f slavery; ~**handel** m
slave trade; ~**treiber** m slave-driver.
Sklaverei [sklaːvə'raɪ] f no pl (lit, fig) slavery no art.
Sklavin ['sklaːvɪn] f slave.
sklavisch ['sklaːvɪʃ] adj slavish.
Sklerose f -n sclerosis.
Skonto nt or m, pl -s or **Skonti** cash discount.
Skorbut m no pl scurvy.
Skorpion m -e (Zool) scorpion; (Astrol) Scorpio.
Skrupel m - usu pl scruple. er hatte keine ~, das
zu tun he had no scruples about doing it; ohne ~
without scruples.
Skrupel-: **s~los** adj unscrupulous; ~**losigkeit** f
unscrupulousness.
Skulptur f sculpture.
Skunk m -s skunk.
skurril adj (geh) droll, comical.
S-Kurve ['ɛs-] f S-bend.
Slalom m -s slalom.
Slang [slɛŋ] m no pl slang.
Slawe m (wk) -n, -n, **Slawin** f Slav.
slawisch adj Slavonic, Slavic.
Slip m -s (pair of) briefs pl.
Slipper m - slip-on (shoe).
Slogan ['sloːgn] m -s slogan.
Slum [slam] m -s slum.
Smaragd m -e emerald.
Smog m -s smog.
Smoking ['smoːkɪŋ] m -s dinner-jacket, tuxedo
(US).
Snob m -s snob.
snobistisch adj snobbish.
SO = Südosten SE.
s.o. = siehe oben.
so 1 adv (a) (mit adj, adv) so; (mit vb: ~ sehr) so
much, ~ groß etc so big etc; eine ~ große Frau
such a big woman; ~ groß wie ... as big as ...; ~
gut es geht as best as I/he etc can; er ist nicht ~
dumm, das zu glauben he's not so stupid as to
believe that; das hat ihn ~ geärgert, daß ... that
annoyed him so much that ...; ~ ein Fehler such
a mistake; ~ ein Idiot! what an idiot!; hast du ~
etwas schon einmal gesehen? have you ever
seen anything like it?; na ~ was! well I never!; ~
etwas Schönes such a beautiful thing; ~ einer
wie ich somebody like me.
(b) (auf diese Weise) like this/that. mach es
nicht ~ don't do it like that; mach es ~, wie er es

vorgeschlagen hat do it the way he suggested; ~
ist sie nun einmal that's the way she is; (ach) ~
ist das! I see!; ~ oder/und ~ in one way or the
other; und ~ weiter and so on; gut ~! fine!; das
ist gut ~ that's fine; mir ist (es) ~, als ob ... it
seems to me as if ...; das kam ~: ... this is what
happened ...; es verhält sich ~: ... the facts are
as follows ...; das habe ich nur ~ gesagt I didn't
really mean it.
(c) (etwa) about, or so. ich komme ~ um 8
Uhr I'll come at 8 or so.
(d) (col: umsonst) for nothing.
(e) (als Füllwort) nicht übersetzt. ~ beeil dich
doch! do hurry up!; ~ mancher a number of
people pl.
2 conj (a) ~ daß so that. (b) ~ wie es jetzt ist
as things are at the moment. (c) ~ klein er auch
sein mag however small he may be.
3 interj so; (wirklich) oh, really; (abschließend)
well, right. er ist schon da — ~ he's here already
— is he?; ~, ~! well well.
sobald conj as soon as.
Socke f -n sock. sich auf die ~n machen (col) to
get going (col).
Sockel m - base; (von Denkmal, Statue) pedestal.
Soda nt no pl soda.
Sodawasser nt soda water.
Sodbrennen nt heartburn.
Sodomie f buggery, bestiality.
soeben adv just (this moment).
Sofa nt -s sofa, settee (esp Brit).
sofern conj provided (that). ~ ... nicht if ... not.
soff pret of **saufen**.
sofort adv immediately. komm hierher, und zwar
~! come here this instant!; (ich) komme ~!
(I'm) just coming!
Soforthilfe f emergency relief or aid.
sofortig adj immediate, instant.
Sofortmaßnahme f immediate measure.
Soft|eis ['sɔft-] nt soft ice-cream.
Software ['sɔftwɛːə] f -s (Comp) software.
sog pret of **saugen**.
sog. = sogenannt.
Sog m -e (saugende Kraft) suction; (von Strudel)
vortex; (fig) maelstrom.
sogar adv even. schön, ~ sehr schön beautiful, in
fact very beautiful.
sogenannt adj attr so-called.
sogleich adv = sofort.
Sohle f -n (a) (Fuß~ etc) sole; (Einlage) insole. auf
leisen ~n softly. (b) (Boden) bottom.
Sohn m ⸚e (lit, fig) son.
Soja f, pl **Sojen** soy.
Soja-: ~**bohne** f soybean; ~**soße** f soya sauce.
solang(e) conj as long as, so long as.
Solar- in cpds solar.
solch adj inv, **solche(r, s)** adj such. ein ~es
Mensch such a person; wir haben ~en Durst
we're so thirsty; ~ ein langer Weg such a long
way; ~es that kind of thing; Rechtsanwälte gibt
es ~e und ~e there are lawyers and lawyers.
solcherlei adj attr inv such.
Sold m no pl (Mil) pay.
Soldat m (wk) -en, -en soldier. ~ spielen to play
soldiers.
Soldaten-: ~**friedhof** m military cemetery;
~**sprache** f military slang; ~**tum** nt soldiery
no art; (Tradition) military tradition; ~**verband**
m ex-servicemen's association.
soldatisch adj (militärisch) military; (soldatenge-
mäß) soldierly.
Söldner m - mercenary.
Söldnertruppe f mercenary force.
Sole f -n brine, salt water.
Solei ['zoːl|aɪ] nt pickled egg.
solidarisch adj sich mit jdm ~ erklären to declare one's solidarity with sb; ~ mit jdm handeln to act in solidarity with sb.

solidarisieren* vr sich ~ mit to show (one's) solidarity with.

Solidarität f solidarity.

Solidaritätsstreik m sympathy strike.

solid(e) adj Haus, Möbel etc solid, sturdy; Arbeit, Wissen, Handwerker sound; Mensch, Lokal respectable; Firma solid; Preise reasonable.

Solist(in f) m (Mus) soloist.

Soll nt -(s) (Schuld) debit; (Schuldseite) debit side. ~ **und Haben** debit and credit; **sein** ~ **erfüllen** to meet one's target.

sollen 1 modal aux pret **sollte**, ptp ~ (a) (bei Befehl, Anordnung, Absicht) to be (supposed) to. **was soll ich/er tun?** what shall or should I/should he do?; **er weiß nicht, was er tun soll** he doesn't know what to do; **sie sagte ihm, er solle draußen warten** she told him to wait outside; **was ich (nicht) alles tun/wissen soll!** the things I'm supposed to do/know!; **es soll nicht wieder vorkommen** it won't happen again; **er soll reinkommen** tell him to come in; **niemand soll sagen, daß ...** let no-one say that ...; **das Haus soll nächste Woche gestrichen werden** the house is to be painted next week; **was sollte ich/er deiner Meinung nach tun?** what do you think I/he should do or ought to do?; **das hättest du nicht tun** ~ you shouldn't have or oughtn't to have done that.

(**b**) (bei Gerücht, Vermutung) to be supposed or meant to. **sie soll verheiratet sein** I've heard she's married; **Xanthippe soll zänkisch gewesen sein** Xanthippe is said to have been quarrelsome; **das soll gar nicht so einfach sein** they say it's not that easy; **was soll das heißen?** what's that supposed to mean?; **mir soll es gleich sein** it's all the same to me; **so etwas soll es geben** these things happen; **man sollte glauben, daß ...** you would think that ...; **sollte das möglich sein?** can that be possible?

(**c**) **sollte das passieren, ...** if that should happen ...; **er sollte sie nie wiedersehen** he was never to see her again.

2 vti pret **sollte**, ptp **gesollt** was soll das? what's all this?; (warum denn das) what's that for?; **was soll's?** what the hell! (col); **das sollst du nicht** you shouldn't do that; **was man nicht alles soll!** (col) the things you're meant to do!

Söller m - balcony.

Soll-: ~**seite** f (Fin) debit side; ~**stärke** f required strength.

solo adv (Mus) solo; (fig col) on one's own, alone.

Solo nt, pl **Soli** solo.

solvent [zɔl'vɛnt] adj (Fin) solvent.

somit adv consequently, therefore.

Sommer m - summer. **im** ~ in (the) summer; **im nächsten** ~ next summer; ~ **wie Winter** all year round.

Sommer- in cpds summer; ~**abend** m summer('s) evening; ~**anfang** m beginning of summer; ~**ferien** pl summer holidays pl (Brit) or vacation (US); (Jur, Parl) summer recess; ~**gast** m summer guest; ~**haus** nt holiday home; ~**kleidung** f summer clothing.

sommerlich adj summer attr; (sommerartig) summery.

Sommer-: ~**mantel** m summer coat; ~**monat** m summer month; ~**nacht** f summer('s) night; ~**pause** f summer break; (Jur, Parl) summer recess; ~**reifen** m normal tyre (Brit) or tire (US); ~**saison** f summer season; ~**schlußverkauf** m summer sale; ~**semester** nt (Univ) summer semester, ≈ summer term (Brit); ~**sitz** m summer residence; ~**spiele** pl **die Olympischen** ~**spiele** the Summer Olympics; ~**sprosse** f freckle; ~**tag** m summer's day; ~**weizen** m spring wheat; ~**wetter** nt summer weather; ~**zeit** f summer time no art.

Sonate f -n sonata.

Sonde f -n (Space, Med) probe.

Sonder- in cpds special; ~**anfertigung** f special model; ~**angebot** nt special offer; ~**ausgabe** f (a) special edition; (b) ~**ausgaben** pl (Fin) additional or extra expenses pl.

sonderbar adj strange, peculiar, odd.

sonderbarerweise adv strange to say.

Sonder-: ~**beauftragte(r)** mf (Pol) special emissary; ~**fahrt** f special excursion; ~**fall** m special case; (Ausnahme) exception; ~**genehmigung** f special permission; (Schein) special permit; s~**gleichen** adv inv **eine Frechheit** s~**gleichen** an incredible cheek; ~**konto** nt special account.

sonderlich 1 adj attr particular. **ohne** ~**e Begeisterung** without any particular enthusiasm. 2 adv particularly.

Sonderling m eccentric.

Sonder-: ~**marke** f special issue (stamp); ~**maschine** f special plane; ~**meldung** f (Rad, TV) special announcement.

sondern[1] conj but.

sondern[2] vt (geh) to separate; siehe gesondert.

Sonder-: ~**preis** m special reduced price; ~**recht** nt (special) privilege; ~**regelung** f special provision; ~**schicht** f special shift; (zusätzlich) extra shift; ~**schule** f special school; ~**stellung** f special position; ~**stempel** m (bei der Post) special postmark; ~**wünsche** pl special requests pl; ~**zug** m special train.

sondieren* vti to sound out. **das Terrain** ~ to spy out the land; **die Lage** ~ to find out how the land lies.

Sondierungsgespräch nt exploratory talk.

Sonett nt -e sonnet.

Sonnabend m Saturday; siehe Dienstag.

sonnabends adv on Saturdays, on a Saturday.

Sonne f -n sun. **an die** ~ **gehen** to go out in the sun; **geh mir aus der** ~! (col) get out of the way!; (aus dem Licht) get out of the light!

sonnen vr to sun oneself. **sich in etw** (dat) ~ (fig) to bask in sth.

Sonnen-: ~**anbeter** m (lit, fig) sun-worshipper; ~**aufgang** m sunrise; ~**bad** nt sunbathing no pl; **ein** ~**bad nehmen** to sunbathe; ~**batterie** f solar battery.

Sonnenblume f sunflower.

Sonnenblumen-: ~**kern** m sunflower seed; ~**öl** nt sunflower oil.

Sonnen-: ~**brand** m sunburn no art; ~**bräune** f suntan; ~**brille** f (pair of) sunglasses pl; ~**deck** nt (Naut) sundeck; ~**energie** f solar energy; ~**finsternis** f solar eclipse; ~**fleck** m (Astron) sunspot; s~**gebräunt** adj suntanned; ~**gott** m sungod; ~**hut** m sunhat; ~**jahr** nt (Astron) solar year; s~**klar** adj (col) crystal clear; ~**kollektor** m solar panel; ~**kult** m sun cult; ~**licht** nt sunlight; ~**öl** nt suntan oil; ~**schein** m sunshine; **bei strahlendem** ~**schein** in brilliant sunshine; ~**schirm** m sunshade; ~**schutz** m protection against the sun; ~**seite** f (lit, fig) sunny side; ~**stand** m position of the sun; ~**stich** m sunstroke no art; **du hast wohl einen** ~**stich!** (col) you must have been out in the sun too long!; ~**strahl** m sunbeam; ~**system** nt solar system; ~**uhr** f sundial; ~**untergang** m sunset; ~**wende** f solstice.

sonnig adj sunny.

Sonntag m Sunday; siehe Dienstag.

sonntäglich adj Sunday attr. ~ **gekleidet** dressed in one's Sunday best.

sonntags adv on Sundays, on a Sunday.

Sonntags- in cpds Sunday; ~**arbeit** f Sunday working; ~**ausflug** m Sunday trip; ~**beilage** f Sunday supplement; ~**dienst** m (von Polizist etc) Sunday duty; ~**dienst haben** (Apotheke) to be open on Sundays; ~**fahrer** m (pej) Sunday driver; ~**maler** m Sunday painter; ~**zeitung** f Sunday paper.

sonor adj sonorous.

sonst 1 *adv* **(a)** *(außerdem)* *(mit pron, adv)* else; *(mit n)* other. ~ **noch Fragen?** any other questions?; **wer/wie** *etc* **(denn)** ~**?** who/how *etc* else?; **er denkt, er ist** ~ **wer** *(col)* he thinks he's somebody special; ~ **noch etwas?** is that all?, anything else?; **wo warst du** ~ **noch?** where else did you go?; ~ **geht's dir gut?** *(iro col)* are you feeling okay? *(col).* **(b)** *(andernfalls)* otherwise. **(c)** *(in anderen Beziehungen)* in other ways. **wenn ich Ihnen** ~ **noch behilflich sein kann** if I can help you in any other way. **(d)** *(gewöhnlich)* usually. **genau wie es** ~ **ist** just as it usually is; **genau wie/anders als** ~ the same as/different from usual; **alles war wie** ~ everything was as it always used to be. **2** *conj* otherwise, or (else).

sonstig *adj attr* other; **Fragen, Auskünfte** *etc* further. „**S**~**es**" "other".

sonst-: ~**wann** *adv (col)* some other time; ~**was** *indef pron (col)* **da kann ja** ~**was passieren** anything could happen; **ich habe** ~**was versucht** I've tried everything; ~**wie** *adv (col)* (in) some other way; *(sehr)* like mad *(col);* ~**wo** *adv (col)* somewhere else; ~**wohin** *adv (col)* somewhere else.

so|oft *conj* whenever.

Sopran *m* -e soprano; *(von Jungen)* treble.

Sopranistin *f* soprano.

Sorge *f* -**n (a)** worry. **keine** ~**!** *(col)* don't worry!; **wir betrachten diese Entwicklung mit** ~ **we** view this development with concern; ~**n haben** to have problems; **ich habe solche** ~ I'm so worried; **du hast** ~**n!** *(iro)* you think you've got troubles! *(col);* **jdm** ~**n machen** *(Kummer bereiten)* to cause sb a lot of worry; **machen Sie sich** *(dat)* **deshalb keine** ~**n** don't worry about that; **lassen Sie das meine** ~ **sein** let me worry about that; **das ist nicht meine** ~ that's not my problem; **dafür** ~ **tragen, daß** ... *(geh)* to see to it that ... **(b)** *(Für*~, *Jur)* care.

sorgen 1 *vi* ~ **für** *(sich kümmern um)* to look after; *(vorsorgen für)* to provide for; *(herbeischaffen) Proviant, Musik* to provide; *(bewirken)* to ensure; **dafür** ~, **daß** ... to see to it that ...; **dafür ist gesorgt** that's taken care of. **2** *vr* to worry. **sich** ~ **um** to worry about.

Sorgen-: **s**~**frei** *adj* free of care; *(heiter)* carefree; ~**kind** *nt (col)* problem child; **s**~**voll** *adj* worried; *Leben* full of worries.

Sorgerecht *nt (Jur)* custody.

Sorgfalt *f no pl* care. **ohne** ~ **arbeiten** to work carelessly; **viel** ~ **auf etw** *(acc)* **verwenden** to take a lot of care over sth.

sorgfältig *adj* careful.

sorglos *adj* carefree; *(leichtfertig)* careless.

Sorglosigkeit *f siehe adj* carefreeness; carelessness.

sorgsam *adj* careful.

Sorte *f* -**n (a)** type, kind; *(Qualität, Klasse)* grade; *(Marke)* brand. **beste** ~ top quality. **(b)** *(Fin) usu pl* foreign currency.

sortieren* *vt* to sort. **etw in einen Schrank** ~ to tidy sth away into a cupboard.

Sortierer(in *f) m* - sorter.

Sortiermaschine *f* sorting machine.

Sortiment *nt (a)* assortment. **(b)** *(Buchhandel)* retail book trade.

Sortimentsbuchhandlung *f* retail bookshop *(Brit)* or bookstore *(US).*

SOS [ɛsoːˈɛs] *nt* -, - SOS.

sosehr *conj* however much, no matter how much.

soso *interj* ~**!** I see!; *(erstaunt)* well well!; *(drohend)* well!

Soße *f* -**n** sauce; *(Braten~)* gravy; *(pej col)* gunge *(col).*

Souffleur [zuˈfløːɐ] *m,* **Souffleuse** [zuˈfløːzə] *f (Theat)* prompter.

soufflieren* [zuˈfliːrən] *vti (Theat)* to prompt *(jdm sb).*

so|undso *adv* ~ **lange** for such and such a time; ~ **viele** so and so many; **Paragraph** ~ **article** such-and-such; **er sagte, mach das** ~ he said, do it in such and such a way.

so|undsovielte(r, s) *adj* umpteenth. **am S**~**n** *(Datum)* on such and such a date.

Souterrain [ˈzuːtɛrɛ̃] *nt* -**s** basement.

Souvenir [zuvəˈniːɐ] *nt* -**s** souvenir.

souverän [zuvəˈrɛːn] *adj* sovereign *no adv; (fig)* supremely good; *(überlegen)* (most) superior *no adv.* **sein Gebiet** ~ **beherrschen** to have a commanding knowledge of one's field.

Souveränität [zuvəreniˈtɛːt] *f* sovereignty.

soviel 1 *adv* so much. **halb** ~ half as much; ~ **wie** ... as much as ...; **noch einmal** ~ *(doppelt* ~*)* twice as much; ~ **für heute!** that's all for today. **2** *conj* as far as. ~ **ich weiß, nicht!** not as far as I know.

sovielmal *adv* so many times.

soweit 1 *adv* **(a)** on the whole; *(bis jetzt)* up to now; *(bis zu diesem Punkt)* thus far. ~ **wie möglich** as far as possible. **(b)** ~ **sein** to be finished *or (bereit)* ready; **es ist bald** ~ it's nearly time. **2** *conj* as far as; *(insofern)* in so far as.

sowenig *adv* no more, not any more *(wie* than*).* ~ **wie möglich** as little as possible.

sowie *conj* **(a)** *(sobald)* as soon as. **(b)** *(und auch)* as well as.

sowieso *adv* anyway. **das** ~**!** obviously!

sowjetisch *adj* Soviet.

Sowjet- *in cpds* Soviet; ~**republik** *f* Soviet Republic; ~**russe** *m* Soviet Russian; ~**union** *f* Soviet Union.

sowohl *conj* ~ **X als** *or* **wie** **(auch)** **Y** both X and Y, X as well as Y.

Sozi *m* -**s** *(esp pej col)* Socialist.

sozial *adj* social; *(*~ *eingestellt)* public-spirited. ~**er Wohnungsbau** ≃ council housing *(Brit),* state-subsidized housing.

Sozial-: ~**abgaben** *pl* (social) welfare contributions *pl;* ~**amt** *nt* (social) welfare office; ~**arbeit** *f* social work; ~**arbeiter** *m* social worker; ~**beruf** *m* caring profession; ~**demokrat** *m* social democrat; ~**demokratie** *f* social democracy; **s**~**demokratisch** *adj* social-democratic; ~**einrichtungen** *pl* social facilities *pl;* ~**fall** *m* hardship case; ~**gericht** *nt* (social) welfare tribunal; ~**hilfe** *f* welfare (aid).

Sozialisation *f (Psych, Sociol)* socialization.

Sozialismus *m* socialism.

Sozialist(in *f) m* socialist.

sozialistisch *adj* socialist.

Sozial-: ~**politik** *f* social policy; ~**versicherung** *f* social security; ~**wohnung** *f* ≃ council flat *(Brit),* state-subsidized apartment.

Sozio-: ~**loge** *m (wk),* ~**login** *f* sociologist; ~**logie** *f* sociology; **s**~**logisch** *adj* sociological.

Sozius *m* -**se (a)** *(Beifahrer)* pillion rider. **(b)** *(Partner)* partner.

Soziussitz *m* pillion (seat).

sozusagen *adv* so to speak, as it were.

Spachtel *m (Werkzeug)* spatula.

Spachtelmasse *f* filler.

spachteln 1 *vt Mauerfugen, Ritzen* to fill (in). **2** *vi (col: essen)* to tuck in.

Spagat *m or nt* -**e** splits *pl.* ~ **machen** to do the splits.

Spaghetti [ʃpaˈgɛti] *pl* spaghetti *sing.*

spähen *vi* to peer.

Spähtrupp *m (Mil)* reconnaissance party.

Spalier *nt* -**e** *(von Menschen)* row, line; *(zur Ehrenbezeigung)* guard of honour *(Brit)* or honor *(US).* ~ **stehen/ein** ~ **bilden** to form a guard of honour.

Spalt *m* -**e (a)** *(Öffnung)* gap, opening; *(Riß)* crack; *(Fels*~*)* crevice. **das Fenster einen** ~ **öffnen** to open the window slightly. **(b)** *(fig: Kluft)* split.

spaltbar *adj (Phys) Atomkerne* fissionable.

Spaltbreit *m:* **etw einen** ~ **öffnen** to open sth

slightly.
Spalte f **-n (a)** (esp Geol) fissure; (in Wand) crack. **(b)** (Typ, Press) column.
spalten ptp auch **gespalten** vt (lit, fig) to split; Holz to chop. **bei dieser Frage sind die Meinungen gespalten** opinions are divided on this question; siehe **gespalten.**
Spaltung f (lit, fig) splitting; (in Partei etc) split.
Span m **-e** (Hobel~) shaving; (Metall~) filing.
Spanferkel nt sucking pig.
Spange f **-n** clasp; (Haar~) hair slide (Brit), barrette (US); (Schuh~) strap; (Arm~) bangle; (Zahn~) brace.
Spanien ['ʃpaːniən] nt Spain.
Spanier(in f) ['ʃpaːniɐ, -iərɪn] m - Spaniard. **die ~** the Spanish, the Spaniards.
spanisch adj Spanish. **~e Wand** (folding) screen; **das kommt mir ~ vor** (col) that seems odd to me; siehe **deutsch.**
Spanisch(e) nt decl as adj Spanish.
Spankorb m chip basket.
Spann m **-e** instep.
spann pret of **spinnen.**
spannen 1 vt **(a)** Saite, Seil to tighten; Bogen to draw; Muskeln to flex. **(b)** (straff befestigen) Werkstück to clamp; Wäscheleine to put up; Netz, Plane to stretch. **(c)** (anschirren) to hitch (up) (vor +acc to). **2** vr **(a)** (Haut, Muskeln) to go or become taut. **(b) sich über etw** (acc) **~** (Brücke) to span sth. **3** vi (Kleidung) to be (too) tight.
spannend adj exciting; (stärker) thrilling. **mach's nicht so ~!** (col) don't keep me/us in suspense.
Spanner m **- (a)** (Hosen~) hanger; (Schuh~) shoetree. **(b)** (col: Voyeur) peeping Tom.
Spannkraft f (von Feder) tension; (von Muskel) tone; (fig) vigour (Brit), vigor (US).
Spannung f (lit, fig) tension; (Elec auch) voltage; (Mech) stress. **mit großer/atemloser ~ with** great/breathless excitement; **etw mit ~ erwarten** to await sth full of suspense.
Spannungs-: ~feld nt (lit) electric field; (fig) area of conflict; **~gebiet** nt (Pol) flashpoint, area of tension; **~prüfer** m voltage detector.
Spannweite f (von Flügeln, Aviat) (wing)span.
Spanplatte f chipboard.
Spar-: ~buch nt savings book; **~büchse** f moneybox.
sparen 1 vt to save. **keine Kosten/Mühe ~ to** spare no expense/effort; **spar' dir deine guten Ratschläge!** (col) you can keep your advice!; **diese Mühe/diese Kosten hätten Sie sich** (dat) **~ können** you could have saved or spared yourself the trouble/this expense. **2** vi to save; (haushalten) to economize. **an etw** (dat) **~** to be sparing with sth; (mit etw haushalten) to save or economize on sth; **er hatte nicht mit Lob gespart** he was lavish in his praise; **für** or **auf etw** (acc) **~** to save up for sth.
Sparer(in f) m - (bei Bank etc) saver.
Sparflamme f low flame. **auf ~** (fig col) just ticking over (col).
Spargel m **-** asparagus.
Spar-: ~groschen m nest egg; **~guthaben** nt savings account; **~kasse** f savings bank; **~konto** nt savings account, deposit account (Brit).
spärlich adj sparse; Ausbeute, Reste, Kleidung, Kenntnisse scanty; Beleuchtung poor. **~ bevölkert** sparsely populated.
Spar-: ~maßnahme f economy measure; **~packung** f economy size; **~prämie** f savings premium.
sparsam adj thrifty; (haushälterisch) economical. **~ im Verbrauch** economical; **~ verwenden** to use sparingly.
Sparsamkeit f thrift; (das Haushalten) economizing.
Sparschwein nt piggy bank.
spartanisch adj Spartan. **~ leben** to lead a Spar-

tan life.
Sparte f **-n (a)** (Comm) (Branche) line of business; (Teilgebiet) area. **(b)** (Rubrik) column.
Spar-: ~vertrag m savings agreement; **~zinsen** pl interest no pl.
Spaß m **-e** (no pl: Vergnügen) fun; (Scherz) joke; (Streich) prank. **~ beiseite** joking apart; **viel ~!** have fun! (auch iro); **an etw** (dat) **~ haben** to enjoy sth; **es macht mir ~/keinen ~** it's fun/no fun; **Hauptsache, es macht ~** the main thing is to have fun; **(nur so,) zum ~** for fun; **etw im ~ sagen** to say sth in fun; **da hört der ~ auf** that's going beyond a joke; **ein teurer ~** an expensive business; **~ muß sein** there's no harm in a joke; **es war ein ~,** ihm bei der Arbeit zuzusehen it was a joy to see him at work; **sich** (dat) **einen ~ daraus machen, etw zu tun** to get enjoyment out of doing sth; **seinen ~ mit jdm treiben** to make fun of sb; **er versteht keinen ~!** he has no sense of humour (Brit) or humor (US); **da verstehe ich keinen ~!** I won't stand for any nonsense.
spaßen vi **mit Blutvergiftung ist nicht zu ~** blood poisoning is no joke; **mit ihm ist nicht zu ~** he doesn't stand for any nonsense.
spaßeshalber adv for the fun of it, for fun.
spaßig adj funny, droll.
Spaß-: ~macher m joker; **~verderber** m - spoilsport; **~vogel** m joker.
Spastiker(in f) m - spastic.
spastisch adj spastic. **~ gelähmt** suffering from spastic paralysis.
spät adj late; Reue, Ruhm, Glück belated. **am ~en Nachmittag** in the late afternoon; **~ in der Nacht/am Tage** late at night/in the day; **heute abend wird es ~** it'll be a late night tonight; (nach Hause kommen) I/he etc will be late this evening; **von früh bis ~** from morning till night; **wie ~ ist es?** what's the time?; **zu ~** too late; **er kommt morgens regelmäßig fünf Minuten zu ~** he's always five minutes late in the mornings; **wir sind ~ dran** we're late.
Spaten m **-** spade.
Spatenstich m **den ersten ~ tun** to turn the first sod.
Spät|entwickler m late developer.
später comp of **spät** adj later; (zukünftig) future. **was will er denn ~** (einmal) **werden?** what does he want to do later (on)?; **an ~ denken** to think of the future; **bis ~!** see you later!
spätestens adv at the latest. **~ morgen** tomorrow at the latest; **~ um 8** by 8 at the latest; **bis ~ in einer Woche** in one week at the latest.
Spät-: ~geburt f late birth; **~herbst** m late autumn, late fall (US); **~lese** f late vintage; **~nachmittag** m late afternoon; **~schicht** f late shift; **~sommer** m late summer.
Spatz m (wk) **-en, -en (a)** sparrow. **wie ein ~ essen** to peck at one's food. **(b)** (col: Kind) tot (col).
Spätzle pl (Cook) home-made pasta.
Spätzünder m (hum col) **~ sein** to be slow on the uptake.
spazieren* vi aux sein to stroll. **wir waren ~** went for a walk or stroll.
spazieren-: ~fahren sep irreg **1** vi aux sein to go for a drive; **2** vt jdn **~fahren** to take sb for a drive; **das Baby (im Kinderwagen) ~fahren** to take the baby for a walk (in the pram); **~gehen** vi sep irreg aux sein to go for a walk.
Spazier-: ~fahrt f drive; **eine ~fahrt machen** to go for a run; **~gang** m walk; **einen ~gang machen** to go for a walk; **~gänger** m - stroller; **~stock** m walking stick.
SPD [espeː'deː] f = Sozialdemokratische Partei Deutschlands.
Specht m **-e** woodpecker.
Speck m **-e** (Schweine~) bacon fat; (Schinken~, durchwachsener ~) bacon. **~ ansetzen** (col) to

get fat; **mit** ~ **fängt man Mäuse** *(Prov)* you need a sprat to catch a mackerel *(prov)*; **ran an den** ~ *(col)* let's get stuck in *(col)*.

speckig *adj* greasy.

Speckschwarte *f* bacon rind.

Spediteur [ʃpedi'tøːrə] *m* haulage contractor; *(Umzugsfirma)* furniture remover *(Brit)* or mover.

Spedition *f (auch* ~**sfirma)** haulage contractor; *(Umzugsfirma)* removal firm *(Brit)*, furniture movers *pl (US)*.

Speer *m* -**e** spear; *(Sport)* javelin.

Speer-: ~**spitze** *f (lit, fig)* spearhead; ~**werfen** *nt (Sport)* das ~**werfen** throwing the javelin.

Speiche *f* -**n** (a) spoke. (b) *(Anat)* radius.

Speichel *m no pl* saliva, spittle.

Speichel-: ~**drüse** *f* salivary gland; ~**lecker** *m* - *(pej col)* bootlicker *(col)*.

Speicher *m* - *(Lagerhaus)* storehouse; *(im Haus)* loft; *(Wasser~)* tank; *(Comp)* memory. **auf dem** ~ in the loft.

Speicherkapazität *f* storage capacity; *(Comp)* memory capacity.

speichern 1 *vt Vorräte, Energie, Daten* to store. 2 *vr* to accumulate.

Speicherung *f* storing, storage.

speien *pret* **spie,** *ptp* **gespie(e)n** *vti* to spit; *Lava, Feuer* to spew (forth); *Wasser* to spout.

Speise *f* -**n** *(geh: Nahrung)* food; *(Gericht)* dish. **kalte und warme** ~**n** hot and cold meals.

Speise-: ~**eis** *nt* icecream; ~**fett** *nt* cooking fat; ~**kammer** *f* larder; ~**karte** *f* menu.

speisen 1 *vti (geh)* to eat, to dine *(form)*. 2 *vt (liter, Tech)* to feed.

Speise-: ~**öl** *nt* salad oil; *(zum Braten)* cooking oil; ~**reste** *pl* left-overs *pl*; ~**röhre** *f (Anat)* gullet; ~**saal** *m* dining hall; *(in Hotel etc)* dining room; ~**schrank** *m* larder; ~**wagen** *m (Rail)* dining car.

Spektakel *m* - *(col: Lärm)* row; *(Aufregung)* fuss.

spektakulär *adj* spectacular.

Spektralfarbe *f* colour *(Brit)* or color *(US)* of the spectrum.

Spektrum *nt, pl* **Spektren** spectrum.

Spekulant(in *f)* *m* speculator.

Spekulation *f (auch Fin)* speculation *(mit in)*. ~ **mit Grundstücken** property speculation; ~**en anstellen** to make speculations.

Spekulatius [ʃpeku'laːtsiʊs] *m* -, - spiced biscuit *(Brit)* or cookie *(US)*.

spekulativ *adj* speculative.

spekulieren* *vi (auch Fin)* to speculate *(mit in)*. **auf etw (acc)** ~ *(col)* to have hopes of sth.

Spelze *f* -**n** *(Bot)* husk.

spendabel *adj (col)* generous, open-handed.

Spende *f* -**n** donation; *(Beitrag)* contribution.

spenden *vti Lebensmittel, Blut, Geld* to donate; *(beitragen) Geld* to contribute; *Trost* to give.

Spendenkonto *nt* donations account.

Spender(in *f)* *m* - donator; *(Beitragleistender)* contributor; *(Med)* donor.

spendieren* *vt* to buy, to get *(jdm etw* sb sth, sth for sb). **spendierst du mir einen?** *(col)* are you going to buy me a drink?

Sperling *m* sparrow.

Sperma *nt, pl* **Spermen** *or* -**ta** sperm.

sperr|angelweit *adv (col)* ~ **offen** wide open.

Sperrbezirk *m* no-go area.

Sperre *f* -**n** (a) *(Schlagbaum, Bahnsteig~ etc)* barrier; *(Polizei~)* roadblock; *(Tech)* locking device. (b) *(Verbot, Sport)* ban; *(Comm)* embargo; *(Nachrichten~)* (news) blackout.

sperren 1 *vt* (a) *(schließen) Grenze, Straße etc* to close; *(Comm) Konto* to freeze; *Einfuhr, Ausfuhr, (Sport)* to ban; *(Tech)* to lock. **etw für jdn/etw** ~ to close sth to sb/sth; **jdm das Gehalt** ~ to stop sb's salary; **jdm den Strom/das Telefon** ~ to cut off sb's electricity/telephone. (b) *(einschließen)* **jdn in etw (acc)** ~ to lock sb in sth. (c) *(Typ)* to space out. 2 *vr* **sich (gegen etw)** ~ to ba(u)lk (at sth). 3

vi (Sport) to obstruct.

Sperr-: ~**feuer** *nt (Mil, fig)* barrage; ~**frist** *f* waiting period *(auch Jur)*; *(Sport)* (period of) suspension; ~**gebiet** *nt* no-go area; ~**gut** *nt* bulky freight; ~**holz** *nt* plywood.

sperrig *adj* bulky; *(unhandlich)* unwieldy.

Sperr-: ~**kette** *f* chain; *(an Haustür)* safety chain; ~**konto** *nt* blocked account; ~**müll** *m* bulky refuse; ~**sitz** *m (im Kino)* back seats *pl*; *(im Zirkus)* front seats *pl*; ~**stunde** *f* closing time.

Sperrung *f* (a) *siehe vt* (a) closing; freezing; banning; locking. (b) *(Verbot, Sport)* ban.

Spesen *pl* expenses *pl*. **auf** ~ **reisen/essen** to travel/eat on expenses; **außer** ~ **nichts gewesen** *(col)* there was nothing doing *(col)*.

Spesen-: **s~frei** *adj* free of charge; ~**konto** *nt* expense account.

Spezial-: ~**ausbildung** *f* specialized training; ~**ausführung** *f* special model; ~**fall** *m* special case; ~**gebiet** *nt* special field; ~**geschäft** *nt* specialist shop *(Brit)* or store *(US)*; **ein** ~**geschäft für Sportkleidung** a sportswear specialist.

spezialisieren* *vr* **sich** *(auf etw acc)* ~ to specialize (in sth).

Spezialisierung *f* specialization.

Spezialist(in *f)* *m* specialist *(für in)*.

Spezialität *f* speciality *(Brit)*, specialty *(US)*.

speziell 1 *adj* special. 2 *adv* (e)specially.

spezifisch *adj* specific.

spezifizieren* *vt* to specify.

Sphäre *f* -**n** *(lit, fig)* sphere.

sphärisch *adj* spherical; *Klänge, Musik* celestial.

Sphinx *f* -**e** sphinx.

spicken *vt (Cook) Braten* to lard. **mit Fehlern gespickt** peppered with mistakes.

Spickzettel *m* crib.

spie *pret of* **speien.**

Spiegel *m* - (a) *(lit, fig)* mirror. **jdm den** ~ **vorhalten** *(fig)* to hold up a mirror to sb. (b) *(Wasser~, Alkohol~, Zucker~)* level.

Spiegel-: ~**bild** *nt (lit, fig)* reflection; *(seitenverkehrtes Bild)* mirror image; **s~bildlich** *adj* Zeichnung etc mirror-image; **s~blank** *adj* shining.

Spiegel|ei *nt* fried egg.

Spiegel-: ~**fechterei** *f (fig)* shadow-boxing; *(Vortäuschung)* bluff; **s~glatt** *adj* like glass.

spiegeln 1 *vi* to reflect; *(glitzern)* to gleam. 2 *vt* to reflect. 3 *vr* to be reflected or mirrored.

Spiegel-: ~**reflexkamera** *f* reflex camera; ~**schrift** *f* mirror writing; **etw in** ~**schrift schreiben** to write sth backwards.

Spiegelung *f* reflection; *(Luft~)* mirage.

Spiel *nt* -**e** (a) game; *(Wettkampfs~ auch)* match; *(Theat: Stück)* play. **im** ~ **sein** *(fig)* to be at work; **das** ~ **verloren geben** *(fig)* to throw in the towel; **sein Geld beim** ~ **verlieren** to lose one's money gambling. (b) *(Bewegung, Zusammenspiel)* play. **das (freie)** ~ **der Kräfte** the (free) (inter)play of forces. (c) *(Spielzubehör)* game; *(Karten)* deck, pack; *(Satz)* set. (d) *(fig)* **leichtes** ~ **(mit** *or* **bei jdm) haben** to have an easy job of it (with sb); **jdm das** ~ **verderben** to spoil sb's little game; **das** ~ **ist aus** the game's up; **die Finger im** ~ **haben** to have a hand in affairs; **jdn/etw aus dem** ~ **lassen** to leave sb/sth out of it; **etw aufs** ~ **setzen** to put sth at stake; **auf dem** ~**(e) stehen** to be at stake; **sein** ~ **mit jdm treiben** to play games with sb.

Spiel-: ~**automat** *m* gambling machine; *(zum Geldgewinnen)* fruit machine *(Brit)*; ~**ball** *m (fig)* plaything; **ein** ~**ball der Wellen sein** *(geh)* to be at the mercy of the waves; ~**bank** *f* casino; ~**dose** *f* musical box *(Brit)*, music box *(US)*.

spielen 1 *vt* to play. **jdm einen Streich** ~ to play a trick on sb; **Klavier** ~ to play the piano; **was wird heute im Theater/Kino gespielt?** what's on at the theatre/cinema today?; **den Beleidigten** ~

to act all offended; **was wird hier gespielt?** *(col)* what's going on here? 2 *vi* to play; *(Theaterstück, Film)* to be on; *(beim Glücksspiel)* to gamble. **seine Beziehungen ~ lassen** to bring one's connections to bear; **das Stück spielt im 18. Jahrhundert** the play is set in the 18th century; **mit dem Gedanken ~, etw zu tun** to toy with the idea of doing sth.

spielend 1 *adj* playing. 2 *adv* easily. **das ist ~ leicht** that's very easy.

Spieler(in *f) m* - player; *(Glücks~)* gambler.

Spielerei *f no pl (Kinderspiel)* child's play *no art.* **das ist nur ~** I am/he is *etc* just playing about.

spielerisch 1 *adj (verspielt)* Geste, Katze etc playful. **(b)** *(Sport)* playing; *(Theat)* acting. **~es Können** playing/acting ability. 2 *adv* **(a)** *(verspielt)* playfully. **(b)** *(Sport)* in playing terms; *(Theat)* in acting terms.

Spiel-: ~**feld** *nt* field, pitch *(Brit)*; *(Tennis, Basketball)* court; ~**figur** *f* piece; ~**film** *m* feature film; ~**folge** *f (Sport)* order of play; *(Theat)* programme *(Brit)*, program *(US)*; ~**gefährte** *m* playmate; ~**geld** *nt* **(a)** *(Einsatz)* stake; **(b)** *(unechtes Geld)* toy money; ~**hölle** *f* gambling den; ~**kamerad** *m* playmate; ~**karte** *f* playing-card; ~**kasino** *nt* (gambling) casino; ~**klasse** *f* division; ~**leidenschaft** *f* gambling mania; ~**macher** *m* key player; ~**mannszug** *m* (brass) band; ~**minute** *f* minute (of play); ~**plan** *m (Theat, Film)* programme *(Brit)*, program *(US)*; **ein Stück vom ~plan absetzen** to drop a play; ~**platz** *m (für Kinder)* playground; ~**raum** *m* room to move; *(fig)* scope; *(zeitlich)* time; *(bei Planung etc)* leeway; *(Tech)* clearance, (free) play; ~**regel** *f (lit, fig)* rule of the game; **sich an die ~regeln halten** *(lit, fig)* to play the game; **gegen die ~regeln verstoßen** *(lit, fig)* not to play the game; ~**sachen** *pl* toys *pl*; ~**saison** *f (Theat, Sport)* season; ~**schuld** *f* gambling debt; ~**stand** *m* score; **bei einem ~stand von ...** with the score at ...; ~**tag** *m* day; ~**tisch** *m (beim Glücksspiel)* gaming table; ~**trieb** *m* play instinct; ~**uhr** *f* musical box *(Brit)*, music box *(US)*; ~**verbot** *nt (Sport)* ban; ~**verbot haben** to be banned; ~**verderber(in** *f) m* - spoilsport; ~**verlängerung** *f* extra time *(Brit)*, overtime *(US)*; ~**verlauf** *m* action; ~**warengeschäft** *nt* toy shop *(Brit)* or store *(US)*; ~**weise** *f* way of playing; ~**werk** *nt* musical mechanism; ~**wiese** *f* playing field; *(fig)* playground; ~**zeit** *f* **(a)** *(Saison)* season; **(b)** *(~dauer)* playing time.

Spielzeug *nt* toy; toys *pl*; *(fig auch)* plaything.

Spielzeug- *in cpds* toy; ~**eisenbahn** *f* toy train set.

Spielzimmer *nt* playroom.

Spieß *m* -e **(a)** spear; *(Brat~)* spit; *(kleiner)* skewer. **am ~ gebraten** spitroast(ed); **wie am ~(e) schreien** *(col)* to squeal like a stuck pig; **den ~ umdrehen** *(fig)* to turn the tables. **(b)** *(Mil col)* sarge *(col)*.

Spießbraten *m* joint roasted on a spit.

Spießbürger *m* (petit) bourgeois.

spießbürgerlich *adj* (petit) bourgeois.

spießen *vt* **etw auf etw** *(acc)* ~ *(auf Pfahl)* to impale sth on sth; *(auf Gabel)* to skewer sth on sth.

Spießer *m* - *(col)* (petit) bourgeois.

Spießgeselle *m (hum: Komplize)* crony *(col)*.

spießig *adj (col)* (petit) bourgeois.

Spießrute *f* ~**n laufen** *(fig)* to run the gauntlet.

Spikes [ʃpaiks, sp-] *pl (Sportschuhe)* spikes *pl*; *(Autoreifen)* studded tyres *pl (Brit)* or tires *pl (US)*; *(Stifte an Reifen)* studs *pl.*

Spinat *m no pl* spinach.

Spind *m* or *nt* -e locker.

Spindel *f* -n spindle; *(Treppen~)* newel.

spindeldürr *adj (pej)* spindly, thin as a rake.

Spinett *nt* -e *(Mus)* spinet.

Spinne *f* -n spider.

spinnefeind *adj pred (col)* **sich** *or* **einander** *(dat)* ~

sein to be deadly enemies.

spinnen *pret* **spann**, *ptp* **gesponnen** 1 *vti* to spin; **Lügen** to concoct, to invent. 2 *vi (col) (leicht verrückt sein)* to be crazy; *(Unsinn reden)* to talk rubbish. **ich denk' ich spinne** I don't believe it; **du spinnst wohl!, spinnst du?** you must be crazy!

Spinnen-: ~**faden** *m* spider's thread; ~**netz** *nt* cobweb.

Spinner(in *f) m* - **(a)** *(col)* nutcase *(col)*, screwball *(esp US col)*. **(b)** spinner.

Spinnerei *f* **(a)** *(Spinnwerkstatt)* spinning mill. **(b)** *(col)* crazy behaviour *(Brit)* or behavior *(US) no pl*; crazy thing; *(Unsinn)* rubbish.

Spinn-: ~**faser** *f* spinning fibre *(Brit)* or fiber *(US)*; ~**gewebe** *nt* cobweb; ~**rad** *nt* spinning-wheel; ~**webe** *f* -n spider's web.

Spion *m* -e spy; *(col: Guckloch)* peephole.

Spionage [ʃpioˈnaːʒə] *f no pl* espionage. ~ **treiben** to spy.

Spionage-: ~**abwehr** *f* counter-intelligence; ~**ring** *m* spy-ring.

spionieren* *vi* to spy; *(col: nachforschen)* to snoop about *(col)*.

Spionin *f* (woman) spy.

Spirale *f* -n spiral; *(Med)* coil.

Spiralfeder *f* coil spring.

Spiritismus *m* spiritualism.

spiritistisch *adj* spiritualist.

spirituell *adj* spiritual.

Spirituosen *pl* spirits *pl.*

Spiritus *m* -, *no pl (Alkohol)* spirit. **mit ~ kochen** to cook with a spirit stove; **etw in ~ legen** to put sth in alcohol.

Spiritus-: ~**kocher** *m* spirit stove; ~**lampe** *f* spirit lamp.

spitz *adj* **(a)** *(mit einer Spitze)* pointed; *Bleistift, Nadel etc* sharp; *(Math) Winkel* acute. ~ **zulaufen** to taper; **etw mit ~en Fingern anfassen** *(col)* to pick sth up gingerly. **(b)** *(gehässig) Bemerkung* pointed, barbed; *Zunge* sharp.

Spitz *m* -e *(Hund)* spitz.

Spitz-: ~**bart** *m* goatee; **s~bekommen*** *vt sep irreg (col)* **etw s~bekommen** to get wise to sth *(col)*; ~**bub(e)** *m* villain, rogue; *(col: Schlingel)* scamp *(col)*; **s~bübisch** *adj* mischievous.

Spitze *f* -n **(a)** point; *(Finger~, Nasen~, Bart~, Schuh~)* tip; *(Berg~, Fels~, Baum~, Turm~)* top. **auf der ~ stehen** to be upside-down; **etw auf die ~ treiben** to carry sth too far; **einer Sache** *(dat)* **die ~ nehmen** *(fig)* to take the sting out of sth. **(b)** *(Führung)* head; *(vorderes Ende)* front; *(Tabellen~)* top; *(fig: Höchstwert)* peak. **an der ~ stehen** to be at the head; **an der ~ liegen** *(Sport, fig)* to be in the lead; **sich an die ~ setzen** to take the lead. **(c)** *(fig: Stichelei)* dig. **das ist eine ~ gegen Sie** that's a dig at you. **(d)** *(Gewebe)* lace. **(e)** *(col: prima)* great *(col)*.

Spitzel *m* - informer; *(Spion)* spy; *(Schnüffler)* snooper; *(Polizei~)* police informer.

spitzen *vt (spitz machen) Bleistift* to sharpen; *Lippen, Mund* to purse; *(zum Küssen)* to pucker; *Ohren (lit, fig)* to prick up.

Spitzen- *in cpds* top; *(aus Spitze)* lace; ~**belastung** *f* peak load; ~**bluse** *f* lace blouse; ~**erzeugnis** *nt* top(-quality) product; ~**feld** *nt (Sport)* leading group; ~**funktionär** *m* top official; ~**gehalt** *nt* top salary; ~**geschwindigkeit** *f* top speed; ~**höschen** *nt* lace panties *pl*; ~**kandidat** *m* top candidate; ~**klasse** *f* top class; Sekt der ~**klasse** top-class champagne; ~**leistung** *f* top performance; *(von Maschine, Auto)* peak performance; *(bei der Herstellung von Produkten, Energie)* peak output; ~**lohn** *m* top wage(s *pl*); ~**position** *f* leading position; ~**qualität** *f* top quality; ~**reiter** *m (Sport)* leader; *(fig) (Kandidat)* frontrunner; *(Ware)* top seller; *(Schlager)* number one; ~ ~**sportler** *m* top(-class) sportsman; ~**stellung** *f* leading position; ~**verband** m leading organization; ~**verdiener** m top earner; ~**verkehrszeit** f peak period; ~**wein** m top-quality wine; ~**wert** m peak; ~**zeit** f *(Sport)* record time.

Spitzer m sharpener.

Spitz-: s~**findig** adj over-subtle; ~**findigkeit** f over-subtlety; ~**hacke** f pick-axe *(Brit)*, pickax *(US)*; s~**kriegen** vt sep *(col)* = s~**bekommen**; ~**maus** f shrew; ~**name** m nickname; **mit dem** ~**namen** ... nicknamed ...; s~**züngig** adj sharptongued.

Spleen [ʃpliːn] m -s *(col)* *(Angewohnheit)* crazy habit; *(Idee)* crazy idea; *(Fimmel)* obsession. **du hast ja einen** ~! you're off your head *(col)*.

spleenig ['ʃpliːnɪç] adj *(col)* crazy, nutty *(col)*.

Splint n -e cotter (pin), split pin.

Splitt m -e stone chippings pl; *(Streumittel)* grit.

Splitter m - splinter; *(Granat~)* fragment.

Splitter-: ~**bombe** f *(Mil)* fragmentation bomb; ~**gruppe** f *(Pol)* splinter group.

splittern vi aux sein or haben *(Holz, Glas)* to splinter.

splitternackt adj stark naked.

Splitterpartei f *(Pol)* splinter party.

sponsern [ʃp-, sp-] vti to sponsor.

Sponsor [ʃp-, sp-] m -en sponsor.

spontan adj spontaneous.

Spontaneität [ʃpontanei'tɛːt] f spontaneity.

sporadisch adj sporadic.

Spore f -n *(Biol)* spore.

Sporen pl *(auch Zool, Bot)* spurs. **einem Pferd die** ~ **geben** to spur a horse; **sich** *(dat)* **die (ersten)** ~ **verdienen** *(fig)* to win one's spurs.

Sport m no pl sport. **treiben Sie** ~? do you do any sport?; **etw zum** ~ **betreiben** *(als Hobby)* to do sth as a hobby.

Sport-: ~**abzeichen** nt sports certificate; ~**angler** m angler; ~**art** f (kind of) sport; ~**artikel** m ~**artikel** pl sports equipment *with sing vb;* ~**arzt** m sports physician; s~**begeistert** adj keen on sport; ~**bericht** m sports report; ~**ereignis** nt sporting event; ~**fest** nt sports festival; ~**flieger** m amateur pilot; ~**flugzeug** nt sporting aircraft; ~**freund** m sport(s)-fan; ~**geschäft** nt sports shop *(Brit)* or store *(US)*; ~**halle** f sports hall; ~**hemd** nt sports or sport *(US)* shirt; ~**hochschule** f college of physical education; ~**kleidung** f sportswear; ~**klub** m sports club; ~**lehrer(in** f) m sports instructor; *(Sch)* PE or physical education teacher.

Sportler m - sportsman, athlete.

Sportlerin f sportswoman, (woman) athlete.

sportlich adj **(a)** *Mensch, Auto* sporty; *Veranstaltung, Wettkampf* sporting; *(durchtrainiert)* athletic. **(b)** *(fair)* sportsmanlike no adv. **(c)** *Kleidung* smart but casual; *(wie Sportkleidung aussehend)* sporty.

Sportlichkeit f **(a)** *(von Menschen)* sportiness; *(Durchtrainiertheit)* athleticism. **(b)** *(Faireß)* sportsmanship.

Sport-: ~**medizin** f sports medicine; ~**nachrichten** pl sports news *with sing vb* or reports pl; ~**platz** m sports field; ~**rad** nt sports bike *(col)*; ~**reportage** f sports report.

Sports-: ~**freund** m *(fig col)* buddy *(col)*; ~**kanone** f *(col)* sporting ace *(col)*.

Sport-: ~**veranstaltung** f sporting event; ~**verein** m sports club; ~**wagen** m sports *(Brit)* or sport *(US)* car; *(für Kind)* push-chair *(Brit)*, (baby-)stroller *(US)*; ~**zeitung** f sports paper.

Spot [spɔt] m -s commercial, advertisement.

Spott m no pl mockery, ridicule. **seinen** ~ **mit jdm treiben** to make fun of sb.

Spott-: ~**bild** nt *(fig)* travesty; s~**billig** adj dirtcheap *(col)*.

spötteln vi to mock *(über jdn/etw sb/sth)*.

spotten vi to mock. **über jdn/etw** ~ to mock sb/sth; **das spottet jeder Beschreibung** that

simply defies description.

Spötter(in f) m - mocker.

Spott-: ~**figur** f joke figure; **eine** ~**figur sein** to be an object of ridicule; ~**gedicht** nt satirical poem.

spöttisch adj mocking.

Spott-: ~**lied** nt satirical song; ~**name** m derisive nickname; ~**preis** m ridiculously low price; ~**rede** f satirical speech; ~**vers** m satirical verse.

sprach pret of **sprechen**.

Sprach-: ~**barriere** f language barrier; s~**begabt** adj good at languages; ~**begabung** f talent for languages.

Sprache f -n language; *(das Sprechen, Sprechweise)* speech; *(Fähigkeit zu sprechen)* faculty of speech. **eine** ~ **sprechen** to speak a language; **in französischer** etc ~ in French etc; **heraus mit der** ~! *(col)* come on, out with it!; **zur** ~ **kommen** to be mentioned; **etw zur** ~ **bringen** to bring sth up; **hast du die** ~ **verloren?** have you lost your tongue?; **es verschlägt einem die** ~ it takes your breath away.

Sprachenschule f language school.

Sprach-: ~**fehler** m speech defect; ~**forscher** m linguist; ~**forschung** f linguistic research; ~**führer** m phrase-book; ~**gebiet** nt language area; **ein französisches** etc ~**gebiet** a French-speaking etc area; ~**gebrauch** m usage; **moderner deutscher** ~**gebrauch** modern German usage; ~**gefühl** nt feeling for language; ~**gemeinschaft** f speech community; ~**genie** nt linguistic genius; ~**geschichte** f linguistic history; s~**gewandt** adj articulate; ~**kenntnisse** pl linguistic proficiency sing; **mit englischen** ~**kenntnissen** with a knowledge of English; **haben Sie irgendwelche** ~**kenntnisse?** do you know any languages?; ~**kurs(us)** m language course; ~**labor** nt language laboratory; ~**lehrer** m language teacher.

sprachlich adj linguistic; *Unterricht, Schwierigkeiten* language attr; *Fehler* grammatical. ~ **falsch/richtig** grammatically incorrect/correct.

sprachlos adj speechless. **ich bin** ~! I'm speechless.

Sprachlosigkeit f speechlessness.

Sprach-: ~**rohr** nt *(Megaphon)* megaphone; *(fig)* mouthpiece; ~**schöpfung** f linguistic innovation; ~**schule** f language school; ~**störung** f speech disorder; ~**studium** nt study of language; ~**übung** f language exercise; ~**unterricht** m language teaching; ~**wissenschaft** f linguistics sing; ~**wissenschaftler** m linguist; s~**wissenschaftlich** adj linguistic.

sprang pret of **springen**.

Spray [ʃpreː, spreː] m or nt -s spray.

Spraydose f [ʃpreː-, 'spreː-] f aerosol (can), spray.

sprayen ['ʃpreːən, sp-] vti to spray.

Sprech-: ~**anlage** f intercom; ~**chor** m chorus; *(fig)* chorus of voices; ~**einheit** f *(Telec)* unit.

sprechen pret **sprach**, ptp **gesprochen 1** vi to speak *(über +acc, von* about); *(reden, sich unterhalten auch)* to talk *(über +acc, von* about). **viel** ~ to talk a lot; **frei** ~ to extemporize; **er spricht wenig** he doesn't say very much; **im Schlaf** ~ to talk in one's sleep; **es spricht/es** ~ ... **the speaker is/the speakers are** ...; **nicht gut auf jdn zu** ~ **sein** to be on bad terms with sb; **wie sprichst du mit mir?** who do you think you're talking to?; **wir** ~ **nicht mehr miteinander** we are no longer on speaking terms; **mit wem spreche ich?** to whom am I speaking, please?; **darüber spricht man nicht** one doesn't talk about such things; **wovon** ~ **Sie eigentlich?** what are you talking about?; **wir von etwas anderem** let's change the subject; **es wird kaum noch von ihm gesprochen** he's hardly mentioned now; **es spricht für jdn/etw(, daß** ...) it says something for sb/sth (that ...); **das**

spricht für ihn that's a point in his favour *(Brit)* or favour *(US)*; **das spricht für sich (selbst)** that speaks for itself; **es spricht vieles dafür** there's a lot to be said for it; **es spricht vieles dafür, daß ...** there is every reason to believe that ...; **was spricht dafür/dagegen?** what is there to be said for/against it?; **er sprach vor den Studenten** he spoke to the students; **ganz allgemein gesprochen** generally speaking.

2 *vt* **(a)** *(sagen)* to say, to speak; *eine Sprache* to speak; *Gebet, Gedicht* to say. **~ Sie Japanisch?** do you speak Japanese?; **hier spricht man Spanisch** Spanish spoken. **(b)** *(mit jdm reden)* to speak to. **kann ich bitte Herrn Kurz ~?** may I speak to Mr Kurz, please?; **er ist nicht zu ~** he can't see anybody; **wir ~ uns noch!** you haven't heard the last of this! **(c)** *Urteil* to pronounce.

Sprecher(in) *f)* *m* - speaker; *(Nachrichten~)* newsreader; *(für Dokumentarfilme etc)* narrator; *(Ansager)* announcer; *(Wortführer)* spokesman.

Sprech-: **s~faul** *adj* taciturn; **~funk** *m* radiotelephone system; **~funkgerät** *nt* radiotelephone; **~gebühr** *f (Telec)* call charge; **~muschel** *f (Telec)* mouthpiece; **~organ** *nt* speech organ; **~probe** *f* voice trial; **~rolle** *f* speaking part; **~schulung** *f* voice training; **~stunde** *f* consultation (hour); *(von Arzt)* surgery *(Brit)*, doctor's office *(US)*; **~stunden** consultation hours; *(von Arzt)* surgery *(Brit)*; **~stundenhilfe** *f* receptionist; **~übung** *f* speech exercise; **~weise** *f* way of speaking; **~werkzeuge** *pl* organs of speech; **~zeit** *f (Telec)* call time; **~zimmer** *nt* consulting room.

spreizen 1 *vt* to spread. **2** *vr (sich sträuben)* to kick up *(col)*.

Spreng|arbeiten *pl* blasting operations *pl*.

sprengen *vt* **(a)** to blow up; *Fels* to blast. **(b)** *Tür* to force (open); *Tresor* to break open; *Bande, Fesseln, (Spiel)bank* to break; *Versammlung* to break up. **(c)** *(bespritzen)* to sprinkle.

Spreng-: **~kapsel** *f* detonator; **~kopf** *m* warhead; **~körper** *m* explosive device; **~kraft** *f* explosive force; **~ladung** *f* explosive charge; **~satz** *m* explosive device.

Sprengstoff *m* explosive.

Sprengstoff|anschlag *m* bomb attack. **auf ihn wurde ein ~ verübt** he was the subject of a bomb attack.

Sprengung *f* blowing-up; *(von Fels)* blasting; *(von Versammlung)* breaking-up.

Sprenkel *m* - *(Tupfen)* spot, speckle.

sprenkeln *vt Farbe* to sprinkle spots of; *siehe* **gesprenkelt.**

Spreu *f no pl* chaff. **die ~ vom Weizen trennen** *(fig)* to separate the wheat from the chaff.

Sprichwort *nt* ⁼er proverb.

sprichwörtlich *adj (lit, fig)* proverbial.

sprießen *pret* **sproß** *or* **sprießte,** *ptp* **gesprossen** *vi aux sein (aus der Erde)* to spring up; *(Knospen)* to shoot.

Springbrunnen *m* fountain.

springen *pret* **sprang,** *ptp* **gesprungen** *vi aux sein* **(a)** *(lit, fig, Sport, bei Brettspielen)* to jump; *(mit Schwung auch)* to leap; *(beim Stabhochsprung)* to vault; *(Raubtier)* to pounce; *(sich springend fortbewegen)* to bound; *(hüpfen, seilhüpfen)* to skip; *(Ball etc)* to bounce; *(Wassersport)* to dive. **die Kinder kamen gesprungen** the children came running. **(b)** *etw ~ lassen (col)* to fork out for sth *(col)*; *Geld* to fork out sth *(col)*; **für jdn etw ~ lassen** *(col)* to treat sb to sth. **(c)** *(Saite, Glas)* to break; *(Risse bekommen)* to crack.

Springen *nt* - *(Sport)* jumping; *(Stabhoch~)* vaulting.

springend *adj* **der ~e Punkt** the crucial point.

Springer(in) *f)* *m* - **(a)** *(Sport)* jumper; *(Stabhoch~)* vaulter. **(b)** *(Chess)* knight. **(c)** *(Ind)* stand-in.

Spring-: **~flut** *f* spring tide; **~form** *f* *(Cook)*

---

springform *nt* jumper; **~pferd** *nt* jumper; **~reiten** *nt* show jumping; **~turnier** *nt* show jumping competition.

Sprinkler *m* - sprinkler.

Sprint *m* - sprint.

sprinten *vti aux sein* to sprint.

Sprit *m* -e *(col: Benzin)* gas *(col)*, juice *(col)*.

Spritz-: **~beutel** *m* icing bag; **~düse** *f* nozzle.

Spritze *f* -n syringe; *(Feuer~, Garten~)* hose; *(Injektion)* injection. **eine ~ bekommen** to have an injection.

spritzen 1 *vti* **(a)** to spray; *(verspritzen) Wasser, Schmutz etc* to splash; *(aus Wasserpistole etc)* to squirt. **(b)** *Wein* to dilute with soda water/mineral water. **(c)** *(injizieren) Serum etc* to inject; *Heroin etc auch* to shoot *(col)*. **wir müssen (dem Kranken) Morphium ~** we have to give (the patient) a morphine injection. **2** *vi aux haben or sein (heißes Fett)* to spit; *(in einem Strahl)* to spurt; *(aus einer Tube etc)* to squirt.

Spritzer *m* - *(Farb~, Wasser~)* splash.

spritzig *adj Wein* tangy; *Aufführung, Dialog etc* sparkling; *(witzig)* witty.

Spritz-: **~lack** *m* spray paint; **~pistole** *f* spray-gun; **~tour** *f (col)* spin *(col)*; **~tülle** *f* nozzle.

spröd(e) *adj Glas, Haar* brittle; *Haut* rough; *Stimme* thin; *(abweisend)* aloof.

sproß *pret of* **sprießen.**

Sproß *m* -sse shoot.

Sprosse *f* -n *(lit, fig)* rung.

Sprossenwand *f (Sport)* wall bars *pl*.

Sprößling *m* shoot; *(fig hum)* offspring.

Spruch *m* ⁼e **(a)** saying; *(Wahl~)* motto; *(Bibel~)* quotation. ~e *(col: Gerede)* patter *no pl (col)*; **~e klopfen** *(col)* to talk fancy *(col)*; **das sind doch nur ~e!** that's just talk. **(b)** *(Richter~)* judgement; *(Urteils~)* verdict; *(Schieds~)* ruling.

Spruchband *nt* banner.

Sprücheklopfer *m (col)* patter-merchant *(col)*.

spruchreif *adj (col)* **die Sache ist noch nicht ~** it's not definite yet.

Sprudel *m* - mineral water.

sprudeln *vi* **(a)** *(lit, fig)* to bubble; *(Sekt, Limonade)* to fizz. **(b)** *aux sein (hervor~) (Wasser etc)* to bubble; *(fig: Worte)* to pour out.

sprudelnd *adj Getränke* fizzy; *(fig)* effervescent.

Sprudhose *f* spray (can).

sprühen 1 *vi* **(a)** *aux haben or sein* to spray; *(Funken)* to fly. **(b)** *(fig) (vor Witz etc)* to bubble over; *(Augen: vor Freude etc)* to sparkle. **2** *vt* to spray.

sprühend *adj Laune, Temperament etc* bubbling, effervescent; *Witz* sparkling, bubbling.

Sprühregen *m* drizzle.

Sprung *m* ⁼e **(a)** jump; *(schwungvoll, fig: Gedanken~ auch)* leap; *(Hüpfer)* skip; *(von Raubtier)* pounce; *(Stabhoch~)* vault; *(Wassersport)* dive. **ein großer ~ nach vorn** *(fig)* a great leap forward; **damit kann man keine großen ~e machen** *(col)* you can't exactly live it up on that *(col)*; **immer auf dem ~ sein** *(col)* to be always on the go *(col)*; *(aufmerksam)* to be always on the ball *(col)*; **jdm auf die ~e helfen** *(wohlwollend)* to give sb a (helping) hand; *(drohend)* to show sb what's what. **(b)** *(col: kurze Strecke)* **auf einen ~ bei jdm vorbeikommen** to drop in to see sb *(col)*. **(c)** *(Riß)* crack. **einen ~ haben/bekommen** to be cracked/ to crack.

Sprung-: **~brett** *nt (lit, fig)* springboard; **~feder** *f* spring; **s~haft 1** *adj* **(a)** *Charakter* volatile; *Denken* disjointed; **(b)** *(rapide)* rapid; **2** *adv ansteigen, sich entwickeln* by leaps and bounds; **~schanze** *f* *(Ski)* ski-jump; **~turm** *m* diving platform.

Spucke *f no pl (col)* spittle, spit. **da bleibt einem die ~ weg!** it's flabbergasting *(col)*; **mit Geduld und ~** *(col)* with blood, sweat and tears *(col)*.

spucken *vti* to spit; *(fig col) Lava, Flammen* to spew (out). **in die Hände ~** *(fig)* to roll up one's sleeves.

Spucknapf m spittoon.

Spuk m -e *(Geistererscheinung)* apparition. **dem ~ ein Ende bereiten** *(fig)* to put an end to the nightmare.

spuken vi to haunt. **es spukt auf dem Friedhof** the cemetery is haunted; **das spukt noch immer in den Köpfen** that still has a hold on people's minds.

Spuk-: **~geschichte** f ghost story; **s~haft** adj eerie.

Spül|automat m (automatic) dishwasher.

Spule f -n spool, reel; *(Nähmaschinen~, Ind)* bobbin; *(Elec)* coil.

Spüle f -n sink.

spulen vt to spool, to reel.

spülen vti **(a)** *(aus~, ab~)* to rinse; *(Med)* to irrigate; *(abwaschen) Geschirr* to wash up *(Brit)*, to wash the dishes; *(auf der Toilette)* to flush. **(b) etw an Land ~** to wash sth ashore.

Spül-: **~maschine** f dishwasher; **~mittel** nt washing-up liquid *(Brit)*, dish-washing liquid; **~schüssel** f washing-up bowl; **~tisch** m sink (unit).

Spülung f rinsing; *(Wasser~)* flush; *(Med)* irrigation.

Spülwasser nt *(beim Abwaschen)* dishwater.

Spund m -e **(a)** bung, spigot. **(b) junger ~** *(dated col)* young pup *(dated col)*.

Spundloch nt bunghole.

Spur f -en **(a)** track; *(Anzeichen, Beweisstück)* trace, sign. **von den Tätern fehlt jede ~** the criminals left no trace; **jds ~ aufnehmen** to take up sb's trail; **jdm auf der ~ sein** to be on sb's trail; **auf der richtigen ~ sein** *(lit, fig)* to be on the right track; **jdm auf die ~ kommen** to get onto sb; **(seine) ~en hinterlassen** *(fig)* to leave its mark. **(b)** *(fig: kleine Menge, Überrest)* trace; *(von Vernunft, Anstand etc)* scrap. **von Anstand/Takt keine ~** *(col)* no decency/tact at all; **keine ~** *(col)* not at all/nothing at all; **eine ~ zu laut/grell** a shade too loud/garish. **(c)** *(Fahrbahn)* lane. **auf der linken ~ fahren** to drive in the left-hand lane; **in der ~ bleiben** to keep in lane.

spürbar adj noticeable, perceptible.

spuren vi *(col)* to obey; *(sich fügen)* to toe the line.

spüren **1** vt to feel; *(ahnen auch)* to sense. **sie spürte, daß der Erdboden leicht bebte** she felt the earth trembling underfoot; **sie ließ mich ihr Mißfallen ~** she let me know that she was displeased; **etw zu ~ bekommen** *(lit)* to feel sth; *(fig)* to feel the (full) force of sth. **2** vti *(Hunt)* *(nach)* etw **~** to track sth.

Spuren-: **~element** nt trace element; **~sicherung** f securing of evidence.

Spürhund m tracker dog; *(col: Mensch)* sleuth.

spurlos adj without trace. **~ an jdm vorübergehen** to have no effect on sb.

Spür-: **~nase** f *(Hunt)* nose; **~sinn** m *(Hunt, fig)* nose; *(fig: Gefühl)* feel.

Spurt m -s spurt.

spurten vi *aux sein (Sport)* to spurt; *(col: rennen)* to sprint.

sputen vr *(dated col)* to hurry.

St. = **Stück; Sankt** St.

Staat m -en **(a)** state; *(Land)* country. **beim ~ arbeiten** to be employed by the government. **(b)** *(von Insekten)* colony. **(c)** *(fig)* *(Pracht)* pomp; *(Kleidung, Schmuck)* finery. **damit ist kein ~ zu machen** that's nothing to write home about *(col)*.

Staaten-: **~bund** m confederation; **s~los** adj stateless.

staatlich **1** adj state attr. **2** adv by the state. **~ geprüft** state-certified.

Staats-: **~affäre** f **(a)** *(lit)* affair of state; **(b)** *(fig)* major operation; **~akt** m *(lit)* state occasion; **~aktion** f major operation; **~amt** nt public office; **~angehörige(r)** mf decl as adj national; **~angehörigkeit** f nationality; **~anleihe** f

government bond; **~anwalt** m prosecuting attorney *(US)*, public prosecutor; **~apparat** m apparatus of state; **~archiv** nt state archives pl; **~aufsicht** f state control; **~ausgaben** pl public spending sing; **~bank** f national bank; **~bankrott** m national bankruptcy; **~beamte(r)** m public servant; **~begräbnis** nt state funeral; **~besitz** m state property; **(in) ~besitz sein** to be state-owned; **~besuch** m state visit; **~betrieb** m state-owned enterprise; **~bibliothek** f national library; **~bürger** m citizen; **~chef** m head of state; **~dienst** m civil service; **s~eigen** adj state-owned; **~eigentum** nt state property no art; **~empfang** m state reception; **~examen** nt = university degree; **~feiertag** m national holiday; **~feind** m enemy of the state; **~finanzen** pl public finances pl; **~flagge** f national flag; **~form** f type of state; **~gebiet** nt national territory no art; **~geheimnis** nt *(lit, fig hum)* state secret; **~gelder** pl public funds pl; **~gewalt** f authority of the state; **~grenze** f state frontier; **~haushalt** m national budget; **~hoheit** f sovereignty; **~interesse** nt interests pl of (the) state; **~kasse** f treasury; **~kirche** f state church; **~kosten** pl public expenses pl; **auf ~kosten** at the public expense; **~mann** m statesman; **s~männisch** adj statesmanlike; **~oberhaupt** nt head of state; **~präsident** m president; **~recht** nt **(a)** national law; **(b)** *(Verfassungsrecht)* constitutional law; **~regierung** f state government; **~religion** f state religion; **~rente** f state pension; **~schuld** f *(Fin)* national debt; **~sekretär** m *(BRD: Beamter)* ≃ permanent secretary *(Brit)*, senior official in government department; **~sicherheit** f national security; **~streich** m coup (d'état).

Stab m -e **(a)** rod; *(Gitter~)* bar; *(Bischofs~)* crosier; *(Hirten~)* crook; *(Dirigenten~, für Staffellauf)* baton; *(als Amtzeichen)* mace; *(für ~hochsprung)* pole; *(Meß~)* (measuring) rod; *(Zauber~)* wand. **(b)** *(Mitarbeiter~, Mil)* staff; *(von Experten)* panel.

Stäbchen nt dim of **Stab** *(Eß~)* chopstick.

Stab-: **~hochspringer** m pole-vaulter; **~hochsprung** m pole vault.

stabil adj *Möbel, Schuhe* sturdy, robust; *Währung, Beziehung, Charakter* stable; *Gesundheit* sound.

Stabilisator [ʃtabiliˈzaːtɔr, st-] m stabilizer.

stabilisieren* vtr to stabilize.

Stabilität f stability.

Stabreim m alliteration.

Stabs-: **~arzt** m *(Mil)* captain in the medical corps; **~chef** m *(Mil col)* chief of staff; **~offizier** m *(Mil)* staff officer; *(Rang)* field officer.

stach pret of **stechen**.

Stachel m -n *(von Rosen etc)* thorn; *(von Kakteen, Igel)* spine; *(von ~schwein)* quill, spine; *(auf ~draht)* barb; *(zum Viehantrieb)* goad; *(Gift~: von Bienen etc)* sting. **einer Sache (dat) den ~ nehmen** *(geh)* to take the sting out of sth.

Stachel-: **~beere** f gooseberry; **~draht** m barbed wire.

stach(e)lig adj *Rosen* thorny; *Kaktus, Igel* spiny;- *(sich ~ anfühlend)* prickly; *Kinn, Bart* bristly.

Stachelschwein nt porcupine.

Stadion nt, pl **Stadien** [-iən] stadium.

Stadium nt, pl **Stadien** [-iən] stage. **im vorgerückten/letzten ~** *(Med)* at an advanced/terminal stage.

Stadt f -e **(a)** town; *(Groß~)* city. **die ~ Paris** the city of Paris; **~ und Land** town and country; **in die ~ gehen** to go into town. **(b)** *(~verwaltung)* (town) council; *(von Groß~)* corporation. **die ~ Ulm** Ulm Corporation.

Stadt-: **s~auswärts** adv out of town; **~autobahn** f urban motorway *(Brit)* or freeway *(US)*; **~bad** nt municipal swimming pool; **~bahn** f suburban railway *(Brit)*, city railroad *(US)*; **s~be-**

kannt adj known all over town; **~bewohner** m town-dweller; (von Groß~) city-dweller; **~bezirk** m municipal district; **~bücherei** f town/city library.

Städtebau m urban development.

stadt|einwärts adv into town.

Städteplanung f town planning.

Städter(in f) m - town-dweller; (Groß~) city-dweller.

Stadt-: **~flucht** f exodus from the cities; **~gebiet** nt municipal area; **~gespräch** nt (das) **~gespräch sein** to be the talk of the town; **~grenze** f town/city boundary; **~gue(r)rilla** f urban guerrilla.

städtisch adj municipal, town/city attr; (nach Art einer Stadt) urban.

Stadt-: **~kämmerer** m town/city treasurer; **~kasse** f town/city treasury; **~kern** m town/city centre (Brit) or center (US); **~kreis** m town/city borough; **~mauer** f city wall; **~mitte** f town/city centre (Brit) or center (US); **~park** m municipal park; **~parlament** nt city council; **~plan** m (street) map; **~planung** f town planning; **~rand** m outskirts pl (of a/the town/city); **am ~rand** on the outskirts (of the town/city); **~rat** m (Behörde) (town/city) council; **~rundfahrt** f (sightseeing) tour of a/the town/city; **~staat** m city state; **~streicher(in** f) m - (town/city) tramp; **~teil** m district, part of town; **~theater** nt municipal theatre (Brit) or theater (US); **~tor** nt town/city gate; **~verwaltung** f (Behörde) municipal authority; **~viertel** nt part of town; **~zentrum** nt town/city centre (Brit) or center (US).

Staffel f **-n (a)** echelon; (Aviat: Einheit) squadron. **(b)** (Sport) relay (race); (Mannschaft) relay team. **~ laufen/schwimmen** to run/swim in a relay (race).

Staffelei f easel.

Staffellauf m relay (race).

staffeln vt Gehälter, Fahrpreise to grade; Anfangszeiten, Startplätze to stagger.

Staff(e)lung f siehe vt grading; staggering.

Stagnation f stagnation.

stagnieren* vi to stagnate.

stahl pret of **stehlen.**

Stahl m **-e** or **=e** steel. **Nerven wie ~** nerves of steel.

Stahl- in cpds steel; **~bau** m steel-girder construction; **~beton** m reinforced concrete; **~blech** nt sheet-steel.

stählen vt to harden, to toughen.

stählern adj steel; (fig) Muskeln, Wille of iron, iron attr; Nerven of steel.

Stahl-: **~feder** f steel nib; **~gerüst** nt tubular steel scaffolding; (Gerippe) steel-girder frame; **s~hart** adj (as) hard as steel; **~rohr** nt tubular steel; (Stück) steel tube; **~roß** nt (hum) bike (col); **~träger** m steel girder; **~werk** nt steelworks sing or pl; **~wolle** f steel wool.

stak (geh) pret of **stecken 1.**

Stalinismus m Stalinism.

Stalin|orgel f multiple rocket launcher.

Stall m **=e (a)** (Pferde~, Gestüt, Aut: Renn~) stable; (Kuh~) cowshed, (cow) barn (US); (Hühner~) hen-house; (Kaninchen~) hutch; (Schweine~) (pig)sty, (pig)pen (US). **(b)** (col: Hosenschlitz) flies pl.

Stallung(en pl) f stables pl.

Stamm m **=e (a)** (Baum~) trunk. **(b)** (Ling) stem. **(c)** (Volks~) tribe; (Abstammung) line; (Bakterien~) strain. **(d)** (Personal, Kunden) regulars pl; (Arbeiter) regular workforce; (Angestellte) permanent staff pl. **zum ~ gehören** to be one of the regulars etc.

Stamm-: **~baum** m family tree; (von Zuchttieren) pedigree; **~buch** nt book of family events with some legal documents, ≈ family bible; **jdm etw ins ~buch schreiben** (fig) to make sb take note of sth.

stammeln vti to stammer.

stammen vi to come (von, aus from); (zeitlich) to date (von, aus from). **die Uhr stammt von seinem Großvater** the watch was handed down from his grandfather.

Stamm-: **~form** f base form; **~gast** m regular; **~gericht** nt standard meal.

stämmig adj stocky, thickset no adv; (kräftig) sturdy.

Stamm-: **~kapital** nt (Fin) ordinary share or common stock (US) capital; **~kneipe** f (col) local (Brit col); **~kunde** m regular (customer); **~lokal** nt favourite (Brit) or favorite (US) café/restaurant etc; (Kneipe) local (Brit), favorite bar (US); **~personal** nt permanent staff pl; **~platz** m usual seat; **~tisch** m (Tisch in Gasthaus) table reserved for the regulars; (~tischrunde) group of regulars.

stampfen 1 vi **(a)** (laut auftreten) to stamp. **mit dem Fuß ~** to stamp one's foot. **(b)** aux sein (gehen) to tramp; (wütend) to stamp; (stapfen) to trudge. **2** vt **(a)** (festtrampeln) Lehm, Sand to stamp; Trauben to press; (mit den Füßen) to tread. **(b)** (mit Stampfer) to mash.

Stampfer m - (Stampfgerät) pounder.

stand pret of **stehen.**

Stand m **=e (a)** no pl (das Stehen) standing position. **aus dem ~** from a standing position; **bei jdm** or **gegen jdn einen schweren ~ haben** (fig) to have a hard time of it with sb. **(b)** (Markt~ etc) stand; (Taxi~) rank (Brit), stand (US). **(c)** no pl (Lage) state; (Niveau) level; (Zähler~ etc) reading, level; (Konto~) balance; (Spiel~) score. **beim jetzigen ~ der Dinge** the way things stand at the moment; **etw auf den neuesten ~ bringen** to bring sth up to date. **(d)** (soziale Stellung) station, status; (Klasse) rank, class; (Beruf, Gewerbe) profession.

Standard- in cpds standard.

standardisieren* vt to standardize.

Standardisierung f standardization.

Standarte f **-n** (Mil, Pol) standard.

Standbild nt statue.

Ständchen nt serenade. **jdm ein ~ bringen** to serenade sb.

Ständer m - stand; (Pfeiler) upright.

Standes-: **~amt** nt registry office (Brit); **s~amtlich** adj **s~amtliche Trauung** registry office (Brit) wedding; **sich s~amtlich trauen lassen** to get married in a registry office (Brit), to have a civil marriage (US); **~beamte(r)** m registrar; **~bewußtsein** nt status consciousness; **~dünkel** m snobbery; **s~gemäß 1** adj befitting one's rank; **2** adv in a manner befitting one's rank; **~organisation** f professional association; **~unterschied** m class difference.

Stand-: **s~fest** adj Tisch, Leiter stable, steady; (fig) steadfast; **~festigkeit** f stability (auch Sci); (fig auch) steadfastness; **~foto** nt still (photograph); **~gericht** nt (Mil) drumhead court martial; **vor ein ~gericht kommen** to be summarily court-martialled (Brit) or court-martialed (US); **s~haft** adj steadfast; **sie blieb s~haft im Glauben** her faith did not falter; **er weigerte sich s~haft** he steadfastly refused; **s~halten** vi sep irreg (Mensch) to resist attack; (Gebäude, Brücke etc) to hold; (+dat) to stand up to; **Versuchungen** (dat) **s~halten** to resist temptation; **einer Prüfung s~halten** to stand up to close examination.

ständig adj **(a)** (dauernd) permanent; Mitglied full. **~er Ausschuß** standing committee. **(b)** (unaufhörlich) constant. **sie kommt ~ zu spät** she's always late; **müssen Sie mich ~ unterbrechen?** do you have to keep on interrupting me?

Standlicht nt sidelights pl. **mit ~ fahren** to drive on sidelights.

Stand|ort m location; (von Schütze, Schiff, fig) position; (Mil) garrison; (Bot) habitat.

Stand-: ~**pauke** *f (col)* lecture *(col)*; **jdm eine** ~**pauke halten** to give sb a lecture *(col)*; ~**platz** *m* stand; ~**punkt** *m (Meinung)* point of view; **auf dem** ~**punkt stehen, daß** ... to take the view that ...; **von seinem** ~**punkt aus** from his point of view; **s**~**rechtlich** *adj* **s**~**rechtlich erschießen** to put before a firing squad; **s**~**sicher** *adj* stable; *Mensch* steady (on one's feet/skis *etc*); ~**spur** *f (Aut)* hard shoulder; ~**uhr** *f* grandfather clock.

Stange *f* -**n (a)** *(langer, Stab)* pole; *(Querstab, Ballett*~*)* bar; *(Kleider*~*, Teppich*~*)* rail; *(Gardinen*~*)* rod; *(Vogel*~*)* perch. **(b)** *(länglicher Gegenstand)* stick. **eine** ~ **Zigaretten** a carton of 200 cigarettes. **(c) ein Anzug von der** ~ a suit off the peg; **jdm die** ~ **halten** *(col)* to stick up for sb *(col)*; **eine schöne** ~ **Geld** *(col)* a tidy sum *(col)*.

Stangen-: ~**bohne** *f* runner bean; ~**brot** *nt* French bread; *(Laib)* French loaf; ~**spargel** *m* asparagus spears *pl*.

stank *pret of* **stinken.**

stänkern *vi (col)* to stir things up *(col)*.

Stanniol *nt* -**e** silver foil.

Stanniolpapier *nt* silver paper.

Stanze *f* -**n** die, stamp; *(Loch*~*)* punch.

stanzen *vt* to press; *(prägen)* to stamp; *Löcher* to punch.

Stapel *m* - **(a)** stack, pile. **(b)** *(Naut: Schiffs*~*)* stocks *pl*. **vom** ~ **laufen** to be launched.

Stapellauf *m (Naut)* launching.

stapeln 1 *vt* to stack; *(lagern)* to store. **2** *vr* to pile up.

stapfen *vi aux sein* to trudge, to plod.

Star[1] *m* -**e** *(Orn)* starling.

Star[2] *m* -**e** *(Med)* **grauer/grüner** ~ cataract/glaucoma.

Star[3] *m* -**s** *(Film etc)* star.

starb *pret of* **sterben.**

Star-: ~**besetzung** *f* star cast; ~**gast** *m* star guest.

stark *comp* ⁺**er**, *superl* ⁺**ste(r, s)** *or (adv)* **am** ⁺**sten 1** *adj* **(a)** *(kräftig, konzentriert)* strong. **sich für etw** ~ **machen** *(col)* to stand up for sth; **das ist ein** ~**es Stück** *(col)* that's a bit much! **(b)** *(dick)* thick; *(euph: korpulent)* Dame, Herr large. **(c)** *(heftig)* Schmerzen, Kälte severe; Regen, Verkehr, Raucher, Druck heavy; Sturm, Abneigung violent; Erkältung bad, heavy; Wind, Strömung, Eindruck strong; Beifall hearty, loud; Übertreibung great. **(d)** *(leistungsfähig)* Motor powerful; Sportler able; Mannschaft, Brille, Arznei strong. **(e)** *(zahlreich)* Nachfrage great, big. **zehn Mann** ~ ten strong; **das Buch ist 300 Seiten** ~ the book is 300 pages long. **(f)** *(col: hervorragend)* Leistung, Werk great *(col)*. **2** *adv (mit vb)* a lot; *(mit adj, mit vb)* very; *(mit adj, mit vb)* beschädigt etc badly; vergrößert, verkleinert greatly. ~ **wirken** to have a strong effect; ~ **gesalzen/gewürzt** very salty/highly spiced; ~**er befahrene Straßen** busier roads; **er ist** ~ **erkältet** he has a bad cold.

Starkbier *nt* strong beer.

Stärke[1] *f* -**n (a)** strength *(auch fig)*. **(b)** *(Dicke)* thickness; *(Macht)* power. **(c)** *(von Leid)* intensity; *(von Sturm, Abneigung)* violence. **(d)** *(Anzahl)* *(von Mannschaft)* size; *(von Nachfrage)* amount; *(Auflage)* size.

Stärke[2] *f* -**n** *(Chem)* starch.

Stärkemehl *nt (Cook)* thickening agent.

stärken 1 *vt* **(a)** *(lit, fig)* to strengthen; Selbstbewußtsein to boost; Gesundheit to improve. **(b)** *(erfrischen)* to fortify. **(c)** Wäsche to starch. **2** *vi* to be fortifying. ~ **des Mittel** tonic. **3** *vr* to fortify oneself.

Starkstrom *m (Elec)* heavy current.

Starkstrom- *in cpds* power; ~**leitung** *f* power

line.

Stärkung *f* **(a)** strengthening *(auch fig)*; *(des Selbstbewußtseins)* boosting. **(b)** *(Erfrischung)* refreshment. **eine** ~ **zu sich nehmen** to take some refreshment.

Stärkungsmittel *nt (Med)* tonic.

starr *adj* **(a)** stiff; *(unbeweglich)* rigid. ~ **vor Frost** stiff with frost. **(b)** *(unbewegt)* Augen glassy; Blick auch fixed. **(c)** *(regungslos)* paralyzed. **(d)** *(nicht flexibel)* Regelung, Prinzip inflexible, rigid.

Starre *f no pl* stiffness, rigidity.

starren *vi* **(a)** *(starr blicken)* to stare *(auf + acc* at*)*. **ins Leere** ~ to stare into space; **vor sich (acc) hin** ~ to stare straight ahead. **(b)** *(steif sein)* to be stiff *(von, vor + dat* with*)*. **vor Dreck** ~ to be filthy.

Starrheit *f siehe adj* **(a)** stiffness; rigidity.

Starr-: ~**kopf** *m (Mensch)* stubborn mule; **s**~**köpfig** *adj* stubborn; ~**köpfigkeit** *f* stubbornness; ~**krampf** *m (Med)* tetanus, lockjaw; **s**~**sinnig** *adj* stubborn, mulish.

Start *m* -**s (a)** *(Sport)* start. **einen guten/schlechten** ~ **haben** *(lit, fig)* to get (off to) a good/bad start. **(b)** *(Aviat)* take-off; *(Raketen*~*)* launch.

Start-: ~**automatik** *f (Aut)* automatic choke; ~**bahn** *f (Aviat)* runway; **s**~**bereit** *adj (Sport, fig)* ready to go; *(Aviat)* ready for take-off; ~**block** *m (Sport)* starting block.

starten 1 *vi aux sein* to start; *(Aviat)* to take off; *(zum Start antreten)* to take part. **2** *vt* Satelliten, Rakete to launch; Motor to start.

Starter *m* - *(Aut, Sport)* starter.

Start-: ~**erlaubnis** *f (Sport)* permission to take part; *(Aviat)* clearance for take-off; ~**hilfe** *f (Aviat)* rocket-assisted take-off; *(fig)* initial aid; **jdm** ~**hilfe geben** to help sb get off the ground; ~**hilfekabel** *nt* jump leads *pl (Brit)*, jumper cables *pl (US)*; **s**~**klar** *adj (Aviat)* clear for take-off; *(Sport)* ready to start; ~**kommando** *nt (Sport)* starting signal; ~**linie** *f (Sport)* starting line; ~**loch** *nt (Sport)* **in den** ~**löchern** on their marks; ~**rampe** *f (Space)* launching pad; ~**schuß** *m (Sport)* starting signal; *(fig)* signal *(zu* for*)*; **den** ~**schuß geben** to fire the pistol; *(fig: Erlaubnis geben)* to give the go-ahead; ~**verbot** *nt (Aviat)* ban on take-off; *(Sport)* ban; ~**verbot bekommen** to be banned.

Statik *[ˈʃtaːtɪk, st-]* *f* **(a)** *(Sci)* statics *sing*. **(b)** *(Build)* structural engineering.

Statiker(in) *m* - *(Tech)* structural engineer.

Station *f* **(a)** station; *(Haltestelle)* stop; *(fig: Abschnitt: von Reise)* stage. ~ **machen** to stop off. **(b)** *(Kranken*~*)* ward.

stationär *[ʃtatsioˈnɛːɐ]* *adj (Astron, Sociol)* stationary; *(Med)* in-patient *attr*. ~**er Patient** in-patient; ~ **behandeln** to treat in hospital.

stationieren* *[ʃtatsioˈniːrən]* *vt* Truppen to station; Atomwaffen etc to deploy.

Stationierung *[ʃtatsioˈniːrʊŋ]* *f siehe vt* stationing; deployment.

Stations-: ~**arzt** *m* ward doctor; ~**schwester** *f* ward sister; ~**vorsteher** *m (Rail)* station-master.

statisch *[ˈʃtaːtɪʃ, st-]* *adj (lit, fig)* static.

Statist *m (Film)* extra; *(Theat)* supernumerary; *(fig)* cipher.

Statistenrolle *f (lit, fig)* minor role.

Statistik *f* statistics *sing*. **eine** ~ a set of statistics.

Statistiker(in *f)* *m* - statistician

statistisch *adj* statistical.

Stativ *nt* tripod.

statt 1 *prep* +*gen* instead of. ~**dessen** instead; ~ **meiner/seiner** in my/his place. **2** *conj* instead of. ~ **zu bleiben** instead of staying.

Statt *f no pl (form)* stead *(form)*, place. **an Kindes** ~ **annehmen** *(Jur)* to adopt.

Stätte *f* -**n** *(liter)* place.

Statt-: **s**~**finden** *vi sep irreg* to take place; **s**~**haft** *adj pred* permitted; ~**halter** *m* governor.

stattlich adj (hochgewachsen, groß) Tier magnificent; Bursche strapping; Erscheinung imposing; Gebäude, Park splendid; Sammlung impressive; Familie large; Summe handsome.

Statue f -n statue.

statuieren* vt **ein Exempel (an jdm)** ~ to make an example (of sb); **ein Exempel mit etw** ~ to use sth as a warning.

Statur f build.

Status m - status. ~ **quo** status quo.

Statussymbol nt status symbol.

Statut nt -en statute.

Stau m -s (Wasserstauung) build-up; (Verkehrsstauung) tailback (Brit), line of cars.

Staub m, pl -e or **Stäube** dust; (Bot) pollen. ~ **saugen** to vacuum; ~ **wischen** to dust; **sich vor jdm in den** ~ **werfen** to throw oneself at sb's feet; **sich aus dem** ~**e machen** (col) to clear off (col).

Staubecken nt reservoir.

stauben vi to be dusty; (Staub machen) to make a lot of dust.

stäuben vt **Mehl auf etw** (acc) ~ to sprinkle flour on sth.

Staub-: ~**fänger** m (col) dust collector; ~**flocke** f piece of fluff.

staubig adj dusty.

Staub-: ~**korn** nt speck of dust; ~**lappen** m duster; ~**lunge** f (Med) dust on the lung; (von Kohlenstaub) black lung; **s~saugen** vi insep, ptp **s~gesaugt** to vacuum; ~**sauger** m vacuum cleaner; ~**tuch** nt duster.

stauchen vt to compress (auch Tech).

Staudamm m dam.

Staude f -n (Busch) shrub; (Bananen~, Tabak~) plant.

stauen 1 vt Wasser to dam; Blut to stop the flow of. **2** vr (sich anhäufen) to pile up; (ins Stocken geraten) to get jammed; (Wasser, Blut, fig) to build up. **der Verkehr staute sich über eine Strecke von 2 km** there was a 2 km tailback (Brit) or a 2 km line of cars.

Staumauer f dam wall.

staunen vi to be astonished (über +acc at). ~**d in** astonishment; **da kann man nur noch** ~ it's just amazing; **da staunst du, was?** (col) you didn't expect that, did you!

Staunen nt no pl astonishment, amazement (über +acc at). **jdn in** ~ **versetzen** to amaze sb.

Stausee m reservoir, artificial lake.

Stauung f (a) (Stockung) pile-up; (von Verkehr) tailback (Brit), line of cars. **(b)** (von Wasser) build-up (of water). **(c)** (Blut~) congestion no pl. **Std.** = **Stunde** hr.

Steak [ste:k] nt -s steak.

stechen pret **stach**, ptp **gestochen** 1 vti (Dorn, Stachel etc) to prick; (Insekt) to sting; (Mücken) to bite; (mit Messer etc) to stab (nach at). **2** vi (a) (Sonne) to beat down. **(b)** (Cards) to play a trump. **Karo sticht** diamonds are trumps. **3** vt (a) (Cards) to trump. **(b)** Spargel, Torf to cut. **4** vr to prick oneself (an +dat on, mit with). **sich** (acc or dat) **in den Finger** ~ to prick one's finger. **5** vti impers **es sticht** it is prickly.

Stechen nt - (a) (Sport) play-off/jump-off etc. **(b)** (Schmerz) sharp pain.

stechend adj piercing; Schmerz sharp; (durchdringend) Augen auch penetrating; (beißend) Geruch pungent.

Stech-: ~**karte** f clocking-in card; ~**mücke** f gnat; ~**uhr** f time-clock.

Steck-: ~**brief** m "wanted" poster; (fig) personal description; **s~brieflich** adv **s~brieflich gesucht werden** to be wanted; ~**dose** f (Elec) socket (Brit), outlet (US).

stecken 1 vi ret **steckte** or **stak** (geh), ptp **gesteckt (a)** (festsitzen) to be stuck; (an- or eingesteckt sein) to be; (Nadel, Splitter etc) to be

(sticking); (Brosche etc) to be (pinned). **der Schlüssel steckt** the key is in the lock. **(b) wo steckt er?** where has he got to?; **darin steckt viel Mühe a** lot of work has gone into that; **da steckt etwas dahinter** (col) there's something behind it; **zeigen, was in einem steckt** to show what one is made of; **in einer Krise** ~ to be in the throes of a crisis.

2 vt pret **steckte**, ptp **gesteckt (a)** to put; Haare to pin up; Brosche to pin (an +acc onto). **die Hände in die Taschen** ~ to put one's hands in one's pockets; **das Hemd in die Hose** ~ to tuck one's shirt in (one's trousers); **jdn ins Gefängnis** ~ (col) to stick sb in prison (col). **(b)** (Sew) to pin. **(c)** (col: investieren) Geld, Mühe to put (in +acc into); Zeit to devote (in +acc to). **(d)** (pflanzen) to set.

Stecken-: **s~bleiben** vi sep irreg aux sein to get stuck; (in Rede) to falter; **etw bleibt jdm im Halse s~** (lit, fig) sth sticks in sb's throat; **s~lassen** vt sep irreg **den Schlüssel s~lassen** to leave the key in the lock; ~**pferd** nt (lit, fig) hobby-horse.

Stecker m - (Elec) plug.

Steckling m (Hort) cutting.

Stecknadel f pin. **man hätte eine** ~ **fallen hören können** you could have heard a pin drop; **eine** ~ **im Heuhaufen suchen** (fig) to look for a needle in a hay-stack.

Steck-: ~**nadelkissen** nt pincushion; ~**rübe** f swede, rutabaga (US); turnip; ~**schloß** nt bicycle lock; ~**schlüssel** m box spanner (Brit) or wrench (US); ~**zwiebel** f bulb.

Steg m -e (a) (Brücke) footbridge; (Landungs~) landing stage (Brit), jetty. **(b)** (Mus, Brillen~) bridge.

Stegreif m **eine Rede aus dem** ~ **halten** to make an impromptu speech or a speech off the cuff.

Stegreif-: ~**rede** f impromptu speech; ~**spiel** nt (Theat) improvisation.

Steh- in cpds stand-up.

Steh|aufmännchen nt (Spielzeug) tumbler. **er ist ein richtiges** ~ (fig) he always bounces back.

stehen pret **stand**, ptp **gestanden** aux haben or (S Ger, Aus Sw) sein 1 vi (a) to stand; (col: fertig sein) to be finished; (col: geregelt sein) to be settled. **gebückt/krumm** ~ to slouch; **so wahr ich hier stehe** as sure as I'm standing here; **mit jdm/etw** ~ **und fallen** to depend on sb/sth. (wesentlich sein für) to stand or fall by sb/sth.

(b) (sich befinden) to be. **meine alte Schule steht noch** my old school is still there; **die Sonne steht abends im Westen** the sun in the evening is in the West; **unter Schock** ~ to be in a state of shock; **unter Drogeneinwirkung** ~ to be under the influence of drugs; **vor einer Entscheidung** ~ to be faced with a decision; **ich tue, was in meinen Kräften steht** I'll do everything I can.

(c) (geschrieben, angezeigt sein) to be. **wo steht das?** (lit) where does it say that?; **was steht da?** what does it say?; **das steht im Gesetz** the law says so; **es stand im „Kurier"** it was in the "Courier"; **das steht in der Bibel** it says that in the Bible; **der Zeiger steht auf 4 Uhr** the clock says 4 (o'clock); **es steht 2:1 für München** the score is 2-1 to Munich; **wie steht das Pfund?** how does the pound stand?; **die Sache steht mir bis hier** (col) I'm sick and tired of it (col).

(d) (angehalten haben) to have stopped. **meine Uhr steht** my watch has stopped; **der ganze Verkehr steht** all traffic is at a complete standstill.

(e) (Gram) (bei Satzstellung) to come; (bei Zeit, Fall, Modus) to be. **mit dem Dativ** ~ to take the dative.

(f) (passen zu) **jdm** ~ to suit sb.

(g) (Belohnung, Strafe etc) **auf Betrug steht eine Gefängnisstrafe** the penalty for fraud is imprisonment.

(h) *(Redewendungen)* **zu seinem Versprechen** ~ to stand by one's promise; **zu dem, was man gesagt hat,** ~ to stick to what one has said; **zu jdm** ~ to stand by sb; **wie** ~ **Sie dazu?** what are your views on that?; **für etw** ~ to stand for sth; **auf jdn/etw** ~ *(col)* to be mad about sb/sth *(col)*, to be into sb/sth *(col)*; **hinter jdm/etw** ~ to be behind sb/sth.

2 *vr* **sich gut/schlecht** ~ to be well-off/badly off; **sich mit jdm/etw gut/schlecht** ~ to be well-off/badly off with sb/sth.

3 *vi impers* **es steht schlecht/gut um jdn** *(bei Aussichten)* things look bad/good for sb; *(gesundheitlich, finanziell)* sb is doing badly/well; **wie steht's?** how are things?; **wie steht es damit?** how about it?

4 *vt Posten, Wache* to stand. **sich** *(acc)* **müde** ~, **sich** *(dat)* **die Beine in den Bauch** *(col)* ~ to stand until one is ready to drop.

Stehen *nt no pl* standing. **zum** ~ **bringen** to stop; **zum** ~ **kommen** to stop.

stehenbleiben *vi sep irreg aux sein (anhalten)* to stop; *(nicht weitergehen) (Mensch, Tier)* to stay; *(Zeit)* to stand still; *(Auto, Zug)* to stand.

stehend *adj attr Fahrzeug* stationary; *Gewässer* stagnant; *(ständig) Heer* regular. **~e Redensart** stock phrase.

stehenlassen *ptp* ~ *or* **stehengelassen** *vt sep irreg* to leave; *(Cook)* to let stand. **alles stehen- und liegenlassen** to drop everything; **jdn einfach** ~ to leave sb standing (there); **sich** *(dat)* **einen Bart** ~ to grow a beard.

Steh-: **~imbiß** *m* stand-up snack-bar; **~kneipe** *f* stand-up bar; **~lampe** *f* standard lamp *(Brit)*, floor lamp *(US)*; **~leiter** *f* stepladder.

stehlen *pret* **stahl**, *ptp* **gestohlen 1** *vti* to steal. **jdm die Zeit** ~ to waste sb's time. **2** *vr* to steal. **sich aus dem Haus** ~ to steal out of the house.

Steh-: **~platz** *m* ich bekam nur noch einen **~platz** I had to stand; **ein ~platz kostet 10 Mark** a standing ticket costs 10 marks; **~pult** *nt* high desk; **~vermögen** *nt* staying power, stamina.

steif *adj (lit, fig)* stiff; *Penis* erect; *Empfang* formal; *(gestärkt)* starched. ~ **und fest auf etw** *(dat)* **beharren** to insist stubbornly on sth.

steifen *vt* to stiffen; *Wäsche* to starch.

Steifftier ® *nt* soft toy (animal).

steigen *pret* **stieg**, *ptp* **gestiegen** *aux sein* **1** *vi* **(a)** *(klettern)* to climb. **auf einen Berg** ~ to climb (up) a mountain; **aufs Fahrrad** ~ to get on(to) one's bicycle; **vom Fahrrad** ~ to get off one's bicycle; **aus dem Zug** ~ to get off the train. **(b)** *(sich aufwärts bewegen)* to rise; *(Flugzeug, Straße)* to climb; *(Nebel)* to lift; *(Fieber)* to go up. **Drachen** ~ **lassen** to fly kites; **das Blut stieg ihm in den Kopf** the blood rushed to his head; **in jds Achtung** *(dat)* ~ to rise in sb's estimation. **2** *vt Treppen, Stufen* to climb (up).

Steiger *m -* *(Min)* pit foreman.

steigern 1 *vt* **(a)** to increase; *(verschlimmern) Übel, Zorn* to aggravate. **(b)** *(Gram)* to form the comparative and superlative of. **2** *vi* to bid *(um* for). **3** *vr* **(a)** *(sich erhöhen)* to increase; *(Farben)* to be intensified; *(Zorn, Übel)* to be aggravated. **(b)** *(sich verbessern)* to improve.

Steigerung *f* **(a)** *siehe vt* **(a)** *(das Steigern)* increase *(gen* in*)*; aggravation. **(b)** *(Verbesserung)* improvement. **(c)** *(Gram)* comparison.

Steigung *f (Hang)* slope; *(von Hang, Straße, Math)* gradient.

Steigungsgrad *m* gradient.

steil *adj* **(a)** steep. **eine ~e Karriere** *(fig)* a rapid rise. **(b)** *(senkrecht)* upright. **sich** ~ **aufrichten** to sit/stand up straight. **(c)** *(Sport)* **~er Paß** through ball.

Steil-: **~hang** *m* steep slope; **~küste** *f* steep coast; **~paß** *m (Sport)* through ball.

Stein *m* **-e** **(a)** stone; *(Ziegel~)* brick; *(in Uhr)*

jewel; *(Spiel~)* piece. **der** ~ **der Weisen** *(lit, fig)* the philosophers' stone; **es blieb kein** ~ **auf dem anderen** not a stone was left standing; **mir fällt ein** ~ **vom Herzen!** *(fig)* that's a load off my mind!; **bei jdm einen** ~ **im Brett haben** *(fig col)* to be well in with sb *(col)*; **den ersten** ~ **(auf jdn) werfen** to cast the first stone (at sb); **es friert** ~ **und Bein** *(fig col)* it's freezing cold outside; ~ **und Bein schwören** *(fig col)* to swear blind *(col)*.

Stein-: **~adler** *m* golden eagle; **s~alt** *adj* as old as the hills; **~bock** *m* **(a)** *(Zool)* ibex; **(b)** *(Astrol)* Capricorn; **~bohrer** *m* masonry drill; *(Gesteinsbohrer)* rock drill; **~bruch** *m* quarry.

steinern *adj* stone; *(fig)* stony.

Stein-: **~erweichen** *nt* **zum ~erweichen weinen** to cry heartbreakingly; **~frucht** *f* stone fruit; **~fußboden** *m* stone floor; **~garten** *m* rockery; **~gut** *nt* stoneware; **s~hart** *adj* rock hard.

steinig *adj* stony.

steinigen *vt* to stone.

Steinkohle *f* hard coal.

Steinkohlenbergbau *m* coal mining.

Stein-: **~krug** *m (Kanne)* stoneware jug; *(Becher)* stoneware mug; **~meißel** *m* stone chisel; **~metz** *m (wk)* **-en, -en** stonemason; **~obst** *nt* stone fruit; **~pilz** *m* type of mushroom; **~platte** *f* stone slab; *(zum Pflastern)* flagstone; **s~reich** *adj (col)* stinking rich *(col)*; **~salz** *nt* rock salt; **~schlag** *m* rockfall; **„Achtung ~schlag"** "danger falling stones"; **~tafel** *f* stone tablet; **~topf** *m* stoneware pot; **~wurf** *m (fig)* stone's throw; **~wüste** *f* stony desert; *(fig)* concrete jungle; **~zeit** *f* Stone Age.

Steißbein *nt (Anat)* coccyx.

Stellage [ʃtɛˈlaːʒə] *f* **-n** *(col: Gestell)* rack, frame.

Stelldichein *nt* **-(s)** *(dated)* rendezvous.

Stelle *f* **-n** **(a)** place; *(Fleck: rostend, naß, faul etc)* patch. **an dieser** ~ in this place; **eine kahle** ~ **am Kopf** a bald patch on one's head; **eine empfindliche** ~ *(lit)* a sensitive spot or place; *(fig)* a sensitive point; **eine schwache** ~ a weak spot; **auf der** ~ **treten** *(lit)* to mark time; *(fig)* not to make any headway; **auf der** ~ *(fig: sofort)* on the spot; **kommen, gehen** straight away; **nicht von der** ~ **kommen** not to make any progress; **sich nicht von der** ~ **rühren** to refuse to move; **zur** ~ **sein** to be on the spot; *(bereit, etw zu tun)* to be at hand.

(b) *(in Buch etc)* place; *(Abschnitt)* passage; *(Text~, etw beim Zitieren)* reference; *(Bibel~)* verse; *(Mus)* passage. **an dieser** ~ here; **an anderer** ~ elsewhere.

(c) an erster ~ in the first place; **(bei jdm) an erster/letzter** ~ **kommen** to come first/last (for sb); **an führender** ~ **stehen** to be in a leading position; **an** ~ **von** *or (+gen)* in place of; **an jds** *(acc)*/**an die** ~ **einer Sache** *(gen)* **treten** to take sb's place; **ich möchte jetzt nicht an seiner** ~ **sein** I wouldn't like to be in his position; **an deiner** ~ **würde ich ...** if I were you I would ...

(d) *(Math)* digit; *(hinter Komma)* place. **drei ~n hinter dem Komma** three decimal places.

(e) *(Posten)* job; *(Ausbildungs~)* place; *(Dienst~)* office; *(Behörde)* authority. **eine freie** *or* **offene** ~ a vacancy; **ohne** ~ without a job.

stellen 1 *vt* **(a)** *(hin~)* to put. **jdm etw auf den Tisch** ~ to put sth on the table for sb; **auf sich** *(acc)* **selbst gestellt sein** *(fig)* to have to fend for oneself. **(b)** *(arrangieren)* Szene to arrange; *Aufnahme* to pose. **eine gestellte Pose** a pose. **(c)** *(zur Verfügung* ~*)* to provide. **(d)** *(ein~)* to set *(auf +acc* at*)*; *Uhr etc* to set *(auf +acc* for*)*. **das Radio lauter/leiser** ~ to turn the radio up/down. **(e)** *(finanziell)* **gut/besser gestellt** well/better off. **(f)** *Verbrecher* to catch; *(fig col)* to corner. **(g)** *Aufgabe, Bedingung* to set *(jdm* sb*)*; *Frage* to put *(jdm, an jdn* to sb*)*; *Antrag, Forderung* to make. **jdn vor ein Problem** ~ to confront sb with a problem.

2 vr **(a)** to (go and) stand (an +acc at, by); (sich auf~, sich einordnen) to position oneself; (sich aufrecht hin~) to stand up. **sich gegen jdn/ etw ~** (fig) to oppose sb/sth; **sich hinter jdn/etw ~** (fig) to support sb/sth.
(b) (fig: sich verhalten) **sich anders zu etw ~** to have a different attitude towards sth; **wie stellst du dich zu ...?** how do you regard ...?; **sich gut mit jdm ~** to put oneself on good terms with sb.
(c) (sich ein~: Gerät etc) to set itself (auf +acc at).
(d) (sich ausliefern, antreten) to give oneself up (jdm to sb). **sich den Journalisten ~** to make oneself available to the reporters; **sich einer Herausforderung ~** to take up a challenge.
(e) (sich ver~) **sich krank/schlafend** etc ~ to pretend to be ill/asleep etc.
Stellen-: ~**angebot** nt offer of employment; „~**angebote"** "situations vacant"; ~**anzeige** f job advertisement or ad (col); ~**gesuch** nt advertisement seeking employment; „~**gesuche"** "situations wanted"; ~**markt** m job market; (in Zeitung) appointments section; ~**vermittlung** f employment bureau; s~**weise** adv in places; s~**weise Schauer** showers in places; ~**wert** m (fig) status.
Stellung f (lit, fig, Mil) position; (Posten auch) post. **in ~ bringen/gehen** to bring/get into position; **die ~ halten** (Mil) to hold one's position; (hum) to hold the fort; ~ **beziehen** (Mil) to move into position; (fig) to make it clear where one stands; **zu etw ~ nehmen** to give one's opinion on sth; **für/gegen jdn/etw ~ nehmen** or **beziehen** to come out in favour (Brit) or favor (US) of/to come out against sb/sth; **in führender ~** in a leading position; **die rechtliche ~ des Mieters** the legal status of the tenant; **ohne ~ sein** (arbeitslos) to be unemployed.
Stellungnahme f -**n** statement (zu on). **eine ~ zu etw abgeben** to make a statement on sth.
Stellungs-: ~**krieg** m positional warfare no indef art; s~**los** adj unemployed; ~**suche** f search for employment; **auf ~suche sein** to be looking for employment.
Stell-: s~**vertretend** adj (von Amts wegen) deputy attr; (vorübergehend) acting attr; s~**vertretend für jdn** acting for sb; s~**vertretend für jdn handeln** to act for sb; ~**vertreter** m (acting) representative; (von Amts wegen) deputy; ~**werk** nt (Rail) signal box (Brit) or tower (US).
Stelze f -**n** stilt.
stelzen vi aux sein (col) to stalk.
Stemmeisen nt crowbar.
stemmen 1 vt **(a)** (stützen) to press; Ellenbogen to prop. **die Arme in die Seiten** or **Hüften gestemmt** with arms akimbo. **(b)** (hoch~) to lift (above one's head). **(c)** (meißeln) to chisel. **2** vr **sich gegen etw ~** to brace oneself against sth; (fig) to set oneself against sth.
Stempel m - **(a)** (Gummi~) (rubber-)stamp. **(b)** (Abdruck) stamp; (Post~) postmark. **jdm/einer Sache einen/seinen ~ aufdrücken** (fig) to make a/one's mark on sb/sth. **(c)** (Tech) (Präge~) die; (stangenförmig, Loch~) punch. **(d)** (Bot) pistil.
Stempel-: ~**farbe** f stamping ink; ~**geld** nt (col) dole (money) (col); ~**kissen** nt ink pad.
stempeln 1 vt to stamp; Brief to postmark; Briefmarke to frank. **jdn zum Lügner ~** (fig) to brand sb as a liar. **2** vi (col) **(a)** ~ **gehen** to be/go on the dole (col). **(b)** (Stempeluhr betätigen) to clock in; (beim Hinausgehen) to clock out.
Stempeluhr f time-clock.
Stengel m - stem, stalk. **vom ~ fallen** (col) (Schwächeanfall haben) to collapse; (überrascht sein) to be staggered (col).
Steno f no pl (col) shorthand.
Steno-: ~**gramm** nt text in shorthand; (Diktat)

shorthand dictation; ~**grammblock** m shorthand pad; ~**graph(in** f) m (im Büro) shorthand secretary; (esp in Gericht, bei Konferenz etc) stenographer; ~**graphie** f shorthand; s~**graphieren** * 1 vt to take down in shorthand; 2 vi to do shorthand; s~**graphisch** adj shorthand attr; ~**typist(in** f) m shorthand typist.
Steppdecke f quilt.
Steppe f -**n** steppe.
steppen vti (Sew) to quilt.
Steppjacke f quilted jacket.
Step-: ~**tanz** m tap-dance; ~**tänzer** m tap dancer.
Sterbe-: ~**bett** nt death-bed; ~**fall** m death; ~**hilfe** f euthanasia; ~**kasse** f death benefit fund.
sterben pret **starb**, ptp **gestorben** vti aux sein to die. **einen schnellen Tod/eines natürlichen Todes ~** to die quickly/to die a natural death; **an einer Krankheit/Verletzung ~** to die of an illness/from an injury; **er stirbt vor Angst** (fig) he's frightened to death; **er ist für mich gestorben** (fig col) he might as well be dead.
Sterben nt no pl death. **Angst vor dem ~** fear of death; **im ~ liegen** to be dying.
Sterbens-: ~**angst** f (col) mortal fear; s~**elend** adj (col) wretched; s~**krank** adj mortally ill; s~**langweilig** adj (col) deadly boring; ~**wörtchen** nt (col) **er hat kein ~wörtchen gesagt** he didn't say a word.
Sterbe-: ~**stunde** f dying hour; ~**urkunde** f death certificate; ~**ziffer** f death rate.
sterblich adj mortal.
Sterbliche(r) mf decl as adj mortal.
Sterblichkeit f mortality; (Zahl) death-rate.
Stereo nt **in ~** in stereo.
stereo adj pred (in) stereo.
Stereo-: in cpds stereo; (s~skopisch) stereoscopic; ~**anlage** f stereo unit; ~**aufnahme** f stereo recording; ~**gerät** nt stereo unit; ~**kamera** f stereoscopic camera; s~**phon 1** adj stereophonic; **2** adv stereophonically; ~**skop** nt -**e** stereoscope; s~**typ** adj (fig) stereotyped.
steril adj (lit, fig) sterile.
Sterilisation f sterilization.
sterilisieren * vt to sterilize.
Sterilisierung f sterilization.
Sterilität f (lit, fig) sterility.
Stern m -**e** star. **das steht (noch) in den ~en** (fig) it's in the lap of the gods; **nach den ~en greifen** (fig) to reach for the stars; **sein ~ ist im Sinken** his star is on the decline; **mein guter ~** my lucky star; **unter einem glücklichen ~ geboren sein** to be born under a lucky star; **unter einem guten ~ stehen** to be blessed with good fortune.
Sternbild nt (Astron) constellation; (Astrol) sign.
Sternchen nt dim of **Stern (a)** little star. **(b)** (Typ) asterisk.
Sterndeuter m astrologer.
Sternen-: ~**banner** nt Stars and Stripes sing; ~**himmel** m starry sky.
Stern-: ~**fahrt** f (Mot, Pol) rally; s~**förmig** adj star-shaped; s~**hagelvoll** adj (col) rolling drunk (col); ~**kunde** f astronomy; ~**marsch** m (Pol) protest march; ~**schnuppe** f shooting star; ~**stunde** f great moment; ~**system** nt galaxy; ~**warte** f observatory; ~**zeichen** nt (Astrol) sign of the zodiac; **im ~zeichen der Jungfrau** under the sign of Virgo.
stet adj constant.
Stethoskop nt -**e** stethoscope.
stetig adj steady; (Math) Funktion continuous.
stets adv always.
Steuer¹ nt - (Naut) helm, tiller; (Aut) (steering-)wheel; (Aviat) controls pl. **am ~ stehen** (Naut) or **sein** (Naut, fig) to be at the helm; **am ~ sitzen** (col) (Aut) to be at the wheel; (Aviat) to be at the controls; **das ~ übernehmen** (lit, fig) to take over; **das ~ fest in der Hand haben** (fig) to be firmly in control; **das ~ herumrei-**

ßen *(fig)* to turn the tide of events.
Steuer[2] *f* **-n** *(Abgabe)* tax; *(Gemeinde~)* rates *pl* *(Brit)*, local tax *(US)*. **~n** tax; *(Arten von* **~n)** taxes; **~n zahlen** to pay tax.
Steuer-: **~beamte(r)** *m* tax officer; **s~begünstigt** *adj Investitionen, Hypothek* tax-deductible; *Waren* taxed at a lower rate; **~behörde** *f* tax authorities *pl*, inland *(Brit)* or internal *(US)* revenue authorities *pl*; **~berater** *m* tax consultant; **~bescheid** *m* tax assessment; **~betrug** *m* tax evasion; **~bord** *nt no pl (Naut)* starboard; **s~bord(s)** *adv (Naut)* to starboard; **~einnahmen** *pl* revenue from taxation; **~erklärung** *f* tax return; **~erlaß** *m* tax exemption; **~erstattung** *f* tax rebate; **~flucht** *f* tax evasion; **s~frei** *adj* tax-free; **~freiheit** *f* tax exemption; **~gelder** *pl* tax money; **~gerät** *nt* tuneramplifier; **~hinterziehung** *f* tax evasion; **~inspektor** *m* tax inspector; **~jahr** *nt* tax year; **~karte** *f* tax notice; **~klasse** *f* tax bracket; **~knüppel** *m* control column.
steuerlich *adj* tax *attr.* **~e Belastung** tax burden.
steuerlos *adj* out of control; *(fig)* leaderless.
Steuer-: **~mann** *m pl* **~männer** *or* **~leute** helmsman; *(als Rang)* (first) mate; **~marke** *f* revenue stamp; *(für Hunde)* dog licence disc *(Brit)*, dog tag *(US)*; **~moral** *f* tax-payer honesty.
steuern **1** *vt* to steer; *Schiff auch* to navigate; *Flugzeug* to pilot; *(fig) Wirtschaft, Politik, (Comp)* to control. **staatlich gesteuert** state-controlled; **einen Kurs ~** *(lit, fig)* to steer a course. **2** *vi (aux sein* to head. **(b)** *(am Steuer sein) (Naut)* to be at the helm; *(Aut)* to be at the wheel; *(Aviat)* to be at the controls.
Steuer-: **~oase** *f* tax haven; **~pflicht** *f* liability to tax; **s~pflichtig** *adj Einkommen* taxable, liable to tax; **~politik** *f* tax policy; **~progression** *f* progressive taxation; **~prüfer** *m* tax inspector; **~prüfung** *f* tax inspector's investigation; **~rad** *nt (Aviat)* control wheel; *(Aut)* (steering-)wheel; **~recht** *nt* tax law; **~reform** *f* tax reform; **~ruder** *nt* rudder; **~satz** *m* rate of taxation; **~schuld** *f* tax liability.
Steuerung *f* **(a)** *no pl (das Steuern) (von Schiff)* navigation; *(von Flugzeug)* piloting. **(b)** *(Steuervorrichtung) (Aviat)* controls *pl*; *(Tech)* steering apparatus. **automatische ~** *(Aviat)* autopilot; *(Tech)* automatic steering (device).
Steuer-: **~vorteil** *m* tax advantage; **~zahler** *m* taxpayer.
Steven ['ʃteːvn] *m* **-** *(Naut) (Vorder~)* prow; *(Achter~)* stern.
Stewardeß ['stjuːɹɛdɛs] *f* **-ssen** stewardess.
StGB [esteːgeːˈbeː] *nt* = **Strafgesetzbuch.**
stibitzen* *vt (hum)* to swipe *(col)*, to pinch *(col)*.
Stich *m* **-e (a)** *(Insekten~)* sting; *(Mücken~)* bite; *(Nadel~)* prick; *(Messer~)* stab. **(b)** *(Schmerz)* stabbing pain; *(Seiten~)* stitch; *(fig)* pang. **(c)** *(Sew)* stitch. **(d)** *(Kupfer~, Stahl~)* engraving. **(e)** *(Schattierung)* shade *(in +acc of)*; *(Tendenz)* suggestion *(in +acc of)*. **ein ~ ins Rote** a tinge of red. **(f)** *(Cards)* trick. **einen ~ machen** to get a trick. **(g) jdn im ~ lassen** to let sb down; *(verlassen)* to desert sb. **(h) einen ~ haben** *(Eßwaren)* to be bad *or* off *(Brit)*; *(Milch)* to be sour; *(col: Mensch: verrückt sein)* to be nuts *(col)*.
Stichel *m* **-** *(Art)* gouge.
Stichelei *f (pej col: boshafte Bemerkung)* dig. **deine ständigen ~en kannst du dir sparen** stop getting at me.
sticheln *vi (pej col)* to make snide remarks *(col)*.
Stich-: **~flamme** *f* tongue of flame; **s~haltig** *adj* valid; *Beweis* conclusive; **~haltigkeit** *f no pl* validity; conclusiveness.
Stichling *m (Zool)* stickleback.
Stich-: **~probe** *f* spot check; **~tag** *m* qualifying date; **~waffe** *f* stabbing weapon; **~wahl** *f (Pol)* final ballot, run-off *(US)*.

Stichwort *nt* **(a)** *pl* **-wörter** *(in Lexikon)* headword. **(b)** *pl* **-worte** *(Theat, fig)* cue. **(c)** *pl* **-worte** *usu pl* notes *pl*.
Stichwort-: **s~artig** *adj* abbreviated; **etw s~artig zusammenfassen** to summarize the main points of sth; **~katalog** *m* classified catalogue; **~verzeichnis** *nt* index.
Stichwunde *f* stab wound.
Stick|arbeit *f* embroidery.
sticken *vti* to embroider.
Stickerei *f* embroidery.
stickig *adj Luft, Zimmer* stuffy; *Klima* humid.
Stickstoff *m* nitrogen.
stieben *pret* **stob** *or* **stiebte,** *ptp* **gestoben** *or* **gestiebt** *vi (geh) aux haben or sein (sprühen) (Funken, Staub, Schnee)* to fly; *(Wasser)* to spray.
Stiefbruder *m* stepbrother.
Stiefel *m* **- (a)** boot. **(b)** *(Trinkgefäß)* large, boot-shaped beer glass.
Stiefel-: **~absatz** *m* (boot-)heel; **~knecht** *m* bootjack.
stiefeln *vi aux sein (col)* to hoof it *(col)*; *siehe* **gestiefelt.**
Stief-: **~eltern** *pl* step-parents *pl*; **~kind** *nt* stepchild; *(fig)* poor cousin; **~mutter** *f* stepmother; **~mütterchen** *nt (Bot)* pansy; **s~mütterlich** *adj (fig)* **jdn/etw s~mütterlich behandeln** to pay little attention to sb/sth; **~schwester** *f* stepsister; **~sohn** *m* stepson; **~tochter** *f* stepdaughter; **~vater** *m* stepfather.
stieg *pret of* **steigen.**
Stiege *f* **-n** *(Treppe)* (narrow) flight of stairs.
Stieglitz *m* **-e** goldfinch.
Stiel *m* **-e (a)** *(Griff)* handle; *(Pfeifen~, Glas~)* stem. **(b)** *(Stengel)* stalk.
Stiel|augen *pl (fig col)* **er machte ~** his eyes (nearly) popped out of his head.
stier *adj (stumpfsinnig) Blick* vacant, blank.
Stier *m* **-e (a)** bull; *(junger~)* bullock. **wütend wie ein ~** beside oneself with rage. **(b)** *(Astrol)* Taurus.
stieren *vi* to stare *(auf +acc at)*.
Stier-: **~kampf** *m* bull-fight; **~kampfarena** *f* bullring; **~kämpfer** *m* bull-fighter.
stieß *pret of* **stoßen.**
Stift *m* **-e (a)** *(Metall~)* pin; *(Nagel)* tack. **(b)** *(Blei~)* pencil. **(c)** *(col: Lehrling)* apprentice (boy).
stiften *vt* **(a)** *(spenden)* to donate; *(gründen) Kirche* to found. **(b)** *Verwirrung* to cause; *Unfrieden, Frieden* to bring about; *Ehe* to arrange.
stiftengehen *vi sep irreg aux sein (col)* to hop it *(col)*.
Stifter(in *f)* *m* **-** *(Gründer)* founder; *(Spender)* donator.
Stiftung *f* **(a)** *(Gründung)* foundation; *(Schenkung)* donation. **(b)** *(Organisation)* foundation.
Stiftzahn *m* post crown.
Stigma *nt* **-men** *or* **-ta** *(Bio, Rel, fig)* stigma.
Stil *m* **-e** style; *(Eigenart)* way, manner. **im großen ~** in a big way; **schlechter ~** bad style; **das ist schlechter ~** *(fig)* that is bad form.
Stil-: **~blüte** *f (hum)* stylistic howler; **~bruch** *m* stylistic incongruity.
Stilett *nt* **-e** stiletto.
Stil-: **~fehler** *m* stylistic lapse; **~gefühl** *nt* feeling for style.
stilisieren* *vt* to stylize.
Stilistik *f (Liter)* stylistics *sing.*
stilistisch *adj* stylistic.
still *adj* **(a)** *(ruhig)* quiet, silent; *Seufzer, Plätzchen* quiet; *Gebet, Vorwurf, Beobachter* silent. **~ werden** to go quiet; **im Saal wurde es ~** the room fell silent; **um ihn ist es ~ geworden** you don't hear anything about him any more; **~ weinen/leiden** to cry quietly/to suffer in silence; **in ~er Trauer** in silent grief; **im ~en** quietly; **ich dachte mir im ~en** I thought to myself; **sich** *(dat)* **~**

gegenübersitzen to sit opposite one another in silence; **die S~en im Lande** the quiet ones; **sei doch ~!** be quiet; **~e Messe** silent mass. **(b)** *(unbewegt) Luft* still. **der S~e Ozean** the Pacific (Ocean); **~ sitzen** to sit still; **die Füße ~ halten** to keep one's feet still; **er ist ein ~es Wasser** he's a deep one. **(c)** *(heimlich)* secret. **im ~en** in secret. **(d)** *(Comm) Teilhaber* sleeping *(Brit)*, silent *(US)*; *Reserven, Rücklagen* hidden. **~e Beteiligung** sleeping partnership *(Brit)*, non-active interest.

Stille *f no pl* **(a)** *(Ruhe)* quiet(ness), peace(fulness); *(Schweigen)* silence. **die Beerdigung fand in aller ~ statt** it was a quiet funeral. **(b)** *(Unbewegtheit)* calm(ness); *(der Luft)* stillness. **(c)** *(Heimlichkeit)* secrecy. **in aller ~** secretly.

Stilleben ['ʃtɪleːbn] *nt* still life.

stillegen *vt sep* to close down.

Stillegung *f* closure.

Stillehre *f* stylistics *sing*.

stillen 1 *vt* **(a)** *(zum Stillstand bringen) Tränen* to stop; *Schmerzen* to ease. **(b)** *(befriedigen) Neugier, Hunger* to satisfy; *Durst auch* to quench. **(c)** *Säugling* to breast-feed. **2** *vi* to breast-feed.

Stillhalte|abkommen *nt (Fin, fig)* moratorium.

stillhalten *vi sep irreg* to keep still; *(fig)* to keep quiet.

stilliegen *vi sep irreg aux sein or haben* **(a)** *(außer Betrieb sein)* to be shut down. **(b)** *(lahmliegen)* to be at a standstill.

Stillschweigen *nt* silence. **über etw** *(acc)* **~ bewahren** to observe silence about sth; **etw mit ~ übergehen** to pass over sth in silence.

stillschweigend *adj* silent; *Einverständnis* tacit. **über etw** *(acc)* **~ hinweggehen** to pass over sth in silence.

stillsitzen *vi sep irreg aux sein or haben* to sit still.

Stillstand *m* standstill; *(in Entwicklung)* halt. **zum ~ kommen** *(Verkehr)* to come to a standstill; **etw zum ~ bringen** to stop sth.

stillstehen *vi sep irreg aux sein or haben* **(a)** *(Produktion, Handel etc)* to be at a standstill; *(Herz)* to have stopped. **(b)** *(stehenbleiben)* to stop; *(Maschine)* to stop working.

stillvergnügt *adj* contented.

Stil-: **~mittel** *nt* stylistic device; **~möbel** *pl* period furniture *sing*; **s~voll** *adj* stylish; **~wörterbuch** *nt* dictionary of correct usage.

Stimm-: **~abgabe** *f* voting; **~band** *nt usu pl* vocal chord; **s~berechtigt** *adj* entitled to vote; **~berechtigte(r)** *mf decl as adj* person entitled to vote; **~bezirk** *m* constituency; **~bruch** *m* **er ist im ~bruch** his voice is breaking.

Stimme *f* **-n (a)** *(lit, fig)* voice; *(Mus: Part)* part; *(Orgel~)* register. **mit leiser/lauter ~** in a soft/loud voice; **zweite ~** *(in Chor)* second part; **bei einem Lied die erste/zweite ~ singen** to sing the top part of/descant to a song; **die ~n mehren sich, die ...** there is a growing body of opinion that ...; **der ~ des Gewissens folgen** to follow one's conscience. **(b)** *(Wahl~)* vote. **eine/keine ~ haben** to have the vote/not to be entitled to vote; *(Mitspracherecht)* to have a/no say; **seine ~ abgeben** to vote; **jdm seine ~ geben** to vote for sb.

stimmen 1 *vi* **(a)** *(richtig sein)* to be right. **stimmt es, daß ...?** is it true that ...?; **hier stimmt was nicht!** there's something wrong here; **stimmt so!** that's all right. **(b)** *(zusammenpassen)* to go (together). **(c)** *(wählen, sich entscheiden)* to vote. **für/gegen jdn/etw ~** to vote for/against sb/sth. **2** *vt Instrument* to tune. **jdn froh/traurig ~** to make sb (feel) cheerful/sad.

Stimmen-: **~gewirr** *nt* babble of voices; **~gleichheit** *f* tied vote; **bei ~gleichheit in** the event of a tie; **~mehrheit** *f* majority of votes.

Stimm-: **~enthaltung** *f* abstention; **~gabel** *f* tuning fork; **s~haft** *adj (Ling)* voiced; **s~haft ausgesprochen werden** to be voiced.

stimmlich *adj* vocal. **ihre ~en Qualitäten** the quality of her voice.

Stimm-: **s~los** *adj (Ling)* unvoiced; **s~los ausgesprochen werden** not to be voiced; **~recht** *nt* right to vote.

Stimmung *f* **(a)** *(auch St Ex)* mood; *(Moral)* morale. **in (guter)/gehobener ~** in a good mood/in high spirits; **in ~ kommen** to liven up; **ich bin nicht in der ~ dazu** I'm not in the mood for that. **(b)** *(Meinung)* opinion. **~ gegen/für jdn/etw machen** to stir up (public) opinion against/in favour *(Brit)* or favor *(US)* of sb/sth.

Stimmungs-: **~kanone** *f (col)* life and soul of the party; **~mache** *f no pl (pej)* cheap propaganda; **~musik** *f* light music; **~umschwung** *m* change of atmosphere; *(Pol)* swing (in public opinion); **s~voll** *adj Bild* idyllic; *Atmosphäre* tremendous; *Gedicht* full of atmosphere.

Stimm-: **~vieh** *nt (pej)* gullible voters *pl*; **~volk** *nt* voters *pl*, electorate; **~zettel** *m* ballot paper.

stimulieren* *vt (Med, fig)* to stimulate.

Stinkbombe *f* stink bomb.

stinken *pret* **stank,** *ptp* **gestunken** *vi* to stink *(nach* of*)*. **er stinkt nach Kneipe** he smells of drink; **er stinkt vor Faulheit** he's bone-idle; **das stinkt zum Himmel** it's an absolute scandal; **die Sache stinkt mir** *(col)* I'm fed up to the back teeth (with it) *(col)*.

Stink-: **s~faul** *adj (col)* bone-lazy; **s~langweilig** *adj (col)* deadly boring; **s~reich** *adj (col)* stinking rich *(col)*; **~tier** *nt* skunk; **~wut** *f (col)* raging temper; **eine ~wut (auf jdn) haben** to be livid (with sb).

Stipendium *nt* grant; *(als Auszeichnung etc erhalten)* scholarship.

Stirn *f* **-en** forehead. **es steht ihm auf der ~ geschrieben** *(geh)* it is written in his face; **die ~ haben zu ...** to have the nerve to ...; **jdm/einer Sache die ~ bieten** *(geh)* to stand up to sb.

Stirn-: **~band** *nt* headband; **~falte** *f* wrinkle (on one's forehead); **~glatze** *f* receding hair-line; **~runzeln** *nt no pl* frown.

stob *pret of* **stieben.**

stöbern *vi* to rummage *(in +dat* in, *durch* through*)*.

stochern *vi* to poke *(in +dat* at*)*; *(im Essen)* to pick *(in +dat* at*)*. **sich** *(dat)* **in den Zähnen ~** to pick one's teeth.

Stock *m* **-e (a)** stick; *(Rohr~)* cane; *(Takt~)* baton; *(Zeige~)* pointer; *(Billard~)* cue. **am ~ gehen** *(lit)* to walk with a stick; **da gehst du am ~** *(col)* you'll be flabbergasted *(col)*. **(b)** *(Pflanze)* *(Reb~)* vine; *(Rosen~)* rose-bush; *(Blumen~)* pot-plant. **über ~ und Stein** up hill and down dale. **(c)** *pl* **- (~werk)** floor, storey *(Brit)*, story *(US)*. **im ersten ~** on the first floor *(Brit)*, on the second floor *(US)*.

Stock-: **s~betrunken** *(col) adj* blind drunk; **s~blind** *adj (col)* as blind as a bat; **s~dunkel** *adj (col)* pitch-dark.

Stöckelschuh *m* stiletto-heeled shoe.

stocken *vi* **(a)** *(Herz, Puls)* to miss a beat; *(nicht vorangehen) (Arbeit, Entwicklung)* to make no progress; *(Unterhaltung)* to flag; *(innehalten)* to falter; *(im Satz)* to break off; *(Verkehr)* to be held up. **ihm stockte das Herz/der Puls** his heart/pulse missed a beat; **ihm stockte der Atem** he caught his breath; **ins S~ geraten** *(Gespräch)* to begin to flag. **(b)** *(stagnieren) (Verhandlungen)* to break off; *(Geschäfte, Handel)* to drop off. **(c)** *(gerinnen: Blut)* to thicken. **das Blut stockte ihm in den Adern** *(geh)* the blood froze in his veins.

stockend *adj* faltering, hesitant.

Stock-: **s~finster** *adj (col)* pitch-black; **~fisch** *m* dried cod; **s~konservativ** *adj (col)* arch-conservative; **s~nüchtern** *adj (col)* stone-cold sober *(col)*; **s~sauer** *adj (col)* pissed-off *(col)*; **~schlag** *m* blow (from a stick); *(mit Rohr~)* stroke of the cane; **s~steif** *adj (col)* as stiff as a poker.

Stockung f (a) hold-up (gen, in +dat in); (Verkehrs~) traffic-jam. (b) (Pause) (im Gespräch) lull; (in der Rede) hesitation.

Stockwerk nt floor, storey (Brit), story (US). im 5. ~ on the 5th (Brit) or 6th (US) floor; **ein Haus mit vier ~en** a four-storeyed (Brit) or four-storied (US) building.

Stoff m -e (a) material, fabric; (als Materialart) cloth. (b) (no pl: Materie) matter. (c) (Substanz, Chem) substance; (Papier~) pulp. (d) (Thema) subject (matter); (Unterhaltungs~, Diskussions~) topic; (Material) material. ~ **zum Lesen** reading matter. (e) (col: Rauschgift) dope (col).

Stoff-: ~**bahn** f length of material; ~**ballen** m roll of cloth.

Stoffel m - (pej col) lout (col), boor.

stoff(e)lig adj (pej col) uncouth, boorish.

Stoffhandschuh m fabric glove.

stofflich adj (Philos) material; (den Inhalt betreffend) as regards subject matter.

Stoff-: ~**puppe** f rag doll; ~**rest** m remnant. **Stoffwechsel** m metabolism.

Stoffwechselstörung f metabolic disturbance.

stöhnen vi to groan. ~**d with a groan.

stoisch adj stoic(al); (Philos) Stoic.

Stola ['ʃtoːla, st-] f, pl **Stolen** stole.

Stollen m - (a) (Min, Mil) gallery, tunnel. (b) (Cook) fruit loaf (eaten at Christmas), stollen (US).

stolpern vi aux sein to stumble, to trip (über +acc over); (fig: zu Fall kommen) to come a cropper (col). **über einen Hinweis** ~ (fig) to stumble upon a clue.

stolz adj (a) proud (auf +acc of). **darauf kannst du** ~ **sein** that's something to be proud of. (b) (imposant) Bauwerk majestic; (iro: stattlich) Preis princely.

Stolz m no pl pride. **sein Garten ist sein ganzer** ~ his garden is his pride and joy.

stolzieren* vi aux sein to strut; (hochmütig) to stalk.

stopfen 1 vt (a) (füllen) to stuff; Pfeife, Loch to fill. **jdm das Maul** (col) ~ to silence sb; **gierig stopfte er alles in sich hinein** he greedily stuffed down everything. (b) (ausbessern, flicken) Loch, Strümpfe etc to darn. 2 vi (a) (Speisen) (ver~) to cause constipation. (b) (flicken) to darn.

Stopf-: ~**garn** nt darning thread; ~**nadel** f darning needle.

Stopp m -s stop, halt; (Lohn~) freeze.

Stoppball m dropshot.

Stoppel f -n (Getreide~, Bart~) stubble.

Stoppel-: ~**bart** m stubbly beard; ~**feld** nt stubble-field.

stopp(e)lig adj Bart stubbly; Kinn auch bristly.

stoppen 1 vt to stop; Zeit, Läufer to time. **er hat die Zeit genau gestoppt** he timed exactly how long it took. 2 vi to stop.

Stopper m - (Ftbl) centre half.

Stopp-: ~**licht** nt stop-light, red light; ~**schild** nt stop sign; ~**uhr** f stop-watch.

Stöpsel m - plug; (Pfropfen) stopper.

stöpseln vti (Telec) to connect.

Stör m -e (Zool) sturgeon.

Stör-: ~**aktion** f disruptive action no pl; **s~anfällig** adj susceptible to interference.

Storch m ⁼e stork.

Store [ʃtoːɐ] m -s usu pl net curtain.

stören 1 vt (a) Schlaf, öffentliche Ordnung, Frieden etc to disturb; Verhältnis, Harmonie etc to spoil; Rundfunkempfang to interfere with; (absichtlich) to jam. **jds Pläne** ~ to upset sb's plans. (b) Prozeß, Vorlesung to disrupt. (c) (unangenehm berühren) to disturb, to bother. **was mich an ihm/daran stört** what I don't like about him/it; **lassen Sie sich nicht** ~**!** don't let me disturb you; **stört es Sie, wenn ich rauche?** do you mind if I smoke?; **sie läßt sich durch nichts** ~ she doesn't

let anything bother her.

2 vr **sich an etw** (dat) ~ to be bothered about sth; **ich störe mich an seiner Unpünktlichkeit** I take exception to his unpunctuality.

3 vi (a) (lästig, im Weg sein) to get in the way; (unterbrechen) to interrupt; (Belästigung darstellen: Musik, Lärm etc) to be disturbing. **bitte nicht** ~**!** please do not disturb!; **ich möchte nicht** ~ **I** don't want to be in the way; **etw als** ~**d empfinden** to find sth bothersome. (b) (unangenehm auffallen) to spoil the effect.

Störenfried m -e, **Störer** m - trouble-maker.

Störmanöver nt disruptive action.

stornieren* vti (Comm) Auftrag to cancel; Buchungsfehler to reverse.

Storno m or nt, pl **Storni** (Comm) (von Buchungsfehler) reversal; (von Auftrag) cancellation.

störrisch adj stubborn, obstinate; Kind unmanageable; Pferd restive.

Störsender m (Rad) jamming transmitter.

Störung f (a) disturbance; (von Ablauf, Verhandlungen etc) disruption; (Verkehrs~) hold-up. (b) (Tech) fault. (c) (Rad) interference; (absichtlich) jamming. (d) (Med) disorder. **nervöse** ~**en** nervous trouble.

Störungs-: **s~frei** adj trouble-free; (Rad) free from interference; ~**stelle** f (Telec) faults service.

Stoß m ⁼e (a) push, shove; (leicht) poke; (mit Faust) punch; (mit Fuß) kick; (mit Ellbogen) nudge; (mit Kopf, Hörnern) butt; (Dolch~ etc) stab; (Fechten) thrust; (Atem~) gasp. **seinem Herzen einen** ~ **geben** to pluck up courage. (b) (Anprall) impact; (Erd~) tremor; (eines Wagens) jolt. (c) (Stapel) pile, stack. (d) (Trompeten~ etc) blast (in +acc on).

Stoßdämpfer m (Aut) shock absorber.

Stößel m - pestle; (Aut: Ventil~) tappet.

stoß|empfindlich adj susceptible to shock.

stoßen pret **stieß**, ptp **gestoßen** 1 vt (a) to push, to shove; (leicht) to poke; (mit Faust) to punch; (mit Fuß) to kick; (mit Ellbogen) to nudge; (mit Kopf, Hörnern) to butt; (stechen) Dolch to plunge; (Sport) Kugel to put. **sich** (dat) **den Kopf etc** ~ to hit one's head etc; **jdn von sich** ~ to push sb away; (fig) to cast sb aside; **er stieß den Ball mit dem Kopf ins Tor** he headed the ball into the goal. (b) (zerkleinern) Zimt, Pfeffer to pound.

2 vr to bump oneself. **sich an etw** (dat) ~ (lit) to bump oneself on sth; (fig) to take exception to sth.

3 vi (a) (mit den Hörnern) to butt (nach at). (b) (Tech) to butt (an +acc against). (c) (Gewichtheben) to jerk. (d) aux sein **an etw** (acc) ~ to bump into sth; (grenzen) to border on sth; **gegen etw** ~ to run into sth; **zu jdm** ~ to meet up with sb; **auf jdn** ~ to bump into sb; **auf etw** (acc) ~ (Schiff) to hit sth; (fig: entdecken) to come across sth; **auf Erdöl** ~ to strike oil; **auf Widerstand** ~ to meet with resistance.

Stoß-: ~**gebet** nt quick prayer; **ein** ~**gebet zum Himmel schicken** to say a quick prayer; ~**seufzer** m deep sigh; **s~sicher** adj shock-proof; ~**stange** f (Aut) bumper; ~**trupp** m (Mil) raiding party; ~**verkehr** m rush-hour (traffic); ~**waffe** f thrust weapon; **s~weise** adv (a) (ruckartig) by fits and starts; (b) (stapelweise) by the pile; ~**zahn** m tusk; ~**zeit** f (im Verkehr) rush-hour; (in Geschäft etc) peak period.

stottern vti to stutter; (Motor) to splutter. **leicht/stark** ~ to stutter slightly/badly; **ins S~ kommen** to start stuttering.

Stövchen nt (teapot- etc) warmer.

Str. = **Straße** St.

Straf-: ~**anstalt** f penal institution, prison; ~**antrag** m legal proceedings pl; ~**antrag stellen** to institute legal proceedings; ~**anzeige** f ~**anzeige gegen jdn erstatten** to bring a charge against sb; ~**arbeit** f (Sch) lines pl, imposition; ~**bank** f (Sport) penalty bench.

strafbar adj Vergehen punishable. ~**e Handlung** punishable offence; **sich** ~ **machen** to commit an offence (Brit) or offense (US).

Strafe f **-n** punishment; (Jur, Sport) penalty; (Geld~) fine; (Gefängnis~) sentence. ... **bei** ~ **verboten** ... forbidden; **etw unter** ~ **stellen** to make sth a punishable offence (Brit) or offense (US); **unter** ~ **stehen** to be a punishable offence (Brit) or offense (US); **seine** ~ **absitzen** to serve one's sentence; ~ **zahlen** to pay a fine; **100 Dollar** ~ **zahlen** to pay a $100 fine; **zur** ~ as a punishment; ~ **muß sein!** discipline is necessary; **seine gerechte** ~ **bekommen** to get one's just deserts; **er hat seine** ~ **weg** (col) he's had his punishment.

strafen vti to punish. **mit etw gestraft sein** to be cursed with sth; **sie ist vom Schicksal gestraft** she is cursed by fate; **er ist gestraft genug** he has been punished enough.

strafend adj attr punitive; Blick reproachful.

Straf-: ~**entlassene(r)** mf decl as adj ex-convict; ~**erlaß** m remission (of sentence); ~**expedition** f punitive expedition.

straff adj Seil tight, taut; Haut smooth; (fig: streng) Disziplin, Organisation strict. ~ **sitzen** to fit tightly; **etw** ~ **spannen** to tighten sth; **das Haar** ~ **zurückkämmen** to comb one's hair back severely.

straffällig adj ~ **werden** to commit a criminal offence (Brit) or offense (US).

Straffällige(r) mf decl as adj offender.

straffen 1 vt to tighten; (raffen) Darstellung to tighten up. 2 vr to tighten; (Haut) to become smooth.

Straf-: s~**frei** adj s~**frei ausgehen** to go unpunished; ~**freiheit** f impunity; ~**gebühr** f surcharge; ~**gefangene(r)** mf decl as adj prisoner; ~**gericht** nt criminal court; **ein** ~**gericht abhalten** to hold a trial; **das göttliche** ~**gericht** divine judgement; ~**gesetz** nt penal law; ~**gesetzbuch** nt Criminal Code; ~**justiz** f criminal justice no art; ~**kolonie** f penal colony; ~**kompanie** f (Mil) punishment battalion.

sträflich 1 adj (lit, fig) criminal. 2 adv vernachlässigen etc criminally.

Sträfling m prisoner.

Sträflingskleidung f prison clothing.

Straf-: ~**mandat** nt ticket; ~**maß** nt sentence; **das höchste** ~**maß** the maximum penalty; s~**mildernd** adj mitigating; ~**minute** f (Sport) penalty minute; ~**porto** nt excess postage; ~**predigt** f dressing-down (col); **jdm eine** ~**predigt halten** to give sb a dressing-down; ~**prozeß** m criminal proceedings pl; ~**punkt** m (Sport) penalty point; ~**raum** m (Sport) penalty area; ~**recht** nt criminal law; s~**rechtlich** adj criminal; **jdn/etw** s~**rechtlich verfolgen** to prosecute sb/sth; ~**richter** m criminal judge; ~**sache** f criminal matter; ~**stoß** m (Ftbl etc) penalty (kick); (Hockey etc) penalty (shot); ~**tat** f criminal offence (Brit) or offense (US); ~**täter** m offender; ~**verfahren** nt criminal proceedings pl; ~**verfolgung** f criminal prosecution; s~**versetzen*** vt insep Beamte to transfer for disciplinary reasons; ~**verteidiger** m counsel for the defence (Brit) or defense (US); ~**vollzug** m penal system; ~**vollzugsanstalt** f (form) penal institution; s~**würdig** adj (form) criminal; ~**wurf** m (Sport) penalty throw; ~**zettel** m (col) ticket.

Strahl m **-en** (lit, fig) ray; (Radio~, Laser~ etc) beam; (Wasser~, Luft~) jet.

strahlen vi (Sonne, Licht etc) to shine; (Sender, fig: Gesicht) to beam; (Kernreaktor etc) to radiate. **er strahlte (übers ganze Gesicht)** he was beaming all over his face.

strahlend adj radiant; Wetter, Tag bright. ~**es**

Lachen beaming smile; **mit** ~**em Gesicht** with a beaming face.

Strahlen-: s~**förmig** adj radial; s~**geschädigt** adj suffering from radiation damage; ~**krankheit** f radiation sickness; ~**schäden** pl radiation injuries pl; ~**schutz** m radiation protection; ~**therapie** f radiotherapy.

Strahltriebwerk nt jet engine.

Strahlung f radiation.

Strähne f **-n** (Haar~) strand. **ich habe schon eine weiße** ~ I already have a white streak.

strähnig adj Haar straggly.

stramm adj (straff) Seil, Hose tight; (schneidig) Haltung, Soldat erect; (kräftig, drall) Mädchen, Junge strapping; Junge, Beine sturdy; Brust firm; (col) (tüchtig) Marsch, Arbeit hard; (überzeugt) staunch. ~ **sitzen** (Kleidung) to be tight; ~**e Haltung annehmen** to stand to attention; ~ **marschieren** (col) to march hard.

stramm-: ~**stehen** vi sep irreg (Mil col) to stand to attention; ~**ziehen** vt sep irreg Seil, Hose to pull tight; **jdm den Hosenboden** ~**ziehen** (col) to give sb a good hiding.

Strampelhöschen [-'hø:sçən] nt rompers pl.

strampeln vi (a) to thrash about. (b) aux sein (col: radfahren) to pedal.

Strand m **=e** (Meeres~) beach; (Seeufer) shore. **am** ~ on the beach.

Strand-: ~**anzug** m beach suit; ~**bad** nt (seawater) swimming pool; (Badeort) bathing resort.

stranden vi aux sein to run aground; (fig) to fail; (Mädchen) to go astray.

Strand-: ~**gut** nt (lit, fig) flotsam and jetsam; ~**hafer** m marram (grass); ~**hotel** nt seaside hotel; ~**kleidung** f beachwear; ~**korb** m wicker beach chair with a hood; ~**promenade** f promenade; ~**räuber** m beachcomber.

Strang m **=e** (Nerven~, Muskel~) cord; (Rail: Schienen~) track. **der Tod durch den** ~ death by hanging; **am gleichen** ~ **ziehen** (fig) to be in the same boat; **über die** ~**e schlagen** to run riot.

strangulieren* vt to strangle.

Strapaze f **-n** strain.

strapazieren* 1 vt to be a strain on; Kleidung to be hard on; (fig col) Begriff to flog (col); Nerven to strain. 2 vr to tax oneself.

strapazierfähig adj Schuhe, Kleidung hard-wearing; (fig col) Nerven tough.

strapaziös adj (lit, fig) wearing, exhausting.

Straße f **-n (a)** road; (in Stadt, Dorf) street, road (Brit); (kleine Land~) lane. **an der** ~ by the roadside; **auf der** ~ in the street; **auf die** ~ **gehen** (lit) to go out on the street; (als Demonstrant) to take to the streets; **auf der** ~ **liegen** (fig col) to be out of the work; **auf die** ~ **gesetzt werden** (col) to be turned out (onto the streets); **über die** ~ **gehen** to cross the road/street); **er wohnt drei** ~**n weiter** he lives three blocks further on; **dem Druck der** ~ **nachgeben** (fig) to give in to the demands of demonstrators. **(b)** (Meerenge) strait(s pl). **(c)** (Tech) (Fertigungs~) (production) line.

Straßenarbeiten pl roadworks (Brit) pl, roadwork (US).

Straßenbahn f (Wagen) tram (Brit), streetcar (US).

Straßenbahn-: ~**fahrer** m tram (Brit) or streetcar (US) driver; ~**haltestelle** f tram (Brit) or streetcar (US) stop; ~**linie** f tramline (Brit), streetcar line (US).

Straßen-: ~**bau** m road construction; ~**bauarbeiten** pl roadworks (Brit) pl, roadwork (US); ~**benutzungsgebühr** f (road) toll; ~**decke** f road surface; ~**ecke** f street corner; ~**gabelung** f fork (in a/the road); ~**glätte** f slippery road surface; ~**graben** m ditch; ~**händler** m street trader; ~**junge** m (pej) street urchin; ~**kampf** m street fighting no pl; ~**karte** f road map; ~**kehrer** m - road sweeper; ~**kreuzer** m - (col) limousine; ~**kreuzung** f crossroads *sing or pl,* intersection *(US);* ~**laterne** f street lamp; ~**mädchen** nt streetwalker; ~**netz** nt road network; ~**rand** m roadside; ~**raub** m mugging; ~**räuber** m mugger; ~**reinigung** f street cleaning; ~**rennen** nt road race; ~**sammlung** f street collection; ~**schild** nt street sign; ~**schuh** m walking shoe; ~**seite** f side of a/the road; ~**sperre** f road block; ~**strich** m (col) street-walking; **auf den** ~**strich gehen** to walk the streets; ~**theater** nt street theatre *(Brit)* or theatre *(US);* ~**überführung** f footbridge; ~**unterführung** f underpass; ~**verhältnisse** pl road conditions pl; ~**verkauf** m street-trading; takeaway *(Brit)* or take-out *(US)* sales pl; ~**verkäufer** m street vendor; ~**verkehr** m traffic; ~**verkehrsordnung** f *(Jur)* Road Traffic Act; ~**verzeichnis** nt index of street names; ~**wacht** f road patrol; ~**zustand** m road conditions pl; ~**zustandsbericht** m road report.

Stratege m (wk) -n, -n strategist.
Strategie f strategy.
strategisch adj strategic.
Stratosphäre f no pl stratosphere.
sträuben 1 vr **(a)** *(Haare, Fell)* to stand on end; *(Gefieder)* to become ruffled. **da** ~ **sich einem die Haare** it's enough to make your hair stand on end. **(b)** *(fig)* to struggle *(gegen* against*).* **es sträubt sich alles in mir, das zu tun** I am most reluctant to do it. 2 vt *Gefieder* to ruffle.
Strauch m, pl **Sträucher** bush, shrub.
straucheln vi aux sein **(a)** *(geh: stolpern)* to stumble. **(b)** *(fig)* to transgress; *(Mädchen)* to go astray.
Strauchwerk nt no pl *(Gebüsch)* bushes pl, shrubs pl; *(Gestrüpp)* undergrowth.
Strauß[1] m -e *(Orn)* ostrich.
Strauß[2] m, pl **Sträuße** bunch; *(Blumen~)* bunch of flowers; *(als Geschenk)* bouquet, bunch of flowers.
Strebe f -n brace, strut; *(Decken~)* joist.
Strebebalken m diagonal brace.
streben vi *(geh)* **(a)** *(sich bemühen)* to strive *(nach* for*);* *(Sch pej)* to swot *(col).* **danach** ~**, etw zu tun** to strive to do sth. **(b)** aux sein *(sich bewegen)* **nach** or **zu etw** ~ to make one's way to sth.
Streben nt no pl *(Drängen)* striving *(nach* for*);* *(nach Ruhm, Geld)* aspiration *(nach* to*);* *(Bemühen)* efforts pl.
Strebepfeiler m buttress.
Streber m - *(pej col)* pushy person; *(Sch)* swot *(col).*
strebsam adj assiduous, industrious.
Strebsamkeit f no pl assiduity, industriousness.
Strecke f -n **(a)** *(Entfernung)* distance; *(Math)* line. **eine** ~ **zurücklegen** to cover a distance. **(b)** *(Abschnitt)* *(von Straße, Fluß)* stretch; *(von Bahnlinie)* section. **(c)** *(Weg, Route)* route; *(Straße)* road; *(Bahnlinie, Sport: Bahn)* track; *(fig: Passage)* passage. **für die** ~ **London-Glasgow brauchen wir 5 Stunden** the journey from London to Glasgow will take us 5 hours; **auf der** ~ **Paris-Brüssel** on the way from Paris to Brussels; **auf der** ~ **bleiben** *(fig)* to fall by the wayside. **(d)** *(Hunt)* zur ~ **bringen** to bag.
strecken 1 vt **(a)** *Arme, Beine* to stretch; *Hals* to crane. **die Zunge aus dem Mund** ~ to stick out one's tongue; **die Beine von sich** ~ to stretch out one's legs; **den Kopf aus dem Fenster** ~ to stick one's head out of the window. **(b)** *(Med)* Bein, Arm to straighten. **(c)** *(col: absichtlich verlängern)* Vorräte, Geld to eke out; Arbeit to drag out *(col);* Essen to make go further. 2 vr **(a)** *(sich recken)* to stretch. **sich ins Gras** ~ to stretch out on the grass. **(b)** *(sich hinziehen)* to drag on.
Strecken-: ~abschnitt m *(Rail)* track section; ~**netz** nt rail network; **s~weise** adv in parts.
Streich m -e *(Schabernack)* prank, trick. **jdm**

einen ~ **spielen** *(lit)* to play a trick on sb; *(fig: Gedächtnis etc)* to play tricks on sb.
streicheln vti to stroke. **jdm die Wange** ~ to stroke sb's cheek.
streichen pret strich, ptp gestrichen 1 vt **(a)** to stroke. **etw glatt**~ to smooth sth (out); **sich** *(dat)* **die Haare aus der Stirn** ~ to push one's hair back from one's forehead; *siehe* **gestrichen. (b)** *(auftragen)* Butter, Brot etc to spread; Salbe, Farbe etc to apply, to put on. **(c)** *(an~: mit Farbe)* to paint. **frisch gestrichen!** wet paint. **(d)** *(tilgen)* Zeile, Satz to delete; Auftrag, Zug etc to cancel; Schulden to write off; Zuschuß etc to cut. **jdn/etw von der Liste** ~ to take sb/sth off the list.
2 vi **(a)** *(über etw hinfahren)* to stroke. **mit der Hand über etw** *(acc)* ~ to stroke sth; **sie strich ihm über das Haar** she stroked his hair. **(b)** aux sein *(streifen)* to brush past *(an etw* dat*)* sth*)*. **um/ durch etw** ~ *(herum~)* to prowl around/through sth; **die Katze strich mir um die Beine** the cat rubbed against my legs. **(c)** *(malen)* to paint.
Streicher pl *(Mus)* strings pl.
Streich-: s~fähig adj easy to spread; ~**holz** nt match; ~**holzschachtel** f matchbox; ~**instrument** nt string(ed) instrument; ~**käse** m cheese spread; ~**orchester** nt string orchestra.
Streichung f *(Tilgung)* *(von Zeile, Satz)* deletion; *(Kürzung)* cut; *(von Auftrag, Zug)* cancellation.
Streifband nt wrapper.
Streifbandzeitung f newspaper sent at printed paper rate.
Streife f -n *(Patrouille)* patrol. **auf** ~ **gehen/sein** to go/be on patrol; **ein Polizist auf** ~ a policeman on his beat.
streifen 1 vt **(a)** to touch, to brush (against); *(Kugel)* to graze; *(Auto)* to scrape. **jdn mit einem Blick** ~ to glance fleetingly at sb. **(b)** *(flüchtig erwähnen)* to touch (up)on. **(c)** *(ab~, überziehen)* **die Schuhe von den Füßen** ~ to slip one's shoes off; **sich** *(dat)* **die Handschuhe über die Finger** ~ to pull on one's gloves. 2 vi *(geh)* **(a)** aux sein *(wandern)* to roam; *(Fuchs)* to prowl. **(b)** aux sein *(Blick etc)* **sie ließ ihren Blick über die Menge** ~ she scanned the crowd.
Streifen m - **(a)** *(Stück, Band)* strip; *(Loch~, Klebe~* etc*)* tape. **ein** ~ **Land** a strip of land. **(b)** *(Strich)* stripe. **ein goldener** ~ **am Horizont** a streak of gold on the horizon. **(c)** *(Tresse)* braid; *(Mil)* stripe. **(d)** *(Film)* film *(Brit),* movie *(esp US).*
Streifen-: ~dienst m patrol duty; ~**wagen** m patrol car.
Streif-: ~licht nt *(fig)* highlight; **ein** ~**licht auf etw** *(acc)* **werfen** to highlight sth; ~**schuß** m graze; ~**zug** m *(Bummel)* expedition; *(fig: kurzer Überblick)* brief survey *(durch of).*
Streik m -s strike. **zum** ~ **aufrufen** to call a strike; **in den** ~ **treten** to come out on strike, to strike.
Streik-: ~aufruf m strike call; ~**brecher** m - strikebreaker, scab *(pej).*
streiken vi to be on strike; *(in den Streik treten)* to strike; *(hum col)* *(nicht funktionieren)* to pack up *(col);* *(Gedächtnis)* to fail. **der Computer streikt** the computer's packed up *(col),* the computer's on the blink *(col);* **da streike ich** *(col)* I refuse!
Streikende(r) mf decl as adj striker.
Streik-: ~geld nt strike pay; ~**kasse** f strike fund; ~**posten** m picket; ~**posten aufstellen** to put up pickets; ~**recht** nt right to strike; ~**welle** f wave of strikes.
Streit m -e argument *(über +acc* about*);* *(leichter)* quarrel; *(Auseinandersetzung)* dispute. **wegen etw mit jdm (einen)** ~ **haben** to argue with sb about sth; ~ **anfangen** to start an argument; **mit jdm in** ~ **liegen** to be at loggerheads with sb.
Streit|**axt** f *(Hist)* battleaxe *(Brit),* battleax *(US).*
streiten pret stritt, ptp gestritten 1 vi *(über +acc* about, over*)* to argue; *(leichter)* to quarrel.

darüber läßt sich ~ that's debatable; **die** ~**den Parteien** *(Jur)* the litigants. **2** *vr* to argue, to quarrel. **wir wollen uns deswegen nicht** ~! don't let's fall out over that!

Streit-: ~**fall** *m* dispute, conflict; *(Jur)* case; **im** ~**fall** in case of dispute; **im** ~**fall Müller gegen Braun** in the case of Müller versus Braun; ~**frage** *f* dispute; ~**gespräch** *nt* debate; ~**hahn** *m (col)* squabbler.

streitig *adj* **jdm das Recht auf etw** *(acc)* ~ **machen** to dispute sb's right to sth.

Streitigkeiten *pl* quarrels *pl*, squabbles *pl*.

Streit-: ~**kräfte** *pl* armed forces *pl*; **s**~**lustig** *adj (aggressiv)* aggressive; ~**macht** *f* armed forces *pl*; ~**punkt** *m* contentious issue; ~**sache** *f* dispute; *(Jur)* case; ~**sucht** *f* quarrelsomeness; **s**~**süchtig** *adj* quarrelsome.

streng *adj* strict; *Blick, Bestrafung, Anforderung, Winter* severe; *Geruch, Geschmack* pungent. ~ **gegen jdn/etw vorgehen** to deal severely with sb/sth; ~ **aber gerecht** severe but just; **etw** ~ **befolgen** to keep strictly to sth; ~ **geheim** top secret; ~ **vertraulich** strictly confidential; ~ **nach Vorschrift** strictly according to regulations; ~ **verboten!** strictly prohibited.

Strenge *f no pl siehe adj* strictness; severity; pungency.

streng-: ~**genommen** *adv* strictly speaking; *(eigentlich)* actually; ~**gläubig** *adj* strict.

Streß *m* -sse stress. **im** ~ **sein** to be under stress.

stressen *vt* to put under stress. **gestreßt sein** to be under stress.

Streu *f no pl* straw; *(aus Sägespänen)* sawdust.

streuen 1 *vt Futter, Samen* to scatter; *Dünger, Sand* to spread; *Gewürze, Zucker etc* to sprinkle; *Straße* to grit; to salt. **2** *vi (mit Streumittel)* to grit; to put down salt.

Streuer *m* - shaker; *(Salz~)* cellar; *(Pfeffer~)* pot.

Streufahrzeug *nt* gritter, sander.

streunen *vi* **(a)** to roam about; *(Hund, Katze)* to stray. ~**de Katzen** stray cats. **(b)** *aux sein* **durch etw** ~ to roam through sth.

Streusand *m* sand; *(für Straße)* grit.

Streusel *nt* - *(Cook)* crumble (mixture).

Streuselkuchen *m thin sponge cake with crumble topping*.

Streuung *f (Statistik)* mean variation; *(Phys)* scattering.

strich *pret of* **streichen**.

Strich *m* -e **(a)** line; *(Quer~)* dash; *(Schräg~)* oblique, slash *(esp US)*; *(Feder~, Pinsel~)* stroke; *(von Land)* stretch. **jdm einen** ~ **durch die Rechnung machen** to thwart sb's plans; **einen** ~ **(unter etw acc) machen** *(fig)* to forget sth; **unterm** ~ **sein** *(col)* not to be up to scratch; **sie ist nur noch ein** ~ *(col)* she's as thin as a rake now. **(b)** *(von Teppich)* pile; *(von Gewebe)* nap; *(von Fell, Haar)* direction of growth. **gegen den** ~ **bürsten** *(lit)* to brush the wrong way; **es geht (mir) gegen den** ~ *(col)* it goes against the grain; **nach** ~ **und Faden** *(col)* good and proper *(col)*. **(c)** *(Mus: Bogen~)* stroke, bow. **(d)** *(col) (Prostitution)* prostitution *no art*; *(Bordellgegend)* red-light district. **auf den** ~ **gehen** to be/go on the game *(col)*.

stricheln *vti (schraffieren)* to hatch. **eine gestrichelte Linie** a broken line.

Strich-: ~**junge** *m (col)* male prostitute; ~**mädchen** *nt (col)* tart *(col)*; **s**~**weise** *adv (Met)* **s**~**weise Regen** rain in places.

Strick *m* -e rope. **jdm aus etw einen** ~ **drehen** to use sth against sb.

stricken *vti* to knit.

Strickerei *f* knitting *no indef art, no pl*.

Strick-: ~**jacke** *f* cardigan; ~**leiter** *f* rope ladder; ~**maschine** *f* knitting machine; ~**nadel** *f* knitting needle; ~**waren** *pl* knitwear *sing*; ~**wolle** *f* knitting wool; ~**zeug** *nt* knitting.

Striegel *m* - currycomb.

striegeln 1 *vt* to curry(comb); *(fig col: kämmen)* to comb. **2** *vr (col)* to spruce oneself up.

Strieme *f* -n weal.

strikt *adj* strict.

Strippe *f* -n *(col)* **(a)** *(Bindfaden)* string. **(b)** *(Telefonleitung)* phone. **an der** ~ **hängen** to be on the phone.

stritt *pret of* **streiten**.

strittig *adj* controversial. **noch** ~ still in dispute.

Stroh *nt no pl* straw; *(Dach~)* thatch.

Stroh-: ~**ballen** *m* bale of straw; **s**~**blond** *adj* *Mensch* flaxen-haired; *Haare* flaxen; ~**blume** *f* strawflower; ~**dach** *nt* thatched roof; **s**~**dumm** *adj* thick *(col)*; ~**feuer** *nt*: **ein** ~ **feuer sein** *(fig)* to be a passing fancy; ~**halm** *m* straw; **sich an einen** ~**halm klammern** to clutch at a straw; ~**hut** *m* straw hat; ~**kopf** *m (col)* blockhead *(col)*; ~**mann** *m*, *pl* ~**männer** *(fig)* front man; ~**sack** *m* heiliger ~**sack!** *(col)* good(ness) gracious (me)!; ~**witwe** *f* grass widow; ~**witwer** *m* grass widower.

Strolch *m* -e *(pej)* rogue, rascal.

Strom *m* ⁼e **(a)** (large) river; *(Strömung)* current; *(von Besuchern)* stream. **ein reißender** ~ a raging torrent; **in** ~**en regnen** to be pouring with rain; **der Wein floß in** ~**en** the wine flowed like water; **mit dem/gegen den** ~ **schwimmen** *(lit, fig)* to swim with/against the current. **(b)** *(Elec)* current; *(Elektrizität)* electricity. ~ **führen** to be live; **unter** ~ **stehen** *(lit)* to be live; **der** ~ **ist ausgefallen** the power is off.

Strom-: **s**~**ab** *adv* downstream; **s**~**abwärts** *adv* downstream; ~**anschluß** *m* ~**anschluß haben** to be connected to the electricity mains; **s**~**auf(wärts)** *adv* upstream; ~**ausfall** *m* power failure.

strömen *vi aux sein* to stream; *(heraus~)* to pour *(aus* from*)*. **bei** ~**dem Regen** in (the) pouring rain.

Strom-: ~**kabel** *nt* electric cable; ~**kreis** *m* (electrical) circuit; ~**leitung** *f* electric cables *pl*; ~**linienform** *f* streamlined design; **s**~**linienförmig** [-li:niən-] *adj* streamlined; ~**netz** *nt* power supply system; ~**quelle** *f* source of power; ~**schnelle** *f* rapids *pl*; ~**speicher** *m* (storage) battery; ~**sperre** *f* power cut.

Strömung *f* current.

Strom-: ~**verbrauch** *m* power consumption; ~**versorgung** *f* power supply; ~**zähler** *m* electricity meter.

Strophe *f* -n verse.

strotzen *vi* to abound *(von, vor +dat* with*)*; *(von Kraft, Gesundheit)* to be bursting *(von* with*)*. **von Schmutz** ~ to be thick with dirt.

strubb(e)lig *adj (col) Haar, Fell* tousled.

Strudel *m* - **(a)** *(lit, fig)* whirlpool. **(b)** *(Cook)* strudel.

strudeln *vi* to whirl, to swirl.

Struktur *f* structure; *(von Stoff etc)* texture.

strukturell *adj* structural.

strukturieren* *vt* to structure.

Strumpf *m* ⁼e sock; *(Damen~)* stocking. **ein Paar** ⁼**e** a pair of socks/stockings.

Strumpf-: ~**band** *nt* garter; ~**geschäft** *nt* hosiery shop *(Brit)* or store *(US)*; ~**halter** *m* - suspender *(Brit)*, garter *(US)*; ~**hose** *f* tights *pl (Brit)*, panty-hose; **eine** ~**hose** a pair of tights *(Brit)* or panty-hose; ~**waren** *pl* hosiery *sing*.

struppig *adj* unkempt; *Tier* shaggy.

Stube *f* -n room. **die gute** ~ the parlour *(Brit)* or parlor *(US)* (dated).

Stuben-: ~**arrest** *m* confinement to one's room or *(Mil)* quarters; ~**arrest haben** to be confined to one's room/quarters; ~**fliege** *f (common)* housefly; ~**hocker** *m* - *(pej col)* stay-at-home *(col)*; **s**~**rein** *adj Katze, Hund* house-trained; *(hum) Witz* clean.

Stuck *m no pl* stucco.

Stück *nt* **-e** *or (nach Zahlenangaben)* - **(a)** piece; *(von Vieh, Wild)* head; *(von Zucker)* lump; *(Seife)* bar; *(von Land)* plot. **ich nehme fünf ~** I'll take five; **20 ~ Vieh** 20 head of cattle; **sechs ~ von diesen Apfelsinen** six of these oranges; **10 Pfennig das ~** 10 pfennigs each; **am ~** in one piece; **aus einem ~** in one piece; **~ für ~** *(ein Exemplar nach dem andern)* one by one; **ein ~ Garten** a patch of garden; **das ist unser bestes ~** *(hum)* that is our pride and joy. **(b)** *(Teil, Abschnitt)* piece, bit; *(von Buch, Rede)* part. **~ für ~** *(einen Teil um den andern)* bit by bit; **in ~e gehen** to be broken to pieces; **etw in ~e schlagen** to smash sth to pieces; **ich komme ein ~ (des Weges) mit** I'll come part of the way with you; **ein ~ spazierengehen** to go for a walk; **das ist ein starkes ~!** *(col)* that's a bit much *(col)*; **große ~e auf jdn halten** to think highly of sb; **aus freien ~en** of one's own free will. **(c)** *(Bühnen~)* play; *(Musik~)* piece.

Stückeschreiber *m* dramatist, playwright.

Stück-: **~gut** *nt (Rail)* parcel service; **etw als ~gut schicken** to send sth as a parcel; **~lohn** *m* piece(work) rate; **~preis** *m* unit price; **s~weise** *adv* bit by bit; **s~weise verkaufen** to sell individually; **~werk** *nt no pl* incomplete work; **~werk sein/bleiben** to be/remain incomplete; **~zahl** *f* number of pieces.

Student *m* student.

Studenten-: **~ausweis** *m* student card; **~bewegung** *f* student movement; **~bude** *f (col)* student digs *pl*; **~futter** *nt* nuts and raisins; **~gemeinde** *f* student religious society; **~schaft** *f* student body; **~verbindung** *f* students' society; **~werk** *nt* student administration; **~wohnheim** *nt* hall of residence.

Studentin *f* student.

studentisch *adj attr* student *attr*.

Studie ['ʃtuːdiə] *f* study *(über +acc of)*.

Studien- ['ʃtuːdən-]: **~abschluß** *m* completion of a course of study; **~aufenthalt** *m* study visit; **~beratung** *f* course guidance service; **~fach** *nt* subject; **~fahrt** *f* study trip; *(Sch)* educational trip; **~förderung** *f* study grant; *(an Universität)* university grant; **~gang** *m* course of studies; **~gebühren** *pl* tuition fees *pl*; **~jahr** *nt* academic year; **~jahre** *pl* university/college years *pl*; **~platz** *m* university place; **ein ~platz in Medizin** a place to study medicine; **~rat** *m*, **~rätin** *f* teacher at a secondary school; **~referendar** *m* student teacher; **~reform** *f* university/college reform; **~zeit** *f* **(a)** student days *pl*; **(b)** *(Dauer)* duration of a/one's course of studies.

studieren* **1** *vi* to study. **ich studiere an der Universität Bonn** I am at Bonn University; **wo haben Sie studiert?** what university/college did you go to?; **bei jdm ~e** to study under sb. **2** *vt* to study; *(genau betrachten)* to scrutinize.

Studio *nt* **-s** studio.

Studiobühne *f* studio theatre *(Brit)* or theater *(US)*.

Studium *nt* study; *(Hochschul~)* studies *pl*. **das ~ hat fünf Jahre gedauert** the course of study lasted five years; **während seines ~s** while he is/was *etc* a student.

Stufe *f* **-n (a)** step; *(Mus: Ton~)* degree; *(im Haar)* layer. **(b)** *(fig)* stage; *(Niveau)* level; *(Rang)* grade. **sich mit jdm/etw auf eine ~ stellen** to put oneself on a level with sb/sth.

stufen *vt Schüler, Preise* to grade.

Stufen-: **s~förmig** **1** *adj (lit)* stepped; *Landschaft* terraced; *(fig)* gradual. **2** *adv (lit)* in steps; *angelegt* in terraces; *(fig)* in stages; **~leiter** *f (fig)* ladder *(gen* to*)*; **s~los** *adj Übergang* direct; *(fig: gleitend)* smooth; *(Tech)* infinitely variable; **~plan** *m* graduated plan *(zu* for*)*; **s~weise 1** *adv* step by step; **2** *adj attr* gradual.

Stufung *f* gradation.

Stuhl *m* **-e (a)** chair. **zwischen zwei ~en sitzen** *(fig)* to fall between two stools; **das haut einen vom ~** *(col)* it knocks you sideways *(col)*; **jdm den ~ vor die Tür setzen** *(fig)* to kick sb out *(col)*. **(b)** *(Königs~)* throne. **der Heilige ~** the Holy See. **(c)** *(~gang)* bowel movement; *(Kot)* stool.

Stuhl-: **~bein** *nt* chair leg; **~gang** *m no pl* bowel movement; **~lehne** *f* back of a chair.

Stuka *m* **-s** = **Sturzkampfflugzeug.**

Stukkateur [ʃtʊka'tøːɐ] *m* plasterer.

Stukkatur *f* stucco, ornamental plasterwork.

stülpen *vt* **den Kragen nach oben ~** to turn up one's collar; **etw auf/über etw** *(acc)* **~** to put sth on/over sth.

stumm *adj* **(a)** *(lit, fig)* dumb; *(schweigend)* mute. **die ~e Kreatur** *(geh)* the dumb creatures *pl*; **~ vor Schmerz** in silent agony; **sie sah mich ~ an** she looked at me without speaking; **~ bleiben** to stay silent. **(b)** *Rolle* non-speaking; *Film, Szene* silent.

Stummel *m* **-** **(a)** *(Zigaretten~, Kerzen~)* stub; *(von Gliedmaßen, Zahn)* stump. **(b)** *(Stummelschwanz)* dock.

Stummfilm *m* silent film *(Brit)* or movie *(esp US)*.

Stümper(in *f***)** *m* **-** *(pej)* amateur; *(Pfuscher)* bungler.

Stümperei *f (pej)* amateur work; *(Pfuscherei)* bungling; *(stümperhafte Arbeit)* botched job.

stümperhaft *adj (pej)* amateurish.

stümpern *vi* **bei einer Arbeit ~** to do a job in an amateur way.

stumpf *adj* **(a)** blunt; *Nase* snub, turned-up. **(b)** *(fig) Haar, Farbe, Mensch* dull. **~ vor sich hin brüten** to sit brooding impassively. **(c)** *(Math)* *Winkel* obtuse.

Stumpf *m* **-e** stump; *(Bleistift~)* stub. **etw mit ~ und Stiel ausrotten** to eradicate sth root and branch.

Stumpf-: **~sinn** *m* mindlessness; *(Langweiligkeit)* tedium; **s~sinnig** *adj* mindless; *(langweilig)* tedious.

Stunde *f* **-n (a)** hour. **eine viertel/halbe/dreiviertel ~** a quarter of an hour/half an hour/three-quarters of an hour; **eine halbe ~ Pause** a half-hour break; **um ~** an hour after hour; **von ~ zu ~** by the hour; **90 Meilen in der ~** 90 miles per hour. **(b)** *(Augenblick, Zeitpunkt)* time. **zu dieser ~** at this/that time; **zu später ~** at a late hour; **bis zur ~** up to the present moment; **eine schwere ~** a time of difficulty; **seine ~ hat geschlagen** *(fig)* his hour has come; **die ~ der Entscheidung** the moment of decision. **(c)** *(Unterricht, Sch)* lesson.

stunden *vt* **jdm etw ~** to give sb time to pay sth.

Stunden-: **~geschwindigkeit** *f* speed per hour; **eine ~geschwindigkeit von 90 km** a speed of 90 km per hour; **~glas** *nt* hour-glass; **~kilometer** *pl* kilometres *(Brit)* or kilometers *(US)* per hour *pl*.

stundenlang 1 *adj* lasting several hours. **nach ~em Warten** after hours of waiting. **2** *adv* for hours.

Stunden-: **~lohn** *m* hourly wage; **~lohn bekommen** to be paid by the hour; **~plan** *m (Sch)* timetable; **s~weise** *adv (pro Stunde)* by the hour; *(stündlich)* every hour; **Kellner s~weise gesucht** part-time waiters required; **~zeiger** *m* hour-hand.

stündlich 1 *adj* hourly. **2** *adv* hourly, every hour.

Stunk *m no pl* **~ machen** *(col)* to kick up a stink *(col)*.

stupid(e) *adj (geh)* mindless.

Stups *m* **-e** nudge.

stupsen *vt* to nudge.

Stupsnase *f* snub nose.

stur *adj* stolid; *Nein, Arbeiten* dogged; *(hartnäckig)* stubborn; *(querköpfig)* cussed. **~ weitermachen** *etc* to carry on regardless; **er fuhr ~ geradeaus** he just carried straight on; **sich ~ stellen, auf ~**

stellen (col) to dig one's heels in; **ein ~er Bock** (col) a pig-headed fellow.

Sturheit f siehe adj stolidness; doggedness; stubbornness; cussedness.

Sturm m ~e **(a)** (lit,fig) storm. **die Zeichen stehen auf ~** (fig) there's a storm brewing; **die Ruhe vor dem ~** the calm before the storm; **ein ~ im Wasserglas** (fig) a storm in a teacup; **~ läuten** to keep one's finger on the doorbell; **ein ~ der Begeisterung** a wave of enthusiasm. **(b)** (Angriff) attack. **etw im ~ nehmen** (Mil, fig) to take sth by storm; **zum ~ blasen** (Mil,fig) to sound the attack; **gegen etw ~ laufen** (fig) to be up in arms against sth; **ein ~ auf die Banken** a run on the banks.

Sturm-: ~angriff m (Mil) assault (auf +acc on); **~bö** f squall.

stürmen 1 vi **(a)** (Meer) to rage; (Sport, Mil) to attack. **(b)** aux sein (rennen) to storm. **2** vi impers to be blowing a gale. **3** vt (Mil,fig) to storm; Bank etc to make a run on.

Stürmer m - (Sport) forward.

Sturm-: ~flut f storm tide; **s~frei** adj (Mil) unassailable; **eine s~freie Bude** (col) a room free from disturbance.

stürmisch adj **(a)** Meer rough; Wetter blustery; (mit Regen) stormy. **(b)** (fig) tempestuous; Entwicklung rapid; Liebhaber passionate; Beifall tumultuous. **nicht so ~** take it easy.

Sturm-: ~schritt m (Mil,fig) double-quick pace; **im ~schritt** at the double; **~warnung** f gale warning; **~wind** m whirlwind.

Sturz m ~e fall; (in Temperatur, Preis auch) drop; (Pol: durch Coup) overthrow.

Sturzbach m (lit) fast-flowing stream.

stürzen 1 vi aux sein **(a)** to fall (auch Pol). **ins Wasser ~** to plunge into the water; **vom Pferd ~** to fall off a/one's horse; **er ist schwer gestürzt** he had a bad fall. **(b)** (rennen) to dash. **sie kam ins Zimmer gestürzt** she burst into the room. **2** vt **(a)** (werfen) to fling, to hurl. **jdn ins Unglück ~** to bring disaster upon sb. **(b)** (kippen) to turn upside down. **„nicht ~!"** "this side up". **(c)** (Pol) Regierung etc to bring down; (durch Coup) to overthrow; König to dispose. **3** vr sich zu Tode ~ to fall to one's death; (absichtlich) to jump to one's death; **sich aus dem Fenster ~** to fling or hurl oneself out of the window; **sich auf jdn/etw ~** to pounce on sb/sth; auf Essen to fall on sth; **sich in Schulden ~** to plunge into debt; **sich ins Unglück ~** to plunge headlong into disaster; **sich in Unkosten ~** to go to great expense.

Sturz-: ~flug m (nose)dive; **~helm** m crash helmet; **~kampfflugzeug** nt dive bomber.

Stuß m no pl (col) nonsense, rubbish (col).

Stute f -n mare.

Stütze f -n **(a)** support; (Pfeiler) pillar; (Buch~) rest. **(b)** (Halt) support; (Fuß~) foot-rest. **(c)** (fig) (Hilfe) help, aid (für to); (Beistand) support; (wichtiger Mensch) mainstay. **die ~n der Gesellschaft** the pillars of society.

stutzen¹ vi to stop short; (zögern) to hesitate.

stutzen² vt to trim; Flügel, Hecke to clip; Schwanz to dock.

Stutzen m - **(a)** (Gewehr) carbine. **(b)** (Rohrstück) connecting piece; (Endstück) nozzle.

stützen 1 vt (Halt geben) to support; Gebäude, Mauer to shore up. **einen Verdacht auf etw** (acc) **~** to base a suspicion on sth; **die Ellbogen auf den Tisch ~** to prop one's elbows on the table. **2** vr sich auf jdn/etw **~** (lit) to lean on sb/sth; (fig) to count on sb/sth; (Beweise, Theorie) to be based on sb/sth.

Stutzer m - (pej) fop, dandy.

stutzig adj pred **~ werden** (argwöhnisch) to become suspicious; **jdn ~ machen** to make sb suspicious.

Stütz-: ~mauer f retaining wall; **~pfeiler** m supporting pillar; **~punkt** m (Mil, fig) base.

Stützung f support.

s.u. = siehe unten.

sub|altern adj (pej) Stellung subordinate.

Subjekt nt -e **(a)** subject. **(b)** (pej: Mensch) character (col).

subjektiv adj subjective.

Subjektivität [-vɪ'tɛːt] f subjectivity.

Sub-: ~kontinent m subcontinent; **~kultur** f subculture.

sublimieren* vt (Psych, Chem) to sublimate.

substantiell [zʊpstan'tsiɛl] adj (fig geh: bedeutsam) fundamental.

Substantiv ['zʊpstantiːf] nt -e noun.

Substanz [zʊp'stants] f **(a)** substance. **(b)** (Fin) capital assets pl. **von der ~ zehren** to live on one's capital.

subtil adj (geh) subtle.

subtrahieren* [zʊptra'hiːrən] vti to subtract.

Subtraktion f subtraction.

subtropisch ['zʊptroːpɪʃ] adj subtropical.

Subvention [zʊpvɛn'tsioːn] f subsidy.

subventionieren* [zʊpvɛntsio'niːrən] vt to subsidize.

subversiv [zʊpvɛr'ziːf] adj subversive. **sich ~ betätigen** to engage in subversive activities.

Such-: ~aktion f search operation; **~dienst** m missing persons tracing service.

Suche f no pl search (nach for). **auf die ~ nach jdm/etw gehen** to go in search of sb/sth.

suchen 1 vt **(a)** to look for; (stärker, intensiv) to search for. **Verkäufer(in) gesucht** sales person wanted; **was suchst du hier?** what are you doing here?; **du hast hier nichts zu ~** you have no business being here; **seinesgleichen ~** to be unparalleled. **(b)** (streben nach) to seek. **ein Gespräch ~** to try to have a talk. **2** vi to search, to hunt. **nach etw ~** to look for sth; (stärker) to search for sth; **nach Worten ~** to search for words; (sprachlos sein) to be at a loss for words; **such!** (zu Hund) seek!, find!; **gesucht!** wanted (wegen for).

Sucher m - (Phot) viewfinder.

Such-: ~mannschaft f search party; **~meldung** f SOS message; **~scheinwerfer** m searchlight.

Sucht f ~e addiction (nach to); (fig) obsession (nach with). **eine krankhafte ~ haben, etw zu tun** (fig) to be obsessed with doing sth; **an einer ~ leiden** to be an addict.

süchtig adj addicted (nach to). **~ machen** (Droge) to be addictive.

Süchtige(r) mf decl as adj addict.

Sud m -e liquid; (esp von Fleisch, für Suppe) stock.

Süd m no pl (Naut, Met, liter) south.

Süd- in cpds south; **~afrika** nt South Africa; **~amerika** nt South America.

Sudan [zu'daːn, 'zuːdan] m **der ~** the Sudan.

Sudanese m (wk) -n, -n, **Sudanesin** f Sudanese.

Süd-: s~deutsch adj South German; **~deutschland** nt South(ern) Germany.

Süden m no pl south; (von Land) South. **aus dem ~, vom ~ her** from the south; **nach ~ hin** to the south; **weiter im ~** further south.

Süd-: ~europa nt Southern Europe; **~früchte** pl citrus and tropical fruit(s pl); **~küste** f south(ern) coast; **~lage** f southern aspect; **~länder** m - southerner; Mediterranean or Latin type; **s~ländisch** adj southern; (italienisch, spanisch etc) Latin.

südlich 1 adj (a) southern; Kurs, Richtung southerly. **(b)** (mediterran) Mediterranean, Latin; Temperament Latin. **2** adv (to the) south. **~ von Wien (gelegen)** (to the) south of Vienna; **es liegt weiter ~** it is further (to the) south. **3** prep +gen (to the) south of.

Süd|ost m (Met, Naut) south-east.

Süd|osten m south-east; (von Land) South East. **aus** or **von ~** from the south-east; **nach ~ to the**

south-east.

süd|östlich 1 *adj Gegend* south-eastern; *Wind* south-east(erly). **2** *adv* south-east. **3** *prep +gen* (to the) south-east of.

Süd-: ~**pol** *m* South Pole; ~**polarmeer** *nt* Antarctic Ocean; ~**see** *f* South Seas *pl*; ~**seite** *f* south side; *(von Berg)* south(ern) face.

südwärts *adv* south(wards).

Südwest *m (Naut, Met)* south-west.

Südwesten *m* south-west; *(von Land)* South West. **aus** *or* **von** ~ from the south-west; **nach** ~ to the south-west.

südwestlich 1 *adj Gegend* south-western; *Wind* south-west(erly). **2** *adv* (to the) south-west. **3** *prep +gen* (to the) south-west of.

Südwind *m* south wind.

Suezkanal *m* Suez Canal.

Suff *m no pl (col)* **dem** ~ **verfallen sein** to be on the bottle *(col)*; **etw im** ~ **sagen** to say sth when one is tight *(col)*.

süffeln *vi (col)* to tipple *(col)*.

süffig *adj* light and sweet.

süffisant *adj* smug, complacent.

Suffix *nt* -e suffix.

suggerieren* *vt* to suggest. **jdm etw** ~ to influence sb by suggesting sth; **jdm** ~, **daß** ... to get sb to believe that ...

Suggestion *f* suggestion.

Suggestivfrage *f* suggestive question.

suhlen *vr (lit, fig)* to wallow.

Sühne *f* -n *(Rel, geh)* atonement; *(von Schuld)* expiation. ~ **leisten** to atone *(für for)*.

sühnen 1 *vt Unrecht, Verbrechen* to atone for; *Schuld* to expiate. **2** *vi* to atone.

Sühnetermin *m (Jur)* conciliatory hearing.

Sulfat *nt* sulphate *(Brit)*, sulfate *(US)*.

Sultan *m* -e sultan.

Sultanat *nt* sultanate.

Sultanine *f (Rosine)* sultana.

Sülze *f* -n brawn.

summarisch *adj (auch Jur)* summary. **etw** ~ **zusammenfassen** to summarize sth.

Sümmchen *nt* dim of **Summe. ein schönes** ~ *(hum)* a tidy sum, a pretty penny *(col)*.

Summe *f* -n sum; *(fig)* sum total.

summen 1 *vt Melodie etc* to hum. **2** *vi* to buzz; *(Mensch, Motor)* to hum.

Summer *m* - buzzer.

summieren* 1 *vt* to sum up. **2** *vr* to mount up. **das summiert sich** it (all) adds up.

Summton *m* buzz, buzzing sound.

Sumpf *m* ⁼e marsh; *(Morast)* mud; *(in tropischen Ländern)* swamp.

Sumpf-: ~**boden** *m* marshy ground; ~**fieber** *nt* malaria.

sumpfig *adj* marshy, swampy.

Sumpf-: ~**land** *nt* marshland; *(in tropischen Ländern)* swampland; ~**pflanze** *f* marsh plant; ~**vogel** *m* wader.

Sund *m* -e sound, straits *pl*.

Sünde *f* -n sin. **eine** ~ **begehen** to sin, to commit a sin.

Sünden-: ~**bekenntnis** *nt* confession of one's sins; *(Gebet)* confession (of sins); ~**bock** *m (col)* scapegoat; ~**fall** *m (Rel)* Fall; ~**register** *nt (fig)* list of sins; **jds** ~**register** the list of sb's sins.

Sünder(in *f)* *m* -s, - sinner. **armer** ~ *(fig)* poor wretch.

sündhaft *adj (lit)* sinful; *(fig col) Preise* wicked. ~ **teuer** *(col)* wickedly expensive.

sündig *adj* sinful.

sündigen *vi* to sin *(an +dat* against); *(hum)* to indulge.

Super *nt no pl (Benzin)* four-star (petrol) *(Brit)*, premium *(US)*, super.

super *(col)* **1** *adj inv* super *(col)*. **2** *adv (mit vb)* incredibly well *(col)*.

Super- *in cpds* super-; *(sehr)* ultra-; ~**-8-Film** *m*

super-8 film.

superklug *adj (iro col)* brilliant. **du bist ein S**~**er** *(Besserwisser)* you are a (real) know-all *(col)*.

Superlativ *m (Gram, fig)* superlative.

Super-: ~**macht** *f* superpower; ~**mann** *m, pl* ~**männer** superman; ~**markt** *m* supermarket; **s**~**modern** *adj (col)* ultramodern; ~**star** *m (col)* superstar.

Suppe *f* -n soup; *(sämig mit Einlage)* broth; *(klare Brühe)* bouillon; *(fig col: Nebel)* pea-souper *(col)*. **du mußt die** ~ **auslöffeln, die du dir eingebrockt hast** *(col)* you've made your bed, now you must lie on it *(prov)*; **jdm die** ~ **versalzen** *(col)* to put a spoke in sb's wheel *(col)*.

Suppen- *in cpds* soup; ~**fleisch** *nt* meat for making soup; ~**gemüse** *nt* vegetables *pl* for making soup; ~**grün** *nt* herbs and vegetables *pl* for making soup; ~**huhn** *nt* boiling fowl; ~**kasper** *m (col)* poor eater; ~**kelle** *f* soup ladle; ~**löffel** *m* soup spoon; ~**schüssel** *f* tureen; ~**tasse** *f* soup bowl; ~**teller** *m* soup plate; ~**würfel** *m* stock cube; ~**würze** *f* soup seasoning.

surfen ['sœrfn] *vi* to surf.

Surfing ['sœrfiŋ] *nt no pl (Sport)* surfing.

Surrealismus *m no pl* surrealism.

surrealistisch *adj* surrealist(ic).

surren *vi* to hum; *(Insektenflügel)* to whirr.

suspekt [zʊs'pɛkt] *adj* suspicious. **jdm** ~ **sein** to seem suspicious to sb.

suspendieren* [zʊspɛn'diːrən] *vt* to suspend *(von* from).

süß *adj (lit, fig)* sweet. **gern** ~ **essen** to have a sweet tooth; **das** ~ **e Leben** the good life; **(mein)** **S**~**er/meine S**~**e** *(col)* my sweetheart.

süßen 1 *vt* to sweeten; *(mit Zucker) Tee, Kaffee* to sugar. **2** *vi* mit **Honig** *etc* ~ to use honey *etc* as a sweetener.

Süßholz *nt* liquorice *(Brit)*, licorice *(US)*. ~ **raspeln** *(fig)* to turn on the blarney.

Süßigkeit *f* **(a)** *no pl (lit, fig)* sweetness. **(b)** ~**en** *pl* sweets *pl (Brit)*, candy *(US)*.

Süßkirsche *f* sweet cherry.

süßlich *adj* sweetish; *(unangenehm süß)*, *(fig) Töne, Miene* sickly sweet; *(kitschig)* mawkish.

Süß-: ~**most** *m* unfermented fruit juice; **s**~**sauer** *adj* sweet-and-sour; *Gurken etc* pickled; *(fig: gezwungen) Lächeln* forced; *Miene* artificially friendly; ~**speise** *f* sweet dish; ~**stoff** *m* sweetener; ~**waren** *pl* confectionery *sing*; ~**warengeschäft** *nt* sweetshop *(Brit)*, candy store *(US)*; ~**wasser** *nt* freshwater; ~**wasserfisch** *m* freshwater fish.

SW = Südwesten SW.

Swimming-pool ['svɪmɪŋpuːl] *m* -s swimming pool.

Symbol *nt* -e symbol.

Symbolik *f* symbolism.

symbolisch *adj* symbolic(al) *(für of)*.

symbolisieren* *vt* to symbolize.

Symbolismus *m* symbolism.

Symmetrie *f* symmetry.

symmetrisch *adj* symmetric(al).

Sympathie [zʏmpa'tiː] *f (Zuneigung)* liking; *(Mitgefühl, Solidaritätsgefühl)* sympathy. **für jdn/etw** ~ **haben** to have a liking for/a certain amount of sympathy with sb/sth; **durch seine Unverschämtheit hat er sich** *(dat)* **alle** ~**(n) verscherzt** he has turned everyone against him with his rudeness.

Sympathie-: ~**kundgebung** *f* demonstration of support; ~**streik** *m* sympathy strike.

Sympathisant(in *f)* *m* sympathizer.

sympathisch *adj* pleasant, nice. **er ist mir** ~ I like him.

sympathisieren* *vi* to sympathize *(mit with)*.

Symphonie [zʏmfo'niː] *f* symphony.

symphonisch *adj* symphonic.

Symposium [zʏm'poːziʊm] *nt, pl* **Symposien**

[zym'po:ziən] symposium.
Symptom *nt* -e symptom.
symptomatisch *adj* symptomatic *(für* of*)*.
Synagoge *f* -n synagogue.
synchron [zyn'kro:n] *adj* synchronous.
Synchrongetriebe [zyn'kro:n-] *nt (Aut)* synchromesh gearbox.
Synchronisation [zynkroniza'tsio:n] *f (Film, TV)* dubbing; *(Tech)* synchronization.
synchronisieren* [zynkroni'zi:rən] *vt Film* to dub; *(Tech)* to synchronize.
Syndikat *nt (Kartell)* syndicate.
Syndrom *nt* -e syndrome.
Synkope [zyn'ko:pə] *f* -n *(Mus)* syncopation.
Synode *f* -n *(Eccl)* synod.
Synonym [zyno'ny:m] *nt* -e synonym.
synonym [zyno'ny:m] *adj* synonymous.
Synonymwörterbuch *nt* dictionary of synonyms, thesaurus.
syntaktisch *adj* syntactic(al).
Sytnax *f no pl* syntax.
Synthese *f* -n synthesis.
Synthetics *pl* synthetics *pl.*
synthetisch *adj* synthetic.
Syphilis ['zy:fılıs] *f no pl* syphilis.

Syrer(in *f) m* - Syrian.
Syrien ['zy:riən] *nt* Syria.
syrisch *adj* Syrian.
System [zys'te:m] *nt* -e system. **etw mit ~ machen** to do sth systematically; **hinter dieser Sache steckt ~** there's method behind it; **~ in etw** *(acc)* **bringen** to get some system into sth; **ein ~ von Straßen/Kanälen** a road/canal system.
System-: **~analyse** *f* systems analysis; **~analytiker** *m* systems analyst.
Systematik *f no pl* system.
systematisch *adj* systematic.
System-: **~kritiker** *m* critic of the system; **s~kritisch** *adj* critical of the system.
Szene *f* -n *(Theat, fig)* scene; *(Theat: Bühnenausstattung)* set. **hinter der ~** backstage; *(fig)* behind the scenes; **etw in ~ setzen** *(lit, fig)* to stage sth; **sich in ~ setzen** to play to the gallery; **die ~ beherrschen** *(fig)* to dominate the scene *(gen* in*)*; *(meistern)* to control things; **sich in der ~ auskennen** *(col)* to know the scene; **(jdm) eine ~ machen** to make a scene (in front of sb).
Szenenwechsel *m* scene change.
Szenerie *f (Theat, fig)* scenery.
Szepter ['stseptɐ] *nt* - sceptre *(Brit)*, scepter *(US)*.

T

T, t [te:] *nt* -, - T, t.

t = **Tonne.**

Tabak ['ta:bak, 'tabak] *m* -e tobacco; *(Schnupf~)* snuff.

Tabak- *in cpds* tobacco; **~händler** *m* tobacconist; **~laden** *m* tobacconist's *(Brit)*, tobacco store *(US)*.

Tabaks-: **~beutel** *m* tobacco pouch; **~dose** *f* tobacco tin; **~pfeife** *f* pipe.

Tabak-: **~steuer** *f* duty on tobacco; **~waren** *pl* tobacco goods.

tabellarisch 1 *adj* tabular; *Lebenslauf* in tabular form. **2** *adv* in tables/a table.

Tabelle *f* table; *(Diagramm)* chart.

Tabellen-: **~form** *f:* **in ~form** in tabular form; as a chart; **~führer** *m (Sport)* league leaders *pl;* **~platz** *m (Sport)* position in the league.

Tablett *nt* -s *or* -e tray. **jdm etw auf einem silbernen ~ servieren** *(fig: einfach machen)* to hand sb sth on a plate.

Tablette *f* tablet, pill.

Tabu *nt* -s taboo.

tabu *adj pred* taboo.

tabuisieren* *vt* to make taboo.

Tabulator *m* tabulator, tab *(col)*.

Tach(e)les *no art (col;* **(mit jdm)** **~ reden** to have a talk with sb.

Tacho *m* -s *(col)* speedo *(Brit col)*, speedometer.

Tachometer *m or nt* - speedometer.

Tadel *m* - *(Verweis)* reprimand; *(Vorwurf)* reproach; *(Kritik)* criticism; *(geh: Makel)* blemish; *(Sch: Eintrag)* black mark. **ein Leben ohne jeden ~** *(geh)* a spotless life.

tadellos 1 *adj* perfect; *(col)* splendid. **2** *adv* perfectly; *gekleidet* immaculately.

tadeln *vt jdn* to reprimand; *jds Benehmen* to criticize.

tadelnd *adj attr* reproachful.

tadelnswert *adj (geh)* reprehensible.

Tadels|antrag *m (Parl)* motion of censure.

Tafel *f* -n **(a)** *(Platte)* slab; *(Holz~)* panel; *(Wand~)* (black)board; *(Schreib~)* slate; *(Schokoladen~)* bar; *(Gedenk~)* plaque; *(Elec: Schalt~)* control panel, console; *(Anzeige~)* board. **(b)** *(Bildseite)* plate. **(c)** *(form: festlicher Speisetisch)* table; *(Festmahl)* meal; *(mittags)* luncheon *(form); (abends)* dinner. **die ~ aufheben** to officially end the meal.

Tafel-: **~apfel** *m* eating apple; **~besteck** *nt* (best) silver; **t~fertig** *adj* ready to serve; **~freuden** *pl* culinary delights *pl;* **~geschirr** *nt* tableware; **~lappen** *m* (blackboard) duster.

tafeln *vi (geh)* to feast.

täfeln *vt Wand* to wainscot; *Decke* to panel.

Tafel-: **~obst** *nt* (dessert) fruit; **~öl** *nt* cooking/ salad oil; **~salz** *nt* table salt; **~silber** *nt* silver.

Täf(e)lung *f siehe* **täfeln** wainscoting; (wooden) panelling *(Brit)* or paneling *(US)*.

Tafel-: **~wasser** *nt* mineral water; **~wein** *m* table wine.

Taft *m* -e taffeta.

Tag *m* -e **(a)** day. **an dem/diesem ~** on that/this day; **am ~(e) des/der ... (on) the day of ...; am ~** during the day; **alle ~e** *(col)*, **jeden ~** every day; **am vorigen ~(e)** the day before; **auf den ~ (genau)** to the day; **auf ein paar ~e** for a few

days; **auf seine alten ~e** at his age; **den ganzen ~ (lang)** *(lit, fig)* all day long; **eines ~es** one day; **sich** *(dat)* **einen schönen/faulen ~ machen** to have a nice/lazy day; **~ für ~** day by day; **von ~ zu ~** from day to day; **welcher ~ ist heute?** what day is it today?; **guten ~!** hello; *(esp bei Vorstellung)* how do you do; *(vormittags auch)* good morning; *(nachmittags auch)* good afternoon; **~!** *(col)* hello, hi *(col)*; **zweimal am ~(e)** *or* **pro ~** twice a day; **von einem ~ auf den anderen** overnight; **seinen guten/schlechten ~ haben** to have a good/bad day; **in den ~ hinein leben** to take each day as it comes; **~ und Nacht** night and day; **bei ~(e) ankommen** while it's light; *arbeiten, reisen* during the day; **es wird schon ~** it's getting light already; **an den ~ kommen** *(fig)* to come to light; **er legte großes Interesse an den ~** he showed great interest. **(b)** *(col: Menstruation)* **ihre ~e** her period. **(c)** *(Min)* **über/unter ~e arbeiten** to work above/below ground.

tag|aus *adv* **~, tagein** day in, day out.

Tagdienst *m* day duty.

Tage-: **~bau** *m* -e *(Min)* open-cast mining; **~blatt** *nt* daily (news)paper; **~buch** *nt* diary; **(über etw** *acc)* **~ buch führen** to keep a diary (of sth); **~geld** *nt* daily allowance; **t~lang** *adj* lasting for days; **er war t~lang verschwunden** he disappeared for days; **~löhner(in** *f)* *m* - day labourer *(Brit)*, day laborer *(US)*.

tagen *vi impers (geh)* **es tagt** day is breaking. **2** *vi (konferieren)* to sit.

Tages-: **~anbruch** *m* daybreak, dawn; **~arbeit** *f* day's work; **~ausflug** *m* day trip; **~creme** *f* day cream; **~decke** *f* bedspread; **~fragen** *pl* issues of the day; **~gespräch** *nt* talk of the town; **~karte** *f* **(a)** *(Speisekarte)* menu of the day; **(b)** *(Fahr-, Eintrittskarte)* day ticket; **~kasse** *f* **(a)** *(Theat)* box-office; **(b)** *(Econ)* day's takings *pl;* **~klinik** *f* day clinic; **~lauf** *m* day; **~leistung** *f* daily workload; *(von Maschine, Schriftsteller etc)* daily output; **~licht** *nt no pl* daylight; **ans ~licht kommen** *(fig)* to come to light; **~lohn** *m* day's wages; **~marsch** *m* day's march; **~mutter** *f* child minder; **~nachrichten** *pl* (today's) news; **~ordnung** *f* agenda; **etw auf die ~ordnung setzen** to put sth on the agenda; **auf der ~ordnung stehen** to be on the agenda; **zur ~ordnung übergehen** to proceed with business as usual *(fig)* to carry on as usual; **an der ~ordnung sein** *(fig)* to be the order of the day; **~ordnungspunkt** *m* item on the agenda; **~presse** *f* daily newspapers; **~reise** *f* **(a)** *(Entfernung)* day's journey; **(b)** *(Ausflug)* day trip; **~satz** *m* daily rate; **~zeit** *f* time (of day); **zu jeder ~- und Nachtzeit** at all hours of the day and night; **~zeitung** *f* daily (paper).

Tage-: **t~weise** *adv* on a daily basis; **~werk** *nt (geh)* day's work.

taghell *adj* (as) bright as day. **es war schon ~** it was already broad daylight.

täglich 1 *adj; (attr: gewöhnlich)* everyday. **das reicht gerade fürs ~e Leben** it's just about enough to get by on; **sein ~(es) Brot verdienen** to earn a living. **2** *adv* every day. **einmal ~** once a day.

414

tags adv ~ **zuvor** the day before, the previous day; ~ **darauf** or **danach** the next or following day.

Tagschicht f day shift. ~ **haben** to be on day shift.

tags|über adv during the day.

Tag-: t~**täglich** 1 adj daily; 2 adv every (single) day; ~**traum** m daydream; ~**undnachtgleiche** f equinox.

Tagung f conference; (von Ausschuß) sitting, session.

Tagungsort m venue (of a/the conference).

Taifun m -e typhoon.

Taille ['taljə] f -n waist. **auf seine** ~ **achten** to watch one's waistline.

Takel nt - (Naut) tackle.

Takelage [takə'la:ʒə] f -n (Naut) rigging, tackle.

Takt m -e (a) (Mus) bar; (Phon, Poet) foot. (b) (Rhythmus) time. **den** ~ **schlagen** to beat time; **gegen den** ~ out of time; **den** ~ **angeben** to give the beat. (c) (Aut) stroke. (d) (Ind) phase. (e) no pl (Taktgefühl) tact.

Taktgefühl nt (a) sense of tact. (b) (Mus) sense of rhythm.

taktieren* vi to manoeuvre (Brit), to maneuver (US). **so kann man nicht** ~ you can't use those tactics.

Taktik f tactics pl. **eine** ~ tactics pl.

Taktiker(in f) m - tactician.

taktisch adj tactical. ~ **klug vorgehen** to use good tactics.

Takt-: t~**los** adj tactless; ~**losigkeit** f tactlessness; ~**stock** m baton; ~**strich** m (Mus) bar (line); t~**voll** adj tactful.

Tal nt -ër valley.

tal|ab(wärts) adv down into the valley.

Talar m -e (Univ) gown; (Jur, Eccl) robe(s).

tal|aufwärts adv up the valley.

Tal-: ~**brücke** f bridge over a valley; ~**enge** f gorge.

Talent nt -e (a) (Begabung) talent (zu for). **ein großes** ~ **haben** to be very talented; **sie hat viel** ~ **zum Singen/zur Schauspielerin** she has a great talent for singing/acting. (b) (Mensch) talented person. **junge** ~**e** young talent.

talentiert adj talented, gifted.

Talfahrt f descent; (fig) decline.

Talg m -e tallow; (Cook) suet; (Haut~) sebum.

Talisman m -e talisman, (lucky) charm; (Maskottchen) mascot.

Talk m no pl talc(um).

Talkessel m basin, hollow.

Talkpuder m or nt talcum powder.

Tal-: ~**senke** f hollow (of a/the valley); ~**sohle** f bottom of a/the valley; (fig) rock bottom; **in der** ~**sohle** (fig) at rock bottom; ~**sperre** f dam; t~**wärts** adv down to the valley.

Tambour ['tambu:ɐ] m -e drummer.

Tamburin nt -e tambourine.

Tampon [tam'po:n] m -s tampon.

tamponieren* vt to plug, to tampon.

Tamtam nt -s (a) (Mus) tomtom. (b) (col: Wirbel) fuss, ballyhoo (col); (Lärm) din (col).

Tand m no pl (liter) knick-knacks pl; (fig) dross.

tändeln vi (liter) (flirten) to flirt; (herumspielen) to play around; (trödeln) to dilly-dally.

Tandem nt -s tandem.

Tang m -e seaweed.

Tangens ['tangɛns] m - (Math) tan(gent).

Tangente [taŋ'gɛntə] f -n (Math) tangent; (Straße) ring-road, expressway.

tangieren* [taŋ'gi:rən] vt Problem to touch on; (betreffen) to affect; (col: kümmern) to bother.

Tango ['taŋgo] m -s tango.

Tank m -s or -e tank.

tanken vti (a) (bei Auto) to fill up; (bei Rennwagen, Flugzeug) to refuel. **wo kann man hier** ~? where can I get petrol (Brit) or gas (US) around here?;

wir hielten an, um zu ~ we stopped for petrol/gas; **was tankst du?** — **ich tanke nur Super** what grade (of petrol/gas) do you use? — I only use 4 star; **ich tanke nur für 10 Mark** I'll just put 10 marks' worth in. (b) (col) frische Luft, neue Kräfte to get. **er hat ganz schön getankt** he's had a few.

Tanker m - (Naut) tanker.

Tank-: ~**fahrzeug** nt (Aut) tanker; ~**lager** nt oil or petrol depot; ~**laster** m tanker; ~**säule** f petrol pump (Brit), gas(oline) pump (US); ~**schiff** nt tanker; ~**stelle** f petrol (Brit) or gas(oline) (US) station; ~**uhr** f fuel gauge; ~**verschluß** m petrol (Brit) or gas (US) cap; ~**wagen** m tanker; (Rail) tank wagon or car; ~**wart** m petrol pump (Brit) or gas station (US) attendant.

Tanne f -n fir, pine; (Holz) pine.

Tannen-: ~**baum** m fir-tree, pine-tree; (Weihnachtsbaum) Christmas tree; ~**zapfen** m fir cone, pine cone.

Tante f -n (a) (Verwandte) aunt, aunty. (b) (pej col: Frau) old girl (col). (c) (baby-talk: Frau) lady.

Tante-Emma-Laden m (col) corner shop.

tantenhaft adj (a) (col) old-maidish. (b) (pej: betulich) twee.

Tantieme [tã'tie:mə] f -n fee; (für Künstler) royalty.

Tanz m -e dance. **dort ist heute abend** ~ there's a dance there this evening; **jdn zum** ~ **auffordern** to ask sb to dance.

Tanz-: ~**abend** m dance; ~**bar** f bar with dancing; ~**bär** m dancing bear; ~**bein** nt: **das** ~**bein schwingen** (hum) to trip the light fantastic (hum); ~**boden** m (~fläche) dance floor; (Saal) dance hall; ~**café** nt restaurant with dancing.

tänzeln vi aux haben or (bei Richtungsangabe) sein to mince; (Boxer) to skip; (Pferd) to step delicately.

tanzen vti aux haben or (bei Richtungsangabe) sein to dance; (Boot auch) to bob; (Kreisel) to spin; (hüpfen) to hop. ~ **gehen** to go dancing.

Tänzer(in f) m - dancer; (Partner) (dancing) partner.

tänzerisch adj dance-like. ~ **veranlagt sein** to have a talent for dancing; **sein** ~**es Können** his dancing ability.

Tanz-: ~**fläche** f dance floor; ~**gruppe** f dance group; ~**kapelle** f dance band; ~**kurs(us)** m dancing course; ~**lehrer** m dancing teacher; ~**lokal** nt café with dancing; ~**musik** f dance music; ~**saal** m dance hall; (in Hotel etc) ballroom; ~**schritt** m (dance) step; ~**schule** f dancing school; ~**stunde** f dancing class; ~**turnier** nt dancing competition.

Tapet nt: **etw aufs** ~ **bringen** (col) to bring sth up.

Tapete f -n wallpaper no pl. **die** ~**n wechseln** (fig col) to have a change of surroundings.

Tapeten-: ~**bahn** f strip of wallpaper; ~**rolle** f roll of wallpaper; ~**wechsel** m (col) change of surroundings.

Tapezierer m - paperhanger, decorator.

tapezieren* vt to (wall)paper. **neu** ~ to repaper.

tapfer adj brave, courageous; (wacker) steadfast. **sich** ~ **schlagen** (col) to put on a brave show.

Tapferkeit f siehe adj bravery, courage; steadfastness.

tappen vi (a) aux sein (tapsen) to go/come falteringly; (Bär) to lumber; (dial: gehen) to wander. **er ist in eine Pfütze getappt** (col) he walked smack into a puddle (col). (b) (tasten) **nach etw** ~ to grope for sth; **im dunkeln** ~ (fig) to grope in the dark.

tapsen vi aux sein (col) (Kind) to toddle; (Bär) to lumber; (Kleintier) to waddle.

tapsig adj (col) awkward, clumsy.

Tara f, pl **Taren** (Comm) tare.

Tarantel f -n tarantula. **wie von der** ~ **gestochen** as if stung by a bee.

Tarif m -e rate; (Wasser~, Gas~, Verkehrs~ etc auch) tariff. **die Gewerkschaft hat die** ~**e gekün-**

digt the union has put in a new wage claim; **nach/über/unter ~ bezahlen** to pay according to/above/below the (union) rate(s).

Tarif-: **~autonomie** f free collective bargaining; **~gruppe** f grade; **~kommission** f joint working party on pay.

tariflich adj agreed, union. **der ~e Mindestlohn** the agreed minimum wage.

Tarif-: **~lohn** m standard wage; **~partner** m die **~partner** union and management; **~verhandlungen** pl pay negotiations pl; **~vertrag** m pay agreement.

tarnen 1 vti to camouflage; (fig) Absichten, Identität etc to disguise. **2** vr (Tier) to camouflage itself; (Mensch) to disguise oneself.

Tarnfarbe f camouflage colour (Brit) or color (US)/paint.

Tarnung f camouflage; (von Agent etc) disguise.

Tarock m or nt -s tarot.

Tasche f **-n (a)** (Hand~) bag (Brit), purse (US); (Reise~, Schul~ etc) bag; (Akten~) (brief)case; (Backen~) pouch. **(b)** (bei Kleidungsstücken) pocket. **in die eigene ~ wirtschaften** to line one's own pockets; **etw in der ~ haben** (col) to have sth in the bag (col); **jdm das Geld aus der ~ ziehen** to get sb to part with his money; **etw aus der eigenen ~ bezahlen** to pay for sth out of one's own pocket; **jdm auf der ~ liegen** (col) to live off sb; **die Hände in die ~n stecken** (lit) to put one's hands in one's pockets; (fig) to stand idly by; **jdn in die ~ stecken** (col) to put sb in the shade (col).

Taschen-: **~ausgabe** f pocket edition; **~buch** nt paperback (book); **~dieb** m pickpocket; **~diebstahl** m pickpocketing; **~format** nt pocket size; **~geld** nt pocket-money; **~lampe** f torch (Brit), flashlight (US); **~messer** nt pocket-knife, penknife; **~rechner** m pocket calculator; **~schirm** m collapsible umbrella; **~spieler** m conjurer; **~spielertrick** m (fig) sleight of hand no indef art, no pl; **~tuch** nt handkerchief; (aus Papier) tissue; **~uhr** f pocket watch.

Tasse f **-n** cup; (Suppen~) bowl. **eine ~ Kaffee** a cup of coffee; **er hat nicht alle ~n im Schrank** (col) he's not all there.

Tastatur f keyboard.

Taste f **-n** key; (Knopf an Gerät auch) button. **auf die ~n hauen** (col) to hammer away at the keyboard.

tasten 1 vi to feel. **nach etw ~** (lit, fig) to feel or grope for sth; **~de Schritte** (lit, fig) tentative steps. **2** vr to feel or grope one's way. **3** vti (drücken) to press; Telex, (Typ: setzen) to key.

Tasten-: **~instrument** nt (Mus) keyboard instrument; **~telefon** nt pushbutton telephone.

Tast-: **~organ** nt organ of touch; **~sinn** m sense of touch.

Tat f **-en** (das Handeln) action; (Einzel~ auch) act; (Helden~, Un~) deed; (Leistung) feat; (Verbrechen) crime. **eine gute/böse ~** a good/wicked deed; **etw in die ~ umsetzen** to put sth into action; **zur ~ schreiten** to act; **in der ~** indeed; (wider Erwarten) actually.

tat pret of **tun**.

Tatbestand m (Jur) facts (of the case) pl.

Taten-: **~drang** m energy; **t~los** adj idle; **t~los herumstehen** to stand idly by; **wir mußten t~los zusehen** we could only stand and watch.

Täter(in f) m - culprit; (Jur) perpetrator (form). **als ~ verdächtigt werden** to be a suspect; **wer war der ~?** who did it?

Täterschaft f guilt. **die ~ leugnen/zugeben** to deny/admit one's guilt.

tätig adj **(a)** attr active. **~e Nächstenliebe** practical charity. **(b)** (arbeitend) **~ sein** to work; **er ist im Bankwesen ~** he's in banking.

tätigen vt (Comm) to conclude; (geh) Einkäufe to carry out; (geh) Anruf to make.

Tätigkeit f activity; (Beschäftigung) occupation; (Arbeit) work; (Beruf) job. **in/außer ~ setzen** Maschine to start up/to stop.

Tätigkeits-: **~bereich** m field of activity; **~bericht** m progress report.

Tat-: **~kraft** f no pl energy, drive; **t~kräftig** adj energetic; Hilfe active.

tätlich adj violent. **gegen jdn ~ werden** to assault sb.

Tat|ort m scene of the crime.

tätowieren* vt to tattoo.

Tätowierung f tattooing; (Darstellung) tattoo.

Tatsache f fact. **~? (col)** really?, no!; **das ist ~ (col)** that's a fact; **jdn vor vollendete ~n stellen** to present sb with a fait accompli.

Tatsachenbericht m documentary (report).

tatsächlich 1 adj attr real, actual. **2** adv actually, really, in fact. **willst du das ~ tun?** are you really or actually going to do it?; **da kommt er! — ~!** he's coming! — so he is!

tätscheln vt to pat.

Tattergreis m (pej col) old dodderer (pej).

tatt(e)rig adj (col) Mensch doddery; Hände, Schriftzüge shaky.

Tat-: **~verdacht** m suspicion (of having committed a crime); **unter ~verdacht stehen** to be under suspicion; **t~verdächtig** adj suspected.

Tatze f **-n** (lit, fig) paw.

Tau[1] m no pl dew.

Tau[2] nt **-e** (Seil) rope; (Naut auch) hawser.

taub adj deaf; Glieder numb; Ähre unfruitful; Nuß empty. **sich ~ stellen** to pretend not to hear; **gegen or für etw ~ sein** (fig) to be deaf to sth.

Taube f **-n (a)** (Zool) pigeon; (Turtel~, fig) dove.

Taubenschlag m dovecot(e). **hier geht es zu wie im ~** (fig) it's like Waterloo Station here (Brit col), it's like Grand Central Station here (US col).

Taube(r) mf decl as adj deaf person. **die ~n** the deaf.

Taubheit f deafness; (von Körperteil) numbness.

Taub-: **t~stumm** adj deaf and dumb, deaf-mute attr; **~stumme(r)** mf deaf-mute.

tauchen 1 vi aux haben or sein to dive (nach for); (als Sport auch) to skin-dive; (kurz ~) to duck under; (unter Wasser sein) to stay under water; (U-Boot auch) to submerge; (aux sein: auf ~) to emerge (aus out of, from). **2** vt (kurz ~) to dip; Menschen, Kopf to duck; (ein~) to immerse.

Taucher(in f) m - diver.

Taucher-: **~anzug** m diving suit; **~brille** f diving goggles pl; **~glocke** f diving bell.

Tauch-: **~sieder** m - immersion coil (for boiling water); **~sport** m (skin-)diving; **~station** f auf **~station gehen** (U-Boot) to dive; (fig: sich verstecken) to make oneself scarce; **auf ~station sein** (U-Boot) to be submerged.

tauen vti (vi: aux haben or sein) (Schnee) to melt, to thaw. **es taut** it is thawing.

Taufbecken nt font.

Taufe f **-n** baptism; (Kindes~ auch) christening; (Schiffs~) launching (ceremony).

taufen vt to baptize; (nennen) Kind, Schiff etc to christen. **sich ~ lassen** to be baptized; **jdn auf den Namen Rufus ~** to christen sb Rufus.

Täufer m -: **Johannes der ~** John the Baptist.

Tauf-: **~pate** m godfather; **~patin** f godmother; **~schein** m certificate of baptism; **~zeuge** m godparent.

taugen vi **(a)** (geeignet sein) to be suitable (zu, für for). **er taugt zu gar nichts** he is useless; **er taugt nicht zum Arzt** he wouldn't make a good doctor. **(b)** (wert sein) etwas/nichts **~** to be all right/to be no good.

Taugenichts m -e good-for-nothing.

tauglich adj (zu for) suitable; (Mil) fit.

Tauglichkeit f suitability; (Mil) fitness (for service).

Taumel *m no pl (geh: Schwindel)* (attack of) dizziness; *(liter: Rausch)* frenzy. **wie im ~** in a daze.

taumeln *vi aux sein* to stagger; *(zur Seite)* to sway.

Tausch *m* **-e** exchange, swap; *(~handel)* barter.
im ~ gegen etw in exchange for sth; **einen guten/schlechten ~ machen** to get a good/bad deal.

tauschen 1 *vt (gegen for)* to exchange, to swap; *Güter* to barter; *(aus~) Briefmarken etc* to swap; *Geld* to change *(in+acc* into). **2** *vi* to swap; *(in Handel)* to barter. **ich möchte nicht mit ihm ~** I wouldn't like to be in his place.

täuschen 1 *vt* to deceive; *Vertrauen* to betray. **wenn mich mein Gedächtnis nicht täuscht** if my memory serves me right; **wenn mich nicht alles täuscht** unless I'm completely wrong. **2** *vr* to be wrong *or* mistaken *(in+dat, über+acc* about). **3** *vi (irreführen: Aussehen etc)* to be deceptive.

täuschend 1 *adj Nachahmung* remarkable; *Ähnlichkeit auch* striking. **2** *adv* **sich** *(dat)* **~ ähnlich sehen/sein** to look/be remarkably alike *or* almost identical.

Tauschgeschäft *nt* exchange; *(Handel)* barter.

Tauschung *f* **(a)** *(das Täuschen)* deception. **(b)** *(Irrtum)* mistake, error; *(falsche Wahrnehmung)* illusion; *(Selbst~)* delusion. **er gab sich einer ~** *(dat)* **hin** he was deluding himself.

Täuschungsmanöver *nt (Sport)* feint; *(col)* ploy.

tausend *num* a *or* one thousand; *siehe* **hundert.**

Tausender *m* **-** **(a)** *(Zahl)* **ein ~** a figure in the thousands; **die ~** the thousands. **(b)** *(Geldschein)* thousand.

tausenderlei *adj inv* a thousand kinds of.

Tausend-: **~füßler** *m* - centipede; **~jahrfeier** *f* millenary; **t~jährig** *adj attr* thousand year old; *(t~ Jahre lang)* thousand year (long); **t~mal** *adv* a thousand times; **~sas(s)a** *m* **-s** *(col)* hell of a guy *(col).*

tausendste(r, s) *adj* thousandth.

Tau-: **~werk** *nt no pl (Naut)* rigging; **~wetter** *nt* thaw; *(fig auch)* relaxation; **es ist ~wetter** it is thawing; **~ziehen** *nt no pl (lit, fig)* tug-of-war.

Taxi *nt* **-s** taxi, cab. **~ fahren** to drive a taxi; *(als Fahrgast)* to go by taxi.

Taxi-: **~fahrer** *m* taxi *or* cab driver, cabby *(col)*; **~fahrt** *f* taxi ride; **~stand** *m* taxi rank *(Brit)* or stand *(US).*

Tb [te:'be:] **-s** = **Tuberkulose** TB.

Teak(holz) ['ti:k-] *nt* teak. **ein Tisch aus ~** a teak table.

Team|arbeit ['ti:m-] *f* teamwork.

Technik *f* **(a)** *(no pl: Technologie)* technology. **(b)** *(Arbeitsweise, Verfahren)* technique. **(c)** *(no pl: Funktionsweise)* mechanics *pl.*

Techniker(in *f)* *m* - engineer; *(Beleuchtungs~, Labor~, fig: Fußballspieler, Künstler)* technician.

Technikum *nt, pl* **Technika** college of technology.

technisch *adj* technical; *(technologisch)* technological. **er ist ~ begabt** he is technically minded; **T~e Hochschule** polytechnic.

Technokrat *m (wk)* **-en, -en** technocrat.

Technologie *f* technology.

technologisch *adj* technological.

Techtelmechtel *nt* - *(col)* affair, carry-on *(col).*

Teddy ['tɛdi] *m* **-s** *(auch ~bär)* teddy (bear).

Tee *m* **-s** tea. **einen im ~ haben** *(col)* to be tipsy *(col).*

Tee-: **~beutel** *m* tea bag; **~gebäck** *nt no pl* sweet biscuits *pl*; **~glas** *nt* tea-glass; **~kanne** *f* teapot; **~kessel** *m* kettle; **~licht** *nt* night-light; **~löffel** *m* teaspoon; *(Menge)* teaspoonful; **~mischung** *f* blend of tea.

Teen [ti:n] *m* **-s** *(col)* teenager.

Teepause *f* tea break.

Teer *m* **-e** tar.

Teerdecke *f* tarred (road) surface.

teeren *vt* to tar.

Teer-: **~gehalt** *m* tar content; **t~haltig** *adj* **eine wenig/stark t~haltige Zigarette** a low/high tar cigarette; **~pappe** *f* roofing felt.

Tee-: **~service** *nt* tea-set; **~sieb** *nt* tea-strainer; **~stube** *f* tea-room; **~tasse** *f* teacup.

Teich *m* **-e** pond.

Teig *m* **-e** dough; *(Blätter~ etc)* pastry.

teigig *adj* doughy.

Teigwaren *pl (Nudeln)* pasta *sing.*

Teil[1] *m* **-e** **(a)** part. **zum ~** partly; **zum größten ~** for the most part, mostly; **er hat die Bücher darüber zum großen/größten ~ gelesen** he has read many/most of the books about that. **(b)** *(auch nt: An~)* share. **zu gleichen ~en erben** to get an equal share of an inheritance; **er hat seinen ~ dazu beigetragen** he did his bit *or* share; **sich** *(dat)* **sein(en) ~ denken** *(col)* to draw one's own conclusions. **(c)** *(auch nt)* **ich für mein(en) ~ ... ...** I, for my part ...

Teil[2] *nt* **-e (a)** part; *(Bestand~ auch)* component; *(Ersatz~)* spare, (spare) part. **etw in seine ~e zerlegen** to take sth apart *or* to pieces. **(b)** = **Teil**[1] **(b,c).**

Teil-: **t~bar** *adj* divisible; **~bereich** *m* part; **~betrag** *m* part (of an amount); *(auf Rechnung)* item; *(Rate)* instalment *(Brit)*, installment *(US)*; *(Zwischensumme)* subtotal.

Teilchen *nt* particle; *(dial: Gebäckstück)* cake.

teilen 1 *vt* **(a)** to divide *(durch* by). **geteilter Meinung sein** to have different opinions; **darüber sind die Meinungen geteilt** opinions differ on that. **(b)** *(auf~)* to share (out) *(unter +dat* amongst). **etw mit jdm ~** to share sth with sb. **(c)** *(an etw teilhaben)* to share. **sie haben Freud und Leid miteinander geteilt** they shared the rough and the smooth; **sie teilten unser Schicksal** they shared the same fate as us. **2** *vr* **(a)** *(in Gruppen)* to split up. **(b)** *(Straße, Fluß)* to fork, to divide. **(c)** **sich** *(dat)* **etw ~** to share sth; **teilt euch das!** share that between you. **3** *vi* to share. **er teilt nicht gern** he doesn't like sharing.

Teil-: **~erfolg** *m* partial success; **~gebiet** *nt (Bereich)* branch; *(räumlich)* area; **t~haben** *vi sep irreg (geh)* **an etw** *(dat)* **t~haben** to have a part in sth; **~haber(in** *f)* *m* - *(Comm)* partner.

Teilkaskoversicherung *f* insurance covering more than third party liability but giving less than fully comprehensive coverage.

Teilnahme *f no pl* **(a)** *(Anwesenheit)* attendance *(an+dat* at); *(Beteiligung)* participation *(an +dat* in). **(b)** *(Interesse)* interest *(an+dat* in); *(Mitgefühl)* sympathy. **jdm seine herzliche ~ aussprechen** to offer sb one's heartfelt condolences.

teilnahmeberechtigt *adj* eligible.

teilnahms-: **~los** *adj (gleichgültig)* indifferent, apathetic; *(stumm leidend)* listless; **~voll** *adj* compassionate, sympathetic.

teilnehmen *vi sep irreg* **an etw** *(dat)* **~** *(sich beteiligen)* to take part in sth; **an einem Ausflug ~** to go on an outing; **am Unterricht ~** to attend school.

Teilnehmer(in *f)* *m* - participant; *(bei Wettbewerb)* competitor, contestant; *(Kurs~)* student.

teils *adv* partly. **bist du zufrieden? — ~, ~** are you happy? — sort of *(col).*

Teil-: **~strecke** *f* stage; *(von Straße)* stretch; *(bei Bus etc)* fare-stage; **~stück** *nt* part.

Teilung *f* division.

teilweise 1 *adv* partly; *(manchmal)* sometimes. **~ sind sie interessiert** to a certain extent they are interested. **2** *adj attr* partial.

Teil-: **~zahlung** *f* hire-purchase *(Brit)*, installment plan *(US)*; *(Rate)* instalment *(Brit)*, installment *(US)*; **auf ~zahlung** on hire purchase/the installment plan; **~zeitarbeit** *f* part-time job/ work.

Teint [tɛ̃:] *m* **-s** complexion.

Tel. = **Telefon.**

Telebrief m facsimile, fax.
Telefon nt -e (tele)phone; **am ~ on the phone; ans ~ gehen** to answer the phone.
Telefon- in cpds (tele)phone; **~anruf** m (tele)phone call; **~apparat** m telephone.
Telefonat nt (tele)phone call.
Telefon-: **~buch** nt (tele)phone book; **~gebühr** f call charge; (Grundgebühr) telephone rental; **~gespräch** nt (tele)phone call.
telefonieren* vi to make a (tele)phone call. **er telefoniert gerade** he's on the phone; **bei jdm ~** to use sb's phone; **mit jdm ~** to speak to sb on the phone.
telefonisch adj **~e Auskunft/Beratung** telephone information/advice service; **eine ~e Mitteilung** a (tele)phone message; **jdm etw ~ mitteilen** to tell sb sth over the phone; **etw ~ bestellen** to order sth on the phone or by phone; **ich bin ~ zu erreichen** I can be contacted by phone.
Telefonist(in f) m telephone operator; (in Betrieb auch) switchboard operator.
Telefon-: **~leitung** f telephone line; **~netz** nt telephone network; **~nummer** f (tele)phone number; **~rechnung** f (tele)phone bill; **~verbindung** f telephone line; (zwischen Orten) telephone link; **~zelle** f (tele)phone box (Brit) or booth; **~zentrale** f (telephone) switchboard.
Telegraf m (wk) -en, -en telegraph.
Telegrafie f telegraphy.
telegrafieren* vti to telegram, to cable.
telegrafisch adj telegraphic. **jdm ~ Geld überweisen** to wire sb money.
Telegramm nt -e telegram.
Tele- ['tele-]: **~kolleg** nt ≈ Open University (Brit); **~objektiv** nt (Phot) telephoto lens; **~pathie** f telepathy; **~pathisch** adj telepathic.
Teleskop nt -e telescope.
Telex nt -e telex.
Teller m - plate. **ein ~ Suppe** a plate of soup.
Tellerwäscher m dishwasher.
Tempel m - temple (auch fig).
Temperament nt (a) (Wesensart) temperament. **ein hitziges ~ haben** to be hot-tempered. (b) no pl (Lebhaftigkeit) vitality, vivacity. **viel/kein ~ haben** to be very/not to be lively; **sein ~ ist mit ihm durchgegangen** he went over the top.
temperament-: **~los** adj lifeless; **~voll** adj vivacious, lively; Aufführung auch spirited.
Temperatur f temperature. **erhöhte ~ haben** to have a temperature; **die ~en sind angestiegen/gesunken** the temperature has risen/fallen.
Temperatur-: **~anstieg** m rise in temperature; **~regler** m thermostat; **~rückgang** m fall in temperature; **~schwankung** f variation in temperature.
temperieren* vt etw ~ (anwärmen) to warm sth up; **der Raum ist angenehm temperiert** the room is at a pleasant temperature.
Tempo nt -s speed; (Arbeits~, Schritt~ auch) pace. **~!** (col) hurry up!; **nun mach mal ein bißchen ~!** (col) get a move on! (col); **~ 100 fahren** to be doing 100; **das ~ angeben** (fig) to set the pace.
Tendenz f trend; (Neigung) tendency; (Absicht) intention; (no pl: Parteilichkeit) bias, slant. **die ~ haben, zu ...** to have a tendency to ...; **er hat nationalistische ~en** he has nationalist leanings.
tendenziell adj **eine ~e Veränderung** a change in direction; **nur ~e Unterschiede** merely differences in emphasis.
tendenziös adj tendentious.
tendieren* vi **dazu ~, etw zu tun** to tend to do sth; **zum Kommunismus ~** to have communist leanings or tendencies.
Tennis nt -, no pl tennis.
Tennis- in cpds **~platz** m tennis court; **~schläger** m tennis racket.

Tenor m -̈e (Mus) tenor.
Teppich m -e carpet; (Wand~) tapestry. **etw unter den ~ kehren** (lit, fig) to sweep sth under the carpet.
Teppich-: **~boden** m fitted carpet(s); **~kehrmaschine** f carpet-sweeper; **~klopfer** m carpet-beater.
Termin m -e date; (für Fertigstellung) deadline; (Comm: Liefertag) delivery date; (bei Arzt, Besprechung etc) appointment; (Jur: Verhandlung) hearing. **die ~e besprechen** to discuss the schedule; **der letzte ~** the deadline; (bei Bewerbung etc) the closing date; **sich (dat) einen ~ geben lassen** to make an appointment; **schon einen anderen ~ haben** to have a prior engagement.
Terminal ['tœrminəl] nt or m -s terminal.
Termin-: **t~gerecht** adj on schedule; **~geschäfte** pl futures; **~kalender** m (appointments or engagements) diary.
terminlich adj **etw ~ einrichten** to fit sth in (to one's schedule); **~e Verpflichtungen** commitments.
Terminologie f terminology.
Termite f -n termite.
Terpentin nt -e turpentine; (col: ~öl) turps (col).
Terrain [tɛ|rɛ̃ː] nt -s land, terrain; (fig) territory. **das ~ sondieren** (Mil) to reconnoitre the terrain; (fig) to see how the land lies.
Terrasse f -n terrace; (Dach~) roof garden.
terrassenförmig 1 adj terraced. 2 adv in terraces.
Territorium nt territory.
Terror m no pl terror; (Terrorismus) terrorism; (~herrschaft) reign of terror; (Einschüchterung) intimidation. **blutiger ~** terrorism and bloodshed; **~ machen** (col) to raise hell (col).
Terror-: **~anschlag** m terrorist attack; **~herrschaft** f reign of terror.
terrorisieren* vt to terrorize.
Terrorismus m terrorism.
Terrorist(in f) m terrorist.
Terror|organisation f terrorist organization.
Tertia ['tɛrtsia] f, **Tertien** ['tɛrtsiən] (Sch) (Unter-/Ober~) fourth/fifth year of German secondary school.
Tertianer(in f) [tɛrtsi'aːnɐ, -ərɪn] m - (Sch) pupil in fourth/fifth year of German secondary school.
Terz f -en (Mus) third; (Fechten) tierce.
Tesafilm ® m Sellotape ® (Brit), Scotch tape ® (esp US).
Test m -s or -e test.
Testament nt (a) (Jur) will; (fig) legacy. **sein ~ machen** to make one's will. (b) (Bibl) **Altes/Neues ~** Old/New Testament.
testamentarisch adj testamentary. **etw ~ festlegen** to write sth in one's will.
Testbild nt (TV) testcard.
testen vt to test (auf+acc for). **jdn auf seine Intelligenz ~** to test sb's intelligence.
Test-: **~fahrer** m test driver; **~fall** m test case; **~person** f subject (of a test); **~pilot** m test-pilot.
teuer adj expensive, dear usu pred; (fig) dear. **etw ~ kaufen/verkaufen** to buy/sell sth for a high price; **etw für teures Geld kaufen** to pay good money for sth; **in Tokio lebt man ~** life is expensive in Tokyo; **das wird ihn ~ zu stehen kommen** (fig) that will cost him dear; **einen Sieg ~ erkaufen** to pay dearly for a victory.
Teuerung f rise in prices.
Teufel m - (a) (lit, fig) devil. (b) (col) **scher dich zum ~** go to hell (col!); **jdn zum ~ jagen** to send sb packing (col); **wer zum ~?** who the devil (col) or the hell (col!)?; **zum ~ mit dem Ding!** damn (col) or blast (col) the thing!; **den ~ an die Wand malen** (schwarzmalen) to imagine the worst; (Unheil heraufbeschwören) to tempt fate or providence; **wenn man vom ~ spricht** (prov) talk of the devil; **das müßte schon mit dem ~ zugehen**

that really would be a stroke of bad luck; **in ~s Küche kommen** to get into a mess; **sich den ~ um etw kümmern** not to give a damn about sth *(col)*.

Teufels-: ~**arbeit** *f (col)* hell of a job *(col)*; ~**austreibung** *f* casting out of devils *no pl*, exorcism; ~**kerl** *m (dated)* devil of a fellow *(dated)*; ~**kreis** *m* vicious circle.

teuflisch *adj* fiendish, devilish, diabolical.

Text *m* -e text; *(einer Urkunde auch, eines Gesetzes)* wording; *(von Lied)* words *pl*; *(von Schlager)* lyrics *pl*; *(von Film, Rede etc)* script; *(Bild~)* caption; *(auf Plakat)* words *pl*.

Text-: ~**buch** *nt* script; *(für Lieder)* songbook; ~**dichter** *m* songwriter; *(bei Oper)* librettist.

texten 1 *vt* to write. 2 *vi siehe* **Texter(in)** to write songs/copy.

Texter(in *f)* *m* - *(für Schlager)* songwriter; *(für Werbesprüche)* copywriter.

Textil- *in cpds* textile; ~**arbeiter** *m* textile worker; ~**branche** *f* textile trade.

Textilien [-ion] *pl* textiles *pl*.

Textilindustrie *f* textile industry.

Text-: ~**kritik** *f* textual criticism; ~**stelle** *f* passage; ~**system** *nt* word-processor; ~**verarbeitung** *f* word-processing; ~**verarbeitungssystem** *nt* word-processor.

TH [teː'haː] *f* **-s** = **Technische Hochschule**.

Thailand *nt* Thailand.

Thailänder(in *f)* *m* - Thai.

Theater *nt* - **(a)** theatre *(Brit)*, theater *(US)*; *(~kunst auch)* drama; *(Schauspielbühne)* theatre *(Brit)* or theater *(US)* company. **beim/im ~ arbeiten** to be on the stage/work in the theatre; **zum ~ gehen** to go on the stage; **ins ~ gehen** to go to the theatre. **(b)** *(fig)* carry-on *(col)*, fuss. **(ein)** ~ **machen** to make a (big) fuss *(mit jdm of sb)*.

Theater- *in cpds* theatre *(Brit)*, theater *(US)*; ~**aufführung** *f* stage production; *(Vorstellung, Darbietung)* performance; ~**besucher** *m* theatregoer *(Brit)*, theatergoer *(US)*; ~**kritiker** *m* drama critic; ~**stück** *nt* (stage) play.

theatralisch *adj* theatrical, histrionic.

Theke *f* **-n** *(Schanktisch)* bar; *(Ladentisch)* counter. **etw unter der ~ verkaufen** to sell sth under the counter.

Thema *nt, pl* **Themen** *or* **-ta** subject, topic; *(Leitgedanke, Mus)* theme. **beim ~ bleiben/vom ~ abschweifen** to stick to/wander off the subject; **das ~ wechseln** to change the subject.

Thematik *f* topic.

thematisch *adj* thematic.

Themenkreis *m* topic.

Theologe *m*, **Theologin** *f* theologian.

Theologie *f* theology.

theologisch *adj* theological.

Theoretiker(in *f)* *m* - theorist, theoretician.

theoretisch *adj* theoretical. ~ **gesehen** in theory, theoretically.

Theorie *f* theory.

Therapeut(in *f)* *m (wk)* **-en, -en** therapist.

therapeutisch *adj* therapeutic(al).

Therapie *f* therapy.

Thermal-: ~**bad** *nt (Badeort)* spa; ~**quelle** *f* thermal spring.

thermisch *adj attr (Phys)* thermal.

Thermo- *in cpds* thermo-.

Thermometer *nt* - thermometer.

Thermosflasche *f* thermos (flask) ®.

Thermostat *m* -e thermostat.

These *f* **-n** hypothesis, thesis.

Thron *m* -e throne. **von seinem ~ herabsteigen** *(fig)* to come down off one's high horse.

thronen *vi* to sit enthroned; *(fig: in exponierter Stellung sitzen)* to sit in state.

Thron-: ~**erbe** *m*, ~**erbin** *f* heir to the throne; ~**folge** *f* line of succession; ~**folger(in** *f)* *m* - heir

to the throne, heir apparent.

Thunfisch *m* tuna (fish).

Thymian *m* -e thyme.

tick *interj* tick. ~ **tack** tick-tock.

Tick *m* -s tic; *(col: Schrulle)* quirk. **Uhren sind sein** ~ he has a thing about clocks *(col)*; **einen ~ haben** *(col)* to be crazy.

ticken *vi* to tick (away). **du tickst ja nicht richtig** you're off your rocker! *(col)*.

tief 1 *adj* deep; *(niedrig)* Ton, Ausschnitt low; *(tiefgründig auch)* profound; Schmerz intense; Not dire; Elend utter. ~**er Teller** soup plate; **die** ~**en Ursachen** the underlying causes; **aus** ~**stem Herzen/~ster Seele** from the bottom of one's heart/the depths of one's soul; **bis ~ in die Nacht hinein** late into the night; ~ **im Wald** deep in the forest; **im ~en Winter** in the depths of winter; ~ **in der Nacht** at dead of night.

2 *adv* **(a)** *(weit nach unten, innen etc)* deep; *untersuchen* in depth; *sich bücken* low. ~ **in etw** *(acc)* **einsinken** to sink deep into sth; **3 m ~ fallen** to fall 3 metres; ~ **sinken** *(fig)* to sink low; **(ganz)** ~ **unter uns** a long way below us, far below us; ~ **verschneit** deep with snow; ~ **in Gedanken (versunken)** deep in thought; ~ **in Schulden stecken** to be deep in debt; ~ **in die Tasche greifen müssen** *(col)* to have to dig deep in one's pocket. **(b)** *(schwer, stark)* deeply; *erschrecken* terribly. ~ **atmen** to breathe deeply; **im Winter steht die Sonne ~er** the sun is lower (in the sky) in winter.

Tief *nt* -e *(Met)* depression; *(fig)* low. **ein moralisches** ~ *(fig)* a low.

Tief-: ~**bau** *m* civil engineering *(excluding the construction of buildings)*; **t~betrübt** *adj attr* deeply distressed.

Tiefdruck *m* **(a)** *(Met)* low pressure. **(b)** *(Typ)* gravure.

Tiefe *f* **-n** *siehe* tief depth; lowness; profundity. **unten in der** ~ far below.

Tiefebene *f* lowland plain.

Tiefen-: ~**psychologie** *f* depth psychology; psychoanalysis; ~**wirkung** *f* deep action.

Tief-: ~**flug** *m* low-level *or* low-altitude flight; ~**gang** *m (Naut)* draught *(Brit)*, draft *(US)*; *(fig col)* depth; ~**garage** *f* underground car park *(Brit)* or parking lot *(US)*; **t~gekühlt** *adj (gefroren)* frozen; **t~gründig** *adj* profound, deep; *(durchdacht)* well-grounded.

Tiefkühl-: ~**fach** *nt* freezer compartment; ~**kost** *f* frozen food; ~**truhe** *f* deep-freeze.

Tief-: ~**lader** *m* low-loader; ~**land** *nt* lowlands *pl*; **t~liegend** *adj attr* Gegend, Häuser low-lying; Augen deep-set; *(nach Krankheit)* sunken; ~**parterre** *nt* basement; ~**punkt** *m* low; ~**schlag** *m* *(Boxen, fig)* hit below the belt; ~**see** *f* deep sea; ~**sinn** *m* profundity; **t~sinnig** *adj* profound; ~**stand** *m* low; **t~stapeln** *vi sep* to understate the case; *(in bezug auf eigene Leistung)* to be modest.

Tiegel *m* - (sauce)pan; *(Chem)* crucible.

Tier *nt* -e animal; *(Haus~ auch)* pet; *(col: grausamer Mensch)* brute. **hohes** ~ *(col)* big shot *(col)*.

Tier- *in cpds* animal; *(Med)* veterinary; ~**arzt** *m* vet, veterinary surgeon *(form)*, veterinarian *(US)*; ~**freund** *m* animal lover; ~**garten** *m* zoo; ~**halter** *m (von Haustier)* pet-owner; *(von Nutztieren)* livestock owner; ~**handlung** *f* pet shop *(Brit)* or store *(US)*; ~**heim** *nt* animal home.

tierisch *adj* animal *attr*; *(fig)* Roheit bestial. ~**er Ernst** *(col)* deadly seriousness.

Tier-: ~**kreis** *m* zodiac; ~**kreiszeichen** *nt* sign of the zodiac; ~**kunde** *f* zoology; ~**liebe** *f* love of animals; **t~liebend** *adj* fond of animals, animal-loving *attr*; ~**medizin** *f* veterinary medicine; ~**park** *m* zoo; ~**pfleger** *m* zoo-keeper; ~**quälerei** *f* cruelty to animals; ~**reich** *nt* animal kingdom; ~**schutz** *m* protection of animals; ~**schutzverein** *m* society for the prevention of

cruelty to animals; ~**versuch** m animal experiment.
Tiger m - tiger.
Tigerin f tigress.
tilgen vt (geh) Schulden to pay off.
Tilgung f (von Schulden) repayment.
Tinnef m no pl (col) rubbish, trash (col).
Tinte f -n ink. **in der ~ sitzen** (col) to be in the soup (col).
Tinten-: ~**faß** nt inkpot; ~**fisch** m cuttlefish; (Kalmar) squid; (achtarmig) octopus; ~**fleck** m ink stain; ~**klecks** m ink blot.
Tip m -s (Sport, St Ex) tip; (Andeutung) hint; (an Polizei) tip-off. **kannst du mir einen ~ geben, wo ich ...?** can you give me an idea where I ...?
Tippelbruder m (col) tramp, gentleman of the road (hum).
tippeln vi aux sein (col) (gehen) to foot it (col); (auf Zehenspitzen) to tiptoe.
tippen vti (a) to tap (an/auf/gegen etw (acc) sth); (zeigen) to touch (auf or an etw (acc) sth). **jdm auf die Schulter ~** to tap sb on the shoulder; **sich** (dat) **an die Stirn ~** to tap one's forehead. (b) (col: auf der Schreibmaschine) to type (an etw (dat) sth). (c) (wetten) to fill in one's coupon; (im Toto auch) to do the pools. **im Lotto ~** to do the lottery; **ich tippe auf Kohl** (col) I'll put my money on Kohl.
Tippfehler m typing error.
Tippse f -n (pej) typist.
tipptopp (col) **1** adj immaculate; (prima) first-class. **2** adv immaculately; (prima) really well.
Tippzettel m (im Toto) football pools coupon; (im Lotto) lottery coupon.
Tirol nt the Tyrol.
Tiroler(in f) m - Tyrolese, Tyrolean.
Tisch m -e table; (Schreib~) desk. **bei ~** at table; **bitte zu ~!** lunch/dinner is served!; **vor/nach ~** before/after the meal; **unter den ~ fallen** (col) to go by the board; **jdn unter den ~ trinken** to drink sb under the table; **es wird gegessen, was auf den ~ kommt!** you'll eat what you're given; **vom ~ sein** (fig) to be cleared out of the way.
Tisch- in cpds table; ~**dame** f dinner partner; ~**decke** f tablecloth; ~**herr** m dinner partner; ~**karte** f place card; ~**kasten** m drawer in the table.
Tischler m - joiner, carpenter; (Möbel~) cabinet-maker.
Tischlerei f (Werkstatt) joiner's or carpenter's/cabinet-maker's workshop.
Tischlerhandwerk nt joinery, carpentry; cabinet-making.
tischlern vi (col) to do woodwork.
Tisch-: ~**nachbar** m neighbour (Brit) or neighbor (US) (at table); ~**ordnung** f seating plan; ~**rechner** m desk calculator; ~**rede** f after-dinner speech; ~**tennis** nt table tennis; ~**tuch** nt tablecloth; ~**wein** m table wine.
Titel m - title. **jdn mit ~ ansprechen** to address sb by his/her title; **unter dem ~** under the title.
Titel-: ~**bild** nt cover (picture); ~**blatt** nt title page; ~**kampf** m (Sport) finals pl; (Boxen) title fight; ~**rolle** f title role; ~**schutz** m copyright (of a title); ~**seite** f (von Zeitschrift) cover; (von Zeitung) front page; ~ **verteidiger** m title holder.
titulieren* vt jdn to address (mit as).
tja interj well.
Toast [toːst] m -e (a) (Brot) toast. **ein ~** some toast. (b) (Trinkspruch) toast.
toasten ['toːstn] **1** vi to drink a toast (auf+acc to). **2** vt Brot to toast.
toben vi (a) (wüten) to rage; (Mensch) to throw a fit; (vor Begeisterung etc) to go wild (vor with). (b) (ausgelassen spielen) to rollick (about).
Tobsucht f (bei Tieren) madness; (bei Menschen) maniacal rage. **er hat wieder mal die ~** (col) he's gone raving mad again (col).

Tochter f ⁼ daughter; (~firma) subsidiary.
Tochtergesellschaft f subsidiary (company).
Tod m -e death. **~ durch Ersticken** death by suffocation; **eines natürlichen/gewaltsamen ~es sterben** to die of natural causes/to die a violent death; **sich zu ~e trinken** to drink oneself to death; **sich** (dat) **den ~ holen** to catch one's death (of cold); **sich zu ~(e) langweilen** to be bored to death; **zu ~e betrübt sein** to be in the depths of despair.
tod|ernst adj (col) deadly serious.
Todes-: ~**angst** f fear of death; ~**ängste ausstehen** (col) to be scared to death (col); ~**anzeige** f obituary (notice); ~**fall** m death; (in der Familie auch) bereavement; ~**jahr** nt year of sb's death; ~**kampf** m death throes pl; t~**mutig** adj absolutely fearless; ~**opfer** nt death, casualty, fatality; ~**qualen** pl final agony; ~**qualen ausstehen** (fig) to suffer agonies; ~**stoß** m death-blow; **jdm/einer Sache den ~stoß versetzen** (lit, fig) to deal sb/sth the deathblow; ~**strafe** f death penalty; ~**tag** m day of sb's death; (Jahrestag) anniversary of sb's death; ~**ursache** f cause of death; ~**urteil** nt death sentence; ~**verachtung** f (col) **mit ~verachtung** with utter disgust.
Tod-: ~**feind** m deadly or mortal enemy; t~**krank** adj dangerously or critically ill.
tödlich adj fatal; Gefahr mortal; Gift deadly, lethal; (col) Langeweile deadly. **~ verunglücken** to be killed in an accident.
Tod-: t~**müde** adj (col) dead tired (col); t~**schick** adj (col) dead smart (col); t~**sicher** (col) **1** adj dead certain (col); Methode, Tip sure-fire (col); **2** adv for sure; ~**sünde** f mortal or deadly sin.
Toilette [toa'lɛta] f (a) (Abort) toilet. **öffentliche ~** public conveniences pl (Brit), comfort station (US). **auf die ~ gehen/auf der ~ sein** to go to/be in the toilet. (b) no pl (geh: Körperpflege) toilet.
Toiletten- [toa'lɛtn-] in cpds toilet; ~**artikel** m usu pl toiletry; ~**beutel** m toilet bag; ~**papier** nt toilet paper; ~**schrank** m bathroom cabinet; ~**wasser** nt toilet water.
tolerant adj tolerant (gegen of).
Toleranz f tolerance (gegen of).
tolerieren* vt to tolerate.
toll adj (a) (wild, ausgelassen) wild, mad. (b) (col: verrückt) mad, crazy. (c) (col: schlimm) terrible. (d) (col: großartig) fantastic (col), great (col) no adv.
tollen vi to romp about; (aux sein: laufen) to rush about.
Toll-: t~**kühn** adj daredevil attr, daring; ~**wut** f rabies; t~**wütig** adj rabid.
Tolpatsch m -e (col) clumsy creature.
Tölpel m - (col) fool.
Tomate f -n tomato. **du treulose ~!** (col) you're a fine friend!
Tomaten- in cpds tomato; ~**mark,** ~**püree** nt tomato puree.
Ton¹ m -e (Erdart) clay.
Ton² m ⁼e (a) (Laut) sound; (von Zeitzeichen, im Telefon, Klangfarbe) tone; (Mus: note) note. **den ~ angeben** (Mus) to give an A; (fig: Mensch) to set the tone; **keinen ~ herausbringen** not to be able to say a word; **keinen ~ sagen** not to make a sound; **hast du ~e!** (col) did you ever! (col); **dicke** or **große ~e spucken** (col) to talk big. (b) (Betonung) stress; (Tonfall) intonation. (c) (Redeweise, Umgangston) tone. **den richtigen ~ finden** to strike the right note; **ich verbitte mir diesen ~** I will not be spoken to like that; **einen anderen ~ anschlagen** to change one's tune; **der gute ~** good form. (d) (Farb~) tone; (Nuance) shade.
Ton-: ~**abnehmer** m pick-up; ~**arm** m pick-up arm; ~**art** f (Mus) key; (fig: Tonfall) tone.
Tonband nt tape; (col: Gerät) tape recorder.
Tonband-: ~**aufnahme** f tape recording; ~**gerät**

nt tape recorder.

tönen[1] *vi (lit, fig: klingen)* to sound; *(schallen auch)* to resound; *(großspurig reden)* to sound off.

tönen[2] *vt* to tint. **etw leicht rot** *etc* ~ **to tinge sth** (with) red *etc*.

Ton|erde *f* aluminium oxide.

tönern *adj attr* clay. **auf ~en Füßen stehen** *(fig)* to be shaky.

Ton-: ~**fall** *m* tone of voice; *(Intonation)* intonation; ~**film** *m* sound film, talkie *(col)*; ~**folge** *f* sequence of notes/sounds; ~**geschirr** *nt* earthenware; ~**höhe** *f* pitch; ~**ingenieur** *m* sound engineer; ~**kopf** *m* recording head; ~**lage** *f* pitch (level); *(~umfang)* register; ~**leiter** *f* scale; t~**los** *adj* toneless.

Tonne *f* -n **(a)** *(Behälter)* barrel; *(aus Metall)* drum; *(Müll~)* bin *(Brit)*, trash can *(US)*; *(col: Mensch)* fatso *(col)*. **(b)** *(Gewicht)* metric tonne. **(c)** *(Register~)* (register) ton.

Ton-: ~**störung** *f* sound interference; ~**taube** *f* clay pigeon; ~**waren** *pl* earthenware *sing*.

Top- *in cpds* top.

Topas *m* -e topaz.

Topf *m* ⁻e pot; *(Koch~ auch)* (sauce)pan; *(Nacht~)* potty *(col)*; *(col: Toilette)* loo *(Brit col)*, john *(US col)*. **alles in einen** ~ **werfen** *(fig)* to lump everything together.

Topfblume *f* potted flower.

Töpfer(in *f)* *m* - potter.

Töpferei *f* pottery.

töpfern **1** *vi* to do pottery. **2** *vt* to make (in clay).

Töpfer-: ~**scheibe** *f* potter's wheel; ~**waren** *pl* pottery *sing*; *(irden)* earthenware *sing*.

Topfhandschuh *m* ovenglove.

topfit ['tɔp'fɪt] *adj pred* in top form.

Topf-: ~**lappen** *m* ovencloth; ~**pflanze** *f* potted plant.

Tor *nt* -e **(a)** *(lit, fig, Ski)* gate; *(Durchfahrt etc)* gateway; *(von Garage, Scheune)* door. **(b)** *(Sport)* goal. **im** ~ **stehen** to be in goal.

Tor-: ~**bogen** *m* arch, archway; ~**einfahrt** *f* entrance gate.

Toresschluß *m:* *(kurz)* **vor** ~ right at the last minute.

Torf *m* no pl peat.

Torf-: ~**boden** *m* peat; ~**erde** *f* peat.

torfig *adj* peaty.

Torf-: ~**moor** *nt* peat bog *or (trocken)* moor; ~**stecher** *m* - peat-cutter.

Torheit *f* foolishness; *(Handlung)* foolish action.

töricht *adj* foolish; *Wunsch, Hoffnung* idle.

torkeln *vi aux sein* to stagger, to reel.

Tor-: ~**latte** *f* crossbar; ~**lauf** *m* slalom; ~**linie** *f* goal-line; ~**mann** *m, pl* ~**männer** goalkeeper, goalie *(col)*.

Tornister *m* - *(Mil)* knapsack; *(dated: Schulranzen)* satchel.

torpedieren* *vt (Naut, fig)* to torpedo.

Torpedo *m* -s torpedo.

Tor-: ~**pfosten** *m* gatepost; *(Sport)* goalpost; ~**schluß** *m (fig) siehe* ~**esschluß;** ~**schlußpanik** *f (col)* last minute panic; *(von Unverheirateten)* fear of being left on the shelf; ~**schütze** *m* (goal) scorer.

Torte *f* -n cake, gâteau; *(Obst~)* flan *(Brit)*, tart.

Torten-: ~**boden** *m* flan *(Brit) or* tart *(US)* base; ~**guß** *m* glaze; ~**heber** *m* - cake slice; ~**platte** *f* cake plate; ~**schaufel** *f* cake slice.

Tortur *f* torture; *(fig auch)* ordeal.

Tor-: ~**verhältnis** *nt* score; ~**wart** *m* goalkeeper.

tosen *vi* to roar, to thunder; *(Wind, Sturm)* to rage. ~**der Beifall** thunderous applause.

tot *adj (lit, fig)* dead; *Augen* sightless; *Haus, Stadt* deserted; *Gegend, Landschaft etc* bleak; *Wissen* useless; *Vulkan* extinct; *Farbe* lifeless; *(Rail) Gleis* disused. **mehr** ~ **als lebendig** *(fig col)* more dead than alive; ~ **geboren werden** to be stillborn; ~ **umfallen** to drop dead; **er war auf der**

Stelle ~ he died instantly; **ein** ~**er Briefkasten** a dead-letter box; **der** ~**e Winkel** the blind spot; **ein** ~**er Punkt** *(Stillstand)* a standstill; *(in Verhandlungen)* deadlock; *(körperliche Ermüdung)* low point; **ein** ~**es Rennen** *(lit, fig)* a dead heat; **ein** ~**er Mann** *(fig col)* a goner *(col)*.

total **1** *adj* total. **2** *adv* totally.

Totalausverkauf *m* clearance sale.

totalitär *adj* totalitarian.

Totalität *f* totality, entirety.

Total-: ~**operation** *f* extirpation; *(von Gebärmutter)* hysterectomy; ~**schaden** *m* write-off.

töt-: ~**arbeiten** *vr sep (col)* to work oneself to death; ~**ärgern** *vr sep (col)* to be/become livid.

töten *vti (lit, fig)* to kill. **das kann einem den Nerv** ~ *(fig col)* he/that really gets on my/one's *etc* nerves.

Toten-: ~**bett** *nt* deathbed; t~**blaß** *adj* deathly pale; ~**glocke** *f* death knell; ~**gräber** *m* gravedigger; ~**hemd** *nt* shroud; ~**klage** *f* lamentation of the dead; *(Liter)* dirge, lament; ~**kopf** *m* skull; *(als Zeichen)* death's-head; *(auf Piratenfahne, Arzneiflasche etc)* skull and crossbones; ~**messe** *f* requiem mass; ~**reich** *nt (Myth)* kingdom of the dead; ~**schein** *m* death certificate; t~**still** *adj* deathly silent; ~**starre** *f* rigor mortis; ~**wache** *f* wake.

Tote(r) *mf decl as adj* dead person, dead man/woman; *(bei Unfall etc)* fatality, casualty. **die** ~**n** the dead; **es gab 3** ~ 3 people were killed.

Tot-: t~**geboren** *adj attr* stillborn; **ein** t~**geborenes Kind sein** *(fig)* to be doomed to failure; ~**geburt** *f* stillbirth; *(Kind)* stillborn baby; ~**gesagte(r)** *mf decl as adj* person *or* man/woman *etc* who has been declared dead; t~**kriegen** *vt sep (col)* **nicht** t~**zukriegen sein** to go on for ever; t~**lachen** *vr sep (col)* to die laughing *(col)*.

Toto *m or nt* -s (football) pools. **(im)** ~ **spielen** to do the pools.

Toto- *in cpds* pools; ~**zettel** *m* pools coupon.

Tot-: ~**schlag** *m (Jur)* manslaughter; *(US)* homicide; t~**schlagen** *vt sep irreg (lit, fig)* to kill; *(col) Menschen auch* to beat to death; ~**schläger** *m* cudgel, club; t~**schweigen** *vt sep irreg* to hush up *(col)*; t~**stellen** *vr sep* to pretend to be dead.

toupieren* [tu'piːrən] *vt* to backcomb.

Tour [tuːɐ] *f* -en **(a)** *(Fahrt)* trip, outing; *(Ausflugs~)* tour; *(Spritz~)* *(mit Auto)* drive; *(mit Rad)* ride; *(Wanderung)* walk; *(Berg~)* climb. **eine** ~ **machen** to go on a trip *or* outing/tour; to go for a drive/ride/walk/climb. **(b)** *(Umdrehung)* revolution, rev *(col)*. **auf** ~**en kommen** *(Auto)* to reach top speed; *(fig col)* to get into top gear; *(sich aufregen)* to get worked up *(col)*; **auf vollen** ~**en laufen** *(lit)* to run at full speed; *(fig)* to be in full swing; **in einer** ~ *(col)* the whole time. **(c)** *(col: Art und Weise)* ploy. **mit der** ~ **brauchst du mir gar nicht zu kommen** don't try that one on me; **auf die krumme** ~ by dishonest means.

Touren- ['tuːrən-]: ~**rad** *nt* tourer; ~**zähler** *m* rev counter.

Tourismus [tu'rɪsmʊs] *m* tourism.

Tourist [tu'rɪst] *m* tourist; ~**industrie** tourist industry.

Touristik [tu'rɪstɪk] *f* tour industry.

Tournee [tur'neː] *f* -n [-eːən] *or* -s tour.

Trab *m* no pl *no pl.* **im** ~ at a trot; **(im)** ~ **reiten** to trot; **auf** ~ **sein** *(col)* to be on the go *(col)*; **jdn auf** ~ **bringen** *(col)* to make sb get a move on *(col)*.

Trabant *m (Astron, fig)* satellite.

Trabantenstadt *f* satellite town.

traben *vi* **(a)** *aux haben or sein* to trot. **(b)** *aux sein (col: laufen)* to trot.

Tracht *f* -en *(Kleidung)* dress; *(Volks~ etc)* costume; *(Schwestern~)* uniform. **eine** ~ **Prügel** a good thrashing.

trachten *vi (geh)* to strive *(nach* for, after). **jdm nach dem Leben** ~ to be after sb's blood.

trächtig *adj Tier* pregnant; *(fig geh)* laden *(von* with).

Tradition [tradi'tsio:n] f tradition.
traditionell [traditsio'nɛl] adj usu attr traditional.
traf pret of **treffen.**
Trafo m -s (col) transformer.
tragbar adj (a) Apparat, Gerät portable; Kleid wearable. **(b)** (annehmbar) acceptable (für to); (erträglich) bearable.
Trage -n (Bahre) litter; (Tragkorb) pannier.
träge adj (a) sluggish; Mensch, Bewegung auch lethargic. **(b)** (Phys) Masse inert.
tragen pret **trug**, ptp **getragen 1** vt (a) to carry; (an einen Ort bringen) to take. **etw mit sich ~ to** carry sth with one. **(b)** Kleid, Brille etc to wear; (im Moment auch) to have on; Bart, Gebiß to have; Waffen to carry. **getragene Kleider** second-hand clothes; (abgelegt) cast-offs. **(c)** (stützen, halten, fig) to support; Schicksal, Leid etc to bear, to endure. **(d)** Zinsen to yield; Ernte auch to produce; (lit, fig) Früchte to bear. **(e)** (trächtig sein) to be carrying. **(f)** Verluste to absorb; Kosten to bear, to carry; Risiko, Folgen to take; (unterhalten) Verein to support, to back. **(g)** Titel, Aufschrift etc to bear, to have; Vermerk to contain.
2 vi (a) (Baum, Acker etc) to produce a crop. **(b)** (reichen: Geschütz, Stimme) to carry. **(c)** (Eis) to take weight. **(d)** schwer an etw (dat) ~ to have a job carrying sth; (fig) to find sth hard to bear. **(e)** zum T~ kommen to come to fruition; (nützlich werden) to come in useful.
3 vr (a) sich leicht ~ to be easy to carry; der Anzug trägt sich gut this suit feels comfortable (on). **(b)** (finanziell) to be self-supporting.
tragend adj Säule, Bauteil load-bearing; Idee, Motiv fundamental.
Träger m - (a) (an Kleidung) strap; (Hosen~) braces pl (Brit), suspenders pl (US). **(b)** (Holz~, Beton~) (supporting) beam; (Stahl~, Eisen~) girder. **(c)** (Tech: Stütze von Brücken etc) support. **(d)** (Mensch) (von Lasten) bearer, porter; (von Namen) bearer. **(e)** (fig) (der Kultur, Staatsgewalt etc) representative; (einer Veranstaltung) sponsor.
Träger-: ~**kleid** nt pinafore dress (Brit), jumper (US); ~**rakete** f carrier rocket.
Tragetasche f carrier bag (Brit), carry-all (US).
Trag-: t~**fähig** adj (Brücke, Balken) able to take a load; (Kompromiß, Beschluß) acceptable; ~**fläche** f wing; (von Boot) hydrofoil; ~**flächenboot** nt hydrofoil.
Trägheit f siehe adj sluggishness; lethargy; (Faulheit) laziness; (Phys) inertia.
Tragik f tragedy.
Tragiker m - tragedian.
Tragikomödie f tragicomedy.
tragisch adj tragic. **etw ~ nehmen** (col) to take sth to heart; **das ist nicht so ~** (col) it's not the end of the world.
Trag-: ~**korb** m pannier; ~**last** f load.
Tragödie [-iə] f (Liter, fig) tragedy.
Trag-: ~**pfeiler** m load-bearing pillar; (von Brücke) support; ~**riemen** m strap; ~**weite** f (von Geschütz) range; (fig) consequences pl: (von Gesetz) scope; **von großer ~weite sein** to have far-reaching consequences.
Trainer(in f) ['trɛːnɐ, 'trɛː-] m - coach, trainer; (bei Fußball) manager.
trainieren* [trɛ'niːrən, trɛː'n-] **1** vt to train; Mannschaft, Sportler auch to coach; Sprung, Übung to practise (Brit), to practice (US). **ein (gut) trainierter Sportler** an athlete who is in training; **jdn auf or für etw** (acc) ~ to train or coach sb for sth. **2** vi (Sportler) to train; (Übungen machen) to exercise; (üben) to practise (Brit), to practice (US). **auf or für etw** (acc) ~ to train/practise for sth. **3** vr to train (auf+acc for); (üben) to practise (Brit), to practice (US).
Training ['trɛːnɪŋ, 'trɛːn-] nt -s training no pl; (Fitneß~) exercise no pl; (fig: Übung) practice.

Trainings-: ~**anzug** m track-suit; ~**hose** f track-suit trousers pl; ~**jacke** f track-suit top; ~**schuh** m trainer; ~**zeit** f practice time.
Trakt m -e (Gebäudeteil) section; (Flügel) wing.
Traktat m or nt -e (Abhandlung) treatise; (Flugschrift, religiöse Schrift) tract.
traktieren* vt (col) (schlecht behandeln) to maltreat; (quälen) Geschwister, Tiere to torment.
Traktor m -en tractor.
Trampel m or nt - clumsy clot (col).
trampeln 1 vi (a) to stamp. **(b)** aux sein (schwerfällig gehen) to stamp along. **über die Wiese ~ to** tramp across the meadow. **2** vt Weg to trample. **jdn zu Tode ~** to trample sb to death.
Trampel-: ~**pfad** m track, path; ~**tier** nt (Zool) (Bactrian) camel; (col) clumsy oaf (col).
trampen ['trɛmpn] vi to hitch-hike, to hitch (col).
Tramper(in f) ['trɛmpɐ, -ərɪn] m - hitch-hiker.
Trampolin nt -e trampoline.
Tran m -e (a) (von Fischen) train oil. **(b)** (col) **im ~ dop(e)y** (col); (leicht betrunken) merry (col). **das habe ich im ~ ganz vergessen** it completely slipped my mind.
tranchieren [trã'ʃiːrən] vt to carve.
Tranchier-: ~**gabel** f carving-fork; ~**messer** nt carving-knife.
Träne f -n tear; (einzelne ~) tear(drop). **den ~n nahe sein** to be on the verge of tears; ~**n lachen** to laugh till one cries; **deswegen vergieße ich keine ~n** (fig) I'm not going to shed any tears over that; **bittere ~n weinen** to weep bitterly.
tränen vi to water.
Tränen-: ~**drüse** f lachrymal gland; **der Film drückt sehr auf die ~drüsen** the film is a real tear-jerker; ~**gas** nt tear gas.
Tranfunzel f (col) slowcoach (Brit col), slowpoke (US col).
tranig adj (col) slow, sluggish.
Trank m ːe (liter) drink, draught (liter).
trank pret of **trinken.**
Tränke f -n drinking trough.
tränken vt Tiere to water; (durchnässen) to soak.
Trans|aktion f transaction.
trans|atlantisch adj transatlantic.
Transformation f transformation.
Transformator m transformer.
transformieren* vt to transform.
Transfusion f transfusion.
Transistorradio nt transistor (radio).
Transit m -e transit.
transitiv adj (Gram) transitive.
Transitverkehr m transit traffic.
transparent [transpa'rɛnt] adj transparent; (fig geh) Argument lucid, clear. **eine Entscheidung ~ machen** to make a decision-making process open.
Transparent [transpa'rɛnt] nt -e (Reklameschild etc) neon sign; (Durchscheinbild) transparency; (Spruchband) banner.
Transparentpapier nt waxed tissue paper; (zum Pausen) tracing paper.
Transparenz [transpa'rɛnts] f siehe adj transparency; lucidity, clarity.
Transplantation [transplanta'tsio:n] f (Med) transplant; (von Haut) graft; (Bot) grafting.
Transport [trans'pɔrt] m -e (a) transport. **ein ~ auf dem Landweg** road transport; **ein ~ des Kranken ist ausgeschlossen** moving the patient is out of the question. **(b)** (Fracht) consignment, shipment; (Menschen) transport.
transportabel [transpɔr'taːbl] adj transportable.
Transport|arbeiter m transport worker.
Transporter [trans'pɔrtɐ] m - (Schiff) cargo ship; (Flugzeug) transport plane; (Auto) van.
Transporteur [transpɔr'tøːɐ] m removal man (Brit), furniture mover.
transportfähig adj moveable.
transportieren* [transpɔr'tiːrən] **1** vt to trans-

budget

port; *Patienten* to move; *Film* to wind on. **2** *vi* (*Förderband*) to move; (*Kamera*) to wind on.

Transport- [trans'pɔrt-]: ~**kosten** *pl* freight costs *pl;* ~**schiff** *nt* cargo ship; (*Mil*) transport ship; ~**unternehmen** *nt* haulier, haulage firm.

Transuse *f* -**n** (*col*) slowcoach (*Brit col*), slowpoke (*US col*).

Transvestit [transvɛs'tiːt] *m* (*wk*) -**en**, -**en** transvestite.

transzendent(al) *adj* transcendent(al).

Trapez *nt* -**e** (*von Artisten*) trapeze.

trappeln *vi aux sein* to clatter; (*Pony*) to clip-clop.

Trara *nt* -**s** (*fig col*) hullabaloo (*col*) (*um* about).

trat *pret of* **treten**.

Tratsch *m no pl* (*col*) gossip, scandal.

tratschen *vi* (*col*) to gossip.

Tratsch-: ~**maul** *nt*, ~**tante** *f* (*pej col*) scandalmonger, gossip.

Tratte *f* -**n** (*Fin*) draft.

Traube *f* -**n** (*Beere*) grape; (*ganze Frucht*) bunch of grapes; (*Menschen*~) bunch. ~**n** (*Fruchtart*) grapes.

Trauben-: ~**lese** *f* grape harvest; ~**saft** *m* grape juice; ~**zucker** *m* glucose, dextrose.

trauen 1 *vi+dat* to trust. **ich traute meinen Augen nicht** I couldn't believe my eyes. **2** *vr* to dare. **ich trau' mich nicht** I daren't, I dare not; **sich auf die Straße** ~ to dare to go out (of doors). **3** *vt* to marry. **sich** ~ **lassen** to get married.

Trauer *f no pl* (*das Trauern*, ~**zeit**, ~**kleidung**) mourning; (*Schmerz, Leid*) sorrow, grief.

Trauer-: ~**anzeige** *f* obituary, death notice; ~**fall** *m* bereavement, death; ~**feier** *f* funeral service; ~**flor** *m* black ribbon; ~**gemeinde** *f* mourners *pl;* ~**kleidung** *f* mourning; ~**kloß** *m* (*col*) wet blanket (*col*); ~**marsch** *m* funeral march; ~**miene** *f* (*col*) long face.

trauern *vi* to mourn (*um jdn/etw* sb/sth).

Trauer-: ~**schleier** *m* black veil; ~**spiel** *nt* tragedy; (*fig col*) fiasco; ~**weide** *f* weeping willow; ~**zug** *m* funeral procession.

Traufe *f* -**n** eaves *pl.*

träufeln *vt* to dribble.

traulich *adj* cosy (*Brit*), cozy (*US*).

Traum *m*, *pl* **Träume** (*lit,fig*) dream. **aus der** ~**!** it's all over; **das fällt mir nicht im** ~ **ein** I wouldn't dream of it.

Trauma *nt*, *pl* **Traumen** *or* -**ta** (*lit,fig*) trauma.

traumatisch *adj* (*lit,fig*) traumatic.

Traum-: ~**beruf** *m* dream job; ~**deutung** *f* interpretation of dreams.

träumen *vti* (*lit,fig*) to dream. **von jdm/etw** ~ to dream about sb/sth; **das hätte ich mir nicht** ~ **lassen** I'd never have thought it possible.

Träumer(in *f*) *m* - dreamer.

träumerisch *adj* dreamy.

traumhaft *adj* (*phantastisch*) fantastic; (*wie im Traum*) dreamlike.

traurig *adj* sad; *Leben auch* unhappy; *Leistung, Rekord* pathetic, sorry; *Wetter* miserable.

Traurigkeit *f* sadness.

Trau-: ~**ring** *m* wedding ring; ~**schein** *m* marriage certificate.

Trauung *f* wedding.

Trauzeuge *m* witness (*at marriage ceremony*).

Treck *m* -**s** trek, trail; (*Leute*) train.

Treff *m* -**s** (*col*) (*Treffen*) meeting, get-together (*col*); (~**punkt**) haunt, rendezvous.

treffen *pret* **traf**, *ptp* **getroffen 1** *vt* (**a**) (*durch Schlag etc*) to hit (*an/in+dat* on, *in+acc* in); (*Blitz, Faust auch, Unglück*) to strike. **auf dem Photo bist du gut getroffen** (*col*) that's a good photo of you. (**b**) (*betreffen*) to hit, to affect. **er fühlte sich getroffen** he took it personally. (**c**) (*jdm begegnen*) to meet; (*an*~) to hit. (**d**) (*finden*) to hit upon, to find; (*lit, fig*) *Ton* to hit. (**e**) **es mit dem Wetter gut/schlecht** ~ to be lucky/unlucky

with the weather. (**f**) *Vereinbarung* to reach; *Entscheidung* to make, to take; *Maßnahmen* to take. **2** *vi* (**a**) (*Schlag, Schuß etc*) to hit. **nicht** ~ to miss. (**b**) *aux sein* (*stoßen*) **auf jdn/etw** ~ to meet sb/ sth. (**c**) (*verletzen*) to hurt. **3** *vr* (*zusammen*~) to meet. **4** *vr impers* **es trifft sich, daß** ... **it** (just) **happens that** ...; **das trifft sich gut/schlecht, daß** ... **it is convenient/inconvenient that** ...

Treffen *nt* - meeting; (*Sport, Mil*) encounter.

treffend *adj* apt; *Ähnlichkeit* striking.

Treffer *m* - hit; (*Tor*) goal; (*fig: Erfolg*) hit; (*Gewinnlos*) winner.

Treff-: ~**punkt** *m* meeting place; **t**~**sicher** *adj* accurate; *Urteil* sound.

Treibeis *nt* drift ice.

treiben *pret* **trieb**, *ptp* **getrieben 1** *vt* (**a**) (*lit, fig*) to drive; (*auf Treibjagd*) *Wild* to beat; *Teig* to make rise; (*fig: drängen*) to rush; (*an*~) to push. **jdn zum Wahnsinn** ~ to drive sb mad; **jdn zur Eile/ Arbeit** ~ to make sb hurry up/work; **die** ~**de Kraft** the driving force; **jdm den Schweiß/das Blut ins Gesicht** ~ to make sb sweat/blush. (**b**) *Geschäfte, Sport* to do; *Studien, Politik* to pursue; *Gewerbe* to carry on; *Unsinn* to be up to; *Aufwand* to create. **was treibst du?** what are you up to?; **Handel mit etw/jdm** ~ to trade in sth/with sb. (**c**) (*col*) **wenn du es weiter so treibst** ... if you carry on like that ...; **es toll** ~ to have a wild time; **es zu weit** ~ to go too far; **es mit jdm** ~ to have sex with sb. (**d**) *Blüten etc* to sprout; (*im Treibhaus*) to force. **2** *vi* (**a**) *aux sein* (*sich fortbewegen*) to drift. **sich** ~ **lassen** (*lit, fig*) to drift. (**b**) (*wachsen*) to sprout. (**c**) (*Hefe*) *Teig* to make dough *etc* rise. ~**de Medikamente** diuretics.

Treiben *nt* - (*Getriebe*) hustle and bustle; (*von Schneeflocken*) swirling.

Treiber *m* - (*Hunt*) beater; (*Vieh*~) drover.

Treib-: ~**gas** *nt* propellant; ~**haus** *nt* hothouse; ~**holz** *nt* driftwood; ~**jagd** *f* shoot (*in which game is sent up by beaters*); (*fig*) witchhunt; ~**mittel** *nt* (*in Sprühdosen*) propellant; (*Cook*) raising agent; ~**sand** *m* quicksand; ~**stoff** *m* fuel.

Trend *m* -**s** trend.

trennbar *adj* separable.

trennen 1 *vt* (**a**) to separate (*von* from); *Kopf, Glied etc* to sever; (*abmachen*) to detach (*von* from); *Aufgenähtes* to take off, to remove; *Saum, Naht* to undo; *Begriffe* to distinguish (between); (*nach Rasse, Geschlecht*) to segregate. **jetzt kann uns nichts mehr** ~ now nothing can ever come between us. (**b**) (*in Bestandteile zerlegen*) *Kleid* to take to pieces; *Wort* to split; (*Chem*) *Gemisch* to separate (out). **2** *vr* (*auseinandergehen*) to separate; (*Partner, Eheleute etc auch*) to split up; (*Abschied nehmen*) to part; (*Wege, Flüsse*) to divide. **sich von jdm/der Firma** ~ to leave sb/the firm; **die zwei Mannschaften trennten sich 2:2** the final score was 2:2; **sich von etw** ~ to part with sth; **hier** ~ **sich unsere Wege** (*fig*) now we must go our separate ways.

Trennschärfe *f* selectivity.

Trennung *f* separation; (*Abschied*) parting; (*in Teile*) division; (*von Wort*) division; (*Rassen*~, *Geschlechter*~) segregation.

Trenn(ungs)-: ~**strich** *m* hyphen; ~**wand** *f* partition (wall); ~**zeichen** *nt* hyphen.

trepp|auf *adv:* ~, **treppab** up and down stairs.

Treppe *f* -**n** stairs *pl*, staircase; (*im Freien*) steps *pl.* **eine** ~ a staircase, a flight of stairs/steps; **sie wohnt zwei** ~**n höher** she lives two flights up.

Treppen-: ~**absatz** *m* half-landing; ~**geländer** *nt* banister; ~**haus** *nt* stairwell; **im** ~**haus** on the stairs; ~**stufe** *f* step, stair.

Tresen *m* - (*Theke*) bar; (*Ladentisch*) counter.

Tresor *m* -**e** safe; (*Raum*) strongroom, vault.

Tret-: ~**auto** *nt* pedal car; ~**boot** *nt* pedal boat, pedalo.

treten *pret* **trat**, *ptp* **getreten 1** *vi* (**a**) **gegen etw**

~ to kick sth. **(b)** *aux sein* to step. **näher an etw** *(acc)* ~ to move *or* step closer to sth; **jdm auf die Füß** ~ to step *or* tread on sb's foot; **jdm auf die Füße** ~ *(fig)* to tread on sb's toes; **aufs Gas(pedal)** ~ to press the accelerator; *(col: schnell fahren)* to step on it *(col).* **(c) der Schweiß trat ihm auf die Stirn** sweat appeared on his forehead; **der Fluß trat über die Ufer** the river overflowed its banks. **(d)** *aux sein* **in den Streik** ~ to go on strike; **in den Stand der Ehe** ~ to enter into the state of matrimony. **2** *vt* to kick; *(Sport)* **Ecke, Freistoß** to take. **jdn ans Bein** ~ to kick sb on the leg; **jdn mit dem Fuß** ~ to kick sb.

Tret-: ~**mine** *f (Mil)* (anti-personnel) mine; ~**mühle** *f (lit, fig)* treadmill; **in der** ~**mühle sein** to be in a rut *(col);* ~**roller** *m* scooter.

treu 1 *adj* **Freund, Sohn, Kunde** *etc* loyal; **Hund, Gatte** *etc* faithful; **Abbild** true; *(~herzig)* trusting; **Miene** innocent. ~ **sein/bleiben** to be/ remain faithful to sb; **seinen Grundsätzen** ~ **bleiben** to stay true to one's principles. **2** *adv* faithfully; **sorgen** devotedly; *(~herzig)* trustingly; **ansehen** innocently.

Treu-: ~**bruch** *m* breach of faith; **t**~**brüchig** *adj* faithless, false; **t**~**doof** *adj (col)* naive.

Treue *f no pl siehe* **treu** faithfulness; *(eheliche ~)* faithfulness, fidelity.

Treu|eid *m* oath of allegiance.

Treueprämie *f* long-service bonus.

Treu-: ~**händer(in** *f)* *m* trustee; ~**handgesellschaft** *f* trust company; **t**~**herzig** *adj* trusting; **t**~**los** *adj* disloyal, faithless; **t**~**los an jdm handeln** to fail sb; ~**losigkeit** *f* disloyalty, faithlessness.

Triangel *m* - triangle.

Tribunal *nt* -**e** tribunal.

Tribüne *f* -**n** *(Redner~)* platform; *(Zuschauer~, Zuschauer)* stand; *(Haupt~)* grandstand.

Tribut *m* -**e** *(lit, fig)* tribute; *(Opfer)* toll.

Trichine *f* trichina.

Trichter *m* - funnel; *(Bomben~)* crater; *(von Trompete etc)* bell; *(von Hörgerät)* trumpet; *(von Lautsprecher)* cone; *(Einfüll~)* hopper. **auf den** ~ **kommen** *(col)* to catch on *(col).*

Trick *m* -**s** trick. **keine faulen** ~**s!** no funny business! *(col);* **das ist der ganze** ~ that's all there is to it; **der** ~ **dabei ist, ...** the trick is to ...; **jdm einen** ~ **verraten** to give sb a tip.

Trick-: ~**betrug** *m* confidence trick; ~**film** *m* trick film; *(Zeichen~)* cartoon (film); **t**~**reich** *adj (col)* tricky; *(raffiniert)* clever.

trieb *pret of* **treiben**.

Trieb *m* -**e** **(a)** *(Psych, Natur~)* drive; *(Drang, Verlangen)* urge; *(Neigung, Hang)* inclination; *(Selbsterhaltungs~)* instinct. **(b)** *(Bot)* shoot.

Trieb-: ~**feder** *f (fig)* motivating force *(gen* behind); **t**~**haft** *adj* **Handlungen** compulsive; **sie ist ein t**~**hafter Mensch** she is ruled by her physical desires; ~**kraft** *f (Mech)* motive power; *(fig)* driving force; ~**leben** *nt (Geschlechtsleben)* sex life; ~**rad** *nt* driving wheel; ~**täter** *m* sexual offender; ~**wagen** *m (Rail)* railcar; ~**werk** *nt* power plant; *(in Uhr)* mechanism.

triefen *vi* to be dripping wet; *(Nase)* to run; *(Auge)* to water. ~ **vor** to be dripping with; *(fig pej)* to gush with; ~**d** soaking (wet).

triezen *vt (col)* **jdn** ~ to pester sb; *(schuften lassen)* to drive sb hard.

triftig *adj* cogent.

Trigonometrie *adj* trigonometry.

Trikolore *f* -**n** tricolour *(Brit),* tricolor *(US).*

Trikot [tri'ko:, 'triko] *nt* -**s** *(Hemd)* shirt, jersey.

Triller *m* - *(Mus)* trill.

trillern *vti* to warble, to trill.

Trillerpfeife *f* (pea-)whistle.

Trillion *f* -**en** trillion *(Brit),* quintillion *(US).*

Trilogie *f* trilogy.

Trimester *nt* - term.

Trimm-: ~**-Aktion** *f* keep-fit campaign; ~**-dich-Gerät** *nt* keep-fit apparatus; ~**-dich-Pfad** *m* keep-fit trail.

trimmen 1 *vt* **Hund, Schiff, Flugzeug** to trim; *(col)* **Mensch, Tier** to teach, to train. **2** *vr* to do keep-fit (exercises). **trimm dich durch Sport** keep fit with sport.

trinkbar *adj* drinkable.

trinken *pret* **trank**, *ptp* **getrunken** *vti* to drink; **ein Bier, Tasse Tee, Flasche Wein** *auch* to have. **er trinkt gern einen** *(col)* he likes his drink; **jdm zu** ~ **geben** to give sb something to drink; **auf jdn/etw** ~ to drink to sb/to sth.

Trinker(in *f)* *m* - drinker.

Trinker|anstalt *f* detoxification centre *(Brit) or* center *(US).*

Trink-: t~**fest** *adj* **ich bin nicht sehr t**~**fest** I can't hold my drink very well; ~**geld** *nt* tip; **jdm** ~**geld geben** to tip sb, to give sb a tip; ~**halle** *f (Kiosk)* refreshment kiosk; ~**halm** *m* drinking straw; ~**milch** *f* milk; ~**schokolade** *f* drinking chocolate; ~**spruch** *m* toast; ~**wasser** *nt* drinking water.

Triole *f* -**n** *(Mus)* triplet.

trippeln *vi aux haben or (bei Richtungsangabe) sein* to trip; *(Kind, alte Dame)* to toddle.

Tripper *m* - gonorrhoea *no art (Brit),* gonorrhea *no art (US).*

trist *adj* dreary, dismal; **Farbe** dull.

Tritt *m* -**e (a)** *(Schritt)* step. **im** ~ **marschieren/**~ **halten** to march/keep in step. **(b)** *(Fuß~)* kick. **jdm einen** ~ **geben** to give sb a kick, to kick sb; *(fig) (entlassen etc)* to kick sb out *(col); (col: anstacheln)* to give sb a kick up the backside *(col).* **(c)** *(bei ~leiter, Stufe)* step; *(Gestell)* steps *pl.*

Tritt-: ~**brett** *nt (Auto)* running board; ~**brettfahrer** *m (fig col)* free-rider *(col);* **er ist ein politischer** ~**brettfahrer** he has jumped on the political bandwagon; ~**leiter** *f* stepladder.

Triumphbogen *m* triumphal arch.

triumphieren* *vi (frohlocken)* to rejoice, to exult. **über jdn/etw** ~ *(geh)* to triumph over sb/sth.

Triumphzug *m* triumphal procession.

trivial [tri'via:l] *adj* trivial.

Trivialliteratur [tri'via:l-] *f* light fiction.

trocken *adj (lit, fig)* dry. **da bleibt kein Auge** ~ everyone is moved to tears; ~ **aufbewahren/lagern** to keep/store in a dry place; **sich** ~ **rasieren** to use an electric razor; **auf dem** ~**en sitzen** *(col)* to be in a tight spot *(col).*

Trocken-: ~**automat** *m* tumble dryer; ~**boden** *m* drying room *(in attic);* ~**dock** *nt* dry dock; ~**futter** *nt* dried food; ~**haube** *f* (salon) hairdryer.

Trockenheit *f (lit, fig)* dryness; *(Dürre)* drought.

Trocken-: ~**kurs** *m (Ski)* ski training course using dry slopes; **t**~**legen** *vt sep* **(a) Baby** to change; **(b) Sumpf** to drain; ~**milch** *f* dried milk; ~**zeit** *f (Jahreszeit)* dry season.

trocknen 1 *vt* to dry. **2** *vi aux sein* to dry.

Troddel *f* -**n** tassel.

Trödel *m no pl (col)* junk.

Trödelmarkt *m (col)* flea market.

trödeln *vi* to dawdle.

Trödler *m* - **(a)** *(Händler)* junk dealer. **(b)** *(col: langsamer Mensch)* dawdler.

Trog *m* -̈**e** trough; *(Wasch~)* tub.

trog *pret of* **trügen**.

trollen *vr (col)* to push off *(col).*

Trommel *f* -**n** *(Mus, Tech)* drum. **die** ~ **rühren** *(fig col)* to drum up support.

Trommel-: ~**bremse** *f* drum brake; ~**fell** *nt* eardrum; ~**feuer** *nt* drumfire, heavy barrage.

trommeln 1 *vi* to drum; *(Regen)* to beat (down). **mit den Fingern** ~ to drum one's fingers. **2** *vt* **Marsch, Lied** to play on the drum/drums.

Trommel-: ~**schlag** *m* drum beat; *(das Trommeln)* drumming; ~**stöcke** *pl* drumsticks *pl.*

Trommler(in *f)* *m* - drummer.

Trompete f -n trumpet.

trompeten* 1 vi to trumpet. 2 vt Marsch to play on the trumpet.

Trompeter(in f) m - trumpeter.

Tropen pl tropics pl.

Tropen- in cpds tropical; ~helm m pith-helmet, topee.

Tropf m ⁼e (col) (a) (Schelm) rogue, rascal. armer ~ poor devil. (b) no pl (Infusion) drip (col).

tröpfeln 1 vi (Leitung, aux sein: Flüssigkeit) to drip; (Nase) to run. 2 vt to drip.

tropfen vi to drip; (Nase) to run.

Tropfen m - drop; (Schweiß~ auch) bead; (fallender ~) drip; (col: kleine Menge) drop. ~ pl (Medizin) drops; ein guter or edler ~ (col) a good wine; bis auf den letzten ~ to the last drop; ein ~ auf den heißen Stein (fig col) a drop in the ocean.

Tropf-: t~naß adj dripping wet; ~steinhöhle f cave with stalactites/stalagmites.

Trophäe [troˈfɛːə] f -n trophy.

tropisch adj tropical.

Trost m no pl consolation, comfort. ein ~, daß jetzt alles vorbei ist it is a relief that everything is over; das ist ein schwacher (iro) ~ some comfort that is!

trösten vt to comfort. sich/jdn über etw (acc) ~ to get over sth/to help sb to get over sth.

tröstlich adj cheering, comforting.

trostlos adj hopeless; Jugend, Verhältnisse miserable, wretched; (öde, trist) dreary.

Trost-: ~pflaster nt consolation; ~preis m consolation prize.

Trott m no pl (slow) trot; (fig) routine. im ~ at a (slow) trot.

Trottel m - (col) idiot, dope (col).

trotten vi aux sein to trot along.

trotz prep+gen (geh) or +dat (col) in spite of, despite.

Trotz m no pl defiance; (trotziges Verhalten) contrariness. jdm/einer Sache zum ~ in defiance of sb/sth.

Trotz|alter nt defiant age.

trotzdem adv nevertheless. (und) ich mache das ~! I'll do it all the same.

trotzen vi (a)+dat to defy; der Kälte, Klima etc to withstand; der Gefahr to brave. (b) (trotzig sein) to be awkward.

trotzig adj defiant; Kind etc difficult, awkward.

Trotz-: ~kopf m (col) contrary so-and-so (col); ~reaktion f act of defiance.

trüb(e) adj (a) dull; Flüssigkeit cloudy; Sonne, Licht dim. im ~en fischen (col) to fish in troubled waters. (b) (fig: bedrückend, unerfreulich) Zeiten bleak; Erfahrung grim. ~e Tasse (col) drip (col).

Trubel m no pl hurly-burly.

trüben 1 vt (a) Flüssigkeit to make cloudy; Glas, Metall to dull; Blick to cloud. sie sieht aus, als könnte sie kein Wässerlein ~ (col) she looks as if butter wouldn't melt in her mouth. (b) (fig) Glück, Verhältnis to spoil; Bewußtsein, Verstand to dull. 2 vr (Flüssigkeit) to go cloudy; (Spiegel, Metall) to become dull; (geh) (Verstand) to become dulled; (Augen) to dim; (Himmel) to cloud over; (Glück, Freude) to be marred.

Trüb-: ~sal f gloom; ~sal blasen (col) to mope; t~selig adj gloomy; Behausung, Wetter miserable; ~sinn m no pl gloom, melancholy.

trudeln vi aux sein or haben (Aviat) to spin.

Trüffel¹ f -n (Pilz) truffle.

Trüffel² m - truffle.

Trug m no pl (liter) deception; (der Sinne) illusion.

trug pret of tragen.

trügen pret trog, ptp getrogen 1 vt to deceive. wenn mich nicht alles trügt unless I am very much mistaken. 2 vi to be deceptive.

trügerisch adj (irreführend) deceptive.

Trugschluß m fallacy.

Truhe f -n chest.

Trümmer pl rubble sing; (Ruinen, fig: von Glück etc) ruins pl; (von Schiff, Flugzeug etc) wreckage sing; (Überreste) remnants pl. etw in ~ schlagen to smash sth to pieces.

Trümmerfeld nt expanse of rubble/ruins; (fig) scene of devastation.

Trumpf m -ë (Cards) (~karte, auch fig) trump card; (Farbe) trumps pl. ~ sein to be trumps; (fig col: modisch sein) to be in (col); den ~ in der Hand haben/aus der Hand geben (fig) to hold the/throw away one's trump card.

trumpfen 1 vt to trump. 2 vi to play a trump (card).

Trumpf-: ~farbe f trumps pl; ~karte f trump (card).

Trunk m ⁼e (a) (old, liter) draught (old, liter). (b) dem ~ verfallen sein to have taken to drink.

Trunken-: ~bold m -e (pej) drunkard; ~heit f drunkenness; ~heit am Steuer drunken driving.

Trunksucht f alcoholism.

Trupp m -s (Einheit) group; (Mil) squad.

Truppe f -n (a) (Mil) army, troops pl; (Panzer~ etc) corps sing. ~n pl troops. nicht von der schnellen ~ sein (col) to be slow. (b) (Künstler~) troupe, company.

Truppen-: ~gattung f corps sing; ~übung f field exercise; ~übungsplatz m military training area.

Trut-: ~hahn m turkey(cock); ~henne f turkey(hen); ~huhn nt usu pl turkey.

Tschechе m (wk) -n, -n, **Tschechin** f Czech.

tschechisch adj Czech.

Tschechoslowake m (wk) -n, -n, **Tschechoslowakin** f Czechoslovak.

Tschechoslowakei f die ~ Czechoslovakia.

tschüs interj (col) cheerio (Brit col), so long (col).

Tsetsefliege f tsetse fly.

TU [teːˈʔuː] f - = **Technische Universität.**

Tube f -n tube. auf die ~ drücken (col) to get a move on (col).

Tuberkulose f -n tuberculosis.

tuberkulosekrank adj tubercular.

Tuch nt ⁼er (a) cloth; (Hals~, Kopf~) scarf. das wirkt wie ein rotes ~ auf ihn it's like a red rag to a bull. (b) pl -e (old: Stoff) cloth.

Tuch-: ~fabrik f textile factory; ~fühlung f physical contact; ~händler m cloth merchant; ~macher m clothworker.

tüchtig 1 adj (a) (fähig) competent (in+dat at); (fleißig) efficient. etwas T~es lernen/werden (col) to get a proper training/job; ~, ~! not bad! (b) (col: groß) Portion big. 2 adv (a) (fleißig, fest) hard; essen heartily. hilf ~ mit give us a hand. (b) (col: sehr) good and proper (col). ~ regnen to pelt down (col); ~ zulangen to tuck in (col).

Tüchtigkeit f (Fähigkeit) competence; (von Arbeiter etc) efficiency.

Tücke f -n (a) (no pl: Bosheit) malice, spite. (b) (Gefahr) danger, peril; (von Krankheit) perniciousness. voller ~n stecken to be difficult; (gefährlich) to be treacherous; seine ~n haben (Maschine etc) to be temperamental. (c) (des Schicksals) vagary usu pl.

tückisch adj Mensch malicious, spiteful;Berge, Strom treacherous; Krankheit pernicious.

tüfteln vi (col) to puzzle; (basteln) to fiddle about (col). an etw (dat) ~ to fiddle about with sth; (geistig) to puzzle over sth.

Tüftler(in f) m - (col) person who likes doing fiddly or finicky things.

Tugend f -en virtue.

Tugend-: ~bold m -e (pej) paragon of virtue; t~haft adj virtuous.

Tüll m -e tulle; (für Gardinen) net.

Tulpe f -n (Bot) tulip; (Glas) tulip glass.

tummeln vr (a) to romp (about). (b) (sich beeilen) to hurry.

Tummelplatz m play area; (fig) hotbed.

Tümmler *m* - (bottle-nosed) dolphin.
Tumor *m* **-en** [tu'moːrən] tumour *(Brit)*, tumor *(US)*.
Tümpel *m* - pond.
Tumult *m* **-e** commotion.
tun *pret* **tat,** *ptp* **getan 1** *vt* **(a)** to do; *Blick, Schritt* to take. **was ~?** what shall we do?; **du kannst ~ und lassen, was du willst** you can do as you please; **tu, was du nicht lassen kannst** well, if you must; **damit ist es noch nicht getan** and that's not all; **etwas gegen etw ~** to do something about sth; **Sie müssen etwas für sich ~** you should treat yourself; *(sich schonen)* you should take care of yourself; **so etwas tut man nicht!** that's just not done; **es tat einen Knall** there was a bang; **das hat nichts mit ihm zu ~** that is nothing to do with him; **ich habe mit mir (selbst) genug zu ~** I have enough problems of my own; **es mit jdm zu ~ bekommen** *(col)* to get into trouble with sb; **er hat es mit der Leber zu ~** *(col)* he has liver trouble; **was tut's?** what difference does it make?; **jdm etwas ~** to do something to sb *(stärker)* to harm *or* hurt sb.
(b) *(col: an bestimmten Ort legen)* to put. **etw in die Tasche ~** to put sth in one's pocket.
(c) *(col: funktionieren)* **die Uhr tut es nicht mehr** this watch has had it *(col)*; **das Radio tut es wieder** the radio is going again.
2 *vr (geschehen)* **es tut sich etwas** there is something happening; **hat sich in dieser Hinsicht schon etwas getan?** has anything been done about this?
3 *vi* **(a) zu~ haben** *(beschäftigt sein)* to be busy, to have work to do; **in der Stadt zu ~ haben** to have things to do in town; **mit jdm zu ~ haben** to deal with sb. **(b)** *(sich benehmen)* to act. **so ~, als ob...** to pretend that ...; **tust du nur so dumm?** are you just acting stupid?; **sie tut nur so** she's only pretending. **(c) Sie täten gut daran, früh zu kommen** you would do well to come early.
Tünche *f* **-n** whitewash; *(fig)* veneer.
tünchen *vt* to whitewash.
Tunesien [-iən] *nt* Tunisia.
Tunichtgut *m* **-e** good-for-nothing.
Tunke *f* **-n** sauce; *(Braten~)* gravy.
tunken *vt* to dip; *(stippen)* to dunk *(col)*; **jdn** to duck.
tunlichst *adv* if possible. **ich werde es ~ vermeiden, ihm meine Meinung zu sagen** I'll do my best to avoid telling him what I think.
Tunnel *m* - *or* **-s** tunnel.
Tunte *f* **-n** *(col)* fairy *(pej col)*.
Tüpfel *m or nt* **-, Tüpfelchen** *nt* dot.
tupfen *vt* to dab. **getupft** spotted.
Tupfen *m* - spot; *(klein)* dot.
Tupfer *m* - swab.
Tür *f* **-en** door; *(Garten~)* gate. **in der ~** in the doorway; **an die ~ gehen** to answer the door; **Weihnachten steht vor der ~** Christmas is just around the corner; **jdn vor die ~ setzen** *(col)* to throw sb out; **jdm die ~ weisen** to show sb the door; **ein jeder kehre vor seiner ~** *(prov)* everyone should set his own house in order; **mit der ~ ins Haus fallen** *(col)* to blurt it/things out; **zwischen ~ und Angel** in passing.
Tür|angel *f* (door) hinge.
Turban *m* **-e** turban.
Turbine *f* turbine.
Turbinenflugzeug *nt* turbo-jet.
Turbomotor *m* turbocharged engine.
turbulent *adj* turbulent.
Turbulenz *f* turbulence *no pl.*
Tür-: **~drücker** *m* doorknob; *(col: Öffner)* buzzer; **~flügel** *m* door *(of a pair of doors)*.
Türke *m* *(wk)* **-n, -n, Türkin** *f* Turk.
Türkei *f* **die ~** Turkey.
türken *vt* *(col) Papiere, Zahlen* to fiddle.

Türkis *m* **-e** *(Edelstein)* turquoise.
türkis *adj* turquoise.
türkisch *adj* Turkish.
Tür-: **~klinke** *f* door handle; **~klopfer** *m* doorknocker.
Turm *m* **-e (a)** tower; *(spitzer Kirch~)* spire. **(b)** *(Chess)* castle, rook.
türmen 1 *vt* to pile up. **2** *vr* to pile up; *(Wolken)* to build up; *(Wellen)* to tower up. **3** *vi aux sein (col: davonlaufen)* to run off.
Turm-: **~falke** *m* kestrel; **~schwalbe** *f* swift; **~uhr** *f* clock (on a/the tower); *(Kirch~)* church clock.
Turnanzug *m* gym costume.
turnen *vi* **(a)** to do gymnastics; *(Sch)* to do gym. **am Reck ~** to do exercises on the horizontal bar. **(b)** *aux sein (herumklettern)* to climb about; *(Kind)* to romp.
Turnen *nt no pl* gymnastics *sing.*
Turner(in *f)* *m* - gymnast.
Turn-: **~fest** *nt* gymnastics display; *(von Schule)* sports day; **~gerät** *nt* (piece of) gymnastic equipment; **~halle** *f* gym(nasium); **~hemd** *nt* gym shirt; **~hose** *f* gym shorts *pl.*
Turnier *nt* **-e** tournament; *(Tanz~)* competition; *(Reit~)* show.
Turnierpferd *nt* show horse.
Turn-: **~lehrer** *m* gym teacher; **~schuh** *m* gym shoe; **~stunde** *f* gym lesson; **~übung** *f* gymnastic exercise.
Turnus *m* **-se** rota. **im (regelmäßigen) ~** in rotation.
Turn-: **~verein** *m* gymnastics club; **~zeug** *nt* gym kit.
Tür-: **~öffner** *m* buzzer; **~pfosten** *m* doorpost; **~rahmen** *m* doorframe; **~schild** *nt* doorplate; **~schloß** *nt* door lock; **~schwelle** *f* threshold.
Turteltaube *f* *(lit, fig col)* turtle-dove.
Türvorleger *m* doormat.
Tusch *m* **-e** *(Mus)* flourish.
Tusche *f* **-n** *(Auszieh~)* Indian ink; *(~farbe)* water colour *(Brit)* or color *(US)*.
tuscheln *vti* to whisper. **hinter seinem Rücken über jdn ~** to talk about sb behind his/her back.
tuschen *vt* to draw in Indian ink. **sich** *(dat)* **die Wimpern ~** to put one's mascara on.
Tusch-: **~farbe** *f* water colour *(Brit)* or color *(US)*; **~zeichnung** *f* pen-and-ink drawing.
Tüte *f* **-n** bag; *(Eis~)* cornet, cone; *(col: für Alkoholtest)* breathalyzer. **in die ~ blasen** *(col)* to be breathalyzed; **~n kleben** *(col)* to be in clink *(col)*; **das kommt nicht in die ~!** *(col)* no way! *(col)*.
tuten *vti* to toot; *(Schiff)* to sound its horn. **von T~ und Blasen keine Ahnung haben** *(col)* not to have a clue *(col)*.
TÜV [tyf] *m* **-s** = **Technischer Überwachungs-Verein** ≈ MOT *(Brit)*. **das Auto ist durch den ~ gekommen** the car passed its MOT.
Twen *m* **-s** *person in his/her twenties.*
Typ *n* **-en** type; *(von Auto auch)* model; *(col: Mensch)* person, character; *(col: Mann, Freund)* guy *(col)*. **er ist nicht mein ~** *(col)* he's not my type *(col)*; **dein ~ wird verlangt** *(col)* you're wanted; **dein ~ ist nicht gefragt** *(col)* you're not wanted around here.
Type *f* **-n (a)** *(Druckbuchstabe)* character. **~n** *(Schrift)* type *sing;* **~n gießen** to set type. **(b)** *(col: Mensch)* character.
Typhus *m no pl* typhoid (fever).
Typhuskranke(r) *mf* typhoid case.
typisch *adj* typical *(für of)*. **~ deutsch** typically German.
Typographie *f* typography.
Tyrann(in *f)* *m* *(wk)* **-en, -en** tyrant.
Tyrannei *f* tyranny.
tyrannisch *adj* tyrannical.
tyrannisieren* *vt* to tyrannize.

U

U, u [uː] *nt* -, - U, u.
u. = und.
u.a. = **und andere(s); unter anderem/anderen.**
U-Bahn ['uː] *f* underground *(Brit)*, subway *(US)*; *(in London)* tube.
U-Bahnhof ['uː] *m* underground *etc* station.
übel 1 *adj* bad; *Erkältung etc auch* nasty; *(moralisch auch)* wicked, evil. **er war übler Laune** he was in a bad mood; **das ist eine üble Sache!** it's a bad business; **in übler** *or* **~ster Weise** in a most unpleasant way; **mir wird ~** I feel ill *or* sick. **2** *adv* badly. **etw ~ aufnehmen** to take sth badly; **das schmeckt gar nicht so ~** it doesn't taste so bad; **ich hätte nicht ~ Lust, jetzt nach Paris zu fahren** I wouldn't mind going to Paris now.
Übel *nt* - evil. **ein notwendiges/das kleinere ~** a necessary/the lesser evil; **das alte ~** the old trouble; **von ~ sein** to be a bad thing, to be bad; **zu allem ~ ...** to make matters worse ...
übelgelaunt *adj attr* sullen, morose.
Übelkeit *f (lit, fig)* nausea.
Übel-: **ü~launig** *adj* ill-tempered; **ü~nehmen** *vt sep irreg* **(jdm) etw ü~nehmen** to take sth amiss; **ü~riechend** *adj* foul-smelling, evil-smelling; **~täter** *m (geh)* wrongdoer.
üben *vtir* to practise *(Brit)*, to practice *(US)*; *(Mil)* to drill; *Gedächtnis, Muskeln etc* to exercise. **mit geübtem Auge** with a practised eye; **Kritik an etw** *(dat)* **~** to criticize sth; **sich in etw** *(dat)* **~** to practise sth.
über 1 *prep* **(a)**+*acc (räumlich)* over; *(quer ~ auch)* across; *(weiter als)* beyond. **er lachte ~ das ganze Gesicht** he was beaming all over his face.
(b)+*dat (räumlich) (Lage, Standort)* over, above; *(jenseits)* over, across. **zwei Grad ~ Null** two degrees above zero; **~ jdm stehen** *(fig)* to be over *or* above sb.
(c)+*dat (zeitlich: bei, während)* over. **~ der Arbeit einschlafen** to fall asleep over one's work.
(d)+*acc* **Macht ~ jdn haben** to have power over sb; **sie liebt ihn ~ alles** she loves him more than anything; **das geht mir ~ den Verstand** that's beyond my understanding.
(e)+*acc (vermittels, auf dem Wege ~)* via. **die Nummer erfährt man ~ die Auskunft** you'll get the number from *or* through *or* via directory enquiries; **nach Köln ~ Aachen** to Cologne via Aachen.
(f)+*acc (zeitlich)* over. **~ Weihnachten** over Christmas; **den ganzen Sommer ~** all summer long; **~ Wochen** for weeks on end; **die ganze Zeit ~** all the time; **~ kurz oder lang** sooner or later.
(g)+*acc (bei Zahlenangaben)* **ein Scheck ~ DM 20** a cheque for 20 DM; **Kinder ~ 14 Jahre** children over 14 years *or* of 14 and over.
(h)+*acc (betreffend)* about. **ein Buch ~ ...** a book about *or* on ...; **~ jdn/etw lachen** to laugh about *or* at sb/sth; **sich ~ etw freuen/ärgern** to be pleased/angry about *or* at sth.
(i)+*acc (steigernd)* **Fehler ~ Fehler** mistake upon *or* after mistake.
2 *adv* **~ und ~** all over; **er wurde ~ und ~ rot** he went red all over.
über|all *adv* everywhere. **~ wo wherever; ~**

Bescheid wissen *(wissensmäßig)* to have a wide-ranging knowledge; **es ist ~ dasselbe** it's the same wherever you go.
über|all-: **~her** *adv* from all over; **~hin** *adv* everywhere.
Über-: **~angebot** *nt* surplus *(an+dat* of); **ü~ängstlich** *adj* overanxious; **ü~anstrengen*** *insep* **1** *vt* to overstrain; *Kräfte* to overtax; *Augen* to strain; **2** *vr* to overstrain oneself; **~anstrengung** *f* overexertion; **eine ~anstrengung der Nerven/Augen** a strain on the nerves/eyes; **ü~arbeiten*** *insep* **1** *vt* to rework; **in einer ü~arbeiteten Fassung** published in a revised edition; **2** *vr* to overwork; **~arbeitung** *f no pl* **(a)** revision; **(b)** *(~anstrengung)* overwork; **ü~aus** *adv* extremely; **ü~backen*** *vt insep irreg* to put in the oven/under the grill; **ü~backene Käseschnitten** cheese on toast.
Überbau *m -e (Build, Philos)* superstructure.
überbauen* *vt insep* to build over; *(mit einem Dach)* to build a roof over.
Über-: **ü~beanspruchen*** *vt insep* **(a)** *Menschen, Körper, Maschine* to overtax; **(arbeitsmäßig) ü~beansprucht sein** to be overworked; **(b)** *Einrichtungen, Dienste* to overburden; **ü~belegen*** *vt insep usu ptp* to overcrowd; *Kursus, Fach etc* to oversubscribe; **ü~belichten*** *vt insep (Phot)* to overexpose; **~beschäftigung** *f* overemployment; **ü~besetzt** *adj Abteilung* overstaffed; **ü~betonen*** *vt insep (fig)* to overemphasize; **ü~betrieblich** *adj* industry-wide; **~bevölkerung** *f* overpopulation; **ü~bewerten*** *vt insep (lit)* to overvalue; *(fig auch)* to overrate; *Schulleistung etc* to mark too high; *Äußerungen* to attach too much importance to; **~bezahlung** *f* overpayment; **ü~bieten*** *insep irreg* **1** *vt (bei Auktion)* to outbid *(um* by); *(fig)* to outdo; *Leistung, Rekord* to beat; **das ist kaum noch zu ü~bieten** *(Frechheit etc)* it's outrageous; **2** *vr* **sich ~ etw** *(dat)* **(gegenseitig) ü~bieten** to vie with each other in sth; **~bleibsel** *nt* - remnant; *(Speiserest)* leftovers *pl*; *(Brauch, Angewohnheit etc)* survival, hangover.
Überblick *m (über+acc* of) **(a)** *(freie Sicht)* view. **(b)** *(Einblick)* overview. **er hat keinen ~** he has no overall picture; **den ~ verlieren** to lose track (of things). **(c)** *(Abriß)* survey; *(Übersicht)* synopsis, summary. **sich** *(dat)* **einen ~ verschaffen** to get a general idea.
überblicken* *vt insep* **(a)** *(lit)* Platz, Stadt to overlook. **(b)** *(fig)* to see; *Lage etc auch* to grasp.
überbraten* *vt insep irreg (Cook)* to fry lightly.
überbringen* *vt insep irreg* **jdm etw ~** to bring sb sth.
Überbringer(in *f)* *m* - bringer; *(von Scheck)* bearer.
überbrücken* *vt insep Kluft, Zeitraum* to bridge; *Krisenzeiten* to get over; *Gegensätze* to reconcile.
Überbrückung *f* **100 Mark zur ~** 100 marks to tide me/him *etc* over.
Überbrückungskredit *m* bridging loan.
Über-: **ü~dachen*** *vt insep* to cover; **ü~dauern*** *vt insep* to survive; **~decke** *f* bedspread; **ü~decken[1]** *vt sep* to cover up *or* over; *(col) Tischtuch* to put on; **ü~decken[2]*** *vt insep Riß, Geschmack* to cover up; **ü~dehnen*** *vt insep Muskel**

427

überdies etc to strain; *Gummi*, *(fig)* *Begriff* to over-
stretch; **ü~denken*** *vt insep irreg* to think over.
überdies *adv (geh) (außerdem)* moreover; *(ohnehin)* anyway.
Über-: **ü~dimensional** *adj* colossal, oversize;
~dosis *f* overdose, OD *(col); (zu große Zumessung)*
excessive amount; **ü~drehen*** *vt insep Uhr etc* to
overwind; *Gewinde* to strip; **~druck** *m*, *pl*
~drücke *(Tech)* excess pressure *no pl*.
Überdruß *m no pl (Übersättigung)* surfeit
(an+dat of); (Widerwille) aversion *(an +dat* to).
bis zum ~ ad nauseam.
überdrüssig *adj jds/einer Sache (gen) ~* **sein/
werden** to be/grow weary of sb/sth.
über-: **~durchschnittlich 1** *adj* above-average;
2 *adv* exceptionally; **~eifrig** *adj* overzealous;
~eignen* *vt insep (geh)* **jdm etw ~eignen** to
make sth over to sb; **~eilen*** *vtr insep* to rush;
~eilen Sie nichts! don't rush things!; **~eilt** *adj*
hasty.
über|einander *adv* **(a)** *(räumlich)* on top of each
other; *hängen* one above the other. **(b)** *reden etc*
about each other.
über|einander-: **~legen** *vt sep* to put one on top
of the other; **~liegen** *vi sep irreg* to lie on top of
each other; **~schlagen** *vt sep irreg* **die Beine
~schlagen** to cross one's legs.
über|einkommen *vi sep irreg aux sein* to agree.
Über|einkunft *f* **~e** agreement. **eine ~ treffen/
erzielen** to make/reach an agreement.
über|einstimmen *vi sep* to agree; *(Angaben,
Meßwerte etc)* to tally; *(Farben, Stile etc)* to match;
(mit Tatsachen) to fit. **mit jdm in etw** *(dat)* **~** to
agree with sb on sth.
über|einstimmend 1 *adj* corresponding; *Mei-
nungen* concurring; *Farben* matching. **nach ~en
Meldungen** according to all reports. **2** *adv* **alle
erklärten ~, daß** ... everybody agreed that ...
Über|einstimmung *f* correspondence, agree-
ment; *(von Meinung)* agreement. **zwei Dinge in ~
bringen** to bring two things into line; **darin besteht bei allen Beteiligten ~** all parties involved
are agreed on that; **in ~ mit jdm/etw** in agreement with sb/in accordance with sth.
über-: **~empfindlich** *adj (gegen* to) oversensitive, hypersensitive *(auch Med);* **~erfüllen*** *vt
insep Norm, Soll* to exceed *(um* by); **~ernähren***
vt insep to overfeed; **~essen**[1] *vt sep irreg* **sich
(dat) etw ~essen** to grow sick of sth; **~essen**[2]
pret **~aß**, *ptp* **~gessen** *vr insep* to overeat; **sich
an Käse ~essen** to eat too much cheese.
überfahren[1] *sep irreg* **1** *vt (mit Boot etc)* to take *or*
ferry across. **2** *vi aux sein* to cross over.
überfahren[2]* *vt insep irreg* **(a)** *jdn, Tier* to run
over, to knock down. **(b)** *(hinwegfahren über)* to
go *or* drive over. **(c)** *Ampel* to jump.
Überfahrt *f* crossing.
Überfall *m* attack *(auf+acc* on); *(auf offener
Straße auch)* mugging *(auf+acc* of); *(auf Bank etc)*
raid *(auf+acc* on).
überfallen* *vt insep irreg* **(a)** to attack; *(auf offener Straße auch)* to mug; *Bank, Lager* to raid. **(b)**
(fig geh: Gefühle, Müdigkeit) to come over.
Über-: **ü~fällig** *adj* overdue *usu pred;* **~fallkom-
mando** *nt* flying squad; **ü~fliegen*** *vt insep irreg*
(a) to fly over, to overfly; **(b)** *(flüchtig ansehen)*
Buch etc to take a quick look at; **ü~fließen** *vi sep
irreg aux sein (Gefäß)* to overflow; *(fig: vor Dank
etc auch)* to gush *(vor+dat* with); **ü~flügeln*** *vt
insep* to outdo.
Überfluß *m no pl* abundance *(an +dat* of); *(Luxus)*
affluence. **Arbeit im ~** plenty of work; **zu allem
or zum ~** *(unnötigerweise)* superfluously; *(obendrein)* to crown it all *(col).*
überflüssig *adj* superfluous; *(frei, entbehrlich)*
spare; *(unnötig)* unnecessary; *(zwecklos)* useless.
überflüssigerweise *adv* superfluously.
Über-: **ü~fluten*** *vt insep (lit, fig)* to flood; *(fig*

auch) to inundate; **ü~fordern*** *vt insep* to
overtax; *jdn auch* to ask too much of; **ü~fragt** *adj
pred* stumped; **da bin ich ü~fragt** there you've
got me; **ü~führen**[1] *vt sep* to transfer; *Wagen* to
drive; **ü~führen**[2]* *vt insep* **(a)** *siehe* **ü~führen**[1];
(b) *Täter* to convict *(gen* of), to find guilty *(gen*
of); **(c) einen Fluß mit einer Brücke ü~führen** to
build a bridge over a river; **~führung** *f* **(a)** transportation; **(b)** *no pl (Jur)* conviction; **(c)** *(Brücke
über Straße etc)* bridge *(auch Rail)*, overpass;
(Fußgänger~) footbridge; **ü~füllt** *adj* overcrowded; *Kurs* oversubscribed; *(Comm) Lager*
overstocked; **ü~füttern*** *vt insep* to overfeed.
Übergabe *f no pl* handing over *no pl; (von Neubau)*
opening; *(Mil)* surrender.
Übergang *m* **(a)** *(das Überqueren)* crossing. **(b)**
(Fußgänger~) crossing, crosswalk *(US)*;
(Brücke) footbridge; *(Rail)* level *(Brit) or*
grade *(US)* crossing. **(c)** *(fig: Wechsel)* transition.
Übergangs-: **ü~los** *adj* without a transition;
~zeit *f* transitional period.
übergeben* *insep irreg* **1** *vt* to hand over *(jdm* to
sb); *(Mil auch)* to surrender. **eine Straße dem
Verkehr ~** to open a road to traffic. **2** *vr (sich
erbrechen)* to vomit, to be sick *(Brit).*
übergehen[1] *vi sep irreg aux sein* **(a) in etw** *(acc)* **~**
to turn *or* change into sth; *(Farben)* to merge into
sth; **in jds Besitz** *(acc)* **~** to become sb's property. **(b) auf jdn ~** *(geerbt, übernommen werden)*
to pass to sb. **(c) zu jdm ~** *(überwechseln)* to go
over to sb.
übergehen[2]* *vt insep irreg jdn* to pass over; *Einwände etc auch* to ignore.
Über-: **ü~geordnet** *adj Behörde* higher; **ü~ge-
schnappt** *adj (col)* crazy; **~gewicht** *nt* overweight; *(fig)* predominance; **~gewicht haben** to
be overweight; **ü~gießen*** *vt insep irreg* to pour
over; *jdn* to douse; *Braten* to baste; **jdn/sich
mit etw ü~gießen** to pour sth over sb/oneself;
ü~glücklich *adj* overjoyed; **ü~greifen** *vi sep
irreg (auf Rechte etc)* to encroach *(auf+acc* on);
(Feuer, Streik, Krankheit etc) to spread *(auf
+acc* to); **ineinander ü~greifen** to overlap;
ü~greifend *adj (fig) Überlegungen* general;
~griff *m (Einmischung)* encroachment *(auf
+acc* on); *(Mil)* incursion *(auf+acc* into);
~größe *f (bei Kleidung)* outsize; **ü~haben*** *vt
sep irreg (col)* **(a)** *(satt haben)* to be sick of *(col);*
(b) *(übrig haben)* to have left (over); **für etw
nichts ü~haben** not to like sth.
überhandnehmen *vi sep irreg* to get out of hand.
Über-: **~hang** *m* **(a)** *(Fels~)* overhang; **(b)**
(Comm: Überschuß) surplus *(an+dat* of); **ü~hän-
gen** *sep* **1** *vi irreg aux haben or sein* to overhang;
2 *vt sep (dat)* **einen Mantel ü~hängen** to put
a coat over one's shoulders; **ü~hastet** *adj* overhasty; **ü~hastet sprechen** to speak too fast;
ü~häufen* *vt insep irreg jdn* to overwhelm; **jdn mit
Geschenken/Vorwürfen ü~häufen** to heap
presents/reproaches on sb.
überhaupt *adv* **(a)** *(in Fragen, Verneinungen)* at
all. **~ nicht** not at all; **~ kein Grund** no reason at
all *or* whatsoever; **hast du denn ~ keinen Anstand?** have you no decency at all?; **das habe ich
ja ~ nicht gewußt** I had no idea at all. **(b)**
(sowieso, im allgemeinen) in general; *(überdies,
außerdem)* anyway, anyhow. **er ist ~ sehr
schüchtern** he's very shy in general; **er sagt ~
immer sehr wenig** he never says very much
anyway *or* anyhow. **(c)** *(erst, eigentlich)* **waren
Sie ~ schon in dem neuen Film?** have you actually been to the latest film?; **wenn ~** if at all; **wie
ist das ~ möglich?** how is that (even) possible?;
wer sind Sie ~? who do you think you are?
über-: **~heblich** *adj* arrogant; **~hitzen*** *vt insep* to
overheat; **~hitzt** *adj (fig) Diskussion* very heated;
~höht *adj Forderungen, Preise* exorbitant.
überholen* *vti insep* **(a)** *Fahrzeug* to overtake

(Brit), to pass; (fig: übertreffen) to overtake. **(b)** Motor etc to overhaul.

Überhol-: ~spur f fast lane; ~verbot nt restriction on overtaking (Brit) or passing; (als Schild etc) no overtaking (Brit), no passing.

überhören* vt insep not to hear; (nicht hören wollen) to ignore. **das möchte ich überhört haben!** (I'll pretend) I didn't hear that!

Über-Ich nt superego.

über-: ~irdisch adj celestial, heavenly; ~kandidelt adj (col) eccentric; ~kippen vi sep aux sein to topple over; ~kleben* vt insep **die Kiste** ü~kleben to stick something over the box; ~kochen vi sep aux sein (lit, fig) to boil over; ~kommen* vt insep irreg (geh: ergreifen) to come over; **Furcht** etc ~kam ihn he was overcome with fear etc; ~kriegen vt sep (col) **(a)** (ü~drüssig werden) to get fed up with (col); **(b) eins** ~kriegen to get landed one (col); ~laden* 1 vt insep irreg to overload; (reichlich geben) to shower; (zu stark verzieren auch) to clutter; **sich** (dat) **den Magen** ~laden to overeat; 2 adj Wagen overloaded; (fig) Stil over-ornate; Bild cluttered; ~lagern* insep 1 vt **(a)** Schichten to overlie; Sender to blot out; **(b)** Konflikt etc to eclipse; 2 vr (sich überschneiden) to overlap; ~lang adj too long; ~lappen* vir insep to overlap.

überlassen* vt insep irreg **jdm etw** ~ (haben lassen) to let sb have sth; (in Obhut geben) to leave sth in sb's care; **es jdm** ~, **etw zu tun** to leave it up to sb to do sth; **das bleibt Ihnen** ~ that's up to you; **jdn sich** (dat) **selbst** ~ to leave sb to his/her own devices; **jdn seinem Schicksal** ~ to leave or abandon sb to his fate.

überlasten* vt insep to put too great a strain on; jdn to overtax; (Elec) Telefonnetz, (durch Gewicht) to overload. **überlastet sein** to be under too great a strain; (überfordert sein) to be overtaxed; (Elec etc) to be overloaded.

überlaufen¹* vt insep irreg (Angst etc) to seize. **es überlief ihn kalt** a cold shiver ran down his spine.

überlaufen² vi sep irreg aux sein **(a)** (Wasser) to overflow; (überkochen) to boil over. **(b)** (Mil: überwechseln) to desert (zu to).

überlaufen³ adj overcrowded; Stadt (mit Touristen) overrun.

Überläufer m (Mil) deserter.

überleben* insep 1 vti **(a)** to survive; **die Nacht** auch to last, to live through. **(b)** (länger leben als) to outlive. **2** vr **das hat sich überlebt** that's had its day.

Überlebende(r) mf decl as adj survivor.

überlebensgroß adj larger-than-life.

überlebt adj outmoded, out-of-date.

überlegen¹ insep 1 vi (nachdenken) to think. **hin und her** ~ to deliberate; **ohne zu** ~ without thinking; (ohne zu zögern) without thinking twice. 2 vt to think over or about, to consider. **das werde ich mir** ~ I'll think it over, I'll think about it; **ich habe es mir anders/noch mal überlegt** I've changed my mind; **wenn man es sich** (dat) **recht überlegt** when you think about it; **das hätten Sie sich** (dat) **vorher** ~ **müssen** you should have thought of that sooner.

überlegen² 1 adj superior; Sieg convincing. **jdm** ~ **sein** to be superior to sb. **2** adv in a superior manner.

Überlegenheit f no pl superiority.

überlegt 1 adj considered. **2** adv in a considered way.

Überlegung f consideration, thought; (Bemerkung) observation. ~en anstellen to make observations (zu about or on).

Über-: **ü~leiten** insep 1 vt Abschnitt etc to link up (in +acc with); 2 vi **zu etw ü~leiten** to lead up to sth; ~leitung f connection; (zur nächsten Frage,

(Mus) transition; **ü~lesen*** vt insep irreg **(a)** (flüchtig lesen) to glance through; **(b)** (übersehen) to overlook, to miss; **ü~liefern*** vt insep Brauch to hand down; ~lieferung f tradition; schriftliche ~lieferungen (written) records; **ü~listen*** vt insep to outwit.

übern = über den.

Über-: ~macht f no pl superior strength; **ü~mächtig** adj Gewalt superior; Feind powerful; Wunsch overpowering; **ü~malen*** vt insep to paint over; ~maß nt no pl excess (an+acc of); im ~maß to excess; **er hat Zeit im** ~maß he has more than enough time; **ü~mäßig** 1 adj excessive; Schmerz, Sehnsucht violent; Freude intense; **das war nicht ü~mäßig** that was not too brilliant; **2** adv excessively; essen, trinken auch to excess; ~mensch m superman; **ü~menschlich** adj superhuman; **ü~mitteln*** vt insep to convey (jdm to sb); (telefonisch etc) to transmit; **ü~morgen** adv the day after tomorrow; **ü~müden*** vt insep usu ptp to overtire; ~mut m high spirits pl; **ü~mütig** adj (ausgelassen) high-spirited; (zu mutig) cocky (col).

übern = über den.

übernächste(r, s) adj attr **das** ~ **Haus** the next house but one; **die** ~ **Woche** the week after next; **er kommt** ~**en Freitag** he's coming Friday week.

Über-: ~nachten* vi insep to sleep; (in Hotel) to stay; (eine Nacht) to stay the night; **ü~nächtigt** adj bleary-eyed;'~nachtung f overnight stay; ~nachtung mit Frühstück bed and breakfast; ~nahme f -n takeover; (von Ausdruck, Ansicht) adoption; (von Zitat, Wort) borrowing; (von Amt) assumption; **durch** ~nahme dieser Aufgabe by taking on this task; **ü~natürlich** adj supernatural; **ü~nehmen*** insep irreg 1 vt **(a)** Aufgabe, Verantwortung, (Jur) Fall to take on; Amt to assume; Klasse to take charge of; **lassen Sie mal, das ü~nehme ich!** let me take care of that; **den Befehl ü~nehmen** to take (over) command; **(b)** (stellvertretend, ablösend) to take over (von from); Zitat, Wort to take; 2 vr to take on too much; (sich überanstrengen) to overdo it; (beim Essen) to overeat; **ü~ordnen** vt sep jdn jdm **ü~ordnen** to put sb over sb; **etw einer Sache** (dat) **ü~ordnen** to give sth precedence over sth; **ü~parteilich** adj Zeitung independent; (Parl) Problem all-party attr; Amt, Präsident etc above party politics; ~produktion f overproduction; **ü~prüfen*** vt insep (auf+acc for) to check; Entscheidung, Lage, Frage to examine; Ergebnisse, Teilnehmer etc to scrutinize; (Pol) jdn to screen.

Überprüfung f **(a)** no pl siehe vt checking; examination; scrutiny; (Pol) screening. **(b)** (Kontrolle) check.

über-: ~quellen vi sep irreg aux sein to overflow (von, mit with); (Reis) to boil over; ~queren* vt insep to cross; ~ragen* vt insep to tower above; (fig: übertreffen) to outshine (an+dat, in +dat in); ~ragend adj outstanding; Bedeutung paramount; ~raschen* vt insep to surprise; (überrumpeln auch) to take by surprise; **jdn bei etw** ~raschen to surprise or catch sb doing sth; ~raschend adj surprising; Besuch surprise attr; Tod, Weggang unexpected; ~rascht adj surprised (über+acc at); **jdn** ~rascht ansehen to look at sb in surprise.

Überraschung f surprise. **zu meiner** ~ to my surprise.

Überraschungs|angriff m surprise attack.

überreden* vt insep to persuade. **jdn** ~, **etw zu tun** to persuade sb to do sth, to talk sb into doing sth; **jdn zu etw** ~ to talk sb into sth.

Überredung f persuasion.

Überredungskunst f powers of persuasion pl.

Über-: **ü~regional** adj national; Zeitung, Sender auch nationwide; **ü~reich** adj lavish, abundant; (zu reich) overabundant; **ü~reich an etw** (dat)

overflowing with sth; **ü~reichen*** *vt insep* (jdm)
etw ~ to hand sth over (to sb); **ü~reichlich** *adj*
ample, abundant; *(zu reichlich)* overabundant; **in**
ü~reichlichem Maße in abundance; **ü~reif** *adj*
overripe; **ü~reizen*** *insep* 1 *vt* Nerven, Augen to
overstrain; 2 *vtr* (Cards) to overbid; **ü~reizt** *adj*
Augen overstrained; *(nervlich)* overwrought; *(zu*
erregt) overexcited; **ü~rennen*** *vt insep irreg* to
run down; *(Mil)* to overrun; **~rest** *m* remnant,
remains *pl*; **ü~rollen*** *vt insep* to run down; *(Mil,*
fig) to overrun; **ü~rumpeln*** *vt insep* *(col)* to take
by surprise, to catch unawares; *(überwältigen)* to
overpower; **ü~runden*** *vt insep* (Sport) to lap;
(fig) to outstrip.
übers = **über das.**
Über-: ü~säen* *vt insep* to strew; **ü~sät** strewn;
(mit Abfall etc) littered; *(mit Sternen)* Himmel
studded; **ü~sättigen*** *vt insep* to satiate; Markt to
oversaturate; **~schall-** in *cpds* supersonic;
ü~schatten* *vt insep (geh)* (lit, fig) to over-
shadow; *(fig: trüben)* to cast a shadow over;
ü~schätzen* *vt insep* to overestimate;
ü~schaubar *adj* Plan easily comprehensible,
clear; **damit die Abteilung ü~schaubar bleibt**
so that one can keep track of the department;
ü~schäumen *vi sep aux sein* to froth over; *(fig)* to
bubble over *(vor +dat* with); *(vor Wut)* to seethe;
~schicht *f* (Ind) extra shift; **ü~schlafen*** *vt in-*
sep irreg Problem to sleep on.
Überschlag *m* **(a)** *(Berechnung)* (rough) estimate. **(b)** *(Drehung)* somersault.
überschlagen¹* *insep irreg* 1 *vt* **(a)** *(auslassen)* to
skip (over). **(b)** Kosten etc to estimate (roughly).
2 *vr* **(a)** to somersault; *(Mensch: versehentlich)* to
go head over heels; *(fig: Ereignisse)* to come thick
and fast. **(b)** *(Stimme)* to crack.
überschlagen² *sep irreg* 1 *vt* Beine to cross; Arme
to fold; Decke to fold back. 2 *vi aux sein* **(a)**
(Wellen) to break. **(b)** *(Stimmung etc)* **in etw** *(acc)*
~ to turn into sth.
Über-: ü~schnappen *vi sep aux sein* (Stimme)
to break; *(col: Mensch)* to crack up *(col)*;
ü~schneiden* *vr insep irreg* (unerwünscht) to
clash; *(Linien)* to intersect; **ü~schreiben*** *vt*
insep irreg **(a)** *(betiteln)* to head; **(b)** etw auf
jdn **ü~schreiben** to make sth over to sb;
ü~schreiten* *vt insep irreg* to cross; *(fig)* to exceed; Höhepunkt, Alter to pass; **~schrift** *f* heading; *(Schlagzeile)* headline; **~schuh** *m* overshoe;
ü~schuldet *adj* heavily in debt; Grundstück
heavily mortgaged; **Ü~schuß** *m* surplus (an
+dat of); **ü~schüssig** *adj* surplus; **ü~schütten***
vt insep jdn/etw mit etw **ü~schütten** to cover
sb/sth with sth; *(mit Flüssigkeit)* to pour sth onto
sb/sth; jdn mit etw **ü~schütten** *(fig: über-*
häufen) to heap sth on sb; **~schwang** *m no pl*
exuberance; **ü~schwappen** *vi sep aux sein* to
splash over; **ü~schwemmen*** *vt insep* (lit, fig) to
flood; *(Touristen)* Land etc auch to overrun; *(mit*
Aufträgen) to swamp, to inundate; **~schwem-**
mung *f* flood; **ü~schwenglich** *adj* effusive,
gushing *(pej)*.
Übersee *no art* **in/nach** ~ overseas; **aus/von** ~
from overseas.
Übersee-: ~dampfer *m* ocean liner; **~hafen** *m*
international port; **~handel** *m* overseas trade.
überseeisch ['yːbzeːɪʃ] *adj* overseas.
Überseeverkehr *m* overseas traffic.
übersehbar *adj* (fig) Folgen, Zusammenhänge etc
clear; Kosten, Dauer etc assessable.
übersehen* *vt insep irreg* (fig) Folgen, Zusammenhänge, Sachlage to see clearly; Fachgebiet to have
an overall view of; *(abschätzen)* Schaden, Kosten,
Dauer to assess. **(b)** *(ignorieren, nicht erkennen)* to
overlook; *(nicht bemerken)* to miss.
übersein *vi sep irreg aux sein* (col) **jdm ist etw über**
sb is fed-up with sth *(col)*.
übersenden* *vt insep irreg* to send.

übersetzen¹* *vti insep* **(a)** to translate. **aus dem** *or*
vom Englischen ins Deutsche ~ to translate
from English into German; **etw falsch** ~ to mis-
translate sth; **sich leicht/schwer** ~ lassen to be
easy/hard to translate. **(b)** *(Tech: übertragen)* to
transmit.
übersetzen² *sep* 1 *vi aux sein* to cross (over). 2 *vt*
(mit Fähre) to take *or* ferry across.
Übersetzer(in *f***)** *m* - translator.
Übersetzung *f* **(a)** translation. **(b)** *(Tech: Über-*
tragung) transmission.
Übersetzungsbüro *nt* translation bureau *or*
agency.
Übersicht *f* **(a)** *no pl (Überblick)* overall view. **die**
~ **verlieren** to lose track. **(b)** *(Abriß, Resümee)*
survey; *(Tabelle)* table.
übersichtlich *adj* Gelände etc open; Darstellung
etc clear.
Übersichtskarte *f* general map.
übersiedeln *sep*, **übersiedeln*** *insep vi aux sein*
to move *(von* from, *nach, in+acc* to).
über-: ~sinnlich *adv* supersensory; *(übernatür-*
lich) supernatural; **~spannen** *vt insep* **(a)**
(Brücke etc) to span; **(b)** *(zu stark spannen)* to put
too much strain on; **~spannt** *adj* Ideen, Forderungen wild, extravagant; *(exaltiert)* eccentric;
(hysterisch) hysterical; Nerven overexcited;
~spielen* *vt insep* **(a)** *(verbergen)* to cover (up);
(b) *(übertragen)* Aufnahme to transfer; **~spitzt** 1
adj (zu spitzfindig) oversubtle; *(übertrieben)* exaggerated; 2 *adv* oversubtly; in an exaggerated
fashion.
überspringen¹* *vt insep irreg* **(a)** Hindernis, Höhe
to jump, to clear. **(b)** *(auslassen)* to skip.
überspringen² *vi sep irreg aux sein* (Begeisterung)
to spread quickly *(auf+acc* to).
über-: ~sprudeln *vi sep aux sein* (lit, fig) to bubble
over *(vor* with); **~stehen*** *vt insep irreg (durch-*
stehen) to come *or* get through; *(überleben)* to
survive; Gewitter to weather, to ride out; Krankheit to get over; **~steigen*** *vt insep irreg* **(a)** to
climb over; **(b)** *(hinausgehen über)* to exceed, to
go beyond; **~steigert** *adj* excessive; **~steuern***
vi insep (Aut) to oversteer; **~stimmen** *vt insep* to
outvote; Antrag to vote down; **~strapazieren***
insep 1 *vt* to wear out; 2 *vr* to wear oneself out;
~streichen* *vt insep irreg* to paint/varnish over;
~streifen *vt sep* (sich dat) etw **~streifen** to slip
sth on.
überströmen¹* *vt insep (überfluten)* to flood. **von**
Blut überströmt sein to be streaming with blood.
überströmen² *vi sep aux sein (lit, fig)* to overflow
(vor+dat with).
überstülpen *vt sep* **sich** (dat) etw ~ to put on sth;
jdm/einer Sache etw ~ to put sth on sb/sth.
Überstunde *f* hour of overtime. **~n** overtime
sing; **~n machen** to do overtime.
über-: ~stürzen* *insep* 1 *vt* to rush into; 2 *vr (Ereig-*
nisse etc) to happen in a rush; *(Nachrichten)* to
come fast and furious; **~stürzt** *adj* overhasty;
~tariflich *adj*, *adv* above the agreed *or* union
rate; **~tippen*** *vt insep* to type over; **~tölpeln*** *vt*
insep to take in; **~tönen*** *vt insep* to drown.
Übertrag *m* **-e** amount carried forward.
übertragbar *adj* transferable; Methode, Maßstab
applicable *(auf+acc* to); Krankheit infectious;
(durch Berührung) contagious.
übertragen¹* *insep irreg* 1 *vt* **(a)** to transfer;
Krankheit, *(Tech)* Bewegung to transmit; Daten to
communicate. **(b)** *(übersetzen)* Text to render (in
+acc into). **(c)** *(anwenden)* Methode to apply *(auf*
+acc to). **(d)** Verantwortung etc to give *(jdm* sb);
(auftragen) Aufgabe to assign *(jdm* to sb). **(e)** (TV,
Rad) to broadcast; (TV auch) to televise. 2 *vr*
(Eigenschaft, Krankheit etc, Tech) to be trans-
mitted *(auf+acc* to); *(Heiterkeit etc)* to spread
(auf+acc to).
übertragen² *adj* Bedeutung etc figurative.

Überträger *m (Med)* carrier.

Übertragung *f siehe vt* (a) transference; transmission. (b) rendering. (c) application. (d) *(Aufgabe)* assignment. (e) *(TV, Rad)* transmission.

übertreffen* *insep irreg* 1 *vt* to surpass *(an+dat* in); *(mehr leisten als auch)* to outdo; *(übersteigen auch)* to exceed. 2 *vr* **sich selbst** ~ to surpass *or* excel oneself.

übertreiben* *vti insep irreg* to exaggerate. **es mit der Sauberkeit** ~ to carry cleanliness too far; **man kann es auch** ~ you can overdo things.

Übertreibung *f* exaggeration.

übertreten[1] *vi sep irreg aux sein* (a) *(Fluß)* to break its banks. (b) *(zu anderer Partei etc)* to go over *(zu* to).

übertreten[2]* *vt insep irreg Gesetz* to break.

Übertretung *f (von Gesetz etc)* violation; *(Jur: strafbare Handlung)* misdemeanour *(Brit)*, misdemeanor *(US)*.

Über-: **ü~trieben** *adj* exaggerated; *(übermäßig)* Vorsicht, Training excessive; ~**tritt** *m (über Grenze)* crossing *(über+acc* of); *(zu anderem Glauben)* conversion; *(von Abtrünnigen, esp zu anderer Partei)* defection; **ü~trumpfen*** *vt insep (Cards)* to overtrump; *(fig)* to outdo; **ü~tünchen*** *vt insep* to whitewash; *(mit Farbton)* to distemper; *(fig)* to cover up; ~**völkerung** *f* overpopulation; **ü~voll** *adj* overfull *(von* with); **ü~vorteilen*** *vt insep* to cheat; *(beobachten)* to keep a watch on; *(kontrollieren)* to supervise; *(beobachten)* to keep a watch on; *(Verdächtigen)* to keep under surveillance; *(auf Monitor, mit Radar, fig)* to monitor; **ü~wältigen*** *vt insep (lit)* to overpower; *(zahlenmäßig)* to overwhelm; *(bezwingen, fig: Schlaf, Angst)* to overcome; **ü~wältigend** *adj* overwhelming; Schönheit stunning; Gestank, Gefühl auch overpowering; **ü~wechseln** *vi sep* to move *(in+acc* to); *(zu Partei etc)* to go over *(zu* to); *(Wild)* to cross over; ~**weg** *m* ~**weg für Fußgänger** pedestrian crossing; **ü~weisen*** *vt insep irreg (an +acc* to) Geld to transfer; Patienten to refer; ~**weisung** *f (Geld~)* (credit) transfer; ~**weite** *f* large size.

überwerfen[1]* *vr insep irreg* **sich (mit jdm)** ~ to fall out (with sb).

überwerfen[2] *vt sep irreg* to put over; *Kleidungsstück* to put on; *(sehr rasch)* to throw on.

Über-: **ü~wiegen*** *insep irreg* 1 *vt* to outweigh; 2 *vi (das Übergewicht haben)* to predominate; **ü~wiegend** 1 *adj* predominant; *Mehrheit* vast; 2 *adv* predominantly, mainly; **ü~winden*** *insep irreg* 1 *vt* to overcome; 2 *vr* to overcome one's inclinations; **sich ü~winden, etw zu tun** to force oneself to do sth; ~**windung** *f* overcoming; *(Selbstüberwindung)* will power; **das hat mich viel** ~**windung gekostet** that was a real effort of will for me; **ü~wintern*** *vi insep* to (spend the) winter; *(col: Winterschlaf halten)* to hibernate; **ü~wuchern*** *vt insep* to overgrow; *(fig)* to obscure; **ü~wunden** *adj* Standpunkt, Haltung etc of the past; *Angst* conquered; ~**wurf** *m (Kleidungsstück)* wrap; ~**zahl** *f no pl* **in der** ~**zahl sein** to be in the majority; *(Feind)* to be superior in number; **ü~zählig** *adj (überschüssig)* surplus; *(überflüssig)* superfluous; *(übrig)* spare.

überzeugen* *insep* 1 *vt* to convince; *(Jur)* to satisfy. **ich bin davon überzeugt, daß** ... I am convinced that ...; **er ist sehr von sich überzeugt** he is very sure of himself. 2 *vi* to be convincing. 3 *vr* **sich (selbst)** ~ to convince oneself *(von* of); *(mit eigenen Augen)* to see for oneself.

überzeugt *adj attr* Anhänger, Vegetarier etc dedicated; *Christ, Moslem* devout.

Überzeugung *f* (a) *(das Überzeugen)* convincing. (b) *(Überzeugtsein)* conviction; *(Prinzipien)* convictions *pl.* **meiner** ~ **nach** ... I am convinced (that) ...; **zu der** ~ **gelangen, daß** ... to become

convinced that ...

überziehen[1]* *insep irreg* 1 *vt* (a) *(bedecken)* to cover; *(mit Schicht, Belag)* to coat; *(mit Metall)* to plate; *(mit Zuckerguß)* to ice, to frost *(esp US)*. **ein Bett frisch** ~ to change the sheets; Polstermöbel neu ~ **lassen** to have furniture re-covered. (b) *Konto* to overdraw *(um +acc* by). (c) *Redezeit etc* to overrun. 2 *vi (Fin)* to overdraw one's account. 3 *vr (Himmel)* to cloud over.

überziehen[2] *vt sep irreg* (a) *(sich dat)* **etw** ~ to put sth on. (b) *jdm* **eins** ~ *(col)* to give sb a clout *(col)*.

Über-: **ü~züchten*** *vt insep* to overbreed; **ü~zuckern*** *vt insep* to sugar; *(zu stark zuckern)* to put too much sugar in/on; ~**zug** *m* (a) *(Beschichtung)* coat(ing); *(aus Metall)* plating; *(für Kuchen, esp aus Zuckerguß)* icing, frosting *(esp US)*; (b) *(von Bett, Sessel etc)* cover; *(von Kopfkissen auch)* (pillow)slip.

üblich *adj* usual; *(herkömmlich)* customary; *(typisch, normal)* normal. **wie** ~ as usual; **das ist bei ihm so** ~ that's usual for him; **allgemein** ~ **sein** to be common practice.

üblicherweise *adv* usually, normally.

U-Boot *nt* submarine, sub *(col)*.

übrig *adj* (a) *attr (verbleibend)* remaining; *(andere auch)* other. **meine** ~**en Sachen** the rest of my things. (b) *pred* left (over); *(zu entbehren)* spare. **etw** ~ **haben** to have sth left/to spare. (c) *(mögen)* **für jdn/nichts** ~ **haben** to have no time for sb; **für jdn/etw etwas** ~ **haben** to be fond of sb/sth. (d) *(substantivisch)* **das** ~**e** the rest, the remainder; **im** ~**en** moreover, also.

übrig-: ~**behalten*** *vt sep irreg* to have left over; ~**bleiben** *vi sep irreg aux sein* to be left over, to remain; **wieviel ist** ~ **geblieben?** how much is left?; **was blieb mir anderes** ~ **als** ...? what choice did I have but ...?

übrigens *adv* incidentally, by the way.

übriglassen *vt sep irreg* to leave *(jdm* for sb). **(einiges)/viel zu wünschen** ~ *(col)* to leave something/a lot to be desired.

Übung *f* practice; *(Mil, Sport, Sch)* exercise; *(Feuerwehr~)* exercise, drill; *(Univ: Kursus)* seminar. **aus der** ~ **kommen/außer** ~ **sein** to get/be out of practice; **zur** ~ as practice; ~ **macht den Meister** *(Prov)* practice makes perfect *(Prov)*.

Übungs-: ~**arbeit** *f (Sch)* mock test; ~**aufgabe** *f (Sch)* exercise; ~**heft** *nt (Sch)* exercise book; ~**platz** *m* training ground; *(Mil)* drill ground.

UdSSR [uːdeː|ɛs|ɛs|ˈɛr] *f* = **Union der Sozialistischen Sowjetrepubliken. die** ~ the USSR.

Ufer *nt - (Fluß~)* bank; *(See~)* shore. **direkt am** ~ **gelegen** right on the waterfront; **etw ans** ~ **spülen** to wash sth ashore; **das sichere** ~ **erreichen** to reach dry land.

Ufer-: ~**befestigung** *f* bank reinforcement; ~**böschung** *f* embankment; **u~los** *adj* endless; *(grenzenlos)* boundless; **ins u~lose gehen** *(Debatte etc)* to go on forever; *(Kosten)* to go up and up; ~**mauer** *f* sea wall; ~**straße** *f* lakeside/riverside road.

Ugander(in *f) m* - Ugandan.

U-Haft *f (col)* custody.

Uhr *f* -en clock; *(Armband~, Taschen~)* watch; *(Anzeiger)* gauge, dial. **nach meiner** ~ by my watch; **um drei (~)** at three (o'clock); **ein** ~ **dreißig** half past one, one-thirty; **wieviel** ~ **ist es?** what time is it?, what's the time?; **um wieviel** ~? at what time?

Uhr(arm)band *nt* watch strap; *(aus Metall)* watch bracelet.

Uhr-: ~**feder** *f* watch spring; ~**kette** *f* watch chain; ~**macher(in** *f) m* watchmaker; ~**macherei** *f* clock-/watchmaker's; ~**werk** *nt* clockwork mechanism *(auch fig)*, movements *pl*; ~**zeiger** *m* (clock/watch) hand; ~**zeigersinn** *m* **im** ~**zeigersinn** clockwise; **entgegen dem** ~**zeigersinn** anticlockwise *(Brit)*,

counterclockwise *(US)*; ~zeit *f* time (of day).
Uhu ['u:hu] *m* -s eagle-owl.
Ukrainer(in *f) m* - Ukrainian.
UKW [u:ka:'ve:] = **Ultrakurzwelle** ≈ FM.
Ulk *m* -e *(col)* lark *(col)*; *(Streich)* practical joke; *(Spaß)* fun *no pl, no indef art.* **mit jdm seinen ~ treiben** *(Streiche spielen)* to play tricks on sb.
ulkig *adj (col)* funny.
Ulme *f* -n elm.
ultimativ *adj Forderung etc* given as an ultimatum. **jdn ~ zu etw auffordern** to give sb an ultimatum to do sth.
Ultimatum *nt, pl* -s *or* **Ultimaten** ultimatum. **jdm ein ~ stellen** to give sb an ultimatum.
Ultra *m* -s *(pej)* extremist.
Ultra- *in cpds* ultra; **u~kurz** *adj (Phys)* ultrashort.
Ultrakurzwelle *f (Phys)* ultra-short wave; *(Rad)* ≈ very high frequency, ≈ frequency modulation.
Ultra-: **u~modern** *adj* ultramodern; **~schall** *m (Phys)* ultrasound.
um 1 *prep+acc* **(a)** ~ ... **(herum)** around; ~ **sich schauen** to look around (one) *or* about one; ~ **Weihnachten/Ostern** around Christmas/Easter; ~ **acht** at eight. **(b)** *(betreffend, über)* about. **es geht ~ das Prinzip** it's a question of principles; **der Kampf ~ den Titel** the battle for the title; ~ **Geld spielen** to play for money; **die Sorge ~ die Zukunft** concern for *or* about the future. **(c)** *(bei Differenzangaben)* by. ~ **10% teurer** 10% more expensive; ~ **einiges besser** quite a bit better; **etw ~ 4 cm verkürzen** to shorten sth by 4cm. **(d)** *(bei Verlust)* **jdn ~ etw bringen** to deprive sb of sth. **(e)** *(nach)* after, upon. **Stunde ~ Stunde** hour after *or* upon hour.
2 *prep+gen* ~ ... **willen** for the sake of; ~ **Gottes willen!** for goodness *or* *(stärker)* God's sake!
3 *conj* **(a)** ~ ... **zu** (in order) to; **intelligent genug/zu intelligent,** ~ ... **zu** intelligent enough/ too intelligent to ...; **er studierte jahrelang Jura,** ~ **dann Taxifahrer zu werden** he studied law for several years only to become a taxi-driver. **(b)** *(desto)* ~ **so besser/schlimmer!** so much the better/worse!; **je mehr,** ~ **so besser** the more the better; ~ **so mehr, als** ... all the more considering ...
4 *adv* **(a)** *(ungefähr)* ~ **(die) 30 Schüler** about *or* around the 30 pupils. **(b)** **die zwei Stunden sind jetzt** ~ the two hours are now up.
um|adressieren* *vt sep* to readdress.
um|ändern *vt sep* to alter.
um|arbeiten *vt sep* to alter; *Buch etc* to rewrite; *Metall etc* to rework.
um|armen* *vt insep* to embrace; *(fester)* to hug.
Umbau *m siehe vt* rebuilding, renovation; conversion; alterations *pl (+gen, von* to); modification; reorganization; changing.
umbauen¹ *sep* **1** *vt Gebäude (gründlich renovieren)* to rebuild, to renovate; *(zu etw anderem)* to convert *(zu* into); *(umändern)* to alter; *Maschine etc* to modify; *(fig: Organisation)* to reorganize; *(Theat) Kulissen* to change. **2** *vi* to rebuild.
umbauen²* *vt insep* to enclose.
umbenennen* *vt sep irreg* to rename *(in etw* sth).
umbesetzen* *vt sep (Theat)* to recast; *Mannschaft* to change; *Posten, Stelle* to find someone else for.
umbestellen* *vi sep* to change one's order.
umbetten *vt sep Kranken* to move (to another bed).
umbilden *vt sep (fig)* to reorganize; *(Pol) Kabinett* to reshuffle *(Brit)*, to shake up *(US)*.
umbinden *vt sep irreg* to put on; *(mit Knoten)* to tie on. **sich** *(dat)* **einen Schal** ~ to put a scarf on.
umblättern *vti sep* to turn over.
umblicken *vr sep* to look around *(nach* at).
umbringen *sep irreg* **1** *vt* to kill *(auch fig col)*,

to murder. **2** *vr* to kill oneself.
Umbruch *m* **(a)** radical change. **(b)** *(Typ)* makeup.
umbuchen *sep* **1** *vi* to change one's reservation. **2** *vt* to change.
umdenken *vi sep irreg* to change one's ideas.
umdirigieren* *vt sep* to redirect.
umdisponieren* *vi sep* to change one's plans.
umdrängen* *vt insep* to crowd around; *(stärker)* to mob.
umdrehen *sep* **1** *vt* to turn over; *(auf den Kopf)* to turn up (the other way); *(mit der Vorderseite nach hinten)* to turn around; *(von innen nach außen) Tasche etc* to turn inside out; *(um die Achse)* to turn around; *Schlüssel* to turn. **einem Vogel/ jdm den Hals** ~ to wring a bird's/sb's neck; **jdm den Arm** ~ to twist sb's arm. **2** *vr* to turn around *(nach* to look at); *(im Bett etc)* to turn over. **3** *vi* to turn around.
Umdrehung *f* turn; *(Phys, Mot)* revolution.
um|einander *adv* about each other; *(räumlich)* around each other.
um|erziehen* *vt sep irreg (Pol euph)* to re-educate *(zu* to become).
umfahren¹ *vt sep irreg* to run over, to knock down.
umfahren²* *vt insep irreg* to travel around; *(mit dem Auto)* to drive around; *(auf Umgehungsstraße)* to bypass; *(um etw zu vermeiden)* to make a detour around.
umfallen *vi sep irreg aux sein* to fall over *or* down; *(fig col: nachgeben)* to give in. **zum U~ müde sein** to be fit to drop.
Umfang *m, pl* **Umfänge** **(a)** *(von Kreis etc)* perimeter, circumference *(auch Geom)*; *(von Baum auch, Bauch~)* girth. **(b)** *(Fläche)* area; *(Rauminhalt)* capacity; *(Größe)* size; *(von Gepäck etc)* amount. **das Buch hat einen** ~ **von 800 Seiten** the book extends to 800 pages. **(c)** *(fig) (Ausmaß)* extent; *(Reichweite)* range; *(von Untersuchung etc)* scope; *(von Verkehr, Verkauf etc)* volume. **in großem** ~ on a large scale; **in vollem** ~ fully.
umfangen* *vt insep irreg* **(a)** *(geh: umarmen)* to embrace. **(b)** *(fig: umgeben)* to envelop.
umfangreich *adj* extensive; *(geräumig)* spacious; *Buch* thick.
umfassen* *vt insep* **(a)** to grasp, to clasp; *(umarmen)* to embrace. **(b)** *(einschließen) Zeitperiode* to cover; *(enthalten)* to contain.
umfassend *adj* extensive; *(vieles enthaltend)* comprehensive; *Vorbereitung* thorough; *Geständnis* full, complete.
Umfeld *nt* zum ~ **von etw gehören** to be associated with sth.
umfliegen* *vt insep irreg* to fly around.
umformen *vt sep* **(a)** to reshape *(in+acc* into). **(b)** *(Elec)* to convert.
Umfrage *f (Social)* survey; *(esp Pol)* (opinion) poll. **eine** ~ **halten** to carry out a survey/an opinion poll; ~ **halten** to ask around.
umfüllen *vt sep* to transfer into another bottle/ container *etc.*
umfunktionieren* *vt sep etw in (+acc) or zu etw* ~ to change *or* turn sth into sth.
Umgang *m no pl* contact; *(Bekanntenkreis)* acquaintances *pl*, friends *pl.* **schlechten** ~ **haben** to keep bad company; **keinen** ~ **mit jdm haben** to have nothing to do with sb; **er ist kein** ~ **für dich** he's not fit company for you. **(b)** **im** ~ **mit Jugendlichen** in dealing with young people; **an den** ~ **mit Kindern gewöhnt sein** to be used to children.
umgänglich *adj (entgegenkommend)* obliging; *(gesellig)* friendly.
Umgangs-: **~formen** *pl* manners *pl*; **~sprache** *f* colloquial language; **u~sprachlich** *adj* colloquial.
umgeben* *vt insep irreg* to surround *(auch fig).* **mit einer Mauer/einem Zaun** ~ **sein** to be walled/

fenced in, to be surrounded by a wall/fence.
Umgebung f (Umwelt) surroundings pl; (Nach-barschaft) vicinity; (gesellschaftlicher Hinter-grund) background; (Freunde etc) people pl about one. **in der näheren/weiteren ~ Münchens** on the outskirts/in the environs of Munich.
umgehen[1] vi sep irreg aux sein **(a)** (Gerücht, Grippe etc) to go around or about; (Gespenst) to walk. **(b) mit jdm/etw ~ können** to know how to handle sb/sth; **sorgsam/verschwenderisch mit etw ~ to** be careful/lavish with sth.
umgehen[2]* vt insep irreg to go around; (ver-meiden) to avoid; (Straße) to bypass; (Mil) to outflank; (fig) to avoid; Gesetz to get around.
umgehend 1 adj immediate. **2** adv immediately.
Umgehungsstraße f by-pass.
umgekehrt 1 adj reversed; Reihenfolge reverse; (gegenteilig) opposite; (anders herum) the other way around. **nein, ~!** no, the other way around; **genau ~!** just the opposite!; **im ~en Verhältnis zu etw stehen** or **sein** to be in inverse proportion to sth. **2** (anders herum) the other way around; (dagegen) conversely; proportional in-versely. **... und ~ ...** and vice versa; **~ als** or **wie** (col) ... the other way around to what ...
umgestalten* vt sep to alter; (reorganisieren) to reorganize; (umbilden) to remodel; (umordnen) to rearrange.
umgewöhnen* vr sep to re-adapt.
umgraben vt sep irreg to dig over; Erde to turn.
umgrenzen* vt insep to surround; (umfassen auch) to enclose; (fig) to delimit.
umgruppieren* vt sep Möbel etc to rearrange; Mitarbeiter to regroup.
umgucken vr sep = **umsehen**.
umhaben vt sep irreg (col) to have on.
Umhang m, pl **Umhänge** cape; (länger) cloak; (Umhängetuch) shawl, wrap.
umhängen vt sep Rucksack etc to put on; Jacke, Schal etc to drape around. **sich** (dat) **etw ~** to put sth on; to drape sth around one.
Umhängetasche f shoulder bag.
umhauen vt sep irreg **(a)** to cut down. **(b)** (col: umwerfen) to knock flying (col) or over. **(c)** (col: erstaunen) to bowl over (col).
umhegen* vt insep (geh) to care for lovingly.
umher adv around, about. **weit ~** all around.
umher- pref siehe auch **herum-** around, about; **~fahren** vi sep irreg aux sein to travel around; (mit Auto) to drive around; **~gehen** vi sep irreg aux sein to walk around; **~irren** vi sep irreg (in etw dat) sth) to wander around; (Blick, Augen) to roam about; **~laufen** vi sep irreg aux sein to walk around; (rennen) to run around; **im Garten ~laufen** to walk/run around the garden; **~wandern** vi sep aux sein to wander about (in etw dat) sth); **~ziehen** vi sep irreg aux sein to travel around (in etw dat) sth).
umhinkönnen vi sep irreg **er kann nicht umhin, das zu tun** he can't avoid doing it; (einem Zwang folgend) he can't help doing it.
umhören vr sep to ask around.
umhüllen* vt insep to wrap (up) (mit in).
umkämpfen* vt insep Entscheidung to dispute; Wahlkreis, Sieg to contest. **die Stadt wurde wochenlang umkämpft** the battle for the city lasted weeks.
Umkehr f no pl **(a)** (lit) turning back. **jdn zur ~ zwingen** to force sb to turn back. **(b)** (fig geh: Änderung) change.
umkehren sep **1** vi aux sein to turn back; (fig) to change one's ways. **2** vt Kleidungsstück to turn inside out; Reihenfolge to reverse, to invert (auch Gram, Mus). **das ganze Zimmer ~** (col) to turn the whole room upside down (col). **3** vr (Verhältnisse) to become reversed.
umkippen sep **1** vt to tip over, to upset; Auto, Boot to overturn; Leuchter, Vase to knock over. **2** vi

aux sein **(a)** to tip or fall over; (Auto, Boot) to overturn; (volles Gefäß, Bier) to be upset. **(b)** (es sich anders überlegen) to come around. **(c)** (Fluß, See) to become polluted.
umklammern* vt insep to wrap one's arms/legs around; (mit Händen) to clasp; (festhalten) to cling to; (Ringen) to hold.
umklappen sep **1** vt to fold down. **2** vi aux sein (col) to pass out.
Umkleidekabine f changing cubicle (Brit), dressing room (US).
umkleiden vr sep to change (one's clothes).
Umkleideraum m changing room.
umknicken sep **1** vt Ast to snap; Papier to fold (over). **2** vi aux sein (Ast) to snap; (Halm) to get bent over. **mit dem Fuß ~** to twist one's ankle.
umkommen vi insep irreg aux sein to die, to be killed. **ich komme um vor Hitze** (col) the heat is killing me (col).
Umkreis m **im ~ das Flughafens** in the airport area; **im näheren/weiteren ~** in the immediate/general vicinity; **im ~ von 20 km** within a radius of 20 km.
umkreisen* vt insep to circle; (Space) to orbit.
umkrempeln vt sep **(a)** to turn up; (mehrmals) to roll up. **(b)** (umwenden) to turn inside out; Betrieb to shake up (col). **jdn ~** (fig col) to change sb's ways.
umladen vt sep irreg to transfer; (Naut) to trans-ship.
Umlage f **eine ~ machen** to split the cost.
umlagern[1]* vt insep to besiege.
umlagern[2] vt sep to transfer (in+acc into).
Umland nt no pl surrounding countryside.
Umlauf m, pl **Umläufe (a)** (von Erde etc) revo-lution; (das Kursieren) circulation (auch fig). **im ~ sein** to be in circulation; **in ~ bringen** to circu-late; Geld to put in circulation. **(b)** (Rund-schreiben) circular.
Umlaufbahn f orbit.
umlaufen vt sep irreg aux sein to circulate.
Umlaut m umlaut.
umlegen vt sep **(a)** (umhängen) to put around; Verband to put on. **(b)** Mauer, Baum to bring down. **(c)** (umklappen) to tilt (over); Kragen to turn down. **(d)** (verlegen) Kranke to transfer; Leitung to re-lay. **(e)** Termin to change (auf+acc to). **(f)** (verteilen) **die 20 Mark wurden auf uns fünf umgelegt** the five of us each had to pay a contribution towards the 20 marks. **(g)** (col: ermorden) to do in (col).
umleiten vt sep to divert (Brit), to detour.
Umleitung f diversion (Brit), detour.
umlernen vi sep to retrain; (fig) to change one's ideas.
umliegend adj surrounding.
ummelden vtr sep jdn/sich **~** to notify (the police of) a change in sb's/one's address.
Umnachtung f **geistige ~** mental derangement.
um|ordnen vt sep to rearrange.
um|organisieren* vt sep to reorganize.
um|orientieren* vr sep (fig) to reorientate one-self.
umpflanzen vt sep to transplant.
umpflügen vt sep to plough up.
umquartieren* vt sep to move; Truppen to re-quarter.
umrahmen* vt insep to frame.
umranden* vt insep to edge, to border.
umräumen sep **1** vt (anders anordnen) to re-arrange; (an anderen Platz bringen) to move. **2** vi to rearrange the furniture.
umrechnen vt sep to convert (in+acc into).
Umrechnung f conversion.
Umrechnungskurs m exchange rate.
umreißen[1] vt sep irreg to tear down; (umwerfen) to knock over.
umreißen[2]* vt insep irreg to outline.

umrennen vt sep irreg to (run into and) knock down.

umringen* vt insep to surround.

Umriß m outline; (Kontur) contour(s pl).

umrühren vt sep to stir.

umrüsten vt sep (a) (Tech) to adapt (auf+acc to). (b) (Mil) to re-equip.

ums = um das.

umsatteln sep 1 vt Pferd to resaddle. 2 vi (col: beruflich) to change jobs.

Umsatz m (Comm) sales pl, turnover. 500 Mark ~ machen (col) to do 500 marks' worth of business.

Umsatz-: ~beteiligung f commission; ~steuer f sales tax.

umsäumen* vt insep to line; (Sew) to edge. von Bäumen umsäumt tree-lined.

umschalten sep 1 vt (auf+acc to) Schalter to flick; Hebel to throw; Strom to convert; Gerät to switch over. 2 vi to flick the/a switch; to push/pull a/the lever; (auf anderen Sender) to change over (auf +acc to); (Aut) to change (Brit), to shift (in +acc to). „wir schalten jetzt um nach Hamburg" "and now we go over to Hamburg".

Umschalttaste f shift-key.

Umschau f no pl (fig) review. ~ halten to look around (nach for).

umschauen vr sep = umsehen.

umschichten vt sep to restack.

umschichtig adv on a shift basis.

umschiffen* vt insep to sail around; Erde auch to circumnavigate.

Umschlag m (a) (Veränderung) (sudden) change (+gen in, in +acc into). (b) (Hülle) cover; (Brief~) envelope; (als Verpackung) wrapping; (Buch~) jacket. (c) (Med) compress; (Packung) poultice. (d) (Ärmel~) cuff; (Hosen~) turn-up (Brit), cuff (US). (e) (umgeschlagene Gütermenge) volume of traffic.

umschlagen sep irreg 1 vt (a) Seite etc to turn over; Ärmel, Hosenbein, Saum to turn up; Teppich, Decke to turn back; Kragen to turn down. (b) (um die Schultern) Schal to put on. (c) (absetzen) Güter to handle. 2 vi aux sein (sich ändern) to change (suddenly); (Wind auch) to veer; (Stimme) to break. in etw (acc) ~ to change or turn into sth.

Umschlag-: ~entwurf m jacket design; ~hafen m port of transshipment; ~platz m trade centre (Brit) or center (US).

umschlingen* vt insep irreg (Pflanze) to twine around. jdn (mit den Armen) ~ to embrace sb.

umschmeißen vt sep irreg (col) (a) siehe um-hauen (b, c). (b) (col) Pläne to screw up (col).

umschreiben¹ vt sep irreg (a) Text etc to rewrite; (bearbeiten) Theaterstück etc to adapt (für for). (b) Hypothek etc to transfer (auf +acc to).

umschreiben²* vt insep irreg (mit anderen Worten) to paraphrase; (darlegen) to outline; (verhüllen) Sachverhalt to refer to obliquely.

Umschuldung f rescheduling (of debts).

umschulen vt sep (a) to retrain; (Pol euph) to re-educate. (b) (auf andere Schule) to transfer (to another school).

umschütten vt sep (verschütten) to spill, to upset.

Umschweife pl ohne ~ straight out, plainly; mach keine ~! come (straight) to the point.

umschwenken vi sep (a) aux sein or haben (An-hänger, Kran) to swing out; (fig) to do an about-turn. (b) (Wind) to veer.

Umschwung m (a) (Gymnastik) circle. (b) (fig) (Veränderung) drastic change; (ins Gegenteil) about-turn.

umsegeln* vt insep to sail around; Erde auch to circumnavigate.

umsehen vr sep irreg to look around (nach for); (rückwärts) to look back. sich in der Stadt ~ to have a look around town; sich in der Welt ~ to see something of the world; ich möchte mich nur mal ~ (in Geschäft) I'm just looking; ohne mich

wird er sich noch ~ (col) he's not going to find it easy without me.

umsein vi sep irreg aux sein (Zeit) to be up.

umseitig adj overleaf pred.

umsetzen sep 1 vt (a) Pflanzen to transplant; Schüler to move. (b) Waren to turn over. (c) etw in etw (acc) ~ to convert sth into sth; etw in die Tat ~ to translate sth into action. 2 vr (Schüler) to change places.

Umsicht f circumspection.

umsichtig adj circumspect.

umsiedeln vti sep (vi: aux sein) to resettle. von einem Ort an einen anderen ~ to move from one place and settle in another.

Umsiedler m resettler.

umso siehe um 3.

umsonst adv (a) (unentgeltlich) free. (b) (vergebens) in vain, to no avail. (c) (ohne Grund) for nothing.

umsorgen* vt insep to care for.

umspringen vi sep irreg aux sein to change; (Wind) to veer around (nach to). so kannst du nicht mit ihr ~! (col) you can't treat her like that!

Umstand m, pl Umstände (a) circumstance; (Tatsache) fact. den Umständen entsprechend much as one would expect (under the circum-stances); die näheren Umstände further details; in anderen Umständen sein to be expecting; unter diesen/keinen Umständen under these/no circumstances; unter Umständen possibly. (b) Umstände pl (Mühe, Schwierigkeiten) bother sing; trouble sing; (Förmlichkeit) fuss sing; jdm Um-stände machen to cause sb bother; machen Sie bloß keine Umstände! please don't go to any bother.

umständehalber adv owing to circumstances. „~ zu verkaufen" "forced to sell".

umständlich adj Arbeitsweise, Methode (awk-ward) and involved; (langsam und ungeschickt) ponderous; Vorbereitung elaborate; Erklärung, Übersetzung, Anleitung long-winded; Abfertigung laborious; Arbeit, Reise awkward. er ist fürch-terlich ~ he always makes such heavy weather of everything; etw ~ machen to make heavy weather of doing sth; etw ~ beschreiben to describe sth in a roundabout way.

Umstands-: ~kleid nt maternity dress; ~krämer m (col) fusspot (col), fussbudget (US col); ~wort nt adverb.

umstehend adj attr (a) standing round about. die U~en the bystanders. (b) (umseitig) overleaf.

umsteigen vi sep irreg aux sein (a) to change (nach for). (b) (fig col) to change over, to switch (over) (auf+acc to).

umstellen¹ sep 1 vti (a) Möbel to rearrange. (b) Hebel to throw; Fernsehgerät to switch over; Radio to switch to another station; Uhr to alter, to put back/forward. auf etw (acc) ~ (Betrieb) to go or switch over to sth; auf Erdgas etc to convert to sth. 2 vr to move about; (fig) to get used to a different lifestyle. sich auf etw (acc) ~ to adjust to sth.

umstellen²* vt insep to surround.

Umstellung f (a) (von Möbeln etc) rearrange-ment. (b) (von Hebel) throwing; (von Uhr) put-ting back/forward. (c) (fig: das Sichumstellen) adjustment (auf+acc to).

umstimmen vt sep (a) Instrument to retune. (b) jdn ~ to change sb's mind.

umstoßen vt sep irreg Gegenstand to knock over; (fig) Plan etc to change; (Umstände) to upset.

umstritten adj (fraglich) controversial; (wird noch debattiert) disputed.

umstrukturieren* vt sep to restructure.

umstülpen vt sep to turn upside down; Tasche to turn out.

Umsturz m coup (d'état).

umstürzen sep 1 vt to overturn; (fig) Staat to overthrow; Demokratie to destroy. 2 vi aux sein to fall; (Möbelstück, Wagen etc) to overturn.

Umtausch m exchange. diese Waren sind vom ~ ausgeschlossen these goods cannot be exchanged.

umtauschen vt sep to exchange; Geld to change (in+acc into).

umtopfen vt sep Blumen etc to repot.

umtreten vt sep irreg to tread down.

Umtriebe pl machinations pl. subversive ~ subversive activities.

umverteilen* vt sep or insep to redistribute.

umwälzend adj (fig) radical; Veränderungen auch sweeping; Ereignisse revolutionary.

Umwälzung f (fig) radical change.

umwandeln vt sep to transform (in +acc into); (Comm, Fin, Sci) to convert (in +acc to); (Jur) Strafe to commute (in+acc to).

umwechseln vt sep Geld to change (in +acc to, into).

Umweg ['umveːk] m detour; (fig) roundabout way. einen ~ machen/fahren to go a long way around; (absichtlich auch) to make a detour.

Umwelt f no pl environment.

Umwelt- in cpds environmental; ~belastung f ecological damage; u~feindlich adj damaging to the environment; u~freundlich adj pollution-free; ~freundlich hergestellt manufactured without harm to the environment; u~gestört adj (Psych) maladjusted; ~politik f ecological policy; u~schädlich adj harmful to the environment; ~schutz m conservation no art; ~schützer m environmentalist; ~sünder m (col) polluter of the environment; ~verschmutzung f pollution (of the environment).

umwenden sep irreg 1 vt to turn over. 2 vr to turn (around) (nach to).

umwerben* vi insep irreg to court.

umwerfen vt sep irreg (a) Gegenstand to knock over. (b) (fig: ändern) to upset. (c) jdn (körperlich) to knock down; (Ringen) to throw down; (fig col) to bowl over. (d) sich (dat) etw ~ to put sth around one's shoulders.

umwerfend adj fantastic. von ~er Komik hilarious.

umwickeln* vt insep to wrap around; (mit Schnur) to wind around.

umzäunen* vt insep to fence around.

Umzäunung f fencing.

umziehen sep irreg 1 vi aux sein to move (nach to). 2 vr to change.

umzingeln* vt insep to surround, to encircle.

Umzug ['umtsuːk] m (a) (Wohnungs~) move. (b) (Festzug) procession; (Demonstration) parade.

un|ab|änderlich adj (a) unalterable; Entschluß, Urteil auch irrevocable. ~ feststehen to be absolutely certain. (b) (ewig) Gesetze immutable.

un|abdingbar adj indispensable; Recht inalienable.

un|abhängig adj independent (von of). ~ davon, was Sie meinen irrespective of what you think; sich ~ machen to go one's own way; sich von jdm/etw ~ machen to become independent of sb/sth.

Un|abhängigkeit f independence.

un|abkömmlich adj (geh) busy.

un|ablässig adj continual; Versuche, Bemühungen unremitting.

un|absehbar adj (a) (fig) Folgen etc unforeseeable; Schaden incalculable. auf ~e Zeit for an indefinite period. (b) (lit) interminable.

un-: ~abweisbar adj irrefutable; ~achtsam adj (unaufmerksam) inattentive; (nicht sorgsam) careless, (unbedacht) thoughtless; ~ähnlich adj dissimilar; einer Sache/jdm ~ähnlich sein to be unlike sth/sb; ~anfechtbar adj Urteil incontestable; Argument

etc unassailable; Beweis irrefutable; ~angebracht adj Bemerkung uncalled-for; Sparsamkeit auch misplaced; (unzweckmäßig) Maßnahmen inappropriate; ~angefochten adj unchallenged no adv; Testament, Wahlkandidat, Urteil uncontested; ~angemeldet adj unannounced no adv; Besucher unexpected; Patient etc without an appointment.

un|angemessen adj (zu hoch) unreasonable; (unzulänglich) inadequate. einer Sache (dat) ~ sein to be inappropriate to sth.

un|angenehm adj unpleasant; (peinlich) Zwischenfall, Begegnung embarrassing. das ist mir immer so ~ I don't like that at all.

un-: ~angetastet adj untouched; ~angetastet bleiben (Rechte) not to be violated; ~angreifbar adj unassailable; Festung, Land impregnable; ~annehmbar adj unacceptable.

Un|annehmlichkeit f usu pl trouble no pl. ~en haben/bekommen to be in/to get into trouble.

un|ansehnlich adj unsightly; Frau etc plain; Tapete, Möbel shabby.

un|anständig adj (a) (unerzogen) ill-mannered; (unverschämt) rude. (b) (anstößig) dirty; Kleidung indecent.

un-: ~antastbar adj inviolable, sacrosanct; ~appetitlich adj (lit, fig) unappetizing.

Un|art f bad habit.

un|artig adj naughty.

Un-: u~ästhetisch adj Anblick not aesthetically (Brit) or esthetically (US) pleasing; u~aufdringlich adj unobtrusive; Parfüm auch discreet; Mensch unassuming; u~auffällig 1 adj inconspicuous; (unscheinbar, schlicht) unobtrusive; 2 adv unobtrusively, discreetly; u~auffindbar adj nowhere to be found; u~aufgefordert 1 adj unsolicited (esp Comm); 2 adv without being asked; u~aufgefordert zugesandte Manuskripte unsolicited manuscripts; u~aufhaltsam adj (a) (unaufhaltbar) unstoppable; (b) (unerbittlich) inexorable; u~aufhörlich adj continual, incessant; u~auflösbar adj Ehe indissoluble; u~aufmerksam adj inattentive; u~aufrichtig adj insincere; u~aufrichtigkeit f insincerity; u~aufschiebbar adj urgent; u~ausbleiblich adj inevitable, unavoidable; u~ausgeglichen adj unbalanced; u~ausgegoren adj immature; Idee, Plan half-baked (col); u~ausgeschlafen adj tired; u~ausgesetzt adj incessant, constant; u~ausgesprochen adj unspoken; u~ausgewogen adj unbalanced; u~ausrottbar adj Unkraut indestructible; (fig) Vorurteile etc ineradicable; u~aussprechlich adj (a) Wort unpronounceable; (b) Schönheit,Leid etc inexpressible; u~ausstehlich adj intolerable; u~ausweichlich adj inevitable; Folgen auch inescapable.

un|bändig adj (a) Kind boisterous. (b) (ungezügelt) unrestrained no adv; Haß, Zorn etc auch unbridled no adv; Hunger enormous.

un-: ~bar adj (Comm) etw ~bar bezahlen not to pay sth in cash; ~barmherzig adj merciless; ~beabsichtigt adj unintentional.

unbe|achtet adj unnoticed; Warnung, Vorschläge unheeded. wir wollen die weniger wichtigen Punkte zunächst ~ lassen let's leave aside the less important points for the time being.

un-: ~bebaut adj Land undeveloped; Feld uncultivated; ~bedacht adj rash; ~bedarft adj (col) clueless (col); ~bedeckt adj bare; ~bedenklich adj (ungefährlich) completely harmless; ~bedeutend adj insignificant; (geringfügig) Änderung etc minor.

unbedingt 1 adj attr absolute. 2 adv jeden Fall really; nötig, erforderlich absolutely. müßt ihr denn ~ in meinem Arbeitszimmer spielen? do you have to play in my study?; ~! absolutely!; nicht ~ not necessarily.

Un-: u~**beeindruckt** adj unimpressed; u~**beein-flußt** adj uninfluenced (von by); u~**befahrbar** adj Straße impassable; Gewässer unnavigable; u~**befahren** adj Straße, Seeweg unused; u~**befangen** adj (a) (unparteiisch) impartial; (b) (natürlich) natural; (ungehemmt) uninhibited; ~**befangenheit** f siehe adj impartiality; naturalness; uninhibitedness; u~**befriedigend** adj unsatisfactory; u~**befriedigt** adj (frustriert) unsatisfied; (unerfüllt auch) unfulfilled; (unzufrieden) dissatisfied; u~**befristet** adj permanent; u~**befugt** adj unauthorized; **Eintritt für** ~**befugte verboten** no admittance to unauthorized persons; u~**beglichen** adj unpaid, unsettled.

unbegreiflich adj incomprehensible. **es wird mir immer** ~ **bleiben, wie/daß ...** I shall never understand how/why ...

unbegreiflicherweise adv inexplicably.

unbegrenzt adj unlimited; Möglichkeiten, Energie etc auch limitless; Land, Meer etc boundless; Zeitspanne, Frist indefinite. **zeitlich** ~ indefinite; ~, **auf** ~**e Zeit** indefinitely; „~" **haltbar** "will keep indefinitely".

unbegründet adj unwarranted.

unbehaart adj hairless; (auf dem Kopf) bald.

Unbehagen nt uneasiness; (Unzufriedenheit) discontent (an+dat with); (körperlich) discomfort.

unbehaglich adj uncomfortable; Gefühl uneasy.

un-: ~**behelligt** adj (unbelästigt) unmolested; (unkontrolliert) unchecked; **jdn** ~**behelligt lassen** to leave sb alone; ~**beherrscht** adj uncontrolled; (Mensch) lacking self-control; (gierig) greedy; ~**behindert** adj unimpeded; ~**beholfen** adj clumsy, awkward; (hilflos) helpless; ~**beirrbar** adj unwavering; ~**beirrt** adj unflustered.

unbekannt adj unknown; Gesicht auch unfamiliar. **das war mir** ~ I was unaware of that; **Angst ist ihm** ~ he doesn't know what fear is; ~**e Größe** (Math, fig) unknown quantity; **nach** ~ **verzogen** moved - address unknown; ~**e Täter** person or persons unknown.

Unbekannte f (wk) **-n, -n** (Math) unknown.

Unbekannte(r) mf decl as adj stranger.

unbekannterweise adv grüße sie ~ von mir give her my regards although I don't know her.

unbekleidet adj bare. **sie war** ~ she had nothing on.

unbekümmert adj (a) (unbesorgt) unconcerned. **sei ganz** ~ don't worry. **(b)** (sorgenfrei) carefree.

unbelastet adj (a) (ohne Last) unloaded, unladen. **(b)** (ohne Schulden) unencumbered. **(c)** (Pol: ohne Schuld) guiltless. **(d)** (ohne Sorgen) free from worries.

un-: ~**belebt** adj Straße quiet; Natur inanimate; ~**belehrbar** adj fixed in one's views; Rassist etc dyed-in-the-wool attr; ~**beleuchtet** adj unlit; Fahrzeug without lights; ~**beliebt** adj unpopular (bei with); ~**bemannt** adj Raumflug unmanned; Fahrzeug driverless; ~**bemerkbar** adj imperceptible; ~**bemerkt** adj unnoticed; ~**bemittelt** adj without means; ~**benommen** adj pred (form) **es bleibt** or **ist Ihnen** ~**benommen, zu ...** you are at liberty to ...; ~**beobachtet** adj unobserved, unnoticed; **wenn er sich** ~**beobachtet fühlt ...** when he thinks nobody is looking ...; ~**bequem** adj (ungemütlich) uncomfortable; (lästig) Situation awkward; Aufgabe unpleasant; (mühevoll) difficult; **der Regierung** ~**bequem sein** to be an embarrassment to the government; ~**berechenbar** adj unpredictable; u~**berechtigt** adj unwarranted; Sorge, Kritik etc unfounded; (unbefugt) unauthorized.

unberücksichtigt adj unconsidered. **etw** ~ **lassen** not to consider sth.

unberührbar adj untouchable.

unberührt adj (a) ~ (untouched; Wald etc virgin; Natur unspoiled. ~ **sein** (Mädchen) to be a virgin. **(b)** (mitleidlos) unmoved. **(c)** (unbetroffen) unaffected.

unbeschadet prep+gen (form) regardless of.

unbeschädigt adj undamaged; Siegel unbroken. ~ **bleiben** not to be damaged/broken; (seelisch etc) to come off unscathed

unbeschäftigt adj (müßig) idle; (arbeitslos) not working.

unbescheiden adj presumptuous.

un-: ~**bescholten** adj (geh) respectable; Ruf spotless; ~**beschrankt** adj (Rail) without gates.

unbeschränkt adj unlimited; Macht absolute.

unbeschreiblich adj indescribable.

un-: ~**beschrieben** adj blank; ~**beschwert** adj (a) (sorgenfrei) carefree; Melodien light; (b) (ohne Gewicht) unweighted.

unbesehen adv indiscriminately; (ohne es anzusehen) without looking at it/them.

un-: ~**besetzt** adj vacant; Stuhl, Platz auch unoccupied; Bus, Zug empty; Schalter closed; ~**besiegbar** adj Armee etc invincible; (Sport auch) unbeatable; ~**besonnen** adj rash.

unbesorgt 1 adj unconcerned. **Sie können ganz** ~ **sein** you can set your mind at rest. **2** adv without worrying.

un-: ~**beständig** adj Wetter changeable; Mensch erratic; (launisch) moody; Liebhaber inconstant; ~**bestechlich** adj (a) Mensch incorruptible; (b) Urteil, Blick unerring; ~**bestimmbar** adj indeterminable; ~**bestimmt** adj (ungewiß) uncertain; Gefühl, Erinnerung vague; (Gram) indefinite; **auf** ~**bestimmte Zeit** indefinitely.

unbestreitbar adj Tatsache indisputable; Verdienste, Fähigkeiten unquestionable.

unbestritten adj undisputed, indisputable.

unbeteiligt adj (a) (uninteressiert) indifferent. **(b)** (nicht teilnehmend) uninvolved no adv (an +dat, bei in); (Jur, Comm) disinterested.

un-: ~**betont** adj unstressed; ~**beugsam** adj uncompromising; Wille unshakeable; ~**bewacht** adj (lit, fig) unguarded; Parkplatz unattended; ~**bewaffnet** adj unarmed; ~**beweglich** adj immovable; (steif) (geistig) rigid, inflexible; (bewegungslos) motionless; ~**bewegt** adj motionless; (fig: unberührt) unmoved; ~**bewiesen** adj unproven; ~**bewohnbar** adj uninhabitable; ~**bewohnt** adj Gegend uninhabited; Haus unoccupied; ~**bewußt** adj unconscious; Reflex involuntary; ~**bezahlbar** adj (a) (zu teuer) prohibitively expensive; (b) (fig) (komisch) priceless; (nützlich) invaluable; ~**bezahlt** adj unpaid; ~**bezähmbar** adj Optimismus etc irrepressible; Verlangen uncontrollable; ~**bezwinglich** adj unconquerable; Gegner invincible; Festung impregnable; Drang uncontrollable; ~**blutig** 1 adj bloodless; **2** adv without bloodshed; ~**brauchbar** adj (nutzlos) useless; (nicht zu verwenden) unusable; ~**bürokratisch** adj without any red tape.

und conj and. ~? well?; ~ **dann?** then what?; **ich** ~ **ihm Geld leihen?** (col) me, lend him money?; **er konnte** ~ **konnte nicht aufhören** he simply couldn't stop; ... ~ **wenn ich selbst bezahlen muß** ... even if I have to pay myself.

Undank m ingratitude. ~ **ernten** to get little thanks; ~ **ist der Welt Lohn** (Prov) never expect thanks for anything.

undankbar adj ungrateful; Arbeit thankless.

Undankbarkeit f ingratitude.

un-: ~**definierbar** adj indefinable; ~**denkbar** adj unthinkable, inconceivable.

undeutlich adj indistinct; Erinnerung vague; Schrift illegible; Ausdrucksweise unclear. ~ **sprechen** to speak indistinctly, to mumble.

undicht adj not air-/water-tight. **das Rohr ist** ~ the pipe leaks; **das Fenster ist** ~ the window lets in a draught (Brit) or draft (US); **eine** ~**e Stelle haben** (Rohr etc) to leak; (Reifen) to have a hole.

undifferenziert *adj* simplistic.

Unding *nt no pl* **es ist ein ~, ...** it is absurd ...

Un-: **u~diplomatisch** *adj* undiplomatic; **u~diszipliniert** *adj* undisciplined; **u~duldsam** *adj* intolerant *(gegen of)*; **~duldsamkeit** *f no pl* intolerance *(gegen of)*; **u~durchdringlich** *adj Urwald* impenetrable; *Gesicht* inscrutable; **u~durchführbar** *adj* impracticable, unworkable; **u~durchlässig** *adj* impermeable *(gegen to)*; **u~durchschaubar** *adj* unfathomable; *Mensch* inscrutable; **u~durchsichtig** *adj Fenster* opaque; *Papier Stoff* non-transparent; *(fig pej) Mensch, Methoden* devious; *Motive* obscure.

un|eben *adj* uneven; *Straße auch* bumpy.

Unebenheit *f siehe adj* unevenness; bumpiness. **kleine ~en** uneven patches.

un-: **~echt** *adj* false; *Schmuck, Edelstein, Blumen etc* artifical, fake *(usu pej)*; **~edel** *adj Metalle* base; **~ehelich** *adj* illegitimate; **~ehelich geboren sein** to be illegitimate; **~ehrenhaft** *adj* dishonourable *(Brit)*, dishonorable *(US)*; **~ehrlich** *adj* dishonest; **~ehrlich spielen** to cheat; **~eigennützig** *adj* unselfish, selfless.

un|eingeschränkt *adj* absolute, total; *Rechte, Handel* unrestricted; *Zustimmung* unqualified.

Un-: **u~einheitlich** *adj* non-uniform; *Preise* unsteady; **u~einheitlich sein** to vary; **u~einig** *adj* in disagreement; *Familie* divided; **über etw** *(acc)* **u~einig sein** to disagree about sth; **~einigkeit** *f* disagreement *(gen between)*; **u~einnehmbar** *adj* impregnable.

un|eins *adj pred* divided. **(mit jdm) ~ sein/werden** to disagree with sb.

un-: **~empfänglich** *adj (für to)* not susceptible; *(für Eindrücke, Atmosphäre)* insensitive; **~empfindlich** *adj (gegen to)* insensitive; *Bazillen etc* immune; *Pflanzen* hardy; *Textilien* practical.

un|endlich 1 *adj* infinite; *(zeitlich)* endless. **2** *adv* endlessly; *(fig: sehr)* terribly. **~ lange diskutieren** to argue endlessly.

Un|endlichkeit *f* infinity; *(zeitlich)* endlessness.

un-: **~entbehrlich** *adj* indispensable; **~entgeltlich** *adj* free of charge.

un|entschieden *adj* undecided; *(entschlußlos)* indecisive; *(Sport)* drawn. **~ enden** to end in a draw; **ein ~es Rennen** a dead heat.

Un|entschieden *nt -* *(Sport)* draw.

un|entschlossen *adj* undecided; *(entschlußlos) Mensch* indecisive.

un|entschuldbar *adj* inexcusable.

un|entschuldigt 1 *adj* unexcused. **~es Fernbleiben von der Arbeit/Schule** absenteeism/truancy. **2** *adv* without an excuse.

un|entwegt 1 *adj* constant, untiring. **einige U~e** a few stalwarts. **2** *adv* constantly, without tiring; **weiterarbeiten** unceasingly.

un|erbittlich *adj* relentless.

Un-: **u~erfahren** *adj* inexperienced; **u~erfindlich** *adj* incomprehensible; **u~erforschlich** *adj* impenetrable; *Wille* unfathomable; **u~erfreulich** *adj* unpleasant; **~erfreuliches** *(schlechte Nachrichten)* bad news *sing*; *(Übles)* bad things *pl*; **u~erfüllbar** *adj* unrealizable; **u~erfüllt** *adj* unfulfilled; **u~ergiebig** *adj Quelle, Thema* unproductive; *Boden, Ernte, Nachschlagewerk* poor; **u~ergründlich** *adj* unfathomable; **u~erheblich** *adj* insignificant; **u~erhofft** *adj* unexpected.

un|erhört¹ 1 *adj attr (ungeheuer)* enormous; *(empörend)* outrageous; *Frechheit* incredible. **2** *adv* incredibly. **~ viel a** tremendous amount (of).

un|erhört² *adj Bitte* unanswered.

un-: **~erkannt** *adj* unrecognized; **~erklärlich** *adj* inexplicable; **~erklärt** *adj Phänomen* unexplained; *Krieg, Liebe* undeclared; **~erläßlich** *adj* imperative.

un|erlaubt *adj* forbidden; *Betreten, Parken* unauthorized; *(ungesetzlich)* illegal.

un|erledigt *adj* unfinished; *Post* unanswered; *Rechnung* outstanding; *(schwebend)* pending.

un-: **u~ermeßlich** *adj* immense, vast; **~ermüdlich** *adj* untiring; **u~erprobt** *adj* untested, untried; **u~erreichbar** *adj Ziel* unattainable; *Ort* inaccessible; *(telefonisch)* unobtainable; **~erreicht** *adj* unequalled; *Ziel* unattained; **~ersättlich** *adj* insatiable; **~erschlossen** *adj Land* undeveloped; *Boden* unexploited; *Vorkommen, Markt* untapped; **~erschöpflich** *adj* inexhaustible; **~erschrocken** *adj* intrepid, courageous; **~erschütterlich** *adj* unshakeable; *Ruhe* imperturbable; **~erschwinglich** *adj* exorbitant, prohibitive; **für jdn ~erschwinglich sein** to be beyond sb's means; **~ersetzlich** *adj* irreplaceable; **~erträglich** *adj* unbearable; **~erwartet** *adj* unexpected; **~erwünscht** *adj Kind* unwanted; *Besuch, Effekt* unwelcome; **~erzogen** *adj* ill-mannered; *Kind auch* badly brought up.

un|fachmännisch *adj* unprofessional.

unfähig *adj* **(a)** *attr* incompetent. **(b)** **~ sein, etw zu tun** to be incapable of doing sth.

Unfähigkeit *f* **(a)** *(Untüchtigkeit)* incompetence. **(b)** *(Nichtkönnen)* inability.

Unfall *m, pl* **Unfälle** accident.

Unfall-: **~arzt** *m* specialist for accident injuries; **~flucht** *f* failure to stop after an accident; **~flucht begehen** to commit a hit-and-run offence *(Brit)* or offense *(US)*; **~folge** *f* result of an/the accident; **u~frei 1** *adj* accident-free; *Auto* with no accident damage; **2** *adv* without an accident; **~klinik** *f* accident hospital; **~opfer** *nt* casualty; **~ort** *m* scene of an/the accident; **~station** *f* accident or emergency ward; **~wagen** *m* car involved in an/the accident; *(col: Rettungswagen)* ambulance; **~zahl, ~ziffer** *f* number of accidents.

unfaßbar, unfaßlich *adj* incomprehensible.

un-: **~fehlbar 1** *adj* infallible; **2** *adv* without fail; **~fein** *adj* unrefined; **das ist ~fein** that's bad manners; **~fertig** *adj* unfinished, incomplete; *Mensch* immature; **~folgsam** *adj* disobedient; **~förmig** *adj (formlos)* shapeless; *(groß)* cumbersome; *Füße, Gesicht* unshapely; **~frankiert** *adj* unstamped.

unfrei *adj* **(a)** not free. **(b)** *(befangen)* constrained, uneasy. **(c)** *Brief* unfranked.

unfreiwillig *adj* compulsory; *Witz, Fehler* unintentional. **ich war ~er Zeuge** I was an unwilling witness.

unfreundlich *adj* unfriendly *(zu, gegen to)*; *Landschaft, Zimmer, Farbe* cheerless; *Akt* hostile.

Unfriede(n) *m* strife.

un-: **~frisiert** *adj Haare* uncombed; *Mensch* with one's hair all over the place; **~fruchtbar** *adj* infertile; *(fig) Debatte etc* fruitless; **die ~fruchtbaren Tage** *(Med)* the days of infertility.

Unfug ['ʊnfuːk] *m no pl* nonsense. **~ treiben** to get up to mischief.

Ungar(in *f*) ['ʊŋɡar(ɪn)] *m (wk)* **-n, -n** Hungarian.

ungarisch ['ʊŋɡarɪʃ] *adj* Hungarian.

Ungarn ['ʊŋɡarn] *nt* Hungary.

ungastlich *adj* inhospitable.

unge|achtet *prep+gen* in spite of, despite.

un-: **~geahndet** *adj (Jur)* unpunished; **~geahnt** *adj* undreamt-of; **~gebärdig** *adj* unruly; **~gebeten** *adj* uninvited; **~gebildet** *adj* uncultured; *(ohne Bildung)* uneducated; **~geboren** *adj* unborn; **~gebräuchlich** *adj* uncommon; **~gebrochen** *adj* unbroken.

ungebührlich *adj* improper. **sich ~ aufregen** to get unduly excited.

ungebunden *adj* **(a)** *Buch* unbound; *Blumen* loose. **(b)** **in ~er Rede** in prose. **(c)** *Leben* (fancy-)free; *(unverheiratet)* unattached; *(Pol)* independent. **frei und ~** footloose and fancy-free.

ungedeckt *adj* **(a)** *(schutzlos)* unprotected; *(Sport) Tor* undefended; *Spieler* unmarked;

Scheck uncovered. **(b)** *Tisch* unlaid *(Brit)*, not set *pred.*

Ųngeduld *f* impatience. **vor** ~ with impatience; **voller** ~ impatiently.

ụngeduldig *adj* impatient.

ụnge|eignet *adj* unsuitable.

ụngefähr 1 *adj attr* approximate, rough. **2** *adv* roughly, approximately. **(so)** ~ **dreißig** about *or* approximately thirty; **das kommt nicht von** ~ it's no accident; **wo** ~? whereabouts?; **so** ~! more or less!; **damit ich** ~ **weiß,** ... so that I have a rough idea ...; ~ **(so) wie** a bit like.

ụn-: ~**gefährdet** *adj* safe; ~**gefährlich** *adj* safe; *Tier, Krankheit, Arzneimittel etc* harmless; ~**gefällig** *adj Mensch* unobliging; ~**gefärbt** *adj Haare, Stoff* undyed; *Lebensmittel* without colouring *(Brit) or* coloring *(US)*; ~**gefedert** *adj* without springs; ~**gegliedert** *adj Körper* unjointed; *(fig)* disjointed; *Satz, Aufsatz etc* unstructured; ~**gehalten** *adj* indignant *(über +acc* about).

Ųngeheuer *nt* - monster.

ụngeheuer 1 *adj* **(a)** *(riesig)* enormous, immense. **(b)** = **ungeheuerlich. 2** *adv (sehr)* enormously, tremendously; *(negativ)* terribly.

ụngeheuerlich *adj* monstrous; *Verdacht, Dummheit* dreadful; *Leichtsinn* outrageous, appalling.

ụn-: ~**gehindert** *adj* unhindered; ~**gehobelt** *adj Mensch* boorish; ~**gehörig** *adj* impertinent; ~**gehorsam** *adj* disobedient; ~**gekämmt** *adj Haar* uncombed; ~**gekämmt aussehen** to look unkempt; ~**geklärt** *adj Abwasser* untreated; *Frage, Verbrechen* unsolved; *Ursache* unknown; ~**gekocht** *adj* raw; *Flüssigkeit* unboiled; *Obst etc* uncooked; ~**gekünstelt** *adj* natural; ~**gekürzt** *adj* not shortened; *Buch* unabridged; *Film* uncut; *Ausgaben* not cut back.

ụngelegen *adj* inconvenient. **komme ich (Ihnen)** ~? is this an inconvenient time for you?

Ųngelegenheiten *pl* inconvenience *sing.* **jdm** ~ **bereiten** to inconvenience sb.

ụn-: ~**gelehrig** *adj* unteachable; ~**gelenkig** *adj* stiff; *(fig col: nicht flexibel)* inflexible; ~**gelernt** *adj attr* unskilled; ~**gelogen** *adv* honestly.

ụngemein *adj* immense, tremendous.

ụngemustert *adj* plain.

ụn-: ~**gemütlich** *adj* uncomfortable; *Mensch* awkward; *Land, Wetter, Wochenende* unpleasant; **mir wird es hier** ~**gemütlich** I'm getting a bit uncomfortable; **er kann** ~**gemütlich werden** he can get nasty; ~**genannt** *adj* anonymous; ~**genau** *adj* inaccurate; *(vage)* vague; *(ungefähr)* approximate.

ụngeniert ['ʊnʒeniːɐt] **1** *adj* free and easy; *(bedenkenlos, taktlos)* uninhibited. **2** *adv* openly; *(bedenkenlos, taktlos)* without any inhibition.

ụngenießbar *adj (nicht zu essen)* inedible; *(nicht zu trinken)* undrinkable; *(unschmackhaft)* unpalatable; *(col) Mensch* unbearable.

ụngenügend *adj* inadequate, insufficient; *(Sch)* unsatisfactory.

Ụn-: **u**~**genutzt** *adj* unused; **eine Chance u**~**genutzt lassen** to miss an opportunity; **u**~**geordnet** *adj* disordered; **u**~**gepflegt** *adj Mensch* untidy; *Park, Hände etc* neglected; **sich u**~**gepflegt ausdrücken** to talk in a common way; **u**~**gerade** *adj* odd; **u**~**geraten** *adj Kind* ill-bred; **u**~**gerecht** *adj* unjust; **u**~**geregelt** *adj* irregular; **u**~**gereimt** *adj Verse* unrhymed; *(fig)* inconsistent; ~**gereimtheit** *f (fig)* inconsistency.

ụngern *adv* reluctantly. **(höchst)** ~! if I/we really have to!

ụn-: ~**gerufen** *adj* without being called; ~**gerührt** *adj* unmoved; ~**gesagt** *adj* unsaid; **etw** ~**gesagt machen** to pretend sth has never been said; ~**geschehen** *adj* undone; **etw** ~**geschehen machen** to undo sth; ~**geschickt** *adj* clumsy, awkward; *(unbedacht)* careless; ~**geschlechtlich** *adj* asexual; ~**geschliffen** *adj Edelstein* uncut; *Mes-*

ser blunt; *(fig) Benehmen* uncouth; ~**geschmäckt** *adj* undiminished; ~**geschmeidig** *adj Stoff, Leder* rough; *Haar* coarse; ~**geschminkt** *adj* without make-up; *(fig) Wahrheit* unvarnished.

ụngeschoren *adj* unshorn; *(fig)* spared. **jdn** ~ **lassen** *(col)* to spare sb; *(ungestraft)* to let sb off.

ụn-: ~**geschult** *adj* untrained; ~**geschützt** *adj* unprotected; *(Mil) Einheit* exposed; ~**gesetzlich** *adj* illegal; ~**gesichert** *adj* unsecured, not secured; *Schußwaffe* with the safety catch off; ~**gesittet** *adj* uncivilized; ~**gestört** *adj* undisturbed; *(Rad, TV etc)* without interference; ~**gestraft** *adv* with impunity.

ụngestüm ['ʊngəʃtyːm] *adj* impetuous.

ụn-: ~**gesund** *adj* unhealthy; ~**getan** *adj* undone; ~**getrübt** *adj* clear; *Glück* perfect.

Ųngetüm *nt* -e monster.

ụn-: ~**geübt** *adj* unpractised *(Brit)*, unpracticed *(US)*; *Mensch* out of practice; ~**gewandt** *adj* awkward.

ụngewiß *adj* uncertain; *(vage)* vague. **jdn (über etw** *acc)* **im ungewissen lassen** to leave sb in the dark (about sth).

Ųngewißheit *f* uncertainty.

ụngewöhnlich 1 *adj* unusual. **2** *adv* unusually.

ụngewohnt *adj* unusual; *(fremdartig)* strange, unfamiliar. **das ist mir** ~ I am not used to it.

ụngewollt *adj* unintentional.

Ųngeziefer *nt no pl* vermin.

ụngezogen *adj* ill-mannered.

Ụngezogenheit *f* bad manners *no indef art.*

ụn-: ~**gezügelt 1** *adj (unbeherrscht)* unbridled; *(ausschweifend)* dissipated; **2** *adj* without restraint; ~**gezwungen** *adj* casual, informal; **sich** ~**gezwungen bewegen** to feel quite free; ~**giftig** *adj* non-poisonous.

ụnglaubhaft *adj* incredible, unbelievable.

ụngläubig 1 *adj* unbelieving; *(zweifelnd)* doubting. ~**er** Thomas doubting Thomas. **2** *adv* doubtingly, in disbelief.

Ụngläubige(r) *mf* unbeliever.

ụnglaublich *adj* unbelievable, incredible.

ụnglaubwürdig *adj* implausible; *Dokument* dubious; *Mensch* unreliable. **sich** ~ **machen** to lose credibility.

ụngleich 1 *adj Charaktere* dissimilar; *Größe, Farbe* different; *(nicht gleichwertig, nicht vergleichbar)* *Mittel, Waffen* unequal; *(Math)* not equal. **2** *adv* much, incomparably.

ụngleichartig *adj* dissimilar.

Ụngleich-: **u**~**mäßig** *adj* uneven; *Atemzüge, Gesichtszüge, Puls* irregular; ~**mäßigkeit** *f siehe adj* unevenness; irregularity.

Ụnglück *nt* -e *(Unfall, Vorfall)* accident; *(Schicksalsschlag)* disaster, tragedy; *(Unheil)* misfortune; *(Pech, im Aberglauben, bei Glücksspiel)* bad luck; *(Unglücklichsein)* unhappiness. **das ist auch kein** ~ that's not a disaster; **das** ~ **wollte es, daß** ... as (bad) luck would have it, ...; **zu allem** ~ to make matters worse; **ein** ~ **kommt selten allein** *(Prov)* it never rains but it pours *(Prov)*.

ụnglücklich *adj* **(a)** *(traurig)* unhappy; *Liebe* unrequited. **ich U**~**(r)!** poor me! **(b)** *(bedauerlich)* sad, unfortunate. ~ **enden** to turn out badly.

ụnglücklicherweise *adv* unfortunately.

ụnglückselig *adj (liter)* unfortunate; *(armselig)* miserable; *(unglückbringend)* disastrous.

Ụnglücks-: ~**fall** *m* accident; ~**rabe** *m (col)* unlucky thing *(col)*; ~**zahl** *f* unlucky number.

Ųngnade *f* **bei jdm in** ~ **fallen** to fall out of favour *(Brit) or* favor *(US)* with sb.

ụngnädig *adj* ungracious.

ụngültig *adj* invalid; *(Sport) Tor* disallowed. **etw für** ~ **erklären** to declare sth null and void; **eine Ehe für** ~ **erklären** to annul a marriage.

ụngünstig *adj* unfavourable *(Brit)*, unfavorable *(US)*, disadvantageous; *Termin* inconvenient; *Augenblick, Wetter* bad; *(nicht preiswert)*

expensive.
ungut *adj* bad. **ein ~es Gefühl haben** to have an uneasy *or* bad feeling; **nichts für ~!** no offence *(Brit) or* offense *(US)!*
un-: **~haltbar** *adj Zustand* intolerable; *Vorwurf, Behauptung etc* untenable; *Torschuß* unstoppable; **~handlich** *adj* unwieldy.
Unheil *nt no pl* disaster. **~ stiften** to do damage.
unheilbar *adj* incurable.
Unheil-: **u~bringend** *adj* fateful, ominous; **~stifter** *m* mischief-maker; **u~voll** *adj* disastrous.
unheimlich 1 *adj* **(a)** *(angsterregend)* frightening, sinister. **das/er ist mir ~** it/he gives me the creeps *(col)*. **(b)** *(col)* tremendous *(col)*. **2** *adv (col: sehr)* incredibly *(col)*. **~ viele Menschen** an incredible number of people.
un-: **~höflich** *adj* impolite; **~hörbar** *adj* silent; *Frequenzen* inaudible.
Uni *f* **-s** *(col)* university.
uni [y'ni:] *adj pred* self-coloured *(Brit)*, self-colored *(US)*, plain.
Uniform *f* **-en** uniform.
uniformieren* *vt (einheitlich machen)* to make uniform.
un-: **~interessant** *adj* uninteresting; **sein Angebot ist für uns ~interessant** we're not interested in his offer; **~interessiert** *adj (neutral)* disinterested; *(nicht interessiert)* uninterested.
Union *f* **-en** union. **die ~** *(BRD Pol)* the CDU and CSU.
Unionsparteien *pl (BRD Pol)* CDU and CSU parties *pl*.
universal, universell [univer-] *adj* universal.
Universal- [univer'za:l-] *in cpds* universal; *Bildung etc* general; **~genie** *nt* universal genius.
Universität [univerzi'te:t] *f* university. **die ~ Freiburg, die Freiburger ~** the University of Freiburg, Freiburg University; **auf die ~ gehen, die ~ besuchen** to go to university.
Universitäts- *in cpds* university; **~klinik** *f* university clinic *or* hospital.
Universum [uni'verzʊm] *nt no pl* universe.
Unkenruf *m (fig)* prophecy of doom.
unkenntlich *adj* unrecognizable; *Inschrift etc* indecipherable.
Unkenntlichkeit *f siehe adj* unrecognizableness; indecipherability. **bis zur ~** beyond recognition.
Unkenntnis *f no pl* ignorance. **in ~ über etw** *(acc)* **sein** to be ignorant about sth.
unklar *adj* hazy; *Wetter* hazy. **ich bin mir darüber noch im ~en** I'm not quite clear about that yet; **jdn über etw** *(acc)* **im ~en lassen** to leave sb in the dark about sth; **nur ~ zu erkennen sein** not to be easily discernible.
Unklarheit *f* lack of clarity; *(über Tatsachen)* uncertainty. **darüber herrscht noch ~** it is still unclear.
un-: **~klug** *adj* unwise; **~kollegial** *adj* uncooperative; **~kompliziert** *adj* straightforward, uncomplicated; **~kontrollierbar** *adj* uncontrollable; **~kontrollierbar werden** *(Mißbrauch etc)* to get out of hand; **~kontrolliert** *adj* unchecked; **~korrekt** *adj* **(a)** improper; **(b)** *(unrichtig)* incorrect.
Unkosten *pl* costs *pl*; *(Ausgaben)* expenses *pl*. **sich in ~ stürzen** *(col)* to go to a lot of expense.
Unkraut *nt* weed. **von ~ übersät** overgrown with weeds; **~ vergeht nicht** *(Prov)* it would take more than that to finish me/him *etc* off!
Unkraut-: **~bekämpfung** *f* weed control; **~vertilgungsmittel** *nt* weed killer.
unkündbar *adj* permanent; *Vertrag* binding. **in ~er Stellung** in a permanent position.
unkundig *adj (geh)* ignorant *(+gen of)*. **des Lesens/Schreibens ~ sein** to be illiterate.
un-: **~längst** *adv (geh)* recently; **~lauter** *adj* dishonest; *Wettbewerb* unfair; **~leserlich** *adj* unreadable; *Handschrift etc auch* illegible;

~leugbar *adj* undeniable; indisputable; **~lieb** *adj:* **es ist mir nicht ~lieb, daß ... I am quite glad that ...;** **~liebsam** *adj* unpleasant; **~lösbar** *adj Problem,* *(Chem)* insoluble; *(untrennbar)* indissoluble; *Widerspruch* irreconcilable.
Unlust *f no pl* **(a)** *(Widerwille)* reluctance. **(b)** *(Lustlosigkeit)* listlessness.
unlustig *adj (gelangweilt)* bored; *(widerwillig)* reluctant.
unmännlich *adj* unmanly.
Unmasse *f (col)* load *(col)*. **eine ~ Leute** loads of people.
unmaßgeblich *adj* inconsequential. **nach meiner ~en Meinung** *(hum)* in my humble opinion *(hum)*.
unmäßig *adj* excessive, immoderate.
Unmenge *f* vast number; *(bei unzählbaren Begriffen)* vast amount. **~n von Leuten** vast numbers of people.
Unmensch *m* monster.
unmenschlich *adj* inhuman.
un-: **~merklich** *adj* imperceptible; **~mißverständlich** *adj* unequivocal.
unmittelbar 1 *adj* direct; *Nähe etc* immediate. **2** *adv* immediately; *(direkt)* directly. **~ vor** *(+dat) (zeitlich)* immediately before; *(räumlich)* right *or* directly in front of.
un-: **~möbliert** *adj* unfurnished; **~modern** *adj* old-fashioned.
unmöglich 1 *adj* impossible. **das ist mir ~** that is impossible for me; **U~es/das U~e** the impossible; **~ aussehen** *(col)* to look ridiculous. **2** *adv (keinesfalls)* not possibly; *(pej col: unpassend)* impossibly. **ich kann es ~ tun** I cannot possibly do it.
Un-: **~moral** *f* immorality; **u~moralisch** *adj* immoral; **u~mündig** *adj (minderjährig)* underage; **wir wollen nicht länger wie ~mündige behandelt werden** we don't want to go on being treated as though we were incapable of thinking for ourselves.
Unmut *m* ill-humour *(Brit)*, ill-humor *(US)*; *(Unzufriedenheit)* displeasure *(über+acc at)*.
un-: **~nachahmlich** *adj* inimitable; **~nachgiebig** *adj* inflexible; *(fig) Mensch auch* intransigent; **~nachsichtig 1** *adj* severe; *Strenge* unrelenting; **2** *adv* hinrichten mercilessly; *bestrafen* severely; **~nahbar** *adj* unapproachable; **~natürlich** *adj* unnatural; **~normal** *adj* abnormal; **~nötig** *adj* unnecessary; **~nötigerweise** *adv* unnecessarily, needlessly.
unnütz *adj* useless; *Geschwätz* idle.
UNO ['u:no] *f no pl* **die ~** the UN *sing*.
unordentlich *adj* untidy; *Lebenswandel* disorderly.
Un|ordnung *f* disorder *no indef art;* *(in Zimmer etc auch)* untidiness *no indef art;* *(Durcheinander)* mess. **mach nicht so eine ~!** don't make such a mess!
un-: **~organisch** *adj* inorganic; **~organisiert** *adj* disorganized; **~orthodox** *adj* unorthodox; **~pädagogisch** *adj* educationally unsound; *Lehrer etc* bad (as a teacher).
unparteiisch *adj* impartial.
Unparteiische(r) *mf decl as adj* neutral person. **der ~** *(Sport)* the referee.
Un-: **u~passend** *adj* unsuitable; *Zeit auch* inconvenient; **u~päßlich** *adj (geh)* indisposed *(form)*; **~person** *f* persona non grata; **u~persönlich** *adj* impersonal *(auch Ling)*; *Mensch* aloof; **u~praktisch** *adj Mensch* unpractical; *Maschine, Lösung* impractical; **u~problematisch** *adj* unproblematic; *(einfach)* uncomplicated; **u~produktiv** *adj* unproductive; **u~pünktlich** *adj Mensch* unpunctual; *Zug* not on time; **~pünktlich kommen/abfahren** to come/leave late; **u~qualifiziert** *adj* unqualified; *Äußerung* incompetent.
Unrast *f no pl (geh)* restlessness.

Unrat ['unraːt] *m no pl (geh)* refuse; *(fig)* filth.
un-: ~**rationell** *adj* inefficient; ~**ratsam** *adj* inadvisable; ~**recht** *adj* wrong; **das ist mir gar nicht so** ~**recht I** don't really mind.
Unrecht *nt no pl* wrong, injustice. **zu** ~ *verdächtigt* wrongly, unjustly; **nicht zu** ~ not without good reason; **im** ~ **sein** to be wrong; **u**~ **haben** to be wrong; **jdm u**~ **tun** to do sb an injustice.
unrechtmäßig *adj* unlawful, illegal.
un-: ~**redlich** *adj* dishonest; ~**reell** *adj* unfair; *(unredlich)* dishonest; *Preis* unreasonable.
unregelmäßig *adj* irregular.
Unregelmäßigkeit *f* irregularity.
Un-: **u**~**reif** *adj* immature; *Obst* unripe; ~**reife** *f siehe adj* immaturity; unripeness.
unrein *adj* not clean; *Ton* impure; *Atem, Haut* bad; *Gedanken, Taten* impure. **etw ins** ~**e schreiben** to write sth out in rough.
unrentabel *adj* unprofitable.
unrichtig *adj* incorrect.
Unruhe *f* -**n** **(a)** *no pl* restlessness; *(Nervosität)* agitation; *(Besorgnis)* disquiet. **(b)** *no pl (Lärm)* noise, disturbance; *(Geschäftigkeit)* bustle. **(c)** *no pl (Unfrieden)* unrest *no pl*, trouble. ~ **stiften** to create unrest; *(in Familie, Schule)* to make trouble.
Unruhestifter(in *f)* *m* - troublemaker.
unruhig *adj* restless; *(nervös auch)* fidgety *no adv; (laut, belebt)* noisy; *Schlaf* fitful; *Zeit etc, Meer* troubled.
unrühmlich *adj* inglorious.
uns **1** *pers pron acc, dat of* **wir** us; *(dat auch)* to/for us. **bei** ~ *(zu Hause, im Betrieb etc)* at our place; *(in unserer Beziehung)* between us; *(in unserem Land)* in our country; **ein Freund von** ~ a friend of ours. **2** *refl pron acc, dat* ourselves; *(einander)* each other, one another. ~ **selbst** ourselves; **unter** ~ **gesagt** between you and me; **mitten unter** ~ in our midst; **hier sind wir unter** ~ we are alone here; **das bleibt unter** ~ it won't go any further.
unsachgemäß *adj* improper.
unsachlich *adj* unobjective; *(fehl am Platz)* uncalled-for. ~ **werden** to become personal.
unsanft *adj* rough; *(unhöflich)* rude.
unsauber *adj* **(a)** *(schmutzig)* dirty. **(b)** *Handschrift, Arbeit* untidy; *(nicht exakt) Schuß, Schnitt* inaccurate; *Klang* impure. **(c)** *(unmoralisch)* shady; *Spielweise* dirty.
unschädlich *adj* harmless; *Bombe auch* safe. **jdn** ~ **machen** *(col)* to take care of sb *(col)*.
unscharf *adj* blurred, fuzzy; *Foto auch* out of focus; *(Rad)* unclear.
unschätzbar *adj* incalculable; *Hilfe* invaluable. **von** ~**em Wert** invaluable; *Schmuck* priceless.
unscheinbar *adj* inconspicuous; *(unattraktiv) Mensch* unprepossessing.
unschicklich *adj* unseemly, improper.
unschlagbar *adj* unbeatable.
unschlüssig *adj* undecided. **er ist sich** *(dat)* **noch** ~ he's still undecided, he hasn't made up his mind yet.
unschön *adj (häßlich)* unsightly; *(stärker)* ugly; *Gesicht* plain; *(unangenehm)* unpleasant. ~**e Szenen** ugly scenes.
Unschuld *f no pl* innocence; *(Jungfräulichkeit)* virginity; *(fig: Mädchen)* innocent.
unschuldig *adj* innocent *(an +dat* of). **schuldig oder** ~ guilty or not guilty; **sie ist noch** ~ she is still a virgin.
Unschulds-: ~**engel** *m (col)* little innocent; ~**miene** *f* innocent expression.
unschwer *adv* easily, without difficulty.
unselbständig **1** *adj Denken, Handeln* lacking in independence; *Mensch auch* dependent, unable to stand on one's own two feet. **Einkünfte aus** ~**er Arbeit** income from (salaried) employment. **2** *adv (mit fremder Hilfe)* not independently.

Unselbständige(r) *mf decl as adj (Fin)* employed person.
unselig *adj* unfortunate; *(verhängnisvoll)* ill-fated.
unser *poss pron* our.
unser|einer, unser|eins *indef pron (col)* the likes of us *(col)*.
uns(e)re(r, s) *poss pron (substantivisch)* ours. **der/die/das** ~ *(geh)* ours; **wir tun das U**~ *(geh)* we are doing our bit; **die U**~**n** *(geh)* our family.
unser(er)seits *adv (auf unserer Seite)* for our part; *(von unserer Seite)* on our part.
uns(e)resgleichen *indef pron* people like us.
uns(e)rige(r, s) *poss pron (old,geh)* **der/die/das** ~ ours; *siehe* **uns(e)re(r, s).**
unseriös *adj* **(a)** not serious. **(b)** *(unehrlich)* not straight, untrustworthy.
unsert-: ~**halben,** ~**wegen** *adv* on our behalf; ~**willen** *adv:* **um** ~**willen** for our sake.
unsicher *adj* **(a)** *(gefährlich)* dangerous, unsafe. **die Gegend** ~ **machen** *(fig col)* to knock about the district *(col)*. **(b)** *(nicht selbstbewußt)* insecure. **(c)** *(ungewiß, zweifelhaft)* unsure, uncertain; *Verhältnisse* unstable. **(d)** *(ungeübt, ungefestigt)* unsure; *Hand* unsteady; *Kenntnisse* shaky. ~ **auf den Beinen** unsteady on one's feet.
Unsicherheit *f siehe adj* **(a)** danger. **(b)** insecurity. **(c)** uncertainty; instability.
unsichtbar *adj (lit, fig)* invisible.
Unsinn *m no pl* nonsense *no indef art,* rubbish *no indef art.* ~ **machen** to do silly things; ~ **reden** to talk nonsense; **laß den** ~! stop fooling about!
unsinnig *adj (sinnlos)* nonsensical; *(ungerechtfertigt)* unreasonable.
Unsitte *f (schlechte Gewohnheit)* bad habit.
unsittlich *adj* immoral.
unsolid(e) *adj Mensch* free-living; *(unredlich) Firma* unreliable.
un-: ~**sozial** *adj Verhalten* antisocial; *Politik* unsocial; ~**spezifisch** *adj* non-specific; ~**sportlich** *adj* unathletic; *(unfair)* unsporting; ~**statthaft** *adj (form)* inadmissible; *(~gesetzlich)* illegal; *(Sport)* not allowed.
unsterblich **1** *adj* immortal; *Liebe* undying. **jdn** ~ **machen** to immortalize sb. **2** *adv (col)* utterly.
Unsterblichkeit *f* immortality.
unstet *adj Glück, Liebe* fickle; *Mensch* restless; *(wankelmütig)* changeable; *Entwicklung* unsteady; *Leben* unsettled.
Un-: **u**~**stillbar** *adj Durst* unquenchable; *Sehnsucht, Hunger* insatiable; ~**stimmigkeit** *f (Streit)* difference; **u**~**streitig** *adv* indisputably; ~**summe** *f* vast sum.
unsympathisch *adj* unpleasant, disagreeable. **das/er ist mir** ~ I don't like that/him.
untad(e)lig *adj* impeccable; *Mensch* beyond reproach.
Untat *f* atrocity.
untätig *adj (müßig)* idle; *(nicht handelnd)* passive; *Vulkan* inactive, dormant.
un-: ~**tauglich** *adj (zu, für* for) unsuitable *(für Wehrdienst)* unfit; ~**teilbar** *adj* indivisible.
unten *adv* at the bottom; *(tiefer, drunten)* (down) below; *(an der Unterseite)* underneath; *(in Gebäude)* downstairs. ~ **am Berg/im Glas** at the bottom of the mountain/glass; **nach** ~ down; **bis** ~ to the bottom; **dort** *or* **da/hier** ~ down there/ here; **weiter** ~ further down; ~ **bleiben** to stay down; **rechts/links** ~ down on the right/left; *siehe* ~ see below; **er ist bei mir** ~ **durch** *(col)* I'm through with him *(col)*.
unten-: ~**an** *adv (am unteren Ende)* at the far end; *(in Reihenfolge: lit, fig)* at the bottom; **(bei jdm)** ~**an stehen** *(fig)* to be at the bottom of sb's list; ~**drunter** *adv (col)* underneath.
unter *prep* **(a)**+*dat* under; *(drunter)* underneath, below; *(zwischen, innerhalb)* among(st). ~ **18 Jahren** under 18 years (of age); **Temperaturen**

~ **25 Grad** temperatures below 25 degrees; **sie waren** ~ **sich** (*dat*) they were by themselves; **jdn** ~ **sich haben** to have sb under one; ~ **anderem** among other things. (**b**)+*acc* under. **bis** ~ **das Dach voll mit** ... full to the rafters with...

Unter-: ~**abteilung** *f* subdivision; ~**arm** *m* forearm; ~**art** *f* (*esp Biol*) subspecies; ~**bau** *m, pl* **-ten** (*von Gebäude*) foundations *pl*; (*bei Straßen*) (road)bed; **ʉ**~**belegt** *adj Hotel etc* not full; *Kurs* under-subscribed; **ʉ**~**belichten*** *vti insep* (*Phot*) to underexpose; **ʉ**~**besetzt** *adj* understaffed; **ʉ**~**bewerten*** *vt insep* to underrate; **ʉ**~**bewußt** *adj* subconscious; ~**bewußtsein** *nt* subconscious; **im** ~**bewußtsein** subconsciously; **ʉ**~**bezahlen*** *vt insep* to underpay; **ʉ**~**bieten*** *vt insep irreg Konkurrenten* to undercut; (*fig*) to surpass; **ʉ**~**binden*** *vt insep irreg* to stop, to prevent; **ʉ**~**bleiben*** *vi insep irreg aux sein* (**a**) (*aufhören*) to stop; **in Zukunft muß das ʉ**~**bleiben** that must not happen again in the future; (**b**) (*versäumt werden*) to be omitted; **ʉ**~**brechen*** *vt insep irreg* to interrupt; *Reise, Eintönigkeit* to break; (*langfristig*) to break off; *Telefonverbindung* to disconnect; *Spiel* to suspend, to stop; **wir sind ʉ**~**brochen worden** (*am Telefon*) we've been cut off; ~**brecherkontakte** *pl* points *pl*; ~**brechung** *f* interruption; break (+*gen* in); (*von Telefonverbindung*) disconnection; (*von Spiel*) stoppage;**ohne** ~**brechung** without a break; **ʉ**~**breiten*** *vt insep Plan* to present; (**jdm**) **einen Vorschlag ʉ**~**breiten** to make a proposal (to sb).

ʉnterbringen *vt sep irreg* (**a**) to put; *Arbeitslose etc* to fix up (*bei* with). **ich kann nicht alles im Schrank** ~ I can't put *or* get everything in the cupboard; **ich kenne ihn, aber ich kann ihn nirgends** ~ (*col*) I know him, but I just can't place him. (**b**) (*Unterkunft geben*) *Menschen* to accommodate; (*in Haus, Hotel etc auch*) to put up. **gut/ schlecht untergebracht sein** to have good/bad accommodation (*Brit*) *or* accommodations (*US*); (*versorgt werden*) to be well/badly looked after.

Unterbringung *f* accommodation (*Brit*), accommodations *pl* (*US*).

ʉnterbuttern *vt sep* (*col*) (**a**) (*zuschießen*) to throw in. (**b**) (*unterdrücken*) to ride roughshod over.

unterderhand *adv* secretly; *verkaufen* privately.

unterdessen *adv* (in the) meantime, meanwhile.

unterdrücken* *vt insep* (**a**) *Neugier, Lachen* to suppress; *Gähnen* to stifle; *Tränen, Bemerkung* to hold back. (**b**) (*beherrschen*) *Menschen* to oppress; *Freiheit, Revolution* to suppress.

Unterdrücker(in *f*) *m* - oppressor.

ʉnterdurchschnittlich *adj* below average.

unter|einander *adv* (**a**) (*gegenseitig*) each other; (*miteinander*) among ourselves/themselves *etc*. (**b**) (*räumlich*) one below the other.

unter|einander- *pref* (**a**) (*durcheinander-*) together. (**b**) (*örtlich*) one below the other.

ʉnter|entwickelt *adj* underdeveloped.

untere(r, s) *adj, superl* **unterste(r, s)** lower.

Unter-: ʉ~**ernährt** *adj* undernourished; ~**ernährung** *f* malnutrition.

Unterfangen *nt* - (*geh*) venture, undertaking.

Unterführung *f* underpass.

Untergang *m* (**a**) (*von Schiff*) sinking. (**b**) (*von Gestirn*) setting. (**c**) (*das Zugrundehen*) (*allmählich*) decline; (*völlig*) destruction; (*der Welt etc*) (*von Individuum*) downfall, ruin. **dem** ~ **geweiht sein** to be doomed.

Untergebene(r) *mf decl as adj* subordinate.

ʉntergegangen *adj Volk etc* extinct.

ʉntergehen *vi sep irreg aux sein* (**a**) (*versinken*) to sink; (*Schiff auch*) to go down; (*fig: im Lärm etc*) to be drowned. (**b**) (*Gestirn*) to set. (**c**) (*Kultur, Welt*) to come to an end; (*Individuum*) to perish; (*im Existenzkampf*) to go under.

Unter-: ʉ~**geordnet** *adj Dienststelle* subordinate;

Bedeutung secondary; ~**geschoß** *nt* basement; ~**gewicht** *nt* ~**gewicht haben** to be underweight; **ʉ**~**gliedern*** *vt insep* to subdivide; **ʉ**~**graben*** *vt insep irreg* to undermine.

Untergrund *m no pl* (**a**) (*Geol*) subsoil. (**b**) (*farblicher Hintergrund*) background. (**c**) (*Pol etc*) underground. **in den** ~ **gehen** to go underground.

Untergrund- in *cpds* (*Pol etc*) underground; ~**bahn** *f* underground (*Brit*), subway (*US*).

Unter-: ~**gruppe** *f* subgroup; **ʉ**~**haken** *vr sep* **sich bei jdm ʉ**~**haken** to link arms with sb.

ʉnterhalb 1 *prep*+*gen* below. **2** *adv* below.

Unterhalt *m no pl* (**a**) (*Lebens*~) keep, maintenance (*esp Jur*). **seinen** ~ **verdienen** to earn one's living; **seinen** ~ **haben** to earn enough. (**b**) (*Instandhaltung*) upkeep.

unterhalten* *insep irreg* **1** *vt* (**a**) (*versorgen*) to support. (**b**) *Geschäft, Kfz*, to run; *Konto* to have. (**c**) (*pflegen*) *Kontakte* to maintain. (**d**) *Gäste, Publikum* to entertain. **2** *vr* (**a**) (*sprechen*) to talk (*mit* to, with). **sich mit jdm (über etw** *acc*) ~ to (have a) talk with sb (about sth). (**b**) (*sich vergnügen*) to enjoy oneself.

Unterhalter(in *f*) *m* - (**a**) entertainer. (**b**) (*Verdiener*) breadwinner.

unterhaltsam *adj* entertaining.

Unterhaltskosten *pl* maintenance costs *pl*.

Unterhaltung *f* (**a**) (*Gespräch*) talk, conversation. (**b**) (*Amüsement*) entertainment. (**c**) *no pl* (*Instandhaltung*) upkeep; (*von Gebäuden auch, von Kfz, Maschinen*) maintenance.

Unterhaltungs-: ~**elektronik** *f* (*Industrie*) entertainment electronics *sing*; (*Geräte*) audio systems *pl*; ~**literatur** *f* light fiction; ~**programm** *nt* light entertainment programme (*Brit*) *or* program (*US*).

Unterhändler *m* negotiator.

Unterhaus *nt* House of Commons (*Brit*), Lower House.

Unterhemd *nt* vest (*Brit*), undershirt (*US*).

unterhöhlen* *vt insep* to hollow out; (*fig*) to undermine.

Unterholz *nt no pl* undergrowth.

Unterhose *f* (*Herren*~) (pair of) underpants *pl*; (*Damen*~) (pair of) pants *pl*. **lange** ~**n** long johns *pl*.

unter|irdisch *adj* underground.

unter|jochen* *vt insep* to subjugate.

unterjubeln *vt sep* (*col*) **jdm etw** ~ (*andrehen*) to palm sth off on sb (*col*); (*anlasten*) to pin sth on sb (*col*).

unterkellern* *vt insep* to build with a cellar.

Unter-: ~**kiefer** *m* lower jaw; ~**klasse** *f* (**a**) subclass; (**b**) (*Sociol*) lower class; ~**kleidung** *f* underwear, underclothes *pl*.

ʉnterkommen *vi sep irreg aux sein* (**a**) (*Unterkunft finden*) to find accommodation (*Brit*) *or* accommodations (*US*); (*col: Stelle finden*) to find a job (*als as, bei* with, at). **bei jdm** ~ to stay at sb's (place). (**b**) **so etwas ist mir noch nie untergekommen!** (*col*) I've never come across anything like it!

Unterkommen *nt* - (*Obdach*) accommodation (*Brit*), accommodations (*US*). **bei jdm ein** ~ **finden** to be put up at sb's (place).

Unter-: ~**körper** *m* lower part of the body; **ʉ**~**kriegen** *vt sep* (*col*) **sich nicht ʉ**~**kriegen lassen** not to let things get one down; **ʉ**~**kühlen*** *vt insep Körper* to expose to subnormal temperatures; **ʉ**~**kühlt** *adj Körper* affected by hypothermia; (*fig*) *Atmosphäre, Mensch* cool; ~**kühlung** *f* (*Med*) hypothermia.

Unterkunft *f, pl* **Unterkünfte** (**a**) accommodation (*Brit*), accommodations (*US*). ~ **und Verpflegung** board and lodging. (**b**) (*von Soldaten etc*) quarters *pl*; (*esp in Privathaus*) billet.

Unterlage *f* (**a**) base; (*für Teppich*) underlay; (*im*

Bett) drawsheet. **(b)** *usu pl (Papiere)* document, paper.

unterlassen* *vt insep irreg (nicht tun)* to refrain from; *(nicht durchführen)* not to carry out; *(auslassen)* to omit; *etwas Dummes etc* to refrain from doing. **er hat es ~, mich zu benachrichtigen** he failed *or* omitted to notify me.

Unterlassung *f (Versäumnis)* omission (of sth), failure (to do sth).

Unterlauf *m* lower reaches (of a river).

unterlaufen[1]* *insep irreg* **1** *vi+dat aux sein* **mir ist ein Fehler ~** I made a mistake. **2** *vt Bestimmungen* to get around.

unterlaufen[2] *adj* **mit Blut ~** bloodshot.

unterlegen *adj* inferior; *(besiegt)* defeated. **jdm ~ sein** to be inferior to sb.

Unterlegene(r) *mf decl as adj* underdog.

Unterleib *m* abdomen.

Unterleibs- *in cpds* abdominal; **~krebs** *m* cancer of the abdomen; cancer of the womb.

unterliegen* *vi insep irreg aux sein* **(a)** *(besiegt werden)* to be defeated *(+dat* by*)*. **(b)**+*dat (unterworfen sein)* to be subject to; *einer Gebühr, Steuer* to be liable to. **es unterliegt keinem Zweifel, daß ...** it's not open to any doubt that ...

Unterlippe *f* bottom *or* lower lip.

unterm = unter dem.

untermalen* *vt insep (mit Musik)* to provide with background music.

untermauern* *vt insep (Build, fig)* to underpin.

Untermensch *m* subhuman creature.

Untermiete *f* subtenancy. **bei jdm zur ~ wohnen** to rent a room from sb.

Untermieter(in *f)* *m* lodger, subtenant *(Jur)*.

unterminieren* *vt insep (lit, fig)* to undermine.

untern = unter den.

unternehmen* *vt insep irreg* to do; *(durchführen auch)* to undertake; *Versuch, Vorstoß, Reise* to make. **etwas/nichts gegen jdn/etw ~** to do something/nothing about sb/sth.

Unternehmen *nt* - **(a)** *(Firma)* business, enterprise. **(b)** *(Aktion, Vorhaben)* undertaking, enterprise; *(Mil)* operation.

Unternehmens-: **~berater** *m* management consultant; **~leitung** *f* management.

Unternehmer(in *f)* *m* - (business) employer; *(alten Stils)* entrepreneur. **die ~** the employers.

unternehmerisch *adj* entrepreneurial.

Unternehmer-: **~kreise** *pl* in/aus **~kreisen** in/ from business circles; **~verband** *m* employers' association.

Unternehmung *f* **(a)** *siehe* **Unternehmen.** **(b)** *(Transaktion)* undertaking.

Unternehmungs-: **~geist** *m no pl* enterprise; **~lust** *f no pl* enterprise; **u~lustig** *adj* enterprising.

Unter-: **~offizier** *m* non-commissioned officer, NCO; **u~ordnen** *sep* **1** *vt* to subordinate *(+dat* to*)*; **2** *vr* to subordinate oneself *(+dat* to*)*; **~ordnung** *f* **(a)** *no pl* subordination; **(b)** *(Biol)* sub-order; **~organisation** *f* subsidiary organization; **u~privilegiert** *adj* underprivileged.

unterreden* *vr insep* **sich (mit jdm) ~** to confer (with sb).

Unterredung *f* discussion; *(Pol auch)* talks *pl.*

Unterricht *m no pl* lessons *pl*, classes *pl.* **~ in Mathematik/Englisch** maths/English lessons *or* classes; **seine Art des ~s** his way of teaching; **(jdm) ~ geben** to teach (sb) *(in etw (dat)* sth*)*; **am ~ teilnehmen** to attend classes; **zu spät zum ~ kommen** to be late for class.

unterrichten* *insep* **1** *vt* **(a)** *Schüler, Fach* to teach. **jdn in etw** *(dat)* **~** to teach sb sth. **(b)** *(informieren)* to inform *(von, über+acc* about*)*. **gut ~e Kreise** well-informed circles. **2** *vi* to teach. **3** *vr* **sich über etw** *(acc)* **~** to inform oneself about sth.

Unterrichts-: **~einheit** *f* teaching unit; **~fach** *nt*

subject; **u~frei** *adj Stunde, Tag* free; **der Montag ist u~frei** there are no classes on Monday; **~gegenstand** *m* topic, subject; **~methode** *f* teaching method; **~mittel** *nt* teaching aid; **~stoff** *m* subject matter; **~zwecke** *pl* **zu ~zwecken** for teaching purposes.

Unterrock *m* underskirt, slip.

unters = unter das.

untersagen* *vt insep* to forbid, to prohibit. **jdm etw ~** to forbid sb sth.

Untersatz *m* mat; *(für Blumentöpfe etc)* base.

unterschätzen* *vt insep* to underestimate.

unterscheiden* *insep irreg* **1** *vt* to distinguish. **A nicht von B ~ können** to be unable to tell the difference between A and B, to be unable to tell A from B. **2** *vi* to differentiate, to distinguish. **3** *vr* **sich von etw ~** to differ (from) sth.

Unterscheidung *f* differentiation; *(Unterschied)* difference, distinction. **eine ~ treffen** to make a distinction.

Unterschenkel *m* lower leg.

Unterschicht *f (Sociol)* lower class.

unterschieben[1]* *vt insep irreg (col: unterstellen)* **jdm etw ~** to attribute sth to sb; **du unterschiebst mir immer, daß ich schwindle** you're always accusing me of cheating.

unterschieben[2] *vt sep irreg* **(a)** *(lit)* **etw unter etw** *(acc)* **~** to push sth under(neath) sth. **(b)** *(fig)* **jdm etw ~** to foist sth on sb.

Unterschied *m* **-e** difference; *(Unterscheidung auch)* distinction. **einen ~ (zwischen zwei Dingen) machen** to make a distinction (between two things); **das macht keinen ~** that makes no difference; **im ~ zu jdm/etw** in contrast to sb/sth; **alle ohne ~ halfen mit** everyone without exception lent a hand; **es wurden alle ohne ~ getötet** everyone was killed indiscriminately.

unterschiedlich *adj* different; *(veränderlich)* variable; *(gemischt)* varied, patchy. **das ist sehr ~** it varies a lot; **~ gut/lang** of varying quality/length.

unterschiedslos *adv* indiscriminately; *(gleichmäßig)* on an equal basis.

unterschlagen* *vt insep irreg Geld* to embezzle; *Brief, Beweise* to withhold; *(col) Nachricht etc* to keep quiet about.

Unterschlagung *f (von Geld)* embezzlement.

Unterschlupf *m, pl* **Unterschlüpfe** *(Obdach)* shelter; *(Versteck)* hiding place.

unterschlüpfen *vi sep aux sein (col)* to take cover or shelter; *(Versteck finden)* to hide out *(col) (bei jdm* at sb's*)*.

unterschreiben* *vti insep irreg* to sign. **das kann ich ~!** *(fig)* I'll subscribe to that!

unterschreiten* *vt insep irreg* to fall short of; *Temperatur, Zahlenwert* to fall below.

Unterschrift *f* **(a)** signature. **seine ~ leisten** to give one's signature; **jdm etw zur ~ vorlegen** to give sb sth to sign; **eigenhändige ~** personal signature. **(b)** *(Bild~)* caption.

unterschrifts-: **~berechtigt** *adj* authorized to sign; **~reif** *adj Vertrag* ready to be signed.

unterschwellig *adj* subliminal.

Unterseeboot *nt* submarine.

unterseeisch [-zeːɪʃ] *adj* undersea, submarine.

Unter-: **~seite** *f* underside; **~setzer** *m* - *siehe* **~satz;** **u~setzt** *adj* stocky; **~stadt** *f* lower part of a/the town; **~stand** *m* shelter; *(Mil)* dugout.

unterstehen* *insep irreg* **1** *vi+dat* to be under; *jdm* to be subordinate to; *(in Firma)* to report to; **dem Gesetz ~** to be subject to. **2** *vr* to dare. **untersteh dich (ja nicht)!** (don't) you dare!

unterstellen[1]* *vt insep* **(a)** *(unterordnen)* to subordinate *(dat* to*)*. **jdm/etw unterstellt sein** to be under sb/sth; *(in Firma)* to report to sb/sth; **jdm etw ~** to put sb in charge of sth. **(b)** *(annehmen)* to assume, to suppose. **(c)** *(pej: unterschieben)* **jdm etw ~** to insinuate that sb has done/said sth.

unterstellen² *sep* **1** *vt (abstellen, unterbringen)* to keep; *Möbel auch* to store. **2** *vr* to take shelter. **Unterstellung** *f (falsche Behauptung)* misrepresentation; *(Andeutung)* insinuation. **das ist eine ~!** what are you insinuating!

unterste(r, s) *adj superl of* **untere(r, s)** lowest; *(tiefste auch)* bottom; *(letzte)* last. **das U~ zuoberst kehren** to turn everything upside down.

untersteuern* *vi insep* to understeer.

Unter-: **u~streichen*** *vt insep irreg (lit, fig)* to underline; **~strömung** *f (lit, fig)* undercurrent; **~stufe** *f (Sch)* lower school, lower grade *(US)*.

unterstützen* *vt insep* to support.

Unterstützung *f* **(a)** *no pl* support *(zu, für* for*)*. **(b)** *(Zuschuß)* assistance, aid; *(col: Arbeitslosen~)* unemployment benefit *(Brit)*, welfare *(US)*.

unterstützungsbedürftig *adj* needy.

untersuchen* *vt insep* **(a)** to examine *(auf+acc* for*)*; *(erforschen)* to look into, to investigate; *(chemisch, technisch etc)* to test *(auf +acc* for*)*. **sich ärztlich ~ lassen** to have a medical or a check-up; **etw gerichtlich ~** to try sth (in court). **(b)** *(nachprüfen)* to check, to verify.

Untersuchung *f siehe vt* **(a)** examination; investigation *(gen, über+acc* into*)*; test; *(ärztlich)* examination, check-up. **(b)** check, verification.

Untersuchungs-: **~ausschuß** *m* fact-finding committee; *(nach Unfall etc)* committee of inquiry; **~ergebnis** *nt (Jur)* findings *pl*; *(Med)* result of an/the examination; *(Sci)* test result; **~gefangene(r)** *mf* prisoner awaiting trial; **~haft** *f* custody; **~richter** *m* examining magistrate.

Untertage- *in cpds* underground; **~arbeiter** *m* (coal)face worker; **~bau** *m no pl* underground mining.

Untertan *m (wk)* **-en, -en** *(old: Staatsbürger)* subject; *(pej)* underling *(pej)*.

untertan *adj pred* subject *(+dat* to*)*.

untertänig *adj* subservient, submissive. **jdn ~st bitten** to ask sb most humbly.

Unter-: **u~tariflich** *adj Bezahlung* below the agreed or union rate; **~tasse** *f* saucer; **~tauchen** *sep* **1** *vi aux sein* to dive (under); *(fig)* to disappear; **2** *vt* to immerse; *jdn* to duck; **~teil** *nt or m* bottom or lower part; **~teilen*** *vt insep* to subdivide *(in+acc* into*)*; **~teller** *m* saucer; **~titel** *m* subtitle; *(für Bild)* caption; **~ton** *m (Mus, fig)* undertone; **u~treiben*** *insep irreg* **1** *vt* to understate; **2** *vi* to play things down; **~treibung** *f* understatement; **u~tunneln*** *vt insep* to tunnel under; **u~vermieten*** *vti insep* to sublet, to sublease; **u~wandern*** *vt insep* to infiltrate.

Unterwäsche *f no pl* underwear *no pl*.

Unterwasser- *in cpds* underwater.

unterwegs *adv* on the way *(nach, zu* to*)*; *(auf Reisen)* away. **bei denen ist wieder ein Kind ~** they've got another child on the way.

unterweisen* *vt insep irreg (geh)* to instruct *(in +dat* in*)*.

Unterwelt *f (lit, fig)* underworld.

unterwerfen* *insep irreg* **1** *vt* **(a)** *Volk* to subjugate. **(b)** *(unterziehen)* to subject *(dat* to*)*. **einer Sache** *(dat)* **unterworfen sein** to be subject to sth. **2** *vr (lit, fig)* **sich jdm/einer Sache ~** to submit to sb/sth.

unterworfen *adj* **der Mode ~ sein** to be subject to fashion.

unterwürfig *adj (pej)* obsequious.

unterzeichnen* *vt insep (form)* to sign. **Unterzeichner** *m* - signatory.

unterziehen¹* *insep irreg* **1** *vr* **sich einer Sache** *(dat)* **~** to undergo sth; **sich einer Prüfung** *(dat)* **~** to take an examination. **2** *vt* to subject *(dat* to*)*.

unterziehen² *vt sep irreg Kleidung* to put on underneath.

Untiefe *f (seichte Stelle)* shallow.

Untier *nt* monster.

untragbar *adj* intolerable, unbearable.

untreu *adj Liebhaber etc* unfaithful; *(einer Sache)* disloyal *(dat* to*)*. **sich** *(dat)* **selbst ~ werden** to be untrue to oneself.

Untreue *f siehe adj* unfaithfulness; disloyalty.

untröstlich *adj* inconsolable *(über +acc* about*)*.

untrüglich *adj Gedächtnis* infallible; *Zeichen* unmistakable

Untugend *f* vice; *(Angewohnheit)* bad habit.

un-: **~überbietbar** *adj Preis, Rekord etc* unbeatable; *Frechheit, Eifer* unparalleled; **~überbrückbar** *adj (fig) Gegensätze etc* irreconcilable; *Kluft* unbridgeable; **~überlegt** *adj* rash; **~übersehbar** *adj Schaden etc* incalculable; *Menge* vast, immense; *(auffällig) Fehler etc* obvious; **~übersichtlich** *adj Gelände* broken; *Kurve* blind; *System, Plan* confused; **~übertrefflich 1** *adj* matchless; *Rekord* unbeatable; **2** *adv* superbly, magnificently; **~übertroffen** *adj* unsurpassed; **~überwindlich** *adj* insurmountable; *Gegner, Heer* invincible; *Festung* impregnable.

un|umgänglich *adj* essential; *(unvermeidlich)* inevitable. **~ herrschen** to have absolute rule.

un|umschränkt *adj* unlimited. **~ herrschen** to have absolute rule.

un|umstößlich *adj Tatsache* incontrovertible; *Entschluß* irrevocable. **~ feststehen** to be absolutely definite.

un-: **~umstritten** *adj* indisputable, undisputed; **~umwunden** *adv* frankly; **~unterbrochen** *adj* uninterrupted; *(unaufhörlich)* incessant; **~veränderlich** *adj* unchanging; *(unwandelbar)* unchangeable; **~verändert** *adj* unchanged; **du siehst ~verändert jung aus** you look just as young as ever; **~verantwortlich** *adj* irresponsible; **~verarbeitet** *adj (lit, fig)* raw; **~veräußerlich** *adj Rechte* inalienable; **~verbesserlich** *adj* incorrigible; **~verbindlich** *adj* **(a)** *(nicht bindend)* not binding; *Besichtigung* free; *sich* *(dat)* **etw ~verbindlich schicken lassen** to have sth sent without obligation; **(b)** *(vage, allgemein)* non-committal; *(nicht entgegenkommend)* abrupt; **~verbleit** *adj Benzin* unleaded; **~verblümt** *adj* blunt; **~verbraucht** *adj (fig)* unspent; **~verbürgt** *adj* unconfirmed; **~verdächtig** *adj* unsuspicious; *(nicht unter Verdacht stehend)* unsuspected, above suspicion; **~verdaulich** *adj (lit, fig)* indigestible; **~verdient** *adj* undeserved; **~verdorben** *adj (lit, fig)* unspoilt, pure; **~verdrossen** *adj* undeterred; *(unermüdlich)* untiring; **~verdünnt** *adj* undiluted; **~vereinbar** *adj* incompatible; **~verfälscht** *adj (lit, fig)* unadulterated; *Dialekt* pure; *Natürlichkeit* unaffected; *Natur* unspoilt; **~verfänglich** *adj* harmless.

unverfroren *adj* insolent.

unvergänglich *adj* immortal; *Eindruck, Erinnerung* everlasting.

unvergessen *adj* unforgotten.

unvergeßlich *adj* unforgettable. **das wird mir ~ bleiben** I'll never forget that.

un-: **~vergleichlich** *adj* unique, incomparable; **~verhältnismäßig** *adv* disproportionately; *(übermäßig)* excessively; **~verheiratet** *adj* unmarried; **~verhofft** *adj* unexpected; **~verhohlen** *adj* open, unconcealed; **~verhüllt** *adj* **(a)** *Tatsachen* undisguised; **(b)** *siehe* **~verhohlen**; **~verkäuflich** *adj* unsaleable; „**~verkäuflich**" "not for sale"; **~verkennbar** *adj* unmistakable; **~verlangt** *adj* unsolicited; **~verletzlich** *adj (fig) Rechte* inviolable; *(lit)* invulnerable; **~vermeidlich** *adj* inevitable; *(nicht zu umgehen)* unavoidable; **~vermindert** *adj* undiminished; **~vermischt** *adj* unmixed; *(rein)* pure; **~vermittelt** *adj (plötzlich)* sudden, unexpected.

Unvermögen *nt no pl* inability.

unvermögend *adj (arm)* without means.

unvermutet *adj* unexpected.

Unvernunft f *(Torheit)* stupidity; *(mangelnder Verstand)* irrationality; *(Uneinsichtigkeit)* unreasonableness.

unvernünftig *adj siehe* n stupid; irrational; unreasonable.

unverrichtet *adj:* ~er Dinge empty-handed.

unverrückbar *adj (fig)* unshakeable. ~ **feststehen** to be absolutely definite.

unverschämt *adj* outrageous; *Mensch, Frage, Benehmen etc* impudent, impertinent; *Lüge auch* blatant, barefaced.

Unverschämtheit f **(a)** *no pl* outrageousness. **(b)** *(Bemerkung)* impertinence; *(Tat)* outrageous thing. **das ist eine** ~! it's outrageous!

unverschuldet *adj* occurring through no fault of one's own.

unversehens *adv* suddenly; *(überraschend)* unexpectedly.

un-: ~**versehrt** *adj Mensch (lit, fig)* unscathed; ~**versöhnlich** *adj* irreconcilable.

Unverstand m lack of judgement; *(Torheit)* folly.

unverstanden *adj* not understood; *(mißverstanden)* misunderstood.

unverständlich *adj* incomprehensible.

Unverständnis *nt no pl* lack of understanding; *(für Kunst etc)* lack of appreciation.

un-: ~**versucht** *adj:* **nichts** ~**versucht lassen** to try everything; ~**verträglich** *adj* **(a)** *(streitsüchtig)* quarrelsome; **(b)** *(unverdaulich)* indigestible; *(Med: mit anderer Substanz etc)* incompatible; ~**verwandt** *adv* fixedly, steadfastly; ~**verwechselbar** *adj* ummistakable, distinctive; ~**verwüstlich** *adj* indestructible; *Gesundheit* robust; *Mensch* irrepressible; ~**verzagt** *adj* undaunted; ~**verzeihlich** *adj* unforgivable; ~**verzichtbar** *adj attr Recht* inalienable; *Anspruch* indisputable; *Bedingung* indispensible; ~**verzinslich** *adj* interest-free; ~**verzollt** *adj* duty-free; ~**verzüglich 1** *adj* immediate; **2** *adv* immediately; ~**vollendet** *adj* unfinished; ~**vollkommen** *adj (unvollständig)* incomplete; *(fehlerhaft, mangelhaft)* imperfect.

unvollständig *adj* incomplete. **er hat das Formular** ~ **ausgefüllt** he didn't fill the form out properly.

un-: ~**vorbereitet** *adj* unprepared *(auf +acc* for*)*; **eine** ~**vorbereitete Rede halten** to make an impromptu speech; ~**voreingenommen** *adj* unbiased, unprejudiced; ~**vorhergesehen** *adj* unforeseen; *Besuch* unexpected; ~**vorschriftsmäßig** *adj* not in keeping with the regulations; ~**vorsichtig** *adj* careless; *(voreilig)* rash; ~**vorstellbar** *adj* inconceivable; ~**vorteilhaft** *adj* disadvantageous; *Kleid, Frisur etc* unbecoming; ~**vorteilhaft aussehen** not to look one's best.

Un-: **u**~**wahr** *adj* untrue; **u**~**wahrhaftig** *adj* untruthful; *Gefühle* insincere; ~**wahrheit** f untruth.

unwahrscheinlich 1 *adj* improbable; *(col: groß)* incredible *(col)*. **2** *adv (col)* incredibly *(col)*.

unwandelbar *adj (geh)* unalterable; *Treue* unwavering.

unwegsam *adj Gelände etc* rough.

unweiblich *adj* unfeminine.

unweigerlich 1 *adj attr Folge* inevitable. **2** *adv* inevitably.

unweit *prep+gen, adv* not far from.

Unwesen *nt no pl (übler Zustand)* terrible state of affairs. **sein** ~ **treiben** *(Mörder etc)* to be at large.

unwesentlich *adj* irrelevant; *(unwichtig)* unimportant, insignificant.

Unwetter *nt* (thunder)storm. **ein** ~ **brach los a** storm broke.

un-: ~**wichtig** *adj* unimportant; *(belanglos)* irrelevant; *(verzichtbar)* non-essential; ~**widerleglich** *adj* irrefutable; ~**widerruflich** *adj* irrevocable; **es steht** ~**widerruflich fest, daß** ... it is absolutely definite that ...; ~**widersprochen** *adj Behauptung* unchallenged; ~**widersteh-**

lich *adj* irresistible; ~**wiederbringlich** *adj (geh)* irretrievable.

Unwille(n) m *no pl* displeasure *(über +acc* at*)*; *(Ungeduld)* irritation. **jds** ~**n erregen** to incur sb's displeasure.

unwillig *adj* indignant *(über +acc* about*)*; *(widerwillig)* unwilling, reluctant.

unwillkommen *adj* unwelcome.

unwillkürlich *adj* spontaneous; *(instinktiv)* instinctive.

Un-: **u**~**wirklich** *adj* unreal; **u**~**wirksam** *adj* ineffective; *Vertrag etc* void; **u**~**wirsch** *adj* surly, gruff; *Bewegung* brusque; **u**~**wirtlich** *adj* inhospitable; **u**~**wissend** *adj* ignorant; *(ahnungslos)* unsuspecting; *(unerfahren)* inexperienced; ~**wissenheit** f *no pl siehe adj* ignorance; unsuspectingness; inexperience; **u**~**wissenschaftlich** *adj* unscientific; *Ausdrucksweise* unacademic; **u**~**wissentlich** *adv* unwittingly, unknowingly.

unwohl *adj (unpäßlich)* unwell; *(unbehaglich)* uneasy. **mir ist** ~ I don't feel well.

Unwohlsein *nt* indisposition; *(unangenehmes Gefühl)* unease.

un-: ~**wohnlich** *adj Zimmer etc* uncomfortable; ~**würdig** *adj* unworthy *(+gen* of*)*; *Verhalten* undignified; *Situation* degrading.

Unzahl f **eine** ~ **von a** host of.

unzählbar *adj* innumerable, countless.

unzählig 1 *adj* innumerable, countless. ~**e Male** countless times, time and again. **2** *adv* ~ **viele** huge numbers.

unzähmbar *adj* untameable; *(fig auch)* indomitable.

Unze f **-n** ounce.

un-: ~**zeitgemäß** *adj (altmodisch)* old-fashioned; ~**zerstörbar** *adj* indestructible; ~**zertrennlich** *adj* inseparable.

Unzucht f *no pl (esp Jur)* sexual offence *(Brit)* or offense *(US)*. ~ **mit jdm treiben** to fornicate with sb.

unzüchtig *adj (esp Jur)* indecent; *Reden* obscene.

Un-: **u**~**zufrieden** *adj* discontent; ~**zufriedenheit** f *no pl* discontent; **u**~**zugänglich** *adj Gegend* inaccessible; *Mensch* inapproachable; *(unaufgeschlossen gegen)* deaf *(+dat* to*)*; **u**~**zulänglich** *adj* insufficient, inadequate; ~**zulänglichkeit** f **(a)** insufficiency, inadequacy; **(b)** *usu pl* shortcomings *pl*; **u**~**zulässig** *adj (auch Jur)* inadmissible; *Gebrauch* improper; *Belastung, Geschwindigkeit* excessive; **u**~**zumutbar** *adj* unreasonable; **u**~**zurechnungsfähig** *adj* not responsible for one's actions; **jdn für u**~**zurechnungsfähig erklären lassen** *(Jur)* to have sb certified (insane); **u**~**zureichend** *adj* insufficient, inadequate; **u**~**zustellbar** *adj* undeliverable; **u**~**zuträglich** *adj jds Gesundheit* u~**zuträglich sein** to be bad for sb's health; **u**~**zutreffend** *adj* inapplicable; *(unwahr)* incorrect; ~**zutreffendes bitte streichen** delete as applicable; **u**~**zuverlässig** *adj* unreliable; ~**zuverlässigkeit** f unreliability; **u**~**zweckmäßig** *adj (nicht ratsam)* unadvisable; *(unpraktisch)* impractical; *(ungeeignet)* unsuitable; **u**~**zweideutig** *adj* unambiguous, unequivocal; *(fig: unanständig)* explicit; **er sagte mir u**~**zweideutig, daß** ... he told me in no uncertain terms that ...; **u**~**zweifelhaft 1** *adj* indubitable, unquestionable; **2** *adv* without doubt.

üppig *adj Wachstum* luxuriant; *Vegetation auch* lush; *Haar* thick; *Mahl, Ausstattung* sumptuous; *Gehalt* lavish; *Figur, Frau* voluptuous; *Leben* luxurious; *Phantasie* rich. ~ **leben** to live in style.

Ur- *in cpds (erste)* first; *(ursprünglich)* original; ~**abstimmung** f ballot; ~**ahn(e)** m *(Vorfahr)* forefather; *(~großvater)* great-grandfather; ~**ahne** f *(Vorfahr)* forebear; *(~großmutter)* great-grandmother; **u**~**alt** *adj* ancient.

Uran nt no pl uranium.
ur|aufführen vt ptp **uraufgeführt** to give the first performance of; Film to premiere.
Ur|aufführung f premiere; (von Theaterstück etc auch) first night or performance.
urbar adj die Wüste/Land ~ **machen** to to reclaim the desert/to cultivate land.
Ur-: ~**bevölkerung** f original inhabitants pl; ~**christentum** nt early Christianity; **u~eigen** adj very own; ~**einwohner** m original inhabitant; (in Australien und Neuseeland) Aborigine; ~**enkel** m great-grandchild, great-grandson; ~**enkelin** f great-granddaughter; ~**fassung** f original version; ~**geschichte** f prehistory; ~**gewalt** f elemental force.
Urgroß-: ~**eltern** pl great-grandparents pl; ~**mutter** f great-grandmother; ~**vater** m great-grandfather.
Urheber(in f) m - originator; (Jur: Verfasser) author.
Urheber-: ~**recht** nt copyright (an+dat on); **u~rechtlich** adj **u~rechtlich geschützt** copyright.
urig adj (col) Mensch earthy.
Urin m -e urine.
urinieren* vi to urinate.
Ur-: ~**knall** m (Astron) big bang; **u~komisch** adj (col) screamingly funny (col).
Urkunde f -n document; (Kauf~) deed; (Gründungs~ etc) charter; (Sieger~, Diplom, Bescheinigung etc) certificate.
urkundlich adj documentary. ~ **verbürgt** authenticated; ~ **erwähnt** mentioned in a document, documented.
Urlaub m -e (Ferien) holiday(s) (Brit), vacation (US); (esp Mil) leave. ~ **haben** to have a holiday or vacation/to have leave; **in** ~ **fahren** to go on holiday or vacation/on leave; (sich dat) **einen Tag** ~ **nehmen** to take a day off.
Urlauber(in f) m - holiday-maker (Brit), vacationist (US).
Urlaubs-: ~**geld** nt holiday (Brit) or vacation (US) money; **u~reif** adj (col) ready for a holiday (Brit) or vacation (US); ~**reise** f holiday (Brit) or vacation (US) trip; ~**tag** m (one day of) holiday (Brit) or vacation (US); **ich habe noch drei** ~**tage gut** I've still got three days' holiday to come; ~**zeit** f holiday (Brit) or vacation (US) period.
Urmensch m primeval man; (col) caveman (col).
Urne f -n urn; (Los~) box; (Wahl~) ballot-box. **zur** ~ **gehen** to go to the polls.
Ur-: ~**oma** f (col) great-granny (col); ~**opa** m (col) great-grandpa (col); ~**pflanze** f primordial plant; **u~plötzlich** adv (col) all of a sudden.
Ursache f -n cause; (Grund) reason; (Beweggrund) motive. ~ **und Wirkung** cause and effect; **keine** ~**!** (auf Dank) don't mention it, you're welcome; (auf Entschuldigung) that's all right; **ohne** (jeden) ~ for no reason (at all); **jdm** ~ **geben, etw zu tun** to give sb cause to do sth; **alle/keine** ~ **haben, etw zu tun** to have every/no reason to do sth.
Ur-: ~**schrei** m (Psych) primal scream; ~**schrift** f

original (text).
Ursprung m, pl **Ursprünge** origin.
ursprünglich 1 adj (a) attr original; (anfänglich) initial, first. (b) (urwüchsig) natural; Natur unspoilt. **2** adv originally; (anfänglich) initially.
Ursprungsland nt (Comm) country of origin.
Urteil nt -e (a) judgement; (Entscheidung) decision; (Meinung) opinion. **nach meinem** ~ in my judgement/opinion; **ich kann darüber kein** ~ **abgeben** I am no judge of this; **sich** (dat) **ein** ~ **über etw** (acc) **erlauben/ein** ~ **über etw fällen** to pass judgement on sth; **sich** (dat) **kein** ~ **über etw** (acc) **erlauben können** to be in no position to judge sth; **zu dem** ~ **kommen, daß** ... to come to the conclusion that ...; **sich** (dat) **ein** ~ **über jdn/etw bilden** to form an opinion about sb/sth. **(b)** (Jur: Gerichts~) verdict; (Richterspruch) judgement; (Strafmaß) sentence; (Schiedsspruch) award; (Scheidungsspruch) decree. **das** ~ **über jdn sprechen** (Jur) to pass judgement or opinion on sb.
urteilen vi to judge (nach by). **über etw** (acc) ~ to judge sth; (seine Meinung äußern) to give one's opinion on sth.
Urteils-: ~**begründung** f (Jur) opinion; **u~fähig** adj competent to judge; (umsichtig) discriminating; ~**findung** f (Jur) reaching a verdict no art; ~**kraft** f no pl power of judgement; (Umsichtigkeit) discrimination; ~**spruch** m (Jur) judgement; (von Geschworenen) verdict; (von Strafgericht) sentence; (von Schiedsgericht) award; ~**verkündung** f (Jur) pronouncement of judgement; ~**vermögen** nt siehe ~**kraft**.
Ur-: ~**text** m original (text); ~**trieb** m basic drive; **u~tümlich** adj siehe **u~wüchsig**; ~**typ(us)** m, pl ~**typen** prototype.
Ur|ur- in cpds great-great-.
Ur-: ~**vater** m forefather; **u~verwandt** adj Wörter cognate; ~**viech**, ~**vieh** nt (col) real character; ~**wald** m primeval forest; (in den Tropen) jungle; ~**welt** f primeval world; **u~weltlich** adj primeval, primordial; **u~wüchsig** adj natural; Natur unspoilt; (urweltlich) Flora primeval; (ursprünglich) original; (bodenständig) rooted to the soil; (unberührt) Land etc untouched; (urgewaltig) Kraft elemental; (derb, kräftig) sturdy; Mensch rugged; Humor, Sprache earthy; ~**zeit** f primeval times pl; **seit** ~**zeiten** since primeval times; (col) for donkey's years (col); **u~zeitlich** adj primeval; ~**zustand** m primordial state.
USA [u:|ɛs'|a:] pl die ~ the USA sing.
usf. = und so fort.
Usurpator m (liter) usurper.
usurpieren* vt (liter) to usurp.
usw. = und so weiter etc.
Utensil nt -ien [-iən] utensil, implement.
utilitaristisch adj utilitarian.
Utopie f utopia.
utopistisch adj (pej) utopian.
u.U. = unter Umständen.
Ü-Wagen m (Rad, TV) outside broadcast vehicle.
uzen vti (col) to tease, to kid (col).
Uzname m (col) nickname.

V

V, v [faʊ] *nt* -, - V, v.
V = Volt; Volumen.
Vagabund [vaga'bʊnt] *m (wk)* -en, -en vagabond.
vag(e) [vaːk,'vaːgə] *adj* vague.
Vagheit ['vaːkhaɪt] *f* vagueness.
Vakuum ['vaːkuʊm] *nt, pl* **Vakuen** ['vaːkuən] *(lit, fig)* vacuum. **unter/im** ~ in a vacuum.
Vakuum- ['vaːkuʊm-] *in cpds* vacuum; **~pumpe** *f* vacuum pump; **v~verpackt** *adj* vacuum-packed.
Valentinstag ['vaːlentiːns-] *m* (St) Valentine's Day.
Vampir [vam'piːɐ] *m* -e vampire.
Vandalismus [vanda'lɪsmʊs] *m no pl* vandalism.
Vanille [va'nɪljə, va'nɪlə] *f no pl* vanilla.
Vanille-: ~**eis** *nt* vanilla ice-cream; ~**geschmack** *m* vanilla flavour *(Brit)* or flavor *(US)*; **mit** ~**geschmack** vanilla-flavoured *(Brit)* or -flavored *(US)*; ~**zucker**, **Vanillinzucker** *m* vanilla sugar.
variabel [va'riaːbl] *adj* variable.
Variable [va'riaːblə] *f (wk)* -n, -n variable.
Variante [va'riantə] *f* -n variant *(zu* on).
Variation [varia'tsioːn] *f* variation. ~**en zu einem Thema** variations on a theme.
Varieté [varie'teː] *nt* -s **(a)** variety, vaudeville *(US)*. **(b)** *(Theater)* variety theatre *(Brit)*, music hall *(Brit)*, vaudeville theater *(US)*.
variieren* [vari'iːrən] *vti* to vary.
Vasall [va'zal] *m (wk)* -en, -en *(Hist, fig)* vassal.
Vase ['vaːzə] *f* -n vase.
Vater *m* = *(lit, fig)* father. ~ **unser** *(Rel)* Our Father; **unsere** ~ *pl (geh: Vorfahren)* our (fore)fathers; **wie der** ~, **so der Sohn** *(prov)* like father, like son *(prov)*; ~ **Staat** *(hum)* the State.
Vater-: ~**figur** *f* father figure; ~**freuden** *pl* joys of fatherhood *pl*; ~**haus** *nt* parental home.
Vaterland *nt* native country; *(esp Deutschland auch)* Fatherland. **unser** ~ our country.
vaterländisch *adj* national; *(patriotisch)* patriotic.
Vaterlands-: ~**liebe** *f* patriotism; **v~liebend** *adj* patriotic; ~**verräter** *m* traitor.
väterlich *adj* paternal, fatherly.
väterlicherseits *adv* on one's father's side. **meine Großeltern** ~ my paternal grandparents.
Vater-: ~**liebe** *f* fatherly love; **v~los** *adj* fatherless; ~**recht** *nt* patriarchy.
Vaterschaft *f* fatherhood *no art; (esp Jur)* paternity.
Vaterschaftsklage *f* paternity suit.
Vater-: ~**stelle** *f* **bei jdm** ~**stelle vertreten** to take the place of sb's father; ~**tag** *m* Father's Day; ~**unser** *nt* - **das** ~**unser** the Lord's Prayer.
Vati *m* -s *(col)* dad(dy) *(col)*.
Vatikan [vati'kaːn] *m* Vatican.
Vatikanstadt [vati'kaːn-] *f* Vatican City.
V-Ausschnitt ['faʊ-] *m* V-neck.
v. Chr. = **vor Christus** BC.
Vegetarier(in *f)* [vege'taːriɐ, -iərɪn] *m* - vegetarian.
vegetarisch [vege'taːrɪʃ] *adj* vegetarian. ~ **leben** to be a vegetarian.
Vegetation [vegeta'tsioːn] *f* vegetation.
vegetieren* [vege'tiːrən] *vi* to vegetate; *(kärglich leben)* to eke out a bare existence.
Vehikel [ve'hiːkl] *nt* - *(pej col)* boneshaker *(col)*.
Veilchen *nt* violet; *(col: blaues Auge)* shiner *(col)*,

black eye. **blau wie ein** ~ *(col)* roaring drunk *(col)*.
Velours [və'luːɐ, ve'luːɐ] *m* - *(Tex)* velour(s).
Velours(leder) *nt* - [və'luːɐ-, ve'luːɐ-] suede.
Vene ['veːnə] *f* -n vein.
Venedig [ve'neːdɪç] *nt* Venice.
Venezolaner(in *f)* [venetso'laːnɐ, -ərɪn] *m* - Venezuelan.
venezolanisch [venetso'laːnɪʃ] *adj* Venezuelan.
Venezuela [vene'tsueːla] *nt* Venezuela.
Ventil [vɛn'tiːl] *nt* -e valve; *(fig)* outlet.
Ventilation [vɛntila'tsioːn] *f* ventilation.
Ventilator [vɛnti'laːtɔr] *m* ventilator.
Venus ['veːnʊs] *f no pl (Myth, Astron)* Venus.
ver|abreden* **1** *vt* to arrange; *Termin auch* to agree; *Straftat* to collude in; *Hochverrat* to conspire in. **es war eine verabredete Sache** it was arranged beforehand; **wir haben verabredet, daß wir uns um 5 Uhr treffen** we have arranged to meet at 5 o'clock; **schon verabredet sein** *(für on)* to have a prior engagement *(esp form)*, to have something else on; **mit jdm verabredet sein** to have arranged to meet sb. **2** *vr* **sich mit jdm/miteinander** ~ to arrange to meet sb/to meet.
Ver|abredung *f (Vereinbarung)* arrangement, agreement; *(Treffen)* appointment; *(esp mit Freund)* date. **ich habe eine** ~ I'm meeting somebody.
ver|abreichen* *vt Tracht Prügel etc* to give; *Arznei auch* to administer *(form)* (jdm to sb).
ver|abscheuen* *vt* to detest, to abhor, to loathe.
ver|abscheuungswürdig *adj* detestable.
ver|abschieden* **1** *vt* to say goodbye to; *(entlassen)* to discharge; *(Pol)* Haushaltsplan to adopt; *Gesetz* to pass. **2** *vr* **sich (von jdm)** ~ to say goodbye (to sb), to take one's leave (of sb).
ver|achten* *vt* to despise; *(liter)* Tod, Gefahr to scorn. **nicht zu** ~ *(col)* not to be scoffed at.
ver|achtenswert *adj* despicable, contemptible.
ver|ächtlich *adj* contemptuous; *(verachtenswert)* despicable, contemptible.
Ver|achtung *f no pl* contempt *(von* for). **jdn mit** ~ **strafen** to treat sb with contempt.
ver|albern* *vt (col)* to make fun of.
ver|allgemeinern* *vti* to generalize.
Ver|allgemeinerung *f* generalization.
ver|alten* *vi aux sein* to become obsolete; *(Mode)* to go out of date.
ver|altet *adj* obsolete; *Mode* out-of-date.
Veranda [ve'randa] *f, pl* **Veranden** veranda, porch.
ver|änderlich *adj* variable; *Wetter, Mensch* changeable.
ver|ändern* **1** *vt* to change. **2** *vr* to change; *(Stellung wechseln)* to change one's job; *(Wohnung wechseln)* to move. **verändert aussehen** to look different.
Ver|änderung *f* change. **eine berufliche** ~ a change of job.
ver|ängstigen* *vt (erschrecken)* to frighten; *(einschüchtern)* to intimidate.
ver|ankern* *vt (Naut, Tech)* to anchor; *(fig)* to embed (in *in+dat* in).
ver|anlagen* *vt* to assess *(mit* at).
ver|anlagt *adj* **melancholisch** ~ seir to have a

446

melancholy disposition; **praktisch ~ sein** to be practically minded; **künstlerisch ~ sein** to be artistic; **zu** or **für etw ~ sein** to be cut out for sth.

Ver|anlagung f **(a)** (körperlich, esp Med) predisposition; (charakterlich) nature, disposition; (Hang) tendency; (allgemeine Fähigkeiten) natural abilities pl; (künstlerisches, praktisches etc Talent) bent. **(b)** (von Steuern) assessment.

ver|anlassen* vt **(a)** etw ~ to arrange for sth; (befehlen) to order sth. **(b)** auch vi (bewirken) to give rise (zu to). **jdn zu etw ~, jdn (dazu) ~, etw zu tun** to cause sb to do sth.

Ver|anlassung f cause, reason. **auf ~ von** or **+gen** at the instigation of; **keine ~ zu etw haben/ keine ~ haben, etw zu tun** to have no cause or reason for sth/to do sth.

ver|anschaulichen* vt to illustrate (an +dat, mit with). **sich** (dat) **etw ~** to visualize sth.

ver|anschlagen* vt to estimate (auf +acc at). **etw zu hoch/niedrig ~** to overestimate/underestimate sth.

ver|anstalten* vt to organize, to arrange; (kommerziell) Konzerte etc to promote; Party to hold.

Ver|anstalter(in f) m - organizer; (Comm: von Konzerten etc) promoter.

Ver|anstaltung f **(a)** event (von organized by); (feierlich, öffentlich) function. **(b)** no pl (das Veranstalten) organization.

ver|antworten* 1 vt to accept responsibility for; die Folgen auch, sein Tun to answer for (vor +dat to). **wie könnte ich es denn ~, ...?** it would be most irresponsible of me ...; **eine nicht zu ~de Fahrlässigkeit** inexcusable negligence. 2 vr **sich für** or **wegen etw ~** to justify sth (vor+dat to).

ver|antwortlich adj responsible; (haftbar) liable. **jdm (gegenüber) ~ sein** to be responsible to sb; **jdn für etw ~ machen** to hold sb responsible for sth.

Ver|antwortung f responsibility (für for). **auf eigene ~** on one's own responsibility; **auf deine ~!** you take the responsibility!; **jdn zur ~ ziehen** to call sb to account.

Ver|antwortungs-: v~bewußt adj responsible; ~bewußtsein nt sense of responsibility; v~los adj irresponsible; v~voll adj responsible.

ver|arbeiten* vt to use (zu etw to make sth); (Tech, Biol, Comp) to process; Ton, Gold etc to work; (verbrauchen) to consume; Erlebnis etc to assimilate, to digest. **~de Industrie** processing industries pl; **etw geistig ~** to assimilate or digest sth.

ver|arbeitet adj gut ~ Rock etc well finished.

Ver|arbeitung f **(a)** (von Rohstoffen etc) processing. **(b)** (Ausführung) finish.

ver|ärgern* vt to annoy.

ver|armen* vi aux sein (lit, fig) to become impoverished. **verarmt** impoverished.

ver|arschen* vt (col!) to take the piss out of (col!); (für dumm verkaufen) to mess around (col).

ver|arzten* vt (col) to fix up (col).

ver|ästeln* vr to branch out; (fig) to ramify.

ver|ausgaben* vr to overexert oneself; (finanziell) to overspend. **ich habe mich total verausgabt** (finanziell) I'm completely spent out.

ver|äußern* vt (form: verkaufen) to dispose of.

Verb [verp] nt -en verb.

verbal [vɛrˈbaːl] adj verbal.

verballhornen* vt to parody; (unabsichtlich) to get wrong.

Verband m -e **(a)** (Med) dressing; (mit Binden) bandage. **(b)** (Bund) association. **(c)** (Mil) unit.

Verband(s)-: ~kasten m first-aid box; ~päckchen nt gauze bandage; ~stoff m dressing; ~zeug nt dressing.

verbannen* vt to banish (auch fig), to exile (aus from, auf to).

Verbannte(r) mf decl as adj exile.

verbarrikadieren* 1 vt to barricade. 2 vr sich in (in etw (dat) sth).

verbauen* vt **(a)** (versperren) to obstruct, to block. **sich** (dat) **alle Chancen ~** to spoil one's chances. **(b)** (verbrauchen) Holz, Geld to use in building. **(c)** (schlecht bauen) to construct badly.

verbeißen* irreg 1 vt (fig col) sich (dat) etw ~ Schmerz to hide sth; sich (dat) das Lachen ~ to keep a straight face. 2 vr sich in etw (acc) ~ (fig) to become obsessed with sth; siehe verbissen.

verbergen* vtr irreg (lit, fig) to hide (vor +dat from).

verbessern* 1 vt **(a)** to improve; Leistung, Bestzeit to improve on; die Welt to reform. **eine neue, (b)** (korrigieren) to correct. 2 vr to improve, to get better; (beruflich, finanziell) to better oneself; (sich korrigieren) to correct oneself.

Verbesserung f **(a)** improvement (von in); (beruflich, finanziell) betterment. **(b)** (Berichtigung) correction.

verbeugen* vr to bow (vor +dat to).

Verbeugung f bow.

verbeulen* vt to dent.

verbiegen* vtr irreg to bend; (Holz) to warp; siehe verbogen.

verbieten* vt irreg to forbid; (amtlich auch) to prohibit; Zeitung, Partei to ban. **jdm ~, etw zu tun** to forbid sb to do sth; (amtlich auch) to prohibit sb from doing sth; siehe verboten.

verbilden* vt (fig) jdn to bring up badly; Geschmack, Charakter to spoil.

verbilligen* 1 vt to reduce the cost of; Kosten, Preis to reduce. **verbilligte Waren** reduced goods. 2 vr to become cheaper.

verbinden* irreg 1 vt **(a)** to connect. **jdn (mit jdm) ~** (Telec) to put sb through (to sb); **falsch verbunden!** wrong number; **die damit verbundenen Kosten** the costs involved; **uns verbindet nichts** we have nothing in common; siehe verbunden. **(b)** **ich verbinde die Geschäftsreise mit einem Kurzurlaub** I'll combine the business trip with a short holiday; **was ~ Sie mit diesem Begriff?** what do you associate with this concept? **(c)** (Med) to dress; (mit Binden) to bandage. **jdm die Augen ~** to blindfold sb. 2 vr **(a)** to combine (zu to form). **(b)** (assoziiert werden) to be associated; (hervorgerufen werden) to be evoked (mit by). 3 vi **ich verbinde!** I'll put you through. **(b)** (emotional) to form a bond.

verbindlich adj **(a)** obliging. **(b)** (verpflichtend) obligatory, compulsory; Regelung, Zusage binding; (verläßlich) Auskunft reliable. **~ zusagen** to accept definitely.

Verbindlichkeit f siehe adj **(a)** obligingness. **~en** polite words pl. **(b)** no pl obligatory nature; binding nature; reliability. **(c)** **~en** pl (Comm, Jur) obligations pl; (finanziell auch) liabilities pl.

Verbindung f **(a)** connection; (einflußreiche Beziehung auch, Kontakt) contact (zu, mit with). **in ~ mit** (zusammen mit) in conjunction with; (im Zusammenhang mit) in connection with; **jdn/eine mit etw in ~ bringen** to connect sb/sth with sth; (assoziieren) to associate sb/sth with sth; **~ mit jdm aufnehmen** to contact sb; **(mit jdm) in ~ treten** to get in touch or contact (with sb), to contact sb; **mit jdm in ~ stehen** to be in touch or contact with sb.
(b) (Telec: Anschluß) line. **telefonische ~** telephone link; **eine ~ (zu einem Ort) bekommen** to get through (to a place).
(c) (Kombination) combination.
(d) (Vereinigung, Bündnis) association; (ehelich) union; (Univ: Burschenschaft) fraternity.
(e) (Chem) (Prozeß) combination; (Ergebnis) compound (aus of).

Verbindungs- in cpds (esp Tech, Archit) connecting; ~**mann** *m, pl* ~**leute** *or* ~**männer** intermediary; *(Agent)* contact; ~**stelle** *f* join; *(von Gleisen)* junction; *(Amt)* liaison office.

verbissen *adj* grim; *Arbeiter, Gesicht* determined. **das darfst du nicht so ~ sehen** *(col)* you shouldn't be so rigid about it.

verbitten *vr irreg* **das verbitte ich mir!** I won't have it!

verbittern* **1** *vt* to embitter, to make bitter. **2** *vi aux sein* to become embittered *or* bitter. **verbittert** embittered, bitter.

Verbitterung *f* bitterness.

verblassen* *vi aux sein (lit, fig)* to fade; *(Mond)* to pale.

verbleiben* *vi irreg aux sein* to remain. **verbleibe ich Ihr ...** *(form)* ... I remain, Yours sincerely ...; **wir sind so verblieben, daß wir ...** we agreed to ...

verbleien* *vt Benzin* to lead.

verblüffen* *vt (erstaunen)* to amaze; *(verwirren)* to baffle. **sich durch** *or* **von etw ~ lassen** to be taken in by sth.

verblühen* *vi aux sein (lit, fig)* to fade.

verbluten* *vi aux sein* to bleed to death.

verbogen *adj* bent; *Rückgrat* curved.

verbohren* *vr (col)* **sich in etw** *(acc)* **~** to become obsessed with sth.

verbohrt *adj Haltung* stubborn, obstinate.

verborgen¹* *vt* to lend out *(an+acc* to).

verborgen² *adj* hidden. **etw/sich ~ halten** to hide sth/to hide; **im V~en leben** to live hidden away; **im ~en liegen** to be not yet known.

Verbot *nt -e* ban *(etw zu tun* on doing sth). **er ging trotz meines ~s** he went even though I had forbidden him to do so.

verboten *adj* forbidden; *(amtlich auch)* prohibited; *(gesetzeswidrig) Handel* illegal; *Zeitung, Partei, Buch etc* banned. **Rauchen/Parken ~** no smoking/parking; **er sah ~ aus** *(col)* he looked a real sight *(col)*.

Verbots-: ~**schild** *nt,* ~**tafel** *f* sign (prohibiting something); *(im Verkehr)* prohibition sign.

verbrämen* *vt (geh) Kleidungsstück* to trim; *(fig) Rede* to pad; *Wahrheit* to gloss over; *Kritik* to veil *(mit* in).

verbrannt *adj* burnt; *(fig) Erde* scorched.

Verbrauch *m no pl* consumption *(von, an +dat* of); *(von Geld)* expenditure; *(von Kräften)* drain *(von, an+dat* on).

verbrauchen* *vt* **(a)** to use; *Vorräte* to use up; *Nahrungsmittel etc auch* to consume. **der Wagen verbraucht 10 Liter Benzin auf 100 km** the car does 10 kms to the litre. **(b)** *(abnützen) Kräfte etc* to exhaust; *Kleidung etc* to wear out. **sich ~** to wear oneself out; **verbrauchte Luft** stale air.

Verbraucher *m* - consumer.

Verbraucher- *in cpds* consumer; **v~gerecht** *adj Verpackung* handy; ~**schutz** *f* consumer protection; ~**verband** *m* consumer council.

Verbrauchsgüter *pl* consumer goods *pl.*

Verbrechen *nt* - *(lit, fig)* crime *(an +dat* against). **verbrechen** *vt irreg* **etwas ~** to commit a crime; *(col: anstellen)* to be up to something *(col).*

Verbrecher(in *f) m* - criminal.

Verbrecherbande *f* gang of criminals.

verbrecherisch *adj* criminal.

Verbrecherkartei *f* criminal records *pl.*

verbreiten* **1** *vt* to spread; *Zeitung* to circulate; *Wärme, Ruhe* to radiate; *Licht* to shed. **eine (weit) verbreitete Ansicht** a widely held opinion. **2** *vr* to spread. **sich über ein Thema ~** to expound on a subject.

verbreitern* *vtr* to widen.

verbrennen* *irreg* **1** *vt* to burn; *(einäschern) Tote* to cremate; *(versengen) Haar* to singe; *(verbrühen)* to scald. **sich** *(dat)* **den Mund ~** *(lit)* to burn one's mouth; *(fig)* to say too much. **2** *vr* to burn oneself; *(sich verbrühen)* to scald oneself. **3** *vi aux sein* to burn; *(Mensch, Tier)* to burn to

death; *(Haus etc)* to burn down; *(durch Sonne, Hitze)* to be scorched. **alles verbrannte** everything was destroyed in the fire.

Verbrennung *f* **(a)** *no pl* burning; *(von Treibstoff)* combustion; *(von Leiche)* cremation. **(b)** *(Brandwunde)* burn; *(Verbrühung)* scald.

Verbrennungs-: ~**anlage** *f* incineration plant; ~**motor** *m* internal combustion engine.

verbriefen* *vt* to document. **verbriefte Rechte** attested rights.

verbringen *vt irreg* to spend.

verbrühen* **1** *vt* to scald. **2** *vr* to scald oneself.

Verbrühung *f* scalding; *(Wunde)* scald.

verbuchen* *vt* to enter. **Erfolge (für sich) ~** to notch up successes *(col).*

verbummeln* *(col)* **1** *vt (verlieren)* to lose; *Zeit* to waste, to fritter away; *Verabredung* to miss. **2** *vi aux sein (herunterkommen)* to go to seed.

verbunden *adj (form: dankbar)* **jdm (für etw) ~ sein** to be obliged to sb (for sth).

verbünden *vr* to form an alliance.

Verbundenheit *f no pl (von Völkern)* solidarity; *(mit Menschen, Natur)* closeness *(mit* to); *(mit Land, Tradition)* attachment *(mit* to).

Verbündete(r) *mf decl as adj* ally.

verbürgen* *vtr* to guarantee. **sich für jdn/etw ~** to vouch for sb/sth; **verbürgte Nachricht** confirmed report; **ein verbürgtes Recht** an established right.

verbüßen* *vt* to serve.

verchromt* [fɛɐˈkroːmt] *adj* chromium-plated.

Verdacht *m no pl* suspicion. **jdn in ~ haben** to suspect sb; **im ~ stehen, etw getan zu haben** to be suspected of having done sth; **jdn wegen ~s einer Sache** *(gen)* **festnehmen** to arrest sb on suspicion of sth; **(gegen jdn) ~ schöpfen** to become suspicious (of sb); **es besteht ~ auf Krebs** *(acc)* cancer is suspected.

verdächtig *adj* suspicious. **sich ~ machen** to arouse suspicion; **einer Sache** *(gen)* **~ sein** to be suspected of sth.

verdächtigen* *vt* to suspect *(gen* of).

Verdächtige(r) *mf decl as adj* suspect.

verdammen* *vt* to damn; *(verurteilen)* to condemn.

verdammt *(col)* **1** *adj, adv* damned *(col).* **das tut ~ weh** that hurts like hell *(col);* **mir geht's ~ schlecht** I'm in a pretty bad way *(col).* **2** *interj* ~**!** damn *(it) (col);* ~ **noch mal!** *(col!)* bloody hell *(Brit col!),* damn *(col).*

verdampfen* *vti (vi: aux sein)* to vaporize; *(Cook)* to boil away.

verdanken* *vt* **jdm etw ~** to owe sth to sb; **das haben wir ihm zu ~** that's thanks to him.

verdarb *pret* of **verderben**.

verdauen* *vti (lit, fig)* to digest.

verdaulich *adj* digestible. **leicht ~** easy to digest.

Verdauung *f* digestion *no indef art.*

Verdauungs- *in cpds* digestive; ~**spaziergang** *m* constitutional; ~**störung** *f usu pl* indigestion *no pl.*

Verdeck *nt -e (von Kinderwagen)* canopy; *(von Auto)* soft top; *(von Schiff)* sundeck.

verdecken* *vt* to hide, to conceal; *(zudecken)* to cover (up); *Sicht* to block.

verdenken* *vt irreg* **ich kann es ihm nicht ~(, daß er es getan hat)** I can't blame him (for doing it).

verderben* *pret* **verdarb,** *ptp* **verdorben 1** *vt* to spoil; *(stärker)* to ruin; *Luft* to pollute; *(moralisch)* to corrupt; *(verwöhnen)* to spoil. **jdm etw ~** to ruin sth for sb; **sich** *(dat)* **den Magen ~** to give oneself an upset stomach; **sich** *(dat)* **die Augen ~** to ruin one's eyes; **die Preise ~** to force prices down/up; **jdm die Freude an etw** *(dat)* **~** to spoil sb's enjoyment of sth; **es (sich** *dat)* **mit jdm ~** to fall out with sb. **2** *vi aux sein (Material)* to become spoiled/ruined; *(Nahrungsmittel)* to go bad; *(Ernte)* to be ruined; *(Mensch)* to become depraved.

Verderben nt no pl (a) ruin. in sein ~ rennen to be heading for disaster. (b) (von Material) spoiling, ruining; (von Nahrungsmittel) going off.
verderblich adj pernicious; Lebensmittel perishable.
verdeutlichen* vt (deutlicher machen) to clarify; (erklären) to explain. sich (dat) etw ~ to think sth out for oneself.
verdeutschen* vt to translate into German; (eindeutschen) to Germanize.
verdichten* 1 vt (Phys, fig) to compress; Gefühle to intensify, to heighten. 2 vr to thicken; (Gas) to become compressed; (fig: häufen) to increase; (Verdacht, Eindruck) to deepen.
Verdichter m - compressor.
verdicken* 1 vt to thicken. 2 vr to thicken; (anschwellen) to swell.
verdienen* 1 vt (a) (einnehmen) to earn; (Gewinn machen) to make (an+dat on). sich (dat) etw ~ to earn the money for sth. (b) (fig) Lob, Strafe to deserve. er verdient es nicht anders he doesn't deserve anything else. 2 vi to earn; (Gewinn machen) to make (a profit) (an +dat on). er verdient gut he earns a lot; am Krieg ~ to profit from war.
Verdiener* m - wage-earner.
Verdienst¹ m -e income; (Profit) profit.
Verdienst² nt -e (a) merit; (Dank) credit. es ist sein ~/das ~ der Wissenschaftler (, daß...) it is thanks to him/the scientists (that ...); nach ~ on merit. (b) usu pl (um to) (Leistung) contribution; (um Wissenschaft, Staat) service.
Verdienst-: ~ausfall m loss of earnings; ~orden m order of merit; v~voll adj commendable.
verdient adj (a) Lohn, Strafe rightful; Ruhe, Lob well-deserved. (b) Wissenschaftler, Politiker, Sportler of outstanding merit. sich um etw ~ machen to render outstanding services to sth.
verdonnern* vt (col: zu Haft etc) to sentence (zu to). jdn zu etw ~, jdn dazu ~, etw zu tun to order sb to do sth as a punishment.
verdoppeln* vtr to double.
verdorben 1 ptp of verderben. 2 adj Lebensmittel bad; Magen upset; Stimmung, Urlaub, Freude spoiled, ruined; (moralisch) corrupt; (verzogen) Kind spoiled.
verdorren* vi aux sein to wither.
verdrängen* vt jdn to drive out; Gegner auch to oust; (ersetzen) to replace; (Phys) Wasser to displace; (Met) to drive; (fig) Sorgen to dispel; (Psych) to repress, to suppress.
verdrecken* vt (vi: aux sein) (col) to get filthy.
verdrehen* vt (lit, fig) to twist; (verknacksen) to sprain; Hals to crick; Augen to roll. das Recht ~ to pervert the course of justice; sich (dat) den Hals ~ (fig col) to crane one's neck.
verdreht adj (col) crazy (col); Bericht confused.
verdreifachen* vtr to treble, to triple.
verdrießen pret verdroß, ptp verdrossen vt jdn to annoy. sich (dat) den Abend durch etw ~ lassen to let sth spoil one's evening.
verdrießlich adj morose; Arbeit irksome.
verdroß pret of verdrießen.
verdrossen 1 ptp of verdrießen. 2 adj (schlechtgelaunt) morose; (unlustig) Mensch, Gesicht unwilling, reluctant.
Verdrossenheit f (schlechte Laune) moroseness; (Lustlosigkeit) unwillingness, reluctance.
verdrucken* vr (col) to make a misprint.
verdrücken* 1 vt Kleider to crumple; (col) Essen to polish off (col). 2 vr (col) to beat it (col). sich heimlich ~ to slip away.
Verdruß m -sse frustration. ~ mit jdm haben to get frustrated with sb; zu jds ~ to sb's annoyance.
verduften* vi aux sein (col) to beat it (col).
verdummen* 1 vt jdn ~ (für dumm verkaufen) to make sb out to be stupid; (dumm machen) to dull

sb's mind. 2 vi aux sein to become stultified.
verdunkeln* 1 vt to darken; Bühne auch, (im Krieg) to black out; (fig) Zusammenhänge etc to obscure. die Sonne ~ (Mond) to eclipse the sun; (Wolken) to obscure the sun. 2 vr to darken.
verdünnen* 1 vt to thin (down); (mit Wasser) to water down; Lösung to dilute. den Teig mit Wasser ~ to add water to the dough. 2 vr (Lösung) to become diluted; (schmaler werden) to become thinner.
Verdünner m - thinner.
verdunsten* vi aux sein to evaporate.
Verdunster m - humidifier.
verdursten* vi aux sein to die of thirst.
verdüstern* vtr to darken.
verdutzt adj, adv (col) taken aback; (verwirrt) baffled.
ver|ebben* vi aux sein to subside.
ver|edeln* vt Metalle, Erdöl to refine; Fasern to finish; Boden, Geschmack to improve.
ver|ehren* vt to admire; (anbeten) to worship.
Ver|ehrer(in f) m - admirer.
ver|ehrt adj (sehr) ~e Anwesende/Gäste/~es Publikum Ladies and Gentlemen.
Ver|ehrung f admiration; (von Heiligen) worship; (Liebe) adoration.
ver|eidigen* vt to swear in. jdn auf etw (acc) ~ to make sb swear on sth; vereidigter Übersetzer sworn translator.
Ver|ein m -e organization, society; (Sport~) club; (col) crowd. ein wohltätiger ~ a charity; im ~ mit in conjunction with.
ver|einbar adj compatible; Aussagen consistent.
ver|einbaren* vt (a) to agree; Zeit auch, Treffen to arrange. (es) ~, daß ... to agree/arrange that ... (b) etw mit etw ~ to reconcile sth with sth; mit etw zu ~ sein to be compatible with sth.
Ver|einbarung f siehe vt (a) (das Vereinbaren) agreeing; arranging; (Abmachung) agreement; arrangement. laut ~ as agreed; nach ~ by arrangement.
ver|einen* 1 vt to unite; Ideen, Prinzipien to reconcile. vereint handeln to act together; Vereinte Nationen United Nations sing. 2 vr to unite.
ver|einfachen* vt to simplify.
Ver|einfachung f simplification.
ver|einheitlichen* vt to standardize.
ver|einigen* 1 vt to unite; Kräfte, Eigenschaften to combine; Firmen to merge (zu into); Kapital to pool. etw mit etw ~ to combine sth with sth; (vereinbaren) to reconcile sth with sth; in einer Hand vereinigt sein to be held by the same person; alle Stimmen auf sich (acc) ~ to collect all the votes; Vereinigtes Königreich United Kingdom; Vereinigte Staaten United States. 2 vr to unite; (sich verbünden auch) to join forces; (Firmen) to merge; (zusammenkommen) to combine; (Flüsse) to meet; (sich versammeln) to assemble.
Ver|einigung f (a) siehe vt uniting; combining; merging; pooling; (körperliche, eheliche ~) union. (b) (Organisation) organization.
ver|einnahmen* vt (geh) to take. jdn ~ (fig) to make demands on sb; (Beruf) to occupy sb.
ver|einsamen* vi aux sein to become lonely.
Ver|einsmeier m - (col) er ist ein richtiger ~ all he thinks about is his club.
ver|einzelt 1 adj occasional; Regenfälle auch isolated. 2 adv occasionally.
ver|eisen* vi aux sein to freeze; (Straße, Fenster-scheibe) to ice over.
ver|eist adj Straßen, Fenster icy; Bäche frozen; Türschloß iced-up; Land covered in ice.
ver|eiteln* vt to thwart, to foil.
ver|eitern* vi aux sein to go septic.
ver|elenden* vi aux sein to become impoverished.
ver|enden* vi aux sein to perish, to die.

ver|engen* **1** _vr_ to narrow; _(Gefäße, Pupille)_ to contract; _(Kleid, Taille)_ to go in. **2** _vt_ to make narrower; _Kleid_ to take in.

ver|erben* **1** _vt_ **(a)** _Besitz_ to leave, to bequeath _(dat, an +acc to)_. **(b)** _Anlagen_ to pass on _(dat, auf +acc to)_; _Krankheit_ to transmit. **2** _vr_ to be passed on/transmitted _(auf +acc to)_.

ver|ewigen* **1** _vt_ to immortalize; _Zustand, Verhältnisse_ to perpetuate. **2** _vr (lit, fig)_ to immortalize oneself.

verfahren[1]*** _vi irreg aux sein (vorgehen)_ to act, to proceed.

verfahren[2]*** _irreg_ **1** _vt Geld, Zeit_ to spend in travelling _(Brit)_ or traveling _(US)_; _Benzin_ to use up. **2** _vr_ to lose one's way; _(fig)_ to get muddled.

verfahren[3] _adj Angelegenheit_ muddled.

Verfahren _nt_ - _(Vorgehen)_ actions _pl_; _(~sweise)_ procedure; _(Tech)_ process; _(Methode)_ method; _(Jur)_ proceedings _pl_. **ein ~ gegen jdn einleiten** to take legal proceedings against sb.

Verfall _m no pl_ **(a)** _(Zerfall)_ decay; _(von Gebäude)_ dilapidation; _(gesundheitlich, geistig, sittlich, von Kultur)_ decline. **(b)** _(von Anspruch, Rechnung etc)_ lapsing; _(von Scheck, Fahrkarte)_ expiry.

verfallen[1]*** _vi irreg aux sein_ **(a)** _(zerfallen)_ to decay; _(Bauwerk)_ to fall into disrepair; _(Zellen)_ to die; _(körperlich und geistig)_ to deteriorate; _(Sitten, Reich)_ to decline. **(b)** _(Geldscheine)_ to become invalid; _(Scheck, Fahrkarte)_ to expire; _(Termin, Anspruch)_ to lapse. **(c)** _(abhängig werden)_ **jdm/einer Sache ~/~ sein** to become/be a slave to sb/sth; **jdm völlig ~ sein** to be completely under sb's spell. **(d) auf etw** _(acc)_ **~** to think of sth; _(aus Verzweiflung)_ to resort to sth. **(e) in etw** _(acc)_ **~** to sink into sth; **in einen tiefen Schlaf ~** to fall into a deep sleep; **in einen Fehler ~** to make a mistake.

verfallen[2] _adj Gebäude_ dilapidated, ruined; _Mensch (körperlich)_ emaciated; _(geistig)_ senile; _(abgelaufen)_ _Fahrkarten, Briefmarken_ invalid; _Strafe_ lapsed; _Scheck_ expired.

Verfalls-: ~datum _nt_ expiry date; _(der Haltbarkeit)_ best before date; ~tag _m_ expiry date.

verfälschen* _vt_ to falsify; _Lebensmittel, Wein_ to adulterate.

verfangen* _irreg_ **1** _vr_ to get caught. **sich in Widersprüchen ~** to contradict oneself. **2** _vi_ to be accepted. **bei jdm nicht ~** not to cut any ice with sb _(col)_.

verfänglich _adj Situation_ awkward, embarrassing; _Aussage, Beweismaterial, Blicke_ incriminating; _(gefährlich)_ dangerous; _Angewohnheit_ insidious; _Frage_ tricky.

verfärben* _vr_ to change colour _(Brit)_ or color _(US)_; _(Metall, Stoff)_ to discolour _(Brit)_, to discolor _(US)_. **sich grün/rot ~** to turn green/red.

verfassen* _vt_ to write; _Gesetz, Urkunde_ to draw up.

Verfasser(in _f)_ _m_ - writer, author.

Verfassung _f_ **(a)** _(Pol)_ constitution. **(b)** _(Zustand)_ state; _(körperlich)_ state of health; _(seelisch)_ state of mind. **sie ist in guter/schlechter ~** she is in good/bad shape.

Verfassungs-: ~änderung _f_ constitutional amendment; v~feindlich _adj_ anticonstitutional; ~schutz _m_ defence _(Brit)_ or defense _(US)_ of the constitution; _(Amt)_ office responsible for defending the constitution; v~treu _adj_ loyal to the constitution; v~widrig _adj_ unconstitutional.

verfaulen* _vi aux sein_ to decay, to rot; _(fig)_ to degenerate.

verfault _adj_ decayed; _Fleisch, Obst etc_ rotten; _Körper_ decomposed.

verfechten* _vt irreg_ to defend; _Lehre_ to advocate.

Verfechter(in _f)_ _m_ - advocate, champion.

verfehlen* _vt (nicht treffen)_ to miss. **den Zweck ~** not to achieve its purpose; **das Thema ~** to be completely off the subject.

verfehlt _adj_ unsuccessful; _(unangebracht)_ inappropriate.

Verfehlung _f_ **(a)** _(des Ziels)_ missing. **(b)** _(Vergehen)_ misdemeanour _(Brit)_, misdemeanor _(US)_; _(Sünde)_ transgression.

verfeinden* _vr_ to quarrel. **sich mit jdm ~** to make an enemy of sb; **verfeindet sein** to be on bad terms.

verfeinern* **1** _vt_ to improve; _Methode auch_ to refine. **2** _vr_ to improve; _(Methoden auch)_ to become refined.

verfeinert _adj Methode, Geräte_ sophisticated.

Verfeinerung _f_ refinement.

verfestigen* **1** _vt_ to harden; _Flüssigkeit_ to solidify; _(verstärken)_ to strengthen. **2** _vr_ to harden; _(Flüssigkeit)_ to solidify; _(Kenntnisse)_ to be reinforced; _(Ideen, Gewohnheiten)_ to become set.

Verfettung _f (von Organ, Muskeln)_ fatty degeneration.

verfeuern* _vt_ to burn; _Munition_ to fire; _(restlos)_ to use up.

verfilmen* _vt_ to film, to make a film of.

Verfilmung _f_ film (version).

verfilzen* _vi aux sein (Wolle)_ to become felted; _(Haare)_ to become matted. **verfilzt** felted/matted.

verfinstern* **1** _vt_ to darken; _Sonne, Mond_ to eclipse. **2** _vr (lit, fig)_ to darken.

verflachen* **1** _vi aux sein_ to flatten out; _(fig: Diskussion)_ to become superficial. **2** _vr (Gelände)_ to flatten out.

verflechten* _irreg_ **1** _vt_ to interweave; _Methoden_ to combine; _Firmen_ to interlink. **eng mit etw verflochten sein** _(fig)_ to be closely linked with sth. **2** _vr_ to interweave; _(sich verwirren)_ to become entangled _(mit in)_; _(Methoden)_ to combine.

verfliegen* _irreg_ **1** _vi aux sein_ to vanish; _(Zeit)_ to fly (past). **2** _vr_ to stray; _(Pilot, Flugzeug)_ to lose one's/its bearings.

verfließen* _vi irreg aux sein (geh)_ to go by, to pass.

verflixt _(col)_ **1** _adj_ darned _(col)_; _(kompliziert)_ tricky. **2** _adv_ darned _(col)_. **3** _interj_ ~! blow! _(col)_.

verfluchen* _vt_ to curse.

verflucht _(col)_ **1** _adj_ damn _(col)_. **~ (noch mal)!** damn (it) _(col)_. **2** _adv_ damned _(col)_.

verflüchtigen* **1** _vt_ to evaporate. **2** _vr (Alkohol etc)_ to evaporate; _(Duft)_ to disappear; _(Gase)_ to volatilize.

verflüssigen* _vtr_ to liquefy.

verfolgen* _vt_ jdn, Ziel, Karriere etc to pursue; _Idee, Gedanken_ to follow up; _(politisch, religiös)_ to persecute. **jdn politisch ~** to persecute sb for political reasons; **jdn gerichtlich ~** to prosecute sb; **jdn mit den Augen ~** to follow sb with one's eyes.

Verfolger(in _f)_ _m_ - pursuer; _(politisch)_ persecutor.

Verfolgte(r) _mf decl as adj (politisch)_ victim of persecution.

Verfolgung _f_ pursuit; _(politische)_ persecution _no pl._ **die ~ aufnehmen** to take up the chase; **strafrechtliche ~** prosecution.

Verfolgungs-: ~jagd _f_ chase, pursuit; ~rennen _nt (Sport)_ pursuit race; ~wahn _m_ persecution mania.

verformen* **1** _vt_ to distort _(zu into)_; _(umformen)_ to work. **verformt sein** to be out of shape; _(Mensch, Gliedmaßen)_ to be deformed. **2** _vr_ to go out of shape.

verfrachten* _vt_ to ship. **etw in eine Kiste ~** _(col)_ to dump sth in a crate.

verfremden* _vt_ to make unfamiliar.

verfressen* _(col!)_ **1** _vt irreg_ to blow on food _(col)._ **2** _adj_ greedy, piggish _(col)._

verfroren _adj_ sensitive to cold; _(durchgefroren)_ frozen.

verfrüht _adj (zu früh)_ premature; _(früh)_ early.

verfügbar _adj_ available.

verfugen* vt to fit flush.

verfügen* **1** vi über etw (acc) ~ to have sth at one's disposal; (besitzen) to have sth; über jdn/ etw ~ (bestimmen über) to be in charge of sb/sth; du kannst doch nicht über mich ~ you can't tell me what to do; über etw (acc) frei ~ können to be able to do as one wants with sth; ich kann im Moment über meine Zeit nicht frei ~ I am not master of my own time just now; ~ Sie über mich I am at your disposal. **2** vt to order; (gesetzlich) to decree.

Verfügung f (a) no pl jdm etw zur ~ stellen to put sth at sb's disposal; etw zur ~ haben to have sth at sb's disposal; (jdm) zur ~ stehen (verfügbar sein) to be available (to sb); etw zur ~ haben to have sth at one's disposal. (b) (behördlich) order; (von Gesetzgeber) decree; (testamentarisch) provision; (Anweisung) instruction.

Verfügungsgewalt f (Jur) right of disposal.

verführen* vt to tempt; (esp sexuell) to seduce; die Jugend, das Volk etc to lead astray.

Verführer m - seducer.

Verführerin f seductress, temptress.

verführerisch adj seductive; (verlockend) tempting.

Verführung f seduction; (von Jugend, Volk) tempting; (Verlockung) enticement.

verfüttern* vt etw an die Vögel ~ to feed sth to the birds.

Vergabe f -n (von Arbeiten) allocation; (von Stipendium, Auftrag etc) award.

vergällen* vt (geh) jdm die Freude/das Leben ~ to spoil sb's fun/to sour sb's life.

vergaloppieren* vr (col: sich irren) to be on the wrong track.

vergammeln* (col) **1** vi aux sein (Speisen) to go bad; (verlottern) to go to the dogs (col). vergammelt aussehen to look scruffy. **2** vt Zeit to waste.

vergangen adj (a) (letzte) last. (b) Jahre past; Zeiten, Bräuche bygone. das V~e the past.

Vergangenheit f past; (Gram) past (tense). der ~ angehören to be a thing of the past.

Vergangenheitsbewältigung f coming to terms with the past.

vergänglich adj transitory.

vergasen* vt (töten) to gas.

Vergaser m - (Aut) carburettor (Brit), carburetor (US).

vergaß pret of **vergessen**.

vergeben* irreg **1** vt (a) Auftrag, Preis to award (an+acc to); Studienplätze, Stellen to allocate; (fig) Chance, Möglichkeit to throw away. ein Amt an jdn ~ to appoint sb to an office; zu ~ sein to be available; ~ sein (Wohnung, Plätze) to have been taken; (Stelle) to have been filled. (b) (verzeihen) to forgive. jdm etw ~ to forgive sb (for) sth. **2** vr sich (dat) etwas/nichts ~ to lose/ not to lose face.

vergebens adj pred, adv in vain.

vergeblich **1** adj futile; Bitten, Mühe auch vain attr, in vain. **2** adv in vain.

Vergebung f no pl forgiveness.

vergegenwärtigen* vr sich (dat) etw ~ to imagine sth.

Vergehen nt - (Verstoß) offence (Brit), offense (US). das ist doch kein ~, oder? that's not a crime, is it?

vergehen* irreg **1** vi aux sein (a) to pass; (Liebe, Leidenschaft auch) to die; (Zeit, Jahre etc auch) to go by; (Schönheit, Glück) to fade. wie doch die Zeit vergeht how time flies; mir ist der Appetit vergangen I have lost my appetite. (b) vor etw (dat) ~ to be dying of sth; vor Angst ~ to be scared to death; vor Sehnsucht ~ to pine away. **2** vr sich an jdm ~ to do sb wrong; (unsittlich) to assault sb indecently; sich gegen das Gesetz ~ to violate the law.

vergeistigt adj cerebral, spiritual.

vergelten vt to repay. jdm etw ~ to repay sb for sth.

Vergeltung f (Rache) retaliation.

Vergeltungsmaßnahme f retaliatory measure.

vergesellschaften* vt (Pol) to nationalize.

vergessen pret vergaß, ptp ~ **1** vti to forget; (liegenlassen auch) to leave (behind). ... und nicht zu ~ seine Ehrlichkeit ... and not forgetting his honesty; das werde ich dir nie ~ I will never forget that. **2** vr (Mensch) to forget oneself.

Vergessenheit f no pl oblivion. in ~ geraten to fall into oblivion.

vergeßlich adj forgetful.

vergeuden* vt to waste, to squander.

vergewaltigen* vt to rape.

Vergewaltigung f rape.

vergewissern* vr to make sure. sich einer Sache (gen) or über etw (acc) ~ to make sure of sth.

vergießen* vt irreg Kaffee, Wasser to spill; Blut auch, Tränen to shed.

vergiften* vt (lit, fig) to poison.

vergilben* vi aux sein to go yellow. **vergilbt** yellowed.

Vergißmeinnicht nt -(e) forget-me-not.

vergittert adj Fenster barred.

verglasen* vt to glaze.

Vergleich m -e (a) comparison. ~e ziehen to make comparisons; im ~ zu or mit in comparison with; in keinem ~ zu etw stehen to be out of all proportion to sth; (Leistungen) not to compare with sth; dem ~ mit jdm standhalten, den ~ mit jdm aushalten to bear comparison with sb. (b) (Jur) settlement.

vergleichbar adj comparable.

vergleichen* irreg **1** vt to compare. etw mit etw ~ to compare sth to sth; (prüfend) to compare sth with sth; vergleiche oben compare above. **2** vr (a) sich mit jdm ~ to compare oneself with sb. (b) (Jur) to reach a settlement, to settle.

vergleichsweise adv comparatively.

verglimmen* vi irreg aux sein (Zigarette) to go out; (Licht, Feuer auch) to die away.

verglühen* vi aux sein (Feuer) to die away; (Draht) to burn out; (Raumkapsel, Meteor etc) to burn up.

vergnügen* vr to enjoy oneself. sich mit jdm/etw ~ to amuse oneself with sth/sb; sich mit Lesen ~ to amuse oneself by reading.

Vergnügen nt - (Freude, Genuß) pleasure; (Spaß) fun no indef art; (Erheiterung) amusement. das macht or bereitet mir ~ I enjoy it, it gives me pleasure; nur zum ~ just for pleasure or for the fun of it; das war ein teures ~ (col) that was an expensive bit of fun; viel ~! enjoy yourself/ yourselves (auch iro).

vergnüglich adj enjoyable; (erheiternd) amusing.

vergnügt adj Stunden enjoyable; Mensch, Stimmung cheerful.

Vergnügung f pleasure; (Veranstaltung) entertainment.

Vergnügungs-: ~industrie f entertainment industry; ~park m amusement park; ~reise f pleasure trip; ~steuer f entertainment tax; ~sucht f craving for pleasure; ~viertel nt entertainments district.

vergolden* vt (mit Blattgold) to gild; (mit Gold) to gold-plate; (fig: verschönern) to enhance.

vergönnen* vt (geh) es war ihr noch vergönnt, das zu sehen she was granted the privilege of seeing it.

vergöttern* vt to idolize.

vergraben* irreg **1** vt to bury. **2** vr (lit, fig) to bury oneself.

vergrämt adj (kummervoll) Gesicht troubled.

vergreifen* vr irreg (a) to make a mistake. sich im Ton/Ausdruck ~ (fig) to adopt the wrong tone/use the wrong expression. (b) sich an etw (dat) ~ (stehlen) to misappropriate sth; sich an jdm ~ (*angreifen*) to lay hands on sb.

vergreisen* *vi aux sein* (*Bevölkerung*) to age; (*Mensch*) to become senile.

vergriffen *adj* unavailable; *Buch* out of print.

vergröbern* *vtr* to coarsen.

vergrößern 1 *vt* to enlarge; *Gelände auch* to extend; *Firma, Absatzmarkt* to expand; *Anzahl, Probleme, Einfluß* to increase; (*Lupe, Brille*) to magnify. **2** *vr* to increase; (*räumlich*) to be extended; (*Firma, Absatzmarkt*) to expand; (*Organ*) to become enlarged.

Vergrößerung *f siehe vb* enlargement; extension; expansion; increase; magnification. **in 1.000facher** ~ magnified 1,000 times.

Vergrößerungsglas *nt* magnifying glass.

vergucken* *vr* da hab ich mich verguckt (*col*) I didn't see it properly.

vergünstigt *adj Lage* improved; *Preis* reduced.

Vergünstigung *f* (*Vorteil*) privilege; (*Preisermäßigung*) reduction.

vergüten* *vt* jdm etw ~ *Unkosten* to reimburse sb for sth; *Arbeit, Leistung* to pay sb for sth.

Vergütung *f* reimbursement.

verh. = **verheiratet.**

verhaften* *vt* to arrest. **Sie sind verhaftet!** you are under arrest!

Verhaftete(r) *mf decl as adj* person under arrest.

Verhaftung *f* arrest.

verhallen* *vi aux sein* (*Geräusch etc*) to die away.

verhalten[1]* *vr irreg* **1** (**a**) to behave; (*handeln*) to act. **sich ruhig** ~ to keep quiet; (*sich nicht bewegen*) to keep still. (**b**) (*Sachen, Marktlage*) to be; (*Chem*) to react. **wie verhält sich die Sache?** how do things stand? **2** *vr impers* **wie verhält es sich damit?** (*wie ist die Lage?*) how do things stand?; (*wie wird das gehandhabt?*) how do you go about it?; **damit verhält es sich anders** the situation is different; **wenn sich das so verhält,** ... if that is the case ...

verhalten[2] **1** *adj* restrained; *Stimme* muted; *Atem* bated; *Wut* suppressed; *Tempo, Rhythmus* measured. **2** *adv* with restraint; *laufen* at a measured pace.

Verhalten *nt no pl* (*Benehmen*) behaviour (*Brit*), behavior (*US*); (*Vorgehen*) conduct; (*Chem*) reaction.

Verhaltens-: ~**forschung** *f* behaviourism (*Brit*), behaviorism (*US*); **v**~**gestört** *adj* disturbed; ~**maßregel** *f* rule of conduct; ~**weise** *f* behaviour (*Brit*), behavior (*US*).

Verhältnis *nt* (**a**) (*Proportion*) proportion; (*Math, Mischungs*~) ratio. **im** ~ **zu** in relation *or* proportion to; **im** ~ **zu früher** in comparison with earlier times; **in keinem** ~ **zu etw stehen** to be out of all proportion to sth. (**b**) (*Beziehung*) relationship; (*zwischen Ländern, innerhalb einer Gruppe*) relations *pl* (*zu* with); (*Einstellung*) attitude (*zu* to). (**c**) (*Liebes*~) affair. (**d**) ~**se** *pl* conditions *pl*; (*finanzielle*) circumstances *pl*; **so wie die** ~**se liegen** as things stand; **aus welchen** ~**sen kommt er?** what sort of background does he come from?; **über seine** ~**se leben** to live beyond one's means; **für klare** ~**se sorgen, klare** ~**se schaffen** to get things straight.

Verhältnis-: **v**~**mäßig** relatively; ~**wahl(recht** *nt*) *f* proportional representation *no art*.

verhandeln* 1 *vi* (**a**) to negotiate (*über*+*acc* about); (*col: diskutieren*) to argue. **über den Preis läßt sich** ~ (*col*) we can discuss the price. (**b**) (*Jur*) **gegen jdn/in einem Fall** ~ to hear sb's/a case. **2** *vt* (**a**) to negotiate. (**b**) (*Jur*) *Fall* to hear.

Verhandlung *f* (**a**) negotiations *pl*; (*das Verhandeln*) negotiation. ~**en führen** to negotiate. (**b**) (*Jur*) hearing; (*Straf*~) trial.

Verhandlungs-: ~**basis** *f* basis for negotiation(s); ~**basis DM 2.500** DM 2,500 *or* near offer; **v**~**bereit** *adj* ready to negotiate; ~**partner** *m* negotiating party; **wer war Ihr** ~**partner?** who were you negotiating with?; ~**tisch** *m* negotiating table.

verhangen *adv* overcast.

verhängen* *vt* (**a**) *Embargo, Strafe* to impose (*über*+*acc* on); *Ausnahmezustand* to declare (*über* +*acc* in). (**b**) (*zuhängen*) to cover (*mit* with).

Verhängnis *nt* fate. **jdm zum** ~ **werden** to be sb's undoing.

verhängnisvoll *adj* disastrous, fatal; *Tag* fateful.

verharmlosen* *vt* to play down.

verharren* *vi aux haben or sein* to pause; (*in einer bestimmten Stellung*) to remain. **auf einem Standpunkt** ~ to adhere to a viewpoint.

verharschen* *vi aux sein* (*Schnee, Piste*) to crust.

verhaßt *adj* hated; *Arbeit, Pflicht* hateful. **sich** ~ **machen** to make oneself hated (*bei* by).

verhätscheln* *vt* to spoil, to pamper.

Verhau *m or nt* -**e** (*zur Absperrung*) barrier; (*Käfig*) coop.

verhauen* *irreg* (*col*) **1** *vt* (**a**) (*verprügeln*) to beat up; (*zur Strafe*) to beat. (**b**) *Prüfung etc* to muff (*col*). **2** *vr* (**a**) (*sich verprügeln*) to have a fight. (**b**) (*beim Schreiben etc*) to make a mistake. (**c**) (*sich irren*) to slip up (*col*).

verheben* *vr irreg* to hurt oneself lifting something.

verheddern* *vr* (*col: lit, fig*) to get into a tangle.

verheerend *adj Sturm, Folgen* devastating, disastrous; *Anblick* ghastly.

verhehlen* *vt* to conceal (*jdm* from sb).

verheilen* *vi aux sein* (*lit, fig*) to heal.

verheimlichen* *vt* to keep secret, to conceal (*jdm* from sb). **ich habe nichts zu** ~ I have nothing to hide.

verheiraten* 1 *vt* to marry (*mit* to). **2** *vr* to get married, to marry. **sich mit jdm** ~ to marry sb, to get married to sb.

verheiratet *adj* married.

verheißen* *vt irreg* (*geh*) to promise.

verheißungsvoll *adj* promising; *Blicke* alluring.

verheizen* *vt* to burn, to use as fuel. **Soldaten** ~ (*col*) to send soldiers to the slaughter.

verhelfen* *vi irreg* jdm zu etw ~ to help sb to get sth.

verherrlichen* *vt* to glorify.

verheult *adj Augen, Gesicht* puffy. **du siehst** ~ **aus** you look as though you've been crying.

verhexen* *vt* to bewitch; (*col*) *Maschine etc* to put a jinx on (*col*). **das ist doch wie verhext** (*col*) it's maddening (*col*).

verhindern* *vt* to prevent; *Versuch, Plan* to foil. **ich konnte es nicht** ~, **daß er die Wahrheit erfuhr** I couldn't prevent him from finding out the truth; **das läßt sich leider nicht** ~ it can't be helped, unfortunately; **er war an diesem Abend** (**dienstlich**) **verhindert** he was unable to come that evening (for reasons of work); **ein verhinderter Politiker** (*col*) a would-be politician.

verhöhnen* *vt* to mock, to deride.

verhökern* *vt* (*col*) to get rid of (*col*).

Verhör *nt* -**e** questioning, interrogation.

verhören* 1 *vt* to question, to interrogate. **2** *vr* to mishear.

verhüllen* 1 *vt* to veil; *Haupt, Körperteil* to cover. **2** *vr* to disguise oneself; (*Frau*) to veil oneself.

verhüllend *adj Ausdruck* euphemistic.

verhungern* *vi aux sein* (*lit, fig*) to starve, to die of starvation.

verhunzen* *vt* (*col*) to ruin.

verhüten* *vt* to prevent.

verhütten *vt* to smelt.

Verhütung *f* prevention; (*Empfängnis*~) contraception.

Verhütungsmittel *nt* contraceptive.

verhutzelt *adj Gesicht, Männlein* wizened; *Haut* wrinkled; *Obst* shrivelled (*Brit*), shriveled (*US*).

verifizieren* [verifi'tsiːrən] *vt* to verify.

ver|innerlichen* *vt* to internalize.

ver|irren* *vr* to get lost, to lose one's way; *(fig)* to go astray; *(Tier, Kugel)* to stray.

Ver|irrung *f* losing one's way *no art; (fig)* aberration.

verjagen* *vt (lit, fig)* to chase away.

verjähren* *vi aux sein* to come under the statute of limitations; *(Anspruch)* to lapse.

Verjährung *f* limitation; *(von Anspruch)* lapse.

verjubeln* *vt (col) Geld* to blow *(col)*.

verjüngen* **1** *vt* to rejuvenate; *(jünger aussehen lassen)* to make look younger; *Baumbestand* to regenerate. **eine Mannschaft** ~ to build up a younger team. **2** *vr* **(a)** to become younger; *(Haut, Erscheinung)* to become rejuvenated; *(jünger aussehen)* to look younger. **(b)** *(dünner werden)* to taper.

verkabeln *vt Leitung* to lay; *Haus* to wire; *(col) Stadtteil* to wire up for cable television.

verkalken* *vi aux sein (Arterien)* to become hardened; *(Gewebe)* to calcify; *(Wasserleitung etc)* to fur up; *(col: Mensch)* to become senile.

verkalkt *adj (col)* senile.

verkalkulieren* *vr* to miscalculate.

verkannt *adj* unrecognized.

verkappt *adj attr* hidden; *(Med)* undiagnosed.

verkatert *adj (col)* hung-over *(col)*.

Verkauf *m, pl* **Verkäufe** sale. **zum** ~ **stehen** to be up for sale.

verkaufen* **1** *vti (lit, fig)* to sell *(für, um* for*)*. „zu ~" "for sale"; **jdm etw** *or* **etw an jdn** ~ to sell sb sth, to sell sth to sb. **2** *vr (Ware)* to sell; *(Mensch)* to sell oneself.

Verkäufer(in *f)* *m* - seller; *(in Geschäft)* sales assistant *(Brit)*, sales clerk *(US)*; *(im Außendienst)* salesman/saleswoman, salesperson.

verkäuflich *adj* sal(e)able, marketable; *(zu verkaufen)* for sale. **leicht/schwer** ~ easy/hard to sell.

Verkaufs- *in cpds* sales; ~**abteilung** *f* sales department; ~**förderung** *f* sales promotion; ~**leiter** *m* sales manager; **v**~**offen** *adj* open for business; ~**personal** *nt* sales personnel; ~**preis** *m* retail price; ~**schlager** *m* big seller.

Verkehr *m no pl* **(a)** traffic; *(Beförderung, Verkehrsmittel)* transport. **für den** ~ **freigeben** *Straße etc* to open to traffic; *Transportmittel* to bring into service; **aus dem** ~ **ziehen** to withdraw from service. **(b)** *(Verbindung)* contact, communication; *(Umgang)* company; *(Geschlechts~)* intercourse. **(c)** *(Umlauf)* circulation. **etw in (den)** ~ **bringen/aus dem** ~ **ziehen** to put sth into/withdraw sth from circulation.

verkehren* **1** *vi* **(a)** *aux haben or sein (fahren)* to run; *(Flugzeug)* to fly. **(b)** *(Gast sein, Kontakt pflegen)* **bei jdm** ~ to frequent sb's house; **mit jdm** ~ to associate with sb; **in Künstlerkreisen** ~ to move in artistic circles; **mit jdm brieflich/schriftlich** ~ *(form)* to correspond with sb; **mit jdm (geschlechtlich)** ~ to have (sexual) intercourse with sb. **2** *vtr* to turn *(in+acc* into*)*. **etw ins Gegenteil** ~ to reverse sth.

Verkehrs- *in cpds* traffic; ~**ampel** *f* traffic lights *pl (Brit)*, traffic light *(US)*; **v**~**arm** *adj Zeit, Straße* quiet; **ein v**~**armes Gebiet** an area with little traffic; ~**aufkommen** *nt* volume of traffic; ~**behinderung** *f (Jur)* obstruction (of traffic); ~**betriebe** *pl* transport services *pl*; ~**büro** *nt* tourist information office; ~**delikt** *nt* traffic offence *(Brit) or* offense *(US)*; ~**erziehung** *f* road safety training; ~**flugzeug** *nt* commercial aircraft; ~**funk** *m* radio traffic service; ~**gefährdung** *f (durch Fahrer)* dangerous driving; **v**~**günstig** *adj* convenient; ~**hindernis** *nt* (traffic) obstruction; ~**insel** *f* traffic island; ~**knotenpunkt** *m* traffic junction; ~**kontrolle** *f* traffic check; ~**minister** *m* minister of transport; ~**mittel** *nt* means of transport *sing*; **öffentliche/private** ~**mittel** public/private transport; ~**netz** *nt*

traffic network; ~**opfer** *nt* road casualty; ~**polizei** *f* traffic police *pl*; ~**regel** *f* traffic regulation; **v**~**reich** *adj Straße* busy; **v**~**reiche Zeit** peak (traffic) time; ~**schild** *nt* road sign; **v**~**schwach** *adj Zeit* off-peak; **v**~**sicher** *adj Fahrzeug* roadworthy; *Brücke* safe (for traffic); ~**stau** *m* traffic jam; ~**stockung** *f* traffic hold-up; ~**sünder** *m (col)* traffic offender; ~**teilnehmer** *m* road-user; ~**tote(r)** *mf* road casualty; **v**~**tüchtig** *adj Fahrzeug* roadworthy; *Mensch* fit to drive; ~**unfall** *m* road accident; ~**unternehmen** *nt* transport company; ~**unterricht** *m* road safety instruction; ~**verbindung** *f* public transport facilities *pl*; *(Anschluß)* connection; ~**verbund** *m* transport association; ~**verein** *m* tourist information office; ~**verhältnisse** *pl* traffic situation *sing*; *(Straßenzustand)* road conditions *pl*; ~**wesen** *nt* transport and communications *no art*; **v**~**widrig** *adj* contrary to road traffic regulations; ~**zeichen** *nt* road sign.

verkehrt **1** *adj* wrong; *Welt* topsy-turvy. **2** *adv* wrongly. **etw** ~ **(herum) anhaben** to have sth on the wrong way around; **das V**~**este, was du tun könntest** the worst thing you could do.

verkeilen* *vr* to become wedged together.

verkennen* *vt irreg* to misjudge. **es ist nicht zu** ~, **daß** ... it is undeniable that ...; *siehe* **verkannt**.

verketten* *vt Tür, Kiste* to put a chain on; *(fig)* to link.

Verkettung *f* **eine** ~ **unglücklicher Umstände** an unfortunate chain of events.

verkitten* *vt* to cement; *Fenster* to putty around.

verklagen* *vt* to sue *(wegen* for*)* **jdn auf etw** *(acc)* ~ to take sb to court for sth.

verklammern* *vt* to staple together; *(fig)* to link.

verklärt *adj* transfigured.

verklausulieren* *vt Vertrag* to hedge in with (restrictive) clauses.

verkleben* **1** *vt (zusammenkleben)* to stick together; *(zukleben)* to cover *(mit* with*)*. **2** *vi aux sein (Wunde)* to close; *(Augen)* to get gummed up; *(Briefmarken, Bonbons)* to stick together; *(Haare)* to become matted. **mit etw** ~ to stick to sth.

verklebt *adj* sticky; *Augen* gummed up; *Haare* matted.

verkleckern* *vr (col)* to spill.

verkleiden* **1** *vt* **(a)** to disguise; *(kostümieren)* to dress up. **(b)** *Schacht, Tunnel* to line; *(vertäfeln)* to panel; *Heizkörper* to cover in. **2** *vr* to disguise oneself; *(sich kostümieren)* to dress (oneself) up.

Verkleidung *f* **(a)** *(Kleidung)* disguise; *(Kostüm)* fancy dress. **(b)** *siehe vt* **(b)** lining; panelling *(Brit)*, paneling *(US)*; covering.

verkleinern* **1** *vt* to reduce; *Raum, Gebiet, Firma* to make smaller. **2** *vr* to be reduced; *(Raum, Gebiet, Firma)* to become smaller.

Verkleinerung *f* reduction.

verklemmen* *vr* to get stuck.

verklemmt *adj (col) Mensch* inhibited; *Beine* crossed.

verklingen* *vi irreg aux sein* to die away.

verklumpen* *vi aux sein* to get lumpy.

verknacksen* *vt (col)* **(sich** *dat)* **den Fuß** ~ to twist one's ankle.

verknallen* *vr (col)* **sich (in jdn)** ~ to fall for sb.

verknappen* *vt* to cut back.

verkneifen* *vt irreg (col)* **sich** *(dat)* **etw** ~ to stop oneself (from) saying/doing *etc* sth; **ich konnte mir das Lachen nicht** ~ I couldn't help laughing.

verkniffen *adj Gesicht (angestrengt)* strained; *(verbittert)* pinched.

verknöchert* *adj (fig)* fossilized.

verknoten* **1** *vt* to tie, to knot; *(col) Paket* to tie up. **2** *vr* to become knotted.

verknüpfen* *vt* **(a)** to tie (together). **(b)** *(fig)* to combine; *(in Zusammenhang bringen)* to link, to connect; *Gedanken* to associate. **so ein Umzug ist immer mit großen Ausgaben verknüpft** moving house always involves a lot of expense.

verkochen* *vti (vi: aux sein) (Flüssigkeit)* to boil away; *(Kartoffeln, Gemüse)* to overboil.

verkohlen* 1 *vi aux sein* to become charred. 2 *vt* **(a)** *Holz* to char. **(b)** *(col)* **jdn** ~ to have sb on *(col).*

verkommen[1]* *vi irreg aux sein* **(a)** *(Mensch)* to go to the dogs; *(moralisch)* to become dissolute; *(Kind)* to run wild. **zu etw** ~ to degenerate into sth. **(b)** *(Gebäude, Auto)* to fall to pieces; *(Stadt)* to become run-down; *(Gelände)* to run wild; *(Begabung)* to go to waste; *(Lebensmittel)* to go bad.

verkommen[2] *adj Mensch* depraved; *Auto, Gebäude* dilapidated; *Garten* wild.

verkoppeln* *vt* to connect, to couple; *(Space)* to link (up).

verkorken* *vt* to cork (up).

verkorkst *adj (col)* ruined; *Magen* upset. **eine** ~e **Sache** a mess.

verkörpern* *vt* to embody; *(Theat)* to play.

Verkörperung *f* embodiment.

verköstigen* *vt* to feed.

verkrachen* *vr (col)* **sich (mit jdm)** ~ to fall out (with sb).

verkracht *adj (col) Leben* ruined; *Typ* dead-beat *(col).* **sie sind** ~ *(zerstritten)* they have fallen out with each other.

verkraften* *vt* to cope with; *(seelisch)* to come to terms with; *(finanziell, col: essen, trinken können)* to manage.

verkrampfen* *vr* to become cramped; *(Hände)* to clench up; *(Mensch)* to go tense. **verkrampft** *(fig)* tense.

verkriechen* *vr irreg* to creep away; *(fig)* to hide (oneself away). **sich unter den** or **dem Tisch** ~ to crawl or creep under the table.

verkrümeln* 1 *vr (col)* to disappear. 2 *vt* to crumble.

verkrümmen* *vtr* to bend; *(Rückgrat)* to become curved; *(Holz)* to warp; *(Baum)* to grow crooked.

Verkrümmung *f* bend *(gen in); (von Fingern, Knochen, Bäumen)* crookedness *no pl.* ~ **der Wirbelsäule** curvature of the spine.

verkrüppeln* 1 *vt* to cripple. 2 *vi aux sein* to become crippled; *(Zehen, Füße)* to become deformed; *(Baum etc)* to grow stunted.

verkrusten* *vir (vi: aux sein)* to become encrusted.

verkümmern* *vi aux sein (Glied, Organ)* to atrophy; *(Pflanze)* to die; *(Talent)* to go to waste; *(Mensch)* to waste away. **emotionell/geistig** ~ to become emotionally/intellectually stunted.

verkünden[2]* *vt* to announce; *Urteil* to pronounce; *Evangelium* to preach; *Gesetz* to promulgate.

Verkünder(in *f)* *m* - **ein** ~ **des Evangeliums** a preacher of the gospel.

verkündigen* *vt* to proclaim; *(iro)* to announce; *Evangelium auch* to preach.

verkupfert *adj* copper-plated.

verkuppeln* *vt (pej)* to pair off. **jdn an jdn** ~ *(Zuhälter)* to procure sb for sb.

verkürzen* 1 *vt* to shorten; *Strecke, Wege etc auch* to cut; *Aufenthalt* to cut short; *Haltbarkeit* to reduce; *Leiden* to end. **sich (dat) die Zeit** ~ to pass the time; **verkürzte Arbeitszeit** shorter working hours. 2 *vr* to be shortened; *(Strecke, Zeit auch)* to be cut; *(Haltbarkeit)* to be reduced; *(Leiden)* to be ended; *(Urlaub, Aufenthalt)* to be cut short.

verladen* *vt irreg* to load.

Verlag *m* -e publisher. **in** or **bei welchem** ~ **ist das erschienen?** who published it?

verlagern* *vtr (lit, fig)* to shift.

Verlagerung *f* shift.

Verlags-: ~**anstalt** *f* publishing firm; ~**buchhandel** *m* publishing trade; ~**wesen** *nt* publishing *no art.*

verlangen* 1 *vt* **(a)** *(fordern)* to demand; *(wollen)* to want; *Preis* to ask; *Qualifikationen, Erfahrung* to

require. **(b)** *(erwarten)* to ask *(von of).* **es wird von jdm verlangt, daß** ... it is required or expected of sb that ...; **das ist nicht zuviel verlangt** it's not asking too much. **(c)** *(fragen nach)* to ask for. **Sie werden am Telefon verlangt** you are wanted on the phone; **ich verlange den Geschäftsführer (zu sprechen)** I want to see the manager. 2 *vi* ~ **nach** to ask for; *(sich sehnen nach)* to long for.

Verlangen *nt* - *(nach for)* desire; *(Sehnsucht)* yearning, longing; *(Begierde)* craving; *(Forderung)* request. **auf** ~ on demand; **auf** ~ **der Eltern** at the parents' request.

verlängern* 1 *vt* to extend; *(zeitlich) Wartezeit, Schmerzen etc* to prolong; *Hosenbein, Ärmel etc* to lengthen; *Paß, Abonnement etc* to renew. **ein verlängertes Wochenende** a long weekend. 2 *vr* to be extended; *(zeitlich auch, Leiden etc)* to be prolonged.

Verlängerung *f* **(a)** *siehe vt* extension; prolongation; lengthening; renewal. **(b)** *(von Spielzeit)* extra time *(Brit),* overtime *(US).*

Verlängerungs-: ~**kabel** *nt,* ~**schnur** *f (Elec)* extension lead.

verlangsamen* *vtr* to slow down or up. **das Tempo** ~ to slow down.

Verlaß *m no pl* **auf ihn ist kein** ~ there's no relying on him.

verlassen[1]* *irreg* 1 *vt* to leave; *(fig: Mut etc)* to desert; *(im Stich lassen)* to desert, to abandon. 2 *vr* **sich auf jdn/etw** ~ to rely or depend on sb/sth; **darauf können Sie sich** ~ you can depend on that.

verlassen[2] *adj* deserted; *Auto* abandoned; *(öd)* desolate; *(einsam)* lonely. **einsam und** ~ so all alone.

verläßlich *adj* reliable.

Verlauf *m, pl* **Verläufe** course; *(Ausgang)* end. **im** ~**(e) des Tages** etc during the course of the day etc. **einen guten/schlechten** ~ **nehmen** to go well/badly.

verlaufen* *irreg* 1 *vi aux sein* **(a)** *(Tag, Prüfung)* to go; *(Kindheit)* to pass; *(Untersuchung)* to proceed. **(b)** *(sich erstrecken)* to run. **(c)** *(auseinanderfließen)* to run. **die Spur verlief im Sand** the track disappeared in the sand. 2 *vr* **(a)** *(sich verirren)* to get lost, to lose one's way. **(b)** *(Menschenmenge)* to disperse; *(Spur, Weg)* to disappear.

verlautbaren* *vti (form)* to announce.

Verlautbarung *f* announcement.

verlauten* 1 *vi* **etwas** ~ **lassen** to give an indication. 2 *vi impers* **es verlautet, daß** ... it is reported that ...; **wie aus Bonn verlautet** according to reports from Bonn.

verleben* *vt* to spend. **eine schöne Zeit** ~ to have a nice time.

verlegen[1]* 1 *vt* **(a)** *(an anderen Ort)* to transfer, to move. **(b)** *(verschieben)* to postpone *(auf +acc until); (vorverlegen)* to bring forward *(auf +acc to).* **(c)** *(an falschen Platz legen)* to mislay. **(d)** *Kabel, Fliesen etc* to lay. **(e)** *(drucken lassen)* to publish. 2 *vr* **sich auf etw** *(acc)* ~ to resort to sth; **sich aufs Unterrichten** ~ to take up teaching.

verlegen[2] *adj* embarrassed *no adv.* **um Worte** ~ **sein** to be at a loss for words.

Verlegenheit *f* **(a)** *no pl* embarrassment. **jdn in** ~ **bringen** to embarrass sb; **in** ~ **kommen** or **geraten** to get embarrassed. **(b)** *(unangenehme Lage)* embarrassing situation.

Verleger *m* - publisher.

verleiden* **jdm etw** ~ to put sb off sth.

Verleih *m* -e **(a)** *(Unternehmen)* rental or hire *(Brit)* company; *(Auto~)* car rental or hire *(Brit); (Film~)* distributor(s). **(b)** *(das Verleihen)* renting (out), hiring (out) *(Brit); (Film~)* distribution. **der** ~ **von Büchern** the lending of books.

verleihen* *vt irreg* **(a)** *(verborgen)* to lend *(an jdn* to sb); *(gegen Gebühr)* to rent, to hire *(Brit).* **(b)**

(zuerkennen) to award *(jdm* (to) *sb)*; *Titel, Ehren-bürgerrechte* to confer *(jdm* on *sb)*. **(c)** *(geben, verschaffen)* to give.

Verleiher m - hire *(Brit)* or rental firm; *(von Filmen)* distributor; *(von Büchern)* lender.

Verleihung f siehe vt *(a, b)* **(a)** lending; renting, hiring *(Brit)*. **(b)** award(ing), conferment.

verleimen* vt to glue.

verleiten* vt **(a)** *(verlocken)* to tempt; *(verführen)* to lead astray. **jdn dazu ~, die Schule zu schwänzen** to encourage sb to play truant. **(b)** *(veranlassen)* **jdn zu etw ~** to lead sb to sth.

verlernen* vt to forget. **das Tanzen ~** to forget how to dance.

verlesen* irreg **1** vt **(a)** *(vorlesen)* to read (out). **(b)** *Gemüse etc* to sort. **2** vr **ich habe mich wohl ~** I must have misread it.

verletzen* 1 vt **(a)** to injure; *(in Kampf etc, mit Kugel, Messer)* to wound; *(fig)* jdn to hurt, to offend; *jds Schönheitssinn etc* to offend. **(b)** *Gesetz* to break; *Pflicht, Rechte, Intimsphäre* to violate. **2** vr to injure oneself.

verletzend adj *Bemerkung* hurtful.

verletzlich adj vulnerable.

Verletzte(r) mf decl as adj injured person; *(Unfall~ auch)* casualty; *(bei Kampf)* wounded man. **die ~n** the injured/the wounded.

Verletzung f siehe vt **(a)** injuring; wounding; *(fig)* hurting, offending. **(b)** breaking; violation. **(c)** *(Wunde)* injury.

verleugnen* vt to deny; *Kind* to disown. **er läßt sich immer ~** he always pretends not to be there; **sich (selbst) ~** to deny one's own self.

verleumden* vt to slander; *(schriftlich)* to libel.

verleumderisch adj siehe vt slanderous; libellous *(Brit)*, libelous *(US)*.

Verleumdung f *(Bemerkung)* slander; *(Bericht)* libel.

verlieben* vr to fall in love *(in +acc* with).

verliebt adj *Benehmen, Blicke, Worte* amorous. **(in jdn) ~ sein** to be in love (with sb).

verlieren pret **verlor**, ptp **verloren 1** vti to lose. **kein Wort über jdn/etw ~** not to say a word about sb/sth; **das/er hat hier nichts verloren** *(col)* that/he has no business to be here; **sie hat an Schönheit verloren** she has lost some of her beauty; **sie/die Altstadt** *etc* **hat sehr verloren** she/the old town *etc* is not what she/it *etc* used to be; **durch etw ~** to lose (something) by sth. **2** vr *(Menschen)* to lose each other; *(verschwinden)* to disappear; *(verhallen)* to fade away. **sich in etw** *(dat)* **~** to get lost in sth; *(fig)* to become absorbed in sth; *siehe* **verloren.**

Verlierer(in f) m - loser

Verlies nt -e dungeon

verloben* vr to get engaged *(mit* to). **verlobt sein** to be engaged.

Verlobte(r) mf decl as adj **mein ~r** my fiancé; **meine ~** my fiancée; **die ~n** the engaged couple.

Verlobung f engagement.

Verlobungs- in cpds engagement.

verlocken* vti to entice, to tempt.

Verlockung f enticement.

verlogen adj *Mensch* lying; *Komplimente, Versprechungen* false; *Moral, Gesellschaft* hypocritical.

verlor pret of **verlieren.**

verloren 1 ptp of **verlieren. 2** adj lost; *(Cook) Eier* poached. **jdn/etw ~ geben** to give sb/sth up for lost; **auf ~em Posten kämpfen** or **stehen** to be fighting a losing battle.

verlorengehen vi sep irreg aux sein to be lost. **an ihm ist ein Sänger verlorengegangen** he would have made a good singer.

verlöschen* vi aux sein to go out; *(Inschrift, Farbe, Erinnerung)* to fade.

verlosen* vt to raffle (off).

Verlosung f *(das Verlosen)* raffling; *(Lotterie)* raffle.

verlöten* vt to solder.

verlottern* vi aux sein *(col) (Stadt, Restaurant)* to become run down; *(Garten)* to run wild; *(Mensch)* to go to the dogs; *(moralisch)* to go to the bad.

verlottert adj *(col) Stadt* run-down; *Garten* wild; *Mensch, Aussehen* scruffy; *(moralisch)* dissolute.

Verlust m -e loss. **mit ~ verkaufen** to sell at a loss.

Verlust-: **~anzeige** f "lost" notice; **~betrieb** m loss-maker; **v~bringend** adj loss-making; **v~bringend arbeiten** to work at a loss; **~geschäft** nt **das war ein ~geschäft** I/he etc made a loss; **~liste** f *(Mil)* casualty list; **v~reich** adj with heavy losses.

vermachen* vt **jdm etw ~** to leave or bequeath sth to sb.

Vermächtnis nt bequest, legacy; *(fig)* legacy.

vermählen* *(form)* **1** vt to marry. **frisch vermählt sein** to be newly married. **2** vr **sich (mit jdm) ~** to marry (sb).

Vermählte(r) mf decl as adj **die beiden ~n** the newly-weds; **die/der soeben ~** the bride/groom.

vermasseln* vt *(col)* to mess up *(col)*.

vermauern* vt to wall or brick up.

vermehren* 1 vt to increase; *(fortpflanzen)* to breed. **diese Fälle treten vermehrt auf** these cases are happening increasingly often. **2** vr to increase; *(sich fortpflanzen)* to reproduce, to breed; *(Bakterien)* to multiply; *(Pflanzen)* to propagate.

vermeidbar adj avoidable.

vermeiden* vt irreg to avoid. **~, daß etw passiert** to avoid letting sth happen; **es läßt sich nicht ~, daß ...** it is inevitable or unavoidable that ...

vermeidlich adj avoidable.

vermeintlich adj attr putative.

vermengen* vt to mix; *(fig col: durcheinanderbringen)* to mix up.

vermenschlichen* vt to humanize.

Vermerk m -e note, remark; *(im Kalender)* entry; *(in Paß)* observation; *(Stempel)* stamp.

vermerken* vt to make a note of; *(in Paß, Karte)* to record. **sich** *(dat)* **etw ~** to make a note of sth; **jdm etw übel ~** to take sth amiss.

vermessen[1]* vt irreg to measure; *Land, Gelände* to survey.

vermessen[2] adj *(anmaßend)* presumptuous; *(kühn) Unterfangen* bold.

Vermessung f measurement; *(von Land, Gelände)* survey.

Vermessungs-: **~amt** nt land survey(ing) office; **~ingenieur** m land surveyor.

vermiesen* vt *(col)* **jdm etw ~** to spoil sth for sb.

vermietbar adj rentable. **schlecht ~** difficult to rent.

vermieten* vti to rent (out), to let (out) *(Brit)*; *Boot, Auto* to rent (out), to hire (out) *(Brit)*. **Zimmer zu ~** room to let *(Brit)* or for rent.

Vermieter m - lessor; *(von Wohnung)* landlord.

Vermieterin f landlady.

vermindern* 1 vt to reduce, to decrease; *Ärger etc* to lessen; *Schmerzen* to ease. **2** vr siehe vt to decrease; to lessen; to ease.

Verminderung f siehe vb reduction *(gen* of); lessening; easing.

verminen* vt to mine.

vermischen* 1 vt to mix; *Teesorten etc* to blend. **vermischte Schriften** miscellaneous writings. **2** vr to mix; *(Elemente, Klänge, Farben)* to blend.

vermissen* vt to miss. **vermißt werden** to be missing; **vermißt sein**, **als vermißt gemeldet sein** to be reported missing; **etw an jdm ~** to find sb lacking in sth; **wir haben dich bei der Party vermißt** we didn't see you at the party; **etw ~ lassen** to be lacking in sth.

Vermißten|anzeige f missing persons report.

Vermißte(r) mf decl as adj missing person.

vermitteln* 1 vt to arrange (jdm for sb); Stelle, Privatschüler to find (jdm for sb); Aushilfskräfte, Lehrer etc to place; (Telec) Gespräch to connect; Lösung etc to negotiate; Gefühl, Bild, Idee to convey, to give (jdm to sb); Wissen to impart (jdm to sb). **jdm etw ~ to** get sth for sb. **2** vi to mediate. **~de Worte** conciliatory words.

Vermittler(in f) m - (a) mediator. (b) (Comm) agent; (Fin, Heirats~) broker; (von Anleihe) negotiator; (Stellen~) clerk in an employment agency.

Vermittlung f (a) siehe vt arranging; finding; placing; connection; negotiation; conveying; imparting. **durch seine freundliche ~** with his kind help. **(b)** (Schlichtung) mediation. **(c)** (Stelle, Agentur) agency; (Heirats~) marriage bureau; (Wohnungs~) estate agent's (Brit), realtor (US); (Arbeits~) employment agency. **(d)** (Telec) exchange; (in Firma etc) switchboard.

Vermittlungs-: ~**gebühr** f commission; ~**stelle** f agency; (Telec) (telephone) exchange; (in Firma etc) switchboard.

vermodern* vi aux sein to moulder, to decay.

vermögen vt aux (geh) etw zu tun ~, (es) ~, etw zu tun to be able to do sth; **Geduld vermag viel bei ihm** patience works wonders with him.

Vermögen nt - (a) (Reichtum, viel Geld) fortune. **~ haben** to have money. **(b)** (Besitz) property. **mein ganzes ~ besteht aus ...** my entire assets consist of ... **(c)** (Können) ability, capacity.

vermögend adj (reich) wealthy, well-off.

Vermögens-: ~**abgabe** f property levy; ~**bildung** f wealth creation; ~**steuer** f wealth tax; ~**verhältnisse** pl financial circumstances pl; ~**werte** pl assets pl; v~**wirksam** adj profitable; **sein Geld** v~**wirksam anlegen** to invest one's money profitably; v~**wirksame Leistungen** employers' contributions to tax-deductible savings scheme.

vermummen* vr (a) to wrap up (warm). (b) (sich verkleiden) to disguise.

Vermummung f disguise.

vermurksen* vt (col) etw ~ to make a mess of sth.

vermuten* vt to suspect. **ich vermute es nur** that's only an assumption; **wir haben ihn dort nicht vermutet** we didn't expect to find/see etc him there; **es ist zu ~, daß ...** it may be supposed that ...

vermutlich 1 adj attr presumable; Täter suspected. **2** adv presumably.

Vermutung f (Annahme) supposition, assumption; (Verdacht) suspicion. **die ~ liegt nahe, daß ...** there are grounds for assuming that ...; **meine ~en waren doch richtig** my guess was right.

vernachlässigen* 1 vt to neglect; (Schicksal) jdn to be unkind to. **das können wir ~** (nicht berücksichtigen) we can ignore that. **2** vr to neglect one's appearance.

Vernachlässigung f neglect.

vernageln* vt to nail up. **etw mit Brettern ~** to board sth up.

vernähen* vt Wunde, Saum to stitch (up).

vernarben* vi aux sein to heal or close (up).

vernarren* vr (col) **sich in jdn/etw ~** to fall for sb/sth; **in jdn/etw vernarrt sein** to be crazy about sb/sth (col).

vernaschen* vt Süßigkeiten to eat up; Geld to spend on sweets (Brit) or candy (US); (col) Mädchen, Mann to make it with (col).

vernebeln* vt (Mil) to cover with a smoke screen; (fig) Tatsachen to obscure; (col) Zimmer to fug up.

vernehmbar adj (hörbar) audible.

vernehmen* vt irreg (a) (hören, erfahren) to hear. **(b)** (Jur) Zeugen, Angeklagte to examine; (Polizei) to question.

Vernehmen nt: **dem ~ nach** from what I/we etc hear.

vernehmlich adj clear, audible.

Vernehmung f (Jur: von Zeugen, Angeklagten) examination; (durch Polizei) questioning.

verneigen* vr to bow. **sich vor jdm/etw ~** (lit) to bow to sb/sth; (fig) to bow down before sb/sth.

verneinen* vti Frage to answer in the negative; (leugnen) Tatsache, Existenz Gottes etc to deny; These to dispute; (Gram, Logik) to negate. **die verneinte Form** the negative (form).

verneinend adj (auch Gram) negative.

Verneinung f (Leugnung) denial; (von These etc) disputing; (Gram, Philos) negation; (verneinte Form) negative.

vernichten* vt (lit, fig) to destroy.

vernichtend adj devastating; Niederlage crushing. **jdn ~ schlagen** (Mil, Sport) to annihilate sb.

Vernichtung f destruction.

Vernichtungs-: ~**krieg** m war of extermination; ~**lager** nt extermination camp; ~**schlag** m devastating blow; ~**waffe** f doomsday weapon.

verniedlichen* vt to trivialize.

vernieten* vt to rivet.

Vernunft f no pl reason. **zur ~ kommen** to come to one's senses; ~ **annehmen** to see reason; etw **mit/ohne ~ tun** to do sth sensibly/foolishly.

Vernunft-: v~**begabt** adj rational; v~**gemäß** adv rationally; ~**glaube(n)** m rationalism; ~**gründe** pl rational grounds pl; ~**heirat** f marriage of convenience.

vernünftig 1 adj sensible; (logisch denkend) rational; (col: ordentlich, anständig) decent; Vorschlag reasonable. **2** adv siehe adj sensibly; rationally; decently; reasonably; (tüchtig) properly (col).

Vernunft-: v~**los** adj irrational; ~**mensch** m rational person; v~**widrig** adj irrational.

ver|öffentlichen* vti to publish.

Ver|öffentlichung f publication.

ver|ordnen* vt to prescribe (jdm etw sth for sb).

Ver|ordnung f (a) (Med) prescription. (b) (Verfügung) decree.

verpachten* vt to lease, to rent out (an +acc to).

Verpachtung f lease.

verpacken* vt to pack; (verbrauchergerecht) to package; (einwickeln) to wrap.

Verpackung f siehe vt packing; packaging; wrapping.

verpassen* vt (a) (versäumen) to miss. (b) (col: zuteilen) **jdm etw ~** to give sb sth; (aufzwingen) to make sb have sth; **jdm eine Ohrfeige ~** to clout sb one (col).

verpatzen* vt (col) to spoil; Examen to make a mess of. **sich** (dat) **etw ~** to spoil sth/mess sth up (col).

verpennen* (col) **1** vt (verpassen) to miss by oversleeping; (schlafend verbringen) Tag, Morgen etc to sleep through. **2** vir to oversleep.

verpesten* vt to pollute.

verpetzen* vt (col) to tell on (bei to).

verpfänden* vt to pawn; (Jur) to mortgage.

verpfeifen* vt irreg (col) to grass on (bei to) (col).

verpflanzen* vt (lit, fig) to transplant; Haut to graft.

verpflegen* 1 vt to feed. **2** vr **sich (selbst) ~** to feed oneself; (selbst kochen) to cook for oneself.

Verpflegung f (a) (das Verpflegen) catering; (Mil) rationing. (b) (Essen) food; (Mil) rations pl.

verpflichten* 1 vt to oblige; (vertraglich) to commit. **verpflichtet sein, etw zu tun, zu etw verpflichtet sein** to be obliged/committed to do sth; **jdm verpflichtet sein** to be under an obligation to sb; ~**d** Zusage binding. (b) (einstellen) to engage; Sportler to sign on. **2** vi to involve a commitment. **das verpflichtet zu nichts** there's no obligation involved. **3** vr to commit oneself. **sich zu etw ~** to commit oneself to doing sth.

Verpflichtung f (a) obligation (zu etw to do sth); (Pflicht auch, finanzielle ~) commitment (zu etw to do sth); *(Aufgabe)* duty. **(b)** *(Einstellung)* engaging; *(von Sportlern)* signing on.

verpfuschen* *vt (col)* to make a mess of.

verplanen* 1 *vt Zeit* to book up; *Geld* to budget. **jdn ~** *(col)* to fill up all sb's spare time (for him/her). **2** *vr* to plan badly; *(falsch berechnen)* to miscalculate.

verplappern* *vr (col)* to open one's big mouth *(col)*.

verplempern* *vt (col)* to waste, to fritter away.

verpönt *adj* frowned upon *(bei* by).

verprassen* *vt* to blow *(col) (für* on).

verprellen* *vt* to put off, to intimidate.

verprügeln* *vt* to thrash, to beat up.

verpuffen* *vi aux sein* to (go) pop; *(fig)* to fall flat.

Verputz *m no pl* plaster; *(Rauhputz)* roughcast.

verputzen* *vt* **(a)** to plaster; *(mit Rauhputz)* to roughcast. **(b)** *(col: aufessen)* to polish off *(col)*.

verqualmen* *vt Zimmer* to fill with smoke.

verrammeln* *vt* to barricade.

verramschen* *vt (col)* to sell off cheap.

Verrat *m no pl* betrayal *(an* +*dat* of); *(Jur)* treason *(an* +*dat* against). **~ an jdm üben** to betray sb.

verraten* *irreg* **1** *vt* to betray; *(bekanntgeben, ausplaudern)* to tell; *(fig: erkennen lassen)* to show. **nichts ~!** don't say a word!; **er hat es ~** he let it out. **2** *vr* to give oneself away.

Verräter(in *f)* *m* - traitor (+*gen* to).

verräterisch *adj* treacherous; *(Jur)* treasonable; *Blick etc* telltale *attr*.

verrauchen* 1 *vi aux sein (fig: Zorn)* to blow over. **2** *vt Zimmer* to fill with smoke; *Geld* to spend on smoking.

verräuchern* *vt* to fill with smoke.

verrechnen* 1 *vt (begleichen)* to settle; *Scheck* to clear; *Gutschein* to redeem. **etw mit etw ~** *(gegeneinander aufrechnen)* to balance sth with sth. **2** *vr* to miscalculate; *(col: sich täuschen)* to be mistaken. **sich um eine Mark ~** to be out by one mark.

Verrechnungsscheck *m* crossed *(Brit)* or non negotiable cheque *(Brit)* or check *(US)*.

verrecken* *vi aux sein (col!)* to die; *(elend sterben)* to die a wretched death. **er ist elend verreckt** he died like a dog *(col)*.

verregnet *adj* rainy, wet.

verreiben* *vt irreg* to rub *(auf* +*dat* into).

verreisen* *vi aux sein* to go away (on a trip). **er ist geschäftlich verreist** he's away on business.

verreißen* *vt irreg (kritisieren)* to tear to pieces.

verrenken* 1 *vt* to dislocate; *Hals* to crick. **2** *vr* to contort oneself.

verrennen* *vr irreg* **sich in etw** *(acc)* **~** to get stuck on sth.

verrichten* *vt Arbeit* to carry out.

verriegeln* *vt* to bolt.

verringern* 1 *vt* to reduce. **2** *vr* to decrease; *(Qualität, Leistungen)* to deteriorate.

Verringerung *f* siehe *vb* reduction; decrease; deterioration.

verrinnen* *vi irreg aux sein (Wasser)* to trickle away *(in* +*dat* into); *(Zeit)* to elapse.

Verriß *m* -sse slating review.

verrohen* *vi aux sein* to become brutalized.

Verrohung *f* brutalization.

verrosten* *vi aux sein* to rust. **verrostet** rusty.

verrotten* *vi aux sein* to rot; *(organisch)* to decompose.

verrucht *adj* despicable; *(verrufen)* disreputable.

verrücken* *vt* to move.

verrückt *adj* mad. **~ auf** (+*acc)* or **nach** *(col)* crazy or mad about *(col)*; **wie ~** like mad or crazy *(col)*; **die Leute kamen wie ~** *(col)* loads of people came *(col)*; **jdn ~ machen** *(col)* to drive sb crazy or mad; **~ werden** *(col)* to go crazy; **~ spielen** *(col)* to play up *(col)*.

Verrückte(r) *mf decl as adj (col)* lunatic.

Verruf *m no pl* **in ~ kommen** to fall into disrepute.

verrufen *adj* disreputable.

verrühren* *vt* to mix, to stir.

verrußen* *vi aux sein* to get sooty.

verrutschen* *vi aux sein* to slip.

Vers [fɛrs] *m* -e verse *(auch Bibl)*; *(Zeile)* line.

versachlichen* *vt* to objectify.

versacken* *vi aux sein* **(a)** *(lit)* to sink. **(b)** *(fig col) (herunterkommen)* to go downhill; *(lange zechen)* to get involved in a booze-up *(col)*.

versagen* 1 *vt* **jdm/sich etw ~** to deny sb/oneself sth; *(verweigern)* to refuse sb sth. **2** *vi* to fail. **die Beine/Nerven** *etc* **versagten ihm** his legs/nerves *etc* gave way.

Versagen *nt no pl* failure; *(von Maschine)* breakdown. **menschliches ~** human error.

Versager *m* - failure, flop *(col)*.

versalzen[1]* *vt irreg* to put too much salt in/on; *(col: verderben)* to spoil.

versalzen[2] *adj Essen* too salty.

versammeln* 1 *vt* to assemble. **2** *vr* to assemble; *(Parliament)* to sit; *(Ausschuß, Verein)* to meet.

Versammlung *f* meeting, assembly.

Versammlungs-: **~freiheit** *f* freedom of assembly; **~lokal** *nt* meeting place.

Versand *m no pl* dispatch; *(das Vertreiben)* distribution.

Versand-: **~abteilung** *f* dispatch department; **~artikel** *m* article for dispatch; **~bahnhof** *m* dispatch station; **v~bereit** *adj* ready for dispatch.

versanden* *vi aux sein* to silt (up); *(fig)* to peter out.

Versand-: **~gut** *nt* goods pl for dispatch; **~handel** *m* mail order business; **~haus** *nt* mail order firm; **~kosten** *pl* transport(ation) costs *pl*.

Versandweg *m* **auf dem ~** by mail order.

versauen* *vt (col)* to mess up *(col)*.

versaufen* *irreg (col)* **1** *vt Geld* to spend on booze *(col)*. **2** *vi aux sein (ertrinken)* to drown.

versäumen* *vt* to miss; *Zeit* to lose; *Pflicht* to neglect. **(es) ~, etw zu tun** to fail to do sth; **das Versäumte** what one has missed; **die versäumte Zeit aufholen** to make up for lost time.

Versäumnis *nt (Fehler)* failing; *(Unterlassung)* omission.

verschachern* *vt* to sell off.

verschachtelt *adj Satz* encapsulated, complex.

verschaffen* 1 *vt* **jdm etw ~** to provide sb with sth; *Erleichterung, Genugtuung* to give sb sth; *Respekt* to earn sb sth. **2** *vr* **sich** *(dat)* **etw ~** to obtain sth; *Ansehen, Vorteil* to gain sth; *Ruhe, Respekt* to get sth; **sich mit Gewalt Zutritt ~** to force an entry.

verschalen* *vt Wand* to panel; *Heizung etc* to box in.

verschämt *adj* coy.

verschandeln* *vt* to ruin.

verschanzen* 1 *vt (Mil)* to fortify. **2** *vr (Mil,fig)* to entrench oneself *(hinter*+*dat* behind); *(sich verbarrikadieren)* to barricade oneself in *(in etw* *(dat)* sth).

verschärfen* 1 *vt (erhöhen) Tempo* to increase; *Gegensätze* to intensify; *(verschlimmern) Lage* to aggravate; *(strenger machen) Kontrollen, Gesetze* to tighten up. **2** *vr siehe vt* to increase; to intensify; to become aggravated; to become tighter.

verscharren* *vt* to bury.

verschätzen* *vt* to miscalculate *(in etw (dat)* sth).

verschenken* *vt (lit, fig)* to give away.

verscherzen* *vt* **sich** *(dat)* **etw ~** to forfeit sth; **es sich** *(dat)* **mit jdm ~** to spoil things with sb.

verscheuchen* *vt* to scare off; *(fig) Sorgen etc* to drive away.

verschicken* *vt (versenden)* to send out; *(zur Kur etc)* to send away; *(deportieren)* to deport.

verschieben* *irreg* **1** *vt* **(a)** *(verrücken)* to move, to shift; *(Rail)* to shunt. **(b)** *(auf später)* to postpone *(um* for, *auf* +*acc* until). **(c)** *(col) Waren,*

Devisen to traffic in. **2** *vr* to shift; *(zeitlich)* to be postponed.

Verschiebung *f (zeitlich)* postponement.

verschieden 1 *adj* **(a)** *(unterschiedlich)* different. **die ~sten Sorten** many different kinds; **das ist ganz ~** *(wird ~ gehandhabt)* that varies, that just depends. **(b)** *attr (mehrere, einige)* various, several. **(c)** *(substantivisch)* **~e** *pl* various *or* several people; **~es** several things; **V~es** *(in Zeitung, Liste)* miscellaneous. **2** *adv* differently. **die Häuser sind ~ hoch** the houses vary in height.

verschieden|artig *adj* different; *(mannigfaltig)* various, diverse. **die ~sten Dinge** all sorts of things.

Verschiedenheit *f* difference *(gen* of, in); *(Unähnlichkeit)* dissimilarity.

verschießen* *vt irreg Munition* to use up.

verschiffen* *vt* to ship; *Sträfling* to transport.

verschimmeln* *vi aux sein (Nahrungsmittel)* to go mouldy *(Brit)* or moldy *(US)*; *(Leder, Papier etc)* to go mildewy. **verschimmelt** *(lit)* mouldy *(Brit)*, moldy *(US)*; mildewy.

verschlafen* *irreg* **1** *vir* to oversleep. **2** *vt Termin* to miss by oversleeping; *Tag* to sleep through. **3** *adj* sleepy; *(trottelig)* dozy *(col)*.

Verschlag *m ~e (Schuppen)* shed; *(für Kaninchen)* hutch.

verschlagen¹* *vt irreg* **(a) etw mit Brettern ~** to board sth up; **etw mit Nägeln ~** to nail sth up. **(b)** *Atem* to take away. **das hat mir die Sprache ~** it left me speechless. **(c)** *(geraten lassen)* to bring. **an einen Ort ~ werden** to end up somewhere. **(d)** *(Sport)* Ball to mishit. **(e)** *(verblättern) Seite, Stelle* to lose.

verschlagen² *adj Mensch, Blick etc* sly.

Verschlagenheit *f* slyness.

verschlammen* *vi aux sein* to silt up.

verschlampen* *(col)* **1** *vt (verlieren)* to lose *(col)*. **2** *vi aux sein (Mensch)* to go to seed *(col)*.

verschlechtern* **1** *vt* to make worse. **2** *vr* to get worse; *(gehaltlich)* to take a lower-paid job. **sich beruflich ~** to take a worse job.

Verschlechterung *f* worsening.

verschleiern* **1** *vt* to veil; *(fig)* to disguise; *Blick* to blur. **2** *vr (Frau)* to veil oneself; *(Himmel)* to become hazy; *(Blick)* to become blurred.

Verschleiß *m ~e (lit, fig)* wear and tear; *(Verbrauch)* consumption. **ein ~ deiner Kräfte** a drain on your strength.

verschleißen *pret* **verschliß**, *ptp* **verschlissen 1** *vt* to wear out; *(verbrauchen)* to use up. **2** *vi aux sein* to wear out. **3** *vr* to wear out; *(Menschen)* to wear oneself out.

verschleppen* *vt* **(a)** *(entführen) jdn* to abduct; *Kunstschätze etc* to carry off. **(b)** *(verbreiten) Seuche* to spread. **(c)** *(hinauszögern)* to protract; *(Pol) Gesetzesänderung etc* to delay.

verschleudern* *vt (Comm)* to dump; *(vergeuden)* to squander.

verschließen* *irreg* **1** *vt* **(a)** *(abschließen)* to lock up; *(fig)* to close, to shut; *(versperren)* to bar; *(mit Riegel)* to bolt. **(b)** *(zumachen)* to close; *(mit Pfropfen) Flasche* to cork. **die Augen (vor etw dat) ~** to shut one's eyes (to sth). **2** *vr (Reize, Sprache, Möglichkeit)* to be closed *(dat* to); *(Mensch: reserviert sein)* to shut oneself off *(dat* from). **sich einer Sache** *(dat)* **or gegen etw ~** to close one's mind to sth.

verschlimmbessern *vt insep (hum)* to make worse.

verschlimmern *vtr* to worsen.

verschlingen* *irreg* **1** *vt* **(a)** *(lit, fig)* to devour; *(Wellen etc, verbrauchen)* to swallow up. **(b)** *(verknoten)* to entwine; *Arme* to fold. **ein verschlungener Pfad** a winding path. **2** *vr* to become entwined.

verschliß *pret of* **verschleißen**.

verschlissen 1 *ptp of* **verschleißen**. **2** *adj* worn

(out).

verschlossen *adj* closed; *(fig: unzugänglich)* reserved. **etw bleibt jdm ~ sth** is a closed book to sb; **wir standen vor ~er Tür** we were left standing on the doorstep.

Verschlossenheit *f (von Mensch)* reserve.

verschlucken* **1** *vt* to swallow; *Geld* to swallow up; *Schall* to deaden. **2** *vr* to swallow the wrong way; *(fig)* to splutter.

Verschluß *m ~sse* **(a)** *(Schloß)* lock; *(luft-, wasserdicht, für Zoll)* seal; *(Deckel, Klappe)* top, lid; *(Pfropfen, Stöpsel)* stopper; *(an Kleidung)* fastener. **etw unter ~ halten** to keep sth under lock and key. **(b)** *(Phot)* shutter.

verschlüsseln* *vt* to (put into) code, to encode.

verschmachten* *vi aux sein* to languish *(vor +dat* for). **(vor Durst/Hitze) ~** *(col)* to be dying of thirst/heat *(col)*.

verschmähen* *vt* to spurn.

verschmälern* *vtr* to narrow.

verschmelzen* *irreg* **1** *vi aux sein* to melt together; *(Metalle)* to fuse; *(Farben)* to blend; *(fig)* to blend *(zu* into). **2** *vt Metalle* to fuse; *Farben* to blend; *(fig)* to unify *(zu* into).

verschmerzen* *vt* to get over.

verschmieren* **1** *vt* **(a)** *Salbe, Schmiere* to spread *(in +dat* over). **(b)** *(verputzen) Löcher* to fill in. **(c)** *(verwischen) Fenster, Gesicht* to smear; *Geschriebenes, Schminke* to smudge. **2** *vi* to smudge.

verschmiert *adj Hände* smeary; *Schminke* smudged.

verschmitzt *adj* mischievous.

verschmutzen* **1** *vt* to dirty; *Umwelt* to pollute; *Gewehr, Zündkerze* to foul; *Fahrbahn* to make muddy; *(Hund) Bürgersteig* to foul. **2** *vi aux sein* to get dirty; *(Umwelt)* to become polluted.

verschmutzt *adj* dirty, soiled; *Luft etc* polluted.

verschnaufen* *vir* *(col)* to have a breather.

verschneiden* *vt irreg* **(a)** *Rum etc* to blend. **(b)** *Flügel, Hecke* to clip. **(c)** *(falsch schneiden)* to cut wrongly. **(d)** *Tiere* to castrate.

verschneit *adj* snow-covered. **tief ~** thick with snow.

Verschnitt *m* **(a)** *(von Rum etc)* blend. **(b)** *(Abfall)* clippings *pl*.

verschnörkelt *adj* ornate.

verschnupft *adj (col)* **~ sein** to have a cold; *(beleidigt)* to be peeved *(col)*.

verschnüren* *vt* to tie up.

verschollen *adj* missing; *Literaturwerk* forgotten.

verschonen* *vt* to spare *(jdn von etw sb sth)*. **von etw verschont bleiben** to escape sth.

verschöne(r)n* *vt* to improve (the appearance of); *Wohnung* to brighten up.

Verschönerung *f* siehe *vt* improvement; brightening up.

verschränken* *vt* to cross over; *Arme* to fold; *Beine* to cross; *Hände* to clasp.

verschrauben* *vt* to screw together.

verschreckt *adj* frightened, scared.

verschreiben* *irreg* **1** *vt* **(a)** *(verordnen)* to prescribe. **(b)** *Papier* to use up. **2** *vr* **(a)** *(falsch schreiben)* to make a slip (of the pen). **(b)** **sich einer Sache** *(dat)* **~** to devote oneself to sth.

verschrie(e)n *adj* notorious.

verschroben *adj* eccentric, odd.

verschrotten* *vt* to scrap.

verschrumpeln* *vi aux sein* to shrivel.

verschüchtern* *vt* to intimidate.

verschulden* **1** *vt* to be to blame for. **2** *vi aux sein (in Schulden geraten)* to get into debt. **verschuldet sein** to be in debt.

Verschulden *nt no pl* fault. **ohne sein/mein ~** through no fault of his/my own.

verschütten* *vt* **(a)** *Flüssigkeit* to spill. **(b)** *(zuschütten) Brunnen* to fill in. **(c) verschüttet wer-**

den *(Mensch)* to be buried (alive); *(fig)* to be submerged.

verschwägert *adj* related (by marriage) *(mit* to).

verschweigen* *vt irreg Tatsachen, Wahrheit etc* to conceal *(jdm etw sth* from *sb).*

verschweißen* *vt* to weld together.

verschwenden* *vt* to waste *(auf or* an +acc on).

Verschwender(in *f) m* - spendthrift.

verschwenderisch *adj* wasteful; *Leben* extravagant; *(üppig)* lavish.

Verschwendung *f* waste.

Verschwendungs-: ~**sucht** *f* no *pl* extravagance; v~**süchtig** *adj* extravagant.

verschwiegen *adj Mensch* discreet; *Ort* secluded.

Verschwiegenheit *f* no *pl* (von *Mensch*) discretion. **zur** ~ **verpflichtet** bound to secrecy.

verschwimmen* *vi irreg aux sein* to become blurred. **ineinander** ~ to merge into one another; *siehe* **verschwommen.**

verschwinden*vi *irreg aux sein* to disappear, to vanish. **verschwinde!** clear off! *(col);* neben jdm/etw ~ *(in bezug auf Größe)* to look minute beside sb/sth.

Verschwinden *nt no pl* disappearance.

verschwindend *adj Anzahl, Menge* insignificant. ~ **wenig** very, very few; ~ **klein** minute.

verschwistert *adj* (miteinander) ~ **sein** to be brother and sister; *(Brüder)* to be brothers; *(Schwestern)* to be sisters; *(Städte)* to be twinned.

verschwitzen* *vt* (a) *Kleidung* to make sweaty. (b) *(fig col)* to forget.

verschwitzt *adj* sweat-stained; *Mensch* sweaty.

verschwommen *adj Foto, Umrisse* blurred; *Berge* hazy; *Begriffe, Erinnerung* vague.

verschworen *adj Gesellschaft* sworn.

verschwören* *vr irreg* (a) to conspire, to plot *(mit* with, gegen against). **sich zu etw** ~ to plot sth; **alles hat sich gegen mich verschworen** *(fig)* there's a conspiracy against me. (b) **sich einer Sache** *(dat)* ~ to give oneself over to sth.

Verschwörer(in *f) m* - conspirator.

Verschwörung *f* conspiracy, plot.

verschwunden *adj* missing.

versehen* *irreg* **1** *vt* (a) *Amt, Stelle* to hold; *Dienst* to perform; *(sich kümmern um)* to look after. (b) *(ausstatten)* **jdn mit etw** ~ to provide or supply sb with sth; **etw mit etw** ~ to put sth on/in sth; *(montieren)* to fit sth with sth; **mit etw** ~ **sein** to have sth; **jdn mit einer Vollmacht** ~ to invest sb with full powers. **2** *vr* (a) *(sich irren)* to make a mistake. (b) **sich mit etw** ~ *(sich versorgen)* to provide oneself with sth; *(sich ausstatten)* to equip oneself with sth. (c) **ehe man sich's versieht** before you know what's happening.

Versehen *nt* - mistake, error; *(Unachtsamkeit)* oversight. **aus** ~ by mistake, inadvertently.

versehentlich 1 *adj attr* inadvertent; *(irrtümlich)* erroneous. **2** *adv* inadvertently, by mistake.

Versehrte(r) *mf decl as adj* disabled person.

verselbständigen* *vr* to become independent.

versenden* *vt irreg or reg* to send.

versengen* *vt* (a) to scorch; *(Feuer)* to singe. (b) *(col: verprügeln)* to wallop *(col).*

versenken* *vt* (a) *Schiff etc* to sink; *Leiche, Sarg* to lower; *das eigene Schiff* to scuttle. (b) *Schraube* to countersink; *Tischplatte* to fold away. **2** *vr* **sich in etw** *(acc)* ~ to become immersed in sth.

Versenkung *f* (a) *siehe vt* (a) sinking; lowering; scuttling. (b) *(das Sichversenken)* immersion. **innere/mystische** ~ inner/mystic contemplation. (c) **in der** ~ **verschwinden** *(col)* to vanish; **aus der** ~ **auftauchen** to re-appear.

versessen *adj* **auf etw** *(acc)* ~ **sein** to be very keen on sth.

versetzen* **1** *vt* (a) to move, to shift; *(nicht geradlinig anordnen)* to stagger; *(beruflich)* to transfer, to move. (b) *(Sch: in höhere Klasse)* to move up.

(c) *(col)* *(verkaufen)* to flog *(Brit col),* to sell; *(verpfänden)* to pawn. (d) *(col: nicht erscheinen)* **jdn** ~ to stand sb up *(col).* (e) **etw in Bewegung** ~ to set sth in motion; **jdn in Wut/in fröhliche Stimmung** ~ to send sb into a rage/to put sb in a cheerful mood; **jdn in Angst** ~ to frighten sb; **jdn in die Lage** ~, **etw zu tun** to put sb in a position to do sth; **jdn in seine Jugend** ~ to take sb back to his/her youth. **(f)** *Stoß, Schlag, Tritt etc* to give. **jdm einen Stich** ~ *(fig)* to cut sb to the quick, to wound sb (deeply).

2 *vr* *(sich an andere Stelle setzen)* to move (to another place). **sich in jdn/in jds Lage** ~ to put oneself in sb's place; **sich in eine frühere Zeit etc** ~ to imagine oneself back in an earlier period.

Versetzung *f* (a) *(beruflich)* transfer. (b) *(Sch)* moving up. **seine** ~ **ist gefährdet** he's in danger of having to stay down. (c) *(nicht geradlinige Anordnung)* staggering. (d) *(Vermischung)* mixing.

verseuchen* *vt* to contaminate.

Versfuß *m (Poet)* (metrical) foot.

Versicherer *m* - insurer; *(bei Schiffen)* underwriter.

versichern* **1** *vt* (a) *(beteuern)* **jdm** ~, **daß ...** to assure sb that ...; **jdm etw** ~, **jdn einer Sache** *(gen)* ~ to assure sb of sth; **seien Sie versichert, daß ...** rest assured that ... (b) *(gegen Diebstahl etc)* to insure. **2** *vr* (a) to insure oneself *(mit* for).
(b) *(sich vergewissern)* to make sure or certain.

Versicherung *f siehe vt* (a) assurance. (b) insurance; *(~sgesellschaft)* insurance company.

Versicherungs-: ~**beitrag** *m* insurance premium; *(bei staatlicher Versicherung etc)* insurance contribution; ~**betrug** *m* insurance fraud; ~**dauer** *f* period of insurance; ~**gesellschaft** *f* insurance company; ~**nehmer** *m (form)* policy holder; ~**pflicht** *f* compulsory insurance; ~**police** *f* insurance policy; ~**prämie** *f* insurance premium; ~**schutz** *m* insurance cover; ~**summe** *f* sum insured; ~**vertreter** *m* insurance agent; ~**wert** *m* insurance value; ~**wesen** *nt* insurance (business).

versickern* *vi aux sein* to seep away; *(fig: Interesse etc)* to peter out.

versiegeln* *vt* to seal.

versiegen* *vi aux sein (lit, fig)* to dry up; *(Interesse)* to peter out; *(Humor, Kräfte)* to fail.

versiert [vɛr-] *adj* **in etw** *(dat)* ~ **sein** to be experienced or *(in bezug auf Wissen)* well versed in sth.

versilbern* *vt* to silver-(plate).

versinken* *vi irreg aux sein* to sink. **ich hätte im Boden/vor Scham** ~ **mögen** I wished the ground would swallow me up; **in etw** *(acc)* ~ *(fig) in Trauer, Melancholie* to sink into sth; *in Anblick, Gedanken, Musik* to lose oneself in sth.

versinnbildlichen* *vt* to symbolize.

Version [vɛr'zioːn] *f* version.

versklaven* [fɛɐ'sklaːvn] *vt (lit, fig)* to enslave.

Vers-: ~**lehre** *f* study of verse; ~**maß** *nt* metre *(Brit),* meter *(US).*

versohlen* *vt (col)* to belt *(col).*

versöhnen* **1** *vt* to reconcile; *(besänftigen)* jdn, Götter to placate. ~**de Worte** conciliatory words. **2** *vr* to be(come) reconciled; *(Streitende)* to make it up. **sich mit etw** ~ to reconcile oneself to sth.

versöhnlich *adj Mensch* conciliatory; *(nichts nachtragend)* forgiving.

Versöhnung *f* reconciliation; *(Beschwichtigung)* appeasement.

versonnen *adj Gesichtsausdruck* pensive, thoughtful; *(träumerisch)* Blick dreamy.

versorgen* **1** *vt* (a) *(sich kümmern um)* to look after. (b) *(beliefern)* to supply. (c) *(unterhalten)* Familie to provide for, to support. **2** *vr* **sich mit etw** ~ to provide oneself with sth; **sich selbst** ~ to look after oneself.

Versorger(in *f) m* - **(a)** *(Ernährer)* provider, breadwinner. **(b)** *(Belieferer)* supplier.

Versorgung *f* **(a)** *(Pflege)* care. **(b) die ~ dieses Gebiets mit Bussen** the bus service for this district. **(c)** *(Unterhalt)* **die ~ im Alter** providing for one's old age.

Versorgungs-: v~**berechtigt** *adj* entitled to maintenance; *(durch Staat)* entitled to benefit; ~**betrieb** *m* public utility; ~**güter** *pl* supplies *pl;* ~**netz** *nt (Wasser~, Gas~ etc)* (supply) grid; *(von Waren)* supply network.

verspachteln* *vt Risse* to fill in.

verspannen* 1 *vt* to brace. **2** *vr (Muskeln)* to tense up.

verspäten* *vr (zu spät kommen)* to be late.

verspätet* *adj Zug, Flugzeug* delayed, late *pred; Ankunft, Frühling, Entwicklung* late; *Glückwunsch* belated.

Verspätung *f (von Verkehrsmitteln)* delay; *(von Mensch)* late arrival; *(von Glückwunsch etc)* be-latedness. **(10 Minuten) ~ haben** to be (10 minutes) late; **eine zweistündige ~ a** delay of two hours; **die ~ aufholen** to catch up lost time; **mit zwanzig Minuten ~** twenty minutes late.

verspeisen* *vt (geh)* to consume.

versperren* *vt* to block.

verspielen* 1 *vt (lit, fig) Geld, Chancen* to gamble away; *Vorteile* to bargain away. **2** *vi (fig)* **jetzt hast du (bei ihr) verspielt** you've had it now (with her) *(col).*

verspielt *adj Kind, Katze* playful; *Frisur, Muster* pretty.

versponnen *adj* airy-fairy.

verspotten* *vt* to mock.

versprechen* *irreg* **1** *vt* to promise *(jdm etw* sb sth). **nichts Gutes ~** to be ominous. **2** *vr* **(a) sich** *(dat)* **viel/wenig von jdm/etw ~** to have high hopes/no great hopes of sb/sth. **(b)** *(etwas Nicht-Gemeintes sagen)* to make a slip of the tongue.

Versprechen *nt* - promise.

Versprecher *m* - *(col)* slip (of the tongue).

Versprechung *f* promise.

verspritzen* *vt* **(a)** to spray; *(versprengen)* to sprinkle; *(zuspritzen) Fugen* to seal by injection moulding *(Brit)* or molding *(US).* **(b)** *(verkleckern) Farbe, Kleidung* to sp(l)atter. **(c)** *(verbrauchen) Wasser, Farbe etc* to use.

versprühen* *vt* to spray; *Funken* to send out; *(verbrauchen)* to use. **Witz/Geist ~** *(fig)* to scintillate.

verspüren* *vt* to feel, to be conscious of.

verstaatlichen* *vt* to nationalize.

Verstaatlichung *f* nationalization.

verstädtern* 1 *vt* to urbanize. **2** *vi aux sein* to become urbanized.

Verstand *m no pl (Fähigkeit zu denken)* reason; *(Intellekt)* mind, intellect; *(Vernunft)* (common) sense; *(Urteilskraft)* (powers *pl* of) judgement. **den ~ verlieren** to lose one's mind; **nicht recht** *or* **ganz bei ~ sein** not to be in one's right mind; **das geht über meinen ~** it's beyond me; **etw ohne ~ tun** to do sth mindlessly.

verstandesmäßig *adj* rational.

verständig *adj (vernünftig)* sensible; *(einsichtig)* understanding.

verständigen* 1 *vt* to notify. **2** *vr* to communicate; *(sich einigen)* to come to an understanding.

Verständigung *f no pl* **(a)** *(Benachrichtigung)* notification. **(b)** *(das Sichverständigen)* communication *no indef art.* **(c)** *(Einigung)* understanding.

verständlich *adj (begreiflich)* understandable; *(intellektuell erfaßbar)* comprehensible; *(hörbar)* audible. **schwer ~** hard to understand; **jdm etw ~ machen** to make sb understand sth; *(erklären)* to explain sth to sb; **sich ~ machen** to make oneself understood; *(sich klar ausdrücken)* to make oneself clear.

verständlicherweise   *adv*   understandably

(enough).

Verständnis *nt no pl* understanding *(für* of*); (Mitgefühl)* sympathy *(für* for*).* **für etw kein ~ haben** to have no understanding of/sympathy for sth; *für Kunst etc* to have no appreciation of sth; *für Unordnung etc* to have no time for sth; **dafür hast du mein vollstes ~** you have my fullest sympathy.

verständnis-: ~**los** *adj* uncomprehending; *(ohne Mitgefühl)* unsympathetic *(für* towards*); (für Kunst)* unappreciative *(für* of*);* ~**voll** *adj* understanding; *Blick* knowing *no pred.*

verstärken* 1 *vt* to strengthen, to reinforce; *Truppen* to reinforce; *Spannung, Zweifel* to increase; *(Elec, Mus)* to amplify. **2** *vr (fig)* to intensify; *(sich vermehren)* to increase.

Verstärker *m* - *(Rad, Elec)* amplifier.

Verstärkung *f siehe vt* strengthening; reinforcement; increase; amplification.

verstauben* *vi aux sein* to get dusty; *(fig)* to gather dust. **verstaubt** dusty; *(fig) Ansichten* fuddy-duddy *(col).*

verstauchen* vt sich *(dat)* **die Hand/den Fuß ~** to sprain one's hand/foot.

verstauen* *vt Gepäck* to load *(in +dat* in*).*

Versteck *nt* -e hiding-place; *(von Verbrechern)* hide-out. **~ spielen** to play hide-and-seek.

verstecken* 1 *vt* to hide, to conceal *(vor* from*).* **2** *vr* to hide. **sich vor jdm ~** to hide from sb; **sich vor jdm nicht zu ~ brauchen** *(fig)* not to need to fear comparison with sb.

Versteckspiel *nt (lit, fig)* hide-and-seek.

versteckt *adj* **(a)** hidden; *(nicht leicht sichtbar) Eingang, Tür* concealed; *(abgelegen auch)* Ort secret. **(b)** *(fig) Lächeln, Blick* furtive; *Andeutung* veiled; *Bedeutung* hidden.

verstehen 1 *vti* **(a)** to understand. **etw unter etw** *(dat)* **~** to understand sth by sth; **wie soll ich das ~?** how am I supposed to take that?; **das ist nicht wörtlich zu ~** that isn't to be taken literally; **jdn/etw falsch ~** to misunderstand sb/sth; **jdm zu ~ geben, daß ...** to give sb to understand that ... **(b)** *(können, beherrschen)* to know. **es ~, etw zu tun** to know how to do sth; **es mit Kindern ~** to be good with children; **etwas von etw ~** to know something about sth. **2** *vr* **(a)** to understand each other; *(auskommen)* to get on. **(b)** *(klar sein)* to go without saying. **das versteht sich von selbst** that goes without saying; **die Preise ~ sich einschließlich Lieferung** prices are inclusive of delivery. **(c)** *(auffassen)* **sich als etw ~** to see oneself as sth. **(d) sich auf etw** *(acc)* **~** to be an expert at sth.

versteifen* 1 *vt* to strengthen, to reinforce. **2** *vr* to stiffen up; *(fig: Haltung, Gegensätze)* to harden. **sich auf etw** *(acc)* **~** *(fig)* to become set on sth.

versteigen* vr *irreg* **er hat sich zu der Behauptung verstiegen, daß ...** he presumed to claim that ...

versteigern* *vt* to auction (off). **etw ~ lassen** to put sth up for auction.

Versteigerung *f* auction.

versteinern* 1 *vi aux sein (Pflanzen, Tiere)* to fossilize; *(Holz)* to petrify. **2** *vr (fig) Miene* to harden.

verstellbar *adj* adjustable.

verstellen* 1 *vt* **(a)** *(anders einstellen)* to adjust; *Möbel* to move; *(in Unordnung bringen)* to put in the wrong place; *(falsch einstellen)* to adjust wrongly; *Radio* to alter the tuning of; *Uhr* to set wrong. **(b)** *Stimme* to disguise. **(c)** *(versperren)* to block, to obstruct. **2** *vr* to move (out of position); *(fig)* to act a part.

versteuern* *vt* to pay tax on. **versteuert** taxed; **zu ~n** taxable.

verstiegen *adj (fig: überspannt)* extravagant, fantastic.

verstimmen* *vt* to put out of tune; *(fig)* to put out.

verstimmt adj Klavier etc out of tune; (fig) Magen upset; (verärgert) put out, disgruntled.
Verstimmung f disgruntlement; (zwischen Parteien) ill-feeling, ill-will.
verstockt adj obstinate, stubborn; Sünder unrepentant.
verstohlen adj furtive, surreptitious.
verstopfen* vt to stop up; Straße to block, to jam.
verstopft adj blocked; Straßen auch jammed; Mensch constipated.
Verstopfung f blockage; (Med) constipation.
Verstorbene(r) mf decl as adj deceased.
verstört adj disturbed; (vor Angst) distraught.
Verstoß m -̈e violation (gegen of).
verstoßen* irreg 1 vt jdn to disown, to repudiate; (ausschließen) to expel (aus from). 2 vi gegen etw ~ to offend against sth.
Verstoßene(r) mf decl as adj outcast.
verstrahlt adj radioactively contaminated, irradiated.
Verstrebung f (Strebebalken) support(ing beam).
verstreichen* irreg 1 vt Salbe, Farbe to put on; Butter to spread (auf +dat on); Riß to fill in; (verbrauchen) to use. 2 vi aux sein (Zeit) to pass (by); (Frist) to expire.
verstreuen* vt to scatter; (versehentlich) to spill.
verstricken* 1 vt (a) Wolle to use. (b) (fig) to involve. 2 vr (fig) to become entangled.
verströmen* vt (lit, fig) to exude.
verstümmeln* vt to mutilate, to maim; (fig) Nachricht to distort.
verstummen* vi aux sein (Mensch) to go silent; (Geräusch, Beifall) to stop; (langsam verklingen) to die away; (fig: sich legen) to subside. **jdn/etw zum V~ bringen** to silence sb/sth.
Versuch m -e attempt (zu tun at doing, to do); (wissenschaftlich) experiment, test. **einen ~ machen** to make an attempt; to do an experiment or a test; **das käme auf einen ~ an** we'll have to have a try.
versuchen* 1 vt (a) (auch vi) to try. **es mit jdm/etw ~** to give sb/sth a try; **versuchter Mord** attempted murder; **das Unmögliche ~** to attempt the impossible. (b) (in Versuchung führen) to tempt. 2 vr sich an or in etw (dat) ~ to try one's hand at sth.
Versucher(in f) m - tempter/temptress.
Versuchs-: ~anstalt f research institute; ~ballon m sounding balloon; **einen ~ballon steigen lassen** (fig) to fly a kite; ~bohrung f experimental drilling; ~kaninchen nt (fig) guinea-pig; ~objekt nt test object; (fig: Mensch) guinea-pig; ~person f experimental subject; ~reihe f series of experiments; ~stadium nt experimental stage; ~strecke f test track; ~tier nt laboratory animal; **v~weise** adv as a trial, on a trial basis.
Versuchung f temptation. **jdn in ~ führen** to lead sb into temptation.
versumpfen* vi aux sein (a) (Gebiet) to become marshy. (b) (fig col) (verwahrlosen) to go to pot (col); (zechen) to get involved in a booze-up (col).
versündigen* vr (geh) sich an jdm/etw ~ to sin against sb/sth.
versunken adj sunken, submerged; Kultur submerged; (fig) engrossed. **in Gedanken ~** lost in thought.
versüßen* vt (fig) to sweeten (jdm etw sth for sb).
vertagen* 1 vti to adjourn; (verschieben) to postpone (auf+acc until). 2 vr to adjourn.
vertauschbar adj exchangeable (gegen for); (miteinander) interchangeable.
vertauschen* vt to exchange (gegen or mit for); (miteinander) to interchange. **vertauschte Rollen** reversed roles. (b) (verwechseln) Mäntel etc to mix up.
Vertauschung f (Austausch) exchange.
verteidigen* 1 vti to defend. 2 vr to defend oneself; (vor Gericht) to conduct one's own

defence (Brit) or defense (US).
Verteidiger(in f) m - defender; (Anwalt) defence (Brit) or defense (US) lawyer. **der ~ des Angeklagten** the counsel for the defence.
Verteidigung f defence (Brit), defense (US). **zur ~ von** or +gen in defence of.
Verteidigungs- in cpds defence (Brit), defense (US); ~krieg m defensive war; ~minister m Minister of Defence (Brit), Defense Secretary (US); ~ministerium nt Ministry of Defence (Brit), Defense Department (US); ~schlacht f defensive battle; ~spieler m defence (Brit) or defense (US) player; ~stellung f defensive position; ~system nt defence (Brit) or defense (US) system; ~waffe f defensive weapon.
verteilen* 1 vt (an+acc to, unter +acc among) to distribute; Essen to dish out; (Theat) Rollen to cast; Investitionen, Lehrstoff to spread (über +acc over); (Mil) to deploy; (verstreuen) to spread out; (streichen) Farbe etc to spread; (streuen) Sand to sprinkle. 2 vr (Menschen, Flüssigkeiten) to spread out; (Reichtum etc) to be spread or distributed; (zeitlich) to be spread (über+acc over).
Verteiler m - (Comm, Aut) distributor.
Verteilung f distribution.
verteuern* 1 vt to make more expensive. 2 vr to become more expensive.
Verteuerung f increase in price.
verteufeln* vt to condemn.
verteufelt (col) 1 adj Lage devilish (col), tricky. 2 adv (mit adj) damned (col).
vertiefen* 1 vt (lit, fig) to deepen; (Sch) Lehrstoff to consolidate. 2 vr (lit, fig) to deepen; (fig: Lehrstoff) to be consolidated. **sich in etw (acc) ~** (fig) to become engrossed in sth.
Vertiefung f (a) siehe vt deepening; consolidation. (b) (in Oberfläche) depression. (c) (in Arbeit etc) absorption.
Vertikale [vɛrtiˈkaːlə] f -n vertical line.
vertilgen* vt (a) Unkraut etc to eradicate. (b) (col: aufessen) to demolish (col).
Vertilgungsmittel nt weed-killer; (Insekten~) pesticide.
vertippen* vr (col) to make a typing error.
vertonen* vt to set to music; Film etc to add a sound-track to.
Vertrag m -̈e contract; (Abkommen) agreement; (Pol: Friedens~) treaty. **unter ~ stehen** to be under contract.
vertragen* irreg 1 vt to take; (aushalten auch) to stand. **Eier vertrage ich nicht** eggs don't agree with me; **synthetische Stoffe vertrage ich nicht** I can't wear synthetics; **viel ~ können** (col: Alkohol) to be able to hold one's drink. 2 vr sich (mit jdm) ~ to get along (with sb); **sich wieder ~** to be friends again; **sich mit etw ~** (Nahrungsmittel, Farbe) to go with sth; (Aussage, Verhalten) to be consistent with sth.
verträglich 1 adj contractual. 2 adv by contract; festgelegt in the/a contract.
verträglich adj (friedlich, umgänglich) peaceable, easy-going; Speise digestible; (bekömmlich) wholesome; Medikament well tolerated (für by). **gut ~** easily digestible.
Verträglichkeit f no pl siehe adj easy-going nature; digestibility; wholesomeness.
Vertrags-: ~bruch m breach of contract; breaking of an/the agreement; breaking of a/the treaty; **v~gemäß** adj, adv as stipulated in the contract/agreement/treaty; ~händler m concessionary; **v~schließend** adj contracting; ~werkstätte f authorized repair shop; **v~widrig** 1 adj contrary to the contract/agreement/treaty; 2 adv in breach of contract/the agreement/the treaty.
vertrauen* vi jdm/einer Sache ~ to trust sb/sth; **auf jdn/etw ~** to trust in sb/sth.
Vertrauen nt no pl trust, confidence (zu, in +acc,

auf +*acc* in); *(Pol)* confidence. **im ~ (gesagt)** strictly in confidence; **im ~ darauf, daß ...** confident that ...; **~ zu jdm fassen** to gain confidence in sb; **jdn ins ~ ziehen** to take sb into one's confidence.

Vertrauens-: ~**bruch** *m* breach of confidence; ~**mann** *m, pl* ~**leute** *or* ~**männer** intermediary; ~**person** *f* someone to confide in, confidant(e); ~**sache** *f (vertrauliche Angelegenheit)* confidential matter; *(Frage des Vertrauens)* question of trust; **v~selig** *adj* trusting; **v~voll** *adj* trusting; ~**votum** *nt (Parl)* vote of confidence; **v~würdig** *adj* trustworthy.

vertraulich 1 *adj* **(a)** *(geheim)* confidential. **(b)** *(freundschaftlich)* friendly; *(plump ~)* familiar. **~ werden** to take liberties. **2** *adv* **(a)** confidentially. **(b)** in a friendly way.

Vertraulichkeit *f* confidentiality.

verträumt *adj* dreamy; *Städtchen etc* sleepy.

vertraut *adj* intimate; *(bekannt) Gesicht, Umgebung* familiar. **sich mit etw ~ machen** to familiarize oneself with sth; **sich mit dem Gedanken ~ machen, daß ...** to get used to the idea that ...; **mit jdm ~ werden** to become friendly with sb.

Vertraute(r) *mf decl as adj* close friend.

Vertrautheit *f no pl siehe adj* intimacy; familiarity.

vertreiben* *vt irreg Tiere, Menschen, Sorgen* to drive away; *(aus Haus, Land)* to drive out *(aus* of); *(aus Amt, von Stellung)* to oust *(aus* from); *Feind* to drive off; *(Comm) Waren* to sell. **jdm/sich die Zeit mit etw ~** to help sb pass the time/to pass the time with sth.

Vertreibung *f (aus* from) expulsion; *(aus Amt etc)* ousting; *(von Feind)* repelling.

vertretbar *adj* justifiable; *Theorie* tenable.

vertreten* *vt irreg* **(a)** *(ersetzen)* to replace; *Kollegen auch* to stand in for. **(b)** *jds Interessen, Firma, Wahlkreis* to represent; *Sache* to stand after; *(Jur) Fall* to plead. **~ sein** to be represented. **(c)** *(Comm)* to be the agent for; *(Angestellter)* to represent. **(d)** *(verfechten) Standpunkt* to support; *Meinung* to hold; *Kunstrichtung* to represent; *(rechtfertigen)* to justify *(vor* to). **(e) sich** *(dat)* **den Fuß ~** to twist one's ankle; **sich** *(dat)* **die Beine** *or* **Füße ~** *(col)* to stretch one's legs.

Vertreter(in *f)* *m* - **(a)** representative; *(Comm) (Firma)* agent; *(Angestellter)* (sales) representative, rep *(col)*. **(b)** *(Ersatz)* replacement; *(im Amt)* deputy. **(c)** *(Verfechter) (von Doktrin)* supporter, advocate; *(von Meinung)* holder.

Vertretung *f siehe vt (a-d)* **(a)** replacement. **die ~ (für jdn) übernehmen** to stand in (for sb); **in ~ +gen** on behalf of; *(in Briefen)* pp. **(b)** representation. **X übernimmt die ~ des Falles X** is pleading the case. **(c)** *(Comm)* agency. **(d)** supporting; holding; representation.

Vertretungs-: ~**stunde** *f (Sch)* stand-in class; **v~weise** *adv* as a replacement; *(bei Amtsperson)* as a deputy.

Vertrieb *m* -**e** *no pl* sales *pl*. **der ~ eines Produktes** the sale of a product; **den ~ für eine Firma haben** to have the (selling) agency for a firm.

Vertriebene(r) *mf decl as adj* exile.

Vertriebs-: ~**abteilung** *f* sales department; ~**gesellschaft** *f* marketing company; ~**kosten** *pl* marketing costs *pl*.

vertrinken* *vt irreg* to spend on drink.

vertrocknen* *vi aux sein* to dry out; *(Eßwaren)* to go dry; *(Pflanzen)* to shrivel; *(Quelle)* to dry up.

vertrödeln* *vt (col)* to fritter away.

vertrösten* *vt* to put off *(auf* +*acc* until). **jdn auf ein andermal/auf später ~** to put sb off.

vertun* *irreg* **1** *vt Zeit etc* to waste. **2** *vr (col)* to make a mistake.

vertuschen* *vt* to hush up. **etw vor jdm ~** to keep sth from sb.

ver|übeln* *vt* **jdm etw ~** not to be at all pleased with sb for doing sth; **das kann ich dir nicht ~ I** can't blame you for that.

ver|üben* *vt* to commit.

ver|ulken* *vt (col)* to make fun of.

ver|unglimpfen* *vt jdn* to disparage.

ver|unglücken* *vi aux sein (Mensch)* to have an accident; *(Fahrzeug)* to crash; *(fig col: mißlingen)* to go wrong. **mit dem Flugzeug ~** to be in a plane crash.

ver|unglückt *adj (fig) Versuch etc* unsuccessful.

Ver|unglückte(r) *mf decl as adj* casualty, victim.

ver|unreinigen* *vt Fluß etc* to pollute; *(beschmutzen)* to dirty; *(Hund etc)* to foul.

Ver|unreinigung *f siehe vt* pollution; dirtying; fouling.

ver|unsichern* *vt* to make unsure *(in* +*dat* of). **sie versuchten, ihn zu ~** they tried to throw him.

ver|unstalten* *vt* to disfigure.

ver|untreuen* *vt* to embezzle.

Ver|untreuung *f* embezzlement.

ver|ursachen* *vt* to cause.

Ver|ursacher(in *f)* *m* - person responsible *(gen* for), perpetrator *(gen* of).

ver|urteilen* *vt* to condemn *(Jur)*; *(für schuldig befinden)* to convict *(für* of); *(zu Strafe)* to sentence *(zu* to). **jdn zu einer Geldstrafe von 1.000 DM ~** to fine sb DM 1,000.

Ver|urteilte(r) *mf decl as adj* convicted man/woman. **der zum Tode ~** the condemned man.

Ver|urteilung *f* condemnation; *(Jur)* conviction.

vervielfachen* *vtr* to multiply.

vervielfältigen* *vt* to duplicate.

Vervielfältigung *f* duplication; *(Abzug)* copy.

vervierfachen* *vtr* to quadruple.

vervollkommnen* **1** *vt* to perfect. **2** *vr* to make oneself perfect.

vervollständigen* **1** *vt* to complete. **2** *vr* to be completed.

Vervollständigung *f* completion.

verwachsen[1]* *vi irreg aux sein* **(a)** *(zusammenwachsen)* to grow together; *(Narbe, Wunde)* to heal; *(Knochen)* to knit. **mit etw ~** to grow into sth. **(b)** *(fig: Menschen)* to grow closer (together). **zu etw ~** to grow into sth; **mit etw ~ mit** *Aufgabe, Traditionen* to become caught up in sth; **mit etw ~** to have very close ties with sth.

verwachsen[2] *adj* **(a)** *Mensch* deformed; *(verkümmert)* stunted. **(b)** *(überwuchert)* overgrown.

verwackeln* *vt* to blur.

verwählen* *vr* to dial the wrong number.

verwahren* **1** *vt (aufbewahren)* to keep safe. **2** *vr* **sich gegen etw ~** to protest against sth.

verwahrlosen* *vi aux sein* to go to pot *(col)*; *(Gebäude auch)* to fall into disrepair; *(Mensch)* to let oneself go; *(verwildern)* to run wild.

verwahrlost *adj* neglected. **sittlich ~** decadent.

Verwahrung *f* **(a)** *no pl (von Geld etc)* keeping; *(von Täter)* custody, detention. **jdm etw in ~ geben** to give sth to sb for safekeeping; **etw in ~ nehmen** to take sth into safekeeping; *(Behörde)* to take possession of sth; **jdn in ~ nehmen** to take sb into custody. **(b)** *(Einspruch)* protest.

verwaist* *adj* orphaned; *(fig)* deserted.

verwalten* *vt* to manage; *Amt* to hold; *(Pol) Provinz etc* to govern; *(Beamte)* to administer; *(Rel)* to administer. **sich selbst ~** *(Pol)* to be self-governing.

Verwalter(in *f)* *m* - administrator.

Verwaltung *f* **(a)** *siehe vt* management; holding; government; administration. **(b)** *(Behörde, Abteilung)* administration; *(Haus~)* management. **städtische ~** municipal authorities *pl*.

Verwaltungs-: ~**angestellte(r)** *mf* administrative employee; ~**apparat** *m* administrative machinery; ~**beamte(r)** *m* government official; ~**bezirk** *m* administrative district; ~**gericht** *nt* Administrative Court; ~**weg** *m* **auf dem ~weg**

through administrative channels.
verwandeln* 1 *vt* to change, to transform. **jdn/ etw in etw** *(acc)* ~ to turn sb/sth into sth; **ein Gebäude in einen Trümmerhaufen** ~ to reduce a building to a pile of rubble; **er ist wie verwandelt** he's a changed man. **2** *vi (Sport sl)* **zum 1:0** ~ to make it 1-0. **3** *vr* to change. **sich in etw** *(acc)* or **zu etw** ~ to change or turn into sth.
Verwandlung *f* change, transformation. **eine** ~ **durchmachen** to undergo a transformation.
verwandt *adj (lit, fig)* related *(mit* to). **geistig** ~ **sein** *(fig)* to be kindred spirits.
Verwandte(r) *mf decl as adj* relation, relative.
Verwandtschaft *f* relationship; *(die Verwandten)* relations *pl*, relatives *pl*; *(fig)* affinity.
verwandtschaftlich *adj* family *attr.*
verwarnen* *vt* to caution, to warn.
Verwarnung *f* caution, warning.
verwaschen *adj* faded; *(verwässert) Farbe* watery.
verwässern* *vt (lit, fig)* to water down.
verwechseln* *vt* to confuse, to mix up. **jdn (mit jdm)** ~ to confuse sb with sb; *(für jdn halten auch)* to mistake sb for sb; **sie sind sich zum V~ ähnlich** it's impossible to tell the difference between them.
Verwechslung *f* confusion; *(Irrtum)* mistake. **das muß eine** ~ **sein** there must be some mistake.
verwegen *adj* daring, bold; *(tollkühn)* foolhardy; *(keck)* saucy.
verwehen* 1 *vt Rauch* to blow away; *Spur* to cover over. **2** *vi aux sein (Spur)* to be covered over.
verwehren* *vt (geh)* **jdm etw** ~ to refuse or deny sb sth; **jdm** ~**, etw zu tun** to bar sb from doing sth.
Verwehung *f* drift.
verweichlichen* 1 *vt* **jdn** ~ to make sb soft; **ein verweichlichter Mensch** a weakling. **2** *vi aux sein* to get soft.
verweigern* *vt* to refuse; *Befehl* to refuse to obey; *Kriegsdienst* to refuse to do. **jdm etw** ~ to refuse or deny sb sth.
Verweigerung *f* refusal. ~ **des Kriegsdienstes** refusal to do (one's) military service; ~ **des Gehorsams** disobedience.
verweilen* *vi (geh) (Mensch)* to stay; *(Blick, Gedanken)* to dwell. **bei einer Sache** ~ to dwell on sth.
verweint *adj Augen* tear-swollen; *Gesicht* tear-stained.
Verweis *m* **-e** *(a) (Rüge)* reprimand. **jdm einen** ~ **erteilen** to reprimand sb. **(b)** *(Hinweis)* reference *(auf* +*acc* to).
verweisen* *irreg* **1** *vt (a) (hinweisen)* **jdn auf etw** *(acc)*/**an jdn** ~ to refer sb to sth/sb. **(b)** *(von der Schule)* to expel. **jdn des Landes** ~ to expel sb (from the country); **jdm vom Platz** or **des Spielfeldes** ~ to send sb off; **jdn auf den zweiten Platz** ~ *(Sport)* to relegate sb to second place. **(c)** *(Jur)* to refer *(an* +*acc* to). **2** *vi auf etw* *(acc)* ~ to refer to sth.
verwelken* *vi aux sein (Blumen)* to wilt; *(fig)* to fade. **ein verwelktes Gesicht** a worn face.
verweltlichen* *vt* to secularize.
verwendbar *adj* usable *(zu* for). **das ist nur einmal** ~ it can be used once only.
Verwendbarkeit *f no pl* usability.
verwenden 1 *vt* to use. **Mühe auf etw** *(acc)* ~ to put effort into sth; **Zeit auf etw** *(acc)* ~ to spend time on sth. **2** *vr* **sich (bei jdm) für jdn** ~ to approach sb on sb's behalf.
Verwendung *f* use; *(von Zeit, Geld)* expenditure *(auf* +*acc* on).
Verwendungs-: ~**möglichkeit** *f* (possible) use; ~**weise** *f* manner of use; ~**zweck** *m* use, purpose.
verwerfen* *irreg vt (ablehnen)* to reject; *(Jur)*

Klage, Antrag to dismiss; Urteil to quash; *(kritisieren) Handlungsweise* to condemn.
verwerflich *adj* reprehensible.
verwertbar *adj* usable.
verwerten* *vt (verwenden)* to utilize; *Erfindung, Material etc* to exploit.
Verwertung *f siehe vt* utilization; exploitation.
verwesen* *vi aux sein* to decay; *(Fleisch)* to rot.
Verweser *m* **-** *(old, liter)* administrator.
Verwesung *f no pl* decay.
verwickeln* 1 *vt Fäden etc* to tangle (up). **jdn in etw** *(acc)* ~ to involve sb in sth. **2** *vr (Fäden etc)* to get tangled up. **sich in etw** *(acc)* ~ *(lit, fig)* to become entangled in sth.
verwickelt *adj (fig col: schwierig)* involved, complicated.
Verwicklung *f* involvement *(in* +*acc in)*; *(Komplikation)* complication; *(Verwirrung)* confusion.
verwildern* *vi aux sein (Garten)* to become overgrown; *(Pflanzen)* to grow wild; *(Haustier)* to become wild.
verwildert *adj* wild; *Garten* overgrown; *Aussehen* unkempt.
verwirken *vt (geh)* to forfeit.
verwirklichen* 1 *vt* to realize. **2** *vr* to be realized; *(Mensch)* to fulfil *(Brit)* or fulfill *(US)* oneself.
Verwirklichung *f no pl* realization.
verwirren* 1 *vt* **(a)** *Haar* to tousle; *Fäden etc* to get tangled up. **(b)** *(durcheinanderbringen)* to confuse; *(konfus machen)* to bewilder. **2** *vr (Fäden etc)* to become tangled up; *(Haare)* to become tousled; *(fig)* to become confused.
Verwirrung *f (Durcheinander)* confusion.
verwirtschaften* *vt* to squander away.
verwischen* 1 *vt (verschmieren)* to smudge; *(lit, fig) Spuren* to cover over; *(fig) Erinnerungen* to blur. **2** *vr (lit, fig)* to become blurred.
verwittern* *vi aux sein* to weather.
verwitwet *adj* widowed.
verwöhnen* 1 *vt* to spoil; *(Schicksal)* to be good to. **2** *vr* to spoil oneself.
verwöhnt *adj* spoilt; *Kunde, Geschmack* discriminating.
verworfen *adj (geh)* depraved.
verworren *adj* confused, muddled; *(verwickelt)* intricate.
verwundbar *adj (lit, fig)* vulnerable.
verwunden* *vt* to wound.
verwunderlich *adj* surprising; *(sonderbar)* strange, odd.
verwundern* 1 *vt* to astonish. **2** *vr* to be astonished *(über* +*acc* at).
Verwunderung *f no pl* astonishment.
Verwundete(r) *mf decl as adj* casualty. **die** ~**n** *(Mil)* the wounded.
Verwundung *f* wound.
verwünschen* *vt* **(a)** *(verfluchen)* to curse. **(b)** *(in Märchen: verzaubern)* to enchant.
verwurzelt *adj* ~ **sein** *(Pflanze)* to be rooted; *(fest)* **in** or **mit etw** ~ *(fig)* deeply rooted in sth.
verwüsten* *vt* to devastate, to ravage.
Verwüstung *f* devastation *no pl*, ravaging *no pl*.
verzagen* *vi (geh)* to lose heart.
verzagt *adj* disheartened.
verzählen* *vt* to miscount.
verzahnen* *vt* to dovetail; *Zahnräder* to cut teeth in. **ineinander verzahnt sein** *(lit, fig)* to mesh.
verzapfen* *vt (col) Unsinn* to come out with.
verzärteln* *vt (pej)* to mollycoddle, to pamper.
verzaubern* *vt* to cast a spell on; *(bezaubern)* to enchant. **jdn in etw** *(acc)* ~ to turn sb into sth.
verzehnfachen* *vtr* to increase ten-fold.
Verzehr *m no pl* consumption.
verzehren* *vt (form: lit, fig)* to consume.
verzeichnen* *vt* to record; *(in einer Liste auch)* to enter. **einen Erfolg zu** ~ **haben** to have scored a success.

Verzeichnis nt index; *(Tabelle)* table; *(Namens~, esp amtlich)* register; *(Aufstellung)* list.

verzeihen pret **verzieh,** ptp **verziehen** vti *(vergeben)* to forgive; *(entschuldigen)* to excuse, to pardon. **jdm (etw)** ~ to forgive sb (for sth); ~ **Sie!** excuse me!

verzeihlich adj forgivable; *(zu entschuldigen)* excusable.

Verzeihung f no pl forgiveness; *(Entschuldigung)* pardon. ~! excuse me!; **(jdn) um** ~ **bitten** *(sich entschuldigen)* to apologize (to sb).

verzerren* 1 vti *(lit, fig)* to distort; *Gesicht* to contort; *Sehne, Muskel* to strain, to pull. **etw verzerrt darstellen** *(fig)* to present a distorted picture of sth. 2 vr to become distorted; *(Gesicht etc)* to become contorted *(zu in)*.

Verzerrung f *(lit, fig)* distortion; *(von Gesicht)* contortion.

verzetteln* 1 vt to waste. 2 vr to waste a lot of time; *(bei Aufgabe)* to get bogged down.

Verzicht m -e renunciation *(auf +acc of)*; *(auf Anspruch)* abandonment *(auf +acc of)*; *(Opfer)* sacrifice; *(auf Thron)* abdication *(auf +acc of)*. **ein** ~, **der mir nicht schwerfällt** that's something I can easily do without.

verzichten* vi to do without; *(Opfer bringen)* to make sacrifices. **der Kandidat hat zugunsten eines Jüngeren verzichtet** the candidate stepped down in favour of a younger man; **auf jdn/etw** ~ *(ohne auskommen müssen)* to do without sb/sth; *(aufgeben)* to renounce sth; *auf Erbschaft* to renounce sth; *(von etw absehen) auf Kommentar, Anzeige etc* to abstain from sth; *auf Amt* to refuse sth; **auf den Thron** ~ to abdicate.

verzieh pret of **verzeihen.**

verziehen¹* irreg 1 vt (a) *Mund, Züge etc* to twist *(zu into)*. **das Gesicht** ~ to pull a face; **den Mund** ~ to turn up one's mouth; **keine Miene** ~ not to turn a hair. **(b)** *Stoff* to pull out of shape; *Holz* to warp. **(c)** *(verwöhnen)* to spoil. 2 vr **(a)** *(Stoff)* to go out of shape; *(Holz)* to warp. **(b)** *(Mund, Gesicht etc)* to twist *(zu into)*. **(c)** *(verschwinden)* to disappear; *(Gewitter)* to pass; *(Nebel, Wolken)* to disperse. 3 vi aux sein to move *(nach to)*. **verzogen** *(Vermerk)* no longer at this address.

verziehen² ptp of **verzeihen.**

verzieren* vt to decorate; *(verschönern)* to embellish.

Verzierung f siehe vt decoration; embellishment.

verzinsen* 1 vt to pay interest on. **das Geld wird mit 3% verzinst** 3% interest is paid on the money. 2 vr **sich (mit 6%)** ~ to yield (6%) interest.

verzinslich adj interest-bearing attr. **~/fest** ~ **sein** to yield interest/a fixed rate of interest; **nicht** ~ interest-free.

verzogen adj Kind spoilt.

verzögern* 1 vt to delay; *(verlangsamen)* to slow down. 2 vr to be delayed.

Verzögerung f **(a)** delay, hold-up. **(b)** no pl *(das Verzögern)* delaying; *(Verlangsamung)* slowing down.

verzollen* vt to pay duty on. **haben Sie etwas zu** ~? have you anything to declare?; **verzollt** dutypaid.

verzuckern* 1 vi aux sein *(Honig etc)* to crystallize. 2 vt to put too much sugar on.

verzückt adj enraptured, ecstatic.

Verzückung f no pl rapture, ecstasy. **in** ~ **geraten** to go into ecstasies *(wegen over)*.

Verzug m delay; *(Fin)* arrears pl. **bei** ~ **(der Zahlungen)** on default of payment; **mit etw in** ~ **geraten** to fall behind with sth; *mit Zahlungen auch* to fall into arrears with sth.

verzweifeln* vi aux sein to despair *(an +dat of)*. **es ist zum V~!** it drives you to despair!

verzweifelt adj desperate; *Blick, Stimme etc auch* despairing.

Verzweiflung f *(Gemütszustand)* despair; *(Ratlosigkeit)* desperation. **jdn zur** ~ **treiben** to drive sb to despair.

verzweigen* vr to branch.

verzweigt adj Baum, Firma with a lot of branches; *Verkehrsnetz* complex.

verzwickt adj *(col)* tricky.

Vesper f -n *(Eccl)* vespers pl.

Veteran [vete'ra:n] m *(wk)* **-en, -en** *(Mil, fig)* veteran.

Veto ['ve:to] vt **-s** veto.

Vetorecht ['ve:to-] nt right of veto.

Vetter m -n cousin.

Vetternwirtschaft f *(col)* nepotism.

vgl. = vergleiche cf.

v.H. = vom Hundert per cent.

via ['vi:a] adv via.

Viadukt [via'dʊkt] m -e viaduct.

Vibration [vibra'tsio:n] f vibration.

vibrieren* [vi'bri:rən] vi to vibrate; *(Stimme)* to tremble.

Video ['vi:deo] nt **-s** video. **auf** ~ **aufnehmen** to video.

Video-: ['vi:deo-] in cpds video; **~aufnahme** f video (recording); **~band** nt video-tape; **~gerät** nt video; **~kassette** f video (cassette); **~recorder** m video recorder; **~technik** f video technology; **~text** m viewdata sing.

Vieh nt no pl **(a)** *(Nutztiere)* livestock; *(Rinder auch)* cattle pl. **(b)** *(col: Tier)* animal.

Vieh-: **~bestand** m livestock; **~futter** nt animal fodder; **~handel** m livestock/cattle trade.

viehisch adj brutish; *Schmerzen* beastly.

Vieh-: **~markt** m livestock/cattle market; **~seuche** f livestock disease; **~zeug** nt *(col)* animals pl; **~zucht** f (live)stock/cattle breeding.

viel indef pron, adj, comp **mehr,** superl **meiste(r, s)** or *(adv)* **am meisten (a)** sing *(adjektivisch)* a lot of; *(fragend, verneint auch)* much; *(substantivisch)* a lot; *(fragend, verneint auch)* much. **~es** a lot of things; **sehr** ~ **Geld** a lot of money, a very large sum of money; **in** ~**em** in many respects; **mit** ~**em** with a lot of things; **noch (ein)mal so** ~ *(Zeit etc)* as much (time etc) again; **gleich** ~ *(Gewinn etc)* the same amount (of profit etc); **einer zu** ~ one too many; ~ **Neues/Schönes** etc a lot of or many new/beautiful etc things; **das** ~**e/sein** ~**es Geld** all that/all his money.

(b) ~**e** pl *(adjektivisch)* many, a lot of; **gleich** ~**e** *(Angestellte/Anteile etc)* the same number (of employees/shares etc); **so/zu** ~**e** *(Menschen/Fehler etc)* so/too many *(people/mistakes etc)*; **aufgrund der** ~**en Fehler** because of all the mistakes; ~**e hundert Menschen** many hundreds of people.

(c) *(adverbial: mit vb)* a lot, a great deal; *(fragend, verneint auch)* much. ~**er arbeitet** ~/**nicht** ~ he works a lot/doesn't work much; **er arbeitet zu/so** ~ he works too/so much or such a lot; **die Straße wird (sehr/nicht)** ~ **befahren** this street is (very/not very) busy; **sich** ~ **einbilden** to think a lot of oneself.

(d) *(adverbial: mit adj, adv)* much, a lot. ~ **größer** much or a lot bigger; ~ **zu ... much too ...;** ~ **zu** ~**e** far too many.

Viel-: **v~beschäftigt** adj attr very busy; **v~deutig** adj ambiguous; **v~diskutiert** adj attr much discussed; **~eck** nt polygon.

vielerlei adj inv **(a)** all sorts of. **(b)** *(substantivisch)* all sorts of things.

vielerorts adv in many places.

vielfach 1 adj multiple attr. **ein** ~**er Millionär** a multimillionaire; **auf** ~**e Weise** in many various ways; **um ein** ~**es besser** many times better. **2** adv many times; *(in vielen Fällen)* in many cases; *(col: häufig)* frequently. ~ **bewährt** tried and tested many times.

Vielfache(s) nt decl as adj *(Math)* multiple. **um**

ein ~s many times over; **er verdient ein** ~s **von dem, was ich verdiene** his salary is many times larger than mine.
Vielfalt f (great) variety.
vielfältig adj varied, diverse.
Viel-: v~farbig adj multicoloured (Brit), multicolored (US); **~fraß** m -e glutton; **v~gehaßt** adj attr much-hated; **v~geliebt** adj attr much-loved; **v~geprüft** adj attr (hum) sorely tried; **v~gereist** adj attr much-travelled (Brit), much-traveled (US); **~götterei** f polytheism; **v~köpfig** adj (col) Familie, Schar large.
vielleicht adv (a) perhaps; (in Bitten auch) by any chance. **ja,** ~ yes, perhaps or maybe; ~ **sagst du mir mal, warum** you'd better tell me why; **hat er sich** ~ **verirrt/weh getan?** maybe he has got lost/hurt himself; **hast du ihm das** ~ **erzählt?** did you perhaps tell him that?; (entsetzt: denn etwa) **you didn't tell him that, did you?;** ~, **daß** ... it could be that ... (b) (col) **soll ich** ~ **24 Stunden arbeiten?!** am I supposed to work 24 hours then?; **du bist** ~ **ein Idiot!** you really are an idiot!; **ich war** ~ **nervös!** I wasn't half nervous! (col), was I nervous!
vielmalig adj attr repeated.
vielmals adv danke ~! many thanks!; **ich bitte** ~ **um Entschuldigung!** I do apologize!; **er läßt** ~ **grüßen** he sends his best regards.
vielmehr adv rather; (sondern, nur) just.
Viel-: v~sagend adj meaningful, significant; **jdn v~sagend ansehen** to give sb a meaningful look; **v~schichtig** adj (fig) complex; **~schreiber** m **er ist ein richtiger ~schreiber** (pej) he really churns out the stuff (col); **v~seitig** adj (lit) many-sided; Mensch, Gerät versatile; Interessen varied; Ausbildung all-round attr; **auf v~seitigen Wunsch** by popular request; **v~sprachig** adj multilingual, polyglot; **v~stimmig** adj many-voiced; **v~versprechend** adj promising; **~völkerstaat** m multinational state; **~weiberei** f polygamy; **~zahl** f multitude.
Vielzweck- in cpds multipurpose.
vier num four. **sie ist** ~ (**Jahre**) she's four (years old); **mit** ~ (**Jahren**) at the age of four; **es ist** ~ (**Uhr**) it's four (o'clock); ~ **Uhr** ~ four minutes past four; **für** or **auf** ~ **Tage** for four days; **in** ~ **Tagen** in four days, in four days' time; **wir waren** ~ there were four of us; **jdn unter** ~ **Augen sprechen** to speak to sb in private; ~ **Augen sehen mehr als zwei** (prov) two heads are better than one (prov); **alle** ~**e von sich strecken** (col: ausgestreckt liegen) to stretch out; **auf allen** ~**en** (col) on all fours.
Vier f **-en** four. **die Herz** ~ the four of hearts.
Vier-: ~beiner m - (hum) four-legged friend (hum); **v~beinig** adj four-legged; **v~blätt(e)rig** adj four-leaved; **~eck** nt four-sided figure; (Rechteck) rectangle; **v~eckig** adj square; **v~einhalb** num four and a half.
Vierer m - (Rudern, Sch) four; (Golf) foursome.
Vierer-: ~bande f gang of four; **~bob** m fourman bob; **v~lei** adj inv (a) attr Brot, Käse, Wein four kinds or sorts of; Möglichkeiten, Größen four different; (b) (substantivisch) four different things; (vier Sorten) four different kinds.
vierfach 1 adj fourfold, quadruple. **die** ~**e Größe** four times the size; **in** ~**er Ausfertigung** in quadruplicate. **2** adv four times, fourfold. **das Papier** ~ **legen** to fold the paper in four.
Vierfache(s) nt decl as adj four times the amount, quadruple. **um das** ~ **zunehmen** to quadruple.
Vier-: ~farbendruck m (Verfahren) four-colour (Brit) or four-color (US) printing; (Erzeugnis) four-colour (Brit) or four-color (US) print; **~farb(en)stift** m four-colour (Brit) or four-color (US) pen; **v~füßig** adj four-legged; **~gangge-triebe** nt four-speed gearbox; **v~geschossig** adj

four-storey attr (Brit), four-story attr (US); **v~händig** adv for four hands.
vierhundert num four hundred.
vierhundertste(r, s) adj four hundredth.
Vier-: v~kant adj, adv (Naut) square; **~kant** m or nt -e (Tech) square; **v~kantig** adj square(-headed); **v~köpfig** adj Ungeheuer four-headed; **eine v~köpfige Familie** a family of four.
Vierling m quadruplet, quad.
Viermächte|abkommen nt four-power agreement.
Vier-: v~mal adj four times; **v~malig** adj nach v~maligem Versuch after the fourth attempt; **~master** m - (Naut) four-master; **v~motorig** adj four-engined; **v~räd(e)rig** adj four-wheel attr, four-wheeled; **v~seitig** adj four-sided; Abkommen, Verhandlungen quadripartite; Broschüre four-page attr; **~sitzer** m - four-seater; **v~sitzig** adj four-seater attr; **v~spurig** adj four-lane attr; **v~stellig** adj four-figure attr; **v~stimmig** adj four-part attr, for four voices.
viert adj **wir gingen zu** ~ four of us went.
Vier-: ~tagewoche f four-day week; **v~tausend** num four thousand; **~tausender** m - (Berg) four-thousand-metre (Brit) or -meter (US) mountain.
vierte adj siehe **vierte(r, s)**.
vierteilig adj four-piece attr; Roman four-part attr.
Viertel¹ ['fɪrtl] nt - quarter. **ein** ~ **Leberwurst/ Wein** a quarter of liver sausage/wine; (ein) ~ **nach/vor sechs** (a) quarter past/to six; (ein) ~ **sechs** (a) quarter past five; **drei** ~ **sechs** (a) quarter to six.
Viertel² ['fɪrtl] nt - (Stadtbezirk) quarter, district.
viertel ['fɪrtl] adj inv quarter. **ein** ~ **Liter/Pfund** a quarter (of a) litre/pound; **drei** ~ **Liter** three quarters of a litre.
Viertelfinale nt quarter-finals pl.
Vierteljahr nt three months pl, quarter (Comm, Fin).
Vierteljahres- in cpds quarterly; **~schrift** f quarterly.
Viertel- [fɪrtl-]: **~jahrhundert** nt quarter of a century; **v~jährig** adj attr Kind etc three-month-old; Aufenthalt, Frist three months; **v~jährlich 1** adj quarterly; Kündigung three months' attr; **2** adv quarterly, every three months.
vierteln ['fɪrtln] vt (in vier Teile teilen) to divide into four; Summe, Gewinn to divide by four.
Viertel- ['fɪrtl-]: **~note** f crotchet (Brit), quarter note (US); **~pfund** nt = quarter (of a pound); **~stunde** f quarter of an hour; **v~stündig** adj attr Abstand quarter-hour; **v~stündlich** adv every quarter of an hour; **~ton** m quarter tone.
viertens adv fourth(ly), in the fourth place.
Vierte(r) mf decl as adj fourth. **Karl IV** or **der** ~ Charles IV or the Fourth.
vierte(r, s) adj fourth. **der** ~ **Oktober** the fourth of October; **der** ~ **Stock** the fourth (Brit) or fifth (US) floor; **er war** ~r **im Rennen** he was or came fourth in the race; **du bist der** ~, **der mich das fragt** you're the fourth person to ask me that.
vier-: ~türig adj four-door attr; **~undzwanzig** num twenty-four.
Vierviertaltakt [-'fɪrtl-] m four-four or common time.
Vierwaldstätter See m Lake Lucerne.
vier-: ~wöchentlich adj, adv every four weeks; **~wöchig** adj four-week attr.
vierzehn ['fɪrtseːn] num fourteen. ~ **Uhr** 2 p.m.; (auf Fahrplan, Mil) fourteen hundred hours, 14.00; ~ **Tage** two weeks, a fortnight sing (Brit).
vierzehn- ['fɪrtseːn-]: **~tägig** adj two-week attr, lasting two weeks; **~täglich** adj, adv fortnightly (Brit), every two weeks.
Vierzehntel ['fɪrtseːntl] nt - fourteenth.
vierzehnte(r, s) ['fɪrtseːntə(r, s)] adj fourteenth.

vierzig ['fɪrtsɪç] *num* forty. **mit ~ (km/h) fahren** to drive at forty (kilometres an hour); **Mitte (der) V~** in one's mid-forties.

vierziger ['fɪrtsɪgɐ] *adj attr inv* **die ~ Jahre** the forties.

Vierziger(in *f*) ['fɪrtsɪgɐ, -ərɪn] *m* - *(Mensch)* forty-year-old; *(Wein)* wine of vintage forty. **er ist Mitte der ~** he is in his mid-forties; **er ist in den ~n** he is in his forties.

vierzigmal *adv* forty times.

Vierzigstel ['fɪrtsɪçstl] *nt* - fortieth.

vierzigstel ['fɪrtsɪçstl] *adj inv* fortieth.

vierzigste(r, s) ['fɪrtsɪçstə(r, s)] *adj* fortieth.

Vierzigstundenwoche [fɪrtsɪç-] *f* forty-hour week.

Vierzimmerwohnung *f* four-room flat *(Brit)* or apartment.

Vietnam [viɛt'nam] *nt* Vietnam.

Vietnamese [viɛtna'meːzə] *m (wk)* **-n, -n, Vietnamesin** *f* Vietnamese.

Vikar [vi'kaːɐ] *m* curate.

Villa ['vɪla] *f, pl* **Villen** villa.

Villenviertel ['vɪlən-] *nt* exclusive residential area.

violett [vio'lɛt] *adj* violet.

Violine [vio'liːnə] *f* violin.

Violinist(in *f*) [violi'nɪst(ɪn)] *m* violinist.

Violin- [vio'liːn-]: **~konzert** *nt* violin concerto; *(Darbietung)* violin concert; **~schlüssel** *m* treble clef.

Viper ['viːpɐ] *f* **-n** viper, adder.

Viren ['viːrən] *pl of* **Virus.**

virtuos [vɪr'tuoːs] *adj* virtuoso *attr.* **~ spielen** to give a virtuoso performance.

Virtuose [vɪr'tuoːzə] *m (wk)* **-n, -n, Virtuosin** *f* virtuoso.

Virus ['viːrʊs] *nt or m, pl* **Viren** virus.

Virus|infektion *f* virus infection.

Visage [vi'zaːʒə] *f* **-n** *(pej)* face, (ugly) mug *(col).*

vis-à-vis [viza'viː] *(dated)* **1** *adv* opposite *(von* to*).* **2** *prep* +*dat* opposite (to).

Visier [vi'ziːɐ] *nt* **-e (a)** *(am Helm)* visor. **(b)** *(an Gewehren)* sight.

Vision [vi'zioːn] *f* vision.

Visite [vi'ziːtə] *f* **-n** *(Med)* round. **um 9 Uhr ist ~** the doctors do their rounds at 9 o'clock.

Visitenkarte [vi'ziːtn-] *f (lit, fig)* visiting *or* calling *(US)* card.

visuell [vi'zuɛl] *adj* visual.

Visum ['viːzʊm] *nt, pl* **Visa** *or* **Visen** visa.

Visumzwang ['viːzʊm-] *m* obligation to hold a visa.

vital [vi'taːl] *adj* energetic; *(lebenswichtig)* vital.

Vitalität [vitali'tɛːt] *f* vitality, vigour *(Brit)*, vigor *(US).*

Vitamin [vita'miːn] *nt* **-e** vitamin.

Vitamin- [vita'miːn-]: **v~arm** *adj* low in vitamins; **~bedarf** *m* vitamin requirement; **v~haltig** *adj* containing vitamins; **v~haltig sein** to contain vitamins; **~mangel** *m* vitamin deficiency; **v~reich** *adj* rich in vitamins.

Vitrine [vi'triːnə] *f (Schrank)* glass cabinet; *(Schaukasten)* showcase, display case.

Vivisektion [vivizɛk'tsioːn] *f* vivisection.

Vize ['fiːtsə] *m* - *(col)* number two *(col)*; *(~meister)* runner-up.

Vize- ['fiːtsə-] *in cpds* vice-; **~kanzler** *m* vice-chancellor; **~könig** *m* viceroy; **~meister** *m* runner-up; **~präsident** *m* vice-president.

Vlies [fliːs] *nt* **-e** fleece.

V-Mann ['fau-] *m* = **Verbindungsmann.**

Vogel *m* - *(lit, fig)* bird. **ein seltsamer etc ~** *(col)* a queer bird *(col)*; **ein lustiger ~** *(col)* a lively character *(col)*; **den ~ abschießen** *(col)* to surpass everyone *(iro)*; **einen ~ haben** *(col)* to have a screw loose *(col)*; **jdm den ~ zeigen** *(col)* ≈ to give sb the V sign *(Brit)* or the finger *(US).*

Vogel-: **~bauer** *nt* bird-cage; **~beere** *f (auch*

~beerbaum) rowan(-tree), mountain ash; *(Frucht)* rowan(-berry); **~dreck** *m* bird droppings *pl*; **~ei** *nt* bird's egg; **v~frei** *adj (Hist)* outlawed; **~futter** *nt* bird food; *(Samen)* birdseed; **~käfig** *m* bird-cage; **~kirsche** *f (wilde Süßkirsche)* wild cherry; **~kunde** *f* ornithology. **~nest** *nt* bird's nest; **~perspektive** *f* bird's-eye view; **~scheuche** *f (lit, fig col)* scarecrow; **~schutz** *m* protection of birds; **~-Strauß-Politik** *f* head-in-the-sand policy; **~warte** *f* ornithological station; **~zug** *m* bird migration.

Vokabel [vo'kaːbl] *f* **-n** word. **~n** *pl* vocabulary *sing.*

Vokabular [vokabu'laːɐ] *nt* **-e** vocabulary.

Vokal [vo'kaːl] *m* **-e** vowel.

Vokalmusik [vo'kaːl-] *f* vocal music.

Volk *nt* **-̈er** people *pl*; *(~sstamm)* people *sing*; *(Zool)* colony; *(col: Gruppe)* crowd *pl*; *(pej: Pack)* rabble *pl.* **das ~ verlangt, daß ...** the people demand that ...; **viel ~** lots of people *pl*; **etw unters ~ bringen** *Nachricht* to spread sth; *Geld* to spend sth; **da verkehrt vielleicht ein ~!** there's a really strange crowd there!

Völkchen *nt (col: Gruppe)* lot *(col)*, crowd. **ein ~ für sich** sein to be a race apart.

Völker-: **~bund** *m (Hist)* League of Nations; **~kunde** *f* ethnology; **~mord** *m* genocide; **~recht** *nt* international law; **v~rechtlich 1** *adj Vertrag, Anerkennung* under international law; *Frage, Thema, Standpunkt* of international law; **2** *adv* according to international law; **~verständigung** *f* international understanding.

volkreich *adj* populous.

Volks- *in cpds* popular; *(auf ein Land bezogen)* national; *(Pol, esp DDR)* people's; **~abstimmung** *f* plebiscite; **~armee** *f (DDR)* People's Army; **~ausgabe** *f* popular edition; **~befragung** *f* public opinion poll; **~belustigung** *f* public entertainment; **~bibliothek** *f* public library; **~bildung** *f* national education; *(Erwachsenenbildung)* adult education; **~deutsche(r)** *mf* ethnic German; **~dichter** *m* poet of the people; **v~eigen** *adj (DDR)* nationally-owned; *(in Namen)* People's Own; **~einkommen** *nt* national income; **~empfinden** *nt* public feeling; **das gesunde ~empfinden** popular sentiment; **~entscheid** *m* referendum; **~erhebung** *f* national uprising; **~feind** *m* enemy of the people; **v~feindlich** *adj* hostile to the people; **~fest** *nt* public festival; *(Jahrmarkt)* fair; **~front** *f (Pol)* popular front; **~gemeinschaft** *f (NS)* national community; **~gerichtshof** *m (NS)* People's Court; **~gesundheit** *f* public health; **~glaube(n)** *m* popular belief; **~gruppe** *f* ethnic group; **~held** *m* popular hero; *(Held des Landes)* national hero; **~hochschule** *f* adult education centre *(Brit)* or center *(US)*; **~kunde** *f* folklore; **~lied** *nt* folk song; **~märchen** *nt* folktale; **~meinung** *f* public or popular opinion; **~menge** *f* crowd, mob *(pej)*; **~mund** *m* vernacular; **~musik** *f* folk music; **~partei** *f* people's party; **~polizei** *f (DDR)* People's Police; **~republik** *f* people's republic; **~sage** *f* folk legend; **~schicht** *f* level of society; **~schule** *f (dated)* ≈ elementary school; **~seuche** *f* epidemic; **~stamm** *m* tribe; **~stimme** *f* voice of the people; **~stück** *nt* dialect folk play; **~tanz** *m* folk dance; **~theater** *nt* folk theatre *(Brit)* or theater *(US)*; **~tracht** *f* traditional costume; **~tum** *nt* national traditions *pl*, folklore; **v~tümlich** *adj* folk *attr*, folksy *(col)*; *(traditionell, überliefert)* traditional; *(beliebt)* popular; **~vermögen** *nt* national wealth; **~versammlung** *f* people's assembly; *(Kundgebung)* public gathering; **~vertreter** *m* representative of the people; **~wahl** *f* direct election(s *pl*); **~wirt** *m* economist; **~wirtschaft** *f* national economy; *(Fach)* economics *sing*, political economy; **~wirtschaftler** *m* economist; **~zählung** *f* (national) census;

~**zugehörigkeit** f ethnic origin.
voll 1 adj full; *Haar* thick; *Satz, Service, Erfolg*
complete; *Wahrheit* whole. ~ **von** or **mit etw** full
of sth; *(bedeckt mit)* covered with sth; **mit** ~**em**
Mund with one's mouth full; **aus dem** ~**en schöp-**
fen to draw on unlimited resources; **die Uhr**
schlägt nur alle ~**en Stunden** the clock only
strikes the full hour; **die Zahl ist** ~ the numbers
are complete; **in** ~**er Fahrt** at full speed; **in** ~**er**
Größe *(Bild)* life-size; ~**e Gewißheit über etw** *(acc)*
etc) large as life; ~**e Gewißheit über etw** *(acc)*
haben to be fully certain about sth; **jdn nicht für**
~ **nehmen** not to take sb seriously; ~ **sein** *(col)*
(satt) to be full (up); *(betrunken)* to be plastered
(col). **2** adv fully. ~ **und ganz** completely, wholly;
eine Rechnung ~ **bezahlen** to pay a bill in full.
volladen vt sep irreg to load up. **vollgeladen** fully-
laden.
voll|auf adv fully, completely. **das genügt** ~
that's quite enough; ~ **zu tun haben** to have quite
enough to do.
vollaufen vi sep irreg aux sein to fill up. **etw** ~
lassen to fill sth (up); **sich** ~ **lassen** *(col)* to get
tanked up *(col)*.
Voll-: v~**automatisch** adj fully automatic; ~**bad**
nt (proper) bath; ~**bart** m (full) beard; **v**~**be-**
kommen* vt sep irreg to (manage to) fill; **v**~**be-**
rechtigt adj attr with full rights;
~**beschäftigung** f full employment; ~**besitz** m:
im ~**besitz**+gen in full possession of.
Vollblut nt no pl thoroughbred.
Vollblut- in cpds (lit: *Tier*) thoroughbred; *(fig)* full-
blooded.
Voll-: ~**blüter** m - thoroughbred; **v**~**blütig** adj
thoroughbred; *(fig)* full-blooded; ~**bremsung** f
emergency stop; **eine** ~**bremsung machen** to
slam on the brakes *(col)*; **v**~**bringen*** vt insep
irreg *(ausführen)* to accomplish, to achieve; *Wun-*
der to perform; **v**~**busig** adj full-bosomed;
~**dampf** m *(Naut)* **mit** ~**dampf** at full steam.
voll|enden* insep **1** vt to complete. **2** vr *(zum*
Abschluß kommen) to come to an end; *(vollkom-*
men werden) to be completed.
voll|endet adj *(vollkommen)* completed; *Tugend,*
Schönheit perfect; *Mensch* accomplished. **nach**
~**em 18. Lebensjahr** upon completion of one's
18th year.
vollends adv **(a)** *(völlig)* completely. **(b)** *(beson-*
ders) especially.
Voll|endung f no pl completion; *(Vollkommenheit)*
perfection.
voller adj full *(gen* of).
Völlerei f gluttony.
voll-: ~**essen** vr sep irreg *(col)* to gorge oneself;
~**fett** adj full-fat.
vollführen* vt insep to execute, to perform.
Voll-: ~**gas** nt no pl full speed or throttle; ~**gas**
geben to go flat out *(col)*; ~**gefühl** nt: **im** ~**gefühl**
+gen fully aware of; ~**genuß** m: **im** ~**genuß**
+gen in full enjoyment of; **v**~**gießen** vt sep irreg
to fill (up); **v**~**gültig** adj attr *Paß* fully valid;
Ersatz completely satisfactory; ~**gummi** nt or m
solid rubber; ~**idiot** m *(col)* complete idiot.
völlig 1 adj complete. **2** adv completely. **es genügt**
~ that's quite enough; **er hat** ~ **recht** he's absolutely right.
Voll-: v~**jährig** adj of age; **v**~**jährig werden/sein**
to come/be of age; ~**jährige(r)** mf decl as adj
major; ~**jährigkeit** f majority no art;
v~**kaskoversichert** adj comprehensively insured; ~**kasko(versicherung** f) nt fully comprehensive insurance; **v**~**klimatisiert** adj fully
air-conditioned.
vollkommen 1 adj perfect; *(völlig)* complete,
absolute. **sein Glück war** ~ his happiness was
complete. **2** adv completely.
Vollkommenheit f no pl siehe adj perfection;
completeness.

Voll-: ~**kornbrot** nt wholemeal *(Brit)* or wholewheat *(US)* bread; **v**~**machen** vt sep **(a)** *Gefäß* to
fill (up); *Zahl, Dutzend* to make up; **(b)** *(col)* Hosen, Windeln to fill; ~**macht** f -en power, authority no pl, no indef art; *(Urkunde)* power of attorney; ~**matrose** m able-bodied seaman; ~**milch**
f full-cream milk; ~**mond** m full moon; **heute**
ist ~**mond** there's a full moon today; **v**~**mun-**
dig adj *Wein* full-bodied; ~**narkose** f general
anaesthetic *(Brit)* or anesthetic *(US)*; **v**~**packen**
vt sep *(lit, fig)* to pack full; *jdn* to load up; ~**pen-**
sion f full board *(Brit)*, American plan *(US)*;
v~**pumpen** vt sep to fill (up); ~**rausch** m drunken
stupor; **einen** ~**rausch haben** to be in a drunken
stupor; **v**~**reif** adj fully ripe; **v**~**saugen** vr sep
irreg to become saturated; **v**~**schlank** adj plump,
stout; **v**~**schmieren** sep **1** vt to mess up; **2** vr to
make oneself all messy; **v**~**schreiben** vt sep irreg
Heft, Seite to fill; *Tafel* to cover (with writing).
vollständig 1 adj complete; *Adresse* full
attr. **etw** ~ **machen** to complete sth. **2** adv
completely, entirely.
Vollständigkeit f no pl completeness.
vollstopfen vt sep to cram full.
vollstrecken* vt insep to execute.
Voll-: v~**tanken** vti sep to fill up; **v**~**tönend** adj
resonant, sonorous; ~**treffer** m *(lit, fig)* bull's
eye; **v**~**trunken** adj completely drunk; ~**ver-**
sammlung f general meeting; ~**waise** f orphan;
v~**wertig** adj full attr; *Stellung* equal; *Ersatz* fully
adequate; **v**~**zählig** adj usu pred complete;
v~**zählig anwesend** all present.
vollziehen* insep irreg **1** vt to carry out, to execute; *Trauung* to perform; *Bruch* to make. **die**
~**de Gewalt** the executive (power). **2** vr to take
place; *(jds Schicksal)* to be fulfilled.
Vollziehung f, **Vollzug** m no pl siehe vt carrying
out, execution; performance; making.
Volontär(in f) *(volɔn'tɛːɐ, -'tɛːərɪn)* m trainee.
Volt *(vɔlt)* nt - volt.
Volt- *(vɔlt-)*: ~**meter** nt voltmeter; ~**zahl** f voltage.
Volumen *(vo'luːmən)* nt, pl - *(lit, fig)* volume.
vom = von dem. ~ **10. September an** from the
10th September.
von prep +dat **(a)** *(Ausgangspunkt)* from. **nördlich**
~ **to the north of;** ~ **... an** from ...; **Waren** ~ **5**
Mark an or ab goods from 5 marks; ~ **heute ab**
from today (on); ~ **... aus** from ...; ~ **dort aus**
from there; **etw** ~ **sich aus tun** to do sth of one's
own accord; ~ **... bis from ...** to; ~ **morgens bis**
abends from morning till night; ~ **... zu** from ...
to; **etw** ~ **etw nehmen/abreißen** to take/tear sth
off sth; ~ **einem Bus abspringen** to jump off a
bus; ~ **wo/wann ...?** where/when ... from?
(b) *(Ursache, Urheberschaft, im Passiv)* by. **das**
Gedicht ist ~ **Schiller** the poem is by Schiller;
ein Kind ~ **jdm kriegen** to have a child by sb;
~ **etw müde** tired from sth.
(c) *(als Genitiv)* of. **jeweils zwei** ~ **zehn** two
out of every ten; **ein Riese** ~ **einem Mann** *(col)* a
giant of a man; **nett** ~ **dir** nice of you; **die Kö-**
nigin ~ **England** the queen of England; **der Ge-**
burtstag ~ **meinem Vater** my father's birthday;
ein „~ **(und zu)"** **sein** to have a handle to one's
name.
(d) *(über)* about. **er erzählte vom Urlaub** he
talked about his holiday; **da weiß ich nichts** ~
(col) I don't know anything about it.
(e) *(col)* ~ **wegen** no way! *(col)*.
von|einander adv from each other; *wissen* of
each other.
vonnöten adj: ~ **sein** to be necessary.
vonstatten adv: ~ **gehen** *(stattfinden)* to take
place; **alles ging gut** ~ everything went well.
vor 1 prep+acc or dat **(a)**+dat *(räumlich)* in front
of; *(außerhalb von)* outside; *(~ Hintergrund)*
against; *(in jds Achtung)* in the eyes of; *(bei Rei-*
henfolge) before. ~ **der Kirche rechts abbiegen**

turn right before the church; ~ **allen Dingen,** ~
allem above all. **(b)**+*acc (Richtung)* in front of;
(außerhalb von) outside. **(c)** +*dat (zeitlich)* before. **zwanzig (Minuten)** ~ **drei** twenty
(minutes) to three; **das liegt noch** ~ **uns** this is
still to come; ~ **fünf Jahren** five years ago. **(d)**
+*acc* ~ **sich hin summen** to hum to oneself; ~
sich hin schreiben/arbeiten to write/work away.
(e) +*dat* ~ **sich her** before one, in front of one.
(f)+*dat (Ursache angebend)* with. ~ **Kälte zittern** to shiver with cold; ~ **Hunger sterben** to die
of hunger; ~ **lauter Arbeit** because of work. **(g)**
sich ~ **jdm** verstecken to hide from sb. **2** *adv* ~
und zurück backwards and forwards; **alle
kleinen Kinder** ~! all small children to the
front!

vor|ab *adv* to begin with.

Vor-: ~**abdruck** *m* preprint; ~**abend** *m* evening
before; **am** ~**abend der Revolution** *(fig)* on the
eve of revolution; ~**ahnung** *f* premonition.

voran *adv* **(a)** *(vorn, an der Spitze)* first. **ihm/ihr** ~
in front of him/her; **mit dem Kopf** ~ **fallen** to fall
head first. **(b)** *(vorwärts)* forwards. **nur** *or* **immer**
~ keep going.

voran- *pref siehe auch* **voraus-;** ~**bringen** *vt sep*
irreg to make progress with; ~**gehen** *vi sep irreg*
aux sein **(a)** *(an der Spitze gehen)* to go first *or* in
front; *(fig: Einleitung etc)* to precede *(dat* sth*)*;
jdm ~**gehen** to go ahead of sb; **(b)** *(zeitlich vor*
jdm gehen) to go on ahead; **einer Sache** *(dat)*
~**gehen** to precede sth; **(c)** *auch vi impers (Fort-*
schritte machen) to make progress *or* headway;
~**kommen** *vi sep irreg aux sein* to get on.

Vor|anschlag *m* estimate.

voran-: ~**stellen** *vt sep* to put in front *(dat* of*)*; *(fig)*
to give precedence *(dat* over*)*; ~**treiben** *vt sep*
irreg to drive forward.

Vor-: ~**arbeit** *f* preliminary work, groundwork;
v~**arbeiten** *sep* **1** *vi* to work in advance; **2** *vr*
to work one's way forward; ~**arbeiter(in** *f)*
m foreman; forewoman.

voraus *adv* **(a)** *(voran)* in front (+*dat* of*)*. **er ist den
anderen/seiner Zeit** ~ he is ahead of the others/
his time. **(b)** *(vorher)* **im** ~ in advance.

Voraus-: **v**~**blicken** *vi sep* to look ahead;
v~**blickend 1** *adj* foresighted; **2** *adv* with regard
to the future; **v**~**eilen** *vi sep aux sein (lit, fig)* to
hurry on ahead; **v**~**fahren** *vi sep irreg aux sein (an*
der Spitze) to drive/go in front *(dat* of*)*; *(früher)* to
drive/go on ahead; **v**~**gehen** *vi sep irreg aux sein*
siehe **vorangehen (a, b);** **v**~**gesetzt** *adj*
v~**gesetzt, (daß)** ...; provided (that) ...; **v**~ **haben**
vt sep irreg **jdm viel v**~**haben** to have a great
advantage over sb; **v**~**laufen** *vi sep irreg aux sein*
(an der Spitze) to run in front *(dat* of*)*; *(früher)* to
run on ahead; **v**~**planen** *vti sep* to plan ahead;
v~**sagen** *vt sep* to predict *(jdm* for sb*)*; **Wetter** to
forecast; **jdm die Zukunft v**~**sagen** to foretell
sb's future; **v**~**schicken** *vt sep* to send on ahead
(dat of*)*; *(fig: vorher sagen)* to say in advance *(dat*
of*)*; **v**~**sehen** *vt sep irreg* to foresee.

voraussetzen *vt sep* to presuppose; *(als selbstver-*
ständlich, sicher annehmen) to take for granted;
(erfordern) to require, to demand. **etw als bekannt** ~ to assume that everyone knows sth.

Voraussetzung *f* prerequisite; *(Qualifikation)*
qualification; *(Erfordernis)* requirement; *(An-*
nahme) assumption. **unter der** ~, **daß** ... on condition that ...

Voraus-: ~**sicht** *f* foresight; *(Erwartung)* anticipation; **aller** ~**sicht nach** in all probability;
v~**sichtlich 1** *adj* expected; **2** *adv* probably; **er
wird v**~**sichtlich gewinnen** he is expected to
win; ~**zahlung** *f* advance payment.

Vorbau *m* porch; *(Balkon)* balcony.

vorbauen *sep* **1** *vt (anbauen)* to build on (in front).
2 *vi (Vorkehrungen treffen)* to take precautions.

Vorbedacht *m*: **mit/ohne** ~ *(Überlegung)* with/

without due consideration; *(Absicht)* inten-
tionally/unintentionally.

Vorbedingung *f* precondition.

Vorbehalt *m* **-e** reservation. **unter dem** ~, **daß** ...
with the reservation that ...

vorbehalten* *vt sep irreg* **sich** *(dat)* **etw** ~ to
reserve sth (for oneself); **Recht** to reserve sth;
diese Entscheidung bleibt ihm ~ this decision is
left up to him; **alle Rechte** ~ all rights reserved;
Änderungen (sind) ~ subject to alterations.

vorbehaltlich *prep*+*gen (form)* subject to.

vorbehaltlos *adj* unconditional, unreserved.

vorbei *adv* **(a)** *(räumlich)* past, by. ~ **an** (+*dat*)
past. **(b)** *(zeitlich)* ~ **sein** to be past; *(Sorgen)* to
be over; *(Schmerzen)* to be gone; **damit ist es nun**
~ that's all over now; **aus und** ~ over and done.

vorbei- *pref (vorüber)* past; *(zu Besuch)* over;
~**bringen** *vt sep irreg (col)* to drop off; ~**dürfen** *vi*
sep irreg (col) to be allowed past; **dürfte ich bitte**
~? could I get past *or* by, please?; ~**fahren** *vi sep*
irreg aux sein to pass *(an jdm/etw* sb/sth*)*; **bei jdm**
~**fahren** to call in on sb; ~**gehen** *vi sep irreg*
aux sein **(a)** *(lit, fig) (an jdm/etw* sb/sth*)* to go past,
to pass; **an etw** *(dat)* ~**gehen** *(fig: nicht beachten)*
to overlook sth; **bei jdm** ~**gehen** *(col)* to drop in
on sb; **(b)** *(vergehen)* to pass; **(c)** *(verfehlen)* to
miss *(an etw (dat)* sth*)*; ~**kommen** *vi sep irreg aux*
sein **(a)** *(an jdm/etw* sb/sth*)* to pass, to go past; *(an*
einem Hindernis) to get past *or* by; **an einer Aufgabe nicht** ~**kommen** to be unable to avoid a
task; **(b) bei jdm** ~**kommen** *(col)* to drop *or* call in
on sb; ~**können** *vi sep irreg* to be able to get past
or by *(an etw (dat)* sth*)*; ~**lassen** *vt sep irreg* to let
past *(an jdm/etw* sb/sth*)*; ~**laufen** *vi sep irreg aux*
sein (an jdm/etw sb/sth*)* to run past; *(col:* ~**gehen**)
to go *or* walk past; ~**marschieren*** *vi sep aux sein*
to march past; ~**müssen** *vi sep irreg (an jdm/etw*
sb/sth*)* to have to go past; **bei jdm** ~**müssen** *(col)*
to have to call in at sb's; ~**reden** *vi sep* **an etw**
(dat) ~**reden** to talk around sth; **aneinander**
~**reden** to talk at cross purposes; ~**ziehen** *vi sep*
irreg aux sein to file past *(an jdm/etw* sb/sth*)*.

vorbelastet *adj* handicapped; *(voreingenommen)*
biased (**von** because of*)*.

Vorbemerkung *f* introductory remark.

vorbereiten* *vtr sep* to prepare *(auf* +*acc* for*)*.

vorbereitend *adj attr* preparatory, preliminary.

Vorbereitung *f* preparation. ~**en (für** *or* **zu etw)**
treffen to make preparations (for sth).

Vorbereitungs- *in cpds* preparatory.

Vor-: ~**besprechung** *f* preliminary meeting;
v~**bestellen*** *vt sep* to book (in advance), to reserve; **v**~**bestraft** *adj* previously convicted; **er
ist schon einmal v**~**bestraft** he has a previous
conviction; **v**~**beten** *sep* **1** *vi* to lead the prayer/
prayers; **2** *vt* **jdm etw v**~**beten** *(fig col)* to keep
spelling sth out for sb *(col)*.

Vorbeugehaft *f* preventive custody.

vorbeugen *sep* **1** *vi* to prevent *(einer Sache (dat)*
sth*)*. **2** *vtr* to bend forward.

vorbeugend *adj* preventive.

Vorbeugung *f* prevention *(gegen, von* of*)*.

Vorbeugungs- *in cpds* preventive.

Vorbild *nt* model; *(Beispiel)* example *(für jdn* to
sb*)*. **er/sein Verhalten kann uns zum** ~ **dienen**
he/his behaviour is an example to us; **sich** *(dat)*
jdn zum ~ **nehmen** to model oneself on sb.

vorbildlich *adj* exemplary; **sich benehmen** in an
exemplary fashion.

Vor-: ~**bildung** *f* educational background; ~**bote**
m (fig) herald.

vorbringen *vt sep irreg* **Plan** to propose; **Meinung,
Wunsch, Forderung** to express, to state; **Einwand,
Beschwerde** to make; **Entschuldigung** to offer.

Vor-: **v**~**christlich** *adj* pre-Christian; ~**dach** *nt*
canopy; **v**~**datieren*** *vt sep* to postdate.

Vorder-: ~**achse** *f* front axle; ~**ansicht** *f* front
view; ~**asien** *nt* Near East; ~**bein** *nt* foreleg.

Vordere(r) *mf decl as adj* person in front.
vordere(r, s) *adj* front.
Vorder-: ~**front** *f* frontage; ~**fuß** *m* forefoot; ~**grund** *m* foreground; *(fig)* fore(front); **sich in den** ~**grund drängen** to push oneself to the fore; **im** ~**grund stehen** *(fig)* to be to the fore; **v**~**gründig** *adj (oberflächlich)* superficial; ~**mann** *m, pl* ~**männer** person in front; **etw auf** ~**mann bringen** *(fig col)* to get sth into shape; ~**pfote** *f* front paw; ~**rad** *nt* front wheel; ~**seite** *f* front; *(von Münze)* head; ~**sitz** *m* front seat.
vorderste(r, s) *adj superl of* **vordere(r, s)** front(most). **der/die V~ in der Schlange** the first person in the queue *(Brit) or* line *(US)*.
Vorder-: ~**teil** *m or nt* front; ~**tür** *f* front door; ~**zahn** *m* front tooth; ~**zimmer** *nt* front room.
vordrängen *vr sep* to push to the front. **sich in der Schlange** ~ to jump the queue *(Brit)*, to push to the front of the line *(US)*.
vordringen *vi sep irreg aux sein* to advance. **bis zu jdm/etw** ~ to get as far as sb/sth.
vordringlich *adj* urgent, pressing.
Vordruck *m* form.
vor|ehelich *adj attr* premarital.
vor|eilig *adj* rash. ~**e Schlüsse ziehen** to jump to conclusions.
vor|einander *adv (räumlich)* in front of each other; *(einander gegenüber)* face to face.
vor|eingenommen *adj* prejudiced, biased.
Vor|eingenommenheit *f no pl* prejudice, bias.
vor|enthalten* *vt sep irreg* **jdm etw** ~ to withhold sth from sb.
Vor|entscheidung *f* preliminary decision.
vor|erst *adv* for the time being.
Vorfahr *m (wk)* -en, -en forefather, ancestor.
vorfahren *sep irreg* **1** *vi aux sein* **(a)** to go or move forward. **(b)** *(ankommen)* to drive up. **(c)** *(früher fahren)* to go on ahead. **(d)** *(an der Spitze fahren)* to drive in front. **2** *vt* **(a)** *(weiter nach vorn fahren)* to move up or forward. **(b)** *(vor den Eingang fahren)* to drive up.
Vorfahrt *f no pl* right of way. „~ (be)achten" "give way" *(Brit)*, "yield" *(US)*; **jdm die** ~ **nehmen** to ignore sb's right of way.
Vorfahrts-: **v**~**berechtigt** *adj* **v**~**berechtigt sein** to have (the) right of way; ~**regel** *f* rule on (the) right of way; ~**schild** *nt* give way *(Brit) or* yield *(US)* sign; ~**straße** *f* major road.
Vorfall *m* incident, occurrence.
vorfallen *vi sep irreg aux sein* to occur, to happen.
Vor-: ~**feld** *nt (fig)* run-up (+*gen* to); **v**~**fertigen** *vt sep* to prefabricate; ~**film** *m* short; **v**~**finden** *vt sep irreg* to find, to discover; ~**freude** *f* anticipation; ~**frühling** *m* early spring.
vorfühlen *vi sep (fig)* to put out feelers. **bei jdm** ~ to sound sb out.
vorführen *vt sep* **(a)** *(zeigen)* to present; *Film* to show; *Mode* to model; *Übung, (Vertreter) Gerät* to demonstrate *(dat* to); *Theaterstück auch, Kunststücke* to perform *(dat* to, in front of). **(b)** *Angeklagten* to bring forward.
Vorführung *f* presentation; *(von Filmen)* showing; *(von Mode)* modelling *(Brit)*, modeling *(US)*; *(von Geräten, Modellen, Übungen)* demonstration; *(von Theaterstück, Kunststücken)* performance.
Vorgang *m* **(a)** *(Ereignis)* event, occurrence; *(Ablauf, Hergang)* series of events. **(b)** *(Sci)* process.
Vorgänger(in *f) m* - predecessor.
Vorgarten *m* front garden.
vorgaukeln *vt sep* **jdm etw** ~ to lead sb to believe in sth; **jdm** ~, **daß** ... to lead sb to believe that ...
vorgeben *vt sep irreg (vortäuschen)* to pretend; *(fälschlich beteuern)* to profess.
Vorgebirge *nt* foothills *pl*.
vorgefaßt *adj Meinung* preconceived.
Vorgefühl *nt* anticipation; *(böse Ahnung)* presentiment.

vorgehen *vi sep irreg aux sein* **(a)** *(handeln)* to act, to proceed. **gerichtlich gegen jdn** ~ to take legal action against sb. **(b)** *(geschehen, vor sich gehen)* to go on, to happen. **(c)** *(Uhr) (spätere Zeit anzeigen)* to be fast; *(zu schnell gehen)* to gain. **(d)** *(nach vorn gehen)* to go forward. **(e)** *(vorangehen)* to go first; *(früher gehen)* to go on ahead. **(f)** *(den Vorrang haben)* to come first, to have priority.
Vorgehen *nt no pl* action.
Vor-: **v**~**gerückt** *adj Stunde* late; *Alter* advanced; ~**geschichte** *f* **(a)** *(eines Falles)* past history; **(b)** *(Urgeschichte)* prehistory, prehistoric times *pl*; ~**geschmack** *m (fig)* foretaste.
Vorgesetzte(r) *mf decl as adj* superior.
vorgestern *adv* the day before yesterday. **von** ~ *(fig)* antiquated.
vorgreifen *vi sep irreg* to anticipate; *(verfrüht handeln)* to act prematurely. **jdm** ~ to forestall sb; **einer Sache** *(dat)* ~ to anticipate sth.
vorhaben *vt sep irreg* to intend; *(planen)* to have planned. **was haben Sie heute vor?** what are your plans for today?, what do you have on today?
Vorhaben *nt* plan; *(Absicht)* intention.
Vorhalle *f (Diele)* entrance hall; *(von Parlament)* lobby.
vorhalten *sep irreg* **1** *vt* **(a)** **jdm etw** ~ *(vorwerfen)* to reproach sb for sth; *(als Beispiel)* to hold sth up to sb. **(b)** *(vor den Körper halten)* to hold up; *(beim Niesen etc)* to put in front of one's mouth. **mit vorgehaltener Pistole** at gunpoint. **2** *vi (anhalten)* to last.
vorhanden *adj (verfügbar)* available; *(existierend)* existing.
Vorhang *m, pl* **Vorhänge** curtain.
Vorhängeschloß *nt* padlock.
Vorhaut *f* foreskin.
vorher *adv* before(hand); *(früher)* before. **am Tage** ~ the day before, the previous day.
vorher-: ~**bestimmen*** *vt sep* to determine in advance; *Schicksal* to predetermine; *(Gott)* to preordain; **es war ihm** ~**bestimmt** ... he was predestined ...; ~**gehen** *vi sep irreg aux sein* to go first or in front; *(fig)* to precede; ~**gehend** *adj Tag, Ereignisse* preceding.
vorherig [foːɐˈheːrɪç] *adj attr* prior, previous; *(ehemalig)* former.
Vorherrschaft *f* predominance, supremacy.
vorherrschen *vi sep* to predominate, to prevail.
vorherrschend *adj* predominant; *(weitverbreitet)* prevalent.
Vorher-: ~**sage** *f* forecast; **v**~**sagen** *vt sep* to predict; **v**~**sehen** *vt sep irreg* to foresee.
vorhin *adv* a little while ago.
vorhinein *adv:* **im** ~ in advance.
Vor-: ~**hof** *m* forecourt; ~**hut** *f* -en *(Mil)* advance guard.
vorig *adj attr* previous; *Jahr, Woche etc* last.
Vor-: ~**jahr** *nt* previous year, year before; **v**~**jährig** *adj* of the previous year; **v**~**jammern** *vti sep* **jdm (etwas) v**~**jammern** to moan to sb *(von* about); ~**kämpfer(in** *f) m* pioneer *(für* of); **v**~**kauen** *vt sep Nahrung* to chew; **jdm etw v**~**kauen** *(fig col)* to spoonfeed sth to sb *(col)*.
Vorkehrung *f* ~**en treffen** to take precautions.
Vorkenntnis *f* previous knowledge *no pl*.
vorknöpfen *vt sep (fig col)* **sich** *(dat)* **jdn** ~ to take sb to task.
vorkommen *vi sep irreg aux sein* **(a)** *auch vi impers (sich ereignen)* to happen. **das soll nicht wieder** ~ it won't happen again; **so was soll** ~! that's life! **(b)** *(vorhanden sein, auftreten)* to occur; *(Pflanzen, Tiere)* to be found. **(c)** *(erscheinen)* to seem *(jdm* to sb). **sich** *(dat)* **überflüssig** ~ to feel superfluous; **sich** *(dat)* **klug** ~ to think one is clever. **(d)** *(nach vorn kommen)* to come forward.
Vorkommen *nt* - *(no pl: das Auftreten)* occurrence; *(Min)* deposit.
Vorkriegs- *in cpds* pre-war; ~**zeit** *f* pre-war

period.

vorladen vt sep irreg (bei Gericht) to summons.

Vorlage f -n (a) no pl (von Dokument, Scheck etc) presentation; (von Beweismaterial) submission. **(b)** (Muster) (zum Stricken, Nähen) pattern; (Liter) model. **etw nach einer ~ machen** to model sth on sth. **(c)** (Entwurf) draft; (Parl: Gesetzes~) bill.

vorlassen vt sep irreg **(a)** (col) **jdn ~** (nach vorn gehen lassen) to let sb go in front; (überholen lassen) to let sb pass. **(b)** (Empfang gewähren) to allow in.

Vorlauf m (Sport) preliminary heat/round.

vorlaufen vi sep irreg aux sein (col) (vorauslaufen) to run on ahead; (nach vorne laufen) to run to the front.

Vorläufer m forerunner (auch Ski), precursor.

vorläufig 1 adj temporary; (provisorisch) provisional. **2** adv (einstweilig) temporarily; (fürs erste) for the time being.

vorlaut adj cheeky, impertinent.

Vorleben nt past (life).

Vorlegebesteck nt serving cutlery; (Tranchierbesteck) carvers pl.

vorlegen sep vt **(a)** to present; Paß, Zeugnisse to produce; Beweismaterial to submit; (Pol) Entwurf to table (Brit), to introduce. **(b)** Speisen to serve; (hinlegen) Futter to put down (dat for). **(c)** Riegel to put across.

Vorleger m - mat; (Bett~ auch) (bedside) rug.

vorlehnen vr sep to lean forward.

Vorleistung f (Econ) (Vorausbezahlung) advance (payment); (Vorarbeit) preliminary work; (Pol) prior concession.

vorlesen vti sep irreg to read aloud. **jdm (etw) ~** to read (sth) to sb.

Vorlesung f (Univ) lecture; (Vorlesungsreihe) course (of lectures). **über etw** (acc) **~en halten** to give (a course of) lectures on sth; **~en hören** to go to lectures.

Vorlesungsverzeichnis nt lecture timetable.

vorletzte(r, s) adj last but one, penultimate. **~n Jahr** the year before last.

Vorliebe f predilection. **etw mit ~ tun** to particularly like doing sth.

vorliebnehmen vi sep irreg **mit jdm/etw ~** to make do with sb/sth.

vorliegen vi sep irreg (zur Verfügung stehen) to be available; (Urteil) to be known; (eingereicht, vorgelegt sein) to have come in. **jdm ~** (Unterlagen, Akten etc) to be with sb; **etw liegt gegen jdn vor** sb is charged with sth; **hier liegt ein Irrtum vor** there is an error here.

vorliegend adj attr Gründe existing; Akten, Unterlagen on hand; Frage at issue; Ergebnisse available.

vorlügen vt sep irreg **jdm etwas ~** to lie to sb.

vormachen vt sep **(a) jdm etw ~** (zeigen) to show sb how to do sth. **(b)** (fig) **jdm etwas ~** (täuschen) to fool sb; **er läßt sich** (dat) **von niemandem etwas ~** nobody can fool him; **mach mir doch nichts vor** don't try and fool me.

Vormacht(stellung) f supremacy (gegenüber over).

Vormarsch m (Mil) advance. **im ~ sein** to be on the advance.

vormerken vt sep to make a note of; (bei Bestellung auch) to take an order for; Plätze to book. **sich für einen Kursus ~ lassen** to put oneself down for a course.

Vormittag m morning. **am ~** in the morning.

vormittag adv heute/gestern/morgen ~ this/yesterday/tomorrow morning.

vormittags adv in the morning; (jeden Morgen) in the morning(s).

Vormund m -e guardian. **ich brauche keinen ~** (fig) I don't need anyone to tell me what to do.

Vormundschaft f guardianship. **jdn unter ~**

stellen to place sb under the care of a guardian.

vorn adv **(a)** in front; (am vorderen Ende, auf der Vorderseite) at the front. **von ~** from the front; **nach ~** (ganz nach ~) to the front; (weiter nach ~) forwards; **von weit ~** from the very front; **~ im Buch/in der Schlange/auf der Liste** at the front of the book/queue/at the top of the list; **sich ~ anstellen** to join the front of the queue (Brit) or line (US); **~ im Bild** in the front of the picture; **von ~** from the front; **jdn von ~ sehen** to see sb's face; **~ im Auto/Bus** in the front of the car/bus; **das Buch ist ~ schmutzig** the front of the book is dirty; **das Auto da ~** the car in front or ahead there; **sie waren ziemlich weit ~** they were quite far ahead.

(b) (am Anfang) **von ~** from the beginning; **von ~ anfangen** to start from the beginning; (von neuem) to start (all) over again; (neues Leben) to make a fresh start; **er betrügt sie von ~ bis hinten** he deceives her right, left and centre (Brit) or center (US).

Vorname m Christian name, first name.

vornehm adj **(a)** (von hohem Rang) Familie, Kreise distinguished; (von adliger Herkunft) aristocratic; (kultiviert) Herr, Dame posh (col); Manieren, Art, Benehmen refined; (edel) Gesinnung, Charakter, Handeln noble. **die ~e Gesellschaft** high society; **in ~en Kreisen** in polite society. **(b)** (elegant, luxuriös) smart, posh (col); Geschäft exclusive, posh (col); Kleid, Äußeres elegant, stylish.

vornehmen vt sep irreg **(a)** (ausführen) to carry out. **(b)** sich (dat) **etw ~** (in Angriff nehmen) to get to work on sth; (planen, vorhaben) to intend to do sth; (Vorsatz fassen) to have resolved to do sth; **sich** (dat) **zuviel ~** to take on too much. **(c)** sich (dat) **jdn ~** (col) to have a word with sb.

vornehmlich adv (hauptsächlich, vor allem) principally; (vorzugsweise) first and foremost.

vorneigen vtr sep to lean forward.

vorn(e)weg adv in front; (als erstes) first.

vorn-: **~herein** adv: **von ~herein** from the outset; **~über** adv forwards.

Vor|ort m (Vorstadt) suburb.

Vor|ortzug m suburban train; (im Berufsverkehr) commuter train.

Vor-: **~platz** m forecourt; **~posten** m (Mil) outpost; **v~programmieren*** vt sep (lit, fig) to preprogramme (Brit), to preprogram (US); **v~programmiert** adj Erfolg, Antwort automatic.

Vorrang m no pl ~ **haben** to have priority; (vor +dat vor); **jdm/einer Sache (den) ~ geben** or **einräumen** to give sb/a matter priority.

vorrangig 1 adj of prime importance, priority attr. **2** adv as a matter of priority.

Vorrangstellung f pre-eminence no indef art.

Vorrat m, pl **Vorräte** (an +dat of) stock; (von Waren) stocks pl. **etw auf ~ kaufen** to stock up with sth; **Vorräte anlegen** to lay in a stock; **solange der ~ reicht** (Comm) while stocks last.

vorrätig adj in stock; (verfügbar) available. **etw nicht mehr ~ haben** to be out of sth.

Vorrats-: **~kammer** f store cupboard; (für Lebensmittel) larder; **~raum** m store room; (in Geschäft) stock room.

Vorraum m anteroom; (Büro) outer office.

vorrechnen vt sep **jdm etw ~** to calculate sth for sb; (als Kritik) to point sth out to sb.

Vorrecht nt prerogative; (Vergünstigung) privilege.

Vorrede f introductory speech; (Theat) prologue.

Vorredner m (vorheriger Redner) previous speaker.

Vorreiter m (fig) precursor.

vorrennen vi sep irreg aux sein (col) (voraus) to race ahead; (nach vorn) to run forward.

Vorrichtung f device, gadget.

vorrücken sep **1** vt to move forward. **2** vi aux sein to move forward; *(Mil)* to advance; *(Uhrzeiger)* to move on. **mit dem Stuhl** ~ to move one's chair forward; *siehe* **vorgerückt**.

Vorrunde *f (Sport)* preliminary round.

vorsagen *sep (Sch)* **1** *vt Lösung* to tell. **2** *vi* **jdm** ~ to tell sb the answer.

Vorsaison *f* low season, early season.

Vorsatz *m* (firm) intention. **den** ~ **haben, etw zu tun** to intend to do sth.

vorsätzlich *adj* deliberate; *(Jur)* wilful; *Mord* premeditated. **jdn** ~ **töten** to kill sb intentionally.

Vorschau *f* preview; *(Film)* trailer; *(Wetter~)* forecast.

Vorschein *m* **zum** ~ **bringen** *(lit: zeigen)* to produce; *(fig: deutlich machen)* to bring to light; **zum** ~ **kommen** *(lit: sichtbar werden)* to appear; *(fig: entdeckt werden)* to come to light.

vorschieben *vt sep irreg* **(a)** *(davorschieben)* to push in front; *Riegel* to put across; *(nach vorn schieben)* to push forward. **(b)** *(Mil)* **vorgeschobener Posten** advance party. **(c)** *(fig: vorschützen)* to put forward as an excuse. **(d)** **jdn** ~ to put sb forward as a front man.

vorschießen *sep irreg* **1** *vt* **jdm Geld** ~ to advance sb money. **2** *vi aux sein* to shoot forward.

Vorschlag *m* suggestion; *(Rat)* advice; *(Pol: von Kandidaten)* proposal. **auf** ~ **von** *or* +*gen* at *or* on the suggestion of.

vorschlagen *vt sep irreg* to suggest. **jdn für ein Amt** ~ to propose sb for a post; **jdm** ~, **daß er etw tut** to suggest to sb that he do(es) sth.

Vorschlaghammer *m* sledgehammer.

vorschreiben *vt sep irreg (befehlen)* to stipulate. **ich lasse mir nichts** ~ I won't be dictated to.

vorschreiten *vi sep irreg aux sein* to progress. **im vorgeschrittenen Alter** at an advanced age; **zu vorgeschrittener Stunde** at a late hour.

Vorschrift *f* -**en** rule, regulation; *(Anweisung)* instruction. **nach** ~ **des Arztes** according to doctor's orders; **jdm** ~**en machen** to give sb orders.

vorschrifts-: ~**gemäß,** ~**mäßig 1** *adj Signal, Verhalten* correct, proper *attr*; **2** *adv* according to (the) regulations; *(laut Anordnung)* as instructed; ~**widrig** *adj, adv* contrary to regulations.

Vorschub *m:* **jdm/einer Sache** ~ **leisten** to encourage sb/sth.

vorschulisch *adj* pre-school *attr*.

Vorschuß *m* advance.

vorschützen *vt sep* to put forward as a pretext; *Unwissenheit* to plead. **er schützte vor, daß ... he** pretended that ...

vorschwärmen *vti sep* **jdm von jdm/etw** ~ to go into raptures over sb/sth.

vorschweben *vi sep* **jdm schwebt etw vor** sb has sth in mind.

vorschwindeln *vt sep* **jdm etwas** ~ to lie to sb.

vorsehen *sep irreg* **1** *vt* to provide for; *(planen)* to plan; *Zeit* to allow. **etw für etw** ~ *(bestimmen)* to intend sth for sth; *Geld* to earmark sth for sth; **jdn für etw** ~ *(bestimmen)* to designate sb for sth; **er ist für dieses Amt vorgesehen** we have him in mind for this post. **2** *vr (sich in acht nehmen)* to take care. **sich vor jdm/etw** ~ to beware of sb/sth.

Vorsehung *f no pl* **die** ~ Providence.

vorsetzen *vt sep* **(a)** to move forward; *Fuß* to put forward; *Schüler* to move (up) to the front. **(b)** *(davorsetzen)* to put in front *(vor* +*acc of)*. **(c)** **jdm etw** ~ *(anbieten)* to serve sth up for sb.

Vorsicht *f no pl* care; *(bei Gefahr)* caution; *(Behutsamkeit)* wariness. **(jdn) zur** ~ **(er)mahnen** to advise sb to be careful/cautious/wary; „~ **Stufe"** "mind the step"; **mit** ~ carefully; cautiously; warily; **was er sagt ist mit** ~ **zu genießen** *(hum col)* you have to take what he says with a pinch of salt *(col)*; **dieser Wein ist mit** ~ **zu genießen** *(col)* I should be a bit wary of this

wine; ~ **ist besser als Nachsicht** *(Prov)* better safe than sorry.

vorsichtig *adj* careful; *(besonnen)* cautious; *(mißtrauisch)* wary; *Schätzung* conservative.

Vorsichts-: **v**~**halber** *adv* as a precaution; ~**nahme** *f* precaution; ~**maßnahmen** **treffen** to take precautions.

Vor-: ~**silbe** *f* prefix; **v**~**singen** *sep irreg* **1** *vti* **jdm (etw) v**~**singen** to sing (sth) to sb. **2** *vi (zur Prüfung)* to have a singing test; **v**~**sintflutlich** *adj (col)* antiquated.

Vorsitz *m* chairmanship; *(Amt eines Präsidenten)* presidency. **den** ~ **haben** *or* **führen (bei etw)** to be chairman *or* chairperson (of sth); *(bei Sitzung)* to chair sth.

Vorsitzende(r) *mf decl as adj* chairman/chairwoman, chairperson; *(von Verein)* president.

Vorsorge *f no pl (Vorsichtsmaßnahme)* precaution; *(vorherplanende Fürsorge)* provision(s *pl)* no *def art.* **zur** ~ as a precaution; ~ **treffen** to take precautions; *(fürs Alter)* to make provisions.

vorsorgen *vi sep* to make provisions *(daß so* that). **für etw** ~ to make provisions for sth.

vorsorglich **1** *adj* precautionary; *Mensch* cautious. **2** *adv* as a precaution.

Vorspann *m* -**e** *(Film, TV)* opening credits *pl*.

vorspannen *vt sep Pferde* to harness.

Vorspeise *f* starter.

vorspiegeln *vt sep* to sham. **jdm** ~**(, daß ...)** to pretend to sb (that ...).

Vorspiegelung *f* pretence *(Brit)*, pretense *(US)*. **das ist** ~ **falscher Tatsachen** it's false pretences.

Vorspiel *nt (Einleitung)* prelude; *(Ouvertüre)* overture; *(Theat)* prologue; *(Sport)* preliminary match; *(bei Geschlechtsverkehr)* foreplay.

vorspielen *sep* **1** *vt* **jdm etw** ~ *(Mus)* to play sth to sb; *(Theat)* to act sth to sb; *(fig)* to act out a sham of sth in front of sb. **2** *vi (vor Zuhörern)* to play; *(Mus, Theat) (zur Prüfung)* to do one's practical (exam). **jdm** ~ *(Mus)* to play for sb; *(Theat)* to act (a role) in front of sb.

vorsprechen *sep irreg* **1** *vt (vortragen)* to recite. **jdm etw** ~ to pronounce sth for sb. **2** *vi* **(a)** *(form: jdn aufsuchen)* to call *(bei jdm on* sb). **(b)** *(Theat)* to audition. **jdn** ~ **lassen** to audition sb.

vorspringen *vi sep irreg aux sein* to leap out; *(vorwärts)* to jump forward; *(herausragen)* to jut out; *(Nase, Kinn)* to be prominent.

vorspringend *adj* projecting; *Nase, Kinn* prominent.

Vorsprung *m* **(a)** *(Archit)* projection; *(Fels~)* ledge. **(b)** *(Sport, fig: Abstand)* lead *(vor* +*dat over)*; *(Vorgabe)* start. **einen** ~ **vor jdm haben** to be ahead of sb.

Vor-: ~**stadt** *f* suburb; **v**~**städtisch** *adj* suburban.

Vorstand *m (leitendes Gremium)* board; *(von Verein)* committee; *(von Partei)* executive.

Vorstandssitzung *f (von Firma)* board meeting.

vorstecken *vt sep* to put forward; *Kopf* to stick out.

vorstehen *vi sep irreg aux haben or sein* **(a)** *(hervorragen)* to project; *(Zähne)* to protrude; *(Knochen, Kinn, Nase)* to be prominent. **(b)** *dem Haushalt* to preside over; *einer Firma, einer Partei* to be the chairman of; *einem Geschäft* to manage; *einer Abteilung* to head (up); *einem Amt* to hold.

Vorsteher(in *f) m* - *(von Abteilung)* head; *(von Gefängnis)* governor *(Brit)*, warden *(US)*; *(Bahnhofs~)* station-master.

vorstellbar *adj* conceivable. **das ist nicht** ~ it's inconceivable.

vorstellen *sep* **1** *vt* **(a)** *Tisch, Stuhl, Auto* to move forward; *Bein* to put out; *Uhr* to put forward *(um* by*)*. **(b)** *(col: davorstellen)* **etw** ~ to put sth in front. **(c)** *(darstellen)* to represent; *(bedeuten)* to mean. **etwas** ~ *(fig: Ansehen haben)* to count for something. **(d)** *(bekannt machen)* **jdn jdm** ~ to

introduce sb to sb. **(e)** *(bekanntmachen, vorführen)* to present. **jdm etw ~** to show sb sth.

2 *vr* **(a)** **sich** *(dat)* **etw ~** to imagine sth; **sich** *(dat)* **etw unter etw** *(dat)* **~** *Begriff, Wort* to understand sth by sth; **darunter kann ich mir nichts ~** it doesn't mean anything to me; **stell dir das nicht so einfach vor** don't think it's so easy; **so stelle ich mir einen gelungenen Urlaub vor** that's my idea of a successful holiday. **(b)** *(sich nach vorn stellen)* to move forward. **(c)** *(sich bekannt machen)* to introduce oneself *(jdm* to sb); *(bei Bewerbung)* to go for an interview.

Vorstellung *f* **(a)** *(Gedanke)* idea; *(bildlich)* picture; *(Einbildung)* illusion; *(~skraft)* imagination. **sich** *(dat)* **eine ~ von etw machen** to form an idea *or* *(Bild)* picture of sth; **du machst dir keine ~, wie schwierig das ist** you have no idea how difficult that is. **(b)** *(Theat etc)* performance. **(c)** *(das Bekanntmachen) (zwischen Leuten)* introduction; *(Vorführung)* presentation; *(bei Bewerbung)* interview *(bei* with).

Vorstellungs-: **~gespräch** *nt* interview; **~kraft** *f* imagination; **~vermögen** *nt* powers of imagination *pl*.

Vorstoß *m* *(Vordringen)* venture; *(Mil)* advance; *(fig: Versuch)* attempt.

vorstoßen *vt irreg* **1** *vt* to push forward. **2** *vi aux sein* to venture; *(Sport)* to attack; *(Mil)* to advance.

Vorstrafe *f* previous conviction.

vorstrecken *vt sep* to stretch forward; *Hände to* stretch out; *(fig) Geld* to advance *(jdm* sb).

Vorstufe *f* preliminary stage; *(von Entwicklung)* early stage.

vorstürmen *vi sep aux sein* to rush forward.

Vortag *m* day before.

vortäuschen *vt sep Krankheit* to feign; *Schlag to* fake.

Vortäuschung *f* pretence *(Brit)*, pretense *(US)*, fake. **unter ~ falscher Tatsachen** under false pretences.

Vorteil *m* **-e** advantage *(auch Sport)*. **die Vor- und Nachteile** the pros and cons; **auf seinen ~ bedacht sein** to have an eye to one's own interests; **jdm gegenüber im ~ sein** to have an advantage over sb; **sich zu seinem ~ ändern** to change for the better; **von ~ sein** to be advantageous.

vorteilhaft *adj* advantageous; *Kleider* flattering; *Geschäft* lucrative. **~ aussehen** to look one's best; **etw ~ verkaufen** to sell sth for a profit.

Vortrag *m, pl* **Vorträge** *m* talk. **einen ~ halten** to give a talk. **(b)** *(Darbietung)* performance; *(von Gedicht)* reading.

vortragen *vt sep irreg (berichten)* to report; *(förmlich mitteilen) Fall, Forderung* to present; *Beschwerde* to lodge; *Meinung, Wunsch* to express; *(einen Vortrag halten über)* to give a talk on; *(vorsprechen) Gedicht* to recite; *(Mus)* to perform.

Vortrags-: **~abend** *m* lecture evening; *(mit Gedichten)* poetry evening; *(mit Musik)* recital; **~reihe** *f* series of lectures.

vortrefflich *adj* splendid, superb.

vortreten *vi sep irreg aux sein* **(a)** *(lit)* to step forward. **(b)** *(hervorragen)* to project; *(Augen)* to protrude.

Vortritt *m no pl* priority. **jdm den ~ lassen** *(lit, fig)* to let sb go first.

vorüber *adv* **~ sein** *(räumlich, Jugend)* to be past; *(Gewitter etc)* to be over; *(Schmerz)* to have gone.

vorüber- *pref siehe auch* **vorbei-;** **~gehen** *vi sep irreg aux sein* to pass *(an etw* (dat) sth); *(Gewitter)* to blow over; **~gehend** *adj (flüchtig)* momentary; *Krankheit* short; *(zeitweilig)* temporary.

Vor|urteil *nt* prejudice *(gegenüber* against). **~e haben** to be prejudiced.

vor|urteils-: **~frei,** **~los** **1** *adj* unprejudiced; **2** *adv* without prejudice.

Vor-: **~väter** *pl* forefathers *pl*; **~verkauf** *m*

advance booking; **sich** *(dat)* **Karten im ~verkauf besorgen** to buy tickets in advance.

vorverlegen* *vt sep* **(a)** *Termin* to bring forward. **(b)** *(Mil) Front, Gefechtslinie* to push forward.

vorwagen *vr sep* to venture forward.

Vorwahl *f* **(a)** preliminary election; *(US)* primary. **(b)** *(Telec)* area code.

Vorwahlnummer *f* area code.

vorwärmen *vt sep* to pre-heat; *Teller* to heat.

Vorwarnung *f* (advance) warning.

vorwärts *adv* forwards, forward. **~!** *(col)* let's go *(col)*; *(Mil)* forward march!; **weiter ~** further on.

Vorwärts-: **~bewegung** *f* forward movement; **~gang** *m* forward gear; **v~gehen** *sep irreg aux sein (fig)* **1** *vi* to progress; **2** *vi impers* **mit etw geht es v~** sth is going well; **v~kommen** *vi sep irreg aux sein (fig)* to get on *(in,* mit with).

Vorwäsche *f,* **Vorwaschgang** *m* prewash.

vorweg *adv (an der Spitze)* at the front; *(vorher)* before(hand); *(von vornherein)* at the outset.

Vorweg-: **~nahme** *f* **-n** anticipation; **v~nehmen** *vt sep irreg* to anticipate.

Vorweihnachtszeit *f* pre-Christmas period.

vorweisen *vt sep irreg* to show; *Zeugnisse* to produce. **etw ~ können** *(fig)* to possess sth.

vorwerfen *vt sep irreg* **(a)** *(fig)* **jdm etw/Unpünktlichkeit ~** to reproach sb for sth/for being unpunctual; *(beschuldigen)* to accuse sb of sth/of being unpunctual; **das wirft er mir heute noch vor** he still holds it against me; **ich habe mir nichts vorzuwerfen** my conscience is clear. **(b)** *(lit) Tieren/Gefangenen* **etw ~** to throw sth down for the animals/prisoners.

vorwiegend **1** *adj attr* predominant. **2** *adv* predominantly.

Vorwissen *nt* previous knowledge.

vorwitzig *adj (keck)* cheeky; *(vorlaut)* forward.

Vorwort *nt* **-e** foreword, preface.

Vorwurf *m, pl* **Vorwürfe** reproach; *(Beschuldigung)* accusation. **jdm/sich große Vorwürfe machen** to reproach sb/oneself; **ich habe mir keine Vorwürfe zu machen** my conscience is clear; **jdm etw zum ~ machen** to reproach sb with sth.

vorwurfsvoll *adj* reproachful.

Vorzeichen *nt (Omen)* omen; *(Med)* early symptom; *(Math)* sign. **positives/negatives ~** *(Math)* plus/minus (sign); **mit umgekehrtem ~** *(fig)* the other way around.

vorzeichnen *vt sep Linien etc* to sketch (out). **jdm etw ~** *(fig)* to map sth out for sb.

vorzeigen *vt sep* to show, to produce.

Vorzeit *f* prehistoric times *pl*.

vorzeitig *adj* early; *Geburt, Altern etc* premature.

vorzeitlich *adj* prehistoric; *(fig)* archaic.

vorziehen *vt sep irreg* **(a)** *(hervorziehen)* to pull out; *(nach vorne ziehen) Stuhl etc* to pull up; *(zuziehen) Vorhänge* to draw. **etw hinter/unter etw** *(dat)* **~** to pull sth out from behind/under sth. **(b)** *(fig) (lieber mögen)* to prefer; *(bevorzugen) jdn* to favour *(Brit)*, to favor *(US)*. **etw einer anderen Sache ~** to prefer sth to sth else; **es ~, etw zu tun** to prefer to do sth. **(c)** *(zuerst behandeln, abfertigen)* to give priority to.

Vorzimmer *nt* anteroom; *(Büro)* outer office.

Vorzug *m, pl* **Vorzüge** preference; *(Vorteil)* advantage; *(gute Eigenschaft)* asset. **einer Sache** *(dat)* **den ~ geben** *(form)* to prefer sth.

vorzüglich *adj* excellent.

vorzugsweise *adv* preferably; *(hauptsächlich)* chiefly. **etw ~ trinken** to prefer to drink sth.

Votum ['voːtʊm] *nt, pl* **Voten** vote.

vulgär [vʊl'gɛːɐ] *adj* vulgar.

Vulkan [vʊl'kaːn] *m* **-e** volcano. **ein Tanz auf dem ~** playing with fire.

Vulkan|ausbruch [vʊl'kaːn-] *m* volcanic eruption.

vulkanisch [vʊl'kaːnɪʃ] *adj* volcanic.

W

W, w [ve:] *nt* -, - W, w.
W = Westen.
Waage *f* -**n** (a) *(Gerät)* scales *pl*; *(Feder~, Apotheker~)* balance. **eine ~** a pair of scales; **sich** *(dat)* **die ~ halten** *(fig)* to balance one another. **(b)** *(Astrol)* Libra.
Waag(e)-: w~recht *adj* horizontal; **~rechte** *f* horizontal.
Waagschale *f* (scale) pan. **(schwer) in die ~fallen** *(fig)* to carry weight; **seine Autorität in die ~ werfen** *(fig)* to bring one's authority to bear.
wabb(e)lig *adj Pudding* wobbly; *Mensch* flabby.
Wabe *f* -**n** honeycomb.
wach *adj* awake *pred*; *(fig: aufgeweckt)* alert. **in ~em Zustand** in the waking state; **~ werden** to wake up.
Wach-: ~ablösung *f* changing of the guard; *(fig: Regierungswechsel)* change of government; *(Mensch)* relief guard; **~boot** *nt* patrol boat; **~dienst** *m* look-out; *(Mil)* guard (duty); *(Naut)* watch; **~dienst haben/machen** to be on guard (duty); *(Naut)* to have the watch.
Wache *f* -**n (a)** *no pl (Wachdienst)* guard (duty). **(bei jdm) ~ halten** to keep watch (over sb); *(Kranken~)* to keep watch (at sb's bedside); **~ stehen** *or* **schieben** *(col)* to be on guard (duty); *(Dieb, Schüler etc)* to keep a look-out. **(b)** *(Mil)* *(Wachposten)* guard; *(Gebäude)* guardhouse. **(c)** *(Naut: Personen, Dauer)* watch. **~ haben** to be on watch. **(d)** *(Polizei~)* (police) station.
wachen *vi* **(a)** *(wach sein)* to be awake. **(b)** *(Wache halten)* to keep watch. **bei jdm ~** to sit up with sb; **über etw** *(acc)* **~** to (keep) watch over sth; *über Verkehr* to supervise sth.
Wach-: w~habend *adj attr* duty; **w~halten** *vt sep irreg (fig) Interesse etc* to keep alive; **~hund** *m (lit, fig)* watchdog; *(lit auch)* guard-dog; **~mannschaft** *f* guards *pl*; *(Naut)* watch.
Wacholder *m* - *(Bot)* juniper (tree).
Wacholder-: ~beere *f* juniper berry; **~schnaps** *m* spirit made from juniper berries, ≈ gin.
wach-: ~rufen *vt sep irreg (fig) Erinnerung etc* to evoke; **~rütteln** *vt sep (fig)* to (a)rouse.
Wachs [vaks] *nt* -**e** wax. **weich wie ~** as soft as butter.
wachsam *adj* vigilant; *(vorsichtig)* on one's guard.
Wachsamkeit *f no pl* vigilance; *(Vorsichtigkeit)* guardedness.
Wachschiff *nt* patrol ship.
wachsen[1] ['vaksn] *pret* **wuchs** [vu:ks], *ptp* **gewachsen** *vi aux sein* to grow. **in die Breite/Länge ~** to broaden (out)/to lengthen; **sich** *(dat)* **einen Bart ~ lassen** to grow a beard; **gut gewachsen** *Baum* well-grown; *Mensch* having a good figure.
wachsen[2] ['vaksn] *vt* to wax.
Wachs-: ~farbe *f* **(a)** *(Farbstift)* wax crayon; **(b)** *(Farbstoff)* wax dye; **~figur** *f* wax figure; **~kerze** *f* wax candle; **~malstift** *m*, **~malkreide** *f* wax crayon; **~papier** *nt* waxed paper; **~stift** *m* wax crayon.
Wachstube ['vaxʃtu:bə] *f* guard-room; *(von Polizei)* duty room.
Wachstum ['vakstu:m] *nt no pl* growth. **im ~ zurückgeblieben** stunted.
Wachstums-: w~hemmend *adj* growth-inhibiting; **~störung** *f* disturbance of growth.
Wachtel *f* -**n** quail.
Wächter *m* - guardian; *(Nacht~)* watchman.
Wachtposten *m* sentry; *(Schüler, Dieb etc)* lookout.
Wach(t)turm *m* watch-tower.
Wach- und Schließgesellschaft *f* security corps.
wack(e)lig *adj* wobbly; *(fig) Firma* shaky. **~ auf den Beinen sein** *(col: Patient)* to be wobbly on one's legs; **~ stehen** *(lit)* to be unsteady; *(fig: Unternehmen, Schüler)* to be shaky.
Wackelkontakt *m* loose connection.
wackeln *vi* **(a)** to wobble; *(zittern)* to shake; *(Zahn, Schraube)* to be loose; *(beim Fotografieren)* to move. **mit den Ohren/Hüften/dem Kopf/Schwanz ~** to waggle one's ears/wiggle one's hips/wag one's head/its tail. **(b)** *aux sein (langsam, unsicher gehen)* to totter.
wacker *adj (tapfer)* brave, valiant. **sich ~ schlagen** *(col)* to put up a brave fight.
Wade *f* -**n** calf.
Waden-: ~bein *nt* fibula; **~krampf** *m* cramp in one's calf; **~strumpf** *m* half stocking; **~wickel** *m (Med)* compress around the leg.
Waffe *f* -**n** *(lit, fig)* weapon; *(Schuß~)* gun; *(Mil: Waffengattung)* arm. **~n** *(Mil)* arms; **~n tragen** to carry arms; **die ~n strecken** *(lit, fig)* to surrender; **jdn mit seinen eigenen ~n schlagen** *(fig)* to beat sb at his own game.
Waffel *f* -**n** waffle; *(Keks, Eis~)* wafer; *(Eistüte)* cornet.
Waffel|eisen *nt* waffle iron.
Waffen- *in cpds* arms; **~arsenal** *nt* arsenal; *(von Staat)* stockpile; **~gattung** *f (Mil)* arm of the service; **~gewalt** *f* force of arms; **mit ~gewalt** by force of arms; **~hilfe** *f* military assistance; **~lager** *nt (von Armee)* ordnance depot; *(von Terroristen)* cache; **~los** *adj* unarmed; **~ruhe** *f* ceasefire; **~schein** *m* firearms *or* gun licence *(Brit)* *or* license *(US)*; **~schmuggel** *m* gunrunning, arms smuggling; **~stillstand** *m* armistice.
wagemutig *adj* daring, bold.
wagen 1 *vt* to venture; *(sich getrauen)* to dare. **es ~, etw zu tun** to venture to do sth; to dare (to) do sth; **wage nicht, mir zu widersprechen!** don't you dare (to) contradict me! **2** *vr* to dare. **sich an etw** *(acc)* **~** to venture to do sth; **sich auf ein Gebiet ~** to venture into an area.
Wagen *m* - *(Personen~)* car; *(Liefer~)* van; *(von Pferden gezogen)* wag(g)on, cart; *(Kutsche)* coach; *(Kinder~)* pram *(Brit)*, baby carriage *(US)*; *(Hand~)* (hand)cart; *(Kofferkuli, Einkaufs~)* trolley *(Brit)*, cart *(US)*; *(Schreibmaschinen~)* carriage; *(Eisenbahn~)* car, carriage *(Brit)*.
wägen *pret* **wog**, *ptp* **gewogen** *vt (old)* to weigh.
Wagen-: ~abteil *nt (Rail)* compartment; **~führer** *m* driver; **~heber** *m* jack; **~ladung** *f (von Lastwagen)* lorryload *(Brit)*, truckload; *(von Eisenbahn)* wag(g)onload; **~park** *m* fleet of cars; **~rad** *nt* cartwheel; **~wäsche** *f* carwash.
Waggon [va'gɔŋ] *m* -**s** (goods) wag(g)on *(Brit)*, freight car *(US)*; *(Ladung)* wag(g)onload/carload.
Wag-: ~hals *m* daredevil; **w~halsig** *adj* fool-

473

hardy, daredevil *attr*.
Wagnis *nt* hazardous business; *(Risiko)* risk.
Wahl *f* **-en (a)** *(Auswahl)* choice. **die ~ fiel auf ihn**
he was chosen; **aus freier ~** of one's own free
choice; **wir hatten keine (andere) ~(, als)** we had
no alternative *or* choice (but); **jdm die ~ lassen**
to leave (it up to) sb to choose; **jdm etw zur ~**
stellen to give sb a choice of sth; **seine ~ treffen**
to make one's selection; **wer die ~ hat, hat die**
Qual *(Prov)* he is/you are *etc* spoilt for choice.
(b) *(Pol etc)* election; *(Abstimmung)* vote;
(geheim) ballot. **seine ~ in den Vorstand/zum**
Präsidenten his election to the board/as president; **zur ~ gehen** to go to the polls; **jdn zur ~**
aufstellen to put sb up as a candidate; **sich zur ~**
stellen to stand, to run (for parliament *etc*); **die**
~ annehmen to accept the vote.
(c) *(Qualität)* **erste ~** top quality; *(Gemüse,*
Eier) grade one; **Waren erster ~** top-quality
goods; **Gemüse zweiter ~** grade-two vegetables.
wählbar *adj* eligible (for office).
Wahl-: **~benachrichtigung** *f* polling card;
w~berechtigt *adj* entitled to vote; **~beteiligung**
f poll, turnout; **~bezirk** *m* ward.
wählen 1 *vt* **(a)** to choose *(von* from, out of); *siehe*
gewählt. (b) *(Telec)* Nummer to dial. **(c)** *(Pol)* to
elect; *(sich entscheiden für)* Partei to vote for. **jdn**
ins Parlament ~ to elect sb to Parliament; **jdn**
zum Präsidenten ~ to elect sb president. **2** *vi* **(a)**
(auswählen) to choose. **(b)** *(Telec)* to dial. **(c)**
(Stimme abgeben) to vote.
Wähler(in *f)* *m* - *(Pol)* elector, voter.
Wahl|ergebnis *nt* election result.
wählerisch *adj* particular; *Geschmack, Kunde*
discriminating. **sei nicht so ~!** don't be so
choosy *(col)*.
Wähler-: **~stimme** *f* vote; **~verzeichnis** *nt*
electoral roll.
Wahl-: **~fach** *nt* *(Sch)* optional subject; **~gang** *m*
ballot; **~geheimnis** *nt* secrecy of the ballot;
~geschenk *nt* pre-election vote-catching gimmick; **~gesetz** *nt* electoral law; **~heimat** *f*
country of adoption; **~helfer** *m* *(im ~kampf)*
election assistant; *(bei der Wahl)* polling officer;
~kabine *f* polling booth; **~kampf** *m*
election(eering) campaign; **~kreis** *m* constituency; **~lokal** *nt* polling station; **w~los 1** *adj* indiscriminate; **2** *adv* at random, haphazardly;
(nicht wählerisch) indiscriminately; **~mann** *m, pl*
~männer delegate; **~möglichkeit** *f* option;
~ordnung *f* election regulations *pl*; **~periode** *f*
lifetime of a/the parliament; **~pflicht** *f* electoral
duty; **~recht** *nt* (right to) vote; **allgemeines**
~recht universal franchise; **das aktive ~recht**
the right to vote; **das passive ~recht** eligibility
(for political office); **~rede** *f* election speech;
~reform *f* electoral reform.
Wählscheibe *f* dial.
Wahl-: **~schein** *m* polling card; **~spruch** *m* motto; **~system** *nt* electoral system; **~tag** *m* election day; **~urne** *f* ballot box; **~verfahren** *nt*
electoral procedure; **~versammlung** *f* election
meeting; **~versprechungen** *pl* election
promises *pl*; **~vorschlag** *m* election proposal;
w~weise *adv* alternatively; **w~weise Kartof-**
feln oder Reis a choice of potatoes or rice.
Wählzeichen *nt* *(Telec)* dialling tone.
Wahn *m no pl* illusion, delusion; *(Manie)* mania. **in**
dem ~ leben, daß ... to labour *(Brit)* or labor
(US) under the delusion that ...
Wahnsinn *m no pl* madness. **das ist doch (heller)**
~, so ein ~! that's sheer madness.
wahnsinnig 1 *adj (col)* *(verrückt)* mad, crazy;
(attr: sehr groß, viel) awful, dreadful. **eine ~e**
Arbeit a crazy amount of work; **das macht mich**
~ *(col)* it's driving me crazy; **~ werden** to go
mad *(col)*; **ich werde ~!** it's mind-blowing! *(col)*.
2 *adv (col)* incredibly *(col)*. **~ verliebt** madly in

love; **~ viele/viel** an incredible number/amount
(col).
Wahnsinnige(r) *mf decl as adj* lunatic.
Wahnsinns- *in cpds (col: verrückt)* crazy; *(col: pri-*
ma) incredible *(col)*.
Wahn-: **~vorstellung** *f* delusion; **w~witzig 1** *adj*
crazy *attr*; **2** *adv* terribly.
wahr *adj* Geschichte, Liebe, Glaube *etc* true; *(echt)*
Kunst, *(attr: wirklich)* real, veritable. **im ~sten**
Sinne des Wortes in the true sense of the word;
daran ist kein Wort ~ *or* **kein ~es Wort** there's
not a word of truth in it; **da ist etwas W~es daran**
there's some truth in that; **da hast du ein ~es**
Wort gesprochen *(col)* there's a lot of truth in
that; **etw ~ machen** Pläne to make sth a reality;
Versprechung, Drohung to carry sth out; **~ wer-**
den to come true; **so ~ mir Gott helfe!** so help
me God!; **das darf** *or* **kann doch nicht ~ sein!**
(col) it can't be true!; **das ist nicht das W~e** *(col)*
it's no great shakes *(col)*.
wahren *vt* Interessen, Rechte to look after; *Autori-*
tät, Ruf, Würde to preserve, to keep; *Geheimnis* to
keep; *gute Manieren* to adhere to, to observe.
währen *vi (geh)* to last.
während 1 *prep +gen or dat* during. **~ eines**
Zeitraums over a period of time. **2** *conj* while.
währenddessen *adv* meanwhile.
Wahr-: **w~haben** *vt sep irreg* **etw nicht w~haben**
wollen not to want to admit sth; **w~haft 1** *adj*
real; **2** *adv* really, truly; **w~haftig** *adv* really;
(tatsächlich) actually.
Wahrheit *f* truth. **in ~** in reality; **die ~ sagen** to
tell the truth.
wahrheits-: **~getreu** *adj* Bericht truthful; *Dar-*
stellung faithful; **~liebend** *adj* truth-loving;
(ehrlich) truthful.
Wahr-: **w~nehmbar** *adj* perceptible; **mit bloßem**
Auge w~nehmbar visible to the naked eye;
w~nehmen *vt sep irreg* **(a)** *(sinnlich)* to perceive;
Veränderungen etc to be aware of; **nichts mehr**
um sich herum w~nehmen to be no longer
aware of anything around one; **(b)** *Frist, Termin*
to observe; *Gelegenheit* to take; *Interessen, Rech-*
te to look after; **~nehmung** *f siehe* **vt (a)** perception; awareness; **(b)** *(von Frist)* observing;
(von Interessen) looking after; **w~sagen** *vi sep or*
insep to tell fortunes; **aus den Karten w~sagen**
to read cards; **~sager(in** *f)* *m* - fortuneteller.
wahrscheinlich 1 *adj* probable, likely; *(glaub-*
haft) plausible. **2** *adv* probably.
Wahrscheinlichkeit *f* probability; *(Glaubhaftig-*
keit) plausibility. **mit großer ~, aller ~ nach, in**
aller ~ in all probability.
Währung *f* currency.
Währungs- *in cpds* currency; **~einheit** *f* monetary unit; **~fonds** *m* Monetary Fund; **~krise**
f monetary crisis; **~reform** *f* currency reform.
Wahrzeichen *nt* *(von Stadt, Verein)* emblem; *(Ge-*
bäude, Turm etc) symbol.
Waid- *in cpds* = **Weid-**.
Waise *f* **-n** orphan.
Waisen-: **~haus** *nt* orphanage; **~kind** *nt* orphan;
~knabe *m* **gegen dich ist er ein ~knabe** *(col)* he's
no match for you; **~rente** *f* orphan's allowance.
Wal *m* **-e** whale.
Wald *m* **-er** wood (*s pl)*; *(großer)* forest; *(no pl:*
~land) woodland(s *pl)*. **er sieht den ~ vor lauter**
Bäumen nicht he can't see the wood for the
trees.
Wald-: **~ameise** *f* red ant; **~arbeiter** *m* forestry
worker; **~blume** *f* woodland flower; **~brand** *m*
forest fire; **~erdbeere** *f* wild strawberry.
waldig *adj* wooded, woody.
Wald-: **~land** *nt* woodland(s *pl)*; **~lauf** *m* cross-
country running; *(einzelner Lauf)* cross-country
run; **~lehrpfad** *m* nature trail; **~meister** *m* *(Bot)*
woodruff; **w~reich** *adj* densely wooded; **~ster-**
ben *nt no pl* loss of trees due to pollution.

Wald- und Wiesen- *in cpds (col)* common-or-garden *(col)*.

Wald-: ~**weg** *m* woodland/forest path; ~**wiese** *f* glade.

Wal-: ~**fang** *m* whaling; ~**fänger** *m* whaler.

Waliser(in *f)* *m* - Welshman; Welsh woman.

walisisch *adj* Welsh.

Wall *m* ⁼e embankment; *(Mil)* rampart; *(fig)* bulwark.

Wallach *m* -e gelding.

Wallfahrer(in *f)* *m* - pilgrim.

Wallfahrt *f* pilgrimage.

Wallone *m (wk)* -n, -n, **Wallonin** *f* Walloon.

Walnuß *f* walnut.

Walroß *nt* -sse walrus.

walten *vi (geh)* to reign *(in* +dat over); *(wirken: Mensch, Naturkräfte)* to be at work. **über jdm/etw** ~ to rule (over) sb/sth; **Vernunft** ~ **lassen** to let reason prevail; **Vorsicht** ~ **lassen** to exercise caution.

Walzblech *nt* sheet metal.

Walze *f* -n roller.

walzen *vt* to roll.

wälzen 1 *vt* **(a)** *(rollen)* to roll. **(b)** *(col) Akten, Bücher* to pore over; *Probleme, Gedanken, Pläne* to turn over in one's mind. **die Verantwortung auf jdn** ~ to shift the responsibility onto sb. **2** *vr* to roll; *(schlaflos im Bett)* to toss and turn; *(fig: Menschenmenge, Wassermassen)* to surge.

walzenförmig *adj* cylindrical.

Walzer *m* - waltz.

Wälzer *m* - *(col)* heavy *or* weighty tome *(hum)*.

Walz-: ~**straße** *f* rolling train; ~**werk** *nt* rolling mill.

wand *pret of* **winden**.

Wand *f* ⁼e wall; *(nicht gemauerte Trenn~)* partition (wall); *(von Gefäß, Behälter, Schiff)* side; *(Fels~)* (rock) face; *(fig)* barrier, wall. **spanische** ~ (folding) screen; ~ **an** ~ wall to wall; **in seinen vier** ⁓**en** *(fig)* within one's own four walls; **weiß wie die** ~ as white as a sheet; **jdn an die** ~ **spielen** to put sb in the shade; *(Sport auch)* to outplay sb; **jdn an die** ~ **drücken** *(fig)* to push sb to the wall; **jdn an die** ~ **stellen** *(fig)* to send sb before the firing squad; **er lachte, daß die** ⁓**e wackelten** *(col)* he raised the roof (with his laughter) *(col)*; **das ist, um die** ⁓**e hochzugehen** *(col)* it's enough to drive you up the wall *(col)*.

Wand-: ~**behang** *m* wall hanging; ~**bekleidung** *f* wall covering; *(aus Holz)* panelling *(Brit)*, paneling *(US)*; ~**bord**, ~**brett** *nt* (wall) shelf.

Wandel *m no pl* change. **im** ~ **der Zeiten** throughout the ages.

Wandel-: w~**bar** *adj* changeable; ~**halle** *f* foyer; *(im Parlament)* lobby.

wandeln¹ *vtr (ändern)* to change.

wandeln² *vi aux sein (geh: gehen)* to walk, to stroll. **ein** ~**des Wörterbuch** *(hum)* a walking dictionary.

Wander-: ~**ameise** *f* army ant; ~**ausstellung** *f* touring exhibition; ~**bühne** *f* touring company; ~**düne** *f* shifting dune.

Wanderer *m* - hiker; *(esp in Verein)* rambler.

Wander-: ~**falke** *m* peregrine (falcon); ~**freund(in** *f)* *m* hiker; ~**karte** *f* map of walks; ~**kleidung** *f* hiking outfit; ~**leben** *nt* roving *or* wandering life; *(fig)* unsettled life; ~**lied** *nt* hiking song; ~**lust** *f* wanderlust.

wandern *vi aux sein* to hike; *(in Verein)* to ramble; *(umherschweifen)* to roam; *(Wanderbühne)* to travel; *(Tiere, Völker)* to migrate; *(Wolken)* to drift; *(weitergegeben werden)* to be passed on; *(col: in den Papierkorb)* to land.

Wander-: ~**niere** *f* floating kidney; ~**pokal** *m* challenge cup; ~**prediger** *m* itinerant preacher; ~**preis** *m* challenge trophy; ~**ratte** *f* brown rat.

Wanderschaft *f no pl* travels *pl.* **auf (der)** ~ **sein** to be on one's travels; **auf** ~ **gehen** to go off on one's travels.

Wander-: ~**schauspieler** *m* travelling *(Brit)* or traveling *(US)* actor; ~**schuhe** *pl* walking shoes *pl*; ~**truppe** *f* touring company.

Wanderung *f* **(a)** *(Ausflug)* walk. **eine** ~ **machen** to go on a ramble. **(b)** *(von Tieren, Völkern)* migration.

Wander-: ~**verein** *m* rambling club; ~**weg** *m* trail, (foot)path; ~**zirkus** *m* travelling *(Brit)* or traveling *(US)* circus.

Wand-: ~**gemälde** *nt* mural, wall-painting; ~**kalender** *m* wall calendar; ~**karte** *f* wall map; ~**lampe** *f* wall lamp; ~**leuchter** *m* wall bracket.

Wandlung *f (Wechsel, Wandel)* change; *(völlige Um~)* transformation. **eine** ~ **durchmachen** to undergo a change.

Wand-: ~**malerei** *f* mural painting; ~**schirm** *m* screen; ~**schrank** *m* wall cupboard; ~**tafel** *f* (black)board.

wandte *pret of* **wenden**.

Wand-: ~**teller** *m* wall plate; ~**teppich** *m* tapestry, wall hanging; ~**uhr** *f* wall clock; ~**verkleidung** *f* wall covering; *(aus Holz)* panelling *(Brit)*, paneling *(US)*; ~**zeitung** *f* (wall) news-sheet.

Wange *f* -n cheek.

wankelmütig *adj* fickle, inconstant.

wanken *vi* **(a)** *(Mensch, Gebäude)* to sway; *(Knie)* to shake, to wobble; *(unsicher sein/werden)* to waver. **(b)** *aux sein (gehen)* to stagger; *(alter Mensch)* to totter.

wann *interrog adv* when. ~ **(auch) immer** whenever; **seit** ~ **bist/hast du ...?** how long have you been/have you had ...?; *(entrüstet etc)* since when are you/do you have ...?

Wanne *f* -n bath; *(Öl~)* reservoir.

Wanze *f* -n *(Zool, col: Abhörgerät)* bug.

Wappen *nt* - coat of arms.

Wappen-: ~**kunde** *f* heraldry; ~**tier** *nt* heraldic animal.

wappnen *vr (fig)* **sich (gegen etw)** ~ to prepare (oneself) (for sth); **gewappnet sein** to be forearmed.

war *pret of* **sein¹** was.

warb *pret of* **werben**.

Ware *f* -n product; *(einzelne* ~*)* article; *(als Sammelbegriff)* goods *pl.* ~ **n** *pl* goods *pl*.

Waren-: ~**angebot** *nt* range of goods for sale; ~**aufzug** *m* goods hoist; ~**haus** *nt* (department) store; ~**lager** *nt* warehouse; *(Bestand)* stocks *pl*; ~**probe** *f* trade sample; ~**sendung** *f* trade sample (sent by post); ~**zeichen** *nt* trademark.

warf *pret of* **werfen**.

warm *adj comp* ⁼**er**, *superl* ⁼**ste(r, s)** *adv)* **am** ⁼**sten** *(lit, fig)* warm; *(col: homosexuell)* queer *(col)*. **mir ist** ~ I'm warm; **das Essen** ~ **machen** to heat up the food; **das Essen** ~ **stellen** to keep the food hot; **sich** ~ **anziehen** to dress up warmly; **sich** ~ **laufen** to warm up; **jdn/etw** ⁓**stens empfehlen** to recommend sb/sth warmly; **mit jdm** ~ **werden** *(col)* to get close to sb.

Warm-: ~**blüter** *m* warm-blooded animal; w~**blütig** *adj* warm-blooded.

Wärme *f no pl (lit, fig)* warmth; *(von Wetter etc, Phys)* heat. **10 Grad** ~ 10 degrees above zero; **ist das eine** ~! isn't it warm!

wärmen 1 *vt* to warm; *Essen* to heat up. **2** *vi (Kleidung, Sonne)* to be warm. **3** *vr* to warm up. **sich gegenseitig** ~ to keep each other warm.

Wärme-: ~**regler** *m* thermostat; ~**technik** *f* heat technology; ~**verlust** *m* heat loss.

Wärmflasche *f* hot-water bottle.

Warm-: ~**front** *f* (Met) warm front; w~**herzig** *adj* warm-hearted; w~**laufen** *vi sep irreg aux sein* **den Motor** w~**laufen lassen** to warm up the engine; ~**luft** *f* warm air.

Warmwasser-: ~**heizung** *f* hot-water central heating; ~**leitung** *f* hot-water pipe; ~**speicher** *m* hot-water tank.

Warn-: ~anlage f warning system; ~blinkanlage f (Aut) hazard warning lights pl; ~dreieck nt warning triangle.

warnen vti to warn (vor +dat of). **jdn (davor)** ~, **etw zu tun** to warn sb not to do sth.

Warn-: ~kreuz nt warning cross; ~schild nt warning sign; ~schuß m warning shot; ~streik m token strike.

Warnung f warning (vor +dat of).

Warn-: ~vorrichtung f warning system; ~zeichen nt warning sign; (hörbar) warning signal.

Warschau nt Warsaw. **~er Pakt** Warsaw Pact.

Warte f -n observation point; (fig) viewpoint. **von jds** ~ **(aus)** (fig) from sb's standpoint.

Warte-: ~frist f waiting period; (für Lieferung) delivery time; ~halle f waiting room; ~liste f waiting list.

warten[1] vi to wait (auf +acc for). **warte mal!** wait a minute; (überlegend) let me see; **na warte!** (col) just you wait!; **mit dem Essen auf jdn** ~ to wait for sb before eating; **lange auf sich** ~ **lassen** to be a long time (in) coming.

warten[2] vt Auto, Maschine to service.

Wärter(in f) m - attendant; (Tier~) keeper; (Gefängnis~) warder/wardress (Brit), guard.

Warte-: ~saal m waiting room; ~zeit f waiting period; ~zimmer nt waiting room.

Wartung f (von Auto, Maschine) servicing. **das Auto muß zur** ~ the car has to go in for a service.

warum interrog adv why. ~ **nicht gleich so!** that's better.

Warze f -n wart; (Brust~) nipple.

was 1 interrog pron **(a)** what. ~ **ist, kommst du mit?** well, are you coming?; ~ **denn?** what is it?; (ungläubig) what?; **wenn nicht das,** ~ **denn?** if not that, what then?; **wenn ein Unfall passiert,** ~ **dann?** what if there's an accident?; ~ **haben wir gelacht!** (col) how we laughed! **(b)** (col: warum) what ... for. **(c)** ~ **für** ... what sort or kind of ...; ~ **für ein schönes Haus!** what a lovely house! **2** rel pron (auf Satz bezogen) which. **das,** ~ ... **that which** ..., **what** ...; **ich weiß,** ~ **ich/er tun soll** I know what to do/what he should do; ~ **auch (immer)** whatever; **alles,** ~ ... everything or all (that)...; **lauf,** ~ **du kannst!** (col) run as fast as you can! **3** (col) indef pron abbr of **etwas** something; (fragend, verneint) anything; (Teil einer Menge) some; any. **(na,) so** ~! well I never!; siehe **etwas.**

Wasch-: ~anlage f (für Autos) carwash; **w~bar** adj washable; ~bär m rac(c)oon; ~becken nt wash-basin (Brit), washbowl (US); ~beutel m sponge bag; ~brett nt wash-board; ~creme f cream detergent.

Wäsche f no pl **(a)** washing; (Schmutz~) laundry. **große** ~ **haben** to have a large amount of washing (to do); **in der** ~ in the wash. **(b)** (Bett~, Küchen~) linen; (Unter~) underwear. **dumm aus der** ~ **gucken** (col) to look stupid.

Wäschebeutel m dirty clothes bag.

wasch|echt adj Farbe fast; (fig) genuine.

Wäsche-: ~klammer f clothespeg (Brit), clothespin (US); ~korb m dirty clothes basket; ~leine f (clothes-)line.

waschen pret **wusch,** ptp **gewaschen 1** vt to wash; Gold etc to pan. **(Wäsche)** ~ to do the washing; **etw** (acc) **warm/kalt** ~ to wash sth in hot/cold water; **sich** (dat) **die Hände** ~ to wash one's hands. **2** vr to wash (oneself/itself); (Stoff) to wash. **eine Geldbuße, die sich gewaschen hat** (col) a really heavy fine.

Wäscherei f laundry.

Wäsche-: ~sack m laundry bag; ~schleuder f spin-drier (Brit), dryer; ~schrank m linen cupboard; ~ständer m clothes-horse; ~stärke f starch; ~trockner m (Ständer) clothes-horse; (Trockenautomat) drier.

Wasch-: ~gang m stage of the washing programme (Brit) or program (US); ~gelegenheit f washing facilities pl; ~haus nt wash-house, laundry; ~kessel m (wash-)boiler; ~küche f washroom; ~lappen m flannel (Brit), washcloth (US); (col: Feigling) softy (col); ~lauge f suds pl; ~maschine f washing-machine; **w~maschinenfest** adj machine-washable; ~mittel nt detergent; ~pulver nt washing-powder (Brit), soap powder; ~salon m launderette (Brit), laundromat (US); ~schüssel f wash-basin (Brit), washbowl (US); ~wasser nt washing water; ~zettel m (Typ) blurb; ~zeug nt toilet or washing things pl; ~zuber m wash-tub.

Wasser nt - **(a)** no pl water. **das ist** ~ **auf seine Mühle** (fig) this is all grist to his mill; **dort wird auch nur mit** ~ **gekocht** (fig) they're no different from anybody else (there); **ihr kann er nicht das** ~ **reichen** (fig) he can't hold a candle to her; **unter** ~ **stehen** to be flooded; **ins** ~ **fallen** (fig) to fall through; **sich über** ~ **halten** (fig) to keep one's head above water; **mit allen** ~**n gewaschen sein** (col) to be a shrewd customer; **ein Boot zu** ~ **lassen** to launch a boat; **nahe am** ~ **gebaut haben** (col) to be a cry-baby (col); ~ **lassen** (euph) to pass water. **(b)** pl **÷** (Flüssigkeit) (Abwasch~ etc) water; (medizinisch) lotion; (Parfüm) cologne; (Mineral~) mineral water. **das** ~ **läuft mir im Mund zusammen** my mouth is watering.

Wasser-: **w~abstoßend** adj water-repellent; **w~arm** adj arid; ~ball m **(a)** (no pl: Spiel) water polo; **(b)** (Ball) beach-ball; (fürs ~ballspiel) water-polo ball; ~bett nt water-bed.

Wässerchen nt er sieht aus, als ob er kein ~ trüben könnte he looks as if butter wouldn't melt in his mouth.

Wasser-: ~dampf m steam; **w~dicht** adj (lit, fig) watertight; Uhr, Stoff etc waterproof; ~enthärter m water-softener; ~fahrzeug nt water-craft; ~fall m waterfall; ~farbe f watercolour (Brit), watercolor (US); **w~fest** adj waterproof; ~floh m water-flea; ~flugzeug nt seaplane; **w~gekühlt** adj water-cooled; ~glas nt (Trinkglas) tumbler; ~glätte f aquaplaning; ~graben m (Sport) water-jump; (um Burg) moat; ~hahn m tap, faucet (US); ~härte f hardness of water.

wässerig adj (lit, fig) watery. **jdm den Mund** ~ **machen** (col) to make sb's mouth water.

Wasser-: ~kessel m kettle; (Tech) boiler; ~klosett nt water-closet; ~kraft f water-power; ~kraftwerk nt hydroelectric power station; ~kreislauf m water cycle; ~kühlung f water-cooling; **mit** ~**kühlung** water-cooled; ~lassen nt passing water; ~lauf m watercourse; ~leiche f drowned body; ~leitung f (Rohr) water pipe; (Anlagen) plumbing no pl; ~lilie f water-lily; **w~löslich** adj water-soluble; ~mann m, pl ~männer (Astrol) Aquarius no art; ~melone f water-melon; ~mühle f water-mill.

wassern vi (Aviat) to land on water.

wässern vti to water; Erbsen etc to soak. **mir** ~ **die Augen** my eyes are watering.

Wasser-: ~pfeife f hookah; ~pflanze f aquatic plant; ~pistole f water-pistol; ~rad nt waterwheel; ~ratte f water-rat or -vole; (col: Schwimmer) water-baby; **w~reich** adj Gebiet abounding in water; Fluß containing a lot of water; ~rohr nt water-pipe; ~scheide f watershed; **w~scheu** adj scared of water; ~schildkröte f turtle; ~schutz polizei f (auf Flüssen, ~wegen) river police; (im Hafen) harbour (Brit) or harbor (US) police; (auf der See) coastguard service; ~ski nt water-skiing; ~spiegel m (Oberfläche f) surface of the water; (~stand) water-level; ~sport m der ~sport water sports pl; ~spülung f flush; ~stand m water-level; **niedriger/hoher** ~stand low/high water.

Wasserstoff m hydrogen.

Wasserstoffbombe f H-bomb.

Wasser-: ~**straße** f waterway; ~**sucht** f dropsy; ~**tank** m water-tank; ~**tier** nt aquatic animal; ~**träger** m water-carrier; ~**treten** nt (Med) paddling (in cold water as therapy); ~**tropfen** m drop of water; ~**turm** m water-tower; ~**uhr** f watermeter; ~**verbrauch** m water consumption no def art; ~**versorgung** f water-supply; ~**vogel** m waterfowl; ~**waage** f spirit-level; ~**weg** m waterway; **auf dem** ~**weg** by water or (Meer) sea; ~**werfer** m water-cannon; ~**werk** nt waterworks sing or pl; ~**wirtschaft** f water-supply (and distribution); ~**zähler** m water-meter; ~**zeichen** nt watermark.

wäßrig adj = **wässerig**.

waten vi aux sein to wade.

watscheln vi aux sein to waddle.

Watt[1] nt - (Elec) watt.

Watt[2] nt -en (Geog) mud-flats pl.

Watte f -n cotton wool (Brit), absorbent cotton (US); (zur Polsterung) wadding.

Wattebausch m cotton ball.

Wattenmeer nt mud-flats pl.

Wattestäbchen nt cotton swab.

wattieren* vt to pad; (füttern) to line with padding; (und absteppen) Stoff to quilt.

Wattzahl f wattage.

WC [veːˈtseː] nt -s WC.

weben pret **webte** or (liter, fig) **wob**, ptp **gewebt** or (liter, fig) **gewoben** vti (lit, fig) to weave; Spinnennetz to spin.

Weber(in f) m - weaver.

Weberei f (a) (Betrieb) weaving mill. (b) (Zeug) woven article.

Web-: ~**stuhl** m loom; ~**waren** pl woven goods pl.

Wechsel [ˈvɛksl] m - (a) change; (abwechselnd) alternation; (Geld~) exchange. (b) (Staffel~) change-over; (Ftbl etc) substitution. (c) (Fin) bill (of exchange).

Wechsel- [ˈvɛksl-]: ~**bäder** pl (lit) alternating hot and cold baths pl; ~**beziehung** f correlation, interrelation; ~**fälle** pl vicissitudes pl; ~**geld** nt change; **w**~**haft** adj changeable; ~**jahre** pl menopause sing; **in die** ~**jahre kommen** to start the menopause; ~**kurs** m exchange rate.

wechseln [ˈvɛksln] **1** vt to change (in +acc into); (austauschen) to exchange. **die Schule/das Hemd** ~ to change schools/one's shirt; **die Farbe** ~ to change colour; **Briefe** ~ to correspond (mit with); **können Sie (mir) 10 Mark** ~? can you change 10 marks (for me)? **2** vi (a) to change; (einander ablösen) to alternate. **ich kann leider nicht** ~ I'm sorry, I don't have any change. (b) **über die Straße** ~ to cross the road.

wechselnd [ˈvɛkslnt] adj changing; (einander ablösend) alternating; Stimmungen changeable; Winde, Bewölkung variable. **mit** ~**em Erfolg** with varying (degrees of) success.

Wechsel [ˈvɛksl-]: ~**rahmen** m clip-on picture frame; **w**~**seitig** adj reciprocal; ~**strom** m alternating current, A.C.; ~**stube** f currency exchange, bureau de change; **w**~**voll** adj varied; ~**wirkung** f interaction.

Wechsler [ˈvɛkslɐ] m - (Automat) change dispenser.

wecken vt to wake (up); (fig) to arouse; Bedarf to create; Erinnerungen to revive.

Wecker m - alarm clock. **jdm auf den** ~ **fallen** (col) to get on sb's nerves.

Weck-: ~**glas** ® nt preserving jar; ~**radio** nt radio-alarm clock; ~**ruf** m (Telec) alarm call.

Wedel m - (Staub~) feather duster.

wedeln vi (mit dem Schwanz) ~ to wag its tail; **mit etw** ~ (winken) to wave sth.

weder conj ~ ... **noch** ... neither ... nor ...

weg adv away. ~ **sein** to have or be gone; (nicht hier, entfernt) to be away; (col: eingeschlafen) to be out like a light (col); (col: begeistert) to be taken

(von with); (über etw (acc)) ~ **sein** (emotional) to have got over sth; **über den Tisch** ~ across the table; **nichts wie** or **nur** ~ **von hier!** let's get out of here; ~ **da!** (get) out of the way!; ~ **damit!** (mit Schere etc) put it away!; **Hände** ~! hands off!; **in einem** ~ (col) non-stop.

Weg m -e (a) (Pfad, fig) path. **am** ~**e** by the wayside; **jdm den** ~ **versperren** to block sb's way; **jdm/einer Sache im** ~ **stehen** (fig) to stand in the way of sb/sth; **jdm Steine in den** ~ **legen** (fig) to put obstructions in sb's way; **jdm nicht über den** ~ **trauen** (fig) not to trust sb an inch; **etw aus dem** ~ **räumen** (fig) to get sth out of the way; **den** ~ **des geringsten Widerstandes gehen** to follow the line of least resistance.

(b) (lit, fig: Route) way; (Entfernung) distance; (Reise) journey; (zu Fuß) walk. **ich muß diesen** ~ **jeden Tag zweimal gehen** I have to walk this stretch twice a day; **den richtigen** ~ **einschlagen** (lit) to follow the right road; **jdm einen guten Rat mit auf den** ~ **geben** to give sb good advice to follow in life; **jdm/einer Sache aus dem** ~ **gehen** (lit) to get out of sb's way/the way of sth; **jdm über den** ~ **laufen** (fig) to run into sb; **etw in die** ~**e leiten** to arrange sth; **auf dem besten** ~ **sein**, **etw zu tun** to be well on the way to doing sth.

(c) (Mittel, Art und Weise) way. **auf diesem** ~**e** this way; **auf diplomatischem** ~**e** through diplomatic channels; **auf legalem** ~**e** legally.

wegbekommen* vt sep irreg to get rid of (von from); Fleck to get off; (von bestimmtem Ort) jdn to get away (von from).

Weg-: ~**bereiter** m precursor, forerunner; ~**bereiter einer Sache** (gen) or **für etw sein** to pave the way for sth; ~**biegung** f turn, bend.

weg-: ~**blasen** vt sep irreg to blow away; **wie** ~**geblasen sein** (fig) to have vanished; ~**bleiben** vi sep irreg aux sein to stay away; **mir bleibt die Spucke** ~! (col) I'm absolutely flabbergasted!; ~**bringen** vt sep irreg to take away; (zur Reparatur) to take in; ~**denken** vt sep irreg: **das Auto ist aus unserem Leben nicht mehr** ~**zudenken** life today without the car is something that cannot be imagined; ~**dürfen** vi sep irreg to be allowed to leave; (col: ausgehen dürfen) to be allowed to go out.

Wegelagerer m - highwayman; (zu Fuß) footpad.

wegen prep +gen because of. **von** ~! (col) you must be joking!

Wegerich m -e (Bot) plantain.

wegfahren vi sep irreg aux sein (abfahren) to leave; (Auto, Fahrer) to drive off; (im Boot) to sail away; (zum Einkaufen, als Ausflug) to go out; (verreisen) to go away.

wegfallen vi sep irreg aux sein to be discontinued; (Bestimmung) to cease to apply; (unterbleiben) to be lost; (überflüssig werden) to become unnecessary; (ausgelassen werden) to be omitted. ~ **lassen** to discontinue; (auslassen) to omit.

weg-: ~**fegen** vt sep (lit, fig) to sweep away; ~**fliegen** vi sep irreg aux sein to fly away; (Hut) to fly off; (mit Flugzeug) to leave; ~**führen** vt sep to lead away.

Weggabelung f fork (in the road).

weggeben vt sep irreg (verschenken) to give away. **seine Wäsche (zum Waschen)** ~ to have one's washing done.

weggehen vi sep irreg aux sein to go, to leave; (verreisen, umziehen etc) to go away; (ausgehen) to go out; (col: Fleck) to come off; (col: Ware) to sell.

weggucken vi sep to look away.

weghaben vt sep irreg (col) (erledigt haben) to have got done; (bekommen, verstanden haben) to have got. **du hast deinen Denkzettel weg** you have had your punishment; **einen** ~ (col: verrückt sein) to have a screw loose (col).

weg-: ~**helfen** vi sep irreg **jdm von irgendwo** ~**helfen** to help sb get away from a place;

~**holen** *vt sep* to take away; *(abholen)* to fetch; ~**hören** *vi sep* not to listen; ~**jagen** *vt sep* to chase away.

wegkommen *vi sep irreg aux sein (col)* **(a)** *(abhanden kommen)* to disappear; *(weggehen können)* to get away; *(aus dem Haus)* to get out. **mach, daß du wegkommst!** hop it! *(col)*; **gut/schlecht (bei etw)** ~ to come off well/badly (with sth). **(b)** = **hinwegkommen**.

Weg-: ~**kreuzung** *f* crossroads; ~**krümmung** *f* bend in the road.

weg-: ~**lassen** *vt sep irreg (auslassen)* to leave out; *(col: gehen lassen)* to let go; ~**laufen** *vi sep irreg aux sein* to run away *(vor +dat* from*);* **das läuft (dir) nicht** ~! *(fig hum)* that can wait; ~**legen** *vt sep* to put away; *(zum späteren Verbrauch)* to put aside.

wegmachen *vt sep (col)* to get rid of.

wegmüssen *vi sep irreg* to have to go; *(entfernt werden)* to have to be removed. **ich muß eine Zeitlang aus New York weg** I must get out of New York for a while.

wegnehmen *vt sep irreg* to take; *(fortnehmen, entziehen)* to take away; *Platz* to take up. **Gas** ~ *(Aut)* to ease off the accelerator *or* gas *(US);* **jdm die Frau** ~ to steal sb's wife.

weg-: ~**packen** *vt sep* to pack away; ~**putzen** *vt sep* to wipe away; *(col: essen)* to polish off.

Wegrand *m* wayside.

weg-: ~**räumen** *vt sep* to clear away; *(in Schrank)* to put away; ~**reißen** *vt sep irreg* to tear away *(jdm* from sb*);* ~**rennen** *vi sep irreg aux sein (col)* to run away; ~**rücken** *vti sep (vi: aux sein)* to move away; ~**rufen** *vt sep irreg* to call away; ~**rutschen** *vi sep aux sein (aus der Hand etc)* to slip away; *(auf Eis etc)* to slide away; ~**schaffen** *vt sep (beseitigen)* to get rid of; *(~räumen)* to clear away; *(~tragen)* to remove; ~**schicken** *vt sep Brief, jdn* to send away; *(um etwas zu holen etc)* to send off; ~**schleichen** *vir sep irreg (vi: aux sein)* to creep *or* steal away; ~**schleppen** *vt sep* to drag away *or* off; *(tragen)* to carry off; ~**schließen** *vt sep irreg* to lock away; ~**schmeißen** *vt sep irreg (col)* to chuck away *(col);* ~**schnappen** *vt sep (col)* **jdm etw** ~**schnappen** to snatch sth (away) from sb; **jdm die Freundin** ~**schnappen** to pinch sb's girl-friend *(col);* ~**schütten** *vt sep* to tip away; ~**schwemmen** *vt sep* to wash away; ~**sehen** *vi sep irreg* to look away; ~**setzen** *vt sep* to move (away); *(wegstellen)* to put away; ~**sollen** *vi sep irreg (col)* **das soll** ~ that is to go; **ich soll von London** ~ I am (supposed) to leave London; ~**spülen** *vt sep* to wash away; ~**stecken** *vt sep* to put away; *(col: einkraften)* to cope with; ~**stehlen** *vr sep irreg* to steal away; ~**stellen** *vt sep* to put away; ~**sterben** *vi sep irreg aux sein (col)* to die off; ~**stoßen** *vt sep irreg* to push away; *(mit Fuß)* to kick away; ~**tragen** *vt sep irreg* to carry away; ~**treiben** *sep irreg* **1** *vt Tier etc* to drive away; **2** *vi aux sein* to drift away; ~**treten** *vi sep irreg aux sein (Mil)* to fall out; ~**treten!** dismiss!; **geistig** ~**getreten sein** *(col: geistesabwesend)* to be away with the fairies *(col);* ~**tun** *vt sep irreg* to put away; ~**wehen** *vti sep (vi: aux sein)* to blow away.

Weg-: **w**~**weisend** *adj* pioneering *attr*, revolutionary; ~**weiser** *m* - sign; *(an einem Pfosten)* signpost; *(fig: Buch etc)* guide.

Wegwerf- *in cpds* disposable.

weg-: ~**werfen** *vt sep irreg* to throw away; **das ist** ~**geworfenes Geld** that's throwing money away; ~**werfend** *adj* disdainful; ~**wischen** *vt sep* to wipe off; ~**wollen** *vi sep irreg (verreisen)* to want to go away; *(~gehen: von Party etc)* to want to leave; *(hinausgehen)* to want to go out; ~**zaubern** *vt sep* to make disappear; ~**ziehen** *sep irreg* **1** *vt* to pull away *(jdm* from sb*);* **2** *vi aux sein* to move away.

weh *adj (wund)* sore. ~ **tun** *(lit, fig)* to hurt; **mir tut**

der Rücken ~ my back hurts; **sich/jdm** ~ **tun** *(lit, fig)* to hurt oneself/sb.

wehe *interj* ~ **(dir), wenn du das tust** you'll regret it if you do that; **darf ich das anfassen?** — ~ **(dir)!** I can I touch? — you dare!

Wehe *f* -**n (a)** *(Schnee*~ *etc)* drift. **(b)** *(Geburts*~*)* ~**n** *pl (lit)* contractions; **in den** ~**n liegen** to be in labour *(Brit)* or labor *(US).*

wehen 1 *vi (Wind)* to blow; *(Fahne)* to flutter; *(Haare)* to blow about. **2** *vt* to blow *(von* off*);* *(sanft)* to waft.

Weh-: **w**~**leidig** *adj* oversensitive to pain; *(jammernd)* whining *attr*; *(voller Selbstmitleid)* self-pitying; **sei nicht so w**~**leidig!** stop feeling sorry for yourself; ~**mut** *f no pl (geh)* melancholy; *(Sehnsucht)* wistfulness; **w**~**mütig** *adj siehe n* melancholy; wistful.

Wehr[1] *f* -**en (a)** *(Feuer*~*)* fire brigade *(Brit)* or department *(US).* **(b) sich zur** ~**setzen** to defend oneself.

Wehr[2] *nt* -**e** weir.

Wehr- *in cpds* defence *(Brit)*, defense *(US);* ~**dienst** *m* military service; **jdn zum** ~**dienst einberufen** to call sb up, to draft sb *(US);* ~**dienstverweigerer** *m* conscientious objector.

wehren 1 *vr* to defend oneself; *(aktiv kämpfen)* to (put up a) fight. **2** *vi +dat (geh)* **wehret den Anfängen!** these things must be nipped in the bud.

Wehr-: ~**etat** *m* defence *(Brit)* or defense *(US)* budget; **w**~**fähig** *adj* fit for military service; **w**~**haft** *adj (geh)* able to put up a fight; *Stadt etc* well-fortified; **w**~**los** *adj* defenceless *(Brit),* defenseless *(US);* *(fig: hilflos)* helpless; **jdm w**~**los ausgeliefert sein** to be at sb's mercy; ~**pflicht** *f* *(allgemeine)* ~**pflicht** (universal) conscription; **w**~**pflichtig** *adj* liable for military service; ~**pflichtige(r)** *mf decl as adj* person liable for military service; ~**sold** *m* (military) pay; ~**übung** *f* reserve duty training exercise.

Wehwehchen *nt (col)* (minor) complaint.

Weib *nt* -**er** woman, female *(pej)*, broad *(US col).*

Weibchen *nt* little woman; *(Zool)* female.

Weiber-: ~**feind** *m* woman-hater, misogynist; ~**geschichten** *pl* sexploits *pl (hum);* ~**geschwätz** *nt (pej)* women's talk; ~**held** *m (pej)* womanizer.

weibisch *adj* effeminate.

weiblich *adj* female; *(Gram, fraulich)* feminine.

Weiblichkeit *f* femininity; *(Frauen)* women.

weich *adj* soft *(auch fig*, Ling, Phot*);* Ei soft-boiled; *Fleisch, Gemüse* tender. ~ **werden** *(lit, fig)* to soften; **die Knie wurden mir** ~ my knees turned to jelly; ~ **machen** to soften.

Weiche[1] *f* -**n** *(Seite)* side; *(von Tier auch)* flank.

Weiche[2] *f* -**n** *(Rail)* points *pl (Brit),* switch *(US).* **die** ~**n stellen** *(lit)* to switch the points; *(fig)* to set the course.

weichen[1] *vti (vi: aux haben or sein) (ein*~*)* to soak.

weichen[2] *pret* **wich**, *ptp* **gewichen** *vi aux sein (a)* to give way *(dat* to*);* *(zurück*~*)* to retreat *(dat, vor* +*dat* from*);* **(nicht) von jdm** *or* **jds Seite** ~ (not) to leave sb's side. **(b)** *(Schmerz)* to go.

Weich-: **w**~**gekocht** *adj attr* Ei soft-boiled; *Fleisch, Gemüse* boiled until tender; **w**~**herzig** *adj* soft-hearted; ~**käse** *m* soft cheese.

weichlich *adj (lit, fig)* soft; *Charakter* weak.

Weichling *m (pej)* softy *(col).*

Weich-: **w**~**machen** *vt sep (fig)* to soften up; ~**macher** *m (Chem)* softener; **w**~**spülen** *vt sep* to condition; *Wäsche* to use softener on; ~**spüler** *m* conditioner; ~**teile** *pl* soft parts *pl;* ~**tier** *nt* mollusc.

Weide[1] *f* -**n** *(Bot)* willow.

Weide[2] *f* -**n** *(Agr)* pasture; *(Wiese)* meadow. **auf der** ~ sein to be grazing.

weiden 1 *vi* to graze. **2** *vt* to (put out to) graze. **3** *vr* **sich an etw** *(dat)* ~ *(fig)* to gloat over sth.

Weiden-: ~**baum** *m* willow tree; ~**busch** *m* willow bush; ~**kätzchen** nt willow catkin; ~**korb** m wicker basket; ~**rost** m cattle grid.

Weideplatz m pasture.

weidlich adv (mit adj) pretty. **etw** ~ **ausnutzen** to make full use of sth.

Weid-: ~**mann** m, pl ~**männer** (liter) huntsman, hunter; **w**~**männisch 1** adj huntsman's attr; **das ist nicht w**~**männisch** that's not done in hunting; **2** adv like a professional hunter.

weigern vr to refuse.

Weigerung f refusal.

Weihe f **-n** (Eccl) consecration; (Priester~) ordination.

weihen vt **(a)** (Eccl) to consecrate. **jdn zum Bischof/Priester** ~ to consecrate sb bishop/ordain sb priest. **(b)** (widmen) **etw jdm/einer Sache** ~ to dedicate sth to sb/sth; **dem Untergang geweiht** (liter) doomed.

Weiher m - pond.

Weihnachten nt - Christmas. **fröhliche** ~! happy or merry Christmas!; **(an)** ~ **at** Christmas; ~ **nach Hause fahren** to go home for Christmas; **etw zu** ~ **bekommen/schenken** to get sth for Christmas/to give sth as a Christmas present; **weiße/grüne** ~ **(a)** white Christmas/(a) Christmas without snow.

weihnachten vi impers (poet, iro) **es weihnachtet sehr** Christmas is very much in evidence.

weihnachtlich adj Christmassy (col).

Weihnachts- in cpds Christmas; ~**baum** m Christmas tree; ~**einkauf** m Christmas shopping no pl; ~**feier** f Christmas celebration(s pl); ~**(feier)tag** m (erster) Christmas Day; (zweiter) Boxing Day (Brit); ~**fest** nt Christmas; ~**gans** f Christmas goose; **jdn ausnehmen wie eine** ~**gans** (col) to fleece sb (col), to take sb to the cleaners (col); ~**geld** nt Christmas bonus; ~**geschenk** nt Christmas present; ~**karte** f Christmas card; ~**lied** nt carol; ~**mann** m, pl ~**männer** Father Christmas, Santa Claus; (pej col) clown (pej col); ~**markt** m Christmas fair; ~**zeit** f Christmas time.

Weih-: ~**rauch** m incense; ~**wasser** nt holy water.

weil conj because.

Weilchen nt **ein** ~ a while.

Weile f no pl while. **eine** ~ for a while.

Weiler m - hamlet.

Weimarer Republik f Weimar Republic.

Wein m -e wine. **jdm reinen** ~ **einschenken** to tell sb the truth.

Wein- in cpds (auf Getränk bezogen) wine; (auf Pflanze bezogen) vine; ~**bau** m wine-growing; ~**bauer** m wine-grower; ~**berg** m vineyard; ~**bergschnecke** f snail; ~**brand** m brandy; ~**brennerei** f brandy distillery.

weinen vti to cry; (aus Trauer auch) to weep (um for, über +acc over). **sich** (dat) **die Augen rot** ~ to cry one's eyes out; **es ist zum W**~! it's enough to make you weep!

weinerlich adj whining, whiny (col).

Wein-: ~**ernte** f grape harvest; ~**essig** m wine vinegar; ~**faß** nt wine cask; ~**garten** m vineyard; ~**gegend** f wine-growing area; ~**geist** m (ethyl)alcohol; ~**gut** nt wine-growing estate; ~**händler** m wine dealer; ~**handlung** f wine shop (Brit) or store; ~**karte** f wine list; ~**keller** m wine-cellar; (Lokal) wine bar; ~**kelter** f wine press; ~**kenner** m wine connoisseur.

Weinkrampf m crying fit.

Wein-: ~**küfer** m cellarman; ~**land** nt wine-growing country; ~**laub** nt vine leaves pl; ~**lese** f grape harvest; ~**lokal** nt wine bar; ~**panscherei** f wine-adulterating; ~**probe** f wine-tasting; ~**rebe** f vine; **w**~**rot** adj wine-red; ~**säure** f (Chem) tartaric acid; **w**~**selig** adj merry with wine; ~**stock** m vine; ~**traube** f grape.

weise adj wise.

Weise f **-n (a)** (Verfahren etc) manner. **auf diese** ~ in this way; **auf geheimnisvolle** etc ~ in a mysterious way; **in gewisser/keiner** ~ in a/no way; **in der** ~, **daß** ... in such a way that ... **(b)** (liter: Melodie) melody.

weisen pret **wies**, ptp **gewiesen** (geh) **1** vt **jdm etw** ~ (lit, fig) to show sb sth; **jdn aus dem Lande** ~ to expel sb; **jdn vom Platz** ~ (Sport) to order sb off (the field); **jdn von der Schule** ~ to expel sb (from school); **etw (weit) von sich** ~ (fig) to reject sth (emphatically). **2** vi to point (nach to(wards), auf+acc at).

Weise(r) m decl as adj wise man.

Weisheit f (a) no pl wisdom. **das ist auch nicht der** ~ **letzter Schluß** that's not exactly the ideal solution; **er hat die** ~ **nicht mit Löffeln gefressen** he's not so bright. **(b)** (weiser Spruch) wise saying; (iro) pearl of wisdom.

Weisheitszahn m wisdom tooth.

weismachen vt sep **er wollte uns** ~, **daß** ... he would have us believe that ...; **das kannst du mir nicht** ~! you can't expect me to believe that.

weiß adj white. **ein** ~**es** (Blatt) **Papier** a blank sheet of paper; **ein** ~**er Fleck auf der Landkarte**) a blank area (on the map); **das W**~**e Haus** the White House; **das W**~**e im Auge** the whites of one's eyes; **das W**~**e vom Ei** the white of an egg.

Weiß nt - white.

weissagen vt insep to foretell.

Weiß-: ~**blech** nt tinplate; **w**~**blond** adj ashblond(e); ~**brot** nt white bread; (Laib) white loaf; ~**buch** nt (Pol) white paper.

weißen vt to whiten; (tünchen) to whitewash.

Weiße(r) mf decl as adj white, white man/woman.

Weiß-: ~**glut** f **jdn zur** ~**glut bringen** to make sb see red; **w**~**haarig** adj white-haired; ~**herbst** m ≈ rosé; ~**kohl** m white cabbage; **w**~**lich** adj whitish; ~**metall** nt white metal; ~**wal** m white whale; ~**waren** pl linen sing; ~**wein** m white wine; ~**wurst** f veal sausage.

Weisung f directive; (Jur) ruling. **auf** ~ on instructions.

weit siehe auch **weiter 1** adv **(a)** far. **es ist noch** ~ **bis Bremen** there's still a long way to go till Bremen; ~ **zurückliegen** to be far behind; (zeitlich) to be a long time ago; ~ **nach Mitternacht** well after midnight; ~ **und breit** for miles around; **ziemlich** ~ **am Ende** fairly near the end; **von** ~**em** from a long way off; ~ **entfernt** a long way away; ~**er entfernt** farther away; **ich bin** ~ **davon entfernt, das zu tun** I have no intention of doing that; ~ **gefehlt!** far from it; ~ **offen** wide open; ~ **herumkommen** to get around a lot; ~ **verbreitet** widespread.

(b) (in Entwicklung) ~ **fortgeschritten** well advanced; **wie** ~ **bist du?** how far have you got?; **er hat es** ~ **gebracht** he has come a long way; **es so** ~ **bringen, daß** ... to bring it about that ...

(c) (fig: erheblich) (mit adj, adv) far; (mit vb) by far. ~ **besser** far better; **bei** ~**em nicht so gut** etc (wie...) not nearly as good etc (as ...); ~ **über 60** well over 60.

(d) **das ist nicht** ~ **her** (col) that's not up to much (col); **das würde zu** ~ **führen** that would be taking things too far; **zu** ~ **gehen** to go too far; **das geht zu** ~ that's going too far; **etw zu** ~ **treiben** to carry sth too far.

2 adj **(a)** wide; (fig) Begriff, Horizont etc broad; Meer open; Herz big. **im** ~**eren Sinne** in the broader or wider sense; **das ist ein** ~**es Feld** (fig) that is a big subject. **(b)** (lang) Reise, Wurf etc long. **in** ~**en Abständen** at long intervals; **man hat hier einen** ~**en Blick** you can see a long way from here; **in** ~**er Ferne** in the far distance; **das liegt in** ~**er Ferne** it's still a long way away.

Weit-: **w**~**ab** adv **w**~**ab von** far (away) from; **w**~**aus** adv far; **w**~**aus besser** far better; **w**~**ausholend** adj Geste etc expansive; (fig)

Erzählung etc long-drawn-out; ~**blick** *m (fig)* far-sightedness; **w**~**blickend** *adj (fig)* far-sighted.
Weite *f* **-n** *(Ferne)* distance; *(Länge)* length; *(Größe)* expanse; *(Durchmesser)* width. **etw in der** ~ **ändern** to alter the width of sth.
weiten *vtr* to widen; *(Pupille)* to dilate.
weiter **1** *adj* further; *(andere)* other. **2** *adv (noch hinzu)* further; *(außerdem)* furthermore; *(sonst)* otherwise; *(nachher)* afterwards. **nichts** ~ *(darüber hinaus nichts)* nothing further; ~ **nichts?** is that all?; ~ **nichts als …** nothing but …; **ich brauche** ~ **nichts** that's all I need; **wenn es** ~ **nichts ist, …** well, if that's all (it is), …; **außer uns war** ~ **niemand da** there was nobody else there besides us; **das hat** ~ **nichts zu sagen** that doesn't really matter; **etw** ~ **tun** to continue to do sth; **immer** ~ on and on; *(Anweisung)* keep on (going); **was geschah (dann)** ~**?** what happened then?
weiter-: ~**arbeiten** *vi sep* to work on; **an einer Sache** *(dat)* ~**arbeiten** to do some more work on sth; ~**bewegen*** *vtr sep* to move further; ~**bilden** *vr sep* to continue one's education; ~**bringen** *vt sep irreg* to take further; **das bringt uns auch nicht** ~ that doesn't get us any further; ~**denken** *vi sep irreg* to think it out; *(an Zukünftiges)* to think ahead; ~**empfehlen*** *vt sep irreg* to recommend (to one's friends *etc*); ~**erzählen*** *vt sep Geheimnis etc* to pass on.
Weitere(s) *nt decl as adj* further details *pl.* **das** ~ the rest; **alles** ~ all the rest; **bis auf w**~**s** for the time being.
Weiter-: **w**~**fahren** *vi sep irreg aux sein (Fahrt fortsetzen)* to travel on; **w**~**fliegen** *vi sep irreg aux sein* to fly on; **die Maschine fliegt in 10 Minuten w**~ the plane will take off again in 10 minutes; **w**~**führen** *vti sep* to continue; **das führt nicht w**~ *(fig)* that doesn't get us anywhere; **w**~**führend** *adj Schule* secondary; **w**~**geben** *vt sep irreg* to pass on; **w**~**gehen** *vi sep irreg aux sein* to go on; **so kann es nicht w**~**gehen** *(fig)* things can't go on like this; **wie soll es nun w**~**gehen?** what's going to happen now?; **w**~**helfen** *vi sep irreg* to help (along) *(jdm sb)*; **w**~**kommen** *vi sep irreg aux sein* to advance; **nicht w**~**kommen** *(fig)* to be stuck down; **w**~**können** *vi sep irreg* to be able to carry on; **ich kann nicht w**~ I can't go on; **w**~**laufen** *vi sep irreg aux sein* to run/walk on; *(Film, Produktion)* to go on; *(Gehalt)* to continue to be paid; **w**~**leben** *vi sep* to live on; **w**~**leiten** *vt sep* to pass on *(an +acc to)*; *(senden)* to forward; **w**~**machen** *vti sep* to carry on *(etw* with sth*)*; **w**~**reichen** *vt sep* to pass on; ~**reise** *f* continuation of the/one's journey; **auf der** ~**reise nach …** when I *etc* was travelling *(Brit)* or traveling *(US)* on to …; **w**~**sagen** *vt sep* to pass on; **nicht w**~**sagen!** don't tell anyone!; **w**~**senden** *vt sep irreg* to forward; **w**~**verarbeiten*** *vt sep* to process; **w**~**verfolgen*** *vt sep Idee* to follow up; ~**verkauf** *m* resale; **w**~**verkaufen*** *vti sep* to resell; **w**~**vermieten*** *vt sep* to sublet; **w**~**wissen** *vi sep irreg* **nicht (mehr) w**~**wissen** *(verzweifelt sein)* to be at one's wits' end; **w**~**wollen** *vi sep irreg* to want to go on; **w**~**wursteln** *vi sep (col)* to muddle on.
Weit-: **w**~**gehend** **1** *adj Vollmachten etc* far-reaching, extensive; *Übereinstimmung etc* a large degree of; **2** *adv* to a large extent; **w**~**gereist** *adj attr* widely travelled *(Brit)* or traveled *(US)*; **w**~**her** *adv (auch von w*~**her)** from far away; **w**~**hergeholt** *adj* far-fetched; **w**~**herzig** *adj* charitable; **w**~**hin** *adv* widely; *(weitgehend)* to a large extent; **w**~**hin unbekannt** largely unknown; **w**~**läufig** *adj (a) Park, Gebäude* spacious; *Dorf* sprawling *attr*; *(fig) Erzählung* long-drawn-out; **(b)** *Verwandte* distant; **w**~**maschig** *adj Netz* wide-meshed; **w**~**reichend** *adj (fig)* far-reaching; **w**~**schweifig** *adj* long-winded; ~**sicht** *f (fig)* far-sightedness; **w**~**sich-**

tig *adj (lit, fig)* far-sighted; ~**sichtigkeit** *f* far-sightedness; ~**sprung** *m (Sport)* the long jump *cr* broad jump *(US)*; **w**~**verbreitet** *adj attr* widespread; *Zeitung* with a wide circulation; **w**~**verzweigt** *adj attr Straßensystem* extensive.
Weizen *m no pl* wheat.
Weizen-: ~**brot** *nt* wheat bread; ~**keime** *pl (Cook)* wheatgerm *sing*; ~**mehl** *nt* wheat flour; ~**schrot** *m or nt* wheatmeal.
welch *interrog pron inv (geh)* **(a)** ~ **friedliches Bild!** what a peaceful scene! **(b)** *(in indirekten Fragesätzen)* ~ **ein(e)** what.
welche(r, s) **1** *interrog pron* **(a)** *(adjektivisch)* what; *(bei Auswahl)* which. ~**r Mensch könnte behaupten …?** what person could claim …?; ~ **Kleid soll ich anziehen?** which dress shall I wear? **(b)** *(substantivisch)* which (one). ~**r von den beiden?** which (one) of the two?; ~**s sind die Symptome dieser Krankheit?** what are the symptoms of this illness? **(c)** *(in Ausrufen)* ~ **Freude!** what joy! **2** *indef pron* some; *(in Fragen)* any. **ich habe keine Äpfel, haben Sie** ~? I don't have any apples, do you have any? **3** *rel pron (Mensch)* who; *(Sache)* which, that. ~**(r, s) auch immer** whoever/whichever/whatever.
welcher|art *interrog adj inv (geh) (attributiv)* what kind of; *(substantivisch)* of what kind.
welk *adj Pflanze* wilted, faded; *Blatt* dead; *Gesicht* tired-looking.
welken *vi aux sein (lit, fig)* to fade, to wilt.
Wellblech *nt* corrugated iron.
Welle *f* **-n (a)** wave; *(Rad: Frequenz)* wavelength. **weiche** ~ *(col)* soft line; *(hohe)* ~**n schlagen** *(fig)* to create (quite) a stir. **(b)** *(Tech)* shaft.
wellen *vt* to wave. **gewelltes Haar** wavy hair.
Wellen-: ~**bad** *nt* wave pool; ~**bereich** *m (Phys, Telec)* frequency range; *(Rad)* waveband; ~**brecher** *m* breakwater; **w**~**förmig** **1** *adj* wave-like; *Linie* wavy; **2** *adv* in the form of waves; ~**gang** *m no pl* waves *pl*, swell; **starker** ~**gang** heavy sea(s) or swell; ~**länge** *f (Phys, Telec)* wavelength; **die gleiche** ~**länge haben** *(col)* to be on the same wavelength *(col)*; ~**linie** *f* wavy line; ~**reiten** *nt (Sport)* surfing; ~**sittich** *m* budgerigar, budgie *(col)*.
Wellfleisch *nt* boiled pork.
wellig *adj Haar etc* wavy; *Oberfläche* uneven; *Hügelland* rolling.
Wellpappe *f* corrugated cardboard.
Welpe *m (wk)* **-n, -n** pup, whelp; *(von Wolf etc)* cub.
Wels *m* **-e** catfish.
Welt *f* **-en** *(lit, fig)* world. **die (große) weite** ~ the big wide world; **der höchste Berg der** ~ the highest mountain in the world; **die Alte/Neue/Freie/Dritte** ~ the Old/New/Free/Third World; **die** ~ **der Oper** the world of opera; **eine** ~ **brach für ihn zusammen** his whole world collapsed about him; **das ist doch nicht die** ~ it isn't as important as all that; **deswegen geht die** ~ **nicht unter** *(col)* it isn't the end of the world; **das kostet doch nicht die** ~ it won't cost the earth; **zwischen ihnen liegen** ~**en** they are worlds apart; **auf der** ~ in the world; **aus aller** ~ from all over the world; **aus der** ~ **schaffen** to eliminate; **in aller** ~ all over the world; **warum in aller** ~ …? why on earth …?; **um nichts in der** ~ not for anything on earth; **ein Kind in die** ~ **setzen** to bring a child into the world; **ein Mann/eine Dame von** ~ a man/woman of the world; **vor aller** ~ in front of everybody; **zur** ~ **bringen** to give birth to; **auf die** ~ **kommen** to be born.
Welt- *in cpds* world; ~**all** *nt no pl* universe; **w**~**anschaulich** *adj* ideological; ~**anschauung** *f (Philos, Pol)* world view; ~**ausstellung** *f* world exhibition; ~**bank** *f* World Bank; **w**~**berühmt** *adj* world-famous; **w**~**beste(r, s)** *adj attr* world's best; **w**~**bewegend** *adj* world-shattering; ~**bild** *nt* conception of the world; *(jds Ansichten)* phi-

losophy; ~**bürger** m citizen of the world.
Weltenbummler m globetrotter.
Weltergewicht nt (Boxen) welterweight.
Welt-: w~**fremd** adj unworldly; ~**frieden** m
world peace; ~**geschichte** f world history;
w~**geschichtlich** adj von w~**geschichtlicher**
Bedeutung of great significance in world history; ~**gesundheitsorganisation** f World Health
Organization; ~**handel** m world trade; ~**herrschaft** f world domination; ~**karte** f map of the
world; ~**kirchenrat** m World Council of Church-
es; ~**klasse** f ~**klasse sein** to be world-class;
~**krieg** m world war; **der Erste/Zweite** ~**krieg**
World War One/Two, the First/Second World
War; ~**kugel** f globe; w~**lich** adj worldly; (säku-
lar) secular; ~**literatur** f world literature;
~**macht** f world power; w~**männisch** adj urbane; ~**markt** m world market; ~**meer** nt ocean;
~**meister** m world or world's (US) champion;
~**meisterschaft** f world or world's (US) championship; (Ftbl) World Cup; w~**offen** adj liberal-
minded; ~**ordnung** f world order; ~**politik** f
world politics pl; w~**politisch** adj **die** w~**politische Entwicklung** the development of world
politics; **von** w~**politischer Bedeutung** of
importance in world politics.
Weltraum m (outer) space.
Weltraum- in cpds space; ~**fahrer** m space
traveller (Brit) or traveler (US); ~**forschung** f
space research; ~**station** f space station; ~**waffen** pl space weapons pl.
Welt-: ~**reich** nt empire; ~**reise** f world tour; **eine**
~**reise machen** to go around the world; ~**rekord**
m world record; ~**religion** f world religion;
~**revolution** f world revolution; ~**ruf** m world-
wide reputation; ~**ruhm** m world fame; ~**si-
cherheitsrat** m (Pol) (United Nations) Security
Council; ~**sprache** f world language; ~**stadt** f
cosmopolitan city; w~**städtisch** adj cosmopolitan; ~**umseglung** f circumnavigation of the
globe; ~**untergang** m (lit, fig) end of the
world; ~**verbesserer** m starry-eyed idealist;
w~**weit** adj world-wide; ~**wirtschaft** f world
economy; ~**wirtschaftskrise** f world economic
crisis; ~**wunder** nt **die sieben** ~**wunder** the
Seven Wonders of the World.
wem dat of **wer** interrog pron who ... to, to whom.
mit ~ ... who ... with, with whom; ~ **von euch soll
ich den Schlüssel geben?** which (one) of you
should I give the key to?
wen acc of **wer** 1 interrog pron who, whom. **an** ~
hast du geschrieben? who did you write to?; ~
von den Schülern kennst du? which (one) of
these pupils do you know?
Wende f **-n** turn; (Veränderung) change.
Wendekreis m (**a**) tropic. (**b**) (Aut) turning
circle.
wenden pret **wendete** or **wandte**, ptp
gewendet or **gewandt** 1 vt to turn; (auf die
andere Seite) to turn (over); (Cook) to toss. **bitte**
~**!** please turn over; **wie man es auch wendet** ...
whichever way you look at it ... 2 vr to turn
(around); (Wetter, Glück) to change. **sich nach
links** ~ to turn to the left; **sich zu jdm/etw** ~ to
turn towards sb/sth; **sich zum Besseren/Schlim-
meren** ~ to take a turn for the better/worse; **sich
an jdn** ~ (um Auskunft) to consult sb; (um Hilfe) to
turn to sb; (Buch etc) to be directed at sb; **sich
gegen jdn/etw** ~ to come out against sb/sth. 3 vi
to turn (auch Sport); (umkehren) to turn around.
Wende-: ~**platz** m turning place; ~**punkt** m
turning point.
wendig adj (lit, fig) agile; Auto etc manoeuvrable
(Brit), maneuverable (US).
Wendigkeit f siehe adj agility; manoeuvrability
(Brit), maneuverability (US).
Wendung f (**a**) turn; (Veränderung) change. **eine**
~ **zum Besseren nehmen** to take a turn for the

better. (**b**) (Rede~) expression, phrase.
wenig 1 adj, indef pron (**a**) sing (a) little. **ich habe**
~ **I have only a little; hast du Zeit?** — ~**! have you
got time?** — not much; **das** ~**e, was er übrig
hatte** the little he had left; **es fehlte (nur)** ~, **und
er wäre überfahren worden** he was very nearly
run over; **er gibt sich mit** ~ **zufrieden** (verlangt
nicht viel) he is satisfied with a little; (ist selten
zufrieden) not much satisfies him; **sie hat zu** ~
Geld etc she doesn't have enough money etc; **ein
Exemplar zu** ~ one copy too few; **£ 20 zu** ~ £20
too little. (**b**) ~**e** pl (ein paar) a few; (nicht viele)
few; **in** ~**en Tagen** in (just) a few days; **einige** ~**e**
Leute a few people. (**c**) (auch adv) **ein** ~ a little;
ein ~ **Salz** a little salt.
2 adv little. ~ **besser** little better; ~ **bekannt**
little-known attr, little known pred; **sie kommt
(nur)** ~ **raus** she doesn't get out very often.
weniger comp of **wenig** 1 adj, indef pron less; pl
fewer. ~ **werden** to get less and less. 2 adv less.
das finde ich ~ **schön!** that's not so nice!; **je
mehr** ... **desto** ~ ... the more ... the less ...; **sieben**
~ **drei ist vier** seven less three is four.
wenigstens adv at least.
wenigste(r, s) superl of **wenig** adj, indef pron, **am**
~**n** adv least; pl fewest. **er hat von uns allen am**
~**n Geld/Sorgen** he has the least money/the fewest worries of any of us; **diese Farbe ist am** ~**n**
schön this colour is the least attractive one; **die**
~**n glauben das** very few believe that.
wenn conj (**a**) (konditional, bei Wünschen) if. **selbst
or und** ~ even if; ~ ... **auch** ... even though or if
...; ~ **er auch noch so dumm sein mag**, ... however stupid he may be, ...; ~ **schon!** so what?
(col); ~ **es schon sein muß** well, if that's the way
it's got to be; ~ **wir erst die neue Wohnung
haben** once we get the new flat; ~ **ich doch** ... if
only I ...; **außer** ~ except if, unless. (**b**) (zeitlich)
when. **immer** ~ whenever; **außer** ~ except
when.
Wenn nt: **das** ~ **und Aber** (the) ifs and buts; **ohne**
~ **und Aber** unequivocally.
wennschon adv (col) (**na**,) ~**!** what of it?; ~,
dennschon! in for a penny, in for a pound!
wer 1 interrog pron who. ~ **von** ... which (one) of ...
2 rel pron (derjenige, der) the person who; (jeder,
der) anyone or anybody who. ~ ... **auch (immer)**
whoever ... 3 indef pron (col: jemand) somebody,
someone. **ist da** ~**?** is somebody there?; ~ **sein** to
be somebody (col).
Werbe- in cpds advertising; ~**abteilung** f publicity department; ~**agentur** f advertising agency; ~**aktion** f advertising campaign; ~**antwort** f
business reply card; ~**etat** m advertising
budget; ~**fernsehen** nt commercial television;
~**film** m promotional film; (Spot) (filmed) commercial; ~**funk** m radio commercials pl; ~**gag** m
publicity stunt or gimmick; ~**geschenk** nt gift
(from company), freebie (col); (zu Gekauftem) free
gift; ~**kampagne** f publicity campaign; ~**muster** nt advertising sample.
werben pret **warb**, ptp **geworben** 1 vt Mitglieder, Soldaten to recruit; Kunden, Stimmen to
attract, to win. 2 vi to advertise. **für etw** ~ to
advertise sth; **für eine Partei** ~ to try to get
support for a party; **um Unterstützung** ~ to try
to enlist support; **um junge Wähler** ~ to try to
attract young voters; **um ein Mädchen** ~ to
court a girl.
Werbe-: ~**schrift** f publicity leaflet; ~**schriften**
promotional literature sing; ~**slogan** m publicity
slogan; ~**spot** m commercial; ~**text** m advertising copy no pl; ~**texter** m copywriter; ~**träger** m
carrier of advertising; ~**trommel** f: **die** ~**trommel (für etw) rühren** (col) to beat the big drum
(for sth) (col); w~**wirksam** adj w~**wirksam sein**
to be good publicity; ~**wirksamkeit** f publicity
value.

Werbung f (esp Comm) advertising; (für Produkt auch) publicity, promotion; (Werbeabteilung) publicity department. ~ **für etw machen** to advertise sth.

Werbungskosten pl (von Mensch) professional outlay sing or expenses pl; (von Firma) business expenses pl.

werden pret **wurde**, ptp **geworden** aux sein 1 vi to become; (mit adj auch) to get. **blind** ~ to go blind; **krank** ~ to fall ill; **rot** ~ to turn red; **es wird kalt** it's getting cold; **mir wird warm** I'm getting warm; **mir wird schlecht** I feel bad; **anders** ~ to change; **die Fotos sind gut geworden** the photos have come out nicely; **aus ihm ist ein großer Komponist geworden** he has become a great composer; **ich will Lehrer** ~ I want to be a teacher; **Erster** ~ to come or be first; **was soll das** ~? — **das wird ein Pullover** what's that going to be? — it's going to be a pullover; **daraus ist nichts geworden** it came to nothing; **es wird bald ein Jahr, daß ...** it's almost a year since ...; **es wird Zeit, daß er kommt** it's time (that) he came; **es wird Nacht/Tag** it's getting dark/light; **es wird Winter** winter is coming; **er wird am 8. Mai 36** he is 36 on the 8th of May; **er ist gerade 40 geworden** he has just turned 40; **was soll nun** ~? so what's going to happen now?; **es wird schon** ~ (col) it'll come all right in the end; **er wird mal wie sein Vater** he's going to be like his father; **wie soll der Pullover** ~? what's the pullover going to be like?

2 aux (a) (bei Futur und Konjunktiv) **er wird es tun** he will do it, he'll do it; **er wird das nicht tun** he will not or won't do that; **es wird gleich regnen** it's going to rain; **wer wird denn gleich!** (col) come on, now!; **das würde ich gerne tun** I would or I'd gladly do that. (b) (bei Vermutung) **sie wird wohl in der Küche sein** she will be in the kitchen; **er wird (wohl) ausgegangen sein** he will have gone out. (c) (bei Passiv) ptp **worden gebraucht** ~ to be used; **er ist erschossen worden** he was shot/he has been shot; **hier wird nicht geraucht!** there's no smoking here; **mir wurde gesagt, daß ... I** was told ...

werdend adj ~**e Mutter** expectant mother.

werfen pret **warf**, ptp **geworfen** 1 vt to throw (nach at); Tor, Korb to score. **Bomben** ~ (von Flugzeug) to drop bombs; **eine Münze** ~ to toss a coin; „**nicht** ~" "handle with care"; **Bilder an die Wand** ~ to project pictures onto the wall; **etw auf jdn/etw** ~ to throw sth at sb/sth; **etw auf den Boden** ~ to throw sth to the ground; **billige Waren auf den Markt** ~ to dump cheap goods on the market; **jdn aus der Firma** ~ to throw sb out (of the firm); **jdn ins Gefängnis** etc ~ to throw sb into prison etc; **etw in den Briefkasten** ~ to put sth in the letter box. **2** vi (a) to throw. **mit etw (auf jdn/etw)** ~ to throw sth (at sb/sth); **mit Geld um sich** ~ to throw one's money about; **mit Fremdwörtern um sich** ~ to bandy foreign words about. (b) (Tier) to have its young. **3** vr to throw oneself (auf +acc (up)on, at).

Werft f -en shipyard; (für Flugzeuge) hangar.

Werft|arbeiter m shipyard worker.

Werg nt no pl tow.

Werk nt -e (a) (Arbeit) work no indef art; (geh: Tat) deed, act; (Kunst~, Buch) work; (Gesamt~) works pl. **das** ~ **eines Augenblicks** the work of a moment; **das ist sein** ~ this is his doing; **das** ~ **jahrelanger Arbeit** the product of many years of work; **gute** ~**e tun** to do good works; **ein** ~ **der Nächstenliebe** an act of charity; **ans** ~ **gehen** to set to work. (b) (Betrieb, Fabrik) works sing or pl, plant. **ab** ~ (Comm) ex works. (c) (Trieb~) works pl.

Werk- in cpds works, factory; siehe auch **Werk(s)-**; ~**bank** f workbench.

werkeln vi (col) to potter about.

werken vi to be busy. **W**~ (Sch) handicrafts.

Werk-: ~**halle** f factory building; ~**meister** m foreman.

Werk(s)-: ~**angehörige(r)** mf factory employee; ~**arzt** m works or company doctor.

Werkschutz m works security service.

Werks-: **w**~**eigen** adj company attr; ~**fahrer** m company or factory driver; ~**feuerwehr** f factory fire service; ~**gelände** nt factory premises pl; ~**kantine** f works canteen; ~**küche** f works kitchen; ~**leiter** m works director or manager; ~**leitung** f factory management; ~**spionage** f industrial espionage.

Werk-: ~**statt** f workshop (auch fig); (für Autoreparaturen) garage; (von Künstler) studio; ~**stoff** m material; ~**stück** nt workpiece; ~**student** m working student.

Werk(s)-: ~**verkehr** m company transport; ~**wohnung** f company flat (Brit) or apartment.

Werktag m working day, workday.

werktags adv on working days.

Werk-: ~**tisch** m work-table; ~**unterricht** m woodwork/metalwork etc instruction.

Werkzeug nt (lit, fig) tool.

Werkzeug-: ~**kasten** m toolbox; ~**macher** m toolmaker; ~**maschine** f machine tool.

Wermut m no pl (~wein) vermouth.

Wermutstropfen m (fig geh) drop of bitterness.

wert adj (a) **etw** ~ **sein** to be worth sth; **nichts** ~ **sein** to be worthless; **Glasgow ist eine Reise** ~ Glasgow is worth a visit; **es ist der Mühe** ~ it's worth the trouble; **es ist nicht der Rede** ~ it's not worth mentioning; **er ist es nicht** ~, **daß man ihm vertraut** he doesn't deserve to be trusted. (b) (nützlich) useful. **ein Auto ist viel** ~ a car is very useful; **das ist schon viel** ~ (erfreulich) that's very encouraging.

Wert m -e value; (esp menschlicher) worth; (von Banknoten, Briefmarken) denomination. ~**e** pl (Ergebnisse) results pl; **im** ~**e von** to the value of; **an** ~ **verlieren** to decrease in value; **etw unter** ~ **verkaufen** to sell sth for less than its true value; **sie hat innere** ~**e** she has certain inner qualities; ~ **auf etw** (acc) **legen** (fig) to attach importance to sth.

Wert-: ~**angabe** f declaration of value; ~**arbeit** f craftsmanship; **w**~**beständig** adj stable in value.

werten vti (einstufen) to rate (als as); Klassenarbeit etc to grade; (beurteilen) to judge (als to be); (Sport) (als gültig ~) to allow; (Punkte geben) to give a score. **ein Tor nicht** ~ (Ftbl etc) to disallow a goal.

Wert-: ~**gegenstand** m object of value; ~**gegenstände** pl valuables pl; **w**~**frei** value-free; **w**~**los** adj worthless; ~**losigkeit** f worthlessness; ~**marke** f stamp; (Gutschein) voucher; ~**maßstab** m standard; ~**papier** nt bond; ~**papiere** pl stocks and shares pl; ~**papierbörse** f stock market.

Wertung f evaluation; (von Jury etc) judging; (Punkte) score.

Wert-: ~**urteil** nt value judgement; **w**~**voll** adj valuable; ~**vorstellung** f moral concept.

Wesen nt - (a) no pl nature; (Wesentliches) essence. **es liegt im** ~ **einer Sache ...** it's in the nature of a thing ... (b) (Geschöpf) being. **ein weibliches/männliches** ~ a female/male.

Wesens-: **w**~**art** f nature; **w**~**gleich** adj essentially alike; **w**~**verwandt** adj related in character; ~**zug** m trait.

wesentlich 1 adj (hauptsächlich) essential; (grundlegend) fundamental; (wichtig) important. **das W**~**e** the essential thing; (von Text, Rede) the gist; **im** ~**en** essentially; (im großen) in the main. **2** adv fundamentally; (erheblich) considerably. **es ist mir** ~ **lieber, wenn wir ...** I would much rather we ...

weshạlb 1 *interrog adv* why. **2** *rel adv* **der Grund,** ~ ... the reason why ...

Wẹspe *f* -n wasp.

Wẹspen-: ~**nest** *nt* wasps' nest; **in ein** ~**nest stechen** *(fig)* to stir up a hornets' nest; ~**stich** *m* wasp sting.

wẹssen *pron* **1** *gen of* **wer** *interrog* whose. **2** *gen of* **was** *(liter)* ~ **hat man dich angeklagt?** of what have you been accused?

Wẹst *m no pl (Naut, Met, liter)* west.

Wẹst- *in cpds (in Ländernamen) (politisch)* West; *(geographisch auch)* the West of ..., Western; ~**-Berlin,** ~**berlin** *nt* West Berlin; ~**berliner** *adj attr* West Berlin; ~**berliner(in** *f)* *m* West Berliner; **w**~**deutsch** *adj* West German; ~**deutsche(r)** *mf* West German; ~**deutschland** *nt* West Germany.

Wẹste *f* -n waistcoat *(Brit)*, vest *(US)*. **eine reine** ~ **haben** *(fig)* to have a clean slate.

Wẹsten *m no pl* west; *(von Land)* West. **der** ~ *(Pol)* the West.

Wẹstentasche *f* waistcoat *(Brit)* or vest *(US)* pocket. **etw wie seine** ~ **kennen** *(col)* to know sth like the back of one's hand *(col)*.

Wẹstern *m* - western.

wẹst|europäisch *adj* West(ern) European. ~**e Zeit** Greenwich Mean Time.

Westfale *m (wk)* **-n, -n, Westfälin** *f* Westphalian.

Westfalen *nt* Westphalia.

westfälisch *adj* Westphalian.

wẹstlich 1 *adj* western; *Wind, Richtung* westerly; *(Pol)* Western. **der** ~**ste Ort** the westernmost place. **2** *adv* (to the) west *(von of)*. **3** *prep* +*gen* (to the) west of.

Wẹst-: ~**mächte** *pl (Pol)* **die** ~**mächte** the western powers *pl*; ~**mark** *f (col)* West German mark; **w**~**östlich** *adj* west-to-east; **in w**~**östlicher Richtung** from west to east; ~**politik** *f* western policy; ~**sektor** *m* western sector; **w**~**wärts** *adv* westward(s); ~**wind** *m* west wind.

weswegen *interrog adv* why.

wẹtt *adj pred* ~ **sein** to be quits.

Wẹttbewerb *m* competition. **mit jdm in** ~ **stehen/treten** to be in/enter into competition with sb.

Wẹttbewerbs-: ~**beschränkung** *f* restraint of trade; **w**~**fähig** *adj* competitive; ~**teilnehmer** *m* competitor.

Wẹttbüro *nt* betting office.

Wẹtte *f* -n bet *(auch Sport)*, wager. **eine** ~ **abschließen** to make a bet; **darauf gehe ich jede** ~ **ein** I'll bet you anything you like; **was gilt die** ~? what are you betting?; **die** ~ **gilt!** done!, you're on! *(col)*; **um die** ~ **laufen** to run a race (with each other); **sie schreien um die** ~ they're having a screaming competition.

wẹtt|eifern *vi insep* **mit jdm um etw** ~ to compete with sb for sth.

wẹtten *vti* to bet. **(wollen wir)** ~? (do you) want to bet?; ~, **daß ich recht habe?** (I) bet you I'm right!; **so haben wir nicht gewettet!** that's not part of the bargain!; **auf etw** *(acc)* ~ to bet on sth; **mit jdm** ~ to bet with sb; **(mit jdm) um 5 Mark** ~ to bet (sb) 5 marks; **ich wette 100 gegen 1(, daß ...)** I'll bet 100 to 1 (that ...).

Wẹtter[1] *m* - better.

Wẹtter[2] *nt* **- (a)** weather *no indef art.* **bei jedem** ~ in all weathers; **das ist vielleicht ein** ~! *(col)* what weather!; **was haben wir heute für** ~? what's the weather like today?; **wir haben herrliches** ~ the weather's marvellous. **(b)** *usu pl (Min)* air. **schlagende** ~ *pl* firedamp *sing*.

Wẹtter-: ~**amt** *nt* met office; ~**aussichten** *pl* weather outlook; ~**beobachtung** *f* meteorological observation; ~**bericht** *m* weather report; ~**besserung** *f* improvement in the weather; **w**~**beständig** *adj* weatherproof; ~**dienst**

m meteorological service; **w**~**empfindlich** *adj* sensitive to the weather; ~**fahne** *f* weather vane; **w**~**fest** *adj* weatherproof; **w**~**fühlig** *adj* sensitive to the weather; ~**häuschen** *nt* weather house; ~**karte** *f* weather chart; ~**lage** *f* weather situation; ~**leuchten** *nt no pl* sheet lightning; ~**meldung** *f* meteorological report.

wẹttern *vi* to curse and swear. **gegen etw** ~ to rail against sth.

Wẹtter-: ~**regel** *f* weather saying; ~**satellit** *m* weather satellite; ~**schaden** *m* weather damage; ~**seite** *f* windward side; ~**station** *f* weather station; ~**störung** *f* meteorological disturbance; ~**umschlag** *m* sudden change in the weather; ~**verhältnisse** *pl* weather conditions *pl*; ~**vorhersage** *f* weather forecast; ~**warte** *f* weather station; **w**~**wendisch** *adj (fig)* moody; ~**wolke** *f* storm cloud.

Wẹtt-: ~**fahrt** *f* race; ~**kampf** *m* competition; ~**kämpfer** *m* competitor; ~**lauf** *m* race; **einen** ~**lauf machen** to run a race; **ein** ~**lauf mit der Zeit** a race against time; ~**läufer** *m* runner (in a/the race).

wẹttmachen *vt sep* to make up for; *Verlust etc* to make good.

Wẹtt-: ~**rennen** *nt (lit, fig)* race; ~**rüsten** *nt* arms race; ~**schein** *m* betting slip; ~**schuld** *f* betting debt; ~**streit** *m* competition.

wẹtzen **1** *vt* to whet. **2** *aux sein (col)* to scoot *(col)*.

Wẹtzstein *m* whetstone.

Whisky ['vɪski] *m* **-s** whisky, whiskey *(US)*.

wịch *pret of* **weichen**[2].

wịchsen ['vɪksn] **1** *vti Schuhe* to polish; *Boden etc* to wax. **2** *vi (col!: onanieren)* to jerk or toss off *(col!)*.

Wịcht *m* **-e** *(Kobold)* goblin; *(kleiner Mensch)* titch *(col)*; *(fig: verachtenswerter Mensch)* scoundrel.

wịchtig *adj* important. **eine** ~ **Miene machen** to try to look important; **er will sich nur** ~ **machen** he just wants to get attention; **sich selbst/etw (zu)** ~ **nehmen** to take oneself/sth (too) seriously; **sich** *(dat)* ~ **vorkommen** to be full of oneself; **alles W**~**e** everything of importance; **W**~**eres zu tun haben** to have more important things to do; **nichts W**~**eres zu tun haben** nothing better to do.

Wịchtigkeit *f* importance.

Wịchtigtuer(in *f)* *m* - *(pej)* pompous ass *(col)*.

wịchtigtuerisch *adj* pompous.

Wịcke *f* -n *(Bot)* vetch; *(Garten*~*)* sweet pea.

Wịckel *m* - **(a)** *(Med)* compress. **(b)** *(Rolle)* reel; *(Locken*~*)* curler. **(c)** *(col)* **jdn am** ~ **kriegen/haben** to grab/have sb by the scruff of the neck; *(fig)* to give sb a good talking to *(col)*.

Wịckel-: ~**bluse** *f* wrap-around blouse; ~**kind** *nt* babe-in-arms; ~**kleid** *nt* wrap-around dress.

wịckeln 1 *vt* **(a)** *(schlingen)* to wind *(um* around); *Verband etc* to bind; *Haare* to put in curlers. **sich** *(dat)* **eine Decke um die Beine** ~ to wrap a blanket around one's legs; **da bist du schief gewickelt!** *(fig col)* you're very much mistaken. **(b)** *(einwickeln)* to wrap *(in* +*acc* in*)*; *(mit Verband)* to dress. **einen Säugling** ~ to put on a baby's nappy *(Brit)* or diaper *(US)*. **2** *vr* to wrap oneself (*in* +*acc* in*)*. **sich um etw** ~ to wrap itself around sth; *(Schlange, Pflanze)* to wind itself around sth.

Wịckeltisch *m* baby's changing table.

Wịdder *m* - ram; *(Astrol)* Aries.

wịder *prep* +*acc (geh)* against. ~ **Erwarten** contrary to expectations.

widerfahren* *vi, vi impers insep irreg aux sein* +*dat (geh)* to happen *(jdm* to sb*)*.

Wịder-: ~**haken** *m* barb; ~**hall** *m* echo; **(bei jdm) keinen** ~**hall finden** *(Interesse)* to meet with no response (from sb).

widerlẹgbar *adj* refutable. **nicht** ~ irrefutable.

widerlẹgen* *vt insep* to refute; *jdn* to prove wrong.

Wịder-: **w**~**lich** *adj* revolting; ~**ling** *m (pej col)* repulsive creep *(col)*; w~**natürlich** *adj* unnatural; w~**rechtlich** *adj* unlawful; **sich** *(dat)* **etw w~rechtlich aneignen** to misappropriate sth; ~**rede** *f* contradiction; **keine** ~**rede!** don't argue!

Widerruf *m siehe vb* withdrawal; retraction; cancellation; withdrawal. **bis auf** ~ until revoked.

widerrufen* *insep irreg* **1** *vt Erlaubnis etc* to withdraw; *Aussage* to retract; *Befehl* to cancel. **2** *vi (bei Verleumdung etc)* to withdraw.

Wider-: ~**sacher**(in *f*) *m* - adversary; w~**setzen** *vr insep* **sich jdm/einer Sache** w~**setzen** to oppose sb/sth; *der Polizei, Festnahme* to resist sb/sth; *einem Befehl* to refuse to comply with sth; w~**sinnig** *adj* absurd; w~**spenstig** *adj* unruly; *(störrisch)* stubborn; *Haar* unmanageable; ~**spenstigkeit** *f siehe adj* unruliness; stubbornness; w~**spiegeln** *sep* **1** *vt (lit, fig)* to reflect; **2** *vr (lit, fig)* to be reflected; ~**spieg(e)lung** *f* reflection.

widersprechen* *insep irreg* **1** *vi* **jdm/einer Sache** ~ to contradict sb/sth; **das widerspricht meinen Grundsätzen** that goes against my principles. **2** *vr (einander)* ~ to contradict one another. **sich (selbst)** ~ to contradict oneself.

Widerspruch *m* **(a)** *(Gegensätzlichkeit)* contradiction. **ein** ~ **in sich** a contradiction in terms; **im** ~ **zu** contrary to; **in** ~ **zu etw geraten** to come into conflict with sth; **in** *or* **im** ~ **zu etw stehen** to conflict with sth. **(b)** *(Widerrede)* contradiction; *(Ablehnung)* opposition. **kein** ~**!** don't argue!; **er duldet keinen** ~ he won't have any argument; **es erhob sich** ~ there was opposition *(gegen* to*)*; ~ **erheben** to protest.

widersprüchlich *adj* contradictory, inconsistent.

widerspruchs-: ~**frei** *adj Theorie* consistent; ~**los** **1** *adj Zustimmung* unopposed; **2** *adv* without opposition; **etw** ~**los hinnehmen** to accept sth unquestioningly; ~**voll** *adj* full of inconsistencies.

Widerstand *m* ⁺e resistance; *(Ablehnung)* opposition. **jdm/einer Sache** ~ **leisten** to resist sb/sth.

Widerstands-: ~**bewegung** *f* resistance movement; w~**fähig** *adj* robust; *Pflanze* hardy; *(Med, Tech etc)* resistant *(gegen* to*)*; ~**fähigkeit** *f siehe adj* robustness; hardiness; resistance *(gegen* to*)*; ~**kämpfer** *m* resistance fighter; w~**los** *adj, adv* without resistance; ~**nest** *nt (Mil)* pocket of resistance.

widerstehen* *vi insep irreg +dat* **einer Sache** ~ to resist sth; *einem Erdbeben etc* to withstand sth.

widerstreben* *vi insep +dat* **jds sittlichem Empfinden** ~ to go against sb's moral sense; **es widerstrebt mir, so etwas zu tun** I am reluctant to do anything like that.

Widerstreben *nt no pl* reluctance.

widerstrebend *adj (gegensätzlich) Interessen* conflicting; *(widerwillig)* reluctant.

widerwärtig *adj* disgusting. **er ist mir** ~ he disgusts me.

Widerwille *m (Abscheu, Ekel)* disgust *(gegen* for*)*, revulsion; *(Abneigung)* distaste *(gegen* for*)*; *(Widerstreben)* reluctance.

widerwillig *adj* reluctant, unwilling.

Widerworte *pl* answering back *sing.* **er tat es ohne** ~ he did it without protest.

widmen **1** *vt* **jdm etw** ~ to dedicate sth to sb. **2** *vr +dat* to devote oneself to; **den Gästen, einer Aufgabe** to attend to.

Widmung *f (in Buch etc)* dedication *(an +acc* to*)*.

widrig *adj* adverse.

wie 1 *interrog adv* how. ~ **anders ...?** how else ...?; ~ **wär's (mit uns beiden** *etc) (col)* how about it? *(col)*; ~ **wär's mit einem Whisky?** *(col)* how about a whisky?; ~ **ist er (denn)?** what's he like?; **Sie wissen ja,** ~ **das so ist** well, you know how it is; ~ **nennt man das?** what is that called?; ~

bitte? pardon?; ~ **bitte?!** *(entrüstet)* I beg your pardon!; **das macht dir Spaß,** ~**?** you like that, don't you?; **und** ~**!, aber** ~**!** and how! *(col)*; ~ **groß er ist!** isn't he big!

2 *adv* **(a)** *(relativ)* **die Art,** ~ **sie geht the way she walks. (b)** *(in Verbindung mit auch)* ~ **stark du auch sein magst** however strong you may be. **3** *conj* **(a)** *(vergleichend)* **so ...** ~ **as ... as; weiß** ~ **Schnee** (as) white as snow; **ein Mann** ~ **er a man like him; in einer Lage** ~ **diese(r)** in a situation like this; **ich fühle mich** ~ **im Traum** I felt as if I was dreaming; ~ **du weißt** as you know; ~ **noch nie** as never before. **(b)** *(zum Beispiel)* ~ **(zum Beispiel)** such as (for example). **(c)** *(bei Verben der Wahrnehmung)* **er sah,** ~ **es geschah** he saw it happen; **er hörte,** ~ **der Regen fiel** he heard the rain falling. **(d)** *(zeitlich: als)* ~ **ich mich umdrehte, sah ich ...** as I turned around I saw ...

Wie *nt no pl* **das** ~ **und Wann werden wir später besprechen** we'll talk about how and when later.

Wiedehopf *m* -e hoopoe.

wieder *adv* again. ~ **nüchtern** sober again; **immer** ~ again and again; ~ **ist ein Jahr vorbei** another year has passed; **wie, schon** ~**?** what, again?; **das ist auch** ~ **wahr** that's true; **da sieht man mal** ~**, ...** it just shows ...; **das fällt mir schon** ~ **ein** I'll remember it again.

Wieder- *pref* re; *(bei Verben) (erneut)* again; *(zurück)* back; ~**aufbau** *m (lit, fig)* reconstruction; w~**aufbauen** *vti sep* to reconstruct; w~**aufbereiten*** *vt sep* to recycle; *Atommüll* to reprocess; ~**aufbereitungsanlage** reprocessing plant; w~**aufforsten** *vti sep* to reforest; w~**aufführen** *vt sep Theaterstück* to revive; *Film* to rerun; w~**aufladen** *vt sep irreg* to recharge; w~**aufleben** *vi sep aux sein* to revive; ~**aufleben** *nt* revival; ~**aufnahme** *f* **(a)** *(von Tätigkeit etc)* resumption; **(b)** *(in Verein etc)* readmittance; *(von Patienten)* readmission; w~**aufnehmen** *vt sep irreg* **(a)** to resume; *Gedanken, Hobby* to take up again; *Thema* to revert to; *(Jur) Verfahren* to reopen; **(b)** *Menschen* to take back; *(in Verein, Klinik)* to readmit; w~**aufrüsten** *vti sep* to rearm; ~**aufrüstung** *f* rearmament; w~**bekommen*** *vt sep irreg* to get back; w~**beleben*** *vt sep irreg* to revive; ~**belebung** *f* revival; w~**beschaffen*** *vt sep* to recover; ~**beschaffung** *f* recovery; w~**bewaffnen*** *vr sep* to rearm; ~**bewaffnung** *f* rearmament; w~**bringen** *vt sep irreg* to bring back; w~**einführen** *vt sep* to reintroduce; ~**einführung** *f* reintroduction; ~**einnahme** *f (Mil)* recapture; w~**einnehmen** *vt sep irreg (Mil)* to recapture; w~**einsetzen** *sep* **1** *vt* to reinstate *(in +acc* in*)*; **2** *vi (Regen)* to start up again; *(Med: Fieber, Schmerzen)* to recur; ~**einsetzung** *f* reinstatement; w~**einstellen** *vt sep* to re-engage; ~**einstellung** *f* re-engagement; w~**entdecken*** *vt sep (lit, fig)* to rediscover; ~**entdeckung** *f* rediscovery; w~**ergreifen*** *vt sep irreg* to recapture; ~**ergreifung** *f* recapture; w~**erkennen*** *vt sep irreg* to recognize; **er war nicht** w~**zuerkennen** he was unrecognizable; w~**eröffnen*** *vti sep* to reopen; *(Buch etc)* to be republished; w~**erstatten*** *vt sep Unkosten etc* to refund *(jdm etw* sb for sth*)*; ~**erstattung** *f* reimbursement; w~**finden** *sep irreg* **1** *vt* to find again; *(fig) Selbstachtung etc* to regain; **2** *vr (nach Schock)* to recover; **sich irgendwo** w~**finden** to find oneself somewhere.

Wiedergabe *f* **(a)** *(von Rede, Ereignis)* account, report; *(Wiederholung)* repetition. **(b)** *(Darbietung: von Stück, Konzert)* performance; *(Interpretation)* interpretation. **(c)** *(Reproduktion)* reproduction.

Wiedergabegerät *nt* playback unit.

wiedergeben *vt sep irreg* **(a)** *Gegenstand, Geld* to give back. **jdm ein Buch** ~ to give a book back to sb. **(b)** *(erzählen)* to give an account of; *(wiederholen)* to repeat. **(c)** *Gedicht* to recite; *Musikstück etc* to perform. **(d)** *(reproduzieren)* to reproduce.

Wieder-: ~**geburt** *f* rebirth; **w**~**gewinnen*** *vt sep irreg (lit, fig)* to regain; *Land, Rohstoffe etc* to reclaim; *Geld, Selbstvertrauen* to recover; **w**~**gutmachen** *vt sep* to make good; *Schaden* to compensate for; *(Pol)* to make reparations for; *(Jur)* to redress; ~**gutmachung** *f* compensation; *(Pol)* reparations *pl*; *(Jur)* redress; **w**~**haben** *vt sep irreg (col)* to have (got) back; **w**~**herstellen** *vt sep Gebäude, Frieden, jds Gesundheit* to restore; ~**herstellung** *f* restoration.

wiederholbar *adj* repeatable. **schwer** ~ hard to repeat.

wiederholen[1]***** *insep* **1** *vti* to repeat; *(mehrmals) Forderung etc* to reiterate; *Lernstoff* to revise; *Spiel* to replay. **eine Klasse** ~ *(Sch)* to repeat a year. **2** *vr (Mensch)* to repeat oneself; *(Thema, Ereignis)* to recur.

wiederholen[2] *vt sep* to get back.

wiederholt *adj* repeated. **zum** ~**en Male** once again.

Wiederholung *f* repetition; *(von Aufführung)* repeat performance; *(von Sendung)* repeat; *(in Zeitlupe)* replay; *(von Lernstoff)* revision; *(von Spiel)* replay.

Wiederholungs-: ~**kurs** *m* refresher course; ~**spiel** *nt (Sport)* replay; ~**täter** *m (Jur)* second-time offender; *(mehrmalig)* persistent offender; ~**zeichen** *nt (Mus)* repeat (mark).

Wieder-: ~**hören** *nt (auf)* ~**hören!** goodbye!; **w**~**käuen** *vti sep* to ruminate; *(fig col)* to go over again and again; ~**käuer** *m* - ruminant.

Wiederkehr *f no pl (geh) (Rückkehr)* return; *(wiederholtes Vorkommen)* recurrence; *(von Ereignis)* anniversary.

wiederkehren *vi sep aux sein* to return; *(sich wiederholen)* to recur.

wiederkehrend *adj* recurrent.

Wieder-: **w**~**kennen** *vt sep irreg (col)* to recognize; **w**~**kommen** *vi sep irreg aux sein* to come back; **komm doch mal w**~**!** you must come again!; **w**~**sehen** *vt sep irreg* to see again; ~**sehen** *nt* (another) meeting; *(nach längerer Zeit)* reunion; **sie hofften auf ein baldiges** ~**sehen** they hoped to meet again soon; **(auf)** ~**sehen!** goodbye!; **w**~**tun** *vt sep irreg* to do again.

wiederum *adv* **(a)** *(andrerseits)* on the other hand; *(allerdings)* though. **(b)** *(seinerseits etc)* in turn. **er** ~ **wollte ...** he, for his part, wanted ...

Wieder-: **w**~**vereinigen*** *sep* **1** *vt Menschen* to reunite; *Land* to reunify; **2** *vr* to reunite; ~**vereinigung** *f* reunification; **w**~**verheiraten*** *vr sep* to remarry; ~**verheiratung** *f* remarriage; ~**verkauf** *m* resale; **w**~**verkaufen*** *vt sep* to resell; **w**~**verwendbar** *adj* reusable; **w**~**verwenden*** *vt sep* to reuse; ~**verwendung** *f* re-use; **w**~**verwerten*** *vt sep* to reutilize; ~**verwertung** *f* reutilization; ~**wahl** *f* re-election; **w**~**wählen** *vt sep* to re-elect.

Wiege *f* -n cradle. **es ist ihm auch nicht an der** ~ **gesungen worden, daß ...** no-one could have foreseen that ...

wiegen[1] **1** *vt* to rock; *Kopf* to shake (slowly); *Hüften* to sway. **2** *vr sich in trügerischen Hoffnungen** ~ to nurture false hopes.

wiegen[2] *pret* **wog**, *ptp* **gewogen** *vti* to weigh. **schwer** ~ *(fig)* to carry a lot of weight; *(Irrtum)* to be serious; *siehe* **gewogen.**

Wiegenlied *nt* lullaby.

wiehern *vi* to neigh. **(vor Lachen)** ~ to bray with laughter.

Wien *nt* Vienna.

Wiener *adj attr* Viennese. ~ **Würstchen** frankfurter, wiener (sausage) *(esp US)*; ~ **Schnitzel**

Wiener schnitzel.

Wiener(in *f)* *m* - Viennese.

wies *pret of* **weisen.**

Wiese *f* -n meadow; *(col: Rasen)* lawn. **auf der grünen** ~ *(fig)* in the open countryside.

Wiesel *nt* - weasel. **schnell** *or* **flink wie ein** ~ quick as a flash.

Wiesenblume *f* meadow flower.

wieso *interrog adv* why. ~ **gehst du nicht?** how come you're not going? *(col);* ~ **weißt du das?** how do you know that?

wieviel *interrog adv* how much; *(bei Mehrzahl)* how many.

wievielmal *interrog adv* how many times.

wievielte(r, s) *interrog adj* **das** ~ **Kind ist das jetzt?** how many children is that now?; **den** ~**n Platz hat er im Wettkampf belegt?** where did he come in the competition?; **das** ~ **Mal bist du schon in England?** how often have you been to England?; **ich habe morgen Geburtstag! — der** ~ **ist es denn?** it's my birthday tomorrow! — how old will you be?; **den W**~**n haben wir heute?** what's the date today?

wieweit *conj* to what extent.

Wikinger *m* - Viking.

wild *adj* wild; *Stamm* savage; *(ausgelassen)* boisterous; *(heftig) Kampf, (zornig) Blick* fierce; *(ungesetzlich) Parken etc* illegal; *Streik* wildcat *attr,* unofficial. **den** ~**en Mann spielen** *(col)* to come the heavy *(col);* **der W**~**e Westen** the Wild West; **in** ~**er Ehe leben** *(dated, hum)* to live in sin; ~ **durcheinanderliegen** to be strewn all over the place; **dann ging alles** ~ **durcheinander** there was chaos then; **wie** ~ **rennen** to run like mad; ~ **drauflosreden** to talk nineteen to the dozen; **seid nicht so** ~**!** calm down a bit!; **einen Hund** ~ **machen** to drive a dog wild; ~ **werden** to go wild *(auch col);* **ich könnte** ~ **werden** *(col)* I could scream *(col);* ~ **entschlossen** *(col)* dead set *(col).*

Wild *nt no pl* game; *(Rot~)* deer; *(Fleisch von Rot~)* venison.

Wild-: ~**bach** *m* torrent; ~**bahn** *f* **in freier** ~**bahn** in the wild; ~**bestand** *m* game population; ~**braten** *m* roast venison; ~**bret** *nt no pl* game; *(von Rotwild)* venison; ~**dieb** *m* poacher; ~**diebstahl** *m* poaching; ~**ente** *f* wild duck.

Wilde(r) *mf decl as adj* savage; *(fig)* maniac.

Wilderer *m* - poacher.

wildern *vi (Mensch)* to poach; *(Hund etc)* to kill game.

Wild-: ~**esel** *m* wild ass; ~**fang** *m* little rascal; **w**~**fremd** *adj (col)* **w**~**fremde Leute** complete strangers; ~**gans** *f* wild goose; ~**hüter** *m* gamekeeper; ~**katze** *f* wildcat; **w**~**lebend** *adj attr* living in the wild; ~**leder** *nt* suede.

Wildnis *f (lit, fig)* wilderness. **in der** ~ **leben** to live in the wild.

Wild-: ~**park** *m* game park; *(für Rotwild)* deer park; ~**reservat** *nt* game reserve; ~**schaden** *m* damage caused by game; ~**schutzgebiet** *nt* game preserve; ~**schwein** *nt* wild boar; **w**~**wachsend** *adj attr* wild(-growing); ~**wasser** *nt* white water; ~**wechsel** *m* „~**wechsel**" "wild animals"; ~**west** *no art* the wild west; ~**westfilm** *m* western; ~**westroman** *m* western; ~**wuchs** *m (geh)* rank growth; *(fig)* proliferation.

Wille *m* -ns, *no pl* will; *(Absicht)* intention. **nach jds** ~**n** as sb wanted/wants; **wenn es nach ihrem** ~**n ginge** if she had her way; **das geschah gegen meinen** ~**n** that was done against my will; **jds** ~**n tun** to do sb's will; **seinen** ~**n durchsetzen** to get one's (own) way; **jdm seinen** ~**n lassen** to let sb have his own way; **seinen eigenen** ~**n haben** to be self-willed; **beim besten** ~**n nicht** not with the best will in the world; **es war kein böser** ~ there was no ill-will intended; **der gute** ~ good will.

willen *prep siehe* **um 2.**

willenlos adj weak-willed. **völlig ~ sein** to have no will of one's own; **jds ~es Werkzeug sein** to be the mere tool of sb.

willens adj (geh) **~ sein** to be willing.

Willens-: **~äußerung** f expression of will; **~freiheit** f freedom of will; **~kraft** f willpower; **w~schwach** adj weak-willed; **~schwäche** f weakness of will; **w~stark** adj strong-willed; **~stärke** f willpower.

willentlich adj wilful (Brit), willful (US), deliberate.

willig adj willing.

willkommen adj welcome. **du bist (mir) immer ~** you are always welcome; **jdn ~ heißen** to welcome sb; **herzlich ~ welcome** (in +dat to); **es ist mir ganz ~, daß ...** I quite welcome the fact that ...

Willkommen nt - welcome.

Willkommensgruß m greeting, welcome.

Willkür f no pl capriciousness; (politisch) despotism; (bei Handlungen) arbitrariness. **das ist reinste ~** that is purely arbitrary.

Willkür-: **~akt** m despotic act; **~herrschaft** f tyranny.

willkürlich adj arbitrary; Herrscher autocratic.

wimmeln vi auch vi impers **der See wimmelt von Fischen** the lake is teeming with fish; **hier wimmelt es von Mücken/Menschen** this place is swarming with midges/people.

wimmern vi to whimper.

Wimpel m - pennant.

Wimper f -n (eye)lash. **ohne mit der ~ zu zucken** (fig) without batting an eyelid.

Wimperntusche f mascara.

Wind m -e (a) wind. **bei ~ und Wetter** in all weathers; **der ~ dreht sich** the wind is changing direction; **merken, woher der ~ weht** (fig) to see the way the wind is blowing; **daher weht der ~!** (fig) so that's the way the wind is blowing; **seither weht ein anderer/frischer ~** (fig) things have changed since then; **viel ~ um etw machen** (col) to make a lot of fuss about sth; **den Mantel** or **das Fähnchen nach dem ~ hängen** to trim one's sails to the wind; **jdm den ~ aus den Segeln nehmen** (fig) to take the wind out of sb's sails; **sich** (dat) **den ~ um die Ohren wehen lassen** to see a bit of the world; **etw in den ~ schlagen** to turn a deaf ear to sth; **in alle (vier) ~e** to the four winds; **von etw ~ bekommen** (fig col) to get wind of sth. (b) (Med: Blähung) wind.

Wind-: (b) **~beutel** m (a) cream puff; (b) (col: Mensch) rake; **~bö(e)** f gust of wind.

Winde¹ f -n (Tech) winch, windlass.

Winde² f -n (Bot) bindweed, convulvulus.

Windel f -n nappy (Brit), diaper (US).

windelweich adj **jdn ~ schlagen** (col) to beat the living daylights out of sb (col).

winden pret **wand,** ptp **gewunden 1** vt to wind; **Kranz** to bind. **2** vr (Bach, Schlange, Pflanze) to wind; (Mensch) (durch Menge etc) to wind (one's way); (vor Schmerzen) to writhe (vor with, in); (fig: ausweichen) to try to wriggle out.

Windesieile f **etw in ~ tun** to do sth in no time (at all); **sich in** or **mit ~ verbreiten** to spread like wildfire.

Wind-: **w~geschützt 1** adj sheltered (from the wind); **2** adv in a sheltered place; **~geschwindigkeit** f wind speed; **~hauch** m breath of wind; **~hose** f vortex; **~hund** m (a) (Hund) greyhound; (b) (fig pej) rake.

windig adj windy; (fig) Sache dodgy (col).

Wind-: **~jacke** f windcheater (Brit), windbreaker ® (US); **~jammer** m - (Naut) windjammer; **~mühle** f windmill; **gegen ~mühlen (an)kämpfen** (fig) to tilt at windmills; **~mühlenflügel** m windmill sail; **~pocken** pl chickenpox sing; **~richtung** f wind direction; **~rose** f (Naut) compass card; (Met) wind rose; **~schatten** m lee;

(von Autos) slipstream; **w~schief** adj crooked; **~schirm** m windbreak; **~schutzscheibe** f windscreen (Brit), windshield (US); **~seite** f windward side; **~skala** f wind scale; **~stärke** f (Met) wind-force; **w~still** adj windless; **Ecke** etc sheltered; **wenn es völlig w~still ist** when there is no wind at all; **~stille** f calm; **~stoß** m gust of wind.

Windung f (von Weg, Fluß etc) meander; (von Schlange, Spule) coil; (von Schraube) thread.

Wink m -e (Zeichen) sign; (mit der Hand) wave (mit of); (mit dem Kopf) nod (mit of); (Hinweis, Tip) hint, tip.

Winkel m - (a) angle. (b) (fig: Ecke) corner; (Plätzchen) place, spot. **jdn/etw in allen (Ecken und) ~n suchen** to look high and low for sb/sth.

Winkel-: **~advokat** m (pej) incompetent lawyer; **~eisen** nt angle iron.

wink(e)lig adj Haus, Altstadt full of nooks and crannies; Gasse twisty, windy.

Winkelmesser m - protractor.

winken ptp **gewinkt** or (col) **gewunken 1** vi to wave (jdm to sb). **sie winkte mit einem Fähnchen** she waved a flag; **einem Taxi ~** to hail a taxi; **dem Sieger winkt eine Reise nach Italien** the winner will receive (the attractive prize of) a trip to Italy. **2** vt to wave; Abseits to signal; Taxi to hail; Kellner to call. **jdn zu sich ~** to beckon sb over to one.

winseln vti to whimper; (pej) to grovel.

Winter m - winter. **es ist/wird ~** winter is here/is coming; **im/über den ~** in (the)/over the winter; **über den ~ kommen** to get through the winter.

Winter- in cpds winter; **~anfang** m beginning of winter; **~einbruch** m onset of winter; **w~fest** adj winterproof; (Bot) hardy; **~garten** m winter garden; **~getreide** nt winter crop; **~halbjahr** nt winter; **~kleid** nt winter dress; (Zool) winter coat; **~kleidung** f winter clothing; **w~lich** adj wintry; **~kleidung** f Kleidung winter attr; **w~lich gekleidet** dressed for winter; **~obst** nt winter fruit; **~pause** f winter break; **~quartier** nt winter quarters pl; **~reifen** m winter tyre (Brit) or tire (US); **~saat** f winter seed; **~sachen** pl winter clothes pl; **~schlaf** m hibernation; **~schlaf halten** to hibernate; **~schlußverkauf** m winter sale; **~semester** nt winter semester; **~spiele** pl (Olympische) **~spiele** Winter Olympics pl; **~sport** m winter sports pl; (Sportart) winter sport; **~zeit** f winter time; (Jahreszeit) winter.

Winzer(in f) m - wine-grower; (Weinleser) grape-picker.

winzig adj tiny. **~ klein** minute, tiny little attr.

Wipfel m - treetop.

Wippe f -n seesaw.

wippen vi (auf und ab) to bob up and down; (hin und her) to teeter. **~der Gang** bouncing gait.

wir pers pron we. **~ alle/beide/drei** all/both/the three of us; **~ Armen** we poor people; **wer ist da?** — **~ (sind's)** who's there? — (it's) us; **trinken ~ erst mal einen** let's have a drink first.

Wirbel m - (a) (lit, fig) whirl; (in Fluß etc) whirlpool, eddy; (der Ereignisse) turmoil. **einen ~ um jdn/etw machen** to make a fuss about sb/sth. (b) (Haar~) crown. (c) (Anat) vertebra. (d) (Trommel~) (drum) roll.

wirbellos adj (Zool) invertebrate. **die W~en** the invertebrates.

wirbeln vi (a) (aux sein) to whirl. (b) **mir wirbelt der Kopf** (col) my head is reeling. (c) (Trommeln etc) to roll. **2** vt to whirl.

Wirbel-: **~säule** f (Anat) spinal column; **~sturm** m whirlwind; **~tier** nt vertebrate; **~wind** m whirlwind.

wirken¹ 1 vi (a) (Wirkung haben) to have an effect. **die Arznei hat nicht gewirkt** the medicine did not work; **schalldämpfend ~** to have a sound-proofing effect; **das Bild wirkt hier nicht richtig** the picture doesn't fit in here; **etw auf sich** (acc)

~ lassen to take sth in. **(b)** *(erscheinen)* to seem, to appear. **nervös (auf jdn)** ~ to give (sb) the impression of being nervous; **sie wirkt abstoßend auf mich** I find her repulsive. **(c)** *(geh: tätig sein) (Mensch)* to work; *(Einflüsse, Kräfte etc)* to be at work. **2** *vt (geh: tun)* Gutes to do; Wunder to work.

wirken² *vt* Teppiche, Stoffe to weave.

wirklich *adj* real. **im ~en Leben** in real life. **2** *adv* really. **~?** really?

Wirklichkeit *f* reality. **~ werden** to come true; **in ~** in reality.

wirklichkeits-: **~fremd** *adj* unrealistic; **~getreu** *adj* realistic; **etw ~getreu abbilden** to paint a realistic picture of sth.

wirksam *adj* effective. **mit (dem)/am 1. Januar ~ werden** *(form: Gesetz)* to take effect on *or* from January 1st.

Wirksamkeit *f* effectiveness.

Wirkstoff *m (esp Physiol)* active substance.

Wirkung *f* effect *(bei* on*)*; *(von Tabletten etc)* effects *pl*. **seine ~ tun** to have an effect; *(Droge)* to take effect; **ohne ~ bleiben** to have no effect; **seine ~ verfehlen** not to have the desired effect; **mit ~ vom 1. Januar** *(form)* with effect from January 1st.

Wirkungs-: **~bereich** *m* field of activity/interest *etc)*; *(Domäne)* domain; **w~los** *adj* ineffective; **~losigkeit** *f* ineffectiveness; **w~voll** *adj* effective; **~weise** *f (von Medikament)* action; **die ~weise eines Kondensators** the way a condenser works.

Wirkwaren *pl* knitwear *sing*.

wirr *adj* confused; Blick crazed; *(unordentlich)* Haare tangled; Gedanken weird. **er ist ~ im Kopf** he is confused in his mind; **mach mich nicht ~** don't confuse me; **alles lag ~ durcheinander** everything was in chaos.

Wirren *pl* confusion *sing*, turmoil *sing*.

Wirrkopf *m (pej)* muddle-head.

Wirrwarr *m no pl* confusion; *(von Stimmen)* hubbub; *(von Fäden, Haaren etc)* tangle.

Wirsing *m no pl* savoy cabbage.

Wirt *m -e (Gastwirt, Vermieter)* landlord.

Wirtin *f* landlady; *(Gastgeberin)* hostess.

Wirtschaft *f* **(a)** *(Volks~)* economy; *(Geschäftsleben)* industry and commerce; *(Finanzwelt)* business world. **freie ~** free market economy. **(b)** *(Gast~)* ≈ pub *(Brit)*, saloon *(US)*. **(c)** *(col: Zustände)* **eine schöne/saubere ~** *(iro)* a fine state of affairs.

wirtschaften 1 *vi* **(a)** *(sparsam sein)* to economize. **gut ~ können** to be economical. **(b)** *(col: sich betätigen)* to busy oneself. **2** *vt* jdn/etw zugrunde ~ to ruin sb/sth financially.

Wirtschafter(in *f)* *m -* **(a)** *(Verwalter)* manager. **(b)** *(im Haushalt, Heim etc)* housekeeper.

wirtschaftlich *adj* economic; *(sparsam)* economical.

Wirtschaftlichkeit *f* economy.

Wirtschafts- *in cpds* economic; **~berater** *m* economic advisor; **~form** *f* economic system; **~gebäude** *nt* working quarters *pl*; **~geld** *nt* housekeeping (money); **~gemeinschaft** *f* economic community; **~güter** *pl* economic goods *pl*; **~hilfe** *f* economic aid; **~krieg** *m* economic war/warfare; **~kriminalität** *f* white-collar crime; **~krise** *f* economic crisis; **~lage** *f* economic situation; **~minister** *m* minister of economic affairs; **~ministerium** *nt* ministry of economic affairs; **~ordnung** *f* economic order; **~politik** *f* economic policy; **~prüfer** *m* accountant; *(zum Überprüfen der Bücher)* auditor; **~recht** *nt* commercial *or* business law; **~spionage** *f* industrial espionage; **~system** *nt* economic system; **~verband** *m* business association; **~wissenschaft** *f* economics *sing*; **~wissenschaftler** *m* economist; **~wunder** *nt*

economic miracle; **~zeitung** *f* financial paper; **~zweig** *m* branch of industry.

Wirts-: **~haus** *nt* ≈ pub *(Brit)*, saloon *(US)*; *(esp auf dem Land)* inn; **~leute** *pl* landlord and landlady; **~stube** *f* lounge.

Wisch *m -e (pej col)* piece of paper; *(mit Gedrucktem)* piece of bumph *(Brit col)*.

wischen 1 *vti* to wipe. **Staub ~** to dust; **mit einem Tuch über eine Schallplatte ~** to wipe a record with a cloth; **sie wischte sich** *(dat)* **den Schweiß von der Stirn** she wiped the sweat from her brow; **Bedenken** *(einfach)* **vom Tisch ~** *(fig)* to brush aside misgivings; **jdm eine ~** *(col)* to clout sb one *(col)*; **eine gewischt bekommen** *(col: elektrischen Schlag)* to get a shock. **2** *vi aux sein (sich schnell bewegen)* to whisk.

Wischer *m -* *(Aut)* wiper.

Wischerblatt *nt (Aut)* wiper blade.

Wischiwaschi *nt no pl (pej col)* drivel *(col)*.

Wischlappen *m* cloth; *(für Fußboden)* floorcloth.

Wisent *m -e* bison.

wispern *vti* to whisper.

Wißbegier(de) *f* thirst for knowledge.

wißbegierig *adj* Kind eager to learn.

wissen *pret* **wußte**, *ptp* **gewußt** *vti* **(a)** to know *(von* about*)*. **ich weiß (es)** I know; **er weiß von nichts** he doesn't know anything about it; **weißt du schon das Neuste?** have you heard the latest?; **als ob ich das wüßte!** how should I know?; **von jdm/etw nichts ~ wollen** not to be interested in sb/sth; **er weiß es nicht anders/besser** he doesn't know any different/better; **das mußt du (selbst) ~** it's your decision; **das hättest du ja ~ müssen!** you ought to have realized that; **man kann nie ~** you never know; **weiß Gott** *(col)* God knows *(col)*; **sie hält sich für wer weiß wie klug** *(col)* she doesn't half think she's clever *(col)*; **... oder was weiß ich** *(col)* **...** or something; **er ist wieder wer weiß wo** *(col)* goodness knows where he's got to again *(col)*; **nicht, daß ich wüßte** not as far as I know; **gewußt wie/wo** etc! sheer brilliance!; **ich weiß sie in Sicherheit** I know that she is safe. **(b)** *(sich erinnern)* to remember; *(sich vor Augen führen)* to realize. **ich weiß seine Adresse nicht mehr** I can't remember his address; **du mußt ~, daß** ... you must realize that ...

Wissen *nt no pl* knowledge. **meines ~s** to my knowledge; **etw gegen (sein) besseres ~ tun** to do sth against one's better judgement; **nach bestem ~ und Gewissen** to the best of one's knowledge and belief.

Wissenschaft *f* science.

Wissenschaftler(in *f)* *m -* scientist; *(Geistes~)* academic.

wissenschaftlich *adj* scientific; *(geistes~)* academic. **W~er Assistent** assistant lecturer.

Wissens-: **~durst** *m (geh)* thirst for knowledge; **~gebiet** *nt* field (of knowledge); **~stoff** *m* material; **w~wert** *adj* worth knowing.

wissentlich 1 *adv* knowingly, deliberately. **2** *adj* deliberate.

wittern 1 *vi (Wild)* to sniff the air. **2** *vt* to scent.

Witterung *f* **(a)** *(Wetter)* weather. **bei günstiger ~** if the weather is good. **(b)** *(Hunt) (Geruch)* scent *(von* of*)*; *(Geruchssinn)* sense of smell.

Witterungs- *in cpds* weather; **~einflüsse** *pl* effects *pl* of the weather; **~umschlag** *m* change in the weather.

Witwe *f -n* widow. **~ werden** to be widowed.

Witwen-: **~geld** *nt* widow's allowance; **~rente** *f* widow's pension; **~stand** *m* widowhood.

Witwer *m -* widower.

Witz *m -e (a)* *(Äußerung)* joke *(über +acc* about*)*. **einen ~ machen** to make a joke; **mach keine ~e!** don't be funny; **das ist doch wohl ein ~** he/you *etc* must be joking; **die Prüfung war ein ~** *(col)* the exam was a joke. **(b)** *(Geist)* wit. **der ~ an der Sache ist, daß** ... the great thing about it is that ...

Witz-: ~**blatt** nt joke book; ~**bold** m -e joker; **du bist vielleicht ein** ~**bold!** (iro) you're a great one! (iro).

witzeln vi to joke (über +acc about).

Witzfigur f (fig col) figure of fun.

witzig adj funny.

witzlos adj (col: unsinnig) pointless, futile.

wo 1 interrog, rel adv where; (irgendwo) somewhere. **überall,** ~ **wherever;** ~ **immer** ... **wherever** ...; **ach** ~! (col) nonsense! **2** conj ~ **nicht/möglich** if not/possible; ~ **er doch wußte, daß ich nicht kommen konnte** when he knew I couldn't come.

wo-: ~**anders** adv somewhere else; ~**andersher** adv from somewhere else; ~**andershin** adv somewhere else.

wob pret of **weben.**

wobei adv (a) interrog ~ **ist das passiert?** how did that happen?; ~ **hast du ihn erwischt?** what did you catch him at or doing? (b) rel ... **sagte er,** ~ **er mich scharf ansah** ..., he said with a penetrating look; ..., ~ **er das Buch aufschlug** ... opening the book; ..., ~ **mir gerade einfällt** which reminds me.

Woche f -n week. **zweimal in der** ~ twice a week; **in dieser** ~ this week.

Wochenbett nt im ~ **sterben** to die after childbirth; **während sie im** ~ **lag** during the period after the birth of her child.

Wochen|end- in cpds weekend.

Wochen|ende nt weekend. **schönes** ~! have a nice weekend; **verlängertes** ~ long weekend.

Wochen-: ~**karte** f weekly ticket; **w**~**lang** adj, adv for weeks; ~**lohn** m weekly wage; ~**markt** m weekly market; ~**schau** f newsreel; ~**tag** m weekday (including Saturday); **was ist heute für ein** ~**tag?** what day is it today?; **w**~**tags** adv on weekdays.

wöchentlich 1 adj weekly. **2** adv weekly; (einmal pro Woche) once a week. **sich** ~ **abwechseln** to take turns every week.

Wochen-: **w**~**weise** adv by the week; ~**zeitschrift** f weekly; ~**zeitung** f weekly (paper).

Wöchnerin f woman who has recently given birth.

Wodka m -s vodka.

wodurch adv (a) interrog how. (b) rel as a result of which.

wofür adv (a) interrog for what, what ... for. (b) rel for which, which ... for.

wog pret of **wiegen**².

Woge f -n wave; (fig auch) surge.

wogegen adv (a) interrog against what, what ... against. (b) rel against which, which ... against.

woher adv (a) interrog where ... from. ~ **weißt du das?** how do you (come to) know that?; ~ **kommt es eigentlich, daß** ... how is it that ...? (b) rel from which, where ... from.

wohin adv (a) interrog where. (b) rel where. ~ **man auch schaut** wherever you look.

wohingegen conj whereas, while.

wohinter adv (a) interrog what or where ... behind. (b) rel behind which.

wohl 1 adv (a) (angenehm zumute) happy; (gesund) well. **sich** ~/~**er fühlen** to feel happy/happier; (gesundheitlich) to feel well/better; **bei dem Gedanken ist mir nicht** ~ I'm not very happy at the thought; ~ **oder übel** whether one likes it or not; ~ **dem, der** ... happy the man who ... (b) (wahrscheinlich) probably; (iro: bestimmt) surely. **er ist** ~ **schon zu Hause** he's probably at home by now; **das ist doch** ~ **nicht dein Ernst!** surely you're not serious! (c) (vielleicht) perhaps; (etwa) about. **das mag** ~ **sein** that may well be; **ob das** ~ **stimmt?** I wonder if that's true; **willst du das** ~ **lassen!** I wish you'd stop (doing) that. (d) (durchaus) well. **ich denke, ich verstehe dich sehr** ~! I think I understand you very well. **2** conj (zwar) **er hat es** ~ **versprochen, aber** ...

he may have promised, but ....

Wohl nt no pl welfare, well-being. **das öffentliche** ~ the public good; **zu eurem** ~ for your benefit or good; **zum** ~! cheers!; **auf dein** ~! your health!; **auf jds** ~ **trinken** to drink sb's health.

Wohl-: **w**~**auf** adj pred in good health; ~**befinden** nt well-being; **w**~**begründet** adj well-founded; Maßnahme, Strafe well-justified; ~**behagen** nt feeling of well-being; **w**~**behalten** adj Mensch safe and sound; Gegenstand intact; **w**~**bekannt** adj well-known; **w**~**beleibt** adj (hum) stout, portly; **w**~**durchdacht** adj well thought out; ~**ergehen** nt no pl welfare; **w**~**erzogen** adj (geh) well-mannered.

Wohlfahrt f no pl welfare.

Wohlfahrts-: ~**einrichtung** f social service; ~**marke** f charity stamp; ~**organisation** f charity; ~**pflege** f welfare work; **freie** ~**pflege** voluntary welfare work; ~**staat** m welfare state.

Wohl-: ~**gefallen** nt no pl pleasure; **sich in** ~**gefallen auflösen** (hum) (Gegenstände, Probleme) to vanish into thin air; (zerfallen) to fall apart; **w**~**gefällig** adj (gefallend) pleasing. **w**~**geformt** adj well-shaped; Körperteil shapely; Satz well-formed; ~**gefühl** nt sense of well-being; **w**~**gemeint** adj well-intentioned; **w**~**gemerkt** adv mark you; **w**~**genährt** adj well-fed; **w**~**geraten** adj (geh) Kind fine; Werk successful; ~**geruch** m (geh) pleasant smell ~**geschmack** m (geh) pleasant taste; **w**~**gesinnt** adj (geh) well-disposed (dat towards); **w**~**habend** adj well-to-do.

wohlig adj pleasant; (gemütlich) cosy (Brit), cozy (US). ~ **warm** nice and warm.

Wohl-: **w**~**klang** m (geh) melodious sound; **w**~**klingend** adj melodious; ~**leben** nt (geh) life of luxury; **w**~**meinend** adj well-meaning; **w**~**riechend** adj fragrant.

Wohlstand m no pl affluence, prosperity.

Wohlstandsgesellschaft f affluent society.

Wohltat f (a) (Genuß) relief. (b) (Gefallen) favour (Brit), favor (US); (gute Tat) good deed. **jdm eine** ~ **erweisen** to do sb a favour.

Wohltäter(in f) m benefactor; benefactress.

wohltätig adj charitable. **für** ~**e Zwecke** for charity.

Wohltätigkeits-: ~**basar** m charity bazaar; ~**verein** m charity.

Wohl-: **w**~**tuend** adj pleasant; **w**~**tun** vi sep irreg (angenehm sein) to do good (jdm sb); **das tut w**~ that's good; **w**~**überlegt** adj etw **w**~**überlegt machen** to do sth after careful consideration; **w**~**verdient** adj well-deserved; ~**verhalten** nt good conduct; ~**wollen** nt no pl goodwill; **w**~**wollend** adj benevolent.

Wohn-: ~**anhänger** m caravan (Brit), trailer (US); ~**bau** m, pl -**ten** residential building; ~**block** m, pl -**s** block of flats (Brit), apartment house (US).

wohnen vi to live; (vorübergehend) to stay. **er wohnt in (der) Friedrichstraße 11** he lives at (number) 11 Friedrichstraße; **wir** ~ **da sehr schön** it's very nice where we live.

Wohn-: ~**fläche** f living space; ~**gebiet** nt residential area; ~**geld** nt a rent allowance; ~**gemeinschaft** f (Menschen) people sharing a/the flat (Brit) or apartment/house; **in einer** ~**gemeinschaft leben** to share a flat etc; ~**haus** nt residential building; ~**heim** nt (esp für Arbeiter) hostel; (für Studenten) hall (of residence), dormitory (US); (für Senioren) home; ~**komfort** m mit sämtlichem ~**komfort** with all mod cons; ~**komplex** m housing estate; ~**küche** f kitchen-cum-livingroom; ~**kultur** f style of home décor; **w**~**lich** adj cosy (Brit), cozy (US); **es sich** (dat) **w**~**lich machen** to make oneself comfortable; ~**mobil** nt motor caravan (Brit) or trailer (US); ~**ort** m place of residence; ~**siedlung** f housing estate (Brit), development; ~**sitz**

m domicile; **ohne festen** ~**sitz** of no fixed abode; ~**stadt** *f* residential town.
Wohnung *f* flat *(Brit)*, apartment. **1.000 neue** ~**en** 1,000 new homes.
Wohnungs-: ~**amt** *nt* housing office; ~**bau** *m no pl* house building *no def art*; ~**besetzer(in** *f) m* - squatter; ~**inhaber** *m* householder; *(Eigentümer auch)* owner-occupier; **w**~**los** *adj* homeless; ~**makler** *m* estate agent *(Brit)*, realtor *(US)*; ~**mangel** *m* housing shortage; ~**markt** *m* housing market; ~**not** *f* serious housing shortage; ~**suche** *f* flat-hunting *(Brit)*; **auf** ~**suche sein** to be looking for a flat *(Brit)* or an apartment; ~**tür** *f* door (to the flat *(Brit)* or apartment); ~**wechsel** *m* change of address.
Wohn-: ~**viertel** *nt* residential area; ~**wagen** *m* caravan *(Brit)*, trailer *(US)*; ~**zimmer** *nt* living-room.
wölben 1 *vt* to curve; *Dach* to vault. **2** *vr* to curve; *(Tapete)* to bulge out; *(Decke, Brücke)* to arch.
Wölbung *f* curvature; *(kuppelförmig)* dome; *(bogenförmig)* arch; *(von Körperteil)* curve.
Wolf *m* ⁼**e (a)** *m* wolf. **ein** ~ **im Schafspelz** a wolf in sheep's clothing; **mit den** ~**en heulen** *(fig)* to run with the pack. **(b)** *(Tech)* shredder; *(Fleisch*~*)* mincer *(Brit)*, grinder *(US)*.
Wolfram *nt no pl (Chem)* tungsten.
Wolfs-: ~**hund** *m* Alsatian *(Brit)*, German shepherd; **irischer** ~**hund** Irish wolfhound; ~**milch** *f* *(Bot)* spurge; ~**rachen** *m* *(Med)* cleft palate; ~**rudel** *nt* pack of wolves.
Wolke *f* -**n** *(lit, fig)* cloud. **aus allen** ~**n fallen** *(fig)* to be flabbergasted *(col)*.
Wolken-: ~**bank** *f* cloudbank; ~**bruch** *m* cloudburst; **w**~**bruchartig** *adj* torrential; ~**decke** *f* cloud cover; ~**kratzer** *m* skyscraper; ~**kuckucksheim** *nt* cloud-cuckoo-land; **w**~**los** *adj* cloudless; **w**~**verhangen** *adj* overcast.
wolkig *adj* cloudy.
Wolldecke *f* (woollen *(Brit)* or woolen *US*) blanket.
Wolle *f* -**n** wool. **sich mit jdm in die** ~**kriegen** *(fig col)* to start squabbling with sb.
wollen¹ *adj attr* woollen *(Brit)*, woolen *(US)*.
wollen² **1** *modal aux ptp* ~ to want to. **er will ein Haus kaufen** he wants to buy a house; **etw gerade tun** ~ to be going to do sth; **wolltest du gerade weggehen?** were you just leaving?; **es sieht aus, als wollte es regnen** it looks as if it's going to rain; **es will einfach nicht klappen** it just won't work; **keiner will es gewesen sein** nobody will admit to it; **er will ihn gesehen haben** he claims to have seen him; **und so jemand** *or* **etwas** *(col)* **will Lehrer sein!** and he calls himself a teacher; **ich wollte, ich wäre ...** I wish I were ...; **darauf** ~ **wir mal anstoßen!** let's drink to that; **das will alles gut überlegt sein** that needs a lot of thought.
2 *vti* to want. **kommt er nun? — nein, er will nicht** is he coming? — no, he doesn't want to; **ich will nach Hause** I want to go home; **oh, das hab ich nicht gewollt** oh, I didn't mean to do that; **ich will, daß du genau zuhörst** I want you to listen carefully; **ob du willst oder nicht** whether you like it or not; **er hat nichts zu** ~ he has no say; **ich weiß nicht, was er will** *(verstehe ihn nicht)* I don't know what he's on about; *siehe* **gewollt**.
Woll-: ~**faser** *f* wool fibre *(Brit)* or fiber *(US)*; ~**garn** *nt* woollen *(Brit)* or woolen *(US)* yarn. **wollig** *adj* woolly.
Woll-: ~**jacke** *f* cardigan; ~**knäuel** *nt* ball of wool; ~**sachen** *pl* woollens *pl (Brit)*, woolens *pl (US)*; ~**stoff** *m* woollen *(Brit)* or woolen *(US)* material.
Wollust *f no pl (geh) (Sinnlichkeit)* sensuality; *(Lüsternheit)* lust.
wollüstig *adj (geh) (sinnlich)* sensual; *(lüstern)* lascivious.
Wollwaren *pl* woollens *pl (Brit)*, woolens *pl (US)*.

womit *adv* **(a)** *interrog* with what, what ... with. ~ **kann ich dienen?** what can I do for you? **(b)** *rel* with which; *(auf ganzen Satz bezüglich)* by which. **das ist es,** ~ **ich nicht einverstanden bin** that's what I don't agree with; ~ **ich nicht sagen will, daß ...** by which I don't mean that ...
womöglich *adv* possibly.
wonach *adv* **(a)** *interrog* after what, what ... after. ~ **sollen wir uns richten?** what should we go by? **(b)** *rel* **das war es,** ~ **ich mich erkundigen wollte** that was what I wanted to ask about.
Wonne *f* -**n** *(geh) (Glückseligkeit)* bliss *no pl; (Vergnügen)* joy, delight. **die** ~**n der Liebe** the joys of love; **es ist eine wahre** ~ it's a sheer delight.
wonnevoll *adj Gefühl* blissful; *Kind, Anblick* delightful. ~ **lächeln** to smile with delight.
wonnig *adj* delightful; *Gefühl* blissful.
woran *adv* **(a)** *interrog* ~ **liegt das?** what's the reason for it? **(b)** *rel* by which. **das,** ~ **ich mich gerne erinnere** what I like to recall; ~ **ich merkte, daß ...** which made me realize that ...
worauf *adv* **(a)** *interrog (räumlich)* on what, what ... on. ~ **wartest du?** what are you waiting for? **(b)** *rel (zeitlich)* whereupon. ~ **er einen Wutanfall bekam** whereupon he flew into a rage; ~ **du dich verlassen kannst** of that you can be sure.
woraus *adv* **(a)** *interrog* out of what, what ... out of. **(b)** *rel* out of which, which ... out of. ~ **ich schließe, daß ...** from which I conclude that ...
worden *ptp of* **werden 2 (c)**.
worin *adv* **(a)** *interrog* in what, what ... in. ~ **war das eingewickelt?** what was it wrapped in? **(b)** *rel* in which, ... in. **das ist etwas,** ~ **wir nicht übereinstimmen** that's something we don't agree on.
Wort *nt* -**e (a)** *pl usu* ⁼**er** *(Vokabel)* word. ~ **für** ~ word for word.
(b) *(Äußerung)* word. **genug der** ~**e!** enough talk!; ~**en Taten folgen lassen** to suit the action to the word(s); **mit einem** ~ in a word; **mit anderen** ~**en** in other words; **hast du (da noch)** ~**e!** it leaves you speechless; **mir fehlen die** ~**e** words fail me; **kein** ~ **von etw sagen** not to say one word about sth; **ich verstehe kein** ~! I don't understand a word (of it); *(hören)* I can't hear a word (that's being said); **ein** ~ **mit jdm sprechen** to have a word with sb; **ein ernstes** ~ **mit jdm reden** to have a serious talk with sb; **davon hat man mir kein** ~ **gesagt** they didn't tell me anything about it; **man kann sein eigenes** ~ **nicht (mehr) verstehen** you can't hear yourself speak; **um nicht viel(e)** ~ **zu machen** to make it brief; **jdm das** ~ **im Mund (her)umdrehen** to twist sb's words; **die passenden** ~**e für etw finden** to find the right words for sth; **jdm aufs** ~ **glauben** to believe sb implicitly; **jdm aufs** ~ **gehorchen** to obey sb's every word; **dabei habe ich auch (noch) ein** ~ **mitzureden** I (still) have something to say about that too; **jdn beim** ~ **nehmen** to take sb at his word; **ich gebe Ihnen mein** ~ **darauf** I give you my word on it; **sein** ~ **halten** to keep one's word.
(c) *no pl* **das große** ~ **führen** *(col)* to shoot one's mouth off *(col)*; **das** ~ **an jdn richten** to address (oneself to) sb; **jdm ins** ~ **fallen** to interrupt sb; **zu** ~ **kommen** to get a chance to speak; **sich zu** ~ **melden** to ask to speak; **jdm das** ~ **erteilen** to allow sb to speak.
(d) *(Ausspruch)* saying; *(Zitat)* quotation. *(Rel)* Word. **ein** ~ **Goethes** a quotation from Goethe.
(e) *(Text)* words *pl.* **in** ~**en** in words; **in** ~ **und Bild** in words and pictures; **in** ~ **und Schrift** in speech and writing; **etw in** ~**e fassen** to put sth into words.
Wort-: ~**art** *f (Gram)* part of speech; ~**bruch** *m* **das wäre ein** ~**bruch** that would be breaking your/my *etc* word; **w**~**brüchig** *adj* false; **w**~**brü-**

chig werden to break one's word.
Wörtchen nt dim of **Wort da habe ich wohl ein** ~ **mitzureden** (col) I think I have some say in that.
Wörter-: ~**buch** nt dictionary; ~**verzeichnis** nt vocabulary; (von Spezialbegriffen) glossary.
Wort-: ~**führer** m spokesman; ~**gebühr** f (Telec) rate per word; ~**gefecht** nt battle of words; **w**~**getreu** adj, adv verbatim; **w**~**gewandt** adj eloquent; **w**~**karg** adj taciturn; ~**klauberei** f quibbling; ~**laut** m wording; **im** ~**laut** verbatim.
wörtlich adj Bedeutung literal; Rede direct. **etw** ~ **wiedergeben** to repeat sth word for word; **das hat er** ~ **gesagt** those were his very words.
Wort-: **w**~**los** 1 adj silent; 2 adv without saying a word; ~**meldung** f **wenn es keine weiteren** ~**meldungen gibt** if nobody else wishes to speak; **w**~**reich** adj Rede, Erklärung etc wordy; Sprache rich in vocabulary; ~**schatz** m vocabulary; ~**spiel** nt pun; ~**stellung** f (Gram) word order; ~**wahl** f choice of words; ~**wechsel** m verbal exchange; **w**~**wörtlich** 1 adj word-for-word; 2 adv quite literally.
worüber adv (a) interrog about what, what ... about; (örtlich) over what, what ... over. (b) rel about which, which ... about; (örtlich) over which, which ... over.
worum adv (a) interrog about what, what ... about. ~ **handelt es sich?** what's it about? (b) rel about which, which ... about.
worunter adv (a) interrog under what, what ... under. (b) rel under which, which ... under.
wovon adv (a) interrog from what, what ... from. (b) rel from which, which ... from. **das ist ein Gebiet,** ~ **er viel versteht** that is a subject he knows a lot about.
wovor adv (a) interrog (örtlich) before what, what ... before. ~ **fürchtest du dich?** what are you afraid of? (b) rel before which, which ... before.
wozu adv (a) interrog to what, what ... to; (warum) why. ~ **soll das gut sein?** what's the point of that? (b) rel to which, which ... to. **das,** ~ **ich am meisten neige** that what I'm most inclined to do.
Wrack nt -s wreck.
wringen pret **wrang**, ptp **gewrungen** vti to wring.
Wucher m no pl profiteering. **das ist der reinste** ~! that's daylight robbery! (col).
Wucherer(in f) m - profiteer.
Wuchergeschäft nt profiteering no pl.
wucherisch adj profiteering; Zinsen etc extortionate.
wuchern vi (a) aux sein or haben (Pflanzen) to grow rampant. (b) (Kaufmann etc) to profiteer.
wuchernd adj Pflanzen rampant.
Wucherpreis m exorbitant price.
Wucherung f rank growth; (Med) growth.
Wucherzins m exorbitant interest no pl.
wuchs [vu:ks] pret of **wachsen**[1].
Wuchs [vu:ks] m no pl (Wachstum) growth; (von Mensch) stature.
Wucht f no pl force. **mit voller** ~ with full force; **er ist eine** ~! (col) he's smashing! (col).
wuchten vti to heave.
wuchtig adj massive; Schlag powerful.
wühlen 1 vi (a) (nach for) to dig; (Maulwurf etc) to burrow; (Schwein, Vogel) to root. **in den Haaren** ~ to run one's fingers through one's hair. (b) (suchen) to rummage (nach etw for sth). **in den Schubladen** ~ to rummage through the drawers. (c) (Untergrundarbeit leisten) to stir things up. 2 vr **sich durch etw** ~ to burrow one's way through sth.
Wühlmaus f vole.
Wulst m or f -e bulge.
wulstig adj bulging; Rand, Lippen thick.
wund adj sore. **sich** (dat) **die Füße** ~ **laufen** (lit) to get sore feet from walking; (fig) to walk one's legs off; **ein** ~**er Punkt** a sore point.

Wundbrand m gangrene.
Wunde f -n (lit, fig) wound. **alte** ~**n wieder aufreißen** (fig) to open up old sores; **an eine alte** ~ **rühren** (fig geh) to touch on a sore point; **Salz in eine/jds** ~ **streuen** (fig) to turn the knife in the wound.
Wunder nt - miracle (auch Rel), wonder. ~ **wirken** to work miracles; **das grenzt an ein** ~ it verges on the miraculous; **die** ~ **der Natur** the wonders of nature; **es ist ein/kein** ~**, daß** ... it's a wonder/small wonder that ...; **ist es ein** ~**, daß er dick ist?** is it any wonder that he's fat?
wunder adv inv **meine Eltern denken** ~ **was passiert ist** my parents think goodness knows what has happened; **er glaubt,** ~ **wer er ist** he thinks he's so fantastic.
wunderbar adj (a) wonderful. (b) (übernatürlich) miraculous.
wunderbarerweise adv miraculously.
Wunder-: ~**droge** f wonder drug; **w**~**gläubig** adj **w**~**gläubig sein** to believe in miracles; ~**heiler** m faith-healer; ~**kerze** f sparkler; ~**kind** nt child prodigy; ~**land** nt wonderland; **w**~**lich** adj (a) (merkwürdig) strange, odd; (b) (w~sam) wondrous; ~**mittel** nt miracle cure.
wundern 1 vr to be surprised (über +acc at). **du wirst dich** ~! you'll be amazed!; **ich wundere mich über gar nichts mehr** nothing surprises me any more; **dann darfst du dich nicht** ~**, wenn** ... then don't be surprised if ... 2 vt, vt impers to surprise. **es wundert mich, daß er noch nicht hier ist** I'm surprised that he is not here yet; **das würde mich nicht** ~ I shouldn't be surprised.
Wunder-: **w**~**schön** adj beautiful; ~**täter** m miracle worker; **w**~**tätig** adj miraculous; Leben, Heilige miracle-working; ~**tüte** f surprise packet; **w**~**voll** adj marvellous (Brit), marvelous (US); ~**waffe** f wonder weapon; ~**werk** nt miracle.
Wund-: ~**fieber** nt traumatic fever; ~**infektion** f wound infection; ~**liegen** vr sep irreg to get bedsores; ~**pflaster** nt adhesive plaster; ~**salbe** f ointment; ~**starrkrampf** m tetanus.
Wunsch m -e (a) (sehnliches Verlangen) desire; (Bitte) request. **ein Pferd war schon immer mein** ~ I've always wanted a horse; **haben Sie** (sonst) **noch einen** ~? (beim Einkauf etc) is there anything else you'd like?; **alles geht nach** ~ everything is going smoothly; **auf** ~ on request; **auf jds (besonderen/ausdrücklichen)** ~ **hin** at sb's (special/express) request. (b) usu pl (Glückwunsch) wish.
Wunsch-: ~**bild** nt ideal; ~**denken** nt wishful thinking.
Wünschelrute f divining rod.
wünschen 1 vt (a) **sich** (dat) **etw** ~ to want sth; (den Wunsch äußern) to ask for sth; **ich wünsche mir das** I would like that; **ich wünsche mir, daß du** ... I would like you to ...; **das habe ich mir von meinen Eltern zu Weihnachten gewünscht** I asked my parents to give me that for Christmas; **er wünscht sich** (dat) **diesen Mann als Lehrer** he wishes that this man was his teacher; **was wünschst du dir?** what would you like?; **du darfst dir etwas** ~ you may make a wish; **sie haben alles, was man sich** (dat) **nur** ~ **kann** they have everything you could possibly wish for.
(b) **jdm etw** ~ to wish sb sth; **jdm einen guten Morgen** ~ to wish sb good morning; **wir** ~ **dir gute Besserung/eine gute Reise** we hope you get well soon/have a pleasant journey; **ich wünschte, ich hätte dich nie gesehen** I wish I'd never seen you.
(c) (begehren, verlangen) to want. **was** ~ **Sie?** (in Geschäft) what can I do for you?; (in Restaurant) what would you like?; **wen** ~ **Sie zu sprechen?** to whom would you like to speak?
2 vi to wish. **Sie** ~? what can I do for you?;

ganz wie Sie ~ (just) as you wish; **zu ~/viel zu ~ übrig lassen** to leave something/a great deal to be desired.

wünschenswert adj desirable.

Wunsch-: **w~gemäß** adv as requested; **~kind** nt planned child; **~konzert** nt (Rad) musical request programme (Brit) or program (US); **w~los** adj Mensch content(ed); **w~los glücklich** perfectly happy; **~sendung** f (Rad) request programme (Brit) or program (US); **~traum** m dream; **das ist doch bloß ein ~traum** that's just a pipe-dream; **~zettel** m list of things one would like.

wurde pret of **werden.**

Würde f **-n** (a) no pl dignity. **unter aller ~ sein** to be beneath contempt; **unter jds ~ sein** to be beneath sb or sb's dignity. **(b)** (Auszeichnung) honour (Brit), honor (US); (Titel) title; (Amt) rank.

würdelos adj undignified.

Würdenträger(in f) m - dignitary.

würdevoll adj = **würdig (a).**

würdig adj (a) dignified. **sich ~ verhalten** to behave with dignity. **(b)** (wert) worthy. **jds/ einer Sache** (gen) **~/nicht ~ sein** to be worthy/unworthy of sb/sth.

würdigen vt (a) to appreciate; (lobend erwähnen) to acknowledge. **etw zu ~ wissen** to appreciate sth. **(b)** (geh) **jdn einer Sache** (gen) **~** to deem sb worthy of sth; **jdn keines Blickes ~** not to deign to look at sb.

Würdigung f (a) siehe vt appreciation; acknowledgement; (Ehrung) honour (Brit), honor (US). **(b)** (Rede, Artikel) appreciation.

Wurf m **=e (a)** throw; (beim Kegeln etc) bowl. **mit dem Film ist ihm ein großer ~ gelungen** this film is a big hit for him (col). **(b)** no pl (das Werfen) throwing. **(c)** (Zool) litter.

Würfel m - (a) dice. **~** to play at dice; **die ~ sind gefallen** the die is cast. **(b)** (Math) cube; (Zucker~) lump.

Würfel-: **~becher** m shaker; **w~förmig** adj cube-shaped.

würfeln vti to throw; (Würfel spielen) to play at dice. **um etw ~** to throw dice for sth.

Würfel-: **~spiel** nt (Partie) game of dice; (Spielart) dice; **~zucker** m cube sugar.

Wurf-: **~geschoß** nt projectile; **~messer** nt throwing knife; **~pfeil** m dart; **~ring** m quoit; **~sendung** f circular; **~speer** m javelin; **~waffe** f missile.

Würgegriff m (lit, fig) stranglehold.

würgen 1 vt jdn to throttle; (fig: Angst) to choke. **2** vi **(a)** to choke. **an etw** (dat) **~** to choke on sth, to gag. **(b)** (beim Erbrechen) to retch. **mit Hängen und W~** by the skin of one's teeth.

Wurm m **=er** worm; (Made) maggot; (col: Kind) (little) mite. **da steckt der ~ drin** (fig col) there's something wrong somewhere; (verdächtig) there's something fishy about it (col).

wurmen vt, vt impers (col) to rankle with.

wurmig adj Obst maggoty.

Wurm-: **~mittel** nt vermifuge; **w~stichig** adj Holz full of worm-holes; (madig auch) Obst maggoty.

Wurst f **=e** sausage; (col: Kot) turd (col!). **jetzt geht es um die ~** (fig col) the moment of truth has come; **das ist mir ~** (col) I don't give a damn (col).

Wurst-: **~aufschnitt** m assortment of sliced sausage; **~brot** nt open sausage sandwich; (zusammengeklappt) sausage sandwich.

Würstchen nt (a) dim of **Wurst** small sausage. **heiße** or **warme ~** hot sausages. **(b)** (pej: Mensch) squirt (col), nobody. **ein armes ~** (fig) a poor soul.

Würstchen-: **~bude** f, **~stand** m sausage stand; hot-dog stand.

wursteln vi (col) to muddle along. **sich durchs Leben ~** to muddle through life.

Wurst-: **~finger** pl (pej col) podgy fingers pl; **~salat** m sausage salad; **~waren** pl sausages pl; **~zipfel** m sausage end.

Würze f **-n** (Gewürz) seasoning, spice; (Aroma) aroma; (fig: Reiz) spice.

Wurzel f **-n (a)** (lit, fig) root. **etw mit der ~ ausrotten** (fig) to eradicate sth; **~n schlagen** (lit) to root; (fig) to put down roots. **(b)** (Math) root. **~n ziehen** to find the roots; **(die) ~ aus 4 ist 2** the square root of 4 is 2.

Wurzel-: **~gemüse** nt root vegetables pl; **w~los** adj (lit, fig) rootless.

wurzeln vi (lit, fig) to be rooted.

Wurzel-: **~werk** nt no pl root system; **~zeichen** nt (Math) radical sign.

würzen vt (lit, fig) to season.

würzig adj Speise tasty; (scharf) spicy; Luft tangy; Wein, Bier full-bodied.

wusch pret of **waschen.**

Wuschelhaar nt (col) mop of curly hair.

wusch(e)lig adj (col) Tier shaggy; Haare fuzzy.

Wuschelkopf m (Mensch) fuzzy-head (col).

wußte pret of **wissen.**

Wust m no pl (col) (Durcheinander) jumble; (Menge) pile.

wüst adj (a) (öde) desert attr, desolate. **(b)** (unordentlich) wild. **~ aussehen** to look a real mess. **(c)** (ausschweifend) wild. **~ feiern** to have a wild party. **(d)** (rüde) Beschimpfung vile. **jdn ~ beschimpfen** to use vile language to sb.

Wüste f **-n** (lit, fig) desert; (Ödland) waste. **die ~ Gobi** the Gobi Desert; **jdn in die ~ schicken** (fig) to send sb packing (col).

Wüsten-: **~fuchs** m desert fox; **~könig** m (poet) king of the desert (poet); **~schiff** nt (poet) ship of the desert (poet).

Wüstling m lecher.

Wut f no pl (a) (Zorn, Raserei) rage. **(auf jdn/etw) eine ~ haben** to be furious (with sb/sth); **eine ~ im Bauch haben** (col) to be seething; **eine ~ haben** to be in a rage; **in ~ geraten** to fly into a rage; **jdn in ~ versetzen** to infuriate sb. **(b)** (Verbissenheit) frenzy. **mit einer wahren ~** like crazy (col).

Wut-: **~anfall** m fit of rage; (esp von Kind) tantrum; **~ausbruch** m outburst of fury.

wüten vi (lit, fig) (toben) to rage; (zerstörerisch hausen) to cause havoc.

wütend adj furious, enraged; Menge angry. **auf jdn/etw** (acc) **~ sein** to be mad at sb/sth.

wut|entbrannt adj furious, enraged. **~ hinauslaufen** to leave in a rage.

Wüterich m brute.

wutverzerrt adj distorted with rage.

Wwe. = **Witwe.**

X

X, x [ɪks] *nt* -, - X, x. **Herr X** Mr X; **jdm ein X für ein U vormachen** to put one over on sb *(col)*.
Xanthippe [ksan'tɪpə] *f* -n *(fig col)* shrew.
X-Beine ['ɪks-] *pl* knock-knees *pl*.
x-beinig ['ɪks-] *adj* knock-kneed.
x-beliebig [ɪks-] *adj* any old *(col)*. **wir können uns an einem ~en Ort treffen** we can meet anywhere you like *or* any old place you like *(col)*.

xerographieren* *vti insep* to Xerox.
xerokopieren* *vti insep* to Xerox.
x-fach ['ɪks-] *adj* **die ~e Menge** *(Math)* n times the amount.
x-mal ['ɪks-] *adv (col)* n (number of) times *(col)*.
x-te ['ɪkstə] *adj (Math, col)* nth. **zum ~n Male** for the nth *or* umpteenth time *(col)*.
Xylophon *nt* -e xylophone.

Y

Y, y ['ʏpsilɔn] *nt* -, - Y, y.
Yen [jɛn] *m* -(s) yen.
Yoga ['joːɡa] *m or nt no pl* yoga.

Yogi ['joːɡi] *m* -s yogi.
Ypsilon ['ʏpsilɔn] *nt* -s y.
Yucca ['jʊka] *f* -s yucca.

Z

Z, z [tsɛt] *nt* -, - Z, z.
Zack *m no pl (col)* **auf ~ sein** to be on the ball *(col)*.
zack *interj (col)* pow, zap *(col)*. **~ ~!** chop-chop! *(col)*; **bei uns muß alles ~, ~ gehen** we have to do everything chop-chop *(col)*.
Zacke *f* -n point; *(von Gabel)* prong; *(von Kamm)* tooth; *(Berg~)* jagged peak.
zackig *adj* **(a)** *(gezackt)* jagged. **(b)** *(col) Soldat* smart; *Tempo, Musik* brisk. **... aber ein bißchen ~!** ... and make it snappy *(col)*!
zaghaft *adj* timid.
Zaghaftigkeit *f* timidity.
zäh *adj* tough; *(dickflüssig)* glutinous; *Verkehr etc* slow-moving; *(ausdauernd)* dogged. **ein ~es Leben haben** to have a tenacious hold on life; *(fig: Idee etc)* to die hard.
zähflüssig *adj* viscous; *Verkehr* slow-moving.
Zähigkeit *f* toughness; *(Ausdauer)* doggedness.
Zahl *f* -en number; *(in Statistik, als Größe auch)* figure. **~en nennen** to give figures; **eine fünfstellige ~** a five-figure number; **in großer ~** in great numbers.
zahlbar *adj* payable *(an +acc* to).
zählbar *adj* countable.
zählebig *adj* hardy; *Vorurteil* persistent.
zahlen *vti* to pay. **Herr Ober, (bitte) ~!** waiter, the bill *or* check (US) please; **dort zahlt man gut/schlecht** they pay well/badly; **wenn er nicht bald zahlt, dann ...** if he doesn't pay up soon, then **...; laß mal, ich zahl's** no no, I'll pay; **ich zahle dir ein Bier** I'll buy you a beer.

zählen 1 *vi* **(a)** to count. **(b)** *(gehören)* **er zählt zu den besten Schriftstellern unserer Zeit** he ranks as one of the best authors of our time; **zählt Aids zu den unheilbaren Krankheiten?** is AIDS an incurable disease? **(c)** *(sich verlassen)* **auf jdn/ etw ~** to count on sb/sth. **(d)** *(gelten)* to count. **2** *vt* to count. **seine Tage sind gezählt** his days are numbered; **der König zählt 5 Punkte** *(Cards)* the King counts as 5 points.
Zahlen-: **~angabe** *f* figure; **ich kann keine genauen ~angaben machen** I can't quote any precise figures; **~folge** *f* order of numbers; **~gedächtnis** *nt* memory for numbers; **~material** *nt* figures *pl*; **~schloß** *nt* combination lock; **~verhältnis** *nt* (numerical) ratio.
Zähler *m* - **(a)** *(Math)* numerator. **(b)** *(Meßgerät)* meter.
Zählerstand *m* meter reading.
Zahl-: **~grenze** *f* fare stage; **~karte** *f* transfer form; **z~los** *adj* countless, innumerable; **~meister** *m* *(Naut)* purser; **z~reich** *adj* numerous; **~stelle** *f* payments office; **~tag** *m* payday.
Zahlung *f* payment. **in ~ geben/nehmen** to give/ take in part-exchange; **gegen eine ~ von $ 500 erhalten Sie ...** on payment of $500 you will receive ... __
Zählung *f* count.
Zahlungs-: **~anweisung** *f* transfer order; **~aufforderung** *f* request for payment; **~aufschub** *m* extension (of credit); **~bedingungen** *pl* terms (of payment) *pl*; **~befehl** *m* order to pay; **~bi-**

lanz *f* balance of payments; ~**empfänger** *m* payee; **z**~**fähig** *adj* able to pay; *Firma* solvent; ~**fähigkeit** *f* ability to pay; solvency; ~**frist** *f* period allowed for payment; **z**~**kräftig** *adj* wealthy; ~**mittel** *nt* means *sing* of payment; *(Münzen, Banknoten)* currency; **gesetzliches** ~**mittel** legal tender; **z**~**pflichtig** *adj* obliged to pay; ~**schwierigkeiten** *pl* financial difficulties *pl*; **z**~**unfähig** *adj* unable to pay; *Firma* insolvent; ~**unfähigkeit** *f* inability to pay; insolvency; **z**~**unwillig** *adj* unwilling to pay; ~**verkehr** *m* payments *pl*; ~**verpflichtung** *f* obligation to pay; ~**verzug** *m* default; ~**weise** *f* method of payment; **z**~**willig** *adj* willing to pay.
Zählwerk *nt* counter.
Zahlwort *nt* numeral.
zahm *adj* tame.
zähmen *vt* to tame; *(fig) Leidenschaft* to control.
Zahn *m* ⁻**e** tooth; *(von Briefmarke)* perforation; *(Rad*~*)* cog. **künstliche** ~**e** false teeth *pl*; ~**e bekommen** to cut one's teeth; **die ersten/zweiten** ~**e** one's milk teeth/second set of teeth; **die dritten** ~**e** *(hum)* false teeth; **diese Portion reicht** *or* **ist für den hohlen** ~ *(col)* that's hardly enough to satisfy a mouse *(col)*; **der** ~ **der Zeit** the ravages *pl* of time; **die** ⁻**e zeigen** to bare one's teeth; *(fig col)* to show one's teeth; **jdm einen** ~ **ziehen** *(lit)* to pull a tooth out; *(fig)* to put an idea out of sb's head; **jdm auf den** ~ **fühlen** *(aushorchen)* to sound sb out; *(streng befragen)* to give sb a grilling; **einen** ~ **draufhaben** *(col: Geschwindigkeit)* to be going like the clappers *(col)*.
Zahn-: ~**arzt** *m* dentist; **z**~**ärztlich** *adj* dental; ~**belag** *m* plaque; ~**bürste** *f* tooth brush; ~**creme** *f* toothpaste.
zähne-: ~**fletschend** *adj attr*, *adv* snarling; ~**knirschend** *adj attr*, *adv (fig)* gnashing one's teeth.
zahnen *vi* to teethe.
Zahn-: ~**ersatz** *m* dentures *pl*; ~**fleisch** *nt* gum(s *pl*); **auf dem** ~**fleisch gehen** *(col)* to be all in *(col)*, to be on one's last legs *(col)*; ~**fleischbluten** *nt* bleeding of the gums; ~**füllung** *f* filling; ~**heilkunde** *f* dentistry; ~**höhle** *f* pulp cavity; ~**klinik** *f* dental hospital; ~**krone** *f* crown; **z**~**los** *adj* toothless; ~**lücke** *f* gap between one's teeth; ~**medizin** *f* dentistry; ~**pasta** *f* toothpaste; ~**pflege** *f* dental hygiene; ~**rad** *nt* cogwheel; ~**radbahn** *f* rack-railway *(Brit)*, rack-railroad *(US)*; ~**radgetriebe** *nt* gear mechanism; ~**schmelz** *m* (tooth) enamel; ~**schmerz** *m usu pl* toothache *no pl*; ~**spange** *f* brace; ~**stein** *m* tartar; ~**stocher** *m* - toothpick; ~**techniker** *m* dental technician; ~**weh** *nt* toothache; ~**wurzel** *f* root (of a/the tooth).
Zange *f* -**n** *(Flach*~*, Rund*~*)* (pair of) pliers *pl*; *(Beiß*~*)* (pair of) pincers *pl*; *(Greif*~*, Zucker*~*)* (pair of) tongs *pl*; *(von Tier)* pincers *pl*. **jdn in die** ~ **nehmen** *(fig)* to put the screws on sb *(col)*.
Zank *m no pl* squabble. ~ **und Streit** trouble and strife.
Zank\apfel *m (fig)* bone of contention.
zanken *vr* to squabble.
zänkisch *adj* quarrelsome; *Weib* nagging *attr*.
Zäpfchen *nt (Gaumen*~*)* uvula.
Zapfen *m* - *(Spund)* bung; *(Tannen*~ *etc)* cone; *(Holzverbindung)* tenon.
zapfen *vt* to tap, to draw.
Zapfenstreich *m (Mil)* tattoo.
Zapf-: ~**hahn** *m* tap; ~**säule** *f* petrol pump *(Brit)*, gas pump *(US)*.
zapp(e)lig *adj* wriggly; *(unruhig)* fidgety.
zappeln *vi* to wriggle; *(unruhig sein)* to fidget. **jdn** ~ **lassen** *(fig col)* to keep sb in suspense.
Zar *m (wk)* -**en**, -**en** Tzar, Czar.
Zarin *f* Tzarina, Czarina.
zart *adj Haut, Töne* soft; *Braten, Gemüse* tender; *Gebäck, Teint, Kind, Gefühle* delicate; *Berührung*

gentle. **im** ~**en Alter von** ... at the tender age of ...; ~ **besaitet sein** to be very sensitive.
Zart-: **z**~**besaitet** *adj attr* highly sensitive; **z**~**bitter** *adj Schokolade* plain; **z**~**fühlend** *adj* sensitive; ~**gefühl** *nt* delicacy of feeling, sensitivity.
Zartheit *f siehe adj* softness; tenderness; delicacy; gentleness.
zärtlich *adj* tender, affectionate.
Zärtlichkeit *f* (a) *no pl* affection, tenderness. (b) *(Liebkosung)* caress. ~**en** *(Worte)* loving words.
Zaster *m no pl (col)* lolly *(col)*.
Zäsur *f* caesura; *(fig)* break.
Zauber *m* - *(lit, fig)* magic. **fauler** ~ *(col)* humbug *no indef art*.
Zauberei *f no pl* magic.
Zauberer *m*, **Zauberin** *f* - magician.
Zauber-: **z**~**haft** *adj* enchanting; ~**künstler** *m* conjurer; ~**kunststück** *nt* conjuring trick; ~**mittel** *nt* magical cure; *(Trank)* magic potion.
zaubern 1 *vi* to do magic; *(Kunststücke vorführen)* to do conjuring tricks. **ich kann doch nicht** ~! *(col)* I'm not a magician! 2 *vt* **etw aus etw** ~ to conjure sth out of sth.
Zauber-: ~**spruch** *m* spell; ~**stab** *m* wand; ~**trank** *m* magic potion; ~**trick** *m* conjuring trick; ~**wort** *nt* magic word.
Zauderer *m* - vacillator.
zaudern *vi* to vacillate. **etw ohne zu** ~ **tun** to do sth without hesitating.
Zaum *m*, *pl* **Zäume** bridle. **jdn/etw im** ~ **halten** *(fig)* to keep a tight rein on sb/sth; **seine Ungeduld im** ~**e halten** *(fig)* to control one's impatience.
zäumen *vt* to bridle.
Zaun *m*, *pl* **Zäune** fence. **einen Streit vom** ~ **brechen** to pick a quarrel.
Zaun-: ~**gast** *m* mere onlooker; ~**könig** *m (Orn)* wren; ~**pfahl** *m* (fencing) post; **jdm einen Wink mit dem** ~**pfahl geben** to drop sb a broad hint.
zausen *vt* to ruffle; *Haare* to tousle.
z.B. = **zum Beispiel** eg.
ZDF [tsɛtdeːˈɛf] = **Zweites Deutsches Fernsehen**.
Zebra *nt* -s zebra.
Zebrastreifen *m* zebra crossing *(Brit)*, crosswalk *(US)*.
Zeche *f* -**n** (a) *(Rechnung)* bill, check *(US)*. **die (ganze)** ~ **(be)zahlen** *(lit, fig)* to foot the bill. (b) *(Bergwerk)* (coal-)mine.
zechen *vi* to booze *(col)*, to drink.
Zecher(in *f) m* - boozer *(col)*, drinker.
Zech-: ~**kumpan** *m* drinking-pal *(col)*; ~**preller** *m* - person who leaves a bar/restaurant without paying the bill; ~**prellerei** *f* skipping payment in restaurants *etc*; ~**tour** *f (col)* pub-crawl *(esp Brit col)*, bar hop *(US col)*.
Zeder *f* -**n** cedar.
Zeh *m* -**en**, **Zehe** *f* -**n** toe; *(Knoblauch*~*)* clove. **jdm auf die** ~**en treten** *(lit, fig)* to tread on sb's toes.
Zehen-: ~**nagel** *m* toenail; ~**spitze** *f* tip of the toe; **auf (den)** ~**spitzen** on tiptoe; **auf (den)** ~**spitzen gehen** to tiptoe.
zehn *num* ten; *siehe* **vier**.
Zehn *f* -**en** ten; *siehe* **Vier**.
Zehner *m* - (a) *(Math)* ten. (b) *(col) (Groschen)* ten-pfennig piece; *(Schein)* tenner *(col)*.
Zehner-: ~**packung** *f* packet of ten; ~**system** *nt* decimal system.
Zehn-: ~**fingersystem** *nt* touch-typing method; ~**kampf** *m (Sport)* decathlon; ~**markschein** *m* ten mark note *(Brit)* or bill *(US)*.
zehntausend *num* ten thousand. **Z**~**e von Menschen** tens of thousands of people.
Zehntel *nt* - tenth.
zehnte(r, s) *adj* tenth; *siehe* **vierte(r, s)**.
zehren *vi* (a) **von etw** ~ *(lit)* to live off sth; *(fig)* to feed on sth. (b) **an jdm/etw** ~ *an Menschen, Kraft etc* to wear sb/sth out; *an Gesundheit* to

undermine sth.
Zeichen nt - sign; (Sci, auf Landkarte) symbol; (Schrift~) character; (Hinweis, Signal) signal; (Erkennungs~) identification; (Vermerk) mark. **es ist ein ~ unserer Zeit, daß ...** it is a sign of the times that ...; **als ~ von etw as a sign of sth; als ~ der Verehrung** as a token of respect; **jdm ein ~ geben to give sb a signal; unser/Ihr ~** (form) our/your reference; **unter dem ~ von etw stehen** (fig: Konferenz etc) to take place against a background of sth.

Zeichen-: ~**block** m sketch pad; ~**brett** nt drawing-board; ~**erklärung** f (auf Fahrplänen etc) key (to the symbols); (auf Landkarte) legend; ~**lehrer** m art teacher; ~**papier** nt drawing paper; ~**saal** m art-room; ~**setzung** f punctuation; ~**sprache** f sign language; ~**stift** m drawing pencil; ~**stunde** f art lesson; ~**system** nt notation; ~**tisch** m drawing table; ~**trickfilm** m (animated) cartoon; ~**unterricht** m art; (Unterrichtsstunde) art lesson.

zeichnen 1 vt (a) to draw; (entwerfen) Plan to draft. (b) (kennzeichnen) to mark. 2 vi to draw.
gezeichnet: XY signed, XY.
Zeichner(in f) m - draughtsman/-woman (Brit), draftsman/-woman (US); (Art auch) artist.
zeichnerisch 1 adj Darstellung graphic(al). **sein ~es Können** his drawing ability. 2 adv ~ **begabt sein** to have a talent for drawing.
Zeichnung f (a) drawing. (b) (Muster) pattern; (von Gefieder, Fell) markings pl.
zeichnungsberechtigt adj authorized to sign.
Zeigefinger m index finger, forefinger.
zeigen 1 vi to point (auf +acc to). 2 vt to show. **jdm etw ~** to show sb sth or sth to sb; **dem werd' ich's (aber) ~!** (col) I'll show him!; **zeig mal, was du kannst!** let's see what you can do! 3 vr to appear; (Gefühle) to show. **in dem Kleid kann ich mich doch nicht ~** I can't be seen in a dress like that; **er zeigte sich befriedigt** he was satisfied; **es zeigt sich, daß ...** it turns out that ...; **es wird sich ~, wer recht hat** we shall see who's right.
Zeiger m - pointer; (Uhr~) hand.
Zeigestock m pointer.
Zeile f -n line. **vielen Dank für Deine ~n** many thanks for your letter; **zwischen den ~n** between the lines.
Zeilen-: ~**abstand** m line spacing; ~**schalter** m line spacer.
Zeisig m -e (Orn) siskin.
Zeit f -en (a) time; (Epoche) age. **die gute alte ~** the good old days; **das waren noch ~en!** those were the days; **die ~ Goethes** the age of Goethe; **für alle ~en** for ever; **mit der ~ gehen** to move with the times; **die ~ wird knapp** time is running out, it's getting tight; **die ~ wurde mir lang** time hung heavy on my hands; **eine Stunde ~ haben** to have an hour (to spare); **haben Sie vielleicht einen Augenblick ~?** do you have a moment?; **sich** (dat) **für jdn/etw ~ nehmen** to devote time to sb/sth; **damit hat es noch ~** there's no hurry; **das hat ~ bis morgen** that can wait until tomorrow; **laß dir ~** take your time; **auf unbestimmte ~** for an indefinite period; **in letzter ~** recently; **die ganze ~ über** the whole time; **mit der ~** (allmählich) in time; **nach ~ bezahlt werden** to be paid by the hour; **auf ~ spielen** (Sport) to play for time; **es wird ~, daß wir gehen** it's about time we left; **Soldat auf ~** soldier serving for a set time; **seit dieser ~** since then; **zur ~ Königin Viktorias** in Queen Victoria's times; **zu der ~, als ...** (at the time) when ...; **von ~ zu ~** from time to time; **zur ~** at the moment. (b) (Ling) tense.
zeit prep +gen **~ meines Lebens** in my lifetime.
Zeit-: ~**abschnitt** m period (of time); ~**alter** nt age; ~**angabe** f time; (Datum) date; ~**ansage** f (Rad) time check; (Telec) speaking clock; ~**arbeit** f temporary work/job; ~**aufwand** m time

(needed for a task); ~**bombe** f time bomb; ~**druck** m pressure of time; **unter ~druck** under pressure; ~**frage** f question of time; ~**geist** m spirit of the times; **z~gemäß** adj up-to-date; **z~gemäß sein** to be in keeping with the times; ~**genosse** m contemporary; **z~genössisch** adj contemporary.
zeitig adj, adv early.
zeitigen vt (geh) Ergebnis to bring about.
Zeit-: ~**karte** f season ticket; **z~kritisch** adj Aufsatz full of comment on contemporary issues; ~**lang** f **eine ~lang** a while, a time; **eine ~lang ist das ganz schön** for a while it's quite nice; **z~lebens** adv all one's life.
zeitlich 1 adj temporal; Reihenfolge chronological. **in kurzem ~em Abstand** at short intervals (of time); **das Z~e segnen** (euph) to depart this life. 2 adv timewise (col). **das kann sie ~ nicht einrichten** she can't find (the) time for that; **das ist ~ ungünstig** that's bad timing; ~ **unmöglich not possible timewise; ist das ~ begrenzt?** is there a time limit?
Zeit-: **z~los** adj timeless; ~**lupe** f slow motion no art; **Wiederholung in ~lupe** slow-motion replay; ~**lupentempo** nt **im ~lupentempo** (fig) at a snail's pace; ~**mangel** m aus ~**mangel** for lack of time; ~**not** f shortage of time; **in ~not sein** to be pressed for time; ~**plan** m schedule; ~**punkt** m time; **zu diesem ~punkt** at that time; ~**raffer** m no pl time-lapse photography; **z~raubend** adj time-consuming; ~**raum** m period of time; **in einem ~raum von ...** over a period of ...; ~**rechnung** f calendar; ~**schrift** f magazine; (wissenschaftlich) journal; ~**spanne** f period of time; **z~sparend** adj timesaving; ~**tafel** f chronological table.
Zeitung f (news)paper.
Zeitungs- in cpds newspaper; ~**anzeige** f newspaper advertisement; (Familienanzeige) announcement in the paper; ~**ausschnitt** m newspaper cutting; ~**austräger** m paperboy/-girl; ~**beilage** f newspaper supplement; ~**händler** m newsagent (Brit), news vendor (US); ~**junge** m paperboy; ~**korrespondent** m newspaper correspondent; ~**leser** m newspaper reader; ~**papier** nt newsprint; (als Altpapier) newspaper; ~**redakteur** m newspaper editor; ~**ständer** m newspaper rack; ~**verleger** m newspaper publisher.
Zeit-: ~**unterschied** m time difference; ~**verlust** m loss of time; **ohne ~verlust** without losing any time; ~**verschwendung** f waste of time; ~**vertreib** m way of passing the time; (Hobby) pastime; **z~weilig** adj temporary; **z~weise** adv at times; ~**wort** nt verb; ~**zeichen** nt time signal; ~**zünder** m time fuse.
zelebrieren* vt to celebrate.
Zelle f -n cell (auch Sci, Pol); (Kabine) cabin; (Telefon~) box (Brit), booth.
Zell-: ~**gewebe** nt cell tissue; ~**kern** m nucleus (of a/the cell).
Zellophan nt no pl cellophane.
Zellstoff m cellulose.
Zelluloid [auch -'lɔyt] nt no pl celluloid.
Zellulose f -n cellulose.
Zelt nt -e tent; (Zirkus~) big top. **seine ~e aufschlagen/abbrechen** (fig) to settle down/to pack one's bags.
Zelt-: ~**bahn** f strip of canvas; ~**dach** nt tent-roof.
zelten vi to camp.
Zelt-: ~**lager** nt camp; ~**mast** m tent pole; ~**pflock** m tent peg (Brit) or stake (US); ~**plane** f tarpaulin; ~**platz** m camp site; ~**stange** f tent pole.
Zement m -e cement.
zementieren* vt to cement; (fig) to reinforce.
Zementmaschine f cement mixer.
Zenit m no pl (lit, fig) zenith. **die Sonne steht im ~**

the sun is at its zenith.

zensieren* vt **(a)** auch vi (benoten) to mark. **(b)** (Bücher etc) to censor.

Zensor m censor.

Zensur f **(a)** (no pl) censorship no indef art; (Prüf-stelle) censors pl. **einer ~ unterliegen** to be cen-sored. **(b)** (Note) mark.

Zenti-: **~meter** m or nt centimetre (Brit), centi-meter (US); **~metermaß** nt (metric) tape measure.

Zentner m - (metric) hundredweight; (Aus, Sw) 100kg.

zentral adj (lit,fig) central.

Zentral- in cpds central; **~bank** f central bank.

Zentrale f **-n** head office; (für Taxis etc) head-quarters sing or pl; (Telefon~) exchange

Zentralheizung f central heating.

Zentralisation f centralization.

zentralisieren* vt to centralize.

zentralistisch adj centralist.

Zentralkomitee nt central committee.

zentrieren* vti (Typ) to centre (Brit), to center (US).

zentrifugal adj centrifugal.

Zentrifuge f **-n** centrifuge.

Zentrum nt, pl **Zentren** (lit, fig) centre (Brit), center (US).

Zeppelin m **-e** zeppelin.

Zepter nt - sceptre (Brit), scepter (US). **das ~ führen** to wield the sceptre.

zerbeißen* vt irreg to chew; Bonbon, Keks etc to crunch; (beschädigen) to chew to pieces.

zerbersten* vi irreg aux sein to burst.

zerbeulen* vt to dent. **zerbeult** battered.

zerbomben* vt to flatten with bombs. **zerbombt** Stadt bombed.

zerbrechen* irreg **1** vt (lit) to break into pieces; Glas, Porzellan etc to smash; Ketten (lit, fig) to break. **2** vi aux sein to break into pieces; (Glas, Porzellan etc) to smash; (fig) to be destroyed (an +dat by).

zerbrechlich adj fragile.

Zerbrechlichkeit f fragility.

zerbröckeln* vti to crumble.

zerdrücken* vt to squash; Gemüse to mash; (zer-knittern) to crush.

Zeremonie f ceremony.

zeremoniell adj ceremonial.

Zeremonienmeister [-'moːniən-] m master of ceremonies.

zerfahren adj scatty; (unkonzentriert) distracted.

Zerfahrenheit f siehe adj scattiness; distraction.

Zerfall m no pl disintegration; (von Gebäude auch, von Atom) decay; (von Leiche, Holz etc) decompo-sition; (von Kultur, Gesundheit) decline.

zerfallen* **1** vi irreg aux sein **(a)** to disintegrate; (Atomkern) to decay; (Leiche, Holz etc) to decom-pose; (Reich, Moral, Gesundheit) to decline. **(b)** (sich gliedern) to fall (in +acc into). **2** adj Haus tumble-down.

zerfetzen* vt to tear to pieces.

zerfetzt adj Hose tattered; Arm lacerated.

zerfleddert adj (col) tattered.

zerfleischen* vt to tear to pieces.

zerfließen* vi irreg aux sein (Tinte, Makeup etc) to run.

zerfranst adj frayed.

zerfressen* vt irreg to eat away; (Motten, Mäuse etc) to eat. **(von Motten/Würmern)** ~ **sein** to be moth-/worm-eaten.

zerfurchen* vt to furrow.

zergehen* vi irreg aux sein to dissolve; (schmel-zen) to melt. **auf der Zunge** ~ (Gebäck etc) to melt in the mouth.

zergliedern* vt (Biol) to dissect; (fig) to analyse.

zerhauen* vt irreg to chop in two; (in viele Stücke) to chop up.

zerkauen* vt to chew.

zerkleinern* vt to cut up.

zerklüftet adj Küste jagged. **tief ~es Gestein** deeply fissured rock.

zerknirscht adj overcome with remorse.

zerknittern* vt to crease, to crumple.

zerknüllen* vt to crumple up.

zerkratzen* vt to scratch.

zerkrümeln* vt to crumble.

zerlaufen* vi irreg aux sein to melt.

zerlegbar adj die Möbel waren leicht ~ the furni-ture could easily be taken apart.

zerlegen* vt to take apart; (zerschneiden) to cut up; (Fleisch) to carve up; (Biol) to dissect. **etw in seine Einzelteile** ~ to take sth to pieces.

zerlumpt adj ragged.

zermahlen* vt to grind.

zermalmen* vt to crush.

zermartern* vt sich (dat) **das Hirn** ~ to rack one's brains.

zermürben* vt (fig) jdn ~ to wear sb down; **~d** wearing.

zernagen* vt to gnaw to pieces.

zerpflücken* vt to pick to pieces.

zerplatzen* vi aux sein to burst.

zerquetschen* vt to crush; Kartoffeln to mash. **10 Mark und ein paar Zerquetschte** (col) 10 marks something (or other), 10 marks odd.

Zerrbild nt (fig) caricature.

zerreden* vt to flog to death (col).

zerreiben* vt irreg (lit,fig) to crush.

zerreißen* irreg **1** vt to tear up; (aus Versehen) to tear; Faden, Seil etc to break; (zerfleischen) to tear apart. **2** vi aux sein (Stoff) to tear; (Band, Seil etc) to break.

Zerreißprobe f (lit) pull test; (fig) real test.

zerren **1** vt to drag; Sehne to pull. **2** vi **an etw** (dat) ~ to tug at sth.

zerrinnen* vi irreg aux sein (lit,fig) to melt away; (Geld) to disappear.

zerrissen adj (fig) Volk, Partei strife-torn; Mensch torn.

Zerrissenheit f (von Volk, Partei) disunity no pl; (innere ~) (inner) conflict.

Zerrspiegel m (lit) distorting mirror; (fig) tra-vesty.

Zerrung f eine ~ a pulled ligament/muscle.

zerrütten* vt (lit,fig) to destroy; Nerven to shat-ter. **eine zerrüttete Ehe** a broken marriage.

Zerrüttung f destruction; (von Nerven) shatter-ing; (von Ehe) breakdown.

Zerrüttungsprinzip nt principle of irretriev-able breakdown.

zersägen* vt to saw up.

zerschellen* vi aux sein (Schiff, Flugzeug) to be smashed to pieces.

zerschlagen* irreg **1** vt **(a)** (Mensch) to smash (to pieces). **(b)** (fig) Opposition to crush; Vereinigung to break up. **2** vr (Plan etc) to fall through; (Hoff-nung) to be shattered. **3** adj pred washed out (col); (nach Anstrengung) shattered (col), worn out.

Zerschlagung f (fig) (von Bewegung, Opposition) crushing; (von Plänen etc) failure.

zerschlissen adj Kleider tattered.

zerschmelzen* vi irreg aux sein to melt.

zerschmettern* **1** vt to shatter; Feind to crush. **2** vi aux sein to shatter.

zerschneiden* vt irreg to cut; (in Stücke) to cut up.

zersetzen* **1** vt to decompose; (Säure etc) to corrode; (fig) to subvert. **2** vr to decompose; (durch Säure) to corrode.

zersetzend adj (fig) subversive.

Zersetzung f (Chem) decomposition; (durch Säure) corrosion; (fig: Untergrabung) subversion.

zerspalten* vt to split; Gemeinschaft to split up.

zersplittern* **1** vt to shatter; Holz to splinter; (fig) Kräfte, Zeit to dissipate. **2** vi aux sein to shatter; (Holz) to splinter; (fig) to split up. **3** vr *(fig)* to dissipate one's energies; *(Gruppe, Partei)* to become fragmented.

zerspringen* *vi irreg aux sein* to shatter; *(einen Sprung bekommen)* to crack.

zerstampfen* *vt (zertreten)* to stamp on; *(zerkleinern)* to crush.

zerstäuben* *vt* to spray.

Zerstäuber *m* - spray; *(Parfüm~ auch)* atomizer.

zerstechen* *vt irreg* **(a)** *(Mücken)* to bite (all over). **(b)** *Material, Haut* to puncture; *Finger* to prick.

zerstieben* *vi irreg aux sein* to scatter; *(Wasser)* to spray.

zerstören* *vt* to destroy; *(Rowdys)* to vandalize; *Gesundheit* to ruin.

Zerstörer *m* - *(Naut)* destroyer.

zerstörerisch *adj* destructive.

Zerstörung *f no pl* destruction *no pl.*

Zerstörungswut *f* destructive mania.

zerstoßen* *vt irreg* to crush.

zerstreiten* *vt irreg* to quarrel, to fall out.

zerstreuen* **1** *vt* **(a)** to scatter *(in +dat* over); *(fig)* to dispel. **(b)** *jdn* ~ to take sb's mind off things. **2** *vr* **(a)** *(sich verteilen)* to scatter; *(fig)* to be dispelled. **(b)** *(sich ablenken)* to take one's mind off things.

zerstreut *adj (fig) Mensch* absent-minded.

Zerstreutheit *f no pl* absent-mindedness.

Zerstreuung *f* **(a)** *no pl siehe vt* scattering. **(b)** *(Ablenkung)* diversion. **zur** ~ as a diversion.

zerstritten *adj* estranged. **mit jdm** ~ **sein** to be on very bad terms with sb.

zerstückeln* *vt (lit)* to cut up; *Leiche* to dismember; *Land* to carve up.

zerteilen* *vt* to split up.

Zertifikat *nt* certificate.

zertrampeln* *vt* to trample on.

zertrennen* *vt* to sever; *(auftrennen) Nähte* to undo.

zertreten* *vt irreg* to crush (underfoot); *Rasen* to ruin.

zertrümmern* *vt* to smash; *Einrichtung* to smash up; *Ordnung* to wreck.

Zervelatwurst [tsɛrvə'laːt-] *f* German salami, cervelat.

zerwühlen* *vt* to ruffle up, to tousle; *Bett* to rumple (up); *(aufwühlen) Erdboden* to churn up.

zerzaust *adj* dishevelled *(Brit)*, disheveled *(US)*.

Zeter *nt:* ~ **und Mordio schreien** to scream blue murder.

zetern *vi (pej)* to clamour *(Brit)*, to clamor *(US)*; *(keifen)* to scold.

Zettel *m* - piece of paper; *(Notiz~)* note; *(Kartei~)* card; *(Kassen~)* receipt; *(Formular)* form.

Zettel-: ~**kartei** *f* card index; ~**kasten** *m* file-card box; ~**wirtschaft** *f (pej)* **eine** ~**wirtschaft haben** to have bits of paper everywhere.

Zeug *nt no pl (col)* stuff *no indef art, no pl; (Unsinn)* nonsense, rubbish *(col); (Kleidung)* things *pl (col)*. **altes** ~ junk, trash; **das** ~ **zu etw haben** to have (got) what it takes to be sth; **jdm etwas am** ~ **flicken** *(col)* to find fault with sb; **was das** ~ **hält** for all one is worth; *laufen* like mad; *fahren* like the blazes *(col)*; **sich ins** ~ **legen** to go flat out *(col)*; **dummes** ~ **reden** to talk a lot of nonsense.

Zeuge *m (wk)* -**n**, -**n** *(Jur, fig)* witness *(gen* to). ~ **eines Unfalls sein** to be a witness to an accident.

zeugen[1] *vt Kind* to father.

zeugen[2] *vi* **(a) von etw** ~ to show sth. **(b)** *(aussagen)* to testify *(vor +dat* to).

Zeugen-: ~**aussage** *f* testimony; ~**bank** *f,* ~**stand** *m* witness box *(Brit)*, witness stand *(US)*.

Zeugin *f* witness.

Zeugnis *nt* **(a)** *(Bescheinigung)* certificate; *(Schul~)* report; *(von Arbeitgeber)* reference. **jdm ein** ~ **ausstellen** to give sb a reference. **(b)** *(esp liter: Zeugenaussage)* evidence. **für/gegen jdn** ~ **ablegen** to testify for/against sb.

Zeugnis-: ~**konferenz** *f (Sch)* staff meeting to decide on marks etc; ~**papiere** *pl* certificates *pl; (von Arbeitgeber)* references *pl.*

Zeugungs-: **z**~**fähig** *adj* fertile; ~**fähigkeit** *f* fertility; **z**~**unfähig** *adj* sterile; ~**unfähigkeit** *f* sterility.

z.H(d). = **zu Händen** att, attn.

Zicke *f* -**n** **(a)** nanny goat. **(b)** *(pej col: Frau)* old bag *(col)*.

Zicken *pl (col)* nonsense *no pl.* **mach bloß keine** ~**!** no nonsense now!; ~ **machen** to make trouble.

zickig *adj (albern)* silly; *(prüde)* prudish.

Zickzack *m* -**e** zigzag. **z**~ *or* **im** ~ **laufen** to zigzag.

Zickzack-: ~**kurs** *m* zigzag course; ~**linie** *f* zigzag.

Ziege *f* -**n** **(a)** goat. **(b)** *(pej col: Frau)* cow *(col!).*

Ziegel *m* - *(Backstein)* brick; *(Dach~)* tile. **ein Dach mit** ~**n decken** to tile a roof.

Ziegel-: ~**bau** *m, pl* -**ten** brick building; ~**brenner** *m* brickmaker; *(von Dachziegeln)* tilemaker; ~**dach** *nt* tiled roof.

Ziegelei *f* brickworks *sing or pl; (für Dachziegel!)* tile-making works *sing or pl.*

Ziegelstein *m* brick.

Ziegen-: ~**bart** *m (hum: Bart)* goatee (beard); ~**bock** *m* billy goat; ~**fell** *nt* goatskin; ~**käse** *m* goat's milk cheese; ~**leder** *nt* kid(-leather), kidskin; ~**milch** *f* goat's milk; ~**peter** *m* mumps *sing.*

Zieh-: ~**brücke** *f* drawbridge; ~**brunnen** *m* well; ~**eltern** *pl* foster parents *pl.*

ziehen *pret* **zog**, *ptp* **gezogen** **1** *vt* **(a)** to pull; *(schleppen)* to drag; *Hut* to raise; *Handbremse* to put on; *(heraus~)* to pull out *(aus* of); *Fäden* to take out. **den Ring vom Finger** ~ to pull one's ring off (one's finger); **die Mütze tiefer ins Gesicht** ~ to pull one's hat further down over one's face; **er zog noch einen Pullover übers Hemd** he put on a pullover over his shirt; **unangenehme Folgen nach sich** ~ to have unpleasant consequences. **(b)** *(zeichnen, anlegen) Kreis, Linie* to draw; *Graben, Furchen* to dig; *Mauer* to build; *Grenze* to set up. **(c)** *(herstellen) Draht, Kerzen* to make; *(züchten) Pflanzen* to grow; *Tiere* to breed.

2 *vi* **(a)** to pull. **an etw** *(dat)* ~ to pull (on *or* at) sth. **(b)** *aux sein (um~)* to move. **nach Bayern/in eine größere Wohnung** ~ to move to Bavaria/ into a bigger flat; **zu jdm** ~ to move in with sb. **(c)** *aux sein (sich bewegen)* to move, to go; *(Soldaten)* to march; *(durchstreifen)* to roam. **in den Krieg** ~ to go to war. **(d)** *(mit Spielfigur)* to move. **mit dem Turm** ~ to move the rook; **wer zieht?** whose move is it? **(e)** *(Cook) (Tee, Kaffee)* to draw; *(in Kochwasser)* to simmer. **(f)** *(col: Eindruck machen)* **so was zieht bei mir nicht** I don't like that sort of thing.

3 *vi impers* **es zieht** there's a draught *(Brit)* or draft *(US)*; **wenn es dir zieht** if you're in a draught; *(von Schmerzen)* **mir zieht's im Rücken** my back hurts.

4 *vt impers* **es zog ihn in die weite Welt** he felt drawn towards the big wide world.

5 *vr* **(a)** *(sich erstrecken, verlaufen)* to stretch. **dieses Thema zieht sich durch das ganze Buch** this theme runs throughout the whole book. **(b)** *(sich dehnen)* to stretch; *(Holz)* to warp; *(Metall)* to bend.

Ziehen *nt no pl (Schmerz)* ache.

Ziehharmonika *f* concertina.

Ziehung *f* draw.

Ziel *nt* -**e** **(a)** *(Reise~)* destination; *(Absicht, Zweck)* goal, aim; *(von Wünschen, Spott)* object. **mit dem** ~ **zu gewinnen** with the aim of winning; **jdm/sich ein** ~ **stecken** to set sb/oneself a goal; **sich** *(dat)* **etw zum** ~ **setzen** to set sth as one's goal; **zum** ~ **kommen** *(fig)* to reach one's goal; **am** ~ **sein** to be at one's destination; *(fig)* to have reached one's goal. **(b)** *(Sport)* finish. **durchs** ~

gehen to cross the finishing line. **(c)** *(Mil etc)* target. **ins ~ treffen** to hit the target; **über das ~ hinausschießen** *(fig)* to overshoot the mark. **Ziel-: ~band** *nt* finishing-tape; **z~bewußt** *adj* purposeful.

zielen *vi* to aim *(auf +acc, nach at)*; *(fig)* to be aimed *(auf +acc at)*. **ich weiß, worauf deine Bemerkungen ~** I know what you're driving at.

Ziel-: ~fernrohr *nt* telescopic sight; **~gruppe** *f* target group; **~hafen** *m* port of destination; **~linie** *f (Sport)* finishing-line; **z~los** *adj* aimless; **~losigkeit** *f* lack of purpose; **~ort** *m* destination; **~scheibe** *f* target; **z~sicher** *adj* unerring; *Handeln* purposeful; **z~strebig 1** *adj* single-minded; **2** *adv* single-mindedly, full of determination; **~strebigkeit** *f* single-mindedness; **~vorstellung** *f* objective.

ziemen *vr, vr impers (geh)* **das/es ziemt sich nicht (für dich)** it is not proper (for you).

ziemlich 1 *adv* **(a)** quite, pretty *(col)*; *sicher, genau* reasonably. **wir haben uns ~ beeilt** we've hurried quite a bit; **~ lange** quite a long time; **~ viel** quite a lot. **(b)** *(col: beinahe)* almost, nearly. **so ~** more or less; **so ~ alles** just about everything; **so ~ dasselbe** pretty much the same. **2** *adj* *attr Anzahl, Strecke* fair; *Vermögen* sizeable. **eine ~e Anstrengung** quite an effort.

Zierat *m* **-e** *(geh)* decoration.

Zierde *f* **-n** ornament, decoration; *(Schmuckstück)* adornment. **zur ~** for decoration; **das alte Haus ist eine ~ der Stadt** the old house is one of the beauties of the town.

zieren 1 *vt* to adorn; *(fig: auszeichnen)* to grace. **2** *vr (sich bitten lassen)* to need a lot of pressing; *(sich gekünstelt benehmen)* to be affected. **zier dich nicht!** don't be shy or silly *(col)*.

Zier-: ~fisch *m* ornamental fish; **~garten** *m* ornamental garden; **~leiste** *f* border; *(an Auto)* trim; *(an Wand, Möbeln)* moulding *(Brit)*, molding *(US)*.

zierlich *adj* dainty; *Frau* auch petite.

Zierlichkeit *f siehe adj* daintiness; petiteness.

Zierpflanze *f* ornamental plant.

Ziffer *f* **-n (a)** digit; *(Zahl)* figure, number. **römische/arabische ~n** roman/arabic numerals; **eine Zahl mit drei ~n** a three-figure number. **(b)** *(eines Paragraphs)* clause.

Zifferblatt *nt (an Uhr)* dial; *(hum: Gesicht)* face.

zig *adj inv (col)* umpteen *(col)*.

Zigarette *f* cigarette.

Zigaretten- *in cpds* cigarette; **~automat** *m* cigarette machine; **~dose** *f* cigarette box; **~etui** *nt* cigarette case; **~kippe** *f* cigarette end; **~pause** *f* break for a cigarette; **~schachtel** *f* cigarette packet or pack; **~spitze** *f* cigarette-holder.

Zigarillo *m or nt* **-s** cigarillo.

Zigarre *f* **-n (a)** cigar. **(b)** *(col: Verweis)* **jdm eine ~ verpassen** to give sb a dressing-down.

Zigarren- *in cpds* cigar; **~kiste** *f* cigar-box; **~spitze** *f* cigar-holder; **~stummel** *m* cigar butt.

Zigeuner(in *f)* *m* - gipsy.

Zigeunerschnitzel *nt (Cook)* cutlet served in a spicy sauce with green and red peppers.

zigmal *adv (col)* umpteen times *(col)*.

Zimmer *nt* - room. **~ frei** vacancies.

Zimmer-: ~antenne *f* indoor aerial *(Brit)* or antenna *(US)*; **~arbeit** *f* carpentry job; **~brand** *m* fire in a/the room; **~flucht** *f* suite of rooms; **~handwerk** *nt* carpentry; **~kellner** *m* room-waiter; **~lautstärke** *f* **bitte auf ~lautstärke stellen** please keep volume down; **~mädchen** *nt* chambermaid *(Brit)*, maid *(US)*; **~mann** *m, pl* **~leute** carpenter.

zimmern 1 *vt* to make from wood. **2** *vi* to do woodwork.

Zimmer-: ~pflanze *f* house plant; **~suche** *f* room hunting; **auf ~suche sein** to be looking for rooms/a room; **~temperatur** *f* room temperature; **~vermittlung** *f* accommodation *(Brit)* or

accommodations *(US)* agency.

zimperlich *adj* squeamish; *(prüde)* prissy; *(wehleidig)* soft. **sei doch nicht so ~** don't be so silly; **da darf man nicht so ~ sein** you can't afford to be soft.

Zimt *m* **-e** *(Gewürz)* cinnamon.

Zimt-: ~stange *f* stick of cinnamon; **~ziege** *f (col)* stupid cow *(col!)*.

Zink *nt no pl* zinc.

Zinke *f* **-n** *(von Gabel)* prong; *(von Kamm, Harke)* tooth.

Zinken *m* - **(a)** *(col: Nase)* hooter *(col)*. **(b)** = **Zinke**.

zinken *vt Karten* to mark.

Zinn *nt no pl* **(a)** tin. **(b)** *(Legierung)* pewter. **(c)** *(~produkte)* pewter, pewterware.

Zinnbecher *m* pewter tankard.

zinnoberrot *adj* vermilion.

Zinnsoldat *m* tin soldier.

Zins *m* **-en** *usu pl (Geld~)* interest *no pl*. **~en bringen** to earn interest; *(fig)* to pay dividends; **Darlehen zu 10% ~en** loan at 10% interest; **jdm etw mit ~en heimzahlen** *(fig)* to pay sb back for sth with interest.

Zinseszins *m* compound interest.

Zins-: z~frei *adj* interest-free; **~fuß** *m* interest rate; **z~los** *adj* interest-free; **~rechnung** *f* calculation of interest; **~satz** *m* interest rate; **~senkung** *f* reduction in the interest rate.

Zionismus *m* Zionism.

zionistisch *adj* Zionist.

Zipfel *m* - *(von Tuch)* corner; *(von Mütze)* point; *(von Jacke)* tail; *(von Wurst)* end; *(von Land)* tip.

Zipfelmütze *f* pointed cap or hat.

zirka *adv* about.

Zirkel *m* - *(Gerät)* pair of compasses, compasses *pl*; *(Stech~)* pair of dividers, dividers *pl*.

zirkulieren* *vi* to circulate.

Zirkus *m* **-se (a)** circus. **(b)** *(col: Getue)* fuss, to-do *(col)*.

Zirkus- *in cpds* circus; **~zelt** *nt* big top.

zirpen *vi* to chirp, to cheep.

Zirrhose [tsi'ro:zə] *f* **-n** cirrhosis.

zischeln *vti* to whisper.

zischen 1 *vi* to hiss; *(Limonade)* to fizz; *(Fett)* to sizzle. **2** *vt* **(a)** *(~d sagen)* to hiss. **(b)** *(col: ohrfeigen)* **jdm eine ~** to belt or clout sb one *(col)*.

Zischlaut *m (Ling)* sibilant.

ziselieren* *vt* to engrave.

Zitadelle *f* citadel.

Zitat *nt* **-e** quotation, quote. **ein falsches ~** a misquotation; **~ ... Ende des ~s** quote ... unquote.

Zither *f* **-n** zither.

zitieren* *vt* **(a)** to quote. **(b)** *(vorladen, rufen)* to summon *(vor +acc before, an +acc, zu to)*.

Zitronat *nt* candied lemon peel.

Zitrone *f* **-n** lemon; *(Getränk)* lemon drink. **jdn wie eine ~ auspressen** to squeeze sb dry.

Zitronen-: z~gelb *adj* lemon yellow; **~limonade** *f* lemonade; **~melisse** *f* (lemon) balm; **~saft** *f* lemon juice; **~säure** *f* citric acid; **~schale** *f* lemon peel.

Zitrusfrucht *f* citrus fruit.

Zitter-: ~aal *m* electric eel; **~greis** *m (col)* old dodderer *(col)*.

zitt(e)rig *adj* shaky.

zittern *vi* to tremble *(vor +dat with)*. **am ganzen Körper ~** to shake all over; **mir ~ die Knie** my knees are trembling; **vor jdm ~** to be terrified of sb.

Zittern *nt no pl* shaking, trembling. **mit ~ und Zagen** in fear and trembling.

Zitze *f* **-n** teat.

zivil [tsi'vi:l] *adj* **(a)** civilian; *Schaden* non-military. **~er Bevölkerungsschutz** civil defence *(Brit)* or defense *(US)*. **(b)** *(col: anständig)* civil; *Preise* reasonable.

Zivil [tsi'vi:l] *nt no pl* **in ~ Soldat** in civilian clothes,

in civvies; **Polizist in** ~ plain-clothes policeman.
Zivil-: ~**beruf** m civilian profession/trade; ~**bevölkerung** f civilian population; ~**courage** f
courage (to stand up for one's beliefs);
~**dienst** m alternative service (for conscientious
objectors); ~**ehe** f civil marriage; ~**flughafen**
m civil airport; ~**gericht** nt civil court.
Zivilisation [tsiviliza'tsio:n] f civilization.
Zivilisationskrankheit [tsiviliza'tsio:ns-] f illness
caused by civilization.
zivilisatorisch [tsiviliza'to:rɪʃ] adj of civilization.
zivilisiert [tsivili'zi:ɐt] adj civilized.
Zivilist [tsivi'lɪst] m civilian.
Zivil-: ~**kleidung** f = Zivil; ~**leben** nt civilian life,
civvy street (col); ~**person** f civilian; ~**prozeß** m
civil action; ~**recht** nt civil law; ~**richter** m civil
court judge; ~**sache** f matter for a civil court;
~**schutz** m civil defence (Brit) or defense (US).
ZK [tset'ka:] nt -s = **Zentralkomitee.**
Zobel m - (Zool, Pelz) sable.
Zofe f -n lady's maid; (von Königin) lady-in-
waiting.
zog pret of **ziehen.**
zögern vi to hesitate. **er zögerte lange mit der
Antwort** he hesitated a long time before re-
plying.
Zögern nt no pl hesitation. **nach langem** ~ after
hesitating a long time.
Zölibat nt or m no pl celibacy. **im** ~ **leben** to lead a
life of celibacy.
Zoll¹ m - (Measure) inch.
Zoll² m -̃e **(a)** (Waren~) customs duty; (Brücken~,
Straßen~) toll. **darauf wird** ~ **erhoben** there is
duty to pay on that. **(b)** (Stelle) **der** ~ customs pl.
Zoll-: ~**amt** nt customs house or office; ~**beam-
te(r)** m customs officer or official; ~**behörde** f
customs authorities pl, customs pl; ~**bestimmung** f usu pl customs regulation.
zollen vt jdm Anerkennung/Achtung ~ to
acknowledge/respect sb.
Zoll-: ~**erklärung** f customs declaration; ~**fahndung** f customs investigation department;
z~frei adj duty-free; **etw z~frei einführen** to
import sth free of duty; ~**gebiet** nt customs area
or territory; ~**grenze** f customs border; ~**kontrolle** f customs check; ~**papiere** pl customs
documents pl; **z~pflichtig** adj dutiable;
~**schranke** f customs barrier; ~**stock** m inch
rule; ~**tarif** m customs tariff; ~**union** f customs
union.
Zone f -n zone; (von Fahrkarte) fare stage.
Zonen-: ~**grenze** f zonal border; **die** ~**grenze** (col)
the border (with East Germany); ~**randgebiet**
nt border area (with East Germany).
Zoo [tso:] m -s zoo.
Zoologe [tsoo'lo:gə] m (wk) -n, -n, **Zoologin** f zoologist.
Zoologie [tsoolo'gi:] f zoology.
zoologisch [tsoo'lo:gɪʃ] adj zoological.
Zoom [zu:m] nt -s zoom shot; (Objektiv) zoom lens.
Zoowärter m zoo keeper.
Zopf m -̃e pigtail. **das Haar in** ~**e flechten** to plait
one's hair; **ein alter** ~ (fig) an antiquated
custom.
Zopf-: ~**band** nt hair ribbon; ~**spange** f clip.
Zorn m no pl anger. **der** ~ **Gottes** the wrath of God;
jds ~ **heraufbeschwören** to incur sb's wrath; **in**
~ **geraten** to fly into a rage; **im** ~ **in a rage; in**
gerechtem ~ **in righteous indignation; einen**
~ **auf jdn haben** to be furious with sb.
Zorn(es)ausbruch m fit of anger or rage.
zornig adj angry, furious. **(leicht)** ~ **werden** to
lose one's temper (easily); **auf jdn** ~ **sein** to be
angry with sb.
Zote f -n dirty joke.
Zotte f -n, **Zottel** f -n (col) rat's tail (col).
Zottelhaar nt (col) shaggy hair.
zottelig adj (col) Haar shaggy.

zottig adj Fell shaggy.
z.T. = **zum Teil.**
zu 1 prep +dat **(a)** (örtlich) to. ~**m Bahnhof** to the
station; ~**m Arzt gehen** to go to the doctor's
(Brit) or doctor; **bis** ~ as far as; **(bis)** ~**m Bahnhof sind es 5 km** it's 5 kms to the station; ~**r
Schule/Kirche gehen** to go to school/church; ~**m
Film/Ballett gehen** to go into films/to join the
ballet; ~**m Fenster herein/hinaus** in (at)/out of
the window; ~**r Decke sehen** to look (up) at the
ceiling; ~**jdm/etw hinaufsehen** to look up at
sb/sth; **sie sah** ~ **ihm hin** she looked towards
him; **das Zimmer liegt** ~**r Straße hin** the room
looks out onto the street; **ein Zimmer mit Blick**
~**m Meer** a room with a view of the sea; **die Tür**
~**m Keller** the door to the cellar; ~**r Stadtmitte hin** towards the town/city centre; ~ **meiner Linken** to or on my left; ~ **Lande und** ~
Wasser on land and sea; **der Dom** ~ **Köln** Cologne
Cathedral.
(b) (zeitlich) at. ~ **später Stunde** at a late
hour; ~ **Mittag** (am Mittag) at noon; (bis Mittag)
by midday; ~ **Ostern** at Easter; **rechtzeitig** ~**m
Essen kommen** to be in time for dinner; **bis** ~
15. April until 15th April; (nicht später als) by
15th April; **der Wechsel ist** ~**m 15. April fällig**
the bill is due on 15th April; ~**m 31. Mai
kündigen** to give in one's notice for May 31st.
(c) (Zusatz, Zusammengehörigkeit) with. **Wein**
~**m Essen trinken** to drink wine with one's meal;
~**r Gitarre singen** to sing to a/the guitar; **die
Melodie** ~ **dem Lied** the tune of the song; **Vor-
wort/Anmerkungen** ~ **etw** preface/notes to sth;
~ **dem kommt noch, daß ich ...** on top of that I ...;
etw ~ **etw legen** to put sth with sth; **sich** ~ **jdm
setzen** to sit down beside sb; **setz dich doch** ~
uns (come and) sit with us; **Liebe** ~ **jdm** love for
sb; **sein Verhältnis** ~ **ihr** his relationship with
her.
(d) (Zweck) for. **Wasser** ~**m Waschen** water
for washing; **Papier** ~**m Schreiben** paper to
write on; **er sagte das nur** ~ **ihrer Beruhigung**
he said that just to set her mind at rest; **etw** ~**m
Geburtstag/** ~ **Weihnachten bekommen** to get
sth for one's birthday/for Christmas; **jdm** ~ **etw
gratulieren** to congratulate sb on sth; **Ausstellung** ~**m Jahrestag der Revolution** exhibition
to mark the anniversary of the revolution; ~
dieser Frage möchte ich folgendes sagen I
should like to say the following to this question.
(e) (Folge, Umstand, Art und Weise) ~ **seinem
Besten** for his own good; ~**m Glück** luckily; ~
meiner Freude etc to my joy etc; ~/~**m Tode** to
death; **es ist** ~**m Weinen** it's enough to make you
(want to) weep; ~ **Fuß/Pferd** on foot/horseback;
~ **Schiff** by ship or sea.
(f) (Veränderung) into. ~ **etw werden** to turn
into sth; **Leder** ~ **Handtaschen verarbeiten** to
make handbags out of leather; **jdn/etw** ~ **etw
machen** to make sb/sth (into) sth; ~ **Asche verbrennen** to burn to ashes; **jdn** ~**m König wählen**
to choose sb as king; **jdn** ~ **etw ernennen** to
nominate sb sth.
(g) (bei Zahlen) **drei** ~ **zwei** (Sport) three-two;
drei Sätze ~ **zwei** (Tennis) three sets to two;
Äpfel das Stück ~ **30 Pfennig** apples at 30
pfennigs each; ~**m halben Preis** at half price;
~**m ersten Male** for the first time.
2 adv **(a)** (allzu) too. ~ **sehr** too much; **das war
einfach** ~ **dumm!** (col) it was so stupid! **(b)**
(geschlossen) shut, closed. **auf,** ~ (an Hähnen
etc) on, off; **Tür** ~! (col) shut the door; **die Geschäfte haben jetzt** ~ the shops are closed now.
(c) (col: los, weiter) **dann mal** ~! right, off we go!;
nur ~! just keep on!; **mach** ~! hurry up! **(d)**
(örtlich) toward(s). **auf den Wald** ~ towards
the forest.
3 conj **(a)** (mit Infinitiv) to. **etw** ~ **essen** sth to

eat; **der Fußboden ist noch ~ fegen** the floor still has to be swept; **er hat ~ gehorchen** he has to obey; **ohne es ~ wissen** without knowing it; **um besser sehen ~ können** in order to see better; **ich komme, um mich ~ verabschieden** I've come to say goodbye. **(b)** (*mit Partizip*) **noch ~ bezahlende Rechnungen** bills that are still to be paid; **nur winzige, leicht ~ übersehende Punkte** only very small points (that are) easily overlooked.
4 *adj* (*col: geschlossen*) **eine ~e Tür** a closed door; **siehe zusein.**
zu|aller-: ~erst *adv* first of all; **~letzt** *adv* last of all.
zubauen *vt sep Lücke* to fill in; *Platz, Gelände* to build up.
Zubehör *nt* -**e** equipment *no pl*; (*Zusatzgeräte, ~teile*) accessories *pl*. **Küche mit allem ~** fully equipped kitchen.
Zubehörteil *nt* accessory.
zubeißen *vi sep irreg* to bite.
zubekommen* *vt sep irreg* (*col*) *Tür, Fenster* to get shut *or* closed. **ich bekomm' den Reißverschluß nicht zu** I can't get my zip done up.
Zuber *m* - (wash)tub.
zubereiten* *vt sep* to prepare.
Zubereitung *f* preparation.
zubilligen *vt sep* **jdm etw ~** to allow sb sth.
zubinden *vt sep irreg* to tie up. **jdm die Augen ~** to blindfold sb.
zubringen *vt sep irreg* **(a)** (*verbringen*) to spend.
(b) (*herbeibringen*) to bring to, to take to.
Zubringer *m* - **(a)** (*Tech*) conveyor. **(b)** (*Straße*) feeder road. **(c)** **~(bus)** shuttle (bus); (*zum Flughafen*) airport bus.
Zubrot *nt* (*hum*) extra income. **ein kleines ~ verdienen** to earn a bit on the side (*col*).
Zucchini [tsu'ki:ni] *f* - courgette (*Brit*), zucchini (*US*).
Zucht *f* **(a)** (*Disziplin*) discipline. **~ und Ordnung** discipline. **(b)** (*Aufzucht*) (*von Tieren*) breeding; (*von Pflanzen*) cultivation. **(c)** (*~generation*) stock.
Zuchtbulle *m* breeding bull.
züchten *vt* to breed; *Bienen* to keep; *Pflanzen* to grow; *Perlen, Bakterien* to cultivate.
Züchter(in *f*) *m* - (*von Tieren*) breeder; (*von Pflanzen*) cultivator; (*von Bienen*) keeper.
Zuchthaus *nt* (*Gebäude*) prison (*for capital offenders*), penitentiary (*US*).
Zuchthäusler *m* - (*col*) convict.
Zuchthengst *m* breeding stallion.
züchtig *adj* (*liter*) chaste; (*tugendhaft*) virtuous.
züchtigen *vt* (*geh*) to beat.
Züchtigung *f* beating. **körperliche ~** corporal punishment.
Zucht-: ~perle *f* cultured pearl; **~stute** *f* broodmare; **~tier** *nt* breeding animal; **~vieh** *nt* breeding cattle.
zucken 1 *vi* **(a)** (*nervös*) to twitch; (*vor Schreck*) to start; (*vor Schmerzen*) to flinch; (*verwundetes Tier*) to thrash about. **er zuckte ständig mit dem Mund** his mouth kept twitching; **mit den Schultern ~** to shrug (one's shoulders). **(b)** (*aufleuchten*) (*Blitz*) to flash; (*Flammen*) to flare up. **2** *vt* **die Schultern ~** to shrug (one's shoulders).
zücken *vt Schwert* to draw; (*col*) *Notizbuch, Brieftasche* to take out.
Zucker *m no pl* **(a)** sugar. **ein Stück ~** a lump of sugar. **(b)** (*Med*) (*~gehalt*) sugar; (*Krankheit*) diabetes *sing*. **~ haben** (*col*) to be a diabetic.
Zucker-: ~dose *f* sugar bowl; **~erbse** *f* mangetout (pea); **~gehalt** *m* sugar content, **~guß** *m* icing, frosting (*esp US*); **mit ~guß überziehen** to ice, to frost (*esp US*); **~hut** *m* sugarloaf.
zuck(e)rig *adj* sugary.
Zucker-: z~krank *adj* diabetic; **~lecken** *nt*: **das ist kein ~lecken** (*col*) it's no picnic (*col*).

zuckern *vt* to sugar. **zu stark gezuckert** too sweet.
Zucker-: ~rohr *nt* sugar-cane; **~rübe** *f* sugar beet; **~spiegel** *m* (*Med*) (blood) sugar level; **~stange** *f* stick of rock (*Brit*) *or* candy (*US*); **z~süß** *adj* (*lit, fig*) sugar-sweet, sugary; **~watte** *f* candy floss; **~zange** *f* sugar tongs *pl*.
Zuckung *f* twitch; (*krampfhaft*) convulsion.
zudecken *vt sep* to cover; (*im Bett*) to tuck up *or* in. **jdn/sich (mit etw) ~** to cover sb/oneself up (with sth); to tuck sb/oneself up (in sth).
zudem *adv* (*geh*) moreover.
zudrehen *sep* **1** *vt Wasserhahn etc* to turn off; (*zuwenden*) to turn (*dat to*). **2** *vr* to turn (*dat to*).
zudringlich *adj Mensch* pushy (*col*); *Nachbarn* intrusive. **~ werden** (*zu einer Frau*) to make advances (*zu to*).
Zudringlichkeit *f* siehe *adj* pushiness (*col*); intrusiveness; (*einer Frau gegenüber*) advances *pl*.
zudrücken *vt sep* to press shut. **jdm die Kehle ~** to throttle sb.
zu|eilen *vi sep aux sein* **auf jdn/etw ~** to rush towards sb/sth.
zu|einander *adv* (*gegenseitig*) to each other; *Vertrauen* in each other; (*zusammen*) together. **~ passen** to go together; (*Menschen*) to suit each other.
zu|erkennen* *vt sep irreg Preis* to award (*jdm to* sb); *Recht* to grant; (*vor Gericht*) *Entschädigung* to award (*jdm etw* sb sth).
zu|erst *adv* first; (*anfangs*) at first. **~ an die Reihe kommen** to be first.
zufahren *vi sep irreg aux sein* **(a)** **auf jdn/etw ~** to drive/ride towards sb/sth. **(b)** **fahren Sie doch zu!** go on then!
Zufahrt *f* approach (road); (*zu einem Haus*) drive(way). „**keine ~ zum Krankenhaus**" "no access to hospital".
Zufahrtsstraße *f* access road; (*zur Autobahn*) approach road.
Zufall *m* chance; (*Zusammentreffen*) coincidence. **das ist ~** it's pure chance; **durch ~** (quite) by chance; **es ist kein ~, daß** ... it's no accident that ...; **es war ein glücklicher ~, daß** ... it was lucky that ...; **welch ein ~!** what a coincidence!; **etw dem ~ überlassen** to leave sth to chance.
zufallen *vi sep irreg aux sein* **(a)** (*sich schließen: Fenster etc*) to close. **die Tür fiel laut zu** the door slammed shut; **die Augen fielen ihm zu** he fell asleep. **(b)** **jdm ~** (*Preis etc*) to go to sb; (*Aufgabe*) to fall to sb.
zufällig 1 *adj* chance *attr*; *Zusammentreffen auch* coincidental. **das war rein ~** it was pure chance. **2** *adv* **(a)** by chance. **er ging ~ vorüber** he happened to be passing; **wenn Sie das ~ wissen sollten** if you (should) happen to know. **(b)** (*in Fragen*) by any chance.
Zufalls- *in cpds* chance; **~bekanntschaft** *f* chance acquaintance; **~treffer** *m* fluke; **einen ~treffer machen** to make a lucky choice.
zufassen *vi sep* **(a)** (*zugreifen*) to take hold of it/them; (*fig: schnell handeln*) to seize an/the opportunity. **(b)** (*helfen*) to lend a hand.
zufliegen *vi sep irreg aux sein* **(a)** **auf etw** (*acc*) **~** to fly towards sth. **(b)** +*dat* to fly to. **der Vogel ist uns zugeflogen** the bird flew into our house/flat *etc*; **ihm fliegt alles nur so zu** (*fig*) everything comes so easily to him. **(c)** (*col: Fenster, Tür*) to slam shut.
zufließen *vi sep irreg aux sein* +*dat* to flow to(wards); (*fig: Geld*) to flow into.
Zuflucht *f* refuge (*vor* +*dat from*). **du bist meine letzte ~** (*fig*) you are my last hope; **zu etw ~ nehmen** (*fig*) to resort to sth.
Zufluchtsstätte *f* place of refuge.
Zufluß *m* **(a)** *no pl* influx; (*Mech: Zufuhr*) supply. **(b)** (*Nebenfluß*) tributary; (*zu Binnensee*) inlet.
zuflüstern *vti sep* **jdm etw (etw) ~** to whisper (sth) to sb.

zufolge prep +dat (gemäß) according to; (auf Grund) as a result of. **dem Bericht** ~ according to the report.

zufrieden adj contented, content. **ein** ~**es Gesicht machen** to look pleased; ~ **lächeln** to smile contentedly; **mit jdm/etw** ~ **sein** to be satisfied or happy with sb/sth; **er ist mit nichts** ~ nothing pleases him.

Zufrieden-: z~**geben** vr sep irreg **sich mit etw** z~**geben** to be satisfied with sth; ~**heit** f contentment, contentedness; (Befriedigtsein) satisfaction; **zur allgemeinen** ~**heit** to everyone's satisfaction; z~**lassen** vt sep irreg to leave alone; **laß mich damit** z~! (col) shut up about it! (col); z~**stellen** vt sep to satisfy; **schwer** z~**zustellen sein** to be hard to please.

zufrieren vi sep irreg **aux sein** to freeze (over).

zufügen vt sep (a) **Leid** to cause. **jdm Schaden** ~ to harm sb; **jdm etw** ~ to cause sb sth. **(b)** (col) = **hinzufügen.**

Zufuhr f -**en** (Versorgung) supply (in +acc, nach to); (Mil) supplies pl; (Met) influx.

zuführen sep 1 vt +dat (a) (versorgen mit) to supply. **jdm etw** ~ to supply sb with sth. **(b)** (bringen) to bring. **jdn der gerechten Strafe** ~ to give sb the punishment he/she deserves. 2 vi **auf etw** (acc) ~ to lead to sth.

Zug[1] m -̈e (a) (Luft~) draught (Brit), draft (US); (Atem~) breath; (an Zigarette etc) puff, drag; (Schluck) mouthful. **einen** ~ **machen** (an Zigarette etc) to take a drag; **das Glas in einem** ~ **leeren** to empty the glass with one gulp; **etw in vollen** ~**en genießen** to enjoy sth to the full; **in den letzten** ~**en liegen** (col) to be at one's last gasp.

(b) no pl (von Vögeln, Menschen) migration; (der Wolken) drifting. **im** ~**e** (im Verlauf) in the course (gen of); **das liegt im** ~ **der Zeit** it's a sign of the times.

(c) (beim Schwimmen) stroke; (beim Rudern) pull (mit at); (bei Brettspiel) move. **einen** ~ **machen** (beim Schwimmen) to do a stroke; ~ **um** ~ (fig) step by step; **zum** ~ **kommen** (col) to get a look-in (col); **du bist am** ~ (bei Brettspiel, fig) it's your move; **etw in groben** ~**en darstellen/ umreißen** to outline sth.

(d) no pl (Ziehen) pull, tug (an +dat on, at).

(e) (Gruppe) (von Menschen) procession; (Mil) platoon; (Abteilung) section.

Zug[2] m -̈e (Eisenbahn~) train; (Last~) truck and trailer. **mit dem** ~ **fahren** to go/travel by train.

Zug[3] m -̈e (Gesichts~, Charakter~) feature; (brutal etc) streak; (Anflug) touch. **das war kein schöner** ~ **von dir** that wasn't nice of you.

Zugabe f extra, bonus; (Comm) free gift; (Theat) encore. ~! encore!

Zugang m (a) (Eingang, Einfahrt) entrance; (Zutritt) access (zu to). **er hat keinen** ~ **zur Musik** music doesn't mean anything to him. **(b)** (von Patienten) admission; (von Schülern) intake; (von Büchern) acquisition.

zugange adj pred: **mit jdm/etw** ~ **sein** (col) to be busy with sb/sth; (euph: sexuell) to be carrying on with sb (col).

zugänglich adj (dat, für to) (erreichbar) Gelände, Ort accessible; öffentliche Einrichtungen open; (umgänglich) Mensch, Vorgesetzter approachable. **etw der Allgemeinheit** ~ **machen** to open sth to the public; **für etw leicht/nicht** ~ **sein** to respond/not to respond to sth.

Zugänglichkeit f (Erreichbarkeit) accessibility; (Verfügbarkeit) availability; (Umgänglichkeit) approachability.

Zug-: ~**begleiter** m (Rail) guard (Brit), conductor (US); ~**brücke** f drawbridge.

zugeben vt sep irreg (a) (zugestehen, einräumen) to admit. **er gab zu, es getan zu haben** he admitted (to) having done it; **jdm gegenüber etw** ~ to confess sth to sb; **zugegeben** granted. **(b)** (hinzu-

fügen) to add. **(c)** (zusätzlich geben) to give as an extra. **jdm etw** ~ to give sb sth extra.

zugegebenermaßen adv admittedly.

zugegen adv (geh) ~ **sein** to be present.

zugehen sep irreg **aux sein** 1 vi (a) (Tür, Deckel) to shut. **der Koffer geht nicht zu** the case won't shut. **(b)** auf **jdn/etw** ~ to go towards sb/sth; **direkt auf jdn/etw** ~ to go straight up to sb/sth; **es geht auf den Winter zu** winter is drawing in; **er geht schon auf die Siebzig zu** he's getting on for seventy; **dem Ende** ~ to draw to a close. **(c)** +dat (Nachricht etc) to reach. **der Brief ist uns noch nicht zugegangen** the letter hasn't reached us yet. 2 vi impers **dort geht es ... zu** things are .. there; **hier geht es nicht mit rechten Dingen zu** there's something odd going on here.

zugehörig adj attr (geh) accompanying; (verbunden) affiliated (dat to).

Zugehörigkeit f (a) (zu Land, Glauben) affiliation; (Mitgliedschaft) membership (zu of). **(b)** (Zugehörigkeitsgefühl) sense of belonging.

zugeknöpft adj (fig col) Mensch reserved.

Zügel m - rein (auch fig). **die** ~ **anziehen** (lit) to draw in the reins; (fig) to keep a tighter rein (bei on); **die** ~ **fest in der Hand behalten** (fig) to keep things firmly in hand; **die** ~ **locker lassen** (fig) to give free rein (bei to); **die** ~ **an sich** (acc) **reißen** (fig) to seize the reins.

zugelassen adj authorized; Arzt registered; Kfz licensed. **amtlich/staatlich** ~ **sein** to be authorized/to be state-registered; **eine nicht** ~**e Partei** an illegal party; **als Kassenarzt** ~ **sein** ≈ to be registered as a GP.

Zügel-: z~**los** adj (fig) unbridled no adv, unrestrained; ~**losigkeit** f (fig) lack of restraint; (in sexueller Hinsicht) promiscuity.

zügeln 1 vt Pferd to rein in; (fig) to curb, to check. 2 vr to restrain oneself.

Zugeständnis nt concession (dat, an +acc to). ~**se machen** to make allowances.

zugestehen* vt sep irreg (einräumen) Recht to concede, to grant; (zugeben) to admit. **jdm etw** ~ (einräumen) to grant sb sth.

zugetan adj **jdm/einer Sache** ~ **sein** to be fond of sb/sth.

Zugezogene(r) mf decl as adj newcomer.

Zug-: ~**folge** f (Rail) order of incoming trains; z~**frei** adj Raum draught-free (Brit), draft-free (US); ~**führer** m (Rail) chief guard (Brit) or conductor (US).

zugig adj draughty (Brit), drafty (US).

zügig adj swift, speedy; Handschrift smooth.

zugkräftig adj (fig) Werbetext, Titel eye-catching. Stück crowd-pulling attr, popular.

zugleich adv (auch ebenso) at the same time.

Zug-: ~**luft** f draught (Brit), draft (US); ~**maschine** f towing vehicle; (von Sattelschlepper) traction engine; ~**personal** nt (Rail) train personnel; ~**pferd** nt draught (Brit) or draft (US) horse; (fig) crowd puller.

zugreifen vi sep irreg (a) to grab it/them; (fig) to act fast or quickly; (bei Tisch) to help oneself. **(b)** (Polizei) to step in quickly.

Zugriff m (a) **durch raschen** ~ by acting fast; **sich dem** ~ **der Polizei entziehen** to evade justice. **(b)** (Comp) access.

Zugriffszeit f (Comp) access time.

zugrunde adv (a) ~ **gehen** to perish; **jdn/etw** ~ **richten** to destroy sb/sth; (finanziell) to ruin sb/ sth; **er wird daran nicht** ~ **gehen** he'll survive; (finanziell) it won't ruin him. **(b)** **einer Sache** (dat) ~ **liegen** to form the basis of sth; **etw einer Sache** (dat) ~ **legen** to base sth on sth.

Zugtier nt draught (Brit) or draft (US) animal.

zugucken vi sep = **zusehen.**

Zug|unglück nt train accident.

zugunsten prep **von** or +gen in favour of (Brit), in favor of (US).

zugute *adv* jdm etw ~ halten to grant sb sth; *(Verständnis haben)* to make allowances for sth; einer Sache/jdm ~ kommen to come in useful for sth/to sb; *(Geld, Erlös)* to benefit sth/sb.

Zug-: ~verbindung *f* train connection; ~verkehr *m (Rail)* rail services *pl*; starker ~verkehr heavy rail traffic; ~vieh *nt no pl* draught *(Brit)* or draft *(US)* cattle; ~vogel *m* migratory bird; ~zwang *m (Chess)* zugzwang; unter ~zwang stehen *(fig)* to be in a tight spot.

zuhaben *vi sep irreg (col: Geschäft)* to be closed.

zuhalten *sep irreg* **1** *vt* to hold shut. sich *(dat)* die Nase ~ to hold one's nose; sich *(dat)* die Augen/ Ohren ~ to put one's hands over one's eyes/ears. **2** *vi* auf etw *(acc)* ~ to head straight for sth.

Zuhälter(in *f) m* - pimp, procurer.

zuhängen *vt sep* to cover up or over.

zuhauen *sep irreg* **1** *vt* Baumstamm to hew; Stein to trim. **2** *vi* to strike out.

zuhause *adv* at home.

Zuhause *nt no pl* home.

zuheilen *vi sep aux sein* to heal up.

Zuhilfenahme *f:* unter ~ von *or* +gen with the aid of.

zuhinterst *adv* right at the back.

zuhören *vi sep* to listen *(dat* to*)*. hör mal zu! *(drohend)* now (just) listen (to me)!

Zuhörer *m* listener. die ~ *(das Publikum)* the audience *sing*.

zujubeln *vi sep* jdm ~ to cheer sb.

zukehren *vt sep (zuwenden)* to turn. jdm das Gesicht ~ to turn to face sb; jdm den Rücken ~ *(lit, fig)* to turn one's back on sb.

zuklappen *sep* **1** *vt* Buch, Deckel to close. **2** *vi aux sein (Tür etc)* to click shut.

zukleben *vt sep* Briefumschlag to stick down.

zuknallen *vti sep (vi: aux sein) (col)* to slam or bang (shut).

zukneifen *vti sep irreg* to pinch; Augen to screw up; Mund to shut tight(ly).

zuknöpfen *vt sep* to button (up); *siehe* zugeknöpft.

zukommen *vi sep irreg aux sein* **(a)** auf jdn/etw ~ to come toward(s) *or (direkt)* up to sb/sth; die Aufgabe, die nun auf uns zukommt the task which now confronts us; die Dinge auf sich *(acc)* ~ lassen to take things as they come. **(b)** jdm etw ~ lassen Brief etc to send sb sth; *(schenken auch)*, Hilfe to give sb sth. **(c)** +dat *(geziemen)* to befit, to become. diesem Treffen kommt große Bedeutung zu this meeting is of the utmost importance.

zukriegen *vt sep (col)* = zubekommen.

Zukunft *f no pl (auch Gram)* future. in ferner/ naher ~ in the distant/near future; unsere gemeinsame ~ our future together.

zukünftig **1** *adj* future. meine Z~e *(col)*/mein Z~er *(col)* my future wife/husband. **2** *adv* in future.

Zukunfts-: ~aussichten *pl* future prospects *pl*; ~glaube *m* belief in the future; ~gläubig *adj* believing in the future; ~musik *f (fig col)* pie in the sky *(col)*; ~pläne *pl* plans *pl* for the future; ~roman *m* novel dealing with the future; *(Science-fiction)* science fiction novel; z~weisend *adj* forward-looking.

zulächeln *vi sep* jdm ~ to smile at sb.

Zulage *f* **(a)** *(Geld~)* extra pay *no indef art*. eine ~ von 100 Mark an extra 100 marks pay. **(b)** *(Gehaltserhöhung)* rise *(Brit)*, raise *(US)*.

zulande *adv* bei uns ~ in our country.

zulangen *vi sep (col: Dieb, beim Essen)* to help oneself.

zulassen *vt sep irreg* **(a)** *(Zugang gewähren)* to admit; *(amtlich)* to authorize; Arzt to register; Kraftfahrzeug to license; Rechtsanwalt, Prüfling to admit. **(b)** *(dulden, gestatten)* to allow, to permit. ~, daß etw passiert to allow sth to happen. **(c)**

(geschlossen lassen) to leave closed.

zulässig *adj* permissible, permitted. ~es Gesamtgewicht *(Mot)* maximum laden weight; ~e Höchstgeschwindigkeit (upper) speed limit.

Zulassung *f* **(a)** *no pl (Erlaubnis, Gewährung von Zugang)* admission; *(amtlich)* authorization; *(von Kfz)* licensing; *(als Arzt)* registration. **(b)** *(Dokument)* papers *pl*; *(Lizenz)* licence *(Brit)*, license *(US)*.

Zulauf *m no pl* großen ~ haben *(Geschäft)* to be very popular.

zulaufen *vi sep irreg aux sein* **(a)** auf jdn/etw ~ to run towards sb/sth. **(b)** *(auslaufen)* spitz ~ to taper. **(c)** *(Wasser etc)* laß noch etwas kaltes Wasser ~ run in some more cold water. **(d)** *(Tier)* jdm ~ to stray into sb's house/place; eine zugelaufene Katze a stray (cat).

zulegen *sep* **1** *vt* **(a)** *(dazulegen)* to put on. **(b)** Geld to add; *(bei Verlustgeschäft)* to lose. die fehlenden 20 DM legte meine Mutter zu my mother made up the remaining DM 20. **(c)** etwas Tempo ~ *(col)* to get a move on *(col)*. **2** *vi (col)* **(a)** *(an Gewicht)* to put on (weight). **(b)** *(sich mehr anstrengen) (col)* to pull one's finger out *(col)*; *(Sport)* to step up the pace *(col)*. **3** *vr* sich *(dat)* etw/jdn ~ *(col)* to get oneself sth/sb.

zuleide *adv* jdm etwas ~ tun to harm sb.

zuleiten *vt sep* Wasser etc to supply; Post, Waren to send on.

Zuleitung *f (Tech)* supply.

zuletzt *adv* **(a)** in the end. ~ kam sie doch she came in the end; wir blieben bis ~ we stayed to the very end; ganz ~ at the very last moment. **(b)** *(als letzte(r, s), an letzter Stelle)* last. ich kam ~ I came last; ganz ~ last of all; nicht ~ wegen not least because of.

zuliebe *adv* jdm ~ tun to do sth for sb's sake.

Zulieferbetrieb *m (Econ)* supplier.

Zulu ['tsu:lu] *mf -(s)* Zulu.

zum = zu dem.

zumachen *sep* **1** *vt (schließen)* to close; *(col: auflösen)* Laden etc to close (down). **2** *vi (col)* **(a)** *(den Laden ~)* to close (down); *(fig)* to call it a day. **(b)** *(sich beeilen)* to hurry up.

zumal **1** *conj* ~ *(da)* especially as. **2** *adv (besonders)* especially.

zumauern *vt sep* to brick up, to wall up.

zumeist *adv* mostly.

zumessen *vt sep irreg* Zeit to allocate *(dat* for*)*; Schuld to attribute *(jdm* to sb*)*; Bedeutung to attach *(dat* to*)*.

zumindest *adv* at least.

zumutbar *adj* reasonable. es ist mir nicht ~, das zu tun I can't be expected to do that.

zumute *adv* mir ist traurig ~ I feel sad; mir ist gar nicht lächerlich ~ I'm not in a laughing mood.

zumuten *vt sep* jdm etw ~ to expect sth of sb; Sie wollen mir doch wohl nicht ~, diesen Unsinn zu lesen you surely don't expect me to read this nonsense; sich *(dat)* zuviel ~ to take on too much.

Zumutung *f* unreasonable demand; *(Unverschämtheit)* nerve *(col)*. das ist eine ~! that's a bit much!

zunächst *adv* **(a)** *(zuerst)* first (of all). ~ einmal first of all. **(b)** *(vorläufig)* for the time being.

zunageln *vt sep* Fenster etc to nail up; *(mit Brettern, Pappe etc)* to board up; Kiste etc to nail down.

zunähen *vt sep* to sew up.

Zunahme *f* - increase *(gen, an +dat* in*)*.

Zuname *m* surname, last name.

zünden **1** *vi* to ignite; *(Streichholz)* to light; *(Motor)* to fire; *(Sprengkörper)* to go off; *(fig)* to kindle enthusiasm. **2** *vt* to ignite; Rakete to fire; Sprengkörper to detonate; Feuerwerkskörper to let off.

zündend *adj (fig)* stirring.

Zunder *m* - tinder. ~ kriegen/jdm ~ geben *(col)* to

get/to give sb a good hiding *(col)*.

Zünder *m* - igniter; *(für Sprengstoff, Bombe etc)* fuse; *(für Mine)* detonator.

Zünd-: ~**flamme** *f* pilot light; ~**holz** *nt* match; ~**hütchen** *nt* percussion cap; ~**kabel** *nt (Aut)* plug lead; ~**kapsel** *f* detonator; ~**kerze** *f (Aut)* spark plug; ~**plättchen** *nt* cap; ~**schloß** *nt (Aut)* ignition lock; ~**schlüssel** *m (Aut)* ignition key; ~**schnur** *f* fuse; ~**spule** *f* ignition coil; ~**stoff** *m* inflammable matter; *(Sprengstoff)* explosives *pl*; *(fig)* inflammatory stuff.

Zündung *f* ignition. **die ~ einstellen** *(Aut)* to adjust the timing.

zunehmen *vi sep irreg* **1** *vi* to increase; *(an Weisheit etc)* to gain *(an +dat* in); *(an Gewicht)* to put on weight; *(Mond)* to wax. **2** *vt (Mensch: an Gewicht)* to gain.

zunehmend 1 *adj* increasing, growing. **bei ~em Alter** with advancing age; **wir haben ~en Mond** there is a crescent moon; **in ~em Maße** to an increasing degree. **2** *adv* increasingly.

zuneigen *sep +dat* **1** *vi* to be inclined towards. **jdm zugeneigt sein** *(geh)* to be well disposed towards sb. **2** *vr* to lean towards. **sich dem Ende ~** *(geh)* to be drawing to a close; *(Vorräte etc)* to be running out.

Zuneigung *f* affection *(zu* for*)*.

Zunft *f* -e *(Hist)* guild; *(hum col)* brotherhood.

zünftig *adj* Kleidung professional; *(col: ordentlich)* proper. **eine ~e Ohrfeige** a hefty box on the ears.

Zunge *f* -n tongue; *(von Waage)* pointer. **das brennt auf der ~** that burns the tongue; **jdm die ~ herausstrecken** to stick one's tongue out at sb; **eine spitze/lose ~ haben** to have a sharp/loose tongue; **böse ~n behaupten, ...** malicious gossip has it ...; **mir liegt das Wort auf der ~** the word is on the tip of my tongue; **mir hängt die ~ zum Hals heraus** *(col)* my tongue is hanging out; *(erschöpft)* I'm exhausted.

züngeln *vi (Flammen)* to lick.

Zungen-: ~**brecher** *m* tongue-twister; **z~fertig** *adj (geh)* fluent; *(pej)* glib; ~**kuß** *m* French kiss; ~**spitze** *f* tip of the tongue; ~**wurst** *f* tongue sausage.

Zünglein *nt:* **das ~ an der Waage sein** *(fig)* to tip the scales.

zunichte *adv* ~ **machen/werden** *(geh)* to ruin/to be ruined.

zunicken *vi sep* jdm ~ to nod to sb; **jdm freundlich ~** to give sb a friendly nod.

zunutze *adv* **sich** *(dat)* **etw ~ machen** *(verwenden)* to make use of sth; *(ausnutzen)* to take advantage of sth.

zu|oberst *adv* right at the top.

zu|ordnen *vt sep +dat* to assign to.

zupacken *vi sep (col)* **(a)** *(zugreifen)* to make a grab for it *etc*. **(b)** *(bei der Arbeit)* to get down to it. **(c)** *(helfen)* **mit ~** to give me/them *etc* a hand.

zupfen *vti* to pick; Unkraut, Fäden to pull. **jdn am Ärmel** *etc* ~ to tug at sb's sleeve *etc;* **sich** *(dat or acc)* **am Bart ~** to pull at one's beard.

Zupf|instrument *nt (Mus)* plucked string instrument.

zuprosten *vi sep* jdm ~ to drink sb's health.

zur = **zu der.**

zuraten *vi sep irreg* jdm ~, **etw zu tun** to advise sb to do sth.

zurechnen *vt sep* **(a)** *(col: dazurechnen)* to add to. **(b)** *(fig: zuordnen)* to class *(dat* with*)*; Kunstwerk *etc* to ascribe *(dat* to*)*.

Zurechnungs-: **z~fähig** *adj* of sound mind; *(esp Jur, fig col)* compos mentis *pred;* ~**fähigkeit** *f* soundness of mind; **verminderte ~fähigkeit** diminished responsibility.

zurecht-: ~**biegen** *vt sep irreg* to bend into shape; *(fig)* to twist; **er hat alles wieder ~gebogen** *(col)* he has straightened everything out again;

~**finden** *vr sep irreg* to find one's way *(in +dat* around*)*; **sich in der Welt nicht mehr ~finden** not to be able to cope with the world any longer; ~**kommen** *vi sep irreg aux sein* **(a)** *(fig)* to get on; *(schaffen)* to cope; *(genug haben)* to have enough; **(b)** *(rechtzeitig kommen)* to come in time; **(c)** *(finanziell)* to manage; ~**legen** *vt sep irreg* to lay out ready; **sich** *(dat)* **etw ~legen** to get sth out ready; *(fig)* to work sth out; ~**machen** *vt sep (col)* **(a)** Zimmer, Essen *etc* to prepare; Bett to make up; **(b)** *(anziehen)* to dress; *(schminken)* to make up; **sich ~machen** to get ready; to put on one's make-up; ~**rücken** *vt sep (lit, fig)* to put straight; Brille, Hut *etc* to adjust; ~**stutzen** *vt sep* to trim; *(fig)* to lick into shape; ~**weisen** *vt sep irreg (form)* to rebuke; *(Schüler etc* to reprimand; **Z~weisung** *f siehe vt* rebuke; reprimand.

zureden *vi sep* jdm ~ to encourage sb; *(überreden)* to persuade sb; **wenn du ihm gut zuredest, hilft er dir** if you talk to him nicely, he'll help you.

zureiten *sep irreg* **1** *vt* Pferd to break in. **2** *vi aux sein* **auf jdn/etw ~** to ride toward(s) sb/sth.

zurichten *vt sep* **(a)** Essen *etc* to prepare. **(b)** *(verunstalten)* to make a mess of; *(verletzen)* to injure; **jdn übel ~** to knock sb about.

zürnen *vi (geh)* jdm ~ to be angry with sb.

zurück *adv* back; *(mit Zahlungen)* behind; *(fig: zurückgeblieben: von Kind)* backward. **in Mathematik (sehr) ~ sein** *(fig)* to be (really) behind in maths; **~! get back!;** ~ **an Absender** return to sender; **hinter jdm ~ sein** *(fig)* to lie behind sb; **es gibt kein Z~ (mehr)** there's no going back.

zurück-: ~**behalten** *vt sep irreg* to keep (back); **er hat Schäden ~behalten** he suffered lasting damage; ~**bekommen** *vt sep irreg* to get back; ~**berufen** *vt sep irreg* to recall; ~**bewegen** *vtr sep* to move back; ~**bilden** *vr sep (Geschwür)* to recede; *(Muskel)* to become wasted; *(Biol)* to regress.

zurückbleiben *vi sep irreg aux sein* **(a)** to stay behind. **(b)** *(übrigbleiben)* to be left, to remain. **ihm ist eine Narbe zurückgeblieben** he has been left with a scar. **(c)** *(nicht Schritt halten)* to fall behind; *(in Entwicklung)* to be retarded; *(Sport)* to be behind. **ihre Leistung blieb hinter meinen Erwartungen zurück** her performance did not come up to my expectations; **siehe zurückgeblieben.**

zurück-: ~**blicken** *vi sep* to look back *(auf +acc* at*)*; *(fig)* to look back *(auf +acc* on*)*; ~**bringen** *vt sep irreg* to bring back; *(wieder wegbringen)* to take back; ~**denken** *vi sep irreg* to think back *(an +acc* to*)*; **so weit ich ~denken kann** as far as I can recall; ~**drängen** *vt sep* to force back; *(Mil, to drive back;* ~**drehen** *vt sep* to turn back; ~**dürfen** *vi sep irreg (col)* to be allowed back; ~**erhalten*** *vt sep irreg* to get back; ~**erinnern*** *vr sep* to remember; ~**erobern*** *vt sep (Mil* to recapture; ~**erstatten*** *vt sep* to reimburse; ~**fahren** *sep irreg* **1** *vi aux sein* to return; **2** *vt* to drive back; ~**fallen** *vi sep irreg aux sein* to fall back; *(Sport)* to drop back; *(in Leistungen)* to fall behind; *(fig) (an Besitzer)* to revert *(an +acc* on*)*; *(Schande, Vorwurf etc)* to reflect *(auf +acc* on*)*; ~**finden** *vi sep irreg* to find the way back; ~**fliegen** *vti sep irreg (vi aux sein)* to fly back; ~**fließen** *vi sep irreg aux sein (lit, fig)* to flow back; ~**fordern** *vt sep* **etw ~fordern** to ask for sth back; ~**fragen** *vi sep* to ask a question back; *(wegen Auskunft)* to check (back) with.

zurückführen *sep* **1** *vt* **(a)** *(zurückbringen)* to lead back. **(b)** *(ableiten aus)* to put down to. **2** *vi* to lead back. **es führt kein Weg zurück** *(fig)* there's no going back.

zurückgeben *vt sep irreg* to give back; Ball, Beleidigung to return.

zurückgeblieben *adj* geistig/körperlich ~

mentally/physically retarded.
zurückgehen *vi sep irreg aux sein* **(a)** to go back *(nach, in +acc* to, *fig: auf +acc* to). **er ging zwei Schritte zurück** he took two steps back; **Waren/ Essen ~ lassen** to send back goods/food. **(b)** *(zurückweichen)* to retreat, to fall back; *(fig: abnehmen)* to go down; *(Geschäft, Umsatz)* to fall off; *(Schmerz, Blutung)* to ease
zurück-: ~**gezogen** *adj Mensch* retiring; *Lebensweise* secluded; **er lebt sehr ~gezogen** he lives a very secluded life; ~**greifen** *vi sep irreg (fig)* to fall back *(auf +acc* on); *(zeitlich)* to go back *(auf +acc* to); ~**haben** *vt sep irreg (col)* to have back; **ich will mein Geld ~haben** I want my money back.
zurückhalten *sep irreg* **1** *vt* to hold back; *(aufhalten) jdn* to hold up; *(nicht freigeben) Informationen* to withhold; *(unterdrücken) Tränen* to keep back. **jdn von etw** *(dat)* ~ to keep sb from sth. **2** *vr (sich beherrschen)* to restrain oneself; *(im Hintergrund bleiben)* to keep in the background; *(bei Verhandlung etc)* to keep a low profile. **Sie müssen sich beim Essen sehr** ~ you must cut down a lot on what you eat. **3** *vi* **mit etw** ~ *(verheimlichen)* to hold sth back.
zurückhaltend *adj* restrained; *(reserviert)* reserved; *Empfang, Nachfrage* low-key. **sich ~ über etw** *(acc)* **äußern** to be restrained in one's comments about sth.
Zurück-: ~**haltung** *f siehe adj* restraint; reserve; z~**holen** *vt sep* to fetch back; z~**kaufen** *vt sep* to buy back; z~**kehren** *vi sep aux sein* to return *(von, aus* from; *nach, zu* to); z~**kommen** *vi sep irreg aux sein* to come back; **ich kann nicht mehr z~** *(fig)* there's no going back!; z~**kriegen** *vt sep (col)* to get back; z~**lassen** *vt sep irreg* **(a)** to leave; *(liegenlassen, fig: übertreffen)* to leave behind; **(b)** *(col: z~kehren lassen)* to allow back; z~**laufen** *vi sep irreg aux sein* to run back; *(z~gehen)* to walk back.
zurücklegen *sep* **1** *vt* **(a)** to put back. **(b)** *Kopf* to lay or lean back. **(c)** *(aufbewahren)* to put aside; *(sparen)* to lay aside. **jdm etw** ~ to keep sth for sb. **(d)** *Strecke* to cover, to do. **2** *vr* to lie back.
Zurück-: z~**lehnen** *vtr sep* to lean back; z~**liegen** *vi sep irreg* **der Unfall liegt etwa eine Woche z~** the accident was about a week ago; z~**melden** *vtr sep* to report back; z~**müssen** *vi sep irreg (col)* to have to go back; ~**nahme** *f -n siehe* z~**nehmen** taking back; revoking; reversal; withdrawal; z~**nehmen** *vt sep irreg* **(a)** to take back; *Verordnung* to revoke; *Entscheidung* to reverse; *Angebot* to withdraw; **sein Wort z~nehmen** to go back on one's word; z~**prallen** *vi sep aux sein* to bounce back; z~**reichen** *vi sep (Tradition etc)* to go back *(in +acc* to); z~**reißen** *vt sep irreg* to pull back; z~**rollen** *vti sep (vi: aux sein)* to roll back; z~**rufen** *vti sep irreg* to call back; *Botschafter, fehlerhafte Autos* to recall; **jdn ins Leben z~rufen** to bring sb back to life; **jdm/sich etw ins Gedächtnis z~rufen** to remind sb of sth/to recall sth; z~**schalten** *vi sep* to change back; z~**schauen** *vi sep* to look back *(auf +acc (lit)* at, *(fig)* on); z~**schicken** *vt sep* to send back; z~**schieben** *vt sep irreg* to push back.
zurückschlagen *sep irreg* **1** *vt* **(a)** *Ball* to return; *Angriff etc* to repulse. **(b)** *Decke* to fold back; *Kragen* to turn back. **2** *vi* to hit back.
zurück-: ~**schrauben** *vt sep* **seine Ansprüche ~schrauben** to lower one's sights; ~**schrecken** *vi sep irreg aux sein or haben (fig)* to shy away *(vor +dat* from); **vor nichts ~schrecken** to stop at nothing; ~**sehen** *vi sep irreg* to look back *(auf +acc (lit)* at, *(fig)* on); ~**sehnen** *vr sep* to long to return *(nach* to); **sich nach der guten alten Zeit ~sehnen** to long for the good old days; ~**senden** *vt sep irreg* to send back.

zurücksetzen *sep* **1** *vt (nach hinten)* to move back; *(an früheren Platz)* to put back. **2** *vr* to sit back. **3** *vi (mit Fahrzeug)* to reverse, to back.
Zurück-: ~**setzung** *f (fig: Benachteiligung)* neglect; z~**sinken** *vi sep irreg aux sein* to sink back *(in +acc* into); z~**spielen** *vti sep (Sport)* to play back; z~**stecken** *sep* **1** *vt* to put back; **2** *vi* **(a)** *(weniger Ansprüche stellen)* to lower one's expectations; **(b)** *(nachgeben)* to backtrack.
zurückstehen *vi sep irreg* **(a)** *(Haus etc)* to stand back. **(b)** *(hintangesetzt werden)* to take second place *(hinter +dat* to).
zurückstellen *vt sep* **(a)** *(an seinen Platz, Uhr)* to put back; *(nach hinten)* to move back. **(b)** *Waren* to put aside or by. **(c)** *(fig) Schüler* to keep down. **jdn vom Wehrdienst** ~ to defer sb's military service. **(d)** *(fig: verschieben)* to defer; *Bedenken etc* to put aside. **persönliche Interessen hinter etw** *(dat)* ~ to put one's personal interests after sth.
Zurück-: ~**stellung** *f (Aufschub, Mil)* deferment; z~**stoßen** *vt sep irreg* to push back; *(fig)* to reject; z~**stufen** *vt sep* to downgrade; z~**tragen** *vt sep irreg* to carry back; z~**treiben** *vt sep irreg* to drive back.
zurücktreten *sep irreg* **1** *vi aux sein* **(a)** to step back; *(fig: Hochwasser)* to go down. **bitte ~!** stand back, please!; **einen Schritt ~** to take a step back. **(b)** *(Regierung)* to resign; *(von einem Amt)* to step down. **(c)** *(von einem Vertrag etc)* to decrease; *(Wald)* to recede. **hinter jdm/etw ~** to come second to sb/sth. **2** *vti (mit Fuß)* to kick back.
Zurück-: z~**verfolgen*** *vt sep (fig)* to trace back; z~**verlangen*** *vt sep* to demand back; z~**verlegen*** *vt sep (zeitlich)* to set back; **(b)** *Front etc, Wohnsitz* to move back; z~**versetzen*** *sep* **1** *vt* **(a)** *(in alten Zustand)* to restore *(in +acc* to); *(in andere Zeit)* to take back *(in +acc* to); **(b)** *Beamte etc* to transfer back; **2** *vr* to think oneself back *(in +acc* to); z~**verweisen*** *vt sep irreg* to refer back; *(Parl) Gesetzentwurf* to recommit; z~**weichen** *vi sep irreg aux sein* to shrink back *(vor +dat* from); z~**weisen** *vt sep irreg* to reject; *Bittsteller* to turn away; *(an der Grenze)* to turn back; ~**weisung** *f siehe vt* rejection; turning away; turning back; z~**werfen** *vt sep irreg Ball, Kopf* to throw back; *Feind auch* to repel; *Strahlen, Schall* to reflect; *(fig: wirtschaftlich)* to set back *(um* by); z~**wollen** *vi sep (col)* to want to go back; z~**zahlen** *vt sep* to pay back.
zurückziehen *sep irreg* **1** *vt* to pull back; *Antrag, Klage etc* to withdraw. **2** *vr* to withdraw *(von* from); *(von Tätigkeit)* to retire; *siehe* **zurückgezogen.** **3** *vi aux sein* to move back.
Zuruf *m* shout; *(aufmunternd)* cheer.
zurufen *vi sep irreg* **jdm etw ~** to shout sth to sb.
Zusage *f* **-n (a)** *(Verpflichtung)* commitment. **(b)** *(Annahme)* acceptance. **(c)** *(Versprechen)* promise.
zusagen *vi sep* **(a)** *(annehmen)* **(jdm)** ~ to accept. **(b)** *(gefallen)* **jdm** ~ to appeal to sb.
zusammen *adv* together. **wir hatten ~ 100 Mark zum Ausgeben** between us we had 100 marks to spend; **er verdient mehr als wir alle ~** he earns more than the rest of us put together; **das macht ~ 50 Mark** that makes 50 marks altogether.
Zusammen-: ~**arbeit** *f* co-operation; z~**arbeiten** *vi sep* to co-operate; ~**ballung** *f* accumulation; ~**bau** *m no pl* assembly; z~**bauen** *vt sep* to assemble; **etw wieder z~bauen** to reassemble sth; z~**beißen** *vt sep irreg* **die Zähne z~beißen** *(lit)* to clench one's teeth; *(fig)* to grit one's teeth; z~**bekommen*** *vt sep irreg* to get together; *Wortlaut etc* to remember; z~**binden** *vt sep irreg* to tie together; z~**bleiben** *vi sep irreg aux sein* to stay

together; **z~brauen** sep 1 vt (col) to concoct; 2 vr (Gewitter, Unheil etc) to be brewing.

zusammenbrechen vi sep irreg aux sein to collapse; (Mensch auch, Verhandlungen, Telefonverbindungen) to break down; (Verkehr etc) to come to a standstill.

zusammenbringen vt sep irreg to collect; Geld to raise; (ins Gedächtnis zurückrufen) to remember; (bekannt machen) Menschen to bring together.

Zusammenbruch m (von Beziehungen, Kommunikation, Nerven~) breakdown; (fig) collapse.

zusammen-: ~**drängen** vtr to crowd together; ~**drücken** vt sep to press together; **z~fahren** sep irreg 1 vi aux sein (a) (~stoßen) to collide; (b) (erschrecken) to start; 2 vt (col) Fahrzeug to wreck; ~**fallen** vi sep irreg aux sein (a) (einstürzen) to collapse; (b) (Ereignisse) to coincide; ~**falten** vt sep to fold up.

zusammenfassen sep 1 vt to combine (zu in). 2 vti (das Fazit ziehen) to summarize. ~**d kann man sagen,** ... to sum up, one can say ...

Zusammen-: ~**fassung** f (a) combination; (b) (Überblick) summary; **z~fegen** vt sep to sweep together; **z~fließen** vi sep irreg aux sein to meet; (Farben) to run together; ~**fluß** m confluence; **z~fügen** sep 1 vt to join together; (Tech) to fit together; **etw zu etw z~fügen** to join/fit sth together to make sth; 2 vr to fit together; **z~führen** vt sep to bring together; Familie to reunite; **z~gehen** vi sep irreg aux sein (sich vereinen) to unite; (Linien etc) to meet; **z~gehören*** vi sep to belong together; (Gegenstände) to go together, to match; **z~gehörig** adj Kleidungsstücke etc matching; ~**gehörigkeit** f (Einheit) unity; ~**gehörigkeitsgefühl** nt sense of belonging; (in Familie) sense of a common bond; **z~gesetzt** adj aus etw ~ gesetzt sein to be composed of sth; **z~gewürfelt** adj motley; **z~haben** vt sep irreg (col) etw z~haben to have got sth together; ~**halt** m no pl cohesion; (Tech) (cohesive) strength.

zusammenhalten sep irreg 1 vt to hold together; (col) Geld etc to hold on to. 2 vi to hold together; (fig: Freunde, Gruppe etc) to stick together.

Zusammenhang m connection (von, zwischen +dat between); (im Text) context. **etw mit etw in ~ bringen** to connect sth with sth; **im or in ~ mit etw stehen** to be connected with sth; **etw aus dem ~ reißen** to take sth out of its context.

zusammenhängen vi sep irreg to be joined (together); (fig) to be connected. ~**d** Erzählung coherent.

zusammenhang(s)los 1 adj disjointed. 2 adv incoherently.

Zusammen-: **z~hauen** vt sep irreg (col) (zerstören) to smash to pieces; **jdn z~hauen** to beat sb up; **z~heften** vt sep to staple together; **z~heilen** vi sep aux sein to heal (up); (Knochen) to knit (together); **z~kehren** vt sep to sweep together; **z~klappbar** adj folding; **z~klappen** sep 1 vt to fold up; Schirm to shut; 2 vi aux sein (a) (Stuhl etc) to collapse; (b) (fig col: vor Erschöpfung) to flake out (col); **z~kleben** vti sep (vi: aux haben or sein) to stick together; **z~kneifen** vt sep irreg Lippen etc to press together; Augen to screw up; **z~knüllen** vt sep to crumple up; **z~kommen** vi sep irreg aux sein to meet; (Umstände) to combine; (Geld) to be collected; **er kommt viel mit Menschen zusammen** he meets a lot of people; **z~kratzen** vt sep to scrape together; **z~kriegen** vt sep (col) = **z~bekommen**; ~**kunft** f, pl ~**künfte** meeting; (zwanglos) get-together; **z~lassen** vt sep irreg to leave together.

zusammenlaufen vi sep irreg aux sein (a) (an eine Stelle laufen) to gather; (Flüssigkeit) to collect. (b) (Farben) to run together; (Linien) to intersect. (c) (Stoff) to shrink.

zusammenleben vi sep to live together.

Zusammenleben nt living together no art. **das ~ der Menschen** the social life of man; **das menschliche ~** social existence.

zusammen-: ~**legen** vt sep (a) to fold (up); (b) (stapeln) to pile together; (c) (vereinigen) to put together, to combine; Grundstücke to join; Termine to hold together; **sie legten ihr Geld ~** they pooled their money; ~**nähen** vt sep to sew or stitch together.

zusammennehmen sep irreg 1 vt to gather up; Mut to summon up; Gedanken to collect. **alles zusammengenommen** all in all. 2 vr to pull oneself together.

Zusammen-: **z~packen** vt sep to pack up together; **pack (deine Sachen) z~!** get packed!; **z~passen** vi sep to be suited to each other; (Farben, Stile) to go together; **z~pferchen** vt sep to herd together; ~**prall** m collision; (fig) clash; **z~prallen** vi sep aux sein to collide; (fig) to clash; **z~pressen** vt sep to press together; **z~raffen** sep 1 vt (a) (fig) Mut to summon up; (b) (fig pej: anhäufen) to amass, to pile up; 2 vr to pull oneself together; **z~rechnen** vt sep to add up; **z~reimen** vt sep (col) **das kann ich mir nicht z~reimen** I can't make head or tail of this; **z~reißen** vr sep irreg to pull oneself together; **z~rollen** sep 1 vt to roll up; 2 vr to curl up; (Schlange) to coil up; **z~rotten** vr sep (pej) to gang up (gegen against); (in aufrührerischer Absicht) to form a mob; **z~rücken** sep 1 vt Möbel etc to move closer together; 2 vi aux sein to move up closer; **z~rufen** vt sep irreg to call together; **z~scharen** vr sep to gather; **z~schießen** vt sep irreg to shoot up; 2 vi (col) das kann ich mir nicht z~reimen; **z~schlagen** sep irreg 1 vt (a) (aneinanderschlagen) to knock together; Hacken to click; **die Hände überm Kopf z~schlagen** to throw up one's hands in horror; (b) (verprügeln) to beat up; (zerschlagen) to smash up; 2 vi aux sein über jdm/etw z~schlagen (Wellen etc) to close over sb/sth; **z~schließen** vr sep irreg to combine; (Comm, Pol) to merge; ~**schluß** m siehe vr combining; merger; **z~schmelzen** vti siehe vi combining; (a) (verschmelzen) to fuse; (b) (zerschmelzen) to melt (away); (Anzahl) to dwindle; **z~schreiben** vt sep irreg (a) Wörter to write together; (b) (pej: verfassen) was der für einen Mist zusammenschreibt what a load of rubbish he writes; **z~schrumpfen** vi sep aux sein to shrivel up; (fig) to dwindle (auf +acc to).

zusammensein vi sep irreg aux sein mit jdm ~ to be with sb; (col: befreundet) to be going out with sb; (euph: mit jdm schlafen) to sleep with sb.

Zusammensein nt (a) being together. (b) (Zusammenkunft) get-together.

zusammensetzen sep 1 vt to put together. 2 vr (a) to sit together; (um etwas zu tun) to get together. (b) sich ~ aus to consist of.

Zusammen-: ~**setzung** f (Struktur) composition; (Mischung) mixture; **das Team in dieser** ~**setzung** the team in this line-up; **z~sinken** vi sep irreg aux sein (in sich) **z~sinken** to slump; (Gebäude) to cave in; **z~sparen** vt sep to save up; ~**spiel** nt teamwork; (von Kräften etc) interaction; **z~stauchen** vt sep (col) to give a dressing-down (col); **z~stecken** sep 1 vt Einzelteile to fit together; (mit Nadeln etc) to pin together; **die Köpfe z~stecken** (col) to put their heads together; (flüstern) to whisper to each other; 2 vi (col) to be together; **z~stehen** vi sep irreg aux sein to stand together; (Gegenstände) to stand together; (fig) to stand by each other.

zusammenstellen vt sep to put together; (nach System) to arrange; Liste to draw up.

Zusammenstellung f (a) siehe vt putting together; arranging; drawing up. (b) (nach System) arrangement; (Liste) list; (Zusammensetzung) composition; (Übersicht) survey.

Zusammenstoß m collision, crash; (Mil, fig:

Streit) clash.

zusammenstoßen sep irreg **1** vi aux sein (z~prallen) to collide; (Mil, fig: sich streiten) to clash. **mit jdm ~** to collide with sb; (fig) to clash with sb; **sie stießen mit den Köpfen zusammen** they banged their heads together. **2** vt to knock together.

Zusammen-: **z~streichen** vt sep irreg to cut (down) (auf +acc to); **z~strömen** vi sep aux sein (Menschen) to flock together; **z~stürzen** vi sep aux sein (einstürzen) to collapse; **z~suchen** vt sep to collect (together); **sich** (dat) **etw z~suchen** to find sth; **z~tragen** vt sep irreg to collect; **z~treffen** vi sep irreg aux sein (Menschen) to meet; (Ereignisse) to coincide; **mit jdm z~treffen** to meet sb; **z~treten** vi sep irreg aux sein (Vorstand etc) to meet; **z~trommeln** vt sep (col) to round up (col); **z~tun** sep irreg **1** vt (col) to put together; (vermischen) to mix; **2** vr to get together; **z~wachsen** vi sep irreg aux sein to grow together; (Wunde) to close; (Knochen) to knit; **z~wirken** vi sep to combine; **z~zählen** vt sep to add up.

zusammenziehen sep irreg **1** vt (a) to draw together; (verengen) to narrow; Augenbrauen to knit. (b) (fig) Truppen, Polizei to assemble. (c) (kürzen) Wörter etc to contract; Zahlen to add together. **2** vr (esp Biol, Sci) to contract; (Gewitter) to be brewing. **3** vi aux sein to move in together.

zusammenzucken vi sep aux sein to start.

Zusatz m addition; (zu Gesetz) rider; (Beimischung) additive.

Zusatz- in cpds supplementary; ~**bestimmung** f supplementary provision; ~**gerät** nt attachment.

zusätzlich 1 adj additional. **2** adv in addition.

Zusatz-: ~**mittel** nt, ~**stoff** m additive.

zuschanzen vt sep (col) jdm etw ~ to make sure sb gets sth.

zuschauen vi sep = **zusehen.**

Zuschauer m - spectator; (TV) viewer; (Theat) member of the audience; (Beistehender) onlooker. **die ~** pl the spectators pl; (TV) the viewers pl; (Theat) the audience sing.

Zuschauer-: ~**raum** m auditorium; ~**tribüne** f (esp Sport) stand.

zuschicken vt sep jdm etw ~ to send sth to sb or sb sth; **sich** (dat) **etw ~ lassen** to send for sth.

zuschieben vt sep irreg (a) jdm etw ~ to push sth over to sb; **jdm die Schuld ~** to put the blame on sb. (b) (schließen) to push shut.

zuschießen sep irreg **1** vt (a) jdm den Ball ~ to kick the ball (over) to sb. (b) Geld etc to contribute. **Geld für etw ~** to put money towards sth. **2** vi aux sein (col) **auf jdn ~** to shoot up to sb.

Zuschlag m (a) (Erhöhung) surcharge (esp Comm, Econ); (Rail) supplement (für +acc on). (b) **er erhielt den ~** (bei Auktion) it went to him; (bei Auftragsvergabe) he won the order.

zuschlagen sep irreg **1** vt (a) Tür, Fenster to slam (shut). (b) Gebiet to annex (dat to). **2** vi (a) (kräftig schlagen) to strike (auch fig). **schlag zu!** hit me/him/it etc! (b) aux sein (Tür) to slam (shut).

Zuschlag(s)- (Rail): ~**karte** f supplementary ticket; **z~pflichtig** adj Zug subject to a supplement.

zuschließen vt sep irreg to lock; Laden to lock up.

zuschmieren vt sep (col) to smear over; Löcher to fill in.

zuschnappen vi sep (a) der Hund schnappte zu the dog snapped at me/him etc. (b) aux sein (Schloß) to snap shut.

zuschneiden vt sep irreg to cut to size; (Sew) to cut out. **auf etw** (acc) **zugeschnitten sein** (fig) to be geared to sth.

Zuschneider m cutter.

zuschneien vi sep aux sein to snow in.

Zuschnitt m (a) no pl cutting. (b) (Form) cut; (fig)

calibre (Brit), caliber (US).

zuschnüren vt sep to tie up; Schuhe, Mieder to lace up. **die Angst schnürte ihm die Kehle zu** he was choked with fear.

zuschrauben vt sep Hahn etc to screw shut; Deckel etc to screw on.

zuschreiben vt sep irreg (fig) to ascribe (dat to). **das hast du dir selbst zuzuschreiben** you've only got yourself to blame for that; **das ist nur seiner Dummheit zuzuschreiben** that can only be put down to his stupidity.

Zuschrift f letter; (auf Anzeige) reply.

zuschulden adv: **sich** (dat) **etwas ~ kommen lassen** to do something wrong.

Zuschuß m contribution; (staatlich) subsidy, grant.

Zuschußbetrieb m loss-making concern.

zuschütten vt sep to fill in; (hin~) to add.

zusehen vi sep irreg (a) to watch; (unbeteiligter Zuschauer sein) to look on; (etw dulden) to sit back (and watch). **jdm/(bei) einer Sache ~** to watch sb/sth; (etw dulden) to sit back and watch sth; **jdm bei der Arbeit ~** to watch sb working; **ich kann doch nicht ~, wie er ...** (dulden) I can't sit back and watch him ... (b) (dafür sorgen) ~, **daß** ... to see to it that ...

zusehends adv visibly; (rasch) rapidly.

zusein vi sep irreg aux sein (col) to be shut.

zusenden vt sep irreg to send, to forward.

zusetzen sep **1** vt (hinzufügen) to add. **2** vi jdm ~ (unter Druck setzen) to lean on sb (col); dem Gegner to harass sb; (schwer treffen) to hit sb hard; (Kälte, Krankheit etc) to take a lot out of sb.

zusichern vt sep jdm etw ~ to assure sb of sth; **mir wurde zugesichert, daß** ... I was assured that ...

Zusicherung f assurance.

zuspielen vt sep Ball to pass (dat to). **jdm etw ~** (fig) to pass sth on to sb; (der Presse) to leak sth to sb.

zuspitzen sep **1** vt Stock etc to sharpen. **2** vr to be pointed; (fig: Lage) to become acute.

zusprechen sep irreg **1** vt (Jur) Preis, Gewinn etc to award; Kind to grant custody of. **jdm Mut/Trost ~** (fig) to encourage/comfort sb. **2** vi dem Essen tüchtig ~ to tuck into the food.

zuspringen vi sep irreg aux sein (a) (Schloß, Tür) to snap shut. (b) **auf jdn ~** to leap towards sb.

Zuspruch m no pl (a) (Worte) words pl; (Aufmunterung) encouragement; (tröstlich) comfort. (b) (großen) ~ **finden** to be (very) popular.

Zustand m state; (von Haus, Ware, Med) condition; (Lage) state of affairs. **Zustände** pl conditions; **in gutem/schlechtem ~** in good/poor condition; (Haus) in good/bad repair; **in ungepflegtem/baufälligem ~** in a state of neglect/disrepair; **Zustände bekommen or kriegen** (col) to have a fit (col); **das sind ja schöne Zustände!** (iro) that's a fine state of affairs! (iro).

zustande adv (a) ~ **bringen** to manage; Arbeit to get done; Ereignis, Frieden etc to bring about. (b) ~ **kommen** (erreicht werden) to be achieved; (geschehen) to come about.

zuständig adj responsible; Behörde etc appropriate. **dafür ist er** ~ that's his responsibility.

Zuständigkeit f (Kompetenz) competence; (Verantwortlichkeit) responsibility.

Zuständigkeitsbereich m area of responsibility.

zustatten adj jdm ~ **kommen** (geh) to come in useful for sb.

zustecken vt sep (a) Kleid etc to pin up. (b) jdm etw ~ to slip sb sth.

zustehen vi sep irreg ihm stehen 6 Wochen Urlaub zu he is entitled to 6 weeks' holiday.

zusteigen vi sep irreg aux sein to get on, to board. **noch jemand zugestiegen?** (in Zug) tickets please!

zustellen vt sep (a) Brief to deliver. (b) Tür etc to block.

Zusteller(in f) m - deliverer; (Briefträger) postman (Brit), mailman (US).

Zustellung f delivery.

zusteuern sep 1 vi aux sein auf etw (acc) ~ (geh) to head for sth; (beim Gespräch) to steer toward(s) sth. 2 vt (beitragen) to contribute (zu to).

zustimmen vi sep (einer Sache dat) ~ to agree (to sth); (einwilligen) to consent (to sth); jdm (in einem Punkt) ~ to agree with sb (on a point).

Zustimmung f (Einverständnis) agreement, assent; (Einwilligung) consent; (Beifall) approval. **allgemeine** ~ **finden** to meet with general approval.

zustopfen vt sep to stop up.

zustöpseln vt sep Flasche to stopper; (mit Korken) to cork.

zustoßen sep irreg 1 vt Tür etc to push shut. 2 vi (a) to plunge a/the knife/sword etc in; (Stier etc) to strike. (b) (passieren) aux sein jdm ~ to happen to sb.

Zustrom m no pl (fig: Menschenmenge) stream (of visitors etc); (hineinströmend) influx; (Met) inflow.

zuströmen vi sep aux sein +dat (Fluß) to flow toward(s); (fig: Menschen) to stream toward(s).

zustürzen vi sep aux sein auf jdn/etw ~ to rush up to sb/sth

zutage adj etw ~ **fördern** to unearth sth; ~ **kommen** to come to light.

Zutaten pl (Cook) ingredients pl; (fig) accessories pl.

zuteil adv (geh) jdm wird etw ~ sb is granted sth, sth is granted to sb.

zuteilen vt sep (jdm to sb) to allocate; Arbeitskraft to assign.

Zuteilung f siehe vt allocation; assignment.

zutiefst adv deeply.

zutragen sep irreg 1 vt (fig: weitersagen) to report (jdm to sb). 2 vr (liter) to take place.

zuträglich adj good (dat for), beneficial (dat to).

zutrauen vt sep jdm etw ~ (Aufgabe, Tat) to believe sb (is) capable of (doing) sth; **sich** (dat) **zuviel** ~ to overrate one's own abilities; **sich** (dat) **nichts** ~ to have no confidence in oneself; **das hätte ich ihm nie zugetraut!** I would never have thought him capable of it!; **jdm viel/wenig** ~ to think/not to think a lot of sb.

Zutrauen nt no pl confidence (zu in). **zu jdm** ~ **fassen** to begin to trust sb.

zutraulich adj Kind trusting; Tier friendly.

zutreffen vi sep irreg (gelten) to apply (auf +acc, für to); (stimmen) to be correct, to be true. **das trifft zu** that is so.

zutreffend adj accurate. **Z~es bitte unterstreichen** underline where applicable.

zutreten vi sep irreg (a) to kick him/it etc. (b) aux sein auf jdn/etw ~ to step up to sb/sth.

zutrinken vi sep irreg jdm ~ to drink to sb; (mit Trinkspruch) to toast sb.

Zutritt m no pl (Einlaß) admittance; (Zugang) access. **kein** ~, ~ **verboten** no admittance; **sich** ~ **verschaffen** to gain admission; (Dieb) to gain access.

Zutun nt no pl **es geschah ohne mein** ~ I did not have a hand in the matter.

zu|ungunsten prep +gen to the disadvantage of.

zu|unterst adv at the bottom.

zuverlässig adj reliable.

Zuverlässigkeit f reliability.

Zuversicht f no pl confidence; (religiös) faith.

zuversichtlich adj confident.

zuviel adj, adv too much; (col: zu viele) too many. **viel** ~ far too much; **da krieg' ich** ~ (col) I blow my top (col); **einer/zwei** etc ~ one/two etc too many; **was** ~ **ist, ist** ~ that's just too much.

zuvor adv before. **im Jahr** ~ the year before.

zuvorderst adv right at the front.

zuvorkommen vi sep irreg aux sein +dat to anticipate; (verhindern) einer Gefahr etc to forestall. **jemand ist uns zuvorgekommen** somebody beat us to it.

zuvorkommend adj obliging; (hilfsbereit) helpful.

Zuwachs ['tsu:vaks] m, pl **Zuwächse (a)** no pl (Wachstum) growth (an +dat of). (b) (Ansteigen) increase (an +dat in). ~ **bekommen** (col: ein Baby) to have an addition to the family.

zuwachsen ['tsu:vaksən] vi sep irreg aux sein (a) (Loch) to grow over; (Garten) to become overgrown. (b) (Wunde) to heal (over).

Zuwachsrate ['tsu:vaks-] f rate of increase.

Zuwanderer m immigrant.

zuwandern vi sep aux sein to immigrate.

Zuwanderung f immigration.

zuwege adv etw ~ **bringen** to manage sth; (erreichen) to achieve sth; **mit etw** ~ **kommen** to (be able to) cope with sth.

zuweilen adv (geh) (every) now and then.

zuweisen vt sep irreg to allocate (jdm etw sth to sb).

zuwenden sep irreg 1 vt (lit, fig) to turn (dat to, towards); 2 vr **sich jdm/einer Sache** ~ (lit,fig) to turn to sb/sth; (sich widmen, liebevoll) to devote oneself to sb/sth.

Zuwendung f (a) (Liebe) care. (b) (Geldsumme) sum (of money).

zuwenig adj too little; (col: zu wenige) too few. **du schläfst** ~ you don't get enough sleep; **zwei** ~ two too few.

zuwerfen vt sep irreg (a) (hinwerfen) jdm etw ~ to throw sth to sb; jdm einen Blick ~ to cast a glance at sb; jdm einen bösen Blick ~ to look daggers at sb. (b) (schließen) Tür to slam (shut).

zuwider adj er/das ist mir ~ I detest or loathe him/that.

Zuwider-: z~handeln vi sep +dat (geh) to go against; einem Verbot, Befehl to defy; dem Gesetz to contravene; ~handlung f (form) contravention; z~laufen vi sep irreg aux sein +dat to run counter to.

zuwinken vi sep jdm ~ to wave to sb.

zuzahlen sep 1 vt **10 Mark** ~ to pay another 10 marks. 2 vi to pay extra.

zuzählen vt sep (col) to add; (einbeziehen) to include (zu in).

zuziehen sep irreg 1 vt (a) Vorhang to draw; Tür to pull shut; Knoten to tighten; Arzt etc to consult. (b) sich (dat) jds Zorn ~ to incur sb's anger; sich (dat) eine Verletzung ~ (form) to sustain an injury. 2 vr (Schlinge etc) to tighten. 3 vi aux sein to move into the area.

Zuzug m (Zustrom) influx; (von Familie etc) move (nach to).

zuzüglich prep +gen plus.

zuzwinkern vi sep jdm ~ to wink at sb.

zwang pret of **zwingen**.

Zwang m =e compulsion; (Gewalt) force; (Verpflichtung) obligation. **gesellschaftliche** ~e social constraints; **unter** ~ (dat) **stehen** to be under duress; **etw ohne** ~ **tun** to do sth without being forced to; **auf jdn** ~ **ausüben** to exert pressure on sb; **darf ich rauchen?** — **tu dir keinen** ~ **an** may I smoke? — feel free; **der** ~ **der Verhältnisse** the force of circumstances.

zwang-: z~haft adj (Psych) compulsive; ~los adj (ohne Förmlichkeit) informal; (locker) casual; (frei) free; **da geht es recht** ~los zu things are very informal there.

Zwangs-: ~abgabe f (Econ) compulsory levy; ~ernährung f force feeding; ~jacke f (lit, fig) straitjacket; ~lage f predicament; z~läufig adj inevitable; **das mußte ja z~läufig so kommen**

that had to happen; ~**läufigkeit** f inevitability; ~**maßnahme** f compulsory measure; (Pol) sanction; ~**räumung** f compulsory evacuation; ~**verkauf** m forced sale; ~**versteigerung** f compulsory auction; ~**vollstreckung** f execution; ~**vorstellung** f (Psych) obsession.

zwanzig num twenty; siehe **vierzig**.

Zwanziger(in f) m - (a) man/woman in his/her twenties. (b) (col: Geldschein) twenty (mark note (Brit) or bill US).

Zwanzigmarkschein m twenty mark note (Brit) or bill (US).

zwanzigste(r, s) adj twentieth.

zwar adv (a) (wohl) sie ist ~ sehr schön, aber ... it's true she's very beautiful but ... (b) **und ~** in fact, actually; **er ist tatsächlich gekommen, und ~ um 4 Uhr** he really did come, at 4 o'clock actually; **er hat mir das anders erklärt, und ~ so:** ... he explained it differently to me(, like this) ...; **mach deine Hausaufgaben, und ~ sofort** get on with your homework, now!

Zweck m -e (a) purpose. **einem ~ dienen** to serve a purpose; **Spenden für wohltätige ~e** donations to charity; **seinen ~ erfüllen** to serve its/one's purpose; **zu welchem ~?** for what purpose?; **einen ~ verfolgen** to have a specific aim. (b) (Sinn) point. **was soll das für einen ~ haben?** what's the point of that?; **es hat keinen ~, darüber zu reden** there is no point (in) talking about it.

Zweck-: ~**bau** m -ten functional building; z~**dienlich** adj appropriate; (nützlich) useful; z~**dienliche Hinweise** (any) relevant information.

Zweck-: z~**entfremden*** vt insep to use sth for another purpose; **etw als etw z~entfremden** to use sth as sth else; ~**entfremdung** f misuse; z~**entsprechend** adj appropriate; z~**frei** adj Forschung etc pure; z~**gebunden** adj for a specific purpose; z~**los** adj pointless; **es ist z~los, hier zu bleiben** it's pointless staying here; ~**losigkeit** f no pl pointlessness; z~**mäßig** adj (nützlich) useful; (wirksam) effective; (ratsam) advisable; (z~entsprechend) Arbeitskleider etc suitable; ~**mäßigkeit** f (Nützlichkeit) usefulness.

zwecks prep +gen (form) for (the purpose of).

zwei num two. **dazu gehören ~** (col) it takes two; siehe **vier**.

Zwei f -en two; siehe **Vier**.

Zwei-: z~**beinig** adj two-legged; ~**bettzimmer** nt twin room; z~**deutig** adj ambiguous; (schlüpfrig) suggestive; z~**dimensional** adj two-dimensional; ~**drittelmehrheit** f (Parl) two-thirds majority; z~**eiig** adj Zwillinge non-identical.

Zweier m - two; (Zweipfennigstück) two pfennig piece; siehe **Vierer**.

Zweier- (Sport): ~**bob** m two-man bob; ~**kajak** m or nt (Kanu) double kayak; (Disziplin) kayak pairs.

zweierlei adj inv attr Brot, Käse two kinds or sorts of; Möglichkeiten, Größen two different. **auf ~ Art** in two different ways; ~ **Handschuhe/ Strümpfe** etc odd gloves/socks etc.

zweifach adj double; (zweimal) twice; siehe **vierfach**.

Zwei-: ~**familienhaus** nt two-family house; z~**farbig** adj two-colour (Brit), two-color (US).

Zweifel m - doubt. **außer ~** beyond doubt; **im ~ in** doubt; **ohne ~** without doubt; **über allen ~ erhaben** beyond all doubt; **es besteht kein ~, daß ...** there is no doubt that ...; **da habe ich meine ~** I have my doubts; **etw in ~ ziehen** to call sth into question; **ich bin mir im ~, ob ich das tun soll** I'm in two minds whether I should do that.

zweifelhaft adj doubtful.

zweifellos adv undoubtedly.

zweifeln vi to doubt. **an etw/jdm ~** to doubt sth/sb.

Zweifelsfall m difficult case. **im ~ in** case of doubt.

Zweifler(in f) m - sceptic.

Zweifrontenkrieg m war/warfare on two fronts.

Zweig m -e (a) (Ast) branch; (dünner, kleiner) twig. (b) (fig) branch; (Abteilung) department.

Zweig-: ~**betrieb** m branch; ~**gesellschaft** f subsidiary (company).

zweigleisig adj double-track attr. ~ **argumentieren** to argue along two different lines.

Zweig-: ~**linie** f branch line; ~**niederlassung** f subsidiary; ~**stelle** f branch (office); ~**werk** nt (Fabrik) branch.

zwei-: ~**händig** adj two-handed; (Mus) for two hands; ~**höck(e)rig** adj Kamel two-humped.

zweihundert num two hundred.

zweijährig adj attr Kind etc two-year-old attr, two years old; (Dauer) two-year attr, of two years.

Zweikampf m single combat; (Duell) duel.

zweimal adv twice. **sich** (dat) **etw ~ überlegen** to think twice about sth; **das lasse ich mir nicht ~ sagen** I don't have to be told twice.

zweimalig adj attr nach ~**er Aufforderung** after being told twice.

Zwei-: ~**markstück** nt two-mark piece; z~**motorig** adj twin-engined; ~**parteiensystem** nt two-party system; ~**pfennigstück** nt two-pfennig piece; ~**rad** nt two-wheeler; z~**räd(e)rig** adj two-wheeled; z~**reihig** 1 adj double-row attr, in two rows; Anzug double-breasted; 2 adv in two rows; ~**samkeit** f (liter, hum) togetherness; z~**schneidig** adj (lit, fig) double-edged; **das ist ein z~schneidiges Schwert** (fig) it cuts both ways; z~**seitig** 1 adj Vertrag etc bilateral; Kleidungsstück reversible; 2 adv on two sides; ~**sitzer** m - (Aut, Aviat) two-seater; z~**sprachig** adj bilingual; z~**spurig** adj double-tracked, double-track attr; Autobahn two-lane attr; ~**spur(ton-band)gerät** nt twin-track (tape) recorder; z~**stellig** adj Zahl two-digit attr, with two digits; z~**stimmig** adj (Mus) for two voices; z~**stimmig singen** to sing in two parts; z~**stöckig** adj two-storey attr (Brit), two-story attr (US); z~**stündig** adj two-hour attr.

zweit adv: **zu ~** (in Paaren) in twos; **wir gingen zu ~ spazieren** the two of us went for a walk; **das Leben zu ~** living with someone; siehe **vier**.

Zwei-: z~**tägig** adj two-day attr, of two days; ~**taktmotor** m two-stroke engine.

Zweit-: z~**älteste(r, s)** second eldest; ~**ausfertigung** f (form) copy; z~**beste(r, s)** adj second best.

zwei-: ~**teilen** vt sep, infin, ptp only to divide (into two); ~**teilig** adj Roman two-part attr, in two parts; Kleidungsstück two-piece.

zweitens adv secondly.

zweite(r, s) adj second. ~ **Klasse** (Rail etc) second class; **Bürger ~r Klasse** second-class citizen(s); **jeder ~** (lit, col: sehr viele) every other; **zum ~n** secondly; **ein ~r Caruso** another Caruso; siehe **vierte(r, s)**.

Zweite(r) mf decl as adj (Sport etc) runner-up. **wie kein z~r** like nobody else.

Zweit-: ~**gerät** nt (Rad, TV) second set; z~**größte(r, s)** adj second biggest/largest; z~**klassig** adj (fig) second-class, second-rate (pej); z~**letzte(r, s)** adj last but one; ~**schlüssel** m duplicate key; ~**stimme** f second vote.

zweitürig adj two-door.

Zweit-: ~**wagen** m second car; ~**wohnung** f second home.

Zwei-: ~**vierteltakt** m (Mus) two-four time; z~**wöchig** adj two-week attr, of two weeks, fortnightly (Brit); ~**zeiler** m (Liter) couplet; z~**zeilig** adj two-lined; (Typ) Abstand double-spaced; z~**zeilig schreiben** to double-space; ~**zimmerwohnung** f two-room(ed) flat (Brit) or apartment; z~**zylindrig** adj two cylinder attr.

Zwerchfell nt (Anat) diaphragm.
Zwerg(in f) m -e dwarf; (fig: Knirps) midget; (pej: unbedeutender Mensch) squirt (col).
zwergenhaft adj dwarfish; (fig) diminutive.
Zwerg-: ~**huhn** nt bantam; ~**pinscher** m pet terrier; ~**schule** f (Sch col) village school; ~**staat** m miniature state; ~**wuchs** m dwarfism; z~**wüchsig** adj attr dwarfish.
Zwetsch(g)e f -n plum.
Zwetsch(g)enschnaps m plum brandy.
zwicken 1 vt (col) to pinch; (leicht schmerzen) to hurt. **2** vt impers **es zwickt mich in der Schulter** I've a twinge in my shoulder.
Zwicker m - pince-nez.
Zwickmühle f **in der** ~ **sitzen** (fig) to be in a dilemma.
Zwieback m -e or ⁻e ≈ rusk.
Zwiebel f -n onion; (Blumen~) bulb; (hum col: Uhr) watch.
Zwiebel-: z~**förmig** adj onion-shaped; ~**kuchen** m onion tart; ~**ring** m onion ring; ~**suppe** f onion soup; ~**turm** m onion tower.
Zwie-: ~**gespräch** nt dialogue; ~**licht** nt no pl twilight; (morgens) half-light; **ins** ~**licht geraten sein** (fig) to appear in an unfavourable (Brit) or unfavorable (US) light; z~**lichtig** adj (fig) shady; ~**spalt** m (der Gefühle etc) conflict; (zwischen Menschen) rift, gulf; z~**spältig** adj Gefühle mixed, conflicting attr; **ein** z~**spältiger Mensch** a man/woman of contradictions; ~**sprache** f (geh) ~**sprache mit jdm halten** to commune with sb; ~**tracht** f no pl discord; ~**tracht säen** to sow discord.
Zwilling m -e twin; (Gewehr) double-barrelled (Brit) or double-barreled (US) gun. ~**e** (Astrol) Gemini.
Zwillings-: ~**bruder** m twin brother; ~**geburt** f twin birth; ~**paar** nt twins pl; ~**schwester** f twin sister.
Zwinge f -n (Tech) (screw) clamp; (an Stock, Schirm) tip; (an Werkzeuggriff) ferrule.
zwingen pret **zwang**, ptp **gezwungen 1** vt to force. **jdn** ~, **etw zu tun** to force sb to do sth; **jdn zu etw** ~ to force sb to do sth; **jdn zum Handeln** ~ to force sb to act; **die Regierung wurde zum Rücktritt gezwungen** the government was forced to step down; siehe **gezwungen**. **2** vr to force oneself. **3** vi **zum Handeln/Umdenken** ~ to force or compel us/them etc to act/re-think.
zwingend adj Notwendigkeit urgent; (logisch notwendig) necessary; Schluß, Beweis conclusive; Argument, Gründe cogent.
Zwinger m - (Käfig) cage; (Hunde~) kennels pl.
zwinkern vi to blink; (als Zeichen) to wink; (lustig) to twinkle. **mit den Augen** ~ to blink (one's eyes).
zwirbeln vt Bart to twirl; Schnur to twist.
Zwirn m -e (strong) thread, yarn.
Zwirnsfaden m thread.
zwischen prep +dat or (mit Bewegungsverben) +acc between; (bei mehreren auch) among. **mitten** ~ right in the midst of.
Zwischen-: ~**akt** m (Theat) intermission; ~**aufenthalt** m stopover; ~**bemerkung** f interjection; **wenn Sie mir eine kurze** ~**bemerkung erlauben** if I may just interrupt; ~**bericht** m interim report; ~**bescheid** m provisional notification no indef art; ~**bilanz** f (Comm) interim

balance; ~**deck** nt (Naut) 'tween deck; **im** ~**deck** 'tween decks; ~**ding** nt cross (between the two); z~**durch** adv (a) (zeitlich) in between times; (inzwischen) meantime; (nebenbei) on the side; (b) (örtlich) here and there; ~**ergebnis** nt interim result; (Sport) latest score; ~**fall** m incident; (Cook) entrée; ~**größe** f in-between size; ~**handel** m wholesaling; ~**händler** m middleman; z~**landen** vi sep (Aviat) to stop over; ~**landung** f (Aviat) stopover; ~**lösung** f temporary solution; ~**mahlzeit** f snack (between meals); z~**menschlich** adj attr interpersonal; ~**musik** f interlude; ~**produkt** nt intermediate product; ~**prüfung** f intermediate examination; ~**raum** m gap, space; (zeitlich) interval; ~**ruf** m interruption; ~**rufe** heckling; ~**rufer(in** f) m - heckler; ~**runde** f intermediate round; z~**schalten** vt sep (Elec) to insert; (fig) to interpose; ~**schalter** m (Elec) circuit breaker; ~**spiel** nt (Mus) intermezzo; (Theat, fig) interlude; ~**spurt** m (Sport) short burst (of speed); z~**staatlich** adj attr international; ~**stadium** nt intermediate stage; ~**station** f (intermediate) stop; **in London machten wir** ~**station** we stopped off in London; ~**stecker** m (Elec) adapter; ~**stück** nt connecting piece; ~**summe** f subtotal; ~**text** m inserted text; ~**ton** m (Farbe) shade; ~**töne** (fig) nuances; ~**wand** f dividing wall; (Stellwand) partition; ~**zeit** f (a) (Zeitraum) interval; **in der** ~**zeit** (in the) meantime; (b) (Sport) intermediate time. z~**zeitlich** adv in between; (inzwischen) (in the) meantime; ~**zeugnis** nt (Sch) interim report.
Zwist m (rare) - (geh) discord; (Fehde, Streit) strife no indef art. **mit jdm in** ~ (acc) **geraten** to become involved in a dispute with sb.
Zwistigkeit f usu pl dispute.
zwitschern vti to twitter. **einen** ~ (col) to have a drink.
Zwitter m - hermaphrodite; (fig) cross (aus between).
zwo num (Telec, col) two.
zwölf num twelve. ~ **Uhr mittags/nachts** (12 o'clock) midday/midnight; **fünf Minuten vor** ~ (fig) at the eleventh hour; siehe **vier**.
Zwölf-: z~**fach** adj twelve-fold; (adv) twelvefold; ~**fingerdarm** m duodenum; ~**kampf** m (Sport) twelve-exercise event.
zwölftens adv twelfth(ly), in the twelfth place.
zwölfte(r, s) adj twelfth; siehe **vierte(r, s)**.
Zyankali [tsyan'ka:li] nt no pl (Chem) potassium cyanide.
zyklisch 1 adj cyclic(al). **2** adv cyclically.
Zyklon m -e cyclone.
Zyklus ['tsy:klʊs] m -, **Zyklen** ['tsy:klən] cycle.
Zylinder m - (a) (Math, Tech) cylinder. (b) (Hut) top-hat.
zylindrisch adj cylindrical.
Zyniker(in f) ['tsy:nikɐ, -ərɪn] m - cynic.
zynisch ['tsy:nɪʃ] adj cynical.
Zynismus m cynicism.
Zypern ['tsy:pɐn] nt Cyprus.
Zypresse f (Bot) cypress.
Zypriot(in f) m (wk) -en, en Cypriot.
zypriotisch, zyprisch ['tsy:prɪʃ] adj Cyprian, Cypriot.
Zyste ['tsʏstə] f -n cyst.
z.Z(t). = **zur Zeit**.

A

A, a [eɪ] *n* A, a *nt; (Sch: as a mark)* sehr gut; *(Mus)* A, a *nt.* **to get from A to B** von A nach B kommen; **A sharp/flat** *(Mus)* Ais, ais *nt/*As, as *nt.*

a [eɪ, ə] *indef art, before vowel* **an (a)** ein; *(before feminine noun)* eine. **so large ~ country** ein so großes Land; **an unusual feeling** ein merkwürdiges Gefühl. **(b)** *(in negative constructions)* **not ~** kein(e); **he didn't want ~ present** er wollte kein Geschenk. **(c)** *(with profession, nationality etc)* **he's ~ doctor/Frenchman** er ist Arzt/Franzose; **he's ~ famous doctor/Frenchman** er ist ein berühmter Arzt/Franzose. **(d)** *(per)* pro. **£4~head** £4 pro Person; **50p ~ kilo** 50 Pence das or pro Kilo; **twice ~ month** zweimal im or pro Monat.

aback [ə'bæk] *adv:* **to be taken ~** erstaunt sein; *(upset)* betroffen sein.

abandon [ə'bændən] **1** *vt* **(a)** *(leave, forsake)* verlassen; *wife, family also* im Stich lassen; *baby* aussetzen; *car* (einfach) stehenlassen. **to ~ ship** das Schiff verlassen. **(b)** *(give up)* aufgeben. **to ~ play** das Spiel abbrechen. **(c)** *(fig)* **to ~ oneself to sth** sich einer Sache *(dat)* hingeben. **2** *n* **with ~** mit ganzer Seele.

abandoned [ə'bændənd] *adj* **(a)** *(dissolute)* verkommen. **(b)** *(unrestrained)* hingebungsvoll.

abashed [ə'bæʃd] *adj* beschämt.

abate [ə'beɪt] *vi* nachlassen.

abatement [ə'beɪtmənt] Nachlassen *nt.* **the noise ~ society** die Gesellschaft zur Bekämpfung von Lärm.

abattoir ['æbətwɑːʳ] *n* Schlachthof *m.*

abbey ['æbɪ] *n* Abtei *f; (church)* Klosterkirche *f.*

abbot ['æbət] *n* Abt *m.*

abbreviate [ə'briːvɪeɪt] *vt* abkürzen *(to* mit*).*

abbreviation [ə,briːvɪ'eɪʃən] *n* Abkürzung *f.*

abdicate ['æbdɪkeɪt] **1** *vt* verzichten auf *(+acc).* **2** *vi (monarch)* abdanken.

abdication [,æbdɪ'keɪʃən] *n* Abdankung *f.* **his ~ of the throne** sein Verzicht auf den Thron.

abdomen ['æbdəmen] *n* Unterleib *m; (of insects)* Hinterleib *m.*

abdominal [æb'dɒmɪnl] *adj* Unterleibs-.

abduct [æb'dʌkt] *vt* entführen.

abduction [æb'dʌkʃən] *n* Entführung *f.*

abductor [æb'dʌktəʳ] *n* Entführer(in *f) m.*

aberration [,æbə'reɪʃən] *n* Anomalie *f; (in statistics)* Abweichung *f; (mistake)* Irrtum *m; (moral)* Verirrung *f.* **in a moment of (mental) ~** *(col)* in einem Augenblick geistiger Verwirrung.

abet [ə'bet] *vt see* **aid** 2.

abeyance [ə'beɪəns] *n no pl* **to be in ~** *(law, rule, issue)* ruhen; *(custom, office)* nicht mehr ausgeübt werden.

abhor [əb'hɔːʳ] *vt* verabscheuen.

abhorrence [əb'hɒrəns] *n* Abscheu *f (of* vor *+dat).*

abhorrent [əb'hɒrənt] *adj* abscheulich.

abide [ə'baɪd] *vt (usu neg, interrog) person* ausstehen; *(endure)* aushalten. **I cannot ~ living here** ich kann es nicht ertragen, hier zu leben.

♦ **abide by** *vi +prep obj decision, law etc* sich halten an *(+acc).* **I ~ ~ what I said** ich bleibe bei dem, was ich gesagt habe.

ability [ə'bɪlɪtɪ] *n* Fähigkeit *f.* **to the best of my ~** nach (besten) Kräften; *(with mental activities)* so gut ich kann; **a man of many abilities** ein sehr vielseitiger Mensch.

abject ['æbdʒekt] *adj state, liar, thief* elend, erbärmlich; *poverty* bitter; *apology* demütig.

ablaze [ə'bleɪz] *adv, adj pred* in Flammen. **to be ~ in Flammen stehen; to be ~ with light** hell erleuchtet sein.

able [eɪbl] *adj* **(a)** *person* fähig, kompetent; *piece of work, exam paper, speech* gekonnt. **(b) to be ~ to** do sth etw tun können; *(be in a position to)* in der Lage sein, etw zu tun.

able-bodied [,eɪbl'bɒdɪd] *adj* (gesund und) kräftig; *(Mil)* tauglich.

able(-bodied) seaman *n* Vollmatrose *m.*

ablutions [ə'bluːʃənz] *npl (lavatory)* sanitäre Einrichtungen *pl.*

ably ['eɪblɪ] *adv* gekonnt, fähig.

abnormal [æb'nɔːməl] *adj* anormal; *(deviant, Med)* abnorm.

abnormality [,æbnɔː'mælɪtɪ] *n* Anormale(s) *nt; (deviancy, Med)* Abnormität *f.*

abnormally [æb'nɔːməlɪ] *adv* **(a)** *see adj.* **(b)** *(exceptionally)* außergewöhnlich.

aboard [ə'bɔːd] **1** *adv (on plane, ship)* an Bord. **all ~!** alle an Bord!; *(on train, bus)* alles einsteigen!; **to go ~** an Bord gehen. **2** *prep* **~ the ship** an Bord des Schiffes.

abode [ə'bəʊd] *n (liter: dwelling)* Aufenthalt *m.* **a humble ~** *(iro)* eine bescheidene Hütte *(iro);* **of no fixed ~** ohne festen Wohnsitz.

abolish [ə'bɒlɪʃ] *vt* abschaffen; *law also* aufheben.

abolition [,æbəʊ'lɪʃən] *n* Abschaffung *f.*

abominable [ə'bɒmɪnəbl] *adj* gräßlich, abscheulich. **A~ Snowman** Schneemensch *m.*

abominably [ə'bɒmɪnəblɪ] *adv* gräßlich, abscheulich. **~ rude** furchtbar unhöflich.

abomination [ə,bɒmɪ'neɪʃən] *n (a) no pl* Verabscheuung *f.* **to be held in ~ by sb** von jdm verabscheut werden. **(b)** *(thing)* Scheußlichkeit *f.*

aborigine [,æbə'rɪdʒɪnɪ] *n* Ureinwohner(in *f) m* (Australiens).

abort [ə'bɔːt] **1** *vi (Med: mother)* eine Fehlgeburt haben. **2** *vt (Med) foetus* abtreiben; *(break off) mission etc* abbrechen.

abortion [ə'bɔːʃən] *n* Abtreibung *f.* **to have an ~** abtreiben lassen.

abortive [ə'bɔːtɪv] *adj (unsuccessful) attempt* gescheitert. **to be ~** scheitern, fehlschlagen.

abound [ə'baʊnd] *vi* im Überfluß vorhanden sein; *(persons)* sehr zahlreich sein. **to ~ in** reich sein an *(+dat).*

about [ə'baʊt] **1** *adv* **(a)** *(here and there)* herum, umher; *(present)* in der Nähe. **to walk ~** herum- or umhergehen; **with flowers all ~** mit Blumen ringsumher; **to be (up and) ~** again wieder auf den Beinen sein; **there's a lot of measles ~** die Masern gehen um; **there's nobody ~** es ist keiner da; **he's/it's ~ somewhere** es ist irgendwo in der Nähe; **it's the other way ~** es ist gerade umgekehrt.

(b) to be ~ to im Begriff sein zu; *(esp US col: intending)* vorhaben, zu ...; **I was ~ to go out** ich wollte gerade ausgehen; **it's ~ to rain** es regnet gleich; **we are ~ to run out of petrol** uns geht gleich das Benzin aus; **are you ~ to tell me ...?** willst du mir etwa erzählen ...?

(c) *(approximately)* ungefähr. **he's ~ 40** er ist ungefähr 40 or um die 40; **he is ~ the same,**

doctor sein Zustand hat sich kaum geändert, Herr Doktor; **that's ~ it** das ist so ziemlich alles, das wär's *(col)*; **I've had ~ enough of this** jetzt reicht es mir aber allmählich *(col)*. **2** *prep* **(a)** um *(... herum)*; *(in)* in *(+dat)* *(... herum)*. **the fields ~ the house** die Felder ums Haus; **scattered ~ the room** über das ganze Zimmer verstreut; **somewhere ~ here** hier irgendwo; **to do jobs ~ the house** sich im Haus nützlich machen; **he looked ~ him** er schaute sich um; **there's something ~ him** er hat so etwas an sich *(dat)*; **while you're ~ it** wenn du schon dabei bist; **you've been a long time ~ it** du hast lange dazu gebraucht. **(b)** *(concerning)* über *(+acc)*. **what's the film ~?** wovon handelt der Film?; **what's it all ~?** worum geht es eigentlich?; **he's promised to do something ~ it** er hat versprochen, (in der Sache) etwas zu unternehmen; **they fell out ~ money** sie haben sich wegen Geld zerstritten; **how *or* what ~ me?** und ich?, und was ist mit mir? *(col)*; **how *or* what ~ going to the pictures?** wollen wir ins Kino gehen?; **(yes,) what ~ it/him?** ja *or* na und(, was ist damit/mit ihm)?

about-face [ə‚baʊt'feɪs], **about-turn** [ə‚baʊt'tɜːn] *n* *(Mil)* Kehrtwendung *f*; *(fig also)* Wendung *f* um hundertachtzig Grad. **to do an ~** kehrtmachen; *(fig)* sich um hundertachtzig Grad drehen.

above [ə'bʌv] **1** *adv* oben; *(in a higher position)* darüber. **from ~** von oben; **the flat ~** die Wohnung oben *or* *(~ that one)* darüber.
2 *prep* über *(+dat)*; *(with motion)* über *(+acc)*; *(upstream of)* oberhalb *(+gen)*. **~ all** vor allem; **I couldn't hear ~ the din** ich konnte bei dem Lärm nichts hören; **to be ~ sb/sth** über jdm/etw stehen; **~ criticism/praise** über jede Kritik/jedes Lob erhaben; **he's ~ that sort of thing** er ist über so etwas erhaben; **he's not ~ a bit of blackmail** er ist sich *(dat)* nicht zu gut *or* zu schade für eine kleine Erpressung; **it's ~ my head** *or* **me** das ist mir zu hoch; **to be/get ~ oneself** *(col)* größenwahnsinnig werden.
3 *adj attr* **the ~ figures** die obengenannten Zahlen; **the ~ paragraph** der obige Abschnitt.

above: ~ board *adj pred* korrekt; **~-mentioned** *adj* obenerwähnt.

abrasion [ə'breɪʒən] *n* *(Med)* (Haut)abschürfung *f*.

abrasive [ə'breɪsɪv] **1** *adj* *surface* rauh; *(fig)* *personality, person* aggressiv; *tongue, voice* scharf. **2** *n* *(cleanser)* Scheuermittel *nt*; *(~ substance)* Schleifmittel *nt*.

abrasiveness [ə'breɪsɪvnɪs] *n* *(of personality)* Aggressivität *f*.

abreast [ə'brest] *adv* Seite an Seite. **to march four ~** im Viererglied *(Mil)* *or* zu viert nebeneinander marschieren; **to keep ~ of the news** mit den Nachrichten auf dem laufenden bleiben.

abridged [ə'brɪdʒd] *adj* gekürzt.

abroad [ə'brɔːd] *adv* **(a)** im Ausland. **to go ~** ins Ausland gehen; **from ~** aus dem Ausland. **(b)** **there is a rumour ~ that ...** es geht das Gerücht, daß ...; **to get ~** an die Öffentlichkeit dringen.

abrupt [ə'brʌpt] *adj* abrupt; *descent, drop* jäh; *manner, reply* schroff.

abruptness [ə'brʌptnɪs] *n* abrupte Art; *(of person)* schroffe Art; *(of descent, drop)* Steilheit *f*; *(of reply)* Schroffheit *f*.

abscess ['æbses] *n* Abszeß *m*.

abscond [əb'skɒnd] *vi* sich (heimlich) davonmachen; *(schoolboys also)* durchbrennen.

absence ['æbsəns] *n* **(a)** Abwesenheit *f*; *(from school, work etc also)* Fehlen *nt*. **in the ~ of the chairman** in Abwesenheit des Vorsitzenden; **in his ~** in seiner Abwesenheit. **(b)** *(lack)* Fehlen *nt*. **~ of enthusiasm** Mangel *m* an Enthusiasmus; **in the ~ of further evidence** in Ermangelung weiterer Beweise.

absent ['æbsənt] **1** *adj* **(a)** abwesend, nicht da. **to be**

~ from school/work in der Schule/am Arbeitsplatz fehlen. **(b)** *expression, look* (geistes)abwesend. **2** [æb'sent] *vr* **to ~ oneself (from)** *(not go, not appear)* fernbleiben *(+dat, von)*; *(leave temporarily)* sich zurückziehen.

absentee [‚æbsən'tiː] *n* Abwesende(r) *mf*. **there were a lot of ~s** es fehlten viele.

absenteeism [‚æbsən'tiːɪzəm] *n* häufige Abwesenheit; *(of workers also)* Nichterscheinen *nt* am Arbeitsplatz; *(pej)* Krankfeiern *nt*; *(Sch)* Schwänzen *nt*.

absently ['æbsəntlɪ] *adv* (geistes)abwesend.

absent-minded [‚æbsənt'maɪndɪd] *adj* *(lost in thought)* geistesabwesend; *(forgetful)* zerstreut.

absent-mindedness [‚æbsənt'maɪndɪdnɪs] *n* *see adj* Geistesabwesenheit *f*; Zerstreutheit *f*.

absolute ['æbsəluːt] *adj* absolut; *idiot* ausgemacht.

absolutely ['æbsəluːtlɪ] *adv* absolut; *prove* eindeutig; *agree, trust also, true, correct* vollkommen, völlig; *deny, refuse* strikt; *forbidden* streng; *stupid also* völlig. **~!** genau!; **do you agree? — ~** sind Sie einverstanden? — vollkommen; **do you insist?** muß das unbedingt sein? **~ amazing** wirklich erstaunlich.

absolution [‚æbsə'luːʃən] *n* *(Eccl)* Absolution *f*.

absolve [əb'zɒlv] *vt* *(from sins)* lossprechen *(from* von)*; *(from blame)* freisprechen *(from* von)*.

absorb [əb'sɔːb] *vt* absorbieren; *liquid also* aufsaugen; *knowledge, news also* in sich *(acc)* aufnehmen; *shock* dämpfen; *costs etc* tragen. **to be/get ~ed in a book** in ein Buch vertieft sein/sich in ein Buch vertiefen; **she was completely ~ed in her family/job** sie ging völlig in ihrer Familie/Arbeit auf.

absorbency [əb'sɔːbənsɪ] *n* Saugfähigkeit *f*.

absorbent [əb'sɔːbənt] *adj* saugfähig, absorbierend.

absorbent cotton *n (US)* Watte *f*.

absorbing [əb'sɔːbɪŋ] *adj* fesselnd.

absorption [əb'sɔːpʃən] *n see vt* Absorption *f*; Aufsaugen *f*; Aufnahme *f*; Dämpfung *f*.

abstain [əb'steɪn] *vi* **(a)** sich enthalten *(from gen)*. **(b)** *(in voting)* sich der Stimme enthalten.

abstemious [əb'stiːmɪəs] *adj* *person, life* enthaltsam; *meal, diet* bescheiden.

abstention [əb'stenʃən] *n* **(a)** *no pl* Enthaltung *f*; *(from alcohol also)* Abstinenz *f*. **(b)** *(in voting)* (Stimm)enthaltung *f*.

abstinence ['æbstɪnəns] *n* Abstinenz, Enthaltung *f* *(from* von)*.

abstract[1] ['æbstrækt] **1** *adj* abstrakt. **in the ~** abstrakt. **2** *n* *(kurze)* Zusammenfassung *f*.

abstract[2] [æb'strækt] *vt* abstrahieren; *information* entnehmen *(from* aus)*; *metal etc* trennen.

abstruse [æb'struːs] *adj* abstrus.

absurd [əb'sɜːd] *adj* absurd. **don't be ~!** sei nicht albern; **you're just being ~** du bist ja nicht recht bei Trost!

absurdity [əb'sɜːdɪtɪ] *n* Absurde(s) *nt* *no pl* *(of an +dat)*; *(thing etc also)* Absurdität *f*.

abundance [ə'bʌndəns] *n* Fülle *f* *(of* von, gen)*. **in ~** in Hülle und Fülle; **an ~ of raw materials** großer Reichtum an Rohstoffen.

abundant [ə'bʌndənt] *adj* reich; *time, proof* reichlich; *energy, self-confidence etc* ungeheuer.

abundantly [ə'bʌndəntlɪ] *adv* reichlich. **to make it ~ clear that ...** überdeutlich zu verstehen geben, daß ...

abuse [ə'bjuːs] **1** *n* **(a)** *no pl* *(insults)* Beschimpfungen *pl*. **a term of ~** ein Schimpfwort *nt*. **(b)** *(misuse)* Mißbrauch *m*; *(unjust practice)* Mißstand *m*. **the system is open to ~** das System kann leicht mißbraucht werden. **2** [ə'bjuːz] *vt* **(a)** *(revile)* beschimpfen. **(b)** *(misuse)* mißbrauchen; *one's health* Raubbau treiben mit.

abusive [ə'bjuːsɪv] *adj* beleidigend. **~ language** Beschimpfungen *pl*; **to become ~ (with sb)** (jdm gegenüber) beleidigend *or* ausfallend werden.

abysmal [ə'bɪzməl] adj (fig) entsetzlich; performance, work etc miserabel.

abyss [ə'bɪs] n (lit, fig) Abgrund m.

academic [ˌækə'demɪk] **1** adj (a) akademisch, wissenschaftlich. ~ **year** Studienjahr. (b) (theoretical) out of ~ **interest** aus rein akademischem Interesse; it's purely ~ **now** das ist jetzt nur noch eine rein theoretische Frage. **2** n Akademiker(in f) m; (Univ) Hochschullehrer m.

academy [ə'kædəmɪ] n Akademie f.

accede [æk'siːd] vi (a) to ~ to the throne den Thron besteigen. (b) (agree) zustimmen (to dat). (c) to ~ to a treaty einem Pakt beitreten.

accelerate [æk'seləreɪt] **1** vt beschleunigen. **2** vi beschleunigen; (driver also) Gas geben; (speed, change, growth, inflation etc) zunehmen.

acceleration [æk,selə'reɪʃən] n Beschleunigung f.

accelerator [æk'seləreɪtəʳ] n (a) (Aut) Gaspedal, Gas (col) nt. (b) (Phys) Beschleuniger m.

accent ['æksənt] n Akzent m; (stress also) Betonung f. to speak without/with an ~ akzentfrei or ohne/ mit Akzent sprechen; to put the ~ on sth (fig) den Akzent auf etw (acc) legen.

accentuate [æk'sentjʊeɪt] vt betonen; (in speaking, Mus) akzentuieren.

accept [ək'sept] **1** vt annehmen; suggestion, work also, report, findings, person akzeptieren; responsibility übernehmen; (recognize) need einsehen, anerkennen; (allow, put up with) behaviour, fate, conditions hinnehmen. it is generally ~ed that ... es ist allgemein anerkannt, daß ...; we must ~ the fact that ... wir müssen uns damit abfinden, daß ...; it's the ~ed thing es ist allgemein or so üblich. **2** vi annehmen; (with offers also) akzeptieren; (with invitations) zusagen.

acceptable [ək'septəbl] adj annehmbar (to für), akzeptabel (to für); behaviour zulässig; (suitable) gift passend.

acceptance [ək'septəns] n see vt Annahme f; Akzeptierung f; Übernahme f. to meet with general ~ allgemeine Anerkennung finden.

access ['ækses] **1** n Zugang m (to zu); (to room, private grounds etc also) Zutritt m (to zu). this location offers easy ~ to shops and transport facilities von hier sind Läden und Verkehrsmittel leicht zu erreichen; the thieves gained ~ through the window die Diebe gelangten durch das Fenster hinein; ~ road Zufahrt(sstraße) f. **2** vt (Comp) file, data Zugriff haben auf (+acc).

accessible [æk'sesəbl] adj information, person zugänglich (to dat); place also (leicht) zu erreichen (to für).

accession [æk'seʃən] n (a) (to an office) Antritt m (to gen); (also ~ to the throne) Thronbesteigung f. (b) (consent: to treaty, demand) Zustimmung f (to zu), Annahme f (to gen) f.

accessory [æk'sesərɪ] n (a) Extra nt; (in fashion) Accessoire nt. **accessories** pl Zubehör nt. (b) (Jur) Mitschuldige(r) mf (to an +dat).

accident ['æksɪdənt] n (Mot, in home, at work) Unfall m; (Rail, Aviat, disaster) Unglück nt; (mishap) Mißgeschick nt; (chance occurrence) Zufall m. she has had an ~ sie hat einen Unfall gehabt or (caused it) gebaut (col); (by car, train etc also) sie ist verunglückt; by ~ (by chance) durch Zufall, zufällig; (unintentionally) aus Versehen.

accidental [ˌæksɪ'dentl] adj (unplanned) zufällig, Zufalls-; (unintentional) versehentlich. ~ **death** Tod durch Unfall.

accidentally [ˌæksɪ'dentlɪ] adv (by chance) zufällig; (unintentionally) versehentlich.

accident-prone ['æksɪdənt,prəʊn] adj vom Pech verfolgt.

acclaim [ə'kleɪm] **1** vt (applaud) feiern (as als). to ~ **sb the winner** jdn zum Sieger erklären. **2** n Beifall m.

acclamation [ˌæklə'meɪʃən] n Beifall m no pl; (of critics also) Anerkennung f.

acclimatization [ə,klaɪmətaɪ'zeɪʃən], (US) **acclimation** [ˌæklaɪ'meɪʃən] n Akklimatisierung f (to an +acc).

acclimatize [ə'klaɪmətaɪz], (US) **acclimate** [ə'klaɪmət] vt gewöhnen (to an +acc). to become ~d sich akklimatisieren.

accommodate [ə'kɒmədeɪt] vt (a) (provide lodging for) unterbringen. (b) (hold, have room for) Platz haben für. (c) theory, plan, forecasts Rechnung f tragen (+dat). (d) (form: oblige) dienen (+dat); wishes entgegenkommen (+dat).

accommodating [ə'kɒmədeɪtɪŋ] adj entgegenkommend.

accommodation [ə,kɒmə'deɪʃən] n (US ~s pl) Unterkunft f; (room also) Zimmer nt; (flat also) Wohnung f. "~" „Fremdenzimmer"; they found ~ in a youth hostel sie kamen in einer Jugendherberge unter; ~ **bureau** Wohnungsvermittlung f; **seating** ~ Sitzplätze.

accompaniment [ə'kʌmpənɪmənt] n Begleitung f (also Mus).

accompanist [ə'kʌmpənɪst] n Begleiter(in f) m.

accompany [ə'kʌmpənɪ] vt begleiten (also Mus).

accomplice [ə'kʌmplɪs] n Komplize m, Komplizin f.

accomplish [ə'kʌmplɪʃ] vt schaffen. he ~ed a great deal in his short career er hat in der kurzen Zeit seines Wirkens Großes geleistet; that didn't ~ anything damit war nichts erreicht.

accomplished [ə'kʌmplɪʃt] adj (skilled) player fähig; performance vollendet.

accomplishment [ə'kʌmplɪʃmənt] n (skill) Fertigkeit f; (achievement) Leistung f.

accord [ə'kɔːd] **1** n Übereinstimmung, Einigkeit f. of one's/its own ~ von selbst; with one ~ geschlossen; sing, cheer, say etc wie aus einem Mund(e); to be in ~ with sth mit etw in Einklang sein. **2** vt gewähren (sb sth jdm etw). **3** vi to ~ with sth einer Sache (dat) entsprechen.

accordance [ə'kɔːdəns] n in ~ with entsprechend (+dat), gemäß (+dat); to be in ~ with sth einer Sache (dat) entsprechen.

accordingly [ə'kɔːdɪŋlɪ] adv (correspondingly) (dem)entsprechend; (so, therefore also) folglich.

according to [ə'kɔːdɪŋ'tuː] prep entsprechend (+dat), nach. ~ **this** danach; ~ **the map** der Karte zufolge; ~ **Peter** laut Peter, Peter zufolge; **what he says** seiner Aussage nach; **we did it** ~ **the rules** wir haben uns an die Regeln gehalten.

accordion [ə'kɔːdɪən] n Akkordeon nt.

accost [ə'kɒst] vt ansprechen, anpöbeln (pej).

account [ə'kaʊnt] n (a) (description) Darstellung f; (report also) Bericht m. to keep an ~ of one's expenses über seine Ausgaben Buch führen; by all ~s nach allem, was man hört; to give an ~ of sth über etw (acc) Bericht erstatten; to give an ~ of oneself Rede und Antwort stehen; to give a good ~ of oneself sich bewähren.

(b) (consideration) to take ~ of sb/sth, to take sb/sth into ~ jdn/etw in Betracht ziehen; to take no ~ of sb/sth, to leave sb/sth out of ~ jdn/etw außer Betracht lassen; on no ~, not on any ~ auf (gar) keinen Fall; on this/that ~ deshalb; on ~ of him/the weather seinetwegen/wegen des Wetters; on my/his/their ~ meinet-/seinet-/ihretwegen; on one's own ~ für sich (selbst).

(c) (benefit) to turn sth to (good) ~ (guten) Gebrauch von etw machen, etw (gut) nützen.

(d) (importance) of no ~ ohne Bedeutung.

(e) (Fin, Comm) (at bank, shop) Konto nt (with bei); (bill) Rechnung f. to buy sth on ~ etw auf (Kunden)kredit kaufen; please charge it to my ~ stellen Sie es mir bitte in Rechnung; £50 on ~ £50 als Anzahlung; ~ **number** Kontonummer f; ~s **department** Buchhaltung f; (of shop) Kreditbüro nt.

(f) ~s pl (of company, club) (Geschäfts)bü-

cher *pl.* **to keep the** ~s die Bücher führen.
♦ **account for** *vi* +*prep obj* **(a)** *(explain)* erklären; *(give account of) actions, expenditure* Rechenschaft ablegen über (+*acc*). **all the children were** ~ed ~ man wußte, wo alle Kinder waren; **there's no** ~**ing** ~ **taste** über Geschmack läßt sich (nicht) streiten. **(b) this area alone** ~s ~ **some 25% of the population** allein in diesem Gebiet leben etwa 25% der Bevölkerung. **(c)** *(be cause of death, downfall)* zur Strecke bringen; *(illness)* fertigmachen, den Rest geben (+*dat*).
accountability [ə,kaʊntə'bɪlətɪ] *n* Verantwortlichkeit *f* (*to sb* jdm gegenüber).
accountable [ə'kaʊntəbl] *adj* verantwortlich (*to sb* jdm). **to hold sb** ~ **(for sth)** jdn (für etw) verantwortlich machen.
accountancy [ə'kaʊntənsɪ] *n* Buchhaltung *f*.
accountant [ə'kaʊntənt] *n* Buchhalter(in *f*) *m*; *(external financial adviser)* Wirtschaftsprüfer(in *f*) *m*; *(tax* ~*)* Steuerberater(in *f*) *m*.
accredited [ə'kredɪtɪd] *adj* (offiziell) zugelassen.
accrue [ə'kruː] *vi* **(a)** *(accumulate)* sich ansammeln; *(Fin: interest)* auflaufen. **(b) to** ~ **to sb** *(honour, costs etc)* jdm erwachsen (geh) *(from* aus).
accumulate [ə'kjuːmjʊleɪt] **1** *vt* ansammeln, anhäufen; *evidence* sammeln. **2** *vi* sich ansammeln; *(possessions, wealth also)* sich anhäufen; *(evidence)* sich häufen.
accumulation [ə,kjuːmjʊ'leɪʃən] *n see vi* Ansammlung *f*; Anhäufung *f*; Häufung *f*.
accuracy ['ækjʊrəsɪ] *n* Genauigkeit *f*.
accurate ['ækjʊrɪt] *adj* genau. **his aim was** ~ er hat genau gezielt.
accusation [,ækjʊ'zeɪʃən] *n* Anschuldigung *f*; *(Jur)* Anklage *f*; *(reproach)* Vorwurf *m*.
accusative [ə'kjuːzətɪv] *n* Akkusativ *m*.
accuse [ə'kjuːz] *vt* **(a)** *(Jur)* anklagen *(of wegen, gen)*. **(b) to** ~ **sb of doing sth** jdn beschuldigen *or* bezichtigen, etw getan zu haben; **are you accusing me of lying?** willst du (damit) vielleicht sagen, daß ich lüge?; **to** ~ **sb of being untidy** jdm vorwerfen, unordentlich zu sein.
accused [ə'kjuːzd] *n* the ~ der/die Angeklagte; die Angeklagten *pl.*
accusing [ə'kjuːzɪŋ] *adj* anklagend.
accustom [ə'kʌstəm] *vt* **to be** ~**ed to sth/to doing sth** an etw *(acc)* gewöhnt sein/gewöhnt sein, etw zu tun; **to become** ~**ed to sth/to doing sth** sich an etw *(acc)* gewöhnen/sich daran gewöhnen, etw zu tun.
ace [eɪs] *n (Cards, Tennis, col: expert)* As *nt*. **the** ~ **of clubs** das Kreuzas; **he came within an** ~ **of winning** er hätte um ein Haar gesiegt.
ache [eɪk] **1** *n* Schmerz *m*. **I have an** ~ **in my side** ich habe Schmerzen in der Seite; **just a few little** ~**s and pains** nur ein paar Wehwehchen *(col)*. **2** *vi* **(a)** weh tun, schmerzen. **my head/stomach** ~**s** mir tut der Kopf/Magen weh; **it makes my heart** ~ **to see him** *(fig)* es tut mir in der Seele weh, wenn ich ihn sehe. **(b)** *(fig: yearn)* **to** ~ **to do sth** sich danach sehnen, etw zu tun.
achieve [ə'tʃiːv] *vt* erreichen, schaffen; *success* erzielen; *victory* erringen; *rank also, title* erlangen. **she** ~**d a great deal** *(did a lot of work)* sie hat eine Menge geleistet; *(was quite successful)* sie hat viel erreicht.
achievement [ə'tʃiːvmənt] *n* **(a)** *(act) see vt* Erreichen *nt*; Erzielen *nt*; Erringen *nt*; Erlangen *nt*. **(b)** *(thing achieved)* Leistung *f*; *(of civilization, technology)* Errungenschaft *f*. **that's quite an** ~! das ist wirklich eine Leistung! *(also iro)*.
acid ['æsɪd] **1** *adj (sour, Chem)* sauer; *(fig)* ätzend. ~ **rain** Saurer Regen; ~ **test** *(fig)* Feuerprobe *f*. **2** *n (Chem)* Säure *f*.
acidity [ə'sɪdɪtɪ] *n* Säure *f*; *(Chem)* Säuregehalt *m*.
acknowledge [ək'nɒlɪdʒ] *vt* anerkennen; *truth, fault, defeat etc* eingestehen, zugeben; *(note*

receipt *of) letter etc* bestätigen; *(respond to)* greetings, cheers *etc* erwidern. **to** ~ **oneself beaten** sich geschlagen geben; **to** ~ **sb's presence** jds Anwesenheit zur Kenntnis nehmen.
acknowledged [ək'nɒlɪdʒd] *adj attr* anerkannt.
acknowledgement [ək'nɒlɪdʒmənt] *n see vt* Anerkennung *f*; Eingeständnis *nt*; Bestätigung *f*; Erwiderung *f*. **in** ~ **of** in Anerkennung (+*gen*).
acme ['ækmɪ] *n* Höhepunkt, Gipfel *m*.
acne ['æknɪ] *n* Akne *f*.
acorn ['eɪkɔːn] *n* Eichel *f*.
acoustic [ə'kuːstɪk] *adj* akustisch.
acoustics [ə'kuːstɪks] *n sing or pl* Akustik *f*.
acquaint [ə'kweɪnt] *vt* **(a)** *(make familiar)* bekannt machen. **to be** ~**ed/thoroughly** ~**ed with sth** mit etw bekannt/vertraut sein; **to become** ~**ed with sth** etw kennenlernen; **to** ~ **oneself with sth** sich mit etw vertraut machen. **(b)** *(with person)* **to be** ~**ed with sb** mit jdm bekannt sein; **to become** *or* **get** ~**ed** sich (näher) kennenlernen.
acquaintance [ə'kweɪntəns] *n* **(a)** *(person)* Bekannte(r) *mf*. **(b)** *(with person)* Bekanntschaft *f*; *(with subject etc)* Kenntnis *f* *(with gen)*. **to make sb's** ~ jds Bekanntschaft machen; **it improves on** ~ man kommt mit der Zeit auf den Geschmack.
acquiesce [,ækwɪ'es] *vi* einwilligen *(in in* +*acc*); *(submissively)* sich fügen *(in dat)*.
acquiescence [,ækwɪ'esns] *n see vi* Einwilligung *f (in in* +*acc*); Fügung *f (in in* +*acc*).
acquiescent [,ækwɪ'esnt] *adj* fügsam.
acquire [ə'kwaɪə'] *vt* erwerben; *habit* annehmen. **to** ~ **a taste for sth** Geschmack an etw *(dat)* finden; **it's an** ~**d taste** das ist (nur) was für Kenner.
acquisition [,ækwɪ'zɪʃən] *n* **(a)** *(act)* Erwerb *m*. **(b)** *(thing acquired)* Anschaffung *f*.
acquisitive [ə'kwɪzɪtɪv] *adj* auf Erwerb aus, habgierig *(pej)*.
acquit [ə'kwɪt] **1** *vt* freisprechen. **2** *vr* **he** ~**ted himself well** er hat seine Sache gut gemacht.
acquittal [ə'kwɪtl] *n* Freispruch *m*.
acre ['eɪkə'] *n* ≈ Morgen *m*.
acrid ['ækrɪd] *adj taste* bitter; *(of wine)* sauer; *comment, smoke* beißend.
acrimonious [,ækrɪ'məʊnɪəs] *adj discussion, argument* erbittert; *person, words* bissig.
acrimony ['ækrɪmənɪ] *n see* **acrimonious** erbitterte Schärfe; Bissigkeit *f*.
acrobat ['ækrəbæt] *n* Akrobat(in *f*) *m*.
acrobatic [,ækrəʊ'bætɪk] *adj* akrobatisch.
acrobatics [,ækrəʊ'bætɪks] *npl* Akrobatik *f*.
across [ə'krɒs] **1** *adv* **(a)** *(direction) (to the other side)* hinüber; *(from the other side)* herüber; *(crosswise)* (quer)durch. **to cut sth** ~ etw (quer) durchschneiden; **he was already** ~ er war schon drüben; ~ **from your house** gegenüber von eurem Haus; **the stripes go** ~ es ist quer gestreift. **(b)** *(measurement)* breit; *(of round object)* im Durchmesser. **how far is it** ~? wie groß ist der Durchmesser? **(c)** *(in crosswords)* waagerecht.
2 prep (a) *(direction)* über (+*acc*); *(diagonally* ~*)* quer durch (+*acc*). **to run** ~ **the road** über die Straße laufen; **a tree fell** ~ **the path** ein Baum fiel quer über den Weg. **(b)** *(position)* über (+*dat*). **a tree lay** ~ **the path** ein Baum lag quer über dem Weg; **from** ~ **the sea** von jenseits des Meeres *(geh)*, von der anderen Seite des Meeres; **he lives** ~ **the street from us** er wohnt uns gegenüber; **from** ~ **the hall** von der anderen Seite der Halle.
across-the-board [ə'krɒsðə'bɔːd] *adj attr* allgemein.
act [ækt] **1** *n* **(a)** *(deed, thing done)* Tat *f*; *(official, ceremonial)* Akt *m*. **an** ~ **of mercy** ein Gnadenakt *m*; **an** ~ **of God** höhere Gewalt *no pl*; **an** ~ **of folly/madness** reine Dummheit/reiner Wahnsinn. **(b) to be in the** ~ **of doing sth** (gerade)

dabei sein; etw zu tun; **to catch sb in the ~** jdn auf frischer Tat ertappen. **(c)** ~ **(of Parliament)** Gesetz *nt.* **(d)** *(Theat) (of play, opera)* Akt *m; (turn)* Nummer *f.* **to get in on the ~** *(fig col)* mit von der Partie sein. **(e)** *(fig: pretence)* **it's all an** ~ das ist alles nur Theater *or* Schau *(col).*
     2 *vt part* spielen; *play* aufführen. **to ~ the fool** herumalbern, den Clown spielen.
     3 *vi* **(a)** *(Theat) (perform)* spielen; *(to be an actor, fig)* schauspielern, Theater spielen. **he's only ~ing** er tut (doch) nur so; **to ~ stupid/ innocent** den Dummen/Unschuldigen spielen *or* markieren *(col).* **(b)** *(function) (brakes etc)* funktionieren; *(drug)* wirken. **to ~ as ... wirken als ...;** *(have function)* fungieren als ...; **it ~s as a deterrent** das wirkt abschreckend; **to ~ for sb** jdn vertreten. **(c)** *(behave)* sich verhalten. ~ **like a man!** sei ein Mann!; **she ~ed as though she was surprised** sie tat so, als ob sie überrascht wäre. **(d)** *(take action)* handeln. **he ~ed to stop it** er unternahm etwas dagegen.
♦ **act on** *or* **upon** *vi* +*prep obj* **(a)** *(affect)* wirken auf (+*acc*). **(b)** *(take action on)* warning, report handeln auf (+*acc*) ... hin; *suggestion, advice* folgen (+*dat*).
♦ **act out** *vt sep fantasies etc* durchspielen. **the affair was ~ed ~ at** ... die Affäre spielte sich in ... ab.
♦ **act up** *vi (col) (bad knee etc)* Ärger machen; *(person also)* Theater machen *(col); (to attract attention)* sich aufspielen; *(machine also)* verrückt spielen *(col).*

acting ['æktɪŋ] **1** *adj* **(a)** stellvertretend *attr.* **(b)** *attr (Theat)* schauspielerisch. **2** *n (Theat: profession)* Schauspielerei *f.* **what was the/his ~ like?** wie waren die Schauspieler/wie hat er gespielt?; **I didn't like his ~** ich mochte seine Art zu spielen nicht.

action ['ækʃən] *n* **(a)** *no pl (activity)* Handeln *nt; (of play, novel etc)* Handlung *f.* **now is the time for ~** die Zeit zum Handeln ist gekommen; **a man of ~** ein Mann der Tat; **to take ~** etwas *or* Schritte unternehmen; **course of ~** Vorgehen *nt.*
     (b) *(deed)* Tat *f.*
     (c) *(motion, operation)* **in/out of** ~ *(machine)* in/außer Betrieb; *(operational)* einsatzfähig/ nicht einsatzfähig; **to go into** ~ in Aktion treten; **to put a plan into** ~ einen Plan in die Tat umsetzen; **to put out of** ~ außer Gefecht setzen.
     (d) *(exciting events)* Action *f (col).* **a novel full of** ~ ein handlungsgeladener Roman.
     (e) *(Mil) (fighting)* Aktionen *pl; (battle)* Kampf *m,* Gefecht *nt.* **enemy** ~ feindliche Handlungen *or* Aktionen *pl;* **killed in** ~ gefallen; **he saw ~ in the desert** er war in der Wüste im Einsatz; **they never went into** ~ sie kamen nie zum Einsatz.
     (f) *(way of operating) (of machine)* Arbeitsweise *f; (of piano etc)* Mechanik *f; (of watch, gun)* Mechanismus *m; (way of moving: of athlete etc)* Bewegung *f.*
     (g) *(esp Chem, Phys: effect)* Wirkung *f (on* auf +*acc).*
     (h) *(Jur)* Klage *f.* **to bring an** ~ **(against sb)** eine Klage (gegen jdn) anstrengen.

actionable ['ækʃnəbl] *adj* verfolgbar; *statement* klagbar.

action: ~ **group** *n* Initiative *f;* ~**-packed** *adj film, book* aktions- *or* handlungsgeladen; ~ **replay** *n* Wiederholung *f.*

activate ['æktɪveɪt] *vt* betätigen; *(automatically) alarm etc* auslösen; *(lever)* in Gang setzen.

active ['æktɪv] *adj* aktiv *(also Gram); mind, social life* rege; *volcano also* tätig; *dislike* offen. **to be ~ in politics** politisch aktiv *or* tätig sein; **to be under** ~ **consideration** ernsthaft erwogen werden; **on** ~ **service** *(Mil)* im Einsatz; **he played an** ~ **part** in er war aktiv daran beteiligt.

actively ['æktɪvlɪ] *adv* aktiv.
activist ['æktɪvɪst] *n* Aktivist(in *f) m.*
activity [æk'tɪvɪtɪ] *n* **(a)** *no pl* Aktivität *f; (in classroom, station, on beach etc also)* reges Leben; *(in market, town, office)* Geschäftigkeit *f.* **(b)** *(pastime)* Betätigung *f.* **the church organizes many activities** die Kirche organisiert viele Veranstaltungen; **business/social activities** geschäftliche/gesellschaftliche Unternehmungen *pl.*
actor ['æktə^r] *n (lit, fig)* Schauspieler *m.*
actress ['æktrɪs] *n (lit, fig)* Schauspielerin *f.*
actual ['æktjʊəl] *adj* eigentlich; *reason, price also, result* tatsächlich; *case, example* konkret. **in** ~ **fact** eigentlich; **what were his** ~ **words?** was hat er genau gesagt?; **this is the** ~ **house** das ist hier das Haus.
actuality [ˌæktjʊ'ælɪtɪ] *n (reality)* Wirklichkeit *f.*
actually ['æktjʊəlɪ] *adv* **(a)** *(to tell the truth, in actual fact)* eigentlich; *(by the way)* übrigens. **you don't know him, do you?** — ~ **I do** Sie kennen ihn (doch) nicht, oder? — doch, ich kenne ihn (tatsächlich); **I'm going soon, tomorrow** ~ ich gehe bald, genauer gesagt morgen; **you're never home** — ~ **I was home last night** du bist nie zu Hause — doch, gestern abend war ich da. **(b)** *(truly, in reality, showing surprise)* tatsächlich. **don't tell me you're** ~ **going now!** sag bloß, du gehst jetzt tatsächlich *or* wirklich!; **oh, you're** ~ **in!** oh, du bist sogar da!; **I wasn't** ~ **there, but** ... ich war zwar selbst nicht dabei aber ...; **as far** ~ **working** ... was die Arbeit selbst betrifft ...
actuary ['æktjʊərɪ] *n (Insur)* Aktuar *m.*
actuate ['æktjʊeɪt] *vt (lit)* auslösen; *(fig)* treiben.
acumen ['ækjʊmen] *n* Scharfsinn *m.* **business/ political** ~ Geschäftssinn *m/*politische Klugheit.
acupuncture ['ækjʊˌpʌŋktʃə^r] *n* Akupunktur *f.*
acute [ə'kjuːt] *adj* **(a)** *(intense, serious, Med)* akut; *pleasure* intensiv. **(b)** *eyesight* scharf; *hearing also, sense of smell* fein. **(c)** *(shrewd)* scharf; *person* scharfsinnig; *child* aufgeweckt. **(d)** *(Math)* angle spitz.
acutely [ə'kjuːtlɪ] *adv* **(a)** *(intensely)* akut; *feel* intensiv; *embarrassed, uncomfortable* äußerst. **(b)** *(shrewdly)* scharfsinnig; *observe* scharf.
acuteness [ə'kjuːtnɪs] *n* **(a)** *(of problem)* Dringlichkeit *f.* **(b)** *see adj (b)* Schärfe *f;* Feinheit *f.* **(c)** *see adj (c)* Schärfe *f;* Scharfsinn *m;* Aufgewecktheit *f.*
AD = **Anno Domini** A.D., a.D.
ad [æd] = **advertisement** Anzeige *f,* Inserat *nt.* **small** ~**s** Kleinanzeigen *pl.*
Adam ['ædəm] *n* ~**'s apple** Adamsapfel *m;* **I don't know him from** ~ *(col)* ich habe keine Ahnung, wer er ist *(col).*
adamant ['ædəmənt] *adj* hart. **since you're** ~ **da** Sie darauf bestehen; **he was** ~ **about going or** bestand hartnäckig darauf zu gehen.
adapt [ə'dæpt] **1** *vt* anpassen *(to* dat); *machine* umstellen *(for* auf +*acc); vehicle, building* umbauen *(to, for* für); *text, book etc* adaptieren, bearbeiten *(for* für). **2** *vi* sich anpassen *(to* dat).
adaptability [əˌdæptə'bɪlɪtɪ] *n see adj* Anpassungsfähigkeit *f;* Vielseitigkeit *f;* Flexibilität *f.*
adaptable [ə'dæptəbl] *adj person* anpassungsfähig; *vehicle* vielseitig; *schedule* flexibel.
adaptation [ˌædæp'teɪʃən] *n (process)* Adaptation *f (to* +*acc); (of person, plant, animal)* Anpassung *f (to* an +*acc); (of machine)* Umstellung *f (to* auf +*acc); (of vehicle, building)* Umbau *m; (of text)* Bearbeitung *f.*
adapter, adaptor [ə'dæptə^r] *n (Elec)* Adapter *m; (for several plugs)* Doppel-/Dreifachstecker *m,* Mehrfachstecker *m.*
add [æd] **1** *vt* **(a)** *(Math)* addieren; *(~ up)* several numbers *also* zusammenzählen. **(b)** hinzufügen

(to zu*)*; *ingredients, money also* dazutun *(to* zu*)*; *(say in addition also)* dazusagen; *(build on)* anbauen. ~**ed to which** ... hinzu kommt, daß ... 2 *vi (Math)* addieren.

♦ **add to** *vi* +*prep obj (expand) collection* erweitern; *(increase) problems* vergrößern; *(improve) flavour* steigern, verfeinern.

♦ **add up 1** *vt sep* zusammenzählen. **2** *vi* **(a)** *(figures etc)* stimmen; *(fig: make sense)* sich reimen. **it's beginning to** ~ ~ jetzt wird so manches klar. **(b) to** ~ ~ **to** *(column, figures, fig)* ergeben; *(expenses also)* sich belaufen auf (+*acc*); **it doesn't** ~ ~ **to much** *(fig)* das ist nicht berühmt *(col)*.

adder ['ædə^r] *n* Otter *f*.

addict ['ædɪkt] *n (lit, fig)* Süchtige(r) *mf*. **he's a TV/heroin** ~ er ist fernseh-/heroinsüchtig.

addicted [ə'dɪktɪd] *adj* süchtig. **to be/become** ~ **to heroin** heroinsüchtig sein/werden; **he's** ~ **to it** *(fig)* das ist bei ihm schon zur Sucht geworden.

addiction [ə'dɪkʃən] *n* Sucht *f (to* nach*)*; *(no pl: state of dependence also)* Süchtigkeit *f*. ~ **to alcohol** Trunksucht *f*.

addictive [ə'dɪktɪv] *adj* **to be** ~ *(lit)* süchtig machen; *(fig)* zu einer Sucht werden können.

addition [ə'dɪʃən] *n* **(a)** *(Math)* Addition *f*. **the** ~ **of Greece to the EEC** die Erweiterung der EG durch Griechenland. **(b)** *(thing added)* Zusatz *m (to* zu*)*; *(to list)* Ergänzung *f (to* zu*)*. **they are expecting an** ~ **to their family** *(col)* sie erwarten (Familien)zuwachs. **(c)** **in** ~ außerdem, obendrein; **in** ~ **to sth** zusätzlich zu etw.

additional [ə'dɪʃənl] *adj* zusätzlich. ~ **charge** Aufpreis *m*; **an** ~ **chapter** ein weiteres Kapitel.

additive ['ædɪtɪv] *n* Zusatz *m*.

address [ə'dres] **1** *n* **(a)** Adresse *f*. **home** ~ Privatadresse *f*; *(when travelling)* Heimatanschrift *f*. **(b)** *(speech)* Ansprache *f*. **(c)** **form of** ~ *(Form f* der*)* Anrede *f*. **2** *vt* **(a)** *letter, parcel* adressieren *(to* an +*acc*). **(b)** *(direct) complaints, speech, remarks* richten *(to* an +*acc*). **(c)** *(speak to) meeting* sprechen zu; *jury* sich wenden an *(+acc)*; *person* anreden. **3** *vr* **to** ~ **oneself to sb** *(speak to)* jdn ansprechen; **to** ~ **oneself to a task** *(form)* sich einer Aufgabe widmen.

address book *n* Adreßbuch *nt*.

addressee [ˌædre'siː] *n* Empfänger(in *f*) *m*.

adenoids ['ædɪnɔɪdz] *npl* Rachenmandeln *pl*.

adept ['ædept] **1** *n* Meister(in *f*) *m (in, at* in +*dat*). **2** *adj* ~ **at sewing** geschickt im Nähen.

adequate ['ædɪkwɪt] *adj* adäquat, angemessen; *(sufficient) supply, heating system* ausreichend; *time* genügend *inv*. **to be** ~ *(sufficient)* (aus)reichen; *(good enough)* angemessen sein; **this is just not** ~ das ist einfach unzureichend.

adhere [əd'hɪə^r] *vi* haften *(to* an +*dat*).

♦ **adhere** *vi* +*prep obj* festhalten an (+*dat*).

adherence [əd'hɪərəns] *n* Festhalten *nt (to* an +*dat*).

adherent [əd'hɪərənt] *n* Anhänger(in *f*) *m (of* gen*)*.

adhesive [əd'hiːzɪv] **1** *n* Klebstoff *m*. **2** *adj* haftend; *(more firmly)* klebend. ~ **plaster** Heftpflaster *nt*; ~ **tape** Klebstreifen *m*.

ad hoc [ˌæd'hɒk] *adj, adv* ad hoc *inv*.

adjacent [ə'dʒeɪsənt] *adj* angrenzend; *room also, angles* Neben-. **to be** ~ **to sth** an etw *(acc)* angrenzen, neben etw *(dat)* liegen.

adjective ['ædʒektɪv] *n* Adjektiv, Eigenschaftswort *nt*.

adjoin [ə'dʒɔɪn] **1** *vt* grenzen an *(+acc)*. **2** *vi* aneinander grenzen.

adjoining [ə'dʒɔɪnɪŋ] *adj room* Neben-, Nachbar-; *field* angrenzend; *(of two things)* nebeneinanderliegend. **in the** ~ **office** im Büro nebenan.

adjourn [ə'dʒɜːn] **1** *vt* **(a)** vertagen *(until* auf +*acc*). **he** ~**ed the meeting for three hours** er unterbrach die Konferenz für drei Stunden. **(b)** *(US: end)* beenden. **2** *vi* **(a)** sich vertagen *(until*

auf +*acc*). **to** ~ **for lunch/one hour** für die Mittagspause/für eine Stunde unterbrechen. **(b) to** ~ **to the lounge** sich ins Wohnzimmer begeben.

adjournment [ə'dʒɜːnmənt] *n* Vertagung *f (until* auf +*acc*); *(within a day)* Unterbrechung *f*.

adjudicate [ə'dʒuːdɪkeɪt] **1** *vt claim* entscheiden; *competition* Preisrichter sein bei. **2** *vi* entscheiden, urteilen *(on, in* bei*)*; *(in dispute)* Schiedsrichter sein *(on* bei, in +*dat*); *(in competition, dog-show etc)* als Preisrichter fungieren.

adjudicator [ə'dʒuːdɪkeɪtə^r] *n (in competition)* Preisrichter(in *f*) *m*; *(in dispute)* Schiedsrichter(in *f*) *m*.

adjust [ə'dʒʌst] **1** *vt (set) machine, carburettor, brakes, knob etc* einstellen; *(alter) plan, terms* ändern; *height, speed* verstellen; *(correct, readjust)* nachstellen; *height, speed, flow* regulieren; *hat, tie* zurechtrücken. **to** ~ **sth to new requirements/conditions** etw neuen Erfordernissen/Bedingungen anpassen. **2** *vi (to new circumstances)* sich anpassen *(to* dat*)*; *(to new requirements, demands)* sich einstellen *(to* auf +*acc*).

adjustable [ə'dʒʌstəbl] *adj tool, angle* verstellbar; *shape* veränderlich, variabel; *speed, temperature* regulierbar; *tax, rate of production* beweglich, flexibel; *person, animal, plant* anpassungsfähig. ~ **spanner** Engländer *m*.

adjustment [ə'dʒʌstmənt] *n* **(a)** *see vt* Einstellung *f*; Änderung *f*; Verstellen *nt*; Nachstellen *nt*; Regulierung *f*. **to make an** ~ **to sth** etw einstellen/verstellen/nachstellen etc; **to make** ~**s** Änderungen vornehmen. **(b)** *(socially etc)* Anpassung *f*.

ad-lib [æd'lɪb] **1** *adv* aus dem Stegreif. **2** *adj* improvisiert, Stegreif-. **3** *vti* improvisieren.

administer [əd'mɪnɪstə^r] *vt* **(a)** *institution, funds* verwalten; *business, affairs* führen; *(run) company, department* die Verwaltungsangelegenheiten regeln *(+gen)*. **(b)** *(to sb)* jdm) *medicine* verabreichen; *sacraments* spenden. **to** ~ **an oath to sb** jdm einen Eid abnehmen.

administration [əd,mɪnɪs'treɪʃən] *n* **(a)** *no pl* Verwaltung *f*; *(of a project etc)* Organisation *f*. **(b)** **the Schmidt** ~ die Regierung Schmidt. **(c)** *no pl (of remedy)* Verabreichung *f*; *(of sacrament)* Spenden *nt*. **the** ~ **of an oath** die Vereidigung; **the** ~ **of justice** die Rechtsprechung.

administrative [əd'mɪnɪstrətɪv] *adj* administrativ.

administrator [əd'mɪnɪstreɪtə^r] *n* Verwalter *m*.

admirable ['ædmərəbl] *adj* bewundernswert, erstaunlich; *(excellent)* ausgezeichnet.

admiral ['ædmərəl] *n* Admiral *m*.

Admiralty ['ædmərəltɪ] *n (Brit)* britisches Marineministerium.

admiration [ˌædmə'reɪʃən] *n* Bewunderung *f*.

admire [əd'maɪə^r] *vt* bewundern.

admissible [əd'mɪsəbl] *adj* zulässig.

admission [əd'mɪʃən] *n* **(a)** *(entry)* Zutritt *m*; *(to club also, university)* Zulassung *f*; *(price)* Eintritt *m*; *(to hospital)* Einlieferung *f*. **(b)** *(confession)* Eingeständnis *nt*. **by his own** ~ nach eigenem Eingeständnis; **that would be an** ~ **of failure** das hieße, sein Versagen einzugestehen.

admit [əd'mɪt] *vt* **(a)** *(let in)* hinein-/hereinlassen; *(permit to join)* zulassen *(to* zu*)*, aufnehmen *(to* in +*acc*). **to be** ~**ted to hospital** ins Krankenhaus eingeliefert werden; **children not** ~**ted** kein Zutritt für Kinder. **(b)** *(acknowledge)* zugeben. **he** ~**ted himself** beaten er gab sich geschlagen.

admittance [əd'mɪtəns] *n (to building)* Zutritt *(to* zu*)*.

admittedly [əd'mɪtɪdlɪ] *adv* zugegebenermaßen.

ad nauseam [ˌæd'nɔːsɪæm] *adv* bis zum Überdruß, bis zum Gehtnichtmehr *(col)*.

ado [ə'duː] *n* **without further** ~ ohne weiteres.

adolescence [ˌædəʊ'lesns] n Jugend f; (puberty) Pubertät f.

adolescent [ˌædəʊ'lesnt] 1 n Jugendliche(r) mf. 2 adj Jugend-; (in puberty) Pubertäts-; (immature) unreif. **he is so** ~ er steckt noch in der Pubertät.

adopt [ə'dɒpt] vt (a) child adoptieren; family, city die Patenschaft übernehmen für. (b) suggestion, method übernehmen; mannerisms annehmen. (c) (Pol) motion annehmen; candidate nominieren.

adopted [ə'dɒptɪd] adj son, daughter Adoptiv-, adoptiert; country Wahl-.

adoption [ə'dɒpʃən] n (a) (of child) Adoption f; (into the family) Aufnahme f. (b) (of method, idea) Übernahme f; (of mannerisms: law, candidate) Annahme f.

adorable [ə'dɔːrəbl] adj bezaubernd, hinreißend.

adoration [ˌædə'reɪʃən] n (grenzenlose) Liebe (of für); (of God) Anbetung f.

adore [ə'dɔːʳ] vt über alles lieben.

adorn [ə'dɔːn] vt schmücken.

adrenalin(e) [ə'drenəlɪn] n Adrenalin nt. **when the** ~'s going he ... wenn er richtig aufgedreht ist, ... er ...

Adriatic (Sea) [ˌeɪdrɪ'ætɪk'siː)] n Adria f.

adrift [ə'drɪft] adv, adj pred to be ~ (Naut) treiben; **to come** ~ (wire, hair etc) sich lösen; (plans) fehlschlagen; (theory) zusammenbrechen.

adroit [ə'drɔɪt] adj gewandt; mind scharf.

adulation [ˌædju'leɪʃən] n Verherrlichung f.

adult ['ædʌlt] 1 n Erwachsene(r) mf. 2 adj person erwachsen; film für Erwachsene; (mature) decision reif. ~ **education** Erwachsenenbildung f.

adulterate [ə'dʌltəreɪt] vt drink panschen; food, (fig) text verhunzen (col).

adultery [ə'dʌltərɪ] n Ehebruch m. **to commit** ~ Ehebruch begehen.

advance [əd'vɑːns] 1 n (a) (progress) Fortschritt m. (b) (of science) Weiterentwicklung f; (of ideas, sea) Vordringen nt. **recent** ~s jüngste Entwicklungen; **with the** ~ **of old age** mit fortschreitendem Alter. (c) (Mil) Vorrücken nt. (d) (money) Vorschuß m (on auf +acc). (e) (amorous, fig) ~s pl Annäherungsversuche pl. (f) **in** ~ im voraus; (temporal also) vorher; **to send sb on in** ~ jdn vorausschicken; **to arrive in** ~ **of the others** vor den anderen ankommen.

2 vt (a) (move forward) date, time vorverlegen. (b) (further) work, project voranbringen; cause, interests fördern; growth vorantreiben. (c) suggestion, opinion vorbringen. (d) (pay beforehand) (sb jdm) (als) Vorschuß geben, vorschießen (col); (lend) als Kredit geben.

3 vi (a) (Mil) vorrücken. (b) (move forward) vorankommen. **to** ~ **towards sb/sth** auf jdn/etw zugehen/-kommen; **to** ~ **upon sb** drohend auf jdn zukommen. (c) (fig: progress) Fortschritte machen.

advance booking n Reservierung f; (Theat) Vorverkauf m.

advanced [əd'vɑːnst] adj student, level, age fortgeschritten; studies, mathematics etc höher; technology also, ideas fortschrittlich; version, model verbessert, neu(er); level of civilization hoch; position, observation post etc vorgeschoben. ~ **in years** in fortgeschrittenem Alter.

advancement [əd'vɑːnsmənt] n (furtherance) Förderung f.

advance: ~ **notice** or **warning** n frühzeitiger Bescheid; (of sth bad) Vorwarnung f; ~ **party** n (Mil, fig) Vorhut f; ~ **payment** n Vorauszahlung f.

advantage [əd'vɑːntɪdʒ] n Vorteil m (also Tennis). **to have an** ~ **(over sb)** (jdm gegenüber) im Vorteil sein; **he had the** ~ **of greater experience** er war durch seine größere Erfahrung im Vorteil; **that gives you an** ~ **over me** damit sind Sie mir gegenüber im Vorteil; **to take** ~ **of sb/sth** jdn/etw ausnutzen; **he took** ~ **of her** (euph) er hat

sie mißbraucht; to turn sth to (good) ~ Nutzen aus etw ziehen; **it would be to our** ~ es wäre vorteilhaft für uns.

advantageous [ˌædvən'teɪdʒəs] adj vorteilhaft.

advent ['ædvənt] n (a) (of era) Beginn, Anbruch m; (of jet plane etc) Aufkommen nt. (b) (Eccl) A~ Advent m.

adventure [əd'ventʃəʳ] n Abenteuer nt. **an** ~ **into** the unknown ein Vorstoß ins Unbekannte.

adventurer [əd'ventʃərəʳ] n Abenteurer(in f) m.

adventurous [əd'ventʃərəs] adj person abenteuerlustig; journey abenteuerlich; scheme gewagt.

adverb ['ædvɜːb] n Adverb, Umstandswort nt.

adversary ['ædvəsərɪ] n Widersacher(in f) m; (in contest) Gegner(in f) m.

adverse ['ædvɜːs] adj ungünstig; criticism, comment, reaction negativ; effect nachteilig.

adversity [əd'vɜːsɪtɪ] n no pl Not f. **in** ~ im Unglück, in der Not.

advert ['ædvɜːt] n (Brit) = **advertisement**.

advertise ['ædvətaɪz] vti (a) (publicize) Werbung or Reklame machen (für), werben (für). (b) (in paper etc) flat, table etc inserieren; job, post also ausschreiben. **to** ~ **for sb** jdn (per Anzeige) suchen.

advertisement [əd'vɜːtɪsmənt] n (a) (Comm) Werbung, Reklame f no pl; (in paper also) Anzeige f. (b) (announcement) Anzeige f; (in paper also) Inserat nt. **to put an** ~ **in the paper (for sb/sth)** eine Anzeige (für jdn/etw) in die Zeitung setzen.

advertiser ['ædvətaɪzəʳ] n (in paper) Inserent(in f) m.

advertising ['ædvətaɪzɪŋ] n Werbung, Reklame f. **he is in** ~ er ist in der Werbung (tätig).

advertising in cpds Werbe-; ~ **agency** n Werbeagentur f; ~ **campaign** n Werbekampagne f.

advice [əd'vaɪs] n (a) no pl Rat m no pl. **a piece of** ~, **some** ~ ein Rat(schlag) m; **to take sb's** ~ jds Rat (be)folgen; **take my** ~ hör auf mich. (b) (Comm) Bescheid m. ~ **note** (Brit) Benachrichtigung f.

advisable [əd'vaɪzəbl] adj ratsam.

advise [əd'vaɪz] vti (a) (give advice to) raten (+dat); (professionally) beraten. **to** ~ **caution** zur Vorsicht raten; **I would** ~ **you to do it/not to do it** ich würde dir zuraten/abraten; **to** ~ **sb against sth/doing sth** jdm von etw abraten/jdm abraten, etw zu tun. (b) (Comm) unterrichten.

advisedly [əd'vaɪzɪdlɪ] adv richtig. **and I use the word** ~ ich verwende bewußt dieses Wort.

adviser [əd'vaɪzəʳ] n Ratgeber(in f) m; (professional) Berater(in f) m.

advisory [əd'vaɪzərɪ] adj beratend. **to act in a purely** ~ **capacity** rein beratende Funktion haben.

advocate ['ædvəkɪt] 1 n (a) (of cause etc) Verfechter, Befürworter m. (b) (esp Scot: Jur) (Rechts)anwalt m/-anwältin f. 2 ['ædvəkeɪt] vt eintreten für; plan etc befürworten.

Aegean [iː'dʒiːən] n the ~ (Sea) das Ägäische Meer.

aerial ['ɛərɪəl] 1 n (esp Brit) Antenne f. 2 adj Luft-.

aerial: ~ **photograph** n Luftbild nt, Luftaufnahme f; ~ **photography** n Luftaufnahmen pl.

aero- ['ɛərəʊ] pref aero- (form), Luft-.

aerobatics ['ɛərəʊ'bætɪks] npl Kunstfliegen nt.

aerobics [ɛər'əʊbɪks] n sing Aerobic nt.

aerodrome ['ɛərədrəʊm] n (Brit) Flugplatz m.

aerodynamic ['ɛərəʊdaɪ'næmɪk] adj aerodynamisch.

aerodynamics ['ɛərəʊdaɪ'næmɪks] n sing Aerodynamik f.

aerofoil ['ɛərəʊfɔɪl] n Tragflügel m; (on racing cars) Spoiler m.

aeronautic(al) [ˌɛərə'nɔːtɪk(əl)] adj Luftfahrt-. ~ **engineering** Flugzeugbau m.

aeronautics [ˌɛərə'nɔːtɪks] n sing Luftfahrt f.

aeroplane ['ɛərəpleɪn] n (Brit) Flugzeug nt.

aerosol ['ɛərəsɒl] n (can) Spraydose f; (mixture)

Aerosol nt.

aerospace in cpds Raumfahrt-.

aesthete, (US) **esthete** ['iːsθiːt] n Ästhet(in f) m.

aesthetic(al), (US) **esthetic(al)** [iːs'θetɪk(əl)] adj ästhetisch.

aesthetics, (US) **esthetics** [iːs'θetɪks] n sing Ästhetik f.

afar [ə'faːʳ] adv (liter) weit. **from ~** aus der Ferne.

affable ['æfəbl] adj umgänglich, freundlich.

affair [ə'fɛəʳ] n **(a)** Sache, Angelegenheit f. **the Watergate ~** die Watergate-Affäre; **the state of ~s with the economy** die Lage der Wirtschaft; **in the present state of ~s** beim gegenwärtigen Stand der Dinge; **there's a fine state of ~s!** das sind ja schöne Zustände!; **~s of state** Staatsangelegenheiten pl; **it's not your ~ what I do in the evenings** was ich abends tue, geht dich nichts an; **that's my/his ~!** das ist meine/seine Sache! **(b)** (love ~) Verhältnis nt, Affäre f.

affect¹ [ə'fekt] vt **(a)** (have effect on) sich auswirken auf (+acc); decision, sb's life also beeinflussen; health, person schaden (+dat). **(b)** (concern) betreffen. **(c)** (emotionally) berühren.

affect² vt (feign) vortäuschen, vorgeben.

affectation [ˌæfek'teɪʃən] n (pretence) Vortäuschung f; (artificiality) Affektiertheit f no pl.

affected [ə'fektɪd] adj person, clothes affektiert; behaviour, style, accent also gekünstelt.

affection [ə'fekʃən] n (fondness) Zuneigung f no pl (for, towards zu). **I have a great ~ for her** ich mag sie sehr gerne; **you could show a little more ~ towards me** du könntest etwas liebevoller (zu mir) sein; **children who lacked ~** Kinder, denen die Liebe fehlte.

affectionate [ə'fekʃənɪt] adj liebevoll, zärtlich.

affidavit [ˌæfɪ'deɪvɪt] n (Jur) eidesstattliche Versicherung f.

affiliated [ə'fɪlɪeɪtɪd] adj angeschlossen, Schwester-.

affiliation [əˌfɪlɪ'eɪʃən] n Angliederung f (to, with an +acc). **what are his political ~s?** wie steht es mit seiner politischen Zugehörigkeit?

affinity [ə'fɪnɪtɪ] n **(a)** (liking) Neigung f (for, to zu); (for person) Verbundenheit f (for, to mit). **(b)** (resemblance, connection) Verwandtschaft f.

affirm [ə'fɜːm] vt versichern; (very forcefully) beteuern.

affirmation [ˌæfə'meɪʃən] n see vt Versicherung f; Beteuerung f.

affirmative [ə'fɜːmətɪv] adj bejahend, positiv. **to answer in the ~** bejahend or mit „ja" antworten.

afflict [ə'flɪkt] vt person, zusetzen (+dat); (emotionally, mentally also) belasten; (troubles, inflation, injuries) heimsuchen. **the ~ed** die Leidenden pl.

affliction [ə'flɪkʃən] n (distress) Not f; (pain) Leiden pl; (illness) Beschwerde f.

affluence ['æfluəns] n Reichtum, Wohlstand m.

affluent ['æfluənt] adj reich, wohlhabend. **the ~ society** die Wohlstandsgesellschaft.

afford [ə'fɔːd] vt **(a)** (also non-financially) sich (dat) leisten. **I can't ~ to buy both of them** ich kann es mir nicht leisten, beide zu kaufen. **(b)** (liter: provide) (sb sth jdm etw) gewähren, bieten; pleasure bereiten.

affray [ə'freɪ] n (esp Jur) Schlägerei f.

affront [ə'frʌnt] **1** vt beleidigen. **2** n Beleidigung f (to sb jds, to sth für etw), Affront m (to gegen).

Afghanistan [æf'gænɪstæn] n Afghanistan nt.

afield [ə'fiːld] adv **further ~** weiter entfernt.

afloat [ə'fləut] adj pred, adv (Naut) **to be ~** schwimmen; **the largest navy ~** die größte Flotte auf See; **to get a business ~** (fig) ein Geschäft auf die Beine stellen.

afoot [ə'fut] adv im Gange. **what's ~?** was geht hier vor?

aforementioned [əˌfɔː'menʃənd], **aforesaid** [əˌfɔː'sed] adj attr (form) obengenannt.

afraid [ə'freɪd] adj pred **(a)** (frightened) **to be ~ (of sb/sth)** (vor jdm/etw) Angst haben, sich (vor jdm/etw) fürchten; **don't be ~!** keine Angst!; **I am ~ of hurting him** or **that I might hurt him** ich fürchte, ihm weh zu tun or ich könnte ihm weh tun; **I was ~ of waking the children** ich wollte die Kinder nicht wecken; **he's not ~ to say what he thinks** er scheut sich nicht, zu sagen, was er denkt; **that's what I was ~ of, I was ~ that would happen** das habe ich befürchtet. **(b)** (expressing polite regret) **I'm ~ I can't do it** leider kann ich es nicht machen; **I'm ~ you'll have to wait** Sie müssen leider warten; **I'm ~ not/I'm ~ so** leider nicht/ja, leider.

afresh [ə'freʃ] adv noch einmal von vorn.

Africa ['æfrɪkə] n Afrika nt.

African ['æfrɪkən] **1** n Afrikaner(in f) m. **2** adj afrikanisch.

aft [ɑːft] (Naut) adv sit achtern; go nach achtern.

after 1 prep nach (+dat). **~ that** danach; **the week ~** next übernächste Woche; **to run ~ sb** hinter jdm herlaufen; **he shut the door ~ her** er machte die Tür hinter ihr zu; **~ what has happened** nach allem, was geschehen ist; **to do sth ~ all** etw schließlich doch tun; **~ all our efforts!** und das, nachdem wir uns soviel Mühe gegeben haben!; **you tell me lie ~ lie** du erzählst mir eine Lüge nach der anderen; **~ El Greco** in der Art von El Greco; **to be ~ sb/sth** hinter jdm/etw hersein; **what are you ~?** was willst du?; (looking for) was suchst du?

2 adv (time, order) danach. **the year/week ~** das Jahr/die Woche danach or darauf.

3 conj nachdem. **~ finishing it I will/I went ...** wenn ich das fertig habe, werde ich .../als ich das fertig hatte, ging ich ...; **~ arriving they went ...** nachdem sie angekommen waren, gingen sie ...

4 ~s pl (Brit col) Nachtisch m.

after: **~birth** n Nachgeburt f; **~-care** n (of convalescent) Nachbehandlung f; **~-dinner** adj speech, speaker Tisch-; **~-effect** n Nachwirkung f; **~-life** n Leben nt nach dem Tode; **~math** n Nachwirkungen pl; **in the ~math of sth** nach etw.

afternoon ['ɑːftə'nuːn] n Nachmittag m. **in the ~** am Nachmittag, nachmittags; **at three o'clock in the ~** (um) drei Uhr nachmittags; **on Sunday ~** (am) Sonntag nachmittag; **this/tomorrow ~** heute/morgen nachmittag; **good ~!** Guten Tag!

after: **~-pains** npl Nachwehen pl; **~-sales service** n (Brit) Kundendienst m; **~ shave (lotion)** n After-shave, Rasierwasser nt; **~-thought** n nachträgliche Idee.

afterwards ['ɑːftəwədz] adv nachher; (after that, after some event etc) danach, anschließend.

again [ə'gen] adv **(a)** wieder. **~ and ~** immer wieder; **to do sth ~** etw noch (ein)mal tun; **not to do sth ~** etw nicht wieder tun; **I'll ring ~ tomorrow** ich rufe morgen noch einmal an; **never ~** nie wieder; **if that happens ~** wenn das noch einmal passiert; **all over ~** noch (ein)mal von vorn; **not ~!** schon wieder! **(b)** (in quantity) **as much ~** doppelt soviel, noch (ein)mal soviel. **(c)** (on the other hand) wiederum; (besides, moreover) außerdem. **but then ~, it may not be true** vielleicht ist es aber auch gar nicht wahr.

against [ə'genst] prep gegen (+acc). **he's ~ her** going er ist dagegen, daß sie geht; **to have something ~ sb/sth** etwas gegen jdn/etw haben; **~ their wish** entgegen ihrem Wunsch; **the advantages of flying (as) ~ going by boat** die Vorteile von Flugreisen gegenüber Schiffsreisen.

age [eɪdʒ] **1** n **(a)** Alter nt. **what is her ~, what ~ is she?** wie alt ist sie?; **he is ten years of ~ or** ist zehn Jahre alt; **at the ~ of 15** im Alter von 15 Jahren, mit 15 Jahren; **when I was your ~** als ich

in deinem Alter war; **but he's twice your** ~ aber er ist doppelt so alt wie du; **over** ~ zu alt; **be** *or* **act your** ~! sei nicht kindisch! **(b)** *(length of life)* Lebensdauer *f*. **(c)** *(Jur)* **to come of** ~ volljährig *or* mündig werden, die Volljährigkeit erlangen; **under** ~ minderjährig, unmündig. **(d)** *(period, epoch)* Zeit(alter *nt*) *f*. **the** ~ **of technology** das technologische Zeitalter; **down the** ~s durch alle Zeiten. **(e)** *(col: long time)* **I haven't seen him for** ~s, **it's been** ~s **since I saw him** ich habe ihn eine Ewigkeit *or* ewig nicht gesehen *(col)*; **it/he takes** ~s das dauert ewig/er braucht ewig *(col)*. **2** *vi* alt werden, altern.
3 *vt (worry, experience etc)* altern lassen; *(dress, hairstyle etc)* älter machen.

aged [eɪdʒd] **1** *adj* **(a)** im Alter von, ... Jahre alt, -jährig. **a boy** ~ **ten** ein zehnjähriger Junge. **(b)** ['eɪdʒɪd] *person* bejahrt, betagt. **2** ['eɪdʒɪd] *npl* **the** ~ die alten Menschen, die Alten *pl*.

age: ~ **difference** *or* **gap** *n* Altersunterschied *m*; ~-**group** *n* Altersgruppe *f*; ~ **limit** *n* Altersgrenze *f*.

agency ['eɪdʒənsɪ] *n* **(a)** *(Comm)* Agentur *f*. **typing/ tourist** ~ Schreib-/Reisebüro *nt*; **they have the Citroën** ~ sie haben die Citroën-Vertretung. **(b) through the** ~ **of friends** durch die Vermittlung *or* mit Hilfe von Freunden.

agenda [ə'dʒendə] *n* Tagesordnung *f*. **on the** ~ auf dem Programm.

agent ['eɪdʒənt] *n* **(a)** *(Comm)* *(person)* Vertreter(in *f*) *m*; *(organization)* Vertretung *f*. **(b)** *(literary, press, secret* ~ *etc)* Agent(in *f*) *m*; *(Pol)* Wahlkampfleiter(in *f*) *m*. **you're a free** ~ du bist dein eigener Herr. **(c)** *(Chem, means)* Mittel *nt*.

age-old ['eɪdʒəʊld] *adj* uralt.

aggravate ['ægrəveɪt] *vt* **(a)** *(worsen)* verschlimmern. **(b)** *(annoy)* aufregen; *(deliberately)* reizen.

aggravating ['ægrəveɪtɪŋ] *adj* ärgerlich; *noise, child* lästig.

aggravation [ˌægrə'veɪʃən] *n* **(a)** Verschlimmerung *f*. **(b)** *(annoyance)* Ärger *m*. **her constant** ~ **made him** ... sie reizte ihn so, daß er ...

aggregate ['ægrɪgət] **1** *n* **(a)** Summe, Gesamtheit *f*. **they won on** ~ sie wurden Gesamtsieger. **(b)** *(Build)* Zuschlagstoffe *pl*. **2** *adj* gesamt, Gesamt-.

aggression [ə'greʃən] *n* Aggression *f*; *(of person: aggressiveness)* Aggressivität *f*. **an act of** ~ eine aggressive Handlung.

aggressive [ə'gresɪv] *adj* aggressiv; *salesman, businessman etc* dynamisch, aufdringlich *(pej)*.

aggressiveness [ə'gresɪvnɪs] *n see adj* Aggressivität *f*; Dynamik, Aufdringlichkeit *(pej) f*.

aggressor [ə'gresə'] *n* Angreifer(in *f*) *m*.

aggrieved [ə'griːvd] *adj (offended)* verletzt *(at, by durch)*.

aghast [ə'gɑːst] *adj pred* entgeistert *(at* über *+acc)*.

agile ['ædʒaɪl] *adj person, thinker* beweglich; *body movements* geschmeidig; *animal* flink. **she has an** ~ **mind** sie ist geistig rege.

agility [ə'dʒɪlɪtɪ] *n see adj* Beweglichkeit *f*; Geschmeidigkeit *f*; Flinkheit *f*.

agitate ['ædʒɪteɪt] **1** *vt* **(a)** *(excite, upset)* aufregen, aus der Fassung bringen. **(b)** *(lit: shake)* liquid schütteln. **2** *vi* agitieren. **to** ~ **for sth** sich für etw stark machen.

agitated ['ædʒɪteɪtɪd] *adj* aufgeregt, erregt. **to get** ~ sich aufregen.

agitation [ˌædʒɪ'teɪʃən] *n* **(a)** *(anxiety, worry)* Erregung *f*. **(b)** *(incitement)* Agitation *f*.

agitator ['ædʒɪteɪtə'] *n (person)* Agitator(in *f*) *m*.

AGM = **annual general meeting**.

agnostic [æg'nɒstɪk] **1** *adj* agnostisch. **2** *n* Agnostiker(in *f*) *m*.

agnosticism [æg'nɒstɪsɪzəm] *n* Agnostizismus *m*.

ago [ə'gəʊ] *adv* vor. **years/a week/a little while** ~ vor Jahren/einer Woche/kurzem; **that was**

years/a week ~ das ist schon Jahre/eine Woche her; **how long** ~ **is it since you last saw him?** wann haben Sie ihn das letzte Mal gesehen?; **how long** ~? wie lange ist das her?; **that was long** ~ das ist schon lange her; **as long** ~ **as 1950** schon 1950; **no longer** ~ **than yesterday** erst gestern (noch).

agog [ə'gɒg] *adj pred* gespannt.

agonize ['ægənaɪz] *vi* sich *(dat)* den Kopf zermartern *(over* über *+acc)*.

agonizing ['ægənaɪzɪŋ] *adj* qualvoll.

agony ['ægənɪ] *n* **(a)** Qual *f*; *(mental also)* Leid *nt*. **that's** ~ das ist eine Qual; **to be in** ~ schreckliche Schmerzen haben; **put him out of his** ~ *(lit)* mach seiner Qual ein Ende; *(fig)* nun spann ihn doch nicht länger auf die Folter.

agony column *n (Brit col)* Kummerkasten *m*.

agree [ə'griː] *pret, ptp* ~**d 1** *vt (a) price, date etc* vereinbaren, abmachen. **we all** ~ **that** ... wir sind alle der Meinung, daß ...; **it was** ~**d that** ... man einigte sich darauf *or* es wurde beschlossen, daß ...; **to** ~ **to differ** sich *(dat)* verschiedene Meinungen zugestehen. **(b)** *(consent)* **to** ~ **to do sth** sich bereit erklären, etw zu tun. **(c)** *(admit)* zugeben. **I** ~ **(that) I was wrong** ich gebe zu, daß ich mich geirrt habe.
2 *vi* **(a)** *(hold same opinion) (two or more people)* übereinstimmen; *(one person)* der gleichen Meinung sein. **to** ~ **with sb** jdm zustimmen; **I quite** ~ ganz meine Meinung!; **it's too late now, don't you** ~? meinen Sie nicht auch, daß es jetzt zu spät ist?; **to** ~ **with the figures** *(accept)* die Zahlen akzeptieren. **(b)** *(come to an agreement)* sich einigen, Einigkeit erzielen *(about* über *+acc)*. **(c)** *(people: get on together)* miteinander auskommen. **(d)** *(statements, figures, Gram)* übereinstimmen. **(e)** **I don't** ~ **with children drinking wine** ich bin nicht damit einverstanden, daß Kinder Wein trinken. **(f)** *(food, climate etc)* **whisky doesn't** ~ **with me** Whisky bekommt mir nicht.

agreeable [ə'griːəbl] *adj* **(a)** *(pleasant)* angenehm. **(b)** *pred* **are you** ~ **to that?** sind Sie damit einverstanden?

agreed [ə'griːd] *adj* **(a)** *pred* **are we all** ~? sind wir uns da einig?; *(on course of action)* sind alle einverstanden. **(b)** *(arranged)* vereinbart; *price also* festgesetzt; *time also* verabredet. **it's all** ~ es ist alles abgesprochen; ~? einverstanden?

agreement [ə'griːmənt] *n* **(a)** *(understanding, arrangement)* Abmachung, Übereinkunft *f*; *(treaty, contract)* Übereinkommen *nt*, Vertrag *m*. **to reach an** ~ **(with sb)** (mit jdm) zu einer Einigung kommen. **(b)** *(sharing of opinion)* Einigkeit *f*. **by mutual** ~ in gegenseitigem Einvernehmen; **to be in** ~ **with sb** mit jdm einer Meinung sein; **to be in** ~ **with/about sth** mit etw übereinstimmen/ über etw *(acc)* einig sein. **(c)** *(consent)* Zustimmung *f (to zu)*. **(d)** *(between figures, Gram etc)* Übereinstimmung *f*.

agricultural [ˌægrɪ'kʌltʃərəl] *adj produce, tool etc* landwirtschaftlich; *studies* Landwirtschafts-. ~ **worker** Landarbeiter(in *f*) *m*.

agriculture ['ægrɪkʌltʃə'] *n* Landwirtschaft *f*.

aground [ə'graʊnd] *adv* **to go** *or* **run** ~ auflaufen, auf Grund laufen.

ahead [ə'hed] *adv* **(a)** **there's some thick cloud** ~ da vorne ist eine große Wolke; **the German runner was/drew** ~ der deutsche Läufer lag vorn/ zog nach vorne; **he is** ~ **by about two minutes** er hat etwa zwei Minuten Vorsprung; **we sent him on** ~ wir schickten ihn voraus; **in the months** ~ in den bevorstehenden Monaten; **I can see problems** ~ ich sehe Probleme auf mich/uns *etc* zukommen. **(b)** ~ **of sb/sth** vor jdm/etw; **walk** ~ **of me** geh voran; **we arrived ten minutes** ~ **of time** wir kamen zehn Minuten vorher an; **to be** ~ **of one's time** *(fig)* seiner Zeit voraus sein.

ahoy [əˈhɔɪ] *interj* (*Naut*) ahoi. **ship** ~! Schiff ahoi!

aid [eɪd] **1** *n* **(a)** *no pl* (*help*) Hilfe *f*. (*foreign*) ~ Entwicklungshilfe *f*; **with the** ~ **of** mit Hilfe; (*+gen*) **to come to sb's** ~ jdm zu Hilfe kommen; **a sale in** ~ **of the blind** ein Verkauf zugunsten der Blinden; **what's all this wiring in** ~ **of?** (*col*) wozu sind all diese Drähte da *or* gut? **(b)** (*useful person, thing*) Hilfe *f* (*to* für); (*piece of equipment*) Hilfsmittel *nt*; (*teaching* ~) Lehrmittel *nt*. **2** *vt* unterstützen, helfen (*+dat*). **to** ~ **sb's recovery** jds Heilung fördern; **to** ~ **and abet sb** (*Jur*) jdm Beihilfe leisten; (*after crime*) jdn begünstigen.

aide [eɪd] *n* Helfer(in*f*) *m*; (*adviser*) Berater(in*f*) *m*.

AIDS [eɪdz] *n* Aids *nt*.

ailing [ˈeɪlɪŋ] *adj* (*lit*) kränklich; (*fig*) *industry, economy etc* krankend, krank.

ailment [ˈeɪlmənt] *n* Gebrechen, Leiden *nt*. **minor** ~**s** leichte Beschwerden *pl*.

aim [eɪm] **1** *n* **(a)** Zielen *nt*. **to take** ~ zielen (*at auf* +*acc*); **his** ~ **was good** er zielte gut. **(b)** (*purpose*) Ziel *nt*, Absicht *f*. **what is your** ~ **in life?** was ist Ihr Lebensziel?; **what is your** ~ **in doing that?** was wollen Sie damit bezwecken?

2 *vt* **(a)** *guided missile, camera* richten (*at auf* +*acc*); *stone etc* zielen mit (*at auf* +*acc*). **to** ~ **a pistol at sb/sth** eine Pistole auf jdn/etw richten, mit einer Pistole auf jdn/etw zielen. **(b)** (*fig*) *remark, insult, criticism* richten (*at gegen*). **this programme is** ~**ed at the general public** dieses Programm ist für die breite Öffentlichkeit gedacht; **to be** ~**ed at sth** (*cuts, measure, new law etc*) auf etw (*acc*) abzielen.

3 *vi* **(a)** (*with gun, punch etc*) zielen (*at, for auf* +*acc*). **(b)** (*try, strive for*) **to** ~ **high** sich (*dat*) hohe Ziele setzen; **isn't that** ~**ing a bit high?** wollen Sie nicht etwas zu hoch hinaus?; **to** ~ **at** *or* **for sth** etw anstreben, auf etw (*acc*) abzielen; **he** ~**s at only spending £10 per week** er hat es sich zum Ziel gesetzt, mit £10 pro Woche auszukommen. **(c)** (*col: intend*) **to** ~ **to do sth** vorhaben, etw zu tun.

aimless [ˈeɪmlɪs] *adj* ziellos.

ain't [eɪnt] (*incorrect*) = **am not**; **is not**; **are not**; **has not**; **have not**.

air [ɛəʳ] **1** *n* **(a)** Luft *f*. **to go for a breath of (fresh)** ~ frische Luft schnappen (gehen); **by** ~ per *or* mit dem Flugzeug; (*transport*) auf dem Luftweg. **(b)** (*fig phrases*) **there's something in the** ~ es liegt etwas in der Luft; **it's still all up in the** ~ (*col*) es ist noch alles offen; **to clear the** ~ die Atmosphäre reinigen; **to be walking on** ~ wie auf Wolken gehen.

(c) (*Rad, TV*) **to be on the** ~ (*programme*) gesendet werden; (*station*) senden; **he's on the** ~ **every day** er ist jeden Tag im Radio zu hören; **to go off the** ~ das Programm beenden.

(d) (*facial expression*) Miene *f*; (*appearance*) Aussehen *nt*; (*atmosphere*) Atmosphäre *f*. **there was an** ~ **of mystery about her** sie hatte etwas Geheimnisvolles an sich (*dat*).

(e) ~**s** *pl* Getue, Gehabe *nt*; **to give oneself** ~**s** vornehm tun; ~**s and graces** Allüren *pl*.

(f) (*Mus*) Weise *f* (*old*); (*tune also*) Melodie *f*.

2 *vt* **(a)** *clothes, bed, room* (aus)lüften. **(b)** *anger, grievance* Luft machen (*+dat*); *opinion* darlegen.

3 *vi* (*clothes etc*) (*after washing*) nachtrocknen; (*after storing*) (aus)lüften.

air *in cpds* Luft-; ~ **base** *n* Luftwaffenstützpunkt *m*; ~**borne** *adj troops* Luftlande-; **to be** ~**borne** sich in der Luft befinden; ~ **brake** *n* (*on truck*) Druckluftbremse *f*; ~**bus** *n* Airbus *m*; ~**-conditioned** *adj* klimatisiert; ~**-conditioning** *n* (*plant*) Klimaanlage *f*; ~**-cooled** *adj* luftgekühlt; ~**craft** *n*, *pl* ~**craft** Flugzeug *nt*, Maschine *f*; ~**craft carrier** *n* Flugzeugträger *m*; ~**drome** *n* (*US*) Flugplatz *m*; ~**field** *n* Flugplatz *m*; ~ **force** *n* Luftwaffe *f*; ~**-freight 1** *n*

Luftfracht *f*; **2** *vt* per Luftfracht senden; ~ **hostess** *n* Stewardeß *f*.

airing [ˈɛərɪŋ] *n* **to give sth an** ~ etw gut durch- *or* auslüften lassen; (*fig col*) *idea* etw darlegen.

airing cupboard *n* (*Brit*) (Wäsche)trockenschrank *m*.

air: ~ **intake** *n* Lufteinlaß *m*; (*for engine*) Luftansaugstutzen *m*; (*quantity*) Luftmenge *f*; ~**lane** *n* Flugroute *f*; ~**less** *adj* (*lit*) *space* luftleer; (*stuffy*) *room* stickig; (*with no wind*) *day* windstill; ~ **letter** *n* Luftpostbrief *m*; ~**lift** *n* Luftbrücke *f*; ~**line** *n* Fluggesellschaft, Fluglinie *f*; ~**lock** *n* (*in spacecraft etc*) Luftschleuse *f*; (*in pipe*) Luftsack *m*; ~**mail** *n* Luftpost *f*; **to send sth (by)** ~ etw per *or* mit Luftpost schicken; ~**plane** *n* (*US*) Flugzeug *nt*; ~ **pocket** *n* Luftloch *nt*; ~**port** *n* Flughafen *m*; ~ **raid** *n* Luftangriff *m*; ~ **rifle** *n* Luftgewehr *nt*; ~**-sea rescue service** *n* Seenotrettungsdienst *m*; ~**ship** *n* Luftschiff *nt*; ~**sick** *adj* luftkrank; ~**space** *n* Luftraum *m*; ~**strip** *n* Start- und Landebahn *f*; ~ **terminal** *n* Terminal *m*; ~**tight** *adj* luftdicht; ~**-to-**~ *adj* (*Mil*) Luft-Luft-; ~**-to-ground** *adj* (*Mil*) Luft-Boden-; ~**-traffic controller** *n* Fluglotse *m*; ~ **waybill** *n* Luftfrachtbrief *m*; ~**worthy** *adj* flugtüchtig.

airy [ˈɛərɪ] *adj* (+*er*) **(a)** *room* luftig. **(b)** (*casual*) *manner, gesture* lässig, nonchalant; (*vague*) *promise* vage; *theory* versponnen.

airy-fairy [ˈɛərɪˈfɛərɪ] *adj* (*col*) versponnen; *excuse* windig; *talk also* larifari *inv* (*col*).

aisle [aɪl] *n* Gang *m*; (*in church*) Seitenschiff *nt*; (*central* ~) Mittelgang *m*. **he had them rolling in the** ~**s** die Leute kugelten sich vor Lachen.

ajar [əˈdʒɑːʳ] *adj, adv* angelehnt.

akimbo [əˈkɪmbəʊ] *adv*: **with arms** ~ die Arme in die Hüften gestemmt.

akin [əˈkɪn] *adj pred* verwandt (*to* mit).

à la carte [ɑːlɑːˈkɑːt] *adj, adv* à la carte.

alacrity [əˈlækrɪtɪ] *n* **to accept with** ~ ohne zu zögern annehmen.

alarm [əˈlɑːm] **1** *n* **(a)** (*warning*) Alarm *m*. **to give/sound the** ~ Alarm geben *or* (*fig*) schlagen. **(b)** (*device*) Alarmanlage *f*. **(c)** **to cause a good deal of** ~ große Unruhe auslösen. **2** *vt* **(a)** (*worry*) beunruhigen; (*frighten*) erschrecken. **don't be** ~**ed** erschrecken Sie nicht. **(b)** (*warn*) warnen; *fire brigade etc* alarmieren.

alarm *in cpds* Alarm-; ~ **call** *n* (*Telec*) Weckruf *m*; ~ **clock** *n* Wecker *m*.

alarming [əˈlɑːmɪŋ] *adj* (*worrying*) beunruhigend; (*frightening*) erschreckend; *news* alarmierend.

alarmist [əˈlɑːmɪst] *n* Unheilsprophet *m*.

alas [əˈlæs] *interj* leider.

Albania [ælˈbeɪnɪə] *n* Albanien *nt*.

Albanian [ælˈbeɪnɪən] **1** *adj* albanisch. **2** *n* **(a)** Albaner(in *f*) *m*. **(b)** (*language*) Albanisch *nt*.

albatross [ˈælbətrɒs] *n* Albatros *m*.

albeit [ɔːlˈbiːɪt] *conj* (*liter*) obgleich, wenn auch.

albino [ælˈbiːnəʊ] **1** *n* Albino *m*. **2** *adj* Albino-.

album [ˈælbəm] *n* Album *nt*.

alchemy [ˈælkɪmɪ] *n* Alchemie, Alchimie *f*.

alcohol [ˈælkəhɒl] *n* Alkohol *m*.

alcoholic [ˌælkəˈhɒlɪk] **1** *adj drink* alkoholisch. **2** *n* **to be an** ~ Alkoholiker(in) sein.

alcoholism [ˈælkəhɒlɪzm] *n* Alkoholismus *m*.

alcove [ˈælkəʊv] *n* Nische *f*.

ale [eɪl] *n* (*old*) Ale, Bier *nt*.

alert [əˈlɜːt] **1** *adj* aufmerksam; (*as character trait*) aufgeweckt; *mind* scharf, hell. **2** *vt* warnen (*to vor* +*dat*). **3** *n* Alarm *m*. **to put troops on the** ~ Truppen in Alarmbereitschaft versetzen; **to be on (the)** ~ einsatzbereit sein; (*be on lookout*) auf der Hut sein (*for vor* +*dat*).

A level [ˈeɪˌlevl] *n* (*Brit*) ≈ Abitur *nt no pl*.

alfresco [ælˈfreskəʊ] *adj, adv* im Freien.

algebra [ˈældʒɪbrə] *n* Algebra *f*.

Algeria [ælˈdʒɪərɪə] *n* Algerien *nt*.

Algerian [ælˈdʒɪərɪən] **1** *n* Algerier(in *f*) *m*. **2** *adj* algerisch.

alias ['eɪlɪæs] **1** *adv* alias. **2** *n* Deckname *m*.

alibi ['ælɪbaɪ] *n* Alibi *nt*.

alien ['eɪlɪən] **1** *n* (*esp Pol*) Ausländer(in *f*) *m*; (*Sci-Fi*) außerirdisches Wesen. **2** *adj* (*foreign*) ausländisch; (*Sci-Fi*) außerirdisch; (*different*) fremd. **to be** ~ **to sb's nature** jdm fremd sein.

alienate ['eɪlɪəneɪt] *vt people* befremden. **to be** ~**d from sb** jdm entfremdet sein.

alienation [,eɪlɪə'neɪʃən] *n* Entfremdung *f*.

alight¹ [ə'laɪt] *vi* (**a**) (*form: person*) aussteigen (*from* aus). (**b**) (*bird*) sich niederlassen (*on* auf +*dat*).

alight² *adj pred* **to be** ~ brennen; **to keep the fire** ~ das Feuer in Gang halten; **to set sth** ~ etw in Brand setzen *or* stecken.

align [ə'laɪn] *vt* (**a**) *wheels of car, gun sights etc* ausrichten; (*bring into line also*) in eine Linie bringen. (**b**) (*Fin, Pol*) *currencies, policies* aufeinander abstimmen. **to** ~ **oneself with a party** sich einer Partei anschließen.

alignment [ə'laɪnmənt] *n* Ausrichtung *f*; (*of policies etc also*) Orientierung *f* (*with* nach). **to be out of** ~ (*wheels etc*) nicht richtig ausgerichtet sein; (*views, policies*) nicht übereinstimmen; **the new** ~ **of world powers** die Neugruppierung der Weltmächte.

alike [ə'laɪk] *adj pred, adv* gleich; (*similar*) ähnlich. **you men are all** ~! ihr Männer seid doch alle gleich!; **winter and summer** ~ Sommer wie Winter.

alimentary [,ælɪ'mentərɪ] *adj* (*Anat*) Verdauungs-. ~ **canal** Verdauungskanal *m*.

alimony ['ælɪmənɪ] *n* Unterhaltszahlung *f*. **to pay** ~ Unterhalt zahlen.

alive [ə'laɪv] *adj* (**a**) *pred* (*living*) lebendig, lebend *attr*. **dead or** ~ tot oder lebendig; **to be** ~ leben; **the greatest violinist** ~ der größte lebende Geiger; **it's good to be** ~ das Leben ist schön; **to stay** ~ am Leben bleiben; **to keep sb/sth** ~ (*lit, fig*) jdn/etw am Leben erhalten. (**b**) (*lively*) lebendig. (**c**) *pred* (*aware*) **to be** ~ **to sth** sich (*dat*) einer Sache (*gen*) bewußt sein. (**d**) **to be** ~ **with** *tourists/fish/insects etc* von Touristen/Fischen/ Insekten *etc* wimmeln.

alkali ['ælkəlaɪ] *n*, *pl* -**(e)s** Base, Lauge *f*.

all [ɔːl] **1** *adj* (*with pl n*) alle *no art*; (*with sing n*) ganze(r, s), alle(r, s) *no art.* ~ **the books/people** alle Bücher/Leute, die ganzen Bücher; ~ **the tobacco/milk/fruit** der ganze Tabak/die ganze Milch/das ganze Obst; ~ **my books/friends/ strength** all(e) meine Bücher/Freunde/meine ganze Kraft; ~ **my life** mein ganzes Leben (lang); ~ **Spain** ganz Spanien; **we** ~ **sat down** wir setzten uns alle; ~ **day** (**long**) den ganzen Tag (lang); **I don't understand** ~ **that** ich verstehe das alles nicht; **in** ~ **respects** in jeder Hinsicht; **why me of** ~ **people?** warum ausgerechnet ich?; **of** ~ **the idiots!** so ein Idiot!; **with** ~ **possible speed** so schnell wie möglich.

2 *pron* (**a**) (*everything*) alles; (*everybody*) alle *pl.* ~ **of them/of it** (sie) alle/alles; ~ **of Paris/of the house** ganz Paris/das ganze Haus; **the score was two** ~ es stand zwei zu zwei. (**b**) (*phrases*) **at** ~ überhaupt; **nothing at** ~ überhaupt *or* gar nichts; **it's not bad at** ~ das ist gar nicht schlecht; **for** ~ **I know she could be ill** was weiß ich, vielleicht ist sie krank; **in** ~ insgesamt; ~ **in** ~ alles in allem; **happiest of** ~ am glücklichsten; **the best car of** ~ das allerbeste Auto.

3 *adv* (**a**) (*quite, entirely*) ganz. **dressed** ~ **in white** ganz in Weiß (gekleidet); **an** ~ **wool carpet** ein reinwollener Teppich; ~ **along the road** die ganze Straße entlang; **I'll tell you** ~ **about it** ich erzähl dir alles; **that's** ~ **very well** das ist alles ganz schön und gut; **it's not as bad as** ~ **that** so schlimm ist es nun auch wieder nicht; **if at** ~ **possible** wenn irgend möglich; **to be** ~ **in** (*col*)

total erledigt sein (*col*); **he's** ~/**not** ~ **there** (*col*) er ist voll da/er ist nicht ganz da (*col*).

(**b**) ~ **but fast; he** ~ **but died** er wäre fast gestorben.

(**c**) (*with comp*) ~ **the happier** noch glücklicher; ~ **the sadder because** ... um so trauriger, weil ...; ~ **the more so since** ... besonders weil ..., zumal ...

4 *n* **one's** ~ alles.

allay [ə'leɪ] *vt* verringern; *doubt, fears, suspicion* (weitgehend) zerstreuen.

all-clear *n* Entwarnung *f*.

allegation [,ælɪ'geɪʃən] *n* Behauptung *f*.

allege [ə'ledʒ] *vt* behaupten. **he is** ~**d to have said that** ... er soll angeblich gesagt haben, daß ...

alleged *adj*, ~**ly** *adv* [ə'ledʒd, ə'ledʒɪdlɪ] angeblich.

allegiance [ə'liːdʒəns] *n* Treue *f* (*to dat*).

allegory ['ælɪgərɪ] *n* Allegorie *f*.

all-embracing [,ɔːlɪm'breɪsɪŋ] *adj* (all)umfassend.

allergic [ə'lɜːdʒɪk] *adj* (*lit, fig*) allergisch (*to* gegen).

allergy ['ælədʒɪ] *n* Allergie *f* (*to* gegen).

alleviate [ə'liːvɪeɪt] *vt* lindern.

alley ['ælɪ] *n* (*between buildings*) (enge) Gasse.

alliance [ə'laɪəns] *n* Verbindung *f*; (*of institutions also, of states*) Bündnis *nt*; (*in historical contexts*) Allianz *f*.

Allied ['ælaɪd] *adj* **the** ~ **forces** die Alliierten.

alligator ['ælɪgeɪtə'] *n* Alligator *m*.

all: ~**-important** *adj* außerordentlich wichtig; **the** ~**-important question** die Frage, auf die es ankommt; ~**-in** *adj* (**a**) (*inclusive*) Inklusiv-; (**b**) (*Sport*) ~**-in wrestling** Freistilringen *nt*.

alliteration [ə,lɪtə'reɪʃən] *n* Alliteration *f*.

all-night [,ɔːl'naɪt] *adj attr café* durchgehend geöffnet. **to have an** ~ **party** die ganze Nacht durchfeiern.

allocate ['æləʊkeɪt] *vt* (*allot*) zuteilen, zuweisen (*to sb* jdm); (*apportion*) verteilen (*to* auf +*acc*); *tasks* vergeben (*to* an +*acc*). **to** ~ **money to** *or* **for a project** Geld für ein Projekt bestimmen.

allocation [,æləʊ'keɪʃən] *n* (*sum*) Zuwendung *f*.

allot [ə'lɒt] *vt* zuteilen (*to sb/sth* jdm/etw); *time* vorsehen (*to* für); *money* bestimmen (*to* für).

allotment [ə'lɒtmənt] *n* (*Brit: land*) Schrebergarten *m*.

all-out [,ɔːl'aʊt] **1** *adj strike* total; *attack* massiv; *effort* äußerste(r, s). **to make an** ~ **attempt** alles daransetzen. **2** *adv* mit aller Kraft. **to go** ~ **to do sth** alles daransetzen, etw zu tun.

allow [ə'laʊ] **1** *vt* (**a**) (*permit*) etw erlauben, gestatten. **to** ~ **sb sth/to do sth** jdm etw erlauben/ jdm erlauben, etw zu tun; **to be** ~**ed to do sth** etw tun dürfen; **smoking is not** ~**ed** Rauchen ist nicht gestattet; **to** ~ **oneself sth** sich (*dat*) etw erlauben; (*treat oneself*) sich (*dat*) etw gönnen; ~ **me!** gestatten Sie (*form*); **to** ~ **sth to happen** zulassen, daß etw geschieht; **to** ~ **sb in/out** jdn hinein-/hinauslassen; **to be** ~**ed in/out/past** hinein-/hinaus-/vorbeidürfen. (**b**) (*recognize, accept*) *claim* anerkennen; *goal* also geben. (**c**) (*allocate, grant*) *discount* geben; *space* lassen; *time* einplanen, einberechnen; (*in tax, Jur*) zugestehen. ~ (*yourself*) **an hour** rechnen Sie mit einer Stunde; ~ **5 cms extra** geben Sie 5 cm zu.

2 *vi* **if time** ~**s** falls es zeitlich möglich ist.

♦ **allow for** *vi* +*prep obj* berücksichtigen.

allowance [ə'laʊəns] *n* (**a**) finanzielle Unterstützung; (*paid by state*) Beihilfe *f*; (*father to child*) Unterhaltsgeld *nt*; (*for unsociable hours, overseas* ~ *etc*) Zulage *f*; (*on business trip*) Spesen *pl*; (*spending money*) Taschengeld *nt*. **clothing** ~ Kleidungsgeld *nt*. (**b**) (*Fin: tax* ~) Freibetrag *m*. (**c**) (*Fin, Comm: discount*) (Preis)nachlaß *m* (*on* für). (**d**) **to make** ~(**s**) **for sth** etw berücksichtigen; **you have to make** ~**s** Sie müssen (gewisse) Zugeständnisse machen.

alloy ['ælɔɪ] *n* Legierung *f*.

all: ~-**powerful** *adj* allmächtig; ~-**purpose** *adj* All-zweck-.

all right ['ɔːl'raɪt] **1** *adj pred* in Ordnung, okay (*col*). **it's** ~ (*not too bad*) es geht; (*working properly*) es ist in Ordnung; **that's** *or* **it's** ~ (*after thanks, apology*) schon gut; **to taste** ~ ganz gut schmecken; **is it** ~ **for me to leave early?** kann ich früher gehen?; **it's** ~ **for you** du hast's gut; **are you** ~? (*healthy*) geht es Ihnen gut?; (*unharmed*) ist Ihnen etwas passiert?; **are you feeling** ~? **fehlt Ihnen was?**; (*iro*) sag mal, fehlt dir was? **2** *adv* (**a**) (*satisfactory*) ganz gut, ganz ordentlich; (*safely*) gut. **did I do it** ~? habe ich es richtig gemacht?; **did you get home** ~? bist du gut nach Hause gekommen?; **did you get/find it** ~? haben Sie es denn bekommen/gefunden? (**b**) (*certainly*) schon. **he'll come** ~ er wird schon kommen; **that's the boy** ~ das ist der Junge; **he's a clever man** ~ er ist schon intelligent; **oh yes, we heard you** ~ o ja, und ob wir dich gehört haben. **3** *interj* okay (*col*); (*in agreement also*) in Ordnung. ~, ~! **I'm coming** schon gut, schon gut, ich komme ja!

all: ~-**round** *adj* **athlete** Allround-; *improvement* in jeder Beziehung; ~-**rounder** *n* Allroundmann *m*; (*Sport*) Allroundsportler(in *f*) *m*; **A**~ **Saints' Day** *n* Allerheiligen *nt*; ~-**time** *adj* **record** ungebrochen; **an** ~-**time high/low** der höchste/niedrigste Stand aller Zeiten.

allude to [ə'luːd] *vi* +*prep obj* anspielen auf (+*acc*).

allure [ə'ljʊə'] *n* Reiz *m*.

alluring [ə'ljʊərɪŋ] *adj* verführerisch.

allusion [ə'luːʒən] *n* Anspielung *f* (*to* auf +*acc*).

ally ['ælaɪ] **1** *n* Verbündete(r) *mf*, Bundesgenosse *m*; (*Hist*) Alliierte(r) *m*. **2** [ə'laɪ] *vr* **to** ~ **o.s. with sb** sich mit jdm verbünden.

almanac ['ɔːlmənæk] *n* Almanach *m*.

almighty [ɔːl'maɪtɪ] **1** *adj* allmächtig; (*col*) Mords-, gewaltig. **2** *n* **the A**~ der Allmächtige.

almond ['ɑːmənd] *n* Mandel *f*; (*tree*) Mandelbaum *m*.

almost ['ɔːlməʊst] *adv* beinahe, fast. **he** ~ **fell** er wäre fast gefallen.

alms [ɑːmz] *npl* Almosen *pl*.

aloft [ə'lɒft] *adv* (*into the air*) empor; (*in the air*) hoch droben.

alone [ə'ləʊn] **1** *adj pred* allein(e). **we're not** ~ **in thinking that** wir stehen mit dieser Meinung nicht allein. **2** *adv* allein(e). **to live on bread** ~ von Brot allein leben; **the hotel** ~ **cost £35** das Hotel allein kostete (schon) £ 35, schon das Hotel kostete £ 35.

along [ə'lɒŋ] **1** *prep* (*direction*) entlang (+*acc*), lang (+*acc*) (*col*); (*position*) entlang (+*dat*). **he walked** ~ **the river** er ging den Fluß entlang; **somewhere** ~ **here/there** irgendwo hier/dort (*herum*); (*in this/that direction*) irgendwo in dieser Richtung/der Richtung. **2** *adv* **to move** ~ weitergehen; **he was just strolling** ~ er ist bloß so dahingeschlendert; **run** ~ nun lauf!; **he'll be** ~ **soon** er muß gleich da sein; **I'll be** ~ **about eight** ich komme ungefähr um acht; ~ **with** zusammen mit; **to come/sing** ~ **with sb** mit jdm mitkommen/mitsingen; **take an umbrella** ~ nimm einen Schirm mit.

alongside [ə'lɒŋ'saɪd] **1** *prep* neben (+*dat*). **we were moored** ~ **the pier** wir lagen am Pier vor Anker; **the houses** ~ **the river** die Häuser am Fluß; **he works** ~ **me** (*with*) er ist ein Kollege von mir; (*next to*) er arbeitet neben mir. **2** *adv* daneben; (*Naut*) längsseits. **a police car drew up** ~ ein Polizeiauto fuhr neben mich/ihn *etc* heran; **they brought their dinghy** ~ sie brachten ihr Dingi heran.

aloof [ə'luːf] **1** *adv* (*lit, fig*) abseits. **to remain** ~ sich abseits halten. **2** *adj* unnahbar.

aloud [ə'laʊd] *adv* laut.

alphabet ['ælfəbet] *n* Alphabet *nt*.

alphabetic(al) [ˌælfə'betɪk(əl)] *adj* alphabetisch. **in** ~ **order** in alphabetischer Reihenfolge.

alpine ['ælpaɪn] *adj* alpin; *flowers, scenery* Alpen-, Gebirgs-.

Alps [ælps] *npl* Alpen *pl*.

already [ɔːl'redɪ] *adv* schon, bereits.

alright ['ɔːl,raɪt] *adj, adv* = **all right**.

Alsace ['ælsæs] *n* Elsaß *nt*.

Alsace-Lorraine ['ælsæslə'reɪn] *n* Elsaß-Lothringen *nt*.

alsatian [æl'seɪʃən] *n* (*Brit: dog*) Schäferhund *m*.

Alsatian [æl'seɪʃən] *adj* elsässisch.

also ['ɔːlsəʊ] *adv* (**a**) auch. (**b**) (*moreover*) ~, **I must explain that** ... außerdem muß ich erklären, daß ...

also-ran [ˌɔːlsəʊ'ræn] *n* **to be an** ~ (*Sport, fig*) unter „ferner liefen" kommen.

altar ['ɒltə'] *n* Altar *m*.

alter ['ɒltə'] **1** *vt* ändern; (*modify also*) abändern. **to** ~ **sth completely** etw vollkommen verändern. **2** *vi* sich (ver)ändern.

alteration [ˌɒltə'reɪʃən] *n* Änderung *f*; (*modification also*) Abänderung *f*; (*of appearance*) Veränderung *f*; (*to building*) Umbau *m*. **to make** ~**s in** *or* **to sth** Änderungen an etw (*dat*) vornehmen.

alternate [ɒl'tɜːnɪt] **1** *adj* (**a**) **on** ~ **days** jeden zweiten Tag; **they put down** ~ **layers of brick and mortar** sie schichteten abwechselnd Ziegel und Mörtel aufeinander. (**b**) (*alternative*) Alternativ-. ~ **route** Ausweichstrecke *f*. **2** ['ɔːltəneɪt] *vi* (sich) abwechseln.

alternating ['ɒltɜːneɪtɪŋ] *adj* wechselnd. ~ **current** Wechselstrom *m*.

alternative [ɒl'tɜːnətɪv] **1** *adj* Alternativ-; *route* Ausweich-. **2** *n* Alternative *f*.

alternatively [ɒl'tɜːnətɪvlɪ] *adv* **or** ~ oder aber.

alternator ['ɒltɜːneɪtə'] *n* (*Elec*) Wechselstromgenerator *m*; (*Aut*) Lichtmaschine *f*.

although [ɔːl'ðəʊ] *conj* obwohl, obgleich.

altitude ['æltɪtjuːd] *n* Höhe *f*. **at this** ~ in dieser Höhe.

alto ['æltəʊ] *n* Alt *m*, Altstimme *f*; (*person*) Alt *m*; (*also* ~ **saxophone**) Altsaxophon *nt*.

altogether [ˌɔːltə'geðə'] **1** *adv* (**a**) im ganzen, insgesamt. **taken** ~, *or* ~ **it was very pleasant** alles in allem war es sehr nett. (**b**) (*wholly*) vollkommen, ganz und gar. **he wasn't** ~ **wrong/pleased** er hatte nicht ganz unrecht/war nicht besonders zufrieden. **2** *n* **in the** ~ (*hum col*) hüllenlos, im Adams-/Evaskostüm.

altruism ['æltruɪzəm] *n* Altruismus *m*.

altruistic [ˌæltru'ɪstɪk] *adj* altruistisch.

aluminium [ˌælju'mɪnɪəm], (*US*) **aluminum** [ə'luːmɪnəm] *n* Aluminium *nt*. ~ **foil** Alufolie *f*.

always ['ɔːlweɪz] *adv* (**a**) immer. (**b**) **we could** ~ **go by train** wir könnten doch auch den Zug nehmen.

am [æm] *1st pers sing pres of* **be**.

amalgam [ə'mælgəm] *n* Amalgam *nt*; (*fig also*) Gemisch *nt*, Mischung *f*.

amalgamate [ə'mælgəmeɪt] **1** *vt companies* fusionieren; *departments* zusammenlegen. **2** *vi* (*companies*) fusionieren; (*metals*) amalgamieren.

amass [ə'mæs] *vt* anhäufen; *money* also scheffeln.

amateur ['æmətə'] **1** *n* Amateur *m*; (*pej*) Dilettant(in *f*) *m*. **2** *adj attr* Amateur-; *photographer* also, *painter* Hobby-; *dramatics* also Laien-.

amateurish ['æmətərɪʃ] *adj* (*pej*) dilettantisch, laienhaft; *performance, work* also laienhaft.

amaze [ə'meɪz] *vt* erstaunen. **to be** ~**d at sth** über etw (*acc*) erstaunt sein.

amazement [ə'meɪzmənt] *n* Erstaunen *nt*. **much to my** ~ zu meinem großen Erstaunen.

amazing [ə'meɪzɪŋ] *adj* erstaunlich; (*col*) *holiday etc* toll (*col*).

amazingly [ə'meɪzɪŋlɪ] *adv* erstaunlich; *simple*,

obvious also verblüffend. ~ **enough** erstaunlicherweise.
Amazon ['æməzən] *n* Amazonas *m*; *(Myth, fig)*
Amazone *f*.
ambassador [æm'bæsədəʳ] *n* Botschafter(in *f*) *m*;
(fig) Repräsentant(in *f*), Vertreter(in *f*) *m*.
amber ['æmbəʳ] **1** *n (substance)* Bernstein *m*;
(colour) Bernsteingelb *nt*; *(Brit: in traffic lights)*
Gelb *nt*. **2** *adj* (~-coloured) bernsteinfarben.
ambidextrous [ˌæmbɪ'dekstrəs] *adj* mit beiden
Händen gleich geschickt, beidhändig.
ambiguity [ˌæmbɪ'gjuɪtɪ] *n* Zweideutigkeit *f*.
ambiguous [æm'bɪgjuəs] *adj* zweideutig.
ambition [æm'bɪʃən] *n* **(a)** *(desire)* Ambition *f*. she
has ~s in that direction/for her son sie hat
Ambitionen in dieser Richtung/ehrgeizige Pläne
für ihren Sohn. **(b)** *(ambitious nature)* Ehrgeiz *m*.
ambitious [æm'bɪʃəs] *adj* ehrgeizig, ambitiös *(pej)*.
she is ~ for her husband sie hat ehrgeizige Pläne
für ihren Mann.
ambivalent [æm'bɪvələnt] *adj* ambivalent.
amble ['æmbl] *vi* schlendern.
ambulance ['æmbjuləns] *n* Krankenwagen *m*.
ambulance: ~ **driver** *n* Krankenwagenfahrer *m*;
~**man** *n* Sanitäter *m*.
ambush ['æmbuʃ] **1** *n* Überfall *m* (aus dem
Hinterhalt). **to lie in** ~ **for sb** *(Mil, fig)* jdm im
Hinterhalt auflauern. **2** *vt* (aus dem Hinterhalt)
überfallen.
ameba *n (US)* = **amoeba**.
amelioration [əˌmiːlɪə'reɪʃən] *n (form)* Verbesserung *f*.
amen [ˌɑː'men] **1** *interj* amen. **2** *n* Amen *nt*.
amenable [ə'miːnəbl] *adj* zugänglich *(to dat)*.
amend [ə'mend] *vt* ändern.
amendment [ə'mendmənt] *n* Änderung *f (to gen)*.
the First/Second *etc* **A~** *(US Pol)* das Erste/
Zweite *etc* Amendement, Zusatz 1/2 *etc*.
amends [ə'mendz] *npl* **to make** ~ **(for sth)** etw
wiedergutmachen.
amenity [ə'miːnɪtɪ] *n (public)* ~ öffentliche
Einrichtung; **the lack of amenities in many parts
of the city** der Mangel an Einkaufs-,
Unterhaltungs- und Transportmöglichkeiten in
vielen Teilen der Stadt; **close to all amenities in**
günstiger (Einkaufs- und Verkehrs)lage.
America [ə'merɪkə] *n* Amerika *nt*.
American [ə'merɪkən] **1** *adj* amerikanisch. ~ **plan**
(US) Vollpension *f*. **2** *n* Amerikaner(in *f*) *m*.
americanize [ə'merɪkənaɪz] *vt* amerikanisieren.
amethyst ['æmɪθɪst] *n* Amethyst *m*; *(colour)* Ame-
thystblau *nt*.
amiable ['eɪmɪəbl] *adj* liebenswürdig.
amicable ['æmɪkəbl] *adj* freundlich; *relations*
freundschaftlich; *(Jur)* settlement gütlich.
amid(st) [ə'mɪd(st)] *prep* inmitten (+*gen*).
amiss [ə'mɪs] **1** *adj pred* **there's something** ~ da
stimmt irgend etwas nicht. **2** *adv* **to take sth** ~
(jdm) etw übelnehmen; **a drink would not go** ~
etwas zu trinken wäre gar nicht verkehrt.
ammonia [ə'məunɪə] *n* Ammoniak *nt*.
ammunition [ˌæmju'nɪʃən] *n (lit,fig)* Munition *f*. ~
dump *n* Munitionslager *nt*.
amnesia [æm'niːzɪə] *n* Amnesie *f (form)*, Gedächt-
nisschwund *m*.
amnesty ['æmnɪstɪ] *n* Amnestie *f*.
amoeba, *(US)* **ameba** [ə'miːbə] *n* Amöbe *f*.
amok [ə'mɒk] *adv* = **amuck.**
among(st) [ə'mʌŋ(st)] *prep* unter (+*acc or dat*). ~
other things unter anderem; **this habit is widespread** ~ **the French** diese Sitte ist bei den
Franzosen weitverbreitet; **there were ferns** ~
the trees zwischen den Bäumen wuchs Farnkraut.
amoral [æ'mɒrəl] *adj* amoralisch.
amorous ['æmərəs] *adj* amourös; *look also* verliebt.
amorphous [ə'mɔːfəs] *adj* amorph, formlos; *style*,
ideas, play, novel strukturlos.

amount [ə'maunt] **1** *vi* **(a)** *(total)* sich belaufen *(to*
auf +*acc*). **(b)** *(be equivalent)* gleichkommen *(to*
+*dat*). **it** ~**s to the same thing** das läuft *or* kommt
aufs gleiche hinaus; **he will never** ~ **to much** aus
ihm wird nie etwas werden. **2** *n* **(a)** *(of money)*
Betrag *m*. **total** ~ Gesamtsumme *f*, Endbetrag
m; **a large/small** ~ **of money** eine große/geringe
Summe. **(b)** *(quantity)* Menge *f*; *(of luck,*
intelligence, skill etc) Maß *nt* *(of* an +*dat*). **an**
enormous ~ **of work** sehr viel Arbeit; **any** ~ **of**
food jede Menge Essen.
amp(ère) ['æmp(ɛəʳ)] *n* Ampere *nt*.
amphetamine [æm'fetəmiːn] *n* Amphetamin *nt*.
amphibian [æm'fɪbɪən] *n* Amphibie *f*; *(vehicle)*
Amphibienfahrzeug *nt*.
amphibious [æm'fɪbɪəs] *adj* animal, *(Mil)* amphibisch; *vehicle*, *aircraft* Amphibien-.
amphitheatre, *(US)* **amphitheater** ['æmfɪ-
ˌθɪətəʳ] *n* Amphitheater *nt*.
ample ['æmpl] *adj (+er)* **(a)** *(plentiful)* reichlich.
more than ~ überreichlich; ~ **time** genügend
Zeit. **(b)** *(large)* figure, proportions üppig; *boot of*
car etc geräumig; *garden* weitläufig, ausgedehnt.
amplifier ['æmplɪfaɪəʳ] *n (Rad)* Verstärker *m*.
amplify ['æmplɪfaɪ] *vt (Rad)* verstärken. **(b)**
(expand) statement, *idea* näher ausführen.
amply ['æmplɪ] *adv* reichlich.
amputate ['æmpjuteɪt] *vti* amputieren.
amputation [ˌæmpju'teɪʃən] *n* Amputation *f*.
amuck [ə'mʌk] *adv*: **to run** ~ Amok laufen.
amuse [ə'mjuːz] **1** *vt* **(a)** *(cause mirth)* amüsieren,
belustigen. **I was** ~**d to hear** ... es hat mich
amüsiert *or* belustigt zu hören ...; **he was not** ~**d**
er fand es überhaupt nicht komisch. **(b)**
(entertain) unterhalten. **let the children do it if it**
~**s them** laß die Kinder doch, wenn es ihnen
Spaß macht; **I have no problem keeping myself**
~**d** ich habe keinerlei Schwierigkeiten, mir die
Zeit zu vertreiben. **2** *vr* **the children can** ~
themselves die Kinder können sich
eine Zeitlang selbst beschäftigen.
amusement [ə'mjuːzmənt] *n* **(a)** *(enjoyment, fun)*
Vergnügen *nt*; *(pastime)* Zeitvertreib *m*. **the toys**
were a great source of ~ das Spielzeug bereitete
großen Spaß; **I see no cause for** ~ ich sehe
keinen Grund zur Heiterkeit; **to my great** ~/**to**
everyone's ~ zu meiner großen/zur allgemeinen
Belustigung, Unterhaltung *f*. **(c)** ~**s** *pl (place of*
entertainment) Vergnügungsstätte *f usu pl*; *(at*
fair) Attraktionen *pl*.
amusement: ~ **arcade** *n* Spielhalle *f*; ~ **park** *n*
Vergnügungspark *m*.
amusing [ə'mjuːzɪŋ] *adj* amüsant. **I don't find that**
very ~ das finde ich gar nicht lustig.
an [æn, ən, n] *indef art see* **a.**
anachronism [ə'nækrənɪzəm] *n* Anachronismus
m.
anaemia, *(US)* **anemia** [ə'niːmɪə] *n* Anämie, Blut-
armut *f*.
anaemic, *(US)* **anemic** [ə'niːmɪk] *adj* **(a)** anä-
misch, blutarm. **(b)** *(fig)* saft- und kraftlos.
anaesthetic, *(US)* **anesthetic** [ˌænɪs'θetɪk] *n*
Narkose, Anästhesie *(spec)* *f*; *(substance)*
Narkosemittel *nt*. **general** ~ Vollnarkose *f*; **local**
~ örtliche Betäubung, Lokalanästhesie *(spec) f*;
under the ~ in der Narkose.
anaesthetist, *(US)* **anesthetist** [æ'niːsθɪtɪst] *n*
Anästhesist(in *f*) *m*.
anagram ['ænəgræm] *n* Anagramm *nt*.
analog computer = **['ænəlɒgkəm'pjuːtəʳ]** *n* Analogrechner *m*.
analogous [ə'næləgəs] *adj* analog *(to, with* zu).
analogue ['ænəlɒg] *n* Gegenstück *n*, Parallele *f*.
analogy [ə'nælədʒɪ] *n* Analogie *f*. **to draw an** ~ eine
Analogie herstellen; **on the** ~ **of** analog zu.
analyse, *(US)* **analyze** ['ænəlaɪz] *vt* analysieren.
analysis [ə'næləsɪs] *n, pl* **analyses** [ə'næləsiːz] **(a)**

Analyse f; **in the final** ~ letzten Endes; **on (closer)** ~ bei genauerer Untersuchung. **(b)** (psycho~) Psychoanalyse, Analyse (col) f.

analyst ['ænəlɪst] n Analytiker m.

analytic(al) [,ænə'lɪtɪk(əl)] adj analytisch.

analyze ['ænəlaɪz] vt (US) = **analyse.**

anarchist ['ænəkɪst] n Anarchist(in f) m.

anarchy ['ænəkɪ] n Anarchie f.

anathema [ə'næθɪmə] n no art (fig) it is ~ **to me** das ist mir ein Greuel.

anatomical [,ænə'tɒmɪkəl] adj anatomisch.

anatomy [ə'nætəmɪ] n Anatomie f.

ancestor ['ænsestəʳ] n Vorfahr, Ahne m.

ancestral [æn'sestrəl] adj Ahnen-, seiner/ihrer Vorfahren. ~ **home** Stammsitz m.

ancestry ['ænsɪstrɪ] n (descent) Abstammung, Herkunft f; (ancestors) Ahnenreihe, Familie f.

anchor ['æŋkəʳ] **1** n (Naut) Anker m. **to drop** ~ vor Anker gehen; **to weigh** ~ den Anker lichten; **to be** or **lie at** ~ vor Anker liegen. **2** vt (Naut, fig) verankern. **3** vi (Naut) ankern.

anchorage ['æŋkərɪdʒ] n (Naut) Ankerplatz m.

anchorman ['æŋkəʳ,mæn] n (TV etc) Koordinator(in f) m; (in team) Zentralfigur f; (last person in relay race) Letzte(r) mf.

anchovy ['æntʃəvɪ] n Sardelle, An(s)chovis f.

ancient ['eɪnʃənt] adj alt; (col) person, clothes etc uralt. **in** ~ **times** im Altertum; (Greek, Roman also) in der Antike; ~ **Rome** das alte Rom; ~ **monument** (Brit) historisches Denkmal, historische Stätte.

ancillary [æn'sɪlərɪ] adj (secondary) Neben-; (auxiliary) service, troops Hilfs-.

and [ænd, ənd, nd, ən] conj und. **nice** ~ **early/warm** schön früh/warm; **try** ~ **come** versuch zu kommen; ~/**or** und/oder; ~ **so on** und so weiter; **better** ~ **better** immer besser; **I tried** ~ **tried** ich habe es immer wieder versucht; **three hundred** ~ **ten** dreihundert(und)zehn.

Andes ['ændiːz] npl **the** ~ die Anden pl.

anecdote ['ænɪkdəʊt] n Anekdote f.

anemia etc (US) = **anaemia** etc.

anemone [ə'nemənɪ] n (Bot) Anemone f, Buschwindröschen nt; (sea ~) Seeanemone f.

anesthetic etc (US) = **anaesthetic** etc.

anew [ə'njuː] adv aufs neue. **to start** ~ noch einmal or wieder von vorn anfangen.

angel ['eɪndʒəl] n (lit, fig) Engel m. **be an** ~ **and ...** sei so lieb und ...

angelic [æn'dʒelɪk] adj **(a)** (of angel) Engels-; hosts himmlisch. **(b)** (like an angel) engelhaft.

anger ['æŋgəʳ] **1** n Ärger m; (wrath: of gods etc) Zorn m. **a fit of** ~ ein Wutanfall m; **red with** ~ rot vor Wut; **public** ~ öffentliche Entrüstung. **2** vt verärgern.

angina [æn'dʒaɪnə] n Angina, Halsentzündung f. ~ **pectoris** Angina pectoris f.

angle¹ ['æŋgl] n **(a)** Winkel m. **at an** ~ **of 40°** in einem Winkel von 40°; **at an** ~ schräg; (hat) schief. **(b)** (projecting corner) Ecke f. **(c)** (of problem etc: aspect) Seite f. **(d)** (point of view) Standpunkt m, Position f.

angle² vi (Fishing) angeln.

♦ **angle for** vi +prep obj (fig) **to** ~ ~ **sth** auf etw (acc) aus sein.

angler ['æŋgləʳ] n Angler(in f) m.

Anglican ['æŋglɪkən] **1** n Anglikaner(in f) m. **2** adj anglikanisch.

anglicism ['æŋglɪsɪzəm] n Anglizismus m.

anglicize ['æŋglɪsaɪz] vt anglisieren.

angling ['æŋglɪŋ] n Angeln nt.

Anglo- ['æŋgləʊ] pref Anglo-; (between two countries) Englisch-; ~**-German** adj deutsch-englisch.

angora [æŋ'gɔːrə] n Angora(wolle f) nt.

angrily ['æŋgrɪlɪ] adv wütend.

angry ['æŋgrɪ] adj (+er) **(a)** böse; letter, look also, animal wütend. **to be** ~ **with** or **at sb** jdm or auf

jdn böse sein; **to be/get** ~ **at** or **about sth** sich über etw (acc) ärgern; **don't get** ~**!** reg dich nicht auf!; **to make sb** ~ jdn verärgern; **it makes me so** ~ es ärgert mich furchtbar. **(b)** (fig) sea aufgewühlt; sky, clouds bedrohlich, finster; (inflamed) wound entzündet, böse.

anguish ['æŋgwɪʃ] n Qual f.

anguished ['æŋgwɪʃt] adj qualvoll; look gequält.

angular ['æŋgjʊləʳ] adj shape eckig; face, features kantig.

animal ['ænɪməl] **1** n Tier nt; (brutal person also) Bestie f. **man is a social** ~ der Mensch ist ein soziales Wesen. **2** adj attr story, picture Tier-; products, fat, lust tierisch. ~ **kingdom** Tierreich nt, Tierwelt f; ~ **magnetism** körperliche Anziehungskraft.

animate ['ænɪmeɪt] vt (enliven) beleben.

animated ['ænɪmeɪtɪd] adj lebhaft, rege; discussion also angeregt. ~ **cartoon** Zeichentrickfilm m.

animation [,ænɪ'meɪʃən] n Lebhaftigkeit f; (Film) Animation f.

animosity [,ænɪ'mɒsɪtɪ] n Animosität (geh), Feindseligkeit f (towards gegenüber, gegen).

aniseed ['ænɪsiːd] n Anis m.

ankle ['æŋkl] n Knöchel m.

annals ['ænəlz] npl Annalen pl.

annex [ə'neks] **1** vt annektieren. **2** ['æneks] n **(a)** (to document etc) Anhang m. **(b)** (building) Nebengebäude nt; (extension) Anbau m.

annexation [,ænek'seɪʃən] n Annexion f.

annexe ['æneks] n = **annex 2 (b).**

annihilate [ə'naɪəleɪt] vt (lit, fig) vernichten; (col) person, team fertigmachen (col).

annihilation [ə,naɪə'leɪʃən] n (lit, fig) Vernichtung f. **our team's** ~ die vollständige Niederlage unserer Mannschaft.

anniversary [,ænɪ'vɜːsərɪ] n Jahrestag m; (wedding ~) Hochzeitstag m. **the** ~ **of his death** sein Todestag m.

announce [ə'naʊns] vt (lit, fig: person) bekanntgeben, verkünden; arrival, departure, radio programme ansagen; (over intercom) durchsagen; (formally) birth, marriage etc anzeigen; coming of spring etc ankündigen. **to** ~ **sb** jdn melden.

announcement [ə'naʊnsmənt] n (public declaration) Bekanntgabe, Bekanntmachung f; (of impending event, speaker) Ankündigung f; (over intercom etc) Durchsage f; (on radio etc) Ansage f; (written: of birth, marriage etc) Anzeige f.

announcer [ə'naʊnsəʳ] n (Rad, TV) Ansager(in f), Radio-/Fernsehsprecher(in f) m.

annoy [ə'nɔɪ] vt ärgern; (noise, questions etc) aufregen; (pester) belästigen. **to be** ~**ed that ...** ärgerlich or verärgert sein, weil ...; **to be** ~**ed with sb/about sth** sich über jdn/etw ärgern, (mit) jdm/über etw (acc) verärgert sein.

annoyance [ə'nɔɪəns] n **(a)** no pl (irritation) Ärger m. **to his** ~ zu seinem Ärger. **(b)** (nuisance) Plage, Belästigung f, Ärgernis nt.

annoying [ə'nɔɪɪŋ] adj ärgerlich; habit lästig.

annual ['ænjʊəl] **1** n **(a)** (Bot) einjährige Pflanze. **(b)** (book) Jahrbuch nt. **2** adj (happening once a year) jährlich; salary etc Jahres-. ~ **general meeting** (Brit) Jahreshauptversammlung f; ~ **report** Geschäftsbericht m.

annually ['ænjʊəlɪ] adv jährlich.

annuity [ə'njuːɪtɪ] n (Leib)rente f.

annul [ə'nʌl] vt annullieren; law, decree, judgement aufheben; contract, marriage also auflösen.

annulment [ə'nʌlmənt] n see vt Annullierung f. Aufhebung f; Auflösung f.

Annunciation [ə,nʌnsɪ'eɪʃən] n (Bibl) Mariä Verkündigung f.

anode ['ænəʊd] n Anode f.

anoint [ə'nɔɪnt] vt salben.

anomalous [ə'nɒmələs] adj ano(r)mal, ungewöhnlich.

anomaly [ə'nɒməlɪ] *n* Anomalie *f*; *(in law etc)* Besonderheit *f*.

anonymity [ˌænə'nɪmɪtɪ] *n* Anonymität *f*.

anonymous [ə'nɒnɪməs] *adj* anonym.

anorak ['ænəræk] *n (Brit)* Anorak *m*.

anorexia (nervosa) [ænə'reksɪə(nɔː'vəʊsə)] *n* Magersucht *f*.

another [ə'nʌðəʳ] **1** *adj* **(a)** *(additional)* noch eine(r, s). ~ **one** noch eine(r, s); **take** ~ **ten** nehmen Sie noch (weitere) zehn; **I don't want** ~ **drink!** ich möchte nichts mehr trinken; ~ **20 years and he...** noch 20 Jahre, und er ...; **without** ~ **word** ohne ein weiteres Wort; **and (there's)** ~ **thing** und noch eins, und (da ist) noch etwas; ~ **Shakespeare** ein zweiter Shakespeare. **(b)** *(different)* ein anderer, eine andere, ein anderes. **that's quite** ~ **matter** das ist etwas ganz anderes. **2** *pron* ein anderer, eine andere, ein anderes. **have** ~**!** nehmen Sie (doch) noch einen/eins *etc*; **tell me** ~**!** *(col)* das glaubst du doch wohl selbst nicht!; **what with one thing and** ~ bei all dem Trubel; **is this** ~ **of your brilliant ideas!** ist das wieder so eine deiner Glanzideen!

answer ['ɑːnsəʳ] **1** *n* **(a)** Antwort *f (to* auf *+acc)*. **there was no** ~ *(to telephone, doorbell)* es hat sich niemand gemeldet; **the** ~ **to our prayers** ein Geschenk des Himmels; **there's no** ~ **to that** *(col)* was soll man da groß machen/sagen! *(col)*; **in** ~ **to your letter/my question** in Beantwortung Ihres Briefes *(form)*/auf meine Frage hin. **(b)** *(solution)* Lösung *f (to* gen). **his** ~ **to any difficulty is ...** seine Reaktion auf jede Schwierigkeit ist ...

2 *vt* **(a)** antworten auf *(+acc)*, erwidern auf *(+acc) (geh)*; *person* antworten *(+dat)*; *exam questions* beantworten, antworten auf *(+acc)*; *objections, criticism also* beantworten. **will you** ~ **that?** *(phone/door)* gehst du ran/hin?; **to** ~ **the telephone/bell** *or door* das Telefon abnehmen, ans Telefon gehen/die Tür aufmachen. **(b)** *(fulfil) description* entsprechen *(+dat)*; *prayer (God)* erhören; *need* befriedigen. **(c)** *(Jur) charge* sich verantworten wegen *(+gen)*.

3 *vi (also react)* antworten. **if the phone rings, don't** ~ wenn das Telefon läutet, geh nicht ran *or* nimm nicht ab.

♦ **answer back** *vi* widersprechen; *(children also)* freche Antworten geben. **don't** ~ ~**!** keine Widerrede!

♦ **answer for** *vi +prep obj* **(a)** *(be responsible for)* verantwortlich sein für; *(person also)* verantworten; *mistakes also* einstehen für. **he has a lot to** ~ ~ er hat eine Menge auf dem Gewissen. **(b)** *(guarantee)* sich verbürgen für; *(speak for also)* sprechen für.

♦ **answer to** *vi +prep obj* **(a)** *(be accountable to)* to ~ ~ **sb for sth** jdm für etw Rechenschaft schuldig sein. **(b)** to ~ ~ **a description** einer Beschreibung entsprechen. **(c)** to ~ ~ **the name of ...** auf den Namen ... hören.

answerable ['ɑːnsərəbl] *adj* **(a)** *(responsible)* to be ~ **to sb (for sth)** jdm gegenüber für etw verantwortlich sein. **(b)** *question* zu beantworten.

answering machine ['ɑːnsərɪŋməˈʃiːn] *n* (automatischer) Anrufbeantworter.

ant [ænt] *n* Ameise *f*.

antagonism [æn'tægənɪzəm] *n* Antagonismus *m*; *(towards sb, ideas)* Feindseligkeit *f (to(wards)* gegenüber).

antagonist [æn'tægənɪst] *n* Gegner, Antagonist *m*.

antagonistic [æn,tægə'nɪstɪk] *adj* feindselig. **to be** ~ **towards sb/sth** jdm/gegen etw feindselig gesinnt sein.

antagonize [æn'tægənaɪz] *vt* gegen sich aufbringen.

antarctic [ænt'ɑːktɪk] **1** *adj* antarktisch. **A**~ **Circle** südlicher Polarkreis; **A**~ **Ocean** Südpolarmeer *nt*. **2** *n* **the A**~ die Antarktis.

Antarctica [ænt'ɑːktɪkə] *n* die Antarktis.

ante- *pref* vor-.

anteater ['ænt,iːtəʳ] *n* Ameisenbär *m*.

antecedent [ˌæntɪ'siːdənt] *n* ~**s** *(of person) (past history)* Vorleben *nt*; *(ancestry)* Abstammung *f*; *(of event)* Vorgeschichte *f*.

ante-: ~**date** *vt document, cheque* vordatieren *(to* auf *+acc)*; *event* vorausgehen *(+dat) (by* um); ~**diluvian** *adj (lit, fig col)* vorsintflutlich.

antelope ['æntɪləʊp] *n* Antilope *f*.

antenatal ['æntɪ'neɪtl] *adj* vor der Geburt, pränatal *(form)*. ~ **care/excercises** Schwangerschaftsfürsorge/-gymnastik *f*; ~ **clinic** Klinik *f* für werdende Mütter.

antenna [æn'tenə] *n* **(a)** *pl* **-e** [æn'teniː] *(Zool)* Fühler *m*. **(b)** *pl* **-e** *or* **-s** *(Rad, TV)* Antenne *f*.

anteroom ['æntɪruːm] *n* Vorzimmer *nt*.

anthem ['ænθəm] *n* Hymne *f*; *(by choir)* Chorgesang *m*.

anthology [æn'θɒlədʒɪ] *n* Anthologie *f*.

anthracite ['ænθrəsaɪt] *n* Anthrazit *m*.

anthropoid ['ænθrəʊpɔɪd] *n* Anthropoid *m (spec)*; *(ape)* Menschenaffe *m*.

anthropologist [ˌænθrə'pɒlədʒɪst] *n* Anthropologe *m*, Anthropologin *f*.

anthropology [ˌænθrə'pɒlədʒɪ] *n* Anthropologie *f*.

anti ['æntɪ] *prep (col)* gegen *(+acc)*. ~ **everything** grundsätzlich gegen alles.

anti- *in cpds* anti-, gegen-; ~**-aircraft** *adj* gun, rocket Flugabwehr-; ~**ballistic missile** *n* Anti-(Raketen)-Rakete *f*; ~**biotic** *n* Antibiotikum *nt*; ~**body** *n* Antikörper *m*.

anticipate [æn'tɪsɪpeɪt] **1** *vt* **(a)** *(expect)* erwarten. **(b)** *(see in advance)* vorhersehen; *(see in advance and cater for)* objection, need etc zuvorkommen *(+dat)*. **(c)** *(do before sb else)* zuvorkommen *(+dat)*. **2** *vi (chess-player etc)* vorauskalkulieren.

anticipation [æn,tɪsɪ'peɪʃən] *n* **(a)** *(expectation)* Erwartung *f*. **thanking you in** ~ herzlichen Dank im voraus; **to wait in** ~ gespannt warten. **(b)** his **uncanny** ~ **of every objection** die verblüffende Art, in der er jedem Einwand zuvorkam; **the driver showed good** ~ der Fahrer zeigte ein gutes Reaktionsvermögen. **(c)** *(of discovery, discoverer)* Vorwegnahme *f*.

anti: ~**climax** *n* Enttäuschung *f*; ~**clockwise** *adv* nach links, gegen den Uhrzeigersinn.

antics ['æntɪks] *npl* Eskapaden *pl*; *(tricks)* Streiche *pl*.

anti: ~**cyclone** *n* Hoch(druckgebiet) *nt*; ~**depressant** *n* Mittel *nt* gegen Depressionen; ~**dote** *n (Med, fig)* Gegenmittel *nt (for* gegen); ~**freeze** *n* Frostschutz *m*; ~**histamine** *n* Antihistamin *nt*; ~**missile** *adj* Raketenabwehr-.

antipathy [æn'tɪpəθɪ] *n* Antipathie, Abneigung *f (towards* gegen).

antipodes [æn'tɪpədiːz] *npl* die entgegengesetzten Teile der Erde. **A**~ *(Brit)* Australien und Neuseeland.

antiquated ['æntɪkweɪtɪd] *adj* antiquiert; *machines, ideas also* überholt; *institutions also* veraltet.

antique [æn'tiːk] **1** *adj* antik. **2** *n* Antiquität *f*.

antique dealer *n* Antiquitätenhändler(in *f*) *m*.

antiquity [æn'tɪkwɪtɪ] *n* das Altertum; *(Roman, Greek* ~) die Antike; *(great age)* großes Alter.

anti: ~**rust** *adj* Rostschutz-; ~**-Semitic** *adj* antisemitisch; ~**Semitism** *n* Antisemitismus *m*; ~**septic** **1** *n* Antiseptikum *nt*; **2** *adj* antiseptisch; ~**social** *adj* unsozial; *(Psych)* asozial; **in an** ~**social mood** nicht in Gesellschaftslaune.

antithesis [æn'tɪθɪsɪs] *n, pl* **antitheses** [æn'tɪθɪsiːz] *(direct opposite)* genaues Gegenteil *(to, of* gen); *(contrast)* Gegensatz *m*.

antler ['æntləʳ] *n* Geweihsprosse *f*. **(set** *or* **pair of)** ~**s** Geweih *nt*.

antonym ['æntənɪm] *n* Antonym *nt*.

anus ['eɪnəs] n After m.

anvil ['ænvɪl] n Amboß m.

anxiety [æŋg'zaɪətɪ] n (a) Sorge f. to suffer from ~ unter Angst leiden. (b) (keen desire) in his ~ to get away weil er unbedingt wegkommen wollte.

anxious ['æŋkʃəs] adj (a) (worried) besorgt; person (as character trait) ängstlich. to be ~ about sb/sth sich (dat) um jdn/etw Sorgen machen, um jdn/ etw besorgt sein. (b) (worrying) moment, minutes der Angst, bang (geh). it's been an ~ time for us all wir alle haben uns (in dieser Zeit) große Sorgen gemacht. (c) to be ~ to do sth etw unbedingt wollen; they were ~ for news sie warteten auf Nachricht; we are ~ for a settlement uns ist an einer Klärung sehr gelegen; I am ~ for him to do it mir liegt viel daran, daß er es tut.

anxiously ['æŋkʃəslɪ] adv (a) besorgt. (b) (keenly) begierig.

any ['enɪ] 1 adj (a) (in interrog, conditional, neg sentences) not translated; (emph: ~ at all) (with sing n) irgendein(e); (with pl n) irgendwelche; (with uncountable n) etwas. do you have ~ wine/ cigarettes? haben Sie Wein/Zigaretten?; not ~ kein/keine; not any ... at all überhaupt kein/ keine ...; if I had any plan/ideas/money (at all) wenn ich irgendeinen Plan/irgendwelche Ideen/ (auch nur) etwas Geld hätte; without ~ difficulty (at all) ohne jede Schwierigkeit; hardly ~ difference at all kaum ein Unterschied.
(b) (no matter which) jede(r, s) (beliebige); (with pl or uncountable n) alle. ~ one will do es ist jede(r, s) recht; you can have ~ book/books you find du kannst jedes Buch/alle Bücher haben, das/die du findest; take ~ two points wähle zwei beliebige Punkte; ~ one you like was du willst; ~ one of us jeder von uns.
2 pron (a) (in interrog, conditional, neg sentences) (replacing sing n) ein(e), welche(r, s); (replacing pl n) einige, welche; (replacing uncountable n) etwas, welche. I need some butter/stamps, do you have ~? ich brauche Butter/Briefmarken, haben Sie welche?; have you seen ~ of my ties? haben Sie eine von meinen Krawatten gesehen?; haven't you ~ (at all)? haben Sie (gar) keinen/keine/keines?; the profits, if ~ die eventuellen Gewinne; if ~ of you can sing wenn (irgend) jemand or (irgend)einer/-eine von euch singen kann; few, if ~, will come wenn überhaupt, werden nur wenige kommen. (b) (no matter which) alle. ~ I have ... alle, die ich habe ...
3 adv if it gets ~ colder wenn es (noch) kälter wird; not ~ colder/bigger nicht kälter/größer; it won't get ~ colder es wird nicht mehr kälter; we can't go ~ further wir können nicht mehr weitergehen; are you feeling ~ better? geht es dir etwas besser?; do you want ~ more soup? willst du noch etwas Suppe?; I don't want ~ more ich möchte nichts mehr.

anybody ['enɪˌbɒdɪ] 1 pron (a) (irgend) jemand, (irgend)eine(r). not ... ~ niemand, keine(r); don't tell ~ erzähl das niemandem(em) or keinem. (b) (no matter who) jede(r). ~ will tell you the same jeder wird dir dasselbe sagen. 2 n she'll never be ~ sie wird es nie zu etwas bringen; he's not just ~ er ist nicht einfach irgend jemand.

anyhow ['enɪhaʊ] adv (a) ~, that's what I think das ist jedenfalls meine Meinung; it's no trouble, I'm going there ~ es ist keine Mühe, ich gehe sowieso hin; I told him not to, but he did it ~ ich habe es ihm verboten, aber er hat es trotzdem gemacht; who cares, ~? überhaupt, wen kümmert es denn schon? (b) (carelessly) irgendwie; (at random also) aufs Geratewohl.

anyone ['enɪwʌn] pron, n = anybody.

anyplace ['enɪpleɪs] adv (US col) = anywhere.

anything ['enɪθɪŋ] 1 pron (a) (irgend) etwas. not ~

nichts; (euph) gar or überhaupt nichts. (b) (no matter what) alles. ~ you like (alles,) was du willst; they eat ~ sie essen alles; not just ~ nicht bloß irgend etwas; I wouldn't do it for ~ ich würde es um keinen Preis tun. 2 adv (col) it isn't ~ like him das sieht ihm überhaupt nicht ähnlich; it didn't cost ~ like £100 es kostete bei, weitem keine £ 100; not ~ like as wet as ... nicht annähernd so naß wie ...; she's been working like ~ (col) sie hat wie verrückt gearbeitet.

anyway ['enɪweɪ] adv = anyhow (a).

anywhere ['enɪwɛər] adv (a) be, stay, live irgendwo; go, travel irgendwohin. not ~ nirgends/ nirgendwohin; I haven't found ~ to live yet ich habe noch nichts gefunden, wo ich wohnen kann; he'll never get ~ er wird es zu nichts bringen; I wasn't getting ~ ich kam (einfach) nicht weiter. (b) (no matter where) be, stay, live überall; go, travel überallhin. they could be ~ sie könnten überall sein; ~ you like wo/wohin du willst.

aorta [eɪ'ɔːtə] n Aorta f.

apart [ə'pɑːt] adv (a) auseinander. to sit with one's legs ~ mit gespreizten Beinen dasitzen; I can't tell them ~ ich kann sie nicht auseinanderhalten; to live ~ getrennt leben; to come or fall ~ entzweigehen, auseinanderfallen; to take sth ~ etw auseinandernehmen. (b) (to one side) zur Seite, beiseite; (on one side) abseits (from gen). a class/thing ~ eine Klasse/Sache für sich. (c) (excepted) abgesehen von, bis auf (+acc). these problems ~ abgesehen von diesen Problemen; ~ from that abgesehen davon.

apartheid [ə'pɑːteɪt] n Apartheid f.

apartment [ə'pɑːtmənt] n (a) (Brit: room) Raum m. (b) ~s pl (Brit: suite of rooms) Appartement nt. (c) (esp US: flat) Wohnung f. ~ house Wohnblock m.

apathetic [ˌæpə'θetɪk] adj apathisch, teilnahmslos.

apathy ['æpəθɪ] n Apathie, Teilnahmslosigkeit f.

ape [eɪp] 1 n (lit, fig) Affe m. 2 vt nachäffen (pej), nachmachen.

aperitif [ə,perɪ'tiːf] n Aperitif m.

aperture ['æpətʃjʊər] n Öffnung f; (Phot) Blende f.

apex ['eɪpeks] n Spitze f; (fig) Höhepunkt m.

aphorism ['æfərɪzəm] n Aphorismus m.

aphrodisiac [ˌæfrəʊ'dɪzɪæk] n Aphrodisiakum nt.

apiary ['eɪpɪərɪ] n Bienenhaus nt.

apiece [ə'piːs] adv pro Stück; (per person) pro Person. I gave them two ~ ich gab ihnen je zwei; they had two ~ sie hatten jeder zwei.

aplomb [ə'plɒm] n Gelassenheit f.

Apocalypse [ə'pɒkəlɪps] n Apokalypse f.

apocryphal [ə'pɒkrɪfəl] adj (untrue) erfunden.

apologetic [ə,pɒlə'dʒetɪk] adj gesture, look entschuldigend attr. he was most ~ (about it) er entschuldigte sich vielmals (dafür).

apologize [ə'pɒlədʒaɪz] vi sich entschuldigen (to bei).

apology [ə'pɒlədʒɪ] n Entschuldigung f. to make or offer sb an ~ jdn um Verzeihung bitten; to make one's apologies sich entschuldigen; Mr Jones sends his apologies Herr Jones läßt sich entschuldigen; ~ for a breakfast ein erbärmliches Frühstück.

apoplexy ['æpəpleksɪ] n Schlaganfall m.

apostle [ə'pɒsl] n (lit, fig) Apostel m.

apostrophe [ə'pɒstrəfɪ] n (Gram) Apostroph m.

appal, (US also) **appall** [ə'pɔːl] vt entsetzen. to be ~led (at or by sth) (über etw acc) entsetzt sein.

appalling [ə'pɔːlɪŋ] adj entsetzlich.

apparatus [ˌæpə'reɪtəs] n (lit, fig) Apparat m; (equipment also) Ausrüstung f; (in gym) Geräte pl. a piece of ~ ein Gerät nt.

apparent [ə'pærənt] adj (a) (obvious) offensichtlich. to be ~ to sb jdm klar sein; to become ~ sich (deutlich) zeigen. (b) (seeming) scheinbar.

apparently [ə'pærəntlɪ] adv anscheinend.

apparition [,æpə'rɪʃən] n (a) (ghost, hum: person) Erscheinung f. (b) (appearance) Erscheinen nt.

appeal [ə'piːl] 1 n (a) (request: for help, money etc) Appell m, Bitte f (for um); (for mercy) Gesuch nt (for um). ~ for funds Spendenaufruf m or -aktion f; to make an ~ to sb (to do sth)/to sb for sth an jdn appellieren(, etw zu tun)/jdn um etw bitten. (b) (against decision) Einspruch m; (Jur: against sentence) Berufung f; (actual trial) Berufungsverhandlung f. he lost his ~ er verlor in der Berufung; right of ~ Einspruchsrecht nt; (Jur) Berufungsrecht nt; Court of A~ Berufungsgericht nt. (c) (attraction) Reiz m (to für). his music has a wide ~ seine Musik findet großen Anklang.
2 vi (a) (make request) to ~ to sb for sth jdn um etw bitten; to ~ to the public to do sth die Öffentlichkeit (dazu) aufrufen, etw zu tun. (b) (against decision: to authority etc) Einspruch erheben (to bei); (Jur) Berufung einlegen (to bei). (c) (apply: for support, decision) appellieren (to an +acc); (Sport) Einspruch erheben (to bei). to ~ to sb's better nature an jds besseres Ich appellieren. (d) (be attractive) reizen (to sb jdn), zusagen (to sb jdm); (plan, candidate, idea) zusagen (to sb jdm); (book, magazine) ansprechen (to sb jdn). how does that ~? wie gefällt dir/ Ihnen das?; the story ~ed to his sense of humour die Geschichte sprach seinen Sinn für Humor an.

appealing [ə'piːlɪŋ] adj (attractive) attraktiv, reiz-voll; character, smile ansprechend, gewinnend.

appear [ə'pɪər] vi (a) erscheinen; (unexpectedly) auftauchen; (personality, ghost also) sich zeigen; (Theat) auftreten. to ~ in court vor Gericht erscheinen; to ~ for sb jdn vertreten. (b) (seem) scheinen. he ~ed (to be) tired er schien müde zu sein; it ~s that ... anscheinend ...; so it ~s, so it would ~ so scheint es; it ~s not anscheinend nicht, es sieht nicht so aus; it ~s from his statement that ... aus seiner Bemerkung geht hervor, daß ...

appearance [ə'pɪərəns] n (a) Erscheinen nt; (unexpected) Auftauchen nt no pl; (Theat) Auftritt m. many successful court ~s viele erfolgreiche Auftritte vor Gericht; to put in or make an ~ sich sehen lassen. (b) (look) Aussehen nt; (of person also) Äußere(s) nt, äußere Erscheinung. ~s (outward signs) der äußere (An)schein; in ~ dem Aussehen nach; at first ~ auf den ersten Blick; for the sake of ~s um den Schein zu wahren; (as good manners) der Form halber; to keep up ~s den (äußeren) Schein wahren; ~s are often deceptive der Schein trügt oft; to all ~s allem Anschein nach.

appease [ə'piːz] vt person, anger beschwichtigen, besänftigen; hunger, curiosity stillen.

appeasement [ə'piːzmənt] n (esp Pol) Beschwichtigung f.

append [ə'pend] vt notes etc anhängen (to an +acc), hinzufügen; signature setzen (to under +acc).

appendage [ə'pendɪdʒ] n (fig) Anhängsel nt.

appendicitis [ə,pendɪ'saɪtɪs] n Blinddarmentzündung f.

appendix [ə'pendɪks] n, pl **appendices** (a) (Anat) Blinddarm m. to have one's ~ out sich (dat) den Blinddarm herausnehmen lassen. (b) (to book etc) Anhang, Appendix m.

appetite ['æpɪtaɪt] n (for auf etw +acc) Appetit m; (fig: desire) Lust f. to have a good ~ einen guten or gesunden Appetit haben.

appetizer ['æpɪtaɪzər] n (food) Appetitanreger m; (drink) appetitanregendes Getränk.

appetizing ['æpɪtaɪzɪŋ] adj appetitlich (also fig); smell lecker.

applaud [ə'plɔːd] vti (lit, fig) applaudieren (+dat); (fig) efforts, courage loben; decision begrüßen.

applause [ə'plɔːz] n no pl (lit fig) Beifall m.

apple ['æpl] n Apfel m. to be the ~ of sb's eye jds Liebling sein.

apple in cpds Apfel-; ~-pie n ≃ gedeckter Apfelkuchen; ~-tree n Apfelbaum m; ~ turnover n Apfeltasche f.

appliance [ə'plaɪəns] n Vorrichtung f; (household ~) Gerät nt.

applicable [ə'plɪkəbl] adj anwendbar (to auf +acc); (on forms) zutreffend (to für). that isn't ~ to you das trifft auf Sie nicht zu.

applicant ['æplɪkənt] n (for job) Bewerber(in f) m (for um, für); (for loan etc) Antragsteller(in f) m (for für).

application [,æplɪ'keɪʃən] n (a) (for job etc) Bewerbung f (for um, für); (for grant, loan etc) Antrag m (for auf +acc). ~ form Bewerbung(sformular nt) f; Antrag(sformular nt) m; (for course, exhibition etc) Anmeldeformular nt. (b) (act of applying) see apply 1 Anwendung f; Auftragen nt; Anlegen nt; Betätigung f; Verwertung f. (c) (diligence, effort) Fleiß, Eifer m.

applied [ə'plaɪd] adj attr maths etc angewandt.

apply [ə'plaɪ] 1 vt anwenden (to auf +acc); paint etc auftragen (to auf +acc); dressing anlegen; brakes betätigen; results, findings verwerten (to für). to ~ oneself or one's mind (to sth) sich (bei etw) anstrengen. 2 vi (a) sich bewerben (for um, für). to ~ for a loan einen Kredit beantragen. (b) (be applicable) gelten (to für).

appoint [ə'pɔɪnt] vt (a) (to a position) einstellen; (to a post) ernennen. to ~ sb sth jdn zu etw ernennen. (b) (designate, ordain) bestimmen. at the ~ed time zur vereinbarten Zeit.

-appointed [-ə'pɔɪntɪd] adj suf well-~ gut ausgestattet.

appointment [ə'pɔɪntmənt] n (a) Verabredung f; (business ~, with doctor, lawyer etc) Termin m (with bei). to make an ~ with sb mit jdm eine Verabredung treffen; einen Termin mit jdm vereinbaren; do you have an ~? sind Sie angemeldet?; by ~ auf Verabredung; (on business, to see doctor, lawyer etc) mit (Vor)anmeldung, nach Vereinbarung. (b) (act of appointing) see vt (a) Einstellung f; Ernennung f. (c) (post) Stelle f. ~s (vacant) Stellenangebote pl.

apportion [ə'pɔːʃən] vt aufteilen. to ~ sth to sb jdm etw zuteilen.

apposite ['æpəzɪt] adj treffend, passend.

appraisal [ə'preɪzəl] n see vt Schätzung f; Beurteilung f.

appraise [ə'preɪz] vt schätzen; character, ability beurteilen.

appreciable [ə'priːʃəbl] adj beträchtlich, deutlich; difference, change also merklich.

appreciate [ə'priːʃɪeɪt] 1 vt (a) (be aware of) sich (dat) bewußt sein (+gen); (understand) sb's wishes, reluctance etc also Verständnis haben für. I ~ that you can't come ich habe Verständnis dafür, daß ihr nicht kommen könnt. (b) (value, be grateful for) zu schätzen wissen. thank you, I ~ it vielen Dank, sehr nett von Ihnen; I would really ~ that das wäre mir wirklich sehr lieb. (c) (enjoy) art, music, poetry schätzen. 2 vi (Fin) im Wert steigen, an Wert gewinnen.

appreciation [ə,priːʃɪ'eɪʃən] n (a) (awareness) Erkennen nt. (b) (esteem, respect) Anerkennung f; (of abilities, efforts also) Würdigung f; (of person also) Wertschätzung f; (gratitude) Dankbarkeit f. in ~ of sth in Anerkennung (+gen), zum Dank für etw. (c) (enjoyment, understanding) Verständnis nt; (of art) Sinn m (of für). (d) (Fin: increase) (Wert)steigerung f.

appreciative [ə'priːʃɪətɪv] adj anerkennend; audience dankbar; (grateful) dankbar. to be ~ of sth etw zu schätzen wissen; of music, art Sinn für etw haben.

apprehend [,æprɪ'hend] vt (arrest) festnehmen.
apprehension [,æprɪ'henʃən] n (a) (fear) Besorgnis, Befürchtung f. **a feeling of** ~ eine dunkle Ahnung. (b) (arrest) Festnahme f.
apprehensive [,æprɪ'hensɪv] adj ängstlich. **to be** ~ **of sth/that** ... etw befürchten/fürchten, daß ...
apprentice [ə'prentɪs] n Lehrling m, Auszubildende(r) mf.
apprenticeship [ə'prentɪʃɪp] n Lehre f.
approach [ə'prəʊtʃ] **1** vi (physically) sich nähern, näherkommen; (date, summer etc) nahen.
  2 vt (a) (come near) sich nähern (+dat); (Aviat also) anfliegen; (in quality, stature) herankommen an (+acc). **to** ~ **thirty** auf die Dreißig zugehen. (b) person, committee herantreten an (+acc) (about wegen). **he is easy/difficult to** ~ **er** ist leicht/nicht leicht ansprechbar. (c) (tackle) problem angehen.
  3 n (a) (drawing near) (Heran)nahen nt; (of troops, in time also) Heranrücken nt; (of night) Einbruch m; (Aviat) Anflug m (to auf +acc). (b) **to make** ~**es/an** ~ **to sb** (with request) an jdn herantreten; (man to woman) Annäherungsversuche machen. (c) (way of tackling, attitude) Ansatz m (to zu). **an easy** ~ **to maths** ein einfacher Weg, Mathematik zu lernen; **his** ~ **to the problem** sein Problemansatz m; **you've got the wrong** ~ du machst das verkehrt; **try a different** ~ versuch's doch mal anders. (d) (access) Zugang, Weg m; (road also) Zufahrt(sstraße) f.
approachable [ə'prəʊtʃəbl] adj (a) person umgänglich, zugänglich. (b) place zugänglich.
approach road n (to city etc) Zufahrtsstraße f; (to motorway) Zubringer m.
approbation [,æprə'beɪʃən] n Billigung f; (from critics) Beifall m.
appropriate¹ [ə'prəʊprɪɪt] adj (a) (suitable, fitting) passend, geeignet (for, to für); name, remark also treffend. (b) (relevant) entsprechend; body, authority also zuständig. **where** ~ wo es angebracht ist/war, an gegebener Stelle; **delete as** ~ Nichtzutreffendes streichen.
appropriate² [ə'prəʊprɪeɪt] vt (authorities) beschlagnahmen; (take for oneself) sich (dat) aneignen, mit Beschlag belegen.
appropriately [ə'prəʊprɪɪtlɪ] adv treffend; dressed passend (for, to für); (to fit particular needs) designed, equipped zweckmäßig (for, to für).
approval [ə'pruːvəl] n Zustimmung (of zu), Billigung f. **to meet with sb's** ~ jds Zustimmung or Beifall finden; **to show one's** ~ **of sth** zeigen, daß man einer Sache (dat) zustimmt or etw billigt; **on** ~ (Comm) auf Probe; (to look at) zur Ansicht.
approve [ə'pruːv] **1** vt decision billigen, gutheißen; minutes, motion annehmen; project genehmigen. **an** ~**d campsite** ein empfohlener Campingplatz. **2** vi **I don't** ~ **of him/it** ich halte nichts von ihm/davon; **I don't** ~ **of children smoking** ich finde es nicht richtig, daß Kinder rauchen; **do you** ~? findest du das richtig or in Ordnung?
approved school [ə'pruːvd'skuːl] n (Brit) Erziehungsheim nt.
approximate¹ [ə'prɒksɪmɪt] **1** adj ungefähr. **2** [ə'prɒksɪmeɪt] vti to ~ (to) sth einer Sache (dat) in etwa entsprechen.
approximately [ə'prɒksɪmɪtlɪ] adv ungefähr.
approximation [ə,prɒksɪ'meɪʃən] n Annäherung f (of, to an +acc); (figure, sum etc) (An)näherungswert m.
apricot ['eɪprɪkɒt] n Aprikose f.
April ['eɪprəl] n April m. ~ **fool!** ≈ April, April!; ~ **Fool's Day** der erste April; see **September.**
apron ['eɪprən] n Schürze f; (Aviat) Vorfeld nt. **to be tied to one's mother's** ~**-strings** seiner Mutter (dat) am Schürzenzipfel hängen (col).
apse [æps] n Apsis f.
apt [æpt] adj (a) (suitable, fitting) passend; comparison, remark also treffend. (b) (able,

intelligent) begabt (at für). (c) (liable) **to be** ~ **to do sth** dazu neigen, etw zu tun.
aptitude ['æptɪtjuːd] n Begabung f. ~ **test** Eignungsprüfung f.
aptly ['æptlɪ] adv passend.
aqualung ['ækwəlʌŋ] n Tauchgerät nt.
aquarium [ə'kwɛərɪəm] n Aquarium nt.
Aquarius [ə'kwɛərɪəs] n Wassermann m.
aquatic [ə'kwætɪk] adj Wasser-.
aqueduct ['ækwɪdʌkt] n Aquädukt m or nt.
aquiline ['ækwɪlaɪn] adj nose Adler-, gebogen.
Arab ['ærəb] **1** n Araber m (also horse), Araberin f. **2** adj attr arabisch; policies, ideas also der Araber.
arabesque [,ærə'besk] n Arabeske f.
Arabia [ə'reɪbɪə] n Arabien nt.
Arabian [ə'reɪbɪən] adj arabisch. **tales of the** ~ **Nights** Märchen aus Tausendundeiner Nacht.
Arabic ['ærəbɪk] **1** n Arabisch nt. **2** adj arabisch.
arable ['ærəbl] adj land bebaubar; (being used) Acker-.
arbitrary ['ɑːbɪtrərɪ] adj willkürlich.
arbitrate ['ɑːbɪtreɪt] **1** vt dispute schlichten. **2** vi vermitteln.
arbitration [,ɑːbɪ'treɪʃən] n Schlichtung f. **to go to** ~ vor eine Schlichtungskommission gehen; (dispute) vor eine Schlichtungskommission gebracht werden.
arbitrator ['ɑːbɪtreɪtər] n Vermittler m; (esp Ind) Schlichter m.
arc [ɑːk] n Bogen m.
arcade [ɑː'keɪd] n (Archit) Arkade f; (shopping ~) Passage f.
arcane [ɑː'keɪn] adj obskur.
arch¹ [ɑːtʃ] **1** n (a) Bogen m. (b) (Anat) fallen ~**es** Senkfuß m. **2** vi sich wölben; (arrow etc) einen Bogen beschreiben. **3** vt back krümmen. **the cat** ~**ed his back** die Katze machte einen Buckel.
arch² adj attr Erz-. ~ **traitor** Hochverräter m.
archaeological, (US) **archeological** [,ɑːkɪə'lɒdʒɪkəl] adj archäologisch.
archaeologist, (US) **archeologist** [,ɑːkɪ-'ɒlədʒɪst] n Archäologe m, Archäologin f.
archaeology, (US) **archeology** [,ɑːkɪ'ɒlədʒɪ] n Archäologie f.
archaic [ɑː'keɪɪk] adj word etc veraltet, archaisch (spec); (col) vorsintflutlich.
arch: ~**angel** ['ɑːk,eɪndʒəl] n Erzengel m; ~**bishop** n Erzbischof m; ~**duke** n Erzherzog m.
arched [ɑːtʃt] adj gewölbt; window (Rund)bogen-.
arch-enemy [,ɑːtʃ'enɪmɪ] n Erzfeind m.
archeological etc (US) = **archaeological** etc.
archer ['ɑːtʃər] n Bogenschütze m.
archery ['ɑːtʃərɪ] n Bogenschießen nt.
archetypal ['ɑːkɪtaɪpəl] adj archetypisch (geh); (typical) typisch.
archetype ['ɑːkɪtaɪp] n Urbild nt, Urtyp m.
archipelago [,ɑːkɪ'pelɪgəʊ] n, pl -(e)s Archipel m.
architect ['ɑːkɪtekt] n (lit, fig) Architekt(in f) m.
architectural [,ɑːkɪ'tektʃərəl] adj architektonisch.
architecture ['ɑːkɪtektʃər] n Architektur f; (of building also) Baustil m.
archives ['ɑːkaɪvz] npl Archiv nt.
archway ['ɑːtʃweɪ] n Torbogen m.
arc lamp ['ɑːk,læmp] n Bogenlampe f.
arctic ['ɑːktɪk] **1** adj (lit, fig) arktisch. **A**~ **Circle** nördlicher Polarkreis; **A**~ **Ocean** Nordpolarmeer nt. **2** n the **A**~ die Arktis.
ardent ['ɑːdənt] adj leidenschaftlich; supporter also begeistert; admirer also glühend.
ardour, (US) **ardor** ['ɑːdər] n (of person) Leidenschaft f; (of feelings also) Heftigkeit f; (passion) Leidenschaftlichkeit f.
arduous ['ɑːdjʊəs] adj beschwerlich, mühsam; course, work anstrengend; task mühselig.
are [ɑːr] 2nd pers sing, 1st, 2nd, 3rd pers pl pres of **be.**
area ['ɛərɪə] n (a) (measure) Fläche f. (b) (region, district) Gebiet nt; (neighbourhood,

vicinity) Gegend *f*; *(separated off, piece of ground etc)* Gelände *nt*; *(on plan, diagram etc)* Bereich *m*; *(slum* ~, *residential* ~, *commercial* ~ *also)* Viertel *nt*. in the ~ in der Nähe; **dining/sleeping** ~ Eß-/Schlafbereich *m*; **no smoking/reception** ~ Nichtraucherzone *f*/Empfangsbereich *m*; **this** ~ **is for directors' cars** dieser Platz ist für die Direktorenwagen vorgesehen; **the infected** ~**s of the lungs** die befallenen Lungenpartien; **in the** ~ **of the station** in der Bahnhofsgegend; **in the London** ~ im Raum London, im Londoner Raum; ~ **code** *(Telec)* Vorwahl(nummer) *f*; ~ **office** Bezirksbüro *nt*. **(c)** *(fig)* Bereich *m*. **his** ~ **of responsibility** sein Verantwortungsbereich *m*; **the** ~**s in which we agree** die Bereiche, in denen wir übereinstimmen; ~ **of interest/study** Interessen-/Studiengebiet *nt*; **in the** ~ **of £100** um die hundert Pfund.

arena [ə'riːnə] *n (lit, fig)* Arena *f*.

aren't [ɑːnt] = **are not; am not;** *see* **be.**

Argentina [,ɑːdʒən'tiːnə] *n* Argentinien *nt*.

Argentinian [,ɑːdʒən'tɪnɪən] **1** *n (person)* Argentinier(in *f*) *m*. **2** *adj* argentinisch.

arguable ['ɑːɡjʊəbl] *adj* **(a)** *(capable of being maintained)* vertretbar. **it is** ~ **that** ... es läßt sich der Standpunkt vertreten, daß ... **(b)** *(doubtful)* **it is** ~ **whether** ... es ist (noch) die Frage, ob ...

arguably ['ɑːɡjʊəblɪ] *adv* **this is** ~ **his best book** dies dürfte (wohl) sein bestes Buch sein.

argue ['ɑːɡjuː] **1** *vi* **(a)** *(dispute)* streiten; *(quarrel)* sich streiten. **don't** ~ **(with me)!** keine Widerrede! **(b)** *(present reasons)* **he** ~**s that** ... er vertritt den Standpunkt, daß ..., er behauptet, daß ...; **to** ~ **for** *or* **in favour of sth** für etw sprechen; *(in book)* sich für etw aussprechen; **to** ~ **against sth** gegen etw sprechen; *(in book)* sich gegen etw aussprechen; **to** ~ **from a position of** ... von einem Standpunkt (+*gen*) aus argumentieren. **2** *vt (debate)* issue diskutieren, erörtern; *(Jur, present)* case vertreten. **a well** ~**d case** ein gut dargelegter Fall.

argument ['ɑːɡjʊmənt] *n* **(a)** *(discussion)* Diskussion *f*. **for the sake of** ~ rein theoretisch; **this is open to** ~ darüber läßt sich streiten. **(b)** *(quarrel)* Auseinandersetzung *f*. **to have an** ~ sich streiten. **(c)** *(reason)* Argument *nt*; *(line of reasoning)* Argumentation, Beweisführung *f*; *(statement of proof)* Beweis *m*. **(d)** *(theme: of play, book etc)* Aussage *f*; *(claim)* These *f*.

argumentative [,ɑːɡjʊ'mentətɪv] *adj* streitsüchtig.

aria ['ɑːrɪə] *n* Arie *f*.

arid ['ærɪd] *adj* dürr; *(fig)* subject trocken.

Aries ['ɛəriːz] *n (Astrol)* Widder *m*.

arise [ə'raɪz] *pret* **arose** [ə'rəʊz], *ptp* **arisen** [ə'rɪzn] *vi* **(a)** *(occur)* entstehen; *(misunderstanding, problem also)* aufkommen; *(protest, cry)* sich erheben; *(question)* sich stellen. **(b)** *(result)* **to** ~ **from sth** sich aus etw ergeben. **(c)** *(old, liter: get up)* sich erheben *(liter)*.

aristocracy [,ærɪs'tɒkrəsɪ] *n* Aristokratie *f*.

aristocrat ['ærɪstəkræt] *n* Aristokrat(in *f*) *m*, Adlige(r) *mf*.

aristocratic [,ærɪstə'krætɪk] *adj (lit, fig)* aristokratisch, adlig; *(fig also)* vornehm.

arithmetic [ə'rɪθmətɪk] *n* Rechnen *nt*. **could you check my** ~? kannst du das mal nachrechnen?

ark [ɑːk] *n* Arche *f*. **Noah's** ~ die Arche Noah.

arm¹ [ɑːm] *n* **(a)** Arm *m*. **under one's** ~ unter dem *or* unterm Arm; **to take sb in one's** ~**s** jdn in die Arme nehmen; **to put one's** ~**s around sb** jdn umarmen; ~ **in** ~ Arm in Arm; *(fig: linked)* eingehakt, untergehakt; **to keep sb at** ~**'s length** *(fig)* jdn auf Distanz halten; **with open** ~**s** mit offenen Armen; **within** ~**'s reach** in Reichweite. **(b)** *(sleeve)* Arm, Ärmel *m*; *(of river)* (Fluß)arm

m; *(of armchair)* (Arm)lehne *f*; *(of record player)* Tonarm *m*.

arm² **1** *vt person, nation etc* bewaffnen. **to** ~ **sth with sth** etw mit etw ausrüsten; **to** ~ **oneself with sth** *(lit, fig)* sich mit etw bewaffnen; *(fig: non-aggressively)* sich mit etw wappnen; **he came** ~**ed with an excuse** er hatte eine Ausrede parat. **2** *vi* aufrüsten. **to** ~ **for war** zum Krieg rüsten.

armament ['ɑːmənənt] *n* **(a)** ~**s** *pl (weapons)* Ausrüstung *f*. **(b)** *(preparation)* Aufrüstung *f* no *pl*.

armchair [,ɑːm'tʃɛəʳ] *n* Sessel, Lehnstuhl *m*.

armed [ɑːmd] *adj* bewaffnet.

armed: ~ **forces** *pl* Streitkräfte *pl*; ~ **robbery** bewaffneter Raubüberfall.

armful ['ɑːmfʊl] *n* Armvoll *m no pl*, Ladung *f (col)*.

armistice ['ɑːmɪstɪs] *n* Waffenstillstand *m*.

armour, *(US)* **armor** ['ɑːməʳ] *n* **(a)** Rüstung *f*; *(of animal)* Panzer *m*. **suit of** ~ Rüstung *f*. **(b)** *(no pl: steel plates)* Panzerplatte(n *pl*) *f*. **(c)** *(vehicles)* Panzerfahrzeuge *pl*.

armoured ['ɑːməd] *adj* division Panzer-. ~ **car** Panzerwagen.

armour: ~**-piercing** *adj* panzerbrechend; ~**-plated** *adj* gepanzert.

armoury, *(US)* **armory** ['ɑːmərɪ] *n* Arsenal, Waffenlager *nt*; *(US: factory)* Munitionsfabrik *f*.

arm: ~**pit** *n* Achselhöhle *f*; ~**rest** *n* Armlehne *f*.

arms [ɑːmz] *npl* **(a)** *(weapons)* Waffen *pl*. **to be up in** ~ *(about sth) (fig col)* (über etw acc) empört sein; ~ **race** Wettrüsten *nt*. **(b)** *(Her)* Wappen *nt*.

army ['ɑːmɪ] **1** *n (a)* Armee *f*, Heer *nt*. **to join the** ~ zum Militär gehen. **(b)** *(fig)* Heer *nt*. **(c)** *(division)* Armee(korps *nt*) *f*. **2** *attr* Militär-; *discipline* militärisch; *life, slang* Soldaten-. ~ **officer** Offizier *m* (in der Armee).

aroma [ə'rəʊmə] *n* Duft *m*, Aroma *nt*.

aromatic [,ærəʊ'mætɪk] *adj* aromatisch.

arose [ə'rəʊz] *pret of* **arise.**

around [ə'raʊnd] **1** *adv* herum, rum *(col)*. **with gardens all** ~ mit Gärten ringsherum; **I looked all** ~ ich sah mich nach allen Seiten um; **books were lying all** ~ überall lagen Bücher herum; **for miles** ~ meilenweit im Umkreis; **is he** ~? ist er da?; **he's been** ~! der kennt sich aus!; **it's been** ~ **for ages** das ist schon uralt; **see you** ~! *(col)* bis bald! **2** *prep* **(a)** *(movement, position)* um (+*acc*); *(in a circle)* um (+*acc*) ... herum. **(b)** *(in, through)* **to wander** ~ **the city** durch die Stadt spazieren; **to talk** ~ **a subject** um ein Thema herumreden. **(c)** *(approximately) (with date)* um (+*acc*); *(with time of day)* gegen (+*acc*); *(with weight, price)* etwa, um die *(col)*; *see also* **round.**

arousal [ə'raʊzəl] *n (sexual)* Erregung *f*.

arouse [ə'raʊz] *vt* **(a)** *(lit liter)* wecken. **(b)** *(excite)* erregen; *interest, suspicion etc also* (er)wecken.

arrange [ə'reɪndʒ] *vt* **(a)** *(order)* ordnen; *furniture, objects* aufstellen, hinstellen; *flowers* arrangieren; *room* einrichten. **(b)** *(fix)* vereinbaren, ausmachen; *details* regeln; *party* arrangieren, organisieren. **I have** ~**d for a car to pick you up** ich habe Ihnen einen Wagen bestellt, der Sie abholt; **if you could** ~ **to be there at five** wenn du es einrichten kannst, um fünf Uhr da zu sein; **that's easily** ~**d** das läßt sich leicht einrichten *or* arrangieren; **a meeting has been** ~**d for next month** nächsten Monat ist ein Treffen angesetzt; **good, that's** ~**d then** gut, das ist abgemacht!; **but you** ~**d to meet me!** aber du wolltest dich doch mit mir treffen! **(c)** *(Mus)* bearbeiten; *light music* arrangieren.

arrangement [ə'reɪndʒmənt] *n* **(a)** Anordnung *f*; *(of room)* Einrichtung *f*. **a floral** ~ ein Blumenarrangement *nt*. **(b)** *(agreement)* Vereinbarung *f*; *(to meet)* Verabredung *f*; *(esp shifty)* Arrangement *nt*. **a special** ~ eine Sonderregelung; **to have an** ~ **with sb** eine Regelung mit jdm getroffen haben; **to make an** ~ **with sb** eine

arrant Vereinbarung or Absprache mit jdm treffen; **to come to an ~ with sb** eine Regelung mit jdm treffen; (settle dispute) sich mit jdm einigen. **(c)** **~s** pl (plans) Pläne pl; (preparations) Vorbereitungen pl. **to make ~s for sth** für etw Vorbereitungen treffen; **to make ~s for sth to be done** veranlassen, daß etw getan wird. **(d)** (Mus) Bearbeitung f; (light music) Arrangement nt.

arrant ['ærənt] adj ~ **nonsense** barer Unsinn.

array [ə'reɪ] n (collection) Ansammlung f, Aufgebot nt. **in battle ~** in Kampfaufstellung.

arrears [ə'rɪəz] npl Rückstände pl. **to be in ~ with sth** mit etw im Rückstand sein.

arrest [ə'rest] 1 vt **(a)** festnehmen, verhaften. **(b)** (check) hemmen; sth unwanted (Ein)halt gebieten (+dat). 2 n Festnahme, Verhaftung f. **you are under ~** Sie sind festgenommen/verhaftet; **to put sb under ~** jdn festnehmen/verhaften.

arresting [ə'restɪŋ] adj (striking) atemberaubend; features markant.

arrival [ə'raɪvəl] n **(a)** (coming) Ankunft f no pl; (of person also) Kommen, Eintreffen nt no pl; (of train also, of goods, news) Eintreffen nt no pl. **on ~** bei Ankunft. **(b)** (person) new ~ Neuankömmling m; (at school also) Neue(r) mf.

arrive [ə'raɪv] vi ankommen, eintreffen (geh). **to ~ home** nach Hause kommen; **the great day ~d** der große Tag kam.

♦ **arrive at** vi +prep obj decision gelangen zu; price sich einigen auf (+acc).

arrogance ['ærəgəns] n Arroganz, Überheblichkeit f.

arrogant ['ærəgənt] adj arrogant, überheblich.

arrow ['ærəu] n (weapon, sign) Pfeil m.

arse [ɑːs] (col!) Arsch m (col!).

♦ **arse about** vi (col) rumblödeln (col).

arsenal ['ɑːsɪnl] n (Mil) (store) Arsenal nt; (factory) Waffen-/Munitionsfabrik f.

arsenic ['ɑːsnɪk] n Arsen nt.

arson ['ɑːsn] n Brandstiftung f.

arsonist ['ɑːsənɪst] n Brandstifter(in f) m.

art [ɑːt] n **(a)** Kunst f. **there's an ~ to it** das ist eine Kunst; **~s and crafts** Kunsthandwerk, Kunstgewerbe nt. **(b)** **~s** (Univ) Geisteswissenschaften pl; **Faculty of A~s** Philosophische Fakultät.

art college n Kunsthochschule f.

artefact (Brit), **artifact** ['ɑːtɪfækt] n Artefakt nt.

arteriosclerosis [ɑː'tɪərɪəusklɪ'rəusɪs] n (Med) Arteriosklerose, Arterienverkalkung f.

artery ['ɑːtərɪ] n **(a)** (Anat) Arterie f, Schlagader f. **(b)** (also traffic ~) Verkehrsader f.

artful ['ɑːtful] adj person, trick raffiniert, schlau.

art gallery n Kunstgalerie f.

arthritic [ɑː'θrɪtɪk] adj arthritisch. **she is ~** sie hat Arthritis.

arthritis [ɑː'θraɪtɪs] n Arthritis, Gelenkentzündung f.

artichoke ['ɑːtɪtʃəuk] n Artischocke f.

article ['ɑːtɪkl] n **(a)** (item) Gegenstand m; (in list) Posten m; (Comm) Ware f, Artikel m. **~s of clothing** Kleidungsstücke pl; **toilet ~s** Toilettenartikel pl. **(b)** (in newspaper) Artikel, Beitrag m; (encyclopedia entry) Eintrag m. **(c)** (of constitution) Artikel m; (of treaty, contract) Paragraph m. **~s of association** Gesellschaftsvertrag m. **(d)** (Gram) Artikel m. **(e)** (of articled clerk) **to be under ~s** (Rechts)referendar sein.

articulate [ɑː'tɪkjulɪt] 1 adj sentence, book leicht verständlich. **to be ~** sich gut or klar ausdrücken können; **clear and ~** klar und deutlich. 2 [ɑː'tɪkjuleɪt] vt (a) (pronounce) artikulieren. **(b)** (state) reasons, views etc darlegen. **(c)** **~d lorry** (Brit) or truck Sattelschlepper m.

articulation [ɑː,tɪkju'leɪʃən] n (of speech) Artikulation f.

artifact n = artefact.

artifice ['ɑːtɪfɪs] n (guile) List f no pl.

artificial [,ɑːtɪ'fɪʃəl] adj (lit, fig) künstlich; (pej) smile gekünstelt, unecht. **~ insemination** n künstliche Befruchtung; **~ limb** Prothese f.

artificiality [,ɑːtɪfɪʃɪ'ælɪtɪ] n **(a)** Künstlichkeit f. **(b)** (insincerity, unnaturalness) Gekünsteltheit f.

artillery [ɑː'tɪlərɪ] n (weapons, troops) Artillerie f.

artisan ['ɑːtɪzæn] n Handwerker m.

artist ['ɑːtɪst] n Künstler(in f) m.

artiste [ɑː'tiːst] n Künstler(in f) m; (circus ~) Artist(in f) m.

artistic [ɑː'tɪstɪk] adj künstlerisch; (tasteful) arrangements kunstvoll; (appreciative of art) kunstverständig. **~ temperament** Künstlertemperament nt; **she's very ~** sie ist künstlerisch veranlagt.

artistry ['ɑːtɪstrɪ] n (lit, fig) Kunst f.

artless ['ɑːtlɪs] adj unschuldig.

Art Nouveau ['ɑːnuː'vəu] n Jugendstil m.

art school n Kunsthochschule f.

arty ['ɑːtɪ] adj (+er) (col) Künstler-; type also, tie, clothes verrückt (col); person künstlerisch angehaucht (col); decoration, style auf Kunst getrimmt (col); film, novel geschmäcklerisch.

arty-farty ['ɑːtɪ'fɑːtɪ] adj (hum col) see **arty**.

as [æz, əz] 1 conj **(a)** (when, while) als; (two parallel actions) während als, indem. **~ he got older** mit zunehmendem Alter; **~ a child** als Kind. **(b)** (since) da. **~ it's late** da es spät ist. **(c)** (although) rich/big ~ he is und wenn er noch so reich/groß ist; **much ~ I admire her, ...** so sehr ich sie auch bewundere, ...; **try ~ he might** so sehr er sich auch bemüht/bemühte. **(d)** (manner) wie. ~ **I said** wie gesagt; **do ~ you like** machen Sie, was Sie wollen; **leave it ~ it is** lassen Sie es so; **he drinks enough ~ it is** er trinkt sowieso schon genug; **~ it were** sozusagen. **(e)** (phrases) **~ if** or **though** als ob; **he rose ~ if to go** er erhob sich, als wollte er gehen; **it isn't ~ if he didn't see me** schließlich hat er mich ja gesehen; **~ for him/ you** (und) was ihn/dich angeht; **~ from** or **of the 5th/now** vom Fünften an/von jetzt an.
2 adv ~ ... ~ ... so ... wie; **not ~ ...** ~ nicht so ... wie; **twice ~ old** doppelt so alt; **just ~ nice** genauso nett; **late ~ usual!** wie immer zu spät!; **is it ~ difficult ~ that?** ist das denn so schwierig?; **~ many/much ~ I could** so viele/ soviel ich (nur) konnte.
3 prep (in the capacity of) als. **to be employed as a ...** als ... angestellt sein.

asap = as soon as possible.

asbestos [æz'bestəs] n Asbest m.

ascend [ə'send] 1 vi (rise) aufsteigen. **in ~ing order** in aufsteigender Reihenfolge. 2 vt stairs hinaufsteigen; mountain, throne besteigen.

ascendancy [ə'sendənsɪ] n **to gain the ~ over sb** die Vorherrschaft über jdn gewinnen.

ascendant [ə'sendənt] n **to be in the ~** (Astrol) im Aszendenten stehen; (fig) im Aufstieg begriffen sein.

Ascension [ə'senʃən] n **the ~** (Christi) Himmelfahrt f; **~ Day** Himmelfahrt(stag m) nt.

ascent [ə'sent] n Besteigung f, Aufstieg m (of auf +acc).

ascertain [,æsə'teɪn] vt ermitteln, feststellen.

ascetic [ə'setɪk] 1 adj asketisch. 2 n Asket m.

asceticism [ə'setɪsɪzəm] n Askese f.

ascribe [ə'skraɪb] vt zuschreiben (sth to sb jdm etw).

ash¹ [æʃ] n (also ~ tree) Esche f.

ash² n **(a)** Asche f. **~es** Asche f; **to reduce sth to ~es** etw total or völlig niederbrennen; (in war) etw in Schutt und Asche legen. **(b)** (Cricket) **the A~es** Testmatch nt zwischen Australien und England.

ashamed [ə'ʃeɪmd] adj beschämt. **to be** or **feel ~ (of sb/sth)** sich schämen (für jdn/für or wegen etw); **it's nothing to be ~ of** deswegen braucht man sich nicht zu schämen; **... I'm ~ to say ...,**

muß ich leider zugeben; **you ought to be ~ (of yourself)** du solltest dich (was) schämen!
ashore [ə'ʃɔːʳ] *adv* an Land. **to go ~** an Land gehen.
ash: ~tray *n* Aschenbecher *m*; **A~ Wednesday** *n* Aschermittwoch *m*.
Asia ['eɪʃə] *n* Asien *nt*.
Asian ['eɪʃn] **1** *adj* asiatisch. **2** *n* Asiat(in *f*) *m*.
aside [ə'saɪd] **1** *adv* **(a)** *(with verb)* zur Seite, beiseite. **to turn ~** sich zur Seite drehen, sich abwenden *(esp fig)*. **(b)** *(Theat etc)* beiseite. **(c) ~ from außer; this criticism, ~ from being wrong, is** ... diese Kritik ist nicht nur falsch, sondern auch ... **2** *n (Theat)* **to say sth in an ~** etw beiseite sprechen.
asinine ['æsɪnaɪn] *adj* idiotisch.
ask [ɑːsk] **1** *vt* **(a)** *(inquire)* fragen; *question* stellen.
to ~ sb the way/the time/his opinion jdn nach dem Weg/der Uhrzeit/seiner Meinung fragen; **to ~ if** ... (nach)fragen, ob ...; **he ~ed me where I'd been** er fragte mich, wo ich gewesen sei; **if you ~ me** wenn du mich fragst; **don't ~ me!** *(col)* was weiß ich! *(col)*, da bin ich überfragt!; **I ~ you!** *(col)* ich muß schon sagen! **(b)** *(invite)* einladen; *(in dancing)* auffordern. **to ~ sb to lunch** jdn zum (Mittag)essen einladen; **to ~ sb in/up** jdn hereinbitten/heraufbitten. **(c)** *(request)* bitten *(sb for sth* jdn um etw*)*; *(require, demand)* verlangen *(sth of sb* etw von jdm*)*. **to ~ sb to do sth** jdn darum bitten, etw zu tun; **you don't ~ for much, do you?** *(iro)* sonst noch was? *(iro)*; **it's not ~ing much** das ist nicht (zu)viel verlangt. **(d)** *(Comm)* **price** verlangen, fordern. **~ing price** Verkaufspreis *m*.
2 *vi* **(a)** *(inquire)* fragen. **to ~ about sb/sth** sich nach jdm/etw erkundigen; **~ away!** frag nur!; **well may you ~** das fragt man sich mit Recht. **(b)** *(request)* bitten *(for sth* um etw*)*. **I'm not ~ing for sympathy** ich will kein Mitleid; **it's yours for the ~ing** du kannst es haben; **that's ~ing for trouble** das kann ja nicht gutgehen; **you ~ed for it** *(col)* du hast es ja so gewollt; **to ~ for Mr X** Herrn X verlangen.
♦ **ask after** *vi +prep obj* sich erkundigen nach. **tell her I was ~ing ~ her** grüß sie schön von mir.
♦ **ask out** *vt sep* einladen.
askance [ə'skɑːns] *adv* **to look ~ at sb** jdn entsetzt ansehen.
askew [ə'skjuː] *adv* schief.
asleep [ə'sliːp] *adj pred* **to be (fast) ~ (fest)** schlafen; **to fall ~** einschlafen *(also euph)*.
asparagus [əs'pærəgəs] *n no pl* Spargel *m*.
aspect ['æspekt] *n* **(a)** *(of question etc)* Aspekt *m*, Seite *f*. **(b)** *(of building)* **to have a southerly ~** Südlage haben.
aspersion [əs'pɜːʃən] *n*: **to cast ~s upon sb/sth** abfällige Bemerkungen über jdn/etw machen.
asphalt ['æsfælt] *n* Asphalt *m*.
asphyxia [æs'fɪksɪə] *n* Erstickung *f*.
asphyxiate [æs'fɪksɪeɪt] *vti* ersticken. **to be ~d** ersticken.
aspic ['æspɪk] *n (Cook)* Aspik, Gelee *m or nt*.
aspiration [,æspə'reɪʃən] *n* Ziel, Bestreben *nt*.
aspire [ə'spaɪəʳ] *vi* **to ~ to sth** nach etw streben; **~ to do sth** danach streben, etw zu tun.
aspirin ['æsprɪn] *n* Kopfschmerztablette *f*.
aspiring [ə'spaɪərɪŋ] *adj* aufstrebend.
ass[1] [æs] *(lit, fig col)* Esel *m*.
ass[2] *n (US col)* = **arse**.
assail [ə'seɪl] *vt (lit, fig)* angreifen; *(fig: with questions etc)* überschütten, bombardieren.
assailant [ə'seɪlənt] *n* Angreifer(in *f*) *m*.
assassin [ə'sæsɪn] *n* Attentäter(in *f*), Mörder(in *f*) *m*.
assassinate [ə'sæsɪneɪt] *vt* ein Attentat *or* einen Mordanschlag verüben auf *(+acc)*. **JFK was ~d in Dallas** JFK wurde in Dallas ermordet.
assassination [ə,sæsɪ'neɪʃən] *n* (geglücktes) Attentat, (geglückter) Mordanschlag *(of* auf

+*acc)*. **~ attempt** Attentat *nt*; **to plan an ~ ein** Attentat planen.
assault [ə'sɔːlt] **1** *n* **(a)** *(Mil)* Sturm(angriff) *m (on* auf *+acc)*; *(fig)* Angriff *m (on gegen)*. **(b)** *(Jur)* Körperverletzung *f*. **~ and battery** Körperverletzung *f*; **indecent/sexual ~** Notzucht *f*. **2** *vt* angreifen; *(Jur)* tätlich werden gegen; *(sexually)* herfallen über *(+acc)*; *(rape)* sich vergehen an *(+dat)*.
assemble [ə'sembl] **1** *vt* zusammenbauen; *car, machine etc also* montieren. **2** *vi* sich versammeln.
assembly [ə'semblɪ] *n* **(a)** *(gathering)* Versammlung *f*. **(b)** *(Sch)* Morgenandacht *f*; Versammlung *f*. **(c)** *(putting together)* Zusammenbau *m*; *(of machine, cars also)* Montage *f*.
assembly: ~ hall *n (Sch)* Aula *f*; **~ line** *n* Montageband *nt*.
assent [ə'sent] **1** *n* Zustimmung *f*. **2** *vi* **to ~ to sth** einer Sache *(dat)* zustimmen.
assert [ə'sɜːt] *vt* **(a)** *(declare)* behaupten; *one's innocence* beteuern. **(b)** **to ~ one's authority** seine Autorität geltend machen; **to ~ one's rights** sein Recht behaupten; **to ~ oneself** sich behaupten *or* durchsetzen *(over* gegenüber*)*.
assertion [ə'sɜːʃən] *n* Behauptung *f*.
assertive [ə'sɜːtɪv] *adj* bestimmt.
assess [ə'ses] *vt* **(a)** einschätzen; *proposal, advantages* abwägen. **(b)** *property* schätzen; *person (for tax purposes)* veranlagen *(at* mit*)*; *tax* festsetzen *(at* auf *+acc)*; *damages* schätzen *(at* auf *+acc)*.
assessment [ə'sesmənt] *n see vt* **(a)** Einschätzung *f*; Abwägen *nt*. **what's your ~ of the situation?** wie beurteilen Sie die Lage? **(b)** Schätzung *f*; Veranlagung *f*. **(c)** Festsetzung *f*; Schätzung *f*.
assessor [ə'sesəʳ] *n* Schätzer *m*.
asset ['æset] *n* **(a)** *usu pl* Vermögenswert *m*; *(on balance sheet)* Aktivposten *m*. **~s** Vermögen *nt*; *(on balance sheet)* Aktiva *pl*; **~ stripping** *Aufkauf von finanziell gefährdeten Firmen und anschließender Verkauf ihrer Vermögenswerte*. **(b)** *(fig)* **to be an ~** zu vorteilhaft sein für; **the new man is an ~ to the company** der neue Mann ist ein Gewinn für die Firma.
assiduous [ə'sɪdjuəs] *adj* gewissenhaft.
assign [ə'saɪn] *vt* **(a)** *(allot)* zuweisen, zuteilen *(to sb* jdm*)*; *(Jur)* übertragen *(to sb* jdm*)*; *room* bestimmen *(to* für*)*; *meaning* zuordnen *(to* dat*)*; *(attribute)* novel, play, music zuschreiben *(to* dat*)*. **she was ~ed to this school** sie wurde an diese Schule berufen.
assignation [,æsɪg'neɪʃən] *n (lovers')* Rendezvous *nt*.
assignment [ə'saɪnmənt] *n* **(a)** *(task)* Aufgabe *f*. **(b)** *(to post etc)* Berufung *f*. **(c)** *(Jur)* Übertragung *f*.
assimilate [ə'sɪmɪleɪt] *vt food, knowledge* aufnehmen; *(fig: into society etc also)* integrieren.
assimilation [ə,sɪmɪ'leɪʃən] *n see vt* Aufnahme *f*; Integration *f*. **his powers of ~** seine geistige Aufnahmefähigkeit.
assist [ə'sɪst] **1** *vt* helfen *(+dat)*; *(act as an assistant to)* assistieren *(+dat)*. **to ~ sb in doing or to do sth** jdm helfen, etw zu tun. **2** *vi* helfen. **to ~ with** sth bei etw helfen.
assistance [ə'sɪstəns] *n* Hilfe *f*. **to come to sb's ~** jdm zu Hilfe kommen; **can I be of any ~?** kann ich irgendwie behilflich sein?
assistant [ə'sɪstənt] **1** *n* Assistent(in *f*) *m*; *(Brit: shop ~)* Verkäufer(in *f*) *m*. **2** *adj attr manager etc* stellvertretend.
associate [ə'səʊʃɪɪt] **1** *n (colleague)* Kollege *m*, Kollegin *f*; *(Comm)* Partner *m*; *(accomplice)* Komplize *m*, Komplizin *f*; *(of a society)* außerordentliches Mitglied. **~ professor** *n (US)* außerordentlicher Professor. **2** [ə'səʊʃɪeɪt] *vt* assoziieren *(also Psych)*. **to ~ oneself with sb/sth** sich jdm/

einer Sache anschließen; **to be** ~**d with sb/sth** mit jdm/einer Sache in Verbindung gebracht *or* assoziiert werden; **I don't** ~ ... **with sport bei** ... denke ich nicht an Sport. **3** [ə'səʊʃɪeɪt] *vi* **to** ~ **with** verkehren mit.

association [ə,səʊsɪ'eɪʃən] *n* **(a)** *no pl (with people)* Verkehr, Umgang *m*; *(co-operation)* Zusammenarbeit *f*. **he has had a long** ~ **with the party** er hat seit langem Verbindung zur Partei. **(b)** *(organization)* Verband *m*. **(c)** *(mental)* Assoziation *f (with an +acc) (also Psych).* ~ **of ideas** Gedankenassoziation *f*.

assorted [ə'sɔːtɪd] *adj (mixed)* gemischt.

assortment [ə'sɔːtmənt] *n* Mischung *f*; *(of goods)* Auswahl *f (of an +dat)*, Sortiment *nt (of von)*.

assuage [ə'sweɪdʒ] *vt hunger etc* stillen, befriedigen; *anger etc* beschwichtigen; *grief* lindern.

assume [ə'sjuːm] *vt* **(a)** annehmen; *(presuppose)* voraussetzen. **let us** ~ **that you are right** nehmen wir an *or* gehen wir davon aus, Sie hätten recht; **assuming (that)** ... angenommen(, daß) ... **(b)** *power, control* übernehmen; *(forcefully)* ergreifen. **(c)** *(take on) title, guise, shape* annehmen. **under an** ~**d name** unter anderem Namen.

assumption [ə'sʌmpʃən] *n* **(a)** Annahme *f*; *(presupposition)* Voraussetzung *f*. **to go on the** ~ **that** ... von der Voraussetzung ausgehen, daß ...; **that's just an** ~ das ist nur eine Vermutung. **(b)** *(of power, role etc)* Übernahme *f*; *(forcefully)* Ergreifen *nt*. **(c)** *(of guise, false name etc)* Annahme *f*. **(d)** *(Eccl)* **the A~** Mariä Himmelfahrt *f*.

assurance [ə'ʃʊərəns] *n* **(a)** Versicherung *f*; *(promise also)* Zusicherung *f*. **he gave me his** ~ **that it would be done** er versicherte mir, daß es erledigt würde; **you have my** ~ **that** ... Sie können versichert sein, daß ... **(b)** *(self-confidence)* Sicherheit *f*. **(c)** *(confidence)* Zuversicht *f*. **(d)** *(esp Brit: life* ~*)* (Lebens)versicherung *f*.

assure [ə'ʃʊə'] *vt* **(a)** versichern *(+dat)*; *(promise)* zusichern *(+dat)*. **to** ~ **sb of sth** *(of love, willingness etc)* jdn einer Sache *(gen)* versichern; *(of service, support, help)* jdm etw zusichern; ... **I** ~ **you** ... das versichere ich Ihnen. **(b)** *(make certain of) success, happiness, future* sichern. **(c)** *(esp Brit: insure) life* versichern.

assured [ə'ʃʊəd] *adj* sicher; *income, future also* gesichert. **to rest** ~ **that** ... sicher sein, daß ...

asterisk ['æstərɪsk] *n* Sternchen *nt*.

astern [ə'stɜːn] *(Naut) adv* achtern; *(towards the stern)* nach achtern; *(backwards)* achteraus.

asteroid ['æstərɔɪd] *n* Asteroid *m*.

asthma ['æsmə] *n* Asthma *nt*.

asthmatic [æs'mætɪk] *n* Asthmatiker(in *f*) *m*.

astigmatism [æs'tɪgmətɪzəm] *n* Astigmatismus *m*.

astonish [ə'stɒnɪʃ] *vt* erstaunen, überraschen. **I was** ~**ed to learn that** ... ich war sehr erstaunt, als ich hörte, daß ...

astonishing [ə'stɒnɪʃɪŋ] *adj* erstaunlich.

astonishingly [ə'stɒnɪʃɪŋlɪ] *adv* erstaunlich. ~ **(enough)** erstaunlicherweise.

astonishment [ə'stɒnɪʃmənt] *n* Erstaunen *nt (at über +acc)*. **look of** ~ erstaunter Blick; **she looked at me in** ~ sie sah mich erstaunt an; **to my** ~ zu meinem Erstaunen.

astound [ə'staʊnd] *vt* in Erstaunen versetzen. **to be** ~**ed (at)** höchst erstaunt sein *(über +acc)*.

astounding [ə'staʊndɪŋ] *adj* erstaunlich.

astray [ə'streɪ] *adj* verloren. **to go** ~ *(person) (lit)* vom Weg abkommen; *(fig: morally)* auf Abwege geraten; *(letter, object)* verlorengehen; **to lead sb** ~ *(fig)* jdn vom rechten Weg abbringen; *(mislead)* jdn irreführen.

astride [ə'straɪd] *prep* rittlings auf.

astrologer [əs'trɒlədʒə'] *n* Astrologe *m*, Astrologin *f*.

astrology [əs'trɒlədʒɪ] *n* Astrologie *f*.

astronaut ['æstrənɔːt] *n* Astronaut(in *f*) *m*.

astronomer [əs'trɒnəmə'] *n* Astronom(in *f*) *m*.

astronomical [,æstrə'nɒmɪkəl] *adj (fig also* **astronomic)** astronomisch.

astronomy [əs'trɒnəmɪ] *n* Astronomie *f*.

astrophysics [,æstrəʊ'fɪzɪks] *n sing* Astrophysik *f*.

astute [ə'stjuːt] *adj* schlau; *remark also* scharfsinnig; *mind* scharf.

astuteness [əs'tjuːtnɪs] *n see adj* Schlauheit *f*; Scharfsinnigkeit *f*; Schärfe *f*.

asylum [ə'saɪləm] *n* **(a)** **to ask for (political)** ~ um *(politisches)* Asyl bitten. **(b)** *(lunatic* ~*)* (Irren)anstalt *f*.

asymmetric(al) [,eɪsɪ'metrɪk(əl)] *adj* asymmetrisch.

at [æt] *prep* **(a)** *(position)* an *(+dat)*, bei *(+dat)*; *(with place)* in *(+dat)*. ~ **the window/corner** am *or* beim Fenster/an der Ecke; ~ **university/school/the hotel/the zoo** an *or* auf der Universität/in der Schule/im Hotel/im Zoo; ~ **my brother's** bei meinem Bruder; ~ **a party auf** *or* bei einer Party; ~ **the station** am Bahnhof.
  (b) *(direction)* **to aim/point** *etc* ~ **sb/sth auf** jdn/etw zielen/zeigen *etc*; **to look/growl** *etc* ~ **sb** jdn ansehen/anknurren *etc*.
  (c) *(time, frequency, order)* ~ **ten o'clock** um zehn Uhr; ~ **night** bei Nacht; ~ **Christmas/Easter** zu Weihnachten/Ostern; ~ **your age/16** in deinem Alter/mit 16; **three** ~ **a time** drei auf einmal; ~ **the start/end of sth** am Anfang/am Ende einer Sache.
  (d) *(activity)* ~ **play/work** beim Spiel/bei der Arbeit; **good/bad/an expert** ~ **sth** gut/schlecht/ein Experte in etw *(dat)*; **while we are** ~ **it** *(col)* wenn wir schon mal dabei sind.
  (e) *(as a result of, upon)* auf *(+acc)* ... *(hin).* ~ **his request** auf seine Bitte *(hin)*; ~ **her death** bei ihrem Tod; ~ **that/this he left the room** daraufhin verließ er das Zimmer.
  (f) *(cause: with)* delighted *etc* über *(+acc)*.
  (g) *(rate, value, degree)* ~ **50 km/h** mit 50 km/h; ~ **50p a pound** für 50 Pence pro Pfund; ~ **5% interest** zu 5% Zinsen; **when the temperature is** ~ **90** wenn die Temperatur auf 90° ist.

ate [et, eɪt] *pret of* **eat.**

atheism ['eɪθɪɪzəm] *n* Atheismus *m*.

atheist ['eɪθɪɪst] *n* Atheist(in *f*) *m*.

Athens ['æθɪnz] *n* Athen *nt*.

athlete ['æθliːt] *n* Athlet(in *f*) *m*; *(in track and field events)* Leichtathlet(in *f*) *m*. **he is a natural** ~ er ist der geborene Sportler; ~**'s foot** Fußpilz *m*.

athletic [æθ'letɪk] *adj* sportlich; *build* athletisch.

athletics [æθ'letɪks] *n sing or pl* Leichtathletik *f*. ~ **meeting** Leichtathletikwettkampf *m*.

Atlantic [ət'læntɪk] *n (also* ~ **Ocean)** Atlantik *m*, Atlantischer Ozean.

atlas ['ætləs] *n* Atlas *m*.

atmosphere ['ætməsfɪə'] *n (lit, fig)* Atmosphäre *f*. *(fig: of novel also)* Stimmung *f*.

atmospheric [,ætməs'ferɪk] *adj* atmosphärisch; *(full of atmosphere) description* stimmungsvoll.

atmospherics [,ætməs'ferɪks] *npl (Rad)* atmosphärische Störungen *pl*.

atom ['ætəm] *n* Atom *nt*. ~ **bomb** Atombombe *f*.

atomic [ə'tɒmɪk] *adj* atomar.

atomic *in cpds* Atom-; ~ **age** *n* Atomzeitalter *nt*; ~ **bomb** *n* Atombombe *f*.

atomizer ['ætəmaɪzə'] *n* Zerstäuber *m*.

atone [ə'təʊn] *vi* ~ **for sth** für etw sühnen *or* büßen.

atonement [ə'təʊnmənt] *n* Sühne, Buße *f*. **to make** ~ **for sth** für etw sühnen *or* Buße tun; **the A~** *(Eccl)* das Sühneopfer (Christi).

atrocious [ə'trəʊʃəs] *adj* grauenhaft.

atrocity [ə'trɒsɪtɪ] *n* Grausamkeit *f*; *(act also)* Greueltat *f*.

atrophy ['ætrəfɪ] **1** *n* Atrophie *f*; *(Med)* Schwund *m*. **2** *vi* verkümmern, schwinden.

attach [ə'tætʃ] *vt* **(a)** *(join)* festmachen, befestigen *(to an +dat).* **please find** ~**ed** ... beiliegend finden Sie ...; **is he/she** ~**ed?** ist er/sie schon vergeben? **(b) to be** ~**ed to sb/sth** *(be fond of)* an jdm/etw hängen. **(c)** *(attribute) value, importance* beimessen, zuschreiben *(to dat).*

attaché [ə'tæʃeɪ] *n* Attaché *m.* ~ **case** Aktenkoffer *m.*

attachment [ə'tætʃmənt] *n* **(a)** *(accessory)* Zusatzteil, Zubehörteil *nt.* **(b)** *(fig: affection)* Zuneigung *f (to zu).* **(c) he's (working) here on** ~ er ist *(vorübergehend)* hierher versetzt worden.

attack [ə'tæk] **1** *n* **(a)** *(Mil, Sport, fig)* Angriff *m (on* auf *+acc).* **to be under** ~ angegriffen werden; *(fig also)* unter Beschuß stehen; **to leave oneself open to** ~ Angriffsflächen bieten. **(b)** *(Med etc)* Anfall *m.* **2** *vt* **(a)** *(Mil, Sport, fig)* angreifen; *(from ambush, in robbery etc)* überfallen. **(b)** *(tackle) task, problem* in Angriff nehmen.

attacker [ə'tækəʳ] *n* Angreifer *m.*

attain [ə'teɪn] *vt rank, age* erreichen; *knowledge* erlangen; *happiness, power* gelangen zu.

attainment [ə'teɪnmənt] *n* **(a)** *(act)* Erreichen *nt; (of knowledge, happiness, prosperity, power)* Erlangen *nt.* **(b)** *(usu pl: accomplishment)* Fertigkeit *f.*

attempt [ə'tempt] **1** *vt* versuchen; *task* sich versuchen an *(+dat).* ~**ed murder** Mordversuch *m.* **2** *n* Versuch *m.* **an** ~ **on the record** ein Versuch, den Rekord zu brechen; **to make an** ~ **on sb's life** einen Anschlag auf jdn *or* jds Leben verüben; **he made no** ~ **to help us** er unternahm keinen Versuch, uns zu helfen; **at the first** ~ auf Anhieb, beim ersten Versuch.

attend [ə'tend] **1** *vt* **(a)** *classes, church, meeting* besuchen; *wedding, funeral* anwesend sein bei *(+dat).* **(b)** *(wait on) queen etc* bedienen. **2** *vi* **(a)** *(be present)* anwesend sein. **are you going to** ~? gehen Sie hin? **(b)** *(pay attention)* aufpassen.
♦ **attend to** *vi +prep obj (see to)* sich kümmern um; *(pay attention to) work etc* Aufmerksamkeit schenken *(+dat); customers* bedienen. **are you being** ~**ed** ~? werden Sie schon bedient?; **that's being** ~**ed** ~ das wird (bereits) erledigt.

attendance [ə'tendəns] *n* **(a)** Anwesenheit *f (at* bei). **regular** ~ **at school** regelmäßiger Schulbesuch. **(b)** *(number present)* Teilnehmerzahl *f.*

attendant [ə'tendənt] *n (in art galleries, museums)* Aufseher(in *f), Wärter(in *f) *m; (in public toilets)* Toilettenwart *m,* Toilettenfrau *f; (in swimming baths)* Bademeister(in *f) *m.*

attention [ə'tenʃən] *n* **(a)** *no pl* Aufmerksamkeit *f.* **to call** *or* **draw sb's** ~ **to sth** jdn auf etw *(acc)* aufmerksam machen; **to attract sb's** ~ jdm auffallen; *(by waving etc)* jdn auf sich *(acc)* aufmerksam machen; **to turn one's** ~ **to sb/sth** jdm/ einer Sache seine Aufmerksamkeit zuwenden; **to pay** ~/**no** ~ **to sb/sth** jdn/etw beachten/nicht beachten; **to pay** ~ **to the teacher** dem Lehrer zuhören; **to hold sb's** ~ jdn fesseln; **your** ~, **please** ich bitte um Aufmerksamkeit; *(over tannoy)* Achtung, Achtung!; **it has come to my** ~ **that** ... ich habe feststellen müssen, daß ...; **it has been brought to my** ~ **that** ... es ist mir zu Ohren gekommen, daß ...; **the bodywork needs a little** ~ an der Karosserie muß etwas getan werden. **(b)** ~**s** *pl (kindnesses)* Aufmerksamkeiten *pl.* **(c)** *(Mil)* **to stand at** ~ stillstehen; ~! stillgestanden! **(d)** *(Comm)* **for the** ~ **of** ... zu Händen von ...

attentive [ə'tentɪv] *adj* aufmerksam.

attenuating [ə'tenjueɪtɪŋ] *adj:* ~ **circumstances** mildernde Umstände.

attest [ə'test] *vt (certify)* bestätigen, bescheinigen; *signature also* beglaubigen.
♦ **attest to** *vi +prep obj* bezeugen.

attic [ˈætɪk] *n* Dachboden, Speicher *m; (lived-in)* Mansarde *f.* **in the** ~ auf dem (Dach)boden.

attire [ə'taɪəʳ] *n no pl* Kleidung *f.* **ceremonial** ~

Festtracht *f; (of priest)* Ornat *nt.*

attitude [ˈætɪtjuːd] *n (way of thinking)* Einstellung *f (to, towards* zu); *(way of acting, posture, manner)* Haltung *f (to, towards* gegenüber). **well, if that's your** ~ ja, wenn du so denkst.

attorney [ə'tɜːnɪ] *n (US: lawyer)* (Rechts)anwalt *m,* (Rechts)anwältin *f.* ~ **general** *(US) (of state government)* ≃ Generalstaatsanwalt *m; (of federal government)* ≃ Generalbundesanwalt *m; (Brit)* ≃ Justizminister *m.*

attract [ə'trækt] *vt (also Phys)* anziehen; *sb's attention* auf sich *(acc)* ziehen *or* lenken; *(idea, music, place etc)* ansprechen. **she feels** ~**ed to him/to the idea** sie fühlt sich zu ihm hingezogen/die Idee reizt sie.

attraction [ə'trækʃən] *n* **(a)** *(Phys, fig)* Anziehungskraft *f.* **to lose its** ~ seinen Reiz verlieren; **to have an** ~ **for sb** eine Anziehungskraft *or* einen Reiz auf jdn ausüben; **the** ~ **of the city** der Reiz der Großstadt. **(b)** *(attractive thing)* Attraktion *f.*

attractive [ə'træktɪv] *adj* attraktiv, reizvoll.

attractiveness [ə'træktɪvnɪs] *n* Attraktivität *f; (of house, furnishing, view etc)* Reiz *m.*

attributable [ə'trɪbjʊtəbl] *adj* **to be** ~ **to sb/sth** jdm/einer Sache zuzuschreiben sein.

attribute [ə'trɪbjuːt] **1** *vt* **to** ~ **sth to sb** *play, remark etc* jdm etw zuschreiben; *intelligence, feelings etc* jdm etw zusprechen; **to** ~ **sth to sth** *success, accident etc* etw auf etw *(acc)* zurückführen. **2** [ˈætrɪbjuːt] *n (quality)* Merkmal *nt,* Eigenschaft *f.*

attributive [ə'trɪbjutɪv] *(Gram) adj* attributiv.

attrition [ə'trɪʃən] *n* Zermürbung *f.* **war of** ~ *(Mil)* Zermürbungskrieg *m.*

aubergine [ˈəʊbəʒiːn] *n (Brit)* Aubergine *f.*

auburn [ˈɔːbən] *adj hair* rotbraun, rostrot.

auction [ˈɔːkʃən] **1** *n* Auktion, Versteigerung *f.* **2** *vt (also* ~ **off)** versteigern.

auctioneer [ˌɔːkʃəˈnɪəʳ] *n* Auktionator *m.*

audacious [ɔː'deɪʃəs] *adj* **(a)** *(impudent)* dreist, unverfroren. **(b)** *(bold)* kühn.

audacity [ɔː'dæsɪtɪ] *n* **(a)** *(impudence)* **to have the** ~ **to do sth** die Dreistigkeit *or* Unverfrorenheit besitzen, etw zu tun. **(b)** *(boldness)* Kühnheit *f.*

audible [ˈɔːdɪbl] *adj* hörbar, (deutlich) vernehmbar. **she was hardly** ~ man konnte sie kaum hören.

audience [ˈɔːdɪəns] *n* **(a)** Publikum *nt no pl; (Theat, TV also)* Zuschauer *pl; (of speaker also)* Zuhörer *pl; (Rad, Mus also)* Zuhörerschaft *f.* **(b)** *(formal interview)* Audienz *f.*

audio [ˈɔːdɪəʊ] *adj attr* Audio-.

audio: ~ **typist** *n* Phonotypistin *f;* ~**-visual** *adj* audiovisuell.

audit [ˈɔːdɪt] **1** *n* Buchprüfung *f.* **2** *vt* prüfen.

audition [ɔː'dɪʃən] **1** *n* Vorsprechprobe *f; (Mus)* Probespiel *nt; (of singer)* Vorsingen *nt.* **2** *vt* vorsprechen/vorspielen/vorsingen lassen.

auditor [ˈɔːdɪtəʳ] *n* Wirtschaftsprüfer *m.*

auditorium [ˌɔːdɪˈtɔːrɪəm] *n* Auditorium *or* Zuschauerraum *m; (in theatre, cinema)* Zuschauerraum *m.*

au fait [ˌəʊˈfeɪ] *adj* vertraut.

augment [ɔːg'ment] **1** *vt* vermehren; *income also* vergrößern. **2** *vi* zunehmen.

augur [ˈɔːgəʳ] *vi* **to** ~ **well/ill** etwas Gutes/nichts Gutes verheißen.

august [ɔː'gʌst] *adj* illuster; *occasion* erhaben.

August [ˈɔːgəst] *n* August *m; see* **September.**

aunt [ɑːnt] *n* Tante *f.*

auntie, aunty [ˈɑːntɪ] *n (col)* Tante *f.*

au pair [ˌəʊˈpeəʳ] *n, pl* - **-s** *(also* ~ **girl)** Au-pair(-Mädchen) *nt.*

aura [ˈɔːrə] *n* Aura *f (geh),* Ausstrahlung *f.* **she has an** ~ of ... sie strahlt ... aus.

auspices [ˈɔːspɪsɪz] *npl* **under the** ~ **of** unter der Schirmherrschaft *(+gen).*

auspicious [ɔːs'pɪʃəs] *adj* günstig; *start* vielversprechend. **an** ~ **occasion** ein feierlicher Anlaß.

Aussie ['ɒzɪ] *(col)* Australier(in *f*) *m.*

austere [ɒs'tɪə^r] *adj* streng; *way of life also* asketisch; *room* schmucklos.

austerity [ɒs'terɪtɪ] *n* **(a)** *(severity)* Strenge *f*; *(simplicity)* strenge Einfachheit, Schmucklosigkeit *f*. **(b)** *(hardship)* **after the ~ of the war years** nach den Entbehrungen der Kriegsjahre; **a life of ~** ein Leben der Entsagung; **~ measures** Sparmaßnahmen *pl.*

Australasia [ˌɔːstrə'leɪsjə] *n* Australien und Ozeanien *nt.*

Australia [ɒs'treɪlɪə] *n* Australien *nt.*

Australian [ɒs'treɪlɪən] **1** *n* Australier(in *f*) *m.* **2** *adj* australisch.

Austria ['ɒstrɪə] *n* Österreich *nt.*

Austrian ['ɒstrɪən] **1** *n* Österreicher(in *f*) *m*; *(dialect)* Österreichisch *nt.* **2** *adj* österreichisch.

authentic [ɔː'θentɪk] *adj* echt; *document etc* authentisch; *claim* berechtigt.

authenticate [ɔː'θentɪkeɪt] *vt* bestätigen; *signature, document* beglaubigen; *manuscript, work of art* für echt befinden.

authenticity [ˌɔːθen'tɪsɪtɪ] *n* Echtheit, Authentizität *(geh) f*; *(of claim to title)* Berechtigung *f.*

author ['ɔːθə^r] *n* Autor(in *f*), Schriftsteller(in *f*) *m*; *(of report, pamphlet)* Verfasser(in *f*) *m*; *(fig)* Urheber(in *f*) *m.*

authoritarian [ˌɔːθɒrɪ'teərɪən] *adj* autoritär.

authoritative [ɔː'θɒrɪtətɪv] *adj* **(a)** *(commanding)* bestimmt, entschieden. **(b)** *(definitive)* maßgeblich, maßgebend.

authority [ɔː'θɒrɪtɪ] *n* **(a)** *(power)* Autorität *f*; *(right, entitlement)* Befugnis *f*; *(specifically delegated power)* Vollmacht *f*; *(permission)* Erlaubnis *f.* **people who are in ~** Menschen, die Autorität haben; **the person in ~** der Zuständige or Verantwortliche; **to be in** or **have ~ over sb** jdm übergeordnet sein; **on one's own ~** auf eigene Verantwortung; **by what ~ do you claim the right to ...?** mit welcher Berechtigung verlangen Sie, daß ...?; **to have the ~ to do sth** berechtigt or befugt sein, etw zu tun; **to do sth on sb's ~** etw in jds Auftrag *(dat)* tun; **to have** or **carry (great) ~** viel gelten *(with bei)*; **to speak/ write with ~** mit Sachkenntnis sprechen/ schreiben.

(b) *(also pl: ruling body)* Behörde *f*; *(body of people)* Verwaltung *f*; **the authorities** die Behörden *pl*; **the university authorities** die Universitätsverwaltung; **the local ~** die Gemeinde-/Stadtverwaltung.

(c) *(expert)* Autorität *f*, Fachmann *m (on auf dem Gebiet +gen)*; *(definitive book etc)* (anerkannte) Autorität; *(source)* Quelle *f.* **to have sth on good ~** etw aus zuverlässiger Quelle wissen; **this book is the ~ on** spelling dieses Buch ist maßgebend für die Rechtschreibung.

authorization [ˌɔːθəraɪ'zeɪʃən] *n* Genehmigung *f*; *(delegated authority)* Vollmacht *f*; *(right)* Recht *nt.*

authorize ['ɔːθəraɪz] *vt* **(a)** *(empower)* berechtigen, ermächtigen. **to be ~d to do sth** *(have right)* das Recht haben, etw zu tun; **he was specially ~d to ...** er hatte eine Sondervollmacht, zu ... **(b)** *(permit)* genehmigen; *money, claim etc* bewilligen; *translation, biography etc* autorisieren. **the A~d Version** englische Bibelfassung von 1611.

autistic [ɔː'tɪstɪk] *adj* autistisch.

auto ['ɔːtəu] *n (US)* Auto *nt*, Pkw *m.*

auto- ['ɔːtəu] *pref* auto-, Auto-.

autobiography [ˌɔːtəubaɪ'ɒgrəfɪ] *n* Autobiographie *f.*

autocratic [ˌɔːtəu'krætɪk] *adj* autokratisch.

autocue ['ɔːtəukjuː] *n (Brit TV)* Neger *m.*

autograph ['ɔːtəgrɔːf] **1** *n* Autogramm *nt.* **2** *vt* signieren.

automat ['ɔːtəmæt] *n (US)* Automatenrestaurant *nt.*

automate ['ɔːtəmeɪt] *vt* automatisieren.

automatic [ˌɔːtə'mætɪk] **1** *adj (lit, fig)* automatisch; **~ choke** Startautomatik *f*; **the ~ model** das Modell mit Automatik; **~ pilot** Autopilot *m.* **2** *n (car)* Automatikwagen *m.*

automatically [ˌɔːtə'mætɪkəlɪ] *adv* automatisch.

automation [ˌɔːtə'meɪʃən] *n* Automatisierung *f.*

automaton [ɔː'tɒmətən] *n, pl -s or automata* [-ətə] *(robot)* Roboter *m*; *(fig also)* Automat *m.*

automobile ['ɔːtəməbiːl] *n* Auto(mobil), Kraftfahrzeug *nt.*

autonomous [ɔː'tɒnəməs] *adj* autonom.

autonomy [ɔː'tɒnəmɪ] *n* Autonomie *f.*

autopilot [ˌɔːtəu'paɪlət] *n* Autopilot *m.*

autopsy ['ɔːtɒpsɪ] *n* Autopsie, Obduktion *f.*

autumn ['ɔːtəm] *(esp Brit)* **1** *n (lit, fig)* Herbst *m.* **in (the) ~** im Herbst. **2** *adj attr* Herbst-, herbstlich.

autumnal [ɔː'tʌmnəl] *adj* herbstlich, Herbst-.

auxiliary [ɔːg'zɪlɪərɪ] **1** *adj* Hilfs-; *(emergency also)* Not-; *(additional) engine, generator etc* Zusatz-. **~ nurse** Schwesternhelferin *f.* **2** *n* **(a)** *(Mil)* **auxiliaries** *pl* Hilfstruppe(n *pl*) *f.* **(b)** *(general: assistant)* Hilfskraft *f*, Helfer(in *f*) *m.* **(c)** *(~ verb)* Hilfsverb *nt.*

avail [ə'veɪl] **1** *vr* **to ~ oneself of sth** von etw Gebrauch machen. **2** *n* **of no ~** erfolglos, ohne Erfolg; **to no ~** vergebens, vergeblich.

availability [əˌveɪlə'bɪlɪtɪ] *n see adj* Erhältlichkeit *f*; Lieferbarkeit *f*; Verfügbarkeit *f*; *(presence: of secretarial staff, mineral ore etc)* Vorhandensein *nt.* **the market price is determined by ~** der Marktpreis richtet sich nach dem vorhandenen Angebot; **the ~ of jobs** *etc* das Angebot an Stellen *etc.*

available [ə'veɪləbl] *adj object* erhältlich; *(Comm) (from supplier also)* lieferbar; *(free) time, seats etc* frei; *(at one's disposal) means, resources etc* verfügbar. **to be ~** *(at one's disposal)* zur Verfügung stehen; *(can be reached)* erreichbar sein; *(for discussion)* zu sprechen sein; **to make sth ~ to sb** jdm etw zur Verfügung stellen; *(accessible) knowledge etc* jdm etw zugänglich machen; **the best dictionary ~, the best ~ dictionary** das beste Wörterbuch, das es gibt; **to try every ~ means (to achieve sth)** nichts unversucht lassen(, um etw zu erreichen).

avalanche ['ævəlɑːnʃ] *n (lit, fig)* Lawine *f.*

avant-garde ['ævɑ̃ː'gɑːd] **1** *n* Avantgarde *f.* **2** *adj* avantgardistisch.

avarice ['ævərɪs] *n* Habgier *f.*

avaricious [ˌævə'rɪʃəs] *adj* habgierig.

avenge [ə'vendʒ] *vt* rächen. **to ~ oneself on sb (for sth)** sich an jdm (für etw) rächen.

avenue ['ævənjuː] *n* **(a)** *(tree-lined)* Allee *f*; *(broad street)* Boulevard *m.* **(b)** *(fig)* **~s of approach** Verfahrensweisen; **to explore every ~** alle sich bietenden Wege prüfen.

average ['ævərɪdʒ] **1** *n* (Durch)schnitt *m.* **to do an ~ of 50 miles a day** durchschnittlich or im (Durch)schnitt 50 Meilen pro Tag fahren; **on ~** durchschnittlich, im (Durch)schnitt; *(normally)* normalerweise; **above/below ~** überdurchschnittlich, unter dem Durchschnitt. **2** *adj* durchschnittlich; *(ordinary)* Durchschnitts-; *(not good or bad)* mittelmäßig. **he's a ~ man, Mr A~** der Durchschnittsbürger; **he's a man of ~ height** er ist von mittlerer Größe. **3** *vt* **we ~d 80 km/h** wir sind durchschnittlich 80 km/h gefahren; **the factory ~s 500 cars a week** die Fabrik produziert im (Durch)schnitt 500 Autos pro Woche.

♦ **average out** *vi* durchschnittlich ausmachen *(at acc)*; *(balance out)* sich ausgleichen. **how does it ~ ~ on a weekly basis?** wieviel ist das durchschnittlich pro Woche?

averse [ə'vɜːs] *adj pred* **I am not ~ to a glass of wine** einem Glas Wein bin ich nicht abgeneigt.

aversion [ə'vɜːʃən] *n* Abneigung, Aversion *f (to*

gegen). ~ **therapy** Schocktherapie f.

avert [ə'vɜːt] vt **(a)** eyes abwenden. **(b)** (prevent) verhindern; suspicion ablenken.

aviary ['eɪvɪərɪ] n Vogelhaus nt.

aviation [ˌeɪvɪ'eɪʃən] n Luftfahrt f. the art of ~ die Kunst des Fliegens.

avid ['ævɪd] adj **(a)** (desirous) gierig (for nach). **(b)** (keen) begeistert, passioniert. **I am an ~ reader** ich lese leidenschaftlich gern.

avionics [ˌeɪvɪ'ɒnɪks] n sing Avionik f.

avocado [ˌævə'kɑːdəʊ] n, pl **-s** Avocado f.

avoid [ə'vɔɪd] vt vermeiden; damage, accident also verhüten; person, danger meiden, aus dem Weg gehen (+dat); obstacle ausweichen (+dat); difficulty, duty, truth umgehen. **in order to ~ being seen** um nicht gesehen zu werden; **I'm not going if I can possibly ~ it** wenn es sich irgendwie vermeiden läßt, gehe ich nicht hin.

avoidable [ə'vɔɪdəbl] adj vermeidbar. **if it's (at all) ~** wenn es sich (irgend) vermeiden läßt.

avoidance [ə'vɔɪdəns] n Vermeidung f.

avowed [ə'vaʊd] adj erklärt.

avuncular [ə'vʌŋkjʊləʳ] adj onkelhaft.

await [ə'weɪt] vt erwarten; future events, decision etc entgegensehen (+dat). **the long ~ed day** der langersehnte Tag.

awake [ə'weɪk] pret **awoke**, ptp **awoken** or **awaked** [ə'weɪkt] **1** vi (lit, fig) erwachen. **to ~ to sth** (fig) (realize) sich (dat) einer Sache (gen) bewußt werden. **2** vt wecken; (fig) suspicion, interest etc also erwecken. **3** adj pred (lit, fig) wach. **to be/stay ~** wach sein/bleiben; **to keep sb ~** jdn wachhalten; **wide ~** (lit, fig) hellwach; **to be ~ to sth** (fig) sich (dat) einer Sache (gen) bewußt sein.

awaken [ə'weɪkən] vti = **awake 1, 2.**

awakening [ə'weɪknɪŋ] n (lit, fig) Erwachen nt. **a rude ~** (lit, fig) ein böses Erwachen.

award [ə'wɔːd] **1** vt prize etc zusprechen (to sb jdm); (present) prize, degree, medal etc verleihen (to sb jdm); penalty, free kick geben. **to be ~ed damages** Schadenersatz zugesprochen bekommen. **2** n **(a)** (prize) Preis m; (for bravery) Auszeichnung f. **(b)** (Univ) Stipendium nt.

aware [ə'wɛəʳ] adj esp pred bewußt. **to be/become ~ of sb/sth** sich (dat) jds/einer Sache bewußt sein/werden; (notice) jdn bemerken/etw merken; **I was not ~ (of the fact) that ...** es war mir nicht klar or bewußt, daß ...; **are you ~ that ...?** ist dir eigentlich klar, daß ...?; **not that I am ~ (of)** nicht daß ich wüßte; **as far as I am ~** soviel ich weiß; **to make sb more ~/~ of sth** jds Bewußtsein wecken/jdm etw bewußt machen; **she's very ~ of language** sie ist sehr sprachbewußt.

awareness [ə'wɛənɪs] n Bewußtsein nt.

awash [ə'wɒʃ] adj pred decks, rocks etc überspült; cellar unter Wasser.

away [ə'weɪ] adv **1 (a)** weg. **three miles ~ (from here)** drei Meilen (entfernt) von hier; **to look ~** wegsehen; **~ we go!** los (geht's)! **(b)** (absent) fort, weg. **he's ~ from work (with a cold)** er fehlt (wegen einer Erkältung); **he's ~ in London** er ist in London; **when I have to be ~** wenn ich nicht da sein kann. **(c)** (Sport) **to play ~** auswärts spielen. **(d)** to **put/give ~** weglegen/weggeben; **to gamble/die ~** verspielen/verhallen; **to work/knit etc ~** vor sich hin arbeiten/stricken etc; **ask ~!** frag nur!, schieß los (col). **(e)** (col) **he's ~ again** (talking, giggling, drunk etc) es geht wieder los; **~ with you!** ach wo! **2** adj attr (Sport) **team** auswärtig, Gast-; match, win Auswärts-.

awe [ɔː] **1** n Ehrfurcht f. **to be** or **stand in ~ of sb** Ehrfurcht vor jdm haben; (feel fear) große Furcht vor jdm haben. **2** vt **~d by the beauty/silence** von der Schönheit/der Stille ergriffen.

awe-inspiring [ˈɔːɪnˌspaɪərɪŋ], **awesome** ['ɔːsəm] adj ehrfurchtgebietend.

awful ['ɔːfəl] adj (col) schrecklich, furchtbar. **you are ~!** du bist wirklich schrecklich!; **it's not an ~ lot better** das ist nicht viel besser.

awfully ['ɔːflɪ] adv (col) furchtbar (col), schrecklich (col).

awkward ['ɔːkwəd] adj **(a)** (difficult) schwierig; time, moment, angle, shape ungünstig. **(b)** (embarrassing) peinlich. **(c)** (embarrassed) verlegen; silence betreten. **the ~ age** das schwierige Alter; **to feel ~ in sb's company** sich in jds Gesellschaft (dat) nicht wohl fühlen. **(d)** (clumsy) unbeholfen.

awning ['ɔːnɪŋ] n (on window, of shop) Markise f.

awoke [ə'wəʊk] pret of **awake.**

awoken [ə'wəʊkən] ptp of **awake.**

awry [ə'raɪ] adj pred, adv schief. **to go ~** (plans etc) schiefgehen.

axe, (US) **ax** [æks] **1** n Axt f, Beil nt. **to have an/no ~ to grind** (fig) ein/kein persönliches Interesse haben. **2** vt plans, jobs streichen; person entlassen.

axiom ['æksɪəm] n Axiom nt.

axiomatic [ˌæksɪəʊ'mætɪk] adj axiomatisch.

axis ['æksɪs] n, pl **axes** ['æksiːz] Achse f. **the A~ (powers)** (Hist) die Achsenmächte pl.

axle ['æksl] n Achse f.

aye [aɪ] interj (esp Scot, dial) ja. **~, ~ Sir** jawohl, Herr Kapitän etc.

azalea [ə'zeɪlɪə] n Azalee f.

azure ['æʒəʳ] **1** n Azur(blau nt) m. **2** adj azurblau.

B

B, b [biː] n **(a)** B, b nt. **(b)** (Mus) H, h nt. ~ **flat/sharp** B, b nt/His, his nt.

BA = **Bachelor of Arts.**

babble ['bæbl] **1** n **(a)** Gemurmel nt; (of baby, excited person etc) Geplapper nt. ~ (of voices) Stimmengewirr nt. **(b)** (of stream) Murmeln nt no pl (liter). **2** vi **(a)** (person) plappern. **(b)** (stream) murmeln (liter).

baboon [bə'buːn] n Pavian m.

baby ['beɪbɪ] n **(a)** Kind, Baby nt; (of animal) Junge(s) nt. **to have a ~ ein Kind** or **Baby bekommen; I've known him since he was a ~ ich kenne ihn von Kindesbeinen an; the ~ of the family das Nesthäkchen; don't be such a ~! stell dich nicht so an!** (col); **he's a big ~ er ist ein großes Kind; to be left holding the ~ der Dumme sein** (col), **die Sache ausbaden müssen** (col); **to throw out the ~ with the bathwater das Kind mit dem Bade ausschütten. (b)** (col: girlfriend, boyfriend) Schatz m. **(c)** (esp US col: as address) Schätzchen nt (col); (man to man) Junge m.

baby in cpds **(a)** (for baby) Baby-, Säuglings-. **(b)** (little) Klein-. **(c)** (of animal) ~ **crocodile** Krokodiljunge(s) nt.

baby: ~ **boy** n Junge m; ~ **carriage** n (US) Kinderwagen m; ~ **clothes** npl Babywäsche f; ~ **face** n Kindergesicht nt; (of adult male) Milchgesicht nt; ~ **girl** nt Töchterchen nt; ~ **grand (piano)** n Stutzflügel m.

babyhood ['beɪbɪhʊd] n Säuglingsalter nt.

babyish ['beɪbɪʃ] adj kindisch.

baby: ~**-minder** n Tagesmutter f; ~**-sit** pret, ptp ~**-sat** vi babysitten; **she** ~**-sits for her sie geht bei ihr babysitten;** ~**-sitter** n Babysitter(in f) m.

bachelor ['bætʃələʳ] n **(a)** Junggeselle m. **(b)** (Univ) **B~ of Arts/Science** = Magister m der Geisteswissenschaften/Naturwissenschaften.

bachelor: ~ **flat** n Junggesellenwohnung f; ~ **girl** n Junggesellin f.

bacillus [bə'sɪləs] n, pl **bacilli** [bə'sɪlaɪ] Bazillus m.

back [bæk] **1** n **(a)** (of person, animal, book) Rücken m; (of chair also) (Rücken)lehne f. **with one's ~ to the engine** entgegen der Fahrtrichtung; **to break one's ~** (fig) sich abrackern; **we've broken the ~ of the job** wir sind mit der Arbeit übern Berg (col); **behind sb's ~** (fig) hinter jds Rücken (dat); **to put one's ~ into sth** (fig) bei etw Einsatz zeigen; **to put** or **get sb's ~ up** jdn gegen sich aufbringen; **to turn one's ~ on sb** (lit, fig) sich von jdm abwenden; **he's at the ~ of all the trouble** er steckt hinter dem ganzen Ärger; **get these people off my ~** (col) schaff mir diese Leute vom Hals! (col); **to have one's ~ to the wall** (fig) in die Enge getrieben sein; **I was pleased to see the ~ of them** (col) ich war froh, sie endlich los zu sein (col).

(b) (as opposed to front) Rück- or Hinterseite f; (of hand, dress) Rücken m; (of house, page, cheque) Rückseite f; (of material) linke Seite. **I know London like the ~ of my hand** ich kenne London wie meine Westentasche; **at the ~ of the book** hinten im Buch; **he drove into the ~ of me** er ist mir hinten reingefahren (col); **in the ~ (of a car)** hinten (im Auto); **one consideration was at the ~ of my mind** ich hatte dabei eine Überlegung im Hinterkopf; **there's one other worry at the ~ of my mind** da ist noch etwas, das mich beschäftigt; **at the ~ of beyond** am Ende der Welt, j.w.d. (hum).

(c) (Ftbl) Verteidiger m.

2 adj wheel, yard Hinter-; rent ausstehend.

3 adv zurück. ~ **and forth** hin und her; **to pay sth ~** etw zurückzahlen; **to come/go** ~ zurückkommen/-gehen; **there and** ~ hin und zurück; **I'll never go** ~ da gehe ich nie wieder hin; **a week** ~ vor einer Woche; **as far** ~ **as the 18th century** (dating back) bis zurück ins 18. Jahrhundert.

4 prep (US) ~ **of** hinter.

5 vt **(a)** (support) unterstützen. **I will** ~ **you** whatever you do egal, was du tust, ich stehe hinter dir. **(b)** (Betting) setzen auf (+acc). **(c)** (cause to move) car zurücksetzen. **he** ~**ed his car into the tree/garage** er fuhr rückwärts gegen den Baum/in die Garage.

6 vi (car, train) zurücksetzen. **the car** ~**ed into the garage** das Auto fuhr rückwärts in die Garage; **she** ~**ed into me** sie fuhr rückwärts in mein Auto.

♦ **back away** vi zurückweichen (from vor +dat).
♦ **back down** vi (fig) nachgeben, klein beigeben.
♦ **back on to** vi +prep obj hinten angrenzen an (+acc).
♦ **back out** vi **(a)** (car etc) rückwärts herausfahren. **(b)** (fig: of contract, deal etc) aussteigen (of, from aus) (col). **2** vt sep vehicle rückwärts herausfahren or -setzen.
♦ **back up** vi **(a)** (car etc) zurücksetzen. **to** ~ ~ **to sth** rückwärts an etw (acc) heranfahren. **(b)** (US: drains) **to have** ~**ed** ~ verstopft sein. **2** vt sep (support) unterstützen; (confirm) story bestätigen; (in discussion etc also) den Rücken stärken (+dat); claim, theory untermauern. **he can** ~ **me** ~ **in this** er kann das bestätigen.

back: ~**ache** n Rückenschmerzen pl; ~**bencher** n (esp Brit) Abgeordnete(r) mf (auf den hinteren Reihen im britischen Parlament); ~**bone** n (lit, fig) Rückgrat nt; ~**-breaking** adj äußerst anstrengend; ~**chat** n no pl Widerrede f; ~**cloth** n Hintergrund m; ~**comb** vt hair toupieren; ~ **copy** n alte Ausgabe; ~**date** vt (zu)rückdatieren; ~**dated** to May rückwirkend ab Mai; ~ **door** n (lit, fig) Hintertür f; ~**drop** n = ~**-cloth.**

backer ['bækəʳ] n **(a)** (supporter) his ~**s** (die,) ihn unterstützen. **(b)** (Comm) Geldgeber m.

back: ~**fire** n **1** n (Aut) Fehlzündung f. **2** vi **(a)** (Aut) Fehlzündung haben; **(b)** (col: plan etc) ins Auge gehen (col); **it** ~**fired on us** der Schuß ging nach hinten los (col); ~**gammon** n Backgammon nt; ~ **garden** n Garten m (hinterm Haus).

background ['bækgraʊnd] **1** n **(a)** (of painting etc, fig) Hintergrund m. **to stay in the** ~ sich im Hintergrund halten. **(b)** (educational etc) Werdegang m; (social) Verhältnisse pl; (family ~) Herkunft f no pl. **he comes from a** ~ **of poverty** er kommt aus ärmlichen Verhältnissen. **(c)** (of case, event, problem etc) Zusammenhänge, Hintergründe pl. **the** ~ **to the crisis** die Hintergründe der Krise. **2** cpds: ~ **information** Hintergrundinformationen pl; ~ **music** Musikuntermalung f; ~ **reading** Sekundärliteratur f.

back: ~**hand 1** *n (Sport)* Rückhand *f no pl; (one stroke)* Rückhandschlag *m;* **2** *adj stroke* Rückhand-; **3** *adv* mit der Rückhand; ~**handed** *adj compliment* zweifelhaft; *shot* Rückhand-; ~**hander** *n (col: bribe)* Schmiergeld *nt;* **to give sb a** ~**hander** jdn schmieren *(col).*
backing ['bækɪŋ] *n* **(a)** *(support)* Unterstützung *f.* **(b)** *(Mus)* Begleitung *f.* **(c)** *(for picture frame, for strengthening)* Rücken(verstärkung *f*) *m.*
back: ~**lash** *n (fig)* Gegenreaktion *f;* ~**log** *n* Rückstände *pl;* **I have a** ~**log of work** ich bin mit der Arbeit im Rückstand; ~ **number** *n (of paper)* alte Ausgabe *or* Nummer; ~**pack** *n* Rucksack *m;* ~ **pay** *n* Nachzahlung *f;* ~**-pedal** *vi (lit)* rückwärts treten; *(fig col)* einen Rückzieher machen; ~ **room** *n* Hinterzimmer *nt;* ~ **seat** *n* Rücksitz *m;* **to take a** ~ **seat** *(col)* sich zurückhalten; ~**seat driver** *n* **she is a terrible** ~**seat driver** sie redet beim Fahren immer rein; ~**side** *n (col)* Hinterteil *nt (col);* ~**-space** *vi (Typing)* zurücksetzen; ~**stage** *adv, adj* hinter den Kulissen; *(in dressing-room area)* in der Garderobe; ~ **street** *n* Seitensträßchen *nt;* **he comes from the** ~ **streets of Liverpool** er kommt aus dem ärmeren Teil von Liverpool; ~**-street abortionist** *n* Engelmacher(in *f*) *m (col);* ~**stroke** *n (Swimming)* Rückenschwimmen *nt;* ~ **to** ~ *adv* Rücken an Rücken; *(things)* mit den Rückenseiten aneinander; ~ **to front** *adv* verkehrt herum; *read* von hinten nach vorne; ~**-up 1** *n* Unterstützung *f;* **2** *adj troops* Hilfs-.
backward ['bækwəd] **1** *adj* **(a)** ~ **and forward movement** Vor- und Zurückbewegung *f;* **a** ~ **glance** ein Blick zurück. **(b)** *(fig)* **a** ~ **step/move** ein Schritt *m* zurück/eine (Zu)rückentwicklung. **(c)** *(retarded) child* zurückgeblieben; *region, country* rückständig. **2** *adv* = **backwards.**
backwards ['bækwədz] *adv* rückwärts. **to fall** ~ nach hinten fallen; **to walk** ~ **and forwards** hin und her gehen; **to bend over** ~ **to do sth** *(col)* sich *(dat)* ein Bein ausreißen, um etw zu tun *(col);* **I know it** ~ das kenne ich in- und auswendig.
back: ~**water** *n (lit)* Stauwasser *nt; (fig)* rückständiges Nest; **this town is a cultural** ~**water** kulturell gesehen ist diese Stadt tiefste Provinz; ~**yard** *n* **(a)** Hinterhof *m;* **(b)** *(US)* = ~ **garden.**
bacon ['beɪkən] *n* Speck *m.* ~ **and eggs** Eier mit Speck; **to save sb's** ~ *(col)* jds Rettung sein.
bacteria [bæk'tɪərɪə] *npl* Bakterien *pl.*
bacterial [bæk'tɪərɪəl] *adj* Bakterien-, bakteriell.
bacteriology [bæk,tɪərɪ'ɒlədʒɪ] *n* Bakteriologie *f.*
bad [bæd] *adj, comp* **worse,** *superl* **worst (a)** schlecht; *risk* hoch; *word* unanständig; *(immoral, wicked also)* böse; *(naughty, misbehaved)* unartig, ungezogen; *dog* böse. **you** ~ **boy!** du Lümmel!; **I didn't mean that word in a** ~ **sense** ich habe mir bei dem Wort nichts Böses gedacht; **to go** ~ schlecht werden; **to be** ~ **for sb/sth** schlecht für jdn/etw sein; **he's** ~ **at tennis** er spielt schlecht Tennis; **it would not be a** ~ **thing** das wäre nicht schlecht; **(that's) too** ~! *(indignant)* so was!; *(*~ *luck)* Pech!; **too** ~ **you couldn't make it** wirklich schade, daß Sie nicht kommen konnten. **(b)** *(serious) wound, situation* schlimm. **to have it** ~ **for sb** *(col)* schwer in jdn verknallt sein *(col);* **things are going from** ~ **to worse** es wird immer schlimmer. **(c)** *(in poor health, sick) stomach* krank; *leg, knee, hand* schlimm. **he/the economy is in a** ~ **way** es geht ihm schlecht/es steht schlecht mit der Wirtschaft; **to feel** ~ sich nicht wohl fühlen; **I feel** ~ mir geht es nicht gut; **how is he?** — **he's not so** ~ wie geht es ihm? — nicht schlecht. **(d)** *(regretful)* **I feel really** ~ **about not having told him** ich habe ein schlechtes Gewissen, daß ich ihm das nicht gesagt habe; **don't feel** ~ **about it** mach dir keine Gedanken (darüber).

baddie ['bædɪ] *n (col)* Schurke, Bösewicht *m.*
bade [beɪd] *pret of* **bid.**
badge [bædʒ] *n* Abzeichen *nt; (made of metal: women's lib, joke* ~ *etc)* Button *m,* Plakette *f.* ~ **of office** Dienstmarke *f.*
badger ['bædʒə^r^] **1** *n* Dachs *m.* **2** *vt* zusetzen (+*dat*).
badly ['bædlɪ] *adv* **(a)** schlecht. **the party went** ~ die Party war ein Reinfall *(col).* **(b)** *wounded, mistaken* schwer. ~ **beaten** *(Sport)* vernichtend geschlagen; *person* schwer verprügelt. **(c)** *(very much)* äußerst, sehr; *in debt, overdrawn* hoch. **to want sth** ~ etw unbedingt wollen; **he** ~ **needs a haircut** er muß dringend zum Friseur.
bad-mannered [,bæd'mænəd] *adj* unhöflich; *child also* ungezogen.
badminton ['bædmɪntən] *n* Federball *nt; (on court)* Badminton *nt.*
bad-tempered [,bæd'tempəd] *adj* schlechtgelaunt *attr.* **to be** ~ schlechte Laune haben; *(as characteristic)* ein reizbarer Mensch sein.
baffle ['bæfl] *vt (confound, amaze)* verblüffen; *(cause incomprehension)* vor ein Rätsel stellen. **a** ~**d look** ein verdutzter Blick; **it really** ~**s me how** ... es ist mir wirklich ein Rätsel, wie ...
baffling ['bæflɪŋ] *adj case* rätselhaft; *complexity* verwirrend; *mystery* unergründlich.
bag [bæg] *n* Tasche *f; (with drawstrings, pouch)* Beutel *m; (for school)* Schultasche *f; (made of paper, plastic)* Tüte *f; (sack)* Sack *m; (suitcase)* Reisetasche *f.* ~**s** *(Reise)*gepäck *nt;* **to be a** ~ **of bones** *(fig col)* nur Haut und Knochen sein *(col);* **it's in the** ~ *(fig col)* das ist gelaufen *(col);* ~**s under the eyes** *(black)* Ringe *pl* unter den Augen; *(of skin)* Tränensäcke *pl;* ~**s of** *(col: a lot)* jede Menge *(col);* **(old)** ~ *(pej col: woman)* (alte) Ziege *(pej col).*
baggage ['bægɪdʒ] *n (luggage)* (Reise)gepäck *nt.*
baggage: ~ **car** *n* Gepäckwagen *m;* ~ **checkroom** *n (US)* Gepäckaufbewahrung *f;* ~ **claim** *n* Gepäckausgabe *f.*
baggy ['bægɪ] *adj (+er) (ill-fitting)* (zu) weit; *skin* schlaff; *(out of shape) trousers, suit* ausgebeult; *jumper* ausgeleiert.
bagpipes (*pl*) ['bægpaɪp(s)] *n* Dudelsack *m.*
bag-snatcher ['bæg,snætʃə^r^] *n* Handtaschendieb *m.*
Bahamas [bə'hɑːməz] *npl* **die** ~ die Bahamas.
bail¹ [beɪl] *n (Jur)* Kaution *f.* **to stand** ~ **for sb** für jdn *(die)* Kaution stellen; **to grant** ~ **die** Freilassung gegen Kaution bewilligen; **to let sb out on** ~ jdn gegen Kaution freilassen.
♦ **bail out** *vt sep* **(a)** *(Jur)* gegen Kaution freibekommen. **(b)** *(fig)* aus der Patsche helfen (+*dat*) *col.*
bail² *vti* = **bale².**
bailiff ['beɪlɪf] *n* **(sheriff's)** ~ Amtsdiener *m; (for property)* Gerichtsvollzieher *m; (in court)* Gerichtsdiener *m; (on estate)* (Guts)verwalter *m.*
bait [beɪt] **1** *n (lit, fig)* Köder *m.* **to swallow the** *or* **rise to the** ~ *(lit, fig)* anbeißen. **2** *vt* **(a)** *hook, trap* mit einem Köder versehen. **(b)** *(torment) animal* (mit Hunden) hetzen; *person* quälen.
baize [beɪz] *n* Fries *m.* **green** ~ Billardtuch *nt.*
bake [beɪk] *vt* **(a)** *(Cook)* backen. ~**d beans** *pl* gebackene Bohnen *pl;* ~**d potatoes** *pl* in der Schale gebackene Kartoffeln *pl.* **(b)** *pottery, bricks* brennen; *(sun) earth* ausdörren.
baker ['beɪkə^r^] *n* Bäcker(in *f*) *m.* ~**'s (shop)** *(Brit)* Bäckerei *f;* ~**'s dozen** 13 (Stück).
bakery ['beɪkərɪ] *n* Bäckerei *f.*
baking ['beɪkɪŋ] *n* **(a)** *(Cook)* Backen *nt; (of earthenware)* Brennen *nt.*
baking: ~ **day** *n* Backtag *m;* ~ **dish** *n* Backform *f;* ~ **powder,** ~ **soda** *n* Backpulver *nt;* ~ **tin** *n* Backform *f.*
Balaclava [,bælə'klɑːvə] *n* Kapuzenmütze *f.*
balance ['bæləns] **1** *n* **(a)** *(apparatus)* Waage *f.* **to be** *or* **hang in the** ~ *(fig)* in der Schwebe sein. **(b)**

(counterpoise) Gegengewicht *nt (to* zu); *(fig also)* Ausgleich *m (to* für). **(c)** *(lit, fig: equilibrium)* Gleichgewicht *nt.* **to keep/lose one's** ~ das Gleichgewicht halten/verlieren; **to throw sb off (his)** ~ jdn aus dem Gleichgewicht bringen; **the** ~ **of power** das Gleichgewicht der Kräfte; **to strike the right** ~ den goldenen Mittelweg finden; **on** ~ *(fig)* alles in allem. **(d)** *(Comm, Fin: state of account)* Saldo *m; (with bank also)* Kontostand *m; (of company)* Bilanz *f.* ~ **carried forward** Saldoübertrag *m;* ~ **due** *(banking)* Soll *nt; (Comm)* Rechnungsbetrag *m;* ~ **of payments/ trade** Zahlungs-/Handelsbilanz *f.* **(e)** *(fig: remainder)* Rest *m.*
   2 *vt* **(a)** *(keep level, in equilibrium)* im Gleichgewicht halten; *(as trick)* ball *etc* balancieren; *(bring into equilibrium)* ins Gleichgewicht bringen. **(b)** *(weigh in the mind)* two solutions *(gegeneinander)* abwägen. **to** ~ **sth against sth** etw einer Sache *(dat)* gegenüberstellen. **(c)** *(equal, make up for)* ausgleichen. **(d)** *(Comm, Fin) account (add up)* abschließen; *(make equal)* ausgleichen. **to** ~ **the books** die Bilanz ziehen.
   3 *vi* **(a)** *(be in equilibrium)* Gleichgewicht halten; *(scales)* sich ausbalancieren. **he** ~**d on one foot** er balancierte auf einem Bein. **(b)** *(Comm, Fin: of accounts)* ausgeglichen sein. **the books don't** ~ **the books** die Abrechnung stimmt nicht.
♦ **balance out 1** *vt sep* ausgleichen. **they** ~ **each other** ~ sie halten sich die Waage; *(personalities)* sie gleichen sich aus. **2** *vi* sich ausgleichen.
balanced ['bælənst] *adj* ausgewogen; *personality* ausgeglichen.
balance sheet *n (Fin)* Bilanz *f.*
balancing trick ['bælənsɪŋ,trɪk] *n* Balancekunststück *m.*
balcony ['bælkənɪ] *n* **(a)** Balkon *m.* **(b)** *(Theat)* oberster Rang.
bald [bɔːld] *adj (+er)* **(a)** *person* kahl, glatzköpfig; *type* abgefahren. **he is** ~ er hat eine Glatze; **to go** ~ eine Glatze bekommen; ~ **patch** kahle Stelle. **(b)** *style, statement* knapp.
baldly ['bɔːldlɪ] *adv (fig: bluntly)* unverblümt.
baldness ['bɔːldnɪs] *n* **(a)** Kahlheit *f.* **(b)** *(of style, statement)* Knappheit *f.*
bale[1] [beɪl] *n (of hay)* Ballen *m.*
bale[2] *vti (Naut)* schöpfen.
♦ **bale out 1** *vi* **(a)** *(Aviat)* abspringen, aussteigen *(col) (of aus).* **(b)** *(Naut)* schöpfen. **2** *vt sep (Naut)* water schöpfen; *ship* ausschöpfen.
Balearic [,bælɪ'ærɪk] *adj* **the** ~ **Islands** die Balearen *pl.*
baleful ['beɪlfʊl] *adj (evil)* böse; *(sad)* traurig.
balk, baulk [bɔːk] *vi (person)* zurückschrecken *(at vor +dat); (horse)* scheuen *(at bei).*
Balkan ['bɔːlkən] **1** *adj* Balkan-. **2** *n* **the** ~**s** der Balkan, die Balkanländer *pl.*
ball[1] [bɔːl] *n* **(a)** Ball *m; (Billiards)* Kugel *f; (of wool, string)* Knäuel *m; (US: baseball)* Baseball *nt.* **to keep the** ~ **rolling** *(fig)* das Ganze in Gang halten; **to start** *or* **set the** ~ **rolling** *(fig)* den Stein ins Rollen bringen; **the** ~ **is with you** *or* **in your court** *(fig)* Sie sind am Ball *(col);* **to be on the** ~ *(fig col)* auf Zack *or* Draht sein *(col);* ~ **of the foot/thumb** Fuß-/Handballen *m.* **(b)** *(col!: testicle)* Ei *nt usu pl (col!).* ~**s!** *(nonsense)* red keinen Scheiß! *(col!).*
ball[2] *n (dance)* Ball *m.* **to have a** ~ *(col)* sich prima amüsieren *(col).*
ballad ['bæləd] *n (Mus, Liter)* Ballade *f.*
ballast ['bæləst] *n (Naut, Aviat, fig)* Ballast *m.*
ball: ~**-bearing** *n* Kugellager *nt;* ~**-cock** *n* Schwimmerhahn *m.*
ballerina [,bælə'riːnə] *n* Ballerina *f.*
ballet ['bæleɪ] *n* Ballett *nt.*
ballet: ~**-dancer** *n* Ballettänzer(in *f) m;* ~**shoe** *n* Ballettschuh *m.*
ballistic [bə'lɪstɪk] *adj* ballistisch. ~ **missile** Raketengeschoß *nt.*

ballistics [bə'lɪstɪks] *n sing* Ballistik *f.*
balloon [bə'luːn] *n* Ballon *m; (toy also)* Luftballon *m; (in cartoon)* Sprechblase *f.*
balloonist [bə'luːnɪst] *n* Ballonfahrer(in *f) m.*
ballot ['bælət] **1** *n* (geheime) Abstimmung. **to decide sth by** ~ über etw *(acc)* (geheim) abstimmen; **to take** *or* **hold a** ~ abstimmen. **2** *vt members* abstimmen lassen.
ballot: ~**-box** *n* Wahlurne *f;* ~**-paper** *n* Stimmzettel *m.*
ball: ~**park** *n (US)* Baseballstadion *nt;* ~**-point (pen)** *n* Kugelschreiber *m;* ~**room** *n* Ballsaal *m;* ~**room dancing** *n* Gesellschaftstänze *pl.*
balm [bɑːm] *n (lit, fig)* Balsam *m.*
balmy ['bɑːmɪ] *adj (+er) (fragrant)* wohlriechend; *(mild)* sanft. ~ **breezes** linde Lüfte *(geh).*
balsa ['bɔːlsə] *n (also* ~ **wood)** Balsa(holz) *nt.*
Baltic ['bɔːltɪk] *adj* Ostsee-. ~ **(Sea)** Ostsee *f;* **the** ~ **States** *(Hist)* das Baltikum.
balustrade [,bælə'streɪd] *n* Balustrade *f.*
bamboo [bæm'buː] *n* Bambus *m.*
bamboozle [bæm'buːzl] *vt (col) (baffle)* verblüffen; *(trick)* hereinlegen *(col).*
ban [bæn] **1** *n* Verbot *nt.* **to put a** ~ **on sth** etw verbieten; **a** ~ **on smoking** Rauchverbot *nt.* **2** *vt (prohibit)* verbieten; *footballer etc* sperren. **she was** ~**ned from driving** ihr wurde Fahrverbot erteilt.
banal [bə'nɑːl] *adj* banal.
banality [bə'nælɪtɪ] *n* Banalität *f.*
banana [bə'nɑːnə] *n* Banane *f.* ~ **republic** Bananenrepublik *f.*
bananas [bə'nɑːnəz] *adj pred (col: crazy)* bescheuert *(col).* **this is driving me** ~ dabei dreh' ich noch durch *(col).*
banana skin *n* Bananenschale *f.*
band[1] [bænd] *n* **(a)** *(of cloth, iron)* Band *nt; (of leather)* Band *nt,* Riemen *m; (waist* ~) Bund *m; (on machine)* Riemen *m.* **(b)** *(stripe)* Streifen *m.*
band[2] *n* **(a)** Schar *f; (of robbers etc)* Bande *f; (of workers)* Trupp *m* Kolonne *f.* **(b)** *(Mus)* Band *f; (dance* ~) Tanzkapelle *f; (brass* ~, *Mil etc)* (Musik)kapelle *f.*
♦ **band together** *vi* sich zusammenschließen.
bandage ['bændɪdʒ] **1** *n* Verband *m; (strip of cloth)* Binde *f.* **2** *vt (also* ~ **up)** *cut* verbinden; *broken limb* bandagieren.
B & B [,biːənd'biː] *n* = **bed and breakfast.**
bandit ['bændɪt] *n* Bandit, Räuber *m.*
bandsman ['bændzmən] *n, pl* -**men** [-mən] Musiker *m. military* ~ Mitglied *nt* eines Musikkorps.
band: ~**stand** *n* Musikpavillon *m;* ~**wagon** *n:* **to jump** *or* **climb on the** ~**wagon** auf den fahrenden Zug aufspringen; ~**width** *n (Rad)* Bandbreite *f.*
bandy ['bændɪ] *adj* krumm. ~ **legs** *(of people)* O-Beine.
♦ **bandy about** *or* **around** *vt sep story* herumerzählen; *words, technical expressions* um sich werfen mit; *sb's name* immer wieder nennen.
bandy-legged [,bændɪ'legd] *adj* mit krummen Beinen; *person* O-beinig.
bane [beɪn] *n (cause of distress)* Fluch *m.* **he's the** ~ **of my life** er macht mir ihm bin ich geschlagen.
bang [bæŋ] **1** *n (noise)* Knall *m; (of sth falling)* Plumps *m.* **there was a** ~ **outside** draußen hat es geknallt; **to go off with a** ~ mit lautem Knall losgehen; *(col: be a success)* ein Bombenerfolg sein *(col).* **2** *adv* **(a) to go** ~ knallen; *(gun also, balloon)* peng machen *(col); (balloon)* zerplatzen. **(b)** *(col)* **his answer was** ~ **on** seine Antwort war genau richtig; **she came** ~ **on time** sie war auf die Sekunde pünktlich. **3** *interj* peng. ~ **went a £10 note** *(col)* und schon war ein 10-Pfund-Schein futsch *(col).* **4** *vt* **(a)** *(thump)* schlagen, knallen *(col).* **he** ~**ed his fist on the table** er schlug mit der Faust auf den Tisch. **(b)** *(shut noisily)* door zuknallen *(col).* **(c)** to ~ **one's head** *etc* on sth sich *(dat)* den Kopf *etc* an etw *(dat)* anschlagen. **5** *vi*

(a) *(door: shut)* zuknallen *(col); (fireworks, gun)* knallen. **(b) to ~ on** *or* **at sth gegen** *or* **an etw** *(acc)* schlagen.

♦ **bang down** *vt sep* (hin)knallen *(col)*. **to ~ ~ the receiver** den Hörer aufknallen *(col)*.

banger ['bæŋə^r] *n* **(a)** *(col: sausage)* Wurst *f*. **(b)** *(col: old car)* Kiste *f (col)*. **(c)** *(Brit: firework)* Knallkörper *m*.

bangle ['bæŋgl] *n* Armreif *m; (for ankle)* Fußreif *m*.

bangs [bæŋz] *n pl (US: in hair)* Franse *f*.

banish ['bænɪʃ] *vt person* verbannen; *cares, fear* vertreiben.

banisters ['bænɪstəz] *npl* Geländer *nt*.

banjo ['bændʒəʊ] *n, pl* **-es**, *(US)* **-s** Banjo *nt*.

bank[1] [bæŋk] **1** *n* **(a)** *(of earth, sand)* Wall, Damm *m; (slope)* Böschung *f*, Abhang *m; (on racetrack)* Kurvenüberhöhung *f*. **(b)** *(of river, lake)* Ufer *nt*. **(c)** *(of clouds)* Wand, Bank *f*. **2** *vi (Aviat)* eine Kurve fliegen.

bank[2] **1** *n (Fin, Med)* Bank *f*. **2** *vt money* einzahlen. **3** *vi* **where do you ~?** bei welcher Bank sind Sie?

♦ **bank (up)on** *vi* +*prep obj* sich verlassen auf *(+acc)*.

bank: ~ account *n* Bankkonto *nt; ~* **book** *n* Sparbuch *nt; ~* **charges** *pl (Brit)* Bankgebühren *pl; ~* **clerk** *n* Bankangestellte(r) *mf*.

banker ['bæŋkə^r] *n (Fin)* Bankier *m; (gambling)* Bankhalter *m*.

banker's card ['bæŋkəz,kɑːd] *n* Scheckkarte *f*.

bank holiday *n (Brit)* öffentlicher Feiertag; *(US)* Bankfeiertag *m*.

banking ['bæŋkɪŋ] *n* **he wants to go into ~** er will ins Bankfach gehen.

banking hours *npl* Schalterstunden *pl*.

bank: ~loan *n* Darlehen *nt; ~* **manager** *n* Filialleiter(in *f*) *m; ~* **note** *n (Brit)* Banknote *f*, Geldschein *m; ~* **rate** *n* Diskontsatz *m*.

bankrupt ['bæŋkrʌpt] *adj (Jur)* bankrott. **to go ~** Bankrott machen; **to be ~** bankrott *or* pleite *(col)* sein.

bankruptcy ['bæŋkrəptsɪ] *n (lit, fig)* Bankrott *m*.

bank statement *n* Kontoauszug *m*.

banner ['bænə^r] *n* Banner *(also fig)* nt; *(in processions)* Transparent *nt*.

bannisters ['bænɪstəz] *n* = **banisters**.

banns [bænz] *npl (Eccl)* Aufgebot *nt*. **to read the ~** das Aufgebot verlesen.

banquet ['bæŋkwɪt] *n (lavish feast)* Festessen *nt; (ceremonial dinner)* Bankett *nt*.

bantam ['bæntəm] *n* Bantamhuhn *nt*.

bantamweight ['bæntəm,weɪt] *n* Bantamgewicht *nt*.

banter ['bæntə^r] *n* Geplänkel *nt*. **enough of this foolish ~** lassen wir das alberne Gerede!

baptism ['bæptɪzəm] *n* Taufe *f*. **~ of fire** *(fig)* Feuertaufe *f*.

Baptist ['bæptɪst] *n* Baptist(in *f*) *m*. **John the ~** Johannes der Täufer.

baptize [bæp'taɪz] *vt* taufen.

bar[1] [bɑː^r] **1** *n* **(a)** *(of metal, wood)* Stange *f; (of toffee etc)* Riegel *m; (of electric fire)* Element *nt*. **~ of gold/silver** Gold-/Silberbarren *m;* **a ~ of chocolate, a chocolate ~** *(slab)* eine Tafel Schokolade; *(smaller)* ein Schokoladenriegel *m;* **a ~ of soap** ein Stück *nt* Seife. **(b)** *(of window, cage)* (Gitter)stab *m; (of door)* Stange *f*. **behind ~s** hinter Gittern. **(c)** *(fig: obstacle)* Hindernis *(to* für) *nt*. **to be a ~ to sth** einer Sache *(dat)* im Wege stehen. **(d)** *(for drinks)* Bar *f; (counter)* Theke *f*, Tresen *m*. **(e)** *(Jur)* **the B~** die Anwaltschaft; **to be called** *or* **admitted** *(US)* **to the B~** als Anwalt zugelassen werden; **"prisoner at the ~"** „Angeklagter!" **(f)** *(Mus)* Takt *m*.

2 *vt* **(a)** *(obstruct)* road versperren. **(b)** *(fasten)* door verriegeln. **(c)** *(exclude, prohibit)* person ausschließen; *action, thing* verbieten. **to ~ sb from a competition** jdn von (der Teilnahme

an) einem Wettbewerb ausschließen.

bar[2], **barring** *prep* **barring accidents** falls nichts passiert; **bar none** ohne Ausnahme.

barb [bɑːb] *n (of fish-hook, arrow)* Widerhaken *m*.

Barbados [bɑː'beɪdɒs] *n* Barbados *nt*.

barbarian [bɑː'beərɪən] **1** *n (Hist, fig)* Barbar(in *f*) *m*. **2** *adj (Hist, fig)* barbarisch.

barbaric [bɑː'bærɪk] *adj* barbarisch; *guard etc* grausam, roh; *(fig col)* conditions grauenhaft.

barbarous ['bɑːbərəs] *adj (Hist, fig)* barbarisch; *(cruel)* grausam.

barbecue ['bɑːbɪkjuː] **1** *n (Cook: grid)* Grill *m; (occasion)* Grillparty *f; (meat)* Grillfleisch *nt/* -wurst *f etc*. **2** *vt* grillen.

barbed wire ['bɑːbd'waɪə^r] *n* Stacheldraht *m*.

barber ['bɑːbə^r] *n* (Herren)friseur *m*. **at/to the ~'s** *(Brit)* beim/zum Friseur.

barbiturate [bɑː'bɪtjʊrɪt] *n* Barbiturat *nt*.

bard [bɑːd] *n (old)* Barde *m*.

bare [beə^r] **1** *adj* (+*er*) **(a)** *skin, floor* nackt, bloß; *countryside, room* kahl. **~ patch** kahle Stelle; **to lay ~ one's heart** sein Innerstes bloßlegen; **with his ~ hands** mit bloßen Händen; **a ~ statement of the facts** eine reine Tatsachenfeststellung. **(b)** *(scanty, mere)* knapp. **a ~ majority** eine knappe Mehrheit; **with just the ~st hint of garlic** nur mit einer winzigen Spur Knoblauch. **2** *vt parts of the body* entblößen; *(at doctor's)* freimachen; *end of a wire* freilegen.

bare: ~back *adv, adj* ohne Sattel; **~faced** *adj* liar unverfroren, schamlos; **~foot** *adv* barfuß; **~headed** *adj* ohne Kopfbedeckung.

barely ['beəlɪ] *adv (scarcely)* kaum. **we ~ know him** wir kennen ihn kaum.

bargain ['bɑːgɪn] **1** *n* **(a)** *(transaction)* Handel *m*, Geschäft *nt*. **to make** *or* **strike a ~** sich einigen; **I'll make a ~ with you, if you…** ich mache Ihnen ein Angebot, wenn Sie…; **it's a ~!** abgemacht!; **you drive a hard ~** Sie stellen ja harte Forderungen!; **then it started raining into the ~** dann hat es (obendrein) auch noch angefangen zu regnen. **(b)** *(cheap offer)* Sonderangebot *nt; (thing bought)* Gelegenheitskauf *m*. **what a ~!** das ist aber günstig! **2** *vi* handeln *(for* um); *(in negotiations)* verhandeln.

♦ **bargain for** *vi* +*prep obj (col: expect)* erwarten. **I hadn't ~ed ~ that** damit hatte ich nicht gerechnet; **I got more than I ~ed ~** ich habe vielleicht mein blaues Wunder erlebt! *(col)*.

barge [bɑːdʒ] **1** *n (for freight)* Last- *or* Frachtkahn *m; (unpowered)* Schleppkahn *m; (ceremonial)* Barkasse *f*. **2** *vt* **he ~d me out of the way** er hat mich weggestoßen.

♦ **barge in** *vi (col)* hinein-/hereinplatzen *(col); (interrupt)* dazwischenplatzen *(col) (on* bei).

♦ **barge into** *vi* +*prep obj (a) (knock against)* person *(hinein)*rennen in *(+acc) (col); (shove)* (an)rempeln; *thing* rennen gegen *(col)*. **(b)** *(col)* room, party, conversation (hinein-/herein)platzen in *(+acc) (col)*.

barge pole *n:* **I wouldn't touch it/him with a ~** *(Brit col)* von so etwas/so jemandem lasse ich die Finger *(col); (because disgusting, unpleasant)* das/den würde ich noch nicht mal mit der Kneifzange anfassen *(col)*.

baritone ['bærɪtəʊn] *n (voice, singer)* Bariton *m*.

barium ['beərɪəm] *n* Barium *nt*. **~ meal** Bariumbrei, Kontrastbrei *m*.

bark[1] [bɑːk] *n (of tree)* Rinde, Borke *f*.

bark[2] **1** *n (dog)* Bellen *nt*. **his ~ is worse than his bite** *(Prov)* Hunde, die bellen, beißen nicht *(Prov)*. **2** *vi* bellen. **to ~ at sb** jdn anbellen; *(person)* jdn anfahren; **to be ~ing up the wrong tree** *(fig col)* auf dem Holzweg sein *(col)*.

♦ **bark out** *vt sep* orders bellen.

barley ['bɑːlɪ] *n* Gerste *f*. **~ sugar** *n* Malzzucker *m; (sweet)* Malzbonbon *nt*.

bar: ~maid *n* Bardame *f; ~* **man** *n* Barkeeper *m*.

barmy ['bɑːmɪ] adj (Brit col) bekloppt (col).
barn [bɑːn] n Scheune f.
barn: ~ **owl** n Schleiereule f; ~**yard** n (Bauern)hof m.
barometer [bə'rɒmɪtə'] n (lit, fig) Barometer nt.
baron ['bærən] n (lit, fig) Baron m.
baroque [bə'rɒk] 1 adj barock, Barock-. 2 n (style) Barock m or nt.
barracks ['bærəks] npl (often with sing vb) (Mil) Kaserne f; (fig pej also) Mietskaserne f.
barrage ['bærɑːʒ] n (a) (across river) Wehr nt; (larger) Staustufe f. (b) (Mil) Sperrfeuer nt. **under this** ~ **of stones** ... unter diesem Steinhagel ... (c) (fig: of questions etc) Hagel m.
barrel ['bærəl] n (a) Faß nt; (for rainwater etc) Tonne f; (measure: of oil) Barrel nt. **they've got us over a** ~ (col) sie haben uns in der Zange (col). (b) (of handgun) Lauf m; (of cannon etc) Rohr nt.
barrel organ n Drehorgel f, Leierkasten m.
barren ['bærən] adj (lit, fig) unfruchtbar; land also karg; landscape kahl, öde.
barricade [,bærɪ'keɪd] 1 n Barrikade f. 2 vt verbarrikadieren.
barrier ['bærɪə'] n (lit, fig) Barriere f; (railing etc) Schranke f; (crash ~) Leitplanke f. **ticket** ~ Sperre f.
barrier cream n (Haut)schutzcreme f.
barring ['bɑːrɪŋ] prep = **bar**[2].
barrister ['bærɪstə'] n (Brit) Rechtsanwalt m/ -anwältin f (bei Gericht).
barrow ['bærəʊ] n Karre(n m) f.
bartender ['bɑːtendə'] n (US) Barkeeper m.
barter ['bɑːtə'] 1 vt tauschen (for gegen). 2 vi tauschen; (as general practice also) Tauschhandel treiben. **to** ~ **for sth** um etw handeln. 3 n (Tausch)handel m.
♦ **barter away** vt sep one's rights verspielen.
base[1] [beɪs] 1 n (a) (lowest part) Basis f; (support for statue etc) Sockel m; (of lamp, mountain) Fuß m. (b) (main ingredient) Hauptbestandteil m. (c) (Mil) Stützpunkt m; (for holidays) Standort m. (d) (Chem) Lauge, Base f. 2 vt (a) stellen. **to be** ~**d on** ruhen auf (+dat); (statue) stehen auf (+dat); **something to** ~ **it on** eine Unterlage dafür. (b) (fig) opinion, theory basieren (on auf +acc); hopes setzen (on auf +acc); relationship bauen (on auf +acc). **to be** ~**d on sb/sth** auf jdm/etw basieren. (c) (Mil) stationieren. **the company/my job is** ~**d in London** die Firma hat ihren Sitz in London/ich arbeite in London.
base[2] adj (+er) adj motive niedrig; person, action gemein, niederträchtig. (b) metal unedel.
baseball ['beɪsbɔːl] n Baseball m or nt.
base camp n Basislager nt.
-based [beɪst] adj suf **London-**~ mit Sitz in London.
base line n (Tennis) Grundlinie f.
basement ['beɪsmənt] n (in building) Untergeschoß nt; (in house also) Keller m. ~ **flat** Kellerwohnung f.
bash [bæʃ] (col) 1 n (a) Schlag m. **the bumper has had a** ~ die Stoßstange hat 'ne Delle abgekriegt (col). (b) (fig) **I'll have a** ~ (at it) ich probier's mal (col). 2 vt person (ver)hauen (col); ball knallen (col); car, wing einbeulen (col). **to** ~ **one's head/shin** (against or on sth) sich (dat) den Kopf/ das Schienbein (an etw dat) anschlagen; **to** ~ **sb on the head with sth** jdm etw auf den Kopf hauen (col).
♦ **bash in** vt sep (col) door einschlagen. **to** ~ **sb's head** ~ jdm den Schädel einschlagen (col).
♦ **bash up** vt sep (Brit col) person vermöbeln (col).
bashful ['bæʃfʊl] adj schüchtern; (on particular occasion) verlegen.
basic ['beɪsɪk] 1 adj (a) (fundamental) Grund-; problem also, reason, issue Haupt-; points, issues wesentlich. **there's no** ~ **difference** es besteht kein grundlegender Unterschied; **must you be so** ~! müssen Sie sich denn so direkt ausdrücken?; ~ **salary** Grundgehalt nt; ~ **English** englischer Grundwortschatz. (b) (original) zu Grunde liegend. (c) (essential) notwendig. 2 npl the ~s das Wesentliche.
basically ['beɪsɪkəlɪ] adv im Grunde; (mainly) im wesentlichen.
basil ['bæzl] n (Bot) Basilikum nt.
basin ['beɪsn] n (a) (vessel) Schüssel f; (wash~) (Wasch)becken nt. (b) (Geog) Becken nt.
basis ['beɪsɪs] n (foundation) Basis f; (for assumption) Grund m. **we're working on the** ~ **that** ... wir gehen von der Annahme aus, daß ...; **on the** ~ **of this evidence** aufgrund dieses Beweismaterials.
bask [bɑːsk] vi (in sun) sich aalen (in in +dat).
basket ['bɑːskɪt] n Korb m; (for rolls, fruit etc) Körbchen nt.
basket: ~**ball** n Basketball m; ~**work chair** n Korbstuhl m.
Basle [bɑːl] n Basel nt.
bass [beɪs] (Mus) 1 n Baß m. 2 adj Baß-. ~ **clef** Baßschlüssel m; ~ **drum** große Trommel.
bassoon [bə'suːn] n Fagott nt.
bastard ['bɑːstəd] n (a) (lit) uneheliches Kind; (fig: hybrid) Kreuzung f. (b) (col!: person) Scheißkerl m (col!). **poor** ~ armes Schwein (col).
baste[1] [beɪst] vt (Sew) heften.
baste[2] vt (Cook) (mit Fett) beträufeln.
bat[1] [bæt] n (Zool) Fledermaus f. (as) **blind as a** ~ blind wie ein Maulwurf.
bat[2] (Sport) 1 n (Baseball, Cricket) Schlagholz nt; (Table-tennis) Schläger m. **off one's own** ~ (fig) auf eigene Faust (col). 2 vi (Baseball, Cricket) Schlagmann sein.
bat[3] vt without ~**ting an eyelid** ohne mit der Wimper zu zucken; **he didn't** ~ **an eyelid** er blieb seelenruhig.
batch [bætʃ] n (of loaves) Schub m; (of prisoners, recruits also) Trupp m; (of things dispatched) Sendung f; (of letters, work) Stoß, Stapel m.
bated ['beɪtɪd] adj: **with** ~ **breath** mit angehaltenem Atem.
bath [bɑːθ] 1 n (a) Bad nt. **to have or take a** ~ baden; **a room with** ~ ein Zimmer mit Bad. (b) (bathtub) (Bade)wanne f. (c) (swimming) ~s pl (Schwimm)bad nt; (public) ~s pl Badeanstalt f; (Hist) Bäder pl. 2 vt (Brit) baden. 3 vi (Brit) (sich) baden.
bath: ~**chair** n Rollstuhl m; ~**cube** n Würfel m Badesalz.
bathe [beɪð] 1 vt baden; (with cottonwool etc) waschen. **to be** ~**d in light/sweat** in Licht/Schweiß gebadet sein. 2 vi (US) (sich) baden.
bather ['beɪðə'] n Badende(r) mf.
bathing ['beɪðɪŋ] ~**cap** n Badekappe f; ~**costume** n (Brit) Badeanzug m; ~**trunks** npl (Brit) Badehose f.
bath: ~**mat** n Badematte f; ~**robe** n Bademantel m; ~**room** n Bad(ezimmer) nt; (euph: lavatory) Toilette f; ~**salts** npl Badesalz nt; ~**towel** n Badetuch nt; ~**tub** n Badewanne f.
baton ['bætən] n (a) (Mus) Taktstock m; (Mil) (Kommando)stab m. (b) (of policeman) Schlagstock m; (for directing traffic) Stab m. (c) (in relay race) Staffelholz nt, Stab m.
battalion [bə'tælɪən] n (Mil, fig) Bataillon nt.
batter[1] ['bætə'] n (Cook) Teig m.
batter[2] 1 vt (a) einschlagen auf (+acc); wife, baby (ver)prügeln. **the house was** ~**ed by the wind** der Wind rüttelte unentwegt am Haus. (b) (damage) übel zurichten; car also, metal zeror verbeulen. (c) (col) opponent eins draufgeben (+dat) (col). 2 vi **to** ~ **at the door** an die Tür hämmern (col).
♦ **batter down** vt sep door einschlagen.
battered ['bætəd] adj übel zugerichtet; wife, baby mißhandelt; object verbeult; furniture ramponiert (col); nerves zerrüttet.

battering ram ['bætərɪŋ,ræm] n Rammbock m.

battery ['bætərɪ] n Batterie f; (fig: of arguments etc) Reihe f.

battery: ~-charger n Ladesatz m; ~ farming n (Hühner- etc) batterien pl; ~ hen n (Agr) Batteriehenne f.

battle ['bætl] 1 n (lit) Schlacht f; (fig) Kampf m. to give ~ sich zum Kampf stellen; to fight a ~ eine Schlacht schlagen; killed in ~ (im Kampf) gefallen; ~ of words/wits Wortgefecht nt/ geistiger Wettstreit; that's half the ~ damit ist schon viel gewonnen. 2 vi kämpfen (for um).

battle: ~-axe, ~-ax (US) (col: woman) Drachen m (col); ~field, ~ground n Schlachtfeld nt.

battlements ['bætlmənts] npl Zinnen pl.

battleship ['bætl,ʃɪp] n Schlachtschiff nt.

batty ['bætɪ] adj (+er) (col) verrückt.

bauble ['bɔːbl] n Flitter m no pl. ~s Flitterzeug nt.

baulk [bɔːk] vi = **balk.**

bauxite ['bɔːksaɪt] n Bauxit m.

Bavaria [bə'vɛərɪə] n Bayern nt.

Bavarian [bə'vɛərɪən] 1 n (a) (person) Bayer(in f) m. (b) (dialect) Bayrisch nt. 2 adj bay(e)risch.

bawdy ['bɔːdɪ] adj (+er) derb.

bawl [bɔːl] vi (a) (shout) brüllen, schreien; (sing) grölen (col). (b) (col: weep) heulen (col).

♦ **bawl out** vt sep (a) order brüllen; song grölen (pej col). (b) (col: scold) ausschimpfen.

bay[1] [beɪ] n Bucht f; (of sea also) Bai f.

bay[2] n (a) (Archit) Erker m. (b) (loading ~) Ladeplatz m.

bay[3] 1 n (of dogs) Bellen nt no pl; (Hunt) Melden nt no pl. to keep or hold sb/sth at ~ jdn/etw in Schach halten. 2 vi bellen; (Hunt also) melden.

bay[4] adj horse (kastanien)braun.

bayleaf ['beɪliːf] n Lorbeerblatt nt.

bayonet ['beɪənɪt] 1 n Bajonett, Seitengewehr nt. 2 vt mit dem Bajonett aufspießen.

bay window n Erkerfenster nt.

bazaar [bə'zɑːʳ] n Basar m.

BBC = **British Broadcasting Corporation** BBC f.

BC = **before Christ** v. Chr.

be [biː] pres **am, is, are,** pret **was, were,** ptp **been** 1 (a) (with adj, n) sein. he is a soldier/a German er ist Soldat/Deutscher; who is that? — it's me/that's Mary wer ist das? — ich bin's/das ist Mary; if I were you wenn ich Sie wäre; ~ sensible! sei vernünftig! (b) how are you? wie geht's?; I'm better now es geht mir jetzt besser; to ~ hungry/thirsty Hunger/Durst haben; I am hot/cold mir ist heiß/kalt. (c) (age) sein. he'll ~ three wird drei (Jahre alt). (d) (cost) kosten. how much is that? wieviel or was kostet das?; (altogether) wieviel macht das? (e) (Math) sein. two times two is or are four zwei mal zwei ist or sind vier. (f) (with poss) gehören (+dat). that book is your brother's das Buch gehört Ihrem Bruder. (g) (in exclamations) sein. was I pleased to hear it! er war vielleicht froh, das zu hören!

2 aux (a) (+prp: continuous tenses) what are you doing? was machst du da?; she is always complaining sie beklagt sich dauernd; they're coming tomorrow sie kommen morgen; will you ~ seeing her tomorrow? treffen Sie sie morgen?; I'll ~ starting soon ich fange gleich an; I have been waiting for you for half an hour ich warte schon seit einer halben Stunde auf Sie.

(b) (+ptp: passive) werden. the box had been opened die Schachtel war geöffnet worden; the car is to ~ sold das Auto soll verkauft werden.

(c) he is to ~ pitied/not to ~ envied er ist zu bedauern/nicht zu beneiden; not to ~ confused with nicht zu verwechseln mit.

(d) (intention, obligation, command) sollen. I am to look after my mother ich soll mich um meine Mutter kümmern; he is not to open it er soll es nicht öffnen.

(e) (~ destined) sollen. she was never to return sie sollte nie zurückkehren.

(f) (suppositions, wishes) if it were or was to snow falls or wenn es schneien sollte; I would ~ surprised if ... ich wäre überrascht, wenn ...

(g) (in tag questions, short answers) he's always late, isn't he? — yes he is er kommt doch immer so spät, nicht? — ja, das stimmt; he's never late, is he? — no he is never late, is er kommt nie zu spät, oder? — o, doch.

3 vi (a) sein; (remain) bleiben. to ~ or not to ~ Sein oder Nichtsein; the powers that ~ die zuständigen Stellen; let me/him ~ laß mich/ihn (in Ruhe); ~ that as it may wie dem auch sei. (b) (be situated) sein; (town, country, carpet etc also) liegen; (car, bottle, chair also) stehen. (c) (visit, call) I've been to Paris ich war schon (ein)mal in Paris; the postman has already been der Briefträger war schon da. (d) now you've been and done it (col) jetzt hast du aber was angerichtet! (col).

4 vb impers (a) sein. it is dark/morning es ist dunkel/Morgen; it's 5 km to the nearest town es sind 5 km bis zur nächsten Stadt. (b) (emphatic) it was us or we (form) who found it wir haben das gefunden. (c) (wishes etc) were it not for him, if it weren't or wasn't for him wenn er nicht wäre.

beach [biːtʃ] n Strand m. on the ~ am Strand.

beach: ~ball n Wasserball m; ~ buggy n Strandbuggy m; ~comber n Strandgutsammler m; ~wear n Badesachen pl.

beacon ['biːkən] n (fire, light) Leuchtfeuer nt; (radio ~) Funkfeuer nt; (one of a series of lights, radio ~s) Bake f.

bead [biːd] n (also sweat) Perle f. (string of) ~s Perlenschnur f; (necklace) Perlenkette f.

beady ['biːdɪ] adj I've got my ~ eye on you (col) ich beobachte Sie genau!

beak [biːk] n Schnabel m.

beaker ['biːkəʳ] n Becher m; (Chem etc) Becherglas nt.

beam [biːm] 1 n (a) (Build) Balken m. (b) to be broad in the ~ (ship) sehr breit sein; (person) breit gebaut sein. (c) (of light etc) Strahl m. on main ~ mit Fernlicht. (d) (radio ~) Leitstrahl m. (e) (smile) Strahlen nt. 2 vi strahlen. to ~ down (sun) niederstrahlen; her face was ~ing with joy sie strahlte übers ganze Gesicht; to ~ at sb jdn anstrahlen. 3 vt (Rad, TV) ausstrahlen.

bean [biːn] n Bohne f. to be full of ~s (col) putzmunter sein (col).

bean: ~pole n (lit, fig) Bohnenstange f; ~sprout n Sojabohnensprosse f.

bear[1] [bɛəʳ] n (a) Bär m; (fig: person) Brummbär m (col). (b) (Astron) the Great/Little B~ der Große/Kleine Bär.

bear[2] pret **bore,** ptp **borne** 1 vt (a) burden, weight, responsibility, fruit tragen; gift, message bei sich tragen. he was borne along by the crowd die Menge trug ihn mit (sich). (b) inscription, signature, name, title tragen; mark, traces also, likeness, relation aufweisen. (c) (have in heart or mind) love, hatred, grudge empfinden. (d) (endure, tolerate) ertragen; criticism, noise etc also vertragen. could you ~ to stay a little longer? können Sie es noch ein bißchen länger hier aushalten?; it doesn't ~ thinking about man darf gar nicht daran denken. (e) (give birth to) gebären; see **born.**

2 vi (a) (move) to ~ right/left/north sich rechts/links/nach Norden halten. (b) (fruit-tree etc) tragen. to bring one's mind to ~ on sth seinen Verstand or Geist für etw anstrengen; to bring pressure to ~ on sb/sth Druck auf jdn/etw ausüben.

3 vr sich halten. he bore himself with dignity er hat Würde gezeigt.

♦ **bear down** vi to ~ ~ on sb/sth (driver etc) auf

jdn/etw zuhalten.
♦ **bear out** vt sep bestätigen.
♦ **bear up** vi sich halten. **he bore ~ well under the death of his father** er trug den Tod seines Vaters mit Fassung; **how are you? — ~ing ~!** wie geht's? — man lebt!
♦ **bear with** vi +prep obj tolerieren. **if you would ~ ~ me for a couple of minutes** wenn Sie sich vielleicht noch zwei Minuten gedulden wollen.
bearable ['bɛərəbl] adj erträglich.
beard [bɪəd] 1 n Bart m; (full-face) Vollbart m. 2 vt **to ~ the lion in his den** (fig) sich in die Höhle des Löwen wagen.
bearded ['bɪədɪd] adj man, animal bärtig.
bearer ['bɛərə^r] n (carrier) Träger(in f) m; (of news, banknote) Überbringer m; (of passport) Inhaber(in f) m.
bearing ['bɛərɪŋ] n (a) (posture) Haltung f; (behaviour) Verhalten nt. (b) (relevance) **to have some/no ~ on sth** von Belang/belanglos für etw sein; (be/not be connected with) einen gewissen/ keinen Bezug zu etw haben. (c) (direction) **to take a compass ~** den Kompaßkurs feststellen; **to lose one's ~s** die Orientierung verlieren; **to get one's ~s** sich orientieren. (d) (Tech) Lager nt.
beast [biːst] n (a) Tier nt. (b) (col: person) Biest, Ekel nt. **it's a ~ (of a problem)** das (Problem) hat's in sich (col).
beastly ['biːstlɪ] adj (col) scheußlich (col); person, conduct also gemein.
beat [biːt] (vb: pret ~, ptp ~en) 1 n (a) (of heart etc) (single ~) Schlag m; (repeated beating) Schlagen nt. (b) (of policeman, sentry) Runde f, Rundgang m; (district) Revier nt. **to be on one's ~** seine Runde machen. (c) (Mus, Poet) Takt m; (of metronome, baton) Taktschlag m.
2 vt (a) (hit) schlagen; person (ver)prügeln; carpet klopfen. **~ it!** (fig col) hau ab! (col), verschwinde! (b) (hammer) metal hämmern. (c) (defeat) schlagen; record brechen. **to ~ sb at chess/tennis** jdn im Schach/Tennis schlagen; **coffee ~s tea any day** Kaffee ist allemal besser als Tee; **that ~s everything** das ist doch wirklich der Gipfel (col); (is very good) darüber geht nichts; **that ~s me** (col) das ist mir ein Rätsel (col). (d) (be before) budget, crowds zuvorkommen (+dat). **to ~ sb to it** jdm zuvorkommen. (e) **the bird ~s its wings** der Vogel schlägt mit den Flügeln. (f) (Mus) **to ~ time** den Takt schlagen. (g) cream, eggs schlagen.
3 vi (a) (heart etc) schlagen. **to ~ on the door (with one's fists)** (mit den Fäusten) gegen die Tür hämmern; **with ~ing heart** mit pochendem or klopfendem Herzen. (b) (wind, waves) schlagen; (rain also) trommeln; (sun) brennen.
4 adj (a) (col: exhausted) **to be (dead) ~** total geschafft or erledigt sein (col). (b) (col: defeated) **to be ~(en)** aufgeben müssen (col), sich geschlagen geben müssen; **this problem's got me ~** mit dem Problem komme ich nicht klar (col).
♦ **beat back** vt sep flames, enemy zurückschlagen.
♦ **beat down** 1 vi (rain) herunterprasseln; (sun) herunterbrennen. 2 vt sep (a) prices herunterhandeln; opposition kleinkriegen (col). **I managed to ~ him ~** ich konnte den Preis herunterhandeln. (b) (flatten) door einrennen.
♦ **beat off** vt sep attack, attacker abwehren.
♦ **beat out** vt sep fire ausschlagen; dent aushämmern; rhythm schlagen; (on drum) trommeln.
♦ **beat up** vt sep (a) person zusammenschlagen. (b) (Cook) eggs, cream schlagen.
beaten ['biːtn] 1 ptp of **beat**. 2 adj (a) metal gehämmert. (b) **to be off the ~ track** abgelegen sein.
beater ['biːtə^r] n (carpet ~) Klopfer m; (egg ~) Schneebesen m.

beating ['biːtɪŋ] n (a) (series of blows) Schläge, Prügel pl. **to give sb a ~** jdn verprügeln; **to get a ~** verprügelt werden; (as punishment also) Prügel bekommen. (b) (of drums, heart, wings) Schlagen nt. (c) (defeat) Niederlage f. **to take a ~** eine Schlappe einstecken (col). (d) **to take some ~** seines-/ihresgleichen suchen.
beat-up ['biːtʌp] adj (col) ramponiert (col).
beautiful ['bjuːtɪfʊl] adj schön; weather also, idea, meal herrlich; piece of work hervorragend.
beautifully ['bjuːtɪfəlɪ] adv schön; warm, simple herrlich; (well) sew, sing hervorragend.
beautify ['bjuːtɪfaɪ] vt verschönern.
beauty ['bjuːtɪ] n (a) Schönheit f. **~ is only skin-deep** (prov) der äußere Schein kann trügen; **~ is in the eye of the beholder** (Prov) schön ist, was gefällt; **the ~ of it is that ...** das Schöne daran ist, daß ... (b) (beautiful person) Schönheit f. (c) (good example) Prachtexemplar nt.
beauty in cpds Schönheits-; **~ contest** n Schönheitswettbewerb m; **~ queen** n Schönheitskönigin f; **~ spot** n (a) Schönheitsfleck m; (b) (place) schönes or hübsches Fleckchen (Erde).
beaver ['biːvə^r] n Biber m. **to work like a ~** wie ein Wilder/eine Wilde arbeiten.
becalm [bɪ'kɑːm] vt (Naut) **to be ~ed** in eine Flaute geraten.
became [bɪ'keɪm] pret of **become**.
because [bɪ'kɒz] 1 conj weil. **it was the more surprising ~ we were not expecting it** es war um so überraschender, als wir es nicht erwartet hatten. 2 prep **~ of** wegen (+gen or (col) dat); **I only did it ~ of you** ich habe es nur deinetwegen getan.
beckon ['bɛkən] vti winken. **he ~ed me in/back/ over** er winkte mich herein/zurück/herüber.
become [bɪ'kʌm] pret **became**, ptp **~** 1 vi werden. **to ~ old/fat/tired** alt/dick/müde werden; **to ~ accustomed to sb/sth** sich an jdn/etw gewöhnen; **to ~ interested in sb/sth** anfangen, sich für jdn/ etw zu interessieren; **to ~ king/a doctor** König/ Arzt werden; **what has ~ of him?** was ist aus ihm geworden? 2 vt (suit) stehen (+dat); (befit) sich schicken für.
becoming [bɪ'kʌmɪŋ] adj (fitting) schicklich; (flattering) vorteilhaft. **that dress/colour is very ~** das Kleid/die Farbe steht ihr/dir etc sehr gut.
bed [bɛd] 1 n (a) Bett nt. **to go to ~** zu or ins Bett gehen; **to go to ~ with sb** mit jdm ins Bett gehen; **to put sb to ~** jdn ins Bett bringen; **he must have got out of ~ on the wrong side** (col) er ist wohl mit dem linken Fuß zuerst aufgestanden; **to be in ~** im Bett sein; **his life is not exactly a ~ of roses** er ist nicht gerade auf Rosen gebettet; **can I have a ~ for the night?** kann ich hier/bei euch etc übernachten? (b) (sea ~) Grund, Boden m; (river ~) Bett nt. (c) (oyster ~, coral ~) Bank f. (d) (flower ~) Beet nt. 2 vt plant setzen, pflanzen.
♦ **bed down** vi sein Lager aufschlagen.
bed and breakfast n Übernachtung f mit Frühstück. **"~ ~"** "Fremdenzimmer".
bed in cpds Bett-; **~-bath** n (Kranken)wäsche f im Bett; **to give sb a ~-bath** jdn im Bett waschen; **~-bug** n Wanze f; **~-clothes** npl Bettzeug nt; **~-cover** n Bettdecke f.
bedding ['bɛdɪŋ] n Bettzeug nt; (for horses) Streu f.
bedevil [bɪ'dɛvl] vt erschweren. **~led by misfortune/bad luck** vom Schicksal/Pech verfolgt.
bedfellow ['bɛd,fɛləʊ] n **to be** or **make strange ~s** (fig) ein merkwürdiges Gespann sein.
bedlam ['bɛdləm] n Chaos nt. **it was sheer ~ in the class** in der Klasse ging es zu wie im Irrenhaus.
bed: ~-linen n Bettwäsche f; **~-pan** n Bettpfanne f; **~-post** n Bettpfosten m.
bedraggled [bɪ'dræɡld] adj (wet) trief- or tropfnaß; (dirty) verdreckt; (untidy) person, appearance ungepflegt.

bed-ridden ['bedrɪdn] *adj* bettlägerig.

bedroom ['bedruːm] *n* Schlafzimmer *nt*.

bedroom *in cpds* Schlafzimmer-; ~ **slipper** *n* Hausschuh *m*.

bedside ['bedsaɪd] *n* **to be/sit at sb's** ~ an jds Bett (*dat*) sein/sitzen.

bedside: ~ **lamp** *n* Nachttischlampe *f*; ~ **manner** *n* **he has a good/bad** ~ **manner** er kann gut/nicht gut mit den Kranken umgehen; ~ **rug** *n* Bettvorleger *m*; ~ **table** *n* Nachttisch *m*.

bed: ~**-sit(ter)** (*col*), ~**-sitting room** *n* (*Brit*) möbliertes Zimmer; ~**time** *n* **it's** ~**time** es ist Schlafenszeit; **his** ~**time is 10 o'clock** er geht um 10 Uhr schlafen; **it's past your** ~**time** du müßtest schon lange im Bett sein; ~**time story** *n* Gutenachtgeschichte *f*; ~**-wetting** *n* Bettnässen *nt*.

bee [biː] *n* Biene *f*. **he's got a** ~ **in his bonnet about cleanliness** er hat einen Sauberkeitstick (*col*).

beech [biːtʃ] *n* (*tree, wood*) Buche *f*.

beef [biːf] **1** *n* (**a**) (*meat*) Rindfleisch *nt*. **roast** ~ Roastbeef *nt*. (**b**) (*col*) (*flesh*) Speck *m* (*col*); (*muscles*) Muskeln *pl*. **2** *vi* (*col: complain*) meckern (*col*) (*about* über +*acc*).

beef: ~**burger** *n* Hamburger *m*; ~**eater** *n* (**a**) Beefeater *m*; (**b**) (*US col*) Engländer(in *f*) *m*; ~**steak** *n* Beefsteak *nt*.

beefy ['biːfɪ] *adj* (+*er*) fleischig.

bee: ~**hive** *n* (**a**) Bienenstock *m*; (*dome-shaped*) Bienenkorb *m*; (**b**) (*hairstyle*) toupierte Hochfrisur; ~**keeper** *n* Bienenzüchter(in *f*), Imker(in *f*) *m*; ~**-line** *n* **to make a** ~**-line for sb/sth** schnurstracks auf jdn/etw zugehen.

been [biːn] *ptp of* **be**.

beer [bɪəʳ] *n* Bier *nt*. **two** ~**s, please** zwei Bier, bitte.

beer *in cpds* Bier-; ~**-bottle** *n* Bierflasche *f*; ~ **can** *n* Bierdose *f*; ~ **glass** *n* Bierglas *nt*; ~**mat** *n* Bierdeckel *m*.

beeswax ['biːzwæks] *n* Bienenwachs *nt*.

beet [biːt] *n* Rübe *f*.

beetle ['biːtl] *n* Käfer *m*.

beetle-browed ['biːtl,braud] *adj* mit buschigen Augenbrauen.

beetroot ['biːt,ruːt] *n* (*Brit*) rote Bete *or* Rübe.

befall [bɪ'fɔːl] *pret* **befell** [bɪ'fel], *ptp* **befallen** [bɪ'fɔːlən] *vt* widerfahren (+*dat*) (*dated*).

befitting [bɪ'fɪtɪŋ] *adj* geziemend (*dated*). ~ **for a lady** für eine Dame schicklich.

before [bɪ'fɔːʳ] **1** *prep* (**a**) (*earlier than*) vor (+*dat*). **the day** ~ **yesterday** vorgestern; ~ **Christ** (*abbr* **BC**) vor Christi Geburt (*abbr* v. Chr.); ~ **now** früher; ~ **long** bald. (**b**) (*in place, rank, in the presence of*) vor (+*dat*). ~ **my** (*very*) **eyes** vor meinen Augen; **the question** ~ **us** die uns vorliegende Frage; **ladies** ~ **gentlemen** Damen haben den Vortritt; **to appear** ~ **a court/judge** vor Gericht/einem Richter erscheinen. (**c**) (*rather than*) he would die ~ betraying his country er würde eher sterben als sein Land verraten.

2 *adv* (**a**) (*in time*) (~ *that*) davor; (*at an earlier time,* ~ *now*) vorher. **I have read** *etc* **this** ~ ich habe das schon einmal gelesen *etc*; **it has never happened** ~ das ist noch nie passiert; **two days** ~ zwei Tage davor or zuvor. (**b**) (*indicating order*) davor. **that chapter and the one** ~ dieses Kapitel und das davor.

3 *conj* (**a**) (*in time*) bevor. ~ **doing sth** bevor man etw tut; **it will be a long time** ~ **he comes back** es wird lange dauern, bis er zurückkommt. (**b**) (*rather than*) **he will die** ~ **he surrenders** eher will er sterben als sich geschlagen geben.

beforehand [bɪ'fɔːhænd] *adv* im voraus. **you must tell me** ~ Sie müssen mir vorher Bescheid sagen.

befriend [bɪ'frend] *vt* sich annehmen (+*gen*).

befuddled [bɪ'fʌdld] *adj* (*confused*) durcheinander (*pred*).

beg [beg] **1** *vt* (**a**) *money, alms* betteln um. (**b**) *forgiveness, mercy* bitten um. **he** ~**ged to be allowed to ...** er bat darum, ... zu dürfen; **I** ~ **to differ** ich erlaube mir, anderer Meinung zu sein. (**c**) (*entreat*) *sb* anflehen. (**d**) **to** ~ **the question** an der eigentlichen Frage vorbeigehen. **2** *vi* (**a**) (*beggar*) betteln; (*dog*) Männchen machen. (**b**) (*for help, time etc*) bitten (*for* um). (**c**) (*entreat*) **I** ~ **of you** ich bitte Sie. (**d**) **to go** ~**ging** (*col*) noch zu haben sein; (*to be unwanted*) keine Abnehmer finden.

began [bɪ'gæn] *pret of* **begin**.

beggar ['begəʳ] *n* (**a**) Bettler(in *f*) *m*. ~**s can't be choosers** (*prov*) wer arm dran ist, kann nicht wählerisch sein. (**b**) (*col*) Kerl *m* (*col*). **poor** ~! armer Kerl! (*col*); **a lucky** ~ ein Glückspilz *m*.

begin [bɪ'gɪn] *pret* **began**, *ptp* **begun 1** *vt* (**a**) beginnen, anfangen; *song also* anstimmen; *bottle* anbrechen; *book* anfangen; *rehearsals, work* anfangen mit; *task* in Angriff nehmen. **to** ~ **to do sth** *or* **doing sth** anfangen *or* beginnen, etw zu tun; **that doesn't even** ~ **to compare with ...** das läßt sich nicht mal annähernd mit ... vergleichen; **I can't** ~ **to thank you for what you've done** ich kann Ihnen gar nicht genug dafür danken, was Sie getan haben. (**b**) (*initiate*) anfangen; *fashion, custom, policy* einführen; *society, firm, movement* gründen; (*cause*) *war* auslösen.

2 *vi* anfangen, beginnen; (*new play etc*) anlaufen; (*custom*) entstehen; (*river*) entspringen. **to** ~ **by doing sth** etw zuerst (einmal) tun; **he began by saying that ...** er sagte einleitend, daß ...; ~**ning from Monday** ab Montag, von Montag an; **to** ~ **with there were only three** anfänglich waren es nur drei; **to** ~ **with, this is wrong, and ...** erstens einmal ist das falsch, dann ...; **to** ~ **on sth** mit etw anfangen *or* beginnen; **since the world began** seit (An)beginn *or* Anfang der Welt.

beginner [bɪ'gɪnəʳ] *n* Anfänger(in *f*) *m*. ~**'s luck** Anfängerglück *nt*.

beginning [bɪ'gɪnɪŋ] *n* Anfang *m*. (*temporal also*) Beginn *m*; (*of custom, movement*) Entstehen *nt* *no pl*; (*of river*) Ursprung *m*. **at the** ~ **of sth** am Anfang *or* (*temporal also*) zu Beginn einer Sache (*gen*); **the** ~ **of time/the world der** Anbeginn der Welt; **in the** ~ (*Bibl*) am Anfang; **from the** ~ von Anfang an; **from** ~ **to end** von vorn bis hinten; (*temporal*) von Anfang bis Ende; **to begin at the** ~ ganz vorn anfangen; **Nazism had its** ~**s in Germany** der Nazismus hatte seine Anfänge in Deutschland.

begonia [bɪ'gəunɪə] *n* Begonie *f*.

begrudge [bɪ'grʌdʒ] *vt* (**a**) (*be reluctant*) **to** ~ **doing sth** etw widerwillig tun. (**b**) (*envy*) mißgönnen (*sb sth* jdm etw). **no one** ~**s you your good fortune** wir gönnen dir ja dein Glück. (**c**) (*give unwillingly*) nicht gönnen (*sb sth* jdm etw). **I shan't** ~ **you £5** du sollst die £ 5 haben.

beguile [bɪ'gaɪl] *vt* (*deceive*) betören (*geh*).

begun [bɪ'gʌn] *ptp of* **begin**.

behalf [bɪ'hɑːf] *n* **on** ~ **of** (*as spokesman*) im Namen von; (*as authorized representative*) im Auftrag von.

behave [bɪ'heɪv] **1** *vi* sich verhalten; (*people also*) sich benehmen. **to** ~ **well towards sb** jdn gut behandeln; ~! benimm dich!; **the car** ~**s well at high speeds** das Auto zeigt bei hoher Geschwindigkeit ein gutes Fahrverhalten. **2** *vt* **to** ~ **oneself** sich benehmen; ~ **yourself!** benimm dich!

behaviour, (*US*) **behavior** [bɪ'heɪvjəʳ] *n* (**a**) (*manner, bearing*) Benehmen *nt*; (*esp of children also*) Betragen *nt*. **to be on one's best** ~ sich von seiner besten Seite zeigen. (**b**) (*towards others, of car*) Verhalten *nt* (*to(wards*) gegenüber).

behaviourism, (*US*) **behaviorism** [bɪ'heɪvjərɪzəm] *n* Behaviorismus *m*.

behead [bɪ'hed] vt enthaupten, köpfen.

beheld [bɪ'held] prep, ptp of **behold**.

behest [bɪ'hest] n (liter) Geheiß nt (liter). **at his** ~ auf sein Geheiß hin (liter).

behind [bɪ'haɪnd] **1** prep **(a)** (stationary) hinter (+dat); (with motion) hinter (+acc). ~ **from** ~ **the door** komm hinter der Tür (her)vor; **he came up** ~ **me** er trat von hinten an mich heran; **he has the Communists** ~ **him** er hat die Kommunisten hinter sich (dat); **to be** ~ **an idea** eine Idee unterstützen; **what is** ~ **this?** was steckt dahinter? **(b)** (more backward than) **to be** ~ **sb** hinter jdm zurücksein. **(c)** (in time) **to be** ~ **time** (train etc) Verspätung haben; (with work etc) im Rückstand sein; **to be** ~ **schedule** im Verzug sein; **to be** ~ **the times** (fig) hinter seiner Zeit zurück(geblieben) sein. **2** adv **(a)** (in or at rear) hinten; (~ this, sb etc) dahinter. **from** ~ von hinten; **to look** ~ zurückblicken. **(b)** (late) **to be** ~ **with one's studies/payments** mit seinen Studien/Zahlungen im Rückstand sein. **3** n (col) Hintern m (col).

behold [bɪ'həʊld] pret, ptp **beheld** vt (liter) sehen, erblicken (liter). ~**!** und siehe (da); (Rel) siehe.

beige [beɪʒ] **1** adj beige. **2** n Beige nt.

being [ˈbiːɪŋ] n **(a)** (existence) Dasein, Leben nt. **to come into** ~ entstehen; (club etc also) ins Leben gerufen werden; **to bring into** ~ ins Leben rufen. **(b)** (that which exists) Geschöpf nt. **2** vi (have a religious faith) an Gott glauben.

belabour, (US) **belabor** [bɪ'leɪbəʳ] vt einschlagen auf (+acc); (with insults etc) überhäufen.

belated [bɪ'leɪtɪd] adj verspätet.

belch [beltʃ] **1** vi (person) rülpsen, aufstoßen; (volcano) Lava ausstoßen; (smoke, fire) herausquellen. **2** vt (also ~ **forth** or **out**) smoke, flames ausstoßen. **3** n Rülpser m (col).

beleaguer [bɪ'liːgəʳ] vt belagern; (fig) umgeben.

belfry ['belfrɪ] n Glockenstube f.

Belgian ['beldʒən] **1** n Belgier(in f) m. **2** adj belgisch.

Belgium ['beldʒəm] n Belgien nt.

belie [bɪ'laɪ] vt **(a)** (prove false) words, proverb Lügen strafen, widerlegen. **(b)** (give false impression of) hinwegtäuschen über (+acc).

belief [bɪ'liːf] n **(a)** Glaube m (in an +acc). **it is beyond** ~ es ist nicht zu glauben; **in the** ~ **that ...** im Glauben, daß ...; **it is my** ~ **that ...** ich bin der Überzeugung, daß ...; **strong** ~**s** feste Überzeugungen.

believe [bɪ'liːv] **1** vt **(a)** sth glauben; sb glauben (+dat). **I don't** ~ **you** das glaube ich (Ihnen) nicht; **don't you** ~ **it** wer's glaubt, wird selig (col); **I would never have** ~**d it of him** das hätte ich nie von ihm geglaubt; **he could hardly** ~ **his eyes/ears** er traute seinen Augen/Ohren nicht. **(b)** (think) glauben. **I** ~ **so/not** ich glaube schon/nicht. **2** vi (have a religious faith) an Gott glauben.

♦ **believe in** vi +prep obj glauben an (+acc). **he doesn't** ~ ~ **medicine/doctors** er hält nicht viel von Medikamenten/Ärzten.

believer [bɪ'liːvəʳ] n **(a)** (Rel) Gläubige(r) mf. **(b)** **to be a (firm)** ~ **in sth** (grundsätzlich) für etw sein.

belittle [bɪ'lɪtl] vt herabsetzen.

bell [bel] n **(a)** Glocke f; (small: on toys etc) Glöckchen nt, Schelle f; (school ~, door~, of cycle) Klingel f; (Boxing) Gong m. **(b)** (sound of ~) Läuten nt; (of door~, telephone etc) Klingeln nt. **was that the** ~? hat es gerade geklingelt or geläutet?

bell: ~**-bottomed trousers**, ~**-bottoms** npl ausgestellte Hosen; ~**-boy** n (US) Page, Hoteljunge m.

belle [bel] n Schöne, Schönheit f. **the** ~ **of the ball** die Ballkönigin.

bellhop ['bel,hɒp] n (US) = **bell-boy**.

bellicose ['belɪkəʊs] adj nation, mood kriegerisch.

belligerent [bɪ'lɪdʒərənt] **1** adj **(a)** nation kriege-

---

risch; person, attitude streitlustig; speech aggressiv. **(b)** (waging war) kriegführend. **2** n (nation) kriegführendes Land; (person) Streitende(r) mf.

bell-jar ['beldʒɑːʳ] n (Glas)glocke f.

bellow ['beləʊ] **1** vi (animal, person) brüllen; (singing also) grölen (col). **2** vt (also ~ **out**) brüllen; song also grölen (col). **3** n Brüllen nt.

bellows ['beləʊz] npl Blasebalg m.

bell: ~**push** n Klingel f; ~**-ringer** n Glöckner m; ~**-shaped** adj glockenförmig, kelchförmig; ~**tower** n Glockenturm m.

belly ['belɪ] n Bauch m.

belly: ~**-ache** n (col) Bauchweh nt (col), Bauchschmerzen pl; **2** vi (col: complain) murren (about über +acc); ~ **button** n (col) Bauchnabel m.

belong [bɪ'lɒŋ] vi **(a)** gehören (to sb jdm). **who does it** ~ **to?** wem gehört es?; **the lid** ~**s to this box** der Deckel gehört zu dieser Schachtel; **to** ~ **to a club** einem Club angehören. **(b)** (be in right place) gehören. **to feel that one doesn't** ~ das Gefühl haben, daß man nicht dazugehört; **where does this one** ~? wo gehört das hin?

belongings [bɪ'lɒŋɪŋz] npl Besitz m, Habe f (geh). **personal** ~ persönlicher Eigentum, persönlicher Besitz; **all his** ~ sein ganzes Hab und Gut.

beloved [bɪ'lʌvd] **1** adj geliebt; memory lieb, teuer. **2** n Geliebte(r) mf.

below [bɪ'ləʊ] **1** prep **(a)** (under) unterhalb (+gen); (with line, level etc also) unter (+dat or with motion +acc). **the sun disappeared** ~ **the horizon** die Sonne verschwand hinter dem Horizont; **to be** ~ **sb** (in rank) (rangmäßig) unter jdm stehen. **(b)** (downstream from) unterhalb (+gen). **2** adv unten. **they live one floor** ~ sie wohnen ein Stockwerk tiefer; **the flat** ~ die Wohnung darunter; (below us) die Wohnung unter uns; **see** ~ siehe unten; **15 degrees** ~ 15 Grad unter Null, 15 Grad minus.

belt [belt] **1** n **(a)** (on clothes) Gürtel m; (for holding etc, seat~) Gurt m. **that was below the** ~ das war ein Schlag unter die Gürtellinie; **to tighten one's** ~ (fig) (sich dat) den Gürtel or Riemen enger schnallen (col). **(b)** (Tech) (Treib)riemen m; (conveyor ~) Band nt. **(c)** (tract of land) Gürtel m. **industrial** ~ Industriegürtel m. **(d)** (col: hit) Schlag m. **2** vt (col: hit) knallen (col). **she** ~**ed him one in the eye** sie verpaßte ihm eins aufs Auge (col). **3** vi (col: rush) rasen (col). **to** ~ **out** hinaus-/herausrasen (col); **we were really** ~**ing along** wir sind wirklich gerast (col).

♦ **belt out** vt sep (col) tune schmettern (col).

♦ **belt up 1** vt sep jacket den Gürtel (+gen) zumachen. **2** vi **(a)** (col) die Klappe (col) halten; (stop making noise) mit dem Krach aufhören (col). **(b)** (hum: put seatbelt on) sich anschnallen.

bemoan [bɪ'məʊn] vt beklagen.

bemused [bɪ'mjuːzd] adj (puzzled) verwirrt.

bench [bentʃ] n **(a)** (seat) Bank f. **(b)** (Jur: office of a judge) Richteramt nt; (judges generally) Richter pl; (court) Gericht nt. **to be on the** ~ (permanent office) Richter sein; (when in court) der Richter sein. **(c)** (show ~) Werkbank f; (in lab) Experimentiertisch m.

bend [bend] (vb: pret, ptp **bent**) **1** n (in river, tube etc) Krümmung, Biegung f; (in road also) Kurve f. **to drive sb round the** ~ (col) jdn verrückt or wahnsinnig machen (col). **2** vt **(a)** biegen; arm, knee also beugen; (forwards) back also, head beugen. **on** ~**ed knees** auf Knien; (fig also) kniefällig. **(b)** (fig) rules frei auslegen. **3** vi **(a)** sich biegen; (pipe, rail also) sich krümmen; (forwards also) (tree, corn etc) sich neigen; (person) sich beugen. **this metal** ~**s easily** (a bad thing) dieses Metall verbiegt sich leicht; (a good thing) dieses Metall läßt sich leicht biegen. **(b)** (river) eine Biegung machen; (road also) eine Kurve machen. **(c)** (fig: submit) sich beugen, sich fügen (to dat).

♦ **bend down** vi (person) sich bücken.
♦ **bend over 1** vi (person) sich bücken. **2** vt sep umbiegen.
bends [bendz] n the ~ Taucherkrankheit f.
beneath [bɪ'niːθ] **1** prep **(a)** unter (+dat or with motion +acc); (with line, level etc also) unterhalb (+gen); see **below 1 (a)**. **(b)** (unworthy of) it is ~ him das ist unter seiner Würde. **2** adv unten; see also **below 2**.
benediction [,benɪ'dɪkʃən] n Segen m; (act of blessing) Segnung f.
benefactor ['benɪfæktəʳ] n Wohltäter m; (giver of money also) Gönner m.
beneficial [,benɪ'fɪʃəl] adj gut (to für); climate also zuträglich (geh) (to dat); influence also vorteilhaft; advice nützlich (to für).
beneficiary [,benɪ'fɪʃərɪ] n Nutznießer(in f) m; (of will, insurance etc) Begünstigte(r) mf.
benefit ['benɪfɪt] **1** n **(a)** (advantage) Vorteil m; (profit) Gewinn m. **for the** ~ **of your health** Ihrer Gesundheit zuliebe; **it is for his** ~ **that this was done** das ist seinetwegen geschehen; **to give sb the** ~ **of the doubt** im Zweifel zu jds Gunsten entscheiden. **(b)** (allowance) Unterstützung f; (sickness ~) Krankengeld nt; (social security ~) Sozialhilfe f. **(c)** (special performance) Benefizveranstaltung f. **2** vt nützen (+dat); (healthwise) guttun (+dat). **3** vi profitieren (from, by von); (from experience also) Nutzen ziehen (from aus). **who will** ~ **from that?** wem wird das nützen?
Benelux ['benɪlʌks] n Beneluxländer pl.
benevolence [bɪ'nevələns] n see adj Wohlwollen nt; Gutmütigkeit f; Güte f.
benevolent [bɪ'nevələnt] adj wohlwollend; smile gutmütig; (as character trait) gütig.
benign [bɪ'naɪn] adj **(a)** gütig; influence günstig; climate mild. **(b)** (Med) gutartig.
bent [bent] **1** pret, ptp of **bend**. **2** adj **(a)** metal etc gebogen; (out of shape) verbogen. **(b)** (Brit col: dishonest) person korrupt. **(c)** (col: homosexual) andersrum pred (col). **(d) to be** ~ **on sth/doing sth** etw unbedingt wollen/tun wollen. **3** n (aptitude) Neigung f (for zu); (type of mind, character) Schlag m.
bequeath [bɪ'kwiːð] vt vermachen; (fig also) hinterlassen (to sb jdm).
bequest [bɪ'kwest] n (legacy) Nachlaß m; (to museum) Stiftung f.
berate [bɪ'reɪt] vt (liter) schelten.
bereaved [bɪ'riːvd] npl the ~ die Hinterbliebenen pl.
bereavement [bɪ'riːvmənt] n (death in family) Trauerfall m. **to feel a sense of** ~ **at sth** etw als schmerzlichen Verlust empfinden.
bereft [bɪ'reft] adj **to be** ~ **of sth** einer Sache (gen) bar sein (geh); ~ **of reason** ohne jede Vernunft.
beret ['bereɪ] n Baskenmütze f.
Berlin [bɜː'lɪn] n Berlin nt. **the** ~ **wall** die Mauer.
Bermuda [bɜː'mjuːdə] n Bermuda nt. ~ **shorts** Bermudashorts pl.
berry ['berɪ] n Beere f. **as brown as a** ~ ganz braungebrannt.
berserk [bə'sɜːk] adj wild. **to go** ~ wild werden; (audience) zu toben anfangen; (go mad) überschnappen (col).
berth [bɜːθ] **1** n **(a)** (on ship) Koje f; (on train) Bett nt. **(b)** (Naut: place for ship) Liegeplatz m. **to give sb/sth a wide** ~ (fig) einen (weiten) Bogen um jdn/etw machen. **2** vi anlegen.
beseech [bɪ'siːtʃ] pret, ptp ~ed or (liter) **besought** vt person anflehen, beschwören.
beset [bɪ'set] pret, ptp ~ vt (difficulties, dangers) (von allen Seiten) bedrängen; (doubts) befallen; (temptations, trials) heimsuchen. **to be** ~ **with danger** (journey etc) voller Gefahren sein.
besetting [bɪ'setɪŋ] adj his ~ **sin** eine ständige Untugend von ihm.

beside [bɪ'saɪd] prep **(a)** neben (+dat or with motion +acc); (at the edge of) am Rand (+dat or with motion +acc). ~ **the road** am Straßenrand. **(b)** (compared with) neben (+dat). **(c) to be** ~ **oneself** (with anger) außer sich sein (with vor).
besides [bɪ'saɪdz] **1** adv außerdem. **have you got any others** ~? haben Sie noch andere or noch welche? **2** prep außer (+dat). **others** ~ **ourselves** außer uns noch andere; ~ **which he was unwell** außerdem fühlte er sich nicht wohl.
besiege [bɪ'siːdʒ] vt (Mil, fig) belagern; (with offers) überhäufen; (pester) bestürmen.
besotted [bɪ'sɒtɪd] adj völlig vernarrt (with in +acc).
besought [bɪ'sɔːt] (liter) pret, ptp of **beseech**.
bespatter [bɪ'spætəʳ] vt bespritzen.
bespectacled [bɪ'spektɪkld] adj bebrillt.
bespoke [bɪ'spəʊk] **1** prep, ptp of **bespeak**. **2** adj garment Maß-. **a** ~ **tailor** ein Maßschneider m.
best [best] **1** adj, superl of **good** beste(r,s) attr; (most favourable) route, price also günstigste(r, s) attr. **to be** ~ am besten/günstigsten sein; **the** ~ **thing about her** das Beste an ihr; **may the** ~ **man win!** dem Besten der Sieg!; **the** ~ **part of the year** fast das ganze Jahr.
   2 adv, superl of **well (a)** am besten; like am liebsten; enjoy am meisten. **the** ~ **known title** der bekannteste Titel; ~ **of all** am allerbesten/-liebsten/-meisten; **I helped him as** ~ **I could** ich half ihm, so gut ich konnte; **do as you think** ~ tun Sie, was Sie für richtig halten; **you know** ~ Sie müssen es (am besten) wissen. **(b) you had** ~ **go now** am besten gehen Sie jetzt.
   3 n **(a) the** ~ der/die/das beste; **the** ~ **of the bunch** (col) der/die/das beste; **he can sing with the** ~ **of them** er kann sich im Singen mit den Besten messen; **to be in one's (Sunday)** ~ im Sonntagsstaat sein. **(b) to do one's (level)** ~ sein Bestes or möglichstes tun; **to make the** ~ **of it/a bad job** das Beste daraus machen; **the** ~ **of it is that ...** das beste daran ist, daß ...; **I meant it for the** ~ ich habe es doch nur gut gemeint; **to the** ~ **of my ability** so gut ich kann/konnte; **to the** ~ **of my knowledge** meines Wissens; **to look one's** ~ besonders gut aussehen; **he is at his** ~ **at about 8 in the evening** so gegen 8 Uhr abends ist seine beste Zeit; **at** ~ bestenfalls; **all the** ~ alles Gute!
bestial ['bestɪəl] adj acts, cruelty bestialisch; person, appearance brutal; (carnal) tierisch.
best man n Trauzeuge m (des Bräutigams).
bestow [bɪ'stəʊ] vt (on or upon sb jdm) (grant, give) schenken; honour erweisen; title, medal verleihen.
best-seller [,best'seləʳ] n Verkaufs- or Kassenschlager m; (book) Bestseller m.
bet [bet] (vb: pret, ptp ~) **1** n Wette f (on auf +acc); (money etc staked) Wetteinsatz m. **to have a** ~ **with sb** mit jdm wetten; **it's a safe** ~ **that ...** (fig) höchstwahrscheinlich ... **2** vt **(a)** wetten, setzen (against gegen, on auf +acc). **I** ~ **him £5** ich habe mit ihm (um) £ 5 gewettet. **(b)** (col) wetten. **you can** ~ **your boots or your bottom dollar that ...** Siekönnen Gift darauf nehmen, daß ... (col). **3** vi wetten. **to** ~ **on a horse** auf ein Pferd setzen; **you** ~! und ob! (col).
betray [bɪ'treɪ] vt verraten (also Pol) (to dat or (Pol) an +acc); trust enttäuschen; sb's secrets also preisgeben. **his accent** ~ed him as a foreigner sein Akzent verriet, daß er Ausländer war.
betrayal [bɪ'treɪəl] n Verrat m (of an +acc); (instance) Verrat m (of trust) Enttäuschung f; (of friends also) Untreue f (of gegenüber); (of plans also) Preisgabe f.
betrothal [bɪ'trəʊðəl] n (liter, hum) Verlobung f.
better [better] **1** adj, comp of **good** besser; route, way also günstiger. **he's much** ~ es geht ihm viel besser; **that's** ~! (approval) so ist es besser!; (relief etc) endlich!; **the** ~ **part of an hour** fast eine Stunde;

to go one ~ einen Schritt weiter gehen; *(in offer)* höher gehen.
2 *adv, comp of* **well (a)** besser; *like* lieber; *enjoy* mehr. ~ **they are** ~ **off than we are** sie sind besser dran als wir; **all the** ~**, so much the** ~ um so besser; **to think** ~ **of it** es sich *(dat)* noch einmal überlegen. **(b) I had** ~ **go** ich gehe jetzt wohl besser; **you'd** ~ **do what he says** tun Sie lieber, was er sagt.
3 *n* **(a) one's** ~**s** Leute, die über einem stehen; *(socially also)* Höhergestellte. **(b)** *(person, object)* **the** ~ der/die/das Bessere. **(c) it's a change for the** ~ es ist eine Wendung zum Guten; **it's done now, for** ~ **or worse** so oder so, es ist geschehen; **to get the** ~ **of sb** *(person)* jdn unterkriegen *(col)*; *(illness)* jdn erwischen *(col)*; *(problem etc)* jdm schwer zu schaffen machen.
4 *vt (improve on)* verbessern; *(surpass)* übertreffen.
5 *vr* **to** ~ **oneself** sich verbessern.

betting: ~ **man** *n* **I'm not a** ~ **man** ich wette eigentlich nicht; ~ **shop** *n* Wettannahme *f.*

between [bɪ'twiːn] **1** *prep* **(a)** zwischen *(+dat)*; *(with movement)* zwischen *(+acc)*. **sit down** ~ **those two boys** setz dich zwischen diese beiden Jungen; **in** ~ zwischen *(+dat/acc)*; ~ **now and next week we must** ... bis nächste Woche müssen wir ...; **there's nothing** ~ **them** *(they're equal)* sie sind gleich gut; *(no feelings, relationship)* zwischen ihnen ist nichts. **(b)** *(amongst)* unter *(+dat/ acc)*. **we shared an apple** ~ **us** wir teilten uns *(dat)* einen Apfel; ~ **you and me** he is not very clever unter uns *(dat)* (gesagt), er ist nicht besonders gescheit; **that's just** ~ **ourselves** das bleibt aber unter uns; **we have a car** ~ **the two/three of us** wir haben zu zweit/dritt ein Auto. **2** *adv (place)* dazwischen; *(time also)* zwischendurch. **in** ~ dazwischen; **the space/time** ~ der Zwischenraum/die Zwischenzeit, der Raum/ die Zeit dazwischen.

bevelled edge ['bevld'edʒ] Schrägkante *f.*

beverage ['bevərɪdʒ] *n* Getränk *nt.*

bevy ['bevɪ] *n (of girls)* Schar *f.*

bewail [bɪ'weɪl] *vt (deplore)* beklagen; *(lament also)* bejammern; *sb's death also* betrauern.

beware [bɪ'weəʳ] *vti imper and infin only* **to** ~ **(of)** **sb/sth** sich vor jdm/etw hüten, sich vor jdm/etw in acht nehmen; ~ **of falling** passen Sie auf, daß Sie nicht fallen; "~ **of the dog**" „Vorsicht, bissiger Hund".

bewilder [bɪ'wɪldəʳ] *vt (confuse)* verwirren; *(baffle)* verblüffen.

bewildered [bɪ'wɪldəd] *adj* verwirrt; *(baffled)* verblüfft, perplex *(col).*

bewildering [bɪ'wɪldərɪŋ] *adj see vt* verwirrend; verblüffend.

bewilderment [bɪ'wɪldəmənt] *n see vt* Verwirrung *f*; Verblüffung *f.* **in** ~ verwundert.

bewitch [bɪ'wɪtʃ] *vt* verzaubern; *(fig)* bezaubern.

beyond [bɪ'jɒnd] **1** *prep* **(a)** *(on the other side of)* hinter *(+dat)*, jenseits *(+gen) (geh)*; *(further than)* über *(+acc)* ... hinaus, weiter als. ~ **the Alps** jenseits der Alpen. **(b)** *(in time)* ~ **6 o'clock** nach 6 Uhr; ~ **the middle of June/the week** nach Mitte Juni/über die Woche hinaus. **(c) a task** ~ **her abilities** eine Aufgabe, die über ihre Fähigkeiten geht; **that's almost** ~ **belief** das ist fast unglaublich or nicht zu glauben; **that's** ~ **me** *(I don't understand)* das geht über meinen Verstand. **2** *adv (on the other side of)* jenseits davon *(geh)*. **the world** ~ das Jenseits.

bi- [baɪ] *pref* bi, Bi-.

biannual [baɪ'ænjʊəl] *adj* halbjährlich.

bias ['baɪəs] *(vb: pret, ptp* ~**(s)ed)** **1** *n* **(a)** Voreingenommenheit *f*; *(of course, newspaper etc)* (einseitige) Ausrichtung *f (towards* auf *+acc)*; *(of person)* Vorliebe *f (towards* für). **to have a** ~ **against sth** *(course, newspaper etc)* gegen etw

eingestellt sein; *(person)* ein Vorurteil *nt* gegen etw haben; **to have a left-wing/right-wing** ~ nach links/rechts ausgerichtet sein. **(b)** *(Sew)* on the ~ schräg zum Fadenlauf. **2** *vt report, article* einseitig färben.

bias(s)ed ['baɪəst] *adj* voreingenommen.

bib [bɪb] *n* Latz *m*; *(for baby)* Lätzchen *nt.*

Bible ['baɪbl] *n* Bibel *f.*

biblical ['bɪblɪkəl] *adj* biblisch.

bibliography [ˌbɪblɪ'ɒgrəfɪ] *n* Bibliographie *f.*

bicarbonate of soda [baɪˌkɑːbənɪtəv'səʊdə] *n (Cook)* Natron *nt*; *(Chem)* doppelt kohlensaures Natrium.

bi-: ~**centenary,** *(US)* ~**centennial** *n* Zweihundertjahrfeier *f (of gen).*

biceps ['baɪseps] *n* Bizeps *m.*

bicker ['bɪkəʳ] *vi* sich zanken. **they are always** ~**ing** sie liegen sich dauernd in den Haaren.

bicycle ['baɪsɪkl] *n* Fahrrad *nt.* **to ride a** ~ Fahrrad fahren, radfahren; *see* **cycle.**

bid [bɪd] **1** *vti* **(a)** *pret, ptp* ~ *(at auction)* bieten *(for* auf *+acc).* **(b)** *pret, ptp* ~ *(Cards)* reizen, bieten. **(c)** *pret* **bade,** *ptp* ~**den** *(say)* **to** ~ **sb good-morning** jdm einen guten Morgen wünschen; **to** ~ **farewell to sb** jdm Lebewohl sagen *(geh).* **2** *vi pret* **bad,** *ptp* ~**den everything** ~**s fair to be successful** es sieht alles recht erfolgversprechend aus. **3** *n* **(a)** *(at auction)* Gebot *nt (for* auf *+acc)*; *(Comm)* Angebot *nt (for* für). **(b)** *(Cards)* Ansage *f.* **(c)** *(attempt)* Versuch *m.* **to make a** ~ **for power** nach der Macht greifen; **to make a** ~ **for freedom** versuchen, die Freiheit zu erlangen.

bidden ['bɪdn] *ptp of* **bid.**

bidder ['bɪdəʳ] *n* Bietende(r) *mf.* **to sell to the highest** ~ an den Meistbietenden verkaufen.

bidding ['bɪdɪŋ] *n* **(a)** *(at auction)* Steigern, Bieten *nt.* **(b)** *(Cards)* Bieten, Reizen *nt.*

bide [baɪd] *vt* **to** ~ **one's time** den rechten Augenblick abwarten.

bidet ['biːdeɪ] *n* Bidet *nt.*

biennial [baɪ'enɪəl] **1** *adj (every two years)* zweijährlich. **2** *n (Bot)* zweijährige Pflanze.

bier [bɪəʳ] *n* Bahre *f.*

biff [bɪf] *n (col)* Stoß, Puff *(col) m.* **a** ~ **on the nose** eins auf die Nase *(col).*

bifocal [baɪ'fəʊkəl] **1** *adj* Bifokal-. **2** *n* ~**s** *pl* Bifokalbrille *f.*

big [bɪg] **1** *adj (+er)* groß. **a** ~ **man** ein großer, schwerer Mann; **my** ~ **brother** mein großer Bruder; **that's really** ~ **of you** *(iro)* wirklich nobel von dir *(iro)*; **he is too** ~ **for his boots** *(col)* der ist ja größenwahnsinnig; **to have a** ~ **head** *(col)* eingebildet sein; **to earn** ~ **money** das große Geld verdienen *(col)*; **to have** ~ **ideas** große Pläne haben *(col)*; **to have a** ~ **mouth** *(col)* eine große Klappe haben *(col)*; **to do things in a** ~ **way** alles im großen (Stil) tun; ~ **deal!** *(iro col)* na und? *(col)*; *(that's not much effort)* ist ja toll! *(iro col).* **2** *adv* **to talk** ~ große Töne spucken *(col)*; **to think** ~ im großen (Maßstab) planen.

bigamist ['bɪgəmɪst] *n* Bigamist *m.*

bigamy ['bɪgəmɪ] *n* Bigamie *f.*

big: ~ **business** *n (high finance)* Großkapital *nt;* ~ **dipper** *n (Brit: at fair)* Achterbahn *f;* ~ **game** *n (Hunt)* Großwild *nt;* ~**head** *n (col: person)* Angeber *m (col);* ~**headed** *adj (col)* angeberisch *(col);* ~ **noise** *n (col)* hohes Tier *(col).*

bigoted ['bɪgətɪd] *adj* engstirnig.

big: ~ **shot** *n* hohes Tier *(col);* ~**-time** *n (col)* **to make** *or* **hit the** ~**-time** groß einsteigen *(col);* ~ **toe** *n* große Zehe; ~ **top** *n (circus)* Zirkus *m; (main tent)* Hauptzelt *nt;* ~ **wheel** *n* **(a)** *(US col)* = ~ **shot;** **(b)** *(Brit: at fair)* Riesenrad *nt;* ~**wig** *n (col)* hohes Tier *(col).*

bike [baɪk] *(col)* **1** *n (Fahr)rad nt; (motor* ~*)* Motorrad *nt.* **2** *vi* radeln *(col).*

bikini [bɪ'kiːnɪ] *n* Bikini *m.*

bilateral [baɪ'lætərəl] *adj* bilateral.

bilberry ['bɪlbərɪ] *n* Heidelbeere *f*.

bile [baɪl] *n (Med)* Galle *f*.

bilingual [baɪ'lɪŋwəl] *adj* zweisprachig.

bilious ['bɪlɪəs] *adj (Med)* Gallen-. ~ **attack** Gallen-kolik *f*.

bill¹ [bɪl] **1** *n (of bird, turtle)* Schnabel *m*. **2** *vi* to ~ **and coo** *(birds)* schnäbeln und gurren.

bill² **1** *n* **(a)** *(statement of charges)* Rechnung *f*. **could we have the ~ please** zahlen bitte!, wir möchten bitte zahlen. **(b)** *(US: banknote)* Bank-note *f*, Schein *m*. **(c)** *(poster)* Plakat *nt*; *(on notice board)* Anschlag *m*; *(public announcement)* Aus-hang *m*; **"stick no ~s"** „Plakate ankleben ver-boten". **(d)** *(Theat)* Programm *nt*. **to top the** ~ **Star** *m* des Abends/der Saison sein; *(act)* die Hauptattraktion sein. **(e)** ~ **of fare** Speisekarte *f*. **(f)** *(Parl)* Gesetzentwurf *m*. **(g)** *(Comm)* ~ **of lading** Frachtbrief *m*; ~ **of exchange** Wechsel *m*; ~ **of sale** Verkaufsurkunde *f*; **to fit** *or* **fill the** ~ *(fig)* der/die/das richtige sein, passen.

    2 *vt* **(a)** *customers* eine Rechnung ausstellen (+*dat*). **(b)** *play, actor* ankündigen. **he's ~ed at the Apollo** er tritt im Apollo auf.

billboard ['bɪlbɔːd] *n* Reklametafel *f*.

billet ['bɪlɪt] **1** *n (Mil)* Quartier *nt*, Unterkunft *f*. **2** *vt (Mil)* einquartieren *(on sb* bei jdm).

billfold ['bɪl,fəʊld] *n (US)* Brieftasche *f*.

billiards ['bɪljədz] *n* Billard *nt*.

billion ['bɪljən] *n* **(a)** *(Brit)* Billion *f*. **(b)** *(US)* Mil-liarde *f*.

billow ['bɪləʊ] **1** *n (of smoke)* Schwaden *m*. **2** *vi (sail)* sich blähen; *(dress etc)* sich bauschen.

billy(-goat) ['bɪlɪ(gəʊt)] *n* Ziegenbock *m*.

bin [bɪn] *n (esp Brit) (for bread)* Brotkasten *m*; *(rubbish~)* Mülleimer *m*; *(dust~)* Mülltonne *f*; *(litter-~)* Abfallbehälter *m*.

binary ['baɪnərɪ] *adj* binär.

bind [baɪnd] *pret, ptp* **bound 1** *vt* **(a)** *(make fast, tie together)* binden *(to an* +*acc); person* fesseln; *(fig)* verbinden *(to* mit). **bound hand and foot an Händen und Füßen gefesselt. (b)** *wound, arm etc* verbinden; *bandage* wickeln. **(c)** *(secure edge of)* einfassen. **(d)** *book* binden. **(e)** *(oblige)* **to ~ sb to sth/to do sth** jdn zu etw verpflichten/jdn verpflichten, etw zu tun; *see* **bound³**. **2** *n (col: nuisance)* **to be** (a bit of) a ~ recht lästig sein.

◆ **bind over** *vt sep (Jur)* **to ~ sb ~ (to keep the peace)** jdn verwarnen; **he was bound ~ for six months** er bekam eine sechsmonatige Bewäh-rungsfrist.

◆ **bind together** *vt sep (lit)* zusammenbinden; *(fig)* verbinden.

◆ **bind up** *vt sep wound* verbinden; *hair* hoch-binden. **to be bound ~ in** *(work etc)* verwachsen sein mit; **to be bound ~ with** *(person)* eng ver-bunden sein mit.

binder ['baɪndə^r] *n* **(a)** *(machine)* Bindemaschine *f*. **(b)** *(for papers)* Hefter *m*.

binding ['baɪndɪŋ] **1** *n (of book)* Einband *m*; *(Sew)* Band *nt*; *(on skis)* Bindung *f*. **2** *adj agreement* bindend, verbindlich *(on* für).

binge [bɪndʒ] *n (col)* Gelage *nt*. **to go on a ~** *(drink-ing)* auf Sauftour *(col)* gehen; *(eating)* eine Freß-tour *(col)* machen.

bingo ['bɪŋgəʊ] *n* Bingo *nt*.

bin liner *n* Mülltüte *f*.

binoculars [bɪ'nɒkjuləz] *npl* Fernglas *nt*.

bio- [baɪəʊ-]: **~chemist** *n* Biochemiker(in *f*) *m*; **~chemistry** *n* Biochemie *f*; **~degradable** *adj* biologisch abbaubar.

biographer [baɪ'ɒgrəfə^r] *n* Biograph(in *f*) *m*.

biographic(al) [,baɪəʊ'græfɪk(əl)] *adj* biogra-phisch.

biography [baɪ'ɒgrəfɪ] *n* Biographie *f*.

biological [baɪə'lɒdʒɪkəl] *adj* biologisch.

biologist [baɪ'ɒlədʒɪst] *n* Biologe *m*, Biologin *f*.

biology [baɪ'ɒlədʒɪ] *n* Biologie *f*.

biophysics [,baɪəʊ'fɪzɪks] *n sing* Biophysik *f*.

birch [bɜːtʃ] *n* Birke *f*; *(for whipping)* Rute *f*.

bird [bɜːd] *n* **(a)** Vogel *m*. **a little ~ told me** *(col)* das hat mir mein kleiner Mann im Ohr erzählt; **the early ~ catches the worm** Morgenstund hat Gold im Mund *(Prov)*; **a ~ in the hand is worth two in the bush** *(Prov)* der Spatz in der Hand ist besser als die Taube auf dem Dach *(Prov)*; **they are ~s of a feather** sie sind vom gleichen Schlag; **~s of a feather flock together** gleich und gleich gesellt sich gern; **to tell sb about the ~s and the bees** jdm erzählen, wo die kleinen Kinder herkommen. **(b)** *(Brit col: girl)* Biene *f (col)*. **(c)** **he's an odd ~** *(col)* er ist ein komischer Kauz.

bird ~-cage *n* Vogelkäfig *m*; **~ sanctuary** *n* Vogel-schutzgebiet *nt*; **~seed** *n* Vogelfutter *nt*.

bird's: **~-eye view** *n* Vogelperspektive *f*; ~ **nest** *n* Vogelnest *nt*.

bird watcher *n* Vogelbeobachter(in *f*) *m*.

Biro ® ['baɪərəʊ] *n (Brit)* Kugelschreiber, Kuli *(col) m*.

birth [bɜːθ] *n* **(a)** Geburt *f*. **to give ~ to** zur Welt bringen; **to give ~** entbinden; *(animal)* jungen. **(b)** *(parentage)* Abstammung, Herkunft *f*. **Scottish by ~** gebürtiger Schotte, gebürtige Schottin; **of good/low** *or* **humble ~** aus guter Familie/von niedriger Geburt. **(c)** *(fig)* Geburt *f*; *(of movement, fashion etc)* Aufkommen *nt*; *(of nation, party, company also)* Entstehen *nt*; *(of new era)* Anbruch *m*; *(of planet)* Entstehung *f*.

birth: **~ certificate** *n* Geburtsurkunde *f*; **~ con-trol** *n* Geburtenkontrolle *f*.

birthday ['bɜːθdeɪ] *n* Geburtstag *m*. **what did you get for your ~?** was hast du zum Geburtstag bekommen?

birthday: **~ cake** *n* Geburtstagskuchen *m or* -torte *f*; **~ card** *n* Geburtstagskarte *f*; **~ party** *n* Geburtstagsfeier *f*; *(with dancing etc)* Geburts-tagsparty *f*; *(for child)* Kindergeburtstag *m*; **~ present** *n* Geburtstagsgeschenk *nt*; **~ suit** *n (col)* Adams-/Evaskostüm *nt (col)*.

birth: **~mark** *n* Muttermal *nt*; **~place** *n* Ge-burtsort *m*; **~rate** *n* Geburtenrate *or* -ziffer *f*; **~right** *n (fig: right)* angeborenes Recht.

biscuit ['bɪskɪt] *n* **(a)** *(Brit)* Keks *m*. **that takes/ you take the ~!** *(col)* das übertrifft alles; *(negatively)* das schlägt dem Faß den Boden aus! **(b)** *(US)* Brötchen *nt*. **2** *adj (colour)* beige.

bisect [baɪ'sekt] *vt* in zwei Teile teilen; *(Math)* halbieren.

bishop ['bɪʃəp] *n* Bischof *m*; *(Chess)* Läufer *m*.

bison ['baɪsn] *n (American)* Bison *m*; *(European)* Wisent *m*.

bit¹ [bɪt] *n* **(a)** *(for horse)* Gebiß(stange *f*) *nt*. **(b)** *(of drill)* Bohrer *m*.

bit² **1** *n* **(a)** *(piece)* Stück *nt*; *(smaller)* Stückchen *nt*; *(of glass also)* Scherbe *f*; *(part or place in book etc)* Stelle *f*. **a ~** *(not much, small amount)* ein bißchen, etwas; **would you like a ~ of ice cream?** möchten Sie etwas Eis?; **there's a ~ of truth in what he says** daran ist schon etwas Wahres; **a ~ of advice/news** ein Rat *m*/eine Neuigkeit; **we had a ~ of trouble** wir hatten ein wenig Ärger; **it wasn't a ~ of help/use** das war überhaupt keine Hilfe/hat überhaupt nichts genützt; **there's quite a ~ of bread left** es ist noch eine ganze Menge Brot übrig; **in ~s and pieces** in tausend Stücken; **bring all your ~s and pieces** bring deine Siebensachen; **to come** *or* **fall to ~s** kaputtgehen.

    (b) *(with time)* **a ~** ein Weilchen *nt*.

    (c) *(with cost)* **a ~** eine ganze Menge.

    (d) **to do one's ~** sein(en) Teil tun.

    (e) **he's a ~ of a rogue/musician/expert** er ist ein ziemlicher Schlingel/er ist gar kein schlechter Musiker/er versteht einiges davon.

    (f) ~ **by ~** Stück für Stück; *(gradually)* nach und nach; **he's every ~ a soldier** er ist durch und

durch Soldat; it/he is every ~ as good as ... es/er ist genauso gut wie ...; not a ~ of it keine Spur *(col)*.
(g) when it comes to the ~ wenn es drauf ankommt.
(h) *(coin) (Brit)* Stück *nt*, Münze *f*. **2/4/6 ~s** *(US)* 25/50/75 Cent(s).
(i) *(Comp)* Bit *nt*.
2 *adv* **a** ~ ein bißchen, etwas; **I'm not a** ~ **surprised** das wundert mich kein bißchen *(col)* or keineswegs; **he's improved quite a** ~ er hat sich ziemlich gebessert.

bit³ *pret of* **bite.**

bitch [bɪtʃ] **1** *n* **(a)** *(of dog)* Hündin *f*. **terrier** ~ weiblicher Terrier. **(b)** *(col: woman)* Miststück *nt (col)*; *(spiteful)* Hexe *f*. **2** *vi* *(col: complain)* meckern *(col) (about* über +*acc)*.

bitchy ['bɪtʃɪ] *adj* (+*er*) *(col)* woman gehässig, gemein; *remark also* bissig.

bite [baɪt] *vb: pret* **bit,** *ptp* **bitten) 1** *n* **(a)** Biß *m*. **(b)** *(insect* ~) Stich *m*; *(flea* ~) Biß *m*; *(love* ~) (Knutsch)fleck *m (col)*. **(c)** *(Fishing)* **I think I've got a** ~ ich glaube, es hat einer angebissen. **(d)** *(of food)* Happen *m*. **there's not a** ~ **to eat** es ist überhaupt nichts zu essen da; **do you fancy a** ~ **(to eat)?** möchten Sie etwas essen? **2** *vt (person, dog)* beißen; *(insect)* stechen. **to** ~ **one's nails** an den Nägeln kauen; **to** ~ **the dust** *(col)* ins Gras beißen *(col)*; **once bitten twice shy** *(Prov)* (ein) gebranntes Kind scheut das Feuer *(Prov)*. **3** *vi (dog etc)* beißen; *(insects)* stechen; *(fish, fig col)* anbeißen.

♦ **bite into** *vi* +*prep obj (person)* (hinein)beißen in (+*acc)*; *(teeth)* (tief) eindringen in (+*acc)*; *(acid, saw)* sich hineinfressen in (+*acc)*; *(screw, drill)* sich hineinbohren in (+*acc)*.

♦ **bite off** *vt sep* abbeißen. **he won't** ~ **your head** ~ er wird dir schon nicht den Kopf abreißen; **to** ~ **more than one can chew** *(prov)* sich *(dat)* zuviel zumuten.

♦ **bite through** *vt insep* durchbeißen.

biting ['baɪtɪŋ] *adj* beißend; *cold, wind also* schneidend.

bitten ['bɪtʃɪ] *ptp of* **bite.**

bitter ['bɪtəʳ] **1** *adj* (+*er*) bitter; *weather, wind* eisig; *enemy, struggle, opposition* erbittert. **it was a** ~ **pill to swallow** das war eine bittere Pille; **he's still** ~ **about it** er nimmt es mir/ihnen *etc* noch übel; **to the** ~ **end** bis zum bitteren Ende. **2** *n (Brit: beer)* ≈ Altbier *nt*.

bitterly ['bɪtəlɪ] *adv* bitter; *complain also, weep* bitterlich; *oppose* erbittert; *criticize* scharf; *jealous* sehr; *(showing embitteredness)* verbittert; *criticize* erbittert.

bitterness ['bɪtənɪs] *n see adj* Bitterkeit *f*; eisige Kälte; Erbitterheit *f*.

bitter-sweet ['bɪtə,swiːt] *adj (lit, fig)* bittersüß.

bitty ['bɪtɪ] *adj* (+*er*) *(Brit col: scrappy)* zusammengestückelt *(col)*.

bitumen ['bɪtjʊmɪn] *n* Bitumen *nt*.

bivouac ['bɪvʊæk] *(vb: pret, ptp* ~**ked) 1** *n* Biwak *nt*. **2** *vi* biwakieren.

bizarre [bɪ'zaːʳ] *adj* bizarr.

blab [blæb] *vi* quatschen *(col)*; *(talk fast, tell secret)* plappern; *(criminal)* singen *(col)*.

black [blæk] **1** *adj* (+*er*) **(a)** schwarz. ~ **man/ woman** Schwarze(r) *mf*; **a** ~ **eye** ein blaues Auge; ~ **and blue** grün und blau; ~ **and white film** Schwarzweißfilm *m*; **he's not so** ~ **as he's painted** *(prov)* er ist nicht so schlecht wie sein Ruf. **(b)** *future, prospects, mood* düster, finster. **things are looking** ~ es sieht düster aus. **(c)** *(fig: angry) looks* böse. **he looked as** ~ **as thunder** er machte ein bitterböses Gesicht.

2 *n* **(a)** *(colour)* Schwarz *nt*. **he is dressed in** ~ er trägt Schwarz; **to wear** ~ **for sb** für jdn Trauer tragen; **it's written down in** ~ **and white** es steht schwarz auf weiß geschrieben; **in the** ~

(Fin) in den schwarzen Zahlen. **(b)** *(negro)* Schwarze(r) *mf*.
3 *vt* **(a)** schwärzen. **to** ~ **sb's eye** jdm ein blaues Auge schlagen. **(b)** *(Brit: trade union)* bestreiken; *goods* boykottieren.

♦ **black out 1** *vi* das Bewußtsein verlieren, ohnmächtig werden. **2** *vt sep* **(a)** *building, stage* verdunkeln. **(b)** *(with ink, paint)* schwärzen.

black: ~**berry** *n* Brombeere *f*; ~**bird** *n* Amsel *f*; ~**board** *n* Tafel *f*; **to write sth on the** ~**board** etw an die Tafel schreiben; ~ **box** *n (Aviat)* Flugschreiber *m*; ~**currant** *n* schwarze Johannisbeere; **B**~ **Death** *n (Hist)* Schwarzer Tod.

blacken ['blækən] **1** *vt* schwarz machen; *one's face* schwarz anmalen; *(fig) character* verunglimpfen. **to** ~ **sb's name** jdn schlechtmachen. **2** *vi* schwarz werden.

black: **B**~ **Forest** *n* Schwarzwald *m*; ~**head** *n* Mitesser *m*; ~ **hole** *n (Astron)* schwarzes Loch; ~ **humour** *(Brit) or* **humor** *(US)* *n* schwarzer Humor; ~ **ice** *n* Glatteis *nt*; ~**jack** *n (Cards)* Siebzehn und Vier; ~**leg** *(Brit Ind)* *n* Streikbrecher(in *f*) *m*; ~ **list** *n* schwarze Liste; ~ **magic** *n* Schwarze Magie *f*; ~**mail** **1** *n* Erpressung *f*; **2** *vt* erpressen; **to** ~**mail sb into doing sth** jdn durch Erpressung dazu zwingen, etw zu tun; **B**~ **Maria** *n* grüne Minna *(col)*; ~ **mark** *n* Tadel *m*; *(in school register)* Eintrag *m*; ~ **market 1** *n* Schwarzmarkt *m*; **2** *adj attr* Schwarzmarkt-.

blackness ['blæknɪs] *n* Schwärze *f*.

black: ~**out** *n* **(a)** *(Med)* Ohnmacht(sanfall *m*) *f no pl*; **(b)** *(light failure)* Stromausfall *m*; *(during war)* Verdunkelung *f*; *(TV)* Ausfall *m*; **(c)** *(news* ~*out)* (Nachrichten)sperre *f*; ~ **pudding** *n* ≈ Blutwurst *f*; **B**~ **Sea** *n* Schwarzes Meer; ~ **sheep** *n (fig)* schwarzes Schaf; **B**~**shirt** *n* magic *n* Schwarze ~**smith** *n* Schmied *m*; ~ **spot** *n (also accident* spot*)* Gefahrenstelle *f*; "~ **tie"** *n (on invitation)* Abendanzug *m*.

bladder ['blædəʳ] *n (Anat, Bot)* Blase *f*.

blade [bleɪd] *n (of knife, tool)* Klinge *f*; *(of oar, saw, propeller)* Blatt *nt*; *(of plough)* Schar *f*; *(of turbine, paddle wheel)* Schaufel *f*; *(of grass, corn)* Halm *m*.

blame [bleɪm] **1** *vt* **(a)** *(hold responsible)* die Schuld geben (+*dat)*. **to** ~ **sb for sth/sth on sb** jdm die Schuld an etw *(dat)* geben; **you only have yourself to** ~ du bist ganz allein (daran) schuld; **I'm to** ~ **for this** daran bin ich schuld. **(b)** *(reproach)* Vorwürfe machen *(sb for* jdm für *or* wegen*)*. **nobody is blaming you** es macht Ihnen ja niemand einen Vorwurf. **(c)** **he decided to turn down the offer — well, I can't say I** ~ **him** er entschloß sich, das Angebot abzulehnen — das kann man ihm wahrhaftig nicht verdenken. **2** *n (responsibility)* Schuld *f*. **to put the** ~ **for sth on sb** jdm die Schuld an etw *(dat)* geben; **to take the** ~ die Schuld auf sich *(acc)* nehmen; *(for sb's mistakes also)* den Kopf hinhalten; **the** ~ **lies with** him er hat or ist schuld daran.

blameless ['bleɪmlɪs] *adj* schuldlos; *life* untadelig.

blanch [blɑːntʃ] **1** *vt (Cook) vegetables* blanchieren. **2** *vi (with* +*dat) (person)* blaß werden.

bland [blænd] *adj* (+*er*) **(a)** *person* verbindlich; *face* ausdruckslos-höflich. **(b)** *food* mild, fade *(pej)*. **(c)** *(mild, lacking distinction)* nichtssagend.

blandishment ['blændɪʃmənt] *n* Schmeichelei *f*.

blank [blæŋk] **1** *adj* (+*er*) **(a)** *piece of paper, page, wall* leer; ~ **cheque** Blankoscheck *m*; *(fig)* Freibrief *m*; **there is a** ~ **space after each question** nach jeder Frage ist eine Lücke (gelassen). **(b)** *(expressionless) face, look* ausdruckslos; *(stupid)* verständnislos; *(puzzled)* verdutzt, verblüfft. **he just looked** ~ er guckte mich nur groß an *(col)*; **my mind went** ~ ich hatte Mattscheibe *(col)*. **(c)** ~ **verse** Blankvers *m*. **2** *n* **(a)** *(in document)* freier Raum, leere Stelle; *(~ document)* Formular *nt*; *(gap)* Lücke *f*. **(b)** **my mind was/went a complete** ~ ich hatte totale Mattscheibe *(col)*; **to**

draw a ~ kein Glück haben. **(c)** *(also ~ cartridge)* Platzpatrone f.

blanket ['blæŋkɪt] **1** n *(lit, fig)* Decke f. **a ~ of snow/fog** eine Schnee-/Nebeldecke. **2** *adj attr statement* pauschal; *insurance etc* umfassend. **3** *vt (snow, smoke)* zudecken.

blare [blɛəʳ] **1** n *(of car horn etc)* lautes Hupen; *(of trumpets etc)* Schmettern nt. **2** vi *see* n laut hupen; schmettern. **the music ~d through the hall** die Musik schallte durch den Saal.

♦ **blare out 1** vi *(loud voice, music)* schallen; *(trumpets)* schmettern. **2** vt sep *(trumpets)* tune schmettern; *(radio) music* plärren; *(person) order, warning etc* brüllen.

blasé ['blɑːzeɪ] *adj* blasiert.

blaspheme [blæs'fiːm] vi Gott lästern.

blasphemous ['blæsfɪməs] *adj (lit, fig)* blasphemisch; *(lit also)* gotteslästerlich.

blasphemy ['blæsfɪmɪ] n *see adj* Blasphemie f; Gotteslästerung f.

blast [blɑːst] **1** n **(a)** Windstoß m; *(of hot air)* Schwall m. **(b)** *(sound: of trumpets)* Geschmetter nt; *(of foghorn)* Tuten nt. **(c)** *(noise, explosion)* Explosion f; *(shock wave)* Druckwelle f. **to get the full ~ of sb's anger** jds Wut in voller Wucht abbekommen. **(d)** *(in quarrying etc)* Sprengung f. **(e) at full ~** *(lit, fig)* auf Hochtouren; **with the radio turned up (at) full ~** mit dem Radio voll aufgedreht. **2** vt hole sprengen; *rocket* schießen. **3** interj *(col)* ~ **(it)!** verdammt! *(col)*.

♦ **blast off** vi *(rocket, astronaut)* abheben, starten.

♦ **blasted** ['blɑːstɪd] *adj (col)* verdammt *(col)*.

blast furnace n Hochofen m.

blasting ['blɑːstɪŋ] n *(Tech)* Sprengen nt. **"danger ~ in progress"** „Achtung! Sprengarbeiten!"

blast-off ['blɑːstɒf] n Abschuß m.

blatant ['bleɪtənt] *adj (very obvious)* offensichtlich; *injustice also* eklatant; *error also* kraß; *liar* unverfroren; *disregard* offen.

blaze¹ [bleɪz] **1** n *(fire)* Feuer nt; *(of building etc also)* Brand m; *(of sun)* Glut f. **a ~ of lights/colour** ein Lichtermeer nt/Meer nt von Farben; **he went out in a ~ of glory** er trat mit Glanz und Gloria ab; **go to ~s** *(col)* scher dich zum Teufel! *(col)*; **what/ how the ~s ...?** *(col)* was/wie zum Teufel ...? *(col)*; **like ~s** *(col)* wie verrückt *(col)*. **2** vi **(a)** *(sun)* brennen; *(fire also)* lodern. **to ~ with anger** vor Zorn glühen. **(b)** *(guns)* feuern.

♦ **blaze away** vi **(a)** *(soldiers, guns)* drauflos feuern *(at* auf *+acc)*. **(b)** *(fire etc)* lodern.

♦ **blaze up** vi auflodern.

blaze² vt **to ~ a trail** *(fig)* den Weg bahnen.

blazer ['bleɪzəʳ] n Blazer m.

blazing ['bleɪzɪŋ] *adj building etc* brennend; *fire, torch* lodernd; *(hot)* brennend; *(fig) eyes* funkelnd *(with* vor *+dat)*; *red* knall-, leuchtend.

bleach [bliːtʃ] **1** n Bleichmittel nt. **2** vt linen, bones, hair bleichen.

bleachers ['bliːtʃəz] npl *(US)* unüberdachte Zuschauertribüne.

bleak [bliːk] *adj (+er)* **(a)** öde, trostlos. **(b)** *weather, wind* rauh, kalt. **(c)** *(fig) future etc* trostlos.

bleary ['blɪərɪ] *adj (+er) eyes* trübe; *(after sleep)* verschlafen.

bleary-eyed ['blɪərɪˌaɪd] *adj (after sleep)* verschlafen.

bleat [bliːt] vi *(sheep, calf)* blöken; *(goat, fig col)* meckern.

bleed [bliːd] *pret, ptp* **bled** [bled] vi bluten. **to ~ to death** verbluten; **my heart ~s for you** *(iro)* mir blutet das Herz; **ignorance is ~** *(prov)* was ich nicht weiß, macht mich nicht heiß *(prov)*. fang' gleich an zu weinen. **2** vt **(a)** *person* zur Ader lassen. **(b)** *(fig col)* schröpfen *(col) (for* um*)*. **(c)** *(Aut)* brakes lüften.

bleeding ['bliːdɪŋ] **1** n **(a)** *(loss of blood)* Blutung f. **(b)** *(taking blood)* Aderlaß m. **(c)** *(of brakes)* Lüftung f. **2** *adj* **(a)** *wound* blutend; *(fig) heart* gebrochen. **(b)** *(Brit col)* verdammt *(col)*. **just a ~ minute** nu mal sachte *(col)*.

bleep [bliːp] **1** n *(Rad, TV)* Piepton m. **2** vi *(transmitter)* piepen. **3** vt *(in hospital)* doctor rufen.

bleeper ['bliːpəʳ] n Funkrufempfänger m.

blemish ['blemɪʃ] **1** n *(lit, fig)* Makel m. **2** vt object beschädigen; *work* beeinträchtigen; *reputation* beflecken.

blend [blend] **1** n Mischung f. **2** vt **(a)** teas, colours etc *(ver)*mischen. **(b)** *(Cook) (stir)* einrühren; *(in blender)* liquids mixen; *semi-solids* pürieren. **3** vi **(a)** *(voices, colours)* verschmelzen. **(b)** *(also ~ in: go together, harmonize)* harmonieren *(with* mit*)*, passen *(with* zu*)*.

blender ['blendəʳ] n Mixer m, Mixgerät nt.

bless [bles] vt segnen. **~ you, you're an angel** *(col)* du bist wirklich ein Engel *(col)*; **~ you!** *(to sneezer)* Gesundheit!; **~ my soul!** *(col)* du meine Güte! *(col)*; **to be ~ed with** gesegnet sein mit.

blessed ['blesɪd] **1** *adj* **(a)** *(Rel)* heilig. **B~ Virgin** Heilige Jungfrau (Maria). **(b)** *(euph col: cursed)* verflixt *(col)*. **the whole ~ day** den lieben langen Tag *(col)*. **2** n **the ~, the Blest** die Seligen pl.

blessing ['blesɪŋ] n *(Rel, fig)* Segen m. **he can count his ~s** da kann er von Glück sagen; **what a ~ that** ... welch ein Segen or Glück, daß ...; **it was a ~ in disguise** es war Glück im Unglück.

blew [bluː] *pret of* **blow**².

blight [blaɪt] **1** n *(on plants)* Braunfäule f. **these slums are a ~ upon the city** diese Slums sind ein Schandfleck für die Stadt. **2** vt plants zerstören; *(fig) hopes* zunichte machen.

blind [blaɪnd] **1** *adj (+er) person, obedience, fury* blind; *corner* unübersichtlich. **a ~ man/woman** ein Blinder/eine Blinde; **~ in one eye** auf einem Auge blind; **he was ~ to her faults** er sah ihre Fehler einfach nicht; **to be ~ to the possibilities** die Möglichkeiten nicht sehen; **to turn a ~ eye to sth** bei etw ein Auge zudrücken; **but he didn't take a ~ bit of notice** *(col)* aber er hat sich nicht die Spur darum gekümmert *(col)*. **2** vt blenden; *(love, hate etc)* blind machen *(to* für, gegen*)*. **he was ~ed to the war** er ist kriegsblind; **to ~ sb with science** jdn mit Fachjargon beeindrucken (wollen). **3** n **(a)** **the ~** die Blinden pl; **it's the ~ leading the ~** *(fig)* das hieße, einen Lahmen einen Blinden führen lassen. **(b)** *(window shade) (cloth)* Rollo nt; *(slats)* Jalousie f; *(outside)* Rolladen m. **4** *adv* **(a)** *(Aviat)* fly blind. **(b)** ~ **drunk** *(col)* sinnlos betrunken.

blind: ~ alley n *(lit, fig)* Sackgasse f; **~ date** n Rendezvous nt mit einem/einer Unbekannten.

blindfold ['blaɪndfəʊld] **1** vt die Augen verbinden *(+dat)*. **2** n Augenbinde f. **3** *adj* mit verbundenen Augen. **I could do it ~** *(col)* das mach' ich mit links *(col)*.

blindly ['blaɪndlɪ] *adv (lit, fig)* blind(lings).

blind man's buff n Blindekuh no art.

blindness ['blaɪndnɪs] n *(lit, fig)* Blindheit f *(to* gegenüber*)*.

blind spot n *(Med)* blinder Fleck; *(Aut, Aviat)* toter Winkel; *(Rad)* tote Zone.

blink [blɪŋk] **1** n Blinzeln nt. **to be on the ~** *(col)* kaputt sein *(col)*. **2** vi blinzeln; *(light)* blinken. **3** vt **to ~ one's eyes** mit den Augen zwinkern.

blinkers ['blɪŋkəz] npl Scheuklappen pl.

blinkered ['blɪŋkəd] *adj (fig)* engstirnig. **they are all so ~** sie laufen alle mit Scheuklappen herum.

bliss [blɪs] n Glück nt, **this is ~!** das ist eine Wohltat!; **a life of marital ~** ein glückliches Eheleben; **ignorance is ~** *(prov)* was ich nicht weiß, macht mich etc nicht heiß *(prov)*.

blissful ['blɪsfʊl] *adj time* herrlich; *respite also* wohltuend; *happiness* höchste(s); *state, look, smile* glück)selig; *moments* selig.

blissfully ['blɪsfəlɪ] *adv stretch* wohlig; *peaceful* herrlich; *smile* selig. **~ happy** überglücklich; **to be ~ ignorant** herrlich ahnungslos sein.

blister ['blɪstəʳ] **1** n *(on skin, paint)* Blase f. **2** vi *(skin)* Blasen bekommen; *(paintwork, metal)* Blasen werfen. **3** *vt* Blasen hervorrufen auf *(+dat)*.

blithely ['blaɪðlɪ] *adv* ignore, carry on munter. **he ~ ignored the problem** er setzte sich ungeniert über das Problem hinweg.

blitz [blɪts] **1** *n* **(a)** Blitzkrieg *m*; *(aerial)* Luftangriff *m*. **the B~** *deutscher Luftangriff auf britische Städte 1940-41.* **(b)** *(fig col)* Blitzaktion *f*. **2** *vt* heftig bombardieren.

blizzard ['blɪzəd] *n* Schneesturm, Blizzard *m*.

bloated ['bləʊtɪd] *adj* aufgedunsen. **I feel absolutely ~** *(col)* ich bin zum Platzen voll *(col)*.

blob [blɒb] *n (of water, honey, wax)* Tropfen *m*; *(of ink)* Klecks *m*; *(of paint)* Tupfer *m*; *(of ice-cream, mashed potatoes)* Klacks *m*.

bloc [blɒk] *n* **(a)** *(Pol)* Block *m*. **(b) en ~** en bloc.

block [blɒk] **1** *n* **(a)** Block, Klotz *m*. **(b)** *(building, of shares, seats, for notes)* Block *m*. **~ of flats** *(Brit)* Wohnblock *m*; **to take a stroll around the ~** einen Spaziergang um den Block machen; **she lived in the next ~/three ~s from us** *(esp US)* sie wohnte im nächsten Block/drei Blocks *or* Straßen weiter. **(c)** *(obstruction: in pipe, Med)* Verstopfung *f*. **I've a mental ~ about it** dabei habe ich total Mattscheibe *(col)*. **(d)** *(col: head)* **to knock sb's ~ off** jdm eins überziehen *(col)*. **2** *vt* road blockieren; *traffic also, progress* aufhalten; *pipe* verstopfen; *(Ftbl)* blocken; *ball* stoppen; *credit* sperren. **to ~ sb's way/view** jdm den Weg/die Sicht versperren.

♦ **block off** *vt sep* street absperren; *fireplace* abdecken.

♦ **block out** *vt sep* **(a)** *(obscure)* light nicht durchlassen; *sun also* verdecken. **(b)** *(obliterate)* part of picture wegretuschieren.

♦ **block up** *vt sep* **(a)** *(obstruct)* gangway blockieren; *pipe* verstopfen. **my nose is all ~ed ~** meine Nase ist völlig verstopft. **(b)** *(close, fill in)* window zumauern; *hole* zustopfen.

blockade [blɒ'keɪd] **1** *n* *(Mil)* Blockade *f*. **2** *vt* blockieren, sperren.

blockage ['blɒkɪdʒ] *n* Verstopfung *f*.

block: ~ and tackle *n* Flaschenzug *m*; **~ booking** *n* Gruppenbuchung *f*; **~** *(Theat)* Gruppenbestellung *f*; **~ capitals** *npl* Blockschrift *f*.

bloke [bləʊk] *n* *(Brit col)* Kerl *(col)*, Typ *(col) m*.

blond [blɒnd] *adj* man, hair blond.

blonde [blɒnd] **1** *adj* woman blond. **2** *n* *(woman)* Blondine *f*.

blood [blʌd] *n* Blut *nt*. **to give ~** Blut spenden; **it makes my ~ boil** das macht mich rasend; **she's after his ~** sie will ihm an den Kragen *(col)*; **his ~ ran cold** es lief ihm eiskalt über den Rücken; **it's like trying to get ~ out of a stone** *(prov)* das ist verlorene Liebesmüh; **there is bad ~ between them** sie haben ein gestörtes Verhältnis; **it's in his ~** das liegt ihm im Blut; **~ is thicker than water** *(prov)* Blut ist dicker als Wasser *(prov)*.

blood *in cpds* Blut-; **~ bank** *n* Blutbank *f*; **~ bath** *n* Blutbad *nt*; **~ brother** *n* Blutsbruder *m*; **~ clot** *n* Blutgerinnsel *nt*; **~curdling** *adj* grauenerregend; **~ donor** *n* Blutspender(in *f*) *m*; **~ group** *n* Blutgruppe *f*; **~hound** *n* **(a)** *(Zool)* Bluthund *m*; **(b)** *(fig: detective)* Schnüffler *m* *(col)*.

bloodless ['blʌdlɪs] *adj* victory, coup unblutig; *(pallid)* blutleer, bleich.

blood: ~ money *n* schmutziges Geld; **~ orange** *n* Blutorange *f*; **~-poisoning** *n* Blutvergiftung *f*; **~ pressure** *n* Blutdruck *m*; **to have (high) ~ pressure** hohen Blutdruck haben; **~-red** *adj* blutrot; **~shed** *n* Blutvergießen *nt*; **~shot** *adj* blutunterlaufen; **~ sports** *npl* Jagdsport, Hahnenkampf *etc*; **~stain** *n* Blutfleck *m*; **~stained** *adj* blutig, blutbefleckt; **~stream** *n* Blut *nt*, Blutkreislauf *m*; **~ test** *n* Blutprobe *f*; **~thirsty** *adj* blutrünstig; **~ transfusion** *n* (Blut)transfusion *f*; **~ vessel** *n* Blutgefäß *nt*.

bloody ['blʌdɪ] **1** *adj (+er)* **(a)** *(lit)* blutig. **(b)** *(Brit col!: damned)* verdammt *(col)*, Scheiß- *(col!)*; *(in positive sense)* genius, wonder echt *(col)*, verdammt *(col)*. **~ hell!** verdammt nochmal! *(col)*; **he is a ~ marvel** er ist verdammt gut *(col)*. **2** *adv* *(Brit col!)*; verdammt *(col)*; cold, stupid sau- *(col)*; *(in positive sense)* good, brilliant echt *(col)*, verdammt *(col)*.

bloody-minded ['blʌdɪ'maɪndɪd] *adj* (Brit col) stur *(col)*.

bloom [bluːm] **1** *n* **(a)** Blüte *f*. **to be in (full) ~** in (voller) Blüte stehen; **in the ~ of youth** in der Blüte der Jugend. **(b)** *(on fruit)* satter Schimmer; *(on peaches)* Flaum *m*. **2** *vi (lit, fig)* blühen.

bloomers ['bluːməz] *npl* Pumphose *f*.

blossom ['blɒsəm] **1** *n* Blüte *f*. **in ~** in Blüte. **2** *vi (lit, fig)* blühen; *(person, trade etc also)* aufblühen. **to ~ into sth** zu etw aufblühen.

♦ **blossom out** *vi (fig)* aufblühen *(into zu)*.

blot [blɒt] **1** *n* **(a)** *(of ink)* (Tinten)klecks *m*. **(b)** *(fig: on honour, reputation)* Fleck *m (on auf +dat)*. **a ~ on the landscape** ein Schandfleck in der Landschaft. **2** *vt* **(a)** *(make ink spots on)* beklecksen. **to ~ one's copybook** *(fig)* sich danebenbenehmen; *(with sb)* es sich *(dat)* verderben. **(b)** *(dry)* ink, page löschen.

♦ **blot out** *vt sep* **(a)** *(lit)* words verschmieren. **(b)** *(hide from view)* landscape verdecken; *(obliterate)* memories auslöschen.

blotch [blɒtʃ] *n (on skin)* Fleck *m*; *(of ink, colour also)* Klecks *m*.

blotchy ['blɒtʃɪ] *adj (+er)* skin fleckig; drawing, paint klecksig.

blotting paper ['blɒtɪŋ,peɪpə'] *n* Löschpapier *nt*.

blouse [blaʊz] *n* Bluse *f*.

blow¹ [bləʊ] *n (lit, fig)* Schlag *m (for, to für)*. **to come to ~s** handgreiflich werden; **at one ~** *(fig)* mit einem Schlag *(col)*.

blow² *(vb: pret* **blew**, *ptp* **~n)* **1** *vi* **(a)** *(wind)* wehen, blasen. **(b)** *(person)* blasen, pusten *(col)* *(on auf +acc)*. **(c)** *(move with the wind)* fliegen. **the door blew open/shut** die Tür flog auf/zu. **(d)** *(bugle)* blasen; *(whistle)* pfeifen. **(e)** *(fuse, light bulb)* durchbrennen; *(gasket)* platzen.

2 *vt* **(a)** *(breeze)* wehen; *(strong wind, draught)* blasen; *(gale etc)* treiben; *(person)* blasen, pusten *(col)*. **the wind blew the ship off course** der Wind trieb das Schiff vom Kurs ab; **to ~ sb a kiss** jdm eine Kußhand zuwerfen; **to ~ one's nose** sich *(dat)* die Nase putzen. **(b)** *glass, trumpet* blasen; *bubbles* machen; *(Hunt, Mil)* horn blasen in *(+acc)*. **the referee blew his whistle** der Schiedsrichter pfiff. **(c)** *(burn out, ~ up)* safe, bridge etc sprengen; *valve, gasket* platzen lassen; *transistor* zerstören. **I've ~n a fuse/light bulb** mir ist eine Sicherung/Birne durchgebrannt; **to be ~n to pieces** *(bridge, car)* in die Luft gesprengt werden; *(person)* zerfetzt werden. **(d)** *(col: spend extravagantly)* money verpulvern *(col)*. **(e)** *(col: reveal)* secret verraten. **~! Mist!** *(col)*; **~ the expense** das doch wurscht, was es kostet *(col)*.

♦ **blow away 1** *vi (hat, paper etc)* wegfliegen. **2** *vt sep* wegblasen; *(breeze also)* wegwehen.

♦ **blow down 1** *vi (tree etc)* umgeweht werden. **2** *vt sep (tree etc)* umwehen.

♦ **blow in 1** *vi* **(a)** *(lit)* *(be blown down: window etc)* eingedrückt werden; *(be ~n inside: dust etc)* hereingeweht werden; *(wind)* hereinwehen, hereinblasen. **(b)** *(col: arrive unexpectedly)* hereinschneien *(col)* *(+prep obj, -to in +acc)*. **2** *vt sep window, door etc* eindrücken; *dust etc* hereinwehen *(+prep obj, -to in +acc)*.

♦ **blow off 1** *vi* wegfliegen. **2** *vt sep (+prep obj)* blasen von. **3** *vt insep (fig)* steam ablassen *(col)*.

♦ **blow out 1** *vt (candle etc)* ausgehen. **2** *vt sep candle* ausblasen; *cheeks* aufblasen. **to ~ one's brains ~** sich *(dat)* eine Kugel durch den Kopf

jagen. **3** vr (wind, storm) sich legen.
♦ **blow over** vi (lit, fig: storm, dispute) sich legen.
♦ **blow up 1** vi (be exploded) in die Luft fliegen; (bomb) explodieren; (gale, crisis, row) ausbrechen; (fig col: person) explodieren (col). **2** vt sep mine, bridge, person in die Luft jagen; tyre, balloon aufblasen; photo vergrößern; (exaggerate) event aufbauschen (into zu).
blow: ~-**by**-~ adj account detailliert; ~-**dry 1** n to have a ~-**dry** sich fönen lassen; **2** vt fönen; ~**lamp** n Lötlampe f.
blown [bləʊn] ptp of **blow**².
blow: ~-**out** n (a) (col: meal) Schlemmerei f; (b) (burst tyre) he had a ~-**out** ihm ist ein Reifen geplatzt; (c) (Elec) there's been a ~-**out** die Sicherung ist durchgebrannt; ~ **pipe** n (weapon) Blasrohr nt.
blowy [ˈbləʊɪ] adj (+er) windig.
blubber [ˈblʌbəʳ] **1** n Walfischspeck m. **2** vi (col) flennen (col), heulen (col).
blue [bluː] **1** adj (+er) **(a)** blau. ~ **with cold** blau vor Kälte; **until you're** ~ **in the face** (col) bis zur Vergasung (col); **once in a** ~ **moon** alle Jubeljahre (einmal). **(b)** (col: miserable) melancholisch, trübsinnig. **to feel** ~ niedergeschlagen sein. **(c)** (col: obscene) joke schlüpfrig; film Porno-, Sex-. **(d)** (Pol) konservativ. **2** n **(a)** Blau nt. **(b)** (liter: sky) Himmel m. **out of the** ~ (fig col) aus heiterem Himmel (col). **(c)** (Pol) Konservative(r) mf. **(d)** (col) **to have (a fit of) the** ~**s** den Moralischen haben (col). **(e)** (Mus) **the** ~**s** pl der Blues.
blue: ~ **baby** n Baby nt mit angeborenem Herzfehler; ~**bell** n Sternhyazinthe f; (Scot) Glockenblume f; ~**berry** n Blau- or Heidelbeere f; ~ **blood** n blaues Blut; ~**bottle** n Schmeißfliege f; ~ **cheese** n Blauschimmelkäse m; ~-**collar** adj ~-**collar worker/union/jobs** Arbeiter m/Arbeitergewerkschaft f/Stellen pl für Arbeiter; ~-**eyed** adj blauäugig; **sb's** ~-**eyed boy** (fig) jds Liebling m; ~**print** n Blaupause f; (fig) Plan, Entwurf m; ~**tit** n Blaumeise f.
bluff¹ [blʌf] **1** n (headland) Kliff nt; (inland) Felsvorsprung m. **2** adj rauh aber herzlich (col); honesty, answer aufrichtig.
bluff² **1** vti bluffen. **2** n Bluff m. **to call sb's** ~ **es** darauf ankommen lassen; (make prove) jdn auf die Probe stellen.
♦ **bluff out** vt sep **to** ~ **it** ~ sich rausreden (col).
blunder [ˈblʌndəʳ] **1** n Schnitzer m (col); (socially) Fauxpas m. **to make a** ~ einen Bock schießen (col); (socially) einen Fauxpas begehen. **2** vi **(a)** einen Bock schießen (col); (socially) sich blamieren. **(b)** (move clumsily) tappen (into gegen).
blunt [blʌnt] **1** adj (+er) **(a)** stumpf. **with a** ~ **instrument** mit einem stumpfen Gegenstand. **(b)** (outspoken) person geradeheraus pred; speech unverblümt; fact nackt. **to be** ~ **about sth** sich unverblümt zu etw äußern. **2** vt knife etc stumpf machen; (fig) palate, senses abstumpfen.
bluntly [ˈblʌntlɪ] adv speak freiheraus.
bluntness [ˈblʌntnɪs] n **(a)** (of blade) Stumpfheit f. **(b)** (outspokenness) Unverblümtheit f
blur [blɜːʳ] **1** n verschwommener Fleck. **2** vt **(a)** inscription verwischen; writing also verschmieren; outline, photograph unscharf machen; sound verzerren. **to be/become** ~**red** undeutlich sein/werden; (image etc also) verschwommen sein/verschwimmen. **(b)** (fig) senses, mind trüben; meaning verwischen.
blurb [blɜːb] n Material nt, Informationen pl; (on book cover) Klappentext m.
blurt (out) [blɜːt(ˈaʊt)] vt sep herausplatzen mit (col).
blush [blʌʃ] **1** vi rot werden (with vor +dat). **2** n Erröten nt no pl. **with a** ~ errötend.

bluster [ˈblʌstəʳ] vi (wind) toben; (person) ein großes Geschrei machen; (angrily also) toben.
blustery [ˈblʌstərɪ] adj wind, day stürmisch.
BO [ˌbiːˈəʊ] (col) = **body odour** Körpergeruch m.
boa [ˈbəʊə] n Boa f. ~ **constrictor** Boa constrictor f.
boar [bɔːʳ] n (male pig) Eber m; (wild) Keiler m.
board [bɔːd] **1** n **(a)** Brett nt; (black~) Tafel f; (notice~) Schwarzes Brett; (sign~) Schild nt; (floor~) Diele(nbrett nt) f. **(b)** (provision of meals) Verpflegung f. ~ **and lodging** Kost und Logis; **full/half** ~ (Brit) Voll-/Halbpension f. **(c)** (group of officials) Ausschuß m; (with advisory function, ~ of trustees) Beirat m; (permanent official institution: gas~, harbour ~ etc) Behörde f; (of company: also ~ of directors) Vorstand m; (including shareholders, advisers) Aufsichtsrat m. **B**~ **of Trade** (Brit) Handelsministerium nt. **(d)** (Naut, Aviat) **on** ~ an Bord; **to go on** ~ an Bord gehen. **(e)** (fig phrases) **across the** ~ (fig) allgemein, pauschal; **to go by the** ~ (dreams, hopes) zunichte werden; (principles) über Bord geworfen werden.
2 vt ship, plane besteigen, an Bord (+gen) gehen/kommen; train, bus einsteigen in (+acc); (Naut: in attack) entern.
3 vi **(a)** (live) in Pension sein (with bei). **(b)** (Sch) Internatsschüler(in f) m sein. **(c)** (Aviat) die Maschine besteigen. **flight ZA173 now** ~**ing through gate 13** Aufruf für Passagiere des Fluges ZA173, sich zum Flugsteig 13 zu begeben.
♦ **board up** vt sep mit Brettern vernageln.
boarder [ˈbɔːdəʳ] n **(a)** Pensionsgast m. **(b)** (Sch) Internatsschüler(in f) m.
boarding [ˈbɔːdɪŋ-]: ~ **card** n Bordkarte f; ~ **house** n Pension f; ~ **party** n (Naut) Enterkommando nt; ~ **school** n Internat nt.
board: ~ **meeting** n Vorstandssitzung f; ~**room** n Sitzungssaal m; ~**walk** n (US) Holzsteg m; (on beach) hölzerne Uferpromenade.
boast [bəʊst] **1** n Prahlerei f. **it is their** ~ **that ... sie** rühmen sich, daß ... **2** vi angeben (about, of mit, to sb jdm gegenüber). **don't** ~ gib nicht so an. **3** vt (possess) sich rühmen (+gen) (geh).
boaster [ˈbəʊstəʳ] n Angeber(in f) m.
boastful [ˈbəʊstfʊl] adj angeberisch.
boasting [ˈbəʊstɪŋ] n Angeberei f.
boat [bəʊt] n Boot nt; (sea-going, passenger ~) Schiff nt; (pleasure steamer etc) Dampfer m. **by** ~ mit dem Schiff; **to miss the** ~ (fig col) den Anschluß verpassen; **we're all in the same** ~ (fig col) wir sitzen alle im gleichen Boot.
boater [ˈbəʊtəʳ] n **(a)** (hat) steifer Strohhut. **(b)** (person boating) Bootsfahrer(in f) m.
boat: ~**hook** n Bootshaken m; ~ **race** n Regatta f.
boatswain, bosun, bo's'n [ˈbəʊsn] n Bootsmann m.
boat train n Zug m mit Fährenanschluß.
bob¹ [bɒb] vi sich auf und ab bewegen; (rabbit) hoppeln; (bird's tail) wippen; (boxer) tänzeln. **to** ~ (**up and down**) **in** or **on the water** auf dem Wasser schaukeln.
♦ **bob up** vi (lit, fig) auftauchen.
bob² n, pl - (Brit col) Shilling m. **that will cost a few** ~ das wird einiges kosten.
bob³ n (haircut) Bubikopf m.
bob⁴ n (sleigh) Bob m.
bobbin [ˈbɒbɪn] n Spule f; (cotton reel) Rolle f.
bobble [ˈbɒbl] n Bommel f, Pompon m.
bobby [ˈbɒbɪ] n (dated Brit col) Bobby m.
bob: ~**cat** n (US) Luchs m; ~**sleigh 1** n Bob m; **2** vi Bob fahren.
bode [bəʊd] vi: **to** ~ **well/ill** ein gutes/schlechtes Zeichen sein.
bodice [ˈbɒdɪs] n **(a)** (of dress) Oberteil nt. **(b)** (vest) Unterhemd nt.
bodily [ˈbɒdɪlɪ] **1** adj (physical) körperlich. ~

needs leibliche Bedürfnisse pl; ~ harm Körperverletzung f. 2 adv (forcibly) gewaltsam.

body ['bɒdɪ] n (a) Körper m; (of human also) Leib m (geh). to keep ~ and soul together Leib und Seele zusammenhalten. (b) (corpse) Leiche f. (c) (of plane, ship) Rumpf m; (of speech, army) Hauptteil m. the main ~ of his readers/the students das Gros seiner Leser/der Studenten. (d) (of car) Karosserie f. (e) (group of people) Gruppe f. the student ~ die Studentenschaft. (f) (organization) Organ nt; (committee) Gremium nt; (corporation) Körperschaft f. (g) (of wine) Körper m; (of hair, paper, cloth) Festigkeit f.

body: ~building n Bodybuilding nt; ~guard n (one person) Leibwächter m; (group) Leibwache f; ~work n (Aut) Karosserie f.

bog [bɒg] n (a) Sumpf m; (peat ~) (Torf)moor nt. (b) (Brit col: toilet) Klo nt (col).

♦ **bog down** vt sep to be or get ~ged ~ (lit) steckenbleiben; (fig) sich festgefahren haben; (in details) sich verzettelt haben.

boggle ['bɒgl] vi (col) the mind ~s (faced with fact) da bist du baff (col) or platt (col); (faced with possibility) das kann man sich (dat) kaum ausmalen.

bogus ['bəʊgəs] adj doctor falsch; money, pearls gefälscht; company Schwindel-; claim erfunden.

Bohemia [bəʊ'hiːmɪə] n Böhmen nt.

Bohemian [bəʊ'hiːmɪən] 1 n (a) Böhme m, Böhmin f. (b) (fig) b~ Bohemien m. 2 adj (a) böhmisch. (b) (fig) b~ lifestyle unkonventionell, unbürgerlich.

boil[1] [bɔɪl] n (Med) Furunkel m.

boil[2] 1 vi (a) kochen; (water also, Phys) sieden. the kettle is ~ing das Wasser kocht. (b) (fig col: be angry) kochen, schäumen (with or +dat). 2 vt kochen. ~ed/hard ~ed egg weich-/hartgekochtes Ei; ~ed potatoes Salzkartoffeln pl. 3 n to bring to the ~ zum Kochen bringen; he's gone off the ~ (fig col) er hat kein Interesse mehr.

♦ **boil down** 1 vt sep eindicken lassen. 2 vi (a) (jam etc) dickflüssig werden. (b) (fig) what it ~s ~ to is that ... das läuft darauf hinaus, daß ...

♦ **boil over** vi (a) (lit) überkochen. (b) (fig) (situation, quarrel) den Siedepunkt erreichen.

boiler ['bɔɪlə[r]] n (a) (domestic) Boiler, Warmwasserbereiter m; (in ship, engine) (Dampf)kessel m. (b) (chicken) Suppenhuhn nt.

boiler: ~maker n Kesselschmied m; ~suit n Overall, Blaumann (col) m.

boiling ['bɔɪlɪŋ]: ~ hot (col) kochendheiß; I'm ~ hot mir ist schrecklich heiß; ~ point n (lit, fig) Siedepunkt m.

boisterous ['bɔɪstərəs] adj (exuberant) person ausgelassen; game etc also wild.

bold [bəʊld] adj (+er) (a) (valiant) kühn. (b) (impudent) dreist. to make so ~ as to ... sich erlauben, zu ... (c) (striking) colours etc kräftig; handwriting, style kraftvoll. (d) (Typ) fett. ~ type Fettdruck m.

boldness ['bəʊldnɪs] n see adj Kühnheit (geh) f; Dreistigkeit f; Kräftigkeit f.

Bolivia [bə'lɪvɪə] n Bolivien m.

bollard ['bɒlɑːd] n (on quay) Poller m.

Bolshevik ['bɒlʃəvɪk] 1 n Bolschewik m. 2 adj bolschewistisch.

Bolshevism ['bɒlʃəvɪzəm] n Bolschewismus m.

bolshy ['bɒlʃɪ] (col) adj (+er) (uncooperative) stur, störrisch; (aggressive) pampig (col).

bolster ['bəʊlstə[r]] 1 n (on bed) Nackenrolle f. 2 vt (also ~ up) (fig) person Mut machen (+dat); status aufbessern; currency stützen.

bolt [bəʊlt] 1 n (a) (on door etc) Riegel m. (b) (Tech) Bolzen m. (c) (of lightning) Blitzstrahl m. it came/was like a ~ from the blue (fig) das war wie ein Blitz aus heiterem Himmel. (d) (of crossbow) Bolzen m. (e) (of rifle) Kammer f. (f) (sudden

dash) Satz m (col). he made a ~ for the door er machte einen Satz zur Tür; to make a ~ for it abhauen (col). 2 adv: ~ upright kerzengerade. 3 vi (a) (horse) durchgehen; (person) Reißaus nehmen (col), abhauen (col). (b) (move quickly) sausen, rasen. 4 vt (a) door, window verriegeln. (b) (Tech) machine parts verschrauben (to mit). to ~ together verschrauben. (c) (also ~ down) one's food hinunterschlingen.

bomb [bɒm] 1 n Bombe f. his party went like a ~ (col) seine Party war ein Bombenerfolg (col); the car goes like a ~ (col) der Wagen läuft verdammt gut (col). 2 vt town bombardieren.

bombard [bɒm'bɑːd] vt (Mil, fig) bombardieren (with mit); (Phys) beschießen.

bombardment [bɒm'bɑːdmənt] n (Mil) Bombardierung f (also fig), Bombardement nt.

bombastic [bɒm'bæstɪk] adj bombastisch.

bomb disposal squad n Bombenräumtrupp m.

bomber ['bɒmə[r]] n (a) (aircraft) Bomber m, Bombenflieger m. (b) (person) (Aviat) Bombenschütze m; (terrorist) Bombenattentäter(in f) m.

bomber jacket n Blouson m or nt.

bomb: ~shell n this news was a ~shell die Nachricht schlug wie eine Bombe ein; ~ site n Trümmergrundstück nt.

bona fide ['bəʊnə'faɪdɪ] adj bona fide; traveller, word, antique echt. it's a ~ offer es ist ein Angebot auf Treu und Glauben.

bonanza [bə'nænzə] n (a) (US Min) reiche Erzader. (b) (fig) Goldgrube f. the oil ~ der Ölboom.

bond [bɒnd] 1 n (a) (agreement) Übereinkommen nt. to enter into a ~ with sb ein Übereinkommen mit jdm treffen. (b) (fig: link) Band nt (geh), Bindung f. (c) ~s pl (lit, fig: chains) Bande pl (geh). (d) (Comm, Fin) Obligation f, Pfandbrief m. government ~ Staatsanleihe f. (e) (Comm: custody of goods) Zollverschluß m. goods in ~ Zollgut nt. (f) (adhesion between surfaces) Haftfestigkeit f. 2 vt (Comm) goods unter Zollverschluß nehmen. 3 vi (glue) binden.

bondage ['bɒndɪdʒ] n (a) (lit) Sklaverei f; (in Middle Ages) Leibeigenschaft f. (b) (fig liter) Versklavung f.

bonded warehouse ['bɒndɪd'wɛəhaʊs] Zollager nt.

bone [bəʊn] 1 n Knochen m; (of fish) Gräte f. ~s pl (of the dead) Gebeine pl; chilled to the ~ völlig durchgefroren; ~ of contention Zankapfel m; to have a ~ to pick with sb (col) mit jdm ein Hühnchen zu rupfen haben (col); he made no ~s about saying what he thought (col) er hat kein Blatt vor den Mund genommen; I can feel it in my ~s ich spüre es in den Knochen. 2 vt die Knochen lösen aus; fish entgräten.

bone china n feines Porzellan.

bone: ~-dry adj (col) knochentrocken; ~-idle adj (col) stinkfaul (col); ~ meal n Knochenmehl nt.

bonfire ['bɒnfaɪə[r]] n Feuer nt; (as beacon) Leuchtfeuer nt.

bonnet ['bɒnɪt] n (a) (woman's) Haube f; (baby's) Häubchen nt; (esp Scot) Mütze f. (b) (Brit Aut) Motor- or Kühlerhaube f.

bonny ['bɒnɪ] adj (esp Scot) schön; baby prächtig.

bonus ['bəʊnəs] n (a) Prämie f; (on output, production also) Zulage f; (cost-of-living ~) Zuschlag m; (Christmas ~) Gratifikation f. (b) (Fin: on shares) Extradividende f. (c) (fig: sth extra) Zugabe f.

bony ['bəʊnɪ] adj (+er) (of bone) knöchern; (like bone) knochenartig; person, knee, hips knochig; fish mit viel Gräten; meat mit viel Knochen.

boo [buː] 1 interj buh. he wouldn't say ~ to a goose (col) er ist ein schüchternes Pflänzchen. 2 vt actor, play, speaker ausfeifen, ausbuhen. to be ~ed off the stage ausgepfiffen or ausgebuht werden. 3 vi buhen. 4 n Buhruf m.

boob [buːb] 1 n (a) (Brit col: mistake) Schnitzer m.

(b) (col: woman's breast) Brust f. **2** vi (Brit col) einen Schnitzer machen; (fail) Mist bauen (col).

booby: ~ **prize** n Trostpreis m für den schlechtesten Teilnehmer; ~ **trap 1** n **(a)** (als Schabernack versteckt angebrachte) Falle f; **(b)** (Mil etc) versteckte Bombe; **2** vt **the suitcase was ~-trapped** in dem Koffer war eine Bombe versteckt.

book [bʊk] **1** n **(a)** Buch nt; (exercise ~) Heft nt. **to bring sb to** ~ jdn zur Rechenschaft ziehen; **he does everything by the** ~ er hält sich bei allem strikt an die Vorschriften; **to be in sb's good/bad** ~**s** bei jdm gut/schlecht angeschrieben sein (col); **to throw the** ~ **at sb** (col) jdn fertigmachen (col); **in my** ~ für mich; **he knows every trick in the** ~ (col) er ist mit allen Wassern gewaschen (col). **(b)** (of tickets) Heft nt; (thicker) Block m; (of matches) Briefchen nt. **(c)** (Comm, Fin) ~**s** pl Buch er pl; **to keep the** ~**s of a firm** die Bücher einer Firma führen. **2** vt **(a)** bestellen; seat, room buchen; artiste engagieren. **(b)** driver aufschreiben (col); einen Strafzettel verpassen (+dat) (col); football player verwarnen. **3** vi see vt **(a)** bestellen; buchen.

♦ **book in 1** vi (in hotel etc) sich eintragen. **we ~ed** ~ **at the Hilton** wir sind im Hilton abgestiegen. **2** vt sep **(a)** (register) eintragen. **(b)** (make reservation for) to ~ **sb** ~**to a hotel** jdm ein Hotelzimmer reservieren lassen.

♦ **book up 1** vi buchen. **2** vt sep (usu pass) reservieren lassen. **to be (fully) ~ed** ~ **(voll)** ausgebucht sein.

book: ~**case** n Bücherregal nt; (with doors) Bücherschrank m; ~**end** n Buchstütze f.
bookie ['bʊkɪ] n (col) Buchmacher m.
booking ['bʊkɪŋ] n (Brit) Buchung, Reservierung f; (of artiste) Engagement nt. **to make a** ~ buchen.
booking: ~**clerk** n Fahrkartenverkäufer(in f) m; ~ **office** n (Brit) (Rail) Fahrkartenschalter m; (Theat) Theaterkasse f.
bookish ['bʊkɪʃ] adj gelehrt (pej, hum); language, expression (pej) trocken.
book: ~**keeper** n Buchhalter(in f) m; ~**keeping** n Buchhaltung or -führung f.
booklet ['bʊklɪt] n Broschüre f.
book: ~**maker** n Buchmacher m; ~**mark** n Lesezeichen nt; ~**seller** n Buchhändler(in f) m; ~**shelf** n Bücherbord or -regal nt; ~**shop** (Brit), ~**store** (US) n Buchhandlung f; ~**stall** n Bücherstand m; ~**token** n Büchergutschein m; ~**worm** n Bücherwurm m.

boom[1] [buːm] n (across river etc) Sperre f; (factory gate etc) Schranke f; (Naut) Baum m; (jib of crane) Ausleger m; (for microphone) Galgen m.

boom[2] **1** n (of sea, waves, wind) Brausen nt; (of thunder) Grollen nt; (of guns) Donnern nt; (of organ, voice) Dröhnen nt. **2** vi **(a)** (sea, wind) brausen; (thunder) grollen. **(b)** (also ~ **out**) (organ, person, voice) dröhnen; (guns) donnern. **3** interj bum.

♦ **boom out 1** vi see boom[2] **2 (b)**. **2** vt sep (person) order brüllen.

boom[3] **1** vi (trade, sales) einen Aufschwung nehmen. **business is ~ing** das Geschäft blüht or floriert. **2** n (of business, fig) Boom, Aufschwung m; (period of economic growth) Hochkonjunktur f.
boomerang ['buːməræŋ] **1** n (lit, fig) Bumerang m. **2** vi (fig col: words, actions) wie ein Bumerang zurückkommen (on zu).
boom town n Goldgräberstadt f.
boon [buːn] n (blessing, advantage) Segen m.
boor [bʊəʳ] n Rüpel, Flegel m.
boorish ['bʊərɪʃ] adj rüpelhaft, flegelhaft.
boost [buːst] **1** n Auftrieb m no pl; (Elec, Aut) Verstärkung f; (of rocket) Zusatzantrieb m. **to give sb/sth a** ~ jdm/einer Sache Auftrieb geben. **2** vt production, economy ankurbeln; electric charge, heart etc verstärken; confidence, sb's ego stärken; morale heben.

booster ['buːstəʳ] n **(a)** (Elec) Puffersatz m; (Rad) Zusatzverstärker m; (TV) Zusatzgleichrichter m; (Aut) (supercharger) Kompressor m; (for heating) Gebläse nt; (~ rocket) Booster m. **(b)** (Med: also ~ **shot**) Wiederholungsimpfung f.
boot [buːt] **1** n **(a)** Stiefel m. **the** ~ **is on the other foot** (fig) es ist genau umgekehrt; **to give sb the** ~ (fig col) jdn rausschmeißen (col). **(b)** (Brit: of car) Kofferraum m. **2** vt **(a)** (col: kick) einen (Fuß)tritt geben (+dat); ball kicken. **(b)** (Comp) laden.
booth [buːð] n **(a)** (at fair) (Markt)bude f. **(b)** (telephone ~) Zelle f; (polling ~, in language laboratory) Kabine f.
boot: ~**lace** n Schnürsenkel m; ~**leg** adj whisky etc schwarz gebrannt; ~**legger** n (US) Bootlegger m; (producer also) Schwarzbrenner m; ~ **polish** n Schuhcreme f.
booty ['buːtɪ] n (lit, fig) Beute f.
booze [buːz] (col) **1** n Alkohol m. **bring some** ~ bring was zu trinken mit. **2** vi saufen (col).
boozer ['buːzəʳ] n **(a)** (pej col: drinker) Säufer(in f) (pej col) m. **(b)** (Brit col: pub) Kneipe f (col).
border ['bɔːdəʳ] **1** n **(a)** (edge, side) Rand m. **(b)** (boundary, frontier) Grenze f. **north/south of the** ~ (Brit) in/nach Schottland/England; ~ **dispute** Grenzstreitigkeit f; (incident) Grenzzwischenfall m. **(c)** (in garden) Rabatte f. **(d)** (edging: on dress) Bordüre f; (of carpet) Einfassung f; (of picture) Umrahmung f. **black** ~ (on notepaper) schwarzer Rand, Trauerrand m. **2** vt **(a)** road säumen; garden etc begrenzen; (on all sides) umschließen. **(b)** (land etc) grenzen an (+acc).
♦ **border on** vi +prep obj (lit, fig) grenzen an (+acc).
border: ~**line 1** n (lit, fig) Grenzlinie, Grenze f; **to be on the** ~**line** an der Grenze liegen; **2** adj ~**line case** Grenzfall m; ~ **town** n Grenzstadt f.
bore[1] [bɔːʳ] **1** vt hole etc bohren. **2** vi bohren (for nach). **3** n (hole) Bohrloch nt; (of tube, pipe) Durchmesser m; (of shotgun, cannon) Kaliber nt.
bore[2] **1** n **(a)** (person) Langeweiler m. **the club/office** ~ der Langweiler vom Dienst. **(b)** (thing, profession, situation etc) **to be a** ~ langweilig sein. **(c)** (nuisance) **don't be a** ~ nun hab dich doch nicht so!; **oh what a** ~! das ist aber auch zu dumm! **2** vt langweilen. **to** ~ **sb stiff** or **to death** or **to tears** jdn zu Tode langweilen; **I'm ~d** ich langweile mich.
bore[3] pret of **bear**[1].
boredom ['bɔːdəm] n Lang(e)weile f.
boring ['bɔːrɪŋ] adj langweilig.
born [bɔːn] adj **to be** ~ geboren werden; (fig) entstehen; (idea) geboren werden; **I was** ~ **in 1948** ich bin 1948 geboren; **I wasn't** ~ **yesterday** (col) ich bin nicht von gestern (col); **he is Chicago-**~ er ist ein gebürtiger Chicagoer; **high-/low-**~ von vornehmer/niedriger Geburt; **he is a** ~ **poet/teacher** er ist der geborene Dichter/Lehrer; **an Englishman** ~ **and bred** in echter or waschechter (col) Engländer.
borne [bɔːn] ptp of **bear**[1].
borough ['bʌrə] n (also municipal ~) Bezirk m.
borrow ['bɒrəʊ] vt **(a)** sich (dat) leihen (from sb); library book ausleihen; word entlehnen; (fig) idea übernehmen (from von). **to** ~ **money from the bank** einen Kredit bei der Bank aufnehmen.
borrower ['bɒrəʊəʳ] n (of books) Entleiher(in f) m; (of capital, loan etc) Kreditnehmer(in f) m.
borrowing ['bɒrəʊɪŋ] n see vt Leihen nt; Ausleihen nt; Entlehnung f; Übernahme f. ~**s** pl (Fin) Anleihen pl.
borstal ['bɔːstl] n (Brit Jur) Besserungsanstalt f.
bosom ['bʊzəm] **1** n (lit, fig: of person) Busen m. **in the** ~ **of his family** im Schoß der Familie. **2** adj attr friend etc Busen-.
boss [bɒs] n Chef, Boß (col) m. **industrial/union** ~**es** Industrie-/Gewerkschaftsbosse pl (col);

OK, you're the ~ okay, du bestimmst.

♦ **boss about** or **around** vt sep (col) rumkommandieren (col).

bossy ['bɒsɪ] adj (+er) herrisch. **don't you get ~ with me!** kommandier mich nicht so rum! (col).

botanical [bə'tænɪkəl] adj botanisch, Pflanzen-. **~ gardens** botanischer Garten.

botanist ['bɒtənɪst] n Botaniker(in f) m.

botany ['bɒtənɪ] n Botanik, Pflanzenkunde f.

botch [bɒtʃ] (col) vt (also ~ **up**) verpfuschen (col).

both [bəʊθ] **1** adj beide. ~ **(the) boys** beide Jungen. **2** pron beide; (two different things) beides. ~ **of them** were there, they were ~ there sie waren (alle) beide da; **come in** ~ **of** you kommt beide herein. **3** adv ~ ... and ... sowohl ... als auch ...; ~ you and I wir beide; **John and I ~ came** John und ich sind beide gekommen; **she was ~ laughing and crying** sie lachte und weinte zugleich or gleichzeitig; **is it black or white?** — ~ **ist es** schwarz oder weiß? — beides.

bother ['bɒðə'] **1** vt (a) (pester) belästigen; (worry) Sorgen machen (+dat); (back, teeth etc) zu schaffen machen (+dat); (problem, question) beschäftigen. **I'm sorry to ~ you but ...** es tut mir leid, daß ich Sie damit belästigen muß, aber ...; **I shouldn't let it ~ you** machen Sie sich mal keine Sorgen; **don't ~ me!** laß mich in Frieden!; **could I ~ you for a light?** dürfte ich Sie vielleicht um Feuer bitten?; **what's ~ing you?** was haben Sie denn? (b) **I can't be ~ed with doing that** ich habe einfach keine Lust dazu; **do you want to stay or go?** — **I'm not ~ed** willst du blei ben oder gehen? — das ist mir egal.

2 vti sich kümmern (about um). **don't ~!** nicht nötig!; (sarcastic) machen Sie sich (dat) keine Mühe!; **she didn't even ~ to ask/check** sie hat nicht einmal gefragt/nachgesehen; **you needn't ~ to come** Sie brauchen wirklich nicht (zu) kommen; **I didn't ~ about lunch** ich habe das Mittagessen ausgelassen.

3 n (a) (nuisance) Plage f. **it's such a ~** das ist wirklich lästig; **I've forgotten it, what a ~** ich habe es vergessen, wie ärgerlich. (b) (trouble etc) Ärger m; (difficulties) Schwierigkeiten pl. **we had a spot or bit of ~ with the car** wir hatten Ärger mit dem Auto; **it wasn't any ~** (don't mention it) gern geschehen; (not difficult) das war ganz einfach; **the children were no ~ at all** wir hatten mit den Kindern überhaupt keine Probleme; **to go to a lot of ~ to do sth** sich (dat) mit etw viel Mühe geben.

4 interj so was Dummes! (col).

bottle ['bɒtl] **1** n Flasche f. **a ~ of wine** eine Flasche Wein; **to take to the ~** zur Flasche greifen. **2** vt in Flaschen abfüllen. **~d in ...** abgefüllt in ...

♦ **bottle up** vt sep aufstauen in sich (dat) aufstauen.

bottled ['bɒtld] adj wine in Flaschen (abgefüllt); beer Flaschen-; fruit eingemacht.

bottle: ~ **bank** n Altglasbehälter m; ~-**feed** vt mit der Flasche ernähren; ~ **green** adj flaschengrün; ~**neck** n (fig) Engpaß m; ~ **opener** n Flaschenöffner m; ~ **party** n Bottle-Party f.

bottom ['bɒtəm] **1** n (a) (of receptacle) Boden m; (of mountain, pillar, spire) Fuß m; (of well, canyon) Grund m; (of page, screen, wall) (unteres) Ende; (of list, road) Ende nt. **at the ~** (of) unten (an/in +dat); **to be (at the) ~ of the class** der/die Letzte in der Klasse sein; ~**s up!** hoch die Tassen (col); **at ~** (fig) im Grunde; **the ~ fell out of his world** (col) für ihn brach eine Welt zusammen. (b) (underneath, underside) Unterseite f, untere Seite. (c) (of sea, lake, river) Grund, Boden m. (d) (of person) Hintern (col), Po (col) m; (of trousers etc) Hosenboden m. (e) (fig: cause) **to be at the ~ of sth** (person) hinter etw (dat) stecken; (thing) einer Sache (dat) zugrunde liegen; **to get to the ~ of sth** einer Sache (dat) auf den Grund kommen. (f) (Brit Aut: gear) **in ~** im ersten Gang.

2 adj attr (lower) untere(r, s); (lowest) unterste(r, s); (Fin) Tiefst-; **pupil** schlechteste(r, s). ~ **half** (of box) untere Hälfte; (of list, class) zweite Hälfte.

bottom: ~ **drawer** n (Brit) **to put sth away in one's ~ drawer** etw für die Aussteuer sparen; ~ **gear** n (Brit Aut) erster Gang; ~**less** adj (lit) bodenlos; **a ~less pit** (fig) ein Faß ohne Boden; ~**most** adj allerunterste(r, s).

bough [baʊ] n Ast m.

bought [bɔːt] pret, ptp of **buy**.

boulder ['bəʊldə'] n Felsblock, Felsbrocken m.

bounce [baʊns] **1** vi (a) (ball etc) springen; (Sport: ball) aufspringen. **the child ~d up and down on the bed** das Kind hüpfte auf dem Bett herum. (b) (col: cheque) platzen (col). **2** vt aufprallen lassen, prellen (Sport). **he ~d the baby on his knee** er ließ das Kind auf den Knien reiten. **3** n (a) (of ball: rebound) Aufprall m. (b) no pl (of ball) Sprungkraft f; (of rubber) Elastizität f; (col: of person) Schwung m (col).

♦ **bounce back** vi abprallen, zurückprallen; (fig col: person) sich nicht unterkriegen lassen (col).

♦ **bounce off** vt always separate **to ~ sth ~ sth** von etw abprallen lassen; **to ~ an idea ~ sb** eine Idee an jdm testen (col).

bouncer ['baʊnsə'] n (col) Rausschmeißer m (col).

bouncing ['baʊnsɪŋ] adj ~ **baby** strammes Baby.

bouncy ['baʊnsɪ] adj (+er) (a) ball gut springend; mattress federnd; springs elastisch; ride holpernd. (b) (fig col: exuberant) übermütig.

bound[1] [baʊnd] **1** n usu pl (lit, fig) Grenze f. **to keep within the ~s** of propriety im Rahmen bleiben; **within the ~s of probability** im Bereich des Wahrscheinlichen; **there are no ~s to his ambition** sein Ehrgeiz kennt keine Grenzen; **out of ~s** gesperrt. **2** vt usu pass country begrenzen.

bound[2] **1** n Sprung, Satz m. **2** vi springen; (rabbit) hoppeln. **the dog came ~ing up** der Hund kam angesprungen.

bound[3] **1** pret, ptp of **bind**. **2** adj (a) (prisoner, book) gebunden. ~ **hand and foot** an Händen und Füßen gebunden. (b) (sure) **to be ~ to do sth** etw bestimmt tun; **he's ~ to be late** er kommt garantiert zu spät; **it's ~ to happen** das muß so kommen. (c) (obliged) person verpflichtet; (by contract, word, promise) gebunden. **but I'm ~ to say ...** (col) aber ich muß schon sagen ...

bound[4] adj pred **to be ~ for London** (heading for) auf dem Weg nach London sein; **where are you ~ for?** wohin geht die Reise?, wohin wollen Sie?; **we were northward-/California-~** wir waren nach Norden/Kalifornien unterwegs.

boundary ['baʊndərɪ] n Grenze f.

boundless ['baʊndlɪs] adj (lit, fig) grenzenlos.

bountiful ['baʊntɪfʊl] adj großzügig; sovereign, god gütig; harvest, gifts (über)reich.

bounty ['baʊntɪ] n (a) (generosity) Freigebigkeit f; (of nature) reiche Fülle (geh). (b) (reward money) Kopfgeld nt. ~ **hunter** Kopfgeldjäger m.

bouquet ['bʊkeɪ] n (a) Strauß m, Bukett nt (geh). (b) (of wine) Bukett nt, Blume f.

bourgeois ['bʊəʒwɑː] **1** n Bürger(in f) m; (pej) Spießbürger(in f) m. **2** adj bürgerlich; (pej) spießbürgerlich.

bourgeoisie [ˌbʊəʒwɑː'ziː] n Bürgertum nt, Bourgeoisie f.

bout [baʊt] n (a) (of flu etc) Anfall m; (of negotiations) Runde f. **a ~ of fever** ein Fieberanfall m; **a drinking ~** eine Zecherei. (b) (Boxing, Wrestling, Fencing) Kampf m.

boutique [buː'tiːk] n Boutique f.

bow[1] [bəʊ] n (a) (for arrows, Mus) Bogen m. **a ~ and arrow** Pfeil und Bogen pl. (b) (of ribbon etc) Schleife f.

bow[2] [baʊ] **1** n (with head, body) Verbeugung f; (by young boy) Diener m. **2** vi (a) sich verbeugen (to sb vor jdm); (young boy) einen Diener machen.

~ **and scrape** katzbuckeln (pej). **(b)** (bend: branches etc) sich biegen. **(c)** (fig: defer, submit) sich beugen (before vor +dat, under unter +dat, to dat). **to** ~ **to the inevitable** sich in das Unvermeidliche fügen. **3** vt **to** ~ **one's head** den Kopf senken; (in prayer) sich verneigen.

♦ **bow out** vi (fig) sich verabschieden.

bow³ [baʊ] n (also: ~s) Bug m. **on the port** ~ backbord voraus.

bowel ['baʊəl] n usu pl (Anat) (of person) Eingeweide nt usu pl; (of animal also) Innereien pl. **a** ~ **movement** Stuhl(gang) m; **the** ~**s of the earth** das Erdinnere.

bowl¹ [baʊl] n **(a)** Schüssel f; (smaller, shallow also, finger~) Schale f; (for sugar etc) Schälchen nt; (for animals, prisoners also) Napf m. **(b)** (of pipe) Kopf m; (of lavatory) Becken nt. **(c)** (Geog) Becken nt. **(d)** (US: stadium) Stadion nt.

bowl² **1** n (Sport: ball) Kugel f. **2** vi (Cricket) (mit gestrecktem Arm) werfen. **3** vt **(a)** (roll) ball rollen; hoop also treiben. **(b)** (Cricket) ball werfen; batsman ausschlagen.

♦ **bowl over** vt sep (lit, fig) umwerfen. **he was** ~**ed** ~ **by the news** die Nachricht hat ihn überwältigt or umgehauen (col).

bow-legged [,bəʊ'legɪd] adj O-beinig.

bowler ['bəʊləʳ] n **(a)** (Cricket) Werfer m. **(b)** (Brit: also ~ **hat**) Melone f.

bowling ['bəʊlɪŋ] n **(a)** (Cricket) Werfen nt. **(b)** (tenpin ~) Bowling nt; (skittles) Kegeln nt. **to go** ~ bowlen/kegeln gehen.

bowling: ~ **alley** n Kegelbahn f; ~ **green** n Rasenfläche f für Bowling.

bowls [bəʊlz] n sing Bowling nt.

bow: ~ **tie** n Fliege f; ~ **window** n Erkerfenster nt.

box¹ [bɒks] **1** vti (Sport) boxen. **to** ~ **sb's ears** jdn ohrfeigen, jdm eine Ohrfeige geben. **2** n **a** ~ **on the ear** eine Ohrfeige.

box² n **(a)** (cardboard ~) Karton m; (smaller) Schachtel f; (snuff~, cigarette ~ etc, biscuit tin) Dose f; (chocolates etc) Schachtel f; (jewellery ~) Schatulle f, Kasten m; (collection ~) (Sammel)büchse f; (in church) Opferbüchse f; (fixed to wall etc) Opferstock m. **(b)** (two-dimensional) (umrandetes) Feld; (Baseball) Box f; (in road junction) gelb schraffierter Kreuzungsbereich. **(c)** (Theat) Loge f; (jury ~) Geschworenenbank f; (witness ~) Zeugenstand m; (press ~) Pressekabine f. **(d)** (Tech: housing) Gehäuse nt. **gear** ~ Getriebe nt. **(e)** (sentry ~) Schilderhaus nt; (signal ~) Häuschen nt. **(f)** (horse ~) Box f. **(g)** PO B~ Postfach nt. **(h)** (Brit: phone ~) Zelle f. **(i)** (Brit col: TV) Glotze f (col).

♦ **box in** vt sep player in die Zange nehmen; parked car einklemmen; (fig) einengen.

boxer ['bɒksəʳ] n (Sport, dog) Boxer m.

boxing ['bɒksɪŋ] n Boxen nt.

boxing in cpds Box-; ~ **Day** n (Brit) zweiter Weihnachts(feier)tag; ~ **match** n Boxkampf m; ~ **ring** n Boxring m.

box: ~ **number** n (at post office) Postfach nt; ~ **office** n Kasse, Theater-/Kinokasse f; ~**room** n (Brit) Abstellraum m.

boy [bɔɪ] n Junge m; (lift~) Boy m. ~**s will be** ~**s** Jungen sind nun mal so; **a school for** ~**s** eine Jungenschule; **the old** ~ (boss) der Alte (col); (father) mein etc alter Herr; **old** ~ (col) alter Junge (col); **oh** ~! (col) Junge, Junge! (col).

boycott ['bɔɪkɒt] **1** n Boykott m. **2** vt boykottieren.

boy: ~**friend** n Freund m; ~**hood** n Kindheit f; (as teenager) Jugend(zeit) f.

boyish ['bɔɪɪʃ] adj jungenhaft; (of woman) figure, appearance knabenhaft.

Boy Scouts n sing Pfadfinder pl.

BR = **British Rail.**

bra [brɑː] n = **brassière** BH m.

brace¹ [breɪs] n, pl - (pair: of pheasants etc) Paar nt.

brace² **1** n **(a)** (Build) Strebe f. **(b)** (tool) (wheel ~) Radschlüssel m; (to hold bit) Bohrwinde f. ~ **and bit** Bohrer m (mit Einsatz). **(c)** (on teeth) Klammer, Spange f; (Med) Stützapparat m. **2** vt **(a)** (ab)stützen; (horizontally) verstreben; (in vice etc) verklammern. **3** vr **to** ~ **oneself for sth** sich auf etw (acc) gefaßt machen.

bracelet ['breɪslɪt] n Armband nt; (bangle) Armreif m.

braces ['breɪsɪz] npl (Brit) Hosenträger pl.

bracing ['breɪsɪŋ] adj anregend; climate Reiz-.

bracken ['brækən] n Adlerfarn m.

bracket ['brækɪt] **1** n **(a)** (angle ~) Winkelträger m; (Archit) Konsole f. **(b)** (Typ) Klammer f. **in** ~**s** in Klammern. **(c)** (group) Gruppe, Klasse f. **the lower income** ~ die untere Einkommensgruppe. **2** vt **(a)** (put in ~s) einklammern. **(b)** (also ~ **together**) mit einer Klammer versehen; (fig: group together) zusammenfassen.

brackish ['brækɪʃ] adj water brackig.

brag [bræg] vti prahlen, angeben (about, of mit).

braggart ['brægət] n Prahler, Angeber m.

braid [breɪd] **1** n **(a)** (of hair) Zopf m. **(b)** (trimming) Borte f; (self-coloured) Litze f. **(c)** (Mil) Tressen pl. **gold** ~ Goldtressen pl. **2** vt (plait) hair, straw etc flechten.

braille [breɪl] n Blinden- or Brailleschrift f.

brain [breɪn] **1** n **(a)** (Anat, of machine) Gehirn nt. **he's got cars on the** ~ (col) er hat nur Autos im Kopf. **(b)** ~**s** pl (Anat) Gehirn nt; (Cook) Hirn nt. **(c)** (mind) Verstand m. ~**s** pl (intelligence) Intelligenz f, Grips m (col), Köpfchen nt (col). **he didn't have the** ~**s to warn us** er ist nicht einmal darauf gekommen, uns zu warnen; **he's the** ~**s of the family** er ist das Genie in der Familie. **2** vt **stop it or I'll** ~ **you!** (col) hör auf oder ich knall dir eine! (col).

brain: ~**child** n (invention) Erfindung f; ~**less** adj plan, idea hirnlos, dumm; person also unbedarft; ~**storm** n (a) (Brit) **to have a** ~**storm** geistig weggetreten sein (col); **(b)** (US: ~wave) Geistesblitz m; ~ **teaser** n Denksportaufgabe f; ~**tumour** (Brit) or **tumor** (US) n Gehirntumor m; ~**wash** vt einer Gehirnwäsche (dat) unterziehen; **to** ~**wash sb into believing that** ... jdm (ständig) einreden, daß ...; ~**washing** n Gehirnwäsche f; ~**wave** n (Brit) Geistesblitz m.

brainy ['breɪnɪ] adj (+er) (col) gescheit, helle pred (col).

braise [breɪz] vt (Cook) schmoren.

brake [breɪk] **1** n (Tech) Bremse f. **to put the** ~**s on** (lit, fig) bremsen; **to put the** ~**s on sth** (fig) etw bremsen. **2** vi bremsen.

brake in cpds Brems-; ~ **drum** n Bremstrommel f; ~**light** n Bremslicht nt; ~ **lining** n Bremsbelag m.

braking ['breɪkɪŋ] n Bremsen nt. ~ **distance** Bremsweg m.

bramble ['bræmbl] n **(a)** (thorny shoot) Dornenzweig m. **(b)** (blackberry) Brombeere f; (bush) Brombeerstrauch m.

bran [bræn] n Kleie f.

branch [brɑːntʃ] **1** n **(a)** (Bot) Zweig m; (growing straight from trunk) Ast m. **(b)** (of river, pipe, duct) Arm m; (of road) Abzweigung f; (of family, race, language) Zweig m; (of railway) Abzweig m. **(c)** (Comm) Filiale f; (of company, bank also) Geschäftsstelle f. ~ **manager** Filialleiter m/ Geschäftsstellenleiter m. **2** vi (divide: river, road etc) sich gabeln; (more than two) sich verzweigen.

♦ **branch off** vi (road) abzweigen; (driver) abbiegen.

♦ **branch out** vi (company) sein Geschäft erweitern or ausdehnen (into auf +acc). **to** ~ ~ **on one's own** sich selbständig machen.

branch: ~ **line** n (Rail) Zweiglinie, Nebenlinie f; ~ **office** n Filiale, Geschäftsstelle f.

brand [brænd] **1** n **(a)** (make) Marke f. **(b)** (mark) (on cattle) Brandzeichen nt; (on criminal, prisoner, fig) Brandmal nt. **2** vt **(a)** (Comm) goods mit seinem Warenzeichen versehen. **(b)** cattle, property mit einem Brandzeichen kennzeichnen. **(c)** (stigmatize) person brandmarken.

brandish ['brændɪʃ] vt schwingen, fuchteln mit (col).

brand: ~ **name** n Markenname m; ~-**new** adj nagelneu, brandneu (col).

brandy ['brændɪ] n Weinbrand m.

brash [bræʃ] adj (+er) frech, dreist; (tasteless) colour etc aufdringlich.

brass [brɑːs] **1** n **(a)** Messing nt. **(b)** the ~ (Mus) die Blechbläser pl. **(c)** (col) the top ~ die hohen Tiere (col). **(d)** (col: money) Moos nt (col), Kies m (col). **2** adj (made of ~) Messing-. ~ **section** Blechbläser pl; to get down to ~ tacks (col) zur Sache kommen.

brass band n Blaskapelle f.

brassière ['bræsɪəʳ] n (dated, form) Büstenhalter m.

brat [bræt] n (pej col) Balg m or nt (col), Gör nt (col).

bravado [brə'vɑːdəʊ] n (showy bravery) Wagemut m; (hiding fear) gespielte Tapferkeit.

brave [breɪv] **1** adj (+er) mutig, unerschrocken; (suffering pain) smile tapfer. be ~! nur Mut!; (more seriously) sei tapfer! **2** n (Indian) Krieger m. **3** vt die Stirn bieten (+dat); weather trotzen (+dat); death tapfer ins Auge sehen (+dat).

♦ **brave out** vt sep you have to ~ it ~ das mußt du durchstehen.

bravery ['breɪvərɪ] n see adj Mut m; Tapferkeit f.

bravo [brɑː'vəʊ] interj bravo!

brawl [brɔːl] **1** vi sich schlagen. **2** n Schlägerei f.

brawn [brɔːn] n **(a)** (Cook) Preßkopf m, Sülze f. **(b)** Muskeln pl, Muskelkraft f.

brawny ['brɔːnɪ] adj (+er) muskulös, kräftig.

bray [breɪ] **1** n (of ass) (Esels)schrei m. **2** vi (ass) schreien; (col: person) wiehern.

brazen ['breɪzn] adj (impudent) unverschämt, dreist; lie schamlos.

♦ **brazen out** vt sep to ~ it ~ durchhalten; (by lying) sich durchmogeln (col).

brazier ['breɪzɪəʳ] n (Kohlen)feuer nt (im Freien); (container) Kohlenbecken nt.

brazil [brə'zɪl] n (also ~ nut) Paranuß f.

Brazil [brə'zɪl] n Brasilien nt.

Brazilian [brə'zɪlɪən] **1** n Brasilianer(in f) m. **2** adj brasilianisch.

breach [briːtʃ] **1** n **(a)** (of law) Übertretung f (of gen), Verstoß m (of gegen). a ~ of contract ein Vertragsbruch m; ~ of the peace (Jur) öffentliche Ruhestörung. **(b)** (in friendship etc) Bruch m. **(c)** (in wall etc, in security) Lücke f. to step into the ~ (fig) in die Bresche springen. **2** vt wall eine Bresche schlagen (in +acc); defences, security durchbrechen.

bread [bred] **1** n **(a)** Brot nt. a piece of ~ and butter ein Butterbrot nt; it's my ~ and butter (fig) davon lebe ich; he knows which side his ~ is buttered (on) er weiß, wo was zu holen ist; to earn one's daily ~ (sich dat) sein Brot verdienen. **(b)** (col: money) Moos nt (col), Kohle f (col). **2** vt panieren.

bread: ~**bin** n Brotkasten m; ~**board** n Brot(schneide)brett nt; ~**crumb** n Brotkrume f or -krümel m; ~**crumbs** npl (Cook) Paniermehl nt; ~**knife** n Brotmesser nt; ~**line** n to be on the ~**line** (fig) nur das Allernotwendigste zum Leben haben.

breadth [bretθ] n Breite f; (of ideas, of theory) (Band)breite f. a hundred metres in ~ hundert Meter breit; his ~ of outlook (open-mindedness) seine Aufgeschlossenheit; (variety of interests) seine Vielseitigkeit.

breadwinner ['bredwɪnəʳ] n Ernährer m.

break [breɪk] (vb: pret **broke**, ptp **broken**) **1** n **(a)**

(in bone, pipe, end of relations etc) Bruch m; (in wall, line) Lücke f; (in clouds) Spalt m. ~ in the circuit Stromkreisunterbrechung f. **(b)** (pause, rest: Brit Sch) Pause f. without a ~ ununterbrochen; to take or have a ~ (eine) Pause machen. **(c)** (change) (in contest etc) Wende f; (holiday, change of activity etc) Abwechslung f. it makes a nice ~ das ist mal etwas anderes; ~ in the weather Wetterumschwung m. **(d)** at ~ of day bei Tagesanbruch. **(e)** (col: escape) Ausbruch m. they made a ~ for it sie versuchten zu entkommen. **(f)** (col: luck, opportunity) to have a good/bad ~ Glück or Schwein (col) nt/Pech nt haben; we had a few lucky ~s wir haben ein paarmal Glück or Schwein (col) gehabt; give me a ~! gib mir ein Chance! **(g)** (Snooker) Ballfolge, Serie f.

2 vt **(a)** brechen; stick, glass zerbrechen; window einschlagen; egg aufschlagen; surface, shell durchbrechen. to ~ a leg sich (dat) das Bein brechen; to ~ surface (submarine) auftauchen. **(b)** rule verletzen; appointment nicht einhalten. **(c)** journey, current, silence etc unterbrechen; monotony, routine auflockern. **(d)** sound barrier durchbrechen. **(e)** he couldn't ~ the habit of smoking er konnte sich das Rauchen nicht abgewöhnen. **(f)** code entziffern; (Sport) serve durchbrechen. to ~ sb (financially) jdn ruinieren; (with grief) jdn seelisch brechen; to ~ the bank die Bank sprengen. **(g)** fall dämpfen, abfangen. **(h)** jail, one's bonds ausbrechen aus. **(i)** news mitteilen. how can I ~ it to her? wie soll ich es ihr bloß beibringen?

3 vi **(a)** brechen; (rope) zerreißen; (smash) kaputtgehen; (cup, glass etc) zerbrechen. **(b)** (stop working etc: toy, watch) kaputtgehen. **(c)** (pause) (eine) Pause machen. **(d)** (wave) sich brechen. **(e)** (day, dawn) anbrechen; (suddenly: storm) losbrechen. **(f)** (change: weather, luck) umschlagen. **(g)** (disperse: clouds) aufreißen. **(h)** (stamina) gebrochen werden; (under interrogation etc) zusammenbrechen. after 6 months her health broke nach 6 Monaten war ihre Gesundheit ruiniert. **(i)** (voice: with emotion) brechen. his voice is beginning to ~ (boy) er kommt in den Stimmbruch. **(j)** (story, news, scandal) bekannt werden. **(k)** to ~ even seine (Un)kosten decken. **(l)** he's broken with her er hat mit ihr Schluß gemacht.

♦ **break away 1** vi **(a)** (chair leg, handle etc) abbrechen (from von); (railway coaches, boats) sich losreißen (from von). **(b)** (dash away) weglaufen (from von); (prisoner) sich losreißen (from von); (Ftbl) sich freispielen. **(c)** (cut ties) sich trennen (from von). **2** vt sep abbrechen (from von).

♦ **break down 1** vi **(a)** (vehicle) eine Panne haben; (machine) ausfallen. **(b)** (negotiations, plan) scheitern; (communications) zum Erliegen kommen; (law and order) zusammenbrechen. **(c)** (argument, resistance, person: start crying) zusammenbrechen. **(d)** (be analysed) (expenditure) sich aufschlüsseln or -gliedern; (theory) sich aufgliedern (lassen). **2** vt sep **(a)** door einrennen; wall niederreißen; opposition brechen; reserve, shyness überwinden; suspicion zerstreuen. **(b)** expenditure aufschlüsseln; theory, argument untergliedern; substance aufspalten.

♦ **break in 1** vi **(a)** (interrupt) unterbrechen (on sb/sth jdn/etw). **(b)** (enter illegally) einbrechen. **2** vt sep **(a)** door aufbrechen. **(b)** horse zureiten; shoes einlaufen.

♦ **break into** vi +prep obj **(a)** house einbrechen in (+acc); safe, car aufbrechen. **(b)** (use part of) savings, £5 note anbrechen. **(c)** (begin suddenly) to ~ ~ song/a trot zu singen/traben anfangen.

♦ **break off 1** vi abbrechen; (stop also) aufhören. we ~ ~ at 5 o'clock wir hören um 5 Uhr auf. **2** vt *sep* abbrechen; *engagement* lösen. **she's broken it ~** sie hat sich von ihm getrennt.

♦ **break out** *vi* **(a)** *(epidemic, fire, war)* ausbrechen. **(b) to ~ ~ in a rash/in(to) spots** einen Ausschlag/Pickel bekommen; **he broke ~ in a cold sweat** ihm brach der Angstschweiß aus. **(c)** *(escape)* ausbrechen *(from, of* aus*)*.

♦ **break through** *vi* durchbrechen.

♦ **break up 1** *vi* **(a)** *(road)* aufbrechen; *(ice also)* bersten; *(ship in storm)* zerbersten. **(b)** *(clouds)* sich lichten; *(crowd, group)* auseinanderlaufen; *(meeting, partnership)* sich auflösen; *(marriage, relationship)* in die Brüche gehen; *(friends, partners)* sich trennen. **(c)** *(Brit Sch) (school)* aufhören. **when do you ~ ~?** wann hört bei euch die Schule auf? **2** *vt sep* **(a)** *ground, road* aufbrechen; *ship (in breaker's yard)* abwracken. **(b)** *estate* aufteilen; *room also, paragraph, sentence* unterteilen; *empire* auflösen; *lines, expanse of colour (make more interesting)* auflockern. **(c)** *marriage, home* zerstören; *meeting* auflösen; *crowd (police)* zerstreuen, auseinandertreiben. **~ it ~!** auseinander!

breakable ['breɪkəbl] **1** *adj* zerbrechlich. **2** *n* ~**s** *pl* zerbrechliche Ware.

breakage ['breɪkɪdʒ] *n* Bruch *m*. **to pay for ~s** für zerbrochene Ware bezahlen.

breakaway ['breɪkə,weɪ] **1** *n* **(a)** *(Pol)* Absplitterung *f*; *(of state also)* Loslösung *f*. **(b)** *(Sport)* Aus- *or* Durchbruch *m*. **(c)** *(US Sport: false start)* Fehlstart *m*. **2** *adj* ~ **group** Splittergruppe *f*.

breakdown ['breɪkdaʊn] *n* **(a)** *(of machine)* Betriebsschaden *m*; *(of vehicle)* Panne *f*. **(b)** *(of communications, Med)* Zusammenbruch *m*. **(c)** *(of figures, expenditure etc)* Aufschlüsselung *f*; *(of thesis, theory etc)* Auf- *or* Untergliederung *f*. **(d)** *(Chem)* Aufspaltung *f*.

breakdown: ~ service *n* *(Brit)* Pannendienst *m*; **~ truck** *or* **van** *n* *(Brit)* Abschleppwagen *m*.

breaker ['breɪkə'] *n* *(wave)* Brecher *m*.

breakfast ['brekfəst] **1** *n* Frühstück *nt*. **to have ~** frühstücken, Frühstück essen; **for ~** zum Frühstück. **2** *vi* frühstücken.

break-in ['breɪkɪn] *n* Einbruch *m*.

breaking ['breɪkɪŋ] *n* ~ **and entering** *(Jur)* Einbruch *m*.

breaking point *n* **(a)** *(Tech)* Festigkeitsgrenze *f*. **(b)** *(fig)* **she is at ~** sie ist nervlich am Ende.

break: ~neck *adj*: **at ~neck speed** mit halsbrecherischer Geschwindigkeit; **~out** *n* Ausbruch *m*; **~through** *n* *(Mil, fig)* Durchbruch *m*; **~up** *n* **(a)** *(lit) (of ship)* Zerbersten *nt*; *(of ice)* Bersten *nt*; **(b)** *(fig) (of friendship)* Bruch *m*; *(of marriage)* Zerrüttung *f*; *(of political party)* Zersplitterung *f*; *(of partnership, meeting)* Auflösung *f*; **~water** *n* Wellenbrecher *m*.

breast [brest] *n* *(lit, fig)* Brust *f*.

breast: ~fed *adj* **to be ~fed** gestillt werden; **~feed** *vti* stillen; **~ stroke** *m* Brustschwimmen *nt*; **to do the ~ stroke** brustschwimmen.

breath [breθ] *n* **(a)** Atem *m*. **to take a deep ~** einmal tief Luft holen; **bad ~** Mundgeruch *m*; **with one's dying ~** mit dem letzten Atemzug; **out of ~** außer Atem, atemlos; **in the same ~** im selben Atemzug; **to take sb's ~ away** jdm den Atem verschlagen; **to say sth under one's ~** etw vor sich *(acc)* hin murmeln; **to go out for a ~ of (fresh) air** an die frische Luft gehen. **(b)** *(slight stirring)* **~ of wind** Lüftchen *nt*, Hauch *m*.

breathalyzer ['breθəlaɪzə'] *n* *(Brit)* Röhrchen *nt* *(col)*. **to give sb a ~** jdn ins Röhrchen blasen lassen.

breathe [briːð] **1** *vi* atmen; *(col: rest)* verschnaufen, Luft holen. **now we can ~ again** jetzt können wir wieder aufatmen; *(have more space)* jetzt haben wir wieder Luft. **2** *vt air* einatmen. **to ~ one's last** seinen letzten Atemzug tun; **he ~d**

garlic all over me er verströmte einen starken Knoblauchgeruch; **he ~d new life into the firm** er brachte neues Leben in die Firma; **don't ~ a word** sag kein Sterbenswörtchen!

♦ **breathe in** *vi, vt sep* einatmen.

♦ **breathe out** *vi, vt sep* ausatmen.

breather ['briːðə'] *n* *(short rest)* Atempause, Verschnaufpause *f*.

breathing ['briːðɪŋ] *n* *(respiration)* Atmung *f*. **~ space** *(fig)* Atempause, Ruhepause *f*.

breathless ['breθlɪs] *adj* atemlos; *(with exertion also)* außer Atem. **it left me ~** *(lit, fig)* es verschlug mir den Atem.

breathtaking ['breθteɪkɪŋ] *adj* atemberaubend.

bred [bred] *pret, ptp of* **breed**.

breeches ['brɪtʃɪz] *npl* Kniehose *f*; *(riding ~)* Reithose *f*.

breed [briːd] *(vb: pret, ptp* **bred***)* **1** *n* *(lit, fig) (species)* Art, Sorte *f*. **2** *vt* **(a)** *animals, flowers* züchten. **(b)** *(fig: give rise to)* erzeugen. **3** *vi* *(animals)* Junge haben; *(birds)* brüten.

breeder ['briːdə'] *n* **(a)** *(person)* Züchter *m*. **(b)** *(Tech: also ~ reactor)* Brutreaktor, Brüter *m*.

breeding ['briːdɪŋ] *n* **(a)** *(reproduction)* Fortpflanzung und Aufzucht *f* der Jungen. **(b)** *(rearing)* Zucht *f*. **(c)** *(upbringing, good manners: also* **good ~***)* gute Erziehung, Kinderstube *f*.

breeze [briːz] **1** *n* Brise *f*. **2** *vi* **to ~ in/out** fröhlich angetrabt kommen/vergnügt abziehen *(of* aus*)*.

breezy ['briːzɪ] *adj (+er)* **(a)** *weather, day* windig; *corner also* luftig. **(b)** *manner* forsch-fröhlich.

brevity ['brevɪtɪ] *n* Kürze *f*.

brew [bruː] **1** *n* *(beer)* Bräu *nt*; *(of tea)* Tee *m*, Gebräu *nt* *(iro)*; *(of herbs)* Kräutermischung *f*. **witch's ~** Zaubertrank *m*. **2** *vt* *beer* brauen; *tea* aufgießen; *(fig) scheme, plot* ausbrüten. **3** *vi* *(beer)* gären; *(tea)* ziehen; *(make beer)* brauen. **there's something ~ing** da braut sich etwas zusammen.

brewery ['bruːərɪ] *n* Brauerei *f*.

bribe [braɪb] **1** *n* Bestechung *f*; *(money)* Bestechungsgeld *nt*. **to take a ~** sich bestechen lassen. **2** *vt* bestechen. **to ~ sb to do sth** jdn bestechen, damit er etw tut.

bribery ['braɪbərɪ] *n* Bestechung *f*.

bric-à-brac ['brɪkəbræk] *n* Nippes *m*.

brick [brɪk] *n* **(a)** Ziegel- *or* Backstein *m*. **he came down on me like a ton of ~s** *(col)* er hat mich völlig fertiggemacht *(col)*; **to drop a ~** *(fig col)* ins Fettnäpfchen treten; **to drop sb/sth like a hot ~** *(col)* jdn/etw wie eine heiße Kartoffel fallenlassen. **(b)** *(toy)* (Bau)klotz *m*. **box of (building) ~s** Baukasten *m*.

♦ **brick in** *or* **up** *vt sep door, window* zumauern.

brick: ~layer *n* Maurer *m*; **~ wall** *n* *(fig col)* **I might as well be talking to a ~ wall** ich könnte genausogut gegen eine Wand reden.

bridal ['braɪdl] *adj* Braut-; *procession, feast* Hochzeits-.

bride [braɪd] *n* Braut *f*. **the ~ and groom** Braut und Bräutigam, das Hochzeitspaar.

bridegroom ['braɪdgruːm] *n* Bräutigam *m*.

bridesmaid ['braɪdzmeɪd] *n* Brautjungfer *f*.

bridge¹ ['brɪdʒ] **1** *n* **(a)** *(lit, fig)* Brücke *f*. **(b)** *(Naut)* (Kommando)brücke *f*. **2** *vt river, railway* eine Brücke schlagen *or* bauen über *(+acc)*; *(fig)* überbrücken. **to ~ the gap** *(fig)* die Zeit überbrücken; *(between people)* die Kluft überbrücken.

bridge² *n* *(Cards)* Bridge *nt*.

bridgehead ['brɪdʒhed] *n* Brückenkopf *m*.

bridging loan ['brɪdʒɪŋ,ləʊn] *n* *(Brit)* Überbrückungskredit *m*.

bridle ['braɪdl] **1** *n* *(of horse)* Zaum *m*. **2** *vt horse* aufzäumen; *(fig) emotions* im Zaum halten.

bridlepath ['braɪdl,pɑːθ] *n* Reitweg *m*.

brief [briːf] **1** *adj* *(+er)* kurz; *(curt also) manner* kurz angebunden. **in ~** kurz (und gut). **2** *n* **(a)**

briefcase — column 1

(Jur) Auftrag *m (an einen Anwalt); (document)* Unterlagen *pl* zu dem/einem Fall; *(instructions)* Instruktionen *pl.* **(b)** *(instructions)* Auftrag *m.* **3** *vt (employ) lawyer* beauftragen; *(give instructions to)* instruieren *(on* über +*acc); (give information)* informieren *(on* über +*acc).*

briefcase ['bri:fkeɪs] *n* (Akten)tasche *f.*

briefing ['bri:fɪŋ] *n (instructions)* Instruktionen *pl,* Anweisungen *pl; (also* ~ **session)** Einsatzbesprechung *f.*

briefly ['bri:flɪ] *adv* kurz.

briefs [bri:fs] *npl* Slip *m.* **a pair of** ~ ein Slip.

brigade [brɪ'geɪd] *n (Mil)* Brigade *f.*

brigadier (general) [ˌbrɪgə'dɪə('dʒenərəl)] *n* Brigadegeneral *m.*

bright [braɪt] *adj (+er)* **(a)** hell; *colour* leuchtend; *sunshine also, eyes* strahlend; *day, weather* heiter. ~ **red** knallrot; ~ **intervals** *or* **periods** *(Met)* Aufheiterungen *pl;* **the** ~ **lights** *(col)* Großstadtluft *f.* **(b)** *(cheerful) person, smile* fröhlich, heiter. **I wasn't feeling too** ~ es ging mir nicht besonders gut; ~ **and early** in aller Frühe. **(c)** *(intelligent) person* intelligent; *child* aufgeweckt; *idea* glänzend; *(iro)* intelligent. **(d)** *future, prospects* glänzend.

brighten (up) ['braɪtn(ʌp)] **1** *vt (sep)* **(a)** *(make cheerful)* spirits, *person* aufheitern; *room, atmosphere* aufhellen; *prospects, situation* verbessern. **(b)** *(make bright) colour, hair* aufhellen; *metal* aufpolieren. **2** *vi (weather, sky, face)* sich aufheitern; *(person)* fröhlicher werden; *(eyes)* aufleuchten; *(prospects)* besser werden; *(future)* freundlicher aussehen.

brightly ['braɪtlɪ] *adv shine* hell; *smile* fröhlich.

brightness ['braɪtnɪs] *n see adj* **(a)** Helligkeit *f;* Leuchten *nt;* Strahlen *nt;* Heiterkeit *f.* **(b)** Fröhlichkeit, Heiterkeit *f.* **(c)** Intelligenz *f;* Aufgeweckheit *f.*

brilliance ['brɪljəns] *n* **(a)** *(of light)* heller Glanz, Strahlen *nt.* **(b)** *(of idea, achievement)* Großartigkeit *f; (of person)* Brillanz *f.* **a man of such** ~ ein Mann von so hervorragender Intelligenz.

brilliant ['brɪljənt] *adj* **(a)** *sunshine, colour* strahlend. **(b)** *idea etc* großartig *(also iro); scientist, achievement also* glänzend, brilliant. **she is a** ~ **woman** sie ist eine sehr intelligente Frau.

brim [brɪm] **1** *n (of cup)* Rand *m; (of hat also)* Krempe *f.* **2** *vi* sprühen *(with* von *or* vor +*dat).* **her eyes were** ~**ming with tears** ihre Augen standen voll Tränen.

♦ **brim over** *vi (lit, fig)* überfließen *(with* vor +*dat).*

brimful ['brɪm'fʊl] *adj (lit)* randvoll; *(fig)* voll *(of, with* von). **he is** ~ **of energy** er sprüht vor Energie.

brine [braɪn] *n* **(a)** *(salt water)* Sole *f; (for pickling)* Lake *f.* **(b)** *(sea water)* Salzwasser *nt.*

bring [brɪŋ] *pret, ptp* **brought** *vt* **(a)** bringen; *(also* ~ **with one)** mitbringen. **did you** ~ **your guitar?** haben Sie Ihre Gitarre mitgebracht?; **to** ~ **tears to sb's eyes** jdm die Tränen in die Augen treiben. **(b)** **I cannot** ~ **myself to speak to him** ich kann es nicht über mich bringen, mit ihm zu sprechen.

♦ **bring about** *vt sep* **(a)** *(cause)* herbeiführen, verursachen. **(b)** *(Naut)* wenden.

♦ **bring back** *vt sep* **(a)** *(lit) person, object, memories* zurückbringen. **(b)** *custom, hanging* wieder einführen; *government* wiederwählen. **to** ~ **sb** ~ **to life** jdn wieder lebendig machen.

♦ **bring down** *vt sep* **(a)** *(out of air) (shoot down) bird, plane* herunterholen; *(land) plane, kite* herunterbringen. **(b)** *opponent, government* zu Fall bringen; *(by shooting) animal* zur Strecke bringen; *person* niederschießen. **(c)** *(reduce) temperature, prices* senken; *swelling* zurückgehen lassen.

♦ **bring forward** *vt sep* **(a)** *(lit) person, chair* nach

briefcase — column 2

vorne bringen. **(b)** *(fig: present) witness* vorführen; *evidence, argument* vorbringen. **(c)** *(advance time of) meeting* vorverlegen. **(d)** *(Comm)* figure übertragen.

♦ **bring in** *vt sep* **(a)** *(lit) person, object* hereinbringen *(prep obj, -to* in +*acc); harvest* einbringen. **(b)** *(fig: introduce) fashion, custom* einführen. **(c)** *(involve, call in) police etc* einschalten *(on* bei). **(d)** *(Fin) income, money* (ein)bringen *(-to* sb jdm); *(Comm)* business bringen. **(e)** *(Jur: jury) verdict* fällen.

♦ **bring off** *vt sep* **(a)** *people from wreck* retten, wegbringen *(prep obj* von). **(b)** *(succeed with)* plan zustande *or* zuwege bringen. **he brought it** ~! er hat es geschafft! *(col).*

♦ **bring on** *vt sep* **(a)** *(cause) illness, quarrel* herbeiführen, verursachen; *attack* also auslösen. **(b)** *(help develop) pupil* weiterbringen. **(c)** *(Theat) person* auftreten lassen; *thing* auf die Bühne bringen; *(Sport) player* einsetzen. **(d)** **you brought it** ~ **yourself** das hast du dir selbst zuzuschreiben.

♦ **bring out** *vt sep (lit, fig)* herausbringen; *(also* ~ ~ **on strike)** *workers* in den Streik treten lassen.

♦ **bring round** *vt sep* **(a)** *(to one's house etc)* vorbeibringen. **(b)** *discussion* bringen *(to* auf +*acc).* **(c)** *unconscious person* wieder zu Bewußtsein bringen. **(d)** *(convert)* herumkriegen *(col).*

♦ **bring to** *vt always separate unconscious person* wieder zu Bewußtsein bringen.

♦ **bring up** *vt sep* **(a)** *(to a higher place)* heraufbringen. **(b)** *(raise, increase) amount* erhöhen *(to* auf +*acc); level, standards* anheben. **to** ~ **sb** ~ **to a certain standard** jdn auf ein gewisses Niveau bringen. **(c)** *(rear) child, animal* groß- *or* aufziehen; *(educate)* erziehen. **a well brought-**~ **child** ein gut erzogenes Kind. **(d)** *(vomit up)* brechen. **(e)** *(mention) fact, problem* erwähnen.

brink [brɪŋk] *n (lit, fig)* Rand *m.* **on the** ~ **of sth/ doing sth** *(lit, fig)* am Rande von etw/nahe daran, etw zu tun.

briny ['braɪnɪ] **1** *adj* salzhaltig, salzig. **2** *n (col)* See *f.*

brisk [brɪsk] *adj (+er)* **(a)** *person, way of speaking* forsch; *walk, pace* flott. **(b)** *(fig) trade, betting* lebhaft, rege. **(c)** *wind, weather* frisch.

bristle ['brɪsl] **1** *n (of brush, boar etc)* Borste *f; (of beard)* Stoppel *f.* **2** *vi* **(a)** *(animal's hair)* sich sträuben. **(b)** *(fig: person)* zornig werden. **to** ~ **with anger** vor Wut schnauben. **(c)** *(fig)* **to be bristling with police** von Polizisten wimmeln; **bristling with difficulties** mit Schwierigkeiten gespickt.

bristly ['brɪslɪ] *adj (+er) animal, hair* borstig; *chin* Stoppel-, stoppelig.

Britain ['brɪtn] *n* Großbritannien *nt.*

British ['brɪtɪʃ] **1** *adj* britisch. **I'm** ~ ich bin Brite/ Britin; **the** ~ **Isles** die Britischen Inseln. **2** *n* **the** ~ *pl* die Briten *pl.*

Britisher ['brɪtɪʃə'] *n (US)* Brite *m,* Britin *f.*

Briton ['brɪtən] *n* Brite *m,* Britin *f.*

Brittany ['brɪtnɪ] *n* die Bretagne.

brittle ['brɪtl] *adj* spröde, zerbrechlich. ~ **bones** schwache Knochen.

broach [brəʊtʃ] *vt* **(a)** *barrel* anstechen, anzapfen. **(b)** *subject, topic* anschneiden.

broad [brɔːd] *adj (+er)* **(a)** *(wide)* breit. **it's as** ~ **as it is long** *(fig)* es ist Jacke wie Hose *(col).* **(b)** *(widely applicable) theory* umfassend; *(general)* allgemein. **(c)** *(not detailed) idea, outline* grob; *sense* weit. **as a very** ~ **rule** als Faustregel. **(d)** *(liberal) mind, attitude* großzügig, tolerant. **(e)** *hint* deutlich. **(f)** *(strongly marked) accent* stark.

broad bean *n* dicke Bohne, Saubohne *f.*

broadcast ['brɔːdkɑːst] *(vb: pret, ptp* ~) **1** *n (Rad, TV)* Sendung *f; (of match etc)* Übertragung *f.* **2** *vt* **(a)** *(Rad, TV)* senden, ausstrahlen; *football* match, event übertragen. **(b)** (fig) news, rumour etc verbreiten. **3** vi (Rad, TV: station) senden.

broadcaster ['brɔːdkɑːstəʳ] n (Rad, TV) (announcer) Rundfunk-/Fernsehsprecher(in f) m; (personality) Mitarbeiter(in f) m beim Rundfunk/Fernsehen.

broadcasting ['brɔːdkɑːstɪŋ] **1** n (Rad, TV) Sendung f; (of event) Übertragung f. **2** attr (Rad) Rundfunk-; (TV) Fernseh-. ~ **station** (Rad) Rundfunkstation f; (TV) Fernsehstation f.

broaden (out) ['brɔːdn(aʊt)] **1** vt (sep) road etc verbreitern. **to** ~ **one's mind/one's horizons** (fig) seinen Horizont erweitern. **2** vi breiter werden, sich verbreitern.

broadly ['brɔːdlɪ] adv **(a)** (in general terms) allgemein, in großen Zügen. ~ **speaking** ganz allgemein gesprochen. **(b)** (greatly, widely) differ beträchtlich. **(c)** grin, smile, laugh breit.

broad: ~**-minded** adj großzügig, tolerant; ~**sheet** n Flugblatt nt; ~**-shouldered** adj breitschult(e)rig; ~**side** (Naut) n Breitseite f; (fig also) Attacke f; **to fire a** ~**side** eine Breitseite abfeuern.

brocade [brəʊˈkeɪd] n Brokat m.

broccoli ['brɒkəlɪ] n Brokkoli pl.

brochure ['brəʊʃjʊəʳ] n Broschüre f, Prospekt m.

brogue [brəʊg] n (Irish accent) irischer Akzent.

broil [brɔɪl] vti (Cook) grillen.

broke [brəʊk] **1** pret of **break. 2** adj pred (col) abgebrannt (col), pleite (col).

broken ['brəʊkən] **1** ptp of **break. 2** adj **(a)** kaputt (col); twig geknickt; bone gebrochen; rope also gerissen; (smashed) cup, glass etc also zerbrochen. **(b)** heart, spirit, man, promise gebrochen; health, marriage zerrüttet. **from a** ~ **home** aus zerrütteten Familienverhältnissen. **(c)** road, surface, ground uneben; coastline zerklüftet. **(d)** (interrupted) journey, line on road unterbrochen; line on paper gestrichelt; sleep unruhig. **(e)** English, German etc gebrochen.

broken: ~**-down** adj machine, car kaputt (col); ~**-hearted** adj untröstlich.

broker ['brəʊkəʳ] n Makler m.

brolly ['brɒlɪ] n (Brit col) (Regen)schirm m.

bromide ['brəʊmaɪd] n (Chem) Bromid nt.

bronchial ['brɒŋkɪəl] adj bronchial. ~ **tubes** Bronchien pl.

bronchitis [brɒŋˈkaɪtɪs] n Bronchitis f.

bronze [brɒnz] **1** n Bronze f. **2** vi (person) braun werden. **3** vt face, skin bräunen. **4** adj Bronze-.

Bronze Age n Bronzezeit f.

bronzed [brɒnzd] adj (sonnen)gebräunt.

brooch [brəʊtʃ] n Brosche f.

brood [bruːd] **1** n (lit, fig) Brut f. **2** vi **(a)** (bird) brüten. **(b)** (fig: person) grübeln.

♦ **brood over** or **(up)on** vi +prep obj nachgrübeln über (+acc); (despondently also) brüten über (+dat).

broody ['bruːdɪ] adj **(a) the hen is** ~ die Henne gluckt; **she is feeling** ~ (hum col) sie will (unbedingt) ein Kind. **(b)** person grüblerisch.

brook [brʊk] n Bach m.

broom [bruːm] n Besen m. **a new** ~ **sweeps clean** (Prov) neue Besen kehren gut (Prov).

broom: ~ **cupboard** n Besenschrank m; ~**stick** n Besenstiel m.

Bros npl (Comm) = **Brothers** Gebr.

broth [brɒθ] n Fleischbrühe f; (thickened soup) Suppe f.

brothel ['brɒθl] n Bordell nt, Puff m (col).

brother ['brʌðəʳ] n **(a)** Bruder m. **my/his** ~**s and sisters** meine/seine Geschwister; **oh** ~! (esp US col) Junge, Junge! (col). **(b)** (in trade unions) Kollege m.

brother: ~**hood** n **(a)** Brüderlichkeit f; **(b)** (organization) Bruderschaft f; ~**hood of man** Gemeinschaft f der Menschen; ~**-in-law** n, pl ~**s-in-law** Schwager m.

brotherly ['brʌðəlɪ] adj brüderlich.

brought [brɔːt] pret, ptp of **bring.**

brow [braʊ] n **(a)** (eyebrow) Braue f. **(b)** (forehead) Stirn f. **(c)** (of hill) (Berg)kuppe f.

browbeat ['braʊbiːt] pret ~, ptp ~**en** vt unter Druck setzen.

brown [braʊn] **1** adj (+er) braun. **2** n Braun nt. **3** vt (sun) skin, person bräunen; (Cook) (an)bräunen; meat also anbraten. **4** vi braun werden.

♦ **brown off** vt **to be** ~**ed** ~ **with sb/sth** (esp Brit col) jdn/etw satt haben (col).

brown: ~ **ale** n Malzbier nt; ~ **bear** n Braunbär m; ~ **bread** n Grau- or Mischbrot nt; (from wholemeal) Vollkornbrot nt; (darker) Schwarzbrot nt.

brownie ['braʊnɪ] n **(a)** (fairy) Heinzelmännchen nt. **(b) B**~ Pfadfinderin f.

brownish ['braʊnɪʃ] adj bräunlich.

brown: ~**owl** n **(a)** (Orn) Waldkauz m; **(b) B**~ **Owl** (in Brownies) die Weise Eule; ~ **paper** n Packpapier nt; ~ **rice** n ungeschälter Reis.

browse [braʊz] **1** vi **to** ~ **among the books in** den Büchern schmökern; **to** ~ **(around)** sich umsehen. **2** n **to have a** ~ **(around)** sich umsehen.

bruise [bruːz] **1** n blauer Fleck; (on fruit) Druckstelle f. **2** vt person einen blauen Fleck/blaue Flecke(n) schlagen (+dat); fruit beschädigen; (fig) feelings verletzen. **3** vi he ~**s easily** er bekommt leicht blaue Flecken.

brunette [bruːˈnet] **1** n Brünette f. **2** adj brünett.

brunt [brʌnt] n **to bear the** ~ **of the costs/attack** die Hauptlast der Kosten tragen/die volle Wucht des Angriffs mitbekommen.

brush [brʌʃ] **1** n **(a)** Bürste f; (artist's ~, paint ~, shaving ~) Pinsel m; (with dustpan) Handbesen or -feger m. **(b)** (action) **to give sth a** ~ etw bürsten; jacket, shoes etw abbürsten. **(c)** (light touch) leichte Berührung. **(d)** (Mil: skirmish) Zusammenstoß m. **to have a** ~ **with sb** mit jdm aneinandergeraten. **2** vt jdn bürsten; (with hand) wischen. **to** ~ **one's teeth/hair** sich (dat) die Zähne putzen/das Haar bürsten. **(b)** (sweep) dirt fegen, kehren; (with hand, cloth) wischen. **(c)** (touch lightly) streifen.

♦ **brush against** vi +prep obj streifen.

♦ **brush aside** vt sep obstacle, person (einfach) zur Seite schieben; objections (einfach) abtun.

♦ **brush away** vt sep abbürsten; (with hand, cloth) wegwischen; insects verscheuchen.

♦ **brush off** vt sep (a) mud, snow abbürsten; insect verscheuchen. **(b)** (col: reject) person abblitzen lassen (col); suggestion, criticism zurückweisen.

♦ **brush past** vi streifen (prep obj acc).

♦ **brush up** vt sep **(a)** crumbs, dirt auffegen, aufkehren. **(b)** (fig: also ~ **on**) subject, one's German etc auffrischen.

brush: ~**-off** n (col) Abfuhr f; **to give sb the** ~**-off** jdn abblitzen lassen (col), jdm einen Korb geben (col); ~**work** n (Art) Pinselführung f.

brusque [bruːsk] adj (+er) brüsk, schroff.

brusqueness ['bruːsknɪs] n Schroffheit f.

Brussels ['brʌslz] n Brüssel nt. ~ **sprouts** Rosenkohl m.

brutal ['bruːtl] adj brutal.

brutality [bruːˈtælɪtɪ] n Brutalität f.

brute [bruːt] **1** n **(a)** Tier, Vieh (pej) nt. **(b)** (person) brutaler Kerl; (savage) Bestie f. **(c)** (col: thing) **it's a** ~ **of a thing to lift** es ist verdammt schwer, das hochzuheben (col). **2** adj attr strength nackt; passion tierisch. **by** ~ **force** mit roher Gewalt.

BSc = **Bachelor of Science.**

bubble ['bʌbl] **1** n Blase f. **to blow** ~**s** Blasen machen. **2** vi (liquid) sprudeln; (wine) perlen; (gas) Blasen bilden.

♦ **bubble over** vi (lit) überschäumen; (fig) übersprudeln (with vor +dat).

bubble: ~ **bath** n Schaumbad nt; ~ **gum** n Kaugummi m or nt.

bubbly ['bʌblɪ] 1 *adj* (+*er*) (*lit*) sprudelnd; (*fig col*) *personality* temperamentvoll, lebendig. 2 *n* (*col*) Schampus *m* (*col*).

buck [bʌk] *n* (a) (*male of deer*) Bock *m*. (b) (*US col: dollar*) Dollar *m*. (c) **to pass the ~** den Schwarzen Peter weitergeben; (*responsibility also*) die Verantwortung abschieben.

♦ **buck up** (*col*) 1 *vi* (a) (*hurry up*) sich ranhalten (*col*), rasch *or* fix machen (*col*). ~ ~! halt dich ran! (*col*). (b) (*cheer up*) aufleben. ~ ~! Kopf hoch! 2 *vt sep* (a) (*make cheerful*) aufmuntern. (b) **to ~ one's ideas ~** sich zusammenreißen (*col*).

bucket ['bʌkɪt] 1 *n* Eimer *m*; (*of excavator*) Schaufel *f*. **a ~ of water** ein Eimer Wasser. 2 *vi* (*col*) **it's ~ing!, the rain is ~ing (down)!** es gießt wie aus Kübeln (*col*).

buckle ['bʌkl] 1 *n* (a) (*on belt, shoe*) Schnalle, Spange *f*. (b) (*in metal etc*) Beule *f*; (*concave also*) Delle *f*. 2 *vt* (a) *belt, shoes* zuschnallen. (b) *wheel, girder etc* verbiegen; (*dent*) verbeulen. 3 *vi* (a) (*belt, shoe*) mit einer Schnalle *or* Spange geschlossen werden, geschnallt werden. (b) (*wheel, metal*) sich verbiegen.

♦ **buckle down** *vi* (*col*) sich dranmachen (*to an* +*dat*) (*col*).

buck: **~skin** *n* Wildleder *nt*; **~tooth** *m* vorstehender Zahn; **~wheat** *n* Buchweizen *m*.

bud [bʌd] 1 *n* Knospe *f*. **to be in ~** knospen, Knospen treiben. 2 *vi* (*plant, flower*) knospen, Knospen treiben; (*tree also*) ausschlagen.

Buddha ['budə] *n* Buddha *m*.

Buddhism ['budɪzəm] *n* Buddhismus *m*.

Buddhist ['budɪst] 1 *n* Buddhist(in *f*) *m*. 2 *adj* buddhistisch.

budding ['bʌdɪŋ] *adj* knospend; (*fig*) *poet etc* angehend.

buddy ['bʌdɪ] *n* (*US col*) Kumpel *m*.

budge [bʌdʒ] 1 *vi* (a) (*move*) sich rühren, sich bewegen. (b) (*fig: give way*) nachgeben, weichen. **I will not ~ an inch** ich werde keinen Fingerbreit nachgeben. 2 *vt* (*move*) (von der Stelle) bewegen. **we can't ~ him** (*fig*) er läßt sich durch nichts erweichen.

budgerigar ['bʌdʒərɪgɑːʳ] *n* Wellensittich *m*.

budget ['bʌdʒɪt] 1 *n* Etat *m*, Budget *nt*; (*Parl also*) Haushalt(splan) *m*. 2 *vi* wirtschaften.

♦ **budget** *vt* +*prep obj* (im Etat) einplanen.

budgie ['bʌdʒɪ] *n* (*col*) = **budgerigar**.

buff [bʌf] 1 *n* (a) (*colour*) Gelbbraun *nt*. (b) (*col: movie ~ etc*) Fan *m*. 2 *adj* gelbbraun.

buffalo ['bʌfələu] *n*, *pl* **-es**, *collective pl* - Büffel *m*.

buffer ['bʌfəʳ] *n* (*lit, fig*) Puffer *m*; (*Rail: at terminus*) Prellbock *m*; (*Comp*) Pufferspeicher *m*. **old ~** (*col*) alter Heini (*col*).

buffer state *n* (*Pol*) Pufferstaat *m*.

buffet[1] ['bʌfɪt] 1 *n* (*blow*) Schlag *m*. 2 *vt* hin und her werfen. **~ed by the wind** vom Wind gerüttelt.

buffet[2] ['bufeɪ] *n* Büfett *nt*; (*Brit Rail*) Speisewagen *m*; (*meal*) Stehimbiß *m*; (*cold ~*) kaltes Büfett.

buffet car ['bufeɪ-] *n* (*Brit Rail*) Speisewagen *m*.

buffet ['bufeɪ-]: **~ lunch/supper** *n* Stehimbiß *m*.

bug [bʌg] 1 *n* (a) Wanze *f*; (*col: any insect*) Käfer *m*. **~s** *pl* Ungeziefer *nt*. (b) (*bugging device*) Wanze *f*. (c) (*col: germ, virus*) Bazillus *f*. **he picked up a ~ while on holiday** er hat sich (*dat*) im Urlaub eine Krankheit geholt. (d) (*col: obsession*) **she's got the travel ~** die Reiselust hat sie gepackt. (e) (*col: fault*) Fehler *m*. 2 *vt* (a) *room, building* Wanzen *pl* einbauen in (+*acc*) (*col*); *conversation, telephone lines* abhören. (b) (*col*) (*worry*) stören; (*annoy*) nerven (*col*), den Nerv töten (+*dat*) (*col*). **don't let it ~ you** mach dir nichts draus (*col*).

bugbear ['bʌgbeəʳ] *n* Schreckgespenst *nt*.

bugger ['bʌgəʳ] 1 *n* (*col!*) Scheißkerl *m* (*col!*), Arschloch *nt* (*col!*); (*when not contemptible*) Kerl (*col*), Typ *m* (*col*); (*thing*) Scheißding *nt* (*col!*). **you**

lucky ~! du hast vielleicht ein Schwein! (*col*); **to play silly ~s** (*col*) Scheiß machen (*col*). 2 *interj* (*col!*) Mist! (*col*). **~ him** dieser Scheißkerl (*col!*).

♦ **bugger off** *vi* (*Brit col!*) abhauen (*col*).

♦ **bugger up** *vt sep* (*Brit col!*) versauen (*col!*).

bugle ['bjuːgl] *n* Signalhorn *nt*.

build [bɪld] (*vb: pret, ptp* **built**) 1 *n* Körperbau *m*. 2 *vt* (a) bauen. **the house is being built** das Haus ist im Bau. (b) (*fig*) *new nation, relationship etc* aufbauen; *a better future* schaffen. 3 *vi* bauen.

♦ **build on** 1 *vt sep* anbauen. 2 *vi* +*prep obj* bauen auf (+*acc*).

♦ **build up** 1 *vi* (a) entstehen; (*anticyclone, atmosphere also*) sich aufbauen; (*increase*) zunehmen; (*Tech: pressure*) sich erhöhen. **the music ~s ~ to a huge crescendo** die Musik steigert sich zu einem gewaltigen Crescendo. (b) (*traffic*) sich verdichten; (*queue, line of cars*) sich bilden. 2 *vt sep* (a) aufbauen (*into zu*); *finances* aufbessern. **to ~ ~ a reputation** sich (*dat*) einen Namen machen. (b) (*increase*) *ego, muscles* aufbauen; *production, pressure* steigern, erhöhen; *forces* (*mass*) zusammenziehen; *health* kräftigen; *sb's confidence* stärken. **to ~ ~ sb's hopes** jdm Hoffnung(en) machen. (c) (*with houses*) *area, land* (ganz) bebauen. (d) (*publicize*) *person* aufbauen.

builder ['bɪldəʳ] *n* (*worker*) Bauarbeiter(in *f*) *m*; (*contractor*) Bauunternehmer *m*.

building ['bɪldɪŋ] *n* (a) Gebäude *nt*; (*usually big also*) Bau *m*. (b) (*act of constructing*) Bau *m*, Bauen *nt*.

building: **~ contractor** *n* Bauunternehmer *m*; **~ site** *n* Baustelle *f*; **~ society** *n* (*Brit*) Bausparkasse *f*; **~ trade** *n* Baugewerbe *nt*.

build-up ['bɪldʌp] *n* (a) (*publicity*) Werbung *f*. **they gave the play a good ~** sie haben das Stück ganz groß herausgebracht (*col*). (b) (*of pressure*) Steigerung *f*; (*Tech also*) Verdichtung *f*. **~ of troops** Truppenmassierungen *pl*.

built [bɪlt] *pret, ptp of* **build**.

built: **~in** *adj* (a) *cupboard etc* eingebaut, Einbau-; (b) (*instinctive*) instinktmäßig; **~up area** *n* bebautes Gebiet; (*Mot*) geschlossene Ortschaft.

bulb [bʌlb] *n* (a) Zwiebel *f*. (b) (*Elec*) (Glüh)birne *f*. (c) (*of thermometer etc*) Kolben *m*.

bulbous ['bʌlbəs] *adj* *nose* Knollen-; *growth etc* knotig, Knoten-.

Bulgaria [bʌl'geərɪə] *n* Bulgarien *f*.

Bulgarian [bʌl'geərɪən] 1 *adj* bulgarisch. 2 *n* (a) Bulgare *m*, Bulgarin *f*. (b) (*language*) Bulgarisch *nt*.

bulge [bʌldʒ] 1 *n* (*in surface*) Wölbung *f*; (*irregular*) Unebenheit *f*, Buckel *m* (*col*); (*in line*) Bogen *m*; (*in tyre*) Wulst *m*; (*in birth rate etc*) Zunahme *f* (*in gen*). 2 *vi* (a) (*also* **~ out**) (*swell*) (an)schwellen; (*metal, sides of box*) sich wölben; (*stick out*) vorstehen. (b) (*pocket, sack*) prall gefüllt sein; (*with mit*).

bulk [bʌlk] *n* (a) (*size*) Größe *f*; (*large shape*) (*of thing*) massige Form; (*of person, animal*) massige Gestalt. (b) (*also* **great ~**) größter Teil; (*of debt, loan also*) Hauptteil *m*; (*of work, mineral deposits also*) Großteil *m*; (*of people, votes also*) Gros *nt*; (*of property, legacy etc also*) Masse *f*. (c) (*Comm*) **in ~** im großen, en gros.

bulky ['bʌlkɪ] *adj* (+*er*) *object* sperrig; *book* dick; *sweater* unförmig; *person* massig, wuchtig.

bull [bul] *n* (a) Stier *m*; (*for breeding*) Bulle *m*. **to take the ~ by the horns** (*fig*) den Stier bei den Hörnern packen; **like a ~ in a china shop** (*col*) wie ein Elefant im Porzellanladen (*col*). (b) (*male of elephant, whale etc*) Bulle *m*.

bulldog ['buldɒg] *n* Bulldogge *f*.

bulldoze ['buldəuz] *vt* **to ~ sb into doing sth** jdn zwingen, etw zu tun; **she ~d her way through the crowd** sie boxte sich durch die Menge.

bulldozer ['buldəuzəʳ] *n* Planierraupe *f*, Bulldozer *m*.

bullet ['bʊlɪt] n Kugel f. ~hole Einschuß(loch nt) m.

bulletin ['bʊlɪtɪn] n Bulletin nt, amtliche Bekanntmachung. health ~ Krankenbericht m, Bulletin nt; ~ board (US) Schwarzes Brett.

bullet: ~proof adj kugelsicher; ~ wound n Schußwunde or -verletzung f.

bull: ~fight n Stierkampf m; ~fighter n Stierkämpfer m; ~finch n Dompfaff, Gimpel m; ~frog n Ochsenfrosch m.

bullion ['bʊljən] n no pl Gold-/Silberbarren pl.

bull-necked ['bʊlnekt] adj stiernackig.

bullock ['bʊlək] n Ochse m.

bull: ~ring n Stierkampfarena f; ~'s eye n (of target) Scheibenmittelpunkt m, Scheibenzentrum nt; (hit) Schuß m ins Schwarze or Zentrum; ~shit n (col!) Scheiß (col) m.

bully ['bʊlɪ] 1 n Tyrann m; (esp Sch) Rabauke m. you great big ~ du Rüpel. 2 vt tyrannisieren, schikanieren; (using violence) drangsalieren, traktieren. to ~ sb into doing sth jdn so unter Druck setzen, daß er etc etw tut.

♦ **bully about** or **around** vt sep herumkommandieren, tyrannisieren.

bulrush ['bʊlrʌʃ] n Rohrkolben m.

bulwark ['bʊlwək] n (lit, fig) Bollwerk nt.

bum[1] [bʌm] n (esp Brit col) Hintern m (col).

bum[2] (col) n (a) (good-for-nothing) Rumtreiber m (col); (young) Gammler m; (down-and-out) Penner m (col). (b) (despicable person) Saukerl m (col).

♦ **bum about** or **around** vi (col) rumgammeln (col).

bumble-bee ['bʌmblbiː] n Hummel f.

bumf [bʌmf] n (Brit col) Papierkram m (col).

bump [bʌmp] 1 n (a) (blow, noise, jolt) Bums m (col); (of sth falling also) Plumps m (col). to get a ~ on the head sich (dat) den Kopf anschlagen. (b) (on any surface) Unebenheit f; (on head, knee etc) Beule f; (on car) Delle f. 2 vt stoßen; car wing etc, one's own car eine Delle fahren in (+acc); another car auffahren auf (+acc). to ~ one's head sich (dat) den Kopf anstoßen or anschlagen (on, against an +dat). 3 vi (move jointingly) holpern. 4 adv to go ~ bumsen (col).

♦ **bump into** vi +prep obj (a) stoßen gegen; (driver, car) fahren gegen; another car fahren auf (+acc). (b) (col: meet) zufällig treffen.

♦ **bump off** vt sep (col) abmurksen (col).

bumper ['bʌmpə'] 1 n (of car) Stoßstange f. 2 adj ~ crop Rekordernte f.

bumpkin ['bʌmpkɪn] n (also country ~) (Bauern)tölpel m.

bumpy ['bʌmpɪ] adj (+er) surface holp(e)rig; flight unruhig.

bun [bʌn] n (a) (bread) süßes Brötchen; (iced ~ etc) süßes Teilchen. to have a ~ in the oven (col) ein Kind kriegen (col). (b) (hair) Knoten m.

bunch [bʌntʃ] n (a) (of flowers) Strauß m; (of radishes) Bund m; (of bananas) Büschel m. a ~ of grapes eine (ganze) Weintraube; ~ of keys Schlüsselbund m; to wear one's hair in ~es Rattenschwänze haben. (b) (col: of people) Haufen m (col).

♦ **bunch together** 1 vt sep ~ed ~ dicht zusammen. 2 vi (people) einen Haufen bilden.

♦ **bunch up** vi (a) Haufen bilden. (b) (material) sich bauschen.

bundle ['bʌndl] 1 n Bündel nt. he is a ~ of nerves er ist ein Nervenbündel; that child is a ~ of mischief das Kind hat nichts als Unfug im Kopf. 2 vt (a) bündeln. 2 vt (put, send hastily) things stopfen; people verfrachten, schaffen; (into vehicle) packen (col).

♦ **bundle off** vt sep he was ~d ~ to Australia er wurde nach Australien verfrachtet.

♦ **bundle up** vt sep (tie into bundles) bündeln.

bung [bʌŋ] 1 n (of cask) Spund(zapfen) m. 2 vt (Brit col: throw) schmeißen (col).

♦ **bung up** vt sep (col) pipe verstopfen. I'm all ~ed ~ meine Nase ist verstopft.

bungalow ['bʌŋgələʊ] n Bungalow m.

bungle ['bʌŋgl] vt verpfuschen.

bungler ['bʌŋglə'] n Stümper m.

bungling ['bʌŋglɪŋ] adj person ungeschickt, dusselig (col); attempt stümperhaft.

bunk[1] [bʌŋk] n: to do a ~ (col) türmen (col).

bunk[2] n (in ship) Koje f; (in train, dormitory) Bett nt.

bunk-beds [bʌŋk'bedz] npl Etagenbett nt.

bunker ['bʌŋkə'] n (Naut, Golf, Mil) Bunker m.

bunkum ['bʌŋkəm] n (col) Quatsch (col) m.

bunny ['bʌnɪ] n (also ~ rabbit) Hase m, Häschen nt.

bunting ['bʌntɪŋ] n (flags) bunte Fähnchen pl, Wimpel pl.

buoy [bɔɪ] n Boje f.

♦ **buoy up** vt sep (lit) über Wasser halten; (fig) person Auftrieb geben (+dat); hopes beleben.

buoyancy ['bɔɪənsɪ] n (a) (of ship, object) Schwimmfähigkeit f. (b) (fig: cheerfulness) Schwung, Elan m.

buoyant ['bɔɪənt] adj (a) ship, object schwimmend. (b) (fig) person, mood heiter; (energetic) step federnd. (c) market rege.

burden ['bɜːdn] 1 n (a) (lit) Last f. beast of ~ Lasttier nt. (b) (fig) Belastung f (on, to für). I don't want to be a ~ on you ich möchte Ihnen nicht zur Last fallen; the ~ of proof lies with him er muß den Beweis dafür erbringen; (Jur) er trägt die Beweislast. 2 vt belasten.

bureau [bjʊə'rəʊ] n (a) (Brit: desk) Sekretär m. (b) (US: chest of drawers) Kommode f. (c) (office) Büro nt. (d) (government department) Amt nt.

bureaucracy [bjʊə'rɒkrəsɪ] n Bürokratie f.

bureaucrat ['bjʊərəʊkræt] n Bürokrat m.

bureaucratic [,bjʊərəʊ'krætɪk] adj bürokratisch.

burger ['bɜːgə'] n (col) Hamburger m.

burglar ['bɜːglə'] n Einbrecher(in f) m. ~ alarm Alarmanlage f.

burglarize ['bɜːgləraɪz] vt (US) einbrechen in (+acc). he was ~d bei ihm wurde eingebrochen.

burglary ['bɜːglərɪ] n Einbruch m.

burgle ['bɜːgl] vt einbrechen in (+acc). he was ~d bei ihm wurde eingebrochen.

burial ['berɪəl] n Beerdigung f; (~ ceremony also) Begräbnis nt; (in cemetery also) Beisetzung f (form).

burlesque [bɜː'lesk] n (a) (parody) Parodie f; (Theat) Burleske f. (b) (US Theat) Varieté nt; (show) Varietévorstellung f.

burly ['bɜːlɪ] adj (+er) kräftig, stramm.

Burma ['bɜːmə] n Birma nt.

Burmese [bɜː'miːz] 1 adj birmanisch. 2 n Birmane m, Birmanin f; (language) Birmanisch nt.

burn (vb: pret, ptp ~ed or ~t) 1 n (on skin) Brandwunde f; (on material) verbrannte Stelle, Brandfleck m. severe ~s schwere Verbrennungen pl. 2 vt (a) verbrennen; village, building niederbrennen. to ~ oneself sich verbrennen; to be ~t to death (at stake) verbrannt werden; (in accident) verbrennen; to ~ a hole in sth ein Loch in etw (acc) brennen; to ~ one's boats or bridges (fig) alle Brücken hinter sich (dat) abbrechen; to ~ the midnight oil (fig) bis tief in die Nacht arbeiten. (b) meat, toast etc verbrennen lassen; (slightly) anbrennen lassen. (c) (acid) ätzen. (d) (use as fuel: ship etc) befeuert werden mit; (use up) petrol, electricity verbrauchen.

3 vi (a) brennen. (b) (meat, pastry etc) verbrennen; (slightly) anbrennen. she ~s easily sie bekommt leicht einen Sonnenbrand. to be ~ing to do sth darauf brennen, etw zu tun; he was ~ing with anger er kochte wor Wut. (d) (Space: rockets) zünden.

♦ **burn down** 1 vi (a) (house etc) ab- or niederbrennen. (b) (fire, candle, wick) herunterbrennen. 2 vt sep ab- or niederbrennen.

♦ **burn off** *vt sep paint etc* abbrennen.

♦ **burn out 1** *vi (fire, candle)* ausgehen; *(fuse)* durchbrennen; *(rocket)* den Treibstoff verbraucht haben. **2** *vr* **(a)** *(candle, lamp)* herunterbrennen; *(fire)* ab- *or* ausbrennen. **(b)** *(fig col)* to ~ **oneself** ~ sich völlig verausgaben. **3** *vt sep usu pass* ~t ~ **lorries/houses** ausgebrannte Lastwagen/Häuser.

♦ **burn up 1** *vi* **(a)** *(fire etc)* auflodern. **(b)** *(rocket etc)* verglühen. **2** *vt sep rubbish* verbrennen; *fuel, energy* verbrauchen; *excess fat also* abbauen.

burner ['bɜːnə^r] *n (of cooker, lamp)* Brenner *m*.

burning ['bɜːnɪŋ] **1** *adj (lit, fig)* brennend. **2** *n* **I can smell** ~ es riecht verbrannt.

burnish ['bɜːnɪʃ] *vt metal* polieren.

burnt [bɜːnt] *adj* verbrannt.

burp [bɜːp] *(col)* **1** *vi* rülpsen *(col); (baby)* aufstoßen. **2** *vt baby* aufstoßen lassen. **3** *n* Rülpser *m (col)*.

burrow ['bʌrəʊ] **1** *n (of rabbit etc)* Bau *m*. **2** *vti (rabbits, dogs etc)* graben, buddeln *(col); (person: in papers etc)* wühlen.

bursar ['bɜːsə^r] *n* Schatzmeister *m*.

bursary ['bɜːsərɪ] *n* **(a)** *(grant)* Stipendium *nt*. **(b)** *(office)* Schatzamt *nt*.

burst [bɜːst] *(vb: pret, ptp* ~*)* **1** *n* **(a)** *(of shell etc)* Explosion *f*. **(b)** *(in pipe etc)* Bruch *m*. **(c)** *(of anger, enthusiasm, activity etc)* Ausbruch, Anfall *m*. ~ **of laughter** Lachsalve *f*; ~ **of applause** Beifallsturm *m*; ~ **of speed** Spurt *m; (of cars etc)* Riesenbeschleunigung *f (col)*; **a** ~ **of automatic gunfire** eine Maschinengewehrsalve.

2 *vi* **(a)** platzen. **to** ~ **open** *(box, door etc)* aufspringen; *(abscess, wound)* aufplatzen. **(b)** *(be very full)* platzen. **to fill sth to** ~**ing point** etw bis zum Platzen füllen; **to be** ~**ing with pride** vor Stolz platzen; **he was** ~**ing to tell us** *(col)* er brannte darauf, uns das zu sagen; **I'm** ~**ing** *(col)* ich platze gleich *(col)*. **(c)** **to** ~ **into tears/ flames** in Tränen ausbrechen/in Flammen aufgehen; **he** ~ **into song** er fing plötzlich an zu singen; **the** ~ **into the room** er platzte ins Zimmer; **the sun** ~ **through the clouds** die Sonne brach durch die Wolken; **to** ~ **out laughing/ crying** in Gelächter/Tränen ausbrechen.

3 *vt balloon, bubble* zum Platzen bringen, platzen lassen; *boiler, pipe, dyke* sprengen; **the river has** ~ **its banks** der Fluß ist über die Ufer getreten; **to** ~ **one's sides with laughter** vor Lachen platzen.

bury ['berɪ] *vt* **(a)** *person, animal, differences* begraben; *(with ceremony also)* beerdigen; *(hide in earth)* treasure, bones vergraben; *(put in earth)* end of post, roots eingraben. **buried by an avalanche** von einer Lawine verschüttet *or* begraben; **to** ~ **one's head in the sand** *(fig)* den Kopf in den Sand stecken; **to** ~ **one's face in one's hands** das Gesicht in den Händen vergraben. **(b)** *(put, plunge)* hands, fingers vergraben *(in in +dat);* claws, teeth schlagen *(in in +acc);* dagger stoßen *(in in +acc)*. **(c)** **to** ~ **oneself in one's books** sich in seinen Büchern vergraben; **buried in thought** in Gedanken versunken.

bus [bʌs] *n, pl* **-es** *or (US)* **-ses** (Omni)bus *m*. **by** ~ mit dem Bus.

bus: ~ **conductor** *n* Busschaffner *m;* ~ **depot** *n* Busdepot *nt;* ~ **driver** *n* Busfahrer(in *f*) *m*.

bush [bʊʃ] *n* **(a)** *(shrub)* Busch, Strauch *m; (thicket: also* ~**es)** Gebüsch *nt.* **to beat about the** ~ *(fig)* wie die Katze um den heißen Brei herumschleichen. **(b)** *(in Africa, Australia)* Busch *m*.

bushy ['bʊʃɪ] *adj (+er)* buschig.

busily ['bɪzɪlɪ] *adv* eifrig.

business ['bɪznɪs] *n, pl* -es *n* **(a)** Geschäft *nt; (enterprise also)* Betrieb *m; (line of* ~*)* Branche *f*. **to be in the plastics/insurance** ~ in der Plastikbranche/im Versicherungsgewerbe sein; **to set up in** ~ ein Geschäft gründen; **to go out of** ~ zumachen; **to**

do ~ **with sb** Geschäfte *pl* mit jdm machen; ~ **is** ~ Geschäft ist Geschäft; **he is here/away on** ~ er ist geschäftlich hier/unterwegs; **to get down to** ~ zur Sache kommen; **now we're in** ~ *(fig col)* jetzt kann's losgehen *(col);* **to mean** ~ *(col)* es ernst meinen. **(b)** *(concern, col: affair)* Sache *f; (task, duty also)* Aufgabe *f.* **that's my** ~ das ist meine Sache *or* Angelegenheit; **that's none of my/your** ~ das geht mich/dich nichts an; **to make it one's** ~ **to do sth** es sich *(dat)* zur Aufgabe machen, etw zu tun; **you've no** ~ **doing that** du hast kein Recht, das zu tun.

business: ~ **address** *n* Geschäftsadresse *f;* ~ **card** *n* Visitenkarte *f;* ~ **expenses** *npl* Spesen *pl;* ~ **hours** *npl* Geschäftsstunden *pl*, Geschäftszeit *f.*

businesslike ['bɪznɪslaɪk] *adj (good at doing business)* geschäftüchtig; *person, manner* geschäftsmäßig; *prose* nüchtern.

business: ~**man** *n* Geschäftsmann *m;* ~ **sense** *n* Geschäftssinn *m;* ~ **studies** *npl* Wirtschaftslehre *f;* ~ **trip** *n* Geschäftsreise *f;* ~**woman** *n* Geschäftsfrau *f.*

busker ['bʌskə^r] *n* Straßenmusikant *m.*

bus: ~**man** *n:* **a** ~**man's holiday** *(fig)* Fortsetzung *f* der Arbeit im Urlaub; ~ **service** *n* Busverbindung *f; (network)* Busverbindungen *pl;* ~ **shelter** *n* Wartehäuschen *nt;* ~ **station** *n* Busbahnhof *m;* ~ **stop** *n* Bushaltestelle *f.*

bust¹ [bʌst] *n* Büste *f; (Anat also)* Busen *m.* ~ **measurement** Brustumfang *m*, Oberweite *f.*

bust² *(vb: pret, ptp* ~*) (col)* **1** *adj* **(a)** *(broken)* kaputt *(col)*. **(b)** *(bankrupt)* pleite *(col)*. **2** *adv (bankrupt)* **to go** ~ pleite gehen *or* machen *(col)*. **3** *vt* kaputtmachen *(col); drugs ring* auffliegen lassen *(col)*.

bustle ['bʌsl] **1** *n* Betrieb *m (of* in *+dat); (of fair, streets also)* reges Treiben *(of* auf *or* in *+dat)*. **2** *vi* **to** ~ **about** geschäftig hin und her eilen.

bustling ['bʌslɪŋ] *adj person* geschäftig; *place, scene* belebt, voller Leben.

busy ['bɪzɪ] **1** *adj (+er)* **(a)** *(occupied)* person beschäftigt. **a very** ~ **man** ein vielbeschäftigter Mann; **are you** ~? haben Sie gerade Zeit?; **I was** ~ **studying when you called** ich war gerade beim Lernen, als Sie kamen; **let's get** ~ an die Arbeit! **(b)** *(active)* life, time bewegt; *place, street, town* belebt; *street (with traffic)* stark befahren. **it's been a** ~ **day/week** heute/diese Woche war viel los. **(c)** *telephone line* besetzt. **2** *vr* **to** ~ **oneself doing sth** sich damit beschäftigen, etw zu tun; **to** ~ **oneself with sth** sich mit etw beschäftigen.

busybody ['bɪzɪ'bɒdɪ] *n* **don't be such a** ~ misch dich nicht überall ein.

but [bʌt] **1** *conj* **(a)** aber. **(b)** **not X** ~ **Y** nicht X sondern Y. **(c)** **never a week passes** ~ **she is ill** keine Woche vergeht, ohne daß sie krank ist.

2 *adv* **she's** ~ **a child** sie ist doch noch ein Kind; **I cannot (help)** ~ **think that** ... ich kann nicht umhin, zu denken, daß ...; **you can** ~ **try** du kannst es immerhin versuchen; **she left** ~ **a few minutes ago** sie ist erst vor ein paar Minuten gegangen.

3 *prep* **no one** ~ **me could do it** niemand außer mir konnte es tun; **anything** ~ **that!** (alles,) nur das nicht!; **he/it was nothing** ~ **trouble** er/das hat nichts als *or* hat nur Schwierigkeiten gemacht; **the last house** ~ **one/two/three** das vorletzte/vorvorletzte/drittletzte Haus; **the next street** ~ **one** die übernächste Straße; ~ **for you I would be dead** ohne Sie wäre ich tot, wenn Sie nicht gewesen wären, wäre ich tot.

4 *n* **no** ~**s about it** kein Aber *nt.*

butane ['bjuːteɪn] *n* Butan *nt.*

butch [bʊtʃ] *adj (col)* maskulin.

butcher ['bʊtʃə^r] **1** *n* **(a)** Fleischer, Metzger *m.* ~**'s (shop)** *(Brit)* Fleischerei, Metzgerei *f;* **at the**

~'s (*Brit*) beim Fleischer *or* Metzger. **(b)** (*fig:* *murderer*) Schlächter *m*. **2** *vt animals* schlachten; *people* abschlachten.

butchery ['bʊtʃərɪ] *n* (*slaughter*) Gemetzel *nt*.

butler ['bʌtləʳ] *n* Butler *m*.

butt¹ [bʌt] *n* (*for wine*) großes Faß; (*for rainwater*) Tonne *f*.

butt² *n* (*also* ~ **end**) dickes Ende; (*of rifle*) (Gewehr)kolben *m*; (*of cigarette*) Stummel *m*.

butt³ *n* (*US col: cigarette*) Kippe *f* (*col*).

butt⁴ *n* **(a)** (*target*) Schießscheibe *f*. **(b)** *usu pl* (*on shooting range*) Schießstand *m*. **(c)** (*fig: person*) **she's always the** ~ **of his jokes** sie ist immer (die) Zielscheibe seines Spottes.

butt⁵ **1** *n* (Kopf)stoß *m*. **2** *vt* mit dem Kopf stoßen; (*goat also*) mit den Hörnern stoßen.

♦ **butt in** *vi* sich einmischen (*on* in +*acc*).

butter ['bʌtəʳ] **1** *n* Butter *f*. **she looks as if** ~ **wouldn't melt in her mouth** sie sieht aus, als ob sie kein Wässerchen trüben könnte. **2** *vt bread etc* mit Butter bestreichen, buttern.

butter: ~ **bean** *n* Mondbohne *f*; ~**cup** *n* Butterblume *f*, Hahnenfuß *m*; ~**dish** *n* Butterdose *f*; ~**fingers** *n sing* (*col*) Schussel *m* (*col*).

butterfly ['bʌtəflaɪ] *n* Schmetterling *m*. **I've got/ I get butterflies (in my stomach)** mir ist/wird ganz flau im Magen (*col*).

butterfly stroke *n* Schmetterlingsstil *m*.

buttock ['bʌtək] *n* (Hinter)backe, Gesäßhälfte (*form*) *f*. ~**s** *pl* Gesäß *nt*, Hintern *m* (*col*).

button ['bʌtn] **1** *n* Knopf *m*. **2** *vt garment* zuknöpfen. **3** *vi* (*garment*) geknöpft werden.

♦ **button up** *vt sep* zuknöpfen.

button: ~**hole 1** *n* **(a)** (*in garment*) Knopfloch *nt*; **(b)** (*flower*) Blume *f* im Knopfloch; **2** *vt* (*fig*) zu fassen bekommen, sich (*dat*) schnappen (*col*); ~**mushroom** *n* junger Champignon.

buttress ['bʌtrɪs] *n* (*Archit*) Strebepfeiler *m*; (*fig*) Pfeiler *m*.

buxom ['bʌksəm] *adj* drall.

buy [baɪ] (*vb: pret, ptp* **bought**) **1** *vt* **(a)** kaufen; (*Rail*) *ticket also* lösen. **(b)** (*fig*) *victory, fame* sich (*dat*) erkaufen; *time* gewinnen. **the victory was dearly bought** der Sieg war teuer erkauft. **(c)** **to** ~ **sth** (*col*) (*accept*) etw akzeptieren; (*believe*) jdm etw abnehmen (*col*) *or* abkaufen (*col*); **I'll** ~ **that** das ist o.k. (*col*); (*believe*) ja, das glaube ich. **2** *vi* kaufen. **3** *n* (*col*) Kauf *m*. **to be a good** ~ ein guter Kauf sein; (*clothes also, food*) preiswert sein.

♦ **buy back** *vt sep* zurückkaufen.

♦ **buy in** *vt sep* (*acquire supply of*) *goods* einkaufen.

♦ **buy off** *vt sep* (*col: bribe*) kaufen (*col*).

♦ **buy out** *vt sep shareholders etc* auszahlen; *firm* aufkaufen.

♦ **buy up** *vt sep* aufkaufen.

buyer ['baɪəʳ] *n* Käufer *m*; (*agent*) Einkäufer *m*. ~'s **market** Käufermarkt *m*.

buzz [bʌz] **1** *vi* summen. **my head is** ~**ing** mir schwirrt der Kopf; (*from noise*) mir dröhnt der Kopf; **the town is** ~**ing** in der Stadt ist viel los. **2** *vt* **(a)** (*call*) *secretary* (mit dem Summer) rufen. **(b)** (*col: telephone*) anrufen. **(c)** (*plane*) *plane, building* dicht vorbeifliegen an (+*dat*). **3** *n* **(a)** Summen *nt*. **(b)** (*of conversation*) Stimmengewirr *nt*. **(c)** (*col*) **to give sb a** ~ jdn anrufen; *secretary etc* jdn (mit dem Summer) rufen.

♦ **buzz off** *vi* (*Brit col*) abzischen (*col*).

buzzard ['bʌzəd] *n* Bussard *m*.

buzzer ['bʌzəʳ] *n* Summer *m*.

buzz word *n* Modewort *nt*.

by [baɪ] **1** *prep* **(a)** (*close to*) bei, an (+*dat*); (*with movement*) an (+*acc*); (*next to*) neben (+*dat*); (*with movement*) neben (+*acc*). **a holiday** ~ **the sea** Ferien *pl* an der See; **come and sit** ~ **me** komm,

setz dich neben mich. **(b)** (*via*) über (+*acc*). **(c)** (*past*) **to go/rush** *etc* ~ **sb/sth** an jdm/etw vorbeigehen/-eilen *etc*. **(d)** (*time: during*) ~ **day/night** bei Tag/Nacht. **(e)** (*time: not later than*) bis. **can you do it** ~ **tomorrow?** kannst du es bis morgen machen?; ~ **tomorrow I'll be in France** morgen werde ich in Frankreich sein; ~ **the time I got there** ... bis ich dorthin kam ...; ~ **that time** *or* ~ **then it will be too late** bis dahin *or* dann ist es schon zu spät; ~ **now** inzwischen. **(f)** (*indicating amount*) ~ **the metre/kilo/hour** meter-/kilo-/stundenweise; **one** ~ **one** einer nach dem anderen. **(g)** (*indicating agent, cause*) von, durch. **killed** ~ **a bullet** durch eine *or* von einer Kugel getötet; **a painting** ~ **Picasso** ein Bild von Picasso; **surrounded** ~ umgeben von. **(h)** (*indicating method, means, manner*) ~ **bus/ car** mit dem *or* per Bus/Auto; ~ **land and** (~) **sea** zu Land und zu Wasser; **to pay** ~ **cheque** mit Scheck bezahlen; **made** ~ **hand/machine** handgearbeitet/maschinell hergestellt; ~ **daylight/moonlight** bei Tag(eslicht)/im Mondschein; **to know sb** ~ **sight** jdn vom Sehen her kennen; **to be known** ~ **the name of** ... unter dem Namen ... bekannt sein; **to lead** ~ **the hand** an der Hand führen; **to grab sb** ~ **the collar** jdn am Kragen packen; **he had a daughter** ~ **his first wife** von seiner ersten Frau hatte er eine Tochter; ~ **myself/himself** *etc* allein; ~ **saving hard he managed to** ... durch eisernes Sparen gelang es ihm, zu ...; ~ **saying that I didn't mean** ... ich habe damit nicht gemeint ... **(i)** (*according to*) nach. **to judge** ~ **appearances** allem Anschein nach; **it's all right** ~ **me** von mir aus gern. **(j)** (*measuring distance*) um. **broader** ~ **a meter** um einen Meter breiter; **it missed me** ~ **inches** es verfehlte mich um Zentimeter. **(k)** (*Math, Measure*) **to divide/multiply** ~ dividieren durch/multiplizieren mit; **a room 20 metres** ~ **30** ein Zimmer 20 auf *or* mal 30 Meter. **(l)** (*points of compass*) **South** ~ **South West** Südsüdwest. **(m)** (*in oaths*) bei. **I swear** ~ **Almighty God** ich schwöre beim allmächtigen Gott. **(n)** ~ **the way** *or* **by(e)** übrigens. **2** *adv* **(a)** (*past*) **to pass/wander/rush** *etc* ~ vorbei- *or* vorüberkommen/-wandern/-eilen *etc*. **(b)** (*in reserve*) **to put** *or* **lay** ~ beiseite legen. **(c)** (*phrases*) ~ **and** ~ irgendwann; (*with past tense*) nach einiger Zeit; ~ **and large** im großen und ganzen.

bye [baɪ] *interj* (*col*) tschüs. ~ **for now!** bis bald!

bye-bye ['baɪ'baɪ] **1** *interj* (*col*) Wiedersehen (*col*). **2** *n* **to go** ~**s** (*baby-talk*) in die Heia gehen (*baby-talk*).

by(e)-election [baɪɪ'lekʃən] *n* Nachwahl *f*.

bygone ['baɪgɒn] **1** *adj* längst vergangen. **2** *n* **to let** ~**s be** ~**s** die Vergangenheit ruhen lassen.

by: ~**law** *n* (*also* **bye-law**) Verordnung *f*; ~**pass 1** *n* (*road*) Umgehungsstraße *f*; (*Tech: pipe etc*) Bypass *m*; **2** *vt town, village* umgehen; (*Tech*) *fluid, gas* umleiten; (*fig*) *person* übergehen; *intermediate stage also* überspringen; *difficulties* umgehen; ~**pass operation** *n* Bypass-Operation *f*; ~**product** *n* (*lit, fig*) Nebenprodukt *nt*; ~**stander** *n* Zuschauer *m*.

byte [baɪt] *n* (*Comp*) Byte *nt*.

by: ~**way** *n* Seitenweg *m*; ~**word** *n* **to be/become a** ~**word for sth** gleichbedeutend mit etw sein/ werden.

Byzantium [baɪ'zæntɪəm] *n* Byzanz *nt*.

C

C, c [siː] C, c *nt.* **C sharp/flat** Cis, cis *nt*/Ces, ces *nt.*
c = (a) **cent** c, ct. (b) **circa** ca.
CA = **chartered accountant.**
cab [kæb] *n* (a) *(taxi)* Taxi *nt.* (b) *(of lorry etc)* Führerhaus *nt.*
cabaret ['kæbəreɪ] *n* Varieté *nt*; *(satire)* Kabarett *nt.*
cabbage ['kæbɪdʒ] *n* (a) Kohl *m.* (b) *(col: person)* **to become a** ~ *(sick person)* dahinvegetieren.
cabby ['kæbɪ] *n (col: of taxi)* Taxifahrer *m.*
cabin ['kæbɪn] *n* (a) *(hut)* Hütte *f.* (b) *(Naut)* Kabine *f.* (c) *(of lorries, buses etc)* Führerhaus *nt.* (d) *(Aviat)* Passagierraum *m.*
cabin-: ~**boy** *n* Schiffsjunge *m*; *(steward)* Kabinensteward *m*; ~ **crew** *n (Aviat)* Flugpersonal *nt*; ~ **cruiser** *n* Kajütboot *nt.*
cabinet ['kæbɪnɪt] *n* (a) Schränkchen *nt*; *(for display)* Vitrine *f*; *(for TV, record-player)* Schrank *m*; *(loudspeaker ~)* Box *f.* (b) *(Pol)* Kabinett *nt.*
cabinet: ~**maker** *n* (Möbel)schreiner *m*; ~ **meeting** *n* Kabinettssitzung *f*; ~ **minister** *n* Mitglied *nt* des Kabinetts.
cable ['keɪbl] **1** *n* (a) Tau *nt*; *(of wire)* Drahtseil *nt.* (b) *(Elec)* Kabel *nt.* (c) *(~gram)* Telegramm *nt.* **2** *vt information* telegrafisch durchgeben. **to** ~ **sb** jdm telegrafieren. **3** *vi* telegrafieren, ein Telegramm schicken.
cable: ~**car** *n (hanging)* Drahtseilbahn *f*; *(streetcar)* Straßenbahn *f*; ~ **laying** *n* Kabelverlegung *f*; ~ **television** *n* Kabelfernsehen *nt.*
caboodle [kə'buːdl] *n*: **the whole** ~ *(col)* der ganze Kram *(col).*
cache [kæʃ] **1** *n* geheimes (Waffen-/Proviant)lager *nt.* **2** *vt* verstecken.
cack-handed ['kæk'hændəd] *adj (Brit col)* tolpatschig *(col).*
cackle ['kækl] **1** *n (of hens)* Gackern *nt*; *(laughter)* meckerndes Gelächter. **2** *vi (hens)* gackern; *(laugh)* meckernd lachen.
cacophony [kæ'kɒfənɪ] *n* Mißklang *m.*
cactus ['kæktəs] *n* Kaktus *m.*
cad [kæd] *n (dated)* Schurke *m (dated).*
cadaver [kə'deɪvər] *n* Kadaver *m*; *(of humans)* Leiche *f.*
cadaverous [kə'dævərəs] *adj (corpse-like)* Kadaver-, Leichen-; *(gaunt)* ausgemergelt; *(pale)* leichenblaß.
caddie ['kædɪ] *n (Golf~)* Caddie, Golfjunge *m.*
caddy ['kædɪ] *n (tea ~)* Behälter *m*, Dose *f.*
cadence ['keɪdəns] *n (Mus)* Kadenz *f*; *(of voice)* Tonfall *m*, Melodie *f*; *(rhythm)* Rhythmus *m*, Melodie *f.*
cadenza [kə'denzə] *n (Mus)* Kadenz *f.*
cadet [kə'det] *n (Mil etc)* Kadett *m.*
cadge [kædʒ] **1** *vt (or re)*betteln, schnorren *(col) (from sb bei or von jdm).* **could I** ~ **a lift?** könnten Sie mich vielleicht mitnehmen? **2** *vi* schnorren *(col).*
cadger ['kædʒər] *n* Schnorrer *(col) m.*
Caesar ['siːzər] *n* Cäsar *m*; *(emperor)* Kaiser *m.*
Caesarean, Caesarian [siː'zeərɪən] *n, adj* **(section)** *(Med)* Kaiserschnitt *m.*
café ['kæfeɪ] *n* Café *nt.*
cafeteria [,kæfɪ'tɪərɪə] *n* Cafeteria *f.*
caffein(e) ['kæfiːn] *n* Koffein *nt.*
caftan ['kæftæn] *n* Kaftan *m.*

cage [keɪdʒ] **1** *n* (a) Käfig *m*; *(small bird~)* Bauer *nt or m.* (b) *(of lift)* Aufzug *m*; *(Min)* Förderkorb *m.* **2** *vt (also* ~ **up)** in einen Käfig sperren.
cagey ['keɪdʒɪ] *adj (col)* vorsichtig; *(evasive)* ausweichend. **what are you being so** ~ **about?** warum tust du so geheimnisvoll?
cagily ['keɪdʒɪlɪ] *adv see* **cagey.**
caginess ['keɪdʒɪnɪs] *n (col)* Vorsicht *f*; *(evasiveness)* ausweichende Art.
cagoule [kə'guːl] *n* Windhemd *nt.*
cahoots [kə'huːts] *n (col):* **to be in** ~ **with sb** mit jdm unter einer Decke stecken.
Cairo ['kaɪərəʊ] *n* Kairo *nt.*
cajole [kə'dʒəʊl] *vt* gut zureden (+*dat*), beschwatzen *(col).* **to** ~ **sb into doing sth** jdn dazu bringen, etw zu tun.
cake [keɪk] **1** *n* (a) Kuchen *m*; *(gateau)* Torte *f.* **a piece of** ~ *(fig col)* ein Kinderspiel *nt*, ein Klacks *m (col);* **to sell like hot** ~**s** weggehen wie warme Semmeln *(col);* **you can't have your** ~ **and eat it** *(prov)* man kann nicht beides (gleichzeitig) haben. (b) *(of soap)* Stück *nt*; *(of chocolate)* Tafel *f.* **2** *vt* überkrusten. **my shoes are** ~**d with mud** meine Schuhe sind dreckverkrustet. **3** *vi* eine Kruste bilden.
cake: ~ **shop** *n* Konditorei *f*; ~ **tin** *n (for baking)* Kuchenform *f*; *(for storage)* Kuchendose *f.*
calamine ['kæləmaɪn] *n* Galmei *m.* ~ **lotion** Galmeilotion *f.*
calamity [kə'læmɪtɪ] *n* Katastrophe *f.*
calcify ['kælsɪfaɪ] **1** *vt* Kalk *m* ablagern auf/in (+*dat*). **2** *vi* verkalken.
calcium ['kælsɪəm] *n* Kalzium *nt.*
calculate ['kælkjʊleɪt] **1** *vt* (a) *costs* berechnen. (b) *(fig: estimate)* kalkulieren, schätzen. (c) **to be** ~**d to do sth** *(be intended)* auf etw *(acc)* abzielen. (d) *(US col: suppose)* schätzen. **2** *vi (Math)* rechnen.
♦ **calculate on** *vi +prep obj* rechnen mit. **I had** ~**d** ~ **finishing by this week** ich hatte damit gerechnet, noch in dieser Woche fertig zu werden.
calculated ['kælkjʊleɪtɪd] *adj (deliberate)* berechnet. **to take a** ~ **risk** ein kalkuliertes Risiko eingehen.
calculating ['kælkjʊleɪtɪŋ] *adj* berechnend.
calculation [,kælkjʊ'leɪʃən] *n* Berechnung *f*; *(critical estimation)* Schätzung *f.* **to do a quick** ~ die Sache schnell überschlagen.
calculator ['kælkjʊleɪtər] *n* Rechner *m.*
calculus ['kælkjʊləs] *n (Math)* Differential- und Integralrechnung *f.*
calendar ['kæləndər] *n* (a) Kalender *m.* ~ **month** Kalendermonat *m.* (b) *(schedule)* Terminkalender *m.* **Church** ~ Kirchenkalender *m.*
calf[1] [kɑːf] *n, pl* **calves** (a) Kalb *nt.* **a cow in or with** ~ eine trächtige Kuh. (b) *(young elephant, seal etc)* Elefanten-/Robbenjunge(s) *etc nt.* (c) *(leather)* Kalb(s)leder *nt.*
calf[2] *n, pl* **calves** *(Anat)* Wade *f.*
caliber *n (US)* = **calibre.**
calibrate ['kælɪbreɪt] *vt gun* kalibrieren; *meter, instrument* eichen.
calibration [,kælɪ'breɪʃən] *n see vt* Kalibrieren *nt*; Eichen *nt*; *(mark)* Kalibrierung *f*; Eichung *f.*
calibre, (US) caliber ['kælɪbər] *n (lit)* Kaliber *nt*; *(fig also)* Format *nt.* **a man of his** ~ ein Mann

seines Kalibers.
calico ['kælɪkəʊ] n Kattun m.
California [kælɪ'fɔːnɪə] n Kalifornien nt.
calipers ['kælɪpəz] npl (US) = **callipers**.
call [kɔːl] 1 n (a) (shout, cry) (of person, bird etc) Ruf
m; (of bugle) Signal nt. **to give sb a ~** jdn
(herbei)rufen; (wake sb) jdn wecken; **within ~** in
Rufweite f; **a ~ for help** (lit, fig) ein Hilferuf m.
   (b) (telephone ~) Anruf m. **I'll give you a ~**
ich rufe Sie an; **to take a ~** ein Gespräch
entgegennehmen.
   (c) (fig: summons) Aufruf m; (of religion) Berufung f; (fig: lure) Verlockung f. **to be on ~**
(Bereitschafts)dienst haben; **the ~ of duty** der
Ruf der Pflicht.
   (d) (visit) Besuch m. **to make** or **pay a ~ on sb**
jdn besuchen; **port of ~** Anlaufhafen m; (fig)
Station f; **to pay a ~** (euph) mal verschwinden
(col).
   (e) (demand, claim) Beanspruchung f; (Comm)
Nachfrage f (for nach). **to have many ~s on one's**
purse/time finanziell/zeitlich sehr in Anspruch
genommen sein.
   (f) at or **on ~** (Fin) auf Abruf.
   (g) (need, occasion) Grund m, Veranlassung f.
there is no ~ for you to worry es besteht kein
Grund zur Sorge; **there was no ~ for that!** das
war wirklich nicht nötig!
   (h) (Cards) Ansage f.
   2 vt **(a)** (shout out) rufen. **(b)** (name, consider)
nennen. **to be ~ed** heißen; **what's he ~ed?** wie
heißt er?; **what's this ~ed in German?** wie heißt
das auf deutsch?; **~ it £5** sagen wir £ 5; **would**
you ~ German a difficult language? würden Sie
Deutsch als schwierige Sprache bezeichnen? **(c)**
(summon) person, doctor rufen; meeting einberufen; strike ausrufen; (Jur) witness aufrufen;
(subpoena) vorladen; (waken) wecken. **(d)** (telephone) anrufen. **(e)** (Fin) bond aufrufen; loan
abrufen.
   3 vi **(a)** (shout: person, animal) rufen. **to ~ for**
help um Hilfe rufen; **to ~ to sb** jdm zurufen. **(b)**
(visit) vorbeigehen/-kommen. **(c)** (Telec)
anrufen. **who's ~ing, please?** wer spricht bitte?;
London ~ing! (Rad) hier ist London; **thanks for**
~ing vielen Dank für den Anruf.
♦ **call aside** vt sep person beiseite rufen.
♦ **call at** vt +prep obj (person) vorbeigehen bei;
(Rail) halten in (+dat); (Naut) anlaufen.
♦ **call away** vt sep weg- or abrufen. **I was ~ed ~**
on business ich wurde geschäftlich abgerufen.
♦ **call back** vti sep zurückrufen. **2** vi (come back)
I'll ~ ~ later ich komme später noch einmal
wieder.
♦ **call by** vi vorbeikommen.
♦ **call for** vi +prep obj **(a)** (send for) person rufen;
food, drink kommen lassen; (ask for) verlangen
(nach). **(b)** (need: courage, endurance) erfordern.
that ~s ~ a drink/celebration! darauf müssen
wir einen trinken!/das muß gefeiert werden! **(c)**
(collect) person, goods abholen. **"to be ~ed ~"**
(goods sent by rail) „bahnlagernd"; (by post)
„postlagernd"; (in shop) „wird abgeholt".
♦ **call in** vt sep **(a)** doctor zu Rate ziehen. **(b)**
(withdraw) aus dem Verkehr ziehen. **2** vi vor-
beischauen (at, on bei).
♦ **call off** vt sep **(a)** (cancel) absagen; deal
rückgängig machen; engagement lösen. **(b)** dog
zurückrufen.
♦ **call on** vi +prep obj **(a)** (visit) besuchen. **(b)** =
call upon.
♦ **call out 1** vi rufen. **2** vt sep **(a)** names aufrufen;
(announce) ansagen. **(b)** doctor rufen; troops, fire
brigade alarmieren. **(c)** (order to strike) zum
Streik aufrufen.
♦ **call out for** vi +prep obj food, drink verlangen;
help rufen um.
♦ **call round** vi (col) vorbeikommen.

♦ **call up 1** vt sep **(a)** (Mil) reservist einberufen;
reinforcements mobilisieren. **(b)** (Telec) anrufen.
(c) (fig) (herauf)beschwören; memories wachrufen. **2** vi (Telec) anrufen.
♦ **call upon** vi +prep obj **(a)** (ask) **to ~ ~ ~ sb to do**
sth jdn bitten, etw zu tun. **(b)** (invoke) **to ~ ~ ~ sb's**
generosity an jds Großzügigkeit (acc) appellieren; **to ~ ~ God** Gott anrufen.
callbox ['kɔːl‚bɒks] n (Brit) Telefonzelle f.
caller ['kɔːlə'] n **(a)** (visitor) Besuch(er) m. **(b)**
(Telec) Anrufer m.
callgirl ['kɔːlgɜːl] n Callgirl nt.
calligraphy [kə'lɪgrəfɪ] n Kalligraphie, Schön-
schreibkunst f.
callipers ['kælɪpəz] npl **(a)** (Tast-
zirkel m. **(b)** (Med) Beinschienen pl.
callous ['kæləs] adj (cruel) gefühllos.
callousness ['kæləsnɪs] n Gefühllosigkeit f.
callow ['kæləʊ] adj unreif.
calm [kɑːm] **1** adj (+er) ruhig; weather windstill.
keep ~! bleib ruhig! **2** n Ruhe f; (at sea) Flaute f;
(of wind) Windstille f. **the ~ before the storm** (lit,
fig) die Ruhe vor dem Sturm. **3** vt beruhigen.
♦ **calm down 1** vt sep beruhigen. **2** vi sich beruhigen; (wind) abflauen.
calmly ['kɑːmlɪ] adv speak, act ruhig, gelassen.
calorie ['kælərɪ] n Kalorie f.
calorific [‚kælə'rɪfɪk] adj wärmeerzeugend. **~**
value Heizwert m.
calumny ['kæləmnɪ] n Verunglimpfung f.
calve [kɑːv] vi kalben.
calves [kɑːvz] pl of **calf**[1], **calf**[2].
cam [kæm] n Nocken m.
camber ['kæmbə'] n Wölbung f.
Cambodia [kæm'bəʊdɪə] n Kambodscha nt.
came [keɪm] pret of **come.**
camel ['kæməl] n Kamel nt.
camel in cpds (colour) kamelhaarfarben.
camellia [kə'miːlɪə] n Kamelie f.
cameo ['kæmɪəʊ] n **(a)** (jewellery) Kamee f. **(b)** ~
part Mini(atur)rolle f.
camera[1] ['kæmərə] n Kamera f; (for stills also)
Fotoapparat m.
camera[2] n (Jur): **in ~** unter Ausschluß der
Öffentlichkeit; (fig) hinter verschlossenen
Türen.
cameraman ['kæmərə'mæn] n, pl **-men** [-mən]
Kameramann m.
camomile ['kæməʊmaɪl] m Kamille f. **~ tea** Kamillentee f.
camouflage ['kæməflɑːʒ] **1** n (Mil, fig) Tarnung f. **2**
vt (Mil, fig) tarnen.
camp[1] [kæmp] **1** n (lit, fig) Lager nt. **to pitch ~** ein
Lager aufschlagen; **to strike** or **break ~** das
Lager abbrechen. **2** vi zelten, campen; (Mil)
lagern. **to go ~ing** zelten (gehen).
♦ **camp out** vi zelten.
camp[2] adj (theatrical, stagey) übertrieben; person's
appearance aufgedonnert; (homosexual) schwul
(col).
campaign [kæm'peɪn] **1** n **(a)** (Mil) Feldzug m. **(b)**
(fig) Kampagne f. **2** vi **(a)** (Mil) einen Feldzug
unternehmen. **(b)** (fig) (for für, against gegen)
sich einsetzen; (politician, candidate) den
Wahlkampf führen.
campaigner [kæm'peɪnə'] n **(a)** (Mil) Krieger m.
old ~ Kriegsveteran m; (fig) alter Hase (col). **(b)**
(fig) Befürworter(in f) m (for gen); Gegner(in f)
m (against gen); (Pol) Wahlwerber(in f) m.
camp bed n (Brit) Campingliege f.
camper ['kæmpə'] n Camper(in f) m (col); (vehicle)
Campingwagen m.
camp: **~fire** n Lagerfeuer nt; **~ follower** n
Marketender(in f) m; **~ followers** (fig) Gefolge nt no pl.
camphor ['kæmfə'] n Kampfer m.
camping ['kæmpɪŋ] n Zelten, Camping nt.
camping in cpds Camping-; **~ site** n (also **camp**

site) Campingplatz *m*.

campus ['kæmpəs] *n* Campus *m*, Universitätsgelände *nt*.

camshaft ['kæmʃɑːft] *n* Nockenwelle *f*.

can[1] [kæn] *pret* **could** *modal aux* können; *(may also)* dürfen. ~ **you speak German?** können *or* sprechen Sie Deutsch?; ~ **I come too?** kann ich mitkommen?; ~ **you hear me?** hören Sie mich?; **how** ~/**could you say such a thing!** wie können/ konnten Sie nur so etwas sagen!; **he could be on the next train** er könnte im nächsten Zug sein; **you could have told me** das hättest du mir sagen können; **she was as happy as could be** sie war über alle Maßen glücklich; **he** ~'**t couldn't have done that** er kann das unmöglich getan haben; **as soon as it** ~ **be arranged** sobald es sich machen läßt.

can[2] **1** *n* **(a)** *(container)* Kanister *m*; *(milk*~*)* Kanne *f*; *(esp US: garbage* ~*)* (Müll)eimer *m*. **to carry the** ~ *(fig col)* die Sache ausbaden *(col)*. **(b)** *(tin)* Dose *f*; *(of food also)* Büchse *f*. **a** ~ **of beer** eine Dose Bier. **2** *vt foodstuffs* in Dosen füllen.

Canada ['kænədə] *n* Kanada *nt*.

Canadian [kə'neɪdɪən] **1** *adj* kanadisch. **2** *n* Kanadier(in *f*) *m*.

canal [kə'næl] *n* **(a)** Kanal *m*. **(b)** *(Anat)* Gang *m*.

Canaries [kə'nɛərɪz] *npl* Kanarische Inseln *pl*.

canary [kə'nɛərɪ] *n* Kanarienvogel *m*.

canary *in cpds (colour: also* ~ **yellow)** kanariengelb.

cancel ['kænsəl] *vt* **(a)** *(call off)* absagen; *(Comm)* stornieren; *plans* aufgeben; *train, bus* streichen; *invitation, deal* rückgängig machen; *subscription* kündigen. **the last train has been** ~**led der** letzte Zug fällt aus. **(b)** *cheque* entwerten; *(cross out) name etc* (durch)streichen. **(c)** *(Math)* kürzen.

♦**cancel out 1** *vt* **each other** aufheben; *(fig)* zunichte machen. **to** ~ **each other** ~ *(Math)* sich aufheben; *(fig)* sich die Waage halten. **2** *vi (Math)* sich aufheben.

cancellation [ˌkænsə'leɪʃən] *n see vt* **(a)** Absage *f*; Stornierung *f*; Aufgabe *f*; Streichung *f*; Kündigung *f*. **(b)** Entwertung *f*. **(c)** *(Math)* Kürzung *f*.

cancer ['kænsə'] *n (Med)* Krebs *m*; *(fig)* Krebsgeschwür *nt*. **C**~ *(Astrol)* Krebs *m*; ~ **research** Krebsforschung *f*.

cancerous ['kænsərəs] *adj* krebsartig.

candelabra [ˌkændɪ'lɑːbrə] *n* Leuchter *m*.

candid ['kændɪd] *adj* offen, ehrlich.

candidacy ['kændɪdəsɪ] *n* Kandidatur *f*.

candidate ['kændɪdeɪt] *n (Pol)* Kandidat(in *f*) *m*.

candle ['kændl] *n* Kerze *f*. **he's burning the** ~ **at both ends** er arbeitet Tag und Nacht; **he can't hold a** ~ **to his brother** *(col)* er kann seinem Bruder nicht das Wasser reichen.

candle *in cpds* Kerzen-; ~**light** *n* Kerzenlicht *nt*; ~**stick** *n* Kerzenhalter *m*.

candour, *(US)* **candor** ['kændə'] *n* Offenheit, Ehrlichkeit *f*.

candy ['kændɪ] **1** *n (US) (sweet)* Bonbon *m or nt*; *(sweets)* Süßigkeiten *pl*; *(bar of chocolate)* (Tafel) Schokolade *f*; *(individual chocolate)* Praline *f*. **2** *vt sugar* kristallisieren lassen; *fruit etc* kandieren.

candy: ~**floss** *n (Brit)* Zuckerwatte *f*; ~ **store** *n (US)* Süßwarenhandlung *f*.

cane [keɪn] **1** *n* **(a)** *(stem of bamboo, sugar etc)* Rohr *nt*; *(of raspberry)* Zweig *m*; *(for supporting plants)* Stock *m*. **a chair made of** ~ ein Rohrstuhl *m*. **(b)** *(walking stick)* (Spazier)stock *m*; *(instrument of punishment)* (Rohr)stock *m*. **to get the** ~ Stockschläge bekommen. **2** *vt* mit dem Stock schlagen.

canine ['keɪnaɪn] **1** *n* **(a)** *(animal)* Hund *m*. **(b)** *(also* ~ **tooth)** Eckzahn *m*. **2** *adj* Hunde-.

canister ['kænɪstə'] *n* Behälter *m*.

cannabis ['kænəbɪs] *n* Cannabis *m*.

canned [kænd] **(a)** *food* Dosen-, in Dosen. ~ **music** *(col)* Musikberieselung *f* *(col)*. **(b)** *(col: drunk)* voll *(col)*.

cannibal ['kænɪbəl] **1** *n (person)* Kannibale, Menschenfresser *m*. **2** *adj* kannibalisch.

cannibalism ['kænɪbəlɪzəm] *n* Kannibalismus *m*.

cannibalize ['kænɪbəlaɪz] *vt old car etc* ausschlachten.

cannon ['kænən] *n (Mil)* Kanone *f*.

♦**cannon into** *vi* +*prep obj* prallen gegen.

cannon: ~**ball** *n* Kanonenkugel *f*; ~ **fodder** *n* Kanonenfutter *nt*.

cannot ['kænɒt] = **can not**.

canoe [kə'nuː] **1** *n* Kanu *m*. **2** *vi* Kanu fahren.

canoeist [kə'nuːɪst] *n* Kanufahrer(in *f*) *m*.

canon[1] ['kænən] *n (all senses)* Kanon *m*.

canon[2] *n (priest)* Kanoniker *m*.

canonize ['kænənaɪz] *vt (Eccl)* heiligsprechen.

can opener *n* Dosen- *or* Büchsenöffner *m*.

canopy ['kænəpɪ] *n (awning)* Markise *f*; *(over entrance)* Vordach *nt*; *(of bed, throne)* Baldachin *m*.

can't [kɑːnt] = **can not**.

cantankerous [kæn'tæŋkərəs] *adj* verdrießlich.

canteen [kæn'tiːn] *n* **(a)** *(restaurant)* Kantine *f*. **(b)** *(Mil) (flask)* Feldflasche *f*; *(mess tin)* Kochgeschirr *nt*. **(c)** *(of cutlery)* Besteckkasten *m*.

canter ['kæntə'] **1** *n* Kanter *m*. **2** *vi* langsam galoppieren.

cantilever ['kæntɪliːvə'] *n* Ausleger *m*; *(support also)* Freiträger *m*.

cantilever *in cpds* Ausleger-; ~ **bridge** *n* Auslegerbrücke *f*.

canton ['kæntɒn] *n* Kanton *m*.

canvas ['kænvəs] *n* Leinwand *f*; *(for sails)* Segeltuch *nt*; *(set of sails)* Segel *pl*; *(painting)* Gemälde *nt*. **under** ~ *(in a tent)* im Zelt; *(Naut)* mit gehißtem Segel.

canvass ['kænvəs] **1** *vt* **(a)** *(Pol) district* Wahlwerbung machen in (+*dat*). **to** ~ **voters** Wahlwerbung machen. **(b)** *customers, citizens etc* werben; *district* bereisen; *(sound out) opinions* erforschen. **2** *vi* **(a)** *(Pol)* um Stimmen werben *(for sb für* jdn). **(b)** *(Comm)* eine Werbekampagne durchführen.

canvasser ['kænvəsə'] *n* **(a)** *(Pol)* Wahlhelfer(in *f*) *m*. **(b)** *(Comm)* Vertreter(in *f*) *m*.

canyon ['kænjən] *n* Cañon *m*.

cap [kæp] **1** *n* **(a)** *(hat)* Mütze *f*; *(nurse's* ~*)* Haube *f*; *(for swimming)* Badekappe *f*. ~ **in hand** *(fig)* kleinlaut; **if the** ~ **fits(, wear it)** *(prov)* wem der Schuh paßt(, der soll ihn sich anziehen); **he's got his** ~ **for England, he's an English** ~ *(Sport)* er ist/war in der englischen Nationalmannschaft. **(b)** *(lid, cover: of bottle)* Deckel *m*; *(of fountain pen)* (Verschluß)kappe *f*; *(Mil: of shell, fuse)* Kapsel *f*; *(Aut: petrol* ~, *radiator* ~*)* Verschluß *m*. **(c)** *(contraceptive)* Pessar *m*. **(d)** *(of tooth)* (Jacket)krone *f*.

2 *vt* **(a)** *(put* ~ *on) bottle etc* verschließen. **(b)** *(do or say better)* übertreten. **and then to** ~ **it all** ... und um dem Ganzen die Krone aufzusetzen, ... **(c)** **he's been** ~**ped twice for England** er war zweimal in der englischen Nationalmannschaft.

capability [ˌkeɪpə'bɪlɪtɪ] *n (potential ability)* Fähigkeit *f* *(nobl: capableness also)* Kompetenz *f*.

capable ['keɪpəbl] *adj* **(a)** *(skilful, competent)* fähig. **(b) to be** ~ **of doing sth** etw tun können; **it's** ~ **of speeds of up to ...** es erreicht Geschwindigkeiten bis zu ...; **thank you but I'm quite** ~ **of doing that myself** danke, ich bin durchaus imstande, das allein zu machen.

capacitor [kə'pæsɪtə'] *n* Kondensator *m*.

capacity [kə'pæsɪtɪ] *n* **(a)** *(cubic content etc)* Fassungsvermögen *nt*; *(maximum output)* Kapazität *f*; *(maximum weight)* Höchstlast *f*; *(Aut: engine* ~*)* Hubraum *m*. **filled to** ~ randvoll; *(hall)* bis an den letzten Platz besetzt; **seating** ~ **of 400** 400 Sitzplätze; **working at full** ~ voll ausgelastet; **to play to a** ~ **audience** vor ausverkauftem Saal spielen. **(b)** *(ability)* Fähigkeit *f*. **this work is**

beyond his ~ diese Arbeit übersteigt seine Fähigkeiten. **(c)** *(role, position)* Eigenschaft *f*. **in my** ~ **as a doctor** (in meiner Eigenschaft) als Arzt.

cape¹ [keɪp] *n* Cape *nt*, Umhang *m*.

cape² *n (Geog)* Kap *nt*.

caper¹ ['keɪpəʳ] **1** *vi* herumtollen. **2** *n (prank)* Kapriole *f*. **all this** ~ **with the garage** *(col)* das ganze Theater mit der Werkstatt *(col)*.

caper² *n (Bot, Cook)* Kaper *f*.

capillary [kə'pɪlərɪ] **1** *adj* kapillar, Kapillar-. ~ **action** Kapillarwirkung *f*. **2** *n* Kapillare *f*.

capital ['kæpɪtl] **1** *n* **(a)** *(also* ~ **city)** Hauptstadt *f*. **(b)** *(also* ~ **letter)** Großbuchstabe *m*. **please write in** ~**s** bitte in Blockschrift schreiben. **(c)** *no pl (Fin)* Kapital *nt*. **to make** ~ **out of sth** *(fig)* aus etw Kapital schlagen. **2** *adj* **(a)** *letter* Groß-. **(b)** *(dated: excellent)* prächtig.

capital *in cpds* Kapital-; ~ **expenditure** *n* Kapitalaufwendungen *pl*; ~ **gains tax** *n* Kapitalertragssteuer *f*; ~ **goods** *npl* Investitionsgüter *pl*; ~**-intensive** *adj* kapitalintensiv.

capitalism ['kæpɪtəlɪzəm] *n* Kapitalismus *m*.

capitalist ['kæpɪtəlɪst] **1** *n* Kapitalist(in *f*) *m*. **2** *adj* kapitalistisch.

capitalize ['kæpɪtə,laɪz] *vt* **(a)** *(Fin)* kapitalisieren. **(b)** *(Typ) word* groß schreiben.

♦ **capitalize on** *vi +prep obj (fig)* Kapital schlagen aus.

capital: ~ **offence** *(Brit) or* **offense** *(US) n* Kapitalverbrechen *nt*; ~ **punishment** *n* Todesstrafe *f*.

capitulate [kə'pɪtjʊleɪt] *vi* kapitulieren *(also Mil)* (*to* vor +*dat*), aufgeben (*to* gegenüber).

caprice [kə'priːs] *n* Laune(nhaftigkeit), Kaprice *(geh) f*.

capricious [kə'prɪʃəs] *adj* launisch, kapriziös *(geh)*.

Capricorn ['kæprɪkɔːn] *n* Steinbock *m*.

capsize [kæp'saɪz] **1** *vi* kentern. **2** *vt* zum Kentern bringen.

capstan ['kæpstən] *n* Poller *m*.

capsule ['kæpsjuːl] *n* Kapsel *f*.

captain ['kæptɪn] *(abbr* **Capt)** **1** *n (Mil)* Hauptmann *m*; *(Naut, Aviat, Sport)* Kapitän *m*; *(US: in restaurant)* Oberkellner *m*. ~ **of industry** Industriekapitän *m*. **2** *vt (Sport) team* anführen; *(Naut) ship* befehligen. **he** ~**ed the team for years er** war jahrelang Kapitän der Mannschaft.

caption ['kæpʃən] *n* Überschrift *f*; *(under cartoon)* Bildunterschrift *f*; *(Film: subtitle)* Untertitel *m*.

captivate ['kæptɪveɪt] *vt* bezaubern.

captivating ['kæptɪveɪtɪŋ] *adj* bezaubernd.

captive ['kæptɪv] **1** *n* Gefangene(r) *mf*. **to take sb** ~ jdn gefangennehmen. **2** *adj: person* gefangen. a ~ **audience** unfreiwillige Zuhörer/Zuschauer *pl*.

captivity [kæp'tɪvɪtɪ] *n* Gefangenschaft *f*.

captor ['kæptəʳ] *n* **his** ~**s** **were** British er wurde von Briten gefangengehalten; **his** ~**s treated him kindly** er wurde nach seiner Gefangennahme gut behandelt.

capture ['kæptʃəʳ] **1** *vt* **(a)** *town* einnehmen, erobern; *person* gefangennehmen; *animal* (ein)fangen. **(b)** *(fig: painter etc)* atmosphere einfangen; *attention, sb's interest* erregen. **2** *n* Eroberung *f*; *(of soldier, escapee)* Gefangennahme *f*; *(of animal)* Einfangen *nt*.

car [kɑːʳ] *n* **(a)** Auto *nt*, Wagen *m*. **by** ~ mit dem Auto. **(b)** *(Rail, tram~)* Wagen *m*. **(c)** *(US: of elevator)* Fahrkorb *m*.

carafe [kə'ræf] *n* Karaffe *f*.

caramel ['kærəməl] *n (substance)* Karamel *m*; *(sweet)* Karamelbonbon *nt or m*.

carat ['kærət] *n* Karat *nt*. **nine** ~ **gold** neunkarätiges Gold.

caravan ['kærəvæn] *n* **(a)** *(Brit: Aut)* Wohnwagen, Caravan *m*. **(b)** *(gipsy* ~) Zigeunerwagen *m*. **(c)** *(desert* ~) Karawane *f*.

caravanning ['kærəvænɪŋ] *n (Brit)* Urlaub *m* im Wohnwagen.

caravan site *n (Brit)* Campingplatz *m* für Wohnwagen.

caraway ['kærəweɪ] *n* Kümmel *m*.

carbohydrate ['kɑːbəʊ'haɪdreɪt] *n* Kohlehydrat *nt*.

carbolic [kɑː'bɒlɪk] *adj* ~ **acid** Karbolsäure *f*.

carbon ['kɑːbən] *n (Chem)* Kohlenstoff *m*.

carbon: ~ **copy** *n* Durchschlag *m*; **to be a** ~ **copy of sth/sb** einer Sache/jdm aufs Haar gleichen *(col)*; ~ **dioxide** *n* Kohlendioxyd *nt*.

carbonize ['kɑːbənaɪz] *vt* karbonisieren.

carbon: ~ **monoxide** *n* Kohlenmonoxyd *nt*; ~ **paper** *n* Kohlepapier *nt*.

carbuncle ['kɑː,bʌŋkl] *n (Med)* Karbunkel *m*.

carburettor, *(US)* **carburetor** [,kɑːbə'retəʳ] *n* Vergaser *m*.

carcass ['kɑːkəs] *n* **(a)** *(corpse)* Leiche *f*; *(of animal)* Kadaver *m*; *(at butcher's)* Rumpf *m*. **(b)** *(of ship)* Skelett *nt*.

carcinogenic [,kɑːsɪnə'dʒenɪk] *adj* krebserregend.

card [kɑːd] *n* **(a)** *no pl (~board)* Pappe *f*. **(b)** *(greetings, visiting* ~ *etc)* Karte *f*. **(c)** *(Spiel)karte f*. **to play** ~**s** Karten spielen. **(d)** *(fig uses)* **to put one's** ~**s on the table** seine Karten auf den Tisch legen; **to play one's** ~**s right** taktisch geschickt vorgehen; **it's on the** ~**s es ist zu erwarten.**

card: ~**board** *n* Karton *m*, Pappe *f*; ~**board box** *n* (Papp)karton *m*; ~ **game** *n* Kartenspiel *nt*.

cardiac ['kɑːdɪæk] *adj* Herz-. ~ **arrest** Herzstillstand *m*.

cardigan ['kɑːdɪgən] *n* Strickjacke *f*.

cardinal ['kɑːdɪnl] *n (Eccl)* Kardinal *m*.

cardinal: ~ **number** *n* Kardinalzahl *f*; ~ **sin** *n* Todsünde *f*.

card index *n* Kartei *f*; *(in library)* Katalog *m*.

cardiology [,kɑːdɪ'ɒlədʒɪ] *n* Kardiologie *f*.

care [keəʳ] **1** *n* **(a)** *(worry, anxiety)* Sorge *f (of* um). **he hasn't a** ~ **in the world** er hat keinerlei Sorgen.

(b) *(carefulness, attentiveness)* Sorgfalt *f*. **to drive with due** ~ **and attention** umsichtig fahren; **"fragile, with** ~**", "handle with** ~**"** „Vorsicht, zerbrechlich"; **to take** ~ aufpassen, achtgeben; **bye-bye, take** ~ tschüs, mach's gut; **to take** ~ **to do sth** sich bemühen, etw zu tun; **take** ~ **not to drop it** paß auf, daß du es nicht fallenläßt; **you should take more** ~ **with or over the details** Sie sollten sich sorgfältiger mit den Einzelheiten befassen.

(c) *(of teeth, car etc)* Pflege *f*. **to take** ~ **of sth** auf etw *(acc)* aufpassen; *of one's appearance, hair, car* etw pflegen; *(not treat roughly) car, health* etw schonen.

(d) *(of old people, children)* Fürsorge *f*. **he needs medical** ~ er muß ärztlich behandelt werden; **to take** ~ **of sb** sich um jdn kümmern; *of patients* jdn versorgen; *of one's family* für jdn sorgen; **he can take** ~ **of himself** *(in a fight)* er kann sich verteidigen.

(e) ~ **of** *(abbr c/o)* bei; **to take a child into** ~ ein Kind in Pflege nehmen.

(f) to take ~ **of sb/sth** *(see to)* sich um jdn/etw kümmern; *of arrangements also* etw erledigen.

(g) *(caringness, concern) (of person)* Anteilnahme *f*; *(of state, council)* soziale Einstellung.

2 *vi (be concerned)* sich kümmern *(about* um). **money is all he** ~**s about** er interessiert sich nur fürs Geld; **he** ~**s deeply about her** sie bedeutet ihm sehr viel; **I don't** ~ das ist mir egal; **for all I** ~ meinetwegen, von mir aus; **who** ~**s?** na und?

3 *vt (a) (mind, be concerned)* **I don't** ~ **what people say** es ist mir egal, was die Leute sagen; **what do I** ~? was geht mich das an?; **I couldn't** ~ **less** es ist mir doch völlig egal. **(b)** *(like)* **would you** ~ **to take off your coat?** möchten Sie nicht

(Ihren Mantel) ablegen?

♦ **care for** vi +prep obj **(a)** (look after) sich kümmern um; invalid also versorgen; hands, furniture etc pflegen. **(b)** (like) **I don't ~ ~ your tone of voice** wie reden Sie denn mit mir?; **would you ~ ~ a cup of tea?** hätten or möchten Sie gerne eine Tasse Tee?; **I never have much ~d ~ his films** ich habe mir noch nie viel aus seinen Filmen gemacht.

career [kə'rɪəʳ] **1** n Karriere f; (profession) Beruf m; (working life) Laufbahn f. **~s officer** Berufsberater(in f) m; **to make a ~ for oneself** Karriere machen. **2** attr Karriere-; soldier, diplomat Berufs-. **~ woman** Karrierefrau f. **3** vi rasen. **to ~ along** rasen.

carefree ['kɛəfriː] adj sorglos; song heiter.

careful ['kɛəful] adj sorgfältig; (with money etc) sparsam. **~!** Vorsicht!; **to be ~** aufpassen (of auf +acc); **be ~ what you do** nimm dich in acht; **be ~ (that) they don't hear you** gib acht, daß sie dich nicht hören.

carefully ['kɛəfəlɪ] adv see adj.

careless ['kɛəlɪs] adj (negligent, heedless) nachlässig; driver unvorsichtig; driving leichtsinnig; remark gedankenlos. **~ mistake** Flüchtigkeitsfehler m.

carelessly ['kɛəlɪslɪ] adv see adj.

carelessness ['kɛəlɪsnɪs] n see adj Nachlässigkeit f; Unvorsicht(igkeit) f, Leichtsinn m; Gedankenlosigkeit f.

caress [kə'rɛs] **1** n Liebkosung f, Streicheln nt no pl. **2** vt streicheln, liebkosen.

care: **~taker** n Hausmeister m; **~taker government** n geschäftsführende Regierung; **~worn** adj von Sorgen gezeichnet.

car ferry n Autofähre f.

cargo ['kɑːgəʊ] n (Schiffs)ladung f. **~ boat** Frachter m, Frachtschiff nt.

Caribbean [ˌkærɪ'biːən, (US) kə'rɪbiːən] **1** adj karibisch. **~ Sea** Karibisches Meer. **2** n Karibik f.

caricature ['kærɪkətjʊəʳ] **1** n Karikatur f. **2** vt karikieren.

caries ['kɛəriːz] n Karies f.

caring ['kɛərɪŋ] adj person liebevoll; government, society sozial eingestellt.

carnage ['kɑːnɪdʒ] n Gemetzel nt.

carnal ['kɑːnl] adj fleischlich, körperlich.

carnation [kɑː'neɪʃən] n Nelke f.

carnival ['kɑːnɪvəl] n Karneval m; (in SGer) Fasching m.

carnivore ['kɑːnɪvɔːʳ] n (animal) Fleischfresser m; (plant) fleischfressende Pflanze.

carnivorous [kɑː'nɪvərəs] adj fleischfressend.

carol ['kærəl] n Lied nt. **Christmas ~** Weihnachtslied nt; **~ singers** npl ≈ Sternsinger pl.

carouse [kə'raʊz] vi (old) zechen.

carousel [ˌkæruː'sɛl] n = **car(r)ousel**.

carp¹ [kɑːp] n (fish) Karpfen m.

carp² vi etwas auszusetzen haben (at an +dat).

car park n (Brit) (open air) Parkplatz m; (covered) Parkhaus m.

carpenter ['kɑːpɪntəʳ] n Zimmermann m; (for furniture) Tischler m.

carpentry ['kɑːpɪntrɪ] n Zimmerhandwerk nt; (as hobby) Tischlern nt.

carpet ['kɑːpɪt] **1** n (lit, fig) Teppich m; (fitted ~) Teppichboden m. **2** vt floor (mit Teppichen/ Teppichboden) auslegen.

carpet: **~ slippers** npl Pantoffeln pl; **~ sweeper** n Teppichkehrer m.

carport ['kɑːpɔːt] n Einstellplatz m.

carriage ['kærɪdʒ] n **(a)** (horse-drawn vehicle) Kutsche f; (esp US: baby ~) Kinderwagen m. **(b)** (Brit Rail) Wagen m. **(c)** (Comm: conveyance) Beförderung f. **~ free** frachtfrei; **~ paid** frei Haus. **(d)** (Typ) Wagen m. **~ return** Rücklauftaste f. **(e)** (of person: bearing) Haltung f.

carriageway ['kærɪdʒweɪ] n (Brit) Fahrbahn f.

carrier ['kærɪəʳ] n **(a)** (goods haulier) Spediteur m. **(b)** (of disease) Überträger m. **(c)** (aircraft ~) Flugzeugträger m; (troop ~) Transportflugzeug nt/-schiff nt. **(d)** (Chem) Träger(substanz f) m. **(e)** (Brit also ~ bag) Tragetüte f.

carrion ['kærɪən] n Aas nt. **~ crow** Rabenkrähe f.

carrot ['kærət] n Karotte, Möhre f; (fig) Köder m.

car(r)ousel [ˌkæruː'sɛl] n Karussell nt.

carry ['kærɪ] **1** vt **(a)** tragen; message (über)bringen.

(b) (vehicle: convey) befördern. **the wind carried the sound to him** der Wind trug die Laute zu ihm hin.

(c) (have on person) documents, money bei sich haben.

(d) (fig) **his voice carries conviction** seine Stimme klingt überzeugend; **the offence carries a penalty of £5** darauf steht eine Geldstrafe von £5; **it carries interest at 8%** es wirft 8% Zinsen ab; **you're ~ing things too far** (fig) du treibst es zu weit; **he carries himself well** er hat eine gute Haltung.

(e) (bridge etc: support) tragen. **he carries his drink well** er kann viel vertragen.

(f) (Comm) goods, stock führen, (auf Lager) haben; (newspaper) story bringen.

(g) (Tech: pipe) führen; (wire) (weiter)leiten.

(h) (win) einnehmen, erobern. **to ~ the day** den Sieg davontragen; **the motion was carried unanimously** der Antrag wurde einstimmig angenommen.

2 vi (voice, sound) tragen. **the sound of the alphorn carried for miles** der Klang des Alphorns war meilenweit zu hören.

♦ **carry away** vt sep **(a)** (lit) (hin)wegtragen; (torrent, flood) (hin)wegspülen. **(b)** (fig) **to get carried ~** sich nicht mehr bremsen können; **don't get carried ~!** übertreib's nicht!

♦ **carry back** vt sep (fig) person zurückversetzen (to in +acc).

♦ **carry forward** vt sep (Fin) vortragen.

♦ **carry off** vt sep **(a)** (seize, carry away) wegtragen. **(b)** (win) prizes, medals gewinnen. **(c) to ~ it ~** es hinkriegen (col).

♦ **carry on** vi **(a)** (continue) weitermachen; (life) weitergehen. **(b)** (col) (talk) reden und reden; (make a scene) ein Theater machen (col). **to ~ ~ about sth** sich über etw (acc) auslassen. **(c)** (have an affair) etwas haben (col) (with sb mit jdm). **2** vt sep **(a)** (continue) tradition fortführen. **(b)** (conduct) conversation, correspondence führen; profession, trade ausüben.

♦ **carry out** vt sep **(a)** (lit) heraustragen. **(b)** order ausführen; plan, experiment durchführen; threats wahrmachen.

♦ **carry through** vt sep (carry out) zu Ende führen.

carry: **~-all** n (Reise)tasche f; **~cot** n (Brit) Babytragetasche f; **~-on** n (col) Theater nt (col).

carsick ['kɑːsɪk] adj **I get ~** mir wird beim Autofahren immer übel.

cart [kɑːt] **1** n Wagen, Karren m; (US) (in supermarket) Einkaufswagen m; (for baggage) Gepäckwagen m. **to put the ~ before the horse** (prov) das Pferd am Schwanz aufzäumen (prov). **2** vt (fig col) mit sich schleppen.

♦ **cart away** or **off** vt sep abtransportieren.

carte blanche [kɑːt'blɑ̃ʃ] n no pl **to give sb ~** jdm (eine) Blankovollmacht geben.

cartel [kɑː'tɛl] n Kartell nt.

carthorse ['kɑːthɔːs] n Zugpferd nt.

cartilage ['kɑːtɪlɪdʒ] n Knorpel m.

cartography [kɑː'tɒgrəfɪ] n Kartographie f.

carton ['kɑːtən] n Karton m; (of cigarettes) Stange f; (of milk) Tüte f.

cartoon [kɑː'tuːn] n **(a)** (in newspaper etc) Karikatur f; (strip ~) Comics pl. **(b)** (Film, TV)

(Zeichen)trickfilm *m.*
cartoonist [ˌkɑːˈtuːnɪst] *n* (a) *(in newspaper etc)* Karikaturist(in *f*) *m.* (b) *(Film, TV)* Trickzeichner(in *f*) *m.*
cartridge ['kɑːtrɪdʒ] *n (for rifle, pen)* Patrone *f*; *(Phot, for tape recorder)* Kassette *f*; *(for record player)* Tonabnehmer *m.*
cartridge paper *n* Zeichenpapier *nt.*
cartwheel ['kɑːtwiːl] *n (lit)* Wagenrad *nt*; *(Sport)* Rad *nt.* **to turn** *or* **do** ~**s** radschlagen.
carve [kɑːv] **1** *vt* (a) *(Art: cut)* wood schnitzen; stone etc (be)hauen. **to** ~ **sth on a stone** etw in einen Stein einmeißeln. (b) *(Cook)* tranchieren. **2** *vi (Cook)* tranchieren.
♦ **carve out** *vt sep* **to** ~ ~ **a career for oneself** sich *(dat)* eine Karriere aufbauen.
♦ **carve up** *vt sep meat* aufschneiden; body, *(fig)* country zerstückeln.
carving ['kɑːvɪŋ] *n (Art) (thing carved)* Skulptur *f*; *(in wood)* Holzschnitt *m.* ~ **knive** Tranchiermesser *nt.*
cascade [kæsˈkeɪd] **1** *n* Kaskade *f.* **2** *vi (also* ~ **down)** *(onto* auf *+acc)* (in Kaskaden) herabfallen; *(hair)* wallend herabfallen; *(boxes etc)* herunterpurzeln *(col).*
case[1] [keɪs] *n* (a) *(Med, Jur, instance)* Fall *m.* **if that's the** ~ wenn das der Fall ist; **as the** ~ **may be** je nachdem; **it's a clear** ~ **of lying** das ist eindeutig gelogen; **in** ~ falls; **(just) in** ~ für alle Fälle; **in** ~ **of emergency** im Notfall *m*; **in any** ~ sowieso; **in this/that** ~ in dem Fall; **the** ~ **for the defence/prosecution** die Verteidigung/Anklage; **in the** ~ **Higgins v Schwarz** in der Sache Higgins gegen Schwarz; **the** ~ **for/against the abolition of capital punishment** die Argumente für/gegen die Abschaffung der Todesstrafe; **to put the** ~ **for sth** etw vertreten; **you've got a good** ~ was Sie sagen, ist durchaus gerechtfertigt; **there's a strong** ~ **for legalizing pot** es spricht viel für die Legalisierung von Marihuana.
(b) *(Gram)* Fall, Kasus *m.* **in the genitive** ~ im Genitiv.
(c) *(col: person)* Type *f (col).* **he's a** ~ das ist vielleicht 'ne Type *(col)*; **a hard** ~ ein schwieriger Fall.
case[2] *n* (a) *(suit* ~*)* Koffer *m*; *(crate, packing* ~*)* Kiste *f*; *(display* ~*)* Vitrine *f.* (b) *(box)* Schachtel *f*; *(for spectacles)* Etui *nt*; *(pillow* ~*)* Bezug *m*; *(for musical instrument)* Kasten *m.*
case: ~ **history** *n (Med)* Krankengeschichte *f*; *(Sociol, Psych)* Vorgeschichte *f*; ~ **study** *n* Fallstudie *f*; ~ **work** *n (Sociol)* ≈ Sozialarbeit *f.*
cash [kæʃ] **1** *n* (a) *(Med)* Bargeld *nt.* ~ **in hand** Barbestand *m*; **to pay (in)** ~ bar bezahlen; **ready** ~ verfügbares Geld. (b) *(immediate payment)* Barzahlung *f*; *(not credit)* Sofortzahlung *f.* ~ **on delivery** per Nachnahme. (c) *(money)* Geld *nt.* **to be short of** ~ knapp bei Kasse sein *(col).* **2** *vt cheque* einlösen.
♦ **cash in 1** *vt sep* einlösen. **2** *vi* **to** ~ ~ **on sth** aus etw Kapital schlagen.
cash: ~**-and-carry 1** *adj* Cash-and-carry-; **2** *n (for retailers)* Cash and Carry *m*; *(for public)* Verbrauchermarkt *m*; ~ **desk** *n* Kasse *f*; ~ **dispenser** *n* Geldautomat *m.*
cashew [kæˈʃuː] *n (tree)* Nierenbaum *m*; *(nut)* Cashewnuß *f.*
cashflow ['kæʃfləʊ] *n* Cash-flow *m.* ~ **problems** Liquiditätsprobleme.
cashier [kæˈʃɪəʳ] *n* Kassierer(in *f*) *m.*
cashless ['kæʃləs] *adj* bargeldlos.
cashmere [kæʃˈmɪəʳ] *n* Kaschmir *m.*
cash: ~ **payment** *n* Barzahlung *f*; ~ **prize** *n* Geldpreis *m*; ~ **register** *n* Registrierkasse *f.*
casing ['keɪsɪŋ] *n (Tech)* Gehäuse *nt.*
casino [kəˈsiːnəʊ] *n (Spiel)*kasino *nt.*
cask [kɑːsk] *n* Faß *nt.*
casket ['kɑːskɪt] *n* Schatulle *f*; *(US: coffin)* Sarg *m.*

casserole ['kæsərəʊl] **1** *n (Cook)* Kasserolle *f.* **2** *vt (Brit)* schmoren.
cassette [kæˈset] *n* Kassette *f.* ~ **deck** Kassettendeck *nt*; ~ **recorder** Kassettenrecorder *m.*
cassock ['kæsək] *n* Soutane *f.*
cast [kɑːst] *(vb: pret, ptp* ~*)* **1** *n* (a) *(of dice, net, line)* Wurf *m.* (b) *(mould)* (Guß)form *f*; *(object moulded)* Abdruck *m*; *(in metal)* (Ab)guß *m.* ~ **iron** Gußeisen *nt.* (c) *(plaster* ~*)* Gipsverband *m.* (d) *(Theat)* Besetzung *f.* ~ **(in order of appearance)** Mitwirkende *pl* (in der Reihenfolge ihres Auftritts). (e) ~ **of mind** Gesinnung *f.* (f) *(Med: squint)* schielender Blick. **2** *vt* (a) wood, stone etc schnitzen. anchor, net auswerfen; vote abgeben. **to** ~ **one's eyes over sth** einen Blick auf etw *(acc)* werfen. (b) *(shed)* **to** ~ **its skin** sich häuten. (c) *(Tech, Art)* gießen. (d) *(Theat)* parts, play besetzen. **he was** ~ **for the part of Hamlet** er sollte den Hamlet spielen. **3** *vi* (a) *(Fishing)* die Angel auswerfen. (b) *(Theat)* die Rollen verteilen.
♦ **cast about** *or* **around for** *vi +prep obj* suchen nach; for new job etc sich umsehen nach.
♦ **cast aside** *vt sep* cares, inhibitions ablegen; old clothes etc ausrangieren.
♦ **cast away** *vt sep* wegwerfen. **to be** ~ ~ *(Naut)* gestrandet sein.
♦ **cast down** *vt sep* eyes niederschlagen. **to be** ~ ~ *(fig)* niedergeschlagen sein.
♦ **cast off 1** *vt sep* (a) *(get rid of)* abwerfen; friends fallenlassen. (b) *stitches* abketten. (c) *(Naut)* losmachen. **2** *vi* (a) *(Naut)* ablegen. (b) *(in knitting)* abketteln.
♦ **cast on** *vti sep (Knitting)* anschlagen.
♦ **cast up** *vt sep* **to** ~ ~ **sth** ~ **at sb** jdm etw vorhalten.
castanets [ˌkæstəˈnets] *npl* Kastagnetten *pl.*
castaway ['kɑːstəweɪ] *n (lit, fig)* Schiffbrüchige(r) *mf.*
caste [kɑːst] *n* Kaste *f.*
caster ['kɑːstəʳ] *n* = **castor.**
castigate ['kæstɪgeɪt] *vt person (old: physically)* züchtigen; *(verbally)* geißeln.
casting vote ['kɑːstɪŋˈvəʊt] *n* ausschlaggebende Stimme.
cast-iron ['kɑːstˌaɪən] *adj* (a) *(lit)* gußeisern. (b) *(fig)* will, constitution eisern; case, alibi hieb- und stichfest.
castle ['kɑːsl] **1** *n* (a) Schloß *nt*; *(fortress)* Burg *f.* **to build** ~**s in the air** Luftschlösser bauen. (b) *(Chess)* Turm *m.* **2** *vi (Chess)* rochieren.
cast: ~**-off 1** *adj* clothes abgelegt *attr*; **2** *npl* ~**-offs** *(col)* abgelegte Kleider.
castor ['kɑːstəʳ] *n* (a) *(Brit: for sugar, salt etc)* Streuer *m.* (b) *(wheel)* Rolle *f*, Rad *nt.*
castor: ~ **oil** *n* Rizinus(öl) *nt*; ~ **sugar** *n (Brit)* Kristallzucker *m.*
castrate [kæsˈtreɪt] *vt* kastrieren.
casual ['kæʒʊl] **1** *adj* (a) *(not planned)* zufällig; acquaintance, glance flüchtig. (b) *(offhand, careless)* lässig; attitude gleichgültig; remark beiläufig. (c) *(informal)* zwanglos; clothes leger. ~ **wear** Freizeitkleidung *f.* (d) *(irregular) work, labourer* Gelegenheits-. **2** *n* ~ *(worker)* Gelegenheitsarbeiter(in *f*) *m.* ~**s** Aushilfen *pl.*
casually ['kæʒʊlɪ] *adv (without planning)* zufällig; *(in an offhand manner)* beiläufig; *(informally)* zwanglos; dressed leger.
casualty ['kæʒʊltɪ] *n* (a) *(lit, fig)* Opfer *nt*; *(injured also)* Verletzte(r) *mf*; *(dead also)* Tote(r) *mf.* (b) *(also* ~ **ward)** Unfallstation *f.*
cat [kæt] *n* Katze *f.* **to let the** ~ **out of the bag** die Katze aus dem Sack lassen; **they fight like** ~ **and dog** die vertragen sich wie Hund und Katze; **there isn't room to swing a** ~ **(in)** *(col)* man kann sich nicht rühren(, so eng ist es); **to be like a** ~ **on hot bricks** (wie) auf glühenden Kohlen sitzen; **that's put the** ~ **among the pigeons!** da hast du etc aber was (Schönes) angerichtet!; **when the**

~'s away the mice will play (prov) wenn die Katze aus dem Haus ist, tanzen die Mäuse.
cataclysm ['kætəklızəm] n Verheerung f; (fig) Umwälzung f.
catacombs ['kætəkuːmz] npl Katakomben pl.
catalogue ['kætəlɒg] 1 n Katalog m. 2 vt katalogisieren.
catalyst ['kætəlɪst] n (lit, fig) Katalysator m.
catamaran [,kætəmə'ræn] n Katamaran m.
catapult ['kætəpʌlt] 1 n (slingshot) Schleuder f; (Mil, Aviat) Katapult nt or m. 2 vt schleudern; (Aviat) katapultieren.
cataract ['kætərækt] n (a) (rapids) Katarakt m. (b) (Med) grauer Star.
catarrh [kə'tɑːʳ] n Katarrh m.
catastrophe [kə'tæstrəfɪ] n Katastrophe f.
catastrophic [,kætə'strɒfɪk] adj katastrophal.
cat: ~ **burglar** n Fassadenkletterer m; ~**call** n (Theat) ~**calls** Pfiffe und Buhrufe pl.
catch [kætʃ] (vb: pret, ptp **caught**) 1 n (a) (of ball etc) **to make a (good)** ~ (gut) fangen. (b) (Fishing, Hunt) Fang m. (c) (trick, snag) Haken m. **there's a** ~ **in it somewhere** die Sache hat irgendwo einen Haken; **a** ~**-22 situation** (col) eine Zwickmühle; ~ **question** Fangfrage f. (d) (device for fastening) Verschluß(vorrichtung f) m; (hook) Haken m; (latch) Riegel m.
  2 vt (a) fangen; thief fassen, schnappen (col); (col: manage to see) erwischen (col). **to** ~ **sight/a glimpse of sb/sth** jdn/etw erblicken/flüchtig zu sehen bekommen; **he caught the waiter's eye** er machte den Ober auf sich aufmerksam; **this dress caught my eye** das Kleid ist mir ins Auge gefallen; **to** ~ **one's breath** (after exercise etc) Luft holen, verschnaufen (col).
  (b) (take by surprise) erwischen, ertappen. **to** ~ **sb at sth** jdn bei etw erwischen; **you won't** ~ **me doing that again!** (col) das mache ich bestimmt nicht wieder!; **caught in the act** auf frischer Tat ertappt.
  (c) train, bus erreichen, kriegen (col).
  (d) (get entangled) coat hängenbleiben mit. **I caught my finger in the car door** ich habe mir den Finger in der Wagentür eingeklemmt.
  (e) (understand, hear) mitkriegen (col).
  (f) **to** ~ **an illness** sich (dat) eine Krankheit holen (col); **he's always** ~**ing cold(s)** er erkältet sich leicht.
  (g) (hit) treffen. **the blow/ball caught him on the arm** der Schlag/Ball traf ihn am Arm; **you'll** ~ **it!** (col) du kannst was erleben!
  3 vi (a) (with ball) fangen. (b) (fire) in Gang kommen; (wood etc) Feuer fangen; (Cook) anbrennen. (c) (get stuck) sich verklemmen; (get entangled) hängenbleiben. **her dress caught in the door** sie blieb mit ihrem Kleid in der Tür hängen.
♦ **catch on** vi (col) (a) (become popular) (gut) ankommen. (b) (understand) kapieren (col).
♦ **catch out** vt sep (fig) durchschauen; (with trick question etc) hereinlegen (col). **I caught you** ~ **there!** du bist durchschaut; (with trick question) jetzt bist du aber reingefallen (col).
♦ **catch up 1** vi aufholen. **to** ~ ~ **on sth** etw nachholen; **to** ~ ~ **on one's sleep** Schlaf nachholen; **to** ~ ~ **with sb** (running, in work etc) jdn einholen. **2** vt sep (a) **to** ~ **sb** ~ (walking, working etc) jdn einholen. (b) **to get caught** ~ **in sth** (entangled) sich in etw (dat) verfangen; in traffic in etw (acc) geraten; in discussion in etw (acc) verwickelt werden.
catching ['kætʃɪŋ] adj (Med, fig) ansteckend.
catchment area ['kætʃmənt'ɛərɪə] n Einzugsgebiet nt.
catch phrase n Slogan m.
catchy ['kætʃɪ] adj (+er) tune eingängig.
catechism ['kætɪkɪzəm] n (book) Katechismus m.
categorical [,kætɪ'gɒrɪkəl] adj kategorisch.

categorize ['kætɪgəraɪz] vt kategorisieren.
category ['kætɪgərɪ] n Kategorie f.
cater ['keɪtəʳ] vi (provide food) die Speisen und Getränke liefern.
♦ **cater for** vi +prep obj (a) (serve) mit Speisen und Getränken versorgen; functions ausrichten. (b) eingestellt sein auf (+acc); (also cater to) needs, tastes gerecht werden (+dat). **we** ~ ~ **all sizes** wir führen alle Größen; **this magazine** ~**s** ~ **all ages** diese Zeitschrift hat jeder Altersgruppe etwas zu bieten; **a dictionary which** ~**s** ~ **the user** ein benutzerfreundliches Wörterbuch.
catering ['keɪtərɪŋ] n Versorgung f mit Speisen und Getränken (for gen); (trade) Gastronomie f. **who's doing the** ~? welche Firma liefert das Essen?; ~ **trade** (Hotel- und) Gaststättengewerbe nt.
caterpillar ['kætəpɪləʳ] n (Zool) Raupe f; (Tech) Raupe(nkette) f; (vehicle) Raupenfahrzeug nt. ~**-track** Raupenkette f.
caterwauling ['kætəwɔːlɪŋ] n Gejaule nt.
cathedral [kə'θiːdrəl] n Dom m, Kathedrale f.
Catherine wheel ['kæθərɪn,wiːl] n Feuerrad nt.
cathode ['kæθəʊd] n Kathode f. ~**-ray tube** Kathodenstrahlröhre f.
catholic ['kæθəlɪk] adj (varied, all-embracing) vielseitig. **he's a man of very** ~ **tastes** er ist (ein) sehr vielseitig interessiert(er Mensch).
Catholic 1 adj (Eccl) katholisch. **the** ~ **Church** die katholische Kirche. **2** n Katholik(in f) m.
Catholicism [kə'θɒlɪsɪzəm] n Katholizismus m.
cat: ~**kin** n (Bot) Kätzchen nt; ~'s **eye** n Katzenauge nt.
cattle ['kætl] npl Rind(vieh) nt. ~ **breeding** Rinderzucht f; ~ **market** (lit) Viehmarkt m; (fig col) Fleischbeschau f (col).
catty ['kætɪ] adj (+er) gehässig, boshaft.
catwalk ['kætwɔːk] n Steg m; (for models) Laufsteg m.
Caucasian [kɔː'keɪzɪən] 1 adj kaukasisch. 2 n Kaukasier(in f) m.
caucus ['kɔːkəs] n (committee) Gremium nt; (US: meeting) Sitzung f.
caught [kɔːt] pret, ptp of **catch**.
cauldron ['kɔːldrən] n großer Kessel.
cauliflower ['kɒlɪflaʊəʳ] n Blumenkohl m.
cause [kɔːz] 1 n (a) Ursache f (of für). ~ **and effect** Ursache und Wirkung. (b) (reason) Grund m. **there's no** ~ **for alarm** es besteht kein Grund zur Aufregung. (c) (purpose, ideal) Sache f. **in the** ~ **of justice** im Namen der Gerechtigkeit; **it's all in a good** ~ es ist für eine gute Sache. **2** vt verursachen. **to** ~ **grief to sb** jdm Kummer machen; **to** ~ **sb to do sth** jdn veranlassen, etw zu tun.
causeway ['kɔːzweɪ] n Damm m.
caustic ['kɔːstɪk] adj (Chem, fig) ätzend; remark bissig. ~ **soda** Ätznatron nt.
cauterize ['kɔːtəraɪz] vt (Med) ausbrennen.
caution ['kɔːʃən] 1 n (a) Vorsicht f. "~!" "Vorsicht!"; **to act with** ~ umsichtig or vorsichtig vorgehen. (b) (warning) Warnung f; (official) Verwarnung f. **2** vt (warn) **to** ~ **sb** jdn warnen (against vor +dat); (officially) jdn verwarnen.
cautious ['kɔːʃəs] adj vorsichtig (of in bezug auf +acc).
cavalier [,kævə'lɪəʳ] 1 n Kavalier m. 2 adj person, nature unbekümmert.
cavalry ['kævəlrɪ] n Kavallerie f.
cave [keɪv] n Höhle f.
♦ **cave in** vi (col) (a) (become popular) (ground, ceiling) einstürzen.
cave: ~**-in** n Einsturz m; ~**man** n Höhlenmensch m.
cavern ['kævən] n Höhle f.
cavernous ['kævənəs] adj pit tief; hole gähnend; eyes tiefliegend; cheeks eingefallen.
caviar(e) ['kævɪɑːʳ] n Kaviar m.

cavil ['kævɪl] vi kritteln. **to ~ at sth** an etw (dat) herumkritteln.

cavity ['kævɪtɪ] n Hohlraum m; (in tooth) Loch nt. **nasal/chest ~** (Anat) Nasen-/Brusthöhle f; **~ wall** Hohlwand f; **~ wall insulation** Schaumisolierung f.

cavort [kə'vɔːt] vi tollen, toben.

caw [kɔː] **1** vi krächzen. **2** n (heiserer) Schrei.

cayenne pepper ['keɪen'pepəʳ] n Cayennepfeffer m.

CB = Citizens' Band CB.

CBI (Brit) = Confederation of British Industry ≃ BDI.

cc = cubic centimetre ccm, cm³.

cease [siːs] **1** vi aufhören. **2** vt beenden; fire, production einstellen. **to ~ to exist** aufhören zu bestehen; **~ fire!** Feuer halt!

ceasefire [,siːs'faɪəʳ] n Feuerpause f; (longer) Waffenruhe f.

ceaseless ['siːslɪs] adj unaufhörlich; (relentless) vigilance unablässig.

cedar ['siːdəʳ] n (tree) Zeder f.

cede [siːd] vt territory abtreten (to an +acc). **to ~ a point** in einem Punkt nachgeben.

ceiling ['siːlɪŋ] n (a) (Zimmer)decke f. (b) (Aviat) (cloud ~) Wolkengrenze f; (aircraft's ~) maximale Flughöhe. (c) (fig: upper limit) ober(st)e Grenze. **to put a ~ on sth** etw nach oben begrenzen.

celebrate ['selɪbreɪt] **1** vt (a) feiern. (b) mass, ritual zelebrieren. **2** vi feiern.

celebrated ['selɪbreɪtɪd] adj berühmt (for für).

celebration [,selɪ'breɪʃən] n (a) (party, festival) Feier f. (b) (of mass) Zelebration f.

celebrity [sɪ'lebrɪtɪ] n Berühmtheit f; (person also) berühmte Persönlichkeit.

celeriac [sə'lerɪæk] n (Knollen)sellerie m.

celery ['selərɪ] n Stangensellerie m.

celestial [sɪ'lestɪəl] adj (heavenly) himmlisch; (Astron) Himmels-.

celibacy ['selɪbəsɪ] n Zölibat nt or m; (fig) Enthaltsamkeit f.

celibate ['selɪbɪt] adj (Rel) ehelos; (fig) enthaltsam.

cell [sel] n Zelle f.

cellar ['seləʳ] n Keller m.

cellist ['tʃelɪst] n Cellist(in f) m.

cello, 'cello ['tʃeləʊ] n Cello nt.

cellophane ® ['seləfeɪn] n Cellophan ® nt.

cellular ['seljʊləʳ] adj zellular, Zell-. **~ phone** drahtloses Telefon.

celluloid ['seljʊlɔɪd] n Zelluloid nt.

cellulose ['seljʊləʊs] **1** n Zellulose f. **2** adj Zellulose-.

Celsius ['selsɪəs] adj Celsius.

Celt [kelt, selt] n Kelte m, Keltin f.

Celtic ['keltɪk, 'seltɪk] adj keltisch.

cement [sə'ment] **1** n (a) (Build) Zement m. **~ mixer** Betonmischmaschine f. (b) (glue) Klebstoff m; (for holes etc, fig) Kitt m. **2** vt (Build, fig) zementieren; (glue) kleben; holes kitten.

cemetery ['semɪtrɪ] n Friedhof m.

cenotaph ['senətɑːf] n Kriegerdenkmal nt.

censor ['sensəʳ] **1** n Zensor m. **2** vt zensieren.

censorship ['sensəʃɪp] n Zensur f.

censure ['senʃəʳ] **1** vt tadeln. **2** n Tadel m. **vote of ~** Tadelsantrag m.

census ['sensəs] n Volkszählung f. **traffic ~** Verkehrszählung f.

cent [sent] n Cent m. **I haven't a ~** (US) ich habe keinen Pfennig.

centenarian [,sentɪ'neərɪən] n Hundertjährige(r) mf.

centenary [sen'tiːnərɪ] n (anniversary) hundertster Jahrestag; (birthday) hundertster Geburtstag; (100 years) Jahrhundert nt.

centennial [sen'tenɪəl] **1** adj hundertjährig, hundertjährlich. **2** n (esp US) Hundertjahrfeier f.

center n (US) = centre.

centigrade ['sentɪgreɪd] adj Celsius-. **one degree ~** ein Grad Celsius.

centimetre, (US) centimeter ['sentɪˌmiːtəʳ] n Zentimeter m or nt.

centipede ['sentɪpiːd] n Tausendfüßler m.

central ['sentrəl] **1** adj (a) zentral, Zentral-; (main, chief) Haupt-. **~ station** Hauptbahnhof m; **~ government** Zentralregierung f. (b) (fig) wesentlich; importance, figure zentral. **2** n (US: exchange, operator) (Telefon)zentrale f.

central: C~ America n Mittelamerika nt; **C~ Europe** n Mitteleuropa nt; **~ heating** n Zentralheizung f.

centralize ['sentrəlaɪz] vt zentralisieren.

central: ~ nervous system n Zentralnervensystem nt; **~ reservation** n (Brit) Mittelstreifen m; (with grass) Grünstreifen m.

centre, (US) center ['sentəʳ] **1** n (a) Zentrum nt. (b) (middle) Mitte f; (of circle) Mittelpunkt m; (town ~) Stadtmitte f. **~ of gravity** Schwerpunkt m; **~ of attraction** Hauptattraktion f; **he always wants to be the ~ of attraction** er will immer im Mittelpunkt stehen. **2** vt (a) (put in the middle, Typ) zentrieren; ball zur Mitte spielen or flanken. (b) (concentrate) konzentrieren.

♦ **centre (up)on** vi +prep obj (thoughts, talk etc) sich drehen um.

centre-forward ['sentə'fɔːwəd] n (Sport) Mittelstürmer m.

centrifugal [,sentrɪ'fjuːgəl] adj zentrifugal. **~ force** Zentrifugalkraft, Fliehkraft f.

centrifuge ['sentrɪfjuːʒ] n (Tech) Zentrifuge f.

centurion [sen'tjʊərɪən] n Zenturio m.

century ['sentjʊrɪ] n Jahrhundert nt. **in the 20th ~** im 20. Jahrhundert.

ceramic [sɪ'ræmɪk] **1** adj keramisch, Keramik-. **2** n Keramik f.

ceramics [sɪ'ræmɪks] n (a) sing (art) Keramik f. (b) pl (articles) Keramiken pl.

cereal ['sɪərɪəl] n (a) (crop) Getreide nt. (b) (food) Getreideprodukt nt; (breakfast ~) Corn-flakes, Haferflocken etc, Cerealien pl.

cerebral ['serɪbrəl] adj (Physiol) zerebral; (intellectual) geistig. **~ haemorrhage** Gehirnblutung f.

ceremonial [,serɪ'məʊnɪəl] **1** adj zeremoniell. **2** n Zeremoniell nt.

ceremonious [,serɪ'məʊnɪəs] adj förmlich.

ceremony ['serɪmənɪ] n (a) (event etc) Zeremonie f. (b) (formality) Förmlichkeit(en pl) f. **to stand on ~** förmlich sein.

cert [sɜːt] n (col) a (dead) **~** eine todsichere Sache (col).

certain ['sɜːtən] adj (a) (positive, convinced) sicher; (inevitable, guaranteed) bestimmt. **is he ~** weiß er das genau?; **I don't know for ~, but ...** ich bin mir nicht ganz sicher, aber ...; **I can't say for ~** ich kann das nicht mit Sicherheit sagen; **he is ~ to come** er wird ganz bestimmt kommen; **to make ~ of sth** (check) etw nachprüfen; (ensure) für etw sorgen; **be ~ to tell him** vergessen Sie bitte nicht, ihm das zu sagen; **that was ~ to happen** das mußte ja so kommen. (b) (attr: not named or specified) gewiß; reason, conditions bestimmt. a **~ gentleman** ein gewisser Herr; **to a ~ extent** in gewissem Maße.

certainly ['sɜːtənlɪ] adv (admittedly) sicher(lich); (positively, without doubt) bestimmt. **~ not!** ganz bestimmt nicht!; **~!** gewiß!

certainty ['sɜːtəntɪ] n (sure fact) Gewißheit f. **to know for a ~ that ...** mit Sicherheit wissen, daß ...; **the ultimate ~ of death** die Gewißheit des Todes.

certifiable [,sɜːtɪ'faɪəbl] adj (a) fact, claim nachweisbar. (b) (Psych) unzurechnungsfähig; (col: mad) nicht ganz bei Trost (col).

certificate [sə'tɪfɪkɪt] n Bescheinigung f; (of qualifications, health) Zeugnis nt.

certify ['sɜːtɪfaɪ] vt (a) bescheinigen; (Jur) beglaubigen. **this is to ~ that** ... hiermit wird bescheinigt or bestätigt, daß ...; **certified public accountant** (US) geprüfter Buchhalter; **by certified mail** (US) per Einschreiben. **(b)** (Psych) für unzurechnungsfähig erklären.

cervical ['sɜːvɪkəl] adj zervikal (spec). **~ cancer** Gebärmutterhalskrebs m; **~ smear** Abstrich m.

cervix ['sɜːvɪks] n (of uterus) Gebärmutterhals m.

cessation [se'seɪʃən] n Ende nt; (of hostilities) Einstellung f.

cesspit ['sespɪt] n = **cesspool** (a).

cesspool ['sespuːl] n (a) Senkgrube f. **(b)** (fig) Sumpf m.

cf = **confer** vgl.

chafe [tʃeɪf] **1** vt (rub) (auf)scheuern. **his shirt ~d** his neck sein (Hemd)kragen scheuerte. **2** vi (a) (rub) sich aufscheuern; (cause soreness) scheuern. **her skin ~s easily** ihre Haut wird leicht wund. **(b)** (fig) sich ärgern, wütend werden (at, against über +acc).

chaff [tʃɑːf] n (a) (husks of grain) Spreu f. **(b)** (straw) Häcksel m or nt.

chaffinch ['tʃæfɪntʃ] n Buchfink m.

chagrin ['ʃægrɪn] **1** n Verdruß m. **2** vt verdrießen.

chain [tʃeɪn] **1** n (a) (lit, fig) Kette f. **~s** (lit, fig: fetters) Ketten pl. **(b)** (of mountains) (Gebirgs)kette f. **2** vt (lit, fig) anketten. **to ~ sb/sth to sth** jdn/etw an etw (acc) ketten.

chain: **~ reaction** n Kettenreaktion f; **~saw** n Kettensäge f; **~-smoke** vi eine nach der anderen rauchen (col); **~-smoker** n Kettenraucher(in f) m; **~ store** n Ladenkette f; (individual shop) Geschäft m einer Ladenkette.

chair [tʃɛəʳ] **1** n (a) (seat) Stuhl m; (arm~) Sessel m. **b** (in committees etc) Vorsitz m. **to be in/take the ~** den Vorsitz führen. **(c)** (professorship) Lehrstuhl m (of für). **(d)** (electric ~) (elektrischer) Stuhl. **2** vt meeting den Vorsitz führen bei.

chair: **~lift** n Sessellift m; **~man** n Vorsitzende(r) mf; **~manship** n Vorsitz m; **~person** n Vorsitzende(r) mf; **~woman** n Vorsitzende f.

chalet ['ʃæleɪ] n Chalet nt.

chalice ['tʃælɪs] n (poet, Eccl) Kelch m.

chalk [tʃɔːk] **1** n Kreide f. **not by a long ~** (Brit col) bei weitem nicht; **they're as different as ~ and cheese** sie sind so verschieden wie Tag und Nacht. **2** vt message etc mit Kreide schreiben.

♦ **chalk up** vt sep (a) (lit) (mit Kreide) aufschreiben. **(b)** (fig) success, victory verbuchen. **(c)** (fig: mark up as credit) anschreiben (col).

challenge ['tʃælɪndʒ] **1** n (a) (to duel, match etc) Herausforderung f (to an +acc); (fig: demands) Anforderung(en pl) f. **to issue a ~ to sb** jdn herausfordern; **the ~ of the unknown** der Reiz des Unbekannten. **(b)** (bid: for leadership etc) Griff m (for nach). **a direct ~ to his authority** eine direkte Infragestellung seiner Autorität. **(c)** (Mil: of sentry) Anruf m. **(d)** (Jur: of witness) Ablehnung f. **2** vt (a) person herausfordern; world record etc überbieten wollen. **(b)** (fig: make demands on) fordern. **(c)** (fig) remarks, sb's authority in Frage stellen. **(d)** (sentry) anrufen. **(e)** (Jur) witnesses ablehnen; evidence, verdict anfechten.

challenger ['tʃælɪndʒəʳ] n (to duel, match etc) Herausforderer m.

challenging ['tʃælɪndʒɪŋ] adj (provocative) herausfordernd; (thought-provoking) reizvoll; book anregend; (demanding) anspruchsvoll. **I don't find this work very ~** diese Arbeit fordert mich nicht genügend.

chamber ['tʃeɪmbəʳ] n (a) (old: room) Kammer f (old). **(b)** C**~ of Commerce** Handelskammer f; **the Upper/Lower C~** (Parl) die Erste/Zweite Kammer. **(c)** (Anat) (Herz)kammer f.

chamber: **~maid** n (Brit) Zimmermädchen nt; **~ music** n Kammermusik f; **~ pot** n Nachttopf m.

chameleon [kə'miːlɪən] n (Zool, fig) Chamäleon nt.

chamois ['ʃæmwɑː] n (a) also ['ʃæmɪ] (leather) Gamsleder nt. **a ~ (leather)** ein Ledertuch nt, ein Fensterleder nt. **(b)** (Zool) Gemse f.

champagne [ʃæm'peɪn] n Sekt m; (French ~) Champagner m.

champion ['tʃæmpjən] **1** n (a) (Sport) Meister(in f) m. **~s** (team) Meister m; **world ~** Weltmeister(in f) m. **(b)** (of a cause) Verfechter m. **2** adj (a) (prize-winning) siegreich; show animal preisgekrönt. **~ boxer** Boxmeister. **(b)** (N Engl col) klasse inv (col). **3** vt person, action, cause sich engagieren für.

championship ['tʃæmpjənʃɪp] n (a) (Sport) Meisterschaft f. **(b)** ~s pl (event) Meisterschaftskämpfe pl. **(c)** (support) Engagement nt (of für).

chance [tʃɑːns] **1** n (a) (coincidence) Zufall m; (luck, fortune) Glück nt. **by ~** zufällig; **would you by any ~ be able to help?** könnten Sie mir vielleicht behilflich sein?

(b) (possibility) Chance(n pl) f; (probability, likelihood) Möglichkeit f. **the ~s are that ...** wahrscheinlich ...; **he has not much/a good ~ of winning** er hat wenig/gute Aussicht zu gewinnen; **to be in with a ~** ein Chance haben; **he doesn't stand a ~** er hat keine Chance(n); **no ~!** (col) (das) ist nicht drin (col), nichts zu machen (col); **the ~ of a lifetime** eine einmalige Chance; **you won't get another ~** das ist eine einmalige Gelegenheit; **now's your ~!** das ist deine Chance!; **give me a ~!** nun mach aber mal langsam! (col); **you never gave me a ~ to explain** du hast mir ja nie Gelegenheit gegeben, das zu erklären.

(c) (risk) Risiko nt. **to take a ~** ein Risiko eingehen.

2 attr zufällig. **~ meeting** zufällige Begegnung.

3 vt **I'll ~ it!** (col) ich versuch's mal (col); **to ~ one's luck** (have a try) sein Glück versuchen; (risk) das Glück herausfordern.

♦ **chance (up)on** vi +prep obj person zufällig treffen; thing zufällig stoßen auf (+acc).

chancel ['tʃɑːnsəl] n Chor, Altarraum m.

chancellor ['tʃɑːnsələʳ] n (Jur, Pol, Univ) Kanzler m. **C~ (of the Exchequer)** (Brit) Schatzkanzler m.

chancy ['tʃɑːnsɪ] adj (col) riskant.

chandelier [ˌʃændə'lɪəʳ] n Kronleuchter m.

change [tʃeɪndʒ] **1** n (a) Veränderung f; (modification) Änderung f (to gen). **a ~ of air** eine Luftveränderung; **a ~ is as good as a rest** (prov) Abwechslung wirkt Wunder; **no ~** unverändert; **a ~ for the better/worse** eine Verbesserung/Verschlechterung; **the ~ of life** die Wechseljahre pl; **he needs a ~ of clothes** er müßte sich mal was anderes anziehen. **(b)** (variety) Abwechslung f. **(just) for a ~** zur Abwechslung (mal); **that makes a ~** das ist mal was anderes; (iro) das ist ja was ganz Neues! **(c)** (of one thing for another) Wechsel m. **a ~ of government** ein Regierungswechsel. **(d)** no pl (money) Wechselgeld nt; (small ~) Kleingeld nt. **can you give me ~ for a pound?** können Sie mir ein Pfund wechseln?; **keep the ~** stimmt so!; **you won't get much ~ out of £5** von £5 wird nicht viel übrigbleiben.

2 vt (a) (replace) wechseln; address, name ändern. **to ~ train/buses** etc umsteigen; **to ~ one's clothes** sich umziehen; **to ~ a wheel/the oil** ein Rad/das Öl wechseln; **to ~ hands** den Besitzer wechseln; **to ~ places with sb** mit jdm den Platz tauschen. **(b)** (alter) ändern; (transform) verwandeln. **to ~ sb/sth into sth** jdn/etw in etw (acc) verwandeln. **(c)** (exchange: in shop etc) umtauschen. **(d)** money wechseln; (into other currency also) (um)tauschen. **(e)** (Aut) **to ~ gear** schalten.

3 vi (a) sich ändern; (town, person also) sich

verändern. **you've ~d!** du hast dich aber verändert!; **to ~ into sth/sb** sich in etw (acc)/jdn verwandeln. **(b)** (~ *clothes*) sich umziehen. **she ~d into an old skirt** sie zog sich (dat) einen alten Rock an. **(c)** (~ *trains etc*) umsteigen. **all ~!** Endstation!, alles aussteigen! **(d)** (~ *gear*) schalten. **(e)** (*from one thing to another*) (*seasons*) wechseln. **to ~ to a different system** zu einem anderen System übergehen.

♦ **change down** *vi* (*Aut*) in einen niedrigeren Gang schalten.

♦ **change over** *vi* **(a)** (*change to sth different*) sich umstellen auf (+*acc*). **(b)** (*exchange places, activities etc*) wechseln. **do you mind if I ~ ~?** (*TV*) hast du was dagegen, wenn ich umschalte?

♦ **change up** *vi* (*Aut*) in einen höheren Gang schalten.

changeable ['tʃeɪndʒəbl] *adj weather* unbeständig, wechselhaft; *person* wankelmütig.

changing ['tʃeɪndʒɪŋ] **1** *adj* sich verändernd. **2** *n* **the ~ of the Guard** die Wachablösung.

changing-room ['tʃeɪndʒɪŋˌruːm] *n* (*Brit*) (*in store*) Ankleideraum *m*; (*Sport*) Umkleideraum *m*.

channel ['tʃænl] **1** *n* **(a)** (*watercourse*) (Fluß)bett *nt*; (*strait*) Kanal *m*; (*deepest part of river etc*) Fahrrinne *f*. **the (English) C~** der Ärmelkanal; **C~ Islands** Kanalinseln *pl*. **(b)** (*fig, usu pl*) (*of bureaucracy etc*) Dienstweg *m*; (*of information etc*) Kanal *m*; (*of thought, interest etc*) Bahn *f*. **if you go through the right ~s** wenn Sie sich an die richtigen Stellen wenden. **(c)** (*groove*) Rinne *f*. **(d)** (*TV, Rad*) Kanal *m*, Programm *nt*. **2** *vt* **(a)** (*dig out, furrow*) way, course sich (dat) bahnen. **(b)** (*direct*) water, river (hindurch)leiten (*through* durch). **(c)** (*fig*) efforts, interest lenken (*into* auf +*acc*).

chant [tʃɑːnt] **1** *n* (*Eccl, Mus*) Gesang *m*; (*monotonous song*) Sprechgesang *m*; (*of football fans*) Sprechchor *m*. **2** *vt* im (Sprech)chor rufen; (*Eccl*) singen. **3** *vi* Sprechchöre anstimmen; (*Eccl*) singen.

chaos ['keɪɒs] *n* Chaos, Durcheinander *nt*.

chaotic [keɪ'ɒtɪk] *adj* chaotisch.

chap¹ [tʃæp] *n* (*Med: of skin*) **he's got ~s on his hands** seine Hände sind aufgesprungen.

chap² *n* (*Brit col: man*) Kerl (*col*), Typ (*col*) *m*. **old ~** alter Junge (*col*). **the poor little ~** der arme Kleine.

chapel ['tʃæpəl] *n* Kapelle *f*.

chaperon(e) ['ʃæpərəʊn] **1** *n* **(a)** (*for propriety*) Anstandsdame *f*. **(b)** (*escort*) Begleiter(in *f*) *m*. **2** *vt* **(a)** (*for propriety*) Anstandsdame spielen bei. **(b)** (*escort*) begleiten.

chaplain ['tʃæplɪn] *n* Kaplan *m*.

chapter ['tʃæptə'] *n* (*of book*) Kapitel *nt*. **to give ~ and verse (for sth)** (*fig*) etw genau belegen; **a ~ of accidents** eine Serie von Unfällen.

char¹ [tʃɑː'] *vt* (*burn black*) verkohlen.

char² (*Brit col*) **1** *n* (*charwoman*) Putzfrau *f*. **2** *vi* putzen.

character ['kærɪktə'] *n* **(a)** (*nature*) Charakter *m*; (*of people*) Wesen *nt no pl*. **it is out of ~ for him to behave like that** solches Benehmen ist untypisch für ihn; **to be of good/bad ~** ein guter/ schlechter Mensch sein; **a man of ~** ein Mann von Charakter; **he's quite a ~** er ist ein Original. **(b)** *no pl* (*individuality*) (*of towns etc*) Charakter *m*; (*of person*) Persönlichkeit *f*. **(c)** (*in novel, Theat*) Figur *f*. **(d)** (*Typ*) Buchstabe *m*.

character actor *n* Charakterdarsteller *m*.

characteristic ['kærɪktə'rɪstɪk] **1** *adj* charakteristisch, typisch (*of* für). **2** *n* (typisches) Merkmal.

characterization [ˌkærɪktəraɪ'zeɪʃən] *n* (*in a novel etc*) Personenbeschreibung *f*; (*of one character*) Charakterisierung *f*.

characterize ['kærɪktəraɪz] *vt* (*be characteristic of*) kennzeichnen, charakterisieren; (*describe*) beschreiben.

charade [ʃə'rɑːd] *n* Scharade *f*; (*fig*) Farce *f*.

charcoal ['tʃɑːkəʊl] *n* Holzkohle *f*; (*drawing*) Kohlezeichnung *f*; (*pencil*) Kohle(stift *m*) *f*.

charge [tʃɑːdʒ] **1** *n* **(a)** (*Jur: accusation*) Anklage *f* (*of wegen*). **to bring a ~ against sb** gegen jdn Anklage erheben; **he was arrested on a ~ of murder** er wurde wegen Mordverdacht festgenommen; **to be on a ~** (*soldier*) eine Disziplinarstrafe verbüßen. **(b)** (*attack: of soldiers, bull etc*) Angriff *m*. **(c)** (*fee*) Gebühr *f*. **what's the ~?** was kostet das?; **free of ~** kostenlos. **(d)** (*explosive ~*) (Spreng)ladung *f*; (*in firearm, Elec, Phys*) Ladung *f*. **(e)** (*position of responsibility*) Verantwortung *f* (*of* für). **to be in ~** verantwortlich sein; **who's in ~ here?** wer ist hier der Verantwortliche?; **the children were placed in their aunt's ~** die Kinder wurden ihrer Tante anvertraut; **to take ~ of sth** etw übernehmen; **he took ~ of the situation** er nahm die Sache in die Hand. **2** *vt* **(a)** (*with gen*) (*Jur*) anklagen; (*fig*) beschuldigen. **(b)** (*attack*) stürmen; *troops* angreifen. **(c)** (*ask in payment*) berechnen. **I won't ~ you for that** dafür berechne ich Ihnen nichts. **(d)** (*record as debt*) in Rechnung stellen. **~ it to the company** stellen Sie das der Firma in Rechnung. **(e)** *firearm* laden; (*Phys, Elec*) *battery* (auf)laden. **3** *vi* **(a)** (*attack*) stürmen; (*at people*) angreifen (*at sb* jdn). **~!** vorwärts! **(b)** (*col: rush*) rennen. **he ~d into the room/upstairs** er stürmte ins Zimmer/die Treppe hoch.

charge account *n* Kunden(kredit)konto *nt*.

chargé d'affaires ['ʃɑːʒeɪdæ'feə'] *n* Chargé d'affaires *m*.

charger ['tʃɑːdʒə'] *n* (*battery ~*) Ladegerät *nt*.

chariot ['tʃærɪət] *n* Streitwagen *m*.

charisma [kæ'rɪzmə] *n* Charisma *nt*.

charitable ['tʃærɪtəbl] *adj* gütig; *organization* Wohltätigkeits-; (*financially generous, tolerant*) großzügig; *thought, remark etc* freundlich.

charity ['tʃærɪtɪ] *n* **(a)** (*Christian virtue*) Nächstenliebe *f*; (*tolerance, kindness*) Güte *f*. **~ begins at home** (*Prov*) man sollte zuerst an seine eigene Familie/sein eigenes Land etc denken; **to live on ~** von Almosen leben. **(b)** (*charitable society*) Wohltätigkeitsverein *m*; (*charitable purposes*) Wohlfahrt *f*. **a collection for ~** eine Sammlung für wohltätige Zwecke.

charm [tʃɑːm] **1** *n* **(a)** (*attractiveness*) Charme *m no pl*; (*of village, countryside*) Reiz *m*. **feminine ~s** weibliche Reize *pl*; **to turn on the ~** seinen (ganzen) Charme spielen lassen. **(b)** (*spell*) Bann *m*. **it worked like a ~** das hat hervorragend geklappt. **(c)** (*amulet*) Talisman *m*; (*trinket*) Anhänger *m*; **~ bracelet** Armband *nt* mit Anhängern. **2** *vt* (*attract, please*) bezaubern. **(b)** **to lead a ~ed life** einen Schutzengel haben.

charming ['tʃɑːmɪŋ] *adj* reizend, charmant. **~!** (*iro*) wie reizend! (*iro*).

chart [tʃɑːt] **1** *n* **(a)** Tabelle *f*; (*graph*) Schaubild *nt*; (*map, weather ~*) Karte *f*. **(b)** **~s** *pl* (*top twenty*) Hitliste *f*. **2** *vt* (*make a map of*) kartographisch erfassen; (*record progress of*) auswerten; (*keep a ~ of*) aufzeichnen; (*plan*) festlegen.

charter ['tʃɑːtə'] **1** *n* **(a)** Charta *f*; (*of a society*) Satzung *f*; (*permission to become established*) Charter *f or m*, Freibrief *m*. **(b)** (*Naut, Aviat: hire*) **on ~** gechartert. **2** *vt plane, bus etc* chartern. **~ed accountant** (*Brit*) Bilanzbuchhalter *m*; **~ flight** *n* Charterflug *m*.

charwoman ['tʃɑːˌwʊmən] *n* (*Brit*) Putzfrau *f*.

chary ['tʃeərɪ] *adj* (*+er*) (*cautious*) vorsichtig; (*sparing*) zurückhaltend (*of* mit). **he is ~ of giving praise** er spart mit Lob.

chase [tʃeɪs] **1** *n* Verfolgungsjagd *f*; (*Hunt*) Jagd *f*. **to give ~** die Verfolgung aufnehmen. **2** *vt* jagen; (*follow*) verfolgen. **he's been chasing that**

woman for months er ist schon seit Monaten hinter der Frau her. **3** *vi* to ~ **after sb** hinter jdm herrennen *(col)*; *(in vehicle)* hinter jdm herrasen *(col)*; **to** ~ **around** herumrasen *(col)*.

♦ **chase away** *or* **off 1** *vi* losrasen *(col)*. **2** *vt sep* wegjagen; *(fig)* sorrow *etc* vertreiben.

♦ **chase up** *vt sep* person rankriegen *(col)*; information *etc* ranschaffen *(col)*.

chasm ['kæzəm] *n (Geol, fig)* Kluft *f*. **a yawning** ~ ein gähnender Abgrund.

chassis ['ʃæsɪ] *n* Chassis *nt*; *(Aut)* Fahrgestell *nt*.

chaste [tʃeɪst] *adj (+er)* keusch.

chastening ['tʃeɪsnɪŋ] *adj* experience ernüchternd.

chastise [tʃæs'taɪz] *vt* züchtigen *(geh)*; *(scold)* schelten.

chastity ['tʃæstɪtɪ] *n* Keuschheit *f*.

chat [tʃæt] *n* Unterhaltung *f*. **could we have a** ~ **about it?** können wir uns mal darüber unterhalten?; **she dropped in for a** ~ sie kam zu einem Schwätzchen rein *(col)*.

♦ **chat up** *vt sep (col)* person einreden auf *(+acc)*; girl, boy sich heranmachen an *(+acc)*, anmachen *(col)*.

chat show *n (Brit)* Talkshow *f*.

chattels ['tʃætlz] *npl* **all his (goods and)** ~ seine gesamte Habe.

chatter ['tʃætə^r] **1** *n (of person)* Geschwätz *nt*; *(of birds)* Gezwitscher *nt*; *(of teeth)* Klappern *nt*. **2** *vi* *see n* schwatzen; zwitschern; klappern.

chatterbox ['tʃætəbɒks] *n* Quasselstrippe *f (col)*.

chatty ['tʃætɪ] *adj (+er)* person geschwätzig.

chauffeur ['ʃəʊfə^r] *n* Chauffeur *m*.

chauvinism ['ʃəʊvɪnɪzəm] *n* Chauvinismus *m*.

chauvinist ['ʃəʊvɪnɪst] *n (jingoist)* Chauvinist(in *f*) *m*. **(male)** ~ **pig** Pascha *(col)*, Chauvi *(col)* *m*.

cheap [tʃiːp] *adj,adv (+er)* billig. **to buy sth on the** ~ *(col)* etw für einen Pappenstiel kaufen *(col)*; **it's** ~ **at the price** es ist spottbillig; **to feel** ~ sich *(dat)* schäbig vorkommen.

cheapen ['tʃiːpən] **1** *vt (lit, fig)* herabsetzen. **2** *vi* billiger werden.

cheaply ['tʃiːplɪ] *adv see adj*.

cheapskate ['tʃiːpskeɪt] *n (col)* Knicker *m (col)*.

cheat [tʃiːt] **1** *vt* betrügen. **to** ~ **sb out of sth** jdn um etw betrügen. **2** *vi* betrügen; *(in exam, game etc)* mogeln *(col)*, schummeln *(Sch sl)*. **3** *n (a) (person)* Betrüger(in *f*) *m*; *(in exam, game etc)* Mogler(in *f*) *(col)*, Schummler(in *f*) *(Sch sl)* *m*. **(b)** *(dishonest trick)* Betrug *m*.

check [tʃek] **1** *n (a) (examination)* Kontrolle *f*. **a random** ~ eine Stichprobe; **to keep a** ~ **on sb/sth** jdn/etw überwachen *or* kontrollieren. **(b)** *(restraint)* Hemmnis *nt*. **to keep one's temper in** ~ sich beherrschen; **to act as a** ~ **on sth** etw unter Kontrolle *(dat)* halten. **(c)** *(pattern)* Karomuster *nt*; *(square)* Karo *nt*. **(d)** *(Chess)* Schach *nt*. **to be in** ~ im Schach stehen; **to put sb in** ~ jdm Schach bieten. **(e)** *(US) (cheque)* Scheck *m*; *(bill)* Rechnung *f*. ~ **please** bitte (be)zahlen! **2** *vt (a) (examine)* überprüfen; *(in book)* nachschlagen; tickets kontrollieren. **(b)** *(act as control on)* kontrollieren; anger unterdrücken. **(c)** *(Chess)* Schach bieten *(+dat)*. **(d)** *(US: tick)* abhaken. **3** *vi (make sure)* nachprüfen; *(ask also)* nachfragen *(with bei)*; *(have a look)* nachsehen.

♦ **check in 1** *vi (at airport)* einchecken; *(at hotel)* sich anmelden. **2** *vt sep (at airport)* luggage abfertigen lassen; *(at hotel)* person anmelden.

♦ **check out 1** *vi* sich abmelden; *(leave hotel)* abreisen. **2** *vt sep* figures, facts überprüfen.

♦ **check up** *vi* überprüfen.

♦ **check up on** *vi +prep obj* überprüfen; *(keep a check on)* sb kontrollieren.

checkered *adj (US)* = **chequered**.

checkers ['tʃekəz] *n (US)* Damespiel *nt*.

check-in (desk) ['tʃekɪn('desk)] *n* Abfertigung *f*.

checking account ['tʃekɪŋə'kaʊnt] *n (US)*

Girokonto *nt*.

check: ~ **list** *n* Prüf- *or* Checkliste *f*; ~**mate** *n* Schachmatt *nt*; ~**-out** *n (in supermarket)* Kasse *f*; ~**point** *n* Kontrollpunkt *m*; ~**room** *n (US) (Theat)* Garderobe *f*; *(Rail)* Gepäckaufbewahrung *f*; ~**-up** *n (Med)* Untersuchung *f*; **to have a** ~**-up** sich untersuchen lassen.

cheddar ['tʃedə^r] *n* Cheddar(käse) *m*.

cheek [tʃiːk] *n (a)* Backe, Wange *(geh) f*. **(b)** *(buttock)* Backe *f*. **(c)** *(impudence)* Frechheit *f*. **what (a)** ~! was für eine *or* so eine Frechheit!

cheeky ['tʃiːkɪ] *adj (+er)* frech.

cheep [tʃiːp] **1** *n* Piepser *m*. **2** *vi* piepsen.

cheer [tʃɪə^r] **1** *n* Beifallsruf *m*; *(cheering)* Hurrageschrei *nt*. **three** ~**s for Mike!** ein dreifaches Hurra für Mike!; ~**s!** *(Brit col) (your health)* prost!; *(goodbye)* tschüs! *(col)*; *(thank you)* danke schön! **2** *vt (a)* person zujubeln. **(b)** *(gladden)* aufmuntern. **3** *vi* jubeln.

♦ **cheer on** *vt sep* anfeuern.

♦ **cheer up 1** *vt sep* aufmuntern; room, place freundlicher gestalten. **2** *vi* **he** ~**ed** ~ seine Stimmung hob sich; ~ ~! laß den Kopf nicht hängen!

cheerful ['tʃɪəfʊl] *adj* vergnügt; colour *etc* heiter; room freundlich; prospect, news erfreulich; *(iro)* heiter. **you're a** ~ **one!** *(iro)* du bist vielleicht ein Miesmacher! *(col)*.

cheerio ['tʃɪərɪ'əʊ] *interj (esp Brit col)* Wiedersehen *(col)*; *(to friends)* tschüs *(col)*; *(your health)* prost.

cheerless ['tʃɪəlɪs] *adj* person trübselig; prospect trübe; scenery grau.

cheery ['tʃɪərɪ] *adj (+er)* fröhlich.

cheese [tʃiːz] *n* Käse *m*.

cheese *in cpds* Käse-; ~**board** *n* Käsebrett *nt*; *(course)* Käseplatte *f*; ~**burger** *n* Cheeseburger *m*; ~**cake** *n (Cook)* Käsekuchen *m*; ~**cloth** *n (Tex)* Baumwollkrepp *m*.

cheesed-off [tʃiːzd'ɒf] *adj (Brit col)* angeödet *(col)*.

cheetah ['tʃiːtə] *n* Gepard *m*.

chef [ʃef] *n* Küchenchef *m*; *(as profession)* Koch *m*.

chemical ['kemɪkəl] **1** *adj* chemisch. **2** *n* Chemikalie *f*.

chemist ['kemɪst] *n (a) (scientist)* Chemiker(in *f*) *m*. **(b)** *(Brit: in shop)* Drogist(in *f*) *m*; *(dispensing)* Apotheker(in *f*) *m*. ~**'s shop** Drogerie *f*; Apotheke *f*.

chemistry ['kemɪstrɪ] *n* Chemie *f*.

cheque, *(US)* **check** [tʃek] *n* Scheck *m*. **a** ~ **for £10** ein Scheck über £10; **to pay by** ~ mit (einem) Scheck bezahlen; ~**book** Scheckbuch *nt*; ~ **card** *(Brit)* Scheckkarte *f*.

chequered, *(US)* **checkered** ['tʃekəd] *adj (lit)* kariert; *(fig)* career, history bewegt.

cherish ['tʃerɪʃ] *vt (a)* person liebevoll sorgen für. **(b)** feelings, hope hegen.

cherry ['tʃerɪ] *n* Kirsche *f*. ~ **brandy** Cherry Brandy *m*; ~ **red** kirschrot.

cherub ['tʃerəb] *n (fig: baby)* Engelchen *nt*.

chess [tʃes] *n* Schach(spiel) *nt*. ~ **board** Schachbrett *nt*; ~**man** Schachfigur *f*.

chest[1] [tʃest] *n (for tea, tools etc)* Kiste *f*; *(piece of furniture)* Truhe *f*. ~ **of drawers** Kommode *f*.

chest[2] *n (Anat)* Brust *f*. **to get sth off one's** ~ *(fig col)* sich *(dat)* etw von der Seele reden; **to have a weak** ~ schwach auf der Brust sein *(col)*; ~ **specialist** Facharzt *m* für Lungenkrankheiten.

chestnut ['tʃesnʌt] **1** *n (a) (nut, tree)* Kastanie *f*. **(b)** *(colour)* Kastanienbraun *nt*. **(c)** *(horse)* Fuchs *m*. **(d)** **old** ~ *(joke)* olle Kamelle *(col)*. **2** *adj (colour)* hair kastanienbraun.

chew [tʃuː] *vt* kauen.

♦ **chew over** *vi +prep obj (col)* facts, problem sich *(dat)* durch den Kopf gehen lassen.

♦ **chew up** *vt sep* pencil *etc* zerkauen; ground, road surface zerstören.

chewing gum ['tʃuːɪŋɡʌm] *n* Kaugummi *m or* nt.

chewy ['tʃuːwɪ] *adj meat* zäh.
chic [ʃiːk] *adj* (+*er*) schick, elegant.
chick [tʃɪk] *n* (*of chicken*) Küken *nt*; (*young bird*) Junge(s) *nt*; (*col: girl*) Mädchen *nt*.
chicken ['tʃɪkɪn] **1** *n* **(a)** Huhn *nt*; (*for roasting, frying*) Hähnchen *nt*. **she's no** ~ (*col*) sie ist nicht mehr die Jüngste; **don't count your** ~**s (before they're hatched)** (*Prov*) man soll den Tag nicht vor dem Abend loben (*Prov*). **(b)** (*col: coward*) feiges Huhn (*col*). **2** *adj* (*col*) feig.
♦ **chicken out** *vi* (*col*) kneifen (*col*).
chicken *in cpds* Hühner-; ~**feed** *n* **(a)** (*lit*) Hühnerfutter *nt*; **(b)** (*col: insignificant sum*) ein Pappenstiel (*col*); ~**pox** *n* Windpocken *pl*.
chickpea ['tʃɪkˌpiː] *n* Kichererbse *f*.
chicory ['tʃɪkərɪ] *n* Chicorée *f or m*; (*in coffee*) Zichorie *f*.
chief [tʃiːf] **1** *n*, *pl* -**s** (*of department or organization*) Leiter *m*; (*of tribe*) Häuptling *m*; (*of gang*) Anführer *m*; (*col: boss*) Chef *m*. ~ **of police** Polizeipräsident *m*; ~ **of staff** (*Mil*) Stabschef *m*. **2** *adj* **(a)** (*most important*) Haupt-, wichtigste(r, s). **the** ~ **thing** die Hauptsache. **(b)** (*most senior*) Haupt-. ~ **clerk** Bürochef *m*; ~ **constable** (*Brit*) Polizeipräsident *m*; ~ **justice** (*Brit*) ≃ Oberrichter *m*; (*US*) Oberster Bundesrichter.
chiefly ['tʃiːflɪ] *adv* hauptsächlich, vor allem.
chieftain ['tʃiːftən] *n* (*of tribe*) Häuptling *m*.
chiffon ['ʃɪfɒn] **1** *n* Chiffon *m*. **2** *adj* Chiffon-.
chilblain ['tʃɪlbleɪn] *n* Frostbeule *f*.
child [tʃaɪld] *n*, *pl* **children** (*lit, fig*) Kind *nt*. **when I was a** ~ in meiner Kindheit.
child: ~ **bearing** *adj of* ~-**bearing age** im gebärfähigen Alter; ~**birth** *n* Geburt *f*; **to die in** ~**birth** bei der Geburt sterben; ~ **care** *n* Kinderpflege *f*; ~**hood** *n* Kindheit *f*.
childish ['tʃaɪldɪʃ] *adj* (*pej*) kindisch.
child: ~ **labour** (*Brit*) *or* **labor** (*US*) *n* Kinderarbeit *f*; ~**less** *adj* kinderlos; ~**like** *adj* kindlich; ~**minder** *n* Tagesmutter *f*.
children ['tʃɪldrən] *pl of* **child.**
child: ~ **prodigy** *n* Wunderkind *nt*; ~**'s play** *n* ein Kinderspiel *nt*; ~ **welfare** *n* Jugendfürsorge *f*.
Chile ['tʃɪlɪ] *n* Chile *nt*.
Chilean ['tʃɪlɪən] **1** *adj* chilenisch. **2** *n* Chilene *m*, Chilenin *f*.
chill [tʃɪl] **1** *n* **(a)** Kälte *f*. **there's quite a** ~ **in the air** es ist ziemlich frisch draußen. **(b)** (*Med*) fieberhafte Erkältung; (*shiver*) Schauder *m*. **to catch a** ~ sich verkühlen. **2** *adj* (*lit, fig*) kühl. **3** *vt* **(a)** (*lit*) *wine etc* kalt stellen. **(b)** ~**ed to the bone** *etc* die Kälte ging mir bis auf die Knochen. **(b)** (*fig*) *blood* gefrieren lassen.
chil(l)i ['tʃɪlɪ] *n* Peperoni *pl*; (*spice, meal*) Chili *m*.
chilly ['tʃɪlɪ] *adj* (+*er*) (*lit, fig*) kühl. **I feel** ~ mir ist kühl.
chime [tʃaɪm] **1** *n* Geläut *nt*; (*of door-bell*) Läuten *nt* *no pl*. **2** *vt* schlagen. **3** *vi* läuten.
♦ **chime in** *vi* (*col*) sich einschalten.
chimney ['tʃɪmnɪ] *n* Schornstein *m*.
chimney: ~**pot** *n* Schornsteinkopf *m*; ~ **sweep** *n* Schornsteinfeger *m*.
chimp [tʃɪmp] (*col*), **chimpanzee** [ˌtʃɪmpænˈziː] *n* Schimpanse *m*.
chin [tʃɪn] *n* Kinn *nt*. **keep your** ~ **up!** Kopf hoch!; **he took it on the** ~ (*fig col*) er hat's mit Fassung getragen.
China ['tʃaɪnə] *n* China *nt*. **the People's Republic of** ~ die Volksrepublik China.
china ['tʃaɪnə] **1** *n* Porzellan *nt*. **2** *adj* Porzellan-.
china: ~ **clay** *n* Kaolin *m*; **C**~**man** *n* Chinese *m*.
Chinese [tʃaɪˈniːz] **1** *n* **(a)** (*person*) Chinese *m*, Chinesin *f*. **(b)** (*language, fig: gibberish*) Chinesisch *nt*. **2** *adj* chinesisch.
chink [tʃɪŋk] *n* **(a)** Ritze *f*; (*in door*) Spalt *m*. **(b)** (*pej, hum: Chinaman*) **C**~ Schlitzauge *m* (*col*).
chink² **1** *n* (*sound*) Klimpern *nt*. **2** *vt* klimpern mit. **3** *vi* klimpern.

chintz [tʃɪnts] **1** *n* Chintz *m*. **2** *attr* Chintz-.
chip [tʃɪp] **1** *n* **(a)** Splitter *m*; (*of wood*) Span *m*. **he's a** ~ **off the old block** er ist ganz der Vater; **to have a** ~ **on one's shoulder** einen Komplex haben (*about wegen*). **(b)** (*Brit: potato* ~) ~**s** Pommes frites *pl*; (*US: crisps*) Chips *pl*. **(c)** (*in crockery, furniture etc*) abgeschlagene Stelle *f*. **(d)** (*in poker etc*) Chip *m*. **when the** ~**s are down** wenn es drauf ankommt. **(e)** (*micro*~) Chip *m*. **2** *vt cup, stone* anschlagen; *varnish, paint* abstoßen. **3** *vi* (*cup, china etc*) angeschlagen werden; (*paint, varnish*) abspringen.
♦ **chip in** *vi* (*col*) **(a)** (*interrupt*) sich einschalten. **(b)** (*contribute*) **he** ~**ped** ~ **with £3** er steuerte £3 bei.
♦ **chip off 1** *vt sep paint etc* wegschlagen; *piece of china* abschlagen. **2** *vi* (*paint etc*) absplittern.
chipboard ['tʃɪpbɔːd] *n* Spanholz *nt*.
chipmunk ['tʃɪpmʌŋk] *n* Backenhörnchen *nt*.
chiropodist [kɪˈrɒpədɪst] *n* Fußpfleger(in *f*) *m*.
chiropody [kɪˈrɒpədɪ] *n* Fußpflege *f*.
chirp [tʃɜːp] *vi* (*birds*) zwitschern; (*crickets*) zirpen.
chirpy ['tʃɜːpɪ] *adj* (+*er*) (*col*) munter.
chirrup ['tʃɪrəp] = **chirp.**
chisel ['tʃɪzl] **1** *n* Meißel *m*; (*for wood*) Beitel *m*. **2** *vt* meißeln; (*in wood*) stemmen. **her finely** ~**led features** ihr fein geschnittenes Gesicht.
chit [tʃɪt] *n* (*also* ~ **of paper**) Zettel *m*.
chivalrous ['ʃɪvəlrəs] *adj* ritterlich.
chivalry ['ʃɪvəlrɪ] *n* Ritterlichkeit *f*.
chives [tʃaɪvz] *n* Schnittlauch *m*.
chloride ['klɔːraɪd] *n* Chlorid *nt*.
chlorinate ['klɒrɪneɪt] *vt water* chloren.
chlorine ['klɔːriːn] *n* Chlor *nt*.
chloroform ['klɒrəfɔːm] *n* Chloroform *nt*.
chlorophyll ['klɒrəfɪl] *n* Chlorophyll *nt*.
choc-ice ['tʃɒkaɪs] *n* Eis *nt* mit Schokoladenüberzug.
chock [tʃɒk] *n* Bremskeil *m*.
chock-a-block ['tʃɒkəblɒk], **chock-full** ['tʃɒkful] *adj* (*col*) gerammelt voll (*col*).
chocolate ['tʃɒklɪt] **1** *n* **(a)** Schokolade *f*. **a** ~ eine Praline; **a box of** ~**s** eine Schachtel Pralinen. **2** *adj* Schokoladen-; (*also* ~-**coloured** (*Brit*) *or* ~-**colored** *US*) schokoladenbraun.
choice [tʃɔɪs] **1** *n* **(a)** Wahl *f*. **to make a** ~ eine Wahl treffen; **he had no** ~ es blieb ihm nichts anderes übrig, als zu …; **take your** ~ such dir etwas/eine *etc* aus; **it was your** ~ du wolltest es ja so. **(b)** (*variety to choose from*) Auswahl *f* (*of an* +*dat, von*). **2** *adj goods, fruit, wine* Qualitäts-. ~ **fruit** Obst *nt* erster Wahl.
choir ['kwaɪə'] *n* Chor *m*. ~**boy** Sängerknabe *m*.
choke [tʃəʊk] **1** *vt* **(a)** (*stifle*) ersticken; (*throttle*) (er)würgen, erdrosseln. **(b)** (*fig*) *pipe etc* verstopfen. **2** *vi* ersticken (*on an* +*dat*). **3** *n* (*Aut*) Choke *m*.
♦ **choke back** *vt sep tears, reply* unterdrücken.
choker ['tʃəʊkə'] *n* (*collar*) Vatermörder *m*; (*of velvet etc*) enganliegendes Halsband.
cholera ['kɒlərə] *n* Cholera *f*.
cholesterol [kɒˈlestərɒl] *n* Cholesterin *nt*.
choose [tʃuːz] *pret* **chose**, *ptp* **chosen** **1** *vt* (*aus*)wählen. **to** ~ **to do sth** es vorziehen, etw zu tun. **2** *vi* **to** ~ (*between or among/from*) wählen (*zwischen* +*dat/aus or unter* +*dat*); **there is nothing to** ~ **between them** sie sind gleich gut; **I'll do it when I** ~ ich mache es, wann es mir paßt (*col*).
choos(e)y ['tʃuːzɪ] *adj* (+*er*) wählerisch.
chop¹ [tʃɒp] **1** *n* **(a)** (*blow*) Schlag *m*. **(b)** (*Cook*) Kotelett *nt*. **(c)** (*col*) **to get the** ~ (*be axed*) gestrichen werden; (*be fired*) rausgeschmissen werden. **2** *vt* hacken; *meat, vegetables etc* kleinschneiden.
♦ **chop down** *vt sep tree* fällen.
♦ **chop off** *vt sep* abhacken.

chop² vi (fig) **to ~ and change** ständig seine Meinung ändern.

chopper ['tʃɒpə'] n (a) (axe) Hackbeil nt. (b) (col: helicopter) Hubschrauber m. (c) (bicycle ®) Fahrrad nt.

chopping ['tʃɒpɪŋ]: **~ block** n Hackklotz m; (for wood) Block m; **~ board** n Hackbrett nt.

choppy ['tʃɒpɪ] adj (+er) sea kabbelig; wind böig.

chopstick ['tʃɒpstɪk] n Stäbchen nt.

choral ['kɔːrəl] adj Chor-. **~ society** Gesangverein m.

chord [kɔːd] n (Mus) Akkord m. **to strike the right/a sympathetic ~** (fig) den richtigen Ton treffen/auf Verständnis stoßen.

chore [tʃɔː'] n lästige Pflicht. **~s** pl Hausarbeit f; **to do the ~s** den Haushalt machen.

choreographer [ˌkɒrɪˈɒɡrəfə'] n Choreograph(in f) m.

choreography [ˌkɒrɪˈɒɡrəfɪ] n Choreographie f.

chortle ['tʃɔːtl] vi glucksen.

chorus ['kɔːrəs] **1** n (a) (refrain) Refrain m. (b) Chor m; (dancers) Tanzgruppe f. **in ~** im Chor. **2** vi im Chor singen/sprechen/rufen.

chorus girl n (Revue)tänzerin f.

chose [tʃəʊz] pret of **choose**.

chosen ['tʃəʊzn] **1** ptp of **choose**. **2** adj **the ~ people** das auserwählte Volk.

chowder ['tʃaʊdə'] n (US) sämige Fischsuppe.

Christ [kraɪst] n Christus m.

christen ['krɪsn] vt taufen.

christening ['krɪsnɪŋ] n Taufe f.

Christian ['krɪstɪən] **1** n Christ m. **2** adj (lit, fig) christlich.

Christianity [ˌkrɪstɪˈænɪtɪ] n (faith, religion) Christentum nt; (body of Christians) Christenheit f.

Christian name n Vorname m.

Christmas ['krɪsməs] n Weihnachten nt. **happy** or **merry ~!** fröhliche Weihnachten!

Christmas: **~ card** n Weihnachtskarte f; **~ carol** n Weihnachtslied nt; **~ Day** n der erste Weihnachtstag; **~ Eve** n Heiligabend m; **~ present** n Weihnachtsgeschenk nt; **~ tree** n Weihnachtsbaum, Christbaum m.

chromatic [krə'mætɪk] adj (Art, Mus) chromatisch.

chrome [krəʊm] n Chrom nt. **~-plated** verchromt.

chromosome ['krəʊməsəʊm] n Chromosom nt.

chronic ['krɒnɪk] adj (a) (Med, fig) chronisch. (b) (col: terrible) miserabel (col).

chronicle ['krɒnɪkl] **1** n Chronik f. **2** vt aufzeichnen.

chronological [ˌkrɒnə'lɒdʒɪkəl] adj chronologisch.

chronology [krə'nɒlədʒɪ] n zeitliche Abfolge; (list of dates) Zeittafel f.

chrysalis ['krɪsəlɪs] n, pl -es (Biol) Puppe f.

chrysanthemum [krɪ'sænθəməm] n Chrysantheme f.

chubby ['tʃʌbɪ] adj (+er) pummelig, rundlich.

chuck [tʃʌk] vt (col) (a) (throw) schmeißen (col). (b) (also: **~ away**) wegschmeißen (col). (c) (also: **~ in**) boyfriend Schluß machen mit (col); job hinschmeißen (col).

♦ **chuck out** vt sep (col) rausschmeißen (col); old clothes etc wegschmeißen.

chuckle ['tʃʌkl] **1** n leises Lachen. **2** vi in sich (acc) hineinlachen.

chuffed [tʃʌft] adj (Brit col) vergnügt und zufrieden; (flattered) gebauchpinselt (col) (about wegen).

chug [tʃʌg] **1** n Tuckern nt. **2** vi tuckern.

♦ **chug along** vi dahintuckern.

chum [tʃʌm] n (col) Kamerad, Kumpel (col) m.

chunk [tʃʌŋk] n großes Stück; (of stone) Brocken m.

chunky ['tʃʌŋkɪ] adj (+er) (col) legs, arms stämmig; knitwear grob gestrickt; meat grob geschnitten; book, format kompakt; glasses solide.

church [tʃɜːtʃ] n Kirche f; (service) die Kirche. **to go to ~** in die Kirche gehen; **the C~ of England** die Anglikanische Kirche; **he has entered the C~** er ist Geistlicher geworden.

church in cpds Kirchen-; **~-goer** n Kirchgänger(in f) m; **~ service** n Gottesdienst m; **~yard** n Kirchhof m.

churlish ['tʃɜːlɪʃ] adj ungehobelt.

churn [tʃɜːn] **1** n (for butter) Butterfaß nt; (Brit: milk-~) Milchkanne f. **2** vt **to ~ butter** buttern. **3** vi (water) wirbeln.

♦ **churn out** vt sep am laufenden Band produzieren.

♦ **churn up** vt sep aufwühlen.

chute [ʃuːt] n (a) Rutsche f; (garbage ~) Müllschlucker m. (b) (in playground) Rutschbahn f.

chutney ['tʃʌtnɪ] n Chutney m.

CIA = **Central Intelligence Agency** CIA m.

cicada [sɪ'kɑːdə] n Zikade f.

CID = **Criminal Investigation Department**.

cider ['saɪdə'] n Apfelwein, Cidre m.

cigar [sɪ'gɑː'] n Zigarre f.

cigarette [sɪgə'ret] n Zigarette f.

cigarette: **~ case** n Zigarettenetui nt; **~ end** n Zigarettenstummel m; **~ lighter** n Feuerzeug nt.

cinch [sɪntʃ] n (col) **it's a ~** (easy) das ist ein Klacks (col); (esp US: certain) es ist todsicher (col).

cinder ['sɪndə'] n **~s** pl Asche f. **burnt to a ~** (fig) verkohlt.

Cinderella [ˌsɪndə'relə] n Aschenputtel nt.

cinder track n Aschenbahn f.

cine-camera [ˌsɪnɪ'kæmərə] n (Brit) (Schmal)filmkamera f.

cinema ['sɪnəmə] n (esp Brit) Kino nt. **at/to the ~** im/ins Kino.

cinnamon ['sɪnəmən] n Zimt m.

cipher ['saɪfə'] n (a) Ziffer f; (zero) Null f. (b) (code) Chiffre f.

circle ['sɜːkl] **1** n (a) Kreis m. **we're just going around in ~s** (fig) wir bewegen uns nur im Kreis; **to come full ~** (fig) zum Ausgangspunkt zurückkehren; **the family ~** der engste Familienkreis; **he's moving in different ~s** now er verkehrt jetzt in anderen Kreisen. (b) (Brit: Theat) Rang m. **2** vt (a) (surround) umgeben. (b) (move around) kreisen um. **3** vi (fly in a ~) kreisen.

circuit ['sɜːkɪt] n (a) (journey around etc) Rundgang m/-fahrt f/-reise f (of um). **three ~s of the racetrack** drei Runden auf der Rennbahn. (b) (Elec) Stromkreis m; (apparatus) Schaltung f. (c) (Sport: track) Rennbahn f.

circuit: **~ breaker** n Stromkreisunterbrecher m; **~ diagram** n Schaltplan m.

circuitous [sɜː'kjuːtəs] adj umständlich.

circular ['sɜːkjʊlə'] **1** adj object rund. **~ saw** Kreissäge f; **~ tour** Rundfahrt f/-reise f; **~ letter** Rundschreiben nt, Rundbrief m. **2** n (in firm) Rundschreiben nt; (advertisement) Wurfsendung f.

circulate ['sɜːkjʊleɪt] **1** vi (blood, money) zirkulieren; (rumour) kursieren; (news) sich verbreiten; (person: at party) die Runde machen. **2** vt memo etc zirkulieren lassen.

circulation [ˌsɜːkjʊ'leɪʃən] n (a) (Med) Kreislauf m; (of traffic) Fluß m; (of money) Umlauf m; (of news, rumour) Kursieren nt. **to have poor ~** Kreislaufstörungen haben; **to put notes into ~** Banknoten in Umlauf bringen; **new words which come into ~** neue Wörter, die in den Sprachgebrauch eingehen; **he's back in ~** now (col) er mischt wieder mit (col). (b) (of newspaper etc) Auflage(nziffer) f.

circumcise ['sɜːkəmsaɪz] vt beschneiden.

circumcision [ˌsɜːkəm'sɪʒən] n Beschneidung f.

circumference [sə'kʌmfərəns] n Umfang m.

circumflex ['sɜːkəmfleks] n Zirkumflex m.

circumscribe ['sɜːkəmskraɪb] vt (a) (Math) einen

Kreis beschreiben um. **(b)** *(restrict)* eingrenzen.
circumspect ['sɜːkəmspekt] *adj* umsichtig.
circumstance ['sɜːkəmstəns] *n* Umstand *m*. **in** *or* **under the** ~**s** unter diesen Umständen; **under no** ~**s** unter gar keinen Umständen; **in certain** ~**s** unter Umständen.
circumstantial [ˌsɜːkəm'stænʃəl] *adj* **(a)** *report* ausführlich. **(b)** *(Jur)* ~ **evidence** Indizien/-beweis *m*.
circumvent [ˌsɜːkəm'vent] *vt* umgehen.
circus ['sɜːkəs] *n* Zirkus *m*; *(in place names)* Platz *m*.
cirrhosis [sɪ'rəusɪs] *n* Zirrhose *f*.
cissy ['sɪsɪ] *n* = **sissy**.
cistern ['sɪstən] *n* Zisterne *f*; *(of WC)* Spülkasten *m*.
citadel ['sɪtədl] *n* Zitadelle *f*.
cite [saɪt] *vt (quote)* zitieren.
citizen ['sɪtɪzn] *n* Bürger(in *f*) *m*.
citizenship ['sɪtɪznʃɪp] *n* Staatsbürgerschaft *f*.
citric ['sɪtrɪk] *adj* Zitrus-. ~ **acid** Zitronensäure *f*.
citrus ['sɪtrəs] ~ **fruits** Zitrusfrüchte *pl*.
city ['sɪtɪ] *n* **(a)** Großstadt *f*. **the** ~ **of Glasgow** die Stadt Glasgow. **(b)** *(in London)* **the C**~ die City, das Banken- und Börsenviertel.
city: ~ **centre** *(Brit) or* **center** *(US) n* Stadtmitte *f*; ~ **hall** *n* Rathaus *nt*; ~ **page** *n (Brit)* Wirtschaftsseite *f*; ~ **slicker** *n (pej col)* feiner Pinkel aus der (Groß)stadt *(pej col)*.
civic ['sɪvɪk] *adj rights* bürgerlich, Bürger-; *authorities* Stadt-, städtisch. ~ **centre** *(Brit)* Verwaltungszentrum *nt* einer Stadt.
civil ['sɪvl] *adj* **(a)** *(of society)* bürgerlich; *duties* Bürger-. **(b)** *(polite)* höflich. **(c)** *(Jur)* zivilrechtlich.
civil: ~ **defence** *(Brit) or* **defense** *(US) n* ziviler Bevölkerungsschutz; ~ **disobedience** *n* ziviler Ungehorsam; ~ **engineer** *n* Hoch- und Tiefbauingenieur *m*; ~ **engineering** *n* Hoch- und Tiefbau *m*.
civilian [sɪ'vɪlɪən] **1** *n* Zivilist *m*. **2** *adj* zivil, Zivil-. **in** ~ **clothes** in Zivil.
civility [sɪ'vɪlɪtɪ] *n* Höflichkeit *f*.
civilization [ˌsɪvɪlaɪ'zeɪʃən] *n* **(a)** Zivilisation *f*. **(b)** *(of Greeks etc)* Kultur *f*.
civilize ['sɪvɪlaɪz] *vt* zivilisieren.
civilized ['sɪvɪlaɪzd] *adj* **(a)** zivilisiert. **(b)** *(cultured) lifestyle etc* kultiviert.
civil: ~ **law** *n* Bürgerliches Recht; ~ **marriage** *n* standesamtliche Trauung; ~ **rights** *npl* (staats)bürgerliche Rechte *pl*; ~ **servant** *n* ≃ Staatsbeamte(r) *mf*; ~ **service** *n* ≃ Staatsdienst *m (ohne Richter und Lehrer)*; *(~ servants collectively)* Beamtenschaft *f*; ~ **war** *n* Bürgerkrieg *m*.
clad [klæd] **1** *(old) pret, ptp of* **clothe**. **2** *adj (liter)* gekleidet.
claim [kleɪm] **1** *vt* **(a)** *(demand as one's own or due)* Anspruch erheben auf *(+acc)*; *benefits, sum of money (apply for)* beantragen; *lost property* abholen. **he** ~**ed diplomatic immunity** er berief sich auf seine diplomatische Immunität. **(b)** *(profess, assert)* behaupten. **the advantages** ~**ed for this technique** die Vorzüge, die man dieser Methode zuschreibt.
2 *vi* **(a)** *(Insur)* Ansprüche geltend machen; *(for damage done by people)* Schadenersatz verlangen. **(b)** *(for expenses etc)* **to** ~ **for sth** sich *(dat)* etw zurückzahlen lassen; **you can** ~ **for your travelling expenses** Sie können sich *(dat)* Ihre Reisekosten (zurück)erstatten lassen.
3 *n* **(a)** Anspruch *m*; *(pay~, Ind)* Forderung *f*. **to lay** ~ **to the title/property** *etc* Anspruch auf den Titel/das Grundstück *etc* erheben; **to put in a** ~ **(for sth)** etw beantragen; **he put in an expenses** ~ **for £100** er reichte Spesen in Höhe von £100 ein; **the** ~**s were all paid** *(Insur)* der Schaden wurde voll ersetzt. **(b)** *(assertion)* Behauptung *f*. **the book makes no** ~ **to be original** das Buch erhebt keinen Anspruch auf

Originalität.
♦ **claim back** *vt sep* zurückfordern. **to** ~ **sth** ~ **(as expenses)** sich *(dat)* etw zurückzahlen *or* -erstatten lassen.
claimant ['kleɪmənt] *n (for social security etc)* Antragsteller(in *f*) *m*; *(for inheritance etc)* Anspruchsteller(in *f*) *m (to auf +acc)*; *(Jur)* Kläger(in *f*) *m*.
claim form *n* Antragsformular *nt*.
clairvoyant [kleə'vɔɪənt] **1** *n* Hellseher(in *f*) *m*. **2** *adj* hellseherisch.
clam [klæm] *n* Venusmuschel *f*.
♦ **clam up** *vi (col)* keinen Piep (mehr) sagen *(col)*.
clamber ['klæmbəʳ] *vi* klettern. **to** ~ **up a hill** einen Berg hinaufklettern.
clammy ['klæmɪ] *adj (+er)* feucht, klamm.
clamour, *(US)* **clamor** ['klæməʳ] **1** *n* **(a)** *(noise)* Lärm *m*. **(b)** *(demand)* lautstark erhobene Forderung *(for nach)*. **2** *vi* **to** ~ **for sth** lautstark etw fordern.
clamp [klæmp] **1** *n* Schraubzwinge *f*; *(Med, Elec)* Klemme *f*. **2** *vt* (ein)spannen.
♦ **clamp down** *vt sep (lit)* festmachen. **2** *vi (fig col: on expenses etc)* gewaltig bremsen *(col)*; *(police, government)* rigoros durchgreifen.
♦ **clamp down on** *vi +prep obj (col) person an die* Kandare nehmen; *expenditure, activities* einen Riegel vorschieben *(+dat)*; *crime etc* zum Schlag ausholen gegen.
clan [klæn] *n (lit, fig)* Clan *m*.
clandestine [klæn'destɪn] *adj* geheim.
clang [klæŋ] **1** *n* Klappern *nt*; *(of hammer)* Dröhnen *nt*. **2** *vi* klappern; *(hammer)* dröhnen. **3** *vt* mit etw klappern.
clanger ['klæŋəʳ] *n (Brit col)* Schnitzer *(col) m*. **to drop a** ~ ins Fettnäpfchen treten *(col)*.
clank [klæŋk] **1** *n* Klirren *nt*. **2** *vt* klirren mit. **3** *vi* klirren.
clap klæp **1** *n* Klatschen *nt no pl; (no pl: applause)* (Beifall)klatschen *nt*. **a** ~ **of thunder** ein Donnerschlag *m*. **2** *vt* **(a)** *(applaud)* Beifall klatschen *(sb* jdm*)*. **(b)** **to** ~ **one's hands** in die Hände klatschen. **(c)** **to** ~ **sb into prison** jdn ins Gefängnis stecken; **to** ~ **eyes on sb/sth** *(col)* jdn/etw zu Gesicht bekommen. **3** *vi* (Beifall) klatschen.
clapping ['klæpɪŋ] *n* Klatschen *nt*.
claptrap ['klæptræp] *n (col)* Geschwafel *nt (col)*.
claret ['klærət] *n (wine)* roter Bordeauxwein.
clarification [ˌklærɪfɪ'keɪʃən] *n* Klarstellung *f*.
clarify ['klærɪfaɪ] *vt* klären; *text* erklären.
clarinet [ˌklærɪ'net] *n* Klarinette *f*.
clarity ['klærɪtɪ] *n* Klarheit *f*.
clash [klæʃ] **1** *vi* **(a)** *(armies, demonstrators)* zusammenstoßen. **(b)** *(colours)* sich beißen; *(interests)* aufeinanderprallen; *(programmes, films)* sich überschneiden. **(c)** *(cymbals etc: also* ~ **together)** aneinanderschlagen; *(metal)* klirren. **2** *vt cymbals* schlagen. **3** *n* **(a)** *(of armies, demonstrators etc)* Zusammenstoß *m*. **(b)** *(of personalities)* grundsätzliche Verschiedenheit. **it's such a** ~ **of personalities** sie sind charakterlich grundverschieden. **(c)** *(of swords)* Aufeinanderprallen *nt*; *(between people)* Konflikt *m*. **there's a** ~ **of dates** die Termine überschneiden sich.
clasp [klɑːsp] **1** *n* **(a)** *(on brooch, purse etc)* (Schnapp)verschluß *m*. **(b)** *(with one's arms)* Umklammerung *f*; *(with hand)* Griff *m*. **2** *vt* **(a)** (er)greifen. **with his hands** ~**ed** mit gefalteten Händen; **to** ~ **sb in one's arms** jdn in die Arme schließen. **(b)** *(to fasten with a* ~*)* befestigen.
class [klɑːs] **1** *n* **(a)** *(group, division)* Klasse *f*. **in a** ~ **by himself/itself** weitaus der/das Beste. **(b)** *(social rank)* Schicht, Klasse *f*. **(c)** *(Sch, Univ)* Klasse *f*. **to give** *or* **take a Latin** ~ Latein unterrichten; **the French** ~ *(lesson)* die Französischstunde; *(people)* die Französischklasse; **an evening** ~ ein Abendkurs *m*. **(d)** *(col:*

quality, tone) Stil *m*. **to have** ~ Stil haben; *(person)* Format haben. **2** *vt* einordnen, klassifizieren.

class: ~ **conscious** *adj* klassenbewußt, standesbewußt; ~ **distinction** *n* Klassenunterschied *m*.

classic ['klæsɪk] **1** *adj (lit, fig)* klassisch. **2** *n* Klassiker *m*.

classical ['klæsɪkəl] *adj* klassisch; *education* humanistisch.

classics ['klæsɪks] *n sing (Univ)* Altphilologie *f*.

classification [,klæsɪfɪ'keɪʃən] *n* Klassifizierung *f*.

classified ['klæsɪfaɪd] *adj* in Klassen eingeteilt. ~ **ad(vertisement)** Kleinanzeige *f*; ~ **information** *(Mil)* Verschlußsache *f*; *(Pol)* Geheimsache *f*.

classify ['klæsɪfaɪ] *vt* klassifizieren.

class: ~**less** *adj* klassenlos; ~**room** *n* Klassenzimmer *nt*; ~ **war(fare)** *n* Klassenkrieg *m*.

classy ['klɑːsɪ] *adj (+er) (col)* nobel *(col)*. ~ **woman** Klassefrau *f*.

clatter ['klætə^r] **1** *n* Klappern *nt*. **2** *vi* klappern. **the cart** ~**ed over the cobbles** der Wagen rumpelte über das Pflaster.

clause [klɔːz] *n* **(a)** *(Gram)* Satz *m*. **(b)** *(Jur etc)* Klausel *f*.

claustrophobia [,klɔːstrə'fəʊbɪə] *n* Platzangst *f*.

claustrophobic [,klɔːstrə'fəʊbɪk] *adj* klaustrophob(isch) *(Psych)*. **I get this** ~ **feeling** ich kriege Platzangst *(col)*.

claw [klɔː] **1** *n* Kralle *f*; *(of lions, birds of prey also)* Klaue *f*; *(of lobster etc)* Schere *f*. **to get one's** ~**s into sb** *(col)* jdn in die Krallen bekommen *(col)*. **2** *vt* kratzen. **he** ~**ed back the sheets** er riß die Laken weg. **3** *vi* **to** ~ **at sth** sich an etw *(acc)* krallen.

clay [kleɪ] *n* Lehm *m*. **potter's** ~ Ton *m*.

clay: ~ **pigeon shooting** *n* Tontaubenschießen *nt*; ~ **pipe** *n* Tonpfeife *f*.

clean [kliːn] **1** *adj (+er)* sauber. **to wipe sth** ~ **etw** abreiben; ~ **licence** Führerschein *m* ohne Strafeintrag; **to make a** ~ **start** ganz von vorne anfangen; *(in life)* ein neues Leben anfangen; **to make a** ~ **breast of sth** sich *(dat)* etw von der Seele reden; **to give sb a** ~ **bill of health** *(doctor)* jdm gute Gesundheit bescheinigen; *(authorities)* jdn für unbedenklich erklären.

2 *adv* glatt. **I** ~ **forgot** das habe ich glatt(weg) vergessen *(col)*; **he got** ~ **away** er verschwand spurlos; **I'm** ~ **out of cigarettes** *(col)* meine Zigaretten sind alle *(col)*; **to cut** ~ **through sth** etw ganz durchschneiden/durchschlagen *etc*; **to come** ~ *(col)* auspacken *(col)*.

3 *vt* saubermachen; *carpets, clothes, buildings* reinigen; *window, shoes* putzen; *fish, wound* säubern; *chicken* ausnehmen; *car* waschen. **to** ~ **one's teeth** *(col)* die Zähne putzen.

♦ **clean off** *vt sep (wash)* abwaschen; *(wipe)* abwischen.

♦ **clean out** *vt sep* **(a)** *(lit)* gründlich saubermachen. **(b)** *(col: leave penniless) person* ausnehmen *(with one* Weihnachtsgans) *(col)*.

♦ **clean up 1** *vt sep* saubermachen; *old building, old painting* reinigen. **2** *vi (tidy up)* aufräumen. *(wash)* sich waschen; *(col: make money)* absahnen *(col)*.

cleaner ['kliːnə^r] *n* **(a)** *(person)* Raumpfleger (in *f*) *m*. **a firm of office** ~**s** eine Büroreinigungsfirma. **(b)** *(shop)* ~**'s** Reinigung *f*; **to take sb to the** ~**'s** *(col)* jdn übers Ohr hauen *(col)*. **(c)** *(substance)* Reinigungsmittel *nt*.

cleaning lady ['kliːnɪŋ'leɪdɪ] *n* Raumpflegerin, Putzfrau *(col) f*.

cleanliness ['klenlɪnɪs] *n* Reinlichkeit *f*.

cleanness ['kliːnnɪs] *n* Sauberkeit *f*.

cleanse [klenz] *vt* reinigen; *(spiritually)* läutern *(of von)*.

cleanser ['klenzə^r] *n* Reinigungsmittel *nt*.

clean-shaven ['kliːn'ʃeɪvn] *adj* glattrasiert.

cleansing ['klenzɪŋ] *adj agent* Reinigungs-.

clear [klɪə^r] **1** *adj (+er)* **(a)** klar; *complexion, con-*

science rein; *photograph* scharf. **on a** ~ **day** bei klarem Wetter.

(b) *(distinct, obvious)* klar. **it's still not** ~ **to me why** es ist mir immer noch nicht klar, warum; **to make it** ~ **to sb that ...** es jdm klarmachen, daß ...; **let's get this** ~, **I'm the boss** eins wollen wir mal klarstellen: ich bin hier der Chef; **as** ~ **as day** sonnenklar; **as** ~ **as mud** *(col)* klar wie Kloßbrühe *(col)*.

(c) to be ~ **on sth** über etw *(acc)* im klaren sein; **I'm not** ~ **on the implications** ich bin mir nicht sicher, was das bedeutet.

(d) *road, way* frei. **I want to keep the weekend** ~ ich möchte mir das Wochenende freihalten; **all** ~! *(alles)* frei!; **is it all** ~ **now?** ist alles in Ordnung?; **at last we were** ~ **of London** endlich hatten wir London hinter uns; **the mortars landed well** ~ **of us** die Mörser schlugen ein ganzes Stück neben uns ein; **a** ~ **profit** ein Reingewinn *m*; **three** ~ **days** drei volle Tage; **a** ~ **majority** eine Mehrheit; **to have a** ~ **lead** klar führen.

2 *n* **to be in the** ~ nichts zu verbergen haben; **we're not in the** ~ **yet** *(not out of debt, difficulties)* wir sind noch nicht aus allem heraus; **this puts Harry in the** ~ damit ist Harry entlastet.

3 *adv* **to keep** ~ **of sb/sth** jdm aus dem Wege gehen/etw meiden; **keep** ~ **of the testing area** Versuchsgebiet nicht betreten!; **stand** ~ **of the doors!** bitte von den Türen zurücktreten!

4 *vt* **(a)** *(remove obstacles etc from) pipe* reinigen; *blockage* beseitigen; *road, snow* räumen; *one's conscience* erleichtern. **to** ~ **the table** den Tisch abräumen; **to** ~ **a space for sth** für etw Platz schaffen; **to** ~ **the way for sb/sth** den Weg für jdn/etw freimachen; **to** ~ **the ground for further talks** den Boden für weitere Gespräche bereiten.

(b) *(free from guilt etc, Jur: find innocent) person* freisprechen; *one's/sb's name* reinwaschen.

(c) *(get past or over)* **he** ~**ed the bar** easily er übersprang die Latte mit Leichtigkeit.

(d) *debt* begleichen; *profit* machen.

(e) *(pass, OK)* abfertigen; *ship* klarieren; *expenses, appointment* bestätigen; *goods* zollamtlich abfertigen. **he's been** ~**ed by security** er ist von den Sicherheitsbehörden für unbedenklich erklärt worden; **you'll have to** ~ **that with the boss** das müssen Sie mit dem Chef abklären.

(f) *(Sport)* **to** ~ **the ball** klären.

5 *vi (weather)* aufklaren; *(mist)* sich lichten.

♦ **clear off 1** *vt sep debts* begleichen; *stock* räumen. **2** *vi.(col)* verschwinden *(col)*.

♦ **clear out 1** *vt sep cupboard, room* ausräumen. **2** *vi (col)* verschwinden *(col)*.

♦ **clear up 1** *vt sep* **(a)** *point, matter* klären; *mystery, crime* aufklären. **(b)** *(tidy)* aufräumen. **2** *vi* **(a)** *(weather)* sich aufklären; *(rain)* aufhören. **(b)** *(tidy up)* aufräumen.

clearance ['klɪərəns] *n* **(a)** *(act of clearing)* Beseitigung *f*. **slum** ~ Slumsanierung *f*. **(b)** *(free space)* Spielraum *m*; *(headroom)* lichte Höhe. **(c)** *(by customs)* Abfertigung *f*; *(by security)* Unbedenklichkeitserklärung *f*; *(authorization)* Genehmigung *f*. ~ **for take-off** Startfreigabe *f*. **(d)** *(Sport)* Klärung *f*.

clearance sale *n (Comm)* Räumungsverkauf *m*.

clear-cut ['klɪə'kʌt] *adj* klar.

clearing ['klɪərɪŋ] *n (in forest)* Lichtung *f*.

clearing bank *n* Clearingbank *f*.

clearly ['klɪəlɪ] *adv* **(a)** *(distinctly)* klar. ~ **visible** gut zu sehen; **to stand out** ~ **from the rest** sich deutlich von den anderen abheben. **(b)** *(obviously)* eindeutig. ~ **we cannot allow ...** wir können keinesfalls zulassen, ...

cleavage ['kliːvɪdʒ] *n* **(a)** *(split)* Spalte *f*; *(fig)*

cleaver Kluft f. (b) (of woman's breasts) Dekolleté nt.
cleaver ['kliːvəʳ] n Hackbeil nt.
clef [klef] n (Noten)schlüssel m.
cleft [kleft] adj gespalten. ~ **palate** Gaumenspalte f; **to be in a** ~ **stick** in der Klemme sitzen (col). 2 n Spalte f.
clemency ['klemənsɪ] n (of person) Nachsicht f (towards sb jdm gegenüber); (of weather) Milde f.
clench [klentʃ] vt fist ballen; teeth zusammenbeißen. **to** ~ **sth between one's teeth** etw zwischen die Zähne klemmen; **to** ~ **sth in one's hands** etw mit den Händen umklammern.
clergy ['klɜːdʒɪ] npl Klerus m, Geistlichkeit f.
clergyman ['klɜːdʒɪmən] n, pl **-men** [-mən] Geistlicher m.
clerical ['klerɪkəl] adj (a) (Eccl) geistlich. (b) ~ **staff** Büropersonal nt; ~ **error** Versehen nt.
clerk [klɑːk, (US) klɜːrk] n (a) (Büro)angestellte(r) mf. (b) **C~ of the Court** (Jur) Protokollführer(in f) m. (c) (US: in shop) Verkäufer(in f) m.
clever ['klevəʳ] adj (a) (mentally bright) klug; machine also clever. **to be** ~ **at French** gut in Französisch sein; **how** ~ **of you to remember my birthday!** wie aufmerksam von dir, daß du an meinen Geburtstag gedacht hast! (b) (ingenious, skilful) **to be** ~ **at sth** Geschick zu etw haben, in etw (dat) geschickt sein; **to be** ~ **with one's hands** geschickte Hände haben. (c) (cunning, smart) schlau, clever (col).
cleverly ['klevəlɪ] adv geschickt; (wittily) schlau.
cleverness ['klevənɪs] n see adj (a) Klugheit f. (b) Geschicktheit f. (c) Schläue, Cleverness f.
cliché ['kliːʃeɪ] n Klischee nt.
click [klɪk] 1 n Klicken nt; (of latch, key in lock) Schnappen nt; (of tongue) Schnalzen nt. 2 vi (a) see n klicken; schnappen; schnalzen. (b) (col: be understood) funken (col). **suddenly it all** ~**ed (into place)** plötzlich hatte es gefunkt (col). (c) (col: get on well) **they** ~**ed right from the moment they first met** zwischen ihnen hatte es vom ersten Augenblick an gefunkt (col). 3 vt heels zusammenklappen; fingers schnippen mit; tongue schnalzen mit. **to** ~ **sth into place** etw einschnappen lassen.
client ['klaɪənt] n Kunde m, Kundin f; (of lawyer) Mandant m, Mandantin f.
clientele [ˌkliːɑːnˈtel] n Kundschaft f. **the regular** ~ die Stammkundschaft.
cliff [klɪf] n Klippe f; (inland also) Felsen m. **the** ~**s of Dover** die Felsen von Dover.
cliffhanger ['klɪfˌhæŋə] n Superthriller m (col).
climate ['klaɪmɪt] n (lit, fig) Klima nt. **the two countries have very different** ~**s** die beiden Länder haben (ein) unterschiedliches Klima; **to move to a warmer** ~ in eine wärmere Gegend ziehen; **the** ~ **of popular opinion** das öffentliche Klima.
climax ['klaɪmæks] n (all senses) Höhepunkt m.
climb [klaɪm] 1 vt (a) (also ~ up) klettern auf (+acc); wall also, hill steigen auf (+acc); Everest besteigen; ladder, steps hinaufsteigen; pole, cliffs hochklettern. **my car can't** ~ **that hill** mein Auto schafft den Berg nicht; **to** ~ **a rope** an einem Seil hochklettern. (b) (also ~ over) wall etc steigen or klettern über (+acc). 2 vi klettern; (into train, car etc) steigen; (road) ansteigen; (aircraft) (auf)steigen. 3 n (a) **the long** ~ **up Pitt Street** die lange Kletterei die Pittstraße hinauf; **we're going out for a** ~ wir machen eine Klettertour; **this face is a difficult** ~ diese Steilwand ist schwer zu besteigen. (b) (of aircraft) Steigflug m. **the plane went into a steep** ~ das Flugzeug zog steil nach oben.
♦**climb down** vi (a) (lit) (person) (from tree, wall) herunterklettern; (from horse, mountain) absteigen. (b) (admit error) klein beigeben.
climber ['klaɪməʳ] n (a) (mountaineer) Bergsteiger(in f) m. (b) (socially) Aufsteiger m.

climbing ['klaɪmɪŋ] 1 adj club Berg(steiger)-. ~ **frame** Klettergerüst nt; ~ **plant** Kletterpflanze f. 2 n Bergsteigen nt; (rock ~) Klettern nt. **we did a lot of** ~ wir sind viel geklettert.
clinch [klɪntʃ] 1 vt argument zum Abschluß bringen. **to** ~ **the deal** den Handel perfekt machen; **that** ~**es it** damit ist der Fall erledigt. 2 n (Boxing) Clinch m.
cling [klɪŋ] pret, prep **clung** vi (hold on tightly) sich festklammern (to an +dat); (to opinion also) festhalten (to an +dat); (remain close) sich halten (to an +acc); (clothes, fabric) eng anliegen; (smell) haften (to an +dat). **the boat clung to the shoreline** das Schiff hielt sich dicht an die Küste.
clinging ['klɪŋɪŋ] adj garment enganliegend. **she's the** ~ **sort** sie ist wie eine Klette (col).
clinic ['klɪnɪk] n Klinik f.
clinical ['klɪnɪkəl] adj (a) (Med) klinisch. (b) (fig) nüchtern.
clink[1] [klɪŋk] 1 vt klirren lassen. **to** ~ **glasses with sb** mit jdm anstoßen. 2 vi klirren; (jingle) klimpern. 3 n no pl Klirren nt; Klimpern nt. **the** ~ **of glasses** das Klingen der Gläser.
clink[2] n (col: prison) Knast m (col).
clip[1] [klɪp] 1 n (a) (for holding things) Klammer f. (b) (jewel) Klips m. 2 vt **to** ~ **on** anklemmen; papers anheften.
clip[2] 1 vt scheren; dog trimmen; hedge, fingernails schneiden; wings stutzen; (Brit) ticket entwerten. 2 n (a) see vt Scheren nt; Trimmen nt; Schneiden nt; Stutzen nt. (b) (from film) Ausschnitt m. (c) **to give sb a** ~ **on the ear** jdm eine Ohrfeige geben.
clip: ~**board** n Klemmbrett nt; ~**-on** adj brooch mit Klips; ~**-on earrings** Clips pl.
clipped [klɪpt] adj accent abgehackt.
clipper ['klɪpəʳ] n (Naut) Klipper m.
clippers ['klɪpəz] npl (also **pair of** ~s) Schere f; (for fingernails) Zwicker m.
clipping ['klɪpɪŋ] n (newspaper ~) Ausschnitt m.
clique [kliːk] n Clique f.
cloak [kləʊk] 1 n (lit) Umhang m; (fig: disguise) Deckmantel m; (veil: of secrecy etc) Schleier m. **under the** ~ **of darkness** im Schutz der Dunkelheit. 2 vt (fig) hüllen.
cloak: ~**-and-dagger** adj mysteriös; **a** ~**-and-dagger operation** eine Nacht-und-Nebel-Aktion; ~**room** n (a) (for coats) Garderobe f; (b) (Brit euph) Waschraum m (euph).
clock [klɒk] 1 n (a) Uhr f. **around the** ~ rund um die Uhr; **to work against the** ~ gegen die Uhr arbeiten. (b) (col) (speedometer, milometer) Tacho m (col); (of taxi) Uhr f. **it's got 100 on the** ~ es hat einen Tachostand von 100. 2 vt (Sport) **he's** ~**ed the fastest time this year** er ist die schnellste Zeit dieses Jahres gelaufen/gefahren.
♦**clock in** or on vi (den Arbeitsbeginn) stempeln.
♦**clock off** or out vi (das Arbeitsende) stempeln.
♦**clock up** vt sep (a) (athlete, competitor) time laufen, schwimmen etc. (b) speed, distance zurücklegen. (c) (col) success verbuchen.
clock in cpds Uhr(en)-; ~ **face** n Zifferblatt nt; ~**-radio** n Radiouhr f; ~**wise** adj, adv im Uhrzeigersinn; ~**work 1** n (of clock) Uhrwerk nt; (of toy) Aufziehmechanismus nt, like ~**work** wie am Schnürchen; 2 attr train, car zum Aufziehen.
clod [klɒd] n (of earth) Klumpen m.
clog [klɒg] 1 n (shoe) Holzschuh m. ~**s** (modern) Clogs pl. 2 vt (also ~ **up**) pipe, drain etc verstopfen; mechanism, wheels blockieren. 3 vi (also ~ **up**) (pipe etc) verstopfen; (mechanism etc) blockiert werden.
cloister ['klɔɪstəʳ] n (a) (covered walk) Kreuzgang m. (b) (monastery) Kloster nt.
cloistered ['klɔɪstəd] adj (fig) weltabgeschieden.
clone [kləʊn] n Klon m. 2 vt klonen.
close[1] [kləʊs] 1 adj (+er) (a) (near) in der Nähe (to gen, von); (in time) nahe (bevorstehend); (fig)

friend, co-operation, connection etc eng; relative nahe; resemblance stark; fight, result knapp. **is Glasgow ~ to Edinburgh?** liegt Glasgow in der Nähe von Edinburgh?; in ~ **proximity** in unmittelbarer Nähe (to gen); **it's ~r to what we want** das kommt unseren Vorstellungen näher; **you're very ~** (in guessing etc) du bist dicht dran; ~ **combat** Nahkampf m.
(b) (not spread out) handwriting, print eng; ranks geschlossen.
(c) examination, study eingehend; translation originalgetreu. **to keep a ~ watch on sb** jdn scharf bewachen; **now pay ~ attention to me** jetzt hör mir gut zu!
(d) (stuffy) schwül; (inside) stickig.
(e) ~ **on** nahezu; ~ **on sixty/midnight** an die sechzig/kurz vor Mitternacht.
2 adv (+er) nahe; (spatially also) dicht. ~ **by** in der Nähe; **stay ~ to me** bleib dicht bei mir; ~ **to the water/ground** nahe or dicht am Wasser/Boden; **to be ~ to tears** den Tränen nahe sein.

close² [kləʊz] **1** vt **(a)** schließen, zumachen; (col) factory stillegen. **to ~ one's eyes/ears to sth** sich einer Sache gegenüber blind/taub stellen. **(b)** (bring to an end) meeting schließen, beenden; bank account etc auflösen. **2** vi (shut, come together) sich schließen; (door, box, lid also) zugehen; (shop, factory) schließen; (come to an end) schließen; (tourist season) zu Ende gehen. **3** n Ende nt. **to come to a ~** zu Ende gehen; **to bring sth to a ~** etw beenden.

♦**close down 1** vi **(a)** (business, shop etc) schließen, zumachen (col); (factory: permanently) stillgelegt werden. **(b)** (Rad, TV) das Programm beenden. **2** vt sep shop etc schließen; factory (permanently) stillegen.

♦**close in** vi (night, darkness) hereinbrechen; (days) kürzer werden; (enemy etc) bedrohlich nahekommen. **the police are closing ~ on him** die Polizei zieht das Netz um ihn zu.

♦**close off** vt sep (ab)sperren; (separate off) abteilen.

♦**close up 1** vi **(a)** (line of people) zusammenrücken. **(b)** (lock up) ab- or zuschließen. **2** vt sep **(a)** shop zumachen; house verschließen. **(b)** (block up) hole zumachen.

closed-circuit television ['kləʊz,sɜːkɪt-'telɪ,vɪʒən] n interne Fernsehanlage; (for supervision) Fernsehüberwachungsanlage f.

close-down ['kləʊzdaʊn] n **(a)** (of shop, business etc) (Geschäfts)schließung f; (of factory) Stillegung f. **(b)** (Rad, TV) Sendeschluß m.

closed shop ['kləʊzd'ʃɒp] n Closed Shop m. **we have a ~** wir haben Gewerkschaftszwang.

closely ['kləʊslɪ] adv eng, dicht; work, connect eng; related nah(e); follow (in time) dicht; (attentively) watch, listen etc genau; guard scharf, streng.

closeness ['kləʊsnɪs] n (nearness, in time) Nähe f; (fig) (of friendship) Innigkeit f; (of examination, interrogation) Genauigkeit f; (of translation) Texttreue f; (of air, atmosphere) Schwüle f; (indoors) stickige Luft.

closet ['klɒzɪt] (vb: pret, ptp ~ed ['klɒzɪtɪd]) **1** n Wandschrank m. **to come out of the ~** (fig col) sich als Homosexueller bekennen. **2** vt **to be ~ed** hinter verschlossenen Türen sitzen (with sb mit jdm).

close-up ['kləʊsʌp] n Nahaufnahme f. **in ~** in Nahaufnahme; (of face) in Großaufnahme.

closing ['kləʊzɪŋ] adj remarks abschließend. ~ **time** Ladenschluß m; (Brit: in pub) Polizeistunde f; ~ **prices** (St Ex) Schlußnotierungen pl.

closure ['kləʊʒə'] n **(a)** Schließung f; (of road) Sperrung f; (of factory, mine etc also) Stillegung f. **(b)** (object, stopper) Verschluß m.

clot [klɒt] **1** n **(a)** (of blood) (Blut)gerinnsel nt. **(b)** (col: person) Trottel m. **2** vi (blood, milk) gerinnen.

cloth [klɒθ] n Tuch nt; (for cleaning) Lappen m;

(table~) Tischdecke f. **a gentleman of the ~** ein geistlicher Herr.

clothe [kləʊð] pret, ptp **clad** (old) or ~**d** vt (usu pass: dress) kleiden.

clothes [kləʊðz] npl (garments) Kleider pl; (clothing, outfit also) Kleidung f no pl. **to put on/take off one's ~** sich anziehen/ausziehen.

clothes: ~ **hanger** n Kleiderbügel m; ~ **horse** n Wäscheständer m; ~**line** n Wäscheleine f; ~ **peg** (Brit), ~ **pin** (US) n Wäscheklammer f; ~ **shop** n Bekleidungsgeschäft nt.

clothing ['kləʊðɪŋ] n Kleidung f.

cloud [klaʊd] **1** n Wolke f. **to have one's head in the ~s** in höheren Regionen schweben; **to be on ~ nine** (col) im siebten Himmel sein (col); ~ **of dust/smoke** Staub-/Rauchwolke f; **he's been under a ~ for weeks** (under suspicion) seit Wochen haftet ein Verdacht an ihm; (in disgrace) er ist seit Wochen in einem schlechten Ruf. **2** vt **(a)** (lit) sky, view verhängen (geh); mirror trüben. **a ~ed sky** ein bewölkter Himmel. **(b)** (fig) prospect, sb's enjoyment, mind, judgement etc trüben; friendship, sb's future überschatten. **to ~ the issue** (complicate) die Dinge unnötig kompliziert machen.

♦**cloud over** vi (sky) sich bewölken; (mirror etc) sich beschlagen.

cloud: ~**burst** n Wolkenbruch m; ~**-cuckoo-land** n Wolkenkuckucksheim nt.

cloudless ['klaʊdlɪs] adj sky wolkenlos.

cloudy ['klaʊdɪ] adj (+er) sky bewölkt; liquid trüb.

clout [klaʊt] **1** n **(a)** (col: blow) Schlag m. **(b)** influence Schlagkraft f. **2** vt (col) hauen (col). **to ~ sb one** jdm eine runterhauen (col).

clove [kləʊv] n **(a)** Gewürznelke f. **(b)** ~ **of garlic** Knoblauchzehe f.

clover ['kləʊvə'] n Klee m. ~ **leaf** (Bot, Mot) Kleeblatt nt.

clown [klaʊn] n **1** n Clown m; (pej) Trottel m. **to act the ~** den Hanswurst spielen. **2** vi (also ~ **about** or **around**) herumblödeln (col).

club [klʌb] **1** n **(a)** (weapon) Knüppel m; (golf~) Golfschläger m. **(b)** (Cards); ~**s** pl Kreuz nt; (Bridge) Treff nt. **nine of ~s** (die) Kreuz-/Treff-Neun. **(c)** (society) Klub, Verein m. **to be in the ~** (col) ein Kind kriegen (col). **2** vt einknüppeln auf (+acc).

♦**club together** vi zusammenlegen.

clubhouse ['klʌb,haʊs] n Klubhaus nt.

cluck [klʌk] vi (hen) glucken.

clue [kluː] n Anhaltspunkt m; (in crosswords) Frage f. **I'll give you a ~** ich gebe dir einen Tip; **I haven't a ~!** (ich hab') keine Ahnung!

clued-up [,kluːd'ʌp] adj (col) im Bilde; (about subject) vertraut (about mit).

clueless ['kluːlɪs] adj (col) unbedarft (col).

clump [klʌmp] n (of trees, flowers etc) Gruppe f; (of earth) Klumpen m. **2** vi **to ~ about** herumtrampeln.

clumsy ['klʌmzɪ] adj (+er) **(a)** ungeschickt. **(b)** (unwieldy) plump; tool unhandlich; (ungainly) schwerfällig.

clung [klʌŋ] pret, ptp of **cling.**

cluster ['klʌstə'] n (of trees, flowers, houses) Gruppe f; (of grapes) Traube f.

♦**cluster around** vi +prep obj sich scharen (um +acc).

clutch [klʌtʃ] n **(a)** (Aut) Kupplung f. **to let in/out the ~** ein-/auskuppeln. **(b)** (fig) **to fall into sb's ~es** jdm in die Hände fallen. **2** vt umklammern.

♦**clutch at** vi +prep obj (lit) schnappen nach (+dat); (fig) sich klammern an (+acc).

clutter ['klʌtə'] **1** n (confusion) Durcheinander nt; (disorderly articles) Kram m (col). **2** vt (also ~ **up**) cupboard vollstopfen. **to be ~ed up with sth** mit etw vollgestopft sein; (floor, desk etc) mit etw übersät sein.

CND = Campaign for Nuclear Disarma-

ment.
Co = (a) **company** KG f. (b) **county.**
c/o = **care of** bei, c/o.
co- [kəu-] pref Mit-, mit-.
coach [kəutʃ] **1** n (a) (horsedrawn) Kutsche f; (state ~) (Staats)karosse f; (Rail) (Eisenbahn)wagen m; (motor ~) (Reise)bus m. (b) (tutor) Nachhilfelehrer(in f) m; (Sport) Trainer m. **2** vt (a) (Sport) trainieren. (b) to ~ sb for an exam jdn aufs Examen vorbereiten.
coagulate [kəu'ægjuleɪt] **1** vi gerinnen. **2** vt gerinnen lassen.
coal [kəul] n Kohle f. **to carry** ~s **to Newcastle** (Prov) Eulen nach Athen tragen (Prov).
coal in cpds Kohlen-; ~ **black** adj kohlrabenschwarz; ~-**cellar** n Kohlenkeller m; ~-**face** n: **to work at the** ~-**face** vor Ort arbeiten; ~**field** n Kohlenrevier nt; ~ **fire** n Kamin m.
coalition [,kəuə'lɪʃən] n Koalition f.
coal: ~**man** n Kohlenauslieferer m; ~-**mine** n Grube, Zeche f; ~-**miner** n Bergmann, Kumpel (col) m; ~-**mining** n Kohle(n)bergbau m; ~ **scuttle** n Kohleneimer m; ~**shed** n Kohlenschuppen m.
coarse [kɔ:s] adj (+er) (a) (in texture) grob. (b) (uncouth) gewöhnlich; person, manners ungehobelt; joke, language derb.
coarsen ['kɔ:sn] **1** vt derb(er) machen; skin gerben. **2** vi (person) derb(er) werden.
coast [kəust] **1** n Küste f. **at/on the** ~ an der Küste; **the** ~ **is clear** (fig) die Luft ist rein. **2** vi (car, cyclist) (in neutral) im Leerlauf fahren; (cruise effortlessly) dahinrollen.
coastal [kəustəl] adj Küsten-.
coaster ['kəustər] n (a) (Naut) Küstenmotorschiff nt. (b) (drip mat) Untersetzer m.
coast: ~**guard** n Küstenwache f; ~**line** n Küste f.
coat [kəut] **1** n (a) Mantel m; (doctor's ~ etc also) (Arzt)kittel m; (jacket of suit etc) Jacke f. (b) (Her) ~ **of arms** Wappen nt. (c) (of animal) Fell nt. (d) (of paint) Anstrich m. **2** vt (with paint etc) streichen; (with chocolate, icing etc) überziehen. ~**ed tongue** belegte Zunge.
coat-hanger ['kəut,hæŋər] n Kleiderbügel m.
coating ['kəutɪŋ] n Überzug m; (of paint) Anstrich m.
co-author ['kəu,ɔ:θər] n Mitverfasser m.
coax [kəuks] vt: **to** ~ **sb into doing sth** jdn dazu bringen, etw zu tun; **to** ~ **sth out of sb** jdm etw entlocken.
cobalt ['kəubɒlt] n Kobalt nt.
cobble ['kɒbl] **1** n (also ~**stone**) Kopfstein m. **2** vt **a** ~**d street** eine Straße mit Kopfsteinpflaster.
♦cobble together vt sep (col) essay etc zusammenschustern.
cobbler ['kɒblər] n Schuster m.
cobra ['kəubrə] n Kobra f.
cobweb ['kɒbweb] n Spinn(en)webe f.
cocaine [kə'keɪn] n Kokain nt.
cock [kɒk] **1** n (a) (rooster) Hahn m. (b) (male bird) Männchen m. (c) (tap) (Wasser)hahn m. **fuel** ~ Treibstoffhahn m. (d) (col!: penis) Schwanz m (col!). **2** vt ears spitzen; gun entsichern. **the parrot** ~**ed its head on one side** der Papagei legte seinen Kopf schief.
cock: ~-**a-doodle-doo** interj Kikeriki; ~-**a-hoop** adj ganz aus dem Häuschen; ~-**and-bull** adj: ~-**and-bull story** Lügengeschichte f.
cockatoo [,kɒkə'tu:] n Kakadu m.
cockchafer ['kɒk,tʃeɪfər] n Maikäfer m.
cockerel ['kɒkərəl] n junger Hahn.
cock-eyed [,kɒk'aɪd] adj (col) (a) (crooked) schief. (b) (absurd) verrückt.
cockle ['kɒkl] n (shellfish) Herzmuschel f.
cockney ['kɒknɪ] n Cockney nt; (person) Cockney m.
cockpit ['kɒkpɪt] n (Aviat, Naut, of racing car) Cockpit nt.

cockroach ['kɒkrəutʃ] n Küchenschabe f.
cocksure ['kɒk'ʃuər] adj fest überzeugt.
cocktail ['kɒkteɪl] n (a) Cocktail m. (b) **fruit** ~ Obstsalat m.
cocktail in cpds Cocktail-; ~ **bar** n Cocktail-Bar f; ~ **cabinet** n Hausbar f.
cock-up ['kɒkʌp] n (Brit col!) **to make a** ~ **of sth** bei etw Scheiße bauen (col!).
cocky ['kɒkɪ] adj (+er) (col) großspurig.
cocoa ['kəukəu] n Kakao m.
coconut ['kəukənʌt] **1** n Kokosnuß f. **2** attr Kokos-. ~ **matting** Kokosmatte f; ~ **palm**, ~ **tree** Kokospalme f.
cocoon [kə'ku:n] **1** n Kokon m; (fig: of scarves, blankets etc) Hülle f. **2** vt einhüllen.
COD = **cash** (Brit) or **collect** (US) **on delivery** per Nachnahme.
cod [kɒd] n Kabeljau m.
coddle ['kɒdl] vt child verhätscheln.
code [kəud] n (a) (cipher) Kode, Code m. **in** ~ verschlüsselt; **to put into** ~ verschlüsseln; ~-**name** Deckname m; ~-**number** Kennziffer f. (b) (rules) ~ **of honour/behaviour** Ehren-/Sittenkodex m. (c) post (Brit) or zip (US) ~ Postleitzahl f.
codeine [kəudi:n] n Kodein nt.
codger ['kɒdʒər] n (col): **old** ~ alter Kauz.
cod-liver-oil ['kɒdlɪvər'ɔɪl] n Lebertran m.
co-driver ['kəudraɪvər] n Beifahrer m.
co-ed, coed ['kəu'ed] n (col) (Brit: school) gemischte Schule; (US: girl student) Schülerin f einer gemischten Schule.
coeducation ['kəu,edju'keɪʃən] n Koedukation f.
coerce [kəu'ɜ:s] vt zwingen. **to** ~ **sb into doing sth** jdn zwingen, etw zu tun.
coercion [kəu'ɜ:ʃən] n Zwang m; (Jur) Nötigung f.
coexist [,kəuɪg'zɪst] vi nebeneinander bestehen.
coexistence [,kəuɪg'zɪstəns] n Koexistenz f.
C of E = **Church of England.**
coffee ['kɒfɪ] n Kaffee m. **two** ~**s, please** zwei Kaffee, bitte.
coffee in cpds Kaffee-; ~ **bar** n (Brit) Café nt; ~ **break** n Kaffeepause f; ~ **pot** n Kaffeekanne f; ~ **table** n Couchtisch m.
coffin ['kɒfɪn] n Sarg m.
cog [kɒg] n Zahn m; (~**wheel**) Zahnrad m. **he's only a** ~ **in the wheel** (fig) er ist nur ein Rädchen im Getriebe.
cogent ['kəudʒənt] adj argument, reason zwingend; reasoning überzeugend.
cogitate ['kɒdʒɪteɪt] vi nachsinnen.
cognac ['kɒnjæk] n Kognak m; (French) Cognac m.
cognate ['kɒgneɪt] adj verwandt.
cohabit [kəu'hæbɪt] vi (esp Jur) in eheähnlicher Gemeinschaft leben.
coherence [kəu'hɪərəns] n (a) (lit) Kohärenz f. (b) (of community) Zusammenhalt m; (of essay, symphony etc) Geschlossenheit f. **his speech lacked** ~ seiner Rede (dat) fehlte der Zusammenhang.
coherent [kəu'hɪərənt] adj (a) (comprehensible) verständlich. (b) (cohesive) zusammenhängend; logic, reasoning etc schlüssig.
cohesive [kəu'hi:sɪv] adj (fig) geschlossen.
coil [kɔɪl] **1** n (a) (of rope, wire etc) Rolle f; (on loop) Windung; f (of smoke) Kringel m. ~ **spring** Sprungfeder f. (b) (Elec) Spule f. (c) (contraceptive) Spirale f. **2** vt (also ~ **up**) aufwickeln. **to** ~ **sth around sth** etw um etw wickeln; **the python** ~**ed itself up** die Pythonschlange rollte sich zusammen. **3** vi sich ringeln; (river) sich schlängeln.
coin [kɔɪn] n Münze f. ~-**box** (telephone) Münzfernsprecher m; ~-**operated** Münz-; **the other side of the** ~ (fig) die Kehrseite der Medaille. **2** vt money, phrase prägen. ..., **to** ~ **a phrase** ..., um es mal so auszudrücken.
coincide [,kəuɪn'saɪd] vi (in time, place) zusammenfallen; (in area) sich decken; (agree)

übereinstimmen.
coincidence [kəʊ'ɪnsɪdəns] n Zufall m.
coke [kəʊk] n Koks m.
Coke ® [kəʊk] n (col) Cola f, Coke ® nt.
colander ['kʌləndəʳ] n Durchschlag m, Sieb nt.
cold [kəʊld] **1** adj (+er) kalt (also fig); reception, personality kühl. **I am** ~ ich friere; **my hands are** ~/**are getting** ~ ich habe/bekomme kalte Hände; **to be** ~ **to sb** jdn kühl behandeln; **that leaves me** ~ das läßt mich kalt; **to be out** ~ bewußtlos sein; (knocked out) k.o. sein; **in** ~ **blood** kaltblütig; **to have** ~ **feet** (fig col) kalte Füße gekriegt haben (col); **to give sb the** ~ **shoulder** (col) jdm die kalte Schulter zeigen. **2** n **(a)** Kälte f. **to feel the** ~ kälteempfindlich sein; **to be left out in the** ~ (fig) ausgeschlossen werden. **(b)** (Med) Erkältung f; (runny nose) Schnupfen m. **to have a** ~ erkältet sein; **to get** or **catch a** ~ sich erkälten.
cold: ~-**blooded** adj (Zool, fig) kaltblütig; ~ **cream** n Cold Cream f or nt, Feuchtigkeitscreme f; ~-**hearted** adj kaltherzig.
coldly ['kəʊldlɪ] adv (lit, fig) kalt; answer, receive betont kühl.
cold: ~-**shoulder** vt (col) links liegenlassen (col); ~ **storage** n to put sth into ~ **storage** (lit) food etw kühl lagern; (fig) idea, plan etw auf Eis legen.
coleslaw ['kəʊlslɔː] n Krautsalat m.
collaborate [kə'læbəreɪt] vi **(a)** zusammenarbeiten. **(b)** (with enemy) kollaborieren.
collaboration [kə,læbə'reɪʃən] n **(a)** Zusammenarbeit f; (of one party) Mitarbeit f. **(b)** (with enemy) Kollaboration f.
collaborator [kə'læbəreɪtəʳ] n **(a)** Mitarbeiter(in f) m. **(b)** (with enemy) Kollaborateur(in f) m.
collapse [kə'læps] **1** vi (lit, fig) zusammenbrechen; (building, wall, roof) einstürzen; (negotiations) scheitern. **they all** ~**d with laughter** sie konnten sich alle vor Lachen nicht mehr halten; **his whole world** ~**d about him** für ihn brach eine Welt zusammen. **2** n Zusammenbruch m; (heart attack) Kollaps m; (of building etc) Einsturz m; (of negotiations) Scheitern nt.
collapsible [kə'læpsəbl] adj bicycle, chair zusammenklappbar, Klapp-.
collar ['kɒləʳ] **1** n Kragen m; (for dogs) Halsband nt; (Mech: on pipe etc) Bund m. ~**bone** n Schlüsselbein nt. **2** vt (capture) fassen.
collate [kɒ'leɪt] vt vergleichen.
collateral [kɒ'lætərəl] n (Fin) (zusätzliche) Sicherheit.
colleague ['kɒliːg] n Kollege m, Kollegin f.
collect ['kɒlekt] **1** vt **(a)** stamps etc, one's thoughts, money, facts sammeln; (accumulate) ansammeln; (furniture) dust etc anziehen; empty glasses, tickets etc einsammeln; litter aufsammeln; belongings zusammenpacken; taxes einziehen; rent, fares kassieren. **(b)** (pick up, fetch) abholen (from bei). **2** vi (gather) sich ansammeln; (dust) sich absetzen; (~ money) kassieren; (for charity) sammeln. **3** adj (esp US) ~ **call** R-Gespräch nt. **4** adv (esp US) **to call** ~ ein R-Gespräch führen.
collected [kə'lektɪd] adj **(a)** the ~ **works of Oscar Wilde** Oscar Wildes gesammelte Werke. **(b)** (calm) ruhig, gelassen.
collection [kə'lekʃən] n **(a)** (group of people, objects) Ansammlung f; (of stamps, coins etc) Sammlung f. **(b)** (collecting) (of facts, information) Zusammentragen nt; (of goods) Abholung f; (from letterbox) Leerung nt; (of stamps, coins) Sammeln nt; (of money, jumble for charity) Sammlung f; (in church) Kollekte f; (of rent, fares) Kassieren nt; (of taxes) Einzug m. **(c)** (Fashion) Kollektion f.
collective [kə'lektɪv] **1** adj kollektiv, Kollektiv-. ~ **bargaining** Tarifverhandlungen pl. **2** n Kollektiv nt.
collector [kə'lektəʳ] n **(a)** (of taxes) Einnehmer(in f) m; (of rent, cash) Kassierer(in f) m; (ticket ~)

Fahrkartenkontrolleur m. **(b)** (of stamps, coins etc) Sammler(in f) m. ~'**s item** Sammler-; price Liebhaber-.
college ['kɒlɪdʒ] n **(a)** (Univ) College nt. **to go to** ~ (university) studieren. **(b)** (of music, technology) Fachhochschule f. ~ **of Art** Kunstakademie f.
collide [kə'laɪd] vt zusammenstoßen.
collie ['kɒlɪ] n Collie m.
colliery ['kɒlɪərɪ] n Grube, Zeche f.
collision [kə'lɪʒən] n (lit) Zusammenstoß m; (fig) Konflikt m, Kollision f. **on a** ~ **course** (lit, fig) auf Kollisionskurs.
colloquial [kə'ləʊkwɪəl] adj umgangssprachlich.
collusion [kə'luːʒən] n (geheime) Absprache.
Cologne [kə'ləʊn] n Köln nt.
cologne [kə'ləʊn] n Kölnisch Wasser nt.
colon[1] ['kəʊlən] n (Anat) Dickdarm m.
colon[2] n (Gram) Doppelpunkt m.
colonel ['kɜːnl] n Oberst m.
colonial [kə'ləʊnɪəl] **1** adj Kolonial-, kolonial. **2** n Bewohner(in f) m einer Kolonie/der Kolonien.
colonialism [kə'ləʊnɪəlɪzəm] n Kolonialismus m.
colonist ['kɒlənɪst] n Siedler(in f) m.
colonize ['kɒlənaɪz] vt kolonisieren.
colony ['kɒlənɪ] n (also Zool) Kolonie f; (of ants, bees) Staat m.
color etc (US) = **colour** etc.
Colorado beetle [,kɒlə'rɑːdəʊ'biːtl] n Kartoffelkäfer m.
colossal [kə'lɒsl] adj riesig; prices, mistake gewaltig.
colour, (US) **color** ['kʌləʳ] **1** n **(a)** (lit, fig) Farbe f. **what** ~ **is it?** welche Farbe hat es?; **let's see the** ~ **of your money first** (col) zeig erst mal dein Geld her (col). **(b)** (complexion) (Gesichts)farbe f. **to get one's** ~ **back** wieder Farbe bekommen. **(c)** (racial) Hautfarbe f. **(d)** (flag) ~**s** Fahne f; **to nail one's** ~**s to the mast** (fig) Farbe bekennen; **to show one's true** ~**s** (fig) sein wahres Gesicht zeigen. **2** vt **(a)** (lit) anmalen. **(b)** (fig) beeinflussen; (bias) färben. **3** vi **(a)** (leaves) sich (ver)färben. **(b)** (person: also ~ **up**) rot werden.
♦ **colour in** vt sep anmalen; (Art) kolorieren.
colour in cpds Farb-; (racial) Rassen-; (Mil) Fahnen-. ~-**bar** n Rassenschranke f; ~-**blind** adj farbenblind.
coloured, (US) **colored** ['kʌləd] **1** adj **(a)** bunt. **(b)** (fig: biased) gefärbt. **(c)** person, race farbig. **2** n Farbige(r) mf.
-**coloured,** (US) -**colored** adj suf straw-/dark-~ strohfarben/dunkel.
colourful, (US) **colorful** ['kʌləfʊl] adj **(a)** (lit) bunt. **(b)** account etc anschaulich; life bewegt; personality schillernd.
colouring, (US) **coloring** ['kʌlərɪŋ] n (complexion) Gesichtsfarbe f; (substance) Farbstoff m; (coloration) Farben pl. ~ **book** Malbuch nt.
colourless, (US) **colorless** ['kʌlələs] adj (lit, fig) farblos.
colour: ~ **photograph** n Farbfoto nt; ~ **scheme** n Farbzusammenstellung f; ~ **supplement** n (Press) Farbbeilage; ~ **television** n Farbfernsehen nt; (set) Farbfernseher m.
colt [kəʊlt] n Fohlen nt.
column ['kɒləm] n **(a)** (Archit, of smoke) Säule f. **(b)** (division of page) Spalte; (article in newspaper) Kolumne f.
columnist ['kɒləmnɪst] n Kolumnist(in f) m.
coma ['kəʊmə] n Koma nt. **to go into a** ~ ins Koma fallen; **to be in a** ~ im Koma liegen.
comatose ['kəʊmətəʊs] adj im Koma.
comb [kəʊm] **1** n Kamm m. **2** vt (a) kämmen. **to** ~ **one's hair** sich (dat) die Haare kämmen. **(b)** (search) durchkämmen.
combat ['kɒmbæt] **1** n Kampf m. **2** vt (lit, fig) bekämpfen.
combatant ['kɒmbətənt] n (lit, fig)) Kämpfer m.
combination [,kɒmbɪ'neɪʃən] n **(a)** Kombination f;

(*combining: of organizations, people etc*) Zusammenschluß *m*; (*of events*) Verkettung *f*. in ~ zusammen. (**b**) (*for lock*) Kombination *f*. ~ **lock** Kombinationsschloß *nt*.

combine [kəm'baɪn] **1** *vt* verbinden, kombinieren. **2** *vi* sich zusammenschließen; (*Chem*) sich verbinden. **3** ['kɒmbaɪn] *n* (**a**) Konzern *m*; (*in socialist countries*) Kombinat *nt*. (**b**) (*also* ~ **harvester**) Mähdrescher *m*.

combined [kəm'baɪnd] *adj* gemeinsam; *talents, efforts* vereint. ~ **with** in Kombination mit; (*esp clothes, furniture*) kombiniert mit.

combustible [kəm'bʌstɪbl] *adj* brennbar.

combustion [kəm'bʌstʃən] *n* Verbrennung *f*. ~ **chamber** Verbrennungsraum *m*.

come [kʌm] *pret* **came**, *ptp* ~ **1** *vi* (**a**) kommen. ~ **and see me soon** besuchen Sie mich bald einmal; **he has** ~ **a long way** er kommt von weit her; (*fig*) er ist weit gekommen; **the project has** ~ **a long way** das Projekt ist schon ziemlich weit; **he came running/hurrying into the room** er kam ins Zimmer gerannt/er eilte ins Zimmer; **coming!** ich komme; ~ ~**!**, ~ **now!** (*fig*) komm, komm; **Christmas is coming** bald ist Weihnachten; **they came to a town/castle** sie kamen in eine Stadt/an ein Schloß; **it came into my head that** ... ich habe mir gedacht, daß ...; **May** ~**s before June** Mai kommt vor Juni; **it came as a shock to me** es war ein Schock für mich; ~ **what may** ganz gleich, was geschieht; **you could see it coming** das war ja zu erwarten; **she had it coming to her** (*col*) das mußte so kommen; **people were coming and going all day** es war den ganzen Tag ein Kommen und Gehen; **to** ~ **for sb** (*collect*) jdn abholen; **we'll** ~ **after you** wir kommen nach; **he came third in the race** er wurde Dritter in dem Rennen; **it all came right in the end** am Ende ergab sich alles; **how** ~**?** (*col*) wieso?

(**b**) (*be, become*) werden. **his dreams came true** seine Träume wurden wahr; **no good will** ~ **of it** das wird nicht gut ausgehen; **nothing came of it** es wurde nichts daraus; **that's what** ~**s of being careless** das kommt davon, wenn man unvorsichtig ist; **the handle has** ~ **loose** der Griff hat sich gelockert.

(**c**) (*Comm: be available*) erhältlich sein. **milk now** ~**s in plastic bottles** es gibt jetzt Milch in Plastikflaschen.

(**d**) **I have** ~ **to believe him** mittlerweile glaube ich ihm; **I'm sure you will** ~ **to agree with me** ich bin sicher, daß du mir schließlich zustimmst; (*now I*) ~ **to think of it** wenn ich es mir recht überlege; **the years/weeks to** ~ die kommenden Jahre/Wochen; **the life to** ~ das ewige Leben.

(**e**) (*col uses*) ~ **next week** nächste Woche; **I've known him for three years** ~ **January** im Januar kenne ich ihn drei Jahre; ~ **again?** wie bitte?; **she is as vain as they** ~ sie ist so eingebildet wie nur was (*col*).

2 *vt* **don't** ~ **the innocent with me** (*col*) komm mir bloß nicht auf die unschuldige Tour (*col*)!

♦ **come about** *vi impers* (*happen*) passieren.

♦ **come across 1** *vi* (**a**) (*cross*) herüberkommen. (**b**) (*be understood*) verstanden werden; (*message, speech*) ankommen. (**c**) (*make an impression*) wirken. **2** *vi* +*prep obj* (*find*) finden. **if you** ~ ~ **my watch** wenn du zufällig meine Uhr siehst.

♦ **come along** *vi* (**a**) ~ ~**!** (nun) komm doch! (**b**) (*accompany*) mitkommen. (**c**) (*progress*) to be coming ~ sich machen; **my play isn't coming** ~ **at all well** mein Stück macht überhaupt keine Fortschritte; **how's the thesis coming** ~**?** was macht die Doktorarbeit?

♦ **come apart** *vi* auseinandergehen; (*to be able to be taken apart*) zerlegbar sein.

♦ **come around** *vi* (**a**) (*call round*) vorbei-

kommen. (**b**) (*recur*) **Christmas has** ~ ~ **again** nun ist wieder Weihnachten. (**c**) (*change one's opinions*) es sich (*dat*) anders überlegen. **eventually he came** ~ **to our way of thinking** schließlich schloß er sich unserer Auffassung an. (**d**) (*regain consciousness*) wieder zu sich (*dat*) kommen.

♦ **come away** *vi* (**a**) (*leave*) (weg)gehen. ~ ~ **from there!** komm da weg! (**b**) (*become detached*) abgehen.

♦ **come back** *vi* (**a**) zurückkommen. **can I** ~ ~ **to you on that one?** kann ich später darauf zurückkommen? (**b**) (*return to one's memory*) **ah yes, it's all coming** ~ ach ja, jetzt fällt mir alles wieder ein; **your German will very quickly** ~ ~ du wirst ganz schnell wieder ins Deutsche reinkommen (*col*).

♦ **come by** *vi* (**a**) +*prep obj* kommen zu; **idea** kommen auf (+*acc*). **2** *vi* (*visit*) vorbeikommen.

♦ **come down** *vi* (**a**) (*from ladder, stairs*) herunterkommen. (**b**) (*be demolished: building etc*) abgerissen werden; (*fall down*) herunterfallen. (**c**) (*drop: prices*) sinken; (*seller*) heruntergehen (*to auf* +*acc*). (**d**) (*be a question of*) ankommen (*to auf* +*acc*). **it all** ~**s to something very simple** das ist im Grunde ganz einfach. (**e**) (*lose social rank*) sinken. **you've** ~ ~ **in the world** du bist aber ganz schön tief gesunken.

♦ **come down on** *vi* +*prep obj* (*rebuke*) zusammenstauchen (*col*).

♦ **come down with** *vi* +*prep obj* **illness** bekommen.

♦ **come forward** *vi* (**a**) sich melden. (**b**) **to** ~ ~ **with help/money** Hilfe/Geld anbieten.

♦ **come in** *vi* (**a**) hereinkommen. ~ ~**!** herein! (**b**) (*arrive*) ankommen; (*train*) einfahren; (*ship*) einlaufen. (**c**) (*be received as income*) **he has £10,000 coming** ~ **every year** er hat £ 10.000 im Jahr. (**d**) (*have a part to play*) **where do I** ~ ~**?** welche Rolle spiele ich dabei?; **that will** ~ ~ **useful** das kann ich/man gut gebrauchen.

♦ **come in for** *vi* +*prep obj* **attention, admiration** erregen; **criticism etc** einstecken müssen.

♦ **come into** *vi* +*prep obj* (**a**) **legacy etc** (*inherit*) erben. **to** ~ ~ **one's own** zeigen, was in einem steckt. (**b**) (*be involved*) **I don't see where I** ~ ~ **all this** ich verstehe nicht, was ich mit der ganzen Sache zu tun habe; **money doesn't** ~ ~ **it** das hat nichts mit Geld zu tun.

♦ **come off 1** *vi* (**a**) (*off bicycle etc*) herunterfallen. (**b**) (*button, handle, paint etc*) abgehen; (*stains, marks*) weggehen. (**c**) (*take place*) **her wedding didn't** ~ ~ **after all** aus ihrer Hochzeit ist nun doch nichts geworden. (**d**) (*col: succeed*) klappen (*col*). (**e**) (*acquit oneself*) abschneiden. **2** *vi* +*prep obj* (**a**) **bicycle, horse etc** fallen von. (**b**) (*button, paint, stain*) abgehen von. (**c**) (*col*) ~ ~ **it!** nun mach mal halblang! (*col*).

♦ **come on 1** *vi* (**a**) (*follow*) nachkommen. (**b**) ~ ~**! komm!; ~ on!** komm schon! (**c**) (*continue to advance*) zukommen (*towards auf* +*acc*). (**d**) (*start*) (*night*) hereinbrechen; (*storm*) einsetzen. **I feel a cold coming** ~ ich spüre die ersten Anzeichen einer Erkältung. (**e**) (*actor*) auftreten. (**f**) (*col*) **to** ~ ~ **strong** groß auftreten (*col*). (**g**) = ~ **along** (*q.v.*).

♦ **come out** *vi* (**a**) herauskommen; (*book, magazine also*) erscheinen; (*new product*) auf den Markt kommen; (*film*) (in den Kinos) anlaufen. (**b**) (*exam results, news also*) bekannt werden. (**b**) (*Ind*) **to** ~ ~ **on strike** in den Streik treten. (**c**) (*Phot: film, photograph*) let's hope the photos ~ ~ hoffentlich sind die Bilder etwas geworden. (**d**) (*stains, dye etc*) herausgehen. (**e**) **he came** ~ **in a rash** er bekam einen Ausschlag; **to** ~ ~ **against/in favour of sth** sich gegen/für etw aussprechen; **to** ~ ~ **of sth badly/well** bei etw schlecht/nicht schlecht wegkommen.

♦ **come out with** vi +prep obj truth, facts herausrücken mit; (col) remarks, nonsense von sich geben.

♦ **come over 1** vi herüberkommen. he came ~ to England er kam nach England; he came ~ to our side er trat auf unsere Seite über; she came ~ giddy (col) ihr wurde schwindelig; it came ~ cloudy es bewölkte sich. **2** vi +prep obj (feelings) überkommen. what's ~ ~ you? was ist denn in dich gefahren?

♦ **come round** vi = come around.

♦ **come through 1** vi (a) (phone-call, order) durchkommen. your papers haven't ~ ~ yet (be cleared) Ihre Papiere sind noch nicht fertig. (b) (survive) durchkommen. **2** vi +prep obj (survive) illness, danger überstehen.

♦ **come to 1** vi (regain consciousness) wieder zu sich (dat) kommen. **2** vi +prep obj (a) he will never ~ ~ much aus ihm wird nie etwas werden. (b) (impers) if it ~s ~ that we're sunk wenn es dazu kommt, sind wir verloren; ~ ~ that or if it ~s ~ that, he's just as good was das betrifft, ist er genauso gut; when it ~s ~ mathematics wenn es um Mathematik geht; it ~s ~ the same thing das läuft auf dasselbe hinaus. (c) (price, bill) how much does it ~ ~? wieviel macht das? (d) (touch on) point, subject etc kommen auf (+acc); (tackle) problem, job etc herangehen an (+acc).

♦ **come together** vi zusammenkommen. he and his wife have ~ ~ again er ist wieder mit seiner Frau zusammen.

♦ **come under** vi +prep obj (a) to ~ ~ sb's influence unter jds Einfluß geraten; this shop has ~ ~ new management dieser Laden hat eine neue Geschäftsführung. (b) category, heading kommen unter (+acc).

♦ **come up** vi (a) (lit) hochkommen; (diver, submarine) nach oben kommen; (sun, moon) aufgehen. you've ~ ~ in the world du bist ja richtig vornehm geworden!; he came ~ to me with a smile er kam lächelnd auf mich zu. (b) (Jur) (case) verhandelt werden; (accused) vor Gericht stehen. (c) (for discussion) aufkommen; (name) erwähnt werden. (d) (number in lottery etc) gewinnen. to ~ ~ for sale/auction zum Verkauf/ zur Auktion etc kommen. (e) (post, job) frei werden.

♦ **come up against** vi +prep obj stoßen auf (+acc); opposing team treffen auf (+acc). the new teacher keeps coming ~ ~ the headmaster der neue Lehrer gerät ständig mit dem Direktor aneinander.

♦ **come (up)on** vi +prep obj (find) stoßen auf (+acc).

♦ **come up to** vi +prep obj (a) (reach up to) gehen or reichen bis zu or an (+acc). (b) expectations entsprechen (+dat). (c) (col: approach) it's just coming ~ ~ 10 es ist gleich 10.

♦ **come up with** vi +prep obj answer haben; plan sich (dat) ausdenken; suggestion machen; money (raise) aufbringen; (pay) herausrücken (col).

comeback ['kʌmbæk] n (a) (Theat etc, fig) Comeback nt. (b) (col: redress) Anspruch m auf Schadenersatz; (reaction) Reaktion f. we have no ~ wir können nichts machen.

comedian [kə'miːdɪən] n Komiker m.

comedienne [kə,miːdɪ'en] n Komikerin f.

comedown ['kʌmdaʊn] n (col) Abstieg m. that's a bit of a ~ for you du bist ganz schön heruntergekommen (col).

comedy ['kɒmɪdɪ] n Komödie f.

comer ['kʌməʳ] n "open to all ~s" „Teilnahme für jedermann".

comet ['kɒmɪt] n Komet m.

come-uppance [,kʌm'ʌpəns] n (col): to get one's ~ die Quittung kriegen (col).

comfort ['kʌmfət] **1** n (a) Komfort m no pl. to live in ~ komfortabel leben; that car was a little too

close for ~ für meine Begriffe ist dieses Auto zu nahe herangefahren. (b) (consolation) Trost m. to take ~ from the fact that ... sich damit trösten, daß ...; your presence is a great ~ to me es beruhigt mich sehr, daß Sie da sind; small ~ schwacher Trost. (c) (US) ~ station öffentliche Toilette. **2** vt (console) trösten.

comfortable ['kʌmfətəbl] adj (a) armchair, shoes, life bequem; room, hotel etc komfortabel; temperature angenehm. to make sb/oneself ~ es jdm/sich bequem machen; (make at home) es jdm/sich gemütlich machen. (b) (fig) income, pension ausreichend; life angenehm; majority, lead sicher. I don't feel too ~ about it mir ist nicht ganz wohl bei dem Gedanken.

comfortably ['kʌmfətəblɪ] adv (a) sit, dress etc bequem; furnished komfortabel. (b) (fig) win, lead sicher; live angenehm; afford gut und gern; claim, say ruhig. they are ~ off es geht ihnen gut.

comforter ['kʌmfətəʳ] n (US) (on bed) Deckbett nt; (scarf) Wollschal m.

comforting ['kʌmfətɪŋ] adj tröstlich.

comfy ['kʌmfɪ] adj (+er) (col) bequem; room gemütlich.

comic ['kɒmɪk] **1** adj komisch. ~ strip Comic strip m. **2** n (a) (person) Komiker(in f) m. (b) (magazine) Comic-Heft(chen) nt. (c) (US) ~s Comics pl.

comical ['kɒmɪkəl] adj komisch.

coming ['kʌmɪŋ] **1** n Kommen nt. ~ and going/~s and goings Kommen und Gehen nt. **2** adj (lit, fig) kommend.

comma ['kɒmə] n Komma nt.

command [kə'mɑːnd] **1** vt (a) befehlen. (b) army, ship befehligen. (c) resources, vocabulary verfügen über (+acc). to ~ sb's admiration/ respect jdm Bewunderung/Respekt abnötigen; he ~s our admiration wir bewundern ihn. (d) view bieten (of über +acc). **2** n (a) (order) Befehl m. at/by the ~ of auf Befehl +gen; on ~ auf Befehl. (b) (Mil: power, authority) Kommando m. to be in ~ das Kommando haben (of über +acc); to take ~ das Kommando übernehmen (of gen). (c) (fig: possession, mastery) Beherrschung f. he has a ~ of three foreign languages er beherrscht drei Fremdsprachen; to have sb/sth at one's ~ jdm/etw verfügen; I am at your ~ ich stehe zu Ihrer Verfügung.

commandant ['kɒmən'dænt] n (Mil) Kommandant m.

commandeer [,kɒmən'dɪəʳ] vt (Mil) men einziehen; (lit, fig) stores, ship, car beschlagnahmen.

commander [kə'mɑːndəʳ] n Führer m; (Mil, Aviat) Kommandant m; (Naut) Fregattenkapitän m. ~/~s-in-chief Oberbefehlshaber m/pl.

commanding [kə'mɑːndɪŋ] adj (a) ~ officer (Mil) befehlshabender Offizier. (b) personality, voice, tone gebieterisch. (c) (of place) beherrschend.

commandment [kə'mɑːndmənt] n (Bibl) Gebot nt.

command module n (Space) Kommandokapsel f.

commando [kə'mɑːndəʊ] n, pl -s (Mil: soldier) Angehöriger m eines Kommando(trupp)s.

command performance n (Theat) königliche Galavorstellung.

commemorate [kə'meməreɪt] vt gedenken (+gen).

commemoration [kə,memə'reɪʃən] n Gedenken nt. in ~ of zum Gedenken an (+acc).

commemorative [kə'memərətɪv] adj Gedenk-. ~ plaque Gedenktafel f.

commence [kə'mens] vti (form) beginnen.

commencement [kə'mensmənt] n (form) Beginn m.

commend [kə'mend] **1** vt (praise) loben; (recommend) empfehlen. **2** vr to ~ itself sich empfehlen (to dat).

commendable [kə'mendəbl] adj lobenswert.

commendation [,kɒmen'deɪʃən] n (award) Auszeichnung f.

commensurate [kə'menʃərɪt] *adj* entsprechend *(with dat)*. **to be ~ with** sth einer Sache *(dat)* entsprechen.

comment ['kɒment] **1** *n (remark)* Bemerkung *f (on, about* über *+acc,* zu*); (official)* Kommentar *m (on* zu*).* **no ~** kein Kommentar! **2** *vi* sich äußern *(on* über *+acc,* zu*).* **3** *vt* bemerken.

commentary ['kɒmntərɪ] *n* Kommentar *m (on* zu*).*

commentate ['kɒmenteɪt] *vi (Rad, TV)* Reporter(in) sein *(on* bei*).*

commentator ['kɒmenteɪtəʳ] *n (Rad, TV)* Reporter(in *f) m.* **political ~** politischer Kommentator.

commerce ['kɒmɜːs] *n* Handel *m.*

commercial ['kə'mɜːʃəl] **1** *adj* Handels-; *ethics, training* kaufmännisch; *premises, vehicle* Geschäfts-; *production, radio, project, success, attitude etc* kommerziell. **the ~ world** die Geschäftswelt. **2** *n (Rad, TV)* Werbespot *m.*

commercial: ~ art *n* Werbegraphik *f;* **~ college** *n* Fachschule *f* für kaufmännische Berufe.

commercialism [kə'mɜːʃəlɪzəm] *n* Kommerzialisierung *f.*

commercialize [kə'mɜːʃəlaɪz] *vt* kommerzialisieren.

commercial: ~ television *n* Werbefernsehen *nt;* **~ traveller** *(Brit) or* **traveler** *(US) n* Handelsvertreter(in *f) m.*

commiserate [kə'mɪzəreɪt] *vi* mitfühlen *(with* mit*).*

commiseration [kə,mɪzə'reɪʃən] *n* (An)teilnahme *f no pl.* **my ~s** herzliches Beileid *(on* zu*).*

commission [kə'mɪʃən] **1 (a)** *(for building, painting etc)* Auftrag *m.* **(b)** *(Comm: payment)* Provision *f.* **on ~** auf Provision. **(c)** *(Mil)* Patent *nt.* **(d)** *(special committee)* Kommission *f.* **the (EEC) C~** die EG-Kommission. **(e)** *(use)* **in/out of ~** in/außer Betrieb. **2** *vt* **(a)** *person* beauftragen; *book, painting* in Auftrag geben. **to ~ sb to do sth** jdn damit beauftragen, etw zu tun. **(b)** *(Mil) sb* zum Offizier ernennen. **~ed officer** Offizier *m.* **(c)** *(Naut) ship* in Dienst stellen.

commissionaire [kə,mɪʃə'neəʳ] *n* Portier *m.*

commissioner [kə'mɪʃənəʳ] *n* **(a)** *(member of commission)* Ausschußmitglied *nt.* **(b)** *(of police)* Polizeipräsident *m.*

commit [kə'mɪt] **1** *vt* **(a)** *crime, suicide* begehen. **(b) to have sb ~ted (to an asylum)** jdn in eine Anstalt einweisen lassen; **to ~ sb for trial** jdn einem Gericht überstellen; **to ~ to writing** zu Papier bringen. **2** *vr* sich festlegen *(to* auf *+acc).* **to ~ oneself on an issue** sich in einer Frage festlegen; **... without ~ting myself to the whole contract** ... ohne damit an den ganzen Vertrag gebunden zu sein.

commitment [kə'mɪtmənt] *n (obligation)* Verpflichtung *f; (dedication)* Engagement *nt.*

committed [kə'mɪtɪd] *adj (dedicated)* engagiert.

committee [kə'mɪtɪ] *n* Ausschuß *m,* Komitee *nt.* **~ meeting** Ausschußsitzung *f;* **~ member** Ausschußmitglied *nt.*

commodity [kə'mɒdɪtɪ] *n* Ware *f; (agricultural)* Erzeugnis *nt.* **~ market** Rohstoffmarkt *m.*

common ['kɒmən] **1** *adj (+er)* **(a)** *(shared by many)* gemeinsam. **it is ~ knowledge that** ... es ist allgemein bekannt, daß ... **(b)** *(frequently seen or heard etc)* häufig; *word* geläufig; *experience also* allgemein; *belief, custom, animal, bird* (weit)verbreitet; *(customary, usual)* normal. **(c)** *(ordinary)* gewöhnlich. **the ~ man** der Normalbürger; **the ~ people** die einfachen Leute; **it's only ~ decency** das gehört sich einfach. **(d)** *(vulgar, low-class)* gewöhnlich. **2** *n* **(a)** *(land)* Gemeindewiese *f.* **(b) to have sth in ~** etw miteinander gemein haben.

common denominator *n (Math, fig)* gemeinsamer Nenner.

commoner ['kɒmənəʳ] *n* Bürgerliche(r) *mf.*

common-law ['kɒmənlɔː] *adj* **she is his ~-law wife** sie lebt mit ihm in eheähnlicher Gemeinschaft.

commonly ['kɒmənlɪ] *adv* **(a)** *(often)* häufig; *(widely)* weithin. **a ~ held belief** eine weitverbreitete Ansicht. **(b)** *(vulgarly)* ordinär.

common: C~ Market *n* Gemeinsamer Markt; **~-or-garden** *adj* Durchschnitts-, Feld-, Wald- und Wiesen- *(esp pej col); topic, novel etc* ganz gewöhnlich; **~place 1** *adj* alltäglich; *(banal)* *remark* banal; **2** *n* Gemeinplatz *m;* **~room** *n* Aufenthaltsraum *m; (for teachers)* Lehrerzimmer *nt; (Univ)* Dozentenzimmer *nt.*

Commons ['kɒmənz] *npl* **the ~** *(Parl)* das Unterhaus.

common: ~ sense *n* gesunder Menschenverstand; **~sense** *adj* vernünftig; **C~wealth** *n* **the (British) C~wealth,** **the C~wealth of Nations** das Commonwealth.

commotion [kə'məʊʃən] *n* Aufruhr *f; (noise)* Lärm *m.* **to cause a ~** Aufsehen erregen.

communal ['kɒmjuːnl] *adj* **(a)** *(of a community)* Gemeinde-. **~ life** Gemeinschaftsleben *nt.* **(b)** *(owned, used in common)* gemeinsam.

commune ['kɒmjuːn] **1** *n* Kommune *f.* **2** [kə'mjuːn] *vi* **to ~ with nature** mit der Natur Zwiesprache halten.

communicable [kə'mjuːnɪkəbl] *adj disease* übertragbar.

communicant [kə'mjuːnɪkənt] *n (Eccl)* Kommunikant(in *f) m.*

communicate [kə'mjuːnɪkeɪt] **1** *vt news etc* übermitteln; *ideas, feelings* vermitteln; *illness* übertragen *(to* auf *+acc).* **2** *vi* **(a)** *(be in communication)* in Verbindung stehen. **(b)** *(convey or exchange thoughts)* sich verständigen. **he can't ~** er hat keine Kommunikationsfähigkeit. **(c)** *(rooms)* verbunden sein. **communicating rooms** Zimmer *pl* mit einer Verbindungstür.

communication [kə,mjuːnɪ'keɪʃən] *n* **(a)** Kommunikation *f; (of ideas, information)* Vermittlung *f; (of disease)* Übertragung *f; (between people)* Verständigung *f; (contact)* Verbindung *f.* **to be in ~ with sb** mit jdm in Verbindung stehen *(about* wegen*);* **to get into ~ with sb about sth** sich mit jdm wegen etw in Verbindung setzen. **(b)** *(letter, message)* Mitteilung *f.* **(c)** **~s** *(roads, railways, telegraph lines etc)* Kommunikationswege *pl; (Telec)* Nachrichtenwesen *nt.*

communication: ~ cord *n (Brit Rail)* ≈ Notbremse *f;* **~ network** *n* Kommunikationsnetz *nt;* **~s satellite** *n* Nachrichtensatellit *m;* **~s studies** *npl* Kommunikationswissenschaften *pl.*

communicative [kə'mjuːnɪkətɪv] *adj* gesprächig. **~ skills** Kommunikationsfähigkeit *f.*

communion [kə'mjuːnɪən] *n* **(a)** *(intercourse, exchange of feelings etc)* Zwiesprache *f.* **(b)** *(Eccl: also C~)* *(Protestant)* Abendmahl *nt; (Catholic)* Kommunion *f.* **to receive or take ~** die Kommunion/das Abendmahl empfangen.

communiqué [kə'mjuːnɪkeɪ] *n* Kommuniqué *nt,* *(amtliche)* Verlautbarung.

communism ['kɒmjʊnɪzəm] *n* Kommunismus *m.*

communist ['kɒmjʊnɪst] **1** *n* Kommunist(in *f) m.* **2** *adj* kommunistisch.

community [kə'mjuːnɪtɪ] *n* **(a)** *(social etc group)* Gemeinde *f.* **(b)** *(the public)* Allgemeinheit *f.*

community: ~ centre *(Brit) or* **center** *(US) n* Gemeindezentrum *nt;* **~ chest** *n (US)* Hilfsfonds *m;* **~ relations** *npl* das Verhältnis zwischen den Bevölkerungsgruppen; **~ spirit** *n* Gemeinschaftsgeist *m.*

commute [kə'mjuːt] **1** *vt* umwandeln. **2** *vi (be commuter)* pendeln.

commuter [kə'mjuːtəʳ] *n* Pendler(in *f) m.* **~ train** Pendlerzug *m;* **the ~ belt** das Einzugsgebiet.

compact¹ [kəm'pækt] *adj (+er)* kompakt; *soil, snow* fest. **~ disk** Compact-disc *f.*

compact² ['kɒmpækt] *n* **(a)** *(powder ~)* Puderdose

f. **(b)** *(US: car)* Kompaktauto *nt.*

compact³ ['kɒmpækt] *n (form: agreement)* Übereinkunft *f.*

companion [kəm'pænjən] *n* **(a)** Begleiter(in *f*) *m.* **travelling** ~ Reisegefährte *m,* Reisegefährtin *f.* **(b)** *(friend)* Freund(in *f*) *m.* **(c)** *(one of pair of objects)* Pendant *nt.* **(d)** *(lady's)* Betreuerin *f.*

companionable [kəm'pænjənəbl] *adj* freundlich.

companionship [kəm'pænjənʃɪp] *n* Gesellschaft *f.*

company ['kʌmpənɪ] **1** *n* Gesellschaft *f;* *(guests)* Besuch *m;* *(Comm also)* Firma *f;* *(Theat)* (Schauspiel)truppe *f.* **ship's** ~ *(Naut)* Besatzung *f;* **to keep sb** ~ jdm Gesellschaft leisten; **she is not fit** ~ **for your sister** sie ist nicht der richtige Umgang für deine Schwester; **to get into bad** ~ **in** schlechte Gesellschaft geraten; **we have** ~ **this evening** wir haben heute abend Besuch. **2** *attr* ~ **car** Firmenwagen *m;* ~ **secretary** *(Brit)* ≃ Prokurist *m.*

comparable ['kɒmpərəbl] *adj* vergleichbar *(with, to* mit*).*

comparative [kəm'pærətɪv] *adj* **(a)** *religion, philology etc* vergleichend. **the** ~ **form** *(Gram)* der Komparativ. **(b)** *(relative)* relativ. **to live in** ~ **luxury** relativ luxuriös leben.

comparatively [kəm'pærətɪvlɪ] *adv (relatively)* verhältnismäßig.

compare [kəm'pɛəʳ] **1** *vt* vergleichen *(with, to* mit*).* ~**d with** verglichen mit; **they cannot be** ~**d man** kann sie nicht vergleichen; **to** ~ **notes** Eindrücke/Erfahrungen austauschen. **2** *vi* sich vergleichen lassen *(with* mit*).* **it** ~**s badly/well es** schneidet vergleichsweise schlecht/gut ab. **3** *n:* **beyond** ~ unvergleichlich.

comparison [kəm'pærɪsn] *n* Vergleich *m (to* mit*).* **in** ~ **with** im Vergleich zu.

compartment [kəm'pɑːtmənt] *n (in fridge, desk etc)* Fach *nt;* *(Rail)* Abteil *nt.*

compass ['kʌmpəs] *n* **(a)** Kompaß *m.* **(b)** ~**es** *pl* **pair of** ~**es** Zirkel *m.* **(c)** *(fig: extent)* Rahmen *m;* *(of human mind, experience)* Bereich *m.*

compassion [kəm'pæʃən] *n* Mitgefühl *nt (for* mit*).*

compassionate [kəm'pæʃnɪt] *adj* mitfühlend. **on** ~ **grounds** aus familiären Gründen; ~ **leave** Beurlaubung *f* wegen einer dringenden Familienangelegenheit.

compatibility [kəm,pætɪ'bɪlɪtɪ] *n* Vereinbarkeit *f;* *(Med)* Verträglichkeit *f;* *(Tech)* Kompatibilität *f.*

compatible [kəm'pætɪbl] *adj* vereinbar; *(Med)* verträglich; *people* zueinander passend; *colours,* *furniture* passend; *(Tech)* kompatibel.

compatriot [kəm'pætrɪət] *n* Landsmann *m,* Landsmännin *f.*

compel [kəm'pel] *vt* zwingen. **I feel** ~**led to tell you** ... ich sehe mich (dazu) gezwungen, Ihnen mitzuteilen, ...

compelling [kəm'pelɪŋ] *adj* *reason* zwingend; *performance* bezwingend.

compendium [kəm'pendɪəm] *n* Handbuch *nt.*

compensate ['kɒmpənseɪt] *vt* *(recompense)* entschädigen.

♦ **compensate for** *vi* +*prep obj (in money etc)* ersetzen; *(make up for, offset)* wieder wettmachen.

compensation [,kɒmpən'seɪʃən] *n* *(damages)* Entschädigung *f;* *(fig)* Ausgleich *m.*

compère ['kɒmpɛəʳ] *(Brit)* **1** *n* Conférencier *m.* **2** *vt* **to** ~ **a show** bei einer Show der Conférencier sein.

compete [kəm'piːt] *vi* **(a)** konkurrieren. **to** ~ **with each other** sich (gegenseitig) Konkurrenz machen; **he can't** ~ **with her** er kann sich nicht mit ihr messen. **(b)** *(Sport)* teilnehmen.

competence ['kɒmpɪtəns], **competency** ['kɒmpɪtənsɪ] *n* Fähigkeit *f;* *(of doctor etc also)* Kompetenz *f.*

competent ['kɒmpɪtənt] *adj* fähig, befähigt *(in* zu*);* *(in a particular field)* kompetent.

competition [,kɒmpɪ'tɪʃən] *n* **(a)** *no pl* Konkurrenz *f (for* um*).* **(b)** *(contest)* Wettbewerb *m;* *(in newspapers etc)* Preisausschreiben *nt.* **beauty** ~ Schönheitswettbewerb *m.*

competitive [kəm'petɪtɪv] *adj* **(a)** *person, attitude* vom Konkurrenzdenken geprägt; *sport* (Wett)kampf-. **a** ~ **examination** eine Auswahlprüfung. **(b)** *(Comm)* *business, prices, salaries* konkurrenzfähig.

competitor [kəm'petɪtəʳ] *n* **(a)** Teilnehmer(in *f*) *m.* **(b)** *(Comm)* **our** ~**s** unsere Konkurrenten.

compile [kəm'paɪl] *vt* zusammenstellen; *material* zusammentragen; *dictionary* verfassen.

complacency [kəm'pleɪsnsɪ] *n* Selbstgefälligkeit *f.*

complacent [kəm'pleɪsənt] *adj* selbstgefällig.

complain [kəm'pleɪn] *vi* sich beklagen *(about* über +*acc); (to make a formal complaint)* sich beschweren *(about* über +*acc, to* bei*).* **(I) can't** ~ *(col)* ich kann nicht klagen *(col).*

complaint [kəm'pleɪnt] *n* **(a)** Klage *f; (formal* ~*)* Beschwerde *f.* **(b)** *(illness)* Beschwerden *pl.* **a very rare** ~ eine sehr seltene Krankheit.

complement ['kɒmplɪmənt] **1** *n* **(a)** *(also Gram)* Ergänzung *f (to* gen*).* **(b)** *(full number)* volle Stärke; *(crew of ship)* Besatzung *f.* **2** ['kɒmplɪment] *vt* ergänzen. **to** ~ **each other** sich ergänzen.

complementary [,kɒmplɪ'mentərɪ] *adj* **they have** ~ **interests** ihre Interessen ergänzen sich.

complete [kəm'pliːt] **1** *adj* **(a)** *(entire, whole)* ganz *attr; wardrobe, deck of cards* komplett; *(having the required numbers)* vollzählig; *edition* Gesamt-. ~ **with** komplett mit; **the** ~ **works of Shakespeare** die gesammelten Werke Shakespeares; **my happiness was** ~ mein Glück war vollkommen. **(b)** *attr (total, absolute)* völlig; *failure, disaster, victory* total; *satisfaction, approval* voll. **a** ~ **idiot** ein Vollidiot *m;* **we were** ~ **strangers** wir waren uns völlig fremd. **(c)** *(finished)* fertig. **2** *vt* **(a)** *(make whole)* collection, set* vervollständigen. **(b)** *(fig)* happiness* vollkommen machen. **and to** ~ **their misery** ... und zu allem Unglück ... **(c)** *(finish)* abschließen. **(d)** *form, questionnaire* ausfüllen.

completely [kəm'pliːtlɪ] *adv* völlig, vollkommen.

completion [kəm'pliːʃən] *n* *(finishing)* Fertigstellung *f; (of project, course, education)* Abschluß *m.* **on** ~ **of the contract/sale** bei Vertrags-/Kaufabschluß.

complex ['kɒmpleks] **1** *adj* komplex. **2** *n* **(a)** Komplex *m.* **industrial** ~ Industriekomplex. **(b)** *(Psych)* Komplex *m.* **he has a** ~ **about his big ears** er hat Komplexe wegen seiner großen Ohren.

complexion [kəm'plekʃən] *n* **(a)** Teint *m; (skin colour)* Gesichtsfarbe *f.* **(b)** *(fig: aspect)* Aspekt *m.* **to put a new/different/sinister etc** ~ **on sth** etw in einem neuen/anderen/düsteren *etc* Licht erscheinen lassen.

complexity [kəm'pleksɪtɪ] *n* Komplexität *f.*

compliance [kəm'plaɪəns] *n* Einverständnis *nt; (with rules etc)* Einhalten *nt (with* gen*).* **in** ~ **with the law/our wishes** *etc* dem Gesetz/unseren Wünschen *etc* gemäß.

complicate ['kɒmplɪkeɪt] *vt* komplizieren.

complicated ['kɒmplɪkeɪtɪd] *adj* kompliziert.

complication [,kɒmplɪ'keɪʃən] *n* Komplikation *f; (condition)* Kompliziertheit *f.*

complicity [kəm'plɪsɪtɪ] *n* Mittäterschaft *f (in* bei*).*

compliment ['kɒmplɪmənt] **1** *n* **(a)** Kompliment *nt (on* zu, wegen*).* **to pay sb a** ~ jdm ein Kompliment machen. **(b)** *(form)* ~**s** *pl* Grüße *pl;* **the** ~**s of the season** „frohes Fest"; **"with the** ~**s of Mr X/the management"** „mit den besten Empfehlungen von Herrn X/der Geschäftsleitung"; ~**s slip** *(Comm)* Empfehlungszettel *m.* **2** ['kɒmplɪment] *vt* ein Kompliment/Komplimente machen (+*dat) (on* wegen, zu*).*

complimentary [,kɒmplɪ'mentərɪ] *adj* **(a)** *(prais-*

ing) schmeichelhaft. ~ **close** (*in letter*) Schlußformel *f*. **(b)** (*gratis*) *seat, ticket* Frei-.

comply [kəm'plaɪ] *vi* (*person*) einwilligen; (*object, system etc*) den Bedingungen entsprechen. **to ~ with a request/a wish/instructions** einer Bitte/ einem Wunsch/den Anordnungen entsprechen (*form*).

component [kəm'pəʊnənt] *n* Bestandteil *m*; (*Chem, Phys*) Komponente *f*.

compose [kəm'pəʊz] *vt* **(a)** *music* komponieren; *letter, poem* verfassen. **(b)** (*constitute, make up*) bilden. **to be ~d of** sich zusammensetzen aus. **(c) to ~ oneself** sich sammeln.

composed [kəm'pəʊzd] *adj* gefaßt.

composer [kəm'pəʊzə^r] *n* **(a)** (*Mus*) Komponist(in *f*) *m*. **(b)** (*of letter, poem etc*) Verfasser(in *f*) *m*.

composition [ˌkɒmpə'zɪʃən] *n* **(a)** (*act*) (*of music*) Komponieren *nt*; (*of letter, poem etc*) Verfassen *nt*. **(b)** (*arrangement, Mus, Art*) Komposition *f*. **(c)** (*Sch: essay*) Aufsatz *m*. **(d)** (*constitution, make-up*) Zusammensetzung *f*. **(e)** ~ **soles** Kunststoffsohlen *pl*.

compositor [kəm'pɒzɪtə^r] *n* (*Typ*) (Schrift)setzer(in *f*) *m*.

compost ['kɒmpɒst] *n* Kompost *m*.

composure [kəm'pəʊʒə^r] *n* Fassung *f*.

compote ['kɒmpəʊt] *n* Kompott *nt*.

compound ['kɒmpaʊnd] **1** *n* (*Chem*) Verbindung *f*; (*Gram*) zusammengesetztes Wort; (*enclosed area*) Lager *nt*. **2** *adj* ~ **interest** Zinseszins *m*; ~ **fracture** komplizierter Bruch. **3** [kəm'paʊnd] *vt* (*make worse*) verschlimmern.

comprehend [ˌkɒmprɪ'hend] *vt* verstehen.

comprehensible [ˌkɒmprɪ'hensəbl] *adj* verständlich.

comprehension [ˌkɒmprɪ'henʃən] *n* (*understanding*) Verständnis *nt*; (*school exercise*) Fragen *pl* zum Textverständnis.

comprehensive [ˌkɒmprɪ'hensɪv] *adj* umfassend, ausführlich; *measures, knowledge* umfassend. ~ **school** (*Brit*) Gesamtschule *f*; ~ **policy** (*Insur*) Vollkasko(versicherung *f*) *nt*.

compress[1] [kəm'pres] **1** *vt* komprimieren (*into* auf +*acc*); *materials* zusammenpressen (*into* zu). **2** *vi* sich komprimieren lassen.

compress[2] ['kɒmpres] *n* (*Med*) Kompresse *f*.

compressed air [kəm'prest'ɛə^r] *n* Preßluft *f*.

compression [kəm'preʃən] *n* Kompression *f*.

compressor [kəm'presə^r] *n* Kompressor *m*.

comprise [kəm'praɪz] *vt* umfassen.

compromise ['kɒmprəmaɪz] **1** *n* Kompromiß *m*. **2** *adj attr* Kompromiß-. ~ **solution** Kompromißlösung *f*. **3** *vi* Kompromisse schließen (*about* in +*dat*). **not prepared to** ~ nicht kompromißbereit. **4** *vt* kompromittieren.

compulsion [kəm'pʌlʃən] *n* Zwang *m*; (*Psych*) innerer Zwang. **under** ~ unter Druck; **you are under no** ~ niemand zwingt Sie.

compulsive [kəm'pʌlsɪv] *adj* Zwangs-; *behaviour* zwanghaft. **he is a** ~ **eater** er leidet an einem Eßzwang; **he is a** ~ **liar** er hat einen krankhaften Trieb zu lügen; **he's a** ~ **smoker** das Rauchen ist bei ihm zur Sucht geworden; **it makes** ~ **viewing** das muß man unbedingt sehen.

compulsory [kəm'pʌlsərɪ] *adj* obligatorisch; *measures* Zwangs-; *subject* Pflicht-. **that is** ~ das ist Pflicht; **education is** ~ es besteht (allgemeine) Schulpflicht; ~ **purchase** Enteignung *f*.

compunction [kəm'pʌŋkʃən] *n* (*liter*) Schuldgefühle *pl*. **with no** ~ ohne sich schuldig zu fühlen.

computation [ˌkɒmpjʊ'teɪʃən] *n* Berechnung *f*.

compute [kəm'pjuːt] *vt* berechnen (*at* auf +*acc*).

computer [kəm'pjuːtə^r] *n* Computer, Rechner *m*.

computerization [kəmˌpjuːtəraɪ'zeɪʃən] *n* (*of information etc*) Computerisierung *f*. **the** ~ **of the factory** die Umstellung der Fabrik auf Computer.

computerize [kəm'pjuːtəraɪz] *vt* *information*

computerisieren; *company, accounting methods* auf EDV umstellen.

computer: ~-**operated** *adj* computergesteuert; ~ **program** *n* Programm *nt*; ~ **programmer** *n* Programmierer(in *f*) *m*; ~ **science** *n* Informatik *f*.

comrade ['kɒmrɪd] *n* Kamerad *m*; (*Pol*) Genosse *m*, Genossin *f*.

con [kɒn] (*col*) **1** *n* Schwindel *m*. ~ **man** Schwindler *m*. **2** *vt* hereinlegen (*col*). **he** ~**ned her out of all her money** er hat sie um ihr ganzes Geld gebracht.

concave ['kɒn'keɪv] *adj* konkav; *mirror* Hohl-.

conceal [kən'siːl] *vt* (*hide*) verbergen; (*keep secret*) verheimlichen.

concealed [kən'siːld] *adj* verborgen; *lighting* indirekt; *entrance* verdeckt.

concede [kən'siːd] *vt* **(a)** (*yield*) *privilege* aufgeben; *lands* abtreten (*to* an +*acc*); (*Sport*) *corner, penalty* verursachen. **to** ~ **victory to sb** vor jdm kapitulieren; **to** ~ **a point to sb** (*in debate*) jdm in einem Punkt recht geben. **(b)** (*admit, grant*) einräumen. **to** ~ **defeat** sich geschlagen geben.

conceit [kən'siːt] *n* (*pride*) Einbildung *f*.

conceited [kən'siːtɪd] *adj* eingebildet.

conceivable [kən'siːvəbl] *adj* denkbar. **the worst** ~ **thing to say** das denkbar Schlechteste, was man sagen kann.

conceivably [kən'siːvəblɪ] *adv* **she may** ~ **be right** es ist durchaus denkbar, daß sie recht hat.

conceive [kən'siːv] **1** *vt* **(a)** *child* empfangen. **(b)** (*imagine*) sich (*dat*) vorstellen; *idea, plan* haben; *novel* die Idee haben zu. **I can't** ~ **why** ich verstehe nicht, warum. **2** *vi* (*woman*) empfangen.

concentrate ['kɒnsəntreɪt] **1** *vt* konzentrieren (*on* auf +*acc*). **2** *vi* **(a)** (*give one's attention*) sich konzentrieren. **(b)** (*people*) sich sammeln. **3** *n* (*Chem*) Konzentrat *nt*.

concentration [ˌkɒnsən'treɪʃən] *n* Konzentration *f*. **powers of** ~ Konzentrationsfähigkeit *f*.

concentration camp *n* Konzentrationslager, KZ *nt*.

concept ['kɒnsept] *n* Begriff *m*; (*conception*) Vorstellung *f*.

conception [kən'sepʃən] *n* **(a)** (*idea*) Vorstellung *f*; (*way sth is conceived*) Auffassung *f*. **the writer's powers of** ~ die Vorstellungskraft des Schriftstellers. **he has no** ~ **of how difficult it is** er macht sich (*dat*) keinen Begriff davon, wie schwer das ist. **(b)** (*of child*) die Empfängnis.

concern [kən'sɜːn] **1** *n* **(a)** (*connection*) **to have no** ~ **with sth** mit etw nichts zu tun haben. **(b)** (*business, affair*) Angelegenheit(en *pl*) *f*; (*matter of importance to a person*) Anliegen *nt*. **it's no** ~ **of his** das geht ihn nichts an; **what** ~ **is it of yours?** was geht Sie das an? **(c)** (*Comm*) Konzern *m*. **(d)** (*anxiety*) Sorge *f*. **a look of** ~ ein besorgter Blick; **there's some/no cause for** ~ es besteht Grund/ kein Grund zur Sorge; **he showed great** ~ **for your safety** er zeigte sich sehr um Ihre Sicherheit besorgt.

2 *vt* **(a)** (*be about*) handeln von. **(b)** (*be the business of, involve*) angehen, betreffen. **that doesn't** ~ **you** das betrifft Sie nicht; (*as snub*) das geht Sie nichts an; **to whom it may** ~ (*on letter*) an den betreffenden Sachbearbeiter; (*on certificate*) Bestätigung *f*; (*on reference*) Zeugnis *nt*; **as far as I'm** ~**ed** was mich betrifft; **as far as I'm** ~**ed you can do what you like** von mir aus kannst du tun und lassen, was du willst; **the persons** ~**ed** die Betroffenen.

(c) (*interest*) **he is only** ~**ed with facts** ihn interessieren nur die Fakten, (*is only dealing with*) ihm geht es nur um die Fakten.

(d) (*worry*) **there's no need for you to** ~ **yourself about** it darum brauchen Sie sich nicht zu kümmern; **to be** ~**ed about sth** sich (*dat*) um etw Sorgen machen, um etw besorgt sein;

don't ~ **yourself** machen Sie sich keine Sorgen; **I was very** ~**ed about** *or* **for your safety** ich war sehr um Ihre Sicherheit besorgt.

concerning [kən'sɜːnɪŋ] *prep* bezüglich (+*gen*), hinsichtlich (+*gen*). ~ **your request** ... was Ihre Anfrage betrifft ...

concert ['kɒnsət] *n* (*Mus*) Konzert *nt*. **in** ~ (*fig*) gemeinsam.

concerted [kən'sɜːtɪd] *adj efforts* vereint; *action* gemeinsam.

concert: ~**goer** *n* Konzertbesucher(in *f*) *m*; ~ **grand** *n* Konzertflügel *m*; ~ **hall** *n* Konzertsaal *m*.

concertina [,kɒnsə'tiːnə] *n* Konzertina *f*.

concertmaster ['kɒnsətmæstə^r] *n* (*esp US*) Konzertmeister *m*.

concerto [kən'tʃɜːtəʊ] *n* Konzert, Concerto *nt*.

concert: ~ **pianist** *n* Pianist(in *f*) *m*: ~ **pitch** *n* Kammerton *m*; ~ **tour** *n* Konzerttournee *f*.

concession [kən'seʃən] *n* Zugeständnis *nt* (*to an* +*acc*); (*Comm*) Konzession *f*.

concessionary [kən'seʃənərɪ] *adj* (*Comm*) Konzessions-.

conciliate [kən'sɪlɪeɪt] *vt* (**a**) (*placate*) besänftigen. (**b**) (*reconcile*) *opposing views* in Einklang bringen.

conciliatory [kən'sɪlɪətərɪ] *adj* versöhnlich; (*placatory*) beschwichtigend.

concise [kən'saɪs] *adj* präzis(e). ~ **dictionary** Handwörterbuch *nt*.

conclude [kən'kluːd] **1** *vt* (**a**) (*end*) *meeting, letter, speech* schließen. (**b**) (*arrange*) *treaty, deal* abschließen. (**c**) (*decide*) **to** ~ **that** ... zu dem Schluß kommen, daß ...; **what do you** ~ **from this?** was schließen Sie daraus? **2** *vi* (*meetings, events*) enden; (*letter, speech*) schließen. **the concluding paragraph** der letzte Abschnitt.

conclusion [kən'kluːʒən] *n* (**a**) (*end, settling*) Abschluß *m*; (*of essay, novel etc*) Schluß *m*. **in** ~ zum (Ab)schluß. (**b**) (*deduction*) Schluß(folgerung *f*) *m*. **to come to the** ~ **that** ... zu dem Schluß kommen, daß ...

conclusive [kən'kluːsɪv] *adj* (*convincing*) überzeugend; (*decisive, final*) endgültig; (*Jur*) *evidence* einschlägig; *proof* schlüssig.

concoct [kən'kɒkt] *vt* (**a**) (*Cook etc*) zusammenstellen. (**b**) (*fig*) sich (*dat*) zurechtlegen; *new dress, hat* zaubern; *story, alibi* sich (*dat*) ausdenken.

concoction [kən'kɒkʃən] *n* (*food*) Zusammenstellung *f*; (*drink*) Gebräu *nt*; (*story*) Lügengeschichte *f*; (*fashion*) Spielerei *f*.

concord ['kɒŋkɔːd] *n* (*harmony*) Eintracht *f*.

concourse ['kɒŋkɔːs] *n* (*place*) Eingangshalle *f*. **station** ~ Bahnhofshalle *f*.

concrete[1] ['kɒŋkriːt] *adj object, example* konkret.

concrete[2] *n* (*Build*) Beton *m*. ~ **mixer** Betonmischmaschine *f*. **2** *adj* Beton-. **3** *vt wall, floor* betonieren.

concur [kən'kɜː^r] *vi* (**a**) (*agree*) übereinstimmen; (*with a suggestion etc*) beipflichten (*with dat*). **I** ~ **with that** ich pflichte dem bei. (**b**) (*happen together*) zusammentreffen.

concurrent [kən'kʌrənt] *adj* gleichzeitig.

concuss [kən'kʌs] *vt* (*usu pass*) **to be** ~**ed** eine Gehirnerschütterung haben.

concussion [kən'kʌʃən] *n* Gehirnerschütterung *f*.

condemn [kən'dem] *vt* (**a**) (*censure, Jur, fig*) verurteilen. **to** ~ **sb to death** jdn zum Tode verurteilen. (**b**) (*declare unfit*) *building, slums* für abbruchreif erklären; *food* für den Verzehr ungeeignet erklären.

condemnation [,kɒndem'neɪʃən] *n* Verurteilung *f*.

condensation [,kɒnden'seɪʃən] *n* (**a**) (*of vapour*) Kondensation *f*; (*liquid formed*) Kondensat *nt*. **the windows/walls are covered with** ~ die Fenster/Wände sind beschlagen. (**b**) (*short form*) Kurzfassung *f*.

condense [kən'dens] **1** *vt* (**a**) kondensieren. ~**d milk** (gesüßte) Kondensmilch *f*. (**b**) (*Phys*) *gas* kondensieren; (*compress*) verdichten. (**c**) (*shorten*) zusammenfassen. **2** *vi* (*gas*) kondensieren.

condenser [kən'densə^r] *n* (*Elec, Phys*) Kondensator *m*.

condescend [,kɒndɪ'send] *vi* sich herablassen.

condescending [,kɒndɪ'sendɪŋ] *adj* (*pej*) herablassend.

condescension [,kɒndɪ'senʃən] *n* (*pej*) Herablassung *f*.

condition [kən'dɪʃən] **1** *n* (**a**) (*determining factor*) Bedingung *f* (*also Jur, Comm*); (*prerequisite*) Voraussetzung *f*. **on** ~ **that** ... unter der Voraussetzung, daß ...; **on no** ~ auf keinen Fall; **to make** ~**s** Bedingungen stellen.

(**b**) ~**s** *pl* (*circumstances*) Verhältnisse *pl*; **working** ~**s** Arbeitsbedingungen *pl*; **living** ~**s** Wohnverhältnisse *pl*.

(**c**) *no pl* (*state*) Zustand *m*. **he is in good/bad** ~ er ist in guter/schlechter Verfassung; **it is in good/bad** ~ es ist in gutem/schlechtem Zustand; **you're in no** ~ **to drive** du bist nicht fahrtüchtig; **to be in/out of** ~ eine gute/keine Kondition haben; **to keep in/get into** ~ in Form bleiben/kommen.

(**d**) (*Med*) Beschwerden *pl*. **he has a heart** ~ er ist herzkrank.

2 *vt* (**a**) (*esp pass: determine*) bedingen. **to be** ~**ed by** bedingt sein durch. (**b**) (*Psych etc: train*) konditionieren; (*accustom*) gewöhnen. ~**ed reflex** bedingter Reflex.

conditional [kən'dɪʃənl] *adj* (**a**) mit Vorbehalt, bedingt. **to be** ~ (*up*)**on sth** von etw abhängen. (**b**) (*Gram*) konditional, Bedingungs-. **the** ~ **mood/tense** das Konditional.

conditioner [kən'dɪʃənə^r] *n* (*for hair*) Haarshampoo *nt*; (*for fabrics*) Weichspüler *m*.

condolence [kən'dəʊləns] *n* Beileid *nt no pl*.

condom ['kɒndəm] *n* Kondom *nt* or *m*.

condominium [,kɒndə'mɪnɪəm] *n* (*US*) Eigentumswohnung *f*; (*block*) Eigentumsblock *m*.

condone [kən'dəʊn] *vt* (*overlook*) hinwegsehen über (+*acc*); (*tacitly approve*) (stillschweigend) dulden.

conducive [kən'djuːsɪv] *adj* dienlich (*to dat*).

conduct ['kɒndʌkt] **1** *n* (**a**) (*behaviour*) Verhalten, Benehmen *nt* (*towards* gegenüber). (**b**) (*management*) Führung *f*. **2** [kən'dʌkt] *vt* (**a**) (*guide*) führen. ~**ed tour** (**of**) (*Brit*) (*of country*) Gesellschaftsreise *f* (durch); (*of building*) Führung *f* (durch). (**b**) (*direct, manage*) führen; *meeting* leiten; *investigation* durchführen. (**c**) (*Mus*) dirigieren. (**d**) (*Phys, Physiol*) leiten; *lightning* ableiten. **3** [kən'dʌkt] *vt* **to** ~ **oneself** sich benehmen.

conduction [kən'dʌkʃən] *n* (*Phys*) Leitung *f*.

conductivity [,kɒndʌk'tɪvɪtɪ] *n* (*Phys*) Leitfähigkeit *f*.

conductor [kən'dʌktə^r] *n* (**a**) (*Mus*) Dirigent(in *f*) *m*. (**b**) (*bus, tram* ~) Schaffner *m*; (*US Rail: guard*) Zugführer *m*. (**c**) (*Phys*) Leiter *m*; (*lightning* ~) Blitzableiter *m*.

conductress [kən'dʌktrɪs] *n* (*on bus etc*) Schaffnerin *f*.

conduit ['kɒndɪt] *n* Leitungsrohr *nt*.

cone [kəʊn] *n* (**a**) Kegel *m*. (**b**) (*Bot*) Zapfen *m*. (**c**) (*ice-cream* ~) (Eis)tüte *f*.

cone-shaped ['kəʊnʃeɪpt] *adj* kegelförmig.

confab ['kɒnfæb] *n* (*col*) kleine Besprechung *f*.

confectioner's [kən'fekʃənəz] *n* (*Brit*) Süßwarenladen *m*.

confectionery [kən'fekʃənərɪ] *n* Süßwaren *pl*; (*chocolates*) Konfekt *nt*.

confederate [kən'fedərɪt] **1** *adj system* konföderiert; *nations* verbündet. **2** *n* (*Pol: ally*) Verbündete(r) *m*; (*pej: accomplice*) Komplize *m* (*pej*).

confederation [kən‚fedə'reɪʃən] n (a) (Pol) (alliance) Bündnis nt; (system of government) Staatenbund m. **the Swiss C~** die Schweizer Eidgenossenschaft. **(b)** (association) Bund m. **C~ of British Industry** Bund m britischer Industrieller.

confer [kən'fɜː^r] **1** vt title, degree verleihen (on, upon sb jdm). **2** vi sich beraten.

conference ['kɒnfərəns] n Konferenz f; (more informal) Besprechung f.

confess [kən'fes] **1** vt (a) (acknowledge) gestehen. **(b)** (Eccl) sins bekennen; (to priest) beichten; (priest) penitent die Beichte abnehmen (+dat). **2** vi (a) gestehen (to acc). **to ~ to sth** etw gestehen. **(b)** (Eccl) beichten.

confession [kən'feʃən] n (a) Eingeständnis nt; (of guilt, crime etc) Geständnis nt. **I have a ~ to make** ich muß jdm etwas gestehen. **(b)** (Eccl: of sins) Beichte f. **~ of faith** Glaubensbekenntnis nt; **to make one's ~** seine Sünden bekennen.

confessional [kən'feʃənl] n Beichtstuhl m.

confessor [kən'fesə^r] n (Eccl) Beichtvater m.

confetti [kən'fetiː] n no pl Konfetti nt.

confidant [‚kɒnfɪ'dænt] n Vertraute(r) m.

confidante [‚kɒnfɪ'dænt] n Vertraute f.

confide [kən'faɪd] **1** vt anvertrauen (to sb jdm). **2** vi **to ~ in sb** jdn ins Vertrauen ziehen.

confidence ['kɒnfɪdəns] n (a) (trust) Vertrauen nt; (confident expectation) Zuversicht f. **to have (every/no) ~ in sb/sth** (volles/kein) Vertrauen zu jdm/etw haben; **I have every ~ that ...** ich bin ganz zuversichtlich, daß ...; **to give/ask for a vote of ~** (Parl) das Vertrauen aussprechen/die Vertrauensfrage stellen; **motion/vote of no ~** Mißtrauensantrag m/-votum nt. **(b)** (self-~) (Selbst)vertrauen nt. **(c)** (confidential relationship) Vertrauen nt. **in (strict) ~** (streng) vertraulich; **to take sb into one's ~** jdn ins Vertrauen ziehen. **(d)** (information confided) vertrauliche Mitteilung.

confidence: ~ trick, ~trickster n = **con trick, con-man.**

confident ['kɒnfɪdənt] adj (a) (sure) überzeugt; look etc zuversichtlich. **(b)** (self-assured) (selbst)sicher.

confidential [‚kɒnfɪ'denʃəl] adj information vertraulich. **~ secretary** Privatsekretär(in f) m.

confidentially [‚kɒnfɪ'denʃəlɪ] adv im Vertrauen.

confine [kən'faɪn] vt (a) (keep in) (ein)sperren. **~d to bed/the house** ans Bett/ans Haus gefesselt; **to be ~d to barracks** Kasernenarrest haben. **(b)** (limit) beschränken (to auf +acc). **to ~ oneself to doing sth** sich darauf beschränken, etw zu tun.

confined [kən'faɪnd] adj space beschränkt; atmosphere beengend.

confinement [kən'faɪnmənt] n (a) (imprisonment) (act) Einsperren nt; (in jail) Haft f. **(b)** (dated: childbirth) Niederkunft f (dated) f.

confines ['kɒnfaɪnz] npl Grenzen pl.

confirm [kən'fɜːm] vt (a) (verify) bestätigen. **(b)** (strengthen) bestärken; one's resolve bekräftigen. **(c)** (Eccl) konfirmieren; Roman Catholic firmen.

confirmation [‚kɒnfə'meɪʃən] n (a) Bestätigung f. **(b)** (Eccl) Konfirmation f; (of Roman Catholics) Firmung f.

confirmed [kən'fɜːmd] adj erklärt; bachelor eingefleischt.

confiscate ['kɒnfɪskeɪt] vt beschlagnahmen.

conflict ['kɒnflɪkt] **1** n Konflikt m; (between two accounts etc) Widerspruch m; (fighting) Zusammenstoß m. **to come into ~ with sb/sth** mit jdm/etw in Konflikt geraten; **~ of interests/opinions** Interessen-/Meinungskonflikt m. **2** [kən'flɪkt] vi im Widerspruch stehen (with zu).

conflicting [kən'flɪktɪŋ] adj widersprüchlich.

conform [kən'fɔːm] vi (things: comply with) ent-

sprechen (to dat); (people: socially) sich anpassen (to an +acc); (things, people: to rules etc) sich richten (to nach).

conformity [kən'fɔːmɪtɪ] n (a) (uniformity) Konformismus m. **(b)** (compliance) Übereinstimmung f; (socially) Anpassung f (with an +acc). **to be in ~ with sth** einer Sache (dat) entsprechen; **in ~ with** entsprechend (+dat).

confound [kən'faʊnd] vt (amaze) verblüffen; (throw into confusion) verwirren. **~ it!** (col) verflixt noch mal! (col).

confounded [kən'faʊndɪd] adj (col) verflixt (col); noise Heiden- (col).

confront [kən'frʌnt] vt (a) (face) gegenübertreten (+dat); (problems, decisions) sich stellen (+dat). **(b)** (bring face to face with) konfrontieren. **to ~ sb with sb/sth** jdn mit jdm/etw konfrontieren.

confrontation [‚kɒnfrən'teɪʃən] n Konfrontation f (also Pol); (with witnesses, evidence etc) Gegenüberstellung f.

confuse [kən'fjuːz] vt (a) (bewilder, perplex) verwirren, durcheinanderbringen. **(b)** (mix up) verwechseln.

confused [kən'fjuːzd] adj (muddled) konfus; person also verwirrt; (through old age, after anaesthetic etc) wirr im Kopf; idea, report, situation verworren.

confusing [kən'fjuːzɪŋ] adj verwirrend.

confusion [kən'fjuːʒən] n (a) (disorder) Durcheinander nt; (jumble) Wirrwarr m. **(b)** (perplexity) Verwirrung f; (mental ~: after drugs, blow on head etc) Verwirrtheit f; (through old age etc) Wirrheit f. **in the ~ of the moment** im Eifer des Gefechts. **(c)** (mixing up) Verwechslung f.

congeal [kən'dʒiːl] vi erstarren; (glue, mud) hart werden; (blood) gerinnen.

congenial [kən'dʒiːnɪəl] adj (pleasant) angenehm.

congenital [kən'dʒenɪtl] adj deficiency, disease angeboren. **~ defect** Geburtsfehler m; **~ idiot** (col) Vollidiot m (col).

congested [kən'dʒestɪd] adj überfüllt; (with traffic) verstopft.

congestion [kən'dʒestʃən] n (traffic, pedestrians) Stau m; (overpopulation) Übervölkerung f; (Med) Blutstau m.

conglomerate [kən'glɒmərɪt] n (also Geol, Comm) Konglomerat nt.

conglomeration [kən‚glɒmə'reɪʃən] n Ansammlung f.

congratulate [kən'grætjʊleɪt] vt gratulieren (+dat) (on zu).

congratulations [kən‚grætjʊ'leɪʃənz] **1** npl Glückwünsche pl. **2** interj (ich) gratuliere!; **~ (on your success)!** herzlichen Glückwunsch (zu deinem Erfolg)!

congregate ['kɒŋgrɪgeɪt] vi sich sammeln; (on a particular occasion) sich versammeln.

congregation [‚kɒŋgrɪ'geɪʃən] n (a) Versammlung f. **(b)** (Eccl) Gemeinde f.

congress ['kɒŋgres] n (a) (meeting) Kongreß m; (b) (political party) Parteitag m. **(b)** **C~** (US etc Pol) der Kongreß.

Congressman ['kɒŋgresmən] n, pl -men [-mən] Kongreßabgeordnete(r) m.

Congresswoman ['kɒŋgres‚wʊmən] n, pl -women [-‚wɪmɪn] Kongreßabgeordnete f.

conic ['kɒnɪk] adj (a) (Math) konisch. **~ section** Kegelschnitt m. **(b)** (also **~al**) kegelförmig.

conifer ['kɒnɪfə^r] n Nadelbaum m. **~s** Nadelhölzer pl.

coniferous [kə'nɪfərəs] adj tree, forest Nadel-.

conjecture [kən'dʒektʃə^r] **1** vt mutmaßen (geh). **2** vi Mutmaßungen anstellen. **3** n Mutmaßung f.

conjugal ['kɒndʒʊgəl] adj bliss, duties ehelich.

conjugate ['kɒndʒʊgeɪt] vt (Gram) konjugieren.

conjugation [‚kɒndʒʊ'geɪʃən] n (Gram) Konjugation f.

conjunction [kən'dʒʌŋkʃən] n (a) (Gram) Konjunktion *f*. **(b)** *(association)* Verbindung *f*. in ~ zusammen.

conjunctivitis [kən,dʒʌŋktɪ'vaɪtɪs] *n* (*Med*) Bindehautentzündung *f*.

conjure ['kʌndʒəʳ] *vti* zaubern.

♦ **conjure up** *vt sep* (*host, spirits* beschwören; *(fig)* memories *etc* heraufbeschwören.

conjurer, conjuror ['kʌndʒərəʳ] *n* Zauberkünstler(in *f*) *m*.

conjuring ['kʌndʒərɪŋ] *n* Zaubern *nt*; ~ **set** Zauberkasten *m*; ~ **trick** Zauberkunststück *nt*.

♦ **conk out** [,kɒŋk'aʊt] *vi* (*col*) den Geist aufgeben; *(person)* umkippen *(col)*.

conker ['kɒŋkəʳ] *n* (*Brit col*) (Roß)kastanie *f*.

con-man ['kɒnmæn] *n*, *pl* **-men** [-men] *(col)* Schwindler *m*; (*pretending to have social status*) Hochstapler *m*; (*promising marriage*) Heiratsschwindler *m*.

connect [kə'nekt] **1** *vt* **(a)** (*join*) verbinden *(to, with* mit*)*; (*Elec etc: also* ~ **up**) *appliances, subscribers* anschließen *(to* an +*acc*). **I'll** ~ **you** (*Telec*) ich verbinde (Sie); **to be** ~**ed** (*two things*) miteinander verbunden sein. **(b)** (*fig: associate*) in Verbindung bringen. **(c)** (*esp pass: link*) *ideas, theories etc* verbinden. **to be** ~**ed with** eine Beziehung haben zu; (*be related to*) verwandt sein mit. **2** *vi* (*rooms*) eine Verbindung haben *(to, with* zu*)*; (*train, plane*) Anschluß haben (*with* an +*acc*). **his punch didn't** ~ sein Schlag hat nicht getroffen.

connection, connexion [kə'nekʃən] *n* **(a)** Verbindung *f* (*to, with* zum, mit*)*; (*wire*) Leitung *f*; (*to mains*) Anschluß *m* (*to* an +*acc*); (*connecting part*) Verbindung(sstück *nt*) *f*. **parallel/series** ~ Parallel-/Reihenschaltung *f*. **(b)** (*fig: link*) Zusammenhang *m*. **the two events are not** ~**ed** zwischen den beiden Ereignissen besteht kein Zusammenhang; **in this** ~ in diesem Zusammenhang; **in** ~ **with** in Zusammenhang mit. **(c)** (*relationship, business* ~) Beziehung *f* (*with* zu*)*; (*family* ~) familiäre Beziehung. **to have** ~**s** Beziehungen haben; **there is some family** ~ **between them** sie sind weitläufig miteinander verwandt. **(d)** (*Rail etc*) Anschluß *m*.

conning tower ['kɒnɪŋtaʊəʳ] *n* Kommandoturm *m*.

connivance [kə'naɪvəns] *n* (*tacit consent*) stillschweigendes Einverständnis.

connive [kə'naɪv] *vi* **(a)** (*conspire*) sich verschwören. **(b)** (*deliberately overlook*) **to** ~ **at sth** etw stillschweigend dulden.

connoisseur [,kɒnə'sɜːʳ] *n* Kenner *m*.

connotation [,kɒnəʊ'teɪʃən] *n* Assoziation *f*.

conquer ['kɒŋkəʳ] *vt* **(a)** (*lit*) *country, the world* erobern; *enemy, nation* besiegen. **(b)** (*fig*) *mountain* bezwingen; *people, sb's heart* erobern.

conquering ['kɒŋkərɪŋ] *adj hero* siegreich.

conqueror ['kɒŋkərəʳ] *n* (*of country, heart*) Eroberer *m*; (*fig*) Sieger *m* (*of* über +*acc*); (*of mountain*) Bezwinger *m* (*of gen*).

conquest ['kɒŋkwest] *n* Eroberung *f*; (*of enemy etc, disease*) Sieg *m* (*of* über +*acc*); (*col: person*) Eroberung *f*; (*of mountain*) Bezwingung *f*.

conscience ['kɒnʃəns] *n* Gewissen *nt*. **to have a clear/easy/bad** ~ ein reines/gutes/schlechtes Gewissen haben (*about* wegen*)*; **to have sth on one's** ~ mit etw auf dem Gewissen haben; **with an easy** ~ mit ruhigem Gewissen; **in (all)** ~ allen Ernstes.

conscience-stricken ['kɒnʃəns,strɪkən] *adj* schuldbewußt.

conscientious [,kɒnʃɪ'enʃəs] *adj* (*diligent*) gewissenhaft; (*conscious of one's duty*) pflichtbewußt. ~ **objector** Kriegsdienstverweigerer *m* (*aus Gewissensgründen*).

conscientiousness [,kɒnʃɪ'enʃəsnɪs] *n* Gewissenhaftigkeit *f*; (*sense of duty*) Pflichtbewußtsein *nt*.

conscious ['kɒnʃəs] *adj* **(a)** (*Med*) bei Bewußtsein.

(b) (*aware*) bewußt (*also Psych*). **to be/become** ~ **of sth** (*dat*) einer Sache (*gen*) bewußt sein/ werden. **(c)** (*deliberate*) bewußt.

consciousness ['kɒnʃəsnɪs] *n* **(a)** (*Med*) Bewußtsein *nt*. **to lose/regain** ~ das Bewußtsein verlieren/wiedererlangen. **(b)** (*awareness*) Wissen *nt* (*of* um*)*.

conscript [kən'skrɪpt] **1** *vt* einziehen; *army* ausheben. **2** ['kɒnskrɪpt] *n* Wehrpflichtige(r) *m*.

conscription [kən'skrɪpʃən] *n* Wehrpflicht *f*; (*act of conscripting*) Einberufung *f*; (*of army*) Aushebung *f*.

consecrate ['kɒnsɪkreɪt] *vt* (*lit, fig*) weihen.

consecration [,kɒnsɪ'kreɪʃən] *n* Weihe *f*; (*in mass*) Wandlung *f*.

consecutive [kən'sekjʊtɪv] *adj* aufeinanderfolgend; *numbers* fortlaufend. **on four** ~ **days** vier Tage hintereinander.

consensus [kən'sensəs] *n* Übereinstimmung *f*. **the** ~ **is that** ... man ist allgemein der Meinung, daß ...; **that's the** ~ **of opinion** das ist die allgemeine Meinung.

consent [kən'sent] **1** *vi* zustimmen (*to dat*). **to** ~ **to do sth** sich bereit erklären, etw zu tun. **2** *n* Zustimmung *f* (*to* zu*)* *f*. **by mutual** ~ in gegenseitigem Einverständnis; **the age of** ~ das Ehemündigkeitsalter; **she's below the age of** ~ sie ist noch minderjährig.

consequence ['kɒnsɪkwəns] *n* **(a)** (*result, effect*) Folge *f*. **in** ~ folglich; **in** ~ **of** infolge (+*gen*); **in** ~ **of which** infolgedessen; **to take the** ~**s** die Konsequenzen tragen. **(b)** (*importance*) Bedeutung *f*. **it's of no** ~ das spielt keine Rolle.

consequent ['kɒnsɪkwənt] *adj attr* daraus folgend; (*temporal*) darauffolgend.

consequently [,kɒnsə'vəɪʃən] *adv* folglich.

conservation [,kɒnsə'veɪʃən] *n* (*preservation*) Erhaltung *f*. ~ **area** (*in the country*) Naturschutzgebiet *nt*; (*in town*) unter Denkmalschutz stehendes Gebiet.

conservationist [,kɒnsə'veɪʃənɪst] *n* Umweltschützer(in *f*) *m*; (*as regards old buildings etc*) Denkmalpfleger(in *f*) *m*.

conservative [kən'sɜːvətɪv] *adj* (*also Pol*) konservativ. **at a** ~ **estimate** bei vorsichtiger Schätzung.

conservatory [kən'sɜːvətrɪ] *n* **(a)** (*Hort*) Wintergarten *m*; (*esp US: Mus*) Konservatorium *nt*.

conserve [kən'sɜːv] *vt* erhalten; (*one's strength*) schonen; *energy* sparen.

consider [kən'sɪdəʳ] *vt* **(a)** (*reflect upon*) *plan, idea, offer* nachdenken über (+*acc*). **I'll** ~ **the matter** ich werde mir die Sache durch den Kopf gehen lassen; **have you** ~**ed the possibility of ...?** haben Sie an die Möglichkeit gedacht, zu...?; **I wouldn't even** ~ **it!** ich denke nicht daran! **(b)** (*bear in mind*) in Erwägung ziehen; (*take into account*) denken an (+*acc*), berücksichtigen; *person, feelings also* Rücksicht nehmen auf (+*acc*). ~ **how much you owe him** bedenken Sie, wieviel Sie ihm schulden; **all things** ~**ed** alles in allem. **(c)** (*regard as*) betrachten als; *person* halten für. **to** ~ **oneself lucky** sich glücklich schätzen.

considerable [kən'sɪdərəbl] *adj* beträchtlich.

considerably [kən'sɪdərəblɪ] *adv* beträchtlich.

considerate [kən'sɪdərɪt] *adj* rücksichtsvoll (*to/wards* gegenüber); (*kind*) aufmerksam.

consideration [kən,sɪdə'reɪʃən] *n* **(a)** *no pl* (*careful thought*) Überlegung *f*. **I'll give it my** ~ ich werde es mir überlegen. **(b)** *no pl* (*regard, account*) **to take sth into** ~ etw berücksichtigen; **to leave sth out of** ~ etw außer acht lassen; **he's under** ~ **for the job** er wird für die Stelle in Erwägung gezogen; **it's under** ~ es wird zur Zeit geprüft. **(c)** *no pl* (*thoughtfulness*) Rücksicht *f* (*for auf* +*acc*). **to have** ~ **for sb's feelings** Rücksicht auf jds Gefühle nehmen; **his lack of** ~ **(for others)** seine Rücksichtslosigkeit *(anderen gegenüber)*. **(d)** *(sth taken into account)* Faktor *m*. **money is no** ~ **Geld** spielt keine Rolle; **his first** ~ **is his family** seine Familie spielt für ihn die größte Rolle. **(e)** *(payment)* **for a** ~ gegen Entgelt.

considered [kən'sɪdəd] *adj attr opinion* ernsthaft.

considering [kən'sɪdərɪŋ] **1** *prep* ~ **my age** für mein Alter, wenn man mein Alter bedenkt. **2** *conj* ~ **(that) he's been ill ...** wenn man bedenkt, daß er krank war ...

consign [kən'saɪn] *vt* **(a)** *(Comm: send)* versenden. **(b)** *(entrust)* anvertrauen *(to +dat)*.

consignee [ˌkɒnsaɪ'niː] *n* Empfänger *m*.

consignment [kən'saɪnmənt] *n* *(Comm)* *(goods)* Sendung *f*; *(bigger)* Ladung *f*. ~ **note** Frachtbrief *m*.

consist [kən'sɪst] *vi* **to** ~ **of** bestehen aus; **to** ~ **in sth in etw** *(dat)* bestehen.

consistency [kən'sɪstənsɪ] *n* **(a)** *see adj* **(a)** Konsequenz *f*; Übereinstimmung *f*; Folgerichtigkeit *f*; Beständigkeit *f*. **his statements lack** ~ **seine** Aussagen widersprechen sich. **(b)** *(of substance)* Konsistenz *f*.

consistent [kən'sɪstənt] *adj* **(a)** konsequent; *statements* übereinstimmend; *argument* folgerichtig; *quality* beständig. **(b)** *(in agreement)* **to be** ~ **with sth einer Sache** *(dat)* entsprechen.

consistently [kən'sɪstəntlɪ] *adv* **(a)** *argue* konsequent. **(b)** *(uniformly)* durchweg. **(c)** *(in agreement)* entsprechend *(with dat)*.

consolation [ˌkɒnsə'leɪʃən] *n* Trost *m no pl.* **words of** ~ tröstende Worte; ~ **prize** Trostpreis *m*.

console¹ [kən'səʊl] *vt* trösten.

console² ['kɒnsəʊl] *n* **(a)** *(control panel)* (Kontroll)pult *nt*; *(of organ)* Spieltisch *m*. **(b)** *(cabinet)* Schrank *m*. **(c)** *(ornamental bracket)* Konsole *f*.

consolidate [kən'sɒlɪdeɪt] *vt* **(a)** *(confirm)* festigen. **(b)** *(combine)* zusammenlegen; *companies* zusammenschließen; *funds, debts* konsolidieren.

consolidation [kənˌsɒlɪ'deɪʃən] *n see vt* **(a)** Festigung *f*. **(b)** Zusammenlegung *f*; Zusammenschluß *m*; Konsolidierung *f*.

consommé [kɒn'sɒmeɪ] *n* Kraftbrühe *f*.

consonant ['kɒnsənənt] *n (Phon)* Konsonant *m*. ~ **shift** Lautverschiebung *f*.

consort ['kɒnsɔːt] **1** *n (form: spouse)* Gemahl(in *f*) *m (form)*. **2** [kən'sɔːt] *vi (form)* verkehren *(with mit)*.

consortium [kən'sɔːtɪəm] *n* Konsortium *nt*.

conspicuous [kən'spɪkjʊəs] *adj* auffällig; *road signs* deutlich sichtbar; *lack of sth* offensichtlich; *bravery* bemerkenswert. **to be/make oneself** ~ auffallen; **to be/not to be** ~ **for sth** sich/sich nicht gerade durch etw auszeichnen; **he was** ~ **by his absence** er glänzte durch Abwesenheit.

conspiracy [kən'spɪrəsɪ] *n* Verschwörung *f*. **a** ~ **of silence** ein verabredetes Schweigen.

conspirator [kən'spɪrətə'] *n* Verschwörer *m*.

conspire [kən'spaɪə'] *vi* sich verschwören *(against gegen)*; *(events)* zusammenkommen.

constable ['kʌnstəbl] *n (Brit: police* ~*)* Polizist(in *f*) *m*.

constabulary [kən'stæbjʊlərɪ] *n (Brit)* Polizei *f no pl*.

constant ['kɒnstənt] **1** *adj* **(a)** *(continuous)* ständig. **(b)** *(unchanging)* gleichbleibend, konstant. **(c)** *(steadfast)* beständig. **2** *n (Math, Phys, fig)* Konstante *f*.

constantly ['kɒnstəntlɪ] *adv* ständig.

constellation [ˌkɒnstə'leɪʃən] *n* Sternbild *nt*.

consternation ['kɒnstə'neɪʃən] *n (dismay)* Bestürzung *f*; *(worry)* Sorge *f*; *(confusion)* Aufruhr *m*. **to my great** ~ zu meiner großen Bestürzung; **with a look of** ~ **on his face** mit bestürzter Miene; **the news filled me with** ~ ich war bestürzt, als ich das hörte.

constipated ['kɒnstɪpeɪtɪd] *adj* verstopft. **he is** ~

er hat Verstopfung.

constipation [ˌkɒnstɪ'peɪʃən] *n no pl* Verstopfung *f*.

constituency [kən'stɪtjʊənsɪ] *n (Pol)* Wahlkreis *m*.

constituent [kən'stɪtjʊənt] **1** *n* **(a)** *(Pol)* Wähler(in *f*) *m*. **(b)** *(part, element)* Bestandteil *m*. **2** *adj* **(a)** *(Pol)* *assembly* konstituierend. **(b)** *attr part, element* einzeln.

constitute ['kɒnstɪtjuːt] *vt* **(a)** *(make up)* bilden. **(b)** *(amount to)* darstellen. **(c)** *(set up)* gründen.

constitution [ˌkɒnstɪ'tjuːʃən] *n* **(a)** *(Pol)* Verfassung *f*; *(of club etc)* Satzung *f*. **(b)** *(of person)* Konstitution *f*. **(c)** *(way sth is made)* Aufbau *m*; *(what sth is made of)* Zusammensetzung *f*. **(d)** *(setting up)* Gründung *f*.

constitutional [ˌkɒnstɪ'tjuːʃənl] **1** *adj* **(a)** *(Pol)* *reform, crisis* Verfassungs-; *monarchy* konstitutionell; *government, action* verfassungsmäßig. ~ **law** Verfassungsrecht *nt*; **it's not** ~ **das ist** verfassungswidrig. **(b)** *(Med)* konstitutionell. **2** *n (hum col)* Spaziergang *m*.

constrain [kən'streɪn] *vt* zwingen; *one's temper* zügeln. **to find oneself/feel** ~**ed to ...** sich gezwungen sehen/fühlen, zu ...

constraint [kən'streɪnt] *n* **(a)** *(compulsion)* Zwang *m*. **(b)** *(restriction)* Beschränkung *f*. **to place** ~**s on sth einer Sache** *(dat)* Zwänge auferlegen. **(c)** *(in manner etc)* Gezwungenheit *f*; *(embarrassment)* Befangenheit *f*.

constrict [kən'strɪkt] *vt* **(a)** einengen; *muscle* zusammenziehen; *vein* verengen. **(b)** *movements* einschränken *(also fig)*.

constriction [kən'strɪkʃən] *n* **(a)** *(of muscles)* Zusammenziehen *nt*. **(b)** *(of movements etc)* Einschränkung *f*.

construct [kən'strʌkt] *vt* bauen; *geometrical figure* konstruieren; *sentence* bilden; *theory* entwickeln.

construction [kən'strʌkʃən] *n* **(a)** *see vt* Bau *m*; Konstruktion *f*; Entwicklung *f*. **under** ~ in or im Bau. **(b)** *(way sth is constructed)* Struktur *f*; *(of building)* Bauweise *f*; *(of machine, bridge)* Konstruktion *f*. **(c)** *(sth constructed)* Bau *m*; *(bridge, machine)* Konstruktion *f*. **(d)** *(interpretation)* Deutung *f*. **to put a wrong** ~ **on sth** etw falsch auffassen. **(e)** *(Gram)* Konstruktion *f*. **sentence** ~ Satzbau *m*.

construction industry *n* Bauindustrie *f*.

constructive [kən'strʌktɪv] *adj* konstruktiv.

construe [kən'struː] *vt (interpret)* auffassen.

consul ['kɒnsəl] *n* Konsul *m*.

consular ['kɒnsjʊlə'] *adj* konsularisch.

consulate ['kɒnsjʊlɪt] *n* Konsulat *nt*.

consult [kən'sʌlt] **1** *vt* sich besprechen mit; *lawyer, doctor etc* konsultieren; *dictionary* nachschlagen in *(+dat)*; *map* nachsehen auf *(+dat)*; *oracle* befragen; *horoscope* nachlesen. **he did it without** ~**ing anyone** er hat das getan, ohne jemanden zu fragen. **2** *vi (confer)* sich beraten *(with mit)*.

consultancy [kən'sʌltənsɪ] *n (act)* Beratung *f*; *(business)* Beratungsbüro *nt*.

consultant [kən'sʌltənt] **1** *n* **(a)** *(Brit Med)* Facharzt *m*, Fachärztin *f*. ~ **gynaecologist** Facharzt/ -ärztin für Frauenkrankheiten. **(b)** *(other professions)* Berater(in *f*) *m*. **2** *adj attr* beratend.

consultation [ˌkɒnsəl'teɪʃən] *n* Besprechung *f*; *(of doctor, lawyer)* Konsultation *f (of gen)*. **in** ~ **with** in gemeinsamer Beratung mit.

consulting [kən'sʌltɪŋ] *adj* ~ **hours/room** *(Brit)* Sprechstunde *f*/-zimmer *nt*.

consume [kən'sjuːm] *vt* **(a)** *food, drink* zu sich nehmen; *(Econ)* konsumieren. **(b)** *(destroy)* vernichten; *(use up)* verbrauchen. **he was** ~**d with jealousy** er wurde von Eifersucht verzehrt *(geh)*.

consumer [kən'sjuːmə'] *n* Verbraucher(in *f*) *m*.

consumer *in cpds* Verbraucher-; ~ **durables** *npl* Gebrauchsgüter *pl*; ~ **goods** *npl* Konsumgüter *pl*; ~ **protection** *n* Verbraucherschutz *m*;

~s' advice centre *(Brit) or* center *(US) n* Verbraucherzentrale *f*; ~ society *n* Konsumgesellschaft *f*.

consummate [kən'sʌmɪt] 1 *adj* vollendet. with ~ ease mit spielender Leichtigkeit. 2 ['kɒnsəmeɪt] *vt marriage* vollziehen.

consumption [kən'sʌmpʃən] *n* (a) Konsum *m*; *(of non-edible products)* Verbrauch *m*. this letter is for private ~ only *(col)* der Brief ist nur für den privaten Gebrauch; not fit for human ~ zum Verzehr ungeeignet. (b) *(Med old)* Schwindsucht *f*.

contact ['kɒntækt] 1 *n* (a) Kontakt *m*; *(communication also)* Verbindung *f*. to be in ~ with sb/sth *(be touching)* jdn/etw berühren; *(in communication)* mit jdm/etw in Kontakt stehen; to come into ~ with sb/sth *(lit, fig)* mit jdm/etw in Berührung kommen; he has no ~ with his family er hat keinen Kontakt zu seiner Familie; to make ~ with sb/sth *(get in touch with)* sich mit jdm/etw in Verbindung setzen; I finally made ~ with him at his office ich habe ihn schließlich im Büro erreicht; to lose ~ (with sb/sth) den Kontakt (zu jdm/etw) verlieren; point of ~ *(Math, fig)* Berührungspunkt *m*.
(b) *(Elec) (act)* Kontakt *m*; *(equipment)* Kontaktstück *nt*. to make/break ~ den Kontakt herstellen/unterbrechen.
(c) *(person)* Kontaktperson *f (also Med)*; *(in espionage)* Verbindungsmann, V-Mann *m*. ~s *pl* Kontakte *pl*; to make ~s Kontakte herstellen.
2 *vt person, agent* sich in Verbindung setzen mit. I've been trying to ~ you for hours ich versuche schon seit Stunden, Sie zu erreichen.

contact: ~ adhesive *n* Kontaktklebstoff *m*; ~-breaker *n* Unterbrecher *m*; ~ lens *n* Kontaktlinse *f*.

contagion [kən'teɪdʒən] *n (contact)* Ansteckung *f*; *(disease)* Ansteckungskrankheit *f*; *(epidemic)* Seuche *f (also fig)*; *(fig: spreading influence)* schädlicher Einfluß.

contagious [kən'teɪdʒəs] *adj (Med, fig)* ansteckend.

contain [kən'teɪn] *vt* (a) *(hold within itself)* enthalten. (b) *(have capacity for)* fassen. (c) *emotions, oneself* beherrschen; *disease, inflation* in Grenzen halten; *epidemic, flood* unter Kontrolle bringen.

container [kən'teɪnəʳ] 1 *n* (a) Behälter *m*. (b) *(Comm)* Container *m*. 2 *adj attr* Container-.

containerize [kən'teɪnəraɪz] *vt freight* in Container verpacken; *port* auf Container umstellen.

contaminate [kən'tæmɪneɪt] *vt* verunreinigen; *(poison)* vergiften; *(radioactivity)* verseuchen; *(fig) mind* verderben.

contd = continued Forts., Fortsetzung *f*.

contemplate ['kɒntempleɪt] *vt* (a) *(look at)* betrachten. (b) *(reflect upon)* nachdenken über *(+acc)*; *(consider) a purchase, action* in Erwägung ziehen; *a holiday* denken an *(+acc)*.

contemplation [ˌkɒntem'pleɪʃən] *n* (a) *(looking)* Betrachtung *f*. (b) *(thinking)* Nachdenken *nt (of* über *+acc)*; *(deep thought)* Betrachtung, Kontemplation *(esp Rel) f*.

contemplative [kən'templətɪv] *adj look* nachdenklich; *life* beschaulich, kontemplativ *(esp Rel)*.

contemporary [kən'tempərərɪ] 1 *adj* (a) *(of the same time) events* gleichzeitig; *literature* zeitgenössisch; *(of the same age)* gleich alt. (b) *(of the present time) life* heutig; *art* zeitgenössisch, modern. 2 *n* Altersgenosse *m*/-genossin *f*; *(in history)* Zeitgenosse *m*/-genossin *f*.

contempt [kən'tempt] *n* (a) Verachtung *f*; *(disregard also)* Geringschätzung *f (for* von). to hold in ~ verachten; beneath ~ unter aller Kritik. (b) *(Jur: also ~ of court)* Mißachtung *f* des Gerichts.

contemptible [kən'temptəbl] *adj* verachtenswert.

contemptuous [kən'temptjʊəs] *adj manner, look* verächtlich. to be ~ of sb/sth jdn/etw verachten.

contend [kən'tend] 1 *vi* (a) kämpfen. to ~ for sth um etw kämpfen; then you'll have me to ~ with dann bekommst du es mit mir zu tun. (b) *(cope)* to ~ with sb/sth mit jdm/etw fertig werden. 2 *vt* behaupten.

contender [kən'tendəʳ] *n* Anwärter(in *f) m (for* auf *+acc)*; *(Sport)* Wettkämpfer(in *f) m (for* um).

content¹ [kən'tent] 1 *adj* zufrieden *(with* mit). 2 *n* Zufriedenheit *f*; *see* heart (a). 3 *vt person* zufriedenstellen. to ~ oneself with sich zufriedengeben mit.

content² ['kɒntent] *n* (a) ~s *pl* Inhalt *m*; *(table of)* ~s Inhaltsverzeichnis *nt*. (b) *no pl (substance)* Gehalt *m*.

contented [kən'tentɪd] *adj* zufrieden.

contention [kən'tenʃən] *n* (a) *(dispute)* Streit *m*. the matter in ~ die strittige Angelegenheit. (b) *(assertion)* Behauptung *f*.

contentment [kən'tentmənt] *n* Zufriedenheit *f*.

contest ['kɒntest] 1 *n* Kampf *m (for* um*)*; *(beauty ~ etc)* Wettbewerb *m*. boxing ~ Boxkampf *m*; election ~ Wahlkampf *m*. 2 [kən'test] *vt* (a) *(fight over)* kämpfen um; *(Pol: candidate) seat* sich bewerben um; *(oppose)* kämpfen gegen. (b) *statement* bestreiten; *(Jur) will* anfechten.

contestant [kən'testənt] *n* (Wettbewerbs)teilnehmer(in *f) m*; *(Parl, in quiz)* Kandidat(in *f) m*; *(Sport)* (Wettkampf)teilnehmer(in *f) m*. the ~s in the election die Wahlkandidaten.

context ['kɒntekst] *n* Zusammenhang *m*. out of ~ aus dem Zusammenhang gerissen.

continent ['kɒntɪnənt] *n* Kontinent *m*; *(mainland)* Festland *nt*. the C~ *(Brit)* Kontinentaleuropa *nt*; on the C~ auf dem europäischen Festland.

continental [ˌkɒntɪ'nentl] 1 *adj* (a) *(Geog)* kontinental. (b) *(Brit: European)* europäisch. 2 *n* (Festlands)europäer(in *f) m*.

continental: ~ breakfast *n* kleines Frühstück *(Kaffee und Brötchen)*; ~ quilt *n (Brit)* Federbett *nt*.

contingency [kən'tɪndʒənsɪ] *n* möglicher Fall. in this ~ in diesem Fall; ~ fund Eventualfonds *m*; a ~ plan ein Ausweichplan *m*.

contingent [kən'tɪndʒənt] 1 *adj* ~ upon *(form)* abhängig von; to be ~ upon abhängen von. 2 *n* Kontingent *nt*; *(Mil)* Trupp *m*.

continual [kən'tɪnjʊəl] *adj (frequent)* dauernd; *(unceasing)* ununterbrochen.

continuance [kən'tɪnjʊəns] *n* (a) *(duration)* Dauer *f*. (b) *(continuation)* Fortsetzung *f*.

continuation [kən,tɪnju'eɪʃən] *n* Fortsetzung *f*.

continue [kən'tɪnjuː] 1 *vt* fortsetzen. to ~ to read, to ~ reading weiterlesen; to be ~d Fortsetzung folgt. 2 *vi (go on) (person)* weitermachen; *(crisis, speech)* (an)dauern; *(weather)* anhalten; *(road etc)* sich fortsetzen; *(concert etc)* weitergehen. he ~s (to be) optimistic er ist nach wie vor optimistisch.

continuity [ˌkɒntɪ'njuːɪtɪ] *n* (a) Kontinuität *f*. the story lacks ~ der Geschichte fehlt der rote Faden. (b) *(Film)* ~ girl Scriptgirl *nt*.

continuous [kən'tɪnjʊəs] *adj* dauernd, ständig; *line* ununterbrochen; ~ performance *(Film)* durchgehende Vorstellung.

continuously [kən'tɪnjʊəslɪ] *adv see adj* dauernd, ständig; ununterbrochen.

contort [kən'tɔːt] *vt features* verziehen *(into* zu*)*; *limbs* verrenken. a face ~ed by pain ein schmerzverzerrtes Gesicht.

contortion [kən'tɔːʃən] *n (esp of acrobat)* Verrenkung *f*; *(of features)* Verzerrung *f*.

contortionist [kən'tɔːʃənɪst] *n* Schlangenmensch *m*.

contour ['kɒntʊəʳ] *n* Kontur *f*.

contour: ~ line *n (Geog)* Höhenlinie *f*; ~ map *n* Höhenlinienkarte *f*.

contraband

contraband ['kɒntrəbænd] **1** *n* no *pl (goods)* Schmuggelware *f; (form: smuggling)* Schleichhandel *m.* **2** *adj* Schmuggel-.
contraception [ˌkɒntrə'sepʃən] *n* Empfängnisverhütung.
contraceptive [ˌkɒntrə'septɪv] **1** *n* empfängnisverhütendes Mittel. **2** *adj* empfängnisverhütend; *pill* Antibaby-.
contract¹ ['kɒntrækt] **1** *n* **(a)** Vertrag *m; (Comm: order)* Auftrag *m.* **to enter into a ~ (with sb)** (mit jdm) einen Vertrag schließen; **to put work out to ~** Arbeiten außer Haus machen lassen. **(b)** *(Bridge)* Kontrakt *m.* **~ bridge** Kontrakt-Bridge *nt.* **2** *adj price, date* vertraglich festgelegt. **3** [kən'trækt] *vt* **(a)** *debts* machen; *illness* erkranken an (+*dat*). **(b)** *(enter into) marriage, alliance* eingehen. **4** [kən'trækt] *vi (Comm)* **to ~ to do sth** sich vertraglich verpflichten, etw zu tun.
♦ **contract in** *vi* sich anschließen *(-to dat); (into insurance scheme)* beitreten *(-to dat).*
♦ **contract out** **1** *vi (withdraw)* austreten *(of aus); (not join)* sich nicht anschließen *(of dat); (of insurance scheme)* nicht beitreten *(of dat).* **2** *vt sep (Comm) work* vergeben *(to an +acc).*
contract² [kən'trækt] **1** *vt* zusammenziehen. **2** *vi (muscle, metal etc)* sich zusammenziehen.
contraction [kən'trækʃən] *n* **(a)** *(shrinking)* Zusammenziehung *f.* **(b)** *(in childbirth)* Wehe *f.*
contractor [kən'træktər] *n (individual)* Auftragnehmer *m; (building ~)* Bauunternehmer *m.*
contractual [kən'træktʃʊəl] *adj* vertraglich.
contradict [ˌkɒntrə'dɪkt] *vt* widersprechen (+*dat*).
contradiction [ˌkɒntrə'dɪkʃən] *n* Widerspruch *m (of zu).* **full of ~s** voller Widersprüchlichkeiten.
contradictory [ˌkɒntrə'dɪktərɪ] *adj* widersprüchlich.
contra-flow ['kɒntrə'fləʊ] *n (Mot)* Gegenverkehr *m.*
contralto [kən'træltəʊ] **1** *n (voice)* Alt *m.* **2** *adj voice* Alt-. **the ~ part** die Altstimme.
contraption [kən'træpʃən] *n (col)* Apparat *m (col); (vehicle)* Vehikel *nt (col).*
contrary¹ ['kɒntrərɪ] **1** *adj (opposite)* entgegengesetzt. **2** *n* Gegenteil *nt.* **on the ~** im Gegenteil; **do you have information to the ~?** liegen Ihnen gegenteilige Informationen vor?; **unless you hear to the ~** sofern Sie nichts Gegenteiliges hören. **3** *adv* **~ to expectations** wider Erwarten; **~ to what he said** im Gegensatz zu dem, was er gesagt hat.
contrary² [kən'treərɪ] *adj (awkward)* widerspenstig.
contrast ['kɒntrɑːst] **1** *n* **(a)** Gegensatz *m (with, to zu); (visual)* Kontrast *m (with, to zu).* **by** or **in ~** im Gegensatz dazu. **(b)** *(Art, Phot, TV)* Kontrast *m.* **2** [kən'trɑːst] *vt* gegenüberstellen *(with dat).* **3** [kən'trɑːst] *vi* im Gegensatz stehen *(with zu); (colours)* sich abheben *(with von).*
contrasting [kən'trɑːstɪŋ] *adj* gegensätzlich.
contravene [ˌkɒntrə'viːn] *vt* verstoßen gegen.
contravention [ˌkɒntrə'venʃən] *n* Verstoß *m (of gegen).* **to act in ~ of sth** einer Sache (*dat*) zuwiderhandeln.
contretemps ['kɒntrətɒŋ] *n* no *pl* Zwischenfall *m.*
contribute [kən'trɪbjuːt] **1** *vt* beitragen *(to zu); money, supplies* beisteuern *(to zu); (to charity)* spenden *(to für).* **to ~ one's share** sein(en) Teil (dazu) beitragen. **2** *vi* beitragen *(to zu); (to pension fund etc, to newspaper)* einen Beitrag leisten *(to zu); (to present)* beisteuern *(to zu); (to charity)* spenden *(to für).*
contribution [ˌkɒntrɪ'bjuːʃən] *n* Beitrag *m (to zu); (to charity)* Spende *f.* **the beer is my ~** das Bier stelle ich.
contributor [kən'trɪbjʊtər] *n (to magazine)* Mitarbeiter(in *f*) *m (to an +dat); (of goods, money)* Spender(in *f*) *m.*

contributory [kən'trɪbjʊtərɪ] *adj* **(a)** **that's a ~ factor** dieser Faktor spielt eine Rolle; **~ negligence** *(Jur)* Mitverschulden *nt.* **(b)** *pension scheme* beitragspflichtig.
con trick *n (col)* Schwindel *m.*
contrite ['kɒntraɪt] *adj* reuig.
contrition [kən'trɪʃən] *n* Reue *f.* **act of ~** *(Eccl)* Buße *f.*
contrivance [kən'traɪvəns] *n (device)* Vorrichtung *f; (mechanical)* Gerät *nt.*
contrive [kən'traɪv] *vt* **(a)** *plan* ersinnen. **to ~ a means of doing sth** einen Weg finden, etw zu tun. **(b)** *(manage, arrange)* bewerkstelligen. **to ~ to do sth** *(also iro)* es fertigbringen, etw zu tun; **he always ~s to get his own way** er versteht (es) immer, seinen Kopf durchzusetzen.
contrived [kən'traɪvd] *adj* gestellt; *style* gekünstelt.
control [kən'trəʊl] **1** *n* no *pl (supervision)* Aufsicht *f (of über +acc); (of situation, emotion)* Beherrschung *f (of gen); (authority, power)* Gewalt *f (over über +acc); (of prices)* Kontrolle *f (of gen); (of traffic)* Regelung *f (of gen)* etc. **to be in ~ of sth** *business, office* etw leiten; *group of children* etw beaufsichtigen; **to have sth under ~** etw in der Hand haben; **to be in ~ of one's emotions** Herr seiner Gefühle sein; **to have no ~ over sb** keinen Einfluß auf jdn haben; **to lose ~ (of sth)** (über etw *acc*) die Gewalt verlieren; **to lose ~ of the situation** nicht mehr Herr der Lage sein; **to be/get out of ~** *(child, class)* außer Rand und Band sein/geraten; *(situation)* außer Kontrolle sein/geraten; **the car went out of ~** das Auto geriet außer Kontrolle; **under state ~** unter staatlicher Aufsicht; **to be under ~** unter Kontrolle sein; **he was beyond parental ~** er war seinen Eltern über den Kopf gewachsen; **circumstances beyond our ~** außerhalb unserer Hand liegende Umstände; **his ~ of the ball** seine Ballführung.
(b) *(check)* Kontrolle *f (on gen,* über +*acc*).
wages/price ~s Lohn-/Preiskontrolle *f.*
(c) *(~ room)* die Zentrale; *(Aviat)* der Kontrollturm.
(d) *(knob, switch)* Regler *m; (of vehicle, machine)* Schalter *m.* **to be at the ~s** *(of spaceship, airliner)* am Kontrollpult sitzen; *(of small plane, car)* die Steuerung haben; **to take over the ~s** die Steuerung übernehmen.
(e) *(Sci: group)* Kontrollgruppe *f.* **~ experiment** Kontrollversuch *m.*
2 *vt* **(a)** *(direct, manage)* kontrollieren; *business* führen; *organization* in der Hand haben; *child, class* fertigwerden mit; *car* lenken; *traffic* regeln; *emotions* beherrschen; *hair* bändigen. **to ~ oneself/one's temper** sich beherrschen; **~ yourself!** nimm dich zusammen! **(b)** *(regulate) temperature, speed* regulieren; *prices etc* kontrollieren; *disease* unter Kontrolle bringen; *population* eindämmen.
control column *n* Steuerknüppel *m.*
controlled [kən'trəʊld] *adj emotion* beherrscht; *conditions* kontrolliert; *prices* gebunden; *temperature* geregelt.
controller [kən'trəʊlər] *n* **(a)** *(Rad)* Intendant *m; (Aviat)* (Flug)lotse *m.* **(b)** *(Tech)* Regler *m.*
controlling [kən'trəʊlɪŋ] *adj attr factor* beherrschend; *body* Aufsichts-. **~ interest** Mehrheitsanteil *m.*
control: ~ panel *n* Schalttafel *f; (on aircraft, TV)* Bedienungsfeld *nt; (on car)* Armaturenbrett *nt;* **~ point** *n* Kontrollpunkt *m;* **~ room** *n* Kontrollraum *m; (Mil)* (Operations)zentrale *f; (of police)* Zentrale *f;* **~ tower** *n (Aviat)* Kontrollturm *m.*
controversial [ˌkɒntrə'vɜːʃəl] *adj* umstritten.
controversy ['kɒntrəvɜːsɪ, kən'trɒvəsɪ] *n* Kontroversen *pl.* **to give rise to ~** Anlaß zu Kontroversen geben.

contusion [kən'tjuːʒən] n Quetschung f.

conundrum [kə'nʌndrəm] n (lit, fig) Rätsel nt.

conurbation [ˌkɒnɜː'beɪʃən] n Ballungsgebiet nt.

convalesce [ˌkɒnvə'les] vi genesen (from, after von).

convalescence [ˌkɒnvə'lesəns] n Genesung f; (period) Genesungszeit f.

convalescent [ˌkɒnvə'lesənt] 1 n Genesende(r) mf. 2 adj genesend. to be ~ auf dem Wege der Besserung sein; ~ home Genesungsheim nt.

convection [kən'vekʃən] n Konvektion f.

convector [kən'vektər] n (also ~ heater) Heizlüfter m.

convene [kən'viːn] 1 vt meeting einberufen. 2 vi sich versammeln.

convener [kən'viːnər] n Person, die Versammlungen einberuft.

convenience [kən'viːnɪəns] n (a) no pl (usefulness) Annehmlichkeit f; (expediency) Zweckmäßigkeit f. ~ foods Fertiggerichte pl. (b) no pl these chairs are for the ~ of customers diese Stühle sind für unsere Kunden gedacht; at your own ~ wann es Ihnen paßt; at your earliest ~ (Comm) möglichst bald. (c) (convenient thing, amenity) Annehmlichkeit f. a house with every ~ ein Haus mit allem Komfort. (d) (Brit form: public ~) (öffentliche) Toilette.

convenient [kən'viːnɪənt] adj (useful) praktisch; area, house (for shops etc) günstig gelegen; time günstig. if it is ~ for you wenn es Ihnen (so) paßt; is tomorrow ~ (for you)? paßt (es) Ihnen morgen?; the trams are very ~ (nearby) die Straßenbahnhaltestellen liegen sehr günstig; (useful) die Straßenbahn ist sehr praktisch.

conveniently [kən'viːnɪəntlɪ] adv günstigerweise; situated günstig; (usefully) designed praktisch.

convent ['kɒnvənt] n (Frauen)kloster nt. ~ school Klosterschule f.

convention [kən'venʃən] n (a) Sitte f; (social rule) Konvention f. it's a ~ that ... es ist so üblich or Sitte, daß ... (b) (conference) Tagung f; (Pol) Konvent m.

conventional [kən'venʃənl] adj dress konventionell; beliefs herkömmlich; style traditionell.

converge [kən'vɜːdʒ] vi (road, lines) zusammenlaufen (at in +dat); (fig: views etc) sich aneinander annähern. to ~ on sb/sth/New York von überallher zu jdm/etw/nach New York strömen.

convergence [kən'vɜːdʒəns] n see vi Zusammenlaufen nt; Annäherung f. point of ~ Schnittpunkt m; (of rays) Brennpunkt m.

conversation [ˌkɒnvə'seɪʃən] n Gespräch nt; (Sch) Konversation f. to make ~ sich unterhalten; to get into/be in ~ with sb mit jdm ins Gespräch kommen/im Gespräch sein; deep in ~ ins Gespräch vertieft; his ~ is so amusing er ist ein unterhaltsamer Gesprächspartner; a subject of ~ ein Gesprächsthema nt; ~ piece Gesprächsgegenstand m; that was a ~-stopper (col) das hat uns die Sprache verschlagen (col); the art of ~ die Kunst des (guten) Gespräch(e)s.

conversational [ˌkɒnvə'seɪʃənl] adj tone, style Unterhaltungs-. ~ German gesprochenes Deutsch.

conversationalist [ˌkɒnvə'seɪʃnəlɪst] n guter Gesprächspartner, gute Gesprächspartnerin.

converse¹ [kən'vɜːs] vi (form) sich unterhalten.

converse² ['kɒnvɜːs] 1 adj umgekehrt; opinions etc gegenteilig. 2 n (opposite) Gegenteil nt.

conversely [kɒn'vɜːslɪ] adv umgekehrt.

conversion [kən'vɜːʃən] n (a) Konversion f (into in +acc); (Rugby, US Ftbl) Verwandlung f; (of measures) Umrechnung f (into in +acc); (of building) Umbau m (into zu). ~ table Umrechnungstabelle f. (b) (Rel, fig) Bekehrung f (to zu).

convert ['kɒnvɜːt] 1 n (lit, fig) Bekehrte(r) mf; (to another denomination) Konvertit m. 2 [kən'vɜːt] vt

(a) konvertieren (into in +acc); (Rugby, US Ftbl) verwandeln; measures umrechnen (into in +acc); attic ausbauen (into zu); building umbauen (into zu). (b) (Rel, fig) bekehren (to zu); (to another denomination) konvertieren. 3 [kən'vɜːt] vi sich verwandeln lassen (into in +acc).

converter [kən'vɜːtər] n (Elec) Konverter m; (for AC/DC) Stromgleichrichter m.

convertible [kən'vɜːtəbl] 1 adj verwandelbar; currency konvertibel. ~ sofa Bettcouch f. 2 n (car) Kabriolett nt.

convex [kɒn'veks] adj lens, mirror konvex.

convey [kən'veɪ] vt (a) befördern; goods spedieren; water leiten. (b) idea vermitteln; meaning klarmachen; best wishes übermitteln. words cannot ~ what I feel was ich empfinde, läßt sich nicht mit Worten ausdrücken; the name ~s nothing to me der Name sagt mir nichts. (c) (Jur) property übertragen (to auf +acc).

conveyance [kən'veɪəns] n (transport) Beförderung f. ~ of goods Güterverkehr m; means of ~ Beförderungsmittel nt.

conveyancing [kən'veɪənsɪŋ] n (Jur) (Eigentums)übertragung f.

conveyor [kən'veɪər] n (of message etc) Überbringer(in f) m; (Tech) Förderer m. ~ belt Fließband nt; (for transport, supply) Förderband nt.

convict ['kɒnvɪkt] 1 n Strafgefangene(r) mf. 2 [kən'vɪkt] vt (Jur) person verurteilen (of wegen). a ~ed criminal ein überführter Verbrecher. 3 [kən'vɪkt] vt jdn verurteilen.

conviction [kən'vɪkʃən] n (a) (Jur) Verurteilung f. (b) (belief, act of convincing) Überzeugung f. to carry ~ überzeugend klingen; see courage.

convince [kən'vɪns] vt überzeugen.

convincing adj, **~ly** adv [kən'vɪnsɪŋ, -lɪ] überzeugend.

convivial [kən'vɪvɪəl] adj heiter und unbeschwert; (sociable) gesellig.

convoluted ['kɒnvəluːtɪd] adj (involved) verwickelt; style gewunden.

convoy ['kɒnvɔɪ] n (a) (escort) Geleit nt. under ~ mit Geleitschutz; to be on ~ duty als Geleitschutz abgeordnet sein. (b) (vehicles under escort, fig) Konvoi m. in ~ im Konvoi.

convulse [kən'vʌls] vt land erschüttern; muscles krampfhaft zusammenziehen. to be ~d with laughter/pain sich vor Lachen schütteln/vor Schmerzen krümmen.

convulsion [kən'vʌlʃən] n (a) (Med) Schüttelkrampf m no pl. (b) (caused by social upheaval etc) Erschütterung f. (c) (col: of laughter) to go into/be in ~s sich biegen vor Lachen.

convulsive [kən'vʌlsɪv] adj Krampf-. ~ laughter Lachkrämpfe pl.

coo [kuː] 1 vi (pigeon, fig) gurren. 2 n Gurren nt.

cook [kʊk] 1 n Koch m, Köchin f. too many ~s spoil the broth (Prov) viele Köche verderben den Brei (Prov). 2 vt (a) food, meal zubereiten; (in water, milk etc) kochen; (fry, roast) braten; pie, pancake backen. to ~ sb's goose (fig) jdm die Suppe versalzen. (b) (col: falsify) accounts frisieren (col). 3 vi (person, food) kochen; (fry, roast) braten; (pie) backen. what's ~ing? (fig col) was ist los?

♦**cook up** vt sep (fig col) story, excuse zurechtbasteln (col). **~ed** ~ story Lügenmärchen nt.

cookbook ['kʊkbʊk] n Kochbuch nt.

cooker ['kʊkər] n (Brit) (a) (stove) Herd m. (b) (apple) Kochapfel m.

cookery ['kʊkərɪ] n Kochen nt (also Sch). ~ book Kochbuch nt.

cookhouse ['kʊkhaʊs] n (Naut) Kombüse f; (Mil) Feldküche f.

cookie, cooky ['kʊkɪ] n (a) (US: biscuit) Keks m. (b) (col: smart person) Typ m. he's a pretty sharp ~ er ist ein richtiger Schlauberger.

cooking ['kʊkɪŋ] n Kochen nt; (food) Essen nt.
plain ~ Hausmannskost f; **French** ~ die französische Küche.
cooking in cpds Koch-; ~ **apple** n Kochapfel m; ~ **chocolate** n Blockschokolade f.
cookout ['kʊkaʊt] n (US) Kochen nt am Lagerfeuer; (on charcoal brazier) Grillparty f.
cool {kuːl] 1 adj (+er) **(a)** weather, drink kühl; person besonnen; clothes luftig. "keep in a ~ place" „kühl aufbewahren"; keep ~! reg dich nicht auf!; to be ~ to(wards) sb sich jdm gegenüber kühl verhalten; play it ~! immer mit der Ruhe! **(b)** (audacious) unverfroren. a ~ customer (col) ein lässiger Typ (col); that was very ~ of him da hat er sich ein starkes Stück geleistet. **(c)** (col: of money) glatt (col). he earns a ~ ten thousand a year er verdient glatte zehntausend im Jahr (col). **(d)** disco, dress etc stark (col). ~ **jazz** Cool Jazz m.
2 n **(a)** (lit, fig) Kühle f. the ~ of the evening die Abendkühle. **(b)** (col) keep your ~! reg dich nicht auf!; to lose one's ~ durchdrehen (col).
3 vt **(a)** kühlen; (~ down) abkühlen; wine kaltstellen. **(b)** ~ it! (relax) reg dich ab; (don't cause trouble) mach keinen Ärger! (col).
4 vi (lit, fig) abkühlen; (anger) sich legen; (interest) nachlassen.
♦ **cool down** 1 vi **(a)** (lit) abkühlen. **(b)** (feelings, fig: person) sich abkühlen; (critical situation) sich beruhigen. to let things ~ ~ die Sache etwas ruhen lassen. 2 vt sep food, drink abkühlen; (let ~ ~) abkühlen lassen.
♦ **cool off** vi **(a)** (liquid, food) abkühlen; (person) sich abkühlen. **(b)** (fig) (sich) abkühlen; (enthusiasm, interest) nachlassen; (become less angry) sich abreagieren; (become less friendly) kühler werden (towards sb jdm gegenüber).
coolant ['kuːlənt] n Kühlmittel nt.
cool: ~ **bag** n Kühltasche f; ~ **box** n Kühlbox f.
cooler ['kuːlə'] n **(a)** (for wine) Kühler m. **(b)** (col: solitary) Bau m (col).
cooling ['kuːlɪŋ] adj drink, shower kühlend.
cooling-off ['kuːlɪŋ'ɒf] 1 n (in relationship etc) Abkühlung f. 2 adj ~ **period** Zeitraum für Schlichtungsverhandlungen (bei Arbeitskämpfen).
cooling tower n Kühlturm m.
coolly ['kuːlɪ] adv **(a)** (calmly) ruhig, gefaßt. **(b)** (unenthusiastically, in an unfriendly way) kühl. **(c)** (audaciously) unverfroren.
coolness ['kuːlnɪs] n see adj kühl; Besonnenheit f; Luftigkeit f. **(b)** Unverfrorenheit f.
coop [kuːp] n (also hen ~) Hühnerstall m.
♦ **coop up** vt sep person einsperren; several people zusammenpferchen.
co-op ['kəʊ'ɒp] n Genossenschaft f; (shop) Coop m.
cooperate [kəʊ'ɒpəreɪt] vi zusammenarbeiten; (not be awkward) mitmachen.
cooperation [kəʊ,ɒpə'reɪʃən] n Kooperation, Zusammenarbeit f; (help) Mitarbeit f.
cooperative [kəʊ'ɒpərətɪv] 1 adj **(a)** (willing to comply) kooperativ; (willing to help) hilfsbereit. **(b)** ~ **society** Genossenschaft f; ~ **farm** Bauernhof m auf Genossenschaftsbasis. 2 n Genossenschaft f; (also ~ **farm**) Bauernhof m auf Genossenschaftsbasis.
coopt [kəʊ'ɒpt] vt (hinzu)wählen. he was ~ed onto the committee er wurde vom Komitee dazugewählt.
coordinate [kəʊ'ɔːdɪnɪt] 1 n (Math etc) Koordinate f. ~s (clothes) Kleidung f zum Kombinieren. 2 [kəʊ'ɔːdɪneɪt] vt koordinieren.
coordination [kəʊ,ɔːdɪ'neɪʃən] n Koordination f.
coordinator [kəʊ'ɔːdɪneɪtə'] n Koordinator m.
cop [kɒp] n **(a)** (col: policeman) Polizist(in f), Bulle (pej col) m. **(b)** (Brit col) it's not much ~ das ist nichts Besonderes. 2 vt (col: catch) sb schnappen (col). you'll ~ it when your dad gets home warte nur, bis dein Vater nach Haus kommt!;

hey, ~ a load of this! he, hör/sieh dir das mal an! (col).
♦ **cop out** vi (col) aussteigen (of aus).
cope [kəʊp] vi zurechtkommen; (with work) es schaffen. to ~ with fertigwerden mit; she can't ~ with the stairs any more sie schafft die Treppe nicht mehr.
Copenhagen [,kəʊpn'heɪgən] n Kopenhagen nt.
copier ['kɒpɪə'] n (copyist) Kopist(in f) m; (machine) Kopierer m, Kopiergerät nt.
co-pilot ['kəʊˌpaɪlət] n Kopilot m.
copious ['kəʊpɪəs] adj supply reichlich; (information, illustrations zahlreich.
copper ['kɒpə'] n **(a)** (metal) Kupfer nt. **(b)** (colour) Kupferrot nt. **(c)** (coin) Pfennig m. ~s Kleingeld nt. **(d)** (col: policeman) Polizist(in f), Bulle (pej col) m.
copper: ~ **beech** n Rotbuche f; ~-**coloured** (Brit) or ~-**colored** (US) adj kupferfarben.
copse [kɒps] n Wäldchen nt.
copulate ['kɒpjʊleɪt] vi kopulieren.
copulation [,kɒpjʊ'leɪʃən] n Kopulation f.
copy ['kɒpɪ] 1 n **(a)** Kopie f; (carbon) Durchschlag m; (Phot) Abzug m. to write out a fair ~ etw ins reine schreiben. **(b)** (of book etc) Exemplar m. **(c)** (Press etc) (material) Stoff m; (text) Text m. that's always good ~ das zieht immer. **(d)** (in advertising) Werbetext m. 2 vi **(a)** (imitate) nachahmen. **(b)** (Sch etc) abschreiben. 3 vt **(a)** (make a ~ of) sb or sth kopieren; einen Durchschlag machen von; abziehen; (write out again) abschreiben. **(b)** (imitate) nachmachen; accent etc nachahmen. **(c)** (Sch etc) sb else's work abschreiben.
copy: ~**book** 1 n Schönschreibheft nt; 2 adj attr mustergültig; ~**cat** n (col) she's a terrible ~**cat** sie macht immer alles nach.
copyright ['kɒpɪraɪt] 1 n Urheberrecht, Copyright nt. 2 adj urheberrechtlich geschützt.
copy: ~ **typist** n Schreibkraft f; ~**writer** n Werbetexter(in f) m.
coral ['kɒrəl] n **(a)** Koralle f. **(b)** (colour) Korallenrot nt.
coral in cpds Korallen-; ~ **necklace** n Korallenkette f; ~ **reef** n Korallenriff nt.
cord [kɔːd] n **(a)** Schnur f; (for clothes) Kordel f. **(b)** ~**s** pl (also a pair of ~**s**) Kordhosen pl. **(c)** (Tex) = **corduroy.**
cordial ['kɔːdɪəl] 1 adj herzlich. 2 n (soft drink) Fruchtkonzentrat nt; (alcoholic) Fruchtlikör m.
cordon ['kɔːdn] n Postenkette f. to put a ~ around sth etw (hermetisch) abriegeln.
♦ **cordon off** vt sep area, building abriegeln.
corduroy ['kɔːdərɔɪ] n Kordsamt m. ~**s** Kordhosen pl.
core [kɔː'] 1 n (lit, fig) Kern m; (of apple, pear) Kerngehäuse nt; (of rock) Innere(s) nt. rotten/English to the ~ (fig) durch und durch schlecht/englisch; to get to the ~ of the matter (fig) zum Kern der Sache kommen. 2 vt fruit entkernen; apple, pear das Kerngehäuse aus- schneiden.
co-respondent ['kəʊrɪs'pɒndənt] n (Jur) Mitbeklagte(r) mf (im Scheidungsprozeß).
coriander [,kɒrɪ'ændə'] n Koriander m.
cork [kɔːk] 1 n **(a)** no pl (substance) Kork m. **(b)** (stopper) Korken m. **(c)** (Fishing: also ~ **float**) Schwimmer m. 2 vt (also ~ **up**) bottle, wine verkorken. 3 adj Kork-.
corked [kɔːkt] adj the wine is ~ der Wein schmeckt nach Kork.
cork: ~**screw** n Korkenzieher m; ~**screw curls** npl Korkenzieherlocken pl; ~ **tile** n Korkfliese f; ~-**tipped** adj cigarette mit Korkfilter; ~ **tree** n Korkbaum m.
corn¹ [kɔːn] n **(a)** no pl (Brit: cereal) Getreide nt. **(b)** (seed of ~) Korn nt. **(c)** no pl (esp US: sweet ~) Mais m; ~ **on the cob** Maiskolben m.

corn² *n* Hühnerauge *nt*. ~ **plaster** Hühneraugenpflaster *nt*.

cornea ['kɔːnɪə] *n* Hornhaut *f*.

corned beef ['kɔːnd'biːf] *n* Corned beef *nt*.

corner ['kɔːnəʳ] **1** *n* **(a)** Ecke *f*; *(of sheet)* Zipfel *m*; *(of mouth, eye)* Winkel *m*; *(in road)* Kurve *f*. **at** *or* **on the** ~ an der Ecke; **it's just around the** ~ es ist gleich um die Ecke; **to turn the** ~ *(lit)* um die Ecke biegen; **we've turned the** ~ **now** *(fig)* wir sind jetzt über den Berg; **out of the** ~ **of one's eye** aus dem Augenwinkel (heraus); **to cut** ~**s** *(lit)* Kurven schneiden; *(fig)* das Verfahren abkürzen; **to drive sb into a** ~ *(fig)* jdn in die Enge treiben; **to drive** ~**s of the world** die ganze Welt. **(b)** *(out-of-the-way place)* Winkel *m*. **(c)** *(Ftbl)* Eckball *m*, Ecke *f*. **to take a** ~ eine Ecke ausführen.
2 *vt* **(a)** *(lit, fig: trap)* in die Enge treiben. **(b)** *(Comm)* **the market** monopolisieren.
3 *vi* *(take a* ~*)* *(person)* Kurven/die Kurve nehmen. **this car** ~**s well** dieses Auto hat eine gute Kurvenlage.

corner *in cpds* Eck-; ~ **cupboard** *n* Eckschrank *m*; ~ **kick** *n* (Ftbl) Eckstoß *m*; ~ **seat** *n* (Rail) Eckplatz *m*; ~ **shop** *n* Laden *m* an der Ecke; ~**stone** *n* *(lit, fig)* Eckstein *m*.

cornet ['kɔːnɪt] *n* **(a)** *(Mus)* Kornett *nt*. **(b)** *(icecream* ~*)* (Eis)tüte *f*.

corn: ~**field** *n* (Brit) Weizenfeld *nt*; *(US)* Maisfeld *nt*; ~**flakes** *npl* Corn-flakes ® *pl*; ~**flour** *n* (Brit) Stärkemehl *nt*; ~**flower** *n* Kornblume *f*.

cornice ['kɔːnɪs] *n* (Archit: *of wall, column)* (Ge)sims *nt*; *(fig: of snow)* Wächte *f*.

Cornish ['kɔːnɪʃ] **1** *adj* aus Cornwall. **2** *n* *(dialect)* Kornisch *nt*.

corn: ~**meal** *n* (US) Maismehl *nt*; ~ **oil** *n* (Mais)keimöl *nt*; ~ **pone** *n* (US) Maisbrot *nt*; ~**starch** *n* (US) Stärkemehl *nt*; ~ **whiskey** *n* (US) Maiswhiskey *m*.

corny ['kɔːnɪ] *adj* (+er) *(col)* joke blöd *(col)*; *(sentimental)* kitschig. **what a** ~ **old joke!** der Witz hat (so) einen Bart *(col)*.

corollary [kə'rɒlərɪ] *n* (logische) Folge, Korollar *nt* *(also Math)*.

coronary ['kɒrənərɪ] **1** *adj* (Med) Koronar- *(spec)*. ~ **thrombosis** Herzinfarkt *m*. **2** *n* Herzinfarkt *m*.

coronation [,kɒrə'neɪʃən] *n* Krönung *f*.

coroner ['kɒrənəʳ] *n* Beamter, der Todesfälle untersucht, die nicht eindeutig eine natürliche Ursache haben.

coronet ['kɒrənɪt] *n* Krone *f*; *(jewellery)* Krönchen *nt*.

corporal¹ ['kɔːpərəl] *n* *(abbr* **corp)** *(Mil)* Stabsunteroffizier *m*.

corporal² *adj* körperlich. ~ **punishment** Prügelstrafe *f*.

corporate ['kɔːpərɪt] *adj* **(a)** *(of a group)* gemeinsam. **(b)** *(of a corporation)* korporativ; *(of a company)* Firmen-. ~ **body** Körperschaft *f*.

corporation [,kɔːpə'reɪʃən] *n* **(a)** *(municipal* ~*)* Gemeinde *f*. **(b)** *(Brit Comm: incorporated company)* Handelsgesellschaft *f*; *(US Comm: limited liability company)* Gesellschaft *f* mit beschränkter Haftung. **(c)** *(Brit hum: large belly)* Schmerbauch *m*.

corps [kɔːʳ] *n, pl -* (Mil) Korps *nt*. ~ **de ballet** Corps de ballet *nt*.

corpse [kɔːps] *n* Leiche *f*.

corpulence ['kɔːpjuləns] *n* Korpulenz *f*.

corpulent ['kɔːpjulənt] *adj* korpulent.

corpuscle ['kɔːpʌsl] *n* Korpuskel *nt* *(spec)*. **blood** ~ Blutkörperchen *nt*.

correct [kə'rekt] **1** *adj* *(right)* richtig; *(proper)* korrekt. **am I** ~ **in thinking ...?** gehe ich recht in der Annahme, daß ...; **you are** ~ Sie haben recht; **it's the** ~ **thing to do** das gehört sich so. **2** *vt* korrigieren; *bad habit* sich/jdm abgewöhnen. ~ **me if I'm wrong** Sie können mich gern berich-

tigen; **I stand** ~**ed** ich nehme alles zurück.

correction [kə'rekʃən] *n* see *vt* Korrektur *f*; Abgewöhnung *f*.

correctly [kə'rektlɪ] *adv* richtig; *behave* korrekt.

correlate ['kɒrɪleɪt] **1** *vt two things* zueinander in Beziehung setzen. **to** ~ **sth with sth** etw mit etw in Beziehung setzen. **2** *vi* *(two things)* sich entsprechen. **to** ~ **with sth** mit etw in Beziehung stehen.

correlation [,kɒrɪ'leɪʃən] *n* *(interdependence)* Wechselbeziehung *f*; *(Math, Statistics)* Korrelation *f*.

correspond [,kɒrɪs'pɒnd] *vi* **(a)** *(be equivalent)* entsprechen *(to, with dat)*; *(to one another)* sich entsprechen. **(b)** *(exchange letters)* korrespondieren *(with mit)*.

correspondence [,kɒrɪs'pɒndəns] *n* **(a)** *(agreement, equivalence)* Übereinstimmung *f* *(between zwischen, with mit)*. **(b)** *(letter-writing, letters)* Korrespondenz *f*. **to be in** ~ **with sb** mit jdm in Briefwechsel stehen.

correspondence: ~ **column** *n* (Press) Leserbriefspalte *f*; ~ **course** *n* Fernkurs *m*.

correspondent [,kɒrɪs'pɒndənt] *n* **(a)** *(letterwriter)* Briefschreiber(in *f*) *m*. **to be a bad** ~ schreibfaul sein. **(b)** *(Press)* Korrespondent(in *f*) *m*.

corresponding [,kɒrɪs'pɒndɪŋ] *adj* entsprechend.

corridor ['kɒrɪdɔːʳ] *n* Korridor *m*; *(in train, bus)* Gang *m*.

corroborate [kə'rɒbəreɪt] *vt* bestätigen.

corroboration [kə,rɒbə'reɪʃən] *n* Bestätigung *f*.

corrode [kə'rəud] **1** *vt metal* zerfressen; *(fig)* zerstören. **2** *vi (metal)* korrodieren.

corrosion [kə'rəuʒən] *n* Korrosion *f*; *(fig)* Zerstörung *f*.

corrosive [kə'rəuzɪv] **1** *adj* korrosiv; *(fig)* zerstörend. **2** *n* Korrosion verursachendes Mittel.

corrugated ['kɒrəgeɪtɪd] *adj* gewellt. ~ **cardboard** dicke Wellpappe; ~ **iron** Wellblech *nt*.

corrupt [kə'rʌpt] **1** *adj* verdorben; *(open to bribery)* korrupt. **2** *vt* *(morally)* verderben; *(ethically)* korrumpieren; *(form: bribe)* bestechen.

corruption [kə'rʌpʃən] *n* **(a)** *(act: of person)* Korruption *f*. **(b)** *(corrupt nature)* Verdorbenheit *f*; *(by bribery)* Bestechlichkeit *f*; *(of morals)* Verfall *m*.

corset ['kɔːsɪt] *n* *(also* ~**s**) Korsett *nt*. **surgical** ~ Stützkorsett *nt*.

Corsica ['kɔːsɪkə] *n* Korsika *nt*.

Corsican ['kɔːsɪkən] **1** *adj* korsisch. **2** *n* Korse *m*, Korsin *f*.

cortège [kɔː'teɪʒ] *n* *(retinue)* Gefolge *nt*; *(procession)* Prozession *f*; *(funeral* ~*)* Leichenzug *m*.

cortisone ['kɔːtɪzəun] *n* Kortison *nt*.

cos [kɒs] *n* *(also* ~ **lettuce)* römischer Salat.

cosh [kɒʃ] *(Brit col)* **1** *vt* eins über den Schädel ziehen *(+dat) (col)*. **2** *n* *(instrument)* Totschläger *m*.

cosmetic [kɒz'metɪk] **1** *adj* kosmetisch. **she's had** ~ **surgery** sie hat eine Schönheitsoperation gehabt. **2** *n* Kosmetikum *nt*.

cosmic ['kɒzmɪk] *adj* kosmisch.

cosmonaut ['kɒzmənɔːt] *n* Kosmonaut(in *f*) *m*.

cosmopolitan [,kɒzmə'pɒlɪtən] **1** *adj* kosmopolitisch. **2** *n* Kosmopolit *m*.

cosmos ['kɒzmɒs] *n* Kosmos *m*.

cosset ['kɒsɪt] *vt* verwöhnen.

cost [kɒst] *(vb: pret, ptp* ~*)* **1** *vt* **(a)** *(lit, fig)* kosten. **how much does it** ~? wieviel kostet es?; **how much will it** ~ **to have it repaired?** wieviel kostet die Reparatur?; **it** ~ **(ihn) a lot of money** das hat (ihn) viel Geld gekostet; **it** ~ **him a great effort** es kostete ihn viel Mühe; ~ **what it may** koste es, was es wolle; **politeness doesn't** ~ **(you) anything** kostet (dich) nichts, höflich zu sein. **(b)**

co-star *(Comm: put a price on) pret, ptp* ~ed *articles for sale* auszeichnen *(at* zu)*; piece of work* veranschlagen *(at* mit).
2 *n* (a) Kosten *pl (of* für). **to bear the** ~ **of sth** die Kosten für etw tragen; **to buy sth at** ~ etw zum Selbstkostenpreis kaufen. (b) *(fig)* Preis *m.*
at all ~s um jeden Preis; **whatever the** ~ kostet es, was es wolle; **at the** ~ **of one's health/job/ marriage** *etc* auf Kosten seiner Gesundheit/ Stelle/Ehe *etc;* **he found out to his** ~ **that ... er** machte die bittere Erfahrung, daß ... (c) *(Jur)* ~s *pl* Kosten *pl;* **to be ordered to pay** ~s zur Übernahme der Kosten verurteilt werden.
co-star ['kəʊstɑːʳ] **1** *n (Film, Theat)* einer der Hauptdarsteller. **2** *vi* **she was** ~**ring with Robert Redford** sie spielte neben Robert Redford in einer der Hauptrollen.
cost: ~**-conscious** *adj* kostenbewußt; ~**-effective** *adj* rentabel.
costing ['kɒstɪŋ] *n* Kalkulation *f.*
costly ['kɒstlɪ] *adj* kostspielig.
cost: ~ **of living** *n* Lebenshaltungskosten *pl;* ~**-of-living index** *n* Lebenshaltungskostenindex *m;* ~ **price** *n (Brit)* Selbstkostenpreis *m.*
costume ['kɒstjuːm] *n* Kostüm *nt; (bathing* ~) Badeanzug *m.* **national** ~ Nationaltracht *f.*
costume: ~ **ball** *n* Kostümfest *nt;* ~ **jewellery** *(Brit) or* **jewelry** *(US) n* Modeschmuck *m.*
cosy, *(US)* **cozy** ['kəʊzɪ] **1** *adj* (+er) *room, atmosphere* behaglich; *(warm)* mollig warm. **warm and** ~ mollig warm. **2** *n (tea* ~) Wärmer *m.*
cot [kɒt] *n (esp Brit: child's bed)* Kinderbett *nt; (US: camp bed)* Feldbett *nt.*
cottage ['kɒtɪdʒ] *n* Cottage, Häuschen *nt; (US: in institution)* Wohneinheit *f.*
cottage: ~ **cheese** *n* Hüttenkäse *m;* ~ **hospital** *n (Brit) kleines Krankenhaus für leichtere Fälle;* ~ **industry** *n* Heimindustrie *f.*
cotter-pin ['kɒtəpɪn] *n* Splint *m.*
cotton ['kɒtn] **1** *n* Baumwolle *f; (plant)* Baumwollstrauch *m; (sewing thread)* (Baumwoll)garn *nt.* **absorbent** ~ *(US)* Watte *f.* **2** *adj* Baumwoll-.
♦ **cotton on** *vi (col)* es kapieren *(col).*
cotton *in cpds* Baumwoll-; ~ **batting** *n (US)* Gaze *f;* ~ **candy** *n (US)* Zuckerwatte *f;* ~ **mill** *n* Baumwollspinnerei *f;* ~**-picking** *adj (US col)* verdammt *(col);* ~ **print** *n (fabric)* bedruckter Baumwollstoff; ~**tail** *n (US)* Kaninchen *nt;* ~**wool** *n (Brit)* Watte *f;* **to wrap sb in** ~**wool** *(fig)* jdn in Watte packen.
couch [kaʊtʃ] **1** *n* Couch *f.* **2** *vt (put in words)* formulieren.
couchette [kuːˈʃet] *n (Rail)* Liegewagenplatz *m.*
cough [kɒf] **1** *n* Husten *m.* **2** *vti* husten.
♦ **cough up 1** *vt sep (lit)* aushusten. **2** *vt insep (fig col) money* rausrücken *(col).* **3** *vi (fig col)* blechen *(col).*
cough: ~ **drop** *n* Hustenpastille *f;* ~ **mixture** *n* Hustensaft *m;* ~ **sweet** *n* Hustenbonbon *nt.*
could [kʊd] *pret of* **can¹**.
couldn't ['kʊdnt] = **could not.**
council ['kaʊnsl] **1** *n* Rat *m.* **city/town** ~ Stadtrat *m.* **2** *attr estate (Brit)* ≃ des sozialen Wohnungsbaus. ~ **house/housing** ≃ *(Brit)* Sozialwohnung *f/*sozialer Wohnungsbau; ~ **chamber** *n* Sitzungssaal *m* des Rats; ~**man** *n (US)* = **councillor;** ~ **meeting** *n* Ratssitzung *f.*
councillor, *(US)* **councilor** ['kaʊnsələʳ] *n* Ratsmitglied *nt; (town* ~) Stadtrat *m/*-rätin *f.*
counsel ['kaʊnsl] **1** *n* (a) *(form: advice)* Rat(schlag) *m.* (b) *(Jur)* Rechtsanwalt *m.* ~ **for the defence/prosecution** Verteidiger(in *f) m/*Vertreter(in *f)* der Anklage, ≃ Staatsanwalt *m/*-anwältin *f.* **2** *vt (form) person* beraten; *course of action* raten zu.
counsellor, *(US)* **counselor** ['kaʊnsələʳ] *n* (a) *(adviser)* Berater(in *f) m.* (b) *(US, Ir: lawyer)* Rechtsanwalt *m/*-anwältin *f.*

count¹ [kaʊnt] **1** *n* (a) Zählung *f; (of votes)* (Stimmen)auszählung *f.* **she lost** ~ **when she was interrupted** sie kam mit dem Zählen durcheinander, als sie unterbrochen wurde; **I've lost all** ~ ich habe völlig die Übersicht verloren; **he was out for the** ~ *(Sport)* er wurde ausgezählt; *(fig)* er war k.o. (b) *(Jur: charge)* Anklagepunkt *m.* **on that** ~ *(fig)* in dem Punkt; **on all** ~s in jeder Hinsicht.
2 *vt* (a) (ab)zählen; *(*~ *again)* nachzählen; *votes* (aus)zählen. **to** ~ **the cost** *(lit)* auf die Kosten achten. (b) *(consider)* betrachten; *(include)* mitzählen. **to** ~ **sb among one's friends** jdn zu seinen Freunden zählen; ~ **yourself lucky that** ... Sie können von Glück sagen, daß ...; **ten people** ~**ing the children** zehn Leute, die Kinder mitgerechnet.
3 *vi* (a) zählen. ~**ing from today** von heute an (gerechnet). (b) *(be considered)* betrachtet werden; *(be included)* mitgezählt werden; *(be important)* wichtig sein. **that doesn't** ~ das zählt nicht; **to** ~ **against sb** gegen jdn sprechen.
♦ **count in** *vt sep* mitzählen. **you can** ~ **me** ~! da bin ich dabei.
♦ **count on** *vi* +*prep obj (depend on)* rechnen mit. **you can** ~ ~ **him to help you** du kannst auf seine Hilfe zählen.
♦ **count out** *vt sep* (a) *(Sport)* auszählen. (b) *money, books etc* abzählen. (c) *(col: exclude)* **(you can)** ~ **me** ~ **(of that)!** ohne mich!, da mache ich nicht mit!
♦ **count up** *vt sep* zusammenzählen.
♦ **count upon** *vi* +*prep obj* = **count on.**
count² *n* Graf *m.*
countable ['kaʊntəbl] *adj* zählbar *(also Gram).*
countdown ['kaʊntdaʊn] *n* Countdown *m.* **to start the** ~ mit dem Countdown beginnen.
countenance ['kaʊntɪnəns] **1** *n (old, form: face)* Antlitz *nt (old).* **to keep one's** ~ *(fig)* die Haltung bewahren. **2** *vt behaviour* gutheißen.
counter ['kaʊntəʳ] **1** *n* (a) *(in shop)* Ladentisch *m; (in cafe)* Theke *f; (in bank, post office)* Schalter *m.* **under-the-**~ **dealings** *(fig)* undurchsichtige Geschäfte. (b) *(for games)* Spielmarke *f.* (c) *(Tech)* Zähler *m.* **2** *vt (retaliate against)* antworten auf (+*acc).* **3** *vi* kontern *(also Sport).* **4** *adv* ~ **to** gegen (+*acc);* **to run** ~ **to sb's wishes** jds Wünschen *(dat)* zuwiderlaufen.
counter: ~**act** *vt (make ineffective)* neutralisieren; *(act in opposition to)* entgegenwirken (+*dat); disease* bekämpfen; ~**action** *n see vt* Neutralisierung *f;* Gegenwirkung *f;* Bekämpfung *f;* ~**attack 1** *n* Gegenangriff *m;* **2** *vi* einen Gegenangriff starten; ~**balance 1** *n* Gegengewicht *nt;* **2** *vt* ausgleichen; ~**clockwise** *adj, adv (US)* = **anti-clockwise;** ~**espionage** *n* Gegenspionage *f.*
counterfeit ['kaʊntəfiːt] **1** *adj* gefälscht; *(fig)* falsch. ~ **money** Falschgeld *nt.* **2** *n* Fälschung *f.* **3** *vt* fälschen.
counterfoil ['kaʊntəfɔɪl] *n (Brit)* Kontrollabschnitt *m.*
counterintelligence [,kaʊntərɪn'telɪdʒəns] *n* Gegenspionage *f.*
countermand ['kaʊntəmɑːnd] *vt order* aufheben; *attack, plan* rückgängig machen.
counter: ~**measure** *n* Gegenmaßnahme *f;* ~**offensive** *n (Mil)* Gegenoffensive *f;* ~**-offer** *n* Gegenangebot *nt;* ~**pane** *n* Tagesdecke *f;* ~**part** *n (equivalent)* Gegenüber *nt; (complement)* Gegenstück *nt;* ~**-productive** *adj* widersinnig; *measures* destruktiv; **that'd be** ~**-productive** das würde den Zweck verfehlen; **that runs the risk of being** ~**-productive** es besteht die Gefahr, daß dadurch das Gegenteil bewirkt wird; ~**sign** *vt cheque etc* gegenzeichnen; ~**sink** *vt hole* senken; *screw* versenken; ~**weight** *n* Gegengewicht *nt.*
countess ['kaʊntɪs] *n* Gräfin *f.*

countless ['kaʊntlɪs] adj unzählig attr, zahllos attr.

country ['kʌntrɪ] n (a) (state) Land nt. his own ~ seine Heimat; to die for one's ~ für sein Land sterben; to go to the ~ (Pol) Wahlen ausschreiben. (b) no pl (as opposed to town) Land nt. in/to the ~ auf dem/aufs Land; the surrounding ~ die Umgebung; there's some lovely ~ up north die Gegend im Norden ist herrlich.

country in cpds Land-; ~-and-western n Countrymusic f; ~ **bumpkin** n (pej) Bauerntölpel (col) m; (girl) Bauerntrampel m (col); ~ **cousin** n Vetter m/Cousine f vom Lande; ~ **dancing** n Volkstanz m; ~ **dweller** n Landbewohner(in f) m; ~ **house** n Landhaus nt; ~**man** n (a) Landsmann m; his **fellow** ~**men** seine Landsleute; (b) (countrydweller) Landbewohner m; ~ **people** npl Leute pl vom Land(e); ~**side** n (scenery) Landschaft f; it's beautiful ~**side** das ist eine herrliche Landschaft; ~ **town** n Kleinstadt f; ~-**wide** adj landesweit; ~**woman** n (a) Landsmännin f; (b) (country dweller) Landbewohnerin f.

county ['kaʊntɪ] n (Brit) Grafschaft f; (US) (Verwaltungs)bezirk m.

county: ~ **council** n (Brit) Grafschaftsrat m; ~ **town** n (Brit) Hauptstadt f einer Grafschaft.

coup [kuː] n (a) (successful action) Coup m. (b) (~ d'état) Staatsstreich m.

coupé ['kuːpeɪ] n (car) Coupé nt.

couple ['kʌpl] 1 n (a) (pair) Paar nt; (married ~) Ehepaar nt. (b) (col) a ~ (two) zwei; (several) ein paar; a ~ of friends ein paar Freunde; a ~ of times ein paarmal. 2 vt ideas etc verbinden; carriages etc koppeln.

coupling ['kʌplɪŋ] n (a) (linking) Verbindung f; (of carriages etc) Kopplung f. (b) (device) Kupplung f.

coupon ['kuːpɒn] n (a) (voucher) Gutschein m. (b) (Ftbl) Wettschein m.

courage ['kʌrɪdʒ] n Mut m. I haven't the ~ to refuse ich habe einfach nicht den Mut, nein zu sagen; to have the ~ of one's convictions Zivilcourage haben; to take one's ~ in both hands sein Herz in beide Hände nehmen.

courageous [kə'reɪdʒəs] adj mutig.

courgette ['kʊəʒet] n (Brit) Zucchini f.

courier ['kʊrɪəʳ] n (messenger) Kurier m; (tourist guide) Reiseleiter(in f) m.

course[1] [kɔːs] n (a) (direction) Kurs m; (of river, history) Lauf m; (fig: of illness) Verlauf m. to set ~ for a place Kurs auf einen Ort nehmen; to change ~ den Kurs ändern; to be on/off ~ auf Kurs sein/vom Kurs abgekommen sein; to let sth take its ~ einer Sache (dat) ihren Lauf lassen; the ~ of true love ne'er did run smooth (prov) Liebe geht oft seltsame Wege (prov); which ~ of action did you take? wie sind Sie vorgegangen?; the best ~ would be ... das beste wäre ...; we have no other ~ (of action) but to ... es bleibt uns nichts anderes übrig als zu ...

(b) in the ~ of his life/the next few weeks/the meeting etc während seines Lebens/der nächsten paar Wochen/der Versammlung etc; in the ~ of time/the conversation im Laufe der Zeit/ Unterhaltung; in the ordinary ~ of things unter normalen Umständen; in the ~ of construction im Bau.

(c) of ~ (admittedly) natürlich; (obviously) selbstverständlich; of ~ I will! aber natürlich; of ~ I'm coming natürlich komme ich.

(d) (Sch, Univ) Kurs(us) m; (at work) Lehrgang m; (Med: of treatment) Kur f. to go to/on a French ~ einen Französischkurs(us) besuchen; a ~ of lectures eine Vorlesungsreihe; a ~ of treatment eine Behandlung.

(e) (Sports) (race ~) Kurs m; (golf ~) Platz m.

(f) (Cook) Gang m. a three-~ meal ein Essen mit drei Gängen.

course[2] vi (blood, tears) strömen.

court [kɔːt] 1 n (a) (Jur) Gericht nt; (room) Gerichtssaal m. to appear in ~ vor Gericht erscheinen; his suggestion was ruled out of ~ (fig) sein Vorschlag wurde verworfen; to take sb to ~ jdn vor Gericht bringen. (b) (royal) Hof m. (c) (Sport) Platz m. 2 vt (a) (dated) woman den Hof machen (+dat). (b) (fig) danger herausfordern. 3 vi (dated) she's ~ing sie hat einen Freund; ~ing couple Liebespaar nt.

court card n (Brit) Bildkarte f.

courteous ['kɜːtɪəs] adj höflich.

courtesy ['kɜːtɪsɪ] n Höflichkeit f. **by** ~ **of** ... freundlicherweise zur Verfügung gestellt von ...; you might have had the ~ to ... sie hätten doch so freundlich sein können und ...

courtesy: ~ **coach** n gebührenfreier Bus; ~ **light** n (Aut) Innenleuchte f; ~ **visit** n Höflichkeitsbesuch m.

courthouse ['kɔːthaʊs] n (Jur) Gerichtsgebäude nt.

courtier ['kɔːtɪəʳ] n Höfling m.

court-martial ['kɔːt'mɑːʃəl] 1 n (Mil) Kriegsgericht nt. 2 vt vor das/ein Kriegsgericht stellen.

courtship ['kɔːtʃɪp] n (dated) (Braut)werbung f (dated) (of um).

court: ~ **shoe** n Pumps m; ~**yard** n Hof m.

cousin ['kʌzn] n (male) Vetter, Cousin m; (female) Cousine f.

cove[1] [kəʊv] n (Geog) (kleine) Bucht.

cove[2] n (dated Brit col: fellow) Kerl m (col).

covenant ['kʌvɪnənt] 1 n Schwur m; (Bibl) Bund m; (Jur) Verpflichtung f zu regelmäßigen Spenden. 2 vt to ~ to do sth durch ein Abkommen versprechen, etw zu tun.

Coventry ['kɒvəntrɪ] n: to send sb to ~ (Brit col) jdn schneiden (col).

cover ['kʌvəʳ] 1 n (a) (lid) Deckel m; (of lens) (Schutz)kappe f; (on chair etc) Bezug m; (for typewriter etc) Hülle f; (on lorries, tennis court) Plane f; (over merchandise) Decke f; (quilt) (Bett)decke f.

(b) (of book) Einband m; (of magazine) Umschlag m. to read a book from ~ to ~ ein Buch von der ersten bis zur letzten Seite lesen.

(c) (Comm: envelope) Umschlag m. **under separate** ~ mit getrennter Post.

(d) no pl (shelter, protection) Schutz m (from vor +dat, gegen); (Mil) Deckung f (from vor +dat, gegen). to take ~ (from rain) sich unterstellen; (Mil) in Deckung gehen (from vor +dat); under the ~ of the trees im Schutz der Bäume; under ~ of darkness im Schutz(e) der Dunkelheit; to give sb ~ (Mil) jdm Deckung geben.

(e) (Hunt) Deckung f. to break ~ aus der Deckung hervorbrechen.

(f) (place at meal) Gedeck nt.

(g) (Comm, Fin) Deckung f; (insurance ~) Versicherung f. to take out ~ against fire eine Feuerversicherung abschließen; do you have adequate ~? sind Sie ausreichend versichert?

2 vt (a) bedecken; (cover over) zudecken; (with loose cover) beziehen; etc beziehen. to ~ oneself in or with glory (iro) sich mit Ruhm bekleckern (iro col); ~ed in or with shame zutiefst beschämt.

(b) (hide) verbergen.

(c) (Mil, Sport, Chess: protect) decken. he only said that to ~ himself er hat das nur gesagt, um sich zu decken; I'll keep you ~ed ich gebe dir Deckung.

(d) (point a gun at etc) door etc sichern; sb in Schach halten; (be on guard near) sichern. to keep sb ~ed jdn in Schach halten; I've got you ~ed! (with gun etc) ich hab auf dich angelegt; (fig: Chess etc) ich hab' dich.

(e) (Fin) loan decken; (Insur) versichern. will £3 ~ the petrol? reichen £3 für das Benzin?; we've ~ed most eventualities wir haben die meisten Eventualitäten abgedeckt.

(f) (Press: report on) berichten über (+acc).
(g) (travel) miles, distance zurücklegen; (deal with) topics behandeln. **we've ~ed a lot today** wir haben heute viel geschafft.
(h) (salesman etc) territory zuständig sein für.
♦ **cover for** vi + prep obj vertreten.
♦ **cover over** vt sep zudecken.
♦ **cover up 1** vi **(a)** (wrap up) sich einmummen. **(b)** (conceal a fact) alles vertuschen. **to ~ ~ for sb** jdn decken. **2** vt sep **(a)** child zudecken. **(b)** (hide) truth, facts vertuschen.
coverage ['kʌvərɪdʒ] n no pl **(a)** (in media) Berichterstattung f (of über +acc). **to give full ~ to an event** ausführlich über ein Ereignis berichten. **(b)** (Insur) Versicherung f.
cover: ~**all** n usu pl (US) Overall m; ~ **charge** n Kosten pl für ein Gedeck; ~ **girl** n Titelmädchen nt.
covering ['kʌvərɪŋ] n Decke f; (floor ~) Belag m. **a** ~ **of dust/snow** eine Staub-/Schneedecke.
covering letter n Begleitbrief m.
cover note n vorläufiger Versicherungsschein.
covert ['kʌvət] adj threat, attack versteckt; glance verstohlen.
cover-up ['kʌvərʌp] n Vertuschung f.
covet ['kʌvɪt] vt begehren.
covetous ['kʌvɪtəs] adj begehrlich.
cow[1] [kaʊ] n **(a)** Kuh f. ~ **elephant** Elefantenkuh f; **you'll be waiting till the ~s come home** (fig col) da kannst du warten, bis du schwarz wirst (col). **(b)** (pej col: woman) (stupid) Kuh f (col); (nasty) gemeine Ziege (col).
cow[2] vt person, animal einschüchtern. **she had a** ~**ed look about her** sie machte einen eingeschüchterten Eindruck.
coward ['kaʊəd] n Feigling m.
cowardice ['kaʊədɪs], **cowardliness** ['kaʊədlɪnɪs] n Feigheit f.
cowardly ['kaʊədlɪ] adj feig(e).
cow: ~**boy** n Cowboy m; ~**catcher** n (Rail) Schienenräumer m.
cower ['kaʊə'] vi sich ducken; (squatting) kauern.
cowhide ['kaʊhaɪd] n **(a)** (untanned) Kuhhaut f; (no pl: leather) Rindsleder nt. **(b)** (US: whip) Lederpeitsche f.
cowl [kaʊl] n **(a)** (monk's hood) Kapuze f. **(b)** (chimney ~) (Schornstein)kappe f.
cowman ['kaʊmən] n, pl **-men** [-mən] (farm labourer) Stallbursche m; (US: cattle rancher) Viehzüchter m.
cow: ~**shed** n Kuhstall m; ~**slip** n (Brit: primrose) Schlüsselblume f; (US: kingcup) Sumpfdotterblume f.
cox [kɒks] **1** n Steuermann m. **2** vt crew Steuermann sein für. **3** vi steuern.
coy [kɔɪ] adj (+er) (affectedly shy) verschämt; (coquettish) kokett.
cozy adj (US) = **cosy**.
crab [kræb] n Krabbe f.
crab apple n Holzapfel m.
crack [kræk] **1** n **(a)** Riß m; (between floorboards etc) Ritze f; (wider hole etc) Spalte f; (in pottery etc) Sprung m. **at the ~ of dawn** in aller Frühe. **(b)** (sharp noise) (of wood etc breaking) Knacks m; (of gun, whip) Knall(en nt no pl) m; (of thunder) Schlag m. **(c)** (sharp blow) Schlag m. **to give sb/oneself a ~ on the head** jdm eins auf den Kopf geben/sich (dat) den Kopf anschlagen. **(d)** (col) (gibe) Stichelei f; (joke) Witz m. **(e)** (col: attempt) **to have a ~ at sth** etw mal probieren (col).
2 adj attr erstklassig; (Mil) Elite-. ~ **shot** Meisterschütze m.
3 vt nuts, (col) safe, (fig) code knacken; problem, case lösen; joke reißen; whip knallen mit. **I think I've ~ed it** ich glaub, ich hab's.
4 vi **(a)** (get a ~) (pottery) springen; (ice, road) einen Riß/Risse bekommen; (lips, skin) spröde

werden; (bones) einen Knacks bekommen (col); (break) brechen. **(b)** (twigs, joints) knacken; (whip, gun) knallen. **(c)** (col) **to get ~ing** loslegen (col).
♦ **crack down** vi (clamp down) hart durchgreifen (on bei).
♦ **crack up 1** vi **(a)** (break into pieces) zerbrechen. **(b)** (fig col: person) zusammenbrechen. **2** vt sep (col) **he's not all he's ~ed ~ to be** so toll ist er dann auch wieder nicht.
cracked [krækt] adj **(a)** plate gesprungen; rib angebrochen; walls rissig. **(b)** (col: mad) übergeschnappt (col).
cracker ['krækə'] n **(a)** (biscuit) Kräcker m. **(b)** (fire~) Knallkörper m; (Christmas ~) Knallbonbon m.
crackers ['krækəz] adj pred (Brit col) übergeschnappt (col).
crackle ['krækl] **1** vi (dry leaves, paper) rascheln; (fire) knistern; (twigs, telephone line) knacken. **2** n (crackling noise) see vi Rascheln nt; Knistern nt; Knacken nt.
crackling ['kræklɪŋ] n no pl **(a)** = **crackle 2. (b)** (Cook) Kruste f (des Schweinebratens).
cradle ['kreɪdl] **1** n Wiege f; (of phone) Gabel f. **from the ~ to the grave** von der Wiege bis zur Bahre. **2** vt (hold closely) an sich (acc) drücken. **he was cradling his injured arm** er hielt sich (dat) seinen verletzten Arm; **to ~ sb/sth in one's arms** jdn/etw fest in den Armen halten.
cradle-song ['kreɪdlsɒŋ] n Wiegenlied nt.
craft [krɑːft] n **(a)** (handicraft) Kunst f; (trade) Handwerk nt; (weaving, pottery etc) Kunstgewerbe nt. **(b)** no pl (skill) Geschick(lichkeit f) nt, Kunstfertigkeit f. **(c)** no pl (cunning) List f. **(d)** pl - (boat) Boot nt.
craftsman ['krɑːftsmən] n, pl **-men** [-mən] Handwerker m.
craftsmanship ['krɑːftsmənʃɪp] n Handwerkskunst f; (of person) handwerkliches Können.
crafty ['krɑːftɪ] adj (+er) (shrewd) schlau; (sly) durchtrieben.
crag [kræg] n Fels m.
craggy ['krægɪ] adj (+er) (rocky) felsig; (jagged) zerklüftet; face kantig.
cram [kræm] **1** vt **(a)** (fill) vollstopfen; (stuff in) hineinstopfen (in/to in +acc); people hineinzwängen (in/to in +acc). **the room was ~med** der Raum war gestopft voll; **he ~med his hat (down) over his eyes** er zog sich (dat) den Hut tief ins Gesicht. **(b)** Latin etc pauken (col), büffeln (col); pupil pauken mit (col). **2** vi (swot) pauken (col), büffeln (col).
cramp [kræmp] **1** n (Med) Krampf m. **2** vt (also ~ **up**) persons zusammenpferchen. **to ~ sb's style** jdm im Weg sein.
cramped [kræmpt] adj **(a)** space beschränkt. **we are very ~ (for space)** wir sind räumlich sehr beschränkt. **(b)** position verkrampft.
cranberry ['krænbərɪ] n Preiselbeere f.
crane [kreɪn] **1** n **(a)** Kran m. ~ **driver** n Kranführer m. **(b)** (Orn) Kranich m. **2** vt: **to ~ one's neck** den Hals recken. **3** vi (also ~ **forward**) den Hals or den Kopf recken.
crank[1] [kræŋk] n (eccentric) Spinner(in f) m (col); (US: cross person) Griesgram m.
crank[2] **1** n (Mech) Kurbel f. **2** vt (also: ~ **up**) ankurbeln.
crankshaft ['kræŋkʃɑːft] n (Aut) Kurbelwelle f.
cranky ['kræŋkɪ] adj (+er) **(a)** (eccentric) verrückt. **(b)** (US: bad-tempered) griesgrämig.
crap [kræp] n (lit, fig: col!) Scheiße f (col!). **to go for a** ~ aufs Scheißhaus gehen (col!).
crap game n (US) Würfelspiel nt (mit zwei Würfeln).
crappy ['kræpɪ] adj (col!) beschissen (col!).
crash [kræʃ] **1** n **(a)** (noise) Krach(en nt) m no pl (of thunder etc) Schlag m. **(b)** (accident) Unfall m;

crash out *(collision also)* Zusammenstoß *m*; *(with several cars)* Karambolage *f*; *(plane* ~*)* (Flugzeug)unglück *nt*. **to have a** ~ *(mit dem Auto)* verunglücken. **(c)** *(Fin)* Zusammenbruch *m*. **2** *vt car* einen Unfall haben mit; *plane* abstürzen mit. **to** ~ **one's car/plane into sth** mit dem Auto/ Flugzeug gegen etw krachen. **3** *vi* **(a)** *(have an accident)* verunglücken; *(plane)* abstürzen. **to** ~ **into sth** gegen etw krachen. **(b)** *(move with a* ~*)* krachen. **to** ~ **to the ground/through sth** zu Boden/durch etw krachen; **his whole world** ~**ed about him** eine Welt brach für ihn zusammen. **(c)** *(Fin)* pleite machen *(col)*; *(stock market)* zusammenbrechen.

♦ **crash out** *vi (col: fall asleep)* sich hinhauen *(col)*; *(without meaning to)* wegtreten *(col)*.

crash: ~ **barrier** *n (Brit)* Leitplanke *f*; ~ **course** *n* Intensivkurs *m*; ~ **diet** *n* Radikalkur *f*; ~ **dive** 1 *n* Schnelltauchmanöver *nt*; **2** *vti* schnelltauchen; ~ **helmet** *n* Sturzhelm *m*; ~-**land** *vi* eine Bruchlandung machen; ~-**landing** *n* Bruchlandung *f*.

crass [kræs] *adj (+er) (unsubtle)* kraß.

crate [kreɪt] *n (also col: car, plane)* Kiste *f*; *(of bottles)* Kasten *m*.

crater ['kreɪtə'] *n* Krater *m*.

cravat(te) [krə'væt] *n* Halstuch *nt*.

crave [kreɪv] *vt (liter: beg)* erbitten; *attention, drink etc* sich sehnen nach.

craving ['kreɪvɪŋ] *n* Verlangen *nt*. **to have a** ~ **for sth** Verlangen nach etw haben.

crawfish ['krɔːfɪʃ] *n* Languste *f*.

crawl [krɔːl] **1** *n* **(a)** *(on hands and knees)* Kriechen *nt*; *(slow speed)* Kriechtempo *nt*. **(b)** *(swimming stroke)* Kraulstil *m*. **to do the** ~ kraulen. **2** *vi* **(a)** kriechen; *(baby, insects)* krabbeln. **(b)** *(be infested)* wimmeln *(with von)*. **the place is** ~**ing!** hier wimmelt es von Ungeziefer! **(c)** *(col: suck up)* kriechen *(to vor +dat)*.

crawler lane ['krɔːlələɪn] *n (Brit Aut)* Kriechspur *f*.

crayfish ['kreɪfɪʃ] *n* **(a)** *(freshwater)* Flußkrebs *m*. **(b)** *(saltwater: also* **crawfish**) Languste *f*.

crayon ['kreɪən] *n (pencil)* Buntstift *m*; *(wax* ~*)* Wachs(mal)stift *m*; *(chalk* ~*)* Pastellstift *m*.

craze [kreɪz] **1** *n (of person)* Fimmel *m (col)*. **it's the latest** ~ es ist jetzt in *(col)*. **2** *vt* **(a)** *(make insane)* **to be half** ~**d with grief** vor Schmerz halb wahnsinnig sein; **he had a** ~**d look** er sah wie wahnsinnig aus. **(b)** *glazing* rissig machen.

crazy ['kreɪzɪ] *adj (+er)* **(a)** verrückt *(with vor +dat)*. **to drive sb** ~ jdn verrückt machen; **to go** ~ verrückt werden. **(b)** *(col: enthusiastic)* verrückt *(col)*. **to be** ~ **about sb/sth** ganz verrückt auf jdn/etw sein *(col)*. **(c)** *angle, tilt* unwahrscheinlich.

crazy paving *n* Mosaikpflaster *nt*.

creak [kriːk] **1** *n* Knarren *nt no pl*; *(of hinges, bed)* Quietschen *nt no pl*; *(of knees etc)* Knacken *nt no pl*. **2** *vi* knarren; *(hinges, bed)* quietschen; *(knees etc)* knacken.

cream [kriːm] **1** *n* **(a)** Sahne *f*; *(~ pudding, artificial* ~*)* Creme *f*. ~ **of tomato/chicken soup** Tomaten-/Hühnercremesuppe *f*. **(b)** *(lotion)* Creme *f*. **(c)** *(colour)* Creme(farbe *f*) *nt*. **(d)** *(fig: best)* **the** ~ die Besten; *(of society)* die Elite *f*. **2** *adj (colour)* cremefarben. **3** *vt* **(a)** *(put* ~ *on) face etc* eincremen. **(b)** *butter etc* cremig rühren; *potatoes* pürieren. ~**ed potatoes** Kartoffelpüree *nt*. **(c)** *milk* entrahmen.

♦ **cream off** *vt sep (lit)* abschöpfen; *(fig)* absahnen.

cream: ~ **cake** *n* Sahnetorte *f*; ~ **cheese** *n* (Doppelrahm)frischkäse *m*.

creamery ['kriːmərɪ] *n* Molkerei *f*.

creamy ['kriːmɪ] *adj (+er) (tasting of cream)* sahnig; *(smooth)* cremig.

crease [kriːs] **1** *n* Falte *f*. **to put a** ~ **in a pair of** trousers eine Falte in eine Hose bügeln. **2** *vt (deliberately) clothes* Falten/eine Falte machen in *(+acc)*; *paper* falzen; *(unintentionally)* zerknittern. **3** *vi* knittern. **his face** ~**d with laughter** er fing an zu lachen.

crease-resistant ['kriːsrɪzɪstənt] *adj* knitterfrei.

create [kriː'eɪt] **1** *vt* **(a)** schaffen; *fashion* kreieren; *the world, man* erschaffen; *fuss* verursachen; *difficulties, impression* machen. **to** ~ **a sensation** eine Sensation sein; **to** ~ **a fuss** Theater machen *(col)*. **(b)** *peer* ernennen. **2** *vi (Brit col)* Theater machen *(col)*.

creation [kriː'eɪʃən] *n* **(a)** *no pl see vt* Schaffung *f*; Kreation *f*; Erschaffung *f*; Verursachung *f*; Ernennung *f*. **(b)** *no pl* **the C~** die Schöpfung. **(c)** *(Art)* Werk *nt*; *(Fashion)* Kreation *f*.

creative [kriː'eɪtɪv] *adj* kreativ.

creativity [,kriːeɪ'tɪvɪtɪ] *n* Kreativität *f*.

creator [kriː'eɪtə'] *n* Schöpfer(in *f*) *m*.

creature ['kriːtʃə'] *n* Geschöpf *nt*. **she's a poor/ funny** ~ sie ist ein armes/komisches Geschöpf.

creature comforts *npl* leibliches Wohl.

crèche [kreɪʃ] *n (Brit)* (Kinder)krippe *f*.

credentials [krɪ'denʃəlz] *npl (references)* Referenzen *pl*; *(papers of identity)* (Ausweis)papiere *pl*.

credibility [,kredə'bɪlɪtɪ] *n* Glaubwürdigkeit *f*. **there's a** ~ **gap** es besteht ein Mangel an Glaubwürdigkeit.

credible ['kredɪbl] *adj* glaubwürdig.

credit ['kredɪt] **1** *n* **(a)** *no pl (Fin)* Kredit *m*. **the bank will let me have £5,000** ~ die Bank räumt mir einen Kredit von £ 5.000 ein; **his** ~ **is good** er ist kreditwürdig; **to give sb** ~ jdm Kredit geben; **to be in** ~ Geld auf dem Konto haben. **(b)** *no pl (honour)* Ehre *f*; *(recognition)* Anerkennung *f*; *(Sch, Univ: distinction)* Auszeichnung *f*. **he's a** ~ **to his family** er macht seiner Familie Ehre; **that's to his** ~ das muß man ihm hoch anrechnen; **to take the** ~ **for sth** das Verdienst für etw in Anspruch nehmen; **I gave you** ~ **for more sense** ich habe Sie für vernünftiger gehalten. **(c)** *(esp US Univ)* Schein *m*. **(d)** ~**s** *pl (Film etc)* Vor-/Nachspann *m*.

2 *vt* **(a)** *(believe)* glauben. **would you** ~ **it!** ist das denn die Möglichkeit! **(b)** *(attribute)* zuschreiben *(+dat)*. **I** ~**ed him with more sense** ich habe ihn für vernünftiger gehalten; **it's** ~**ed with (having) magic powers** ihm werden Zauberkräfte zugeschrieben. **(c)** *(Fin)* gutschreiben. **to** ~ **a sum to sb's account** jds Konto *(dat)* einen Betrag gutschreiben.

creditable ['kredɪtəbl] *adj (praiseworthy)* lobenswert.

credit: ~ **card** *n* Kreditkarte *f*; ~ **facilities** *npl* Kreditmöglichkeiten *pl*; ~ **note** *n (Brit)* Gutschrift *f*.

creditor ['kredɪtə'] *n* Gläubiger *m*.

credit: ~ **squeeze** *n* Kreditbeschränkung *f*; ~ **terms** *npl* Kreditbedingungen *pl*; ~-**worthy** *adj* kreditwürdig.

credulity [krɪ'djuːlɪtɪ] *n no pl* Leichtgläubigkeit *f*.

credulous ['kredjʊləs] *adj* leichtgläubig.

creed [kriːd] *n (Eccl)* Glaubensbekenntnis *nt*.

creek [kriːk] *n (esp Brit: inlet)* (kleine) Bucht; *(US: brook)* Bach *m*. **to be up the** ~ *(col: be in trouble)* in der Tinte sitzen *(col)*.

creep [kriːp] *(vb: pret, ptp* **crept**) **1** *vi* **(a)** schleichen; *(crawl)* kriechen. **ivy is a** ~**ing plant** Efeu ist eine Kletterpflanze; **time's** ~**ing on** die Zeit verrinnt. **(b)** **the story made my flesh** ~ bei der Geschichte überlief es mich kalt. **2** *n* **(a)** *(col: unpleasant person)* fieser Typ *(col)*. **(b)** **this old house gives me the** ~**s** *(col)* in dem alten Haus kriege ich das kalte Grausen *(col)*.

♦ **creep in** *vi (mistakes, new tone etc)* sich einschleichen *(-to* in *+acc)*.

♦ **creep over** *vi +prep obj (pleasant feeling)* überkommen.

♦ **creep up** vi (a) (person) sich heranschleichen (on an +acc); (prices) (in die Höhe) klettern. (b) to ~ ~ **on sb** (time, exam) langsam auf jdn zukommen; **old age is** ~**ing** ~ **on him** er wird langsam alt.

creeper ['kriːpəʳ] n (a) (plant) (along ground) Kriechpflanze f; (upwards) Kletterpflanze f. (b) ~s pl (US: shoes) Leisetreter pl (col).

creepy ['kriːpɪ] adj (+er) (frightening) unheimlich.

creepy-crawly ['kriːpɪ'krɔːlɪ] (col) n Krabbeltier nt (col).

cremate [krɪ'meɪt] vt einäschern.

cremation [krɪ'meɪʃən] n Einäscherung f.

crematorium [ˌkreməˈtɔːrɪəm], (esp US) **crematory** ['kremə,tɔːrɪ] n Krematorium nt.

creosote ['krɪəsəʊt] 1 n Kreosot nt (ein Holzschutzmittel). 2 vt mit Kreosot streichen.

crêpe [kreɪp]: ~ **bandage** n elastischer Verband; ~ **paper** n Kreppapier nt; ~ **rubber** 1 n Kreppgummi m; 2 adj Kreppgummi-; ~**-soled** [kreɪp'səʊld] adj mit Kreppsohle(n).

crept [krept] pret, ptp of **creep**.

crescendo [krɪ'ʃendəʊ] n (Mus) Crescendo nt; (fig) Zunahme f.

crescent ['kresnt] 1 n Halbmond m; (street) Straße f (halbmondförmig verlaufend). 2 adj ~**-shaped** adj halbmondförmig; **the** ~ **moon** die Mondsichel.

cress [kres] n (Garten)kresse f; (water~) Brunnenkresse f.

crest [krest] n (a) (of bird) Haube f; (of cock) Kamm m; (on hat etc) Federbusch m. (b) (Her) Helmzierde f; (coat of arms) Wappen nt. (c) (of wave, hill, Anat: of horse etc) Kamm m; (fig: of excitement, popularity) Höhepunkt m; (Phys: of oscillation) Scheitel(punkt) m. **he's riding on the** ~ **of a wave** (fig) er schwimmt im Augenblick oben.

crestfallen ['krest,fɔːlən] adj niedergeschlagen.

Crete [kriːt] n Kreta nt.

cretin ['kretɪn] n (Med) Kretin m; (col) Schwachkopf m (col).

crevasse [krɪ'væs] n (Gletscher)spalte f.

crevice ['krevɪs] n Spalte f.

crew[1] [kruː] 1 n (a) Mannschaft (also Sport) f; (including officers: of ship also, of plane, tank) Besatzung f. **50 passengers and 20** ~ 50 Passagiere und 20 Mann Besatzung; **the ground** ~ (Aviat) das Bodenpersonal. (b) (col: gang) Bande f. **they were a motley** ~ sie waren ein bunt zusammengewürfelter Haufen (col). 2 vt yacht die Mannschaft sein von. 3 vi to ~ **for sb** (Sailing) bei jdm den Vorschotmann machen.

crew[2] (old) pret of **crow**.

crew-cut ['kruːkʌt] n Bürstenschnitt m.

crib [krɪb] 1 n (a) (manger, nativity scene) Krippe f; (US: cot) Kinderbett nt. (b) (Sch: cheating aid) Spickzettel m (col). 2 vti (esp Sch col) spicken (col).

crick [krɪk] 1 n a ~ **in one's neck** ein steifes Genick. 2 vt to ~ **one's neck** sich (dat) ein steifes Genick zuziehen.

cricket[1] ['krɪkɪt] n (insect) Grille f.

cricket[2] ['krɪkɪt] n (Sport) Kricket nt. **that's not** ~ (fig col) das ist nicht fair.

cricket in cpds Kricket-; ~ **bat** n (Kricket)schlagholz nt.

crime [kraɪm] n Straftat f; (robbery etc also, fig) Verbrechen nt. **it's a** ~ **to throw away all that good food** es ist eine Sünde, all das gute Essen wegzuwerfen.

crime: ~ **prevention** n Verbrechensverhütung f; ~ **rate** n Verbrechensrate f; ~ **wave** n Welle f von Straftaten.

criminal ['krɪmɪnl] 1 n Straftäter(in f) m; (guilty of capital crimes also, fig) Verbrecher(in f) m. 2 adj (a) kriminell, verbrecherisch. **C**~ **Investi-**

gation Department Kriminalpolizei f; ~ **code** Strafgesetzbuch nt; ~ **lawyer** m für Strafsachen; (specializing in defence) Strafverteidiger m; **to have a** ~ **record** vorbestraft sein. (b) (fig) kriminell.

criminology [ˌkrɪmɪ'nɒlədʒɪ] n Kriminologie f.

crimson ['krɪmzn] 1 adj purpurrot; sky blutrot. **to turn** ~ (person, face) knallrot (col) or dunkelrot anlaufen. 2 n Purpurrot nt.

cringe [krɪndʒ] vi (a) (shrink back) zurückschrecken (at vor +dat); (fig) schaudern. **to** ~ **before sb** vor jdm zurückschrecken; **he** ~**d at the thought** er or ihn schauderte bei dem Gedanken; **his jokes make me** ~ bei seinen Witzen kriege ich zuviel. (b) (fawn) kriechen (to vor +dat).

cringing **behaviour** kriecherisches Benehmen.

crinkle ['krɪŋkl] 1 n (Knitter)falte f. 2 vt paper, dress etc (zer)knittern. 3 vi (paper, foil, dress etc) knittern; (face, skin) (Lach)fältchen bekommen; (edges of paper) sich wellen; (curl: hair) sich krausen.

crinkly ['krɪŋklɪ] adj (+er) (col) paper etc zerknittert; hair kraus.

cripple ['krɪpl] 1 n Krüppel m. 2 vt person zum Krüppel machen; legs etc verkrüppeln; ship, plane aktionsunfähig machen; (fig) industry lahmlegen. **the ship was** ~**d** das Schiff war nicht mehr aktionsfähig; ~**d with rheumatism** von Rheuma praktisch gelähmt.

crippling ['krɪplɪŋ] adj taxes erdrückend.

crisis ['kraɪsɪs] n, pl **crises** ['kraɪsiːz] Krise f.

crisp [krɪsp] 1 adj (+er) apple, lettuce knackig; bread, biscuits, bacon knusprig; snow verharscht; leaves trocken; appearance adrett; style knapp; air frisch. 2 n (Brit: potato ~) Chip m usu pl.

crispbread ['krɪspbred] n Knäckebrot nt.

criss-cross ['krɪskrɒs] 1 adv kreuz und quer. 2 adj pattern Kreuz-. 3 vi (lines) sich kreuzen.

criterion [kraɪ'tɪərɪən] n, pl **criteria** [kraɪ'tɪərɪə] Kriterium nt.

critic ['krɪtɪk] n Kritiker(in f) m.

critical ['krɪtɪkəl] adj kritisch. **to be** ~ **of sb/sth** (criticize) jdn/etw kritisieren; (have ~ attitude) jdm/einer Sache kritisch gegenüberstehen; **that's** ~ (crucial) das ist entscheidend.

critically ['krɪtɪkəlɪ] adv (a) kritisch. (b) ill schwer.

criticism ['krɪtɪsɪzəm] n Kritik f.

criticize ['krɪtɪsaɪz] vti kritisieren.

critique [krɪ'tiːk] n Kritik f.

croak [krəʊk] 1 n (of frog) Quaken nt no pl; (of raven, person) Krächzen nt no pl. 2 vti (frog) quaken; (raven, person) krächzen.

croaky ['krəʊkɪ] adj (+er) (col) voice heiser.

crochet ['krəʊʃeɪ] 1 n Häkelei f. ~ **hook** Häkelnadel f. 2 vti häkeln.

crock[1] [krɒk] n (jar) Topf m.

crock[2] n (col) (vehicle) Kiste f (col); (person) Wrack nt (col).

crockery ['krɒkərɪ] n (Brit) Geschirr nt.

crocodile ['krɒkədaɪl] n (a) Krokodil nt. ~ **tears** Krokodilstränen. (b) (Brit Sch) **to walk in a** ~ zwei und zwei hintereinandergehen.

crocus ['krəʊkəs] n Krokus m.

croft [krɒft] n (esp Scot) kleines Pachtgrundstück; (house) Kate f.

crofter ['krɒftəʳ] n (esp Scot) Kleinpächter(in f) m.

croissant ['krwaːsɒŋ] n Hörnchen nt.

crony ['krəʊnɪ] n Freund(in f) m.

crook [krʊk] 1 n (a) (dishonest person) Gauner(in f) m (col). (b) (of shepherd) Hirtenstab m; (of bishop) Bischofsstab m. (c) (bend: in road, river) Biegung f; (in arm) Beuge f. 2 vt finger krümmen; arm beugen.

crooked ['krʊkɪd] adj (lit) (bent) smile schief; (fig col: dishonest) method krumm; person unehrlich.

croon [kruːn] vti (sing softly) leise singen; (sentimentally) schmalzig singen (pej col).

crooner ['kruːnəʳ] n Schnulzensänger m (pej col).

crop [krɒp] **1** n **(a)** (produce) Ernte f; (species grown) (Feld)frucht f; (fig: large number) Schwung m. **a good ~ of potatoes** eine gute Kartoffelernte. **(b)** (of bird) Kropf m. **(c)** (of whip) Stock m; (hunting ~) Reitpeitsche f. **(d)** (hairstyle) Kurzhaarschnitt m. **2** vt hair stutzen.
♦ **crop up** vi aufkommen. **something's ~ped ~ es ist** etwas dazwischengekommen.

cropper ['krɒpəʳ] n (col) to come a ~ (lit: fall) hinfliegen (col); (fig: fail) auf die Nase fallen.

crop spraying n Schädlingsbekämpfung f (durch Besprühen).

croquet ['krəʊkeɪ] n Krocket(spiel) nt.

croquette [krəʊˈket] n Krokette f.

cross¹ [krɒs] **1** n **(a)** Kreuz nt. **we all have our ~ to bear** wir haben alle unser Kreuz zu tragen. **(b)** (bias) on the ~ schräg. **(c)** (hybrid) Kreuzung f; (fig) Mittelding nt.
2 attr (transverse) street etc Quer-.
3 vt **(a)** road, river, Channel überqueren; (on foot) überschreiten; country, desert durchqueren. **to ~ the road** über die Straße gehen; **to ~ sb's path** (fig) jdm über den Weg laufen; **it ~ed my mind that …** es fiel mir ein, daß …; **we'll ~ that bridge when we come to it** lassen wir das Problem erst mal auf uns zukommen. **(b)** (intersect) kreuzen. **to ~ one's legs** die Beine übereinanderschlagen; **the lines are ~ed** (Telec) die Leitungen überschneiden sich; **I'm keeping my fingers ~ed for you** (col) ich drücke dir die Daumen (col). **(c)** to ~ oneself sich bekreuzigen; **~ my/your heart** (col) Ehrenwort. **(d)** (mark with a ~) ankreuzen. **~ed cheque** Verrechnungsscheck m. **(e)** (go against) plans durchkreuzen. **to ~ sb** jdn verärgern. **(f)** animal, fruit kreuzen.
4 vi **(a)** (across road) hinübergehen; (across Channel etc) hinüberfahren. **(b)** (lines, letters) sich kreuzen. **our paths have ~ed several times** (fig) unsere Wege haben sich öfters gekreuzt.
♦ **cross off** vt sep streichen (prep obj aus, von).
♦ **cross out** vt sep ausstreichen.

cross² adj (+er) böse. **to be ~ with sb** mit jdm or auf jdn böse sein.

cross: **~bar** n (of bicycle) Stange f; (Sport) Querlatte f; **~breed** (Zool, Biol) **1** n Kreuzung f; **2** vt kreuzen; **~-Channel** attr ferries Kanal-; **~-check 1** n Gegenprobe f; **2** vt facts, figures überprüfen; **~-country 1** adj Querfeldein-; **2** adv querfeldein; skiing Langlauf m; **~-examination** n Kreuzverhör nt (of über +acc); **~-examine** vt ins Kreuzverhör nehmen; **~-eyed** adj schielend; **~fire** n Kreuzfeuer nt; **to be caught in the ~fire** (lit, fig) ins Kreuzfeuer geraten.

crossing ['krɒsɪŋ] n **(a)** (act) Überquerung f; (sea ~) Überfahrt f. **(b)** (~ place) Übergang m; (crossroads) Kreuzung f.

cross-legged [ˌkrɒsˈlegɪd] adj, adv mit gekreuzten Beinen; (on ground) im Schneidersitz.

crossly ['krɒslɪ] adv böse, verärgert.

cross: **~patch** n (col) Brummbär m (col); **~-purposes** npl to be at ~-purposes aneinander vorbeireden; **~-reference** n Querverweis m (to auf +acc); **~roads** n sing or pl (lit) Kreuzung f; (fig) Scheideweg m. **~-section** n Querschnitt m (of durch); **~walk** n (US) Fußgängerüberweg m; **~wind** n Seitenwind m; **~word (puzzle)** n Kreuzworträtsel m.

crotch [krɒtʃ] n **(a)** (in tree etc) Gabelung f. **(b)** (of trousers) Schritt m; (Anat) Unterleib m.

crotchet ['krɒtʃɪt] n (Mus) Viertelnote f.

crouch [kraʊtʃ] vi sich zusammenkauern. **to ~ down** sich niederkauern.

croupier ['kruːpɪeɪ] n Croupier m.

crouton ['kruːtɒn] n Crouton m.

crow¹ [krəʊ] n (Orn) Krähe f. **as the ~ flies** (in der) Luftlinie.

crow² **1** n (of cock, baby) Krähen nt. **2** vi **(a)** pret **~ed** or (old) **crew**, ptp **~ed** (cock) krähen. **(b)** pret, ptp **~ed** (baby) krähen; (boast) sich brüsten (about mit).

crowbar ['krəʊbɑːʳ] n Brecheisen nt.

crowd [kraʊd] **1** n **(a)** Menschenmenge f; (Sport, Theat) Zuschauermenge f. **~s of people** Menschenmassen pl; **~ scene** (Theat) Massenszene f. **(b)** (set) Clique f. **the university** ~ die Leute von der Uni; **they're a nice** ~ sie sind alle sehr nett. **(c)** no pl (the masses) **the** ~ die (breite) Masse; **to go with** or **follow the** ~ mit der Herde laufen. **2** vi (sich) drängen. **to ~ together/in** sich zusammendrängen/(sich) hereindrängen; **to ~ around** sb/sth (sich) um jdn/etw herumscharen. **3** vt **to ~ the streets** die Straßen bevölkern.
♦ **crowd out** vt sep (not let in) wegdrängen. **the pub was ~ed** ~ das Lokal war gerammelt voll (col).

crowded ['kraʊdɪd] adj train etc überfüllt.

crown [kraʊn] **1** n **(a)** Krone f. **the C~** die Krone. **(b)** (of head) Wirbel m; (of hat) Kopf m; (of road) Wölbung f; (of tooth) Krone f. **2** vt **(a)** (lit, fig) krönen. **he was ~ed king** er ist zum König gekrönt worden; **~ed head** gekröntes Haupt; **to be ~ed with success** von Erfolg gekrönt sein; **to ~ it all it began to snow** (col) zur Krönung des Ganzen begann es zu schneien. **(b)** (in draughts etc) eine Dame bekommen mit. **(c)** tooth eine Krone machen für. **(d)** (col: hit) I'll ~ you! ich hau dir gleich eine runter! (col).

crown court n (Brit) Bezirksgericht nt für Strafsachen.

crowning ['kraʊnɪŋ] **1** n Krönung f. **2** adj achievement krönend.

crown: **~ jewels** npl Kronjuwelen pl; **~ prince** n Kronprinz m; **~ princess** n Kronprinzessin f; **~ witness** n (Brit) Zeuge m/Zeugin f der Anklage.

crow's: **~ feet** npl Krähenfüße pl; **~ nest** n (Naut) Mastkorb m; (on foremast) Krähennest nt.

crucial ['kruːʃəl] adj **(a)** (decisive) entscheidend (to für). **(b)** (col: very important) sehr wichtig.

crucible ['kruːsɪbl] n (Schmelz)tiegel m.

crucifix ['kruːsɪfɪks] n Kruzifix nt.

crucifixion [ˌkruːsɪˈfɪkʃən] n Kreuzigung f.

crucify ['kruːsɪfaɪ] vt **(a)** kreuzigen. **(b)** (fig) play, author verreißen; person in der Luft zerreißen (col). **(c)** (mortify) the flesh abtöten.

crude [kruːd] adj (+er) **(a)** (unprocessed) Roh-. **(b)** expression etc ordinär. **(c)** implement primitiv; manners ungehobelt, grob.

crudeness ['kruːdnɪs], **crudity** ['kruːdɪtɪ] n **(a)** (vulgarity) Derbheit f. **(b)** see adj (c) Primitivität f; Ungehobelte(s) nt (of gen, in +dat).

cruel ['kruːəl] adj grausam (to zu). **that is ~ to animals** das ist Tierquälerei.

cruelty ['kruːəltɪ] n Grausamkeit f (to gegenüber). **~ to children** Kindesmißhandlung f; **~ to animals** Tierquälerei f; **physical/mental** ~ Grausamkeit f/seelische Grausamkeit.

cruet ['kruːɪt] n (set) Gewürzständer m; (for oil) Krug m.

cruise [kruːz] **1** vi eine Kreuzfahrt/Kreuzfahrten machen; (ship) kreuzen; (car) Dauergeschwindigkeit fahren. **cruising speed** (Aut) Reisegeschwindigkeit f. **2** n Kreuzfahrt f. **to go for a** ~ eine Kreuzfahrt machen.

cruise missile n Cruise-Missile nt, Marschflugkörper m.

cruiser ['kruːzəʳ] n (Naut) Kreuzer m; (pleasure ~) Vergnügungsjacht f.

crumb [krʌm] **1** n **(a)** (of bread) Krümel m; (inside of loaf) Krume f. **a few ~s of information** ein paar Informationsbrocken; **that's one ~ of comfort** das ist (wenigstens) ein winziger Trost. **(b)** (col: fool) Depp m (col). **2** interj **~s!** (col)

Mensch! *(col)*.
crumble ['krʌmbl] **1** *vt* zerkrümeln. **2** *vi (brick)* bröckeln; *(bread etc)* krümeln; *(also ~ away) (earth, building)* zerbröckeln; *(opposition)* sich auflösen. **3** *n (Cook)* Obst *nt* mit Streusel; *(topping)* Streusel *pl*.
crumpet ['krʌmpɪt] *n* **(a)** *(Cook)* kleiner dicker Pfannkuchen. **(b)** *(esp Brit col: women)* Miezen *pl (col)*.
crumple ['krʌmpl] **1** *vt (also ~ up) paper, dress* zerknittern; *(screw up)* zusammenknüllen; *metal* eindrücken. **2** *vi (lit, fig: collapse)* zusammenbrechen.
crumple zone *n* Knautschzone *f*.
crunch [krʌntʃ] **1** *vt apple, biscuit etc* mampfen *(col)*. **2** *vi (gravel, snow etc)* knirschen; *(gears)* krachen. **3** *n (sound)* Krachen *nt*; *(of footsteps, gravel etc)* Knirschen *nt*. **when it comes to the ~** wenn es darauf ankommt.
crunchy ['krʌntʃɪ] *adj (+er) apple* knackig; *biscuit* knusprig; *snow* verharscht.
crusade [kruː'seɪd] *n (Hist, fig)* Kreuzzug *m*.
crusader [kruː'seɪdəʳ] *n (Hist)* Kreuzritter *m*.
crush [krʌʃ] **1** *n* **(a)** *(crowd)* Gedrängel *nt*. **~ barrier** Absperrung *f*. **(b)** *(col)* **to have a ~ on sb** für jdn schwärmen. **2** *vt* **(a)** *(squeeze)* quetschen; *fruit etc* zerdrücken; *(kill)* zu Tode quetschen; *spices, garlic* (zer)stoßen; *stone* zerkleinern; *scrap metal* zusammenpressen; *(crease)* zerknittern; *(screw up)* zerknüllen. **(b)** *(fig) hopes, sb* vernichten; *people* unterdrücken. **3** *vi (clothes)* knittern.
crushing ['krʌʃɪŋ] *adj defeat, reply* vernichtend.
crust [krʌst] *n (all senses)* Kruste *f*. **the earth's ~** die Erdkruste.
crustacean [krʌs'teɪʃən] *n* Schalentier *nt*.
crusty ['krʌstɪ] *adj (+er)* knusprig; *(fig: irritable)* barsch.
crutch [krʌtʃ] **(a)** *n (for walking)* Krücke *f*. **(b)** = **crotch (b)**.
crux [krʌks] *n (of problem)* Kern *m*. **the ~ of the matter** der springende Punkt.
cry [kraɪ] **1** *n* **(a)** Schrei *m*; *(call)* Ruf *m*. **to utter a ~** einen Schrei ausstoßen; **a ~ of pain** ein Schmerzensschrei *m*; **a ~ for help** ein Hilferuf *m*. **(b)** *(slogan)* Parole *f*. **(c)** *(weep)* **a ~ will do you good** weine ruhig, das wird dir guttun. **2** *vi* **(a)** *(weep)* weinen; *(baby)* schreien. **she was ~ing for her mother** sie weinte nach ihrer Mutter. **(b)** *(call)* rufen; *(louder, animal, bird)* schreien. **to ~ for help** um Hilfe rufen/schreien. **3** *vt* **(a)** *(shout out)* rufen; *(louder)* schreien. **(b)** *bitter tears etc* weinen. **to ~ one's heart out** herzzerreißend weinen; **to ~ oneself to sleep** sich in den Schlaf weinen.
♦ **cry off** *vi* einen Rückzieher machen.
♦ **cry out** *vi* **(a)** aufschreien. **to ~ ~ to sb** jdm etwas zuschreien. **(b)** *(fig)* **this door is ~ing ~ for a coat of paint** diese Tür schreit danach, gestrichen zu werden.
crying ['kraɪɪŋ] **1** *adj (fig) injustice* schreiend; *need* dringend. **it is a ~ shame** es ist ein Jammer. **2** *n (weeping)* Weinen *nt*.
crypt [krɪpt] *n* Krypta *f*; *(burial ~)* Gruft *f*.
cryptic ['krɪptɪk] *adj remark* hintergründig; *riddle* verschlüsselt.
crystal ['krɪstl] **1** *n* **(a)** *(Chem, Rad)* Kristall *m*. **(b)** *(on watch)* (Uhr)glas *nt*. **(c)** *(~ glass)* Kristall *nt*. **2** *adj* **(a)** *(crystalline)* kristallen; *(~-glass)* Kristall-; *(quartz)* Quarzkristall-. **(b)** *(fig) waters, lake* kristallklar.
crystal: **~ ball** *n* Glaskugel *f*; **~-clear** *adj (lit, fig)* glasklar; **~-gazing** *n* Hellseherei *f*.
crystallization [‚krɪstəlaɪˈzeɪʃən] *n* Kristallisierung *f*.
crystallize ['krɪstəlaɪz] **1** *vt (lit)* zum Kristallisieren bringen; *(fig)* feste Form geben *(+dat)*. **2** *vi (lit)* kristallisieren; *(fig)* feste Form annehmen.

crystallized ['krɪstəlaɪzd] *adj fruit* kandiert.
cub [kʌb] *n* **(a)** *(of animal)* Junge(s) *nt*. **(b)** *(also ~ scout)* Wölfling *m*.
Cuba ['kjuːbə] *n* Kuba *nt*.
cubby-hole ['kʌbɪhəʊl] *n* **(a)** *(compartment)* Fach *nt*. **(b)** *(room)* Kabäuschen *nt (col)*.
cube [kjuːb] *n* **(a)** *(shape, object)* Würfel *m*. **~ sugar** Würfelzucker *m*. **(b)** *(Math)* dritte Potenz. **~ root** Kubikwurzel *f*.
cubic ['kjuːbɪk] *adj* **(a)** *(of volume)* Kubik-. **~ capacity** Fassungsvermögen *nt*; *(of engine)* Hubraum *m*. **(b)** *(Math)* kubisch. **~ equation** Gleichung *f* dritten Grades.
cubicle ['kjuːbɪkəl] *n* Kabine *f*.
cubism ['kjuːbɪzəm] *n* Kubismus *m*.
cuckoo ['kʊkuː] **1** *n* Kuckuck *m*. **2** *adj pred (col)* meschugge *(col)*. **~ clock** *n* Kuckucksuhr *f*.
cucumber ['kjuːkʌmbəʳ] *n* (Salat)gurke *f*. **as cool as a ~** seelenruhig.
cud [kʌd] *n* **to chew the ~** *(lit)* wiederkäuen; *(fig)* vor sich hingrübeln.
cuddle ['kʌdl] **1** *n* Liebkosung *f*. **to give sb a ~** jdn in den Arm nehmen; **to have a ~** schmusen. **2** *vt* in den Arm nehmen.
♦ **cuddle down** *vi* sich kuscheln.
♦ **cuddle up** *vi* sich kuscheln *(to, against* an *+acc)*.
cuddly ['kʌdlɪ] *adj (+er) (wanting a cuddle)* anschmiegsam; *(good to cuddle) toy, doll* zum Liebhaben, knuddelig *(col)*.
cudgel ['kʌdʒəl] **1** *n* Knüppel *m*. **to take up the ~s for sb/sth** *(fig)* für jdn/etw eine Lanze brechen. **2** *vt* prügeln. **to ~ one's brains** *(fig)* sich *(dat)* das (Ge)hirn zermartern.
cue [kjuː] *n* **(a)** *(Theat, fig)* Stichwort *nt*; *(action)* (Einsatz)zeichen *nt*; *(Mus)* Einsatz *m*. **to take one's ~ from sb** sich nach jdm richten; **right on ~** *(Theat)* genau aufs Stichwort; *(fig)* wie gerufen. **(b)** *(Billiards)* Queue *nt*.
♦ **cue in** *vt sep* den Einsatz geben *(+dat)*; *(TV, Film) scene* abfahren lassen; *tape etc* (rechtzeitig) einspielen.
cuff¹ [kʌf] *n* **(a)** Manschette *f*. **off the ~** *(fig)* aus dem Stegreif; *remark* aus dem Handgelenk. **(b)** *(US: of trousers)* (Hosen)aufschlag *m*.
cuff² *vt (strike)* einen Klaps geben *(+dat)*.
cuff-link ['kʌflɪŋk] *n* Manschettenknopf *m*.
cuisine [kwɪ'ziːn] *n* Küche *f*.
cul-de-sac ['kʌldəsæk] *n (esp Brit)* Sackgasse *f*.
culinary ['kʌlɪnərɪ] *adj* kulinarisch; *skill etc* Koch-.
cull [kʌl] **1** *n* **(a)** *(selection)* Auswahl *f*. **(b)** *(killing of surplus)* **~ of seals** Robbenschlag *m*. **2** *vt* **(a)** *(pick) flowers* pflücken. **(b)** *(collect)* entnehmen *(from dat)*. **(c)** *(kill as surplus)* **to ~ seals** Robbenschlag *m* betreiben.
culminate ['kʌlmɪneɪt] *vi* gipfeln *(in* in *+dat)*.
culmination [‚kʌlmɪ'neɪʃən] *n* Höhepunkt *m*; *(end)* Ende *nt*.
culottes [kjuː'lɒts] *npl* Hosenrock *m*. **a pair of ~** ein Hosenrock.
culpable ['kʌlpəbl] *adj (form)* schuldig. **~ homicide** *(Jur)* fahrlässige Tötung; **~ negligence** grobe Fahrlässigkeit.
culprit ['kʌlprɪt] *n* Schuldige(r) *mf*; *(Jur)* Täter(in *f*) *m*.
cult [kʌlt] *n (Rel, fig)* Kult *m*. **to make a ~ of sth** (einen) Kult mit etw treiben.
cultivate ['kʌltɪveɪt] *vt* **(a)** *soil* bebauen; *crop* anbauen. **(b)** *(fig) friendship, links etc* pflegen; *skill, taste* entwickeln.
cultivation [‚kʌltɪ'veɪʃən] *n see vt* **(a)** Bebauung *f*; Anbau *m*. **(b)** Pflege *f (of* von*)*; Entwicklung *f*.
cultural ['kʌltʃərəl] *adj* Kultur-; *differences, events* kulturell.
culture ['kʌltʃəʳ] *n* **(a)** Kultur *f*. **(b)** *(Agr, Biol, Med)* Kultur *f*; *(of animals)* Zucht *f*.
cultured ['kʌltʃəd] *adj* kultiviert; *(Agr)* Kultur-; *(Biol, Med)* gezüchtet. **~ pearl** Zuchtperle *f*.
cumbersome ['kʌmbəsəm] *adj clothing* hinder-

lich; *vehicle* schwer zu manövrieren; *suitcases, parcels* sperrig; *procedure* beschwerlich.

cumin ['kʌmɪn] *n* Kreuzkümmel *m*.

cumulative ['kju:mjʊlətɪv] *adj* kumulativ. **the ~ debts of ten years** die Schulden, die sich im Lauf von zehn Jahren angehäuft haben/hatten.

cunning ['kʌnɪŋ] **1** *n (cleverness)* Schlauheit *f*. **2** *adj* schlau; *person also* gerissen; *expression* verschmitzt; *gadget* raffiniert.

cup [kʌp] **1** *n* **(a)** Tasse *f*; *(goblet)* Pokal *m*; *(mug)* Becher *m*. **a ~ of tea** eine Tasse Tee; **that's just/that's not my ~ of tea** *(fig col)* das ist genau/ ist nicht mein Fall *(col)*. **(b)** *(prize, football ~ etc)* Pokal *m*. **(c)** *(of bra)* Körbchen *nt*. **2** *vt hands* hohl machen. **~ped hand** hohle Hand; **he ~ped his chin in his hand** er stützte das Kinn in die Hand; **to ~ one's hands around sth** etw mit der hohlen Hand umfassen.

cupboard ['kʌbəd] *n* Schrank *m*. **~ love** fauler Schmus *(col)*.

cup: C~ Final *n* Pokalendspiel *nt*; **~ful** *n, pl* **~sful** *or* **~fuls** Tasse *f*; **~ size** *n (of bra)* Körbchengröße *f*; **~ tie** *n* Pokalspiel *nt*.

curate ['kjʊərɪt] *n (Catholic)* Kurat *m*; *(Protestant)* Vikar *m*.

curator [kjʊə'reɪtə'] *n (of museum etc)* Kustos *m*.

curb [kɜ:b] **1** *n* **(a)** *(of harness) (lit)* Kandare *f*; *(chain)* Kinnkette *f*. **(b)** *(fig)* Behinderung *f*; *(deliberate)* Beschränkung *f*. **(c)** *(esp US: curbstone)* = **kerb**. **2** *vt horse, (fig)* zügeln; *immigration etc* in Schranken halten.

curd [kɜ:d] *n (often pl)* Quark *m*. **~ cheese** Quark *m*.

curdle ['kɜ:dl] **1** *vt (lit, fig)* gerinnen lassen. **2** *vi* gerinnen. **his blood ~d** das Blut gerann ihm in den Adern.

cure [kjʊə'] **1** *vt* **(a)** *(Med)* illness, person heilen. **to be/get ~d (of sth)** (von etw) geheilt sein/werden; **to ~ sb (of sth)** jdn (von etw) heilen. **(b)** *(fig) inflation, ill etc* abhelfen *(+dat)*. **to ~ sb of sth** jdn von etw kurieren. **(c)** *food* haltbar machen; *(salt)* pökeln; *(smoke)* räuchern; *skins, tobacco* trocknen. **2** *n* *(Med) (remedy)* (Heil)mittel *nt (for gegen)*; *(treatment)* Heilverfahren *nt (for sb* für jdn, *for sth* gegen etw); *(recovery)* Heilung *f*; *(health ~)* Kur *f*; *(fig: remedy)* Mittel *nt (for gegen)*. **to take** *or* **follow a ~** zur *or* in Kur gehen.

cure-all ['kjʊərɔ:l] *n (lit, fig)* Allheilmittel *nt*.

curfew ['kɜ:fju:] *n* Ausgangssperre *f*.

curio ['kjʊərɪəʊ] *n* Kuriosität *f*.

curiosity [,kjʊərɪ'ɒsɪtɪ] *n* **(a)** *no pl (inquisitiveness)* Neugier *f*. **~ killed the cat** *(Prov)* sei nicht so neugierig. **(b)** *(object, person)* Kuriosität *f*.

curious ['kjʊərɪəs] *adj* **(a)** *(inquisitive)* neugierig. **I'm ~ to know what he'll do** ich bin mal gespannt, was er macht; **I'd be ~ to know ...** ich wüßte gern, ... **(b)** *(odd)* sonderbar.

curiously ['kjʊərɪəslɪ] *adv* **(a)** neugierig. **(b)** *behave, speak etc* eigenartig. **~ enough** merkwürdigerweise.

curl [kɜ:l] **1** *n (of hair)* Locke *f*. **a ~ of smoke** ein Rauchkringel *m*. **2** *vt hair* locken; *(with curlers)* in Locken legen; *lips* kräuseln. **3** *vi (hair)* sich locken; *(tightly)* sich kräuseln; *(naturally)* lockig sein. **his lips ~ed** er kräuselte die Lippen.

◆**curl up** *vi (animal)* sich zusammenrollen; *(person)* sich zusammenkuscheln; *(leaf)* sich hochbiegen. **to ~ ~ in an armchair** sich in einen Sessel kuscheln; **to ~ ~ with a good book** es sich *(dat)* mit einem guten Buch gemütlich machen.

curler ['kɜ:lə'] *n (hair ~)* Lockenwickler *m*. **to put one's ~s in** sich *(dat)* die Haare eindrehen.

curlew ['kɜ:lju:] *n* Brachvogel *m*.

curling ['kɜ:lɪŋ] *n (Sport)* Curling, Eisschießen *nt*.

curling-tongs ['kɜ:lɪŋ,tɒŋz] *npl* Lockenschere *f*; *(electric)* Lockenstab *m*.

curly ['kɜ:lɪ] *adj (+er) hair* lockig; *(tighter)* kraus; *tail* Ringel-.

currant ['kʌrənt] *n* **(a)** *(dried fruit)* Korinthe *f*. **~**

---

bun Rosinenbrötchen *nt*. **(b)** *(Bot)* Johannisbeere *f*.

currency ['kʌrənsɪ] *n* **(a)** *(Fin)* Währung *f*. **foreign ~** Devisen *pl*. **(b)** *(of ideas etc)* Verbreitung *f*; *(of expression)* Gebräuchlichkeit *f*. **to be in ~** in Umlauf sein.

current ['kʌrənt] **1** *adj (present)* gegenwärtig; *edition* letzte(r, s); *opinion* verbreitet. **to be no longer ~** nicht mehr aktuell sein; *(coins)* nicht mehr in Umlauf sein; **~ affairs** aktuelle Fragen *pl*; **in ~ use** allgemein gebräuchlich. **2** *n* **(a)** *(Elec)* Strom *m*; *(of water also)* Strömung *f*; *(of air)* Luftströmung *f*. **(b)** *(fig: of events, opinions etc)* Tendenz *f*. **to go against the ~ of popular opinion** gegen den Strom der öffentlichen Meinung anschwimmen.

current: ~ account *n (Brit)* Girokonto *nt*; **~ assets** *npl* Umlaufvermögen *nt*.

currently ['kʌrəntlɪ] *adv* zur Zeit.

curriculum [kə'rɪkjʊləm] *n, pl* **curricula** Lehrplan *m*. **~ vitae** Lebenslauf *m*.

curry¹ ['kʌrɪ] *(Cook) n* Curry *m or nt*. **~-powder** Currypulver *nt*.

curry² *vt horse* striegeln. **to ~ favour** *(Brit) or* **favor** *(US)* **(with sb)** sich (bei jdm) einschmeicheln.

curse [kɜ:s] **1** *n (lit, fig)* Fluch *m*. **to put sb under a ~** jdn mit einem Fluch belegen; **~s!** *(col)* verflucht! *(col)*; **it's the ~ of my life** das ist der Fluch meines Lebens; **the ~** *(col: menstruation)* die Tage *pl (col)*; **she has the ~** sie hat ihre Tage *(col)*. **2** *vt* **(a)** *(to put a curse on)* verfluchen. **~ you/it!** *(col)* verflucht! *(col)*; **~ these trains!** *(col)* diese verfluchten Züge! *(col)*. **(b)** *(swear at or about)* fluchen über *(+acc)*. **(c)** *(fig: to afflict)* **to be ~d with sb/sth** mit jdm/etw gestraft sein. **3** *vi* fluchen.

cursor ['kɜ:sə'] *n (Comp)* Cursor *m*.

cursory ['kɜ:sərɪ] *adj glance* flüchtig.

curt [kɜ:t] *adj (+er) person* kurz angebunden; *nod, refusal* kurz.

curtail [kɜ:'teɪl] *vt* kürzen.

curtain ['kɜ:tn] *n* Vorhang *m (also Theat)*. **to draw the ~s** *(open)* den Vorhang/die Vorhänge aufziehen; *(close)* den Vorhang/die Vorhänge zuziehen; **the ~ rises/falls** der Vorhang hebt sich/ fällt; **if you get caught it'll be ~s for you** *(col)* wenn sie dich erwischen, bist du weg vom Fenster *(col)*.

◆**curtain off** *vt sep* durch einen Vorhang abtrennen.

curtain: ~-call *n (Theat)* Vorhang *m*; **to get/take a ~-call** einen Vorhang bekommen/vor den Vorhang treten; **~ hook** *n* Gardinengleithaken *m*; **~-raiser** *n (Theat)* kurzes Vorspiel; **~ ring** *n* Gardinenring *m*; **~ rod** *n* Gardinenstange *f*.

curts(e)y ['kɜ:tsɪ] *n* Knicks *m*; *(to royalty)* Hofknicks *m*. **to drop a ~** einen Knicks machen.

curvaceous [kɜ:'veɪʃəs] *adj figure, woman* kurvenreich.

curvature ['kɜ:vətʃə'] *n* Krümmung *f*; *(misshapen)* Verkrümmung *f*. **~ of the spine** *(normal)* Rückgratkrümmung *f*; *(abnormal)* Rückgratverkrümmung *f*.

curve [kɜ:v] **1** *n* Kurve *f*; *(of body, vase etc)* Rundung *f*; *(of river)* Biegung *f*; *(of archway)* Bogen *m*. **there's a ~ in the road** die Straße macht einen Bogen. **2** *vt* biegen; *arch, roof* wölben. **3** *vi* **(a)** *(road)* einen Bogen machen; *(river)* eine Biegung machen; **the road ~s around the city** die Straße macht einen Bogen um die Stadt. **(b)** *(be curved) (arch)* sich wölben; *(hips, breasts)* sich runden; *(metal strip etc)* sich biegen.

curved [kɜ:vd] *adj line* gebogen; *arch* gewölbt; *hips* rund.

cushion ['kʊʃən] **1** *n* Kissen *nt*; *(pad, fig: buffer)* Polster *nt*; *(Billiards)* Bande *f*. **2** *vt fall, blow* auffangen. **to ~ sb against sth** jdn gegen etw abschirmen.

cushy ['kʊʃɪ] *adj* (+*er*) (*col*) bequem. **to be onto a ~ number** eine ruhige Kugel schieben (*col*).

custard ['kʌstəd] *n* (*pouring* ~) ≈ Vanillesoße *f*; (*set*) ≈ Vanillepudding *m*.

custard: ~ **cream (biscuit)** *n* Doppelkeks *m* (mit Vanillecremefüllung); ~ **powder** *n* ≈ Vanillepuddingpulver *nt*; ~-**tart** *n* ≈ Puddingteilchen *nt*.

custodian [kʌs'təʊdɪən] *n* (*of park, museum*) Aufseher *m*; (*of treasure*) Hüter *m*.

custody ['kʌstədɪ] *n* (a) (*keeping, guardianship*) Obhut *f*; (*Jur: of children*) Vormundschaft *f* (*of* für, über +*acc*). **to place sth in sb's ~** etw jdm zur Aufbewahrung anvertrauen; **the money is in safe ~** das Geld ist gut aufgehoben; **the mother was awarded ~ of the children** die Kinder wurden der Mutter zugesprochen. (b) (*police*) Haft *f*. **to take sb into ~** jdn verhaften.

custom ['kʌstəm] *n* (a) (*convention*) Sitte *f*, Brauch *m*; (*habit*) (An)gewohnheit *f*. **as was his ~** wie er es gewohnt war. (b) *no pl* (*Comm*) Kundschaft *f*. **to get sb's ~** jdn als Kunden gewinnen. (c) ~s *pl* Zoll *m*; (**the**) **C~s** der Zoll; **to go through ~s** durch den Zoll gehen.

customary ['kʌstəmərɪ] *adj* (*conventional*) üblich; (*habitual*) gewohnt. **it's ~ to wear a tie** man trägt gewöhnlich eine Krawatte.

custom-built ['kʌstəmbɪlt] *adj* spezialgefertigt.

customer ['kʌstəmə'] *n* (a) (*Comm: patron*) Kunde *m*, Kundin *f*. **our ~s** unsere Kundschaft. (b) (*col: person*) Kunde *m* (*col*).

custom-made ['kʌstəmmeɪd] *adj* maßgefertigt; *clothes* maßgeschneidert; *furniture, car* spezialgefertigt.

customs: ~ **clearance** *n* Zollabfertigung *f*; ~ **declaration** *n* Zollerklärung *f*; ~ **duty** *n* Zoll(abgabe *f*) *m*; ~ **inspection** *n* Zollkontrolle *f*; ~ **officer** *n* Zollbeamte(r) *m*.

cut [kʌt] (*vb: pret, ptp* ~) **1** *n* (a) Schnitt *m*. **to make a ~ in sth** in etw (*acc*) einen Einschnitt machen; **the ~ and thrust of politics** das Spannungsfeld der Politik; **the ~ and thrust of the debate** die Hitze der Debatte. (b) (*reduction*) (*in gen*) (*in prices*) Senkung *f*; (*in financial matters*) Kürzung *f*; (*in production, output*) Einschränkung *f*. **he had to take a ~ in** (**his**) **salary** er mußte eine Gehaltskürzung hinnehmen. (c) (*of meat*) Stück *nt*. (d) (*col: share*) Anteil *m*. (e) (*short route*) Abkürzung *f*. (f) (*Elec*) Unterbrechung *f* (*in gen*). **power** ~ Stromausfall *m*. (g) (*Cards*) **it's your** ~ du hebst ab. (h) **he's a** ~ **above the rest of them** er ist den anderen um einiges überlegen.

2 *adj usu attr flowers* Schnitt-; *bread* geschnitten; *grass* gemäht; *prices* herabgesetzt.

3 *vt* (a) schneiden; *grass* mähen; *cake* anschneiden; (~ *out*) *fabric, suit* zuschneiden; (~ *off*) abschneiden. **to ~ one's finger** (*with knife etc*) sich (*dat*) in den Finger schneiden; **to ~ one's nails** sich (*dat*) die Nägel schneiden; **to ~ sth in half/three** etw halbieren/dritteln; **to ~ to pieces** zerstückeln; **to get one's hair ~** sich (*dat*) die Haare schneiden lassen; **to ~ sb free/loose** jdn losschneiden.

(b) (*shape*) *steps* schlagen; *channel, trench* ausheben; *figure* (*in wood*) schnitzen (*in aus*); (*in stone*) hauen (*in aus*); *diamond* schleifen; *key* anfertigen. **to ~ one's coat according to one's cloth** (*Prov*) sich nach der Decke strecken. (c) (*fig: break off*) *electricity* abstellen; *ties, links* abbrechen. **to ~ a long story short** der langen Rede kurzer Sinn. (d) *person* schneiden. **to ~ sb dead** jdn wie Luft behandeln.

(e) *class* schwänzen (*col*).

(f) (*intersect*) schneiden.

(g) (*reduce*) *prices* senken; *expenses, salary* kürzen; *production, output* einschränken.

(h) *part of text or film* streichen.

(i) (*cause pain to*) **it** ~ **me to the quick** es schnitt mir ins Herz.

(j) **to ~ a tooth** einen Zahn bekommen.

(k) (*Cards*) **to ~ the cards/the pack** abheben.

(l) **aren't you** ~**ting it a bit fine?** ist das nicht ein bißchen knapp?

4 *vi* (a) (*knife, scissors*) schneiden. **to ~ both ways** (*fig*) auch umgekehrt zutreffen; (*have disadvantages too*) ein zweischneidiges Schwert sein. (b) (*intersect: lines, roads*) sich schneiden. (c) (*Cards*) abheben. (d) **to ~ and run** abhauen (*col*).

♦ **cut away** *vt sep* wegschneiden.

♦ **cut back 1** *vi* (a) (*go back*) zurückgehen/-fahren. (b) (*reduce expenditure etc*) sich einschränken. **to ~ on smoking** weniger rauchen. **2** *vt sep* (a) *plants, shrubs* zurückschneiden. (b) *production* zurückschrauben.

♦ **cut down 1** *vt sep* (a) *tree* fällen. (b) *number, expenses* einschränken. **to ~ sb ~ to size** jdn auf seinen Platz verweisen. **2** *vi* (*reduce intake, expenditure etc*) sich einschränken. **to ~ ~ on sth** etw einschränken.

♦ **cut in** *vi* (a) (*interrupt*) sich einschalten. (b) (*Aut*) **to ~ ~ in front of sb** jdn schneiden.

♦ **cut into** *vi* +*prep obj savings* ein Loch reißen in (+*acc*).

♦ **cut off** *vt sep* (a) (*lit, fig*) abschneiden; *allowance* sperren. **to ~ ~ the enemy's retreat** dem Feind den Rückzug abschneiden; **we're very ~ ~ out here** wir leben hier draußen sehr abgeschieden. (b) (*disinherit*) enterben. **to ~ sb ~ without a penny** jdn völlig enterben. (c) (*disconnect*) *telephone etc* abstellen. **operator, I've been ~ ~** wir sind unterbrochen worden.

♦ **cut out 1** *vi* (*engine*) aussetzen. **2** *vt sep* (a) (*remove by cutting*) ausschneiden; *malignant growth etc* herausschneiden. (b) *dress* zuschneiden. (c) (*delete*) (heraus)streichen; (*not bother with*) verzichten auf +*acc*; *smoking, swearing etc* aufhören mit. ~ **it** ~! (*col*) laß das (sein)! (*col*). (d) (*fig*) **to be** ~ ~ **for sth** zu etw gemacht sein. (e) **to have one's work** ~ ~ alle Hände voll zu tun haben.

♦ **cut up 1** *vi* **to** ~ ~ **rough** Krach schlagen (*col*). **2** *vt sep* (a) *meat* aufschneiden; *wood* spalten. (b) *pass* (*col: upset*) **he was very** ~ ~ **about it** das hat ihn schwer getroffen.

cut-and-dried [,kʌtən'draɪd] *adj* **it's ~** (*fixed beforehand*) das ist eine abgemachte Sache; (*unchangeable*) das ist festgelegt.

cut-back ['kʌtbæk] *n* (a) Kürzung *f*. (b) (*Film*) Rückblende *f*.

cute [kjuːt] *adj* (+*er*) (a) (*col: sweet*) süß. (b) (*esp US col: clever*) *idea, gadget* dufte (*col*); (*shrewd*) *person, move* clever (*col*).

cut glass *n* geschliffenes Glas.

cuticle ['kjuːtɪkl] *n* (*of nail*) Nagelhaut *f*. ~ **remover** Nagelhautentferner *m*.

cutie ['kjuːtɪ] *n* (*esp US col: attractive*) dufte Biene (*col*).

cutlery ['kʌtlərɪ] *n no pl* (*esp Brit*) Besteck *nt*.

cutlet ['kʌtlɪt] *n* (*boneless chop*) Schnitzel *nt*; (*of chopped meat*) (paniertes) Hacksteak.

cut: ~-**off** *n* (a) (*Tech: device*) Ausschaltmechanismus *m*; (b) (*also* ~-**off point**) Trennlinie *f*; ~-**out** *n* (*of engine*) Aussetzen *nt*; **it has an automatic** ~-**out** es setzt automatisch aus; ~-**price** *adj* (*Brit*), ~-**rate** *adj* (*US*) zu herabgesetzten Preisen.

cut-throat ['kʌtθrəʊt] **1** *n* (*murderous type*) Verbrechertyp (*col*) *m*. **2** *adj* (a) (*competition*) mörderisch. (b) ~ **razor** (offenes) Rasiermesser.

cutting ['kʌtɪŋ] **1** *n* (a) Schneiden *nt*; (~ *off*) Abschneiden *nt*; (*of prices*) Senkung *f*; (*of expenses, salary*) Kürzung *f*; (*of production*) Drosselung *f*; (*of part of text*) Streichung *f*; (*of film*) Schnitt *m*. ~

room *(Film)* Schneideraum *m.* **(b)** *(from newspaper)* Ausschnitt *m.* **(c)** *(Hort)* Ableger *m.* **to take a** ~ einen Ableger nehmen. **2** *adj* **(a)** *edge* scharf. **(b)** *(fig) wind, cold* schneidend; *remark, tongue* spitz.

cuttlefish ['kʌtlfɪʃ] *n* Tintenfisch *m.*

cwt = **hundredweight.**

cyanide ['saɪənaɪd] *n* Zyanid *nt.* ~ **poisoning** Blausäurevergiftung *f.*

cybernetics [,saɪbə'netɪks] *n sing* Kybernetik *f.*

cyclamen ['sɪkləmən] *n* Alpenveilchen *nt.*

cycle ['saɪkl] **1** *n* **(a)** Zyklus *m*; *(of events)* Gang *m.* **(b)** *(bicycle)* (Fahr)rad *nt*; *(col: motorbike)* Maschine *f (col).* ~ **path** Radweg *m*; ~ **race** Radrennen *nt.* **2** *vi* mit dem (Fahr)rad fahren.

cycling ['saɪklɪŋ] *n* Radfahren *nt.* **I enjoy** ~ **ich** fahre gern Rad.

cycling: ~ **holiday** *n* Urlaub *m* mit dem Fahrrad; ~ **tour** *n* Radtour *f.*

cyclist ['saɪklɪst] *n* (Fahr)radfahrer(in *f*) *m.*

cyclone ['saɪkləʊn] *n* Zyklon *m.*

cygnet ['sɪgnɪt] *n* Schwanjunge(s) *nt.*

cylinder ['sɪlɪndəʳ] *n (Math, Aut)* Zylinder *m.* **a four-**~ **car** ein Vierzylinder *m.*

cylinder: ~ **block** *n (Aut)* Zylinderblock *m*; ~ **head** *n (Aut)* Zylinderkopf *m*; ~ **head gasket** *n* Zylinderkopfdichtung *f.*

cylindrical [sɪ'lɪndrɪkəl] *adj* zylindrisch.

cymbal ['sɪmbəl] *n* Beckenteller *m.* ~**s** Becken *nt.*

cynic ['sɪnɪk] *n* Zyniker(in *f*) *m.*

cynical ['sɪnɪkəl] *adj* zynisch.

cynicism ['sɪnɪsɪzəm] *n* **(a)** *no pl* Zynismus *m.* **(b)** *(cynical remark)* zynische Bemerkung.

cypress ['saɪprɪs] *n* Zypresse *f.*

Cypriot ['sɪprɪət] **1** *adj* zypriotisch. **2** *n* Zypriot(in *f*) *m.*

Cyprus ['saɪprəs] *n* Zypern *nt.*

cyst [sɪst] *n* Zyste *f.*

cystitis [sɪs'taɪtɪs] *n* Blasenentzündung *f.*

czar [zɑːʳ] *n* Zar *m.*

czarina [zɑː'riːnə] *n* Zarin *f.*

Czech [tʃek] **1** *adj* tschechisch. **2** *n* **(a)** Tscheche *m*, Tschechin *f.* **(b)** *(language)* Tschechisch *nt.*

Czechoslovakia ['tʃəkeʊslə'vækɪə] *n* die Tschechoslowakei.

Czechoslovak(ian) ['tʃekəʊslə'væk(ɪən)] **1** *adj* tschechoslowakisch. **2** *n* Tschechoslowake *m*, Tschechoslowakin *f.*

D

D, d [diː] *n* D, d *nt*. **D sharp/flat** Dis, dis *nt*/Des, des *nt*.

dab¹ [dæb] **1** *n* Klecks *m*; *(of powder, cream etc)* Tupfer *m*; *(of liquid, perfume, glue etc)* Tropfen *m*; *(of butter)* Klacks *m*. **a** ~ **of ointment** ein bißchen Salbe; **to give sth a** ~ **of paint** etw überstreichen. **2** *vt (with powder etc)* betupfen; *(with towel etc)* tupfen. **to** ~ **one's eyes** sich *(dat)* die Augen tupfen.
♦ **dab at** *vi* +*prep obj* betupfen.
♦ **dab on** *vt sep* auftragen *(prep obj* auf +*acc).*

dab² *adj (col)* **to be a** ~ **hand at sth/doing sth** gut in etw *(dat)* sein/sich darauf verstehen, etw zu tun.

dabble ['dæbl] *vi* **to** ~ **in sth** sich nebenbei mit etw beschäftigen.

dachshund ['dækshʊnd] *n* Dackel *m*.

dad [dæd], **daddy** ['dædɪ] *n (col)* Vater, Papa *(col)*, Vati *m (col)*.

daddy-long-legs [ˌdædɪ'lɒŋlegz] *n, pl* - *(Brit)* Schnake *f*; *(US)* Weberknecht *m*.

daffodil ['dæfədɪl] *n* Osterglocke, Narzisse *f*.

daft [dɑːft] *adj* (+*er*) doof *(col)*, blöd *(col)*. **he's** ~ **about her** *(col)* er ist verrückt nach ihr *(col)*.

dagger ['dægəʳ] *n* Dolch *m*. **to be at** ~**s drawn with sb** *(fig)* mit jdm auf Kriegsfuß stehen; **to look** ~**s at sb** jdn mit Blicken durchbohren.

dago ['deɪɡəʊ] *n (pej)* Südländer *m*.

dahlia ['deɪlɪə] *n* Dahlie *f*.

daily ['deɪlɪ] **1** *adj* täglich; *wage, newspaper* Tages-. ~ **grind** täglicher Trott; **on a** ~ **basis** tageweise. **2** *adv* täglich. **3** *n* **(a)** *(newspaper)* Tageszeitung *f*. **(b)** *(also* ~**s** *help)* Putzfrau *f*.

dainty ['deɪntɪ] *adj* (+*er*) zierlich; *manners* geziert; *lace, handkerchief* fein; *movement, music* anmutig; *food* appetitlich. ~ **morsel** Leckerbissen *m*.

dairy ['dɛərɪ] *n* Molkerei *f*; *(on farm)* Milchkammer *f*; *(shop)* Milchgeschäft *nt*.

dairy: ~ **butter** *n* Markenbutter *f*; ~ **cow** *n* Milchkuh *f*; ~ **farming** *n* Milchviehhaltung *f*; ~ **ice cream** *n* Milchspeiseeis *nt*.

dais ['deɪs] *n* Podium *nt*.

daisy ['deɪzɪ] *n* Gänseblümchen *nt*. **as fresh as a** ~ taufrisch; **to be pushing up the daisies** *(col)* sich *(dat)* die Radieschen von unten besehen *(col)*; ~ **wheel** Typenrad *nt*; *(printer)* Typenraddrucker *m*.

dale [deɪl] *n (N Engl, liter)* Tal *nt*.

dally ['dælɪ] *vi (waste time)* (herum)trödeln.

Dalmatian [dæl'meɪʃən] *n (dog)* Dalmatiner *m*.

dam [dæm] **1** *n (lit, fig)* Damm *m*; *(reservoir)* Stausee *m*. **2** *vt (also* ~ **up)** *river, lake* stauen.

damage ['dæmɪdʒ] **1** *n* **(a)** Schaden *m (to* an +*dat).* **to do a lot of** ~ großen Schaden anrichten; **to do sb/sth a lot of** ~ jdm/einer Sache *(dat)* großen Schaden zufügen; **that did a lot of** ~ **to his reputation** das hat seinem Ruf sehr geschadet. **(b)** *(Jur)* ~**s** Schaden(s)ersatz *m*. **(c)** *(col: cost)* **what's the** ~? was kostet der Spaß? *(col).* **2** *vt* beschädigen; *health, reputation, relations* schaden (+*dat*), **to** ~ **one's eyesight** sich *(dat)* die Augen verderben; **smoking can** ~ **your health** Rauchen schadet Ihrer Gesundheit.

damaging ['dæmɪdʒɪŋ] *adj* schädlich *(to* für).

dame [deɪm] *n* **(a)** D~ britischer Titel. **(b)** *(Theat)* (komische) Alte. **(c)** *(US col)* Weib *nt (col).*

damn [dæm] **1** *interj (col)* verdammt *(col).*
2 *n (col)* **he doesn't care** *or* **give a** ~ **er schert sich einen Dreck (darum)** *(col)*; **I don't give a** ~ das ist mir scheißegal *(col!).*
3 *adj attr (col)* verdammt. **I couldn't see a** ~ **thing** so ein Mist *(col)*, ich konnte überhaupt nichts sehen.
4 *adv (col)* verdammt. **I should** ~ **well hope so** das will ich aber auch stark hoffen; ~**-all** nicht die Bohne *(col)*; **I've done** ~**-all today** ich hab heute überhaupt nichts gemacht *(col).*
5 *vt* **(a)** *(Rel)* verdammen. **(b)** *(judge and condemn)* verurteilen; *book etc also* verreißen. **(c)** *(col)* ~ **him/you!** der kann/du kannst mich mal! *(col)*; ~ **it!** verdammt (noch mal)! *(col)*; **well, I'll be** ~**ed!** Donnerwetter! *(col)*; **I'll be** ~**ed if I'll go there** ich denke nicht daran, da hinzugehen; **I'll be** ~**ed if I know** weiß der Teufel *(col).*

damnation [dæm'neɪʃən] **1** *n (Eccl)* Verdammnis *f*. **2** *interj (col)* verdammt *(col).*

damned [dæmd] **1** *adj* **(a)** *soul* verdammt. **(b)** *(col)* = **damn 3. 2** *adv* = **damn 4.**

damnedest ['dæmdɪst] *n* **to do** *or* **try one's** ~ *(col)* sein möglichstes tun.

damning ['dæmɪŋ] *adj* vernichtend; *evidence* belastend.

damp [dæmp] **1** *adj* (~*er*) feucht. **a** ~ **squib** *(fig)* ein Reinfall *m*. **2** *n* Feuchtigkeit *f*. **3** *vt* **(a)** befeuchten. **(b)** *(fig) enthusiasm etc* dämpfen. **to** ~ **sb's spirits** jdm einen Dämpfer aufsetzen. **(c)** *sounds, vibrations* dämpfen; *(also* ~ **down)** *fire* ersticken.

damp course *n* Dämmschicht, Isolierschicht *f*.

dampen ['dæmpən] *vt* = **damp 3 (a, b).**

damper ['dæmpəʳ] *n* **(a)** *(of chimney)* (Luft)klappe *f*; *(of piano)* Dämpfer *m*. **(b)** **to put a** ~ **on sth** einer Sache *(dat)* einen Dämpfer aufsetzen.

damson ['dæmzən] *n (fruit)* Damaszenerpflaume *f*.

dance [dɑːns] **1** *n* Tanz *m*; *(occasion also)* Tanzabend *m*; *(school etc)* Ball *m*. **she's led him a fine** ~ sie hat ihn ganz schön an der Nase herumgeführt. **2** *vti* tanzen. **to** ~ **for joy** einen Freudentanz aufführen.

dance *in cpds* Tanz-; ~ **band** *n* Tanzkapelle *f*; ~ **floor** *n* Tanzboden *m*; *(in restaurant)* Tanzfläche *f*; ~ **hall** *n* Tanzsaal *m*; ~ **music** *n* Tanzmusik *f*.

dancer ['dɑːnsəʳ] *n* Tänzer(in *f*) *m*.

dancing ['dɑːnsɪŋ] **1** *n* Tanzen *nt*. **2** *attr* Tanz-.

dandelion ['dændɪlaɪən] *n* Löwenzahn *m*.

dandruff ['dændrəf] *n* Schuppen *pl*.

dandy ['dændɪ] **1** *n* Dandy, Geck *m*. **2** *adj (esp US col)* prima *(col).*

Dane [deɪn] *n* Däne *m*, Dänin *f*.

danger ['deɪndʒəʳ] *n* **(a)** Gefahr *f*. **to put sb/sth in** ~ jdn/etw in Gefahr bringen; **to be in** ~ **of doing sth** Gefahr laufen, etw zu tun; **out of** ~ außer Gefahr; **there is no** ~ **that** die Gefahr besteht nicht; **to be a** ~ **to sb/sth** für jdn/etw eine Gefahr bedeuten. **(b)** "~" "Achtung, Lebensgefahr!"; "~, **ice**" "Glatteisgefahr".

danger: ~ **area** *n* Gefahrenzone *f* or -bereich *m*; ~ **list** *n*: **on/off the** ~ **list** in/außer Lebensgefahr; ~ **money** *n* Gefahrenzulage *f*.

dangerous ['deɪndʒrəs] *adj* gefährlich.

dangerously ['deɪndʒrəslɪ] *adv* gefährlich. **the**

deadline is getting ~ **close** der Termin rückt bedenklich nahe; **to be** ~ **ill** schwerkrank sein.
danger: ~ **signal** n (lit, fig) Warnsignal nt; ~ **zone** n Gefahrenzone f.
dangle ['dæŋgl] **1** vt baumeln lassen. **to** ~ **sth before sb** (fig) jdm etw in Aussicht stellen. **2** vi baumeln.
Danish ['deɪnɪʃ] **1** adj dänisch. ~ **blue (cheese)** Edelpilzkäse m; ~ **pastry** Plundergebäck nt. **2** n (language) Dänisch nt.
dank [dæŋk] adj (unangenehm) feucht.
Danube ['dænjuːb] n Donau f.
dapper ['dæpə'] adj gepflegt, gediegen.
dappled ['dæpld] adj gefleckt; (with small flecks) gesprenkelt; horse scheckig.
dare [dɛə'] **1** vi (be bold enough) es wagen; (have the confidence) sich trauen. **he wouldn't** ~**!** er wird sich schwer hüten; **you** ~**!** untersteh dich!; **how** ~ **you!** was fällt dir ein! **2** vt **(a) to** ~ **(to) do sth** (es) wagen, etw zu tun, sich trauen, etw zu tun; **he** ~ **not** or **doesn't** ~ or ~**n't do it** das wagt er nicht; **don't (you)** ~ **say that to me** untersteh dich, das zu mir zu sagen. **(b) I** ~ **say it gets quite cold here in winter** ich nehme an, daß es hier im Winter ziemlich kalt wird; **I** ~ **say he'll be there** es kann (gut) sein, daß er dort ist; **he was very sorry — I** ~ **say** es tat ihm sehr leid — das glaube ich gerne. **(c)** (challenge) **I** ~ **you to jump off** wetten, daß du dich nicht zu springen traust! **3** n **to do sth for a** ~ etw als Mutprobe tun.
daredevil ['dɛə,devl] **1** n Draufgänger m. **2** adj waghalsig.
daring ['dɛərɪŋ] **1** adj kühn; (in physical matters) waghalsig; opinion, dress gewagt. **2** n Kühnheit f; (in physical matters) Waghalsigkeit f.
dark [dɑːk] **1** adj (+er) (lit, fig) dunkel; thoughts, threats finster. **it's getting** ~ es wird dunkel; ~ **blue** dunkelblau; **D** ~ **Ages** finsteres Mittelalter; **to keep sth** ~ etw geheimhalten. **2** n **(a)** Dunkelheit f. **after** ~ nach Einbruch der Dunkelheit; **until** ~ bis zum Einbruch der Dunkelheit. **(b)** (fig) **to be in the** ~ keine Ahnung haben (about von); **he has kept me in the** ~ er hat mich im dunkeln gelassen; **it was a shot in the** ~ das war nur auf gut Glück gesagt/geraten etc.
darken ['dɑːkən] **1** vt dunkel machen; sky also verdunkeln; (before storm) verfinstern; **never** ~ **my door again!** lassen Sie sich hier nicht mehr blicken! **2** vi see vt dunkel werden; sich verdunkeln; sich verfinstern.
dark: ~**-eyed** ['dɑːkaɪd] adj dunkeläugig; ~ **horse** n (fig) stilles Wasser; (unexpected winner) Außenseiter m.
darkly ['dɑːklɪ] adv (lit, fig) dunkel.
darkness ['dɑːknɪs] n Dunkelheit f. **the house was in** ~ das Haus lag im Dunkeln.
dark: ~**room** n (Phot) Dunkelkammer f; ~**-skinned** ['dɑːkskɪnd] adj dunkelhäutig.
darling ['dɑːlɪŋ] **1** n Liebling, Schatz m. **be a** ~ **and ... sei so lieb und ... 2** adj wife etc lieb.
darn[1] [dɑːn] (Sew) **1** n gestopfte Stelle. **2** vt stopfen.
darn[2] (col) **1** adj, adv, interj verflixt (col). **2** vt ~ **him!** zum Kuckuck mit ihm! (col).
darning ['dɑːnɪŋ] n Stopfen nt; (things to be darned) Stopfsachen pl. **I've a lot of** ~ **to do** ich habe viel zu stopfen; ~ **needle** Stopfnadel f.
dart [dɑːt] **1** n **(a)** (movement) **to make a sudden** ~ **at sb/sth** einen plötzlichen Satz auf jdn/etw zu machen. **(b)** (weapon) Pfeil m; (Sport) (Wurf)pfeil m. **(c)** (Sew) Abnäher m. **2** vi flitzen; (fish) schnellen. **to** ~ **out** (person) heraus-/hinausflitzen; (fish, tongue) hervorschnellen; **he** ~**ed behind a bush** er hechtete hinter einen Busch. **3** vt **to** ~ **a glance at sb** jdm einen Blick zuwerfen.
dart board n Dartscheibe f.
darts [dɑːts] n sing Darts, Pfeilwurfspiel nt.

dash [dæʃ] **1** n **(a)** (sudden rush) **he made a** ~ **for the door** er stürzte auf die Tür zu; **she made a** ~ **for it** sie rannte, so schnell sie konnte. **(b)** (style, vigour) Schwung, Elan m. **to cut a** ~ eine Figur machen. **(c)** (small amount) etwas, ein bißchen; (of wine, vinegar, spirits also) Schuß m; (of seasoning etc also) Prise f. **(d)** (Typ) Gedankenstrich m. **(e)** = **dashboard**. **2** vt **(a)** (throw violently) schleudern. **to** ~ **sth to pieces** etw in tausend Stücke zerschlagen; **to** ~ **one's head against sth** mit dem Kopf gegen etw schlagen. **(b)** sb's hopes zunichte machen. **3** vi **(a) to** ~ **into a room** in ein Zimmer stürzen; **to** ~ **away/back/ up** fort-/zurück-/hinaufstürzen. **(b)** (knock, be hurled) schlagen; (waves also) peitschen. **4** interj ~ **(it)!** (col) verflixt! (col).
♦ **dash off 1** vt sep letter hinwerfen. **2** vi losstürzen.
dashboard ['dæʃbɔːd] n Armaturenbrett nt.
dashing ['dæʃɪŋ] adj flott, schneidig.
data ['deɪtə] pl of **datum** usu with sing vb Daten pl. **a piece of** ~ eine Angabe.
data: ~ **bank** n Datenbank f; ~ **base** n Datenbank f; ~ **processing** n Datenverarbeitung f; ~ **protection** n Datenschutz m; ~ **transmission** n Datenübertragung f.
date[1] [deɪt] n (fruit) Dattel f; (tree) Dattelpalme f.
date[2] **1** n **(a)** Datum nt; (historical ~) Jahreszahl f; (for appointment) Termin m. ~ **of birth** Geburtsdatum nt; **what's the** ~ **today?** der wievielte ist heute?, welches Datum haben wir heute?; **what** ~ **is he coming on?** an welchem Tag kommt er?; **to** ~ bis heute. **(b)** (appointment) Verabredung f; **who's his** ~? mit wem trifft er sich?; **to make a** ~ **with sb** sich mit jdm verabreden; **she's out on a** ~ sie hat eine Verabredung. **2** vt **(a)** mit dem Datum versehen; letter etc also datieren. **a coin** ~**d 1390** eine Münze von 1390. **(b)** (establish age of) work of art etc datieren. **that really** ~**s you** daran merkt man, wie alt Sie sind. **(c)** (take out) girlfriend etc ausgehen mit; (regularly also) gehen mit (col). **3** vi **(a) to** ~ **back to** zurückdatieren auf (+acc); **to** ~ **from** zurückgehen auf (+acc). **(b)** (become old-fashioned) veralten.
dated ['deɪtɪd] adj altmodisch, veraltet.
date: ~ **line** n (Geog) Datumsgrenze f; ~ **stamp** n Datumsstempel m.
dative ['deɪtɪv] n Dativ m. **in the** ~ im Dativ.
daub [dɔːb] vt walls, canvas, face beschmieren; paint, slogans, make-up schmieren.
daughter ['dɔːtə'] n Tochter f. ~**-in-law** Schwiegertochter f.
daunt [dɔːnt] vt entmutigen. **nothing** ~**ed** unverzagt.
daunting ['dɔːntɪŋ] adj entmutigend.
dauntless ['dɔːntlɪs] adj unerschrocken, beherzt.
dawdle ['dɔːdl] vi (be too slow) trödeln; (stroll) bummeln.
dawdler ['dɔːdlə'] n Trödler(in f) m.
dawn [dɔːn] **1** n (Morgen)dämmerung f; (time of day) Tagesanbruch m; (fig) Anbruch m. **at** ~ bei Tagesanbruch; **it's almost** ~ es dämmert schon bald; **from** ~ **to dusk** von morgens bis abends. **2** vi **(a) day was already** ~**ing** es dämmerte schon; **the day will** ~ **when ...** (fig) der Tag wird kommen, wo ... **(b)** (fig: new age etc) dämmern, anbrechen. **(c) it suddenly** ~**ed on him that ...** es dämmerte ihm, daß ...
dawn chorus n Morgenkonzert nt der Vögel.
day [deɪ] n **(a)** Tag m. **it will arrive any** ~ **now** es muß jeden Tag kommen; **what** ~ **is it today?** welcher Tag ist heute?; **what** ~ **of the month is it?** der wievielte ist heute?; **the** ~ **before yesterday** vorgestern; **the** ~ **before her birthday** der Tag vor ihrem Geburtstag; **(on) the** ~ **after/ before** am Tag danach/zuvor; **two years ago to the** ~ heute/morgen etc auf den Tag genau vor

zwei Jahren; **one** ~ eines Tages; **one of these** ~s irgendwann (einmal), eines Tages; ~ **in,** ~ **out** tagein, tagaus; **they went to London for the** ~ sie machten einen Tagesausflug nach London; **for** ~s **on end** tagelang; ~ **after** ~ Tag für Tag; ~ **by** ~ jeden Tag, täglich; **the other** ~ neulich; **at the end of the** ~ *(fig)* letzen Endes; **to live from** ~ **to** ~ von einem Tag auf den andern leben; **I remember it to this** ~ daran erinnere ich mich noch heute; **for** ~s **on end** tagelang; **he's fifty if he's a** ~ er ist mindestens fünfzig; **to travel during the** *or* **by** ~ tagsüber *or* am Tag reisen; **good** ~! guten Tag!; *(good-bye)* auf Wiedersehen; **to be paid by the** ~ tageweise bezahlt werden; **let's call it a** ~ machen wir Schluß; **to have a nice/lazy** ~ einen schönen Tag verbringen/einen Tag faulenzen; **have a nice** ~! schönen Tag noch!; **did you have a nice** ~? na, wie war's?; **to have a good/bad** ~ einen guten/schlechten Tag haben; **that'll be the** ~ das möcht' ich sehen *or* erleben.

(b) *(period of time: often pl)* **these** ~s heute, heutzutage; **what are you doing these** ~s? was machst du denn so?; **in this** ~ **and age** heutzutage; **in** ~s **to come** in künftigen Zeiten; **in his younger** ~s als er noch jünger war; **in Queen Victoria's** ~, **in the** ~s **of Queen Victoria** zu Königin Viktorias Zeiten; **the happiest** ~s **of my life** die glücklichste Zeit meines Lebens; **those were the** ~s das waren noch Zeiten; **in the old** ~s früher; **in the good old** ~s in der guten alten Zeit; **it's early** ~s **yet** es ist noch zu früh; **he/this machine has seen better** ~s er/diese Maschine hat (auch) schon bessere Tage gesehen; **to end one's** ~s **in misery** im Elend sterben.

(c) *(with poss adj: lifetime, best time)* **famous in her** ~ in ihrer Zeit berühmt; **it has had its** ~ das hat seine Glanzzeit überschritten; **his** ~ **will come** sein Tag wird kommen.

(d) *no pl (contest, battle)* **to win** *or* **carry the** ~ siegen. **to lose the** ~ (den Kampf) verlieren; **that saved the** ~ das war die Rettung.

day: ~ **boy** *n (Sch)* Externe(r) *m;* ~**break** *n* Tagesanbruch *m;* **at** ~**break** bei Tagesanbruch; ~**dream 1** *n* Tagtraum *m;* **2** *vi* mit offenen Augen träumen; ~ **girl** *n (Sch)* Externe *f.*

daylight ['deɪlaɪt] *n* Tageslicht *nt.* **at** ~ bei Tage; **it is still** ~ es ist noch hell; **it was broad** ~ es war hellichter Tag; **in broad** ~ am hellichten Tage; **I began to see** ~ *(fig) (to understand)* mir ging ein Licht auf; *(to see the end appear)* so langsam habe ich Land gesehen *(col);* **to beat the living** ~s **out of sb** *(col)* jdn windelweich schlagen *(col);* **to scare the living** ~s **out of sb** *(col)* jdm einen fürchterlichen Schreck einjagen *(col).*

daylight: ~ **robbery** *n (col)* Halsabschneiderei *f (col);* ~ **saving time** *n* Sommerzeit *f.*

day: ~ **nursery** *n* Kindertagesstätte *f; (in private house)* Kinderzimmer *nt;* ~ **release course** *n* Fortbildungskurs *m (für den man 1 Tag pro Woche freigestellt wird);* ~ **return (ticket)** *n (Brit Rail)* Tagesrückfahrkarte *f;* ~ **school** *n* Tagesschule *f;* ~ **shift** *n* Tagschicht *f;* **to be on** ~ **shift** Tagschicht arbeiten.

daytime ['deɪtaɪm] **1** *n* Tag *m.* **in the** ~ bei Tage, tagsüber. **2** *attr* am Tage.

day: ~**-to-day** *adj occurrence* alltäglich. **on a** ~**-to-day basis** tageweise; ~ **trip** *n* Tagesausflug *m;* ~ **tripper** *n* Tagesausflügler(in *f) m.*

daze [deɪz] **1** *n* **in a** ~ ganz benommen. **2** *vt* benommen machen.

dazzle ['dæzl] *vt (lig, fig)* blenden.

dazzling ['dæzlɪŋ] *adj (lit)* blendend.

D-day ['diːdeɪ] *n (Hist) Tag der Invasion durch die Alliierten (6.6.44); (fig)* der Tag X.

DDT [diːdiː'tiː] *n* DDT *nt.*

deacon ['diːkən] *n* Diakon *m.*

dead [ded] **1** *adj* **(a)** *(lit, fig)* tot; *plant also* abge-

storben. **to drop (down)** ~ tot umfallen; **over my** ~ **body** *(col)* nur über meine Leiche *(col).* **(b)** *(not sensitive) limbs* abgestorben, taub. **my fingers are** ~ meine Finger sind wie abgestorben; **to be** ~ **from the neck up** *(col)* nur Stroh im Kopf haben *(col),* gehirnamputiert sein *(col);* **to be** ~ **to the world** vollkommen weggetreten sein *(col).* **(c)** *(Elec) cable* stromlos; *(Telec)* tot. **to go** ~ ausfallen; **the line went** ~ die Leitung war plötzlich tot. **(d)** *(burnt out) fire* aus *pred; match* abgebrannt. **(e)** *(absolute, exact)* total, völlig. ~ **silence** Totenstille *f;* ~ **calm** *(Naut)* totale Windstille; **to come to a** ~ **stop** völlig zum Stillstand kommen; **to hit sth** ~ **centre** etw genau in der Mitte treffen. **(f)** *(col: exhausted)* völlig kaputt *(col).*

2 *adv* **(a)** *(exactly)* genau. ~ **straight** schnurgerade; **to be** ~ **on time** auf die Minute pünktlich kommen; ~ **on course** voll *or* genau auf Kurs. **(b)** *(col: very)* total *(col),* völlig. ~ **drunk/tired** total betrunken/todmüde; **you're** ~ **right** Sie haben völlig recht; ~ **slow** ganz langsam; **to be** ~ **certain about sth** bei etw todsicher sein. **(c) to stop** ~ abrupt stehenbleiben *or (talking)* innehalten.

3 *n* **(a) the** ~ *pl* die Toten *pl.* **(b) at** ~ **of night** mitten in der Nacht; **in the** ~ **of winter** mitten im Winter.

dead-beat ['ded'biːt] *adj (col)* völlig kaputt *(col).*

deaden ['dedn] *vt sound, noise* dämpfen; *pain* mildern; *force, blow* abschwächen; *nerve* abtöten.

dead: ~**end** *n* Sackgasse *f;* **a** ~**-end job** ein Job *m* ohne Aufstiegsmöglichkeiten; ~ **heat** *n* totes Rennen; ~**line** *n* (letzter) Termin; *(for application etc)* Abgabetermin *m;* **to set a** ~**line** eine Frist setzen; **to work to a** ~**line** auf einen Termin hinarbeiten; ~**lock** *n* **to reach (a)** ~**lock** sich festfahren; **to break the** ~**lock** aus der Sackgasse herauskommen.

deadly ['dedlɪ] **1** *adj (+er)* **(a)** *tödlich; sin, enemy* Tod-; *wit, sarcasm* vernichtend. **he's in** ~ **earnest** er meint es todernst, es ist sein voller Ernst. **(b)** *(col: boring)* todlangweilig. **2** *adv boring* tod-. ~ **pale** totenbleich.

dead: ~**pan** *adj face* unbewegt; *style, humour* trocken; **D**~ **Sea** *n* Totes Meer.

deaf [def] *adj (+er)* taub. ~ **as** ~ **a (door)post** stocktaub; **to turn a** ~ **ear to sb/sth** sich jdm/einer Sache *(dat)* gegenüber taub stellen.

deaf: ~**-aid** *n* Hörgerät *nt;* ~**-and-dumb** *adj* taubstumm; *language* Taubstummen-.

deafen ['defn] *vt (lit)* taub machen; *(fig)* betäuben.

deafening ['defnɪŋ] *adj noise* ohrenbetäubend; *row* lautstark. **a** ~ **silence** ein eisiges Schweigen.

deaf-mute ['def'mjuːt] *n* Taubstumme(r) *mf.*

deafness ['defnɪs] *n (lit, fig)* Taubheit *f (to* gegenüber).

deal¹ [diːl] **1** *n* **a good** *or* **great** ~ eine Menge, (ziemlich) viel; **not a great** ~ nicht (besonders) viel; **there's a great** *or* **good** ~ **of truth in what he says** es ist schon ziemlich viel Wahres an dem, was er sagt; **and that's saying a good** ~ und damit ist schon viel gesagt; **to mean a great** ~ **to sb** jdm viel bedeuten. **2** *adv* **a good** *or* **great** ~ viel; **not a great** ~ nicht viel.

deal² *(vb: pret, ptp* **dealt)** **1** *n* **(a)** *(Comm: also* **business** ~) Geschäft *nt; (arrangement)* Abmachung *f; (official)* Abkommen *nt.* **to do a** ~ **with sb** mit jdm ein Geschäft abschließen; **it's a** ~ abgemacht!; **I'll make a** ~ **with you** ich schlage Ihnen ein Geschäft vor; **to give sb a fair** ~ jdn anständig behandeln; **a better** ~ **for the lower paid** bessere Bedingungen für die schlechter bezahlten Arbeiter. **(b)** *(Cards)* it's **your** ~ Sie geben. **2** *vti (Cards)* geben, austeilen.

♦ **deal in** *vi* +*prep obj (Comm)* handeln mit.

♦ **deal out** *vt sep gifts, money* verteilen *(to an* +*acc); cards* geben *(to dat).* **to** ~ ~ **justice** Recht sprechen.

♦ **deal with** vi +prep obj **(a)** (do business with) verhandeln mit. **(b)** (manage, handle) sich kümmern um; (with job) sich befassen mit; (successfully) fertigwerden mit; (Comm) orders erledigen; (be responsible for) zuständig sein für. **to know how to ~ ~ sb** wissen, wie man mit jdm umgeht; **I'll ~ ~ you later!** dich knöpf' ich mir später vor (col). **(c)** (be concerned with) (such, film etc) handeln von; (author) sich befassen mit.

deal³ n (wood) Kiefern- or Tannenholz nt.

dealer ['diːləʳ] n (Comm) Händler m. **a ~ in furs** ein Pelzhändler.

dealing ['diːlɪŋ] n **(a)** (trading) Handel m. **there's some crooked ~ involved here** da ist irgend etwas gemauschelt worden (col). **(b) ~s** pl (Comm) Geschäfte pl; (generally) Umgang m; **to have ~s with sb** mit jdm zu tun haben.

dealt [delt] pret, ptp of **deal**².

dean [diːn] n (Eccl, Univ) Dekan m.

dear [dɪəʳ] **1** adj (+er) **(a)** I hold him/it ~ er/es ist mir lieb und teuer; **that is my ~est wish** das ist mein sehnlichster Wunsch; **my ~ chap** mein lieber Freund. **(b)** (in letter-writing) ~ **Daddy/ John** lieber Vati/John!; ~ **Sir/Madam** sehr geehrter Herr X/sehr geehrte Frau X; ~ **Sirs** sehr geehrte Damen und Herren; ~ **Mr Kemp** sehr geehrter Herr Kemp; (less formal) lieber Herr Kemp! **(c)** (expensive) teuer. **2** interj ~ ~!, ~ **me!** (du) meine Güte!; **oh ~!** oje! **3** n **hello/ thank you** ~ hallo/vielen Dank; **yes,** ~ ja, Liebling; **be a** ~ (col) sei so lieb or gut; **poor** ~ der/die Arme. **4** adv (lit, fig) buy, pay, sell teuer.

dearly ['dɪəlɪ] adv **(a)** love von ganzem Herzen. **I should** ~ **like to live here** ich würde für mein Leben gern hier wohnen. **(b)** (lit, fig) pay etc teuer.

dearth [dɜːθ] n Mangel m (of an +dat). ~ **of ideas** Ideenarmut f.

death [deθ] n Tod m; (of plans, hopes etc) Ende nt. **the number of ~s** die Todesfälle; **to be afraid of** ~ sich vor dem Tod fürchten; **a fight to the** ~ ein Kampf auf Leben und Tod; **to put sb to** ~ jdn hinrichten; **to drink oneself to** ~ sich zu Tode trinken; **to be at ~'s door** an der Schwelle des Todes stehen; **it will be the** ~ **of you** (col) das wird dein Tod sein; **he will be the** ~ **of me** (col) (he's so funny) ich lach' mich noch einmal über ihn (col); (he's annoying) er bringt mich noch ins Grab; **to catch one's** ~ (of cold) (col) sich (dat) den Tod holen; **I am sick to** ~ **of all this** (col) das alles hängt mir gründlich zum Halse raus.

death: ~bed n Sterbebett nt; **~-blow** n (lit, fig) Todesstoß m; ~ **certificate** n Totenschein m; ~ **duties** npl (Brit) Erbschaftssteuer f.

deathly ['deθlɪ] **1** adj (+er) ~ hush Totenstille f; ~ **silence** eisiges Schweigen; ~ **pallor** Totenblässe f. **2** adv ~ **pale** totenblaß.

death: ~-mask n Totenmaske f; ~ **penalty** n Todesstrafe f; ~ **rate** n Sterbeziffer f; ~ **sentence** n Todesurteil nt; ~ **throes** npl Todeskampf m; ~**-trap** n Todesfalle f; ~**-watch beetle** n Klopfkäfer m; ~**-wish** n Wunsch m zu sterben.

debar [dɪ'bɑːʳ] vt ausschließen (from von).

debase [dɪ'beɪs] vt person erniedrigen; qualities mindern, herabsetzen; coinage den Wert mindern von; language entstellen.

debatable [dɪ'beɪtəbl] adj fraglich.

debate [dɪ'beɪt] **1** vti debattieren, diskutieren (with mit, about über +acc). **he was debating with himself whether to go or not** er überlegte hin und her, ob er gehen sollte; **debating society** Debattierklub m. **2** n Debatte f. **after much ~** nach langer Debatte or Diskussion.

debauched [dɪ'bɔːtʃt] adj verkommen; life ausschweifend.

debauchery [dɪ'bɔːtʃərɪ] n Ausschweifung f. **a life**

of ~ ein ausschweifendes Leben.

debenture [dɪ'bentʃəʳ] n (Fin) Schuldschein m.

debilitate [dɪ'bɪlɪteɪt] vt schwächen.

debility [dɪ'bɪlɪtɪ] n Schwäche f.

debit ['debɪt] **1** n Debetposten m, Soll nt. ~**s** Debet, Soll nt; ~ **balance** Debetsaldo m; ~ **note** Lastschrift f; **on the** ~ **side there's the weather** (fig) als Minuspunkt ist das Wetter zu erwähnen. **2** vt **to** ~ **sb/sb's account with a sum** jdn/jds Konto mit einem Betrag belasten.

debonair [,debə'neəʳ] adj flott.

debrief [,diː'briːf] vt befragen. **to be ~ed** Bericht erstatten.

debris ['debriː] n Trümmer pl, Schutt m.

debt [det] n Schuld f. ~ **of honour** Ehrenschuld f; **National D~** Staatsschulden pl; **to be in** ~ verschuldet sein (to gegenüber); **to be £5 in** ~ £ 5 Schulden haben (to bei); **to get into** ~ Schulden machen; **to be out of** ~ schuldenfrei sein; **to repay a** ~ (lit, fig) eine Schuld begleichen; **I shall always be in your** ~ das werde ich Ihnen nie vergessen.

debt collector n Inkassobeauftragte(r) mf, Schuldeneintreiber (col) m.

debtor ['detəʳ] n Schuldner(in f) m.

debunk [,diː'bʌŋk] vt claim entlarven; politician vom Sockel stoßen.

début ['deɪbjuː] n (lit, fig) Debüt nt. **to make one's** ~ sein Debüt geben.

débutante ['debjuːtɑːnt] n Debütantin f.

decade ['dekeɪd] n Jahrzehnt nt.

decadence ['dekədəns] n Dekadenz f.

decadent ['dekədənt] adj dekadent.

decaffeinated [,diː'kæfɪneɪtɪd] adj koffeinfrei.

decal [dɪ'kæl] n (US) Aufkleber m.

decamp [dɪ'kæmp] vi (col) sich aus dem Staube machen.

decant [dɪ'kænt] vt umfüllen.

decanter [dɪ'kæntəʳ] n Karaffe f.

decapitate [dɪ'kæpɪteɪt] vt enthaupten, köpfen.

decarbonize [,diː'kɑːbənaɪz] vt dekarbonisieren, entkohlen.

decathlete [dɪ'kæθliːt] n Zehnkämpfer m.

decathlon [dɪ'kæθlɒn] n Zehnkampf m.

decay [dɪ'keɪ] **1** vi verfallen; (rot) verwesen, verfaulen; (food) schlecht werden, verderben; (beauty) verblühen, vergehen; (civilization, race) untergehen; (one's faculties) verkümmern. **2** n see vi Verfall m; Verwesung f; Verderben nt; (of civilization) Untergang m; (of one's faculties) Verkümmern nt. **to fall into** ~ in Verfall geraten.

decease [dɪ'siːs] n (Jur, form) Ableben nt (form).

deceased [dɪ'siːst] (Jur, form) **1** adj verstorben. **2** n: **the** ~ der/die Tote or Verstorbene; **the** Toten or Verstorbenen pl.

deceit [dɪ'siːt] n Betrug m no pl, Täuschung f.

deceitful [dɪ'siːtfʊl] adj falsch, betrügerisch.

deceitfulness [dɪ'siːtfʊlnɪs] n Falschheit f; (deceitful acts) Betrügereien pl.

deceive [dɪ'siːv] vt täuschen, irreführen; one's wife, husband betrügen. **to ~ sb into thinking sth** jdm etw einreden; **are my eyes deceiving me?** täuschen mich meine Augen?; **to ~ oneself** sich (dat) selbst etwas vormachen.

decelerate [diː'seləreɪt] vi (car, train) langsamer werden; (driver) die Geschwindigkeit herabsetzen.

December [dɪ'sembəʳ] n Dezember m; see **September**.

decency ['diːsənsɪ] n Anstand m. **it's only common** ~ **to** ... es gehört sich einfach, zu ...; **have you no sense of** ~? haben Sie denn kein Anstandsgefühl!; **they didn't even have the** ~ ... haben es nicht einmal für nötig gehalten, ...

decent ['diːsənt] adj anständig. **are you** ~? (col) bist du schon angezogen?

decentralization ['diː,sentrəlaɪ'zeɪʃən] n Dezentralisierung f.

decentralize [diː'sentrəlaız] *vti* dezentralisieren.

deception [dɪ'sepʃən] *n* Betrug *m no pl (of* an +*dat); (of public etc)* Täuschung *f.*

deceptive [dɪ'septɪv] *adj* irreführend; *similarity* täuschend; *simplicity* trügerisch. **to be ~** täuschen, trügen *(geh);* **appearances can be ~** der Schein trügt.

deceptively [dɪ'septɪvlɪ] *adv* täuschend.

decibel ['desɪbel] *n* Dezibel *nt.*

decide [dɪ'saɪd] **1** *vt* **(a)** *(come to a decision)* (sich) entscheiden; *(take it into one's head)* beschließen. **did you ~ anything?** habt ihr irgendwelche Entscheidungen getroffen?; **I have ~d we are making a big mistake** ich bin zu der Ansicht gekommen, daß wir einen großen Fehler machen; **I'll ~ what we do!** ich bestimme, was wir tun! **(b)** *(settle) question, war* entscheiden. **that ~s it** damit ist die Sache entschieden; **that eventually ~d me** das hat schließlich für mich den Ausschlag gegeben. **2** *vi* (sich) entscheiden. **I don't know, you ~** ich weiß nicht, entscheiden *or* bestimmen Sie!; **to ~ for/against sth** (sich) für/gegen etw entscheiden.

♦ **decide on** *vi* +*prep obj* sich entscheiden für.

decided [dɪ'saɪdɪd] *adj* **(a)** *(clear, definite)* entschieden; *difference* deutlich. **(b)** *(determined) manner* entschlossen, bestimmt.

decidedly [dɪ'saɪdɪdlɪ] *adv (definitely)* entschieden.

deciding [dɪ'saɪdɪŋ] *adj* **~ tree** Laubbaum *m.*

deciduous [dɪ'sɪdjʊəs] *adj* **~ tree** Laubbaum *m.*

decimal ['desɪməl] **1** *adj* Dezimal-. **to three ~ places** auf drei Dezimalstellen; **~ point** Komma *nt.* **2** *n* Dezimalzahl *f.*

decimate ['desɪmeɪt] *vt* dezimieren.

decipher [dɪ'saɪfə^r] *vt (lit, fig)* entziffern.

decision [dɪ'sɪʒən] *n* **(a)** Entscheidung *f (on* über +*acc),* Entschluß *m; (esp of committee etc)* Beschluß *m.* **to make a ~** eine Entscheidung treffen *or* fällen, einen Entschluß/Beschluß fassen; **it's your ~** das mußt du entscheiden; **to come to a ~** zu einer Entscheidung kommen. **(b)** *no pl (of character)* Entschlossenheit *f.*

decision-maker [dɪ'sɪʒən,meɪkə^r] *n* Entscheidungsträger *m.*

decisive [dɪ'saɪsɪv] *adj* **(a)** entscheidend; *factor also* ausschlaggebend. **(b)** *manner, answer* entschlossen; *person* entschlußfreudig.

deck [dek] **1** *n* **(a)** *(Naut)* Deck *nt.* **on ~** auf Deck; **to go up on ~** an Deck gehen; **to go (down) below ~(s)** unter Deck gehen. **(b)** *(of bus) top or upper* **~** Oberdeck *nt.* **(c)** *(of cards)* Spiel *nt.* **(d)** *(of record-player)* Laufwerk *nt; (part of hi-fi unit)* Plattenspieler *m.* **tape ~** Tape-deck *nt.* **2** *vt (also* **~ out)** schmücken.

deckchair ['dektʃeə^r] *n* Liegestuhl *m.*

declaim [dɪ'kleɪm] *vti* deklamieren.

declaration [deklə'reɪʃən] *n* Erklärung *f.*

declare [dɪ'kleə^r] *vt* erklären; *results* bekanntgeben; *goods* angeben. **have you anything to ~?** haben Sie etwas zu verzollen?; **to ~ one's income** sein Einkommen angeben; **to ~ war (on sb)** (jdm) den Krieg erklären; **to ~ sb the winner** jdn zum Sieger erklären; **he ~d that ...** er behauptete, daß ...

declared [dɪ'kleəd] *adj* erklärt.

declassify [diː'klæsɪfaɪ] *vt information* freigeben.

declension [dɪ'klenʃən] *n (Gram)* Deklination *f.*

decline [dɪ'klaɪn] **1** *n* **(a)** Rückgang *m; (of empire, a party's supremacy)* Untergang, Niedergang *m.* **to be on the ~** *see vi.* **(b)** *(Med)* Verfall *m.* **2** *vt* **(a)** *invitation, honour* ablehnen. **he ~d to come** er hat es abgelehnt, zu kommen. **(b)** *(Gram)* deklinieren. **3** *vi* **(a)** *(prices, value)* sinken; *(popularity, enthusiasm, interest)* abnehmen; *(population, influence, business)* zurückgehen; *(empire)* verfallen; *(fame)* verblassen; *(health)* sich verschlechtern. **in his declining years** gegen Ende

seines Lebens. **(b)** *(refuse, say no)* ablehnen. **(c)** *(Gram)* dekliniert werden.

declutch [diː'klʌtʃ] *vi* auskuppeln.

decode [diː'kəʊd] *vt* entschlüsseln.

decompose [diːkəm'pəʊz] *vi (Chem, Phys)* zerlegt werden, *(rot)* sich zersetzen.

decomposition [diːkɒmpə'zɪʃən] *n (Chem, Phys)* Zerlegung *f; (rotting)* Zersetzung *f.*

decompression [diːkəm'preʃən] *n* Dekompression, Druckverminderung *f.* **~ chamber** *n* Dekompressionskammer *f.*

decontaminate [diːkən'tæmɪneɪt] *vt* entgiften; *(from radioactivity)* entseuchen.

decontrol [diːkən'trəʊl] *vt prices* freigeben.

décor ['deɪkɔː^r] *n (in room)* Ausstattung *f; (Theat)* Bühnenbild *nt.*

decorate ['dekəreɪt] *vt* **(a)** *cake, hat* verzieren; *street, Christmas tree* schmücken; *room* tapezieren; *(paint)* (an)streichen. **(b)** *soldier* dekorieren, auszeichnen.

decoration [dekə'reɪʃən] *n* **(a)** *(act: of room etc)* Tapezieren *nt;* (An)streichen *nt.* **(b)** *(on cake, hat etc)* Verzierung *f; (on Christmas tree, in street)* Schmuck *m no pl.* **Christmas ~s** Weihnachtsdekorationen *pl or* -schmuck *m;* **interior ~** Innenausstattung *f.* **(c)** *(Mil)* Auszeichnung *f.*

decorative ['dekərətɪv] *adj* dekorativ.

decorator ['dekəreɪtə^r] *n (Brit)* Maler und Tapezierer *m.*

decorous ['dekərəs] *adj* schicklich.

decorum [dɪ'kɔːrəm] *n* Anstand *m.*

decoy ['diːkɔɪ] *n (lit, fig)* Köder *m; (person)* Lockvogel *m.*

decrease [diː'kriːs] **1** *vi* abnehmen; *(figures, output, birthrate, production)* zurückgehen; *(strength, enthusiasm, intensity)* nachlassen. **it ~s in value** es verliert an Wert. **2** *vt* verringern, reduzieren. **3** ['diːkriːs] *n see vi* Abnahme *f;* Rückgang *m;* Nachlassen *nt.* **to be on the ~** *see vi.*

decreasingly [diː'kriːsɪŋlɪ] *adv* immer weniger.

decree [dɪ'kriː] **1** *n (Pol, of king etc)* Erlaß *m; (of tribunal, court)* Entscheid *m,* Urteil *nt.* **~ nisi/absolute** vorläufiges/endgültiges Scheidungsurteil. **2** *vt* verordnen, verfügen.

decrepit [dɪ'krepɪt] *adj* altersschwach; *building also* baufällig.

decry [dɪ'kraɪ] *vt* schlechtmachen.

dedicate ['dedɪkeɪt] *vt* **(a)** *church* weihen. **(b)** *book, music* widmen *(to sb* jdm). **to ~ oneself** *or* **one's life to sth** sich *or* sein Leben einer Sache widmen.

dedicated ['dedɪkeɪtɪd] *adj attitude* hingebungsvoll; *service* treu; *teacher etc* engagiert. **she's a ~ nurse** sie ist Krankenschwester mit Leib und Seele.

dedication [dedɪ'keɪʃən] *n* **(a)** *(quality)* Hingabe *f (to* an +*acc); (to work)* Engagement *nt.* **(b)** *(of church)* Weihe *f.* **(c)** *(in book)* Widmung *f.*

deduce [dɪ'djuːs] *vt* folgern, schließen *(from* aus).

deduct [dɪ'dʌkt] *vt* abziehen *(from* von); *(from wages also)* einbehalten. **to ~ sth from the price** etw vom Preis nachlassen.

deductible [dɪ'dʌktəbl] *adj* abziehbar; *(tax* ~) absetzbar.

deduction [dɪ'dʌkʃən] *n* **(a)** *(act of deducting)* Abzug *m; (sth deducted) (from price)* Nachlaß *m; (from wage)* Abzug *m.* **(b)** *(sth deduced)* (Schluß)folgerung *f.*

deed [diːd] *n* **(a)** Tat *f.* **good ~** gute Tat; **in word and ~** in Wort und Tat. **(b)** *(Jur)* Urkunde *f.* **~ of covenant** Vertragsurkunde *f.*

deem [diːm] *vt* **to ~ sb/sth (to be) sth** jdn/etw für etw erachten *(geh)* or halten.

deep [diːp] **1** *adj* (+*er*) tief; *(profound) thinker, book, remark* tiefsinnig; *concern, interest* groß; *sorrow* tief (empfunden). **two metres ~ in snow/water** mit zwei Meter Schnee bedeckt/zwei Meter tief unter Wasser; **to go off (at) the ~ end** *(col)* an die

Decke gehen (col); **to plunge in at the ~ end** (col) sich kopfüber in die Sache stürzen; **to be thrown in at the ~ end** (col) gleich zu Anfang richtig ranmüssen (col); **~ in thought/a book** in Gedanken/in ein Buch vertieft; **he's a ~ one** (col) er ist ein stilles Wasser. **2** adv (+er) tief. **~ into the night** bis tief in die Nacht hinein; **they stood ten ~** sie standen in zehn Reihen hintereinander. **3** n (liter) **the ~** das Meer, die See.

deepen ['diːpən] **1** vt (lit, fig) vertiefen. **2** vi (lit, fig) tiefer werden; (concern, interest) zunehmen; (mystery) größer werden.

deep: ~-freeze 1 n Tiefkühltruhe f; (upright) Gefrierschrank m; **2** vt einfrieren; **~-fry** vt fritieren, in schwimmendem Fett ausbacken.

deeply ['diːplɪ] adv **(a)** dig, cut, breathe tief; think, consider also gründlich. **(b)** grateful, concerned zutiefst; offended also, indebted tief; love innig; interested höchst; aware voll(kommen).

deep: ~-rooted adj (fig) tiefverwurzelt; **~-sea** adj plant, current, animal Meeres-; **~-sea diver** n Tiefseetaucher m; **~-sea fishing** n Hochseefischerei f; **~-seated** adj tiefsitzend; **~-set** adj tiefliegend; **D~ South** n Tiefer Süden.

deer [dɪəʳ] n, pl - Hirsch m; (roe ~) Reh nt. **are there any ~ here?** gibt es hier Wild?

deer: ~skin n Hirsch-/Rehleder nt; **~stalker** n (hat) ≃ Sherlock-Holmes-Mütze f; **~stalking** n Pirschen nt, Pirsch f.

deface [dɪ'feɪs] vt verunstalten.

de facto [deɪ'fæktəʊ] adj, adv de facto.

defamation [ˌdefə'meɪʃən] n Diffamierung, Verleumdung f. **~ of character** Rufmord m.

defamatory [dɪ'fæmətərɪ] adj diffamierend.

default [dɪ'fɔːlt] **1** n **(a)** (failure to appear) (Jur) Nichterscheinen nt vor Gericht; (Sport) Nichtantreten nt; (failure to perform duty) Versäumnis f. **to win by ~** (Sport) kampflos gewinnen. **(b) in ~ of** in Ermangelung (+gen). **2** vi (not appear) (Jur) nicht erscheinen; (Sport) nicht antreten; (not perform duty, not pay) säumig sein. **to ~ in one's payments** seinen Zahlungsverpflichtungen nicht nachkommen.

defeat [dɪ'fiːt] **1** n (defeating) Sieg m (of über +acc); (of motion, bill) Ablehnung f; (being defeated) Niederlage f. **to admit ~** sich geschlagen geben. **2** vt army, team besiegen, schlagen; government also eine Niederlage beibringen (+dat); motion, bill ablehnen; **that would be ~ing the purpose** das würde den Zweck verfehlen.

defeatism [dɪ'fiːtɪzəm] n Defätismus m.

defeatist [dɪ'fiːtɪst] **1** n Defätist m. **2** adj defätistisch.

defecate ['defəkeɪt] vi den Darm entleeren.

defect[1] ['diːfekt] n Fehler, Schaden m; (in mechanism also) Defekt m. **physical ~** Mißbildung f; (less serious) Schönheitsfehler m; **a character ~** ein Charakterfehler m.

defect[2] [dɪ'fekt] vi sich absetzen; (fig) abtrünnig werden. **to ~ to the enemy** zum Feind übergehen or überlaufen.

defection [dɪ'fekʃən] n (Pol) Überlaufen nt, (fig) Abtrünnigkeit f, Abfall m.

defective [dɪ'fektɪv] adj fehlerhaft; machine also defekt; hearing, sight mangelhaft, gestört.

defence, (US) **defense** [dɪ'fens] n Verteidigung f; (Sport also) Abwehr f. **in his ~** zu seiner Verteidigung; **to come to sb's ~** jdn verteidigen; **to put up a stubborn ~** sich hartnäckig verteidigen; **his only ~ was ...** seine einzige Rechtfertigung war ...; **counsel for the ~** Verteidiger(in f) m; **as a ~ against** als Schutz gegen; **~s** (Mil) Verteidigungsanlagen pl; **Ministry of D~** Verteidigungsministerium nt.

defence: ~less adj schutzlos; **~ mechanism** n Abwehrmechanismus m.

defend [dɪ'fend] vt verteidigen (also Jur) (against gegen). **to ~ oneself** sich verteidigen.

---

defendant [dɪ'fendənt] n Angeklagte(r) mf; (in civil cases) Beklagte(r) mf.

defender [dɪ'fendəʳ] n Verteidiger m.

defending [dɪ'fendɪŋ] adj: **~ counsel** Verteidiger(in f) m.

defense etc [dɪ'fens] (US) = **defence** etc.

defensive [dɪ'fensɪv] **1** adj defensiv (also fig), Verteidigungs-. **2** n (Mil) Abwehraktion f. **to be on the ~** (Mil, fig) in der Defensive sein.

defer[1] [dɪ'fɜːʳ] vt (delay) verschieben; event also verlegen. **~red terms** Ratenkauf m.

defer[2] vi **to ~ to sb/sb's wishes** sich jdm beugen or fügen/sich jds Wünschen (dat) fügen.

deference ['defərəns] n Achtung f, Respekt m. **out of ~ to** aus Achtung or Respekt vor (+dat).

deferential [ˌdefə'renʃəl] adj ehrerbietig, respektvoll.

deferment [dɪ'fɜːmənt] n see **defer[1]** Verschiebung f; Verlegung f.

defiance [dɪ'faɪəns] n Trotz m; (of danger) Mißachtung f. **in ~ of sb/sb's orders** jdm/jds Anordnungen zum Trotz.

defiant [dɪ'faɪənt] adj aufsässig; esp child also, answer trotzig; (challenging) attitude herausfordernd.

deficiency [dɪ'fɪʃənsɪ] n Mangel m; (in character, system) Schwäche f.

deficient [dɪ'fɪʃənt] adj unzulänglich. **sb/sth is ~ in sth** jdm/einer Sache fehlt es an etw (dat).

deficit ['defɪsɪt] n Defizit nt.

defile[1] ['diːfaɪl] n Hohlweg m.

defile[2] [dɪ'faɪl] vt (pollute) verschmutzen; (desecrate) schänden, entweihen.

define [dɪ'faɪn] vt **(a)** festlegen, bestimmen; word definieren. **to ~ one's position** seinen Standpunkt klarmachen. **(b) to be clearly ~d against the sky** sich klar gegen den Himmel abzeichnen.

definite ['defɪnɪt] adj answer, decision klar, eindeutig; date, agreement, plan fest, definitiv; improvement, lisp deutlich; manner, tone bestimmt. **is that ~?** ist das sicher?; **the date is not ~ yet** der Termin steht noch nicht fest; **she was very ~ about it** sie war sich (dat) sehr sicher; (insistent) sie bestand darauf; **can't you be more ~?** können Sie sich etwas genauer festlegen?; **~ article** (Gram) bestimmter Artikel.

definitely ['defɪnɪtlɪ] adv bestimmt; decide, arrange fest, definitiv. **he ~ wanted to come** er wollte bestimmt kommen; **that's ~ an improvement** das ist ganz sicherlich eine Verbesserung.

definition [ˌdefɪ'nɪʃən] n **(a)** (of word, concept) Definition f. **(b)** (of powers, duties, boundaries) Festlegung, Bestimmung f. **(c)** (Phot, TV) Bildschärfe f; (Opt: of lens) Schärfe f.

definitive [dɪ'fɪnɪtɪv] adj victory, answer entschieden; (authoritative) book maßgeblich (on für).

deflate [ˌdiː'fleɪt] vt tyre etwas Luft/die Luft ablassen aus. **to ~ the currency** eine Deflation herbeiführen; **he was a bit ~d** es war ein ziemlicher Dämpfer für ihn.

deflation [ˌdiː'fleɪʃən] n (Fin) Deflation f.

deflationary [ˌdiː'fleɪʃənərɪ] adj (Fin) deflationär.

deflect [dɪ'flekt] vt ablenken; (Phys) light beugen.

deflower [ˌdiː'flaʊəʳ] vt entjungfern, deflorieren.

deforestation [diːˌfɒrɪ'steɪʃən] n Abholzung f.

deform [dɪ'fɔːm] vt deformieren, verunstalten.

deformed [dɪ'fɔːmd] adj limb, body mißgebildet.

deformity [dɪ'fɔːmɪtɪ] n Mißbildung f.

defraud [dɪ'frɔːd] vt **to ~ sb of sth** jdn um etw betrügen.

defray [dɪ'freɪ] vt tragen, übernehmen.

defrock [ˌdiː'frɒk] vt aus dem Priesteramt verstoßen.

defrost [ˌdiː'frɒst] vt entfrosten; fridge abtauen; food auftauen.

defroster [ˌdiː'frɒstəʳ] n (US) Gebläse nt.

deft [deft] adj (+er) flink, geschickt.

defunct [dɪ'fʌŋkt] adj institution etc eingegangen; law außer Kraft.

defuse [ˌdiː'fjuːz] vt (lit, fig) entschärfen.

defy [dɪ'faɪ] vt (a) (disobey) person sich widersetzen (+dat); orders, law, death, danger trotzen (+dat). (b) (fig) efforts widerstehen (+dat). to ~ definition sich nicht erklären or definieren lassen; to ~ description jeder Beschreibung spotten. (c) (challenge) I ~ you to do better machen Sie es doch besser, wenn Sie können.

degeneracy [dɪ'dʒenərəsɪ] n Degeneriertheit f.

degenerate [dɪ'dʒenərɪt] 1 adj degeneriert; race, morals also entartet. 2 n degenerierter Mensch. 3 [dɪ'dʒenəreɪt] vi degenerieren; (people, morals also) entarten.

degradation [ˌdegrə'deɪʃən] n Erniedrigung f.

degrade [dɪ'greɪd] vt erniedrigen.

degrading [dɪ'greɪdɪŋ] adj erniedrigend.

degree [dɪ'griː] n (a) Grad m no pl. it was 35 ~s in the shade es waren 35 Grad im Schatten. (b) (extent) to some ~, to a (certain) ~ zu einem gewissen Grad, in gewissem Maße; to a high ~ in hohem Maße; to such a ~ that ... so sehr, daß ...; to what ~ was he involved? wieweit war er verwickelt?; by ~s nach und nach; first/second ~ murder (Jur) Mord m/Totschlag m. (c) (Univ) akademischer Grad. when did you do your ~? wann haben Sie das Examen gemacht?; he has a ~ in English er hat Anglistik studiert; she has a ~ sie hat einen Universitätsabschluß.

dehydrate [ˌdiːhaɪ'dreɪt] vt Wasser entziehen (+dat).

dehydrated [ˌdiːhaɪ'dreɪtɪd] adj vegetables, milk Trocken-; person, skin ausgetrocknet.

de-ice [ˌdiː'aɪs] vt enteisen.

de-icer [ˌdiː'aɪsəʳ] n Enteiser m; (spray for cars) Defroster m.

deign [deɪn] vt to ~ to do sth geruhen or sich herablassen, etw zu tun.

deity ['diːɪtɪ] n Gottheit f. the D~ Gott m.

déjà vu [ˌdeɪʒɑː'vjuː] n Déjà-vu-Erlebnis nt. a feeling of ~ das Gefühl, das schon einmal gesehen or erlebt zu haben.

dejected [dɪ'dʒektɪd] adj niedergeschlagen, deprimiert.

dejection [dɪ'dʒekʃən] n Niedergeschlagenheit f.

de jure [ˌdiː'dʒʊərɪ] adj, adv de jure.

delay [dɪ'leɪ] 1 vt (a) (postpone) verschieben, aufschieben. he ~ed writing the letter er schob den Brief auf. (b) (hold up) person, train aufhalten. the flight was ~ed das Flugzeug hatte Verspätung; (leaving) der Abflug verzögerte sich; we'll be ~ed wir werden uns verspäten. 2 vi to ~ in doing sth es aufschieben, etw zu tun; don't ~! verlieren Sie keine Zeit! 3 n (hold-up) Verzögerung f; (to train, plane) Verspätung f; there are ~s to all trains alle Züge haben Verspätung; without ~ unverzüglich; without further ~ gleich.

delayed-action [dɪ'leɪdˌækʃən] adj attr bomb, mine mit Zeitzünder.

delectable [dɪ'lektəbl] adj köstlich; (fig) reizend.

delegate ['delɪgeɪt] 1 vt delegieren. to ~ sb to do sth jdn damit beauftragen, etw zu tun. 2 vi delegieren. 3 ['delɪgət] n Delegierte(r) mf.

delegation [ˌdelɪ'geɪʃən] n Delegation f (to an +acc).

delete [dɪ'liːt] vt streichen (from von).

deletion [dɪ'liːʃən] n Streichung f.

deliberate [dɪ'lɪbərɪt] 1 adj (a) (intentional) absichtlich; action, insult, lie also bewußt. (b) (cautious, thoughtful) besonnen; action (wohl)überlegt; (slow) movement, step bedächtig. 2 [dɪ'lɪbəreɪt] vi (ponder) nachdenken (on über +acc); (discuss) sich beraten (on über +acc, wegen). 3 [dɪ'lɪbəreɪt] vt (ponder) bedenken, über-

legen; (discuss) beraten.

deliberately [dɪ'lɪbərɪtlɪ] adv (a) absichtlich, bewußt. (b) (purposefully, slowly) bedächtig.

deliberation [dɪˌlɪbə'reɪʃən] n (a) (consideration) Überlegung f. (b) (discussion) Beratungen pl (of, on in +dat, über +acc).

delicacy ['delɪkəsɪ] n see adj (a) Feinheit f; Zerbrechlichkeit f; Zartheit f; Empfindlichkeit f. the ~ of his health seine schwächliche Konstitution. (b) Feinfühligkeit f; Empfindlichkeit f; Empfindsamkeit f. (c) Heikle nt (of an +dat). (d) (food) Delikatesse f.

delicate ['delɪkɪt] adj (a) fabric etc fein, zart; (fragile) zerbrechlich; person zart; liver empfindlich. to have very ~ health sehr anfällig sein. (b) (sensitive) person feinfühlig; instrument empfindlich; playing empfindsam. (c) operation, situation heikel, delikat.

delicatessen [delɪkə'tesn] n Feinkostgeschäft nt.

delicious [dɪ'lɪʃəs] adj köstlich, lecker (col).

delight [dɪ'laɪt] 1 n Freude f. to my ~ zu meiner Freude; he takes great ~ in doing that es bereitet ihm große Freude, das zu tun; he's a ~ to watch es ist eine Freude, ihm zuzusehen. 2 vt erfreuen. 3 vi sich erfreuen (in an +dat).

delighted [dɪ'laɪtɪd] adj to be ~ sich sehr freuen (at über +acc, that daß); I'd be ~ to help you ich würde Ihnen sehr gern helfen.

delightful [dɪ'laɪtfʊl] adj reizend; weather, party, meal wunderbar.

delimit [diː'lɪmɪt] vt abstecken, abgrenzen.

delineate [dɪ'lɪnɪeɪt] vt (draw) skizzieren; (describe) beschreiben.

delinquency [dɪ'lɪŋkwənsɪ] n Kriminalität f.

delinquent [dɪ'lɪŋkwənt] 1 adj (a) straffällig. (b) (US) bill überfällig; account rückständig. 2 n Delinquent m.

delirious [dɪ'lɪrɪəs] adj (Med) im Delirium; (fig) im Taumel. ~ with joy im Freudentaumel.

deliriously [dɪ'lɪrɪəslɪ] adv ~ happy überglücklich.

delirium [dɪ'lɪrɪəm] n (Med) Delirium nt.

deliver [dɪ'lɪvəʳ] 1 vt (a) goods liefern; note, message überbringen; (on regular basis) letters, papers etc zustellen; to ~ sth to sb jdm etw liefern/zustellen; he ~ed me right to the door er brachte mich bis zur Tür; to ~ the goods (fig col) es bringen (col), es schaffen. (b) (liter: rescue) befreien. (c) (pronounce) speech halten; ultimatum stellen; verdict verkünden. (d) baby zur Welt bringen. (e) (aim) blow versetzen. 2 vi liefern.

deliverance [dɪ'lɪvərəns] n (liter) Erlösung (from von) f.

delivery [dɪ'lɪvərɪ] n (a) (of goods) Lieferung f; (of parcels, letters) Zustellung f. to take ~ of sth etw in Empfang nehmen; to pay on ~ bei Empfang zahlen. (b) (Med) Entbindung f. (c) (of speaker) Vortragsweise f.
delivery: ~ boy n Bote m; ~ note n Lieferschein m; ~ van n (Brit) Lieferwagen m.

delphinium [del'fɪnɪəm] n Rittersporn m.

delta ['deltə] n Delta nt. ~ wing Deltaflügel m.

delude [dɪ'luːd] vt täuschen, irreführen (with mit). to ~ sb into thinking sth jdm etw weismachen; to ~ oneself (dat) Illusionen machen, (dat) etwas vormachen.

deluge ['deljuːdʒ] 1 n Überschwemmung f; (of rain) Wolkenbruch m; (fig: of letters etc) Flut f. 2 vt (lit, fig) überschwemmen, überfluten.

delusion [dɪ'luːʒən] n Illusion f, Irrglaube m no pl.

de luxe [dɪ'lʌks] adj Luxus-.

delve [delv] vi sich vertiefen (into in +acc).

demagogue ['deməgɒg] n Demagoge m, Demagogin f.

demand [dɪ'mɑːnd] 1 vt verlangen, fordern (of, from von); (situation, task etc) erfordern; he ~ed to see my passport er verlangte meinen Paß. 2 n

(a) Forderung *f (for* nach). **by popular** ~ **auf allgemeinen Wunsch; to make** ~**s on sb** Forderungen an jdn stellen; **I have many** ~**s on my time** ich habe sehr viele Verpflichtungen. **(b)** *no pl (Comm)* Nachfrage *f,* Bedarf *m (for* nach). **to be in great** ~ *(article, person)* sehr gefragt sein.

demanding [dɪ'maːndɪŋ] *adj child* anstrengend; *task also, teacher, boss* anspruchsvoll. **physically** ~ körperlich anstrengend.

demarcation [,diːmaː'keɪʃən] *n* Abrenzung, Demarkation *f.* ~**-line** Demarkationslinie *f;* ~ **dispute** Streit *m* um den Zuständigkeitsbereich.

demeanour, *(US)* **demeanor** [dɪ'miːnəʳ] *n (behaviour)* Benehmen, Auftreten *nt.*

demented [dɪ'mentɪd] *adj* verrückt, wahnsinnig.

demerara (sugar) [,deməˈrɛərə(ˈʃʊɡəʳ)] *n* brauner Rohrzucker.

demi ['demɪ-] *pref* Halb-, halb-. ~**god** Halbgott *m.*

demilitarize [,diː'mɪlɪtəraɪz] *vt* demilitarisieren.

demise [dɪ'maɪz] *n (form)* Ableben *nt (geh);* *(fig: of institution, newspaper etc)* Ende *nt.*

demist [,diː'mɪst] *vt windscreen* freimachen.

demister [,diː'mɪstəʳ] *n (Brit)* Gebläse *nt.*

demitasse ['demɪtæs] *n (US) (cup)* Mokkatasse *f; (coffee)* Kaffee *m.*

demo ['deməʊ] *n* = **demonstration** Demo(nstration) *f.*

democracy [dɪ'mɒkrəsɪ] *n* Demokratie *f.*

democrat ['deməkræt] *n* Demokrat(in *f) m.*

democratic [,deməˈkrætɪk] *adj* demokratisch.

demography [dɪ'mɒɡrəfɪ] *n* Demographie *f.*

demolish [dɪ'mɒlɪʃ] *vt building* ab- or einreißen; *(fig) opponent, theory* zunichte machen, vernichten; *(hum) cake etc* vertilgen.

demolition [,deməˈlɪʃən] *n* Abbruch *m.*

demon ['diːmən] *n* Dämon *m; (col: child)* Teufel *m.* **to be a** ~ **for work** ein Arbeitstier sein.

demonstrable ['demənstrəbl] *adj* offensichtlich.

demonstrate ['demənstreɪt] **1** *vt* **(a)** *prove,* beweisen. **(b)** *appliance etc* vorführen. **2** *vi (Pol)* demonstrieren.

demonstration [,demən'streɪʃən] *n* **(a)** Beweis *m; (of appliance)* Vorführung *f.* **(b)** *(Pol)* Demonstration *f.*

demonstrative [dɪ'mɒnstrətɪv] *adj* demonstrativ. **he's not very** ~ er zeigt seine Gefühle nicht.

demonstrator ['demənstreɪtəʳ] *n (Pol)* Demonstrant(in *f) m.*

demoralize [dɪ'mɒrəlaɪz] *vt* entmutigen; *troops etc* demoralisieren.

demote [dɪ'məʊt] *vt* degradieren *(to* zu).

demur [dɪ'mɜːʳ] *(form)* **1** *vi* Einwände erheben *(at* gegen). **2** *n* **without** ~ widerspruchslos.

demure [dɪ'mjʊəʳ] *adj (+er)* (coy) spröde; *(sedate)* ernst, gesetzt.

den [den] *n* **(a)** *(of lion etc)* Höhle *f; (of fox)* Bau *m.* ~ **of iniquity** Lasterhöhle *f;* ~ **of thieves** Spelunke, Räuberhöhle *(hum) f.* **(b)** *(room)* Bude *f (col).*

denationalize [,diː'næʃnəlaɪz] *vt* entstaatlichen.

denial [dɪ'naɪəl] *n* **(a)** *(of accusation, guilt)* Leugnen *nt.* **an official** ~ ein offizielles Dementi. **(b)** *(of request etc)* Ablehnung *f; (official)* abschlägiger Bescheid; *(of rights)* Verweigerung *f.*

denier ['denɪəʳ] *n (of stockings)* Denier *nt.*

denigrate ['denɪɡreɪt] *vt* verunglimpfen.

denim ['denɪm] *n* **(a)** Jeansstoff *m.* ~ **jacket** Jeansjacke *f.* **(b)** ~**s** *pl* (Blue) Jeans *pl.*

Denmark ['denmaːk] *n* Dänemark *nt.*

denomination [dɪ,nɒmɪ'neɪʃən] *n* **(a)** *(Eccl)* Konfession *f.* **(b)** *(of money)* Nennwert *m.*

denominator [dɪ'nɒmɪneɪtəʳ] *n (Math)* Nenner *m.*

denote [dɪ'nəʊt] *vt* bedeuten.

dénouement [dɪ'nuːmɒŋ] *n* Ausgang *m.*

denounce [dɪ'naʊns] *vt* **(a)** *(accuse)* anprangern; *(inform against)* anzeigen, denunzieren *(sb to sb* jdn bei jdm). **(b)** *(condemn) alcohol, habit etc* verurteilen.

dense [dens] *adj (+er)* **(a)** dicht. **(b)** *(col: stupid)* beschränkt.

densely ['denslɪ] *adv* ~ **populated** dicht bevölkert.

density ['densɪtɪ] *n* Dichte *f.* **population** ~ Bevölkerungsdichte *f.*

dent [dent] **1** *n (in metal)* Beule, Delle *(col) f.* **that made a** ~ **in his savings** *(col)* das hat ein Loch in seine Ersparnisse gerissen. **2** *vt car* eindellen, verbeulen; *(col) pride* anknacksen *(col).*

dental ['dentl] *adj* Zahn-; *treatment* zahnärztlich. ~ **floss** Zahnseide *f;* ~ **surgeon** Zahnarzt *m/*-ärztin *f.*

dentifrice ['dentɪfrɪs] *n* Zahnpasta *f.*

dentist ['dentɪst] *n* Zahnarzt *m,* Zahnärztin *f.*

dentistry ['dentɪstrɪ] *n* Zahnmedizin *f.*

dentures ['dentʃəz] *npl (partial* ~*)* Zahnprothese *f; (full* ~*)* Gebiß *nt.*

denude [dɪ'njuːd] *vt* entblößen *(of gen).*

denunciation [dɪ,nʌnsɪ'eɪʃən] *n see* **denounce** Anprangerung *f;* Denunziation *f;* Verurteilung *f.*

deny [dɪ'naɪ] *vt* **(a)** *charge, accusation etc* bestreiten, leugnen; *(officially)* dementieren. **do you** ~ **having said that?** leugnen or bestreiten Sie, das gesagt zu haben?; **I don't** ~ **it** das streite ich gar nicht ab. **(b)** *(refuse) to* ~ **sb a request/his rights** jdm eine Bitte abschlagen/jdm seine Rechte vorenthalten; **I can't** ~ **her anything** ich kann ihr nichts abschlagen; **to** ~ **oneself sth** auf etw *(acc)* verzichten. **(c)** *religion, principles* verleugnen.

deodorant [diː'əʊdərənt] *n* De(s)odorant *m.*

depart [dɪ'paːt] *vi* **(a)** *(go away)* weggehen; *(on journey)* abreisen; *(by bus, car etc)* wegfahren; *(train, bus etc)* abfahren. **(b)** *(deviate: from opinion etc)* abweichen, abgehen.

departed [dɪ'paːtɪd] *n* **the (dear)** ~ der/die (liebe) Verstorbene; die (lieben) Verstorbenen *pl.*

department [dɪ'paːtmənt] *n* **(a)** Abteilung *f; (in civil service)* Ressort *nt.* **D**~ **of Employment** *(Brit)* Arbeitsministerium *nt;* **D**~ **of State** *(US)* Außenministerium *nt;* **that's not my** ~ *(fig)* dafür bin ich nicht zuständig. **(b)** *(Univ)* Seminar *nt.*

departmental [,diːpaːt'mentl] *adj* **(a)** Abteilungs-. **(b)** *(Univ)* Seminar-.

department store *n* Kaufhaus, Warenhaus *nt.*

departure [dɪ'paːtʃəʳ] *n* **(a)** *(of person)* Weggang *m; (on journey)* Abreise *f (from* aus); *(of vehicle)* Abfahrt *f; (of plane)* Abflug *m.* ~ **lounge** Abflughalle *f;* **point of** ~ *(fig)* Ausgangspunkt *m.* **(b)** *(fig: from custom, truth)* Abweichen *nt (from* von). **a new** ~ eine neue Richtung.

depend [dɪ'pend] *vi* **(a)** *(hinge on) (on* sb/sth von jdm/etw). **it all** ~**s (on whether ...)** das hängt ganz davon ab(, ob ...); **that** ~**s** das kommt darauf an; ~**ing on his mood/how late we arrive je** nach seiner Laune/je nachdem, wie spät wir ankommen. **(b)** *(rely)* sich verlassen *(on, upon* auf *+acc).* **you can** ~ **(up)on it!** darauf können Sie sich verlassen! **(c)** *(person: be dependent on) to* ~ **on** angewiesen sein auf *(+acc).*

dependable [dɪ'pendəbl] *adj* zuverlässig, verläßlich.

dependant, dependent [dɪ'pendənt] *n* Abhängige(r) *mf.* **do you have** ~**s?** haben Sie (abhängige) Angehörige?

dependence [dɪ'pendəns] *n* Abhängigkeit *f (on* von).

dependent [dɪ'pendənt] *adj* **1** *adj* abhängig *(on, upon* von). **to be** ~ **on sb's good will** auf jds Wohlwollen *(acc)* angewiesen sein. **2** *n* = **dependant.**

depict [dɪ'pɪkt] *vt* schildern.

depilatory [dɪ'pɪlətərɪ] *n* Enthaarungsmittel *nt.*

deplete [dɪ'pliːt] *vt (exhaust)* erschöpfen; *(reduce)* aufbrauchen.

deplorable [dɪ'plɔːrəbl] *adj* beklagenswert, bedauerlich.

deplore [dɪ'plɔːʳ] *vt (regret)* bedauern, beklagen;

(disapprove of) mißbilligen.
deploy [dɪ'plɔɪ] *vt (Mil, fig)* einsetzen.
deployment [dɪ'plɔɪmənt] *n* Einsatz *m*.
depopulate [,diː'pɒpjʊleɪt] *vt* entvölkern.
depopulation ['diː,pɒpju'leɪʃən] *n* Entvölkerung *f*.
deport [dɪ'pɔːt] *vt prisoner* deportieren; *alien* abschieben.
deportation [,diːpɔː'teɪʃən] *n see vt* Deportation *f*; Abschiebung *f*.
deportment [dɪ'pɔːtmənt] *n* Haltung *f*; *(behaviour)* Verhalten, Benehmen *nt*.
depose [dɪ'pəʊz] *vt* absetzen.
deposit [dɪ'pɒzɪt] **1** *vt* **(a)** *(put down)* hinlegen; *(upright)* hinstellen. **(b)** *money, valuables* deponieren *(with bei)*. **2** *n* **(a)** *(Fin: in bank)* Einlage *f*, Guthaben *nt*. **(b)** *(Comm) (part payment)* Anzahlung *f*; *(returnable security)* Kaution *f*; *(for bottle)* Pfand *nt*. **to lose one's** ~ *(Pol)* seine Kaution verlieren. **(c)** *(Chem: in wine, Geol)* Ablagerung *f*; *(of ore, coal, oil)* (Lager)stätte *f*.
deposit account *n (Brit)* Sparkonto *nt*.
depositor [dɪ'pɒzɪtəʳ] *n* Einzahler(in *f*) *m*.
depository [dɪ'pɒzɪtərɪ] *n* Lagerhaus *nt*.
depot ['depəʊ] *n (bus garage etc)* Depot *nt*; *(store also)* Lager(haus) *nt*.
depraved [dɪ'preɪvd] *adj* verkommen.
depravity [dɪ'prævɪtɪ] *n* Verkommenheit *f*.
deprecate ['deprɪkeɪt] *vt (form)* mißbilligen.
depreciate [dɪ'priːʃɪeɪt] *vi* an Wert verlieren; *(currency)* an Kaufkraft verlieren.
depreciation [dɪ,priːʃɪ'eɪʃən] *n* Wertminderung *f*; *(of currency)* Kaufkraftverlust *m*.
depress [dɪ'pres] *vt* **(a)** *person* deprimieren; *(discourage)* entmutigen. **(b)** *(form) lever* niederdrücken.
depressant [dɪ'presnt] *n* Beruhigungsmittel *nt*.
depressed [dɪ'prest] *adj* **(a)** *person* deprimiert. **don't get** ~ sei nicht deprimiert. **(b)** *industry* notleidend. ~ **area** strukturschwaches Gebiet.
depressing [dɪ'presɪŋ] *adj* deprimierend.
depression [dɪ'preʃən] *n* **(a)** Depressionen *pl*. **(b)** *(in ground)* Vertiefung, Senke *f*. **(c)** *(Met)* Tief(druckgebiet) *nt*. **(d)** *(Econ)* Flaute *f*; *(St Ex)* Baisse *f*. **the D**~ die Weltwirtschaftskrise.
deprivation [,deprɪ'veɪʃən] *n* **(a)** *(depriving)* Entzug *m*; *(Psych)* Deprivation *f*; *(of rights)* Beraubung *f*. **(b)** *(state)* Entbehrung *f*.
deprive [dɪ'praɪv] *vt* **to** ~ **sb of sth** jdm etw nehmen; **they had been** ~**d of ...** *(had lacked)* ihnen fehlte ...; **to** ~ **oneself of sth** auf etw *(acc)* verzichten.
deprived [dɪ'praɪvd] *adj* benachteiligt.
dept = **department** Abt.
depth [depθ] *n (lit, fig)* Tiefe *f*. **the** ~**s of the ocean** die Tiefen des Ozeans; **at a** ~ **of 3 metres** in einer Tiefe von 3 Metern, in 3 Meter Tiefe; **to get out of one's** ~ *(lit, fig)* den Boden unter den Füßen verlieren; **sorry, I'm out of my** ~ **there** es tut mir leid, aber da muß ich passen; **with great** ~ **of feeling** sehr gefühlvoll; **in** ~ eingehend, intensiv; **in the** ~**s of despair** in tiefster Verzweiflung; **in the** ~**s of winter/the forest** im tiefsten Winter/Wald; ~ **charge** Wasserbombe *f*.
deputation [,depjʊ'teɪʃən] *n* Abordnung *f*.
deputize ['depjʊtaɪz] *vi* vertreten *(for sb* jdn).
deputy ['depjʊtɪ] **1** *n* Stellvertreter(in *f*) *m*. **2** *adj attr* stellvertretend.
derail [dɪ'reɪl] *vt* zum Entgleisen bringen, entgleisen lassen. **to be** ~**ed** entgleisen.
derailment [dɪ'reɪlmənt] *n* Entgleisung *f*.
deranged [dɪ'reɪndʒd] *adj mind* gestört. **to be** **(mentally)** ~ geistesgestört sein.
Derby ['dɑːbɪ] *n (US: also* ~ **hat)** Melone *f*.
derelict ['derɪlɪkt] *adj (abandoned)* verlassen; *(ruined)* verfallen, heruntergekommen.
dereliction [,derɪ'lɪkʃən] *n* ~ **of duty** Pflichtversäumnis *nt*.
deride [dɪ'raɪd] *vt* verhöhnen.

derision [dɪ'rɪʒən] *n* Hohn, Spott *m*. **object of** ~ Zielscheibe *f* des Spotts.
derisive [dɪ'raɪsɪv] *adj* spöttisch, höhnisch.
derisory [dɪ'raɪsərɪ] *adj* **(a)** *amount, offer* lächerlich. **(b)** = **derisive**.
derivation [,derɪ'veɪʃən] *n* Ableitung *f*.
derivative [dɪ'rɪvətɪv] **1** *adj* abgeleitet; *literary work etc* nachgeahmt, imitiert. **2** *n* Ableitung *f*.
derive [dɪ'raɪv] **1** *vt ideas, names* her- or ableiten *(from* von*); profit* ziehen *(from* aus*); satisfaction, comfort* beziehen *(from* aus*)*. **this word is** ~**d from the Greek** dieses Wort stammt aus dem Griechischen; **to** ~ **pleasure from sth** Freude haben an etw *(dat)*. **2** *vi* **to** ~ **from** sich her- or ableiten von; *(power, fortune)* beruhen auf *(+dat)*, *(ideas)* stammen von.
dermatitis [,dɜːmə'taɪtɪs] *n* Hautentzündung, Dermatitis *f*.
dermatology [,dɜːmə'tɒlədʒɪ] *n* Dermatologie *f*.
derogatory [dɪ'rɒgətərɪ] *adj* abfällig, abschätzig.
derrick ['derɪk] *n* Kran *m*; *(above oilwell)* Bohrturm *m*.
descant ['deskænt] *n (Mus)* Diskant *m*.
descend [dɪ'send] **1** *vi* **(a)** *(go down)* herunter-/hinuntergehen; *(lift, vehicle)* herunter-/hinunterfahren; *(hill)* abfallen. **(b)** *(attack, visit)* **to** ~ **(up)on sb** jdn überfallen. **(c)** *(lower oneself)* **to** ~ **to sth** sich zu etw herablassen; **he even** ~**ed to bribery** er scheute selbst vor Bestechung nicht zurück. **2** *vt* **(a)** *stairs* hinunter-/heruntergehen. **(b)** **to be** ~**ed from** abstammen von.
descendant [dɪ'sendənt] *n* **(a)** Nachkomme *m*. **(b)** *(Astron, Astrol)* **in the** ~ im Deszendenten.
descent [dɪ'sent] *n* **(a)** Abstieg *m*. **(b)** *(ancestry)* Abstammung, Herkunft *f*. **(c)** *(fig: into crime etc)* Absinken *nt (into* +acc*)*.
describe [dɪ'skraɪb] *vt* **(a)** beschreiben. **(b)** *(+ as)* bezeichnen. **he** ~**s himself as a doctor** er bezeichnet sich als Arzt.
description [dɪ'skrɪpʃən] *n* **(a)** Beschreibung *f*. **beyond** ~ unbeschreiblich. **(b)** *(+ as)* Bezeichnung *f*. **(c)** *(sort)* **vehicles of every** ~ Fahrzeuge aller Art.
descriptive [dɪ'skrɪptɪv] *adj* **(a)** beschreibend; *account, adjective, passage* anschaulich. **(b)** *linguistics, science etc* deskriptiv.
desecrate ['desɪkreɪt] *vt* entweihen, schänden.
desert[1] ['dezət] **1** *n (lig, fig)* Wüste *f*. **2** *adj attr* Wüsten-. ~ **island** einsame or verlassene Insel.
desert[2] [dɪ'zɜːt] **1** *vt (leave)* verlassen; *cause, party* im Stich lassen. **the place was** ~**ed** es war niemand da. **2** *vi (Mil)* desertieren. **to** ~ **to the rebels** zu den Rebellen überlaufen.
deserter [dɪ'zɜːtəʳ] *n (Mil, fig)* Deserteur *m*.
desertion [dɪ'zɜːʃən] *n* **(a)** *(act)* Verlassen *nt*; *(Mil)* Fahnenflucht *f*. **(b)** *(state)* Verlassenheit *f*.
deserts [dɪ'zɜːts] *npl* **to get one's just** ~ bekommen, was einem zusteht.
deserve [dɪ'zɜːv] *vt* verdienen. **he** ~**s to win** er verdient den Sieg; **he** ~**s to be punished** er verdient es, bestraft zu werden.
deservedly [dɪ'zɜːvɪdlɪ] *adv* verdientermaßen.
deserving [dɪ'zɜːvɪŋ] *adj person, cause* verdienstvoll. **to be** ~ **of sth** etw verdienen.
desiccated ['desɪkeɪtɪd] *adj* getrocknet; *(fig)* vertrocknet.
design [dɪ'zaɪn] **1** *n* **(a)** Design *nt*, Ausführung *f*; *(of plane, machine)* Konstruktion *f*; *(plan: of building etc)* Entwurf *m*. **a new** ~ *(Aut)* ein neues Modell. **(b)** *(pattern)* Muster *nt*. **(c)** *(intention)* Plan *m*, Absicht *f*. **by** ~ absichtlich; **to have** ~**s on sb/sth** es auf jdn/etw abgesehen haben. **2** *vt* **(a)** entwerfen; *machine* konstruieren. **(b)** *(intend)* **to be** ~**ed for sb/sth** für jdn/etw vorgesehen or bestimmt sein.
designate [dɪ'zɪgneɪt] **1** *vt (appoint)* ernennen. **to** ~ **sb as sth** jdn zu etw ernennen. **2** ['dezɪgnɪt] *adj* **the Prime Minister** ~ der desi-

gnierte Premierminister.
designation [,dezɪg'neɪʃən] *n see vt* Bezeichnung; Ernennung *f*.
designer [dɪ'zaɪnə^r] *n* Designer(in *f*) *m*; *(fashion* ~) Modeschöpfer(in *f*) *m*; *(of machines etc)* Konstrukteur(in *f*) *m*; *(Theat)* Bühnenbildner(in *f*) *m*.
desirable [dɪ'zaɪərəbl] *adj* wünschenswert, erwünscht; *position, offer, house, area* reizvoll, attraktiv; *woman* begehrenswert.
desire [dɪ'zaɪə^r] **1** *n (for* nach*)* Wunsch *m*; *(longing)* Sehnsucht *f*; *(sexual)* Verlangen, Begehren *nt*. **I have no** ~ **to see him** ich habe kein Verlangen, ihn zu sehen; **I have no** ~ **to cause you any trouble** ich möchte Ihnen keine Unannehmlichkeiten bereiten. **2** *vt* wünschen; *woman* begehren; *peace* wollen. **it leaves much to be** ~**d** das läßt viel zu wünschen übrig.
desirous [dɪ'zaɪərəs] *adj* **to be** ~ **of sth** *(form)* nach etw verlangen.
desist [dɪ'zɪst] *vi (form)* Abstand nehmen, absehen *(from doing sth* davon, etw zu tun*)*.
desk [desk] *n* Schreibtisch *m*; *(for pupils, master)* Pult *nt*; *(Brit: in shop, restaurant)* Kasse *f*; *(in hotel)* Empfang *m*. **information** ~ Information(sschalter *m*) *f*; ~ **job** *n* Bürojob *m*.
desolate ['desəlɪt] **1** *adj (a) place (devastated)* verwüstet; *(barren)* trostlos; *(fig)* outlook trostlos. **(b)** *(grief-stricken)* tieftraurig, zu Tode betrübt. **2** ['desəleɪt] *vt country* verwüsten.
desolation [,desə'leɪʃən] *n (a) (by war)* Verwüstung *f*. **(b)** *(of landscape, grief)* Trostlosigkeit *f*.
despair [dɪ'speə^r] **1** *n* Verzweiflung *f (about, at* über *+acc)*. **in** ~ **aus** Verzweiflung. **2** *vi* verzweifeln, alle Hoffnung aufgeben. **to** ~ **of doing sth** alle Hoffnung aufgeben, etw zu tun.
despairing [dɪs'peərɪŋ] *adj* verzweifelt.
despatch [dɪ'spætʃ] *vt, n* = **dispatch**.
desperate ['despərɪt] *adj* verzweifelt; *criminal* zum Äußersten entschlossen; *(urgent)* need *etc* dringend; *measures* extrem. **to get** ~ **verzweifeln, in Verzweiflung geraten; **to be** ~ **for sth** etw dringend brauchen; **I'm/it's not that** ~! so dringend ist es nicht!; **I was** ~ **to get the job** ich wollte die Stelle unbedingt haben; **things are getting** ~ die Lage wird allmählich verzweifelt.
desperately ['despərɪtlɪ] *adv* verzweifelt; *(urgently)* need dringend. ~ **in love** verliebt bis über beide Ohren; ~ **ill** schwer krank; **do you want ...?** — **not** ~ möchten Sie ...? — nicht unbedingt.
desperation [,despə'reɪʃən] *n* Verzweiflung *f*. **an act of** ~ eine Verzweiflungstat; **in (sheer)** ~ **aus (reiner) Verzweiflung; **to drive sb to** ~ jdn zur Verzweiflung bringen.
despicable [dɪ'spɪkəbl] *adj* abscheulich.
despise [dɪ'spaɪz] *vt* verachten.
despite [dɪ'spaɪt] *prep* trotz *(+gen)*. ~ **what she says** trotz allem, was sie sagt.
despondency [dɪ'spɒndənsɪ] *n* Niedergeschlagenheit *f*.
despondent [dɪ'spɒndənt] *adj* niedergeschlagen *(about* wegen*)*.
despot ['despɒt] *n (lit, fig)* Despot *m*.
despotic [des'pɒtɪk] *adj (lit, fig)* despotisch.
despotism ['despətɪzəm] *n* Despotie *f*.
dessert [dɪ'zɜːt] *n* Nachtisch *m*, Dessert *nt*. ~**spoon** Dessertlöffel *m*.
destination [,destɪ'neɪʃən] *n* Reiseziel *nt*; *(of goods)* Bestimmungsort *m*.
destined ['destɪnd] *adj* **to be** ~**d to do sth** dazu bestimmt *or* ausersehen sein, etw zu tun; **we were** ~**d to meet** das Schicksal wollte es, daß wir uns begegnen; **I was** ~**d never to see them again** ich sollte sie nie (mehr) wiedersehen; ~ **for** *(ship)* unterwegs nach.
destiny ['destɪnɪ] *n* Schicksal *nt*.
destitute ['destɪtjuːt] *adj (poverty-stricken)* mittellos. **to be utterly** ~ bettelarm sein.

destroy [dɪ'strɔɪ] *vt* zerstören; *documents, manuscripts etc* vernichten; *(fire also)* verwüsten; *(kill)* vernichten; *animal* töten; *influence, hopes, chances* zunichte machen; *reputation* ruinieren.
destroyer [dɪ'strɔɪə^r] *n (Naut)* Zerstörer *m*.
destruction [dɪ'strʌkʃən] *n* Zerstörung *f*; *(of enemy, people, documents)* Vernichtung *f*.
destructive [dɪ'strʌktɪv] *adj* wind, fire, war zerstörerisch; *tendencies, criticism* destruktiv.
desultory ['desəltərɪ] *adj* reading flüchtig; *manner, attempt* halbherzig; *conversation* zwanglos.
detach [dɪ'tætʃ] *vt (separate, unfasten)* lösen *(from* von*)*; *section of form* abtrennen *(from* von*)*; *part of machine, hood* abnehmen *(from* von*)*. **to become** ~**ed from sth** sich lösen von etw.
detachable [dɪ'tætʃəbl] *adj* abnehmbar.
detached [dɪ'tætʃt] *adj* **(a)** *(unbiased)* objektiv; *(unemotional)* kühl, distanziert. **(b)** ~ **house** Einfamilienhaus *nt*.
detachment [dɪ'tætʃmənt] *n* **(a)** *(emotionlessness)* Distanz *f*; *(objectivity)* Abstand *m*. **(b)** *(Mil)* Sonderkommando *nt*, Abordnung *f*.
detail ['diːteɪl] **1** *n* **(a)** Detail *nt*; *(particular)* Einzelheit *f*; *(part of painting, photo etc)* Ausschnitt *m*; *(insignificant circumstance)* unwichtige Einzelheit. **in** ~ im Detail, in Einzelheiten; **in great** ~ in allen Einzelheiten, ausführlich; **there's one little** ~ **you've forgotten** eine Kleinigkeit haben Sie vergessen; **further** ~**s** nähere *or* weitere Einzelheiten; **to go into** ~**s** ins Detail gehen; **his attention to** ~ seine Sorgfalt. **(b)** *(Mil)* Sondertrupp *m*. **2** *vt* **(a)** ausführlich *or* detailliert beschreiben. **(b)** *(Mil)* troops abkommandieren.
detailed ['diːteɪld] *adj* ausführlich, detailliert.
detain [dɪ'teɪn] *vt* aufhalten; *(police)* in Haft nehmen.
detainee [diːteɪ'niː] *n* Häftling *m*.
detect [dɪ'tekt] *vt* entdecken; *(see, make out)* ausfindig machen; *crime* aufdecken; *a tone of sadness, movement* wahrnehmen; *gas* aufspüren.
detection [dɪ'tekʃən] *n* Entdeckung *f*; *(of gases)* Aufspüren *nt*. **to escape** ~ nicht entdeckt werden.
detective [dɪ'tektɪv] *n* Kriminalbeamte(r) *mf*; *(private* ~*)* Detektiv *m*. ~ **story** Kriminalgeschichte *f*, Krimi *(col) m*.
detector [dɪ'tektə^r] *n (Rad, Tech)* Detektor *m*.
détente [deɪ'tɑːnt] *n* Entspannung *f*.
detention [dɪ'tenʃən] *n (captivity)* Haft *f*, Gewahrsam *m*; *(act)* Festnahme *f*; *(Sch)* Nachsitzen *nt*. **he's in** ~ *(Sch)* er muß nachsitzen.
deter [dɪ'tɜː^r] *vt* **to** ~ **sb from doing sth** jdn davon abhalten, etw zu tun.
detergent [dɪ'tɜːdʒənt] *n (soap powder etc)* Waschmittel *nt*.
deteriorate [dɪ'tɪərɪəreɪt] *vi* sich verschlechtern; *(materials)* verschleißen; *(building)* verfallen.
deterioration [dɪ,tɪərɪə'reɪʃən] *n see vi* Verschlechterung *f*; Verschleiß *m*; Verfall *m*.
determination [dɪ,tɜːmɪ'neɪʃən] *n* **(a)** *(firmness)* Entschlossenheit *f*. **(b)** *(establishing)* Determinierung *f*; *(of character, future also)* Bestimmung *f*; *(of cause, nature, position)* Ermittlung, Bestimmung *f*; *(of frontiers)* Festsetzung *f*.
determine [dɪ'tɜːmɪn] *vt* **(a)** *sb's character, future* bestimmen. **(b)** *(settle, fix)* conditions, price festsetzen. **(c)** *(ascertain)* ermitteln, bestimmen. **(d)** *(resolve)* issue entscheiden.
determined [dɪ'tɜːmɪnd] *adj* entschlossen. **he's** ~ **to make me lose my temper** *(col)* er legt es darauf an, mich wütend zu machen.
deterrent [dɪ'terənt] **1** *n* Abschreckungsmittel *nt*. **2** *adj attr* Abschreckungs-.
detest [dɪ'test] *vt* verabscheuen, hassen.
detestable [dɪ'testəbl] *adj* widerwärtig, abscheulich.
detestation [,diːtes'teɪʃən] *n* Abscheu *m (of* vor

+dat).

detonate ['detəneɪt] *vt* zur Explosion bringen.

detonator ['detəneɪtə'] *n* Zünd- *or* Sprengkapsel *f.*

detour ['diːˌtʊə'] *n* Umweg *m; (for traffic)* Umleitung *f.*

detract [dɪ'trækt] *vi* **to ~ from sth** etw beeinträchtigen; *pleasure, merit also* etw schmälern.

detriment ['detrɪmənt] *n* Schaden, Nachteil *m.* **to the ~ of** zum Schaden *(+gen);* **without ~ to** ohne Schaden für.

detrimental [ˌdetrɪ'mentl] *adj (to health, reputation)* schädlich *(to dat); (effect also* nachteilig *(to für); (to case, cause)* abträglich *(to dat).*

deuce [djuːs] *n* **(a)** *(Cards)* Zwei *f.* **(b)** *(Tennis)* Einstand *m.* **(c) why the ~ ...?** *(col)* warum zum Teufel ...? *(col).*

devaluation [ˌdiːvæljʊ'eɪʃən] *n* Abwertung *f.*

devalue [diː'væljuː] *vt* abwerten.

devastate ['devəsteɪt] *vt (lit) town, land* verwüsten; *(fig) opposition* vernichten. **I was ~d** *(col)* das hat mich umgehauen *(col).*

devastating ['devəsteɪtɪŋ] *adj (lit, fig)* verheerend, vernichtend; *news* niederschmetternd; *wit, humour* umwerfend, überwältigend.

devastatingly ['devəsteɪtɪŋlɪ] *adv beautiful, funny* umwerfend.

devastation [ˌdevə'steɪʃən] *n* Verwüstung *f.*

develop [dɪ'veləp] **1** *vt* **(a)** *(also Phot)* entwickeln. **(b)** *idea, thesis* (weiter)entwickeln; *plot of novel (unfold)* entfalten; *(Mus) theme* durchführen. **(c)** *natural resources, region* erschließen; *old part of town* sanieren; *business (expand)* ausbauen; *(from scratch)* aufziehen. **2** *vi* sich entwickeln. **to ~ into sth** sich zu etw entwickeln; **it later ~ed that ...** später stellte sich heraus, daß ...

developer [dɪ'veləpə'] *n* **(a)** = **property ~.** **(b)** *(Phot)* Entwickler *m.* **(c)** late **~** Spätentwickler *m.*

developing [dɪ'veləpɪŋ] **1** *adj crisis, storm* aufkommend; *industry* neu entstehend; *interest* wachsend. **~ country** Entwicklungsland *nt.* **2** *n (Phot)* Entwickeln *nt.*

development [dɪ'veləpmənt] *n* **(a)** Entwicklung *f.* **to await ~s** die Entwicklung abwarten. **(b)** *(of subject, plot etc)* Ausführung *f; (of interests also)* Entfaltung *f; (of argument etc)* (Weiter)entwicklung *f; (Mus)* Durchführung *f.* **(c)** *(of site, new town)* Erschließung *f; (of old part of town)* Sanierung *f; (of industry) (from scratch)* Entwicklung *f; (expansion)* Ausbau *m.* **we live in a new ~** wir leben in einer neuen Siedlung.

deviant ['diːvɪənt] *adj behaviour* abweichend.

deviate ['diːvɪeɪt] *vi* abweichen *(from von).*

deviation [ˌdiːvɪ'eɪʃən] *n* Abweichung *f.*

device [dɪ'vaɪs] *n* **(a)** *(gadget etc)* Gerät *nt; (extra fitment)* Vorrichtung *f.* **nuclear ~** atomarer Sprengkörper. **(b) to leave sb to his own ~s** jdn sich *(dat)* selbst überlassen.

devil ['devl] *n* **(a)** *(lit, fig col)* Teufel *m.* **be a ~!** riskier mal was!; **he's a ~ for changing his mind** er ändert ständig seine Meinung.
    (b) *(col: as intensifier)* **I had the ~ of a job getting here** es war verdammt schwierig, hierher zu kommen; **how/what/why/who the ~ ...?** wie/was/warum/wer zum Teufel ...?; **to work like the ~** wie ein Pferd schuften *(col);* **the ~ of a noise** ein Höllenlärm; **there will be the ~ to pay** das dicke Ende kommt nach.
    (c) *(in expressions)* **(to be) between the D~ and the deep blue sea** (sich) in einer Zwickmühle (befinden); **go to the ~!** *(col)* scher dich zum Teufel! *(col);* **talk of the ~!** wenn man vom Teufel spricht!; **give the ~ his due** das muß der Neid ihm lassen; **to have the ~'s own luck** *(col)* ein Schweineglück *(col or* unverschämtes Glück haben; **better the ~ you know (than the ~ you don't)** *(prov)* von zwei Übeln wählt man besser das, was man schon kennt; **(the) ~ take the**

hindmost den Letzten beißen die Hunde *(Prov).*

devilish ['devlɪʃ] *adj* **(a)** teuflisch. **(b)** *(col: terrible)* schrecklich.

devil-may-care [ˌdevlmeɪ'kɛə'] *adj* leichtsinnig.

devilment ['devlmənt] *n* **out of sheer ~** aus lauter Übermut.

devil's advocate *n* Advocatus Diaboli *m.*

devious ['diːvɪəs] *adj* **(a)** *path, argumentation* gewunden. **by a ~ route** auf einem Umweg. **(b)** *(dishonest)* krumm *(col),* fragwürdig; *person* verschlagen, hinterhältig.

devise [dɪ'vaɪz] *vt* sich *(dat)* ausdenken.

devoid [dɪ'vɔɪd] *adj:* **~ of** bar *(+gen),* ohne.

devolution [ˌdiːvə'luːʃən] *n* Übertragung *f (from ... to* von ... *auf +acc); (Pol)* Dezentralisierung *f.*

devote [dɪ'vəʊt] *vt* widmen *(to dat); resources* bestimmen *(to für).*

devoted [dɪ'vəʊtɪd] *adj* ergeben; *followers, service* treu; *admirer* eifrig. **she's ~ to him/her family** sie liebt ihn/ihre Familie über alles.

devotee [ˌdevəʊ'tiː] *n* Anhänger(in *f) m; (of a writer)* Verehrer(in *f) m; (of music also, poetry)* Liebhaber(in *f) m.*

devotion [dɪ'vəʊʃən] *n (to friend, wife etc)* Ergebenheit *f (to* gegenüber); *(to work)* Hingabe *f (to an +acc).* **~ to duty** Pflichteifer *m.*

devour [dɪ'vaʊə'] *vt (lit, fig)* verschlingen.

devout [dɪ'vaʊt] *adj (+er) person* fromm; *hope* sehnlich(st).

dew [djuː] *n* Tau *m.* **~drop** *n* Tautropfen *m.*

dewy-eyed ['djuːraɪd] *adj (innocent, naive)* naiv; *(trusting)* vertrauensselig. **to go all ~** feuchte Augen bekommen.

dexterity [deks'terɪtɪ] *n* Geschick *nt.*

dext(e)rous ['dekstrəs] *adj (skilful)* geschickt.

DHSS *(Brit)* = **Department of Health and Social Security.**

diabetes [ˌdaɪə'biːtiːz] *n* Diabetes *m,* Zucker *no art (col).*

diabetic [ˌdaɪə'betɪk] **1** *adj* **(a)** zuckerkrank. **(b)** *beer, chocolate* Diabetiker-. **2** *n* Zuckerkranke(r) *mf,* Diabetiker(in *f) m.*

diabolic(al) [ˌdaɪə'bɒlɪk(əl)] *adj* **(a)** diabolisch, teuflisch. **(b)** *(col) weather, heat* saumäßig *(col).*

diadem ['daɪədem] *n* Diadem *nt.*

diagnose ['daɪəgnəʊz] *vt (Med, fig)* diagnostizieren.

diagnosis [ˌdaɪəg'nəʊsɪs] *n, pl* **diagnoses** [ˌdaɪəg'nəʊsiːz] Diagnose *f.*

diagnostic [ˌdaɪəg'nɒstɪk] *adj* diagnostisch.

diagonal [daɪ'ægənl] **1** *adj* diagonal. **2** *n* Diagonale *f.*

diagonally [daɪ'ægənəlɪ] *adv cut, fold* diagonal. **~ across sth** schräg über etw *(acc);* **~ opposite site sth** einer Sache *(dat)* schräg gegenüber.

diagram ['daɪəgræm] *n* Schaubild *nt,* graphische Darstellung *f; (Math)* Diagramm *nt.*

dial ['daɪəl] **1** *n (of clock)* Zifferblatt *nt; (of speedometer, pressure gauge)* Skala *f; (Telec)* Wählscheibe *f.* **2** *vti (Telec)* wählen. **you can ~ London direct** man kann nach London durchwählen; **to ~ 999** den Notruf wählen.

dialect ['daɪəlekt] *n* Dialekt *m; (local, rural also)* Mundart *f.*

dialling ['daɪəlɪŋ]: **~ code** *n* Vorwahl *f;* **~ tone** *n (Brit Telec)* Amtszeichen *nt.*

dialogue ['daɪəlɒg] *n* Dialog *m.*

dialysis [daɪ'æləsɪs] *n* Dialyse *f.*

diameter [daɪ'æmɪtə'] *n* Durchmesser *m.* **it is one metre in ~** es hat einen Durchmesser von einem Meter.

diametrically [ˌdaɪə'metrɪkəlɪ] *adv* **~ opposed (to)** diametral entgegengesetzt *(+dat).*

diamond ['daɪəmənd] *n (a)* Diamant *m.* **~ wedding** *n* diamantene Hochzeit. **(b) ~s** *(Cards)* Karo *nt;* **the King of ~s** der Karokönig.

diaper ['daɪəpə'] *n (US)* Windel *f.*

diaphanous [daɪ'æfənəs] *adj* durchscheinend.

diaphragm ['daɪəfræm] *n* *(Anat, Phys, Med)* Diaphragma *nt*; *(abdominal also)* Zwerchfell *nt*; *(contraceptive also)* Pessar *nt*.

diarrhoea, *(US)* **diarrhea** [ˌdaɪə'riːə] *n* Durchfall *m*. **to have verbal** ~ die Laberkrankheit haben *(col)*.

diary ['daɪərɪ] *n* *(of personal experience)* Tagebuch *nt*; *(for noting dates)* (Termin)kalender *m*.

diatribe ['daɪətraɪb] *n* Schmährede *f*.

dice [daɪs] **1** *n, pl* - Würfel *m*. **2** *vi* **to** ~ **with death** sein Leben riskieren. **3** *vt* *(Cook)* in Würfel schneiden.

dicey ['daɪsɪ] *adj* *(Brit col)* riskant.

dichotomy [dɪ'kɒtəmɪ] *n* Trennung, Dichotomie *f*.

dicky ['dɪkɪ] *adj* *(col)* heart angeknackst *(col)*.

dickybird ['dɪkɪbɜːd] *n* *(baby-talk)* Piepmatz *m* *(baby-talk)*.

dictate [dɪk'teɪt] **1** *vti* diktieren. **2** ['dɪkteɪt] *n usu pl* Diktat *nt*; *(of reason)* Gebote *pl*.

♦ **dictate to** *vi* +*prep obj* person diktieren (+*dat*), Vorschriften machen (+*dat*). **I won't be** ~**d** ~ ich lasse mir keine Vorschriften machen.

dictation [dɪk'teɪʃən] *n* *(also Sch)* Diktat *nt*.

dictator [dɪk'teɪtə'] *n* *(Pol, fig)* Diktator *m*.

dictatorial [ˌdɪktə'tɔːrɪəl] *adj* *(Pol, fig)* diktatorisch.

dictatorship [dɪk'teɪtəʃɪp] *n* *(Pol, fig)* Diktatur *f*.

diction ['dɪkʃən] *n* *(way of speaking)* Diktion *f*.

dictionary ['dɪkʃənrɪ] *n* Wörterbuch *nt*.

did [dɪd] *pret of* **do**.

didactic [dɪ'dæktɪk] *adj* didaktisch.

diddle ['dɪdl] *vt* *(col)* übers Ohr hauen *(col)*.

didn't ['dɪdənt] = **did not**; *see* **do**.

die[1] [daɪ] **1** *vi* **(a)** sterben *(of sth an etw dat)*; *(love)* vergehen; *(memory)* (ent)schwinden; *(custom)* aussterben. **the secret** ~**d with him** er nahm das Geheimnis mit ins Grab; **old habits** ~ **hard** der Mensch ist ein Gewohnheitstier; **to** ~ **of hunger** verhungern; **to be dying im Sterben liegen**; **never say** ~! nur nicht aufgeben!; **to** ~ **laughing** *(col)* sich totlachen *(col)*. **(b) to be dying to do sth** *(fig)* darauf brennen, etw zu tun; **I'm dying to know what happened** ich will unbedingt wissen, was passiert ist. **2** *vt* **to** ~ **a hero's/a violent death** den Heldentod/eines gewaltsamen Todes sterben.

♦ **die away** *vi* *(sound, voice)* leiser werden; *(wind, anger)* sich legen.

♦ **die down** *vi* nachlassen; *(fire)* herunterbrennen; *(storm, wind also)* sich legen.

♦ **die off** *vi* wegsterben.

♦ **die out** *vi* aussterben.

die[2] *n, pl* **dice**: **the** ~ **is cast** *(fig)* die Würfel sind gefallen.

die-hard ['daɪhɑːd] *adj* zäh; *(pej)* reaktionär; *conservative* Erz-.

diesel ['diːzəl] *n* *(fuel)* Dieselöl *nt*, Diesel *no art*.

diesel: ~ **engine** *n* Dieselmotor *m*; ~ **oil** *n* Dieselkraftstoff *m*; ~ **train** *n* Dieseltriebwagen *m*.

diet ['daɪət] **1** *n* Ernährung *f*; *(special* ~*)* Diät *f*; *(slimming* ~*)* Abmagerungs- *or* Schlankheitskur *f*. **to be/go on a** ~ eine Schlankheitskur machen. **2** *vi* eine Schlankheitskur machen.

dietician [ˌdaɪə'tɪʃən] *n* Ernährungswissenschaftler(in *f*) *m*; *(in hospital)* Diätassistent(in *f*) *m*.

differ ['dɪfə'] *vi* **(a)** *(be different)* sich unterscheiden *(from* von*)*. **tastes** ~ die Geschmäcker sind verschieden. **(b)** *(disagree)* **to** ~ **with sb over sth** über etw *(acc)* anderer Meinung sein als jd.

difference ['dɪfrəns] *n* **(a)** Unterschied *m* *(in, between* zwischen +*dat)*. **that makes a big** ~ **to me** das ist für mich eine große Unterschied; **that makes a big** ~ das ändert die Sache völlig; **what** ~ **does it make if ...?** was macht es schon, wenn ...?; **what** ~ **is that to you?** was macht dir das aus?; **it makes no** ~ **to me** das ist mir egal; **cooperation**

makes all the ~ gute Zusammenarbeit ist alles; **a car with a** ~ *(col)* das besondere Auto. **(b)** *(between numbers, amounts)* Differenz *f*. **(c)** *(quarrel)* **a** ~ **of opinion** eine Meinungsverschiedenheit; **to settle one's** ~**s** die Meinungsverschiedenheiten beilegen.

different ['dɪfrənt] *adj* andere(r, s), anders *pred* *(from, to* als*)*; *two people, things* verschieden, unterschiedlich. **completely** ~ völlig verschieden; *(changed)* völlig verändert; **that's** ~! das ist was anderes!; **in what way are they** ~? worin unterscheiden sie sich?

differential [ˌdɪfə'renʃəl] *n* **(a)** *(difference)* Unterschied *m*. **wage** ~ Gehaltsunterschiede *pl*. **(b)** *(Aut)* Differential(getriebe) *nt*.

differentiate [ˌdɪfə'renʃɪeɪt] *vti* unterscheiden. **to** ~ **between people** einen Unterschied zwischen Menschen machen.

differently ['dɪfrəntlɪ] *adv* anders *(from* als*)*; *(from one another)* verschieden, unterschiedlich.

difficult ['dɪfɪkəlt] *adj* schwierig, schwer; *writer* kompliziert, schwierig; *neighbour, child* schwierig. **I find it** ~ **to believe that** es fällt mir schwer, das zu glauben; **he's just trying to be** ~ er will nur Schwierigkeiten machen; **she is** ~ **to get on with** es ist schwer, mit ihr auszukommen.

difficulty ['dɪfɪkəltɪ] *n* Schwierigkeit *f*. **with/without** ~ mit/ohne Schwierigkeiten *pl*; **a slight** ~ **in breathing** leichte Atembeschwerden *pl*; **there was some** ~ **in finding him** es war schwierig, ihn zu finden; **to get into difficulties** in Schwierigkeiten geraten.

diffidence ['dɪfɪdəns] *n* Bescheidenheit *f*.

diffident ['dɪfɪdənt] *adj* bescheiden; *smile* zaghaft.

diffuse [dɪ'fjuːz] **1** *vt* ausstrahlen; *light* streuen; *knowledge, news* verbreiten. **2** [dɪ'fjuːs] *adj* *(verbose)* style, writer langatmig, weitschweifig.

diffusion [dɪ'fjuːʒən] *n* Ausbreitung *f*; *(of light)* Streuung *f*; *(of knowledge, news)* Verbreitung *f*.

dig [dɪg] *(vb: pret, ptp* **dug**) **1** *vt* **(a)** *ground* graben. **(b)** *(poke, thrust)* bohren *(sth into sth etw in etw acc)*. **(c)** *(col)* *(enjoy)* stehen auf (+*acc)*; *(understand)* kapieren *(col)*. **2** *vi* graben; *(dog, pig also)* wühlen; *(Tech)* schürfen; *(Archeol)* Ausgrabungen machen. **to** ~ **in one's pockets for sth** in seinen Taschen nach etw suchen *or* wühlen. **3** *n* **(a) to give sb a** ~ **in the ribs** jdm einen Rippenstoß geben. **(b)** *(sarcastic remark)* Seitenhieb *m*, Spitze *f*. **to have a** ~ **at sb/sth** eine Spitze gegen jdn loslassen *(col)*. **(c)** *(Archeol)* (Aus)grabung *f*; *(site)* Ausgrabungsstätte *f*.

♦ **dig in 1** *vi* **(a)** *(also* ~ **oneself** ~*)* *(Mil, fig)* sich eingraben. **(b)** *(col: eat)* reinhauen *(col)*. **2** *vt sep* compost untergraben. **to** ~ **one's heels in** *(fig)* sich stur stellen.

♦ **dig out** *vt sep* *(lit, fig)* ausgraben *(of* aus*)*.

♦ **dig up** *vt sep* *(lit, fig)* ausgraben; *earth* aufwühlen; *lawn, garden* umgraben; *weeds* jäten. **where did you** ~ **her** ~? *(col)* wo hast du die denn aufgegabelt *(col)*.

digest [daɪ'dʒest] **1** *vt* *(lig, fig)* verdauen. **2** ['daɪdʒest] *n* *(of book, facts)* Zusammenfassung *f*.

digestible [dɪ'dʒestəbl] *adj* verdaulich.

digestion [dɪ'dʒestʃən] *n* Verdauung *f*.

digestive [dɪ'dʒestɪv] *adj* Verdauungs-. ~ **(biscuit)** *(Brit)* Keks *m* aus Vollkornschrot.

digit ['dɪdʒɪt] *n* *(Math)* Ziffer *f*.

digital ['dɪdʒɪtəl] *adj* Digital-, digital.

dignified ['dɪgnɪfaɪd] *adj* person würdig; *behaviour, manner* würdevoll.

dignitary ['dɪgnɪtərɪ] *n* Würdenträger(in *f*) *m*. **the local dignitaries** die Honoratioren am Ort.

dignity ['dɪgnɪtɪ] *n* Würde *f*. **that would be beneath my** ~ das wäre unter meiner Würde.

digress [daɪ'gres] *vi* abschweifen.

digression [daɪ'greʃən] *n* Abschweifung *f*, Exkurs *(geh)* *m*.

digs [dɪgz] npl (Brit) Bude f (col). **to be in ~** ein möbliertes Zimmer or eine Bude (col) haben.

dike [daɪk] n, vt = **dyke**.

dilapidated [dɪ'læpɪdeɪtɪd] adj house verfallen, baufällig; clothes verschlissen, schäbig.

dilapidation [dɪ,læpɪ'deɪʃən] n Baufälligkeit f, Verfall m.

dilate [daɪ'leɪt] **1** vt weiten. **2** vi (pupils) sich erweitern.

dilation [daɪ'leɪʃən] n (of pupils) Erweiterung f.

dilatory ['dɪlətərɪ] adj **(a)** person langsam; reply verspätet. **to be ~** sich (dat) Zeit lassen. **(b)** action, policy Verzögerungs-, Hinhalte-.

dilemma [daɪ'lemə] n Dilemma nt. **to be in a ~** sich in einem Dilemma befinden, in der Klemme sitzen (col).

dilettante [,dɪlɪ'tæntɪ] m, pl **dilettanti** [,dɪlɪ'tæntɪ] Amateur(in f), Dilettant(in f) m.

diligence ['dɪlɪdʒəns] n Eifer m; (in work also) Fleiß m.

diligent ['dɪlɪdʒənt] adj person eifrig; (in work also) fleißig; search, work sorgfältig, genau.

dilute [daɪ'luːt] vt orange juice etc verdünnen; (fig) mildern, (ab)schwächen.

dim [dɪm] **1** adj (+er) **(a)** light, eyesight, sound schwach; colour matt; memory, outline, shape verschwommen. **the room grew ~** im Zimmer wurde es dunkel. **(b)** (col: stupid) schwer von Begriff. **(c)** (col) **to take a ~ view of sb/sth** nicht viel von jdm/etw halten. **2** vt light abdunkeln. **to ~ one's headlights** (esp US) abblenden. **3** vi (lamps) schwächer werden; (memory) nachlassen.

dime [daɪm] n (US) Zehncentstück nt.

dimension [daɪ'menʃən] n Dimension f; (measurement) Abmessung(en pl) f, Maß nt. **-dimensional** [-daɪ'menʃənl] adj suf -dimensional.

diminish [dɪ'mɪnɪʃ] **1** vt verringern, herabsetzen; value mindern. **~ed responsibility** (Jur) verminderte Zurechnungsfähigkeit; **~ed** (Mus) vermindert. **2** vi sich verringern; (authority, strength also) abnehmen; (value also) sich vermindern.

diminutive [dɪ'mɪnjʊtɪv] **1** adj winzig, klein. **2** n (Gram) Verkleinerungsform f, Diminutiv(um) nt.

dimly ['dɪmlɪ] adv shine schwach; hear, remember also undeutlich; see verschwommen.

dimple ['dɪmpl] n (on cheek, chin) Grübchen nt.

din [dɪn] **1** n Lärm m, Getöse nt. **2** vt **to ~ sth into sb** jdm etw einbleuen.

dine [daɪn] **1** vi speisen, dinieren (geh) (on etw). **2** vt bewirten, beköstigen.

diner ['daɪnər] n **(a)** (person) Speisende(r) mf; (in restaurant) Gast m. **(b)** (US) Eßlokal nt. **(c)** (Rail) Speisewagen m.

dinghy ['dɪŋgɪ] n Ding(h)i nt; (collapsible) Schlauchboot nt.

dingo ['dɪŋgəʊ] n Dingo m, australischer Wildhund.

dingy ['dɪndʒɪ] adj place, furniture schmuddelig.

dining ['daɪnɪŋ]: **~ car** n Speisewagen m; **~ room** n Eßzimmer nt; (in hotel) Speiseraum m; **~ table** n Eßtisch m.

dinner ['dɪnər] n (Haupt)mahlzeit f, Abendessen nt; (formal) (Abend)essen nt; (lunch) Mittagessen nt. **to be at ~** beim Essen sein.

dinner: ~ jacket n Smokingjacke f; **~ party** n Abendgesellschaft f (mit Essen); **to have a small ~ party** ein kleines Essen geben; **~ service** n Tafelservice nt.

dinosaur ['daɪnəsɔːr] n Dinosaurier m.

dint [dɪnt] n **by ~ of** durch.

diocese ['daɪəsɪs] n Diözese f, Bistum nt.

diode ['daɪəʊd] n Diode f.

dioxide [daɪ'ɒksaɪd] n Dioxyd nt.

dip [dɪp] **1** vt **(a)** (in(to) in +acc) (into liquid) tauchen; pen, hand eintauchen; bread (ein)tunken,

stippen (col). **(b)** (into bag, basket) hand stecken. **(c)** (Brit Aut) headlights abblenden. **2** vi (ground) sich senken; (temperature, pointer on scale) fallen. **the sun ~ped behind the mountains** die Sonne verschwand hinter den Bergen. **3** n **(a)** (swim) **to go for a ~** kurz schwimmen gehen. **(b)** (for cleaning animals) Desinfektionslösung f. **(c)** (in ground) Mulde f. **(d)** (Cook) Dip m.

♦ dip into vi +prep obj (a) (lit) **she ~ped ~ her** handbag sie griff in ihre Handtasche. **(b) to ~ ~** one's savings an seine Ersparnisse gehen. **(c)** book einen kurzen Blick werfen in (+acc).

diphtheria [dɪf'θɪərɪə] n Diphtherie f.

diphthong ['dɪfθɒŋ] n Diphthong m.

diploma [dɪ'pləʊmə] n Diplom nt.

diplomacy [dɪ'pləʊməsɪ] n (Pol, fig) Diplomatie f.

diplomat ['dɪpləmæt] n (Pol, fig) Diplomat m.

diplomatic [,dɪplə'mætɪk] adj (lit, fig) diplomatisch.

diplomatic: ~ bag n Diplomatenpost f; **~ corps** n diplomatisches Korps; **~ immunity** n Immunität f; **~ service** n diplomatischer Dienst.

dipsomania [,dɪpsəʊ'meɪnɪə] n Trunksucht f.

dipsomaniac [,dɪpsəʊ'meɪnɪæk] n Trunksüchtige(r) mf.

dipstick ['dɪpstɪk] n Ölmeßstab m.

dire [daɪər] adj schrecklich, furchtbar; poverty äußerste(r, s). **~ necessity** dringende Notwendigkeit; **to be in ~ need of sth** etw dringend brauchen.

direct [daɪ'rekt] **1** adj direkt; train durchgehend; opposite genau. **~ current** Gleichstrom m; **~ hit** Volltreffer m; **~ object** direktes Objekt, Akkusativobjekt nt; **~ speech** direkte Rede. **2** vt **(a)** (address, aim) remark, letter richten (to an +acc); efforts richten (towards auf +acc). **can you ~ me to the town hall?** können Sie mir sagen, wie ich zum Rathaus komme? **(b)** person's work, business leiten, lenken; traffic regeln. **(c)** (order) anweisen (sb to do sth jdn, etw zu tun), befehlen (sb to do sth jdm, etw zu tun); (Jur) jury Rechtsbelehrung erteilen (+dat). **(d)** film, play Regie führen bei; radio/TV programme leiten. **3** adv direkt.

direction [dɪ'rekʃən] n **(a)** (lit, fig: way) Richtung f. **in the wrong/right ~** (of sth) in die falsche/richtige Richtung; **in the ~ of Hamburg** in Richtung Hamburg; **a sense of ~** (lit) Orientierungssinn m; (fig) ein Ziel nt (im Leben). **(b)** (management: of company etc) Leitung f. **(c)** (of film, actors) Regie f; (of radio/TV programme) Leitung f. **(d)** **~s** pl (instructions) Anweisungen pl; (to a place) Angaben pl; (for use) (Gebrauchs)anweisung f.

directive [dɪ'rektɪv] n Direktive, Weisung f.

directly [dɪ'rektlɪ] **1** adv direkt, unmittelbar; (in a short time) sofort, gleich. **2** conj sobald. **he'll come ~ he's ready** er kommt, sobald er fertig ist.

directness [daɪ'rektnɪs] n Direktheit f.

director [dɪ'rektər] n **(a)** (of company) Direktor, Leiter m; (Univ) Rektor m. **(b)** (Rad, TV) Direktor m; (Film, Theat) Regisseur m.

directory [dɪ'rektərɪ] n Adreßbuch nt; (telephone ~) Telefonbuch nt; (trade ~) Branchenverzeichnis nt; **~ enquiries** or (US) **assistance** (Telec) (Fernsprech)auskunft f.

dirge [dɜːdʒ] n Klagegesang m.

dirt [dɜːt] n (lit, fig) Schmutz, Dreck m; (soil) Erde f. **to treat sb like ~** jdn wie (den letzten) Dreck behandeln (col).

dirt cheap ['dɜːt'tʃiːp] adj, adv (col) spottbillig.

dirty ['dɜːtɪ] **1** adj (+er) **(a)** schmutzig; wound verschmutzt. **~ weather** Sauwetter nt (col); **to give sb a ~ look** (col) jdm einen bösen Blick zuwerfen. **(b)** (fig: obscene) schmutzig, unanständig; story, joke also zotig. **to have a ~ mind** eine schmutzige Phantasie haben; **~ old man** geiler Bock (col!); **they're having a ~ weekend**

(col) sie sind zusammen übers Wochenende weggefahren. **2** *vt* beschmutzen. **3** *n* **to do the ~ on sb** *(Brit col)* jdn reinlegen *(col)*.

disability [͵dɪsə'bɪlɪtɪ] *n* Behinderung *f*. **~ pension** *n* Invalidenrente *f*.

disable [dɪs'eɪbl] *vt* *tank*, *gun* unbrauchbar machen; *ship* kampfunfähig machen.

disabled [dɪs'eɪbld] **1** *adj* **(a)** behindert. **(b)** *tank*, *gun* unbrauchbar; *ship* nicht seetüchtig. **2** *npl* the **~ die** Behinderten *pl*.

disadvantage [͵dɪsəd'vɑːntɪdʒ] *n* Nachteil *m*. **to his ~** zu seinem Nachteil. **to be at a ~** sich im Nachteil befinden, benachteiligt sein.

disadvantaged [dɪsəd'vɑːntɪdʒd] *adj* benachteiligt.

disadvantageous *adj* [͵dɪsædvɑːn'teɪdʒəs] nachteilig.

disagree [͵dɪsə'griː] *vi* **(a)** *(with person, views, figures)* nicht übereinstimmen; *(with plan, suggestion etc)* nicht einverstanden sein; *(two people)* sich nicht einig sein. **(b)** *(quarrel)* eine Meinungsverschiedenheit haben. **(c)** *(climate, food)* **to ~ with sb** jdm nicht bekommen.

disagreeable [͵dɪsə'griːəbl] *adj* unangenehm; *person* unsympathisch.

disagreement [͵dɪsə'griːmənt] *n* **(a)** *(with opinion, between opinions)* Uneinigkeit *f*. **(b)** *(quarrel)* Meinungsverschiedenheit *f*. **(c)** *(between reports)* Diskrepanz *f*.

disallow [͵dɪsə'laʊ] *vt* *evidence*, *goal* nicht anerkennen; *claim also* zurückweisen.

disappear [͵dɪsə'pɪəʳ] *vi* verschwinden.

disappearance [͵dɪsə'pɪərəns] *n* Verschwinden *nt*.

disappoint [͵dɪsə'pɔɪnt] *vt* enttäuschen.

disappointed [͵dɪsə'pɔɪntɪd] *adj* enttäuscht.

disappointing [͵dɪsə'pɔɪntɪŋ] *adj* enttäuschend.

disappointment [͵dɪsə'pɔɪntmənt] *n* Enttäuschung *f*.

disapproval [͵dɪsə'pruːvl] *n* Mißbilligung *f*.

disapprove [͵dɪsə'pruːv] **1** *vt* mißbilligen. **2** *vi* dagegen sein. **he ~s of children smoking** er mißbilligt es, wenn Kinder rauchen.

disapproving [͵dɪsə'pruːvɪŋ] *adj* mißbilligend.

disarm [dɪs'ɑːm] **1** *vt* *(lit, fig)* entwaffnen. **2** *vi* *(Mil)* abrüsten.

disarmament [dɪs'ɑːməmənt] *n* Abrüstung *f*.

disarray [͵dɪsə'reɪ] *n* Unordnung *f*.

disaster [dɪ'zɑːstəʳ] *n* Katastrophe *f*; *(Aviat, Min, Rail also)* Unglück *nt*. **~ area** Katastrophengebiet *nt*.

disastrous [dɪ'zɑːstrəs] *adj* katastrophal.

disband [dɪs'bænd] **1** *vt* auflösen. **2** *vi* *(soldiers, club members)* auseinandergehen.

disbelief ['dɪsbə'liːf] *n* in **~** ungläubig.

disbelieve ['dɪsbə'liːv] *vt* nicht glauben.

disc, *(esp US)* **disk** [dɪsk] *n* **(a)** Scheibe *f*; *(Anat)* Bandscheibe *f*. **(b)** *(record)* Platte *f*. **(c)** *(Comp)* Diskette *f*.

discard [dɪ'skɑːd] *vt* *unwanted article* ausrangieren; *person* abschieben; *idea, plan* verwerfen.

disc brake *n* Scheibenbremse *f*.

discern [dɪ'sɜːn] *vt* erkennen.

discerning [dɪ'sɜːnɪŋ] *adj* *clientele, reader* anspruchsvoll, kritisch. **to the ~ eye** für den Kenner.

discernment [dɪ'sɜːnmənt] *n* *(ability to discern)* feines Gespür. **a man of ~** ein Mann mit Geschmack.

discharge [dɪs'tʃɑːdʒ] **1** *vt* **(a)** *prisoner, patient, soldier* entlassen; *accused* freisprechen. **(b)** *(emit)* *(Elec)* entladen; *liquid, gas* (pipe etc) ausstoßen; *(Med)* absondern. **(c)** *(unload)* *ship, cargo* löschen. **(d)** *(gun)* abfeuern. **(e)** *debt* begleichen; *obligation, duty* nachkommen *(+dat)*; *function* erfüllen. **2** *vi* *(wound, sore)* eitern. **3** ['dɪstʃɑːdʒ] *n* **(a)** *(dismissal)* *see vt (a)* Entlassung *f*; Freispruch *m*; *(of soldier)* Abschied *m*. **(b)** *(Elec)*

Entladung *f*; *(of gas)* Ausströmen *nt*; *(of liquid, Med: vaginal ~)* Ausfluß *m*; *(of pus)* Absonderung *f*. **(c)** *(of debt)* Begleichung *f*; *(of obligation, duty, function)* Erfüllung *f*.

disciple [dɪ'saɪpl] *n* *(lit, fig)* Jünger *m*.

disciplinary ['dɪsɪplɪnərɪ] *adj* Disziplinar-, disziplinarisch. **to take ~ action against sb** ein Disziplinarverfahren gegen jdn einleiten.

discipline ['dɪsɪplɪn] **1** *n* Disziplin *f*. **2** *vt* **(a)** *(train, make obedient)* disziplinieren. **(b)** *(punish)* bestrafen; *(physically)* züchtigen.

disc jockey *n* Diskjockey *m*.

disclaim [dɪs'kleɪm] *vt* abstreiten.

disclaimer [dɪs'kleɪməʳ] *n* Dementi *nt*.

disclose [dɪs'kləʊz] *vt* *secret* enthüllen; *intentions, news* bekanntgeben.

disclosure [dɪs'kləʊʒəʳ] *n* **(a)** *see vt* Enthüllung *f*; Bekanntgabe *f*. **(b)** *(fact revealed)* Mitteilung *f*.

disco ['dɪskəʊ] *n* Disko *f*.

discoloration [dɪs͵kʌlə'reɪʃən] *n* *(mark)* Verfärbung *f*.

discomfort [dɪs'kʌmfət] *n* *(lit)* Beschwerden *pl*; *(fig: uneasiness, embarrassment)* Unbehagen *nt*.

disconcert [͵dɪskən'sɜːt] *vt* aus der Fassung bringen.

disconnect ['dɪskə'nekt] *vt* *pipe etc* trennen; *(cut off supply of)* *gas, electricity* abstellen. **I've been ~ed** *(for non-payment)* man hat mir das Telefon/den Strom/das Gas etc abgestellt. **to ~ an appliance** den Stecker eines Geräts herausziehen.

disconsolate [dɪs'kɒnsəlɪt] *adj* niedergeschlagen.

discontent ['dɪskən'tent] *n* Unzufriedenheit *f*.

discontent(ed) ['dɪskən'tent(ɪd)] *adj* unzufrieden *(with, about mit)*.

discontinue ['dɪskən'tɪnjuː] *vt* aufgeben; *class, project, conversation* abbrechen; *(Comm)* *line* auslaufen lassen.

discord ['dɪskɔːd] *n* **(a)** Uneinigkeit *f*. **(b)** *(Mus)* Dissonanz *f*.

discordant [dɪs'kɔːdənt] *adj* *meeting, atmosphere* unharmonisch; *(Mus)* dissonant.

discotheque [dɪskə'utek] *n* Diskothek *f*.

discount ['dɪskaʊnt] **1** *n* Rabatt *m*; *(for cash)* Skonto *nt or m*. **to give a ~ on sth** Rabatt on etw *(acc)* geben. **2** *vt* **(a)** *(Comm)* nachlassen. **(b)** [dɪs'kaʊnt] *(dismiss)* abtun; *person's opinion* unberücksichtigt lassen.

discourage [dɪs'kʌrɪdʒ] *vt* **(a)** *(dishearten)* entmutigen. **(b)** *(dissuade)* **to ~ sb from sth** jdm von etw abraten; *(successfully)* jdn von etw abbringen.

discouragement [dɪs'kʌrɪdʒmənt] *n* **(a)** *(depression)* Mutlosigkeit *f*. **(b)** **to be a ~** entmutigend sein.

discouraging [dɪs'kʌrɪdʒɪŋ] *adj* entmutigend.

discourteous [dɪs'kɜːtɪəs] *adj* unhöflich.

discourtesy [dɪs'kɜːtɪsɪ] *n* Unhöflichkeit *f*.

discover [dɪs'kʌvəʳ] *vt* entdecken; *(notice)* mistake, loss also festellen, bemerken.

discovery [dɪs'kʌvərɪ] *n* Entdeckung *f*.

discredit [dɪs'kredɪt] **1** *vt* **(a)** *report, theory* in Mißkredit bringen. **(b)** *(disbelieve)* keinen Glauben schenken *(+dat)*. **2** *n* **(a)** *no pl* **to bring ~ on sb** jdn in Mißkredit bringen. **(b)** **to be a ~ to sb** eine Schande für jdn sein.

discreet [dɪs'kriːt] *adj* diskret; *(in quiet taste also)* dezent.

discrepancy [dɪs'krepənsɪ] *n* Diskrepanz *f* *(between zwischen +dat)*.

discretion [dɪs'kreʃən] *n* **(a)** Diskretion *f*. **(b)** **to leave sth to sb's ~** etw jdm anheimstellen; **use your own ~** es steht in Ihrem Ermessen.

discriminate [dɪs'krɪmɪneɪt] *vi* **(a)** *(distinguish)* unterscheiden *(between zwischen +dat)*. **(b)** **to ~ against/in favour of sb** jdn diskriminieren/ bevorzugen.

discriminating [dɪs'krɪmɪneɪtɪŋ] *adj* *person, judgement, mind* kritisch.

discrimination [dɪˌskrɪmɪ'neɪʃən] n (a) Diskriminierung f. racial ~ Rassendiskriminierung f; sexual ~ Diskriminierung auf Grund des Geschlechts. **(b)** *(discernment)* kritisches Urteilsvermögen.

discus ['dɪskəs] n Diskus m.

discuss [dɪ'skʌs] vt besprechen; *politics, theory* erörtern, diskutieren.

discussion [dɪ'skʌʃən] n Diskussion f; *(meeting)* Besprechung f.

disdain [dɪs'deɪn] **1** vt verachten. he ~ed to notice them er hielt es für unter seiner Würde, ihnen Beachtung zu schenken. **2** n Verachtung f.

disease [dɪ'ziːz] n *(lit, fig)* Krankheit f.

diseased [dɪ'ziːzd] adj *(lit, fig)* krank.

disembark [ˌdɪsɪm'bɑːk] **1** vt ausschiffen. **2** vi von Bord gehen.

disembarkation [ˌdɪsembɑː'keɪʃən] n Landung f.

disembodied ['dɪsɪm'bɒdɪd] adj körperlos; *voice* geisterhaft.

disenchanted ['dɪsɪn'tʃɑːntɪd] adj to be ~ with sb/sth von jdm/etw enttäuscht sein; I've become ~ with it ich halte nicht mehr viel davon.

disengage [ˌdɪsɪn'geɪdʒ] vt o ~ the clutch *(Aut)* auskuppeln.

disentangle ['dɪsɪn'tæŋgl] vt *(lit, fig)* entwirren.

disfavour, *(US)* **disfavor** [dɪs'feɪvər] n *(displeasure)* Ungnade f; *(dislike)* Mißfallen nt. to fall into/be in ~ in Ungnade fallen/sein *(with bei)*.

disfigure [dɪs'fɪgər] vt verunstalten; *person also* entstellen.

disfigurement [dɪs'fɪgəmənt] n *see vt* Verunstaltung f; Entstellung f.

disgorge [dɪs'gɔːdʒ] vt ausspeien.

disgrace [dɪs'greɪs] **1** n Schande f; *(person)* Schandfleck m *(to gen)*. to be in/fall into ~ in Ungnade (gefallen) sein/fallen *(with bei)*. **2** vt Schande machen *(+dat)*; *country, family also* Schande bringen über *(+acc)*. to ~ oneself sich blamieren.

disgraceful [dɪs'greɪsfʊl] adj erbärmlich *(schlecht)*; *behaviour, performance* skandalös.

disgruntled [dɪs'grʌntld] adj verstimmt.

disguise [dɪs'gaɪz] **1** vt verkleiden; *voice* verstellen; *interest, feelings* verbergen. there's no disguising the fact that ... es läßt sich nicht verhehlen, daß ... **2** n *(lit)* Verkleidung f; *(fig)* Deckmantel m. in ~ verkleidet.

disgust [dɪs'gʌst] **1** n Ekel m; *(at sb's behaviour)* Entrüstung f, Empörung f. **2** vt *(person, sight)* anekeln, anwidern; *(actions)* empören.

disgusted [dɪs'gʌstɪd] adj angeekelt; *(at sb's behaviour)* empört. I am ~ with you ich bin empört über dich.

disgusting [dɪs'gʌstɪŋ] adj widerlich; *(physically nauseating also)* ekelhaft. that's ~ das ist eine Schweinerei *(col)*.

dish [dɪʃ] n **(a)** Schale f; *(for serving also)* Schüssel f. **(b)** ~es pl *(crockery)* Geschirr nt; to do the ~es abwaschen. **(c)** *(food)* Gericht nt.

♦ **dish out** vt sep *(col)* austeilen.

♦ **dish up** vt sep *(lit, fig)* auftischen.

disharmony ['dɪs'hɑːmənɪ] n *(lit, fig)* Disharmonie f.

dishcloth ['dɪʃklɒθ] n Geschirrtuch nt; *(for washing)* Spültuch nt.

dishearten [dɪs'hɑːtn] vt entmutigen. don't be ~ed nur Mut.

disheartening [dɪs'hɑːtnɪŋ] adj entmutigend.

dished [dɪʃt] adj *(Tech)* konkav (gewölbt); *wheels* gestürzt.

dishevelled, *(US)* **disheveled** [dɪ'ʃevəld] adj ramponiert *(col)*, unordentlich; *hair* zerzaust.

dishonest [dɪs'ɒnɪst] adj unehrlich.

dishonesty [dɪs'ɒnɪstɪ] n Unehrlichkeit f.

dishonour, *(US)* **dishonor** [dɪs'ɒnər] n Schande f. to bring ~ upon sb Schande über jdn bringen.

dishonourable, *(US)* **dishonorable** [dɪs'ɒnərəbl]

---

adj unehrenhaft.

dish: ~washer n *(person)* Tellerwäscher(in f) m; *(machine)* Geschirrspülmaschine f; ~water n Abwasch- or Spülwasser nt; this coffee is like ~water der Kaffee schmeckt wie Spülwasser.

dishy ['dɪʃɪ] adj *(+er)* *(Brit col)* dufte *(col)*.

disillusion [ˌdɪsɪ'luːʒən] vt desillusionieren.

disillusionment [ˌdɪsɪ'luːʒənmənt] n Desillusionierung f.

disincentive [ˌdɪsɪn'sentɪv] n Entmutigung f. it acts as a ~ es wirkt abschreckend.

disinclination [ˌdɪsɪnklɪ'neɪʃən] n Abneigung, Unlust f.

disinclined ['dɪsɪn'klaɪnd] adj abgeneigt.

disinfect [ˌdɪsɪn'fekt] vt desinfizieren.

disinfectant [dɪsɪn'fektənt] n Desinfektionsmittel nt.

disinherit ['dɪsɪn'herɪt] vt enterben.

disintegrate [dɪs'ɪntɪgreɪt] vi zerfallen; *(rock, cement)* auseinanderbröckeln; *(car)* sich in seine Bestandteile auflösen; *(group also, institution)* sich auflösen.

disintegration [dɪsˌɪntɪ'greɪʃən] n *see vi* Zerfall m; Auseinanderbröckeln nt; Auflösung f.

disinterested [dɪs'ɪntrɪstɪd] adj *(unbiased)* unvoreingenommen.

disjointed adj [dɪs'dʒɔɪntɪd] zusammenhanglos.

disk n [dɪsk] *(Comp)* Diskette f; *(video etc)* Platte f. ~ drive Diskettenlaufwerk nt; hard ~ Festplatte f.

diskette [dɪs'ket] n Diskette f.

dislike [dɪs'laɪk] **1** vt nicht mögen, nicht gern haben. to ~ doing sth etw ungern tun. I don't ~ him ich habe nichts gegen ihn. **2** n Abneigung f *(of* gegen). to take a ~ to sb/sth eine Abneigung gegen jdn/etw entwickeln.

dislocate [dɪs'ləʊkeɪt] vt *(Med)* verrenken; *(fig)* plans durcheinanderbringen. to ~ one's shoulder sich *(dat)* den Arm auskugeln.

dislodge [dɪs'lɒdʒ] vt *obstruction, stone* entfernen; *(accidentally)* verschieben; *enemy* verdrängen.

disloyal [dɪs'lɔɪəl] adj treulos; *(esp Pol)* illoyal *(to* gegenüber).

disloyalty [dɪs'lɔɪəltɪ] n Treulosigkeit f; *(esp Pol)* Illoyalität f *(to* gegenüber).

dismal ['dɪzməl] adj trübe, trist; *person* trübsinnig; *failure, result* kläglich.

dismantle [dɪs'mæntl] vt auseinandernehmen; *scaffolding* abbauen; *(fig)* system demontieren.

dismay [dɪs'meɪ] **1** n Bestürzung f. in ~ bestürzt. **2** vt bestürzen.

dismiss [dɪs'mɪs] vt **(a)** *(from job)* entlassen. **(b)** *(allow to go)* entlassen; *assembly* auflösen. **(c)** *objection* abtun. **(d)** *(Jur)* accused entlassen; appeal abweisen. to ~ a case eine Klage abweisen.

dismissal [dɪs'mɪsəl] n Entlassung f; *(of assembly)* Auflösung f; *(of objection)* Zurückweisung f; *(of appeal)* Abweisung f.

dismount [dɪs'maʊnt] vi absteigen.

disobedience [ˌdɪsə'biːdɪəns] n Ungehorsam m *(to* gegenüber).

disobedient [ˌdɪsə'biːdɪənt] adj ungehorsam.

disobey ['dɪsə'beɪ] vt nicht gehorchen *(+dat)*; *rule* übertreten.

disobliging [ˌdɪsə'blaɪdʒɪŋ] adj ungefällig.

disorder [dɪs'ɔːdər] n **(a)** Durcheinander nt; *(in room etc also)* Unordnung f. in ~ durcheinander; in Unordnung. **(b)** *(rioting)* Unruhen pl. **(c)** *(Med)* Störung f.

disordered [dɪs'ɔːdəd] adj *room, thoughts* unordentlich; *plans wirr*; *existence* ungeordnet.

disorderly [dɪs'ɔːdəlɪ] adj *desk, room* unordentlich; *life* unsolide; *mind wirr*; *(unruly)* crowd aufrührerisch. ~ conduct *(Jur)* ungebührliches Benehmen.

disorganized [dɪs'ɔːgənaɪzd] adj durcheinander *pred*, desorganisiert; *life, person* chaotisch.

disorientate, *(US)* **disorient** [dɪs'ɔːrɪənteɪtɪd] adj desorientiert.

disown [dɪs'əʊn] vt verleugnen. I'll ~ you if you go

out in that hat wenn du mit dem Hut ausgehst, tue ich so, als ob ich nicht zu dir gehöre.
disparage [dɪ'spærɪdʒ] vt herabsetzen.
disparaging [dɪ'spærɪdʒɪŋ] adj abschätzig.
disparity [dɪ'spærɪtɪ] n Ungleichheit f.
dispassionate [dɪs'pæʃənɪt] adj objektiv.
dispatch [dɪ'spætʃ] 1 vt (a) senden, schicken; person, troops etc also entsenden. (b) (deal with) job etc (prompt) erledigen. (c) (kill) töten. 2 n (a) see vt Senden, Schicken etc; Entsendung f; prompte Erledigung; Tötung f. **date of** ~ Absendedatum nt; **with** ~ prompt. (b) (message) Depesche f; (Press) Bericht m. **to be mentioned in** ~**es** (Mil) in den Kriegsberichten erwähnt werden; ~ **rider** (Mil) Melder m.
dispel [dɪ'spel] vt clouds, fog auflösen, vertreiben; doubts, fears zerstreuen; sorrows vertreiben.
dispensable [dɪ'spensəbl] adj entbehrlich.
dispensary [dɪ'pensərɪ] n (in hospital) (Krankenhaus)apotheke f.
dispensation [ˌdɪspen'seɪʃən] n (handing out) Verteilung f. ~ **of justice** Rechtsprechung f; **by a special** ~ durch besondere Verfügung.
dispense [dɪ'spens] vt (a) verteilen, austeilen (to an +acc). (b) medicine abgeben; prescription zubereiten. **dispensing chemist's** (Brit) Apotheke f.
♦**dispense with** vi +prep obj verzichten auf (+acc).
dispenser [dɪ'spensə^r] n (container) Spender m; (slot-machine) Automat m.
dispersal [dɪ'spɜːsəl] n see vb Verstreuen nt; Verteilung f; Verbreitung f; Auflösung f.
disperse [dɪ'spɜːs] 1 vt (scatter widely) verstreuen; (Bot) seed verteilen; (fig) knowledge etc verbreiten. 2 vi sich auflösen.
dispirited [dɪ'spɪrɪtɪd] adj entmutigt.
displace [dɪs'pleɪs] vt (move) verschieben; (replace) ablösen, ersetzen; water, air verdrängen. ~**d person** Verschleppte(r) mf.
displacement [dɪs'pleɪsmənt] n see vt Verschiebung f; Ablösung f; Verdrängung f.
display [dɪ'spleɪ] 1 vt (a) zeigen; (ostentatiously) new clothes etc also vorführen; exam results, notice aushängen. (b) (Comm) goods ausstellen. 2 n (a) **to make a great** ~ **of sth** etw groß zur Schau stellen; **a** ~ **of temper** ein Wutanfall m. (b) (of paintings etc) Ausstellung f; (dancing ~ etc) Vorführung f; (military, air ~) Schau f. (c) (Comm) Auslage f. **the goods on** ~ die ausgestellte Ware; ~ **case** Vitrine f. (d) (visual ~: on calculator etc) Anzeige f.
displease [dɪs'pliːz] vt mißfallen (+dat), nicht gefallen (+dat).
displeasure [dɪs'pleʒə^r] n Mißfallen nt (at über +acc).
disposable [dɪ'spəʊzəbl] adj (a) (to be thrown away) Wegwerf-; handkerchief, nappy also Papier-; bottle, syringe Einweg-. (b) (available) verfügbar.
disposal [dɪ'spəʊzəl] n (a) see dispose of (a) Loswerden nt; Beseitigung f; Erledigung f. (waste) ~ **unit** Müllschlucker m. (b) **to be at sb's** ~ jdm zur Verfügung stehen; **to put sth at sb's** ~ jdm etw zur Verfügung stellen.
dispose [dɪ'spəʊz] vt (form: arrange) anorden; troops aufstellen. **to be well/ill** ~**d towards sb** jdm wohlwollen/übelwollen.
♦**dispose of** vi +prep obj (a) (get rid of) loswerden; rubbish beseitigen; opponent, difficulties aus dem Weg räumen; matter erledigen. (b) (have at disposal) fortune, time verfügen über (+acc).
disposition [ˌdɪspə'zɪʃən] n (temperament) Veranlagung f. **her cheerful/friendly** ~ ihre fröhliche/freundliche Art.
dispossess [ˌdɪspə'zes] vt enteignen.
disproportionate [ˌdɪsprə'pɔːʃnɪt] adj **a** ~ **amount of money** ein unverhältnismäßig hoher/

niedriger Geldbetrag.
disprove [dɪs'pruːv] vt widerlegen.
disputable [dɪ'spjuːtəbl] adj sehr zweifelhaft.
dispute [dɪ'spjuːt] 1 vt (a) statement bestreiten; claim to sth, will anfechten. (b) **the issue was hotly** ~**d** das Thema wurde heftig diskutiert. (c) (contest) championship jdm streitig machen. 2 vi (argue) streiten. 3 n also ['dɪspjuːt] (a) no pl (arguing, controversy) Disput m, Kontroverse f. **to be beyond** ~ außer Frage stehen; **without** ~ zweifellos; **to be open to** ~ umstritten sein. (b) (argument) Streit m; (debate) Kontroverse f. **industrial** ~ Arbeitskampf m; **to be in** ~ (on strike) im Ausstand sein.
disqualification [dɪs,kwɒlɪfɪ'keɪʃən] n (a) Ausschluß m; (Sport also) Disqualifikation f. ~ (**from driving**) Führerscheinentzug m. (b) (disqualifying factor) Grund m zur Disqualifikation.
disqualify [dɪs'kwɒlɪfaɪ] vt ungeeignet machen (from für); (Sport etc) disqualifizieren. **to** ~ **sb from driving** jdm den Führerschein entziehen.
disquiet [dɪs'kwaɪət] n Unruhe f.
disregard ['dɪsrɪ'gɑːd] 1 vt ignorieren; remark, feelings also nicht beachten (+acc); danger, advice, authority also mißachten. 2 n Mißachtung f (for gen); (for money) Geringschätzung f (for gen).
disrepair ['dɪsrɪ'pɛə^r] n Baufälligkeit f. **in a state of** ~ baufällig; **to fall into** ~ verfallen.
disreputable [dɪs'repjutəbl] adj verrufen, berüchtigt.
disrepute ['dɪsrɪ'pjuːt] n schlechter Ruf. **to bring sth into** ~ etw in Verruf bringen; **to fall into** ~ in Verruf kommen or geraten.
disrespect ['dɪsrɪs'pekt] n Respektlosigkeit f (for gegenüber).
disrespectful adj [ˌdɪsrɪs'pektfʊl] respektlos (to gegenüber).
disrupt [dɪs'rʌpt] vt stören; train service, communications unterbrechen.
disruption [dɪs'rʌpʃən] n see vt Störung f; Unterbrechung f.
disruptive [dɪs'rʌptɪv] adj störend.
dissatisfaction ['dɪs,sætɪs'fækʃən] n Unzufriedenheit f.
dissatisfied [dɪs'sætɪsfaɪd] adj unzufrieden.
dissect [dɪ'sekt] vt plant präparieren; animal also sezieren.
dissection [dɪ'sekʃən] n see vt Präparieren nt; Sezieren nt.
disseminate [dɪ'semɪneɪt] vt verbreiten.
dissension [dɪ'senʃən] n Meinungsverschiedenheit, Differenz f.
dissent [dɪ'sent] 1 vi anderer Meinung sein, differieren (geh). 2 n Meinungsverschiedenheit f. **to voice/express one's** ~ (**with sth**) erklären, daß man (mit etw) nicht übereinstimmt.
dissenter [dɪ'sentə^r] n Abweichler(in f) m.
dissertation [ˌdɪsə'teɪʃən] n wissenschaftliche Arbeit; (PhD) Dissertation f.
disservice [dɪs'sɜːvɪs] n **to do sb a** ~ jdm einen schlechten Dienst erweisen.
dissident ['dɪsɪdənt] 1 n Dissident(in f), Regimekritiker(in f) m. 2 adj regimekritisch.
dissimilar ['dɪ'sɪmɪlə^r] adj verschieden (to von).
dissimilarity [ˌdɪsɪmɪ'lærɪtɪ] n Verschiedenheit f.
dissipate ['dɪsɪpeɪt] vt (a) doubts, fears zerstreuen. (b) energy, fortune verschwenden.
dissipated ['dɪsɪpeɪtɪd] adj behaviour, society zügellos; person also leichtlebig; (in appearance) verlebt; life ausschweifend.
dissipation [ˌdɪsɪ'peɪʃən] n see vt (a) Zerstreuung f. (b) Verschwendung f. (c) (debauchery) Ausschweifung f.
dissociate [dɪ'səʊʃɪeɪt] vt trennen. **to** ~ **oneself from sb/sth** sich von jdm/etw distanzieren.
dissolute ['dɪsəluːt] adj person zügellos; way of life also ausschweifend; appearance verlebt.

dissolution [,dɪsə'luːʃən] n Auflösung f.

dissolve [dɪ'zɒlv] **1** vt auflösen. **2** vi sich (auf)lösen; (fig) sich in nichts auflösen. **it ~s in water** es ist wasserlöslich.

dissuade [dɪ'sweɪd] vt **to ~ sb from doing sth** jdn davon abbringen, etw zu tun.

distance ['dɪstəns] n Entfernung f; (gap, interval) Abstand m; (distance covered) Strecke f, Weg m. **at a ~ of two metres** in zwei Meter(n) Entfernung; **what's the ~ from London to Glasgow?** wie weit ist es von London nach Glasgow?; **in the (far) ~** (ganz) in der Ferne, (ganz) weit weg; **he admired her at a ~** (fig) er bewunderte sie aus der Ferne; **it's within walking ~** es ist zu Fuß erreichbar; **it's no ~** es ist überhaupt nicht weit; **seen from a ~ it looks different** von weitem sieht das ganz anders aus; **quite a ~ (away)** ziemlich weit (entfernt); **the fight went the ~** der Kampf ging über alle Runden; **to go the ~** durchhalten; **to keep one's ~** (lit, fig) auf Distanz bleiben; **at this ~ in time** nach einem so langen Zeitraum; **to keep sb at a ~** jdn auf Distanz halten.

distance: **~ event** n Langstreckenlauf m; **~ runner** n Langstreckenläufer(in f) m.

distant ['dɪstənt] adj **(a)** country weit entfernt, fern. **we had a ~ view of the church** wir sahen in der Ferne die Kirche. **(b)** (with time) age fern, weit zurückliegend; recollection entfernt. **that was in the ~ past** das liegt weit zurück; **in the ~ future** in ferner Zukunft. **(c)** relationship, likeness, cousin entfernt. **(d)** (fig: aloof) person, manner distanziert, reserviert.

distaste [dɪs'teɪst] n Widerwille m (for gegen).

distasteful [dɪs'teɪstfʊl] adj task unangenehm; photo, magazine geschmacklos. **to be ~ to sb** jdm zuwider or unangenehm sein.

distemper¹ [dɪs'tempər] n (paint) Temperfarbe f.

distemper² n (Vet) Staupe f.

distend [dɪ'stend] **1** vt sails, stomach (auf)blähen. **2** vi sich blähen.

distil, (US) **distill** [dɪ'stɪl] vt (Chem) destillieren; whisky etc also brennen.

distiller [dɪ'stɪlər] n Destillateur, (Branntwein)brenner m.

distillery [dɪ'stɪlərɪ] n (Branntwein)brennerei f.

distinct [dɪ'stɪŋkt] adj **(a)** deutlich, klar; landmark, shape also klar erkennbar; accent, likeness also ausgeprägt. **I had the ~ feeling that ...** ich hatte das bestimmte Gefühl, daß ... **(b)** (different) verschieden; (separate) getrennt. **as ~ from** im Unterschied zu.

distinction [dɪ'stɪŋkʃən] n **(a)** (difference) Unterschied m; (act of distinguishing) Unterscheidung f. **to make a ~ (between two things)** (zwischen zwei Dingen) einen Unterschied machen. **(b)** no pl (preeminence) **to win ~** sich hervortun or auszeichnen; **a pianist of ~** ein Pianist von Rang. **(c)** (Sch, Univ: grade) **he got a ~ in French** er hat das Französischexamen mit Auszeichnung bestanden.

distinctive [dɪ'stɪŋktɪv] adj colour, plumage auffällig; (unmistakable) unverkennbar; characteristic, feature besondere(s).

distinctly [dɪ'stɪŋktlɪ] adv deutlich; prefer also, rude ausgesprochen; better entschieden.

distinguish [dɪ'stɪŋgwɪʃ] **1** vt **(a)** unterscheiden. **(b)** (make out) landmark, shape erkennen. **2** vi **~ between** unterscheiden zwischen (+dat). **3** vr **to ~ oneself** sich auszeichnen.

distinguished [dɪ'stɪŋgwɪʃt] adj **(a)** (eminent) pianist, scholar von hohem Rang; career hervorragend. **(b)** (refined, elegant) person, manner distinguiert (geh), vornehm.

distinguishing [dɪ'stɪŋgwɪʃɪŋ] adj kennzeichnend, charakteristisch. **the ~ feature of his work is ...** was seine Arbeit kennzeichnet, ist ...

distort [dɪ'stɔːt] vt verzerren; truth, words ver-

drehen.

distortion [dɪ'stɔːʃən] n see vt Verzerrung f; Verdrehung f.

distract [dɪ'strækt] vt ablenken.

distracted [dɪ'stræktɪd] adj (worried) besorgt, beunruhigt; (distraught) außer sich (with vor +dat).

distraction [dɪ'strækʃən] n **(a)** (from work etc) Ablenkung f. **(b)** (entertainment) Zerstreuung f. **(c)** (anxiety) Ruhelosigkeit, Unruhe f; (distraughtness) Verstörtheit f. **to drive sb to ~** jdn wahnsinnig machen.

distraught [dɪ'strɔːt] adj verzweifelt.

distress [dɪ'stres] **1** n **(a)** (physical) Leiden nt; (mental) Kummer m, Sorge f. **to be in great ~** sehr leiden. **(b)** (danger) **a ship/plane in ~** ein Schiff in Seenot/ein Flugzeug in Not; **~ signal** Notsignal nt. **2** vt Sorge bereiten (+dat). **please don't ~ yourself** machen Sie sich (dat) bitte keine Sorgen!

distressed [dɪ'strest] adj (upset) bekümmert; (grief-stricken) verzweifelt (about über +acc).

distressing [dɪ'stresɪŋ] adj (upsetting) besorgniserregend; (stronger) erschütternd.

distribute [dɪ'strɪbjuːt] vt verteilen; (Comm) goods vertreiben.

distribution [,dɪstrɪ'bjuːʃən] n see vt Verteilung f; Vertrieb m.

distributor [dɪ'strɪbjutər] n Verteiler m (also Aut); (Comm) Großhändler m.

district ['dɪstrɪkt] n Gegend f; (of town also) Viertel nt; (administrative) (Verwaltungs)bezirk m.

district: **~ attorney** n (US) Bezirksstaatsanwalt m; **~ council** n (Brit) Bezirksrat m; **~ manager** n Bezirksleiter m; **~ nurse** n Gemeindeschwester f.

distrust [dɪs'trʌst] **1** vt mißtrauen (+dat). **2** n Mißtrauen nt (of gegenüber).

distrustful [dɪs'trʌstfʊl] adj mißtrauisch (of gegenüber).

disturb [dɪ'stɜːb] **1** vt **(a)** stören. **(b)** (alarm) person beunruhigen. **(c)** waters bewegen; sediment aufwirbeln; papers durcheinanderbringen. **2** vi **"please do not ~"** „bitte nicht stören".

disturbance [dɪ'stɜːbəns] n **(a)** (political) Unruhe f; (in pub, street) (Ruhe)störung f. **to cause a ~** eine Ruhestörung verursachen. **(b)** (in work, routine) Störung f.

disturbed [dɪ'stɜːbd] adj **(a)** (mentally) geistig gestört; (socially) verhaltensgestört. **(b)** (worried) beunruhigt (at, by über +acc, von).

disturbing [dɪ'stɜːbɪŋ] adj (alarming) beunruhigend; (distracting) störend. **some viewers may find these scenes ~** einige Zuschauer könnten an diesen Szenen Anstoß nehmen.

disuse ['dɪs'juːs] n **to fall into ~** nicht mehr benutzt werden.

disused ['dɪs'juːzd] adj building leerstehend; mine, railway line stillgelegt.

ditch [dɪtʃ] **1** n Graben m. **2** vt (col: get rid of) person loswerden; boyfriend abservieren (col); project fallenlassen.

dither ['dɪðər] **1** n **to be all of a ~** ganz aufgeregt sein. **2** vi zaudern, schwanken.

ditto ['dɪtəu] n **I'd like coffee — ~ (for me)** (col) ich möchte Kaffee — ich auch.

ditty ['dɪtɪ] n Liedchen nt.

divan [dɪ'væn] n Diwan m. **~ bed** Liege f.

dive [daɪv] (vb: pret **~d** or (US) **dove**, ptp **~d**) **1** n **(a)** (by swimmer) Sprung m; (by plane) Sturzflug m; (Ftbl) Hechtsprung m. **the deepest ~ yet made** die bisher größte Tauchtiefe; **to make a ~ for sth** (fig col) sich auf etw (acc) stürzen; **the dollar took a ~** (col) der Dollar sackte ab (col). **(b)** (pej col: club etc) Spelunke f (col). **2** vi **(a)** (person) springen; (under water) tauchen; (submarine) untertauchen; (plane) einen Sturzflug machen; (goalkeeper etc) hechten. **to ~**

for pearls nach Perlen tauchen. **(b)** *(col)* he ~d **into the crowd/under the table** er verschwand blitzschnell in der Menge/unter dem Tisch; **to ~ for cover** blitzschnell in Deckung gehen; **he ~d under the sheets** er machte einen Satz unter die Decke.

dive: ~-**bomb** *vt* im Sturzflug bombardieren; ~-**bomber** *n* Sturzkampfbomber, Stuka *m*.

diver ['daɪvəʳ] *n (also bird)* Taucher *m*; *(off high board)* Turmspringer(in *f*) *m*; *(off springboard)* Kunstspringer(in *f*) *m*.

diverge [daɪ'vɜːdʒ] *vi* abweichen *(from* von*)*; *(two things)* auseinandergehen.

divergence [daɪ'vɜːdʒəns] *n* Abweichung *f*.

divergent [daɪ'vɜːdʒənt] *adj opinions etc* auseinandergehend.

diverse [daɪ'vɜːs] *adj* verschieden(artig).

diversify [daɪ'vɜːsɪfaɪ] 1 *vt* abwechslungsreich(er) gestalten; *business etc* diversifizieren *(Comm)*. 2 *vi (Comm)* diversifizieren.

diversion [daɪ'vɜːʃən] *n* **(a)** *(of stream, esp Brit: of traffic)* Umleitung *f*. **(b)** *(relaxation)* Unterhaltung *f*. **(c)** *(Mil, fig)* Ablenkung *f*. **to create a ~** ablenken.

diversity [daɪ'vɜːsɪtɪ] *n* Vielfalt *f*.

divert [daɪ'vɜːt] *vt* **(a)** *traffic, stream* umleiten; *attention* ablenken; *conversation* in eine andere Richtung lenken; *blow* abwenden. **(b)** *(amuse)* unterhalten.

divide [dɪ'vaɪd] 1 *vt* **(a)** *(separate)* trennen. **(b)** *(split into parts: also* ~ **up)** *money, work* teilen *(into* in +*acc)*; *(in order to distribute)* aufteilen. **(c)** *(Math)* dividieren, teilen *(by* durch*)*. **what is 12** ~**d by 3?** wieviel ist 12 (geteilt) durch 3? 2 *vi* **(a)** *(river, road, cells)* sich teilen. **to ~ into groups** sich in Gruppen aufteilen. **(b)** *(Brit Parl)* **the House** ~**d** das Parlament stimmte durch Hammelsprung ab.

♦ **divide off** *vt sep* (ab)trennen.

♦ **divide out** *vt sep* aufteilen *(among* unter +*acc or dat)*.

divided [dɪ'vaɪdɪd] *adj* geteilt. ~ **highway** *(US)* Schnellstraße *f*; **a people** ~ **against itself** ein gespaltenes Volk.

dividend ['dɪvɪdend] *n (Fin)* Dividende *f*. **to pay ~s** *(fig)* sich bezahlt machen.

dividers [dɪ'vaɪdəz] *npl* Stechzirkel *m*.

dividing [dɪ'vaɪdɪŋ] *adj* ~ **wall** Trennwand *f*; ~ **line** *(lit, fig)* Trennungslinie *f*.

divine [dɪ'vaɪn] 1 *adj* **(a)** *(Rel)* göttlich; *(fig col)* bezaubernd. 2 *vt* **(a)** *the future* weissagen, prophezeien; *sb's intentions* erahnen. **(b)** *water, metal* aufspüren.

diving ['daɪvɪŋ] *n (under water)* Tauchen *nt*; *(into water)* Springen *nt*; *(Sport)* Wasserspringen *nt*.

diving: ~-**bell** *n* Taucherglocke *f*; ~-**board** *n* Sprungbrett *nt*; ~-**suit** *n* Taucheranzug *m*.

divinity [dɪ'vɪnɪtɪ] *n* **(a)** *(divine being)* Gottheit *f*. **(b)** *(Sch)* Religion *f*.

divisible [dɪ'vɪzəbl] *adj* teilbar *(by* durch*)*.

division [dɪ'vɪʒən] *n* **(a)** Teilung *f*; *(Math)* Teilen *nt*, Division *f*. **the ~ of labour** die Arbeitsteilung. **(b)** *(Mil)* Division *f*. **(c)** *(in administration)* Abteilung *f*. **(d)** *(in room)* Trennwand *f*; *(fig: between social classes etc)* Schranke *f*; *(dividing line: lit, fig)* Trennungslinie *f*. **(e)** *(fig: discord)* Uneinigkeit *f*. **(f)** *(Brit Parl)* Abstimmung *f* durch Hammelsprung. **(g)** *(Sport)* Liga *f*.

divisive [dɪ'vaɪsɪv] *adj* **to be** ~ Uneinigkeit schaffen.

divorce [dɪ'vɔːs] 1 *n* Scheidung *f (from* von*)*; *(fig)* Trennung *f*. **he wants a** ~ er will sich scheiden lassen; **to get a** ~ *(from sb)* sich (von jdm) scheiden lassen. 2 *vt* **(a)** sich scheiden lassen von. **to get** ~**d** sich scheiden lassen. **(b)** *(fig)* trennen.

divorced [dɪ'vɔːst] *adj* geschieden *(from* von*)*.

divorcee [dɪˌvɔː'siː] *n* geschiedener Mann, ge-

schiedene Frau. **he is a** ~ er ist geschieden.

divulge [daɪ'vʌldʒ] *vt* preisgeben *(sth to sb* jdm etw*)*.

DIY = **do-it-yourself.**

dizziness ['dɪzɪnɪs] *n* Schwindel *m*.

dizzy ['dɪzɪ] *adj* (+*er*) **(a)** *(lit, fig) person* schwind(e)lig; *height* schwindelerregend. ~ **spell** Schwindelanfall *m*; **I feel** ~ mir ist schwindlig. **(b)** *(col: foolish)* verrückt.

DJ = **dinner jacket; disc jockey.**

do [duː] *(vb: pret* did, *ptp* done) 1 *aux* **(a)** ~ **you understand?** verstehen Sie?; **I** ~ **not** *or* **don't understand** ich verstehe nicht; **didn't you know?, did you not know?** haben Sie das nicht gewußt?

     (b) *(for emphasis: with stress on do)* ~ **come!** kommen Sie doch (bitte)!; ~ **shut up!** *(nun)* sei doch (endlich) ruhig!; ~ **I remember him!** und ob ich mich an ihn erinnere!; **but I** ~ **like it** aber es gefällt mir wirklich; **so you** ~ **know them!** Sie kennen sie also tatsächlich!; *(and were lying etc)* Sie kennen sie also doch!

     (c) *(used to avoid repeating vb)* **you speak better than I** ~ Sie sprechen besser als ich; **he likes cheese and so** ~ **I** er ißt gern Käse und ich auch; **neither** ~ **I** ich auch nicht.

     (d) *(in question tags)* oder. **you know him, don't you?** Sie kennen ihn doch, oder?; **he didn't go, did he?** er ist (doch) nicht gegangen, oder?

     (e) *(in answers: replacing vb)* **do you see them often?** — yes, **I** ~/no, **I don't** sehen Sie sie oft? — ja/nein; **they speak French** — oh, ~ **they?** sie sprechen Französisch — ja?, wirklich?; **may I come in?** — ~! darf ich hereinkommen? — ja, bitte; **shall I open the window?** — no, **don't!** soll ich das Fenster öffnen? — nein, bitte nicht!

     2 *vt* **(a)** tun, machen; *puzzle, housework, military service, translation, film* machen. **what are you** ~**ing on Saturday?** was machen Sie am Sonnabend?; **I've got nothing to** ~ ich habe nichts zu tun; **are you** ~**ing anything this evening?** haben Sie heute abend schon etwas vor?; **what shall we** ~ **for money?** wo kriegen wir jetzt (das) Geld her?; **we'll have to** ~ **something about this** wir müssen da etwas unternehmen; **how do you** ~ **it?** wie macht man das?; *(in amazement)* wie machen Sie das bloß?; **what's to be done?** was ist da zu tun?; **what can you** ~**?** was kann man da machen?; **sorry, it can't be done** tut mir leid, es läßt sich nicht machen; **what can I** ~ **for you?** was kann ich für Sie tun?; *(by shop assistant also)* was darf's sein?; **can you** ~ **it by yourself?** schaffst du das allein?; **what do you want me to** ~ *(about it)?* und was soll ich da tun or machen?; **Brecht doesn't** ~ **anything for me** Brecht sagt mir nichts; **that's done it** *(col)* da haben wir's, da haben wir die Bescherung; **that does it!** jetzt reicht's mir!; **now what have you done!** was hast du jetzt wieder angestellt?; **we don't** ~ **lunches** wir haben keinen Mittagstisch.

     (b) *(arrange, fix etc)* **to** ~ **the flowers** die Blumen arrangieren; **to** ~ **one's hair** sich *(dat)* die Haare machen *(col)*; **who does your hair?** zu welchem Friseur gehen Sie?; **to** ~ **one's nails** sich *(dat)* die Nägel schneiden *or (varnish)* lackieren; **you** ~ **the painting and I'll** ~ **the papering** du streichst und ich tapeziere; **I'll** ~ **the talking** ich übernehme das Reden.

     (c) *(Sch etc: study)* **we've done Milton** wir haben Milton durchgenommen; **I've never done any German** ich habe nie Deutsch gelernt.

     (d) *(in pret, ptp only: complete, accomplish)* **the work's done now** die Arbeit ist gemacht *or* getan *or* fertig; **what's done cannot be undone** was geschehen ist, kann man nicht ungeschehen machen; **done!** abgemacht!

     (e) *(visit)* *city, museum* besuchen; *(take in also)* mitnehmen *(col)*.

(f) *(Aut etc)* schaffen, machen *(col)*. **this car does 130** das Auto schafft *or* macht *(col)* 130; **we did London to Edinburgh in 8 hours** wir haben es in 8 Stunden von London bis Edinburgh geschafft.

(g) *(be suitable)* passen *(sb jdm)*; *(be sufficient for)* reichen *(sb jdm)*. **that will ~ me nicely** *(enough)* das reicht dicke *(col)*; *(just right)* das paßt mir gut.

(h) *(take off, mimic)* nachmachen.

(i) *(col: cheat)* übers Ohr hauen *(col)*.

(j) *(Cook)* machen *(col)*. **to ~ the cooking/food** kochen; **how do you like your steak done?** wie möchten Sie Ihr Steak?; **well done** durch(gebraten).

(k) *(col: in prison)* 6 years (ab)sitzen.

3 *vi* **(a)** *(act)* **~ as I ~** mach es wie ich; **he did well to take advice** er tat gut daran, sich beraten zu lassen. **(b)** *(get on, fare)* **how are you ~ing?** wie geht's (Ihnen)?; **the patient is ~ing very well** dem Patienten geht es recht ordentlich; **he's ~ing well at school** er ist gut in der Schule; **his business is ~ing well** sein Geschäft geht gut. **(c)** *(finish)* **the meat, is it done?** ist das Fleisch fertig *or* durch?; **have you done?** sind Sie endlich fertig? **(d)** *(suit, be convenient)* gehen. **that will never ~!** das geht nicht!; **this room will ~** das Zimmer ist in Ordnung; **will she/it ~?** geht die/das?; **this coat will ~ as a cover** dieser Mantel muß als Decke herhalten; **you'll have to make ~ with £10** Sie werden mit £ 10 auskommen müssen. **(e)** *(be sufficient)* reichen. **will £1 ~?** reicht £ 1?; **yes, that'll ~** ja, das reicht; **that'll ~!** jetzt reicht's aber! **(f)** *(col: char)* putzen *(for* bei).

4 *n* *(col)* **(a)** Veranstaltung *f*; *(party)* Fete *f* *(col)*. **(b)** *(in phrases)* **it's a poor ~!** *(col)* das ist ja ein schwaches Bild! *(col)*; **the ~s and don'ts** was man wissen sollte; *(for behaviour)* Verhaltensregeln *pl*; **fair ~s all round** *(col)* gleiches Recht für alle.

♦ **do away with** *vi* +*prep obj* **(a)** *custom, law* abschaffen; *building* abreißen. **(b)** *(kill)* umbringen.

♦ **do by** *vi* +*prep obj* **to ~ well/badly ~ sb** jdn gut/schlecht behandeln.

♦ **do for** *vi* +*prep obj* *(col: finish off)* person fertigmachen *(col)*; *project* zunichte machen. **to be done ~** *(person)* erledigt *or* fertig *(col)* sein; *(project)* gestorben sein *(col)*.

♦ **do in** *vt sep (col)* **(a)** *(kill)* um die Ecke bringen *(col)*. **(b)** **to be done ~** *(exhausted)* fertig sein *(col)*.

♦ **do out** *vt sep* **(a)** *room* auskehren. **(b)** **to ~ sb ~ of a job/£100** jdn um eine Stelle/£ 100 bringen.

♦ **do up 1** *vi (dress etc)* zugemacht werden. **2** *vt sep* **(a)** *(fasten)* zumachen. **(b)** *(parcel together)* goods zusammenpacken. **to ~ sth ~ in a parcel** etw einpacken. **(c)** *house, room* renovieren. **to ~ oneself ~** sich zurechtmachen.

♦ **do with** *vi* +*prep obj* **(a)** *(with can or could: need)* brauchen. **it could ~ ~ a clean** es müßte mal saubergemacht werden. **(b)** **what has that got to ~ ~ it?** was hat das damit zu tun?; **that has nothing to ~ ~ you!** das geht Sie gar nichts an!; **it's to ~ ~ this letter you sent** es geht um den Brief, den Sie geschickt haben; **money has a lot to ~ ~ it** Geld spielt eine große Rolle dabei. **(c)** **what have you done ~ my gloves/your face?** was haben Sie mit meinen Handschuhen/Ihrem Gesicht gemacht? **(d)** **he doesn't know what to ~ ~ himself** er weiß nicht, was er mit sich anfangen soll. **(e)** **to be done ~ sb/sth** *(finished)* mit jdm/ etw fertig sein.

♦ **do without** *vi* +*prep obj* auskommen ohne. **I can ~ ~ your advice** Sie können sich Ihre Ratschläge sparen; **I could have done ~ that!** das hätte mir (wirklich) erspart bleiben können; **you'll have to ~ ~** Sie müssen so zurechtkommen.

docile ['dəʊsaɪl] *adj* sanftmütig; *horse* fromm; *(pej)* *engine* schwach.

dock¹ [dɒk] **1** *n* Dock *nt*; *(for berthing)* Pier, Kai *m*. **~s** *pl* Hafen *m*. **2** *vt* docken; *(Space also)* ankoppeln. **3** *vi (Naut)* anlegen; *(Space)* ankoppeln.

dock² *n (Jur)* Anklagebank *f*.

dock³ *vt* **(a)** *dog's tail* kupieren; *horse's tail* stutzen. **(b)** *wages* kürzen.

docker ['dɒkə^r] *n (Brit)* Hafenarbeiter, Docker *m*.

docket ['dɒkɪt] *n (on parcel etc)* Warenbegleitschein *m*.

docking ['dɒkɪŋ] *n (Space)* Ankoppelung *f*.

dockyard ['dɒkjɑːd] *n* Werft *f*.

doctor ['dɒktə^r] **1** *n* **(a)** *(Med)* Arzt *m*, Ärztin *f*. **D~ Smith** Dr. Schmidt; **it's just what the ~ ordered** *(fig col)* das ist genau das richtige. **(b)** *(Univ etc)* Doktor *m*. **Dear Dr Smith** Sehr geehrter Herr Dr./Sehr geehrte Frau Dr. Smith. **2** *vt* **(a)** *(col: castrate)* kastrieren. **(b)** *(tamper with) accounts* frisieren; *text, document* verfälschen. **the wine's been ~ed** dem Wein ist etwas beigemischt worden.

doctorate ['dɒktərɪt] *n* Doktortitel *m*; *see* **PhD.**

doctrinaire [,dɒktrɪ'neə^r] *adj* doktrinär.

doctrine ['dɒktrɪn] *n* Doktrin, Lehre *f*.

document ['dɒkjʊmənt] **1** *n* Papier *nt*; *(certificate)* Dokument *nt*, Urkunde *f*. **2** *vt* belegen.

documentary [,dɒkjʊ'mentərɪ] *n* Dokumentarfilm *m*.

documentation [,dɒkjʊmen'teɪʃən] *n* Dokumentation *f*.

dodderer ['dɒdərə^r] *n (col)* Tattergreis *(col)* *m*.

doddery ['dɒdərɪ] *adj* tatterig *(col)*. **the ~ old fool** *(col)* der vertrottelte alte Opa *(col)*.

dodge [dɒdʒ] **1** *n (trick)* Trick, Kniff *m*. **to be up to all the ~s** mit allen Wassern gewaschen sein; **a tax ~** ein Steuertrick. **2** *vt blow, question* ausweichen (+*dat*); *tax* umgehen; *(shirk) work, military service* sich drücken vor (+*dat*). **to ~ the issue** dem Problem ausweichen. **3** *vi* **to ~ out of the way** zur Seite springen; *(to escape notice)* blitzschnell verschwinden; **to ~ through the traffic** sich durch den Verkehr schlängeln.

dodgem ['dɒdʒəm] *n (Brit)* (Auto)skooter *m*.

dodgy ['dɒdʒɪ] *adj* (+*er*) *(Brit col: tricky) situation* vertrackt *(col)*; *(dubious)* zweifelhaft; *engine* defekt; *translation, spelling* fehlerhaft.

doe [dəʊ] *n (roe deer)* Ricke *f*; *(red deer)* Hirschkuh *f*; *(rabbit)* Weibchen *nt*.

does [dʌz] *3rd pers sing of* **do.**

doesn't ['dʌznt] = **does not.**

doff [dɒf] *vt hat* ziehen, lüften.

dog [dɒg] **1** *n* **(a)** Hund *m*. **(b)** *(fig phrases)* **it's a ~'s life** es ist ein Hundeleben; **to go to the ~s** vor die Hunde gehen *(col)*; **~ in the manger** Spielverderber(in *f)* *m*; **-in-the-manger attitude** mißgünstige Einstellung; **every ~ has his day** jeder hat einmal Glück; **you can't teach an old ~ new tricks** der Mensch ist ein Gewohnheitstier; **~'s breakfast** *(fig col)* Schlamassel *m* *(col)*. **(c)** *(male fox, wolf)* Rüde *m*. **(d)** *(col: man)* **lucky ~** Glückspilz *m*; **dirty ~** gemeiner Hund; **sly ~** gerissener Hund *(col)*. **2** *vt* **to ~ sb's footsteps** jdm hart auf den Fersen sein/bleiben; **~ged by misfortune** vom Pech verfolgt.

dog: **~ biscuit** *n* Hundekuchen *m*; **~-collar** *n (lit)* Hundehalsband *nt*; *(vicar's)* steifer, hoher Kragen; **~-eared** ['dɒgɪəd] *adj* mit Eselsohren; **~fight** *n (Aviat)* Luftkampf *m*; **~fish** *n* Hundshai *m*; **~ food** *n* Hundefutter *nt*.

dogged ['dɒgɪd] *adj* beharrlich, zäh.

doggerel ['dɒgərəl] *n* Knittelvers *m*.

doggie bag ['dɒgɪ,bæg] *n* Tüte *f* für Essensreste, die nach Hause mitgenommen werden.

doggo ['dɒgəʊ] *adv (col)*: **to lie ~** sich nicht mucksen *(col)*.

dog house *n* **he's in the ~** *(col)* er ist in Ungnade; *(with wife)* bei ihm hängt der Haussegen schief.

dogma ['dɒgmə] n Dogma nt.

dogmatic [dɒg'mætɪk] adj dogmatisch (about in +dat).

do-gooder ['duː'gudəʳ] n (pej) Weltverbesserer m.

dogsbody ['dɒgzbɒdɪ] n she's/he's the general ~ sie/er ist Mädchen für alles.

dog: ~ **tag** n (US Mil col) Hundemarke (col) f; ~**-tired** adj hundemüde.

doing ['duːɪŋ] n this is your ~ das ist dein Werk; that takes some ~ da gehört (schon) etwas dazu; ~s pl Taten pl.

doings ['duːɪŋz] n sing (Brit col) Dingsbums nt (col).

do-it-yourself ['duːɪtjə'self] 1 adj shop Bastler-, Hobby-. 2 n Heimwerken, Do-it-yourself nt.

doldrums ['dɒldrəmz] npl to be in the ~ Trübsal blasen; (business etc) in einer Flaute stecken.

dole [dəʊl] n (Brit col) Arbeitslosenunterstützung f. to go/be on the ~ stempeln (gehen).

♦ **dole out** vt sep austeilen, verteilen.

doleful ['dəʊlful] adj traurig.

doll [dɒl] n (a) Puppe f. ~'s house Puppenhaus nt. (b) (esp US col: girl) Mädchen nt; (pretty girl) Puppe f (col).

♦ **doll up** vt sep (col) to ~ oneself ~, to get ~ed ~ sich herausputzen or aufdonnern (col).

dollar ['dɒləʳ] n Dollar m.

dollop ['dɒləp] n (col) Schlag m (col).

dolly-bird ['dɒlɪbɜːd] n (col) Puppe f (col).

dolphin ['dɒlfɪn] n Delphin m.

dolt [dəʊlt] n Tölpel m.

domain [dəʊ'meɪn] n (a) (estate) Gut nt; (belonging to state, Crown) Domäne f. (b) (fig) Domäne f.

dome [dəʊm] n (Archit) Kuppel f; (of heaven, skull) Gewölbe nt.

domed [dəʊmd] adj forehead gewölbt.

domestic [də'mestɪk] adj (a) bliss, life häuslich. (b) policy Innen-; news Inland-, aus dem Inland; produce einheimisch; trade Binnen-; flight Inlands-. (c) animal Haus-.

domesticate [də'mestɪkeɪt] vt zähmen; (house-train) stubenrein machen.

domesticated [də'mestɪkeɪtɪd] adj zahm; cat, dog stubenrein. she's very ~ sie ist sehr häuslich.

domestic science n Hauswirtschaftslehre f.

domicile ['dɒmɪsaɪl] n (Admin) Wohnsitz m.

dominance ['dɒmɪnəns] n Vorherrschaft, Dominanz f (also Biol) (over über +acc).

dominant ['dɒmɪnənt] 1 adj beherrschend, dominierend; feature also hervorstehend; gene, (Mus) dominant. 2 n (Mus) Dominante f.

dominate ['dɒmɪneɪt] 1 vi dominieren. 2 vt beherrschen; (species, gene) dominieren.

domination [ˌdɒmɪ'neɪʃən] n (Vor)herrschaft f.

domineer [ˌdɒmɪ'nɪəʳ] vi tyrannisieren (over sb jdn).

domineering [ˌdɒmɪ'nɪərɪŋ] adj herrisch; mother-in-law, husband etc also herrschsüchtig.

dominion [də'mɪnɪən] n (a) no pl Herrschaft f (over über +acc). (b) (territory) Herrschaftsgebiet nt; (Brit Pol) Dominion nt.

don[1] [dɒn] n (Brit Univ) Universitätsdozent m.

don[2] vt garment anziehen.

donate [dəʊ'neɪt] vt spenden.

donation [dəʊ'neɪʃən] n Spende f; (large scale) Stiftung f.

done [dʌn] 1 ptp of do. 2 adj (a) (finished) work erledigt; (cooked) vegetables gar; meat durch. to get sth ~ (finished) etw fertigkriegen. (b) it's not the ~ thing das tut man nicht.

donkey ['dɒŋkɪ] n Esel m. ~'s years (col) eine Ewigkeit.

donkey: ~ **jacket** n dicke (gefütterte) Jacke; ~**work** n Routinearbeit, Dreckarbeit (pej) f.

donor ['dəʊnəʳ] n (Med) Spender(in f) m.

don't [dəʊnt] = do not.

donut ['dəʊnʌt] n (esp US) = doughnut.

doodle ['duːdl] 1 vti kritzeln. 2 n Gekritzel nt.

doom [duːm] 1 n (fate) Schicksal nt; (ruin) Verhängnis nt. 2 vt verurteilen, verdammen. to be ~ed verloren sein; the project was ~ed from the start das Vorhaben war von Anfang an zum Scheitern verurteilt.

doomsday ['duːmzdeɪ] n der Jüngste Tag. otherwise we'll be here till ~ (col) sonst sind wir in zwanzig Jahren noch hier.

door [dɔːʳ] n (a) Tür f; (entrance: to cinema etc) Eingang m. was that the ~? hat es geklingelt/geklopft?; to pay at the ~ (Theat etc) an der Kasse zahlen; he lives three ~s away er wohnt drei Häuser weiter. (b) (phrases) to lay sth at sb's ~ jdm etw anlasten; to leave the ~ open for further negotiations die Tür für weitere Verhandlungen offen lassen; to open the ~ to sth einer Sache (dat) Tür und Tor öffnen; to show sb the ~ jdm die Tür weisen; out of ~s im Freien.

door in cpds Tür-; ~**bell** n Türklingel f; ~ **knob** n Türklinke f; ~**keeper**, ~**man** n Portier m; ~**mat** n Fußmatte f; (fig) Fußabtreter m; ~**nail** n: as dead as a ~**nail** mausetot; ~**post** n deaf as a ~**post** stocktaub; ~**step** n (Tür)schwelle f; on my ~**step** (fig) direkt vor meiner Tür; ~**-to-**~ adj (a) ~**-to-**~ salesman Vertreter m; (b) delivery ins Haus; ~**way** n (of room) Tür f; (of building, shop) Eingang m.

dope [dəʊp] 1 n (a) no pl (col: drugs) Stoff m (col), Dope nt (col); (Sport) Aufputschmittel nt. (b) no pl (col: information) Information(en pl) f. (c) (col: stupid person) Esel m (col). 2 vt dopen.

dopey, dopy ['dəʊpɪ] adj (+er) (col) (stupid) bekloppt (col); (sleepy, half-drugged) benebelt (col).

dormant ['dɔːmənt] adj (Zool, Bot) ruhend; volcano untätig; energy verborgen. to lie ~ (evil etc) schlummern.

dormer (window) ['dɔːmə('wɪndəʊ)] n Mansardenfenster nt.

dormitory ['dɔːmɪtrɪ] n Schlafsaal m; (US: building) Wohnheim nt. ~ **town** n Schlafstadt f.

dormouse ['dɔːmaʊs] n, pl **dormice** ['dɔːmaɪs] Haselmaus f.

dorsal ['dɔːsl] adj ~ **fin** Rückenflosse f.

dosage ['dəʊsɪdʒ] n Dose, Dosis f.

dose [dəʊs] 1 n (Med) Dosis f. a ~ of flu eine Grippe; he's all right in small ~s er ist nur (für) kurze Zeit zu ertragen. 2 vt person Arznei geben (+dat). she's always dosing herself sie nimmt or schluckt ständig Medikamente.

doss [dɒs] vi (Brit col: also ~ **down**) pennen (col), sich hinhauen (col).

dosshouse ['dɒshaʊs] n (Brit col) Bleibe f (col).

dossier ['dɒsɪeɪ] n Dossier m or nt.

dot [dɒt] 1 n Punkt m. to arrive on the ~ auf die Minute pünktlich (an)kommen. 2 vt to ~ one's i's and cross one's t's genau sein; ~**ted line** punktierte Linie; to sign on the ~**ted line** (fig) seine Zustimmung geben; a field ~**ted with flowers** ein mit Blumen übersätes Feld; ~**ted about the country** über das ganze Land verstreut.

dotage ['dəʊtɪdʒ] n in one's ~ senil.

♦ **dote on** ['dəʊtɒn] vi +prep obj abgöttisch lieben.

doting ['dəʊtɪŋ] adj her ~ parents ihre Eltern, die sie abgöttisch lieb(t)en.

dot matrix (printer) n Matrixdrucker m.

dotty ['dɒtɪ] adj (+er) (Brit col) kauzig, schrullig.

double ['dʌbl] 1 adj (twice as much) doppelt; (having two similar parts, for two) Doppel-. a ~ whisky ein doppelter Whisky; her salary is ~ what it was ten years ago ihr Gehalt hat sich in den letzten zehn Jahren verdoppelt; ~ **bottom** doppelter Boden; ~ "p" Doppel-p; ~ **seven five four/**~ **seven five** (Telec) siebenundsiebzig vierundfünfzig/sieben sieben fünf; ~ **room** Doppelzimmer nt; it has a ~ **meaning** es ist zwei- or doppeldeutig; ~ **standards** Doppelmoral f; to lead a ~ **life** ein Doppelleben führen.

2 *adv* **(a)** *(twice)* doppelt. **I have ~ what you have** ich habe doppelt soviel wie du; **to see ~** doppelt sehen. **(b) to be bent ~ with pain** sich vor Schmerzen krümmen; **fold the paper ~** falte das Papier (einmal). **3** *n* **(a)** *(twice)* das Doppelte, das Zweifache. **(b)** *(person)* Ebenbild *nt*, Doppelgänger(in *f*) *m*; *(Film, Theat: stand-in)* Double *nt*. **(c) at the ~** *(also Mil)* im Laufschritt; *(fig)* auf der Stelle. **4** *vt (increase twofold)* verdoppeln. **5** *vi* **(a)** sich verdoppeln. **(b)** *(Film, Theat)* **to ~ for sb** jds Double sein, jdn doubeln; **he ~s as the butler and the duke** er hat eine Doppelrolle als Butler und Herzog.

♦ **double back 1** *vi* kehrtmachen; *(road, river)* sich zurückschlängeln. **2** *vt sep blanket* umschlagen.

♦ **double up** *vi* **(a)** *(with pain)* sich krümmen; *(with laughter)* sich biegen. **he ~d ~ when the bullet hit him** er brach zusammen, als die Kugel ihn traf. **(b)** *(share room)* das Zimmer/Büro etc teilen; *(share bed)* in einem Bett schlafen.

double: ~ **agent** *n* Doppelagent *m*; ~ **bar** *n (Mus)* Doppelstrich *m*; **~-barrelled,** *(US)* **~-barreled** [ˌdʌblˈbærəld] *adj surname* Doppel-; **~-barrel(l)ed shotgun** *n* doppelläufiges Gewehr, Zwilling *m*; ~ **bass** *n* Kontrabaß *m*; ~ **bed** *n* Doppelbett *nt*; ~ **bend** *n* S-Kurve *f*; **~-breasted** *adj* zweireihig; **~-breasted jacket/suit** Zweireiher *m*; **~-check** *vti* noch einmal (über)prüfen; ~ **chin** *n* Doppelkinn *nt*; ~ **cream** *n* Schlagsahne *f*; **~-cross** *vt (col)* ein falsches Spiel treiben mit; **~-dealing** *n* Betrügerei(en *pl*) *f*; **~-decker** *n* Doppeldecker *m*; **~-declutch** *vi (Aut)* mit Zwischengas schalten; ~ **dutch** *n (Brit)* Kauderwelsch *nt*; **it's ~ dutch to me** das sind böhmische Dörfer für mich; **~-edged** *adj (lit, fig)* zweischneidig; ~ **entendre** [ˈduːblãːnˈtãːndr] *n* Zweideutigkeit *f*; ~ **fault** *n (Tennis)* Doppelfehler *m*; ~ **glazing** *n* Doppelfenster *pl*; **~-jointed** *adj* sehr gelenkig; ~ **park** *vi* in zweiter Reihe parken; **~-quick** *adj (col)* in **~-quick time** in Null Komma nichts *(col)*.

doubles [ˈdʌblz] *n sing or pl (Sport)* Doppel *nt*.

double: ~ **take** *n* **he did a ~ take** er mußte zweimal hinsehen; **~talk** *n (ambiguous)* doppeldeutiges Gerede; *(deceitful)* doppelzüngiges Gerede.

doubly [ˈdʌblɪ] *adv* doppelt.

doubt [daʊt] **1** *n* Zweifel *m*. **his honesty is in ~** seine Ehrlichkeit wird angezweifelt; **I am in no ~ as to what he means** ich bin mir völlig im klaren darüber, was er meint; **I have my ~s whether he will come** ich bezweifle, daß er kommt; **there's no ~ about it** daran gibt es keinen Zweifel; **I have no ~s about taking the job** ich habe keine Bedenken, die Stelle anzunehmen; **no ~ he will come tomorrow** höchstwahrscheinlich kommt er morgen; **without (a) ~** ohne Zweifel; **yes, no ~** ja, zweifellos; **it's beyond ~ that ...** es steht außer Zweifel, daß ...; **when in ~** im Zweifelsfall. **2** *vt* bezweifeln; *sb's honesty, truth of statement* anzweifeln, Zweifel haben an (+*dat*). **I ~ it (very much)** das bezweifle ich (sehr).

doubter [ˈdaʊtəʳ] *n* Skeptiker, Zweifler *m*.

doubtful [ˈdaʊtfʊl] *adj* **(a)** *(uncertain)* unsicher, zweifelhaft; *outcome, result, future* ungewiß. **to be ~ about sb/sth** wegen jdm/etw Bedenken haben; **I'm a bit ~** ich habe so meine Bedenken; **to look ~** *(person)* skeptisch dreinblicken; **the weather looked a bit ~** es sah nach schlechtem Wetter aus. **(b)** *(of questionable character)* zweifelhaft; *person, affair also* zwielichtig.

doubtfully [ˈdaʊtfəlɪ] *adv* skeptisch.

doubtfulness [ˈdaʊtfʊlnɪs] *n see adj* **(a)** Unsicherheit *f*; Ungewißheit *f*. **(b)** Zweifelhaftigkeit *f*; Zwielichtigkeit *f*.

doubtless [ˈdaʊtlɪs] *adj* zweifelsohne.

douche [duːʃ] *n* Spülung *f*.

dough [dəʊ] *n* Teig *m*; *(col: money)* Kohle *f (col)*.

doughnut [ˈdəʊnʌt] *n* Berliner *m*.

dour [ˈdʊəʳ] *adj* mürrisch, verdrießlich; *struggle* hart, hartnäckig.

douse [daʊs] *vt* **(a)** Wasser schütten über (+*acc*); *plants* reichlich wässern. **(b)** *light* ausmachen.

dove[1] [dʌv] *n (lit, fig)* Taube *f*.

dove[2] [dəʊv] *(US) pret of* **dive**.

dovecot(e) [ˈdʌvkɒt] *n* Taubenschlag *m*.

dovetail [ˈdʌvteɪl] **1** *n* ~ **joint** Schwalbenschwanzverbindung *f*. **2** *vt plans* koordinieren. **3** *vi (plans)* übereinstimmen.

dowager [ˈdaʊədʒəʳ] *n (adelige)* Witwe.

dowdy [ˈdaʊdɪ] *adj (+er)* ohne jeden Schick.

down[1] [daʊn] **1** *adv* **(a)** *(towards speaker)* herunter, herab; *(away from speaker)* hinunter, hinab; *(downstairs also)* nach unten. ~**!** *(to dog)* Platz!; **to jump ~** hinunter-/herunterspringen; ~ **with traitors!** nieder mit den Verrätern!; **on his way ~ from the hilltop** beim Abstieg; **all the way ~ to the bottom** bis ganz nach unten. **(b)** *(position)* unten. ~ **there** da unten; ~ **here** hier unten; **don't kick a man when he's ~** man soll jemanden nicht fertigmachen, wenn es ihm schon schlecht geht; **the sun is ~** die Sonne ist untergegangen; **I'll be ~ in a minute** ich komme sofort runter; **I've been ~ with flu** ich habe mit Grippe im Bett gelegen; **he was (feeling) a bit ~** er fühlte sich ein wenig niedergeschlagen *or* down *(col)*; **they'll be ~ on you** *(police etc)* du bekommst Ärger mit ihnen.

(c) **he came ~ from London yesterday** er kam gestern aus London; ~ **South** im Süden/in den Süden, ~ **here in Italy** hier unten in Italien; **he's ~ at his brother's** er ist bei seinem Bruder; **from 1700 ~ to the present** von 1700 bis zur Gegenwart.

(d) *(in volume, degree, activity, status)* **the tyres are ~** die Reifen sind platt; **his temperature has gone ~** sein Fieber ist zurückgegangen; **the price is ~ on last week** der Preis ist gegenüber der letzten Woche gefallen; **I'm £2 ~ on what I expected** ich habe £ 2 weniger, als ich dachte; **they're still three goals ~** sie liegen immer noch mit drei Toren zurück.

(e) *(in writing, planning)* **I've got it ~ in my diary** ich habe es in meinem Kalender notiert; **to be ~ for the next race** für das nächste Rennen gemeldet sein; **it's ~ for next month** es steht für nächsten Monat auf dem Programm.

(f) **to pay £2 ~** £ 2 anzahlen; **how much do they want ~?** was verlangen sie als Anzahlung?

2 *prep* **(a)** *(indicating movement to)* **to go/come ~ the hill/street** den Berg/die Straße hinunter-gehen/herunterkommen; **she let her hair fall ~ her back** sie ließ ihr Haar über die Schultern fallen; **he ran his finger ~ the list** er ging mit dem Finger die Liste durch. **(b)** *(at a lower part of)* **the other skiers were further ~ the slope** die anderen Skifahrer waren weiter unten; **she lives ~ the street** sie wohnt hier unten in der Straße. **(c)** ~ **the ages/centuries** Jahrhunderte (hindurch). **(d)** *(along)* **he was walking/coming ~ the street** er ging/kam die Straße entlang. **(e)** *(Brit col: to, in, at)* **he's gone ~ the pub** er ist in die Kneipe gegangen; **she's ~ the shops** sie ist einkaufen gegangen.

3 *n* **to have a ~ on sb** *(col)* jdn auf dem Kieker haben *(col)*.

4 *vt opponent* niederschlagen; *beer* runterkippen *(col)*. **to ~ tools** die Arbeit niederlegen.

down[2] *n (feathers)* Daunen, Flaumfedern *pl*; *(youth's beard)* Flaum *m*.

down[3] *n usu pl* **on the ~(s)** im Hügelland.

down: **~-and-out 1** *n (tramp)* Penner *m (col)*; **2** *adj* heruntergekommen; **~cast** *adj* niedergeschlagen; **~fall** *n* **(a)** Sturz, Fall *m*; *(of empire also)*

Untergang *m*; *(cause of ruin: drink etc)* Ruin *m*; **(b)** *(of rain)* heftiger Niederschlag, Platzregen *m*; ~**grade** *vt hotel, job* herunterstufen; *person also* degradieren; ~**-hearted** *adj* niedergeschlagen; ~**hill** *adv* **to go** ~**hill** *(road)* bergab führen *or* gehen; *(fig) (person)* auf dem absteigenden Ast sein; *(work, health)* sich verschlechtern; ~**market** *adj product* Massen-; *area, shop etc* weniger vornehm; ~ **payment** *n* Anzahlung *f*; ~**pour** *n* Wolkenbruch *m*; ~**right** 1 *adj refusal, lie* glatt; *rudeness, scoundrel, liar* ausgesprochen; 2 *adv rude* ausgesprochen; ~**stairs** 1 *adv* go, come nach unten; *be* unten; 2 *adj* **the** ~**stairs rooms** die unteren Zimmer; **our** ~**stairs neighbours** die Nachbarn unter uns; ~**stream** *adv* flußabwärts *(from* von*)*; ~**-to-earth** *adj* nüchtern; *advice* praktisch; ~**town** 1 *adj* ~**town district** Zentrum *nt*, Innenstadt *f*; *(US)* Geschäftsviertel *nt*; 2 *adv* **to go** ~**town** in die Stadt *or* ins Zentrum gehen; ~ **train** *n* Zug, der von der Stadt aufs Land fährt oder von der Hauptstadt abgeht; ~**trodden** *adj* people unterdrückt; ~ **under** *n (Brit col)* Australien *nt*.
downward ['daʊnwəd] 1 *adj movement, pull* nach unten. 2 *adv (also* **downwards)** *go, look* nach unten. **to slope gently** ~ sanft abfallen; **from the President** ~ beim Präsidenten angefangen.
dowry ['daʊrɪ] *n* Mitgift *f*.
doz = **dozen**.
doze [dəʊz] 1 *n* Nickerchen *nt*. 2 *vi* (vor sich hin) dösen.
♦ **doze off** *vi* einschlafen, einnicken.
dozen ['dʌzn] *n* Dutzend *nt*. **half a** ~ ein halbes Dutzend; ~**s** *(fig col)* eine ganze Menge; ~**s of times** *(col)* x-mal *(col)*.
dozy ['dəʊzɪ] *adj (+er) (sleepy)* verschlafen.
DPP = **Director of Public Prosecutions**.
dpt = **department** Abt.
Dr = **doctor** Dr.
drab [dræb] *adj (+er)* trist; *colour also* düster.
draft [drɑːft] 1 *n* **(a)** *(rough outline)* Entwurf *m*. **(b)** *(Fin, Comm)* Wechsel *m*. **(c)** *(US Mil: conscription)* Einberufung (zum Wehrdienst). **(d)** *(US)* = **draught**. 2 *vt* **(a)** *letter, contract* entwerfen. **(b)** *(US Mil) conscript* einberufen.
drag [dræg] 1 *n* **(a)** *(aerodynamic)* Luftwiderstand *m*. **(b)** *(col: hindrance)* **to be a** ~ **on sb** für jdn ein Klotz am Bein sein. **(c)** *(col)* **what a** ~! *(boring)* Mann, ist der/die/das langweilig! *(col)*; *(nuisance)* so'n Mist *(col)*; **(d)** *(col: pull on cigarette)* Zug *m* (on, at an +dat). **(e)** *(women's clothing)* **in** *or* **wearing** ~ in Frauenkleidung. 2 *vt* **(a)** *person, object* schleppen, schleifen. **to** ~ **one's feet** *(fig)* alles/die Sache schleifen lassen; **to** ~ **the truth out of sb** die Wahrheit mühsam aus jdm herausholen. **(b)** *river* absuchen. 3 *vi* *(time, work)* sich hinziehen; *(play, book, conversation)* sich in die Länge ziehen.
♦ **drag along** *vt sep person* mitschleppen.
♦ **drag away** *vt sep (lit, fig)* wegschleppen. **you'll have to** ~ **him** ~ **from the television** den muß man mit Gewalt vom Fernseher wegziehen.
♦ **drag down** *vt sep (lit)* herunterziehen; *(fig)* mit sich ziehen. **to** ~ **sb** ~ **to one's level** *(fig)* jdn auf sein eigenes Niveau herunterziehen.
♦ **drag in** *vt sep (fig) subject* aufs Tapet bringen; *remark* anbringen.
♦ **drag on** *vi* sich in die Länge ziehen; *(meeting, lecture also)* sich hinziehen. **it** ~**ged** ~ **for 3 hours** es zog sich über 3 Stunden hin.
dragon ['drægən] *n (lit, fig col)* Drache *m*.
dragonfly ['drægənflaɪ] *n* Libelle *f*.
drain [dreɪn] 1 *n* **(a)** *(pipe)* Rohr *nt*; *(under sink etc)* Abfluß(rohr *nt*) *m*; *(under the ground)* Kanalisationsrohr *nt*; *(~ cover)* Rost *m*. 2 *vi (system)* Kanalisation *f*; **open** ~ (Abfluß)rinne *f*; **to throw one's money down the** ~ *(fig col)* das Geld zum Fenster hinauswerfen; **this country's going down the** ~ *(col)* dieses Land geht vor die Hunde

(col). **(b)** *(on resources etc)* Belastung *f (on gen)*. **it has been a great** ~ **on her strength** das hat sehr an ihren Kräften gezehrt.
2 *vt* **(a)** *land, marshes* entwässern; *vegetables* abgießen; *reservoir* trockenlegen; *boiler, radiator* das Wasser ablassen aus; *engine oil* ablassen. **(b)** *(fig)* **to feel** ~**ed (of energy)** sich ausgelaugt fühlen; **to** ~ **a country of resources** ein Land ausbeuten; **to** ~ **sb dry** jdn ausnehmen *(col)*. **(c)** *glass* austrinken, leeren.
3 *vi (vegetables, dishes)* abtropfen.
♦ **drain away** *vi (liquid)* ablaufen; *(strength)* dahinschwinden.
♦ **drain off** *vt sep* abgießen.
drainage ['dreɪnɪdʒ] *n* **(a)** *(draining)* Dränage *f*; *(of land also)* Entwässerung *f*. **(b)** *(system)* Entwässerungssystem *nt*; *(in house, town)* Kanalisation *f*. **(c)** *(sewage)* Abwasser *nt*.
drain: ~**ing board**, *(US)* ~ **board** *n* Ablauf *m*; ~ **pipe** *n* Abflußrohr *nt*.
drake [dreɪk] *n* Erpel, Enterich *m*.
drama ['drɑːmə] *n* Drama *nt*. **the** ~ **of the situation** die Dramatik der Situation.
drama: ~ **critic** *n* Theaterkritiker(in *f*) *m*; ~ **student** *n* Schauspielschüler(in *f*) *m*.
dramatic [drə'mætɪk] *adj* dramatisch.
dramatist ['dræmətɪst] *n* Dramatiker(in *f*) *m*.
dramatize ['dræmətaɪz] 1 *vt* **(a)** *novel* für die Bühne/das Fernsehen bearbeiten. **(b)** *(make vivid)* dramatisieren. 2 *vi (exaggerate)* übertreiben.
drank [dræŋk] *pret of* **drink**.
drape [dreɪp] 1 *vt* drapieren; *person* hüllen. 2 *n* ~**s** *pl (US)* Vorhänge *pl*.
draper ['dreɪpə'] *n (Brit)* Textilkaufmann *m*.
drapery ['dreɪpərɪ] *n (Brit) (cloth etc)* Stoff *m*; *(business: also* ~ **shop)** Stoffgeschäft *nt*.
drastic ['dræstɪk] *adj* drastisch. **things are getting** ~ die Sache wird kritisch.
drat [dræt] *interj* ~ **(it)!** verflixt! *(col)*.
draught, *(US)* **draft** [drɑːft] *n* **(a)** *(Luft)*zug *m*; **there's a terrible** ~ **in here** hier zieht es fürchterlich; **are you in a** ~? zieht es Ihnen?; **a nice cool** ~ etwas frische Luft. **(b)** *(swallow, drink)* Zug *m*. **(c)** *(~ beer)* Faß- *or* Schankbier *nt*. **on** ~ vom Faß. **(d)** *(Naut)* Tiefgang *m*. **(e)** *(Brit: game)* ~**s** *(+sing vb)* Damespiel *nt*; *(+pl vb: pieces)* Damesteine *pl*.
draughtsman, *(US)* **draftsman** [drɑːftsmən] *n, pl* -**men** [-mən] *(Tech)* Zeichner *m*.
draughtsmanship, *(US)* **draftsmanship** [drɑːftsmənʃɪp] *n* zeichnerisches Können.
draughty, *(US)* **drafty** [drɑːftɪ] *adj (+er)* zugig. **it's** ~ **in here** hier zieht es.
draw[1] [drɔː] *pret* **drew**, *ptp* **drawn** 1 *vt (lit, fig)* zeichnen; *line* ziehen. **we must** ~ **the line somewhere** *(fig)* irgendwo muß Schluß sein. 2 *vi* zeichnen.
draw[2] *(vb:* pret **drew**, *ptp* **drawn)** 1 *vt* **(a)** *(pull)* ziehen; *bolt* zurückschieben; *bow* spannen; *curtains (open)* aufziehen; *(shut)* zuziehen; *(Med) abscess* schneiden; *cork* herausziehen. **he drew his hat over his eyes** er zog sich *(dat)* den Hut ins Gesicht.
(b) *(obtain from source)* holen; *salary* beziehen. **to** ~ **a bath** das Badewasser einlassen; **to** ~ **money from the bank** Geld (vom Konto) abheben; **he's bitten her — has he** ~**n blood?** er hat sie gebissen — blutet sie?; **to** ~ **comfort from sth** sich mit etw trösten; **to** ~ **a smile from sb** jdm ein Lächeln entlocken; **to** ~ **a (deep) breath** (tief) Luft holen.
(c) *(attract) interest* erregen; *customer, crowd* anlocken. **to feel** ~**n towards sb** sich zu jdm hingezogen fühlen.
(d) **he refuses to be** ~**n** *(will not speak)* aus ihm ist nichts herauszubringen; *(will not be provoked)* er läßt sich auf nichts ein; **I won't be**

~n on that one dazu möchte ich mich nicht äußern.
  (e) *conclusion, comparison* ziehen; *distinction* treffen.
  (f) *(Sport)* to ~ a match unentschieden spielen.
  (g) **France has been** ~n **against Scotland** Frankreich ist für die Begegnung mit Schottland ausgelost worden.
  (h) *(Cook) fowl* ausnehmen.
  2 *vi* **(a)** *(move, come)* kommen. **he drew towards the door** er bewegte sich zur Tür; **he drew to one side** er ging/fuhr zur Seite; **he drew over to the kerb** er fuhr an den Straßenrand; **to ~ around the table** sich um den Tisch versammeln; **to ~ to an end** zu Ende gehen; **he drew ahead of** *or* **away from the other runners** er zog den anderen Läufern davon. **(b)** *(allow airflow: of chimney, pipe)* ziehen. **(c)** *(Sport)* unentschieden spielen. **they drew 2-2** sie trennten sich 2:2 unentschieden. **(d)** *(infuse: tea)* ziehen.
  3 *n* **(a)** *(lottery)* Ziehung, Ausspielung *f*; *(for sports competitions)* Auslosung *f*. **(b)** *(Sport)* Unentschieden *nt*. **the match ended in a ~** das Spiel endete unentschieden. **(c)** *(attraction: play, film etc)* (Kassen)schlager, Knüller *(col)* *m*; *(person)* Attraktion *f*. **(d) to be quick on the ~** *(lit)* schnell mit der Pistole sein; *(fig)* schlagfertig sein.

♦ **draw back 1** *vi* zurückweichen. **2** *vt sep* zurückziehen; *curtains also* aufziehen.

♦ **draw in 1** *vi* **(a)** *(train)* einfahren; **to ~ ~ at the kerb** am Bordstein (an)halten. **(b)** *(get shorter: days)* kürzer werden. **2** *vt sep* **(a)** *breath, air* einziehen. **(b)** *(attract, gain) crowds* anziehen. **(c) to ~ ~ one's claws** *(lit, fig)* die Krallen einziehen.

♦ **draw on 1** *vi* **as the night drew** ~ mit fortschreitender Nacht; **winter** ~s ~ der Winter naht; **time is** ~ing ~ es wird spät. **2** *vi* +*prep obj* *(use as source: also* ~ **upon)** sich stützen auf (+*acc*). **3** *vt sep stockings, gloves* anziehen.

♦ **draw out 1** *vi* **(a)** *(train)* ausfahren; *(car)* herausfahren *(of* aus*)*. **(b)** *(days)* länger werden. **2** *vt sep* **(a)** *(take out)* herausziehen. **(b)** *(prolong)* in die Länge ziehen, hinausziehen. **(c) to ~ sb ~ (of his shell)** jdn aus der Reserve locken.

♦ **draw together** *vt sep threads* miteinander verknüpfen.

♦ **draw up 1** *vi* *(stop: car)* (an)halten. **2** *vt sep* **(a)** *(formulate)* entwerfen; *contract, agreement also, will* aufsetzen; *list* aufstellen. **(b)** *chair* heranziehen; **to ~ oneself** ~ *(to one's full height)* sich (zu seiner vollen Größe) aufrichten. **(c)** *(set in line) troops* aufstellen.

draw: ~**back** *n* Nachteil *m*; ~**bridge** *n* Zugbrücke *f*.

drawer *n* **(a)** [drɔːʳ] *(in desk etc)* Schublade *f*. **(b)** [ˈdrɔːəʳ] *(person: of pictures)* Zeichner *m*. **(c)** [ˈdrɔːəʳ] *(of cheque etc)* Aussteller *m*.

drawing [ˈdrɔːɪŋ] *n* Zeichnung *f*. **I'm no good at** ~ ich kann nicht gut zeichnen.

drawing: ~**-board** *n* Reißbrett *nt*; **well, it's back to the** ~**-board** *(fig)* das muß noch einmal ganz neu überdacht werden; ~**-pin** *n (Brit)* Reißzwecke *f*; ~ **room** *n* Wohnzimmer *nt*; *(in mansion)* Salon *m*.

drawl [drɔːl] **1** *vi* schleppend sprechen. **2** *vt* schleppend aussprechen. **3** *n* schleppende Sprache.

drawn [drɔːn] **1** *ptp of* **draw¹**, **draw²**. **2** *adj* **(a)** *(from tiredness)* abgespannt; *(from worry)* abgehärmt, verhärmt; *(with pain)* schmerzverzerrt. **(b)** *game, match* unentschieden.

dread [dred] **1** *vt* sich fürchten vor (+*dat*), große Angst haben vor (+*dat*). **I** ~ **to think what may happen** ich wage nicht daran zu denken, was passieren könnte. **2** *n* Furcht *f*.

dreadful [ˈdredfʊl] *adj* schrecklich, furchtbar. **I feel** ~ *(ill)* ich fühle mich schrecklich *or* scheußlich; *(mortified)* es ist mir schrecklich peinlich.

dreadfully [ˈdredfəlɪ] *adv* schrecklich.

dream [driːm] *(vb: pret, ptp* **dreamt** *or* ~**ed**) **1** *n* Traum *m*. **to have a bad** ~ schlecht träumen; **sweet** ~s! träum was Schönes!; **to have a** ~ **about sb/sth** von jdm/etw träumen; **in a** ~ *(fig)* wie im Traum; **the house of his** ~s das Haus seiner Träume, sein Traumhaus; **happy beyond her wildest** ~s glücklicher als in ihren kühnsten Träumen; **to have** ~s **of becoming rich** davon träumen, reich zu werden; **it worked like a** ~ *(col)* es hat hervorragend geklappt; **you're a** ~! du bist ein Schatz; **a** ~ **of a hat** ein traumhaft schöner Hut.
  2 *vi (lit, fig)* träumen *(about, of* von*)*. **I'm sorry, I was** ~ing Verzeihung, ich habe gerade geträumt.
  3 *vt (lit, fig)* träumen; *dream* haben. **I wouldn't** ~ **of it** das würde mir nicht im Traum einfallen; **I never** ~t *(that)* **he would come** ich hätte mir nie träumen lassen, daß er kommen würde.
  4 *adj attr car, holiday* Traum-.

♦ **dream up** *vt sep (col) idea* sich *(dat)* ausdenken.

dreamer [ˈdriːməʳ] *n* Träumer(in *f*) *m*.

dreamt [dremt] *pret, ptp of* **dream**.

dreamy [ˈdriːmɪ] *adj (+er)* verträumt.

dreary [ˈdrɪərɪ] *adj (+er)* eintönig; *weather* trüb; *person, speech* langweilig.

dredge [dredʒ] *vt river, canal* ausbaggern.

♦ **dredge up** *vt sep (lit)* ausbaggern; *(fig)* unpleasant facts ausgraben.

dredger [ˈdredʒəʳ] *n* Bagger *m*.

dregs [dregz] *npl* **(a)** *(Boden)satz m*. **(b)** *(fig)* Abschaum *m*.

drenched [drentʃt] *adj* völlig durchnäßt.

dress [dres] **1** *n* **(a)** *(for woman)* Kleid *nt*. **2** *no pl (clothing)* Kleidung *f*. **in eastern** ~ orientalisch gekleidet. **2** *vt* **(a)** *(clothe)* anziehen. **to get** ~ed sich anziehen; **to** ~ **sb in sth** jdm etw anziehen; ~ed **in black** schwarz gekleidet. **(b)** *(Naut) ship* beflaggen. **(c)** *(Cook) salad* anmachen; *chicken* bratfertig machen. **(d)** *skins* gerben; *material* appretieren; *timber* hobeln; *stone* schleifen. **(e)** *wound* verbinden. **3** *vi* sich anziehen, sich kleiden. **to ~ in black** sich schwarz kleiden.

♦ **dress up 1** *vi (smartly)* sich feinmachen; *(in fancy dress)* sich verkleiden. ~ed ~ **as Father Christmas** als Weihnachtsmann (verkleidet). **2** *vt sep (disguise)* verkleiden.

dressage [ˈdresɑːʒ] *n* Dressur *f*.

dress: ~ **circle** *n* erster Rang; ~ **designer** *n* Modezeichner(in *f*) *m*.

dresser¹ [ˈdresəʳ] *n* **(a)** *(Theat)* Garderobier *m*, Garderobiere *f*. **(b) she's a stylish** ~ sie ist immer sehr elegant (gekleidet).

dresser² *n* **(a)** Anrichte *f*. **(b)** *(US: dressing-table)* Frisierkommode *f*.

dressing [ˈdresɪŋ] *n* **(a)** *(Med: bandage, ointment)* Verband *m*. **(b)** *(Cook)* Soße *f*.

dressing: ~ **down** *n* **to give sb a** ~ **down** jdn herunterputzen *(col)*; ~**-gown** *n* Morgenrock *m*; ~**-room** *n (Theat)* (Künstler)garderobe *f*; *(Sport)* Umkleidekabine *f*; ~**-table** *n* Frisierkommode *f*.

dress: ~**maker** *n* (Damen)schneider(in *f*) *m*; ~**making** *n* Schneidern *nt*; ~ **rehearsal** *n (lit, fig)* Generalprobe *f*; ~ **shirt** *n* Frackhemd *nt*; ~ **uniform** *n* Galauniform *f*.

dressy [ˈdresɪ] *adj (+er) (col) person* fein angezogen; *clothes* elegant.

drew [druː] *pret of* **draw¹**, **draw²**.

dribble [ˈdrɪbl] **1** *vi* **(a)** *(liquids)* tropfen; *(baby, person)* sabbern; *(animal)* geifern. **(b)** *(Sport)* dribbeln. **(c)** *(people)* **to** ~ **back/in** nach und nach zurückkommen/hereinkommen. **2** *vt* **(a)** *(Sport)* **to ~ the ball** mit dem Ball dribbeln. **(b)** *(baby etc)* kleckern.

dribs and drabs ['drɪbzən'dræbz] *npl*: in ~ kleckerweise *(col)*.

dried [draɪd] *adj* getrocknet; *fruit also* Dörr-. ~ milk Trockenmilch *f*, Milchpulver *nt*.

drier *n* = dryer.

drift [drɪft] 1 *vi* **(a)** *(Naut)* treiben; *(sand)* wehen. to ~ off course abtreiben; as the smoke ~ed away als der Rauch abzog. **(b)** *(fig: person)* sich treiben lassen. to let things ~ die Dinge treiben lassen; he ~ed into marriage er ist in die Ehe hineingeschlittert *(col)*; the nation was ~ing towards a crisis das Land trieb auf eine Krise zu; young people are ~ing away from the villages junge Leute wandern aus den Dörfern ab; to ~ apart *(people)* sich auseinanderleben. 2 *n* **(a)** *(of air, water)* Strömung *f*; *(of events)* Lauf *m*. **(b)** *(of sand, snow)* Verwehung *f*. **(c)** *(of ship, aircraft)* (Ab)drift, Abweichung *f*. **(d)** *continental* ~ Kontinentalverschiebung *f*. **(e)** *(of questions)* Richtung, Tendenz *f*. if I get your ~ wenn ich Sie recht verstehe.

drifter ['drɪftə'] *n (person)* Gammler *m*. he's a bit of a ~ er hält es nirgends lange aus.

driftwood ['drɪftwʊd] Treibholz *nt*.

drill[1] [drɪl] 1 *n* Bohrer *m*. 2 *vti* bohren *(for* nach*)*.

drill[2] 1 *n no pl (esp Mil, fig)* Drill *m*; *(marching etc)* Exerzieren *nt*. 2 *vt* **(a)** *soldiers* drillen; *(in marching etc)* exerzieren lassen. **(b)** to ~ pupils in grammar den Schülern Grammatik pauken; I ~ed it into him ich habe es ihm eingebleut *(col)*. 3 *vi (Mil)* gedrillt werden; *(marching etc)* exerzieren.

drill[3] *n (Tex)* Drillich *m*.

drilling ['drɪlɪŋ] *n (for oil)* Bohrung *f*. ~ **rig** Bohrturm *m*; *(at sea)* Bohrinsel *f*.

drily ['draɪlɪ] *adv* trocken.

drink [drɪŋk] *(vb: pret* drank*, ptp* drunk*)* 1 *n* **(a)** Getränk *nt*. food and ~ Essen und Getränke; may I have a ~? kann ich etwas zu trinken haben?; would you like a ~ of water? möchten Sie etwas Wasser?; to give sb a ~ jdm etwas zu trinken geben. **(b)** *(alcoholic)* Drink *m*. let's have a ~ trinken wir was; I need a ~! ich brauche was zu trinken!; he likes a ~ er trinkt gern (einen); to ask friends in for ~s Freunde auf ein Glas *or* einen Drink einladen; he's got a few ~s in him *(col)* er hat einige Gläser intus *(col)*. **(c)** *no pl (alcoholic liquor)* Alkohol *m*. he has a ~ problem er trinkt; his worries/she drove him to ~ vor Kummer fing er an zu trinken/sie trieb ihn in den Alkohol; to smell of ~ eine Fahne haben.
2 *vt* trinken. would you like something to ~? möchten Sie etwas zu trinken (haben)?; this coffee isn't fit to ~ diesen Kaffee kann man nicht trinken.
3 *vi* trinken. he doesn't ~ er trinkt nicht; his father drank sein Vater war Trinker; one shouldn't ~ and drive nach dem Trinken soll man nicht fahren; ~ing and driving Alkohol am Steuer; to ~ to sb/sth auf jdn/etw trinken.
♦ **drink in** *vt sep air* tief einatmen; *(fig) a sight, his words etc* (begierig) in sich *(acc)* aufnehmen.
♦ **drink up** *vti* austrinken.

drinkable ['drɪŋkəbl] *adj* trinkbar.

drinker ['drɪŋkə'] *n* Trinker(in *f*) *m*.

drinking ['drɪŋkɪŋ] *n* Trinken *nt*.

drinking: ~ **fountain** *n* Trinkwasserbrunnen *m*; ~-**up time** *n (Brit)* die letzten zehn Minuten vor der Polizeistunde; ~-**water** *n* Trinkwasser *nt*.

drip [drɪp] 1 *vi* tropfen. to be ~ping with sweat/ blood schweißgebadet/blutüberströmt sein. 2 *vt liquid* träufeln, tropfen. you're ~ping paint over my coat du tropfst mir Farbe auf den Mantel. 3 *n* **(a)** *(sound)* Tropfen *nt*. **(b)** *(drop)* Tropfen *m*. **(c)** *(Med)* Tropf *(col) m*. to be on a ~ eine Infusion bekommen, am Tropf hängen *(col)*. **(d)** *(col: silly person)* Flasche *f (col)*.

drip-dry ['drɪp'draɪ] *adj shirt* bügelfrei.

dripping ['drɪpɪŋ] 1 *n (Cook)* Bratenfett *nt*. 2 *adj* **(a)** *tap* tropfend; *washing* tropfnaß. **(b)** *(col: also* ~ **wet)** *coat, clothes* klatschnaß *(col)*.

drive [draɪv] *(vb: pret* drove*, ptp* driven*)* 1 *n* **(a)** *(Aut: journey)* Fahrt *f*. to go for a ~ (ein bißchen) spazierenfahren; to go for a ~ to the coast ans Meer fahren; one hour's ~ from London eine Autostunde von London (entfernt). **(b)** *(into house: also* ~**way)** Einfahrt *f*; *(longer)* Auffahrt, Zufahrt *f*. **(c)** *(Golf, Tennis)* Treibschlag *m*. **(d)** *(Psych etc)* Trieb *m*; *(energy)* Schwung, Elan *m*. sex ~ Sexualtrieb *m*. **(e)** *(Comm, Pol etc)* Aktion *f*; *(Mil)* Offensive *f*. sales ~ Verkaufskampagne *f*. **(f)** *(Mech: power transmission)* Antrieb *m*; *(Comp)* Laufwerk *nt*. **(g)** *(Aut)* Steuerung *f*. left-hand ~ Linkssteuerung *f*.
2 *vt* **(a)** *animals, dust, clouds etc* treiben. to ~ a nail into sth einen Nagel in etw *(acc)* einschlagen; the gale drove the ship off course der Sturm trieb das Schiff vom Kurs ab. **(b)** *car, train* fahren. he ~s a taxi er fährt Taxi; I'll ~ you home ich fahre Sie nach Hause. **(c)** *(provide power for)* *(belt, shaft)* antreiben; *(electricity, fuel)* betreiben. **(d)** *(cause to become)* treiben. to ~ sb mad jdn verrückt machen; to ~ sb to desperation jdn zur Verzweiflung treiben; I was ~n to it ich wurde dazu getrieben. **(e)** *(force to work hard)* you're driving him too hard Sie nehmen ihn zu hart ran; he ~s himself very hard er fordert viel von sich.
3 *vi* **(a)** fahren; *(go by car)* mit dem Auto fahren. he's learning to ~ er lernt Auto fahren. **(b)** the rain was driving in our faces der Regen peitschte uns *(dat)* ins Gesicht.
♦ **drive along** 1 *vi (vehicle, person)* dahinfahren. 2 *vt sep (wind, current) person, boat* (voran)treiben.
♦ **drive at** *vi +prep obj* hinauswollen auf *(+acc)*. what are you driving ~? worauf wollen Sie hinaus?
♦ **drive away** 1 *vi (car, person)* wegfahren. 2 *vt sep (lig, fig) person, cares* vertreiben.
♦ **drive back** 1 *vti (in vehicle)* zurückfahren. 2 *vt sep enemy* zurücktreiben.
♦ **drive home** *vt sep nail, argument* einhämmern. how can I ~ it to him that ...? wie kann ich (es) ihm nur klarmachen, daß ...?
♦ **drive off** 1 *vi (person, car)* weg- *or* abfahren. 2 *vt sep person, enemy* vertreiben.
♦ **drive on** 1 *vi (person, car)* weiterfahren. 2 *vt sep (encourage)* antreiben; *(to sth bad)* anstiften.
♦ **drive out** *vt sep person* hinaustreiben *or* -jagen; *evil thoughts* austreiben.
♦ **drive up** *vi (car, person)* vorfahren.

drive-in ['draɪv,ɪn] *adj* ~ **cinema** Autokino *nt*.

drivel ['drɪvl] *n (pej)* Blödsinn *m*.

driven ['drɪvn] *ptp of* **drive**.

driver ['draɪvə'] *n* Fahrer(in *f*) *m*; *(Brit: of locomotive)* Führer *m*. to be in the ~'s seat *(fig)* die Zügel in der Hand haben.

driver's license *n (US)* Führerschein *m*.

drive: ~ **shaft** *n* Antriebswelle *f*; *(Aut)* Kardanwelle *f*; ~**way** *n* Auffahrt *f*; *(longer)* Zufahrtsstraße *f*.

driving ['draɪvɪŋ] 1 *n* Fahren *nt*. his ~ is awful er fährt kriminell; dangerous ~ *(Jur)* verkehrsgefährdendes (Fahr)verhalten. 2 *adj* the ~ force die treibende Kraft; ~ **rain** peitschender Regen.

driving: ~ **instructor** *n* Fahrlehrer(in *f*) *m*; ~ **lesson** *n* Fahrstunde *f*; ~ **licence** *n (Brit)* Führerschein *m*; ~ **mirror** *n* Rückspiegel *m*; ~ **school** *n* Fahrschule *f*; ~ **test** *n* Fahrprüfung *f*.

drizzle ['drɪzl] 1 *n* Nieselregen *m*. 2 *vi* nieseln.

droll [drəʊl] *adj* drollig, ulkig.

dromedary ['drɒmɪdərɪ] *n* Dromedar *nt*.

drone [drəʊn] 1 *n* **(a)** *(bee, fig)* Drohne *f*. **(b)** *(sound) (of bees)* Summen *nt*; *(of engine)* Brummen *nt*; *(way of speaking)* monotone

Stimme. **2** *vi* (*bee*) summen; (*engine*) brummen; (*speak: also* ~ **away** *or* **on**) eintönig sprechen; (*in reciting*) leiern. **he ~d on for hours** er redete stundenlang in seinem monotonen Tonfall.

drool [druːl] *vi* sabbern.

♦ **drool over** *vi* +*prep obj sb* vernarrt sein in (+*acc*); *sb's remarks* in Ekstase geraten über (+*acc*); *porno magazine* sich aufgeilen an (+*dat*) (*col!*).

droop [druːp] *vi* (**a**) (*lit*) (*person*) vornüber gebeugt stehen; (*shoulders*) herabhängen; (*head*) herunterfallen; (*eyelids*) herunterhängen; (*with sleepiness*) zufallen; (*flowers*) die Köpfe hängen lassen; (*one's hand, breasts*) schlaff herunterhängen. (**b**) (*fig: interest, energy*) erlahmen; (*audience etc*) abschlaffen. **don't let your spirits ~** laß den Mut nicht sinken.

drop [drɒp] **1** *n* (**a**) (*of liquid, also fig*) Tropfen *m*. **a ~ of blood** ein Blutstropfen *m*; **it's a ~ in the ocean** (*fig*) das ist ein Tropfen auf den heißen Stein; **a ~ of wine?** ein Schlückchen Wein?; **he's had a ~ too much** er hat einen über den Durst getrunken. (**b**) (*sweet*) Drops *m*. (**c**) (*fall: in temperature, prices*) Rückgang *m*; (*sudden*) Sturz *m*. **a ~ in prices** ein Preissturz *m*/-rückgang *m*; **a ~ in salary** eine Gehaltseinbuße. (**d**) (*difference in level*) Höhenunterschied *m*; (*fall*) Sturz, Fall *m*; (*parachute jump*) (Ab)sprung *m*. **there's a ~ of ten metres down to the ledge** bis zu dem Felsvorsprung geht es zehn Meter hinunter; **it's a long ~** es geht tief hinunter. (**e**) (*of supplies, arms*) Abwurf *m*.

2 *vt* (**a**) (*allow to fall*) fallen lassen; *bomb, supplies, burden* abwerfen; *parachutist* absetzen; *voice* senken; (*Knitting*) *stitch* fallen lassen; (*lower*) *hemline* herunterlassen. **I ~ped my watch** meine Uhr ist (mir) runtergefallen.

(**b**) (*set down*) (*from car*) *person* absetzen; *thing* abliefern; (*from boat*) *cargo* löschen.

(**c**) (*utter casually*) *remark, name* fallenlassen; *clue* geben; *hint* machen. **he let ~ that ...** (*deliberately*) er erwähnte so nebenbei, daß ...

(**d**) (*send*) *postcard* schreiben.

(**e**) (*omit*) *word, reference* auslassen; (*deliberately also*) weglassen (*from* in +*dat*); *programme* absetzen. **to ~ sb from a team** jdn aus einer Mannschaft nehmen.

(**f**) (*candidate, minister, friend*) fallenlassen; *girlfriend* Schluß machen mit.

(**g**) (*give up*) aufgeben; *idea, plan also* fallenlassen; (*Jur*) *case* niederschlagen. **you'll find it hard to ~ the habit** es wird Ihnen schwerfallen, sich (*dat*) das abzugewöhnen; **let's ~ the subject** lassen wir das Thema; **you'd better ~ the idea** schlagen Sie sich (*dat*) das aus dem Kopf; **~ it!** (*col*) hör auf (damit)!; **~ everything!** (*col*) laß alles stehen und liegen!

(**h**) (*lose*) *money, game, point* verlieren.

3 *vi* (**a**) (*fall: object*) (herunter)fallen. **don't let it ~** laß es nicht fallen; **to ~ to one's knees** auf die Knie fallen *or* sinken; **I'm ready to ~** (*with fatigue*) ich bin zum Umfallen müde; **she ~ped into an armchair** sie ließ sich in einen Sessel fallen; **to ~ (down) dead** tot umfallen. (**b**) (*rate, temperature etc*) sinken; (*wind*) sich legen; (*voice*) sich senken. (**c**) **you can't just let the matter ~** Sie können die Sache nicht einfach auf sich beruhen lassen; **shall we let it ~?** sollen wir es darauf beruhen lassen?

♦ **drop back** *or* **behind** *vi* zurückfallen.

♦ **drop by** *vi* (*col*) vorbeikommen, hereinschauen.

♦ **drop down** *vi* (*fall*) herunterfallen. **we ~ped ~ to the coast for a few days** wir sind für ein paar Tage an die Küste gefahren.

♦ **drop in** *vi* (*col: visit casually*) **to ~ ~ on sb** bei jdm vorbeischauen; **to ~ ~ at the grocer's** beim Lebensmittelgeschäft vorbeigehen.

♦ **drop off 1** *vi* (**a**) (*fall off*) abfallen; (*come off*)

abgehen. (**b**) (*fall asleep*) einschlafen; (*for brief while*) einnicken. (**c**) (*sales*) zurückgehen; (*speed, interest, popularity*) nachlassen. **2** *vt sep* (*from car etc*) *person* absetzen; *parcel* abliefern.

♦ **drop out** *vi* (**a**) (*of box etc*) herausfallen (*of* aus). (**b**) (*from competition etc*) ausscheiden (*of* aus); (*of society*) aussteigen. **to ~ ~ of university** sein Studium abbrechen.

droplet ['drɒplɪt] *n* Tröpfchen *nt*.

dropout ['drɒpaʊt] *n* Aussteiger *m* (*col*).

droppings ['drɒpɪŋz] *npl* Kot *m*.

drop shot *n* (*Tennis*) Stoppball *m*.

dross [drɒs] *n no pl* (*fig*) Tand *m*. **everything else is ~** alles andere ist eitel und nichtig.

drought [draʊt] *n* Dürre *f*.

drove [drəʊv] **1** *pret of* **drive**. **2** *n* (*of animals*) Herde *f*; (*of people*) Schar *f*.

drown [draʊn] **1** *vi* ertrinken. **a ~ing man will clutch at a straw** (*Prov*) dem Verzweifelten ist jedes Mittel recht. **2** *vt* (**a**) *animal, sorrows* ertränken. **to be ~ed** ertrinken. (**b**) (*also ~ out*) *noise, voice* übertönen; *speaker* niederschreien.

drowse [draʊz] *vi* (vor sich (*acc*) hin) dösen.

drowsiness ['draʊzɪnɪs] *n* Schläfrigkeit *f*.

drowsy ['draʊzɪ] *adj* (+*er*) schläfrig; (*after sleep*) verschlafen; *afternoon* träge.

drudge [drʌdʒ] *n* (*person*) Arbeitstier *nt* (*col*).

drudgery ['drʌdʒərɪ] *n* stumpfsinnige Plackerei. **it's sheer ~** es ist eine einzige Plackerei.

drug [drʌg] **1** *n* Medikament, Arzneimittel *nt*; (*addictive*) Droge *f*. **to be on ~s** drogenabhängig sein; (*Med*) Medikamente nehmen. **2** *vt person* betäuben; *food, drink* ein Betäubungsmittel mischen in (+*acc*). **to be in a ~ged sleep** in tiefer Betäubung liegen.

drug: ~ **addict** *n* Drogenabhängige(r) *mf*; ~ **addiction** *n* Drogenabhängigkeit, Drogensucht *f*.

druggist ['drʌgɪst] *n* (US) Drogist(in *f*) *m*.

drugstore ['drʌgstɔːr] *n* (US) Drugstore *m*.

drum [drʌm] **1** *n* (a) (*Mus*) Trommel *f*. **the ~s** (*in pop, jazz*) das Schlagzeug. **2** (*for oil, petrol*) Tonne *f*; (*cylinder, machine part*) Trommel *f*. **2** *vi* (*Mus, with fingers, rain*) trommeln. **the noise is still ~ming in my ears** das Geräusch dröhnt mir noch in den Ohren. **3** *vt* **to ~ one's fingers on the table** mit den Fingern auf den Tisch trommeln.

♦ **drum into** *vt always separate* **to ~ sth ~ sb** jdm etw eintrichtern (*col*).

♦ **drum up** *vt sep enthusiasm* erwecken; *support* auftreiben. **to ~ ~ business** Aufträge anbahnen.

drummer ['drʌmər] *n* Trommler *m*; (*in band, pop-group*) Schlagzeuger *m*.

drumstick ['drʌmstɪk] *n* (**a**) (*Mus*) Trommelschlegel *or* -stock *m*. (**b**) (*on chicken etc*) Keule *f*.

drunk [drʌŋk] **1** *ptp of* **drink**. **2** *adj* betrunken. **to get ~ (on)** betrunken werden (von); (*on purpose*) sich betrinken (mit); **to arrest sb for being ~ and disorderly** (*Jur*) jdn wegen Trunkenheit und ruhestörenden Lärms verhaften; ~ **with success** vom Erfolg berauscht. **3** *n* Betrunkene(r) *mf*; (*habitually*) Trinker(in *f*), Säufer(in *f*) (*col*) *m*.

drunkard ['drʌŋkəd] *n* Säufer(in *f*) *m* (*col*).

drunken ['drʌŋkən] *adj* betrunken; *orgy* feuchtfröhlich, Sauf-; *brawl* mit/von Betrunkenen. ~ **driving** (*Jur*) Trunkenheit *f* am Steuer.

drunkenness ['drʌŋkənnɪs] *n* (*state*) Betrunkenheit *f*; (*habit, problem*) Trunksucht *f*.

dry [draɪ] **1** *n come into the* ~ komm ins Trockene; **to give sth a** ~ etw trocknen. **2** *adj* (+*er*) trocken. **the river ran** ~ der Fluß trocknete aus; **to be on** ~ **land** festen Boden unter den Füßen haben; **as ~ as a bone** *land, clothes* knochentrocken (*col*); *mouth, ditches* völlig ausgetrocknet; **to feel/to be** ~ (*thirsty*) eine trockene Kehle haben (*col*). **3** *vt* trocknen; *skin* austrocknen; *fruit also* dörren; *dishes, one's hands* abtrocknen. **to** ~ **one's eyes** sich (*dat*) die Tränen abwischen; **to** ~ **oneself**

sich abtrocknen. **4** *vi* trocken werden.
♦ **dry off** *vi* trocknen.
♦ **dry out 1** *vi (clothes)* trocknen; *(ground, skin etc)* austrocknen; *(col: alcoholic)* eine Entziehungskur machen. **2** *vt sep clothes* trocknen; *ground, skin* austrocknen.
♦ **dry up 1** *vi* **(a)** *(stream, well)* austrocknen, versiegen; *(moisture)* trocknen; *(inspiration, source of income)* versiegen. **(b)** *(dishes)* abtrocknen. **(c)** *(actor)* steckenbleiben *(col)*. **(d)** *(col: be quiet)* ~ ~! halt den Mund! *(col)*. **2** *vt sep mess* aufwischen; *dishes* abtrocknen.

dry: ~-**clean** *vt* chemisch reinigen; ~-**cleaner** *n* chemische Reinigung; ~ **dock** *n (Naut)* Trockendock *nt*.

dryer, drier ['draɪəʳ] *n (for clothes)* Wäschetrockner *m*; *(spin* ~*)* Wäscheschleuder *f*; *(for hair)* Fön, Haartrockner *m*; *(hood)* Trockenhaube *f*.

dry: ~ **goods** *npl (Comm)* Kurzwaren *pl*; ~ **ice** *n* Trockeneis *nt*.

drying-up ['draɪŋ'ʌp] *n* Abtrocknen *nt*. **to do the** ~ abtrocknen.

dryness ['draɪnɪs] *n* Trockenheit *f*.

dry: ~ **rot** *n* (Haus- *or* Holz)schwamm *m*; ~ **run** *n* Probe *f*; ~ **ski slope** *n* Trockenskipiste *f*.

DTs ['di:'ti:z] **to have the** ~ das Zittern haben.

dual ['djuəl] *adj (double)* doppelt, Doppel-. ~ **carriageway** *(Brit)* Schnellstraße *f*; ~ **nationality** doppelte Staatsangehörigkeit.

duality [dju'ælɪtɪ] *n* Dualität *f*.

dual-purpose ['djuəl'pɜ:pəs] *adj* zweifach verwendbar.

dub dʌb] *vt* **(a)** *(nickname)* taufen. **(b)** *film* synchronisieren.

dubious ['dju:bɪəs] *adj* zweifelhaft; *matter also* dubios; *look* zweifelnd. **I'm very** ~ **about it** ich habe da (doch) starke Zweifel.

dubiously ['dju:bɪəslɪ] *adv look* zweifelnd; *behave* zweifelhaft, fragwürdig.

duchess ['dʌtʃɪs] *n* Herzogin *f*.

duck [dʌk] **1** *n* **(a)** *(bird)* Ente *f*. **he took to it like a** ~ **to water** da war er sofort in seinem Element; **it's like water off a** ~**'s back** das läuft alles an ihm/ihr *etc* ab. **(b)** *(Cricket)* **to be out for a** ~ ohne Punktgewinn aus sein. **2** *vi* **(a)** *(also* ~ **down)** sich ducken. **he** ~**ed under the water** er tauchte (im Wasser) unter. **(b)** **he** ~**ed out of the room** er verschwand aus dem Zimmer. **3** *vt* **(a)** *(push under water)* untertauchen. **(b) to** ~ **one's head** den Kopf einziehen. **(c)** *(avoid)* *difficult question etc* ausweichen (+*dat*).

duckling ['dʌklɪŋ] *n* Entenküken, Entlein *nt*.

duct [dʌkt] *n* **(a)** *(Anat)* Röhre *f*. **tear** ~ Tränenkanal *m*. **(b)** *(for liquid, gas)* Leitung *f*.

dud [dʌd] *(col)* **1** *adj* **(a)** ~ **shell/bomb** Blindgänger *m*. **(b)** *tool* nutzlos; *actor, teacher* mies *(col)*, schlecht; *coin* falsch; *cheque* ungedeckt; *(forged)* gefälscht. ~ **note** Blüte *f (col)*. **2** *n* **(a)** *(shell, bomb)* Blindgänger *m*. **(b)** *(cheque)* ungedeckter or *(forged)* gefälschter Scheck; *(banknote)* Blüte *f (col)*. **(c)** *(person)* Blindgänger *(col)*, Versager *m*.

dudgeon ['dʌdʒən] *n*: **in high** ~ sehr empört.

due [dju:] *(col)* **1** *adj* **(a)** *(to be paid, owing)* fällig. **the sum which is** ~ **to him** die Summe, die ihm zusteht; **the amount** ~ **as compensation** der Betrag, der als Schadensersatz gezahlt werden soll; **to fall** ~ fällig werden or sein; **I am** ~ **six days off/(for) a rise** mir stehen sechs Tage Urlaub zu/mir steht eine Gehaltserhöhung zu. **(b)** *(expected, scheduled)* **to be** ~ **to do sth** etw tun sollen; **the train is** ~ **at midday** der Zug soll laut Fahrplan um zwölf Uhr ankommen; **I'm** ~ **in London tomorrow** ich soll morgen in London sein; **he's** ~ **back tomorrow** er müßte morgen zurück sein; **when is the baby/she** ~? wann soll das Baby kommen/bekommt sie ihr Baby? **(c)** *(proper, suitable)* gebührend. **with all** ~

respect bei allem Respekt; **we'll let you know in** ~ **course** wir werden Sie zu gegebener Zeit benachrichtigen; **he was, in** ~ **course, to become** ... im Laufe der Zeit wurde er ...; **after** ~ **consideration** nach reiflicher Überlegung. **(d)** ~ **to** aufgrund (+*gen*), wegen (+*gen or dat)*; **what's it** ~ **to?** worauf ist dies zurückzuführen?; **it is** ~ **to you that** ... wir haben es euch zu verdanken, daß ... **2** *adv* ~ **west** direkt nach Westen; ~ **east of the village** genau im Osten des Dorfes.

3 *n* **(a)** ~**s** *pl (fees)* Gebühr *f*, Gebühren *pl*. **(b)** *no pl (to)* **give him his** ~, **he did try hard** das muß man ihm lassen, er hat sich wirklich angestrengt.

duel ['djuəl] **1** *n (lit, fig)* Duell *nt*. **2** *vi* sich duellieren.

duet [dju:'et] *n* Duo *nt*; *(for voices)* Duett *nt*.

duffel ['dʌfl] ~ **bag** *n* Matchbeutel *or* -sack *m*; ~-**coat** *n* Dufflecoat *m*.

dug *pret, ptp of* **dig**.

duke [dju:k] *n* Herzog *m*.

dull [dʌl] **1** *adj (+er)* **(a)** *colour, light* trüb, matt; *weather* trüb; *sound* dumpf. **(b)** *(boring)* langweilig; *person, evening also* lahm; *(lacking spirit)* *person, mood* lustlos. **as** ~ **as ditchwater** stinklangweilig *(col)*. **(c)** *(slow-witted)* *person* schwerfällig. **(d)** *blade* stumpf; *pain* dumpf. **(e)** *market* flau; *trade, business* schleppend. **2** *vt* **(a)** *sense, powers of memory* schwächen; *mind* abstumpfen. **(b)** *pain, grief* betäuben; *pleasure* dämpfen. **(c)** *sound* dämpfen. **(d)** *edge, blade* stumpf machen.

duly ['dju:lɪ] *adv* entsprechend; *(properly)* gebührend, wie es sich gehört; *(according to regulations etc)* vorschriftsmäßig. **and the parcel** ~ **arrived the next morning** und das Paket kam dann auch am nächsten Morgen.

dumb [dʌm] *adj (+er)* **(a)** stumm. **the** ~ **die Stummen** *pl*; ~ **animals** die Tiere *pl*; **he was struck** ~ es verschlug ihm die Sprache; ~ **waiter** Speiseaufzug *m*; *(trolley)* Serviertisch *m*, stummer Diener. **(b)** *(esp US col: stupid)* doof *(col)*, dumm.

dumbfound ['dʌmfaʊnd] *vt* verblüffen. **I'm** ~**ed!** ich bin sprachlos!

dumbness ['dʌmnɪs] *n* **(a)** Stummheit *f*. **(b)** *(esp US col: stupidity)* Doofheit *(col)*, Dummheit *f*.

dummy ['dʌmɪ] **1** *n* **(a)** *(sham object)* Attrappe *f*; *(for clothes)* (Kleider)puppe *f*. **(b)** *(Brit: baby's teat)* Schnuller *m*. **(c)** *(Ftbl etc)* Finte *f*. **2** *adj attr* unecht. **a** ~ **rifle** eine Gewehrattrappe; ~ **run** Probe *f*.

dump [dʌmp] **1** *n* **(a)** *(pile of rubbish)* Abfallhaufen *m*; *(place)* Müllkippe *f*. **(b)** *(Mil)* Depot *nt*. **(c)** *(pej col: town)* Kaff *nt (col)*; *(house, building)* Loch *nt (pej col)*. **(d)** *(col)* **to be (down) in the** ~**s** deprimiert sein. **2** *vt* **(a)** *rubbish* abladen; *(col)* *person, girlfriend* abschieben; *car* abstellen, loswerden. **(b)** *(put down)* *load* abladen; *bags etc (drop)* fallen lassen; *(leave)* lassen. **(c)** *(Comm)* *goods* zu Dumpingpreisen verkaufen.

dumpling ['dʌmplɪŋ] *n* **(a)** *(Cook)* Kloß, Knödel *m*. **(b)** *(col: person)* Dickerchen *nt (col)*.

dump truck *n* Kipper *m*.

dumpy ['dʌmpɪ] *adj person* pummelig.

dun [dʌn] *adj* graubraun.

dunce [dʌns] *n (Sch)* langsamer Schüler; *(stupid person)* Dummkopf *m*.

dune [dju:n] *n* Düne *f*.

dung [dʌŋ] **1** *n* Dung *m*. **2** *vt field* düngen.

dungarees [,dʌŋgə'ri:z] *npl* Latzhose *f*.

dungeon ['dʌndʒən] *n* Verlies *nt*, Kerker *m*.

dunk [dʌŋk] *vt (col)*tunken.

dunno [dʌ'nəʊ] = **(I) don't know.**

duodenal [,dju:əʊ'di:nl] *adj* ~ **ulcer** Zwölffingerdarmgeschwür *nt*.

dupe [dju:p] **1** *vt* betrügen. **he was** ~**d into be-**

lieving it er fiel darauf rein. **2** n Betrogene(r) mf.

duplex ['djuːpleks] n (esp US: also: ~ **apartment**) zweistöckige Wohnung.

duplicate ['djuːplɪkeɪt] **1** vt document ein Duplikat nt anfertigen von; (repeat) action wiederholen; (wastefully) doppelt or zweimal machen. **2** ['djuːplɪkɪt] n (of document) Duplikat nt; (of work of art) Kopie f; (of key) Zweitschlüssel m. **3** ['djuːplɪkɪt] adj doppelt, zweifach.

duplication [ˌdjuːplɪ'keɪʃən] n (of efforts, work) Wiederholung f.

duplicity [djuː'plɪsɪtɪ] n Doppelspiel nt.

durability [ˌdjʊərə'bɪlɪtɪ] n (of material) Haltbarkeit f; (of metal) Widerstandsfähigkeit f.

durable ['djʊərəbl] adj friendship dauerhaft; material haltbar; metal widerstandsfähig.

duration [djʊə'reɪʃən] n (of play, war etc) Länge, Dauer f. **for the** ~ bis zum Ende.

duress [djʊə'res] n **under** ~ unter Zwang.

durex ® ['djʊəreks] n Gummi (col) m.

during ['djʊərɪŋ] prep während (+gen).

dusk [dʌsk] n (twilight) (Abend)dämmerung f; (gloom) Finsternis f. **at** ~ bei Einbruch der Dunkelheit.

dusky ['dʌskɪ] adj (+er) maiden dunkelhäutig.

dust [dʌst] **1** n no pl (a) Staub m. **when the** ~ **had settled** (fig) als sich die Wogen wieder etwas geglättet hatten. **(b) to give sth a** ~ etw abstauben. **2** vt **(a)** furniture abstauben; room Staub wischen in (+dat). **(b)** (Cook) bestäuben.

dust: ~**bin** n (Brit) Mülltonne f; ~**bowl** n Trockengebiet nt; ~**cart** n (Brit) Müllauto nt; ~**cover** n (on furniture) Schonbezug m.

duster [dʌstə^r] n Staubtuch nt; (Sch) (Tafel)schwamm m.

dust: ~ **jacket** n (Schutz)umschlag m; ~**man** n (Brit) Müllmann m (col); **the** ~**men come on Fridays** freitags ist Müllabfuhr; ~**pan** n Kehrschaufel f.

dusty [dʌstɪ] adj (er) table, path staubig.

Dutch [dʌtʃ] **1** adj holländisch, niederländisch (esp form). **I need a little** ~ **courage** (col) ich muß mir ein bißchen Mut antrinken; ~ **elm disease** Ulmenkrankheit f; **to talk to sb like a** ~ **uncle** (col) jdm eine Standpauke halten. **2** adv **to go** ~ (col) getrennte Kasse machen. **3** n **(a) the** ~ die Holländer or Niederländer pl. **(b)** (language) Holländisch, Niederländisch (esp form) nt.

Dutchman ['dʌtʃmən] n, pl -**men** [-mən] Holländer, Niederländer (esp form) m. **he did say that or I'm a** ~ (col) ich fresse einen Besen, wenn er das nicht gesagt hat (col).

Dutchwoman ['dʌtʃwʊmən] n, pl -**women** [-ˌwɪmɪn] Holländerin, Niederländerin (esp form) f.

dutiable [djuːtɪəbl] adj zollpflichtig.

dutiful [djuːtɪfʊl] adj child gehorsam; husband, employee pflichtbewußt.

duty ['djuːtɪ] n **(a)** Pflicht f. **to do one's** ~ **by sb** seine Pflicht gegenüber jdm tun or erfüllen; **I am (in)** ~ **bound to say that** ... es ist meine Pflicht zu sagen, daß ...; **to make it one's** ~ **to do** sth es sich (dat) zur Pflicht machen, etw zu tun. **(b)** (often pl: responsibility) Aufgabe, Pflicht f. **to take up one's duties** seine Pflichten aufnehmen; **to be on** ~ (doctor etc) im Dienst sein; (Sch etc) Aufsicht haben; **who's on** ~ **tomorrow?** wer hat morgen Dienst/Aufsicht?; **to be off** ~ nicht im Dienst sein. **(c)** (Fin: tax) Zoll m.

duty: ~**-free 1** adj zollfrei; ~**-free shop** Duty-free-Shop m; **2** n zollfreie Ware; ~ **officer** n Offizier m vom Dienst.

duvet ['djuːveɪ] n (Brit) Daunendecke f.

dwarf [dwɔːf] **1** n, pl **dwarves** [dwɔːvz] Zwerg m. **2** adj tree, star Zwerg-. **3** vt überragen; (through achievements, ability etc) in den Schatten stellen.

dwell [dwel] pret, ptp **dwelt** vi (liter: live) leben, wohnen.

◆ **dwell (up)on** vi +prep obj **(a)** verweilen bei; (stress unnecessarily etc) herumreiten auf (+dat). **(b)** (Mus) note halten.

dwelling ['dwelɪŋ] n (form: also ~ **place**) Wohnsitz m (form), Wohnung f.

dwelt [dwelt] pret, ptp of **dwell**.

dwindle ['dwɪndl] vi (strength, interest) schwinden; (numbers, audiences) zurückgehen; (supplies) zur Neige gehen.

dwindling ['dwɪndlɪŋ] adj schwindend; resources versiegend.

dye [daɪ] **1** n Farbstoff m. **hair** ~ Haarfärbemittel nt; **the** ~ **will come out in the wash** die Farbe geht beim Waschen heraus. **2** vt färben.

dyed-in-the-wool ['daɪdɪnðə‚wʊl] adj durch und durch pred; attitude eingefleischt; conservative Erz-.

dying ['daɪɪŋ] adj person sterbend; tradition, race, civilization aussterbend; embers verglühend. **to my** ~ **day** bis an mein Lebensende; ~ **wish** letzter Wunsch; ~ **words** letzte Worte.

dyke, dike [daɪk] n **(a)** (channel) (Entwässerungs)graben, Kanal m. **(b)** (barrier) Deich, Damm m. **(c)** (col: lesbian) Lesbe f (col).

dynamic [daɪ'næmɪk] adj dynamisch.

dynamism ['daɪnəmɪzəm] n Dynamismus m; (of person) Dynamik f.

dynamite ['daɪnəmaɪt] **1** n (lit) Dynamit nt; (fig) Sprengstoff m. **she's** ~ sie ist eine Wucht (col); **this story's** ~ diese Geschichte wird wie eine Bombe einschlagen. **2** vt bridge sprengen.

dynamo ['daɪnəməʊ] n Dynamo m.

dynasty ['dɪnəstɪ] n Dynastie f.

dysentery ['dɪsɪntrɪ] n Dysenterie, Ruhr f.

dyslexia [dɪs'leksɪə] n Legasthenie f.

dyslexic [dɪs'leksɪk] **1** adj legasthenisch. **2** n Legastheniker(in f) m.

dyspepsia [dɪs'pepsɪə] n Verdauungsstörung f.

E

E, e [iː] n E, e nt; (Mus) E, e nt. **E flat/sharp** Es, es nt/Eis, eis nt.

E = east O.

each [iːtʃ] 1 adj jede(r, s). ~ **one of us/** ~ **and every one of us** jeder einzelne von uns. 2 pron (a) jede(r, s). **a little of** ~ **please** von jedem etwas, bitte; **we** ~ **had our own ideas about it** jeder von uns hatte seine eigene Vorstellung davon. (b) ~ **other einander; they get on** ~ **other's nerves** sie gehen sich (dat) or einander auf die Nerven; **we visit** ~ **other** wir besuchen uns (gegenseitig); **on top of** ~ **other/next to** ~ **other** aufeinander/ nebeneinander. 3 adv je. **two classes of 20 pupils** ~ zwei Klassen mit je 20 Schülern; **the books are £1** ~ die Bücher kosten je £ 1; **carnations at one mark** ~ Nelken zu einer Mark das Stück; **it cost them £10** ~ das hat sie pro Person £ 10 gekostet.

eager ['iːgəʳ] adj eifrig. **to be** ~ **to do sth** etw unbedingt tun wollen; ~ **to learn** lernbegierig; **to be** ~ **for sth** auf etw (acc) erpicht sein; ~ **beaver** (col) Arbeitstier nt (col).

eagerly ['iːgəlɪ] adv eifrig; look, wait gespannt.

eagerness ['iːgənɪs] n Eifer m.

eagle ['iːgl] n Adler m.

eagle-eyed ['iːgl'aɪd] adj **the** ~ **detective** der Detektiv mit seinen Adleraugen.

ear[1] [ɪəʳ] n (Anat, fig) Ohr nt. **to keep one's** ~**s open** die Ohren offenhalten; **to keep an** ~ **to the ground** die Ohren aufsperren; **to be all** ~**s** ganz Ohr sein; **your** ~**s must have been burning** Ihnen müssen die Ohren geklungen haben; **it goes in one** ~ **and out the other** das geht zum einen Ohr hinein und zum anderen wieder heraus; **to be up to the** ~**s in debt** bis über beide Ohren verschuldet sein; **he'll be out on his** ~ (col) dann fliegt er raus (col); **to have a good** ~ **for music** musikalisch sein; **to play by** ~ (lit) nach Gehör spielen; **to play it by** ~ (fig) improvisieren.

ear[2] n (of grain) Ähre f.

ear: ~**ache** n Ohrenschmerzen pl; ~**drum** n Trommelfell nt.

earl [ɜːl] n Graf m.

early ['ɜːlɪ] 1 adj (+er) früh; (sooner than expected) zu früh; fruit, vegetable Früh-. **it was** ~ **in the morning** es war früh am Morgen; **to be an** ~ **riser** Frühaufsteher sein; **in the** ~ **hours** in den frühen Morgenstunden; **in the** ~ **morning/ afternoon** am frühen Morgen/Nachmittag; **in** ~ **spring/summer** zu Beginn des Frühjahrs/im Frühsommer; **in the** ~ **youth** in seiner frühen Jugend; **from an** ~ **age** von frühester Jugend an; **she's in her** ~ **forties** sie ist Anfang Vierzig; **to take** ~ **retirement** sich vorzeitig pensionieren lassen; **at the earliest possible moment** so bald wie (irgend) möglich.

2 adv früh. **you're** ~ **today** Sie sind heute ja früh dran; **sorry, am I** ~? bin ich zu früh?; **earlier on this evening** zuvor am Abend; **I saw him earlier on this week** ich habe ihn Anfang der Woche gesehen; **earlier on that year** Jim had ... Jim hatte früher in dem Jahr ...; **the earliest he can come is** ... er kann frühestens ... kommen; **as** ~ **as 1935** schon 1935; **she left ten minutes** ~ sie ist zehn Minuten früher gegangen.

early: ~ **bird** n (in morning) Frühaufsteher(in f) m;

(arriving etc) Frühankömmling m; ~ **closing** n **it's** ~ **closing today** die Geschäfte haben heute nachmittag geschlossen; ~**-warning system** n Frühwarnsystem nt.

ear: ~**mark** vt (fig) vorsehen; ~**-muffs** npl Ohrenschützer pl.

earn [ɜːn] vt verdienen; (Fin) interest bringen.

earnest ['ɜːnɪst] 1 adj ernsthaft; hope aufrichtig. 2 n **in** ~ (with determination) ernsthaft; (without joking) im Ernst; **this time I'm in** ~ diesmal meine ich es ernst; **it is snowing in** ~ **now** jetzt schneit es richtig.

earnestness ['ɜːnɪstnɪs] n Ernsthaftigkeit f; (of voice) Ernst m.

earnings ['ɜːnɪŋz] npl Verdienst m.

ear: ~**-phones** npl Kopfhörer pl; ~**-plug** n Ohropax ® nt; ~**-ring** n Ohrring m; ~**shot** n: **out of/within** ~**shot** außer/in Hörweite; ~**-splitting** adj ohrenbetäubend.

earth [ɜːθ] 1 n (a) (also Brit Elec) Erde f. **on** ~ auf der Erde; **to the ends of the** ~ bis ans Ende der Welt; **where/who** etc **on** ~? (col) wo/wer etc ... bloß?; **nothing on** ~ **will stop me** now keine Macht der Welt hält mich jetzt noch auf; **you look like nothing on** ~ (col) du siehst unmöglich aus (col); **it cost the** ~ (col) das hat eine schöne Stange Geld gekostet (col); **to bring sb down to** ~ (with a bump) (fig) jdn (unsanft) wieder auf den Boden der Tatsachen zurückholen. (b) (of fox) Bau m. **to go to** ~ im Bau verschwinden; (criminal) untertauchen; **to run sb to** ~ (fig) jdn ausfindig machen. 2 vt (Elec) erden.

earthenware ['ɜːθənweəʳ] 1 n (material) Ton m; (dishes etc) Tongeschirr nt. 2 adj aus Ton, Ton-.

earthly ['ɜːθlɪ] 1 adj (a) irdisch. (b) (col) **there is no** ~ **reason to think** ... es besteht nicht der geringste Grund für die Annahme ... 2 n (col) **she hasn't an** ~ sie hat nicht die geringste Chance.

earth: ~**-moving equipment** n Erdbewegungsmaschinen pl; ~**quake** n Erdbeben nt; ~**worm** n Regenwurm m.

earthy ['ɜːθɪ] adj (+er) (a) taste, smell erdig. (b) person, humour derb.

earwig ['ɪəwɪg] n Ohrwurm m.

ease [iːz] 1 n (a) Behagen nt. **I am never at** ~ **in his company** in seiner Gegenwart bin ich immer etwas befangen; **to put** or **set sb at his** ~ jdm die Befangenheit nehmen; **to put** or **set sb's mind at** ~ jdn beruhigen; **to feel at** ~ **with sb** sich bei jdm wohlfühlen; **(stand) at** ~! (Mil) rührt euch! (b) **with** ~ mit Leichtigkeit; **a life of** ~ ein beschauliches Dasein. 2 vt (a) pain lindern; mind erleichtern. (b) rope, strap lockern; pressure, tension verringern. (c) **to** ~ **in the clutch** (Aut) die Kupplung langsam kommen lassen; **he** ~**d the lid off** er löste behutsam den Deckel. 3 vi nachlassen; (situation) sich entspannen.

♦ **ease off** or **up** vi (slow down, relax) langsamer werden; (driver) verlangsamen; (situation) sich entspannen; (pain, rain) nachlassen. **the doctor told him to** ~ ~ der Arzt riet ihm, etwas kürzer zu treten.

easel ['iːzl] n Staffelei f.

easily ['iːzɪlɪ] adv leicht. **he is** ~ **the best** er ist mit Abstand der beste; **it's** ~ **25 miles** es sind gut und gerne 25 Meilen.

124

easiness ['iːzɪnɪs] n Leichtigkeit f.

east [iːst] **1** n **(a)** Osten m. **in/to the** ~ **im Osten/ nach Osten; from the** ~ **von Osten; to the** ~ **of** östlich von. **(b)** (Geog, Pol) **the E**~ **der Osten; from the E**~ **aus dem Osten. 2** adv **nach Osten,** ostwärts. ~ **of** östlich von. **3** adj östlich, Ost-. ~ **wind** Ostwind m; **E**~ **Berlin** n Ostberlin nt.

Easter ['iːstə'] **1** n Ostern nt. **at** ~ **an** or **zu Ostern. 2** adj attr week, egg Oster-. ~ **Monday** Ostermontag m; ~ **Sunday,** ~ **Day** Ostersonntag m.

easterly ['iːstəlɪ] adj östlich, Ost-.

eastern ['iːstən] adj Ost-, östlich; attitude orientalisch. **the** ~ **bloc** der Ostblock.

east: E~ **German** adj ostdeutsch (dated), DDR-; **E**~ **Germany** n **die DDR;** ~**ward(s)** adv ostwärts, nach Osten.

easy [iːzɪ] **1** adj (+er) **(a)** leicht. **it's** ~ **for you to say that** du hast gut reden; **he was an** ~ **winner** er hat mühelos gewonnen; **he is** ~ **to get on with** mit ihm kann man gut auskommen; ~ **money** leicht verdientes Geld. **(b)** (free from discomfort etc) bequem, leicht; manners, movement ungezwungen; style flüssig. **in** ~ **stages** in bequemen Etappen; **on** ~ **terms** (Comm) zu günstigen Bedingungen; **I'm** ~ (col) mir ist alles recht. **2** adv ~!, ~ **does it!** immer sachte!; **to take things or it** ~ (healthwise) sich schonen; **take it** ~! (don't worry) nimm's nicht so schwer; (don't get carried away, don't rush) immer mit der Ruhe!; **to go** ~ **on sth** sparsam mit etw umgehen; **to go** ~ **on sb** nicht zu hart sein mit jdm sein; **stand** ~! (Mil) rührt euch!

easy: ~ **chair** n Sessel m; ~ **come** ~ **go** interj wie gewonnen, so zerronnen (Prov); ~**-going** adj (not anxious) gelassen; (lax) lässig.

eat [iːt] (vb: pret **ate**, ptp **eaten**) vti (person) essen; (animal) fressen. **to** ~ **one's breakfast** frühstücken; **he's** ~**ing us out of house and home** (col) der frißt uns noch die Haare vom Kopf (col); **to** ~ **one's words** alles zurücknehmen; **he won't** ~ **you** (col) er wird dich schon nicht fressen (col); **what's** ~**ing you?** (col) was hast du denn?

♦ **eat away** vt sep (sea) auswaschen; (acid) zerfressen.

♦ **eat into** vi +prep obj metal anfressen; capital angreifen.

♦ **eat out 1** vi essen gehen. **2** vt sep **to** ~ **one's heart** ~ **Trübsal blasen.**

♦ **eat up 1** vt sep **(a)** aufessen; (animal) auffressen. **(b)** (fig: use up) verbrauchen. **this car** ~ **s** ~ **the miles** der Wagen gibt ganz schön was her (col). **2** vi aufessen.

eatable ['iːtəbl] adj eßbar, genießbar.

eaten ['iːtn] ptp of **eat.**

eater ['iːtə'] n Esser(in f) m.

eating: ~ **apple** n Eßapfel m; ~ **place** n Eßlokal nt.

eau de Cologne ['əʊdəkə'ləʊn] n Kölnisch Wasser nt.

eaves ['iːvz] npl Dachvorsprung m.

eavesdrop ['iːvzdrɒp] vi (heimlich) lauschen. **to** ~ **on a conversation** ein Gespräch belauschen.

ebb [eb] **1** n Ebbe f. ~ **and flow** Ebbe und Flut f; (fig) Auf und Ab nt; **at a low** ~ (fig) in einem Tief. **2** vi **(a)** (tide) zurückgehen. **to** ~ **and flow** (lit, fig) kommen und gehen. **(b)** (fig: also ~ **away)** (enthusiasm etc) verebben.

ebony ['ebənɪ] n Ebenholz nt.

ebullient [ɪ'bʌlɪənt] adj überschwenglich; mood übersprudelnd.

eccentric [ɪk'sentrɪk] **1** adj exzentrisch. **2** n Exzentriker(in f) m.

eccentricity [‚eksən'trɪsɪtɪ] n Exzentrizität f.

ecclesiastical [ɪ‚kliːzɪ'æstɪkəl] adj kirchlich.

echo ['ekəʊ] **1** n Echo nt. **2** vt sound zurückwerfen; (fig) wiedergeben. **3** vi widerhallen (with von); (room) hallen. **it** ~**es in here** hier ist ein Echo.

éclair [eɪ'kleə'] n Eclair nt, Liebesknochen m.

eclipse [ɪ'klɪps] **1** (Astron) ~ **of the sun/moon** Sonnen-/Mondfinsternis f. **2** vt (Astron) verfinstern; (fig) in den Schatten stellen.

ecological [‚iːkəʊ'lɒdʒɪkəl] adj ökologisch.

ecologist [ɪ'kɒlədʒɪst] n Ökologe m, Ökologin f.

ecology [ɪ'kɒlədʒɪ] n Ökologie f.

economic [‚iːkə'nɒmɪk] adj wirtschaftlich, ökonomisch; development, system also, miracle Wirtschafts-.

economical [‚iːkə'nɒmɪkəl] adj wirtschaftlich, ökonomisch; person sparsam. **to be** ~ **with sth** mit etw haushalten; **to be** ~ **(to run)** (car) wirtschaftlich sein.

economics [‚iːkə'nɒmɪks] n **(a)** with sing or pl vb Volkswirtschaft f; (management studies) Betriebswirtschaft f. **(b)** pl (economic aspect) Wirtschaftlichkeit f. **the** ~ **of the situation** die wirtschaftliche Seite der Situation.

economist [ɪ'kɒnəmɪst] n see **economics** Volkswirt(in f); Betriebswirt(in f) m.

economize [ɪ'kɒnəmaɪz] vi sparen.

♦ **economize on** vi +prep obj sparen.

economy [ɪ'kɒnəmɪ] n **(a)** (system) Wirtschaft f no pl; (from a monetary aspect) Konjunktur f. **(b)** (in time, money) Einsparung f. **a false** ~ falsche Sparsamkeit. **(c)** (thrift) Sparsamkeit f. ~ **of effort** geringer Kräfteaufwand.

economy: ~ **class** n Touristenklasse f; ~ **drive** n Sparmaßnahmen pl; ~ **size** n Sparpackung f.

ecstasy ['ekstəsɪ] n Ekstase f. **to go into ecstasies over sth** über etw (acc) in Verzückung geraten.

ecstatic [eks'tætɪk] adj ekstatisch, verzückt.

Ecuador ['ekwədɔː'] n Ecuador, Ekuador nt.

ecumenical [‚iːkjuː'menɪkəl] adj ökumenisch.

eczema ['eksɪmə] n (Haut)ausschlag m.

eddy ['edɪ] **1** n Wirbel m. **2** vi wirbeln.

edge [edʒ] **1** n **(a)** (of knife) Schneide f. **to take the** ~ **off sth** (fig) sensation etw (dat) die Wirkung nehmen; **that took the** ~ **off my appetite** das nahm mir erst einmal den Hunger; **the noise/ taste sets my teeth on** ~ das Geräusch geht mir durch und durch/der Geschmack ist mir widerlich; **to be on** ~ nervös sein; **to have the** ~ **on sb/sth** jdm/etw überlegen sein. **(b)** (outer limit) Rand m; (of cloth, table, of brick) Kante f; (of lake, river also) Ufer nt.

2 vt **(a)** (put a border on) besetzen, einfassen. **(b)** **to** ~ **one's way towards sth** (slowly) sich allmählich auf etw (acc) zubewegen; (carefully) sich vorsichtig auf etw (acc) zubewegen; **she** ~**d her way through the crowd** sie schlängelte sich durch die Menge.

3 vi sich schieben. **to** ~ **away from sb/sth** sich allmählich immer weiter von jdm/etw entfernen; **to** ~ **up to sb** sich an jdn heranmachen; **he** ~**d past me** er schob sich an mir vorbei.

edgeways ['edʒweɪz] adv mit der Schmalseite voran. **I couldn't get a word in** ~ ich bin überhaupt nicht zu Wort gekommen.

edging ['edʒɪŋ] n Borte, Einfassung f.

edgy ['edʒɪ] adj (+er) person nervös.

edible ['edɪbl] adj eßbar, genießbar.

edict ['iːdɪkt] n Erlaß m.

edifice ['edɪfɪs] n Gebäude nt.

edify ['edɪfaɪ] vt erbauen.

edifying ['edɪfaɪɪŋ] adj erbaulich.

edit ['edɪt] vt series, newspaper, magazine herausgeben; book, text redigieren; film, tape schneiden.

edition [ɪ'dɪʃən] n Ausgabe f; (printing) Auflage f.

editor ['edɪtə'] n Herausgeber(in f) m; (publisher's) (Verlags)lektor(in f) m; (Film) Cutter(in f) m. **political/sports** ~ politischer Redakteur/Sportredakteur m.

editorial [edɪ'tɔːrɪəl] **1** adj redaktionell, Redaktions-. ~ **assistant** Redaktionsassistent(in f) m; ~ **office** Redaktion f; (Publishing also) (Verlags)lektorat nt. **2** n Leitartikel m.

educate ['edjʊkeɪt] vt erziehen; the mind schulen; one's tastes (aus)bilden. he was ~d at Eton er ist in Eton zur Schule gegangen.

educated ['edjʊkeɪtɪd] adj gebildet.

education [,edjʊ'keɪʃən] n Erziehung f; (studies, training) Ausbildung f; (knowledge, culture) Bildung f. **College of E**~ Pädagogische Hochschule; (for graduates) Studienseminar nt; ~ **is free** die Schulausbildung ist kostenlos.

educational [edjʊ'keɪʃənl] adj pädagogisch; films, games also Lehr-; publisher also Schulbuch-; experience lehrreich.

educator ['edjʊkeɪtə'] n Pädagoge, Erzieher m.

Edwardian [ed'wɔːdɪən] adj aus der Zeit Eduards VII.

EEC = **European Economic Community** EG f.

eel [iːl] n Aal m.

eerie ['ɪərɪ] adj (+er) unheimlich.

efface [ɪ'feɪs] vt auslöschen.

effect [ɪ'fekt] **1** n **(a)** (result) Wirkung f, Effekt m; (repercussion) Auswirkung f. **the ~ of this is that ... das hat zur Folge, daß ...; to feel the ~s of an accident/of drink** die Folgen eines Unfalls/des Trinkens spüren; **to no ~** ohne Erfolg; **to have an ~ on sb/sth** eine Wirkung auf jdn/etw haben; **to take ~** (drug) wirken. **(b)** (impression) Wirkung f, Effekt m. **to create an ~** eine Wirkung or einen Effekt erzielen; **it's all done solely for ~** das wird alles bloß des Effekts wegen getan. **(c)** (meaning) **an announcement to the ~ that ...** eine Erklärung des Inhalts, daß ...; **... or words to that ~** ... oder etwas in diesem Sinne. **(d)** ~s pl (property) Effekten pl. **(e) in** ~ effektiv. **(f)** (of laws) **to be in** ~ gültig or in Kraft sein; **to come into** ~ in Kraft treten; **to put sth into** ~ etw in Kraft setzen.

2 vt bewirken, herbeiführen; (form) sale tätigen.

effective [ɪ'fektɪv] adj **(a)** wirksam, effektiv. **to become** ~ (law) in Kraft treten; (drug) wirken. **(b)** (creating impression) wirkungsvoll, effektvoll. **(c)** (real) contribution tatsächlich; profit also effektiv.

effectiveness [ɪ'fektɪvnɪs] n see adj **(a)** Wirksamkeit f. **(b)** Wirkung f, Effekt m.

effectual [ɪ'fektjʊəl] adj wirksam.

effeminate [ɪ'femɪnɪt] adj weibisch.

effervesce [efə'ves] vi sprudeln.

effervescence [efə'vesns] n (lit) Sprudeln nt; (fig) überschäumendes Temperament.

effervescent [,efə'vesnt] adj sprudelnd; (fig) überschäumend.

effete [ɪ'fiːt] adj schwach; person saft- und kraftlos.

efficacious [efɪ'keɪʃəs] adj wirksam.

efficacy ['efɪkəsɪ] n Wirksamkeit f.

efficiency [ɪ'fɪʃənsɪ] n (of person) Tüchtigkeit f; (of machine, factory) Leistungsfähigkeit f; (of method, organization) Rationalität, Effizienz (geh) f.

efficient [ɪ'fɪʃənt] adj person fähig; worker, secretary etc also tüchtig; machine, factory, company leistungsfähig; method, organization rationell. **to be** ~ **at sth/at doing sth** etw gut verstehen/es gut verstehen, etw zu tun; **the** ~ **working of a machine** das gute Funktionieren einer Maschine.

efficiently [ɪ'fɪʃəntlɪ] adv gut. **they handled the sale** ~ sie haben den Verkauf gekonnt abgewickelt.

effigy ['efɪdʒɪ] n Bildnis nt.

effluent ['efluənt] (sewage) Abwasser nt.

effort ['efət] n **(a)** (attempt) Bemühung f; (strain, hard work) Anstrengung f, Mühe f. **to make an** ~ **to do sth** sich bemühen or anstrengen, etw zu tun; **to make every possible** ~ **to do sth** sich (dat) die größte Mühe geben, etw zu tun; **he made no** ~ **to be polite** er gab sich (dat) keine Mühe, höflich zu sein; **it's an** ~ es kostet einige Mühe; **if it's not**

too much of an ~ **for you** (iro) wenn es dir nicht zu viel Mühe macht; **come on, make an** ~ komm, streng dich ein bißchen an. **(b)** (col) **it was a poor** ~ das war eine schwache Leistung; **his first** ~ **at making a film** sein erster Versuch, einen Film zu drehen.

effortless ['efətlɪs] adj mühelos, leicht; style flüssig.

effrontery [ɪ'frʌntərɪ] n Unverschämtheit f.

effusive [ɪ'fjuːsɪv] adj überschwenglich.

eg = **for example** z.B.

egalitarian [ɪ,gælɪ'tɛərɪən] adj egalitär (geh); principle also Gleichheits-.

egg [eg] n Ei nt. **to put all one's** ~s **in one basket** (prov) alles auf eine Karte setzen.

♦ **egg on** vt sep anstacheln.

egg: ~-**cup** n Eierbecher m; ~-**head** n (pej col) Intellektuelle(r) mf, Eierkopf m (col); ~-**plant** n Aubergine f; ~-**shell** n Eierschale f; ~-**white** n Eiweiß nt; ~ **yolk** n Eidotter m, Eigelb nt.

ego ['iːgəʊ] n (Psych) Ego, Ich nt; (col) Selbstbewußtsein nt; (conceit) Einbildung f. **this will boost his** ~ das wird ihm Auftrieb geben.

egocentric(al) [egəʊ'sentrɪk(əl)] adj egozentrisch.

egoism ['egəʊɪzəm] n Egoismus m, Selbstsucht f.

egotism ['egəʊtɪzəm] n Egotismus m.

egotist ['egəʊtɪst] n Egotist m.

egotistic(al) [,egəʊ'tɪstɪk(əl)] adj ichbezogen.

ego-trip ['iːgəʊtrɪp] n (col) **he's on one of his** ~s er gibt wieder so an; **it won't last long, it's just some sort of** ~ das dauert nicht lange, er will nur sein Selbstgefühl aufpäppeln.

Egypt ['iːdʒɪpt] n Ägypten nt.

Egyptian [ɪ'dʒɪpʃən] **1** adj ägyptisch. **2** n **(a)** Ägypter(in f) m. **(b)** (language) Ägyptisch nt.

eiderdown ['aɪdədaʊn] n (quilt) Daunendecke f.

eight [eɪt] **1** adj acht. **2** n Acht f; see six.

eighteen ['eɪ'tiːn] adj achtzehn.

eighteenth ['eɪ'tiːnθ] adj achtzehnte(r, s); see sixteenth.

eighth [eɪtθ] **1** adj achte(r, s). **2** n (fraction) Achtel nt; (of series) Achte(r,s); see sixth.

eightieth ['eɪtɪəθ] adj achtzigste(r, s); see sixtieth.

eighty ['eɪtɪ] adj achtzig; see sixty.

Eire ['ɛərə] n Irland nt.

either ['aɪðə'] **1** adj, pron **(a)** (one or other) eine(r, s) (von beiden). **there are two boxes, take** ~ hier sind zwei Schachteln, nimm eine davon. **(b)** (each, both) jede(r, s), beide pl. ~ **day would suit me** beide Tage passen mir; **which bus will you take?** — **das ist egal; on** ~ **side of the street** auf beiden Seiten der Straße; **it wasn't in** ~ (box) es war in keiner der beiden (Kisten); ~ **way we lose** out wir machen auf jeden Fall einen Verlust.

2 adv, conj **(a)** (after neg statement) auch nicht. **he can't act** ~ schauspielern kann er auch nicht; **I haven't** ~ ich auch nicht. **(b)** ~ ... **or** entweder ... oder; (after a negative) weder ... noch; ~ **be quiet or go out!** entweder bist du ruhig oder du gehst!; **I have never been to Paris, nor to Rome** ~ ich bin bisher weder in Paris noch in Rom gewesen.

ejaculate [ɪ'dʒækjʊleɪt] vi aufschreien; (Physiol) ejakulieren.

ejaculation [ɪ,dʒækjʊ'leɪʃən] n (cry) Ausruf m; (Physiol) Ejakulation f, Samenerguß m.

eject [ɪ'dʒekt] **1** vt heckler, tenant hinauswerfen; cartridge auswerfen. **2** vi (pilot) den Schleudersitz betätigen.

ejection [ɪ'dʒekʃən] n Hinauswurf m; (of cartridge) Auswerfen nt.

ejector seat [ɪ'dʒektəsiːt] n (Aviat) Schleudersitz m.

♦ **eke out** ['iːkaʊt] vt sep strecken. **to** ~ ~ **a living** sich recht und schlecht durchschlagen.

elaborate [ɪ'læbərɪt] **1** *adj design, hairstyle, pattern, drawing* kunstvoll; *style (of writing) also* ausführlich, detailliert; *plan* ausgeklügelt; *preparations* kompliziert. **an ~ meal** ein großes Menü. **2** [ɪ'læbəreɪt] *vt (work out)* ausarbeiten; *(describe)* ausführen. **3** [ɪ'læbəreɪt] *vi* **could you ~ (on that)?** könnten Sie das etwas näher ausführen?

elapse [ɪ'læps] *vi* vergehen, verstreichen.

elastic [ɪ'læstɪk] **1** *adj (lit, fig)* elastisch. **~ band** *(Brit)* Gummiband *nt.* **2** *n* Gummi(band *nt*) *m*; *(US: rubber band)* Gummi *m.*

elasticity [ˌiːlæs'tɪsɪtɪ] *n* Elastizität *f.*

elated [ɪ'leɪtɪd] *adj* begeistert.

elation [ɪ'leɪʃən] *n* Begeisterung *f (at* über *+acc).*

elbow ['elbəʊ] **1** *n* Ellbogen *m.* **out at the ~s** an den Ellbogen durchgewetzt. **2** *vt* **he ~ed his way through the crowd** er boxte sich durch die Menge; **to ~ sb aside** jdn beiseite stoßen.

elbow: ~-grease *n (col)* Muskelkraft *f*; **~-room** *n (col: lit, fig)* Ellbogenfreiheit *f (col).*

elder¹ ['eldəʳ] **1** *adj attr comp of* **old** *brother* ältere(r, s). **~ statesman** erfahrener Staatsmann. **2** *n* **(a)** **respect your ~s and betters** du mußt Respekt vor Älteren haben. **(b)** *(of tribe, Church)* Älteste(r) *m.*

elder² ['eldəʳ] *n (Bot)* Holunder *m.*

elderberry ['eldəˌberɪ] *n* Holunderbeere *f.*

elderly ['eldəlɪ] *adj* ältlich, ältere(r, s) *attr.*

eldest ['eldɪst] *adj attr superl of* **old** älteste(r, s).

elect [ɪ'lekt] **1** *vt* **(a)** wählen. **he was ~ed chairman** er wurde zum Vorsitzenden gewählt. **(b)** *(choose)* **to ~ to do sth** sich dafür entscheiden, etw zu tun. **2** *adj* **the president ~** der designierte Präsident.

election [ɪ'lekʃən] *n* Wahl *f.* **~ campaign** Wahlkampf *m.*

electioneering [ɪˌlekʃə'nɪərɪŋ] *n* Wahlkampf *m*; *(propaganda)* Wahlpropaganda *f.*

elector [ɪ'lektəʳ] *n* Wähler(in *f*) *m.*

electoral [ɪ'lektərəl] *adj* Wahl-. **~ college** Wahlmännergremium *nt*; **~ roll** Wählerverzeichnis *nt.*

electorate [ɪ'lektərɪt] *n* Wähler *pl*, Wählerschaft *f.*

electric [ɪ'lektrɪk] *adj* elektrisch. **the atmosphere was ~** es herrschte Hochspannung; **the effect was ~** *(col)* das hatte eine tolle Wirkung.

electrical [ɪ'lektrɪkəl] *adj* Elektro-, elektrisch. **~ engineer** Elektrotechniker *m*; **~ engineering** Elektrotechnik *f.*

electric: ~ blanket *n* Heizdecke *f*; **~ chair** *n* elektrischer Stuhl; **~ cooker** *n* Elektroherd *m*; **~ fire** *n* elektrisches Heizgerät.

electrician [ɪlek'trɪʃən] *n* Elektriker *m.*

electricity [ɪlek'trɪsɪtɪ] *n* Elektrizität *f*; *(electric power for use)* Strom *m.* **to turn off the ~** den Strom abschalten; **~ meter** Stromzähler *m.*

electric: ~ light *n* elektrisches Licht; **~ motor** *n* Elektromotor *m*; **~ shock** *n* elektrischer Schlag; **~ shock treatment** (Elektro)schocktherapie *f.*

electrify [ɪ'lektrɪfaɪ] *vt* **(a)** *(Rail)* elektrifizieren. **(b)** *(charge with electricity)* unter Strom setzen. **(c)** *(fig)* elektrisieren.

electrifying [ɪ'lektrɪfaɪɪŋ] *adj (fig)* elektrisierend.

electrocute [ɪ'lektrəkjuːt] *vt* durch einen (Strom)schlag töten; *(execute)* auf dem elektrischen Stuhl hinrichten.

electrode [ɪ'lektrəʊd] *n* Elektrode *f.*

electrolysis [ɪlek'trɒlɪsɪs] *n* Elektrolyse *f.*

electromagnetic [ɪˌlektrəʊmæg'netɪk] *adj* elektromagnetisch.

electron [ɪ'lektrɒn] *n* Elektron *nt.* **~ microscope** Elektronenmikroskop *nt.*

electronic [ɪlek'trɒnɪk] *adj* elektronisch.

electronics [ɪlek'trɒnɪks] *n* Elektronik *f.*

electroplated [ɪ'lektrəʊpleɪtɪd] *adj (galvanisch)* versilbert/verchromt *etc.*

elegance ['elɪgəns] *n* Eleganz *f.*

elegant ['elɪgənt] *adj* elegant.

elegy ['elɪdʒɪ] *n* Elegie *f.*

element ['elɪmənt] *n (also Elec)* Element *nt*; *(usu pl: of a subject also)* Grundbegriff *m.* **the ~ of chance** das Zufallselement; **to be in one's ~** in seinem Element sein; **to be out of one's ~** *(with people)* sich fehl am Platz fühlen; *(with subject)* sich nicht auskennen.

elementary [ˌelɪ'mentərɪ] *adj* **(a)** *(simple)* einfach, elementar. **(b)** *(basic)* elementar, Grund-. **~ course** Grundkurs *m*; **~ school** Grundschule *f.*

elephant ['elɪfənt] *n* Elefant *m.*

elevate ['elɪveɪt] *vt* **(a)** heben. **(b)** *elevating reading* erbauliche Lektüre.

elevated ['elɪveɪtɪd] *adj* **(a)** *position* hoch(liegend), höher; *platform* erhöht. **(b)** *(fig) position, style* gehoben; *thoughts* erhaben.

elevation [ˌelɪ'veɪʃən] *n* **(a)** *(lit)* Hebung *f.* **(b)** *(of thought)* Erhabenheit *f*; *(of position, style)* Gehobenheit *f.* **(c)** *(above sea level)* Höhe *f* über dem Meeresspiegel; *(hill)* Anhöhe *f.* **(d)** *(Archit: drawing)* Aufriß *m.* **front ~** Frontansicht *f.*

elevator ['elɪveɪtəʳ] *n (US)* Fahrstuhl, Aufzug *m.*

eleven [ɪ'levn] **1** *n* **(a)** *(number)* Elf *f.* **the ~ plus** *(Brit Sch)* Aufnahmeprüfung in eine weiterführende Schule. **(b)** *(Sport)* Elf *f.* **the second ~** die zweite Mannschaft. **2** *adj* *elf; see* **six.**

elevenses [ɪ'levnzɪz] *n sing or pl (Brit)* zweites Frühstück.

eleventh [ɪ'levnθ] *adj* elfte(r, s). **at the ~ hour** *(fig)* in letzter Minute; *see* **sixth.**

elf [elf] *n, pl* **elves** Elf *m*, Elfe *f*; *(mischievous)* Kobold *m.*

elicit [ɪ'lɪsɪt] *vt* entlocken *(from sb* jdm).

eligibility [ˌelɪdʒə'bɪlɪtɪ] *n* Berechtigung *f.* **graded in order of ~** nach Eignung geordnet.

eligible ['elɪdʒəbl] *adj* in Frage kommend; *(for competition etc also)* teilnahmeberechtigt; *(for grants etc also)* berechtigt; *(for membership)* aufnahmeberechtigt. **an ~ bachelor** ein begehrter Junggeselle.

eliminate [ɪ'lɪmɪneɪt] *vt* **(a)** ausschließen; *competitor* ausschalten. **our team was ~d in the second round** unsere Mannschaft schied in der zweiten Runde aus. **(b)** *(kill)* ausschalten, ausschließen.

elimination [ɪˌlɪmɪ'neɪʃən] *n see vt* **(a)** Ausschluß *m*; Ausschaltung *f.* **by (a)** *process of* **~** durch negative Auslese. **(b)** Ausschaltung, Eliminierung *f.*

élite [eɪ'liːt] *n* Elite *f.*

élitism [eɪ'liːtɪzəm] *n* Elitedenken *nt.*

élitist [eɪ'liːtɪst] *adj* elitär.

elixir [ɪ'lɪksəʳ] *n* Elixier *nt*, Auszug *m.*

Elizabethan [ɪˌlɪzə'biːθən] *adj* elisabethanisch.

elk [elk] *n* Elch *m.*

ellipse [ɪ'lɪps] *n* Ellipse *f.*

elm [elm] *n* Ulme *f.*

elocution [ˌelə'kjuːʃən] *n* Sprechtechnik *f.* **~ classes** Sprecherziehung *f.*

elongate ['iːlɒŋgeɪt] *vt* verlängern.

elope [ɪ'ləʊp] *vi* durchbrennen.

elopement [ɪ'ləʊpmənt] *n* Durchbrennen *nt.*

eloquence ['eləkwəns] *n see* **eloquent** Wortgewandtheit *f*; Wohlgesetztheit *f*; Beredtheit *f.*

eloquent ['eləkwənt] *adj* wortgewandt; *speech* wohlgesetzt; *(fig) gesture* beredt, vielsagend.

else [els] *adv* **(a)** *(after pron)* andere(r, s). **anybody ~ would have done it** jeder andere hätte es gemacht; **somebody ~** *(in addition)* sonst jemand; *(somebody different)* jemand anders; **have you anything ~?** haben Sie sonst noch etwas?; **something ~** sonst etwas; etwas anderes; **anywhere ~** sonstwo; **but they haven't got anywhere ~ to go** aber sie können sonst nirgends hingehen; **somewhere ~** woanders, anderswo; *(with motion)* woandershin, anderswohin.

(b) *(after pron, neg)* nobody ~, no one ~ sonst niemand, niemand anders; nobody ~ **understood** niemand anders hat es verstanden; **nothing** ~ sonst nichts, nichts anderes; **nothing** ~, **thank you** danke, nichts weiter; **nowhere** ~ sonst nirgends, nirgendwo anders; **there's nothing** ~ **for it but to go** da gibt es keinen anderen Ausweg, als zu gehen.

(c) *(after interrog)* **where** ~? wo sonst?; **who** ~? wer sonst?; **what** ~? was sonst?; **what** ~ **could I do?** was konnte ich sonst tun?

(d) *(adv of quantity)* **and much** ~ und vieles andere; **there is little** ~ **to be done** da bleibt nicht viel zu tun übrig.

(e) *(otherwise, if not)* sonst, andernfalls. **do it now (or)** ~ **you'll be punished** tu es jetzt oder es setzt Strafe; **you better had, or** ~ ...! mach das bloß, sonst ...!

elsewhere [ˌelsˈwɛəʳ] *adv* woanders, anderswo; *(to another place)* woandershin, anderswohin. **in Wales and** ~ unter anderem in Wales.

elucidate [ɪˈluːsɪdeɪt] *vt text* erklären; *mystery* aufklären.

elude [ɪˈluːd] *vt observation, justice* sich entziehen *(+dat)*; *question* ausweichen *(+dat)*; *police, enemy* entkommen *(+dat)*. **success has** ~**d him** der Erfolg wollte sich nicht einstellen.

elusive [ɪˈluːsɪv] *adj* schwer faßbar; *concept, meaning also* schwer definierbar; *thoughts, memory* flüchtig; *happiness* unerreichbar; *answer* ausweichend; *fox etc* schwer zu fangen.

elves [elvz] *pl of* **elf**.

emaciated [ɪˈmeɪsɪeɪtɪd] *adj* ausgezehrt.

emanate [ˈeməneɪt] *vi* ausgehen *(from* von*)*; *(light also)* ausstrahlen *(from* von*)*; *(documents, instructions etc)* stammen *(from* aus*)*.

emancipate [ɪˈmænsɪpeɪt] *vt (lit,fig)* emanzipieren.

emancipated [ɪˈmænsɪpeɪtɪd] *adj (lit, fig)* emanzipiert.

emancipation [ɪˌmænsɪˈpeɪʃən] *n (lit, fig)* Emanzipation *f*.

embalm [ɪmˈbɑːm] *vt corpse* einbalsamieren.

embankment [ɪmˈbæŋkmənt] *n* Böschung *f*; *(for railway)* Bahndamm *m*; *(holding back water)* Deich *m*; *(road beside a river)* Uferstraße *f*.

embargo [ɪmˈbɑːgəʊ] *n, pl* **-es** Embargo *nt.* **to put an** ~ **on sth** ein Embargo über etw *(acc)* verhängen.

embark [ɪmˈbɑːk] **1** *vt* einschiffen. **2** *vi* **(a)** *(Naut)* sich einschiffen; *(troops)* eingeschifft werden. **(b)** *(fig)* **to** ~ **up(on) sth** mit etw anfangen.

embarkation [ˌembɑːˈkeɪʃən] *n* Einschiffung *f*. ~ **papers** Bordpapiere *pl.*

embarrass [ɪmˈbærəs] *vt* in Verlegenheit bringen; *(generosity etc also)* beschämen. **I feel so** ~**ed about it** das ist mir so peinlich; **she was** ~**ed by the question** die Frage war ihr peinlich.

embarrassed [ɪmˈbærəst] *adj* verlegen.

embarrassing [ɪmˈbærəsɪŋ] *adj* peinlich.

embarrassment [ɪmˈbærəsmənt] *n* Verlegenheit *f*. **to cause** ~ **to sb** jdn in Verlegenheit bringen; **much to my** ~ **she ... sie ...,** was mir sehr peinlich war; *financial* ~ finanzielle Verlegenheit.

embassy [ˈembəsɪ] *n* Botschaft *f.*

embed [ɪmˈbed] *vt* **the screws were so firmly** ~**ded that ...** die Schrauben steckten so fest, daß ...; **to be** ~**ded in sth** *(fig)* fest in etw *(dat)* verwurzelt sein.

embellish [ɪmˈbelɪʃ] *vt (adorn)* schmücken; *(fig) tale, account* ausschmücken; *truth* beschönigen.

embers [ˈembəz] *npl* Glut *f.*

embezzle [ɪmˈbezl] *vt* unterschlagen.

embezzlement [ɪmˈbezlmənt] *n* Unterschlagung *f.*

embittered [ɪmˈbɪtəd] *adj person* verbittert; *relations* vergiftet.

emblem [ˈembləm] *n* Emblem *nt.*

embodiment [ɪmˈbɒdɪmənt] *n* Verkörperung *f.* **to be the** ~ **of virtue** die Tugend in Person sein.

embody [ɪmˈbɒdɪ] *vt* **(a)** *ideal etc* verkörpern. **(b)** *(include)* enthalten.

emboss [ɪmˈbɒs] *vt metal, leather* prägen. ~**ed wallpaper** Prägetapete *f*; **an** ~**ed silver tray** ein Silbertablett mit Relief.

embrace [ɪmˈbreɪs] **1** *vt* **(a)** *(hug)* umarmen, in die Arme schließen. **(b)** *religion* annehmen; *cause* sich annehmen *(+gen).* **(c)** *(include)* umfassen, erfassen. **2** *vi* sich umarmen. **3** *n* Umarmung *f.*

embroider [ɪmˈbrɔɪdəʳ] *vt* **(a)** besticken; *pattern* sticken. **(b)** *(fig) facts, truth* ausschmücken.

embroidery [ɪmˈbrɔɪdərɪ] *n* **(a)** Stickerei *f.* **(b)** *(fig)* Ausschmückungen *pl.*

embroil [ɪmˈbrɔɪl] *vt* **to become** ~**ed in a dispute** in einen Streit verwickelt werden.

embryo [ˈembrɪəʊ] *n (lit,fig)* Embryo *m*; *(fig)* Keim *m.* **in** ~ *(lit,fig)* im Keim.

embryonic [ˌembrɪˈɒnɪk] *adj* embryonisch; *(fig)* keimhaft.

emend [ɪˈmend] *vt text* verbessern, korrigieren.

emerald [ˈemərəld] **1** *n (stone)* Smaragd *m*; *(colour)* Smaragdgrün *nt.* **2** *adj* Smaragd-. **the E**~ **Isle** die Grüne Insel.

emerge [ɪˈmɜːdʒ] *vi* **(a)** auftauchen. **he** ~**d the winner** er ging als Sieger hervor; **we** ~**d into the bright daylight** wir kamen heraus in das helle Tageslicht; **one arm** ~**d from beneath the blanket** ein Arm kam unter der Decke hervor. **(b)** *(come into being: life, new nation)* entstehen. **(c)** *(truth, nature of problem etc)* sich herausstellen. **it now** ~**s that ...** es stellt sich jetzt heraus, daß ...

emergence [ɪˈmɜːdʒəns] *n* Auftauchen *nt*; *(of new nation etc)* Entstehung *f*; *(of school of thought)* Aufkommen *nt.*

emergency [ɪˈmɜːdʒənsɪ] *n* Notfall *m*; *(state of* ~*)* Notlage *f.* **in case of** ~ im Notfall; **to declare a state of** ~ den Notstand ausrufen.

emergency *in cpds* Not-; ~ **brake** *n* Notbremse *f*; ~ **exit** *n* Notausgang *m*; ~ **landing** *n* Notlandung *f*; ~ **service** *n* Notdienst *m*; ~ **stop** *n (Aut)* Vollbremsung *f*; ~ **ward** *n* Unfallstation *f.*

emergent [ɪˈmɜːdʒənt] *adj nations* aufstrebend.

emery [ˈemərɪ] *n* ~ **board** *n* Papiernagelfeile *f*; ~ **paper** *n* Schmirgelpapier *nt.*

emetic [ɪˈmetɪk] *n* Brechmittel *nt.*

emigrant [ˈemɪgrənt] *n* Auswanderer *m*; *(esp for political reasons)* Emigrant(in *f*) *m.*

emigrate [ˈemɪgreɪt] *vi* auswandern; *(esp for political reasons)* emigrieren.

emigration [ˌemɪˈgreɪʃən] *n* Auswanderung *f*; *(esp for political reasons)* Emigration *f.*

émigré [ˈemɪgreɪ] *n* Emigrant(in *f*) *m.*

eminence [ˈemɪnəns] *n* **(a)** *(distinction)* hohes Ansehen. **(b)** *(of ground)* Erhebung *f.* **(c)** *(Eccl)* **His/Your E**~ Seine/Eure Eminenz.

eminent [ˈemɪnənt] *adj person* (hoch)angesehen; *suitability, fairness* ausgesprochen, eminent.

eminently [ˈemɪnəntlɪ] *adv* ausgesprochen.

emissary [ˈemɪsərɪ] *n* Abgesandte(r) *mf.*

emission [ɪˈmɪʃən] *n* Ausstrahlung *f*; *(of heat also, of sound, smoke)* Abgabe *f*; *(of liquid)* Ausströmen *nt*; *(of lava)* Ausstoßen *nt.*

emit [ɪˈmɪt] *vt light* ausstrahlen; *radiation also* emittieren; *heat also, sound, smoke* abgeben; *lava, cry* ausstoßen.

emotion [ɪˈməʊʃən] *n* **(a)** Gefühl *nt*, Emotion *f.* **(b)** *no pl (state of being moved)* Bewegtheit *f.* **to show no** ~ unbewegt bleiben; **in a voice full of** ~ mit bewegter Stimme.

emotional [ɪˈməʊʃənl] *adj* **(a)** emotional, emotionell; *story,film, speech also* gefühlsbetont; *moment, writing also* gefühlvoll; *decision also* gefühlsmäßig; *day, experience* erregend; *letter* erregt. ~ **state** Zustand *m* der Erregung; **it has an** ~ **appeal** es appelliert an das Gefühl. **(b)** *person* (leicht) erregbar, emotional. **don't get so** ~ **about it** reg dich nicht so darüber auf.

emotionalism [ɪˈməʊʃnəlɪzəm] n Gefühlsbetontheit f. **the article was sheer** ~ der Artikel war reine Gefühlsduselei.

emotionally [ɪˈməʊʃnəlɪ] adv behave, react gefühlsmäßig, emotional; (with feeling) speak gefühlvoll; (showing one is upset) erregt. **an** ~ **deprived child** ein Kind nt ohne Nestwärme; **to be** ~ **disturbed** seelisch gestört sein; **I don't want to get** ~ **involved (with her)** ich will mich (bei ihr) nicht ernsthaft engagieren.

emotive [ɪˈməʊtɪv] adj gefühlsbetont; word also emotional gefärbt; force of a word emotional.

empathy [ˈempəθɪ] n Einfühlungsvermögen nt.

emperor [ˈempərər] n Kaiser m.

emphasis [ˈemfəsɪs] n Betonung f. **to say sth with** ~ etw mit Nachdruck betonen; **to lay** ~ or put **the** ~ **on sth** etw betonen; **this year the** ~ **is on** ... dieses Jahr liegt der Akzent auf ...; **there is too much** ~ **on** ...... wird zu sehr betont; **a change of** ~ eine Akzentverschiebung.

emphasize [ˈemfəsaɪz] vt betonen.

emphatic [ɪmˈfætɪk] adj tone, manner nachdrücklich, entschieden; denial also energisch.

emphatically [ɪmˈfætɪkəlɪ] adv state mit Nachdruck, ausdrücklich; deny, refuse strikt, energisch. **most** ~ **not** auf gar keinen Fall.

empire [ˈempaɪər] n Reich nt; (fig: esp Comm) Imperium nt.

empirical [emˈpɪrɪkəl] adj empirisch.

employ [ɪmˈplɔɪ] vt (a) beschäftigen; (take on) anstellen; private detective beauftragen. **he's** ~**ed in a bank** er arbeitet bei einer Bank. (b) (use) method anwenden; time verbringen.

employee [ˌemplɔɪˈiː] n Angestellte(r) mf. ~**s and employers** Arbeitnehmer und Arbeitgeber; **the** ~**s** (of one firm) die Belegschaft.

employer [ɪmˈplɔɪər] n Arbeitgeber(in f) m.

employment [ɪmˈplɔɪmənt] n (a) (work) Stellung, Arbeit f. **to take up** ~ **with sb** eine Stelle bei jdm annehmen; **to seek** ~ **with sb** sich bei jdm bewerben; **to be in** ~ angestellt sein; **place of** ~ Arbeitsplatz m. (b) (act of employing) Beschäftigung f; (taking on) Einstellen nt. (c) (use: of method) Anwendung f; (of word) Verwendung f.

employment: ~ **agency** n Stellenvermittlung f; ~ **exchange** n Arbeitsamt nt.

empower [ɪmˈpaʊər] vt **to** ~ **sb to do sth** jdn ermächtigen, etw zu tun.

empress [ˈemprɪs] n Kaiserin f.

empties [ˈemptɪz] npl Leergut nt.

emptiness [ˈemptɪnɪs] n Leere f.

empty [ˈemptɪ] **1** adj (+er) leer; (not occupied) house leerstehend attr; head hohl. **2** vt leeren; box, room also ausräumen; house räumen; glass, bottle also (by drinking) austrinken. **he emptied it into another container** er goß es in ein anderes Gefäß um. **3** vi (water) abfließen; (rivers) münden (into in +acc); (theatre, streets) sich leeren.

empty: ~-**handed** adj **to return** ~-**handed** mit leeren Händen zurückkehren; ~-**headed** adj strohdumm.

emu [ˈiːmjuː] n Emu m.

emulate [ˈemjʊleɪt] vt nacheifern (+dat).

emulsion [ɪˈmʌlʃən] n (a) Emulsion f. (b) (also ~ paint) Emulsionsfarbe f.

enable [ɪˈneɪbl] vt **to** ~ **sb to do sth** es jdm ermöglichen, etw zu tun.

enact [ɪˈnækt] vt (a) (Pol) law erlassen. (b) (perform) play aufführen. **the drama which was** ~**ed yesterday** (fig) das Drama, das sich gestern abgespielt hat.

enamel [ɪˈnæməl] **1** n Emaille f; (paint) Emaillelack m; (of teeth) Zahnschmelz m. **2** vt emaillieren.

encampment [ɪnˈkæmpmənt] n Lager nt.

encase [ɪnˈkeɪs] vt verkleiden (in mit); wires umgeben (in mit).

enchant [ɪnˈtʃɑːnt] vt (a) (delight) bezaubern,

entzücken. (b) (put under spell) verzaubern.

enchanting adj [ɪnˈtʃɑːntɪŋ] bezaubernd.

enchantment [ɪnˈtʃɑːntmənt] n (a) (delight) Entzücken nt. (b) (charm) Zauber m.

enchantress [ɪnˈtʃɑːntrɪs] n Zauberin f.

encircle [ɪnˈsɜːkl] vt umgeben, umfassen; (troops) einkreisen; building umstellen.

enc(l) = **enclosure(s)** Anl.

enclave [ˈenkleɪv] n Enklave f.

enclose [ɪnˈkləʊz] vt (a) (shut in) einschließen; (surround) umgeben; (with fence etc) einzäunen. **the garden is completely** ~**d** der Garten ist völlig abgeschlossen. (b) (in envelope) beilegen, beifügen. **please find** ~**d** ... in der Anlage übersenden wir Ihnen ...; **to** ~ **sth in a letter** einem Brief etw beilegen; **the** ~**d cheque** der beiliegende Scheck.

enclosure [ɪnˈkləʊʒər] n (a) (for animals) Gehege nt; (on racecourse) Zuschauerbereich m. (b) (act) Einzäunung f. (c) (with letter) Anlage f.

encompass [ɪnˈkʌmpəs] vt (include) umfassen.

encore [ˈɒŋkɔː] **1** interj da capo, Zugabe. **2** n Zugabe f. **to give an** ~ eine Zugabe spielen/singen.

encounter [ɪnˈkaʊntər] **1** vt stoßen auf (+acc); (liter) person begegnen (+dat), treffen. **2** n Begegnung f, Treffen nt; (in battle) Zusammenstoß m.

encourage [ɪnˈkʌrɪdʒ] vt person ermutigen, ermuntern (to zu); (motivate) anregen; arts, industry fördern; team anfeuern; sb's bad habits unterstützen. **you'll only** ~ **him to think there's still hope** er wird dann nur noch eher glauben, daß noch Hoffnung besteht; **this** ~**s me to think that** ... das läßt mich vermuten, daß ...

encouragement [ɪnˈkʌrɪdʒmənt] n Ermutigung f; (motivation) Anregung f; (support) Unterstützung f, Förderung f. **to give sb** ~ jdn ermuntern.

encouraging [ɪnˈkʌrɪdʒɪŋ] adj ermutigend. **you are not very** ~ du machst mir/uns etc nicht gerade Mut.

encroach [ɪnˈkrəʊtʃ] vi **to** ~ (**up)on** land vordringen in (+acc); sphere, rights eingreifen in (+acc); time in Anspruch nehmen.

encrusted [ɪnˈkrʌstɪd] verkrustet; (with pearls etc) besetzt.

encumber [ɪnˈkʌmbər] vt **to be** ~**ed with sth** (person) mit etw beladen sein; with debts mit etw belastet sein; (room) mit etw überladen sein.

encumbrance [ɪnˈkʌmbrəns] n (also Jur) Belastung f.

encyclop(a)edia [ɪnˌsaɪkləʊˈpiːdɪə] n Lexikon nt, Enzyklopädie f.

end [end] **1** n (a) Ende nt; (of finger) Spitze f. **at the** ~ **of the procession** am Schluß der Prozession; **the fourth from the** ~ der/die/das vierte von hinten; **from** ~ **to** ~ von einem Ende zum anderen; **to stand on** ~ (box etc) hochkant stehen; (hair) zu Berge stehen; **for hours on** ~ stundenlang ununterbrochen; ~ **to** ~ mit den En denaneinander; **to change** ~**s** (Sport) die Sei tenwechseln; **to make** ~**s meet** (fig) durchkommen (col).

(b) (remnant) (of rope) Ende nt; (of candle, cigarette) Stummel m. **just a few odd** ~**s left** nur noch ein paar Reste.

(c) (conclusion) Ende nt. **the** ~ **of the month** das Monatsende; **at/towards the** ~ **of December** Ende/gegen Ende Dezember; **is there no** ~ **to this**? hört das denn nie auf?; **we shall never hear the** ~ **of it** das werden wir noch lange zu hören kriegen; **to be at an** ~ zu Ende sein; **to be at the** ~ **of one's patience** mit seiner Geduld am Ende sein; **to see a film/read a book to the** ~ einen Film/ein Buch bis zu Ende sehen/lesen; **that's the** ~ **of him** er ist erledigt; **that's the** ~ **of that** das ist damit erledigt; **to come to an** ~ zu Ende gehen; **in the** ~ schließlich, zum Schluß; **to put**

an ~ to sth einer Sache *(dat)* ein Ende setzen; to come to a bad ~ ein böses Ende nehmen; to meet one's ~ den Tod finden.
 (d) *(col phrases)* no ~ of famous people irrsinnig viele berühmte Leute *(col)*; it's done him no ~ of harm es hat ihm irrsinnig geschadet *(col)*; to think no ~ of sb große Stücke auf jdn halten; you're the ~ du bist wirklich das Letzte.
 (e) *(purpose)* Ziel *nt*, Zweck *m*. with this ~ in view mit diesem Ziel vor Augen; an ~ in itself Selbstzweck *no art*; the ~ justifies the means *(prov)* der Zweck heiligt die Mittel *(prov)*.
 2 *adj attr* letzte(r, s); *house also* End-.
 3 *vt* beenden; *speech, broadcast, series also*, one's days beschließen. the novel to ~ all novels der größte Roman aller Zeiten.
 4 *vi* enden. we'll have to ~ soon wir müssen bald Schluß machen; to be ~ing zu Ende gehen; where's it all going to ~? wo soll das nur enden?
♦ **end up** *vi* enden, landen *(col)*. to ~ ~ doing sth schließlich etw tun; to ~ ~ as a lawyer/an alcoholic schließlich Rechtsanwalt werden/als Alkoholiker enden.
endanger [ɪn'deɪndʒəʳ] *vt* gefährden.
endear [ɪn'dɪəʳ] *vt* beliebt machen *(to bei)*.
endearing [ɪn'dɪərɪŋ] *adj* smile, personality gewinnend; *characteristic also* liebenswert.
endearment [ɪn'dɪəmənt] *n* term of ~ Kosename *m*.
endeavour, *(US)* **endeavor** [ɪn'devəʳ] **1** *n* Anstrengung, Bemühung *f*. to make every ~ to do sth sich nach Kräften bemühen, etw zu tun. **2** *vt* sich bemühen.
endemic [en'demɪk] *adj (lit, fig)* endemisch.
ending ['endɪŋ] *n (of book, events)* Ausgang *m*; *(last part)* Ende *nt*, Schluß *m*; *(of word)* Endung *f*. happy ~ Happy-End *nt*.
endive ['endaɪv] *n* Endiviensalat *m*.
endless ['endlɪs] *adj* endlos; *possibilities* unendlich. this job is ~ diese Arbeit nimmt kein Ende.
endorse [ɪn'dɔːs] *vt* **(a)** *cheque* auf der Rückseite unterzeichnen. **(b)** *(Brit)* driving licence eine Strafe vermerken auf *(+dat)*. **(c)** *(approve)* billigen. I ~ that dem stimme ich zu.
endorsement [ɪn'dɔːsmənt] *n* **(a)** *(on cheque)* Indossament *nt*. **(b)** *(Brit: on driving licence)* Strafvermerk *m* auf dem Führerschein. **(c)** *(of opinion)* Billigung *f*.
endow [ɪn'daʊ] *vt* institution eine Stiftung machen an *(acc)*; prize stiften. ~ed with sth *(fig: with characteristic)* mit etw ausgestattet.
endowment [ɪndaʊmənt] *n* **(a)** Stiftung *f*. **(b)** *(talent)* Begabung *f*; *(physical)* Merkmal *nt*.
end: ~product *n* Endprodukt *nt*; *(fig)* Produkt *nt*; ~ result *n* Endergebnis *nt*.
endurable [ɪn'djʊərəbl] *adj* erträglich.
endurance [ɪn'djʊərəns] *n (powers of ~)* Durchhaltevermögen *nt*. tried beyond ~ über die Maßen gereizt; ~ test Belastungsprobe *f*.
endure [ɪn'djʊəʳ] **1** *vt* **(a)** *(undergo)* pain, insults (er)leiden. **(b)** *(put up with)* ertragen. she can't ~ being laughed at sie kann es nicht vertragen, wenn man über sie lacht. **2** *vi* Bestand haben.
enduring [ɪn'djʊərɪŋ] *adj* value, fame bleibend; *friendship, peace* dauerhaft; *hardship* anhaltend.
enema ['enɪmə] *n* Klistier *nt*.
enemy ['enəmɪ] **1** *n (lit, fig)* Feind *m*. to make enemies sich *(dat)* Feinde machen; he is his own worst ~ er schadet sich *(dat)* selbst am meisten. **2** *adj attr* feindlich; *position, advance, morale* des Feindes. ~ action Feindeinwirkung *f*.
energetic [ˌenə'dʒetɪk] *adj* voller Energie, energiegeladen; *(active)* aktiv; *manager, government* tatkräftig; *dancing, music, prose* schwungvoll; *protest, denial* energisch. she is a very ~ person sie steckt voller Energie.

energize ['enədʒaɪz] *vt* Antrieb geben *(+dat)*; *(Elec)* unter Strom setzen.
energy ['enədʒɪ] *n* Energie *f*; ~ crisis *n* Energiekrise *f*; ~-saving *adj* energiesparend.
enervating ['enɜːveɪtɪŋ] *adj* strapaziös.
enforce [ɪn'fɔːs] *vt* durchführen; one's claims, rights geltend machen; *silence, discipline* sorgen für, schaffen; *obedience* sich *(dat)* verschaffen. the police ~ the law die Polizei sorgt für die Einhaltung der Gesetze.
engage [ɪn'geɪdʒ] **1** *vt* **(a)** *workers* einstellen; *actor* engagieren; *lawyer* sich *(dat)* nehmen. **(b)** *the attention* in Anspruch nehmen. to ~ sb in conversation jdn in ein Gespräch verwickeln. **(c)** *the enemy* angreifen. **(d)** *(Tech)* gears ineinandergreifen lassen. to ~ a gear einen Gang einlegen; to ~ the clutch (ein)kuppeln. **2** *vi* **(a)** to ~ in sth sich an etw *(dat)* beteiligen; to ~ in politics sich politisch betätigen. **(b)** *(gears)* ineinandergreifen; *(clutch)* fassen.
engaged [ɪn'geɪdʒd] *adj* ~ verlobt. to get ~ sich verloben *(to mit)*; the ~ couple die Verlobten *pl*. **(b)** *(occupied)* beschäftigt. **(c)** the parties ~ in this dispute die streitenden Parteien. **(d)** *(Brit)* toilet, phone besetzt. ~ tone Besetztzeichen *nt*.
engagement [ɪn'geɪdʒmənt] *n* **(a)** *(appointment)* Verabredung *f*; *(of actor etc)* Engagement *nt*. public ~s öffentliche Verpflichtungen *pl*. **(b)** *(to marry)* Verlobung *f*. ~ ring Verlobungsring *m*. **(c)** *(form: undertaking)* Verpflichtung *f*. **(d)** *(Mil)* Gefecht *nt*.
engaging [ɪn'geɪdʒɪŋ] *adj* personality einnehmend; smile, look, tone gewinnend.
engender [ɪn'dʒendəʳ] *vt (fig)* erzeugen.
engine ['endʒɪn] *n* **(a)** Maschine *f*; *(of car, plane etc)* Motor *m*. **(b)** *(Rail)* Lokomotive, Lok *f*.
engine driver *n (Brit)* Lok(omotiv)führer(in *f*) *m*.
engineer [ˌendʒɪ'nɪəʳ] **1** *n* **(a)** Techniker(in *f*) *m*; *(with university degree etc)* Ingenieur(in *f*) *m*. the E~s *(Mil)* die Pioniere *pl*. **(b)** *(Naut: on merchant ships)* Maschinist *m*; *(in Navy)* Schiffsingenieur *m*. **(c)** *(US Rail)* Lokführer(in *f*) *m*. **2** *vt* **(a)** konstruieren. **(b)** *(fig)* election, campaign organisieren; *downfall* einfädeln.
engineering [ˌendʒɪ'nɪərɪŋ] *n* Technik *f*; *(mechanical ~)* Maschinenbau *m*; *(engineering profession)* Ingenieurwesen *nt*. the ~ of the Tay Bridge die Konstruktion der Tay-Brücke.
engine room *n (Naut)* Maschinenraum *m*.
England ['ɪŋglənd] *n* England *nt*.
English ['ɪŋglɪʃ] **1** *adj* englisch. he is ~ er ist Engländer. **2** *n* **(a)** the ~ *pl* die Engländer *pl*. **(b)** Englisch *nt*; *(as university subject)* Anglistik *f*. can you speak ~? können Sie Englisch?; he doesn't speak ~ er spricht kein Englisch; they were speaking ~ sie sprachen englisch; in ~ auf englisch; to translate sth into/from (the) ~ etw ins Englische/aus dem Englischen übersetzen.
English: ~ Channel *n* Ärmelkanal *m*; ~man *n* Engländer *m*; ~woman *n* Engländerin *f*.
engrave [ɪn'greɪv] *vt* eingravieren. it is ~d on my memory *(fig)* es hat sich mir (unauslöschlich) eingeprägt.
engraving [ɪn'greɪvɪŋ] *n (picture)* Stich *m*.
engrossed [ɪn'grəʊst] *adj* to be ~ in sth in etw *(dat)* vertieft sein.
engrossing [ɪn'grəʊsɪŋ] *adj* fesselnd.
engulf [ɪn'gʌlf] *vt* verschlingen.
enhance [ɪn'hɑːns] *vt* verbessern; *chances also, price, value, attraction* erhöhen.
enigma [ɪ'nɪgmə] *n* Rätsel *nt*.
enigmatic [ˌenɪg'mætɪk] *adj* rätselhaft.
enjoy [ɪn'dʒɔɪ] **1** *vt* **(a)** genießen. he ~s swimming/reading er schwimmt/liest gern; I ~ed the book/film das Buch/der Film hat mir gefallen; he ~ed the meal das Essen hat ihm gut geschmeckt; I've ~ed talking to you es war mir eine Freude, mich mit Ihnen zu unterhalten; I

didn't ~ **it at all** es hat mir überhaupt keinen Spaß gemacht. **(b)** *good health* sich erfreuen (+*gen*) (*geh*); *rights, advantages* genießen. 2 *vr* to ~ **oneself** sich amüsieren; ~ **yourself!** viel Spaß!

enjoyable [ɪn'dʒɔɪəbl] *adj* nett; *film, book also* unterhaltsam; *evening also, meal* angenehm.

enjoyment [ɪn'dʒɔɪmənt] *n* Vergnügen *nt*, Spaß *m* (*of an* +*dat*). **he got a lot of ~ from this book** das Buch machte ihm großen Spaß.

enlarge [ɪn'lɑːdʒ] **1** *vt* vergrößern; *hole, field of knowledge* erweitern. **2** *vi* to ~ **(up)on sth** sich über etw (*acc*) genauer äußern.

enlargement [ɪn'lɑːdʒmənt] *n* Vergrößerung *f*.

enlighten [ɪn'laɪtn] *vt* aufklären (*on, as to, about* über +*acc*).

enlightened [ɪn'laɪtnd] *adj* aufgeklärt.

enlightening [ɪn'laɪtnɪŋ] *adj* aufschlußreich.

enlightenment [ɪn'laɪtnmənt] *n* Aufklärung *f*. **the age of E~** das Zeitalter der Aufklärung.

enlist [ɪn'lɪst] **1** *vi* (*Mil etc*) sich melden (*in* zu). **2** *vt soldiers* einziehen; *supporters, sympathy, support* gewinnen. **~ed man** (*US*) gemeiner Soldat.

enliven [ɪn'laɪvn] *vt* beleben.

enmity ['enmɪtɪ] *n* Feindschaft *f*.

enormity [ɪ'nɔːmɪtɪ] *n no pl* (*of offence*) ungeheures Ausmaß.

enormous [ɪ'nɔːməs] *adj* gewaltig, enorm; *person* riesig; *patience* enorm. **an ~ number of people** ungeheuer viele Menschen; **an ~ amount of money/time** eine Unmenge Geld/Zeit.

enormously [ɪ'nɔːməslɪ] *adv* enorm, ungeheuer.

enough [ɪ'nʌf] **1** *adj, n* genug, genügend *attr.* **to be** ~ genügen, reichen; **is there ~ milk?** ist genug Milch da?; **will that be ~?** reicht das?; **I've had** ~, **I'm going home** mir reicht's, ich gehe nach Hause; **I've had ~ of your impudence** jetzt habe ich aber genug von deiner Frechheit; **now children, that's ~!** Kinder, jetzt reicht es aber!; **this noise is ~ to drive me mad** dieser Lärm macht mich noch ganz verrückt; ~ **is ~** was zuviel ist, ist zuviel. **2** *adv* (+*adj*) genug; (+*vb also*) genügend. **not big** ~ nicht groß genug; **he knows well** ~ **what I said** er weiß ganz genau, was ich gesagt habe; **she's pleasant** ~ sie ist so weit ganz nett; **he sings well** ~ er singt ganz ordentlich; **funnily** ~ komischerweise; **and sure** ~, **he didn't come** und er kam auch prompt nicht.

enquire [ɪn'kwaɪə'] **1** *vt* **he ~d what/whether/when** *etc* ... er erkundigte sich, was/ob/wann *etc* ... **2** *vi* sich erkundigen (*about* nach).

♦ **enquire into** *vi* +*prep obj* untersuchen.

enquiring [ɪn'kwaɪərɪŋ] *adj* fragend. **he has an** ~ **mind** er ist eine Forschernatur.

enquiry [ɪn'kwaɪərɪ, (*US*) 'ɪnkwɪrɪ] *n* **(a)** (*question*) Anfrage *f* (*about* über +*acc*); (*for tourist information, direction etc*) Erkundigung *f* (*about* über +*acc*, nach). **to make enquiries** Erkundigungen einziehen; (*police etc*) Nachforschungen anstellen (*about sb* über jdn, *about sth* nach etw). **(b)** (*investigation*) Untersuchung *f*.

enrage [ɪn'reɪdʒ] *vt* wütend machen.

enrich [ɪn'rɪtʃ] *vt* bereichern; *soil, food* anreichern.

enrichment [ɪn'rɪtʃmənt] *n* Bereicherung *f*; (*of soil*) Anreicherung *f*.

enrol, (*US*) **enroll** [ɪn'rəʊl] **1** *vt* einschreiben; *members also* aufnehmen; (*Univ*) immatrikulieren. **2** *vi* sich einschreiben; (*in the army*) sich melden (*in* zu); (*for course also, at school*) sich anmelden; (*Univ also*) sich immatrikulieren.

enrolment [ɪn'rəʊlmənt] *n see* **enrol** Einschreibung *f*; Aufnahme *f*; Immatrikulation *f*.

en route [ɒŋ'ruːt] *adv* unterwegs. ~ **to Paris** auf dem Weg nach Paris.

ensconce [ɪn'skɒns] *vr* sich häuslich niederlassen (*in in* +*dat*).

ensemble [ɑːn'sɑːmbl] *n* Ensemble *nt*.

ensign ['ensaɪn] *n* **(a)** (*flag*) Nationalflagge *f*. **(b)**

(*US Naut*) Fähnrich *m* zur See.

enslave [ɪn'sleɪv] *vt* zum Sklaven machen.

ensnare [ɪn'sneə'] *vt* (*lit*) fangen; (*fig*) (*woman*) umgarnen; (*charms*) berücken, bestricken.

ensue [ɪn'sjuː] *vi* folgen (*from* aus).

ensuing [ɪn'sjuːɪŋ] *adj* folgend.

ensure [ɪn'ʃʊə'] *vt* sicherstellen; (*secure*) sichern.

entail [ɪn'teɪl] *vt expense, suffering* mit sich bringen; *risk, difficulty also* verbunden sein mit.

entangle [ɪn'tæŋgl] *vt* **to become ~d in sth** sich in etw (*dat*) verfangen; (*fig*) sich in etw (*acc*) verstricken.

entanglement [ɪn'tæŋglmənt] *n* **(a)** (*barbed wire*) Verhau *m*. **(b)** (*fig: in affair etc*) Verwicklung *f*.

enter ['entə'] **1** *vt* **(a)** (*towards speaker*) hereinkommen in (+*acc*); (*away from speaker*) hineingehen in (+*acc*); (*walk into*) *building etc* also betreten; (*drive into*) *car park, motorway* einfahren in (+*acc*); (*turn into*) *road etc* einbiegen in (+*acc*); (*river etc*) münden in (+*acc*); (*penetrate: bullet etc*) eindringen in (+*acc*); (*climb into*) *bus* einsteigen in (+*acc*); (*cross border of*) *country* einreisen in (+*acc*). **the thought never ~ed my mind** so etwas wäre mir nie eingefallen. **(b) to ~ the Army/Navy** zum Heer/zur Marine gehen; **to** ~ **the Church** Geistlicher werden; **to** ~ **a university** auf die Universität gehen. **(c)** (*write down, record*) eintragen (*in in* +*acc*). **(d)** (*enrol*) *pupil* anmelden; *horse* melden. **(e)** *race, contest* sich beteiligen an (+*dat*). **(f)** (*submit*) *appeal, plea* einlegen.

2 *vi* **(a)** (*towards speaker*) hereinkommen; (*away from speaker*) hineingehen; (*walk in*) eintreten. **(b)** (*Theat*) auftreten. **(c)** (*for race, exam etc*) sich melden (*for* zu).

♦ **enter into** *vi* +*prep obj* **(a)** *negotiations* aufnehmen; *contract, alliance* schließen, eingehen; *conversation* anknüpfen. **(b)** (*figure in*) eine Rolle spielen bei. **that doesn't** ~ ~ **it** das spielt dabei keine Rolle.

♦ **enter (up)on** *vi* +*prep obj* (*begin*) antreten; *new era* eintreten in (+*acc*).

enterprise ['entəpraɪz] *n* Unternehmen *nt*; (*initiative*) Initiative *f*; (*adventurousness*) Unternehmungsgeist *m*. **free/private** ~ freies/privates Unternehmertum.

enterprising ['entəpraɪzɪŋ] *adj* unternehmungslustig; *idea, venture* kühn.

entertain [,entə'teɪn] **1** *vt* **(a)** (*offer hospitality to*) einladen; (*to meal*) bewirten. **to** ~ **sb to dinner** jdn zum Essen einladen. **(b)** (*amuse*) unterhalten. **(c)** *thought* sich tragen mit; *suspicion, doubt* hegen; *hope* nähren; *proposal, offer, idea* in Erwägung ziehen. **2** *vi* (*have visitors*) Gäste haben.

entertainer [,entə'teɪnə'] *n* Entertainer(in *f*) *m*.

entertaining [,entə'teɪnɪŋ] *adj* unterhaltsam. **2** *n* **she does a lot of** ~ sie hat sehr oft Gäste.

entertainment [,entə'teɪnmənt] *n* **(a)** Unterhaltung *f*. **for my own** ~ nur so zum Vergnügen. **(b)** (*performance*) Darbietung *f*. **(c)** (*of guests*) Bewirtung *f*. ~ **allowance** Aufwandspauschale *f*.

enthral(l) [ɪn'θrɔːl] *vt* begeistern; (*exiting story etc also*) fesseln.

enthralling [ɪn'θrɔːlɪŋ] *adj* spannend.

enthuse [ɪn'θjuːz] *vi* schwärmen (*over* von).

enthusiasm [ɪn'θjuːzɪæzəm] *n* Begeisterung *f*, Enthusiasmus *m* (*for* für).

enthusiast [ɪn'θjuːzɪæst] *n* Enthusiast *m*. **sports/ jazz** ~ begeisterter Sport-/Jazzfan *m*.

enthusiastic [ɪn,θjuːzɪ'æstɪk] *adj* begeistert, enthusiastisch. **to be/get** ~ **about sth** von etw begeistert sein/sich für etw begeistern.

entice [ɪn'taɪs] *vt* locken; (*lead astray*) verführen, verleiten. **to** ~ **sb into doing sth** jdn dazu verleiten, etw zu tun; **to** ~ **sb away** jdn weglocken.

enticement [ɪn'taɪsmənt] n (lure) Verlockung f.

enticing [ɪn'taɪsɪŋ] adj verlockend.

entire [ɪn'taɪə^r] adj ganz; set, waste of time vollständig.

entirely [ɪn'taɪəlɪ] adv ganz. **I'm not ~ surprised** das kommt für mich nicht ganz überraschend.

entirety [ɪn'taɪərətɪ] n in its ~ in seiner Gesamtheit.

entitle [ɪn'taɪtl] vt (a) it is ~d ... es hat den Titel ... (b) (give the right) to ~ sb to sth/to do sth jdn zu etw berechtigen/jdn dazu berechtigen, etw zu tun; (to compensation, legal aid) jdm den Anspruch auf etw (acc) geben; **to be ~d to sth/to do sth** das Recht auf etw (acc) haben/das Recht haben, etw zu tun; (to compensation, legal aid, holiday) Anspruch m auf etw (acc) haben.

entitlement [ɪntaɪtlmənt] n Berechtigung f (to zu); (to compensation, holiday etc) Anspruch m (to auf +acc).

entity ['entɪtɪ] n Wesen nt.

entomology [ˌentə'mɒlədʒɪ] n Insektenkunde f.

entourage [ˌɒntʊ'rɑːʒ] n Gefolge nt.

entrails ['entreɪlz] npl Eingeweide pl.

entrance¹ [ɪn'trɑːns] vt in Entzücken versetzen.

entrance² ['entrəns] n (a) (way in) Eingang m; (for vehicles) Einfahrt f; (hall) Eingangshalle f. (b) (entering) Eintritt m; (Theat) Auftritt m. **to make one's ~** (Theat) auftreten; (fig also) erscheinen. (c) (admission) Eintritt m (to in +acc); (to club etc) Zutritt m (to zu).

entrance: ~ **fee** n Eintrittsgeld nt; (for club) Aufnahmegebühr f; ~ **visa** n Einreisevisum nt.

entrancing [ɪn'trɑːnsɪŋ] adj bezaubernd.

entrant ['entrənt] n (in contest) Teilnehmer(in f) m; (in exam) Prüfling m.

entreat [ɪn'triːt] vt anflehen (for um).

entreaty [ɪn'triːtɪ] n dringende Bitte.

entrenched [ɪn'trentʃt] adj idea, belief etc (fest) verwurzelt; position festgefahren.

entrepreneur [ˌɒntrəprə'nɜː^r] n Unternehmer m.

entrepreneurial [ˌɒntrəprə'nɜːrɪəl] adj unternehmerisch.

entrust [ɪn'trʌst] vt anvertrauen (to sb jdm). **to ~ sb with a task** jdn mit einer Aufgabe betrauen.

entry ['entrɪ] n (a) (into in +acc) Eintritt m; (by car etc) Einfahrt f; (into country) Einreise f; (Theat) Auftritt m. **"no ~"** (on door etc) „Zutritt verboten"; (on one-way street) „keine Einfahrt". (b) (way in, doorway) Eingang m; (for vehicles) Einfahrt f. (c) (in diary, account book etc) Eintrag m. (d) (for race etc) Meldung f.

entry: ~ **form** n Anmeldeformular nt; ~ **permit** n Passierschein m; (into country) Einreiseerlaubnis f.

entwine [ɪn'twaɪn] vt ineinanderschlingen.

enumerate [ɪ'njuːməreɪt] vt aufzählen.

enunciate [ɪ'nʌnsɪeɪt] vti artikulieren.

enunciation [ɪˌnʌnsɪ'eɪʃən] n Artikulation f.

envelop [ɪn'veləp] vt einhüllen.

envelope ['envələʊp] n Umschlag m.

enviable ['envɪəbl] adj beneidenswert.

envious ['envɪəs] adj neidisch (of auf +acc).

environment [ɪn'vaɪərənmənt] n Umwelt f; (of town etc, physical surroundings) Umgebung f; (social, cultural also) Milieu nt. **Department of the E~** (Brit) ≃ Umweltministerium nt.

environmental [ɪnˌvaɪərən'mentl] adj Umwelt-.

environmentalist [ɪnˌvaɪərən'mentəlɪst] n Umweltschützer(in f) m.

envisage [ɪn'vɪzɪdʒ] vt sich (dat) vorstellen; (expect) erwarten.

envoy ['envɔɪ] n Bote m; (diplomat) Gesandte(r) mf.

envy ['envɪ] **1** n Neid m. **his house was the ~ of his friends** sein Haus war der Neid seiner Freunde beneideten ihn um sein Haus. **2** vt person beneiden. **to ~ sb sth** jdn um etw beneiden.

enzyme ['enzaɪm] n Enzym, Ferment nt.

ephemeral [ɪ'femərəl] adj flüchtig.

epic ['epɪk] **1** adj poetry episch; film, novel Monumental-; performance, match gewaltig; journey lang und abenteuerlich. **2** n (poem, film) Epos nt; (match) gewaltiges Spiel.

epicentre, (US) **epicenter** ['epɪsentə^r] n Epizentrum nt.

epidemic [epɪ'demɪk] **1** n Epidemie (also fig), Seuche f. **2** adj epidemisch.

epigram ['epɪgræm] n Epigramm, Sinngedicht nt.

epilepsy ['epɪlepsɪ] n Epilepsie f.

epileptic [epɪ'leptɪk] **1** adj ~ fit epileptischer Anfall. **2** n Epileptiker(in f) m.

epilogue ['epɪlɒg] n Epilog m, Nachwort nt.

Epiphany [ɪ'pɪfənɪ] n das Dreikönigsfest.

episcopal [ɪ'pɪskəpəl] adj bischöflich, Bischofs-.

episode ['epɪsəʊd] n Episode f; (of story, TV, Rad) Fortsetzung f; (incident also) Begebenheit f.

epistle [ɪ'pɪsl] n (Bibl) Brief m (to an +acc).

epitaph ['epɪtɑːf] n Epitaph nt; (on grave) Grabinschrift f.

epithet ['epɪθet] n Beiname m.

epitome [ɪ'pɪtəmɪ] n Inbegriff m (of gen, an +dat).

epitomize [ɪ'pɪtəmaɪz] vt verkörpern.

epoch ['iːpɒk] n Zeitalter nt (also Geol), Epoche f.

epoch-making ['iːpɒk'meɪkɪŋ] adj epochemachend, epochal.

equable ['ekwəbl] adj gleichmäßig, ausgeglichen.

equal ['iːkwəl] **1** adj (a) gleich (to +dat). **they are about ~ in value** sie haben ungefähr den gleichen Wert; **to be on ~ terms** auf der gleichen Stufe stehen (with mit); ~ **opportunities** Chancengleichheit f; (all) **other things being ~** unter sonst gleichen Umständen; **now we're ~** jetzt sind wir quitt. (b) **to be ~ to the situation/ task** der Situation/Aufgabe gewachsen sein; **to feel ~ to sth** sich zu etw imstande or in der Lage fühlen.

2 n (in rank) Gleichgestellte(r) mf. **she is his ~** sie ist ihm ebenbürtig; **he has no ~** er hat nicht seinesgleichen; **our ~s** unseresgleichen; **to treat sb as an ~** jdn als ebenbürtig behandeln.

3 vt (be same as, Math) gleichen; (match, measure up to) gleichkommen (+dat); record erreichen. **three times three ~s nine** drei mal drei (ist) gleich neun; **not to be ~led** unvergleichlich.

equality [ɪ'kwɒlɪtɪ] n Gleichheit f.

equalize ['iːkwəlaɪz] vti ausgleichen.

equalizer ['iːkwəlaɪzə^r] n (Sport) Ausgleich m; (Ftbl etc also) Ausgleichstreffer m.

equally ['iːkwəlɪ] adv divide, distribute gleichmäßig. ~ **gifted** gleich begabt pred, gleichbegabt attr. (b) (just as) genauso. (c) **but then,** ~, **one must concede** ... aber dann muß man ebenso zugestehen, daß ...

equanimity [ˌekwə'nɪmɪtɪ] n Gleichmut m.

equate [ɪ'kweɪt] vt (identify) gleichsetzen; (treat as the same) auf die gleiche Stufe stellen.

equation [ɪ'kweɪʒən] n (Math, fig) Gleichung f.

equator [ɪ'kweɪtə^r] n Äquator m.

equestrian [ɪ'kwestrɪən] adj Reit-.

equidistant [ˌiːkwɪ'dɪstənt] adj gleich weit entfernt.

equilibrium [ˌiːkwɪ'lɪbrɪəm] n Gleichgewicht n.

equine ['ekwaɪn] adj Pferde-.

equinox ['iːkwɪnɒks] n Tagundnachtgleiche f.

equip [ɪ'kwɪp] vt ausrüsten; kitchen ausstatten; laboratory einrichten. **he's well ~ped for the job** (fig) er hat das nötige Rüstzeug für die Stelle.

equipment [ɪ'kwɪpmənt] n no pl Ausrüstung f. **office ~** Büroeinrichtung f; **electrical/kitchen ~** Elektro-/Küchengerät pl.

equitable ['ekwɪtəbl] adj fair, gerecht.

equity ['ekwɪtɪ] n (a) Fairneß f. (b) (Brit Fin) **equities** pl Stammaktien pl.

equivalence [ɪ'kwɪvələns] n Entsprechung f.

equivalent [ɪ'kwɪvələnt] **1** adj (a) (equal) gleichwertig. **that's ~ to saying ...** das ist gleichbedeutend damit, zu sagen ... **(b)** *(corresponding)* entsprechend, äquivalent. **it is ~ to £30** das entspricht £ 30; **that's ~ to** lying das ist soviel wie gelogen. **2** *n* Äquivalent *nt*; *(counterpart)* Pendant *nt.* **what is the ~ in German marks?** was ist der Gegenwert in DM?; **the German ~ of the English word** die deutsche Entsprechung des englischen Wortes.

equivocal [ɪ'kwɪvəkəl] *adj* zweideutig; *outcome* nicht eindeutig.

equivocate [ɪ'kwɪvəkeɪt] *vi* ausweichen.

equivocation [ɪˌkwɪvə'keɪʃən] *n* Ausflüchte *pl.*

era ['ɪərə] *n* Ära *f*; *(Geol)* Erdzeitalter *nt.*

eradicate [ɪ'rædɪkeɪt] *vt* ausrotten.

erase [ɪ'reɪz] *vt* ausradieren; *(from tape, computer)* löschen; *(from the mind)* streichen *(from* aus).

eraser [ɪ'reɪzə^r] *n* Radiergummi *nt or m.*

erect [ɪ'rekt] **1** *adj* aufrecht, gerade. **2** *vt* errichten *(to sb* jdm); *flats, factory* bauen; *collapsible furniture, scaffolding* aufstellen; *tent* aufschlagen; *mast* aufrichten.

erection [ɪ'rekʃən] *n* **(a)** *see vt* Errichten *nt*; Bauen *nt*; Aufstellen *nt*; Aufschlagen *nt*; Aufrichten *nt.* **(b)** *(building, structure)* Gebäude *nt*, Bau *m.* **(c)** *(Physiol)* Erektion *f.*

ergonomics [ˌɜːgəʊ'nɒmɪks] *n sing* Ergonomie *f.*

ermine ['ɜːmɪn] *n* Hermelin *nt*; *(fur)* Hermelin *m.*

erode [ɪ'rəʊd] *vt (sea)* auswaschen; *(rust)* zerfressen; *(fig) confidence* untergraben.

erogenous [ɪ'rɒdʒənəs] *adj* erogen.

erosion [ɪ'rəʊʒən] *n (by water)* Erosion *f*; *(fig: of love etc)* Schwinden *nt.*

erotic [ɪ'rɒtɪk] *adj* aufreizend; *book, film* erotisch.

eroticism [ɪ'rɒtɪsɪzəm] *n* Erotik *f.*

err [ɜː^r] *vi* **(a)** sich irren. **it is better to ~ on the side of caution** man sollte im Zweifelsfall lieber zu vorsichtig sein. **(b)** *(sin)* sündigen.

errand ['erənd] *n (shopping etc)* Besorgung *f*; *(to give a message etc)* Botengang *m.* **to run ~s (for sb)** (für jdn) Besorgungen/Botengänge machen; **~ of mercy** Rettungsaktion *f*; **~ boy** Laufjunge *m.*

erratic [ɪ'rætɪk] *adj* unberechenbar; *results* stark schwankend; *work* ungleichmäßig.

erroneous [ɪ'rəʊnɪəs] *adj* falsch; *belief* irrig.

error ['erə^r] *n* Fehler *m.* **to be in ~** sich im Irrtum befinden; **in ~** aus Versehen, irrtümlicherweise; **to see the ~ of one's ways** seine Fehler einsehen.

erstwhile ['ɜːstwaɪl] *adj (old, liter)* ehemalig.

erudite ['erʊdaɪt] *adj* gelehrt; *person also* gebildet.

erudition [ˌerʊ'dɪʃən] *n* Gelehrsamkeit *f.*

erupt [ɪ'rʌpt] *vi (volcano, war)* ausbrechen; *skin* aufbrechen; *(fig: person)* explodieren.

eruption [ɪ'rʌpʃən] *n (of volcano, anger, violence)* Ausbruch *m*; *(rash etc)* Hautausschlag *m.*

escalate ['eskəleɪt] **1** *vt war* ausweiten; *costs* sprunghaft erhöhen. **2** *vi* sich ausweiten, eskalieren; *(costs)* sprunghaft ansteigen.

escalation [ˌeskə'leɪʃən] *n* Eskalation *f.*

escalator ['eskəleɪtə^r] *n* Rolltreppe *f.*

escapade [ˌeskə'peɪd] *n* Eskapade *f.*

escape [ɪ'skeɪp] **1** *vi* **(a)** *(from pursuers)* entkommen *(from* dat); *(from prison, cage)* ausbrechen *(from* aus); *(water)* auslaufen *(from* aus); *(gas)* ausströmen *(from* aus). **he was shot while trying to ~** er wurde bei einem Fluchtversuch erschossen; **an ~d prisoner/tiger** ein entsprungener Häftling/Tiger; **he ~d from the fire** er ist dem Feuer entkommen; **a room which I can ~ to** ein Zimmer, in das ich mich zurückziehen kann. **(b)** *(get off, be spared)* **to ~ with a warning/a few cuts** mit einer Verwarnung/ein paar Schnittwunden davonkommen; **the others were killed, but he ~d** die anderen kamen um, aber er kam mit dem Leben davon.

2 *vt* **(a)** *pursuers* entkommen *(+dat).* **(b)** *(avoid) consequences, punishment, disaster*

entgehen *(+dat).* **he narrowly ~d being run over** er wäre um ein Haar überfahren worden; **but you can't ~ the fact that ...** aber du kannst nicht abstreiten, daß ... **(c)** *his name* ~**s me** sein Name ist mir entfallen; **nothing ~s him** ihm entgeht nichts; **to ~ sb's notice** jdm entgehen.

3 *n* **(a)** *(from prison etc)* Flucht *f.* **to make an ~** ausbrechen; **there's been an ~** jemand ist ausgebrochen; **to have a miraculous ~** *(from accident, illness)* auf wunderbare Weise davonkommen; **fishing is his ~** Angeln ist seine Zuflucht; **there's no ~** *(fig)* es gibt keinen Ausweg. **(b)** *(of water)* Ausfließen *nt*; *(of gas)* Ausströmen *nt*; *(of steam, gas, in a machine)* Entweichen *nt.*

ecape: **~ bid** *n* Fluchtversuch *m*; **~ clause** *n (Jur)* Befreiungsklausel *f*; **~ hatch** *n (Naut)* Notluke *f*; **~ route** *n* Fluchtweg *m*; **~ velocity** *n (Space)* Fluchtgeschwindigkeit *f.*

escapism [ɪ'skeɪpɪzəm] *n* Wirklichkeitsflucht *f.*

escapist [ɪ'skeɪpɪst] *adj* **~ literature** eine Phantasiewelt vorgaukelnde Literatur.

escapologist [ˌeskə'pɒlədʒɪst] *n* Entfesselungskünstler(in *f*) *m.*

escarpment [ɪ'skɑːpmənt] *n* Steilhang *m*; *(as fortification)* Böschung *f.*

escort ['eskɔːt] **1** *n* **(a)** Geleitschutz *m*; *(vehicles, ships etc)* Eskorte *f.* **under ~** unter Bewachung. **(b)** *(male companion)* Begleiter *m*; *(hired female)* Hostess *f.* **2** [ɪ'skɔːt] *vt* begleiten; *(Mil, Naut)* Geleit(schutz) geben *(+dat).*

escort: **~ agency** *n* Hostessenagentur *f*; **~ duty** *n* Geleitdienst *m*; **to be on ~ duty** Geleitschutz geben müssen; **~ vessel** *n (Naut)* Geleitschiff *nt.*

Eskimo ['eskɪməʊ] **1** *adj* Eskimo-. **2** *n* **(a)** Eskimo *m*, Eskimofrau *f.* **(b)** *(language)* Eskimosprache *f.*

esophagus *n (esp US)* = **oesophagus.**

esoteric [ˌesəʊ'terɪk] *adj* esoterisch.

ESP = **extra-sensory perception** außersinnliche Wahrnehmung.

especial [ɪ'speʃəl] *adj* besondere(r, s).

especially [ɪ'speʃəlɪ] *adv* besonders. **you ~ ought to know** gerade du solltest das wissen; **I came ~ to see you** ich bin eigens gekommen, um dich zu besuchen.

espionage [ˌespɪə'nɑːʒ] *n* Spionage *f.*

esplanade [ˌesplə'neɪd] *n* (Strand)promenade *f.*

espouse [ɪ'spaʊz] *vt cause* Partei ergreifen für.

espresso [e'spresəʊ] *n* Espresso *m.*

esquire [ɪ'skwaɪə^r] *n (Brit: on envelope, abbr* **Esq**) James Jones, Esq Herrn James Jones.

essay[1] [e'seɪ] *n (form: attempt)* Versuch *m.*

essay[2] [e'seɪ] *n* Essay *m or nt*; *(esp Sch)* Aufsatz *m.*

essence ['esəns] *n* **(a)** Wesen *nt.* **in ~** im wesentlichen; **speed is of the ~** Geschwindigkeit ist äußerst wichtig. **(b)** *(Chem, Cook)* Essenz *f.* **~ meat** ~ Fleischextrakt *m.*

essential [ɪ'senʃəl] **1** *adj* **(a)** *(necessary, vital)* (unbedingt) erforderlich. **it is ~ that you understand this** du mußt das unbedingt verstehen; **the ~ thing is to ...** wichtig ist vor allem, zu ... **(b)** *(of the essence, basic)* wesentlich; *question* entscheidend. **2** *n* **the ~s** das Wesentliche; *(most important points)* die wichtigen Punkte, die Essentials *pl.* **with only the bare ~s** nur mit dem Allernotwendigsten ausgestattet.

essentially [ɪ'senʃəlɪ] *adv (basically)* im Grunde genommen; *(in essence)* im wesentlichen.

establish [ɪ'stæblɪʃ] **1** *vt* **(a)** *(found, set up)* gründen; *government* bilden; *custom, new procedure* einführen; *relations* aufnehmen; *post* einrichten; *power, authority, reputation* sich *(dat)* verschaffen; *peace* stiften; *order* (wieder)herstellen; *precedent* setzen; *committee* einsetzen. **(b)** *(prove) fact, innocence* beweisen; *claim* unter Beweis stellen. **(c)** *(determine) identity, facts* ermitteln. **(d)** *(gain acceptance for) product, ideas* Anerkennung finden für. **2** *vr (in business)* **to**

~ oneself sich niederlassen.
established [ɪ'stæblɪʃt] *adj* **(a)** *reputation* gefestigt. **well-~** *business* gut eingeführte Firma.
(b) *(accepted) fact* feststehend; *procedure, author* anerkannt; *belief* herrschend; *laws, order* bestehend.
establishment [ɪ'stæblɪʃmənt] *n* **(a)** *see vt (a)* Gründung *f*; Bildung *f*; Einführung *f*; Aufnahme *f*; Einrichtung *f*; *(of power, authority)* Festigung *f*; Stiftung *f*; (Wieder)herstellung *f*; Setzen *nt*; Einsetzen *nt*. **(b)** *(proving)* Beweis *m*. **(c)** *(determining)* Ermittlung *f*. **(d)** *(institution etc)* Institution *f*; *(hospital, school etc also)* Anstalt *f*. **commercial ~** kommerzielles Unternehmen. **(e)** *(Mil, Naut etc: personnel)* Truppenstärke *f*. **(f)** *(Brit)* **the E~** das Establishment.
estate [ɪ'steɪt] *n* **(a)** *(land)* Gut *nt*. **(b)** *(Jur)* Besitz(tümer *pl*) *m*, Eigentum *nt*; *(of deceased)* Nachlaß *m*, Erbmasse *f*. **(c)** *(esp Brit) (housing ~)* Siedlung *f*; *(trading ~)* Industriegelände *nt*.
estate: ~ **agent** *n (Brit)* Immobilienmakler(in *f*) *m*; ~ **car** *n (Brit)* Kombi(wagen) *m*.
esteem [ɪ'stiːm] **1** *vt (form: consider)* betrachten. **2** *n* Wertschätzung *f*. **to hold sb/sth in (high)** ~ von jdm/etw eine hohe Meinung haben.
esthete *etc (US)* = **aesthete** *etc*.
estimate ['estɪmɪt] **1** *n* **(a)** Schätzung *f*. **it's just an** ~ das ist nur geschätzt; **at a rough** ~ grob geschätzt. **(b)** *(Comm: of cost)* (Kosten)voranschlag *m*. **2** ['estɪmeɪt] *vt* schätzen. **his wealth is** ~**d at** ... sein Vermögen wird auf ... geschätzt.
estimation [ˌestɪ'meɪʃən] *n* **(a)** **in my** ~ meiner Einschätzung nach. **(b)** *(esteem)* Achtung *f*. **he went up/down in my** ~ er ist in meiner Achtung gestiegen/gesunken.
estrange [ɪ'streɪndʒ] *vt person* entfremden *(from +dat)*. **to be/become** ~**d from sb** sich jdm entfremdet haben/entfremden.
estrangement [ɪ'streɪndʒmənt] *n* Entfremdung *f (from* von).
estrogen ['iːstrəudʒən] *n (US)* Östrogen *nt*.
estuary ['estjuərɪ] *n* Mündung *f*.
ETA = estimated time of arrival geschätzte Ankunft.
etch [etʃ] *vti* ätzen; *(in copper)* stechen; *(in other metals)* radieren.
etching ['etʃɪŋ] *n see vb* **(a)** Ätzen *nt*; Stechen *nt*; Radieren *nt*. **(b)** *(picture)* Ätzung *f*; Stich *m*; Radierung *f*.
eternal [ɪ'tɜːnl] *adj (lit, fig)* ewig. **the** ~ **triangle** *(fig)* das Dreiecksverhältnis.
eternity [ɪ'tɜːnɪtɪ] *n (lit, fig)* Ewigkeit *f*. **from here to** ~ bis in alle Ewigkeit.
ether ['iːθəʳ] *n (Chem, poet)* Äther *m*.
ethic ['eθɪk] *n* Ethik *f*, Ethos *nt*.
ethical ['eθɪkəl] *adj* ethisch *attr*. **it is not** ~ **to** ... es ist unmoralisch, zu ...
ethics ['eθɪks] *n* **(a)** *sing* Ethik *f*. **(b)** *pl (morality)* Moral *f*. **the** ~ **of abortion** die moralischen Aspekte der Abtreibung.
Ethiopia [ˌiːθɪ'əupɪə] *n* Äthiopien *nt*.
Ethiopian [ˌiːθɪ'əupɪən] **1** *adj* äthiopisch. **2** *n* Äthiopier(in *f*) *m*.
ethnic ['eθnɪk] *adj* ethnisch, Volks-; *atmosphere, pub* urtümlich, urwüchsig. ~ **groups/minority** ethnische Gruppen *pl*/Minderheit *f*.
ethos ['iːθɒs] *n* Gesinnung *f*, Ethos *nt*.
etiquette ['etɪket] *n* Etikette *f*.
etymology [ˌetɪ'mɒlədʒɪ] *n* Etymologie *f*.
eucalyptus [ˌjuːkə'lɪptəs] *n* Eukalyptus *m*.
eulogy ['juːlədʒɪ] *n* Lobensrede *f*.
eunuch ['juːnək] *n* Eunuch *m*.
euphemism ['juːfəmɪzəm] *n* beschönigender Ausdruck, Euphemismus *m*.
euphemistic [ˌjuːfə'mɪstɪk] *adj* euphemistisch.
euphoria [juː'fɔːrɪə] *n* Euphorie *f*.
euphoric [juː'fɒrɪk] *adj* euphorisch.
eureka [juə'riːkə] *interj* heureka, ich hab's!

Eurocrat ['juərəukræt] *n* Eurokrat(in *f*) *m*.
Eurodollar ['juərəudɒləʳ] *n* Eurodollar *m*.
Europe ['juərəp] *n* Europa *nt*.
European [ˌjuərə'piːən] **1** *adj* europäisch. ~ **Economic Community** Europäische Wirtschaftsgemeinschaft. **2** *n* Europäer(in *f*) *m*.
euthanasia [ˌjuːθə'neɪzɪə] *n* Euthanasie *f*.
evacuate [ɪ'vækjueɪt] *vt* räumen; *people* evakuieren.
evacuation [ɪ,vækju'eɪʃən] *n see vt* Räumung *f*; Evakuierung *f*.
evacuee [ɪ,vækju'iː] *n* Evakuierte(r) *mf*.
evade [ɪ'veɪd] *vt blow, question, sb's eyes* ausweichen *(+dat); pursuit, pursuers, justice* sich entziehen *(+dat)*.
evaluate [ɪ'væljueɪt] *vt house, worth etc* schätzen *(at* auf *+acc); chances, usefulness* einschätzen; *evidence, results* auswerten; *pros and cons* (gegeneinander) abwägen; *achievement* bewerten.
evaluation [ɪ,vælju'eɪʃən] *n see vt* Schätzung *f*; Einschätzung *f*; Auswertung *f*; Abwägung *f*; Bewertung *f*.
evangelic(al) [ˌiːvæn'dʒelɪk(əl)] *adj* evangelisch.
evangelist [ɪ'vændʒəlɪst] *n (Bibl)* Evangelist(in *f*) *m*; *(preacher)* Prediger(in *f*) *m*.
evaporate [ɪ'væpəreɪt] **1** *vi (a) (liquid)* verdunsten. **(b)** *(fig: disappear)* sich in Luft auflösen. **2** *vt* ~**d milk** Kondensmilch *f*.
evaporation [ɪ,væpə'reɪʃən] *n* Verdampfen *nt*; *(fig)* Schwinden *nt*.
evasion [ɪ'veɪʒən] *n* Ausweichen *nt (of* vor *+dat)*.
evasive [ɪ'veɪzɪv] *adj answer* ausweichend; *meaning, truth* schwer zu fassen. **he was very** ~ **about it** er wollte (dazu) nicht mit der Sprache herausrücken; **to take** ~ **action** *(Mil, fig)* ein Ausweichmanöver machen.
eve [iːv] *n* Vorabend *m*. **on the** ~ **of** am Tage vor *(+dat)*; **am Vorabend** *(+gen)*.
even ['iːvən] **1** *adj* **(a)** *surface, ground* eben. **to be** ~ **with sth** mit etw abschließen. **(b)** *(regular) layer etc* gleichmäßig; *progress* stetig; *temper* ausgeglichen. **(c)** *quantities, distances, values* gleich. **the score is** ~ es steht unentschieden; **I will get** ~ **with you for that** das werde ich dir heimzahlen; **that makes us** ~ *(in game)* damit steht es unentschieden; *(fig)* damit sind wir quitt. **(d)** *number* gerade.
2 *adv* ~ **sogar, selbst. they** ~ **denied its existence** sie leugneten sogar seine Existenz; ~ **better/more beautiful** sogar (noch) besser/schöner. **(b) not** ~ nicht einmal; **with** **not** ~ **a smile** ohne auch nur zu lächeln. **(c)** ~ **if/though** selbst wenn; ~ **as I spoke** ... noch während ich redete ...; ~ **so** (aber) trotzdem.
♦ **even out** **1** *vi (a) (prices)* sich einpendeln. **(b)** *(ground)* eben werden. **2** *vt sep (a) prices* ausgleichen. **that should** ~ **things** ~ **a bit** dadurch müßte ein gewisser Ausgleich erzielt werden. **(b)** *ground, cement* ebnen.
evening ['iːvnɪŋ] *n* Abend *m*. **in the** ~ abends, am Abend; **this/tomorrow** ~ heute/morgen abend; **one** ~ eines Abends; **every Monday** ~ jeden Montagabend.
evening *in cpds* Abend-; ~ **class** *n* Abendkurs *m*; ~ **dress** *n (men's)* Abendanzug *m*; *(women's)* Abendkleid *nt*.
evenly ['iːvənlɪ] *adv* gleichmäßig. **they were** ~ **matched** sie waren einander ebenbürtig.
evensong ['iːvənsɒŋ] *n* Abendgottesdienst *m*.
event [ɪ'vent] *n* **(a)** *(happening)* Ereignis *nt*. **in the normal course of** ~**s** normalerweise. **(b)** *(function)* Veranstaltung *f*. **what is your best** ~? *(Sport)* in welcher Disziplin sind Sie am besten? **(c) in the** ~ **of war/fire** im Falle eines Krieges/Brandes; **in any** ~ ohnehin, sowieso; **in the** ~ im Endeffekt; **at all** ~**s** auf jeden Fall.
even-tempered ['iːvən'tempəd] *adj* ausgeglichen.
eventful [ɪ'ventful] *adj* ereignisreich.

eventual [ɪ'ventʃʊəl] *adj* the decline and ~ collapse of ... der Niedergang und schließliche vollkommene Zerfall des ...; his ~ arrival ... als er schließlich kam, ...
eventuality [ɪˌventʃʊ'ælɪtɪ] *n* möglicher Fall. be ready for any ~ sei auf alle Eventualitäten gefaßt.
eventually [ɪ'ventʃʊəlɪ] *adv* schließlich, endlich.
ever ['evə^r] *adv* (a) je(mals). not ~ nie; nothing ~ happens es passiert nie etwas; it hardly ~ snows here hier schneit es kaum (jemals); if I ~ catch you doing that again wenn ich dich noch einmal dabei erwische; seldom, if ~ selten, wenn überhaupt; he's a rascal if ~ there was one er ist ein richtiggehender kleiner Halunke; as if I ~ would als ob ich das jemals täte; don't you ~ say that again! sag das ja nie mehr!; have you ~ been to Glasgow? bist du schon einmal in Glasgow gewesen?; more beautiful than ~ schöner denn je; the first ~ der *etc* allererste; the coldest night ~ die kälteste Nacht aller Zeiten.
(b) ~ since then seit der Zeit, seitdem; for ~ für immer; it seemed to go on for ~ (and ~) es schien ewig zu dauern; ~ increasing powers ständig wachsende Macht.
(c) *(intensive)* no government be it ~ so powerful keine noch so mächtige Regierung; the best grandmother ~ die beste Großmutter, die es gibt; did you ~! *(col)* also so was!; why ~ not? warum denn bloß nicht?
(d) *(col)* ~ so/such unheimlich; ~ so slightly drunk ein ganz klein wenig betrunken; I am ~ so sorry es tut mir schrecklich leid; thank you ~ so much ganz herzlichen Dank.
evergreen ['evəgriːn] 1 *adj* immergrün; *(fig)* topic immer aktuell. 2 *n* Nadelbaum *m*.
everlasting [ˌevə'lɑːstɪŋ] *adj (lit, fig)* ewig.
every ['evrɪ] *adj* jede(r, s). he is ~ bit as clever as his brother er ist ganz genauso schlau wie sein Bruder; I have ~ reason to believe that ... ich habe allen Grund anzunehmen, daß ...; I have ~ confidence in him ich habe uneingeschränktes Vertrauen in ihn; we wish you ~ success/happiness wir wünschen Ihnen alles Gute/viel Glück; his ~ word jedes Wort, das er sagte; ~ fifth day, ~ five days jeden fünften Tag, alle fünf Tage; ~ other day jeden zweiten Tag, alle zwei Tage; ~ so often, ~ now and then or again hin und wieder, ab und zu.
everybody ['evrɪbɒdɪ], **everyone** *pron* jeder(mann), alle *pl*. ~ knows ~ else here hier kennt jeder jeden.
everyday ['evrɪdeɪ] *adj* alltäglich; *language* Umgangs-.
everyone ['evrɪwʌn] *pron* = **everybody**.
everything ['evrɪθɪŋ] *n* alles. ~ possible alles Mögliche; ~ you have alles, was du hast.
everywhere ['evrɪweə^r] *adv* überall; *(with direction)* überallhin. from ~ überallher, von überall; ~ you look man auch hinsieht.
evict [ɪ'vɪkt] *vt* tenants zur Räumung zwingen *(from gen)*.
eviction [ɪ'vɪkʃən] *n* Vertreibung *f (from aus)*.
evidence ['evɪdəns] 1 *n* (a) Beweis(e *pl*) *m*; *(Jur) (object)* Beweisstücke *nt*; *(testimony)* Aussage *f*. there wasn't enough ~ die Beweise reichten nicht aus; all the ~ was against his claim alles sprach gegen seine Behauptung; to give ~ (for/against sb) (für/gegen jdn) aussagen; the ~ for the defence die Beweisführung für die Verteidigung. (b) to be in ~ sichtbar sein; ideas which have been very much in ~ recently Ideen, die in letzter Zeit deutlich in Erscheinung getreten sind. 2 *vt* zeugen von.
evident *adj*, ~ly *adv* ['evɪdənt, -lɪ] offensichtlich.
evil ['iːvl] 1 *adj* böse; *person also, reputation, influence* schlecht; *(col)* smell übel. 2 *n* Böse *nt*. an

~ ein Übel *nt*; the lesser of two ~s das kleinere von zwei Übeln; social ~s soziale Mißstände.
evil: ~-doer *n* Übeltäter(in *f*) *m*; ~-minded *adj* bösartig.
evince [ɪ'vɪns] *vt* an den Tag legen.
evocation [ˌevə'keɪʃən] *n* Heraufbeschwören *nt*.
evocative [ɪ'vɒkətɪv] *adj* evokativ *(geh)*. to be ~ of sth etw heraufbeschwören.
evoke [ɪ'vəʊk] *vt* heraufbeschwören; *memory also* wachrufen; *admiration* hervorrufen.
evolution [ˌiːvə'luːʃən] *n* Entwicklung *f*; *(Biol etc)* Evolution *f*.
evolve [ɪ'vɒlv] 1 *vt* entwickeln. 2 *vi* sich entwickeln, sich herausbilden.
ewe [juː] *n* Mutterschaf *nt*.
ex- [eks-] *pref* ehemalig, Ex-. ~-wife frühere Frau, Exfrau *f*.
exacerbate [ek'sæsəbeɪt] *vt* pain, disease verschlimmern; *situation* verschärfen.
exact [ɪg'zækt] 1 *adj* genau; *figures, analysis etc also* exakt. it's the ~ opposite es ist genau umgekehrt. 2 *vt* money, ransom fordern *(from von)*.
exacting [ɪg'zæktɪŋ] *adj* anspruchsvoll. to be too/very ~ with sb zu viel/sehr viel von jdm verlangen.
exactly [ɪg'zæktlɪ] *adj* genau. I'm not ~ sure who he is ich bin mir nicht ganz sicher, wer er ist; it's not ~ a detective story es ist eigentlich keine Kriminalgeschichte; he wasn't ~ pleased er war nicht gerade erfreut.
exaggerate [ɪg'zædʒəreɪt] *vti* übertreiben; *(intensify)* effect verstärken.
exaggerated [ɪg'zædʒəreɪtɪd] *adj* übertrieben. to have an ~ opinion of oneself eine übertrieben hohe Meinung von sich haben.
exaggeration [ɪgˌzædʒə'reɪʃən] *n* Übertreibung *f*.
exalted [ɪg'zɔːltɪd] *adj* position, style hoch.
exam [ɪg'zæm] *n* Prüfung *f*.
examination [ɪgˌzæmɪ'neɪʃən] *n* (a) *(Sch etc)* Prüfung *f*; *(Univ also)* Examen *nt*. (b) *(study, inspection)* Prüfung, Untersuchung *f*; *(of machine, passports)* Kontrolle *f*; *(of question)* Untersuchung *f*; *(of accounts)* Prüfung *f*. the matter is still under ~ die Angelegenheit wird noch geprüft or untersucht. (c) *(of accused, witness)* Verhör *nt*; *(of case)* Untersuchung *f*.
examine [ɪg'zæmɪn] *vt* (a) *(for* auf +acc*)* untersuchen; *document, accounts* prüfen; *machine, passports, luggage* kontrollieren. (b) pupil, candidate prüfen *(in* in +dat, on über +acc*)*. (c) accused, witness verhören.
examiner [ɪg'zæmɪnə^r] *n (Sch, Univ)* Prüfer *m*.
example [ɪg'zɑːmpl] *n* Beispiel *nt*. for ~ zum Beispiel; to set a good/bad ~ ein gutes/schlechtes Beispiel geben; to make an ~ of sb an jdm ein Exempel statuieren.
exasperate [ɪg'zɑːspəreɪt] *vt* zur Verzweiflung bringen. to get ~d verzweifeln *(with* an +dat*)*; ~d at or by verärgert über *(+acc)*.
exasperating [ɪg'zɑːspəreɪtɪŋ] *adj* ärgerlich; *delay, difficulty, job* leidig *attr*. it's so ~! es ist wirklich zum Verzweifeln!
exasperation [ɪgˌzɑːspə'reɪʃən] *n* Verzweiflung *f (with* über +acc*)*.
excavate ['ekskəveɪt] 1 *vt* ground ausschachten; *(machine)* ausbaggern; *(Archeol)* remains ausgraben. 2 *vi (Archeol)* Ausgrabungen machen.
excavation [ˌekskə'veɪʃən] *n (Archeol)* (Aus)grabung *f*; *(of tunnel etc)* Graben *nt*; ~s *(site)* Ausgrabungsstätte *f*.
excavator ['ekskəveɪtə^r] *n (machine)* Bagger *m*.
exceed [ɪk'siːd] *vt (in value, amount, length of time)* übersteigen *(by um)*; *(go beyond)* hinausgehen über *(+acc)*; expectations, desires übertreffen; limits, powers, speed limit überschreiten.
exceedingly [ɪk'siːdɪŋlɪ] *adv* äußerst.
excel [ɪk'sel] 1 *vi* sich auszeichnen, sich hervortun *(in* in +dat, at bei*)*. 2 *vr* to ~ oneself *(oft iro)* sich

selbst übertreffen.
excellence ['eksələns] n Vorzüglichkeit f.
Excellency ['eksələnsı] n Your ~ Eure Exzellenz.
excellent ['eksələnt] adj ausgezeichnet.
except [ık'sept] 1 prep außer (+dat). what can they do ~ wait? was können sie anders tun als warten?; ~ for abgesehen von, bis auf (+acc); ~ that ... außer daß ...; ~ for the fact that abgesehen davon, daß ...; ~ if außer wenn; ~ when außer wenn. 2 conj I'd refuse ~ I need the money ich würde ablehnen, doch ich brauche das Geld. 3 vt ausnehmen. not ~ing X X nicht ausgenommen.
exception [ık'sepʃən] n (a) Ausnahme f. to make an ~ eine Ausnahme machen; with the ~ of mit Ausnahme von; as an ~ ausnahmsweise; the ~ proves the rule (prov) Ausnahmen bestätigen die Regel (prov). (b) to take ~ to sth Anstoß m an etw (dat) nehmen.
exceptional [ık'sepʃənl] adj außergewöhnlich. apart from ~ cases abgesehen von Ausnahmefällen.
exceptionally [ık'sepʃənəlı] adv (outstandingly) außergewöhnlich.
excerpt ['eksɜːpt] n Auszug m.
excess [ık'ses] n (a) Übermaß nt (of an +dat). to drink to ~ übermäßig trinken; to carry sth to ~ etw übertreiben. (b) ~es pl Exzesse pl; (brutalities also) Ausschreitungen pl. (c) (amount left over) Überschuß m. (d) to be in ~ of überschreiten.
excess in cpds weight, production Über-; ~ baggage n Übergewicht nt; ~ fare n Nachlösegebühr f; I had to pay ~ fare ich mußte nachlösen.
excessive [ık'sesıv] adj übermäßig; praise also übertrieben. I think you're being ~ ich finde, Sie übertreiben.
excessively [ık'sesıvlı] adv (a) (to excess) (+vb) eat, drink übermäßig; (+adj) optimistic, severe allzu. (b) (extremely) äußerst.
exchange [ıks'tʃeındʒ] 1 vt books, glances, seats tauschen; foreign currency umtauschen (for in +acc); ideas, experiences etc austauschen. to ~ words/letters/blows einen Wortwechsel haben/ einen Briefwechsel führen/sich schlagen; to ~ one thing for another eine Sache gegen eine andere austauschen or (in shop) umtauschen.
2 n (a) (of goods, stamps) Tausch m; (of prisoners, views) Austausch m; (of one bought item for another) Umtausch m. in ~ dafür; in ~ for money gegen Geld; in ~ for lending me your car dafür, daß Sie mir Ihr Auto geliehen haben. (b) (Fin: logical) Wechselstube f. ~ rate Wechselkurs m. (c) (telephone) ~ Fernamt nt; (in office etc) (Telefon)zentrale f.
3 adj attr student, teacher Austausch-.
exchequer [ıks'tʃekəʳ] n Finanzministerium nt; (esp in GB) Schatzamt nt.
excise ['eksaız] n Verbrauchssteuer f.
excitable [ık'saıtəbl] adj (leicht) erregbar.
excite [ık'saıt] vt aufregen, aufgeregt machen; (rouse enthusiasm in) begeistern; sentiments, (sexually) erregen; imagination anregen.
excited [ık'saıtıd] adj aufgeregt; (worked up, not calm also, sexually) erregt; (enthusiastic) begeistert. don't get ~! (angry etc) reg dich nicht auf!; aren't you ~ about what might happen? sind Sie nicht gespannt, was passieren wird?
excitement [ık'saıtmənt] n Aufregung f; (not being calm etc also, sexual) Erregung f. a mood of ~ eine spannungsgeladene Stimmung; what's all the ~ about? wozu die ganze Aufregung?; his novel has caused great ~ sein Roman hat große Begeisterung ausgelöst.
exciting [ık'saıtıŋ] adj aufregend; story, film, event, adventure also spannend; new author sensationell. isn't that ~! ist das nicht prima?; how ~ for you prima!, wie aufregend (also iro).

exclaim [ık'skleım] vt ausrufen.
exclamation [,eksklə'meıʃən] n Ausruf m (also Gram). ~ mark or point (US) Ausrufezeichen nt.
exclude [ık'skluːd] vt ausschließen. to ~ sb from the team jdn aus der Mannschaft ausschließen; excluding petrol außer or ausgenommen Benzin.
exclusion [ık'skluːʒən] n Ausschluß m (from von). you can't just think about your job to the ~ of everything else du kannst nicht ausschließlich an deine Arbeit denken.
exclusive [ık'skluːsıv] adj (a) group, club etc exklusiv; right, interview also Exklusiv-. they are mutually ~ sie schließen einander aus. (b)(sole) ausschließlich, einzig. (c) from 15th to 20th June ~ vom 15. bis zum 20. Juni ausschließlich; ~ of ausschließlich (+gen), exklusive (+gen).
exclusively [ık'skluːsıvlı] adv ausschließlich.
excommunicate [,ekskə'mjuːnıkeıt] vt exkommunizieren.
excrement ['ekskrımənt] n Kot m, Exkremente pl.
excruciating [ık'skruːʃıeıtıŋ] adj pain, noise gräßlich, entsetzlich.
excruciatingly [ık'skruːʃıeıtıŋlı] adv it was ~ painful es hat scheußlich weh getan (col); ~ funny urkomisch.
excursion [ık'skɜːʃən] n Ausflug m. to go on an ~ einen Ausflug machen; ~ ticket verbilligte Fahrkarte.
excuse [ık'skjuːz] 1 vt (a) entschuldigen. he ~d himself for being late er entschuldigte sich, daß er zu spät kam; to ~ sb for having done sth jdm verzeihen, daß er etwas getan hat; I think I can be ~d for believing him man kann es mir wohl nicht übelnehmen, daß ich ihm geglaubt habe; if you will ~ the expression wenn Sie mir den Ausdruck gestatten; ~ me! (to get attention, sorry) Entschuldigung!, entschuldigen Sie!; (indignant) erlauben Sie mal! (b) (from obligation) to ~ sb from (doing) sth jdn von einer Sache befreien, jdm etw erlassen; you are ~d ihr könnt gehen; can I be ~d? darf ich mal verschwinden (col)?
2 [ıks'kjuːs] n Entschuldigung f. there's no ~ for it dafür gibt es keine Entschuldigung; to make ~s for sb jdn entschuldigen; he's only making ~s er sucht nur nach einer Ausrede; a good ~ for a party ein guter Grund, eine Party zu feiern.
ex-directory [,eksdaı'rektərı] adj (Brit) to be ~ nicht im Telefonbuch stehen.
execute ['eksıkjuːt] vt (a) plan, order ausführen; duties erfüllen. beautifully ~d (concerto) wunderbar gespielt. (b) criminal hinrichten. (c) (Jur) will vollstrecken.
execution [,eksı'kjuːʃən] n (a) see vt (a) Ausführung f; Erfüllung f. in the ~ of his duties bei der Ausübung seines Amtes. (b) (Mus) Vortrag m; (musician's skill) Ausführung f. (c) (as punishment) Hinrichtung f. (d) (Jur: of will) Vollstreckung f.
executioner [,eksı'kjuːʃnəʳ] n Henker m.
executive [ıg'zekjutıv] 1 adj powers, committee etc Exekutiv-; (Comm) geschäftsführend. ~ position leitende Stellung or Position. 2 n (a) leitender Angestellter, leitende Angestellte, Manager m. ~ (brief)case Diplomatenköfferchen nt. (b) (of government) Exekutive f; (of association) Vorstand m.
executor [ıg'zekjutəʳ] n (of will) Testamentsvollstrecker m.
exemplary [ıg'zemplərı] adj vorbildlich, beispielhaft. ~ punishment exemplarische Strafe.
exemplify [ıg'zemplıfaı] vt erläutern.
exempt [ıg'zempt] 1 adj befreit (from von). 2 vt person befreien.
exemption [ıg'zempʃən] n Befreiung f.
exercise ['eksəsaız] 1 n (a) no pl (of right) Wahrnehmung f; (of physical, mental power)

Ausübung *f.* **(b)** *(bodily or mental, drill, Mus etc)* Übung *f.* **to do one's** ~**s in the morning** Morgengymnastik machen. **(c)** *no pl (physical)* Bewegung *f.* **physical** ~ *(körperliche)* Bewegung; **you should take more** ~ Sie sollten mehr Bewegung haben; **what do you do for** ~? wie halten Sie sich fit? **(d)** *(Mil: usu pl)* Übung *f.* 2 *vt* **(a)** *body, mind* üben, trainieren; *(Mil)* *troops* exerzieren; *dog* spazierenführen. **(b)** *(use) control, power also*; *a right also* geltend machen; *tact, discretion* üben. 3 *vi* **if you** ~ **regularly** wenn Sie sich viel bewegen.

exercise book *n* Heft *nt.*

exert [ɪg'zɜːt] 1 *vt pressure* ausüben *(on* auf *+acc);* *authority* geltend machen *(on* bei). 2 *vr* **to** ~ **oneself** sich anstrengen.

exertion [ɪg'zɜːʃən] *n* **(a)** *(effort)* Anstrengung *f.* **after the day's** ~**s** nach des Tages Mühen. **(b)** *(of pressure, influence)* Ausübung *f (on* auf *+acc).*

exeunt ['eksɪʌnt] *(in stage directions)* ab.

ex gratia [eks'greɪʃə] *adj payment* Sonder-.

exhale [eks'heɪl] *vti* ausatmen.

exhaust [ɪg'zɔːst] 1 *vt (use up, tire)* erschöpfen. 2 *n (Aut etc)* Auspuff *m; (gases)* Auspuffgase *pl.*

exhausted [ɪg'zɔːstɪd] *adj* erschöpft.

exhausting [ɪg'zɔːstɪŋ] *adj* anstrengend.

exhaustion [ɪg'zɔːstʃən] *n* Erschöpfung *f.*

exhaustive [ɪg'zɔːstɪv] *adj* erschöpfend.

exhaust: ~ **pipe** *n* Auspuffrohr *nt;* ~ **system** *n* Auspuff *m.*

exhibit [ɪg'zɪbɪt] 1 *vt* **(a)** ausstellen; *merchandise also* auslegen. **(b)** *skill, ingenuity* zeigen, an den Tag legen. 2 *vi* ausstellen. 3 *n (in an exhibition)* Ausstellungsstück *nt; (Jur)* Beweisstück *nt.*

exhibition [ˌeksɪ'bɪʃən] *n* **(a)** Ausstellung *f; (of articles for sale)* Auslage *f.* **(b) to make an** ~ **of oneself** sich danebenbenehmen *(col).*

exhibitionist [ˌeksɪ'bɪʃənɪst] *n* Exhibitionist(in *f) m.*

exhibitor [ɪg'zɪbɪtəʳ] *n* Aussteller *m.*

exhilarate [ɪg'zɪləreɪt] *vt* in Hochstimmung versetzen; *(sea air etc)* beleben, erfrischen.

exhilarated [ɪg'zɪləreɪtɪd] *adj* erregt. **to feel** ~ **in** Hochstimmung sein.

exhilarating [ɪg'zɪləreɪtɪŋ] *adj sensation, speed* erregend; *music* anregend; *air etc* belebend.

exhilaration [ɪgˌzɪlə'reɪʃən] *n* Hochgefühl *nt.*

exhort [ɪg'zɔːt] *vt* ermahnen.

exhume [eks'hjuːm] *vt* exhumieren.

exile ['eksaɪl] 1 *n (person)* Verbannte(r) *mf; (banishment)* Exil *nt,* Verbannung *f.* **in** ~ **im Exil.** 2 *vt* verbannen *(from* aus).

exist [ɪg'zɪst] *vi* **(a)** existieren, bestehen. **it doesn't** ~ das gibt es nicht; **to continue to** ~ fortbestehen; **there** ~**s a tradition that** ... es gibt den Brauch, daß ...; **she** ~**s on very little** sie kommt mit sehr wenig aus; **we manage to** ~ wir kommen gerade aus. **(b)** *(be found: plants, minerals etc)* vorkommen.

existence [ɪg'zɪstəns] *n* **(a)** Existenz *f; (of custom, tradition, institution also)* Bestehen *nt.* **to be in** ~ existieren, bestehen; **to come into** ~ entstehen; *(person)* auf die Welt kommen; **to go out of** ~ zu existieren aufhören; **the only one in** ~ der einzige, den es gibt. **(b)** *(life)* Dasein *nt,* Existenz *f.*

existential [ˌegzɪs'tenʃəl] *adj* existentiell.

existentialism [ˌegzɪs'tenʃəlɪzəm] *n* Existentialismus *m.*

existing [ɪg'zɪstɪŋ] *adj law* bestehend; *director* gegenwärtig.

exit ['eksɪt] 1 *n* Ausgang *m; (for vehicles)* Ausfahrt *f.* **he made a very dramatic** ~ sein Abgang war sehr dramatisch; ~ **visa** Ausreisevisum *nt.* 2 *vi (from stage)* abgehen.

exodus ['eksədəs] *n* Auszug *m; (Bibl, fig)* Exodus *m.* **general** ~ allgemeiner Aufbruch.

exonerate [ɪg'zɒnəreɪt] *vt* entlasten *(from* von).

exorbitant [ɪg'zɔːbɪtənt] *adj price* astronomisch; *demands* maßlos, übertrieben. **that's** ~! das ist Wucher!

exorcism ['eksɔːsɪzəm] *n* Exorzismus *m.*

exorcize ['eksɔːsaɪz] *vt* exorzieren; *evil spirit also* austreiben.

exotic [ɪg'zɒtɪk] *adj* exotisch.

expand [ɪk'spænd] 1 *vt* ausdehnen, erweitern; *ideas* entwickeln. 2 *vi (gases, universe)* sich ausdehnen; *(business)* expandieren, sich ausweiten; *(knowledge, influence, market)* wachsen. **could you** ~ **on that?** könnten Sie das näher ausführen?

expanse [ɪk'spæns] *n* Fläche *f; (of sea)* Weite *f no pl.*

expansion [ɪk'spænʃən] *n (of gas, metal, property)* Ausdehnung *f; (of business, production, knowledge)* Erweiterung *f; (territorial, economic)* Expansion *f; (of subject, idea)* Entwicklung *f; (of experience, influence)* Vergrößerung *f.*

expansionism [ɪk'spænʃənɪzəm] *n* Expansionspolitik *f.*

expansionist [ɪk'spænʃənɪst] *adj* expansionistisch.

expansive [ɪk'spænsɪv] *adj person* mitteilsam.

expatriate [eks'pætrɪət] 1 *adj* im Ausland lebend. 2 *n* im Ausland Lebende(r) *mf.* **the** ~**s in Abu Dhabi** die Ausländer in Abu Dhabi.

expect [ɪk'spekt] 1 *vt* **(a)** *(anticipate)* erwarten; *esp sth bad also* rechnen mit. **that was to be** ~**ed** das war zu erwarten; **I know what to** ~ ich weiß, was mich erwartet; **I** ~**ed as much** das habe ich erwartet; **I was** ~**ing him to come** ich habe eigentlich erwartet, daß er kommt. **(b)** *(suppose)* annehmen. **will they be on time?** — **yes, I** ~ **so** kommen sie pünktlich? — ja, ich glaube schon; **I** ~ **it will rain** es wird wohl regnen; **I** ~ **he turned it down** ich nehme an, er hat abgelehnt; **well, I** ~ **he's right** er wird schon recht haben. **(c)** *(demand)* **to** ~ **sth of** *or* **from sb** etw von jdm erwarten; **to** ~ **sb to do sth** erwarten, daß jd etw tut; **are we** ~**ed to tip the waiter?** müssen wir dem Kellner Trinkgeld geben?; **what do you** ~ **me to do about it?** was soll ich da machen? **(d)** *(await)* erwarten; *baby also* bekommen. **we'll** ~ **you when we see you** *(col)* wenn wir kommt, dann kommt ihr *(col).* 2 *vi* **she's** ~**ing** sie ist in anderen Umständen.

expectancy [ɪk'spektənsɪ] *n* Erwartung *f.*

expectant [ɪk'spektənt] *adj* erwartungsvoll; *mother* werdend.

expectation [ˌekspek'teɪʃən] *n* **(a)** Erwartung *f.* **in** ~ **of** in Erwartung (*+gen*); **contrary to all** ~**(s)** wider Erwarten; **beyond all** ~**(s)** über Erwarten; **to come up to sb's** ~**s** jds Erwartungen entsprechen. **(b)** *(prospect)* Aussicht *f.*

expedience [ɪk'spiːdɪəns], **expediency** [ɪk'spiːdɪənsɪ] *n* **(a)** *(self-interest)* Zweckdenken *nt,* Berechnung *f.* **(b)** *(of measure etc)* Zweckdienlichkeit *f; (advisability)* Ratsamkeit *f.*

expedient [ɪk'spiːdɪənt] *adj (politic)* zweckdienlich; *(advisable)* angebracht, ratsam.

expedite ['ekspɪdaɪt] *vt* beschleunigen.

expedition [ˌekspɪ'dɪʃən] *n* Expedition *f; (Mil)* Feldzug *m.*

expeditionary [ˌekspɪ'dɪʃənrɪ] *adj* ~ **force** Expeditionskorps *nt.*

expel [ɪk'spel] *vt* vertreiben; *(from country)* ausweisen *(from* aus); *(from school)* verweisen *(from* von, *gen); (from party)* ausschließen *(from* aus).

expend [ɪk'spend] *vt time, energy* aufwenden *(on* für); *(use up) resources* verbrauchen.

expendable [ɪk'spendəbl] *adj* entbehrlich; *people* überflüssig.

expenditure [ɪk'spendɪtʃəʳ] *n (money spent)*

Ausgaben pl; (of time, energy) Aufwand m (of an +dat).

expense [ɪk'spens] n (a) Kosten pl. at my ~ auf meine Kosten; at great ~ mit hohen Kosten; it's a big ~ es ist eine große Ausgabe; to go to great ~ to repair the house es sich (dat) etwas kosten lassen, das Haus instand zu setzen; don't go to any ~ of over our visit stürz dich nicht in Unkosten wegen unseres Besuchs; at sb's ~/at the ~ of sth (fig) auf jds Kosten (acc)/auf Kosten einer Sache (gen). (b) (Comm: usu pl) Spesen pl. to incur ~s Unkosten haben; it's on ~s das geht auf Spesen; ~ account Spesenkonto nt.

expensive [ɪk'spensɪv] adj teuer.

experience [ɪk'spɪərɪəns] 1 n (a) Erfahrung f. ~ shows that ... die Erfahrung lehrt, daß ...; from my own personal ~ aus eigener Erfahrung; he has no ~ of living in the country er kennt das Landleben nicht; to have a lot of teaching ~ große Erfahrung als Lehrer haben. (b) (event experienced) Erlebnis nt. I had a nasty ~ mir ist etwas Unangenehmes passiert; to go through or have a painful ~ Schreckliches erleben; to have an ~ eine Erfahrung machen; what an ~! das war vielleicht was!; it was a new ~ for me es war völlig neu für mich.
2 vt (a) erleben; pain, hunger also erfahren; difficult times durchmachen. to ~ difficulties Schwierigkeiten haben. (b) (feel) empfinden.

experienced [ɪk'spɪərɪənst] adj erfahren (in in +dat); eye, ear geschult.

experiment [ɪk'sperɪmənt] 1 n Versuch m, Experiment nt. to do an ~ einen Versuch or ein Experiment machen. 2 vi experimentieren (on mit).

experimental [ɪk,sperɪ'mentl] adj experimentell; also method, science Experimental-; farm, engine, period Versuchs-; theatre, cinema Experimentier-. at the ~ stage im Versuchsstadium.

experimentation [ɪk,sperɪmen'teɪʃən] n Experimentieren nt.

expert ['ekspɜːt] 1 n Fachmann, Experte m, Expertin f; (Jur) Sachverständige(r) mf. 2 adj work ausgezeichnet, geschickt; driver etc erfahren; approach, advice fachmännisch; opinion eines Fachmanns/Sachverständigen. ~ witness sachverständiger Zeuge; the ~ touch die Meisterhand.

expertise [,ekspɜː'tiːz] n Sachkenntnis f (in auf dem Gebiet +gen); (manual) Geschick nt (in bei).

expire [ɪk'spaɪər] vi (a) (passport, time limit) ablaufen. (b) (liter: die) seinen Geist aufgeben (liter).

expiry [ɪk'spaɪərɪ] n Ablauf m. ~ date Ablauftermin m; (of special offer) Verfallsdatum nt.

explain [ɪk'spleɪn] vt erklären (to sb jdm); situation also erläutern; mystery aufklären. he'd better ~ himself ich hoffe, er kann das erklären.
♦ **explain away** vt sep wegerklären (col).

explanation [,eksplə'neɪʃən] n see vt Erklärung f; Erläuterung f; Aufklärung f. what can you say in ~ of this? wie erklären Sie das?

explanatory [ɪk'splænətərɪ] adj erklärend. a few ~ remarks ein paar Worte zur Erklärung.

expletive [ɪk'spliːtɪv] n Kraftausdruck m.

explicit [ɪk'splɪsɪt] adj deutlich, explizit (geh); text, meaning also klar; sex scene deutlich, unverhüllt.

explicitly [ɪk'splɪsɪtlɪ] adv deutlich.

explode [ɪk'spləʊd] 1 vi (lit, fig) explodieren. to ~ with laughter in schallendes Gelächter ausbrechen. 2 vt (a) bomb, mine sprengen; dynamite, gas zur Explosion bringen. (b) (fig) theory, argument zu Fall bringen.

exploit ['eksplɔɪt] 1 n (heroic) Heldentat f. ~s (adventures) Abenteuer pl. 2 [ɪks'plɔɪt] vt coal seam, workers ausbeuten; situation, (pej) friend, good nature ausnutzen; product nutzen.

exploitation [,eksplɔɪ'teɪʃən] n see vt Ausbeutung f; Ausnutzung f; Nutzung f.

exploration [,eksplɔː'reɪʃən] n Erforschung, Erkundung f; (of topic, Med) Untersuchung f. a voyage of ~ (lit, fig) eine Entdeckungsreise.

exploratory [ɪk'splɔːrətərɪ] adj drilling Probe-. ~ operation (Med) Explorationsoperation f; ~ talks Sondierungsgespräche pl.

explore [ɪk'splɔːr] 1 vt (lit, fig) erforschen; (Med) untersuchen. 2 vi to go exploring auf Entdeckungsreise gehen.

explorer [ɪk'splɔːrər] n Forscher(in f) m.

explosion [ɪk'spləʊʒən] n (lit, fig) Explosion f; (fig: of anger) Wutausbruch m.

explosive [ɪk'spləʊzɪv] 1 adj (lit, fig) explosiv. ~ device Sprengkörper m. 2 n Sprengstoff m.

exponent [ɪk'spəʊnənt] n Vertreter(in f) m.

export 1 [ɪk'spɔːt] vti exportieren. 2 ['ekspɔːt] Export m. ~ drive Exportkampagne f.

exporter [ɪk'spɔːtər] n Exporteur m (of von); (country also) Exportland nt (of für).

expose [ɪk'spəʊz] vt (a) rocks, remains freilegen; electric wire, nerve also bloßlegen. to be ~d to view sichtbar sein. (b) (to danger, sunlight, radiation, criticism) aussetzen (to dat). "not to be ~d to heat" „vor Hitze schützen". (c) (display) one's ignorance offenbaren; (indecently) oneself entblößen. (d) abuse, treachery aufdecken; imposter, thief entlarven. to ~ sb/sth to the press jdn/etw der Presse ausliefern. (e) (Phot) belichten.

exposed [ɪk'spəʊzd] adj (a) (to weather) place ungeschützt. ~ to the wind dem Wind ausgesetzt. (b) (insecure) to feel ~ sich allen Blicken ausgesetzt fühlen. (c) (visible) sichtbar. the ~ parts of a motor die freiliegenden Teile eines Motors.

exposition [ekspə'zɪʃən] n (of theory) Darlegung f; (Mus) Exposition f.

expostulate [ɪk'spɒstjʊleɪt] vi protestieren.

expostulation [ɪk,spɒstjʊ'leɪʃən] n Protest m.

exposure [ɪk'spəʊʒər] n (a) (to sunlight, air, danger) Aussetzung f (to dat). to be suffering from ~ an Unterkühlung leiden; to die of ~ erfrieren. (b) (displaying) Entblößung f. indecent ~ Exhibitionismus m. (c) (unmasking) Bloßstellung f; (of thief, murderer) Entlarvung f; (of abuses, vices, scandals, crime) Aufdeckung f. (d) (Phot) Belichtung(szeit) f. ~ meter Belichtungsmesser m. (e) (Media) Publicity f.

expound [ɪk'spaʊnd] vt darlegen, erläutern.

express [ɪk'spres] 1 vt ausdrücken. to ~ oneself sich ausdrücken. 2 adj instructions ausdrücklich; intention bestimmt. 3 adv to send sth ~ etw per Expreß schicken. 4 n (train) Schnellzug m.

expression [ɪk'spreʃən] n Ausdruck m. as an ~ of our gratitude zum Ausdruck unserer Dankbarkeit; you could tell by his ~ that ... man konnte an seinem Gesichtsausdruck erkennen, daß ...

expressionism [ɪk'spreʃənɪzəm] n Expressionismus m.

expressive [ɪk'spresɪv] adj ausdrucksvoll.

expressly [ɪk'spreslɪ] adv deny etc ausdrücklich.

express: ~ train n Schnellzug m; ~way n Schnellstraße f.

expulsion [ɪk'spʌlʃən] n (from country) Ausweisung f (from aus); (from school) Verweisung f (von der Schule); (from party) Ausschluß m (from aus).

expurgate ['ekspɜːgeɪt] vt zensieren. ~d edition gereinigte Fassung.

exquisite [ɪk'skwɪzɪt] adj workmanship ausgezeichnet; dress, painting exquisit; taste gepflegt; view herrlich; food, wine, sense of humour, satisfaction, pleasure köstlich.

extant [ek'stænt] adj noch vorhanden.

extempore [ɪks'tempərɪ] adj to give an ~ speech

eine Rede aus dem Stegreif halten.

extemporize [ɪk'stempəraɪz] *vti* aus dem Stegreif sprechen; *(Mus, with makeshift)* improvisieren.

extend [ɪk'stend] **1** *vt* **(a)** *(stretch out)* arms ausstrecken. **(b)** *line, visit, passport, holidays* verlängern. **(c)** *(enlarge) research, powers, limits, knowledge* erweitern; *house* anbauen an (+*acc*); *frontiers of a country* ausdehnen. **(d)** *(offer) (to sb* jdm*) help* gewähren; *hospitality, friendship* erweisen; *condolences* aussprechen. **to ~ a welcome to sb** jdn willkommen heißen. **2** *vi (wall, garden)* sich erstrecken *(to, as far as* bis*); (over period of time)* sich hinziehen.

extension [ɪk'stenʃən] *n* **(a)** *(of property)* Vergrößerung *f; (of business, knowledge also)* Erweiterung *f; (of powers, franchise, research, frontiers)* Ausdehnung *f; (of road, line, period of time)* Verlängerung *f; (of house)* Anbau *m.* **(b)** *(Telec)* (Neben)anschluß *m.* **~ 3714** Apparat 3714; **~ cable** Verlängerungskabel *nt;* **~ ladder** Ausziehleiter *f.*

extensive [ɪk'stensɪv] *adj land, forest* ausgedehnt; *knowledge, press coverage, research, enquiries, operations, alterations* umfangreich; *damage* beträchtlich; *use* häufig; *plans, reforms, influence* weitreichend.

extensively [ɪk'stensɪvlɪ] *adv* weit; *study, investigate, cover* ausführlich; *altered, reformed, damaged* beträchtlich; *used* häufig, viel; *travel* viel.

extent [ɪk'stent] *n (length)* Länge *f; (size)* Ausdehnung *f; (range, scope)* Umfang *m; (of damage, commitments also)* Ausmaß *nt.* **to some ~** bis zu einem gewissen Grade; **to what ~** inwieweit; **to a certain ~** in gewissem Maße; **to a large ~** in hohem Maße; **to such an ~ that ...** dermaßen, daß ...

extenuating [ɪk'stenjʊeɪtɪŋ] *adj* **~ circumstances** mildernde Umstände *pl.*

exterior [ɪk'stɪərɪə*r*] **1** *adj surface* äußere(r, s), Außen-. **2** *n (of house etc)* Außenseite *f; (of person)* Äußere(s) *nt.* **on the ~** außen.

exterminate [ɪk'stɜːmɪneɪt] *vt* ausrotten.

external [ek'stɜːnl] **1** *adj wall* äußere(r, s), Außen-; *factors, help* extern. **for ~ use only** *(Med)* nur äußerlich (anzuwenden); **~ trade** Außenhandel *m.* **2** *n (fig)* **~s** *pl* Äußerlichkeiten *pl.*

externally [ek'stɜːnəlɪ] *adv* äußerlich.

extinct [ɪk'stɪŋkt] *adj volcano, love* erloschen; *species* ausgestorben.

extinction [ɪk'stɪŋkʃən] *n (of race)* Aussterben *nt; (annihilation)* Vernichtung *f.*

extinguish [ɪk'stɪŋgwɪʃ] *vt fire* löschen; *hopes, passion* zerstören.

extinguisher [ɪk'stɪŋgwɪʃə*r*] *n* Feuerlöscher *m.*

extol [ɪk'stəʊl] *vt* preisen, rühmen.

extort [ɪk'stɔːt] *vt* erpressen *(from* von*).*

extortion [ɪk'stɔːʃən] *n* Erpressung *f.* **this is sheer ~!** *(col)* das ist ja Wucher!

extortionate [ɪk'stɔːʃənɪt] *adj prices* Wucher-; *tax, demand* ungeheuer.

extra ['ekstrə] **1** *adj* zusätzlich. **we need an ~ chair** wir brauchen noch einen Stuhl; **to make an ~ effort** sich besonders anstrengen; **~ charge** Zuschlag *m;* **there will be no ~ charge** das wird nicht extra berechnet; **~ time** *(Brit Ftbl)* Verlängerung *f;* **~ pay** eine Zulage; **for ~ safety** zur größeren Sicherheit; **we need an ~ 10 minutes** wir brauchen 10 Minuten mehr; **I have brought an ~ pair of shoes** ich habe ein extra Paar Schuhe mitgebracht. **2** *adv* **(a)** *(especially)* extra, besonders. **(b)** *(in addition)* extra. **3** *n* **(a)** *(perk)* Zusatzleistung *f; (for car)* Extra *nt.* **they regard it as an ~** sie betrachten es als Luxus. **(b)** **~s** *pl (~ expenses)* zusätzliche Kosten *pl; (in restaurant)* Zusätzliches *nt.* **(c)** *(Film, Theat)* Statist(in *f*) *m.* **(d)** *(remainder)* Rest *m.*

extract [ɪk'strækt] **1** *vt* **(a)** herausziehen *(from* aus*); juice, minerals, oil* gewinnen *(from* aus*);*

tooth ziehen. **(b)** *(fig) information, confession, money* herausholen *(from* aus*).* **(c)** *quotation, passage* herausziehen. **2** ['ekstrækt] *n (from book etc)* Auszug *m. beef* **~** Fleischextrakt *m.*

extraction [ɪk'strækʃən] *n* **(a)** *see vt* Herausziehen *nt;* Gewinnung *f;* Ziehen *nt;* Herausholen *nt.* **he had to have three ~s** ihm mußten drei Zähne gezogen werden. **(b)** **of Spanish ~** spanischer Abstammung.

extracurricular ['ekstrəkə'rɪkjʊlə*r*] *adj* außerhalb des Stundenplans.

extradite ['ekstrədaɪt] *vt* ausliefern.

extradition [,ekstrə'dɪʃən] *n* Auslieferung *f.* **~ treaty** Auslieferungsvertrag *m.*

extramarital ['ekstrə'mærɪtl] *adj* außerehelich.

extramural ['ekstrə'mjʊərəl] *adj* **~ courses** Volkshochschul-.

extraneous [ɪk'streɪnɪəs] *adj influence* extern. **~ to** *(unrelated)* irrelevant für.

extraordinary [ɪk'strɔːdnrɪ] *adj* **(a)** *(beyond what is common)* außerordentlich; *(not usual)* ungewöhnlich. **(b)** *(odd, peculiar)* sonderbar, seltsam; *(amazing)* erstaunlich. **(c)** *(special)* **an ~ meeting** eine Sondersitzung.

extrapolate [ek'stræpəleɪt] *vti* extrapolieren *(from* aus*).*

extrasensory ['ekstrə'sensərɪ] *adj* **~ perception** außersinnliche Wahrnehmung.

extra-special ['ekstrə'speʃəl] *adj* ganz besondere(r, s).

extraterrestrial ['ekstrətɪ'restrɪəl] *adj* außerirdisch.

extravagance [ɪk'strævəgəns] *n* **(a)** Luxus *m no pl.* **her ~** ihre Verschwendungssucht. **(b)** *(wastefulness)* Verschwendung *f.* **(c)** *(of ideas, theories)* Ausgefallenheit *f; (of claim, demand)* Übertriebenheit *f.* **(d)** *(extravagant action)* Extravaganz *f.*

extravagant [ɪk'strævəgənt] *adj* **(a)** *taste, habit* teuer, kostspielig; *wedding, lifestyle* aufwendig; *price* überhöht. **she is ~** sie gibt das Geld mit vollen Händen aus; **go on, be ~** gönn dir doch den Luxus. **(b)** *(wasteful)* verschwenderisch. **(c)** *behaviour* extravagant; *ideas, tie* also ausgefallen; *claim, demand* übertrieben.

extreme [ɪk'striːm] **1** *adj* äußerste(r, s); *(exaggerated, drastic, Pol)* extrem; *praise, flattery* übertrieben; *exaggeration, demands* maßlos; *penalty* höchste(r, s). **to the ~ right** ganz rechts; **~ old age** ein äußerst hohes Alter; **an ~ case** ein Extremfall *m.* **2** *n* Extrem *nt.* **~s of temperature** extreme Temperaturen *pl;* **in the ~** im höchsten Grade; **to go from one ~ to the other** von einem Extrem ins andere fallen; **to go to ~s** es übertreiben; **to drive sb to ~s** jdn zum Äußersten treiben.

extremely [ɪk'striːmlɪ] *adv* äußerst, höchst. **was it difficult? — ~ war es schwierig? — sehr!**

extremist [ɪk'striːmɪst] **1** *adj* extremistisch. **2** *n* Extremist(in *f*) *m.*

extremity [ɪk'stremɪtɪ] *n* **(a)** *(furthest point)* äußerstes Ende. **(b)** *(state of distress)* Not *f.* **(c)** **to resort to extremities** zu extremen Mitteln greifen. **(d)** **extremities** *pl (hands and feet)* Extremitäten *pl.*

extricate ['ekstrɪkeɪt] *vt* befreien *(from* aus*).*

extrovert ['ekstrəvɜːt] **1** *adj* extrovertiert. **2** *n* extrovertierter Mensch.

exuberance [ɪg'zuːbərəns] *n (of person)* Überschwenglichkeit *f; (of joy, youth, feelings)* Überschwang *m; (joy)* überschwengliche Freude *(at* über +*acc*); *(of prose, style)* Vitalität *f.*

exuberant [ɪg'zuːbərənt] *adj* überschwenglich; *style* übersprudelnd, vital; *music* mitreißend.

exude [ɪg'zjuːd] *vt (liquid)* ausscheiden; *confidence* ausstrahlen; *(pej) charm* triefen vor (+*dat*).

exult [ɪg'zʌlt] *vi* frohlocken.

exultant [ɪg'zʌltənt] *adj* jubelnd; *shout also* Jubel-.

to be ~ jubeln.
exultation [,egzʌl'teɪʃən] n Jubel m.
eye [aɪ] **1** n Auge nt; (of needle) Öhr nt. with one's ~s closed/open mit geschlossenen/offenen Augen; (fig) blind/mit offenen Augen; an ~ for an ~ Auge um Auge; to be all ~s große Augen machen; that's one in the ~ for him (col) da hat er eins aufs Dach gekriegt (col); to cast or run one's ~s over sth etw überfliegen; to look sb (straight) in the ~ jdm in die Augen sehen; to set or clap (col) ~s on sb/sth jdn/etw zu Gesicht bekommen; (why don't you) use your ~s! hast du keine Augen im Kopf?; with one's own ~s mit eigenen Augen; before my very ~s (direkt) vor meinen Augen; under the watchful ~ of the guard unter der Aufsicht des Wächters; to keep an ~ on sb/sth (look after) auf jdn/etw aufpassen; to keep one's ~ on the ball/main objective sich auf den Ball/die Hauptsache konzentrieren; never to take one's ~s off sb/sth kein Auge von jdm/etw wenden; he couldn't take his ~s off her/the cake er konnte einfach den Blick nicht von ihr/dem Kuchen lassen; to keep one's ~s open die Augen offenhalten; to keep an ~ out for a hotel nach einem Hotel Ausschau halten; to keep an ~ on expenditure auf seine Ausgaben achten; to open sb's ~s to sb/sth jdm die Augen über jdn/etw öffnen; to close one's ~s to sth die Augen vor etw (dat) verschließen; to see ~ to ~ with sb mit jdm einer Meinung sein; to make ~s at sb jdm schöne Augen machen; to catch sb's ~ jds Aufmerksamkeit erregen; that colour caught my ~ die Farbe fiel mir ins Auge; in the ~s of the law in den Augen des Gesetzes; in my ~s in meinen Augen; with an ~ to the future im Hinblick auf die Zukunft; with an ~ to buying sth in der Absicht, etw zu kaufen; I've got my ~ on you ich beobachte dich genau; to have one's ~ on sth (want) auf etw (acc) ein Auge geworfen haben; to have an ~ on sb for a job jdn für eine Stelle im Auge haben; he has a good ~ for colour er hat ein Auge für Farbe; you need an ~ for detail man muß einen Blick fürs Detail haben; to be up to the ~s in work (col) in Arbeit ersticken (col).

2 vt anstarren. to ~ sb up and down jdn von oben bis unten mustern.

♦ **eye up** vt sep girls, boys mustern, begutachten.
eye in cpds Augen-; ~ball n Augapfel m; ~brow n Augenbraue f; he never raised an ~brow (col) er hat sich nicht einmal gewundert; ~brow pencil n Augenbrauenstift m; ~-catching adj auffallend; publicity, poster also auffällig; ~ drops Augentropfen pl.
eyeful ['aɪfʊl] n (col) to get an ~ (get sth in eye) etw ins Auge bekommen; get an ~ of this guck dir das mal an (col).
eye: ~glasses npl (US) Brille f; ~lash n Augenwimper f; ~let ['aɪlɪt] n Öse f; ~-level adj attr grill in Augenhöhe; ~lid n Augenlid nt; ~ liner n Eyeliner m; ~-opener n that was a real ~-opener to me das hat mir die Augen geöffnet; ~shadow n Lidschatten m; ~sight n Sehkraft f; to have good ~sight gute Augen haben; to lose one's ~sight das Augenlicht verlieren (geh), erblinden; ~sore n Schandfleck m; this carpet is a real ~sore dieser Teppich beleidigt das Auge; ~strain n Überanstrengung f der Augen; ~ tooth n Eckzahn m; ~wash n (fig col) Gewäsch nt (col); (deception) Augenwischerei f; ~witness n Augenzeuge m.
eyrie ['ɪərɪ] n Horst m.

F

F, f [ef] *n* F, f *nt*. ~ **sharp** Fis, fis *nt*.
F = **Fahrenheit** F.
fable ['feɪbl] *n* Fabel *f*; (*fig*: *lie*) Märchen *nt*.
fabric ['fæbrɪk] *n* (**a**) (*Tex*) Stoff *m*. (**b**) (*of building*) Bausubstanz *f*; (*of society*) Struktur *f*.
fabricate ['fæbrɪkeɪt] *vt* (**a**) *story* erfinden. (**b**) (*manufacture*) herstellen.
fabrication [ˌfæbrɪ'keɪʃən] *n* (**a**) (*lie etc*) Erfindung *f*. (**b**) (*manufacture*) Herstellung *f*.
fabulous ['fæbjʊləs] *adj* sagenhaft (*also col*).
façade [fə'sɑːd] *n* (*lit, fig*) Fassade *f*.
face [feɪs] **1** *n* Gesicht *nt*; (*of clock*) Zifferblatt *nt*; (*rock* ~) (Steil)wand *f*; (*coal* ~) Streb *m*; (*of playing card*) Bildseite *f*; (*of coin*) Vorderseite *f*. **I don't want to see your** ~ **here again** ich möchte Sie hier nie wieder sehen; **we were standing** ~ **to** ~ wir standen einander gegenüber; **to bring two people** ~ **to** ~ zwei Leute einander gegenüberstellen; **to come** ~ **to** ~ **with sb/death** jdn treffen/dem Tod ins Auge sehen; **he told him so to his** ~ er sagte ihm das (offen) ins Gesicht; **he shut the door in my** ~ er schlug mir die Tür vor der Nase zu; **he laughed in my** ~ er lachte mir ins Gesicht; **to look/be able to look sb in the** ~ jdn ansehen/jdm in die Augen sehen können; **in the** ~ **of great difficulties** trotz größter Schwierigkeiten; **courage in the** ~ **of the enemy** Tapferkeit vor dem Feind; **to make** *or* **pull a** ~ das Gesicht verziehen; **to make** *or* **pull** ~**s** Grimassen schneiden (*at sb* jdm); **to put a good** ~ **on it** gute Miene zum bösen Spiel machen; **to put a brave** ~ **on it** sich (*dat*) nichts anmerken lassen; (*do sth one dislikes*) (wohl oder übel) in den sauren Apfel beißen; **to save/lose** ~ das Gesicht wahren/verlieren; **to be** ~ **up/down** (*person*) mit dem Gesicht nach oben/unten liegen; (*thing*) mit der Vorderseite nach oben/unten liegen; **to work at the (coal)** ~ vor Ort arbeiten; **the** ~ **of the town** das Stadtbild; **he vanished off the** ~ **of the earth** (*col*) er war wie vom Erdboden verschwunden; **on the** ~ **of it** so, wie es aussieht; **to have the** ~ **to do sth** (*col*) die Stirn haben, etw zu tun.
2 *vt* (**a**) (*be opposite*) gegenübersein/-stehen/ -liegen *etc* (+*dat*); (*window, door*) north, south gehen nach; *street, garden etc* liegen zu; (*building, room*) north, south liegen nach. ~ **this way!** bitte sehen Sie hierher!; **he was facing me at dinner** er saß mir beim Essen gegenüber; **the picture facing page 16** die Abbildung gegenüber Seite 16; **to sit facing the engine** in Fahrtrichtung sitzen.
(**b**) (*fig*) *possibility, prospect* rechnen müssen mit. **to be** ~**d with sth** sich einer Sache (*dat*) gegenübersehen; **he is facing a charge of murder** er steht unter Mordanklage.
(**c**) *situation, danger, criticism* ins Auge sehen (+*dat*); *person, enemy* gegenübertreten (+*dat*). **to** ~ **(the) facts** den Tatsachen ins Auge sehen; **let's** ~ **it** machen wir uns doch nichts vor; **I can't** ~ **it** ich bringe es einfach nicht über mich; **I couldn't** ~ **another drink** ich könnte jetzt nichts Alkoholisches mehr verkraften.
(**d**) *building, wall* verkleiden.
3 *vi* (*house, room*) liegen (*towards park* dem Park zu, *onto road* zur Straße, *away from road*

nicht zur Straße); (*window*) gehen (*onto, towards* auf +*acc*, zu, *away from* nicht auf +*acc*). **in which direction was he facing?** in welche Richtung stand er?
♦ **face up to** *vi* +*prep obj fact, truth* ins Gesicht sehen (+*dat*); *possibility* sich abfinden mit; *responsibility* auf sich (*acc*) nehmen. **he won't** ~ ~ ~ **the fact that** ... er will es nicht wahrhaben, daß ...
face *in cpds* Gesichts-; ~**cloth** *n* (*Brit*) Waschlappen *m*; ~ **cream** *n* Gesichtscreme *f*; ~**less** *adj* (*fig*) anonym; ~**lift** *n* (*lit*) Gesichts(haut)straffung *f*; (*fig*: *for car, building etc*) Verschönerung *f*; **to have a** ~**lift** sich (*dat*) das Gesicht liften lassen; (*fig*) ein neues Aussehen bekommen; ~**pack** *n* Gesichtspackung *f*; ~**-saving** *adj* a ~**-saving excuse** eine Entschuldigung, um das Gesicht zu wahren.
facet ['fæsɪt] *n* (*lit*) Facette *f*; (*fig*) Aspekt *m*.
facetious [fə'siːʃəs] *adj* witzelnd. **to be** ~ (**about sth**) (über etw *acc*) Witze machen.
face: ~**-to-**~ *adj* persönlich; *confrontation* direkt; ~ **value** *n* (*Fin*) Nennwert *m*; **to take sth at (its)** ~ **value** (*fig*) etw für bare Münze nehmen; **to take sb at** ~ **value** jdm unbesehen glauben.
facial ['feɪʃəl] **1** *adj* Gesichts-. **2** *n* (*col*) kosmetische Gesichtsbehandlung.
facile ['fæsaɪl] *adj* (**a**) (*glib, superficial*) oberflächlich. (**b**) (*easy*) *victory* leicht.
facilitate [fə'sɪlɪteɪt] *vt* erleichtern; (*make possible*) ermöglichen.
facility [fə'sɪlɪtɪ] *n* (**a**) Einrichtung *f*; (*possibility*) Möglichkeit *f*. **facilities for the disabled** Einrichtungen für Behinderte; **cooking facilities** Kochgelegenheit *f*. (**b**) *no pl* (*ease*) Leichtigkeit *f*; (*dexterity*) Gewandtheit *f*.
facing ['feɪsɪŋ] *n* (*on wall*) Verkleidung *f*; (*Sew*) Besatz *m*.
facsimile [fæk'sɪmɪlɪ] *n* (**a**) Faksimile *nt*. (**b**) (*Telec*) Telebrief *m*.
fact [fækt] *n* Tatsache *f*. **to know for a** ~ **that** (es) ganz sicher wissen, daß; **the** ~ **is that** ... die Sache ist die, daß ...; **to stick to the** ~**s** bei den Tatsachen bleiben; **is that a** ~? tatsächlich?; **the** ~ **that** ... (die Tatsache,) daß ...; ~ **and fiction** Dichtung und Wahrheit; **founded on** ~ auf Tatsachen beruhend; **to tell sb the** ~**s of life** jdn aufklären; **the** ~**s of the case** der Sachverhalt; **in** ~, **as a matter of** ~ eigentlich; (*to intensify previous statement*) sogar; **I bet you haven't done that!** — **as a matter of** ~ **I have!** du hast das bestimmt nicht gemacht! — oh doch!; **do you know Sir Charles?** — **as a matter of** ~ **he's my uncle** kennen Sie Sir Charles? — ja, er ist nämlich mein Onkel.
fact-finding ['fæktfaɪndɪŋ] *adj commission* Untersuchungs-; *mission* Erkundungs-.
faction ['fækʃən] *n* (*group*) Gruppe *f*; (*Pol*) Fraktion *f*; (*splinter group*) Splittergruppe *f*.
factor ['fæktəʳ] *n* Faktor *m*.
factory ['fæktərɪ] *n* Fabrik *f*.
factory: ~ **farming** *n* Aufzucht *f* von Tieren in automatisierten Farmen; ~ **inspector** *n* Gewerbeaufsichtsbeamte(r) *m*; ~ **worker** *n* Fabrikarbeiter(in *f*) *m*.
factual ['fæktjʊəl] *adj* sachlich, Tatsachen-. ~ **er-**

ror Sachfehler m.

faculty ['fækəltɪ] n (a) Fähigkeit f. ~ of reason Vernunft f; ~ of speech/sight Sprechvermögen/ Sehvermögen nt; to be in (full) possession of one's faculties im Vollbesitz seiner Kräfte sein. (b) (Univ) Fakultät f. the F~ (staff) der Lehrkörper.

fad [fæd] n Tick m (col); (fashion) Masche f (col).

fade [feɪd] vi verblassen; (flower, beauty) verblühen. he ~d from sight er verschwand; see fade away.

♦ **fade away** vi (memory) verblassen; (hopes) zerrinnen; (interest, strength, inspiration) nachlassen; (sound) verklingen; (voice) immer schwächer werden.

♦ **fade in** vt sep (TV, Film) allmählich einblenden.

♦ **fade out 1** vi (a) (TV, Film) abblenden. (b) to ~ ~ of sb's life aus jds Leben verschwinden. 2 vt sep (TV, Film) abblenden.

faeces, (US) **feces** ['fiːsiːz] n pl Kot m.

fag [fæg] n (a) (Brit: cigarette) Zigarette f, Glimmstengel m (col). (b) (Brit Sch) junger Internatsschüler, der einem älteren bestimmte Dienste zu leisten hat. (c) (esp US col: homosexual) Schwule(r) m (col). 2 vt to be ~ged (out) kaputt or geschafft sein (col).

fag end n (a) (Brit col: cigarette end) Kippe f (col). (b) (col: last part) letztes Ende.

faggot, (US) **fagot** ['fægət] n (a) Reisigbündel nt. (b) (Cook) Frikadelle f. (c) (esp US col: homosexual) Schwule(r) m (col).

Fahrenheit ['færənhaɪt] n Fahrenheit nt.

fail [feɪl] 1 vi (a) keinen Erfolg haben; (in mission, life etc) versagen; (plan, experiment, marriage) scheitern; (undertaking, attempt) fehlschlagen; (applicant, application) nicht angenommen werden; (election candidate, in exam, play) durchfallen; (business) eingehen. they ~ed (in doing sth) es gelang ihnen nicht(, etw zu tun); to ~ in one's duty seine Pflicht nicht tun; to ~ by 5 votes (person) um 5 Stimmen geschlagen werden; if all else ~s wenn alle Stricke reißen. (b) (health) sich verschlechtern; (hearing, eyesight) nachlassen. he is ~ing fast sein Zustand verschlechtert sich zusehends. (c) (generator, battery) ausfallen; (brakes, heart) versagen; (supply) ausbleiben. the crops ~ed die Ernte fiel aus.

2 vt (a) candidate durchfallen lassen. to ~ an exam eine Prüfung nicht bestehen. (b) (let down: person, memory) im Stich lassen; (not live up to sb's expectations) enttäuschen. words ~ me mir fehlen die Worte. (c) to ~ to do sth etw nicht tun; (neglect) (es) versäumen, etw zu tun; I ~ to see why es ist mir völlig unklar, warum; (indignantly) ich sehe gar nicht ein, warum.

3 n without ~ ganz bestimmt; (inevitably) garantiert.

failing ['feɪlɪŋ] 1 n Schwäche f. 2 prep ~ an answer mangels (einer) Antwort (geh); ~ him see if Harry knows und wenn er es nicht weiß, versuch es bei Harry; ~ this/that (oder) sonst, und wenn das nicht möglich ist.

fail-safe ['feɪlseɪf] adj device (ab)gesichert.

failure ['feɪljər] n (a) Mißerfolg m; (of plan, experiment, marriage) Scheitern nt; (of undertaking, attempt) Fehlschlag m; (in exam, Theat: of play also) Durchfall m; (of business) Eingehen nt. it ended in ~ es schlug fehl. (b) (person) Versager m, Niete f (col) (at in +dat). (c) (omission, neglect) because of his ~ to reply weil er es versäumt hat zu antworten; to ~ observe a law Nichtbeachtung f eines Gesetzes; that was a ~ on my part das war mein Fehler. (d) (of generator, engine) Ausfall m; (of brakes, heart) Versagen nt; (of supply) Ausbleiben nt. ~ of crops Ernteausfall m.

faint [feɪnt] 1 adj (+er) (a) schwach; voice (feeble) matt; (distant, not loud) leise. I haven't the ~est (idea) ich habe keinen blassen Schimmer (col).

(b) I feel a bit ~ mir ist ganz schwach; she felt ~ ihr wurde schwach; ~ with hunger schwach vor Hunger. 2 n Ohnmacht f. 3 vi ohnmächtig werden (with, from vor +dat).

faint-hearted [ˌfeɪnt'hɑːtɪd] adj zaghaft.

faintly ['feɪntlɪ] adv schwach; hope, sound leise; smell, smile, interested leicht; similar, resemble entfernt.

faintness ['feɪntnɪs] n (dizziness) Schwächegefühl nt.

fair[1] [feər] 1 adj (+er) (a) (just) fair (to/on sb jdm gegenüber, gegen jdn). that's a ~ comment das stimmt; it's only ~ to ask him man sollte ihn fairerweise fragen; it's only ~ to expect ... man kann doch wohl zu Recht erwarten ...; ~ enough! na gut; that's ~ enough das ist nur recht und billig; ~'s ~! wir wollen doch fair bleiben; by ~ means or foul ohne Rücksicht auf Verluste (col); that's a ~ sample of ... das ist ziemlich typisch für ...

(b) (reasonable) ganz ordentlich. only ~ nur mäßig; he's a ~ judge of character er hat eine gute Menschenkenntnis; to have a ~ idea of sth eine ungefähre Vorstellung von etw haben; a ~ chance of success recht gute Erfolgsaussichten pl.

(c) (reasonably large, fast, strong) sum, number ansehnlich; wind frisch. a ~ amount ziemlich viel; at a ~ speed ziemlich schnell.

(d) (fine) weather heiter. the ~ sex das schöne Geschlecht.

(e) person (light-haired) blond; (light-skinned) hell.

2 adv to play ~ (Sport) fair spielen; (fig) fair sein; ~ and square (honestly) offen und ehrlich; (accurately, directly) direkt; it ~ took my breath away (col) das hat mir glatt den Atem verschlagen.

fair[2] n (Jahr)markt m; (Brit: fun ~) Volksfest nt, Rummel m (col); (Comm) Messe f.

fair: ~ copy n Reinschrift f; to write out a ~ copy of sth etw ins reine schreiben; ~ game n (lit) jagdbares Wild; (fig) Freiwild nt; ~ground n see **fair**[2] Markt(platz) m; Rummelplatz m; ~-haired adj blond; ~-haired boy n (US) Liebling m.

fairly ['feəlɪ] adv (a) (justly) gerecht. ~ and squarely beaten nach allen Regeln der Kunst geschlagen. (b) (rather) ziemlich. it's ~ freezing (col) es ist ganz schön kalt (col).

fair-minded ['feəmaɪndɪd] adj gerecht.

fairness ['feənɪs] n (a) Fairneß f. in all ~ fairerweise; in (all) ~ to him, he didn't have the same chance; fairerweise muß man sagen, daß er nicht die gleichen Chancen hatte. (b) (of hair) Blondheit f; (of skin) Hellhäutigkeit f.

fair: ~ play n (Sport, fig) faires Verhalten, Fair play nt; ~-sized adj recht groß; ~-weather adj friends nur in guten Zeiten.

fairy ['feərɪ] n (a) Fee f. (b) (pej col: homosexual) Schwule(r) m (col), Tunte f (col).

fairy: ~ godmother n (lit, fig) gute Fee; ~land n Märchenland nt; ~ lights npl bunte Lichter pl; ~ queen n Elfenkönigin f; ~ story n, ~-tale n (lit, fig) Märchen nt.

fait accompli [ˌfeɪtəˈkɒmpliː] n to present sb with a ~ jdn vor vollendete Tatsachen stellen.

faith [feɪθ] n (a) (trust) Vertrauen nt (in zu); (in human nature, science etc, religious ~) Glaube m (in an +acc). to have ~ in sb jdm (ver)trauen; to have ~ in sth Vertrauen in etw (acc) haben; act of ~ Vertrauensbeweis m; to keep/break ~ with sb jdm treu bleiben/untreu werden; to act in good/bad ~ in gutem Glauben/böser Absicht handeln. (b) (religion) Glaube m no pl.

faithful ['feɪθfʊl] 1 adj (a) treu (to +dat). (b) account, translation getreu. 2 npl the ~ (Rel) die Gläubigen pl.

faithfully ['feɪθfəlɪ] adv (a) treu; promise fest. (b)

report etc genau; *translate* wortgetreu.

faithfulness ['feιθfʊlnιs] n (*loyalty*) Treue *f (to* zu).

faith: ~ **healer** n Gesundbeter(in *f*) m; ~ **healing** n Gesundbeten nt; ~**less** adj treulos.

fake [feιk] **1** n (*object*) Fälschung *f*; (*jewellery*) Imitation *f*; (*person: trickster*) Schwindler(in *f*) m. **2** vt vortäuschen; *picture, document, results etc* fälschen; *bill, burglary, crash* fingieren.

falcon ['fɔːlkən] n Falke m.

fall [fɔːl] (*vb: pret* **fell,** *ptp* **fallen**) **1** n (**a**) Sturz, Fall m; (*of empire etc*) Untergang m. **the F**~ (**of Man**) (*Eccl*) der Sündenfall; **to have a** ~ (hin)fallen, stürzen; **it's a long** ~ **from up here** von hier oben geht es tief hinunter. (**b**) (*of town, fortress etc*) Einnahme *f*; (*of country*) Zusammenbruch m; (*of government*) Sturz m. (**c**) ~ **of rain/snow** Regen-/Schneefall m; ~ **of rock** Steinschlag m. (**d**) (*in gen*) (*lowering*) Sinken nt; (*sudden*) Sturz m; (*in population, membership*) Abnahme *f*; (*of prices, currency*) (*gradual*) Sinken nt; (*sudden*) Sturz m. (**e**) (*of roof, ground*) Gefälle nt; (*steeper*) Abfall m. (**f**) (*water*~: *also* ~s) Wasserfall m. **the Niagara F**~**s** die Niagarafälle. (**g**) (*Wrestling*) Schultersieg m. (**h**) (*US: autumn*) Herbst m. **in the** ~ im Herbst.

2 vi (**a**) fallen; (*Sport, from a height, badly*) stürzen; (*object: to the ground*) herunter-/hinunterfallen.

(**b**) (*temperature, price*) fallen; (*population, membership etc*) abnehmen; (*wind*) sich legen; (*land*) abfallen. **his face fell** er machte ein langes Gesicht; **to** ~ **in sb's estimation** *or* **eyes** in jds Achtung (*dat*) sinken.

(**c**) (*country*) eingenommen werden; (*government, ruler*) gestürzt werden. **three seats fell to the SDP** drei Sitze gingen an die SDP.

(**d**) (*night*) hereinbrechen.

(**e**) (*birthday, Easter etc*) fallen (*on* auf +*acc*). **that** ~**s outside the scope ...** das fällt nicht in den Bereich ...; **to** ~ **into three sections** sich in drei Teile gliedern.

(**f**) (*phrases*) **her eyes fell on a strange object** ihr Blick fiel auf einen merkwürdigen Gegenstand; **the responsibility** ~**s** *on* you Sie tragen die Verantwortung; **it** ~**s to** *or* **on me to ...** es fällt mir zu, zu ...; **the blame for that** ~**s on him** ihn trifft die Schuld daran; **to** ~ **asleep** einschlafen; **to** ~ **ill** krank werden, erkranken (*geh*); **to** ~ **silent** still werden; **it's all** ~**ing into place now** jetzt wird mir das Ganze klar; **to** ~ **into a deep sleep** in tiefen Schlaf fallen; **to** ~ **into bad ways** auf die schiefe Bahn geraten; **to** ~ **to doing sth** anfangen, etw zu tun.

3 vt **to** ~ **a victim to sb/sth** jdm/einer Sache zum Opfer fallen.

♦**fall about** vi (*laughing*) sich krank lachen (*col*).

♦**fall apart** vi auseinanderfallen; (*fig: marriage etc*) auseinanderbrechen.

♦**fall away** vi (**a**) (*ground*) abfallen. (**b**) (*crumble: plaster, river bank*) abbröckeln (*from* von).

♦**fall back** vi zurückweichen (*also* Mil).

♦**fall back on** vi +*prep obj* zurückgreifen auf (+*acc*).

♦**fall behind** vi (*in race, school etc*) zurückbleiben (*prep obj*) hinter +*dat*); (*with rent, work etc*) in Rückstand geraten.

♦**fall down** vi (*person*) hinfallen; (*statue, vase*) herunterfallen; (*house, scaffolding*) einstürzen. **where he/the plan** ~**s** **is ...** (*fig*) woran es ihm/dem Plan fehlt, ist ...; **that was where we fell** ~ (*fig*) daran sind wir gescheitert; **he's been** ~**ing** ~ **on the job** (*fig*) er hat schlechte Arbeit geleistet.

♦**fall for** vi +*prep obj* (**a**) (*fall in love with*) sich verknallen in (+*acc*) (*col*). **I really fell** ~ **him/it** er/das hatte es mir angetan. (**b**) (*be taken in by*) hereinfallen auf (+*acc*).

♦**fall in** vi (**a**) (*into water etc*) hineinfallen. (**b**)

(*collapse*) einstürzen. (**c**) (*Mil*) (in Reih und Glied) antreten; (*one soldier*) ins Glied treten.

♦**fall in with** vi +*prep obj* (**a**) (*meet*) sich anschließen (+*dat*); *bad company* geraten in (+*acc*). (**b**) (*agree to*) mitmachen bei; *request* unterstützen.

♦**fall off** vi (**a**) (*lit*) herunterfallen (*prep obj* von). (**b**) (*decrease*) zurückgehen; (*supporters*) abfallen; (*support, enthusiasm*) nachlassen.

♦**fall out** vi (**a**) (*of bed, boat, window*) herausfallen. **to** ~ ~ **of sth** aus etw fallen. (**b**) (*quarrel*) sich (zer)streiten. (**c**) (*Mil*) wegtreten. (**d**) (*happen*) **just wait and see how things** ~ ~ wart erst mal ab, wie alles wird; **if everything** ~**s** ~ **all right** wenn alles wunschgemäß verläuft.

♦**fall over** vi (**a**) (*person*) hinfallen; (*collapse*) umfallen. (**b**) +*prep obj* (*trip over*) *stone, sb's legs* fallen über (+*acc*). **to** ~ ~ **oneself to do sth** sich (*dat*) die größte Mühe geben, etw zu tun.

♦**fall through** vi (*plan*) ins Wasser fallen.

♦**fall to** vi (*col*) (*start eating*) sich dranmachen (*col*); (*start fighting, working*) loslegen (*col*).

fallacious [fə'leιʃəs] adj irrig; *argument* trugschlüssig.

fallacy ['fæləsι] n Irrtum m; (*in logic*) Trugschluß m.

fallen ['fɔːlən] **1** ptp of **fall. 2** adj *women, angel* gefallen; *leaf* abgefallen. **3** npl **the F**~ (*Mil*) die Gefallenen pl.

fallible ['fæləbl] adj fehlbar.

falling star ['fɔːlιŋ'stɑːᵣ] n Sternschnuppe *f*.

fall-off ['fɔːlɒf] n (*in gen*) Rückgang m; (*in numbers, attendances*) Abfall m; (*in support*) Nachlassen nt.

Fallopian tube [fə'ləʊpιən'tjuːb] n Eileiter m.

fall-out ['fɔːlaʊt] n radioaktiver Niederschlag, Fallout m. ~ **shelter** Atombunker m.

fallow ['fæləʊ] adj *land* brach. **to lie** ~ brachliegen.

false [fɔːls] adj falsch; *lover* treulos; *ceiling, floor* Zwischen-. **under** ~ **pretences** (*Brit*) *or* **pretenses** (*US*) unter Vorspiegelung falscher Tatsachen; **a box with a** ~ **bottom** ein Kiste mit doppeltem Boden.

false alarm n blinder Alarm.

falsehood ['fɔːlshʊd] n (*lie*) Unwahrheit *f*.

falsely ['fɔːlslι] adv falsch; *believe, claim, declare* fälschlicherweise; *accuse* zu Unrecht.

falseness ['fɔːlsnιs] n Falschheit *f*; (*of lover etc*) Untreue *f*.

false: ~ **start** n Fehlstart m; ~ **teeth** npl (*Brit*) (künstliches) Gebiß.

falsetto [fɔːl'setəʊ] **1** n (*voice*) Fistelstimme *f*. **2** adv *sing* im Falsett.

falsies ['fɔːlsιz] npl (*col*) Gummibusen m (*col*).

falsify ['fɔːlsιfaι] vt *records, evidence* fälschen; *report, story* entstellen.

falter ['fɔːltəᵣ] vi (*speaking*) stocken; (*steps, horse*) zögern.

fame [feιm] n Ruhm m. **to win** ~ sich (*dat*) einen Namen machen.

familiar [fə'mιljəᵣ] adj (*surroundings, sight, scene* vertraut; *street, person, feeling, phrase, song* bekannt; *complaint, event* häufig. **his face looks** ~ **es das Gesicht ist mir bekannt; it looks very** ~ **es** kommt mir sehr bekannt vor; **that sounds** ~ **das** habe ich schon mal gehört; **to be on** ~ **ground with sth** in etw (*dat*) zu Hause sein; **to be** ~ **with sb/sth** mit jdm/etw vertraut sein; **to make oneself** ~ **with sth** sich mit etw vertraut machen. (**b**) (*friendly*) *language, gesture* familiär; (*overfriendly*) plump-vertraulich. **the** ~ **term of address** die vertraute Anrede; **to be on** ~ **terms with sb** mit jdm auf vertrautem Fuß stehen; ~ **language/expressions** Umgangssprache *f* umgangssprachliche Ausdrücke pl.

familiarity [fə,mιlι'ærιtι] n (**a**) *no pl* (*knowledge*) Vertrautheit *f*. (**b**) (*between people*) vertrautes Verhältnis; (*of language etc*) Familiarität *f*; (*pej*) plumpe Vertraulichkeit. ~ **breeds contempt**

(Prov) allzu große Vertrautheit erzeugt Verachtung.

familiarize [fə'mɪlɪəraɪz] *vt* **to** ~ **sb/oneself with sth** jdn/sich mit etw vertraut machen.

family ['fæmɪlɪ] *n* Familie *f; (including cousins, aunts etc)* Verwandtschaft *f.* **to start a** ~ eine Familie gründen; **has he any** ~? hat er Familie?; **it runs in the** ~ das liegt in der Familie; **he's one of the** ~ er gehört zur Familie.

family: ~ **allowance** *n* Kindergeld *nt;* ~ **doctor** *n* Hausarzt *m*/-ärztin *f;* ~ **man** *n (home-loving)* häuslich veranlagter Mann; *(with a* ~*)* Familienvater *m;* ~ **planning** *n* Familienplanung *f;* ~ **planning clinic** *n* Familienberatungsstelle *f;* ~**-size** *adj* in Haushaltsgröße; *car, packets* Familien-; ~ **tree** *n* Stammbaum *m.*

famine ['fæmɪn] *n* Hungersnot *f.*

famished ['fæmɪʃt] *adj (col)* **I'm absolutely** ~ ich sterbe vor Hunger *(col).*

famous ['feɪməs] *adj* berühmt *(for* durch, für*).*

famously ['feɪməslɪ] *adv (dated col)* famos *(dated).*

fan¹ [fæn] **1** *n (hand-held)* Fächer *m; (mechanical, extractor* ~*, Aut)* Ventilator *m.* **2** *vt (wind)* umwehen; *(person)* fächeln *(+dat).* **to** ~ **sb/oneself** jdm/sich (Luft) zufächeln; **to** ~ **the flames** *(fig)* Öl ins Feuer gießen.

♦ **fan out** *vi (troops, searchers)* ausschwärmen.

fan² *n (supporter)* Fan *m.*

fanatic [fə'nætɪk] *n* Fanatiker(in *f*) *m.*

fanatic(al) [fə'nætɪk(əl)] *adj* fanatisch.

fanaticism [fə'nætɪsɪzəm] *n* Fanatismus *m.*

fan belt *n* Keilriemen *m.*

fancier ['fænsɪə'] *n* Liebhaber(in *f*) *m.*

fanciful ['fænsɪfʊl] *adj story, idea* phantastisch; *explanation* weit hergeholt; *pattern* phantasievoll.

fan club *n* Fanclub *m.*

fancy ['fænsɪ] **1** *n* **a** *passing* ~ nur so eine Laune; **he's taken a** ~ **to her** sie hat es ihm angetan; **to take** *or* **catch sb's** ~ jdm gefallen; **to tickle sb's** ~ jdn reizen; **just as the** ~ **takes me/you** ganz nach Lust und Laune.

2 *vt* **(a)** ~ **that!** so was!; ~ **seeing you here!** so was, Sie hier zu sehen!; ~ **him winning!** wer hätte gedacht, daß er gewinnt!; **I rather** ~ **he has gone out** ich glaube, er ist weggegangen.

(b) *(like)* **he fancies the idea/her** die Idee/sie gefällt ihm; **he fancies a house on Crete** *(would like to have)* er hätte gern ein Haus auf Kreta; **he fancies a walk/steak** er hat Lust zu einem Spaziergang/auf ein Steak; **I don't** ~ **the idea** ich habe keine Lust dazu; **I didn't** ~ **that job** die Stelle hat mich nicht gereizt; **he fancies his chances** er meint, er hätte Chancen; **I don't** ~ **my chances of getting that job** ich rechne mir keine großen Chancen aus, die Stelle zu bekommen; **he really fancies himself** er ist stark von sich eingenommen; **he fancies himself as an actor** er hält sich für einen (guten) Schauspieler.

3 *adj* *(+er) (elaborate)* hairdo, footwork kunstvoll; *(unusual) food, pattern, cigarettes, furnishings* ausgefallen; *baking, cakes, bread* fein; *(col) gadget, car* etc schick *(col); idea* überspannt; *cure* seltsam; *price* gepfeffert *(col).* **nothing** ~ etwas ganz Einfaches.

fancy: ~ **dress** *n* (Masken)kostüm *nt;* **in** ~ **dress** verkleidet, kostümiert; ~**-dress ball/party** *n* Maskenball *m*/Kostümfest *nt;* ~ **goods** *npl* Geschenkartikel *pl;* ~ **man** *n (col: lover)* Liebhaber *m;* ~ **woman** *n (col)* Freundin *f.*

fanfare ['fænfeə'] *n* Fanfare *f.*

fang [fæŋ] *n* Fang *m; (of snake)* Giftzahn *m.*

fan: ~ **heater** *n* Heizlüfter *m;* ~**light** *n* Oberlicht *nt;* ~ **mail** *n* Verehrerpost *f.*

fantasize ['fæntəsaɪz] *vi* phantasieren.

fantastic [fæn'tæstɪk] *adj* phantastisch.

fantasy ['fæntəzɪ] *n* Phantasie *f.*

far [fɑː'] *see also comp* **further, farther,** *superl*

furthest, farthest 1 *adv* weit. **not** ~ **(away) from here** nicht weit von hier; **I'll go with you as** ~ **as the gate** ich komme/gehe bis zum Tor mit; ~ **and wide** weit und breit; **from** ~ **and wide** von nah und fern; ~ **above** hoch über *(+dat);* ~ **away** weit weg; ~ **away in the distance** weit in der Ferne; ~ **into the jungle** weit in den Dschungel hinein; **I won't be** ~ **away** ich bin ganz in der Nähe; ~ **out** weit draußen; **have you come** ~? kommen Sie von weit her?; **as** ~ **back as I can remember** so weit ich mich erinnern kann; **as** ~ **back as 1945;** schon (im Jahr) 1945; ~ **into the night** bis spät in die Nacht; ~ **longer/better** weit länger/besser; **it's** ~ **beyond what I can afford** das übersteigt meine Mittel bei weitem; **as** ~ **as I'm concerned** was mich betrifft; **it's all right as** ~ **as it goes** das ist soweit ganz gut; **in so** ~ **as insofern als;** ~ **and away the best, by** ~ **the best** bei weitem der/die/das Beste; ~ **from satisfactory** alles andere als befriedigend; ~ **from liking him** I find him quite unpleasant nicht nur, daß ich ihn nicht leiden kann, ich finde ihn sogar ausgesprochen unsympatisch; ~ **from it!** ganz und gar nicht; ~ **be it from me to** ... es sei mir fern, zu ...; **so** ~ *(up to now)* bis jetzt; *(up to this point)* soweit; **so** ~ **so good** so weit, so gut; **so** ~ **and no further** bis hierher und nicht weiter; **to go** ~ *(money, supplies* etc*)* weit reichen; *(person: succeed)* es weit bringen; **I would go so** ~ **as to say** ... ich würde so weit gehen zu sagen ...; **that's going too** ~ das geht zu weit; **to carry a joke too** ~ einen Spaß zu weit treiben; **not** ~ **out** *(in guess)* nicht schlecht; **not** ~ **off** *(in guess, aim)* fast; ~ **gone** *(col: drunk)* schon ziemlich hinüber *(col).*

2 *adj* **country** weit entfernt. **the** ~ **end of the room** das andere Ende des Zimmers; **the** ~ **window/wall** das Fenster/die Wand am anderen Ende des Zimmers; **the** ~ **one** das da drüben; **in the** ~ **distance** in weiter Ferne; **it's a** ~ **cry from** ... *(fig)* das ist etwas ganz anderes als ...; **it's a** ~ **cry from what she promised** at first ursprünglich hat sie etwas ganz anderes versprochen.

faraway ['fɑːrəweɪ] *adj attr place* abgelegen; *(fig: dreamy)* verträumt.

farce [fɑːs] *n (Theat, fig)* Farce *f.*

farcical ['fɑːsɪkəl] *adj (fig: absurd)* absurd.

fare [feə'] **1** *n* **a** *(charge)* Fahrpreis *m; (on plane)* Flugpreis *m; (on boat)* Preis *m* für die Überfahrt; *(money)* Fahrgeld *nt.* **what is the** ~? was kostet die Fahrt/der Flug/die Überfahrt? **(b)** *(old, form: food)* Kost *f.* **2** *vi* **he** ~**d well** es ging ihm gut; **how did you** ~ wie erging es dir?

Far East *n* **the** ~ der Ferne Osten.

fare stage *n* Fahrzone *f.*

farewell [feə'wel] **1** *n* Abschied *m.* **to bid sb** ~ jdm auf Wiedersehen sagen. **2** *interj (old)* leb(e) wohl *(dated).*

farewell *in cpds* Abschieds-.

far: ~**-fetched** *adj* weithergeholt *attr,* weit hergeholt *pred;* ~**-flung** *adj (distant)* abgelegen.

farm [fɑːm] **1** *n* Bauernhof *m; (bigger)* Gut(shof *m*) *nt; (in US, Australia)* Farm *f.* **2** *attr produce, buildings* Landwirtschafts-; *labourer* Land-. ~ **animals** Tiere auf dem Bauernhof. **3** *vt land* bebauen. **4** *vi* Landwirtschaft betreiben.

♦ **farm out** *vt sep work* vergeben *(on, to* an *+acc); children* in Pflege geben *(to* dat, bei*).*

farmer ['fɑːmə'] *n* Bauer *m; (in US, Australia)* Farmer *m; (gentleman* ~*)* Gutsherr *m; (tenant* ~*)* Pächter *m.* ~**'s wife** Bäuerin *f.*

farm: ~**hand** *n* Landarbeiter *m; (living on small farm)* Knecht *m;* ~**house** *n* Bauernhaus *nt.*

farming ['fɑːmɪŋ] *n* Landwirtschaft *f; (animals also)* Viehzucht *f.*

farm: ~ **land** *n* Ackerland *nt;* ~**yard** *n* Hof *m.*

Far North *n* **the** ~ der Hohe Norden.

far: ~**-off** *adj* (weit)entfernt; ~**-reaching** *adj* weitreichend; ~**-sighted** *adj (lit)* weitsichtig;

(fig) person weitblickend; *(taking precautionary measures)* umsichtig; *measures* auf weite Sicht geplant.

fart [faːt] *(col)* **1** *n* Furz *m (col!).* **2** *vi* furzen *(col!).*

farther ['faːðəʳ] *comp of* **far 1** *adv see* **further 1 (a).** **2** *adj* **at the ~ end** am anderen Ende.

farthest ['faːðɪst] *adj, adv superl of* **far** *see* **furthest 1, 2.**

farthing ['faːðɪŋ] *n (old Brit)* Viertelpenny *m.*

fascia ['feɪʃə] *n (Brit Aut)* Armaturentafel *f.*

fascinate ['fæsɪneɪt] *vt* faszinieren. **it ~s me how ...** ich finde es erstaunlich, wie ...

fascinating ['fæsɪneɪtɪŋ] *adj* faszinierend.

fascination [ˌfæsɪ'neɪʃən] *n* Faszination *f.* **to have a ~ for sb** auf jdn einen besonderen Reiz ausüben; **his ~ with the cinema** die Faszination, die das Kino auf ihn ausübt.

fascism ['fæʃɪzəm] *n* Faschismus *m.*

fascist ['fæʃɪst] **1** *n* Faschist(in *f*) *m.* **2** *adj* faschistisch.

fashion ['fæʃən] **1** *n* **(a)** *no pl (manner)* Art (und Weise) *f.* **in the Indian ~** nach Art der Indianer; **in the usual ~** wie üblich; **well, after a ~** na ja, so einigermaßen; **to do sth after** *or* **in a ~** etw schlecht und recht machen. **(b)** *(in clothing, latest style)* Mode *f.* **in ~** modern; **it's the/all the ~** es ist Mode/große Mode; **to come into/go out of ~** in Mode/aus der Mode kommen; **ladies' ~s** die Damenmode. **(c)** *(custom)* **it was the ~ in those days** das war damals Sitte. **2** *vt* gestalten.

fashionable ['fæʃnəbl] *adj clothes, person* modisch; *illness, colour* Mode-; *area, address* vornehm; *pub, artist, author* in Mode. **it's (very) ~** es ist (große) Mode.

fashion *in cpds* Mode-; **~ designer** *n* Modezeichner(in *f*) *m;* **~ model** *n* Mannequin *nt; (man)* Dressman *m;* **~ parade** *n* Mode(n)schau *f;* **~ show** *n* Mode(n)schau *f.*

fast¹ [faːst] **1** *adj (+er)* **(a)** schnell; *film* hochempfindlich. **he's a ~ worker** *(lit)* er arbeitet schnell; *(fig)* er geht mächtig ran *(col);* **to pull a ~ one (on sb)** *(col)* jdn übers Ohr hauen *(col);* **~ lane** Überholspur *f;* **~ train** D-Zug *m.* **(b) to be ~** *(clock, watch)* vorgehen. **(c)** *(fig: immoral)* locker. **~ woman** leichtlebige Frau. **(d)** *(firm)* fest; *friend* gut. **(e)** *colour, dye* farbecht. **2** *adv* **(a)** schnell. **(b)** *(firmly)* fest. **to stick ~** festsitzen; *(with glue)* festkleben; **to hold ~ to sth** an etw *(dat)* festhalten; **to play ~ and loose with sb** mit jdm ein falsches Spiel treiben; **to be ~ asleep** tief schlafen.

fast² [faːst] **1** *vi (not eat)* fasten. **2** *n* Fasten *nt; (period of fasting)* Fastenzeit *f.*

fast breeder reactor *n* schneller Brüter.

fasten ['faːsn] **1** *vt (attach)* befestigen *(to, onto* an *+dat); buttons, dress etc* zumachen; *(lock) door* (ab)schließen. **to ~ two things together** zwei Dinge aneinander befestigen; **to ~ the blame on sb** die Schuld auf jdn schieben. **2** *vi (door etc)* sich schließen lassen. **the dress ~s at the back** das Kleid wird hinten zugemacht; **this piece ~s in here** dieses Teil wird hier befestigt.

♦ **fasten down** *vt sep* festmachen.

♦ **fasten on 1** *vt sep* befestigen *(+prep obj, -to* an *+dat).* **2** *vi +prep obj (fig)* **the teacher always ~s ~ Smith** der Lehrer hackt immer auf Smith herum *(col).*

♦ **fasten onto** *vi +prep obj (fig) to ~ ~ sb* sich an jdn hängen; **to ~ ~ an idea** eine Idee aufgreifen.

♦ **fasten up** *vt sep dress etc* zumachen.

♦ **fastener** ['faːsnəʳ], **fastening** ['faːsnɪŋ] *n* Verschluß *m.*

fastidious [fæs'tɪdɪəs] *adj* wählerisch *(about* in bezug auf *+acc).*

fat [fæt] **1** *n (Anat, Cook)* Fett *nt.* **to live off the ~ of the land** *(fig)* wie die Made im Speck leben *(col);* **to put on ~** Speck ansetzen; **to run to ~** in die Breite gehen *(col).* **2** *adj (+er)* **(a)** dick, fett *(pej).*

to get ~ dick werden. **(b)** *meat* fett. **(c)** *(fig) volume, wallet, cigar* dick; *salary, cheque, profit* üppig, fett *(col); part in play* umfangreich. **(d)** *(iro col)* **a ~ lot of good you are!** Sie sind ja 'ne schöne Hilfe! *(iro col);* **a ~ lot he knows!** er hat doch überhaupt keine Ahnung!; **a ~ chance he's got** da hat er ja Mordschancen *(iro col).*

fatal ['feɪtl] *adj (lit)* tödlich *(to* für*); (fig)* verheerend; *day, decision* schicksalsschwer. **that would be ~** das wäre das Ende *(to gen);* **to deal sb/sth a ~ blow** *(fig)* jdm/einer Sache einen schweren Schlag versetzen; **it's ~ to say that** das ist fatal, so was zu sagen.

fatalism ['feɪtəlɪzəm] *n* Fatalismus *m.*

fatalist ['feɪtəlɪst] *n* Fatalist(in *f*) *m.*

fatalistic [ˌfeɪtə'lɪstɪk] *adj* fatalistisch.

fatality [fə'tælɪtɪ] *n* Todesfall *m; (in accident, war etc)* (Todes)opfer *nt.*

fatally ['feɪtəlɪ] *adv wounded* tödlich. **to be ~ attracted to sb** jdm hoffnungslos verfallen sein.

fate [feɪt] *n* Schicksal *nt.* **to leave sb to his ~** jdn seinem Schicksal überlassen; **to meet one's ~** *(die)* vom Schicksal ereilt werden.

fated ['feɪtɪd] *adj* unglückselig; *project, plan* zum Scheitern verurteilt. **to be ~** unter einem ungünstigen Stern stehen; **they were ~ never to meet again** es war ihnen bestimmt, sich nie wiederzusehen.

fateful ['feɪtfʊl] *adj (disastrous)* verhängnisvoll; *(momentous)* schicksalsschwer.

fathead ['fæthed] *n (col)* Blödian *m (col).*

father ['faːðəʳ] **1** *n (a) (lit, fig)* Vater *m (to sb* jdm*).* **from ~ to son** vom Vater auf den Sohn; **like ~ like son** der Apfel fällt nicht weit vom Stamm; **F~'s Day** Vatertag *m.* **(b)** *(priest)* Pfarrer *m.* **yes, ~** ja, Herr Pfarrer. **2** *vt child* zeugen.

father: F~ Christmas *n* der Weihnachtsmann; **~-figure** *n* Vaterfigur *f;* **~-hood** *n* Vaterschaft *f;* **~-in-law** *n, pl* **~s-in-law** Schwiegervater *m;* **~-land** *n* Vaterland *nt;* **~-less** *adj* vaterlos.

fatherly ['faːðəlɪ] *adj* väterlich.

fathom ['fæðəm] **1** *n* Faden *m.* **2** *vt (also ~ out)* verstehen. **I just can't ~ him (out)** er ist mir ein Rätsel.

fatigue [fə'tiːg] **1** *n (a)* Erschöpfung *f; (metal ~)* Ermüdung *f.* **(b)** *(Mil: ~ duty)* **to be on ~** Arbeitsdienst haben. **2** *vt (tire)* ermüden; *(exhaust)* erschöpfen.

fatigue: ~ dress *n* Arbeitsanzug *m;* **~ party** *n* Arbeitskommando *nt.*

fatso ['fætsəʊ] *n (col)* Dicke(r) *mf (col).*

fatten ['fætn] *vt (also ~ up) animals* mästen; *people* herausfüttern *(col).*

fattening ['fætnɪŋ] *adj* **chocolate is ~** Schokolade macht dick.

fatty ['fætɪ] **1** *adj* fett; *(greasy)* fettig; *acid, tissue* Fett-. **~ degeneration** *(Med)* Verfettung *f.* **2** *n (col)* Dickerchen *nt (col).*

fatuous ['fætjuəs] *adj* blöd.

faucet ['fɔːsɪt] *n (US)* Hahn *m.*

fault [fɔːlt] **1** *n (a) (Tech)* Defekt *m; (Geol)* Verwerfung *f; (Tennis)* Fehler *m.* **generous to a ~** übermäßig großzügig; **to find ~ with sb/sth** etwas an jdm/etw auszusetzen haben; **he/my memory was at ~** er war im Unrecht/mein Gedächtnis hat mich getrogen. **(b)** *no pl* **it's my ~** es ist meine Schuld; **whose ~ is it?** wer ist schuld?; **it's all your own ~** Sie sind selbst schuld. **2** *vt* etwas auszusetzen haben an *(+dat).* **I can't ~ it** ich habe nichts daran auszusetzen; *(can't disprove it)* ich kann es nicht widerlegen.

fault: ~-finder *n* Krittler(in *f*) *m;* **~-finding** *n* Krittelei *f.*

faultless ['fɔːltlɪs] *adj appearance* tadellos; *(without mistakes)* fehlerlos; *English* fehlerfrei.

faulty ['fɔːltɪ] *adj (+er)* fehlerhaft; *(Tech)* defekt.

fauna ['fɔːnə] *n* Fauna *f.*

faux pas [fəʊ'paː] *n* Fauxpas *m.*

favour, *(US)* **favor** ['feɪvə^r] **1** *n* **(a)** *no pl (goodwill)* Gunst *f.* **to find ~ with sb** bei jdm Anklang finden; **to be in ~ with sb** bei jdm gut angeschrieben sein; *(fashion, pop star, writer etc)* bei jdm beliebt sein; **to be/fall out of ~** in Ungnade (gefallen) sein/fallen; *(fashion, pop star, writer etc)* nicht mehr beliebt sein *(with* bei)/nicht mehr ankommen *(with* bei).
  (b) to be in ~ of sth für etw sein; **in his ~** zu seinen Gunsten; **all those in ~ raise their hands** alle, die dafür sind, Hand hoch; **I'm in ~ of staying** ich bin dafür zu bleiben.
  (c) *(partiality)* Vergünstigung *f.* **to show ~ to sb** jdn bevorzugen.
  (d) *(kindness)* Gefallen *m.* **to ask a ~ of sb** jdn um einen Gefallen bitten; **to do sb a ~** jdm einen Gefallen tun; **do me a ~!** *(col)* sei so gut!; **do me the ~ of shutting up!** *(col)* tu mir den Gefallen und halt den Mund!; **as a ~ aus** Gefälligkeit; **as a ~ to him** ihm zuliebe.
  2 *vt* **(a)** *plan, idea (be in ~ of)* für gut halten; *(prefer)* bevorzugen. **(b)** *(oblige, honour)* beehren *(form).* **(c)** *(US: resemble)* ähneln *(+dat).*
favourable, *(US)* **favorable** ['feɪvərəbl] *adj* günstig *(for, to* für); *(expressing approval)* positiv.
favourably, *(US)* **favorably** ['feɪvərəblɪ] *adv see adj* vorteilhaft; positiv.
favoured, *(US)* **favored** ['feɪvəd] *adj* **the/a ~ few** die wenigen Auserwählten/einige (wenige) Auserwählte.
favourite, *(US)* **favorite** ['feɪvərɪt] **1** *n (person)* Liebling *m; (Sport)* Favorit(in *f) m.* **this one is my ~** das habe ich am liebsten; **we sang all the old ~s** wir haben all die alten Lieder gesungen. **2** *adj attr* Lieblings-.
favouritism, *(US)* **favoritism** ['feɪvərɪtɪzəm] *n* **giving it to Daphne was just ~ on his part** Daphne hat es nur deshalb bekommen, weil er seine Lieblingskinder bevorzugt behandelt.
fawn¹ [fɔːn] **1** *n* **(a)** Hirschkalb *nt; (of roe deer)* Rehkitz *nt.* **(b)** *(colour)* Beige *nt.* **2** *adj* beige.
fawn² *vi (dog)* wedeln (mit dem Schwanz) *m; (fig: person)* katzbuckeln (**on** vor *+dat).*
fax [fæks] *n (document, machine)* Fax *nt.*
faze [feɪz] *vt (esp US col)* aus der Fassung bringen.
FBI *(US)* **= Federal Bureau of Investigation** FBI *nt.*
fear [fɪə^r] **1** *n* **(a)** Angst *f (or* vor *+dat).* **in ~ and trembling** mit schlotternden Knien; **to go in ~ of one's life** ständig um sein Leben bangen; **for ~ that ...** aus Angst, daß ...; **she talked quietly for ~ of waking the child** sie sprach leise, um das Kind nicht aufzuwecken; **without ~ or favour** *(Brit)* **or favor** *(US)* ganz gerecht; **to put the ~ of God into sb** *(col)* jdm gewaltig Angst einjagen *(col).* **(b) no ~!** *(col)* nie im Leben! *(col);* **there's no ~ of that happening again** keine Angst, das passiert so leicht nicht wieder; **there's not much ~ of his coming** wir brauchen kaum Angst zu haben, daß er kommt.
  2 *vt* **(be)fürchten;** *God* Ehrfurcht haben vor *(+dat).* **I ~ the worst** ich befürchte das Schlimmste; **he's a man to be ~ed** er ist ein Mann, vor dem man Angst haben muß.
  3 *vi* **to ~ for** fürchten um; **never ~!** keine Angst.
fearful ['fɪəfʊl] *adj* **(a)** *(terrible)* furchtbar. **(b)** *(apprehensive)* ängstlich. **to be ~ for one's/sb's life** um einen/jds Leben fürchten.
fearless ['fɪəlɪs] *adj* furchtlos. **to be ~ of sth** keine Angst vor etw *(dat)* haben.
fearsome ['fɪəsəm] *adj* furchterregend.
feasibility [ˌfiːzə'bɪlɪtɪ] *n* **(a)** *(of plan etc)* Machbarkeit *f.* **~ study** Machbarkeitsstudie *f;* **the ~ of doing sth** die Möglichkeit, etw zu tun. **(b)** *(plausibility: of story etc)* Wahrscheinlichkeit *f.*
feasible ['fiːzəbl] *adj* **(a)** machbar; *plan* realisierbar. **(b)** *(likely)* excuse plausibel.

feast [fiːst] **1** *n* **(a)** Festessen *nt; (Hist)* Festgelage *nt.* **a ~ for the eyes** eine Augenweide. **(b)** *(Eccl)* Fest *nt.* **~ day** *n* Feiertag *m.* **2** *vi (lit)* ein Festgelage halten. **to ~ on sth** sich an etw *(dat)* gütlich tun. **3** *vt* **to ~ one's eyes on sth** seine Augen an etw *(dat)* weiden.
feat [fiːt] *n* Leistung *f; (heroic, courageous etc)* Heldentat *f; (skilful)* Meisterleistung *f.*
feather ['feðə^r] **1** *n* Feder *f.* **~s** *(plumage)* Gefieder *nt;* **as light as a ~** federleicht; **that's a ~ in his cap** das ist ein Ruhmesblatt *nt* für ihn; **you could have knocked me down with a ~** *(col)* ich war wie vom Donner gerührt; **birds of a ~ flock together** *(Prov)* gleich und gleich gesellt sich gern *(Prov).* **2** *vt* **to ~ one's nest** *(fig)* sein Schäfchen ins trockene bringen.
feather: **~-bed** *n* mit Federn gefüllte Matratze; **~brained** *adj* dümmlich; **~ duster** *n* Staubwedel *m;* **~weight** *(Boxing)* **1** *n* Federgewicht *nt; (fig)* Leichtgewicht *nt;* **2** *adj* Federgewicht-.
feature ['fiːtʃə^r] **1** *n* **(a)** *(facial)* (Gesichts)zug *m.* **(b)** *(characteristic)* Merkmal, Kennzeichen *nt.* **a ~ of his style is ...** sein Stil ist durch ... gekennzeichnet; **a ~ of this book is ...** das Buch zeichnet sich durch ... aus. **(c)** *(focal point: of room etc)* Charakteristikum *nt.* **to make a ~ of sth** etw besonders hervorheben. **(d)** *(Press)* (Sonder)beitrag *m; (Rad, TV)* (Dokumentar)bericht *m.* **(e)** *(film)* Spielfilm *m.* **2** *vt (Press)* story, picture bringen. **this film ~s ...** in diesem Film spielt ... mit. **3** *vi* vorkommen; *(Film)* (mit)spielen. **it ~s prominently in ...** es spielt in *(+dat) ...* eine bedeutende Rolle.
feature: **~ fireplace** *n* offener Kamin; **~-length** *adj film* mit Spielfilmlänge; **~less** *adj* ohne besondere Merkmale; **~ story** *n* Sonderbericht *m,* Feature *nt;* **~ writer** *n* Journalist, der Features schreibt.
February ['fεbruərɪ] *n* Februar *m; see* **September.**
feces ['fiːsiːz] *npl (US)* = **faeces.**
feckless ['fεklɪs] *adj* nutzlos.
fed [fεd] *pret, ptp of* **feed.**
federal ['fεdərəl] *adj* **1** *adj* Bundes-; *system etc* föderalistisch. **~ state** *(in US)* (Einzel)staat *m;* **the F~ Republic of Germany** die Bundesrepublik Deutschland. **2** *n (US col)* FBI-Mann *m.*
federation [ˌfεdə'reɪʃən] *n (Admin)* Zusammenschluß *m; (league)* Föderation *f,* Bund *m.*
fed up ['fεd'ʌp] *adj (col)* **I'm ~** ich habe die Nase voll *(col);* **I'm ~ with him/it** er/es hängt mir zum Hals heraus *(col);* **I'm ~ waiting for him** ich habe es satt, auf ihn zu warten.
fee [fiː] *n* Gebühr *f; (of doctor, lawyer, artist, tutor)* Honorar *nt; (of stage performer)* Gage *f.* **(school) ~s** Schulgeld *nt.*
feeble ['fiːbl] *adj (+er)* schwach.
feeble-minded [ˌfiːbl'maɪndɪd] *adj* dümmlich.
feed [fiːd] *(vb: pret, ptp* **fed)** **1** *n (of animals)* Futter *nt; (col: of person)* Essen *nt.* **when is the baby's next ~?** wann wird das Baby wieder gefüttert?; **to have a good ~** *(col)* tüchtig futtern *(col).* **2** *vt* **(a)** *(provide food for)* verpflegen; *family* ernähren. **(b)** *(give food to)* füttern. **to ~ oneself** *(child)* allein essen (können); **to ~ sth to sb/an animal** jdm/einem Tier etw zu essen/fressen geben. **(c)** *machine* versorgen; *furnace* beschicken; *meter* Geld einwerfen in *(+acc); (fig)* hope, imagination nähren. **to ~ sth into a machine** etw in eine Maschine geben; **to ~ sb with information** jdn mit Informationen versorgen; **the data is fed into the computer** die Daten werden in den Computer eingegeben. **(d)** *(Tech: insert)* führen. **3** *vi (animal)* fressen; *(baby)* gefüttert werden.
♦ **feed back** *vt sep information* zurückleiten *(to* an *+acc).*
♦ **feed on 1** *vi* +prep obj sich (er)nähren von. **2** *vt sep* +prep obj animal, baby füttern mit; *person* ernähren mit.

feedback ['fiːdbæk] Reaktion f, Feedback nt. ~ **of information** Rückinformation f; **to provide more ~ about sth** ausführlicher über etw (acc) berichten.

feeding ['fiːdɪŋ]: ~ **bottle** n (Brit) Flasche f; ~ **time** n (for animal) Fütterungszeit f; (for baby) Zeit f für die Mahlzeit.

feel [fiːl] (vb: pret, ptp **felt**) **1** vt **(a)** (touch) fühlen; (examining) befühlen. **to ~ one's way** sich vortasten; **to ~ one's way into sth** sich in etw (acc) einfühlen. **(b)** (be aware of) fühlen, spüren; pain, emotions, loss empfinden; (be affected by) heat, cold, insult leiden unter (+dat). **I can't ~ anything in my left leg** ich habe kein Gefühl im linken Bein; **I felt it move** ich spürte, wie es sich bewegte; **I could ~ him getting angry** ich merkte, daß er wütend wurde; **I bet she felt that!** das hat bestimmt weh getan. **(c)** (think) glauben. **what do you ~ about him/it?** was halten Sie von ihm/davon?; **it was felt that ...** man war der Meinung, daß ...; **he felt it necessary** er hielt es für notwendig; **don't ~ you have to ...** glauben Sie nicht, Sie müßten ...

2 vi **(a)** (physically or mentally) sich fühlen. **to ~ well/ill** sich wohl/elend fühlen; **to ~ convinced/certain** überzeugt/sicher sein; **to ~ hungry/thirsty/sleepy** hungrig/durstig/müde sein; **I ~ hot/cold** mir ist heiß/kalt; **he doesn't ~ quite himself today** er ist heute nicht ganz auf der Höhe; **I felt sad/strange** mir war traurig/komisch zumute; **I felt as though I'd never been away** mir war, als ob ich nie weggewesen wäre; **I felt as if I was going to be sick** ich dachte, mir würde schlecht werden; **how do you ~ about him?** (emotionally) was empfinden Sie für ihn?; **you can imagine how I felt** Sie können sich (dat) vorstellen, wie mir zumute war; **what does it ~ like or how does it ~ to be all alone?** wie fühlt man sich or wie ist das so ganz allein?; **it ~s like flying** es ist wie Fliegen.

(b) (to the touch) sich anfühlen. **to ~ hard** sich hart anfühlen; **the room/air ~s warm** das Zimmer/die Luft kommt einem warm vor.

(c) (think, have opinions) meinen. **how do you ~ about these developments?** was meinen Sie zu dieser Entwicklung?; **that's just how I ~** das meine ich auch.

(d) to ~ like (have desire for) Lust haben auf (+acc); (for food) Appetit haben auf (+acc); **I ~ like eating something/going for a walk** ich könnte jetzt etwas essen/ich habe Lust spazierenzugehen; **I felt like screaming/giving up** ich hätte am liebsten geschrien/aufgegeben; **if you ~ like it** wenn Sie Lust haben.

3 vi **let me have a ~ (of it)!** laß (mich) mal fühlen!; **it has a velvety ~** es fühlt sich samten an; **he recognizes things by their ~** er erkennt Dinge daran, wie sie sich anfühlen; **to get/have a ~ for sth** (fig) ein Gefühl für etw bekommen/haben.

♦ **feel about** or **around** vi umhertasten; (in drawer, bag etc) herumtasten.

♦ **feel for** vi +prep obj **(a)** (sympathize with) Mitgefühl haben mit. **I ~ ~ you** Sie tun mir leid. **(b)** (search for) tasten nach.

♦ **feel up to** vi +prep obj sich gewachsen fühlen (+dat).

feeler ['fiːlə'] n (Zool, fig) Fühler m. **to put out ~s** seine Fühler ausstrecken.

feeling ['fiːlɪŋ] n **(a)** Gefühl nt. **I've lost all ~ in my right arm** ich habe kein Gefühl mehr im rechten Arm; **I've a funny ~ she won't come** ich hab so das Gefühl, daß sie nicht kommt. **(b)** (opinion: also ~s) Meinung, Ansicht f (on zu). **there was a general ~ that ...** man war allgemein der Ansicht, daß ...; **bad/good ~** Verstimmung f/Wohlwollen nt; **there's been a lot of bad ~ about this decision** wegen dieser Entscheidung hat es viel

böses Blut gegeben. **(c)** ~**s** Gefühle pl; **you've hurt his ~s** Sie haben ihn verletzt; **no hard ~s!** ich nehme es dir nicht übel; **no hard ~s?** nimm es mir nicht übel.

fee-paying ['fiːˌpeɪɪŋ] adj school Privat-; pupils deren Eltern Schulgeld zahlen.

feet [fiːt] pl of **foot**.

feign [feɪn] vt vortäuschen.

feint [feɪnt] n (Sport) Finte f.

feline ['fiːlaɪn] adj (lit) Katzen-; (fig) katzenhaft.

fell[1] [fel] pret of **fall**.

fell[2] n (skin) Fell nt.

fell[3] adj **with one ~ blow** mit einem einzigen gewaltigen Hieb; **at one ~ swoop** mit einem Schlag.

fell[4] vt tree fällen; person niederstrecken; animal zur Strecke bringen.

fell[5] n (Brit) Berg m; (moor) Moorland nt.

fellow ['feləʊ] n **(a)** Mann, Typ (col) m. **(b)** (comrade) Kamerad m; (colleague) Kollege m, Kollegin f. **(c)** (of a society) Mitglied nt; (Univ) Fellow m.

fellow: ~ **citizen** n Mitbürger(in f) m; ~ **countryman** n Landsmann m/-männin f; ~ **countrymen** npl Landsleute pl; ~ **feeling** n Mitgefühl nt; (togetherness) Zusammengehörigkeitsgefühl nt; ~ **men** npl Mitmenschen pl; ~ **passenger** n Mitreisende(r) mf.

fellowship ['feləʊʃɪp] n **(a)** no pl Kameradschaft f; (company) Gesellschaft f. **(b)** (society, club etc) Gesellschaft f. **(c)** (Univ: scholarship) Forschungsstipendium nt; (job) Position f eines Fellow.

fellow: ~ **student** n Kommilitone m, Kommilitonin f; ~ **sufferer** n Leidensgenosse m/-genossin f; ~ **traveller** (Brit) or **traveler** (US) n **(a)** (lit) Mitreisende(r) mf; **(b)** (Pol) Sympathisant(in f) m; ~ **worker** n Kollege m, Kollegin f, Mitarbeiter(in f) m.

felon ['felən] n (Schwer)verbrecher m.

felony ['felənɪ] n (schweres) Verbrechen.

felt[1] [felt] pret, ptp of **feel**.

felt[2] n Filz m.

felt-tip (pen) ['felttɪp'pen] n Filzstift m.

female ['fiːmeɪl] **1** adj weiblich; labour, rights Frauen-. **a ~ doctor/student/slave/dog** eine Ärztin/Studentin/Sklavin/Hündin; ~ **impersonator** Frauenimitator m; **a typical ~ attitude** typisch Frau. **2** n **(a)** (animal) Weibchen nt. **(b)** (col: woman) Frau f; (pej) Weib nt (pej).

feminine ['femɪnɪn] **1** adj (also Gram) weiblich, feminin. **2** n (Gram) Femininum nt. **in the ~** in der weiblichen or femininen Form.

femininity [ˌfemɪ'nɪnɪtɪ] n Weiblichkeit f.

feminism ['femɪnɪzəm] n Feminismus m.

feminist ['femɪnɪst] n Feminist(in f) m.

femur ['fiːmə'] n Oberschenkelknochen m.

fen [fen] n Moorland, Sumpfland nt.

fence [fens] **1** n **(a)** Zaun m; (Sport) Hindernis nt. **to sit on the ~** (fig) nicht Partei ergreifen; **don't sit on the ~** entscheiden Sie sich. **(b)** (col: receiver of stolen goods) Hehler m. **2** vt (also ~ **in**) land einzäunen, umzäunen. **3** vi (Sport) fechten.

♦ **fence in** vt sep einzäunen, umzäunen. **to ~ sb ~** (fig) jds Freiheit beschneiden.

♦ **fence off** vt sep piece of land abzäunen.

fencer ['fensə'] n Fechter(in f) m.

fencing ['fensɪŋ] n **(a)** (Sport) Fechten nt. **(b)** (fences) Einzäunung f.

fend [fend] vi **to ~ for oneself** (provide) für sich (selbst) sorgen; **could she ~ for herself in the big city?** könnte sie sich in der großen Stadt allein durchschlagen?

♦ **fend off** vt sep abwehren.

fender ['fendə'] n **(a)** (in front of fire) Kamingitter nt. **(b)** (US Aut) Kotflügel m; (of bicycle etc) Schutzblech nt.

fennel ['fenl] n (Bot) Fenchel m.

ferment ['fɜːment] **1** *n* (*fig*) Unruhe *f*. **the city/he was in a state of** ~ es gärte in der Stadt/in ihm. **2** [fə'ment] *vi* (*lit, fig*) gären. **3** [fə'ment] *vt* (*lit*) fermentieren; (*fig*) anwachsen lassen.

fermentation [,fɜːmen'teɪʃən] *n* Gärung *f*.

fern [fɜːn] *n* Farn(kraut *nt*) *m*.

ferocious [fə'rəʊʃəs] *adj appearance, animal* wild; *glance, look* grimmig; *criticism, competition* scharf; *fight, temper, attack* heftig.

ferocity [fə'rɒsɪtɪ] *n see adj* Wildheit *f*; Grimmigkeit *f*; Schärfe *f*; Heftigkeit *f*.

ferret ['ferɪt] **1** *n* Frettchen *nt*. **2** *vi* (*also* ~ **about** *or* **around**) herumstöbern, herumschnüffeln (*pej*).
♦ **ferret out** *vt sep* aufstöbern.

ferry ['ferɪ] **1** *n* Fähre *f*. **2** *vt* (*by boat: also* ~ **across** *or* **over**) übersetzen; (*by plane, car etc*) transportieren. **to** ~ **sb across a river** jdn über einen Fluß setzen; **to** ~ **sb/sth back and forth** jdn/etw hin- und herbringen.

ferry: ~**boat** *n* Fährboot *nt*; ~**man** *n* Fährmann *m*.

fertile ['fɜːtaɪl] *adj* (*lit, fig*) fruchtbar.

fertility [fə'tɪlɪtɪ] **1** *n* (*lit, fig*) Fruchtbarkeit *f*. **2** *attr cult, symbol* Fruchtbarkeits-. ~ **drug** Fruchtbarkeitspille *f*.

fertilization [,fɜːtɪlaɪ'zeɪʃən] *n* Befruchtung *f*.

fertilize ['fɜːtɪlaɪz] *vt* befruchten; *land* düngen.

fertilizer ['fɜːtɪlaɪzə'] *n* Dünger *m*. **artificial** ~ Kunstdünger *m*.

fervent ['fɜːvənt], **fervid** ['fɜːvɪd] *adj* leidenschaftlich; *tone of voice, expression, prayer* inbrünstig.

fervour, (*US*) **fervor** ['fɜːvə'] *n* Leidenschaft *f*.

fester ['festə'] *vi* (*wound*) eitern.

festival ['festɪvəl] *n* (**a**) (*Eccl etc*) Fest *nt*. (**b**) (*cultural*) Festspiele *pl*; (*esp pop* ~) Festival *nt*.

festive ['festɪv] *adj* festlich. **the** ~ **season** die Festzeit.

festivity [fe'stɪvɪtɪ] *n* (**a**) (*gaiety*) Feststimmung *f*. (**b**) (*celebration*) Feier *f*. **festivities** *pl* Feierlichkeiten *pl*.

festoon [fe'stuːn] *vt* **to** ~ **sb/sth with sth** jdn mit etw behängen/etw mit etw schmücken.

fetal *adj* (*esp US*) = **foetal**.

fetch [fetʃ] *vt* (**a**) (*bring*) holen; (*collect*) *person, thing* abholen. (**b**) *sigh, groan* ausstoßen. (**c**) (*bring in*) *money* (ein)bringen. (**d**) (*col*) **to** ~ **sb a blow/one** jdm eine langen (*col*).
♦ **fetch back** *vt sep* zurückholen.
♦ **fetch in** *vt sep* hereinbringen.
♦ **fetch up 1** *vi* (*col*) landen (*col*). **2** *vt sep* (*Brit: vomit*) brechen.

fetching ['fetʃɪŋ] *adj* bezaubernd, reizend.

fête [feɪt] **1** *n* Fest *nt*. **2** *vt* (*make much of*) *sb, sb's success* feiern.

fetid ['fetɪd] *adj* übelriechend.

fetish ['fetɪʃ] *n* Fetisch *m*. **to have a** ~ **about cleanliness** einen Sauberkeitstick haben (*col*).

fetishist ['fetɪʃɪst] *n* Fetischist *m*.

fetter ['fetə'] **1** *vt prisoner* fesseln; *goat* anpflocken; (*fig*) in Fesseln legen. **2** *n* ~**s** *pl* (Fuß)fesseln *pl*; (*fig*) Fesseln *pl*.

fettle ['fetl] *n* **to be in fine** ~ in bester Form sein.

fetus *n* (*US*) = **foetus**.

feud [fjuːd] **1** *n* (*lit, fig*) Fehde *f*. **2** *vi* (*lit, fig*) sich befehden.

feudal ['fjuːdl] *adj* Feudal-, feudal.

feudalism ['fjuːdəlɪzəm] *n* Feudalismus *m*.

fever ['fiːvə'] *n* (*lit, fig*) Fieber *nt no pl*. **to have a** ~ eine Fieberkrankheit haben; (*high temperature*) Fieber haben; **in a** ~ **of excitement** in fieberhafter Erregung; **to reach** ~ **pitch** am Siedepunkt angelangt sein; **to be working at** ~ **pitch** auf Hochtouren arbeiten.

feverish ['fiːvərɪʃ] *adj* (*Med*) fiebernd *attr*; (*fig*) *activity* fieberhaft. **he's still** ~ er hat noch Fieber.

few [fjuː] *adj* (+*er*), *pron* (**a**) (*not many*) wenige. **we are very** ~ wir sind nur sehr wenige; ~ **and far**

between dünn gesät; **as** ~ **books as you** genauso wenig(e) Bücher wie du; **as** ~ **as six objections** bloß sechs Einwände; **there were 3 too** ~ **es** waren 3 zuwenig da; **he is one of the** ~ **people who ...** er ist einer der wenigen, die ...; **its days are** ~ es hat nur ein kurzes Leben; **the lucky** ~ die wenigen Glücklichen; **as** ~ **as you** genauso wenig wie du; **however** ~ **there may be** wie wenig auch immer da ist; **I've got too** ~ **as it is** ich habe sowieso schon zu wenig(e); **there are too** ~ **of you** ihr seid zu wenige; **the** ~ **who** knew him die wenigen, die ihn kannten.
(**b**) **a** ~ ein paar; **a** ~ **more days** noch ein paar Tage; **a** ~ **times** ein paar Male; **he's had a good** ~ **drinks** er hat ziemlich viel getrunken; **quite a** ~ **books** ziemlich viele Bücher; **in the next** ~ **days** in den nächsten paar Tagen; **every** ~ **days** alle paar Tage.

fewer ['fjuːə'] *adj, pron comp of* **few** weniger. **no** ~ **than** nicht weniger als.

fewest ['fjuːɪst] *adj, pron superl of* **few** die wenigsten.

fiancé [fɪ'ãːŋseɪ] *n* Verlobte(r) *m*.

fiancée [fɪ'ãːŋseɪ] *n* Verlobte *f*.

fiasco [fɪ'æskəʊ] *n* Fiasko *nt*.

fib [fɪb] (*col*) **1** *n* (*that's a*) ~! das ist geflunkert! (*col*); **don't tell** ~**s** flunker nicht! (*col*). **2** *vi* flunkern (*col*).

fibber ['fɪbə'] *n* (*col*) Flunkerer *m* (*col*).

fibre, (*US*) **fiber** ['faɪbə'] *n* Faser *f*. **moral** ~ Charakterstärke *f*.

fibreglass, (*US*) **fiberglass** ['faɪbəglɑːs] **1** *n* Fiberglas *nt*. **2** *adj* Fiberglas-.

fibre optics (*Brit*), **fiber optics** (*US*) *n* Faseroptik *f*.

fibrositis [,faɪbrə'saɪtɪs] *n* Bindegewebsentzündung *f*.

fibrous ['faɪbrəs] *adj* faserig.

fickle ['fɪkl] *adj* unbeständig, launenhaft.

fiction ['fɪkʃən] *n no pl* (*Liter*) Prosaliteratur *f*; (*category*) Belletristik *f*. **work of** ~ Erzählung *f*; (*longer*) Roman *m*; **light** ~ (*leichte*) Unterhaltungsliteratur *f*; **that's pure** ~ (*fig*) das ist frei erfunden.

fictional ['fɪkʃənl] *adj* erfunden. **a** ~ **character** eine Gestalt aus der Literatur.

fictitious [fɪk'tɪʃəs] *adj* (**a**) (*imaginary*) frei erfunden. (**b**) (*false*) falsch.

fiddle ['fɪdl] **1** *n* (**a**) (*Mus col*) Geige *f*. **to play second** ~ (**to sb**) (*fig*) in jds Schatten (*dat*) stehen; **he refuses to play second** ~ (*fig*) er will immer die erste Geige spielen; **as fit as a** ~ kerngesund. (**b**) (*Brit col: cheat*) Schiebung *f*; (*with money*) faule Geschäfte *pl* (*col*). **it's a** ~ das ist Schiebung!; **there are so many** ~**s going on es** wird so viel getrickst (*col*); **tax** ~ Steuermanipulation *f*. **2** *vi* (*fidget, play around*) herumspielen. **to** ~ **with sth an etw** (*dat*) herumspielen (*col*). **3** *vt* (*col*) *accounts, results* frisieren (*col*); *election* manipulieren. **he** ~**d it so that ...** er hat es so getrickst, daß ... (*col*). **4** *interj* ach du liebe Zeit.

fiddler ['fɪdlə'] *n* (**a**) (*Mus col*) Geiger(in *f*) *m*. (**b**) (*col: cheat*) Schwindler(in *f*) *m*.

fiddlesticks ['fɪdlstɪks] *interj* (*nonsense*) Unsinn, Quatsch (*col*); (*bother*) du liebe Zeit.

fiddling ['fɪdlɪŋ] *adj* (*trivial*) läppisch.

fiddly ['fɪdlɪ] *adj* (+*er*) (*col: intricate*) knifflig (*col*).

fidelity [fɪ'delɪtɪ] *n* (**a**) Treue *f* (*to* zu). (**b**) (*Rad etc*) Klangtreue *f*.

fidget ['fɪdʒɪt] **1** *vi* zappeln. **to** ~ **with sth** mit etw herumfummeln; **don't** ~ zappel nicht so rum! *n* (*person*) Zappelphilipp *m* (*col*).

fidgety ['fɪdʒɪtɪ] *adj* zappelig; *audience etc* unruhig.

field [fiːld] **1** *n* (**a**) (*lit, fig*) Feld *nt*; (*for root vegetables*) Acker *m*; (*area of grass*) Wiese *f*; (*for cows, horses etc*) Weide *f*. **he's working in the** ~**s er** arbeitet auf dem Feld *or* Acker; ~ **of battle**

Schlachtfeld *nt*; ~ **of vision** Blickfeld *nt*; **magnetic** ~ Magnetfeld *nt*; **to lead the** ~ führend sein. **(b)** *(Sport: ground)* Platz *m*; *(competitors)* Feld *nt*. **there's a very strong** ~ das Feld der Teilnehmer ist sehr stark; **the rest of the** ~ *(runners)* die übrigen Läufer; **to take the** ~ auf den Platz kommen. **(c)** *(of study, work etc)* Gebiet *nt*. **to be first in the** ~ **with sth** *(Comm)* etw als Erster auf den Markt bringen; **studies in the** ~ **of medicine** Studien auf dem Gebiet der Medizin; **this is, of course, a very broad** ~ das ist natürlich ein weites Feld; **what** ~ **are you in?** auf welchem Gebiet arbeiten Sie?; **to test sth in the** ~ etw in der Praxis ausprobieren.

2 *vt (Cricket, Baseball etc) ball* auffangen und zurückwerfen; *(fig) question etc* abblocken, abwehren; *team, side* aufs Feld *or* auf den Platz schicken.

field day *n* **I had a** ~ ich hatte meinen großen Tag.

fielder ['fi:ldə'] *n (Cricket, Baseball etc)* Fänger *m*.

field: ~ **events** *npl (Athletics)* Sprung- und Wurfdisziplinen *pl*; ~ **glasses** *npl* Feldstecher *m*; ~ **goal** *n (US Ftbl)* Feldtor *nt*; ~ **gun** *n (Mil)* Feldgeschütz *nt*; ~ **hockey** *n (US)* Hockey *nt*; ~ **marshal** *n (Mil)* Feldmarschall *m*; ~**mouse** *n* Feldmaus *f*; ~ **study** *n* Feldforschung *f*; **a** ~ **study** eine Feldstudie; ~**work** *n (of geologist etc)* Arbeit *f* im Gelände; *(of sociologist etc)* Feldarbeit *f*.

fiend [fi:nd] *n* Teufel *m*. **tennis** ~ *(col)* Tennisnarr *m*; **a fresh-air** ~ *(col)* ein Frischluftfanatiker *m*.

fiendish ['fi:ndɪʃ] *adj* teuflisch; *(col) pace, heat* höllisch *(col)*; *problem* verteufelt *(col)*.

fierce [fɪəs] *adj* (+*er*) *appearance* wild; *glance, look* böse, grimmig; *dog* bissig; *criticism, competition* scharf; *fight, resistance, temper, attack (lit, fig)* heftig; *heat, sun* glühend.

fierceness ['fɪəsnɪs] *n* see *adj* Wildheit *f*; Grimmigkeit *f*; Bissigkeit *f*; Schärfe *f*; Heftigkeit *f*; Glut *f*.

fiery ['faɪərɪ] *adj* (+*er*) *(lit, fig)* feurig; *sunset* rotglühend. **to have a** ~ **temper** ein Hitzkopf *m* sein.

fife [faɪf] *n (Mus)* Querpfeife *f*.

fifteen ['fɪf'ti:n] **1** *adj* fünfzehn. **2** *n* Fünfzehn *f*.

fifteenth ['fɪf'ti:nθ] *adj* fünfzehnte(r, s); *see* **sixteenth**.

fifth [fɪfθ] **1** *adj* fünfte(r, s). **2** *n* Fünfte(r, s); *(part, fraction)* Fünftel *nt*; *(Mus)* Quinte *f*; *see* **sixth**.

fiftieth ['fɪftɪɪθ] *adj* fünfzigste(r, s); *see* **sixtieth**.

fifty ['fɪftɪ] **1** *adj* fünfzig. **2** *n* Fünfzig *f*; *see* **sixty**.

fifty-fifty ['fɪftɪ'fɪftɪ] **1** *adj* halbe-halbe, fifty-fifty. **we have a** ~ **chance of success** unsere Chancen stehen fifty-fifty. **2** *adv* **to go** ~ **(with sb)** (mit jdm) halbe-halbe machen.

fig [fɪg] *n* Feige *f*. **I don't care a** ~ *(col)* ich kümmere mich einen Dreck darum *(col)*.

fight [faɪt] *(vb: pret, ptp* **fought)** **1** *n (lit, fig)* Kampf *m*; *(fist* ~, *scrap)* Schlägerei *f*; *(argument, row)* Streit *m*. **to have a** ~ **with sb** sich mit jdm schlagen; *(argue)* sich mit jdm streiten; **to put up a good** ~ *(lit, fig)* sich tapfer schlagen; **he won't give in without a** ~ er ergibt sich nicht kampflos; **there was no** ~ **left in him** sein Kampfgeist war erloschen.

2 *vi* kämpfen mit; *(have punch-up etc)* sich schlagen; *(argue)* sich streiten. **to** ~ **for one's life** um sein Leben kämpfen.

3 *vt person* kämpfen mit; *(have punch-up with)* sich schlagen mit; *fire, disease, cuts, policy* bekämpfen; *decision* ankämpfen gegen. **I'm prepared to** ~ **the government** ich bin bereit, das mit der Regierung durchzukämpfen; **you can't** ~ **the whole company** du kannst es nicht mit der ganzen Firma aufnehmen; **to** ~ **an action at law** einen Prozeß vor Gericht durchfechten; **to** ~ **one's way out of the crowd** sich aus der Menge freikämpfen.

♦ **fight back 1** *vi (in fight)* zurückschlagen; *(Mil)*

sich verteidigen; *(in argument)* sich wehren; *(after illness)* zu Kräften kommen; *(Sport)* einen Gegenangriff unternehmen; *(pull back)* aufholen. **2** *vt sep tears etc* unterdrücken.

♦ **fight down** *vt sep anxiety* unterdrücken.

♦ **fight off** *vt sep (Mil, fig) attack, disease* abwehren; *sleep* ankämpfen gegen; *a cold* ankämpfen gegen.

♦ **fight on** *vi* weiterkämpfen.

♦ **fight out** *vt sep* **to** ~ **it** ~ **es** untereinander ausfechten.

fighter ['faɪtə'] *n* **(a)** Kämpfer *m*; *(Boxing)* Fighter *m*. **he's a** ~ *(fig)* er ist eine Kämpfernatur. **(b)** *(Aviat: plane)* Jagdflugzeug *nt*.

fighter: ~**-aircraft** *n* Kampfflugzeug *nt*; ~**-bomber** *n* Jagdbomber *m*; ~**-interceptor** *n* Abfangjäger *m*; ~**-pilot** *n* Jagdflieger *m*.

fighting ['faɪtɪŋ] *n (Mil)* Kampf *m*; *(punch-ups etc)* Schlägereien *pl*; *(between husband and wife etc)* Streit *m*. ~ **broke out** Kämpfe brachen aus.

fighting: ~ **chance** *n* faire Chancen *pl*; **he's in with** *or* **he has a** ~ **chance** er hat eine Chance, wenn er sich anstrengt; ~ **forces** *npl* Kampftruppen *pl*; ~ **spirit** *n* Kampfgeist *m*; ~ **strength** *n (Mil)* Kampfstärke *f*.

figment ['fɪgmənt] *n* **a** ~ **of the imagination** pure Einbildung.

figurative ['fɪgjʊrətɪv] *adj use, sense* übertragen.

figure ['fɪgə'] **1** *n* **(a)** *(number)* Zahl; *(digit also)* Ziffer *f*; *(sum)* Summe *f*. **he's good at** ~**s** er ist ein guter Rechner; **three-**~ **number** dreistellige Zahl; **he earns well into four** ~**s** er hat gut und gern ein vierstelliges Einkommen. **(b)** *(in geometry, dancing, drawing)* Figur *f*. ~ **of eight** Acht *f*. **(c)** *(human form)* Gestalt *f*. **(d)** *(shapeliness)* Figur *f*. **she has a good** ~ sie hat eine gute Figur; **he's a fine** ~ **of a man** er ist ein Bild von einem Mann. **(e)** *(personality)* Persönlichkeit *f*; *(character in novel etc)* Gestalt *f*. **(f)** ~ **of speech** Redensart *f*.

2 *vt (imagine)* sich *(dat)* vorstellen; *(US col: think, reckon)* schätzen *(col)*.

3 *vi* **(a)** *(appear)* erscheinen. **he** ~**d** prominently in the talks er spielte eine bedeutende Rolle bei den Gesprächen. **(b)** *(col: make sense)* hinkommen *(col)*. **that** ~**s** das hätte ich mir denken können.

♦ **figure on** *vi +prep obj (esp US)* rechnen mit.

♦ **figure out** *vt sep* **(a)** *(understand)* schlau werden aus. **(b)** *(work out)* ausrechnen; *answer, how to do sth* herausbekommen; *solution* finden.

figure: ~**-conscious** *adj* figurbewußt; ~**head** *n (Naut, fig)* Galionsfigur *f*; ~**-skater** *n* Eiskunstläufer(in *f*) *m*; ~**-skating** *n* Eiskunstlaufen *nt*.

Fiji ['fi:dʒi:] *n* Fidschiinseln *pl*.

filament ['fɪləmənt] *n (Elec)* (Glüh)faden *m*.

filch [fɪltʃ] *vt* mausen *(col)*.

file¹ [faɪl] **1** *n (tool)* Feile *f*. **2** *vt* feilen. **to** ~ **one's fingernails** sich *(dat)* die Fingernägel feilen.

file² **1** *n* **(a)** *(holder)* Aktenordner *m*; *(for card index)* Karteikasten *m*. **it's in the** ~**s somewhere** das muß irgendwo bei den Akten sein. **(b)** *(documents, information)* Akte *f (on sb* über jdn, *on sth* zu etw). **on** ~ aktenkundig; **to keep a** ~ **on sb/sth** eine Akte über jdn/etw führen. **(c)** *(Comp)* Datei *f*. **data on** ~ auf Abruf gespeicherte Daten. **2** *vt* **(a)** *letters* ablegen. **(b)** *(Jur) petition* einreichen.

♦ **file away** *vt sep papers* zu den Akten legen.

file³ **1** *n (row)* Reihe *f*. **in single** ~ im Gänsemarsch; *(Mil)* in Reihe. **2** *vi* **to** ~ **in** hereinmarschieren; **they** ~**d out of the classroom** sie gingen/kamen nacheinander aus dem Klassenzimmer; **the troops** ~**d past** die Truppen marschierten am General vorbei.

file clerk *n (US)* Angestellte(r) *mf* in der Registratur.

filial ['fɪlɪəl] *adj* Kindes-. **with due** ~ **respect** mit dem Respekt, den eine Tochter/ein Sohn schuldig ist.

filibuster ['fılıbʌstəʳ] vi (esp US) Obstruktion betreiben.

filigree ['fılıgriː] n Filigran(arbeit f) nt.

filing: ~ **cabinet** n Aktenschrank m; ~ **clerk** n (Brit) Angestellte(r) mf in der Registratur.

filings ['failıŋz] npl Späne pl.

Filipino [fılı'piːnəʊ] n Filipino m.

fill [fıl] **1** vt füllen; pipe stopfen; teeth plombieren; (wind) sails blähen; post, position (employer) besetzen; (employee) einnehmen; need entsprechen (+dat). ~ed with anger/admiration voller Zorn/Bewunderung; the thought ~ed him with horror der Gedanke erfüllte ihn mit Entsetzen. **2** vi sich füllen. **3** n to drink one's ~ seinen Durst löschen; to eat one's ~ sich satt essen; I've had my ~ of him/it (col) ich habe von ihm/davon die Nase voll (col).
♦ **fill in 1** vi to ~ ~ for sb für jdn einspringen. **2** vt sep (a) hole auffüllen; door, fireplace zumauern; (fig) gaps stopfen. (b) form ausfüllen; name, details, missing word eintragen. (c) to ~ sb ~ (on sth) jdn (über etw acc) aufklären or ins Bild setzen.
♦ **fill out 1** vi (a) (sails etc) sich blähen. (b) (person: become fatter) fülliger werden; (cheeks, face) voller werden. **2** vt sep form ausfüllen; essay, article etc strecken.
♦ **fill up 1** vi (Aut) (auf)tanken; (hall, barrel etc) sich füllen. **2** vt sep tank, cup vollfüllen; (driver) volltanken; hole stopfen; (Brit) form ausfüllen. ~ her ~! (Aut col) volltanken bitte!

filler ['fıləʳ] n (for cracks) Spachtelmasse f.

fillet ['fılıt] **1** n Filet nt. ~ **steak** Filetsteak nt. **2** vt filetieren.

filling ['fılıŋ] **1** n (a) (in tooth) Füllung, Plombe f. I had to have three ~s ich mußte mir drei Zähne plombieren lassen. (b) (in pie, tart) Füllung f. **2** adj food sättigend.

filling station n Tankstelle f.

fillip ['fılıp] n (fig) Ansporn m.

filly ['fılı] n Stutfohlen nt; (dated col) Mädel nt (dated).

film [fılm] **1** n (a) Film m; (of dust, of ice) Schicht f; (of mist, on the eye) Schleier m; (thin membrane) Häutchen nt; (on teeth) Belag m. (b) (Phot) Film m. to make a ~ einen Film drehen; to go to the ~s ins Kino gehen. **2** vt play verfilmen; scene filmen; people einen Film machen von.

film: ~ **camera** n Filmkamera f; ~ **clip** n Filmausschnitt m; ~-**maker** n Filmemacher(in f) m; ~ **rights** npl Filmrechte pl; ~ **script** n Drehbuch nt; ~**star** n Filmstar m; ~**strip** n Filmstreifen m; ~ **studio** n Filmstudio nt; ~ **version** n Verfilmung f.

filter ['fıltəʳ] **1** n Filter m; (Brit: for traffic) Abbiegespur f. **2** vt liquids, air filtern. **3** vi (light) durchscheinen. to ~ to the left (Brit Aut) sich links einordnen.
♦ **filter back** vi (refugees, prisoners etc) allmählich zurückkommen.
♦ **filter in** vi (people) allmählich eindringen; (news) durchsickern.
♦ **filter out** vt sep (lit) herausfiltern.
♦ **filter through** vi (liquid, sound, news) durchsickern; (light) durchscheinen.

filter: ~ **lane** n (Brit) Abbiegespur f; ~ **paper** n Filterpapier nt; ~-**tipped** adj cigarette Filter-.

filth [fılθ] n (lit) Schmutz, Dreck m; (fig) Schweinerei f.

filthy ['fılθı] adj (+er) schmutzig, dreckig; (col) weather Sau- (col); day Mist-; temper übel; (obscene) unanständig. don't be ~ du Ferkel!; a ~ habit eine widerliche Angewohnheit; ~ **rich** (col) stinkreich (col).

fin [fın] n (of fish) Flosse f; (Aviat) Seitenflosse f; (of bomb, rocket, ship) Stabilisierungsfläche f.

final ['faınl] **1** adj (last) letzte(r, s); examination,

chord Schluß-; (definite) decision, version endgültig. ~ **score** Schlußstand m; ~ **round/lap** Endrunde f; that's not ~ yet das steht noch nicht endgültig fest; you're not going and that's ~ du gehst nicht, und damit Schluß! **2** n (a) ~s pl (Univ) Abschlußprüfung f. (b) (Sport) Finale nt; (in quiz) Endrunde f. the ~s das Finale.

finale [fı'nɑːlı] n (Mus, fig) Finale nt.

finalist ['faınəlıst] n (Sport) Endrundenteilnehmer(in f), Finalist(in f) m.

finality [faı'nælıtı] n (of decision etc) Endgültigkeit f; (of tone of voice) Entschiedenheit f.

finalize ['faınəlaız] vt fertigmachen; plans, arrangements endgültig festlegen; deal zum Abschluß bringen; draft die endgültige Form geben (+dat). to ~ a decision eine endgültige Entscheidung treffen.

finally ['faınəlı] adv schließlich; (expressing relief etc) endlich.

finance [faı'næns] **1** n Finanzen pl. high ~ Hochfinanz f; it's a question of ~ das ist eine Geldfrage. **2** vt finanzieren.

financial [faı'nænʃəl] adj finanziell; crisis Finanz-; news, page Wirtschafts-. ~ **director** Leiter m der Finanzabteilung; the ~ **year** das Rechnungsjahr.

financier [faı'nænsıəʳ] n Finanzier m.

finch [fıntʃ] n Fink m.

find [faınd] (vb: pret, ptp **found**) **1** vt (a) finden. this flower is found all over England diese Blume findet man in ganz England; do you know where there is a chemist's to be found? wissen Sie, wo hier eine Apotheke ist?; there wasn't one to be found es war keine(r) zu finden; we left everything as we found it wir haben alles so gelassen, wie wir es vorgefunden haben; he was found dead in bed er wurde tot im Bett aufgefunden; where am I going to ~ the money/time? wo nehme ich nur das Geld/die Zeit her?; I ~ myself in an impossible situation ich befinde mich in einer unmöglichen Situation; he awoke to ~ himself in prison/hospital er erwachte und fand sich im Gefängnis/Krankenhaus wieder; I found myself unable/forced to ... ich sah mich außerstande/gezwungen, zu ...

(b) (supply) besorgen (sb sth jdm etw). go and ~ me a needle hol mir doch mal eine Nadel!

(c) (discover, ascertain) feststellen. we found the car wouldn't start es stellte sich heraus, daß das Auto nicht ansprang; if you still ~ you can't do it wenn Sie feststellen, daß Sie es immer noch nicht können.

(d) (consider to be) finden. I ~ **Spain** too hot ich finde Spanien zu heiß; I don't ~ it easy to tell you this es fällt mir nicht leicht, Ihnen das zu sagen; did you ~ her a good worker? fanden Sie, daß sie gut arbeitet?; I ~ it impossible to understand him ich kann ihn einfach nicht verstehen.

(e) £100 per week all found £ 100 pro Woche, (und freie) Kost und Logis.

(f) (Jur) to ~ sb guilty jdn für schuldig befinden; how do you ~ the accused? wie lautet Ihr Urteil?

2 vi (Jur) to ~ for/against the accused den Angeklagten freisprechen/verurteilen.
♦ **find out 1** vt sep answer, sb's secret herausfinden. get found ~ laß dich nicht erwischen; you've been found ~ du bist ertappt. **2** vi es herausfinden. to ~ ~ about sb/sth (learn facts) etwas über jdn/etw erfahren; his wife ~s ~ about it/her wenn seine Frau dahinterkommt, wenn seine Frau davon/von ihr erfährt.

findings ['faındıŋz] n pl Ergebnis(se pl) nt; (medical) Befund m.

fine[1] [faın] **1** n (Jur) Geldstrafe f. **2** vt zu einer Geldstrafe verurteilen. he was ~d £10 er mußte £ 10 Strafe bezahlen; he was ~d for speeding er

mußte Strafe für zu schnelles Fahren zahlen.
fine² adj (+er) **(a)** weather schön. **one** ~ **day** eines
schönen Tages. **(b)** (good) gut; person fein; specimen, chap, woman prächtig; pianist, novel, painting, shot großartig; holiday, meal, view herrlich;
(elegant) clothes, manners etc fein. **a** ~ **time to ...**
(iro) genau der richtige Augenblick, zu ...; **a** ~
friend you are (iro) du bist mir ja ein schöner
Freund!; **that's a** ~ **thing to say** (iro) das ist ja
wirklich nett, so was zu sagen!; **this is a** ~ **state
of affairs** (iro) das sind ja schöne Zustände!;
that's ~ **by me** ich habe nichts dagegen; **(that's)**
~ **gut, in Ordnung; I'm/he is** ~ **now** es geht
mir/ihm wieder gut; **how are you?** — ~ **wie,**
geht's? — **gut.** **(c)** (delicate, thin) workmanship,
dust, distinction fein. **to appeal to sb's** ~**r feelings**
an jds besseres Ich appellieren; **there's a very** ~
line between ... es besteht ein feiner Unterschied zwischen ...
fine art n **(a)** usu pl schöne Künste pl. **(b)** he's **got
it down to a** ~ er hat den Bogen heraus (col).
finely ['faɪnlɪ] adv fein; worked schön.
finery ['faɪnərɪ] n (of dress) Staat m.
finesse [fɪ'nes] (skill) Gewandtheit f; (cunning) Finesse f.
fine-tooth comb ['faɪn'tuːθkəʊm] n: **to go through
sth with a** ~ etw genau unter die Lupe nehmen.
finger ['fɪŋgə'] **1** n Finger m. **she can twist him
around her little** ~ sie kann ihn um den (kleinen)
Finger wickeln; **to have a** ~ **in every pie** überall
die Finger im Spiel haben; **I didn't lay a** ~ **on her**
ich habe sie nicht angerührt; **he wouldn't lift a** ~
to help me er würde keinen Finger rühren, um
mir zu helfen; **he didn't lift a** ~ er hat keinen
Finger krumm gemacht; **I can't put my** ~ **on it,
but ...** ich kann es nicht genau ausmachen, aber
...; **you've put your** ~ **on it there** da haben Sie den
kritischen Punkt berührt; **to get** or **pull one's** ~
out (col) (do properly) Dampf dahinter machen;
(speed up) Dampf dahinter machen (col). **2** vt
anfassen; (toy, meddle with) herumfingern an
(+dat).
finger: ~ **board** n Griffbrett nt; ~**bowl** n Finger-
schale f.
fingering ['fɪŋgərɪŋ] n (Mus) (in the notation) Fin-
gersatz m; (of keys, strings) (Finger)technik f.
finger: ~**mark** n Fingerabdruck m; ~**nail** n Fingernagel m; ~ **print 1** n Fingerabdruck m; **2** vt **to**
~**print sb/sth** jdm Fingerabdrücke pl abneh-
men/von etw Fingerabdrücke pl abnehmen;
~**tip** n Fingerspitze f; **to have sth at one's**
~**tips** (fig) (know very well) etw aus dem Effeff
kennen (col); (have at one's disposal) etw parat
haben; ~**tip control** n (of steering wheel etc) mü-
helose Steuerung.
finicky ['fɪnɪkɪ] adj person schwer zufriedenzustellen, pingelig (col); work, job kniff(e)lig (col);
detail winzig.
finish ['fɪnɪʃ] **1** n **(a)** (end) Schluß m, Ende nt; (of
race) Finish nt; (~ing line) Ziel nt. **to be in at the**
~ (fig) den Schluß miterleben; **to fight to the** ~
bis zum letzten Augenblick kämpfen. **(b)** (of
products) Finish nt; (of material) Appretur f. **paint
with a gloss/matt**~ Farbe mit Hochglanzeffekt/
mattem Glanz; **this one has a better** ~ das ist
besser verarbeitet.
2 vt **(a)** beenden; course, work, business also
abschließen. **to** ~**have** ~**ed doing sth** mit etw
fertig werden/sein; **to** ~ **writing/reading sth** etw
zu Ende schreiben/lesen; **to have** ~**ed sth** etw
fertig haben; task, course mit etw fertig sein;
when do you ~ **work?** wann machen Sie Feierabend?; **give me time to** ~ **my drink** laß
mich austrinken; ~ **what you're doing** mach
das erst fertig; **that last kilometre nearly** ~**ed
me** (col) dieser letzte Kilometer hat mich
beinahe geschafft (col).
(b) (give ~ to) den letzten Schliff geben

(+dat); piece of handiwork verarbeiten; industrial
product ein schönes Finish geben (+dat). **the
paintwork isn't very well** ~**ed** der Lack hat
keine besonders schöne Oberfläche.
3 vi **(a)** zu Ende sein; (person: with task etc)
fertig sein; (come to an end, ~ work) aufhören;
(piece of music, story etc) enden. **when does the
film** ~? wann ist der Film aus?; **we'll** ~ **by**
singing a song wir wollen mit einem Lied schließen, zum Schluß singen wir ein Lied; **I've** ~**ed**
ich bin fertig. **(b)** (Sport) das Ziel erreichen. **to** ~
second als zweiter durchs Ziel gehen.
♦ **finish off 1** vi aufhören, Schluß machen. **2** vt
sep **(a)** piece of work fertigmachen. **a liqueur to** ~
~ **the meal** zum Abschluß des Essens noch einen
Likör. **(b)** food aufessen; drink austrinken. **(c)**
(kill) den Gnadenstoß geben (+dat); (by shooting)
den Gnadenschuß geben (+dat). **(d)** (do for)
person den Rest geben (+dat).
♦ **finish up 1** vi (end up in a place) landen (col).
he ~**ed a nervous wreck** er war zum Schluß
ein Nervenbündel; **I'll just** ~ ~ **by doing it all
again** zum Schluß muß ich doch alles noch mal
machen. **2** vt sep = **finish off 2 (b)**.
♦ **finish with** vi +prep obj **have you** ~**ed** ~ **the
paper?** haben Sie die Zeitung fertiggelesen?;
I've ~**ed** ~ **him** ich will nichts mehr mit ihm zu
tun haben; (with boyfriend) ich habe mit ihm
Schluß gemacht.
finished ['fɪnɪʃt] adj **(a)** item, product fertig; (polished) poliert; performance ausgereift; appearance vollendet. ~ **goods** Fertigprodukte pl;
beautifully ~ **dolls** wunderschön gearbeitete
Puppen. **(b) to be** ~ (person, task etc) fertig sein;
(exhausted, done for etc) erledigt sein; **the wine is**
~ es ist kein Wein mehr da; **I'm** ~ **with politics**
mit der Politik ist es für mich vorbei; **it's all** ~
(between us) es ist alles aus (zwischen uns).
finishing ['fɪnɪʃɪŋ]: ~ **line** n Ziellinie f; ~ **school** n
(Mädchen)pensionat nt.
finite ['faɪnaɪt] adj (limited) begrenzt; number endlich.
Finland ['fɪnlənd] n Finnland nt.
Finn [fɪn] n Finne m, Finnin f.
Finnish ['fɪnɪʃ] **1** adj finnisch. **2** n Finnisch nt.
fiord [fjɔːd] n Fjord m.
fir [fɜː'] n Tanne f; (~ wood) Tanne(nholz nt) f. ~
cone Tannenzapfen m.
fire [faɪə'] **1** n (lit, fig, Mil) Feuer nt; (electric, gas)
Ofen; (destructive: forest ~, house ~) Brand m.
the house was on ~ das Haus brannte; **to set** ~ **to**
sth, **to set sth on** ~ etw anzünden; (so as to destroy) etw in Brand stecken; **to catch** ~ Feuer
fangen; **you're playing with** ~ (fig) du spielst mit
dem Feuer; **there was a** ~ **next door** nebenan hat
es gebrannt; **to come under** ~ (lit, fig) unter
Beschuß geraten.
2 vt **(a)** gun abschießen; shot abfeuern;
rocket zünden. **to** ~ **a gun at sb** auf jdn schießen;
to ~ **questions at sb** Fragen auf jdn abfeuern.
(b) pottery brennen. **(c)** (fig) imagination beflügeln. **(d)** (col: dismiss) feuern (col).
3 vi **(a)** (shoot) schießen (at auf +acc). ~!
Feuer! **(b)** (engine) zünden. **the engine is only
firing on three cylinders** der Motor läuft
nur auf drei Zylindern.
♦ **fire away** vi (col: begin) losschießen (col).
fire: ~ **alarm** n Feueralarm m; (apparatus) Feuermelder m; ~**arm** n Schußwaffe f; ~ **brigade** n
(Brit) Feuerwehr f; ~**cracker** n Knallkörper m;
~ **department** n (US) Feuerwehr f; ~ **drill** n (for
firemen) Feuerwehrübung f; (for passengers etc)
Probealarm m; ~**-eater** n Feuerschlucker m;
~**-engine** n Feuerwehrauto nt; ~ **escape** n
(staircase) Feuertreppe f; (ladder) Feuerleiter f;
~ **extinguisher** n Feuerlöscher m; ~**guard** n
(Schutz)gitter nt (vor dem Kamin); ~ **hazard** n **to
be a** ~ **hazard** feuergefährlich sein; ~**light** n

Schein *m* des Feuers; ~**man** *n* Feuerwehrmann *m*; ~**place** *n* Kamin *m*; ~**power** *n* (*of guns, aircraft, army*) Feuerkraft *f*; ~**proof** *adj* feuerfest; ~**side** *n* **to sit by the** ~**side** am Kamin sitzen; ~ **station** *n* Feuerwehrzentrale *f*; ~**wood** *n* Brennholz *nt*; ~**works** *npl* Feuerwerkskörper *pl*; (*display*) Feuerwerk *nt*; **there'll be** ~**works if he finds out** (*col*) wenn er das erfährt, dann kracht's.

firing ['faɪrɪŋ] *n* (a) (*of pottery*) Brennen *nt*. (b) (*Mil*) Feuer *nt*; (*of gun, shot, rocket*) Abfeuern *nt*. (c) (*Aut: of engine*) Zündung *f*.

firing: ~ **line** *n* (*lit, fig*) Schußlinie *f*; ~ **squad** *n* Exekutionskommando *nt*.

firm¹ [fɜːm] *n* Firma *f*.

firm² 1 *adj* (+*er*) fest. **to be** ~ **with sb** jdm gegenüber bestimmt auftreten. **2** *adv* **to stand** ~ **on sth** (*fig*) fest bei etw bleiben.

firmly ['fɜːmlɪ] *adv* fest; *say* bestimmt.

firmness ['fɜːmnɪs] *n* Festigkeit *f*.

first [fɜːst] **1** *adj* erste(r, s). **who's** ~? wer ist der erste?; **I'm** ~, I've been waiting longer than you ich bin zuerst an der Reihe, ich warte schon länger als Sie; ~ **things** ~ eins nach dem anderen; **you have to put** ~ **things** ~ du mußt wissen, was dir am wichtigsten ist; **he doesn't know the** ~ **thing about it/cars** davon/von Autos hat er keinen blassen Schimmer (*col*); **in the** ~ **place** zunächst einmal; **why didn't you say so in the** ~ **place?** warum hast du denn das nicht gleich gesagt?

2 *adv* (a) zuerst; *arrive, leave* als erste(r, s); (*in listing*) erstens. ~ **come** ~ **served** (*prov*) wer zuerst kommt, mahlt zuerst (*Prov*); **ladies** ~ Ladies first!; **you** ~ du zuerst; **he says** ~ **one thing then another** er sagt mal so, mal so; **my health comes** ~ meine Gesundheit ist mir am wichtigsten; **he always puts his job** ~ seine Arbeit kommt bei ihm immer vor allem anderen; ~ **and foremost** zunächst; **I must finish this** ~ ich muß das erst fertigmachen; **think** ~ überlegen Sie es sich. (b) (*for the* ~ *time*) zum ersten Mal. **when did you** ~ **meet him?** wann haben Sie ihn das erste Mal getroffen?; **when it** ~ **became known that** ... als zuerst bekannt wurde, daß ... (c) (*in preference*) eher, lieber. **I'd die** ~! eher würde ich sterben!

3 *n* (a) **the** ~ der/die/das Erste; **they were the** ~ **to come** sie kamen als erste; **this is the** ~ I've **heard of it** das ist mir ja ganz neu; **at** ~ zuerst; **from the** ~ von Anfang an; **from** ~ **to last** von Anfang bis Ende. (b) (*Brit Univ*) **he got a** ~ **er bestand** (sein Examen) mit „sehr gut". (c) (*Aut*) ~ (**gear**) der erste (Gang). **in** ~ im ersten (Gang); *see* **sixth**.

first: ~ **aid** *n* Erste Hilfe; ~ **aid box** *n* Verbandskasten *m*; ~ **aid post** *n* Sanitätswache *f*; ~**-class 1** *adj* erstklassig; ~**-class compartment** Abteil *nt* erster Klasse; ~**-class mail** *bevorzugt beförderte Post*; **he's** ~**-class at tennis** er ist ein erstklassiger Tennisspieler; **that's absolutely** ~**-class** das ist einfach Spitze (*col*); ~**-class degree** (*Brit*) sehr gutes Examen; **2** *adv travel* erster Klasse; ~ **cousin** *n* Vetter *m* ersten Grades; ~ **edition** *n* Erstausgabe *f*; ~ **form** *n* (*Brit Sch*) erste Klasse; ~**-generation** *adj* citizen, computer der ersten Generation; ~**-hand** *adj, adv* aus erster Hand; **F~ Lady** First Lady *f*.

firstly ['fɜːstlɪ] *adv* erstens, zunächst (einmal).

first: ~ **name** *n* Vorname *m*; ~ **night** *n* (*Theat*) Premiere *f*; ~ **offender** *n* **he is a** ~ **offender** er ist nicht vorbestraft; ~ **officer** *n* (*Naut*) Erster Offizier; ~ **performance** *n* (*Theat*) Premiere *f*; (*first ever*) Uraufführung *f*; ~**-rate** *adj* erstklassig.

firth [fɜːθ] *n* (*Scot*) Meeresarm *m*.

fir tree *n* Tannenbaum *m*.

fiscal ['fɪskəl] *adj* Finanz-.

fish [fɪʃ] **1** *n, pl* - *or* (*esp for different types*) -**es** Fisch *m*. ~ **and chips** Fisch und Pommes

---

frites; **to drink like a** ~ (*col*) wie ein Loch saufen (*col*); **like a** ~ **out of water** wie ein Fisch auf dem Trockenen; **a queer** ~! (*col*) ein komischer Kauz.

2 *vi* fischen; (*with rod*) angeln. **to go** ~**ing** fischen/angeln gehen; **to go** ~ **salmon** ~**ing** auf Lachsfang gehen. **3** *vt* fischen; (*with rod*) angeln; *river* fischen/angeln in (+*dat*).

♦ **fish for** *vi* +*prep obj* fischen/angeln; (*fig*) *compliments* fischen nach. **they were** ~**ing** ~ **information** sie waren auf Informationen aus.

♦ **fish out** *vt sep* herausfischen (*of or from sth* aus etw).

♦ **fish up** *vt sep* (*from water*) herausziehen.

fish: ~**bone** *n* (Fisch)gräte *f*; ~**cake** *n* Fischfrikadelle *f*.

fisherman ['fɪʃəmən] *n*, *pl* -**men** [mən] Fischer *m*; (*amateur*) Angler *m*.

fishery ['fɪʃərɪ] *n* (*area*) Fischereizone *f*; (*industry*) Fischerei *f*.

fish: ~ **farm** *n* Fischzucht *f*; ~ **finger** *n* (*Brit*) Fischstäbchen *nt*; ~**hook** *n* Angelhaken *m*.

fishing ['fɪʃɪŋ] *n* Fischen *nt*; (*with rod*) Angeln *nt*; (*as industry*) Fischerei *f*.

fishing: ~ **boat** *n* Fischerboot *nt*; ~ **grounds** *npl* Fischgründe *pl*; ~ **industry** *n* Fischindustrie *f*; ~**-line** *n* Angelschnur *f*; ~**-net** *n* Fischnetz *nt*; ~ **port** *n* Fischereihafen *m*; ~**-rod** *n* Angelrute *f*; ~ **tackle** *n* (*for sport*) Angelgeräte *pl*; (*for industry*) Fischereigeräte *pl*; ~ **village** *n* Fischerdorf *nt*.

fish: ~ **knife** *n* Fischmesser *nt*; ~**monger** *n* (*Brit*) Fischhändler(in *f*) *m*; ~ **slice** *n* (Braten)wender *m*; ~ **stick** *n* (*US*) Fischstäbchen *nt*.

fishy ['fɪʃɪ] *adj* (+*er*) (a) *smell* Fisch-. (b) (*col*) verdächtig; *excuse, story* faul (*col*).

fission ['fɪʃən] *n* (*Phys*) Spaltung *f*.

fissure ['fɪʃəʳ] *n* Spalt(e *f*) *m*; (*deep*) Kluft *f*.

fist [fɪst] *n* Faust *f*.

fistful ['fɪstful] *n* Handvoll *f*.

fit¹ [fɪt] **1** *adj* (+*er*) (*suitable*) geeignet. ~ **to eat** eßbar; **is this meat still** ~ **to eat?** kann man dieses Fleisch noch essen?; ~ **for habitation** bewohnbar; **to be** ~ **to be seen** sich sehen lassen können; **you're not** ~ **to be spoken to** du verdienst es nicht, daß man sich mit dir unterhält; **I'll do as I think** ~ ich handle, wie ich es für richtig halte; **to see** ~ **to do sth** es für angebracht halten, etw zu tun; **it is only** ~ es ist nur recht und billig; **he did not see** ~ **to apologize** er hat es nicht für nötig gehalten, sich zu entschuldigen; **to be** ~ **to drop (with tiredness)** zum Umfallen müde sein. (b) (*in health*) gesund; *sportsman etc* fit, in Form. **she is not yet** ~ **to travel** sie ist noch nicht reisefähig.

2 *n* (*of clothes*) **it is a very good** ~ es sitzt or paßt sehr gut; **it's a bit of a tight** ~ (*suitcase, parking*) es geht gerade (noch); **in order to ensure a smooth** ~ (*of parts*) damit es genau paßt.

3 *vt* (a) (*cover, sheet, nut etc*) passen auf (+*acc*); (*key etc*) passen in (+*acc*); (*clothes etc*) passen (+*dat*). **this coat** ~**s you better** dieser Mantel paßt Ihnen besser; **to make a ring** ~ **sb** jdm einen Ring anpassen. (b) (*be suitable for*) *sb's plans, a theory etc* passen in (+*acc*). (c) **to** ~ **a dress on sb** jdm ein Kleid anprobieren. (d) (*put on, attach*) anbringen (*to an* +*dat*); *tyre* montieren; (*put in*) einbauen (*in* +*acc*); (*furnish, provide with*) ausstatten. **to** ~ **a key in the lock** einen Schlüssel ins Schloß stecken. (e) (*match*) *description, facts* entsprechen (+*dat*); (*person*) passen auf (+*acc*).

4 *vi* (*clothes, parts*) passen. **the facts don't** ~ die Fakten sind widersprüchlich; **it all** ~**s es** paßt alles zusammen.

♦ **fit in 1** *vt sep* (a) (*find space for*) unterbringen. (b) (*find time for*) *person* einen Termin geben (+*dat*); *meeting* unterbringen. (c) (*make harmonize*) **to** ~ **sth** ~ **with sth** etw mit etw in Einklang bringen. (d) (*fit, put in*) einbauen.

2 *vi* (a) *(go into place)* hineinpassen. (b) *(plans, ideas, word)* passen; *(facts etc)* übereinstimmen; *(match)* dazupassen. **how does this ~ ~?** wie paßt das ins Ganze?; **I see, it all ~s ~ now** jetzt paßt alles zusammen; **does that ~ ~ with your plans?** läßt sich das mit Ihren Plänen vereinbaren?; **he wants everybody to ~ ~ with him** er will, daß sich jedermann nach ihm richtet; **he doesn't ~ ~ here/with the others** er paßt hier nicht her/nicht zu den anderen; **the new director didn't ~ ~** der neue Direktor hat nicht in die Firma gepaßt; **try to ~ ~ (with the others)** versuche, dich den anderen anzupassen.

♦ **fit out** *vt sep (for expedition)* ausrüsten; *person, ship* ausstatten.

fit[2] *n (Med, fig)* Anfall *m*. **~ of coughing/anger** Husten-/Wutanfall *m*; **in a ~ of anger** in einem Anfall von Wut; **in ~s and starts** sporadisch; **to be in ~s of laughter** sich vor Lachen biegen; **he'd have a ~** *(fig col)* er würde (ja) einen Anfall kriegen *(col)*.

fitful ['fɪtfʊl] *adj sleep* unruhig; *enthusiasm* sporadisch.

fitment ['fɪtmənt] *n (furniture)* Einrichtungsgegenstand *m*; *(of machine, car)* Zubehörteil *nt*.

fitness ['fɪtnɪs] *n* (a) *(health)* Gesundheit *f*; *(condition)* Fitness, Fitneß *f*. (b) *(suitability)* Eignung *f*; *(of remark etc)* Angemessenheit *f*.

fitted ['fɪtɪd] *adj garment* tailliert. **~ carpet** Teppichboden *m*; **~ kitchen/cupboards** Einbauküche *f*/Einbauschränke *pl*.

fitter ['fɪtə'] *n (Tech)* Monteur *m*; *(for machines)* (Maschinen)schlosser *m*.

fitting ['fɪtɪŋ] **1** *adj (suitable)* passend. **it is not ~ for a lady ...** es schickt sich nicht für eine Dame ... **2** *n* (a) *(of suit etc)* Anprobe *f*. (b) *(part)* Zubehörteil *nt*. **~s** Ausstattung *f*; *(furniture)* Einrichtung *f*; **bathroom/office ~s** Badezimmer-/Büroeinrichtung *f*; **electrical ~s** Elektroinstallationen.

five [faɪv] **1** *adj* fünf. **2** *n* Fünf *f*; *see* **six**.

five: **~-and-ten** *n (US)* billiges Kaufhaus; **~-o'clock shadow** *n* nachmittäglicher Anflug von Bartstoppeln.

fiver ['faɪvə'] *n (col)* Fünfpfund-/Fünfdollarschein *m*.

fix [fɪks] **1** *vt* (a) *(make firm)* befestigen *(sth to sth* etw an/auf etw +*dat)*; *(install) new aerial, new dynamo* anbringen; *(fig) ideas, images* festsetzen; *attention* richten *(on auf* +*acc)*. **to ~ a stake in the ground** einen Pfahl im Boden verankern; **to ~ sth in one's mind** sich *(dat)* etw fest einprägen; **to ~ one's eyes on sb/sth** jdn/etw fixieren. (b) *(arrange)* arrangieren; *date, price, limit* festsetzen; *(agree on)* ausmachen; *tickets, taxi etc* besorgen. (c) *(straighten out)* regeln. **I'll ~ him** *(col)* dem werd' ich's besorgen *(col)*. (d) *(repair)* in Ordnung bringen; *(put in good order, adjust)* machen *(col)*. (e) *drink, meal* machen. **to ~ one's hair** sich frisieren *(col)*; **race, fight** manipulieren. **the whole thing was ~ed** das war eine abgekartete Sache *(col)*.

2 *n* (a) **to be in a ~** in der Klemme sitzen *(col)*; **to get oneself into a ~** sich *(dat)* eine schöne Suppe einbrocken *(col)*. (b) *(Naut)* **to take a ~ on sth** etw orten. (c) *(col: of drugs)* Fix *m (col)*. **to give oneself a ~** fixen *(col)*. (d) *(col)* **the fight was a ~** der Kampf war eine abgekartete Sache *(col)*.

♦ **fix on** **1** *vt sep* festmachen *(prep obj auf* +*dat)*; *(fit on)* anbringen. **2** *vi* +*prep obj (decide on)* sich entscheiden für; *(US col: intend)* vorhaben.

♦ **fix up** *vt sep* (a) *shelves* anbringen. (b) *(arrange)* arrangieren; *holidays etc* festmachen. **have you got anything ~ed ~ for this evening?** haben Sie (für) heute abend schon etwas vor? (c) **to ~ sb ~ with sth** jdm etw besorgen; **when you get yourself ~ed ~ (with a room)** wenn du ein Zimmer

hast.

fixation [fɪk'seɪʃən] *n (Psych)* Fixierung *f*. **a ~ about cleanliness** ein Sauberkeitsfimmel *m (col)*.

fixative ['fɪksətɪv] *n* Fixativ *nt*.

fixed [fɪkst] *adj* (a) *fest; idea* fix; *smile* starr. **~ assets** feste Anlagen *pl*; **~ capital** Anlagekapital *nt*; **~ price** Festpreis *m*. (b) *(col)* **how are you ~ for money** etc? wie steht's (denn) bei dir mit Geld etc? *(col)*; **how are you ~ for tonight?** was hast du heute abend vor?

fixedly ['fɪksɪdlɪ] *adv stare, look* starr.

fixings ['fɪksɪŋz] *npl (US Cook)* Beilagen *pl*.

fixture ['fɪkstʃə'] *n* (a) *(of a building etc)* ~s and fittings Anschlüsse und unbewegliches Inventar *(form)*. (b) *(Brit Sport)* Spiel *nt*.

fizz [fɪz] *vi (champagne etc)* perlen, sprudeln.

♦ **fizzle out** *vi (firework, enthusiasm)* verpuffen; *(plan)* im Sand verlaufen.

fizzy ['fɪzɪ] *adj* (+*er*) sprudelnd. **to be ~** sprudeln; **a ~ drink** eine Brause.

fjord [fjɔːd] *n* Fjord *m*.

flab [flæb] *n (col)* Speck *m*.

flabbergasted ['flæbəgɑːstɪd] *adj (col)* platt *(col)*.

flabby ['flæbɪ] *adj* (+*er*) schlaff; *(fat) stomach* wabbelig.

flag[1] [flæg] *n* Fahne *f*; *(small, on map, chart, for charity)* Fähnchen *nt*; *(national also, Naut)* Flagge *f*. **to keep the ~ flying** die Fahne hochhalten.

♦ **flag down** *vt sep taxi etc* anhalten.

flag[2] *vi (grow weaker etc)* nachlassen; *(person)* ermüden.

flag[3] *n (also ~stone)* Steinplatte *f*.

flag: **~ day** *n (Brit)* Tag *m*, an dem für einen wohltätigen Zweck gesammelt wird; **F~ Day** *(US)* 14. Juni, Gedenktag der Einführung der amerikanischen Nationalflagge; **~pole** *n* Fahnenstange *f*.

flagrant ['fleɪgrənt] *adj* eklatant, kraß; *injustice* himmelschreiend; *disregard* unverhohlen.

flag: **~ship** *n* Flaggschiff *nt*; **~stone** *n* (Stein)platte *f*; **~ stop** *n (US)* Bedarfshaltestelle *f*.

flail [fleɪl] *vt* **he ~ed his arms about** er schlug (mit den Armen) wild um sich.

flair [fleə'] *n (talent)* Talent *nt*; *(stylishness)* Flair *nt*.

flak [flæk] *n* Flakfeuer *nt*. **~ jacket** kugelsichere Weste.

flake [fleɪk] **1** *n (of snow, soap)* Flocke *f*; *(of paint, rust)* Splitter *m*; *(of skin)* Schuppe *f*. **2** *vi (also ~ off) (plaster)* abbröckeln; *(paint)* abblättern.

♦ **flake out** *vi (col) (pass out, fall over)* aus den Latschen kippen *(col)*; *(fall asleep)* einpennen *(col)*.

flaky ['fleɪkɪ] *adj* (+*er*) **~ pastry** Blätterteig *m*.

flamboyance [flæm'bɔɪəns] *n* Extravaganz *f*; *(of colour)* Pracht *f*.

flamboyant [flæm'bɔɪənt] *adj* extravagant; *colours* prächtig.

flame [fleɪm] *n (also fig col: sweetheart)* Flamme *f*. **the house was in ~s** das Haus stand in Flammen.

flamethrower ['fleɪm,θrəʊə'] *n* Flammenwerfer *m*.

flaming ['fleɪmɪŋ] *adj (lit)* lodernd; *(fig) passion* glühend; *row* heftig. **he was in a ~ temper** *(col)* er kochte vor Wut *(col)*. (b) *(Brit col!: bloody)* verdammt *(col)*.

flamingo [flə'mɪŋgəʊ] *n, pl* **-(e)s** Flamingo *m*.

flammable ['flæməbl] *adj* feuergefährlich.

flan [flæn] *n (Brit)* Kuchen *m*. **fruit ~** Obstkuchen *m*.

Flanders ['flɑːndəz] *n* Flandern *nt*.

flange [flændʒ] *n* Flansch *m*.

flank [flæŋk] **1** *n (of animal, Mil)* Flanke *f*. **2** *vt* flankieren.

flannel ['flænl] **1** *n* (a) Flanell *m*. **~s** *pl (trousers)* Flanellhose *f*. (b) *(Brit: face-~)* Waschlappen *m*. (c) *(Brit col: waffle)* Geschwafel *nt (col)*. **2** *adj trousers etc* Flanell-.

flannelette [,flænə'let] n Baumwollflanell m. ~ **sheet** Biberbettuch nt.

flap [flæp] 1 n (a) (of pocket, Aviat) Klappe f; (of table) ausziehbarer Teil. a ~ of skin (Med) ein Hautlappen m. (b) (sound) (of sails etc) Flattern nt; (of wings) Schlagen nt. (c) to give sth a ~ (shake out) etw ausschütteln. (d) (col) to get in(to) a ~ in Panik geraten; there's a big ~ on es herrscht große Panik. 2 vi (a) (wings) schlagen; (sails, tarpaulin etc) flattern. his ears were ~ping (col) er spitzte die Ohren. (b) (col) in Panik sein. to start to ~ in Panik geraten; don't ~ reg dich nicht auf! 3 vt to ~ its wings mit den Flügeln schlagen.

flare [flɛəʳ] 1 n (a) Auflodern nt. (b) (signal) Leuchtsignal nt; (from pistol) Leuchtrakete f; (landing ~) Leuchtfeuer nt. (c) (Fashion) ausgestellter Schnitt. (d) (solar ~) Sonneneruption f. 2 vi (a) (match, torch) aufleuchten. (b) (nostrils) sich blähen.

♦ **flare up** vi auflodern; (fig) (person) aufbrausen; (fighting, epidemic) ausbrechen.

flared [flɛəd] adj trousers, skirt ausgestellt.

flare: ~ **path** n (Aviat) Leuchtpfad m; ~ **pistol** n Leuchtpistole f; ~**up** n (sudden dispute) (plötzlicher) Krach; (fighting) (plötzlicher) Ausbruch von Kämpfen.

flash [flæʃ] 1 n (a) Aufblinken nt no pl; (very bright) Aufblitzen nt no pl; (of metal, jewels etc) Blinken nt no pl; (Mot) Lichthupe f no pl. to give sb a ~ (Mot) jdn (mit der Lichthupe) anblinken; ~ of lightning Blitz m. (b) (fig: news ~) Kurzmeldung f. ~ of wit/inspiration Geistesblitz m; in a ~ im Nu; as quick as a ~ blitzschnell; a ~ in the pan (col) ein Strohfeuer nt. (c) (Phot) Blitz(licht nt) m. to use a ~ Blitzlicht benutzen. (d) (US col: torch) Taschenlampe f.
2 vi (a) aufblinken; (very brightly) aufblitzen; (repeatedly: indicators etc) blinken; (metal, jewels, eyes) blitzen. (b) (move quickly) (vehicle) sausen. to ~ past or by vorbeisausen; (holidays etc) vorbeifliegen. the thought ~ed through my mind that ... es schoß mir durch den Kopf, daß ...
3 vt (a) light aufblitzen lassen; SOS, message blinken. to ~ one's headlights die Lichthupe betätigen; to ~ one's headlights at sb, to ~ sb jdn mit der Lichthupe anblinken; she ~ed him a look of contempt sie blitzte ihn verächtlich an. (b) (col: show off: also ~ around) protzen mit; diamond ring blitzen lassen. don't ~ all that money around wedel nicht so mit dem vielen Geld herum! (col).

flash: ~**back** n (Film) Rückblende f; ~**cube** n (Phot) Blitz(licht)würfel m.

flasher ['flæʃəʳ] n (Brit col) Exhibitionist m.

flash: ~ **gun** n Elektronenblitzgerät nt; ~ **Harry** n (col) Lackaffe m (pej col); ~**light** n (a) (Phot) Blitzlicht nt; (b) (esp US: torch) Taschenlampe f.

flashy ['flæʃɪ] adj (+er) auffällig.

flask [flɑːsk] n Flakon m; (Chem) Glaskolben m; (vacuum ~) Thermosflasche f.

flat[1] [flæt] 1 adj (+er) (a) flach; tyre, nose, feet platt; surface eben; battery leer. as ~ as a pancake (col) (tyre) total platt; (countryside) total flach; (girl) flach wie ein Brett; to fall ~ on one's face auf die Nase fallen. (b) (fig: dull) fad(e); painting, photo kontrastarm; colour matt; joke abgedroschen; business, market lau; beer, wine schal, abgestanden. she felt a bit ~ sie hatte zu nichts Lust; to fall ~ (joke) nicht ankommen; (play etc) durchfallen. (c) refusal, denial glatt. and that's ~ und damit basta. (d) (Mus) instrument zu tief (gestimmt); voice zu tief. A~ As nt. (e) (Comm) Pauschal-. ~ rate of pay Pauschallohn m; ~ rate Pauschale f.
2 adv (+er) (a) refuse rundweg; tell klipp und klar. in ten seconds ~ in sage und schreibe (nur) zehn Sekunden; ~ broke (Brit col) total pleite

(col). (b) (Mus) to sing/play ~ zu tief singen/spielen. (c) ~ out (col: asleep, drunk) hinüber (col); to go ~ out voll aufdrehen (col); (in car also) Spitze fahren (col); to work or go ~ out auf Hochtouren arbeiten; to be lying ~ out platt am Boden liegen.
3 n (a) (of hand) Fläche f. (b) (Mus) Erniedrigungszeichen, b nt. (c) (Aut) Platte(r) m (col), (Reifen)panne f.

flat[2] n (Brit: apartment) Wohnung f.

flat: ~-**chested** adj flachbrüstig; ~**fish** n Plattfisch m; ~-**footed** adj plattfüßig; ~**let** n (Brit) kleine Wohnung.

flatly ['flætlɪ] adv deny, refuse rundweg; say klipp und klar.

flatmate ['flætmeɪt] n (Brit) Mitbewohner(in f) m.

flatness ['flætnɪs] n (of land etc) Flachheit f.

flat: ~ **race** n Flachrennen nt; ~ **season** n Flachrennsaison f.

flatten ['flætn] 1 vt path, road, field ebnen; (storm etc) crops zu Boden drücken; trees umwerfen; town dem Erdboden gleichmachen. that'll ~ him (fig col) das wird bei ihm die Luft rauslassen (col). 2 vr to ~ oneself against sth sich platt gegen etw drücken.

♦ **flatten out** 1 vi eben(er) werden. 2 vt sep path ebnen; metal glatt hämmern; map, paper, fabric glätten.

flatter ['flætəʳ] vt schmeicheln (+dat). it ~s your figure das ist sehr vorteilhaft; you can ~ yourself on being ... Sie können sich (dat) etwas darauf einbilden, daß Sie ...

flatterer ['flætərəʳ] n Schmeichler(in f) m.

flattering ['flætərɪŋ] adj schmeichelhaft; clothes vorteilhaft.

flattery ['flætərɪ] n Schmeichelleien pl.

flatulence ['flætjʊləns] n Blähung(en pl) f.

flatware ['flætweəʳ] n (US) (cutlery) Besteck nt; (plates etc) Geschirr nt.

flaunt [flɔːnt] vt zur Schau stellen.

flautist ['flɔːtɪst] n Flötist(in f) m.

flavour, (US) flavor ['fleɪvəʳ] 1 n (taste) Geschmack m; (flavouring) Aroma nt; (fig: atmosphere) Atmosphäre f. **20** ~**s** 20 Geschmackssorten. 2 vt Geschmack geben (+dat). pineapple-~ed mit Ananasgeschmack.

flavouring, (US) flavoring ['fleɪvərɪŋ] n (Cook) Aroma nt. vanilla ~ Vanillearoma nt.

flaw [flɔː] n Fehler m; (in diamond) Unreinheit f.

flawless ['flɔːlɪs] adj fehlerlos; complexion makellos; diamond lupenrein.

flax [flæks] n (Bot) Flachs m.

flaxen-haired ['flæksən,heəd] adj flachsblond.

flay [fleɪ] vt (skin) animal abziehen; (whip) auspeitschen; (fig: criticize) kein gutes Haar lassen an (+dat).

flea [fliː] n Floh m.

fleck [flek] 1 n (of red etc) Tupfen m; (of mud, paint) Fleck(en) m. a ~ of dust ein Stäubchen nt. 2 vt sprenkeln; (with mud etc) bespritzen. blue ~ed with white blau mit weißen Tupfen.

fled [fled] pret, ptp of **flee**.

fledg(e)ling ['fledʒlɪŋ] n (bird) Jungvogel m.

flee [fliː] pret, ptp **fled** 1 vi fliehen, flüchten (from vor +dat). 2 vt town, country flüchten aus; danger entfliehen (+dat).

fleece [fliːs] 1 n Vlies nt; (fabric) (natural) Schaffell nt; (artificial) Webpelz m. 2 vt (fig col: rob) schröpfen.

fleecy ['fliːsɪ] adj (+er) blanket, lining flauschig. ~ clouds Schäfchenwolken pl.

fleet [fliːt] n (a) (Naut) Geschwader nt; (entire naval force) Flotte f. (b) (of buses etc) (Fuhr)park m.

fleeting ['fliːtɪŋ] adj flüchtig; beauty vergänglich.

Flemish ['flemɪʃ] 1 adj flämisch. 2 n (a) the ~ pl die Flamen pl. (b) (language) Flämisch nt.

flesh [fleʃ] n Fleisch nt; (of fruit) Fleisch nt.

one's own ~ and blood sein eigen(es) Fleisch und Blut; **it was more than ~ and blood could bear** das war einfach nicht zu ertragen; **in the ~ in Person**; **~pots** *pl* Fleischtöpfe *pl*; **~ wound** Fleischwunde *f*.

fleshy ['fleʃɪ] *adj* (+er) fleischig.

flew [fluː] *pret of* **fly**[2], **fly**[3].

flex [fleks] **1** *n* (Brit) Schnur *f*; (heavy duty) Kabel *nt*. **2** *vt body, knees* beugen; *muscles* (lit, fig) spielen lassen.

flexibility [,fleksɪ'bɪlɪtɪ] *n see adj* Biegsamkeit *f*; Flexibilität *f*.

flexible ['fleksəbl] *adj wire* biegsam; (fig) flexibel. **~ working hours** gleitende Arbeitszeit.

flex(i)time ['fleks(ɪ)taɪm] *n* Gleitzeit *f*.

flick [flɪk] **1** *n* (of tail) kurzer Schlag. **hot water at the ~ of a switch** auf Knopfdruck heißes Wasser; **she gave the room a quick ~ with the duster** sie ging kurz mit dem Staublappen durch das Zimmer. **2** *vt whip* schnalzen mit; *switch* anknipsen; *dust, ash* wegschnipsen; (with cloth) wegwedeln. **she ~ed her hair out of her eyes** sie strich sich (dat) die Haare aus den Augen. **3** *vi* **the snake's tongue ~ed in and out** die Schlange züngelte.

♦ **flick off** *vt sep* wegschnipsen.

♦ **flick through** *vi* +prep obj (schnell) durchblättern.

flicker ['flɪkə[r]] **1** *vi* (flame, candle) flackern; (TV) flimmern; (needle on dial) zittern; (eyelid) zucken. **2** *n see vi* Flackern *nt*; Flimmern *nt*; Zittern *nt*; Zucken *nt*. **a ~ of hope** ein Hoffnungsschimmer *nt*.

flick knife *n* Klappmesser *nt*.

flight[1] [flaɪt] *n* (a) Flug *m*. **in ~** (birds) im Flug; (Aviat) in der Luft; **~s of fancy** geistige Höhenflüge *pl*. **(b) ~** (of stairs) Treppe *f*; **he lives six ~s up** er wohnt sechs Treppen hoch.

flight[2] *n* Flucht *f*. **to put the enemy to ~** den Feind in die Flucht schlagen; **to take (to) ~** die Flucht ergreifen.

flight: ~ deck *n* (Naut) Flugdeck *nt*; (Aviat) Cockpit *nt*; **~ engineer** *n* Bordingenieur *m*; **~less** *adj* nicht flugfähig; **~ path** *n* Flugbahn *f*; (of individual plane) Flugroute *f*; **incoming/ outgoing ~ path** Einflug-/Ausflugschneise *f*; **~ recorder** *n* Flugschreiber *m*.

flighty ['flaɪtɪ] *adj* (+er) (fickle) flatterhaft.

flimsy ['flɪmzɪ] *adj* (+er) *material* dünn; *clothing* dürftig; *house, aircraft* leicht gebaut; *excuse* fadenscheinig.

flinch [flɪntʃ] *vi* zurückzucken. **without ~ing** ohne mit der Wimper zu zucken; **to ~ from a task** vor einer Aufgabe zurückschrecken.

fling [flɪŋ] (vb: pret, ptp **flung**) **1** *n* (fig col) **to have a ~ at sth**, **to give sth a ~** etw (aus)probieren; **to have a ~ at doing sth** einen Anlauf machen, etw zu tun (col); **to have a or one's ~** sich austoben. **2** *vt* (lit, fig) schleudern. **to ~ the window open/shut** das Fenster aufstoßen/zuwerfen; **the door was flung open** die Tür flog auf; **to ~ one's arms around sb's neck** jdm die Arme um den Hals werfen; **to ~ on one's coat** sich (dat) den Mantel überwerfen; **to ~ oneself into a job** sich auf eine Aufgabe stürzen; **to ~ oneself out of the window/into a chair** sich aus dem Fenster stürzen/sich in einen Sessel werfen.

♦ **fling away** *vt sep* wegwerfen; (fig) money verschwenden.

♦ **fling back** *vt sep* one's head zurückwerfen.

♦ **fling down** *vt sep* (lit) herunterwerfen.

♦ **fling out** *vt sep* object wegwerfen; person hinauswerfen.

flint [flɪnt] *n* Feuerstein *m*.

flip [flɪp] **1** *vt* schnippen, schnipsen. **to ~ a book open** ein Buch aufschlagen; **to ~ one's lid** (col) durchdrehen (col). **2** *vi* (col) durchdrehen (col). **3** *interj* (Brit col) verflixt (col).

♦ **flip off** *vt sep* wegschnipsen; ash from cigarette abschnippen.

♦ **flip over 1** *vt sep* umdrehen; pages of book wenden. **2** *vi* sich (um)drehen.

♦ **flip through** *vi* +prep obj book durchblättern.

flip pack *n* Klappschachtel *f*.

flippancy ['flɪpənsɪ] *n* Leichtfertigkeit *f*.

flippant ['flɪpənt] *adj* leichtfertig.

flipper ['flɪpə[r]] *n* Flosse *f*.

flipping ['flɪpɪŋ] *adj, adv* (Brit col) verflixt (col).

flip: ~ side *n* (of record) B-Seite *f*; **~ top** *n* Klappdeckel *m*.

flirt [flɜːt] **1** *vi* flirten; (with idea, death) spielen. **2** *n* **he/she is just a ~** er/sie will nur flirten.

flirtation [flɜː'teɪʃən] *n* Flirt *m*.

flit [flɪt] **1** *vi* (a) (bats, butterflies etc) flattern; (person, image) huschen. **to ~ in and out** (person) rein- und rausflitzen. **(b)** (Brit: move house secretly) sich bei Nacht und Nebel davonmachen. **2** *n* (Brit) **to do a (moonlight) ~** bei Nacht und Nebel umziehen.

float [fləʊt] **1** *n* (a) (on fishing-line, Tech) Schwimmer *m*; (on trawl net) Korken *m*. **(b)** (vehicle) (in procession) Festwagen *m*; (for deliveries) kleiner Elektrolieferwagen. **(c)** (ready cash: in till) Wechselgeld *nt no indef art*; (loan to start business) Startkapital *nt*. **2** *vi* (a) (on water) schwimmen; (move gently) treiben; (in air) schweben. **(b)** (Comm: currency) floaten. **3** *vt* (a) boat zu Wasser bringen. **(b)** (Comm, Fin) company gründen; shares auf den Markt bringen; bond issue ausgeben; currency freigeben, floaten lassen.

♦ **float away** or **off** *vi* (on water) abtreiben; (in air) davonschweben; (fig: person) hinwegschweben.

floating ['fləʊtɪŋ] *adj* raft, logs treibend; population wandernd; kidney Wander-; decimal point Gleit-. **~ voter** Wechselwähler *m*.

flock [flɒk] **1** *n* (of sheep, geese, Eccl) Herde *f*; (of birds, people) Schar *f*. **2** *vi* in Scharen kommen. **to ~ in** hinein-/hereinströmen; **to ~ around sb** um jdn scharen.

floe [fləʊ] *n* Eisscholle *f*.

flog [flɒg] *vt* (a) prügeln; thief, mutineer auspeitschen. **you're ~ging a dead horse** (col) Sie verschwenden Ihre Zeit; **to ~ sth to death** (fig) etw zu Tode reiten. **(b)** (Brit col: sell) verkloppen (col).

flogging ['flɒgɪŋ] *n* Tracht *f* Prügel; (Jur) Prügelstrafe *f*; (of thief, mutineer) Auspeitschen *nt*.

flood [flʌd] **1** *n* (of water, fig) Flut *f*; **~s** Hochwasser *nt*; **the F~** die Sintflut; **the river is in ~** der Fluß führt Hochwasser; **she had a ~ in the kitchen** ihre Küche stand unter Wasser; **she was in ~s of tears** sie war in Tränen gebadet; **bathed in a ~ of light** lichtüberflutet. **2** *vt* (lit, fig, Comm) überschwemmen. **to ~ the carburettor** den Motor absaufen lassen (col); **~ed with light** lichtdurchflutet. **3** *vi* (river) über die Ufer treten; (bath etc) überlaufen. **(b)** (people) strömen.

♦ **flood in** *vi* (lit, fig) hinein-/hereinströmen. **the letters just ~ed in** wir/sie etc hatten eine Flut von Briefen.

♦ **flood out** *vt sep* house überfluten. **the villagers were ~ed** die Dorfbewohner wurden durch das Hochwasser obdachlos.

floodgate ['flʌdgeɪt] *n* Schleusentor *nt*. **to open the ~s** (fig) Tür und Tor öffnen (to dat).

flooding ['flʌdɪŋ] *n* Überschwemmung *f*.

flood: ~light *n* (vb: pret, ptp ~lit) **1** *vt buildings* anstrahlen; football pitch mit Flutlicht beleuchten; **2** *n* **under ~** das or im Flutlicht; **~lit 1** pret, ptp of **~light**; **2** adj **~lit** football Fußball bei Flutlicht; **~tide** *n* Flut *f*.

floor [flɔː[r]] **1** *n* (a) (of room) (Fuß)boden *m*; (dance-~) Tanzboden *m*. **to take the ~** (dance) aufs Parkett gehen; (speak) das Wort ergreifen; **to have the ~** (speaker) das Wort haben; **a question from the ~** ein Frage aus der Zuhörerschaft; *(Parl)* eine Frage aus dem Haus. **(b)** *(storey)* Stock(werk *nt)* m. **first** ~ *(Brit)* erster Stock; *(US)* Erdgeschoß *nt*; **on the second** ~ *(Brit)* im zweiten Stock; *(US)* im ersten Stock. **2** *vt* **(a)** *room etc* mit einem (Fuß)boden versehen. **(b)** *(knock down) opponent* zu Boden schlagen. **(c)** *(silence)* die Sprache verschlagen (+*dat*); *(puzzle)* verblüffen; *(defeat: question, problem etc)* schaffen *(col)*.

floor: ~**board** *n* Diele *f*; ~**cloth** *n* Putzlappen *m*; ~ **polish** *n* Bohnerwachs *nt*; ~ **show** *n* Show *f (im Nachtklub oder Kabarett)*; ~**walker** *n (Comm)* Ladenaufsicht *f*.

flop [flɒp] **1** *vi* **(a)** *(col: person: into chair etc)* sich hinplumpsen lassen. **(b)** *(col: fail)* durchfallen. **2** *n (col: failure)* Reinfall *m*; *(person)* Niete *f*.

floppy ['flɒpɪ] *adj* (+*er*) schlaff; *hat, ears* Schlapp-; *clothes* weit. ~ **disk** Floppy-Disk, Diskette *f*.

flora ['flɔːrə] *n* Flora *f*.

floral ['flɔːrəl] *adj arrangement* Blüten-; *fabric, dress* geblümt.

florid ['flɒrɪd] *adj* **(a)** *complexion* kräftig. **(b)** *style, writing* blumig.

florist ['flɒrɪst] *n* Florist(in *f)* m.

flotilla [flə'tɪlə] *n* Flotille *f*.

flotsam ['flɒtsəm] *n (lit, fig)* ~ **and jetsam** Strandgut *nt*.

flounce[1] [flaʊns] *vi* **to** ~ **in/out** herein-/herausstolzieren.

flounce[2] *n (frill)* Volant *m*, Rüsche *f*.

flounder[1] ['flaʊndə^r] *n (fish)* Flunder *f*.

flounder[2] *vi* **to** ~ **through the mud/snow** sich durch den Schlamm/Schnee schleppen; **to start to** ~ *(speaker etc)* ins Schwimmen kommen.

flour ['flaʊə^r] *n* Mehl *nt*.

flourish ['flʌrɪʃ] **1** *vi (plants, person)* (prächtig) gedeihen; *(business)* blühen, florieren; *(type of literature, painting)* seine Blütezeit haben. **2** *vt (wave about)* schwenken. **3** *n* **(a)** *(curve, decoration etc)* Schnörkel *m*. **(b)** *(movement)* schwungvolle Bewegung. **(c)** *(Mus) (fanfare)* Fanfare *f*; *(decorative passage)* Verzierung *f*.

flourishing ['flʌrɪʃɪŋ] *adj plant, person* blühend *attr; business* florierend *attr*.

flout [flaʊt] *vt* mißachten.

flow [fləʊ] **1** *vi* **(a)** *(lit, fig)* fließen; *(prose)* flüssig sein. **where the river** ~**s into the sea** wo der Fluß ins Meer mündet; **to keep the conversation** ~**ing** das Gespräch in Gang halten; **to keep the traffic** ~**ing** den Verkehr nicht ins Stocken kommen lassen; **to** ~ **in** *(water, people, money)* hinein-/hereinströmen. **(b)** *(tide)* steigen. **2** *n* Fluß *m*. **the** ~ **of** *traffic/information* der Verkehrs-/Informationsfluß; **the tide is on the** ~ die Flut kommt; **the** ~ **of his style** sein flüssiger Stil; ~**chart** Flußdiagramm *nt*.

flower ['flaʊə^r] **1** *n* Blume *f*; *(blossom, fig)* Blüte *f*. **in** ~ in Blüte; **to be in the** ~ **of youth** in der Blüte seiner Jugend stehen. **2** *vi (lit, fig)* blühen.

flower: ~ **arrangement** *n* Blumengesteck *nt*; ~**bed** *n* Blumenbeet *nt*; ~ **garden** *n* Blumengarten *m*; ~**pot** *n* Blumentopf *m*; ~ **power** *n* Flowerpower *f*; ~ **show** *n* Blumenschau *f*.

flowery ['flaʊərɪ] *adj perfume, fig) language* blumig; *dress, material* geblümt.

flown [fləʊn] *ptp of* **fly**[2], **fly**[3].

flu, 'flu [fluː] *n* Grippe *f*. **to have (the)** ~ (die *or* eine) Grippe haben.

fluctuate ['flʌktjʊeɪt] *vi* schwanken.

fluctuation [ˌflʌktjʊ'eɪʃən] *n* Schwankung *f*; *(fig: of opinions)* Schwanken *nt no pl*.

flue [fluː] *n* Rauchabzug *m*.

fluency ['fluːənsɪ] *n* Flüssigkeit *f*; *(of speaker)* Gewandtheit *f*. **because of his** ~ **in English** ... da er fließend Englisch spricht/sprach ....

fluent ['fluːənt] *adj style* flüssig; *speaker, writer* gewandt. **to be** ~ **in Italian, to speak** ~ **Italian** fließend Italienisch sprechen; **his** ~ **Italian sein**

gutes Italienisch.

fluently ['fluːəntlɪ] *adv speak a language* fließend; *express oneself* gewandt.

fluff [flʌf] **1** *n no pl (on young animals)* Flaum *m*; *(from material)* Fusseln *pl*; *(dust)* Staubflocken *pl*. **a bit of** ~ eine Staubflocke/Fussel; *(hum col)* eine Mieze *(col)*. **2** *vt* **(a)** *(also* ~ **out)** *feathers* aufplustern; *pillows* aufschütteln. **(b)** *(col: make mistake in)* vermasseln *(col)*.

fluffy ['flʌfɪ] *adj* (+*er*) *bird* flaumig; *material, toy* kuschelig, weich; *hair* duftig.

fluid ['fluːɪd] **1** *adj substance, style* flüssig; *(fig) situation* ungewiß. **the situation is still** ~ die Dinge sind noch im Fluß. **2** *n* Flüssigkeit *f*.

fluke [fluːk] *n (col)* Dusel *m (col)*. **it was a (pure)** ~ das war (einfach) Dusel.

flung [flʌŋ] *pret, ptp of* **fling**.

flunk [flʌŋk] *vt (col)* **to** ~ **German/an exam** in Deutsch/bei einer Prüfung durchsausen *(col)*.

flunk(e)y ['flʌŋkɪ] *n* Lakai *m*.

fluorescent [flʊə'resənt] *adj* Leucht-; *lighting, tube* Neon-.

fluoride ['flʊəraɪd] *n* Fluorid *nt*. ~ **toothpaste** Fluorzahnpasta *f*.

flurry ['flʌrɪ] *n* **(a)** *(of snow)* Gestöber *nt*; *(of wind)* Stoß *m*. **(b)** *(fig)* **all in a** ~ in großer Aufregung; **a** ~ **of activity** eine Hektik.

flush[1] [flʌʃ] **1** *n* **(a)** *(lavatory* ~) (Wasser)spülung *f*. **(b)** *(blush)* Röte *f*. **hot** ~**es** *(Med)* fliegende Hitze. **(c)** *(of beauty, youth)* Blüte *f*; *(of excitement)* Welle *f*. **in the (first)** ~ **of victory** im (ersten) Siegestaumel; **in the first** ~ **of youth** in der ersten Jugendblüte. **2** *vi (person, face)* rot werden *(with vor +dat)*. **3** *vt* spülen. **to** ~ **the lavatory** spülen; **to** ~ **sth down the lavatory** etw die Toilette hinunterspülen.

♦ **flush away** *vt sep* wegspülen.

♦ **flush out** *vt sep bottle* ausspülen; *dirt* wegspülen; *birds, spies* aufstöbern.

flush[2] *adj pred* **(a)** bündig. ~ **against the wall** direkt an die/der Wand. **(b)** *(col: with money)* **to be** ~ gut bei Kasse sein *(col)*.

flush[3] *n (Cards)* Flöte, Sequenz *f*; *(Poker)* Flush *m*.

flushed [flʌʃt] *adj person* rot *(with vor)*.

fluster ['flʌstə^r] **1** *vt* nervös machen; *(confuse)* durcheinanderbringen. **she got** ~**ed** sie wurde nervös; **das brachte sie durcheinander. 2** *n* **in a (real)** ~ (ganz) nervös; *(confused)* (völlig) durcheinander.

flute [fluːt] *n* Querflöte *f*.

flutter ['flʌtə^r] **1** *vi (flag, wings, heart)* flattern. **to** ~ **away** davonflattern. **2** *vt (birds) wings* flattern mit. **to** ~ **one's eyelashes at sb** mit den Wimpern klimpern. **3** *n* Flattern *nt (also Med)*. **(all)** in or of a ~ *(fig)* in heller Aufregung; **to have a** ~ *(Brit col: gamble)* sein Glück (beim Wetten) versuchen.

flux [flʌks] *n* **in a state of** ~ im Fluß.

fly[1] [flaɪ] *n* Fliege *f*. **he wouldn't hurt a** ~ er könnte keiner Fliege etwas zuleide tun; **he's the** ~ **in the ointment** er ist Sand im Getriebe; **there are no flies on him** *(col)* ihn legt man nicht so leicht rein *(col)*.

fly[2] *(vb: pret* **flew**, *ptp* **flown**) **1** *vi* **(a)** fliegen. **(b)** *(move quickly) (time)* (ver)fliegen; *(people)* sausen *(col)*; *(sparks)* stieben. **time flies!** wie die Zeit vergeht!; **to** ~ **past** *(car, person)* vorbeisausen *(col)*; **I must** ~ ich muß jetzt wirklich sausen *(col)*; **the door flew open** die Tür flog auf; **to** ~ **into a rage** einen Wutanfall bekommen; **to (let)** ~ **at sb** *(col)* auf jdn losgehen; **he really let** ~ er legte kräftig los; **to knock sb/sth** ~**ing** jdn/etw umwerfen. **(c)** *(flag)* wehen. **2** *vt aircraft, route* fliegen; *kite* steigen lassen; *Atlantic* überfliegen; *flag* führen.

♦ **fly away** *vi (person, plane, bird)* wegfliegen; *(fig: cares)* schwinden.

♦ **fly in** *vti sep* einfliegen. **she flew** ~ **from New York** sie ist mit dem Flugzeug aus New York angekommen.

♦ **fly off** *vi* **(a)** *(plane, person)* abfliegen; *(bird)* wegfliegen. **(b)** *(come off: hat, lid etc)* wegfliegen; *(button)* abspringen.

♦ **fly out** *vi* ausfliegen. **I'll ~ ~ and come back by ship** ich werde hin fliegen und mit dem Schiff zurückkommen. **2** *vt sep (to an area)* hinfliegen; *(out of an area)* ausfliegen.

fly³ *pret* **flew**, *ptp* **flown 1** *vi (flee)* fliehen. **to ~ for one's life** um sein Leben laufen/fahren *etc*. **2** *vt* **to ~ the country** aus dem Land flüchten.

fly⁴ *n (on trousers: also* **flies)** (Hosen)schlitz *m*.

fly⁵ *adj (col: crafty)* clever, gerissen.

fly-away ['flaɪəweɪ] *adj* hair fliegend.

flying ['flaɪɪŋ] *n* Fliegen *nt*. **he likes ~** er fliegt gerne.

flying: ~ colours *(Brit)* or **colors** *(US) npl* **to come through/pass** *etc* **with ~ colours** glänzend abschneiden; **~ fish** *n* fliegender Fisch; **~ jump** *n* **to take a ~ jump** einen großen Satz machen; **~ saucer** *n* fliegende Untertasse; **~ start** *n (Sport)* **to get off to a ~ start** *(Sport)* hervorragend wegkommen; *(fig)* einen glänzenden Start haben; **~-time** *n* Flugzeit *f*; **~ visit** *n* Blitzbesuch *m*.

fly: ~leaf *n* Vorsatzblatt *nt*; **~over** *n* Überführung *f*; **~paper** *n* Fliegenfänger *m*; **~-past** *n* Luftparade *f*; **~sheet** *n (entrance)* Überdach *nt*; *(outer tent)* Überzelt *nt*; **~-swat(ter)** *n* Fliegenklatsche *f*; **~weight** *n (Boxing)* Fliegengewicht *nt*; **~wheel** *n* Schwungrad *nt*.

FM = frequency modulation UKW.

foal [fəʊl] *n* Fohlen, Füllen *nt*.

foam [fəʊm] **1** *n* Schaum *m*. **2** *vi* schäumen. **to ~ at the mouth** *(lit)* Schaum vorm Mund/Maul haben; *(fig: person)* schäumen vor Wut.

foam rubber *n* Schaumgummi *m*.

fob ['ɛfəʊbiː] **= free on board.**

♦ **fob off** [fɒb'ɒf] *vt sep* **to ~ sb ~ (with promises)** jdn (mit leeren Versprechungen) abspeisen; **to ~ sb ~ with sth** jdm etw andrehen.

focal ['fəʊkəl] *adj* **~ length** Brennweite *f*; **~ point** *(lit, fig)* Brennpunkt *m*.

fo'c'sle ['fəʊksl] *n* **= forecastle** Vorschiff *nt*.

focus ['fəʊkəs] **1** *n*, *pl* **foci** ['fəʊkɪ] *(Phys, Math, fig)* Brennpunkt *m*; *(of earthquake, Med)* Herd *m*. **in ~ camera** (scharf) eingestellt; **photo** scharf; **out of ~ lit)** camera unscharf eingestellt; **photo** unscharf; **he was the ~ of attention** er stand im Mittelpunkt. **2** *vt* **instrument** einstellen *(on* auf +*acc)*; *(fig)* one's efforts konzentrieren *(on* auf +*acc)*; **to ~ one's attention on sth** sich auf etw *(acc)* konzentrieren. **3** *vi* **to ~ on sth** sich auf etw *(acc)* konzentrieren; **his eyes ~ed on the book** sein Blick richtete sich auf das Buch; **I can't ~ properly** ich kann nicht mehr klar sehen.

fodder ['fɒdəʳ] *n (lit, fig)* Futter *nt*.

foe [fəʊ] *n (liter)* Feind, Widersacher *(geh) m*.

foetal, *(esp US)* **fetal** ['fiːtl] *adj* fötal.

foetus, *(esp US)* **fetus** ['fiːtəs] *n* Fötus *m*.

fog [fɒg] *n* Nebel *m*.

fogbound ['fɒgbaʊnd] *adj* ship, plane durch Nebel festgehalten; airport wegen Nebel(s) geschlossen.

fogey ['fəʊgɪ] *n (col)* **old ~** alter Kauz *(col)*.

foggy ['fɒgɪ] *adj (+er)* neb(e)lig. **I haven't the foggiest (idea)** *(col)* ich habe keinen blassen Schimmer *(col)*.

fog: ~horn *n (Naut)* Nebelhorn *nt*; **~ light** *n* Nebellampe *f*.

foible ['fɔɪbl] *n* Eigenheit *f*.

foil¹ [fɔɪl] *n (metal)* Folie *f*. **to act as a ~ to sb** *(fig)* jdm als Hintergrund dienen.

foil² *n (Fencing)* Florett *nt*.

foil³ *vt* plans durchkreuzen; attempts vereiteln; person einen Strich durch die Rechnung machen (+*dat)*.

foist [fɔɪst] *vt* **to ~ sth (off) on sb** goods jdm etw andrehen; **to ~ oneself on(to) sb** sich jdm auf-

drängen.

fold¹ [fəʊld] **1** *n* Falte *f*. **2** *vt* **paper** (zusammen)falten; **blanket** zusammenlegen. **to ~ sth in two/in half** etw falten/zweimal falten; **to ~ one's arms** die Arme verschränken; **he ~ed the book in some paper** er schlug das Buch in Papier ein. **3** *vi* **(a)** *(chair, table)* sich zusammenklappen lassen. **(b) = fold up.**

♦ **fold away 1** *vi (table, bed)* zusammenklappbar sein. **2** *vt sep* table, bed zusammenklappen; clothes zusammenlegen.

♦ **fold up 1** *vi (business)* eingehen *(col)*; *(play)* abgesetzt werden. **2** *vt sep* paper zusammenfalten.

fold² *n (pen)* Pferch *m*.

foldaway ['fəʊldəweɪ] *adj attr* zusammenklappbar.

folder ['fəʊldəʳ] *n* **(a)** *(for papers)* Aktenmappe *f*. **(b)** *(brochure)* Informationsblatt *nt*.

folding ['fəʊldɪŋ] *adj attr* **~ bed** Klappbett *nt*; **~ chair** Klappstuhl *m*; **~ doors** Falttür *f*.

foliage ['fəʊlɪdʒ] *n* Blätter *pl*; *(of tree)* Laub *nt*.

folk [fəʊk] *npl* Leute *pl*. **the young/old ~** die Jungen/Alten; **my ~s** *(col)* meine Leute *(col)*.

folk: ~-dance *n* Volkstanz *m*; **~lore** *n* Folklore *f*; **~-music** *n* Volksmusik *f*; *(modern)* Folk *m*; **~-singer** *n* Sänger(in *f*) *m* von Volksliedern/ Folksongs; **~-song** *n* Volkslied *nt*; *(modern)* Folksong *m*.

follow ['fɒləʊ] **1** *vt (also understand)* folgen (+*dat)*; *(pursue also)* verfolgen; advice, instructions also befolgen; profession ausüben; career, serial, speech, news verfolgen; athletics etc sich interessieren für. **he ~ed me about** er folgte mir überall hin; **he ~ed me out** er folgte mir nach draußen; **we're being ~ed** wir werden verfolgt; **to have sb ~ed** jdn verfolgen lassen; **the reaction that ~ed this** die darauf folgende Reaktion; **do you ~ me?** können Sie mir folgen?; **which team do you ~?** für welchen Verein sind Sie?

2 *vi* folgen *(on sth* auf etw acc). **as ~s** wie folgt; **what is there to ~?** was gibt es anschließend?; **what ~s** das Folgende. **(b)** *(results, deduction)* folgen *(from* aus). **it doesn't ~ that ...** daraus folgt nicht, daß ...; **that doesn't ~** nicht unbedingt! **(c)** *(understand)* folgen. **I don't ~** das verstehe ich nicht.

♦ **follow on** *vi (come after)* später kommen.

♦ **follow through 1** *vt sep* argument durchdenken; idea, plan (zu Ende) verfolgen. **2** *vi (Sport)* durchschwingen.

♦ **follow up** *vt sep* **(a)** *(take further action on)* request nachgehen (+*dat)*; offer, suggestion aufgreifen. **(b)** matter weiterverfolgen; rumour nachgehen (+*dat)*. **(c)** *(reinforce)* success, victory festsetzen; advantage ausnutzen. **you should ~ the letter with a phonecall** zusätzlich zu dem Brief sollten Sie noch anrufen.

follower ['fɒləʊəʳ] *n (fan etc)* Anhänger(in *f*) *m*.

following ['fɒləʊɪŋ] **1** *adj* **(a)** folgend. **the ~ day** der (darauf)folgende Tag. **(b) a ~ wind** Rückenwind *m*. **2** *n* **(a)** *(followers)* Anhängerschaft *f*. **(b)** **he said the ~** er sagte folgendes.

follow-up ['fɒləʊ,ʌp] *n* Weiterverfolgen *nt*; *(event, programme etc coming after)* Fortsetzung *f (to gen)*. **what was the ~ to this?** was folgte darauf?

follow-up: ~ advertising *n* Nachfaßwerbung *f*; **~ care** *n (Med)* Nachbehandlung *f*; **~ letter** *n* Nachfaßschreiben *nt*.

folly ['fɒlɪ] *n* Torheit *f*.

fond [fɒnd] *adj (+er)* **to be ~ of sb** jdn gern mögen; **to be ~ of sth** etw mögen; **to be ~ of doing sth** etw gern tun. **(b)** *(loving)* liebevoll; hope sehnsüchtig. **(c)** *(vain)* illusion verloren; hope kühn.

fondant ['fɒndənt] *n* Fondant *m*.

fondle ['fɒndl] vt (zärtlich) spielen mit; (stroke) streicheln; person schmusen mit.

fondly ['fɒndlɪ] adv look etc liebevoll. **he ~ believed that ...** er hoffte vergebens, daß ...

fondness ['fɒndnɪs] n Begeisterung f; (for people) Zuneigung f (for zu); (for food, place) Vorliebe f (for für).

font [fɒnt] n **(a)** (Eccl) Taufstein m. **(b)** (Typ) Schrift f.

food [fuːd] n Essen nt; (for animals) Futter nt; (nourishment) Nahrung f; (~stuff) Nahrungsmittel nt; (groceries) Lebensmittel pl. **canned ~s** Konserven pl; **I haven't any ~ in the house** ich habe nichts zu essen im Haus; **to be off one's ~** keinen Appetit haben; **~ for thought** (fig) Stoff m zum Nachdenken.

food: ~ poisoning n Lebensmittelvergiftung f; **~ shop** (Brit) or **store** n Lebensmittelgeschäft nt; **~stuff** n Nahrungsmittel nt.

fool [fuːl] **1** n Dummkopf, Narr (also jester) m. **don't be a ~!** sei nicht (so) dumm!; **some ~ of a civil servant** irgend so ein blöder Beamter; **I was a ~ not to realize** wie konnte ich nur so dumm sein und das nicht merken; **to play** or **act the ~** herumalbern; **to make a ~ of sb** jdn lächerlich machen; **he made a ~ of himself in the discussion** er hat sich in der Diskussion blamiert; **to live in a ~'s paradise** in einem Traumland leben.

2 vi herumalbern. **I was only ~ing** das war doch nur Spaß. **3** vt (trick) hereinlegen (col); (disguise, phoney accent etc) täuschen. **you had me ~ed** ich habe das tatsächlich geglaubt; **they ~ed him into believing that ...** sie haben ihm weisgemacht, daß ...; **you could have ~ed me!** (iro) was du nicht sagst!

♦ **fool about** or **around** vi **(a)** (waste time) herumtrödeln. **(b)** (play the fool) herumalbern. **(c) to ~ with sth** mit etw Blödsinn machen.

foolhardy ['fuːlhɑːdɪ] adj tollkühn.

foolish ['fuːlɪʃ] adj dumm. **he's afraid of looking ~** er will sich nicht blamieren.

foolishly ['fuːlɪʃlɪ] adv ~, **I assumed ...** törichterweise habe ich angenommen, ...

foolishness ['fuːlɪʃnɪs] n Dummheit f.

foolproof ['fuːlpruːf] adj narrensicher.

foolscap ['fuːlskæp] n ≈ Kanzleipapier nt.

foot [fʊt] **1** n, pl **feet (a)** (also bottom, measure) Fuß m. **he was on one's feet** (lit, fig) auf den Beinen sein; **to put sb (back) on his feet (again)** (lit, fig) jdm (wieder) auf die Beine helfen; **on ~** zu Fuß; **the first time he set ~ in the office** als er das erste Mal das Büro betrat; **to rise/jump to one's feet** aufstehen/aufspringen; **to put one's feet up** (lit) die Füße hochlegen; (fig) es sich (dat) bequem machen. **(b)** (fig phrases) **he never puts a ~ wrong** er macht nie einen Fehler; **to catch sb on the wrong ~** jdn überrumpeln; **to put one's ~ down** (act with decision) ein Machtwort sprechen; (forbid, refuse) es strikt verbieten; (Aut) Gas geben; **to put one's ~ in it** ins Fettnäpfchen treten (col); **to put one's best ~ forward** (hurry) die Beine unter den Arm nehmen; (do one's best) sich anstrengen; **to find one's feet** sich eingewöhnen; **to fall on one's feet** auf die Füße fallen; **to have one ~ in the grave** mit einem Bein im Grabe stehen; **to get/be under sb's feet** jdm in Wege stehen; **to get off on the right/wrong ~** einen guten/schlechten Start haben; **to stand on one's own feet** auf eigenen Füßen stehen.

2 vt **bill** bezahlen.

foot-and-mouth (disease) ['fʊtən'maʊθ(dɪ,ziːz)] n Maul- und Klauenseuche f.

football ['fʊtbɔːl] n (also ball) Fußball m. **~ pools** Fußballtoto pl.

footballer ['fʊtbɔːlə^r] n Fußball(spiel)er m.

foot: ~bridge n Fußgängerbrücke f; **~hills** npl (Gebirgs)ausläufer pl; **~hold** n Halt m; (fig) sichere (Ausgangs)position.

footing ['fʊtɪŋ] n **(a)** (lit) Halt m. **to lose one's ~** den Halt verlieren; **to miss one's ~** danebentreten. **(b)** (fig) Basis f; (relationship) Beziehung f. **on an equal ~ (with each other)** auf gleicher Basis.

footlights ['fʊtlaɪts] npl (Theat) Rampenlicht nt.

footling ['fuːtlɪŋ] adj albern, läppisch.

foot: ~loose adj **~loose and fancy-free** frei und ungebunden; **~man** n Lakai m; **~mark** n Fußabdruck m; **~note** n Fußnote f; **~path** n Fußweg m; (Brit: pavement) Bürgersteig m; **~print** n Fußabdruck m; **~prints** npl Fußspuren pl; **~step** n Schritt m; **to follow in sb's ~steps** (fig) in jds Fußstapfen treten; **~wear** n Schuhwerk nt; **~work** n no pl (Boxing) Beinarbeit f.

for [fɔː^r] **1** prep **(a)** für. **what ~?** wofür?, wozu?; **what is this knife ~?** wozu dient dieses Messer?; **he does it ~ pleasure** er macht es zum Vergnügen; **what did you do that ~?** warum haben Sie das getan?; **a room ~ working in** ein Zimmer zum Arbeiten; **this will do ~ a hammer** das kann man als Hammer nehmen; **the train ~ Stuttgart** der Zug nach Stuttgart; **to leave ~ the USA** nach den USA abreisen; **he swam ~ the shore** er schwamm in Richtung Küste; **to make ~ home** sich auf den Heimweg machen; **to do sth ~ oneself** etw alleine tun; **you're ~ it!** (col) jetzt bist du dran! (col); **oh ~ a cup of tea!** jetzt eine Tasse Tee, das wäre schön!

(b) (indicating suitability) **it's not ~ you to blame him** Sie haben kein Recht, ihm die Schuld zu geben; **it's not ~ me to say** es steht mir nicht zu, mich dazu zu äußern.

(c) (representing, instead of) **I'll see her ~ you** if you like wenn Sie wollen, gehe ich an Ihrer Stelle zu ihr; **to act ~ sb** für jdn handeln; **D ~ Daniel** D wie Daniel.

(d) (in defence, in favour of) für. **are you ~ or against it?** sind Sie dafür oder dagegen?; **I'm all ~ it** ich bin ganz dafür.

(e) (with regard to) anxious ~ sb um jdn besorgt; **~ my part** was mich betrifft; **as ~ him/that** was ihn/das betrifft; **young ~ a president** jung für einen Präsidenten; **it's all right** or **all very well ~ you (to talk)** Sie haben gut reden.

(f) (because of) **~ this reason** aus diesem Grund; **he did it ~ fear of being left** er tat es aus Angst, zurückgelassen zu werden; **he is famous ~ his big nose** er ist wegen seiner großen Nase berühmt; **to shout ~ joy** vor Freude jauchzen; **to go to prison ~ theft** wegen Diebstahls ins Gefängnis wandern; **to choose sb ~ his ability** jdn wegen seiner Fähigkeiten wählen; **if it were not ~ him** wenn er nicht wäre; **do it ~ me** tu es für mich.

(g) (in spite of) trotz (+gen or (col) +dat). **~ all his wealth** trotz all seines Reichtums; **~ all that** trotz allem.

(h) (in contrast) **~ one man who would do it** there are ten who wouldn't auf einen, der es tun würde, kommen zehn, die es nicht tun würden.

(i) (in time) seit; (with future tense) für. **I have not seen her ~ two years** ich habe sie viel Jahren nicht gesehen; **he's been here ~ ten days** er ist seit zehn Tagen hier; **then I did not see her ~ two years** dann habe ich sie zwei Jahre lang nicht gesehen; **he walked ~ two hours** er ist zwei Stunden lang marschiert; **I am going away ~ a few days** ich werde (für) ein paar Tage wegfahren; **he won't be back ~ a week** er wird erst in einer Woche zurück sein; **can you get it done ~ Monday/this time next week?** können Sie es bis Montag/bis in einer Woche fertig haben?; **~ a while/time** (für) eine Weile/einige Zeit.

(j) (distance) **the road is lined with trees ~ two miles** die Straße ist auf zwei Meilen mit Bäumen gesäumt; **we walked ~ two miles** wir sind zwei Meilen weit gelaufen.

(k) *(with infin clauses)* ~ this to be possible damit dies möglich wird/wurde; **I brought it** ~ **you to see** ich habe es mitgebracht, damit Sie es sich *(dat)* ansehen können; **the best would be** ~ **you to go** das beste wäre, wenn Sie weggingen; **their one hope is** ~ **him to return** ihre einzige Hoffnung ist, daß er zurückkommt.

2 *conj* denn. ~ **it was he who** ... denn es war er, der ...

forage ['fɒrɪdʒ] *vi* nach Futter suchen; *(fig: rummage)* herumwühlen *(for* nach*)*. ~-**cap** Schiffchen *nt*.

foray ['fɒreɪ] *n* (Raub)überfall *m*; *(fig)* Exkurs *m* *(into* in *+acc)*.

forbad(e) [fə'bæd] *pret of* **forbid**.

forbearance [fɔː'bɛərəns] *n* Nachsicht *f*.

forbid [fə'bɪd] *pret* **forbad(e)**, *ptp* **forbidden** [fə'bɪdn] *vt* verbieten. **to** ~ **sb to do sth** jdm verbieten, etw zu tun; **smoking** ~**den** Rauchen verboten; **it is** ~**den to** ... es ist verboten, zu ...

forbidding [fə'bɪdɪŋ] *adj rocks, cliffs* bedrohlich; *sky* düster; *prospect* grauenhaft; *look, person* streng.

force [fɔːs] **1** *n* **(a)** *no pl (physical strength, power)* Kraft *f*; *(of blow, of impact)* Wucht *f*; *(physical coercion)* Gewalt *f*. **to resort to** ~ Gewalt anwenden; **by** ~ gewaltsam; **a** ~ **5 wind** Windstärke 5; **they came in** ~ sie kamen in großer Zahl; ~**s of Nature** Naturgewalten *pl*; **there are various** ~**s at work here** hier sind verschiedene Kräfte am Werk; **to come into/be in** ~ *(law etc)* in Kraft treten/sein. **(b)** *no pl (of argument)* Überzeugungskraft *f*; *(of music, phrase)* Eindringlichkeit *f*; *(of character)* Stärke *f*; *(of words, habit)* Macht *f*. **(c)** *(body of men)* **the** ~**s** *(Mil)* die Streitkräfte *pl*; **work** ~ Arbeitskräfte *pl*; **sales** ~ Verkaufspersonal *nt*; **the (police)** ~ die Polizei; **to join** *or* **combine** ~**s** sich zusammentun.

2 *vt* **(a)** *(compel)* zwingen. **to** ~ **sb/oneself to do sth** jdn/sich zwingen, etw zu tun; **he was** ~**d to resign** *or* wurde gezwungen zurückzutreten; *(felt obliged to)* er sah sich gezwungen zurückzutreten; **to** ~ **sth (up)on sb** *present, one's company* jdm etw aufdrängen; *conditions* jdm etw auferlegen; *decision, war* jdm etw aufzwingen; **I don't want to** ~ **myself on you** ich möchte mich Ihnen nicht aufdrängen.

(b) *(break open) lock* aufbrechen. **to** ~ **an entry** sich *(dat)* gewaltsam Zutritt verschaffen. **(c)** *(push, squeeze)* **to** ~ **books into a box** Bücher in eine Kiste zwängen; **if it won't go in, don't** ~ **it** versuche es nicht mit Gewalt, wenn es nicht hineinpaßt; **to** ~ **one's way through** sich gewaltsam einen Weg bahnen; **to** ~ **a car off the road** ein Auto von der Fahrbahn drängen.

(d) to ~ **a smile** gezwungen lächeln; **to** ~ **a confession out of sb** ein Geständnis von jdm erzwingen.

♦ **force back** *vt sep* zurückdrängen; *tear* unterdrücken.

♦ **force down** *vt sep food* hinunterquälen; *aeroplane* zur Landung zwingen.

forced [fɔːst] *adj smile, translation* gezwungen. ~ **landing** Notlandung *f*; ~ **march** Gewaltmarsch *m*.

force-feed ['fɔːsfiːd] *vt* zwangsernähren.

forceful ['fɔːsfʊl] *adj person* energisch; *character* stark; *language, style* eindringlich; *argument* wirkungsvoll.

forceps ['fɔːseps] *npl (also* **pair of** ~*)* Zange *f*.

forcible ['fɔːsəbl] *adj* **(a)** *entry* gewaltsam. **(b)** *language, style* eindringlich; *argument, reason* zwingend.

ford [fɔːd] **1** *n* Furt *f*. **2** *vt* durchqueren.

fore [fɔːʳ] **1** *n* **to the** ~ im Vordergrund; **to come to the** ~ ins Blickfeld geraten. **2** *adv (Naut)* ~ **and aft** längsschiffs.

fore: ~**arm** *n* Unterarm *m*; ~**bear** *n* Vorfahr(in *f*),

Ahn(e *f) m*; ~**boding** [fɔː'bəʊdɪŋ] *n (presentiment)* (Vor)ahnung *f*; ~**cast 1** *vt* vorhersagen; **2** *n* Vorhersage *f*; ~**close** *vi (on loan, mortgage)* ein Darlehen/eine Hypothek kündigen; **to** ~**close on sth** etw kündigen; ~**court** *n* Vorhof *m*; ~**father** *n* Ahn, Vorfahr *m*; ~**finger** *n* Zeigefinger *m*; ~**front** *n* **in the** ~ **of** im Vorfeld *(+gen)*; ~**go** *pret* ~**went**, *ptp* ~**gone** verzichten auf *(+acc)*; ~**going** *adj* vorhergehend; ~**gone 1** *ptp of* ~**go**; **2** *adj*: **it was a** ~**gone conclusion** es stand von vornherein fest; ~**ground** *n* Vordergrund *m*; **in the** ~**ground** im Vordergrund; ~**hand** *n (Sport)* Vorhand *f*; ~**head** ['fɒrhed, 'fɔːrɪd] *n* Stirn *f*.

foreign ['fɒrən] *adj* ausländisch; *customs, appearance* fremdartig; *policy, trade* Außen-. **is he** ~? ist er Ausländer?; ~ **countries** das Ausland; **lying is** ~ **to him** Lügen ist ihm fremd.

foreign: ~ **affairs** *npl* Außenpolitik *f*; ~ **currency** *n* Devisen *pl*.

foreigner ['fɒrənəʳ] *n* Ausländer(in *f) m*.

foreign: ~ **exchange** *n* Devisen *pl*; ~ **exchange market** *n* Devisenmarkt *m*; ~ **language** *n* Fremdsprache *f*; ~ **legion** *n* Fremdenlegion *f*; **F~ Minister** *n* Außenminister *m*; **F~ Office** *n (Brit)* Außenministerium *nt*; **F~ Secretary** *n (Brit)* Außenminister *m*.

fore: ~ **leg** *n* Vorderbein *nt*; ~**man** [-mən] *n, pl* ~**men** [-mən] *(in factory)* Vorarbeiter *m*; *(on building site)* Polier *m*; *(Jur: of jury)* Obmann *m*; ~**most** *adj (lit)* erste(r, s), vorderste(r, s); *(fig) writer, politician etc* führend; ~**name** *n* Vorname *m*.

forensic [fə'rensɪk] *adj* forensisch. ~ **science** Kriminaltechnik *f*; ~ **medicine** Gerichtsmedizin *f*; ~ **expert** Spurensicherungsexperte *m*.

fore: ~**play** *n* Vorspiel *nt*; ~**runner** *n* Vorläufer *m*; ~**see** *pret* ~**saw**, *ptp* ~**seen** *vt* vorhersehen; ~**seeable** *adj* voraussehbar; **in the** ~**seeable future** in absehbarer Zeit; ~**shadow** *vt* ahnen lassen, andeuten; ~**shorten** *vt* perspektivisch zeichnen/fotografieren; **this has a** ~**shortening effect** das läßt es kürzer erscheinen; ~**sight** *n* Weitblick *m*; ~**skin** *n* Vorhaut *f*.

forest ['fɒrɪst] *n* Wald *m*. ~ **ranger** *(US)* Förster *m*.

forestall [fɔː'stɔːl] *vt sb, rival* zuvorkommen *(+dat)*; *objection* vorwegnehmen.

forester ['fɒrɪstəʳ] *n* Förster *m*.

forestry ['fɒrɪstrɪ] *n* Forstwirtschaft *f*.

fore: ~**taste** *n* Vorgeschmack *m*; ~**tell** *pret, ptp* ~**told** *vt* vorhersagen; ~**thought** *n* Vorbedacht *m*.

forever [fər'evəʳ] *adv* **(a)** *(constantly)* ständig, ewig *(col)*. **(b)** *(eternally)* ewig.

fore: ~**warn** *vt* vorher warnen; ~**warned is forearmed** *(Prov)* Gefahr erkannt, Gefahr gebannt *(prov)*; ~**went** *pret of* ~**go**; ~**woman** *n, pl* ~**women** Vorarbeiterin *f*; ~**word** *n* Vorwort *nt*.

forfeit ['fɔːfɪt] **1** *vt (esp Jur)* verwirken; *(fig) health, sb's respect* einbüßen. **2** *n (in game)* Pfand *nt*.

forgave [fə'geɪv] *pret of* **forgive**.

forge [fɔːdʒ] **1** *n (workshop)* Schmiede *f*; *(furnace)* Esse *f*. **2** *vt* **(a)** *metal, (fig) friendship* schmieden. **(b)** *signature, banknote* fälschen. **3** *vi* **to** ~ **ahead** vorwärtskommen; *(in one's career)* seinen Weg machen; *(Sport)* sich an die Spitze setzen.

forger ['fɔːdʒəʳ] *n* Fälscher(in *f) m*.

forgery ['fɔːdʒərɪ] *n (act, thing)* Fälschung *f*.

forget [fə'get] *pret* **forgot**, *ptp* **forgotten 1** *vt* vergessen; *ability, language* verlernen. **never to be forgotten** unvergeßlich; **and don't you** ~ **it!** und daß du das ja nicht vergißt!; **I** ~ **his name** sein Name ist mir entfallen; **I** ~ **what I wanted to say** es ist mir entfallen, was ich sagen wollte; **to** ~ **past quarrels** vergangene Streitigkeiten ruhen lassen; ~ **it!** schon gut!; **you might as well** ~ **it** *(col)* das kannst du vergessen *(col)*. **2** *vi* es vergessen. **don't** ~! vergiß es nicht!

♦ **forget about** *vi +prep obj* vergessen.

forgetful [fəˈgetfʊl] *adj (absent-minded)* vergeßlich; *(of one's duties etc)* nachlässig *(of gegenüber)*.

forget-me-not [fəˈgetmɪnɒt] *n* Vergißmeinnicht *nt*.

forgive [fəˈgɪv] *pret* **forgave**, *ptp* **forgiven** [fəˈgɪvn] *vti sth* verzeihen, vergeben *(also Eccl)*. to ~ **sb for sth** jdm etw verzeihen *or* vergeben; to ~ **sb for doing sth** jdm verzeihen *or* vergeben, daß er etw getan hat; ~ **me, but** ... Entschuldigung, aber ...

forgiveness [fəˈgɪvnɪs] *n, no pl (willingness to forgive)* Versöhnlichkeit *f*. to ask/beg (sb's) ~ (jdn) um Verzeihung *or* Vergebung *(esp Eccl)* bitten.

forgiving [fəˈgɪvɪŋ] *adj* versöhnlich.

forgot [fəˈgɒt] *pret of* **forget**.

forgotten [fəˈgɒtn] *ptp of* **forget**.

fork [fɔːk] **1** *n (implement)* Gabel *f*; *(in road)* Gabelung *f*. **2** *vi (roads, branches)* sich gabeln. to ~ **right** *(road)* nach rechts abzweigen; *(driver)* nach rechts abbiegen.

♦ **fork out** *vti sep (col: pay)* blechen *(col)*.

forked [fɔːkt] *adj* branch, road, tail gegabelt; *lightning* zickzackförmig; *tongue* gespalten.

fork-lift truck [ˌfɔːklɪftˈtrʌk] *n* Gabelstapler *m*.

forlorn [fəˈlɔːn] *adj (deserted)* verlassen; *person* einsam und verlassen; *attempt* verzweifelt; *hope* schwach.

form [fɔːm] **1** *n* (a) Form *f*. ~ **of government** Regierungsform *f*; **a human** ~ eine menschliche Gestalt; **in the** ~ **of** in Form von *or* +gen; *(with reference to people)* in Gestalt von *or* +gen; to take ~ *(lit, fig)* Form annehmen; to be in fine/good ~ gut in Form sein, in guter Form sein; to be on/off ~ in/nicht in Form sein; he was in great ~ that evening er war an dem Abend in Hochform; on past ~ auf dem Papier. (b) *no pl (etiquette)* he did it for ~'s sake er tat es der Form halber; it's bad ~ so etwas tut man einfach nicht; what's the ~? *(col)* was ist üblich? (c) *(questionnaire, document)* Formular *nt*. application ~ Bewerbungsbogen *m*. (d) *(esp Brit: bench)* Bank *f*. (e) *(Brit Sch)* Klasse *f*.
2 *vt (a) object, character* formen *(into zu)*. **(b)** *(develop) liking* entwickeln; *friendship* schließen; *opinion* sich *(dat)* bilden; *impression* gewinnen; *plan* entwerfen. **(c)** *(constitute, make up) part, basis, government, circle, queue, (Gram)* bilden; *company* gründen.
3 *vi (take shape)* Gestalt annehmen.

formal [ˈfɔːməl] *adj (a)* formell; *reception, welcome* feierlich; *education, training* offiziell. ~ **dance/dress** Gesellschaftstanz *m*/-kleidung *f*. **(b)** *(in form)* distinction *etc* Form-.

formality [fɔːˈmælɪtɪ] *n (a) no pl (of person, dress etc)* Förmlichkeit *f*. **(b)** *(matter of form)* Formalität *f*. it's a mere ~ es ist (eine) reine Formsache.

formalize [ˈfɔːməlaɪz] *vt rules, grammar* formalisieren; *agreement, relationship* formell machen.

format [ˈfɔːmæt] **1** *n (as regards size)* Format *nt*; *(as regards content)* Aufmachung *f*; *(Rad, TV: of programme)* Struktur *f*. **2** *vt (Comp) text* formatieren.

formation [fɔːˈmeɪʃən] *n (a) (act of forming, of character)* Formung *f*; *(of government, committee; Gram)* Bildung *f*; *(of company, society)* Gründung *f*. **(b)** *(of aircraft, dances)* Formation *f*.

formative [ˈfɔːmətɪv] *adj* formend. it had a ~ influence on him es hat ihn entscheidend geprägt; ~ **years** Entwicklungsjahre *pl*.

former [ˈfɔːməʳ] **1** *adj (a)* früher, ehemalig. in a ~ life in einem früheren Leben; in ~ times/days früher. **(b)** *(first-mentioned)* erstere(r, s). **2** *n* the ~ der/die/das erstere.

formerly [ˈfɔːməlɪ] *adv* früher.

formica ® [fɔːˈmaɪkə] *n* Resopal ® *nt*.

formidable [ˈfɔːmɪdəbl] *adj* person, rock-face furchterregend; *opponent* gefährlich; *obstacles, debts, problems, task* gewaltig, enorm; *piece of work* beeindruckend.

formula [ˈfɔːmjʊlə] *n, pl* -s *or* -e [ˈfɔːmjʊliː] Formel *f*; *(for lotion, medicine, soap powder)* Rezeptur *f*. all his books use the same ~ alle seine Bücher sind nach demselben Rezept geschrieben.

formulate [ˈfɔːmjʊleɪt] *vt* formulieren.

fornicate [ˈfɔːnɪkeɪt] *vi* Unzucht treiben.

forsake [fəˈseɪk] *pret* **forsook** [fəˈsʊk], *ptp* **forsaken** [fəˈseɪkn] *vt* verlassen; *bad habits* aufgeben.

fort [fɔːt] *n (Mil)* Fort *nt*. to hold the ~ *(fig)* die Stellung halten.

forte [ˈfɔːtɪ] *n (strong point)* Stärke *f*.

forth [fɔːθ] *adv* to set ~ *(liter)* ausziehen *(liter)*; from this day ~ *(liter)* von diesem Tag an; and so ~ und so weiter.

forthcoming [ˌfɔːθˈkʌmɪŋ] *adj* (a) *event* bevorstehend; *book* in Kürze erscheinend; *film, play* in Kürze anlaufend. (b) to be ~ *(money)* kommen; *(help)* erfolgen. (c) *(esp Brit: informative)* mitteilsam.

forthright [ˈfɔːθraɪt] *adj* offen.

forthwith [ˌfɔːθˈwɪθ] *adv (form)* umgehend.

fortieth [ˈfɔːtɪɪθ] *adj* vierzigste(r, s); *see* sixtieth.

fortification [ˌfɔːtɪfɪˈkeɪʃən] *n (often pl: Mil)* Festungsanlagen *pl*.

fortify [ˈfɔːtɪfaɪ] *vt (Mil) town* befestigen; *(food, drink)* stärken. **fortified wine** süßer, starker Wein.

fortitude [ˈfɔːtɪtjuːd] *n (inner)* Stärke.

fortnight [ˈfɔːtnaɪt] *n (Brit)* vierzehn Tage.

fortnightly [ˈfɔːtnaɪtlɪ] *(Brit)* **1** *adj* vierzehntägig. **2** *adv* alle vierzehn Tage.

fortress [ˈfɔːtrɪs] *n* Festung *f*.

fortuitous [fɔːˈtjuːɪtəs] *adj* zufällig.

fortunate [ˈfɔːtʃənɪt] *adj* glücklich. to be ~ *(person)* Glück haben; it was ~ that ... es war ein Glück, daß ...

fortunately [ˈfɔːtʃənɪtlɪ] *adv* zum Glück.

fortune [ˈfɔːtʃuːn] *n (a) (fate)* Geschick *nt*; *(chance)* Zufall *m*. he had the good ~ to have rich parents er hatte das Glück, reiche Eltern zu haben; good ~ glücklicherweise. **(b)** *(money)* Vermögen *nt*. to make a ~ ein Vermögen erwerben; it costs a ~ es kostet ein Vermögen.

fortune: ~ **hunter** *n* Mitgiftjäger *m*; ~-**teller** *n* Wahrsager(in *f*) *m*.

forty [ˈfɔːtɪ] **1** *adj* vierzig. to have ~ **winks** *(col)* ein Nickerchen machen *(col)*. **2** *n* Vierzig *f*; *see* sixty.

forum [ˈfɔːrəm] *n* Forum *nt*.

forward [ˈfɔːwəd] **1** *adv (also* ~s*) (ahead)* vorwärts; *(to the front)* nach vorn. please step ~ bitte vortreten; **backward(s) and** ~**(s)** hin und her; from this time ~ *(from then)* seitdem; *(from now)* von jetzt an. **2** *adj (a) (in place)* vordere(r, s); *(in direction)* Vorwärts-. this seat is too far ~ dieser Sitz ist zu weit vorn. **(b)** *planning* Voraus-; *(Comm) buying* Termin-. good ~ **thinking!** gut vorausgedacht! **(c)** *(presumptuous, pert)* dreist; *(precocious)* frühreif. **3** *n (Sport)* Stürmer *m*. **4** *vt (a) (advance) plans* vorantreiben. **(b)** *(dispatch) goods* senden; *(send on) letter* nachsenden; *(to another office etc)* weiterleiten. please ~ **to** nachsenden.

forwarding [ˈfɔːwədɪŋ]: ~ **address** *n* Nachsendeadresse *f*; ~ **agent** *n* Spediteur *m*.

forward-looking [ˈfɔːwədlʊkɪŋ] *adj person* fortschrittlich, progressiv; *plan* vorausblickend.

forwards [ˈfɔːwədz] *adv* = **forward 1**.

fossil [ˈfɒsl] *n* Fossil *nt*. ~ **fuels** fossile Brennstoffe *pl*.

fossilized [ˈfɒsɪlaɪzd] *adj* versteinert; *(fig) customs* verkrustet.

foster [ˈfɒstəʳ] **1** *vt (a) child (parents)* in Pflege nehmen; *(authorities:* ~ **out)** in Pflege geben *(with bei)*. **(b)** *(encourage, promote)* fördern. **2** *adj* *attr father etc* Pflege-.

fought [fɔːt] *pret, ptp of* **fight**.

foul [faʊl] **1** *adj* (+*er*) *smell* übel; *water* faulig; *air* schlecht; *food* verdorben; (*horrible*) *day, weather, mood* ekelhaft; *person, behaviour* gemein, fies (*col*); *language* unflätig. **a lot of ~ play** (*Sport*) eine Menge Fouls; **the police suspect ~ play** es besteht Verdacht auf einen unnatürlichen Tod; **to fall ~ of sb/the law** mit jdm/dem Gesetz in Konflikt geraten. **2** *n* (*Sport*) Foul *nt*. **3** *vt* **(a)** (*pollute*) *air* verpesten; (*dog*) *pavement* verunreinigen. **(b)** (*entangle*) *fishing line* verheddern; (*seaweed etc*) *propeller* sich verheddern in (+*dat*). **(c)** *also vi* (*Sport*) foulen.

foul-mouthed ['faʊlmaʊðd] *adj* unflätig.

found¹ [faʊnd] *pret, ptp of* **find**.

found² *vt* **(a)** (*set up*) gründen. **(b) to ~ sth on sth** *opinion, belief* etw auf etw (*dat*) gründen; **to be ~ed on sth** auf etw (*dat*) basieren.

foundation [faʊn'deɪʃən] *n* **(a)** (*of business, colony*) Gründung *f*. **(b)** (*institution*) Stiftung *f*. **(c) ~s** *pl* (*of house etc*) Fundament *nt*; (*of road*) Unterbau *m*; (*fig: basis*) Grundlage *f*. **it has no ~ in fact** es beruht nicht auf Tatsachen.

foundation: ~ cream *n* Grundierungscreme *f*; **~ stone** *n* Grundstein *m*.

founder¹ ['faʊndə'] *n* (*of school etc*) Gründer(in *f*) *m*; (*of charity, museum*) Stifter(in *f*) *m*.

founder² *vi* (*ship*) sinken; (*fig: project*) scheitern.

Founding Fathers ['faʊndɪŋ,fɑːðəz] *npl* (*US*) Väter *pl*.

foundry ['faʊndrɪ] *n* Gießerei *f*.

fount [faʊnt] *n* **(a)** (*lit liter, fig*) Quelle *f*. **(b)** (*Typ*) Schrift *f*.

fountain ['faʊntɪn] *n* Brunnen *m*; (*with upward jets*) Springbrunnen *m*; (*fig: source*) Quelle *f*.

fountain-pen ['faʊntɪn,pen] *n* Füllfederhalter, Füller *m*.

four [fɔː'] **1** *adj* vier. **2** *n* Vier *f*. **on all ~s** auf allen vieren; *see* **six**.

four: ~-door *attr* viertürig; **~-footed** *adj* vierfüßig; **~-letter word** *n* Vulgärausdruck *m*; **~-poster (bed)** *n* Himmelbett *nt*; **~some** *n* Quartett *nt*; (*Sport*) Viererspiel *nt*; **to go out in a ~some** zu viert ausgehen.

fourteen ['fɔː'tiːn] **1** *adj* vierzehn. **2** *n* Vierzehn *f*.

fourteenth ['fɔː'tiːnθ] *adj* vierzehnte(r, s); *see* **sixteenth**.

fourth [fɔːθ] **1** *adj* vierte(r, s). **2** *n* (*fraction*) Viertel *nt*; (*in series*) Vierte(r, s). **to drive in ~** im vierten Gang fahren; *see* **sixth**.

four-wheel drive ['fɔːwiːl'draɪv] *n* Vierradantrieb *m*.

fowl [faʊl] *n* (*poultry*) Geflügel *nt*; (*one bird*) Huhn *nt*; Gans *f etc*.

fox [fɒks] **1** *n* (*lit, fig*) Fuchs *m*. **2** *vt* (*deceive*) täuschen; (*bewilder*) verblüffen.

fox: ~glove *n* (*Bot*) Fingerhut *m*; **~-hunting** *n* Fuchsjagd *f*; **~ terrier** *n* Foxterrier *m*; **~trot** *n* Foxtrott *m*.

foyer ['fɔɪeɪ] *n* (*in theatre*) Foyer *nt*; (*esp US: in apartment house*) Diele *f*.

fracas ['fræka:] *n* Aufruhr, Tumult *m*.

fraction ['frækʃən] *n* (*Math*) Bruch *m*; (*fig*) Bruchteil *m*. **a ~ bigger/shorter** (um) eine Spur besser/ kürzer; **for a ~ of a second** einen Augenblick lang; **it missed me by a ~ of an inch** es verfehlte mich um Haaresbreite.

fractional ['frækʃənl] *adj* (*fig*) geringfügig.

fractious ['frækʃəs] *adj* verdrießlich.

fracture ['fræktʃə'] **1** *n* Bruch *m*. **2** *vti* brechen. **he ~d his shoulder** er hat sich (*dat*) die Schulter gebrochen; **~d skull** Schädelbruch *m*.

fragile ['frædʒaɪl] *adj* china, glass, relationship zerbrechlich; *material, plant* zart; (*with age*) brüchig; (*fig*) *person (in health)* gebrechlich; *health* anfällig; *ego* labil. **he's feeling a bit ~ this morning** (*col*) er fühlt sich heute morgen ein

bißchen mitgenommen.

fragment ['frægmənt] **1** *n* **(a)** Bruchstück *nt*; (*of china, glass*) Scherbe *f*; (*of paper, letter*) Schnipsel *m*; (*of programme, opera etc*) Bruchteil *m*. **~s of conversation** Gesprächsfetzen *pl*. **(b)** (*esp Liter, Mus: unfinished work*) Fragment *nt*. **2** [fræg'ment] *vi* (*rock, glass*) (zer)brechen.

fragmentary ['frægməntərɪ] *adj* (*lit, fig*) fragmentarisch.

fragrance ['freɪgrəns] *n* Duft *m*.

fragrant ['freɪgrənt] *adj* duftend. **~ smell** Duft *m*.

frail [freɪl] *adj* (+*er*) zart; *health* anfällig; (*fig*) *hope* schwach.

frailty ['freɪltɪ] *n see adj* Zartheit *f*; Anfälligkeit *f*; Schwäche *f*.

frame [freɪm] **1** *n* (*basic structure, of picture, window, door, bicycle*) Rahmen *m*; (*of building, of ship*) Gerippe *nt*; (*of spectacles: also ~s*) Gestell *nt*; (*of human, animal*) Gestalt *f*; (*Film, Phot*) (Einzel)bild *nt*. **his massive ~** sein massiver Körper; **~ of mind** (*mental state*) Verfassung *f*; (*mood*) Stimmung *f*; **~ of reference** Bezugssystem *nt*. **2** *vt* **(a)** *picture* rahmen; (*fig*) *face etc* umrahmen. **(b)** *law, plan* entwerfen; *idea* entwickeln; (*express*) *answer, excuse* formulieren; *sentence* bilden. **(c) he's been ~ed** (*col*) die Sache wurde ihm angehängt (*col*).

frame: ~house *n* Holzhaus *nt*; **~-up** *n* (*col*) Komplott *nt*; **~work** *n* (*lit*) Grundgerüst *nt*; (*fig*) (*of novel etc also*) Gerippe *nt*; (*of society, government etc*) grundlegende Struktur; **within the ~work of ...** im Rahmen (+*gen*) ...; **outside the ~work of ...** außerhalb des Rahmens (+ *gen*) ...

franc [fræŋk] *n* Franc *m*.

France [frɑːns] *n* Frankreich *nt*.

franchise ['fræntʃaɪz] *n* **(a)** (*Pol*) Wahlrecht *nt*. **(b)** (*Comm*) Lizenz *f*. **~ system** Franchise-System *nt*.

Franconia [fræŋ'kəʊnɪə] *n* Franken *nt*.

frank¹ [fræŋk] *adj* (+*er*) offen. **to be (perfectly) ~** ehrlich gesagt.

frank² *vt* *letter* frankieren; (*postmark, cancel*) *stamp, letter* stempeln.

frankfurter ['fræŋk,fɔːtə'] *n* Frankfurter (Würstchen *nt*) *f*.

frankincense ['fræŋkɪnsens] *n* Weihrauch *m*.

frankly ['fræŋklɪ] *adv* offen; (*to tell the truth*) ehrlich gesagt.

frankness ['fræŋknɪs] *n* Offenheit *f*.

frantic ['fræntɪk] *adj* *effort, cry, scream* verzweifelt; *activity* fiebrig; *desire* übersteigert; *person* außer sich (*with vor* +*dat*). **to drive sb ~** jdn zur Verzweiflung treiben.

fraternal [frə'tɜːnl] *adj* brüderlich.

fraternity [frə'tɜːnɪtɪ] *n* **(a)** *no pl* Brüderlichkeit *f*. **(b)** (*community*) Vereinigung *f*; (*US Univ*) Verbindung *f*. **the legal/medical ~** die Juristen *pl*/ Mediziner *pl*.

fraternize ['frætənaɪz] *vi* freundschaftlichen Umgang haben.

fraud [frɔːd] *n* Betrug *m*; (*person*) Betrüger(in *f*) *m*; (*thing*) (*reiner*) Schwindel *m*; (*col*) ~ **squad** Betrugsdezernat *nt*.

fraudulent ['frɔːdjʊlənt] *adj* betrügerisch.

fraught [frɔːt] *adj* geladen (*with* mit); (*col: atmosphere*) gespannt. **~ with danger** gefahrvoll.

fray¹ [freɪ] *n* Schlägerei *f*; (*Mil*) Kampf *m*. **ready for the ~** (*lit, fig*) kampfbereit.

fray² **1** *vt* *cloth* ausfransen; *cuff, rope* durchscheuern. **my nerves are ~ed** ich bin mit den Nerven herunter (*col*); **tempers were ~ed** die Gemüter waren erhitzt. **2** *vi* (*cloth*) (aus)fransen; (*cuff, trouser turn-up, rope*) sich durchscheuern.

freak [friːk] **1** *n* (*plant*) Mißbildung *f*; (*person, animal also*) Mißgeburt *f*; (*event*) außergewöhnlicher Zufall; (*snowstorm etc*) Anomalie *f*; (*col: weird person*) Irre(r) *mf*. **~ of nature** Laune *f* der Natur; **movie ~** (*col*) Kinofan *m*; **health ~** (*col*)

Gesundheitsapostel *m (col)*. **2** *adj weather, conditions* anormal; *(Statistics) values* extrem; *victory* Überraschungs-.

♦ **freak out** *vi (col)* ausflippen *(col); (of society)* aussteigen.

freakish ['friːkɪʃ] *adj* **(a)** *see* **freak 2. (b)** *(changeable) weather* launisch; *person* ausgeflippt *(col); hairstyle, idea* verrückt *(col)*.

freaky ['friːkɪ] *adj (+er) (col)* irre *(col)*.

freckle ['frekl] *n* Sommersprosse *f*.

freckled ['frekld] *adj* sommersprossig.

free [friː] **1** *adj (+er)* **(a)** frei. **to set sb/an animal** ~ jdn/ein Tier freilassen; **he is** ~ **to go** es steht ihm frei zu gehen; **the fishing is** ~ **here** diese Stelle hier ist zum Fischen freigegeben; **you're** ~ **to choose** die Wahl steht Ihnen frei; **you're** ~ **to refuse** Sie können auch ablehnen; **I'm not** ~ **to do it** es steht mir nicht frei, es zu tun; **feel** ~**!** *(col)* bitte, gerne!; **to give sb a** ~ **hand** jdm freie Hand lassen; **are you** ~ **tonight?** hast du heute abend Zeit?; **am I** ~ **to speak here?** kann ich hier unbesorgt reden?; **he left one end of the string** ~ er ließ ein Ende des Bindfadens lose; ~ **from pain/worry** schmerzfrei/sorgenfrei; ~ **from blame/responsibility** frei von Schuld/Verantwortung; ~ **of sth** frei von etw.

  (b) *(costing nothing)* kostenlos; *(Comm)* gratis. **it's** ~ das kostet nichts; **admission** ~ Eintritt frei; **to get sth** ~ etw umsonst bekommen; **we got in** ~ *or* **for** ~ *(col)* wir kamen umsonst rein; ~ **sample** Gratisprobe *f*; ~ **on board** *(Comm)* frei Schiff.

  (c) *(lavish)* großzügig; *language, behaviour* lose; *(over-familiar)* plump-vertraulich.

  2 *vt prisoner (release)* freilassen; *(help escape)* befreien; *nation* befreien; *(untie) person* losbinden; *pipe* freimachen. **to** ~ **oneself from sth** sich von etw frei machen.

freebie ['friːbiː] *n (col)* Werbegeschenk *nt*.

free collective bargaining *n* Tarifautonomie *f*.

freedom ['friːdəm] *n* Freiheit *f*. ~ **of speech** Redefreiheit *f*; ~ **of the press** Pressefreiheit *f*; **the** ~ **of the city** die (Ehren)bürgerrechte *pl*; **to give sb the** ~ **of one's house** jdm sein Haus zur freien Verfügung stellen.

freedom fighter *n* Freiheitskämpfer(in *f*) *m*.

free: ~ **enterprise** *n* freies Unternehmertum; ~**-for-all** *n* Gerangel *nt (col); (fight)* Schlägerei *f*; **wages** ~**-for-all** Tarifgerangel *nt*; ~**hold** *n* to own sth ~**hold** etw besitzen; ~**hold property** *n* (freier) Grundbesitz; ~ **house** *n (Brit) Wirtshaus nt, das nicht an eine bestimmte Brauerei gebunden ist;* ~ **kick** *n (Sport)* Freistoß *m*; ~**lance** **1** *n* Freiberufler(in *f*) *m; (with particular firm)* freier Mitarbeiter, freie Mitarbeiterin; **2** *adj* frei(schaffend); *(work)* freiberuflich; **4** *adv* freiberuflich tätig sein; *(with particular firm)* als freier Mitarbeiter/freie Mitarbeiterin tätig sein; ~**load** *vi (esp US col)* schmarotzen *(col) (on bei)*.

freely ['friːlɪ] *adv* frei; *give* großzügig. **I** ~ **admit ...** ich gebe offen zu ...

free: ~**mason** *n* Freimaurer *m*; ~**-range** *adj (Brit) chicken* Farmhof-; *eggs* Land-.

freesia ['friːzɪə] *n (Bot)* Freesie *f*.

free: ~ **speech** *n* Redefreiheit *f*; ~**style** *n* Kür *f; (Swimming)* Freistil *m*; ~**-trade** *n* Freihandel *m*; ~**way** *n (US)* Autobahn *f*; ~**wheel** *vi im* Freilauf fahren.

freeze [friːz] *(vb: pret* **froze***, ptp* **frozen***)* **1** *vi* **(a)** *(Met)* frieren; *(water)* gefrieren; *(rivers)* zufrieren; *(pipes)* einfrieren. **I'm/my hands are freezing** mir ist/meine Hände sind eiskalt; **to** ~ **to death** *(lit)* erfrieren; *(fig)* sich zu Tode frieren. **(b)** *(fig) (blood, smile)* erstarren. **(c)** *(keep still)* **he froze in his tracks** er blieb wie angewurzelt stehen; ~**!** keine Bewegung! **2** *vt water* gefrieren; *food, wages* einfrieren;

assets festlegen; *(stop) film* anhalten. **3** *n (Met)* Frost *m*. **a wages** ~ **ein** Lohnstopp *m*.

♦ **freeze over** *vi (lake)* überfrieren; *(windows)* vereisen.

♦ **freeze up** *vi* zufrieren; *(lock also, pipes)* einfrieren; *(windows)* vereisen.

freeze-dried ['friːz,draɪd] *adj* gefriergetrocknet.

freezer ['friːzəʳ] *n* Gefriertruhe *f; (upright)* Gefrierschrank *m; (in fridge)* Gefrierfach *nt*.

freezing ['friːzɪŋ] **1** *adj* eiskalt. **2** *n* **below** ~ unter dem Gefrierpunkt.

freight [freɪt] **1** *n* Fracht *f*. **2** *vt (transport)* verfrachten.

freighter ['freɪtəʳ] *n (Naut)* Frachter *m; (Aviat)* Frachtflugzeug *nt*.

freight: ~ **plane** *n* Frachtflugzeug *nt*; ~ **train** *n* Güterzug *m*.

French [frentʃ] **1** *adj* französisch. **2** *n* **(a) the** ~ *pl* die Franzosen *pl*. **(b)** *(language)* Französisch *nt; see* **English**.

French: ~ **bean** *n* grüne Bohne; ~**-Canadian 1** *adj* frankokanadisch; **2** *n* Frankokanadier(in *f*) *m*; ~ **dressing** *n* Vinaigrette *f*; ~ **fries** *npl* Pommes frites *pl*; ~ **horn** *n (Mus)* (Wald)horn *nt*; ~ **letter** *n (Brit col)* Pariser *m (col)*; ~**man** *n* Franzose *m*; ~ **polish** *vt* lackieren; ~ **window(s** *pl) n* Verandatür *f*; ~**woman** *n* Französin *f*.

frenetic [frə'netɪk] *adj* frenetisch, rasend.

frenzy ['frenzɪ] *n* Raserei *f*. **in a** ~ in heller Aufregung.

frequency ['friːkwənsɪ] *n* Häufigkeit *f; (Phys)* Frequenz *f*. **high/low** ~ Hoch-/Niederfrequenz *f*.

frequency: ~ **band** *n* Frequenzband *nt*; ~ **modulation** *n (wavelength)* Ultrakurzwelle *f*.

frequent ['friːkwənt] **1** *adj* häufig. **he's a** ~ **visitor to our house** er kommt uns oft besuchen. **2** [fri'kwent] *vt* oft besuchen.

frequently ['friːkwəntlɪ] *adv* oft, häufig.

fresco ['freskəu] *n* Fresko(gemälde) *nt*.

fresh [freʃ] **1** *adj (+er)* **(a)** *food, breeze* frisch. **it's still** ~ **in my memory** es ist mir noch frisch in Erinnerung; ~ **water** *(not salt)* Süßwasser *nt*; **in the** ~ **air** an der frischen Luft. **(b)** *(new) supplies, sheet of paper, idea, approach, courage* neu. **to make a** ~ **start** einen neuen Anfang machen. **(c)** *(esp US: cheeky)* frech. **don't get** ~ **with me!** werd nicht frech! **2** *adv* **(a)** *baked, picked* frisch. ~ **from the oven** frisch aus dem Ofen; ~ **out of college** frisch von der Schule; **to come** ~ **to sth** neu zu etw kommen.

freshen ['freʃn] *vi (wind)* auffrischen.

♦ **freshen up** *vir* **to** ~ ~ *(person)* sich frischmachen.

fresher ['freʃəʳ] *n (Brit Univ col)* Erstsemester *nt*.

freshly ['freʃlɪ] *adv* frisch.

freshman ['freʃmən] *n, pl* -**men** [-mən] *(US)* = **fresher**.

freshness ['freʃnɪs] *n see adj* **(a)** Frische *f*. **(b)** Neuheit *f*. **(c)** Frechheit *f*.

freshwater ['freʃwɔːtəʳ] *adj attr* Süßwasser-.

fret[1] [fret] *vi* sich *(dat)* Sorgen machen. **don't** ~ beruhige dich; **the child is** ~**ting for his mother** das Kind jammert nach seiner Mutter.

fret[2] *n (on guitar etc)* Bund *m*.

fretful ['fretful] *adj child* quengelig.

fret: ~**saw** *n* Laubsäge *f*; ~**work** *n (in wood)* Laubsägearbeit *f*.

Freudian ['frɔɪdɪən] *adj (Psych, fig)* Freudsch attr. ~ **slip** Freudscher Versprecher *m*.

friar ['fraɪəʳ] *n* Mönch *m*.

fricassee ['frɪkəseɪ] *n* Frikassee *nt*.

friction ['frɪkʃən] **(a)** Reibung *f*. ~ **tape** *(US)* Isolierband *nt*. **(b)** *(fig)* Reibereien *pl*.

Friday ['fraɪdɪ] *n* Freitag *m; see* **Tuesday**.

fridge [frɪdʒ] *n (Brit)* Kühlschrank *m*.

fried [fraɪd] *adj* gebraten; *potatoes, chicken* Brat-; *egg* Spiegel-.

friend [frend] *n* Freund(in *f*) *m; (less intimate)* Bekannte(r) *mf.* **to make** ~**s with sb** sich mit jdm anfreunden; **to be** ~**s with sb** mit jdm befreundet sein; **we're just (good)** ~**s** wir sind nur gut befreundet; **Society of F**~**s** Quäker *pl.*

friendliness ['frendlɪnɪs] *n see adj* Freundlichkeit *f*; Freundschaftlichkeit *f.*

friendly ['frendlɪ] **1** *adj* (+*er*) *person, smile, welcome* freundlich; *advice, feelings* freundschaftlich. **to be** ~ **to sb** zu jdm freundlich sein; **to be** ~ **with sb** mit jdm befreundet sein. **2** *n* (*Sport*) Freundschaftsspiel *nt.*

friendship ['frendʃɪp] *n* Freundschaft *f.*

Friesian ['friːʒən] *adj* friesisch.

frieze [friːz] *n* (*picture*) Fries *m*; (*thin band*) Zierstreifen *m.*

frigate ['frɪgɪt] *n* (*Naut*) Fregatte *f.*

fright [fraɪt] *n* Schreck(en) *m.* **to get a** ~ einen Schreck bekommen; **to give sb a** ~ jdm einen Schreck(en) einjagen; **to take** ~ es mit der Angst zu tun bekommen; **she looks a** ~ (*col*) sie sieht verboten aus (*col*).

frighten ['fraɪtn] *vt* Angst machen (+*dat*); (*give a sudden fright*) erschrecken. **to be** ~**ed of sth** vor etw (*dat*) Angst haben; **to be** ~**ed of doing sth** Angst davor haben, etw zu tun; **I was** ~**ed out of my wits** ich war zu Tode erschrocken.

♦ **frighten away** *or* **off** *vt sep* abschrecken; (*deliberately*) verscheuchen.

frightening ['fraɪtnɪŋ] *adj* furchterregend.

frightful *adj*, ~**ly** *adv* ['fraɪtfʊl, -fəlɪ] furchtbar.

frigid ['frɪdʒɪd] *adj manner, welcome* kühl; (*Physiol, Psych*) frigid(e).

frill [frɪl] *n* (*on dress, shirt etc*) Rüsche *f.* **with all the** ~**s** mit allem Drum und Dran (*col*).

fringe [frɪndʒ] *n* (*on shawl*) Fransen *pl*; (*Brit: hair*) Pony *m*; (*fig: periphery*) Rand *m.* **on the** ~**(s) of society** am Rande der Gesellschaft.

fringe: ~ **benefits** *npl* zusätzliche Leistungen *pl*; ~ **group** *n* Randgruppe *f.*

frisk [frɪsk] **1** *vi* (*leap about*) umhertollen. **2** *vt suspect etc* durchsuchen.

frisky ['frɪskɪ] *adj* (+*er*) verspielt.

fritter[1] ['frɪtə'] *vt* (*also* ~ **away**) *money, time* vergeuden.

fritter[2] (*Cook*) Schmalzgebackene(s) *nt no pl* mit Füllung.

frivolity [frɪ'vɒlɪtɪ] *n* Frivolität *f.*

frivolous ['frɪvələs] *adj* frivol; *person, life, remark* leichtfertig.

frizz(l)y ['frɪz(l)ɪ] *adj* (+*er*) *hair* kraus.

fro [frəʊ] *adv see* **to 4, to-ing and fro-ing.**

frock [frɒk] *n* Kleid *nt*; (*of monk*) Kutte *f.*

frog [frɒg] *n* (a) Frosch *m.* **to have a** ~ **in one's throat** einen Frosch im Hals haben. (b) **F**~ (*Brit pej col: French person*) Franzose *m*, Französin *f.*

frog: ~**man** *n* Froschmann *m*; ~**march** *vt* (*Brit*) (*weg*)schleifen; (*carry*) zu viert wegtragen; **they** ~**marched him in** sie schleppten ihn herein (*col*).

frolic ['frɒlɪk] *vi pret, ptp* ~**ked** (*also* ~ **about** *or* **around**) umhertoben.

from [frɒm] *prep* (a) (*indicating starting place*) von (+*dat*); (*indicating place of origin*) aus (+*dat*). **where has he come** ~ **today?** von wo ist er heute gekommen?; **where is he** ~? woher kommt er?; **he comes** ~ **York** er kommt aus York; ~ **London to Edinburgh** von London nach Edinburgh; ~ **house to house** von Haus zu Haus.

(b) (*indicating time*) (*in past*) seit (+*dat*); (*in future*) ab (+*dat*), von (+*dat*) ... an. ~ **now on** von jetzt an; **commencing as** ~ **the 6th May** vom 6. Mai an.

(c) (*indicating distance*) von (+*dat*) (... *weg*); (*from town etc also*) von (+*dat*) ... entfernt. **the house is 10 km** ~ **the coast** das Haus ist 10 km von der Küste entfernt; **to go away** ~ **home** von zu Haus weggehen.

(d) (*indicating origin*) von (+*dat*); (*out of*) aus (+*dat*). **tell him** ~ **me** richten Sie ihm von mir

aus; **an invitation** ~ **the Smiths** eine Einladung von den Smiths; "~ ..." (*on envelope, parcel*) „Absender ...", „Abs. ..."; **where did you get that** ~?

wo hast du das her?; **I got it** ~ **the library/Gloria** ich habe es aus der Bibliothek/von Gloria; **to drink** ~ **a stream/glass** aus einem Bach/Glas trinken; **a quotation** ~ **Shakespeare** ein Zitat nach Shakespeare; **translated** ~ **the English** aus dem Englischen übersetzt; **painted** ~ **life** nach dem Leben gemalt.

(e) (*indicating lowest amount*) ab (+*dat*). ~ **£2 (upwards)** ab £ 2; **dresses (ranging)** ~ **£20 to £30** Kleider zwischen £ 20 und £ 30; **there were** ~ **10 to 15 people there** es waren zwischen 10 und 15 Leute da.

(f) (*indicating change*) **things went** ~ **bad to worse** es wurde immer schlimmer; **he went** ~ **office boy to director** er stieg vom Laufjungen zum Direktor auf; **a price increase** ~ **1 mark to 1.50 marks** eine Preiserhöhung von 1 DM auf 1,50 DM.

(g) (*indicating difference*) **he is quite different** ~ **the others** er ist ganz anders als die andern; **to tell black** ~ **white** Schwarz und Weiß auseinanderhalten.

(h) (*because of, due to*) **to act** ~ **conviction** aus Überzeugung handeln; **to die** ~ **fatigue** an Erschöpfung sterben; **weak** ~ **hunger** schwach vor Hunger; ~ **experience** aus Erfahrung; ~ **what I heard** nach dem, was ich gehört habe; ~ **what I can see** ... nach dem, was ich sehen kann, ...; ~ **the look of things** ... (*so*) wie die Sache ausschaut, ...

(i) (+*prep*) ~ **above** *or* **over sth** über etw (*acc*) hinweg; ~ **beneath** *or* **underneath sth** unter etw (*dat*) hervor; ~ **out of sth** aus etw heraus; ~ **among the trees** zwischen den Bäumen hervor; ~ **inside/outside the house** von drinnen/ draußen.

front [frʌnt] **1** *n* (a) Vorderseite *f*; (*forward part*) Vorderteil *nt.* **in** ~ vorne; (*in line, race etc also*) an der Spitze; **in** ~ **of sb/sth** vor jdm/etw; **at the** ~ **of** (*inside*) vorne in (+*dat*); (*outside*) vor (+*dat*); (*at the head of*) an der Spitze (+*gen*); **to be in** ~ vorne sein; (*Sport*) vorn(e) liegen; **in** *or* **at the** ~ **of the class** vorne im Klassenzimmer. (b) (*Mil, Pol, Met*) Front *f.* **they were attacked on all** ~**s** (*Mil*) sie wurden an allen Fronten angegriffen; (*fig*) sie wurden von allen Seiten angegriffen; **cold** ~ (*Met*) Kalt(luft)front *f*; **we must present a united** ~ wir müssen eine geschlossene Front bilden. (c) (*Brit: at sea*) Strandpromenade *f.* (d) (*outward appearance*) Fassade *f.* **to put on a bold** ~ eine tapfere Miene zur Schau stellen; **it's just a** ~ das ist nur Fassade; **the fruit shop was just a** ~ das Obstgeschäft diente nur zur Tarnung.

2 *vi* **the house/windows** ~ **onto the steet** die Häuser liegen/die Fenster gehen auf die Straße hinaus.

3 *adj* vorderste(r, s); *row, page also* erste(r, s), *tooth, wheel, view* Vorder-. ~ **seat** Platz *m* in der ersten Reihe; (*Aut*) Vordersitz *m.*

frontage ['frʌntɪdʒ] *n* (*of building*) Front *f.*

frontal ['frʌntl] *adj* (*Mil*) Frontal-. ~ **view** Vorderansicht *f.*

front: ~ **bench** *n* (*Parl*) vorderste *or* erste Reihe (*wo die führenden Politiker sitzen*); ~ **door** *n* Haustür *f.*

frontier ['frʌntɪə'] *n* (*lit, fig*) Grenze *f.*

frontispiece ['frʌntɪspiːs] *n* Titelseite *f*; (*illustration*) Bildseite *f.*

front: ~ **line** *n* Front(linie) *f*; ~ **man** *n* Mann *m* in der Spitze; (*pej*) Strohmann *m*; ~ **page** *n* Titelseite *f*; ~-**page** *adj news* auf der ersten Seite; ~-**runner** *n* (*fig*) Spitzenreiter, Favorit *m.*

frost [frɒst] **1** *n* Frost *m*; (*on leaves etc*) Rauhreif *m.* **ten degrees of** ~ zehn Grad Kälte. **2** *vt* (*esp US*) *cake* glasieren.

frost: ~**bite** n Frostbeulen pl; (more serious) Erfrierungen pl; ~**bitten** adj hands, feet erfroren.

frosted ['frɒstɪd] adj (a) ~ **glass** Milchglas nt; (textured) geriffeltes Glas. (b) (esp US) cake mit Zuckerguß überzogen, glasiert.

frosting ['frɒstɪŋ] n (esp US: icing) Zuckerguß m.

frosty ['frɒstɪ] adj (+er) (lit, fig) frostig.

froth [frɒθ] **1** n (on liquids, Med) Schaum m. **2** vi schäumen. **the dog was ~ing at the mouth** der Hund hatte Schaum vor dem Maul.

frown [fraʊn] **1** n Stirnrunzeln nt no pl. **to give a ~** die Stirn(e) runzeln; **angry ~** finsterer Blick; **worried/puzzled ~** sorgenvoller/verdutzter Gesichtsausdruck. **2** vi (lit, fig) die Stirn(e) runzeln (at über +acc). **to ~ at sb** jdn finster ansehen.

♦ **frown (up)on** vi +prep obj (fig) suggestion, idea mißbilligen.

froze [frəʊz] pret of **freeze**.

frozen ['frəʊzn] **1** ptp of **freeze**. **2** adj river zugefroren. **I'm absolutely ~ stiff** ich bin total steifgefroren; ~ **foods** Tiefkühlkost f; ~ **peas** gefrorene Erbsen pl.

frugal ['fruːgəl] adj person sparsam; meal einfach.

fruit [fruːt] n (as collective) Obst nt; (Bot) Frucht f. **what is your favourite ~?** welches Obst magst du am liebsten?; **to bear ~** (lit, fig) Früchte tragen; **the ~(s) of my labour** die Früchte pl meiner Arbeit.

fruiterer ['fruːtərə'] n (esp Brit) Obsthändler(in f) m.

fruitful ['fruːtfʊl] adj (lit, fig) fruchtbar.

fruition [fruːˈɪʃən] n **to come to ~** sich verwirklichen.

fruitless ['fruːtlɪs] adj (fig) fruchtlos.

fruit: ~ **machine** n (Brit) Spielautomat m; ~ **salad** n Obstsalat m; ~ **tree** n Obstbaum m.

fruity ['fruːtɪ] adj (+er) (like fruit) fruchtartig; taste, wine fruchtig; voice rauchig. **to get ~** (fig col) keck werden.

frump [frʌmp] n (pej) Vogelscheuche f (col).

frustrate [frʌˈstreɪt] vt hopes zunichte machen; plans, plot durchkreuzen; person frustrieren.

frustrated [frʌˈstreɪtɪd] adj person frustriert.

frustrating [frʌˈstreɪtɪŋ] adj frustrierend.

frustration [frʌˈstreɪʃən] n Frustration f no pl; (of hopes, plans, plot) Zerschlagung f.

fry[1] [fraɪ] npl small ~ (unimportant people) kleine Fische pl (col).

fry[2] vt (in der Pfanne) braten; see fried.

frying pan ['fraɪɪŋˌpæn] n Bratpfanne f. **to jump out of the ~ into the fire** (Prov) vom Regen in die Traufe kommen (Prov).

ft = **foot** ft; **feet** ft.

fuchsia ['fjuːʃə] n Fuchsie f.

fuck [fʌk] (col!!) **1** vt **(a)** (lit) ficken (col!!). **(b)** ~ **you!** leck mich am Arsch (col!!). **2** interj (verdammte) Scheiße (col!).

♦ **fuck off** vi (col!!) ~ ~! verpiß dich! (col!!).

fucking ['fʌkɪŋ] adj (col!!) Scheiß- (col!).

fuddled ['fʌdld] adj (muddled) verwirrt; (tipsy) beschwipst.

fudge [fʌdʒ] n (Cook) ≈ Karamel m.

fuel ['fjʊəl] **1** n Brennstoff m; (for vehicle) Kraftstoff m, (petrol) Benzin nt; (Aviat, Space) Treibstoff m. **to add ~ to the flames** (fig) Öl ins Feuer gießen. **2** vt stove, furnace etc (fill) mit Brennstoff versorgen; (drive, propel) antreiben.

fuel: ~ **cell** n Brennstoffzelle f; ~ **gauge** n Benzinuhr f; ~ **injection** n (Benzin)einspritzung f; **engine with ~ injection** Einspritzmotor m; ~ **pump** n Benzinpumpe f; ~ **tank** n Tank m; (for oil) Öltank m.

fug [fʌg] n (esp Brit col) Mief m (col).

fugitive ['fjuːdʒɪtɪv] **1** n Flüchtling m. **he is a ~ from the law** er ist auf der Flucht vor dem Gesetz. **2** adj flüchtig.

fugue [fjuːg] n (Mus) Fuge f.

fulfil, (US) **fulfill** [fʊlˈfɪl] vt erfüllen. **to be ~led**

(wish etc) sich erfüllen; **to feel ~led** Erfüllung finden.

fulfilment, (US) **fulfillment** [fʊlˈfɪlmənt] n Erfüllung f.

full [fʊl] **1** adj (+er) voll; description, report vollständig; understanding, sympathy vollste(r, s); figure, skirt füllig. ~ **of** ... voller (+gen) ...; **he's ~ of good ideas** er steckt voll(er) guter Ideen; **a look ~ of hate** ein haßerfüllter Blick; **I am ~ (up)** (col) ich bin voll bis obenhin (col); **we are ~ up for July** wir sind für Juli völlig ausgebucht; **for the ~er figure** für vollschlanke Damen; **at ~ speed** in voller Fahrt; **to fall ~ length** der Länge nach hinfallen; **roses in ~ bloom** Rosen in voller Blüte; **I waited two ~ hours** ich habe zwei ganze Stunden gewartet; **the ~ particulars** die genauen Einzelheiten; ~ **employment** Vollbeschäftigung f; ~ **member** vollberechtigtes Mitglied; ~ **name** Vor- und Zuname m; **to be ~ of oneself** von sich (selbst) eingenommen sein; **she was ~ of it** sie hat gar nicht mehr aufgehört, davon zu reden; **the papers were ~ of it for weeks** die Zeitungen waren wochenlang voll davon.

2 adv it is a ~ **five miles from here** es sind volle fünf Meilen von hier; **I know ~ well that** ... ich weiß sehr wohl, daß ...; **to hit sb ~ in the face** jdn mitten ins Gesicht schlagen.

3 n in ~ vollständig; **to write one's name in ~** seinen Namen ausschreiben; **to pay in ~** den vollen Betrag bezahlen; **to the ~** vollständig.

full: ~**-back** n (Sport) Verteidiger m; ~**-blooded** [ˌfʊlˈblʌdɪd] adj (vigorous) kräftig; ~**-blown** adj (fig) doctor, theory richtiggehend; ~**-bodied** adj wine vollmundig; ~**-grown** adj ausgewachsen; ~**-length** adj portrait lebensgroß; film abendfüllend; ~ **moon** n Vollmond m.

fullness ['fʊlnɪs] n (of detail) Vollständigkeit f; (of skirt, sound) Fülle f. **in the ~ of time** (eventually) zu gegebener Zeit; (at predestined time) als die Zeit gekommen war.

full: ~**-scale** adj drawing in Originalgröße; operation, search angelegt; revision umfassend; attack General-; ~ **stop** n Punkt m; ~**-time 1** adv work ganztags; **2** adj employment Ganztags-.

fully [fʊlɪ] adv völlig; equipped vollständig; dressed fertig. **it's ~ two years ago** es ist gut zwei Jahre her; **I ~ expected that** ... ich habe fest damit gerechnet, daß ...

fully: ~**-fledged** adj bird flügge; (fig: qualified) richtiggehend; ~**-qualified** adj vollqualifiziert attr.

fulsome ['fʊlsəm] adj praise übertrieben.

fumble ['fʌmbl] **1** vi (also ~ **about**) umhertasten. **to ~ in the dark** im Dunkeln herumtasten; **to ~ in one's pockets** in seinen Taschen wühlen; **to ~ with sth** an etw (dat) herumfummeln. **2** vt verpfuschen (col). **to ~ the ball** den Ball nicht sicher fangen.

fume [fjuːm] **1** vi (liquids) dampfen; (fig col: person) kochen (col). **2** npl ~**s** Dämpfe pl; (of car) Abgase pl.

fumigate ['fjuːmɪgeɪt] vt ausräuchern.

fun [fʌn] n Spaß m. **for** or **in ~** (as a joke) als Scherz; **it's ~** es macht Spaß; **it's no ~** es macht keinen Spaß; **we just did it for ~** wir haben das nur zum Spaß gemacht; **to spoil the ~** den Spaß verderben; **he's good ~** er ist ganz lustig; **have ~!** viel Spaß!; **that should be ~** and **games** das kann ja (noch) heiter werden (col); **to make ~ of** or **poke ~ at sb/sth** sich über jdn/etw lustig machen.

function ['fʌŋkʃən] **1** n **(a)** (purpose, Math) Funktion f. **in his ~ as judge** in seiner Eigenschaft als Richter. **(b)** (reception) Empfang m; (official ceremony) Feier f. **2** vi funktionieren. **to ~ as** fungieren als; (thing also) dienen als.

functional ['fʌŋkʃənəl] adj funktionell.

fund [fʌnd] **1** n **(a)** (Fin) Fonds m. ~**s** pl Mittel pl. **(b)** (of wisdom, humour etc) Schatz (of von),

Vorrat (of an +dat) m. **2** vt scheme, project das Kapital aufbringen für.

fundamental [ˌfʌndə'mentl] **1** adj (basic) grundlegend; indifference, problem grundsätzlich. **to be** ~ **to sth** für etw von grundlegender Bedeutung sein; **our** ~ **needs/beliefs** unsere Grundbedürfnisse pl/Grundüberzeugungen pl. **2** n usu pl Grundlage f.

fundamentally [ˌfʌndə'mentəlɪ] adv grundlegend; (in essence) im Grunde.

funeral ['fjuːnərəl] n Beerdigung f. **well that's your** ~ (col) na ja, das ist dein Problem (col).

funeral: ~ **director** n Beerdigungsunternehmer m; ~ **procession** n Leichenzug m.

funereal [fjuːˈnɪərɪəl] adj trübselig.

funfair ['fʌnfɛəʳ] n (Brit) Kirmes f.

fungus ['fʌŋgəs] n, pl **fungi** ['fʌŋgaɪ] Pilz m.

funicular (railway) [fjuːˈnɪkjʊlə('reɪlweɪ)] n Seilbahn f.

funk [fʌŋk] n **to be in a (blue)** ~ (col) ganz schön Bammel haben (col).

funnel ['fʌnl] n (for pouring) Trichter m; (Naut, Rail) Schornstein m.

funnily ['fʌnɪlɪ] adv ~ **enough** komischerweise.

funny ['fʌnɪ] adj (+er) (a) (comic) komisch. **are you being** ~? das soll wohl ein Witz sein?; **it's not** ~ das ist or das finde ich überhaupt nicht komisch. **(b)** (strange) seltsam, komisch. **it's a** ~ **thing, only last week** ... (das ist doch) komisch, erst letzte Woche ...; ~ **business** (col) faule Sache (col); **I felt all** ~ (col) mir war ganz komisch; ~ **bone** n Musikantenknochen m.

fur [fɜːʳ] **1** n (on animal) Fell nt; (for clothing) Pelz m; (in kettle) Kesselstein m. **2** attr coat, stole Pelz-.

furious ['fjʊərɪəs] adj person wütend; struggle wild; speed rasend. **to be** ~ **with sb** auf jdn wütend sein.

furlong ['fɜːlɒŋ] n Achtelmeile f.

furnace ['fɜːnɪs] n Hochofen m; (Metal) Schmelzofen m.

furnish ['fɜːnɪʃ] vt (a) house einrichten. ~**ed room** möbliertes Zimmer; ~**ing fabrics** Dekorationsstoffe pl. **(b)** information, reason, excuse liefern. **to** ~ **sb with sth** jdn mit etw versorgen.

furnishings ['fɜːnɪʃɪŋz] npl Mobiliar nt; (with carpets etc) Einrichtung f.

furniture ['fɜːnɪtʃəʳ] n Möbel pl. **a piece of** ~ ein Möbelstück nt; **he's part of the** ~ (fig col) er gehört zum Inventar.

furore [fjʊəˈrɔːrɪ], (US) **furor** ['fjʊrɔːʳ] n Protest(e pl) m. **to cause a** ~ einen Skandal verursachen.

furrier ['fʌrɪəʳ] n Kürschner(in f) m.

furrow ['fʌrəʊ] **1** n (Agr) Furche f; (on brow) Runzel f. **2** vt brow runzeln.

furry ['fɜːrɪ] adj (+er) animal Pelz-; toy Plüsch-; tongue belegt.

further ['fɜːðəʳ] **1** adv, comp of **far (a)** (in place, time, fig) weiter. ~ **on** weiter entfernt; ~ **back** (in place, time) weiter zurück; (in time) früher; **nothing is** ~ **from my thoughts** nichts liegt mir ferner. **(b)** (more) **he didn't question me** ~ er hat mich nichts weiter gefragt; **until you hear** ~ bis

auf weiteres; **and** ~ ... und darüber hinaus ...; ~ **to your letter of** ... (Comm) in bezug auf Ihren Brief vom ... (form). **2** adj **(a)** see **farther. (b)** (additional) weiter. **until** ~ **notice** bis auf weiteres; ~ **particulars** nähere Einzelheiten pl; ~ **education** Fortbildung f; (at university) Hochschulausbildung f. **3** vt one's interests, a cause fördern.

furtherance ['fɜːðərəns] n Förderung f.

furthermore ['fɜːðəmɔːʳ] adv außerdem.

furthermost ['fɜːðəməʊst] adj äußerste(r, s).

furthest ['fɜːðɪst] **1** adv the ~ **north you can go** soweit nach Norden wie möglich. **2** adj am weitesten entfernt. **5 km at the** ~ höchstens 5 km.

furtive ['fɜːtɪv] adj action heimlich; behaviour heimlichtuerisch; look verstohlen.

fury ['fjʊərɪ] n (of person) Wut f; (of storm) Ungestüm nt. **she flew into a** ~ sie kam in Rage; **like** ~ (col) wie verrückt (col).

fuse, (US) **fuze** [fjuːz] **1** vt (a) metals verschmelzen. **(b)** (Brit Elec) **to** ~ **the lights** die Sicherung durchbrennen lassen. **2** vi (a) (metals) sich verbinden; (fig) verschmelzen. **(b)** (Brit Elec) durchbrennen. **the lights** ~**d** die Sicherung war durchgebrannt. **3** n (Elec) Sicherung f; (Brit Elec: act of fusing) Kurzschluß m; (in bombs) Zündschnur f.

fuse box n Sicherungskasten m.

fuselage ['fjuːzəlɑːʒ] n (Flugzeug)rumpf m.

fuse wire n Schmelzdraht m.

fusillade [ˌfjuːzɪˈleɪd] n Salve f.

fusion ['fjuːʒən] n (of metal, fig) Verschmelzung f.

fuss [fʌs] **1** n Theater nt (col); (bother) Umstände pl (col), Aufheben(s) nt. **don't go to a lot of** ~ mach dir keine Umstände; **to make a** ~, **to kick up a** ~ Krach schlagen (col); **to make a** ~ **about** or over sth viel Aufhebens um etw machen; **to make a** ~ **of sb** (spoil) VIP, guest um jdn viel Wirbel machen (col); children jdn verwöhnen; **to fuss** ~ **about nothing** viel Lärm um nichts. **2** vi sich (unnötig) aufregen; (get into a ~) Umstände pl machen. **3** vt person nervös machen; (pester) keine Ruhe lassen (+dat).

♦ **fuss about** vi herumfuhrwerken (col).

♦ **fuss over** vi +prep obj sich (dat) große Umstände machen mit.

fussy ['fʌsɪ] adj (+er) (finicky) kleinlich, pingelig (col); (elaborate) dress, pattern verspielt. **what do you want to do?** — **I'm not** ~ was willst du machen? — ist mir egal.

futile ['fjuːtaɪl] adj sinnlos.

futility [fjuːˈtɪlɪtɪ] n Sinnlosigkeit f.

future ['fjuːtʃəʳ] **1** n Zukunft f. **in the near** ~ bald; **there's no** ~ **in it** das hat keine Zukunft. **2** adj zukünftig. **at some** ~ **date** zu einem späteren Zeitpunkt; **the** ~ **tense** (Gram) das Futur, die Zukunft.

futuristic [ˌfjuːtʃəˈrɪstɪk] adj futuristisch.

fuze n (US) = **fuse.**

fuzz [fʌz] n **(a)** (fluff) Flaum m. **(b)** the ~ (col) die Polypen pl (col).

fuzzy ['fʌzɪ] adj (+er) **(a)** hair kraus. **(b)** (col) picture, sound, memory verschwommen.

G

G, g [dʒiː] *n* G, *g nt*. ~ **sharp/flat** Gis, gis *nt*/Ges, ges *nt*.

g = **gram(s), gramme(s)** g.

gab [gæb] *(col)* **1** *n* **to have the gift of the** ~ nicht auf den Mund gefallen sein. **2** *vi* quatschen *(col)*.

gabardine [ˌgæbəˈdiːn] *n* Gabardine *m*.

gabble [ˈgæbl] **1** *vi (geese)* schnattern. **don't** ~ **red'** nicht so schnell. **2** *vt* herunterrasseln *(col)*.

♦ **gabble away** *vi* drauflosschnattern *(col)*.

gable [ˈgeɪbl] *n* Giebel *m*. ~ **end** Giebelwand *f*.

♦ **gad about** [ˈgædəˈbaʊt] *vi (col)* herumziehen. **to** ~ ~ **the country** im Land herumziehen.

gadget [ˈgædʒɪt] *n* Gerät *nt*. **with a lot of** ~**s** mit allen Schikanen *(col)*.

gadgetry [ˈgædʒɪtrɪ] *n* Vorrichtungen *pl; (superfluous equipment)* technische Spielereien *pl*.

Gaelic [ˈgeɪlɪk] **1** *adj* gälisch. **2** *n (language)* Gälisch *nt*.

gaff [gæf] *n*: **to blow the** ~ *(col)* nicht dichthalten *(col)*.

gaffe [gæf] *n* Fauxpas *m; (verbal)* taktlose Bemerkung. **to make a** ~ einen Fauxpas begehen.

gaffer [ˈgæfəʳ] *n (col) (boss)* Boß *(col) m; (old man)* Opa *m (col)*.

gag [gæg] **1** *n* **(a)** Knebel *m*. **(b)** *(col: joke)* Gag *m*. **2** *vt* knebeln *(auch fig)*.

gaga [ˈgɑːˈgɑː] *adj (col) old person* verkalkt *(col)*.

gage [geɪdʒ] *n, vt (US)* = **gauge**.

gaggle [ˈgægl] *n (of geese)* Herde *f*.

gaiety [ˈgeɪɪtɪ] *n* Fröhlichkeit *f*.

gaily [ˈgeɪlɪ] *adv* fröhlich. ~ **coloured** farbenfroh.

gain [geɪn] **1** *n no pl (advantage)* Vorteil *m; (profit)* Gewinn *m; (increase)* Zunahme *f (in gen)*. **it will be to your** ~ es wird zu Ihrem Vorteil sein; **to do sth for** ~ etw des Geldes wegen tun; **his loss is our** ~ wir profitieren von seinem Verlust; **the SDP made several** ~**s** die SDP gewann einige Sitze.

2 *vt* **(a)** *(obtain, win)* gewinnen; *knowledge, wealth* erwerben; *advantage, respect, entry* sich *(dat)* verschaffen. **what does he hope to** ~ **by it?** was erhofft er sich *(dat)* davon?; **to** ~ **experience** Erfahrung sammeln; **we have nothing to** ~ **by staying** wir haben nichts davon, noch länger dazubleiben. **(b)** *(reach) shore, summit* erreichen. **(c)** *(increase)* **to** ~ **height** (an) Höhe gewinnen; **to** ~ **speed** schneller werden; **she has** ~**ed weight** sie hat zugenommen; **as he** ~**ed confidence** als seine Selbstsicherheit zunahm; **my watch** ~**s five minutes each day** meine Uhr geht fünf Minuten pro Tag vor.

3 *vi* **(a)** *(watch)* vorgehen. **(b)** *(profit: person)* profitieren *(by* von*)*. **society/you would** ~ **from that** das wäre für die Gesellschaft/für Sie von Vorteil. **(c)** **to** ~ **in prestige** an Ansehen gewinnen.

♦ **gain on** *vi +prep obj (close gap)* einholen.

gainful [ˈgeɪnfʊl] *adj occupation etc* einträglich. **to be in** ~ **employment** erwerbstätig sein.

gait [geɪt] *n* Gang *m; (of horse)* Gangart *f*.

gal = **gallon(s)**.

gala [ˈgɑːlə] *n (festive occasion)* großes Fest; *(Theat, Film, ball)* Galaveranstaltung *f*. ~ **performance** Galavorstellung *f*.

galaxy [ˈgæləksɪ] *n (Astron)* Milchstraße *f*.

gale [geɪl] *n* Sturm *m*. **it was blowing a** ~ ein Sturm wütete; ~ **force 8** Windstärke 8; ~**-force winds** orkanartige Winde.

gall [gɔːl] **1** *n* **(a)** *(Physiol, Bot)* Galle *f*. **(b)** *(col)* **of all the** ~! so eine Frechheit! **2** *vt (fig: anger)* maßlos ärgern.

gallant [ˈgælənt] *adj (brave)* tapfer; *(chivalrous, noble)* edel, ritterlich; *(to women)* galant.

gallantry [ˈgæləntrɪ] *n (bravery)* Tapferkeit *f; (chivalry)* Edelmut *m; (to women)* Galanterie *f*.

gall bladder *n* Gallenblase *f*.

galleon [ˈgælɪən] *n* Galeone *f*.

gallery [ˈgælərɪ] *n (balcony, Art)* Galerie *f; (Theat)* oberster Rang. **to play to the** ~ *(fig)* sich in Szene setzen.

galley [ˈgælɪ] *n* **(a)** *(Naut) (ship)* Galeere *f; (kitchen)* Kombüse *f*. ~ **slave** Galeerensklave *m*. **(b)** *(Typ) (also* ~ **proof)** Fahne(nabzug *m*) *f*.

Gallic [ˈgælɪk] *adj* gallisch.

galling [ˈgɔːlɪŋ] *adj* äußerst ärgerlich.

gallivant [ˌgælɪˈvænt] *vi* **to** ~ **about** *(col)* sich herumtreiben.

gallon [ˈgælən] *n* Gallone *f*.

gallop [ˈgæləp] **1** *n* Galopp *m*. **at full** ~ im gestreckten Galopp. **2** *vi* galoppieren. **to** ~ **through a book/one's work** ein Buch im Eiltempo lesen *(col)*/seine Arbeit im Eiltempo erledigen *(col)*.

galloping [ˈgæləpɪŋ] *adj (lit, fig)* galoppierend.

gallows [ˈgæləʊz] *n* Galgen *m*.

gallstone [ˈgɔːlstəʊn] *n* Gallenstein *m*.

Gallup poll ® [ˈgæləpˌpəʊl] *n* Meinungsumfrage *f*.

galore [gəˈlɔːʳ] *adv* in Hülle und Fülle.

galvanize [ˈgælvənaɪz] *vt* **(a)** *(Elec)* galvanisieren. **(b)** *(fig)* elektrisieren. **to** ~ **sb into action** jdn plötzlich aktiv werden lassen.

gambit [ˈgæmbɪt] *n* **(a)** *(Chess)* Gambit *nt*. **(b)** *(fig) (Schach)*zug *m*. **his favourite conversational** ~ **is** ... er fängt eine Unterhaltung am liebsten mit ... an.

gamble [ˈgæmbl] **1** *n (fig)* Risiko *nt*. **it's a** ~ es ist riskant; **I'll take a** ~ **on it** ich riskiere es. **2** *vi* **(a)** *(lit)* (um Geld) spielen *(with* mit*); (on horses etc)* wetten. **to** ~ **on the stock exchange** an der Börse spekulieren. **(b)** *(fig)* **she was gambling on him being late** sie hat sich darauf verlassen, daß er sich verspäten würde; **to** ~ **with sth** etw aufs Spiel setzen.

♦ **gamble away** *vt* Geld verspielen.

gambler [ˈgæmbləʳ] *n (lit, fig)* Spieler(in *f*) *m*.

gambling [ˈgæmblɪŋ] *n* Spielen *nt* (um Geld); *(on horses etc)* Wetten *nt*. **to disapprove of** ~ gegen das Glücksspiel/Wetten sein; ~ **debts** Spielschulden *pl*.

gambol [ˈgæmbəl] *vi* herumspringen.

game¹ [geɪm] *n* **(a)** Spiel *nt; (of table tennis)* Satz *m; (of billiards, board-games etc, informal tennis match)* Partie *f*. ~**s** *(Sch)* Sport *m*; **to have** *or* **play a** ~ **of football/tennis/chess** *etc* Fußball/Tennis/Schach *etc* spielen; **he plays a good** ~ er spielt gut; **to have a** ~ **with sb, to give sb a** ~ mit jdm spielen; **to be off one's** ~ nicht in Form sein; ~ **of chance** Glücksspiel *nt*; ~ **set and match to X** Satz und Spiel (geht an) X.

(b) *(fig)* Spiel *nt*. **to play the** ~ sich an die Spielregeln halten; **to play** ~**s with sb** mit jdm spielen; **the** ~ **is up** das Spiel ist aus; **to play sb's**

~ jdm in die Hände spielen; **two can play at that** ~ wie du mir, so ich dir *(col);* **to beat sb at his own** ~ jdn mit seinen/ihren eigenen Waffen schlagen; **to give the** ~ **away** alles verderben; **to spoil sb's little** ~ jdm die Suppe versalzen *(col);* **I wonder what his little** ~ **is?** ich frage mich, was er im Schilde führt. **(c)** *(col: business, profession)* Branche *f.* **how long have you been in this** ~? wie lange machen Sie das schon?; **to be/go on the** ~ auf den Strich gehen *(col).* **(d)** *(Hunt)* Wild *nt; (Cook also)* Wildbret *nt.*

game² *adj (brave)* mutig. **to be** ~ **for sth** (bei) etw mitmachen; **to be** ~ **for anything** für alles zu haben sein *(col).*

game: ~ **bird** *n* Federwild *nt no pl;* ~**keeper** *n* Wildhüter *m.*

gamesmanship ['geɪmzmənʃɪp] *n* Spieltaktik *f.*

gammon ['gæmən] *n* Schinken *m.*

gamut ['gæmət] *n (fig)* Skala *f.* **to run the (whole)** ~ **of emotion(s)** die ganze Skala der Gefühle durchlaufen.

gander ['gændə'] *n* Gänserich *m.*

gang [gæŋ] *n* Schar *f; (of workers, prisoners)* Kolonne *f; (of criminals, youths, terrorists)* Bande *f; (of friends etc, clique)* Clique *f (col).*

♦ **gang up** *vi* sich zusammentun. **to** ~ ~ **on sb** sich gegen jdn verschwören.

gangling ['gæŋglɪŋ] *adj* schlaksig.

gangplank ['gæŋplæŋk] *n* Laufplanke *f.*

gangrenous ['gæŋɡrɪnəs] *adj* brandig.

gangster ['gæŋstə'] *n* Gangster *m.*

gangway ['gæŋweɪ] **1** *n* **(a)** *(Naut) (gangplank)* Landungsbrücke *f; (ladder)* Fallreep *nt.* **(b)** *(aisle)* Gang *m.* **2** *interj* Platz da.

gantry ['gæntrɪ] *n (for crane)* Portal *nt; (on motorway)* Schilderbrücke *f; (Rail)* Signalbrücke *f; (for rocket)* Abschußrampe *f.*

gaol [dʒeɪl] *n, vt =* **jail.**

gap [gæp] *n (lit, fig)* Lücke *f; (chink)* Spalt *m; (in surface)* Ritze *f; (Tech: spark* ~) Abstand *m; (fig) (in conversation, narrative, time)* Pause *f; (gulf)* Kluft *f.*

gape [geɪp] *vi* **(a)** *(person)* den Mund aufreißen; *(chasm etc)* gähnen; *(seam, wound)* klaffen. **(b)** *(stare: person)* starren. **to** ~ **at sb/sth** jdn/etw (mit offenem Mund) anstarren.

gaping ['geɪpɪŋ] *adj* **(a)** klaffend; *chasm* gähnend. **(b)** *(staring)* gaffend; *(astonished)* staunend.

garage ['gærɑːʒ, *(US)* gə'rɑːʒ] *n (for parking)* Garage *f; (for petrol)* Tankstelle *f; (for repairs etc)* (Reparatur)werkstatt *f.*

garb [gɑːb] *n* Gewand *nt; (col)* Kluft *f (col).*

garbage ['gɑːbɪdʒ] *n (lit: esp US)* Abfall, Müll *m; (fig) (useless things)* Schund *m (col); (nonsense)* Quatsch *m (col).*

garbage: ~ **can** *n (US)* Mülleimer *m; (outside)* Mülltonne *f;* ~ **disposal unit** *n* Müllschlucker *m.*

garbled ['gɑːbld] *adj* entstellt. **the message got** ~ **on its way** die Nachricht kam völlig entstellt an; **the facts got a little** ~ die Tatsachen sind etwas durcheinandergeraten.

garden ['gɑːdn] *n* Garten *m; (often pl: park)* Gartenanlagen *pl.*

gardener ['gɑːdnə'] *n* Gärtner(in *f) m.*

gardening ['gɑːdnɪŋ] *n* Gartenarbeit *f.*

garden *in cpds* Garten-; ~ **party** *n* Gartenfest *nt;* ~ **path:** **to lead sb up the** ~ **path** *(col)* jdn an der Nase herumführen; ~ **shears** *npl* Heckenschere *f.*

gargle ['gɑːgl] **1** *vi* gurgeln. **2** *n (liquid)* Gurgelwasser *nt.* **to have a** ~ gurgeln.

gargoyle ['gɑːgɔɪl] *n* Wasserspeier *m.*

garish ['gɛərɪʃ] *adj lights etc* grell; *colour etc also* knallig *(col); clothes* knallbunt.

garland ['gɑːlənd] *n* Kranz *m; (festoon)* Girlande *f.*

garlic ['gɑːlɪk] *n* Knoblauch *m.*

garment ['gɑːmənt] *n* Kleidungsstück *nt.* ~ **industry** *(US)* Bekleidungsindustrie *f.*

garnish ['gɑːnɪʃ] *vt* garnieren.

garret ['gærət] *n* Dachboden *m; (room)* Dachkammer *f.*

garrison ['gærɪsən] **1** *n* Garnison *f.* **2** *vt troops* in Garnison legen; *town* mit einer Garnison belegen.

garrulous ['gærʊləs] *adj* geschwätzig.

garter ['gɑːtə'] *n* Strumpfband *nt; (US: suspender)* Strumpfhalter *m.*

gas [gæs] **1** *n* **(a)** Gas *nt.* **(b)** *(US: petrol)* Benzin *nt.* **(c)** *(anaesthetic)* Lachgas *nt.* **to have** ~ Lachgas bekommen. **2** *vt* vergasen. **to** ~ **oneself** sich mit Gas vergiften. **3** *vi (col: talk)* schwafeln *(col).*

gas *in cpds* Gas-; ~**bag** *n (col)* Schwätzer(in *f) m (col);* ~ **chamber** *n* Gaskammer *f;* ~ **cooker** *n* Gasherd *m;* ~ **fire** *n* Gasofen *m.*

gash [gæʃ] **1** *n (wound)* klaffende Wunde; *(in earth, tree)* (klaffende) Spalte; *(in upholstery)* tiefer Schlitz. **2** *vt* aufschlitzen; *furniture,* wood tief einkerben. **he** ~**ed his knee** er hat sich *(dat)* das Knie aufgeschlagen.

gasket ['gæskɪt] *n (Tech)* Dichtung *f.*

gas: ~ **lighter** *n* Gasanzünder *m;* ~**man** *n* Gasmann *m (col);* ~ **mask** *n* Gasmaske *f;* ~ **meter** *n* Gaszähler *m.*

gasoline ['gæsəʊliːn] *n (US)* Benzin *nt.*

gasometer [gæ'sɒmɪtə'] *n* Gasometer *m.*

gasp [gɑːsp] **1** *n (for breath)* tiefer Atemzug. **to give a** ~ **of surprise** vor Überraschung die Luft anhalten; **to be at one's last** ~ in den letzten Zügen liegen. **2** *vi (continually)* keuchen; *(once)* tief einatmen; *(with surprise etc)* nach Luft schnappen *(col).* **to make sb** ~ jdm den Atem nehmen; **to** ~ **for breath** nach Atem ringen.

gas: ~ **station** *n (US)* Tankstelle *f;* ~ **stove** *n* Gasherd *m;* ~ **tank** *n (US)* Benzintank *m.*

gastric ['gæstrɪk] *adj;* ~ **flu** *n* Darmgrippe *f;* ~ **ulcer** *n* Magengeschwür *nt.*

gastritis [gæs'traɪtɪs] *n* Gastritis *f.*

gastroenteritis ['gæstrəʊˌentə'raɪtɪs] *n* Magen-Darm-Entzündung *f.*

gastronomic [ˌgæstrə'nɒmɪk] *adj* gastronomisch.

gasworks ['gæswɜːks] *n sing or pl* Gaswerk *nt.*

gate [geɪt] *n* **(a)** Tor *nt; (small, garden* ~) Pforte *f; (five-barred* ~) Gatter *nt; (in airport)* Flugsteig *m; (of level-crossing)* Schranke *f; (sports ground entrance)* Einlaß *m.* **(b)** *(Sport) (attendance)* Zuschauerzahl *f; (entrance money)* Einnahmen *pl.*

gateau ['gætəʊ] *n* Torte *f.*

gate: ~**crash** *(col)* **1** *vt* **to** ~**crash a party** in eine Party hineinplatzen; **2** *vi* einfach so hingehen *(col);* ~**crasher** *n* ungeladener Gast; ~**post** *n* Torpfosten *m;* **between you, me and the** ~**post** *(col)* unter uns gesagt; ~**way** *n (lit, fig)* Tor *nt (to* zu); *(archway)* Torbogen *m.*

gather ['gæðə'] **1** *vt* **(a)** *(collect, bring together)* sammeln; *people* versammeln; *flowers, fruit* pflücken; *potatoes, corn etc* ernten; *harvest* einbringen; *taxes* einziehen; *(collect up)* broken glass, pins etc aufsammeln; *one's belongings* (zusammen)packen. **to** ~ **one's strength/thoughts** Kräfte sammeln/seine Gedanken ordnen; **to** ~ **dust** verstauben.

(b) *(increase)* **to** ~ **speed** schneller werden; **to** ~ **strength** stärker werden.

(c) *(infer)* schließen *(from* aus). **I** ~**ed that** das dachte ich mir; **I** ~ **from the papers that he has** ... weil ich aus den Zeitungen ersehe, hat er ...; **as far as I can** ~ *(so)* wie ich es sehe; **I** ~ **she won't be coming** ich nehme an, daß sie nicht kommt; **as you will have/might have** ~**ed** ... wie Sie bestimmt/vielleicht bemerkt haben ...

(d) **she** ~**ed her mink around her** sie hüllte sich in ihren Nerz.

(e) *(Sew)* raffen.

2 *vi* **(a)** *(people)* sich versammeln; *(objects, dust etc)* sich (an)sammeln; *(clouds)* sich zusammenziehen; *(storm)* sich zusammenbrauen.

(b) *(increase: darkness etc)* zunehmen *(in an +dat)*.

♦ **gather around** *vi* come on, children, ~ ~! kommt alle her, Kinder!; they ~ed ~ the fire sie scharten sich um das Feuer.

♦ **gather up** *vt sep* aufsammeln; *one's belongings* zusammenpacken; *hair* hochstecken; *(fig) pieces* auflesen.

gathering ['gæðərɪŋ] *n* Versammlung *f; (meeting)* Treffen *nt.*

gauche [gəʊʃ] *adj* ungeschickt.

gaudy ['gɔːdɪ] *adj (+er)* knallig *(col).*

gauge [geɪdʒ] **1** *n* **(a)** *(instrument)* Meßgerät *nt; (to measure diameter, width etc)* (Meß)lehre *f; (dial)* Anzeiger *m.* **pressure/wind** ~ Druck-/ Windmesser *m;* **oil** ~ Ölstandsanzeiger *m.* **(b)** *(of wire, sheet metal etc)* Stärke *f; (of tube)* Durchmesser *m; (Rail)* Spurweite *f.* **(c)** *(fig)* Maßstab *m (of für).* **2** *vt* **(a)** *(measure)* messen. **(b)** *(fig: appraise)* character beurteilen; *reaction* abschätzen.

gaunt [gɔːnt] *adj (+er)* hager; *(from suffering)* abgezehrt.

gauntlet ['gɔːntlɪt] *n* (Stulpen)handschuh *m; (of armour)* Panzerhandschuh *m.* **to throw down the** ~ *(fig)* den Fehdehandschuh hinwerfen; **to run the** ~ *(fig)* Spießruten laufen; **to (have to) run the** ~ **of** sth einer Sache *(dat)* ausgesetzt sein.

gauze [gɔːz] *n* Gaze *f; (Med also)* Mull *m.*

gave [geɪv] *pret of* **give.**

gawky ['gɔːkɪ] *adj (+er) person, movement* schlaksig, staksig *(col); animal* staksig *(col).*

gawp [gɔːp] *vi (col)* glotzen *(col).* **to** ~ **at** sb/sth jdn/etw anglotzen *(col).*

gay [geɪ] **1** *adj (+er)* **(a)** *(happy)* fröhlich; *colours also* bunt; *company, occasion* lustig; *life* flott. ~ **dog** *(col)* lockerer Vogel *(col).* **(b)** *(homosexual)* schwul *(col).* **2** *n* Schwule(r) *mf.*

gaze [geɪz] **1** *n* Blick *m.* **2** *vi* starren. **to** ~ **at** sb/sth jdn/etw anstarren.

gazelle [gə'zel] *n* Gazelle *f.*

gazette [gə'zet] *n* Zeitung *f; (government publication)* Amtsblatt *nt.*

gazetteer [ˌgæzɪ'tɪər] *n* alphabetisches Ortsverzeichnis *(mit Ortsbeschreibung).*

gazump [gə'zʌmp] *vt (Brit)* entgegen mündlicher Zusage ein Haus an einen Höherbietenden verkaufen.

GB = **Great Britain** GB, Großbritannien *nt.*

GCE *(Brit)* = **General Certificate of Education.**

Gdns = **Gardens.**

GDR = **German Democratic Republic** DDR *f.*

gear [gɪər] **1** *n* **(a)** *(Aut etc)* Gang *m.* ~s *pl (mechanism)* Getriebe *nt; (on bicycle)* Gangschaltung *f;* **to put the car into** ~ einen Gang einlegen; **to leave the car in** ~/out of ~ den Gang eingelegt lassen/das Auto im Leerlauf lassen; **to change** ~ schalten; **to change into third** ~ in den dritten Gang schalten. **(b)** *(equipment)* Ausrüstung *f; (tools)* Gerät *nt; (belongings, clothes)* Sachen *pl.* **2** *vt (fig)* **to be** ~ed **to** sth auf etw *(acc)* ausgerichtet sein; *(have facilities for)* auf etw *(acc)* eingerichtet sein.

gear: ~**box** *n* Getriebe *nt;* ~**lever** *n (Brit)* Schaltknüppel *m; (column-mounted)* Schalthebel *m;* ~ **shift** *(esp US) n* = ~ **lever;** ~ **wheel** *n* Zahnrad *nt.*

gee [dʒiː] *interj* **(a)** *(esp US col)* Mann! *(col).* ~ **whiz!** Mensch Meier! *(col).* **(b)** ~ **up!** hü!

geese [giːs] *pl of* **goose.**

Geiger counter ['gaɪgəˌkaʊntər] *n* Geigerzähler *m.*

gel [dʒel] **1** *n* Gel *nt.* **2** *vi* gelieren; *(fig: plan, idea)* Gestalt annehmen.

gelatin(e) ['dʒelətiːn] *n* Gelatine *f.*

gelding ['geldɪŋ] *n (horse)* Wallach *m.*

gelignite ['dʒelɪgnaɪt] *n* Plastiksprengstoff *m.*

gem [dʒem] *n* Edelstein *m; (cut also)* Juwel *nt; (fig)*

(person) Juwel *nt; (of collection etc)* Prachtstück *nt.* **be a** ~ **and ... sei ein Schatz und ...; it's a real** ~ *(fig)* es ist einmalig gut.

Gemini ['dʒemɪniː] *n* Zwillinge *pl.* **he's a** ~ er ist Zwilling.

gen [dʒen] *n (Brit col)* Informationen *pl.*

gender ['dʒendər] *n* Geschlecht *nt.*

gene [dʒiːn] *n* Gen *nt,* Erbfaktor *m.*

genealogy [ˌdʒiːnɪ'ælədʒɪ] *n* Stammbaumforschung *f; (ancestry)* Stammbaum *m.*

general ['dʒenərəl] **1** *adj* **(a)** allgemein; *view, enquiry also* generell; *agency* General-; *user, reader* Durchschnitts-; *(vague)* unbestimmt. **as a** ~ **rule** im allgemeinen; **in** ~ **use** allgemein in Gebrauch; **for** ~ **use** für den allgemeinen Gebrauch; *(for use by everybody)* für die Allgemeinheit; ~ **headquarters** *(Mil)* Generalhauptquartier *nt;* **to explain sth in** ~ **terms** etw allgemein erklären; **the** ~ **idea is that ...** wir/sie *etc* hatten uns/sich *(dat)* das so gedacht, daß ...; **that was the** ~ **idea** so war das (auch) gedacht; **the** ~ **idea is to wait and see** wir/sie *etc* wollen einfach mal abwarten; **to give sb a** ~ **idea of** sth jdm eine ungefähre Vorstellung von etw geben; **OK, I've got the** ~ **idea** OK, ich hab' verstanden, um was es geht.
(b) *(after official title)* Ober-. **Consul** ~ Generalkonsul *m.*
2 *n* **(a)** **in** ~ im allgemeinen. **(b)** *(Mil)* General *m; (Caesar, Napoleon etc)* Feldherr *m.*

general: ~ **anaesthetic** *(Brit),* ~ **anesthetic** *(US) n* Vollnarkose *f;* ~ **delivery** *adv (US)* postlagernd; ~ **election** *n* Parlamentswahlen *pl.*

generality [ˌdʒenə'rælɪtɪ] *n* **to talk in generalities** ganz allgemein sprechen.

generalization [ˌdʒenərəlaɪ'zeɪʃən] *n* Verallgemeinerung *f.*

generalize ['dʒenərəlaɪz] *vti* verallgemeinern. **to** ~ **about** sth etw verallgemeinern.

general knowledge *n* Allgemeinbildung *f.*

generally ['dʒenərəlɪ] *adv (usually)* im allgemeinen; *(for the most part also)* im großen und ganzen; *(widely, not in detail)* allgemein. ~ **speaking** im großen und ganzen.

general: ~ **practitioner** *n* praktischer Arzt, praktische Ärztin; ~ **public** *n* Öffentlichkeit *f;* ~-**purpose** *adj* Mehrzweck-; ~ **staff** *n (Mil)* Generalstab *m;* ~ **store** *n* Gemischtwarenhandlung *f;* ~ **strike** *n* Generalstreik *m.*

generate ['dʒenəreɪt] *vt (lit, fig)* erzeugen. **generating station** Kraftwerk *nt.*

generation [ˌdʒenə'reɪʃən] *n* **(a)** *(lit, fig)* Generation *f.* ~ **gap** Generationsunterschied *m.* **(b)** *(act of generating)* Erzeugung *f.*

generator ['dʒenəreɪtər] *n* Generator *m.*

generic [dʒɪ'nerɪk] *adj (Biol)* Gattungs-. ~ **name** or **term** Oberbegriff *m.*

generosity [ˌdʒenə'rɒsɪtɪ] *n* Großzügigkeit *f.*

generous ['dʒenərəs] *adj* **(a)** großzügig. **(b)** *(large, plentiful)* reichlich; *figure* üppig.

genesis ['dʒenɪsɪs] *n* Entstehung *f.* **(the Book of)** G~ die Schöpfungsgeschichte.

genetic [dʒɪ'netɪk] *adj* genetisch. ~ **engineering** experimentelle Genetik.

genetics [dʒɪ'netɪks] *n sing* Genetik *f.*

Geneva [dʒɪ'niːvə] *n* Genf *nt.* **Lake** ~ der Genfer See; ~ **Convention** Genfer Konvention *f.*

genial ['dʒiːnɪəl] *adj (lit, fig)* freundlich; *company* angenehm.

geniality [ˌdʒiːnɪ'ælɪtɪ] *n* Freundlichkeit *f.*

genitals ['dʒenɪtlz] *npl* Geschlechtsorgane *pl.*

genitive ['dʒenɪtɪv] *n (Gram)* Genitiv *m.* **in the** ~ im Genitiv.

genius ['dʒiːnɪəs] *n, pl* -**es** or **genii** Genie *nt; (mental or creative capacity also)* schöpferische Kraft. **a man of** ~ ein genialer Mensch; **to have a** ~ **for** sth eine besondere Gabe für etw haben; **he has a** ~ **for saying the wrong thing** er hat ein

Talent dafür, immer das Falsche zu sagen.

genocide ['dʒenəʊsaɪd] *n* Völkermord *m*.

genre ['ʒãːrə] *n* Gattung *f*.

gent [dʒent] *n (col)* = **gentleman.** **~s' shoes** *(Comm)* Herrenschuhe *pl*; **"G~s"** *(Brit)* „Herren"; **where is the ~s?** wo ist die Herrentoilette?

genteel [dʒen'tiːl] *adj* vornehm, fein.

gentile ['dʒentaɪl] **1** *n* Nichtjude *m.* **2** *adj* nichtjüdisch.

gentle ['dʒentl] *adj* (+*er*) sanft; *smack, breeze also, exercise* leicht; *knock, sound* leise; *rebuke also, heat* mild; *person, disposition* sanftmütig; *animal* zahm. **the ~ sex** das zarte Geschlecht; **to be ~ with sb** mit jdm sanft umgehen; **to be ~ with sth** mit etw behutsam umgehen.

gentleman ['dʒentlmən] *n, pl* **-men** [-mən] *(man)* Herr *m*; *(well-mannered, well-born)* Gentleman *m.* **gentleman's agreement** Gentlemen's Agreement *nt*; **gentlemen!** meine Herren!

gentlemanly ['dʒentlmənlı] *adj* zuvorkommend.

gently ['dʒentlɪ] *adv see adj.* **to handle sb/sth ~** mit jdm/etw behutsam umgehen; **~ does it!** sachte, sachte!

gentry ['dʒentrɪ] *npl* (niederer) Adel *m.*

genuine ['dʒenjʊɪn] *adj* echt; *manuscript* Original-; *offer* ernstgemeint; *(sincere)* aufrichtig.

genuinely ['dʒenjʊɪnlɪ] *adv* wirklich; *(sincerely also)* aufrichtig.

genus ['dʒenəs] *n, pl* **genera** *(Biol)* Gattung *f.*

geographer [dʒɪ'ɒgrəfəʳ] *n* Geograph(in *f*) *m.*

geographical [dʒɪə'græfɪkəl] *adj* geographisch.

geography [dʒɪ'ɒgrəfɪ] *n* Geographie *f*; *(Sch also)* Erdkunde *f.*

geological [dʒɪəʊ'lɒdʒɪkəl] *adj* geologisch.

geologist [dʒɪ'ɒlədʒɪst] *n* Geologe *m*, Geologin *f.*

geology [dʒɪ'ɒlədʒɪ] *n* Geologie *f.*

geometric(al) [dʒɪəʊ'metrɪk(əl)] *adj* geometrisch.

geometry [dʒɪ'ɒmɪtrɪ] *n* Geometrie *f.*

geophysics [,dʒɪ:əʊ'fɪzɪks] *n sing* Geophysik *f.*

Georgian ['dʒɔːdʒɪən] *adj (Brit Hist)* georgianisch.

geranium [dʒɪ'reɪnɪəm] *n* Geranie *f.*

geriatric [,dʒerɪ'ætrɪk] **1** *adj* geriatrisch; *nurse, nursing* Alten-; *home* Alters-; *patient* der Geriatrie. **~ medicine** Altersheilkunde *f.* **2** *n* alter Mensch.

geriatrics [,dʒerɪ'ætrɪks] *n sing* Geriatrie *f.*

germ [dʒɜːm] *n (lit, fig)* Keim *m*; *(of particular illness)* Krankheitserreger *m*; *(esp of cold)* Bazillus *m.* **don't spread your ~s around** behalte deine Bazillen für dich.

German ['dʒɜːmən] **1** *adj* deutsch. **2** *n* **(a)** Deutsche(r) *mf*. **(b)** *(language)* Deutsch *nt*; *see* **English.**

German Democratic Republic *n* Deutsche Demokratische Republik.

Germanic [dʒɜː'mænɪk] *adj* germanisch.

German: ~ measles *n sing* Röteln *pl*; **~ shepherd** *n* deutscher Schäferhund.

Germany ['dʒɜːmənɪ] *n* Deutschland *nt.*

germinate ['dʒɜːmɪneɪt] *vi (lit, fig)* keimen.

germination [,dʒɜːmɪ'neɪʃən] *n* Keimung *f.*

germ warfare *n* bakteriologische Kriegführung.

gerund ['dʒerənd] *n* Gerundium *nt.*

gestation [dʒe'steɪʃən] *n (of animals)* Trächtigkeit *f*; *(of humans)* Schwangerschaft *f*; *(fig)* Reifwerden *nt.*

gesticulate [dʒe'stɪkjʊleɪt] *vi* gestikulieren.

gesture ['dʒestʃəʳ] **1** *n (lit, fig)* Geste *f.* **as a ~ of support** als Zeichen der Unterstützung. **to ~** *vi* gestikulieren. **to ~ to sb to do sth** jdm bedeuten, etw zu tun.

get [get] *pret* **got**, *ptp* **got** *or (US)* **gotten 1** *vt* **(a)** *(receive)* bekommen, kriegen *(col)*; *wealth, glory* kommen zu; *time, personal characteristics, idea* haben *(from* von). **where did you ~ it (from)?** woher hast du das?; **this country ~s very little rain** in diesem Land regnet es sehr wenig; **where**

do you ~ that idea (from)? wie kommst du denn auf die Idee?; **I got quite a surprise/shock** ich war ziemlich überrascht/ich habe einen ziemlichen Schock bekommen *or* gekriegt *(col)*; **I don't ~ much from his lectures** seine Vorlesungen geben mir nicht viel; **he's only in it for what he can ~** er will nur dabei profitieren; **you'll ~ it!** *(col: be in trouble)* du wirst was erleben! *(col).*

(b) *(obtain by one's own efforts) object* sich *(dat)* besorgen; *visa, money* sich *(dat)* beschaffen; *(find) staff, partner, job* finden; *(buy)* kaufen; *(buy and keep) large item, car, cat* sich *(dat)* anschaffen. **not to be able to ~ sth** etw nicht bekommen *or* kriegen *(col)*; **to ~ sb/oneself sth, to ~ sth for sb/oneself** jdm/sich etw besorgen; **to need to ~ sth** etw brauchen; **I've still three to ~** ich brauche noch drei; **you'll have to ~ a job/flat** Sie müssen zusehen, daß Sie eine Stelle/ Wohnung bekommen *or* finden; **why don't you ~ a flat of your own?** warum schaffen Sie sich *(dat)* nicht eine eigene Wohnung an?; *(rent)* warum nehmen Sie sich *(dat)* nicht eine eigene Wohnung?; **what are you ~ting her for Christmas?** was schenkst du ihr zu Weihnachten?; **I got her a doll for Christmas** ich habe für sie eine Puppe zu Weihnachten besorgt; **we could ~ a taxi** wir könnten (uns *dat)* ein Taxi nehmen; **could you ~ me a taxi?** könnten Sie mir ein Taxi besorgen?; **could you ~ that?** *(telephone)* gehst du ran?; *(door)* gehst du?

(c) *(fetch) person, doctor, object* holen. **to ~ sb from the station** jdn vom Bahnhof abholen; **I got him a drink** ich habe ihm etwas zu trinken geholt; **can I ~ you a drink?** möchten Sie etwas zu trinken?

(d) *(catch)* bekommen, kriegen *(col)*; *cold, illness also* sich *(dat)* holen; *(hit)* treffen, erwischen *(col).* **to ~ sb by the arm/leg** jdn am Arm/Bein packen; **to ~ sb/sth ~s** me tut hier weh; **~ him/it!** *(to dog)* faß!; **the bullet got him in the neck** die Kugel traf ihn in den Hals; **(I've) got him/it!** *(col)* ich hab' ihn/ich hab's *(col)*; **got you!** *(col)* hab' dich (erwischt)! *(col)*; **he's out to ~ you** *(col)* er hat's auf dich abgesehen *(col)*; **we'll ~ them yet!** *(col)* die werden wir schon noch kriegen! *(col)*; **I'll ~ you for that!** *(col)* das wirst du mir büßen!; **you've got me there!** *(col)* da bin ich überfragt!

(e) *(Telec) (contact)* erreichen; *number* bekommen; *(put through to, get for sb)* geben. **~ me Mr Johnston please** verbinden Sie mich bitte mit Herrn Johnston.

(f) *(prepare) meal* machen. **I'll ~ you some breakfast** ich mache dir etwas zum Frühstück.

(g) *(send, take)* bringen. **to ~ sb to hospital** jdn ins Krankenhaus bringen; **to ~ sth to sb** jdm etw zukommen lassen; *(take sth oneself)* jdm etw bringen; **where does this ~ us?** *(col)* was bringt uns *(dat)* das? *(col)*; **this discussion isn't ~ting us anywhere** diese Diskussion führt zu nichts; **we'll ~ you there somehow** irgendwie kriegen wir dich schon dahin *(col)*; **how am I going to ~ myself home?** wie komme ich nach Hause?

(h) *(manage to move)* kriegen *(col)*. **we'll never ~ this piano upstairs** das Klavier kriegen wir nie nach oben *(col).*

(i) *(understand)* kapieren *(col)*; *(hear)* mitbekommen, mitkriegen *(col)*. **I don't ~ it/you** *(col)* da komme ich nicht mit *(col)*/ich verstehe nicht, was du meinst; **~ it?** kapiert? *(col).*

(j) *(col) (annoy)* ärgern, aufregen; *(upset)* an die Nieren gehen (+*dat) (col).*

(k) **to ~ sb to do sth** *(have sth done by sb)* etw von jdm machen lassen; *(persuade sb)* jdn dazu bringen, etw zu tun; **I'll ~ him to phone you back** ich sage ihm, er soll Sie zurückrufen; **you'll never ~ him to understand** du wirst es nie schaffen, daß er das versteht.

(l) to ~ sth done *(do)* etw machen; *(cause to be done)* etw machen lassen; **to ~ one's hair cut** sich *(dat)* die Haare schneiden lassen; **I'll ~ the grass cut soon** der Rasen wird bald gemäht; *(by sb else)* ich lasse bald den Rasen mähen; **I'm not going to ~ much done** ich werde nicht viel schaffen; **to ~ things done** etwas fertigkriegen *(col)*; **you'll ~ me thrown out** du bringst es noch so weit, daß ich hinausgeworfen werde.

(m) I can't ~ the car to start/door to open ich kriege das Auto nicht an *(col)*/die Tür nicht auf *(col)*; **once I've got this machine to work** wenn ich die Maschine erst einmal zum Laufen gebracht habe; **to ~ sb talking** jdn zum Sprechen bringen; **to ~ sth clean/shut** etw sauber-/zukriegen *(col)*; **that'll ~ it clean/shut** damit wird es sauber/geht es zu; **to ~ sb drunk** jdn betrunken machen; **to ~ one's arm broken** sich *(dat)* den Arm brechen; **to ~ one's hands dirty** sich *(dat)* die Hände schmutzig machen; **to ~ one's things packed** seine Sachen packen.

(n) to have got sth *(have)* etw haben.

2 *vi* **(a)** *(go, arrive)* kommen; gehen. **to ~ home/here** nach Hause kommen/hier ankommen; **I've got as far as page 16** ich bin auf Seite 16; **~ lost)!** verschwinde!; **to ~ there** *(succeed)* es schaffen *(col)*; *(understand)* dahinterkommen *(col)*; **now we're ~ting there** *(to the truth)* jetzt kommt's raus! *(col)*; **to ~ somewhere/nowhere** *(in job, career etc)* es zu etwas/nichts bringen; *(with work, in discussion etc)* weiterkommen/nicht weiterkommen; **to ~ somewhere/nowhere (with sb)** (bei jdm) etwas/ nichts erreichen.

(b) *(become, be, to form passive)* werden. **to ~ old/tired/paid** *etc* alt/müde/bezahlt *etc* werden; **I'm/the weather is ~ting cold/warm** mir wird es/es wird kalt/warm; **to ~ dressed/shaved/ washed** *etc* sich anziehen/rasieren/waschen *etc*; **you could ~ killed** du riskierst dein Leben; **how do people ~ that way?** *(col)* wie wird man nur so? *(col)*.

(c) *(start)* **I got to like him** er ist mir sympathisch geworden; **to ~ to like sth** an etw *(dat)* Gefallen finden; **to ~ to be ...** (mit der Zeit) ... werden; **to ~ working/scrubbing** *etc* anfangen zu arbeiten/schrubben *etc*; **I got talking to him** ich kam mit ihm ins Gespräch; **let's ~ started** fangen wir an!; **we got to talking about that** wir kamen darauf zu sprechen; **I got to thinking ...** ich habe mir überlegt, ...

(d) *(~ chance to)* **to do sth** die Möglichkeit haben, etw zu tun; **to ~ to see sb** jdn zu sehen bekommen.

(e) *(be obliged to)* **to have got to do sth** etw tun müssen; **I've got to** ich muß.

♦ **get about** *vi* **(a)** *(after illness)* auf den Beinen sein; *(socially)* herumkommen; *(news, rumour)* sich verbreiten *(prep obj* in +dat).

♦ **get across** *vi* **(a)** *(cross)* hinüber-/herüberkommen; *(+prep obj)* road, river kommen über *(+acc)*. **(b)** *(play, comedian etc)* ankommen *(to* bei); *(teacher etc)* sich verständlich machen *(to dat)*; *(idea, meaning)* klarwerden *(to dat)*. **2** *vt always separate* **(a)** *(transport)* hinüber-/ herüberbringen. **to ~ sth ~ sth** etw über etw *(acc)* (hinüber-/herüber)bringen. **(b)** *(communicate)* klarmachen *(to sb* jdm).

♦ **get along** *vi* **(a)** gehen. **I must be ~ting ~** ich muß jetzt gehen; **~ ~ with you!** *(col)* jetzt hör aber auf! *(col)*. **(b)** *(manage)* zurechtkommen. **(c)** *(progress)* vorankommen; *(work, patient, wound etc)* sich machen. **(d)** *(be on good terms)* auskommen *(with* mit). **they ~ ~ quite well** sie kommen ganz gut miteinander aus.

♦ **get around 1** *vi* +*prep obj* problem *etc* herumkommen um; *law, regulations* umgehen. **to ~**

~ **the conference table** sich an einen Tisch setzen. **2** *vt* *always separate* **(a)** *(make agree)* herumbringen *or* -kriegen *(col)*. **I'm sure I can ~ her ~ to my way of thinking** ich bin sicher, daß ich sie überzeugen kann. **(b)** +*prep obj* **to ~ people (together) ~ the conference table** Leute an einem Tisch zusammenbringen.

♦ **get around to** *vi* +*prep obj* *(col)* **to ~ ~ ~ sth/doing sth** zu etw kommen/dazu kommen, etw zu tun.

♦ **get at** *vi* +*prep obj* **(a)** *(gain access to, reach)* herankommen an *(+acc)*; *town, house* erreichen; *(take, eat etc)* food, money gehen an *(+acc)*. **put it where the dog/child won't ~ ~** it stellen Sie es irgendwohin, wo der Hund/das Kind nicht drankommt *(col)*; **let me ~ ~ him!** *(col)* na, wenn ich den erwische! *(col)*; **the mice have been ~ting ~ the cheese** again die Mäuse waren wieder am Käse. **(b)** *(ascertain)* truth herausfinden; *facts* kommen an *(+acc)*. **(c)** *(col: mean)* **what are you ~ting ~?** worauf wollen Sie hinaus? **(d)** **to ~ sb** *(col)* *(criticize)* an jdm etwas auszusetzen haben *(col)*; *(nag)* an jdm herumnörgeln *(col)*.

♦ **get away** *vi* *(leave)* wegkommen; *(prisoner, thief)* entkommen *(from sb* jdm). **there's no ~ting ~ from the fact that ...** man kommt nicht um die Tatsache herum, daß ...; **to ~ ~ from it all** sich von allem frei machen; **~ ~ (with you)!** *(col)* ach, hör auf! *(col)*.

♦ **get away with** *vi* +*prep obj* **(a)** *(steal)* entkommen mit. **(b)** *(col: escape punishment)* **you'll/he'll** *etc* **never ~ ~ ~** that das wird nicht gutgehen; **he got ~ ~ it** er ist ungeschoren davongekommen *(col)*; **the things he ~s ~ ~!** was er sich *(dat)* alles erlauben kann!

♦ **get back 1** *vi* zurückkommen; zurückgehen. **I must be ~ting ~ (home)** ich muß nach Hause; **~ ~!** zurück(treten)! **2** *vt sep* **a)** *possessions* zurückbekommen; *strength* zurückgewinnen. **now that I've got you/it ~** jetzt, wo ich dich/es wiederhabe. **(b)** *(bring back)* zurückbringen.

♦ **get back at** *vi* +*prep obj (col)* sich rächen an *(+dat)*. **to ~ ~ ~ sb for sth** jdm etw heimzahlen *(col)*.

♦ **get back to** *vi* +*prep obj (esp Comm)* sich wieder in Verbindung setzen mit. **I'll ~ ~ ~ you on that** ich werde darauf zurückkommen.

♦ **get behind** *vi* *(with work, payments)* in Rückstand kommen.

♦ **get by** *vi* **(a)** *(move past)* vorbeikommen *(prep obj* an +*dat)*. **(b)** *(manage)* **she ~s ~ on very little money** sie kommt mit sehr wenig Geld aus; **I can just about ~ ~ in German** ich komme mit meinem Deutsch gerade so durch.

♦ **get down 1** *vi* **(a)** *(descend)* hinunter-/heruntersteigen *(prep obj, from* von); *(from horse, bicycle)* absteigen *(from* von). **~ ~!** runter! *(col)*. **(b)** *(leave table)* aufstehen. **2** *vt sep* **(a)** *(take down)* herunternehmen. **(b)** *(reduce)* inflation *etc* herunterbekommen *(to auf* +*acc)*. **(c)** *(swallow)* food hinunterbringen. **~ this ~ (you)!** *(col)* trink/iß das! **(d)** *(make a note of)* aufschreiben. **(e)** *(col: depress)* fertigmachen *(col)*. **don't let it ~ you ~** laß dich davon nicht unterkriegen *(col)*.

♦ **get down to** *vi* +*prep obj* sich machen an *(+acc)*; *(find time to do)* kommen zu.

♦ **get in 1** *vi* **(a)** *(enter)* hinein-/hereinkommen *(prep obj, -to* in +*acc)*; *(into car, train etc)* einsteigen *(prep obj, -to* in +*acc)*. **to ~ ~ (to) the bath** in die Badewanne steigen; **he can't ~ ~** er kommt nicht herein/hinein. **(b)** *(arrive: train, bus)* ankommen. **(c)** *(be admitted)* angenommen werden; *(be elected)* gewählt werden. **(d)** *(get home)* nach Hause kommen. **2** *vt* *sep* *(bring in)* hinein-/hereinbringen *(prep obj, -to* in +*acc)*; *(fetch)* herein-/hineinholen *(-to* in +*acc)*; *(col)* groceries, drink, supplies sich eindecken mit. **(b)** *sep* *(submit)* forms einreichen. **(c)** *sep* *(insert into,* *find room for)* hineinbringen; *(fig) punch, request, words* anbringen. **(d)** *sep (send for) doctor etc* holen. **(e)** *always separate* **to** ~ **one's eye/hand** ~ in Übung kommen.

♦ **get in on** *vi* +*prep obj (col)* mitmachen bei. **to** ~ ~ ~ **the act** mitmachen.

♦ **get into 1** *vi* +*prep obj* **(a)** *rage, debt, company* geraten in (+*acc*). **what's got** ~ **him?** *(col)* was ist bloß in ihn gefahren? *(col)*. **(b)** *bad habits* sich *(dat)* angewöhnen. **(c)** *(get involved in) book* sich einlesen bei; *work* sich einarbeiten in (+*acc*). **(d)** *(put on) clothes* anziehen. **2** *vt* +*prep obj always separate* **you'll** ~ **me** ~ **difficulties** wegen dir komme ich noch in Schwierigkeiten; **to** ~ **sb** ~ **bad habits** jdm schlechte Angewohnheiten beibringen.

♦ **get in with** *vi* +*prep obj bad company* geraten in (+*acc*); *(ingratiate)* sich gut stellen mit.

♦ **get off 1** *vi* **(a)** *(from bus, train etc)* aussteigen *(prep obj* aus*); (from bicycle, horse)* absteigen *(prep obj* von*).* ~ ~ **the grass!** gehen Sie vom Rasen runter!; **to tell sb where to** ~ ~ *(col)* jdm gründlich die Meinung sagen *(col);* **he knows where he can** ~ ~! *(col)* der kann mich mal! *(col!).* **(b)** *(leave)* wegkommen. **it's time you got** ~ **to school** es ist Zeit, daß ihr in die Schule geht; **to** ~ ~ **to a good/bad start** einen guten/ schlechten Anfang machen. **(c)** *(escape, be let off)* davonkommen *(col).* **to** ~ ~ **with a fine** mit einer Geldstrafe davonkommen; **I got** ~ **having to do the work** ich bin um die Arbeit herumgekommen. **(d)** *(fall asleep)* **to** ~ ~ **(to sleep)** einschlafen. **(e)** *(from work etc)* gehen können. **what time do you** ~ ~ **work?** wann hören Sie mit der Arbeit auf?

2 *vt* **(a)** *sep (remove)* wegbekommen, wegkriegen *(col) (prep obj* von*); clothes, shoes* ausziehen; *lid, wrapping* abmachen *(prep obj* von*); (manage to* ~ ~*)* abbekommen *(prep obj* von*); stains* herausmachen *(prep obj* aus*); (manage to* ~ ~*)* herausbekommen *or* -kriegen *(col) (prep obj* aus*).* ~ **your dirty hands** ~ **that** nimm deine schmutzigen Hände da weg! **(b)** *always separate (send off) mail, children* losschicken. **to** ~ **sb/sth** ~ **to a good start** jdm/einer Sache zu einem guten Start verhelfen; **when she'd got the children** ~ **to school** als sie die Kinder versorgt und in die Schule geschickt hatte; **to** ~ **sb** ~ **(to sleep)** jdn zum Schlafen bringen. **(c)** *sep (lawyer) accused* freibekommen. **(d)** *always separate (from work etc) day, afternoon* freibekommen.

♦ **get off with** *vi* +*prep obj (col: start a relationship with)* aufreißen *(col).*

♦ **get on 1** *vi* **(a)** *(climb on)* hinauf-/heraufsteigen *(prep obj* auf +*acc*); *(on bus, train etc)* einsteigen *(prep obj, -to* in +*acc*); *(on bicycle, horse etc)* aufsteigen *(prep obj, -to* auf +*acc*). **to** ~ ~ **sth** auf etw *(acc)* aufsteigen etc.

(b) *(continue: with work etc)* weitermachen. ~ ~ **with it!** nun mach schon! *(col);* **this will do to be** ~**ting** ~ **with** das tut's wohl für den Anfang *(col).*

(c) *(get late, old)* **time is** ~**ting** ~ es wird langsam spät; **he is** ~**ting** ~ **(in years)** er wird langsam alt; **he's** ~**ting** ~ **for 40** er geht auf die 40 zu; **there were** ~**ting** ~ **for 60** es waren fast 60.

(d) = **get along (a).**

(e) *(progress)* vorankommen; *(work also, patient,pupil)* Fortschritte machen. **to** ~ ~ **in the world** es zu etwas bringen; **how did you** ~ ~ **in the exam?** wie ging's (dir) in der Prüfung?; **how are you** ~**ting** ~? wie geht's?; **to** ~ ~ **without sb/sth** ohne jdn/etw zurechtkommen.

(f) *(have a good relationship)* sich verstehen, auskommen *(with* mit*).* **they don't** ~ ~ **(with each other)** sie kommen nicht miteinander aus.

2 *vt sep (prep obj* auf +*acc*) *clothes, shoes* anzie-

hen; *hat, kettle* aufsetzen; *lid, cover* drauftun.

♦ **get on to** *vi* +*prep obj (col)* **(a)** *new subject* übergehen zu. **(b)** *(contact)* sich in Verbindung setzen mit. **I'll** ~ ~ ~ **him about it** ich werde ihn daraufhin ansprechen.

♦ **get out 1** *vi* **(a)** *heraus-/hinauskommen (of* aus*); (climb out)* hinaus-/heraussteigen *(of* aus*); (of bus, train, car)* aussteigen *(of* aus*); (of business, contract)* aussteigen *(col) (of* aus*).* **he has to** ~ ~ **of the country** er muß das Land verlassen; **let's** ~ ~ **(of here)!** bloß weg hier! *(col);* ~ ~ **(of my room)!** raus (aus meinem Zimmer)! *(col);* **to** ~ ~ **of bed** aufstehen; **I don't** ~ ~ **much these days** ich komme in letzter Zeit nicht viel raus *(col).* **(b)** *(lit, fig: escape, leak out) (of* aus*)* herauskommen; *(animal, prisoner also)* entkommen; *(news)* an die Öffentlichkeit dringen.

2 *vt sep* **(a)** *(remove) (of* aus*) cork,* splinter, *stain etc* herausmachen; *people* hinaus-/herausbringen; *(send out)* hinausschicken. ~ **him** ~ **of my house** schaff mir ihn aus dem Haus! **(b)** *(take out) car, wallet* herausholen *(of* aus*).* **(c)** *(withdraw) money* abheben *(of* von*).* **(d)** *(borrow from library)* ausleihen *(of* aus*).* **(e)** **you only** ~ ~ **what you put in** Sie bekommen nur das zurück, was Sie hineinstecken.

♦ **get out of 1** *vi* +*prep obj see also* **get out 1** *duty, obligation* herumkommen um; *difficulty* herauskommen aus. **you can't** ~ ~ **it now** jetzt kannst du nicht mehr zurück. **2** *vt* +*prep obj always separate see also* **get out 2 (a-c)** *words, confession, truth* herausbekommen *or* -kriegen *(col)* aus; *profit* machen bei; *benefit, little, nothing* haben von; *pleasure* haben an (+*dat*). **to** ~ **the best/most** ~ **sth** etw voll ausnutzen; **and what I** ~ ~ ~ **it?** und was habe ich davon?

♦ **get over 1** *vi* **(a)** *(cross)* hinüber-/herübergehen *(prep obj* über +*acc*); *(climb over)* hinüber-/ herübersteigen; *(+prep obj)* steigen über (+*acc*). **they got** ~ **to the other side** sie gelangten auf die andere Seite. **(b)** +*prep obj (lit, fig: recover from) disappointment, loss, fact, experience* (hin)wegkommen über (+*acc*); *shock, illness* sich erholen von. **I can't** ~ ~ **the fact that** ... ich komme gar nicht darüber hinweg, daß ...; **I can't** ~ ~ **it** *(col)* da komm ich nicht drüber weg *(col).* **(c)** +*prep obj (overcome) problem, nervousness* überwinden.

2 *vt* **(a)** *always separate (transport across)* hinüber-/herüberbringen *(prep obj* über +*acc*); *(fetch)* holen; *(help sb to cross, climb)* hinüber-/ herüberhelfen *(sb* jdm*) (prep obj* über +*acc*). **(b)** *(get information, ideas etc* verständlich machen *(to* dat*); (impress upon)* klarmachen *(to* dat*).* **she** ~**s her songs** ~ **well** sie kommt mit ihren Liedern gut an.

♦ **get over with** *vt always separate* hinter sich *(acc)* bringen. **let's** ~ **it** ~ (~) bringen wir's hinter uns.

♦ **get round (to)** = **get around (to).**

♦ **get through 1** *vi* **(a)** *(person, thing)* durchkommen *(prep obj* durch*); (news)* durchdringen; *(Telec)* durchkommen *(col) (to sb* zu jdm, *to London* nach London*).* **to** ~ ~ **to the second round/final** in die zweite Runde/ Endrunde kommen. **(b)** *(communicate, be understood) (person)* durchdringen zu; *(idea etc)* klarwerden *(to* dat*).* **(c)** +*prep obj (finish) work* fertigmachen, erledigen; *(manage to* ~ ~*)* schaffen *(col); book* fertiglesen, auslesen. **when I've got** ~ **this** wenn ich damit fertig bin. **(d)** +*prep obj (survive) days, time* herumbekommen, herumkriegen *(col).* **(e)** +*prep obj (consume, use up)* verbrauchen; *clothes, shoes* abnutzen; *food* aufessen; *fortune* durchbringen *(col).*

2 *vt always separate* **(a)** *person, object, proposal* durchbekommen, durchbringen *(prep obj* durch); *message* durchgeben *(to dat); supplies* durchbringen. it was his English that got him ~ er hat das nur aufgrund seines Englisch geschafft; he got the team ~ to the finals er hat die Mannschaft in die Endrunde gebracht. (b) *(make understand)* to ~ sth ~ (to sb) jdm etw klarmachen.

♦ **get through** *with* vi +prep obj (col: finish) hinter sich bringen; *job also, formalities, subject* erledigen; *(col) person* fertig werden mit.

♦ **get to** vi +prep obj **(a)** *(arrive at)* kommen zu; *hotel, town also* ankommen in *(+dat)*. where have you got ~ with that book? wie weit seid ihr mit dem Buch? **(b)** *(col: annoy, upset)* aufregen.

♦ **get together 1** vi zusammenkommen; *(estranged couple)* sich versöhnen; *(combine forces)* sich zusammenschließen. to ~ ~ ~ about sth zusammenkommen und etw beraten; why don't we ~ ~ later and have a drink? warum treffen wir uns nicht später und trinken einen? **2** vt sep *people, parts, collection* zusammenbringen; *documents* zusammensuchen; *thoughts, ideas* sammeln. to ~ one's things ~ seine Sachen zusammenpacken; to ~ it ~ *(col)* es bringen *(col)*.

♦ **get up 1** vi **(a)** *(stand up, get out of bed)* aufstehen. **(b)** *(climb up)* hinauf-/heraufsteigen *(prep obj* auf *+acc)*. **(c)** *(wind)* aufkommen; *(sea)* stürmisch werden. **2** vt **(a)** *always separate (get out of bed)* aus dem Bett holen; *(help stand up)* aufhelfen *(+dat)*. **(b)** *sep steam* aufbauen. to ~ ~ speed sich beschleunigen. **(c)** *sep (organize)* organisieren; *play also* auf die Beine stellen *(col)*. **(d)** *always separate (dress up)* zurechtmachen. to ~ oneself ~ as sb/sth sich als jd/etw verkleiden; to ~ sth ~ to look like sth etw als etw aufmachen.

♦ **get up to** vi +prep obj **(a)** *(lit, fig: reach)* erreichen; *standard* herankommen an *(+acc)*; *page* kommen bis. **(b)** *(be involved in)* anstellen *(col)*. to ~ ~ ~ mischief etwas anstellen; what have you been ~ting ~ ~? was hast du getrieben? *(col)*.

get: ~-at-able [,get'ætəbl] adj *(col)* leicht erreichbar; ~away 1 n Flucht f; to make one's ~away sich davonmachen *(col)*; 2 adj attr Flucht-; ~-together n Treffen nt; ~-up n *(col)* Aufmachung f *(col)*; ~-up-and-go n *(col)* Elan m.

geyser ['giːzəʳ] n **(a)** *(Geol)* Geiser, Geysir m. **(b)** *(domestic ~)* Durchlauferhitzer m.

Ghana ['gɑːnə] n Ghana nt.

Ghanaian [gɑːˈneɪən] **1** adj ghanaisch. **2** n *(person)* Ghanaer(in f) m.

ghastly ['gɑːstlɪ] adj **(a)** *crime etc* entsetzlich; *mistake* schrecklich. **(b)** *(col: awful)* gräßlich *(col)*, scheußlich *(col)*.

gherkin ['gɜːkɪn] n Gewürzgurke f.

ghetto ['getəʊ] n G(h)etto nt.

ghettoblaster ['getəʊblɑːstəʳ] n *(col)* großes Kofferradio.

ghost [gəʊst] **1** n *(apparition)* Gespenst nt; *(of sb)* Geist m. **I haven't the** ~ **of a chance** ich habe nicht die geringste Chance; to give up the ~ *(col)* den Geist aufgeben *(col)*. **2** vt to ~ sb's speeches für jdn Reden (als Ghostwriter) schreiben.

ghostly ['gəʊstlɪ] adj *(+er)* gespenstisch.

ghost *in cpds* Geister-; ~ **story** n Gespenstergeschichte f; ~ **town** n Geisterstadt f; ~**writer** n Ghostwriter m.

ghoulish ['guːlɪʃ] adj makaber; *laughter, interest* schaurig.

G.I. n GI, US-Soldat m.

giant ['dʒaɪənt] **1** n Riese m; *(fig)* Größe f; *(company)* Gigant m. **2** adj riesig, Riesen-. ~ **(-size)** pack-et Riesenpackung f; ~ **panda** n Großer Panda n.

gibber ['dʒɪbəʳ] vi *(ape)* schnattern; *(idiot)* brabbeln. ~**ing idiot** *(col)* Blödmann m *(col)*.

gibberish ['dʒɪbərɪʃ] n Kauderwelsch nt.

gibbet ['dʒɪbɪt] n Galgen m.

gibbon ['gɪbən] n Gibbon m.

gibe [dʒaɪb] **1** n Stichelei f. **2** vi sticheln. to ~ at sb/sth höhnische Bemerkungen über jdn/etw machen.

giblets ['dʒɪblɪts] npl Geflügelinnereien pl.

Gibraltar [dʒɪˈbrɔːltəʳ] n Gibraltar nt.

giddiness ['gɪdɪnɪs] n Schwindelgefühl nt.

giddy ['gɪdɪ] adj *(+er)* schwind(e)lig; *feeling* Schwindel-. **I feel** ~ mir ist schwind(e)lig.

gift [gɪft] n **(a)** Geschenk nt. a free ~ ein Geschenk nt; it was a ~ *(col: easy)* das war ja geschenkt *(col)*. **(b)** *(talent)* Begabung f. to have a ~ for sth ein Talent für etw haben.

gifted ['gɪftɪd] adj begabt *(in für)*.

gift: ~ **horse** n: don't look a ~ horse in the mouth *(prov)* einem geschenkten Gaul schaut man nicht ins Maul *(prov)*; ~ **token** n Geschenkgutschein m; ~**-wrap** vt in Geschenkpapier einwickeln.

gig [gɪg] n *(col: concert)* Konzert nt.

gigantic [dʒaɪˈgæntɪk] adj riesig, riesengroß.

giggle ['gɪgl] **1** n Gekicher nt no pl. it was a bit of a ~ *(col)* es war ganz lustig; to get the ~s anfangen herumzukichern *(col)*; she's got the ~s sie kann nicht aufhören zu kichern. **2** vi kichern.

gigolo ['ʒɪgələʊ] n Gigolo m.

gild [gɪld] vt vergolden. to ~ the lily des Guten zuviel tun.

gill[1] [gɪl] n *(of fish)* Kieme f.

gill[2] [dʒɪl] n *(Measure)* Gill nt.

gilt [gɪlt] n *(material)* Vergoldung f.

gilt-edged [,gɪltˈedʒd] adj *(Fin)* mündelsicher; *(fig)* solide.

gimlet ['gɪmlɪt] n Vorbohrer m.

gimmick ['gɪmɪk] n Gag m *(col)*; *(gadget)* Spielerei f.

gimmickry ['gɪmɪkrɪ] n Effekthascherei f; *(advertising, sales)* Gags pl; *(gadgetry)* Spielereien pl.

gimmicky ['gɪmɪkɪ] adj effekthascherisch.

gin [dʒɪn] n *(drink)* Gin m. ~ **and tonic** Gin Tonic m.

ginger ['dʒɪndʒəʳ] **1** n Ingwer m. **2** adj *biscuit etc* Ingwer-; *hair* kupferrot; *cat* rötlichgelb.

♦ **ginger up** vt sep *(col)* in Schwung bringen *(col)*.

ginger: ~-**ale** n Ginger Ale nt; ~ **beer** n *(Brit)* Ingwerlimonade f; ~**bread** n Lebkuchen m *(mit Ingwergeschmack.*

gingerly ['dʒɪndʒəlɪ] adv behutsam; *(because sth is cold, hot etc)* zaghaft.

gingham ['gɪŋəm] n Gingan m.

gipsy ['dʒɪpsɪ] n Zigeuner(in f) m.

giraffe [dʒɪˈrɑːf] n Giraffe f.

girder ['gɜːdəʳ] n Träger m.

girdle ['gɜːdl] n *(corset)* Hüfthalter m.

girl [gɜːl] n Mädchen nt; *(daughter also)* Tochter f. **an English** ~ eine Engländerin f; **factory** ~ Fabrikarbeiterin f; **shop** ~ Verkäuferin f; the ~**s** *(colleagues)* die Damen; **the old** ~ die Alte *(col)*; *(col: wife, mother)* meine/seine etc Alte *(col)*.

girl: ~ **Friday** n Allround-Sekretärin f; ~**friend** n Freundin f; ~**guide** n *(Brit)* Pfadfinderin f.

girlish ['gɜːlɪʃ] adj mädchenhaft.

girl scout n *(US)* Pfadfinderin f.

giro ['dʒaɪrəʊ] n *(Brit) (bank)* ~ Giro(verkehr m) nt; *(post-office* ~) Postscheckdienst m.

girth [gɜːθ] n **(a)** *(circumference, of waist)* Umfang m. **(b)** *(harness)* (Sattel)gurt m.

gismo n *(US col)* = gizmo.

gist [dʒɪst] n no pl Wesentliche(s) nt. that was the ~ of what he said das war im wesentlichen, was er gesagt hat.

git [gɪt] n *(Brit col)* Idiot m.

give [gɪv] *(vb: pret gave, ptp given)* **1** vt (a) geben *(sb sth, sth to sb* jdm etw); *(as present)* schenken *(sb sth, sth to sb* jdm etw); *one's name, particulars* angeben; *(let sb know by phone, letter etc)* decision, *results* mitteilen; *(produce) results* bringen; *pleasure, joy, pain* bereiten; *trouble* machen; *one's*

love, attention schenken; *punishment* erteilen. **they gave us roast beef for lunch** sie servierten uns Roastbeef zum (Mittag)essen; **what will you ~ me for it?** was gibst du mir dafür; **what did you ~ for it?** was hast du dafür bezahlt?; **11 o'clock, ~ or take a few minutes** so gegen 11 Uhr; **six foot, ~ or take a few inches** ungefähr sechs Fuß; **to ~ as good as one gets** sich kräftig wehren; **he gave everything he'd got** *(fig)* er holte das Letzte aus sich heraus; **to ~ sb one's cold** *(col)* jdn mit seiner Erkältung anstecken; **I'd ~ a lot/the world/anything to know ...** ich würde viel darum geben, wenn ich wüßte, ...; **what gave you that idea** wie kommst du denn auf die Idee?; **to ~ sb five years** jdm fünf Jahre aufbrummen *(col)*; **~ me Spain (every time)!** *(col)* es geht doch nichts über Spanien; **~ yourself more time/half an hour** lassen Sie sich mehr Zeit/rechnen Sie mit einer halben Stunde; **how long do you ~ that marriage?** wie lange gibst du dieser Ehe? *(col)*; **I'll ~ you that** zugegeben; **he's a good worker, I'll ~ him that** eines muß man ihm lassen, er arbeitet gut; **he wouldn't ~ me his decision/opinion** er wollte mir seine Meinung/Entscheidung nicht sagen.
 (b) *(hold, perform) party, dinner, play* geben; *speech* halten; *song* singen; *toast* ausbringen *(to sb* auf jdn*).* **~ us a song** sing uns was vor; **I ~ you Mary** *(as toast)* auf Mary!; *(as speaker)* ich gebe Mary das Wort.
 (c) *(devote)* widmen *(to dat).* **he has ~n himself entirely to medicine** er hat sich ganz der Medizin verschrieben.
 (d) to ~ a cry/groan/laugh/sigh schreien/stöhnen/lachen/seufzen; **to ~ sb a look/smile** jdn ansehen/anlächeln; **to ~ sb a push/kick** jdm einen Stoß/Tritt geben; **to ~ one's hair a brush/wash** sich *(dat)* die Haare bürsten/waschen.
 2 *vi* **(a)** *(~ money etc)* spenden. **you have to be prepared to ~ and take** man muß zu Kompromissen bereit sein. **(b)** *(also ~ way) (lit, fig: collapse, yield)* nachgeben; *(health, nerve, voice)* versagen; *(break: rope, cable)* reißen. **something's got to ~** *(col)* etwas muß sich einfach ändern. **(c)** *(lit, fig: bend, be flexible)* nachgeben; *(bed)* federn; *(shoe)* sich weiten.
 3 *n* Nachgiebigkeit *f*; *(of floor, bed, chair)* Federung *f*.
♦ **give away** *vt sep* **(a)** *(give present)* verschenken. **at £5 I'm practically giving it ~** ich will £5 dafür, das ist fast geschenkt. **(b)** *bride (als Brautvater etc)* zum Altar führen. **(c)** *(fig: betray)* verraten *(to sb* an jdn*).* **to ~ the game ~** *(col)* alles verraten.
♦ **give back** *vt sep* zurückgeben.
♦ **give in 1** *vi (surrender)* sich ergeben *(to sb* jdm*); (in guessing game etc)* aufgeben; *(accede, back down)* nachgeben *(to dat).* **to ~ ~ to blackmail** auf Erpressung eingehen. **2** *vt sep document, essay* einreichen; *parcel* abgeben.
♦ **give off** *vt sep heat, gas* abgeben; *smell* verbreiten; *rays* ausstrahlen.
♦ **give on to** *vi +prep obj (window)* hinausgehen auf *(+acc)*; *(door) garden* hinausführen in *(+acc)*.
♦ **give out 1** *vi (supplies, strength)* zu Ende gehen or *(in past tense)* sein; *(engine)* versagen. **2** *vt sep* **(a)** *(distribute)* verteilen. **(b)** *(announce)* bekanntgeben. **to ~ oneself ~ as sth** sich als etw ausgeben. **3** *vt insep* = **give off.**
♦ **give over 1** *vt sep* **(a)** *(hand over)* übergeben *(to dat).* **(b)** *(set aside, use)* **to be ~n ~ to sth** für etw beansprucht werden. **2** *vi (col: stop)* ~ ~! hör auf!
♦ **give up 1** *vi* aufgeben. **I ~ ~** ich gebe auf, ich geb's auf *(col).* **2** *vt sep* **(a)** *(abandon); claim also* verzichten auf *(+acc).* **I'm trying to ~ ~ smoking** ich versuche, das Rauchen aufzugeben; **to ~ sb ~ as dead** jdn für tot halten; **I'd**

~n you ~ *(expected visitor etc)* ich hatte nicht mehr damit gerechnet, daß du kommst. **(b)** *land, territory* abgeben *(to dat); seat, place* freimachen *(to* für*); ticket* abgeben *(to* bei*).* **(c)** *(to authorities)* übergeben *(to dat).* **to ~ oneself ~** sich stellen; *(after siege)* sich ergeben. **(d)** *(devote)* widmen. **to ~ ~ one's life to music** sein Leben ganz der Musik widmen. **(e)** *(disclose) secret, treasure* enthüllen *(geh).*
♦ **give way** *vi* **(a)** *(lit)* = **give 2 (b). (b)** *(fig: yield)* nachgeben *(to dat).* **to ~ ~ to intimidation** sich einschüchtern lassen; **don't ~ ~ to despair** überlaß dich nicht der Verzweiflung. **(c)** *(be superseded)* **to ~ ~ to sth** von etw abgelöst werden. **(d)** *(Brit Mot)* **who has to ~ ~ here?** wer hat hier Vorfahrt?; **"~ ~"** „Vorfahrt beachten".
give: **~ and take** *n* Entgegenkommen *nt; (in personal relationships)* Geben und Nehmen *nt;* **~-away** *n (col)* the expression on her face was a **~-away** ihr Gesichtsausdruck verriet alles; **that exam question was a ~-away** diese Prüfungsfrage war geschenkt *(col);* **~-away price** *n (col)* Schleuderpreis *m.*
given ['gɪvn] **1** *ptp of* **give.** **2** *adj* **(a)** *(with indef art)* bestimmt; *(with def art)* angegeben. **(b)** **~ name** *(esp US)* Vorname *m.* **(c) to be ~ to sth** zu etw neigen; **to be ~ to doing sth** gewohnt sein, etw zu tun. **3** *conj* **~ sth** *(with)* vorausgesetzt, man/er *etc* hat etw; *(in view of)* angesichts einer Sache *(gen);* **~ that he ...** *(in view of the fact)* angesichts der Tatsache, daß er ...; *(assuming)* vorausgesetzt *(daß)* er ...; **~ these circumstances/conditions** unter diesen Umständen/Voraussetzungen.
giver ['gɪvə^r] *n* Spender(in *f*) *m.*
gizmo ['gɪzməʊ] *n (US col)* Ding *nt (col).*
glacial ['gleɪsɪəl] *adj (cold) look, wind* eisig.
glacier ['glæsɪə^r] *n* Gletscher *m.*
glad [glæd] *adj (+er)* froh. **to be ~ at or about sth** sich über etw *(acc)* freuen; **I'm so ~!** das freut mich; **you'll be ~ to hear that ...** es wird Sie freuen, daß ...; **we would be ~ of your help** wir wären froh, wenn Sie helfen könnten; **I'd be ~ to** aber gern!
gladden ['glædn] *vt person, heart* erfreuen.
glade [gleɪd] *n* Lichtung *f.*
gladiator ['glædɪeɪtə^r] *n* Gladiator *m.*
gladiolus [,glædɪ'əʊləs] *n, pl* **gladioli** [,glædɪ'əʊlaɪ] Gladiole *f.*
gladly ['glædlɪ] *adv (willingly)* gern.
glamorize ['glæməraɪz] *vt author, war* glorifizieren; *the mundane* idealisiert darstellen.
glamorous ['glæmərəs] *adj* bezaubernd; *film star, life* glamourös; *job* Traum-.
glamour, (US) glamor ['glæmə^r] *n* Glamour *m; (of occasion, situation)* Glanz *m.*
glance [glɑːns] **1** *n* Blick *m.* **at a ~** auf einen Blick; **at first ~** auf den ersten Blick; **to take a (quick) ~ at** einen kurzen Blick auf etw *(acc)* werfen. **2** *vi* **to ~ at sb/sth** einen kurzen Blick auf jdn/etw *(acc)* werfen; **to ~ at/through the newspaper** einen kurzen Blick in die Zeitung werfen; **he ~d around the room** er sah sich kurz im Zimmer um.
♦ **glance off** *vi (bullet etc)* abprallen *(prep obj* von*).*
glancing ['glɑːnsɪŋ] *adj* **to strike sth a ~ blow** etw streifen.
gland [glænd] *n* Drüse *f.*
glandular ['glændjʊlə^r] *adj* Drüsen-. **~ fever** *n* Drüsenfieber *nt.*
glare [gleə^r] **1** *n* **(a)** *(from sun, bulb, lamp also)* greller Schein; *(from sun, bulb, lamp also)* grelles Licht. **the ~ of the sun** das grelle Sonnenlicht; **to avoid the ~ of publicity** das grelle Licht der Öffentlichkeit scheuen. **(b)** *(stare)* stechender Blick. **2** *vi* **(a)** *(light, sun)* grell scheinen; *(headlights)* grell leuchten. **(b)** *(stare)* **to ~ at sb/sth** jdn/etw zornig anstarren.
glaring ['gleərɪŋ] *adj sun, colour* grell; *(fig) omission* eklatant; *mistake* grob; *contrast* kraß;

injustice (himmel)schreiend.
glass [glɑːs] n Glas nt; (dated: mirror) Spiegel m; (barometer) Barometer nt. **a ~ of wine** ein Glas Wein; **~es** pl (spectacles) Brille f; (binoculars) Fernglas nt.
glass in cpds Glas-; **~-blower** n Glasbläser(in f) m; **~ fibre** (Brit) or **fiber** (US) n Glasfaser f; **~house** n (Brit Hort) Gewächshaus nt; (Mil sl) Bau m (col); **~ware** n Glaswaren pl; **~ wool** n Glaswolle f.
glassy ['glɑːsɪ] adj (+er) surface, sea etc spiegelglatt; eye, look glasig.
glaze [gleɪz] **1** n (on pottery, tiles, Cook) Glasur f; (on paper, fabric) Appretur f; (on painting) Lasur f. **2** vt **(a)** door, window verglasen. **(b)** pottery, tiles glasieren; fabric, paper appretieren; painting lasieren. **~d tile** Kachel f. **(c)** (Cook) glasieren. **3** vi (eyes: also **~ over**) glasig werden.
glazier ['gleɪzɪər] n Glaser m.
gleam [gliːm] **1** n **(a)** Schimmer m; (of metal, water) Schimmern nt. **(b)** (fig) **a ~ of humour/ intelligence** ein Anflug m von Humor/ Intelligenz; **he had a ~ in his eye** seine Augen funkelten. **2** vi schimmern; (hair also) glänzen; (eyes) funkeln.
glean [gliːn] vt (lit) corn nachlesen; (fig) facts, news ausfindig machen. **to ~ sth from sb/sth** etw von jdm in Erfahrung bringen/etw einer Sache (dat) entnehmen.
glee [gliː] n Freude f; (malicious) Schadenfreude f. **~ club** (esp US) Chor m.
gleeful ['gliːful] adj fröhlich; (malicious) schadenfroh.
glen [glen] n Tal nt.
glib [glɪb] adj (pej) zungenfertig; reply, remark leichtfertig; talker, speech, style glatt. **don't be so ~** sei nicht so oberflächlich.
glide [glaɪd] vi **(a)** gleiten; (through the air also) schweben. **(b)** (plane) im Gleitflug fliegen; (glider) gleiten.
glider ['glaɪdər] n (Aviat) Segelflugzeug nt.
gliding ['glaɪdɪŋ] n (Aviat) Segelfliegen nt.
glimmer ['glɪmər] **1** n (of light, candle etc) Schimmer m; (of fire) Glimmen nt. **a ~ of hope** ein Hoffnungsschimmer m. **2** vi (light, water) schimmern; (fire) glimmen.
glimpse [glɪmps] **1** n Blick m. **to catch a ~ of sb/sth** einen flüchtigen Blick von jdm/etw erhaschen. **2** vt flüchtig sehen.
glint [glɪnt] **1** n (of light, metal) Glitzern nt no pl; (of cat's eyes) Funkeln nt no pl. **he has a wicked/ merry ~ in his eyes** seine Augen funkeln böse/ lustig. **2** vi glitzern; (eyes) funkeln.
glisten ['glɪsn] vi glitzern.
glitter ['glɪtər] **1** n Glitzern nt; (of eyes, diamonds) Funkeln nt; (fig) Glanz, Prunk m. **2** vi (eyes, diamonds) funkeln. **all that ~s is not gold** (Prov) es ist nicht alles Gold, was glänzt (Prov).
gloat [gləʊt] vi sich großtun (over mit); (over sb's misfortune) sich hämisch freuen (over über +acc). **to ~ over one's possessions** sich an seinen Reichtümern weiden; **there's no need to ~!** das ist kein Grund zur Schadenfreude!
global ['gləʊbl] adj global; peace, war Welt-.
globe [gləʊb] n (sphere) Kugel f; (map) Globus m. **all over the ~** auf der ganzen Erde or Welt; **~-trotter** Globetrotter m.
globule ['glɒbjuːl] n Kügelchen nt; (of oil, water) Tröpfchen nt.
gloom [gluːm] n **(a)** (darkness) Düsterkeit f. **(b)** (sadness) düstere or gedrückte Stimmung. **a life of ~** ein trauriges Leben.
gloomy ['gluːmɪ] adj (+er) room etc düster; atmosphere also gedrückt; thoughts also, character trübsinnig; news also bedrückend; outlook on life pessimistisch. **to take a ~ view of things** schwarzsehen; **to feel ~** bedrückt sein.
glorification [ˌglɔːrɪfɪˈkeɪʃən] n Verherrlichung f.
glorified ['glɔːrɪfaɪd] adj just a ~ **snack-bar** nur

eine bessere Imbißstube.
glorify ['glɔːrɪfaɪ] vt verherrlichen.
glorious ['glɔːrɪəs] adj weather, sky herrlich; deed, victory ruhmreich.
glory ['glɔːrɪ] **1** n **(a)** (honour, fame) Ruhm m. **covered in ~** ruhmbedeckt. **(b)** (beauty, magnificence) Herrlichkeit f. **the rose in all its ~** die Rose in ihrer ganzen Pracht; **the glories of Nature** die Schönheiten der Natur; **Rome at the height of its ~** Rom in seiner Blütezeit. **2** vi **to ~ in one's strength/ability** sich an seiner Kraft/Fähigkeit weiden; **to ~ in one's/sb's success** sich in seinem/jds Erfolg sonnen; **to ~ in the name of ...** den stolzen Namen ... führen.
gloss¹ [glɒs] n Glanz m; (fig: of respectability etc) Schein m.
♦ **gloss over** vt sep (try to conceal) vertuschen; (make light of) beschönigen.
gloss² n (note) Anmerkung f.
glossary ['glɒsərɪ] n Glossar nt.
gloss (paint) n Glanzlack(farbe f) m.
glossy ['glɒsɪ] adj (+er) glänzend; paper, paint Glanz-. **~ (magazine)** Illustrierte f.
glove [glʌv] n Handschuh m. **to fit (sb) like a ~** (jdm) wie angegossen passen; **~ box** or **compartment** Handschuhfach nt; **~ puppet** Handpuppe f.
glow [gləʊ] **1** vi glühen; (colour, hands of clock) leuchten; (lamp also, candle) scheinen. **she/her cheeks ~ed with health** sie hatte ein blühendes Aussehen. **2** n Glühen nt; (of colour, clock hands) Leuchten nt; (of lamp, candle) Schein m; (of fire, sunset, passion) Glut f.
glower ['glaʊər] vi ein finsteres Gesicht machen. **to ~ at sb** jdn finster ansehen.
glowing ['gləʊɪŋ] adj **(a)** glühend; candle, colour, eyes leuchtend; cheeks, complexion blühend. **(b)** (fig) account, description begeistert; praise, report überschwenglich. **to paint sth in ~ colours** (fig) etw in den leuchtendsten Farben schildern.
glow-worm ['gləʊwɜːm] n Glühwürmchen nt.
glucose ['gluːkəʊs] n Traubenzucker m.
glue [gluː] **1** n Klebstoff m. **2** vt kleben. **to ~ sth together** etw zusammenkleben; **to ~ sth down/ on** etw fest-/ankleben; **to ~ sth to sth** etw an etw (acc) kleben; **to keep one's eyes ~d to sb/sth** jdn/etw nicht aus den Augen lassen; **his eyes were ~d to the screen** seine Augen hingen an der Leinwand; **he's ~d to the TV all evening** er hängt den ganzen Abend vorm Fernseher (col); **he stood there as if ~d to the spot** er stand wie angewurzelt da.
glue-sniffing ['gluːˌsnɪfɪŋ] n Schnüffeln nt (col).
glum [glʌm] adj (+er) niedergeschlagen, bedrückt. **to feel ~** bedrückt sein.
glut [glʌt] n (of Comm) market überschwemmen. **2** n Schwemme f; (of manufactured goods also) Überangebot nt (of an +dat). **a ~ of apples** eine Apfelschwemme.
glutinous ['gluːtɪnəs] adj klebrig.
glutton ['glʌtn] n Vielfraß m. **a ~ for work/punishment** ein Arbeitstier nt (col)/Masochist m.
gluttony ['glʌtənɪ] n Völlerei f.
glycerin(e) ['glɪsəriːn] n Glyzerin nt.
gm = **gram(s), gramme(s) g**.
GMT = **Greenwich Mean Time WEZ**.
gnarled [nɑːld] adj tree knorrig; hand knotig.
gnash [næʃ] vt **to ~ one's teeth** mit den Zähnen knirschen.
gnat [næt] n (Stech)mücke f.
gnaw [nɔː] **1** vt nagen. **to ~ at sb/sth** an etw (dat) nagen; (fig) jdn/etw quälen. **2** vt nagen an (+dat); hole nagen.
gnawing ['nɔːɪŋ] adj (fig) quälend.
gnome [nəʊm] n Gnom m.
GNP = **gross national product**.
gnu [nuː] n Gnu nt.
go [gəʊ] (vb: pret **went**, ptp **gone**) **1** vi **(a)** gehen;

(vehicle, by vehicle) fahren; *(plane)* fliegen; *(road)* führen. to ~ to France nach Frankreich fahren; **I have to ~ to the doctor/London** ich muß zum Arzt (gehen)/nach London; **to ~ for a swim** schwimmen gehen; **to ~ fishing/shopping** angeln/einkaufen gehen; **where do we ~ from here?** *(fig)* und was (wird) jetzt?; **you're ~ing too fast for me** *(lit, fig)* du bist mir zu schnell; **just look at him ~!** schau mal, wie schnell er ist! **the favourite is ~ing well** der Favorit liegt gut im Rennen; **to ~ looking for sb/sth** nach jdm/etw suchen; **to ~ for a doctor/newspaper** einen Arzt/ eine Zeitung holen (gehen); **there he ~es!** da ist er ja!; **who ~es there?** *(guard)* wer da?; **you ~ first** geh du zuerst!; **you ~ next** du bist der nächste; **there you ~ again!** *(col)* du fängst ja schon wieder an!; **here we ~ again!** *(col)* jetzt geht das schon wieder los! *(col)*; **~ and shut the door** mach mal die Tür zu; **he's gone and lost his new watch** *(col)* er hat seine neue Uhr verloren; **don't ~ telling him** geh jetzt nicht hin und erzähl ihm das *(col)*.

(b) *(depart)* gehen; *(vehicle, by vehicle also)* (ab)fahren; *(plane, by plane also)* (ab)fliegen. **has he gone yet?** ist er schon weg?; **I must ~ or get ~ing now** ich muß jetzt gehen *or* weg; **when I'm gone** *(left)* wenn ich weg bin; *(dead)* wenn ich (einmal) nicht mehr (da) bin; **~!** *(Sport)* los!; **here ~es!** jetzt geht's los! *(col)*.

(c) *(disappear, vanish)* verschwinden; *(pain, spot, mark etc also)* weggehen; *(be used up)* aufgebraucht werden; *(time)* vergehen. **it has gone** *(disappeared)* es ist weg; *(used up, eaten etc)* es ist alle *(col)*; **where has it gone?** wo ist es hin *or* geblieben?; **gone are the days when ...** die Zeiten sind vorbei, wo ...; **I don't know where the money ~es** ich weiß nicht, wo all das Geld bleibt; **all his money ~es on records** sein ganzes Geld geht für Schallplatten drauf *(col)*; **£30 a week ~es in** *or* **on rent** £30 die Woche sind für die Miete (weg); **how is the time ~ing?** wie steht's mit der Zeit?; **it's just gone three** es ist gerade drei vorbei; **two days to ~ till ...** noch zwei Tage bis ...; **only three more patients to ~** nur noch zwei Patienten; **he'll have to ~** er wird gehen müssen; **that settee will have to ~** das Sofa muß weg.

(d) *(be sold)* **the hats aren't ~ing very well** die Hüte gehen nicht sehr gut; **to be ~ing cheap** billig sein; **it went for £5** es ging für £5 weg; **they are ~ing at 20p each** sie werden zu 20 Pence das Stück verkauft; **~ing, ~ing, gone!** zum ersten, zum zweiten, und zum dritten!

(e) *(prize, 1st place etc)* gehen *(to an* +*acc)*; *(inheritance)* zufallen *(to sb jdm)*.

(f) *(extend)* gehen. **the garden ~es down to the river** der Garten geht bis zum Fluß hinunter; **£5 won't ~ far** mit £5 kommt man nicht weit.

(g) *(run, function)* gehen; *(car, machine also)* laufen; *(workers)* arbeiten. **to get ~ing in** Schwung kommen; **to get sth ~ing, to make sth ~ etw** in Gang bringen; *party* etw in Fahrt bringen; *business* etw auf Vordermann bringen; **to get sb ~ing** jdn in Fahrt bringen; **to get ~ing with sth** etw in Angriff nehmen; **to keep ~ing** *(person)* weitermachen; *(machine, engine, business)* weiterlaufen; *(car)* weiterfahren; **keep ~ing!** weiter!; **this medicine/prospect kept her ~ing** dieses Medikament/diese Aussicht hat sie durchhalten lassen; **here's £50/some work to keep you ~ing** hier hast du erst mal £50/etwas Arbeit.

(h) *(happen, turn out)* *(project, things)* gehen; *(event, evening)* verlaufen. **I've forgotten how the words ~** ich habe den Text vergessen; **how does the story/tune ~?** wie war die Geschichte doch noch mal/wie geht die Melodie?; **the decision went in his favour/against him** die Entscheidung fiel zu seinen Gunsten/Ungunsten aus; **how's it**

~ing?, how ~es it? *(col)* wie geht's (denn so)?; **how did it ~?** wie war's?; **how did the exam/your holiday ~?** wie ging's in der Prüfung/wie war der Urlaub?; **how's the essay ~ing?** was macht der Aufsatz?; **everything is ~ing well** alles läuft gut; **if everything ~es well** wenn alles gutgeht; **we'll see how things ~** *(col)* wir werden sehen, es läuft *(col)*; **she has a lot ~ing for her** sie ist gut dran.

(i) *(fail, break, wear out)* kaputtgehen; *(health, strength, eyesight etc)* nachlassen; *(fail: brakes, steering)* versagen. **the jumper has gone at the elbows** der Pullover ist an den Ärmeln durch *(col)*; **his mind is ~ing** er läßt geistig sehr nach; **there ~es another bulb/button!** schon wieder eine Birne kaputt/ein Knopf ab!

(j) *(be permitted, accepted)* gehen *(col)*. **anything ~es!** alles ist erlaubt; **what I say ~es!** was ich sage, wird gemacht!; **that ~es for me too** *(that applies to me)* das gilt auch für mich; *(I agree with that)* das meine ich auch.

(k) *(be available)* **there are no jobs ~ing** es sind keine Stellen zu haben; **is there any tea ~ing?** gibt es Tee?; **I'll have whatever is ~ing** ich nehme, was es gibt; **he's not bad as boys ~** verglichen mit anderen Jungen ist er nicht übel.

(l) *(be, become)* werden. **to ~ deaf/mad/grey** taub/verrückt/grau werden; **I went cold** mir wurde kalt; **to ~ Labour** Labour wählen.

(m) *(fit)* passen; *(belong, be placed)* hingehören; *(in drawer, cupboard etc)* (hin)kommen. **the books ~ in that cupboard** die Bücher kommen in den Schrank dort; **4 into 3 won't ~** 3 durch 4 geht nicht.

(n) *(match)* dazu passen. **to ~ with sth** zu etw passen.

(o) *(contribute)* **the money ~es to help the poor** das Geld soll den Armen helfen; **the money will ~ towards the holiday** das ist Geld für den Urlaub; **the qualities that ~ to make a great man** die Eigenschaften, die einen großen Mann ausmachen.

(p) *(make a sound or movement)* machen. **to ~ bang/ticktock** peng/ticktack machen; **there ~es the bell** es klingelt; **as the bell went** als es klingelte.

(q) *(US)* **food to ~** Essen zum Mitnehmen.

2 *aux vb* **I'm ~ing to do it** ich werde es tun; **I was ~ing to do it** ich wollte es tun; **I had been ~ing to do it** ich hatte es tun wollen; **I wasn't ~ing to do it (anyway)** ich hätte es sowieso nicht gemacht.

3 *vt* *(col)* **to ~ it** *(~ fast)* ein tolles Tempo draufhaben *(col)*; *(work hard)* sich hineinknien *(col)*; **to ~ it alone** einen Alleingang machen; *(in business)* sich selbständig machen; **I could ~ a beer** ich könnte ein Bier vertragen *(col)*.

4 *n, pl* **-es** *(a)* *(col: energy)* Schwung *m.* **(b) to be on the ~** auf Trab sein *(col)*; **to keep sb on the ~** jdn auf Trab halten; **he's got two books on the ~** er schreibt zwei Bücher gleichzeitig; **it's all ~** es ist immer was los *(col)*. **(c)** *(attempt)* Versuch *m.* **it's your ~** du bist dran *(col)*; **you've had your ~** du warst schon dran *(col)*; **to have a ~** es probieren; **to have a ~ at sb** *(criticize)* jdn runterputzen *(col)*; *(fight)* es mit jdm aufnehmen; **to have a ~ at doing sth** versuchen, etw zu tun; **at** *or* **in one ~** auf einen Schlag *(col)*; *drink* in einem Zug *(col)*; **can I have a ~?** darf ich mal? **(d)** *(success)* **to make a ~ of sth** in etw *(dat)* Erfolg haben; **(it's) no ~** *(col)* das ist nicht drin *(col)*. **(e) from the word ~** von Anfang an; **all systems (are) ~** (es ist) alles klar.

♦**go about 1** *vi* herumgehen; *(by vehicle)* herumfahren; *(rumour, flu etc)* umgehen; *(ship)* wenden. **2** *vi* +*prep obj task, problem* anpacken. **we must ~ it carefully** wir müssen vorsichtig vorgehen; **how does one ~ ~ getting seats?** wie bekommt man Plätze?; **to** ~ ~ **one's business** seinen Geschäften nachgehen.

♦ **go after** *vi* +*prep obj* nachgehen (+*dat*), nachlaufen (+*dat*); (*in vehicle*) nachfahren (+*dat*); *criminal* jagen; *job, girl* sich bemühen um; (*Sport*) *record* einstellen wollen.

♦ **go against** *vi* +*prep obj* **(a)** (*luck*) sein gegen; (*events*) ungünstig verlaufen für; (*evidence, appearance*) sprechen gegen. **the verdict went** ~ **her** das Urteil fiel zu ihren Ungunsten aus. **(b)** (*be contrary to*) im Widerspruch stehen zu; *principles, conscience* gehen gegen.

♦ **go ahead** *vi* **(a)** (*in race*) sich an die Spitze setzen. **(b)** (*work, project*) vorangehen. **he just went** ~ **and did it** er hat es einfach gemacht; ~ ~!; **to** ~ ~ **with sth** etw durchführen.

♦ **go along** *vi* **(a)** (*walk along*) entlanggehen. **as one** ~**es** ~ (*while walking*) unterwegs; (*bit by bit*) nach und nach; (*at the same time*) nebenbei. **(b)** (*accompany*) mitgehen (*with* mit). **(c)** (*agree*) zustimmen (*with dat*).

♦ **go around** *vi* **(a)** (*turn, spin*) sich drehen. **(b)** (*make a detour*) **we went** ~ **by Winchester** wir fuhren bei Winchester herum. **(c)** (*visit*) vorbeigehen (*to* bei). **(d)** (*tour: round museum etc*) herumgehen (*prep obj* in +*dat*). **(e)** (*be sufficient*) (aus)reichen. **there's enough food to** ~ ~ es ist genügend zu essen da. **(f)** = **go about 1.**

♦ **go at** *vi* +*prep obj* (*col: attack*) *person* losgehen auf (+*acc*) (*col*); *task* sich machen an (+*acc*). **he really went** ~ **it** er hat richtig losgelegt (*col*).

♦ **go away** *vi* (weg)gehen; (*for a holiday*) wegfahren.

♦ **go back** *vi* zurückgehen; (*to a subject*) zurückkommen (*to* auf +*acc*); (*revert: to habits, methods etc*) zurückkehren (*to* zu); (*clock: be put back*) zurückgestellt werden. **to** ~ ~ **to the beginning** wieder von vorn anfangen; **there's no** ~**ing** ~ **now** jetzt gibt es kein Zurück mehr; **we** ~ ~ **a long way** wir kennen uns schon seit langem.

♦ **go back on** *vi* +*prep obj* zurücknehmen; *decision* rückgängig machen.

♦ **go before** *vi* (*live before*) in früheren Zeiten leben; (*happen before*) vorangehen.

♦ **go by** *vi* (*person, opportunity*) vorbeigehen (*prep obj* an +*dat*); (*vehicle*) vorbeifahren (*prep obj* an +*dat*); (*time*) vergehen. **as time went** ~ mit der Zeit. **2** *vi* +*prep obj* **(a)** (*base judgement on*) gehen nach; *compass, watch etc* sich richten nach; (*stick to*) *rules* sich halten an (+*acc*). **if that's anything to** ~ ~ wenn man danach gehen kann; ~**ing** ~ **what he said** nach dem, was er sagte; **that's not much to** ~ ~ das will nicht viel heißen. **(b)** to ~ ~ **the name of X** X heißen.

♦ **go down** *vi* **(a)** hinuntergehen (*prep obj acc*); (*by vehicle, lift*) hinunterfahren (*prep obj acc*); (*sun, moon*) untergehen; (*Theat: curtain*) fallen; (*fall: boxer etc*) zu Boden gehen. **(b)** (*ship, person: sink*) untergehen; (*be defeated*) geschlagen werden (*to* von). **(c)** (*Brit Univ*) die Universität verlassen; (*for vacation*) in die Semesterferien gehen. **(d)** (*be accepted, approved*) ankommen (*with* bei). **that won't** ~ ~ **well with him** das wird er nicht gut finden; **he went** ~ **big in the States** (*col*) in den Staaten kam er ganz groß heraus (*col*). **(e)** (*floods, temperature etc*) zurückgehen; (*taxes, value*) weniger werden; (*prices*) sinken; (*balloon, tyre*) Luft verlieren; (*deteriorate: neighbourhood*) herunterkommen. **he has gone** ~ **in my estimation** er ist in meiner Achtung gesunken. **(f)** (*be noted*) vermerkt werden. **to** ~ ~ **to posterity/in history** der Nachwelt überliefert werden/in die Geschichte eingehen. **(g)** to ~ ~ **with a cold** eine Erkältung bekommen.

♦ **go for** *vi* +*prep obj* **(a)** (*col: attack*) losgehen auf (+*acc*) (*col*); (*verbally*) herziehen über (+*acc*). **(b)** (*col: admire, like*) gut finden. **(c)** (*aim at*) zielen auf (+*acc*); (*fig*) aussein auf (+*acc*) (*col*).

♦ **go in** *vi* (*enter, fit in*) hineingehen; (*sun*) verschwinden.

♦ **go in for** *vi* +*prep obj* **(a)** (*enter for*) teilnehmen an (+*dat*). **(b)** (*be interested in*) stehen auf (+*acc*) (*col*); (*as career*) gewählt haben. **to** ~ ~ ~ **sports/tennis** (*play oneself*) Sport treiben/Tennis spielen; (*be interested in*) sich für Sport/Tennis interessieren; **to** ~ ~ ~ **growing vegetables** sich auf den Gemüseanbau verlegen.

♦ **go into** *vi* +*prep obj* **(a)** *house, hospital, politics* gehen in (+*acc*); *the army, navy etc* gehen zu. **to** ~ ~ **teaching** Lehrer werden. **(b)** (*crash into*) *car* (hinein)fahren in (+*acc*); *wall* fahren gegen. **(c)** *explanation, description etc* geben. **(d)** *trance, coma* fallen in (+*acc*). **(e)** (*look into*) sich befassen mit; (*treat, explain at length*) abhandeln. **I don't want to** ~ ~ **that now** darauf möchte ich jetzt nicht (näher) eingehen.

♦ **go off 1** *vi* **(a)** (*leave*) weggehen; (*by vehicle*) wegfahren. **he went** ~ **to the States** er fuhr in die Staaten; **to** ~ ~ **with sth** (*steal*) mit etw auf und davon gehen (*col*). **(b)** (*light*) ausgehen; (*water, electricity, gas*) wegbleiben. **(c)** (*gun, bomb, alarm, alarm clock*) losgehen. **(d)** (*food*) schlecht werden; (*person, work*) nachlassen. **(e)** (*go to sleep*) einschlafen. **(f)** (*take place*) verlaufen. **to** ~ ~ **well/badly** gut/schlecht gehen. **2** *vi* +*prep obj* (*lose liking for*) nicht mehr mögen. **I've gone** ~ **him/it** ich mache mir nichts mehr aus ihm/daraus.

♦ **go on 1** *vi* **(a)** (*walk on etc*) weitergehen; (*by vehicle*) weiterfahren; (*ahead of others*) vorausgehen.

   (b) (*light, power*) angehen.

   (c) (*carry on, continue*) weitergehen; (*person*) weitermachen. **to** ~ ~ **with sth** mit etw weitermachen; **to** ~ ~ **working** weiterarbeiten; **I want to** ~ ~ **being a teacher** ich möchte weiterhin Lehrer bleiben; ~ ~, **tell me/try!** na, sag schon/na, versuch's doch!; **to have enough to be** ~**ing** ~ **with** fürs erste genug haben; **he went** ~ **to say that ...** dann sagte er, daß ...; **I can't** ~ ~ ich kann nicht mehr; **as time** ~**es** ~ im Laufe der Zeit; **don't** ~ ~ (**about it**) nun hör aber (damit) auf; **you do** ~ ~ a bit du weißt manchmal nicht, wann du aufhören solltest; **to** ~ ~ **about sb/sth** (*talk a lot*) stundenlang von jdm/etw erzählen; (*complain*) dauernd über jdn/etw schimpfen; **to** ~ ~ **at sb** an jdm herumnörgeln.

   (d) (*happen*) vor sich gehen; (*party, argument etc*) im Gange sein. **this has been** ~**ing** ~ **for a long time** das geht schon lange so; **what's** ~**ing** ~ **here?** was geht hier vor?

   2 *vi* +*prep obj* (*be guided by*) gehen nach. **we haven't got much to** ~ ~ wir haben nicht viel, worauf wir uns stützen können.

♦ **go on for** *vi* +*prep obj* *fifty, one o'clock* zugehen auf (+*acc*). **there were** ~**ing** ~ ~ **twenty people there** es waren fast zwanzig Leute da.

♦ **go out** *vi* **(a)** (*leave*) hinausgehen. **to** ~ ~ **of a room** aus einem Zimmer gehen. **(b)** (*shopping etc*) weggehen; (*socially, to theatre etc, with girl-/boyfriend*) ausgehen. **to** ~ ~ **for a meal** essen gehen. **(c)** (*fire, light*) ausgehen. **(d)** (*tide*) zurückgehen. **(e)** **my heart went** ~ **to him** ich fühlte mit ihm mit. **(f)** (*Sport: be defeated*) ausscheiden. **(g)** (*circular*) (hinaus)gehen; (*Rad, TV: programme*) ausgestrahlt werden.

♦ **go over 1** *vi* **(a)** (*cross*) hinübergehen; (*by vehicle*) hinüberfahren. **(b)** (*change sides etc*) übergehen (*to* zu); (*to another party*) überwechseln (*to* zu). **(c)** (*TV, Rad: to news desk etc*) umschalten. **(d)** (*be received: play, remarks etc*) ankommen. **2** *vi* +*prep obj* **(a)** (*examine*) *accounts* durchgehen; *house, luggage* durchsuchen;

(medically) person untersuchen; *(see over) house etc* sich *(dat)* ansehen. **(b)** *lesson, facts* durchgehen. **to ~ ~ sth in one's mind** etw überdenken.

♦ **go past** *vi (prep obj* an +*dat)* vorbeigehen; *(vehicle)* vorbeifahren; *(time)* vergehen.

♦ **go round** *vi* = **go around.**

♦ **go through 1** *vi (lit, fig)* durchgehen; *(business deal)* abgeschlossen werden. **2** *vi* +*prep obj* **(a)** *hole, door, customs etc* gehen durch. **(b)** *illness, formalities etc* durchmachen. **(c)** *(examine, discuss)* durchgehen. **(d)** *(search) pocket, suitcase* durchsuchen. **(e)** *(use up)* aufbrauchen; *money* ausgeben; *shoes* durchlaufen *(col).* **he has gone ~ the seat of his trousers** er hat seine Hose durchgesessen.

♦ **go through with** *vi* +*prep obj plan* durchziehen *(col).* **she couldn't ~ ~ ~ it** sie brachte es nicht fertig.

♦ **go together** *vi (harmonize)* zusammenpassen; *(events, conditions)* zusammen auftreten.

♦ **go under 1** *vi (sink)* untergehen; *(businessman)* scheitern; *(company)* eingehen *(col).* **2** *vi* +*prep obj* **to ~ ~ the name of X** als X bekannt sein.

♦ **go up** *vi* **(a)** *(price, temperature etc)* steigen. **(b)** *(climb)* hinaufsteigen *(prep obj acc).* **(c)** *(lift)* hochfahren; *(balloon)* aufsteigen; *(Theat: curtain)* hochgehen; *(be built: new flats etc)* gebaut werden. **(d)** *(explode)* in die Luft gehen. **to ~ ~ in flames** in Flammen aufgehen.

♦ **go without 1** *vi* +*prep obj* **to ~ ~ sth** auf etw *(acc)* verzichten. **2** *vi* darauf verzichten.

goad [gəʊd] *vt (taunt)* aufreizen. **to ~ sb into sth** jdn zu etw anstacheln.

♦ **goad on** *vt sep* anstacheln.

go-ahead [ˈgəʊəhed] **1** *adj* fortschrittlich. **2** *n* **to give sb/sth the ~** jdm/für etw freie Fahrt geben.

goal [gəʊl] *n* **(a)** *(Sport)* Tor *nt.* **(b)** *(aim, objective)* Ziel *nt.*

goalie [ˈgəʊlɪ] *n (col)* Tormann *m.*

goal: ~**keeper** *n* Torwart *m;* ~-**kick** *n* Abstoß *m* (vom Tor); ~-**post** *n* Torpfosten *m;* ~-**scorer** *n* Torschütze *m.*

goat [gəʊt] *n* Ziege *f.* **to get sb's ~** *(col)* jdn auf die Palme bringen *(col).*

gob [gɒb] *n (Brit col!: mouth)* Schnauze *f (col!).*

♦ **gobble down** *vt sep* hinunterschlingen.

♦ **gobble up** *vt sep (lit, fig)* verschlingen.

gobbledygook [ˈgɒbldɪˌguːk] *n (col)* Kauderwelsch *nt.*

go-between [ˈgəʊbɪˌtwiːn] *n* Vermittler(in *f) m.*

goblin [ˈgɒblɪn] *n* Kobold *m.*

god [gɒd] *n* Gott *m.* **G~ forbid** *(col)* Gott behüte; **G~ (only) knows** *(col)* wer weiß; **(my) G~!** *(col),* **good G~!** *(col)* O Gott!, großer Gott! *(col);* **for G~'s sake!** *(col)* um Gottes willen! *(col);* **the ~s** *(Brit Theat col)* die Galerie, der Olymp *(col).*

god: ~**child** *n* Patenkind *nt;* ~**daughter** *n* Patentochter *f.*

goddess [ˈgɒdɪs] *n* Göttin *f.*

god: ~**father** *n* Pate *m;* ~**forsaken** *adj* gottverlassen; ~**less** *adj* gottlos.

godly [ˈgɒdlɪ] *adj (+er)* fromm, gottesfürchtig.

god: ~**mother** *n* Patin *f;* ~**parent** *n* Pate *m,* Patin *f;* ~**send** *n* Geschenk *nt* des Himmels; ~**son** *n* Patensohn *m.*

go-getter [ˈgəʊˌgetəʳ] *n (col)* Tatmensch *m.*

goggle [ˈgɒgl] *vi* **to ~ at sb/sth** jdn/etw anstarren.

goggle-box [ˈgɒglbɒks] *n (Brit col)* Glotze *f (col).*

goggles [ˈgɒglz] *npl* Schutzbrille *f.*

going [ˈgəʊɪŋ] **1** *n* **it's slow ~** es geht nur langsam; **that's good ~** das ist ein flottes Tempo; **the ~ is good/hard** *(in racing)* die Bahn ist gut/hart; **the road was heavy/rough ~** man kam auf der Straße nur schwer/mit Mühe voran; **it's heavy ~ talking to him** es ist sehr mühsam, sich mit ihm zu unterhalten; **while the ~ is good** solange es noch geht. **2** *adj attr business* gutgehend; *price*

aktuell.

goings-on [ˌgəʊɪŋˈzɒn] *npl (col)* Dinge *pl.* **there have been strange ~** da sind seltsame Dinge passiert.

goitre, *(US)* **goiter** [ˈgɔɪtəʳ] *n* Kropf *m.*

go-kart [ˈgəʊˌkɑːt] *n* Go-Kart *m.*

gold [gəʊld] *n* **(a)** Gold *nt.* **(b)** *(colour)* Goldton *m.* **2** *adj* golden; *(made of ~ also)* Gold-.

golden [ˈgəʊldən] *adj (lit, fig)* golden; *opportunity* einmalig. **~ brown** goldbraun; **~ eagle** Steinadler *m;* **~ handshake** *(col)* Abstandssumme *f;* **~ jubilee** goldenes Jubiläum; **~ labrador** Goldener Labrador; **~ rule** goldene Regel; **~ wedding** *(anniversary)* goldene Hochzeit.

gold: ~**finch** *n* Stieglitz, Distelfink *m;* ~**fish** *n* Goldfisch *m;* ~ **medal** *n* Goldmedaille *f;* ~**mine** *n (lit, fig)* Goldgrube *f;* ~ **plate** *n (plating)* Vergoldung *f; (articles)* vergoldetes Gerät; ~**smith** *n* Goldschmied *m.*

golf [gɒlf] *n* Golf *nt.*

golf: ~**ball** *n* Golfball *m; (on typewriter)* Kugelkopf *m;* ~ **club** *n* Golfschläger *m; (association)* Golfklub *m;* ~ **course** *n* Golfplatz *m.*

golfer [ˈgɒlfəʳ] *n* Golfer(in *f),* Golfspieler(in *f) m.*

gondola [ˈgɒndələ] *n* Gondel *f.*

gone [gɒn] *ptp of* **go.**

goner [ˈgɒnəʳ] *n (col)* **to be a ~** *(car etc)* kaputt sein *(col); (patient)* es nicht mehr lange machen; *(professionally: person, company)* weg vom Fenster sein *(col).*

gong [gɒŋ] *n* Gong *m.*

gonorrhoea [ˌgɒnəˈrɪə] *n* Gonorrhö *f,* Tripper *m.*

goo [guː] *n (col)* Papp *m (col).*

good [gʊd] **1** *adj, comp* **better,** *superl* **best (a)** gut. **that's a ~ one!** *(joke)* der ist gut!, das ist ein guter Witz *(also iro); (excuse)* wer's glaubt, wird selig! *(col);* **it's no ~ doing it** like **that** es hat keinen Sinn, das so zu machen; **that's no ~** das ist nichts; **to be ~ at sport/languages** gut im Sport/ in Sprachen sein; **to be ~ at sewing/typing** gut nähen/maschineschreiben können; **I'm not very ~ at** that das kann ich nicht besonders gut; **to be ~ for sb** jdm guttun; *(be healthy also)* gesund sein; **to be ~ for toothache/one's health** gut gegen Zahnschmerzen/für die Gesundheit sein; **to drink more than is ~ for one** mehr trinken, als einem guttut; **to be ~ with people** mit Menschen umgehen können; **it's too ~ to be true** es ist zu schön, um wahr zu sein; **to feel ~** sich wohl fühlen; **I don't feel too ~** ich fühle mich nicht wohl; **that's (not) ~ enough** das reicht (nicht); **if he gives his word, that's ~ enough for me** wenn er sein Wort gibt, reicht mir das; **it's just not ~ enough!** so geht das nicht!; . **his attitude/ behaviour is just not ~ enough** er hat einfach nicht die richtige Einstellung/sein Benehmen ist nicht akzeptabel; **~ morning/afternoon** guten Morgen/Tag; **that's ~!** gut!, prima!; **(it's) ~** to **see you/to be here** (es ist) schön, dich zu sehen/ hier zu sein; **~, I think that'll be all** gut, ich glaube das reicht; **very ~, sir** jawohl; **~ for you/him!** gut!, prima!; *(iro also)* das ist ja toll!

(b) *(favourable) moment, chance, opportunity* günstig, gut. **a ~ day for a picnic** ein guter Tag für ein Picknick; **it's a ~ thing** *or* **job I was there** (nur) gut, daß ich dort war.

(c) *(enjoyable) holiday, evening* schön. **the ~ life** das süße Leben; **to have a ~ time** sich gut amüsieren; **have a ~ time!** viel Spaß *or* Vergnügen!; **did you have a ~ day?** wie ging's (dir) heute?; **have a ~ day!** schönen Tag noch!

(d) *(kind)* gut, lieb. **to be ~ to sb** gut zu jdm sein; **that's very ~ of you** das ist sehr lieb *or* nett von Ihnen; **(it was) ~ of you to come** nett, daß Sie gekommen sind; **would you be ~ enough to tell me ...** wären Sie so nett, mir zu sagen ... *(also iro);* **she was ~ enough to help us** sie war so gut und hat uns geholfen; **with every ~ wish** mit den besten Wünschen.

(e) *(well-behaved, obedient)* artig, brav *(col)*. (as) ~ **as gold** mustergültig; **be a** ~ **girl/boy** sei artig *or* brav *(col)*; **be a** ~ **girl/boy and ... sei so lieb und ...; my** ~ **man** *(dated)* mein guter Mann *(dated)*; ~ **girl/boy!** das ist lieb!; *(well done)* gut!; ~ **old Charles!** der gute alte Charles!

(f) **is his credit** ~? ist er kreditfähig?; **what** *or* **how much is he** ~ **for?** *(will he give us)* mit wieviel kann man bei ihm rechnen?; *(does he have)* wieviel hat er?; **he/the car is** ~ **for another few years** mit ihm kann man noch ein paar Jahre rechnen/das Auto hält *or* tut's *(col)* noch ein paar Jahre.

(g) *(thorough)* gut, gründlich. **to give sth a** ~ **clean** etw gründlich reinigen; **to have a** ~ **laugh** ordentlich lachen; **to take a** ~ **look at sth** sich *(dat)* etw gut ansehen.

(h) *(considerable, not less than)* hour, while gut; amount, distance, way also schön. **it's a** ~ **8 km** es sind gute 8 km; **a** ~ **deal of effort/money** beträchtliche Mühe/ziemlich viel Geld; **a** ~ **many/few people** ziemlich viele/nicht gerade wenig Leute.

(i) **as** ~ **as so gut wie; as** ~ **as new/settled** so gut wie neu/abgemacht; **he was as** ~ **as his word** er hat sein Wort gehalten; **he as** ~ **as called me a liar** er nannte mich praktisch einen Lügner.

2 *adv* schön. **a** ~ **strong stick/old age** ein schön(er) starker Stock/ein schön(es) hohes Alter; ~ **and strong** *(col)* schön stark *(col)*.

3 *n* (a) *(what is morally right)* Gute(s) *nt.* **to do** ~ **Gutes** tun; **to be up to no** ~ *(col)* nichts Gutes im Schilde führen *(col)*.

(b) *(advantage, benefit)* Wohl *nt.* **the common** ~ das Gemeinwohl; **for the** ~ **of the nation** zum Wohl(e) der Nation; **I did it for your own** ~ es war nur zu deinem Besten; **for the** ~ **of one's health** *etc* seiner Gesundheit *etc* zuliebe; **that's all to the** ~ auch gut!; **he'll come to no** ~ mit ihm wird es noch ein böses Ende nehmen; **what's the** ~ **of hurrying?** wozu eigentlich die Eile?; **he's no** ~ **to us** er nützt uns *(dat)* nichts; **it's no** ~ **complaining to me** es ist sinnlos, sich bei mir zu beklagen; **if that is any** ~ **to you** wenn es dir hilft; **the applicant was no** ~ der Bewerber war nicht gut; **he wasn't any** ~ **for the job** er eignete sich nicht für die Arbeit; **is this one any** ~? was ist mit dieser/diesem?; **it's no** ~, **it won't start** es hat keinen Zweck, es springt nicht an; **what** ~ **will that do you?** was hast du davon?; **that won't do you much/any** ~ das hilft dir auch nicht viel/nichts; *(will be unhealthy etc)* das ist nicht gut für dich; **a (fat) lot of** ~ **that will do!** *(iro col)* als ob das etwas helfen würde! *(iro)*.

(c) *(for ever)* **for** ~ **(and all)** für immer (und ewig).

good: ~**bye,** *(US)* ~**by 1** *n* Abschied *m*; **to say** ~**bye (to sb)** sich (von jdm) verabschieden; **to say** ~**bye to sth** einer Sache *(dat)* Lebewohl sagen; **2** *interj* auf Wiedersehen; ~**-for-nothing 1** *n* Nichtsnutz *m*; **2** *adj* nichtsnutzig; **G**~ **Friday** *n* Karfreitag *m*; ~**-humoured,** *(US)* ~**-humored** *adj* gut gelaunt; *(*~*-natured)* gutmütig; ~**-looking** *adj* gutaussehend; ~**-natured** *adj* gutmütig.

goodness ['gudnɪs] *n* Güte *f.* ~ **knows** *(col)* weiß der Himmel *(col)*; **for** ~' **sake** *(col)* um Himmels willen *(col)*; **I wish to** ~ **I had gone** *(col)* wenn ich doch bloß gegangen wäre!; **(my)** ~!, ~ **gracious!** *(col)* ach du meine Güte *(col)*.

goods [gudz] *npl* Güter *pl* (also Comm); *(merchandise also)* Waren *pl*; *(possessions also)* Habe *f* *(geh)*. ~ **train/yard** *(Brit)* Güterzug *m*/-bahnhof *m*; **one's** ~ **and chattels** sein Hab und Gut *(also Jur)*.

good: ~**-sized** *adj* ziemlich groß; ~**-tempered** *adj* person verträglich; *animal* gutartig; ~**will** *n* Wohlwollen *nt*; *(between nations, Comm)* Good-

will *m*; **a gesture of** ~**will** ein Zeichen seines/ ihres *etc* guten Willens; **to gain sb's** ~**will** jds Gunst gewinnen; ~**will mission/tour** Goodwill-reise *f*.

goody-goody ['gudɪ,gudɪ] *n* *(col)* Tugendlamm *nt* *(col)*.

gooey ['guːɪ] *adj* *(+er)* *(sticky)* klebrig; *toffees, centres of chocolates* weich und klebrig.

goof [guːf] *vi* *(col: blunder)* danebenhauen *(col)*.

goose [guːs] *n, pl* **geese** *(lit, fig col)* Gans *f.*

gooseberry ['guzbərɪ] *n* Stachelbeere *f.* **to play** ~ Anstandswauwau spielen *(col)*.

goose: ~**-flesh** *n*, ~**pimples** *npl* Gänsehaut *f*; ~**-step** *n* Stechschritt *m*.

gore[1] [gɔːr] *n* *(liter: blood)* Blut *nt*.

gore[2] *vt* aufspießen.

gorge [gɔːdʒ] **1** *n* *(Geog)* Schlucht *f*. **2** *vr* sich vollessen; *(animal)* gierig fressen. **to** ~ **oneself on sth** etw verschlingen.

gorgeous ['gɔːdʒəs] *adj* großartig, sagenhaft *(col)*.

gorilla [gə'rɪlə] *n* Gorilla *m*.

gormless ['gɔːmlɪs] *adj* *(Brit col)* doof *(col)*.

gorse [gɔːs] *n* Stechginster *m*.

gory ['gɔːrɪ] *adj* *(+er)* battle etc blutig. **the** ~ **details** *(fig)* die peinlichen Einzelheiten.

gosh [gɒʃ] *interj* Mensch! *(col)*, Mann! *(col)*.

go-slow ['gəʊsləʊ] *n* *(Brit)* Bummelstreik *m*.

gospel ['gɒspəl] *n* *(Bibl)* Evangelium *nt*. **to take sth as** ~ etw für bare Münze nehmen *(col)*; **the** ~ **truth** *(col)* die reine Wahrheit.

gossamer ['gɒsəmər'] **1** *n* (a) Spinnfäden *pl*. (b) *(Tex)* hauchdünne Gaze. **2** *adj* hauchdünn.

gossip ['gɒsɪp] **1** *n* (a) Klatsch *(col) m*; *(chat)* Schwatz *m*. **to have a** ~ **with sb** mit jdm schwatzen. (b) *(person)* Klatschbase *f*. **2** *vi* schwatzen *(col)*; *(maliciously)* klatschen.

gossip: ~ **column** *n* Klatschspalte *f*; ~ **columnist** *n* Klatschkolumnist(in *f*) *m*.

got [gɒt] *pret, ptp of* **get**.

Goth [gɒθ] *n* Gote *m*.

Gothic ['gɒθɪk] *adj* gotisch. ~ **novel** Schauerroman *m*.

gotten ['gɒtn] *(esp US)* *ptp of* **get**.

gouge [gaʊdʒ] **1** *n* *(tool)* Hohlmeißel *m*; *(groove)* Furche *f*. **2** *vt* bohren. **the river** ~**d a channel in the mountainside** der Fluß grub sich *(dat)* sein Bett in den Berg.

♦ **gouge out** *vt sep* herausbohren. **to** ~ **sb's eyes** ~ jdm die Augen ausstechen.

goulash ['guːlæʃ] *n* Gulasch *nt*.

gourmand ['guəmənd] *n* Schlemmer *m*.

gourmet ['guəmeɪ] *n* Feinschmecker, Gourmet *m*.

gout [gaʊt] *n* *(Med)* Gicht *f*.

govern ['gʌvən] *vt* (a) *(rule)* country regieren; province, colony, school *etc* verwalten. (b) *(control)* bestimmen; *(legislation)* regeln. (c) *(Mech)* regulieren. (d) *(Gram)* case regieren.

governess ['gʌvənɪs] *n* Gouvernante *f*.

governing ['gʌvənɪŋ] *adj* (a) *(ruling)* regierend. **the** ~ **party** die Regierungspartei; ~ **body** Vorstand *m*. (b) *(guiding, controlling)* entscheidend. ~ **principle** Leitgedanke *m*.

government ['gʌvənmənt] *n* Regierung *f*.

government *in cpds* Regierungs-, der Regierung.

government: ~ **department** *n* Ministerium *nt*; ~ **grant** *n* (staatliche) Subvention; ~ **securities** *npl* *(Fin)* Staatspapiere *pl*.

governor ['gʌvənər'] *n* (a) *(of colony, state etc)* Gouverneur *m*. (b) *(esp Brit: of bank, prison)* Direktor *m*; *(of school)* ≈ Mitglied *nt* des Schulbeirats *m*. **the (board of)** ~**s** *(of Vorstand; (of bank also)* das Direktorium; *(of school)* ≈ der Schulbeirat. (c) *(Brit col)* *(boss)* Chef *m* *(col)*. (d) *(Mech)* Regler *m*.

govt = **government** Reg.

gown [gaʊn] *n* (a) Kleid *nt*; *(evening* ~*)* Abendkleid *nt*. (b) *(academic)* Robe *f*; *(of clergyman, judge)*

Talar *m*.

GP *(Brit)* = **general practitioner**.

grab [græb] **1** *n* **(a)** Griff *m*. **to make a ~ at sth** nach etw greifen. **(b)** *(Mech)* Greifer *m*. **2** *vt (seize)* packen; *(greedily also)* sich *(dat)* schnappen *(col)*; *(take)* wegschnappen *(col)*; *(col: catch)* person schnappen *(col)*; chance beim Schopf ergreifen *(col)*. **he ~bed my sleeve** er packte mich am Ärmel; **to ~ sth away from sb** jdm etw wegreißen; **how does that ~ you?** *(col)* was hältst du davon? **3** *vi* **to ~ at** greifen nach, packen *(+acc)*.

grace [greɪs] **1** *n* Anmut *f*. **to do sth with good/bad ~** etw anstandslos/widerwillig tun; **he took it with good/bad ~** er machte gute Miene zum bösen Spiel/er war sehr ungehalten darüber; **he had the ~ to apologize** er war so anständig, sich zu entschuldigen; **he didn't even have the ~ to apologize** er brachte es nicht einmal fertig, sich zu entschuldigen; **social ~s** (gesellschaftliche) Umgangsformen *pl*; **to give sb a few days' ~** jdm ein paar Tage Zeit lassen; *(Comm)* jdm ein paar Tage Aufschub gewähren; **to say ~** das Tischgebet sprechen; **by the ~ of God** durch die Gnade Gottes; **to fall from ~** in Ungnade fallen; **~ note** *(Mus)* Verzierung *f*.

2 *vt* **(a)** *(adorn)* zieren *(geh)*. **(b)** *(honour)* beehren *(with* mit*) (geh)*. **to ~ the occasion with one's presence** sich *(dat)* die Ehre geben.

graceful ['greɪsfʊl] *adj* anmutig; *outline, appearance also, behaviour* gefällig.

gracefully ['greɪsfəlɪ] *adv see adj accept, give in etc* gelassen. **he gave in ~** er gab gelassen nach.

gracious ['greɪʃəs] **1** *adj* gnädig *(also iro)*; *buildings etc* stilvoll, elegant. **~ living** feudaler Lebensstil. **2** *interj* **(good) ~!** *(col)* du meine Güte!

grade [greɪd] **1** *n* **(a)** *(standard)* Niveau *nt*; *(of goods)* (Güte)klasse *f*. **high-/low-~ goods** hoch-/minderwertige Ware; **to make the ~** *(fig)* es schaffen *(col)*. **(b)** *(job ~)* Position, Stellung *f*; *(Mil)* Rang, (Dienst)grad *m*; *(salary ~)* Klasse, Stufe *f*. **(c)** *(Sch) (mark)* Note *f*; *(esp US: class)* Klasse *f*. **(d)** *(US)* = **gradient**. **2** *vt* **(a)** klassifizieren; *eggs, goods also* sortieren; *students* einstufen. **(b)** *(Sch: mark)* benoten.

grade: ~ crossing *n (US)* Bahnübergang *m*; **~ school** *n (US)* = Grundschule *f*.

gradient ['greɪdɪənt] *n* Neigung *f*; *(upward also)* Steigung *f*; *(downward also)* Gefälle *nt*. **a ~ of 1 in 10** eine Steigung/ein Gefälle von 10%.

gradual ['grædjʊəl] *adj* allmählich; *slope* sanft.

gradually ['grædjʊəlɪ] *adv* nach und nach, allmählich; *slope* sanft.

graduate[1] ['grædjʊɪt] *n (Univ)* (Hochschul)absolvent(in *f*) *m*; *(US Sch)* Schulabgänger(in *f*) *m*. **high-school ~** = Abiturient(in *f*) *m*.

graduate[2] ['grædjʊeɪt] **1** *vi (Univ)* graduieren; *(US Sch)* die Abschlußprüfung bestehen *(from an +dat)*. **2** *vt (mark)* einteilen.

graduation [ˌgrædjʊ'eɪʃən] *n (Univ, US Sch: ceremony)* (Ab)schlußfeier *f (mit feierlicher Überreichung der Zeugnisse)*. **(b)** *(mark)* (Maß)einteilung *f*.

graffiti [grə'fiːtɪ] *npl* Graffiti *pl*.

graft [grɑːft] **1** *n* **(a)** *(Bot)* (Pfropf)reis *nt*; *(Med)* Transplantat *nt*. **(b)** *(col: corruption)* Schiebung *f*. **(c)** *(col: hard work)* Schufterei *(col) f*. **2** *vt (Bot)* (auf)pfropfen *(on auf +acc)*; *(Med)* übertragen *(on auf +acc)*, einpflanzen *(into in +acc)*; *(fig: incorporate)* einbauen *(onto in +acc)*. **3** *vi (col: work hard)* schuften *(col) (at an +dat)*.

grain [greɪn] *n* **(a)** *no pl* Getreide, Korn *nt*. **(b)** *(of corn, sand etc)* Korn *nt*; *(fig)* Spur *f; (of truth also)* Körnchen *nt*. **(c)** *(of leather)* Narben *m; (of cloth)* Strich *m; (of wood, marble)* Maserung *f; (Phot)* Korn *nt*. **it goes against the ~ (with sb)** *(fig)* es geht jdm gegen den Strich.

grainy ['greɪnɪ] *adj (+er) texture* körnig.

gram(me) [græm] *n* Gramm *nt*.

grammar ['græmə'] *n* Grammatik *f*. **that's bad ~** das ist grammat(ikal)isch falsch.

grammar school *n (Brit)* = Gymnasium *nt*.

grammatical [grə'mætɪkəl] *adj* grammat(ikal)isch; *rules, mistakes also* Grammatik-. **this is not ~** das ist grammatisch *or* grammatikalisch falsch.

gramophone ['græməfəʊn] *n (Brit)* Grammophon ® *nt*. **~ record** Schallplatte *f*.

gran [græn] *n (col)* Oma *(col) f*.

granary ['grænərɪ] *n* Getreidespeicher *m*.

grand [grænd] **1** *adj (+er)* großartig; *building, display* prachtvoll; *(lofty) idea* hochfliegend; *(dignified) air, person* würdevoll; *(posh) dinner party, person* vornehm. **to have a ~ time** sich sehr gut amüsieren. **2** *n (col)* = Riese *m (col)* *(1000 Dollar/Pfund)*. **50 ~** 50 Riesen *(col)*.

grand: ~child *n* Enkel(kind *nt*) *m*; **~(d)ad** *n (col)* Opa *(col)*, Opi *(col) m*; **~daughter** *n* Enkelin *f*.

grandeur ['grændjə'] *n (of scenery, music)* Erhabenheit *f; (of manner also)* Würde *f; (of position, event also)* Glanz *m*.

grand: ~father *n* Großvater *m*; **~father clock** *n* Standuhr *f*; **~ finale** *n* großes Finale.

grandiose ['grændɪəʊz] *adj house, idea, speech* grandios *(also pej)*, großartig; *(pej: pompous) style* schwülstig, bombastisch.

grand jury *n (US Jur)* Großes Geschworenengericht.

grand: ~ma *n (col)* Oma *(col) f*; **~mother** *n* Großmutter *f*; **G~ National** *n* Grand National *nt (bedeutendes Pferderennen in GB)*.

grand: ~ opera *n* große Oper; **~pa** *n (col)* Opa *m (col)*; **~parent** *n* Großvater *m*/-mutter *f*; **~parents** *npl* Großeltern *pl*; **~ piano** *n* Flügel *m*; **G~ Prix** *n* Grand Prix *m*; **~ slam** *n* Großschlemm *m*; **~son** *n* Enkel(sohn) *m*; **~stand** *n* Haupttribüne *f*; **to have a ~stand view of sth** (direkten) Blick auf etw *(acc)* haben.

granite ['grænɪt] *n* Granit *m*.

granny, grannie ['grænɪ] *n (a) (col)* Oma *(col) f*. **(b)** *(also ~ knot)* Altweiberknoten *m*.

grant [grɑːnt] **1** *vt* **(a)** gewähren *(sb jdm)*; *privilege also* zugestehen *(sb jdm)*; *prayer* erhören; *honour* erweisen *(sb jdm)*; *permission* erteilen *(sb jdm)*; *(fulfil) wish* erfüllen. **(b)** *(admit, agree)* zugeben, zugestehen. **~ing or ~ed that this is true ...** angenommen, das ist wahr ...; **I ~ you that** da gebe ich dir recht; **to take sb/sth for ~ed** jdn/etw als selbstverständlich hinnehmen; **to take it for ~ed that ...** es als selbstverständlich betrachten, daß ...; **you take too much for ~ed** für dich ist zu vieles (einfach) selbstverständlich. **2** *n (of money)* Subvention *f; (for studying etc)* Stipendium *nt*.

granular ['grænjʊlə'] *adj* körnig.

granulated sugar ['grænjʊleɪtɪd'ʃʊgə'] *n* Zuckerraffinade *f*.

granule ['grænjuːl] *n* Körnchen *nt*.

grape [greɪp] *n* (Wein)traube *f*.

grape: ~fruit *n* Grapefruit *f*; **~vine** *n* Weinstock *m; (col)* Nachrichtendienst *m (col)*; **I heard it on the ~vine** es ist mir zu Ohren gekommen.

graph [grɑːf] *n* Diagramm *nt*, Schaubild *nt*. **~ paper** Millimeterpapier *nt*.

graphic['græfɪk] *adj* **(a)** graphisch. **~ arts** Grafik, Graphik *f*; **~ designer** Graphiker(in *f*) *m*. **(b)** *(vivid) description* anschaulich.

graphics ['græfɪks] *n* **(a)** *pl (drawings)* graphische Darstellungen *pl*. **(b)** *(Comp)* Grafik *f*.

graphite ['græfaɪt] *n* Graphit *m*.

grapple ['græpl] *vi (lit)* ringen, kämpfen. **to ~ with a problem** sich mit einem Problem auseinandersetzen.

grappling iron ['græplɪŋˌaɪən] *n* Haken *m; (Naut)* Enterhaken *m*.

grasp [grɑːsp] **1** *n* **(a)** *(hold)* Griff *m*. **to be within**

sb's ~ (für jdn) in greifbare Nähe gerückt sein. **(b)** (fig: understanding) Verständnis nt. **to have a good** ~ **of sth** etw gut beherrschen; **it is beyond/ within his** ~ das geht über seinen Verstand/das kann er begreifen. **2** vt **(a)** (catch hold of) ergreifen, greifen nach; (hold tightly) festhalten. **(b)** (fig: understand) begreifen, erfassen.

grasping ['grɑːspɪŋ] adj (fig) habgierig.

grass [grɑːs] n **(a)** Gras nt; (lawn) Rasen m; (pasture) Weide(land nt) f. **to let the** ~ **grow under one's feet** lange zögern; **to put out to** ~ auf die Weide führen or treiben. **(b)** (col: marijuana) Gras nt (col). **(c)** (Brit col: informer) Spitzel m (col).

grass: ~**hopper** n Heuschrecke f, Grashüpfer m (col); ~**land** n Grasland nt; ~**roots 1** npl Volk nt; (of a party) Basis f; **2** adj attr an der Basis; **at** ~**-roots level** an der Basis; **a** ~**-roots movement** eine Bürgerinitiative; ~ **snake** n Ringelnatter f; ~ **widow** n Strohwitwe f; ~ **widower** n Strohwitwer m.

grassy ['grɑːsɪ] adj (+er) mit Gras bewachsen.

grate[1] [greɪt] n Gitter nt; (in fire) (Feuer)rost m; (fireplace) Kamin m.

grate[2] **1** vt **(a)** (Cook) reiben; vegetables also raspeln. **(b)** (scrape) streifen; (make a grating noise with) kratzen mit; one's teeth knirschen mit. **2** vi (make a noise) kratzen; (chalk also, rusty door) quietschen. **to** ~ **on sb's nerves** jdm auf die Nerven gehen; **it** ~**s on the ears** es tut in den Ohren weh.

grateful ['greɪtfʊl] adj dankbar (to sb jdm).

grater ['greɪtə^r] n Reibe f; (for vegetable also) Raspel f.

gratification [ˌgrætɪfɪ'keɪʃən] n (pleasure) Genugtuung f; (of desires) Befriedigung f.

gratify ['grætɪfaɪ] vt (give pleasure) erfreuen; (satisfy) befriedigen, zufriedenstellen.

gratifying ['grætɪfaɪɪŋ] adj (sehr) erfreulich.

grating[1] ['greɪtɪŋ] n Gitter nt.

grating[2] adj kratzend; sound (squeaking) quietschend; (rasping) knirschend; voice schrill.

gratis ['grætɪs] adj, adv gratis.

gratitude ['grætɪtjuːd] n Dankbarkeit f (to gegenüber).

gratuitous [grə'tjuːɪtəs] adj überflüssig, unnötig.

gratuity [grə'tjuːɪtɪ] n Gratifikation, (Sonder)zuwendung f; (form: tip) Trinkgeld nt.

grave[1] [greɪv] n (lit, fig) Grab nt. **he's digging his own** ~ (fig) er schaufelt sich selbst sein Grab; **to turn in one's** ~ sich im Grabe herumdrehen.

grave[2] adj (+er) ernst; danger, risk groß; error schwer, gravierend; news schlimm.

grave-digger ['greɪvˌdɪgə^r] n Totengräber m.

gravel ['grævəl] **1** n Kies m; (large chippings) Schotter m. ~ **path** Kiesweg m.

gravelly ['grævəlɪ] adj (fig) voice rauh.

gravely ['greɪvlɪ] adv ernst; mistaken schwer.

grave: ~**stone** n Grabstein m; ~**yard** n Friedhof m.

gravitate ['grævɪteɪt] vi **to** ~ **towards sth** von etw angezogen werden.

gravitation [ˌgrævɪ'teɪʃən] n (Phys) Gravitation, Schwerkraft f; (fig) Tendenz f (towards zu).

gravitational [ˌgrævɪ'teɪʃənl] adj Gravitations-. ~ **field** Gravitations- or Schwerefeld nt; ~ **force** Schwerkraft f; ~ **pull** Anziehungskraft f.

gravity ['grævɪtɪ] n **(a)** (Phys) Schwere, Schwerkraft f. **centre of** ~ Schwerpunkt m; **force of** ~ Schwerkraft f; **specific** ~ spezifisches Gewicht. **(b)** (seriousness) see **grave**[2] Ernst m; Größe f; Schwere f. **such was the** ~ **of the news that ...** die Nachricht war so schlimm, daß ...

gravy ['greɪvɪ] n (juice) Fleischsaft, Bratensaft m; (sauce) Soße f. ~ **boat** Sauciere, Soßenschüssel f. **to get on the** ~ **train** (col) auch ein Stück vom Kuchen abbekommen (col).

gray [greɪ] (esp US) = **grey**.

graze[1] [greɪz] vi (cattle etc) grasen, weiden.

graze[2] **1** vt (touch lightly) streifen. **to** ~ **one's knees** (dat) die Knie aufschürfen. **2** n Schürfwunde f.

grease [griːs] **1** n Fett nt; (lubricant) Schmierfett nt. **2** vt fetten; (Aut, Tech) schmieren.

grease: ~**-gun** n Fettpresse f; ~**paint** n (Theat) (Fett)schminke f; ~**proof paper** n (Brit) Butterbrotpapier nt.

greasy ['griːsɪ] adj (+er) **(a)** fettig; food fett; machinery, axle ölig; hands, clothes schmierig; (slippery) road rutschig. **(b)** (fig pej) person schmierig.

great [greɪt] **1** adj (+er) **(a)** groß. ~ **big** (col) riesig, Mords- (col); **a** ~ **friend of ours** ein guter Freund von uns; **of no** ~ **importance** ziemlich unwichtig; **a** ~ **number of, a** ~ **many** eine große Anzahl, sehr viele; **he lived to a** ~ **age** er erreichte ein hohes Alter; **to take a** ~ **interest** in sich sehr interessieren für; **Frederick the G~** Friedrich der Große; **the** ~ **thing is ...** das Wichtigste ist ...; ~ **minds think alike** (col) große Geister denken gleich. **(b)** (col: excellent) Klasse (col), Spitze (col). **to be** ~ **at football/singing** ein großer Fußballspieler/Sänger sein; **he's a** ~ **one for criticizing others** im Kritisieren anderer ist er (ganz) groß. **2** n usu pl (~ person) Größe f.

great: ~**-aunt** n Großtante f; **G~ Britain** n Großbritannien nt; **G~ Dane** n Dänische Dogge.

greater ['greɪtə^r] adj, comp of **great** größer. **to pay** ~ **attention** besser aufpassen; **G~ London** Groß-London nt.

greatest ['greɪtɪst] adj, superl of **great** größte(r, s). **he's the** ~ (col) er ist der Größte.

great: ~**-grandchild** n Urenkel m; ~**-grandparents** npl Urgroßeltern pl.

greatly ['greɪtlɪ] adv außerordentlich, sehr; improved bedeutend; superior bei weitem.

greatness ['greɪtnɪs] n Größe f.

great: ~**-uncle** n Großonkel m; **the G~ War** n der Erste Weltkrieg.

Grecian ['griːʃən] adj griechisch.

Greece [griːs] n Griechenland nt.

greed [griːd] n Gier f (for nach +dat); (for material wealth also) Habsucht, Habgier f; (gluttony) Gefräßigkeit f. ~ **for power** Machtgier f.

greedy ['griːdɪ] adj (+er) gierig (for auf +acc, nach); (for material wealth also) habgierig; (gluttonous) gefräßig. ~ **for power** machtgierig.

Greek [griːk] **1** adj griechisch. **2** n **(a)** Grieche m, Griechin f. **(b)** (language) Griechisch nt. **it's all** ~ **to me** (col) das sind für mich böhmische Dörfer (col).

green [griːn] **1** adj (+er) (lit, fig, Pol) grün; (gullible) naiv. **to turn** ~ (lit) grün werden; (fig: person) (ganz) grün im Gesicht werden; (with envy) blaß or grün vor Neid werden. **2** n **(a)** (colour) Grün nt. **(b)** (piece of land) Rasen m, Grünfläche f; (Golf) Grün nt; (village ~) (Dorf)wiese f. **(c)** ~**s** pl (Cook) Grüngemüse nt. **(d)** (Pol) Grüne(r) mf.

green: ~**-back** n (US col) Lappen (col), Geldschein m; ~ **belt** n Grüngürtel m.

greenery ['griːnərɪ] n Grün nt; (foliage) grünes Laub.

green: ~ **fingers** npl **to have** ~ **fingers** eine Hand für Pflanzen haben; ~**fly** n Blattlaus f; ~**gage** n Reneklode f; ~**grocer** n (esp Brit) (Obst- und) Gemüsehändler m; ~**house** n Gewächshaus nt.

Greenland ['griːnlənd] n Grönland nt.

green light n **to give sb the** ~ jdm grünes Licht geben.

green pepper n (grüne) Paprikaschote.

greet [griːt] vt (welcome) begrüßen; (receive, meet) empfangen; (say hallo to) grüßen; news, decision aufnehmen. **a terrible sight** ~**ed his eyes/him** ihm bot sich ein fürchterlicher Anblick.

greeting ['griːtɪŋ] n Gruß m; (welcoming) Begrüßung f; (receiving, meeting) Empfang m. **~s card/telegram** Grußkarte f/-telegramm nt.

gregarious [grɪˈgɛərɪəs] adj animal Herden-; person gesellig.

grenade [grɪˈneɪd] n Granate f.

grew [gruː] pret of **grow**.

grey, grey (esp US) **gray** [greɪ] **1** adj (+er) (lit, fig) grau. **to go** or **turn ~** grau werden; **little ~ cells** (col) kleine graue Zellen pl (col); **~ matter** (col) graue Masse or Substanz; **a ~ area** (fig) eine Grauzone. **2** n (colour) Grau nt. **3** vi grau werden. **his ~ing hair** sein graumeliertes Haar.

grey: ~-haired adj grauhaarig; **~hound** n Windhund m.

grid [grɪd] n (grating) Gitter nt; (on barbecue) Rost m; (on map) Gitter, Netz nt; (electricity, gas network) Verteilernetz nt; (Motor-racing: starting ~) Start(platz) m; (US Ftbl) Spielfeld nt. **the (national) ~** (Elec) das Überland(leitungs)netz.

gridiron [ˈgrɪdˌaɪən] n (Cook) (Brat)rost m.

grief [griːf] n Leid nt, Kummer m; (because of loss) große Trauer, Schmerz m. **to come to ~** Schaden erleiden; (be hurt, damaged) zu Schaden kommen; (fail) scheitern.

grievance [ˈgriːvəns] n Beschwerde f; (resentment) Groll m. **~ procedure** Beschwerdeweg m; **to air one's ~s** seine Beschwerden vorbringen.

grieve [griːv] **1** vt Kummer bereiten (+dat), betrüben. **it ~s me to see that ...** es stimmt mich traurig, daß ... **2** vi trauern (at, about über +acc). **to ~ for sb/sth** um jdn/etw trauern.

grievous [ˈgriːvəs] adj **~ bodily harm** (Jur) schwere Körperverletzung.

grill [grɪl] **1** n (a) (on cooker) Grill m; (food) Grillgericht nt. **(b) =** **grille**. **2** vt (a) (Cook) grillen. **(b)** (col: interrogate) in die Zange nehmen (col).

grille [grɪl] n Gitter nt; (on window) Fenstergitter nt; (to speak through) Sprechgitter nt; (Aut) Kühlergrill m.

grilling [ˈgrɪlɪŋ] n strenges Verhör. **to give sb a ~** jdn in die Zange nehmen (col).

grim [grɪm] adj (+er) struggle erbittert, unerbittlich; (stern) face, smile grimmig; (fig) landscape, prospects, weather trostlos; news, tale, task grauenhaft; winter, times hart; determination eisern; necessity, truth bitter. **to look ~** (person) ein grimmiges Gesicht machen; (things, prospects) trostlos aussehen; **to hold on (to sth) like ~ death** sich verbissen (an etw dat) festhalten.

grimace [ˈgrɪməs] **1** n Grimasse f. **to make a ~** eine Grimasse schneiden. **2** vi Grimassen schneiden.

grime [graɪm] n (festsitzender) Schmutz; (on buildings) Ruß m.

grimy [ˈgraɪmɪ] adj (+er) verschmutzt.

grin [grɪn] **1** n see vi Lächeln nt; Grinsen nt. **2** vi (with pleasure) lächeln; (in scorn, cheekily) grinsen. **to ~ and bear it** gute Miene zum bösen Spiel machen; **to ~ at sb** jdn anlächeln/angrinsen.

grind [graɪnd] (vb: pret, ptp **ground**) **1** vt (a) corn, coffee mahlen. **to ~ one's teeth** mit den Zähnen knirschen. **(b)** gem, lens, knife schleifen. **(c)** **ground down by poverty** von Armut niedergedrückt. **2** vi (brakes, teeth, gears) knirschen. **to ~ to a halt** (lit) quietschend zum Stehen kommen; (fig) stocken; (production etc) zum Erliegen kommen; (negotiations) sich festfahren. **3** n (col) **the daily ~** der tägliche Trott; **it's a bit of a ~** das ist ganz schön mühsam (col).

grinder [ˈgraɪndə^r] n (meat~) Fleischwolf m; (coffee~) Kaffeemühle f; (for sharpening) Schleifmaschine f.

grinding [ˈgraɪndɪŋ] adj **~ poverty** drückende Armut.

grindstone [ˈgraɪndstəʊn] n: **to keep one's/sb's nose to the ~** hart arbeiten/jdn hart arbeiten lassen.

grip [grɪp] **1** n (a) Griff m; (on rope also, on road) Halt m. **to get a ~ on oneself** (col) sich zu-

sammenreißen (col); **to have a good ~ of a subject** ein Thema im Griff haben; **to release one's ~ loslassen** (on sth etw); **to lose one's ~** (lit) den Halt verlieren; (fig) nachlassen; **I must be losing my ~** mit mir geht's bergab; **the country is in the ~ of winter** der Winter herrscht im Land; **to get** or **come to ~s with** sth etw in den Griff bekommen; **to get** or **come to ~s with sb** jdm auf den Leib rücken (col). **(b)** (handle) Griff m. **(c)** (travelling-bag) Reisetasche f.

2 vt packen; hand also, (fig: fear etc also) ergreifen; (film, story etc also) fesseln. **the car/tyre ~s the road** der Wagen liegt gut auf der Straße/der Reifen greift gut.

gripe [graɪp] **1** vi (col: grumble) meckern (col). **to ~ at sb** jdn anmotzen (col). **2** n (a) **the ~s pl** Darmkrämpfe pl. **(b)** (col: complaint) Meckerei f (col).

gripping [ˈgrɪpɪŋ] adj story spannend, fesselnd.

grisly [ˈgrɪzlɪ] adj (+er) grausig, gräßlich.

grist [grɪst] n **it's all ~ to his mill** das kann er alles verwerten.

gristle [ˈgrɪsl] n Knorpel m.

grit [grɪt] **1** n (a) (dust, in eye) Staub m; (gravel) Splitt m; (for roads) Streusand m. **(b)** (courage) Mut m. **2** vt (a) road streuen. **(b) to ~ one's teeth** die Zähne zusammenbeißen.

grizzly [ˈgrɪzlɪ] n (also **~ bear**) Grisly(bär), Grizzly(bär) m.

groan [grəʊn] **1** n Stöhnen nt no pl; (of pain also, of planks etc) Ächzen nt no pl. **to let out** or **give a ~** (auf)stöhnen. **2** vi stöhnen (with vor +dat); (with pain also, beneath weight) ächzen (with vor +dat).

grocer [ˈgrəʊsə^r] n Lebensmittelhändler, Kaufmann m.

grocery [ˈgrəʊsərɪ] n (a) Lebensmittelgeschäft nt. **(b) groceries** pl (goods) Lebensmittel pl.

grog [grɒg] n Grog m.

groggy [ˈgrɒgɪ] adj (+er) (col) groggy inv (col).

groin [grɔɪn] n (Anat) Leiste f.

groom [gruːm] **1** n (a) (in stables) Reitknecht m. **(b)** (bride~) Bräutigam m. **2** vt (a) horse striegeln. **well ~ed** (person) gepflegt. **(b) to ~ sb for an office** jdn auf or für ein Amt vorbereiten.

groove [gruːv] n Rille f; (in face) Furche f.

grope [grəʊp] **1** vi (also **~ around** or **about**) (her-um)tasten (for nach); (for words) suchen (for nach). **2** vt (col) girl befummeln (col). **to ~ one's way in/out** sich hinein-/hinaustasten.

gross[1] [grəʊs] n no pl Gros nt.

gross[2] **1** adj (+er) (a) (fat) fett, feist. **(b)** (coarse, vulgar) derb. **(c)** (extreme, flagrant) grob; impertinence ungeheuerlich. **(d)** (total) brutto; income, weight Brutto-. **he earns £250 ~** er verdient £250 brutto; **~ national product** Bruttosozialprodukt nt. **2** vt brutto verdienen.

grotesque [grəʊˈtesk] adj grotesk.

grotto [ˈgrɒtəʊ] n, pl **-(e)s** Grotte f.

grotty [ˈgrɒtɪ] adj (+er) (col) mies (col).

grouch [graʊtʃ] (col) **1** n (a) (complaint) Beschwerde f. **she's always got a ~** sie hat immer was zu meckern (col). **(b)** (person) Meckerer m (col). **2** vi meckern (col).

grouchy [ˈgraʊtʃɪ] adj (+er) griesgrämig.

ground[1] [graʊnd] **1** n (a) (soil, terrain, fig) Boden m. **snow on high ~** Schnee in höheren Lagen; **hilly ~** hügeliges Gelände; **there is common ~ between us** uns verbindet einiges; **to be on dangerous ~** (fig) sich auf gefährlichem Boden bewegen; **to meet sb on his own ~** zu jdm kommen; **to cut the ~ from under sb's feet** jdm den Boden unter den Füßen wegziehen; **to gain/lose ~** Boden gewinnen/verlieren; (disease, rumour) um sich greifen/im Schwinden begriffen sein; **to break new ~** (fig) etwas völlig Neuartiges darstellen; (person) Neuland betreten; **to go over the ~** (fig) alles durchgehen; **to cover a lot of ~** (lit) eine weite Strecke zurücklegen; (fig) eine Menge Dinge

behandeln; **to hold** *or* **stand one's** ~ *(lit)* nicht von der Stelle weichen; *(fig)* seinen Mann stehen, sich nicht unterkriegen lassen; **to shift one's** ~ *(fig)* seine Haltung ändern; **above/below** ~ **über/ unter der Erde;** *(Min)* über/unter Tage; **to fall to the** ~ zu Boden fallen; **to burn sth to the** ~ etw niederbrennen; **it suits me down to the** ~ das paßt mir ausgezeichnet; **to get off the** ~ *(plane etc)* abheben; *(plans, project etc)* ins Rollen kommen; **to get sth off the** ~ etw ins Rollen bringen; **to go to** ~ *(fox)* im Bau verschwinden; *(person)* untertauchen *(col)*; **to run sb/sth to** ~ jdn/etw ausfindig machen; **to run sb/oneself into the** ~ *(col)* jdn/sich selbst fertigmachen *(col)*; **to run a car into the** ~ ein Auto schrottreif fahren.
(b) *(pitch)* Feld *nt*, Platz *m*; *(parade* ~, *drill*~*)* Platz *m*.
(c) ~**s** *pl (premises, land)* Gelände *nt*; *(gardens)* Anlagen *pl*.
(d) ~**s** *pl (sediment)* Satz *m*.
(e) *(US Elec)* Erde *f*.
(f) *(reason)* Grund *m*. **to have** ~**s for sth** Grund zu etw haben; **to be** ~**(s) for sth** Grund für *or* zu etw sein; ~**s for divorce** Scheidungsgrund *m*; **on the** ~**(s) of** aufgrund (+*gen*), auf Grund von; **on the** ~**s that** auf Grund der Tatsache, daß; **on health** ~**s** aus gesundheitlichen Gründen.
2 *vt* **(a)** **ship** auf Grund setzen. **to be** ~**ed** aufgelaufen sein. **(b)** **plane** *(for mechanical reasons)* aus dem Verkehr ziehen; **pilot** sperren. **to be** ~**ed by bad weather** wegen schlechten Wetters nicht starten können. **(c)** *(US Elec)* erden. **(d)** *(base)* **to be** ~**ed on sth** sich auf etw *(acc)* gründen.

ground² **1** *pret, ptp of* **grind. 2** *adj* **coffee** gemahlen. ~ **beef** *(US)* Hackfleisch *m*; ~ **glass** geschliffenes Glas; *(particles)* Glaspulver *nt*; ~ **rice** Reismehl *nt*.

ground: ~ **control** *n (Aviat)* Bodenkontrolle *f*; ~ **crew** *n* Bodenpersonal *nt*; ~ **floor** *n* Erdgeschoß *nt*; ~ **frost** *n* Bodenfrost *m*.

grounding ['graʊndɪŋ] *n (basic knowledge)* Grundwissen *nt*. **to give sb a** ~ **in English** jdm die Grundlagen *pl* des Englischen beibringen.

ground: ~**less** *adj* grundlos, unbegründet; ~ **level** *n* Boden *m*; **below** ~ **level** unter dem Boden; **at** ~ **level** live im Erdgeschoß; ~**nut** *n* Erdnuß *f*; ~ **plan** *n* Grundriß *m*; ~**sheet** *n* Zeltboden(plane *f*) *m*.

groundsman ['graʊndzmən] *n, pl* -**men** *(esp Brit)* Platzwart *m*.

ground: ~ **staff** *n* Bodenpersonal *nt*; ~**-to-air missile** *n* Boden-Luft-Rakete *f*; ~**work** *n* Vorarbeit *f*.

group [gru:p] **1** *n* Gruppe *f*; *(Comm also)* Konzern *m*; *(theatre* ~ *also)* Ensemble *nt*. **2** *attr* Gruppen-; **discussion, activities** in der Gruppe. **3** *vt* gruppieren. **to** ~ **together** *(in one* ~*)* zusammentun; *(in several* ~*s)* in Gruppen einteilen; **the books were** ~**ed according to subject** die Bücher standen nach Sachgruppen geordnet.

group: ~ **captain** *n (Aviat)* Oberst *m*; ~ **therapy** *n* Gruppentherapie *f*.

grouse¹ [graʊs] *n, pl* - Rauhfußhuhn *nt*; *(red* ~*)* Schottisches Moorhuhn *nt*.

grouse² *(col)* **1** *n (complaint)* Klage *f*. **to have a good** ~ herummeckern *(col)*. **2** *vi* meckern *(col) (about* über +*acc)*.

grouting ['graʊtɪŋ] *n* Fugenkitt *m*.

grove [grəʊv] *n* Hain *m*, Wäldchen *nt*.

grovel ['grɒvl] *vi* kriechen *(to sb* vor jdm*)*.

grow [grəʊ] *pret* **grew**, *ptp* **grown 1** *vt* **(a)** **plants** ziehen; *(commercially)* **potatoes, coffee etc** anbauen; *(cultivate)* **flowers** züchten. **(b) to** ~ **one's beard/hair** sich *(dat)* einen Bart/die Haare wachsen lassen. **2** *vi* **(a)** wachsen; *(hair also)* länger werden; *(in numbers)* zunehmen; *(in size also)* sich vergrößern; *(fig: become more mature)* sich

weiterentwickeln. **to** ~ **in stature/wisdom** an Ansehen/Weisheit zunehmen; **to** ~ **in popularity** immer beliebter werden; **it'll** ~ **on you** du wirst schon noch Geschmack daran finden. **(b)** *(become)* werden. **to** ~ **to hate/love sb** jdn hassen/lieben lernen; **to** ~ **to enjoy sth** langsam Gefallen an etw *(dat)* finden.

♦ **grow apart** *vi (fig)* sich auseinanderentwickeln.

♦ **grow away** *vi (fig)* **to** ~ ~ **from sb** sich jdm entfremden.

♦ **grow into** *vi +prep obj* **(a)** **clothes, job** hineinwachsen in (+*acc*). **(b)** *(become)* sich entwickeln zu, werden zu. **to** ~ ~ **a man/woman** zum Mann/ zur Frau heranwachsen.

♦ **grow out of** *vi +prep obj* **(a)** **clothes** herauswachsen aus; **habit** ablegen. **(b)** *(arise from)* entstehen aus.

♦ **grow up** *vi (spend childhood)* aufwachsen; *(become adult)* erwachsen werden; *(fig) (custom, hatred)* aufkommen; *(city)* entstehen. **what are you going to do when you** ~ ~? was willst du mal werden, wenn du groß bist?; ~ ~! werde endlich erwachsen!

grower ['grəʊə'] *n (of fruit, vegetables)* Anbauer *m*; *(of flowers)* Züchter *m*; *(of tobacco, coffee)* Pflanzer *m*.

growing ['grəʊɪŋ] *adj (lit, fig)* wachsend; **child** heranwachsend. ~ **pains** *(Med)* Wachstumsschmerzen *pl*; *(fig)* Kinderkrankheiten *pl*.

growl [graʊl] **1** *n* Knurren *nt no pl*; *(of bear)* Brummen *nt no pl*. **2** *vi* knurren; *(bear)* böse brummen. **to** ~ **at sb** jdn anknurren/ anbrummen.

grown [grəʊn] **1** *ptp of* **grow. 2** *adj* erwachsen. **fully** ~ ausgewachsen.

grown-up [grəʊn'ʌp] **1** *adj* erwachsen; **clothes, shoes** Erwachsenen-. **2** *n* Erwachsene(r) *mf*.

growth [grəʊθ] *n* **(a)** Wachstum *nt*; *(of person also)* Entwicklung *f*; *(increase in quantity, fig: of love, interest etc)* Anwachsen *nt*; *(increase in size also)* Vergrößerung *f*; *(of capital etc)* Zuwachs *m*. ~ **industry** Wachstumsindustrie *f*. **(b) with a two days'** ~ **on his face** mit zwei Tage alten Bartstoppeln. **(c)** *(Med)* Wucherung *f*.

groyne [grɔɪn] *n* Buhne *f*.

grub [grʌb] **1** *n* **(a)** *(larva)* Larve *f*. **(b)** *(col: food)* Fressalien *pl (hum, col)*. ~**('s) up!** antreten zum Essenfassen *(col)*. **2** *vi (also* ~ **about** *or* **around)** wühlen *(in in* +*dat)*.

grubby ['grʌbɪ] *adj (+er)* schmuddelig *(col)*; **hands** dreckig *(col)*.

grudge [grʌdʒ] **1** *n* Groll *m (against* gegen*)*. **to bear sb a** ~, **to have a** ~ **against sb** jdm böse sein; **I bear him no** ~ ich nehme ihm das nicht übel; **to bear** ~**s** nachtragend sein. **2** *vt* **to** ~ **sb sth** jdm etw nicht gönnen; **I don't** ~ **you your success/ these pleasures** ich gönne Ihnen Ihren Erfolg/ das Vergnügen; **to** ~ **doing sth** etw mit Widerwillen tun.

grudging ['grʌdʒɪŋ] *adj* **person, attitude** unwirsch; **contribution, gift** widerwillig gegeben; **admiration, praise, support** widerwillig.

gruel [grʊəl] *n* Schleimsuppe *f*.

gruelling, *(US)* **grueling** ['grʊəlɪŋ] *adj* **task, day etc** aufreibend; **climb, race** äußerst strapaziös.

gruesome ['gru:səm] *adj* grausig, schaurig.

gruff [grʌf] *adj (+er)* barsch, schroff.

grumble ['grʌmbl] **1** *n (complaint)* Murren *nt no pl*. **2** *vi* murren *(about, over* über +*acc)*; *(thunder, gunfire)* grollen.

grumbler ['grʌmblə'] *n* Nörgler(in *f*) *m*.

grumpy ['grʌmpɪ] *adj (+er)* brummig, grantig.

grunt [grʌnt] **1** *n* Grunzen *nt no pl*; *(of pain, in exertion)* Ächzen *nt no pl*. **2** *vi* grunzen; *(with pain, exertion)* ächzen. **3** *vt* reply brummen, knurren.

G-string ['dʒi:strɪŋ] *n (clothing)* Minislip *m*.

guarantee [ˌgærən'ti:] **1** *n* Garantie *f (of für)*. **to**

have a 6-month ~ 6 Monate Garantie haben; while it is under ~ solange noch Garantie darauf ist; that's no ~ that ... das heißt noch lange nicht, daß ...; I give you my ~ das garantiere ich Ihnen. **2** *vt* garantieren. **to be ~d for three months** drei Monate Garantie haben; **I ~ to come tomorrow** ich komme garantiert morgen; **that's a ~d success** das wird garantiert ein Erfolg.

guarantor [ˌgærən'tɔːʳ] *n* Garant *m*; *(Jur)* Bürge *m*.

guard [gaːd] **1** *n* **(a)** *(Mil)* Wache *f*; *(single soldier also)* Wachtposten *m*; *(no pl: squad also)* Wachmannschaft *f*; *(security~)* Sicherheitsbeamte(r) *m*, Sicherheitsbeamtin *f*; *(at factory gates, in park etc)* Wächter(in *f*) *m*; *(esp US: prison ~)* Gefängniswärter(in *f*) *m*; *(Brit Rail)* Schaffner(in *f*) *m*. **the G~s** *(Brit)* das Garderegiment; **~ of honour** *(Brit)* or **honor** *(US)* Ehrenwache *f*; **to change ~** Wachablösung machen; **under ~** unter Bewachung; **to be under ~** bewacht werden; **to keep sb/sth under ~** jdn/etw bewachen; **to be on ~**, **to stand** or **keep ~** Wache halten; **to put a ~ on sb/sth** jdn/etw bewachen lassen. **(b)** *(Boxing, Fencing)* Deckung *f*. **to take ~ in** Verteidigungsstellung gehen; **to drop** or **lower one's ~** *(col)* seine Deckung vernachlässigen; *(fig)* seine Reserve aufgeben; **to catch sb off (his/her) ~** jdn überrumpeln; **to be on one's ~ (against sth)** *(fig)* (vor etw *dat*) auf der Hut sein; **to put sb on his/her ~ (against sth)** jdn (vor etw *dat*) warnen. **(c)** *(safety device, for protection)* Schutz *m (against gegen)*; *(on machinery also)* Schutzvorrichtung *f*; *(fire ~)* Schutzgitter *nt*. **2** *vt prisoner, place, valuables* bewachen; *treasure also, secret* hüten; *luggage* aufpassen auf *(+acc)*; *(protect) person, place* schützen *(from, against* vor *+dat)*.

♦ **guard against** *vi* +*prep obj (take care to avoid) suspicion* sich in acht nehmen vor *(+dat)*; *hasty reaction, bad habit* sich hüten vor *(+dat)*; *illness, misunderstandings* vorbeugen *(+dat)*; *accidents* verhüten. **you must ~ ~ catching cold** Sie müssen aufpassen, daß Sie sich nicht erkälten; **in order to ~ ~ this** um dem vorzubeugen.

guard: **~ dog** *n* Wachhund *m*; **~ duty** *n* Wachdienst *m*; **to be on ~ duty** Wache haben.

guarded [ˈgaːdɪd] *adj reply* zurückhaltend.

guardhouse [ˈgaːdhaus] *n (Mil)* Wachstube *f*; *(for prisoners)* Bunker *m*.

guardian [ˈgaːdɪən] *n* Hüter, Wächter *m*; *(Jur)* Vormund *m*.

guard-rail [ˈgaːdreɪl] *n* Schutzgeländer *nt*.

guardsman [ˈgaːdzmən] *n*, *pl* **-men** [-mən] Wachtposten *m*; *(member of guards regiment)* Gardist *m*; *(US: in National Guard)* Nationalgardist *m*.

guard's van [ˈgaːdzvæn] *n (Brit Rail)* Schaffnerabteil *nt*, Dienstwagen *m*.

guer(r)illa [gə'rɪlə] **1** *n* Guerillakämpfer(in *f*) *m*. **2** *attr* Guerilla-.

guess [ges] **1** *n* Vermutung, Annahme *f*; *(estimate)* Schätzung *f*. **to have a ~ (at sth)** (etw) raten; *(estimate)* (etw) schätzen; **it was just a ~** ich habe nur geraten; **it was just a lucky ~** das war ein Zufallstreffer *m*; **I'll give you three ~es** dreimal darfst du raten; **at a rough ~** grob geschätzt; **my ~ is that ...** ich schätze or vermute, daß ...; **your ~ is as good as mine!** *(col)* da kann ich auch nur raten!; **it's anybody's ~** *(col)* das wissen die Götter *(col)*. **2** *vi* **(a)** raten. **to keep sb ~ing** jdn im ungewissen lassen; **he's only ~ing** das ist eine reine Vermutung von ihm; **you'll never ~!** das wirst du nie erraten; **to ~ at sth** etw raten. **(b)** *(esp US)* **I ~ not** wohl nicht; **he's right, I ~** er hat wohl recht; **is he coming? — I ~ so** kommt er? — ich glaube schon. **3** *vt* raten; *(correctly)* erraten; *(estimate) weight* schätzen. **I ~ed as much** das habe ich mir

schon gedacht; **~ what!** *(col)* stell dir vor! *(col)*.

guesswork [ˈgeswɜːk] *n* (reine) Vermutung.

guest [gest] *n* Gast *m*. **~ of honour** *(Brit)* or **honor** *(US)* Ehrengast *m*; **be my ~** *(col)* nur zu! *(col)*.

guest *in cpds* Gast-; **~appearance** *n* Gastauftritt *m*; **~-house** *n* Pension *f*; **~ list** *n* Gästeliste *f*; **~-room** *n* Gästezimmer *nt*.

guffaw [gʌ'fɔː] **1** *n* schallendes Lachen *no pl*. **2** *vi* schallend (los)lachen.

guidance [ˈgaɪdəns] *n (direction)* Führung, Leitung *f*; *(counselling)* Beratung *f (on* über +*acc)*; *(from superior, parents, teacher etc)* Anleitung *f*. **for your ~** zu Ihrer Orientierung; **~ system** *(on rocket)* Steuerungssystem *nt*.

guide [gaɪd] **1** *n* **(a)** *(person)* Führer(in *f*) *m*; *(fig: indication, pointer)* Anhaltspunkt *m (to* für*)*; *(model)* Leitbild *nt*. **(b)** *(Tech)* Leitvorrichtung *f*. **(c)** *(Brit: girl ~)* Pfadfinderin *f*. **(d)** *(instructions)* Anleitung *f*; *(manual)* Handbuch *nt (to* gen*)*; *(travel ~)* (Reise)führer *m*. **2** *vt people, blind man etc* führen; *discussion also* leiten; *missile, sb's behaviour* lenken. **to ~ a plane in** ein Flugzeug einweisen; **to be ~d by sb/sth** *(person)* sich von jdm/etw leiten lassen.

guide-book [ˈgaɪdbʊk] *n* Reiseführer *m*.

guided missile [ˌgaɪdɪdˈmɪsaɪl] *n* ferngelenktes Geschoß.

guide-dog [ˈgaɪddɒg] *n* Blindenhund *m*.

guided tour [ˌgaɪdɪd'tuəʳ] *n* Führung *f (of* durch*)*.

guidelines [ˈgaɪdlaɪnz] *npl n* Richtlinien *pl*.

guiding [ˈgaɪdɪŋ]: **~ hand** *n* leitende Hand; **~ principle** *n* Leitmotiv *nt*.

guild [gɪld] *n (Hist)* Zunft, Gilde *f*; *(association)* Verein *m*.

guildhall [ˈgɪldhɔːl] *n (townhall)* Rathaus *nt*.

guile [gaɪl] *n* Tücke, (Arg)list *f*.

guillotine [ˌgɪlə'tiːn] *n* Guillotine *f*; *(for paper)* (Papier)schneidemaschine *f*.

guilt [gɪlt] *n* Schuld *f (for, of* an +*dat)*. **to feel ~ about sth** sich wegen etw schuldig fühlen; **~ complex** Schuldkomplex *m*.

guiltless [ˈgɪltlɪs] *adj* schuldlos *(of* an +*dat)*.

guilty [ˈgɪltɪ] *adj* (+*er*) schuldig *(of* gen*)*; *look, voice* schuldbewußt; *conscience, thought* schlecht. **the ~ person/party** der/die Schuldige/ die schuldige Partei; **verdict of ~** Schuldspruch *m*; **to find sb ~/not ~ (of a crime)** jdn (eines Verbrechens) für schuldig/nicht schuldig befinden; **we're all ~ of neglecting the problem** uns alle trifft Schuld, daß das Problem vernachlässigt wurde; **I've been ~ of that myself** den Fehler habe ich auch schon begangen; **I feel very ~ (about ...)** ich habe ein sehr schlechtes Gewissen(, daß ...).

guinea [ˈgɪnɪ] *n (Brit old)* Guinee *f (21 Shillings)*.

guinea-pig [ˈgɪnɪpɪg] *n* Meerschweinchen *nt*; *(fig)* Versuchskaninchen *nt*.

guise [gaɪz] *n* **in the ~ of a clown/swan** als Clown verkleidet/in Gestalt eines Schwans.

guitar [gɪ'taːʳ] *n* Gitarre *f*.

guitarist [gɪ'taːrɪst] *n* Gitarrist(in *f*) *m*.

gulch [gʌltʃ] *n (US)* Schlucht *f*.

gulf [gʌlf] *n (bay)* Golf, Meerbusen *m*; *(lit, fig: chasm)* tiefe Kluft. **G~ stream** Golfstrom *m*; **the (Persian) G~** der Persische Golf.

gull [gʌl] *n (sea~)* Möwe *f*.

gullet [ˈgʌlɪt] *n* Speiseröhre, Kehle *f*.

gullible [ˈgʌlɪbl] *adj* leichtgläubig.

gully [ˈgʌlɪ] *n (ravine)* Schlucht *f*; *(narrow channel)* Rinne *f*.

gulp [gʌlp] **1** *n* Schluck *m*. **at a/one ~** auf einen Schluck. **2** *vt (also ~ down) drink* runterstürzen; *food* runterschlingen; *medicine* hinunterschlucken. **what?, he ~ed** was?, preßte er hervor.

gum¹ [gʌm] *n (Anat)* Zahnfleisch *nt no pl*.

gum² [gʌm] *n (Bot)* Gummi *nt*; *(glue)* Klebstoff *m*; *(chewing ~)* Kaugummi *m*; *(sweet)* Weingummi *m.* **2** *vt (stick together)* kleben; *(spread* ~ *on)* gummieren.

♦ **gum up** *vt sep* verkleben. **to** ~ ~ **the works** *(fig col)* die Sache vermasseln *(col).*

gum: ~**boil** *n* Zahnfleischabszeß *m*; ~**boot** *n* Gummistiefel *m.*

gumption ['gʌmpʃən] *n (col)* Grips *m (col).* **to have the** ~ **to do sth** geistesgegenwärtig genug sein, etw zu tun.

gum: ~-**shield** *n* Zahnschutz *m*; ~-**tree** *n* **to be up a** ~-**tree** *(Brit col)* aufgeschmissen sein *(col).*

gun [gʌn] **1** *n* **(a)** *(cannon etc)* Kanone *f*, Geschütz *nt*; *(rifle)* Gewehr *nt*; *(pistol etc)* Pistole *f.* **to carry a** ~ (mit einer Schußwaffe) bewaffnet sein; **to draw a** ~ **on sb** jdn mit einer Schußwaffe bedrohen; **big** ~ *(fig col)* hohes Tier *(col) (in* +*dat)*; **to stick to one's** ~**s** nicht nachgeben; **to jump the** ~ *(Sport)* Frühstart machen; *(fig)* voreilig sein *or* handeln. **(b)** *(spray~)* Pistole *f.* **grease** ~ Fettpresse *f.* **2** *vi (col)* **to be** ~**ning for sb** *(fig)* jdn auf dem Kieker haben *(col); for opponent* jdn auf die Abschußliste gesetzt haben.

♦ **gun down** *vt sep* niederschießen.

gun: ~**boat** *n* Kanonenboot *nt*; ~ **carriage** *n* Lafette *f*; ~ **crew** *n* Geschützbedienung *f*; ~ **dog** *n* Jagdhund *m*; ~-**fight** *n* Schießerei *f*; *(Mil)* Feuergefecht *nt*; ~**fire** *n* Schießerei *f*, Schüsse *pl*; *(Mil)* Geschützfeuer *nt.*

gunge [gʌndʒ] *n (Brit col)* klebriges Zeug *(col).*

gunman ['gʌnmən] *n, pl* -**men** Bewaffnete(r) *m.* **they saw the** ~ sie haben den Schützen gesehen.

gunner ['gʌnə'] *n (Mil)* Artillerist *m*; *(title)* Kanonier *m*; *(Naut)* Geschützführer *m*; *(in plane)* Bordschütze *m.*

gun: ~**point** *n* **to hold sb at** ~ **point** jdn mit einer Pistole/einem Gewehr bedrohen; **to force sb to do sth at** ~ **point** jdn mit Waffengewalt zwingen, etw zu tun; **to surrender at** ~ **point** sich unter Waffengewalt ergeben; ~ **powder** *n* Schießpulver *nt*; ~**running** *n* Waffenschmuggel *m*; ~**shot** *n* Schuß *m*; *(range)* Schußweite *f*; ~**shot wound** Schußwunde *f*; ~**smith** *n* Büchsenmacher *m*; ~**wale** ['gʌnl] *n* Schandeck *nt.*

gurgle ['gɜːgl] **1** *n (of liquid)* Gluckern *nt no pl.* **2** *vi (liquid)* gluckern; *(person)* glucksen *(with vor* +*dat).*

guru ['guruː] *n* Guru *m.*

gush [gʌʃ] **1** *n (of liquid)* Strahl, Schwall *m*; *(of words)* Schwall *m*; *(of emotion)* Ausbruch *m.* **2** *vi* **(a)** *(also* ~**out)** *(water)* herausprudeln; *(smoke, blood)* hervorquellen; *(flames)* herausschlagen.

(b) *(col: talk)* schwärmen *(col) (about, over von).*

gushing ['gʌʃɪŋ] *adj (fig)* überschwenglich.

gusset ['gʌsɪt] *n (in garment)* Keil, Zwickel *m.*

gust [gʌst] *n (of wind, day)* Böe *f.*

gusto ['gʌstəʊ] *n* Begeisterung *f.* **to do sth with** ~ etw mit Genuß tun.

gusty ['gʌstɪ] *adj (+er)* wind, day böig, stürmisch.

gut [gʌt] **1** *n* **(a)** *(Anat)* Darm *m*; *(stomach, paunch)* Bauch *m*; *(for racket, violin)* Darmsaiten *pl.* **(b)** *usu pl (col: stomach)* Eingeweide *nt usu pl.* **to hate sb's** ~**s** *(col)* jdn auf den Tod nicht ausstehen können *(col)*; ~ **reaction** rein gefühlsmäßige Reaktion. **(c)** *(col: courage)* ~**s** *pl* Mut, Mumm *m (col).* **2** *vt* **(a)** *animal* ausnehmen. **(b) it was completely** ~**ted by the fire** es war völlig ausgebrannt.

gutter ['gʌtə'] **1** *n (on roof)* Dachrinne *f*; *(in street, fig)* Gosse *f.* **2** *vi (candle, flame)* flackern.

gutter: ~-**press** *n* Boulevardpresse *f*; ~**snipe** *n* Gassenkind *nt.*

guttural ['gʌtərəl] *adj* guttural, kehlig.

guy[1] [gaɪ] *n (col: man)* Typ *(col)*, Kerl *(col) m.* **hey you** ~**s** he Leute *(col).*

guy[2] *n (also* ~-**rope)** *(for tent)* Zeltschnur *f.*

guzzle ['gʌzl] *vti (eat)* futtern *(col)*; *(drink)* schlürfen.

gym [dʒɪm] *n (gymnasium)* Turnhalle *f*; *(gymnastics)* Turnen *nt.*

gymkhana [dʒɪm'kɑːnə] *n* Reiterfest *nt.*

gymnasium [dʒɪm'neɪzɪəm] *n* Turnhalle *f.*

gymnast ['dʒɪmnæst] *n* Turner(in *f*) *m.*

gymnastics [dʒɪm'næstɪks] *n* **(a)** *sing (discipline)* Gymnastik *f no pl*; *(with apparatus)* Turnen *nt no pl.* **(b)** *pl (exercises)* Übungen *pl.*

gym: ~ **shoe** *n (Brit)* Turnschuh *m*; ~**slip** *n (Brit)* Schulträgerrock *m.*

gynaecological, *(US)* **gynecological** [ˌgaɪnɪkə-'lɒdʒɪkəl] *adj* gynäkologisch. ~ **illness** Frauenleiden *nt.*

gynaecologist, *(US)* **gynecologist** [ˌgaɪnɪ-'kɒlədʒɪst] *n* Gynäkologe *m*, Gynäkologin *f*, Frauenarzt *m*/-ärztin *f.*

gynaecology, *(US)* **gynecology** [ˌgaɪnɪ'kɒlədʒɪ] *n* Gynäkologie, Frauenheilkunde *f.*

gypsy ['dʒɪpsɪ] *n* Zigeuner(in *f*) *m.*

gyrate [ˌdʒaɪə'reɪt] *vi (rotate)* sich drehen; *(dancer)* sich drehen und winden.

gyrocompass ['dʒaɪərəʊˌkʌmpəs] *n* Kreisel-Magnetkompaß *m.*

gyroscope ['dʒaɪərəˌskəʊp] *n* Gyroskop *nt.*

H

H, h [eɪtʃ] *n* H, h *nt*.

habeas corpus ['heɪbɪəs'kɔːpəs] *n (Jur)* to issue a writ of ~ einen Vorführungsbefehl erteilen.

haberdashery [ˌhæbə'dæʃərɪ] *n (Brit)* Kurzwaren *pl; (US)* Herrenartikel *pl.*

habit ['hæbɪt] *n* **(a)** Gewohnheit *f.* to be in the ~ of doing sth die Angewohnheit haben, etw zu tun; it became a ~ es wurde zur Gewohnheit; out of sheer ~ aus reiner Gewohnheit; I don't make a ~ of asking strangers in (für) gewöhnlich bitte ich Fremde nicht herein; don't make a ~ of it lassen Sie (sich *dat*) das nicht zur Gewohnheit werden; to get into/to get sb into the ~ of doing sth sich/jdm angewöhnen, etw zu tun; to get into bad ~s schlechte Gewohnheiten annehmen; to get out of/to get sb out of the ~ of doing sth sich/jdm abgewöhnen, etw zu tun. **(b)** *(costume)* Gewand *nt; (monk's also)* Habit *nt or m.* **(riding)** ~ Reitkleid *nt.*

habitable ['hæbɪtəbl] *adj* bewohnbar.

habitat ['hæbɪtæt] *n* Heimat *f; (of animals also)* Lebensraum *m; (of plants also)* Standort *m.*

habitation [ˌhæbɪ'teɪʃən] *n* unfit for human ~ für Wohnzwecke nicht geeignet.

habitual [hə'bɪtjʊəl] *adj* gewohnt; *drinker, gambler, liar* gewohnheitsmäßig.

habitually [hə'bɪtjʊəlɪ] *adv* ständig.

habitué [hə'bɪtjʊeɪ] *n* regelmäßiger Besucher, regelmäßige Besucherin.

hack¹ [hæk] **1** *n* **(a)** *(cut)* Kerbe *f; (action)* Hieb *m; (kick)* Tritt *m.* **(b)** *(cough)* trockener Husten. **2** *vt* hacken. to hack sb/sth to pieces jdn zerstückeln/ etw (in Stücke) hacken; to ~ one's way through (sth) sich *(dat)* einen Weg (durch) etw schlagen.
♦ **hack down** *vt sep bushes etc* umhauen; *people also* niedermetzeln.

hack² *n* **(a)** *(hired horse)* Mietpferd *nt; (worn-out horse)* Klepper *m.* **(b)** *(pej: writer)* Schundlite-rat(in *f) m; (journalist also)* Schmierfink *m.*

hacker ['hækə'] *n (Comp)* Hacker *m.*

hacking [hækɪŋ] *adj* **(a)** ~ cough trockener Husten. **(b)** ~ jacket Sportsakko *m or nt; (for riding)* Reitjacke *f.*

hackle [hækl] *n* to get sb's ~s up jdn auf die Palme bringen *(col);* to have one's ~s up auf (hundert)achtzig sein *(col).*

hackney carriage ['hæknɪ,kærɪdʒ] *n (also form: taxi)* Droschke *f.*

hackneyed ['hæknɪd] *adj* abgedroschen.

hacksaw ['hæksɔː] *n* Metallsäge *f.*

had [hæd] *pret, ptp of* have.

haddock ['hædək] *n* Schellfisch *m.*

hadn't ['hædnt] = had not.

haematology, *(US)* **hematology** [ˌhiːmə'tɒlədʒɪ] *n* Hämatologie *f.*

haemoglobin, *(US)* **hemoglobin** [ˌhiːməʊ-'ɡləʊbɪn] *n* Hämoglobin *nt*, roter Blutfarbstoff.

haemophilia, *(US)* **hemophilia** [ˌhiːməʊ'fɪlɪə] *n* Bluterkrankheit *f.*

haemorrhage, *(US)* **hemorrhage** ['heməridʒ] **1** *n* Blutung *f.* **2** *vi* bluten.

haemorrhoids, *(US)* **hemorrhoids** ['hemərɔɪdz] *npl* Hämorrhoiden *pl.*

hag [hæg] *n* Hexe *f.*

haggard ['hæɡəd] *adj* ausgezehrt; *(from tiredness)* abgespannt; *(from worry)* abgehärmt.

haggis ['hæɡɪs] *n schottisches Gericht aus gehackten Schafsinnereien und Haferschrot.*

haggle ['hæɡl] *vi (bargain)* feilschen *(about or over* um); *(argue also)* sich streiten *(over* wegen).

Hague [heɪɡ] *n* the ~ Den Haag *nt.*

hail¹ [heɪl] **1** *n (lit, fig)* Hagel *m.* **2** *vi* hageln.
♦ **hail down** *vi (stones etc)* niederhageln *(on sb/sth* auf jdn/etw).

hail² **1** *vt* **(a)** to ~ sb/sth as sth jdn/etw als etw feiern. **(b)** *(call)* zurufen (+*dat*); *ship* anrufen; *taxi* rufen. **within** ~**ing distance** in Rufweite. **2** *vi* a ship ~ing from London ein Schiff *nt* mit (dem) Heimathafen London; **he** ~**s from Ireland** er stammt aus Irland. **3** *interj* ~ Caesar heil dir Cäsar; the H~ Mary das Ave Maria.

hail-fellow-well-met ['heɪlfeləʊ,wel'met] *adj* plumpvertraulich.

hail: ~**stone** *n* Hagelkorn *nt;* ~**storm** *n* Ha-gel(schlag) *m.*

hair [heə'] **1** *n* Haar *nt; (collective: on head)* Haare *pl,* Haar *nt.* **a fine head of** ~ schönes volles Haar; **to do one's** ~ sich frisieren, sich *(dat)* die Haare (zurecht)machen *(col);* **to have one's** ~ **cut/done** sich *(dat)* die Haare schneiden/frisieren lassen; **her** ~ **is always perfect** sie ist immer sehr gut frisiert; **to let one's** ~ **down** *(fig)* aus sich *(dat)* herausgehen; **keep your** ~ **on!** *(col)* ruhig Blut!; **that film really made my** ~ **stand on end** bei dem Film lief es mir eiskalt den Rücken herunter; **not a** ~ **of his head was harmed** ihm wurde kein Haar gekrümmt; **not a** ~ **out of place** *(fig)* wie aus dem Ei gepellt; *body* ~ Körperbehaarung *f;* **the best cure for a hangover is a** ~ **of the dog (that bit you)** einen Kater kuriert man am be-sten, wenn man mit dem anfängt, womit man aufgehört hat.

2 *attr mattress, sofa* Roßhaar-.

hair: ~**brush** *n* Haarbürste *f;* ~ **clip** *n* Clip *m; (for ponytail etc)* Haarspange *f;* ~ **cream** *n* Haar-pomade *f;* ~**cut** *n* Haarschnitt *m; (hairdo)* Frisur *f;* **to have** *or* **get a** ~**cut** sich *(dat)* die Haare schneiden lassen; **I need a** ~**cut** ich muß mir die Haare schneiden lassen; ~**do** *n (col)* Frisur *f;* ~**dresser** *n* Friseur *m,* Friseuse *f;* ~**drier** *n (hand-held also)* Fön ® *m; (over head also)* Trockenhaube *f;* ~**-grip** *n (Brit)* Haar-klemme *f;* ~**-line** *n* **(a)** Haaransatz *m;* **(b)** *(thin line)* haarfeine Linie; *(in telescope, on sight)* Faden *m;* ~**-line crack** *n* Haarriß *m;* ~**net** *n* Haarnetz *nt;* ~ **oil** *n* Haaröl *nt;* ~**-piece** *n* Haar-teil *nt; (for men)* Toupet *nt;* ~**pin** *n* Haarnadel *f;* ~**pin (bend)** *n* Haarnadelkurve *f;* ~**-raising** *adj* haarsträubend; ~**'s breadth** *n* by a ~**'s breadth** um Haaresbreite; ~**-splitting** 1 *n* Haar-spalterei *f;* 2 *adj* haarspalterisch; ~**spray** *n* Haarspray *nt;* ~**style** *n* Frisur *f.*

hairy ['heərɪ] *adj (+er)* **(a)** stark behaart. **(b)** *(col) situation* brenzlig *(col); film etc* gruselig *(col); driving* kriminell *(col).*

hake [heɪk] *n* Seehecht *m.*

halcyon ['hælsɪən] *adj:* ~ **days** glückliche Tage *pl.*

hale [heɪl] *adj* kräftig. ~ **and hearty** gesund und munter.

half [hɑːf] **1** *n, pl* **halves** **(a)** Hälfte *f.* **to cut in** ~ halbieren; **to break/tear sth in** ~ etw entzwei-brechen/-reißen; ~ **of it/them** die Hälfte davon/

von ihnen; ~ **the book/money** die Hälfte des Buches/Geldes; ~ **a cup/an hour** eine halbe Tasse/Stunde; ~ **a second!** (einen) Augenblick mal!; **to go halves** halbe-halbe machen *(col)*; **he is too clever by** ~ *(col)* das ist ein richtiger Schlaumeier; **not** ~ **enough** längst nicht genug; **one and a** ~ eineinhalb, anderthalb; **an hour and a** ~ eineinhalb *or* anderthalb Stunden; **not to do things by halves** keine halben Sachen machen; ~ **and** ~ halb und halb; **that's not the** ~ **of it** *(col)* und das ist noch nicht einmal die Hälfte *(col)*.
  (b) *(Sport)* *(of match)* Halbzeit *f*; *(player)* Läufer(in *f*) *m*.
  (c) *(of ticket)* Abschnitt *m* der Fahrkarte; *(travel, admission fee)* halbe Karte *(col)*.
  (d) *(beer)* kleines Bier.
  2 *adj* halb. **a** ~ **cup** eine halbe Tasse; **he's not** ~ **the man he used to be** er ist längst nicht mehr das, was er einmal war.
  3 *adv* **(a)** halb. **I** ~ **thought ...** ich hätte fast gedacht ...; **I was** ~ **afraid that ...** ich habe fast befürchtet, daß ...; **the work is only** ~ **done** die Arbeit ist erst zur Hälfte erledigt; **that's** ~ **right** das ist zur Hälfte richtig. **(b)** *(Brit col)* **he's not** ~ **stupid/rich** er ist unheimlich dumm/reich *(col)*; **not** ~ **bad** gar nicht schlecht; **not** ~**!** und wie!, und ob! **(c)** **it's** ~ **past three** *or* ~ **three** es ist halb vier. **(d)** ~ **as big as** halb so groß wie; ~ **as big again** anderthalbmal so groß.
half: ~**-back** *n (Sport)* Läufer(in *f*) *m*; ~**-baked** *adj (fig col)* person, plan blöd; ~**-breed** *n (person)* Mischling *m*; *(animal)* Rassenmischung *f*; *(horse)* Halbblut *n*; ~ **brother** *n* Halbbruder *m*; ~**-caste** *n* Mischling *m*; ~**-cock** *n*: **to go off at** ~**-cock** *(col)* ein Reinfall *m* sein *(col)*; ~**-crown** *n (in old Brit system)* Zweieinhalbschillingstück *nt*; ~**-cut** *adj (Brit col*: drunk) besoffen *(col!)*; ~**-day** *(holiday)* **n** halber freier Tag; **we've got a** ~**-day** *(holiday)* wir haben einen halben Tag frei; ~**-empty** *adj* halbleer *attr*, halb leer *pred*; ~**-fare** *n* 1 halber Fahrpreis; **2** *adv* zum halben Preis; ~**-hearted** *adj* halbherzig; *manner* lustlos; ~**-heartedly** *adv* **agree** mit halbem Herzen; **to do sth** ~**-heartedly** etw ohne rechte Lust tun; ~**-holiday** *n (Brit)* halber Urlaubstag/Feiertag; **we've got a** ~**-holiday tomorrow morning** wir haben morgen vormittag frei; ~**-hour** *n* halbe Stunde; ~**-mast** *n*: **at** ~**-mast** *(also hum)* (auf) halbmast; ~**-moon** *n* Halbmond *m*; ~**-note** *n (US Mus)* halbe Note; ~**penny** ['heɪpnɪ] *n* halber Penny; ~**-pint** *n* **(a)** = Viertelliter *m or nt*; *(of beer also)* kleines Bier; **(b)** *(col: person)* halbe Portion *(col)*; ~**-price** *n* at ~**-price** zum halben Preis; ~**-sister** *n* Halbschwester *f*; ~**-term** *n (Brit)* Ferien *pl* in der Mitte des Trimesters; ~**-timbered** *adj* Fachwerk-; ~**-time** *n* **(a)** *(Sport)* Halbzeit *f*; **(b)** *(Ind)* **to be on** ~**-time** auf Kurzarbeit sein; ~**-truth** *n* Halbwahrheit *f*.
halfway ['hɑːf,weɪ] **1** *adj attr* **when we reached the** ~ **stage on our journey** als wir die Hälfte der Reise hinter uns *(dat)* hatten; **the project is at the** ~ **stage** das Projekt ist zur Hälfte abgeschlossen. **2** *adv* ~**way to** auf halbem Weg nach; **we drove** ~ **to London** wir fuhren die halbe Strecke nach London; ~ **between two points** (in der Mitte *or* genau) zwischen zwei Punkten; ~ **up the hill** auf halber Höhe des Berges; **we went** ~ **up the hill** wir gingen den Berg halb hinauf; ~ **through a book** halb durch ein Buch (durch); **this money will go** ~ **towards paying ...** diese Summe wird die Hälfte der Kosten für ... decken; **to meet sb** ~ *(lit, fig)* jdm (auf halbem Weg) entgegenkommen. **3** *attr* ~ **house** *n (fig)* Zwischending *nt*.
half: ~**-wit** *n (fig)* Schwachkopf *m*; ~**-witted** ['hɑːf,wɪtɪd] *adj* schwachsinnig; ~**-yearly** *adj* halbjährlich.
halibut ['hælɪbət] *n* Heilbutt *m*.

halitosis [,hælɪ'təʊsɪs] *n* Mundgeruch *m*.
hall [hɔːl] *n* **(a)** *(of house)* Flur *m*; *(large)* Diele *f*. **(b)** *(large building)* Halle *f*; *(large room)* Saal *m*; *(village* ~*)* Gemeindehalle *f*; *(school assembly* ~*)* Aula *f*. **(c)** *(mansion)* Herrenhaus *nt*; *(students' also* ~ **of residence)** Studenten(wohn)heim *nt*.
hallelujah [,hælɪ'luːjə] *interj* halleluja.
hallmark ['hɔːlmɑːk] *n* **(a)** (Feingehalts)stempel *m*. **(b)** *(fig)* Kennzeichen *nt (of* gen, für).
hallo [hə'ləʊ] *interj, n* = **hello**.
Hallowe'en [,hæləʊ'iːn] *n* Tag *m* vor Allerheiligen.
hall: ~ **porter** *n* Portier *m*; ~**-stand** *n* (Flur)garderobe *f*; *(treelike)* Garderobenständer *m*.
hallucinate [hə'luːsɪneɪt] *vi* halluzinieren.
hallucination [hə,luːsɪ'neɪʃən] *n* Halluzination *f*.
hallway ['hɔːlweɪ] *n* Korridor *m*.
halo ['heɪləʊ] *n, pl* **-(e)s** *(of saint)* Heiligenschein *m*; *(Astron)* Hof *m*.
halt [hɒlt] **1** *n* **(a)** *(stop)* Pause *f*; *(Mil)* Halt *m*; *(in production)* Stopp *m*. **to come to a** ~ zum Stillstand kommen; **to call a** ~ **to** sth einer Sache *(dat)* ein Ende bereiten; **shall we call a** ~ **now?** wollen wir jetzt Schluß machen?; ~ **sign** Stoppschild *nt*. **(b)** *(small station)* Haltepunkt *m*. **2** *vi* zum Stillstand kommen; *(person)* stehenbleiben; *(Mil)* halten. **to** ~ **briefly** kurz haltmachen. **3** *vt* anhalten; *production, traffic also* zum Stehen bringen. **4** *interj* halt; *(traffic sign)* stop.
halter ['hɒltəʳ] *n (horse's)* Halfter *nt*.
halting ['hɒltɪŋ] *adj walk* unsicher; *speech* stockend; *verse* holp(e)rig.
halve [hɑːv] *vt* **(a)** halbieren. **(b)** *(reduce by one half)* auf die Hälfte reduzieren.
halves [hɑːvz] *pl of* **half**.
ham [hæm] **1** *n* **(a)** *(Cook)* Schinken *m*. **(b)** *(Theat)* Schmierenkomödiant(in *f*) *m*. **(c)** *(Rad col)* Funkamateur *m*. **2** *adj attr acting* übertrieben. **3** *vi (Theat)* chargieren, übertrieben spielen.
♦ **ham up** *vt sep (col)* **to** ~ **it** ~ zu dick auftragen.
hamburger ['hæm,bɜːgəʳ] *n (flache)* Frikadelle *f*; *(with bread)* Hamburger *m*.
ham-fisted [,hæm'fɪstɪd] *adj* ungeschickt.
hamlet ['hæmlɪt] *n* Weiler *m*, kleines Dorf.
hammer ['hæməʳ] **1** *n* Hammer *m*. **to go at it** ~ **and tongs** *(col)* sich ins Zeug legen *(col)*; *(quarrel)* sich in die Haare kriegen *(col)*; **to come under the** ~ *(auction)* unter den Hammer kommen; **in the** ~ *(throwing)* *(Sport)* im Hammerwurf. **2** *vt* **(a)** *nail, metal* hämmern. **to** ~ **a nail into a wall** einen Nagel in die Wand schlagen; **to** ~ **sth into shape** *metal* etw zurechthämmern; *(fig) plan, agreement* etw ausarbeiten; **to** ~ **sth into sb's head, to** ~ **it home to sb** jdm etw einbleuen *(col)*. **(b)** *(col: defeat badly)* eine Schlappe beibringen +*dat (col)*. **3** *vi* hämmern. **to** ~ **(away) at the door** an die Tür hämmern.
♦ **hammer out** *vt sep (fig) plan, solution* ausarbeiten; *tune* hämmern.
hammering ['hæmərɪŋ] *n* **our team took a** ~ *(col)* unsere Mannschaft mußte eine Schlappe einstecken *(col)*.
hammock ['hæmək] *n* Hängematte *f*.
hamper[1] ['hæmpəʳ] *n* Korb *m*; *(as present)* Geschenkkorb *m*.
hamper[2] *vt* behindern. **to be** ~**ed** gehandikapt sein.
hamster ['hæmstəʳ] *n* Hamster *m*.
hamstring ['hæmstrɪŋ] *(vb: pret, ptp* **hamstrung** ['hæmstrʌŋ]) **1** *n (Anat)* Kniesehne *f*. **2** *vt (fig)* **to be hamstrung** außer Gefecht gesetzt sein; *(project)* lahmliegen.
hand [hænd] **1** *n* **(a)** Hand *f*; *(of clock)* Zeiger *m*. **on** ~**s and knees** auf allen vieren; **to take sb by the** ~ jdn bei der Hand nehmen; ~**s up!** Hände hoch!; *(Sch)* meldet euch!; ~**s off** *(col)* Hände weg!; **keep your** ~**s off it** laß die Finger davon!; **made by** ~ handgearbeitet; **to raise an animal by** ~ ein Tier mit der Flasche aufziehen; **to live**

from ~ to mouth von der Hand in den Mund leben; **with a heavy/firm ~** *(fig)* mit harter/ starker Hand.
(b) *(side, direction, position)* Seite *f*. **on the right ~** auf der rechten Seite, rechts; **on my right ~** rechts von mir; **on all ~s** auf allen Seiten; **on the one ~ ... on the other ~ ...** einerseits ..., andererseits ...
(c) *(agency, possession etc)* **it's the ~ of God** das ist die Hand Gottes; **it's in your own ~s what you do now** Sie haben es selbst in der Hand, was Sie jetzt tun; **to put sth into sb's ~s** jdm etw in die Hand geben; **to leave sb/sth in sb's ~s** jdn in jds Obhut lassen/jdm etw überlassen; **I'm in your ~s** ich verlasse mich ganz auf Sie; **to fall into the ~s of sb** jdm in die Hände fallen; **to be in good ~s** in guten Händen sein; **he has too much time on his ~s** er hat zuviel Zeit zur Verfügung; **I've got enough on my ~s** already ich habe schon genug am Hals *(col)*; **to get sb/sth off one's ~s** jdn/etw loswerden; **to take sb/sth off sb's ~s** jdm jdn/etw abnehmen.
(d) *(applause)* **they gave him a big ~** er bekam großen Applaus.
(e) *(worker)* Arbeitskraft *f*; *(Naut)* Besatzungsmitglied *nt*. **to take on ~s** Leute einstellen; *(Naut)* Leute anheuern; **~s** Belegschaft *f*; **all ~s on deck!** alle Mann an Deck!; **to be an old ~** *(at sth)* ein alter Hase (in etw *dat*) sein.
(f) *(Measure: of horse)* ≈ 10 cm.
(g) *(handwriting)* Handschrift *f*.
(h) *(Cards)* Blatt *nt*; *(person)* Mann *m*; *(game)* Runde *f*. **3 ~s** *(people)* 3 Mann.
(i) **Christmas is (close) at ~** Weihnachten steht vor der Tür; **at first/second ~** aus erster/ zweiter Hand; **according to the information on ~** laut den vorliegenden Informationen; **to keep sth at ~** etw in Reichweite haben; **it's quite close at ~** es ist ganz in der Nähe; **he had the situation well in ~** er hatte die Situation im Griff; **to take sb in ~** *(discipline)* jdn zur Räson bringen; *(look after)* nach jdm sehen; **stock in ~** *(Comm)* Warenlager *nt*; **he still had £600/a couple of hours in ~** er hatte £ 600 übrig/noch zwei Stunden Zeit; **the matter in ~** die zur Debatte stehende Angelegenheit; **work in ~** Arbeit, die zur Zeit erledigt wird; **a matter/project etc is in ~** eine Sache/ein Projekt *nt etc* ist in Bearbeitung; **to put sth in ~** zusehen, daß etw erledigt wird; **the children got out of ~** die Kinder waren nicht mehr zu bändigen; **matters got out of ~** die Dinge sind außer Kontrolle geraten; **I don't have the letter to ~** ich habe den Brief gerade nicht zur Hand.
(j) *(phrases)* **to keep one's ~ in** in Übung bleiben; **to eat out of sb's ~** *(lit, fig)* jdm aus der Hand fressen; **to force sb's ~** auf jdn Druck ausüben; **to wait on sb ~ and foot** jdn von vorne und hinten bedienen; **he never does a ~'s turn** er rührt keinen Finger; **to have a ~ in sth** *(in decision)* an etw *(dat)* beteiligt sein; *(in crime)* die Hand bei etw im Spiel haben; **to lend** *or* **give sb a ~** jdn zur Hand gehen; **give me a ~!** hilf mir mal!; **to be ~ in glove with sb** mit jdm unter einer Decke stecken; **to have one's ~s full with sth** mit etw alle Hände voll zu tun haben; **to win ~s down** spielend gewinnen; **he is making money ~ over fist** er scheffelt das Geld nur so; **we're losing money/staff ~ over fist** wir verlieren haufenweise Geld/Personal; **to have the upper ~** die Oberhand behalten; **to gain the upper ~** die Oberhand gewinnen; **to ask for a lady's ~** *(in marriage)* um die Hand einer Dame anhalten.
2 *vt (give)* reichen, geben *(sth to sb, sb sth* jdm etw*)*. **you've got to ~ it to him** *(fig)* das muß man ihm lassen *(col)*.

♦ **hand back** *vt sep* zurückgeben.

♦ **hand down** *vt sep* **(a)** *(lit)* herunter-/hinunterreichen *or* -geben *(to sb* jdm*)*. **(b)** *(fig)* weitergeben; *tradition, story also* überliefern *(to* an +*acc)*; *heirloom etc* vererben *(to* dat*)*.
♦ **hand in** *vt sep* abgeben; *forms, resignation* einreichen.
♦ **hand on** *vt sep* weitergeben *(to* an +*acc)*.
♦ **hand out** *vt sep* austeilen *(to sb* an jdn*)*; *advice* erteilen *(to sb* jdm*)*.
♦ **hand over 1** *vt sep (pass over)* (herüber-/ hinüber)reichen *(to* dat*)*; *(give up)* (her)geben *(to* dat*)*; *(to third party)* (ab)geben *(to* dat*)*; *criminal, prisoner* übergeben *(to* dat*)*; *(from one state to another)* ausliefern; *leadership* abtreten *(to* an +*acc)*; *the controls, business* übergeben *(to* dat, an +*acc)*. **2** *vi* **when the Conservatives ~ed ~ to Labour** als die Konservativen die Regierung an Labour abgaben; **when the chairman ~ed ~ to his successor** als der Vorsitzende das Amt an seinen Nachfolger abgab.
♦ **hand round** *vt sep* herumreichen; *(distribute)* papers austeilen.

hand: **~bag** *n* Handtasche *f*; **~ baggage** *n* Handgepäck *nt*; **~ball** *n* (a) Handball *m*; (b) *(Ftbl: foul)* Handspiel *nt*; **~bill** *n* Handzettel *m*; **~book** *n* Handbuch *nt*; *(tourist's)* Reiseführer *m*; **~brake** *n (Brit)* Handbremse *f*; **~cuff** *vt* Handschellen anlegen (+*dat)*; **~cuffs** *npl* Handschellen *pl*.

handful ['hændful] *n* **(a)** Handvoll *f*; *(of hair, fur)* Büschel *nt*. **by the ~, in ~s** büschelweise. **(b)** *(small number)* Handvoll *f*. **(c)** *(fig)* **those children are a ~** die Kinder können einen ganz schön in Trab halten.

hand-grenade ['hændgrɪneɪd] *n* Handgranate *f*.

handicap ['hændɪkæp] **1** *n* Handikap *nt*; *(in horse racing, golf also)* Vorgabe *f*; *(physical, mental also)* Behinderung *f*. **to be under a great ~** stark gehandikapt sein. **2** *vt* ein Handikap *nt* darstellen für. **to be (physically/mentally) ~ped** (körperlich/geistig) behindert sein; **~ped children** behinderte Kinder *pl*.

handicraft ['hændɪkrɑːft] *n* **(a)** *(work)* Kunsthandwerk *nt*; *(needlework etc)* Handarbeit *f*; *(woodwork, modelling etc)* Werken *nt*. **(b)** *(skill)* Geschick *nt*, Handfertigkeit *f*.

handiness ['hændɪnɪs] *n* *(of shops etc)* günstige Lage.

handiwork ['hændɪwɜːk] *n no pl* **(a)** *(lit)* Arbeit *f*; *(Sch: subject)* Werken *nt*; *(needlework etc)* Handarbeit *f*. **(b)** *(fig)* Werk *nt*; *(pej)* Machwerk *nt*.

handkerchief ['hæŋkətʃɪf] *n* Taschentuch *nt*.

handle ['hændl] **1** *n* Griff *m*; *(of door also)* Klinke *f*; *(of broom, comb)* Stiel *m*; *(of basket, bucket, cup etc)* Henkel *m*. **to fly off the ~** *(col)* an die Decke gehen *(col)*.
2 *vt* **(a)** *(touch, use hands on)* anfassen; *(Ftbl)* ball mit der Hand berühren. **be careful how you ~ that** gehen Sie vorsichtig damit um; **"~ with care"** „Vorsicht Glas/Blumen/lebende Tiere etc".
(b) *(deal with)* person, animal, tool, weapon, machine etc umgehen mit; *legal or financial matters* erledigen; *legal case, order, contract* bearbeiten; *applicant, matter, problem* sich befassen mit; *material for essay etc* bearbeiten; *(tackle)* problem, interview etc anpacken; *(cope with)* child, drunk, situation, problem fertigwerden mit; *vehicle, plane, ship* steuern. **how would you ~ the situation?** wie würden Sie sich in der Situation verhalten?; **you keep quiet, I'll ~ this** sei mal still und laß mich nur machen *(col)*; **who's handling the publicity for this?** wer macht die Öffentlichkeitsarbeit dafür?
3 *vi (ship, plane)* sich steuern lassen; *(car, motorbike)* sich fahren.
4 *vr* **he ~s himself well in a fight** er kann sich in einer Schlägerei behaupten.

handle: ~**bar moustache** n Schnauzbart m; ~**bar(s)** n(pl) Lenkstange f.

handler ['hændlə^r] n (dog–~) Hundeführer m.

handling ['hændlɪŋ] n **(a)** (touching) Berühren nt. **(b)** (of plant, problem) Behandlung f; (of person, patient etc also) Umgang m (of mit); (of tool, weapon, machine) Handhabung f; (of legal or financial matters) Erledigung f; (of order, contract, legal case) Bearbeitung f. **his** ~ **of the situation** die Art, wie er die Situation angepackt hat; **he/it needs careful** ~ man muß vorsichtig mit ihm/ damit umgehen. **(c)** (of vehicle) Fahrverhalten nt. **what's its** ~ **like?** wie fährt es sich?

hand: ~**luggage** n Handgepäck nt; ~**-made** adj handgearbeitet; **this is** ~**-made** das ist Handarbeit; ~**-me-down** n (col) abgelegtes Kleidungsstück; ~**out** n (col: money) (Geld)zuwendung f; (leaflet) Flugblatt nt; (publicity ~) Reklamezettel m; ~**-picked** adj (specially selected) handverlesen; ~**rail** n (of stairs etc) Geländer nt; (of ship) Reling f; ~**shake** n Händedruck m.

handsome ['hænsəm] adj gutaussehend; furniture, building schön; (noble, generous) großzügig, nobel (col); (profit, inheritance etc stattlich, beträchtlich. **he is** ~**/he has a** ~ **face** er sieht gut aus.

handsomely ['hænsəmlɪ] adv **(a)** (elegantly) elegant. **(b)** (generously) großzügig.

hand: ~**-stand** n Handstand m; ~**-to**~ adj ~**-to**-~ **fighting** Nahkampf m; ~**-to-mouth** adj existence kümmerlich, armselig; **to lead a** ~**-to-mouth existence** von der Hand in den Mund leben; ~**writing** n Handschrift f; ~**written** adj handgeschrieben.

handy ['hændɪ] adj (+er) (a) person geschickt. **to be** ~ **at doing sth** ein Geschick nt für etw haben. **(b)** pred (close at hand) in der Nähe (for +gen). **to keep sth** ~ etw griffbereit haben. **(c)** (convenient, useful) praktisch. **it'll come in** ~ das kann ich gut gebrauchen; **he's a very** ~ **person to have around** man kann ihn gut (ge)brauchen (col); **he's very** ~ **about the house** er kann im Haus alles selbst erledigen.

handyman ['hændɪmæn] n, pl **-men** [-mən] (do-it-yourself) Bastler m.

hang [hæŋ] (vb: pret, ptp hung) **1** vt **(a)** hängen; painting aufhängen; door, gate einhängen; wallpaper kleben. **to** ~ **wallpaper** tapezieren; **to** ~ **sth from sth** etw an etw (dat) aufhängen; **the walls were hung with tapestries** die Wände waren mit Gobelins behängt; **to** ~ **one's head** den Kopf hängen lassen. **(b)** pret, ptp **hanged** criminal hängen. **to** ~ **oneself** sich erhängen; ~ **him** (col) zum Kuckuck mit ihm! (col); **I'm** ~**ed if I know** (col) weiß der Kuckuck (col); ~ **it!** (col) so ein Mist! (col).

2 vi **(a)** hängen (on an (+dat), from von); (drapery, clothes, hair) fallen. **time** ~**s heavy on my hands** die Zeit wird mir sehr lang. **(b)** (criminal) gehängt werden. **(c)** **it/he can go** ~! (col) es/er kann mir gestohlen bleiben (col).

3 n **(a)** (of drapery) Fall m; (of suit) Sitz m. **(b)** **you'll soon get the** ~ **of it** (col) du wirst bald den richtigen Dreh (dabei) herauskriegen (col).

♦ **hang about** or **around 1** vi (col) (wait) warten; (loiter) sich herumtreiben (col). **to keep sb** ~**ing** ~ jdn warten lassen; ~ **about, I didn't say that** Moment mal, das habe ich nicht gesagt (col); **he doesn't** ~ ~ (is fast) er ist einer von der schnellen Truppe. **2** vi +prep obj **to** ~ ~ **a place** sich an einem Ort herumtreiben (col).

♦ **hang back** vi (lit) sich zurückhalten; (hesitate) zögern.

♦ **hang in** vi (col) **just** ~ ~ **there!** bleib am Ball (col).

♦ **hang on 1** vi **(a)** (hold) sich festhalten (to sth an etw dat). **(b)** (hold out) durchhalten; (Telec) am Apparat bleiben; (col: wait) warten. ~ ~ **(a minute)** wart mal, einen Augenblick (mal). **2** vi

+prep obj **(a)** **to** ~ ~ **sb's arm** an jds Arm (dat) hängen; **he** ~**s** ~ **her every word** er hängt an ihren Lippen. **(b)** (depend on) **it all** ~**s** ~ **his decision** alles hängt von seiner Entscheidung ab.

♦ **hang on to** vi +prep obj (keep) behalten.

♦ **hang out 1** vi **(a)** (tongue, shirt tails etc) heraushängen (of aus +dat). **(b)** (col: live) sich herumtreiben (be usually found also) sich herumtreiben (col). **(c)** **they hung** ~ **for more pay** sie hielten an ihrer Lohnforderung fest. **(d)** (col) **to let it all** ~ ~ die Sau rauslassen (col). **2** vt sep hinaushängen.

♦ **hang together** vi (people) zusammenhalten; (argument, report) zusammenhängend sein; (alibi etc) keine Widersprüche aufweisen.

♦ **hang up 1** vi (Telec) auflegen. **he hung** ~ **on me** er legte einfach auf. **2** vt sep aufhängen.

hangar ['hæŋə^r] n Flugzeughalle f.

hangdog ['hæŋdɒg] adj look niedergeschlagen; (ashamed) zerknirscht.

hanger ['hæŋə^r] n (for clothes) (Kleider)bügel m; (loop on garment) Aufhänger m.

hanger-on [,hæŋər'ɒn] n, pl **-s-on** (sponger) Schmarotzer m. **he came with all his hangers-on** er kam mit seinem ganzen Gefolge.

hanging ['hæŋɪŋ] **1** n **(a)** Todesstrafe f; (of criminal) Erhängen nt; (event) Hinrichtung f (durch den Strang). **(b)** (curtains etc) ~s pl Vorhänge pl; (on wall) Tapete f; (tapestry) Wandbehang m. **2** attr hängend; bridge Hänge-.

hang: ~**man** n Henker m; ~**-out** n (col) (place where one lives) Bude f (col); (pub, café etc) Stammlokal nt; (of group) Treff m (col); ~**over** n **(a)** Kater (col); **(b)** (sth left over) Überbleibsel nt; ~**up** n (col) Komplex m (about wegen); (obsession) Fimmel m (col) (about mit).

hank [hæŋk] n (of wool etc) Strang m; (of hair, fur) Büschel nt.

hanker ['hæŋkə^r] vi Verlangen haben (for or after sth nach etw).

hankering ['hæŋkərɪŋ] n Verlangen nt. **to have a** ~ **for sth** Verlangen nach etw haben.

hanky ['hæŋkɪ] n (col) Taschentuch nt.

hanky-panky ['hæŋkɪ'pæŋkɪ] n (col) **(a)** (dishonest dealings) Mauscheleien pl (col). **there's some** ~ **going on** hier ist was faul (col). **(b)** (love affair) Techtelmechtel nt (col). **(c)** (sexy behaviour) Gefummel nt (col).

Hanover ['hænəʊvə^r] n Hannover nt.

Hanseatic [,hænzɪ'ætɪk] adj towns Hanse-. ~**League** Hansebund m.

haphazard [,hæp'hæzəd] adj willkürlich.

happen ['hæpən] vi **(a)** geschehen; (special or important event also) sich ereignen; (esp unexpected, unintentional or unpleasant event also) passieren; (process also) vor sich gehen. **it all** ~**ed like this ...** das Ganze war so ...; **it's all** ~**ing here today** (col) heute ist hier ganz schön was los (col); **what's** ~**ing?** was ist los?; **you can't just let things** ~ du kannst die Dinge nicht einfach laufen lassen; **don't let it** ~ **again** daß das nicht noch mal passiert!; **these things** ~ so was kommt (schon mal) vor; **what has** ~**ed to him?** was ist mit ihm passiert? (in accident etc) was ist ihm passiert?; **what's** ~**ed to your leg?** was ist mit deinem Bein passiert?; **if anything should** ~ **to me** wenn mir etwas passieren sollte; **it all** ~**ed so quickly** es ging alles so schnell.

(b) (chance) **how does it** ~ **that ...?** wie kommt es, daß ...?; **it might** ~ **that ...** es könnte sein, daß ...; **how do you** ~ **to know?** wie kommt es, daß du das weißt?; **to** ~ **to do sth** zufälligerweise etw tun; **do you** ~ **to know whether ...?** wissen Sie zufällig, ob ...?; **I just** ~**ed to come along when ...** ich kam zufällig (gerade) vorbei, als ...; **as it** ~**s I'm going there today** zufällig(erweise) gehe ich heute (dort)hin; **he** ~**s to be the boss** er ist nun

einmal der Chef.
♦ **happen (up)on** *vi* +*prep obj* zufällig stoßen auf (+*acc*); *person* zufällig treffen.
happening ['hæpnɪŋ] *n* Ereignis *nt*; *(not planned)* Vorfall *m*; *(Theat)* Happening *nt*.
happily ['hæpɪlɪ] *adv* **(a)** glücklich; *(cheerfully also)* fröhlich; *(contentedly also)* zufrieden. **they lived ~ ever after** *(in fairy-tales)* und wenn sie nicht gestorben sind, dann leben sie noch heute. **(b)** *(fortunately)* glücklicherweise. **(c)** *(worded)* treffend.
happiness ['hæpɪnɪs] *n* Glück *nt*; *(disposition)* Fröhlichkeit *f*.
happy ['hæpɪ] *adj* (+*er*) **(a)** *(about* über +*acc)* glücklich; *(cheerful also)* fröhlich. **a ~ event** ein freudiges Ereignis; **that's all right, ~ to help** schon gut, ich helfe (doch) gern; **yes, I'd be ~ to** ja, sehr gern(e); **to be ~ to do sth** sich freuen, etw tun zu können; **I'm very ~ for you** ich freue mich für dich; **the ~ few** die wenigen Auserwählten. **(b)** *phrase, solution* glücklich. **(c)** *(content)* zufrieden. **we're not ~ with it** wir sind damit nicht zufrieden. **(d)** ~ **anniversary** herzlichen Glückwunsch zum Hochzeitstag; ~ **birthday** alles Gute zum Geburtstag!; ~ **Easter** frohe Ostern; ~ **New Year** ein gutes neues Jahr.
happy-go-lucky ['hæpɪgəʊ'lʌkɪ] *adj* unbekümmert.
harangue [hə'ræŋ] **1** *n* *(scolding)* (Straf)predigt *f*; *(encouraging)* Appell *m*. **2** *vt see n* eine (Straf)predigt halten (+*dat*); einen Appell richten an (+*acc*).
harass ['hærəs] *vt* belästigen; *(mess around)* schikanieren; *(Mil)* immer wieder überfallen. **don't ~ me** dräng mich doch nicht so!; **they eventually ~ed him into resigning** sie setzten ihm so lange zu, bis er schließlich zurücktrat.
harassed ['hærəst] *adj* mitgenommen; *(worried)* von Sorgen gequält.
harassment ['hærəsmənt] *n* *(act)* Belästigung *f*; *(messing around)* Schikanierung *f*; *(state)* Bedrängnis *f*; *(Mil)* Kleinkrieg *m*.
harbour, *(US)* **harbor** ['hɑːbəʳ] **1** *n* Hafen *m*. ~ **master** *n* Hafenmeister *m*. **2** *vt* **(a)** *criminal etc* Unterschlupf gewähren (+*dat*). **(b)** *suspicions, grudge* hegen.
hard [hɑːd] **1** *adj* (+*er*) **(a)** hart; *voice, tone also* schroff. **a ~ man** ein harter Mann; *(ruthless)* ein knallharter Typ *(col)*; **don't be ~ on the boy** sei nicht zu streng zu den Jungen. **(b)** *(difficult)* schwer; *(complicated also)* schwierig; *(~ to endure)* hart. ~ **of hearing** schwerhörig; **I find it ~ to believe that** ... ich kann es kaum glauben, daß ...; **I know it's ~ for you, but** ... ich weiß, es ist hart für Sie, aber ...; **he is ~ to get on with** es ist schwierig, mit ihm auszukommen; **it's ~ going** es ist mühsam; ~ **luck!,** ~ **lines!** (so ein) Pech!
2 *adv* (+*er*) **(a)** mit aller Kraft; *(violently)* heftig; *run* schnell; *breathe, work* schwer. **to listen ~** genau hinhören; **think ~** denk mal scharf nach; **think ~er** denk mal ein bißchen besser nach; **he has obviously thought ~ about this** er hat es sich *(dat)* offensichtlich gut überlegt; **if you try ~** wenn du dich richtig bemühst; **try ~er** gib dir doch ein bißchen mehr Mühe; **you're not trying ~ enough** du strengst dich nicht genügend an; **you're trying too ~** du bemühst dich zu sehr; **he tried as ~ as he could** er hat sich nach Kräften bemüht; **to look ~ at sb/sth** sich jdn/etw genau ansehen; **to be ~ at it** *(col)* schwer am Werk sein *(col)*.
(b) *(in, with difficulty)* **to be ~ put to it to do sth** es sehr schwer finden, etw zu tun; **to be ~ up** *(col)* knapp bei Kasse sein *(col)*; **he's ~ up for ...** *(col)* es fehlt ihm an ... (+*dat*); **to be ~ done by** übel dran sein; **he took it pretty ~** es traf ihn ziemlich schwer; **old traditions die ~** alte Traditionen lassen sich nicht so leicht abschaffen. **(c)** *rain, snow* stark. **it was freezing ~** es herrschte strenger Frost.
hard: ~ **and fast** *adj* fest; *rules also* bindend; ~**-back 1** *adj book* gebunden; **2** *n* gebundene Ausgabe; ~**-bitten** *adj person* abgebrüht; *manager* knallhart *(col)*; ~**board** *n* Hartfaserplatte *f*; ~**-boiled** *adj* **(a)** *egg* hartgekocht; **(b)** *(fig: shrewd)* ausgekocht *(col)*; *(unsentimental)* abgebrüht *(col)*; ~ **cash** *n* Bargeld *nt*; ~ **core** *n* **(a)** *(for road)* Schotter *m*; **(b)** *(fig)* harter Kern; *(pornography)* harter Porno *(col)*; ~ **court** *n* Hartplatz *m*; ~ **disk** *n* *(Comp)* Festplatte *f*; ~ **drinker** *n* starker Trinker; ~ **drug** *n* harte Droge; ~**-earned** *adj wages* sauer verdient; *victory* hart erkämpft.
harden ['hɑːdn] **1** *vt steel* härten; *body, muscles* kräftigen. **this ~ed his attitude** dadurch hat sich seine Haltung verhärtet; **to ~ oneself to sth** *(physically)* sich gegen etw abhärten; *(emotionally)* gegen etw unempfindlich werden. **2** *vi (substance)* hart werden; *(attitude)* sich verhärten.
hardened ['hɑːdnd] *adj steel* gehärtet; *criminal* .Gewohnheits-; *troops* abgehärtet; *sinner* verstockt. **to be ~ to or against the cold/sb's insensitivity/life** gegen die Kälte abgehärtet sein/an jds Gefühllosigkeit *(acc)* gewöhnt sein/vom Leben hart gemacht sein.
hardening ['hɑːdnɪŋ] *n* ~ **of the arteries** Arterienverkalkung *f*.
hard: ~**-fought** *adj battle* erbittert; *game* hart; ~ **hat** *n* Schutzhelm *m*; *(worker)* Bauarbeiter *m*; ~**-headed** *adj* nüchtern; ~**-hearted** *adj* hartherzig *(towards sb* jdm gegenüber*)*; ~ **labour** *(Brit) or* **labor** *(US) n* Zwangsarbeit *f*; ~ **line** *n* harte Linie; **to take a ~ line** eine harte Linie verfolgen; ~**-liner** *n* Vertreter *m* der harten Linie; ~ **liquor** *n* Schnaps *m*.
hardly ['hɑːdlɪ] *adv* kaum. **I need ~ tell you** ich muß Ihnen wohl kaum sagen; ~ **ever** fast nie; **he had ~ gone** *or* **had he gone when** ... er war kaum gegangen, als ...; **he would ~ have said that** das hat er wohl kaum gesagt; ~! (wohl) kaum; ~ **ideal conditions** wohl kaum ideale Bedingungen.
hardness ['hɑːdnɪs] *n* **(a)** Härte *f*. **(b)** *see adj (b)* Schwere *f*; Schwierigkeit *f*; Härte *f*. ~ **of hearing** Schwerhörigkeit *f*.
hard sell *n* aggressive Verkaufstaktik, Hard selling *nt*.
hardship ['hɑːdʃɪp] *n* *(condition)* Not *f*; *(instance)* Härte *f*; *(deprivation)* Entbehrung *f*. **a temporary ~** eine vorübergehende Notlage; **to suffer great ~s** große Not leiden; **if it's not too much (of a) ~ for you** wenn es dir nicht zuviel Mühe macht.
hard: ~ **shoulder** *n (Brit)* Seitenstreifen *m*; ~**top** *n* Hardtop *nt or m*; ~**ware** *n* **(a)** Eisenwaren *pl*; *(household goods)* Haushaltswaren *pl*; **(b)** *(Comp)* Hardware *f*; **(c)** *(Mil)* (Wehr)material *nt*; ~**ware store** *n* Eisenwarenhandlung *f*; *(including household goods)* Haushalt- und Eisenwarengeschäft *nt*; ~**-wearing** *adj* widerstandsfähig; *cloth, clothes* strapazierfähig; ~**-won** *adj* schwer erkämpft; ~**-working** *adj person* fleißig; *engine* leistungsfähig.
hardy ['hɑːdɪ] *adj* (+*er*) **(a)** *(tough)* zäh; *person also* abgehärtet; *plant (frost)* unempfindlich. ~ **annual** winterharte einjährige Pflanze. **(b)** *(bold)* person unerschrocken.
hare [hɛəʳ] **1** *n* (Feld)hase *m*. **2** *vi (col)* flitzen *(col)*.
hare: ~**-brained** *adj* behämmert *(col)*; ~**lip** *n* Hasenscharte *f*.
harem ['hɑːriːm] *n* Harem *m*.
haricot ['hærɪkəʊ] *n* ~ **bean** *(Brit)* Gartenbohne *f*.
hark [hɑːk] *vi* ~! *(liter)* horch!!; ~ **at him!** *(col)* hör sich einer den an! *(col)*.
♦ **hark back** *vi* zurückkommen *(to* auf +*acc*). **he's**

always ~ing ~ to the good old days er fängt immer wieder von der guten alten Zeit an.

harm [hɑːm] 1 n (bodily) Verletzung f; (material, to relations, psychological) Schaden m. to do ~ to sb jdm eine Verletzung zufügen/jdm Schaden zufügen; to do ~ to sth einer Sache (dat) schaden; you will come to no ~ es wird Ihnen nichts geschehen; it will do more ~ than good es wird mehr schaden als nützen; it won't do you any ~ es wird dir nicht schaden; I see no ~ in the odd cigarette ich finde nichts dabei, wenn man ab zu eine Zigarette raucht; to mean no ~ es nicht böse meinen; I don't mean him any ~ ich meine es nicht böse mit ihm; there's no ~ in asking/trying es kann nicht schaden, zu fragen/es zu versuchen; where's or what's the ~ in that? was kann denn das schaden?; out of ~'s way in Sicherheit; to stay out of ~'s way der Gefahr (dat) aus dem Weg gehen.

2 vt schaden (+dat); person verletzen.

harmful ['hɑːmfʊl] adj schädlich (to für); remarks verletzend.

harmless ['hɑːmlɪs] adj harmlos.

harmonica [hɑːˈmɒnɪkə] n Harmonika f.

harmonious [hɑːˈməʊnɪəs] adj harmonisch.

harmonium [hɑːˈməʊnɪəm] n Harmonium nt.

harmonize ['hɑːmənaɪz] 1 vt (Mus) harmonisieren; plans, colours aufeinander abstimmen. 2 vi (notes, colours, people etc) harmonieren; (sing) mehrstimmig singen.

harmony ['hɑːmənɪ] n Harmonie f; (fig: harmonious relations) Eintracht f. to be in/out of ~ with (lit) harmonieren/nicht harmonieren mit; (fig also) in Einklang/nicht in Einklang sein mit; to sing in ~ mehrstimmig singen.

harness ['hɑːnɪs] 1 n Geschirr nt; (of parachute) Gurtwerk nt; (for baby) Laufgurt m. to die in ~ (fig, often hum) in den Sielen sterben. 2 vt (a) horse anschirren. to ~ a horse to a carriage ein Pferd vor einen Wagen spannen. (b) (utilize) river etc nutzbar machen; resources (aus)nutzen.

harp [hɑːp] n Harfe f.

♦ **harp on** vi (col) don't ~ ~ so reite nicht so darauf herum!; to ~ ~ about sth immer wieder mit etw kommen (col).

harpoon [hɑːˈpuːn] 1 n Harpune f. 2 vt harpunieren.

harpsichord ['hɑːpsɪkɔːd] n Cembalo nt.

harrow ['hærəʊ] 1 n Egge f. 2 vt eggen.

harrowed ['hærəʊd] adj look gequält.

harrowing ['hærəʊɪŋ] adj grauenhaft.

harry ['hærɪ] vt zusetzen (+dat).

harsh [hɑːʃ] adj (+er) rauh. (a) (severe) hart; words, tone of voice also barsch; (too strict) streng. don't be too ~ with him sei nicht zu streng mit ihm. (b) colour, light, sound hart; taste herb.

harvest ['hɑːvɪst] 1 n Ernte f; (of wines, berries also) Lese f. 2 vt (also fig) ernten; vines also lesen; (bring in) einbringen. 3 vi ernten.

harvester ['hɑːvɪstəʳ] n (person) Erntearbeiter(in f) m; (machine) Mähmaschine f; (combine ~) Mähdrescher m.

harvest: ~ festival n Erntedankfest nt; ~ time n Erntezeit f.

has [hæz] 3rd pers sing pres of **have**.

has-been ['hæzbiːn] n (pej) vergessene Größe.

hash [hæʃ] n (a) (Cook) Haschee nt. (b) (col: mess) to make a ~ of sth etw verpfuschen (col). (c) (col: hashish) Hasch nt (col).

hashish ['hæʃɪʃ] n Haschisch nt.

hasn't ['hæznt] = **has not**.

hassle ['hæsl] n (col) Ärger m; (bother, fuss) Theater nt (col). getting there is such a ~ es ist so umständlich, dorthin zu kommen; we had a bit of ~ with the police wir hatten ein bißchen Ärger mit der Polizei.

hassock ['hæsək] n Kniekissen nt.

haste [heɪst] n Eile f. to make ~ sich beeilen; more

~ less speed (Prov) eile mit Weile (Prov).

hasten ['heɪsn] 1 vi sich beeilen. I ~ to add that ... ich muß allerdings hinzufügen, daß .... 2 vt beschleunigen. the strain of office ~ed his death die Belastung seines Amtes trug zu seinem vorzeitigen Tod bei; to ~ sb's departure jdn zum Aufbruch drängen.

hastily ['heɪstɪlɪ] adv (a) (hurriedly) hastig. (b) (rashly) vorschnell.

hastiness ['heɪstɪnɪs] n (a) Eile f. (b) (rashness) Voreiligkeit f.

hasty ['heɪstɪ] adj (+er) (a) (hurried) eilig. they made a ~ exit sie gingen eilig hinaus. don't be so ~ nicht so hastig! (b) (rash) vorschnell.

hat [hæt] n (a) Hut m. (b) (fig phrases) I'll eat my ~ if ... ich fresse einen Besen, wenn ... (col); I take my ~ off to him Hut ab vor ihm!; to talk through one's ~ (col) dummes Zeug reden; to keep sth under one's ~ (col) etw für sich behalten; at the drop of a ~ auf der Stelle; that's old ~ (col) das ist ein alter Hut (col); to pass around the ~ for sb für jdn den Hut rumgehen lassen (col).

hatch¹ [hætʃ] (also ~ out) 1 vt ausbrüten; (fig) plot also aushecken. 2 vi (bird) ausschlüpfen. when will the eggs ~? wann schlüpfen die Jungen aus?

hatch² n (Naut) Luke f. (service) ~ (Brit) Durchreiche f. down the ~! (col) hoch die Tassen! (col).

hatchback ['hætʃbæk] n Hecktürmodell nt; (door) Hecktür f.

hatchet ['hætʃɪt] n Beil nt. to bury the ~ das Kriegsbeil begraben; ~ man n (killer) gedungener Mörder; (fig) Vollstreckungsbeamte(r) m.

hatching ['hætʃɪŋ] n (Art) Schraffur f.

hate [heɪt] 1 vt hassen; (detest also) verabscheuen; (dislike also) nicht leiden können. to ~ the sound of sth etw nicht hören können; to ~ to do sth or doing sth es hassen, etw zu tun; (weaker) etw äußerst ungern tun; I ~ seeing her in pain ich kann es nicht ertragen, sie leiden zu sehen; I ~ the idea of leaving der Gedanke, wegzumüssen, ist mir äußerst zuwider; I ~ to bother you es ist mir sehr unangenehm, daß ich Sie belästigen muß; I ~ having to say it but ... es fällt mir sehr schwer, das sagen zu müssen, aber ...; I should ~ to keep you waiting ich möchte Sie auf keinen Fall warten lassen. 2 n Haß m (for, auf + acc). it's one of his pet ~s das kann er auf den Tod nicht ausstehen.

hateful ['heɪtfʊl] adj abscheulich.

hatpin ['hætpɪn] n Hutnadel f.

hatred ['heɪtrɪd] n Haß m (for auf +acc).

hatter ['hætəʳ] n Hutmacher(in f) m; (seller) Hutverkäufer(in f) m.

hat-trick ['hættrɪk] n Hattrick m.

haughty ['hɔːtɪ] adj (+er) hochmütig; (towards people) überheblich.

haul [hɔːl] 1 n (a) (journey) Strecke f. it's a long ~ es ist ein weiter Weg; short/long ~ aircraft Kurz-/Langstreckenflugzeug nt. (b) (Fishing) (Fisch)fang m; (from robbery) Beute f; (col: of presents) Ausbeute f (col). 2 vt ziehen; heavy objects also schleppen.

♦ **haul down** vt sep flag, sail einholen.

haulage ['hɔːlɪdʒ] n (a) Transport m. ~ contractor (firm) Spedition(sfirma) f; (person) Spediteur m. (b) (charges) Transportkosten pl.

haulier ['hɔːlɪəʳ] n Spediteur m; (company) Spedition f.

haunch [hɔːntʃ] n (of person) Hüfte f; (of animal) (hindquarters) Hinterbacke f; (top of leg) Keule f; (Cook) Lendenstück nt. ~es Gesäß nt; (of animal) Hinterbacken pl; he was sitting on his ~es er saß in der Hocke; ~ of venison (Cook) Rehkeule f.

haunt [hɔːnt] 1 vt (a) (ghost) house spuken in (+dat), umgehen in (+dat). (b) (fig: memory etc) verfolgen. the nightmares which ~ed him die Alpträume, die ihn heimsuchten. **(c)** *(frequent)* häufig besuchen. **2** *n* **this is one of his favourite ~s** hier hält er sich sehr gerne auf.

haunted ['hɔːntɪd] *adj* **(a)** Spuk-. **a ~ house** ein Haus *nt*, in dem es spukt; **this place is ~** hier spukt es. **(b)** *look* gehetzt; *person* ruhelos.

haunting ['hɔːntɪŋ] *adj doubt* quälend; *tune, visions, poetry* eindringlich. **these ~ final chords** diese Schlußakkorde, die einen nicht loslassen.

have ['hæv] *pret, ptp* **had,** *3rd pers sing pres* **has 1** *vt* **(a)** *(possess)* haben. **she has (got** *esp Brit)* **blue eyes** sie hat blaue Augen; **~ you (got** *esp Brit)* **or do you ~ a suitcase?** hast du einen Koffer?; **I ~n't (got** *esp Brit)* **or I don't ~ a pen** ich habe keinen Kugelschreiber.

(b) **to ~ breakfast/lunch/dinner** frühstücken/zu Mittag essen/zu Abend essen; **what will you ~?** — **I'll ~ the steak** was möchten Sie gern(e)? — ich möchte gern das Steak; **he had a cigarette/a drink/a steak** er rauchte eine Zigarette/trank etwas/aß ein Steak; **will you ~ some more?** möchten Sie gern (noch etwas) mehr?; **~ another one** nimm noch eine/einen/ eines; **trink noch einen; rauch noch eine.**

(c) *(receive, obtain, get)* haben. **I ~ it from the tax office that ...** ich habe vom Finanzamt erfahren, daß ...; **to let sb ~ sth** jdm etw geben; **it's nowhere to be had** es ist nirgends zu haben *or* kriegen *(col)*; **she's having a baby** sie bekommt ein Kind.

(d) *(maintain, insist)* **he will ~ it that Paul is guilty** er besteht darauf, daß Paul schuldig ist; **he won't ~ it that Paul is guilty** er will nichts davon hören, daß Paul schuldig ist; **as Professor James would ~ it** *(according to)* laut Professor James; *(as he would put it)* um es mit Professor James zu sagen.

(e) *(neg: refuse to allow)* **I won't ~ this nonsense** Unsinn kommt (mir) nicht in Frage!; **I won't ~ it!** das lasse ich mir nicht bieten!

(f) *(hold)* (gepackt) haben. **the dog had (got) him by the ankle** der Hund hatte ihn am Knöchel gepackt; **I ~ (got) him where I want him** ich habe ihn endlich soweit; **I'll ~ you** *(col)* dich krieg ich (beim Kragen); **you ~ me there** da bin ich überfragt.

(g) *(causative)* **to ~ sth done** etw tun lassen; **to ~ one's hair cut/a suit made** sich *(dat)* die Haare schneiden lassen/einen Anzug machen lassen; **to ~ sb do sth** jdn etw tun lassen; **they had him shot** sie ließen ihn erschießen; **I'd ~ you understand ...** Sie müssen nämlich wissen ...; **what would you ~ me say?** was soll ich dazu sagen?; **they soon had the carpet down** sie waren schnell mit dem Teppichverlegen fertig; **when she had the lid off** als sie den Deckel herunterhatte.

(h) *(experience, suffer)* **he had his car stolen** man hat ihm sein Auto gestohlen; **I've had three windows broken** (bei) mir sind drei Fenster eingeworfen worden; **I had my friends turn against me** ich mußte es erleben, wie *or* daß sich meine Freunde gegen mich wandten.

(i) **to ~ a walk** spazierengehen; **to ~ a dream** träumen.

(j) *party* geben, machen; *meeting* abhalten. **are you having a reception?** gibt es einen Empfang?

(k) *(phrases)* **let him ~ it!** gib's ihm! *(col)*; **he/that coat has had it** *(col)* der ist weg vom Fenster *(col)*/der Mantel ist im Eimer *(col)*; **if I miss the last bus, I've had it** *(col)* wenn ich den letzten Bus verpasse, bin ich geliefert *(col)*; **to ~ a pleasant evening** einen netten Abend verbringen; **~ a good time!** viel Spaß!; **you've been had!** *(col)* da hat man dich übers Ohr gehauen *(col)*; **thanks for having me** vielen Dank für Ihre

Gastfreundschaft.

2 *aux* **(a)** haben; *(esp with vbs of motion)* sein. **to ~ been** gewesen sein; **to ~ seen/heard** gesehen/gehört haben; **to ~ gone/run** gegangen/ gelaufen sein; **I ~ /had been** ich bin/war gewesen; **I ~ /had seen** ich habe/hatte gesehen; **had I seen him** hätte ich ihn gesehen; **having seen him** *(since)* da ich ihn gesehen habe/hatte; *(after)* als ich ihn gesehen hatte; **I ~ lived** *or* **~ been living here for 10 years/since January** ich wohne schon 10 Jahre/seit Januar hier; **you** *have* **grown** du bist aber gewachsen.

(b) *(in tag questions etc)* **you've seen her, ~n't you?** du hast sie gesehen, oder nicht?; **you ~n't seen her, ~n't** seen her, **~ you?** du hast sie nicht gesehen, oder?; **you ~n't seen her — yes, I ~** du hast sie nicht gesehen — doch; **you've made a mistake — no I ~n't** du hast einen Fehler gemacht — nein(, hab' ich nicht *col)*; **you've dropped your book — so I ~** du hast dein Buch fallen lassen — tatsächlich!; **I ~ seen a ghost — ~ you?** ich habe ein Gespenst gesehen — tatsächlich?; **I've lost it — you ~n't** *(disbelieving)* ich habe es verloren — das darf doch nicht wahr sein!

3 *modal aux* (+*infin*) **I ~ to do it, I ~ got to do it** *(Brit)* ich muß es tun; **I don't ~ to do it, I ~n't got to do it** *(Brit)* ich muß es nicht tun, ich brauche es nicht zu tun; **do you ~ to go now?, ~ you got to go now?** *(Brit)* müssen Sie jetzt unbedingt gehen?; **you didn't ~ to tell her** das mußten Sie ihr nicht unbedingt sagen; **it has to be a mistake!** das muß wohl ein Irrtum sein!

♦ **have around** *vt always separate* **(a)** *(let sb) to* Besuch haben; *(invite)* einladen. **(b) he's useful to ~ ~** es ist ganz praktisch, ihn zur Hand zu haben.

♦ **have in** *vt always separate* **(a)** *decorators etc* im Haus haben; *doctor* holen. **(b) to ~ it ~ for sb** *(col)* jdn auf dem Kieker haben *(col)*.

♦ **have off** *vt always separate* **to ~ it ~ with sb** *(col)* es mit jdm treiben *(col)*.

♦ **have on 1** *vt sep clothes, radio* anhaben. **2** *vt always separate* **(a)** *(have sth arranged)* vorhaben; *(be busy with)* zu tun haben. **~ you got anything ~ for tonight?** hast du heute abend etwas vor? **(b)** *(col: deceive)* übers Ohr hauen *(col)*; *(tease)* auf den Arm nehmen *(col)*. **(c) to ~ nothing ~ sb** gegen jdn nichts in der Hand haben; **they've got nothing ~ me!** mir kann keiner! *(col)*.

♦ **have out** *vt always separate* **(a) he was having his tonsils ~** ihm wurden die Mandeln herausgenommen. **(b)** *(discuss)* **to ~ it ~ with sb** etw mit jdm ausdiskutieren; **I'll ~ it ~ with him** ich werde mit ihm reden.

♦ **have up** *vt always separate* *(col: in court)* **to be had ~ for sth** wegen etw vor Gericht kommen.

haven ['heɪvn] *n (fig)* Zufluchtsstätte *f*.

haves [hævz] *npl (col)* **the ~ and the have-nots** die Betuchten und die Habenichtse *(col)*.

havoc ['hævək] *n* verheerender Schaden; *(devastation also)* Verwüstung *f*; *(chaos)* Chaos *nt*. **to wreak ~ in** *or* **with sth, to play ~ with sth** bei etw verheerenden Schaden anrichten.

Hawaii [həˈwaɪiː] *n* Hawaii *nt*.

hawk¹ [hɔːk] *n (Orn)* Habicht *m*; *(sparrow ~)* Sperber *m*; *(falcon)* Falke *m*. **the ~s and the doves** *(fig)* die Falken und die Tauben.

hawk² *vt* hausieren (gehen) mit; *(in street)* verkaufen.

hawker ['hɔːkəʳ] *n (pedlar)* *(door-to-door)* Hausierer(in *f)* m; *(in street)* Straßenhändler(in *f)* m.

hawk-eyed ['hɔːkaɪd] *adj* scharfsichtig. **to be ~** Adleraugen haben.

hawser ['hɔːzəʳ] *n (Naut)* Trosse *f*.

hawthorn ['hɔːθɔːn] *n* Weiß- *or* Rotdorn *m*.

hay [heɪ] *n* Heu *nt*. **to make ~** Heu machen; **to hit the ~** *(col)* sich in die Falle hauen *(col)*; **to make**

~ **while the sun shines** (Prov) das Eisen schmieden, solange es heiß ist (Prov).

hay: ~ **fever** n Heuschnupfen m; ~**stack** n Heuhaufen m.

haywire ['heɪwaɪəʳ] adj pred (col) **to be (all)** ~ ein Wirrwarr sein (col); **to go** ~ (plans) durcheinandergeraten; (machinery) verrückt spielen (col).

hazard ['hæzəd] **1** n **(a)** (danger) Gefahr f; (risk) Risiko nt. **it's a fire** ~ es stellt eine Feuergefahr dar. **(b)** (chance) **by** ~ durch Zufall; **game of** ~ Glücksspiel nt. **2** vt life, reputation riskieren, aufs Spiel setzen. **if I might** ~ **a suggestion** wenn ich mir einen Vorschlag erlauben darf; **to** ~ **a guess** (es) wagen, eine Vermutung anzustellen.

hazardous ['hæzədəs] adj gefährlich, risikoreich.

haze [heɪz] n Dunst m.

hazel ['heɪzl] **1** n (Bot) Haselnußstrauch m. **2** adj (colour) haselnußbraun.

hazelnut ['heɪzlnʌt] n Haselnuß f.

hazy ['heɪzɪ] adj (+er) **(a)** dunstig, diesig; mountains im Dunst (liegend). **(b)** (unclear) verschwommen. **I'm** ~ **about what happened** ich kann mich nur verschwommen daran erinnern, was geschah.

he [hiː] **1** pers pron er. **so** ~**'s the one** der (col) or er ist es also!; **Harry Rigg? who's** ~? Harry Rigg? wer ist das denn?; ~ **who** (liter) derjenige, der. **2** n **it's a** ~ (col: baby) es ist ein er.

head [hed] **1** n **(a)** Kopf m. **from** ~ **to foot** von Kopf bis Fuß; ~ **downwards** mit dem Kopf nach unten; **to stand on one's** ~ auf dem Kopf stehen; **you could do it standing on your** ~ (col) das kann man ja im Schlaf machen; **to fall** ~ **over heels in love with sb** sich bis über beide Ohren in jdn verlieben; **to keep one's** ~ **above water** (fig) sich über Wasser halten; **to talk one's** ~ **off** (col) reden wie ein Wasserfall (col); **to shout one's** ~ **off** (col) sich aus dem Leib schreien (col); **I've got some** ~ **this morning** (col) ich habe einen ziemlichen Brummschädel heute morgen (col); **to give sb his** ~ jdn machen lassen; **on your (own)** ~ **be it** auf Ihre eigene Verantwortung; **he gave orders over my** ~ er hat über meinen Kopf (hin)weg Anordnungen gegeben; **to go to one's** ~ einem zu Kopf steigen; **I can't make** ~ **nor tail of it** daraus werde ich nicht schlau.

(b) (mind, intellect) Kopf, Verstand m. **use your** ~ streng deinen Kopf an; **to get sth into one's** ~ (understand) etw begreifen; **he won't get it into his** ~ **that** ... es will ihm nicht in den Kopf, daß ...; **to take it into one's** ~ **to do sth** sich (dat) in den Kopf setzen, etw zu tun; **it never entered his** ~ **that** ... es kam ihm nie in den Sinn, daß ...; **what put that idea into his** ~? wie kommt er denn darauf?; **to get sth out of one's** ~ sich (dat) etw aus dem Kopf schlagen; **he has a good business** ~ er hat einen ausgeprägten Geschäftssinn; **he has a good** ~ **on his shoulders** er ist ein kluger Kopf; **he has an old** ~ **on young shoulders** er ist sehr reif für sein Alter; **two** ~**s are better than one** (prov) besser zwei als einer allein; **we put our** ~**s together** wir haben unsere Köpfe zusammengesteckt; **to be above** or **over sb's** ~ über jds Horizont (acc) gehen; **to keep one's** ~ den Kopf nicht verlieren; **to lose one's** ~ den Kopf verlieren; **he is off his** ~ (col) er ist (ja) nicht (ganz) bei Trost (col); **to be soft in the** ~ (col) einen (kleinen) Dachschaden haben (col).

(c) twenty ~ **of cattle** zwanzig Stück Vieh; **to pay 10 marks a** ~ 10 Mark pro Kopf bezahlen.

(d) (of flower, lettuce, nail, page) Kopf m; (of arrow, spear) Spitze f; (of bed) Kopf(ende nt) m; (on beer) Blume f; (of corn) Ähre f; (of stream) (upper area) Oberlauf m; (source) Ursprung m; (of tape-recorder) Tonkopf m. ~ **of steam** Dampfdruck m; **at the** ~ **of the list/stairs** oben an der

Liste/an der Treppe; **at the** ~ **of the table** am Kopf(ende) des Tisches; **at the** ~ **of the queue/procession** an der Spitze der Schlange/des Zuges; **if things come to a** ~ wenn sich die Sache zuspitzt.

(e) (of family) Oberhaupt nt; (of business, organization) Chef m; (Sch col) Schulleiter m. ~ **of department** (in business) Abteilungsleiter m; (Sch, Univ) Fachbereichsleiter(in f) m; ~ **of state** Staatsoberhaupt nt.

(f) (~ing, in essay etc) Rubrik f.

(g) (of coin) ~**s or tails?** Kopf oder Zahl?; ~**s I win** bei Kopf gewinne ich.

2 vt **(a)** (lead) anführen; (be in charge of also) führen; list also an der Spitze stehen von. **(b)** (direct) steuern (towards, for in Richtung). **(c)** **in the chapter** ~**ed** ... in dem Kapitel mit der Überschrift ...; ~**ed writing paper** Schreibpapier mit Briefkopf. **(d)** (Ftbl) köpfen.

3 vi gehen; fahren. **where are you** ~**ing** or ~**ed?** wo gehen/fahren Sie hin?

♦ **head back** vi zurückgehen/-fahren. **to be** ~**ing** ~ auf dem Rückweg sein.

♦ **head for** vi +prep obj place, person zugehen/zufahren auf (+acc); town, country gehen/fahren in Richtung (+gen); (ship also) Kurs halten auf (+acc). **where are you** ~**ing** or ~**ed** ~? wo gehen/fahren Sie hin?; **you're** ~**ing** ~ **trouble** du bist auf dem besten Weg, Ärger zu bekommen.

♦ **head off** vt sep abfangen; war, strike abwenden.

♦ **head up** vt sep delegation leiten.

head in cpds (top, senior) Ober-; ~**ache** n Kopfschmerzen pl; (col: problem) Problem nt; **to have a** ~**ache** Kopfschmerzen haben; **this is a bit of a** ~**ache** das macht mir/uns ziemliches Kopfzerbrechen; ~**band** n Stirnband nt; ~**dress** n Kopfschmuck m.

header ['hedəʳ] n **(a)** (dive) Kopfsprung m. **(b)** (Ftbl) Kopfball m.

head: ~**first** adv (lit, fig) kopfüber; ~**gear** n Kopfbedeckung f; ~**hunter** n (lit, fig) Kopfjäger m.

heading ['hedɪŋ] n Überschrift f; (on letter, document) Kopf m; (in encyclopedia) Stichwort nt.

head: ~**lamp** n, ~**light** n Scheinwerfer m; ~**land** n Landspitze f; ~**line** n (Press) Schlagzeile f; **to hit the** ~**lines** Schlagzeilen machen; **the news** ~**lines** npl das Wichtigste in Kürze; ~**long** adj, adv fall mit dem Kopf voran; rush Hals über Kopf; ~**master** n Schulleiter m; ~**mistress** n Schulleiterin f; ~ **office** n Zentrale f; ~**-on** adj collision frontal; **2** adv frontal; ~**phones** npl Kopfhörer pl; ~**quarters** n sing or pl (Mil) Hauptquartier nt; (Comm) Zentrale f; (of political party) Parteizentrale f; **police** ~**quarters** Polizeipräsidium nt; ~**rest** n Kopfstütze f; ~**room** n lichte Höhe; (in car) Kopfraum m; ~**scarf** n Kopftuch nt; ~**set** n Kopfhörer pl; ~**start** n Vorsprung m (on sb jdm gegenüber); ~**stone** n (on grave) Grabstein m; ~**strong** adj dickköpfig; ~ **teacher** n (Brit) = ~**master**, ~**mistress**; ~ **waiter** n Oberkellner m; ~**way** n **to make** ~**way** (lit, fig) vorankommen; ~**wind** n Gegenwind m.

heady ['hedɪ] adj (+er) (lit, fig) berauschend.

heal [hiːl] **1** vi (Med, fig) heilen. **2** vt (Med) heilen; (fig) differences etc beilegen.

♦ **heal up** vi verheilen. **2** vt sep zuheilen lassen.

health [helθ] n Gesundheit f. **in good/poor** ~ bei guter/schlechter Gesundheit; **how is his** ~? wie geht es ihm gesundheitlich?; **to be good/bad for one's** ~ gesund/ungesund sein; **Ministry of H**~ Gesundheitsministerium nt; **to drink** (to) **sb's** ~ auf jds Wohl (acc) trinken; **your** ~! zum Wohl!

health: ~ **club** n Fitness-Center nt; ~ **food** n Reformkost f; ~ **food shop** (Brit) or **store** (esp US) n Reformhaus nt; (modern) Bioladen m; ~ **hazard** n Gefahr f für die Gesundheit; ~ **insurance** n

Krankenversicherung f; ~ **resort** n Kurort m;
H~ Service n (Brit) Gesundheitswesen nt; **H~
Service doctor** Kassenarzt m/-ärztin f; ~ **visitor**
n Sozialarbeiter(in f) m (in der Gesundheitsfürsorge).

healthy ['hɛlθɪ] adj (+er) (lit, fig) gesund.

heap [hiːp] **1** n **(a)** Haufen m; (col: old car) Klap-
perkiste f (col). **he fell in a ~ on the floor** er
sackte zu Boden. **(b)** ~s **of** (col) eine Menge
(col); **we've got ~s of time** wir haben jede Menge
Zeit (col). **2** vt häufen. **to ~ praises on sb** jdn mit
Lob überschütten; ~ed **spoonful** gehäufter
Löffel.

♦ **heap up 1** vt sep aufhäufen. **2** vi sich häufen.

hear [hɪəʳ] pret, ptp **heard 1** vt (also learn)
hören. **to make oneself ~d** sich (dat) Gehör verschaffen; **you're not going, do you ~ me!** du
gehst nicht, hörst du (mich)!; **to ~ him speak
you'd think ...** wenn man ihn so reden hört,
könnte man meinen, ...; **I've often ~d say** or **it
said that ...** ich habe oft sagen hören, daß ...; **I ~
(tell) you're going away** ich höre, Sie gehen weg;
I must be ~ing things ich glaube, ich höre nicht
richtig; **to ~ a case** (Jur) einen Fall verhandeln.
2 vi **(a)** hören. ~, ~! (sehr) richtig!; (Parl)
hört!, hört! **(b)** (get news) hören. **yes, so I ~** ja,
ich habe es gehört; **you'll be ~ing from me!**
(threatening) Sie werden noch von mir hören!; **to
~ about sth** von etw hören or erfahren; **have you
~d about John?** he's getting married haben Sie
schon gehört? John heiratet; **never ~d of him/it**
nie (von ihm/davon) gehört; **I've ~d of him** ich
habe schon von ihm gehört; **he was never ~d of**
again man hat nie wieder etwas von ihm gehört;
I've never ~d of such a thing! das ist ja
unerhört!; **I won't ~ of it** (allow) ich will davon
nichts hören.

♦ **hear out** vt sep person ausreden lassen.

heard [hɜːd] pret, ptp of **hear.**

hearing ['hɪərɪŋ] n **(a)** (sense) Gehör nt. **(b)** within/
out of ~ in/außer Hörweite. **(c)** (Pol) Hearing nt,
Anhörung f; (Jur) Verhandlung f. **to give sb a ~**
jdn anhören; **he didn't get a fair ~** man hörte ihn
nicht richtig an; (Jur) er bekam keinen fairen
Prozeß.

hearing aid n Hörgerät nt.

hearsay ['hɪəseɪ] n Gerüchte pl. **to have sth on ~**
etw vom Hörensagen wissen.

hearse [hɜːs] n Leichenwagen m.

heart [hɑːt] n **(a)** (lit, fig) Herz nt. **to break sb's ~**
jdm das Herz brechen; **to break one's ~ over sth**
sich über etw (acc) zu Tode grämen; **you're
breaking my ~** (iro) ich fang' gleich an zu
weinen (iro); **after my own ~** ganz nach meinem
Herzen; **to have a change of ~** sich anders besinnen; **to learn/know sth by ~** etw auswendig
lernen/kennen; **in my ~ of ~s** im Grunde meines
Herzens; **with all my ~** von ganzem Herzen;
from the bottom of one's ~ aus tiefstem Herzen;
to take sth to ~ sich (dat) etw zu Herzen nehmen;
we have your interests at ~ Ihre Interessen
liegen uns am Herzen; **to set one's ~ on sth** sein
Herz an etw (acc) hängen (geh); **to one's ~'s
content** nach Herzenslust; **most men are boys at
~** die meisten Männer sind im Grunde (ihres
Herzens) noch richtige Kinder; **his ~ isn't in it**
er ist nicht mit dem Herzen dabei; **to lose ~** den
Mut verlieren; **to take ~** Mut fassen; **to put new
~ into sb** jdm mit neuem Mut erfüllen; **his ~ is in
the right place** (col) er hat das Herz auf dem
rechten Fleck (col); **to have a ~ of stone** ein Herz
aus Stein haben; **to wear one's ~ on one's sleeve**
(prov) aus seinem Herzen keine Mördergrube
machen (col); **my ~ was in my mouth** (col) mir
schlug das Herz bis zum Hals; **have a ~!** (col) gib
deinem Herzen einen Stoß! (col); **not to have the
~ to do sth** es nicht übers Herz bringen, etw zu
tun; **she has a ~ of gold** sie hat ein goldenes

Herz; **my ~ sank** (apprehension) mir rutschte
das Herz in die Hose (col); (sadness) das
Herz wurde mir schwer; (discouraged) mein
Mut sank; **the ~ of the matter** der Kern der
Sache; **in the ~ of the forest** mitten im Wald.
(b) (Cards) ~s pl Herz nt; (Bridge) Coeur nt;
queen of ~s Herzdame f.

heart: ~**ache** n Kummer m; ~ **attack** n Herzinfarkt m; **I nearly had a ~ attack** (fig col: shock)
ich habe fast einen Herzschlag gekriegt (col);
~**beat** n Herzschlag m; ~**break** n großer
Kummer; ~**breaking** adj herzzerreißend; **it's a
~breaking job** es bricht einem das Herz;
~**broken** adj todunglücklich; ~**burn** n Sodbrennen nt.

heartening ['hɑːtnɪŋ] adj news ermutigend.

heart: ~ **failure** n Herzversagen nt; ~**felt** adj tief
empfunden; sympathy herzlichst.

hearth [hɑːθ] n Feuerstelle f; (whole fireplace)
Kamin m; (fig: home) (häuslicher) Herd. ~**rug**
n Kaminvorleger m.

heartily ['hɑːtɪlɪ] adv herzlich; sing kräftig; eat
herzhaft. **I ~ agree** ich stimme voll und ganz zu.

heart: ~**less** adj herzlos; (cruel also) grausam;
~**rending** adj herzzerreißend; ~-**searching** n
Gewissenserforschung f; ~**strings** npl **to pull** or
tug at the/sb's ~strings auf die/bei jdm auf die
Tränendrüsen drücken (col); ~-**throb** n (col)
Schwarm m (col); ~-**to-~** adj **to have a ~-to-~
talk with sb** sich mit jdm ganz offen aussprechen; ~ **transplant** n Herztransplantation f;
~-**trouble** n Herzbeschwerden pl; ~-**warming**
adj herzerfreuend.

hearty ['hɑːtɪ] adj (+er) herzlich; slap also, meal,
appetite herzhaft, kräftig; dislike tief; person
(robust) kernig; (cheerful) laut und herzlich.

heat [hiːt] **1** n **(a)** (lit, fig) Hitze f; (pleasant, Phys)
Wärme f; (of curry etc) Schärfe f; (~ing) Heizung
f. **in the ~ of the day** wenn es heiß ist; **in the ~ of
the moment** in der Erregung; **to take the ~ out of the
situation** die Situation entschärfen; **to put the ~
on** (col) Druck machen (col); **to put the ~ on sb**
(col) jdn unter Druck setzen; **the ~ is off** (col)
der Druck ist weg (col); (danger is past) die
Gefahr ist vorbei. **(b)** (Sport) Vorlauf m; (Boxing
etc) Vorkampf m. **final ~** Ausscheidungskampf
m. **(c)** (Zool) Brunst f; (of dogs, cats) Läufigkeit f.
on ~ brünstig; läufig. **2** vt erhitzen; room heizen;
pool, house beheizen.

♦ **heat up 1** vi warm werden; (get very hot) sich
erhitzen; (discussion) hitzig werden. **2** vt sep
erwärmen; food heiß machen.

heated ['hiːtɪd] adj (lit) geheizt; pool beheizt; (fig)
words, discussion hitzig, erregt. **things got rather
~** die Gemüter erhitzten sich sehr.

heater ['hiːtəʳ] n Ofen m; (electrical also) Heizgerät
nt; (in car) Heizung f.

heath [hiːθ] n Heide f.

heathen ['hiːðən] **1** adj heidnisch, Heiden-; (fig)
unkultiviert. **2** n Heide m, Heidin f; (fig) un-
kultivierter Mensch.

heather ['hɛðəʳ] n Heidekraut nt, Erika f.

Heath Robinson [,hiːθ'rɒbɪnsən] adj (col) gadget
phantastisch (col).

heating ['hiːtɪŋ] n (in house etc) Heizung f.

heat: ~-**resistant** adj hitzebeständig; ~ **shield** n
Hitzeschild m; ~ **stroke** n Hitzschlag m; ~
treatment n (Med) Wärmebehandlung f; ~**wave**
n Hitzewelle f.

heave [hiːv] **1** vt (lift) (hoch)hieven (onto auf +acc);
(drag) schleppen; (throw) werfen; sigh, sob
ausstoßen. **to ~ anchor** den Anker lichten. **2** vi
(a) (pull) ziehen. **(b)** (bosom, sea) sich heben
und senken; (stomach) sich umdrehen. **(c)**
pret, ptp **hove** (Naut) ~ **in(to) sight** in Sicht
kommen.

♦ **heave to** (Naut) vi beidrehen.

heave ho *interj* hau ruck.

heaven ['hevn] *n* (a) *(lit, fig col)* Himmel *m*. **in** ~ **im Himmel**; **to go to** ~ **in den Himmel kommen**; **he is in (his seventh)** ~ **er ist im siebten Himmel**; **to move** ~ **and earth** Himmel und Hölle in Bewegung setzen; **it was** ~ **es war einfach himmlisch**; **the** ~**s opened** der Himmel öffnete seine Schleusen. **(b)** *(col)* **(good)** ~**s!** (du) lieber Himmel! *(col)*; **would you like to?** — **(good)** ~**s no!** möchten Sie? — um Himmels willen, bloß nicht!; ~ **knows what** ... weiß der Himmel, was ... *(col)*; **for** ~**'s sake!** um Himmels willen!

heavenly ['hevnlɪ] *adj (lit, fig col)* himmlisch. ~ **body** Himmelskörper *m*.

heavily ['hevɪlɪ] *adv* schwer; *move, walk* schwerfällig; *rain, smoke, drink, rely, populated, influenced, in debt* stark; *lose, tax* hoch; *sleep* tief. ~ **built** kräftig gebaut; **time hung** ~ **on his hands** die Zeit verging ihm nur langsam; ~ **committed** stark engagiert; **to be** ~ **subscribed** viele Abonnenten haben.

heaviness ['hevɪnɪs] *n* Schwere *f*.

heavy ['hevɪ] **1** *adj (+er)* (a) schwer; *features* grob; *rain, cold also, traffic, drinker, smoker* stark; *expenses, taxes* hoch; *line* dick; *sleep* tief; *crop* reich; (~**-handed**) *manner, style* schwerfällig; *silence* bedrückend; *weather, air* drückend, schwül; *sky* bedeckt; *(tiring) day* anstrengend. **with a** ~ **heart** schweren Herzens, mit schwerem Herzen; ~ **goods vehicle** Lastkraftwagen *m*; ~ **industry** Schwerindustrie *f*; ~ **artillery** schwere Artillerie; **to be** ~ **on petrol** viel Benzin brauchen; **the going was** ~ wir kamen nur schwer voran; **the conversation was** ~ **going** die Unterhaltung war mühsam; **this book is very** ~ **going** das Buch liest sich schwer. **(b)** *(col: strict)* streng *(on mit)*. **2** *n (col: thug)* Schlägertyp *m*.

heavy: ~**-duty** *adj tyres etc* strapazierfähig; *boots* Arbeits-; *machine* Hochleistungs-; ~**-handed** *adj* ungeschickt; ~**weight** *n (Boxing)* Schwergewicht *nt*; *(fig col)* großes Tier *(col)*.

Hebrew ['hi:bru:] **1** *adj* hebräisch. **2** *n* (a) Hebräer(in *f*) *m*. **(b)** *(language)* Hebräisch *nt*.

Hebrides ['hebrɪdi:z] *npl* Hebriden *pl*.

heck [hek] *interj (col)* oh ~! zum Kuckuck! *(col)*; **I've a** ~ **of a lot to do** ich habe irrsinnig viel zu tun *(col)*.

heckle ['hekl] **1** *vt speaker* (durch Zwischenrufe) stören. **2** *vi* Zwischenrufe machen.

heckler ['heklə^r] *n* Zwischenrufer *m*.

heckling ['heklɪŋ] *n* Zwischenrufe *pl*.

hectare ['hektɑ:^{r}] *n* Hektar *m or nt*.

hectic ['hektɪk] *adj* hektisch.

he'd [hi:d] = **he would; he had.**

hedge [hedʒ] **1** *n* Hecke *f*; *(fig: protection)* Schutz *m*. **2** *vi* Fragen ausweichen, kneifen *(col) (at* bei*)*. **3** *vt investment* absichern. **to** ~ **one's bets** *(lit, fig)* sich absichern.

hedgehog ['hedʒhɒg] *n* Igel *m*.

hedge: ~**hop** *vi* tief fliegen; ~**row** *n* Hecke *f*.

hedonism ['hi:dənɪzəm] *n* Hedonismus *m*.

hedonist ['hi:dənɪst] *n* Hedonist(in *f*) *m*.

heebie-jeebies ['hi:bɪ'dʒi:bɪz] *npl* he gives me the ~ *(col)* wenn ich ihn sehe, bekomm' ich eine Gänsehaut *(col)*.

heed [hi:d] **1** *n* to take ~ achtgeben; **to take** ~/**no** ~ **of sb/sth** jdn/etw beachten/nicht beachten. **2** *vt* beachten; *advice* hören auf *(+acc)*.

heedless ['hi:dlɪs] *adj* rücksichtslos. **to be** ~ **of sth** auf etw *(acc)* nicht achten.

heel [hi:l] **1** *n* (a) Ferse *f*; *(of shoe)* Absatz *m*. **to be right on sb's** ~**s** jdm auf den Fersen folgen; *(fig: chase)* jdm auf den Fersen sein; **to follow hard upon sb's** ~**s** jdm dicht auf den Fersen sein; **to be down at** ~ *(person)* heruntergekommen sein; *(shoes)* abgelaufen sein; **to take to one's** ~**s** sich aus dem Staub(e) machen; ~! *(to dog)* (bei) Fuß!; **to turn on one's** ~ auf dem Absatz kehrtmachen;

to cool *or* **kick one's** ~**s** *(col) (wait)* warten; *(do nothing)* Däumchen drehen; ~ **bar** Absatzbar *f*. **(b)** *(pej col: person)* Scheißkerl *m (col!)*. **2** *vt* **to** ~ **shoes** auf Schuhe neue Absätze machen; **to be well** ~**ed** *(col)* betucht sein *(col)*.

hefty ['heftɪ] *adj (+er) (col)* kräftig; *book* dick; *object, workload* schwer; *sum of money, amount* ganz schön *(col)*.

heifer ['hefə^r] *n* Färse *f*.

height [haɪt] *n* (a) Höhe *f*; *(of person)* Größe *f*. **what** ~ **are you?** wie groß sind Sie? **(b)** *(high place)* ~**s** *pl* Höhen *pl*; **to scale the** ~**s of** Everest den Mount Everest besteigen; **fear of** ~**s** Höhenangst *f*; **to be afraid of** ~**s** nicht schwindelfrei sein. **(c)** *(fig)* Höhe *f*; *(of success, stupidity also)* Gipfel *m*. **at the** ~ **of his power** auf der Höhe seiner Macht; **at the** ~ **of the season** in der Hauptsaison; **at the** ~ **of the storm** als das Gewitter am heftigsten war; **dressed in the** ~ **of fashion** nach der neuesten Mode gekleidet; **at the** ~ **of summer** im Hochsommer.

heighten ['haɪtn] *vt (raise)* höher stellen; *(emphasize) colour etc* hervorheben; *(increase) anger, effect etc* verstärken; *intensity* steigern.

heinous ['heɪnəs] *adj* abscheulich.

heir [ɛə^r] *n* Erbe *m (to gen)*. ~ **apparent** gesetzlicher Erbe; ~ **to the throne** Thronfolger *m*.

heiress ['ɛərɛs] *n* Erbin *f*.

heirloom ['ɛəlu:m] *n* Erbstück *nt*.

heist [haɪst] *n (esp US col)* Raubüberfall *m*.

held [held] *pret, ptp of* **hold.**

helicopter ['helɪkɒptə^r] *n* Hubschrauber *m*.

heliport ['helɪpɔ:t] *n* Hubschrauberlandeplatz *m*.

helium ['hi:lɪəm] *n* Helium *nt*.

hell [hel] *n* (a) Hölle *f*. **to go to** ~ *(lit)* in die Hölle kommen.
(b) *(fig uses)* **all** ~ **was let loose** die Hölle war los; **it's** ~ **working there** es ist die reinste Hölle, dort zu arbeiten; **life became** ~ das Leben wurde zur Hölle; **she made his life** ~ sie machte ihm das Leben zur Hölle; **to give sb** ~ *(col)* jdm die Hölle heiß machen; *(make life unpleasant)* jdm das Leben zur Hölle machen; **there'll be (all)** ~ **when he finds out** *(col)* wenn er das erfährt, ist der Teufel los *(col)*; **to play** ~ **with sth** *(col)* etw total durcheinanderbringen; **for the** ~ **of it** *(col)* nur zum Spaß or aus Jux.
(c) *(col: intensifier)* **a** ~ **of a noise** ein Höllenlärm *(col)*; **to work like** ~ wie wild arbeiten *(col)*; **to run like** ~ laufen, was die Beine hergeben; **we had a** ~ **of a time** *(bad, difficult)* es war grauenhaft; *(good)* wir haben uns prima amüsiert; **a** ~ **of a lot** verdammt viel *(col)*; **that's one** *or* **a** ~ **of a problem/difference/bruise** das ist ein verdammt schwieriges Problem/ein wahnsinniger Unterschied/Bluterguß *(col)*; **to** ~ **with him** hol ihn der Teufel *(col)*, der kann mich mal *(col)*; **to** ~ **with it!**, ~! verdammt noch mal *(col!)*; **go to** ~! scher dich zum Teufel! *(col)*; **what the** ~ **do you want?** was willst du denn, verdammt noch mal? *(col!)*; **oh, what the** ~! ach, was soll's! *(col!)*

he'll [hi:l] = **he shall, he will.**

hellish ['helɪʃ] *adj (col)* höllisch *(col)*; *exams* verteufelt schwer *(col)*.

hello [hə'ləʊ] *interj* hallo. **say** ~ **to your parents (from me)** grüß deine Eltern (von mir).

helm [helm] *n* Ruder *nt*. **to be at the** ~ *(lit, fig)* am Ruder sein.

helmet ['helmɪt] *n* Helm *m*; *(Fencing)* Maske *f*.

help [help] **1** *n* Hilfe *f*. **with the** ~ **of sth** mit Hilfe *(+gen)*; **he is beyond** ~ ihm ist nicht mehr zu helfen; **to go/come to sb's** ~ jdm zu Hilfe eilen/kommen; **to be of** ~ **to sb** jdm behilflich sein; *(thing also)* jdm nützen; **you're a great** ~! *(iro)* du bist mir eine solche Hilfe!; **we are short of** ~ **in the shop** wir haben nicht genügend (Hilfs)kräfte im Geschäft; **there's no** ~ **for it** da ist nichts zu

machen.
2 *vti* **(a)** helfen (+*dat*). **to ~ sb (to) do sth** jdm
(dabei) helfen, etw zu tun; **~!** Hilfe!; **can I ~
you?** kann ich (Ihnen) behilflich sein?; **that
won't ~ you** das wird Ihnen nichts nützen; **this
will ~ the pain** das wird gegen die Schmerzen
helfen; **it will ~ the crops to grow** es wird das
Wachstum des Getreides fördern.

(b) to ~ sb down jdm hinunter-/
herunterhelfen; **to ~ sb off with his coat** jdm
aus dem Mantel helfen; **to ~ sb over the street**
jdm über die Straße helfen; **to ~ sb through a
difficult time** jdm in einer schwierigen Zeit beistehen; **to ~ sb up** (*from floor, chair etc*) jdm
aufhelfen *or* (*up stairs etc*) hinaufhelfen.

(c) she ~ed him to potatoes sie gab ihm
Kartoffeln; **to ~ oneself to sth** sich mit etw
bedienen; **~ yourself!** bedienen Sie sich doch!

(d) he can't ~ it, he was born with it er kann
nichts dafür, das ist angeboren; **he can't ~ it!**
(*col: he's stupid*) er ist nun mal so (doof); **don't say
more than you can ~** sagen Sie nicht mehr als
unbedingt nötig; **not if I can ~** it nicht, wenn ich
es irgendwie vermeiden kann; **I couldn't ~
laughing** ich mußte (einfach) lachen; **I had to do
it, I couldn't ~ myself** ich mußte es einfach tun;
one cannot ~ wondering whether ... man muß
sich wirklich fragen, ob ...; **it can't be ~ed** das ist
nun mal so.
♦ **help out 1** *vi* aushelfen (*with* bei). **2** *vt sep* helfen
(+*dat*) (*with* mit).
helper ['hɛlpə'] *n* Helfer(in *f*) *m*; (*assistant*)
Gehilfe *m*, Gehilfin *f*.
helpful ['hɛlpʊl] *adj person* hilfsbereit; (*useful*)
gadget, advice nützlich. **you have been very ~** Sie
haben mir sehr geholfen.
helpfully ['hɛlpfəlɪ] *adv* hilfreich.
helping ['hɛlpɪŋ] **1** *n* (*at table*) Portion *f*. **to take a
second ~ of sth** sich (*dat*) noch einmal von etw
nehmen. **2** *adj attr* **to lend a ~ hand to sb** jdm
behilflich sein.
helpless ['hɛlplɪs] *adj* hilflos. **she was ~ with
laughter** sie konnte sich vor Lachen kaum
halten.
helter-skelter ['hɛltə'skɛltə'] **1** *adv* Hals über
Kopf (*col*). **2** *n* (*Brit: on fairground*) Rutschbahn *f*.
hem [hɛm] **1** *n* Saum *m*. **2** *vt* säumen.
♦ **hem in** *vt sep troops* einschließen; (*fig*)
einengen.
he-man ['hiːmæn] *n, pl* **-men** [-mɛn] (*col*) sehr
männlicher Typ.
hematology *n* (*US*) = haematology.
hemisphere ['hɛmɪsfɪə'] *n* Hemisphäre *f*.
hemlock ['hɛmlɒk] *n* (*poison*) Schierling(saft) *m*.
hemp [hɛmp] *n* Hanf *m*.
hen [hɛn] *n* Huhn *nt*, Henne *f*; (*female bird*)
Weibchen *nt*.
hence [hɛns] *adv* **(a)** (*for this reason*) also. **~ the
name** daher the Name. **(b)** (*from now*) **two years
~** in zwei Jahren.
henceforth [,hɛns'fɔːθ] *adv* (*from then on*) von da
an; (*from now on*) von nun an.
henchman ['hɛntʃmən] *n, pl* **-men** [-mən] (*pej*)
Kumpan *m*.
henna ['hɛnə] **1** *n* Henna *f*. **2** *vt* mit Henna färben.
hen: ~-party *n* (*col*)=Kaffeeklatsch *m* (*col*);
(*before wedding*) für die Braut arrangierte Da-
mengesellschaft; **~peck** *vt* a **~pecked husband**
ein Pantoffelheld *m* (*col*); **he is ~pecked** er steht
unterm Pantoffel (*col*).
hepatitis [,hepə'taɪtɪs] *n* Hepatitis *f*.
her [hɜː'] **1** *pers pron* **(a)** (*dir obj, with prep* +*acc*)
sie; (*indir obj, with prep* +*dat*) ihr. **with her books
about ~** mit ihren Büchern um sich. **(b) it's ~**
sie ist's; **who, ~?** wer, sie? **2** *poss adj* ihr; *see* **my**.
herald ['hɛrəld] **1** *n* (*Hist*) Herold *m*; (*fig*) (Vor)bote
m (*geh*). **2** *vt* ankündigen.
heraldic [he'rældɪk] *adj* heraldisch, Wappen-.

heraldry ['hɛrəldrɪ] *n* (*science*) Wappenkunde *f*.
herb [hɜːb] *n* Kraut *nt*. **~ garden** Kräutergarten *m*.
herbaceous [hɜː'beɪʃəs] *adj* **~ border** Stauden-
rabatte *f*.
herbal ['hɜːbəl] *adj* Kräuter-.
herd [hɜːd] **1** *n* Herde *f*; (*of deer*) Rudel *nt*. **the
common ~** die breite Masse. **2** *vt* (*drive*) *cattle,
prisoners* treiben; (*tend*) *cattle* hüten.
♦ **herd together 1** *vi* sich zusammendrängen. **2**
vt sep zusammentreiben.
herd instinct *n* Herdentrieb *m*.
here [hɪə'] *adv* **(a)** hier; (*with motion*) hierher; **~ I
am** hier bin ich; **spring is ~** der Frühling ist da;
~ and now auf der Stelle; **this one ~** der/die/das
hier; **I won't be ~ for lunch** ich bin zum Mittagessen nicht da; **~ and there** hier und da; **~,
there and everywhere** überall; **around/about ~**
hier herum; **up/down to ~** bis hierher; **it's in/
over ~** es ist hier (drin)/hier drüben; **put it
in/over ~** stellen Sie es hier herein/hierüber;
from ~ on in (*esp US*) von nun an.
(b) (*phrases*) **~ you are** (*giving sb sth*) hier
(bitte); (*on finding sb*) da bist du ja!; (*on finding
sth*) da ist es ja; **~ we are, home again** so, da
wären wir wieder zu Hause; **~ he comes** da
kommt er ja; **look out, ~ he comes** Vorsicht, er
kommt!; **~ goes!** (*before attempting sth*) dann mal
los; **~, let me do that** komm, laß mich das mal
machen; **~'s to you!** (*in toasts*) auf Ihr Wohl!;
it's neither ~ nor there es spielt keine Rolle.
here: ~abouts ['hɪərəbauts] *adv* hier herum;
~after 1 *adv* (*in books, contracts*) im folgenden. **2**
n **the ~after** das Jenseits; **~by** *adv* (*form*) hiermit.
hereditary [hɪ'redɪtərɪ] *adj* erblich, Erb-.
heredity [hɪ'redɪtɪ] *n* Vererbung *f*.
heresy ['hɛrəsɪ] *n* Ketzerei *f*.
heretic ['hɛrətɪk] *n* Ketzer(in *f*) *m*.
heretical [hɪ'retɪkəl] *adj* ketzerisch.
here: ~upon *adv* daraufhin; **~with** *adv* (*form*)
hiermit.
heritage ['hɛrɪtɪdʒ] *n* (*lit, fig*) Erbe *nt*.
hermaphrodite [hɜː'mæfrədaɪt] *n* Zwitter *m*.
hermetic [hɜː'metɪk] *adj* hermetisch.
hermetically [hɜː'metɪkəlɪ] *adv* **~ sealed** hermetisch verschlossen *or* (*fig*) abgeriegelt.
hermit ['hɜːmɪt] *n* Einsiedler *m* (*also fig*).
hernia ['hɜːnɪə] *n* (Eingeweide)bruch *m*.
hero ['hɪərəʊ] *n, pl* **-es** Held *m*; (*fig: object of hero-
worship also*) Idol *nt*.
heroic [hɪ'rəʊɪk] *adj* heldenhaft; *behaviour, action
also, words* heroisch; *effort* gewaltig.
heroin ['hɛrəʊɪn] *n* Heroin *nt*. **~ addict** Heroin-
süchtige(r) *mf*.
heroine ['hɛrəʊɪn] *n* Heldin *f*.
heroism ['hɛrəʊɪzəm] *n* (Helden)mut *m*.
heron ['hɛrən] *n* Reiher *m*.
hero-worship ['hɪːrəʊ,wɜːʃɪp] **1** *n* Verehrung *f*; (*of
popstar etc*) Schwärmerei *f*. **2** *vt* verehren;
popstar etc schwärmen für.
herring ['hɛrɪŋ] *n* Hering *m*.
herringbone pattern ['hɛrɪŋbəʊn'pætən] *n*
Fischgrät(en)muster *nt*.
hers [hɜːz] *poss pron* ihre(r, s); *see* mine¹.
herself [hɜː'self] *pers pron* **(a)** (*dir and indir obj,
with prep*) sich; *see* **myself**. **(b)** (*emph*) (sie)
selbst.
he's [hiːz] = **he is; he has.**
hesitant ['hɛzɪtənt] *adj answer, smile* zögernd;
person also unentschlossen. **I was rather ~ about
doing it** ich war (mir) ziemlich unschlüssig, ob
ich es tun sollte.
hesitate ['hɛzɪteɪt] *vi* zögern. **he who ~s is lost**
(*Prov*) wer lange zögert, hat das Nachsehen;
even he would ~ at murder selbst er hätte bei
einem Mord Bedenken; **he ~s at nothing** er
schreckt vor nichts zurück; **I am still hesitating
about what to do** ich bin mir immer noch nicht

schlüssig, was ich tun soll; **I wouldn't** ~ **to say so** ich hätte keine Hemmungen, es zu sagen; **don't** ~ **to ask me** fragen Sie ruhig; **please don't** ~ **to get in touch** wenden Sie sich bitte an mich/uns.

hesitation [ˌhezɪ'teɪʃən] n Zögern nt. **without the slightest** ~ ohne auch nur einen Augenblick zu zögern.

hessian ['hesɪən] n Sackleinen nt.

heterogeneous [ˌhetərəʊ'dʒiːnɪəs] adj heterogen.

heterosexual [ˌhetərəʊ'seksjʊəl] **1** adj heterosexuell. **2** n Heterosexuelle(r) mf.

het up ['het ˌʌp] adj (col) aufgeregt.

hew [hjuː] pret ~**ed**, ptp **hewn** or ~**ed** vt hauen; (shape) behauen.

hex [heks] n **to put a** ~ **on sth** etw verhexen.

hexagon ['heksəgən] n Sechseck nt.

hey [heɪ] interj he.

heyday ['heɪdeɪ] n Glanzzeit, Blütezeit f. **in his** ~ in seiner Glanzzeit.

hi [haɪ] interj hallo.

hiatus [haɪ'eɪtəs] n (gap) Lücke f.

hibernate ['haɪbəneɪt] vi Winterschlaf halten.

hibernation [ˌhaɪbə'neɪʃən] n Winterschlaf m.

hiccough, hiccup ['hɪkʌp] n Schluckauf m; (col: in plans etc) kleines Problem. **to have the** ~**s** den Schluckauf haben.

hick [hɪk] n (US col) Hinterwäldler m (col).

hide[1] [haɪd] (vb: pret **hid** [hɪd], ptp **hidden** ['hɪdn] or **hid**) **1** vt (from vor +dat) verstecken; truth, tears, feelings, face verbergen; (from view) moon, rust verdecken. **2** vi sich verstecken (from sb vor jdm). **he was hiding in the cupboard** er hielt sich im Schrank versteckt. **3** n Versteck nt.

♦ **hide away 1** vi sich verstecken. **2** vt sep verstecken.

♦ **hide out** vi sich verstecken.

hide[2] n (of animal) Haut f; (of furry animal) Fell nt; (processed) Leder nt. **I haven't seen** ~ **nor hair of him for weeks** (col) den habe ich in den letzten Wochen nicht mal von weitem gesehen.

hide: ~-**and-seek** n Versteckspiel nt; ~**away** n Versteck nt; ~**bound** adj person, views engstirnig.

hideous ['hɪdɪəs] adj grauenhaft, scheußlich.

hideout ['haɪdaʊt] n Versteck nt.

hiding[1] ['haɪdɪŋ] n **to be in** ~ sich versteckt halten; **to go into** ~ untertauchen; ~ **place** Versteck nt.

hiding[2] n (beating) **to give sb a good** ~ jdm eine Tracht Prügel geben.

hierarchy ['haɪərɑːkɪ] n Hierarchie f.

hieroglyphic ['haɪərə'glɪfɪk] **1** adj hieroglyphisch. **2** n ~**s** pl Hieroglyphen(schrift f) pl.

hi-fi ['haɪˌfaɪ] n Hi-Fi nt; (system) Hi-Fi-Anlage f.

higgledy-piggledy ['hɪgldɪ'pɪgldɪ] adv wie Kraut und Rüben (durcheinander) (col).

high [haɪ] **1** adj (+er) **(a)** hoch pred, hohe(r, s) attr; altitude groß; wind stark; complexion, colour (hoch)rot. **a building 80 metres** ~ ein 80 Meter hohes Gebäude; **on one of the** ~**er floors** in einem der oberen Stockwerke; **the river is quite** ~ der Fluß führt ziemlich viel Wasser; **he left her** ~ **and dry** er hat sie sitzen lassen; **to be left** ~ **and dry** auf dem Trockenen sitzen (col); **on the** ~**est authority** von höchster Stelle; **to act** ~ **and mighty** erhaben tun; **to be on one's** ~ **horse** (fig) auf dem hohen Roß sitzen; **to pay a** ~ **price for sth** (lit, fig) etw teuer bezahlen; **in** ~ **spirits** in Hochstimmung; **to have a** ~ **old time** (col) mächtig Spaß haben (col); **it's** ~ **time you went home** es wird höchste Zeit, daß du nach Hause gehst.

(b) (col) (on drugs) high (col).

(c) meat angegangen.

2 adv (+er) hoch. ~ **up** (position) hoch oben; (motion) hoch hinauf; **one floor** ~**er** ein Stockwerk höher; **to go as** ~ **as £200** bis zu £ 200 (hoch)gehen; **feelings ran** ~ die Gemüter erhitzten sich; **to search** ~ **and low** überall suchen.

3 n **(a) the orders come from on** ~ (hum col) der Befehl kommt von oben. **(b) unemployment has reached a new** ~ die Arbeitslosenziffern haben einen neuen Höchststand erreicht. **(c)** (Met) Hoch nt. **(d)** (US Aut: top gear) **in** ~ im höchsten Gang. **(e)** (US col: high school) Penne f (col).

high: ~ **altar** n Hochaltar m; ~**ball** n (US) Highball m; ~**brow 1** n Intellektuelle(r) mf; **2** adj interests intellektuell; tastes, music anspruchsvoll; ~**chair** n Hochstuhl m; ~-**class** adj hochwertig; ~ **commissioner** n Hochkommissar m; ~ **court** n oberstes Gericht.

higher ['haɪə(r)] adj mathematics, life-forms höher.

high: ~ **explosive** n hochexplosiver Sprengstoff; ~ **flier** n (col) Senkrechtstarter m; ~-**flown** adj style, speech hochtrabend; ~ **frequency** adj Hochfrequenz-; **H**~ **German** n Hochdeutsch nt; ~-**grade** adj hochwertig; ore gediegen; ~-**handed** adj eigenmächtig; character überheblich; ~-**heeled** adj hochhackig; ~ **heels** npl hohe Absätze pl; ~ **jump** n (Sport) Hochsprung m; **to be for the** ~ **jump** (fig col) dran sein (col); **H**~**lands** npl schottisches Hochland; (generally) Berg- or Hochland nt; ~-**level** adj talks auf höchster Ebene; ~ **life** n Leben nt in großem Stil; ~**light 1** n (Art, Phot) Glanzlicht nt; (in hair) Strähne f; (fig) Höhepunkt m; ~**lights** (in hair) Strähnchen pl; **2** vt need, problem hervorheben.

highly ['haɪlɪ] adv hoch-. **to be** ~ **paid** hoch bezahlt werden; **to think** ~ **of sb** eine hohe Meinung von jdm haben; **to speak** ~ **of sb** sich sehr positiv über jdn äußern; ~-**strung** adj nervös.

high: H~ **Mass** n Hochamt nt; ~-**minded** adj hochgeistig; ideals hoch.

highness ['haɪnɪs] n **Her H**~ Ihre Hoheit.

high: ~-**pitched** adj sound hoch; ~-**powered** adj **(a)** car stark, Hochleistungs-; **(b)** (fig) businessman, politician, academic Spitzen-; conversation sehr anspruchsvoll; ~-**pressure** adj **(a)** ~-**pressure area** Hochdruckgebiet nt; **(b)** (fig) salesman aufdringlich; sales technique aggressiv; ~ **priest** n (lit, fig) Hohepriester m; ~-**ranking** adj von hohem Rang; ~-**rise flats** npl Hochhaus n; ~ **school** n (US) Oberschule f; **the** ~ **seas** npl die Meere pl; **on the** ~ **seas** auf hoher See; ~ **society** n High-Society f; ~-**speed** adj Schnell-; drill mit hoher Umdrehungszahl; ~-**speed film** hoch(lich)empfindlicher Film; ~-**spirited** adj in Hochstimmung; ~ **spot** n Höhepunkt m; ~ **street** n (Brit) Hauptstraße f; ~ **summer** n Hochsommer m; ~-**tea** n (frühes) Abendessen; ~-**tension** adj (Elec) Hochspannungs-; ~ **treason** n Hochverrat m; ~**way** n Landstraße f; public ~**way** öffentliche Straße; ~**way code** n Straßenverkehrsordnung f; ~**wayman** n Wegelagerer m.

hijack ['haɪdʒæk] **1** vt entführen; lorry überfallen. **2** n see vt Entführung f; Überfall m (of auf +acc).

hijacker ['haɪdʒækə(r)] n Entführer m.

hike [haɪk] **1** vi wandern. **2** n Wanderung f.

hiker ['haɪkə(r)] n Wanderer m, Wanderin f.

hiking ['haɪkɪŋ] n Wandern nt.

hilarious [hɪ'lɛərɪəs] adj sehr komisch.

hilariously [hɪ'lɛərɪəslɪ] adv ~ **funny** zum Schreien.

hilarity [hɪ'lærɪtɪ] n **his statement caused some** ~ seine Behauptung löste Heiterkeit aus.

hill [hɪl] n Hügel m; (higher) Berg m; (incline) Hang m. **built on a** ~ am Hang or Berg gebaut; **up** ~ **and down dale** bergauf und bergab; **that joke's as old as the** ~**s** der Witz hat so einen Bart; **to be over the** ~ (fig col) die besten Jahre hinter sich (dat) haben.

hillbilly ['hɪlbɪlɪ] n (US col) Hinterwäldler m (pej).

hillock ['hɪlək] n Anhöhe f.

hillside ['hɪlsaɪd] n Hang m.

hilly ['hɪlɪ] adj (+er) hüg(e)lig; (higher) bergig.

hilt [hɪlt] n Heft nt. **up to the ~** (fig) voll und ganz; (involved, in debt also) bis über beide Ohren (col).

him [hɪm] pers pron **(a)** (dir obj, with prep +acc) ihn; (indir obj, with prep +dat) ihm. **with his things around ~** mit seinen Sachen um sich. **(b)** (emph) er. **it's ~** er ist's; **who, ~?** wer, er?

Himalayas [ˌhɪməˈleɪəz] npl Himalaya m.

himself [hɪmˈself] pers pron **(a)** (dir and indir obj, with prep) sich; see **myself**. **(b)** (emph) (er) selbst.

hind¹ [haɪnd] n (Zool) Hirschkuh f.

hind² adj, superl **hindmost** hintere(r, s). **~ legs** Hinterbeine pl; **she could talk the ~ legs off a donkey** (col) sie redet wie ein Buch (col).

hinder [ˈhɪndər] vt (obstruct) behindern; (delay) person aufhalten. **to ~ sb from doing sth** jdn daran hindern, etw zu tun.

Hindi [ˈhɪndiː] n Hindi nt.

hindquarters [ˈhaɪndˌkwɔːtəz] npl Hinterteil nt; (of horse) Hinterhand f.

hindrance [ˈhɪndrəns] n Behinderung f. **to be a ~** hinderlich sein.

hindsight [ˈhaɪndsaɪt] n: **with ~** im nachhinein.

Hindu [ˈhɪnduː] **1** adj hinduistisch, Hindu-. **~ people** Hindu(s) pl. **2** n Hindu m.

Hinduism [ˈhɪnduːɪzəm] n Hinduismus m.

hinge [hɪndʒ] **1** n (of door) Angel f; (of box etc) Scharnier nt. **2** vi (fig) abhängen (on von).

hint [hɪnt] **1** n **(a)** (suggestion) Andeutung f, Wink m. **to give a/no ~ of sth** etw andeuten/nicht andeuten; **give me a ~** gib mir einen Anhaltspunkt; **to drop a ~** eine Andeutung machen; **OK, I can take a ~** schon recht, ich habe den Wink verstanden. **(b)** (trace) Spur f. **a ~ of garlic** eine Spur Knoblauch; **not a ~ of tiredness** keine Spur von Müdigkeit; **with the ~ of a smile** mit dem Anflug eines Lächelns. **(c)** (tip, piece of advice) Tip m. **~s for travellers** Reisetips pl. **2** vt andeuten (to gegenüber). **what are you ~ing (at)?** was wollen Sie damit andeuten?

hip [hɪp] n Hüfte f.

hip in cpds Hüft-; **~ bath** n Sitzbad nt; **~-flask** n Flachmann (col) m; **~ joint** n (Anat) Hüftgelenk nt; **~ pocket** n Gesäßtasche f.

hippopotamus [ˌhɪpəˈpɒtəməs] n, pl **-es** or **hippopotami** [ˌhɪpəˈpɒtəmaɪ] Nilpferd nt.

hippy, hippie [ˈhɪpɪ] n Hippie m.

hire [haɪər] **1** n Mieten nt; (of car also, suit) Leihen nt. **for ~** (taxi) frei; **it's on ~** es ist geliehen/gemietet. **2** vt mieten; cars also, suits leihen; staff einstellen. **~d assassin** gedungener Mörder; **~d car** (Brit) Mietwagen m; **~d hand** Lohnarbeiter m.

♦ **hire out** vt sep vermieten, verleihen.

hire purchase n (Brit) Ratenkauf m. **on ~** auf Raten or Teilzahlung.

his [hɪz] **1** poss adj sein; see **my**. **2** poss pron seine(r, s); see **mine¹**.

hiss [hɪs] **1** vi zischen; (cat) fauchen. **2** vt actor auszischen.

historian [hɪsˈtɔːrɪən] n Historiker(in f) m.

historic [hɪsˈtɒrɪk] adj historisch.

historical [hɪsˈtɒrɪkəl] adj historisch; studies, investigation also geschichtlich, Geschichts-.

history [ˈhɪstərɪ] n Geschichte f. **to make ~** Geschichte machen; **he has a ~ of violence** er hat eine Vorgeschichte als Gewalttäter; **the family has a ~ of heart disease** in der Familie hat es schon immer Fälle von Herzleiden gegeben.

hit [hɪt] (vb: pret, ptp ~) **1** n **(a)** (blow) Schlag m; (on target, Fencing) Treffer m. **(b)** (success, also Theat) Erfolg m, Knüller (col) m; (song) Schlager, Hit m. **to bring** or **make a ~?** with sb bei jdm gut ankommen.

2 vt **(a)** (strike) schlagen; (missile, bullet etc) treffen. **to ~ sb a blow** jdm einen Schlag versetzen; **to ~ one's head against sth** sich (dat) den Kopf an etw (dat) stoßen; **the car ~ a tree** das Auto fuhr gegen einen Baum; **he was ~ by a** stone er wurde von einem Stein getroffen; **he was ~ in the leg** er wurde ins Bein getroffen; **the commandos ~ the town at dawn** die Kommandos griffen die Stadt im Morgengrauen an; **it ~s you** (in the eye) (fig) das springt einem ins Auge; **that ~ home** (fig) das saß (col); **then it ~ me** dann wurde es mir plötzlich klar.

(b) (affect adversely) treffen. **to be hard ~ by** sth von etw schwer getroffen werden; **this tax will ~ the poor** diese Steuer wird die Armen treffen.

(c) (achieve, reach) likeness, top C treffen; speed, level etc erreichen. **to ~ the papers** in die Zeitungen kommen; **we're going to ~ the rush hour** wir geraten direkt in den Stoßverkehr; **the driver ~ a patch of ice** der Fahrer geriet auf eine vereiste Stelle; **to ~ a problem** auf ein Problem stoßen.

(d) (fig col phrases) **to ~ the bottle** zur Flasche greifen; **to ~ the ceiling** or **roof** an die Decke or in die Luft gehen (col); **to ~ the road** sich auf den Weg or die Socken (col) machen.

3 vi **(a)** (strike) schlagen. **he ~s hard** er schlägt hart zu. **(b)** (collide) zusammenstoßen.

♦ **hit back 1** vi (lit, fig) zurückschlagen. **he ~ ~ at his critics** er gab seinen Kritikern Kontra. **2** vt sep zurückschlagen.

♦ **hit off** vt sep **(a)** **he ~ him ~ beautifully** er hat ihn ausgezeichnet getroffen. **(b)** **to ~ it ~ with sb** (col) prima mit jdm auskommen (col).

♦ **hit out** vi (lit) losschlagen (at sb auf jdn); (fig) scharf angreifen (at or against sb jdn).

♦ **hit (up)on** vi +prep obj stoßen auf (+acc).

hit-and-run [ˈhɪtənˈrʌn] n **there was a ~ here last night** hier hat heute nacht jemand einen Unfall gebaut und Fahrerflucht begangen.

hitch [hɪtʃ] **1** n Schwierigkeit f. **without a ~** reibungslos; **but there's one ~** aber die Sache hat einen Haken. **2** vt **(a)** (fasten) anbinden (to an +dat). **(b)** (col) **to get ~ed** heiraten. **(c)** **to ~ a lift** trampen, per Anhalter fahren. **3** vi (~-hike) trampen, per Anhalter fahren.

♦ **hitch up** vt sep **(a)** horses anschirren. **(b)** trousers hochziehen.

hitch: **~-hike** vi per Anhalter fahren, trampen; **~-hiker** n Anhalter(in f), Tramper(in f) m; **~-hiking** n Trampen nt.

hither [ˈhɪðər] adv (obs) hierher. **~ and thither** (liter) hierhin und dorthin.

hitherto [ˌhɪðəˈtuː] adv bisher, bis jetzt.

hit: **~-man** n (col) Killer m (col); **~-or-miss** adj auf gut Glück pred; methods, planning schlampig; **~ parade** n Hitparade f; **~ record** n Schlagerplatte f; **~ song** n Schlager m; **~ tune** n Schlagermelodie f.

hive [haɪv] n (bee ~) Bienenstock m. **the office was a ~ of activity** in dem Büro ging es wie in einem Bienenstock zu.

♦ **hive off 1** vt sep department ausgliedern. **2** vi **(a)** (branch out) sich absetzen. **(b)** (col: slip away) abschwirren (col).

hoard [hɔːd] **1** n Vorrat m; (treasure) Hort m. **a ~ of weapons** ein Waffenlager nt. **2** vt (also **~ up**) food etc hamstern; money horten.

hoarding n (Brit) (fence) Bretterzaun m. (advertisement) ~ Plakatwand f.

hoarfrost [ˈhɔːˈfrɒst] n (Rauh)reif m.

hoarse [hɔːs] adj (+er) heiser.

hoax [həʊks] **1** n (joke) Streich m; (false alarm) blinder Alarm. **2** vt anführen. **he ~ed him into paying money** er hat ihm Geld abgeschwindelt.

hoaxer [ˈhəʊksər] n (in bomb scares etc) jd, der einen blinden Alarm auslöst.

hob [hɒb] n (on modern cooker) Kochmulde f.

hobble [ˈhɒbl] vi humpeln.

hobby [ˈhɒbɪ] n Hobby nt.

hobby-horse [ˈhɒbɪhɔːs] n (lit, fig) Steckenpferd nt.

hobnailed ['hɒbneɪld] adj ~ **boots** genagelte Schuhe pl.

hobnob ['hɒbnɒb] vi **the people he** ~**s with die** Leute mit denen er oft zusammen ist.

hobo ['həʊbəʊ] n (US: tramp) Penner m (col).

hock[1] [hɒk] n (Brit: wine) weißer Rheinwein.

hock[2] n (col) **in** ~ (pawned) versetzt.

hockey ['hɒkɪ] n Hockey nt; (US) Eishockey nt. ~ **stick** Hockeyschläger m.

hocus-pocus ['həʊkəs'pəʊkəs] n Hokuspokus m.

hoe [həʊ] n Hacke f.

hog [hɒg] **1** n (Mast)schwein nt; (US: pig) Schwein nt; (pej col: person) Schwein nt (col); (greedy) Vielfraß m (col). **2** vt (col) in Beschlag nehmen.

Hogmanay [ˌhɒgməˈneɪ] n (Scot) Silvester nt.

hoi polloi ['hɔɪpə'lɔɪ] n (pej) Pöbel m.

hoist [hɔɪst] **1** vt hochheben; (pull up) hochziehen; flag, sails hissen. **to be** ~ **with one's own petard** (prov) in die eigene Falle gehen. **2** n Hebevorrichtung f; (lift) (Lasten)aufzug m.

hoity-toity ['hɔɪtɪ'tɔɪtɪ] (col) adj hochnäsig.

hold [həʊld] (vb: pret, ptp **held**) **1** n (a) Griff m (also Wrestling); (Mountaineering) Halt m; (fig) Einfluß m (over auf +acc). **to seize** or **grab** ~ **of sb/sth** (lit) jdn/etw fassen or packen; **to get** (a) ~ **of sth** sich an etw (dat) festhalten; **to have/catch** ~ **of sth** (lit) etw festhalten/etw fassen or packen; **to get** ~ **of sb** (fig) jdn finden; (on phone etc) jdn erreichen; **to get** or **lay** ~ **of sth** (fig) etw auftreiben (col); **where did you get** ~ **of that idea?** wie kommst du denn auf die Idee?; **to have a** ~ **over** or **on sb** (fig) (großen) Einfluß auf jdn ausüben; **to get** (a) ~ **of oneself** (fig) sich in den Griff bekommen; **get** (a) ~ **of yourself!** reiß dich zusammen! **(b)** (Naut, Aviat) Laderaum m.

2 vt (a) (grasp) halten. **to** ~ **hands** sich an der Hand halten; (lovers, children etc) Händchen halten; **this car** ~**s the road well** dieses Auto hat eine gute Straßenlage; **to** ~ **oneself upright** sich aufrecht halten.

(b) (contain) enthalten; (have capacity of: tank etc) fassen; (bus, hall etc) Platz haben für. **this room** ~**s twenty people** in diesem Raum haben zwanzig Personen Platz; **the box will** ~ **all my books** in die Kiste ist Platz für alle meine Bücher; **what does the future** ~? was bringt die Zukunft?

(c) (believe) meinen; (maintain also) behaupten. **to** ~ **sth to be true/immoral** etc etw für wahr/unmoralisch etc halten; **to** ~ **the belief that ...** glauben, daß ...; **to** ~ **the view that ...** die Meinung vertreten, daß ...; **she held her grandchild dear** ihr Enkelkind bedeutete ihr sehr viel.

(d) (keep back) train aufhalten; one's breath anhalten; suspect, hostages etc festhalten; confiscated goods etc zurückhalten; (discontinue) fire einstellen. **to** ~ **sb** (prisoner) jdn gefangenhalten; **there's no** ~**ing him** er ist nicht zu bremsen (col); ~ **it!** (col) Moment mal (col); (taking photograph) so ist gut; ~ **everything!** (col) stop!

(e) (possess, occupy) post, position innehaben; passport haben; shares besitzen; (Sport) record halten; (Mil) position halten.

(f) (keep, not let go) **to** ~ **its value** seinen Wert behalten; **to** ~ **one's ground** or **own** sich behaupten (können); **I'll** ~ **you to that!** ich werde Sie beim Wort nehmen.

(g) **he can't** ~ **his whisky/liquor** er verträgt keinen Whisky/nichts; **she can** ~ **her drink** sie verträgt was.

(h) meeting abhalten.

3 vi (a) (rope, nail etc) halten. ~ **still!** halt still!; ~ **tight!** festhalten!; **will the good weather** ~? wird sich das gute Wetter wohl halten?; **if his luck** ~**s** wenn ihm das Glück treu bleibt. **(b)** (be valid) gelten.

♦ **hold against** vt always separate **to** ~ **sth** ~ **sb** jdm etw übelnehmen.

♦ **hold back 1** vi sich zurückhalten; (fail to act) zögern. **to** ~ ~ **from doing sth** es unterlassen, etw zu tun. **2** vt sep zurückhalten; floods (auf)stauen; tears also unterdrücken; emotions verbergen, unterdrücken; information geheimhalten. **to** ~ **sb** ~ **from doing sth** jdn daran hindern, etw zu tun; **nothing can** ~ **him** ~ **now** jetzt ist er nicht mehr aufzuhalten; **he was** ~**ing something** ~ **from me** er verheimlichte mir etwas.

♦ **hold down** vt sep (keep on ground) unten halten; (keep in place) (fest)halten; (keep low) prices niedrig halten. **he can't** ~ **any job** ~ **for long** er kann sich in keiner Stellung lange halten.

♦ **hold forth** vi sich auslassen (on über +acc).

♦ **hold in** vt sep stomach einziehen.

♦ **hold off 1** vi (keep away) sich fernhalten (from von); (not act) warten; (enemy) nicht angreifen; (rain, storm) ausbleiben. **I hope the rain** ~**s** ~ ich hoffe, daß es nicht regnet. **2** vt sep enemy, attack abwehren; visitor etc hinhalten.

♦ **hold on 1** vi (maintain grip) sich festhalten; (endure, resist) durchhalten; (wait) warten. ~ ~ **Moment** (mal)!; (Telec) einen Moment bitte. **2** vt sep **to be held** ~ **by sth** mit etw befestigt sein.

♦ **hold on to** vi +prep obj (a) **to** ~ ~ ~ **sth** an etw (dat) festhalten. **(b)** hope nicht aufgeben; idea festhalten an (+dat). **(c)** (keep) behalten. **to** ~ ~ ~ **the lead** in Führung bleiben.

♦ **hold out 1** vi (a) (supplies etc) reichen. **(b)** (endure, resist) durchhalten. **to** ~ ~ **against sb** sich gegen jdn behaupten; **to** ~ ~ **for sth** auf etw (dat) bestehen. **2** vt sep **(a)** ausstrecken. **to** ~ ~ **sth to sb** jdm etw hinhalten; ~ **your hand** ~ halt die Hand auf; **she held** ~ **her arms** sie breitete die Arme aus. **(b)** (fig) prospects bieten. **I don't** ~ ~ **much hope** ich habe nicht mehr viel Hoffnung.

♦ **hold out on** vi +prep obj (col) **you've been** ~**ing** ~ ~ **me** du verheimlichst mir doch was (col).

♦ **hold over** vt sep question, matter vertagen; decision verschieben (until auf +acc).

♦ **hold up 1** vi (a) (tent, wall etc) stehen bleiben; (light fitting, tile etc) halten. **(b)** (belief) standhalten; (theory) sich halten lassen. **2** vt sep **(a)** hochhalten; face nach oben wenden. ~ ~ **your hand** hebt die Hand; **to** ~ **sth** ~ **to the light** etw gegen das Licht halten. **(b)** (support) halten; (from the side) stützen; (from beneath) tragen. **(c)** **to** ~ **sb** ~ **as sth** jdn als etw hinstellen. **(d)** (stop) anhalten; (delay) people aufhalten; talks, delivery verzögern. **(e)** (rob) überfallen.

♦ **hold with** vi +prep obj (col) **I don't** ~ ~ **that** ich bin gegen so was (col).

holdall ['həʊldɔːl] n (Brit) Reisetasche f.

holder ['həʊldə^r] n (of title, office, record, passport) Inhaber(in f) m; (object) Halter m.

holding ['həʊldɪŋ] n (land) Land nt; (with buildings) Gut nt. ~**s** pl (Grund)besitz m; (Fin) ~**s** pl Anteile pl; (stocks) Aktienbesitz m; ~ **company** Dachgesellschaft f.

hold-up ['həʊldʌp] n (a) (delay) Verzögerung f; (Brit: of traffic) Stockung f. **what's the** ~? warum dauert das so lange?; **there's been a** ~ **in our plans** unsere Pläne haben sich verzögert. **(b)** (robbery) bewaffneter Raubüberfall.

hole [həʊl] **1** n Loch nt; (rabbit's, fox's) Bau m, Höhle f; (col) Loch nt (col); (town) Kaff (col) nt. **to make a** ~ **in sb's savings** ein Loch in jds Ersparnisse reißen; **he's talking through a** ~ **in his head** (col) er quatscht lauter Blödsinn (col). **2** vt ein Loch machen in (+acc). **to be** ~**d** ein Loch bekommen; **the ship was** ~**d by an iceberg** der Eisberg schlug das Schiff leck.

♦ **hole up** vi sich verkriechen.

holiday ['hɒlədɪ] n **(a)** (day off) freier Tag; (public ~) Feiertag m. **to take a ~** einen Tag frei nehmen. **(b)** (esp Brit: period) often pl Urlaub m, Ferien pl (esp Sch). **on ~** in den Ferien; **auf** Urlaub; **to go on ~** Urlaub machen; **where are you going for your ~?** wohin fahren Sie in den Ferien or im Urlaub?; **to take a ~** Urlaub nehmen; **I need a ~** ich bin urlaubsreif.

holiday: ~ **camp** n Feriendorf nt; ~**maker** n (esp Brit) Urlauber(in f) m; ~ **resort** n Ferienort m.

holiness ['həʊlɪnɪs] n **His H~** Seine Heiligkeit.

Holland ['hɒlənd] n Holland nt.

hollow ['hɒləʊ] **1** adj (+er) (lit, fig) hohl; person innerlich hohl; life inhaltslos; sympathy, praise unaufrichtig; promise leer; victory wertlos; eyes tiefliegend. **2** adv sound hohl. **they beat us ~** (col) sie haben uns fertiggemacht (col). **3** n (in ground) Mulde f. **the ~ of one's hand** die hohle Hand.
♦ **hollow out** vt sep aushöhlen.

holly ['hɒlɪ] n Stechpalme f.

hollyhock ['hɒlɪhɒk] n Malve f.

holocaust ['hɒləkɔːst] n Inferno nt. **nuclear ~** atomare Katastrophe.

hologram ['hɒləɡræm] n Hologramm nt.

holster ['həʊlstə'] n (Pistolen)halfter nt or f.

holy ['həʊlɪ] adj (+er) heilig; bread, ground geweiht. **~ water** Weihwasser nt; **the H~** Bible die Bibel; **H~ Ghost** Heiliger Geist; **H~ Week** Karwoche f; ~ **smoke** (col) heiliger Strohsack! (col).

homage ['hɒmɪdʒ] n Huldigung f; (for elders) Ehrerbietung f. **to pay ~ to sb** jdm huldigen; **in silent ~** in stummer Ehrerbietung.

home [həʊm] **1** n **(a)** (house) Heim nt; (country, area etc) Heimat f. **gadgets for the ~** praktische Haushaltsgeräte; **his ~ is in Brussels** er ist in Brüssel zu Hause; **Bournemouth is his second ~** Bournemouth ist seine zweite Heimat (geworden); **haven't you got a ~ to go to?** hast du kein Zuhause?; **he invited us around to his ~** er hat uns zu sich (nach Hause) eingeladen; **away from ~** von zu Hause weg; **a long way from ~** weit von zu Hause; **to live away from ~** nicht zu Hause wohnen; **hasn't this hammer got a ~?** gehört der Hammer nicht irgendwohin?; **to find a ~ for sth** etw irgendwo unterbringen; **it's a ~ from ~** es ist wie zu Hause; **at ~** zu Hause; (Sport) auf eigenem Platz; **he doesn't feel at ~ in English** er fühlt sich im Englischen nicht sicher; **to make oneself at ~** es sich (dat) bequem machen; **to make sb feel at ~** es jdm gemütlich machen; ~ **sweet ~** (Prov) trautes Heim, Glück allein (Prov).
(b) (institution) Heim nt.
(c) (Zool, Bot) Heimat f.
2 adv **(a)** (position) zu Hause, daheim; (with verb of motion) nach Hause, heim. **to go ~** nach Hause gehen/fahren; (to country) heimfahren; **on the way ~** auf dem Heimweg or Nachhauseweg; **to return ~ from abroad** aus dem Ausland zurückkommen. **(b)** to drive a nail ~ einen Nagel einschlagen; **to bring** or **get sth ~ to sb** jdm etw klarmachen; **his words went ~** seine Worte hatten ihre Wirkung.
♦ **home in on** vi +prep obj target sich ausrichten auf (+acc); essential point herausgreifen.

home: ~ **address** n Heimatadresse or -anschrift f; (as opposed to business address) Privatanschrift f; ~**brew** n selbstgebrautes Bier; ~ **comforts** npl häuslicher Komfort; ~**coming** n Heimkehr f; **H~ Counties** npl Grafschaften, die an London angrenzen; ~ **economics** n sing Hauswirtschaft(slehre) f; ~ **front** n **on the ~ front** (Mil, Pol) im eigenen Land; (in business contexts) im eigenen Betrieb; (in personal, family contexts) zu Hause; ~ **game** n (Sport) Heimspiel nt; ~ **ground** n (Sport) eigener Platz; **to be on ~ ground** (fig) sich auf vertrautem Terrain bewegen; ~**grown** adj vegetables selbstgezogen;

(not imported) einheimisch; ~ **help** n (Haushalts)hilfe f; ~ **land** n Heimat(land nt) f; ~**less** adj heimatlos; tramp obdachlos; ~ **life** n Familienleben nt.

homely ['həʊmlɪ] adj (+er) **(a)** (home-loving) häuslich; atmosphere heimelig; style anspruchslos; advice einfach. **(b)** (US: plain) person unscheinbar; face reizlos.

home: ~**-made** adj selbstgemacht; ~**maker** n (US) (housewife) Hausfrau f; (social worker) Familienfürsorger(in f) m; ~ **market** n Inlandsmarkt m; ~ **news** n Meldungen pl aus dem Inland; **H~ Office** n (Brit) Innenministerium nt; (with relation to aliens) Einwanderungsbehörde f; **H~ Secretary** n (Brit) Innenminister m; ~**sick** adj **to be ~sick** Heimweh haben (for nach); ~**stead** n **(a)** Heimstätte f; **(b)** (US) Heimstätte f für Siedler; ~ **straight**, ~ **stretch** n (Sport) Zielgerade f; ~ **team** n (Sport) Gastgeber pl; ~ **town** n Heimatort m; ~ **truth** n **to tell sb some ~ truths** jdm die Augen öffnen.

homeward ['həʊmwəd] adj journey, flight Heim-. **we are ~-bound** es geht Richtung Heimat.

homeward(s) ['həʊmwəd(z)] adv nach Hause; (to country also) in Richtung Heimat.

home: ~ **work** n (Sch) Hausaufgaben pl; **to give sb sth for ~work** jdm etw aufgeben; **what have you got for ~work?** was hast du auf?; **he hadn't done his ~work** (fig col) er hatte sich mit der Materie nicht vertraut gemacht.

homey ['həʊmɪ] adj (+er) (US col) gemütlich.

homicidal [,hɒmɪ'saɪdl] adj gemeingefährlich.

homicide ['hɒmɪsaɪd] n Totschlag m. **culpable ~** Mord m; ~ **(squad)** Mordkommission f.

homing ['həʊmɪŋ] adj ~ **pigeon** Brieftaube f; ~ **instinct** Heimfindevermögen nt; ~ **device** Zielsucheinrichtung f.

homoeopath, (US) **homeopath** ['həʊmɪəʊpæθ] n Homöopath(in f) m.

homoeopathy, (US) **homeopathy** [,həʊmɪ'ɒpəθɪ] n Homöopathie f.

homogeneous [,hɒmə'dʒiːnɪəs] adj homogen.

homogenize [hə'mɒdʒənaɪz] vt homogenisieren.

homosexual [,hɒməʊ'seksjʊəl] **1** adj homosexuell. **2** n Homosexuelle(r) mf.

homosexuality [,hɒməʊseksjʊ'ælɪtɪ] n Homosexualität f.

honest ['ɒnɪst] adj ehrlich; business, action also anständig; truth rein. **he made an ~ woman of her** (col) er machte sie zu seiner Frau.

honestly ['ɒnɪstlɪ] adv ehrlich. ~! (in exasperation) also ehrlich!

honesty ['ɒnɪstɪ] n Ehrlichkeit f. **in all ~** ganz ehrlich; ~ **is the best policy** (Prov) ehrlich währt am längsten (Prov).

honey ['hʌnɪ] n Honig m; (col) Schätzchen nt.

honeycomb ['hʌnɪkəʊm] **1** n (Bienen)wabe f. **2** vt usu pass durchlöchern.

honeymoon ['hʌnɪmuːn] n Flitterwochen pl; (trip) Hochzeitsreise f. **to be on one's ~** in den Flitterwochen/auf Hochzeitsreise sein.

honeysuckle ['hʌnɪ,sʌkl] n Geißblatt nt.

honk [hɒŋk] **1** vi (car) hupen; (geese) schreien. **2** vt horn drücken auf (+acc).

honky ['hɒŋkɪ] n (negro pej sl) Weiße(r) mf.

honorary ['ɒnərərɪ] adj secretary ehrenamtlich; member, president Ehren-. ~ **degree** ehrenhalber verliehener akademischer Grad.

honour, (US) **honor** ['ɒnə'] **1** n **(a)** Ehre f. **he made it a point of ~** er betrachtete es als Ehrensache; **you're on your ~** Sie haben Ihr Ehrenwort gegeben; **to put sb on his ~** jdm vertrauen; **man of ~** Ehrenmann m; **to be an ~ to sth** einer Sache (dat) Ehre machen; **in ~ of sb/sth** zu Ehren von jdm/etw; (of dead person, past thing) in Andenken an jdn/etw; **he is ~-bound to do it** es ist Ehrensache für ihn, das zu tun; **to do the ~s** (col) die Honneurs machen. **(b)** (title) Your **H~**

Hohes Gericht; **His H~** das Gericht. **(c)** *(distinction, award)* **~s** Auszeichnung(en *pl*) *f*; *(Univ: also* **~s degree)** *akademischer Grad mit Prüfung im Spezialfach.*
  2 *vt* **(a)** *person* ehren. **to ~ sb with a title** jdm einen Titel verleihen; **I should be ~ed if you ...** ich würde mich geehrt fühlen, wenn Sie ...; **he ~ed us with his presence** *(also iro)* er beehrte uns mit seiner Gegenwart. **(b)** *cheque* annehmen; *obligation* nachkommen *(+dat)*; *commitment* stehen zu.

honourable, *(US)* **honorable** ['ɒnərəbl] *adj* ehrenhaft; *peace, discharge* ehrenvoll. **to receive ~ mention** lobend erwähnt werden; **the H~ member** *(Parl)* Herr/Frau X.

hood [hʊd] *n* **(a)** Kapuze *f*; *(Aut: roof)* Verdeck *nt*; *(US Aut)* (Motor)haube *f*; *(on cooker)* Abzugshaube *f*. **(b)** *(esp US col)* Gangster *m (col)*.

hoodlum ['huːdləm] *n* Rowdy *m*; *(member of gang)* Gangster *m (col)*.

hoodwink ['hʊdwɪŋk] *vt (col)* (he)reinlegen *(col)*.

hoof [huːf] *n, pl* **-s** *or* **hooves** Huf *m*.

hook [hʊk] **1** *n* Haken *m (also Boxing)*. **he swallowed the story ~, line and sinker** er hat die Geschichte tatsächlich ganz geschluckt *(col)*; **by ~ or by crook** auf Biegen und Brechen; **to get sb off the ~** *(col)* jdn herausreißen *(col)*; **that lets me off the ~** *(col)* damit bin ich aus dem Schneider *(col)*; **to leave the phone off the ~** nicht auflegen. **2** *vt* **(a)** **he ~ed the door back** er hakte die Tür fest; **to ~ a trailer to a car** einen Anhänger an ein Auto hängen. **(b)** *fish* an die Angel bekommen; *husband* sich *(dat)* angeln. **(c) to be/get ~ed (on sth)** *(on drugs)* (von etw) abhängig sein/werden; *(on food, place)* auf etw *(acc)* stehen *(col)*; **he's ~ed on the idea** er ist von der Idee besessen.

♦ **hook on 1** *vi* (an)gehakt werden *(to an +acc)*; *(with tow-bar)* angekoppelt werden *(to an +acc)*. **2** *vt sep* **to ~ sth** *(with tow-bar)* etw an etw *(acc)* (an)koppeln.

♦ **hook up 1** *vi (Rad, TV)* **to ~ ~ with sb** sich jdm anschließen. **2** *vt sep dress etc* zuhaken; *(Rad, TV)* anschließen *(with an +acc)*; *trailer* anhängen.

hook and eye *n* Haken und Öse *no art, pl vb*.

hooked nose ['hʊkt 'nəʊz] *n* Hakennase *f*.

hooker ['hʊkə'] *n (esp US col)* Nutte *f (col!)*.

hooligan ['huːlɪgən] *n* Rowdy *m*.

hooliganism ['huːlɪgənɪzəm] *n* Rowdytum *nt*.

hoop [huːp] *n* Reifen *m*; *(on animal)* Ring *m*. **to put sb through the ~s** *(fig col)* jdn durch die Mangel drehen *(col)*.

hoot [huːt] **1** *n* **(a)** *(of owl)* Ruf *m*. **~s of laughter** johlendes Gelächter; **I don't care two ~s** *(col)* das ist mir völlig schnuppe *(col)*; **to be a ~** *(col)* *(person, event etc)* zum Schießen sein *(col)*. **(b)** *(Aut)* Hupen *nt no pl*; *(of train, hooter)* Pfeifen *nt no pl*. **2** *vi* **(a)** *(owl)* schreien. **(b)** *(Aut)* hupen; *(train, factory hooter)* pfeifen.

hooter ['huːtə'] *n* **(a)** *(Brit Aut)* Hupe *f*; *(at factory)* Sirene *f*. **(b)** *(Brit col: nose)* Zinken *m (col)*.

hoover ® ['huːvə'] *(Brit)* **1** *n* Staubsauger *m*. **2** *vti* (staub)saugen.

hooves [huːvz] *pl of* **hoof.**

hop¹ [hɒp] **1** *n* **(a)** (kleiner) Sprung; *(of person, bird also)* Hüpfer *m*; *(of rabbit also)* Satz *m*. **to catch sb on the ~** *(fig col)* jdn überraschen; **to keep sb on the ~** *(fig col)* jdn in Trab halten. **(b)** *(col: dance)* Tanz *m*. **(c)** *(Aviat col)* Sprung *m*. **a short ~** ein Katzensprung *m (col)*. **2** *vi (animal)* hüpfen. **~ in,** **said the driver** steigen Sie ein, sagte der Fahrer; **~ it!** *(col)* zieh Leine *(col)*.

hop² *n (Bot)* Hopfen *m*.

hope [həʊp] **1** *n* Hoffnung *f*. **past or beyond all ~** hoffnungslos; **the patient is beyond all ~** für den Patienten besteht keine Hoffnung mehr; **to have ~s of doing sth** hoffen, etw zu tun; **well, we live in ~** nun, wir hoffen eben (weiter); **there's no ~**

of that da braucht man sich gar keine Hoffnungen zu machen; **to lose ~ of doing sth** die Hoffnung aufgeben, etw zu tun; **what a ~!** *(col)*, **some ~(s)!** *(col)* schön wär's! *(col)*.
  2 *vi* hoffen *(for* auf *+acc)*. **to ~ for the best** das Beste hoffen; **I ~ so/not** hoffentlich/hoffentlich nicht; **to ~ against hope that ...** trotz allem die Hoffnung nicht aufgeben, daß ...
  3 *vt* hoffen. **I ~ to see you** hoffentlich sehe ich Sie; **hoping to hear from you** ich hoffe, von Ihnen zu hören.

hopeful ['həʊpfʊl] **1** *adj* hoffnungsvoll; *situation, sign* vielversprechend. **they weren't very ~** sie hatten keine große Hoffnung; **to be ~ that ...** hoffen, daß ...; **you're ~!** du bist vielleicht ein Optimist! *(col)*. **2** *n (col)* **a young ~** *(hopes to succeed)* ein hoffnungsvoller junger Mensch.

hopefully ['həʊpfəlɪ] *adv* **(a)** hoffnungsvoll. **(b) ~** **it won't rain** hoffentlich regnet es nicht.

hopeless ['həʊplɪs] *adj* situation, outlook hoffnungslos; *liar, drunkard etc* unverbesserlich; *weather, food* unmöglich *(col)*. **it's ~ even to try** es hat gar keinen Wert, es überhaupt zu versuchen; **you're ~** du bist ein hoffnungsloser Fall; **he's ~ at maths** in Mathematik ist er ein hoffnungsloser Fall.

hopelessly ['həʊplɪslɪ] *adv* hoffnungslos. **we were ~ lost** wir hatten uns ganz und gar verirrt.

hopper ['hɒpə'] *n (Tech)* Einfülltrichter *m*.

hopping mad ['hɒpɪŋ'mæd] *adj (col)* fuchsteufelswild *(col)*.

hop: ~scotch *n* Himmel-und-Hölle(-Spiel) *nt*; **~, step and jump** *n* Dreisprung *m*.

horde [hɔːd] *n (of animals, children)* Horde *f*.

horizon [hə'raɪzn] *n (lit, fig)* Horizont *m*. **on the ~** am Horizont.

horizontal [,hɒrɪ'zɒntl] *adj* horizontal.

hormone ['hɔːməʊn] *n* Hormon *nt*.

horn [hɔːn] *n (of cattle, Mus)* Horn *nt*; *(Aut)* Hupe *f*; *(Naut)* (Signal)horn *nt*; *(of snail, insect)* Fühler *m*. **~s** *pl (of deer)* Geweih *nt*; **to sound the ~** *(Aut)* hupen; *(Naut)* das Horn ertönen lassen; **to draw in one's ~s** *(fig: spend less)* den Gürtel enger schnallen.

hornet ['hɔːnɪt] *n* Hornisse *f*.

horn-rimmed ['hɔːn'rɪmd] *adj spectacles* Horn-.

horny ['hɔːnɪ] *adj (+er) hands etc* schwielig; *(col: randy)* geil *(col)*.

horoscope ['hɒrəskəʊp] *n* Horoskop *nt*.

horrendous [hɒ'rendəs] *adj crime* abscheulich; *prices* horrend.

horrible ['hɒrɪbl] *adj* schrecklich. **don't be ~** sei nicht so gemein *(col)*.

horribly ['hɒrɪblɪ] *adv* schrecklich.

horrid ['hɒrɪd] *adj* entsetzlich, schrecklich.

horrific [hɒ'rɪfɪk] *adj* entsetzlich; *documentary* erschreckend.

horrify ['hɒrɪfaɪ] *vt* entsetzen.

horrifying ['hɒrɪfaɪɪŋ] *adj* schrecklich, entsetzlich.

horror ['hɒrə'] **1** *n* Entsetzen *nt*; *(strong dislike)* Horror *m (of* vor *+dat)*; *(of war etc)* Greuel *m*. **she shrank back in ~** sie fuhr entsetzt zurück; **to be a real ~** *(col)* furchtbar sein *(col)*; **you little ~!** *(col)* du kleines Ungeheuer! *(col)*. **2** *attr comics, films* Horror-.

horror-stricken ['hɒrəstrɪkn], **horror-struck** ['hɒrəstrʌk] *adj* von Entsetzen gepackt.

hors d'oeuvre [ɔː'dɜːv] *n* Vorspeise *f*.

horse [hɔːs] *n* Pferd *nt (also Gymnastics)*, Roß *(liter, pej) nt*. **wild ~s would not drag me there** keine zehn Pferde würden mich dahin bringen; **I could eat a ~** ich könnte ein ganzes Pferd essen; **information straight from the ~'s mouth** Informationen aus erster Hand.

horse: ~back: on ~back *adv* zu Pferd; **~-box** *n* Pferdetransporter *m*; **~ chestnut** *n* Roßkastanie *f*; **~hair** *n* Roßhaar *nt*; **~man** *n* Reiter *m*; **~man-**

ship n Reitkunst f; ~**play** n Balgerei f; ~**power** n Pferdestärke f; ~**racing** n (races) Pferderennen pl; ~**radish** n Meerrettich m; ~**shoe** n Hufeisen nt; ~**trading** n (fig) Kuhhandel m; ~**whip** vt auspeitschen; ~**woman** n Reiterin f.

hors(e)y ['hɔːsɪ] adj (+er) (col) (fond of horses) pferdenärrisch; appearance pferdeähnlich.

horticultural [,hɔːtɪ'kʌltʃərəl] adj Garten(bau)-.

horticulture ['hɔːtɪkʌltʃəʳ] n Gartenbau m.

hose[1] [həʊz] **1** n (also ~**pipe**) Schlauch m. **2** vt (also ~ **down**) abspritzen.

hose[2] n no pl (Comm: stockings) Strumpfwaren pl.

hosiery ['həʊʒərɪ] n Strumpfwaren pl.

hospice ['hɒspɪs] n Hospiz nt.

hospitable [hɒs'pɪtəbl] adj gastfreundlich.

hospital ['hɒspɪtl] n Krankenhaus nt, Klinik f. **in** or (US) **in the** ~ im Krankenhaus; **he's got to go to** or (US) **to the** ~ er muß ins Krankenhaus (gehen).

hospitality [,hɒspɪ'tælɪtɪ] n Gastfreundschaft f.

hospitalize ['hɒspɪtəlaɪz] vt ins Krankenhaus einweisen.

host[1] [həʊst] **1** n Gastgeber m; (in own home also) Hausherr m. **2** vt TV programme, games Gastgeber sein bei.

host[2] n Menge f. **for a whole** ~ **of reasons** aus einer ganzen Reihe von Gründen.

hostage ['hɒstɪdʒ] n Geisel f.

hostel ['hɒstəl] n (Wohn)heim nt.

hostess ['həʊstes] n Gastgeberin f; (in own home also) Hausherrin f; (in night-club) Hosteß f; (air-~) Stewardeß f.

hostile ['hɒstaɪl] adj feindlich; person also feindlich gesinnt; reception, looks feindselig. **to be** ~ **to sb** sich jdm gegenüber feindselig verhalten; **don't be so** ~ seien sie nicht so aggressiv!

hostility [hɒs'tɪlɪtɪ] n Feindseligkeit f; (between people) Feindschaft f. **hostilities** pl (warfare) Feindseligkeiten pl.

hot [hɒt] adj (+er) **(a)** heiß; meal, tap warm; curry scharf. **I am** or **feel** ~ mir ist (es) heiß. **(b)** (col: good, competent) stark (col); person also fähig. **he's** ~ **at German** er ist gut in Deutsch; **he/it isn't** ~ (**all**) **that** ~ so umwerfend ist er/das auch wieder nicht (col); **I'm not feeling too** ~ mir geht's nicht besonders (col). **(c)** (fig) ~ **favourite** der große Favorit; ~ **news** das Neueste vom Neuen; **the pace was so** ~ das Tempo war so scharf; **to get into** ~ **water** in Teufels Küche kommen (col); **to be all** ~ **and bothered** (col) ganz aufgeregt sein (about wegen); **to be in** ~ **pursuit of sb** jdm nacheilen; **it's getting too** ~ **for him here** hier wird ihm der Boden unter den Füßen zu heiß. **(d)** (col: stolen) heiß (col).

♦ **hot up** vi (col) (pace) schneller werden; (situation) zuspitzen; (party) in Schwung kommen.

hot: ~ **air** n (fig) leeres Gerede; ~**bed** n (fig) Nährboden m (of für); ~**-blooded** adj heißblütig.

hotchpotch ['hɒtʃpɒtʃ] n Mischmasch m.

hot dog n Hot dog m.

hotel [həʊ'tel] n Hotel nt.

hotelier [həʊ'telɪəʳ] n Hotelier m.

hot: ~**foot** adv eilig; ~**head** n Hitzkopf m; ~**headed** adj hitzköpfig; ~**house** n (lit,fig) Treibhaus nt; ~ **line** n (Pol) heißer Draht.

hotly ['hɒtlɪ] adv contested heiß.

hot: ~**plate** n Kochplatte f; (plate-warmer) Warmhalteplatte f; ~**pot** n (esp Brit) Fleischeintopf m mit Kartoffeleinlage; ~ **potato** n (fig col) heißes Eisen; ~**rod** n (Aut) hoch frisiertes Auto; ~ **seat** n **to be in the** ~ **seat** auf dem Schleudersitz sein; ~ **stuff** n (col) **it's/he's** ~ **stuff** das/er ist große Klasse (col); ~**-tempered** adj jähzornig; ~**-water bottle** n Wärmflasche f.

hound [haʊnd] **1** n (Hunt) (Jagd)hund m; (any dog) Hund m. **the** ~ pl die Meute. **2** vt hetzen.

♦ **hound down** vt sep Jagd machen auf (+acc); (criminal etc) zur Strecke bringen.

♦ **hound out** vt sep vertreiben (of aus).

hour ['aʊəʳ] n Stunde f. ~ **by** ~ mit jeder Stunde; **on the** ~ zur vollen Stunde; **every** ~ **on the** ~ jede volle Stunde; **at an early/a late** ~ früh/spät; **at all** ~**s (of the day and night)** zu jeder (Tages-und Nacht)zeit; **to drive at 80 kilometres an** ~ 80 Stundenkilometer fahren; **to be paid by the** ~ stundenweise bezahlt werden; **for** ~**s** stundenlang; **he took** ~**s to do it** er brauchte stundenlang (dazu); ~**s** pl (of banks, shops etc) Geschäftszeit(en) pl f; **after** ~**s** (in pubs) nach der Polizeistunde; (in office etc) nach Dienstschluß; **the man of the** ~ der Mann der Stunde.

hour: ~ **glass** n Sanduhr f; ~ **hand** n kleiner Zeiger.

hourly ['aʊəlɪ] adj, adv stündlich.

house [haʊs] **1** n, pl **houses** ['haʊzɪz] **(a)** Haus nt. **at my** ~ bei mir (zu Hause); **to my** ~ zu mir (nach Hause); **to set up** ~ einen eigenen Hausstand gründen; (in particular area) sich niederlassen; **to put one's** ~ **in order** (fig) seine Angelegenheiten in Ordnung bringen; **he's getting on like a** ~ **on fire** (col) er kommt prima voran (col); **they get on like a** ~ **on fire** (col) sie kommen ausgezeichnet miteinander aus; **as safe as** ~**s** (Brit) bombensicher (col); **on the** ~ auf Kosten des Hauses; (on the company) auf Kosten der Firma; **he brought the** ~ **down** (col) er riß alle von den Sitzen (col); **full** ~ (Cards) Full House nt.

(b) (Pol) **the upper/lower** ~ das Ober-/Unterhaus; **H~ of Commons/Lords** (Brit) (britisches) Unter-/Oberhaus; **H~ of Representatives** (US) Repräsentantenhaus nt; **the H~s of Parliament** das Parlament(sgebäude).

2 [haʊz] vt people, goods unterbringen.

house in cpds Haus-; ~ **arrest** n Hausarrest m; ~**boat** n Hausboot nt; ~**bound** adj ans Haus gefesselt; ~**breaker** n Einbrecher m; ~**coat** n Morgenmantel m; ~**guest** n (Haus)gast m.

household ['haʊshəʊld] n Haushalt m. ~ **name** or **word** Begriff m.

householder ['haʊs,həʊldəʳ] n Haus-/Wohnungsinhaber(in f) m.

house: ~**-hunting** n Haussuche f; ~**keeper** n Haushälterin f; ~**keeping** n Haushalten nt; (also ~**keeping money**) Haushaltsgeld nt; ~**man** n (Brit) Assistenzarzt m; ~**-proud** adj **she is** ~**-proud** sie ist eine penible Hausfrau; ~**room** n **I wouldn't give it** ~**room** (col) das wollte ich nicht geschenkt haben; **a** ~**-to-**~ **search** eine Suche von Haus zu Haus; ~**-trained** adj stubenrein; ~ **warming** (**party**) n Einzugsparty f; ~**wife** n Hausfrau f; ~**wifely** adj hausfraulich; ~**work** n Hausarbeit f.

housing ['haʊzɪŋ] n **(a)** (act) Unterbringung f. **(b)** (houses) Wohnungen pl; (temporary) Unterkunft f. **(c)** (building of houses) Wohnungsbau m. **(d)** (Tech) Gehäuse nt.

housing in cpds Wohnungs-; ~ **conditions** npl Wohnbedingungen pl; ~ **estate** n (Brit) Wohnsiedlung f.

hove [həʊv] pret, ptp of **heave** (Naut).

hovel ['hɒvəl] n armselige Hütte; (fig pej) Bruchbude f (col).

hover ['hɒvəʳ] vi schweben; (stand around) herumstehen. **a smile** ~**ed on her lips** ein Lächeln lag auf ihren Lippen; **he** ~**ed between two alternatives** er schwankte zwischen zwei Möglichkeiten.

♦ **hover about** or **around** vi (persons) herumlungern; (helicopter etc) (in der Luft) kreisen.

hover: ~**craft** n Luftkissenboot, Hovercraft nt; ~**port** n Anlegestelle f für Hovercrafts.

how [haʊ] adv **(a)** wie. ~ **'s that?**, ~ **come?** (col) wie kommt (denn) das?; ~ **is it that …?** wie kommt es, daß …?; ~ **do you know that?** woher wissen Sie das?; ~ **much** wieviel; **I know** ~ **much he**

loves her ich weiß wie sehr er sie liebt; ~ **many** wie viele; ~ **do you do?** Guten Tag/Abend!, angenehm! *(form)*; ~ **are you?** wie geht es Ihnen?; ~**'s work?** was macht die Arbeit? *(col)*; ~ **are things at school?** wie geht's in der Schule? ~ **about ...** wie wäre es mit ...; ~ **about it?** wie wäre es damit? **(b) and** ~**!** und ob!; ~ **he's grown!** er ist aber groß geworden; ~ **strange!** seltsam!; ~ **kind of him!** wie nett von ihm! **(c)** *(that)* daß. she told me ~ she had seen him there sie sagte mir, daß sie ihn dort gesehen hat.

however [hau'evər] **1** *conj* jedoch, aber. **2** *adv* ~ **strong** he is wie stark er auch ist; ~ **you do it** wie du es auch machst; do it ~ **you like** mach's, wie du willst; ~ **much you cry** und wenn du noch so weinst; ~ **did you manage it?** wie hast du das bloß geschafft?

howl [haul] **1** *n* Schrei *m*; *(of animal, wind)* Heulen *nt no pl.* ~**s of protest** Protestgeschrei *nt*. **2** *vi* brüllen; *(animal)* jaulen; *(wind)* heulen. **to** ~ **with laughter** in brüllendes Gelächter ausbrechen.

♦ **howl down** *vt sep* niederbrüllen.

howler ['haulər] *n (col)* Hammer *m (col)*.

HP, hp = **(a) hire purchase. (b) horse power** ≃ **PS.**

HQ = **headquarters.**

hub [hʌb] *n* (Rad)nabe *f*; *(fig)* Zentrum *nt.*

hubbub ['hʌbʌb] *n* Tumult *m.*

hubcap ['hʌbkæp] *n* Radkappe *f.*

huddle ['hʌdl] **1** *n (of people)* Gruppe *f.* in a ~ dicht zusammengedrängt; **to go into a** ~ *(col)* die Köpfe zusammenstecken. **2** *vi* (sich) kauern.

♦ **huddle together** *vi* sich aneinanderkauern. **to be** ~**d** ~ aneinanderkauern.

♦ **huddle up** *vi* sich zusammenkauern. **to be** ~**d** ~ zusammenkauern.

hue[1] [hju:] *n* Farbe *f*; *(shade, fig)* Schattierung *f.*

hue[2] *n:* ~ **and cry** Zeter und Mordio *nt.*

huff [hʌf] *n* **to be in a** ~ eingeschnappt sein *(col)*; **to go into a** ~ einschnappen *(col)*.

hug [hʌg] **1** *n* Umarmung *f.* **2** *vt* umarmen; *coast etc* sich dicht halten an (+*acc*).

huge [hju:dʒ] *adj* (+*er*) riesig.

hulk [hʌlk] *n (col: person)* Klotz *m (col)*.

hulking ['hʌlkɪŋ] *adj:* ~ **great** massig; **a** ~ **great wardrobe** ein Ungetüm *nt* von einem Kleiderschrank.

hull [hʌl] *n* (*Naut*) Schiffskörper *m.*

hullabaloo [,hʌləbə'lu:] *n (col: noise)* Radau *m.*

hullo [hʌ'ləu] *interj* = **hello.**

hum [hʌm] **1** *n see vi* **(a)** Summen *nt*; Surren *nt*; *(of voices)* Gemurmel *nt.* **2** *vi* **(a)** *(insect, person)* summen; *(small machine, camera etc)* surren. **HQ was** ~**ming with activity** im Hauptquartier ging es zu wie in einem Bienenstock; **to** ~ **and haw** *(col)* herumdrucksen *(col) (over, about um)*. **(b)** *(col: smell)* stinken *(col)*. **3** *vt tune* summen.

human ['hju:mən] **1** *adj* menschlich. **I'm only** ~ ich bin auch nur ein Mensch; ~ **nature** die menschliche Natur. **2** *n (also* ~ **being)** Mensch *m.*

humane [hju:'meɪn] *adj* human, menschlich. ~ **killer** Mittel *nt* zum schmerzlosen Töten.

humanism ['hju:mənɪzəm] *n* Humanismus *m.*

humanist ['hju:mənɪst] **1** *n* Humanist *m.* **2** *adj* humanistisch.

humanitarian [hju:,mænɪ'teərɪən] *adj* humanitär.

humanity [hju:'mænɪtɪ] *n* **(a)** *(mankind)* die Menschheit. **(b)** *(humaneness)* Menschlichkeit *f.* **(c) humanities** *pl* Geisteswissenschaften *pl*; *(Latin and Greek)* Altphilologie *f.*

humanly ['hju:mənlɪ] *adv* menschlich. **to do all that is** ~ **possible** alles menschenmögliche tun.

humble ['hʌmbl] **1** *adj* (+*er*) *(unassuming)* bescheiden; *(meek, Rel)* demütig. **in my** ~ **opinion** meiner bescheidenen Meinung nach; **to eat** ~ **pie** klein beigeben. **2** *vt* demütigen.

humbug ['hʌmbʌg] *n* **(a)** *(col)* Humbug *m.* **(b)** *(Brit: sweet)* Pfefferminzbonbon *nt.*

humdinger ['hʌmdɪŋər] *n (col: person, thing)* **to be a** ~ **Spitze sein** *(col)*.

humdrum ['hʌmdrʌm] *adj* stumpfsinnig.

humid ['hju:mɪd] *adj* feucht.

humidifier [hju:'mɪdɪfaɪər] *n* Luftbefeuchter *m.*

humidity [hju:'mɪdɪtɪ] *n* (Luft)feuchtigkeit *f.*

humiliate [hju:'mɪlɪeɪt] *vt see n* demütigen; beschämen.

humiliation [hju:,mɪlɪ'eɪʃən] *n* Demütigung *f*; *(because of one's own actions)* Beschämung *f no pl.*

humility [hju:'mɪlɪtɪ] *n* Demut *f*; *(unassumingness)* Bescheidenheit *f.*

hummingbird ['hʌmɪŋ,bɜ:d] *n* Kolibri *m.*

humorist ['hju:mərɪst] *n* Humorist(in *f*) *m.*

humorous ['hju:mərəs] *adj person* humorvoll; *story etc also, situation* lustig; *idea* witzig.

humour, (US) humor ['hju:mər] **1** *n* **(a)** Humor *m.* **a sense of** ~ (Sinn *m* für) Humor *m*; **a story full of** ~ eine humorvolle Geschichte. **(b)** *(mood)* Stimmung, Laune *f.* **to be in a good** ~ in guter Stimmung sein; **he took it with good** ~ er nahm es gelassen auf. **2** *vt whims* nachgeben (+*dat*). **to** ~ **sb** jdm seinen Willen lassen.

humourless, (US) humorless ['hju:məlɪs] *adj* humorlos, ohne jeden Humor.

hump [hʌmp] **1** *n* **(a)** *(Anat)* Buckel *m*; *(of camel)* Höcker *m.* **(b)** *(hillock)* Hügel, Buckel *(esp S Ger) m*. **(c)** *(Brit col)* **he's got the** ~ er ist sauer *(col)*. **2** *vt (col: carry)* schleppen.

humpbacked ['hʌmp,bækt] *adj person* buck(e)lig; *(Brit)* bridge gewölbt.

hunch [hʌntʃ] **1** *n (feeling)* Gefühl *nt*, Ahnung *f.* **to have a** ~ **that ...** das (leise) Gefühl haben, daß ... **2** *vt (also* ~ **up)** *back* krümmen; *shoulders* hochziehen. **he was** ~**ed (up) over his desk** er saß über seinen Schreibtisch gebeugt.

hunchback ['hʌntʃ,bæk] *n (person)* Buck(e)lige(r) *mf*; *(back)* Buckel *m.*

hundred ['hʌndrɪd] **1** *adj* hundert. **a or one** ~ **years** (ein)hundert Jahre; **two** ~ **years** zweihundert Jahre; **a or one** ~ **and one** (ein)hundert(und)eins; **not a** ~ **per cent fit** nicht hundertprozentig fit. **2** *n* hundert *num*; *(written figure)* Hundert *f.* ~**s** *(lit, fig)* Hunderte *pl*; **one in a** ~ einer unter hundert; ~**s of times** *(fig)* hundertmal; **they came in their** ~**s** sie kamen zu Hunderten.

hundredth ['hʌndrɪdθ] **1** *adj (in series)* hundertste(r, s). **2** *n (fraction)* Hundertstel *nt.*

hundredweight ['hʌndrɪdweɪt] *n* Zentner *m*; *(Brit)* 50,8 kg; *(US)* 45,4 kg.

hung [hʌŋ] *pret, ptp of* **hang.**

Hungarian [hʌŋ'geərɪən] **1** *adj* ungarisch. **2** *n* **(a)** Ungar(in *f*) *m*. **(b)** *(language)* Ungarisch *nt.*

Hungary ['hʌŋgərɪ] *n* Ungarn *nt.*

hunger ['hʌŋgər] *n (lit, fig)* Hunger *m (for nach)*. **to go on (a)** ~ **strike** in (den) Hungerstreik treten.

hungrily ['hʌŋgrɪlɪ] *adv (lit, fig)* hungrig.

hungry ['hʌŋgrɪ] *adj* (+*er*) *(lit, fig)* hungrig. **to be/ get** ~ Hunger haben/bekommen; **to go** ~ hungern; ~ **for power** machthungrig.

hunk [hʌŋk] *n* Stück *nt.* **a gorgeous** ~ **(of a man)** *(col)* ein Mann! *(col)*.

hunky-dory ['hʌŋkɪ'dɔ:rɪ] *adj (col)* **that's** ~ das ist prima *(col)*.

hunt [hʌnt] **1** *n* Jagd *f*; *(fig: search)* Suche *f.* **to have a** ~ **for sth** nach etw fahnden *(col)*. **2** *vt* jagen; *criminal also* fahnden nach; *missing article, person* suchen. **3** *vi* **(a)** jagen. **to go** ~**ing** jagen, auf die Jagd gehen. **(b)** *(search)* suchen *(for nach)*.

♦ **hunt down** *vt sep* (unerbittlich) Jagd machen auf (+*acc*); *(capture)* zur Strecke bringen.

♦ **hunt out** *vt sep* hervorkramen *(col)*.

♦ **hunt up** *vt sep history, origins* forschen nach.

hunter ['hʌntər] *n* Jäger *m*; *(horse)* Jagdpferd *nt.*

hunting ['hʌntɪŋ] *n* die Jagd. **to go** ~ auf die Jagd gehen.

huntsman ['hʌntsmən] *n, pl* **-men** [-mən] Jagdreiter *m.*

hurdle ['hɜ:dl] (Sport, fig) Hürde f. ~s sing (race) Hürdenlauf m.
hurdler ['hɜ:dlə^r] n (Sport) Hürdenlätufer(in f) m.
hurl [hɜ:l] vt schleudern. **to ~ oneself at sb** sich auf jdn stürzen; **to ~ abuse at sb** jdn wüst beschimpfen (col).
hurly-burly ['hɜ:lɪ'bɜ:lɪ] n Rummel m (col).
hurrah [hʊ'rɑ:], **hurray** [hʊ'reɪ] interj hurra.
hurricane ['hʌrɪkən] n Orkan m; (tropical) Wirbelsturm m. **~ lamp** Sturmlaterne f.
hurried ['hʌrɪd] adj eilig; letter, essay hastig geschrieben; work in Eile gemacht.
hurry ['hʌrɪ] **1** n Eile f. **in my ~ to get it finished** ... vor lauter Eile, damit fertig zu werden ...; **to do sth in a ~** etw hastig tun; **I need it in a ~** ich brauche es dringend; **to be in a ~** es eilig haben; **I won't do that again in a ~!** (col) das mache ich so schnell nicht wieder!; **what's the ~?** warum so eilig?; **is there any ~ for it?** eilt das?; **there's no ~** es eilt nicht.
2 vi sich beeilen; (run/go quickly) laufen. **there's no need to ~** kein Grund zur Eile; **can't you make her ~?** kannst du sie nicht zur Eile antreiben?; **don't ~!** immer mit der Ruhe!; **I must ~ back** ich muß schnell zu rück.
3 vt work etc schneller machen; (do too quickly) überstürzen. **troops were hurried to the spot** es wurden schleunigst Truppen dorthin gebracht; **don't ~ me** hetz mich nicht so!; **don't ~ your meal** lassen Sie sich Zeit beim Essen!
♦ **hurry along 1** vi sich beeilen. **to ~ ~ the road** die Straße entlanglaufen. **2** vt sep person weiterdrängen; (with work etc) zur Eile antreiben; things, work etc vorantreiben.
♦ **hurry away** or **off 1** vi schnell weggehen. **2** vt sep schnell wegbringen.
♦ **hurry on** vi weiterlaufen.
♦ **hurry up 1** vi sich beeilen. **~ ~!** beeil dich! **2** vt sep zur Eile antreiben; work vorantreiben.
hurt [hɜ:t] (vb: pret, ptp ~) **1** vt (a) (lit, fig) weh tun (+dat); (injure) verletzen. **to ~ oneself** sich (dat) weh tun; **to ~ one's arm** sich (dat) am Arm weh tun; (injure) sich (dat) den Arm verletzen. **(b)** (harm) schaden (+dat). **it wouldn't ~ you to say sorry** du solltest dich wirklich entschuldigen; **it won't ~ him to wait** es schadet ihm nicht(s), wenn er etwas warten muß. **2** vi (a) (be painful) weh tun; (fig also) verletzend sein. **that ~s!** (lit, fig) das tut weh! **(b)** but surely a little drink won't ~ aber ein kleines Gläschen kann doch wohl nicht schaden. **3** adj limb, feelings verletzt; tone, look gekränkt.
hurtful ['hɜ:tfʊl] adj verletzend.
hurtle ['hɜ:tl] vi rasen. **he came hurtling around the corner** er kam um die Ecke gerast.
husband ['hʌzbənd] n Ehemann m. **my/her ~** mein/ihr Mann.
hush [hʌʃ] **1** n Stille f. **2** interj pst!
♦ **hush up** vt sep scandal vertuschen.
hushed [hʌʃt] adj voices gedämpft; words leise.
hush-hush ['hʌʃ'hʌʃ] adj (col) streng geheim.
husk [hʌsk] n Schale f; (of rice also) Hülse f.
husky[1] ['hʌskɪ] adj (+er) rauh.
husky[2] n (dog) Schlittenhund m.
hustings ['hʌstɪŋz] npl (Brit) **on the ~** im Wahlkampf; (at election meeting) bei einer Wahlveranstaltung.
hustle ['hʌsl] **1** n **the ~ and bustle** das geschäftige

Treiben. **2** vt **to ~ sb out of the building** jdn schnell aus einem Gebäude bringen; **to ~ things (along)** die Dinge vorantreiben. **3** vi (a) (move busily) hasten, eilen. **(b)** (prostitute) auf den Strich gehen (col). **to ~ for business** (salesman etc) Aufträgen nachjagen.
hut [hʌt] n Hütte f; (Mil) Baracke f.
hutch [hʌtʃ] n Verschlag m.
hyacinth ['haɪəsɪnθ] n Hyazinthe f.
hyaena, hyena [haɪ'i:nə] n Hyäne f.
hybrid ['haɪbrɪd] n (Bot, Zool) Kreuzung f; (fig) Mischform f.
hydrangea [haɪ'dreɪndʒə] n Hortensie f.
hydrant ['haɪdrənt] n Hydrant m.
hydraulic [haɪ'drɒlɪk] adj hydraulisch.
hydraulics [haɪ'drɒlɪks] n sing Hydraulik f.
hydro-: ['haɪdrəʊ-] **~chloric acid** n Salzsäure f; **~electric** adj hydroelektrisch; **~electric power station** n Wasserkraftwerk nt; **~foil** n (boat) Tragflächenboot nt.
hydrogen ['haɪdrɪdʒən] n Wasserstoff m. **~ bomb** Wasserstoffbombe f.
hydrophobia [,haɪdrə'fəʊbɪə] n Wasserscheu f; (rabies) Tollwut f.
hyena [haɪ'i:nə] n = **hyaena**.
hygiene ['haɪdʒi:n] n Hygiene f. **personal ~** Körperpflege f.
hygienic [haɪ'dʒi:nɪk] adj hygienisch.
hymn [hɪm] n Hymne f.
hymnbook ['hɪmbʊk] n Gesangbuch nt.
hyper-: adj pref Hyper-, hyper-, Über-, über-.
hyper-: **~active** adj äußerst aktiv; **~critical** adj übertrieben kritisch; **~market** n (Brit) großer Supermarkt; **~sensitive** adj überempfindlich; **~tension** n Hypertonie f, erhöhter Blutdruck.
hyphen ['haɪfən] n Bindestrich m; (at end of line) Trenn(ungs)strich m.
hyphenate ['haɪfəneɪt] vt mit Bindestrich schreiben; (insert hyphen) trennen.
hypnosis [hɪp'nəʊsɪs] n Hypnose f.
hypnotic [hɪp'nɒtɪk] adj hypnotisch; (hypnotizing, fig) hypnotisierend.
hypnotism ['hɪpnətɪzəm] n Hypnotismus m.
hypnotist ['hɪpnətɪst] n Hypnotiseur m, Hypnotiseuse f.
hypnotize ['hɪpnətaɪz] vt hypnotisieren.
hypochondria [,haɪpəʊ'kɒndrɪə] n Hypochondrie f.
hypochondriac [,haɪpəʊ'kɒndrɪæk] n Hypochonder m.
hypocrisy [hɪ'pɒkrɪsɪ] n Heuchelei f; (pretending innocence) Scheinheiligkeit f.
hypocrite ['hɪpəkrɪt] n Heuchler(in f) m.
hypocritical [,hɪpə'krɪtɪkəl] adj heuchlerisch.
hypodermic (needle) [,haɪpə'dɜ:mɪk (ni:dl)] n Spritze f.
hypotenuse [haɪ'pɒtɪnju:z] n Hypotenuse f.
hypothermia [,haɪpəʊ'θɜ:mɪə] n Unterkühlung f.
hypothesis [haɪ'pɒθɪsɪs] n, pl **hypotheses** [haɪ'pɒθɪsi:z] Hypothese f.
hypothetical [,haɪpəʊ'θetɪkəl] adj hypothetisch. **purely ~** reine Hypothese f.
hysterectomy [,hɪstə'rektəmɪ] n Totaloperation f.
hysteria [hɪ'stɪərɪə] n Hysterie f.
hysterical [hɪ'sterɪkəl] adj hysterisch; (col: very funny) wahnsinnig komisch (col).
hysterics [hɪ'sterɪks] npl hysterischer Anfall m. **to go into ~** (col: laugh) sich (halb) totlachen.

I

I, i [aɪ] *n* I, i *nt*.
I *pers pron* ich. **it is** ~ *(form)* ich bin es.
Iberian [aɪˈbɪərɪən] *adj* ~ **Peninsula** Iberische Halbinsel.
ice [aɪs] **1** *n* **(a)** Eis *nt*; *(on roads)* (Glatt)eis *nt*. **to be as cold as** ~ eiskalt sein; **to keep** *or* **put sth on** ~ *(lit)* etw kalt stellen; *(fig)* etw auf Eis legen; **to break the** ~ *(fig)* das Eis brechen; **to be skating on thin** ~ *(fig)* sich aufs Glatteis begeben; **to cut no** ~ **with sb** *(col)* auf jdn keinen Eindruck machen. **(b)** *(Brit: ice-cream)* (Speise)eis *nt*. **2** *vt cake* glasieren.
♦ **ice over** *vi* zufrieren; *(windscreen)* vereisen.
♦ **ice up** *vi (aircraft wings etc)* vereisen; *(pipes etc)* einfrieren.
ice *in cpds* Eis-; ~ **age** *n* Eiszeit *f*; ~ **axe** *(Brit)* or ~ **ax** *(US)* *n* Eispickel *m*; ~**berg** *n (lit, fig)* Eisberg *m*; ~**bound** *adj port* zugefroren; *ship* vom Eis eingeschlossen; *road* vereist; ~**box** *n (Brit: in refrigerator)* Eisfach *nt*; *(US)* Eisschrank *m*; *(insulated box)* Kühltasche *f*; ~**breaker** *n* Eisbrecher *m*; ~ **bucket** *n* Eiskühler *m*; ~**cap** *n* Eiskappe *f*; ~**-cold** *adj* eiskalt; ~**-cream** *n* Eis *nt*; ~ **cube** *n* Eiswürfel *m*; ~ **hockey** *n* Eishockey *nt*.
Iceland [ˈaɪslənd] *n* Island *nt*.
Icelander [ˈaɪsləndəʳ] *n* Isländer(in *f*) *m*.
Icelandic [aɪsˈlændɪk] **1** *adj* isländisch. **2** *n (language)* Isländisch *nt*.
ice: ~**lolly** *n (Brit)* Eis *nt* am Stiel; ~ **pick** *n* Eispickel *m*; ~ **rink** *n* Schlittschuhbahn *f*; ~**-skate** *vi* Schlittschuh laufen; ~**-skating** *n* Schlittschuhlaufen *nt*.
icicle [ˈaɪsɪkl] *n* Eiszapfen *m*.
icily [ˈaɪsɪlɪ] *adv (lit, fig)* eisig. **to look** ~ **at sb** jdm einen eisigen Blick zuwerfen.
icing [ˈaɪsɪŋ] *n (Cook)* Zuckerguß *m*. ~ **sugar** *(Brit)* Puderzucker *m*.
icon [ˈaɪkɒn] *n* Ikone *f*.
iconoclastic [aɪˌkɒnəˈklæstɪk] *adj* bilderstürmerisch.
icy [ˈaɪsɪ] *adj (+er) (lit, fig)* eisig; *road* vereist.
I'd [aɪd] = I would; I had.
id [ɪd] *n (Psych)* Es *nt*.
idea [aɪˈdɪə] *n* Idee *f*. **good** ~! gute Idee!; **that's not a bad** ~ das ist keine schlechte Idee; **the very** ~! (nein), so was!; **the very** ~ **of eating horsemeat revolts me** der bloße Gedanke an Pferdefleisch ekelt mich; **the** ~ **never entered my head!** auf den Gedanken bin ich überhaupt nicht gekommen; **to hit upon the** ~ **of doing sth** den plötzlichen Einfall haben, etw zu tun; **that gives me an** ~, **we could ...** da fällt mir ein, wir könnten ...; **the** ~ **for the book** die Idee zu dem Buch; **he's somehow got the** ~ **into his head that ...** er bildet sich *(dat)* irgendwie ein, daß ...; **don't go getting** ~**s about promotion** machen Sie sich *(dat)* nur keine falschen Hoffnungen auf eine Beförderung; **to put** ~**s into sb's head** jdm einen Floh ins Ohr setzen; **what's the big** ~? *(col)* was soll das denn?; **that's the** ~ genau (das ist's)!; **if that's your** ~ **of fun** wenn Sie das lustig finden; **he has some very strange** ~**s** er hat merkwürdige Vorstellungen; **his** ~ **of a pleasant evening is ...** seine Vorstellung von einem angenehmen Abend ist, ...; **you've no** ~ **how worried I've been** du kannst dir nicht vorstellen, welche

Sorgen ich mir gemacht habe; **(I've) no** ~ *(ich habe)* keine Ahnung; **I have an** ~ **that ... ich habe so das Gefühl, daß ...; **could you give me an** ~ **of how long ...?** könnten Sie mir ungefähr sagen, wie lange ...?
ideal [aɪˈdɪəl] **1** *adj* ideal. **2** *n* Idealvorstellung *f*, Ideal *nt*.
idealism [aɪˈdɪəlɪzəm] *n* Idealismus *m*.
idealist [aɪˈdɪəlɪst] *n* Idealist(in *f*) *m*.
ideally [aɪˈdɪəlɪ] *adv* ideal. **they are** ~ **suited for each other** sie passen ausgezeichnet zueinander; ~, **... idealerweise** *or* im Idealfall ...
identical [aɪˈdentɪkəl] *adj (exactly alike)* identisch; *(same)* derselbe/dieselbe/dasselbe. ~ **twins** eineiige Zwillinge *pl*.
identification [aɪˌdentɪfɪˈkeɪʃən] *n* Identifizierung *f*; *(papers)* Ausweispapiere *pl*.
identify [aɪˈdentɪfaɪ] **1** *vt* **(a)** identifizieren; *plant, species etc* bestimmen; *(mark identity of)* kennzeichnen; *(recognize, pick)* erkennen *(by* an +*dat)*. **(b)** *(consider as the same)* gleichsetzen *(with* mit). **2** *vr* **(a) to** ~ **oneself** sich ausweisen. **(b) to** ~ **oneself with sb/sth** sich mit jdm/etw identifizieren. **3** *vi (with film hero etc)* sich identifizieren *(with* mit).
identikit [aɪˈdentɪkɪt] *n*: ~ **(picture)** Phantombild *nt*.
identity [aɪˈdentɪtɪ] *n* Identität *f*. **to prove one's** ~ sich ausweisen.
identity: ~ **card** *n* (Personal)ausweis *m*; ~ **parade** *n* Gegenüberstellung *f* (zur Identifikation des Täters).
ideological [ˌaɪdɪəˈlɒdʒɪkəl] *adj* ideologisch.
ideology [ˌaɪdɪˈɒlədʒɪ] *n* Weltanschauung *f*, Ideologie *f*.
idiom [ˈɪdɪəm] *n* idiomatische Wendung.
idiomatic [ˌɪdɪəˈmætɪk] *adj* idiomatisch.
idiosyncrasy [ˌɪdɪəˈsɪŋkrəsɪ] *n* Eigenheit, Eigenart *f*.
idiosyncratic [ˌɪdɪəsɪŋˈkrætɪk] *adj* **he has a very** ~ **way of ...** er hat eine eigene Art zu ...
idiot [ˈɪdɪət] *n* Idiot, Dummkopf *m*. **you (stupid)** ~! du Idiot!; **what an** ~ **I am/was!** ich Idiot!
idiotic [ˌɪdɪˈɒtɪk] *adj* idiotisch. **don't be** ~! sei nicht so blöd!
idle [ˈaɪdl] **1** *adj* **(a)** *(not working) person* untätig. **the** ~ **rich** die reichen Müßiggänger; **in my** ~ **moments** in stillen Augenblicken; ~ **life** faules Leben; *money lying* ~ totes Kapital; **his car was lying** ~ **most of the time** sein Auto stand meistens unbenutzt herum. **(b)** *(lazy)* faul. **(c)** *(in industry) person* unbeschäftigt; *machine* außer Betrieb. **to be made** ~ *(worker)* seine Arbeit einstellen müssen; **the whole factory stood** ~ die ganze Fabrik hatte die Arbeit eingestellt; **the machine stood** ~ die Maschine stand still. **(d)** *promise, words* leer; *(useless)* nutzlos. ~ **curiosity** pure Neugier. **2** *vi (engine)* leerlaufen. **when the engine is idling** wenn der Motor im Leerlauf ist.
♦ **idle away** *vt sep one's time etc* vertrödeln.
idleness [ˈaɪdlnɪs] *n* **(a)** *(not working)* Untätigkeit *f*; *(pleasurable)* Muße *f*. **(b)** *(laziness)* Faulheit *f*.
idler [ˈaɪdləʳ] *n (pej)* Faulenzer(in *f*) *m*.
idly [ˈaɪdlɪ] *adv* **(a)** *(without working)* untätig; *(pleasurably)* müßig. **to stand** ~ **by** untätig herumstehen. **(b)** *(lazily)* faul.

idol ['aɪdl] n (lit) Götzenbild nt; (fig) Idol nt.
idolize ['aɪdəlaɪz] vt vergöttern; (star) zum Idol machen.
I'd've ['aɪdəv] = **I would have.**
idyll ['ɪdɪl] n Idyll nt.
idyllic [ɪ'dɪlɪk] adj idyllisch.
i.e. abbr d.h.
if [ɪf] **1** conj wenn; (in case also) falls; (whether, in indirect clause) ob. **I would be pleased ~ you could do it** wenn Sie das tun könnten, wäre ich sehr froh; **(even) ~ auch** wenn; **(even) ~ they are poor, at least they are happy** sie sind zwar arm, aber wenigstens glücklich; **~ only I had known!** wenn ich das nur gewußt hätte!; **I would like to see him, ~ only for a few hours** ich würde ihn gerne sehen, wenn auch nur für ein paar Stunden; **as ~ als ob; he acts as ~ he were** or **was rich** er tut so, als ob er reich wäre; **~ necessary** falls nötig; **~ so** wenn ja; **~ not** wenn nicht; **~ I were you/him** wenn ich Sie/er wäre. **2** n **it's a big ~** das ist die große Frage; **~s and buts** Wenn und Aber nt.
igloo ['ɪgluː] n Iglu m or nt.
ignite [ɪg'naɪt] **1** vt entzünden. **2** vi sich entzünden.
ignition [ɪg'nɪʃən] n Entzünden nt; (Aut) Zündung f. **to switch on the ~** starten.
ignoble [ɪg'nəʊbl] adj unehrenhaft.
ignominious [ˌɪgnə'mɪnɪəs] adj schmachvoll; behaviour schändlich.
ignominy ['ɪgnəmɪnɪ] n Schmach, Schande f.
ignoramus [ˌɪgnə'reɪməs] n Ignorant m.
ignorance ['ɪgnərəns] n Unwissenheit f; (of particular subject) Unkenntnis f. **to keep sb in ~ of sth** jdn in Unkenntnis über etw (acc) lassen.
ignorant ['ɪgnərənt] adj **(a)** unwissend; (of plan etc) nicht informiert (of plan +acc). **to be ~ of geography** sich in Geographie nicht auskennen; **to be ~ of the facts** die Tatsachen nicht kennen. **(b)** (ill-mannered) ungehobelt.
ignore [ɪg'nɔːʳ] vt ignorieren; (pay no attention to) nicht beachten; remark also übergehen.
ill [ɪl] **1** adj **(a)** pred (sick) krank. **to fall** or **be taken ~** erkranken (with sth an etw dat), krank werden; **to feel ~** sich krank fühlen. **(b)** (bad) schlecht. **~ feeling** böses Blut; **no ~ feeling?** ist es wieder gut?; **no ~ feeling!** (ist) schon vergessen!; **due to ~ health** aus Gesundheitsgründen; **as ~ luck would have it** wie es der Teufel so will; **~ will** böses Blut; **I don't bear them any ~ will** ich trage ihnen nichts nach; **it's an ~ wind (that blows nobody any good)** (Prov) so hat alles seine guten Seiten. **2** n **to think ~ of sb** schlecht von jdm denken; **to speak ~ of sb** schlecht über jdn reden. **3** adv schlecht. **he can ~ afford to refuse** er kann es sich (dat) schlecht leisten abzulehnen.
I'll [aɪl] = **I will; I shall.**
ill: ~-advised adj unklug; **you would be ~-advised to trust her** Sie wären schlecht beraten, wenn Sie ihr trauten; **~-at-ease** adj unbehaglich; **~-bred** adj schlecht erzogen; **~-considered** adj action, words unüberlegt; **~-disposed** adj **to be ~-disposed to(wards) sb** jdm übel gesinnt sein.
illegal [ɪ'liːgəl] adj unerlaubt; (against a specific law) gesetzwidrig; trade, possession etc illegal; (Sport) regelwidrig.
illegality [ˌɪliː'gælɪtɪ] n see adj Ungesetzlichkeit f; Gesetzwidrigkeit f; Illegalität f.
illegally [ɪ'liːgəlɪ] adv **~ imported** illegal eingeführt; **you're ~ parked** Sie stehen im Parkverbot.
illegible [ɪ'ledʒəbl] adj unleserlich.
illegitimate [ˌɪlɪ'dʒɪtɪmɪt] adj **(a)** child unehelich. **(b)** (contrary to law) unzulässig; government unrechtmäßig.
ill: ~-fated adj **(a)** person vom Unglück verfolgt; **(b)** (doomed) unglückselig; **~-founded** adj unbegründet; **~-gotten gains** npl unrechtmäßi-

ger Gewinn; **~-humoured,** (US) **~-humored** adj schlecht gelaunt.
illicit [ɪ'lɪsɪt] adj illegal; spirits schwarz gebrannt.
ill-informed ['ɪlɪnˌfɔːmd] adj person schlecht informiert; criticism, speech wenig sachkundig.
illiterate [ɪ'lɪtərət] **1** adj **to be ~** Analphabet sein; (uncultured) person ungebildet. **2** n Analphabet(in f) m.
ill: ~-mannered adj unhöflich; **~-natured** adj bösartig.
illness ['ɪlnɪs] n Krankheit f.
illogical [ɪ'lɒdʒɪkəl] adj unlogisch.
ill: ~-suited adj (to one another) nicht zusammenpassend; (to sth) ungeeignet (to für); **~-timed** adj ungelegen; **~-treat** vt schlecht behandeln; **~-treatment** n schlechte Behandlung.
illuminate [ɪ'luːmɪneɪt] vt **(a)** room, street beleuchten; (spotlight etc) anstrahlen. **~d sign** Leuchtzeichen nt. **(b)** (fig) question, subject erläutern.
illuminating [ɪ'luːmɪneɪtɪŋ] adj (instructive) aufschlußreich.
illumination [ɪˌluːmɪ'neɪʃən] n **(a)** (of street etc) Beleuchtung f. **(b)** **~s** pl festliche Beleuchtung f. **(c)** (fig) Erläuterung f.
illusion [ɪ'luːʒən] n Illusion f. **to be under an ~** einer Täuschung (dat) unterliegen; **to be under the ~ that ...** sich (dat) einbilden, daß ...; **to have no ~s** sich (dat) keine Illusionen machen.
illusive [ɪ'luːsɪv], **illusory** [ɪ'luːsərɪ] adj trügerisch.
illustrate ['ɪləstreɪt] vt illustrieren; (fig) veranschaulichen. **~d (magazine)** Illustrierte f.
illustration [ˌɪləs'treɪʃən] n (picture) Abbildung f, Illustration f. **by way of ~** als Beispiel.
illustrative ['ɪləstrətɪv] adj veranschaulichend.
illustrator ['ɪləstreɪtəʳ] n Illustrator m.
illustrious [ɪ'lʌstrɪəs] adj glanzvoll, gefeiert; deeds glorreich.
I'm [aɪm] = **I am.**
image ['ɪmɪdʒ] n **(a)** (carved etc) Standbild nt; (painted) Bild nt; (likeness) Ebenbild nt. **(b)** (mental picture) Vorstellung f, Bild nt. **(c)** (public) ~ Image nt.
imagery ['ɪmɪdʒərɪ] n Metaphorik f.
imaginable [ɪ'mædʒnəbl] adj denkbar. **the fastest way ~** der denkbar schnellste Weg.
imaginary [ɪ'mædʒɪnərɪ] adj danger eingebildet; imaginär; characters frei ersonnen, erfunden.
imagination [ɪˌmædʒɪ'neɪʃən] n (creative) Phantasie, Vorstellungskraft f; (self-deceptive) Einbildung f. **to have (a vivid) ~** (eine lebhafte) Phantasie haben; **use your ~** lassen Sie Ihre Phantasie spielen; **it's only (your) ~!** das bilden Sie sich (dat) nur ein!
imaginative [ɪ'mædʒɪnətɪv] adj phantasievoll; plan, idea also einfallsreich.
imagine [ɪ'mædʒɪn] vt **(a)** (picture) sich (dat) vorstellen. **I can't ~ what you mean** ich kann mir nicht vorstellen, was Sie meinen; **you can't ~ how ...** Sie können sich nicht vorstellen, wie ...; **you can't ~ it!** Sie machen sich keine Vorstellungen! **(b)** (be under illusion) sich (dat) einbilden. **don't ~ that ...** bilden Sie sich nur nicht ein, daß ...; **you're (just) imagining things** (col) Sie bilden sich das alles nur ein. **(c)** (suppose) annehmen. **is it time now? — I would ~ so** ist es soweit? — ich denke schon; **I would never have ~d he would have done that** ich hätte nie gedacht, daß er das tun würde.
imbalance [ɪm'bæləns] n Unausgeglichenheit f.
imbecile ['ɪmbəsiːl] n Idiot, Schwachkopf m; (Med) Schwachsinnige(r) mf.
imbibe [ɪm'baɪb] vt (form, hum) trinken, bechern (hum).
imbue [ɪm'bjuː] vt (fig) erfüllen.
IMF = **International Monetary Fund** IWF m, Internationaler Währungsfonds.

imitate ['ɪmɪteɪt] *vt* imitieren, nachahmen.

imitation [,ɪmɪ'teɪʃən] **1** *n* Imitation, Nachahmung *f*. **to do an** ~ **of sb** jdn imitieren *or* nachahmen. **2** *adj* unecht. ~ **leather** Kunstleder *nt*.

imitative ['ɪmɪtətɪv] *adj* imitativ (*geh*).

imitator ['ɪmɪteɪtə'] *n* Nachahmer, Imitator *m*.

immaculate [ɪ'mækjʊlɪt] *adj* tadellos. **the I~ Conception** die Unbefleckte Empfängnis.

immaterial [,ɪmə'tɪərɪəl] *adj* (*unimportant*) unwesentlich. **it is quite** ~ **to me (whether) ... es ist für mich unwichtig, (ob) ...; that's (quite)** ~ **das spielt (überhaupt) keine Rolle.

immature [,ɪmə'tjʊə'] *adj* (*lit, fig*) unreif.

immaturity [,ɪmə'tjʊərɪtɪ] *n* Unreife *f*.

immeasurable [ɪ'meʒərəbl] *adj* unermeßlich.

immediacy [ɪ'miːdɪəsɪ] *n* Unmittelbarkeit *f*; (*urgency*) Dringlichkeit *f*.

immediate [ɪ'miːdɪət] *adj* **(a)** (*instant*) umgehend. **to take** ~ **action** sofort handeln. **(b)** *future etc* unmittelbar; *cause, successor also* direkt; *vicinity also* nächste. **the** ~ **family** die engste Familie.

immediately [ɪ'miːdɪətlɪ] **1** *adv* sofort; *reply, return, depart also* umgehend. ~ **after/before** unmittelbar danach/davor. **2** *conj* (*Brit*) sobald als ...

immemorial [,ɪmɪ'mɔːrɪəl] *adj*: **from time** ~ seit undenklichen Zeiten.

immense [ɪ'mens] *adj* enorm, immens.

immensely [ɪ'menslɪ] *adv* unheimlich (*col*), enorm; *grateful* äußerst.

immensity [ɪ'mensɪtɪ] *n* Unermeßlichkeit *f*.

immerse [ɪ'mɜːs] *vt* eintauchen (*in* in +*acc*). **to be** ~**d in water** unter Wasser sein; **to** ~ **oneself in sth** (*fig*) sich in etw (*acc*) vertiefen.

immersion [ɪ'mɜːʃən] *n* **(a)** Eintauchen *nt*. ~ **heater** (*Brit*) Wasserboiler *m*; (*for jug etc*) Tauchsieder *m*. **(b)** (*fig*) Vertieftsein *nt*.

immigrant ['ɪmɪgrənt] **1** *n* Einwanderer *m*, Einwanderin *f*. **2** *attr* ~ **workers** ausländische Arbeitnehmer *pl*; (*esp BRD also*) Gastarbeiter *pl*.

immigration [,ɪmɪ'greɪʃən] *n* Einwanderung, Immigration *f*; (~ *authorities*) Einwanderungsbehörde *f*. **to go through** ~ die Einwanderungsformalitäten erledigen.

imminent ['ɪmɪnənt] *adj* **to be** ~ nahe bevorstehen.

immobile [ɪ'məʊbaɪl] *adj* unbeweglich; (*not able to move*) *person* bewegungslos.

immobilize [ɪ'məʊbɪlaɪz] *vt* *traffic* zum Erliegen bringen; *army* bewegungsunfähig machen; (*Fin*) *capital* festlegen.

immoderate [ɪ'mɒdərɪt] *adj* *desire* übermäßig; *demands also* überzogen; *views* übersteigert.

immodest [ɪ'mɒdɪst] *adj* unbescheiden.

immodesty [ɪ'mɒdɪstɪ] *n* Unbescheidenheit *f*.

immoral [ɪ'mɒrəl] *adj* *action* unmoralisch; *behaviour also* unsittlich; *person also* sittenlos.

immorality [,ɪmə'rælɪtɪ] *n* Unmoral *f*; (*of person also*) Sittenlosigkeit *f*; (*immoral act*) Unsittlichkeit *f*.

immortal [ɪ'mɔːtl] *adj* unsterblich.

immortality [,ɪmɔː'tælɪtɪ] *n* Unsterblichkeit *f*.

immortalize [ɪ'mɔːtəlaɪz] *vt* unsterblich machen.

immovable [ɪ'muːvəbl] *adj* (*lit*) unbeweglich; (*fig*) *obstacle* unüberwindlich.

immune [ɪ'mjuːn] *adj* (*Med*) immun (*to* gegen); (*fig*) sicher (*from* vor +*dat*).

immunity [ɪ'mjuːnɪtɪ] *n* (*Med, diplomatic*) Immunität *f*; (*fig*) Sicherheit *f*.

immunization [,ɪmjʊnaɪ'zeɪʃən] *n* Immunisierung *f*.

immunize ['ɪmjʊnaɪz] *vt* immunisieren.

immutable [ɪ'mjuːtəbl] *adj* unveränderlich.

imp [ɪmp] *n* Kobold *m*; (*col: child also*) Schlingel *m* (*col*).

impact ['ɪmpækt] *n* Aufprall *m* (*on* auf +*acc*); (*of two moving objects*) Zusammenprall *m*; (*of falling object*) (*on house*) Einschlag *m* (*on* in +*acc*); (*on*

ground) Aufschlag *m* (*on* auf +*dat*); (*force*) Wucht *f*; (*fig*) (*Aus*)wirkung *f* (*on* auf +*acc*). **on** ~ **(with)** beim Aufprall (*auf* +*acc*)/Zusammenprall (*mit*) *etc*; **his speech had a great** ~ **on his audience** seine Rede machte großen Eindruck auf seine Zuhörer.

impair [ɪm'peə'] *vt* beeinträchtigen.

impale [ɪm'peɪl] *vt* aufspießen (*on* auf +*dat*).

impart [ɪm'pɑːt] *vt* **(a)** *information* mitteilen; *knowledge* vermitteln. **(b)** (*bestow*) verleihen (*to* *dat*).

impartial [ɪm'pɑːʃəl] *adj* *person, attitude* unvoreingenommen; *decision also* gerecht.

impartiality [ɪm,pɑːʃɪ'ælɪtɪ] *n see adj* Unvoreingenommenheit *f*; Gerechtigkeit *f*.

impassable [ɪm'pɑːsəbl] *adj* unpassierbar.

impasse [ɪm'pɑːs] *n* (*fig*) Sackgasse *f*. **to have reached an** ~ sich festgefahren haben.

impassioned [ɪm'pæʃnd] *adj* leidenschaftlich.

impassive [ɪm'pæsɪv] *adj* gelassen.

impatience [ɪm'peɪʃəns] *n* Ungeduld *f*; (*intolerance*) Unduldsamkeit *f*.

impatient [ɪm'peɪʃənt] *adj* ungeduldig; (*intolerant*) unduldsam (*of* gegenüber).

impeach [ɪm'piːtʃ] *vt* **(a)** (*Jur: accuse*) *public official* (eines Amtsvergehens) anklagen. **(b)** *sb's character, motives* in Frage stellen.

impeccable [ɪm'pekəbl] *adj* tadellos.

impede [ɪm'piːd] *vt* *person* hindern; *action, traffic* behindern.

impediment [ɪm'pedɪmənt] *n* Hindernis *nt*; (*Med*) Behinderung *f*. **speech** ~ Sprachfehler *m*.

impel [ɪm'pel] *vt* **(a)** (*force*) **to** ~ **sb to do sth** jdn (dazu) nötigen, etw zu tun. **(b)** (*drive on*) (voran)treiben.

impending [ɪm'pendɪŋ] *adj* bevorstehend; *storm also* heraufziehend; *danger* drohend.

impenetrable [ɪm'penɪtrəbl] *adj* undurchdringlich; *fortress* uneinnehmbar; *mind, mystery* unergründlich; *theory* undurchschaubar.

imperative [ɪm'perətɪv] **1** *adj* **to be** ~ unbedingt nötig sein. **2** *n* (*Gram*) Imperativ *m*. **in the** ~ im Imperativ.

imperceptible [,ɪmpə'septəbl] *adj* nicht wahrnehmbar; *difference also* unmerklich.

imperfect [ɪm'pɜːfɪkt] **1** *adj* **(a)** (*faulty*) unvollkommen; (*Comm*) *goods* fehlerhaft. **(b)** (*incomplete*) unvollständig. **2** *n* (*Gram*) Imperfekt *nt*.

imperfection [,ɪmpə'fekʃən] *n* **(a)** *no pl see adj* Unvollkommenheit *f*; Unvollständigkeit *f*. **(b)** (*fault, defect*) Mangel *m*.

imperial [ɪm'pɪərɪəl] *adj* (*of empire*) Reichs-; (*of emperor*) kaiserlich, Kaiser-. **(b)** (*Brit*) *weights, measures* englisch.

imperialism [ɪm'pɪərɪəlɪzəm] *n* Imperialismus *m*.

imperious [ɪm'pɪərɪəs] *adj* gebieterisch.

impermeable [ɪm'pɜːmɪəbl] *adj* undurchlässig.

impersonal [,ɪm'pɜːsnl] *adj* unpersönlich.

impersonate [ɪm'pɜːsəneɪt] *vt* sich ausgeben als; (*take off*) imitieren, nachahmen.

impersonation [ɪm,pɜːsə'neɪʃən] *n see vt* Verkörperung *f*; Imitation, Nachahmung *f*. **he does** ~**s of politicians** er imitiert Politiker.

impersonator [ɪm'pɜːsəneɪtə'] *n* (*Theat*) Imitator(in *f*) *m*.

impertinence [ɪm'pɜːtɪnəns] *n* Unverschämtheit *f*.

impertinent [ɪm'pɜːtɪnənt] *adj* unverschämt (*to* zu, gegenüber).

imperturbable [,ɪmpə'tɜːbəbl] *adj* unerschütterlich.

impervious [ɪm'pɜːvɪəs] *adj* (*fig*) unzugänglich (*to* für); (*criticism*) unberührt (*to* von).

impetuosity [ɪm,petjʊ'ɒsɪtɪ] *n* **(a)** *see adj* Ungestüm *nt*; Impulsivität *f*. **(b)** (*impetuous behaviour*) ungestümes Handeln.

impetuous [ɪm'petjʊəs] *adj* *act, person* ungestüm; *decision* impulsiv.

impetus ['ɪmpɪtəs] *n (lit, fig)* Impuls *m*; *(force)* Kraft *f*; *(momentum)* Schwung *m*.

♦ **impinge on** [ɪm'pɪndʒɒn] *vi* +*prep obj* sich auswirken auf (+*acc*), beeinflussen; *(on sb's rights etc also)* einschränken.

impish ['ɪmpɪʃ] *adj* schelmisch.

implacable [ɪm'plækəbl] *adj* unerbittlich.

implant [ɪm'plɑːnt] **1** *vt* **(a)** *(fig)* einimpfen *(in sb jdm)*. **(b)** *(Med)* einpflanzen. **2** ['ɪmplɑːnt] *n* Implantat *nt*.

implausible [ɪm'plɔːzəbl] *adj* nicht plausibel; *story, excuse also* unglaubwürdig.

implement ['ɪmplɪmənt] **1** *n* Gerät *nt*; *(tool also)* Werkzeug *nt*. **2** [ɪmplɪ'ment] *vt law* vollziehen; *promise* erfüllen; *plan etc* durchführen.

implicate ['ɪmplɪkeɪt] *vt* to ~ sb in sth jdn in etw verwickeln.

implication [ˌɪmplɪ'keɪʃən] *n* Implikation *f*; *(of law, agreement etc also)* Auswirkung *f*. **the possible ~s of his decision** die ganze Tragweite seiner Entscheidung; **by ~** implizit(e).

implicit [ɪm'plɪsɪt] *adj* **(a)** *(implied)* implizit; *threat also* indirekt; *recognition also* stillschweigend. **to be ~ in sth** durch etw impliziert werden; *(in contract etc)* in etw *(dat)* impliziert sein. **(b)** *(unquestioning) confidence* absolut.

implore [ɪm'plɔː'] *vt person* anflehen.

imploring [ɪm'plɔːrɪŋ] *adj* flehend; *beg also* inständig.

imply [ɪm'plaɪ] *vt* **(a)** andeuten, implizieren. **are you ~ing ...?** wollen Sie damit vielleicht andeuten, daß ...?; **it implies that he has changed his mind** das deutet darauf hin, daß er es sich *(dat)* anders überlegt hat. **(b)** *(involve)* bedeuten.

impolite [ˌɪmpə'laɪt] *adj* unhöflich.

impoliteness [ˌɪmpə'laɪtnɪs] *n* Unhöflichkeit *f*.

imponderable [ɪm'pɒndərəbl] *adj* unberechenbar.

import ['ɪmpɔːt] **1** *n* **(a)** *(Comm)* Import *m*, Einfuhr *f*. **(b)** *(meaning)* Bedeutung *f*. **2** [ɪm'pɔːt] *vt goods* einführen, importieren.

importance [ɪm'pɔːtəns] *n* Wichtigkeit *f*; *(significance also)* Bedeutung *f*; *(influence also)* Einfluß *m*. **to be of no (great) ~** nicht (besonders) wichtig sein; **to attach the greatest ~ to sth** einer Sache *(dat)* größte Bedeutung beimessen.

important [ɪm'pɔːtənt] *adj* wichtig; *(significant also)* bedeutend; *(influential)* einflußreich. **it's not ~** *(doesn't matter)* das macht nichts; **to try to look ~** sich *(dat)* ein gewichtiges Aussehen geben.

importantly [ɪm'pɔːtəntlɪ] *adj* **(a)** *(usu pej)* wichtigtuerisch *(pej)*. **(b)** **it is ~ different** das ist entscheidend anders.

import *in cpds* Einfuhr-, Import-; ~ **duty** *n* Einfuhrzoll *m*.

importer [ɪm'pɔːtə'] *n* Importeur(in *f*) *m (of von)*.

import licence *(Brit)* or **license** *(US)* *n* Einfuhrlizenz *f*.

impose [ɪm'pəuz] **1** *vt task, conditions* auferlegen *(on sb jdm)*; *sanctions, fine* verhängen *(on gegen)*; *tax* erheben. **to ~ oneself on sb** sich jdm aufdrängen. **2** *vi* zur Last fallen *(on sb jdm)*. **to ~ on sb's kindness** jds Freundlichkeit ausnützen.

imposing [ɪm'pəuzɪŋ] *adj* beeindruckend; *appearance, building also* stattlich.

imposition [ˌɪmpə'zɪʃən] *n* **(a)** *no pl see vt* Auferlegung *f*; Verhängung *f*. **(b)** *(tax)* Steuer *f (on für, auf +dat)*. **(c)** *(taking advantage)* Zumutung *f*.

impossibility [ɪm,pɒsə'bɪlɪtɪ] *n* Unmöglichkeit *f*.

impossible [ɪm'pɒsəbl] **1** *adj* unmöglich. ~! ausgeschlossen! **2** *n* Unmögliche(s) *nt*. **to ask for the ~** Unmögliches verlangen; **to do the ~** Unmögliches tun.

impostor [ɪm'pɒstə'] *n* Hochstapler(in *f*) *m*.

impotence ['ɪmpətəns] *n see adj* Schwäche *f*; Impotenz *f*; Machtlosigkeit *f*.

impotent ['ɪmpətənt] *adj (physically)* schwach; *(sexually)* impotent; *(fig)* machtlos; *rage* ohnmächtig.

impound [ɪm'paund] *vt* **(a)** *(seize) goods* beschlagnahmen. **(b)** *cattle* einsperren; *car* abschleppen (lassen).

impoverished [ɪm'pɒvərɪʃt] *adj* verarmt; *soil* ausgelaugt.

impracticable [ɪm'præktɪkəbl] *adj* impraktikabel; *design, size* unbrauchbar; *road* schwer befahrbar.

impractical [ɪm'præktɪkəl] *adj* unpraktisch; *scheme also* unbrauchbar.

imprecise [ˌɪmprɪ'saɪs] *adj* ungenau, unpräzis(e).

imprecision [ˌɪmprɪ'sɪʒən] *n* Ungenauigkeit *f*.

impregnable [ɪm'pregnəbl] *adj fortress* uneinnehmbar; *(fig) position* unerschütterlich.

impregnate ['ɪmpregneɪt] *vt* **(a)** *(saturate)* tränken. **(b)** *(Biol: fertilize)* befruchten; *humans also* schwängern.

impresario [ˌɪmpre'sɑːrɪəu] *n* Theater-/Operndirektor *m*.

impress [ɪm'pres] *vt* **(a)** beeindrucken; *(memorably also)* Eindruck machen auf (+*acc*); *(arouse admiration in)* imponieren (+*dat*). **he ~ed me favourably/unfavourably** er hat einen/ keinen guten Eindruck auf mich gemacht. **(b) to ~ a pattern onto sth** ein Muster auf etw *(acc)* aufdrücken.

impression [ɪm'preʃən] *n* **(a)** Eindruck *m*. **to make a good ~ on sb** einen guten Eindruck auf jdn machen; **first ~s** der erste Eindruck; **to give sb the ~ that ...** jdm den Eindruck vermitteln, daß ...; **I was under the ~ that ...** ich hatte den Eindruck, daß ... **(b)** *(on wax etc)* Abdruck *m*. **(c)** *(of book etc)* Nachdruck *m*. **first ~** Erstdruck *m*. **(d)** *(take-off)* Nachahmung, Imitation *f*. **to do an ~ of sb** jdn imitieren.

impressionable [ɪm'preʃnəbl] *adj* für Eindrücke empfänglich. **at an ~ age** in einem Alter, in dem man für Eindrücke besonders empfänglich ist.

impressionism [ɪm'preʃnɪzəm] *n* Impressionismus *m*.

impressionist [ɪm'preʃnɪst] *n* Impressionist(in *f*) *m*.

impressive [ɪm'presɪv] *adj* beeindruckend; *performance, personality also* eindrucksvoll.

imprint [ɪm'prɪnt] **1** *vt seal, paper etc* aufprägen *(on auf* +*acc*); *(on paper)* aufdrucken *(on auf* +*acc*). **to ~ itself on sb's mind** sich jdm einprägen. **2** ['ɪmprɪnt] *n* **(a)** *(on wax etc)* Abdruck *m*. **(b)** *(Typ)* Impressum *nt*.

imprison [ɪm'prɪzn] *(lit)* inhaftieren; *(fig)* gefangenhalten.

imprisonment [ɪm'prɪznmənt] *n* **(a)** *(action)* Inhaftierung *f*; *(state)* Gefangenschaft *f*. **to sentence sb to one month's ~** jdn zu einem Monat Gefängnis verurteilen.

improbability [ɪm,prɒbə'bɪlɪtɪ] *n* Unwahrscheinlichkeit *f*.

improbable [ɪm'prɒbəbl] *adj* unwahrscheinlich.

impromptu [ɪm'prɒmptjuː] **1** *adj* improvisiert. **2** *adv* improvisiert; *perform* aus dem Stegreif.

improper [ɪm'prɒpə'] *adj (unsuitable)* unpassend; *(unseemly)* unschicklich; *(indecent)* unanständig; *use* unsachgemäß; *conduct* unehrenhaft.

impropriety [ˌɪmprə'praɪətɪ] *n* Unschicklichkeit *f*.

improve [ɪm'pruːv] **1** *vt* verbessern; *production* steigern; *knowledge* erweitern; *low salaries* aufbessern. **to ~ one's mind** sich weiterbilden. **2** *vi* *see vt* besser werden; sich steigern. **the patient is improving** dem Patienten geht es besser.

♦ **improve (up)on** *vi* +*prep obj* übertreffen; *offer* überbieten.

improvement [ɪm'pruːvmənt] *n see vt* Verbesserung *f*; Steigerung *f*; Erweiterung *f*; Aufbesserung *f*; *(in health)* Besserung *f*; *(in studies also)* Fortschritte *pl*. **to carry out ~s to a house**

Ausbesserungsarbeiten an einem Haus vorneh-men; **it's an ~ on the old one** es ist eine Verbes-serung gegenüber dem/der alten.

improvisation [ˌɪmprəvaɪ'zeɪʃən] n Improvisation f.

improvise ['ɪmprəvaɪz] vti improvisieren.

imprudent [ɪm'pruːdənt] adj unklug.

impudence ['ɪmpjʊdəns] n Unverschämtheit, Frechheit f.

impudent ['ɪmpjʊdənt] adj unverschämt.

impulse ['ɪmpʌls] n Impuls m. **on ~** aus einem Impuls heraus; **~ buying** spontanes Kaufen.

impulsive [ɪm'pʌlsɪv] adj impulsiv; action, remark also spontan.

impunity [ɪm'pjuːnɪtɪ] n: **with ~** ungestraft.

impure [ɪm'pjʊəʳ] adj water, food verunreinigt; thoughts, motives unsauber.

impurity [ɪm'pjʊərɪtɪ] n see adj Unreinheit f; Un-sauberkeit f.

impute [ɪm'pjuːt] vt zuschreiben (to sb/sth jdm/einer Sache).

in [ɪn] **1** prep **(a)** (position) in (+dat); (with motion) in (+acc). **it was ~ the car** es war im Auto; **he put it ~ the car** er legte es ins Auto; **~ the street** auf der/die Straße; **~ Thompson Street** in der Thompsonstraße; **~ bed/prison** im Bett/Gefängnis; **~ Germany/Iran/Switzerland/the United States** in Deutschland/im Iran/in der Schweiz/in den Vereinigten Staaten.

(b) **we find it ~ Dickens** wir finden das bei Dickens; **rare ~ a child of that age** selten bei einem Kind in diesem Alter; **we've got a good recruit ~ her** sie ist für uns eine gute neue Mitarbeiterin.

(c) (time) in (+dat); (within) innerhalb von. **~ 1974** (im Jahre) 1974; **~ the sixties** in den sech-ziger Jahren; **~ June** im Juni; **~ (the) spring** im Frühling; **~ the morning(s)** morgens, am Mor-gen; **~ the afternoon** am Nachmittag; **~ the daytime** tagsüber; **~ the evening** am Abend; **three o'clock ~ the afternoon** drei Uhr nachmit-tags; **~ those days** damals; **~ a week('s time)** in einer Woche; **I haven't seen him ~ years** ich habe ihn seit Jahren nicht mehr gesehen.

(d) (manner, state, condition) **~ German** auf Deutsch; **to pay ~ dollars** in Dollar bezahlen; **to walk ~ twos** zu zweit gehen; **~ anger** im Zorn; **~ poverty** in Armut; **dressed ~ white** weiß gekleidet; **the lady ~ green** die Dame in Grün; **to write ~ ink** mit Tinte schreiben; **to die ~ hun-dreds** zu Hunderten sterben.

(e) (ratio) **there are 12 inches ~ a foot** ein Fuß hat 12 Zoll; **one ~ ten** jeder zehnte.

(f) (in respect of) **blind ~ the left eye** auf dem linken Auge or links blind; **a rise ~ prices** ein Preisanstieg m; **ten feet ~ height** zehn Fuß hoch; **five ~ number** fünf an der Zahl.

(g) (occupation) **he is ~ the army** er ist beim Militär; **he is ~ banking** er ist im Bankwesen (tätig).

(h) **~ saying this, I ...** wenn ich das sage, ... ich; **~ trying to escape** beim Fluchtversuch; **~ that** insofern als.

2 adv **(a)** da; (at home also) zu Hause. **the train is ~** der Zug ist da or angekommen; **the harvest is ~** die Ernte ist eingebracht; **we were asked ~** wir wurden hereingebeten. **(b)** **miniskirts are ~** Miniröcke sind in (col). **(c)** (phrases) **we are ~ for trouble** wir können uns auf was gefaßt machen (col); **we are ~ for rain** uns (dat) steht Regen bevor; **he's ~ for it!** der kann sich auf was gefaßt machen (col); **you don't know what you are ~ for** Sie wissen nicht, was Ihnen bevorsteht; **he hasn't got it ~ him** er hat nicht das Zeug dazu; **to have it ~ for sb** (col) es auf jdn abgesehen haben (col); **to be ~ on sth** an einer Sache beteiligt sein; on secret etc über etw (acc) Bescheid wissen.

3 adj attr **(a)** "**~**" **tray** Ablage f für Eingänge. **(b)** (col) in inv (col). **an ~ subject** ein Modefach nt; **the ~ thing to is to ...** es ist in (col) or zur Zeit Mode, zu ... **4** n **to know the ~s and outs of a matter** bei einer Sache genau Bescheid wissen.

inability [ˌɪnə'bɪlɪtɪ] n Unfähigkeit f.

inaccessibility ['ɪnæk,sesə'bɪlɪtɪ] n Unzugänglich-keit f.

inaccessible [ˌɪnæk'sesəbl] adj unzugänglich.

inaccuracy [ɪn'ækjʊrəsɪ] n see adj Ungenauigkeit f; Unrichtigkeit f.

inaccurate [ɪn'ækjʊrɪt] adj ungenau; (not correct) unrichtig.

inaction [ɪn'ækʃən] n Untätigkeit f.

inactive [ɪn'æktɪv] adj untätig; volcano erloschen.

inactivity [ˌɪnæk'tɪvɪtɪ] n Untätigkeit f; (of mind) Trägheit f; (Comm) Flaute f.

inadequacy [ɪn'ædɪkwəsɪ] n see adj Unzulänglich-keit f; Unangemessenheit f.

inadequate [ɪn'ædɪkwɪt] adj unzulänglich; sup-plies, reasons also unzureichend; measures unangemessen. **she makes him feel ~** sie gibt ihm das Gefühl der Unzulänglichkeit.

inadmissible [ˌɪnəd'mɪsəbl] adj unzulässig.

inadvertent [ˌɪnəd'vɜːtənt] adj unbeabsichtigt, ungewollt.

inadvertently [ˌɪnəd'vɜːtəntlɪ] adv versehentlich.

inadvisable [ˌɪnəd'vaɪzəbl] adj unratsam.

inane [ɪ'neɪn] adj dumm.

inanimate [ɪn'ænɪmɪt] adj leblos; nature unbelebt.

inanity [ɪ'nænɪtɪ] n Dummheit f.

inapplicable [ɪn'æplɪkəbl] adj answer unzu-treffend; rules nicht anwendbar (to sb auf jdn.).

inappropriate [ˌɪnə'prəʊprɪɪt] adj unpassend; action also unangemessen.

inarticulate [ˌɪnaː'tɪkjʊlɪt] adj essay schlecht or unklar ausgedrückt. **she's very ~** sie kann sich nur schlecht ausdrücken.

inattention [ˌɪnə'tenʃən] n Unaufmerksamkeit f. **~ to detail** Ungenauigkeit f im Detail.

inattentive [ˌɪnə'tentɪv] adj unaufmerksam.

inaudible [ɪn'ɔːdəbl] adj unhörbar.

inaugural [ɪ'nɔːgjʊrəl] adj lecture Antritts-.

inaugurate [ɪ'nɔːgjʊreɪt] vt president, official (feierlich) in sein/ihr Amt einführen; building einweihen; exhibition eröffnen; era einleiten.

inauspicious [ˌɪnɔːs'pɪʃəs] adj unheilverheißend.

in-between [ɪnbɪ'twiːn] (col) adj Mittel-, Zwi-schen-. **it is sort of ~** es ist so ein Mittelding; **~ stage** Zwischenstadium nt; **~ times** zwi-schendurch.

inborn ['ɪn'bɔːn] adj angeboren.

inbreeding ['ɪn'briːdɪŋ] n Inzucht f.

Inc (US) = **Incorporated.**

incalculable [ɪn'kælkjʊləbl] adj amount unermeß-lich; consequences unabsehbar.

incantation [ˌɪnkæn'teɪʃən] n Zauber(spruch) m; (act) Beschwörung f.

incapable [ɪn'keɪpəbl] adj person unfähig; (physically) hilflos. **to be ~ of doing sth** unfähig sein, etw zu tun; **~ of working** arbeitsunfähig; **~ of tenderness** zu Zärtlichkeit nicht fähig.

incapacitate [ˌɪnkə'pæsɪteɪt] vt unfähig machen. **physically ~d** körperlich behindert.

incapacity [ˌɪnkə'pæsɪtɪ] n Unfähigkeit f (for für).

incarcerate [ɪn'kaːsəreɪt] vt einkerkern.

incarnate [ɪn'kaːnɪt] adj (Rel) menschgeworden; (personified) leibhaftig attr, in Person. **the devil ~** der leibhaftige Teufel.

incarnation [ˌɪnkaː'neɪʃən] n (Rel) Menschwerdung f; (fig) Verkörperung f.

incendiary [ɪn'sendɪərɪ] **1** adj (lit) bomb Brand-. **~ device** Brandsatz m. **2** n (bomb) Brandbombe f.

incense[1] [ɪn'sens] vt wütend machen. **~d** wütend, erbost (at, by über +acc).

incense[2] ['ɪnsens] n (Eccl) Weihrauch m.

incentive [ɪn'sentɪv] n Anreiz m. **~ scheme** (Ind)

Leistungsförderungsprogramm nt.

inception [ɪn'sepʃən] n Beginn, Anfang m. **from its ~ von Anfang an.**

incessant [ɪn'sesnt] adj unaufhörlich; noise ununterbrochen.

incest ['ɪnsest] n Inzest m.

incestuous [ɪn'sestjʊəs] adj blutschänderisch.

inch [ɪntʃ] **1** n Zoll, Inch m. **a few ~es** ein paar Zentimeter; **~ by ~** Zentimeter um Zentimeter; **he came within an ~ of** victory er hätte um ein Haar gewonnen; **the lorry missed me by ~es** der Lastwagen hat mich um Haaresbreite verfehlt; **he is every ~ a soldier** er ist vom Scheitel bis zur Sohle ein Soldat; **give him an ~ and he'll take a mile** (prov) wenn man ihm den kleinen Finger gibt, nimmt er die ganze Hand (prov). **2** vi **to ~ forward** sich millimeterweise vorwärtsbewegen; **because prices are ~ing up** weil die Preise allmählich ansteigen; **the Dutch swimmer is ~ing ahead** der holländische Schwimmer schiebt sich langsam an die Spitze.

incidence ['ɪnsɪdəns] n (of crime) Häufigkeit f. **angle of ~** (Opt) Einfallswinkel m.

incident ['ɪnsɪdənt] n (event) Ereignis nt, Vorfall m; (diplomatic etc) Zwischenfall m.

incidental [ˌɪnsɪ'dentl] adj (secondary etc) nebensächlich; remark beiläufig. **~ music** Begleitmusik f; **~ expenses** Nebenkosten pl.

incidentally [ˌɪnsɪ'dentəlɪ] adv (by the way) übrigens.

incinerate [ɪn'sɪnəreɪt] vt verbrennen.

incinerator [ɪn'sɪnəreɪtəʳ] n (Müll)verbrennungsanlage f; (garden ~) Verbrennungsofen m.

incipient [ɪn'sɪpɪənt] adj beginnend.

incision [ɪn'sɪʒən] n Schnitt m; (Med) Einschnitt m.

incisive [ɪn'saɪsɪv] adj prägnant; criticism treffend; mind scharf; person scharfsinnig.

incisor [ɪn'saɪzəʳ] n Schneidezahn m.

incite [ɪn'saɪt] vt aufhetzen (to zu +dat).

incitement [ɪn'saɪtmənt] n Aufhetzung f.

inclement [ɪn'klemənt] adj weather unfreundlich.

inclination [ˌɪnklɪ'neɪʃən] n **(a)** Neigung f. **he follows his (own) ~s** er tut das, wozu er Lust hat; **I have no ~ to see him again** ich habe kein Bedürfnis, ihn wiederzusehen; **he showed no ~ to leave** er schien nicht gehen zu wollen. **(b)** (of hill, slope etc) Gefälle nt.

incline [ɪn'klaɪn] **1** vt **(a)** head, roof neigen. **(b)** (dispose) veranlassen, bewegen. **this ~s me to think that he must be lying** das läßt mich vermuten, daß er lügt. **2** vi **(a)** (slope) sich neigen; (ground also) abfallen. **(b)** (tend) **to ~ to sth** etw neigen. **3** ['ɪnklaɪn] n Neigung f; (of hill) Abhang m; (gradient: Rail etc) Gefälle nt.

inclined [ɪn'klaɪnd] adj **to be ~ to do sth** (wish to) etw tun wollen; (tend to) dazu neigen, etw zu tun; **they are ~ to be late** sie kommen gern zu spät; **I am ~ to think that ...** ich neige zu der Ansicht, daß ...; **if you feel ~** wenn Sie Lust haben; **if you're ~ that way** wenn Ihnen so etwas liegt; **I'm ~ to disagree** ich möchte da doch widersprechen; **it's ~ to break** das bricht leicht.

include [ɪn'kluːd] vt einschließen; (on list, in group etc) aufnehmen. **the tip is not ~d in the bill** Trinkgeld ist in der Rechnung nicht inbegriffen; **the invitation ~s everybody** die Einladung betrifft alle; **the children ~d** einschließlich der Kinder; **does that ~ me?** gilt das auch für mich?

including [ɪn'kluːdɪŋ] prep einschließlich (+gen). **~ service** inklusive Bedienung; **not ~ service** Bedienung nicht inbegriffen; **up to and ~ March 4th** bis einschließlich 4. März.

inclusive [ɪn'kluːsɪv] adj einschließlich; price Pauschal-. **to be ~ of** einschließlich (+gen) sein; **from 1st to 6th May ~** vom 1. bis einschließlich 6. Mai.

incognito [ˌɪnkɒg'niːtəʊ] adv inkognito.

incoherent [ˌɪnkəʊ'hɪərənt] adj style, argument zusammenhanglos; speech, also wirr; drunk etc schwer verständlich. **he was totally ~** man konnte ihn überhaupt nicht verstehen.

income ['ɪnkʌm] n Einkommen nt; (receipts) Einkünfte pl.

income: ~ group n Einkommensklasse f; **~s policy** n Lohnpolitik f; **~ tax** n Lohnsteuer f; **~ tax return** n Steuererklärung f.

incoming ['ɪn,kʌmɪŋ] adj ankommend; train also einfahrend; mail, orders etc eingehend. **~ tide** Flut f.

incommunicado [ˌɪnkəmjʊnɪ'kɑːdəʊ] adj pred abgesondert. **he was held ~** er hatte keinerlei Verbindung zur Außenwelt.

incomparable [ɪn'kɒmpərəbl] adj nicht vergleichbar (with mit); beauty, skill unvergleichlich.

incompatibility ['ɪnkəm,pætə'bɪlɪtɪ] n Unvereinbarkeit f.

incompatible [ˌɪnkəm'pætɪbl] adj characters, ideas unvereinbar; technical systems also nicht zueinander passend; (Comp) nicht kompatibel; blood groups nicht miteinander verträglich. **they are ~** sie passen überhaupt nicht zueinander.

incompetence [ɪn'kɒmpɪtəns] n Unfähigkeit f; (for job) Untauglichkeit f.

incompetent [ɪn'kɒmpɪtənt] adj person unfähig; (for sth) untauglich; piece of work unzulänglich.

incomplete [ˌɪnkəm'pliːt] adj collection, series unvollkommen, unvollständig; (not finished also) painting unfertig.

incomprehensible [ɪn,kɒmprɪ'hensəbl] adj unverständlich; act also unbegreiflich.

inconceivable [ˌɪnkən'siːvəbl] adj unvorstellbar.

inconclusive [ˌɪnkən'kluːsɪv] adj result unbestimmt; action, investigation ergebnislos; (not convincing) argument nicht überzeugend.

incongruous [ɪn'kɒŋgrʊəs] adj couple, mixture nicht zusammenpassend attr; thing to do, behaviour, remark unpassend; (out of place) fehl am Platz.

inconsequential [ɪn,kɒnsɪ'kwenʃəl] adj irrelevant; (not logical) unlogisch; (unimportant) unwichtig.

inconsiderable [ˌɪnkən'sɪdərəbl] adj **a not ~ amount** ein nicht unbedeutender Betrag.

inconsiderate [ˌɪnkən'sɪdərɪt] adj rücksichtslos; (in less critical sense) unaufmerksam.

inconsistency [ˌɪnkən'sɪstənsɪ] n see adj **(a)** Widersprüchlichkeit f. **(b)** Unbeständigkeit f.

inconsistent [ˌɪnkən'sɪstənt] adj **(a)** (contradictory) widersprüchlich. **to be ~ with sth** etw nicht übereinstimmen. **(b)** (uneven, irregular) work unbeständig; person also inkonsequent.

inconsolable [ˌɪnkən'səʊləbl] adj untröstlich.

inconspicuous [ˌɪnkən'spɪkjʊəs] adj unauffällig. **he tried to make himself ~** er versuchte möglichst nicht aufzufallen.

inconstant [ɪn'kɒnstənt] adj person unbeständig.

incontestable [ˌɪnkən'testəbl] adj unbestreitbar.

incontinent [ɪn'kɒntɪnənt] adj (Med) unfähig, Stuhl und/oder Harn zurückzuhalten.

incontrovertible [ɪn,kɒntrə'vɜːtəbl] adj unbestreitbar.

inconvenience [ˌɪnkən'viːnɪəns] **1** n Unannehmlichkeit f (to sb für jdn). **it was something of an ~ not having a car** es war ziemlich lästig, kein Auto zu haben; **I don't want to cause you any ~** ich möchte Ihnen keine Umstände bereiten. **2** vt Umstände bereiten (+dat). **don't ~ yourself** machen Sie keine Umstände.

inconvenient [ˌɪnkən'viːnɪənt] adj time ungelegen; house, design unpraktisch; location ungünstig; journey beschwerlich. **3 o'clock is very ~ for me** 3 Uhr kommt mir sehr ungelegen.

incorporate [ɪn'kɔːpəreɪt] vt **(a)** (integrate) aufnehmen, integrieren (into in +acc). **(b)** (contain) (in sich *dat*) enthalten.

incorporated [ɪn'kɔːpəreɪtɪd] *adj (US Comm)* als Aktiengesellschaft eingetragen.

incorrect [ˌɪnkə'rekt] *adj* **(a)** falsch; *wording, calculation also* fehlerhaft. **that is** ~ das stimmt nicht. **(b)** *dress, behaviour* inkorrekt.

incorrectly [ˌɪnkə'rektlɪ] *adv see adj; assume* fälschlich(erweise).

incorrigible [ɪn'kɒrɪdʒəbl] *adj* unverbesserlich.

increase [ɪn'kriːs] **1** *vi* zunehmen; *(taxes)* erhöht werden; *(strength, friendship)* wachsen; *(price, demand)* steigen; *(business, town)* sich vergrößern. **to** ~ **in volume/weight** an Umfang/Gewicht zunehmen; **to** ~ **in size/number** sich vergrößern/vermehren.
2 *vt* vergrößern; *possessions, riches also* vermehren; *sales also* erweitern; *numbers, taxes, price, speed* erhöhen. **he** ~**d his efforts** er strengte sich mehr an; ~**d standard of living** höherer Lebensstandard; ~**d efficiency** Leistungssteigerung *f.*
3 *n* Zunahme, Steigerung *f; (in size)* Vergrößerung, Erweiterung *f; (in number)* Zuwachs *m*, Zunahme *f; (in speed)* Erhöhung, Steigerung *f (in gen); (of business)* Erweiterung *f; (in sales)* Aufschwung *m; (of effort etc)* Steigerung *f; (of demand)* Steigen *nt; (of violence)* Anwachsen *nt.* **to get an** ~ **of** £15 **per week** eine Lohnerhöhung von £ 15 pro Woche bekommen; **to be on the** ~ ständig zunehmen; **rent** ~ Mieterhöhung *f.*

increasing [ɪn'kriːsɪŋ] *adj* zunehmend, (an)wachsend. **an ever** ~ **number of people are changing to ...** mehr und mehr Leute steigen auf (+*acc*) ... um.

increasingly [ɪn'kriːsɪŋlɪ] *adv* zunehmend, immer mehr.

incredible [ɪn'kredəbl] *adj* unglaublich; *(col also)* unwahrscheinlich gut/schlecht *(col)*. **this music is** ~ diese Musik ist sagenhaft *(col)*; **you're** ~ du bist wirklich unschlagbar.

incredibly [ɪn'kredəblɪ] *adv* unglaublich, unwahrscheinlich.

incredulity [ˌɪnkrɪ'djuːlɪtɪ] *n* Ungläubigkeit, Skepsis *f.*

incredulous [ɪn'kredjʊləs] *adj* ungläubig, skeptisch.

increment ['ɪnkrɪmənt] *n (in salary)* Gehaltserhöhung *f.*

incriminate [ɪn'krɪmɪneɪt] *vt* belasten.

incriminating [ɪn'krɪmɪneɪtɪŋ] *adj* belastend.

incubate ['ɪnkjubeɪt] **1** *vt egg* ausbrüten; *bacteria* züchten. **2** *vi (lit)* ausgebrütet werden.

incubation [ˌɪnkjʊ'beɪʃən] *n see vb* Ausbrüten *nt;* Züchten *nt.* ~ **period** *(Med)* Inkubationszeit *f.*

incubator ['ɪnkjubeɪtəʳ] *n (for babies)* Brutkasten *m; (for chickens)* Brutapparat *m.*

inculcate ['ɪnkʌlkeɪt] *vt* einimpfen *(in sb* jdm).

incumbent [ɪn'kʌmbənt] *(form)* **1** *adj* **to be** ~ **upon sb** jdm obliegen *(form)*. **2** *n* Amtsinhaber *m.*

incur [ɪn'kɜːʳ] *vt anger, injury* sich *(dat)* zuziehen; *loss* erleiden; *debts, expenses* machen.

incurable [ɪn'kjʊərəbl] *adj (Med)* unheilbar; *(fig)* unverbesserlich.

incursion [ɪn'kɜːʃən] *n* Eindringen *nt (into* +*acc)*.

indebted [ɪn'detɪd] *adj* **to be** ~ **to sb for sth** jdm für etw (zu Dank) verpflichtet sein.

indecency [ɪn'diːsnsɪ] *n* Unanständigkeit *f.*

indecent [ɪn'diːsnt] *adj* unanständig, anstößig; *(Jur) act* unsittlich.

indecipherable [ˌɪndɪ'saɪfərəbl] *adj* nicht zu entziffern *pred*, nicht zu entziffernd *attr; handwriting* unleserlich.

indecision [ˌɪndɪ'sɪʒən] *n* Unentschlossenheit *f.*

indecisive [ˌɪndɪ'saɪsɪv] *adj person, manner* unschlüssig, unentschlossen; *discussion* ergebnislos; *argument, battle* nicht entscheidend *attr.*

indeed [ɪn'diːd] *adv* **(a)** tatsächlich, wirklich. **I**

---

feel, ~ **I know he is right** ich habe das Gefühl, ja ich weiß (sogar), daß er recht hat; **isn't that wrong?** — ~ **ist das nicht falsch?** — allerdings; **are you coming?** — ~ **I am!** kommst du? — aber sicher *or* natürlich; **may I open the window?** — you may ~ darf ich das Fenster öffnen? — ja bitte!; **very ...** ~ wirklich sehr ...; **thank you very much** ~ vielen herzlichen Dank. **(b)** *(admittedly)* zwar. **there are** ~ **mistakes in it, but ...** es sind zwar Fehler darin, aber ... **(c)** *(expressing possibility)* **I may** ~ **come** es kann gut sein, daß ich komme.

indefatigable [ˌɪndɪ'fætɪgəbl] *adj* unermüdlich.

indefensible [ˌɪndɪ'fensəbl] *adj behaviour etc* unentschuldbar; *town etc* unhaltbar; *cause, theory* unvertretbar.

indefinable [ˌɪndɪ'faɪnəbl] *adj* undefinierbar; *feeling* unbestimmt.

indefinite [ɪn'defɪnɪt] *adj* unbestimmt; *(vague)* unklar, undeutlich.

indefinitely [ɪn'defɪnɪtlɪ] *adv wait etc* unendlich lange, endlos; *postpone* auf unbestimmte Zeit. **we can't go on like this** ~ wir können nicht immer so weitermachen.

indelible [ɪn'deləbl] *adj ink* wasserfest; *(fig) impression* unauslöschlich. ~ **pencil** Kopierstift *m.*

indelicate [ɪn'delɪkət] *adj person* taktlos; *(crude)* geschmacklos.

indemnify [ɪn'demnɪfaɪ] *vt* **(a)** *(compensate)* entschädigen; *expenses* erstatten. **(b)** *(safeguard)* absichern *(from, against* gegen); *(insure)* versichern *(against, from* gegen).

indemnity [ɪn'demnɪtɪ] *n (a) (compensation) (for damage, loss etc)* Schadensersatz *m*, Entschädigung *f; (after war)* Wiedergutmachung *f.* **(b)** *(insurance)* Versicherung(sschutz *m) f.*

indent [ɪn'dent] *vt (Typ) line* einrücken.

indentation [ˌɪnden'teɪʃən] *n (in border)* Einschnitt *m; (Typ)* Einrückung *f; (in metal)* Delle *f.*

independence [ˌɪndɪ'pendəns] *n see adj* Unabhängigkeit *f (of von)*; Selbständigkeit *f.* **I**~ **Day** *(US)* der Unabhängigkeitstag.

independent [ˌɪndɪ'pendənt] *adj* unabhängig *(of* von) *(also Pol)*; *person (in attitude, spirit also)* selbständig; *development* selbständig. **a man of** ~ **means** ein Mann mit Privateinkommen; ~ **suspension** *(Aut)* Einzel(rad)aufhängung *f.*

independently [ˌɪndɪ'pendəntlɪ] *adv (on own initiative)* von allein(e).

in-depth ['ɪndepθ] *adj* eingehend, gründlich.

indescribable [ˌɪndɪ'skraɪbəbl] *adj* unbeschreiblich; *(col: terrible)* schrecklich.

indestructible [ˌɪndɪ'strʌktəbl] *adj* unzerstörbar.

indeterminate [ˌɪndɪ'tɜːmɪnɪt] *adj* unbestimmt.

index ['ɪndeks] *n* **(a)** *pl* -**es** *(in book)* Register *nt; (of sources)* Quellenverzeichnis *nt.* **(b)** *pl* **indices** *(on scale)* (An)zeiger *m.* ~ **cost-of-living** Lebenshaltungskosten-Index *m.*

index: ~ **card** *n* Karteikarte *f;* ~ **finger** *n* Zeigefinger *m;* ~**-linked** *adj salaries* der Inflationsrate *(dat)* angeglichen; *pensions* dynamisch.

India ['ɪndɪə] *n* Indien *nt.* ~ **ink** Tusche *f.*

Indian ['ɪndɪən] **1** *adj* **(a)** indisch. **(b)** *(American* ~) indianisch, Indianer-. ~ **Ocean** Indischer Ozean; ~ **summer** *m*. Altweibersommer, Spätsommer *m*. **2** *n* **(a)** Inder(in *f) m.* **(b)** *(American* ~) Indianer(in *f) m.*

India rubber *n* Gummi, Kautschuk *m.*

indicate ['ɪndɪkeɪt] **1** *vt* **(a)** *(point out, mark)* zeigen, bezeichnen; *(register) temperature etc* anzeigen. **(b)** *(show) feelings etc* andeuten, zeigen. **(c)** *(be a sign of, suggest)* schließen lassen auf (+*acc*), (hin)deuten auf (+*acc*). **this would definitely** ~ **that ...** das würde bestimmt darauf hindeuten, daß ...; **what does it** ~ **to you?** was schließen Sie daraus? **2** *vi (Aut)* blinken. **to** ~

right rechts blinken.

indication [,ɪndɪ'keɪʃən] n (sign) (An)zeichen nt (also Med) (of für), Hinweis m (of auf +acc). **we had no ~ that** ... es gab kein Anzeichen dafür, daß ...; **if you could give me a rough ~ of** ... wenn Sie mir eine ungefähre Vorstellung davon geben könnten ...

indicative [ɪn'dɪkətɪv] **1** adj (a) **to be ~ of sth** auf etw (acc) schließen lassen; of sb's character für etw bezeichnend sein. **(b)** (Gram) indikativisch. **2** n (Gram) **in the ~** im Indikativ.

indicator ['ɪndɪkeɪtər] n (gauge) Anzeiger m; (needle) Zeiger m; (Aut) Blinker m. **~ board** (Rail) (Anzeige)tafel f.

indices ['ɪndɪsiːz] pl of **index**.

indict [ɪn'daɪt] vt (charge) anklagen, unter Anklage stellen; (US Jur) Anklage erheben gegen (for wegen +gen).

indictable [ɪn'daɪtəbl] adj offence strafbar.

indictment [ɪn'daɪtmənt] n (of person) Anklage, Anschuldigung f. **to be an ~ of sth** (fig) ein Armutszeugnis für etw sein.

indifference [ɪn'dɪfrəns] n see adj **(a)** Gleichgültigkeit f (to, towards gegenüber). **(b)** Mittelmäßigkeit f.

indifferent [ɪn'dɪfrənt] adj **(a)** gleichgültig, indifferent (geh) (to, towards gegenüber). **he is quite ~ to her** sie ist ihm ziemlich gleichgültig. **(b)** (mediocre) mittelmäßig, durchschnittlich.

indigenous [ɪn'dɪdʒɪnəs] adj einheimisch (to in +dat).

indigestible [,ɪndɪ'dʒestəbl] adj unverdaulich.

indigestion [,ɪndɪ'dʒestʃən] n Magenverstimmung f.

indignant [ɪn'dɪgnənt] adj entrüstet, empört (at, about, with über +acc).

indignation [,ɪndɪg'neɪʃən] n Entrüstung, Empörung f (at, about, with über +acc).

indignity [ɪn'dɪgnɪti] n Demütigung f.

indigo ['ɪndɪgəʊ] **1** n Indigo nt or m. **2** adj indigofarben.

indirect [,ɪndɪ'rekt] adj indirekt. **by an ~ route** auf einem Umweg; **to make an ~ reference to sth** auf etw anspielen; **~ object** Dativobjekt nt; **~ speech** or (US) **discourse** indirekte Rede.

indiscreet [,ɪndɪ'skriːt] adj indiskret; (tactless) taktlos.

indiscretion [,ɪndɪ'skreʃən] n see adj Indiskretion f; Taktlosigkeit f; (affair) Affäre f.

indiscriminate [,ɪndɪ'skrɪmɪnɪt] adj wahllos; reader, shopper unkritisch; tastes unausgeprägt.

indispensable [,ɪndɪ'spensəbl] adj unentbehrlich (to für). **~ to life** lebensnotwendig.

indisposed [,ɪndɪ'spəʊzd] adj (unwell) unwohl.

indisputable [,ɪndɪ'spjuːtəbl] adj unbestreitbar; evidence unanfechtbar.

indistinct [,ɪndɪ'stɪŋkt] adj unklar, undeutlich.

indistinguishable [,ɪndɪ'stɪŋgwɪʃəbl] adj nicht unterscheidbar (from von).

individual [,ɪndɪ'vɪdjʊəl] **1** adj **(a)** (separate) einzeln. **~ cases** Einzelfälle pl; **~ tastes differ** die Geschmäcker sind verschieden. **(b)** (own) eigen; (for one person) portion etc einzeln, Einzel-. **(c)** (distinctive) eigen, individuell. **2** n Individuum nt, Einzelne(r) mf.

individualist [,ɪndɪ'vɪdjʊəlɪst] n Individualist(in f) m.

individuality ['ɪndɪ,vɪdjʊ'ælɪti] n Individualität f.

individually [,ɪndɪ'vɪdjʊəlɪ] adv individuell; (separately) einzeln.

indivisible [,ɪndɪ'vɪzəbl] adj unteilbar (also Math).

Indo- ['ɪndəʊ-] pref Indo-. **~-China** n Indochina nt.

indoctrinate [ɪn'dɒktrɪneɪt] vt indoktrinieren.

indoctrination [ɪn,dɒktrɪ'neɪʃən] n Indoktrination f.

indolence ['ɪndələns] n Trägheit f.

indolent ['ɪndələnt] adj träge.

Indonesia [,ɪndəʊ'niːzɪə] n Indonesien nt.

Indonesian [,ɪndəʊ'niːzɪən] **1** adj indonesisch. **2** n **(a)** Indonesier(in f) m. **(b)** (language) Indonesisch nt.

indoor ['ɪndɔːr] adj plant Zimmer-; clothes Haus-; photography Innen-; sport Hallen-; swimming pool Hallen-; (private) überdacht. **~ games** Spiele pl für drinnen; (Sport) Hallenspiele pl.

indoors [ɪn'dɔːz] adv drinnen, innen; (at home) zu Hause. **to stay ~** im Haus bleiben, drin bleiben (col); **to go ~** ins Haus gehen.

induce [ɪn'djuːs] vt **(a)** (persuade) dazu bewegen or bringen. **(b)** reaction bewirken, hervorrufen; sleep herbeiführen; birth einleiten. **this drug ~s sleep** dieses Mittel hat eine einschläfernde Wirkung. **(c)** (Elec) current induzieren.

inducement [ɪn'djuːsmənt] n (no pl: persuasion) Überredung f; (incentive) Anreiz m. **as an added ~** als besonderer Anreiz.

induction [ɪn'dʌkʃən] n **(a)** (of sleep, reaction etc) Herbeiführen nt; (of birth) Einleitung f. **(b)** (Philos, Elec) Induktion f. **~ coil** n (Elec) Induktionsspule f.

indulge [ɪn'dʌldʒ] **1** vt desires etc nachgeben (+dat); person also nachsichtig sein mit; (over~) children verwöhnen. **to ~ oneself in sth** sich (dat) etw gönnen. **2** vi **to ~ in sth** sich (dat) etw gönnen or genehmigen (col); (in vice, drink) einer Sache (dat) frönen. **I don't ~** ich trinke/rauche etc nicht.

indulgence [ɪn'dʌldʒəns] n **(a)** Nachsicht f; (of appetite etc) Nachgiebigkeit f (of gegenüber); (over~) Verwöhnung f. **the ~ of his wishes** das Erfüllen seiner Wünsche. **(b)** (in activity, drink etc) **~ in drink** übermäßiges Trinken. **(c)** (thing indulged in) Luxus m; (food, drink, pleasure) Genuß m.

indulgent [ɪn'dʌldʒənt] adj (to gegenüber) nachsichtig; mother etc also nachgiebig; (to one's own desires etc) zu nachgiebig.

industrial [ɪn'dʌstrɪəl] adj worker, equipment, state Industrie-; production also industriell; training, accident Betriebs-. **~ action** Arbeitskampfmaßnahmen pl; **to take ~ action** in den Ausstand treten; **~ dispute** Auseinandersetzungen pl zwischen Arbeitgebern und Arbeitnehmern; **~ estate** (Brit) Industriegebiet nt; **~ injury** Arbeitsunfall m; **~ relations** Beziehungen pl zwischen Arbeitgebern und Gewerkschaften; (in particular company also) Betriebsklima nt; **I~ Revolution** Industrielle Revolution; **~ tribunal** Arbeitsgericht nt; **~ unrest** Arbeitsunruhen pl.

industrialist [ɪn'dʌstrɪəlɪst] n Industrielle(r) mf.

industrialize [ɪn'dʌstrɪəlaɪz] vti industrialisieren.

industrious [ɪn'dʌstrɪəs] adj fleißig.

industry ['ɪndəstri] n **(a)** Industrie f. **heavy/light ~** Schwer-/Leichtindustrie f. **(b)** (industriousness) Fleiß m.

inebriated [ɪ'niːbrɪeɪtɪd] adj **(a)** (form) unter starkem Alkoholeinfluß (form). **(b)** (fig) berauscht.

inedible [ɪn'edɪbl] adj nicht eßbar; (unpleasant) ungenießbar.

ineffective [,ɪnɪ'fektɪv] adj unwirksam, ineffektiv; person unfähig, untauglich.

ineffectual [,ɪnɪ'fektjʊəl] adj ineffektiv.

inefficiency [,ɪnɪ'fɪʃənsi] n see adj Unfähigkeit f; Inkompetenz f; Leistungsunfähigkeit f.

inefficient [,ɪnɪ'fɪʃənt] adj person unfähig, inkompetent; machine, company leistungsunfähig.

inelegant [ɪn'elɪgənt] adj unelegant; clothes also ohne Schick.

ineligible [ɪn'elɪdʒəbl] adj (for benefits, grant) nicht berechtigt (for zu +dat); (for job) ungeeignet. **~ for a pension** nicht pensionsberechtigt.

inept [ɪ'nept] adj behaviour ungeschickt, linkisch; remark unpassend; attempt plump; comparison ungeeignet.

ineptitude [ɪ'neptɪtjuːd] n see adj Ungeschicktheit

f; Ungeeignetheit f.
inequality [ˌɪnɪ'kwɒlɪtɪ] n Ungleichheit f.
inequitable [ɪn'ekwɪtəbl] adj ungerecht.
inert [ɪ'nɜːt] adj unbeweglich; (Phys) matter träge; (Chem) substance inaktiv. ~ **gas** Edelgas nt.
inertia [ɪ'nɜːʃə] n (lit, fig) Trägheit f. ~**-reel seat belt** Automatikgurt m.
inescapable [ˌɪnɪs'keɪpəbl] adj unvermeidlich.
inevitability [ɪnˌevɪtə'bɪlɪtɪ] n Unvermeidlichkeit f.
inevitable [ɪn'evɪtəbl] adj unvermeidlich.
inexact [ˌɪnɪg'zækt] adj ungenau.
inexcusable [ˌɪnɪks'kjuːzəbl] adj unverzeihlich.
inexhaustible [ˌɪnɪg'zɔːstəbl] adj source nie versiegend; wealth, patience unerschöpflich.
inexorable [ɪn'eksərəbl] adj (relentless) unerbittlich; (not to be stopped) unaufhaltsam.
inexpensive [ˌɪnɪk'spensɪv] adj billig, preisgünstig.
inexperience [ˌɪnɪk'spɪərɪəns] n Unerfahrenheit f.
inexperienced [ˌɪnɪk'spɪərɪənst] adj unerfahren; skier etc ungeübt.
inexplicable [ˌɪnɪk'splɪkəbl] adj unerklärlich.
inexpressible [ˌɪnɪk'spresəbl] adj unbeschreiblich; pain, joy also unsagbar.
inexpressive [ˌɪnɪk'spresɪv] adj face ausdruckslos; word nichtssagend; style ohne Ausdruckskraft.
inextricable [ˌɪnɪk'strɪkəbl] adj tangle unentwirrbar; confusion unüberschaubar; difficulties unlösbar.
infallibility [ɪnˌfælə'bɪlɪtɪ] n Unfehlbarkeit f.
infallible [ɪn'fæləbl] adj unfehlbar.
infamous ['ɪnfəməs] adj berüchtigt, verrufen; deed niederträchtig.
infamy ['ɪnfəmɪ] n see adj Verrufenheit f; Niedertracht f.
infancy ['ɪnfənsɪ] n frühe Kindheit; (fig) Anfangsstadium nt. **data processing is no longer in its** ~ die Datenverarbeitung steckt nicht mehr in den Kinderschuhen.
infant ['ɪnfənt] n (baby) Säugling m; (young child) Kleinkind nt. ~ **mortality** Säuglingssterblichkeit f; ~ **school** (Brit) Grundschule f für die ersten beiden Jahrgänge.
infantile ['ɪnfəntaɪl] adj (childish) kindisch, infantil.
infantry ['ɪnfəntrɪ] n (Mil) Infanterie f.
infatuated [ɪn'fætjueɪtɪd] adj vernarrt, verknallt (col) (with in +acc). **to become** ~ **with sb** sich in jdn verrennen; ~ **with sth** von etw besessen.
infatuation [ɪnˌfætju'eɪʃən] n Vernarrtheit f (with in +acc).
infect [ɪn'fekt] vt wound infizieren; water verseuchen; meat verderben; (fig: with enthusiasm etc) anstecken. **his wound became** ~**ed** seine Wunde entzündete sich.
infection [ɪn'fekʃən] n (illness) Infektion, Entzündung f; (of water) Verseuchung f.
infectious [ɪn'fekʃəs] adj (Med, fig) ansteckend.
infer [ɪn'fɜːʳ] vt (a) schließen, folgern (from aus). (b) (imply) andeuten.
inference ['ɪnfərəns] n Schluß(folgerung f) m.
inferior [ɪn'fɪərɪəʳ] adj (in quality) minderwertig; quality also geringer; person unterlegen; court untergeordnet.
inferiority [ɪnˌfɪərɪ'ɒrɪtɪ] n (in quality) Minderwertigkeit f; (of person) Unterlegenheit f (to gegenüber). ~ **complex** Minderwertigkeitskomplex m.
infernal [ɪn'fɜːnl] adj (lit) Höllen-; (fig) scheme teuflisch; (col) noise höllisch.
inferno [ɪn'fɜːnəʊ] n (hell) Hölle f, Inferno nt; (blazing house etc) Flammenmeer nt. **a blazing** ~ ein flammendes Inferno.
infertile [ɪn'fɜːtaɪl] adj soil, womb unfruchtbar; mind ideenlos.
infertility [ˌɪnfɜː'tɪlɪtɪ] n see adj Unfruchtbarkeit f;

Ideenlosigkeit f.
infest [ɪn'fest] vt (rats) herfallen über (+acc); (plague) befallen. **to be** ~**ed with disease/rats** verseucht/mit Ratten verseucht sein; **to be** ~**ed** (with lice etc) mit Ungeziefer verseucht sein.
infidelity [ˌɪnfɪ'delɪtɪ] n Untreue f.
in-fighting ['ɪnfaɪtɪŋ] n (fig) interner Machtkampf.
infiltrate ['ɪnfɪltreɪt] 1 vt troops infiltrieren; (Pol) organization also unterwandern; spies einschleusen. 2 vi (Mil) eindringen (into in +acc); (spy also) sich einschleusen (into in +acc).
infiltration [ˌɪnfɪl'treɪʃən] n (Mil) Infiltration f; (Pol also) Unterwanderung f.
infinite ['ɪnfɪnɪt] adj (lit) unendlich; (fig also) trouble, pleasure grenzenlos. **an** ~ **amount of time** unendlich viel Zeit.
infinitely ['ɪnfɪnɪtlɪ] adv unendlich; (fig also) grenzenlos; improved ungeheuer; better, worse unendlich viel.
infinitesimal [ˌɪnfɪnɪ'tesɪməl] adj unendlich klein.
infinitive [ɪn'fɪnɪtɪv] n Infinitiv m.
infinity [ɪn'fɪnɪtɪ] n (lit) Unendlichkeit f; (fig also) Grenzenlosigkeit f; (Math) das Unendliche. **to** ~ (bis) ins Unendliche; "~" (Phot) „unendlich".
infirm [ɪn'fɜːm] adj gebrechlich, schwach.
infirmary [ɪn'fɜːmərɪ] n Krankenhaus nt; (in school etc) Krankenzimmer nt; (in prison, barracks) Krankenstation f.
inflame [ɪn'fleɪm] vt (a) (Med) entzünden. **to become** ~**d** sich entzünden. (b) person aufbringen; feelings entflammen; anger erregen.
inflammable [ɪn'flæməbl] adj (lit) feuergefährlich; (leicht) entzündbar; (fig) situation brisant.
inflammation [ˌɪnflə'meɪʃən] n (Med) Entzündung f.
inflammatory [ɪn'flæmətərɪ] adj speech aufrührerisch.
inflatable [ɪn'fleɪtɪbl] adj aufblasbar; dinghy Schlauch-.
inflate [ɪn'fleɪt] vt (a) aufpumpen; (by mouth) aufblasen. (b) (Econ) prices steigern, hochtreiben. (c) (fig) steigern.
inflated [ɪn'fleɪtɪd] adj prices überhöht, inflationär; pride übersteigert; style geschwollen. **to have an** ~ **opinion of oneself** ein übertriebenes Selbstbewußtsein haben.
inflation [ɪn'fleɪʃən] n (Econ) Inflation f. **to fight** ~ die Inflation bekämpfen; **5%** ~ eine Inflationsrate von 5%.
inflationary [ɪn'fleɪʃənərɪ] adj inflationär, inflationistisch (pej). **the** ~ **spiral** die Inflationsspirale.
inflect [ɪn'flekt] vt (Gram) flektieren, beugen.
inflexibility [ɪnˌfleksɪ'bɪlɪtɪ] n (lit) Unbiegsamkeit, Steifheit f; (fig) Unbeugsamkeit f.
inflexible [ɪn'fleksəbl] adj person, attitude, opinion unbeugsam; substance, object unbiegsam, steif.
inflict [ɪn'flɪkt] vt punishment verhängen (on, upon gegen); suffering zufügen (on or upon sb jdm); wound beibringen (on or upon sb jdm). **to** ~ **oneself on sb** sich jdm aufdrängen.
in-flight ['ɪnflaɪt] adj während des Fluges.
influence ['ɪnfluəns] 1 n Einfluß m. **to have an** ~ **on sb/sth** (person) Einfluß auf jdn/etw haben; (put, weather etc also) Auswirkungen pl auf jdn/etw haben; **to have a great deal of** ~ **with sb** großen Einfluß bei jdm haben; **he's been a bad** ~ **on you** er war ein schlechter Einfluß für Sie; **she is a good** ~ **on the pupils** sie hat einen guten Einfluß auf die Schüler; **to exert an** ~ **on sb** Einfluß auf jdn ausüben; **under the** ~ **of drink** unter Alkoholeinfluß; **under the** ~ (col) betrunken. 2 vt beeinflussen. **to be easily** ~**d** leicht beeinflußbar sein.
influential [ˌɪnflu'enʃəl] adj einflußreich.
influenza [ˌɪnflu'enzə] n Grippe f.

influx ['ɪnflʌks] n (of capital) Zufuhr f; (of people) Zustrom m; (of ideas etc) Zufluß m.

inform [ɪn'fɔːm] **1** vt benachrichtigen, informieren (about über +acc); unterrichten. to ~ sb of sth jdn von etw unterrichten, jdn über etw informieren; **I am pleased to ~ you that ...** ich freue mich, Ihnen mitteilen zu können, daß ...; to ~ the police die Polizei benachrichtigen; to keep sb/oneself ~ed jdn/sich auf dem laufenden halten (of über +acc); why was I not ~ed? warum wurde mir das nicht mitgeteilt? **2** vi to ~ against or on sb jdn anzeigen or denunzieren (pej).

informal [ɪn'fɔːməl] adj (not official) meeting informell; visit inoffiziell; (without ceremony) meeting, language ungezwungen; manner leger; restaurant gemütlich. "dress ~" „zwanglose Kleidung".

informality [,ɪnfɔː'mælɪtɪ] n see adj informeller Charakter; inoffizieller Charakter; Ungezwungenheit f; legere Art; Gemütlichkeit f.

informally [ɪn'fɔːməlɪ] adv (unofficially) inoffiziell; (casually, without ceremony) zwanglos, ungezwungen.

informant [ɪn'fɔːmənt] n Informant m.

information [,ɪnfə'meɪʃən] n Auskunft f, Informationen pl. a piece of ~ eine Auskunft, eine Information; for your ~ zu Ihrer Information; (indignantly) damit Sie es wissen!; to give sb ~ about or on sb/sth jdm Auskunft or Informationen über jdn/etw geben; to get ~ about or on sb/sth sich über jdn/etw informieren; detailed ~ Einzelheiten pl.

information: ~ **bureau** n Auskunft(sbüro nt) f, Verkehrsbüro nt; ~ **science** n Informatik f; ~ **technology** Datentechnik f.

informative [ɪn'fɔːmətɪv] adj aufschlußreich; book, lecture also lehrreich. he's not very ~ about his plans er ist nicht sehr mitteilsam, was seine Pläne betrifft.

informed [ɪn'fɔːmd] adj observers informiert, (gut) unterrichtet; (educated) gebildet.

informer [ɪn'fɔːmə'] n Informant, Denunziant (pej) m. police ~ Polizeispitzel m (pej); to turn ~ seine Mittäter verraten.

infra-red ['ɪnfrə'red] adj infrarot.

infrastructure ['ɪnfrə'strʌktʃə'] n Infrastruktur f.

infrequent [ɪn'friːkwənt] adj selten. at ~ intervals in großen Abständen.

infringe [ɪn'frɪndʒ] **1** vt verstoßen gegen; law, copyright also verletzen. **2** vi to ~ (up)on sb's privacy in jds Privatsphäre (acc) eingreifen.

infringement [ɪn'frɪndʒmənt] n (a) an ~ (of a rule) ein Regelverstoß m; ~ of the law Gesetzesverletzung or -übertretung f; ~ of a patent/copyright Patentverletzung f/Verletzung f des Urheberrechts. (b) (of privacy) Eingriff m (of in +acc).

infuriate [ɪn'fjʊərɪeɪt] vt wütend or rasend machen. to be/get ~d wütend or rasend sein/werden.

infuriating [ɪn'fjʊərɪeɪtɪŋ] adj (äußerst) ärgerlich. an ~ habit eine Unsitte; an ~ person ein Mensch, den einen zur Raserei bringen kann.

infuse [ɪn'fjuːz] **1** vt (a) courage etc einflößen (into sb jdm). they were ~d with new hope sie waren von neuer Hoffnung erfüllt. (b) (Cook) tea aufgießen. **2** vi (tea) ziehen.

infusion [ɪn'fjuːʒən] n (a) (of hope etc) Einflößen nt. (b) (Cook) Aufguß m; (tea-like) Tee m. (c) (Med) Infusion f.

ingenious [ɪn'dʒiːnɪəs] adj genial; person also erfinderisch; device also raffiniert.

ingenuity [,ɪndʒɪ'njuːɪtɪ] n Genialität f; (of person also) Einfallsreichtum m; (of device also) Raffiniertheit f.

ingenuous [ɪn'dʒenjʊəs] adj (a) (candid) aufrichtig. (b) (naive) naiv.

ingot ['ɪŋgət] n Barren m.

ingrained [,ɪn'greɪnd] adj (a) habit fest, eingefleischt; belief unerschütterlich. (b) dirt tiefsitzend (attr).

ingratiate [ɪn'greɪʃɪeɪt] vr to ~ oneself with sb sich bei jdm einschmeicheln.

ingratiating [ɪn'greɪʃɪeɪtɪŋ] adj person, speech schmeichlerisch; smile schmeichlerisch süßlich.

ingratitude [ɪn'grætɪtjuːd] n Undank m. sb's ~ jds Undankbarkeit f.

ingredient [ɪn'griːdɪənt] n Bestandteil m; (for recipe) Zutat f. all the ~s of success alles, was man zum Erfolg braucht.

ingrowing ['ɪngrəʊɪŋ] adj toenail eingewachsen.

inhabit [ɪn'hæbɪt] vt bewohnen; (animals) leben in (+dat).

inhabitable [ɪn'hæbɪtəbl] adj bewohnbar.

inhabitant [ɪn'hæbɪtənt] n Bewohner(in f) m; (of island, town also) Einwohner(in f) m.

inhale [ɪn'heɪl] **1** vt einatmen; (Med) inhalieren. **2** vi (in smoking) Lungenzüge machen.

inherent [ɪn'hɪərənt] adj innewohnend. the ~ hardness of diamonds die den Diamanten eigene Härte; the ~ risks of the test die mit dem Test verbundenen Gefahren.

inherently [ɪn'hɪərəntlɪ] adv von Natur aus.

inherit [ɪn'herɪt] vt (lit, fig) erben.

inheritance [ɪn'herɪtəns] n Erbe nt (also fig), Erbschaft f.

inhibit [ɪn'hɪbɪt] vt hemmen. to ~ sb from doing sth jdn daran hindern, etw zu tun.

inhibited [ɪn'hɪbɪtɪd] adj gehemmt.

inhibition [,ɪnhɪ'bɪʃən] n Hemmung f.

inhospitable [,ɪnhɒ'spɪtəbl] adj ungastlich; region unwirtlich.

in-house [ɪn'haʊs] adj hausintern.

inhuman [ɪn'hjuːmən] adj cruelty etc unmenschlich.

inhumane [,ɪnhjuː'meɪn] adj inhuman; (to people also) menschenunwürdig.

inhumanity [,ɪnhjuː'mænɪtɪ] n Unmenschlichkeit f. the ~ of man to man die Unmenschlichkeit der Menschen untereinander.

inimitable [ɪ'nɪmɪtəbl] adj unnachahmlich.

iniquitous [ɪ'nɪkwɪtəs] adj ungeheuerlich.

initial [ɪ'nɪʃəl] adj anfänglich, Anfangs-. my ~ reaction meine anfängliche Reaktion; in the ~ stages im Anfangsstadium. **2** n Initiale f. **3** vt letter mit seinen Initialen unterzeichnen; (Comm) abzeichnen; (Pol) paraphieren.

initially [ɪ'nɪʃəlɪ] adv anfangs, am Anfang.

initiate [ɪ'nɪʃɪeɪt] **1** vt (a) (set in motion) den Anstoß geben zu. (b) (into club) feierlich aufnehmen; (in tribal society) adolescents initiieren. **2** n (in club) Neuaufgenommene(r) mf.

initiation [ɪ,nɪʃɪ'eɪʃən] n (a) (of project etc) Initiierung f. (b) (into society) Aufnahme f; (as tribal member) Initiation f. ~ ceremony Aufnahmezeremonie f.

initiative [ɪ'nɪʃətɪv] n Initiative f. to take the ~ die Initiative ergreifen; on one's own ~ aus eigener Initiative; use your ~! hast du keine Initiative?

inject [ɪn'dʒekt] vt (ein)spritzen; (fig) comment einwerfen; money pumpen. he ~ed new life into the club er brachte neues Leben in den Verein.

injection [ɪn'dʒekʃən] n Injektion, Spritze f. an ~ of capital eine Finanzspritze.

injudicious [,ɪndʒʊ'dɪʃəs] adj unklug.

injunction [ɪn'dʒʌŋkʃən] n Anordnung f; (Jur) gerichtliche Verfügung.

injure ['ɪndʒə'] vt (lit, fig) verletzen. to ~ one's leg sich (dat) das Bein verletzen; he was ~d er verletzte sich; is he ~d? ist er verletzt?; the ~d die Verletzten; the ~d party (Jur) der/die Geschädigte.

injurious [ɪn'dʒʊərɪəs] adj schädlich.

injury ['ɪndʒərɪ] n Verletzung f (to gen); (fig also) Kränkung f (to gen). to do sb/oneself an ~ jdn/

sich verletzen; **to play** ~ **time** *(Brit Sport)* nachspielen.

injustice [ɪn'dʒʌstɪs] *n (unfairness, inequality)* Ungerechtigkeit *f*; *(violation of sb's rights)* Unrecht *nt no pl*. **to do sb an** ~ jdm Unrecht tun.

ink [ɪŋk] *n* Tinte *f*; *(Art)* Tusche *f*.

inkling ['ɪŋklɪŋ] *n* dunkle Ahnung. **he hadn't an** ~ er hatte nicht die leiseste Ahnung; **to give sb an** ~ jdm eine Andeutung geben.

inkpad ['ɪŋkpæd] *n* Stempelkissen *nt*.

inky ['ɪŋkɪ] *adj (+er) (lit)* tintenbeschmiert; *(fig)* darkness tintenschwarz; *black* tintig.

inlaid [ɪn'leɪd] *adj* eingelegt. ~ **table** Tisch *m* mit Einlegearbeit.

inland ['ɪnlænd] **1** *adj waterway, trade* Binnen-; *mail* Inland(s)-. **I**~ **Revenue** *(Brit)* ≈ Finanzamt *nt*. **2** *adv* landeinwärts.

inlaws ['ɪnlɔːz] *npl (parents-in-law)* Schwiegereltern *pl*; *(others)* angeheiratete Verwandte *pl*.

inlet ['ɪnlet] *n* **(a)** *(of sea)* Meeresarm *m*; *(of river)* Flußarm *m*. **(b)** *(Tech)* Zuleitung *f*; *(of ventilator)* Öffnung *f*. ~ **pipe** *n* Zuleitung(srohr *nt*) *f*; ~ **valve** *n* Einlaßventil *nt*.

inmate ['ɪnmeɪt] *n* Insasse *m*, Insassin *f*.

inmost ['ɪnməʊst] *adj* innerst.

inn [ɪn] *n* Gasthaus *nt*; *(old: hotel)* Herberge *f (old)*.

innards ['ɪnədz] *npl* Innereien *pl (also fig)*, Eingeweide *pl*.

innate [ɪ'neɪt] *adj* angeboren.

inner ['ɪnəʳ] *adj* innere(r,s); *surface, door, city, ear also* Innen-; *meaning* verborgen; *life* Seelen-. ~ **harbour** Innenbecken *nt*; **the needs of the** ~ **man** die inneren Bedürfnisse.

innermost ['ɪnəməʊst] *adj* innerst. **in the** ~ **depths of the forest** im tiefsten Wald.

inner tube *n* Schlauch *m*.

innings ['ɪnɪŋz] *n* Innenrunde *f*. **he has had a good** ~ *(fig col)* er war lange an der Reihe; *(life)* er hatte ein langes, ausgefülltes Leben.

innkeeper ['ɪn,kiːpəʳ] *n* (Gast)wirt *m*.

innocence ['ɪnəsəns] *n* **(a)** Unschuld *f*. **in all** ~ in aller Unschuld. **(b)** *(ignorance)* Unkenntnis *f*.

innocent ['ɪnəsənt] *adj* **(a)** unschuldig *(of an* +*dat)*; *mistake* unabsichtlich. **to put on an** ~ **air** eine Unschuldsmiene aufsetzen. **(b)** ~ **of** *(ignorant)* nicht vertraut mit.

innocuous [ɪ'nɒkjʊəs] *adj* harmlos.

innovate ['ɪnəʊveɪt] *vi* Neuerungen einführen.

innovation [,ɪnəʊ'veɪʃən] *n* Innovation *f*; *(introduction also)* Neueinführung *f (of gen)*; *(thing introduced also)* Neuerung *f*.

innovative [ɪnə'veɪtɪv] *adj* innovativ *(geh)*, innovatorisch *(geh)*.

innuendo [,ɪnjʊ'endəʊ] *n, pl* -**es** versteckte Andeutung. **to make** ~**es about sb** über jdn Andeutungen fallenlassen.

innumerable [ɪ'njuːmərəbl] *adj* unzählig.

inoculate [ɪ'nɒkjʊleɪt] *vt person* impfen *(against* gegen*)*.

inoculation [ɪ,nɒkjʊ'leɪʃən] *n* Impfung *f*.

inoffensive [,ɪnə'fensɪv] *adj* harmlos.

inopportune [ɪn'ɒpətjuːn] *adj* inopportun; *moment also* ungelegen. **to be** ~ ungelegen kommen.

inordinate [ɪ'nɔːdɪnɪt] *adj* unmäßig; *number, sum of money* ungeheuer.

inorganic [,ɪnɔː'gænɪk] *adj* anorganisch.

in-patient ['ɪnpeɪʃnt] *n* stationär behandelter Patient/behandelte Patientin.

input ['ɪnpʊt] **1** *n (Comp)* Eingabe *f*, Input *m or nt*; *(power* ~*)* Energiezufuhr *f*; *(of energy, work etc)* Aufwand *m*. **2** *vt (Comp)* eingeben.

inquest ['ɪnkwest] *n (into death)* gerichtliche Untersuchung der Todesursache.

inquire [ɪn'kwaɪəʳ] *etc (esp US)* = **enquire** *etc.*

inquisition [,ɪnkwɪ'zɪʃən] *n (Hist, fig)* Inquisition *f*.

inquisitive [ɪn'kwɪzɪtɪv] *adj* neugierig; *(for knowledge)* wißbegierig.

inquisitiveness [ɪn'kwɪzɪtɪvnɪs] *n* Neugier *f*.

inroad ['ɪnrəʊd] *n (Mil)* Einfall *m (into* in +*acc)*. **to make** ~**s into sth** *into time* etw stark in Anspruch nehmen; *into savings* etw stark angreifen; **the Japanese are making** ~**s into the British market** die Japaner dringen in den britischen Markt ein.

insane [ɪn'seɪn] **1** *adj* geisteskrank; *(fig)* wahnsinnig. **2** *npl* **the** ~ die Geisteskranken *pl*.

insanitary [ɪn'sænɪtərɪ] *adj* unhygienisch.

insanity [ɪn'sænɪtɪ] *n* Geisteskrankheit *f*; *(fig)* Wahnsinn *m*.

insatiable [ɪn'seɪʃəbl] *adj* unersättlich.

inscribe [ɪn'skraɪb] *vt (on sth* in etw *acc) words etc (on ring etc)* eingravieren; *(on stone)* einmeißeln.

inscription [ɪn'skrɪpʃən] *n* Inschrift *f*; *(on coin)* Aufschrift *f*; *(in book)* Widmung *f*.

inscrutable [ɪn'skruːtəbl] *adj* unergründlich. ~ **face** undurchdringlicher Gesichtsausdruck.

insect ['ɪnsekt] *n* Insekt *nt*. ~ **bite** *n* Insektenstich *m*.

insecticide [ɪn'sektɪsaɪd] *n* Insektizid *nt*.

insecure [,ɪnsɪ'kjʊəʳ] *adj* unsicher.

insecurity [,ɪnsɪ'kjʊərɪtɪ] *n* Unsicherheit *f*.

insensible [ɪn'sensəbl] *adj* unempfindlich *(to* gegen*)*.

insensitive [ɪn'sensɪtɪv] *adj* **(a)** *(emotionally)* gefühllos. **(b)** *(unappreciative)* unempfänglich *(to* für*)*. **(c)** *(physically)* unempfindlich. ~ **to pain/light** schmerz-/lichtunempfindlich.

insensitivity [ɪn,sensɪ'tɪvɪtɪ] *n* **(a)** *(emotional)* Gefühllosigkeit *f (towards* gegenüber*)*. **(b)** *(unappreciativeness)* Unempfänglichkeit *f (to* für*)*. **(c)** *(physical)* Unempfindlichkeit *f*.

inseparable [ɪn'sepərəbl] *adj* untrennbar; *friends* unzertrennlich.

insert [ɪn'sɜːt] **1** *vt (stick into)* hineinstecken; *(place in)* hineinlegen; *(place between)* einfügen; *thermometer* einführen; *coin* einwerfen. **to** ~ **a paragraph** einen weiteren Absatz einfügen. **2** ['ɪnsɜːt] *n (in book)* Einlage *f*; *(in magazine)* Beilage *f*.

insertion [ɪn'sɜːʃən] *n see vt* Hineinstecken *nt*; Hineinlegen *nt*; Einfügen *nt*; Einführen *nt*; Einwerfen *nt*.

inset [ɪn'set] *n (also* ~ **map)** Nebenkarte *f*; *(on diagram)* Nebenbild *nt*.

inshore [ɪn'ʃɔːʳ] *adj* Küsten-. ~ **fishing** Küstenfischerei *f*.

inside ['ɪnsaɪd] **1** *n* **(a)** Innere(s) *nt*; *(of pavement)* Innenseite *f*. **on the** ~ innen; **to know a company from the** ~ interne Kenntnisse über eine Firma haben; **locked from the** ~ von innen verschlossen. **(b)** **the wind blew the umbrella** ~ **out** der Wind hat den Schirm umgestülpt; **your jumper's** ~ **out** du hast deinen Pullover verkehrt herum an; **to turn sth** ~ **out** etw umdrehen; *(fig)* flat etc etw auf den Kopf stellen; **to know sth** ~ **out** etw in- und auswendig kennen. **(c)** *(col)* (~**s:** *stomach)* Eingeweide, Innere(s) *nt*.

2 *adj* Innen-, innere(r, s). ~ **information** interne Informationen *pl*; **it looks like an** ~ **job** *(crime)* es sieht nach dem Werk von Insidern aus *(col)*; ~ **lane** *(Sport)* Innenbahn *f*; *(Aut)* Innenspur *f*; ~ **pocket** Innentasche *f*; ~ **story** *(Press)* Inside-Story *f*; ~ **forward** Halbstürmer *m*; ~ **left** Halblinke(r) *m*; ~ **right** Halbrechte(r) *m*.

3 *adv* innen; *(indoors)* drin(nen); *(direction)* nach innen, hinein/herein. **look** ~ sehen Sie hinein; **let's go** ~ gehen wir hinein; **there is something** ~ es ist etwas (innen) drin; **to be** ~ *(col: in prison)* sitzen *(col)*.

4 *prep* **(a)** *(place)* innen in (+*dat*); *(direction)* in (+*acc*) ... (hinein). **he was waiting** ~ **the house** er wartete im Haus; **he went** ~ **the house** er ging ins Haus (hinein). **(b)** *(time)* innerhalb. **he was 5 secs** ~ **the record** er ist 5 Sekunden unter dem Rekord geblieben.

insider [ɪn'saɪdəʳ] *n* Eingeweihte(r) *m*.

insidious [ɪn'sɪdɪəs] *adj* heimtückisch.

insight ['ɪnsaɪt] n his ~ into my problems sein Verständnis nt für meine Probleme; **to gain an ~ into sth** in etw (acc) (einen) Einblick gewinnen.

insignificance [,ɪnsɪg'nɪfɪkəns] n see adj Belanglosigkeit f; Geringfügigkeit f; Unscheinbarkeit f.

insignificant [,ɪnsɪg'nɪfɪkənt] adj belanglos; sum, difference also geringfügig; person unscheinbar.

insincere [,ɪnsɪn'sɪər] adj unaufrichtig.

insincerity [,ɪnsɪn'serɪtɪ] n Unaufrichtigkeit f.

insinuate [ɪn'sɪnjʊeɪt] vt (a) andeuten (sth to sb etw jdm gegenüber). **what are you insinuating?** was wollen Sie damit sagen? **(b) to ~ oneself into sb's favour** sich bei jdm einschmeicheln.

insinuation [ɪn,sɪnjʊ'eɪʃən] n Anspielung f (about auf +acc).

insipid [ɪn'sɪpɪd] adj fad; person, novel also geistlos.

insist [ɪn'sɪst] vti bestehen. **I ~!** ich bestehe darauf!; **if you ~** wenn Sie darauf bestehen; (if you like) wenn's unbedingt sein muß; **I must ~ that you stop** ich muß darauf bestehen, daß Sie aufhören; **he ~s that he is innocent** er behauptet beharrlich, unschuldig zu sein; **I ~ on the best** ich bestehe auf bester Qualität; **if you will ~ on smoking,** ... wenn Sie schon unbedingt rauchen müssen, ...

insistence [ɪn'sɪstəns] n Bestehen nt (on auf +dat). **I did it at his ~** ich tat es, weil er darauf bestand.

insistent [ɪn'sɪstənt] adj (a) person beharrlich; salesman etc aufdringlich. **he was most ~ about it** er beharrte darauf. (b) (urgent) demand, tone nachdrücklich.

insole ['ɪnsəʊl] n Einlegesohle f.

insolence ['ɪnsələns] n Unverschämtheit f.

insolent ['ɪnsələnt] adj unverschämt.

insoluble [ɪn'sɒljʊbl] adj (a) substance unlöslich. **(b)** problem unlösbar.

insolvency [ɪn'sɒlvənsɪ] n Zahlungsunfähigkeit f.

insolvent [ɪn'sɒlvənt] adj zahlungsunfähig.

insomnia [ɪn'sɒmnɪə] n Schlaflosigkeit f.

insomniac [ɪn'sɒmnɪæk] n **to be an ~** an Schlaflosigkeit leiden.

inspect [ɪn'spekt] vt (a) (examine) prüfen. **to ~ sth for sth** etw auf etw (acc) (hin) prüfen. (b) (Mil etc: review) inspizieren.

inspection [ɪn'spekʃən] n (a) Prüfung f; (of school) Inspektion f. **on ~** bei näherer Betrachtung; **for your ~** zur Prüfung. (b) (Mil) Inspektion f.

inspector [ɪn'spektər] n (factory ~, Brit: on buses) Kontrolleur(in f) m; (of schools) Schulrat m, Schulrätin f; (of police) Polizeiinspektor m; (of taxes) Steuerinspektor m.

inspiration [,ɪnspə'reɪʃən] n Inspiration (for zu or für), Eingebung (for zu) f. **he gets his ~ from** ... er läßt sich von ... inspirieren.

inspire [ɪn'spaɪər] vt (a) respect, awe einflößen (in sb jdm). **to ~ sb with confidence** jdm mit Vertrauen erfüllen. (b) (be inspiration to) person inspirieren.

inspired [ɪn'spaɪəd] adj genial. **in an ~ moment** in einem Augenblick der Inspiration; (iro) in einem lichten Moment; **it was an ~ guess** das war genial geraten.

inspiring [ɪn'spaɪərɪŋ] adj speech inspirierend.

instability [,ɪnstə'bɪlɪtɪ] n Instabilität f; (of character also) Labilität f.

install [ɪn'stɔːl] vt installieren; telephone also anschließen; person (in ein Amt) einsetzen.

installation [,ɪnstə'leɪʃən] n (a) see vt Installation f; Anschluß m; Amtseinsetzung f. (b) (machine etc) Anlage f. **(c)** military ~ militärische Anlage.

instalment, (US) **installment** [ɪn'stɔːlmənt] n (a) (of serial) Fortsetzung f; (TV) (Sende)folge f. (b) (Fin) Rate f. **monthly ~** Monatsrate f; **to pay in** or **by ~s** in Raten bezahlen.

installment plan n (US) Ratenzahlung(splan m) f. **to buy on the ~** auf Raten kaufen.

instance ['ɪnstəns] n (example) Beispiel nt; (case)

Fall m. **for ~** zum Beispiel; **in the first ~** zunächst (einmal).

instant ['ɪnstənt] **1** adj (a) unmittelbar; relief, result also sofortig attr. (b) (Cook) Instant-. ~ **coffee** Pulverkaffee m; ~ **food** Schnellgerichte pl. **2** n Augenblick m. **this (very)** ~ sofort; **at that very** ~ genau in dem Augenblick.

instantaneous [,ɪnstən'teɪnɪəs] adj unmittelbar.

instantly ['ɪnstəntlɪ] adv sofort.

instead [ɪn'sted] **1** prep ~ **of** statt (+gen or (col) +dat), anstelle von. ~ **of going to school** (an)statt zur Schule zu gehen; **his brother came** ~ **of him** sein Bruder kam an seiner Stelle. **2** adv statt dessen. **if he doesn't want to go, I'll go** ~ wenn er nicht gehen will, gehe ich statt dessen.

instep ['ɪnstep] n (Anat) Spann m; (of shoe) Blatt nt.

instigate ['ɪnstɪgeɪt] vt anstiften; reform etc initiieren.

instigation [,ɪnstɪ'geɪʃən] n see vt Anstiftung f; Initiierung f. **at sb's ~** auf jds Betreiben.

instil [ɪn'stɪl] vt einflößen (into sb jdm).

instinct ['ɪnstɪŋkt] n Instinkt m. **by** or **from ~** instinktiv.

instinctive [ɪn'stɪŋktɪv] adj instinktiv.

institute ['ɪnstɪtjuːt] **1** vt (a) reforms einführen; search einleiten. (b) (Jur) action einleiten; proceedings anstrengen (against gegen). **2** n Institut nt; (home) Anstalt f.

institution [,ɪnstɪ'tjuːʃən] n (organization, custom) Institution f; (building, home etc) Anstalt f.

institutional [,ɪnstɪ'tjuːʃənl] adj life etc Anstalts-.

instruct [ɪn'strʌkt] vt (a) (teach) person unterrichten. (b) (tell, direct) person anweisen; (command) die Anweisung erteilen (+dat); (appoint) lawyer beauftragen.

instruction [ɪn'strʌkʃən] n (a) (teaching) Unterricht m. (b) (command) Anweisung, Instruktion f; ~**s for use** Gebrauchsanweisung f; ~ **manual** Bedienungsanleitung f.

instructive [ɪn'strʌktɪv] adj aufschlußreich; (of educational value) lehrreich.

instructor [ɪn'strʌktər] n (also Sport) Lehrer m; (US) Dozent m; (Mil) Ausbilder m.

instrument ['ɪnstrʊmənt] n (Mus, Tech) Instrument nt; (domestic) Gerät nt; (person) Werkzeug nt. **to fly an aircraft on** ~**s** ein Flugzeug nach den (Bord)instrumenten fliegen; ~ **panel** n (Aviat, Aut) Armaturenbrett nt.

instrumental [,ɪnstrʊ'mentl] adj (a) **he was** ~ **in getting her the job** er hat ihr zu dieser Stelle verholfen; **to be** ~ **in sth** bei etw mitwirken. (b) music Instrumental-.

instrumentalist [,ɪnstrʊ'mentəlɪst] n Instrumentalist(in f) m.

insubordinate [,ɪnsə'bɔːdənɪt] adj aufsässig.

insubordination ['ɪnsə,bɔːdɪ'neɪʃən] n Aufsässigkeit f; (Mil) Gehorsamsverweigerung f.

insufferable [ɪn'sʌfərəbl] adj unerträglich.

insufficient [,ɪnsə'fɪʃənt] adj ungenügend pred; work, insulation also unzulänglich.

insular ['ɪnsjələr] adj (narrow) engstirnig.

insularity [,ɪnsjʊ'lærɪtɪ] n Engstirnigkeit f.

insulate ['ɪnsjʊleɪt] vt room, (Elec) isolieren; (fig: shelter) abschirmen (from gegen).

insulating tape ['ɪnsjʊleɪtɪŋˌteɪp] n (Brit) Isolierband nt.

insulation [,ɪnsjʊ'leɪʃən] n Isolation f; (material also) Isoliermaterial nt; (fig) Geschütztheit f (from gegen).

insulin ['ɪnsjʊlɪn] n Insulin nt.

insult [ɪn'sʌlt] **1** vt beleidigen; (by words also) beschimpfen. **2** ['ɪnsʌlt] n (to für +acc) Beleidigung f; (with words also) Beschimpfung f. **to add** ~ **to injury** das Ganze noch schlimmer machen.

insulting [ɪn'sʌltɪŋ] adj beleidigend.

insuperable [ɪn'suːpərəbl] adj unüberwindlich.

insupportable [,ɪnsə'pɔːtəbl] adj unerträglich.

insurance [ɪn'ʃʊərəns] n Versicherung f. **to take**

out ~ eine Versicherung abschließen.

insurance: ~ **company** *n* Versicherungsgesellschaft *f*; ~ **policy** *n* Versicherungspolice *f*; *(fig)* Sicherheitsvorkehrung *f*; ~ **salesman** Versicherungsvertreter *m*.

insure [ɪn'ʃʊər] *vt house* versichern (lassen). **to ~ oneself** *or* **one's life** eine Lebensversicherung abschließen.

insurgent [ɪn'sɜːdʒənt] **1** *adj* aufständisch. **2** *n* Aufständische(r) *mf*.

insurmountable [,ɪnsə'maʊntəbl] *adj* unüberwindlich.

insurrection [,ɪnsə'rekʃən] *n* Aufstand *m*.

intact [ɪn'tækt] *adj* unversehrt.

intake ['ɪnteɪk] *n* (*of water, electric current, Sch*) Aufnahme *f*; *(pipe)* Zuflußrohr *nt*. **air ~** Luftzufuhr *f*; **food ~** Nahrungsaufnahme *f*.

intangible [ɪn'tændʒəbl] *adj* (**a**) nicht greifbar. (**b**) *longings* unbestimmbar. (**c**) *(Jur, Comm)* ~ **assets** immaterielle Werte *pl*.

integer ['ɪntɪdʒər] *n* ganze Zahl.

integral ['ɪntɪɡrəl] *adj part* wesentlich.

integrate ['ɪntɪɡreɪt] *vt* integrieren. **to ~ sth into sth** etw in etw *(acc)* integrieren; **to ~ sth with sth** etw auf etw *(acc)* abstimmen.

integrated ['ɪntɪɡreɪtɪd] *adj plan* einheitlich; *school* ohne Rassentrennung. **a fully ~ personality** eine in sich ausgewogene Persönlichkeit; ~ **circuit** integrierter Schaltkreis.

integration [,ɪntɪ'ɡreɪʃən] *n* Integration *f* (*into* in +*acc*). (**racial**) ~ Rassenintegration *f*.

integrity [ɪn'teɡrɪtɪ] *n* (**a**) *(honesty)* Integrität *f*. (**b**) *(wholeness)* Einheit *f*.

intellect ['ɪntɪlekt] *n* Intellekt *m*.

intellectual [,ɪntɪ'lektjʊəl] **1** *adj* intellektuell; *interests also* geistig. **something a little more ~** etwas geistig Anspruchsvolleres. **2** *n* Intellektuelle(r) *mf*.

intelligence [ɪn'telɪdʒəns] *n* (**a**) Intelligenz *f*. (**b**) *(news, information)* Informationen *pl*. (**c**) *(Mil etc)* Geheimdienst *m*.

intelligent [ɪn'telɪdʒənt] *adj* intelligent.

intelligentsia [ɪn,telɪ'dʒentsɪə] *n* Intelligenz *f*.

intelligible [ɪn'telɪdʒəbl] *adj* verständlich.

intemperate [ɪn'tempərɪt] *adj climate* extrem; *person* unmäßig.

intend [ɪn'tend] *vt* (**a**) (+*n*) beabsichtigen, wollen. **I ~ him to go with me** ich habe vor, ihn mitzunehmen; *(insist)* er soll mit mir mitkommen; **I ~ed no harm** es war (von mir) nicht böse gemeint; *(with action)* ich hatte nichts Böses beabsichtigt; **I didn't ~ it as an insult** das sollte keine Beleidigung sein; **that remark was ~ed for you** mit dieser Bemerkung waren Sie gemeint; **this film was never ~ed for children** dieser Film war nie für Kinder bestimmt. (**b**) (+*vb*) beabsichtigen, fest vorhaben. **he ~s to win** er hat fest vor, zu gewinnen; **what do you ~ to do about it?** was beabsichtigen Sie, dagegen zu tun?

intense [ɪn'tens] *adj* intensiv; *disappointment* äußerst groß; *person* ernsthaft.

intensely [ɪn'tenslɪ] *adv angry* äußerst; *study* intensiv.

intensify [ɪn'tensɪfaɪ] **1** *vt* intensivieren; *meaning* verstärken. **2** *vi* zunehmen; *(pain, heat also)* stärker werden.

intensity [ɪn'tensɪtɪ] *n* Intensität *f*; *(of feeling, storm also)* Heftigkeit *f*.

intensive [ɪn'tensɪv] *adj* intensiv, Intensiv-. ~ **care unit** Intensivstation *f*; **they came under ~ fire** sie kamen unter heftigen Beschuß.

intent [ɪn'tent] **1** *n* Absicht *f*. **to all ~s and purposes** im Grunde; **with ~ to** *(Jur)* mit dem Vorsatz zu. **2** *adj look* durchdringend. **to be ~ on achieving sth** fest entschlossen sein, etw zu erreichen.

intention [ɪn'tenʃən] *n* Absicht *f*. **I have every ~ of doing that** ich habe die feste Absicht, das zu tun; **I have no** *or* **haven't the least ~ of staying!** ich

habe nicht die geringste Absicht hierzubleiben; **with the best of ~s** in der besten Absicht; **with the ~ of** ... mit dem Vorsatz zu ...

intentional [ɪn'tenʃənl] *adj* absichtlich, vorsätzlich *(esp Jur)*. **it wasn't ~** das war keine Absicht.

intentionally [ɪn'tenʃnəlɪ] *adv* absichtlich.

inter- ['ɪntər] *pref* zwischen-, Zwischen-.

interact [,ɪntər'ækt] *vi* aufeinander einwirken, *(Phys)* wechselwirken; *(Psychol)* interagieren.

interaction [,ɪntər'ækʃən] *n see vi* gegenseitige Einwirkung, Wechselwirkung *f* (*also Phys*); Interaktion *f*.

intercede [,ɪntə'siːd] *vi* sich einsetzen, sich verwenden *(with bei, on behalf of für)*.

intercept [,ɪntə'sept] *vt message, plane* abfangen; *phone call also* abhören. **they ~ed the enemy** sie schnitten dem Feind den Weg ab.

interception [,ɪntə'sepʃən] *n* Abfangen *nt*.

interchange ['ɪntə,tʃeɪndʒ] **1** *n* (**a**) *(of roads)* Kreuzung *f*; *(of motorways)* (Autobahn)kreuz *nt*. (**b**) *(exchange)* Austausch *m*. **2** [,ɪntə'tʃeɪndʒ] *vt* (**a**) *(switch round)* (aus)tauschen. (**b**) *ideas etc* austauschen *(with mit)*.

interchangeable [,ɪntə'tʃeɪndʒəbl] *adj* austauschbar. **x is ~ with y** x und y sind austauschbar.

interchangeably [,ɪntə'tʃeɪndʒəblɪ] *adv* austauschbar. **they are used ~** sie können ausgetauscht werden.

inter-city [,ɪntə'sɪtɪ] *n* Intercity *m*.

intercom ['ɪntəkɒm] *n* (Gegen)sprechanlage *f*; *(in ship, plane)* Bordverständigungsanlage *f*; *(in schools etc)* Lautsprecheranlage *f*.

intercontinental ['ɪntə,kɒntɪ'nentl] *adj* interkontinental, Interkontinental-.

intercourse ['ɪntəkɔːs] *n* (**sexual**) ~ (Geschlechts)verkehr *m*. **social ~** gesellschaftlicher Verkehr *m*.

interdependent [,ɪntədɪ'pendənt] *adj* wechselseitig voneinander abhängig.

interest ['ɪntrɪst] **1** *n* (**a**) Interesse *nt*. **to take an ~ in sb/sth** sich für jdn/etw interessieren; **just for ~** nur interessehalber; **he has lost ~** er hat das Interesse verloren; **his ~s are** ... er ist interessiert sich für ...; **of vital ~ to the economy** von lebenswichtigem Interesse für die Wirtschaft; **to act in sb's/one's own ~(s)** in jds/im eigenen Interesse handeln; **in the public ~** im öffentlichen Interesse. (**b**) *(Fin)* Zinsen *pl*. **rate of ~,** ~ **rate** Zinssatz *m*; **to bear ~ at 4%** 4% Zinsen tragen, mit 4% verzinst sein. (**c**) *(Comm)* *(share, stake)* Anteil *m*; *(~ group)* Kreise *pl*, Interessentengruppe *f*. **he has a financial ~ in the company** er ist finanziell an der Firma beteiligt; **British trading ~s** britische Handelsinteressen *pl*.

2 *vt* interessieren *(in für, an* +*dat*). **to ~ sb in doing sth** jdn dafür interessieren, etw zu tun; **can I ~ you in a little drink?** kann ich Sie zu etwas Alkoholischem überreden?

interested ['ɪntrɪstɪd] *adj* interessiert *(in an* +*dat*). **I'm not ~** ich bin nicht (daran) interessiert; **to be ~ in sb/sth** sich für jdn/etw interessieren; **I'm going to the cinema, are you ~ (in coming)?** gehe ins Kino, haben Sie Lust mitzukommen?; **she was ~ to see what he would do** sie war gespannt, was er wohl tun würde; **he is an ~ party** er ist daran beteiligt.

interest-free ['ɪntrɪst'friː] *adj loan* zinsfrei.

interesting ['ɪntrɪstɪŋ] *adj* interessant.

interestingly ['ɪntrɪstɪŋlɪ] *adv* ~ **enough,** interessanterweise ...

interface ['ɪntəfeɪs] **1** *n* *(Comp)* Schnittstelle *f*, Interface *nt*; *(fig)* Grenzfläche *f*. **the man/machine** ~ die Interaktion von Mensch und Maschine. **2** ['ɪntə'feɪs] *vt* koppeln.

interfere [,ɪntə'fɪər] *vi* sich einmischen *(in in* +*acc*). **don't ~ with the machine** laß die Finger von der Maschine; **who's been interfering with my books?** wer war an meinen Büchern?; **to ~ with sth** (*disrupt*) etw stören (*also Rad*); **to ~ with sb's plans** jds Pläne durchkreuzen.

interference [,ıntə'fıərəns] n (*meddling*) Einmischung f; (*disruption, Rad*) Störung f (*with gen*).

interfering [,ıntə'fıərıŋ] adj **don't be so ~** misch dich nicht immer ein.

interim ['ıntərım] **1** n **in the ~** in der Zwischenzeit. **2** adj vorläufig; (*arrangements also, government*) Übergangs-; *report, payment* Zwischen-.

interior [ın'tıərıəʳ] **1** adj (*inside*) Innen-; (*inland, domestic*) Binnen-. **2** n (*of country*) Innere(s) nt; (*of house*) Innenausstattung f. **deep in the ~** tief im Landesinneren; **Department of the I~** (*US*) Innenministerium nt.

interior: **~ decorator** n Innenausstatter(in f) m; **~ design** n Innenarchitektur f; **~ designer** n Innenarchitekt(in f) m.

interjection [,ıntə'dʒekʃən] n (*exclamation*) Ausruf m; (*remark*) Einwurf m.

interlocking [,ıntə'lɒkıŋ] adj ineinandergreifend.

interloper ['ıntələupəʳ] n Eindringling m.

interlude ['ıntəlu:d] n Periode f; (*Theat*) Pause f.

intermarry [,ıntə'mærı] vi Mischehen eingehen.

intermediary [,ıntə'mi:dıərı] n (Ver)mittler(in f) m.

intermediate [,ıntə'mi:dıət] adj Zwischen-; *French etc* für fortgeschrittene Anfänger.

interminable [ın'tɜ:mınəbl] adj endlos. **after what seemed an ~ journey** nach einer Reise, die nicht enden zu wollen schien.

intermingle [,ıntə'mıŋgl] vi sich mischen (*with* unter +*acc*).

intermission [,ıntə'mıʃən] n (**a**) Unterbrechung f. (**b**) (*Theat, Film*) Pause f.

intermittent [,ıntə'mıtənt] adj periodisch auftretend; (*Tech*) intermittierend.

intern¹ [ın'tɜ:n] vt *person* internieren.

intern² ['ıntɜ:n] (*US*) n Assistenzarzt m, Assistenzärztin f.

internal [ın'tɜ:nl] adj (*inner*) innere(r, s); *diameter* Innen-; *trade etc* Binnen-; *policy, mail* intern; **~ combustion engine** Verbrennungsmotor m; **I~ Revenue Service** (*US*) Finanzamt nt; **~ affairs** innere Angelegenheiten pl.

internally [ın'tɜ:nəlı] adv innen, im Inneren; (*in body*) innerlich; (*in country*) landesintern; (*in organization*) intern. **"not to be taken ~"** „nicht zur inneren Anwendung".

international [,ıntə'næʃnəl] **1** adj international. **~ law** Völkerrecht nt; **~ money order** Auslandsanweisung f. **2** n (*Sport*) (*match*) Länderspiel nt; (*player*) Nationalspieler(in f) m.

internment [ın'tɜ:nmənt] n Internierung f. **~ camp** Internierungslager nt.

interplanetary [,ıntə'plænıtərı] adj interplanetar.

interplay ['ıntəpleı] n Zusammenspiel nt.

Interpol ['ıntəpɒl] n Interpol f.

interpret [ın'tɜ:prıt] **1** vt (*an understand*) auslegen, interpretieren; (*Theat, Mus*) interpretieren. **how would you ~ what he said?** wie würden Sie seine Worte auffassen? **2** vi dolmetschen.

interpretation [ın,tɜ:prı'teıʃən] n *see vt* (**b**) Auslegung, Interpretation f; Interpretation f.

interpreter [ın'tɜ:prıtəʳ] n Dolmetscher(in f) m; (*Theat, Mus*) Interpret(in f) m.

interrelated [,ıntərı'leıtıd] adj **to be ~** zueinander in Beziehung stehen, zusammenhängen.

interrogate [ın'terəgeıt] vt (*police*) verhören.

interrogation [ın,terə'geıʃən] n Verhör nt.

interrogative [,ıntə'rɒgətıv] adj (*Gram*) Frage-, Interrogativ-.

interrogator [ın'terəgeıtəʳ] n Vernehmungsbeamte(r) mf.

interrupt [,ıntə'rʌpt] vti unterbrechen (*also Elec*);

work also stören. **stop ~ing (me)!** fall mir nicht dauernd ins Wort!

interruption [,ıntə'rʌpʃən] n Unterbrechung f; (*of work also*) Störung f.

intersect [,ıntə'sekt] **1** vt durchschneiden; (*Geometry*) schneiden. **2** vi sich kreuzen; (*Geometry*) sich schneiden.

intersection [,ıntə'sekʃən] n (*crossroads*) Kreuzung f; (*Geometry*) Schnittpunkt m.

intersperse [,ıntə'spɜ:s] vt **woods ~d with fields** Wald mit Feldern dazwischen; **a speech ~d with quotations** eine mit Zitaten gespickte Rede.

interval ['ıntəvəl] n (**a**) (*space, time*) Abstand m. **at ~s** in Abständen; **sunny ~s** Aufheiterungen pl. (**b**) (*Sch, Theat*) Pause f. (**c**) (*Mus*) Intervall nt.

intervene [,ıntə'vi:n] vi (*person*) einschreiten (*in* bei), intervenieren; (*event, fate*) dazwischenkommen. **in the intervening weeks** in den dazwischenliegenden Wochen.

intervention [,ıntə'venʃən] n Eingreifen nt, Intervention f.

interview ['ıntəvju:] **1** n (*for job*) Vorstellungsgespräch nt; (*with authorities etc*) Gespräch nt; (*TV etc*) Interview nt. **2** vt *job applicant* ein/das Vorstellungsgespräch führen mit; (*TV etc*) interviewen. **he is being ~ed on Monday for the job** er hat am Montag sein Vorstellungsgespräch.

interviewer ['ıntəvju:əʳ] n (*for job*) Leiter(in f) m des Vorstellungsgesprächs; (*TV etc*) Interviewer(in f) m.

intestate [ın'testıt] adj (*Jur*) **to die ~** sterben, ohne ein Testament zu hinterlassen.

intestinal [ın'testınl] adj Darm-.

intestine [ın'testın] n Darm m. **small/large ~** Dünn-/Dickdarm m.

intimacy ['ıntıməsı] n Vertrautheit f; (*euph: sexual ~*) Intimität f.

intimate¹ ['ıntımıt] adj *friend* eng, vertraut; (*sexually*) intim; *knowledge* gründlich. **to be on ~ terms with sb** mit jdm auf vertraulichem Fuß stehen; **to be/become ~ with sb** mit jdm vertraut sein/werden.

intimate² ['ıntımeıt] vt andeuten. **he ~d to them that they should stop** er gab ihnen zu verstehen, daß sie aufhören sollten.

intimately ['ıntımıtlı] adv *acquainted* bestens; *speak* vertraulich; *connected* eng; *know* genau.

intimation [,ıntı'meıʃən] n Andeutung f.

intimidate [ın'tımıdeıt] vt einschüchtern.

intimidation [ın,tımı'deıʃən] n Einschüchterung f.

into ['ıntu] prep in (+*acc*); *crash* gegen. **to translate sth ~ French** etw ins Französische übersetzen; **to divide 5 ~ 9** 9 durch 5 teilen; **far ~ the night** bis tief in die Nacht hinein; **it turned ~ a nice day** es wurde ein schöner Tag; **I'm not really ~ the job yet** (*col*) ich bin noch nicht ganz in der Arbeit drin (*col*); **he's (heavily) ~ jazz** (*col*) er steht (schwer) auf Jazz (*col*).

intolerable [ın'tɒlərəbl] adj unerträglich.

intolerance [ın'tɒlərəns] n Intoleranz f (*of gegenüber*).

intolerant [ın'tɒlərənt] adj intolerant (*of gegenüber*).

intonation [,ıntəʊ'neıʃən] n Intonation f.

intoxicate [ın'tɒksıkeıt] vt (*lit, fig*) berauschen.

intoxicated [ın'tɒksıkeıtıd] adj betrunken, berauscht (*also fig*).

intoxication [ın,tɒksı'keıʃən] n Rausch m (*also fig*).

intractable [ın'træktəbl] adj *problem, illness* hartnäckig; *child* widerspenstig.

intransigence [ın'trænsıdʒəns] n Unnachgiebigkeit f.

intransigent [ın'trænsıdʒənt] adj unnachgiebig.

intransitive [ın'trænsıtıv] adj *verb* intransitiv.

intravenous [,ıntrə'vi:nəs] adj intravenös.

intrepid [ın'trepıd] adj unerschrocken.

intricacy ['ıntrıkəsı] n Kompliziertheit f; (*of a law*

etc) Feinheit *f*.
intricate ['ɪntrɪkɪt] *adj* kompliziert; *(involved also)* verwickelt.
intrigue [ɪn'triːg] **1** *vi* intrigieren. **2** *vt (arouse interest of)* faszinieren; *(arouse curiosity of)* neugierig machen. **I'd be ~d to know why ... es** würde mich schon interessieren, warum ... **3** ['ɪntriːg] *n (plot)* Intrige *f*; *(no pl: plotting)* Intrigen(spiel *nt*) *pl*.
intriguing [ɪn'triːgɪŋ] *adj* faszinierend, interessant.
intrinsic [ɪn'trɪnsɪk] *adj value* immanent; *(essential)* wesentlich.
introduce [ˌɪntrə'djuːs] *vt* **(a)** *(to person)* vorstellen *(to sb* jdm*)*, bekannt machen *(to* mit*)*; *(to subject)* einführen *(to* in +*acc*). **have you two been ~d?** hat man Sie bekannt gemacht?; **to ~ oneself** sich vorstellen. **(b)** *reform* einführen; *(Parl) bill* einbringen; *programme, (also TV)* ankündigen. **(c)** *(insert)* einführen *(into* in +*acc*).
introduction [ˌɪntrə'dʌkʃən] *n* **(a)** *(to person)* Vorstellung *f*. **(b)** *(in book)* Einleitung *f (to* zu*)*. **(c)** *(to subject, of reform etc)* Einführung *f (to* in +*acc*); *(of bill)* Einbringen *nt*; *(of programme)* Ankündigung *f*. **(d)** *(insertion)* Einführung *f (into* in +*acc*).
introductory [ˌɪntrə'dʌktərɪ] *adj chapter* einleitend; *remarks* einführend; *talk* Einführungs-.
introspection [ˌɪntrəʊ'spekʃən] *n* Selbstbeobachtung *f*.
introspective [ˌɪntrəʊ'spektɪv] *adj person* selbstbeobachtend; *novel* introspektiv.
introvert ['ɪntrəʊvɜːt] *n* Introvertierte(r) *mf*. **to be an ~** introvertiert sein.
introverted ['ɪntrəʊvɜːtɪd] *adj* introvertiert.
intrude [ɪn'truːd] *vi* sich eindrängen. **to ~ in sb's affairs** sich in jds Angelegenheiten *(acc)* einmischen; **am I intruding?** störe ich?; **to ~ on sb's privacy** jds Privatsphäre verletzen.
intruder [ɪn'truːdə'] *n* Eindringling *m*.
intrusion [ɪn'truːʒən] *n (disturbance)* Störung *f*. **forgive the ~** entschuldigen Sie, wenn ich hier so eindringe.
intrusive [ɪn'truːsɪv] *adj person* aufdringlich.
intuition [ˌɪntjuː'ɪʃən] *n* Intuition *f*; *(of future events etc)* (Vor)ahnung *f (of* von*)*.
intuitive [ɪn'tjuːɪtɪv] *adj* intuitiv; *guess, feeling* instinktiv.
inundate ['ɪnʌndeɪt] *vt (lit, fig)* überschwemmen; *(with work)* überhäufen.
inure [ɪn'jʊə'] *vt* gewöhnen *(to* an +*acc*); *(physically)* abhärten *(to* gegen*)*.
invade [ɪn'veɪd] *vt* einmarschieren in (+*acc*); *(fig)* überfallen; *privacy* eindringen in (+*acc*).
invader [ɪn'veɪdə'] *n* Invasor *m*.
invalid¹ ['ɪnvəlɪd] **1** *adj* krank; *(disabled)* körperbehindert. **~ chair** Rollstuhl *m*; **~ car** Invaliden(kraft)fahrzeug *nt*. **2** *n* Kranke(r) *mf*; *(disabled person)* Invalide, Körperbehinderte(r) *mf*.
♦ **invalid out** *vt sep* **to be ~ed ~ of the army** wegen Dienstuntauglichkeit aus dem Heer entlassen werden.
invalid² [ɪn'vælɪd] *adj* ungültig; *argument* nicht stichhaltig.
invalidate [ɪn'vælɪdeɪt] *vt* ungültig machen; *theory* entkräften.
invaluable [ɪn'væljʊəbl] *adj* unbezahlbar; *service* unschätzbar.
invariable [ɪn'vɛərɪəbl] *adj* unveränderlich.
invariably [ɪn'vɛərɪəblɪ] *adv* ständig.
invasion [ɪn'veɪʒən] *n (lit, fig)* Invasion *f*; *(of privacy etc)* Eingriff *m (of* in +*acc*). **the German ~ of Poland** der Einmarsch der Deutschen in Polen.
invective [ɪn'vektɪv] *n* Beschimpfungen *pl (against gen)*.
invent [ɪn'vent] *vt* erfinden.
invention [ɪn'venʃən] *n* Erfindung *f*.

inventive [ɪn'ventɪv] *adj (creative) mind* schöpferisch; *novel, design* einfallsreich; *(resourceful)* erfinderisch.
inventiveness [ɪn'ventɪvnɪs] *n* Einfallsreichtum *m*.
inventor [ɪn'ventə'] *n* Erfinder(in *f*) *m*.
inventory ['ɪnvəntrɪ] *n* Inventar *nt*, Bestandsaufnahme *f*. **to take an ~ of sth** den Bestand einer Sache *(gen)* aufnehmen.
inverse ['ɪn'vɜːs] *adj* umgekehrt. **in ~ order in** umgekehrter Reihenfolge; **to be in ~ proportion to ...** im umgekehrten Verhältnis zu ... stehen.
inversion [ɪn'vɜːʃən] *n* Umkehrung *f*.
invert [ɪn'vɜːt] *vt* umkehren. **~ed commas** *(Brit)* Anführungszeichen *pl*.
invertebrate [ɪn'vɜːtɪbrɪt] *n* Wirbellose(r) *m*.
invest [ɪn'vest] **1** *vt* **(a)** *(Fin, fig)* investieren *(in* in +*acc or dat)*; *(Fin also)* anlegen *(in* in +*dat)*. **(b)** *(form: in office) president etc* einsetzen. **2** *vi* investieren, Geld anlegen *(in* in +*acc or dat, with* bei*)*. **to ~ in a new car** sich *(dat)* ein neues Auto anschaffen.
investigate [ɪn'vestɪgeɪt] **1** *vt* untersuchen; *(research also)* erforschen; *business affairs* überprüfen; *complaint* nachgehen (+*dat*). **2** *vi* nachforschen; *(police)* Ermittlungen anstellen.
investigation [ɪnˌvestɪ'geɪʃən] *n* **(a)** *(to determine cause)* Untersuchung *f (into* gen*)*; *(by police)* Ermittlungen *pl*; *(of applicants, political beliefs etc)* Überprüfung *f*. **on ~** bei näherer Untersuchung; **to be under ~** überprüft werden; **he is under ~** *(by police)* gegen ihn wird ermittelt. **(b)** *(research)* Forschung *f*; *(of bacteria etc)* Erforschung *f (into* gen*)*.
investigative [ɪn'vestɪgətɪv] *adj journalism* Enthüllungs-.
investigator [ɪn'vestɪgeɪtə'] *n* Ermittler *m*; *(private ~)* (Privat)detektiv *m*.
investiture [ɪn'vestɪtʃə'] *n* Amtseinführung *f*.
investment [ɪn'vestmənt] *n (Fin)* Investition *f*. **to make an ~** investieren *(of* sth etw*)*; **oil is a good ~** Öl ist eine gute (Kapital)anlage.
investor [ɪn'vestə'] *n* Kapitalanleger, Investor *m*. **the small ~** der Kleinanleger.
inveterate [ɪn'vetərɪt] *adj hatred* tief verwurzelt; *enemies* unversöhnlich; *criminal, smoker* Gewohnheits-; *gambler* unverbesserlich.
invidious [ɪn'vɪdɪəs] *adj remark* gehässig; *task* unangenehm; *distinctions* ungerecht.
invigilate [ɪn'vɪdʒɪleɪt] *vti (Brit) exam* Aufsicht führen (bei).
invigilator [ɪn'vɪdʒɪleɪtə'] *n (Brit)* Aufsicht, Aufsichtsperson *f*.
invigorating [ɪn'vɪgəreɪtɪŋ] *adj climate* gesund; *air, shower* erfrischend; *tonic* kräftigend; *(fig) attitude* (herz)erfrischend.
invincible [ɪn'vɪnsəbl] *adj army etc* unbesiegbar; *courage, determination* unerschütterlich.
invisible [ɪn'vɪzəbl] *adj* unsichtbar. **~ earnings** *(Econ)* unsichtbare Einkünfte *pl*; **~ ink** Geheimtinte *f*; **~ mending** Kunststopfen *nt*; **~ to the naked eye** mit dem bloßen Auge nicht erkennbar.
invitation [ˌɪnvɪ'teɪʃən] *n* Einladung *f*. **by ~ (only)** nur auf Einladung; **at sb's ~** auf jds Aufforderung *(acc)* (hin).
invite [ɪn'vaɪt] **1** *vt* **person** einladen; *suggestions* bitten um. **to ~ sb to do sth** jdn bitten, etw zu tun; **to ~ sb in** jdn hereinbitten; **that's inviting trouble** das gibt bestimmt Ärger. **2** ['ɪnvaɪt] *n (col)* Einladung *f*.
♦ **invite out** *vt sep* einladen. **I ~d her ~** ich habe sie gefragt, ob sie mit mir ausgehen möchte.
inviting [ɪn'vaɪtɪŋ] *adj* einladend; *prospect, meal* verlockend.
invoice ['ɪnvɔɪs] **1** *n* Rechnung *f*. **2** *vt goods* in Rechnung stellen, berechnen. **to ~ sb for sth** jdm für etw eine Rechnung ausstellen.

invoke [ɪn'vəuk] vt the law etc anrufen; treaty etc sich berufen auf (+acc).

involuntary [ɪn'vɒləntərɪ] adj unbeabsichtigt; reaction etc unwillkürlich.

involve [ɪn'vɒlv] vt (a) (entangle) verwickeln (sb in sth jdn in etw acc); (include) beteiligen (sb in sth jdn an etw dat); (concern) betreffen. **to get** ~**d in sth** in etw (acc) verwickelt werden; **I didn't want to get** ~**d** ich wollte damit nichts zu tun haben; **I didn't want to get too** ~**d** ich wollte mich nicht zu sehr engagieren; **we are all** ~**d in the battle against inflation** der Kampf gegen die Inflation geht uns alle an; **to be** ~**d with sb** mit jdm zu tun haben; (sexually) mit jdm ein Verhältnis haben; **to get** ~**d with sb** mit jdm Kontakt bekommen; **he got** ~**d with a girl** er hat eine Beziehung mit einem Mädchen angefangen.
(b) (entail) zur Folge haben; (mean) bedeuten. **what does your job** ~? worin besteht Ihre Arbeit?; **to** ~ **a lot of hard work** mit viel Arbeit verbunden sein; **it would** ~ **moving to Germany** das würde bedeuten, nach Deutschland zu ziehen.

involved [ɪn'vɒlvd] adj kompliziert, umständlich (pej); story also verwickelt; style komplex.

involvement [ɪn'vɒlvmənt] n (being concerned with) Beteiligung f (in an +dat); (in quarrel, crime etc) Verwicklung f (in in +acc); (commitment) Engagement nt; (sexually) Verhältnis nt; (complexity) Kompliziertheit f. **the extent of his** ~ **with her/with his work** das Maß, in dem er sich bei ihr/bei seiner Arbeit engagiert hat; **we don't know the extent of his** ~ **in the plot** wir wissen nicht, wie weit er an dem Komplott beteiligt ist/war.

invulnerable [ɪn'vʌlnərəbl] adj unverwundbar; (lit, fig) position unangreifbar.

inward ['ɪnwəd] adj (inner) innere(r, s); life innerlich; thoughts innerste(r, s).

inwardly ['ɪnwədlɪ] adv innerlich.

inward(s) ['ɪnwəd(z)] adv nach innen.

iodine ['aɪədiːn] n Jod nt.

iota [aɪ'əutə] n Jota nt. **not one** ~ nicht ein Jota; **not an** ~ **of truth** kein Körnchen nt Wahrheit.

IOU [,aɪəu'juː] = **I owe you** Schuldschein m.

IQ = **intelligence quotient** IQ, Intelligenzquotient m.

IRA = **Irish Republican Army** IRA f.

Iran [ɪ'rɑːn] n (der) Iran.

Iranian [ɪ'reɪnɪən] **1** adj iranisch. **2** n (a) Iraner(in f) m. (b) (language) Iranisch nt.

Iraq [ɪ'rɑːk] n der Irak.

Iraqi [ɪ'rɑːkɪ] **1** adj irakisch. **2** n Iraker(in f) m.

irascible [ɪ'ræsɪbl] adj reizbar, jähzornig.

irate [aɪ'reɪt] adj zornig; crowd wütend.

Ireland ['aɪələnd] n Irland nt.

iris ['aɪərɪs] n (a) (of eye) Iris f. (b) (Bot) Iris, Schwertlilie f.

Irish ['aɪərɪʃ] **1** adj (a) irisch. ~**man** Ire m; ~ **Sea** Irische See; ~**woman** Irin f. (b) (hum col: illogical) unlogisch. **2** n (a) ~ **the** ~ die Iren pl. (b) (language) Irisch nt.

irksome ['ɜːksəm] adj lästig.

iron ['aɪən] **1** n (a) Eisen nt (also Golf). **a will of** ~ ein eiserner Wille; **to rule with a rod of** ~ mit eiserner Faust herrschen. (b) (electric ~) Bügeleisen nt. **to have more than one** ~ **in the fire** (fig) mehrere Eisen im Feuer haben; **he has too many** ~**s in the fire** er macht zuviel auf einmal; **to strike while the** ~ **is hot** (Prov) das Eisen schmieden, solange es heiß ist (Prov). **2** adj (lit, fig) eisern; (lit also) Eisen-. **3** vt clothes bügeln.
♦ **iron out** vt sep (lit, fig) ausbügeln.

iron: **I**~ **Age** n Eisenzeit f; **I**~ **Curtain** n Eiserner Vorhang; **the I**~ **Curtain countries** die Länder hinter dem Eisernen Vorhang.

ironic(al) [aɪ'rɒnɪk(əl)] adj ironisch; situation paradox.

ironically [aɪ'rɒnɪkəlɪ] adv ironisch. **and then,** ~ **enough, he turned up** komischerweise tauchte er dann auf.

ironing ['aɪənɪŋ] n (process) Bügeln nt; (clothes) Bügelwäsche f. **to do the** ~ (die Wäsche) bügeln; ~ **board** Bügelbrett nt.

iron: ~ **lung** n eiserne Lunge; ~**monger** n (Brit) Eisen(waren)händler(in f) m; ~ **ore** n Eisenerz nt. ~**works** n sing or pl Eisenhütte f.

irony ['aɪərənɪ] n Ironie f no pl. **the** ~ **of it is that ...** das Ironische daran ist, daß ...

irrational [ɪ'ræʃənl] adj irrational; (not sensible) unvernünftig.

irreconcilable [ɪ,rekən'saɪləbl] adj enemy unversöhnlich; differences unvereinbar.

irredeemable [,ɪrɪ'diːməbl] adj sinner (rettungslos) verloren; loss unwiederbringlich.

irrefutable [,ɪrɪ'fjuːtəbl] adj unwiderlegbar.

irregular [ɪ'regjʊləʳ] adj (a) (uneven, Gram) unregelmäßig; surface uneben. **to keep** ~ **hours** keine festen Zeiten haben. (b) behaviour ungehörig. **this is most** ~! das ist äußerst ungewöhnlich!

irregularity [ɪ,regjʊ'lærɪtɪ] n see adj (a) Unregelmäßigkeit f; Unebenheit f. (b) Ungehörigkeit f. **a slight** ~ **in the proceedings** ein kleiner Formfehler.

irrelevance [ɪ'reləvəns] n Irrelevanz f no pl; (of details also) Unwesentlichkeit f; (of titles, individuals) Bedeutungslosigkeit f.

irrelevant [ɪ'reləvənt] adj irrelevant (to für); information unwesentlich; titles etc bedeutungslos. **it is** ~ **whether he agrees or not** es ist belanglos, ob er zustimmt; **that's** ~ das spielt keine Rolle.

irreparable [ɪ'repərəbl] adj damage irreparabel, nicht wiedergutzumachend attr.

irreplaceable [,ɪrɪ'pleɪsəbl] adj unersetzlich.

irrepressible [,ɪrɪ'presəbl] adj urge unbezähmbar; optimism unerschütterlich; person nicht unterzukriegen; delight unbändig.

irreproachable [,ɪrɪ'prəutʃəbl] adj tadellos.

irresistible [,ɪrɪ'zɪstəbl] adj unwiderstehlich.

irresolute [ɪ'rezəluːt] adj unentschlossen.

irrespective [,ɪrɪ'spektɪv] adj: ~ **of** ungeachtet (+gen), unabhängig von; **candidates should be chosen** ~ **of sex** bei der Auswahl der Kandidaten sollte das Geschlecht keine Rolle spielen; ~ **of whether they want to or not** gleichgültig, ob sie wollen oder nicht.

irresponsibility ['ɪrɪ,spɒnsə'bɪlɪtɪ] n see adj Unverantwortlichkeit f; Verantwortungslosigkeit f.

irresponsible [,ɪrɪ'spɒnsəbl] adj behaviour unverantwortlich; person verantwortungslos.

irretrievable [,ɪrɪ'triːvəbl] adj nicht mehr wiederzubekommen; loss unersetzlich. ~ **breakdown of marriage** (unheilbare) Zerrüttung der Ehe.

irretrievably [,ɪrɪ'triːvəblɪ] adv ~ **lost** für immer verloren.

irreverent [ɪ'revərənt] adj behaviour, remark respektlos; (towards religion) ehrfurchtslos.

irreversible [,ɪrɪ'vɜːsəbl] adj judgment unwiderruflich.

irrevocable [ɪ'revəkəbl] adj unwiderruflich.

irrigate ['ɪrɪgeɪt] vt land, crop bewässern.

irrigation [,ɪrɪ'geɪʃən] n (Agr) Bewässerung f. ~ **canal** Bewässerungskanal m.

irritable ['ɪrɪtəbl] adj (as characteristic) reizbar; (on occasion) gereizt.

irritant ['ɪrɪtənt] n (Med) Reizerreger m.

irritate ['ɪrɪteɪt] vt (annoy) ärgern; (deliberately) reizen; (get on nerves) irritieren.

irritating ['ɪrɪteɪtɪŋ] adj ärgerlich; cough lästig. **I find his jokes most** ~ seine Witze regen mich wirklich auf; **you really are the most** ~ **person** du kannst einem wirklich auf die Nerven gehen.

irritation [,ɪrɪ'teɪʃən] n (a) (state) Ärger m; (act)

Ärgern *nt*; *(deliberate)* Reizen *nt*; *(thing that irritates)* Ärgernis *nt.* **(b)** *(Med)* Reizung *f.*

is [ɪz] *3rd person sing pres of* **be.**

Islam ['ɪzlɑːm] *n (religion)* der Islam; *(Moslems collectively)* Mohammedaner *pl.*

Islamic [ɪz'læmɪk] *adj* islamisch.

island ['aɪlənd] *n (lit, fig)* Insel *f.*

islander ['aɪləndəʳ] *n* Inselbewohner(in *f*) *m.*

isle [aɪl] *n (poet)* Eiland *nt (poet).* **the I∼ of Man** die Insel Man.

isn't ['ɪznt] = **is not.**

isolate ['aɪsəʊleɪt] *vt* **(a)** isolieren; *(cut off also)* abschneiden. **to ∼ oneself from the world** sich von der Welt zurückziehen. **(b)** *(pinpoint)* herausfinden; *essential factor* herauskristallisieren.

isolated ['aɪsəʊleɪtɪd] *adj* **(a)** *(cut off)* abgeschnitten, isoliert; *(remote)* abgelegen; *existence* zurückgezogen. **(b)** *(single)* einzeln. **∼ instances** Einzelfälle *pl.*

isolation [ˌaɪsəʊ'leɪʃən] **(a)** *(act)* *(separation)* Absonderung, Isolierung *(esp Med) f*; *(pinpointing)* Herausfinden *nt*; *(of essential factor)* Herauskristallisierung *f.* **(b)** *(state)* Isolation *f*; *(remoteness)* Abgeschiedenheit *f.* **to keep a patient in ∼** einen Patienten isolieren; **to live in ∼** zurückgezogen leben; **to consider sth in ∼** etw gesondert betrachten; **it doesn't make much sense in ∼** ohne Zusammenhang ist es ziemlich unverständlich.

isolation: ∼ hospital *n* Krankenhaus *nt* für ansteckende Krankheiten; **∼ ward** *n* Isolierstation *f.*

isotope ['aɪsəʊtəʊp] *n* Isotop *nt.*

Israel ['ɪzreɪl] *n* Israel *nt.*

Israeli [ɪz'reɪlɪ] **1** *adj* israelisch. **2** *n* Israeli *mf.*

issue ['ɪʃuː] **1** *vt passport* ausstellen; *shares, banknotes, rations* ausgeben; *order, warning* erteilen *(to dat)*; *details* bekanntgeben; *(publish) book* herausgeben. **to ∼ sth to sb/to ∼ sb with sth** etw an jdn ausgeben; **to ∼ sb with a visa** jdm ein Visum ausstellen; **a warrant for his arrest was ∼d** gegen ihn wurde Haftbefehl erlassen.

2 *vi (liquid, gas)* austreten; *(smoke)* (heraus)quellen; *(sound)* (heraus)dringen; *(people etc)* (heraus)strömen.

3 *n* **(a)** *(question)* Frage *f*; *(matter also)* Angelegenheit *f*; *(problematic)* Problem *nt.* **the ∼ is whether ...** die Frage ist, ob ...; **what is at ∼?** worum geht es?; **that's not at ∼** das steht nicht zur Debatte; **to take ∼ with sb over sth** jdm in etw *(dat)* widersprechen; **to make an ∼ of sth** etw aufbauschen; **to evade the ∼** ausweichen; **to face the ∼** den Tatsachen ins Auge sehen.

(b) *(outcome)* Ergebnis *nt.* **that decided the ∼** das war ausschlaggebend; **to force the ∼** eine Entscheidung erzwingen.

(c) *(of banknotes, shares etc)* Ausgabe *f*; *(of shares also)* Emission *f.* **place of ∼** *(of tickets)* Ausgabestelle *f*; *(of passports)* Ausstellungsort *m*; **date of ∼** *(of tickets)* Ausstellungsdatum *nt*; *(of stamps)* Ausgabetag *m.* **the ∼ of blankets/guns to the troops** die Versorgung der Truppen mit Decken/die Ausrüstung der Truppen mit Gewehren.

(d) *(of book etc)* Herausgabe *f*; *(book etc)* Ausgabe *f.*

(e) *(Jur: offspring)* Nachkommenschaft *f.*

it [ɪt] *pron* **(a)** *(when replacing noun) (subject)* er/sie/es; *(dir obj)* ihn/sie/es; *(indir obj)* ihm/ihr/ihm. **of ∼** davon; **behind/over** *etc* **∼** dahinter/darüber *etc*; **who is ∼?** — ∼**'s me** wer ist da? — **ich (bin's); what is ∼?** was ist es *or* das?; *(matter)* was ist los?; **that's not ∼** *(not the trouble)* das ist es (gar) nicht; **the worst of ∼ is that ...** das Schlimmste daran ist, daß ...

(b) *(indef subject)* es. ∼**'s raining** es regnet; **if ∼ hadn't been for her, we would have come** wenn sie nicht gewesen wäre, wären wir gekommen; **why is ∼ always me who has to ...?** warum muß (ausgerechnet) immer ich ...?; **I've known ∼ happen** ich habe es (schon) erlebt; ∼**'s Friday tomorrow** morgen ist Freitag; ∼ **was him who asked her** er hat sie gefragt; ∼**'s his appearance I object to** ich habe nur etwas gegen sein Äußeres; ∼ **was for his sake that she lied** nur um seinetwillen hat sie gelogen.

(c) *(col phrases)* **that's ∼!** *(agreement)* ja, genau!; *(annoyed)* jetzt reicht's mir!; **that's ∼ (then)!** *(achievement)* (so,) das wär's!; *(disappointment)* ja, das war's dann wohl.

IT = information technology.

Italian [ɪ'tæljən] **1** *adj* italienisch. **2** *n* **(a)** Italiener(in *f*) *m.* **(b)** *(language)* Italienisch *nt.*

italic [ɪ'tælɪk] **1** *adj* kursiv. **2** *n* ∼**s** *pl* Kursivschrift *f*; **in** ∼**s** kursiv (gedruckt).

Italy ['ɪtəlɪ] *n* Italien *nt.*

itch [ɪtʃ] **1** *n* **(a)** Jucken *nt*, Juckreiz *m.* **I have an ∼** mich juckt es. **(b)** *(col: urge)* Lust *f.* **I have an ∼ to do sth** es juckt *(col)* mich, etw zu tun. **2** *vi* **(a)** jucken. **my back ∼es** mein Rücken juckt (mich).

(b) *(col)* **he is ∼ing to ...** es juckt *(col)* ihn, zu ...; **he's ∼ing for a fight** er ist auf Streit aus.

itchy ['ɪtʃɪ] *adj (+er) (itching)* juckend. **it's ∼ es** juckt; **I've got ∼ feet** *(col)* ich will hier weg *(col)*; *(want to travel also)* mich packt das Fernweh.

it'd ['ɪtəd] = **it would; it had.**

item ['aɪtəm] *n* **(a)** *(on agenda etc)* Punkt *m*; *(Comm: in account book)* (Rechnungs)posten *m*; *(article)* Gegenstand *m*; *(in catalogue etc)* Artikel *m*; *(Brit: in variety show)* Nummer *f.* **(b)** *(of news)* Bericht *m*; *(short, Rad, TV also)* Meldung *f.* **a short news ∼** eine Zeitungsnotiz/eine Kurzmeldung.

itemize ['aɪtəmaɪz] *vt* einzeln aufführen. ∼**d account** spezifizierte Rechnung.

itinerant [ɪ'tɪnərənt] *adj* umherziehend, Wander-; *worker* Saison-. ∼ **theatre group** Wandertruppe *f.*

itinerary [aɪ'tɪnərərɪ] *n (route)* (Reise)route *f.*

it'll ['ɪtl] = **it will; it shall.**

its [ɪts] *poss adj* sein(e)/ihr(e)/sein(e).

it's [ɪts] = **it is; it has** *(as aux).*

itself [ɪt'self] *pron* **(a)** *(reflexive)* sich. **(b)** *(emph)* selbst. **and now we come to the text ∼** und jetzt kommen wir zum Text selbst; **the frame ∼ is worth £1,000** der Rahmen allein ist £1.000 wert; **the amount in ∼** der Betrag an sich. **(c)** **by ∼** *(alone)* allein; *(automatically)* von selbst, selbsttätig.

ITV *(Brit)* = **Independent Television.**

IUD = intra-uterine device Pessar *nt.*

I've [aɪv] = **I have.**

ivory ['aɪvərɪ] **1** *n (also colour)* Elfenbein *nt.* **2** *adj* elfenbeinern; *(colour)* elfenbeinfarben.

Ivory Coast *n* Elfenbeinküste *f.*

ivory tower *n (fig)* Elfenbeinturm *m.*

ivy ['aɪvɪ] *n* Efeu *m.*

Ivy League *n (US)* Eliteuniversitäten *der* USA.

J

J, j [dʒeɪ] n J, j nt.

jab [dʒæb] **1** vt (with stick, elbow etc) stoßen; (with knife also) stechen. **he ~bed his elbow into my side** er stieß mir den Ellbogen in die Seite; **a sharp ~bing pain** ein scharfer, stechender Schmerz. **2** vi stoßen (at sb with sth mit etw nach jdm). **3** n (with stick, elbow) Stoß m; (with needle, knife) Stich m; (col: injection) Spritze f; (Boxing) (kurze) Gerade.

jabber ['dʒæbər] **1** vt (daher)plappern (col); poem herunterrasseln (col). **2** vi (also ~ away) plappern, quasseln (col). **they were ~ing away in Spanish** sie quasselten (col) Spanisch.

jack [dʒæk] n **(a)** (Aut) Wagenheber m. **(b)** (Cards) Bube m.

♦ **jack in** vt sep (col) job etc aufgeben; girlfriend Schluß machen mit (col).

♦ **jack up** vt sep car aufbocken.

jackal ['dʒækɔːl] n Schakal m.

jackass ['dʒækæs] n (col: person) Esel m (col).

jackdaw ['dʒækdɔː] n Dohle f.

jacket ['dʒækɪt] n **(a)** (garment) Jacke f; (man's ~ also) Jackett nt. **(b)** (of book, US: of record) Hülle f. **(c)** (esp US: for papers etc) Umschlag m. **(d)** ~ **potatoes** in der Schale gebackene Kartoffeln pl. **(e)** (Tech: of boiler etc) Mantel m.

jack: ~-**in-the-box** n Kasteteufel m; ~**knife** vi **the lorry** ~**knifed** der Sattelschlepper hat sich quergestellt; ~-**of-all-trades** n Alleskönner m; **to be (a)** ~-**of-all-trades (and master of none)** (prov) ein Hansdampf m in allen Gassen sein; ~**pot** m Pott m (col); (in lottery etc) Hauptgewinn m; **to hit the** ~**pot** (in lottery) den Hauptgewinn bekommen; (fig) das große Los ziehen; **J~ Robinson** [,dʒæk'rɒbɪnsən] n: **before you could say J~ Robinson** (col) im Nu.

jacuzzi [dʒə'kuːtsɪ] n Whirlpool m.

jade [dʒeɪd] n **1** (stone) Jade m or f; (colour) Jadegrün nt. **2** adj Jade-; (colour) jadegrün.

jaded ['dʒeɪdɪd] adj (physically) abgespannt; (permanently) verbraucht; (mentally) abgestumpft; appearance verbraucht.

jagged ['dʒægɪd] adj zackig; wound, tear ausgefranst; coastline zerklüftet.

jaguar ['dʒægjʊər] n Jaguar m.

jail [dʒeɪl] **1** n (stone) in. in ~ im Gefängnis; **to go to** ~ ins Gefängnis kommen. **2** vt einsperren.

jail: ~**bird** n (col) Knastbruder m (col); ~**break** n Ausbruch m (aus dem Gefängnis).

jailer ['dʒeɪlər] n Gefängniswärter(in f) m.

jalop(p)y [dʒə'lɒpɪ] n (col) alte Mühle (col).

jam[1] [dʒæm] n Marmelade f. **you want** ~ **on it too, do you?** (Brit col) du kriegst wohl nie genug?

jam[2] **1** n **(a)** (crowd) Gedränge nt. **(b)** (traffic ~) (Verkehrs)stau m. **(c)** (blockage in machine etc) Stockung f. **(d)** (col: tight spot) **to be in a** ~ in der Klemme sitzen (col); **to get into a** ~ mit sth mit etw Schwierigkeiten haben; **to get sb out of a** ~ jdm aus der Klemme helfen (col).

2 vt **(a)** (make stick) window etc verklemmen; brakes etc blockieren; (wedge) festklemmen; (between two things) einklemmen. **it's** ~**med** es klemmt; **he** ~**med his finger in the door** er hat sich (dat) den Finger in der Tür eingeklemmt. **(b)** (cram) stopfen, quetschen (into in +acc). **we**

were ~**med together** wir waren zusammengedrängt. **(c)** (block) street etc verstopfen, blockieren; radio station stören. **a street** ~**med with cars** eine verstopfte Straße; **all the lines are** ~**med** alle Leitungen sind besetzt. **3** vi **(a)** **the crowd** ~**med into the bus** die Menschenmenge zwängte sich in den Bus. **(b)** (become stuck) (brake) sich verklemmen; (door etc) klemmen.

♦ **jam in** vt sep **(a)** (wedge in) einkeilen. **he was** ~**med** ~ **by the crowd** er war in der Menge eingekeilt. **(b)** (press in) (herein)stopfen in (+acc).

♦ **jam on** vt sep **to** ~ ~ **the brakes** eine Vollbremsung machen. **2** vi (brakes) klemmen.

Jamaica [dʒə'meɪkə] n Jamaika nt.

Jamaican [dʒə'meɪkən] adj jamaikanisch.

jam: ~ **jar** n Marmeladenglas nt; ~-**packed** adj überfüllt, proppenvoll (col).

jangle ['dʒæŋgl] **1** vi (money) klimpern (col); (bells) bimmeln (col); (chains) rasseln. **2** vt money klimpern mit; keys also, chains rasseln mit.

janitor ['dʒænɪtər] n Hausmeister m; (of flats also) Hauswart m.

January ['dʒænjʊərɪ] n Januar m; see **September**.

Japan [dʒə'pæn] n Japan nt.

Japanese [,dʒæpə'niːz] **1** adj japanisch. **2** n **(a)** Japaner(in f) m. **(b)** (language) Japanisch nt.

jar[1] [dʒɑːr] n (for jam etc) Glas nt; (without handle) Topf m; (with handle) Krug m.

jar[2] **1** n (jolt) Ruck m; (fig) Schock m. **2** vi (note) schauerlich klingen; (colours) sich beißen (col); (ideas) sich nicht vertragen, nicht harmonieren (with mit). **this** ~**s** stylistically das fällt stilmäßig aus dem Rahmen; **this noise** ~**s on my nerves** dieser Lärm geht mir auf die Nerven; **her voice** ~**s on my ears** ihre Stimme geht mir durch und durch. **3** vi building etc erschüttern; back sich (dat) stauchen; (fig) einen Schock versetzen (+dat). **he must have** ~**red the camera** er muß mit dem Fotoapparat gewackelt haben.

jargon ['dʒɑːgən] n Jargon m (pej), Fachsprache f.

jarring ['dʒɑːrɪŋ] adj sound gellend; accent störend; colours sich beißend attr (col).

jasmin(e) ['dʒæzmɪn] n Jasmin m.

jaundice ['dʒɔːndɪs] n Gelbsucht f.

jaundiced ['dʒɔːndɪst] adj **(a)** (lit) gelbsüchtig. **(b)** attitude zynisch. **to take a** ~ **view of sth** in bezug auf etw (acc) zynisch sein.

jaunt [dʒɔːnt] n Trip m, Spritztour f. **to go for a** ~ eine Spritztour machen.

jaunty ['dʒɔːntɪ] adj (+er) fröhlich; hat flott; attitude sorglos, unbekümmert. **he wore his hat at a** ~ **angle** er hatte den Hut keck aufgesetzt.

javelin ['dʒævlɪn] n Speer m. **(throwing) the** ~ Speerwerfen nt.

jaw [dʒɔː] n **(a)** Kiefer m. **with its prey between its** ~**s** mit der Beute im Maul; **the** ~**s of death** die Klauen pl des Todes. **(b)** (of vice) Backe f.

jawbone ['dʒɔːbəʊn] n Kieferknochen m.

jay [dʒeɪ] n Eichelhäher m.

jaywalker ['dʒeɪ,wɔːkər] n unachtsamer Fußgänger, unachtsame Fußgängerin.

jazz [dʒæz] **1** n (Mus) Jazz m. ... **and all that** ~ ... und all so'n Zeug (col). **2** attr band, music Jazz-.

♦ **jazz up** vt sep aufmöbeln (col).

jealous ['dʒeləs] *adj lover etc* eifersüchtig; *(envious: of sb's success etc)* neidisch. **to be ~ of sb** auf jdn eifersüchtig sein/jdn beneiden.

jealousy ['dʒeləsɪ] *n see adj (of* auf *+acc)* Eifersucht *f;* Neid *m*.

jeans [dʒiːnz] *npl* Jeans *pl*.

jeep [dʒiːp] *n* Jeep ® *m*.

jeer [dʒɪəʳ] **1** *n (remark)* höhnische Bemerkung; *(shout)* Buhruf *m; (laughter)* Hohngelächter *nt*. **2** *vi see n* höhnische Bemerkungen machen; buhen; höhnisch lachen. **to ~ at sb** jdn (laut) verhöhnen.

jeering ['dʒɪərɪŋ] **1** *adj* höhnisch. **2** *n see* **jeer 1**.

jelly ['dʒelɪ] *n* Gelee *nt; (esp Brit: dessert)* Wackelpeter *m (col)*.

jellyfish ['dʒelɪfɪʃ] *n* Qualle *f*.

jeopardize ['dʒepədaɪz] *vt* gefährden.

jeopardy ['dʒepədɪ] *n* Gefahr *f*. **in ~** gefährdet; **to put sb/sth in ~** jdn/etw gefährden.

jerk [dʒɜːk] **1** *n* **(a)** Ruck *m; (jump)* Satz *m; (twitch)* Zuckung *f*. **to give sth a ~** einer Sache *(dat)* einen Ruck geben; *rope* an etw *(dat)* ruckartig ziehen; **the train stopped with a ~** der Zug hielt mit einem Ruck an. **(b)** *(col: person)* Trottel *(col) m*. **2** *vt* rucken an *(+dat)*. **the impact ~ed his head forward** beim Aufprall wurde sein Kopf nach vorn geschleudert; **he ~ed the book out of my hand** er riß mir das Buch aus der Hand. **3** *vi (rope)* rucken; *(move jerkily)* ruckeln *(col); (body, muscle)* zucken; *(head)* zurückzucken. **he ~ed away from me** er sprang mit einem Satz von mir weg; **the car ~ed forward** der Wagen machte einen Satz nach vorne; **the car ~ed to a stop** das Auto hielt ruckweise an.

jerky ['dʒɜːkɪ] *adj (+er)* ruckartig; *speech also, style* abgehackt. **a ~ ride** eine holprige Fahrt.

Jerry ['dʒerɪ] *n (col)* Deutsche(r) *m*.

jerry: **~ built** *adj* schlampig gebaut; **~ can** *n* großer (Blech)kanister.

jersey ['dʒɜːzɪ] *n* Pullover *m; (Ftbl etc)* Trikot *nt*.

jest [dʒest] **1** *n (joke)* Scherz, Witz *m*. **in ~** im Spaß. **2** *vi* scherzen. **to ~ about sth** über etw *(acc)* Witze machen.

jester ['dʒestəʳ] *n* **(a)** *(Hist)* Narr *m*. **(b)** *(joker)* Spaßvogel, Witzbold *(col) m*.

Jesuit ['dʒezjuɪt] *n* Jesuit *m*.

Jesus ['dʒiːzəs] *n* Jesus *m*. **~ Christ** Jesus Christus; **~ Christ!** *(col)* Herrgott (noch mal)! *(col)*.

jet¹ [dʒet] *n* **(a)** Strahl *m*. **a ~ of water** ein Wasserstrahl. **(b)** *(nozzle)* Düse *f*. **(c)** *(also ~ plane)* Düsenflugzeug *nt*, Jet *m (col)*.

jet² *n (Miner)* Gagat *m*. **~ black** pechschwarz.

jet: **~ engine** *n* Düsentriebwerk *nt;* **~lag** *n* Schwierigkeiten *pl* durch den Zeitunterschied; **~lagged** *adj* **to be ~lagged** durch den Zeitunterschied völlig fertig sein; **~ plane** *n* Düsenflugzeug *nt;* **~-propelled** *adj* mit Düsenantrieb, Düsen-; **~ set** *n* Jet-set *m*.

jettison ['dʒetɪsn] *vt (lit, fig)* über Bord werfen; *unwanted articles* wegwerfen.

jetty ['dʒetɪ] *n (breakwater)* Hafendamm *m; (landing pier)* Pier *m*, Landungsbrücke *f*.

Jew [dʒuː] *n* Jude *m*, Jüdin *f*.

jewel ['dʒuːəl] *n* **(a)** *(gem)* Edelstein *m*, Juwel *nt (geh); (piece of jewellery)* Schmuckstück *nt*. **(b)** *(of watch)* Stein *m*.

jeweller, *(US)* **jeweler** ['dʒuːələʳ] *n* Juwelier *m; (making jewellery)* Goldschmied *m*.

jewellery, *(US)* **jewelry** ['dʒuːəlrɪ] *n* Schmuck *m no pl*. **a piece of ~** ein Schmuckstück *nt*.

Jewess ['dʒuːɪs] *n* Jüdin *f*.

Jewish ['dʒuːɪʃ] *adj* jüdisch; *(pej col: mean)* knickerig *(col)*.

jib [dʒɪb] **1** *n (of crane)* Dreharm *m; (Naut)* Klüver *m*. **2** *vi* **to ~ at sth** sich gegen etw sträuben.

jibe [dʒaɪb] *n, vi =* **gibe**.

jiffy ['dʒɪfɪ], **jiff** [dʒɪf] *n (col)* Minütchen *nt (col)*. **I won't be a ~** ich komme sofort; *(back soon)* ich

bin sofort wieder da; **in a ~** sofort.

jig [dʒɪg] *n* **(a)** *(dance)* lebhafter Volkstanz. **(b)** *(Tech)* Spannvorrichtung *f*.

jigsaw ['dʒɪgsɔː] *n (also ~ puzzle)* Puzzle(spiel) *nt*.

jilt [dʒɪlt] *vt lover* den Laufpaß geben *(+dat)*. **~ed** verschmäht.

jingle ['dʒɪŋgl] **1** *n* **(a)** *(of keys etc)* Klimpern *nt; (of bells)* Bimmeln *nt*. **(b)** *(catchy verse)* Spruch *m; (for remembering)* Merkspruch *m*. **advertising ~** Werbespruch *m*. **2** *vi (keys etc)* klimpern; *(bells)* bimmeln. **3** *vt keys* klimpern mit; *bells* bimmeln lassen.

jingoism ['dʒɪŋgəʊɪzəm] *n* Hurrapatriotismus *m*.

jinx [dʒɪŋks] *n* **there's a ~ on it** das ist verhext.

jitters ['dʒɪtəz] *npl (col)* **the ~** das große Zittern *(col);* **to give sb the ~** jdn ganz rappelig machen *(col)*.

jittery ['dʒɪtərɪ] *adj (col)* nervös, rappelig *(col)*.

jive [dʒaɪv] **1** *n (dance)* Swing *m*. **2** *vi* Swing tanzen.

job [dʒɒb] *n* **(a)** *(piece of work)* Arbeit *f*. **I have a ~ to do** ich habe zu tun; **it's quite a ~ to paint the house** das Haus zu streichen ist eine Heidenarbeit *(col);* **he's on the ~** *(col: at work)* er ist bei der Arbeit; **he made a good job of it** er hat dabei gute Arbeit geleistet; **we have a lot of ~s on just now** wir haben zur Zeit viele Aufträge; **he knows his ~** er versteht sein Handwerk.

(b) *(employment)* Stelle *f*, Job *m (col)*. **500 ~s lost** 500 Arbeitsplätze verlorengegangen; **to bring new ~s to a region** in einer Gegend neue Arbeitsplätze schaffen.

(c) *(duty)* Aufgabe *f*. **I'm only doing my ~** ich tue nur meine Pflicht.

(d) that's a good ~! so ein Glück; **it's a good ~ I brought my cheque book** nur gut, daß ich mein Scheckbuch mitgenommen habe; **to give sb/sth up as a bad ~** jdn/etw aufgeben; **that should do the ~** das müßte hinhauen *(col);* **this is just the ~** das ist genau das richtige; **she has a ~ getting up the stairs** es ist gar nicht einfach für sie, die Treppe raufzukommen.

(e) *(col: crime)* Ding *nt (col)*. **remember that bank ~?** erinnerst du dich an das große Ding in der Bank? *(col)*.

(f) *(col: person, thing)* Ding *nt*. **his new car's a lovely little ~** sein neues Auto ist wirklich große Klasse *(col)*.

job: **~ centre** *n (Brit)* Arbeitsamt *nt;* **~ creation scheme** *n* Arbeitsbeschaffungsprogramm *nt;* **~ description** *n* Tätigkeitsbeschreibung *f;* **~ hunting** *n* Arbeitssuche *f;* **~less** *1 adj* arbeitslos; **2** *n* **the ~less** *pl* die Arbeitslosen *pl;* **~ lot** *n (Comm)* (Waren)posten *m;* **~ satisfaction** *n* Zufriedenheit *f* am Arbeitsplatz.

jockey ['dʒɒkɪ] **1** *n* Jockey, Rennreiter(in *f*) *m*. **2** *vi* **to ~ for position** *(lit)* sich in eine gute Position zu drängeln versuchen; *(fig)* rangeln.

jockstrap ['dʒɒkstræp] *n* Suspensorium *nt*.

jocular ['dʒɒkjʊləʳ] *adj* lustig, spaßig. **to be in a ~ mood** zu Scherzen aufgelegt sein.

jodhpurs ['dʒɒdpəz] *npl* Reithose(n *pl*) *f*.

jog [dʒɒg] **1** *vt elbow etc* stoßen an *(+acc)* or gegen; *person* anstoßen. **to ~ sb's memory** jds Gedächtnis *(dat)* nachhelfen. **2** *vi* trotten; *(Sport)* Dauerlauf machen, joggen. **3** *n (run)* trabender Lauf, Trott *m; (Sport)* Dauerlauf *m*. **to go for a ~** *(Sport)* einen Dauerlauf machen, joggen gehen.

♦ **jog along** *vi (person, worker, industry)* vor sich *(acc)* hinwursteln *(col); (work)* seinen Gang gehen.

jogging ['dʒɒgɪŋ] *n* Dauerlauf *m*, Joggen *nt*. **he goes ~** er macht Jogging.

join [dʒɔɪn] **1** *vt* **(a)** *(lit, fig: connect)* verbinden *(to* mit); *(attach also)* anfügen *(to* an *+acc)*. **to ~ battle (with the enemy)** den Kampf mit dem Feind aufnehmen; **to ~ hands** *(lit, fig)* sich *(dat)* die Hände reichen.

(b) *(become member of)* army gehen zu; *political party, club* beitreten *(+dat)*, eintreten in *(+acc)*; *university (as student)* anfangen an *(+dat)*; *(as staff)* firm anfangen bei; *group of people* sich anschließen *(+dat)*.

(c) he ~ed us in France er stieß in Frankreich zu uns; I ~ed him at the station ich traf mich mit ihm am Bahnhof; I'll ~ you in five minutes ich bin in fünf Minuten bei Ihnen; *(follow you)* ich komme in fünf Minuten nach; may I ~ you? kann ich mich Ihnen anschließen?; *(sit with you)* darf ich mich zu Ihnen setzen?; will you ~ us? wollen Sie uns nicht Gesellschaft leisten?; *(come with us)* kommen Sie mit?; do ~ us for lunch wollen Sie nicht mit uns essen?; will you ~ me in a drink? trinken Sie ein Glas mit mir?

(d) *(river)* another river, the sea münden or fließen in *(+acc)*; *(road)* another road münden auf *(+acc)*.

2 *vi* **(a)** *(also ~ together)* *(two parts)* *(be attached)* (miteinander) verbunden sein; *(be attachable)* sich (miteinander) verbinden lassen; *(meet, be adjacent)* zusammentreffen; *(estates)* aneinander grenzen; *(rivers)* zusammenfließen; *(roads)* sich treffen. **they** all ~ed together to get her a present sie taten sich alle zusammen, um ihr ein Geschenk zu kaufen. **(b)** *(club member)* beitreten, Mitglied werden.

3 *n* Naht(stelle) *f*; *(in pipe, knitting)* Verbindungsstelle *f*.

♦ **join in** *vi (in activity)* mitmachen *(prep obj bei)*; *(in game also)* mitspielen *(prep obj bei)*; ~ ~, everybody! *(in song etc)* alle (mitmachen)!; everybody ~ed ~ the chorus alle sangen alle zusammen den Refrain.

♦ **join up 1** *vi* **(a)** *(Mil)* zum Militär gehen. **(b)** *(meet: road etc)* sich treffen; *(join forces)* sich zusammenschließen, sich zusammentun *(col)*. **2** *vt sep* (miteinander) verbinden.

joiner ['dʒɔɪnər] *n* Tischler, Schreiner *m*.

joinery ['dʒɔɪnərɪ] *n (trade)* Tischlerei *f*.

joint [dʒɔɪnt] **1** *n* **(a)** *(Anat)* Gelenk *nt*. **(b)** *(join)* *(in woodwork)* Fuge *f*; *(in pipe etc)* Verbindung(sstelle) *f*; *(welded etc)* Naht(stelle) *f*. **(c)** *(Cook)* Braten *m*. **a** ~ **of beef** ein Rinderbraten *m*. **(d)** *(col: place)* Laden *(col) m*. **(e)** *(col: of marijuana)* Joint *m (col)*. **2** *adj attr* gemeinsam; action, work also Gemeinschafts-; owner(ship) Mit-. ~ **account** gemeinsames Konto; **the** essay was a ~ **effort** der Aufsatz ist in Gemeinschaftsarbeit entstanden; ~ **heir** Miterbe *m*, Miterbin *f*; ~ **stock company** Aktiengesellschaft *f*; ~ **venture** Gemeinschaftsunternehmen, Joint-venture *nt*.

jointly ['dʒɔɪntlɪ] *adv* gemeinsam.

joist [dʒɔɪst] *n* Balken *m*.

joke [dʒəʊk] **1** *n* Witz *m*; *(prank)* Streich *m*; *(laughing stock)* Gespött *nt*. for a ~ zum Spaß, aus Jux *(col)*; I don't see the ~ ich möchte wissen, was daran so lustig sein soll; he treats it as a big ~ für ihn ist das ein Witz; he can't take a ~ er versteht keinen Spaß; it's no ~ das ist nicht witzig; this is getting beyond a ~ das geht (langsam) zu weit; the ~ was on me der Spaß ging auf meine Kosten; to play a ~ on sb jdm einen Streich spielen; to make ~s about sth sich über etw lustig machen. **2** *vi* Witze machen *(about über +acc)*; *(pull sb's leg)* Spaß machen. I'm not joking ich meine das ernst; you must be joking! das ist ja wohl nicht Ihr Ernst!

joker ['dʒəʊkər] *n* **(a)** *(person)* Witzbold, Spaßvogel *m*. **(b)** *(Cards)* Joker *m*.

joking ['dʒəʊkɪŋ] **1** *adj* tone scherzhaft, spaßend. **2** *n* Witze *pl*. ~ **apart** Spaß beiseite.

jolly ['dʒɒlɪ] **1** *adj (+er) (merry)* fröhlich, vergnügt. **2** *adv (Brit col)* you are ~ lucky Sie haben vielleicht Glück *(col)*; ~ **good** prima *(col)*; that's ~

kind of you das ist furchtbar nett von Ihnen; you ~ **well will go!** und ob du gehst!

jolt [dʒəʊlt] **1** *vi (vehicle)* holpern; *(give one ~)* einen Ruck machen. to ~ **along** rüttelnd entlangfahren; to ~ **to a halt** ruckweise anhalten. **2** *vt (lit) (shake)* durchrütteln; *(once)* einen Ruck geben *(+dat)*; *(fig)* aufrütteln. it ~ed him into action das hat ihn aufgerüttelt. **3** *n (jerk)* Ruck *m*. it gave me a ~ *(fig)* das hat mir einen Schock versetzt.

Jordan ['dʒɔːdn] *n* Jordanien *nt*; *(river)* Jordan *m*.

joss stick ['dʒɒsstɪk] *n* Räucherstäbchen *nt*.

jostle ['dʒɒsl] **1** *vi* drängeln. he ~d **against me** er rempelte mich an. **2** *vt* anrempeln, schubsen. he was ~d **along with the crowd** die Menge schob ihn mit sich.

jot [dʒɒt] *n (of truth)* Funken *m*, Körnchen *nt*.

♦ **jot down** *vt sep* sich *(dat)* notieren.

♦ **jotter** ['dʒɒtər] *n (note pad)* Notizblock *m*; *(notebook)* Notizheft(chen) *nt*.

jottings ['dʒɒtɪŋz] *npl* Notizen *pl*.

journal ['dʒɜːnl] *n (periodical)* Zeitschrift *f*; *(diary)* Tagebuch *nt*.

journalese [ˌdʒɜːnəˈliːz] *n* Zeitungsjargon *m*.

journalism ['dʒɜːnəlɪzəm] *n* Journalismus *m*.

journalist ['dʒɜːnəlɪst] *n* Journalist(in *f*) *m*.

journey ['dʒɜːnɪ] **1** *n* Reise *f*; *(by train, car also)* Fahrt *f*. to go on a ~ eine Reise machen, verreisen; it is a 50 mile ~ es liegt 50 Meilen entfernt; a two day ~ eine Zwei-Tage-Reise; a train ~ eine Zugfahrt; the ~ home die Heimfahrt. **2** *vi* reisen.

jovial ['dʒəʊvɪəl] *adj* fröhlich; welcome herzlich.

jowl [dʒaʊl] *n (jaw)* (Unter)kiefer *m*; *(often pl: cheek)* Backe *f*.

joy [dʒɔɪ] *n* Freude *f*. to my great ~ zu meiner großen Freude; I wish you ~ (of it)! *(iro)* na dann viel Spaß!; I didn't get much ~ *(Brit col)* ich hatte nicht viel Erfolg; did you get any ~? hat es geklappt? *(col)*.

joyful ['dʒɔɪfʊl] *adj* freudig, froh.

joyous ['dʒɔɪəs] *adj (liter)* freudig, froh.

joy: ~**ride** *n* Spritztour *f (in einem gestohlenen Auto)*; ~**stick** *n (Aviat)* Steuerknüppel *m*; *(Comp)* Joystick *m*.

JP *(Brit)* = **Justice of the Peace.**

Jr = **junior** jr., jun.

jubilant ['dʒuːbɪlənt] *adj mood* Jubel-; crowd jubelnd; face strahlend *attr*. **they gave him a** ~ **welcome** sie empfingen ihn mit Jubel; **he was** ~ **at the news** er war überglücklich, als er die Nachricht hörte.

jubilation [ˌdʒuːbɪˈleɪʃən] *n* Jubel *m*.

jubilee ['dʒuːbɪliː] *n* Jubiläum *nt*.

judge [dʒʌdʒ] **1** *n (Jur)* Richter(in *f*) *m*; *(of competition)* Preisrichter(in *f*) *m*; *(Sport)* Schiedsrichter(in *f*) *m*; *(fig)* Kenner *m*. **to be a good** ~ **of character** ein guter Menschenkenner sein; **to be a good** ~ **of wine** ein Weinkenner sein. **2** *vt* **(a)** *(Jur)* person die Verhandlung führen über *(+acc)*; case verhandeln; *(God)* richten. **(b)** competition beurteilen, bewerten; *(Sport)* Schiedsrichter sein bei. **(c)** *(fig: pass judgement on)* ein Urteil fällen über *(+acc)*. **you shouldn't** ~ **people by appearances** Sie sollten Menschen nicht nach ihrem Äußeren beurteilen. **(d)** *(consider, assess)* halten für. **you can** ~ **for yourself how upset I was** Sie können sich *(dat)* denken, wie bestürzt ich war; **I can't** ~ **whether he was right or wrong** ich kann nicht beurteilen, ob er recht oder unrecht hatte. **(e)** *(estimate)* distance etc einschätzen. **he** ~**d the moment well** er hat den richtigen Augenblick abgepaßt.

3 *vi (Jur)* Richter sein; *(God)* richten; *(at competition)* Preisrichter sein; *(Sport)* Schiedsrichter sein; *(fig)* *(pass judgement)* ein Urteil fällen; *(form an opinion)* (be)urteilen. **as far as one can** ~ soweit man (es) beurteilen kann; **judging by** or

from sth nach etw zu urteilen; **judging by appearances** dem Aussehen nach; **(you can) ~ for yourself** beurteilen Sie das selbst.

judg(e)ment ['dʒʌdʒmənt] n *(Jur)* (Gerichts)urteil nt; *(opinion)* Ansicht f, Urteil nt; *(value ~)* Werturteil nt; *(estimation)* Einschätzung f; *(discernment)* Urteilsvermögen nt. **to pass ~** *(lit, fig)* ein Urteil fällen, das Urteil sprechen *(on* über *+acc)*; **an error of ~** eine Fehleinschätzung; **in my ~** meiner Meinung nach; **against my better ~** gegen meine Überzeugung; **it's a question of ~** das ist Ansichtssache.

Judg(e)ment Day n Tag m des Jüngsten Gerichts.

judicial [dʒuːˈdɪʃəl] adj *(Jur)* gerichtlich, Justiz-.

judiciary [dʒuːˈdɪʃɪərɪ] n *(branch of administration)* Gerichtsbehörden pl; *(judges)* Richterstand m.

judicious [dʒuːˈdɪʃəs] adj klug, umsichtig.

judo ['dʒuːdəu] n Judo nt.

jug [dʒʌg] **1** n **(a)** *(with lid)* Kanne f; *(without lid)* Krug m; *(small)* Kännchen nt. **(b)** *(col: prison)* Knast m (col). **2** vt **~ged hare** ≈ Hasenpfeffer m.

juggernaut ['dʒʌgənɔːt] n *(Brit: lorry)* Schwerlaster m.

juggle ['dʒʌgl] vti jonglieren. **to ~ (with) the figures** die Zahlen so hindrehen, daß sie passen.

juggler ['dʒʌglər] n Jongleur m.

Jugoslavia [ˌjuːgəuˈslɑːvɪə] n = **Yugoslavia.**

jugular ['dʒʌgjulər] n *(also ~ vein)* Drosselvene f.

juice [dʒuːs] n *(lit, fig col)* Saft m.

juicy ['dʒuːsɪ] adj *(+er)* saftig; *story* pikant, schlüpfrig; *scandal also* gepfeffert *(col)*.

jujitsu [ˌdʒuːˈdʒɪtsuː] n Jiu-Jitsu nt.

jukebox ['dʒuːkbɒks] n Musikbox f.

July [dʒuːˈlaɪ] n Juli m; *see* **September.**

jumble ['dʒʌmbl] **1** vt *(also ~ up)* *(lit)* durcheinanderwerfen. **~d up** durcheinander; *(fig) facts* durcheinanderbringen. **2** n **(a)** Durcheinander nt; *(of ideas also)* Wirrwarr m. **(b)** no pl *(for ~ sale)* gebrauchte Sachen pl. **~ sale** *(Brit)* ≈ Flohmarkt m; *(for charity)* Wohltätigkeitsbasar m.

jumbo ['dʒʌmbəu] n *(~ jet)* Jumbo(-Jet) m.

jump [dʒʌmp] **1** n *(lit, fig)* Sprung m; *(with parachute)* Absprung m; *(on race-course)* Hindernis nt; *(of prices)* (sprunghafter) Anstieg. **the movie is full of ~s** der Film ist sprunghaft; **to be one ~ ahead** *(fig)* einen Schritt voraus sein.

2 vi **(a)** springen; *(parachutist)* (ab)springen; *(typewriter)* Buchstaben überspringen; *(prices, shares)* sprunghaft ansteigen. **to ~ for joy** einen Freudensprung machen; **to ~ up and down on the spot** auf der Stelle hüpfen; **to ~ to conclusions** vorschnelle Schlüsse ziehen; **go and ~ in the lake!** *(col)* fahr zum Teufel! *(col)*; **~ to it!** mach schon!; **if you keep ~ing from one thing to another** wenn Sie nie bei einer Sache bleiben. **(b)** *(start)* zusammenzucken. **you made me ~** du hast mich (aber) erschreckt.

3 vt **(a)** *ditch etc* überspringen, hinüberspringen über *(+acc)*. **(b)** *(skip)* überspringen, auslassen. **to ~ the rails** *(train)* entgleisen. **(c)** *(col)* **to ~ bail** abhauen *(col)* *(während man auf Kaution freigelassen ist)*; **to ~ the lights** bei Rot über die Kreuzung fahren; **to ~ the queue** *(Brit)* sich vordrängeln; **to ~ ship** *(Naut)* *(passenger)* das Schiff vorzeitig verlassen; *(sailor)* heimlich abheuern; **they ~ed a train to Acapulco** sie fuhren schwarz nach Acapulco; **to ~ sb** *(attack)* jdn überfallen.

♦ **jump about** *or* **around** vi herumspringen.

♦ **jump at** vi *+prep obj person (lit)* anspringen; *(fig)* anfahren; *object* zuspringen auf *(+acc)*; *offer* sofort zugreifen bei; *chance* sofort beim Schopf ergreifen.

♦ **jump down** vi hinunter-/herunterspringen *(from* von). **to ~ ~ sb's throat** jdn anfahren.

♦ **jump in** vi hineinspringen/hereinspringen. **~ ~!** *(to car)* steig ein!

♦ **jump off** vi herunterspringen *(prep obj* von); *(from train, bus)* aussteigen *(prep obj* aus); *(from bicycle, horse)* absteigen *(prep obj* von).

♦ **jump on** vi *(lit)* *(onto vehicle)* einsteigen *(prep obj, -to* in *+acc)*; *(onto bicycle, horse)* aufsteigen *(prep obj, -to* auf *+acc)*. **he ~ed ~ (to) his bicycle** er schwang sich auf sein Fahrrad.

♦ **jump out** vi hinaus-/heausspringen; *(from vehicle)* aussteigen *(of* aus).

♦ **jump up** vi hochspringen; *(from sitting or lying position also)* aufspringen; *(onto sth)* hinaufspringen *(onto* auf *+acc)*.

jumped-up ['dʒʌmptˈʌp] adj *(col)* **this new ~ manager** dieser kleine Emporkömmling von einem Abteilungsleiter.

jumper ['dʒʌmpər] n **(a)** *(garment)* *(Brit)* Pullover m; *(US: dress)* Trägerkleid nt. **(b)** *(person, animal)* Springer m. **(c)** **~ cables** *(US Aut)* Starthilfekabel nt.

jump: ~ jet n Senkrechtstarter m; **~ leads** npl *(Brit Aut)* Starthilfekabel nt; **~ suit** n Overall m.

jumpy ['dʒʌmpɪ] adj *(+er)* *(col)* person nervös; *(easily startled)* schreckhaft.

Jun = **June; junior** jr., jun.

junction ['dʒʌŋkʃən] n *(Rail)* Gleisanschluß m; *(Brit: of roads)* Kreuzung f. **railway ~** Eisenbahnknotenpunkt m.

juncture ['dʒʌŋktʃər] n: **at this ~** zu diesem Zeitpunkt.

June [dʒuːn] n Juni m; *see* **September.**

jungle ['dʒʌŋgl] n Dschungel m *(also fig)*, Urwald m.

junior ['dʒuːnɪər] **1** adj **(a)** *(younger)* jünger. **Hiram Schwarz, ~** Hiram Schwarz junior; **~ classes** *(Sch)* Unterstufe f; **~ school** *(Brit)* Grundschule f; **~ high (school)** *(US)* ≈ Mittelschule f. **(b)** *employee* untergeordnet; *officer* rangniedriger. **~ clerk** zweiter Buchhalter; **~ Minister** Staatssekretär(in f) m. **2** n **(a)** Jüngere(r) mf. **he is two years my ~** er ist zwei Jahre jünger als ich. **(b)** *(Brit Sch)* Grundschüler(in f) m; *(US Univ)* Student(in f) im vorletzten Studienjahr.

juniper ['dʒuːnɪpər] n Wacholder m. **~ berry** Wacholderbeere f.

junk¹ [dʒʌŋk] n **(a)** *(discarded objects)* Trödel m, Gerümpel nt; *(col: trash)* Schund m; *(pej: food)* Fraß m *(col)*. **(b)** *(col: drugs)* Stoff m *(col)*.

junk² n *(boat)* Dschunke f.

junk foods npl *(pej)* Plastikessen nt *(pej col)*; *(sweets)* Süßkram m *(col)*.

junkie ['dʒʌŋkɪ] n *(col)* Fixer(in f) m *(col)*.

junk: ~ room n Rumpelkammer f; **~ shop** n Trödelladen m.

junta ['dʒʌntə] n Junta f.

Jupiter ['dʒuːpɪtər] n Jupiter m.

jurisdiction [ˌdʒuərɪsˈdɪkʃən] n Gerichtsbarkeit f; *(range of authority)* Zuständigkeit(sbereich m) f. **matters that do not fall under the ~ of this court** Fälle, für die dieses Gericht nicht zuständig ist; **that's not (in) my ~** dafür bin ich nicht zuständig.

juror ['dʒuərər] n Schöffe m, Schöffin f; *(for capital crimes)* Geschworene(r) mf.

jury ['dʒuərɪ] n **(a)** **the ~** die Schöffen pl; *(for capital crimes)* die Geschworenen pl; **to sit on the ~** Schöffe/Geschworener sein. **(b)** *(for competition)* Jury f.

jury: ~box n Schöffen-/Geschworenenbank f; **~ service** n to be called for **~ service** als Schöffe/Geschworener berufen werden.

just¹ [dʒʌst] adj **(a)** *(with time)* gerade, (so)eben. **they have ~ left** sie sind gerade gegangen; **I met him ~ after lunch** ich habe ihn gleich nach dem Mittagessen getroffen; **hurry up, he's ~ going** beeilen Sie sich, er geht gerade; **I'm ~ coming** ich komme ja schon; **I was ~ going to ... ich wollte gerade ...; ~ **as I was going** gerade, als ich gehen wollte.

(b) *(barely, almost not)* gerade noch. **he ~ escaped being run over** er wäre um ein Haar überfahren worden; **I arrived ~ in time** ich bin gerade noch rechtzeitig gekommen.

(c) *(exactly)* genau. **it is ~ five o'clock** es ist genau fünf Uhr; **that's ~ like you** das sieht dir ähnlich; **~ as I expected** genau wie ich es erwartet hatte; **that's ~ it!** das ist es ja gerade!; **that's ~ what I was going to say** genau das wollte ich (auch) sagen; **~ what do you mean by that?** was soll das heißen?; **~ at that moment** genau in dem Augenblick; **everything has to be ~ so** es muß alles seine Ordnung haben.

(d) *(only, simply)* nur, bloß. **~ you and me** nur wir beide; **he's ~ a boy** er ist doch noch ein Junge; **~ like that** einfach so; **it's ~ not good enough** es ist einfach nicht gut genug; **I ~ prefer it this way** ich find's einfach besser so; **~ round the corner** gleich um die Ecke; **~ above the trees** direkt über den Bäumen.

(e) *(absolutely)* einfach, wirklich. **it was ~ fantastic** es war einfach prima; **it's ~ terrible** das ist ja schrecklich!

(f) **~ as** genauso, ebenso; **the blue hat is ~ as nice as the red one** der blaue Hut ist genauso hübsch wie der rote; **it's ~ as well you didn't go out** nur gut, daß Sie nicht weggegangen sind; **it would be ~ as well if you came** es wäre doch besser, wenn Sie kämen; **come ~ as you are** kommen Sie so, wie Sie sind; **~ as you please** wie Sie wollen; **~ as I thought!** ich habe es mir doch gedacht!

(g) **~ about** in etwa, so etwa; **I am ~ about ready** ich bin so gut wie fertig; **did he make it in time? — ~ about** hat er's (rechtzeitig) geschafft? — so gerade; **I am ~ about fed up with it!** (col) so langsam aber sicher hängt es mir zum Hals raus (col).

(h) **~ now** *(in past)* gerade erst; **not ~ now** im Moment nicht; **you can go, but not ~ now** Sie können gehen, aber nicht gerade jetzt;

~ **think** denk bloß; ~ **listen** hör mal; ~ **a moment** *or* **minute!** Moment mal!; **I can ~ see him as a soldier** ich kann ihn mir gut als Soldat vorstellen; **can I ~ finish this?** kann ich das eben noch fertigmachen?; **don't I ~!** und ob!; ~ **watch it** nimm dich bloß in acht; ~ **you dare!** wehe!

just² *adj (+er) person, decision* gerecht *(to gegenüber)*; *anger* berechtigt; *suspicion* begründet. **as (it) is only ~** wie es recht und billig ist.

justice ['dʒʌstɪs] *n* **(a)** *(quality)* Gerechtigkeit *f*; *(system)* Justiz *f*; *(of claims)* Rechtmäßigkeit *f*. **to bring a thief to ~** einen Dieb vor Gericht bringen; **to do him ~** um ihm gegenüber gerecht zu sein; **this photograph doesn't do me ~** auf diesem Foto bin ich nicht gut getroffen; **she never does herself ~** sie kommt nie richtig zur Geltung; **he complained, with ~, that ...** er hat sich zu Recht beklagt, daß ...; **there's no ~, is there?** das ist doch nicht gerecht. **(b)** *(judge)* Richter *m*. **J~ of the Peace** Friedensrichter *m*.

justifiable [,dʒʌstɪ'faɪəbl] *adj* zu rechtfertigen *pred*, berechtigt.

justifiably [,dʒʌstɪ'faɪəblɪ] *adv* zu Recht.

justification [,dʒʌstɪfɪ'keɪʃən] *n* Rechtfertigung *f*.

justify ['dʒʌstɪfaɪ] *vt* **(a)** rechtfertigen *(sth to sb etw jdm gegenüber)*. **am I justified in thinking that ...?** gehe ich recht in der Annahme, daß ...?; **he was justified in doing that** es war gerechtfertigt, daß er das tat; **you're not justified in talking to her like that** Sie haben kein Recht, mit ihr zu reden. **(b)** *(Typ)* justieren.

jut [dʒʌt] *vi (also* ~ **out)** hervorstehen, herausragen.

jute [dʒuːt] *n* Jute *f*.

juvenile ['dʒuːvənaɪl] **1** *n (Admin)* Jugendliche(r) *mf*. **2** *adj (youthful)* jugendlich; *(for young people)* Jugend-, für Jugendliche; *(pej)* kindisch, unreif.

juvenile: ~ court *n* Jugendgericht *nt*; **~ delinquency** *n* Jugendkriminalität *f*; **~ delinquent** *n* jugendlicher Straftäter.

juxtaposition [,dʒʌkstəpə'zɪʃən] *n (act)* Nebeneinanderstellung *f*. **in ~** (direkt) nebeneinander.

K

K, k [keɪ] n K, k nt.
kale [keɪl] n Grünkohl m.
kaleidoscope [kə'laɪdəskəup] n Kaleidoskop nt.
kangaroo [ˌkæŋgə'ruː] n Känguruh nt. **~ court** inoffizielles Gericht.
kaput [kə'pʊt] adj (col) kaputt (col).
karate [kə'rɑːtɪ] n Karate nt.
kebab [kə'bæb] n Kebab m.
keel [kiːl] n (Naut) Kiel m. **to be on an even ~ again** (fig) wieder im Lot sein; **he put the business back on an even ~** er brachte das Geschäft wieder auf die Beine (col).
♦ **keel over** vi (ship) kentern; (fig col) umkippen.
keen [kiːn] adj (+er) **(a)** edge, wind, competition, wit scharf; appetite kräftig; interest stark; desire, pain heftig; sight, hearing gut; (esp Brit) prices günstig. **(b)** (enthusiastic) begeistert; football fan etc also leidenschaftlich; applicant, learner stark interessiert; (hardworking) eifrig. **~ to learn** lernbegierig; **to be ~ on sb** von jdm sehr angetan sein, scharf auf jdn sein (col); **on actor, author** von jdm begeistert sein; **to be ~ on sth** etw sehr gern mögen; **to be ~ on doing sth** (like to do) etw gern tun; **to be ~ to do sth** (want to do) darauf erpicht sein or scharf darauf sein (col), etw zu tun; **to be ~ on mountaineering** sehr gern bergsteigen; **I'm not very ~ on him** ich bin von ihm nicht gerade begeistert; **he's not ~ on her coming** er legt keinen besonderen Wert darauf, daß sie kommt.
keenly ['kiːnlɪ] adv **(a)** (sharply) scharf; feel leidenschaftlich, stark. **(b)** (enthusiastically) mit Begeisterung.
keenness ['kiːnnɪs] n **(a)** (of mind, wind) Schärfe f. **(b)** esp adj (b) Begeisterung f; Leidenschaftlichkeit f; starkes Interesse; Eifer m.
keep [kiːp] (vb: pret, ptp **kept**) **1** vt **(a)** (retain) behalten. **to ~ a place for sb** einen Platz für jdn freihalten; **you can ~ it!** (col) das kannst du dir an den Hut stecken! (col).
(b) shop haben, führen; bees etc halten. **to ~ house for sb** jdm den Haushalt führen.
(c) (support) family etc unterhalten. **I earn enough to ~ myself** ich verdiene genug für mich (selbst) zum Leben; **to ~ sb in clothing** für jds Kleidung sorgen.
(d) (maintain in a state) halten. **to ~ one's dress clean** sein Kleid nicht schmutzig machen; **just to ~ her happy** damit sie zufrieden ist; **to ~ sb waiting** jdn warten lassen; **can't you ~ him talking?** können Sie ihn nicht in ein Gespräch verwickeln?; **to ~ sth tidy** etw sauber or in Ordnung halten; **the garden was well kept** der Garten war (gut) gepflegt; **to ~ a machine running** eine Maschine laufen lassen; **to ~ the conversation going** das Gespräch in Gang halten.
(e) (store, look after) aufbewahren; (put aside) aufheben. **where does he ~ his money?** wo bewahrt er sein Geld auf?; **where do you ~ your spoons?** wo sind die Löffel?; **I've been ~ing it for you** ich habe es für Sie aufgehoben.
(f) promise halten; rule befolgen; treaty, appointment einhalten; obligations nachkommen (+dat).
(g) accounts, diary etc führen (of über +acc).

(h) (detain) aufhalten. **I mustn't ~ you** ich will Sie nicht aufhalten; **what kept you?** wo waren Sie denn so lang?; **to ~ sb in prison** jdn in Haft halten.
(i) (not disclose) can you ~ this from your mother? können Sie das vor Ihrer Mutter geheimhalten?; **~ it to yourself** behalten Sie das für sich.
(j) **to ~ late hours** lange aufbleiben.
2 vi **(a) to ~** (to the) **left** sich links halten; **to ~ to the middle of the road** (Aut) immer in der Mitte der Straße fahren. **(b) to ~ doing sth** (not stop) etw weiter tun; (repeatedly) etw immer wieder tun; (constantly) etw dauernd tun; **to ~ walking** weitergehen; **he kept lying to her** er hat sie immer wieder belogen; **if you ~ complaining** wenn Sie sich weiter beschweren; **she ~s talking about you all the time** sie redet dauernd von Ihnen; **~ going** machen Sie weiter; **~ at it!** bleib am Ball! **(c)** (remain) bleiben. **to ~ quiet** still sein; **to ~ silent** schweigen; **to ~ calm** ruhig bleiben. **(d)** (food etc) sich halten. **(e)** (state of health) **how are you ~ing?** wie geht es Ihnen denn so?; **to ~ well** gesund bleiben; **to ~ fit** fit bleiben; **he's ~ing better now** es geht ihm wieder besser. **(f)** (wait) **that can ~** das kann warten.
3 n **(a)** (livelihood, food) Unterhalt m. **I got £10 a week and my ~** ich bekam £ 10 pro Woche und freie Kost und Logis; **to earn one's ~** (fig) sein Geld verdienen; (machine etc) sich rentieren. **(b)** (in castle) Bergfried m; (as prison) Burgverlies nt. **(c) for ~s** (col) für immer; **it's yours for ~s** das darfst du behalten.
♦ **keep away 1** vi (lit) wegbleiben; (not approach) nicht näher herankommen (from an +acc). **~ ~!** kommen Sie nicht näher!; **I just can't ~ ~** es zieht mich immer wieder hin; **~ ~ from him** lassen Sie die Finger von ihm. **2** vt always separate person, children etc fernhalten (from von). **to ~ sth ~ from sth** etw nicht an etw (acc) kommen lassen.
♦ **keep back 1** vi zurückbleiben. **~ ~!** treten Sie zurück! **2** vt sep **(a)** hair, crowds zurückhalten; water stauen; tears unterdrücken. **to ~ sb ~ from doing sth** jdn davon abhalten, etwas zu tun. **(b)** (withhold) taxes einbehalten; information etc verschweigen (from sb jdm); (from parent, husband etc) verheimlichen (from sb jdm). **(c)** (make late) aufhalten; pupil dabehalten. **(d)** (hold up, slow down) behindern.
♦ **keep down 1** vi unten bleiben. **~ ~!** bleib unten! **2** vt sep **(a)** (hold down) unten halten. **~ your voices** ~ reden Sie leise! **(b)** revolt, one's anger unterdrücken; rabbits, weeds etc unter Kontrolle halten. **you can't ~ a good man ~** ein tüchtiger Mann läßt sich nicht unterkriegen. **(c)** prices niedrig halten; spending einschränken. **to ~ one's weight ~** nicht zunehmen. **(d)** food etc bei sich behalten. **(e)** (Sch) **he was kept ~** er mußte wiederholen.
♦ **keep from 1** vt + prep obj **(a) I couldn't ~ him ~ going there** ich konnte ihn nicht davon abhalten, dort hinzugehen; **the bells ~ me ~ sleeping** die Glocken lassen mich nicht schlafen; **his anorak kept him ~ getting wet** sein Anorak schützte ihn

vor dem Regen; this will ~ the water ~ freezing das verhindert, daß das Wasser gefriert. **(b)** *(withhold)* to ~ sth ~ sb jdm etw verschweigen; *piece of news also* jdm etw vorenthalten. **2** *vi* +*prep obj* to ~ ~ doing sth etw nicht tun; *(avoid doing also)* es vermeiden, etw zu tun; she couldn't ~ ~ laughing sie mußte einfach lachen.

♦ **keep in 1** *vt sep feelings* zügeln; *schoolboy* nachsitzen lassen; *stomach* einziehen. **2** *vi* he's just trying to ~ ~ with her er versucht nur, sich mit ihr gut zu stellen.

♦ **keep off 1** *vi (person)* wegbleiben. if the rain ~s ~ wenn es nicht regnet. **2** *vt sep dog, person* fernhalten *(prep obj* von). "~ ~ the grass" „Betreten des Rasens verboten"; ~ your hands ~ Hände weg! **3** *vi* +*prep obj* vermeiden. ~ ~ the whisky lassen Sie das Whiskytrinken.

♦ **keep on 1** *vi* **(a)** weitermachen. to ~ ~ doing sth etw weiter tun; *(repeatedly)* etw immer wieder tun; *(incessantly)* etw dauernd tun; if you ~ ~ like this wenn du so weitermachst; the rain kept ~ all night es regnete die ganze Nacht durch. **(b)** *(keep going)* weitergehen/-fahren. ~ ~ past the church fahren/gehen Sie immer weiter an der Kirche vorbei. **(c)** to ~ ~ at sb *(col)* dauernd an jdm herummeckern *(col)*; to ~ ~ about sth *(col)* unaufhörlich von etw reden; don't ~ ~ so! *(col)* hören Sie doch endlich auf damit! **2** *vt sep* **(a)** *employee* behalten. **(b)** *coat etc* anbehalten; *hat* aufbehalten.

♦ **keep out 1** *vi (of building)* draußen bleiben; *(of property)* etw nicht betreten. "~ ~" „Zutritt verboten"; to ~ ~ of danger Gefahr meiden; to ~ ~ of debt keine Schulden machen; that child can never ~ ~ of mischief das Kind stellt dauernd etwas an; you ~ ~ of this! halten Sie sich da raus! **2** *vt sep* **(a)** *person* nicht hereinlassen *(of* in +*acc)*; *light, cold, enemy etc* abhalten. **(b)** I wanted to ~ him ~ of this ich wollte nicht, daß er da mit hineingezogen wird; ~ him ~ of my way halte ihn mir vom Leib.

♦ **keep to 1** *vi* +*prep obj* **(a)** ~ ~ the main road bleiben Sie auf der Hauptstraße; to ~ ~ the schedule sich an den Zeitplan halten. **(b)** to ~ (oneself) ~ oneself nicht sehr gesellig sein; they ~ ~ themselves sie bleiben unter sich. **2** *vt* +*prep obj* to ~ sb ~ his word jdn beim Wort nehmen; to ~ sth ~ a minimum etw auf ein Minimum beschränken.

♦ **keep together** *vi (stay together)* zusammenbleiben.

♦ **keep up 1** *vi* **(a)** *(tent)* stehen bleiben. **(b)** *(rain)* (an)dauern; *(weather etc)* anhalten; *(morale, determination)* nicht nachlassen. **(c)** to ~ ~ (with sb/sth) *(in race, work)* (mit jdm/etw) Schritt halten; *(in comprehension)* (jdm/einer Sache) folgen können; to ~ ~ with the Joneses mit den Nachbarn mithalten; to ~ ~ with the times mit der Zeit gehen; to ~ ~ with the news sich auf dem laufenden halten.

2 *vt sep* **(a)** *tent* aufrecht halten. **(b)** *(not stop)* nicht aufhören mit; *study etc* weitermachen; *quality, prices, friendship, tradition, payments* aufrechterhalten; *speed* halten. I try to ~ ~ my French ich versuche, mit meinem Französisch nicht aus der Übung zu kommen; ~ it ~! *(machen Sie)* weiter so!; he couldn't ~ it ~ er hat schlapp gemacht. **(c)** *(maintain)* house unterhalten; *road* instand halten. **(d)** *(prevent from going to bed)* am Schlafengehen hindern. that child kept me ~ all night das Kind hat mich die ganze Nacht nicht schlafen lassen.

keeper ['kiːpə'] *n (zoo)* Wärter(in *f)* m; *(museum)* Aufseher(in *f)* m; *(goal~)* Torhüter m.

keep-fit ['kiːpfɪt] *n* Gymnastik *f*.

keeping ['kiːpɪŋ] *n* **(a)** *(care)* to put sth in sb's ~ jdm etw zur Aufbewahrung übergeben. **(b)** in ~ with in Einklang mit.

keg [keg] *n (barrel)* kleines Faß.

kennel ['kenl] *n* Hundehütte *f*. to put a dog in ~s einen Hund in Pflege geben.

Kenya ['kenjə] *n* Kenia *nt*.

Kenyan ['kenjən] **1** *n* Kenianer(in *f)* m. **2** *adj* kenianisch.

kept [kept] *pret, ptp of* **keep.**

kerb [kɜːb] *n (Brit)* Randstein *m*.

kernel ['kɜːnl] *n (lit, fig)* Kern *m*.

kerosene ['kerəsiːn] *n* Kerosin *nt*; *(paraffin)* Paraffin *nt*.

kestrel ['kestrəl] *n* Turmfalke *m*.

ketchup ['ketʃəp] *n* Ketchup *nt or m*.

kettle ['ketl] *n* Kessel *m*. I'll put the ~ on ich stelle mal eben (Kaffee-/Tee)wasser auf; the ~'s boiling das Wasser kocht; a pretty ~ of fish *(col)* eine schöne Bescherung *(col)*; that's a different ~ of fish *(col)* das ist doch was ganz anderes.

kettledrum ['ketldrʌm] *n* (Kessel)pauke *f*.

key [kiː] **1** *n* **(a)** *(lit, fig)* Schlüssel *m*. the ~ to the mystery der Schlüssel zum Geheimnis. **(b)** *(for maps etc)* Zeichenerklärung *f*. **(c)** *(of piano, typewriter etc)* Taste *f*. **(d)** *(Mus)* Tonart *f*. to sing off ~ falsch singen; change of ~ Tonartwechsel *m*; in the ~ of C in C-Dur/c-Moll. **2** *adj attr (vital)* Schlüssel-. ~ point springender Punkt.

♦ **key in** *vt (Comp)* eingeben.

keyboard ['kiːbɔːd] *n* Tastatur *f*.

keyed up ['kiːd'ʌp] *adj* she was (all) ~ about the interview sie war wegen des Interviews ganz aufgedreht *(col)*.

key: ~hole *n* Schlüsselloch *nt*; ~note speech *n (Pol etc)* programmatische Rede; ~ ring *n* Schlüsselring *m*.

khaki ['kɑːkɪ] **1** *n* K(h)aki *nt*. **2** *adj* k(h)aki(farben).

kibbutz ['kɪ'buts] *n, pl* -**im** Kibbuz *m*.

kick [kɪk] **1** *n* Tritt, Stoß *m*; *(of gun)* Rückstoß *m*. to take a ~ at sb/sth nach jdm/etw treten; to give the door a ~ gegen die Tür treten; it's better than a ~ in the pants *(col)* das ist besser als ein Tritt in den Hintern *(col)*; she gets a ~ out of it *(col)* es macht ihr einen Riesenspaß *(col)*; to do sth for ~s *(col)* als eine Jux *(col)*; this drink has plenty of ~ in it *(col)* dieses Getränk hat es in sich. **2** *vi (person)* treten; *(struggle)* um sich treten; *(animal)* ausschlagen. **3** *vt (person, horse)* sb treten (+*dat)*; *door, ball* treten gegen; *object* einen Tritt versetzen (+*dat)*. to ~ the bucket *(col)* ins Gras beißen *(col)*; I could have ~ed myself *(col)* ich hätte mir in den Hintern treten *(col)* können; to ~ the habit *(col)* es aufgeben.

♦ **kick about** *or* **around 1** *vi (col)* (person) rumhängen *(col)* (prep obj* in +*dat)*; *(thing)* rumliegen *(col)* (prep obj* in +*dat)*. **2** *vt sep* to ~ a ball ~ den Ball herumkicken *(col)*; you shouldn't let them ~ you ~ Sie sollten sich nicht so herumschubsen lassen.

♦ **kick in** *vt sep* door eintreten. to ~ sb's teeth ~ jdm die Zähne einschlagen.

♦ **kick off** *vi (Ftbl)* anstoßen; *(fig col)* anfangen.

♦ **kick out 1** *vi* to ~ ~ at sb nach jdm treten. **2** *vt sep (col)* rauswerfen *(col)* (of* aus).

♦ **kick up** *vt sep* to ~ ~ a fuss *(col)* Krach schlagen *(col)*.

kick: ~-off *n (Sport)* Anpfiff, Anstoß *m*; *(col: beginning)* Beginn *m*. ~-start(er) *n* Kickstarter *m*.

kid [kɪd] **1** *n* **(a)** *(young goat)* Kitz *nt*; *(leather)* Glacéleder *nt*. to handle sb with ~ gloves *(fig)* jdn mit Samthandschuhen anfassen. **(b)** *(col: child)* Kind *nt*. it's ~'s stuff *(for children)* das ist was für kleine Kinder *(col)*; *(easy)* das ist doch ein Kinderspiel; his ~ brother sein kleiner Bruder; OK, ~! okay, Junge/Mädchen! **2** *vt (col)* to ~ sb (on) *(tease)* jdn aufziehen *(col)*; *(deceive)* jdn an der Nase rumführen *(col)*; don't ~ yourself! machen Sie sich doch nichts vor! **3** *vi (col)* Jux machen *(col)*. no ~ding ehrlich *(col)*.

kidnap ['kɪdnæp] *vt* entführen, kidnappen.
kidnapper ['kɪdnæpəʳ] *n* Entführer(in *f*), Kidnapper(in *f*) *m*.
kidnapping ['kɪdnæpɪŋ] *n* Entführung *f*.
kidney ['kɪdnɪ] *n* (*Anat, Cook*) Niere *f*.
kidney: ~ **bean** *n* Gartenbohne *f*; ~ **machine** *n* künstliche Niere.
kill [kɪl] **1** *vt* (**a**) töten, umbringen; (*slaughter*) schlachten; *weeds* vernichten. **to be** ~**ed in battle** im Kampf fallen; **her brother was** ~**ed in a car accident** ihr Bruder ist bei einem Autounfall ums Leben gekommen; **how many were** ~**ed?** wieviel Todesopfer gab es?; **she** ~**ed herself** sie brachte sich um; **don't** ~ **me** lassen Sie mich leben; **he was** ~**ed with poison/a knife** er wurde vergiftet/(mit einem Messer) erstochen; **I'll** ~ **him!** (*also fig*) den bring' ich um (*col*).
(**b**) (*fig*) *feelings, love etc* zerstören; (*spoil*) *flavour, performance* verderben, überdecken; *hopes* zunichte machen; *sound* schlucken; (*Press etc*) *paragraph, story* streichen; (*Tech*) *engine etc* abschalten. **to** ~ **time** die Zeit totschlagen; **we have two hours to** ~ wir haben noch zwei Stunden übrig; **to** ~ **two birds with one stone** (*Prov*) zwei Fliegen mit einer Klappe schlagen (*Prov*); **these stairs are** ~**ing me** (*col*) diese Treppe bringt mich (noch mal) um (*col*); **she was** ~**ing herself (laughing)** (*col*) sie hat sich (fast) totgelacht (*col*); **my feet are** ~**ing me** (*col*) mir brennen die Füße.
2 *vi* töten. **cigarettes can** ~ Zigaretten können tödliche Folgen haben.
3 *n* **to be in at the** ~ (*fig*) den Schlußakt miterleben.
♦ **kill off** *vt sep* vernichten; *cows, pigs* abschlachten; *weeds* vertilgen.
killer ['kɪləʳ] *n* (*person*) Mörder(in *f*) *m*. **this disease is a** ~ diese Krankheit ist tödlich.
killer: the ~ **instinct** *n* (*lit*) der Tötungsinstinkt; **a successful businessman needs the** ~ **instinct** ein erfolgreicher Geschäftsmann muß über Leichen gehen können; ~ **whale** *n* Schwertwal *m*.
killing ['kɪlɪŋ] **1** *n* (*of person*) Töten *nt*. **three more** ~**s in Belfast** drei weitere Todesopfer in Belfast; **to make a** ~ (*fig*) einen Riesengewinn machen. **2** *adj blow etc* tödlich; *pace* mörderisch.
killingly ['kɪlɪŋlɪ] *adv:* ~ **funny** zum Totlachen.
killjoy ['kɪldʒɔɪ] *n* Spielverderber *m*.
kiln [kɪln] *n* (Brenn)ofen *m*; (*for bricks*) Trockenofen *m*.
kilo ['kiːləʊ] *n* Kilo *nt*.
kilobyte ['kɪləʊbaɪt] *n* Kilobyte *nt*.
kilogramme, (*US*) **kilogram** ['kɪləʊgræm] *n* Kilogramm *nt*.
kilometre, (*US*) **kilometer** ['kɪləʊˌmiːtəʳ, kɪ'lɒmɪtəʳ] *n* Kilometer *m*.
kilowatt ['kɪləʊwɒt] *n* Kilowatt *nt*.
kilt [kɪlt] *n* Kilt, Schottenrock *m*.
kin [kɪn] *n* Verwandte *pl*, Verwandtschaft *f*.
kind¹ [kaɪnd] **1** *n* (**a**) Art *f*; (*of coffee etc*) Sorte *f*. **several** ~**s of flour** mehrere Mehlsorten; **this** ~ **of book** diese Art Buch; **what** ~ **of …?** was für ein(e) …?; **the only one of its** ~ das einzige seiner Art; **he is not the** ~ **of man to refuse** er ist nicht der Typ, der nein sagt; **he's not that** ~ **of person** so ist er nicht; **a strange** ~ **of feeling** so ein seltsames Gefühl; **they're two of a** ~ (*people*) sie sind vom gleichen Schlag; **I know your** ~ seinen Typ kenne ich; **this** ~ **of thing** so etwas; **… of all** ~**s** alle möglichen …; **something of the** ~ so etwas ähnliches; **nothing of the** ~ nichts dergleichen; **you'll do nothing of the** ~ du wirst das schön bleiben lassen!; **it's not my** ~ **of holiday** solche Ferien sind nicht mein Fall (*col*); **she's my** ~ **of woman** sie ist mein Typ.
(**b**) **payment in** ~ Bezahlung in Naturalien; **I**

shall pay you in ~ (*fig*) ich werde es Ihnen in gleicher Münze zurückzahlen.
2 *adv* (*col*) **I was** ~ **of disappointed** (*a little*) ich war irgendwie enttäuscht; (*very*) ich war ziemlich enttäuscht.
kind² *adj* (+*er*) nett, freundlich (*to* zu). **would you be** ~ **enough to open the door** wären Sie so nett *or* lieb, die Tür zu öffnen.
kindergarten ['kɪndə,gaːtn] *n* Kindergarten *m*.
kind-hearted ['kaɪnd'haːtɪd] *adj* gütig.
kindle ['kɪndl] *vt fire* anzünden; *passions* entfachen.
kindly ['kaɪndlɪ] **1** *adv speak, act* freundlich, nett; *treat* liebenswürdig. **they** ~ **put me up for a night** sie nahmen mich freundlicherweise für eine Nacht auf; **will you** ~ **do it now** tun Sie das sofort, wenn ich bitten darf!; ~ **shut the door** machen Sie doch bitte die Tür zu!, **I don't take** ~ **to his smoking** sein Rauchen ist mir gar nicht angenehm; **he won't take at all** ~ **to that** das wird ihm gar nicht gefallen. **2** *adj* (+*er*) *person* lieb, nett; *advice* freundlich; *voice* sanft, gütig.
kindness ['kaɪndnɪs] *n no pl* Freundlichkeit, Liebenswürdigkeit *f* (*towards* gegenüber); (*goodness*) Güte *f* (*towards* gegenüber); (*act of* ~) Gefälligkeit, Aufmerksamkeit *f*. **out of the** ~ **of one's heart** aus reiner Nächstenliebe; **to do sb a** ~ jdm eine Gefälligkeit erweisen.
kindred ['kɪndrɪd] **1** *n no pl* (*relatives*) Verwandtschaft *f*. **2** *adj* (*related*) verwandt. ~ **spirit** Gleichgesinnte(r) *mf*.
kinetic [kɪ'netɪk] *adj* kinetisch.
king [kɪŋ] *n* König *m* (*also Chess, Cards*); (*Draughts*) Dame *f*.
kingdom ['kɪŋdəm] *n* Königreich *nt*. **you can go on doing that till** ~ **come** (*col*) Sie können (so) bis in alle Ewigkeit weitermachen.
kingfisher ['kɪŋfɪʃəʳ] *n* Eisvogel *m*.
king: ~**pin** *vt* (*sp: person*) Stütze *f*; ~**-size(d)** *adj* (*col*) in Großformat; *cigarettes* King-size; *bed* extra groß.
kink [kɪŋk] *n* (**a**) (*in rope etc*) Schlaufe *f*; (*in hair*) Welle *f*. (**b**) (*mental peculiarity*) Tick *m* (*col*); (*sexual*) abartige Veranlagung.
kinky ['kɪŋkɪ] *adj* (+*er*) (**a**) *hair* wellig. (**b**) (*col*) *person, ideas* verdreht (*col*); *fashion* verrückt (*col*); (*sexually*) abartig.
kinship ['kɪnʃɪp] *n* Verwandtschaft *f*.
kinsman ['kɪnzmən] *n, pl* **-men** [-mən] Verwandte(r) *m*.
kinswoman ['kɪnzwʊmən] *n, pl* **-women** [-wɪmɪn] Verwandte *f*.
kiosk ['kiːɒsk] *n* Kiosk *m*; (*Brit Telec*) (Telefon)zelle *f*.
kip [kɪp] (*Brit col*) **1** *n* (*sleep*) Schläfchen *nt*. **I've got to get some** ~ ich muß mal 'ne Runde pennen (*col*). **2** *vi* pennen (*col*).
kipper ['kɪpəʳ] *n* Räucherhering *m*.
kiss [kɪs] **1** *n* Kuß *m*. ~ **of life** Mund-zu-Mund-Beatmung *f*; ~ **of death** (*fig*) Todesstoß *m*. **2** *vt* küssen; (*fig: touch gently*) sanft berühren. **to** ~ **sb's cheek** jdn auf die Wange küssen; **they** ~**ed each other** sie küßten sich; **to** ~ **sb goodbye** jdm einen Abschiedskuß geben. **3** *vi* küssen; (~ *each other*) sich küssen.
kit [kɪt] *n* (**a**) (*equipment*) Ausrüstung *f*; (*Brit Sport*) Sportzeug *nt*, Sportsachen *pl*; (*belongings, luggage etc*) Sachen *pl*. (**b**) (*for self-assembly*) Bastelsatz *m*; **model aircraft** ~ Modellflugzeugbaukasten *m*; **in** ~ **form** zum Selberbauen.
♦ **kit out** *vt sep* ausrüsten (*esp Mil*), ausstatten.
kitbag ['kɪtbæg] *n* Seesack *m*.
kitchen ['kɪtʃɪn] *n* Küche *f*. **2** *attr* Küchen-. ~ **unit** Küchenschrank *m*.
kitchenette [,kɪtʃɪ'net] *n* (*separate room*) kleine Küche; (*part of one room*) Kochnische *f*.
kitchen sink *n* Spüle *f*. **I've packed everything**

but the ~ *(col)* ich habe den ganzen Hausrat eingepackt; ~ **drama** Alltagsdrama *nt.*
kite [kaɪt] *n (Orn)* Milan *m; (toy)* Drachen *m.*
kith [kɪθ] *n:* ~ **and kin** Blutsverwandte *pl.*
kitten ['kɪtn] *n* Kätzchen *nt.* **to have** ~**s** *(fig col)* Junge kriegen *(col).*
kitty ['kɪtɪ] *n* **(a)** *(money) (gemeinsame)* Kasse; *(Cards etc also)* Spielkasse *f.* **(b)** *(col: cat)* Mieze *f.*
kleptomaniac [,kleptəʊ'meɪnɪæk] *n* Kleptomane *m,* Kleptomanin *f.*
knack [næk] *n* Trick, Kniff *m.* **there's a (special)** ~ **to opening it** da ist ein Trick dabei, wie man das aufbekommt; **to get the** ~ **of doing sth (es)** herausbekommen, wie man etw macht; **you'll soon get the** ~ **of it** Sie werden den Dreh bald raushaben; **I've lost the** ~ ich bekomme das nicht mehr hin; **she's got a** ~ **of saying the wrong thing** sie hat ein Talent dafür, immer das Falsche zu sagen.
knackered ['nækəd] *adj (Brit col)* kaputt *(col).*
knapsack ['næpsæk] *n* Proviantbeutel *m.*
knead [niːd] *vt dough* kneten.
knee [niː] **1** *n* Knie *nt.* **to be on one's** ~**s** *(lit, fig)* auf den Knien liegen; **on bended** ~**(s)** *(liter, hum)* kniefällig; **to go down on one's** ~**s (to sb)** *(lit, fig)* sich (vor jdm) auf die Knie werfen; **to bring sb to his** ~**s** *(lit, fig)* jdn in die Knie zwingen. **2** *vt* mit dem Knie stoßen.
knee: ~ **cap** *n* Kniescheibe *f;* ~**-deep** *adj* knietief; ~**-high** *adj* in Kniehöhe.
kneel [niːl] *pret, ptp* **knelt** *or* ~**ed** *vi (before vor* +*dat)* knien; *(also* ~ **down)** (sich) hinknien.
knee-length ['niːleŋθ] *adj skirt* knielang; *boots* kniehoch.
knee pad *n* Knieschützer *m.*
knelt [nelt] *pret, ptp of* **kneel.**
knew [njuː] *pret of* **know.**
knickers ['nɪkəz] *npl* Schlüpfer *m.* **don't get your** ~ **in a twist!** *(col!)* dreh nicht gleich durch! *(col).*
knick-knack ['nɪknæk] *n* nette Kleinigkeit *nt.* ~**s** Krimskrams *m.*
knife [naɪf] **1** *n, pl* **knives** Messer *nt.* ~, **fork and spoon** Besteck *nt;* **he's got his** ~ **into me** *(col)* der hat es auf mich abgesehen *(col);* **to be balanced on a** ~ **edge** *(fig)* auf Messers Schneide stehen. **2** *vt* einstechen auf (+*acc); (fatally)* erstechen.
knight [naɪt] **1** *n (title, Hist)* Ritter *m; (Chess)* Springer *m.* **2** *vt* adeln.
knighthood ['naɪthʊd] *n* **to receive a** ~ in den Adelsstand erhoben werden.
knit [nɪt] *pret, ptp* ~**ted** *or* ~ **1** *vt* **(a)** stricken. **(b) to** ~ **one's brow** die Stirn runzeln. **2** *vi* **(a)** stricken. **(b)** *(bones: also* ~ **together)** verwachsen.
knitted ['nɪtɪd] *adj* gestrickt; *cardigan etc* Strick-.
knitting ['nɪtɪŋ] *n* Stricken *nt; (material being knitted)* Strickzeug *nt.* **she was doing her** ~ sie strickte.
knitting: ~ **machine** *n* Strickmaschine *f;* ~ **needle** *n* Stricknadel *f.*
knitwear ['nɪtweəʳ] *n* Strickwaren *pl.*
knives [naɪvz] *pl of* **knife.**
knob [nɒb] *n (on walking stick)* Knauf *m; (on door also)* Griff *m; (on instrument etc)* Knopf *m; (of butter)* Stück *nt.*
knobbly ['nɒblɪ] *adj* (+*er) wood* knorrig. ~ **knees** Knubbelknie *pl (col).*
knock [nɒk] **1** *n* **(a)** *(blow)* Stoß *m; (esp with hand, tool etc)* Schlag *m.* **I got a** ~ **on the head** ich habe einen Schlag auf den Kopf bekommen; **he gave himself a nasty** ~ er hat sich böse angeschlagen. **(b)** *(noise)* Klopfen *nt no pl.* **there was a** ~ **at the door** es hat geklopft. **(c)** *(fig: setback)* (Tief)schlag *m.* ~**s** *(col: criticism)* Kritik *f;* **to (have to) take a lot of** ~**s** viele Tiefschläge einstecken (müssen); *(be criticized)* unter starken Beschuß kommen; **to take a** ~ *(pride etc)* erschüttert werden.

2 *vt* **(a)** *(strike)* stoßen; *(with hand, tool etc)* schlagen; *(jolt)* stoßen gegen; *(collide with: car, driver)* rammen. **to** ~ **one's head** *etc* sich *(dat)* den Kopf *etc* anschlagen; **to** ~ **sb on the head** jdn an *or* auf den Kopf schlagen; **to** ~ **sb to the ground** jdn zu Boden werfen; **to** ~ **sb unconscious** jdn bewußtlos werden lassen; *(person)* jdn bewußtlos schlagen; **to** ~ **holes in an argument** ein Argument zerpflücken; **she** ~**ed the gun out of his hand** sie schlug ihm die Waffe aus der Hand; **she** ~**ed the glass to the ground** sie stieß gegen das Glas, und es fiel zu Boden; **to** ~ **some sense into sb** jdn zur Vernunft bringen. **(b)** *(col: criticize)* (he)runtermachen *(col).*

3 *vi* **(a)** klopfen. **to** ~ **at the door/window** anklopfen/gegen das Fenster klopfen. **(b)** *(collide)* stoßen *(into, against* gegen). **(c) his knees were** ~**ing** ihm zitterten die Knie.

♦ **knock about** *or* **around 1** *vi (col) (prep obj* in +*dat) (person)* herumziehen; *(object)* herumliegen. **2** *vt sep (ill-treat)* verprügeln; *(damage)* ramponieren *(col).* **to** ~ **a ball** ~ ein paar Bälle schlagen.

♦ **knock back** *vt sep (col)* **(a) he** ~**ed** ~ **his whisky** er kippte sich *(dat)* den Whisky hinter die Binde *(col).* **(b)** *(cost)* **this watch** ~**ed me** ~ **£20** ich habe für die Uhr £ 20 hingelegt *(col).*

♦ **knock down** *vt sep person, thing* umwerfen; *opponent* niederschlagen; *(car, driver)* anfahren; *(fatally)* überfahren; *building* abreißen; *door* einschlagen.

♦ **knock in** *vt sep nail* einschlagen.

♦ **knock off 1** *vi (col)* aufhören, Schluß machen *(col).* **let's** ~ **now** Schluß für heute *(col).* **2** *vt sep* **(a)** *(lit) vase, person etc* hinunterstoßen. **the branch** ~**ed the rider** ~ **his horse** der Ast riß dem Reiter vom Pferd. **(b) he** ~**ed £5** ~ **the price** *(col)* er hat £ 5 vom Preis nachgelassen. **(c)** *(col: do quickly) essay* hinhauen *(col).* **(d)** *(Brit col: steal)* klauen *(col).* **(e)** *(col: stop)* aufhören mit. **to** ~ ~ **work** Feierabend machen; ~ **it** ~! nun hör schon auf!

♦ **knock out** *vt sep* **(a)** *tooth* ausschlagen; *nail* herausschlagen *(of aus); pipe* ausklopfen; *contents* herausklopfen *(of aus).* **(b)** *(stun)* bewußtlos werden lassen; *(by hitting)* bewußtlos schlagen, k.o. schlagen *(also Boxing).* **(c)** *(from contest)* besiegen *(of in* +*dat).* **to be** ~**ed** ~ ausscheiden *(of aus).* **(d)** *(col: exhaust)* schaffen *(col).*

♦ **knock over** *vt sep* umwerfen, umstoßen; *(car)* anfahren; *(fatally)* überfahren.

♦ **knock together** *vt sep* **(a)** *(make hurriedly)* auf die Beine stellen *(col).* **(b)** *(lit)* aneinanderstoßen. **I'd like to** ~ **their heads** ~ man sollte die beiden zur Räson bringen.

♦ **knock up** *vt sep* **(a)** *(Brit: wake)* (auf)wecken. **(b)** *meal* auf die Beine stellen *(col).* **(c)** *(col: make pregnant)* ein Kind anhängen (+*dat) (col).*
knockdown ['nɒkdaʊn] *adj* ~ **price** Schleuderpreis *m; (at auction)* Mindestpreis *m.*
knocker ['nɒkəʳ] *n (door* ~) (Tür)klopfer *m.*
knocking ['nɒkɪŋ] *n* Klopfen *nt.*
knock: ~**-kneed** [nɒk'niːd] *adj* **to be** ~**-kneed** X-Beine haben; ~**out** **1** *n (Boxing)* Knockout, K.o. *m; (col: person, thing)* Wucht *f (col);* **2** *attr* ~**out competition** Ausscheidungskampf *m;* ~**-up** *n (Brit Sport)* **to have a** ~ **-up** ein paar Bälle schlagen.
knot [nɒt] **1** *n (lit, fig, Naut)* Knoten *m; (in muscle)* Verspannung *f; (in wood)* Ast *m,* Verwachsung *f.* **to tie/untie a** ~ einen Knoten machen/aufmachen; **to tie oneself (up) in** ~**s** *(fig)* sich immer mehr verwickeln. **2** *vt* einen Knoten machen in (+*acc);* (~ **together)** verknoten. **get** ~**ted!** *(col)* du kannst mich mal! *(col).*
knotty ['nɒtɪ] *adj* (+*er) problem* verwickelt, verzwickt *(col).*
know [nəʊ] *(vb: pret* **knew**, *ptp* **known) 1** *vti* **(a)**

(have knowledge about) wissen; *answer, facts etc also* kennen; *French etc* können. **to ~ how to do sth** *(in theory)* wissen, wie man etw macht; *(in practice)* etw tun können; **she ~s all the answers** sie kennt sich aus; *(pej)* sie weiß immer alles besser; **to let sb ~ sth** *(not keep back)* jdn etw wissen lassen; *(tell, inform)* jdm Bescheid geben; **as far as I ~** soviel ich weiß; **not that I ~** nicht daß ich wüßte; **who ~s?** wer weiß?; **there's no ~ing** what he'll do man weiß nie, was er noch tut; **I'd have you ~ that ...** ich möchte doch sehr betonen, daß ...; **to ~ what one is talking about** wissen, wovon man redet; **before you ~ where you are** ehe man sich's versieht; **he just didn't want to ~** er wollte einfach nicht hören; **I ~!** ich weiß!; *(having a good idea)* ich weiß was!; **I wouldn't ~** *(col)* weiß ich (doch) nicht *(col)*; **I knew it** ich wußte es doch!; **how should I ~** wie soll ich das wissen?; **well, what do you ~!** *(col)* sieh mal einer an!; **you never ~** man kann nie wissen; **you ~, we could ...** weißt du/wissen Sie, wir könnten ...; **he didn't come, you ~** er ist nämlich nicht gekommen; **I ~ better than that** ich bin ja nicht ganz dumm; **I ~ better than to say something like that** ich werde mich hüten, so etwas zu sagen; **he should have ~n better than to do that** es war dumm von ihm, das zu tun; **they don't ~ any better** sie kennen's nicht anders; **OK, you ~ best** okay, Sie müssen's wissen.

(b) *(be acquainted with)* *people, places, book* kennen. **do you ~ him to speak to?** kennen Sie ihn näher?; **if I ~ John, he'll already be there** wie ich John kenne, ist er schon da; **to get to ~ sb/a place** jdn/einen Ort kennenlernen; **to get to ~ sth** *methods etc* etw lernen; *habits, shortcuts etc* etw herausfinden.

(c) *(recognize)* erkennen. **to ~ sb by his voice** *etc* jdn an der Stimme *etc* erkennen; **he ~s a bargain when he sees one** er weiß, was ein guter Kauf ist; **you wouldn't ~ him from his brother** Sie könnten ihn nicht von seinem Bruder unterscheiden; **to ~ the difference between right and wrong** Gut und Böse unterscheiden können; **he wouldn't ~ the difference** das merkt er nicht.

(d) *(experience)* erleben. **I've never ~n it to rain so heavily** so einen starken Regen habe ich noch nie erlebt; **I've never ~n him to smile** ich habe es noch nie erlebt, daß er lächelt; **have you ever ~n such a thing to happen before?** haben Sie je schon so etwas erlebt?

(e) *(in passive)* **to be ~n (to sb)** (jdm) bekannt sein; **it is (well) ~n that ...** es ist (allgemein) bekannt, daß ...; **he is ~n to have been here** man weiß, daß er hier war; **he is ~n as Mr X** man kennt ihn als Herrn X; **to make sb/sth ~n** jdn/ etw bekanntmachen; **to make oneself ~n** sich melden *(to sb* bei jdm); **to become ~n** bekannt werden; *(famous)* berühmt werden.

2 *n (col)* **to be in the ~** Bescheid wissen *(col)*.

♦ **know about** *vi +prep obj* *maths, politics* sich auskennen in *(+dat)*; *Africa* Bescheid wissen über *(+acc)*; *women, cars* sich auskennen mit; *(be aware of)* wissen von. **I didn't ~ ~ that** das wußte ich nicht; **I only knew ~ it yesterday** ich habe erst gestern davon gehört; **did you ~ ~ Maggie?** weißt du über Maggie Bescheid?; **I don't ~ ~ that** *(don't agree)* da bin ich aber nicht so sicher.

♦ **know of** *vi +prep obj* *café, method* kennen; *(have heard of)* sb gehört haben von. **not that I ~ ~** nicht, daß ich wüßte.

know: **~-all** *n* Alleswisser *m*; **~-how** *n* Sachkenntnis *f*, Know-how *nt*.

knowing ['nəʊɪŋ] *adj look* wissend.

knowingly ['nəʊɪŋlɪ] *adv* **(a)** *(consciously)* bewußt, absichtlich. **(b)** *look* wissend.

know-it-all ['nəʊɪtɔːl] *n (US)* = **know-all.**

knowledge ['nɒlɪdʒ] *n* **(a)** Wissen *nt*, Kenntnis *f*. **to have no ~ of** keine Kenntnis haben von; **to (the best of) my ~** meines Wissens; **not to my ~** nicht, daß ich wüßte; **without his ~** ohne sein Wissen; **it has come to my ~ that ...** es ist mir zu Ohren gekommen, daß ... **(b)** *(learning)* Kenntnisse *pl*, Wissen *nt*. **my ~ of English** meine Englischkenntnisse *pl*.

knowledgeable ['nɒlɪdʒəbl] *adj person* bewandert *(about* in *+dat)*; *report* fundiert.

known [nəʊn] **1** *ptp of* **know**. **2** *adj* bekannt; *expert also* anerkannt.

knuckle ['nʌkl] *n* (Finger)knöchel *m*; *(of meat)* Haxe *f*.

♦ **knuckle down** *vi (col)* sich dahinterklemmen *(col)*.

♦ **knuckle under** *vi (col)* spuren *(col)*.

knuckleduster ['nʌkl,dʌstəʳ] *n* Schlagring *m*.

KO *n* K.o.(-Schlag) *m*.

koala [kəʊˈɑːlə] *n (also ~ bear)* Koala(bär) *m*.

Koran [kɒˈrɑːn] *n* Koran *m*.

Korea [kəˈrɪə] *n* Korea *nt*.

kosher ['kəʊʃəʳ] *adj* koscher.

Kraut [kraʊt] *n (esp pej)* Deutsche(r) *mf*.

Kremlin ['kremlɪn] *n*: **the ~** der Kreml.

kudos ['kjuːdɒs] *n* Ansehen *nt*, Ehre *f*.

L

L, l [el] n L, l nt.
L (Brit Mot) = **Learner** L.
l = (a) **litre(s)** l. (b) **left** l.
lab [læb] = **laboratory**.
label ['leɪbl] **1** n (lit, fig) Etikett nt; (showing contents etc) Aufschrift f; (on cage) Schild nt; (tied) Anhänger m; (adhesive) Aufkleber m; (on parcel) Paketadresse f. **on the Pye** ~ bei Pye erschienen. **2** vt (a) etikettieren, mit einem Anhänger/Aufkleber versehen; (write on) beschriften. **the bottle was** ~**led "poison"** die Flasche trug die Aufschrift „Gift". (b) (fig) ideas bezeichnen; (pej) abstempeln.
laboratory [lə'bɒrətərɪ, (US) 'læbrə,tɔːrɪ] n Labor nt. ~ **assistant** Laborant(in f) m.
laborious [lə'bɔːrɪəs] adj task mühsam; style schwerfällig.
labour, (US) **labor** ['leɪbəʳ] **1** n (a) (work in general) Arbeit f; (toil) Mühe; (task) Aufgabe f. **it was a** ~ **of love** ich/er etc tat es aus Liebe zur Sache. (b) (persons) Arbeitskräfte pl. **to withdraw one's** ~ die Arbeit verweigern; **organized** ~ die organisierte Arbeiterschaft. (c) (Brit Pol) **L**~ die Labour Party; **this district is L**~ dies ist ein Labourbezirk. (d) (Med) Wehen pl. **to be in** ~ in den Wehen liegen, die Wehen haben; **to go into** ~ die Wehen bekommen. **2** vt subject auswalzen, breittreten (col). **I won't** ~ **the point** ich will nicht darauf herumreiten. **3** vi (in fields etc) arbeiten; (work hard) sich abmühen (at, with mit). **to** ~ **under a delusion** sich einer Täuschung (dat) hingeben; **to** ~ **up a hill** sich einen Hügel hinaufquälen.
labour: ~ **camp** n Arbeitslager nt; **L**~ **Day** n der Tag der Arbeit.
labourer, (US) **laborer** ['leɪbərəʳ] n (Hilfs)arbeiter m; (farm ~) Landarbeiter m.
labour: L~ **Exchange** n (dated Brit) Arbeitsamt nt; ~ **force** n Arbeiterschaft f; ~**-market** n Arbeitsmarkt m; ~ **movement** n Arbeiterbewegung f; ~ **pains** npl Wehen pl; ~ **relations** npl die Beziehungen pl zwischen Unternehmern und Arbeitern or Gewerkschaften; ~**-saving** adj arbeitssparend.
labyrinth ['læbɪrɪnθ] n (lit, fig) Labyrinth nt.
lace [leɪs] **1** n (a) (fabric) Spitze f; (as trimming) Spitzenbesatz m. (b) (of shoe) Schnürsenkel m. ~**-up** (shoe) Schnürschuh m. **2** vt (a) schnüren. (b) **to** ~ **a drink** einen Schuß Alkohol in ein Getränk geben; ~**d with brandy** mit einem Schuß Weinbrand.
♦**lace up 1** vt sep (zu)schnüren. **2** vi geschnürt werden.
lacerate ['læsəreɪt] vt verletzen; (by glass etc) zerschneiden; painting aufschlitzen. **her knee was badly** ~**d** sie hatte tiefe Wunden am Knie.
laceration [,læsə'reɪʃən] n Fleischwunde f.
lack [læk] **1** n Mangel m. **through** ~ **of sth** aus Mangel an etw (dat); **they failed through** ~ **of support** sie scheiterten, weil es ihnen an Unterstützung mangelte; ~ **of water** Wassermangel m; **there is no** ~ **of money in that family** in dieser Familie fehlt es nicht an Geld. **2** vt **they** ~ **the necessary talent** es fehlt ihnen am richtigen Talent; **we** ~ **time** uns fehlt die nötige Zeit. **3** vi **to be** ~**ing** fehlen; **to be found** ~**ing** zu wünschen

übrig lassen; **he is** ~**ing in confidence** ihm fehlt es an Selbstvertrauen; **he** ~**ed for nothing** es fehlte ihm an nichts.
lackadaisical [,lækə'deɪzɪkəl] adj (lacking energy) schlapp; (idle) saumselig.
lackey ['lækɪ] n (lit, fig) Lakai m.
lacklustre ['læk,lʌstəʳ] adj surface glanzlos; style farblos.
laconic [lə'kɒnɪk] adj lakonisch; prose, style knapp.
lacquer ['lækəʳ] **1** n Lack m; (Brit: hair~) Haarspray nt. **2** vt lackieren; (Brit) hair sprayen.
lacrosse [lə'krɒs] n Lacrosse nt.
lad [læd] n Junge m; (in stable etc) Bursche m. **young** ~ junger Mann; **listen,** ~ hör mir mal zu, mein Junge!; **all together,** ~**s, push!** alle Mann anschieben!; **he's a bit of a** ~ (col) er ist ein ziemlicher Draufgänger; **he likes a night out with the** ~**s** (col) er geht abends gern mal mit seinen Kumpeln weg (col).
ladder ['lædəʳ] **1** n (a) (lit, fig) Leiter f. **the climb up the social** ~ der gesellschaftliche Aufstieg; **it's a first step up the** ~ das ist ein Anfang. (b) (Brit: in stocking) Laufmasche f. ~**proof** maschenfest. **2** vt (Brit) stocking zerreißen. **3** vi (Brit: stocking) Laufmaschen bekommen.
laden ['leɪdn] adj (lit, fig) beladen (with mit).
la-di-da ['lɑːdɪ'dɑː] adj (col) affektiert.
ladle ['leɪdl] **1** n (Schöpf)kelle f, Schöpflöffel m. **2** vt schöpfen.
lady ['leɪdɪ] n (a) Dame f. **"Ladies"** (lavatory) „Damen"; **where is the ladies** or **the ladies' room?** wo ist die Damentoilette?; **ladies and gentlemen!** sehr geehrte Damen und Herren!; **the old** ~ (col) (mother) die alte Dame (col); (wife) meine/seine Alte (col); **his young** ~ seine Freundin; **ladies' man** Charmeur m. (b) (noble) Adlige f. **L**~ (title) Lady f; **Our L**~ die Jungfrau Maria.
lady: ~**bird**, (US) ~**bug** n Marienkäfer m; ~ **doctor** n Ärztin f; ~ **friend** n Dame f; ~**-in-waiting** n Ehrendame f; ~**-killer** n (col) Herzensbrecher m; ~**like** adj damenhaft; ~**ship** n: **Your L**~**ship** Ihre Ladyschaft.
lag[1] [læg] **1** n (time-~) Zeitdifferenz f; (delay) Verzögerung f. **2** vi (time) langsam vergehen, dahinkriechen; (also ~ **behind**) zurückbleiben; **we** ~ **behind in space exploration** in der Raumforschung liegen wir (weit) zurück.
lag[2] vt pipe isolieren.
lager ['lɑːgəʳ] n helles Bier.
lagging ['lægɪn] n Isolierschicht f; (material) Isoliermaterial nt.
lagoon [lə'guːn] n Lagune f.
laid [leɪd] pret, ptp of **lay**[3].
laid-back ['leɪd'bæk] adj (col) gelassen, cool (col).
lain [leɪn] ptp of **lie**[2].
lair [lɛəʳ] n Lager nt; (cave) Höhle f; (den) Bau m.
laity ['leɪɪtɪ] n (Eccl) Laienstand m.
lake [leɪk] n See m.
lamb [læm] **1** n Lamm nt; (meat) Lamm(fleisch) nt. **2** vi lammen. **the** ~**ing season** die Lammungzeit.
lamb chop n Lammkotelett nt.
lambswool ['læmzwʊl] n Lammwolle f.
lame [leɪm] **1** adj (+er) (a) lahm; (as result of stroke etc) gelähmt. **the horse went** ~ das Pferd fing an zu lahmen. (b) (fig) excuse faul; argument schwach. ~ **duck** Niete f (col). **2** vt lähmen; horse

lahm machen.
lament [lə'ment] **1** *n* **(a)** Klage(n *pl*), Wehklage *f*.
(b) *(Mus)* Klagelied *nt*. **2** *vt* beklagen; *misfortune etc* bejammern. **to ~ sb** um jdn trauern. **3** *vi*
(weh)klagen. **to ~ for sb** um jdn trauern; **to ~ over sth** über etw *(acc)* jammern.
lamentable ['læməntəbl] *adj* beklagenswert; *work* erbärmlich.
laminated ['læmɪneɪtɪd] *adj* geschichtet; *windscreen* Verbundglas-; *book cover* laminiert. **~ glass** Verbundglas *nt*; **~ wood** Sperrholz *nt*; **~ plastic** Resopal ® *nt*.
lamp [læmp] *n* Lampe *f*; *(in street)* Laterne *f*; *(on ship)* Licht *nt*; *(torch)* Taschenlampe *f*.
lamp: ~light *n* Lampenlicht *nt*; *(in street)* Licht *nt* der Laterne(n); **by ~light** bei Lampenlicht.
lampoon [læm'puːn] **1** *n* Schmähschrift *f*. **2** *vt* verspotten.
lamp: ~post *n* Laternenpfahl *m*; **~shade** *n* Lampenschirm *m*; **~-standard** *n* = **~post**.
lance [lɑːns] **1** *n* Lanze *f*. **~-corporal** Obergefreite(r) *m*. **2** *vt* (Med) aufschneiden.
lancet ['lɑːnsɪt] *n* (Med) Lanzette *f*.
land [lænd] **1** *n* **(a)** *(not sea)* Land *nt*. **by ~** auf dem Landweg; **to see how the ~ lies** *(fig)* die Lage sondieren. **(b)** *(nation, region, fig)* Land *nt*. **to be in the ~ of the living** unter den Lebenden sein. **(c)** *(as property)* Grund und Boden *m*. **(d)** *(Agr)* Land *nt*; *(soil)* Boden *m*. **to work on the ~** das Land bebauen; **to live off the ~** *(grow own food)* sich von Selbstangebautem ernähren.
2 *vt* **(a)** *passengers* absetzen; *plane, troops* landen; *goods* abladen; *boat, fish on hook* an Land ziehen; *fish at port* anlanden. **(b)** *(col: obtain)* kriegen *(col)*; *contract* sich *(dat)* verschaffen; *prize* sich *(dat)* holen *(col)*. **(c)** *(col)* **he ~ed him a punch on the jaw** er versetzte ihm einen Kinnhaken; **it'll ~ you in jail** das wird dich noch ins Gefängnis bringen; **I've ~ed myself in a real mess** ich bin (ganz schön) in die Klemme geraten *(col)*; **I got ~ed with the job** man hat mir die Arbeit aufgehalst *(col)*; **I got ~ed with him for two hours** ich hatte ihn zwei Stunden lang auf dem Hals.
3 *vi* landen; *(from ship)* an Land gehen. **we're coming in to ~** wir setzen zur Landung an; **to ~ on one's feet** *(lit)* auf den Füßen landen; *(fig)* auf die Füße fallen; **he ~ed awkwardly** er ist ungeschickt aufgekommen.
♦ **land up** *vi (col)* landen *(col)*.
landed ['lændɪd] *adj* **the ~ class** die Großgrundbesitzer *pl*; **~ gentry** Landadel *m*.
landing ['lændɪŋ] *n* **(a)** *(of person, troops, plane)* Landung *f*. **(b)** *(on stairs) (inside house)* Gang *m*; *(outside flat door)* Treppenabsatz *m*.
landing: ~-card *n* Einreisekarte *f*; **~-craft** *n* Landungsboot *nt*; **~-stage** *n* (Brit Naut) Landesteg *m*; **~-strip** *n* Landebahn *f*.
land: ~lady *n* Vermieterin *f*; *(in pub)* Wirtin *f*; **~locked** *adj* von Land eingeschlossen; **a ~locked country** ein Binnenstaat *m*; **~lord** *n* *(of land)* Grundbesitzer *m*; *(of flat etc)* Vermieter *m*; *(of pub)* Wirt *m*; **~mark** *n* Wahrzeichen *nt*; *(fig)* Meilenstein *m*; **~-owner** *n* Grundbesitzer *m*; **~scape** ['lændskeɪp] **1** *n* Landschaft *f*; **2** *vt* *big area* landschaftlich gestalten; *garden* anlegen; **~scape gardening** *n* Landschafts-/Gartengestaltung *f*; **~slide** *n* (lit, fig) Erdrutsch *m*; **a ~slide victory** ein überwältigender Sieg.
lane [leɪn] *n* *(in country)* (Feld)weg *m*; *(in town)* Gasse *f*; Weg *m*; *(sport)* Bahn *f*; *(motorway)* Spur *f*. **"get in ~"** "bitte einordnen".
language ['læŋgwɪdʒ] *n* Sprache *f*. **bad ~** unanständige Ausdrücke *pl*; **strong ~** Kraftausdrücke *pl*; *(forceful)* harte Worte *pl*; **mind your ~!** so was sagt man nicht! *(col)*; **to talk the same ~** *(as sb)* die gleiche Sprache (wie jd) sprechen.
language: ~ course *f* Sprachkurs(us) *m*; **~**

lab(oratory) *n* Sprachlabor *nt*; **~ teacher** *n* Sprachlehrer(in *f*) *m*.
languid ['læŋgwɪd] *adj* träge; *gesture* müde; *appearance, manner* gelangweilt.
languish ['læŋgwɪʃ] *vi* schmachten; *(pine)* sich sehnen *(for nach)*.
languor ['læŋgə'] *n* Trägheit *f*; *(weakness)* Mattigkeit *f*.
languorous ['læŋgərəs] *adj* träge; *feeling* wohlig; *tone, voice* schläfrig.
lank [læŋk] *adj person* hager; *hair* strähnig.
lanky ['læŋkɪ] **1** *adj* (+er) schlaksig. **2** *n* (col) Lange(r) *mf (col)*.
lantern ['læntən] *n* Laterne *f*.
lap[1] [læp] *n* Schoß *m*. **it's in the ~ of the gods** es liegt im Schoß der Götter; **to live in the ~ of luxury** ein Luxusleben führen.
lap[2] *(Sport)* *n (round)* Runde *f*. **we're on the last ~ now** *(fig)* wir haben es bald geschafft.
lap[3] **1** *vt (lick)* lecken. **2** *vi (water)* klatschen *(against gegen)*.
♦ **lap up** *vt sep liquid* auflecken; *praise* genießen; *nonsense* schlucken. **she ~ped it ~** *(fig)* das ging ihr runter wie Honig *(col)*.
lapel [lə'pel] *n* Revers *nt or m*.
Lapland ['læplænd] *n* Lappland *nt*.
lapse [læps] **1** *n* **(a)** *(error)* Fehler *m*; *(moral)* Fehltritt *m*; *(decline)* Absinken *nt no pl*. **he had a ~ of memory** es ist ihm entfallen; **~ in standards** Niveauabfall *m*. **(b)** *(expiry)* Ablauf *m*; *(of claim)* Erlöschen *nt*; *(of time)* Zeitraum *m*. **there was a ~ in the conversation** es gab eine Gesprächspause. **2** *vi (a) (morally)* einen Fehltritt begehen; *(decline)* abgleiten. **to ~ into one's old ways** wieder in seine alten Gewohnheiten verfallen; **he ~d into silence** er verfiel in Schweigen; **his work is lapsing** seine Arbeit läßt nach. **(b)** *(expire)* ablaufen; *(claims)* erlöschen; *(correspondence)* einschlafen.
lapsed [læpst] *adj Catholic* abtrünnig.
larceny ['lɑːsənɪ] *n* (Jur) Diebstahl *m*.
larch [lɑːtʃ] *n* Lärche *f*.
lard [lɑːd] *n* Schweineschmalz *nt*.
larder ['lɑːdə'] *n (room)* Speisekammer *f*; *(cupboard)* Speiseschrank *m*.
large [lɑːdʒ] **1** *adj* (+er) **(a)** *(big)* groß; *person* korpulent. **~ as life** in voller Lebensgröße. **(b)** *(extensive)* weitreichend. **2** *adv* groß. **guilt was written ~ all over his face** die Schuld stand ihm deutlich im Gesicht geschrieben. **3** *n* **at ~** *(in general)* im großen und ganzen; **people at ~** die Allgemeinheit; **to be at ~** *(free)* frei herumlaufen; **strewn at ~** kreuz und quer verstreut.
largely ['lɑːdʒlɪ] *adv (mainly)* zum größten Teil.
large: ~-scale *adj* groß angelegt; **~-scale changes** Veränderungen *pl* in großem Umfang; **a ~-scale producer** ein Großhersteller *m*; **~-scale rioting** Massenunruhen *pl*; **a ~-scale map** eine (Land)karte in großem Maßstab.
lark[1] [lɑːk] *n (Orn)* Lerche *f*. **to get up with the ~** mit den Hühnern aufstehen.
lark[2] *n (col) (joke)* Jux *(col)*, Spaß *m*. **to do sth for a ~** etw (nur) aus Jux machen; **this whole agency ~** die ganze Geschichte mit der Agentur *(col)*.
♦ **lark about** *or* **around** *vi (col)* herumalbern. **to ~ ~ with sth** mit etw herumspielen.
larva ['lɑːvə] *n, pl -e* ['lɑːviː] Larve *f*.
laryngitis [ˌlærɪn'dʒaɪtɪs] *n* Kehlkopfentzündung *f*.
larynx ['lærɪŋks] *n* Kehlkopf *m*.
lascivious [lə'sɪvɪəs] *adj person, behaviour* lüstern.
laser ['leɪzə'] *n* Laser *m*. **~ beam** Laserstrahl *m*.
lash[1] [læʃ] *n (eye~)* Wimper *f*.
lash[2] **1** *n (whip)* Peitsche *f*; *(thong)* Schnur *f*; *(stroke, as punishment)* (Peitschen)schlag *m*; *(~ing) (of tail)* Schlagen *nt*; *(of waves, rain also)* Peitschen *nt*. **2** *vt* **(a)** *(beat)* peitschen; *(as punishment)* auspeitschen; *(rain)* peitschen gegen; *(tail)* schla-

gen mit. **the wind ~ed the sea into a fury** wütend peitschte der Wind die See. **(b)** *(tie)* festbinden *(to an +dat).* **to ~ sth together** etw zusammenbinden.

♦ **lash down 1** *vt sep (tie down)* festbinden. **2** *vi (rain etc)* niederprasseln.

♦ **lash out** *vi* **(a)** *(physically)* (wild) um sich schlagen. **to ~ ~ at sb** auf jdn losgehen. **(b)** *(in words)* vom Leder ziehen *(col).* **to ~ ~ against** *or* **at sb/sth** gegen jdn/etw wettern. **(c)** *(col: with money)* sich in Unkosten stürzen. **to ~ ~ on sth** sich *(dat)* etw was kosten lassen *(col).*

lashing ['læʃɪŋ] *n* **(a)** *(beating)* Prügel *pl; (punishment)* Auspeitschung *f.* **(b)** **~s** *pl (col)* eine Unmenge *(col);* **~s of money** massenhaft Geld *(col).*

lass [læs] *n* (junges) Mädchen.

lasso [læ'suː] **1** *n, pl* **-(e)s** Lasso *m or nt.* **2** *vt* mit dem Lasso einfangen.

last[1] [lɑːst] **1** *adj* letzte(r, s). **he was ~ to arrive** er kam als letzter an; **the ~ person** der letzte; **the ~ but one, the second ~ (one)** der/die/das vorletzte; **~ Monday** letzten Montag; **~ year** letztes Jahr; **during the ~ 20 years** in den letzten 20 Jahren; **to have the ~ laugh** zum Schluß das Lachen haben; **~ but not least** zuletzt; **that's the ~ thing I worry about** das ist das letzte, worüber ich mir Sorgen machen würde; **that was the ~ thing I expected** damit hatte ich am wenigsten gerechnet; **he's the ~ person I want to see** er ist der letzte, den ich sehen möchte. **2** *n* der/die/das letzte. **he was the ~ to leave** er ging als letzter; **each one is better than the ~** eins ist besser als das andere; **this is the ~ of the cake** das ist der Rest des Kuchens; **that was the ~ we heard of him** seitdem haben wir nichts mehr von ihm gehört; **we shall never hear the ~ of it** das werden wir noch lange zu hören kriegen; **at ~** endlich; **to the ~** bis zum Schluß. **3** *adv* **I ~ heard from him a month ago** vor einem Monat habe ich das letztemal von ihm gehört; **he spoke ~** er sprach als letzter.

last[2] **1** *vt* **it will ~ me a lifetime** das hält ein Leben lang; **these cigarettes will ~ me a week** diese Zigaretten reichen mir eine Woche. **2** *vi (continue)* dauern; *(remain intact: flowers, food, marriage)* halten; *(rain)* anhalten. **it's too good to ~** das ist zu schön, um wahr zu sein; **the previous boss ~ed only a week** der letzte Chef blieb nur eine Woche.

last-ditch ['lɑːst,dɪtʃ] *adj attr* in letzter Minute.

lasting ['lɑːstɪŋ] *adj relationship* dauerhaft; *shame etc* anhaltend.

lastly ['lɑːstlɪ] *adv* schließlich, zum Schluß.

last-minute [,lɑːst'mɪnɪt] *adj* in letzter Minute. **it was a ~ decision** er/sie *etc* hat sich in letzter Minute dazu entschlossen.

latch [lætʃ] *n* Riegel *m.* **to leave the door on the ~** die Tür nur einklinken.

♦ **latch on** *vi (col)* **(a)** *(get hold)* sich festhalten *(to sth an etw dat).* **he ~ed ~ to the idea of coming with us** er hat es sich *(dat)* in den Kopf gesetzt, mitzukommen. **(b)** *(attach oneself)* sich anschließen *(to dat).* **she ~ed ~ to me at the party** sie hängte sich auf der Party an mich *(col).* **(c)** *(understand)* kapieren *(col).*

latchkey ['lætʃ,kiː] *n* Haus-/Wohnungsschlüssel *m.* **~ child** Schlüsselkind *nt.*

late [leɪt] **1** *adj (+er)* **(a)** spät. **to be ~ (for sth)** (zu etw) zu spät kommen; **the train was ~** der Zug hatte Verspätung; **I was ~ in getting up this morning** ich bin heute morgen zu spät aufgestanden; **he is ~ with his rent** er hat seine Miete noch nicht bezahlt; **I don't want to make you ~** ich möchte Sie nicht aufhalten; **due to the ~ arrival of ...** wegen der verspäteten Ankunft ... *(+gen).* **(b)** *hour* spät; *opening hours* lang; *bus*

Spät-. **it's ~** es ist spät; **it's getting ~** es ist schon spät; **at this ~ hour** zu so später Stunde; **he keeps very ~ hours** er geht sehr spät ins Bett; **it happened in the ~ eighties** es geschah Ende der achtziger Jahre; **in the ~ morning am späten Vormittag; he came in ~ June** er kam Ende Juni. **(c)** *attr (deceased)* verstorben. **the ~ John F. Kennedy** John F. Kennedy. **(d)** *(former)* **the ~ Prime Minister** der frühere *or* vorige Premierminister.

2 *adv* spät. **to come ~** zu spät kommen; **the train arrived eight minutes ~** der Zug hatte acht Minuten Verspätung; **better ~ than never** besser spät als gar nicht; **to stay up ~** lange aufbleiben; **to work ~ at the office** länger im Büro arbeiten; **~ at night** spät abends; **~ in the afternoon** am späten Nachmittag; **~ in the year** (gegen) Ende des Jahres; **of ~** in letzter Zeit.

latecomer ['leɪtkʌmə[r]] *n* Nachzügler(in *f*) *m.*

lately ['leɪtlɪ] *adv* in letzter Zeit. **till ~** bis vor kurzem.

lateness ['leɪtnɪs] *n (at work etc)* Zuspätkommen *nt; (of train, payments)* Verspätung *f; (of meal)* späte Zeit; *(of harvest, seasons)* spätes Eintreten. **the ~ of the hour** die vorgerückte Stunde.

latent ['leɪtənt] *adj* latent; *ability, strength also* verborgen; *energy* ungenutzt.

later ['leɪtə[r]] **1** *adj* später. **at a ~ date** zu einem späteren Termin; **a ~ edition** eine neuere Auflage; **in his ~ years** in seinem späteren Leben. **2** *adv* später. **~ that night** später in der Nacht; **a moment ~** einen Augenblick später; **see you ~!** bis später!; **not ~ than 1995** spätestens 1995; **~ on** nachher.

lateral ['lætərəl] *adj* seitlich.

latest ['leɪtɪst] **1** *adj* **(a)** späteste(r, s). **what is the ~ date you can come?** wann kannst du spätestens kommen? **(b)** *(most recent) fashion, version* neu(e)ste(r, s). **the ~ news** das Neu(e)ste. **2** *adv* am spätesten. **3** *n* **(a)** **what's the ~ (about John)?** was gibt's Neues (über John)?; **wait till you hear the ~!** warte, bis du das Neueste gehört hast! **(b)** **at the (very) ~** spätestens.

latex ['leɪteks] *n* Latex *(spec),* Milchsaft *m.*

lath [læθ] *n* Latte *f.* **~s** *pl (structure)* Lattenwerk *nt.*

lathe [leɪð] *n* Drehbank *f.* **~ operator** Dreher *m.*

lather ['lɑːðə[r]] **1** *n* **(a)** *(of soap)* (Seifen)schaum *m; (sweat)* Schweiß *m.* **the horse was in a ~** das Pferd war schweißnaß; **to get into a ~ (about sth)** *(col)* sich (über etw *acc*) aufregen. **2** *vt* einschäumen. **3** *vi* schäumen.

Latin ['lætɪn] **1** *adj (Roman) civilization* römisch; *poets also* lateinisch; *temperament* südländisch. **~ language** lateinische Sprache. **2** *n (language)* Latein(isch) *nt.*

Latin America *n* Lateinamerika *nt.*

Latin-American ['lætɪnə'merɪkən] **1** *adj* lateinamerikanisch. **2** *n* Lateinamerikaner(in *f*) *m.*

latitude ['lætɪtjuːd] *n* Breite *f; (fig)* Freiheit *f.*

latrine ['lætrɪn] *n* Latrine *f.*

latter ['lætə[r]] **1** *adj* **(a)** *(second of two)* letztere(r, s). **(b)** *(at the end)* **the ~ part of the book is better** gegen Ende wird das Buch besser; **the ~ part of the week** die zweite Hälfte der Woche; **in his ~ years** in den späteren Jahren seines Lebens. **2** *n* **the ~** der/die/das letztere; der letzteren.

latterly ['lætəlɪ] *adv* in letzter Zeit.

lattice ['lætɪs] *n* Gitter *nt.* **~-work** Gitterwerk *nt.*

laudable ['lɔːdəbl] *adj* lobenswert.

laugh [lɑːf] **1** *n* Lachen *nt.* **she gave a loud ~** sie lachte laut auf; **to have a good ~ about sth** köstlich über etw *(acc)* amüsieren; **it'll give us a ~** *(col)* das wird lustig; **the ~ was on me** der Witz ging auf meine Kosten; **to have the last ~** *(over or on sb)* es jdm zeigen *(col);* **what a ~** (das ist ja) zum Totlachen *(col)!*; **just for a ~** nur (so) aus Spaß; **it'll be a good ~** es wird bestimmt lustig,

he's a ~ er ist zum Schreien (col).
  2 vi lachen (about, at, over über +acc). **to** ~ **at
sb** sich über jdn lustig machen; **to** ~ **up one's
sleeve** sich (dat) ins Fäustchen lachen; **it's
all very well for you to** ~ du hast gut lachen;
you'll be ~**ing on the other side of your face
soon** dir wird das Lachen bald vergehen; **to** ~ **in
sb's face** jdm ins Gesicht lachen; **he who** ~**s
last** ~**s longest** (Prov) wer zuletzt lacht, lacht
am besten (Prov); **don't make me** ~! (iro col)
daß ich nicht lache! (col); **you've got your
own house, you're** ~**ing** (col) du hast ein
eigenes Haus, du hast es gut.
  3 vt **to** ~ **oneself silly** sich tot- or kaputtlachen
(col); **he was** ~**ed out of court** er wurde ausge-
lacht.
♦ **laugh off** vt **(a)** always separate **to** ~ **one's head**
~ sich totlachen (col). **(b)** sep (dismiss) mit
einem Lachen abtun.
laughable ['lɑːfəbl] adj lächerlich.
laughing ['lɑːfɪŋ] **1** adj lachend. **it's no** ~ **matter**
das ist nicht zum Lachen **2** n Lachen nt.
laughing stock n Witzfigur f. **his ideas made him
a** ~ mit seinen Ideen machte er sich lächerlich.
laughter ['lɑːftəʳ] n Gelächter nt. ~ **broke out
among the audience** das Publikum brach in Gelächter aus.
launch [lɔːntʃ] **1** n **(a)** (vessel) Barkasse f.
(~ing) (of ship) Stapellauf m; (of lifeboat)
Aussetzen nt; (of rocket) Abschuß m. **(c)** (~ing)
(of company) Gründung f; (of new product) Einführung f. **2** vt **(a)** new vessel vom Stapel lassen;
lifeboat aussetzen; rocket abschießen. **Lady X**
~**ed the new boat** der Stapellauf fand in Anwesenheit von Lady X statt. **(b)** company
gründen; new product auf den Markt bringen. **to**
~ **an offensive against the enemy** zum Angriff
gegen den Feind übergehen.
♦ **launch into** vi +prep obj (attack) angreifen. **the
author** ~**es straight** ~ **his main theme** der Autor
kommt gleich zum Hauptthema.
♦ **launch out** vi (diversify) sich verlegen (in auf
+acc). **the company** ~**ed** ~ **in several new
directions** die Firma stieg in einige neue Bran-
chen ein.
launching ['lɔːntʃɪŋ] n = **launch 1 (b)**.
launching pad n Abschußrampe f; (fig) Sprungbrett nt.
launder ['lɔːndəʳ] vti waschen und bügeln.
launderette [,lɔːndə'ret] n (Brit) Waschsalon m.
laundromat ['lɔːndrəʊmæt] n (US) Waschsalon m.
laundry ['lɔːndrɪ] n (place) Wäscherei f; (clothes)
(dirty) schmutzige Wäsche; (washed) Wäsche f. **to
do the** ~ (Wäsche) waschen.
laurel ['lɒrəl] n Lorbeer m. **to rest on one's** ~**s** sich
auf seinen Lorbeeren ausruhen.
lava ['lɑːvə] n Lava f.
lavatory ['lævətrɪ] n Toilette f. ~ **seat** Toilettensitz
m.
lavender ['lævɪndəʳ] n (flower) Lavendel m.
lavish ['lævɪʃ] **1** adj gifts großzügig; praise,
affection überschwenglich; banquet, party üppig;
(pej) verschwenderisch. **to be** ~ **with sth** mit etw
verschwenderisch umgehen; **to be** ~ **with one's
money** das Geld mit vollen Händen ausgeben. **2**
vt **to** ~ **sth on sb** jdn mit etw überhäufen.
lavishly ['lævɪʃlɪ] adv give großzügig; praise überschwenglich; put paint on reichlich; entertain üppig. **they entertain** ~ sie geben feudale Feste; ~
furnished aufwendig eingerichtet.
law [lɔː] n Gesetz nt; (system) Recht nt; (as study)
Jura no art. ~ **of nature** Naturgesetz nt; **it's the** ~
das ist Gesetz; **his word is** ~ sein Wort ist Gesetz; **is there a** ~ **against it?** ist das verboten?;
he is a ~ **unto himself** er macht, was er will; **he
is above the** ~ er steht über dem Gesetz; **to keep
within the** ~ sich im Rahmen des Gesetzes
bewegen; **in** ~ vor dem Gesetz; **by** ~ gesetzlich;

to go to ~ vor Gericht gehen; **to take the** ~ **into
one's own hands** das Recht selbst in die Hand
nehmen; ~ **and order** Recht und Ordnung; **I'll
have the** ~ **on you** (col) ich rufe die Polizei.
law: ~-**abiding** adj gesetzestreu; ~**breaker** n
Rechtsbrecher m; ~ **court** n Gericht nt.
lawful ['lɔːfʊl] adj rechtmäßig.
lawless ['lɔːlɪs] adj act gesetzwidrig; person ge-
setzlos; country ohne Gesetzgebung.
lawlessness ['lɔːlɪsnɪs] n Gesetzwidrigkeit f.
lawn [lɔːn] n (grass) Rasen m no pl.
lawn: ~**mower** n Rasenmäher m; ~ **tennis** n Ra-
sentennis nt.
law: ~**school** n (US) juristische Fakultät; ~ **student** n Jurastudent(in f) m; ~**suit** n Prozeß m,
Klage f; **he brought a** ~**suit for damages or**
strengte eine Schadenersatzklage an.
lawyer ['lɔːjəʳ] n (Rechts)anwalt m, (Rechts)an-
wältin f.
lax [læks] adj (+er) lax; discipline lasch; morals
locker. **to be** ~ **about sth** etw vernachlässigen;
he's ~ **about washing** er nimmt's mit dem Waschen nicht so genau.
laxative ['læksətɪv] n Abführmittel nt.
laxity ['læksɪtɪ], **laxness** ['læksnɪs] n Laxheit f;
(carelessness) Nachlässigkeit f.
lay¹ [leɪ] adj Laien-.
lay² pret of **lie**.
lay³ (vb: pret, ptp **laid**) **1** vt **(a)** (place, put) legen
(sth on sth etw auf etw acc). **to** ~ **(one's) hands on**
(get hold of) erwischen; (find) finden; **I never laid
a hand on him** ich habe ihn überhaupt nicht
angefaßt.
  (b) bricks, foundations, track, mines, eggs legen;
cable verlegen; carpet (ver)legen; (prepare) fire
herrichten; (Brit) table decken; plans schmieden.
to ~ **breakfast** den Frühstückstisch decken.
  (c) (non-material things) burden auferlegen
(on sb jdm). **to** ~ **the blame for sth on sb** jdm die
Schuld an etw (dat) geben; **to** ~ **oneself open to
criticism** sich der Kritik aussetzen; **the police
laid a charge of murder against him** die Polizei
erstattete gegen ihn Anzeige wegen Mordes; **he
laid his case before them** er trug ihnen seinen
Fall vor; **to** ~ **a bet on sth** auf etw (acc) wetten.
  (d) ghost anstreiben; fear zerstreuen.
  (e) (col: sexually) aufs Kreuz legen (col).
  2 vi (hen) legen.
♦ **lay aside** vt sep work etc zur Seite legen; (save)
beiseite legen; plans etc auf Eis legen.
♦ **lay down** vt sep **(a)** book, pen etc hinlegen (on auf
+acc). **(b)** (give up) burden ablegen; office niederlegen. **to** ~ ~ **one's arms** die Waffen niederlegen; **to** ~ ~ **one's life** sein Leben opfern. **(c)**
policy festsetzen; rules festlegen. **to** ~ ~ **the
law** (col) Vorschriften machen (to sb jdm).
♦ **lay in** vt sep food etc einlagern; supplies also
anlegen.
♦ **lay into** vi +prep obj (col) **to** ~ ~ **sb** auf jdn
losgehen; (verbally) jdn fertigmachen (col).
♦ **lay off 1** vi (col: stop) aufhören (prep obj mit). ~
it! hör auf damit!; ~ **my little brother, will
you!** laß bloß meinen kleinen Bruder in
Ruhe! **2** vt sep workers entlassen; (temporarily)
Feierschichten machen lassen. **to be laid** ~
entlassen werden; Feierschichten einlegen
müssen.
♦ **lay on** vt sep **(a)** (apply) paint auftragen. **(b)**
hospitality bieten (for sb jdm); entertainment
sorgen für; excursion veranstalten; extra buses
einsetzen; water, electricity anschließen.
♦ **lay out** vt sep **(a)** clothes zurechtlegen; corpse
aufbahren. **(b)** (design, arrange) anlegen; room
aufteilen; rooms in house anordnen; page um-
brechen; (in magazines) das Layout (+gen) machen. **(c)** money ausgeben. **(d)** (knock out) ~
sb jdn erledigen (col).
♦ **lay up** vt sep **(a)** (store) lagern; supply anlegen;

(amass) anhäufen. **he's ~ing ~ trouble for himself in the future** er wird später noch (viel) Ärger bekommen. **(b)** *(immobilize) ship* auflegen; *car* stillegen. **to be laid ~ (in bed)** im Bett liegen.

lay: ~**about** *n* Nichtstuer *m;* ~**by** *n (Brit) (in town)* Parkbucht *f; (in country)* Parkplatz *m; (big)* Rastplatz *m.*

layer ['leɪəʳ] *n* Schicht *(also Geol),* Lage *f.*

lay: ~**man** *n* Laie *m;* **to the** ~**man** für den Laien; ~-**off** *n* **further** ~-**offs were unavoidable** weitere Arbeiter mußten entlassen werden *or (temporarily)* mußten Feierschichten einlegen; ~**out** *n* Anordnung *f; (Typ)* Layout *nt;* **we have changed the** ~**out of this office** wir haben dieses Büro anders aufgeteilt.

laze [leɪz] *vi (also:* ~ **about,** ~ **around)** faulenzen.

laziness ['leɪzɪnɪs] *n* Faulheit *f; (languor)* Trägheit *f.*

lazy ['leɪzɪ] *adj (+er)* faul; *(slow-moving)* langsam; *(lacking activity)* träge. **we had a** ~ **holiday** wir haben im Urlaub nur gefaulenzt.

lazybones ['leɪzɪˌbəʊnz] *n sing (col)* Faulpelz *m.*

lb *n (weight)* ≈ Pfd.

lead¹ [led] *n (metal)* Blei *nt; (in pencil)* Graphit *nt.*

lead² [liːd] *(vb: pret, ptp* **led)** **1** *n* **(a)** *(front position)* Spitzenposition *f; (Sport)* Führung *f; (distance, time ahead)* Vorsprung *m.* **to have two minutes' ~ over sb** zwei Minuten Vorsprung vor jdm haben; **to be in the ~** in Führung liegen; **he took the ~ from the German runner** er ging vor dem deutschen Läufer in Führung; **it's my** *(Cards)* ~ ich fange an. **(b)** *(example)* Beispiel *nt.* **to follow sb's** ~ jds Beispiel folgen. **(c)** *(clue)* Anhaltspunkt *m; (in guessing etc)* Tip *m.* **the police have a ~** die Polizei hat eine Spur. **(d)** *(Theat) (part)* Hauptrolle *f; (person)* Hauptdarsteller(in *f) m.* **to sing the ~** die tragende Partie singen. **(e)** *(leash)* Leine *f.* **on a ~** an der Leine. **(f)** *(Elec)* Leitung *f,* Kabel *nt.*

2 *vt* **(a)** *(conduct) person, animal* führen. **that road will ~ you to the station** auf dieser Straße kommen Sie zum Bahnhof; **to ~ the way** *(lit, fig)* vorangehen; *(fig: be superior)* führend sein.

(b) *(be the leader of, direct)* (an)führen; *expedition, team* leiten; *movement, revolution* anführen; *orchestra (conductor)* leiten; *(first violin)* führen. **to ~ a government** an der Spitze einer Regierung stehen; **to ~ a party** den Parteivorsitz führen.

(c) *(be first in)* anführen. **they led us by 30 seconds** sie lagen 30 Sekunden vor uns *(dat);* **Britain led the world in textiles** Großbritannien war auf dem Gebiet der Textilproduktion führend in der Welt.

(d) *card* ausspielen.

(e) *life* führen. **to ~ a life of luxury** in Luxus leben, ein Luxusleben führen.

(f) *(influence)* **to ~ sb to do sth** jdn dazu bringen, etw zu tun; **what led him to change his mind?** wie kam er dazu, seine Meinung zu ändern?; **he is easily led** er läßt sich leicht beeinflussen; **this led me to the conclusion that ...** daraus schloß ich, daß ...

3 *vi* **(a)** *(go in front)* vorangehen; *(in race)* in Führung liegen. **to ~ by 10 metres** 10 Meter Vorsprung haben. **(b)** *(be a leader)* führen. **(c)** *(Cards)* ausspielen *(with sth etw).* **(d)** *(street etc)* führen. **it ~s into that room** es führt zu diesem Raum. **(e)** *(result in, cause)* führen *(to zu).* **remarks like that could ~ to trouble** solche Bemerkungen können unangenehme Folgen haben; **what will all these strikes ~ to?** wo sollen all diese Streiks hinführen?

♦ **lead away** *vt sep* wegführen; *prisoner* abführen.

♦ **lead off 1** *vt sep* abführen. **a policeman led the drunk man ~ the pitch** ein Polizist führte den Betrunkenen vom Platz. **2** *vi* **several streets led ~ the square** mehrere Straßen gingen vom

Platz ab.

♦ **lead on 1** *vi usu imper* ~ ~, **sergeant!** führen Sie an, Feldwebel! **2** *vt sep (deceive)* hinters Licht führen; *(tease)* aufziehen. **he led us ~ to believe that we would get the money** er hat uns vorgemacht, wir würden das Geld bekommen; **she's just** ~**ing him ~** sie führt ihn nur an der Nase herum.

♦ **lead up** *vi* **the events that led ~ to the war** die Ereignisse, die dem Krieg vorausgingen; **what are you** ~**ing ~ to?** worauf willst du hinaus?; **what's all this** ~**ing ~ to?** was soll das Ganze?

leaded ['ledɪd] *adj window* Bleiglas-.

leader ['liːdəʳ] *n* **(a)** Führer *m; (of union, party also)* Vorsitzende(r) *mf; (military also)* Befehlshaber *m; (of gang, rebels)* Anführer *m; (of expedition, project)* Leiter(in *f) m; (Sport) (in league)* Tabellenführer *m; (in race)* der/die/das Erste; *(Mus) (Brit: of orchestra)* Konzertmeister *m; (of choir)* Leiter *m; (of pop group)* Leader *m.* **to be the** ~**s** *(in race, competition)* in Führung liegen; **the** ~**s** *(in race, competition)* die Spitzengruppe; ~ **of the opposition** Oppositionsführer(in *f) m;* **the product is a** ~ **in its field** dieses Produkt ist auf diesem Gebiet führend. **(b)** *(Brit Press)* Leitartikel *m.* ~ **writer** Leitartikler *m.*

leadership ['liːdəʃɪp] *n* **(a)** Führung *f.* **under the** ~ **of** unter (der) Führung von. **(b)** *(quality)* Führungsqualitäten *pl.*

lead-free ['led'friː] *adj* bleifrei.

leading ['liːdɪŋ] *adj* **(a)** *(first)* vorderste(r, s); *runner also* führend. **(b)** *(most important) person, company* führend; *sportsman, product* Spitzen-; *issue; (Theat) part* Haupt-.

leading: ~ **lady** *n* Hauptdarstellerin *f;* ~ **light** *n (person)* Leuchte *f;* ~ **man** *n* Hauptdarsteller *m;* ~ **question** *n* Suggestivfrage *f.*

lead [led-]: ~ **pencil** *n* Bleistift *m;* ~-**poisoning** *n* Bleivergiftung *f.*

lead story [liːd-] *n* Hauptartikel *m.*

leaf [liːf] **1** *n, pl* **leaves** **(a)** Blatt *nt.* **to be in** ~ grün sein. **(b)** *(of paper)* Blatt *nt.* **to take a** ~ **out of sb's book** sich *(dat)* von jdm eine Scheibe abschneiden; **to turn over a new** ~ einen neuen Anfang machen. **(c)** *(of table)* Ausziehplatte *f.* **2** *vi* **to** ~ **through a book** ein Buch durchblättern.

leaflet ['liːflɪt] *n* Prospekt *m; (with instructions)* Merkblatt *nt; (handout)* Flugblatt *nt; (brochure)* Broschüre *f.*

leafy ['liːfɪ] *adj tree* belaubt; *lane* grün.

league [liːg] *n* **(a)** *(treaty)* Bündnis *nt,* Bund *m; (organization)* Verband *m.* **L~ of Nations** Völkerbund *m;* **to be in** ~ **with sb** mit jdm gemeinsame Sache machen. **(b)** *(Sport)* Liga *f.* **he's not in the same** ~ *(fig)* er hat nicht das gleiche Format.

leak [liːk] **1** *n (lit, fig)* undichte Stelle; *(Naut)* Leck *nt; (escape of liquid)* Leck *nt.* **to have a** ~ undicht sein; **a gas** ~ eine undichte Stelle in der Gasleitung; **there's been a** ~ **to the press** man hat der Presse etwas zugespielt. **2** *vt durchlassen; (fig) information* zuspielen *(to sb jdm).* **3** *vi* **(a)** *(ship, receptacle)* lecken; *(roof, shoes)* nicht dicht sein; *(pen)* auslaufen. **(b)** *(gas)* ausströmen; *(liquid)* auslaufen. **water is** ~**ing (in) through the roof** Wasser sickert durch das Dach.

leakage ['liːkɪdʒ] *n (act)* Auslaufen *nt.* **the ground was polluted by a** ~ **of chemicals** der Boden war durch auslaufende Chemikalien verunreinigt.

leaky ['liːkɪ] *adj (+er)* undicht; *boat also* leck.

lean¹ [liːn] *adj (+er) (a) (thin) person, face, person* schmal; *(through lack of food)* hager; *meat* mager. **(b)** *(poor) year, harvest* mager.

lean² *(vb: pret, ptp* ~**ed** *or* **leant) 1** *vt (put in sloping position)* lehnen *(against gegen, an +acc); (rest)* aufstützen *(on auf +dat or acc).* **to** ~ **one's head on sb's shoulder** seinen Kopf an jds Schulter *(acc)* lehnen; **to ~ one's elbow on sth** sich mit dem Ellbogen auf etw *(acc)* stützen. **2** *vi* **(a)** *(be off vertical)* sich neigen *(to* nach); *(trees)* sich biegen. **he ~t across the counter** er beugte sich über den Ladentisch. **(b)** *(rest)* sich lehnen *(against* gegen +*acc).* **he ~t on the edge of the table** er stützte sich auf die Tischkante. **(c)** *(tend in opinion etc)* **to ~ towards the left/socialism** nach links/zum Sozialismus tendieren.

♦ **lean back** *vi* sich zurücklehnen.

♦ **lean forward** *vi* sich vorbeugen.

♦ **lean on** *vi (depend)* **to ~ ~ sb** sich auf jdn verlassen; *(col: put pressure on)* jdn bearbeiten *(col) or* beknien *(col).*

♦ **lean out** *vi* sich hinauslehnen *(of* aus).

♦ **lean over** *vi (be off vertical)* sich (vor)neigen; *(bend)* sich vorbeugen *(sth* über +*acc).*

leaning ['li:nɪŋ] **1** *adj* schräg, schief. **2** *n* Hang *m.*

leant [lent] *pret, ptp of* **lean.**

lean-to ['li:ntu:] *n* Anbau *m; (shelter)* Wetterschutz *m.*

leap [li:p] *(vb: pret, ptp* ~ed *or* **leapt) 1** *n* Sprung *m.* **in one ~** mit einem Satz; **a great ~ forward** *(fig)* ein großer Sprung nach vorn; **a ~ in the dark** *(fig)* ein Sprung ins Ungewisse; **by ~s and bounds** *(fig)* sprunghaft. **2** *vt* springen über *(+acc).* **3** *vi* springen. **to ~ to one's feet** aufspringen; **my heart leapt** mein Herz machte einen Sprung.

♦ **leap at** *vi +prep obj offer, opportunity* sich stürzen auf *(+acc).*

♦ **leap up** *vi (person)* aufspringen; *(flames)* hochschlagen; *(prices)* sprunghaft ansteigen.

leapfrog ['li:pfrɒg] **1** *n* Bockspringen *nt.* **2** *vi* **he ~ged over him** er machte einen Bocksprung über ihn.

leap year *n* Schaltjahr *nt.*

leapt [lept] *pret, ptp of* **leap.**

learn [lɜ:n] *pret, ptp* ~ed *or* **learnt 1** *vt* lernen; *language also* erlernen; *(be informed)* erfahren. **I ~t (how) to swim** ich habe schwimmen gelernt; **we ~t (how) to write business letters** wir lernten Geschäftsbriefe schreiben. **2** *vi* lernen; *(find out)* erfahren *(about, of* von). **I can't, but I'm hoping to ~** ich kann's nicht, aber ich hoffe, es zu lernen; **he'll never ~!** er lernt es nie!; **to ~ from experience** durch Erfahrung lernen.

learned ['lɜ:nɪd] *adj* gelehrt; *society also, profession* akademisch. **a ~ man** ein Gelehrter *m.*

learner ['lɜ:nə'] *n* Anfänger(in *f) m; (Brit: ~ driver)* Fahrschüler(in *f) m.* **slow ~** lernschwache Schüler.

learning ['lɜ:nɪŋ] *n (act)* Lernen *nt; (erudition)* Gelehrsamkeit *f.* **a man of ~** ein Gelehrter *m.*

learnt [lɜ:nt] *pret, ptp of* **learn.**

lease [li:s] **1** *n (of land, business premises etc)* Pacht *f; (contract)* Pachtvertrag *m; (of house, office)* Miete *f; (contract)* Mietvertrag *m.* **to take a ~ on a house** ein Haus mieten; **to let sth out on ~** etw verpachten/vermieten; **to give sb a new ~ of life** jdm (neuen) Aufschwung geben. **2** *vt (take) (from* von) pachten; mieten; *(give: also ~ out) (to* an +*acc)* verpachten; vermieten.

lease-: ~hold 1 *n (property)* Pachtbesitz *m;* **2** *adj* gepachtet; *property* Pacht-; **~holder** *n* Pächter *m.*

leash [li:ʃ] *n* Leine *f.* **on a ~** an der Leine.

least [li:st] **1** *adj* geringste(r, s). **2** *adv* am wenigsten; **~ possible expenditure** möglichst geringe Kosten; **the ~ expensive car** das billigste Auto; **he's the ~ aggressive of men** er ist nicht im mindesten aggressiv; **not the ~ bit drunk** kein bißchen betrunken. **3** *n* **the ~** der/die/das Geringste; **it's the ~ one can do** es ist das wenigste, was man tun kann; **at ~ it's not raining** wenigstens regnet es nicht; **there were eight at ~** es waren mindestens acht da; **we need three at the very ~** allermindestens

brauchen wir drei; **not in the ~ (upset)** nicht im geringsten (verärgert); **to say the ~ um es milde zu sagen; the ~ said, the better** *(Prov)* je weniger man darüber spricht, desto besser.

leather ['leðə'] **1** *n* Leder *nt.* **2** *adj* Leder-, ledern.

leave [li:v] *(vb: pret, ptp* **left) 1** *n* **(a)** *(permission)* Erlaubnis *f.* **to ask sb's ~** to do sth jdn um Erlaubnis bitten, etw zu tun. **(b)** *(permission to be absent, Mil)* Urlaub *m.* **to be on ~** auf Urlaub sein; **to be on ~ of absence** beurlaubt sein. **(c) to take one's ~** sich verabschieden *(of sb* von jdm*);* **to take ~ of one's senses** den Verstand verlieren.

2 *vt* **(a)** *(depart from, quit) place, person* verlassen. **the train left the station** der Zug fuhr aus dem Bahnhof; **when he left Rome** als er von Rom wegging/wegfuhr *etc;* **to ~ home** von zu Hause weggehen; **to ~ one's job** seine Stelle aufgeben; **I'll ~ you at the station** *(in car)* ich setze dich am Bahnhof ab.

(b) *(allow or cause to remain)* lassen; *mark, message, scar* hinterlassen; *meal* stehenlassen. **who left the window open?** wer hat das Fenster offengelassen?; **this ~s me free for the afternoon** dadurch habe ich den Nachmittag frei; **~ me alone!** laß mich (in Ruhe)!; **to ~ well alone** die Finger davonlassen *(col);* **to ~ sb to himself** jdn allein lassen; **to ~ go of** loslassen; **let's ~ it at that** lassen wir es dabei (bewenden); **I was left with the bill** ich saß mit der Rechnung da.

(c) *(forget)* liegenlassen, stehenlassen.

(d) to be left *(remain, be over)* übrigbleiben; **all I have left is this**, was ich noch habe; **3 from 10 ~s 7** 10 minus 3 (ist) gleich 7; **nothing was left for me but to sell it** mir blieb nichts anderes übrig, als es zu verkaufen.

(e) *(entrust)* überlassen *(up to sb* jdm.). **~ it to me** laß mich nur machen!; **I ~ it to you das** überlasse ich Ihnen; **to ~ sth to chance** etw dem Zufall überlassen.

(f) *(after death) money, person* hinterlassen.

3 *vi (weg)gehen, abfahren; (plane)* abfliegen. **we ~ for Sweden tomorrow** wir fahren morgen nach Schweden.

♦ **leave behind** *vt sep car, children* dalassen; *(outstrip)* hinter sich *(dat)* lassen; *(forget)* liegenlassen, stehenlassen. **we've left all that ~ us** das alles liegt hinter uns.

♦ **leave in** *vt sep piece in play etc* darinlassen.

♦ **leave off 1** *vt sep clothes* nicht anziehen; *lid* nicht darauftun; *lights* auslassen. **you left her name ~ the list** Sie haben ihren Namen nicht in die Liste aufgenommen. **2** *vi +prep obj (col)* aufhören. **we ~ work after lunch** wir haben nach dem Mittagessen Feierabend gemacht; **~ (doing that)!** hör auf (damit)!

♦ **leave on** *vt sep clothes, lights* anlassen.

♦ **leave out** *vt sep* **(a)** *(not bring in)* draußen lassen. **(b)** *(omit)* auslassen; *(exclude) people* ausschließen *(of* von). **you ~ my wife ~ of this** lassen Sie meine Frau aus dem Spiel! **(c)** *(leave available)* dalassen; *(not put away)* liegen lassen. **I'll ~ the books ~ on my desk** ich lasse die Bücher auf meinem Schreibtisch.

♦ **leave over** *vt sep (leave surplus)* übriglassen. **to be left ~** übrig(geblieben) sein.

leaves [li:vz] *pl of* **leaf.**

Lebanon ['lebənən] *n* **the ~** der Libanon.

lecherous ['letʃərəs] *adj* lüstern; *man also* geil.

lecture ['lektʃə'] **1** *n* **(a)** *(Univ)* Vortrag *m;* Vorlesung *f.* **to give a ~** einen Vortrag/eine Vorlesung halten *(to* für, *on sth* über etw *acc).* **(b)** *(scolding)* **to give sb a ~** jdm eine Strafpredigt halten *(about* wegen). **2** *vt* **(a) to ~ sb on sth** jdm einen Vortrag/eine Vorlesung über etw *(acc)* halten; **he ~s us in physics** wir hören bei ihm (Vorlesungen in) Physik. **(b)** *(scold)* abkanzeln.

3 *vi* einen Vortrag halten; *(Univ)* eine Vorlesung halten; *(give* ~ *course)* Vorlesungen halten *(on über +acc).* **he ~s in English** er ist Dozent für Anglistik.

lecture: ~ **hall** *n (Univ)* Hörsaal *nt;* ~ **notes** *npl (professor's)* Manuskript *nt; (student's)* Aufzeichnungen *pl.*

lecturer ['lektʃərəʳ] *n (Univ)* Dozent(in *f) m; (speaker)* Referent(in *f) m.*

led [led] *pret, ptp of* **lead**².

ledge [ledʒ] *n* Leiste, Kante *f; (of window) (inside)* Fensterbrett *nt; (outside)* Sims *nt or m; (shelf)* Ablage *f; (mountain* ~*)* (Fels)vorsprung *m.*

ledger ['ledʒəʳ] *n* Hauptbuch *nt.*

lee [liː] **1** *adj* Lee-. **2** *n* **(a)** *(Naut)* Lee *f.* **(b)** *(shelter)* Windschatten *m.*

leech [liːtʃ] *n* Blutegel *m; (fig)* Blutsauger *m.*

leek [liːk] *n* Porree, Lauch *m.*

leer [lɪəʳ] **1** *n (knowing, sexual)* anzügliches Grinsen; *(evil)* heimtückischer Blick. **2** *vi* anzüglich grinsen; einen heimtückischen Blick haben. **he ~ed at her** er warf ihr lüsterne Blicke zu.

leeward ['liːwəd] **1** *adj* Lee-. **2** *n* Lee(seite) *f.* **to** ~ leewärts.

leeway ['liːweɪ] *n* **(a)** *(Naut)* Leeweg *m.* **(b)** *(fig) (flexibility)* Spielraum *m.* **to make up** ~ den Zeitverlust aufholen.

left¹ [left] *pret, ptp of* **leave**.

left² **1** *adj (also Pol)* linke(r, s). **2** *adv* links *(of* von*).* **turn** ~ *(Aut)* links abbiegen; **keep** ~ links halten. **3** *n* **(a)** Linke(r, s). **on the** ~ links *(of* von*);* **on my** ~ links von mir. **(b)** *(Pol)* Linke *f.* **to be on the** ~ links stehen.

left: ~**-hand** *adj* ~**-hand drive** Linkssteuerung *f;* ~**-hand side** linke Seite; **on his** ~**-hand side** zu seiner Linken; ~**-handed** *adj* linkshändig; *tool* für Linkshänder.

leftie ['leftɪ] *n (pej)* Rote(r) *mf (pej col).*

leftist ['leftɪst] **1** *adj* linke(r, s), linksgerichtet. **2** *n* Linke(r) *mf.*

left: ~**-luggage (office)** *n (Brit)* Gepäckaufbewahrung *f;* ~**-luggage locker** *n* Gepäckschließfach *nt;* ~**-overs** *n (Über)*reste *pl;* ~**-wing 1** *adj (Pol)* linke(r, s); **2** *n* ~ **wing** linker Flügel *(also Sport).*

leg [leg] **1** *n* Bein *nt; (of bed also)* Fuß *m; (Cook)* Keule, Hachse *f.* **to pull sb's** ~ jdn auf den Arm nehmen; **to be on one's last** ~**s** in den letzten Zügen liegen *(col); (person)* auf dem letzten Loch pfeifen *(col);* **he hasn't a** ~ **to stand on** *(fig) (no excuse)* er kann sich nicht herausreden; *(no proof)* das kann er nicht belegen. **2** *vt:* **to** ~ **it** *(col)* laufen.

legacy ['legəsɪ] *n (lit, fig)* Vermächtnis *nt; (fig also)* Erbe *nt; (fig pej)* Hinterlassenschaft *f.*

legal ['liːgl] *adj* **(a)** *(lawful)* legal; *claim* Rechts-; *(according to the law)* tender, limit gesetzlich; *(allowed by law)* speed zulässig; *will, purchase* rechtsgültig. **to become** ~ rechtskräftig werden; **the** ~ **age for marriage** das gesetzliche Heiratsalter; **to have** ~ **status** rechtsfähig sein; *(document)* Rechtskraft haben. **(b)** *(relating to the law)* matters juristisch, Rechts-; *advice, mind* juristisch; *fees, decision* Gerichts-; *act, adviser* Rechts-; *inquiry* gerichtlich. **to take** ~ **action against sb** gegen jdn Klage erheben; ~ **aid** Rechtshilfe *f;* **to take** ~ **advice** juristischen Rat einholen; **the** ~ **profession** die Juristenschaft.

legality [liː'gælɪtɪ] *n* Legalität *f; (of claim)* Rechtmäßigkeit *f; (of will, marriage, purchase)* Rechtsgültigkeit *f.*

legalize ['liːgəlaɪz] *vt* legalisieren.

legally ['liːgəlɪ] *adv (lawfully)* transacted legal; *married* rechtmäßig; *guaranteed* gesetzlich; *indefensible* rechtlich. ~ **binding** rechtsverbindlich; ~ **valid** rechtsgültig.

legation [lɪ'geɪʃən] *n (diplomats)* Gesandtschaft *f; (building)* Gesandtschaftsgebäude *nt.*

legend ['ledʒənd] *n* **(a)** Legende *f; (fictitious)* Sage *f.* **(b)** *(inscription, caption)* Legende *f.*

legendary ['ledʒəndərɪ] *adj* **(a)** legendär. **(b)** *(famous)* berühmt.

-legged [-'legd, -'legɪd] *adj suf* -beinig. **bare-**~ ohne Strümpfe.

leggy ['legɪ] *adj (+er)* langbeinig; *(gawky)* staksig.

legible ['ledʒɪbl] *adj* lesbar; *writing also* leserlich.

legion ['liːdʒən] *n* Legion *f.*

legislate ['ledʒɪsleɪt] *vi* Gesetze/ein Gesetz erlassen. **to** ~ **for sth** *(fig)* etw berücksichtigen.

legislation [,ledʒɪs'leɪʃən] *n (making laws)* Gesetzgebung; *(laws)* Gesetze *pl.*

legislative ['ledʒɪslətɪv] *adj* gesetzgebend. ~ **reforms** Gesetzesreformen *pl.*

legislator ['ledʒɪsleɪtəʳ] *n* Gesetzgeber *m.*

legislature ['ledʒɪsleɪtʃəʳ] *n* Legislative *f.*

legitimate [lɪ'dʒɪtɪmət] *adj (lawful)* rechtmäßig, legitim; *(born in wedlock)* ehelich; *(reasonable)* berechtigt; *excuse* begründet.

legitimize [lɪ'dʒɪtɪmaɪz] *vt* legitimieren; *children* für ehelich erklären.

leg-room ['legruːm] *n* Platz *m* für die Beine.

leisure ['leʒəʳ] *n* Freizeit *f.* **to lead a life of** ~ sich dem (süßen) Nichtstun ergeben; **do it at your** ~ *(in own time)* tun Sie es, wenn Sie Zeit dazu haben; *(at own speed)* lassen Sie sich *(dat)* Zeit damit.

leisure: ~ **activities** *npl* Freizeitbeschäftigungen *pl;* ~ **hours** Freizeit *f.*

leisurely ['leʒəlɪ] *adj* geruhsam. **at a** ~ **pace** gemächlich.

leisure: ~ **time** *n* Freizeit *f;* ~ **wear** *n* Freizeitbekleidung *f.*

lemon ['lemən] *n* **(a)** Zitrone *f; (colour)* Zitronengelb *nt.* **(b)** *(col: fool)* Dussel *m (col).*

lemonade [,lemə'neɪd] *n* Limonade *f.*

lemon: ~ **curd** *n* zähflüssiger Brotaufstrich mit Zitronengeschmack; ~ **tea** *n* Zitronentee *m.*

lend [lend] *pret, ptp* **lent 1** *vt (loan)* leihen *(to sb* jdm*); (banks) money* verleihen *(to* an *+acc).* **to** ~ **a hand** helfen; **it ~s it a certain credibility** das verleiht ihm eine gewisse Glaubwürdigkeit. **2** *vr* **to** ~ **oneself to sth** *(be suitable)* sich für etw eignen.

length [leŋθ] *n* **(a)** Länge *f; (section) (of cloth, pipe)* Stück *nt; (of pool, wallpaper)* Bahn *f.* **to be 4 metres in** ~ 4 Meter lang sein; **what** ~ **is it?** wie lang ist es?; **of some** ~ ziemlich lang; **along the whole** ~ **of the river** den ganzen Fluß entlang; **over all the** ~ **and breadth of England** in ganz England; *(travelling)* kreuz und quer durch ganz England; **at full** ~ in voller Länge; **to win by half a** ~ mit einer halben Länge siegen. **(b)** *(of time)* Dauer *f; (great* ~*)* lange Dauer. **of some** ~ ziemlich lange; **at** ~ *(finally)* schließlich; *(for a long time)* lange, ausführlich. **(c)** **to go to great** ~**s** sich *(dat)* sehr viel Mühe geben; **to go to the** ~ **of ...** so weit gehen, daß ...

lengthen ['leŋθən] **1** *vt* verlängern; *clothes* länger machen. **2** *vi* länger werden.

lengthways ['leŋθweɪz], **lengthwise** ['leŋθwaɪz] *adv* der Länge nach.

lengthy ['leŋθɪ] *adj (+er)* lange; *(dragging on)* langwierig; *speech also* langatmig *(pej).*

lenience ['liːnɪəns], **leniency** ['liːnɪənsɪ] *n see adj* Nachsicht *f;* Milde *f.*

lenient ['liːnɪənt] *adj* nachsichtig *(towards gegenüber); judge* milde.

lens [lenz] *n (Opt)* Linse *f; (in spectacles)* Glas *nt; (camera part)* Objektiv *nt.*

lent [lent] *pret, ptp of* **lend**.

Lent [lent] *n* Fastenzeit *f.*

lentil ['lentl] *n* Linse *f.*

Leo ['liːəʊ] *n (Astrol)* Löwe *m.*

leopard ['lepəd] *n* Leopard *m.*

leotard ['liːəʊtɑːd] *n* Trikot *nt; (gymnastics)* Gymnastikanzug *m.*

leper ['lepə^r] n Leprakranke(r) mf.

leprosy ['leprəsɪ] n Lepra f.

lesbian ['lezbɪən] **1** adj lesbisch. **2** n Lesbierin f.

lesion ['liːʒən] n Verletzung f.

less [les] **1** adj, adv, n weniger. **the minister, no ~** kein Geringerer als der Minister; **~ and ~** immer weniger; **she saw him ~ and ~** (often) sie sah ihn immer seltener; **it's nothing ~ than disgraceful** es ist wirklich eine Schande; **~ quickly** nicht so schnell; **even ~** noch weniger; **none the ~ trotzdem; the ~ said the better** je weniger man darüber spricht, desto besser; **can't you let me have it for ~?** können Sie es mir nicht etwas billiger geben? **2** prep weniger; (Comm) abzüglich. **6 ~ 4 is 2** 6 weniger 4 ist 2.

lessee [le'siː] n Pächter m; (of house, flat) Mieter m.

lessen ['lesn] **1** vt (make less) verringern; cost senken; effect abschwächen; (make less important etc) herabsetzen. **2** vi nachlassen; (value of money) abnehmen.

lessening ['lesnɪŋ] n Nachlassen nt (in sth +gen).

lesser ['lesə^r] adj geringer; (in names) klein. **to a ~ extent** in geringerem Maße.

lesson ['lesn] n (Sch etc) Stunde f; (unit of study) Lektion f; (fig) Lehre f. **~s** Unterricht m; **a French ~** eine Französischstunde; **to give a ~** eine Stunde geben; **to be a ~ to sb** jdm eine Lehre sein; **to teach sb a ~** jdm eine Lektion erteilen.

lessor [le'sɔː^r] n (form) Verpächter m; (of flat etc) Vermieter m.

lest [lest] conj (form) (for fear that) aus Furcht, daß; (in order that ... not) damit ... nicht; (in case) für den Fall, daß. **~ we forget** damit wir nicht vergessen; **I was frightened ~ he should fall** ich hatte Angst, daß er fallen könnte.

let [let] pret, ptp **~** vt (**a**) (permit) lassen. **to ~ sb do sth** jdn etw tun lassen; **~ me help you** kann ich Ihnen behilflich sein?; **~ me know what you think** sagen Sie mir, was Sie davon halten; **to ~ sb be** jdn (in Ruhe) lassen; **to ~ sb/sth go, to ~ go of sb/sth** jdn/etw loslassen; **to ~ oneself go** (neglect oneself) sich gehenlassen; (relax) aus sich herausgehen; **we'll ~ it pass** or **go this once** (disregard) wir wollen es einmal durchgehen lassen; **to ~ sb/sth alone** jdn/etw in Ruhe lassen; **we'd better ~ well alone** wir lassen besser die Finger davon; **~ alone** ... (much less) geschweige denn ...; **to ~ sb through** jdn durchlassen.

(**b**) **~'s go!** gehen wir!; **~ him try (it)!** das soll er nur versuchen!; **~ me think** or **see, where did I put it?** warte mal, wo habe ich das nur hingetan? **~ X be 60 X** sei 60.

(**c**) (esp Brit: hire out) vermieten. **"to ~"** „zu vermieten".

♦ **let down** vt sep (**a**) (lower) rope, person hinunter-/herunterlassen; seat herunterklappen; hair, window herunterlassen. (**b**) **to ~ sb ~** (fail to help) jdn im Stich lassen (over mit); **to feel ~ ~** enttäuscht sein; **to ~ the school/oneself ~** die Schule/sich blamieren.

♦ **let in** vt sep (**a**) water durchlassen. (**b**) (admit) air, visitor hereinlassen. **just ~ yourself ~** geh einfach hinein; **I was just ~ting myself ~** ich schloß gerade die Tür auf. (**c**) (involve in) **to ~ oneself ~ for sth** sich auf etw (acc) einlassen; **to ~ oneself/sb ~ for trouble** sich/jdm Ärger einhandeln. (**d**) (allow to know) **she ~ me ~ on the secret** sie hat es mir verraten. **2** vi (shoes, tent) undicht sein.

♦ **let off 1** vt sep (**a**) arrow abschießen; gun abfeuern; firework, bomb hochgehen lassen; (emit) vapour von sich geben; gases absondern. (**b**) (forgive) **to ~ sb ~** jdm etw durchgehen lassen; **to ~ sb ~ with a warning** jdn mit einer Verwarnung davonkommen lassen; **to be ~ ~ lightly** glimpflich davonkommen. (**c**) (allow to

go) gehen lassen. **2** vi (col: fart) einen fahren lassen (col).

♦ **let on** vi (**a**) also vt don't **~ ~ you know** (col) laß dir bloß nicht anmerken, daß du das weißt. (**b**) (pretend) **to ~ ~ that** ... vorgeben, daß ...

♦ **let out** vt sep (**a**) (allow to go out) hinaus-/herauslassen; (from car) absetzen; (divulge) news bekanntgeben; secret verraten, ausplaudern (col); fire ausgehen lassen. **I'll ~ myself ~** ich finde alleine hinaus; **to ~ ~ a laugh/groan** auflachen/(auf)stöhnen. (**b**) (make larger) dress auslassen. (**c**) (free from responsibility) **that ~s me ~** (of it) da komme ich (schon mal) nicht in Frage. (**d**) (Brit: rent) vermieten.

♦ **let up** vi (cease) aufhören; (ease up) nachlassen. **he never ~s ~ about money** er redet unaufhörlich von Geld.

let-down ['letdaun] n (col: disappointment) Enttäuschung f.

lethal ['liːθəl] adj tödlich.

lethargic [lɪ'θɑːdʒɪk] adj person träge, lethargisch; (uninterested) teilnahmslos.

let's [lets] = **let us**.

letter ['letə^r] n (**a**) (of alphabet) Buchstabe m. **the ~ of the law** der Buchstabe des Gesetzes; **to the ~** sehr genau; (as given) ganz nach Vorschrift. (**b**) (written message) Brief m; (Comm etc) Schreiben nt (to an +acc). **by ~** schriftlich; **~ of credit** Akkreditiv nt. (**c**) (Liter) **~s** Literatur f; **man of ~s** Belletrist m; (writer) Literat m.

letter: **~ bomb** n Briefbombe f; **~ box** n Briefkasten m.

letterhead ['letəhed] n Briefkopf m; (writing paper) Geschäftspapier nt.

lettering ['letərɪŋ] n Beschriftung f.

letterpress ['letəpres] n Hochdruck m.

lettuce ['letɪs] n Kopfsalat m.

let-up ['letʌp] n (col) Pause f; (easing up) Nachlassen nt. **if there is a ~ in the rain** wenn der Regen nachläßt.

leukaemia, leukemia [luː'kiːmɪə] n Leukämie f.

level ['levl] **1** adj (**a**) (flat) surface eben; spoonful gestrichen; (at the same height) auf gleicher Höhe (with mit); (fig) gleich gut. **the two runners are dead ~** die beiden Läufer sind genau auf gleicher Höhe. (**b**) (steady) tone of voice ruhig; (well-balanced) ausgeglichen; judgement abgewogen; head kühl. (**c**) **I'll do my ~ best** ich werde mein möglichstes tun.

2 adv **~ with** in Höhe (+gen); **the pipe runs with the ground** (parallel) das Rohr verläuft parallel zum Boden; **they're running absolutely ~** sie laufen auf genau gleicher Höhe; **to draw ~ with sb** mit jdm gleichziehen.

3 n (**a**) (instrument) Wasserwaage f.

(**b**) (altitude) Höhe f; (standard) Niveau nt. **on a ~ (with)** auf gleicher Höhe (mit); **at eye ~ in** Augenhöhe; **to be on a ~ with** auf gleichem Niveau sein wie; **a high ~ of hydrogen** ein hoher Wasserstoffanteil; **the ~ of alcohol in the blood** der Alkoholgehalt im Blut; **a high ~ of intelligence** ein hoher Intelligenzgrad; **the very high ~ of production** das hohe Produktionsniveau; **a high ~ of civilization** eine hohe Kulturstufe; **the talks were held at a very high ~** die Gespräche fanden auf hoher Ebene statt; **at ministerial ~** auf Ministerebene; **a high-~ meeting** ein Spitzentreffen; **on the moral ~** moralisch gesehen; **on a purely personal ~** auf rein persönlicher Ebene.

(**c**) (col: straightforward, honest) **it's on the ~** (business) es ist reell; **to be on the ~ (with sb)** (jdm gegenüber) ehrlich sein.

4 vt (**a**) ground etc einebnen; building abreißen; town dem Erdboden gleichmachen. (**b**) blow versetzen (at sb jdm); weapon richten (at auf +acc); accusation erheben (at gegen); remark richten (at gegen).

5 *vi* to ~ with sb *(col)* jdm keinen Quatsch erzählen *(col)*.

♦ **level out 1** *vi (also* ~ *off) (ground)* eben werden; *(fig)* sich ausgleichen. **2** *vt sep site* planieren, einebnen; *(fig) differences* ausgleichen.

level: ~ **crossing** *n (Brit)* (beschrankter) Bahnübergang; ~**-headed** *adj person* ausgeglichen; *reply, decision* ausgewogen, überlegt.

lever ['li:və^r, (US) 'levə^r] **1** *n* Hebel *m; (crowbar)* Brechstange *f; (fig)* Druckmittel *nt.* **2** *vt* (hoch)stemmen. **he** ~**ed the box open** er stemmte die Kiste auf.

leverage ['li:vərɪdʒ] *n* Hebelkraft *f; (fig)* Einfluß *m.* **to use sth as** ~ *(fig)* etw als Druckmittel benutzen.

levity ['levɪtɪ] *n* Leichtfertigkeit *f.*

levy ['levɪ] **1** *n (act)* (Steuer)einziehung *f; (tax)* Abgaben *pl.* **2** *vt tax* einziehen; *fine* auferlegen *(on sb* jdm); *army* ausheben.

lewd [luːd] *adj (+er)* unanständig; *(lustful)* lüstern; *remark* anzüglich; *imagination* schmutzig.

liability [ˌlaɪə'bɪlɪtɪ] *n (a) (burden)* Belastung *f; (proneness)* Anfälligkeit *f (to* für); *(responsibility)* Haftung *f.* ~ **for tax** Steuerpflicht *f;* **we accept no** ~ **for ...** wir übernehmen keine Haftung für ... **(b)** *(Fin)* **liabilities** Verbindlichkeiten *pl.*

liable ['laɪəbl] *adj (a) (subject to)* **to be** ~ unterliegen *(for sth* einer Sache *dat);* **to be** ~ **for tax** *(things)* besteuert werden; *(person)* steuerpflichtig sein. **(b)** *(to illness)* anfällig *(to* für *+acc).* **(c)** *(responsible)* **to be** ~ haften *(for* für *+acc).* **(d)** *(likely to)* **we are** ~ **to get wet here** wir können hier leicht naß werden; **is he** ~ **to come?** ist es wahrscheinlich, daß er kommt?; **he's** ~ **to tell the police** es wäre ihm zuzutrauen, daß er es der Polizei meldet; **the computer is still** ~ **to make mistakes** der Computer kann durchaus noch Fehler machen.

liaise [liː'eɪz] *vi* als Verbindungsmann auftreten.

liaison [liː'eɪzɒn] *n (coordination)* Zusammenarbeit *f; (person)* Verbindungsmann *m.*

liaison officer *n* Verbindungsmann *m.*

liar ['laɪə^r] *n* Lügner(in *f*) *m.*

libel ['laɪbəl] **1** *n* (schriftlich geäußerte) Verleumdung *(on gen).* **2** *vt* verleumden.

libellous, *(US)* **libelous** ['laɪbələs] *adj* verleumderisch.

liberal ['lɪbərəl] **1** *adj (a) (generous) offer* großzügig; *helping of food* reichlich. **(b)** *(broad-minded, also Pol)* liberal. **2** *n (Pol:* L~) Liberale(r) *mf.*

liberalism ['lɪbərəlɪzəm] *n* Liberalität *f; (Pol:* L~) der Liberalismus.

liberality [ˌlɪbə'rælɪtɪ] *n (generosity)* Großzügigkeit *f.*

liberalize ['lɪbərəlaɪz] *vt* liberalisieren.

liberally ['lɪbərəlɪ] *adv* liberal; *(generously)* großzügig. **apply the paint** ~ die Farbe reichlich auftragen.

liberal-minded [ˌlɪbərəl'maɪndɪd] *adj person* liberal (eingestellt); *views* liberal.

liberate ['lɪbəreɪt] *vt (free) prisoner* befreien; *gas etc* freisetzen.

liberation [ˌlɪbə'reɪʃən] *n* Befreiung *f; (of gases)* Freisetzung *f.*

liberator ['lɪbəreɪtə^r] *n* Befreier *m.*

liberty ['lɪbətɪ] *n (a)* Freiheit *f.* **basic liberties** Grundrechte *pl;* **to be at** ~ *(criminal etc)* frei herumlaufen; **to be at** ~ **to do sth** *(be permitted)* etw tun dürfen; **I am not at** ~ **to comment** es ist mir nicht gestattet, darüber zu sprechen. **(b)** **I have taken the** ~ **of giving your name** ich habe mir erlaubt, Ihren Namen anzugeben; **to take liberties with sb** sich jdm gegenüber Freiheiten herausnehmen; **what a** ~! *(col)* so eine Frechheit!

libido [lɪ'biːdəʊ] *n* Libido *f.*

Libra ['liːbrə] *n (Astrol)* Waage *f.*

librarian [laɪ'brɛərɪən] *n* Bibliothekar(in *f*) *m.*

library ['laɪbrərɪ] *n* Bibliothek, Bücherei *f.*

library: ~ **book** *n* Leihbuch *nt;* ~ **ticket** *n* Leserausweis *m.*

libretto [lɪ'bretəʊ] *n* Libretto *nt.*

Libya ['lɪbɪə] *n* Libyen *nt.*

Libyan ['lɪbɪən] **1** *adj* libysch. **2** *n* Libyer(in *f*) *m.*

lice [laɪs] *pl of* **louse.**

licence, *(US)* **license** ['laɪsəns] *n (a) (permit)* Genehmigung *f; (Comm)* Lizenz *f; (driving* ~) Führerschein *m; (gun* ~) Waffenschein *m; (marriage* ~) Eheerlaubnis *f; (to sell alcohol)* Schankerlaubnis *f.* **you have to have a (television)** ~ man muß Fernsehgebühren bezahlen; **to manufacture sth under** ~ etw in Lizenz herstellen. **(b)** *(freedom)* Freiheit *f; (excessive freedom)* Zügellosigkeit *f.*

licence: ~ **number** *n (Aut)* (Kraftfahrzeug)kennzeichen *nt;* ~ **plate** *n (Aut)* Nummernschild *nt.*

license ['laɪsəns] **1** *n (US)* = **licence.** **2** *vt* eine Lizenz/Konzession vergeben an *(+acc).* **a car must be** ~**d every year** die Kfz-Steuer muß jedes Jahr bezahlt werden.

licensed ['laɪsənst] *adj* ~ **premises** Lokal *nt* mit Schankerlaubnis.

licensee [ˌlaɪsən'siː] *n (of bar)* Inhaber(in *f*) *m* einer Schankerlaubnis. **postage paid by** ~ Gebühr bezahlt Empfänger.

licensing ['laɪsənsɪŋ] *adj* ~ **hours** Ausschankzeiten *pl.*

licentious [laɪ'senʃəs] *adj life* ausschweifend; *behaviour* anzüglich; *person, look* lüstern.

lick [lɪk] **1** *n (a) (with tongue)* Lecken *nt.* **to give sth a** ~ etw lecken. **(b)** *(col: small quantity)* **it's time we gave the kitchen a** ~ **of paint** die Küche könnte auch mal wieder etwas Farbe vertragen *(col).* **(c)** *(col: pace)* **at full** ~ mit Volldampf *(col).* **2** *vt (a) (with tongue)* lecken; *(flames)* züngeln an *(+dat).* **he** ~**ed the stamp** er leckte an der Briefmarke; **to** ~ **one's lips** sich *(dat)* die Lippen lecken; *(fig)* sich *(dat)* die Finger lecken; **to** ~ **one's wounds** *(fig)* seine Wunden lecken; **to** ~ **sb's boots** *(fig)* vor jdm kriechen. **(b)** *(col: defeat)* in die Pfanne hauen *(col).* **I think we've got it** ~**ed** ich glaube, wir haben die Sache jetzt im Griff.

licorice *n* = **liquorice.**

lid [lɪd] *n (a)* Deckel *m.* **that puts the** ~ **on it** *(col)* das schlägt dem Faß den Boden aus; **the press took the** ~ **off the whole plan** die Presse hat den Plan aufgedeckt. **(b)** *(eye*~*)* Lid *nt.*

lido ['liːdəʊ] *n* Freibad *nt.*

lie¹ [laɪ] **1** *n* Lüge *f.* **to tell a** ~ lügen; **to give the** ~ **to a report** die Unwahrheit eines Berichtes nachweisen; ~ **detector** Lügendetektor *m.* **2** *vi* lügen. **to** ~ **to sb** jdn anlügen. **3** *vt* **to** ~ **one's way out of sth** sich aus etw herauslügen.

lie² *(vb: pret* **lay,** *ptp* **lain)** *vi* liegen; *(*~ *down)* sich hinlegen. **he lay where he had fallen** er blieb liegen, wo er hingefallen war; ~ **on your back** leg dich auf den Rücken; **obstacles** ~ **in the way of our success** unser Weg zum Erfolg ist mit Hindernissen verstellt; **the snow didn't** ~ der Schnee blieb nicht liegen; **the runner who is lying third** der Läufer, der auf dem dritten Platz liegt; **it** ~**s with you to solve the problem** es liegt bei dir, das Problem zu lösen; **that responsibility** ~**s with your department** dafür ist Ihre Abteilung verantwortlich; **to** ~ **asleep** schlafen; **to** ~ **helpless** hilflos daliegen; **to** ~ **dying** im Sterben liegen; **to** ~ **resting** ruhen; **the snow lay deep** es lag tiefer Schnee; **the book lay unopened** das Buch lag ungeöffnet da; **to** ~ **low** untertauchen; **how do things** ~? wie steht die Sache?

♦ **lie about** *or* **around** *vi* herumliegen.

♦ **lie back** *vi (a) (recline)* sich zurücklehnen. **(b)** *(fig: take no action)* sich ausruhen.

♦ **lie down** *vi* sich hinlegen *(on auf +acc).* ~ ~ *(to*

lie in *a dog*) leg dich!; **he won't take that lying ~!** das läßt er sich nicht gefallen!
♦ **lie in** *vi (stay in bed)* im Bett bleiben.
♦ **lie up** *vi (hide)* untertauchen. **the robbers are lying ~** die Räuber sind untergetaucht.

lie-down ['laɪdaʊn] *n (col)* Nickerchen *(col) nt.* **to have a ~** ein Nickerchen machen *(col).*

lie-in ['laɪɪn] *n (col)* **to have a ~** (sich) ausschlafen.

lieu [luː] *n* **in ~ of X** anstelle von X.

lieutenant [lef'tenənt, *(US)* luː'tenənt] *n (US)* Leutnant *m; (Brit)* Oberleutnant *m.*

lieutenant: ~-colonel *n* Oberstleutnant *m;* **~-general** *n* Generalleutnant *m.*

life [laɪf] *n, pl* **lives (a)** Leben *nt.* **bird ~** die Vogelwelt; **drawn from ~** lebensnah; **the battle resulted in great loss of ~** bei der Schlacht kamen viele ums Leben; **this is a matter of ~ and death** hier geht es um Leben und Tod; **a ~ and death struggle** ein Kampf auf Leben und Tod; **to come to ~** *(fig)* lebendig werden; **after half an hour the discussion came to ~** nach einer halben Stunde kam Leben in die Diskussion; **to put new ~ into sb** jdm wieder Auftrieb geben; **they swam for dear ~** sie schwammen um ihr Leben; **at my time of ~** in meinem Alter; **he's got a job for ~** er hat eine Stelle auf Lebenszeit; **to take one's ~ in one's hands** mit dem Leben spielen; **the murderer was imprisoned for ~** der Mörder wurde zu lebenslänglicher Freiheitsstrafe verurteilt; **he's doing ~** *(col)* er ist ein Lebenslänglicher *(col);* **to see ~** *(fig)* die Welt sehen; **there isn't much ~ here in the evenings** hier ist abends nicht viel los; **those children are full of ~!** diese Kinder sind sehr lebhaft!; **he is the ~ and soul of the party** er bringt Leben in die Party.
(b) *(individual life)* **how many lives were lost?** wie viele (Menschen) sind ums Leben gekommen?; **to take sb's ~** jdn umbringen; **to take one's own ~** sich *(dat)* das Leben nehmen; **to save sb's ~** *(lit)* jdm das Leben retten; *(fig)* jdn retten; **early/later in ~** in frühen/späten Jahren; **his ~ won't be worth living!** er wird nichts mehr zu lachen haben!; **all his ~** sein ganzes Leben lang; **I've never been to London in my ~** ich war in meinem ganzen Leben noch nicht in London; **run for your lives!** rennt um euer Leben!; **I can't for the ~ of me ...** *(col)* ich kann beim besten Willen nicht ...; **not on your life!** *(col)* ich bin doch nicht verrückt! *(col).*
(c) *(useful or active life of sth)* Lebensdauer *f.* **during the ~ of the present Parliament** während der Legislaturperiode des gegenwärtigen Parlaments; **there's not much ~ left in the battery** die Batterie macht's nicht mehr lange *(col).*

life: ~ assurance *n (Brit)* Lebensversicherung *f;* **~belt** *n* Rettungsgürtel *m;* **~blood** *n (fig)* Lebensnerv *m;* **~boat** *n* Rettungsboot *nt;* **~buoy** *n* Rettungsring *m;* **~ cycle** *n* Lebenszyklus *m;* **~ expectancy** *n* Lebenserwartung *f;* **~guard** *n (on beach)* Rettungsschwimmer *m;* **~ imprisonment** *n* lebenslängliche Freiheitsstrafe; **~ insurance** *n* Lebensversicherung *f;* **~ jacket** *n* Schwimmweste *f.*

lifeless ['laɪflɪs] *adj* leblos; *planet* ohne Leben; *(fig: dull)* lahm *(col),* langweilig; *hair* schlaff.

life: ~like *adj* lebensecht; *imitation also* naturgetreu; **~line** *n* Rettungsleine *f; (of diver)* Signalleine *f; (fig)* Rettungsanker *m;* **~long** *adj* lebenslang; **they are ~long friends** sie sind schon ihr Leben lang Freunde; **~ raft** *n* Rettungsfloß *nt;* **~saver** *n* **it was a real ~saver!** das hat mich gerettet; **~-size(d)** *adj* in Lebensgröße; **~ support system** *n* Lebenserhaltungssystem *nt;* **~time** *n (a)* Lebenszeit *f; (of battery, machine, animal)* Lebensdauer *f;* **once in a ~time** während im Leben; **during** *or* **in my ~time** während

meines Lebens; **the chance of a ~time** eine einmalige Chance; **the work of a ~time** ein Lebenswerk *nt;* **(b)** *(fig)* Ewigkeit *f.*

lift [lɪft] **1** *n* **(a)** **give me a ~ with this trunk** hilf mir, den Koffer hochzuheben. **(b)** *(fig: emotional uplift)* **to give sb a ~** jdn aufmuntern. **(c)** *(in car etc)* Mitfahrgelegenheit *f.* **to give sb a ~** *(take along)* jdn mitnehmen; *(as special journey)* jdn fahren; **to get a ~ from sb** von jdm mitgenommen/gefahren werden; **thanks for the ~** danke fürs Mitnehmen. **(d)** *(Brit: elevator)* Aufzug *m.* **(e)** *(Aviat)* Auftrieb *m.* **2** *vt* **(a)** *(also ~ up)* hochheben; *window* hochschieben; *feet, head* heben; *eyes* aufschlagen; *hat* ziehen. **it's too heavy to ~** es ist zu schwer zum Hochheben. **(b)** *(fig: also ~ up)* heben; *voice* erheben. **(c)** *(remove) restrictions etc* aufheben. **(d)** *(col: steal)* klauen *(col).* **3** *vi* **(a)** *(mist)* sich lichten. **(b) = ~ up 2.**
♦ **lift down** *vt sep* herunterheben.
♦ **lift off** *vti sep* abheben.
♦ **lift up 1** *vt sep* **= lift 2 (a, b). to ~ ~ one's head** *(fig)* den Kopf hochhalten. **2** *vi* hochgeklappt werden.

lift: ~ attendant *n (Brit)* Fahrstuhlführer *m;* **~-off** *(Space)* Start *m;* **we have ~-off** der Start ist erfolgt; **~shaft** *n* Aufzugsschacht *m.*

ligament ['lɪgəmənt] *n (Anat)* Band *nt.* **he's torn a ~ in his shoulder** er hat einen Bänderriß in der Schulter.

light¹ [laɪt] *(vb: pret, ptp* **lit** *or* **~ ed)** **1** *n* **(a)** Licht *nt.* **at first ~** bei Tagesanbruch; **to shed** *or* **throw ~ on sth** *(fig)* Licht in etw *(acc)* bringen; **to cast fresh ~ on sth** neues Licht auf etw *(acc)* werfen; **to stand in sb's ~** *(lit)* jdm im Licht stehen; **in the cold ~ of day** *(fig)* bei Licht besehen; **this story shows him in a bad ~** diese Geschichte wirft ein schlechtes Licht auf ihn; **it revealed him in a different ~** es ließ ihn in einem anderen Licht erscheinen; **to see sth in a new ~** etw mit anderen Augen betrachten; **in the ~ of** angesichts *(+gen);* **to bring to ~** ans Tageslicht bringen; **to come to ~** ans Tageslicht kommen; **finally I saw the ~** *(col)* endlich ging mir ein Licht auf *(col); (morally)* endlich wurden mir die Augen geöffnet; **according to his ~s** nach bestem Wissen und Gewissen.
(b) *(single ~)* Licht *nt; (lamp)* Lampe *f; (fluorescent ~)* Neonröhre *f.* **to switch the ~ on/off** das Licht anschalten/ausschalten; **(traffic) ~s** Ampel *f;* **the ~s** *(of a car)* die Beleuchtung.
(c) *(flame)* **have you a ~?** haben Sie Feuer?; **to set ~ to sth** etw anzünden.
2 *adj* **(+er)** hell. **~ green dress** ein hellgrünes Kleid; **it is ~ now** es ist jetzt hell *or* Tag.
3 *vt* **(a)** *(illuminate)* beleuchten; *lamp, light* anmachen. **to ~ the way for sb** jdm leuchten; *(fig)* jdm den Weg weisen. **(b)** *(set fire to)* anzünden; *fire also* anmachen.
4 *vi (begin to burn)* brennen.
♦ **light up 1** *vi* **(a)** *(be lit)* aufleuchten. **(b)** *(face)* sich erhellen; *(eyes)* aufleuchten. **2** *vt sep* **(a)** *(illuminate)* beleuchten; *(from inside also)* erhellen. **George Square was all lit ~** der Georgsplatz war hell erleuchtet. **(b)** *cigarette etc* anzünden.

light² **1** *adj* **(+er)** leicht; *taxes* niedrig; *punishment* milde. **to be a ~ eater** kein großer Esser sein; **~ comedy** Lustspiel *nt;* **~ opera** Operette *f;* **~ reading** Unterhaltungslektüre *f;* **as ~ as a feather** federleicht; **to be ~ on one's feet** sich leichtfüßig bewegen; **to make ~ of one's difficulties** seine Schwierigkeiten auf die leichte Schulter nehmen; **to make ~ work of** spielend fertigwerden mit. **2** *adv* **to travel ~** mit leichtem Gepäck reisen.

light: ~ bulb *n* Glühbirne *f;* **~-coloured** *(Brit)* or **~-colored** *(US) adj* hell.

lighten[1] ['laɪtn] **1** vt erhellen; colour, hair aufhellen; gloom aufheitern. **2** vi sich aufhellen.

lighten[2] **1** vt load, (fig) heart leichter machen. **to ~ sb's burden** jds Lage erleichtern. **2** vi (load) leichter werden. **her heart ~ed** ihr wurde leichter ums Herz.

lighter ['laɪtə[r]] n (cigarette ~) Feuerzeug nt.

light: **~-fingered** [,laɪt'fɪŋgəd] adj langfingerig; **~ fitting** n (~bulb holder) Fassung f; **~-haired** adj hellhaarig; **~-headed** adj benebelt (col); (dizzy also) benommen; (frivolous) leichtfertig; **~-hearted** adj unbeschwert; chat zwanglos; reply scherzhaft; book vergnüglich; **~house** n Leuchtturm m.

lighting ['laɪtɪŋ] n Beleuchtung f.

lighting-up time [,laɪtɪŋ'ʌptaɪm] n (Brit) Zeitpunkt m, zu dem Straßen- und Fahrzeugbeleuchtung eingeschaltet werden muß. **when is ~?** wann wird die Beleuchtung angemacht?

lightly ['laɪtlɪ] adv (a) touch, rain, wounded leicht; tread leise. **to sleep ~** einen leichten Schlaf haben; **to get off ~** glimpflich davonkommen. (b) (casually) say leichthin. **he spoke ~ of his illness** ere nahm seine Krankheit auf die leichte Schulter; **to treat sth too ~** etw nicht ernst genug nehmen; **a responsibility not to be ~ undertaken** eine Verantwortung, die man nicht unüberlegt auf sich nehmen sollte.

light meter n Belichtungsmesser m.

lightness[1] ['laɪtnɪs] n Helligkeit f.

lightness[2] n (a) geringes Gewicht; (of task, step) Leichtigkeit f; (of punishment) Milde f; (of soil, cake) Lockerheit f. (b) (lack of seriousness) Leichtfertigkeit f.

lightning ['laɪtnɪŋ] **1** n Blitz m. **as quick as ~, like (greased) ~** wie der Blitz, wie ein geölter Blitz; **~ conductor** or (US) **rod** Blitzableiter m. **2** attr blitzschnell, Blitz-. **~ attack** Blitzangriff m; **~ strike** spontaner Streik.

light: **~weight 1** adj leicht; (boxer) Leichtgewichts-; (fig) schwach; **2** n Leichtgewicht nt (also fig); (boxer) Leichtgewichtler m; **~-year** n Lichtjahr nt.

like[1] [laɪk] **1** adj (a) (similar) ähnlich. (b) (same) of **~ origin** gleicher Herkunft.

2 prep (similar to) ähnlich (+dat); (in comparisons) wie. **to be ~ sb** jdm ähnlich sein; **they are very ~ each other** sie sind sich sehr ähnlich; **who(m) is he ~?** wem sieht er ähnlich?; **what's he ~?** wie ist er?; **what's your new coat ~?** wie sieht dein neuer Mantel aus?; **she was ~ a sister to me** sie war wie eine Schwester zu mir; **that's just ~ him!** das sieht ihm ähnlich!; **it's not ~ him** ist nicht seine Art; **I never saw anything ~ it** so (et)was habe ich noch nie gesehen; **that's more ~ it!** so ist es schon besser!; **there's nothing ~ a nice cup of tea!** es geht nichts über eine gute Tasse Tee!; **the Americans are ~ that** so sind die Amerikaner; **do it ~ this** mach es so; **people ~ that** solche Leute; **it will cost something ~ £10** es wird so ungefähr £ 10 kosten; **that sounds ~ a good idea** das hört sich gut an; **~ mad (col), ~ anything (col)** wie verrückt (col); **he thinks ~ us** er denkt wie wir.

3 adv (col) **it's nothing ~ it** das ist nicht zu vergleichen; **as ~ as not** höchstwahrscheinlich.

4 conj (strictly incorrect) **~ I said** wie gesagt.

5 n (equal etc) **did you ever see the ~?** (col) hast du so was schon gesehen?; **and the ~, and such ~** und dergleichen; **I've met the ~s of you before** solche wie dich kenne ich schon.

like[2] **1** n usu pl **she tried to find out his ~s and dislikes** sie wollte herausbekommen, was er mochte und was nicht.

2 vt (a) person mögen. **how do you ~ him?** wie gefällt er dir?; **I don't ~ him** ich mag ihn nicht; **he is well ~d here** er ist hier sehr beliebt.

(b) **I ~ black shoes** mir gefallen schwarze Schuhe; **I ~ it** das gefällt mir; **I ~ chocolate** ich mag Schokolade; **I ~ football** ich mag Fußball; (playing) ich spiele gerne Fußball; **I ~ this translation** ich finde diese Übersetzung gut; **how would you ~ a walk?** was hältst du von einem Spaziergang?; **well, I ~ that!** (col) das ist ein starkes Stück! (col).

(c) (wish, wish for) **I should ~ more time** ich würde mir gerne noch etwas Zeit lassen; **they should have ~d to come** sie wären gern gekommen; **I should ~ to know why** ich wüßte (gerne), warum; **I should ~ you to do it** ich möchte, daß du es tust; **I didn't ~ to disturb him** ich wollte ihn nicht stören; **what would you ~?** was hätten or möchten Sie gern?; **would you ~ a drink?** möchten Sie etwas trinken?; **how do you ~ your coffee?** wie trinken Sie Ihren Kaffee? **3** vi **as you ~** wie Sie wollen; **if you ~** wenn Sie wollen.

lik(e)able ['laɪkəbl] adj sympathisch.

likelihood ['laɪklɪhʊd] n Wahrscheinlichkeit f. **in all ~** aller Wahrscheinlichkeit nach; **there is no ~ of that** das ist nicht wahrscheinlich; **there is little ~ that ...** es ist kaum anzunehmen, daß ...

likely ['laɪklɪ] **1** adj (+er) (a) (probable) wahrscheinlich. **he is not ~ to come** es ist unwahrscheinlich, daß er kommt; **is it ~ that I would do that?** trauen Sie mir das zu?; **an incident ~ to cause trouble** ein Zwischenfall, der möglicherweise Ärger nach sich zieht; **a ~ explanation** eine wahrscheinliche Erklärung; (iro) **wer's glaubt, wird selig!** (col); **a ~ story!** (iro) das glaubst du doch (wohl) selber nicht! (col). (b) (col: suitable) **a ~ spot for a picnic** ein geeignetes Fleckchen für ein Picknick; **he is a ~ person for the job** er kommt für die Stelle in Frage. **2** adv **not ~!** (col) wohl kaum (col); **as ~ as not** höchstwahrscheinlich; **very ~ they've lost it** höchstwahrscheinlich haben sie es verloren.

like-minded [laɪk'maɪndɪd] adj gleichgesinnt.

liken ['laɪkən] vt vergleichen (to mit).

likeness ['laɪknɪs] n (resemblance) Ähnlichkeit f; (portrait) Bild(nis) nt. **in the ~ of** in der Gestalt (+gen).

likewise ['laɪkwaɪz] adv ebenso. **he did ~** er machte es ebenso; **have a nice weekend — ~** schönes Wochenende! — danke gleichfalls!

liking ['laɪkɪŋ] n (a) (for particular person) Zuneigung f; (for types) Vorliebe f. **to have a ~ for sb** Zuneigung für jdn empfinden; **she took a ~ to him** er war ihr sympathisch. (b) (for thing) Vorliebe f. **to take a ~ to sth** eine Vorliebe für etw bekommen; **to be to sb's ~** nach jds Geschmack m sein.

lilac ['laɪlək] **1** n (a) (plant) Flieder m. (b) (colour) Lila nt. **2** adj fliederfarben, lila.

lilt [lɪlt] n (of song) munterer Rhythmus; (of voice) singender Tonfall.

lily ['lɪlɪ] n Lilie f; (water ~) Seerose f. **~ of the valley** Maiglöckchen nt.

limb [lɪm] n (Anat) Glied nt. **~s** pl Gliedmaßen pl; **life and ~** Leib und Leben nt; **to be out on a ~** (fig) (ganz) allein dastehen.

♦ **limber up** [,lɪmbər'ʌp] vi Lockerungsübungen machen; (fig) sich vorbereiten.

limbo ['lɪmbəʊ] n (Rel) Vorhölle f; (fig) Übergangs- or Zwischenstadium nt. **our plans are in ~** unsere Pläne sind in der Schwebe.

lime[1] [laɪm] n (Geol) Kalk m.

lime[2] n (Bot: linden, also ~ **tree**) Linde(nbaum m) f.

lime[3] n (Bot: citrus fruit) Limone f; (tree) Limonenbaum m.

limelight ['laɪmlaɪt] n Rampenlicht nt. **to be in the ~** im Rampenlicht stehen.

limerick ['lɪmərɪk] n Limerick m.

limestone ['laɪmstəʊn] n Kalkstein m.

limey ['laɪmɪ] n (US col) Engländer m.

limit ['lɪmɪt] **1** n (a) Grenze f; (limitation) Beschränkung f; (speed ~) Geschwindigkeitsbegrenzung f; (Comm) Limit nt. **to put a ~ on sth, to set a ~ to or on sth** etw beschränken; **there's a ~!** alles hat seine Grenzen!; **there is a ~ to what one person can do** ein Mensch kann nur so viel tun und nicht mehr; **there is no ~ to his stupidity** seine Dummheit kennt keine Grenzen; **there's a ~ to the amount of money we can spend** unseren Ausgaben sind Grenzen gesetzt; **it is true within ~s** es ist bis zu einem gewissen Grade richtig; **without ~s** unbegrenzt; **to know no ~s** keine Grenzen kennen; **over the ~** zuviel; (in time) zu lange; **he was driving over the ~** er hat die Geschwindigkeitsbegrenzung überschritten; (after drinking) er hat sich mit zuviel Promille ans Steuer gesetzt.

(b) (col) **that's the ~!** das ist die Höhe! (col); **that child is the ~!** dieses Kind ist eine Zumutung! (col).

2 vt beschränken; freedom, spending einschränken; imagination hemmen. **to ~ sth to sth** etw auf etw (acc) beschränken; **are you ~ed for time?** ist Ihre Zeit begrenzt?

limitation [ˌlɪmɪˈteɪʃən] n Beschränkung f; (of freedom, spending) Einschränkung f; (disadvantage) Handikap nt. **to have/know one's ~s** seine Grenzen haben/kennen.

limited [ˈlɪmɪtɪd] adj begrenzt. **in a ~ sense** in gewissem Maße; **~ company** (Brit) Gesellschaft f mit beschränkter Haftung.

limitless [ˈlɪmɪtlɪs] adj grenzenlos.

limousine [ˈlɪməziːn] n Limousine f.

limp¹ [lɪmp] **1** n Hinken nt. **to walk with a ~** hinken, humpeln. **2** vi hinken. **the ship ~ed into port** das Schiff kam mit Müh und Not in den Hafen.

limp² adj (+er) schlapp, schlaff; flowers welk; material, cloth weich. **let your body go ~** alle Muskeln entspannen.

limpet [ˈlɪmpɪt] n Napfschnecke f. **to stick to sb like a ~** (col) wie eine Klette an jdm hängen.

limpid [ˈlɪmpɪd] adj klar; liquid also durchsichtig.

linchpin [ˈlɪntʃpɪn] n Achs(en)nagel m; (fig) Stütze f. **accurate timing is the ~ of the entire operation** das ganze Unternehmen steht und fällt mit genauer Zeiteinteilung.

linden [ˈlɪndən] n (also ~ **tree**) Linde(nbaum m) f.

line¹ [laɪn] **1** n **(a)** (rope etc, fishing ~) Leine f; (on tennis court etc, on paper) Linie f; (on face) Falte f. **the ~ between right and wrong** die Grenze zwischen Recht und Unrecht; **the ship's graceful ~s** die schnittigen Linien des Schiffes.

(b) (row) Reihe f; (of people, cars also) Schlange f; (of hills) Kette f; (US: queue) Schlange f. **in (a) ~** in einer Reihe; **in a straight ~** geradlinig; **John is next in ~ for promotion** John ist als nächster mit der Beförderung an der Reihe; **he was descended from a long ~ of farmers** er stammte aus einem alten Bauerngeschlecht; **who is fourth in ~ to the throne?** wer steht an vierter Stelle der Thronfolge?; **to be out of ~ with sb/sth** (fig) mit jdm/etw nicht übereinstimmen; **to bring sth into ~ with sth** (fig) etw mit etw in Einklang bringen; **he refused to fall into ~ with the new proposals** er weigerte sich, mit den neuen Vorschlägen konform zu gehen; **to step out of ~** (fig) aus der Reihe tanzen; **to stand in ~** (US) Schlange stehen.

(c) (air~, shipping ~) Linie f.

(d) (Rail) Strecke f. **~s** pl Gleise pl; **to reach the end of the ~** (fig) am Ende sein.

(e) (Telec: cable) Leitung f. **the firm has 52 ~s** die Firma hat 52 Anschlüsse; **this is a very bad ~** die Verbindung ist sehr schlecht; **the ~ went dead** die Leitung war auf einmal tot; **to be on the ~ to sb** mit jdm telefonieren; **hold the ~** bleiben Sie am Apparat!; **can I have an outside ~?** geben Sie mir bitte ein Amt.

(f) (Comp) **on ~** on line.

(g) (written) Zeile f. **~s** (Sch) Strafarbeit f; **~s** (Theat) Text m; **to drop sb a ~** jdm ein paar Zeilen schreiben; **to read between the ~s** zwischen den Zeilen lesen.

(h) (direction, course) ~ **of argument** Argumentation f; **~ of attack** (Mil) Angriffslinie f; (fig) Taktik f; **enemy ~s** (Mil) feindliche Stellungen pl; **to be on the right ~s** (fig) auf dem richtigen Weg sein, richtig liegen (col); **we must take a firm or strong ~ with these people** wir müssen diesen Leuten gegenüber sehr bestimmt auftreten; **to lay it on the ~** (col) die Karten auf den Tisch legen (col); **to lay it on the ~ to sb** jdm reinen Wein einschenken (col); **the ~ of least resistance** der Weg des geringsten Widerstandes; **he took the ~ that ...** er vertrat den Standpunkt, daß ...; **to be along the ~s of** ungefähr so etwas wie ... sein; **I was thinking along the same ~s** ich hatte etwas ähnliches gedacht; **it's all in the ~ of duty** das gehört zu meinen/seinen etc Pflichten.

(i) (fig: business) Branche f; (model) Modell nt. **what ~ is he in?, what's his ~?** was ist er von Beruf?; **that's not in my ~** das liegt mir nicht; **we have a new ~ in spring hats** wir haben eine neue Kollektion Frühjahrshüte.

2 vt **(a)** (cross with ~s) linieren. **worry had ~d his face** sein Gesicht war von Sorgen gezeichnet. **(b)** streets säumen. **a road ~d with trees** eine von Bäumen gesäumte Straße; **the streets were ~d with cheering crowds** eine jubelnde Menge säumte die Straßen.

♦ **line up 1** vi (stand in line) sich aufstellen; (queue) sich anstellen. **2** vt sep **(a)** troops, prisoners antreten lassen; boxes, books etc in einer Reihe aufstellen. **(b)** (prepare, arrange) entertainment sorgen für; speakers verpflichten; support mobilisieren. **have you anything special ~d ~ for today?** haben Sie für heute etwas Besonderes auf dem Programm?; **have you anyone ~d ~ for the job?** haben Sie schon jemanden für die Stelle geplant?

line² vt clothes füttern; box auskleiden. **to ~ one's own pockets** (fig) in die eigene Tasche arbeiten.

line drawing n Zeichnung f.

lined [laɪnd] adj face etc (of old people) faltig; (through worry, etc) gezeichnet; paper liniert.

line printer n Zeilendrucker m.

linen [ˈlɪnɪn] **1** n Leinen nt; (table ~) Tischwäsche f; (sheets, garments etc) Wäsche f. **~ cupboard** Wäscheschrank m. **2** adj Leinen-.

liner [ˈlaɪnəʳ] n (ship) Passagierschiff nt.

linesman [ˈlaɪnzmən], (US also) **lineman** [ˈlaɪmən] n, pl **-men** [-mən] (Sport) Linienrichter m; (Rail) Streckenwärter m.

line-up [ˈlaɪnʌp] n (Sport) Aufstellung f; (cast) Besetzung f; (US: queue) Schlange f.

linger [ˈlɪŋgəʳ] vi (also ~ **on**) (zurück)bleiben; (delay) sich aufhalten; (in dying) zwischen Leben und Tod schweben; (custom) sich halten; (doubts) zurückbleiben; (feeling, pain) anhalten; (memory) bleiben; (chords) nachklingen. **the guests ~ed in the hall** die Gäste standen noch im Flur herum; **to ~ on a subject** bei einem Thema verweilen; **to ~ over a meal** sich bei einer Mahlzeit lange aufhalten.

lingerie [ˈlænʒəriː] n (Damen)unterwäsche f.

lingering [ˈlɪŋgərɪŋ] adj lang; death langsam; illness langwierig; doubt zurückbleibend; look sehnsüchtig; kiss innig.

lingo [ˈlɪŋgəʊ] n (col) Sprache f.

linguist [ˈlɪŋgwɪst] n (speaker of languages) Sprachkundige(r) mf; (specialist in linguistics) Linguist(in f) m. **I'm no ~** ich bin nicht sprachbegabt.

linguistic [lɪŋˈgwɪstɪk] adj **(a)** sprachlich; competence Sprach-. **(b)** (of linguistics) sprachwissenschaftlich.

linguistics [lɪŋ'gwɪstɪks] *n sing* Linguistik *f*.
lining ['laɪnɪŋ] *n (of clothes etc)* Futter *nt; (of brake)* (Brems)belag *m*.
link [lɪŋk] **1** *n (of chain, fig)* Glied *nt; (person)* Verbindungsmann *m*. **he broke all his ~s with his family** er brach alle Beziehungen zu seiner Familie ab; **cultural ~s** kulturelle Beziehungen *pl*. **2** *vt* verbinden; *spaceships also* aneinanderkoppeln. **to ~ arms** sich unterhaken *(with bei)*; **do you think these two murders are ~ed?** glauben Sie, daß zwischen den beiden Morden eine Verbindung besteht?, **3** *vi* **to ~ (together)** *(parts of story)* sich zusammenfügen lassen; *(railway lines)* zusammenlaufen.
♦ **link up** *vi* zusammenkommen; *(people)* sich zusammentun; *(facts)* übereinstimmen; *(companies)* sich zusammenschließen; *(spaceships)* ein Kopplungsmanöver durchführen.
links [lɪŋks] *npl (golf course)* Golfplatz *m*.
link-up ['lɪŋkʌp] *n (Telec, general)* Verbindung *f; (of spaceships)* Kopplung(smanöver *nt) f*.
lino ['laɪnəʊ] *n (Brit)* Linoleum *nt*.
linoleum [lɪ'nəʊlɪəm] *n* Linoleum *nt*.
linseed ['lɪnsiːd] *n* Leinsamen *m*. **~ oil** Leinöl *nt*.
lint [lɪnt] *n* Mull *m*.
lintel ['lɪntl] *n (Archit)* Sturz *m*.
lion ['laɪən] *n* Löwe *m*. **the ~'s share** der Löwenanteil.
lioness ['laɪənɪs] *n* Löwin *f*.
lip [lɪp] *n* **(a)** *(Anat)* Lippe *f; (of jug)* Schnabel *m; (of cup)* Rand *m*. **to keep a stiff upper ~** die Haltung bewahren. **(b)** *(col: cheek)* Frechheit(en *pl) f*. **to give sb a lot of ~** jdm gegenüber eine (freche) Lippe riskieren *(col)*.
lip: ~read *vti* von den Lippen ablesen; **~ service** *n* **to pay ~ service to an idea** ein Lippenbekenntnis zu einer Idee ablegen; **~stick** *n* Lippenstift *m*.
liquefy ['lɪkwɪfaɪ] **1** *vt* verflüssigen. **2** *vi* sich verflüssigen.
liqueur [lɪ'kjʊəʳ] *n* Likör *m*.
liquid ['lɪkwɪd] **1** *adj* flüssig *(also Comm)*. **2** *n* Flüssigkeit *f*.
liquidate ['lɪkwɪdeɪt] *vt* **(a)** *(Comm)* liquidieren; *assets also* flüssig machen; *company also* auflösen. **(b)** *enemy etc* liquidieren.
liquidation [,lɪkwɪ'deɪʃən] *n see vt* **(a)** Liquidation *f; (of company also)* Auflösung *f*. **to go into ~** in Liquidation gehen. **(b)** Liquidierung *f*.
liquid crystal *n* Flüssigkristall *nt*.
liquidity [lɪ'kwɪdɪtɪ] *n* Liquidität *f*.
liquidize ['lɪkwɪdaɪz] *vt* (im Mixer) pürieren.
liquidizer ['lɪkwɪdaɪzəʳ] *n* Mixgerät *nt*.
liquor ['lɪkəʳ] *n (whisky, brandy etc)* Spirituosen *pl; (alcohol)* Alkohol *m*.
liquorice, licorice ['lɪkərɪs] *n* Lakritze *f*.
lisp [lɪsp] **1** *n* Lispeln *nt*. **to speak with a ~** lispeln. **2** *vti* lispeln.
lissom ['lɪsəm] *adj* geschmeidig; *person also* gelenkig.
list[1] [lɪst] **1** *n* Liste *f; (shopping ~)* Einkaufszettel *m*. **it's not on the ~** es steht nicht auf der Liste; **it's on my ~ for tomorrow** es steht für morgen auf dem Programm. **2** *vt* notieren; *item* in die Liste aufnehmen. **it is not ~ed** es ist nicht aufgeführt; **~ed building** Gebäude *nt* unter Denkmalschutz.
list[2] *(Naut)* **1** *n* Schlagseite *f*. **2** *vi* Schlagseite haben.
listen ['lɪsn] *vi* **(a)** hören *(to sth etw acc)*. **to ~ to the radio** Radio hören; **to ~ for sth** auf etw *(acc)* horchen; **to ~ for sb** hören, ob jd kommt; **OK, I'm ~ing** ich höre zu. **(b)** *(heed)* zuhören. **~ to me!** hör mir zu!; **~, I know what we'll do** hör mal, ich weiß, was wir machen; **don't ~ to him** hör nicht auf ihn; **he wouldn't ~** er wollte nicht hören.
♦ **listen in** *vi* (im Radio) hören *(to sth etw acc)*; *(listen secretly)* mithören *(on sth etw acc)*.
listener ['lɪsnəʳ] *n* Zuhörer(in *f) m; (Rad)* Hörer(in *f) m*. **to be a good ~** gut zuhören können.

listless ['lɪstlɪs] *adj* lustlos; *patient* teilnahmslos.
list price *n* Listenpreis *m*.
lists [lɪsts] *npl (Hist)* Schranken *pl*. **to enter the ~** *(fig)* zum Kampf antreten.
lit [lɪt] *pret, ptp of* **light**[1].
litany ['lɪtənɪ] *n* Litanei *f*.
liter *n (US)* = **litre**.
literacy ['lɪtərəsɪ] *n* Fähigkeit *f*, lesen und schreiben zu können. **~ campaign** Alphabetisierungskampagne *f*.
literal ['lɪtərəl] *adj translation* wörtlich; *meaning also* eigentlich. **it was a ~ disaster** es war im wahrsten Sinne des Wortes eine Katastrophe.
literally ['lɪtərəlɪ] *adv (word for word, exactly)* (wort)wörtlich; *(really)* buchstäblich, wirklich. **to take sth ~** etw wörtlich nehmen; **he was ~ a giant** er war im wahrsten Sinne des Wortes ein Riese.
literary ['lɪtərərɪ] *adj* literarisch. **a ~ man** ein Literaturkenner *m; (author)* ein Literat *m*.
literate ['lɪtərɪt] *adj* **to be ~** lesen und schreiben können; *(well-educated)* gebildet sein.
literature ['lɪtrətʃəʳ] *n* Literatur *f; (col: brochures etc)* Informationsmaterial *nt*.
lithe [laɪð] *adj (+er)* geschmeidig.
lithograph ['lɪθəʊgrɑːf] *n* Lithographie *f*, Steindruck *m*.
litigation [,lɪtɪ'geɪʃən] *n* Prozeß, Rechtsstreit *m*.
litmus ['lɪtməs] *n* **~ paper** Lackmuspapier *nt*.
litre, (US) liter ['liːtəʳ] *n* Liter *m or nt*.
litter ['lɪtəʳ] **1** *n* **(a)** *(Zool)* Wurf *m; (bedding for animals)* Streu *f*, Stroh *nt; (cat ~)* Katzenstreu *f*. **2** *vt* **to be ~ed with sth** *(lit, fig)* mit etw übersät sein.
litter: ~ bin *n* Abfalleimer *m; ~ bug (col), ~ lout (col) n* Schmutzfink *(col) m*.
little ['lɪtl] **1** *adj* klein. **a ~ house** ein Häuschen *nt; the ~ ones* die Kleinen *pl; a nice ~ profit* ein hübscher Gewinn; **a ~ while ago** vor kurzem; **it's only a ~ while till I ...** es ist nicht mehr lange, bis ich ...; **in a ~ while** bald.
2 *adv*, *n* **(a)** wenig. **of ~ importance** von geringer Bedeutung; **~ better than** kaum besser als; **~ more than a month ago** vor kaum einem Monat; **~ short of fast schon, beinahe; ~ did I think that ...** ich hätte kaum gedacht, daß ...; **I walk as ~ as possible** ich laufe so wenig wie möglich; **every ~ helps** wir sind froh um jede Kleinigkeit; **I see very ~ of her nowadays** ich sehe sie in letzter Zeit sehr selten; **there was ~ we could do** wir konnten nicht viel tun; **she did what ~ she could** sie tat das Wenige, das sie tun konnte; **~ by ~** nach und nach; **to make ~ of sth** etw herunterspielen; **I could make ~ of this book** ich konnte mit diesem Buch viel anfangen.
(b) **a ~** ein wenig, ein bißchen; **a ~ better** ein bißchen besser; **a ~ effort** mit etwas Anstrengung; **a ~ after five** kurz nach fünf; **we walked on for a ~** wir liefen noch ein bißchen weiter; **after a ~** nach einer Weile.
liturgy ['lɪtədʒɪ] *n* Liturgie *f*.
live[1] [lɪv] **1** *vt* führen. **to ~ life to the full** sein Leben auskosten.
2 *vi* **(a)** leben. **will he ~, doctor?** wird er (über)leben, Herr Doktor?; **don't worry, you'll ~**, it's only a broken ankle reg dich nicht auf, du stirbst schon nicht, du hast nur einen gebrochenen Knöchel; **long ~ Queen Anne!** lang lebe Königin Anne!; **we ~ and learn** man lernt nie aus; **to ~ and let ~** leben und leben lassen; **to ~ like a king** wie Gott in Frankreich leben; **to ~ to a ripe old age** ein hohes Alter erreichen; **his name will ~ for ever** sein Ruhm wird nie vergehen; **his poetry will ~ for ever** seine Dichtung ist unvergänglich; **he ~d through two wars** er hat zwei Kriege miterlebt; **to ~ beyond one's income** über seine Verhältnisse leben; **you'll ~**

to regret it das wirst du noch bereuen!; **you'll just have to ~ with it** du mußt eben damit leben; **the other athletes couldn't ~ with him** die anderen Läufer konnten mit ihm nicht mithalten.

(b) *(reside)* wohnen; *(in town etc)* leben. **he ~s at 19 Marktstraße** er wohnt in der Marktstraße Nr.19; **he ~s with his parents** er wohnt bei seinen Eltern.

♦ **live down** *vt sep humiliation* hinwegkommen über (+*acc*), verwinden; *(actively) scandal* Gras wachsen lassen über (+*acc*). **he'll never ~ it ~** das wird man ihm nie vergessen.

♦ **live in** *vi* im Wohnheim wohnen.

♦ **live off** *vi +prep obj* **to ~ ~ one's interest** von seinen Zinsen leben; **to ~ ~ one's relations** auf Kosten seiner Verwandten leben.

♦ **live on 1** *vi (continue to live)* weiterleben. **2** *vi +prep obj* leben von. **to ~ ~ eggs** sich von Eiern ernähren; **he doesn't earn enough to ~ ~** er verdient nicht genug, um davon zu leben.

♦ **live out 1** *vi* außerhalb (des Wohnheims) wohnen. **2** *vt sep life* verbringen; *winter* überleben. **to ~ ~ one's days** seinen Lebensabend verbringen.

♦ **live together** *vi (cohabit)* zusammenleben; *(share a flat etc)* zusammenwohnen.

♦ **live up** *vt always separate:* **to ~ it ~** *(col)* sich auslehen; *(extravagantly)* in Saus und Braus leben *(col)*.

♦ **live up to** *vi +prep obj* **the holidays ~d ~ ~ our expectations** der Urlaub hielt, was wir uns *(dat)* versprochen hatte; **to ~ ~ ~ one's reputation** seinem Ruf gerecht werden; **it didn't ~ ~ ~ our hopes** es entsprach nicht dem, was wir uns *(dat)* erhofft hatten; **he's got a lot to ~ ~** ~ in ihn werden große Erwartungen gesetzt.

live² [laɪv] **1** *adj* **(a)** *(alive)* lebend; *issue* aktuell. **a real ~ duke** ein waschechter Herzog. **(b)** *(having power or energy) coal* glühend; *match* ungebraucht; *cartridge, shell* scharf; *(Elec)* geladen. **"danger, ~ wires!"** „Vorsicht Hochspannung!"; **she's a real ~ wire** *(fig)* sie ist ein richtiges Energiebündel. **(c)** *(Rad, TV)* live. **a ~ programme** eine Livesendung. **2** *adv (Rad, TV)* live.

livelihood ['laɪvlɪhʊd] *n* Lebensunterhalt *m*. **to earn a ~** sich *(dat)* seinen Lebensunterhalt verdienen.

liveliness ['laɪvlɪnɪs] *n see adj* Lebhaftigkeit *f;* Lebendigkeit *f;* Dynamik *f;* Aufgeweckheit *f.*

lively ['laɪvlɪ] *adj (+er)* lebhaft; *scene, account* lebendig; *campaign* dynamisch; *pace* flott; *mind* aufgeweckt. **things are getting ~** es geht hoch her *(col)*.

♦ **liven up** ['laɪvən'ʌp] **1** *vt sep* beleben, Leben bringen in (+*acc*) *(col)*. **2** *vi* in Schwung kommen; *(person)* aufleben.

liver ['lɪvəʳ] *n (Anat, Cook)* Leber *f.*

liverish ['lɪvərɪʃ] *adj (bad-tempered)* mürrisch. **to be ~** etwas mit der Leber haben; **I felt a bit ~ after the party** mir ging es nach der Party ziemlich mies *(col)*.

livery ['lɪvərɪ] *n* Livree *f; (fig liter)* Kleid *nt.*

lives [laɪvz] *pl of* **life.**

livestock ['laɪvstɒk] *n* Vieh *nt.*

livid ['lɪvɪd] *adj* **(a)** *(col)* fuchsteufelswild *(col)*. **he got ~ with us** er hatte eine Stinkwut auf uns *(col)*. **(b)** *(colour)* bleifarben.

living ['lɪvɪŋ] **1** *adj* lebend; *example, faith* lebendig. **a ~ creature** ein Lebewesen *nt;* **(with)in ~ memory** seit Menschengedenken; **he is ~ proof of ...** er ist der lebende Beweis für ... **2** *n* **(a)** *pl* die Lebenden *pl.* **(b)** *(livelihood)* Lebensunterhalt *m.* **to earn** *or* **make a ~** sich *(dat)* seinen Lebensunterhalt verdienen; **he sells brushes for a ~** er verkauft Bürsten, um sich *(dat)* seinen Lebensunterhalt zu verdienen; **what do you do for a ~?** was machen Sie beruflich?; **to**

work for one's ~ sich selbst unterhalten.

living: ~ conditions *npl* Wohnverhältnisse *pl;* **~ room** *n* Wohnzimmer *nt;* **~ wage** *n* ausreichender Lohn.

lizard ['lɪzəd] *n* Eidechse *f.*

lo [ləʊ] *interj* **~ and behold!** und siehe da.

load [ləʊd] **1** *n* **(a)** *(sth carried, burden)* Last *f; (cargo)* Ladung *f; (on axle etc, fig)* Belastung *f; (Elec)* Spannung *f.* **an arm-~ of shopping** ein Armvoll Einkäufe; **a train-~ of passengers** ein Zug voll Reisender; *(work)* ~ *(Arbeits)*pensum *nt;* **that's a ~ off my mind!** da fällt mir ein Stein vom Herzen!

(b) *(col usages)* **~s of, a ~ of** jede Menge *(col);* **it's a ~ of old rubbish** das ist alles Quatsch! *(col); (book)* das ist alles Mist! *(col);* **get a ~ of this!** *(listen)* hör dir das mal an!; *(look)* guck dir das mal an! *(col).*

2 *vt* **(a)** *goods, software* laden; *lorry etc, (burden: also ~ down)* beladen. **the ship was ~ed with bananas** das Schiff hatte Bananen geladen. **(b)** *gun* laden; *dice* präparieren. **to ~ a camera** einen Film (in einen Fotoapparat) einlegen. **(c)** *(fig)* überhäufen. **to ~ sb with honours** jdn mit Ehrungen überschütten; **we're ~ed (down) with debts** wir stecken bis zum Hals in Schulden; **the dice had been ~ed against him** *(fig)* es war Schiebung *(col)* ein abgekartetes Spiel.

3 *vi* laden. **~ing bay** Ladeplatz *m.*

♦ **load up 1** *vi* aufladen. **2** *vt sep lorry* beladen; *goods* aufladen.

loaded ['ləʊdɪd] *adj* beladen; *dice* präpariert; *camera* mit eingelegtem Film; *gun* geladen. **a ~ question** eine Fangfrage; **he's ~** *(col: rich)* er ist steinreich *(col).*

loaf [ləʊf] *n, pl* **loaves** Brot *nt; (unsliced)* (Brot)laib *m.* **a ~ of bread** ein Brot; **half a ~ is better than none** *(Prov)* (wenig ist) besser als gar nichts; **use your ~!** *(col)* streng deinen Grips an! *(col).*

♦ **loaf about** *or* **around** *vi (col)* faulenzen.

loam [ləʊm] *n* Lehmerde *f.*

loan [ləʊn] **1** *n* **(a)** *(thing lent)* Leihgabe *f; (from bank etc)* Kredit *m,* Darlehen *nt; (public ~)* Anleihe *f.* **I asked for the ~ of the bicycle** ich bat darum, das Fahrrad ausleihen zu dürfen; **he gave me the ~ of his bicycle** er hat mir sein Fahrrad geliehen; **it's on ~** es ist geliehen; *(out on ~)* es ist verliehen. **2** *vt* leihen *(to sb* jdm*).*

loath [ləʊθ] *adj* **to be ~ to do sth** etw ungern tun.

loathe [ləʊð] *vt thing, person* verabscheuen; *jazz etc* nicht ausstehen können. **I ~ doing it** *(in general)* ich hasse es, das zu tun; *(on particular occasion)* es ist mir zuwider, das zu tun.

loathing ['ləʊðɪŋ] *n* Abscheu *m.*

loathsome ['ləʊðsəm] *adj thing, person* abscheulich, widerlich; *task* verhaßt.

loaves [ləʊvz] *pl of* **loaf.**

lob [lɒb] **1** *n (Tennis)* Lob *m.* **2** *vt ball* lobben. **to ~ sth over to sb** jdm etw zuwerfen.

lobby ['lɒbɪ] **1** *n (entrance hall)* Eingangshalle *f; (place in Parliament)* Lobby *f; (Pol)* Interessenverband *m.* **2** *vt* **to ~ one's MP** auf seinen Abgeordneten Einfluß nehmen. **3** *vi* **they are ~ing for this reform** die Lobbyisten versuchen, diese Reform durchzubringen.

lobbyist ['lɒbɪɪst] *n* Lobbyist *m.*

lobe [ləʊb] *n (of ear)* Ohrläppchen *nt.*

lobster ['lɒbstəʳ] *n* Hummer *m.* **~ pot** Hummerkorb *m.*

local ['ləʊkəl] **1** *adj* Orts-; *(in this area)* hiesig; *(in that area)* dortig; *radio station* Regional-; *newspaper* Lokal-; *train* Nahverkehrs-; *politician* Kommunal-; *anaesthetic* örtlich. **he's a ~ man** er ist von hier *(col);* **~ authorities** städtische Behörden *pl; (council)* Stadt-/Gemeinde-/Kreisverwaltung *f;* **~ call** Ortsgespräch *nt;* **~ government** Gemeinde-/Kreisverwaltung *f;* **~ branch** Zweigstelle *f.* **2** *n* **(a)** *(Brit: pub)* the

~ das Stammlokal; *(in village)* die Dorfkneipe *(col)*. **(b)** *(born in)* Einheimische(r) *mf; (living in)* Einwohner(in *f*) *m.*

locality [ləʊˈkælɪtɪ] *n* Gegend *f.* in the ~ of the crime am Ort des Verbrechens.

localize [ˈləʊkəlaɪz] *vt* **(a)** *(detect)* lokalisieren **(b)** ~d *(restricted)* örtlich begrenzt.

locally [ˈləʊkəlɪ] *adv* am Ort. **houses are dear** ~ Häuser sind hier teuer; **the shops are situated** ~ die Geschäfte befinden sich in günstiger Lage; **do you live** ~? wohnen Sie am Ort?

locate [ləʊˈkeɪt] *vt* **(a)** *(position)* legen. **to be** ~**d at** *or* **in sich befinden in** (+*dat*); **the hotel is centrally** ~**d** das Hotel liegt zentral. **(b)** *(find)* ausfindig machen; *submarine* orten.

location [ləʊˈkeɪʃən] *n* **(a)** *(position, site)* Lage *f; (of ship)* Position *f.* this would be an ideal ~ for the road/airport das wäre ein ideales Gelände für die Straße/den Flughafen. **(b)** *(finding)* Auffinden *nt; (of tumour)* Lokalisierung *f; (of star, ship)* Ortung *f.* **(c)** *(Film)* Drehort *m.* **part of the film was done on** ~ **in Mexico** Außenaufnahmen für den Film wurden in Mexiko gedreht.

loch [lɒx] *n (Scot)* See *m; (sea* ~) Meeresarm *m.*

lock¹ [lɒk] *n (of hair)* Locke *f.*

lock² 1 *n* **(a)** *(on door, box, gun)* Schloß *nt.* **to put sb/sth under** ~ **and key** jdn hinter Schloß und Riegel bringen/etw wegschließen; **he offered me the house** ~, **stock and barrel** er bot mir das Haus mit allem Drum und Dran an *(col)*; **they rejected the idea** ~, **stock and barrel** sie lehnten die Idee in Bausch und Bogen ab. **(b)** *(canal* ~*)* Schleuse *f.* **(c)** *(Aut)* Wendekreis *m.* **the steering wheel was on full** ~ das Lenkrad war voll eingeschlagen.

2 *vt door etc* abschließen; *steering wheel* sperren, arretieren; *wheel* blockieren. **the armies were** ~**ed in combat** die Armeen waren in Kämpfe verwickelt; **they were** ~**ed in each other's arms** sie hielten sich fest umschlungen; **this bar** ~**s the wheel in position** diese Stange hält das Rad fest.

3 *vi* schließen; *(wheel)* blockieren. **a suitcase that** ~**s** ein verschließbarer Koffer.

♦ **lock away** *vt sep* wegschließen; *(in safe)* einschließen; *person* einsperren.

♦ **lock in** *vt sep* einschließen. **to be** ~**ed** ~ eingesperrt sein.

♦ **lock out** *vt sep* aussperren.

♦ **lock up** 1 *vt sep* **(a)** *thing, house* abschließen; *person* einsperren. **to** ~ **sth** ~ **in sth** etw in etw *(dat)* einschließen; **he ought to be** ~**ed** ~! den müßte man einsperren! **(b)** *(Comm)* capital fest anlegen. **2** *vi* abschließen.

locker [ˈlɒkəʳ] *n* Schließfach *nt.* ~ **room** Umkleideraum *m.*

locket [ˈlɒkɪt] *n* Medaillon *nt.*

lock: ~ **gate** *n* Schleusentor *nt;* ~ **jaw** *n* Wundstarrkrampf *m;* ~**out** *n* Aussperrung *f;* ~**smith** *n* Schlosser *m;* ~-**up** *n* **(a)** *(shop)* kleiner Laden; *(garage)* Garage *f;* **(b)** *(prison)* Gefängnis *nt.*

locomotion [,ləʊkəˈməʊʃən] *n* Fortbewegung *f.*

locomotive [,ləʊkəˈməʊtɪv] *n* Lokomotive *f.*

locust [ˈləʊkəst] *n* Heuschrecke *f.*

lodge [lɒdʒ] **1** *n (in grounds)* Pförtnerhaus *nt; (skiing etc)* Hütte *f; (porter's* ~*)* Pförtnerloge *f.* **2** *vt person* unterbringen; *complaint* einlegen *(with* bei*); charge* einreichen; *(insert)* spear stoßen; *jewellery, money* deponieren, hinterlegen. **to be** ~**d** *(fest)stecken.* **3** *vi* **(a)** *(live)* (zur *or* in Untermiete) wohnen *(with* sb, at sb's bei jdm*); (at boarding house)* wohnen *(in* in +*dat*). **(b)** *(object, bullet)* steckenbleiben.

lodger [ˈlɒdʒəʳ] *n* Untermieter(in *f*) *m.* **she takes** ~**s** sie vermietet (Zimmer).

lodging [ˈlɒdʒɪŋ] *n* Unterkunft *f.* ~**s** *pl* ein möbliertes Zimmer; möblierte Zimmer *pl;* **we took** ~**s with Mrs B** wir mieteten uns bei Frau B ein;

~ **house** Pension *f.*

loft [lɒft] *n* Dachboden, Speicher *m; (hay*~*)* Heuboden *m.* **in the** ~ auf dem Dachboden.

lofty [ˈlɒftɪ] *adj* (+*er*) **(a)** *(high)* hoch. **(b)** *ideals* hoch; *ambitions* hochfliegend; *sentiments* erhaben; *prose* gehoben. **(c)** *(haughty)* hochmütig.

log¹ [lɒg] *n* Baumstamm *m; (short)* Holzblock *m; (for a fire)* Scheit *nt.* **to sleep like a** ~ wie ein Stein schlafen; ~ **cabin** Blockhütte *f;* ~ **fire** Holzfeuer *nt.*

log² **1** *n (record)* Aufzeichnungen *pl.* **to make** *or* **keep a** ~ of sth über etw *(acc)* Buch führen; *see* ~**book.** **2** *vt* **(a)** Buch führen über (+*acc*); *(Naut)* (ins Logbuch) eintragen. **(b)** *(travel)* zurücklegen.

log³ = **logarithm** log. ~ **tables** Logarithmentafel *f.*

logarithm [ˈlɒgərɪθəm] *n* Logarithmus *m.*

log book *n (Naut)* Logbuch *nt; (Aviat)* Bordbuch *nt; (of lorries)* Fahrtenbuch *nt; (Aut: registration book)* Kraftfahrzeugbrief *m; (in hospitals etc)* Dienstbuch *nt.*

loggerheads [ˈlɒgəhedz] *npl:* **to be at** ~ **(with sb)** Streit (mit jdm) haben; **they were constantly at** ~ **with the authorities** sie standen mit den Behörden dauernd auf Kriegsfuß.

logic [ˈlɒdʒɪk] *n* Logik *f.*

logical [ˈlɒdʒɪkəl] *adj* logisch.

logically [ˈlɒdʒɪkəlɪ] *adv* think, argue logisch. ~, he may be right logisch gesehen könnte er recht haben.

logistics [lɒˈdʒɪstɪks] *n sing* Logistik *f.*

logo [ˈləʊgəʊ] *n* Firmenzeichen *nt.*

loin [lɔɪn] *n* Lende *f.* ~ **cloth** Lendenschurz *m.*

loiter [ˈlɔɪtəʳ] *vi (waste time)* trödeln; *(hang around suspiciously)* herumlungern. **to** ~ **with intent** sich verdächtig machen.

loll [lɒl] *vi* lümmeln. **to** ~ **against sth** sich (lässig) gegen *or* an etw *(acc)* lehnen.

♦ **loll about** *or* **around** *vi* herumlümmeln.

lollipop [ˈlɒlɪpɒp] *n* Lutscher *m; (iced* ~*)* Eis *nt* am Stiel. ~ **man/woman** *(Brit col)* = Schülerlotse *m.*

lolly [ˈlɒlɪ] *n* **(a)** *(Brit col: lollipop)* Lutscher *m.* **an ice** ~ ein Eis *nt* am Stiel. **(b)** *(col: money)* Mäuse *(col)* *pl.*

London [ˈlʌndən] **1** *n* London *nt.* **2** *adj* Londoner.

Londoner [ˈlʌndənəʳ] *n* Londoner(in *f*) *m.*

lone [ləʊn] *adj* einzeln, einsam; *(only)* einzig. ~ **wolf** *(fig)* Einzelgänger *m.*

loneliness [ˈləʊnlɪnɪs] *n* Einsamkeit *f.*

lonely [ˈləʊnlɪ] *adj* (+*er*) einsam.

loner [ˈləʊnəʳ] *n* Einzelgänger(in *f*) *m.*

lonesome [ˈləʊnsəm] *adj (esp US)* einsam.

long¹ [lɒŋ] **1** *adj* (+*er*) **(a)** *(in size)* lang; *glass* hoch; *journey* weit. **it is 6 metres** ~ es ist 6 Meter lang; **to pull a** ~ **face** ein langes Gesicht machen; **it's a** ~ **way to Hamburg** nach Hamburg ist es weit; **to have a** ~ **memory** ein gutes Gedächtnis haben; **to be** ~ **in the tooth** *(col)* nicht mehr der/die Jüngste sein. **(b)** *(in time)* lang; *job* langwierig. **it's a** ~ **time since I saw her** ich habe sie schon seit längerer Zeit nicht mehr gesehen; **will you need it for a** ~ **time?** brauchen Sie es lange?; **he's been here (for) a** ~ **time** er ist schon lange hier; ~ **time no see** *(col)* sieht man dich auch mal wieder? *(col);* **to take a** ~ **look at sth** etw lange betrachten; **how** ~ **is the film?** wie lange dauert der Film?; **to take the** ~ **view** auf lange Sicht betrachten; **a** ~ **drink** *(mixed)* ein Longdrink *m.*

2 *adv* lang(e). **to be** ~ **in doing sth** lange zu etw brauchen; **don't be** ~! beeil dich!; **I shan't be** ~ *(in finishing)* ich bin gleich fertig; *(in returning)* ich bin gleich wieder da; **all night** ~ die ganze Nacht; **something he had** ~ **wished to happen** etwas, was er sich *(dat)* schon lange gewünscht hatte; ~ **ago** vor langer Zeit; **not** ~ **ago** vor kurzem; ~ **before** lange vorher; **not** ~ **before**

that kurz davor; **as ~ as** so lange wie; **we waited as ~ as we could** wir haben gewartet, solange wir konnten; **as ~ as, so ~ as** *(provided that)* solange; **how much ~er can you stay?** wie lange können Sie noch bleiben?; **no ~er** *(not any more)* nicht mehr; **I'll wait no ~er** ich warte nicht länger; **so ~!** *(col)* tschüs *(col)*.

3 *n* **the ~ and the short of it is that ...** der langen Rede kurzer Sinn, ...; **before ~** bald; **are you going for ~?** werden Sie länger weg sein?; **it won't take ~** das dauert nicht lange.

long² *vi* sich sehnen *(for* nach*)*; *(less passionately)* kaum erwarten können *(for* sth etw *acc)*. **I am ~ing to go abroad** ich brenne darauf, ins Ausland zu gehen; **I'm ~ing to see that film** ich will den Film unbedingt sehen.

long: ~-distance 1 *adj* lorry, call Fern-; *flight, race* Langstrecken-; **2** *adv* **to call ~ distance** ein Ferngespräch führen; **~-drawn-out** *adj* speech langatmig; *meeting* in die Länge gezogen; **~-haired** *adj* person langhaarig; *dog etc* Lang-haar-; **~hand** *n* **in ~hand** handschriftlich.

longing ['lɒŋɪŋ] **1** *adj* look sehnsüchtig; *eyes* sehn-suchtsvoll. **2** *n* Sehnsucht *f (for* nach*)*. **to have a ~ to do sth** sich danach sehnen, etw zu tun.

longingly ['lɒŋɪŋlɪ] *adv* sehnsüchtig.

longitude ['lɒŋgɪtjuːd] *n* Länge *f*.

long: ~-legged *adj* langbeinig; **~-lost** *adj* person verloren geglaubt; *ideals etc* verlorengegangen; **~-playing** *adj* Langspiel-; **~-range** *adj* gun weit-tragend; *missile, aircraft* Langstrecken-; *fore-cast* langfristig; **~ shot** *n* **to take a ~ shot** ei-nen gewagten Versuch unternehmen; **not by a ~ shot** bei weitem nicht; **~-sighted** *adj (lit, fig)* weitsichtig; **~-standing** *adj* alt; *friendship also* langjährig; *interest, invitation* schon lange bestehend; **~-suffering** *adj* schwer geprüft; **~-term 1** *adj* langfristig; **2** *n* **in the ~ term** langfristig gesehen; **~ vacation** *n (Univ)* (Sommer)semesterferien *pl*; *(Sch)* große Ferien *pl*; **~-winded** *adj* umständlich; *story* langatmig.

loo [luː] *n (Brit col)* Klo *nt (col)*. **to go to the ~** aufs Klo gehen *(col)*; **in the ~** auf dem Klo *(col)*.

look [lʊk] **1** *n* **(a)** *(glance)* Blick *m*. **she gave me a dirty ~** sie warf mir einen vernichtenden Blick zu; **she gave me a ~ of disbelief** sie sah mich ungläubig an; **to have** *or* **take a ~ at sth** sich *(dat)* etw ansehen; **can I have a ~?** darf ich mal sehen; **have a ~ at this!** sieh dir das mal an!; **let's have a ~** laß mal sehen!; **to take a good ~ at sth** sich *(dat)* etw genau ansehen; **to have a ~ for sth** sich nach etw umsehen; **to have a ~ around** sich umsehen; **shall we have a ~ around the town?** sollen wir uns *(dat)* die Stadt ansehen?

(b) *(air, appearances)* Aussehen *nt*. **there was a ~ of despair in his eyes** ein verzweifelter Blick war in seinen Augen; **I don't like the ~ of him/ this wound** er/die Wunde gefällt mir gar nicht; **by the ~ of him** so, wie er aussieht.

(c) **~s** *pl* Aussehen *nt*; **good ~s** guts man kann nicht nur nach dem Äußeren gehen.

2 *vt* **he is ~ing his age** man sieht ihm sein Alter an; **he's not ~ing himself these days** er sieht in letzter Zeit ganz verändert aus; **to ~ one's best** sein vorteilhaft aussehen; **~ what you've done!** sieh dir mal an, was du da angestellt hast!; **~ where you're going!** paß auf, wo du hintrittst!

3 *vi* **(a)** *(see, glance)* gucken *(col)*, schauen *(dial)*; *(with prep etc also)* sehen; *(search)* suchen, nachsehen. **to ~ carefully** genau hinsehen *etc*; **~ here!** hör *(mal)* zu!; **~, I know you're tired, but ...** ich weiß ja, daß du müde bist, aber ...; **just ~!** guck mal! *(col)*; **to ~ over one's shoulder** über die Schulter sehen; **to ~ over sb's shoulder** jdm über die Schulter sehen; **~ before you leap** *(Prov)* erst wägen, dann wagen *(Prov)*.

(b) *(seem)* aussehen. **it ~s all right to me** es scheint mir in Ordnung zu sein; **it ~s suspicious to me** es kommt mir verdächtig vor; **the car ~s about 10 years old** das Auto sieht so aus, als ob es 10 Jahre alt wäre; **it ~s well on you** es steht dir gut; **to ~ like** aussehen wie; **the picture doesn't ~ like him** das Bild sieht ihm nicht ähnlich; **it ~s like rain** es sieht nach Regen aus; **it ~s as if we'll be late** es sieht (so) aus, als würden wir zu spät kommen.

(c) *(face)* gehen nach. **this window ~s north** dieses Fenster geht nach Norden.

♦ **look after** *vi +prep obj* **(a)** *(take care of)* sich kümmern um. **to ~ ~ oneself** *(cook etc)* für sich selbst sorgen; *(be capable, strong etc)* auf sich *(acc)* aufpassen. **(b)** *bags, children* aufpassen auf *(+acc)*.

♦ **look around** *vi* **(a)** sich umsehen. **(b)** *(in shop etc)* sich umsehen. **let's ~ ~ the garden** sehen wir uns den Garten an.

♦ **look at** *vi +prep obj (also examine)* ansehen, angucken *(col)*; *(view)* betrachten, sehen; *(con-sider)* possibilities sich *(dat)* überlegen; *offer* in Betracht ziehen. **he ~ed ~ his watch** er sah auf die Uhr; **he/it isn't much to ~ ~** *(not attractive)* er/es sieht nicht besonders (gut) aus; *(nothing special)* er/es sieht nach nichts aus.

♦ **look away** *vi* wegsehen.

♦ **look back** *vi* zurücksehen; *(fig)* zurückblicken *(on* sth, *to* sth auf etw *acc)*. **he's never ~ed ~** *(col)* es ist ständig mit ihm bergauf gegangen.

♦ **look down** *vi* hinunter-/heruntersehen *or* -gucken *(col)*. **we ~ed ~ the hole** wir sahen ins Loch hinunter.

♦ **look down on** *vi +prep obj (lit, fig)* herabsehen auf *(+acc)*.

♦ **look for** *vi +prep obj (seek)* suchen. **he's ~ing ~ trouble** er wird sich *(dat)* Ärger einhandeln; *(actively)* er sucht Streit.

♦ **look forward** *vi +prep obj* sich freuen auf *(+acc)*. **I'm so ~ing ~ ~ seeing you again** ich freue mich so darauf, dich wiederzusehen; **I ~ ~ ~ hearing from you** ich hoffe, bald von Ihnen zu hören.

♦ **look in** *vi* **(a)** hinein-/hereinsehen *or* -gucken *(col)*. **(b)** *(visit)* vorbeikommen *(on* sb bei jdm*)*.

♦ **look into** *vi +prep obj* untersuchen; *complaint etc* prüfen.

♦ **look on** *vi* **(a)** *(watch)* zusehen, zugucken *(col)*. **(b)** **to ~ ~ to** *(window)* (hinaus)gehen auf *(+acc)*; *(building)* liegen an *(+dat)*. **(c)** *+prep obj (also* **look upon***)* betrachten, ansehen.

♦ **look out 1** *vi* **(a)** hinaus-/heraussehen *or* -gucken *(col)*. **to ~ ~ (of) the window** zum Fenster hinaussehen, aus dem Fenster sehen; **to ~ ~ for sb/troublemakers** nach jdm Ausschau halten/ auf Unruhestifter achten. **(b)** *(take care)* auf-passen. **~ ~!** paß auf! **2** *vt sep* heraussuchen.

♦ **look over** *vt sep* papers, notes etc durchsehen; *house* sich *(dat)* ansehen.

♦ **look round** *vi* = **look around**.

♦ **look through 1** *vi* durchsehen *or* -gucken *(col)* *(prep obj* durch*)*. **he ~ed ~ the window** er sah zum Fenster hinein/herein; **to ~ straight ~ sb** durch jdn hindurchgucken. **2** *vt sep (examine)* durchsehen.

♦ **look to** *vi +prep obj* **(a)** *(look after)* sich kümmern um. **(b)** *(rely on)* sich verlassen auf *(+acc)*. **they ~ed ~ him to solve the problem** sie verließen sich darauf, daß er das Problem lösen würde.

♦ **look up 1** *vi* **(a)** aufsehen, aufblicken. **(b)** *(im-prove)* besser werden; *(shares, prices)* steigen. **things are ~ing ~** es geht bergauf. **2** *vt sep (lit)* **to ~ sb ~ and down** jdn von oben bis unten an-sehen. **(b)** *(visit)* **to ~ sb ~** bei jdm vor-beischauen. **(c)** *(seek)* word nachschlagen.

looker-on ['lʊkə'(r)ɒn] Schaulustige(r) *mf (pej)*.

look-in ['lʊkɪn] n: he didn't get a ~ (col) er hatte keine Chance.

looking glass ['lʊkɪŋglɑːs] n Spiegel m.

look-out ['lʊk͵aʊt] n (a) (Mil) (tower etc) Ausguck m; (person) Wachtposten m. to keep a ~ for Ausschau halten nach. ~post Beobachtungsposten m. (b) (prospect) Aussichten pl. it's a grim ~ for us es sieht schlecht aus für uns. (c) (col: worry) that's his ~! das ist sein Problem!

loom¹ [luːm] n Webstuhl m.

loom² vi (also ~ ahead or up) (lit, fig) sich abzeichnen; (storm) heraufziehen; (disaster) sich zusammenbrauen; (danger) drohen; (difficulties) sich auftürmen; (exams) bedrohlich näherrücken. the ship ~ed (up) out of the mist das Schiff tauchte aus dem Nebel (auf); to ~ large eine große Rolle spielen.

loony ['luːnɪ] (col) 1 adj (+er) bekloppt (col). 2 n Verrückte(r) (col) mf. ~ bin Klapsmühle f (col).

loop [luːp] 1 n (a) (curved shape) Schlaufe f; (of wire) Schlinge f; (of river) Schleife f. (b) (Aviat) Looping m. to ~ the ~ einen Looping machen. 2 vt rope etc schlingen (around um).

loophole ['luːp͵həʊl] n (fig) Hintertürchen nt. a ~ in the law eine Lücke im Gesetz.

loose [luːs] 1 adj (+er) board, button lose; dress, collar weit; tooth, bandage, knot, screw, soil, weave locker; limbs beweglich. ~ change Kleingeld nt; a ~ connection (Elec) ein Wackelkontakt m; to come or work ~ (screw, handle etc) sich lockern; (button) abgehen. (b) (free) to break or get ~ (person, animal) sich losreißen (from von); (break out) ausbrechen; to run ~ frei herumlaufen; (of children) unbeaufsichtigt herumlaufen; to be at a ~ end (fig) nichts mit sich anzufangen wissen; to turn or set ~ frei herumlaufen lassen; prisoner freilassen; to tie up the ~ ends (fig) ein paar offene Probleme lösen. (c) (not exact, vague) translation frei; account ungenau; connection lose; thinking unlogisch. (d) (too free, immoral) conduct lose; morals locker; person unmoralisch. 2 n (col) to be on the ~ (prisoners, dangerous animals) frei herumlaufen. 3 vt (a) (free) befreien. (b) (untie) losmachen. (c) (slacken) lockern.

loose: ~ covers npl Überzüge pl; ~-fitting adj weit; ~-leaf book n Ringbuch nt; ~-limbed adj (lithe) gelenkig.

loosely ['luːslɪ] adv lose, locker; behave unmoralisch. ~ speaking grob gesagt; I was using the word rather ~ ich habe das Wort ziemlich frei gebraucht.

loosen ['luːsn] 1 vt (a) (free) befreien; tongue lösen. (b) (untie) lösen. (c) (slacken) lockern; collar aufmachen. 2 vi sich lockern.

♦**loosen up** 1 vt sep muscles lockern. 2 vi (muscles) locker werden; (athlete) sich (auf)lockern; (relax) auftauen.

loot [luːt] 1 n Beute f; (col: money) Zaster m (col). 2 vti plündern.

looter ['luːtəʳ] n Plünderer m.

lop [lɒp] vt (also ~ off) abhacken.

lope [ləʊp] vi in großen Sätzen springen; (hare) hoppeln.

lopsided ['lɒp͵saɪdɪd] adj schief; (fig) einseitig.

loquacious [lə'kweɪʃəs] adj redselig.

lord [lɔːd] 1 n (a) (master, ruler) Herr m. ~ and master Herr und Meister m. (b) (Brit) Lord m. the (House of) L~s das Oberhaus; my ~ (to noble) (in English contexts) Mylord; (to judge) Euer Ehren; L~ Chancellor Lordkanzler m; L~ Mayor ≃ Oberbürgermeister m. (c) (Rel) L~ Herr m; the L~'s prayer das Vaterunser; (good) L~! (col) ach, du lieber Himmel! (col); L~ knows (col) wer weiß; L~ knows I've tried often enough ich hab's weiß Gott oft genug versucht. 2

vt to ~ it das Zepter schwingen; to ~ it over sb jdn herumkommandieren.

lordship ['lɔːdʃɪp] n (Brit: title) Lordschaft f. your ~ Eure Lordschaft; (to judge) Euer Ehren.

lore [lɔːʳ] n Überlieferung pl. plant ~ Pflanzenkunde f.

lorry ['lɒrɪ] n (Brit) Last(kraft)wagen, Lkw, Laster (col) m. ~ driver Last(kraft)wagenfahrer(in f) m.

lose [luːz] pret, ptp lost 1 vt (a) verlieren; pursuer abschütteln; one's French verlernen; prize nicht bekommen. the shares have lost 15% in a month die Aktien sind in einem Monat um 15% gefallen; you will ~ nothing by helping them es kann dir nicht schaden, wenn du ihnen hilfst; that mistake lost him the game dieser Fehler kostete ihn den Sieg; to ~ no time in doing sth etw sofort tun; my watch lost three hours in a week meine Uhr ist innerhalb einer Woche drei Stunden nachgegangen. (b) (not catch) train, opportunity verpassen; words nicht mitbekommen. you've lost me now with all this abstract argument bei dieser abstrakten Argumentation komme ich nicht mehr mit. (c) to be lost (things) verschwunden sein; (people) sich verlaufen haben; (driver) sich verfahren haben; (fig) verloren sein; (words) untergehen; I can't follow the reasoning, I'm lost ich kann der Argumentation nicht folgen, ich verstehe nichts mehr; to get lost sich verlaufen; (driver) sich verfahren; get lost! (col) verschwinde! (col); to give sb/sth up for lost jdn verloren geben/etw abschreiben; I'm lost without my watch ohne meine Uhr bin ich verloren or aufgeschmissen (col); classical music is lost on him er hat keinen Sinn für klassische Musik; the remark was lost on her die Bemerkung kam bei ihr nicht an. 2 vi verlieren; (watch) nachgehen. you can't ~ du kannst nichts verlieren

♦**lose out** vi (col) den kürzeren ziehen (on bei) (col).

loser ['luːzəʳ] n Verlierer(in f) m. he's a born ~ er ist der geborene Verlierer; to be a bad ~ ein schlechter Verlierer sein.

losing ['luːzɪŋ] adj team Verlierer-. a ~ battle ein aussichtsloser Kampf.

loss [lɒs] n (a) Verlust m. there was a heavy ~ of life viele kamen ums Leben; the army suffered heavy ~es die Armee erlitt schwere Verluste; his business is running at a ~ er arbeitet mit Verlust; to sell sth at a ~ etw mit Verlust verkaufen; it's your ~ es ist deine Sache; a dead ~ (col) ein böser Reinfall (col); (person) ein hoffnungsloser Fall (col). (b) to be at a ~ nicht mehr weiterwissen; to be at a ~ to explain sth etw nicht erklären können; to be at a ~ for words nicht wissen, was man sagen soll.

lost [lɒst] 1 pret, ptp of **lose.** 2 adj verloren; cause aussichtslos; child verschwunden; opportunity verpaßt. ~-and-found (department) (US), ~ property office (Brit) Fundbüro nt.

lot¹ [lɒt] n (a) (for deciding) Los nt. to cast or draw ~s for sth etw verlosen. (b) (destiny) Los nt. it falls to my ~ to tell him mir fällt die Aufgabe zu, es ihm zu sagen; to throw in one's ~ with sb sich mit jdm zusammentun. (c) (plot) Parzelle f. parking ~ (US) Parkplatz m. (d) (number of articles) Posten m; (at auction) Los nt. where shall I put this ~? wo soll ich das hier hintun?; divide the books up into three ~s teile die Bücher in drei Stapel auf; he's just given me another ~ er hat mir gerade einen neuen Stoß or noch eine Ladung gegeben (col). (e) (col: group) Haufen m. that ~ in the next office die Typen vom Büro nebenan (col). (f) the ~ alle; alles; that's the ~ das ist alles; the whole ~ of them sie alle; he's eaten the ~ er hat alles aufgegessen.

lot² 1 n a ~, ~s viel; a ~ of money viel Geld; a ~ of books, ~s of books viele Bücher; such a ~ so viel; quite a ~ of books ziemlich viele Bücher; he made ~s and ~s of mistakes er hat eine Unmenge Fehler gemacht; we see a ~ of John these days wir sehen John in letzter Zeit sehr oft; I'd give a ~ to know ... ich würde viel darum geben, wenn ich wüßte ...; thanks a ~! (also iro) vielen Dank! 2 adv a ~, ~s viel; things have changed a ~ es hat sich vieles geändert; I feel ~s or a ~ better es geht mir sehr viel besser.

lotion ['ləʊʃən] n Lotion f.

lottery ['lɒtərɪ] n Lotterie f.

loud [laʊd] 1 adj (+er) (a) laut. ~ and clear laut und deutlich. (b) behaviour aufdringlich; colour schreiend; (in bad taste) auffällig. 2 adv laut. to say sth out ~ etw laut sagen.

loudhailer [ˌlaʊd'heɪləʳ] n Megaphon nt; (not hand-held) Lautsprecher m.

loudly ['laʊdlɪ] adv see adj. he was ~ dressed in blue er war in ein grelles Blau gekleidet.

loud-mouthed ['laʊdmaʊðd] adj (col) großmäulig (col).

loudspeaker [ˌlaʊd'spiːkəʳ] n Lautsprecher m; (of hi-fi also) Box f.

lounge [laʊndʒ] 1 n (in house) Wohnzimmer nt; (in hotel) Gesellschaftsraum m; (~ bar) Salon m; (at airport) Warteraum m. 2 vi faulenzen. to ~ about herumliegen/-sitzen/-stehen.

lour, lower ['laʊəʳ] vi (person) ein finsteres Gesicht machen; (clouds) sich türmen. to ~ at sb jdn finster or drohend ansehen.

louse [laʊs] n, pl lice (Zool) Laus f.

lousy ['laʊzɪ] adj (very bad: very bad) saumäßig (col), beschissen (col!); trick etc fies (col). I'm ~ at arithmetic in Mathe bin ich miserabel (col); a ~ $3 lausige 3 Dollar (col).

lout [laʊt] n Rüpel, Flegel m.

lovable ['lʌvəbl] adj liebenswert.

love [lʌv] 1 n (a) (affection) Liebe f. ~ of learning Freude f am Lernen; ~ of books Liebe f zu Büchern; he studies history for the ~ of it er studiert Geschichte aus Liebe zur Sache; to be in ~ (with sb) (in jdn) verliebt sein; to fall in ~ (with sb) sich (in jdn) verlieben; there is no ~ lost between them sie können sich nicht ausstehen; to make ~ (sexually) miteinander schlafen; to make ~ to sb (sexually) mit jdm schlafen. (b) (greetings) all my ~ mit herzlichen Grüßen; give him my ~ grüß ihn von mir; he sends his ~ er läßt grüßen; yes, (my) ~ ja, Liebling. (c) (Tennis) null. fifteen ~ fünfzehn null.
  2 vt lieben; (like) thing gern mögen. I ~ tennis ich mag Tennis sehr gern; (to play) ich spiele sehr gern Tennis; I'd ~ to come ich würde sehr gerne kommen.

love: ~affair n Verhältnis nt; ~ game n (Tennis) Zu-Null-Spiel nt; ~-hate relationship n Haßliebe f; ~ letter n Liebesbrief m; ~ life n Liebesleben nt.

lovely ['lʌvlɪ] adj (+er) (beautiful) schön; object also hübsch; baby niedlich; (delightful) herrlich; (likeable) nett. we had a ~ time es war sehr schön; it's ~ and warm in this room es ist schön warm in diesem Zimmer; it's been ~ to see you es war schön, dich zu sehen.

love-making ['lʌvˌmeɪkɪŋ] n (sexual) Liebe f.

lover ['lʌvəʳ] n (a) (person) Geliebte(r) mf. the ~s das Liebespaar; to be a good ~ gut in der Liebe sein. (b) a ~ of good food ein Freund m von gutem Essen; music ~ Musikliebhaber m.

love: ~sick adj to be ~sick Liebeskummer m haben; ~ story n Liebesgeschichte f.

loving ['lʌvɪŋ] adj liebend; look, disposition liebevoll.

lovingly ['lʌvɪŋlɪ] adv liebevoll.

low¹ [ləʊ] 1 adj (+er) niedrig; form of life nieder;

bow, note, punch tief; density, intelligence gering; food supplies knapp; quality minderwertig; light gedämpft; rank, position also untergeordnet; tastes, manners gewöhnlich, ordinär (pej); company schlecht; joke, song geschmacklos; trick gemein; resistance gering; morale schlecht. to speak in a ~ voice leise sprechen; the lamp was ~ die Lampe brannte schwach; to feel ~ sich nicht wohl or gut fühlen; (emotionally) niedergeschlagen sein.
  2 adv aim nach unten; speak, sing leise; fly, bow tief. I would never sink so ~ as to ... so tief würde ich nie sinken, daß ich ...; share prices went so ~ that ... die Aktienkurse fielen so sehr, daß ...; to run or get ~ knapp werden; we are getting ~ on petrol uns (dat) geht das Benzin aus.
  3 n (a) (Met) Tief nt; (fig also) Tiefpunkt m. to reach a new ~ einen neuen Tiefstand erreichen. (b) (Aut: ~ gear) niedriger Gang.

low: ~brow adj (geistig) anspruchslos; ~-cost adj preiswert; the L~ Countries npl die Niederlande pl; ~-cut adj dress tief ausgeschnitten; ~-down (col) 1 n Informationen pl; he gave me the ~-down on it er hat mich darüber aufgeklärt; 2 adj (esp US) gemein, fies (col).

lower¹ ['ləʊəʳ] 1 adj see low¹ niedriger; tiefer etc; jaw, arm Unter-; limbs, storeys untere(r, s). the ~ school die Unter- und Mittelstufe; hemlines are ~ this year die Röcke sind dieses Jahr länger; the ~ classes die untere(n) Schicht(en).
  2 adv tiefer; leiser. ~ down the mountain weiter unten am Berg; ~ down the scale/the list weiter unten auf der Skala/Liste.
  3 vt load herunter-/hinunterlassen; eyes, gun senken; sail, flag einholen; bicycle saddle niedriger machen; pressure verringern; voice, price senken; morale, resistance schwächen; standard herabsetzen. ~ your voice sprich leiser!; his behaviour ~ed him in my opinion sein Benehmen ließ ihn in meiner Achtung sinken; to ~ the tone of the conversation das Gesprächsniveau senken; to ~ oneself to do sth sich herablassen, etw zu tun.

lower² ['laʊəʳ] vi = lour.

lower case ['ləʊəkeɪs] n Kleinbuchstaben pl.

low: ~-flying adj tieffliegend; ~-grade adj minderwertig; ~ key adj approach gelassen; handling besonnen; production einfach gehalten; reception reserviert; ~land n Flachland nt.

lowly ['ləʊlɪ] adj (+er) bescheiden.

low-lying [ˌləʊ'laɪɪŋ] adj tiefgelegen.

low: ~-pitched adj tief; ~-rise attr niedrig (gebaut); ~-spirited adj niedergeschlagen; ~ tide, ~ water n Niedrigwasser nt.

loyal ['lɔɪəl] adj (+er) treu. he was very ~ to his friends er hielt (treu) zu seinen Freunden.

loyalist ['lɔɪəlɪst] 1 n Loyalist m. 2 adj loyal; troops regierungstreu.

loyally ['lɔɪəlɪ] adv treu.

loyalty ['lɔɪəltɪ] n Treue f; (esp Pol also) Loyalität f. conflicting loyalties nicht zu vereinbarende Treuepflichten; his changing political loyalties seine wechselnden politischen Bekenntnisse.

lozenge ['lɒzɪndʒ] n (a) (Med) Pastille f. (b) (shape) Raute f.

LP = long player, long playing record LP f.

L-plate ['elpleɪt] n Schild nt mit der Aufschrift „L" (für Fahrschüler).

Ltd = Limited GmbH.

lubricant ['luːbrɪkənt] n Schmiermittel nt.

lubricate ['luːbrɪkeɪt] vt (lit, fig) schmieren, ölen. well-~d (hum) gut abgefüllt (col).

lubrication [ˌluːbrɪ'keɪʃən] n Schmieren, Ölen m.

lucid ['luːsɪd] adj (+er) (clear) klar; explanation anschaulich. ~ intervals lichte Augenblicke.

luck [lʌk] n Glück nt. bad ~ Unglück, Pech nt; bad

~! so ein Pech!; **good** ~ Glück *nt;* **good** ~! viel Glück!; **good** ~ **to them** *(iro),* **and the best of (British)** ~! *(iro)* na dann viel Glück!; **no such** ~! schön wär's! *(col);* **just my** ~! Pech (gehabt), wie immer!; **it's the** ~ **of the draw** man muß es eben nehmen, wie's kommt; **with any** ~ mit etwas Glück; **worse** ~ leider; **better** ~ **next time!** vielleicht klappt es beim nächsten Mal!; **to be in** ~ Glück haben; **to be out of** ~ kein Glück haben; **he was a bit down on his** ~ er hatte eine Pechsträhne; **to bring sb bad** ~ jdm Unglück bringen; **as** ~ **would have it** wie es der Zufall wollte; **for** ~ als Glücksbringer; **to try one's** ~ sein Glück versuchen.

luckily ['lʌkɪlɪ] *adv* glücklicherweise. ~ **for me** zu meinem Glück.

lucky [lʌkɪ] *adj (+er) (having, bringing luck) person, number* Glücks-; *coincidence* glücklich. ~ **charm** Glücksbringer *m;* ~ **dip** ≈ Glückstopf *m;* **it must be my** ~ **day** ich habe wohl heute meinen Glückstag; **you** ~ **thing!,** ~ **you!** du Glückliche(r); **to be** ~ Glück haben; **I was** ~ **enough to meet him** ich hatte das Glück, ihn kennenzulernen; **you are** ~ **to be alive** du kannst von Glück sagen, daß du noch lebst; **you were** ~ **to catch him** du hast Glück gehabt, daß du ihn erwischt hast; **you'll be** ~ **to make it in time** wenn du das noch schaffst, hast du (aber) Glück; **I want another £500** — **you'll be** ~! ich will nochmal £ 500 haben — viel Glück!; **it was** ~ **I stopped him in time** zum Glück habe ich ihn rechtzeitig aufgehalten; **that was a** ~ **escape** da habe ich/hast du *etc* nochmal Glück gehabt.

lucrative ['lu:krətɪv] *adj* einträglich, lukrativ.

ludicrous ['lu:dɪkrəs] *adj* grotesk; *sight, words also* lächerlich.

lug [lʌɡ] *vt* schleppen.

luggage ['lʌɡɪdʒ] *n* Gepäck *nt.*

luggage: ~ **rack** *n (Rail etc)* Gepäckablage *f; (Aut)* Gepäckträger *m;* ~ **trolley** *(Brit),* ~ **cart** *(US) n* Kofferkuli *m;* ~ **van** *n (Brit Rail)* Gepäckwagen *m.*

lugubrious [lu:'ɡu:brɪəs] *adj person, song* schwermütig; *expression* kummervoll.

lukewarm ['lu:kwɔːm] *adj (lit, fig)* lauwarm; *support also* mäßig; *friendship* oberflächlich.

lull [lʌl] **1** *n* Pause *f; (Comm)* Flaute *f.* **a** ~ **in the wind** eine Windstille; **a** ~ **in the conversation** eine Gesprächspause. **2** *vt baby* beruhigen; *(fig)* einlullen. **to** ~ **a baby to sleep** ein Baby in den Schlaf wiegen; **he was** ~**ed into a sense of false security** er wiegte sich in trügerischer Sicherheit.

lullaby ['lʌləbaɪ] *n* Schlaflied *nt.*

lumbago [lʌm'beɪɡəʊ] *n* Hexenschuß *m.*

lumber¹ ['lʌmbər] **1** *n* **(a)** *(timber)* (Bau)holz *nt.* **(b)** *(junk)* Gerümpel *nt.* **2** *vt (Brit col)* **to** ~ **sb with sth** jdm etw aufhalsen *(col);* **he got** ~**ed with the job** man hat ihm die Arbeit aufgehalst *(col);* **I got** ~**ed with her for the evening** ich hatte sie den ganzen Abend auf dem Hals *(col).*

lumber² *vi (cart)* rumpeln; *(elephant, person)* trampeln.

lumber: ~**jack** *n* Holzfäller *m;* ~ **room** *n* Rumpelkammer *f;* ~**yard** *n (US)* Holzlager *nt.*

luminous ['lu:mɪnəs] *adj* leuchtend; *paint, dial* Leucht-.

lump [lʌmp] **1** *n* Klumpen *m; (of sugar)* Stück *nt; (swelling)* Beule *f.* **with a** ~ **in one's throat** *(fig)* mit einem Kloß im Hals. **2** *vt (col)* **if he doesn't like it he can** ~ **it** wenn's ihm nicht paßt, hat er eben Pech gehabt *(col).*

♦ **lump together** *vt sep* **(a)** *(put together)* zusammentun; *books* zusammenstellen; *expenses, money* zusammenlegen. **(b)** *(judge together) persons, topics* über einen Kamm scheren. **he** ~**ed all the soldiers** ~ **as traitors** er urteilte all

die Soldaten pauschal als Verräter ab.

lump: ~ **sugar** *n* Würfelzucker *m;* ~ **sum** *n* Pauschalsumme *f;* **to pay sth in a** ~ **sum** etw pauschal bezahlen.

lumpy ['lʌmpɪ] *adj (+er)* klumpig.

lunacy ['lu:nəsɪ] *n* Wahnsinn *m.* **it's sheer** ~! das ist reiner Wahnsinn!

lunar ['lu:nər] *adj* Mond-. ~ **module** Mondfähre *f.*

lunatic ['lu:nətɪk] **1** *adj* verrückt, wahnsinnig. ~ **fringe** radikale Randgruppe. **2** *n* Wahnsinnige(r), Irre(r) *mf.* ~ **asylum** Irrenanstalt *f.*

lunch [lʌntʃ] *n* Mittagessen *nt.* **to have** ~ **(zu)** Mittag essen; **let's** ~ **at** ~ er ist beim Mittagessen.

lunch break *n* Mittagspause *f.*

luncheon ['lʌntʃən] *n (form)* Mittagessen *nt.*

lunch: ~ **hour** *n* Mittagspause *f;* ~**time** *n* Mittagspause *f.*

lung [lʌŋ] *n* Lunge *f.* ~ **cancer** Lungenkrebs *m.*

lunge [lʌndʒ] **1** *n* Satz *m* nach vorn; *(esp Fencing)* Ausfall *m.* **he made a** ~ **at his opponent** er stürzte sich auf seinen Gegner. **2** *vi (sich)* stürzen. **to** ~ **at sb** sich auf jdn stürzen.

lurch¹ [lɜːtʃ] *n:* **to leave sb in the** ~ *(col)* jdn im Stich lassen, jdn hängenlassen *(col).*

lurch² **1** *n* Ruck *m; (of boat)* Schlingern *nt.* **to give a** ~ einen Ruck machen; *(boat)* schlingern. **2** *vi* **(a)** *see* **to give a** ~. **(b)** *(move with* ~*es)* sich ruckartig bewegen; *(boat)* schlingern; *(person)* taumeln. **the train** ~**ed to a standstill** der Zug kam mit einem Ruck zum Stehen; **to** ~ **about** hin und her schlingern/hin und her taumeln.

lure [lʊər] **1** *n (bait)* Köder *m; (person, for hawk)* Lockvogel *m; (general)* Lockmittel *nt; (fig: of city, sea etc)* Verlockungen *pl.* **2** *vt* anlocken. **to** ~ **sb/an animal into a trap** jdn/ein Tier in eine Falle locken; **to** ~ **sb/an animal out** jdn/ein Tier herauslocken.

lurid ['lʊərɪd] *adj (+er) colour, sky* grell; *dress* grellfarben, in grellen Farben; *posters also* schreiend; *language* reißerisch; *account* sensationslüstern; *detail* grausig; *(sordid)* widerlich.

lurk [lɜːk] *vi* lauern. **a doubt still** ~**ed in his mind** ein Zweifel plagte ihn noch.

luscious ['lʌʃəs] *adj* köstlich; *fruit also* saftig; *girl* zum Anbeißen *(col).*

lush [lʌʃ] *adj grass* saftig, satt; *vegetation* üppig.

lust [lʌst] **1** *n (inner sensation)* Wollust *f; (wanting to acquire)* Begierde *f (for* nach*); (greed)* Gier *f (for* nach*).* ~ **for power** Machtgier *f.* **2** *vi* **to** ~ **after, to** ~ **for** *(sexually)* begehren *(+acc); (greedily)* gieren nach.

lustre, *(US)* **luster** ['lʌstər] *n* Schimmer *m; (in eyes)* Glanz *m.*

lustrous ['lʌstrəs] *adj* schimmernd, glänzend.

lusty ['lʌstɪ] *adj (+er) person* gesund und munter; *man also, life* urwüchsig; *appetite* herzhaft; *cheer, cry* kräftig; *push, kick etc* kraftvoll.

lute [lu:t] *n* Laute *f.*

Luxembourg ['lʌksəmbɜːɡ] *n* Luxemburg *nt.*

luxuriant [lʌɡ'zjʊərɪənt] *adj* üppig.

luxurious [lʌɡ'zjʊərɪəs] *adj* luxuriös, Luxus-; *carpet, hotel also* feudal; *food* üppig.

luxury ['lʌkʃərɪ] **1** *n* Luxus *m; (of car, house etc)* luxuriöse Ausstattung. **to live a life of** ~ ein Luxusleben führen; **little luxuries** Luxus *m.* **2** *adj (cruise, tax)* Luxus-.

lying ['laɪɪŋ] **1** *adj* verlogen. **2** *n* Lügen *nt.* **that would be** ~ das wäre gelogen.

lynch [lɪntʃ] *vt* lynchen.

lynching ['lɪntʃɪŋ] *n* Lynchen *nt.*

lynx [lɪŋks] *n* Luchs *m.*

lyre ['laɪər] *n* Leier *f.*

lyric ['lɪrɪk] **1** *adj* lyrisch. **2** *n (poem)* lyrisches Gedicht; *(often pl: words of pop song)* Text *m.*

lyrical ['lɪrɪkəl] *adj* lyrisch; *(fig)* schwärmerisch. **to get** *or* **wax** ~ **about sth** über etw *(acc)* ins Schwärmen geraten.

M

M, m [em] *n* M, *m nt.*
m = **million(s)** Mio; **metre(s)** m; **mile(s).**
MA = **Master of Arts.**
ma [mɑː] *n (col)* Mama *(col)*, Mutti *(col) f.*
mac [mæk] *n (Brit col)* Regenmantel *m.*
macabre [mə'kɑːbrə] *adj* makaber.
macaroni [,mækə'rəʊnɪ] *n* Makkaroni *pl.* ~ **cheese** Käsenudeln *pl.*
macaroon [,mækə'ruːn] *n* Makrone *f.*
mace[1] [meɪs] *n (weapon)* Streitkolben *m; (mayor's)* Amtsstab *m.*
mace[2] *n (spice)* Muskatblüte *f.*
machete [mə'tʃeɪtɪ] *n* Machete *f.*
Machiavellian [,mækɪə'velɪən] *adj* machiavellistisch.
machination [,mækɪ'neɪʃən] *n usu pl* Machenschaften *pl.*
machine [mə'ʃiːn] **1** *n* Maschine *f*, Apparat *m; (vending* ~) Automat *m.* **2** *vt (Tech)* maschinell herstellen; *(treat with machine)* maschinell bearbeiten; *(Sew)* mit der Maschine nähen.
machine: ~ **gun** *n* Maschinengewehr *nt;* ~ **operator** *n* Maschinenarbeiter *m; (skilled)* Maschinist *m.*
machinery [mə'ʃiːnərɪ] *n (lit, fig)* Maschinerie *f; (mechanism)* Mechanismus *m.* **the** ~ **of government** der Regierungsapparat.
machine: ~ **shop** *n* Maschinensaal *m;* ~ **tool** *n* Werkzeugmaschine *f;* ~ **washable** *adj* waschmaschinenfest.
machinist [mə'ʃiːnɪst] *n (Tech) (operator)* Maschinist *m; (Sew)* Näherin *f.*
mackerel ['mækrəl] *n* Makrele *f.*
mackintosh ['mækɪntɒʃ] *n* Regenmantel *m.*
macro- ['mækrəʊ-] *pref* makro-, Makro-.
mad [mæd] **1** *adj (+er)* **(a)** wahnsinnig; *dog* tollwütig; *idea* verrückt. **to go** ~ wahnsinnig werden; **to drive sb** ~ jdn wahnsinnig *or* verrückt machen; **he's as** ~ **as a hatter** *or* **a March hare** *(prov)* er ist total verrückt; **you must be** ~! du bist ja wahnsinnig!; **they made a** ~ **rush for the door** sie stürzten zur Tür; **you** ~ **fool!** du bist ja wahnsinnig! **(b)** *(col: angry)* sauer *(col).* **to be** ~ **at sb** auf jdn sauer *(col)* sein; **to be** ~ **about** *or* **at sth** über etw *(acc)* wütend *or* sauer *(col)* sein. **(c)** *(col: very keen)* **to be** ~ **about** *or* **on sth** auf etw *(acc)* verrückt sein. **2** *adv (col)* **to be** ~ **keen on sb/sth** ganz scharf auf jdn/etw sein *(col);* **to be** ~ **keen to do sth** ganz versessen darauf sein, etw zu tun; **like** ~ wie verrückt.
madam ['mædəm] *n* **(a)** yes, ~ sehr wohl, gnädige Frau *(old, form);* **can I help you,** ~? kann ich Ihnen behilflich sein?; **Dear Sir or M**~ Sehr geehrte Damen und Herren. **(b)** *(col: girl)* kleine Madam. **(c)** *(of brothel)* Bordellwirtin *f.*
madden ['mædn] *vt (make angry)* ärgern.
maddening ['mædnɪŋ] *adj* zum Verrücktwerden; *delay also* lästig; *habit* aufreizend. **isn't it** ~? ist das nicht ärgerlich?
made [meɪd] *pret, ptp of* **make.**
Madeira [mə'dɪərə] *n (wine)* Madeira *m.* ~ **cake** Sandkuchen *m.*
made-to-measure ['meɪdtə'meʒə'] *adj* maßgeschneidert. ~ **suit** Maßanzug *m.*
madly ['mædlɪ] *adv* wie verrückt; *(col: extremely)* wahnsinnig. **to be** ~ **in love (with sb)** total (in

jdn) verschossen sein *(col)* ; **I'm not** ~ **keen** ich bin nicht wahnsinnig scharf darauf *(col).*
madman ['mædmən] *n, pl* **-men** [-mən] Verrückter *m.*
madness ['mædnɪs] *n* Wahnsinn *m.* **it's sheer** ~! das ist heller *or* reiner Wahnsinn!
magazine [,mægə'ziːn] *n* **(a)** Zeitschrift *f*, Magazin *nt.* **(b)** *(in gun)* Magazin *nt.*
maggot ['mægət] *n* Made *f.*
magic ['mædʒɪk] **1** *n* Magie, Zauberei *f; (mysterious charm)* Zauber *m.* **as if by** ~ wie durch Zauberei; **it worked like** ~ *(col)* es lief wie am Schnürchen *(col).* **2** *adj* Zauber-; *powers* magisch; *moment* zauberhaft. **the** ~ **word** *(having special effect)* das Stichwort; *(making sth possible)* das Zauberwort.
magical ['mædʒɪkəl] *adj* magisch.
magician [mə'dʒɪʃən] *n* Zauberer *m; (conjuror)* Zauberkünstler *m.* **I'm not a** ~! ich kann doch nicht hexen!
magistrate ['mædʒɪstreɪt] *n* Friedensrichter *m.* ~**s' court** Schiedsgericht *nt.*
magnanimous [mæg'nænɪməs] *adj* großmütig.
magnate ['mægneɪt] *n* Magnat *m.*
magnesia [mæg'niːʃə] *n* Magnesia *f.*
magnesium [mæg'niːzɪəm] *n* Magnesium *nt.*
magnet ['mægnɪt] *n (lit, fig)* Magnet *m.*
magnetic [mæg'netɪk] *adj (lit)* magnetisch; *charms* unwiderstehlich.
magnetism ['mægnɪtɪzəm] *n* Magnetismus *m; (fig: of person)* Anziehungskraft *f.*
magnetize ['mægnɪtaɪz] *vt* magnetisieren.
magnification [,mægnɪfɪ'keɪʃən] *n* Vergrößerung *f.*
magnificence [mæg'nɪfɪsəns] *n (excellence)* Größe *f; (splendid appearance)* Pracht *f*, Glanz *m.*
magnificent [mæg'nɪfɪsənt] *adj (wonderful, excellent)* großartig; *food, meal* ausgezeichnet; *(of splendid appearance)* prachtvoll.
magnify ['mægnɪfaɪ] *vt* vergrößern; *(exaggerate)* aufbauschen. ~**ing glass** Lupe *f.*
magnitude ['mægnɪtjuːd] *n* Ausmaß *nt; (importance)* Bedeutung *f; (Astron)* Größenklasse *f.* **operations of this** ~ Vorhaben dieser Größenordnung.
magpie ['mægpaɪ] *n* Elster *f.*
mahogany [mə'hɒgənɪ] **1** *n* Mahagoni *m; (tree)* Mahagonibaum *m.* **2** *adj* Mahagoni-.
maid [meɪd] *n (servant)* (Dienst)mädchen *nt; (in hotel)* Zimmermädchen *nt; (lady's* ~) Zofe *f; (old, poet: young girl)* Maid *f (poet).*
maiden ['meɪdn] **1** *n (old, poet)* Mädchen *nt.* **2** *adj flight, voyage etc* Jungfern-.
maiden: ~ **aunt** *n* unverheiratete, ältere Tante; ~ **name** *n* Mädchenname *m;* ~ **speech** *n* Jungfernrede *f.*
maid: ~ **of honour** *(Brit) or* **honor** *(US) n* Brautjungfer *f;* ~**servant** *n* Hausangestellte *f.*
mail [meɪl] **1** *n* Post *f.* **to send sth by** ~ etw mit der Post schicken; **is there any** ~ **for me?** ist Post für mich da? **2** *vt* aufgeben; *(put in letterbox)* einwerfen; *(send by* ~) mit der Post schicken. ~**ing list** Versandliste *f.*
mail: ~**box** *n (US, also electronic)* Briefkasten *m;* ~**man** *n (US)* Briefträger, Postbote *m;* ~**-order catalogue** *n* Versandhauskatalog *m;* ~**-order firm** *n* Versandhaus *nt;* ~**shot** *n* Mailshot *m;*

~ train *n* Postzug *m;* **~ van** *n (on roads)* Postauto *nt; (Brit Rail)* Postwagen *m.*

maim [meɪm] *vt (mutilate)* verstümmeln; *(cripple)* zum Krüppel machen.

main [meɪn] **1** *adj attr* Haupt-. **the ~ thing is to ...** die Hauptsache ist, daß ...; **the ~ thing is you're still alive** Hauptsache, du lebst noch. **2** *n* **(a)** *(pipe)* Hauptleitung *f.* **the ~s** *(of town)* das öffentliche Versorgungsnetz; *(electricity also)* das Stromnetz; **~s operated** für Netzbetrieb; **the electricity was switched off at the ~s** der Hauptschalter für den Strom wurde abgeschaltet. **(b) in the ~** im großen und ganzen.

main: ~ course *n* Hauptgericht *nt;* **~frame** *n (Comp)* Großrechner *m;* **~land** *n* Festland *nt;* **on the ~land of Europe** auf dem europäischen Festland; **~line train** *n* Schnellzug *m.*

mainly ['meɪnlɪ] *adv* hauptsächlich; *(generally)* überwiegend. **the meetings are held ~ on Tuesdays** die Besprechungen finden meistens dienstags statt.

main: ~ road *n* Hauptstraße *f;* **~spring** *n (Mech)* Triebfeder *f; (fig)* treibende Kraft; **~stay** *n (fig)* Stütze *f;* **~stream** *n* Hauptrichtung *f;* **to be in the ~stream of sth** der Hauptrichtung *(+gen)* angehören.

maintain [meɪn'teɪn] *vt* **(a)** *(keep up)* aufrechterhalten; *law and order etc* wahren; *quality also, speed, attitude* beibehalten; *life* erhalten. **(b)** *(support) family* unterhalten. **(c)** *(in good condition) machine* warten; *roads, building* instand halten; *car* pflegen. **(d)** *(claim)* behaupten.

maintenance ['meɪntɪnəns] *n see vt* **(a)** Aufrechterhaltung *f;* Wahrung *f;* Beibehaltung *f;* Erhaltung *f.* **(b)** *(of family)* Unterhalt *m; (social security)* Unterstützung *f.* **he has to pay ~** er ist unterhaltspflichtig. **(c)** Wartung *f;* Instandhaltung *f;* Pflege *f.*

maintenance costs *npl* Unterhaltskosten *pl.*

maisonette [ˌmeɪzə'net] *n (small flat)* Appartement *nt; (small house)* Häuschen *nt.*

maize [meɪz] *n (Brit)* Mais *m.*

majestic [mə'dʒestɪk] *adj* majestätisch; *proportions* stattlich; *music* getragen.

majesty ['mædʒɪstɪ] *n* Majestät *f.* **Her M~** Ihre Majestät; **Your M~** Eure Majestät.

major ['meɪdʒə^r] **1** *adj* Haupt-; *(of greater importance)* bedeutend(er); *(of greater extent)* größer. **a ~ road** eine Hauptverkehrsstraße; **of ~ importance** von großer Bedeutung. **2** *n* **(a)** *(Mil)* Major *m.* **(b)** *(Jur)* **to become a ~** mündig werden. **(c)** *(US) (subject)* Hauptfach *nt.* **3** *vi (US)* **to ~ in sth** etw als Hauptfach studieren.

majority [mə'dʒɒrɪtɪ] *n* **(a)** Mehrheit *f.* **the ~ of cases** die Mehrzahl der Fälle; **to be in a ~** in der Mehrzahl sein; **to have a ~ of 10** eine Mehrheit von 10 Stimmen haben; **by a small ~** mit knapper Mehrheit. **(b)** *(Jur)* Mündigkeit *f.* **to attain one's ~** mündig werden.

majority: ~ decision *n* Mehrheitsbeschluß *m; ~ holding* *n (Fin)* Mehrheitsbeteiligung *f; ~ rule* *n* Mehrheitsregierung *f.*

make [meɪk] *(vb: pret, ptp* **made)** *1 vt* **(a)** machen; *bread* backen; *cars* herstellen; *dress* nähen; *coffee* kochen; *the world* erschaffen; *speech* halten; *choice, arrangements, decision* treffen. **she made it into a suit** sie machte einen Anzug daraus; **it's made of gold** es ist aus Gold; **made in Germany** in Deutschland hergestellt; **to show what one is made of** zeigen, was in einem steckt; **they're made for each other** sie sind wie geschaffen füreinander; **this car wasn't made to carry 8 people** dieses Auto ist nicht dazu gedacht, 8 Leute zu transportieren.

(b) *(cause to be)* machen; *(appoint)* machen zu; *(cause to do or happen)* lassen; *(compel)* zwingen. **to ~ sb happy** *etc* jdn glücklich *etc* machen; **he was made a judge** man ernannte ihn

zum Richter; **it ~s the room look smaller** es läßt den Raum kleiner wirken; **we decided to ~ a day of it** wir beschlossen den ganzen Tag dafür zu nehmen; **let's ~ it Monday** sagen wir Montag; **it all ~s me think that ...** das alles läßt mich denken, daß ...; **to ~ sb laugh** jdn zum Lachen bringen; **what ~s you say that?** warum sagst du das?; **to ~ sb do sth** jdn dazu bringen, etw zu tun; *(force)* jdn zwingen, etw zu tun; **to ~ sth do, to ~ do with sth** mit etw zufrieden sein; **you can't ~ things happen** man kann das nicht erzwingen; **how can I ~ you understand?** wie kann ich es Ihnen verständlich machen?; **that made the cloth shrink** dadurch ging der Stoff ein; **what ~s the engine go?** wie wird der Motor angetrieben?; **what ~s you think you can do it?** weshalb glauben Sie denn, daß Sie es schaffen können?; **the chemical ~s the plant grow faster** die Chemikalie bewirkt, daß die Pflanze schneller wächst; **what made you come to this town?** was hat Sie in diese Stadt geführt?; **to ~ oneself heard/understood** sich *(dat)* Gehör verschaffen/ sich verständlich machen.

(c) *(earn) money* verdienen; *profit, loss, fortune* machen *(on* bei); *name, reputation* sich *(dat)* verschaffen.

(d) *(reach, achieve, also Sport)* schaffen *(col),* erreichen; *connection* schaffen; *summit etc* es schaffen zu *(col).* **we made good time** wir kamen schnell voran; **he just made it** er hat es gerade noch geschafft; **sorry I couldn't ~ your party last night** tut mir leid, ich habe es gestern abend einfach nicht zu deiner Party geschafft; **his first record didn't ~ the charts** seine erste Platte schaffte es nicht bis in die Hitparade; **we've made it!** wir haben es geschafft!; **we'll never ~ the airport in time** wir schaffen es garantiert nicht mehr rechtzeitig zum Flughafen; **the story made the front page** die Geschichte kam auf die Titelseite.

(e) *(cause to succeed)* stars *etc* berühmt machen. **this film made her** dieser Film war für sie der Durchbruch; **you'll be made for life** Sie werden ausgesorgt haben; **he's got it made** *(col)* er hat ausgesorgt; **he's a made man** er ist ein gemachter Mann; **that ~s my day!** das freut mich unheimlich!; *(iro)* das hat mir gerade noch gefehlt!; **he can ~ or break you** er hat dich ganz in der Hand.

(f) *(equal)* sein, ergeben; *(constitute also)* machen. **2 plus 2 ~s 4** 2 und 2 ist 4; **how much does that ~ altogether?** was macht das insgesamt?; **he made a good father** er gab einen guten Vater ab; **he'll never ~ a soldier** aus ihm wird nie ein Soldat.

(g) *(estimate) distance, total* schätzen auf. **what time do you ~ it?** wie spät hast du es?; **I ~ it 3.15** auf meiner Uhr ist es 3¹⁵; **I ~ it 3 miles** ich schätze 3 Meilen; **how many do you ~ it?** wie viele sind es nach deiner Rechnung?

2 vi (a) *(go)* **to ~ towards a place** auf einen Ort zuhalten; *(ship)* Kurs auf einen Ort nehmen; **to ~ after sb** jdm nachsetzen. **(b)** **to ~ as if to do sth** Anstalten machen, etw zu tun; *(as deception)* so tun, als wolle man etw tun.

3 *n* **(a)** *(brand)* Marke *f.* **what ~ of car do you run?** welche (Auto)marke fahren Sie? **(b)** *(pej col)* **on the ~** *(for profit)* profitgierig *(col),* auf Profit aus; *(ambitious)* karrieresüchtig *(col); (sexually)* sexhungrig *(col).*

♦ **make away** *vi* = **make off.**

♦ **make away with** *vi +prep obj (kill)* **to ~ ~ ~ sb/oneself** jdn/sich umbringen.

♦ **make for** *vi +prep obj* **(a)** *(head for)* zuhalten auf *(+acc); (vehicle)* losfahren auf *(+acc); (ship)* Kurs halten auf *(+acc).* **where are you making ~?** wo willst du hin? **(b)** *(promote)* führen zu; *happy marriage etc* den Grund legen für. **the**

trade figures ~ ~ **optimism** die Handelsziffern geben Anlaß zum Optimismus.

♦ **make of** vi +prep obj halten von. **I didn't** ~ **much** ~ **it** ich konnte nicht viel dabei finden.

make off vi sich davonmachen (with sth mit etw).

make out 1 vt sep **(a)** (write out) cheque ausstellen (to auf +acc); list, bill aufstellen; (fill out) form ausfüllen. **to** ~ ~ **a case for sth** für etw argumentieren. **(b)** (see, discern) ausmachen; (decipher) entziffern; (understand) verstehen; person, actions schlau werden aus. **how do you** ~ **that** ~? wie kommst du darauf? **(c)** (imply) **to** ~ ~ **that ...** es so hinstellen, als ob ...; **he made** ~ **that he was hurt** er tat, als sei er verletzt; **to** ~ **sb** ~ **to be a genius** jdn als Genie hinstellen. **2** vi (col) (get on) zurechtkommen; (with people) auskommen; (succeed) es schaffen.

♦ **make over** vt sep (assign) überschreiben (to sb dat); (bequeath) vermachen (to sb dat).

♦ **make up 1** vt sep **(a)** (prepare) food, medicine, bed zurechtmachen; parcel also zusammenpacken; list, accounts, team zusammenstellen. **to** ~ **material** ~ **into sth** Material zu etw verarbeiten. **(b)** (constitute) bilden. **to be made** ~ **of** bestehen aus. **(c)** quarrel beilegen. **to** ~ **it** ~ **(with sb)** sich (mit jdm) wieder vertragen. **(d)** face schminken. **(e) to** ~ ~ **one's mind** (to do sth) sich entschließen(, etw zu tun); **to** ~ ~ **one's mind about sb/sth** sich (dat) eine Meinung über jdn/etw bilden. **(f)** (invent) erfinden. **you're making that** ~! jetzt schwindelst du aber! (col). **(g)** (compensate for) loss ausgleichen; time einholen, aufholen; sleep nachholen. **to** ~ **it** ~ **to sb (for sth)** (compensate) jdn (für etw) entschädigen; (emotionally etc) jdm etw wiedergutmachen. **2** vi **(a)** (after quarrelling) sich wieder vertragen. **(b)** (apply cosmetics) sich schminken. **(c)** (catch up) aufholen. **to** ~ ~ **on sb** jdn einholen.

♦ **make up for** vi +prep obj ausgleichen. **to** ~ ~ ~ **lost time** verlorene Zeit aufholen; **to** ~ ~ ~ **the loss of sb/lack of sth** jdn/etw ersetzen.

♦ **make up to** vi +prep obj (col) sich heranmachen an (+acc).

make-believe ['meɪkbɪˌliːv] **1** adj attr Phantasie-; world also Schein-. **2** n Phantasie f. **a world of** ~ eine Phantasiewelt; **it's only** ~ das ist doch nur eine Geschichte. **3** vt sich (dat) vorstellen.

maker ['meɪkə'] n (manufacturer) Hersteller m. **our M~** unser Schöpfer m.

make: ~**shift** adj improvisiert; repairs behelfsmäßig; ~**up** n **(a)** Make-up nt; (Theat also) Maske f; **(b)** (composition) (of team, party etc) Zusammenstellung f; (character) Veranlagung f; **loyalty is part of his** ~**-up** er ist loyal veranlagt; ~**-up bag** n Schminktäschchen nt.

making ['meɪkɪŋ] n **(a)** (production) Herstellung f; (of food) Zubereitung f. **in the** ~ im Entstehen; **here you can see history in the** ~ hier wird Geschichte gemacht; **it was the** ~ **of him** (made him successful) das hat ihn zu dem gemacht, was er (heute) ist. **(b)** **he has the** ~**s of an actor** etc er hat das Zeug zu einem Schauspieler etc; **the situation has all the** ~**s of a strike** die Situation bietet alle Voraussetzungen für einen Streik.

maladjusted [ˌmælə'dʒʌstɪd] adj (Psych, Sociol) verhaltensgestört.

maladroit [ˌmælə'drɔɪt] adj ungeschickt.

malaise [mæ'leɪz] n Unwohlsein nt; (fig) Unbehagen nt.

malaria [mə'lɛərɪə] n Malaria f.

male [meɪl] **1** adj männlich. ~ **nurse** Krankenpfleger m; ~ **crocodile** Krokodilmännchen nt; ~ **chauvinist pig** (col pej) Chauvi m (col). **2** n (animal) Männchen nt; (col: man) Mann m.

malevolent [mə'levələnt] adj boshaft; action böswillig.

malformed [mæl'fɔːmd] adj mißgebildet.

malfunction [ˌmæl'fʌŋkʃən] **1** n (of liver etc) Funktionsstörung f; (of machine) Defekt m. **2** vi (liver etc) nicht richtig arbeiten; (machine etc) defekt sein; (system) nicht richtig funktionieren.

malice ['mælɪs] n Bosheit f; (of action) Böswilligkeit f. **I bear him no** ~ ich bin ihm nicht böse; **with** ~ **aforethought** (Jur) in böswilliger Absicht.

malicious [mə'lɪʃəs] adj person, words boshaft; slander böswillig; (Jur) damage mutwillig.

malign [mə'laɪn] **1** adj (liter) intent böse; influence unheilvoll. **2** vt verleumden; (run down) schlecht machen. **to** ~ **sb's character** jdm Übles nachsagen.

malignant [mə'lɪgnənt] adj bösartig. **a** ~ **growth** (Med, fig) ein bösartiges Geschwür.

malingerer [mə'lɪŋgərə'] n Simulant m.

malleable ['mælɪəbl] adj formbar (also fig), weich.

mallet ['mælɪt] n Holzhammer m; (croquet) (Krocket)hammer m; (polo) (Polo)schläger m.

malnutrition [ˌmælnjʊ'trɪʃən] n Unterernährung f.

malpractice [ˌmæl'præktɪs] n Berufsvergehen, Amtsvergehen nt.

malt [mɔːlt] n Malz nt. ~ **loaf** ≈ Rosinenbrot nt; ~ **whisky** Malt Whisky m.

Malta ['mɔːltə] n Malta nt.

maltreat [ˌmæl'triːt] vt schlecht behandeln; (using violence) mißhandeln.

mam(m)a [mə'mɑː] n (col) Mama (col).

mammal ['mæməl] n Säugetier nt.

mammoth ['mæməθ] **1** n Mammut m. **2** adj Mammut-; cost, enterprise kolossal.

man [mæn] **1** n, pl **men** Mann m; (human race: also M~) der Mensch; die Menschen; (Chess) Figur f; (in draughts) Stein m. **to make a** ~ **out of sb** einen Mann aus jdm machen; **that's just like a** ~ das ist typisch Mann; **they are** ~ **and wife** sie sind Mann und Frau; **the** ~ **in the street** der Mann auf der Straße; ~ **of property** vermögender Mann; **he's a** ~ **about town** er kennt sich aus; **a** ~ **of the world** ein Mann von Welt; **no** ~ keiner, niemand; **any** ~ jeder; **men say that ...** die Leute sagen, daß ...; **that** ~ **Jones** dieser Jones!; **as one** ~ geschlossen, wie ein Mann; **they are all** ~ **to a** ~ sie sind allesamt Kommunisten; **he's not the** ~ **for the job** er ist nicht der Richtige für diese Aufgabe; **he's not a** ~ **to ...** er ist nicht der Typ, der ...; **he's a family** ~ (home-loving) er ist sehr häuslich; **it's got to be a local** ~ es muß jemand aus dieser Gegend sein; **I'm not a drinking** ~ ich bin kein großer Trinker; **you can't do that,** ~ (col) Mensch or Mann, das kannst du doch nicht machen! (col).

2 vt ship bemannen; fortress besetzen; pump, gun bedienen. **the ship is** ~**ned by a crew of 30** das Schiff hat 30 Mann Besatzung; **there's someone** ~**ning the telephone all day** es ist den ganzen Tag über jemand da, der das Telefon bedient.

manacle ['mænəkl] n usu pl Handfesseln pl.

manage ['mænɪdʒ] **1** vt **(a)** company, organization leiten; affairs regeln; football team, pop group managen. **the election was** ~**d** (pej) die Wahl war manipuliert.

(b) (handle, control) person, animal, car zurechtkommen mit. **I can** ~ **him** mit dem werde ich schon fertig.

(c) task, another portion bewältigen, schaffen (col). **£5 is the most I can** ~ ich kann mir höchstens £5 leisten; **I'll** ~ **it** das werde ich schon schaffen; **can you** ~ **the cases?** kannst du die Koffer (allein) tragen?; **she can't** ~ **the stairs** sie kommt die Treppe nicht hinauf/hinunter; **can you** ~ **8 o'clock?** 8 Uhr, ginge das?; **I couldn't** ~ **another thing** ich könnte keinen Bissen mehr runterbringen; **to** ~ **to do sth** es schaffen, etw zu tun; **he** ~**d not to get his feet wet** es ist ihm gelungen, keine nassen Füße zu bekommen; **how**

did you ~ **to miss that?** wie konnte Ihnen das nur entgehen?; **could you possibly** ~ **to close the door?** *(iro)* wäre es vielleicht möglich, die Tür zuzumachen? **2** *vi* zurechtkommen, es schaffen *(col)*. **can you** ~? geht es?; **how do you** ~? wie machen Sie das bloß?; **to** ~ **without sth/sb** ohne etw/jdn auskommen; **how do you** ~ **on only £20 a week?** wie kommen Sie mit nur £ 20 pro Woche aus?

manageable ['mænɪdʒəbl] *adj child, horse* fügsam; *amount, job* zu bewältigen; *hair* leicht frisierbar; *number* überschaubar; *car* leicht zu handhaben. **pieces of a more** ~ **size** Stücke, die leichter zu handhaben sind.

management ['mænɪdʒmənt] *n* **(a)** *(act: of company)* Leitung, Führung *f.* ~ **studies** Betriebswirtschaft *f;* ~ **and workers** Arbeitgeber und Arbeitnehmer *pl.* **(b)** *(persons)* Unternehmensleitung *f; (of single unit or smaller factory)* Betriebsleitung *f; (non-commercial)* Leitung *f;* "**under new** ~" „neuer Inhaber"; *(shop)* „neu eröffnet".

manager ['mænɪdʒəʳ] *n (Comm etc)* Geschäftsführer *m; (of smaller firm or factory)* Betriebsleiter *m; (of bank, chain store)* Filialleiter *m; (of department)* Abteilungsleiter *m; (of pop group etc)* Manager *m; (of team)* Trainer *m.* **sales/publicity** ~ Verkaufsleiter/Werbeleiter *m.*

manageress [,mænɪdʒə'res] *n* Geschäftsführerin *f; (of department)* Abteilungsleiterin *f; (of chain store)* Filialleiterin *f.*

managerial [,mænə'dʒɪərɪəl] *adj* geschäftlich; *(executive)* Management-; *post* leitend. **he has no** ~ **skills** er ist für leitende Funktionen ungeeignet.

managing director ['mænɪdʒɪŋdɪ'rektəʳ] *n* leitender Direktor.

mandarin ['mændərɪn] *n* **(a)** *(Chinese official)* Mandarin *m.* **(b)** *(language)* **M**~ Hochchinesisch *nt.* **(c)** *(fruit)* Mandarine *f.*

mandate ['mændeɪt] *n* Auftrag *m; (Pol also)* Mandat *nt; (territory)* Mandatsgebiet *nt.* **to give sb a** ~ **to do sth** jdm den Auftrag geben, etw zu tun.

mandatory ['mændətərɪ] *adj* obligatorisch; *(Pol)* mandatorisch. **union membership is** ~ Mitgliedschaft in der Gewerkschaft ist Pflicht.

mandolin(e) ['mændəlɪn] *n* Mandoline *f.*

mane [meɪn] *n (lit, fig)* Mähne *f.*

maneuver *n, vti (US)* = **manoeuvre**.

manful ['mænfʊl] *adj* mannhaft, mutig.

manganese [,mæŋgə'niːz] *n* Mangan *nt.*

mangle[1] ['mæŋgl] *n* Mangel *f.*

mangle[2] *vt (also* ~ **up)** (übel) zurichten.

mango ['mæŋgəʊ] *n (fruit)* Mango *f.*

man: ~**handle** *vt (a)* grob behandeln; **he was** ~**handled into the van** er wurde recht unsanft in den Wagen verfrachtet; **(b)** *piano etc* hieven; ~**hole** *n* Kanalschacht *m.*

manhood ['mænhʊd] *n (state)* Mannesalter *nt.*

man: ~**-hour** *n* Arbeitsstunde *f;* ~**hunt** *n* Fahndung *f; (for criminal also)* Verbrecherjagd *f.*

mania ['meɪnɪə] *n (madness)* Manie *f; (col: enthusiasm)* Manie *f,* Tick *(col) m.* **he has a** ~ **for punctuality** er hat einen Pünktlichkeitsfimmel *(col).*

maniac ['meɪnɪæk] **1** *adj* wahnsinnig. **2** *n* **(a)** Wahnsinnige(r), Irre(r) *mf.* **(b)** *(fig)* **these sports** ~**s** diese Sportfanatiker *pl.*

manic-depressive ['mænɪkdɪ'presɪv] **1** *adj* manisch-depressiv. **2** *n* Manisch-Depressive(r) *mf.*

manicure ['mænɪ,kjʊəʳ] **1** *n* Maniküre *f.* ~ **set** Nagelnecessaire *nt.* **2** *vt* maniküren.

manifest ['mænɪfest] **1** *adj* offenkundig; *(definite also)* eindeutig. **he made it** ~ **that** ... er machte deutlich, daß ... **2** *vt* to ~ **itself** sich zeigen.

manifestation [,mænɪfe'steɪʃən] *n (act of showing)* Ausdruck *m,* Bekundung *f; (sign)* Anzeichen *nt.*

manifestly ['mænɪfestlɪ] *adv* offensichtlich. **it's so** ~ **obvious** es ist so völlig offensichtlich.

manifesto [,mænɪ'festəʊ] *n, pl* **-(e)s** Manifest *nt.*

manifold ['mænɪfəʊld] **1** *adj* vielfältig. ~ **uses** vielseitige Anwendung. **2** *n (Aut: exhaust* ~) Auspuffrohr *nt.*

manipulate [mə'nɪpjʊleɪt] *vt* **(a)** *machine etc* bedienen; *bones* einrenken; *(after fracture)* zurechtrücken. **(b)** *public opinion, prices* manipulieren; *accounts also* frisieren *(col).*

manipulation [mə,nɪpjʊ'leɪʃən] *n* Manipulation *f.*

mankind [mæn'kaɪnd] *n* die Menschheit.

manliness ['mænlɪnɪs] *n* Männlichkeit *f.*

manly ['mænlɪ] *adj (+er)* männlich.

man-made ['mæn'meɪd] *adj* künstlich, Kunst-. ~ **fibres** Kunstfasern *pl.*

manna ['mænə] *n* Manna *nt.*

manned [mænd] *adj satellite etc* bemannt.

mannequin ['mænɪkɪn] *n (fashion)* Mannequin *nt; (Art)* Modell *nt; (dummy)* Schaufensterpuppe *f.*

manner ['mænəʳ] *n* **(a)** *(mode)* Art (und Weise) *f.* **in this** ~ auf diese Art und Weise; **in such a** ~ **that** ... so ..., daß ...; **in a** ~ **of speaking** sozusagen; **as to the** ~ **born** als sei er/sie dafür geschaffen. **(b)** *(behaviour etc)* Art *f.* **he has a very kind** ~ er hat ein sehr freundliches Wesen; **I don't like his** ~ ich mag seine Art nicht. **(c)** ~**s** *pl (good, bad etc)* Manieren *pl;* **that's bad** ~**s** das gehört sich nicht; **it's bad** ~**s to** ... es gehört sich nicht, zu ...; **he has no** ~**s** er hat keine Manieren; **to teach sb some** ~**s** jdm Manieren beibringen. **(d)** *(class, type)* Art *f.* **we saw all** ~ **of interesting things** wir sahen allerlei Interessantes.

mannerism ['mænərɪzəm] *n (in behaviour)* Eigenheit *f; (of style)* Manieriertheit *f.* **his** ~**s** seine Manierismen.

mannerly ['mænəlɪ] *adj* wohlerzogen.

manoeuvrable, *(US)* **maneuverable** [mə'nuːvrəbl] *adj* wendig. **easily** ~ leicht zu manövrieren.

manoeuvre, *(US)* **maneuver** [mə'nuːvəʳ] **1** *n (Mil)* Feldzug *m; (clever plan)* Manöver *nt,* Schachzug *m.* ~**s** Manöver *nt or pl;* **the troops were out on** ~**s** die Truppen befanden sich im Manöver. **2** *vt* manövrieren. **to** ~ **a gun into position** ein Geschütz in Stellung bringen. **3** *vi* manövrieren; *(Mil)* (ein) Manöver durchführen. **to** ~ **for position** *(lit, fig)* sich in eine günstige Position manövrieren; **room to** ~ Manövrierfähigkeit *f.*

manor ['mænəʳ] *n* Gut(shof *m) nt.* **lord of the** ~ Gutsherr *m;* ~ **house** Herrenhaus *nt.*

manpower ['mæn,paʊəʳ] *n* Arbeitskräfte *pl,* Stärke *f.*

mansion ['mænʃən] *n* Villa *f; (of ancient family)* Herrenhaus *nt.*

manslaughter ['mæn,slɔːtəʳ] *n* Totschlag *m.*

mantelpiece ['mæntlpiːs] *n* Kaminsims *nt or m.*

mantle ['mæntl] *n* **(a)** Umhang *m; (fig)* Deckmantel *m.* **a** ~ **of snow** eine Schneedecke. **(b)** *(gas* ~*)* Glühstrumpf *m.*

man-to-man [,mæntə'mæn] *adj, adv* von Mann zu Mann.

manual ['mænjʊəl] **1** *adj* manuell; *labour* körperlich. ~ **worker** (manueller) Arbeiter *m;* ~ **gear change** Schaltgetriebe *nt,* Schaltung *f* von Hand. **2** *n (book)* Handbuch *nt.*

manufacture [,mænjʊ'fæktʃəʳ] **1** *n (act)* Herstellung *f; (pl: products)* Erzeugnisse *pl.* **2** *vt* herstellen. ~**d goods** Fertigware *f.*

manufacturer [,mænjʊ'fæktʃərəʳ] *n* Hersteller *m.*

manufacturing [,mænjʊ'fæktʃərɪŋ] **1** *adj techniques* Herstellungs-; *industry* verarbeitend. **2** *n* Herstellung *f.*

manure [mə'njʊəʳ] **1** *n* Dung *m; (esp artificial)* Dünger *m.* **2** *vt field* düngen.

manuscript ['mænjʊskrɪpt] *n* Manuskript *nt; (ancient also)* Handschrift *f.*

many ['menɪ] *adj, n* viele. ~ **people** viele (Menschen *or* Leute); **there were as ~ as 20** es waren sogar 20 da; **as ~ again** noch einmal so viele; **there's one too ~** einer ist zuviel; **he's had one too ~** er hat einen zuviel getrunken; **they were too ~ for us** sie waren zu viele für uns; **he made one mistake too ~** er hat einen Fehler zuviel gemacht; **~ a good soldier** so mancher gute Soldat; **~ a time** so manches Mal; **a good/great ~ houses** sehr viele Häuser.

many: **~-coloured** *(Brit)*, **~-colored** *(US) adj* vielfarbig; **~-sided** *adj* vielseitig.

map [mæp] **1** *n* (Land)karte *f; (of streets, town)* Stadtplan *m; (showing specific item)* Karte *f.* **this will put Cheam on the ~** *(fig)* das wird Cheam zu einem Namen verhelfen; **it's right off the ~** *(fig)* das liegt (ja) am Ende der Welt; **entire cities were wiped off the ~** ganze Städte wurden ausradiert. **2** *vt (measure)* vermessen; *(make a map of)* eine Karte anfertigen von.
♦ **map out** *vt sep* **(a)** *(lit) see* **map 2. (b)** *(fig: plan)* entwerfen. **our holiday schedule was all ~ped ~ in advance** der Zeitplan für unsere Ferien war schon im voraus genau festgelegt.

maple ['meɪpl] *n (wood, tree)* Ahorn *m.*

mar [mɑː^r] *vt* verderben; *happiness* trüben; *beauty* mindern.

marathon ['mærəθən] **1** *n (lit)* Marathon(lauf) *m; (fig)* Marathon *nt.* **2** *adj* Marathon-.

marauding [mə'rɔːdɪŋ] *adj* plündernd.

marble ['mɑːbl] **1** *n*   Marmor *m; (glass ball)* Murmel *f*, Klicker *m (col).* **2** *adj* Marmor-.

March [mɑːtʃ] *n* März *m; see* **September.**

march [mɑːtʃ] **1** *n* **(a)** *(Mil, Mus)* Marsch *m; (demonstration)* Demonstration *f; (fig: long walk)* Weg *m.* **we had been five days on the ~** wir waren fünf Tage lang marschiert; **it's two days' ~** es ist ein Zwei-Tage-Marsch. **(b)** *(of time, history, events)* Lauf *m.* **(c) to steal a ~ on sb** jdm zuvorkommen. **2** *vt soldiers* marschieren lassen; *distance* marschieren. **to ~ sb off** jdn abführen. **3** *vi* marschieren. **forward ~!** vorwärts(, marsch)!; **quick ~!** im Laufschritt, marsch!; **time ~es on** die Zeit bleibt nicht stehen; **to ~ past sb** an jdm vorbeimarschieren; **she ~ed straight up to him** sie marschierte schnurstracks auf ihn zu.

marching orders ['mɑːtʃɪŋ'ɔːdəz] *npl (Mil)* Marschbefehl *m; (col)* Entlassung *f.* **she gave him his ~** sie hat ihm den Laufpaß gegeben.

marchioness ['mɑːʃənɪs] *n* Marquise *f.*

march past *n* Aufmarsch *m.*

mare [mɛə^r] *n (horse)* Stute *f; (donkey)* Eselin *f.*

margarine ['mɑːdʒəˈriːn], **marge** [mɑːdʒ] *(col) n* Margarine *f.*

margin ['mɑːdʒɪn] *n* **(a)** *(on page)* Rand *m.* **(b)** *(extra amount)* Spielraum *m.* **to allow for a ~ of error** etwaige Fehler mit einkalkulieren; **by a narrow ~** knapp; **(profit) ~** Gewinnspanne *f.*

marginal ['mɑːdʒɪnl] *adj* **(a)** *note* Rand-. **(b)** *improvement, difference* geringfügig; *constituency* mit schwankendem Wählerverhalten.

marginally ['mɑːdʒɪnlɪ] *adv* geringfügig.

marigold ['mærɪɡəʊld] *n* Ringelblume *f.*

marijuana [,mærɪ'hwɑːnə] *n* Marihuana *nt.*

marina [mə'riːnə] *n* Jachthafen *m.*

marinade [,mærɪ'neɪd] *n* Marinade *f.*

marinate ['mærɪneɪt] *vt* marinieren.

marine [mə'riːn] **1** *adj* Meeres-, See-. **~ insurance** Seeversicherung *f;* **~ life** Meeresfauna und -flora *f.* **2** *n* **(a)** *(fleet)* Marine *f.* **merchant ~** Handelsmarine *f.* **(b) the ~s** die Marinetruppen *pl;* **tell that to the ~s!** *(col)* das kannst du deiner Großmutter erzählen! *(col).*

mariner ['mærɪnə^r] *n* Seefahrer, Seemann *m.*

marionette [,mærɪə'net] *n* Marionette *f.*

marital ['mærɪtl] *adj* ehelich. **~ status** Familienstand *m.*

marjoram ['mɑːdʒərəm] *n* Majoran *m.*

mark¹ [mɑːk] *n (Fin)* Mark *f.*

mark² **1** *n* **(a)** *(stain, spot etc)* Fleck *m; (scratch)* Kratzer *m; (on person)* Mal *nt; (on plane, football pitch etc)* Markierung *f.* **to make a ~ on sth** einen Fleck auf etw *(acc)* machen/etw beschädigen; **dirty ~s** Schmutzflecken *pl;* **with not a ~ on it in** makellosem Zustand; **he didn't have a ~ on him** er wies keine Verletzungen auf; **the ~s of violence** die Spuren der Gewalt.
(b) *(in exam)* Note *f.* **high** *or* **good ~s** gute Noten *pl;* **the ~s are out of 100** insgesamt kann/ konnte man 100 Punkte erreichen; **there are no ~s for guessing** *(fig)* das ist ja wohl nicht schwer zu erraten; **he gets full ~s for punctuality** *(fig)* an Pünktlichkeit verdient er eine Eins.
(c) *(sign, indication)* Zeichen *nt.* **it bears the ~s of genius** das trägt geniale Züge; **it's the ~ of a gentleman** daran erkennt man den Gentleman.
(d) *(level)* **expenses have reached the £100 ~** die Ausgaben haben die 100-Pfund-Grenze erreicht.
(e) **Cooper M~ II** Cooper II.
(f) *(phrases)* **to be quick off the ~** *(Sport)* einen guten Start haben; *(fig)* blitzschnell reagieren; **to be up to the ~** den Anforderungen entsprechen; **to leave one's ~ (on sth)** einer Sache *(dat)* seinen Stempel aufdrücken; **to make one's ~** sich *(dat)* einen Namen machen; **on your ~s!** auf die Plätze!; **to be wide of the ~** *(shooting)* danebenschießen; *(fig: in guessing)* danebentippen; **to hit the ~** *(lit, fig)* ins Schwarze treffen.
2 *vt* **(a)** *(adversely)* beschädigen; *(stain)* schmutzig machen; *(scratch)* zerkratzen.
(b) *(for recognition, identity)* markieren; *(label)* beschriften; *(price)* auszeichnen. **the bottle was ~ed "poison"** die Flasche trug die Aufschrift „Gift"; **the teacher ~ed him absent on the map** es ist nicht auf der Karte eingezeichnet.
(c) *(characterize)* kennzeichnen. **the new bill ~s a change of policy** das neue Gesetz deutet auf einen politischen Kurswechsel hin.
(d) *exam, paper* korrigieren (und benoten). **to ~ sth wrong** etw anstreichen.
(e) *(heed)* hören auf (+*acc).* **~ my words** eins kann ich Ihnen sagen; *(threatening, warning)* lassen Sie sich das gesagt sein!
(f) *(Sport)* player, opponent decken.
(g) to ~ time *(Mil, fig)* auf der Stelle treten.
3 *vi (get dirty)* schmutzig werden; *(get scratched)* Kratzer bekommen. **she ~s easily** sie bekommt leicht blaue Flecken.
♦ **mark down** *vt sep (note down)* (sich *dat)* notieren; *prices* herabsetzen.
♦ **mark off** *vt sep* kennzeichnen; *boundary* markieren; *danger area etc* absperren.
♦ **mark out** *vt sep* **(a)** *tennis court etc* abstecken.
(b) *(note)* bestimmen *(for für).* **he's been ~ed ~ for promotion** er ist zur Beförderung vorgesehen.
♦ **mark up** *vt sep (write up)* notieren *(on* auf +*dat); price* heraufsetzen.

marked [mɑːkt] *adj* **(a)** *contrast, accent* deutlich; *improvement* spürbar. **(b) he's a ~ man** er steht auf der schwarzen Liste.

markedly ['mɑːkɪdlɪ] *adv* merklich. **it is ~ better** es ist wesentlich besser.

marker ['mɑːkə^r] *n* **(a)** Marke *f; (to turn at)* Wendemarke *f; (on road)* Schild *nt; (in book)* Lesezeichen *nt.* **(b)** *(for exams)* Korrektor(in *f) m.*

market ['mɑːkɪt] **1** *n* Markt *m.* **at the ~** auf dem Markt; **to go to ~** auf den Markt gehen; **to be in the ~ for sth** an etw *(dat)* interessiert sein; **to be on the ~** auf dem Markt sein; **to come on(to) the ~** auf den Markt kommen; **to put on the ~** auf den Markt bringen; *house* zum Verkauf anbieten; **to create a ~** Nachfrage erzeugen; **to play the ~** (an der Börse) spekulieren. **2** *vt* vertreiben. **to ~ a (new) product** ein (neues) Produkt auf den Markt bringen.

market garden *n (Brit)* Gemüseanbaubetrieb *m.*

marketing ['mɑːkɪtɪŋ] *n* Marketing *nt.*

market: **~place** *n* Marktplatz *m; (world of trade)* Markt *m;* **~ price** *n* Marktpreis *m;* **~ research** *n* Marktforschung *f;* **~ town** *n* Marktstädtchen *nt.*

marking ['mɑːkɪŋ] *n* **(a)** Markierung *f; (on animal)* Zeichnung *f.* **~ink** Wäschetinte *f.* **(b)** *(of exams) (correcting)* Korrektur *f; (grading)* Benotung *f.*

marksman ['mɑːksmən] *n, pl* **-men** [-mən] Schütze *m; (police etc)* Scharfschütze *m.*

mark-up ['mɑːkʌp] *n (amount added)* Preiserhöhung *f.* **~ price** Verkaufspreis *m.*

marmalade ['mɑːməleɪd] *n* Marmelade *f* aus Zitrusfrüchten. **(orange) ~** Orangenmarmelade *f.*

maroon[1] [mə'ruːn] *adj* kastanienbraun.

maroon[2] *vt* **~ed** von der Außenwelt abgeschnitten; **~ed by floods** vom Hochwasser eingeschlossen.

marquee [mɑː'kiː] *n* Festzelt *nt.*

marquess ['mɑːkwɪs] *n* Marquis *m.*

marriage ['mærɪdʒ] *n (state)* die Ehe; *(wedding)* Hochzeit, Heirat *f; (~ ceremony)* Trauung *f.* **relations by ~** angeheiratete Verwandte.

marriageable ['mærɪdʒəbl] *adj* heiratsfähig. **of ~ age** im heiratsfähigen Alter.

marriage: **~ guidance** Eheberatung *f;* **~ vow** *n* Ehegelübde *nt.*

married ['mærɪd] *adj* verheiratet; *life, state* Ehe-. **~ couple** Ehepaar *nt;* **she is a ~ woman** sie ist verheiratet.

marrow ['mærəʊ] *n* **(a)** *(Anat)* (Knochen)mark *nt.* **to be frozen to the ~** völlig durchfroren sein. **(b)** *(Bot)* Gartenkürbis *m.*

marry ['mærɪ] **1** *vt* heiraten; *(priest)* trauen. **2** *vi (also get married)* heiraten. **to ~ into a rich family** in eine reiche Familie einheiraten.
♦ **marry off** *vt sep* verheiraten.

Mars [mɑːz] *n* Mars *m.*

marsh [mɑːʃ] *n* Sumpf *m.*

marshal ['mɑːʃəl] **1** *n (Mil etc)* Marschall *m; (at demo etc)* Ordner *m; (US)* Bezirkspolizeichef *m.* **2** *vt arguments* ordnen; *soldiers* antreten lassen.

marshalling **yard** ['mɑːʃəlɪŋ'jɑːd] *n* Rangierbahnhof *m.*

marsh: **~land** *n* Marschland *nt;* **~mallow** *n (sweet)* Marshmallow *nt; (Bot)* Eibisch *m.*

marshy ['mɑːʃɪ] *adj (+er)* sumpfig.

marsupial [mɑː'suːpɪəl] *n* Beuteltier *nt.*

martial ['mɑːʃəl] *adj music* kriegerisch, Kampf-; *bearing* soldatisch. **the ~ arts** die Kampfkunst; **~ law** Kriegsrecht *nt.*

martin ['mɑːtɪn] *n* Schwalbe *f.*

martyr ['mɑːtə'] **1** *n* Märtyrer(in*f*) *m.* **to be a ~ to arthritis** entsetzlich unter Arthritis zu leiden haben. **2** *vt* martern.

martyrdom ['mɑːtədəm] *n (suffering)* Martyrium *nt; (death)* Märtyrertod *m.*

marvel ['mɑːvəl] **1** *n* Wunder *nt.* **it's a ~ to me how he does it** *(col)* es ist mir einfach schleierhaft, wie er das macht; **you're a ~!** *(col)* du bist ein Engel!; *(clever)* du bist ein Genie! **2** *vi* staunen *(at über +acc).* **to ~ at a sight** einen Anblick bestaunen.

marvellous, *(US)* **marvelous** ['mɑːvələs] *adj* wunderbar, fabelhaft. **isn't it ~?** ist das nicht herrlich?; *(iro)* gut, nicht! *(iro).*

Marxism ['mɑːksɪzəm] *n* der Marxismus.

Marxist ['mɑːksɪst] **1** *adj* marxistisch. **2** *n* Marxist(in*f*) *m.*

marzipan [ˌmɑːzɪ'pæn] *n* Marzipan *nt or m.*

mascara [mæ'skɑːrə] *n* Wimperntusche *f.*

mascot ['mæskət] *n* Maskottchen *nt.*

masculine ['mæskjʊlɪn] **1** *adj* männlich; *woman* maskulin. **2** *n (Gram)* Maskulinum *nt.*

mash [mæʃ] **1** *n* Brei *m; (for animals)* Futterbrei *m.* **2** *vt* zerstampfen. **~ed potatoes** Kartoffelbrei *m or* -püree *nt.*

mask [mɑːsk] **1** *n (lit, fig)* Maske *f.* **2** *vt* maskieren; *(clouds etc)* verdecken; *feelings* verbergen.

masochism ['mæsəʊkɪzəm] *n* Masochismus *m.*

masochist ['mæsəʊkɪst] *n* Masochist(in *f*) *m.*

masochistic [ˌmæsəʊ'kɪstɪk] *adj* masochistisch.

mason ['meɪsn] *n* **(a)** *(builder)* Steinmetz *m.* **(b)** *(free~)* Freimaurer *m.*

masonic [mə'sɒnɪk] *adj* Freimaurer-. **~ lodge** Freimaurerloge *f.*

masonry ['meɪsnrɪ] *n* **(a)** *(stonework)* Mauerwerk *nt.* **(b)** *(free~)* Freimaurertum *nt.*

masquerade [ˌmæskə'reɪd] **1** *n* Maskerade *f.* **2** *vi* **to ~ as ...** sich ausgeben als ...

mass[1] [mæs] *n (Eccl)* Messe *f.* **to go to ~** zur Messe gehen; **to say ~** die Messe lesen.

mass[2] **1** *n (general, Phys)* Masse *f; (of people)* Menge *f.* **a ~ of red hair** ein Wust roter Haare; **he's a ~ of bruises** er ist voller blauer Flecken; **the ~es** die Masse(n *pl*); **the great ~ of the population** die breite Masse der Bevölkerung; **~es (of)** massenhaft, eine Masse *(col).* **2** *vt troops* zusammenziehen. **3** *vi (Mil)* sich massieren; *(clouds)* sich (zusammen)ballen. **they're ~ing for an attack** sie sammeln sich zum Angriff.

massacre ['mæsəkə'] **1** *n* Massaker *nt.* **2** *vt* massakrieren.

massage ['mæsɑːʒ] **1** *n* Massage *f.* **2** *vt* massieren.

masseur [mæ'sɜː'] *n* Masseur *m.*

masseuse [mæ'sɜːz] *n* Masseuse *f.*

massive ['mæsɪv] *adj* riesig, enorm; *wall, heart attack, support* massiv; *task* gewaltig.

mass: **~ media** *npl* Massenmedien *pl;* **~ meeting** *n* Massenveranstaltung *f;* **~-produce** *vt* in Massenproduktion herstellen; **~-produced** *adj* **~-produced items** Massenartikel *pl;* **~ production** *n* Massenproduktion *f.*

mast [mɑːst] *n (Naut)* Mast *m; (Rad etc)* Sendeturm *m.* **10 years before the ~** 10 Jahre auf See.

master ['mɑːstə'] **1** *n* **(a)** *(of the house, dog, servants)* Herr *m.* **to be ~ in one's own house** *(also fig)* Herr im Hause sein; **to be one's own ~** sein eigener Herr sein; **to be ~ of sth** etw beherrschen; **to be ~ of the situation** Herr der Lage sein; **~ of ceremonies** *(at function)* Zeremonienmeister *m; (on stage)* Conférencier *m; (TV)* Showmaster *m.* **(b)** *(Naut)* Kapitän *m.* **(c)** *(musician, painter etc)* Meister *m.* **(d)** *(teacher)* Lehrer *m.* **(e)** *(boy's title)* Master *m.* **(f)** *(Univ)* **M~ of Arts/Science** *n* Magister *m* der philosophischen/naturwissenschaftlichen Fakultät. **2** *vt* meistern; *one's emotions* unter Kontrolle bringen; *technique* beherrschen.

master *in cpds* **~ builder** *n* Baumeister *m;* **~ copy** *n* Original *nt.*

masterful ['mɑːstəfʊl] *adj* meisterhaft; *(dominating) personality* gebieterisch.

master key *n* Haupt- or Generalschlüssel *m.*

masterly ['mɑːstəlɪ] *adj* meisterhaft.

master: **~mind 1** *n* (führender) Kopf; **2** *vt who ~minded the robbery?** wer steckt hinter dem Raubüberfall?; **~piece** *n* Meisterwerk *nt;* **~ switch** *n* Hauptschalter *m.*

mastery ['mɑːstərɪ] *n (of instrument, language etc)* Beherrschung *f; (skill)* Können *nt; (over competitors etc)* Oberhand *f.*

mastiff ['mæstɪf] *n* Dogge *f.*

masturbate ['mæstəbeɪt] *vi* masturbieren, onanieren.

masturbation [ˌmæstə'beɪʃən] *n* Masturbation, Onanie *f.*

mat[1] [mæt] *n* Matte *f; (door~)* Fußabstreifer *m; (on table)* Untersetzer *m.* **place ~** Set *nt.*

mat[2] *adj* **= matt.**

match[1] [mætʃ] *n* Streichholz *nt.*

match[2] **1** *n* **(a)** *(sb/sth similar, suitable etc)* **to be or**

make a good ~ gut zusammenpassen. **(b)** *(equal)* **to be a/no** ~ **for sb** *(be able to compete with)* sich mit jdm messen/nicht messen können; *(be able to handle)* jdm gewachsen/nicht gewachsen sein; **to meet one's** ~ seinen Meister finden. **(c)** *(marriage)* Heirat *f*. **she made a good** ~ sie hat eine gute Partie gemacht. **(d)** *(Sport) (general)* Wettkampf *m; (team game)* Spiel *nt; (Tennis)* Match *nt; (Boxing)* Kampf *m*.

2 *vt* **(a)** *(pair off)* **they're well** ~**ed as man and wife** die beiden passen gut zusammen; **the teams are well** ~**ed** die Mannschaften sind gleichwertig; ~ **each diagram with its counterpart** ordnen Sie die Schaubilder einander *(dat)* zu; **to be** ~**ed against sb** gegen jdn antreten. **(b)** *(equal)* gleichkommen *(+dat) (in an +dat)*. **I can't** ~ **him in chess** im Schach kann ich es mit ihm nicht aufnehmen; **the results did not** ~ **our hopes** die Ergebnisse entsprachen nicht unseren Hoffnungen. **(c)** *(clothes, colours)* passen zu.

3 *vi* zusammenpassen. **with a skirt to** ~, **with a** ~**ing skirt** mit (dazu) passendem Rock.

matchbox ['mætʃbɒks] *n* Streichholzschachtel *f*.

match: ~**maker** *n* Ehestifter(in *f*), Kuppler(in *f*) *(pej) m;* ~ **point** *n (Tennis)* Matchball *m;* ~ **stick** *n* Streichholz *nt*.

mate[1] [meɪt] *(Chess)* **1** *n* Matt *nt*. **2** *vt* matt setzen.

mate[2] **1** *n* **(a)** *(fellow worker)* Kumpel *m; (helper)* Gehilfe *m*. **(b)** *(Naut)* Maat *m*. **(c)** *(of animal) (male)* Männchen *nt; (female)* Weibchen *nt*. **his** ~ das Weibchen. **(d)** *(col: friend)* Kamerad(in *f*) *m*. **listen** ~! hör mal, Freundchen! *(col);* **got a light** ~? hast du Feuer, Kumpel? *(col)*. **2** *vt* *animals* paaren; *female* decken lassen. **3** *vi (Zool)* sich paaren.

material [mə'tɪərɪəl] **1** *adj* **(a)** materiell. ~ **damage** Sachschaden *m*. **(b)** *(esp Jur: important) difference* wesentlich. **2** *n* **(a)** Material *nt; (for report etc)* Stoff *m*. ~**s** Material *nt;* **he's good editorial** ~ er hat das Zeug zum Redakteur. **(b)** *(cloth)* Stoff *m*.

materialism [mə'tɪərɪəlɪzəm] *n* der Materialismus.

materialize [mə'tɪərɪəlaɪz] *vi (idea, plan)* sich verwirklichen; *(promises, hopes etc)* wahr werden.

materially [mə'tɪərɪəlɪ] *adv* wesentlich.

maternal [mə'tɜːnl] *adj* mütterlich. ~ **grandfather** Großvater mütterlicherseits.

maternity [mə'tɜːnɪtɪ] *n* Mutterschaft *f*.

maternity: ~ **benefit** *n* Mutterschaftsgeld *nt;* ~ **dress** *n* Umstandskleid *nt;* ~ **home,** ~ **hospital** *n* Entbindungsheim *nt;* ~ **leave** *n* Schwangerschaftsurlaub *m;* ~ **ward** *n* Entbindungsstation *f*.

math [mæθ] *n (US col)* Mathe *f (col)*.

mathematical [ˌmæθə'mætɪkəl] *adj* mathematisch.

mathematician [ˌmæθəmə'tɪʃən] *n* Mathematiker(in *f*) *m*.

mathematics [ˌmæθə'mætɪks] *n sing* Mathematik *f*.

maths [mæθs] *n sing (Brit col)* Mathe *f (col)*.

matinée ['mætɪneɪ] *n* Matinee *f; (in the afternoon also)* Nachmittagsvorstellung *f*.

mating ['meɪtɪŋ] *n* Paarung *f*.

mating: ~ **call** *n* Lockruf *m;* ~ **season** *n* Paarungszeit *f*.

matriarch ['meɪtrɪɑːk] *n* Matriarchin *f*.

matrices ['meɪtrɪsɪz] *pl of* **matrix.**

matriculate [mə'trɪkjʊleɪt] *vi* sich immatrikulieren.

matrimonial [ˌmætrɪ'məʊnɪəl] *adj vows* Ehe-.

matrimony ['mætrɪmənɪ] *n (form)* Ehe *f*.

matrix ['meɪtrɪks] *n, pl* **matrices** *or* **-es (a)** *(mould)* Matrize *f*. **(b)** *(Geol, Math)* Matrix *f*.

matron ['meɪtrən] *n (in hospital)* Oberschwester *f; (in school)* Schwester *f*.

matronly ['meɪtrənlɪ] *adj* matronenhaft.

matt [mæt] *adj* mattiert. ~ **paint** Mattlack *m*.

matted ['mætɪd] *adj* verfilzt.

matter ['mætə'] **1** *n* **(a)** *(Phys etc: substance)* die Materie. **advertising** ~ Werbung *f;* **printed** ~ Drucksache(n *pl*) *f;* **colouring** ~ Farbstoff(e *pl*) *m;* **reading** ~ Lektüre *f*.
(b) *(Med: pus)* Eiter *m*.
(c) *(content)* Inhalt *m*.
(d) *(question, affair)* Sache, Angelegenheit *f; (topic)* Thema *nt*. **in this** ~ in diesem Zusammenhang; **in the** ~ **of ... was ...** *(+acc)* anbelangt; **in the** ~ **of clothes** *etc* in puncto Kleidung *etc;* **there's the** ~ **of my expenses** da wären noch meine Auslagen; **that's quite another** ~ das ist etwas (ganz) anderes; **it will be no easy** ~ **(to) ...** es wird nicht einfach sein, zu ...; **it's a serious** ~ das ist eine ernste Angelegenheit; **the** ~ **in hand** die vorliegende Angelegenheit; **the** ~ **is closed** der Fall ist erledigt; **for that** ~ eigentlich; **business** ~**s** geschäftliche Dinge *pl,* Geschäftliche(s) *nt;* **money** ~**s** Geldfragen *pl;* **as** ~**s stand** wie die Dinge liegen; **to make** ~**s worse** zu allem Unglück (noch).
(e) **a** ~ **of** eine Sache von; **it's a** ~ **of time** das ist eine Frage der Zeit; **it's a** ~ **of opinion** das ist Ansichtssache; **it will be a** ~ **of a few weeks** es wird ein paar Wochen dauern; **in a** ~ **of minutes** innerhalb von Minuten; **it's a** ~ **of great concern to us** die ganze Sache ist für uns von großer Bedeutung; **it's a** ~ **of increasing the money supply** es geht darum, die Geldzufuhr zu erhöhen; **as a** ~ **of course** selbstverständlich; **no** ~! macht nichts; **I've decided to leave, no** ~ **what** ich gehe, egal was passiert; **no how/what/when** *etc ...* egal, wie/was/wann *etc ...;* **no** ~ **how hot it was** selbst bei der größten Hitze; **something is the** ~ **with sb/sth** etwas ist mit jdm/etw los; *(ill)* etw fehlt jdm; **what's the** ~ **with you?** was ist denn mit dir los?; **what's the** ~ **with smoking?** was ist denn dabei, wenn man raucht?; **something's the** ~ **with the lights** mit dem Licht ist irgend etwas nicht in Ordnung.

2 *vi* **it doesn't** ~ *(es or das)* macht nichts; **what does it** ~? was macht das schon?; **I forgot it, does it** ~? ich hab's vergessen, ist das schlimm?; **does it** ~ **to you if I go?** macht es dir etwas aus, wenn ich gehe?; **it doesn't** ~ **to me what you do** es ist mir (ganz) egal, was du machst.

matter-of-fact ['mætərəv'fækt] *adj* sachlich.

mattress ['mætrɪs] *n* Matratze *f*.

mature [mə'tjʊə'] **1** *adj (+er) person, cheese* reif; *child* vernünftig; *wine* ausgereift. **2** *vi (person)* reifer werden; *(wine, cheese)* reifen.

maturity [mə'tjʊərɪtɪ] *n* Reife *f*. **to reach** ~ *(person)* erwachsen werden; *(legally)* volljährig werden.

maudlin ['mɔːdlɪn] *adj story* rührselig; *person* gefühlvoll.

maul [mɔːl] *vt* übel zurichten.

mausoleum [ˌmɔːsə'lɪəm] *n* Mausoleum *nt*.

mauve [məʊv] *adj* malvenfarben.

maverick ['mævərɪk] *n (dissenter)* Abtrünnige(r) *m; (independent person)* Alleingänger *m*.

mawkish ['mɔːkɪʃ] *adj* rührselig, kitschig.

max = **maximum** max.

maxim ['mæksɪm] *n* Maxime *f*.

maximize ['mæksɪmaɪz] *vt* maximieren.

maximum ['mæksɪməm] **1** *adj attr* Höchst-; *size, costs* maximal. **the** ~ **salary is ...** das höchste Gehalt ist ...; *(top grade)* das Endgehalt ist ... **2** *n, pl* **-s** *or* **maxima** ['mæksɪmə] Maximum *nt*. **up to a** ~ **of £8** bis zu einem Maximum £8; **temperatures reached a** ~ **of 34°** die Höchsttemperatur betrug 34°.

May [meɪ] *n* Mai *m*.

may [meɪ] *vi pret* **might** *(see also* **might**[1]*)* **(a)** *(possibility: also* **might)** können. **it** ~ **rain** vielleicht regnet es; **it** ~ **be that ...** vielleicht ..., es könnte sein, daß ...; **he** ~ **not be hungry** viel-

leicht hat er keinen Hunger; I ~ **have said so es kann** or **könnte sein**, daß ich das gesagt habe; **you ~ be right** (*doubting*) Sie haben vielleicht recht; (*tentatively agreeing*) da könnten Sie recht haben; **yes, I ~ ja**, das ist möglich; **you ~ well ask** das ist eine gute Frage!
(**b**) (*permission*) dürfen. ~ **I go now?** darf ich jetzt gehen?; **yes, you ~** ja, Sie dürfen.
(**c**) **I hope he ~ succeed** ich hoffe, daß es ihm gelingt; **I hoped he might succeed** ich hatte gehofft, es würde ihm gelingen; **you ~** or **might as well go now** du kannst jetzt ruhig gehen; **if they don't have it we ~** or **might as well go to another firm** wenn sie es nicht haben, gehen wir am besten zu einer anderen Firma.
(**d**) (*in wishes*) ~ **you be successful!** (ich wünsche Ihnen) viel Erfolg!; ~ **you be very happy together** ich wünsche euch, daß ihr sehr glücklich miteinander werdet.
maybe ['meɪbiː] *adv* vielleicht.
May: ~ **Day** *n* der 1. Mai; ~**day** *n* (*distress call*) Maydaysignal *nt*, SOS-Ruf *m*.
mayonnaise [ˌmeɪə'neɪz] *n* Mayonnaise *f*.
mayor [mɛəʳ] *n* Bürgermeister(in *f*) *m*.
mayoress ['mɛərɛs] *n* Frau *f* des Bürgermeisters; (*lady mayor*) Bürgermeisterin *f*.
maypole ['meɪpəʊl] *n* Maibaum *m*.
maze [meɪz] *n* Irrgarten *m*; (*fig*) Gewirr *nt*.
MC = **Master of Ceremonies**.
MD = **Doctor of Medicine** Dr. med.
me [miː] *pron* (**a**) (*dir obj, with prep +acc*) mich; (*indir obj, with prep +dat*) mir. **he's older than** ~ er ist älter als ich. (**b**) (*emph*) ich. **who, ~?** wer, ich?; **it's** ~ ich bin's.
meadow ['mɛdəʊ] *n* Wiese *f*.
meagre, (*US*) **meager** ['miːgəʳ] *adj* spärlich; *amount* kläglich; *meal* dürftig.
meal[1] [miːl] *n* (*flour etc*) Schrot(mehl *nt*) *m*.
meal[2] *n* Mahlzeit *f*; (*food*) Essen *nt*. **come around for a** ~ komm zum Essen (zu uns); **to go for a** ~ essen gehen; **to have a** (**good**) ~ (gut) essen; **hot** ~**s** warme Mahlzeiten *pl*; **he really made a** ~ **of it** (*col*) er war nicht mehr zu bremsen (*col*).
meal: ~**-ticket** *n* (*US: lit*) Essensmarke *f*; **she's just his** ~**-ticket** er ist nur des Geldes wegen mit ihr befreundet; ~**time** *n* Essenszeit *f*.
mealy-mouthed ['miːlɪ'maʊðd] *adj* unaufrichtig; *politician* schönfärberisch.
mean[1] [miːn] *adj* (+*er*) (**a**) (*miserly*) geizig. **he's** ~ **with his money** er ist geizig mit seinem Geld. (**b**) (*unkind, spiteful*) gemein. **you** ~ **thing!** du gemeines Stück!, du Miststück! (*col*); **a** ~ **trick** eine Gemeinheit. (**c**) (*vicious*) bösartig; *look* gehässig; *criminal* niederträchtig. (**d**) **he is no** ~ **player** er ist ein beachtlicher Spieler; **that's no** ~ **feat** diese Aufgabe ist nicht zu unterschätzen.
mean[2] *n* Durchschnitt *m*. **the golden** or **happy** ~ der goldene Mittelweg. 2 *adj* mittlere(r, s).
mean[3] *pret, ptp* **meant** *vt* (**a**) bedeuten; (*person: have in mind*) meinen. **what do you** ~ **by that?** was willst du damit sagen?; **I** ~ **it!** ich meine das ernst!; **I** ~ **what I say** es ist mir ernst damit; **the name** ~**s nothing to me** der Name sagt mir nichts; **it** ~**s starting all over again** das bedeutet, daß wir/sie wieder ganz von vorne anfangen müssen; **this will** ~ **great changes** dies wird bedeutende Veränderungen zur Folge haben; **he** ~**s a lot to me** er bedeutet mir viel.
(**b**) (*intend*) beabsichtigen. **to** ~ **to do sth** etw tun wollen; (*do on purpose*) etw absichtlich tun; **to be** ~**t for sb/sth** für jdn/etw bestimmt sein; **to** ~ **sb to do sth** wollen, daß jd etw tut; **sth is** ~**t to be sth** etw soll etw sein; **I** ~ **it as a joke** das sollte ein Witz sein; **you are** ~**t to be on time** du solltest pünktlich sein; **he wasn't** ~**t to be a leader** er war nicht zum Führer bestimmt; **I** ~ **to be obeyed** ich verlange, daß man mir gehorcht; **this pad is** ~**t for drawing** dieser Block ist zum Zeichnen

gedacht; **you weren't** ~**t to see it** du solltest das nicht zu sehen bekommen; **he** ~**s well/no harm** er meint es gut/nicht böse.
meander [mɪ'ændəʳ] *vi* (*river*) sich (dahin)schlängeln; (*go off subject*) (vom Thema) abschweifen; (*walking*) schlendern.
meaning ['miːnɪŋ] *n* Bedeutung *f*; (*sense: of words, poem etc also*) Sinn *m*. **a look full of** ~ ein bedeutsamer Blick; **do you get my** ~? haben Sie mich (richtig) verstanden?; **you don't know the** ~ **of hunger** du weißt ja gar nicht, was Hunger bedeutet; **what's the** ~ **of this?** was soll denn das (heißen)?
meaningful ['miːnɪŋfʊl] *adj* sinnvoll; *film* bedeutungsvoll.
meaningless ['miːnɪŋlɪs] *adj* *sentence* ohne Bedeutung; *life* sinnlos.
meanness ['miːnnɪs] *n* *see adj* (**a**) Geiz *m*. (**b**) Gemeinheit *f*. (**c**) Bösartigkeit *f*; Gehässigkeit *f*; Niedertracht *f*.
means [miːnz] *n* (**a**) *sing* (*method*) Möglichkeit *f*; (*instrument*) Mittel *nt*. **a** ~ **of transport** ein Beförderungsmittel *nt*; **a** ~ **to an end** ein Mittel *nt* zum Zweck; **there is no** ~ **of doing it** es ist unmöglich, das zu tun; **we've no** ~ **of knowing** wir können nicht wissen; **by** ~ **of sth** durch etw; **by** ~ **of doing sth** dadurch, daß man etw tut. (**b**) *sing* **by all** ~! (*aber*) selbstverständlich or natürlich!; **by no** ~ keineswegs; (*under no circumstances*) auf keinen Fall. (**c**) *pl* (*wherewithal*) Mittel *pl*; (*financial* – *also*) Gelder *pl*. **a man of** ~ ein vermögender Mann; **private** ~ private Mittel; **to live beyond/within one's** ~ über seine Verhältnisse leben/seinen Verhältnissen entsprechend leben; ~ **test** Einkommensveranlagung *f*.
meant [mɛnt] *pret, ptp* of **mean**[3].
meantime ['miːntaɪm] 1 *adv* inzwischen. 2 *n* **in the** ~ in der Zwischenzeit, inzwischen.
meanwhile ['miːnwaɪl] *adv* inzwischen.
measles ['miːzlz] *n sing* Masern *pl*.
measly ['miːzlɪ] *adj* (+*er*) (*col*) mick(e)rig (*col*).
measure ['mɛʒəʳ] 1 *n* (**a**) (*unit of measurement*) Maß(einheit *f*) *nt*; (*amount* ~*d*) Menge *f*; (*fig: yardstick*) Maßstab *m* (*of* für). **her joy was beyond** ~ ihre Freude kannte keine Grenzen; **to give sb full/short** ~ (*barman*) richtig/zuwenig ausschenken; **in full** ~ in höchstem Maße; **for good** ~ sicherheitshalber; **it gave us some** ~ **of the difficulty** es gab uns einen Begriff von der Schwierigkeit; **in some** ~ in gewisser Hinsicht; **some** ~ **of** ein gewisses Maß an; **to a** or **in large** ~ in hohem Maße. (**b**) (*step*) Maßnahme *f*. **to take** ~**s to do sth** Maßnahmen ergreifen, um etw zu tun.
2 *vt* messen; *length* abmessen; *room* ausmessen; (*take sb's measurements*) Maß nehmen bei. **to** ~ **one's length** (*fig: fall*) der Länge nach hinfallen.
3 *vi* messen. **what does it** ~? wieviel mißt es?
♦ **measure off** *vt sep* abmessen.
♦ **measure out** *vt sep* abmessen; *weights* abwiegen.
♦ **measure up** *vi* (*be good enough, compare well*) **he didn't** ~ ~ er hat enttäuscht; **to** ~ ~ **to sth** an etw (*acc*) herankommen.
measured ['mɛʒəd] *adj* *tread* gemessen; *tone, way of talking* bedächtig; *words* wohlüberlegt.
measurement ['mɛʒəmənt] *n* (**a**) (*act*) Messung *f*. (**b**) (*measure*) Maß *nt*; (*figure*) Meßwert *m*; (*fig*) Maßstab *m*. **to take sb's** ~**s** bei jdm Maß nehmen.
meat [miːt] *n* Fleisch *nt*. **cold** ~**s** Aufschnitt *m*. **one man's** ~ **is another man's poison** (*Prov*) des einen Freud, des andern Leid (*Prov*).
meat *in cpds* Fleisch-; ~**ball** *n* Fleischkloß *m*.
meaty ['miːtɪ] *adj* (+*er*) (**a**) *taste* Fleisch-. (**b**) (*fig*) *book* aussagestark.
mechanic [mɪ'kænɪk] *n* Mechaniker *m*.

mechanical [mɪ'kænɪkəl] adj (lit, fig) mechanisch. ~ **engineer/engineering** Maschinenbauingenieur m/Maschinenbau m.

mechanics [mɪ'kænɪks] n (a) sing (subject) (engineering) Maschinenbau m; (Phys) Mechanik f. (b) pl (technical aspects) Mechanik f; (of writing etc) Technik f; (of procedure) Mechanismus m.

mechanism ['mekənɪzəm] n Mechanismus m.

mechanize ['mekənaɪz] vt mechanisieren.

medal ['medl] n Medaille f; (decoration) Orden m.

medallist, medalist ['medəlɪst] n gold ~ Goldmedaillengewinner(in f) m.

meddle ['medl] vi (interfere) sich einmischen (in in +acc); (tamper) sich zu schaffen machen (with an +dat). he's not a man to ~ with mit ihm ist nicht gut Kirschen essen (col).

meddler ['medlə'] n he's a terrible ~ er muß sich immer in alles einmischen.

meddlesome ['medlsəm] adj, **meddling** ['medlɪŋ] adj attr she's a ~ old busybody sie mischt sich dauernd in alles ein.

media ['miːdɪə] n, pl of **medium** Medien pl. he works in the ~ er ist im Mediensektor tätig; all the ~ were there Presse, Funk und Fernsehen waren dort.

mediaeval adj = **medieval**.

median strip ['miːdɪən'strɪp] n (US) Mittelstreifen m.

mediate ['miːdɪeɪt] 1 vi vermitteln. 2 vt settlement aushandeln.

mediation [,miːdɪ'eɪʃən] n Vermittlung f.

mediator ['miːdɪeɪtə'] n Vermittler m.

medical ['medɪkəl] 1 adj medizinisch; treatment ärztlich; board, inspector Gesundheits-; student Medizin-. ~ **school** ≃ medizinische Fakultät; ~ **card** (Brit) Krankenversicherungsschein m. 2 n (ärztliche) Untersuchung.

Medicare ['medɪ,keə'] n (US) staatliche Krankenversicherung und Gesundheitsfürsorge.

medicated ['medɪkeɪtɪd] adj medizinisch.

medication [,medɪ'keɪʃən] n (act) (medizinische) Behandlung; (drugs etc) Medikamente pl.

medicinal [me'dɪsɪnl] adj Heil-, heilend.

medicine ['medsɪn, 'medɪsɪn] n (a) Arznei f; (particular preparation) Medikament nt. to give sb a taste of his own ~ (fig) es jdm mit gleicher Münze heimzahlen. (b) (science) Medizin f.

medicine: ~ **chest** n Hausapotheke f; ~**-man** n Medizinmann m.

medieval [,medɪ'iːvəl] adj mittelalterlich.

mediocre [,miːdɪ'əʊkə'] adj mittelmäßig.

mediocrity [,miːdɪ'ɒkrɪtɪ] n Mittelmäßigkeit f.

meditate ['medɪteɪt] vi nachdenken (upon, on über +acc); (Rel, Philos) meditieren.

meditation [,medɪ'teɪʃən] n Nachdenken nt; (Rel, Philos) Meditation f.

Mediterranean [,medɪtə'reɪnɪən] 1 n Mittelmeer nt. 2 adj Mittelmeer-; person südländisch.

medium ['miːdɪəm] 1 adj quality, size etc mittlere(r, s); steak halbdurch; brown, sized etc mittel-. of ~ **height** mittelgroß. 2 n, pl **media** or **-s** (a) (means) Mittel nt. **through the ~ of the press** durch die Presse; **advertising ~** Werbeträger m. (b) (midpoint) Mitte f. **happy ~** goldener Mittelweg. (c) (spiritualist) Medium nt.

medium in cpds mittel-; ~**-sized** adj mittelgroß; ~ **wave** n Mittelwelle f.

medley ['medlɪ] n Gemisch nt; (Mus) Medley nt.

meek [miːk] adj (+er) sanft(mütig); (pej) duckmäuserisch; (uncomplaining) duldsam.

meet [miːt] (vb: pret, ptp **met**) 1 vt (a) (encounter) person treffen; (by arrangement) sich treffen mit; difficulty stoßen auf (+acc); he **met his death in 1800** im Jahre 1800 fand er den Tod; **to arrange to ~ sb** sich mit jdm verabreden; **his eyes met mine** unsere Blicke trafen sich; **there's more to it than ~s the eye** da steckt mehr dahinter, als man auf den ersten Blick meint.

(b) (get to know) kennenlernen. **come and ~ my brother** komm, ich mache dich mit meinem Bruder bekannt; **pleased to ~ you!** angenehm! (form), guten Tag/Abend.

(c) (await arrival, collect) abholen (at an +dat, von). **the car will ~ the train** der Wagen steht am Bahnhof bereit.

(d) expectations, target, deadline erfüllen; requirement gerecht werden (+dat); expenses, needs decken; charge, criticism begegnen (+dat).

2 vi (a) (encounter) (people) sich begegnen; (by arrangement) sich treffen; (society, committee etc) tagen. **haven't we met before somewhere?** sind wir uns nicht schon mal begegnet?; **until we ~ again!** bis zum nächsten Mal! (b) (join etc) sich treffen; (converge) sich vereinigen; (rivers) ineinanderfließen; (intersect) sich schneiden; (fig: come together) sich treffen. **our eyes met** unsere Blicke trafen sich.

3 n (Hunt) Jagd f; (US Sport) Sportfest nt.

♦ **meet up** vi sich treffen.

♦ **meet with** vi +prep obj (a) hostility, problems stoßen auf (+acc); success, accident haben; disaster erleiden; approval, untimely death finden. (b) person treffen; (have a meeting) (zu einer Unterredung) zusammenkommen mit.

meeting ['miːtɪŋ] n (a) Begegnung f; (arranged) Treffen nt; (business ~) Besprechung f. **the minister had a ~ with the ambassador** der Minister traf zu Gesprächen mit dem Botschafter zusammen. (b) (of committee) Sitzung f; (of members, citizens) Versammlung f. **at the last ~** bei der letzten Sitzung; **Mr Jones is in a ~** Herr Jones ist (gerade) in einer Sitzung. (c) (Sport) Veranstaltung f; (between teams, opponents) Begegnung f.

meeting place n Treffpunkt m.

megalomaniac [,megələʊ'meɪnɪæk] n Größenwahnsinnige(r) mf.

megaphone ['megəfəʊn] n Megaphon nt.

melancholy ['melənkəlɪ] 1 adj melancholisch; duty, sight etc traurig. 2 n Melancholie f.

mellow ['meləʊ] 1 adj (+er) fruit, wine ausgereift; colour, light warm; sound, voice weich; person gesetzt; (fig: slightly drunk) angeheitert. 2 vi (wine, fruit) reif werden, (colours, sounds) weicher werden; (person) gesetzter werden.

melodious [mɪ'ləʊdɪəs] adj melodisch.

melodrama ['meləʊ,drɑːmə] n Melodrama nt.

melodramatic [,meləʊdrə'mætɪk] adj melodramatisch.

melody ['melədɪ] n Melodie f.

melon ['melən] n Melone f.

melt [melt] 1 vt schmelzen; butter zerlassen; (fig) heart etc erweichen. **her tears ~ed my anger** beim Anblick ihrer Tränen verflog mein Zorn. 2 vi schmelzen; (butter also) zergehen; (fig: anger) verfliegen. **it just ~s in the mouth** es zergeht einem nur so auf der Zunge; **he ~ed into the crowd** er verschwand in der Menge.

♦ **melt away** vi (lit) (weg)schmelzen; (fig) sich auflösen; (person) dahinschmelzen; (anger) verfliegen; (suspicion, money) zerrinnen.

♦ **melt down** vt sep einschmelzen.

meltdown ['meltdaʊn] n Kernschmelze f.

melting ['meltɪŋ-]: ~ **point** n Schmelzpunkt m; ~ **pot** n (lit, fig) Schmelztiegel m; **to be in the ~ pot** in der Schwebe sein.

member ['membə'] n Mitglied nt; (of tribe, species) Angehörige(r) mf; (Parl) Abgeordnete(r) mf. "~s only" „nur für Mitglieder"; ~ **of the family** Familienmitglied nt; **a ~ of the audience** ein Zuschauer/Zuhörer m; **the ~ countries** die Mitgliedsstaaten pl; ~ **of parliament** Parlamentsmitglied nt.

membership ['membəʃɪp] n Mitgliedschaft f (of in +dat); (number of members) Mitgliederzahl f. ~ **card** Mitgliedskarte f.

membrane ['membreın] n Membran(e) f.
memento [mə'mentəu] n, pl -(e)s Andenken nt (of an +acc).
memo['meməu]n(a) = **memorandum. (b)** ~ **pad** Notizblock m.
memoir ['memwɑː^r] n (a) Kurzbiographie f. (b) ~s pl Memoiren pl.
memorable ['memərəbl] adj unvergeßlich; (important) denkwürdig.
memorandum [‚memə'rændəm] n, pl **memoranda** [‚memə'rændə] (in business) Mitteilung f; (personal reminder) Notiz f.
memorial [mɪ'mɔːrɪəl] 1 adj plaque, service Gedenk-. 2 n Denkmal nt (to für).
memorize ['meməraɪz] vt sich (dat) einprägen.
memory ['memərɪ] n (a) Gedächtnis nt; (faculty) Erinnerungsvermögen nt. **from** ~ aus dem Kopf; **I have a bad** ~ **for faces** ich habe ein schlechtes Personengedächtnis; **if my** ~ **serves me right** wenn ich mich recht entsinne. **(b)** (that remembered) Erinnerung f (of an +acc). **I have no** ~ **of it** ich kann mich nicht daran erinnern. **(c)** (Comp) Speicher m. ~ **bank** Datenspeicher m. **(d) in** ~ **of** zur Erinnerung or zum Gedenken (form) an (+acc).
men [men] pl of **man.**
menace ['menɪs] 1 n (a) Bedrohung f (to gen); (imminent danger) drohende Gefahr. **(b)** (col: nuisance) (Land)plage f. 2 vt bedrohen.
menacing ['menɪsɪŋ] adj drohend.
mend [mend] 1 n to **be on the** ~ auf dem Wege der Besserung sein. 2 vt (repair) reparieren; roof, fence also ausbessern; hole, clothes flicken. **my shoes need** ~**ing** ich muß meine Schuhe reparieren lassen; **to** ~ **one's ways** sich bessern. 3 vi (bone) (ver)heilen.
menfolk ['menfəuk] npl Männer pl.
menial ['miːnɪəl] adj niedrig.
meningitis [‚menɪn'dʒaɪtɪs] n Hirnhautentzündung f.
menopause ['menəupɔːz] n Wechseljahre pl.
menstruate ['menstrʊeɪt] vi die Menstruation haben.
menstruation [‚menstrʊ'eɪʃən] n die Menstruation or Periode.
mental ['mentl] adj (a) geistig; cruelty seelisch. **to make a** ~ **note of sth** sich (dat) etw merken; ~ **arithmetic** Kopfrechnen nt; ~ **health** Geisteszustand m; ~ **home** (Nerven)heilanstalt f; ~ **hospital** psychiatrische Klinik f; ~ **illness** Geisteskrankheit f. **(b)** (col: mad) übergeschnappt (col).
mentality [men'tælɪtɪ] n Mentalität f. **they have an aggressive** ~ sie haben eine aggressive Art.
mentally ['mentlɪ] adv (a) geistig. ~ **handicapped/deficient** geistig behindert/geistesschwach; **he is** ~ **ill** er ist geisteskrank. **(b)** (in one's head) im Kopf.
menthol ['menθɒl] n Menthol nt.
mention ['menʃən] 1 n Erwähnung f. **to get or receive a** ~ erwähnt werden; **to give sth a** ~ etw erwähnen; **there is a/no** ~ **of it** es wird erwähnt/ nicht erwähnt; **it's hardly worth a** ~ es ist kaum erwähnenswert. 2 vt erwähnen (to sb jdm gegenüber). **not to** ~ ... geschweige denn ...; **too numerous to** ~ zu zahlreich, um sie einzeln erwähnen zu können; **don't** ~ **it!** (bitte,) gern geschehen!; ~**ing no names,** ohne irgendwelche Namen nennen zu wollen; ~ **me to your parents!** viele Grüße an Ihre Eltern!
menu ['menjuː] n (a) Speisekarte f. **what's on the** ~? was gibt es heute (zu essen)? **(b)** (Comp) Menü nt. ~**-driven** menügesteuert.
mercenary ['mɜːsɪnərɪ] 1 adj (a) person geldgierig. **(b)** (Mil) troops Söldner-. 2 n Söldner m.
merchandise ['mɜːtʃəndaɪz] n Ware f.
merchant ['mɜːtʃənt] n Kaufmann m. **diamond** ~ Diamantenhändler m.

merchant in cpds Handels-; ~ **bank** n (Brit) Handelsbank f; ~ **navy** n Handelsmarine f; ~ **seaman** n Matrose m in der Handelsmarine.
merciful ['mɜːsɪfʊl] adj gnädig. **his death was a** ~ **release** sein Tod war für ihn eine Erlösung.
mercifully ['mɜːsɪflɪ] adv act barmherzig; treat sb gnädig; (fortunately) glücklicherweise.
merciless ['mɜːsɪlɪs] adj erbarmungslos; destruction schonungslos.
Mercury ['mɜːkjʊrɪ] n Merkur m.
mercury ['mɜːkjʊrɪ] n Quecksilber nt.
mercy ['mɜːsɪ] n no pl (feeling of compassion) Erbarmen nt; (in judgment) Gnade f; (God's ~) Barmherzigkeit f. **to have** ~ **on sb** mit jdm Erbarmen haben; **to show sb** ~/**no** ~ Erbarmen/kein Erbarmen mit jdm haben; **to be at the** ~ **of sb/sth** jdm/einer Sache (dat) ausgeliefert sein; **it's a** ~ **nobody was hurt** (col) man kann von Glück sagen, daß niemand verletzt wurde.
mercy killing n Töten nt aus Mitleid.
mere [mɪə^r] adj bloß; formality also rein. **he's a** ~ **clerk** er ist bloß ein kleiner Angestellter; **but she's a** ~ **child** aber sie ist doch noch ein Kind!
merely ['mɪəlɪ] adv lediglich, bloß.
merge [mɜːdʒ] 1 vi (a) zusammenkommen; (colours) ineinander übergehen; (roads) zusammenlaufen. **to** ~ **with sth** mit etw verschmelzen; (colour) in etw (acc) übergehen; **to** ~ **into sth** in etw (acc) übergehen. **(b)** (Comm) fusionieren. 2 vt (Comm) fusionieren.
merger ['mɜːdʒə^r] n (Comm) Fusion f.
meringue [mə'ræŋ] n Meringe f, Baiser nt.
merit ['merɪt] 1 n (achievement) Leistung f, Verdienst nt; (advantage) Vorzug m. **to look or inquire into the** ~**s of sth** etw auf seine Vorteile untersuchen; **to treat a case on its** ~**s** einen Fall gesondert behandeln. 2 vt verdienen.
meritocracy [‚merɪ'tɒkrəsɪ] n Leistungsgesellschaft f.
mermaid ['mɜːmeɪd] n Nixe, Meerjungfrau f.
merriment ['merɪmənt] n Heiterkeit f; (laughter) Gelächter nt.
merry ['merɪ] adj (+er) (a) (cheerful) fröhlich, vergnügt. **M~ Christmas!** Fröhliche or Frohe Weihnachten! **(b)** (col: tipsy) beschwipst (col).
merry: ~**-go-round** n Karussell nt; ~**making** n Feiern nt.
mesh [meʃ] n (hole) Masche f; (size of hole) Maschenweite f; (wire ~) Maschendraht m. **out of/in** ~ (Mech) nicht im/im Eingriff.
mesmerize ['mezməraɪz] vt hypnotisieren; (fig) fesseln. **the audience sat** ~**d** die Zuschauer saßen wie gebannt.
mess¹ [mes] n Durcheinander nt; (untidy also) Unordnung f; (dirty) Schweinerei f. **to be (in) a** ~ unordentlich sein; (disorganized) ein einziges Durcheinander sein; (fig: one's life, marriage etc) verkorkst sein (col); **to look a** ~ (person) unmöglich aussehen; (untidy also, room) unordentlich aussehen; **to make a** ~ (untidy) eine Schweinerei machen; **to make a** ~ **of sth** (untidy) etw durcheinanderbringen; (dirty) etw verdrecken; (bungle, botch) etw verpfuschen; **the cat made a** ~ **on the** carpet die Katze hat auf den Teppich gemacht.
♦ **mess about or around** (col) 1 vt sep person an der Nase herumführen (col); (boss etc) herumschikanieren; (by delaying) hinhalten. 2 vi (play the fool) herumalbern or -blödeln (col); (do nothing in particular) herumgammeln (col); (fiddle) herumfummeln (col) (with an +dat); (as hobby etc) herumbasteln (with an +dat) (col).
♦ **mess up** vt sep durcheinanderbringen; (make untidy also) in Unordnung bringen; (make dirty) verdrecken; (botch, bungle) verpfuschen, verhunzen (col); marriage kaputtmachen (col); life, person verkorksen (col).
mess² (Mil) n Kasino nt; (on ships) Messe f.

message ['mesɪdʒ] *n* Mitteilung, Nachricht, Botschaft *(form)* *f*. **to take a ~ to** sb jdm eine Nachricht überbringen; **can I take a ~ (for him)?** *(on telephone)* kann ich (ihm) etwas ausrichten?; **to give** sb **a ~** *(verbal)* jdm etwas ausrichten; *(written)* jdm eine Nachricht geben; **would you give John a ~ (for me)?** könnten Sie John etwas (von mir) ausrichten?; **to leave a ~ for** sb *(written)* jdm eine Nachricht hinterlassen; *(verbal)* jdm etwas ausrichten lassen; **to get the ~** *(fig col)* kapieren *(col)*.

messenger ['mesɪndʒəʳ] *n* Bote *(form)*, Überbringer(in *f*) *m*; *(Mil)* Kurier *m*. **~ boy** Laufbursche *m*.

Messiah [mɪ'saɪə] *n* Messias *m*.

Messrs ['mesəz] *pl of* **Mr** *(on letters etc)* **to ~ ... an die Herren ...**

messy ['mesɪ] *adj (+er) (dirty)* dreckig; *(untidy)* unordentlich; *(confused)* durcheinander pred; *(fig: unpleasant)* unschön.

met [met] *pret, ptp of* **meet**.

metal ['metl] *n* Metall *nt*; *(Brit: on road)* Asphalt *m*.

metallic [mɪ'tælɪk] *adj* metallisch.

metallurgy [me'tælədʒɪ] *n* Metallurgie *f*.

metal *in cpds* Metall-; **~ plating** *n* Metallschicht *f*; **~work** *n* Metall *nt*; **we did ~work at school** wir haben in der Schule Metallarbeiten gemacht.

metamorphosis [ˌmetə'mɔːfəsɪs] *n, pl* **metamorphoses** [ˌmetə'mɔːfəsiːz] Metamorphose *f*; *(fig)* Verwandlung *f*.

metaphor ['metəfəʳ] *n* Metapher *f*.

metaphorical [ˌmetə'fɒrɪkəl] *adj* metaphorisch.

metaphysical [ˌmetə'fɪzɪkəl] *adj* metaphysisch.

metaphysics [ˌmetə'fɪzɪks] *n sing* Metaphysik *f*.

♦ **mete out** ['miːt'aʊt] *vt sep* zuteil werden lassen *(to* sb jdm); *praise* austeilen; *rewards* verteilen. **to ~ a punishment to** sb jdn bestrafen.

meteor ['miːtɪəʳ] *n* Meteor *m*.

meteoric [ˌmiːtɪ'ɒrɪk] *adj* meteorisch; *(fig)* kometenhaft.

meteorite ['miːtɪəraɪt] *n* Meteorit *m*.

meteorological [ˌmiːtɪərə'lɒdʒɪkəl] *adj* Wetter-, meteorologisch.

meteorologist [ˌmiːtɪə'rɒlədʒɪst] *n* Meteorologe *m*, Meteorologin *f*.

meteorology [ˌmiːtɪə'rɒlədʒɪ] *n* Meteorologie *f*.

meter¹ ['miːtəʳ] *n* Zähler *m*; *(parking ~)* Parkuhr *f*.

meter² *n (US)* = **metre**.

methane ['miːθeɪn] *n* Methan *nt*.

method ['meθəd] *n* Methode *f*; *(process)* Verfahren *nt*. **~ of payment** Zahlungsweise *f*.

methodology [ˌmeθə'dɒlədʒɪ] *n* Methodik *f*.

meths [meθs] *n sing* Spiritus *m*.

methylated spirits ['meθɪleɪtɪd'spɪrɪts] *n sing* (Brenn)spiritus *m*.

meticulous [mɪ'tɪkjʊləs] *adj* (peinlich) genau. **to be ~ about** sth es mit etw sehr genau nehmen.

metre, *(US)* **meter** ['miːtəʳ] *n* **(a)** *(Measure)* Meter *m or nt*. **(b)** *(Poet)* Metrum *nt*.

metric ['metrɪk] *adj* metrisch. **to go ~** auf das metrische Maßsystem umstellen.

metrication [ˌmetrɪ'keɪʃən] *n* Umstellung *f* auf das metrische Maßsystem.

metropolis [mɪ'trɒpəlɪs] *n* Metropole, Weltstadt *f*; *(capital)* Hauptstadt *f*.

metropolitan [ˌmetrə'pɒlɪtən] *adj* weltstädtisch; der Hauptstadt.

mettle ['metl] *n (spirit)* Stehvermögen *nt*; *(of horse)* Zähigkeit *f*; *(temperament)* Feuer *nt*. **to show one's ~** zeigen, was in einem steckt; **to be on one's ~** auf dem Posten sein.

mew [mjuː] **1** *n* Miau(en) *nt*. **2** *vi* miauen.

Mexican ['meksɪkən] **1** *adj* mexikanisch. **2** *n* Mexikaner(in *f*) *m*.

Mexico ['meksɪkəʊ] *n* Mexiko *nt*.

mezzo-soprano [ˌmetsəʊsə'prɑːnəʊ] *n* Mezzosopran *m*.

miaow [miː'aʊ] **1** *n* Miau(en) *nt*. **2** *vi* miauen.

mica ['maɪkə] *n* Muskovit *m*.

mice [maɪs] *pl of* **mouse**.

mickey ['mɪkɪ] *n (col)*: **to take the ~ (out of** sb**)** jdn auf den Arm *or* auf die Schippe nehmen *(col)*.

micro- ['maɪkrəʊ-] *pref* mikro-, Mikro-.

microbe ['maɪkrəʊb] *n* Mikrobe *f*.

micro: ~biology *n* Mikrobiologie *f*; **~chip** *n* Mikrochip *m*; **~-computer** *n* Mikrocomputer; **~cosm** *n* Mikrokosmos *m*; **~film** *n* Mikrofilm *m*; **~organism** *n* Mikroorganismus *m*; **~phone** *n* Mikrofon *nt*; **~processor** *n* Mikroprozessor *m*; **~scope** *n* Mikroskop *nt*; **~scopic** [ˌmaɪkrə'skɒpɪk] *adj* details, print mikroskopisch; **~scopic creature** mikroskopisch kleines Lebewesen; **~wave** *n* Mikrowelle *f*; **~wave oven** Mikrowellenherd *m*.

mid [mɪd] *adj* mittel-, Mittel-. **in ~ January** Mitte Januar; **in the ~ 1950s** Mitte der fünfziger Jahre; **he's in his mid 30s** er ist Mitte dreißig; **temperatures in the ~ eighties** Temperaturen um 85° Fahrenheit; **in ~ morning** am Vormittag; **in ~ ocean** mitten auf dem Meer; **in ~ air** in der Luft.

midday ['mɪd'deɪ] **1** *n* Mittag *m*. **at ~** mittags, um die Mittagszeit. **2** *adj attr* mittäglich. **~ meal** Mittagessen *nt*.

middle ['mɪdl] **1** *n* Mitte *f*; *(central section: of book, film etc)* mittlerer Teil; *(inside of fruit etc)* Innere(s) *nt*; *(waist)* Taille *f*. **in the ~ of the table** mitten auf dem Tisch; *(in exact centre)* in der Mitte des Tisches; **in the ~ of the night** mitten in der Nacht; **in the ~ of the day** gegen Mittag; **in the ~ of nowhere** am Ende der Welt; **in** *or* **about the ~ of May** Mitte Mai; **we were in the ~ of lunch** wir waren mitten beim Essen; **to be in the ~ of doing** sth mitten dabei sein, etw zu tun; **I'm in the ~ of reading it** ich bin mittendrin. **2** *adj* mittlere(r, s); *part, point, finger* Mittel-.

middle *in cpds* Mittel-, mittel-; **~ age** *n* mittleres Lebensalter; **~-aged** *adj* mittleren Alters; **M~ Ages** *npl* Mittelalter *nt*; **~-class** *adj* bürgerlich, spießig *(pej)*; *(Sociol)* mittelständisch; **~ class(es)** *n* Mittelstand *m or* -schicht *f*; **M~ East** *n* Naher Osten; **~man** *n* Mittelsmann *m*; *(Comm)* Zwischenhändler *m*; **~-of-the-road** *adj* gemäßigt; *policy, politician* der gemäßigten Mitte.

midge [mɪdʒ] *n* Mücke *f*.

midget ['mɪdʒɪt] *n* Liliputaner *m*.

mid: the **M~lands** *npl* die Midlands; **~night** *n* Mitternacht *f*; **at ~night** um Mitternacht.

midriff ['mɪdrɪf] *n* Taille *f*.

midst [mɪdst] *n* **in the ~ of** mitten in.

mid: ~stream *n* **in ~stream** *(lit)* in der Mitte des Flusses; *(fig)* auf halber Strecke; **~summer 1** *n* Hochsommer *m*; **M~summer's Day** Sommersonnenwende *f*; **2** *adj days, nights* Hochsommer-; **~term** *adj* **~-term elections** *(Pol)* Zwischenwahlen *pl*; **~way** *adv* auf halbem Weg; **~way through** sth mitten in etw *(dat)*; **~week** *adv* mitten in der Woche.

midwife ['mɪdwaɪf] *n, pl* **-wives** Hebamme *f*.

midwinter [ˌmɪd'wɪntəʳ] *n* tiefster *f* des Winters.

might¹ [maɪt] *pret of* **may**. **as you ~** expect wie zu erwarten war; **you ~ try Smith's** Sie könnten es ja mal bei Smith versuchen; **he ~ at least have apologized** er hätte sich wenigstens entschuldigen können.

might² *n* Macht *f*. **with all one's ~** mit aller Kraft.

mighty ['maɪtɪ] **1** *adj (+er)* gewaltig; *(wielding power)* mächtig; *warrior* stark. **2** *adv (col)* mächtig *(col)*.

migraine ['miːgreɪn] *n* Migräne *f*.

migrant ['maɪgrənt] **1** *adj* Wander-. **~ bird** Zugvogel *m*; **~ worker** Gastarbeiter *m*. **2** *n* Zugvogel *m*; Gastarbeiter *m*.

migrate [maɪ'greɪt] *vi (animals, workers)* (ab)wandern; *(birds)* nach Süden ziehen.

migration [maɪ'greɪʃən] *n* Wanderung *f*; *(of birds*

also) (Vogel)zug *m; (seasonal)* Zug *m.*

mike [maɪk] *n (col)* Mikrofon, Mikro *(col) nt.*

mild [maɪld] **1** *adj (+er)* mild; *breeze, criticism*
leicht; *character* sanft; *(slight)* leicht. **2** *n (Brit:
beer)* leichtes dunkles Bier.

mildew ['mɪldjuː] *n* Schimmel *m; (on plants)*
Mehltau *m.*

mildly ['maɪldlɪ] *adv* leicht; *say* sanft; *rebuke*
milde. **to put it** ~ gelinde gesagt.

mile [maɪl] *n* Meile *f.* **how many** ~**s per gallon does
your car do?** wieviel verbraucht Ihr Auto?**; a
fifty-**~ **journey** eine Fahrt von fünfzig Meilen;
~**s (and** ~**s)** *(col)* meilenweit; **they live** ~**s away**
sie wohnen meilenweit weg; **it sticks out a** ~ das
sieht ja ein Blinder (mit Krückstock) *(col);* **he's**
~**s better at tennis than she is** er spielt hundertmal besser Tennis als sie *(col).*

mileage ['maɪlɪdʒ] *n* Meilen *pl; (on odometer)*
Meilenstand *m.* **what** ~ **does your car do?** wieviel (Benzin) verbraucht Ihr Auto?**; we got a lot
of** ~ **out of it** *(fig col)* das war uns *(dat)* sehr
dienlich.

mileometer [maɪ'lɒmɪtəʳ] *n (Brit)* Tacho(meter) *m.*

milestone ['maɪlstəʊn] *n (lit, fig)* Meilenstein *m.*

milieu ['miːljɜː] *n* Milieu *nt.*

militant ['mɪlɪtənt] **1** *adj* militant. **2** *n* militantes
Mitglied/militanter Gewerkschaftler *etc.*

militarism ['mɪlɪtərɪzəm] *n* Militarismus *m.*

militaristic [ˌmɪlɪtə'rɪstɪk] *adj* militaristisch.

military ['mɪlɪtərɪ] **1** *adj* militärisch; *government,
band* Militär-. ~ **service** Wehrdienst *m.* **2** *n:* **the**
~ das Militär.

militate ['mɪlɪteɪt] *vi* **to** ~ **against sth** gegen etw
sprechen.

militia [mɪ'lɪʃə] *n* Miliz, Bürgerwehr *f.*

milk [mɪlk] *n* Milch *f.* ~ **of magnesia** Magnesia-
milch *f;* **it's no use crying over spilt** ~ *(prov)* was
passiert ist, ist passiert.

milk *in cpds* Milch-; ~ **chocolate** *n* Vollmilch-
schokolade *f;* ~ **churn** *n* Milchkanne *f;* ~ **float**
n Milchwagen *m.*

milking ['mɪlkɪŋ] *n* Melken *nt.* ~ **machine**
Melkmaschine *f.*

milk: ~**man** *n* Milchmann *m;* ~ **shake** *n* Milch-
shake *m;* ~ **tooth** *n* Milchzahn *m.*

milky ['mɪlkɪ] *adj (+er)* milchig. ~ **coffee** Milch-
kaffee *m.*

Milky Way [ˌmɪlkɪ'weɪ] *n* Milchstraße *f.*

mill [mɪl] **1** *n* Mühle *f; (paper, steel* ~ *etc)* Fabrik *f;
(cotton*~*) (for thread)* Spinnerei *f; (for cloth)*
Weberei *f.* **he really went through the** ~ *(col)* er
hat wirklich viel durchmachen müssen. **2** *vt
flour, coffee etc* mahlen; *metal, paper* walzen.

♦ **mill about** *or* **around** *vi* umherlaufen.

millennium [mɪ'lenɪəm] *n, pl* **-s** *or* **millennia**
[mɪ'lenɪə] *(1,000 years)* Jahrtausend *nt; (state of
perfection)* Tausendjähriges Reich *nt.*

miller ['mɪləʳ] *n* Müller *m.*

millet ['mɪlɪt] *n* Hirse *f.*

milli- ~**gram(me)** *n* Milligramm *nt;* ~**litre, *(US)***
~**liter** *n* Milliliter *m or nt.*

milliner ['mɪlɪnəʳ] *n* Hutmacher(in *f) m.*

million ['mɪljən] *n* Million *f.* **4** ~ **people** 4 Millionen
Menschen; **the starving** ~**s** die Millionen, die
Hunger leiden; **she's one in a** ~ *(col)* so jemanden wie sie findet man sobald nicht wieder;
to feel like a ~ **dollars** *(col)* sich pudelwohl
fühlen.

millionaire [ˌmɪljə'neəʳ] *n* Millionär *m.*

millionairess [ˌmɪljə'neəres] *n* Millionärin *f.*

millipede ['mɪlɪpiːd] *n* Tausendfüßler *m.*

mill: ~**pond** *n* Mühlteich *m;* ~**stone** *n* Mühlstein
m; **it's a** ~**stone around his neck** das ist für ihn
ein Klotz am Bein.

mime [maɪm] **1** *n (acting)* Pantomime *f; (actor)*
Pantomime *m; (ancient play, actor)* Mimus *m.* **2** *vt*
pantomimisch darstellen.

mimic ['mɪmɪk] **1** *n* Imitator *m.* **2** *vt* nachahmen;

(ridicule) nachäffen.

mimicry ['mɪmɪkrɪ] *n* Nachahmung *f.*

min = **minute(s)** min; **minimum** min.

mince [mɪns] **1** *n (Brit)* Hackfleisch, Gehackte(s)
nt. **2** *vt meat* durch den Fleischwolf drehen. **he
doesn't** ~ **his words** er nimmt kein Blatt vor den
Mund. **3** *vi (walk)* tänzeln, trippeln; *(speak)* sich
geziert ausdrücken.

mincemeat ['mɪnsmiːt] *n* süße Gebäckfüllung aus
Dörrobst und Sirup. **to make** ~**meat of sb** *(col)*
(physically) Hackfleisch aus jdm machen *(col);*
(verbally) jdn zur Schnecke machen *(col).*

mincer ['mɪnsəʳ] *n* Fleischwolf *m.*

mind [maɪnd] **1** *n* **(a)** *(intellect)* Geist *(also Philos,
person),* Verstand *m; (type of* ~ *also)* Kopf *m;
(thoughts)* Gedanken *pl; (memory)* Gedächtnis *nt.*
it's a question of ~ **over matter** es ist eine
Willensfrage; **it's all in the** ~ das ist alles
Einbildung; **one of the finest** ~**s of our times**
einer der großen Geister unserer Zeit; **to be
clear in one's** ~ **about sth** sich *(dat)* über etw im
klaren sein; **he had something on his** ~ ihn
beschäftigte etwas; **if you put your** ~ **to it** wenn
du dich anstrengst; **she couldn't get him out of
her** ~ er ging ihr nicht aus dem Kopf; **to take
sb's** ~ **off sth** jdn auf andere Gedanken bringen;
the idea never entered my ~ daran hatte ich
überhaupt nicht gedacht; **to bear** *or* **keep sth in**
~ etw nicht vergessen; *facts also, application* etw
im Auge behalten; **to bear** *or* **keep sb in** ~ an jdn
denken; **it went right out of my** ~ daran habe ich
überhaupt nicht mehr gedacht; **to bring** *or* **call
sth to** ~ etw in Erinnerung rufen.

(b) *(inclination)* Lust *f; (intention)* Absicht *f.* **to
have sb/sth in** ~ an jdn/etw denken; **to have it in**
~ **to do sth** beabsichtigen, etw zu tun; **I've half a**
~**/a good** ~ **to ...** ich hätte Lust/gute Lust, zu ...;
nothing was further from my ~ nichts lag mir
ferner; **his** ~ **is set on that** er hat sich *(dat)* das in
den Kopf gesetzt.

(c) *(opinion)* Meinung, Ansicht *f.* **to change
one's** ~ sich *(dat)* anders überlegen; **to be in
two** ~**s about sth** sich *(dat)* über etw *(acc)* nicht
im klaren sein; **to be of one** *or* **the same** ~
gleicher Meinung sein; **to my** ~ **he's wrong**
meiner Ansicht nach irrt er sich; **to have a** ~ **of
one's own** *(person: not conform)* seinen eigenen
Kopf haben; *(hum: machine etc)* seine Mucken
haben *(col).*

(d) *(sanity)* Verstand *m.* **to go out of** *or* **lose
one's** ~ den Verstand verlieren; **to be out of
one's** ~ nicht bei Verstand sein; *(with worry etc)*
vor Sorgen ganz krank sein.

2 *vt* **(a)** *(look after)* aufpassen auf *(+acc); sb's
chair, seat* freihalten. **I'm** ~**ing the shop** *(fig)* ich
sehe nach dem Rechten.

(b) *(be careful of)* aufpassen (auf *+acc); (pay
attention to)* achten auf *(+acc); (act in accordance
with)* beachten. ~ **the step!** Vorsicht Stufe!; ~
your own business kümmern Sie sich um Ihre
eigenen Angelegenheiten.

(c) *(care, worry about)* sich kümmern um;
(object to) etwas haben gegen. **she doesn't** ~ **it**
es macht ihr nichts aus; *(is not bothered)* es
stört sie nicht; *(is indifferent to)* es ist ihr egal;
would you ~ **opening the door?** wären Sie so
freundlich, die Tür aufzumachen?; **do you** ~ **my
smoking?** macht es Ihnen etwas aus, wenn ich
rauche?; **never** ~ **the expense** (es ist) egal, was
es kostet; **never** ~ **him** kümmere dich nicht um
ihn!; **I wouldn't** ~ **a cup of tea** ich hätte nichts
gegen eine Tasse Tee.

3 *vi* **(a)** *(be careful)* aufpassen. ~ **you get that
done** siehe zu, daß du das fertigbekommst!

(b) ~ **you** allerdings; ~ **you, he did try** er hat
es immerhin versucht.

(c) *(care, worry)* sich kümmern; *(object)* etwas
dagegen haben. **do you** ~? macht es Ihnen etwas

aus?; **do you ~!** *(iro)* ich möchte doch sehr
bitten!; **may I?** — **I don't ~** darf ich? — meinetwegen; **which one do you want?** — **I don't**
~ welches willst du? — das ist mir egal.
(d) **never ~** macht nichts!; *(in exasperation)*
ist ja auch egal!; **never ~, you'll find another**
mach dir nichts draus, du findest bestimmt
einen anderen; **never ~ about that now!** laß das
doch jetzt!
♦ **mind out** *vi* aufpassen *(for auf +acc)*.
mind: **~-blowing** *adj (col)* irre *(col)*; **~-boggling**
adj (col) irrsinnig *(col)*.
-minded *adj suf* **an industrially-~** nation ein auf
Industrie ausgerichtetes Land.
mindful ['maɪndfʊl] *adj* **to be ~ of** sth etw berücksichtigen.
mind: **~less** *adj (stupid)* ohne Verstand; *(sense-*
less) destruction, crime sinnlos; *occupation*
geistlos; **~ reader** *n* Gedankenleser(in *f*) *m*.
mine¹ [maɪn] *poss pron* meine(r, s). **this car is ~**
dieses Auto gehört mir; **is this ~?** gehört das
mir?; **his friends and ~** seine und meine
Freunde; **a friend of ~** ein Freund von mir; **a**
favourite expression of ~ einer meiner Lieb-
lingsausdrücke.
mine² 1 *n* (a) *(Min)* Bergwerk *nt; (copper ~ etc*
also) Mine *f; (coal~ also)* Zeche *f.* **to work down**
the ~s unter Tage arbeiten. (b) *(Mil, Naut etc)*
Mine *f.* **to lay ~s** Minen legen. (c) *(fig)* **the book**
is a ~ of information das Buch ist eine wahre
Fundgrube; **he is a ~ of information** er ist ein
wandelndes Lexikon *(col).* 2 *vt* (a) *coal, metal*
fördern, abbauen. (b) *(Mil, Naut)* verminen;
ship eine Mine befestigen an (+*dat*); *(blow up)*
(mit einer Mine) sprengen. 3 *vi* Bergbau
betreiben. **to ~ for** sth nach etw graben.
mine: **~-detector** *n* Minensuchgerät *nt;* **~field** *n*
Minenfeld *nt.*
miner ['maɪnə*'*] *n* Bergarbeiter, Bergmann *m.*
mineral ['mɪnərəl] 1 *n* Mineral *nt.* 2 *adj deposit,*
resources Mineral-. **~ water** Mineralwasser *nt.*
mine sweeper *n* Minensuchboot *nt.*
mingle ['mɪŋgl] *vi* sich vermischen; *(people,*
groups) sich untereinander vermischen. **to ~**
with the crowd sich unters Volk mischen.
mini- ['mɪnɪ-] *pref* Mini-.
miniature ['mɪnɪtʃə*'*] 1 *n* Miniaturausgabe *f; (Art)*
Miniatur *f.* 2 *adj attr* Miniatur-.
minibus ['mɪnɪ,bʌs] *n* Kleinbus *m.*
minimal ['mɪnɪml] *adj* minimal.
minimize ['mɪnɪmaɪz] *vt expenditure etc* auf ein
Minimum reduzieren.
minimum ['mɪnɪməm] 1 *n* Minimum *nt.* **with a ~ of**
inconvenience mit einem Minimum an Unannehmlichkeiten; **to reduce** sth **to a ~** etw auf ein
Mindestmaß reduzieren. 2 *adj attr* Mindest-. **~**
temperature Tiefsttemperatur *f;* **~ wage** Mindestlohn *m.*
mining ['maɪnɪŋ] *n* (a) *(Min)* Bergbau *m.* (b) *(Mil)*
(of area) Verminen *nt; (of ship)* Sprengung *f* (mit
einer Mine).
mining: **~ engineer** *n* Bergbauingenieur *m;* **~**
industry *n* Bergbau *m.*
miniskirt ['mɪnɪ,skɜ:t] *n* Minirock *m.*
minister ['mɪnɪstə*'*] *n* (a) *(Pol)* Minister *m.* (b)
(Eccl) Pastor *m,* protestantischer Geistlicher.
ministerial [,mɪnɪ'stɪərɪəl] *adj (Pol)* ministeriell,
Minister-.
ministry ['mɪnɪstrɪ] *n* (a) *(Pol)* Ministerium *nt.* **~**
of agriculture Landwirtschaftsministerium. (b)
(Eccl) geistliches Amt. **to join** *or* **go into the ~**
Geistlicher werden.
mink [mɪŋk] *n* Nerz *m.* **~ coat** Nerzmantel *m.*
minor ['maɪnə*'*] 1 *adj* (a) *(of lesser extent)* kleiner;
(of lesser importance) unbedeutend; *offence,*
operation leicht; *importance geringer; position,*
road Neben-. **a ~ role** eine Nebenrolle. (b) *(Mus)*
Moll-. **G ~** g-Moll *nt.* 2 *n* (a) *(Jur)* Minderjäh-

rige(r) *mf.* (b) *(US Univ)* Nebenfach *nt.*
minority [maɪ'nɒrɪtɪ] 1 *n* Minderheit *f.* **to be in a ~**
in der Minderheit sein. 2 *adj attr* Minderheits-. **~**
group Minderheit *f.*
minstrel ['mɪnstrəl] *n* Spielmann *m.*
mint¹ [mɪnt] 1 *n* Münzanstalt, Münze *f.* **to be worth**
a ~ steinreich sein. 2 *adj stamp* ungestempelt. **in**
~ condition in tadellosem Zustand. 3 *vt coin*
prägen.
mint² *n* *(Bot)* Minze *f; (sweet)* Pfefferminz *m.* **~**
sauce Minzsoße *f.*
minuet [,mɪnjʊ'et] *n* Menuett *nt.*
minus ['maɪnəs] 1 *prep* (a) minus, weniger. **£100 ~**
taxes £ 100 abzüglich (der) Steuern. (b) *(without,*
deprived of) ohne. 2 *adj quantity, value* negativ;
sign Minus-; *temperatures* unter Null. **~ three**
degrees drei Grad minus.
minute¹ ['mɪnɪt] *n* (a) *(of time, degree)* Minute *f.* **in a**
~ sofort; **this (very) ~!** auf der Stelle!; **I shan't**
be a ~, it won't take a **~** es dauert nicht lang; **any**
~ jeden Augenblick; **tell me the ~ he comes** sag
mir sofort Bescheid, wenn er kommt; **have you**
got a ~? hast du mal einen Augenblick Zeit?; **at**
the last ~ in letzter Minute. (b) *(official note)*
Notiz *f.* **~s** Protokoll *nt;* **to take the ~s** das
Protokoll führen.
minute² [maɪ'nju:t] *adj (small)* winzig; *(detailed,*
exact) minuziös; *detail* kleinste(r, s).
minute hand *n* Minutenzeiger *m.*
minutely [maɪ'nju:tlɪ] *adv (by a small amount)* ganz
geringfügig; *(in detail)* genauestens.
miracle ['mɪrəkəl] *n* Wunder *nt.* **to work** *or*
perform ~s *(lit)* Wunder vollbringen; **I can't**
work ~s ich kann doch nicht hexen!; **it's a ~ he**
... es ist ein Wunder, daß er ....
miraculous [mɪ'rækjʊləs] *adj* wunderbar; *powers*
Wunder-.
mirage ['mɪrɑːʒ] *n* Fata Morgana *f; (fig)*
Trugbild *nt.*
mirror ['mɪrə*'*] 1 *n* Spiegel *m.* **~ image** *(lit, fig)*
Spiegelbild *nt.* 2 *vt* widerspiegeln.
mirth [mɜːθ] *n* Frohsinn *m; (laughter)* Heiterkeit *f.*
misadventure [,mɪsəd'ventʃə*'*] *n* Mißgeschick *nt.*
death by ~ Tod *m* durch Unfall.
misanthropist [mɪ'zænθrəpɪst] *n* Misanthrop,
Menschenfeind *m.*
misapprehension ['mɪs,æprɪ'henʃən] *n* Mißverständnis *nt.* **I think you are under a ~** ich glaube,
bei Ihnen liegt (da) ein Mißverständnis vor; **he**
was under the ~ that ... er hatte irrtümlicherweise angenommen, daß ...
misappropriate [,mɪsə'prəʊprɪeɪt] *vt* entwenden;
money veruntreuen.
misappropriation ['mɪsə,prəʊprɪ'eɪʃən] *n see vt*
Entwendung *f;* Veruntreuung *f.*
misbehave [,mɪsbɪ'heɪv] *vi* sich schlecht benehmen; *(child also)* ungezogen sein.
misbehaviour, *(US)* **misbehavior** [,mɪs-
bɪ'heɪvjə*'*] *n* schlechtes Benehmen.
miscalculate [,mɪs'kælkjʊleɪt] 1 *vt* falsch berechnen; *(misjudge)* falsch einschätzen. 2 *vi* sich
verrechnen; *(estimate wrongly)* sich verkalkulieren.
miscalculation [,mɪs,kælkjʊ'leɪʃən] *n* Rechen-
fehler *m; (wrong estimation)* Fehlkalkulation *f;*
(misjudgement) Fehleinschätzung *f.*
miscarriage ['mɪs,kærɪdʒ] *n* (a) *(Med)* Fehlgeburt *f.* (b) **~ of justice** Justizirrtum *m.*
miscarry [,mɪs'kærɪ] *vi* (a) *(Med)* eine Fehlgeburt
haben. (b) *(fail: plans)* fehlschlagen.
miscellaneous [,mɪsɪ'leɪnɪəs] *adj* verschieden;
poems verschiedenerlei; *collection, crowd* bunt.
"~" „Verschiedenes".
miscellany [mɪ'selənɪ] *n* *(collection)* (bunte)
Sammlung *f; (variety)* Vielfalt *f.*
mischance [,mɪs'tʃɑːns] *n* **by some ~** durch einen
unglücklichen Zufall.
mischief [,mɪstʃɪf] *n* *(roguery)* Verschmitztheit *f;*

(naughty behaviour) Unfug *m.* he's always getting into ~ er stellt dauernd etwas an; **to keep out of** ~ keine Dummheiten machen; **to make** ~ Unfrieden stiften; **to do sb a** ~ jdm etwas (an)tun.

mischievous ['mɪstʃɪvəs] *adj expression, smile* verschmitzt; *rumour* bösartig; *person* boshaft.

misconception ['mɪskən'sepʃən] *n* fälschliche Annahme; *(no pl: misunderstanding)* Verkennung *f.* **to be under a** ~ **about sth** sich *(dat)* falsche Vorstellungen von etw machen.

misconduct [,mɪs'kɒndʌkt] *n (improper behaviour)* schlechtes Benehmen; *(professional)* Berufsvergehen *nt; (sexual)* Fehltritt *m.*

misconstrue ['mɪskən'struː] *vt* mißverstehen.

misdemeanour, *(US)* **misdemeanor** [,mɪsdɪ'miːnəʳ] *n* schlechtes Benehmen; *(Jur)* Vergehen *nt.*

miser ['maɪzəʳ] *n* Geizhals, Geizkragen *m.*

miserable ['mɪzərəbl] *adj* **(a)** *(unhappy)* unglücklich. **I feel** ~ **today** ich fühle mich heute elend *or* miserabel. **(b)** *headache, weather* fürchterlich; *existence, spectacle* erbärmlich, elend. **(c)** *(contemptible)* miserabel, jämmerlich; *person* gemein, erbärmlich; *failure* kläglich. **a** ~ **£3** miese £ 3 *(col).*

miserably ['mɪzərəblɪ] *adv* **(a)** *(unhappily)* unglücklich. **(b)** *(wretchedly) live, die* jämmerlich; *poor* erbärmlich. **(c)** *(contemptibly) pay* miserabel; *fail* kläglich; *treat, behave* gemein.

miserly ['maɪzəlɪ] *adj* geizig.

misery ['mɪzərɪ] *n (sadness)* Kummer *m,* Trauer *f; (suffering)* Qualen *pl; (wretchedness)* Elend *nt.* **to put an animal out of its** ~ ein Tier von seinen Qualen erlösen; **to put sb out of his** ~ *(fig)* jdn nicht länger auf die Folter spannen.

misfire ['mɪs'faɪəʳ] *vi (engine, rocket)* fehlzünden; *(plan)* fehlschlagen; *(trick)* danebengehen.

misfit ['mɪsfɪt] *n (person)* Außenseiter(in *f) m.*

misfortune ['mɪsfɔːtʃuːn] *n (ill fortune, affliction)* (schweres) Schicksal *or* Los *nt; (bad luck)* Pech *nt no pl; (unlucky incident)* Mißgeschick *nt.* **I had the** ~ **to** ... ich hatte das Pech, zu ....

misgiving [mɪs'gɪvɪŋ] *n* Bedenken *pl.* **I had (certain)** ~**s** about lending him the money mir war bei dem Gedanken, ihm das Geld zu leihen, nicht ganz wohl.

misguided [mɪs'gaɪdɪd] *adj* töricht; *decision also, opinions* irrig; *(misplaced) kindness, enthusiasm* unangebracht.

mishandle [mɪs'hændl] *vt case* falsch handhaben.

mishap ['mɪshæp] *n* Mißgeschick *nt.* he's had a slight ~ ihm ist ein kleines Mißgeschick passiert; **without** ~ ohne Zwischenfälle.

mishear ['mɪs'hɪəʳ] *pret, ptp* **misheard** ['mɪs'hɜːd] **1** *vt* falsch hören. **2** *vi* sich verhören.

mishmash ['mɪʃmæʃ] *n* Mischmasch *m.*

misinform ['mɪsɪn'fɔːm] *vt* falsch informieren. **you've been** ~ed man hat Sie falsch informiert.

misinterpret ['mɪsɪn'tɜːprɪt] *vt* falsch auslegen; *novel* fehlinterpretieren. he ~ed her silence as agreement er deutete ihr Schweigen fälschlich als Zustimmung.

misjudge ['mɪs'dʒʌdʒ] *vt* falsch einschätzen, sich verschätzen in *(+dat); person also* falsch beurteilen.

mislay [mɪs'leɪ] *pret, ptp* **mislaid** [mɪs'leɪd] *vt* verlegen.

mislead [,mɪs'liːd] *pret, ptp* **misled** *vt (give wrong idea)* irreführen. **your description misled me into thinking that** ... aufgrund Ihrer Beschreibung nahm ich (irrtümlich) an, daß...

misleading [,mɪs'liːdɪŋ] *adj* irreführend. **the** ~ **simplicity of his style** die täuschende Einfachheit seines Stils.

misled [,mɪs'led] *pret, ptp of* **mislead.**

mismanage ['mɪs'mænɪdʒ] *vt company, finances* schlecht verwalten; *affair* schlecht handhaben.

misnomer ['mɪs'nəʊməʳ] *n* unzutreffende Bezeichnung.

misogynist [mɪ'sɒdʒɪnɪst] *n* Frauenfeind *m.*

misplace ['mɪs'pleɪs] *vt* **(a)** *file etc* falsch einordnen; *(mislay)* verlegen. **(b) to be** ~**d** *(confidence etc)* unangebracht sein.

misprint ['mɪsprɪnt] *n* Druckfehler *m.*

mispronounce ['mɪsprə'naʊns] *vt* falsch aussprechen.

misquote ['mɪs'kwəʊt] *vt* falsch zitieren.

misread ['mɪs'riːd] *pret, ptp* **misread** ['mɪs'red] *vt* falsch lesen; *(misinterpret)* falsch verstehen.

misrepresent ['mɪs,reprɪ'zent] *vt* falsch darstellen; *ideas* verfälschen.

miss[1] [mɪs] **1** *n (shot)* Fehltreffer *m.* it was a near ~ das war sehr knapp; *(shot)* das war knapp daneben; **to give sth a** ~ *(col)* sich *(dat)* etw schenken.

2 *vt* **(a)** *(fail to hit, catch, find etc)* verpassen; *(not hit, find)* target, ball, vocation, place verfehlen; *(not hear etc)* nicht mitbekommen. **to** ~ **breakfast** nicht frühstücken; *(be too late for)* das Frühstück verpassen; **you haven't** ~ed much! da hast du nicht viel verpaßt!; **they** ~ed each other in the crowd sie verfehlten sich in der Menge; **to** ~ **the boat** *or* **bus** *(fig)* den Anschluß verpassen; **I wouldn't have** ~ed it for anything das hätte ich mir nicht entgehen lassen wollen. **(b)** *(avoid) obstacle* (noch) ausweichen können *(+dat); (escape)* entgehen *(+dat); (leave out)* auslassen; *(overlook)* übersehen. **my heart** ~ed a beat mir stockte das Herz. **(c)** *(notice or regret absence of)* vermissen. **I** ~ **my old car** mein altes Auto fehlt mir.

3 *vi* nicht treffen; *(shooting also)* danebenschießen; *(not catch)* nicht fangen; *(ball also)* danebengehen.

♦ **miss out 1** *vt sep* auslassen, weglassen. **2** *vi (col)* zu kurz kommen. **to** ~ ~ **on sth** etw verpassen; *(get less)* bei etw zu kurz kommen.

miss[2] *n* Fräulein *nt.* **M**~ **Germany 1980** (die) Miß Germany von 1980.

missal ['mɪsəl] *n* Meßbuch *nt.*

missile ['mɪsaɪl] *n* **(a)** *(stone etc)* (Wurf)geschoß *nt.* **(b)** *(rocket)* Rakete *f.* ~ **base** *or* **site** Raketenbasis *f;* ~ **launcher** Startrampe *f; (vehicle)* Raketenwerfer *m.*

missing ['mɪsɪŋ] *adj (not able to be found) person, boat* vermißt; *object* verschwunden; *(not there)* fehlend. **to be** ~ **to have gone** ~ fehlen; *(mountaineer, boat etc)* vermißt werden; **the coat has two buttons** ~ an dem Mantel fehlen zwei Knöpfe; ~ **person** Vermißte(r) *mf;* ~ **link** fehlendes Glied; *(Biol)* Zwischenform *f.*

mission ['mɪʃən] *n (task)* Auftrag *m; (calling)* Berufung *f; (Mil)* Befehl *m; (operation)* Einsatz *m; (journey)* Mission *f.* he's on a secret ~ er ist in geheimer Mission unterwegs; **Kissinger's** ~ **to the Middle East** Kissingers Nahostmission.

missionary ['mɪʃənrɪ] *n* Missionar(in *f) m.*

misspell ['mɪs'spel] *pret, ptp* ~ed *or* **misspelt** *vt* falsch schreiben.

misspent [,mɪs'spent] *adj* vergeudet.

mist [mɪst] *n* Nebel *m; (haze)* Dunst *m; (on glass etc)* Beschlag *m.* **through a** ~ **of tears** durch einen Tränenschleier; **it is lost in the** ~**s of time** das liegt im Dunkel der Vergangenheit.

♦ **mist over** *vi (become cloudy)* sich trüben; *(glass, mirror: also* **mist up** *)* (sich) beschlagen.

mistake [mɪ'steɪk] **1** *n* Fehler *m.* **to make a** ~ *(in calculating etc)* einen Fehler machen; *(be mistaken)* sich irren; **to** ~ *make the* ~ **of asking too much** den Fehler machen, zuviel zu verlangen; **by** ~ aus Versehen, versehentlich; **there must be some** ~ da muß ein Irrtum vorliegen; **there's no** ~ **about it,** ... (es besteht) kein Zweifel, ...; **make no** ~, **I mean what I say** damit wir uns nicht falsch verstehen: mir ist es Ernst; **it's**

freezing and no ~! *(col)* (ich kann dir sagen,) das ist vielleicht eine Kälte! *(col)*.

2 *vt pret* **mistook,** *ptp* **mistaken** *remarks etc* falsch verstehen; *house, time* sich irren *or* vertun *(col)* in *(+dat)*. **to** ~ **sb's meaning** jdn falsch verstehen; **there's no mistaking the urgency of the situation** die Dringlichkeit der Situation steht außer Frage; **to** ~ **A for B** A mit B verwechseln; **to be** ~ **n** sich irren; **if I am not (very much)** ~ **n …** wenn ich mich nicht (sehr) irre …

mistaken [mɪ'steɪkən] *adj (wrong) idea* falsch; *(misplaced)* loyalty, kindness unangebracht. **a case of** ~ **identity** eine Verwechslung.

mistletoe ['mɪsltəʊ] *n* Mistel *f;* *(sprig)* Mistelzweig *m.*

mistook [mɪ'stʊk] *pret of* **mistake.**

mistranslation ['mɪstrænz'leɪʃən] *n* falsche Übersetzung.

mistreat [mɪs'triːt] *vt* schlecht behandeln; *(violently)* mißhandeln.

mistress ['mɪstrɪs] *n* **(a)** *(of house, dog)* Herrin *f.* **(b)** *(lover)* Geliebte. **(c)** *(Brit: teacher)* Lehrerin *f.*

mistrust ['mɪs'trʌst] **1** *n* Mißtrauen *nt (of* gegenüber*).* **2** *vt* mißtrauen *(+dat).*

mistrustful [,mɪs'trʌstfʊl] *adj* mißtrauisch *(of sb/ sth* jdm/einer Sache gegenüber*).*

misty ['mɪstɪ] *adj (+er) day* neblig; *(hazy)* dunstig; *glasses (misted up)* beschlagen.

misunderstand ['mɪsʌndə'stænd] *pret, ptp* **misunderstood** *vt* falsch verstehen, mißverstehen.

misunderstanding ['mɪsʌndə'stændɪŋ] *n* Mißverständnis *nt;* *(disagreement)* Meinungsverschiedenheit *f.*

misunderstood ['mɪsʌndə'stʊd] **1** *ptp of* **misunderstand.** **2** *adj* unverstanden; *artist* verkannt.

misuse ['mɪs'juːs] **1** *n* Mißbrauch *m.* **2** ['mɪs'juːz] *vt* mißbrauchen.

mite [maɪt] *n* **(a)** *(small amount)* bißchen *nt.* **(b)** *(child)* **poor little** ~! armes Wurm! *(col).*

mitigate ['mɪtɪgeɪt] *vt* *punishment* mildern. **mitigating circumstances** mildernde Umstände *pl.*

mitigation [,mɪtɪ'geɪʃən] *n* Milderung *f.*

mitre, *(US)* **miter** ['maɪtə'] *n* **(a)** *(Eccl)* Mitra *f.* **(b)** *(Tech: also* ~*-joint)* Gehrung *f.*

mitt [mɪt] *n* **(a)** = **mitten.** **(b)** *(baseball glove)* Baseballhandschuh *m.*

mitten ['mɪtn] *n* Fausthandschuh *m;* *(with bare fingers)* Handschuh *m* mit halben Fingern.

mix [mɪks] **1** *n* Mischung *f.* **a good social** ~ ein bunt gemischtes Publikum; **cake** ~ Backmischung *f.* **2** *vt* (ver)mischen; *drinks* mixen; *(Cook)* ingredients verrühren. **you shouldn't** ~ **business with pleasure** Dienst ist Dienst und Schnaps ist Schnaps *(prov).* **3** *vi* **(a)** sich mischen lassen; *(chemical substances, races)* sich vermischen. **(b)** *(go together)* zusammenpassen. **(c)** *(people) (get on)* miteinander auskommen; *(associate)* miteinander verkehren. **to** ~ **with sb** mit jdm auskommen; mit jdm verkehren; **to** ~ **well** kontaktfreudig sein.

♦ **mix in** *vt sep egg, water* unterrühren.

♦ **mix up** *vt sep* **(a)** vermischen; *ingredients* verrühren; *medicine* mischen. **(b)** *(get in a muddle)* durcheinanderbringen; *(confuse with sb/ sth else)* verwechseln. **(c)** *(involve)* **to** ~ **sb** ~ **in sth** jdn in etw *(acc)* hineinziehen; **to be** ~ **ed** ~ **in sth** in etw *(acc)* verwickelt sein.

mixed [mɪkst] *adj* gemischt; *(both good and bad)* unterschiedlich. **I have** ~ **feelings about it** ich betrachte die Sache mit gemischten Gefühlen.

mixed: ~ **blessing** *n* it's a ~ **blessing** das ist ein zweischneidiges Schwert; ~ **doubles** *npl (Sport)* gemischtes Doppel; ~ **grill** *n* Grillteller *m;* ~ **metaphor** *n* gemischte Metapher *f;* ~**-up** *adj* durcheinander *pred; (muddled)* person also, ideas

konfus; **she's just a crazy** ~**-up kid** sie ist einfach total verdreht.

mixer ['mɪksə'] *n (a)* *(food* ~*)* Mixgerät *nt; (cement* ~*)* Mischmaschine *f.* **(b)** *(sociable person)* **to be a good** ~ kontaktfreudig sein.

mixture ['mɪkstʃə'] *n* Mischung *f; (Cook)* Gemisch *nt; (cake* ~*, dough)* Teig *m.*

mix-up ['mɪksʌp] *n* Durcheinander *nt.* **there must have been a** ~ da muß irgend etwas schiefgelaufen sein *(col).*

moan [məʊn] **1** *n (groan)* Stöhnen *nt; (grumble)* Gejammer *nt no pl (col).* **2** *vi (groan)* stöhnen; *(grumble)* jammern, schimpfen *(about* über +*acc*).

moat [məʊt] *n* Wassergraben *m; (of castle also)* Burggraben *m.*

mob [mɒb] **1** *n* *(crowd)* Horde *f; (riotous, violent)* Mob *m no pl.* **the** ~ *(pej: the masses)* die Masse(n *pl).* **2** *vt* herfallen über *(+acc).*

mobile ['məʊbaɪl] *adj* person beweglich; *(having means of transport)* beweglich, motorisiert; *(Sociol)* mobil; *X-ray unit etc* fahrbar. ~ **home** Wohnwagen *m;* ~ **library** Fahrbücherei *f.*

mobility [məʊ'bɪlɪtɪ] *n (of person)* Beweglichkeit *f; (of work force, Sociol)* Mobilität *f.*

moccasin ['mɒkəsɪn] *n* Mokassin *m.*

mock [mɒk] **1** *adj attr* emotions gespielt; *battle* Schein-; *examination* Probe-; *Tudor* Pseudo-. **2** *vt (ridicule)* sich lustig machen über *(+acc); (mimic)* nachäffen; *(defy)* trotzen *(+dat).* **3** *vi* **to** ~ **at sb/sth** sich über jdn/etw lustig machen.

mockery ['mɒkərɪ] *n (derision)* Spott *m; (object of ridicule)* Gespött *nt.* **they made a** ~ **of him** sie machten ihn zum Gespött; **to make a** ~ **of sth** etw lächerlich machen; **it was a** ~ **of a trial** der Prozeß war eine einzige Farce.

mocking ['mɒkɪŋ] *adj* spöttisch.

mockingbird ['mɒkɪŋ,bɜːd] *n* Spottdrossel *f.*

mock: ~ **turtle soup** *n* Mockturtlesuppe *f;* ~**-up** *n* Modell *nt* in Originalgröße.

mod cons ['mɒd'kɒnz] = **modern conveniences** Komfort *m.*

mode [məʊd] *n (a) (way)* Art (und Weise) *f; (form)* Form *f.* ~ **of transport** Transportmittel *nt.* **(b)** *(Fashion)* Mode *f.*

model ['mɒdl] **1** *n* Modell *nt; (perfect example)* Muster *nt (of an* +*dat); (fashion* ~*)* Mannequin *nt; (male* ~*)* Dressman *m.* **to make sth on the** ~ **of sth** etw *(acc)* einer Sache *(dat)* nachbilden; **to hold sb up as a** ~ jdn als Vorbild hinstellen. **2** *adj railway* Modell-; *home* Muster-; *(perfect)* vorbildlich, Muster-. **3** *vt (a)* **X is** ~**led on Y** Y dient als Vorlage or Muster für X; **the system was** ~**led on the American one** das System war nach amerikanischem Muster aufgebaut; **to** ~ **oneself on sb** sich *(dat)* jdn zum Vorbild nehmen. **(b)** *(make a* ~*)* modellieren, formen. **(c)** *dress etc* vorführen. **4** *vi (a) (make a* ~*s)* modellieren. **(b)** *(Art, Phot)* als Modell arbeiten; *(fashion)* als Mannequin/Dressman arbeiten. **to** ~ **for sb** jdm Modell stehen/jds Kreationen vorführen.

modem ['məʊdem] *n* Modem *m.*

moderate ['mɒdərɪt] **1** *adj* gemäßigt *(also Pol); appetite, speed* mäßig; *price* vernünftig; *eater* maßvoll; *number, income, success* bescheiden; *punishment, winter* mild. **a** ~ **amount** reingermaßen viel; ~**-sized** mittelgroß. **2** *n (Pol)* Gemäßigte(r) *mf.* **3** ['mɒdəreɪt] *vt* mäßigen. **to have a moderating influence on sb** mäßigend auf jdn wirken. **4** ['mɒdəreɪt] *vi* nachlassen.

moderately ['mɒdərɪtlɪ] *adv* einigermaßen. **a** ~ **expensive suit** ein nicht allzu teurer Anzug; **the house was** ~ **large** das Haus war mäßig groß.

moderation ['mɒdə'reɪʃən] *n* Mäßigung *f.* **in** ~ mit Maß(en).

modern ['mɒdən] *adj* modern *(also Art, Liter); times, world also* heutig; *history* neuere. ~ **languages** neuere Sprachen *pl;* **M**~ **Greek** *etc*

Neugriechisch *etc nt.*

modernity [mɒ'dɜ:nɪtɪ] *n* Modernität *f.*

modernization [ˌmɒdənaɪ'zeɪʃən] *n* Modernisierung *f.*

modernize ['mɒdənaɪz] *vt* modernisieren.

modest ['mɒdɪst] *adj* bescheiden; *requirements* gering; *price* mäßig. **to be ~ about one's successes** nicht mit seinen Erfolgen prahlen.

modesty ['mɒdɪstɪ] *n* Bescheidenheit *f.* **in all ~** bei aller Bescheidenheit.

modicum ['mɒdɪkəm] *n* ein wenig *or* bißchen. **a ~ of truth** ein Körnchen Wahrheit.

modification [ˌmɒdɪfɪ'keɪʃən] *n* (Ver)änderung *f;* *(of design)* Abänderung *f; (of contract, wording)* Modifizierung *f.* **to make ~s to sth** (Ver)änderungen an etw *(dat)* vornehmen; etw abändern; etw modifizieren.

modify ['mɒdɪfaɪ] *vt* **(a)** *(change)* (ver)ändern; *design* abändern; *contract, wording* modifizieren. **(b)** *(moderate)* mäßigen. **(c)** *(Gram)* näher bestimmen.

modular ['mɒdjʊləʳ] *adj* **the ~ design of the furniture** die aus Bauelementen bestehenden Möbel.

modulation [ˌmɒdjʊ'leɪʃən] *n (Mus, Rad)* Modulation *f.*

module ['mɒdjuːl] *n* (Bau)element *nt; (Space)* Raumkapsel *f.*

mohair ['məʊhɛəʳ] *n* Mohair *m.*

Mohammedan [məʊ'hæmɪdən] **1** *adj* mohammedanisch. **2** *n* Mohammedaner(in *f*) *m.*

moist [mɔɪst] *adj (+er)* feucht *(from, with* vor *+dat).*

moisten ['mɔɪsn] *vt* anfeuchten. **to ~ sth with sth** etw mit etw befeuchten.

moisture ['mɔɪstʃəʳ] *n* Feuchtigkeit *f.*

moisturizer ['mɔɪstʃəraɪzəʳ], **moisturizing cream** ['mɔɪstʃəraɪzɪŋ'kriːm] *n* Feuchtigkeitscreme *f.*

molar (tooth) ['məʊləʳ(ˌtuːθ)] *n* Backenzahn *m.*

molasses [məʊ'læsɪz] *n* Melasse *f.*

mold *etc (US)* = **mould** *etc.*

mole¹ [məʊl] *n (Anat)* Leberfleck *m.*

mole² *n (Zool)* Maulwurf *m; (col: secret agent)* Agent *m.*

molecule ['mɒlɪkjuːl] *n* Molekül *nt.*

molest [məʊ'lest] *vt* belästigen.

mollusc ['mɒləsk] *n* Weichtier *nt.*

mollycoddle ['mɒlɪˌkɒdl] *vt* verhätscheln.

molten ['məʊltən] *adj* geschmolzen; *glass, lava* flüssig.

moment ['məʊmənt] *n* **(a)** Augenblick, Moment *m.* **at any ~** jeden Augenblick; **at the ~** im Augenblick, momentan; **not at the ~** im Augenblick *or* zur Zeit nicht; **at the last ~** im letzten Augenblick; **at this (particular) ~** in time momentan; **for the ~** im Augenblick; **for a ~** (für) einen Moment; **not for a** *or* **one ~** ... nie(mals)...; **I didn't hesitate for a ~** ich habe keinen Augenblick gezögert; **in a ~** gleich; **half a ~/one ~!** einen Moment!; **just a ~!**, **wait a ~!** Moment mal!; **I shan't be a ~** ich bin gleich wieder da; *(nearly ready)* ich bin gleich soweit; **I have just this ~ heard of it** ich habe es eben *or* gerade erst erfahren; **not a ~ too soon** keine Minute zu früh; **the ~ it happened** (in dem Augenblick,) als es passierte; **tell me the ~ he comes** sagen Sie mir sofort Bescheid, wenn er kommt; **the man of the ~** der Mann des Tages.

(b) *(Phys)* Moment *nt.*

(c) *(importance)* Bedeutung *f.*

momentarily ['məʊməntərɪlɪ] *adv* **(a)** *(für)* einen Augenblick. **(b)** *(US) (very soon)* jeden Augenblick; *(from moment to moment)* zusehends.

momentary ['məʊməntərɪ] *adj* kurz. **there was a ~ silence** einen Augenblick lang herrschte Stille.

momentous ['məʊ'mentəs] *adj (memorable, important)* bedeutsam; *(of great consequence)* von großer Tragweite.

momentum [məʊ'mentəm] *n (of moving object)* Schwung *m; (at moment of impact)* Wucht *f; (Phys)* Impuls *m; (fig)* Schwung *m.* **to gather** *or* **gain ~** *(lit)* sich beschleunigen, in Fahrt kommen *(col); (fig: idea, movement, plan)* in Gang kommen.

monarch ['mɒnək] *n* Monarch(in *f*) *m.*

monarchist ['mɒnəkɪst] **1** *adj* monarchistisch. **2** *n* Monarchist(in *f*) *m.*

monarchy ['mɒnəkɪ] *n* Monarchie *f.*

monastery ['mɒnəstərɪ] *n* (Mönchs)kloster *nt.*

monastic [mə'næstɪk] *adj* mönchisch, klösterlich; *life* Ordens-.

Monday ['mʌndɪ] *n* Montag *m; see* **Tuesday.**

monetarism ['mʌnɪtərɪzəm] *n* Monetarismus *m.*

monetarist ['mʌnɪtərɪst] **1** *adj* monetaristisch. **2** *n* Monetarist(in *f*) *m.*

monetary ['mʌnɪtərɪ] *adj* **(a)** währungspolitisch; *policy, system* Währungs-; *reserves* Geld-. **(b)** *(pecuniary)* Geld-; *considerations* geldlich.

money ['mʌnɪ] *n* Geld *nt.* **to make ~** *(person)* (viel) Geld verdienen; *(business)* etwas einbringen; **to lose ~** *(person)* Geld verlieren; *(business)* Verluste machen; **there's ~ in it** das ist sehr lukrativ; **that's the one for my ~** ich tippe auf ihn/sie etc; **it's ~ for jam** *(col) or* **old rope** *(col)* da wird einem das Geld ja nachgeworfen *(col);* **to be in the ~** *(col)* Geld wie Heu haben; **to earn good ~** gut verdienen; **to get one's ~'s worth** etwas für sein Geld bekommen; **do you think I'm made of ~?** *(col)* ich bin doch kein Krösus!; **that's throwing good ~ after bad** das ist rausgeschmissenes Geld *(col);* **~ talks** *(col)* mit Geld geht alles; **~ isn't everything** *(prov)* Geld allein macht nicht glücklich *(prov).*

moneybox ['mʌnɪˌbɒks] *n* Sparbüchse *f.*

moneyed ['mʌnɪd] *adj* begütert.

money: ~grubbing *adj* geldgierig; **~lender** *n* Geld(ver)leiher *m;* **~maker** *n (idea)* einträgliche Sache; *(product)* Verkaufserfolg *m;* **~making** *adj idea, plan* einträglich; **~ market** *n* Geldmarkt *m;* **~ order** *n* Zahlungsanweisung *f;* **~spinner** *n (col)* Verkaufsschlager *m (col).*

mongol ['mɒŋgəl] *(Med)* **he's a ~** er ist mongoloid.

mongoose ['mɒŋguːs] *n, pl* **-s** Mungo *m.*

mongrel ['mʌŋgrəl] *n (also* **~ dog)** Promenadenmischung *f; (pej)* Köter *m.*

monitor ['mɒnɪtəʳ] **1** *n* **(a)** *(Sch)* Schüler(in *f*) *m* mit besonderen Pflichten. **book** ~ Bücherwart *m.* **(b)** *(TV, Tech: screen)* Monitor *m; (control, observer)* Überwacher *m; (Rad)* Mitarbeiter(in *f*) *m* am Monitor-Dienst. **2** *vt foreign station* abhören; *product, progress* überwachen.

monk [mʌŋk] *n* Mönch *m.*

monkey ['mʌŋkɪ] *n* Affe *m; (fig: child)* Schlingel *m.*

monkey: ~ business *n (col)* **no ~ business!** mach(t) mir keine Sachen! *(col);* **there's some ~ business going on here** da ist doch irgend etwas faul *(col);* **~-nut** *n* Erdnuß *f;* **~-tricks** *npl* Unfug *m;* **~-wrench** *n* verstellbarer Schraubenschlüssel, Engländer *m.*

mono- ['mɒnəʊ] *pref* Mono-, mono-.

monochrome ['mɒnəkrəʊm] *adj* monochrom; *television* Schwarzweiß-.

monocle ['mɒnəkl] *n* Monokel *nt.*

monogram ['mɒnəgræm] *n* Monogramm *nt.*

monolith ['mɒnəlɪθ] *n* Monolith *m.*

monologue ['mɒnəlɒg] *n* Monolog *m.*

monoplane ['mɒnəʊpleɪn] *n* Eindecker *m.*

monopolize [mə'nɒpəlaɪz] *vt (lit) market* beherrschen; *(fig) place, sb's time etc* in Beschlag nehmen; *conversation* an sich *(acc)* reißen.

monopoly [mə'nɒpəlɪ] *n (lit)* Monopol *nt.* **to have a ~ on sth** *(fig)* etw für sich gepachtet haben *(col).*

mono: ~rail *n* Einschienenbahn *f;* **~syllabic** *adj (lit, fig)* einsilbig; **~syllable** *n* einsilbiges Wort; **to speak/answer in ~syllables** einsilbig sein/ einsilbige Antworten geben.

monotone ['mɒnətəʊn] n monotoner Klang; (voice) monotone Stimme.

monotonous [mə'nɒtənəs] adj (lit, fig) eintönig, monoton.

monotony [mə'nɒtənɪ] n (lit, fig) Eintönigkeit, Monotonie f.

monoxide [mɒ'nɒksaɪd] n Monoxyd nt.

monsoon [mɒn'suːn] n Monsun m.

monster ['mɒnstəʳ] **1** n (big animal, thing) Ungetüm, Monstrum nt; (animal, person also) Ungeheuer nt; (cruel person) Unmensch m. **2** attr (enormous) Riesen-.

monstrosity [mɒn'strɒsɪtɪ] n (quality) Ungeheuerlichkeit f; (thing) Monstrum nt.

monstrous ['mɒnstrəs] adj (huge) ungeheuer (groß); (shocking, horrible) abscheulich; suggestion ungeheuerlich.

month [mʌnθ] n Monat m. in the ~ of October im Oktober; six ~s ein halbes Jahr, sechs Monate; paid by the ~ monatlich bezahlt.

monthly ['mʌnθlɪ] **1** adj monatlich; magazine, ticket Monats-. **2** adv monatlich. twice ~ zweimal im Monat. **3** n Monats(zeit)schrift f.

monument ['mɒnjʊmənt] n Denkmal nt; (big also) Monument nt; (small, on grave etc) Gedenkstein m; (fig) Zeugnis nt (to gen).

monumental [ˌmɒnjʊ'mentl] adj (very great) enorm, monumental (geh); proportions, achievement gewaltig; ignorance ungeheuer.

moo [muː] **1** n Muhen nt. **2** vi muhen.

mooch [muːtʃ] (col) **1** vi to ~ about or around herumgammeln (col). **2** vt (US) abstauben (col).

mood¹ [muːd] n Stimmung f; (of person also) Laune f; (bad ~) schlechte Laune. he was in a good/bad/foul ~ er war gut/schlecht/ fürchterlich gelaunt; to be in a festive ~ feierlich gestimmt sein; to be in a generous ~ in Geberlaune sein; to be in the ~ for sth/to do sth zu etw aufgelegt sein/dazu aufgelegt sein, etw zu tun; I'm not in the ~ for work ich habe keine Lust zum Arbeiten; I'm not in the ~ ich bin nicht in der richtigen Stimmung; he's in a ~ er hat schlechte Laune.

mood² n (Gram) Modus m.

moody ['muːdɪ] adj (+er) launisch; (bad-tempered) schlechtgelaunt attr, schlecht gelaunt pred; look, answer übellaunig.

moon [muːn] n Mond m. you're asking for the ~! du verlangst Unmögliches!; to be over the ~ (col) überglücklich sein.

moon in cpds Mond-; ~beam n Mondstrahl m; ~light **1** n Mondschein m; **2** vi (col) ≈ schwarzarbeiten; ~lit adj object mondbeschienen; night, lawn mondhell; ~shine n (~light) Mondschein m; ~shot n Mondflug m.

moor¹ [mʊəʳ] n (Heide)moor nt.

moor² **1** vt festmachen, vertäuen; (at permanent moorings) muren. **2** vi festmachen, anlegen.

mooring ['mʊərɪŋ] n (place) Anlegeplatz m. ~s (ropes) Verankerung f.

moose [muːs] n Elch m.

moot [muːt] **1** adj: a ~ point or question eine fragliche Sache. **2** vt it has been ~ed whether ... es wurde zur Debatte gestellt, ob ...

mop [mɒp] **1** n (floor ~) Mop m; (dish ~) Spülbürste f; (col: hair) Mähne f. **2** vt floor wischen. to ~ one's face sich (dat) den Schweiß vom Gesicht wischen.

♦ **mop up** vt sep **(a)** aufwischen. **(b)** (Mil) säubern (col).

mope [məʊp] vi Trübsal blasen (col).

♦ **mope about** or **around** vi mit einer Jammermiene herumlaufen.

moped ['məʊped] n Moped nt; (very small) Mofa nt.

moral ['mɒrəl] **1** adj moralisch; principles, philosophy Moral-; (virtuous) moralisch einwandfrei; (sexually) tugendhaft. ~ standards Moral f; ~ courage Charakter m. **2** n (a) (lesson)

Moral f. **(b)** ~s pl (principles) Moralvorstellungen pl.

morale [mɒ'rɑːl] n Moral f. to boost sb's ~ jdm (moralischen) Auftrieb geben.

morality [mə'rælɪtɪ] n Moralität f; (moral system) Moral, Ethik f.

moralize ['mɒrəlaɪz] vi moralisieren. to ~ about sth sich über etw (acc) moralisch entrüsten.

morally ['mɒrəlɪ] adv **(a)** (ethically) moralisch. **(b)** (virtuously) moralisch einwandfrei; (in sexual matters) tugendhaft.

morass [mə'ræs] n Morast, Sumpf (also fig) m.

moratorium [ˌmɒrə'tɔːrɪəm] n Moratorium nt. a ~ on nuclear armament ein Atomwaffenstopp m.

morbid ['mɔːbɪd] adj **(a)** idea etc krankhaft; interest unnatürlich; imagination, humour etc makaber; (gloomy) outlook, thoughts, novel, film düster; person trübsinnig; (pessimistic) schwarzseherisch. **(b)** (Med) morbid; growth krankhaft.

more [mɔːʳ] **1** n, pron **(a)** (greater amount) mehr; (additional amount, things) noch mehr. ~ and ~ immer mehr; a lot ~ viel mehr; (in addition) noch viel mehr; a few ~ ein paar; a little ~ etwas mehr; (in addition) noch etwas mehr; no ~ nichts mehr; (countable) keine mehr; some ~ noch etwas; (countable) noch welche; any ~? noch mehr?; there isn't/aren't any ~ mehr gibt es nicht; (here, left over) es ist nichts mehr da/es sind keine mehr da; is/are there any ~? gibt es noch mehr?; (left over) ist noch etwas da/sind noch welche da?; even ~ noch mehr; what ~ do you want? was willst du denn noch?; there's ~ to it da steckt (noch) mehr dahinter; and what's ~, he ... und obendrein hat er ... (noch) ...

(b) (all) the ~ um so mehr; **the ~ you give him, the ~ he wants** je mehr du ihm gibst, desto mehr verlangt er; **the ~ the merrier** je mehr desto besser.

2 adj mehr; (in addition) noch mehr. two ~ bottles noch zwei Flaschen; one ~ day noch ein Tag; ~ and ~ money immer mehr Geld; a lot/a little ~ money viel/etwas mehr Geld; (in addition) noch viel/noch etwas mehr Geld; a few ~ weeks noch ein paar Wochen; no ~ money kein Geld mehr; no ~ singing! Schluß mit der Singerei; do you want some ~ tea möchten Sie noch etwas Tee?; is there any ~ wine in the bottle? ist noch (etwas) Wein in der Flasche?; the ~ fool you for giving him the money daß du auch so dumm bist, ihm das Geld zu geben.

3 adv **(a)** mehr. ~ and ~ immer mehr; it will grow a bit ~ es wird noch etwas wachsen; £5/2 hours ~ than I thought £5 mehr/2 Stunden länger, als ich dachte; he is ~ than satisfied or ist mehr als zufrieden; it will ~ than meet the demand das wird die Nachfrage mehr als genügend befriedigen; no ~ a duchess than I am genausowenig eine Herzogin wie ich (eine bin); once ~ noch einmal, nochmal (col); never ~ nie mehr or wieder; no ~ am I nicht mehr; if he comes here any ~ ... wenn er noch weiter hierher kommt ...; ~ or less mehr oder weniger. **(b)** (to form comp of adj, adv) -er (than als). ~ beautiful/beautifully schöner; ~ and ~ beautiful immer mehr schöner; no ~ stupid than I am (auch) nicht dümmer als ich.

moreover [mɔː'rəʊvəʳ] adv zudem, außerdem.

morgue [mɔːg] n Leichenschauhaus nt.

moribund ['mɒrɪbʌnd] adj customs, way of life zum Aussterben verurteilt.

morning ['mɔːnɪŋ] **1** n Morgen m; (later part also) Vormittag m. in the ~ am Morgen; am Vormittag; (tomorrow) morgen früh; early in the ~ früh(morgens); (tomorrow) morgen früh; (at) 7 in the ~ (um) 7 Uhr morgens; (tomorrow) morgen (früh) um 7; this/yesterday/tomorrow ~ heute morgen/gestern morgen/morgen früh; heute/

gestern/morgen vormittag; **on the ~ of November 28th** am Morgen des 28. November. **2** *attr* Morgen-; *(train, service etc* Vormittags-; *(early* ~*) train, news* Früh-.

morning: ~ dress *n no pl* Cut *m;* **~ sickness** *n* (Schwangerschafts)übelkeit *f.*

Morocco [mə'rɒkəʊ] *n* Marokko *nt.*

moron ['mɔːrɒn] *n (Med)* Geistesschwache(r) *mf;* *(col)* Dummkopf *(col) m.*

morose [mə'rəʊs] *adj* verdrießlich, mißmutig.

morphine ['mɔːfiːn] *n* Morphium *nt.*

morse [mɔːs] *n (also* **M~ code)** Morseschrift *f.*

morsel ['mɔːsl] *n (food)* Bissen *m; (fig)* bißchen *nt.*

mortal ['mɔːtl] **1** *adj* sterblich; *injury, combat* tödlich. **2** *n* Sterbliche(r) *mf.*

mortality [mɔː'tælɪtɪ] *n* **(a)** Sterblichkeit *f.* **(b)** *(number of deaths)* Todesfälle *pl; (rate)* Sterblichkeit(sziffer) *f.*

mortally ['mɔːtəlɪ] *adv (fatally)* tödlich; *(fig: extremely) shocked* zu Tode; *offended* tödlich.

mortar[1] ['mɔːtəʳ] *n* **(a)** *(bowl)* Mörser *m.* **(b)** *(cannon)* Minenwerfer *m.*

mortar[2] *n (cement)* Mörtel *m.*

mortarboard ['mɔːtəbɔːd] *n (Univ)* Doktorhut *m.*

mortgage ['mɔːgɪdʒ] **1** *n* Hypothek *f (on* auf *+acc/ dat).* **2** *vt house, land* mit einer Hypothek belasten.

mortice *n, vt* = **mortise.**

mortician [ˌmɔː'tɪʃən] *n (US)* Bestattungsunternehmer *m.*

mortification [ˌmɔːtɪfɪ'keɪʃən] *n* **(a)** Beschämung *f; (humiliation)* Demütigung *f.* **(b)** *(Rel)* Kasteiung *f.*

mortify ['mɔːtɪfaɪ] *vt usu pass* **(a)** beschämen. **he was mortified** er empfand das als beschämend. **(b)** *(Rel)* kasteien.

mortise, mortice ['mɔːtɪs] *n* Zapfenloch *nt.* **~ lock** Einsteckschloß *nt.*

mortuary ['mɔːtjʊərɪ] *n* Leichenhalle *f.*

mosaic [məʊ'zeɪɪk] **1** *n* Mosaik *nt.* **2** *attr* Mosaik-.

Moscow ['mɒskəʊ] *n* Moskau *nt.*

Moslem ['mɒzlem] **1** *adj* moslemisch. **2** *n* Moslem *m.*

mosque [mɒsk] *n* Moschee *f.*

mosquito [mɒ'skiːtəʊ] *n, pl* **-es** Stechmücke *f; (in tropics)* Moskito *m.* **~ net** Moskitonetz *nt.*

moss [mɒs] *n* Moos *nt.*

mossy ['mɒsɪ] *adj (+er) (moss-covered)* bemoost; *lawn* vermoost; *(mosslike)* moosartig.

most [məʊst] **1** *adj superl* **(a)** meiste(r, s); *(greatest) satisfaction, pleasure etc* größte(r, s). **who has (the) ~ money?** wer hat am meisten *or* das meiste Geld?; **for the ~ part** größtenteils; *(by and large)* im großen und ganzen. **(b)** *(the majority of)* die meisten. **~ men/people** die meisten (Menschen/Leute).

2 *n, pron* **~ of it/them** das meiste/die meisten; **~ of the money/his friends** das meiste Geld/die meisten seiner Freunde; **~ of the day** fast den ganzen Tag über; **~ of the time** die meiste Zeit; *(usually)* meist(ens); **do the ~ you can** machen Sie soviel (wie) Sie können; **at (the) ~** höchstens; **to make the ~ of sth** *(make good use of)* etw voll ausnützen; *(enjoy)* etw in vollen Zügen genießen.

3 *adv* **(a)** *superl (+vbs)* am meisten; *(+adj)* -ste(r, s); *(+adv)* am -sten. **the ~ beautiful** der/ die/das schönste; **which one did it ~ easily?** wem ist es am leichtesten gefallen?; **what ~ displeased him** ... am meisten mißfiel ihm ...; **~ of all** am allermeisten; **~ of all because** ... vor allem, weil ... **(b)** *(very)* äußerst, überaus. **~ likely** höchstwahrscheinlich.

mostly ['məʊstlɪ] *adv (principally)* hauptsächlich; *(most of the time)* meistens; *(by and large)* zum größten Teil.

MOT *(Brit)* **(a)** = **Ministry of Transport.** **(b)** **~ (test)** der TÜV. **it failed its ~** es ist nicht

durch den TÜV gekommen.

motel [məʊ'tel] *n* Motel *nt.*

motet [məʊ'tet] *n* Motette *f.*

moth [mɒθ] *n* Nachtfalter *m; (wool-eating)* Motte *f.*

moth: ~ball *n* Mottenkugel *f;* **to put in ~balls** *(lit, fig)* einmotten; *ship* stillegen; **~-eaten** *adj (fig)* ausgedient, vermottet *(col).*

mother ['mʌðəʳ] **1** *n* Mutter *f.* **M~'s Day** Muttertag *m;* **to be (like) a ~ to sb** wie eine Mutter zu jdm sein. **2** *vt (care for) young* großziehen; *(cosset)* bemuttern.

mother: ~ country *n (native country)* Vaterland *nt; (head of empire)* Mutterland *nt;* **~hood** *n* Mutterschaft *f;* **~-in-law** *n, pl* **~s-in-law** Schwiegermutter *f.*

motherly ['mʌðəlɪ] *adj* mütterlich.

mother: ~-of-pearl *n* Perlmutt *nt;* **~ ship** *n* Mutterschiff *nt;* **~-to-be** *n, pl* **~s-to-be** werdende Mutter; **~ tongue** *n* Muttersprache *f.*

motif [məʊ'tiːf] *n (Art, Mus)* Motiv *nt.*

motion ['məʊʃən] *n* **(a)** Bewegung *f.* **to be in ~** sich bewegen; *(machine etc)* laufen; *(train etc)* fahren; **to set** *or* **put sth in ~** etw in Gang bringen *or* setzen; **to go through the ~s (of doing sth)** etw der Form halber tun. **(b)** *(proposal)* Antrag *m.* **to propose** *or* **make** *(US)* **a ~** einen Antrag stellen. **2** *vti* **to ~ (to) sb to do sth** jdm ein Zeichen geben, daß er etw tun solle.

motion: ~less *adj* bewegungslos, reg(ungs)los; **~ picture** *n* Film *m.*

motivate ['məʊtɪveɪt] *vt* motivieren.

motivation [ˌməʊtɪ'veɪʃən] *n* Motivation *f.*

motive ['məʊtɪv] **1** *n* Motiv *nt.* **the profit ~** Gewinnstreben *nt.* **I did it from the best of ~s** ich hatte die besten Absichten. **2** *adj force* Antriebs-.

motley ['mɒtlɪ] *adj* kunterbunt; *(varied also)* bunt(gemischt).

motor ['məʊtəʳ] **1** *n* **(a)** Motor *m.* **(b)** *(col: car)* Auto *nt.* **2** *vi* (mit dem Auto) fahren.

motor: ~bike *n* Motorrad *nt;* **~boat** *n* Motorboot *nt;* **~car** *n (form)* Kraftfahrzeug *(form) nt;* **~-cycle** *n* Motorrad *nt;* **~-cyclist** *n* Motorradfahrer(in *f) m.*

motoring ['məʊtərɪŋ] **1** *adj attr accident, offence* Verkehrs-; *correspondent* Auto-. **the ~ public** die Autofahrer *pl.* **2** *n* Autofahren *nt.*

motorist ['məʊtərɪst] *n* Autofahrer(in *f) m.*

motorize ['məʊtəraɪz] *vt* motorisieren.

motor: ~ mechanic *n* Kfz-Mechaniker *m;* **~ racing** *n* Rennsport *m;* **~ scooter** *n* Motorroller *m;* **~ show** *n (Brit)* Automobilausstellung *f;* **~way** *n (Brit)* Autobahn *f;* **~way madness** Geschwindigkeitsrausch *m.*

mottled ['mɒtld] *adj* gesprenkelt; *complexion* fleckig.

motto ['mɒtəʊ] *n, pl* **-es** Motto *nt; (personal also)* Devise *f.*

mould[1]**,** *(US)* **mold** [məʊld] **1** *n (hollow form)* (Guß)form *f; (shape, Cook)* Form *f.* **to be cast in the same ~** *(people)* vom gleichen Schlag sein. **2** *vt formen (into* zu); *(cast)* gießen.

mould[2]**,** *(US)* **mold** *n (fungus)* Schimmel *m.*

moulder, *(US)* **molder** ['məʊldəʳ] *vi (lit)* vermodern; *(food)* verderben; *(building)* zerfallen.

moulding, *(US)* **molding** ['məʊldɪŋ] *n (cast)* Abdruck *m; (ceiling* ~*)* Deckenfries *m.*

mouldy, *(US)* **moldy** ['məʊldɪ] *adj (+er)* ver-schimmelt; *(musty)* mod(e)rig. **to go ~** ver-schimmeln.

moult, *(US)* **molt** [məʊlt] *vi (bird)* sich mausern; *(mammals)* sich haaren.

mound [maʊnd] *n* **(a)** *(hill, burial* ~*)* Hügel *m; (earthwork)* Wall *m; (Baseball)* Wurfmal *nt.* **(b)** *(pile)* Haufen *m; (of books)* Stapel *m.*

mount[1] [maʊnt] *n (poet: mountain, hill)* Berg *m.* **M~ Everest** Mount Everest *m.*

mount[2] **1** *n* **(a)** *(horse etc)* Reittier *nt.* **(b)** *(support, base) (of machine)* Sockel *m; (of colour slide)* Rahmen *m*; *(of jewel)* Fassung *f*; *(of photo, picture)* Passepartout *nt*; *(stamp ~)* Falz *m*. **2** *vt* **(a)** *(climb onto)* besteigen. **(b)** *(place in/on ~)* montieren; picture mit einem Passepartout versehen; *(on backing)* aufziehen; *colour slide* rahmen; *specimen* präparieren; *jewel* (ein)fassen; *stamp* aufkleben. **(c)** *(organize)* play inszenieren; *attack* organisieren. **(d)** to ~ **guard** Wache stehen *(on* vor +*dat)*. **3** *vi* **(a)** *(get on)* aufsteigen; *(on horse also)* aufsitzen. **(b)** *(increase: also* ~ **up)** sich häufen.

mountain ['maʊntɪn] *n (lit, fig)* Berg *m*. in the ~s im Gebirge; **to make a ~ out of a molehill** aus einer Mücke einen Elefanten machen *(col)*; ~ **chain** Gebirgskette *f*.

mountaineer [,maʊntɪ'nɪəʳ] *n* Bergsteiger(in *f*) *m*.

mountaineering [,maʊntɪ'nɪərɪŋ] *n* Bergsteigen *nt*.

mountainous ['maʊntɪnəs] *adj* gebirgig.

mountain: ~ **range** *n* Gebirgszug *m*; ~**side** *n* (Berg)hang *m*.

mounted ['maʊntɪd] *adj (on horseback)* beritten.

mourn [mɔːn] **1** *vt person* trauern um; *sb's death* beklagen, betrauern; *(fig)* nachtrauern (+*dat)*. **2** *vi* trauern. **to ~ for** *or* **over sb/sth** um jdn trauern/ einer Sache *(dat)* nachtrauern.

mourner ['mɔːnəʳ] *n* Trauernde(r) *mf*; *(non-relative at funeral)* Trauergast *m*.

mournful ['mɔːnfʊl] *adj person, occasion* trau-ervoll; *character, voice, look* weinerlich; *sigh, appearance* kläglich; *sound, cry* klagend.

mourning ['mɔːnɪŋ] *n (act)* Trauer *f*, Trauern *nt (of* um). **to be in ~ for sb** um jdn trauern; *(wear ~)* Trauer tragen.

mouse [maʊs] *n, pl* **mice** *(also Comp)* Maus *f*.

mousetrap ['maʊstræp] *n* Mausefalle *f*.

mousse [muːs] *n* Creme(speise) *f*.

moustache, *(US)* **mustache** [məˈstɑːʃ] *n* Schnurrbart *m*.

mousy, **mousey** ['maʊsɪ] *adj (+er) (timid)* schüchtern; *hair* mausgrau.

mouth [maʊθ] *n (of person)* Mund *m*; *(of animal)* Maul *nt*; *(of bottle, cave etc)* Öffnung *f*; *(of river)* Mündung *f*; *(of harbour)* Einfahrt *f*. **to keep one's (big)** ~ **shut** *(col)* die Klappe halten *(col)*; **shut your** ~! *(col!)* halt's Maul! *(col!)*. **2** [maʊð] *vt (say affectedly)* (über)deutlich artikulieren; *(soundlessly)* mit Lippensprache sagen.

mouthful ['maʊθfʊl] *n (of drink)* Schluck *m*; *(of food)* Bissen *m*; *(fig) (difficult word)* Zungenbrecher *m*; *(long word)* Bandwurm *m*.

mouth in cpds Mund-; ~**organ** *n* Mundharmonika *f*; ~**piece** *n* Mundstück *nt*; *(of telephone)* Sprechmuschel *f*; *(fig: medium)* Sprachrohr *nt*; ~**-to-** **resuscitation** *n* Mund-zu-Mund-Beatmung *f*; ~**wash** *n* Mundwasser *nt*; ~**-watering** *adj* lecker; **it's really** ~**-watering** da läuft einem das Wasser im Mund zusammen.

movable ['muːvəbl] *adj* beweglich; *(transportable)* transportierbar.

move [muːv] **1** *n* **(a)** *(in game)* Zug *m*; *(fig) (step, action)* Schritt *m*; *(measure taken)* Maßnahme *f*. **it's my** ~ *(lit, fig)* ich etc bin am Zug!; **to make a/the first** ~ Schritte unternehmen/den er-sten Schritt tun; **that was a bad/good** ~ *(fig)* das war taktisch falsch/das war ein guter Schachzug.

(b) *(movement)* Bewegung *f*. **to be on the** ~ *(fig: things, developments)* im Fluß sein; *(person: in different places)* unterwegs sein; **to get a** ~ **on (with sth)** *(col: hurry up)* sich (mit etw) beeilen; **get a** ~ **on!** nun mach schon! *(col)*; **to make a** ~ **to do sth** *(fig)* Anstalten machen, etw zu tun; **it's time we made a** ~ es wird Zeit, daß wir uns auf den Weg machen.

(c) *(of house etc)* Umzug *m*; *(to different job)* Stellenwechsel *m*; *(to different department)* Wechsel *m*.

2 *vt* **(a)** bewegen; *wheel etc* (an)treiben; *(shift about)* umstellen, umräumen; *(transport)* befördern; *hand* wegziehen; *chess piece etc* ziehen mit; *(out of the way)* wegräumen. **to be unable to** ~ **sth** *(lift)* etw nicht von der Stelle bringen; *screw* etw nicht losbekommen; **I can't** ~ **this handle** der Griff läßt sich nicht bewegen.

(b) *(change location of) offices, troops* ver-legen; *patient* bewegen; *(transport)* transpor-tieren; *employee (to new department)* versetzen. **to ~ house** *(Brit)* umziehen.

(c) *(fig: sway)* **to ~ sb from an opinion** *etc* jdn von einer Meinung *etc* abbringen; **to ~ sb to do sth** jdn veranlassen, etw zu tun; **I shall not be** ~**d** ich bleibe dabei.

(d) *(cause emotion in)* bewegen; *(upset)* er-schüttern, ergreifen. **to ~ sb to tears** jdn zu Tränen rühren.

(e) *(form: propose)* beantragen. **she** ~**d an amendment to the motion** sie stellte einen Abänderungsantrag.

3 *vi* **(a)** sich bewegen; *(vehicle)* fahren; *(traffic)* vorankommen. **nobody** ~**d** niemand rührte sich; **the vehicle began to** ~ das Fahrzeug setzte sich in Bewegung; **don't** ~! stillhalten!; **keep moving** nicht stehenbleiben; **to keep sb/sth moving** jdn/etw in Gang halten; **things are moving at last** endlich kommen die Dinge in Gang; **to** ~ **with the times** mit der Zeit gehen; **they must** ~ **first** sie müssen den ersten Schritt tun; **he has** ~**d to another department** er hat die Abteilung gewechselt; **it's time we were moving** es wird Zeit, daß wir gehen; **that's moving!** *(col: fast)* das ist aber ein ganz schönes Tempo! *(col)*.

(b) *(~ house)* umziehen.

(c) *(in games) (make a ~)* ziehen; *(have one's turn)* am Zug sein.

♦ **move about 1** *vt sep furniture etc* umstellen; *parts of body* (hin und her) bewegen; *employee* versetzen. **2** *vi* sich (hin und her) bewegen; *(fidget)* herumzappeln; *(travel)* unterwegs sein.

♦ **move along 1** *vt sep* weiterrücken; *bystanders etc* zum Weitergehen veranlassen. **2** *vi (along seat etc)* aufrücken; *(along bus etc)* weitergehen; *(cars)* weiterfahren.

♦ **move away 1** *vt sep* wegräumen; *person* weg-schicken. **to ~ sb ~ from sth** jdn von etw entfernen. **2** *vi (move aside)* aus dem Weg gehen; *(leave) (people)* weggehen; *(vehicle)* losfahren; *(move house)* wegziehen *(from* aus, von).

♦ **move back 1** *vt sep (to former place)* zurück-stellen; *people* zurückbringen; *(to the rear) things* zurückschieben; *car* zurückfahren; *people* zu-rückdrängen; *troops* zurückziehen. **2** *vi* **(a)** *(to former place)* zurückkommen; *(into one's house)* wieder einziehen *(into* in +*acc)*. **(b)** *(to the rear)* zurückweichen; *(troops)* sich zurückziehen; *(car)* zurückfahren. ~ ~, **please!** bitte zu-rücktreten!

♦ **move down 1** *vt sep (downwards)* (weiter) nach unten stellen; *(along)* (weiter) nach hinten stellen. **2** *vi* **(a)** *(downwards)* nach unten rücken; *(along)* weiterrücken; *(in bus etc)* nach hinten auf-rücken.

♦ **move forward 1** *vt sep person* vorgehen lassen; *table etc* vorrücken; *chess piece* vorziehen; *car* vorfahren; *troops* vorrücken lassen; *event, date* vorverlegen. **2** *vi (person)* vorrücken; *(crowd)* sich vorwärts bewegen; *(car)* vorwärtsfahren; *(troops)* vorrücken.

♦ **move in 1** *vt sep troops* einsetzen *(-to* in +*dat)*; *(take inside)* herein-/hineinstellen *(-to* in +*acc)*. **2** *vi* **(a)** *(into house)* einziehen *(-to* in +*acc)*. **(b)** *(come closer)* näher herankommen *(on an* +*acc)*; *(police, troops)* anrücken; *(workers)* anfangen. **to** ~ ~ **on sb** gegen jdn vorrücken.

♦ **move off 1** *vt sep people* wegschicken. **2** *vi* **(a)**

(go away) weggehen. **(b)** *(start moving)* sich in Bewegung setzen; *(train, car also)* abfahren.
♦ **move on 1** *vt sep* hands *of clock* vorstellen. **the policeman** ~**d them** ~ der Polizist forderte sie auf, weiterzugehen/weiterzufahren. **2** *vi (people)* weitergehen; *(vehicles)* weiterfahren. **it's about time I was moving** ~ *(fig)* es wird Zeit, daß ich *(mal)* etwas anderes mache; **let's** ~ ~ **to the next point** gehen wir zum nächsten Punkt über.
♦ **move out 1** *vt sep car* herausfahren *(of* aus*); troops* abziehen. ~ **the table** ~ **of the corner** rücken Sie den Tisch von der Ecke weg! **2** *vi (leave accommodation)* ausziehen; *(withdraw: troops)* abziehen.
♦ **move over 1** *vt sep* herüber-/hinüberschieben. **2** *vi* zur Seite rücken. ~ ~**!** rück mal ein Stück! *(col)*.
♦ **move up 1** *vt sep (weiter)* nach oben stellen; *(promote)* befördern; *(Sch)* versetzen; *(Sport)* aufsteigen lassen. **2** *vi (fig)* aufsteigen; *(shares, rates etc)* steigen; *(be promoted)* befördert werden; *(Sch)* versetzt werden; *(move along)* aufrücken. **to** ~ ~ **the social scale** die gesellschaftliche Leiter hinaufklettern.

movement ['muːvmənt] *n* **(a)** Bewegung *f; (fig: trend)* Trend *m (towards* zu*); (of events)* Entwicklung *f.* **a slight upward** ~ eine leichte Aufwärtsbewegung; **the police were investigating his** ~**s** die Polizei stellte Ermittlungen über ihn an. **(b)** *(political etc* ~*)* Bewegung *f.* **(c)** *(Mus)* Satz *m.*

movie ['muːvɪ] *n (esp US)* Film *m.* **(the)** ~**s** der Film; **to go to the** ~**s** ins Kino gehen.
movie *in cpds* Film-; ~ **camera** *n* Filmkamera *f;* ~**goer** *n* Kinogänger(in *f*) *m.*
moving ['muːvɪŋ] *adj* **(a)** beweglich. ~ **staircase** Rolltreppe *f.* **(b)** *(fig: instigating) force* treibend. **(c)** *(causing emotion)* ergreifend; *tribute* rührend.

mow [məʊ] *pret* ~**ed,** *ptp* **mown** *or* ~**ed** *vti* mähen.
MP = **Member of Parliament.**
mpg = **miles per gallon.**
mph = **miles per hour.**
Mr ['mɪstə^r] = **Mister** Herr *m.*
Mrs ['mɪsɪz] *n* Frau *f.*
Ms [mɪz] Frau *f.*
MSc = **Master of Science.**

much [mʌtʃ] **1** *adj, n* **(a)** viel *inv.* **how** ~ wieviel *inv;* **that** ~ so viel; ~ **of this is true** vieles daran ist wahr; **we don't see** ~ **of each other** wir sehen uns nicht oft; **he/it isn't up to** ~ *(col)* er/es ist nicht gerade berühmt *(col)*; **she's not** ~ **of a cook** sie ist keine große Köchin; **that wasn't** ~ **of a party** die Party war nicht gerade besonders; **that's a bit** ~**!** das ist ja ein starkes Stück! *(col)*; **they are** ~ **of a muchness** sie nehmen sich nicht viel.
(b) **too** ~ zuviel *inv;* *(ridiculous)* das Letzte *(col)*; **to be too** ~ **for sb** *(in quantity)* zuviel für jdn sein; *(too expensive)* jdm zuviel sein; **that insult was too** ~ **for me** die Beleidigung ging mir zu weit.
(c) **(just) as** ~ genausoviel *inv;* **not as** ~ nicht soviel; **three times as** ~ dreimal soviel; **as** ~ **as you want/can** *etc* soviel du willst/kannst *etc;* **as** ~ **again** noch einmal soviel; **I feared/thought** *etc* **as** ~ *(genau)* das habe ich befürchtet/mir gedacht *etc;* **it's as** ~ **as I can do to stand up** es fällt mir schwer genug aufzustehen.
(d) **so** ~ soviel *inv;* *(emph so, with following that)* so viel; **it's not so** ~ **a problem of modernization as ...** es ist nicht so sehr ein Problem der Modernisierung, als ...
(e) **to make** ~ **of sb/sth** viel Wind um jdn/etw machen; **I couldn't make** ~ **of that chapter** mit dem Kapitel konnte ich nicht viel anfangen *(col)*.
2 *adv* **(a)** *(with adj, adv)* viel; *(with vb)* sehr; *(with vb of physical action)* drive, sleep, talk *etc* viel; come, visit *etc* oft, viel *(col)*. **so** ~**/too** ~ soviel/zuviel; so sehr/zu sehr; **I like it very/so** ~

es gefällt mir sehr gut/so sehr; **I don't like him/it too** ~ ich kann ihn/es nicht besonders leiden; **thank you very** ~ vielen Dank; **however** ~ **he tries** wie sehr er sich auch bemüht; ~ **to my astonishment** zu meinem großen Erstaunen; ~ **as I should like to** so gern ich möchte; ~ **as I like him** sosehr ich ihn mag.
(b) *(by far)* weitaus, bei weitem. ~ **the biggest** weitaus der/die/das größte; **I would** ~ **rather stay** ich würde viel lieber bleiben.
(c) *(almost)* beinahe. **they are** ~ **the same** sie sind fast gleich.

muck [mʌk] *n (dirt)* Dreck *m; (manure)* Dung *m.* **(b)** *(rubbish)* Mist *m; (food etc)* Zeug *nt (col)*.
♦ **muck about** *or* **around** *(col)* **1** *vt sep to* ~ **sb** ~ jdn herumstoßen *(col); (by not committing oneself)* jdn hinhalten. **2** *vi (lark about)* herumblödeln *(col); (do nothing in particular)* herumgammeln *(col); (tinker with)* herumfummeln *(with* an +*dat).*
♦ **muck in** *vi (col)* mit anpacken *(col).*
♦ **muck up** *vt sep (col)* **(a)** *(dirty)* dreckig machen *(col).* **(b)** *(spoil)* vermasseln *(col).*
muck-raking ['mʌk,reɪkɪŋ] *n (fig col)* Sensationsmache(rei) *f (col).*
mucky ['mʌkɪ] *adj (+er)* dreckig *(col)*, schmutzig.
mucus ['mjuːkəs] *n* Schleim *m.*
mud [mʌd] *n* Schlamm *m.* **his name is** ~ *(col)* er ist unten durch *(col);* **to throw** ~ **at sb/sth** *(fig col)* jdn mit Schmutz bewerfen/etw in den Schmutz ziehen.
mud bath *n* Schlammbad *nt; (Med)* Moorbad *nt.*
muddle ['mʌdl] **1** *n* Durcheinander *nt.* **to get in(to) a** ~ *(things)* durcheinandergeraten; *(person)* konfus werden; **to be in a** ~ völlig durcheinander sein; **to make a** ~ **of sth** etw völlig durcheinanderbringen. **2** *vt (also* ~ **up)** durcheinanderbringen; *(make confused) person also* verwirren.
♦ **muddle along** *or* **on** *vi* vor sich *(acc)* hinwursteln *(col).*
♦ **muddle through** *vi* sich durchschlagen.
muddled ['mʌdld] *adj* konfus; *person also* durcheinander *pred; ideas also* verworren.
muddle-headed ['mʌdl,hedɪd] *adj person* zerstreut; *ideas* verworren.
muddy ['mʌdɪ] *adj (+er) floor, shoes etc* schlammbeschmiert; *ground, liquid* schlammig.
mud: ~**guard** *n (on cycles)* Schutzblech *nt; (on cars)* Kotflügel *m;* ~ **pack** *n* Schlammpackung *f;* ~**-slinging** *n* Schlechtmacherei *f.*
muff[1] [mʌf] *n* Muff *m.*
muff[2] *(col)* *vt* vermasseln *(col); exam also* verhauen *(col); lines, text* verpatzen *(col).*
muffle ['mʌfl] *vt (also* ~ **up)** *(wrap warmly: also* ~ **up)** *person* einmummen. **(b)** *(deaden) shot etc* dämpfen; *noise* abdämpfen; *shouts* ersticken.
muffled ['mʌfld] *adj sound etc* gedämpft; *shouts* erstickt.
muffler ['mʌflə^r] *n* **(a)** *(scarf)* (dicker) Schal. **(b)** *(US Aut)* Auspuff(topf) *m.*
mufti ['mʌftɪ] *n (col)* in ~ in Zivil.
mug [mʌg] **1** *n* **(a)** *(cup)* Becher *m; (for beer)* Krug *m.* **(b)** *(col: fool)* Trottel *m.* **that's a** ~**'s game** das ist doch schwachsinnig. **(c)** *(col: face)* Visage *f (col!).* ~ **shot** Verbrecherfoto *nt (col).* **2** *vt (attack and rob)* überfallen.
♦ **mug up** *vt sep (col)* **(a)** *(also* ~ **on)** pauken *(col).*
mugger ['mʌgə^r] *n* Straßenräuber *m.*
mugging ['mʌgɪŋ] *n* Straßenraub *m no pl.* **a lot of** ~**s** viele Überfälle auf offener Straße.
muggy ['mʌgɪ] *adj (+er)* schwül; *heat* drückend.
mulatto [mjuːˈlætəʊ] *n, pl* **-es** Mulatte *m,* Mulattin *f.*
mulberry ['mʌlbərɪ] *n (fruit)* Maulbeere *f; (tree)* Maulbeerbaum *m.*
mule [mjuːl] *n* Maultier *nt.* **(as)** ~ **stubborn as a** ~ *(so)* störrisch wie ein Maulesel.
mull [mʌl] *vt* ~**ed wine** Glühwein *m.*

♦ **mull over** vt sep sich (dat) durch den Kopf gehen lassen.

multi- ['mʌltɪ] pref mehr-, Mehr-; (with Latin stem in German) Multi-, multi-; ~-**coloured**, (US) ~-**colored** adj mehrfarbig; lights, decorations bunt; bird buntgefiedert.

multifarious [ˌmʌltɪ'fɛərɪəs] adj vielfältig.

multi: ~**lateral** adj (Pol) multilateral; ~**level parking garage** n (US) Parkhaus nt; ~**lingual** adj mehrsprachig; ~**millionaire** n Multimillionär(in f) m; ~**national** 1 n multinationaler Konzern; 2 adj multinational.

multiple ['mʌltɪpl] 1 adj (a) (with sing n: of several parts) mehrfach. ~ **choice** Multiple Choice no art; ~ **crash** Massenkarambolage f. (b) (with pl n: many) mehrere. 2 n (a) (Math) Vielfache(s) nt. (b) (Brit: also ~ **store**) Ladenkette f.

multiple sclerosis n multiple Sklerose.

multiplication [ˌmʌltɪplɪ'keɪʃən] n (a) (Math) Multiplikation f. ~ **table** Multiplikationstabelle f. (b) (fig) Vervielfachung f.

multiplicity [ˌmʌltɪ'plɪsɪtɪ] n Vielzahl f. **for a ~ of reasons** aus vielerlei Gründen.

multiply ['mʌltɪplaɪ] 1 vt (Math) multiplizieren, malnehmen. **4 multiplied by 6 is 24** 4 mal 6 ist 24. 2 vi (a) (Math) multiplizieren. (b) (fig) sich vervielfachen. (c) (breed) sich vermehren.

multi: ~-**purpose** adj Mehrzweck-; ~**racial** adj gemischtrassig; ~-**stor(e)y** adj mehrstöckig; ~-**stor(e)y car-park** (Brit) Parkhaus nt.

multitude ['mʌltɪtjuːd] n Menge f.

mum¹ [mʌm] n, adj (col) ~'**s the word!** nichts verraten! (col); **to keep** ~ den Mund halten (about über +acc) (col).

mum² n (Brit col: mother) Mutter f; (as address) Mutti f (col).

mumble ['mʌmbl] 1 vt murmeln. 2 vi vor sich (acc) hin murmeln; (speak indistinctly) nuscheln.

mummify ['mʌmɪfaɪ] vt mumifizieren.

mummy¹ ['mʌmɪ] n (corpse) Mumie f.

mummy² n (Brit col: mother) Mami f (col).

mumps [mʌmps] n sing Mumps m or f (col) no art.

munch [mʌntʃ] vti mampfen (col).

mundane [ˌmʌn'deɪn] adj (worldly) weltlich; (pej: humdrum) banal.

municipal [mjuː'nɪsɪpəl] adj städtisch; council, elections etc Stadt-, Gemeinde-.

municipality [mjuːˌnɪsɪ'pælɪtɪ] n Gemeinde f.

Munich ['mjuːnɪk] n München nt.

munificence [mjuː'nɪfɪsns] n (form) Großzügigkeit f.

munition [mjuː'nɪʃən] n usu pl Kriegsmaterial nt no pl.

mural ['mjʊərəl] 1 n Wandgemälde nt. 2 adj Wand-.

murder ['mɜːdər] 1 n (a) Mord m. **to commit** ~ einen Mord begehen. (b) (fig col) **it was** ~ es war mörderisch; **to cry blue** ~ ein Mordstheater machen (col); **to get away with** ~ sich (dat) alles erlauben können. 2 vt ermorden, umbringen; (slaughter) morden; (col) opponents haushoch schlagen; (col: ruin) music etc verhunzen (col).

murderer ['mɜːdərər] n Mörder m.

murderous ['mɜːdərəs] adj deed Mord-; (fig) mörderisch.

murky ['mɜːkɪ] adj (+er) trübe; fog dicht; photo, outline etc unscharf; past dunkel.

murmur ['mɜːmər] 1 n Murmeln nt; (of discontent) Murren m; (of water, traffic) Rauschen nt. **there was a** ~ **of approval/disagreement** ein beifälliges/abfälliges Murmeln erhob sich; **not a** ~ kein Laut; **without a** ~ ohne zu murren. 2 vt murmeln; (with discontent) murren. 3 vi murmeln; (with discontent) murren (about über +acc); (fig) rauschen.

muscle ['mʌsl] n Muskel m; (fig: power) Macht f. **to have financial/industrial** ~ finanzkräftig/ wirtschaftlich einflußreich sein; **he never moved a** ~ er rührte sich nicht.

♦ **muscle in** vi (col) **to** ~ ~ (**on sth**) (bei etw) mitmischen.

muscular ['mʌskjʊlər] adj Muskel-; strong muskulös.

muse [mjuːz] 1 vi nachgrübeln (about, on über +acc). 2 vt grüblerisch sagen.

museum [mjuː'zɪəm] n Museum nt. ~ **piece** (lit, hum) Museumsstück nt.

mush [mʌʃ] n Brei m.

mushroom ['mʌʃrʊm] 1 n (eßbarer) Pilz; (button ~) Champignon m. ~ **cloud** Atompilz m. 2 vi (grow rapidly) wie die Pilze aus dem Boden schießen. **his fame** ~**ed** er wurde schlagartig berühmt; **the smoke** ~**ed** der Rauch breitete sich pilzförmig in der Luft aus.

mushy ['mʌʃɪ] adj (+er) matschig; liquid, consistency breiig; (col) film etc schmalzig (col). ~ **peas** Erbsenmus nt.

music ['mjuːzɪk] n Musik f; (written score) Noten pl. **to set sth to** ~ etw vertonen; **to face the** ~ (fig) dafür geradestehen.

musical ['mjuːzɪkəl] 1 adj musikalisch; instrument, evening Musik-; (tuneful) melodisch. ~ **box** Spieluhr or -dose f; ~ **chairs** sing Reise f nach Jerusalem. 2 n Musical nt.

music in cpds Musik-; ~ **centre** (Brit) or **center** (US) n Kompaktanlage f; ~ **hall** n Varieté nt.

musician [mjuː'zɪʃən] n Musiker(in f) m.

musicologist [ˌmjuːzɪ'kɒlədʒɪst] n Musikwissenschaftler(in f) m.

music-: ~ **stand** n Notenständer m; ~**stool** n Klavierhocker m.

musk [mʌsk] n (secretion, smell) Moschus m.

musket ['mʌskɪt] n Muskete f.

musk: ~**rat** n Bisamratte f; ~-**rose** n Moschusrose f.

musky ['mʌskɪ] adj (+er) smell Moschus-.

Muslim ['mʊzlɪm] adj, n = **Moslem**.

musquash ['mʌskwɒʃ] n Bisamratte f.

muss [mʌs] vt (US col: also ~ **up**) durcheinanderbringen (col).

mussel ['mʌsl] n (Mies)muschel f.

must [mʌst] 1 vb aux present tense only (a) müssen. **if you** ~ wenn's sein muß. (b) (in neg sentences) dürfen. **I** ~**n't forget** that ich darf das nicht vergessen. (c) (probability) **he** ~ **be there by now** er ist wohl inzwischen da; (more certain) er ist inzwischen bestimmt da; **I** ~ **have lost it** ich habe es wohl verloren; **you** ~ **have heard of him** Sie haben bestimmt schon von ihm gehört; **he** ~ **be older than that** er muß älter sein; **there** ~ **be a reason for it** es muß doch eine Erklärung dafür geben! 2 n (col) Muß nt. **an umbrella is a** ~ man braucht unbedingt einen Schirm; **this programme is a** ~ **for everyone** dieses Programm muß man einfach gesehen haben.

mustache n (US) = **moustache**.

mustard ['mʌstəd] n Senf m; (colour) Senfgelb nt.

muster ['mʌstər] 1 n (esp Mil: assembly) Appell m. **to pass** ~ (fig) den Anforderungen genügen. 2 vt (a) (summon) zusammenrufen; (esp Mil) antreten lassen. (b) (manage to raise: also ~ **up**) zusammenbekommen; strength, courage aufbringen; all one's strength, courage zusammennehmen. 3 vi sich versammeln; (esp Mil) (zum Appell) antreten.

mustiness ['mʌstɪnɪs] n Muffigkeit f.

mustn't ['mʌsnt] = **must not**.

musty ['mʌstɪ] adj (+er) air muffig; books moderig.

mutate [mjuː'teɪt] vi (Biol) mutieren (to zu).

mutation [mjuː'teɪʃən] n (Biol) Mutation f.

mute [mjuːt] 1 adj stumm (also Ling); amazement, rage sprachlos. 2 n (dumb person) Stumme(r) mf.

muted ['mjuːtɪd] adj gedämpft; (fig) criticism etc leicht.

mutilate ['mjuːtɪleɪt] vt person, animal, story verstümmeln; painting etc verschandeln (col).

mutilation [ˌmjuːtɪ'leɪʃən] n see vt Verstümmelung *f;* Verschandelung *f (col).*

mutineer [ˌmjuːtɪˈnɪəʳ] *n* Meuterer *m.*

mutinous [ˈmjuːtɪnəs] *adj (Naut)* meuterisch; *(fig)* rebellisch.

mutiny [ˈmjuːtɪnɪ] *(Naut, fig)* **1** *n* Meuterei *f.* **2** *vi* meutern.

mutter [ˈmʌtəʳ] **1** *n* Gemurmel *nt; (of discontent)* Murren *nt.* **2** *vt* murmeln, brummeln. **3** *vi* murmeln; *(with discontent)* murren.

mutton [ˈmʌtn] *n* Hammel(fleisch *nt) m.* **leg of ~** Hammelkeule *f;* **she's ~ dressed as lamb** *(col)* sie macht auf jung *(col).*

mutual [ˈmjuːtjʊəl] *adj respect etc* gegenseitig; *satisfaction* beiderseitig; *friends, dislikes etc* gemeinsam. **it would be for our ~ benefit** es wäre für uns beide von Vorteil; **the feeling is ~** das beruht (ganz) auf Gegenseitigkeit.

mutually [ˈmjuːtjʊəlɪ] *adv* beide; *distrust* gegenseitig; *satisfactory, beneficial* für beide Seiten; *agreed* von beiden Seiten.

muzzle [ˈmʌzl] **1** *n* **(a)** *(snout, mouth)* Maul *nt.* **(b)** *(for dog etc)* Maulkorb *m.* **(c)** *(of gun)* Mündung *f; (barrel)* Lauf *m.* **2** *vt animal* einen Maulkorb anlegen *(+dat); (fig) critics, the press* mundtot machen.

muzzy [ˈmʌzɪ] *adj (+er) (dizzy, dazed)* benommen; *(blurred) view, memory etc* veschwommen.

my [maɪ] *poss adj* mein. **I've hurt ~ leg** ich habe mir das Bein verletzt; **~ father and mother** mein Vater und meine Mutter; **in ~ country** bei uns.

myna(h) bird [ˈmaɪnəˌbɜːd] *n* Hirtenstar *m.*

myopia [maɪˈəʊpɪə] *n* Kurzsichtigkeit *f.*

myopic [maɪˈɒpɪk] *adj* kurzsichtig.

myself [maɪˈself] *pers pron* **(a)** *(dir obj, with prep +acc)* mich; *(indir obj, with prep +dat)* mir. **I said to ~** ich sagte mir; **I wanted to see (it) for ~** ich wollte es selbst sehen. **(b)** *(emph)* (ich) selbst. **my wife and ~** meine Frau und ich; **I did it ~** ich habe es selbst gemacht; **(all) by ~** *(ganz)* allein(e); **I'll go there ~** ich gehe selbst hin. **(c)** *(one's normal self)* **I'm not (feeling) ~ today** ich bin heute nicht ganz auf der Höhe.

mysterious [mɪˈstɪərɪəs] *adj* geheimnisvoll; *(puzzling)* mysteriös.

mysteriously [mɪˈstɪərɪəslɪ] *adv vanish, change* auf mysteriöse Weise; *missing* unerklärlicherweise; *(secretively)* geheimnisvoll.

mystery [ˈmɪstərɪ] *n (puzzle)* Rätsel *nt; (secret)* Geheimnis *nt.* **it's a ~ to me** das ist mir ein Rätsel.

mystic [ˈmɪstɪk] **1** *adj* mystisch. **2** *n* Mystiker(in *f) m.*

mystical [ˈmɪstɪkəl] *adj* mystisch.

mysticism [ˈmɪstɪsɪzəm] *n* Mystizismus *m; (of poetry etc)* Mystik *f.*

mystify [ˈmɪstɪfaɪ] *vt* vor ein Rätsel stellen. **I was mystified by the whole business** die ganze Sache war mir ein Rätsel.

mystifying [ˈmɪstɪfaɪɪŋ] *adj* rätselhaft.

mystique [mɪˈstiːk] *n* geheimnisvolle Exotik.

myth [mɪθ] *n* Mythos *m; (fig)* Märchen *nt.*

mythical [ˈmɪθɪkəl] *adj* mythisch; *(fig)* erfunden. **~ figure/character** Sagengestalt *f.*

mythological [ˌmɪθəˈlɒdʒɪkəl] *adj* mythologisch.

mythology [mɪˈθɒlədʒɪ] *n* Mythologie *f.*

myxomatosis [ˌmɪksəʊməˈtəʊsɪs] *n* Myxomatose *f.*

N

N, n [ɛn] *n* N, n *nt.*
N = **north** N.
nab [næb] *vt (col)* **(a)** *(catch, speak to)* erwischen; *(police also)* schnappen *(col)*. **(b)** *(take for oneself)* sich *(dat)* grapschen *(col)*, klauen *(col)*.
nadir [ˈneɪdɪəʳ] *n* **(a)** *(Astron)* Fußpunkt *m.* **(b)** *(fig)* Tiefstpunkt *m.*
nag¹ [næg] **1** *vt* herumnörgeln an (+*dat*). **she** ~**ged me into buying it** sie ließ mir keine Ruhe, bis ich es gekauft hatte. **2** *vi (find fault)* herumnörgeln, meckern *(col)*; *(be insistent)* keine Ruhe geben. **to** ~ **at sb** an jdm herumnörgeln, jdm keine Ruhe lassen. **3** *n (fault-finder)* Nörgler(in *f*) *m.*
nag² *n (old horse)* Klepper *m; (col: horse)* Gaul *m.*
nagging [ˈnægɪŋ] **1** *adj wife* meckernd *(col)*, nörglerisch; *(pestering)* ewig drängend; *pain* dumpf; *worry, doubt* quälend. **2** *n (fault-finding)* Meckern *nt (col)*, Nörgelei *f; (pestering)* ewiges Drängen.
nail [neɪl] **1** *n (Anat, Tech)* Nagel *m.* **as hard as** ~**s** knallhart *(col)*; *(physically)* zäh wie Leder; **to pay on the** ~ *(fig col)* auf der Stelle bezahlen; **to hit the** ~ **on the head** *(fig)* den Nagel auf den Kopf treffen; **to be a** ~ **in sb's coffin** *(fig)* ein Nagel zu jds Sarg sein. **2** *vt* **(a)** nageln. **to** ~ **sth to the wall** etw an die Wand nageln. **(b)** *(fig col)* **to be** ~**ed to the spot** *or* **ground** wie auf der Stelle festgenagelt sein; **to** ~ **sb** sich *(dat)* jdn schnappen *(col)*; *(charge also)* jdn drankriegen *(col)*.
♦ **nail down** *vt sep* **(a)** *(lit) box* zunageln; *carpet, lid* festnageln. **(b)** *person* festnageln *(to* auf +*acc*).
nail *in cpds* Nagel-; ~**-biting** *adj (col) terror* atemberaubend; *suspense also* atemlos; ~**-brush** *n* Nagelbürste *f;* ~**-file** *n* Nagelfeile *f;* ~ **polish** *n* Nagellack *m;* ~ **polish remover** *n* Nagellackentferner *m;* ~ **scissors** *npl* Nagelschere *f;* ~ **varnish** *n (Brit)* Nagellack *m.*
naïve [naɪˈiːv] *adj* (+*er*) naiv.
naïveté, naïvety [naɪˈiːvɪtɪ] *n* Naivität *f.*
naked [ˈneɪkɪd] *adj person* nackt; *branch, countryside* kahl; *flame, light* ungeschützt; *truth, facts* nackt. **to/with the** ~ **eye** für das bloße/mit dem bloßen Auge.
name [neɪm] **1** *n* **(a)** Name *m.* **what's your** ~? wie heißen Sie?, wie ist Ihr Name? *(form);* **my** ~ **is ...** ich heiße ..., mein Name ist ... *(form);* **a man by the** ~ **of** Gunn ein Mann namens Gunn; **I know him only by** ~ ich kenne ihn nur dem Namen nach; **to refer to sb/sth by** ~ jdn/etw namentlich *or* mit Namen nennen; **in** ~ **alone** *or* **only** nur dem Namen nach; **I won't mention any** ~**s** ich möchte keine Namen nennen; **he writes under the** ~ **of X** er schreibt unter dem Namen X; **fill in your** ~(s) **and address(es)** Namen und Adresse eintragen; **in the** ~ **of** im Namen (+*gen*); **in the** ~ **of God** um Gottes willen; **all the big** ~**s were there** alle großen Namen waren da; **I'll put your** ~ **down** *(on list, in register etc)* ich trage dich ein; *(for school, excursion etc)* ich melde dich an *(for* zu*);* **to call sb** ~**s** jdn beschimpfen; **that's the** ~ **of the game** *(col)* darum geht es.
(b) *(reputation)* Name, Ruf *m.* **to have a good/bad** ~ einen guten/schlechten Ruf haben; **to get a bad** ~ in Verruf kommen; **to give sb a bad** ~ jdn in Verruf bringen; **to make a** ~ **for oneself** sich *(dat)* einen Namen machen als; **to have a** ~ **for sth** für etw bekannt sein.

2 *vt* **(a)** *(call by a* ~, *give a* ~ *to, specify)* nennen *(as* als*); new star etc* benennen; *ship* taufen. **a person** ~**d Smith** jemand namens Smith; **to** ~ **a child after** *or (US)* **for sb** ein Kind nach jdm nennen; ~ **your price** nennen Sie Ihren Preis; **to** ~ **the day** den Hochzeitstag festsetzen; **you** ~ **it, he's done it** es gibt nichts, was er noch nicht gemacht hat.
(b) *(appoint, nominate)* ernennen *(as* als, *for* für*).*
name: ~**-drop** *vi (col)* berühmte Bekannte in die Unterhaltung einfließen lassen; **she's always** ~**-dropping** sie muß dauernd erwähnen, wen sie alles kennt; ~**less** *adj (unknown) person* unbekannt; *(undesignated)* namenlos; *(undefined) sensation, emotion* unbeschreiblich; *(shocking) vice, crime* unaussprechlich; **a certain person who shall remain** ~**less** jemand, der nicht genannt werden soll.
namely [ˈneɪmlɪ] *adv* nämlich.
name: ~**-plate** *n* Namensschild *nt; (on business premises)* Firmenschild *nt;* ~**sake** *n* Namensvetter(in *f*) *m.*
nanny [ˈnænɪ] *n* **(a)** Kindermädchen *nt.* **(b)** *(col: also* **nanna**) Oma, Omi *f (col).*
nanny goat *n* Geiß, Ziege *f.*
nap¹ [næp] *n* Nickerchen *nt.* **to have** *or* **take a** ~ ein Nickerchen machen.
nap² *n (Tex)* Flor *m.*
napalm [ˈneɪpɑːm] *n* Napalm *nt.*
nape [neɪp] *n:* ~ **of the neck** Nacken *m*, Genick *nt.*
napkin [ˈnæpkɪn] *n* **(a)** *(table~)* Serviette *f.* ~ **ring** Serviettenring *m.* **(b)** *(for baby)* Windel *f; (US: sanitary* ~) (Damen)binde *f.*
Naples [ˈneɪplz] Neapel *nt.*
nappy [ˈnæpɪ] *n (Brit)* Windel *f.*
narcissus [nɑːˈsɪsəs] *n, pl* **narcissi** *(Bot)* Narzisse *f.*
narcotic [nɑːˈkɒtɪk] *n* Rauschgift *nt.*
nark [nɑːk] *vt (Brit col)* **to get/feel** ~**ed** wütend werden/sich ärgern.
narrate [nəˈreɪt] *vt* erzählen; *events etc* schildern.
narration [nəˈreɪʃən] *n* Erzählung *f; (of events etc)* Schilderung *f.*
narrative [ˈnærətɪv] **1** *n* Erzählung *f.* **three pages of** ~ drei Seiten erzählender Text. **2** *adj* erzählend; *ability etc* erzählerisch.
narrator [nəˈreɪtəʳ] *n* Erzähler(in *f*) *m.*
narrow [ˈnærəʊ] **1** *adj* (+*er*) *g* eng; *road, valley also* schmal. **(b)** *(fig) person, attitudes* engstirnig; *sense* eng; *existence* beschränkt; *majority, victory* knapp; *scrutiny* peinlich genau. **to have a** ~ **mind** engstirnig sein; **to have a** ~ **escape** mit knapper Not davonkommen. **2** *vt road etc* enger machen. **3** *vi* enger werden, sich verengen.
♦ **narrow down** *(to* auf +*acc*) **1** *vi* sich beschränken; *(be concentrated)* sich konzentrieren. **2** *vt sep (limit)* beschränken; *(concentrate)* konzentrieren. **that** ~**s it** ~ **a bit** dadurch wird die Auswahl kleiner.
narrowly [ˈnærəʊlɪ] *adv* **(a)** *beat* knapp; *escape* mit knapper Not. **he** ~ **escaped being knocked down** er wäre um ein Haar überfahren worden; **you** ~ **missed (seeing) him** du hast ihn gerade verpaßt.
(b) *interpret* eng; *examine* peinlich genau.
narrow: ~ **minded** *adj* engstirnig; ~**-mindedness**

n Engstirnigkeit *f.*

nasal ['neɪzəl] *adj sound* nasal, Nasal-; *voice* näselnd.

nastily ['nɑːstɪlɪ] *adv (unpleasantly)* scheußlich; *speak, say* gehässig; *behave also* gemein.

nastiness ['nɑːstɪnɪs] *n no pl* Scheußlichkeit *f; (of person)* Gemeinheit *f; (behaviour)* gemeines Benehmen *(to gegenüber).*

nasturtium [nəs'tɜːʃəm] *n* (Kapuziner)kresse *f.*

nasty ['nɑːstɪ] *adj (+er)* scheußlich, widerlich; *cough, wound* schlimm; *(offensive)* anstößig; *(dirty)* schmutzig; *(dangerous) disease, corner, fog* böse, gefährlich; *person, behaviour* gemein, fies *(col); trick* übel; *(spiteful) remark* gehässig. **she had a ~ fall** sie ist böse hingefallen; **he had a ~ time of** it es ging ihm ganz übel; **to turn ~** unangenehm werden; **he has a ~ temper** mit ihm ist nicht gut Kirschen essen; **he's a ~ piece of work** *(col)* er ist ein übler Typ *(col).*

nation ['neɪʃən] *n* Volk *nt; (people of one country)* Nation *f.*

national ['næʃənəl] **1** *adj* national; *interest, debt, income* Staats-, öffentlich; *strike, scandal* landesweit; *security* Staats-; *team, character* National-; *language* Landes-; *custom, monument* Volks-. **the ~ papers** die überregionale Presse. **2** *n* **(a)** *(person)* Staatsbürger(in *f*) *m.* **foreign ~** Ausländer(in *f*) *m.* **(b)** *(col: newspaper)* überregionale Zeitung.

national: ~ anthem *n* Nationalhymne *f; ~* **costume, ~ dress** *n* Nationaltracht *f;* N~ **Health** *adj attr (Brit)* ≈ Kassen-; N~ **Health (Service)** *n (Brit)* Staatlicher Gesundheitsdienst *m;* **I got it on the N~** Health ≈ das hat die Krankenkasse bezahlt; **~ insurance** *n (Brit)* Sozialversicherung *f.*

nationalism ['næʃnəlɪzəm] *n* Nationalismus *m.*

nationalist ['næʃnəlɪst] **1** *adj* nationalistisch. **2** *n* Nationalist(in *f*) *m.*

nationality [ˌnæʃə'nælɪtɪ] *n* Staatsangehörigkeit, Nationalität *f.* **what ~ is he?** welche Staatsangehörigkeit hat er?

nationalization [ˌnæʃnəlaɪ'zeɪʃən] *n* Verstaatlichung *f.*

nationalize ['næʃnəlaɪz] *vt* verstaatlichen.

nationally ['næʃnəlɪ] *adv (as a nation)* als Nation; *(nation-wide)* landesweit.

national: ~ park *n* Nationalpark *m; ~* **service** *n (Brit)* Wehrdienst *m;* N~ **Socialism** *n* der Nationalsozialismus.

nation-wide ['neɪʃənˌwaɪd] *adj, adv* landesweit.

native ['neɪtɪv] **1** *adj* **(a)** *town* Heimat-; *language* Mutter-; *product, costume, customs, plants* einheimisch; *(associated with natives)* quarters, *labour* Eingeborenen-. **a ~ German** ein gebürtiger Deutscher, eine gebürtige Deutsche; **~ speaker** Muttersprachler(in *f*) *m.* **(b)** *(inborn) wit, quality* angeboren. **2** *n* **(a)** *(person)* Einheimische(r) *mf; (in colonial contexts)* Eingeborene(r) *mf; (original inhabitant)* Ureinwohner(in *f*) *m.* **a ~ of Germany** ein gebürtiger Deutscher, eine gebürtige Deutsche. **(b)** *(to be a ~ of ... (plant, animal)* in ... beheimatet sein.

native: ~ country *n* Heimatland *nt; ~* **land** *n* Vaterland *nt.*

nativity [nə'tɪvɪtɪ] *n* the N~ Christi Geburt *no art; ~* **play** Krippenspiel *nt.*

NATO ['neɪtəʊ] = **North Atlantic Treaty Organization** NATO *f.*

natter ['nætər] *(Brit col)* **1** *vi* schwatzen *(col); (chatter also)* quasseln *(col).* **2** *n* **to have a ~** einen Schwatz halten *(col).*

natural ['nætʃrəl] **1** *adj* **(a)** natürlich; *rights* naturgegeben, Natur-; *laws, phenomena, silk* Natur-. **it is ~ for him to think** ... es ist nur natürlich, daß er denkt ...; **~ resources** Naturschätze *pl;* **the ~ world** die Natur; **in its ~ state** im Naturzustand; **to die a ~ death** *or* of **~ causes** eines natürlichen

Todes sterben; **death from ~ causes** *(Jur)* Tod durch natürliche Ursachen. **(b)** *(inborn) gift, ability* angeboren. **to have a ~ talent for sth** eine natürliche Begabung für etw haben. **2** *n* **(a)** *(Mus) (sign)* Auflösungszeichen *nt; (note)* Note *f* ohne Vorzeichen; B ~/D ~ H, h/D, d. **(b)** *(col: person)* Naturtalent *nt.*

natural: ~ gas *n* Erdgas *nt; ~* **history** *n* Naturkunde *f.*

naturalist ['nætʃrəlɪst] *n* Naturforscher(in *f*) *m.*

naturalization [ˌnætʃrəlaɪ'zeɪʃən] *n* Einbürgerung *f.*

naturalize ['nætʃrəlaɪz] *vt person* einbürgern; *animal, plants* heimisch machen. **to become ~d** eingebürgert werden.

naturally ['nætʃrəlɪ] *adv* **(a)** **he is ~ lazy** er ist von Natur aus faul. **(b)** *(not taught)* natürlich, instinktiv. **it comes ~ to him** das fällt ihm leicht. **(c)** *(unaffectedly)* natürlich, ungekünstelt. **(d)** *(of course)* natürlich.

nature ['neɪtʃər] *n* **(a)** Natur *f.* N~ die Natur; *laws of ~* Naturgesetze *pl;* **to paint from ~** nach der Natur malen. **(b)** *(of person)* Wesen(sart *f*) *nt,* Natur *f.* **to have a jealous/happy ~** eine eifersüchtige/fröhliche Natur haben; **it is not in my ~ to say things like that** es entspricht nicht meiner Art, so etwas zu sagen; **cruel by ~** von Natur aus grausam. **(c)** *(type, sort)* Art *f.* **things of this ~** derartiges; **something in the ~ of an apology** so etwas wie eine Entschuldigung; ... **or something of that ~** ... oder etwas in der Art.

nature: ~ conservancy *n* Naturschutz *m; ~*-**lover** *n* Naturfreund *m; ~* **reserve** *n* Naturschutzgebiet *nt; ~* **study** *n* Naturkunde *f; ~* **trail** *n* Naturlehrpfad *m.*

naturism ['neɪtʃərɪzəm] *n* Freikörperkultur *f,* FKK *no art.*

naturist ['neɪtʃərɪst] *n* Anhänger(in *f*) *m* der Freikörperkultur.

naughtily ['nɔːtɪlɪ] *adv* frech; *(esp of child) remark, behave* ungezogen.

naughtiness ['nɔːtɪnɪs] *n see adj* **(a)** Frechheit *f;* Unartigkeit, Ungezogenheit *f.*

naughty ['nɔːtɪ] *adj (+er)* **(a)** frech; *child* unartig, ungezogen; *dog* ungehorsam. **you ~ boy!** du böser Junge!; **it was ~ of him to break it** das war aber gar nicht lieb von ihm, daß er das kaputtgemacht hat. **(b)** *joke, word, story* unanständig.

nausea ['nɔːsɪə] *n (Med)* Übelkeit *f; (fig)* Ekel *m.*

nauseate ['nɔːsɪeɪt] *vt* **to ~ sb** *(fig)* jdn anwidern.

nauseating ['nɔːsɪeɪtɪŋ] *adj sight, violence, food* ekelerregend; *film, book* gräßlich; *person* widerlich.

nauseous ['nɔːsɪəs] *adj* **(a)** *(Med)* **that made me (feel) ~** dabei wurde mir übel. **(b)** *(fig)* widerlich.

nautical ['nɔːtɪkəl] *adj* nautisch; *superiority* zur See; *tradition, appearance* seemännisch. **~ mile** Seemeile *f.*

naval ['neɪvəl] *adj* Marine-; *base, parade* Flotten-; *battle, forces* See-.

naval: ~ officer *n* Marineoffizier *m; ~* **power** *n* Seemacht *f.*

nave [neɪv] *n (of church)* Haupt- or Mittelschiff *nt.*

navel ['neɪvəl] *n (Anat)* Nabel *m.*

navigable ['nævɪgəbl] *adj waterway* schiffbar.

navigate ['nævɪgeɪt] **1** *vi (in plane, ship)* navigieren; *(in car)* den Fahrer dirigieren. **2** *vt* **(a)** *aircraft, ship* navigieren. **(b)** *(journey through)* durchfahren.

navigation [ˌnævɪ'geɪʃən] **(a)** Navigation *f. ~* **light** Positionslicht *nt.* **(b)** *(shipping)* Schiffsverkehr *m.*

navigator ['nævɪgeɪtər] *n (Naut)* Navigationsoffizier *m; (Aviat)* Navigator *m; (Mot)* Beifahrer *m.*

navvy ['nævɪ] *n (Brit)* Bauarbeiter *m.*

navy ['neɪvɪ] **1** *n* **(a)** *(Kriegs)marine *f.* **(b)** *(also ~*

blue) Marineblau *nt.* **2** *adj* **(a)** *attr* Marine-. **(b)** *(also ~* **blue)** marineblau.

Nazi ['nɑːtsɪ] **1** *n* Nazi *m; (fig pej)* Faschist *m.* **2** *adj* Nazi-.

NB = **nota bene** NB.

NCO = **non-commissioned officer.**

near [nɪəʳ] *(+er)* **1** *adv* **(a)** nahe. **to be ~** *(person, object)* in der Nähe sein; *(event etc)* bevorstehen; *(danger, end, help etc)* nahe sein; **to be very ~** ganz in der Nähe sein; *(in time)* unmittelbar bevorstehen; *(danger etc)* ganz nahe sein; **to be ~er/~est** näher/am nächsten sein; *(event etc)* zeitlich näher liegen/zeitlich am nächsten liegen; **to be ~ at hand** zur Hand sein; *(shops)* in der Nähe sein; *(help)* ganz nahe sein; *(event)* unmittelbar bevorstehen; **he lives quite ~** er wohnt ganz in der Nähe; **that was the ~est I ever got to** seeing him da hätte ich ihn fast gesehen.

(b) *(exactly, accurately)* genau. **as ~ as I can judge** soweit ich es beurteilen kann; **(that's) ~ enough so** geht's ungefähr.

(c) it's **nowhere ~ enough/right** das ist bei weitem nicht genug/das ist weit gefehlt; **nowhere ~ as much** bei weitem nicht soviel; **he is nowhere ~ as clever as you** er ist bei weitem nicht so klug wie du.

2 *prep (also adv: ~* **to) (a)** *(close to) (position)* nahe an *(+dat)*, nahe *(+dat); (with motion)* nahe an *(+acc); (in the vicinity of)* in der Nähe von *or +gen.* **the hotel is very ~ (to) the station** das Hotel liegt ganz in der Nähe des Bahnhofs; **to come** *or* **get ~ (to) sth** nahe an etw herankommen; **to stand ~ (to) the table** neben dem *or* nahe am Tisch stehen; **she stood too ~ (to) the stove** sie stand zu nahe am Herd; **when we got ~ (to) the house** als wir an das Haus herankamen; **~ here/there** hier/dort in der Nähe; **take the chair ~est (to) you** nehmen Sie den Stuhl direkt neben Ihnen.

(b) *(close in time)* gegen. **come back ~er (to) 3 o'clock** kommen Sie gegen 3 Uhr wieder; **~ (to) the end of the play** gegen Ende des Stücks; **I'm ~ (to) the end of the book/my stay** ich habe das Buch fast zu Ende gelesen/mein Aufenthalt ist fast zu Ende.

(c) *(on the point of)* **to be ~ (to) doing sth** nahe daran sein, etw zu tun; **to be ~ (to) tears/despair** *etc* den Tränen/der Verzweiflung *etc* nahe sein; **the project is ~ (to) completion** das Projekt steht vor seinem Abschluß.

(d) *(similar to)* ähnlich *(+dat).* **German is ~er (to) Dutch than English is** Deutsch ist dem Holländischen ähnlicher als Englisch; **nobody comes anywhere ~ him at swimming** im Schwimmen kann es niemand mit ihm aufnehmen *(col).*

3 *adj* **(a)** *(close in space)* nahe. **it looks very ~** es sieht so aus, als ob es ganz nah wäre; **our ~est neighbours are 5 miles away** unsere nächsten Nachbarn sind 5 Meilen entfernt. **(b)** *(relation, friend)* nah. **(c)** *(escape)* knapp; *(resemblance)* groß. **a ~ disaster** beinahe ein Unglück *nt;* **that was a ~ thing** das war knapp; **a ~ contest** ein Wettkampf *m* mit knappem Ausgang; **to be in a state of ~ collapse** einem Zusammenbruch nahe sein; **£50 or ~est offer** Verhandlungsbasis £50; **this is the ~est equivalent** das kommt dem am nächsten.

4 *vt place* sich nähern *(+dat).* **to be ~ing sth** *(fig)* auf etw *(acc)* zugehen; **to ~ completion** kurz vor dem Abschluß stehen.

nearby [nɪə'baɪ] **1** *adv* in der Nähe. **2** *adj* nahe gelegen.

nearly ['nɪəlɪ] *adv* beinahe, fast. **I ~ laughed** ich hätte fast gelacht; **she was ~ in tears** sie war den Tränen nahe; **not ~** bei weitem nicht, nicht annähernd.

nearness ['nɪənɪs] *n* Nähe *f.*

near: ~side 1 *adj* auf der Beifahrerseite, linke(r,

s)/rechte(r, s); **2** *n* Beifahrerseite *f;* **~-sighted** *adj* kurzsichtig.

neat [niːt] *adj (+er)* **(a)** *(tidy) person, house, hairstyle* ordentlich; *worker, work, handwriting also* sauber; *appearance also* gepflegt. **to make a ~ job of sth** etwas tadellos machen. **(b)** *(pleasing)* nett; *clothes also* adrett; *person, figure also* hübsch. **(c)** *(skilful) gadget* gelungen; *style* gewandt; *solution* elegant; *trick* schlau. **that's very ~** das ist sehr schlau. **(d)** *(undiluted) spirits* pur. **(e)** *(US col: excellent)* klasse *inv (col).*

neatly ['niːtlɪ] *adv see adj (a-c)* **(a)** ordentlich; sauber. **(b)** nett; adrett; hübsch. **(c)** gelungen; gewandt; elegant; schlau. **~ put** treffend ausgedrückt.

neatness ['niːtnɪs] *n see adj (a-c)* **(a)** Ordentlichkeit *f;* Sauberkeit *f.* **(b)** Nettheit *f,* nettes Aussehen; Adrettheit *f;* hübsches Aussehen. **(c)** Gelungenheit *f;* Gewandtheit *f;* Eleganz *f;* Schlauheit *f.*

nebulous ['nebjʊləs] *adj (fig)* unklar, nebulös.

necessarily ['nesɪsərɪlɪ] *adv* notwendigerweise, unbedingt. **not ~** nicht unbedingt.

necessary ['nesɪsərɪ] **1** *adj* **(a)** notwendig, nötig *(to, for* für). **it is ~ to ... man muß ...;** **is it ~ for me to come too?** muß ich auch kommen?; **it's not ~ for you to come** Sie brauchen nicht zu kommen; **it is ~ for him to be there** es ist nötig *or* notwendig, daß er da ist, er muß (unbedingt) da sein; **all the ~ qualifications** alle erforderlichen Qualifikationen; **~ condition** Voraussetzung *f;* **to make it ~ for sb to do sth** es erforderlich machen, daß jd etw tut; **if ~** wenn nötig, nötigenfalls; **to make the ~ arrangements** die erforderlichen Anordnungen treffen; **to do what is ~** alles Nötige tun; **to do no more than is ~** nicht mehr tun, als unbedingt nötig ist. **(b)** *(unavoidable) conclusion, result* unausweichlich. **a ~ evil** ein notwendiges Übel.

2 *n* **(a)** *(col: what is needed)* **the ~** das Notwendige; **will you do the ~?** wirst du das Nötige erledigen? **(b)** *(col: money)* **the ~** nötige Kleingeld.

necessitate [nɪ'sesɪteɪt] *vt* notwendig machen, erfordern *(form).*

necessity [nɪ'sesɪtɪ] *n* **(a)** *no pl* Notwendigkeit *f.* **from** *or* **out of ~** aus Not; **of ~** notgedrungen; **it is a case of absolute ~** es ist unbedingt notwendig; **in case of ~** im Notfall. **(b)** *(necessary thing)* Notwendigkeit *f.* **the bare necessities (of life)** das Notwendigste (zum Leben).

neck [nek] **1** *n* Hals *m; (of dress etc)* Ausschnitt *m.* **to break one's ~** sich *(dat)* das Genick brechen; **to risk one's ~** Kopf und Kragen riskieren; **to save one's ~** seinen Hals aus der Schlinge ziehen; **a stiff ~** ein steifer Hals *or* Nacken; **to be up to one's ~ in work** bis über den Hals in der Arbeit stecken; **he's in it up to his ~** *(col)* steckt bis über den Hals drin; **to stick one's ~ out** seinen Kopf riskieren; **in this ~ of the woods** *(col)* in diesen Breiten; **it has a high ~** *(dress etc)* es ist hochgeschlossen. **2** *vi (col)* knutschen *(col).*

neck and neck *(lit, fig)* **1** *adj attr* Kopf-an-Kopf-. **2** *adv* Kopf an Kopf.

necklace ['neklɪs] *n* (Hals)kette *f.*

neck: ~line *n* Ausschnitt *m;* **~tie** *n (esp US)* Krawatte *f,* Schlips *m.*

nectar ['nektəʳ] *n (lit, fig)* Nektar *m.*

nectarine ['nektərɪn] *n (fruit)* Nektarine *f.*

née [neɪ] *adj* **Mrs Smith, ~ Jones** Frau Smith, geborene Jones.

need [niːd] **1** *n* **(a)** *no pl (necessity)* Notwendigkeit *f (for gen).* **if ~ be** nötigenfalls; **in case of ~** notfalls, im Notfall; **(there is) no ~ for sth** etw ist nicht nötig; **there is no ~ for sb to do sth** jd braucht etw nicht zu tun; **there's no ~ to get angry** du brauchst nicht gleich wütend zu werden; **to be (badly) in ~ of sth** *(person)* etw (dringend) brauchen; **to be in ~ of repair** reparaturbedürftig sein; **to have no ~ of sth** etw nicht brauchen; **to have no ~ to do sth** etw nicht zu tun brauchen. **(b)** *no pl (misfortune, poverty)* Not *f.* **in time(s) of ~** in Zeiten der Not; **those in ~** die Notleidenden *pl.* **(c)** *(requirement)* Bedürfnis *nt.* **the body's ~ for oxygen** das Sauerstoffbedürfnis des Körpers; **my ~s are few** ich stelle nur geringe Ansprüche. **2** *vt* **(a)** brauchen. **to ~ no introduction** keine spezielle Einführung brauchen; **much ~ed** dringend notwendig; **just what I ~ed** genau das richtige; **that's all I ~ed** *(iro)* das hat mir gerade noch gefehlt; **it ~s a coat of paint** es muß gestrichen werden; **a visa is ~ed to enter the USA** man braucht für die Einreise in die USA ein Visum; **it ~ed an accident to make him drive carefully** er mußte erst einen Unfall haben, bevor er vernünftig fuhr. **(b)** **sth ~s doing** *or* **to be done** etw muß gemacht werden; **the book ~s careful reading** man muß das Buch genau lesen; **to ~ to do sth** *(have to)* etw tun müssen; **not to ~ to do sth** etw nicht zu tun brauchen; **he doesn't ~ to be told** man braucht es ihm nicht zu sagen; **she ~s to have everything explained to her** man muß ihr alles erklären. **3** *aux* **(a)** *(positive)* müssen. **~ he go?** muß er gehen?; **~ I say more?** mehr brauche ich ja wohl nicht zu sagen; **I ~ hardly say that ...** ich brauche wohl kaum zu erwähnen, daß ...; **you only ~ed (to) ask** du hättest nur (zu) fragen brauchen; **one ~ only look** ein Blick genügt. **(b)** *(negative)* brauchen. **you ~n't wait** du brauchst nicht (zu) warten; **we ~n't have come** wir hätten gar nicht kommen brauchen; **I/you ~n't have bothered** das war nicht nötig. **(c)** *(logical necessity)* **that ~n't be the case** das muß nicht unbedingt der Fall sein; **it ~ not follow that ...** daraus folgt nicht unbedingt, daß ...

needle ['niːdl] **1** *n* Nadel *f.* **it's like looking for a ~ in a haystack** es ist, als ob man eine Stecknadel im Heuhaufen suchte; **to give sb the ~** *(col)* jdn reizen. **2** *vt (col: goad)* ärgern, piesacken *(col).* **what's needling him?** was ist ihm über die Leber gelaufen? *(col).*

needless ['niːdlɪs] *adj* unnötig. **~ to say** natürlich; **~ to say, he didn't come** er kam natürlich nicht.

needlessly ['niːdlɪslɪ] *adv* unnötig(erweise).

needlework ['niːdlwɜːk] *n* Handarbeit *f.*

needy ['niːdɪ] **1** *adj (+er)* ärmlich, bedürftig. **2** *n* **the ~** die Bedürftigen *pl.*

negation [nɪ'ɡeɪʃən] *n* Verneinung *f.*

negative ['neɡətɪv] **1** *adj* negativ; *answer* verneinend; *(Gram) form* verneint. **2** *n* **(a)** *(also Gram)* Verneinung *f.* **to answer in the ~** eine verneinende Antwort geben; *(refuse)* einen abschlägigen Bescheid geben; **his answer was a curt ~** er antwortete mit einem knappen Nein; **put this sentence into the ~** verneinen Sie diesen Satz. **(b)** *(Gram: word)* Negation *f;* *(Math)* negative Zahl. **(c)** *(Phot)* Negativ *nt.* **(d)** *(Elec)* negativer Pol.

neglect [nɪ'ɡlekt] **1** *vt* vernachlässigen; *opportunity* versäumen; *advice* nicht befolgen. **to ~ to do sth** es versäumen, etw zu tun. **2** Vernachlässigung *f;* *(negligence)* Nachlässigkeit *f.* **~ of one's duties** Pflichtversäumnis *nt;* **to be in a state of ~** verwahrlost sein, völlig vernachlässigt sein; **the fire started through (his) ~** das Feuer ist durch seine Nachlässigkeit entstanden.

neglected [nɪ'ɡlektɪd] *adj* vernachlässigt. **to feel ~** sich vernachlässigt fühlen.

neglectful [nɪ'ɡlektfʊl] *adj* nachlässig; *father, government etc* pflichtvergessen. **to be ~ of sb/ sth** jdn/etw vernachlässigen.

négligé(e) ['neɡlɪʒeɪ] *n* Negligé *nt.*

negligence ['neɡlɪdʒəns] *n (carelessness)* Nachlässigkeit *f;* *(causing danger, Jur)* Fahrlässigkeit *f.*

negligent ['neɡlɪdʒənt] *adj* **(a)** nachlässig; *(causing danger, damage)* fahrlässig. **both drivers were ~** beide Fahrer haben sich fahrlässig verhalten. **(b)** *(off-hand)* lässig.

negligible ['neɡlɪdʒəbl] *adj* unwesentlich; *quantity also* geringfügig.

negotiable [nɪ'ɡəʊʃɪəbl] *adj* **(a)** *(Comm) (can be sold)* verkäuflich; *(can be transferred)* übertragbar. **these terms are ~** über diese Bedingungen kann verhandelt werden. **(b)** *road* befahrbar; *river, mountain pass* passierbar; *obstacle, difficulty* überwindbar.

negotiate [nɪ'ɡəʊʃɪeɪt] **1** *vt* **(a)** verhandeln über *(+acc);* *(bring about)* aushandeln. **(b)** *bend, (horse) fence* nehmen; *river, mountain* passieren; *obstacle* überwinden. **2** *vi* verhandeln *(for über +acc).*

negotiation [nɪ,ɡəʊʃɪ'eɪʃən] *n* **(a)** *siehe vt (a)* Verhandlung *f;* Aushandlung *f.* **the matter is still under ~** über diese Sache wird noch verhandelt. **(b)** *usu pl (talks)* Verhandlung *f.* **to enter into ~s with sb** Verhandlungen mit jdm aufnehmen. **(c)** *(of river, mountain)* Passage *f,* Passieren *nt; (of obstacle)* Überwindung *f.*

negotiator [nɪ'ɡəʊʃɪeɪtəʳ] *n* Unterhändler(in *f) m.*

Negress ['niːɡres] *n* Negerin *f.*

Negro ['niːɡrəʊ] **1** *adj* Neger-. **2** *n* Neger *m.*

neigh [neɪ] **1** *vi* wiehern. **2** *n* Wiehern *nt.*

neighbour, *(US)* **neighbor** ['neɪbəʳ] *n* Nachbar(in *f) m; (at table)* Tischnachbar(in *f) m; (Bibl etc)* Nächste(r) *mf.*

neighbourhood, *(US)* **neighborhood** ['neɪbəhʊd] *n (district)* Gegend *f; (people)* Nachbarschaft *f.* **in the ~ of sth** in der Nähe von etw.

neighbouring, *(US)* **neighboring** ['neɪbərɪŋ] *adj house(s), village* benachbart, Nachbar-; *fields, community* Nachbar-.

neighbourly, *(US)* **neighborly** ['neɪbəlɪ] *adj action, relations* gutnachbarlich. **they are ~ people** sie sind gute Nachbarn.

neither ['naɪðəʳ] **1** *adv* **~ ... nor** weder ... noch; **he ~ knows nor cares** er weiß es nicht und will es auch nicht wissen. **2** *conj* auch nicht. **if you don't go, ~ shall I** wenn du nicht gehst, gehe ich auch nicht; **I'm not going — ~ am I** ich gehe nicht — ich auch nicht; **he didn't do it (and) ~ did his sister** weder er noch seine Schwester haben es getan. **3** *adj* keine(r, s) (der beiden). **~ one of them** keiner von beiden. **4** *pron* keiner(r, s). **~ of them** keiner von beiden; **which one will you take? — ~** welches nehmen Sie? — keines (von beiden).

neo- ['niːəʊ-] *pref* neo-, Neo-; **~classical** klassizistisch; **~fascist 1** *adj* neofaschistisch; **2** *n* Neofaschist(in *f) m.*

neolithic [,niːəʊ'lɪθɪk] *adj* jungsteinzeitlich, neolithisch.

neologism [nɪ'ɒlədʒɪzəm] *n (Ling)* (Wort)neubildung *f,* Neologismus *m.*

neon ['niːɒn] *n (Chem)* Neon *nt.* **~ sign** *(name)* Neon- *or* Leuchtschild *nt; (advertisement)* Leuchtreklame *f no pl.*

nephew ['nevjuː, 'nefjuː] *n* Neffe *m.*

nepotism ['nepətɪzəm] *n* Vetternwirtschaft *f.*

nerve ['nɜːv] **1** *n* **(a)** *(Anat)* Nerv *m.* **to suffer from ~s** nervös sein; **to have an attack of ~s** in Panik geraten, durchdrehen *(col);* **his ~s are bad** er hat schlechte Nerven; **to get on sb's ~s** *(col)* jdm auf die Nerven gehen; **to have ~s of steel** Nerven wie Drahtseile haben. **(b)** *no pl (courage)* Mut *m.* **to lose/keep one's ~** die Nerven verlieren/nicht verlieren; **to have the ~ to do sth** sich trauen, etw zu tun; **a test of** ~ eine Nervenprobe. **(c)** *no pl (col: impudence)* Frechheit, Unverschämtheit *f.* **to have the** ~ **to do sth** die Frechheit besitzen, etw zu tun; **he's got a** ~**!** der hat Nerven! *(col).* **2** *vtr* **to** ~ **oneself for sth/to do sth** sich seelisch und moralisch auf etw *(acc)* vorbereiten/darauf vorbereiten, etw zu tun.

nerve-racking ['nɜːvrækıŋ] *adj* nervenaufreibend.

nervous ['nɜːvəs] *adj* **(a)** *(Anat) exhaustion, reflex* nervös. ~ **tension** Nervenanspannung *f.* **(b)** *(apprehensive)* nervös; *(overexcited, tense also)* aufgeregt. **to feel** ~ nervös sein; **I am** ~ **about the exam/him** mir ist bange vor dem Examen/um ihn; **I am rather** ~ **about diving** ich habe einen zeimlichen Bammel vor dem Tauchen *(col).*

nervous *in cpds* Nerven-; ~ **breakdown** *n* Nervenzusammenbruch *m;* ~ **energy** *n* Vitalität *f.*

nervously ['nɜːvəslı] *adv* nervös; *(excitedly also)* aufgeregt.

nervous wreck *n (col)* **to be/look/feel a** ~ mit den Nerven völlig am Ende sein.

nervy ['nɜːvı] *adj (+er)* **(a)** *(Brit: tense)* nervös. **(b)** *(US col: cheeky)* frech.

nest [nest] **1** *n* Nest *nt.* **to leave the** ~ *(lit, fig)* das Nest verlassen; **a** ~ **of tables** ein Satz *m* Tische. **2** *vi* nisten.

nesting-box ['nestıŋbɒks] *n* Nistkasten *m.*

nestle ['nesl] *vi* **to** ~ **down in bed** sich ins Bett kuscheln; **to** ~ **up to sb** sich an jdn kuscheln; **the village nestling in the hills** das Dorf, das zwischen den Bergen eingebettet liegt.

nestling ['neslıŋ] *n* Nestling *m.*

net[1] [net] **1** *n* *(lit, fig)* Netz *nt.* **to be caught in the** ~ *(fig)* in die Falle gehen. **2** *vt* *fish, butterfly* mit dem Netz fangen; *(fig) criminal* fangen.

net[2] **1** *adj* **(a)** *price, income, weight* netto, Netto-. ~ **profit** Reingewinn *m;* **it costs £15** ~ **es kostet £ 15** netto. **(b)** *(fig) result* End-, letztendlich. **2** *vt* netto einnehmen; *(in wages, salary)* netto verdienen; *(deal etc)* einbringen.

net: ~**ball** *n (Brit)* Korbball *m;* ~ **curtain** *n* Tüllgardine *f,* Store *m.*

Netherlands ['neðələndz] *npl* **the** ~ die Niederlande *pl.*

netting ['netıŋ] *n* Netz *nt; (wire* ~) Maschendraht *m.*

nettle ['netl] **1** *n (Bot)* Nessel *f.* **2** *vt (fig col) person* wurmen *(col),* fuchsen *(col).*

network ['netwɜːk] *n* **(a)** *(lit, fig)* Netz *nt.* **(b)** *(Rad, TV)* Sendenetz *nt; (Elec)* Netzwerk *nt.*

neuralgia [njʊə'rældʒə] *n* Neuralgie *f,* Nervenschmerzen *pl.*

neurosis [njʊə'rəʊsıs] *n, pl* **neuroses** [njʊə'rəʊsiːz] Neurose *f.*

neurotic [njʊə'rɒtık] **1** *adj* neurotisch. **to be** ~ **about sth** *(col)* in bezug auf etw *(acc)* neurotisch sein. **2** *n* Neurotiker(in *f) m.*

neuter ['njuːtə[r]] **1** *adj* **(a)** *(Gram)* sächlich. **(b)** *animal, person* geschlechtslos; *(castrated)* kastriert; *plant* ungeschlechtlich. **2** *n* **(a)** *(Gram)* Neutrum *nt.* **(b)** *(animal)* geschlechtloses Wesen; *(castrated)* kastriertes Tier. **3** *vt cat, dog* kastrieren; *female* sterilisieren.

neutral ['njuːtrəl] **1** *adj* neutral. **2** *n (Aut)* Leerlauf *m.* **to be in** ~ im Leerlauf sein.

neutrality [njuː'trælıtı] *n* Neutralität *f.*

neutralize ['njuːtrəlaız] *vt* neutralisieren; *(fig)* ausgleichen.

neutron ['njuːtrɒn] *n* Neutron *nt.*

neutron bomb *n* Neutronenbombe *f.*

never ['nevə[r]] *adv* **(a)** nie. **I have** ~ **seen him** ich habe ihn (noch) nie gesehen; ~ **again** nie wieder; **I'll** ~ **try that again** das werde ich nicht noch einmal versuchen; ~ **before** noch nie; **I have** ~ **seen him before** ich habe ihn noch nie gesehen; ~ **before have men climbed this peak** nie zuvor

haben Menschen diesen Gipfel erklommen; ~ **even nicht einmal;** ~ **ever** gar nie; **I have** ~ **ever been so insulted** ich bin noch nie so beleidigt worden. **(b)** *(emph: not)* **that will** ~ **do!** das geht ganz und gar nicht!; **he** ~ **so much as smiled** er hat nicht einmal gelächelt; **he said** ~ **a word** er hat kein einziges Wort gesagt; **you've** ~ **left it behind!** *(col)* du hast es doch wohl nicht etwa liegenlassen! *(col);* **would you do it again?** — ~**!** würdest du das noch einmal machen? — bestimmt nicht; **Spurs were beaten** — ~**!** *(col)* Spurs sind geschlagen worden — das ist doch nicht möglich!; **well I** ~ **(did)!** *(col)* nein, so was!

never: ~**-ending** *adj* endlos; ~**-never** *n (Brit col):* **on the** ~**-never** auf Pump *(col).*

nevertheless [,nevəðə'les] *adv* trotzdem, dennoch.

new [njuː] *adj (+er)* neu. ~ **moon** Neumond *m;* **there's a** ~ **moon tonight** heute nacht ist Neumond; **that's nothing** ~ das ist nichts Neues; **that's something** ~**!** das ist wirklich ganz was Neues!; **what's** ~? *(col)* was gibt's Neues? *(col);* **dressed in** ~ **clothes** neu eingekleidet; **to make sth (look) like** ~ etw wie neu machen; **as** ~ wie neu; **this system is** ~ **to me** dieses System ist mir neu; **he is a** ~ **man** *(fig)* er ist ein neuer Mensch; **that's a** ~ **one on me** *(col)* das ist mir ja ganz neu; **a** ~ **kind of engine** ein neuartiger Motor; **I'm quite** ~ **to this job** ich bin neu in dieser Stelle; **I am** ~ **to this place** ich bin erst seit kurzem hier.

new: ~**-born** *adj* neugeboren; ~**comer** *n* Neuankömmling *m; (in job, subject etc)* Neuling *m (to* in +*dat).*

new-fangled ['njuː,fæŋgld] *adj* neumodisch.

new-laid ['njuːleıd] *adj* frisch.

newly ['njuːlı] *adv* frisch. ~**-made** ganz neu; *bread, cake etc* frisch gebacken.

newly-weds ['njuːlıwedz] *npl (col)* Frischvermählte *pl.*

newness ['njuːnıs] *n* Neuheit *f.*

news [njuːz] *n no pl* **(a)** *(report, information)* Nachricht *f; (recent development)* Neuigkeit(en *pl) f.* **a piece of** ~ eine Neuigkeit; **I have** ~**/no** ~ **of him** ich weiß Neues/nichts Neues von ihm; **there is no** ~ es gibt nichts Neues; **have you heard the** ~? haben Sie schon das Neueste gehört?; **is there any** ~? gibt es etwas Neues?; **I have** ~ **for you** *(iro)* ich habe eine Überraschung für dich; **bad/good** ~ schlechte/gute Nachricht(en); **that is good** ~ das sind ja gute Nachrichten; **who will break the** ~ **to him?** wer wird es ihm beibringen?; **that is** ~ **to me!** das ist (mir) ganz neu! **(b)** *(Press, Film, Rad, TV)* Nachrichten *pl.* **it was on the** ~ das kam in den Nachrichten; **to be in the** ~ von sich reden machen.

news: ~ **agent** *n (Brit)* Zeitungshändler *m;* ~**cast** *n* Nachrichtensendung *f;* ~**caster** *n* Nachrichtensprecher(in *f) m;* ~ **dealer** *n (US)* Zeitungshändler *m;* ~ **editor** *n* Nachrichtenredakteur *m;* ~**flash** *n* Kurzmeldung *f;* ~**letter** *n* Mitteilungsblatt *nt.*

newspaper ['njuːz,peıpə[r]] *n* Zeitung *f.* **daily/ weekly** ~ Tageszeitung/Wochenzeitung.

newspaper: ~ **article** *n* Zeitungsartikel *m;* ~ **man** *n* Zeitungsverkäufer *m; (journalist)* Journalist *m;* ~ **report** *n* Zeitungsbericht *m.*

news: ~**print** *n* Zeitungspapier *nt;* ~**reader** *n* Nachrichtensprecher(in *f) m;* ~**reel** *n* Wochenschau *f;* ~**room** *n (of newspaper)* Nachrichtenredaktion *f; (TV, Rad)* Nachrichtenstudio *nt;* ~**stand** *n* Zeitungsstand *m;* ~**worthy** *adj* sensationell; **to be** ~**worthy** Neuigkeitswert haben.

newsy ['njuːzı] *adj (+er) (col)* voller Neuigkeiten.

newt [njuːt] *n* Wassermolch *m.*

new: **N**~ **Testament** **1** *n* **the N**~ **Testament** das Neue Testament; **2** *adj attr* des Neuen Testaments; **N**~ **World** *n* Neue Welt.

New Year *n* neues Jahr; (~'s *Day*) Neujahr *nt*. **to see in the ~** das neue Jahr begrüßen; **Happy ~!** (ein) gutes neues Jahr!; ~'s *Day*, (*US also*) ~'s Neujahr *nt*; ~'s *Eve* Silvester *nt*; ~ *resolution* (guter) Vorsatz für das neue Jahr.

New: ~ **Zealand** 1 *n* Neuseeland *nt*; 2 *adj attr* neuseeländisch; ~ **Zealander** *n* Neuseeländer(in *f*) *m*.

next [nekst] 1 *adj* nächste(r, s). **come back ~ week/Tuesday** kommen Sie nächste Woche/ nächsten Dienstag wieder; **he came back the ~ day/week** er kam am nächsten Tag/in der nächsten Woche wieder; **(the)** ~ **time I see him** wenn ich ihn das nächste Mal sehe; **the ~ time I saw him** als ich ihn das nächste Mal sah; **(the)** ~ **moment he was gone** im nächsten Moment war er weg; **from one moment to the** ~ von einem Augenblick auf den anderen; **this time ~ week** nächste Woche um diese Zeit; **the year/week after** ~ übernächstes Jahr/übernächste Woche; **the ~ day but one** der übernächste Tag; **who's ~?** wer ist der nächste?; **you're** ~ Sie sind dran (*col*) *or* an der Reihe; ~ **please!** der nächste bitte!; **the ~ but one** der/die/das übernächste; **the ~ best** der/die/das nächstbeste.

2 *adv* **(a)** (*the* ~ *time*) das nächste Mal; (*afterwards*) danach. **what shall we do ~?** was sollen wir als nächstes machen?; **whatever ~?** (*in surprise*) Sachen gibt's! (*col*); (*despairingly*) wo soll das nur hinführen? **(b)** ~ **to sb/sth** neben jdm/etw; (*with motion*) neben jdn/etw; **the** ~ **to last row** die vorletzte Reihe; **he was ~ to last** er war der vorletzte; **the ~ to bottom shelf** das vorletzte Brett; ~ **to the skin** (direkt) auf der Haut; ~ **to nothing** so gut wie nichts; ~ **to impossible** nahezu unmöglich.

next-door ['neks'dɔ:ʳ] 1 *adv* nebenan. **they live ~ to us** sie wohnen (direkt) neben uns; **the boy ~** der Junge von nebenan. 2 *adj* **the ~ neighbour/house** der Nachbar/die Nachbarin von nebenan/ das Nebenhaus; **we are ~ neighbours** wir wohnen Tür an Tür.

NHS (*Brit*) = **National Health Service.**

nib [nɪb] *n* Feder *f*.

nibble ['nɪbl] 1 *vti* **to ~ (at)** sth an etw (*dat*) knabbern. 2 *vi* (*fig*) sich interessiert zeigen.

nice [naɪs] *adj* (+*er*) **(a)** nett; *voice also* sympathisch; (~-*looking*) *girl, dress, looks etc also* hübsch; *taste, smell, meal* gut; *warmth, weather, feeling, day* schön; (*skilful*) *workmanship, work* gut, schön. **be ~ to him** sei nett zu ihm; **that's not ~!** das ist aber nicht nett; **to have a ~ time** sich gut amüsieren; **I had a ~ rest** ich habe mich gut *or* schön ausgeruht; **how ~ of you to ...** wie nett von Ihnen, zu ...

(b) (*intensifier*) schön. **a ~ long holiday** schön lange Ferien; ~ **and warm/near** schön warm/ nahe; ~ **and easy** ganz leicht.

(c) (*respectable*) nett; *district* fein; *words* schön; *manners* gut.

(d) (*iro*) schön, sauber. **here's a ~ state of affairs!** das sind ja schöne Zustände!; **you're in a ~ mess** du sitzt schön im Schlamassel (*col*).

(e) (*subtle*) *distinction* fein, genau. **that was a ~ point** das war eine gute Bemerkung; **one or two ~ points** ein paar gute Gedanken.

nice-looking ['naɪs'lʊkɪŋ] *adj* gutaussehend; *girl also* hübsch. **to be ~** gut aussehen.

nicely ['naɪslɪ] *adv* (*pleasantly*) nett; (*well*) *go, speak, behave, placed* gut. **to go ~** wie geschmiert laufen (*col*); **that will do ~** das reicht vollauf; **how's it going?** — ~, **thank you** wie geht es so? — danke, ganz gut; **he's getting on ~** ihm geht's ganz gut.

nicety ['naɪsɪtɪ] *n* **(a)** (*subtlety*) Feinheit *f*; (*of judgement also*) Schärfe *f*; (*precision*) (peinliche) Genauigkeit. **(b)** niceties *pl* Feinheiten *pl*.

niche [ni:ʃ] *n* (*Archit*) Nische *f*; (*fig*) Plätzchen *nt*.

nick[1] [nɪk] 1 *n* **(a)** Kerbe *f*. **I got a little ~ on my chin** ich habe mich leicht am Kinn geschnitten. **(b) in the ~ of time** gerade noch (rechtzeitig). **(c)** (*Brit col: condition*) **in good/bad ~** gut/nicht gut in Schuß (*col*). 2 *vt* **(a)** *stick* einkerben. **to ~ oneself** (*col*) sich schneiden. **(b)** (*bullet*) *person, wall* streifen.

nick[2] (*Brit*) 1 *vt* (*col*) **(a)** (*arrest*) einsperren (*col*); (*catch*) schnappen (*col*). **he got ~ed** den haben sie sich (*dat*) geschnappt (*col*). **(b)** (*steal*) klauen (*col*). 2 *n* (*prison*) Knast *m* (*col*); (*police station*) Wache *f*.

nickel ['nɪkl] *n* **(a)** (*metal*) Nickel *nt*. **(b)** (*US*) Fünfcentstück *nt*.

nickname ['nɪkneɪm] 1 *n* Spitzname *m*. 2 *vt person* taufen.

nicotine ['nɪkəti:n] *n* Nikotin *nt*.

niece [ni:s] *n* Nichte *f*.

nifty ['nɪftɪ] *adj* (+*er*) (*col*) flott (*col*); *gadget, tool* schlau (*col*).

Nigeria [naɪ'dʒɪərɪə] *n* Nigeria *nt*.

niggardly ['nɪgədlɪ] *adj person* knaus(e)rig; *amount, portion also* kümmerlich.

nigger ['nɪgəʳ] *n* (*pej*) Nigger *m* (*pej col*).

niggle ['nɪgl] 1 *vi* (*complain*) herumkritisieren (*about* an +*dat*). 2 *vt* (*worry*) plagen, zu schaffen machen (+*dat*).

niggling ['nɪglɪŋ] *adj person* überkritisch; *doubt, pain* quälend; *detail* pingelig (*col*).

night [naɪt] *n* Nacht *f*; (*evening*) Abend *m*. **I saw him last ~** ich habe ihn gestern abend gesehen; **I'll see him tomorrow ~** ich treffe ihn morgen abend; **on Friday ~** Freitag abend/nacht; **on the ~ of (Saturday) the 11th** am (Samstag, dem) 11. nachts; **11/6 o'clock at ~** 11 Uhr nachts/6 Uhr abends; **to travel/see Paris by ~** nachts reisen/ Paris bei Nacht sehen; **far into the ~** bis spät in die Nacht; **in/during the ~** in/während der Nacht; **the ~ before last they were ...** vorgestern abend/vorletzte Nacht waren sie ...; **to spend the ~ at a hotel** in einem Hotel übernachten; **I need a good ~'s sleep** ich muß mal wieder ordentlich schlafen; ~ **after ~** jede Nacht; **all ~ (long)** die ganze Nacht; **to have a ~ out** (abends) ausgehen; **to have a late/an early ~** spät/früh ins Bett kommen, spät/früh schlafen gehen; **to work ~s** nachts arbeiten; ~ **is falling** die Nacht bricht herein; **the last three ~s of Hamlet** die letzten drei Abende von „Hamlet".

night in *cpds* Nacht-; ~-**bird** *n* Nachtvogel *m*; (*fig*) Nachteule *f* (*col*), Nachtschwärmer *m* (*col*); ~**cap** *n* **(a)** (*garment*) Schlafmütze *f*; **(b)** (*drink*) Schlaftrunk *m*; ~-**club** *n* Nachtklub *m*; ~-**dress** *n* (*Brit*) Nachthemd *nt*; ~-**fall** *n* Einbruch *m* der Dunkelheit; ~**gown** *n* Nachthemd *nt*.

nightie ['naɪtɪ] *n* (*Brit: col*) Nachthemd *nt*.

nightingale ['naɪtɪŋgeɪl] *n* Nachtigall *f*.

nightly ['naɪtlɪ] 1 *adj* (*every night*) (all)nächtlich, Nacht-; (*every evening*) (all)abendlich, Abend-. 2 *adv* jede Nacht/jeden Abend. **twice ~** zweimal pro Abend.

night: ~**mare** *n* (*lit, fig*) Alptraum *m*; ~**owl** *n* (*col*) Nachteule *f* (*col*); ~**safe** *n* Nachtsafe *m*; ~-**school** *n* Abendschule *f*; ~-**shift** *n* Nachtschicht *f*; **to be on ~-shift** Nachtschicht haben *or* arbeiten; ~-**spot** *n* Nachtlokal *nt*; ~-**stick** *n* (*US*) Schlagstock *m*; ~-**time** *n* Nacht *f*; **at ~-time** nachts; ~-**watchman** *n* Nachtwächter *m*.

nihilism ['naɪɪlɪzəm] *n* Nihilismus *m*.

nil [nɪl] *n* null (*also Sport*); (*nothing*) nichts. **the score was one—~** es stand eins zu null.

nimble ['nɪmbl] *adj* (+*er*) *fingers* flink, (*agile*) gelenkig, beweglich; (*skilful*) geschickt; *mind* beweglich.

nimbly ['nɪmblɪ] *adv work* flink; *dance* leicht(füßig).

nine [naɪn] 1 *adj* neun. ~ **times out of ten** so gut wie immer. 2 *n* Neun *f*. **dressed up to the ~s** in Schale *(col); see* **six.**

nineteen ['naɪn'tiːn] *adj* neunzehn. **she talks ~ to the dozen** sie redet wie ein Wasserfall *(col).*

nineteenth ['naɪn'tiːnθ] *adj* neunzehnte(r, s); *see* **sixteenth.**

ninety ['naɪntɪ] **1** *adj* neunzig. **2** *n* Neunzig *f; see* **sixty.**

ninth [naɪnθ] **1** *adj* neunte(r, s). **2** *n (as fraction)* Neuntel *nt; (of series)* Neunte(r, s); *see* **sixth.**

nip[1] [nɪp] **1** *n (pinch)* Kniff *m; (bite from animal etc)* Biß *m.* **there's a ~ in the air today** es ist heute ganz schön frisch. **2** *vt* **(a)** *(bite)* zwicken; *(pinch also)* kneifen; *bud, shoot* abknipsen. **to ~ sth in the bud** *(fig)* etw im Keim ersticken. **(b)** *(cold, frost etc) plants* angreifen. **the cold air ~ped our faces** die Kälte schnitt uns ins Gesicht. **3** *vi (Brit col)* sausen *(col)*, flitzen *(col)*. **to ~ up(stairs)/down(stairs)** hoch-/runtersausen *(col);* **I'll just ~ down to the shops** ich gehe mal kurz einkaufen *(col);* **I'll just ~ out for a moment** ich gehe nur mal kurz raus.

nip[2] *n (col: drink)* Schlückchen *nt.*

nipple ['nɪpl] *n (Anat)* Brustwarze *f; (on baby's bottle)* Sauger *m.*

nippy ['nɪpɪ] *adj (+er)* **(a)** *(Brit col)* flink, flott; *car* spritzig. **(b)** *weather* frisch.

nit [nɪt] *n* **(a)** *(Zool)* Nisse *f.* **(b)** *(Brit col)* Dummkopf, Blödmann *(col) m.*

nit-picking ['nɪtpɪkɪŋ] *adj (col)* pingelig *(col).*

nitrogen ['naɪtrədʒən] *n* Stickstoff *m.*

nitroglycerin(e) ['naɪtrəʊ'glɪsəriːn] *n* Nitroglyzerin *nt.*

nitty-gritty ['nɪtɪ'grɪtɪ] *n (col)* **to get down to the ~** zur Sache kommen.

nitwit ['nɪtwɪt] *n (col)* Dummkopf *m.*

No, no = number Nr.

no [nəʊ] **1** *adv* **(a)** *(negative)* nein. **oh ~!** o nein!; **to answer ~** *(to question)* mit Nein antworten; *(to request)* nein sagen; **she can't say ~** sie kann nicht nein sagen. **(b)** *(with comp)* nicht. **I can bear it ~ longer** ich kann es nicht länger ertragen; **I have ~ more money** ich habe kein Geld mehr; **~ fewer than 100** bestimmt 100; **~ later than Monday** spätestens Montag.

2 *adj* kein. **~ one person could do it** keiner könnte das allein tun; **~ two men are alike** zwei Menschen sind immer verschieden; **~ other man** kein anderer; **it's of ~ interest/importance** das ist belanglos/unwichtig; **it's ~ use** *or* **good** das hat keinen Zweck; **~ parking/smoking** Parken/Rauchen verboten; **there's ~ telling what he'll do next** man kann nie wissen, was er als nächstes tun wird; **there's ~ denying it** es läßt sich nicht leugnen; **she's ~ beauty** sie ist nicht gerade eine Schönheit; **I'm ~ expert, but** ... ich bin zwar kein Fachmann, aber ...; **in ~ time** im Nu; **it's ~ small matter** das ist keine Kleinigkeit; **theirs is ~ easy task** sie haben keine leichte Aufgabe; **there is ~ such thing** so etwas gibt es nicht; **it was/we did ~ such thing!** das stimmt überhaupt nicht!

3 *n, pl* **-es** Nein *nt; (~ vote)* Neinstimme *f.* **I won't take ~ for an answer** ich bestehe darauf.

nobble ['nɒbl] *vt (Brit col)* **(a)** *horse* lahmlegen *(col).* **(b)** *(catch)* sich *(dat)* schnappen *(col).* **(c)** *(obtain dishonestly) votes etc* sich *(dat)* kaufen; *money* einsacken *(col).*

Nobel prize ['nəʊbel'praɪz] *n* Nobelpreis *m.*

nobility [nəʊ'bɪlɪtɪ] *n no pl* (Hoch)adel *m.* **she is one of the ~** sie ist eine Adlige.

noble ['nəʊbl] **1** *adj (+er)* **(a)** *person, rank* adlig. **to be of ~ birth** adlig sein. **(b)** *(fine) person, deed etc* edel, nobel; *appearance* vornehm. **(c)** *(col: selfless)* edel, edelmütig. **2** *n* Adlige(r) *mf.*

nobleman ['nəʊblmən] *n, pl* **-men** [-mən] Adlige(r) *m.*

noblewoman ['nəʊblwʊmən] *n, pl* **-women** [-wɪmɪn] Adlige *f.*

nobly ['nəʊblɪ] *adv (aristocratically)* vornehm; *(finely)* edel; *(bravely)* wacker; *(col: selflessly)* nobel, edel(mütig).

nobody ['nəʊbədɪ] **1** *pron* niemand, keiner. **~ knows better than I** niemand *or* keiner weiß besser als ich; **there was ~ else** da war sonst niemand; **~ else could have done it** es kann niemand anders gewesen sein. **2** *n* Niemand *m no pl* **he's a ~** er ist ein Niemand.

nocturnal [nɒk'tɜːnl] *adj* nächtlich; *animal, bird* Nacht-.

nocturne ['nɒktɜːn] *n (Mus)* Nokturne *f.*

nod [nɒd] **1** *n* Nicken *nt.* **to give sb a ~** jdm zunicken; **to answer with a ~** *(zustimmend)* nicken. **2** *vi* nicken. **to ~ to sb** jdm zunicken; **to ~ in agreement** zustimmend nicken. **3** *vt* **to ~ one's head** mit dem Kopf nicken.

♦ **nod off** *vi* einnicken *(col).*

node [nəʊd] *n (all senses)* Knoten *m.*

no-go area ['nəʊ'gəʊˌɛərɪə] *n* Sperrgebiet *nt.*

noise [nɔɪz] *n* Geräusch *nt; (loud, irritating sound)* Lärm, Krach *m; (Elec: interference)* Rauschen *nt.* **what was that ~?** was war das für ein Geräusch?; **the ~ of the traffic/bells** der Straßenlärm/der Lärm der Glocken; **it made a lot of ~** es hat viel Krach gemacht; **don't make a ~!** sei leise!; **stop that ~** hör mit dem Lärm auf; **she made ~s about leaving early** sie wollte unbedingt früh gehen; **a big ~** *(fig col)* ein großes Tier *(col).*

noiseless ['nɔɪzlɪs] *adj* geräuschlos; *step also* lautlos.

noisily ['nɔɪzɪlɪ] *adv see adj.*

noisy ['nɔɪzɪ] *adj (+er)* laut; *protest, debate* lautstark. **don't be so ~** sei nicht so laut, mach nicht so viel Lärm.

nomad ['nəʊmæd] *n* Nomade *m*, Nomadin *f.*

nomadic [nəʊ'mædɪk] *adj* nomadisch; *tribe* Nomaden-.

no-man's-land ['nəʊmænzlænd] *n (lit, fig)* Niemandsland *nt.*

nom de plume ['nɒmdə'pluːm] *n* Pseudonym *nt.*

nomenclature [nəʊ'menklətʃəʳ] *n* Nomenklatur *f.*

nominal ['nɒmɪnl] *adj* nominell.

nominate ['nɒmɪneɪt] *vt (appoint)* ernennen; *(propose)* nominieren, (als Kandidat) aufstellen. **he was ~d chairman** er wurde zum Vorsitzenden ernannt.

nomination [ˌnɒmɪ'neɪʃən] *n (appointment)* Ernennung *f; (proposal)* Nominierung *f.*

nominative [ˌnɒmɪnətɪv] *(Gram)* **1** *n* Nominativ, Werfall *m.* **2** *adj* **(the) ~ case** der Nominativ.

nominee [ˌnɒmɪ'niː] *n* Kandidat(in *f) m.*

non: ~-aggression *n* Nichtangriff *m; ~*-**aggression pact** *n* Nichtangriffspakt *m; ~* **alcoholic** *adj* alkoholfrei; **~-aligned** *adj* bündnisfrei; **~-believer** *n* Nichtgläubige(r) *mf.*

nonchalance ['nɒnʃələns] *n* Lässigkeit, Nonchalance *f.*

nonchalant ['nɒnʃələnt] *adj* lässig, nonchalant.

non: ~-combatant 1 *n* Nichtkämpfer *m; 2 adj* nicht am Kampf beteiligt; **~-commissioned officer** *n* Unteroffizier *m; ~*-**committal** *adj* zurückhaltend; *answer also* unverbindlich; **to be ~-committal about whether** ... sich nicht festlegen, ob ...; **~-conformist 1** *n* Nonkonformist(in *f) m; 2 adj* nonkonformistisch; **~-co-operation** *n* unkooperative Haltung.

nondescript ['nɒndɪskrɪpt] *adj taste, colour* unbestimmbar; *person, appearance* unauffällig, unscheinbar *(pej).*

none [nʌn] **1** *pron* keine(r, s); keine; *(on form)* keine. **~ of them is coming** von ihnen kommt keiner; **~ of the boys/them** keiner der Jungen/von ihnen; **~ of this** nichts davon; **~ of this is any good** das ist alles nicht gut; **do you have any bread/apples?** — **(at all)** haben Sie Brot/Äpfel?— nein, gar keines/keine; **there is ~**

left es ist nichts übrig; **their guest was ~ other than** ... ihr Gast war kein anderer als ...; **(we'll have) ~ of that!** jetzt reicht's aber!; **he would have ~ of it** er wollte davon nichts wissen. **2** *adv* **to be ~ the wiser** auch nicht schlauer sein; **it's ~ too warm** es ist nicht zu warm; **he's ~ the worse for the experience** die Erfahrung hat ihm nichts geschadet; **and ~ too soon** either und auch keineswegs zu früh.

nonentity [nɒ'nentɪtɪ] *n* unbedeutende Figur.

non-essential [nɒnɪ'senʃəl] **1** *adj* unnötig; *workers* nicht unbedingt nötig; *services* nicht lebenswichtig. **2** *n* **~s** *pl* nicht (lebens)notwendige Dinge *pl*.

nonetheless [ˌnʌnðə'les] *adv* nichtsdestoweniger, trotzdem.

non: ~-event *n (col)* Reinfall *m (col)*, Pleite *f (col)*; **~-existence** *n* Nichtvorhandensein *nt*; **~-existent** *adj* nicht vorhanden; **his accent is practically ~-existent** er hat praktisch keinen Akzent; **~-fattening** *adj* nicht dickmachend *attr*; **~-fiction** *n* Sachbücher *pl*; **~-flammable** *adj* nichtentzündbar *attr*, nicht entzündbar; **~-intervention** *n (Pol etc)* Nichteinmischung *f (in* in +*acc)*; **~-iron** *adj* bügelfrei; **~-member** *n* Nichtmitglied *nt*; **open to ~-members** Gäste willkommen; **~-payment** *n* Nichtzahlung *f*.

nonplus ['nɒn'plʌs] *vt* verblüffen.

non: ~-productive *adj* *meeting, discussion etc* unergiebig; **~-productive industries** Dienstleistungssektor *m*; **~-productive worker** Angestellte(r) *mf* im Dienstleistungssektor; **~-profit** *(US)*, **~-profit-making** *adj* keinen Gewinn anstrebend *attr*; *charity etc also* gemeinnützig; **~-resident 1** *adj* nicht ansässig; *(in hotel)* nicht im Hause wohnend; **2** *n* Nicht(orts)ansässige(r) *mf*; *(in hotel)* nicht im Haus wohnender Gast; **open to ~-residents** auch für Nichthotelgäste.

nonsense ['nɒnsəns] *n no pl (also as interjection)* Unsinn, Quatsch *(col) m*; *(verbal also)* dummes Zeug; *(silly behaviour)* Dummheiten *pl*. **a piece of ~** ein Unsinn *or* Quatsch *(col) m*; **that's a lot of ~!** das ist (ja) alles dummes Zeug!; **I've had enough of this ~** jetzt reicht's mir aber; **to make (a) ~ of sth** etw unsinnig *or* sinnlos machen; **no more of your ~!** Schluß mit dem Unsinn!; **he will stand no ~ from anybody** er läßt nicht mit sich spaßen.

nonsensical [nɒn'sensɪkəl] *adj* unsinnig.

non: ~-shrink *adj* nicht einlaufend; **~-skid** *adj* rutschsicher; **~-slip** *adj* rutschfest; **~-smoker** *n* **(a)** *(person)* Nichtraucher(in *f) m*; **(b)** *(Rail)* Nichtraucher(abteil *nt) m*; **~-smoking** *adj area* Nichtraucher-; **~-starter** *n (fig: person, idea)* Blindgänger *m*; **~-stick** *adj pan, surface* kunststoffbeschichtet, Teflon- ®; **~-stop 1** *adj train* durchgehend; *journey* ohne Unterbrechung; *flight, performances* Nonstop-; **2** *adv talk* ununterbrochen; *fly* nonstop; *travel* ohne Unterbrechung; *fly* auch gewaltlos; **~-white 1** *n* Farbige(r) *mf*; **2** *adj* farbig; *area* für Farbige.

noodle ['nuːdl] *n (Cook)* Nudel *f*.

nook [nʊk] *n* Winkel *m*. **in every ~ and cranny** in jedem Winkel.

noon [nuːn] *n* Mittag *m*. **at ~** um 12 Uhr mittags.

no-one ['nəʊwʌn] *pron* = **nobody 1**.

noose [nuːs] *n* Schlinge *f*. **to put one's head in the ~** *(fig)* den Kopf in die Schlinge stecken.

nor [nɔːʳ] *conj* **(a)** noch. **neither ... ~** weder ... noch. **(b)** *(and not)* und ... auch nicht. **I don't like him — ~ do I** ich mag ihn nicht — ich auch nicht.

norm ['nɔːm] *n* Norm *f*.

normal ['nɔːməl] **1** *adj person, situation* normal; *practice, routine also, (customary)* üblich. **it's a perfectly ~ thing** das ist völlig normal; **he is not his ~ self today** er ist heute so anders. **2** *n no pl (of temperature)* Normalwert. **temperatures be-**

low ~ Temperaturen unter dem Durchschnitt; **her temperature is above/below ~** sie hat erhöhte Temperatur/sie hat Untertemperatur; **when things are back to ~** wenn sich alles wieder normalisiert hat.

normality [nɔː'mælɪtɪ] *n* Normalität *f*. **to return to ~** sich wieder normalisieren.

normalize ['nɔːməlaɪz] *vt* normalisieren; *relations* wiederherstellen.

normally ['nɔːməlɪ] *adv (usually)* normalerweise, gewöhnlich; *(in normal way)* normal.

north [nɔːθ] **1** *n* Norden *m*. **in/from the ~** im/aus dem Norden; **to live in the ~** im Norden leben; **to the ~ of** nördlich von, im Norden von; **to veer/go to the ~** in nördliche Richtung *or* nach Norden drehen/gehen; **to face (the) ~** nach Norden liegen; **the N~ (of Scotland/England)** Nordschottland/Nordengland *nt*. **2** *adj attr* Nord-. **3** *adv (towards N~)* nach Norden. **~ of** nördlich *or* im Norden von.

north *in cpds* Nord-; **N~ America** *n* Nordamerika *nt*; **N~ American 1** *adj* nordamerikanisch; **2** *n* Nordamerikaner(in *f) m*.

north: ~-bound *adj carriageway* nach Norden (führend); *traffic* in Richtung Norden; **~-east 1** *adj* Nordost-, nordöstlich; **2** *adv* nach Nordosten; **~-east of** nordöstlich von; **~-easterly** *adj* nordöstlich; **~-eastern** *adj* nordöstlich.

northerly ['nɔːðəlɪ] *adj wind, direction, latitude* nördlich.

northern ['nɔːðən] *adj hemisphere, counties* nördlich; *Germany, Italy etc* Nord-. **N~ Ireland** Nordirland *nt*; **with a ~ outlook** mit Blick nach Norden.

northerner ['nɔːðənəʳ] *n* **(a)** Bewohner(in *f) m* des Nordens; Nordengländer(in *f) m*/-deutsche(r) *mf* etc. **he is a ~** er kommt aus dem Norden des Landes. **(b)** *(US)* Nordstaatler(in *f) m*.

northernmost ['nɔːðənməʊst] *adj* nördlichste(r, s).

north: N~ Pole *n* Nordpol *m*; **N~ Sea 1** *n* Nordsee *f*; **2** *adj* Nordsee-; **N~ Sea gas/oil** Nordseegas *nt*/-öl *nt*; **~-ward** *adj*, **~-wardly** *adj* nördlich; **~-west 1** *adj* Nordwest-, nordwestlich; **2** *adv* nach Nordwest(en); **~-west of** nordwestlich von; **~-westerly 1** *adj* nordwestlich; **2** *n* Nordwestwind *m*; **~-western** *adj* nordwestlich.

Norway ['nɔːweɪ] *n* Norwegen *nt*.

Norwegian [nɔː'wiːdʒən] **1** *adj* norwegisch. **2** *n* **(a)** Norweger(in *f) m*. **(b)** *(language)* Norwegisch *nt*.

nose [nəʊz] **1** *n* **(a)** Nase *f*; *(fig also)* Riecher *m (col)*. **to speak through one's ~** durch die Nase sprechen; **my ~ is bleeding** ich habe Nasenbluten; **follow your ~** immer der Nase nach; **to do sth under sb's very ~** etw vor jds Augen tun; **it was right under his ~ all the time** er hatte es die ganze Zeit direkt vor der Nase; **to lead sb by the ~** jdn an der Nase herumführen; **to poke** *or* **stick one's ~ into sth** *(fig)* seine Nase in etw *(acc)* stecken; **you keep your ~ out of this** *(col)* halt du dich da raus! *(col)*; **to look down one's ~ at sb/sth** auf jdn/etw herabblicken; **to pay through the ~** *(col)* sich dumm und dämlich zahlen *(col)*; **to have a ~ for sth** *(fig)* eine Nase *or* einen Riecher *(col)* für etw haben.

(b) *(of plane)* Nase *f*; *(of car)* Schnauze *f*; *(of boat also)* Bug *m*. **~ to tail** *(cars)* Stoßstange an Stoßstange.

2 *vti* **the ship ~d (its way) through the fog** das Schiff tastete sich durch den Nebel; **to ~ into sb's affairs** *(fig)* seine Nase in jds Angelegenheiten *(acc)* stecken *(col)*.

♦ **nose about** *or* **around** *vi* herumschnüffeln *(col)*; *(press also)* herumspionieren *(col)*.

♦ **nose out 1** *vt sep* aufspüren; *secret, scandal* ausspionieren *(col)*, ausschnüffeln *(col)*. **2** *vi (car)* sich vorschieben.

nose: ~bag *n* Futtersack *m*; **~bleed** *n*

Nasenbluten *nt;* **to have a** ~**bleed** Nasenbluten haben; ~**dive 1** *n (Aviat)* Sturzflug *m;* **to go into a** ~**dive** zum Sturzflug ansetzen; **the company's affairs took a** ~**dive** mit der Firma ging es rapide bergab; **2** *vi (plane)* im Sturzflug herabgehen.

nosey *adj* = **nosy.**

nosh [nɒʃ] *n (Brit col) (food)* Futter *nt (col); (meal)* Schmaus *m.*

nosh-up ['nɒʃʌp] *n (Brit col)* Schmaus *m,* Freßgelage *nt (col).*

nostalgia [nɒ'stældʒɪə] *n* Nostalgie *f (for* nach*).*

nostalgic [nɒ'stældʒɪk] *adj* nostalgisch, wehmütig.

nostril ['nɒstrəl] *n* Nasenloch *nt; (of horse etc)* Nüster *f.*

nosy ['nəʊzɪ] *adj* (+*er*) *(col)* neugierig.

not [nɒt] *adv* **(a)** nicht. **he told me** ~ **to come** er sagte, ich solle nicht kommen; **do** ~ *or* **don't come** kommen Sie nicht; ~ **a sound/word** *etc* nicht *ein* Ton/Wort *etc;* ~ **a bit** kein bißchen; ~ **a sign of ...** keine Spur von ...; ~ **one of them** kein einziger, nicht einer; ~ **a thing** überhaupt nichts; ~ **any more** nicht mehr; ~ **yet** noch nicht.

(b) *(in rhetorical questions)* **it's hot, isn't it?** es ist heiß, nicht wahr *or* nicht?; **isn't it hot?** ist das vielleicht heiß!; **you are coming, aren't you** *or* **are you** ~? Sie kommen doch, oder?; **you are** ~ **angry — or are you?** Sie sind doch nicht etwa böse?

(c) is he coming? — **I hope/I believe** ~ kommt er? — ich hoffe/glaube nicht; **it would appear** ~ anscheinend nicht; **he's decided not to do it** — **I should think/hope** ~ er hat sich entschlossen, es nicht zu tun — das möchte ich auch meinen/hoffen; **are you cold?** — ~ **at all** ist dir kalt? — überhaupt nicht; **thank you very much** — ~ **at all** vielen Dank — keine Ursache; ~ **in the least** überhaupt *or* gar nicht; ~ **that I know of** nicht, daß ich wüßte.

notable ['nəʊtəbl] *adj* **person** bedeutend; *success, event also* bemerkenswert, denkwürdig; *difference, improvement* beträchtlich, beachtlich.

notably ['nəʊtəblɪ] *adv* **(a)** *(strikingly)* auffallend; *improved, different* beträchtlich. **(b)** *(in particular)* hauptsächlich, vor allem.

notary (public) ['nəʊtərɪ('pʌblɪk)] *n* Notar(in *f*) *m.*

notation [nəʊ'teɪʃən] *n (system)* Zeichensystem *nt; (symbols)* Zeichen *pl; (Mus)* Notenschrift *f.*

notch [nɒtʃ] **1** *n* Kerbe *f; (of handbrake etc)* Raste *f; (in belt)* Loch *nt; (on damaged blade etc)* Scharte *f.* **2** *vt* einkerben, einschneiden.

♦ **notch up** *vt sep* **points** erzielen, einheimsen *(col);* **record** verzeichnen; *success* verzeichnen können.

note [nəʊt] **1** *n* **(a)** Notiz *f; (foot~)* Anmerkung, Fußnote *f; (informal letter)* Briefchen *nt,* paar Zeilen *pl.* ~**s** *(summary)* Aufzeichnungen *pl; (plan, draft)* Konzept *nt;* **lecture** ~**s** *(professor's)* Manuskript *nt; (student's)* Aufzeichnungen *pl;* **to speak without** ~**s** ohne Vorlage sprechen; **to take** ~**s** Notizen machen; *(in lecture also, in interrogation)* mitschreiben; **to take** *or* **make a** ~ **of sth** sich *(dat)* etw notieren.

(b) *no pl (notice)* **to take** ~ **of sth** von etw Notiz nehmen; *(heed)* einer Sache *(dat)* Beachtung schenken; **worthy of** ~ beachtenswert, erwähnenswert.

(c) *no pl (importance)* **a man of** ~ ein bedeutender Mann; **nothing of** ~ nichts Erwähnenswertes.

(d) *(Mus) (sign)* Note *f; (sound, on piano etc)* Ton *m.* **to play the right/wrong** ~ richtig/falsch spielen; **to strike the right** ~ *(fig)* den richtigen Ton treffen.

(e) *(quality, tone)* Ton, Klang *m.* **a** ~ **of nostalgia** eine nostalgische Note; **there was a** ~ **of warning in his voice** seine Stimme hatte einen

warnenden Unterton.

(f) *(Brit Fin)* Note *f,* Schein *m.* **a £5** ~**, a five-pound** ~ ein Fünfpfundschein *m.*

2 *vt* bemerken; *(take note of)* zur Kenntnis nehmen; *(pay attention to)* beachten.

notebook ['nəʊtbʊk] *n* Notizbuch *or* -heft *nt.*

noted ['nəʊtɪd] *adj* bekannt *(for* für, wegen*).*

note: ~**pad** *n* Notizblock *m;* ~**paper** *n* Briefpapier *nt.*

noteworthy ['nəʊtwɜːðɪ] *adj* beachtenswert, erwähnenswert.

nothing ['nʌθɪŋ] **1** *n, pron, adv* nichts. **to eat** ~ nichts essen; ~ **could be easier** nichts wäre einfacher; **it was reduced to** ~ es war nichts übrig; **she is** *or* **means** ~ **to him** sie bedeutet ihm nichts; **that came to** ~ da ist nichts draus geworden; **I can make** ~ **of it** das sagt mir nichts; **he thinks** ~ **of doing that** er findet nichts dabei(, das zu tun); **think** ~ **of it** keine Ursache!; **to say** ~ **of ...** ganz zu schweigen von ...; ~ **doing!** *(col)* da ist nichts drin! *(col);* **for** ~ *(free, in vain)* umsonst; **there's** ~ **(else) for it but to leave da** bleibt einem nichts (anderes) übrig als zu gehen; **there's** ~ **in the rumour** das Gerücht ist aus der Luft gegriffen, an dem Gerücht ist nichts (Wahres); **there's** ~ **to it** *(col)* das ist kinderleicht *(col);* ~ **but nur; he does** ~ **but eat** er ißt nur *or* ständig; ~ **else** sonst nichts; ~ **more** sonst nichts; **I'd like** ~ **more than that** ich möchte nichts lieber als das; ~ **much** nicht viel; ~ **if not** polite überaus höflich; ~ **new** nichts Neues; **it was** ~ **like as big** es war lange nicht so groß.

2 *n* **(a)** *(Math)* Null *f.* **(b)** *(thing, person of no value)* Nichts *nt.* **it was a mere** ~ das war doch nicht der Rede wert; **to whisper sweet** ~**s to sb** jdm Zärtlichkeiten ins Ohr flüstern.

nothingness ['nʌθɪŋnɪs] *n* Nichts *nt.*

notice ['nəʊtɪs] **1** *n* **(a)** *(warning, communication)* Bescheid *m,* Benachrichtigung *f; (written notification)* Mitteilung *f; (of forthcoming event, film etc)* Ankündigung *f.* **to give sb** ~ **of sth** jdm etw mitteilen; **without** ~ ohne Ankündigung; *(of arrival also)* unangemeldet; **he didn't give us much** ~, **he gave us rather short** ~ er hat uns nicht viel Zeit gelassen *or* gegeben; **at short** ~ kurzfristig; **at a moment's** ~ jederzeit, sofort; **at three days'** ~ innerhalb von drei Tagen; **until further** ~ bis auf weiteres.

(b) *(public announcement)* Bekanntmachung *f; (on* ~-*board etc)* Anschlag *m; (poster also)* Plakat *nt; (sign)* Schild *nt; (in newspaper)* Mitteilung *f; (short)* Notiz *f; (of wedding, vacancy etc)* Anzeige *f.* **the** ~ **says ...** da steht ...

(c) *(to end employment etc)* Kündigung *f.* ~ **to quit** Kündigung *f;* **to give sb** ~ jdm kündigen; **give in one's** ~ kündigen; **I am under** ~ **(to quit), I got my** ~ mir ist gekündigt worden; **a month's** ~ eine einmonatige Kündigungsfrist.

(d) *(review)* Kritik, Rezension *f.*

(e) *(attention)* **to take** ~ **of sth** von etw Notiz nehmen; *(heed)* etw beachten, einer Sache *(dat)* Beachtung schenken; **to take no** ~ **of sb/sth** von jdm/etw keine Notiz nehmen; **take no** ~! kümmern Sie sich nicht darum!; **that has escaped his** ~ das hat er nicht bemerkt; **to bring sth to sb's** ~ jdn auf etw *(acc)* aufmerksam machen; *(in letter)* jdn von etw in Kenntnis setzen; **it came to his** ~ **that ...** er hat erfahren, daß ...

2 *vt* bemerken; *(perceive also)* wahrnehmen; *(recognize, acknowledge)* zur Kenntnis nehmen; *difference* feststellen; *(realize also)* merken. **without my noticing it** ohne daß ich etwas gemerkt *or* bemerkt habe; **he pretended not to** ~ er tat so, als ob er es nicht bemerken würde; **did he wave?** — **I never** ~**d** hat er gewunken? — ich habe es nicht bemerkt.

noticeable ['nəʊtɪsəbl] *adj* erkennbar, wahrnehmbar; *(visible)* sichtbar; *(obvious, considerable)* deutlich; *(relief, pleasure etc)* sichtlich, merklich. **the stain is very ~** der Fleck fällt ziemlich auf; **it is hardly ~** man merkt es kaum.

notice-board ['nəʊtɪsbɔːd] *n (Brit)* Anschlagbrett *nt; (in school etc also)* Schwarzes Brett.

notification [ˌnəʊtɪfɪ'keɪʃən] *n* Benachrichtigung, Mitteilung *f; (of loss, damage etc)* Meldung *f*. **to send written ~ of sth to sb** jdm etw schriftlich mitteilen.

notify ['nəʊtɪfaɪ] *vt person, candidate* benachrichtigen, unterrichten *(form); (change of address, loss etc* melden. **to ~ sb of sth** jdn von etw benachrichtigen; *authorities etc* jdm etw melden.

notion ['nəʊʃən] *n* **(a)** *(idea, thought)* Idee *f; (conception also)* Vorstellung *f; (vague knowledge also)* Ahnung *f; (opinion)* Meinung *f*. **I have no ~ or not the slightest ~ of what he means** ich habe keine Ahnung *or* nicht die leiseste Ahnung, was er meint; **I have no ~ of time** ich habe überhaupt kein Zeitgefühl; **where did you get the ~ that I ...?** wie kommst du denn auf die Idee, daß ich ...?; **I have a ~ that ...** ich habe den Verdacht, daß ...; **to get/have a ~ to do sth** Lust bekommen/haben, etw zu tun. **(b)** *(esp US col)* **~s** *pl* Kurzwaren *pl*.

notoriety [ˌnəʊtə'raɪətɪ] *n* traurige Berühmtheit.

notorious [nəʊ'tɔːrɪəs] *adj person, fact* berüchtigt; *place also* verrufen; *(well-known) criminal, liar* notorisch. **to be ~ for sth** für etw berüchtigt sein.

notoriously [nəʊ'tɔːrɪəslɪ] *adv* notorisch. **to be ~ violent** für seine Gewalttätigkeit berüchtigt sein.

notwithstanding [ˌnɒtwɪθ'stændɪŋ] *(form)* **1** *prep* ungeachtet (+*gen*) *(form)*. **2** *adv* nichtsdestotrotz *(form)*. **3** *conj* **~ that ...** obgleich ...

nougat ['nuːgaː] *n* Nougat *m*.

nought [nɔːt] *n* Null *f*. **~s and crosses** Kinderspiel *nt mit Nullen und Kreuzen*.

noun [naʊn] *n* Substantiv(um), Hauptwort *nt*.

nourish ['nʌrɪʃ] *vt* nähren; *person* ernähren.

nourishing ['nʌrɪʃɪŋ] *adj* nahrhaft.

nourishment ['nʌrɪʃmənt] *n* Nahrung *f*.

nouveau riche [ˌnuːvəʊ'riːʃ] **1** *n, pl* **-x -s** [ˌnuːvəʊ'riːʃ] Neureiche(r) *mf*. **2** *adj* typisch neureich.

novel[1] ['nɒvəl] *n* Roman *m*.

novel[2] *adj* neu(artig).

novelist ['nɒvəlɪst] *n* Romanschriftsteller(in *f*) *m*.

novelty ['nɒvəltɪ] *n* **(a)** *(newness)* Neuheit *f*. **(b)** *(innovation)* Neuheit *f*, Novum *nt*. **it was quite a ~** das war etwas ganz Neues. **(c)** *(Comm: trinket)* Krimskrams *m*.

November [nəʊ'vembə^r] *n* November *m; see* **September.**

novice ['nɒvɪs] *n (Eccl)* Novize *m*, Novizin *f; (fig)* Neuling, Anfänger(in *f*) *m (at* bei, *in* +*dat)*.

now [naʊ] **1** *adv* **(a)** jetzt, nun; *(immediately)* sofort, gleich; *(at this very moment)* gerade, (so)eben; *(nowadays)* heute, heutzutage. **she ~ realized why ...** da erkannte sie, warum ...; **just ~ gerade; ~ is the time to do it** jetzt ist der richtige Moment dafür; **I'll do it right ~** ich mache es jetzt gleich *or* sofort; **it's ~ or never** jetzt oder nie; **by ~** inzwischen; **for ~** (jetzt) erst einmal, vorläufig; **even ~** selbst jetzt noch; **from ~ on(wards)** von nun an; **in three days from ~** (heute) in drei Tagen; **up to ~, till ~, until ~** bis jetzt; **that's all for ~** das wär's für heute. **(b) ~ ... ~** bald ... bald; **(every) ~ and then, ~ and again** ab und zu, gelegentlich.

2 *conj* **~ (that) you've seen him** jetzt, wo Sie ihn gesehen haben.

3 *interj* also. **~, ~!** na, na!; **well ~** also; **then** also (jetzt); **stop that ~!** Schluß jetzt!; **~, why didn't I think of that?** warum habe ich bloß nicht daran gedacht?

nowadays ['naʊədeɪz] *adv* heute, heutzutage.

nowhere ['nəʊweə^r] *adv* nirgends; *(with verbs of motion)* nirgendwohin. **~ special** irgendwo; *(with motion)* irgendwohin; **to appear from ~** ganz plötzlich auftauchen; **we're getting ~ (fast)** wir kommen nicht weiter; **rudeness will get you ~** Grobheit bringt dir gar nichts ein.

noxious ['nɒkʃəs] *adj* schädlich; *habit* übel.

nozzle ['nɒzl] *n* Düse *f*.

nth [enθ] *adj* **the ~ degree** die n-te Potenz; **for the ~ time** zum x-ten Mal *(col)*.

nuance ['njuːãːns] *n* Nuance *f*.

nubile ['njuːbaɪl] *adj (attractive) girl* gut entwickelt.

nuclear ['njuːklɪə^r] *adj* Kern-, Atom- *(esp Mil); fission, reaction, research* Kern-; *fuel* nuklear, atomar; *attack, testing* Kernwaffen-; Atomwaffen-; *submarine, missile* atomgetrieben, Atom-.

nuclear: ~ deterrent *n* nukleares Abschreckungsmittel; **~ family** *n* Kleinfamilie *f;* **~ physics** *n* Kernphysik *f;* **~ power** *n* Atomkraft, Kernenergie *f;* **~-powered** *adj* atomgetrieben; **~ power station** *n* Kern- *or* Atomkraftwerk *nt;* **~ reactor** *n* Kern- *or* Atomreaktor *m;* **~ war** *n* Atomkrieg *m.*

nucleus ['njuːklɪəs] *n, pl* **nuclei** *(Phys, fig)* Kern *m; (Biol: of cell also)* Nukleus *m.*

nude [njuːd] **1** *adj* nackt; *(Art)* Akt-. **~ figure/portrait** Akt *m.* **2** *n (person)* Nackte(r) *mf; (Art) (painting etc)* Akt *m; (model)* Aktmodell *nt.* **in the ~** nackt.

nudge [nʌdʒ] **1** *vt* stupsen. **2** *n* **to give sb a ~** jdm einen Stups geben.

nudist ['njuːdɪst] *n* Anhänger(in *f*) *m* der Freikörperkultur, FKK-Anhänger(in *f*) *m.* **~ colony** FKK-Kolonie *f.*

nudity ['njuːdɪtɪ] *n* Nacktheit *f.*

nugget ['nʌgɪt] *n (of gold etc)* Klumpen *m.*

nuisance ['njuːsns] *n* **(a)** *(person)* Plage *f; (esp pestering)* Nervensäge *f; (esp child)* Quälgeist *m.* **to make a ~ of oneself** lästig werden. **(b)** *(thing, event)* **to be a ~** lästig sein; *(annoying)* ärgerlich sein; **what a ~,** having to do it again wie ärgerlich, das noch einmal machen zu müssen.

nuke [njuːk] *vt (col)* atomar vernichten.

null [nʌl] *adj:* **~ and void** *(Jur)* (null und) nichtig, ungültig.

nullify ['nʌlɪfaɪ] *vt* annullieren, für (null und) nichtig erklären.

numb [nʌm] **1** *adj* (+*er*) taub, gefühllos; *(emotionally)* benommen, wie betäubt. **hands ~ with cold** Hände, die vor Kälte taub *or* gefühllos sind; **~ with grief** starr *or* wie betäubt vor Schmerz. **2** *vt (cold)* taub *or* gefühllos machen; *(injection, fig)* betäuben.

number ['nʌmbə^r] **1** *n* **(a)** *(Math)* Zahl *f; (numeral)* Ziffer *f; (amount)* Anzahl *f.* **a ~ of applicants** eine Anzahl von Bewerbern; **large ~s of people** books eine große Anzahl von Leuten/eine ganze Menge Bücher; **on a ~ of occasions** des öfteren; **in a small ~ of cases** in wenigen Fällen; **ten in ~** zehn an der Zahl; **in small/large ~s** in kleinen/großen Mengen; **any ~ of cards** etc *(many)* sehr viele Karten *etc.*

(b) *(of house, phone)* Nummer *f; (of page)* Seitenzahl *f; (of car)* (Auto)nummer *f.* **N~ Ten (Downing Street)** Nummer Zehn (Downing Street); **to take a car's ~** die Nummer eines Autos aufschreiben; **I dialled a wrong ~** ich habe mich verwählt; **it was a wrong ~** ich/er *etc* war falsch verbunden; **the ~ one pop star** *(col)* der Popstar Nummer Eins *(col);* **to look after ~ one** *(col)* (vor allem) an sich *(acc)* selbst denken; **his ~'s up** *(col)* er ist dran *(col).*

(c) *(song, act etc)* Nummer *f; (issue of magazine etc also)* Ausgabe *f*, Heft *nt; (dress)* Kreation *f.*

2 *vt* **(a)** *(give a number to)* numerieren; *(count)* zählen. **to be** ~**ed** (limited) begrenzt sein; **his days are** ~**ed** seine Tage sind gezählt. **(b)** (include) zählen (among zu). **we** ~ **them among our friends** wir zählen sie zu unseren Freunden. **(c)** (amount to) zählen. **the group** ~**ed 50** es waren 50 (Leute in der Gruppe).

number: ~**less** adj zahllos, unzählig; ~-**plate** n (Brit) Nummernschild nt.

numbness ['nʌmnɪs] n (of limbs etc) Taubheit f; (fig: of mind, senses) Benommenheit f.

numeracy ['njuːmərəsɪ] n Rechnen nt. **his** ~ seine rechnerischen Fähigkeiten.

numeral ['njuːmərəl] n Ziffer f.

numerate ['njuːmərɪt] adj rechenkundig.

numerical [njuːˈmerɪkəl] adj symbols, equation numerisch, Zahlen-; value Zahlen-; superiority zahlenmäßig. **in** ~ **order** nach Zahlen geordnet.

numerous ['njuːmərəs] adj zahlreich; family kinderreich.

nun [nʌn] n Nonne f.

nuptial ['nʌpʃəl] (liter, hum) **1** adj bliss, vow Ehe-; feast Hochzeits-. **2** n ~**s** pl Hochzeit f.

nurse [nɜːs] **1** n Schwester f; (as professional title) Krankenschwester f; (nanny) Kindermädchen nt. male ~ Krankenpfleger m. **2** vt **(a)** pflegen; (fig) plan hegen; (treat carefully) schonen. **to** ~ **sb back to health** jdn gesundpflegen; **he stood there nursing his bruised arm** er stand da und hielt seinen verletzten Arm. **(b)** (suckle) child stillen; (cradle) (in den Armen) wiegen.

nursemaid ['nɜːsmeɪd] n (nanny, hum: servant) Kindermädchen nt.

nursery ['nɜːsərɪ] n **(a)** (room) Kinderzimmer nt; (in hospital) Säuglingssaal m. **(b)** (institution) Kindergarten m; (all-day) Kindertagesstätte f. **(c)** (Agr, Hort) (for plants) Gärtnerei f; (for trees) Baumschule f.

nursery: ~ **rhyme** n Kinderreim m; ~ **school** n Kindergarten m; ~ **slope** n (Brit) Idiotenhügel (hum), Anfängerhügel m.

nursing ['nɜːsɪŋ] **1** n **(a)** (care of invalids) Pflege f. **(b)** (profession) Krankenpflege f. **she's going in for** ~ sie will in der Krankenpflege arbeiten. **2** adj attr staff Pflege-; abilities pflegerisch. **the** ~ **profession** die pflegerischen Berufe.

nursing: ~ **auxiliary** n (Brit) Schwesternhelferin f; ~ **bottle** n (US) Flasche f; ~ **home** n Privatklinik f; (Brit: maternity hospital) Entbindungsklinik f; (convalescent home) Pflegeheim nt; ~ **mother** n stillende Mutter; ~ **officer** n Oberschwester f.

nut [nʌt] n **(a)** (Bot) Nuß f; (of coal) kleines Stück. **a packet of** ~**s and raisins** eine Tüte Studentenfutter. **(b)** (col: head) Nuß (col), Birne (col) f. **use your** ~! streng deinen Grips an! (col); **to do one's** ~ (Brit col) durchdrehen (col). **(c)** (col: person) Spinner(in f) m (col). **he's a tough** ~ (col) er ist ein harter Brocken (col). **(d)** (Mech) (Schrauben)mutter f.

nut: ~-**case** n (col) Spinner(in f) m (col); ~**cracker(s** pl) n Nußknacker m; ~-**house** n (col) (lit, fig) Irrenhaus nt (col); ~**meg** n Muskat(nuß f) m.

nutrient ['njuːtrɪənt] **1** adj substance nahrhaft; properties Nähr-. **2** n Nährstoff m.

nutrition [njuːˈtrɪʃən] n (diet, science) Ernährung f.

nutritious [njuːˈtrɪʃəs] adj nahrhaft.

nuts [nʌts] adj pred (col) **to be** ~ spinnen (col); **to go** ~ durchdrehen (col); **to be** ~ **about sb/sth** (keen on) ganz wild auf jdn/etw sein (col).

nutshell ['nʌtʃel] n Nußschale f. **in a** ~ (fig) kurz gesagt.

nutty ['nʌtɪ] adj (+er) **(a)** flavour Nuß-. **(b)** (col: crazy) bekloppt (col).

nuzzle ['nʌzl] vi **to** ~ (**up**) **against sb, to** ~ **up to sb** sich an jdn schmiegen or drücken.

nylon ['naɪlɒn] **1** n **(a)** (Tex) Nylon nt. **(b)** ~**s** pl Nylonstrümpfe pl. **2** adj Nylon-.

nymph [nɪmf] n (Myth) Nymphe f.

nymphomaniac [ˌnɪmfəʊˈmeɪnɪæk] n Nymphomanin f.

O

O, o [əʊ] n **(a)** O, o nt. **(b)** [(Brit) əʊ, (US) 'zɪərəʊ] (Telec) Null f.
oaf [əʊf] n, pl -s or **oaves** Flegel, Lümmel m.
oafish ['əʊfɪʃ] adj flegelhaft, lümmelhaft.
oak [əʊk] n Eiche f; (wood also) Eichenholz nt.
oak in cpds Eichen-; ~ **apple** n Gallapfel m.
OAP (Brit) = old-age pensioner.
oar [ɔːʳ] n Ruder nt, Riemen (Rowing) m. **to stick one's** ~ **in** (col) sich einmischen.
oarsman ['ɔːzmən] n Ruderer m.
oasis [əʊ'eɪsɪs] n, pl **oases** [əʊ'eɪsiːz] (lit, fig) Oase f.
oat [əʊt] n usu pl Hafer m. ~**s** pl (Cook) Haferflocken pl; **to sow one's wild** ~**s** (fig) sich (dat) die Hörner abstoßen.
oath [əʊθ] n **(a)** Schwur m; (Jur) Eid m. **to take** or **swear an** ~ schwören; (Jur) einen Eid ablegen or leisten; **to be under** ~ (Jur) unter Eid stehen; **to put sb on** ~ (Jur) jdn vereidigen; **to take the** ~ (Jur) vereidigt werden. **(b)** (curse, profanity) Fluch m.
oatmeal ['əʊtmiːl] n no pl Haferschrot m.
obdurate ['ɒbdjʊrɪt] adj (stubborn) hartnäckig; sinner verstockt; (hardhearted) unerbittlich.
obedience [ə'biːdɪəns] n no pl Gehorsam m. **in** ~ **to the law** dem Gesetz entsprechend.
obedient [ə'biːdɪənt] adj gehorsam; child, dog also folgsam. **to be** ~ gehorchen (to dat).
obelisk ['ɒbɪlɪsk] n (Archit) Obelisk m.
obese [əʊ'biːs] adj fettleibig (form, Med).
obesity [əʊ'biːsɪtɪ] n Fettleibigkeit f (form, Med).
obey [ə'beɪ] **1** vt gehorchen (+dat); law, rules, order befolgen; (machine) reagieren auf (+acc). **2** vi gehorchen; (child, dog also) folgen.
obituary [ə'bɪtjʊərɪ] n Nachruf m. ~ **notice** Todesanzeige f; ~ **column** Sterberegister nt.
object[1] ['ɒbdʒɪkt] n **(a)** (thing) Gegenstand m; (abstract etc) Objekt, Ding nt. **he was an** ~ **of scorn** er war die Zielscheibe der Verachtung. **(b)** (aim) Ziel nt, Absicht f. **with this** ~ **in mind** mit diesem Ziel vor Augen; **with the sole** ~ **(of doing)** mit dem einzigen Ziel (, zu ...); **what's the** ~ **(of staying here)?** wozu (bleiben wir hier)?; **that defeats the** ~ das verfehlt seinen Sinn or Zweck. **(c)** money/distance (is) no ~ Geld/Entfernung spielt keine Rolle. **(d)** (Gram) Objekt nt.
object[2] [əb'dʒekt] **1** vi dagegen sein; (protest) protestieren; (be against: in discussion etc) Einwände haben (to gegen); (raise objection) Einwände erheben (disapprove) sich stören (to an +dat). **to** ~ **to sth** (disapprove) etw mißbilligen; **if you don't** ~ wenn Sie nichts dagegen haben; **do you** ~ **to my smoking?** stört es (Sie), wenn ich rauche?; **I** ~ **to your tone/to people smoking in my living room** ich verbitte mir diesen Ton/ich verbitte mir, daß in meinem Wohnzimmer geraucht wird. **2** vt einwenden.
objection [əb'dʒekʃən] n (reason against) Einwand m (to gegen); (dislike) Abneigung f; (disapproval) Einspruch, Widerspruch m. **to make** or **raise an** ~ einen Einwand erheben; **I have no** ~ **to his going away** ich habe nichts dagegen (einzuwenden), daß er weggeht; **are there any** ~**s?** irgendwelche Einwände?; **I see no** ~ **to it** ich sehe nichts, was dagegen spricht; **I have no** ~ **to him** (as a person) ich habe nichts gegen ihn.
objectionable [əb'dʒekʃənəbl] adj störend; con-

duct, remark, language anstößig; smell übel. **he's a most** ~ **person** er ist unausstehlich.
objective [əb'dʒektɪv] **1** adj objektiv. **2** n (aim) Ziel nt; (esp Comm) Zielvorstellung f; (Mil) Angriffsziel nt.
objectively [əb'dʒektɪvlɪ] adv objektiv.
objectivity [,ɒbdʒek'tɪvɪtɪ] n Objektivität f.
object lesson n (fig) Paradebeispiel nt (in, on für, gen).
objector [əb'dʒektəʳ] n Gegner(in f) m (to gen).
obligation [,ɒblɪ'geɪʃən] n Verpflichtung, Pflicht f. **to be under an** ~ **to do sth** die Pflicht haben, etw zu tun; **without** ~ (Comm) unverbindlich.
obligatory [ɒ'blɪgətərɪ] adj obligatorisch. **biology is** ~ Biologie ist Pflicht; **to make it** ~ **for sb to do sth** vorschreiben, daß jd etw tut.
oblige [ə'blaɪdʒ] vt **(a)** (compel) zwingen; (because of duty) verpflichten (sb to do sth jdn, etw zu tun). **to feel** ~**d to do sth** sich verpflichtet fühlen, etw zu tun; **I was** ~**d to go** ich sah mich gezwungen zu gehen; **you are not** ~**d to do it** Sie sind nicht dazu verpflichtet. **(b)** (do a favour to) einen Gefallen tun (+dat). **could you** ~ **me with a light?** wären Sie so gut, mir Feuer zu geben?; **anything to** ~ **a friend** was tut man nicht alles für einen Freund!; **much** ~**d!** herzlichen Dank!; **I am much** ~**d to you for this** ich bin Ihnen dafür sehr verbunden.
obliging [ə'blaɪdʒɪŋ] adj entgegenkommend, gefällig; personality zuvorkommend.
oblique [ə'bliːk] **1** adj line, look schief, schräg; angle schief; style, reply, hint, reference indirekt. **2** n Schrägstrich m.
obliquely [ə'bliːklɪ] adv schräg; (fig) indirekt.
obliterate [ə'blɪtəreɪt] vt (erase) auslöschen; city also vernichten; (hide) sun, view verdecken.
oblivion [ə'blɪvɪən] n Vergessenheit f. **to sink** or **fall into** ~ in Vergessenheit geraten.
oblivious [ə'blɪvɪəs] adj **to be** ~ **of sth** sich (dat) einer Sache (gen) nicht bewußt sein; **he was quite** ~ **of his surroundings** er nahm seine Umgebung gar nicht wahr.
oblong ['ɒblɒŋ] **1** adj rechteckig. **2** n Rechteck nt.
obnoxious [ɒb'nɒkʃəs] adj widerlich, widerwärtig; person also, behaviour unausstehlich. **an** ~ **person** ein Ekel nt (col).
oboe ['əʊbəʊ] n Oboe f.
obscene [əb'siːn] adj obszön; (non-sexually, repulsive) ekelerregend, widerlich.
obscenity [əb'senɪtɪ] n Obszönität f. **the** ~ **of these crimes** diese ekelerregenden Verbrechen.
obscure [əb'skjʊəʳ] **1** adj (+er) **(a)** style unklar; argument verworren; book schwer verständlich. **(b)** (indistinct) feeling, memory dunkel. **for some** ~ **reason** aus einem unerfindlichen Grund. **(c)** (little known) poet, village unbekannt; beginnings (humble) unbedeutend; life wenig beachtenswert. **2** vt **(a)** (hide) sun, view verdecken. **(b)** (confuse) issue, argument unklar machen.
obscurity [əb'skjʊərɪtɪ] n **(a)** (of night, origins) Dunkel nt; (of style, argument) Unklarheit f. **to live in** ~ zurückgezogen leben; **to sink into** ~ in Vergessenheit geraten.
obsequious [əb'siːkwɪəs] adj unterwürfig (to(wards) gegen, gegenüber).
observance [əb'zɜːvəns] n **(a)** (of law) Befolgung,

Beachtung *f.* **(b)** *(Eccl)* Einhaltung *f.*

observant [əb'zɜːvənt] *adj* aufmerksam, wachsam. **that's very ~ of you** das hast du aber gut bemerkt.

observation [ˌɒbzə'veɪʃən] *n* **(a)** Beobachtung *f*; *(act also)* Beobachten *nt*. **to keep sb/sth under ~** *(by police)* jdn/etw überwachen; **powers of ~** Beobachtungsgabe *f*; **he's in hospital for ~** er ist zur Beobachtung im Krankenhaus; **~ post** Beobachtungsposten *m*. **(b)** *(remark)* Bemerkung *f.*

observatory [əb'zɜːvətrɪ] *n* Sternwarte *f*; *(Met)* Wetterwarte *f.*

observe [əb'zɜːv] *vt* **(a)** *(watch, notice)* beobachten; *difference also* wahrnehmen; *(by police)* überwachen. **(b)** *(obey)* achten auf *(+acc)*; *rule, custom, ceasefire* einhalten.

observer [əb'zɜːvəʳ] *n* *(watcher)* Zuschauer(in *f*) *m*; *(Mil, Pol)* Beobachter(in *f*) *m.*

obsess [əb'ses] *vt* **to be ~ed by** *or* **with sb/sth** von jdm/etw besessen sein.

obsession [əb'seʃən] *n* *(fixed idea)* fixe Idee, Manie *f*; *(fear etc)* Zwangsvorstellung *f*; *(state)* Besessenheit *f (with von)*. **it's an ~ with him** *(hobby etc)* er ist davon besessen; **this ~ with order** dieser Ordnungswahn *m*; **because of his ~ with her** weil er ihr gänzlich verfallen ist/war.

obsessive [əb'sesɪv] *adj* zwanghaft. **to become ~** *(activity)* zum Zwang *or* zur Manie werden; **he is an ~ reader** er liest wie besessen.

obsolescence [ˌɒbsə'lesns] *n* Veralten *nt.*

obsolescent [ˌɒbsə'lesnt] *adj* veraltend. **to be ~** anfangen zu veralten.

obsolete ['ɒbsəliːt] *adj* veraltet, überholt. **to become ~** veralten.

obstacle ['ɒbstəkl] *n (lit, fig)* Hindernis *nt*. **to be an ~ to sb/sth** jdm/einer Sache im Weg(e) stehen; **to put an ~ in sb's way** jdm ein Hindernis in den Weg stellen; **all the ~s to peace** *etc* alles, was den Frieden *etc* behindert.

obstetrician [ˌɒbstə'trɪʃən] *n* Geburtshelfer(in *f*) *m.*

obstetrics [ɒb'stetrɪks] *n sing* Geburtshilfe *f.*

obstinacy ['ɒbstɪnəsɪ] *n* Hartnäckigkeit *f*, Starrsinn *m (pej).*

obstinate ['ɒbstɪnɪt] *adj* hartnäckig, starrsinnig; *nail etc* widerspenstig. **to remain ~** stur bleiben.

obstreperous [əb'strepərəs] *adj* aufmüpfig *(col)*; *child* aufsässig.

obstruct [əb'strʌkt] *vt* **(a)** *(block)* blockieren; *road also, view* versperren; *(Med) artery, pipe also* verstopfen. **you're ~ing my view** Sie versperren mir die Sicht. **(b)** *(hinder)* (be)hindern; *traffic, progress also* aufhalten; *(Sport)* behindern.

obstruction [əb'strʌkʃən] *n see vt* **(a)** Blockierung *f*; *(of view)* Versperren *nt*; Verstopfung *f.* **(b)** Behinderung *f.* **to cause an ~** *(to traffic)* den Verkehr behindern. **(c)** *(obstacle)* Hindernis, Hemmnis *(esp fig) nt.* **there is an ~ in the pipe** das Rohr ist verstopft.

obstructive [əb'strʌktɪv] *adj* obstruktiv *(esp Pol)*, behindernd. **to be ~** *(person)* Schwierigkeiten machen, sich querstellen *(col).*

obtain [əb'teɪn] *vt* erhalten; *result, votes also* erzielen; *information, goods also* beziehen. **to ~ sth by hard work** etw durch harte Arbeit erreichen; **to ~ sth for sb** jdm etw beschaffen.

obtainable [əb'teɪnəbl] *adj* erhältlich.

obtrusive [əb'truːsɪv] *adj person* aufdringlich; *smell also* penetrant; *building, furniture* zu auffällig.

obtuse [əb'tjuːs] *adj* **(a)** *(Geometry)* stumpf. **(b)** *person* begriffsstutzig, beschränkt.

obviate ['ɒbvɪeɪt] *vt* vermeiden; *need* vorbeugen *(+dat).*

obvious ['ɒbvɪəs] *adj* offensichtlich; *difference, fact also* eindeutig; *statement* naheliegend; *reason* (leicht) ersichtlich; *reluctance, surprise*

sichtlich; *(not subtle)* plump. **an ~ truth** eine offenkundige Tatsache; **that's the ~ solution** das ist die naheliegendste Lösung; **he was the ~ choice** es lag nahe, ihn zu wählen; **it's quite ~ he doesn't understand** es ist doch klar, daß er es nicht versteht; **there's no need to make it so ~** man braucht das (doch) nicht so deutlich zu zeigen; **I would have thought that was perfectly ~** das liegt doch auf der Hand; **to state the ~** sagen/schreiben, was sich von selbst versteht.

obviously ['ɒbvɪəslɪ] *adv* offensichtlich, offenbar; *(noticeably)* (offen)sichtlich. **he's ~ French** er ist eindeutig ein Franzose; **he's not ~ French** man merkt ihm nicht an, daß er Franzose ist; **~!** selbstverständlich!

occasion [ə'keɪʒən] **1** *n* **(a)** *(point in time)* Gelegenheit *f*. **on that ~** damals, bei jener Gelegenheit; **on ~** gelegentlich; **to rise to the ~** sich der Lage gewachsen zeigen. **(b)** *(special time)* Ereignis *nt.* **it's an ~** es ist ein besonderes Ereignis. **(c)** *(opportunity)* Gelegenheit *f.* **(d)** *(reason)* Grund *m.* **if you have ~ to ...** sollten Sie Veranlassung haben, zu ... **2** *vt (form)* Anlaß geben zu.

occasional [ə'keɪʒənl] *adj* **(a)** **he likes an ~ cigar** er raucht gelegentlich eine Zigarre. **(b)** **~ table** kleiner Wohnzimmertisch.

occasionally [ə'keɪʒənəlɪ] *adv* gelegentlich, hin und wieder. **very ~** sehr selten.

occult [ɒ'kʌlt] **1** *adj* okkult. **2** *n* Okkulte(s) *nt.*

occupant ['ɒkjʊpənt] *n (of house)* Bewohner(in *f*) *m*; *(of post)* Inhaber(in *f*) *m*; *(of car)* Insasse *m.*

occupation [ˌɒkjʊ'peɪʃən] *n* **(a)** *(employment)* Beruf *m*, Tätigkeit *f.* **he is a joiner by ~** er ist Tischler von Beruf. **(b)** *(pastime)* Beschäftigung *f.* **(c)** *(Mil)* Okkupation *f*; *(act also)* Besetzung *f (of* von*)*; *(state also)* Besatzung *f (of* in *+dat).* **army of ~** Besatzungsheer *nt.* **(d)** *(of house etc)* **ready for ~** bezugsfertig.

occupational [ˌɒkjʊ'peɪʃənl] *adj* Berufs-, beruflich. **~ hazard** *or* **risk** Berufsrisiko *nt*; **~ therapy** Beschäftigungstherapie *f.*

occupier ['ɒkjʊpaɪəʳ] *n (of house)* Bewohner(in *f*) *m*; *(of post)* Inhaber(in *f*) *m.*

occupy ['ɒkjʊpaɪ] *vt* **(a)** *house* bewohnen; *room* belegen. **is this seat occupied?** ist dieser Platz besetzt? **(b)** *(Mil etc)* besetzen. **(c)** *post, position* innehaben, bekleiden *(geh).* **(d)** *(take up)* beanspruchen; *space also* einnehmen; *time also* in Anspruch nehmen. **to ~ one's time** seine Zeit verbringen. **(e)** *(busy)* beschäftigen. **to be occupied (with)** sich beschäftigt sein (mit); **to ~ oneself** sich beschäftigen; **to keep sb occupied** jdn beschäftigen; **he kept his mind occupied or** beschäftigte sich geistig.

occur [ə'kɜːʳ] *vi* **(a)** *(event)* geschehen, vorkommen; *(difficulty)* sich ergeben; *(change)* stattfinden. **that doesn't ~ very often** das kommt nicht oft vor. **(b)** *(be found: disease)* vorkommen. **(c)** **it ~s to me that ...** ich habe den Eindruck, daß ...; **the idea just ~red to me** es ist mir gerade eingefallen; **it never ~red to me** darauf bin ich noch nie gekommen.

occurrence [ə'kʌrəns] *n (event)* Ereignis *nt*, Begebenheit *f*; *(presence, taking place)* Auftreten *nt*; *(of minerals)* Vorkommen *nt.* **an everyday ~** ein alltägliches Ereignis.

ocean ['əʊʃən] *n* Ozean *m*, Meer *nt.*

ocean: ~ bed *n* Meeresboden *or* -grund *m*; **~-going** *adj* Hochsee-.

oceanic [ˌəʊʃɪ'ænɪk] *adj* Meeres-.

oceanography [ˌəʊʃə'nɒɡrəfɪ] *n* Meereskunde *f.*

ochre, *(US)* **ocher** ['əʊkəʳ] *n* Ocker *m or nt.*

o'clock [ə'klɒk] *adv* **at 5 ~** um 5 Uhr; **it is 5 ~** es ist 5 Uhr.

octagon ['ɒktəɡən] *n* Achteck, Oktagon *nt.*

octagonal [ɒk'tæɡənl] *adj* achteckig.

octane ['ɒkteɪn] *n* Oktan *nt.* **high-~ petrol** Benzin *nt* mit hoher Oktanzahl.

octave ['ɒktɪv] n (Mus) Oktave f.
October [ɒk'təʊbəʳ] n Oktober m; see **September**.
octogenarian [ˌɒktəʊdʒɪ'neərɪən] 1 n Achtzigjährige(r) mf. 2 adj achtzigjährig.
octopus ['ɒktəpəs] n Tintenfisch m, Krake f.
oculist ['ɒkjʊlɪst] n Augenspezialist(in f) m.
odd [ɒd] adj (+er) **(a)** (peculiar) merkwürdig, sonderbar; person, thing, idea also eigenartig. **how ~ that we should meet him** (wie) eigenartig etc, daß wir ihn trafen; **the ~ thing about it is that ...** das Merkwürdige etc daran ist, daß ...; **he's got some ~ ways** er hat eine verschrobene Art. **(b)** number ungerade. **(c)** (one of a pair or a set) shoe, glove einzeln. **he is (the) ~ man** or **one out** er ist das fünfte Rad am Wagen; **underline the word which is the ~ man** or **one out** unterstreichen Sie das nicht dazugehörige Wort. **(d)** **600 ~ marks** so um die 600 Mark; **at ~ moments** ab und zu; **~ job** (gelegentlich) anfallende Arbeit; **~ job man** Mädchen nt für alles.
oddity ['ɒdɪtɪ] n **(a)** (of person) Eigenartigkeit f; (of thing) Ausgefallenheit f. **(b)** (odd person) komischer Kauz; (thing) Kuriosität f.
oddly ['ɒdlɪ] adv speak, behave eigenartig, sonderbar. **they are ~ similar** sie sind sich merkwürdig ähnlich; **~ enough she was at home** seltsamerweise war sie zu Hause.
oddment ['ɒdmənt] n usu pl Restposten m; (of cloth) Rest m; (single piece) Einzelstück nt.
oddness ['ɒdnɪs] n Merkwürdigkeit, Seltsamkeit f.
odds [ɒdz] npl **(a)** (Betting) Gewinnquote f; (of bookmaker also) Kurse pl. **the ~ are 6 to 1** die Chancen stehen 6:1; **long/short ~** geringe/hohe Gewinnchancen. **(b)** (chances for or against) Chance(n pl) f. **the ~ were against us** alles sprach gegen uns; **the ~ were in our favour** alles sprach für uns; **against all the ~ he won** wider Erwarten gewann er; **what are the ~ on/against ...?** wie stehen die Chancen, daß .../daß ... nicht?; **to struggle against impossible ~** so gut wie keine Aussicht auf Erfolg haben; **the ~ are that he will come** es sieht ganz so aus, als ob er kommen würde. **(c)** (col) **to pay over the ~** einiges mehr bezahlen. **(d)** (difference) **what's the ~?** was macht das schon (aus)?; **it makes no ~** es spielt keine Rolle. **(e)** (variance) **to be at ~ with sb over sth** mit jdm in etw (dat) nicht übereinstimmen.
odds and ends npl Krimskrams m (col). **bring all your ~** bringen Sie Ihre Siebensachen (col).
odds-on ['ɒdzɒn] adj **he's ~ favourite for the post** er hat die größten Aussichten, die Stelle zu bekommen.
ode [əʊd] n Ode f (to, on an +acc).
odious ['əʊdɪəs] adj person abstoßend, ekelhaft; action abscheulich.
odometer [əʊ'dɒmətəʳ] n (US) Tacho(meter) m.
odour, (US) **odor** ['əʊdəʳ] n (lit, fig) Geruch m; (sweet smell) Duft m; (bad smell) Gestank m. **to be in bad ~ with sb** schlecht bei jdm angeschrieben sein (col).
odourless, (US) **odorless** ['əʊdəlɪs] adj geruchlos.
Odyssey ['ɒdɪsɪ] n (Myth, fig) Odyssee f.
Oedipus ['iːdɪpəs] n Ödipus m. **~ complex** Ödipuskomplex m.
oesophagus, (US) **esophagus** [iː'sɒfəgəs] n Speiseröhre f.
of [ɒv,əv] prep **(a)** von (+dat), use of gen. **the wife ~ the doctor** die Frau des Arztes; **a friend ~ ours** ein Freund von uns; **a painting ~ the Queen** ein Gemälde von der Königin; **a painting ~ the Queen's** (belonging to her) ein Gemälde der Königin; **~ it** davon; **the first ~ May** der erste Mai; **it is very kind ~ you** es ist sehr freundlich von Ihnen; **south ~ Paris** südlich von Paris; **within a month ~ his death** innen Monat nach seinem Tod.

(b) (cause) **he died ~ poison/cancer** er starb an Gift/Krebs; **it tastes ~ garlic** es schmeckt nach Knoblauch.

(c) (material) aus. **dress made ~ wool** Wollkleid nt, Kleid nt aus Wolle.

(d) (quality, identity etc) **man ~ courage** mutiger Mensch; **girl ~ ten** zehnjähriges Mädchen; **the city ~ Paris** die Stadt Paris.

(e) **he is a leader ~ men** er hat die Fähigkeit, Menschen zu führen; **writer ~ legal articles** Verfasser von juristischen Artikeln; **love ~ money** Liebe zum Geld; **how many ~ them do you want?** wie viele möchten Sie (davon)?; **there were six ~ us** wir waren zu sechst; **he is not one ~ us** er gehört nicht zu uns; **today ~ all days** ausgerechnet heute; **you ~ all people ought to know** gerade Sie sollten das wissen; **what do you think ~ him?** was halten Sie von ihm?; **what ~ it?** ja und?

(f) (in temporal phrases) **he's become very quiet ~ late** er ist seit neuestem so ruhig; **they go out ~ an evening** (col) sie gehen abends (schon mal) aus.

off [ɒf] **1** adv **(a)** (distance) **the house is 5km ~** das Haus ist 5 km entfernt; **it's a long way ~** das ist weit weg; (time) das liegt in weiter Ferne; **the exams aren't very far ~** es ist nicht mehr lang bis zu den Prüfungen.

(b) (departure) **to be/go ~** gehen; **he's ~ to school** er ist zur Schule gegangen; **(be) ~ with you!** fort mit dir!; **I must be ~** ich muß gehen; **where are you ~ to?** wohin gehen Sie denn?, wohin geht's denn (col)?; **~ we go!** los!, na denn man los! (col); **he's ~ playing tennis every evening** er geht jeden Abend Tennis spielen.

(c) (removal) **he had his coat ~** er hatte den Mantel aus; **~ with those wet clothes!** raus aus den nassen Kleidern!; **the handle is ~** der Griff ist ab (col) or ist abgegangen; **there are two buttons ~** es fehlen zwei Knöpfe.

(d) (discount) **3% ~** (Comm) 3% Nachlaß; **to give sb £5 ~** jdm £5 Ermäßigung geben.

(e) (not at work) **to have time ~ to do sth** Zeit freibekommen haben, um etw zu tun; **I've got a day ~** ich habe einen Tag frei(bekommen); **she's nearly always ~ on Tuesdays** dienstags hat sie fast immer frei.

(f) (in phrases) **~ and on, on and ~** ab und zu; **right ~ straight ~** gleich; **3 days straight ~** 3 Tage hintereinander.

2 adj **(a)** attr (substandard) schlecht. **I'm having an ~ day today** ich bin heute nicht in Form.

(b) pred (Brit: not fresh) verdorben, schlecht.

(c) pred (cancelled) party, talks abgesagt; (not available: in restaurant) aus. **the agreement is ~** die Abmachung gilt nicht (mehr); **their engagement is ~** ihre Verlobung ist gelöst; **the play is ~** das Stück wurde abgesagt.

(d) TV, light, machine aus(geschaltet); tap zu(gedreht). **the gas/electricity was ~** das Gas/der Strom war abgeschaltet; **the handbrake was ~** die Handbremse war gelöst.

(e) they are badly/well **~** sie sind nicht gut/(ganz) gut gestellt; **how are we ~ for time?** wie sieht es mit der Zeit aus?; **that's a bit ~!** das ist ein dicker Hund! (col).

3 prep **(a)** (indicating motion, removal etc) von (+dat). **he jumped ~ the roof** er sprang vom Dach; **they knocked ~ a chicken** sie verspeisten ein Hühnchen; **he got £2 ~ the shirt** er bekam das Hemd £2 billiger; **the coat has two buttons ~ it** am Mantel fehlen zwei Knöpfe.

(b) a street **~ Piccadilly** eine Nebenstraße von Piccadilly; **he lives just ~ the square** er wohnt gleich am Platz; **2 miles ~ the motorway** 2 Meilen von der Autobahn entfernt; **anchored ~**

the coast vor der Küste liegend.
(c) ~ **the map** nicht auf der Karte; **I'm ~ beer at the moment** Bier kann mich zur Zeit nicht reizen; **I'm right ~ sausages** ich kann keine Wurst mehr sehen.

offal ['ɒfəl] *n no pl* Innereien *pl.*

off: ~**beat** *adj (unusual)* ausgefallen, ungewöhnlich; ~**-centre,** *(US)* ~**-center** *adj (lit)* nicht in der Mitte; ~**-chance** *n* **I just did it on the** ~**-chance** ich habe es auf gut Glück getan; **he bought it on the** ~**-chance that it would come in useful** er kaufte es, weil es vielleicht irgendwann mal nützlich sein könnte; ~**-colour,** *(US)* ~**-color** *adj* **to be** ~**-colour** sich unwohl fühlen.

offence, *(US)* **offense** [ə'fens] *n* **(a)** *(Jur: crime)* Straftat *f*, Delikt *nt*; *(minor also)* Vergehen *nt.* **to commit an** ~ sich strafbar machen; **it is an** ~ **to** ...... ist bei Strafe verboten; **an** ~ **against** ... ein Verstoß *m* gegen ... **(b)** *no pl (to sb's feelings)* Kränkung *f*. **to cause** *or* **give** ~ **to sb** jdn kränken; **to take** ~ **at sth** wegen etw gekränkt sein; **I meant no** ~ ich habe es nicht böse gemeint

offend [ə'fend] **1** *vt* **(a)** *(hurt feelings of)* kränken; *(be disagreeable to)* Anstoß erregen bei. **don't be** ~**ed** nehmen Sie mir *etc* das nicht übel. **(b)** *ear, eye* beleidigen; *sense of justice* verletzen. **2** *vi* **(a)** *(give offence)* beleidigend sein. **(b)** *(do wrong)* Unrecht tun.

offender [ə'fendə^r] *n (law-breaker)* Täter(in *f*) *m*; *(against traffic laws)* Verkehrssünder(in *f*) *m.* **young** ~ jugendlicher Straffälliger.

offensive [ə'fensɪv] **1** *adj* **(a)** *weapon (Jur)* Angriffs-; *(Mil also)* Offensiv-. **(b)** *(unpleasant) smell, sight* übel, abstoßend; *language, film* anstößig; *(insulting) remark, behaviour* beleidigend. **to find sb/sth** ~ jdn/etw abstoßend finden; *behaviour, language* Anstoß an etw *(dat)* nehmen; **he was** ~ **to her** er beleidigte sie. **2** *n (Mil, Sport)* Angriff *m*, Offensive *f.* **to take the** ~ in die Offensive gehen; **on the** ~ in der Offensive.

offensively [ə'fensɪvlɪ] *adv (unpleasantly)* übel, widerlich; *(in moral sense)* anstößig; *(abusively)* beleidigend.

offer ['ɒfə^r] **1** *n* Angebot *nt.* **to make an** ~ **of sth to sb** jdm etw anbieten; **an** ~ **I couldn't refuse** ein Angebot, zu dem ich nicht nein sagen konnte; **on** ~ *(Comm)* im Angebot. **2** *vt* **(a)** anbieten; *reward, prize* aussetzen; *plan, suggestion* unterbreiten; *excuse* vorbringen. **to** ~ **to do sth** anbieten, etw zu tun; **he** ~ **ed to help** er bot seine Hilfe an; **to** ~ **one's services** sich anbieten. **(b)** *resistance* bieten.

offering ['ɒfərɪŋ] *n* Gabe *f*; *(Rel) (collection)* Opfergabe *f*; *(sacrifice)* Opfer *nt.*

offertory ['ɒfətərɪ] *n (Eccl) (part of service)* Opferung *f*; *(collection)* Kollekte *f.*

offhand [ˌɒf'hænd] **1** *adj remark* lässig. **2** *adv* so ohne weiteres, aus dem Stand *(col).* **I couldn't tell you** ~ das könnte ich Ihnen auf Anhieb nicht sagen.

offhandedly [ˌɒf'hændɪdlɪ] *adv* lässig, leichthin.

office ['ɒfɪs] *n* **(a)** Büro *nt*; *(of lawyer)* Kanzlei *f*; *(part of organization)* Abteilung *f*; *(branch also)* Geschäftsstelle *f.* **at the** ~ im Büro. **(b)** *(public position)* Amt *nt.* **to take** ~ sein Amt antreten; *(political party)* die Regierung übernehmen; **to be in** *or* **hold** ~ im Amt sein; *(party)* an der Regierung sein; **to be out of** ~ nicht mehr an der Regierung sein; *(person)* nicht im Amt sein. **(c)** *usu pl* **through his good** ~**s** durch seine guten Dienste; **through the** ~**s of** ... durch Vermittlung von ... **(d)** *(Eccl)* Gottesdienst *m.*

office: ~ **automation** *n* Büroautomatisierung *f*; ~ **bearer** *n* Amtsträger(in *f*) *m*; ~ **block** *n* Bürogebäude *nt*; ~ **hours** *npl* Dienstzeit *f*; *(on sign)* Geschäftszeiten *pl*; ~ **job** *n* Stelle *f* im Büro.

officer ['ɒfɪsə^r] *n (a)* *(Mil, Naut, Aviat)* Offizier *m.* ~**s' mess** Offizierskasino *nt.* **(b)** *(official)*

Beamte(r) *m*, Beamtin *f*; *(police ~)* Polizist *m.* **no,** ~ nein(, Herr Wachtmeister).

office worker *n* Büroangestellte(r) *mf.*

official [ə'fɪʃəl] **1** *adj* offiziell; *report, duties, meeting also* amtlich; *robes, visit* Amts-; *ceremony, style* formell. **is that** ~? ist das amtlich?; *(publicly announced)* ist das offiziell? **2** *n* Beamte(r) *m*, Beamtin *f*; *(of club)* Funktionär(in *f*) *m.*

officialdom [ə'fɪʃəldəm] *n (pej)* Beamtentum *nt.*

officialese [ə,fɪʃə'liːz] *n* Amtssprache *f.*

officially [ə'fɪʃəlɪ] *adv* offiziell.

officiate [ə'fɪʃɪeɪt] *vt* amtieren, fungieren *(at bei).* **to** ~ **at a marriage** eine Trauung vornehmen.

officious [ə'fɪʃəs] *adj* übereifrig.

offing ['ɒfɪŋ] *n:* **in the** ~ in Sicht.

off: ~**-key** *adj (Mus)* falsch; ~**-licence** *n (Brit)* Wein- und Spirituosenhandlung *f*; ~**-load** *vt goods* ausladen, entladen; *passengers* aussteigen lassen; ~**-peak** *adj* ~**-peak charges** verbilligter Tarif; *(Elec)* ≈ Nachttarif *m*; ~**-peak ticket** verbilligte Fahrkarte/Flugkarte außerhalb der Stoßzeit; ~**-putting** *adj (Brit) smell, behaviour* abstoßend; *thought, story* wenig ermutigend; *(daunting)* entmutigend; ~**-season** *n* Nebensaison *f.*

offset ['ɒfset] *(vb: pret, ptp* ~*)* **1** *vt (financially, statistically etc)* ausgleichen; *(make up for)* aufwiegen. **2** *n (Typ)* Offsetdruck *m.*

off: ~**-shoot** *n (of plant)* Ausläufer *m*; **(b)** *(fig: of organization)* Nebenzweig *m*; ~**-shore** *adj fisheries* Küsten-; *island* küstennah; *rig, installations etc* im Meer; ~**-side** **1** *adj* **(a)** *(Sport)* im Abseits; **(b)** *(Aut)* auf der Fahrerseite; **2** *n (Aut)* Fahrerseite *f*; **3** *adv (Sport)* abseits, im Abseits; ~**-spring** *n* Sprößling *m*; *(of animal)* Junge(s) *nt*; ~**-stage** *adv* hinter den Kulissen; ~**-the-cuff** *adj remark, speech* aus dem Stegreif; ~**-the-peg** *adj (Brit) suit* von der Stange; ~**-white** *adj* gebrochen weiß.

often ['ɒfən] *adv* oft, häufig. **not as** ~ **as twice a week** weniger als zweimal in der Woche; **more** ~ **than not, as** ~ **as not** meistens; **every so** ~ von Zeit zu Zeit; **how** ~? wie oft?

ogle ['əʊgl] *vt* kein Auge lassen von, begaffen *(pej)*; *(flirtatiously)* schöne Augen machen *(+dat).*

ogre ['əʊgə^r] *n* Menschenfresser *m*; *(fig)* Unmensch *m.*

oh [əʊ] *interj* ach; *(surprised, disappointed)* oh; *(questioning)* tatsächlich.

OHMS = **On His/Her Majesty's Service.**

oil [ɔɪl] **1** *n (a)* Öl *nt.* **to pour** ~ **on troubled waters** die Wogen glätten; **(b)** *(petroleum)* (Erd)öl *nt.* **to strike** ~ *(lit)* auf Öl stoßen; *(get rich)* das große Los ziehen. **2** *vt* ölen, schmieren.

oil *in cpds* Öl-; ~**can** *n* Ölkanne *f*; ~**field** *n* Ölfeld *nt*; ~**-fired** *adj* Öl-; ~ **lamp** *n* Öllampe *f*; ~ **painting** *n* Ölgemälde *nt*; ~**-producing** *adj* ölproduzierend; ~**-rich** *adj* ölreich; ~ **rig** *n* (Öl)bohrinsel *f*; ~**skin** *n (cloth)* Öltuch *nt*; ~**skins** *npl (clothing)* Ölzeug *nt*; ~ **tanker** *n* (Öl)tanker *m*; *(lorry)* Tankwagen *m*; ~ **well** *n* Ölquelle *f.*

oily ['ɔɪlɪ] *adj (+er)* ölig; *food* fettig; *clothes, fingers* voller Öl; *(fig)* aalglatt.

ointment ['ɔɪntmənt] *n* Salbe *f.*

OK, okay ['əʊ'keɪ] *(col)* **1** *interj* okay *(col)*; *(agreed also)* in Ordnung. ~, ~! ist ja gut! *(col).* **2** *adj* in Ordnung, okay *(col).* **that's** ~ **with** *or* **by me** *(that's convenient)* das ist mir recht, mir ist's recht; **is it** ~ **with you if** ...? macht es (dir) was aus, wenn ...?; **how's your mother? — she's** ~ wie geht's deiner Mutter? — gut *or (not too well)* so einigermaßen; **to be** ~ **(for time/money** *etc*) (noch) genug (Zeit/Geld *etc*) haben; **is that** ~? ist das okay? *(col)*; **he's** ~ er ist in Ordnung *(col).* **3** *adv (well)* gut; *(not too badly)* einigermaßen. **can you mend/manage it** ~? kannst du das reparieren/kommst du damit klar? **4** *vt plan, suggestion* gutheißen, billigen. **5** *n*

Zustimmung *f*, Okay *nt* (*col*).

old [əʊld] **1** *adj* (+*er*) **(a)** alt. ~ **people** *or* **folk(s)** alte Leute *pl*; ~ **Mr Smith** der alte (Herr) Smith; **he is 40 years** ~ er ist 40 (Jahre alt); **two-year-~** Zweijährige(r) *mf*; **the** ~ **part of Ulm** die Ulmer Altstadt; **the** ~ **(part of) town** die Altstadt; **my** ~ **school** meine alte *or* ehemalige Schule. **(b)** (*col: as intensifier*) **she dresses any** ~ **how** die ist vielleicht immer angezogen (*col*); ~ **Mike** der Mike (*col*); **the same** ~ **excuse** die gleiche alte Entschuldigung. **2** *n* **the** ~ die alten Leute; **in days of** ~ in früheren Zeiten; **I know him of** ~ ich kenne ihn von früher.

old: ~ **age** *n* das Alter; **in one's** ~ **age** auf seine alten Tage (*also hum*); **~-age pension** *n* Rente *f*; **~-age pensioner** *n* (*Brit*) Rentner(in *f*) *m*; ~ **boy** *n* (*Brit Sch*) ehemaliger Schüler; **the** ~ **boy network** Beziehungen *pl* (von der Schule her).

olden ['əʊldən] *adj* (*liter*) **in** ~ **times** *or* **days** früher, vordem (*liter*).

old: **O~ English 1** *n* Altenglisch *nt*; **2** *adj* altenglisch; **~-established** *adj* **family, firm** alteingesessen; *custom* seit langem bestehend, alt.

old: **~-fashioned** ['əʊld'fæʃnd] *adj* altmodisch; ~ **girl** *n* (*Brit Sch*) ehemalige Schülerin; ~ **maid** *n* alte Jungfer; ~ **master** *n* alter Meister; ~ **people's home** *n* Altersheim *nt*; ~ **school** *n* (*fig*) alte Schule; **O~ Testament** *n* Altes Testament; **~-timer** *n* Veteran *m*; ~ **wives' tale** *n* Ammenmärchen *nt*; **O~ World** *n* alte Welt.

O Level ['əʊlevl] *n* (*Brit*) Abschluß *m* der Sekundarstufe 1, ≃ mittlere Reife. **to do one's ~s** ≃ die mittlere Reife machen; **3 ~s** die mittlere Reife in 3 Fächern.

oligarchy ['ɒlɪgɑːkɪ] *n* Oligarchie *f*.

olive ['ɒlɪv] **1** *n* **(a)** Olive *f*; (*also* ~ **tree**) Olivenbaum *m*. **(b)** (*colour*) Olive *nt*. **2** *adj* olivgrün.

olive: ~ **branch** *n* (*lit, fig*) Ölzweig *m*; **to hold out the** ~ **branch to sb** jdm seinen Willen zum Frieden bekunden; ~ **oil** *n* Olivenöl *nt*.

Olympic [əʊ'lɪmpɪk] **1** *adj* olympisch. ~ **champion** Olympiasieger(in *f*) *m*. **2** *n* **the ~s** *pl* die Olympiade, die olympischen Spiele.

ombudsman ['ɒmbʊdzmən] *n, pl* -**men** [-mən] Ombudsmann *m*.

omelette, (*US*) **omelet** ['ɒmlɪt] *n* Omelett(e) *nt*.

omen ['əʊmen] *n* Omen, Zeichen *nt*.

ominous ['ɒmɪnəs] *adj* bedrohlich; *sign also* verhängnisvoll. **that sounds** ~ das verspricht nichts Gutes.

ominously ['ɒmɪnəslɪ] *adv* bedrohlich; *say* in einem unheilverkündenden Ton.

omission [əʊ'mɪʃən] *n* Auslassen *nt*; (*word etc left out*) Auslassung *f*; (*failure to do sth*) Unterlassung *f*.

omit [əʊ'mɪt] *vt* **(a)** (*leave out*) auslassen. **(b)** (*fail*) es unterlassen **to do sth** etw zu tun).

omnibus ['ɒmnɪbəs] *n* **(a)** (*form: bus*) Omnibus *m*. **(b)** ~ **edition** (*book*) Sammelband *m*.

omnipotent [ɒm'nɪpətənt] *adj* allmächtig.

omniscient [ɒm'nɪsɪənt] *adj* allwissend.

on [ɒn] **1** *prep* **(a)** (*indicating place, position*) auf (+*dat*); (*with vb of motion*) auf (+*acc*); (*on vertical surface, part of body*) an (+*dat/acc*). **the book is** ~ **the table** das Buch ist auf dem Tisch; **he put the book** ~ **the table** er legte das Buch auf den Tisch; **it was** ~ **the blackboard** es stand an der Tafel; **he hung it** ~ **the wall/nail** er hängte es an die Wand/den Nagel; **he hit his head** ~ **the table/** ~ **the ground** er hat sich (*dat*) den Kopf am Tisch/auf dem *or* am Boden angeschlagen; **I have no money** ~ **me** ich habe kein Geld bei mir; **we had something to eat** ~ **the train** wir haben im Zug etwas gegessen; **a house** ~ **the main road** ein Haus an der Hauptstraße.

(b) (*means*) **we went** ~ **the train** wir fuhren mit dem Zug; ~ **foot/horseback** zu Fuß/Pferd; **he lives** ~ **his income** er lebt von seinem Ein-

kommen.

(c) (*about, concerning*) über (+*acc*). **a book** ~ **German grammar** ein Buch über deutsche Grammatik; **his views** ~ **that** seine Meinung darüber.

(d) (*time*) ~ **Sunday** (am) Sonntag; ~ **Sundays** sonntags; ~ **December the first** am ersten Dezember; ~ **the minute** auf die Minute genau; ~ **my arrival** bei meiner Ankunft; ~ **examination** bei der Untersuchung; ~ **request** auf Wunsch; ~ **hearing** this he left als er das hörte, ging er; ~ (*receiving*) **my letter** nach Erhalt meines Briefes.

(e) **he is** ~ **the committee/the board** er gehört dem Ausschuß/Vorstand an; **I am working** ~ **a new project** ich arbeite gerade an einem neuen Projekt; **we were** ~ **page 72** wir waren auf Seite 72; **this round is** ~ **me** diese Runde geht auf meine Kosten; **prices are up** ~ **last year('s)** im Vergleich zum letzten Jahr sind sie Preise gestiegen; **he played (it)** ~ **the violin/trumpet** er spielte (es) auf der Geige/Trompete; **I'm** ~ **£8,000 a year** ich bekomme £ 8,000 im Jahr; **to be** ~ **a course** (*Sch, Univ*) an einem Kurs teilnehmen; **to be** ~ **drugs/pills** Drogen/Pillen nehmen.

2 *adv see also vb* +*on* **(a)** **he put his hat** ~ er setzte seinen Hut auf; **he put his coat** ~ er zog seinen Mantel an; **she had nothing** ~ sie hatte nichts an; **what did he have** ~? was hatte er an?

(b) (*continuation*) **move** ~! gehen Sie weiter!; **from that day** ~ von diesem Tag an; **it was well** ~ **in the night** es war spät in der Nacht; **to keep** ~ **talking** in einem fort reden; **go** ~ **with your work** machen Sie Ihre Arbeit weiter; **life still goes** ~ das Leben geht weiter; **they talked** ~ **and** ~ sie redeten und redeten; **to read** ~ weiterlesen.

(c) (*in phrases*) **he's always (going)** ~ **at me** to **get my hair cut** er liegt mir dauernd in den Ohren, daß ich mir die Haare schneiden lassen soll; **she's always** ~ **about her experiences in Italy** sie kommt dauernd mit ihren Italienerfahrungen; **what's he** ~ **about?** wovon redet er nun schon wieder?

3 *adj* **(a)** *lights, TV, radio* an; *brake* angezogen; *electricity, gas* an(gestellt). **the** ~ **switch** der Einschalter; **to leave the engine** ~ den Motor laufen lassen.

(b) **to be** ~ (*being performed: film etc*) gezeigt werden; **what's** ~ **tonight?** was läuft heute abend?; **I have nothing** ~ **tonight** ich habe heute abend nichts vor; **what's** ~ **in London?** was ist los in London?

(c) (*valid*) **to be** ~ (*bet, agreement*) gelten; **you're** ~! abgemacht!; **it's just not** ~ (*not acceptable*) das ist einfach nicht drin (*col*).

once [wʌns] **1** *adv* **(a)** (*on one occasion*) einmal. ~ **a week** einmal in der Woche; ~ **again** *or* **more** noch einmal; ~ **again we find that ...** wir stellen erneut fest, daß ...; ~ **or twice** (*fig*) nur ein paarmal; ~ **and for all** ein für allemal; (*every*) ~ **in a while** ab und zu mal; **you can come this** ~ dieses eine Mal können Sie kommen; **for** ~ ausnahmsweise einmal. **(b)** (*in past*) einmal. **he was** ~ **famous** er war früher einmal berühmt; ~ **upon a time there was ...** es war einmal ... **(c)** *at* ~ (*immediately*) sofort, auf der Stelle; (*at the same time*) auf einmal, gleichzeitig; **all at** ~ auf einmal; **they came all at** ~ sie kamen alle gleichzeitig. **2** *conj* wenn; (*with past tense*) als. ~ **you understand, it's easy** wenn Sie es einmal verstehen, ist es einfach.

once-over ['wʌnsəʊvə'] *n* (*col*) **to give sb/sth the** ~ (*appraisal*) jdn/etw mal kurz überprüfen; (*clean*) mal kurz über etw (*acc*) gehen (*col*).

oncoming ['ɒnkʌmɪŋ] *adj car, traffic* entgegenkommend. **the** ~ **traffic** der Gegenverkehr.

one [wʌn] **1** *adj* **(a)** (*number*) ein/eine/ein. ~ **man in**

a thousand einer von tausend; **the baby is ~ (year old)** das Kind ist ein Jahr (alt); **it is ~ (o'clock)** es ist eins, es ist ein Uhr; **there is only ~ way of doing it** es gibt nur eine Möglichkeit, es zu tun.

(b) *(indefinite)* **~ morning/day he realized ...** eines Morgens/Tages bemerkte er ...; **you'll regret it ~ day** Sie werden das eines Tages bereuen; **~ morning next week** nächste Woche einmal morgens.

(c) *(sole, only)* **he is the ~ man to tell you** er ist der einzige, der es Ihnen sagen kann; **no ~ man could do it** niemand konnte es allein tun; **the ~ and only Brigitte Bardot** die unvergleichliche Brigitte Bardot.

(d) *(same)* **they all came in the ~ car** sie kamen alle in dem einen Auto; **they are ~ and the same person** das ist ein und dieselbe Person; **it is ~ and the same thing** das ist ein und dasselbe; **it's all ~** das ist einerlei.

2 *pron* **(a)** eine(r, s). **the ~ who ...** der(jenige), der .../die(jenige), die .../das(jenige), das ...; **do you have ~?** haben Sie einen/eine/ein(e)s?; **the red/big** *etc* **~** der/die/das rote/große *etc;* **a bigger ~** ein größerer/eine größere/ein größeres; **not ~ of them** nicht eine(r, s) von ihnen; **every ~** jede(r, s); **this ~** diese(r, s); **that ~** der/die/das; **which ~?** welche(r, s)?; **I'm not ~ to go out often** ich bin nicht der Typ, der oft ausgeht; **he's never ~ to say no** er sagt nie nein; **he's a great ~ for discipline** der ist ganz groß, wenn's um Disziplin geht; **she is a teacher, and he/her sister wants to be ~ too** sie ist Lehrerin, und er möchte auch gern Lehrer werden/ihre Schwester möchte auch gern eine werden; **I, for ~, think otherwise** ich, zum Beispiel, denke anders; **~ by ~** einzeln; **he is ~ of the family** er gehört zur Familie; **he is ~ of us** er ist einer von uns.

(b) *(impers)* *(nom)* man; *(acc)* einen; *(dat)* einem. **~ must learn to keep quiet** man muß lernen, still zu sein; **to hurt ~'s foot** sich *(dat)* den Fuß verletzen.

3 *n* *(written figure)* Eins *f.* **in ~s and twos** in kleinen Gruppen; **it was bedroom and sitting-room (all) in ~** es war Schlaf- und Wohnzimmer in einem; **to be at ~ with oneself** mit sich selbst im Einklang sein; **to be ~ up on sb** *(col)* *(know more)* jdm eins voraussein; *(have more)* jdm etwas voraushaben.

one another = each other.

one: **~-armed** *adj* einarmig; **~-eyed** *adj* einäugig; **~-legged** *adj* einbeinig; **~-man** *adj* Einmann-; **~-man band** Einmannkapelle *f*; *(fig col)* Einmannbetrieb *m*; **~-off** *adj* *(Brit col)* einmalig; **~-piece** *adj* einteilig.

onerous ['ɒnərəs] *adj* *responsibility* schwer(wiegend); *task, duty* schwer.

oneself [wʌn'self] *pron* **(a)** *(dir and indir, with prep)* sich; *(~ personally)* sich selbst *or* selber. **(b)** *(emph)* (sich) selbst; *see* **myself.**

one: **~-shot** *adj, n* *(US)* einmalig; **~-sided** *adj* einseitig; *judgement, account also* parteiisch; **~-time** *adj* ehemalig; **~-to-one** *adj correlation* eins-zu-eins; **~-track** *adj* **he's got a ~-track mind** der hat immer nur das eine im Sinn; **~-upmanship** [ˌwʌn'ʌpmənʃɪp] *n* **that's just a form of ~-upmanship** damit will er *etc* den anderen nur um eine Nasenlänge voraus sein; **~-way** *adj traffic, street* Einbahn-; **~-way ticket** *(US Rail)* einfache Fahrkarte.

ongoing ['ɒngəʊɪŋ] *adj* *(in progress)* laufend; *(long-term)* development, relationship andauernd.

onion ['ʌnjən] *n* Zwiebel *f.*

online [ɒn'laɪn] **1** *adj attr* On-line-. **2** *adv* on-line. **the computer is operating ~** der Computer arbeitet im On-line-Betrieb.

onlooker ['ɒnlʊkəʳ] *n* Zuschauer(in *f*) *m.*

only ['əʊnlɪ] **1** *adj attr* einzige(r, s). **he's an ~ child**

er ist ein Einzelkind *nt*; **he was the ~ one to leave** *or* **who left** er ist als einziger gegangen; **that's the ~ thing for it/the ~ thing to do** das ist die einzige Möglichkeit; **my ~ wish/regret** das einzige, was ich mir wünsche/was ich bedaure.

2 *adv* nur. **it's ~ five o'clock** es ist erst fünf Uhr; **I ~ wanted to be with you** ich wollte nur mit dir zusammen sein; **~ too true** *etc* nur (all)zu wahr *etc*; **I'd be ~ too pleased to help** ich würde nur zu gerne helfen; **if ~ that hadn't happened** wenn das bloß nicht passiert wäre; **we ~ just caught the train** wir haben den Zug gerade noch gekriegt; **he has ~ just arrived** er ist gerade erst angekommen; **I've ~ just got enough** ich habe gerade genug; **not ~ ... but also ...** nicht nur ..., sondern auch ...

3 *conj* bloß, nur. **I would do it myself, ~ I haven't time** ich würde es selbst machen, ich habe nur keine Zeit.

onomatopoeia [ˌɒnəʊmætəʊ'piːə] *n* Lautmalerei *f.*

onrush ['ɒnrʌʃ] *n* *(of people)* Ansturm *m; (of water)* Schwall *m.*

onset ['ɒnset] *n* Beginn *m; (of cold weather also)* Einbruch *m; (of illness)* Ausbruch *m.*

onslaught ['ɒnslɔːt] *n* *(Mil)* (heftiger) Angriff *(on* auf *+acc)*. **to make an ~ on sb/sth** *(fig)* (verbally) jdn/etw angreifen; *(on work)* einer Sache *(dat)* zu Leibe rücken.

onto ['ɒntʊ] *prep* **(a)** *(upon, on top of)* auf *(+acc); (on sth vertical)* an *(+acc)*. **(b)** *(in verbal expressions)* **to get/come ~ a subject** auf ein Thema zu sprechen kommen; **to be/get ~ or on to sb** *(find sb out)* jdm auf die Schliche gekommen sein/kommen *(col);* **I'll get ~ him about it** ich werde ihn darauf ansprechen.

onus ['əʊnəs] *n no pl* Pflicht *f; (burden)* Last *f.* **to shift the ~ for sth onto sb** jdm die Verantwortung für etw zuschieben; **the ~ to do it is on him** es liegt an ihm, das zu tun.

onward ['ɒnwəd] *adv* *(also ~s)* voran, vorwärts; *march* weiter. **from today/this time ~** von heute/ der Zeit an.

onyx ['ɒnɪks] **1** *n* Onyx *m.* **2** *adj* Onyx-.

ooze [uːz] **1** *n* *(mud)* Schlamm *m.* **2** *vi* triefen; *(wound)* nässen; *(resin, mud, glue)* (heraus)quellen. **3** *vt* **(a)** (aus)schwitzen. **(b)** *(fig)* kindness, charm triefen von *(pej)*, verströmen.

opal ['əʊpəl] *n* *(stone)* Opal *m.*

opaque [əʊ'peɪk] *adj* **(a)** opak; *glass also, liquid* trüb. **(b)** *(fig)* prose undurchsichtig, unklar.

OPEC ['əʊpek] = **Organization of Petroleum Exporting Countries** OPEC *f.*

open ['əʊpən] **1** *adj* offen; *door, bottle, eye, flower also* auf *pred*, geöffnet; *lines of communication, road* frei; *(public)* meeting, trial öffentlich. **to keep/hold the door ~** die Tür offen- *or* auflassen/ offen- *or* aufhalten; **I can't keep my eyes ~** ich kann die Augen nicht offenhalten; **the baker's shop is ~** der Bäckerladen hat geöffnet *or* hat auf *(col);* **to lay oneself ~ to criticism/attack** sich der Kritik/Angriffen aussetzen; **in the ~ air** im Freien; **~ to traffic/shipping** für den Verkehr/die Schiffahrt freigegeben; **to be ~ to sb** *(admission)* jdm freistehen; *(place)* für jdn geöffnet sein; **he was ~ with us** er war ganz offen mit uns; **two possibilities were ~ to him** zwei Möglichkeiten standen ihm offen; **~ day** Tag *m* der offenen Tür; **~ to the public** der Öffentlichkeit zugänglich; **to be ~ to advice/ suggestions** Ratschlägen/Vorschlägen gegenüber offen sein; **I'm ~ to offers** ich lasse gern mit mir reden; **they left the matter ~** sie ließen die Angelegenheit offen; **to keep an ~ mind** alles offen lassen; **to have an ~ mind on sth** einer Sache *(dat)* aufgeschlossen gegenüberstehen.

2 *n* **in the ~** *(outside)* im Freien; *(on ~ ground)* auf freiem Feld; **to bring sth out into the ~** mit etw nicht länger hinterm Berg halten; **to come out into the** ~ *(fig) (person)* Farbe bekennen; *(affair)* herauskommen.

3 *vt* **(a)** *door, mouth, bottle, letter etc* öffnen, aufmachen *(col)*; *book also, newspaper* aufschlagen; *(officially) exhibition* eröffnen; *building* einweihen; *road* dem Verkehr übergeben. **to** ~ **one's heart to sb** sich jdm eröffnen *(geh)*; ~ **your mind to new possibilities** öffnen Sie sich *(dat)* den Blick für neue Möglichkeiten; **to** ~ **fire** *(Mil)* das Feuer eröffnen *(on* auf *+acc)*. **(b)** *shop, trial, school, account* eröffnen.

4 *vi* **(a)** aufgehen; *(door, flower, wound also)* sich öffnen. **(b)** *(shop, museum)* öffnen, aufmachen. **(c)** *(door)* führen *(into* in *+acc)*. **(d)** *(start)* beginnen *(with* mit*)*; *(Cards, Chess)* eröffnen. **the play** ~**s next week** das Stück wird ab nächster Woche gegeben.

◆ **open out 1** *vi (river, street)* sich verbreitern *(into* zu*)*; *(valley also, view)* sich weiten, sich öffnen; *(flower)* sich öffnen, aufgehen. **2** *vt sep (unfold) map etc* auseinanderfalten.

◆ **open up 1** *vi (flower)* sich öffnen, aufgehen; *(fig) (prospects, field, new horizons)* sich erschließen; *(person: become expansive)* gesprächiger werden. **2** *vt sep* **(a)** *territory, prospects* erschließen; *new horizons, field of research etc also* auftun; *(unblock) disused tunnel etc* freimachen. **(b)** *(unlock) house, shop, car etc* aufschließen. **(c)** *(start) business* eröffnen; *shop also* aufmachen.

open: ~**-air** *adj* im Freien; ~**-air swimming pool** *n* Freibad *nt*; ~**-and-shut** *adj* it's an ~**-and-shut case** es ist ein glasklarer Fall; ~**-cast** *adj coalmine* über Tage; ~**-cast** mining Tagebau *m*.

opener ['əupnə'] *n* Öffner *m*.

open: ~**-handed** *adj* freigebig; ~ **house** *n* to keep ~ **house** ein offenes Haus führen.

opening ['əupnɪŋ] **1** *n* **(a)** *(in traffic)* Öffnung *f*; Lücke *f*; *(forest clearing)* Lichtung *f*. **(b)** *(beginning)* Anfang *m*; *(of debate, speech, trial also, Chess, Cards)* Eröffnung *f*. **(c)** *(official* ~*) (of exhibition, stores)* Eröffnung *f*. **O**~ **of Parliament** Parlamentseröffnung *f*. **(d)** *(opportunity)* Möglichkeit *f*, Chance *f*; *(job vacancy)* (freie) Stelle. **2** *attr (initial, first)* erste(r, s); *speech also* Eröffnungs-; *remarks* einführend.

opening: ~ **ceremony** *n* Eröffnungsfeierlichkeiten *pl*; ~ **time** *n* Öffnungszeit *f*; **what are the bank's** ~ **times?** wann hat die Bank geöffnet?

openly ['əupnlɪ] *adv* offen; *(publicly)* öffentlich.

open: ~**-minded** *adj* aufgeschlossen; ~**-mindedness** *n* Aufgeschlossenheit *f*; ~**-mouthed** [,əupn'mauðd] *adj (in surprise or stupidity)* mit offenem Mund; ~**-necked** *adj shirt* mit offenem Kragen.

openness ['əupnɪs] *n (frankness)* Offenheit *f*.

open-plan ['əupən,plæn] *adj office* Großraum-; *flat etc* offen angelegt.

opera ['ɒpərə] *n* Oper *f*. **to go to the** ~ in die Oper gehen.

opera *in cpds* Opern-; ~ **glasses** *npl* Opernglas *nt*; ~ **house** *n* Opernhaus *nt*; ~ **singer** *n* Opernsänger(in *f*) *m*.

operate ['ɒpəreɪt] **1** *vi* operieren *(also Mil, Med)*; *(machine)* funktionieren; *(be in operation)* in Betrieb sein; *(buses, planes)* verkehren; *(theory, plan, law)* sich auswirken; *(organization, system)* arbeiten. **I don't like the way he** ~**s** ich mag seine Methoden nicht; **to be** ~**d on** *(Med)* operiert werden. **2** *vt* **(a)** *machine* bedienen; *(set in operation)* in Betrieb setzen; *brakes etc also* betätigen. **(b)** *business* führen.

operatic [,ɒpə'rætɪk] *adj singer, music* Opern-.

operating ['ɒpəreɪtɪŋ] *adj attr* **(a)** *(Tech, Comm)* pressure, cost Betriebs-. **(b)** *(Med)* Operations-. ~ **theatre** *(Brit) or* **room** *(US)* Operationssaal, OP *m*.

operation [,ɒpə'reɪʃən] *n* **(a)** *(of machine, system)* Funktionieren *nt*; *(act of operating)* Bedienung *f*;

(of small mechanism) Betätigung *f*. **to be in** ~ *(machine)* in Betrieb sein; *(law)* in Kraft sein; *(plan)* durchgeführt werden; **to be out of** ~ außer Betrieb sein; **to come into** ~ *(law)* in Kraft treten; *(plan)* zur Anwendung gelangen; **to bring** *or* **put a law into** ~ ein Gesetz in Kraft setzen. **(b)** *(Med)* Operation *f (on* an *+dat)*. **to have an** ~ operiert werden; **to have an** ~ **for a hernia** wegen eines Bruchs operiert werden. **(c)** *(enterprise)* Unternehmen *nt*; *(task, stage in undertaking)* Arbeitsgang *m*. **(business)** ~**s** Geschäfte *pl*; **to cease** ~**s** den Geschäftverkehr einstellen.

operational [,ɒpə'reɪʃənl] *adj (ready for use)* machine, vehicle betriebsbereit; army unit, aeroplane etc einsatzfähig; *(in use or action)* machine, vehicle etc in Betrieb; army unit etc im Einsatz.

operative ['ɒpərətɪv] **1** *adj* **(a)** *measure, laws* wirksam. **"if"** being the ~ **word** wobei ich „wenn" betone. **(b)** *(Med)* treatment operativ. **2** *n (of machinery)* Maschinenarbeiter(in *f*) *m*.

operator ['ɒpəreɪtə'] *n (Telec)* ≃ Vermittlung *f*; *(person)* Dame *f*/Herr *m* von der Vermittlung; *(of machinery)* (Maschinen)arbeiter(in *f*) *m*; *(of computer etc)* Operator(in *f*) *m*. **to be a smooth** ~ *(col)* raffiniert vorgehen.

ophthalmic [ɒf'θælmɪk] *adj* Augen-.

opinion [ə'pɪnjən] *n* Meinung, Ansicht *f (about, on* zu*)*; *(political, religious)* Anschauung *f*; *(professional advice)* Gutachten *nt*; *(esp Med)* Befund *m*. **in my** ~ meiner Meinung nach; **to be of the** ~ **that** ... der Ansicht sein, daß ...; **to ask sb's** ~ jdn nach seiner Meinung fragen; **it is a matter of** ~ das ist Ansichtssache; **to have a high/poor** ~ **of sb/sth** eine hohe/schlechte Meinung von jdm/etw haben; **to form an** ~ **of sb/sth** sich *(dat)* eine Meinung über jdn/etw bilden; ~ **poll** Meinungsumfrage *f*; **to seek** *or* **get a second** ~ *(esp Med)* ein zweites Gutachten einholen.

opinionated [ə'pɪnjəneɪtɪd] *adj* rechthaberisch.

opium ['əupɪəm] *n (lit, fig)* Opium *nt*.

opponent [ə'pəunənt] *n* Gegner(in *f*) *m*.

opportune ['ɒpətjuːn] *adj time* günstig; *remark* an passender Stelle; *action, event* rechtzeitig.

opportunism [,ɒpə'tjuːnɪzəm] *n* Opportunismus *m*.

opportunist [,ɒpə'tjuːnɪst] *n* Opportunist *m*.

opportunity [,ɒpə'tjuːnɪtɪ] *n* Gelegenheit *f*; *(chance to better oneself)* Chance, Möglichkeit *f*. **at the first** *or* **earliest** ~ bei der erstbesten Gelegenheit; **to take the** ~ **to do sth** *or* **of doing sth** die Gelegenheit nutzen, etw zu tun; **as soon as I get the** ~ sobald sich die Gelegenheit ergibt; **opportunities for promotion** Aufstiegsmöglichkeiten *or* -chancen *pl*.

oppose [ə'pəuz] *vt* ablehnen; *(fight against)* sich entgegenstellen *(+dat)*; *leadership, orders* sich widersetzen *(+dat)*; *government* sich stellen gegen. **he** ~**s our coming** es ist absolut dagegen, daß wir kommen.

opposed [ə'pəuzd] *adj opp to be* ~ **to sb/sth** gegen jdn/etw sein; **I am** ~ **to your going** ich bin dagegen, daß Sie gehen; **as** ~ **to** im Gegensatz zu.

opposing [ə'pəuzɪŋ] *adj team* gegnerisch; *army* feindlich; *characters* gegensätzlich.

opposite ['ɒpəzɪt] **1** *adj* **(a)** *(facing)* gegenüberliegend *attr*, gegenüber *pred*. **to be** ~ gegenüber liegen/stehen/sitzen etc; **on the** ~ **page** auf der Seite gegenüber, auf der gegenüberliegenden Seite. **(b)** *(other) side, end, opinion* entgegengesetzt *(to, from* dat, zu*)*. **the** ~ **sex** das andere Geschlecht; ~ **number** Pendant *nt*; **they've got quite** ~ **characters** sie sind ganz gegensätzliche Charaktere. **2** *n* Gegenteil *nt*; *(contrasting: black/white etc)* Gegensatz *m*. **quite the** ~! ganz im Gegenteil! **3** *adv* gegenüber, auf der gegenüberliegenden Seite. **they sat** ~ sie saßen uns/ihnen/sich etc gegenüber. **4** *prep* gegenüber (+*dat*). ~ **one another** sich gegenüber; **they live** ~ **us** sie wohnen uns gegenüber.

opposition [‚ɒpə'zɪʃən] n **(a)** *(resistance)* Widerstand m; *(people resisting)* Opposition f. **to act in** ~ **to sth** einer Sache *(dat)* zuwiderhandeln. **(b)** *(esp Brit Parl)* O~ Opposition(spartei) f; **to be in** ~ in der Opposition sein.

oppress [ə'pres] vt **(a)** *(tyrannize)* unterdrücken. **(b)** *(weigh down)* bedrücken.

oppression [ə'preʃən] n *(tyranny)* Unterdrückung f.

oppressive [ə'presɪv] adj **(a)** *regime, laws* repressiv; *taxes* (er)drückend. **(b)** *(fig) heat* drückend; *thought* bedrückend.

oppressor [ə'presə'] n Unterdrücker m.

opt [ɒpt] vi **to** ~ **for sth/to do sth** sich für etw entscheiden/sich entscheiden, etw zu tun.

♦ **opt out** vi sich anders entscheiden; *(of awkward situation)* abspringen *(of bei)*; *(of responsibility, invitation)* ablehnen *(of acc)*; *(give up membership)* austreten *(of aus)*; *(of insurance scheme)* kündigen *(of acc)*.

optic ['ɒptɪk] adj *nerve, centre* Seh-.

optical ['ɒptɪkəl] adj optisch. ~ **illusion** optische Täuschung.

optician [ɒp'tɪʃən] n Optiker(in f) m.

optics ['ɒptɪks] n sing Optik f.

optimism ['ɒptɪmɪzəm] n Optimismus m.

optimist ['ɒptɪmɪst] n Optimist(in f) m.

optimistic [‚ɒptɪ'mɪstɪk] adj optimistisch *(about sth* in bezug auf *+acc)*.

optimum ['ɒptɪməm] adj optimal.

option ['ɒpʃən] n **(a)** *(choice)* Wahl f no pl; *(possible course of action also)* Möglichkeit f. **I have no** ~ mir bleibt keine andere Wahl; **he had no** ~ **but to come** ihm blieb nichts andere übrig, als zu kommen; **to leave one's** ~**s open** sich *(dat)* alle Möglichkeiten offenlassen. **(b)** *(Comm)* Option f *(on* auf *+acc)*; *(on house, goods etc also)* Vorkaufsrecht nt *(on an +dat)*; *(on shares)* Bezugsrecht nt *(on* für*)*. **with an** ~ **to buy** mit einer Kaufoption. **(c)** *(Univ, Sch)* Wahlfach nt.

optional ['ɒpʃənl] adj *(not compulsory)* freiwillig; *(Sch, Univ) subject* Wahl-. ~ **extras** Extras pl.

opulence ['ɒpjʊləns] n no pl see adj Reichtum m; Prunk m; Feudalität f; Üppigkeit f.

opulent ['ɒpjʊlənt] adj reich; *clothes* prunkvoll; *chairs, carpets* feudal; *lifestyle* üppig.

opus ['əʊpəs] n, pl **opera** ['ɒpərə] n *(Mus)* Opus m.

or conj oder; *(with neg)* noch. **he could not read** ~ **write** er konnte weder lesen noch schreiben; **you'd better go** ~ **(else) you'll be late** gehen Sie jetzt besser, sonst kommen Sie zu spät; **you'd better do it** ~ **else!** tu das lieber, sonst ...!; **in a day** ~ **two** in ein bis zwei Tagen; **the Congo,** ~ **rather, Zaire** der Kongo, beziehungsweise Zaire.

oracle ['ɒrəkl] n Orakel nt; *(person)* Seher(in f) m; *(fig)* Alleswisser m.

oral ['ɔːrəl] **1** adj **(a)** *(Med)* oral. ~ **vaccination** Schluckimpfung f. **(b)** *(verbal)* mündlich. **to improve one's** ~ **skills in a language** ein Sprache besser sprechen lernen. **2** n Mündliche(s) nt.

orally ['ɔːrəlɪ] adv **(a)** oral. **not to be taken** ~ nicht einnehmen. **(b)** *(verbally)* mündlich.

orange ['ɒrɪndʒ] **1** n *(fruit)* Orange, Apfelsine f; *(tree)* Orangenbaum m. **2** adj *(in colour)* orange inv, orange(n)farben.

orangeade ['ɒrɪndʒ'eɪd] n Orangenlimonade f.

orange: ~**juice** n Orangensaft m; ~ **peel** n Orangenschale f.

orang-utan [ɔː‚ræŋuː'tæn] n Orang-Utan m.

oration [ɒ'reɪʃən] n Ansprache f. **funeral** ~ Grabrede f.

orator ['ɒrətə'] n Redner(in f) m.

oratorio [‚ɒrə'tɔːrɪəʊ] n *(Mus)* Oratorium nt.

oratory ['ɒrətərɪ] n *(art)* Redekunst f.

orbit ['ɔːbɪt] **1** n **(a)** *(Astron, Space)* Umlaufbahn f. **to be in** ~ in der Umlaufbahn sein; **to put a**

satellite into ~ einen Satelliten in die Umlaufbahn schießen; **to go into** ~ in die Umlaufbahn eintreten. **(b)** *(fig: sphere of influence)* Einflußsphäre f. **2** vt umkreisen. **3** vi kreisen.

orchard ['ɔːtʃəd] n Obstgarten m; *(commercial)* Obstplantage f. **apple** ~ Obstgarten m mit Apfelbäumen.

orchestra ['ɔːkɪstrə] n Orchester nt.

orchestral [ɔː'kestrəl] adj Orchester-, orchestral.

orchestra pit n Orchestergraben m.

orchestration [‚ɔːkɪs'treɪʃən] n Orchesterbearbeitung f.

orchid ['ɔːkɪd] n Orchidee f.

ordain [ɔː'deɪn] vt **(a)** *sb* ordinieren. **(b)** *(destine: God, fate)* wollen, bestimmen. **it was** ~**ed das** Schicksal hat es so gefügt.

ordeal [ɔː'diːl] n Tortur f; *(stronger, long-lasting)* Martyrium nt; *(torment, emotional* ~*)* Qual f.

order ['ɔːdə'] **1** n **(a)** *(sequence)* (Reihen)folge f. **word** ~ Wortstellung f; **in** ~ **of preference** etc in der bevorzugten Reihenfolge; **to put sth in (the right)** ~ etw ordnen; **to be in the wrong** ~ or out **of** ~ durcheinander sein; *(one item)* nicht am richtigen Platz sein.

(b) *(system, discipline)* Ordnung f; *(in school also)* Disziplin f. **there's no** ~ **in his work** seiner Arbeit fehlt die Systematik; **it is in the** ~ **of things** es liegt in der Natur der Dinge; **his passport was in** ~ sein Paß war in Ordnung; **to keep** ~ die Ordnung wahren; **to keep the children in** ~ die Kinder unter Kontrolle halten.

(c) *(working condition)* Zustand m. **to be in good/bad** ~ in gutem/schlechtem Zustand sein; *(work well/badly)* in Ordnung/nicht in Ordnung sein; **to be out of/in** ~ *(car, radio, telephone)* nicht funktionieren/funktionieren; *(machine, lift)* außer/in Betrieb sein.

(d) *(command)* Befehl m. **by** ~ **of the minister** auf Anordnung des Ministers; **to be under** ~**s to do sth** Instruktionen haben, etw zu tun.

(e) *(in restaurant etc, for supplies)* Bestellung f; *(for goods, services)* Auftrag m. **made to** ~ auf Bestellung (gemacht); **to place an** ~ **with sb** eine Bestellung bei jdm aufgeben or machen; **jdm einen Auftrag geben; pay to the** ~ of zahlbar an *(+acc)*.

(f) **in** ~ **to do sth** um etw zu tun; **in** ~ **that** damit.

(g) *(correct procedure at meeting, Parl etc)* **a point of** ~ eine Verfahrensfrage; **to be out of** ~ *(fig)* aus dem Rahmen fallen; **to call the meeting to** ~ die Versammlung zur Ordnung rufen; **a drink would seem to be in** ~ ein Drink wäre angebracht; **is it in** ~ **for me to go to Paris?** ist es in Ordnung, wenn ich nach Paris fahre?; **to be the** ~ **of the day** auf dem Programm stehen *(also fig)*; *(Mil)* der Tagesbefehl sein.

(h) *(Biol)* Ordnung f; *(fig: class, degree)* Art f. **intelligence of a high** ~ hochgradige Intelligenz; **something in the** ~ **of ten per cent** in der Größenordnung von zehn Prozent.

(i) *(Eccl) (of monks etc)* Orden m. **to take (holy)** ~**s** die Weihen empfangen.

2 vt **(a)** *(command, decree) sth* befehlen, anordnen; *(prescribe: doctor)* verordnen *(for sb* jdm*)*. **to** ~ **sb to do sth** jdm befehlen, etw zu tun; *(esp Mil)* jdn dazu beordern, etw zu tun; **the referee** ~**ed him off the pitch** der Schiedsrichter verwies ihn des Feldes. **(b)** *(direct, arrange) one's affairs, life* ordnen. **(c)** *(Comm etc) goods, dinner, taxi* bestellen; *(to be manufactured)* in Auftrag geben.

3 vi bestellen.

♦ **order about** or **around** vt sep herumkommandieren.

order: ~ **book** n *(Comm)* Auftragsbuch nt; **to have a full** ~ **book** voll im Geschäft sein; ~ **form** n Bestellformular nt, Bestellschein m.

orderly ['ɔːdəlɪ] **1** adj **(a)** (tidy, methodical) ordentlich. **(b)** (disciplined) ruhig, friedlich. **2** n **(medical)** ~ Pfleger(in f) m; (Mil) Sanitäter m.

ordinal ['ɔːdɪnl] (Math) **1** adj Ordnungs-, Ordinal-. **2** n Ordnungs- or Ordinalzahl f.

ordinance ['ɔːdɪnəns] n (of government) Verordnung f; (Jur) Anordnung f.

ordinarily ['ɔːdnrɪlɪ] adv gewöhnlich; (+adj) normal.

ordinary ['ɔːdnrɪ] **1** adj **(a)** gewöhnlich, normal. in the ~ way I would ... normalerweise or gewöhnlich würde ich ...; my ~ doctor der Arzt, zu dem ich normalerweise gehe. **(b)** (average) durchschnittlich. **2** n out of the ~ außergewöhnlich, außerordentlich.

ordination [,ɔːdɪ'neɪʃən] n Ordination f.

ordnance ['ɔːdnəns] n (Mil) (artillery) Geschütze pl; (supply) Material nt. **O~ Survey map** n (Brit) Meßtischblatt nt.

ore [ɔːʳ] n Erz nt.

organ ['ɔːgən] n **(a)** (Anat) Organ nt. **(b)** (Mus) Orgel f. **(c)** (mouthpiece of opinion) Sprachrohr nt; (newspaper) Organ nt.

organ-grinder ['ɔːgən'graɪndəʳ] n Drehorgelspieler m.

organic [ɔː'gænɪk] adj (lit, fig) organisch; vegetables, farming biodynamisch.

organism ['ɔːgənɪzəm] n Organismus m.

organist ['ɔːgənɪst] n Organist(in f) m.

organization [,ɔːgənaɪ'zeɪʃən] n **(a)** (act) Organisation f (also Pol); (of time) Einteilung f. **(b)** (arrangement) see vt **(a)** Ordnung f; Einteilung f; Aufbau m; Planung f. **(c)** (institution) Organisation f; (Comm) Unternehmen nt.

organize ['ɔːgənaɪz] vt **(a)** (systematize) ordnen; time, work einteilen; essay aufbauen; one's/sb's life planen. **to get (oneself) ~d** (get ready) alles vorbereiten; (sort things out) seine Sachen in Ordnung bringen. **(b)** (arrange) party, meeting etc organisieren; food for party etc sorgen für. **to ~ things so that ...** es so einrichten, daß ...

organized ['ɔːgənaɪzd] adj organisiert; life geregelt. **he isn't very ~** bei ihm geht alles drunter und drüber (col).

organizer ['ɔːgənaɪzəʳ] n Organisator(in f) m; (of event also) Veranstalter(in f) m.

orgasm ['ɔːgæzəm] n Orgasmus m.

orgy ['ɔːdʒɪ] n (lit, fig) Orgie f. **drunken ~** Sauforgie f.

orient ['ɔːrɪənt] n (also **O~**) Orient m; (poet also) Morgenland nt.

oriental [,ɔːrɪ'entl] **1** adj orientalisch. **2** n (person) **O~** Orientale m, Orientalin f.

orientate ['ɔːrɪənteɪt] vt ausrichten (towards auf +acc). **money-~d** materiell ausgerichtet.

orientation [,ɔːrɪən'teɪʃən] n Orientierung f; (fig also) Ausrichtung f.

orienteering [,ɔːrɪən'tɪərɪŋ] n Orientierungslauf m.

orifice ['ɒrɪfɪs] n Öffnung f.

origin ['ɒrɪdʒɪn] n Ursprung m; (of person, family) Herkunft f. **to have its ~ in sth** auf etw (acc) zurückgehen; **country of ~** Herkunftsland nt; **of humble ~s** aus bescheidenen Verhältnissen.

original [ə'rɪdʒɪnl] **1** adj **(a)** (first, earliest) ursprünglich. **~ inhabitants of a country** Ureinwohner pl eines Landes; **~ text/version** Originaltext m/Originalfassung f. **(b)** (not imitative) painting original; idea originell. **~ research** eigene Forschung. **2** n Original nt; (of model) Vorlage f. **he reads Kant in the ~** er liest Kant im Original.

originality [ə,rɪdʒɪ'nælɪtɪ] n Originalität f.

originally [ə,rɪdʒənəlɪ] adv **(a)** ursprünglich. **(b)** (in an original way) originell.

originate [ə'rɪdʒɪneɪt] **1** vt hervorbringen; policy, company eins Leben rufen; product erfinden. **2** vi **(a)** entstehen. **to ~ from** or **with sb** von jdm

stammen. **(b)** (US: bus, train etc) ausgehen (in von).

originator [ə'rɪdʒɪneɪtəʳ] n (of plan, idea) Urheber(in f) m; (of product) Erfinder(in f) m.

ornament ['ɔːnəmənt] **1** n (object) Ziergegenstand m. **2** vt verzieren; room ausschmücken.

ornamental [,ɔːnə'mentl] adj dekorativ; garden, plant etc Zier-.

ornamentation [,ɔːnəmen'teɪʃən] n (ornamental detail) Verzierungen pl; (ornaments) Schmuck m.

ornate [ɔː'neɪt] adj kunstvoll; (of larger objects) prunkvoll; language überladen (pej), reich.

ornithologist [,ɔːnɪ'θɒlədʒɪst] n Ornithologe m, Ornithologin f.

ornithology [,ɔːnɪ'θɒlədʒɪ] n Ornithologie, Vogelkunde f.

orphan ['ɔːfən] **1** n Waise f. **2** vt **to be ~ed** zur Waise werden.

orphanage ['ɔːfənɪdʒ] n Waisenhaus nt.

orthodox ['ɔːθədɒks] adj (Rel, fig) orthodox.

orthodoxy ['ɔːθədɒksɪ] n **(a)** Orthodoxie f. **(b)** (fig) Konventionalität f.

orthography [ɔː'θɒgrəfɪ] n Rechtschreibung, Orthographie f.

orthopaedic, (US) orthopedic [,ɔːθəʊ'piːdɪk] adj orthopädisch.

orthopaedics, (US) orthopedics [,ɔːθəʊ'piːdɪks] n sing Orthopädie f.

orthopaedist, (US) orthopedist [,ɔːθəʊ'piːdɪst] n Orthopäde m, Orthopädin f.

oscillate ['ɒsɪleɪt] vi (lit, fig) schwanken.

oscillation [,ɒsɪ'leɪʃən] n Schwanken nt; (individual movement etc) Schwankung f.

osprey ['ɒspreɪ] n Fischadler m.

ossify ['ɒsɪfaɪ] vi (lit) verknöchern; (fig) erstarren; (mind) unbeweglich werden.

ostensible [ɒ'stensəbl] adj vorgeblich; (alleged) angeblich.

ostentation [,ɒsten'teɪʃən] n (display of wealth etc) Pomp m, Protzerei f (pej); (of skills etc) Angeberei f.

ostentatious [,ɒsten'teɪʃəs] adj **(a)** (pretentious) protzig (col). **(b)** (conspicuous) auffällig.

osteopath ['ɒstɪəpæθ] n Osteopath(in f) m.

ostracism ['ɒstrəsɪzəm] n Ächtung f.

ostracize ['ɒstrəsaɪz] vt ächten.

ostrich ['ɒstrɪtʃ] n Strauß m.

other ['ʌðəʳ] **1** adj **(a)** andere(r, s). **~ people** andere (Leute); **some ~ people will come later** später kommen noch ein paar; **do you have any ~ questions?** haben Sie sonst noch Fragen?; **the ~ day** neulich; **some ~ time** (in future) ein andermal; (in past) ein anderes Mal; **~ people's property** fremdes Eigentum. **(b)** **every ~** (alternate) jede(r, s) zweite. **(c)** **~ than** (except) außer (+dat); (different to) anders als. **(d)** **some time or ~** irgendwann (einmal); **some writer or ~** irgendein Schriftsteller m.

2 pron andere(r, s). **he doesn't like hurting ~s** er mag niemanden verletzen; **there are 6 ~s da** sind noch 6 (andere); **are there any ~s there?** sind noch andere da?; **there were no ~s there** waren sonst keine da; **something/someone or ~** irgend etwas/jemand; **one or ~ of them will** come einer (von ihnen) wird kommen.

3 adv **he could do no ~** (than come) er konnte nicht anders (als kommen); **somehow or ~** irgendwie; **somewhere or ~** irgendwo; **he was none ~ than the Minister** er war niemand anders als der Minister.

otherwise ['ʌðəwaɪz] **1** adv **(a)** (in a different way) anders. **I am ~ engaged** (form) ich bin anderweitig beschäftigt; **except where ~ stated** (form) sofern nicht anders angegeben; **Richard I, ~ (known as) the Lionheart** Richard I., auch bekannt als Löwenherz; **you seem to think ~** Sie scheinen anderer Meinung zu sein. **(b)** (in other respects) sonst, im übrigen. **2** conj (or else) sonst, andernfalls.

other-worldly [ˌʌðə'wɜːldlɪ] *adj attitude* weltfern; *smile, expression* entrückt.

otter ['ɒtəʳ] *n* Otter *m.*

ouch [aʊtʃ] *interj* autsch.

ought [ɔːt] *aux* (a) *(moral obligation)* I ~ **to do it** ich sollte *or* müßte es tun; **he** ~ **to have come** er hätte kommen sollen *or* müssen; **he thought you** ~ **to know** er meinte, Sie sollten das wissen. (b) *(desirability)* **you** ~ **to see that film** den Film sollten Sie sehen; **she** ~ **to have been a teacher** sie hätte Lehrerin werden sollen. (c) *(probability)* **he** ~ **to win the race** er müßte das Rennen gewinnen; **that** ~ **to do** das dürfte wohl *or* müßte reichen; ... **and I** ~ **to know!** ... und ich muß es doch wissen!

ounce [aʊns] *n* Unze *f.* **there's not an** ~ **of truth in it** daran ist kein Fünkchen Wahrheit.

our ['aʊəʳ] *poss adj* unser; *see* **my.**

ours ['aʊəz] *poss pron* unsere(r, s); *see* **mine**[1].

ourselves [ˌaʊə'selvz] *pers pron (dir, indir obj +prep)* uns; *(emph)* selbst; *see* **myself.**

oust [aʊst] *vt object* herausbekommen; *government* absetzen; *politician, colleague etc* absägen *(col)*; *rivals* ausschalten; *(take place of)* verdrängen.

out [aʊt] *see also* ~ **of 1** *adv* (a) *(not in container, car etc)* außen; *(not in building, room)* draußen; *(indicating motion) (seen from inside)* hinaus, raus *(col)*; *(seen from* ~*side)* heraus, raus *(col).* **to be** ~ **weg sein**; *(when visitors come)* nicht da sein; **they are** ~ **shopping** sie sind zum Einkaufen (gegangen); **he's** ~ **in his car** er ist mit dem Auto unterwegs; **it's cold** ~ **here/there** es ist kalt hier/da draußen; **he likes to be** ~ **and about** er ist gern unterwegs; **we had a day** ~ **in London** wir haben einen Tag in London verbracht; **the journey** ~ die Hinreise; *(seen from destination)* die Herfahrt; **the workers are** ~ *(on strike)* die Arbeiter streiken; **the tide is** ~ es ist Ebbe.

(b) *(indicating distance)* **to go** ~ **to China** nach China fahren; ~ **in the Far East** im Fernen Osten; **the boat was ten miles** ~ das Schiff war zehn Meilen weit draußen; **five days** ~ **from Liverpool** *(Naut) (leaving)* fünf Tage nach dem Auslaufen von Liverpool; *(approaching)* fünf Tage vor Liverpool; ~ **at sea** draußen auf dem Meer.

(c) **to be** ~ *(sun)* draußen sein; *(stars, moon)* dasein; *(flowers)* blühen.

(d) *(light, fire, ball, player)* aus; *(not in fashion)* aus der Mode; *(~ of the question)* ausgeschlossen, nicht drin *(col)*; **to be** ~ *(unconscious)* bewußtlos *or* weg *(col)* sein.

(e) **the best car** ~ das beste Auto, das es zur Zeit gibt; **to be** ~ *(be published)* herausgekommen sein; **their secret was** ~ ihr Geheimnis war bekannt geworden; **the results are** ~ die Ergebnisse sind (he)raus; ~ **with it!** heraus damit!; **before the day was** ~ noch am selben Tag; **his calculations were** ~ er hatte sich in seinen Berechnungen geirrt; **you're not far** ~ Sie haben es fast (getroffen); **you're way** ~! you went gefehlt! *(geh)*, da hast du dich völlig vertan *(col)*; **we were £5/20%** ~ wir hatten uns um £ 5/20% verrechnet *or* vertan *(col)*; **speak** ~ **loud** sprechen Sie laut/lauter; **to be** ~ **for a good time** sich amüsieren wollen; **he's** ~ **for all he can get** er will haben, was er nur bekommen kann; **he's** ~ **to get her** er ist hinter ihr her; **he's just** ~ **to make money** er ist nur auf Geld aus; ~ **and away** weitaus, mit Abstand.

2 *n* (a) *see* **in.** (b) *(esp US fig col: way* ~*)* Hintertür *f.*

out-and-out ['aʊtən'aʊt] *adj liar, fool* ausgemacht; *defeat* total.

outback ['aʊtbæk] *(in Australia) n*: **the** ~ das Hinterland.

out: ~**bid** *pret, ptp* ~**bid** *vt* überbieten; ~**board** *adj motor* Außenbord-.

outbreak ['aʊtbreɪk] *n (of war, hostility, disease)* Ausbruch *m.* **a recent** ~ **of fire caused ...** ein Brand verursachte kürzlich ...; **at the** ~ **of war** bei Kriegsausbruch.

outbuilding ['aʊtbɪldɪŋ] *n* Nebengebäude *nt.*

outburst ['aʊtbɜːst] *n (of joy, anger)* Ausbruch *m.*

outcast ['aʊtkɑːst] *n* Ausgestoßene(r) *mf.* **social** ~ Außenseiter *m* der Gesellschaft.

outclass [ˌaʊt'klɑːs] *vt* in den Schatten stellen.

outcome ['aʊtkʌm] *n* Ergebnis *nt.* **what was the** ~? was ist dabei herausgekommen?

outcrop ['aʊtkrɒp] *n* **an** ~ **(of rock)** eine Felsnase.

outcry ['aʊtkraɪ] *n* Aufschrei *m (against state +acc)*; *(public protest)* Protestwelle *f (against* gegen*).* **there was a general** ~ **about the increase in taxes** es gab eine Welle des Protests erhob sich wegen der Steuererhöhung.

out: ~**dated** *adj idea, theory* überholt; *machine, word, custom* veraltet; ~**distance** *vt* hinter sich *(dat)* lassen, abhängen *(col).*

outdo [ˌaʊt'duː] *pret* **outdid** [ˌaʊt'dɪd], *ptp* **outdone** [ˌaʊt'dʌn] *vt* übertreffen, überbieten *(sb in sth* jdn an etw *dat).*

outdoor ['aʊtdɔːʳ] *adj* ~ **shoes** Straßenschuhe *pl*; ~ **clothes** wärmere Kleidung; ~ **type** sportlicher Typ; **the** ~ **life** das Leben im Freien; ~ **swimming pool** Freibad *nt.*

outdoors ['aʊt'dɔːz] **1** *adv* draußen, im Freien. **to go** ~ nach draußen gehen. **2** *n* **the great** ~ *(hum)* die freie Natur.

outer ['aʊtəʳ] *adj attr* äußere(r, s); *door etc also* Außen-. ~ **space** der Weltraum.

outfit ['aʊtfɪt] *n* (a) *(clothes)* Kleidung *f*; *(Fashion)* Ensemble *nt*; *(uniform)* Uniform *f*; *(of scout)* Kluft *f.* (b) *(equipment)* Ausrüstung *f.* (c) *(col: organization)* Verein *(col) m.* (d) *(Mil)* Einheit, Truppe *f.*

outfitter ['aʊtfɪtəʳ] *n (of ships)* Ausrüster *m.* **gentlemen's** ~'s *(esp Brit)* Herrenausstatter *m*; **sports** ~'s *(esp Brit)* Sportartikelgeschäft *nt.*

outgoing ['aʊt'gəʊɪŋ] **1** *adj* (a) *tenant* ausziehend; *office-holder* scheidend; *train, boat* hinausfahrend; *plane* hinausgehend. (b) *personality* kontaktfreudig. **2** *npl* ~**s** *(Brit)* Ausgaben *pl.*

outgrow [ˌaʊt'grəʊ] *pret* **outgrew** [ˌaʊt'gruː], *ptp* **outgrown** [ˌaʊt'grəʊn] *vt clothes* herauswachsen aus; *habit* entwachsen *(+dat).*

outing ['aʊtɪŋ] *n* Ausflug *m.* **to go on an** ~ einen Ausflug machen.

outlandish [ˌaʊt'lændɪʃ] *adj* absonderlich; *behaviour also* befremdend; *wallpaper etc* ausgefallen.

outlast [ˌaʊt'lɑːst] *vt (live longer)* überleben; *(endure longer)* länger durchhalten als; *(thing)* länger halten als; *(idea etc)* überdauern.

outlaw ['aʊtlɔː] **1** *n* Geächtete(r) *mf*; *(in western etc)* Bandit *m.* **2** *vt organization* ächten; *newspaper etc* verbieten.

outlay ['aʊtleɪ] *n* (Kosten)aufwand *m*; *(recurring, continuous)* Kosten *pl.* **the initial** ~ die anfänglichen Aufwendungen; **capital** ~ Kapitalaufwand *m.*

outlet ['aʊtlet] **1** *n* (a) *(for water)* Abfluß *m*; *(for steam)* Abzug *m*; *(US Elec)* Steckdose *f.* (b) *(Comm)* Absatzmarkt *m*; *(merchant)* Abnehmer *m*; *(shop)* Verkaufsstelle *f.* (c) *(fig) (for talents)* Betätigungsmöglichkeit *f*; *(for emotion)* Ventil *m.* **2** *attr pipe* Abfluß-; *(for steam)* Abzugs-; *valve* Auslaß-.

outline ['aʊtlaɪn] **1** *n* (a) *(of objects)* Umriß *m*; *(silhouette)* Silhouette *f*; *(of face)* Züge *pl.* (b) *(fig: summary)* Abriß *m.* **in (broad)** ~ in groben Zügen; **just give (me) the broad** ~**s** skizzieren Sie es mir grob. **2** *vt* (a) **the mountain was** ~**d against the sky** der Berg zeichnete sich gegen den Himmel ab. (b) *(give summary of)* umreißen, skizzieren.

outlive [ˌaʊtˈlɪv] *vt person* überleben. **to have ~d one's usefulness** ausgedient haben; *(method, system)* sich überlebt haben.

outlook [ˈaʊtlʊk] *n* **(a)** *(view)* Aussicht *f (over* über +*acc, on to* auf +*acc)*. **(b)** *(prospects, Met)* Aussichten *pl.* **(c)** *(mental attitude)* Einstellung *f*. **his ~ (up)on life** seine Einstellung zum Leben.

out: ~**lying** *adj (distant)* entlegen, abgelegen; *(outside the town boundary)* umliegend; *district (of town)* Außen-; ~**manoeuvre,** *(US)* ~**maneuver** *vt (Mil, fig)* ausmanövrieren; *(in rivalry)* ausstechen; ~**moded** *adj* unzeitgemäß; *ideas, technology etc also* überholt.

outnumber [ˌaʊtˈnʌmbəʳ] *vt* in der Überzahl sein gegenüber. **we were ~ed five to one** sie waren fünfmal so viele wie wir.

out of *prep* **(a)** *(outside, away from) (position)* nicht in (+*dat)*, außerhalb (+*gen)*; *(motion)* aus (+*dat)*. **to go/be ~ the country** außer Landes gehen/sein; **he walked ~ the room** er ging aus dem Zimmer (hinaus); **he went ~ the door** er ging zur Tür hinaus; **to look ~ the window** aus dem Fenster sehen; **I saw him ~ the window** ich sah ihn durchs Fenster; ~ **danger/sight** außer Gefahr/Sicht; **he feels ~ it** *(col)* er kommt sich *(dat)* ausgeschlossen vor; **you're well ~ it** so ist es auch besser für dich.

(b) *(cause, motive)* aus (+*dat)*. ~ **curiosity** aus Neugier.

(c) *(indicating origins or source)* aus (+*dat)*. **to drink ~ a glass** aus einem Glas trinken; **made ~ silver** aus Silber (gemacht); **to copy sth ~ a book** etw aus einem Buch kopieren.

(d) *(from among)* von (+*dat)*. **in seven cases ~ ten** in sieben von zehn Fällen; **one ~ every four smokers** einer von vier Rauchern.

(e) *(without)* ~ **breath** außer Atem; **we are ~ money/bread** wir haben kein Geld/Brot mehr.

out: ~**-of-date** *adj, pred* ~ **of date** *methods, ideas* überholt; *clothes, records* altmodisch; *customs* veraltet; ~**-of-the-way** *adj, pred* ~ **of the way** *spot* abgelegen; *theory* ungewöhnlich; ~**patient** *n* ambulanter Patient, ambulante Patientin; ~**patient's (department)** Ambulanz *f*; ~**post** *n (Mil, fig)* Vorposten *m*.

output [ˈaʊtpʊt] *n (of machine, factory, person)* Produktion *f; (Elec)* Leistung *f; (capacity of amplifier)* Ausgangsleistung *f; (Comp)* Ausgabe *f*, Output *m or nt*.

outrage [ˈaʊtreɪdʒ] **1** *n (wicked, violent deed)* Schandtat *f; (cruel also)* Greueltat *f; (by police, demonstrators etc)* Ausschreitung *f; (indecency, injustice)* Skandal *m*. **bomb ~** verbrecherischer Bombenanschlag; **an ~ against humanity** ein Verbrechen *nt* gegen die Menschlichkeit; **it's a public ~** es ist ein öffentlicher Skandal; **an ~ against good taste** eine unerhörte Geschmacklosigkeit. **2** [aʊtˈreɪdʒ] *vt sense of decency* beleidigen; *person* empören, entrüsten.

outrageous [aʊtˈreɪdʒəs] *adj (cruel, violent)* grauenhaft; *(unjust)* unerhört; *conduct, nonsense* haarsträubend; *language* entsetzlich; *charge etc* ungeheuerlich; *clothes, make-up* unmöglich; *(indecent)* geschmacklos.

outrageously [aʊtˈreɪdʒəslɪ] *adv* fürchterlich; *exaggerate also* maßlos.

out: ~**ran** *pret of* ~**run**; ~**ride** *pret* ~**rode**, *ptp* ~**ridden** *vt* besser reiten als; *(on bike)* besser fahren als; *(outdistance)* davonreiten (+*dat)*/davonfahren (+*dat)*; ~**rider** *n (on motorcycle)* Kradbegleiter *m*.

outright [aʊtˈraɪt] **1** *adv (at once) kill* auf der Stelle; *(openly)* geradeheraus. **2** [ˈaʊtraɪt] *adj nonsense, disaster* total. **that's ~ arrogance/deception** das ist die reine Arroganz/das ist glatter Betrug; **an ~ error** ganz einfach ein Fehler.

out: ~**rode** *pret of* ~**ride**; ~**run** *pret* ~**ran**, *ptp* ~**run** *vt* schneller laufen als; *(outdistance)* da-

vonlaufen (+*dat)*; ~**set** *n* Anfang *m*; **at the ~set** am Anfang; **from the ~set** von Anfang an; ~**shine** *pret, ptp* ~**shone** *vt (fig)* in den Schatten stellen.

outside [ˈaʊtsaɪd] **1** *n (of house, car, object)* Außenseite *f*. **to open the door from the ~** die Tür von außen öffnen; **to overtake on the ~** außen überholen; **he sees it from the ~** *(fig)* er sieht es als Außenstehender; **at the (very) ~** im äußersten Falle.

2 *adj* **(a)** *(external)* Außen-, äußere(r, s). **an ~ broadcast** eine nicht im Studio produzierte Sendung; **the ~ lane** die äußere Spur; ~ **seat** *(in a row)* Platz *m* am Gang. **(b)** *price* äußerste(r, s). **at an ~ estimate** maximal. **(c)** *(very unlikely)* **an ~ chance** eine kleine Chance; **my horse only has an ~ chance** mein Pferd hat nur Außenseiterchancen.

3 *adv (on the outer side)* außen; *(of house, vehicle)* draußen. **to be/go ~** draußen sein/nach draußen gehen.

4 *prep (also ~ of)* **(a)** *(outside)* außerhalb (+*gen)*. **to be/go ~ sth** außerhalb einer Sache sein/aus etw gehen; **he is waiting ~ the door** er wartet vor der Tür; **it is ~ our agreement** es geht über unsere Vereinbarung hinaus. **(b)** *(apart from)* außer (+*dat)*.

outsider [ˌaʊtˈsaɪdəʳ] *n* Außenseiter(in *f*) *m*.

out: ~**size** *adj* übergroß; ~**size clothes** Kleidung *f* in Übergröße; ~**skirts** *npl (of town)* Außenbezirke *pl*.

outspoken [ˌaʊtˈspəʊkən] *adj person, criticism, book* freimütig; *remark* direkt. **he is ~** er nimmt kein Blatt vor den Mund.

outspread [ˈaʊtspred] *adj* ausgebreitet.

outstanding [ˌaʊtˈstændɪŋ] *adj* **(a)** *(exceptional)* hervorragend; *talent, beauty* außerordentlich; *event* bemerkenswert; *detail* auffallend; *feature* hervorstechend. **(b)** *(Comm, Fin) business, work* unerledigt; *bill, interest* ausstehend.

outstandingly [ˌaʊtˈstændɪŋlɪ] *adv* hervorragend.

out: ~**stay** *vt* **I don't want to** ~**stay my welcome** ich will eure Gastfreundschaft nicht zu lange in Anspruch nehmen; ~**stretched** *adj body* ausgestreckt; ~**strip** *vt* **(a)** überholen. **(b)** *(fig)* übertreffen *(in* an +*dat)*.

outward [ˈaʊtwəd] **1** *adj* **(a)** *appearance, form* äußere(r, s). **it was purely ~** show es war alles nur Theater *or* Mache *(col)*. **(b)** *movement* nach außen gehend; *freight* ausgehend; *journey, voyage* Hin-. **2** *adv* nach außen. **the door opens ~** die Tür geht nach außen auf.

outwardly [ˈaʊtwədlɪ] *adv* nach außen hin.

outwards [ˈaʊtwədz] *adv* nach außen.

out: ~**weigh** *vt* **(fig)** mehr Gewicht haben als; ~**wit** *vt* überlisten; *(in card games etc)* austricksen *(col)*; ~**worn** *adj idea* abgenutzt.

oval [ˈəʊvəl] **1** *adj* oval. ~**-shaped** oval. **2** *n* Oval *nt*.

ovary [ˈəʊvərɪ] *n (Anat)* Eierstock *m; (Bot)* Fruchtknoten *m*.

ovation [əʊˈveɪʃən] *n* Ovation *f*, stürmischer Beifall. **to get an ~** stürmischen Beifall ernten.

oven [ˈʌvn] *n (Cook)* (Back)ofen *m; (cooker)* Herd *m; (Tech: for drying)* (Trocken)ofen *m*. **it's like an ~ in here** hier ist ja der reinste Backofen.

oven: ~**-glove** *n (Brit)* Topfhandschuh *m;* ~**proof** *adj dish* feuerfest; ~**-ready** *adj* bratfertig; ~**ware** *n* feuerfeste Formen *pl*.

over [ˈəʊvəʳ] **1** *prep* **(a)** *(above, across)* über (+*dat)*; *(direction)* über (+*acc)*. **he spread the blanket ~ the bed** er breitete die Decke über das Bett; **he spilled coffee ~ it** er goß Kaffee darüber; **you've got ink all ~ your hands** Ihre Hände sind ganz voller Tinte; **to hit sb ~ the head** jdm auf den Kopf schlagen; **bent ~ one's books** über die Bücher gebeugt; **to look ~ the wall** über die Mauer schauen; **the noise came from ~ the wall** der Lärm kam von der anderen Seite der Mauer; **it's**

~ the page es ist auf der nächsten Seite; **it's just** ~ **the road from us** das ist von uns (aus) nur über die Straße; **the bridge** ~ **the river** die Brücke über den Fluß; **they came from all** ~ **England** sie kamen aus ganz England. **(b)** *(more than, longer than)* über (+*acc*). ~ **and above that** darüber hinaus; **an increase of 15%** ~ **last year** ein Zuwachs von 15% im Vergleich zum letzten Jahr; **that was well** ~ **a year ago** das ist gut ein Jahr her. **(c)** *(during)* während (+*gen*), in (+*dat*). ~ **the weekend** übers Wochenende; ~ **the summer/ Christmas** den Sommer über/über Weihnachten; ~ **the years I've come to realize** … im Laufe der Jahre ist mir klargeworden …; **the visits were spread** ~ **several months** die Besuche verteilten sich über mehrere Monate. **(d) they talked** ~ **a cup of coffee** sie unterhielten sich bei einer Tasse Kaffee; **they'll be a long time** ~ **it** sie werden dazu lange brauchen; **I've got an advantage** ~ **him** ich habe ihm gegenüber einen Vorteil; **he told me** ~ **the phone** er hat es mir am Telefon gesagt; **I heard it** ~ **the radio** ich habe es im Radio gehört; **it's not worth arguing** ~ es lohnt (sich) nicht, darüber zu streiten.

2 *adv* **(a)** *(across) (away from speaker)* hinüber; *(towards speaker)* herüber; *(on the other side)* drüben. **they swam** ~ **to us** sie schwammen zu uns herüber; **he took the fruit** ~ **to his mother** er brachte das Obst zu seiner Mutter hinüber; **he swam** ~ **to the other side** er schwamm auf die andere Seite (hinüber); **come** ~ **tonight** kommen Sie heute abend vorbei; **he is** ~ **here/there** er ist hier/dort drüben; ~ **to you!** Sie sind daran; **and now** ~ **to our reporter in Belfast** und nun schalten wir zu unserem Reporter in Belfast um; ~ **in America** drüben in Amerika. **(b)** *famous* **the world** ~ in der ganzen Welt berühmt; **I've been looking for it all** ~ ich habe überall danach gesucht; **I am aching all** ~ mir tut alles weh; **he was shaking all** ~ er zitterte am ganzen Leib; **that's him/Fred** ~ das ist typisch für ihn/Fred, typisch Fred. **(c)** *to turn an object* ~ einen Gegenstand herumdrehen; **he hit her and** ~ **she went** er schlug sie, und sie fiel um. **(d)** *(ended: film, operation etc)* zu Ende. **the rain is** ~ der Regen hat aufgehört; **the danger was** ~ die Gefahr war vorüber; **when all this is** ~ wenn das alles vorbei ist; **it's all** ~ **between us** es ist aus zwischen uns. **(e)** *(repetition)* **to start (all)** ~ **again** noch einmal (ganz) von vorn anfangen; ~ **and** ~ **(again)** immer (und immer) wieder; **he did it five times** ~ er hat es fünfmal wiederholt. **(f)** *(excessively)* übermäßig, allzu. **(g)** *(remaining)* übrig. **there was no meat (left)** ~ es war kein Fleisch mehr übrig. **(h)** *(more)* **children of 8 and** ~ Kinder über 8; **all results of 5.3 and** ~ alle Ergebnisse von 5,3 und darüber. **(i)** *(Telec)* over. ~ **and out** Ende der Durchsage; *(Aviat)* over and out.

over- *pref* über-.
over: ~**abundant** *adj* überreichlich; ~**act** *vi* übertreiben; ~**active** *adj* zu aktiv.
overall[1] [,əʊvər'ɔːl] **1** *adj* **(a)** *width, total* gesamt, Gesamt-. ~ **dimensions** *(Aut)* Außenmaße *pl*; ~ **majority** absolute Mehrheit. **(b)** *(general)* allgemein. **the** ~ **effect of this was to** … dies hatte das Endergebnis, daß … 2 *adv* **(a)** insgesamt. **(b)** *(in general)* im großen und ganzen.
overall[2] ['əʊvərɔːl] *n* (*Brit*) Kittel *m*.
overalls ['əʊvərɔːlz] *npl* Overall *m*.
over: ~**anxious** *adj* übertrieben besorgt; *(on particular occasion)* übermäßig aufgeregt; **I'm not exactly** ~**anxious to go** ich bin nicht gerade

scharf darauf zu gehen; ~**ate** *pret of* ~**eat**; ~**awe** *vt (intimidate)* einschüchtern; *(impress)* überwältigen; ~**balance 1** *vi* aus dem Gleichgewicht kommen; **2** *vt* umwerfen; *boat* kippen.
overbearing [,əʊvə'bɛərɪŋ] *adj* herrisch.
overboard ['əʊvəbɔːd] *adv* **(a)** *(Naut)* **to fall** ~ über Bord gehen; **man** ~! Mann über Bord! **(b)** *(fig: col)* **to go** ~ übers Ziel hinausschießen, zu weit gehen; **don't go** ~ **about it** übertreibe Sie es nicht.
over: ~**burden** *vt (lit)* überladen; *(fig)* überlasten; ~**came** *pret of* ~**come**; ~**cast** *adj* bedeckt; *sky also* bewölkt; **it's getting rather** ~**cast** es zieht sich zu; ~**cautious** *adj* übervorsichtig.
overcharge [,əʊvə'tʃɑːdʒ] *vt person* zuviel berechnen (+*dat*) *(for fur)*.
overcoat ['əʊvəkəʊt] *n* Mantel *m*.
overcome [,əʊvə'kʌm] *pret* **overcame** [,əʊvə'keɪm], *ptp* ~ *vt enemy* überwältigen; *bad habit* sich *(dat)* abgewöhnen; *shyness etc* überwinden; *temptation* widerstehen (+*dat*); *difficulty, anger* überwinden; *disappointment* hinwegkommen über (+*acc*). **he was** ~ **by the fumes** die giftigen Gase machten ihn bewußtlos; **he was quite** ~ **by grief/emotion** Schmerz/Rührung übermannte ihn; **I'm quite** ~ ich bin ganz ergriffen.
over: ~**confident** *adj* übertrieben selbstsicher; *(too optimistic)* zu optimistisch; ~**crowded** *adj* überfüllt; *(overpopulated)* überbevölkert; ~**crowding** *n* Überfüllung *f*; *(of town)* Überbevölkerung *f*.
overdo [,əʊvə'duː] *pret* **overdid** [,əʊvə'dɪd], *ptp* **overdone** [,əʊvə'dʌn] *vt (exaggerate)* übertreiben. **you are** ~**ing it** *or* **things** Sie übertreiben; *(tiring yourself)* Sie übernehmen sich.
over: ~**done** *adj* **(a)** *(exaggerated)* übertrieben; **(b)** *(Cook)* verkocht; *bacon etc* verbraten; ~**dose** *n* Überdosis *f*; ~**draft** *n* Konto-Überziehung *f*; **to have an** ~**draft of £10** sein Konto um £ 10 überzogen haben; ~**draw** *pret* ~**drew**, *ptp* ~**drawn** *one's account* überziehen; ~**drive** *n (Aut)* Schnellgang(getriebe *nt*) *m*; ~**due** *adj* überfällig; **long** ~**due** schon seit langem fällig; ~**eat** *pret* ~**ate**, *ptp* ~**eaten** *vi* zuviel essen; ~**emphasize** *vt* überbetonen; ~**enthusiastic** *adj* übertrieben begeistert; ~**estimate** *vt price* zu hoch einschätzen; *importance* überbewerten; *chances, danger* überschätzen; ~**excited** *adj* person zu aufgeregt; *children* aufgedreht; ~**exertion** *n* Überanstrengung *f*; ~**expose** *vt (Phot)* überbelichten; ~**feed** *pret, ptp* ~**fed** *vt* überfüttern.
overflow ['əʊvəfləʊ] **1** *n (outlet)* Überlauf *m*; *(excess: of people, population)* Überschuß *m* (*of* an +*dat*). **2** [,əʊvə'fləʊ] *vt area* überschwemmen. **the river has** ~**ed its banks** der Fluß ist über die Ufer getreten. **3** [,əʊvə'fləʊ] *vi (liquid, river etc)* überlaufen. **full to** ~**ing** *(bowl, cup)* zum Überlaufen voll; *(room)* überfüllt; **the crowd at the meeting** ~**ed into the street** die Leute bei der Versammlung standen bis auf die Straße.
over: ~**fly** *pret* ~**flew**, *ptp* ~**flown** *vt* **(a)** *(fly over) town* überfliegen; **(b)** *(fly beyond) runway, airport* hinausfliegen über (+*acc*). ~**generous** *adj* großzügig; ~**grown** *adj* **(a)** überwachsen *(with* von); **(b)** *child* aufgeschossen; **an** ~**grown schoolboy** ein großes Kind; ~**hang** *(vb: pret, ptp* ~**hung)** **1** *vt* hängen über (+*acc*); *(rocks, balcony)* hinausragen über (+*acc*), vorstehen über (+*acc*); **2** *n* Überhang *m*; ~**hanging** *adj* überhängend; ~**haul 1** *vt* Überholung *f*; **2** *vt* *engine* überholen; *plans* überprüfen.
overhead [,əʊvə'hed] **1** *adv* oben; *(in the sky)* am Himmel. **a plane flew** ~ ein Flugzeug flog über uns *etc (acc)* (hinweg). **2** ['əʊvəhed] *adj* ~ **cables** Freileitungen. **3** ['əʊvəhed] *n (US)* = **overheads**.
overheads ['əʊvəhedz] *npl (Brit Comm)* allgemeine Unkosten *pl*.

overhear [ˌəʊvə'hɪəʳ] *pret*, *ptp* **overheard** [ˌəʊvə'hɜːd] *vt* zufällig mit anhören. **he was ~d to say that ...** jemand hat ihn sagen hören, daß ...

over: ~heat *vi (engine)* heißlaufen; **~hung** *pret*, *ptp of* **~hang.**

overindulge [ˈəʊvərɪn'dʌldʒ] *vi* zuviel genießen.

overindulgence [ˈəʊvərɪn'dʌldʒəns] *n (eating)* Völlerei *f.* **~ in wine** übermäßiger Weingenuß.

overjoyed [ˌəʊvə'dʒɔɪd] *adj* überglücklich *(at, by* über *+acc).* **he wasn't exactly ~** er war nicht gerade erfreut.

over: ~kill *n (Mil)* Overkill *m; (fig)* Rundumschlag *m;* **~land** *adv* travel *etc* über Land.

overlap [ˈəʊvəlæp] **1** *n* Überschneidung *f; (of concepts)* teilweise Deckung. **3 inches' ~** 3 Zoll Überlappung; **there's quite a lot of ~ between their work** ihre Arbeitsbereiche überschneiden sich in vielen Punkten. **2** [ˌəʊvə'læp] *vi* **(a)** *(tiles, boards)* einander überdecken. **(b)** *(dates, responsibilities)* sich überschneiden; *(ideas, work)* sich teilweise decken.

over: ~lay *(vb: pret, ptp* **~laid)** [ˌəʊvə'leɪ] *vt* überziehen; **~leaf** *adv* **the illustration ~leaf** die umseitige Abbildung; **~load** *vt* überladen; *lorry, (Elec, Mech)* überlasten.

overlook [ˌəʊvə'lʊk] *vt* **(a)** *(have view onto)* überblicken. **a room ~ing the park** ein Zimmer mit Blick auf den Park; **the garden is not ~ed** niemand kann in den Garten hineinsehen. **(b)** *(fail to notice)* übersehen. **(c)** *(ignore)* mistake hinwegsehen über *(+acc),* durchgehen lassen.

overly [ˈəʊvəlɪ] *adv* übermäßig.

over: ~manning *n* zu große Belegschaft(en *pl);* **~much** *adv* übermäßig viel.

overnight [ˈəʊvə'naɪt] **1** *adv* **(a)** über Nacht. **to stay ~ (with sb)** bei jdm übernachten. **(b)** *(fig)* von heute auf morgen. **the place had changed ~** der Ort hatte sich über Nacht verändert. **2** *adj* **(a)** *journey* Nacht-. **~ stay** Übernachtung *f;* **~bag** Reisetasche *f.* **(b)** *(fig: sudden)* ganz plötzlich. **the play was an ~ success** das Stück wurde über Nacht ein Erfolg.

over: ~paid *pret, ptp of* **~pay;** **~particular** *adj* zu genau, pingelig *(col);* **~pass** *n* Überführung *f;* **~pay** *pret, ptp* **~paid** *vt* überbezahlen; **to pay sb by £50** jdm £ 50 zuviel bezahlen; **~populated** *adj* überbevölkert.

overpower [ˌəʊvə'paʊəʳ] *vt (emotion, heat)* überwältigen.

overpowering [ˌəʊvə'paʊərɪŋ] *adj* überwältigend; *smell* penetrant; *heat* glühend. **he's a bit ~ at times** seine Art kann einem manchmal zuviel werden.

over: ~price *vt* **these goods are ~ priced** diese Waren sind zu teuer; **at £50 it's ~ priced** £ 50 ist zuviel dafür; **~print** *vt stamp, text* überdrucken; *(Phot)* überkopieren; **~produce** *vi* überproduzieren; **~production** *n* Überproduktion *f;* **~protective** *adj parent* überängstlich; **~rate** *vt* überschätzen; *book, system etc* überbewerten; **~reach** *vr* sich übernehmen; **~react** *vi* übertrieben reagieren *(to* auf *+acc).*

override [ˌəʊvə'raɪd] *pret* **overrode** [ˌəʊvə'rəʊd], *ptp* **overridden** [ˌəʊvə'rɪdn] *vt decision, ruling* aufheben, außer Kraft setzen; *objection* ablehnen; *mechanism* abschalten.

overriding [ˌəʊvə'raɪdɪŋ] *adj principle* vorrangig, wichtigste(r, s). **of ~ importance** von allergrößter Wichtigkeit.

overripe [ˌəʊvə'raɪp] *adj* überreif.

overrule [ˌəʊvə'ruːl] *vt* ablehnen; *claim* nicht anerkennen; *verdict, decision* aufheben. **he was ~d by the majority** er wurde überstimmt.

overrun [ˌəʊvə'rʌn] *pret* **overran** [ˌəʊvə'ræn], *ptp* **~ 1** *vt* **(a)** *(weeds)* überwuchern. **~ with tourists** von Touristen überlaufen. **(b)** *(troops etc: invade)* einfallen in *(+dat).* **2** *vi (in time)* überziehen. **his speech overran by ten minutes** seine

Rede dauerte zehn Minuten zu lang.

overseas [ˈəʊvə'siːz] **1** *adj market, state* ausländisch; *(far away)* Übersee-. **our ~ office** unsere Zweigstelle im Ausland/in Übersee; **~ aid** Entwicklungshilfe *f;* **an ~ visitor** ein Besucher aus dem Ausland/aus Übersee. **2** *adv* **to be ~** im Ausland/in Übersee sein; **to go ~** ins Ausland/nach Übersee gehen.

over: ~see *pret* **~saw**, *ptp* **~seen** *vt* beaufsichtigen; **~seer** *n* Aufseher(in *f)* m; *(foreman)* Vorarbeiter(in *f) m;* **~sensitive** *adj* überempfindlich; **~shadow** *vt (lit, fig)* überschatten.

overshoot [ˌəʊvə'ʃuːt] *pret, ptp* **overshot** [ˌəʊvə'ʃɒt] *vt runway* hinausschießen über *(+acc).* **to ~ the mark** *(lit, fig)* übers Ziel hinausschießen.

oversight [ˈəʊvəsaɪt] *n* Versehen *nt.* **by** *or* **through an ~** aus Versehen.

over: ~simplification *n* (zu) grobe Vereinfachung; **~simplify** *vt* grob vereinfachen; **~sleep** *pret, ptp* **~slept** *vi* verschlafen; **~spend** *pret, ptp* **~spent** *vi* zuviel ausgeben; **~spill** *n* *(Brit)* Bevölkerungsüberschuß *m;* **~spill town** Trabantenstadt *f;* **~staffed** *adj* überbesetzt; **~state** *vt facts, case* übertreiben; **~statement** *n* Übertreibung *f;* **~step** *vt* **to ~step the mark** zu weit gehen; **~subscribe** *vt (Fin)* überzeichnen.

overt [əʊ'vɜːt] *adj* offen; *hostility* unverhohlen.

overtake [ˌəʊvə'teɪk] *pret* **overtook** [ˌəʊvə'tʊk], *ptp* **overtaken** [ˌəʊvə'teɪkən] **1** *vt* einholen; *(pass) runner etc, (Brit)* car überholen. **events have ~n us** wir waren auf die Entwicklung der Dinge nicht gefaßt. **2** *vi (Brit)* überholen.

overtaking [ˌəʊvə'teɪkɪŋ] *n (Brit)* Überholen *nt.* **"No ~"** „Überholverbot".

over: ~tax *vt* **(a)** *(fig) person, heart* überlasten; *patience* überfordern; **to ~tax one's strength** sich übernehmen; **(b)** *(lit)* übermäßig besteuern; **~throw** *(vb: pret* **~threw**, *ptp* **~thrown)** **1** [ˈəʊvə'θrəʊ] *n* Sieg *m (of* über *+acc); (being ~thrown)* Niederlage *f; (of dictator etc)* Sturz *m; (of country)* Eroberung *f;* **2** [ˌəʊvə'θrəʊ] *vt (defeat) enemy* besiegen; *dictator* stürzen; *country* erobern.

overtime [ˈəʊvətaɪm] **1** *n* **(a)** Überstunden *pl.* **I am on ~** ich mache Überstunden; **he did four hours' ~** er hat vier (Stunden) Überstunden gemacht. **(b)** *(US Sport)* Verlängerung *f.* **2** *adv* **to work ~** Überstunden machen; **my imagination was working ~** meine Phantasie lief auf Hochtouren *(col).*

overtired [ˌəʊvə'taɪəd] *adj* übermüdet.

overtone [ˈəʊvətəʊn] *n (fig)* Unterton *m.*

overture [ˈəʊvətjʊəʳ] *n (Mus)* Ouvertüre *f.* **to make ~s to sb** Annäherungsversuche bei jdm machen.

overturn [ˌəʊvə'tɜːn] **1** *vt* **(a)** umkippen, umwerfen. **(b)** *regime* stürzen. **2** *vi (chair)* umkippen; *(boat also)* kentern.

over: ~use [ˌəʊvə'juːz] *vt* zu häufig gebrauchen; **~value** *vt goods* zu hoch schätzen; **~view** *n* Überblick *m (of* über *+acc).*

overweight [ˌəʊvə'weɪt] *adj thing* zu schwer; *person* übergewichtig. **this box is 5 kilos ~** diese Schachtel hat 5 Kilo Übergewicht; **you're ~** Sie haben Übergewicht.

overwhelm [ˌəʊvə'welm] *vt* **(a)** *(overpower: strong feelings)* überwältigen. **he was ~ed when they gave him the present** er war zutiefst gerührt, als sie ihm das Geschenk gaben. **(b)** *enemy* überwältigen; *country* besiegen. **(c)** *(fig) (with favours, praise)* überschütten; *(with questions)* bestürmen; *(with work)* überhäufen.

overwhelming [ˌəʊvə'welmɪŋ] *adj* überwältigend; *desire* unwiderstehlich.

overwhelmingly [ˌəʊvə'welmɪŋlɪ] *adv see adj.* **they voted ~ for it** sie haben mit überwältigender Mehrheit dafür gestimmt.

overwork [ˌəʊvəˈwɜːk] **1** *n* Überarbeitung *f.* **2** *vt horse etc* schinden; *person* überanstrengen; *idea, theme* überstrapazieren. **we're** ~**ed** wir sind überarbeitet. **3** *vi* sich überarbeiten.

overwrought [ˌəʊvəˈrɔːt] *adj person* überreizt.

overzealous [ˌəʊvəˈzeləs] *adj* übereifrig.

ovulation [ˌɒvjʊˈleɪʃən] *n* Eisprung *m.*

owe [əʊ] *vt money* schulden, schuldig sein *(sb sth, sth to sb* jdm etw). **I** ~ **him a meal** ich bin ihm noch ein Essen schuldig; **how much do I** ~ **you?** *(in shop etc)* was bin ich schuldig?; **I** ~ **my life to him** ich verdanke ihm mein Leben; **to what do I** ~ **the honour of your visit?** *(iro)* was verschafft mir die Ehre Ihres Besuches?

owing [ˈəʊɪŋ] **1** *adj* unbezahlt. **how much is still** ~? wieviel steht noch aus? **2** *prep* ~ **to** wegen *(+gen or (col) +dat)*, infolge *(+gen)*; ~ **to the circumstances** umständehalber; ~ **to his being foreign** weil er Ausländer ist/war.

owl [aʊl] *n* Eule *f.*

own[1] [əʊn] *vt* **(a)** *(possess)* besitzen. **who** ~**s that?** wem gehört das?; **he looks as if he** ~**s the place** er sieht so aus, als wäre er hier zu Hause. **(b)** *(admit)* zugeben; *(recognize)* anerkennen.

♦ **own up** *vi* es zugeben. **to** ~ ~ **to sth** etw zugeben; **he** ~**ed** ~ **to stealing the money** er gab zu, das Geld gestohlen zu haben.

own[2] **1** *adj attr* eigen. **his** ~ **car** sein eigenes Auto; **one's** ~ **car** ein eigenes Auto; **he's his** ~ **man** er geht seinen eigenen Weg; **he does (all) his** ~ **cooking** er kocht für sich selbst. **2** *pron* **(a)** **that's my** ~ das ist mein eigenes; **those are my** ~ die gehören mir; **my** ~ **is bigger** meine(r, s) ist

größer; **my time is my** ~ ich kann mit meiner Zeit machen, was ich will; **a house of one's** ~ ein eigenes Haus; **I have money of my** ~ ich habe selbst Geld; **it has a beauty all its** ~ *or* **of its** ~ es hat eine ganz eigene Schönheit. **(b)** *(in phrases)* **can I have it for my (very)** ~? darf ich das ganz für mich allein behalten?; **to get one's** ~ **back (on sb)** es jdm heimzahlen; **(all) on one's** ~ **(ganz) allein; on its** ~ von selbst, von allein.

owner [ˈəʊnəʳ] *n* Besitzer(in *f)*, Eigentümer(in *f)* *m*; *(of shop, factory, firm etc)* Inhaber(in *f)* *m*. **who's the** ~ **of this umbrella?** wem gehört dieser Schirm?; **at the** ~**'s risk** auf eigene Gefahr.

owner-occupier [ˌəʊnərˈɒkjʊpaɪəʳ] *n jd,* der ein *Haus/eine Wohnung besitzt und darin wohnt.*

ownership [ˈəʊnəʃɪp] *n* Besitz *m.* **under new** ~ unter neuer Leitung.

ox [ɒks] *n, pl* **-en** Ochse *m.* **as strong as an** ~ bärenstark.

oxidation [ˌɒksɪˈdeɪʃən] *n (Chem)* Oxydation *f.*

oxide [ˈɒksaɪd] *n (Chem)* Oxyd *nt.*

oxidize [ˈɒksɪdaɪz] *vti* oxydieren.

oxtail [ˈɒksteɪl] *n*: ~ **soup** Ochsenschwanzsuppe *f.*

oxyacetylene [ˈɒksɪəˈsetɪliːn] *adj* Azetylensauerstoff-. ~ **burner** Schweißbrenner *m.*

oxygen [ˈɒksɪdʒən] *n* Sauerstoff *m.*

oxygen: ~ **mask** *n* Sauerstoffmaske *f;* ~ **tank** *n* Sauerstoffbehälter *m;* ~ **tent** *n* Sauerstoffzelt *nt.*

oyster [ˈɔɪstəʳ] *n* Auster *f.* **the world's his** ~ die Welt steht ihm offen.

oz = **ounce(s).**

ozone [ˈəʊzəʊn] *n* Ozon *nt.* ~ **layer** Ozonschicht *f.*

P

P, p [piː] *n* P, p *nt*. **to mind one's P's and Q's** *(col)* sich anständig benehmen.

p = **(a)** page S. **(b)** penny, pence.

PA = **(a)** **personal assistant**. **(b)** **public address (system)**.

p.a. = **per annum**.

pace [peɪs] **1** *n* **(a)** *(step)* Schritt *m*. **twelve ~s off** zwölf Schritt(e) entfernt; **to put sb/a new car through his/its ~s** *(fig)* jdn/ein neues Auto auf Herz und Nieren prüfen. **(b)** *(speed)* Tempo *nt*. **at a good** *or* **smart ~** recht schnell; **at a slow ~** langsam; **how long will he keep this ~ up?** wie lange wird er das Tempo durchhalten?; **the present ~ of development** die momentane Entwicklungsrate; **to keep ~** Schritt halten; *(in discussing)* mitkommen; **I can't keep ~ with events** ich komme mit den Ereignissen nicht mehr mit; **to make** *or* **set the ~** das Tempo angeben; **I can't stand the ~ any more** *(col)* ich kann nicht mehr mithalten. **2** *vt (measure) floor, room* mit Schritten ausmessen. **3** *vi* **to ~ up and down** auf und ab gehen.

pace: ~maker *n (Med, Sport, fig)* Schrittmacher *m*; **~-setter** *n (Sport)* Schrittmacher *m*.

Pacific [pəˈsɪfɪk] *n* **the ~** **(Ocean)** der Pazifische Ozean, der Pazifik.

pacifier [ˈpæsɪfaɪəʳ] *n (US: dummy)* Schnuller *m*.

pacifism [ˈpæsɪfɪzəm] *n* Pazifismus *m*.

pacifist [ˈpæsɪfɪst] *n* Pazifist(in *f*) *m*.

pacify [ˈpæsɪfaɪ] *vt baby* beruhigen; *angry person* besänftigen. **just to ~ the unions** nur damit die Gewerkschaften stillhalten.

pack [pæk] **1** *n* **(a)** *(bundle)* Bündel *nt*; *(on animal)* Last *f*; *(rucksack)* Rucksack *m*; *(Mil)* Gepäck *nt no pl*. **(b)** *(packet) (washing powder etc)* Paket *nt*; *(US: of cigarettes)* Schachtel *f*. **in ~s of six** im Sechserpack. **(c)** *(Hunt)* Meute *f*. **(d)** *(of wolves)* Rudel *nt*. **(e)** *(pej: group)* Horde, Meute *f*. **he told us a ~ of lies** er tischte uns einen Sack voll Lügen auf. **(f)** *(of cards)* (Karten)spiel *nt*. **(g)** *(Rugby)* Stürmer *pl*.

2 *vt* **(a)** *container etc* vollpacken; *meat in tin etc* abpacken. **~ed in dozens** im Dutzend abgepackt. **(b)** *case etc, things in case* einpacken. **(c)** *(wrap, put into parcel)* einpacken. **~ed in polythene** in Cellophan verpackt. **(d)** *(crowd)* packen; *articles also* stopfen. **the box was ~ed full of explosives** die Kiste war voll mit Sprengstoff; **the crowds that ~ed the stadium** die Menschenmassen, die sich im Stadium drängten; **to be ~ed** *(full)* gerammelt voll sein *(col)*; **all this information is ~ed into one chapter** all diese Informationen sind in einem Kapitel konzentriert. **(e)** *(make firm) soil etc* festdrücken. **(f)** *(US col: carry)* gun tragen, dabei haben. **(g)** *(col)* **to ~ a (heavy) punch** kräftig zuschlagen.

3 *vi* **(a)** *(items)* passen; *(person)* packen. **it ~s (in) nicely** es läßt sich gut verpacken; **I'm still ~ing** ich bin noch beim Packen. **(b)** *(crowd)* **the crowds ~ed into the stadium** die Menge drängte sich in das Stadion; **we can't all ~ into one Mini** wir können uns nicht alle in einen Mini zwängen. **(c)** *(col)* **to send sb ~ing** jdn kurz abfertigen.

♦ **pack in 1** *vt sep* **(a)** *clothes etc* einpacken. **(b)** *people* hineinpferchen in (+*acc*). **we can't ~ any**

more ~ here *(people)* hier geht keiner mehr rein; *(things)* hier geht nichts mehr rein. **(c)** *(play, actor etc)* in Scharen anziehen. **(d)** *(Brit col: give up) job* hinschmeißen *(col)*; *girlfriend* sausenlassen *(col)*; *work, activity* Feierabend machen mit *(col)*. **~ it ~!** hör auf!, laß es gut sein! **2** *vi* **(a)** *(crowd in)* sich hineindrängen. **(b)** *(Brit col: engine etc)* seinen Geist aufgeben *(hum)*.

♦ **pack off** *vt sep* **she ~ed them ~ to bed/school** sie schickte sie ins Bett/in die Schule.

♦ **pack up 1** *vt sep clothes etc* zusammenpacken. **2** *vi* **(a)** *(prepare luggage)* packen. **(b)** *(col: stop working) (engine)* seinen Geist aufgeben *(hum)*; *(person)* Feierabend machen *(col)*. **(c)** **the tent ~s** easily läßt das Zelt sich gut verpacken.

package [ˈpækɪdʒ] **1** *n* **(a)** *(parcel, esp US: packet)* Paket *nt*; *(of cardboard)* Schachtel *f*. **(b)** *(esp Comm: group, set)* Paket, Bündel *nt*. **2** *vt* **(a)** verpacken. **(b)** *(to enhance sales)* präsentieren.

package: ~ deal *n* Pauschalangebot *nt*; **~ holiday** *n* Pauschalreise *f*.

packaging [ˈpækɪdʒɪŋ] *n see vt* **(a)** Verpackung *f*. **(b)** Präsentation *f*.

packed lunch [ˈpæktˈlʌntʃ] *n* Lunchpaket *nt*.

packet [ˈpækɪt] *n* **(a)** Paket *nt*; *(of cigarettes)* Päckchen *nt*, Schachtel *f*; *(of potato crisps)* Tüte *f*; *(small box)* Schachtel *f*. **(b)** *(Brit col: lot of money)* **that must have cost a ~** das muß ein Heidengeld gekostet haben *(col)*.

pack: ~horse *n* Packpferd *nt*; *(fig)* Packesel *m*; **~ice** *n* Packeis *nt*.

packing [ˈpækɪŋ] *n* **(a)** *(act) (in suitcases)* Packen *nt*; *(in factories etc)* Verpackung *f*. **to do one's ~** packen. **(b)** *(material)* Verpackung *f*.

packing case *n* Kiste *f*.

pact [pækt] *n* Pakt *m*. **to make a ~ with sb** mit jdm einen Pakt schließen.

pad [pæd] **1** *n* **(a)** *(stuffing) (for comfort etc)* Polster *nt*; *(for protection)* Schützer *m*. **(b)** *(of paper)* Block *m*. **(c)** *(for inking)* Stempelkissen *nt*. **(d)** *(of animal's foot)* Ballen *m*. **(e)** *(launching ~)* (Abschuß)rampe *f*. **(f)** *(col: room, home)* Bude *f*. **2** *vt shoulders etc* polstern.

♦ **pad about** *vi* umhertapsen.

♦ **pad out** *vt sep* **(a)** *shoulders* polstern. **(b)** *essay etc* auffüllen; *speech* ausdehnen.

padded [ˈpædɪd] *adj shoulders* wattiert; *dashboard* gepolstert.

padding [ˈpædɪŋ] *n* **(a)** *(material)* Polsterung *f*. **(b)** *(fig: in essay etc)* Füllwerk *nt*.

paddle [ˈpædl] **1** *n* **(a)** *(oar)* Paddel *nt*; *(blade of wheel)* Schaufel *f*; *(wheel)* Schaufelrad *nt*. **(b)** **to go for a ~** durchs Wasser waten. **2** *vti* **(a)** paddeln. **(b)** *(walk in shallow water)* waten.

paddle: ~ boat *n* Raddampfer *m*; *(small, on pond)* Paddelboot *nt*; **~ steamer** *n* Raddampfer *m*.

paddling pool [ˈpædlɪŋˌpuːl] *n (Brit)* Planschbecken *nt*.

paddock [ˈpædək] *n (field)* Koppel *f*; *(of racecourse)* Sattelplatz *m*.

paddy [ˈpædɪ] *n (also ~ field)* Reisfeld *nt*.

padlock [ˈpædlɒk] **1** *n* Vorhängeschloß *nt*. **2** *vt (mit einem Vorhängeschloß)* verschließen.

paediatric, (US) pediatric [ˌpiːdɪˈætrɪk] *adj* Kinder-.

297

pagan ['peɪgən] **1** *adj* heidnisch. **2** *n* Heide *m*, Heidin *f*.

page¹ [peɪdʒ] **1** *n* (*also* ~-**boy**) Page *m*. **2** *vt* **to** ~ **sb** jdn ausrufen lassen.

page² *n* Seite *f*. **on** ~ **14** auf Seite 14; **write on both sides of the** ~ beschreiben Sie beide Seiten.

pageant ['pædʒənt] *n* (*show*) Historienspiel *nt*.

pageantry ['pædʒəntrɪ] *n* Prunk *m*, Gepränge *nt*.

page: ~-**boy** *n* (a) Page *m*; (b) (*hairstyle*) Pagenkopf *m*; ~ **number** *n* Seitenzahl *f*.

pagoda [pə'gəʊdə] *n* Pagode *f*.

paid [peɪd] **1** *pret, ptp of* **pay**. **2** *adj official, work* bezahlt. **to put** ~ **to sth** etw zunichte machen; **that's put** ~ **to him** das war's dann wohl für ihn (*col*).

paid-up ['peɪd'ʌp] *adj share* eingezahlt. **a** ~ **membership of 500** 500 zahlende Mitglieder; **fully** ~ **member** Mitglied *m* ohne Beitragsrückstände.

pail [peɪl] *n* Eimer *m*.

pain [peɪn] **1** *n* (a) (*physical*) Schmerz *m*; (*mental*) Qualen *pl*. **this will help the** ~ das ist gut gegen die Schmerzen; **to be in** ~ Schmerzen haben; **he screamed in** ~ er schrie vor Schmerzen; **I have a** ~ **in my leg** mein Bein tut mir weh. (b) **to be at** (**great**) ~**s to do sth** sich (*dat*) (große) Mühe geben, etw zu tun; **to take** ~**s over sth/to do sth** sich (*dat*) Mühe mit etw geben/sich (*dat*) Mühe geben, etw zu tun. (c) (*penalty*) **on** ~ **of death** bei Todesstrafe. (d) (*col: also* ~ **in the neck** *col*) **to be a** (**real**) ~ einem auf den Wecker gehen (*col*). **2** *vt* (*mentally*) schmerzen. **it** ~**s me to see their ignorance** ihre Unwissenheit tut schon weh.

pained [peɪnd] *adj expression* schmerzerfüllt.

painful ['peɪnfʊl] *adj* (a) (*physically*) schmerzhaft. **is it** ~? tut es weh? (b) *experience, memory* unangenehm. **it is my** ~ **duty to tell you that ...** ich habe die traurige Pflicht, Ihnen mitteilen zu müssen, daß ... (c) (*col: terrible*) peinlich; (*boring*) *party etc* zum Sterben langweilig.

painfully ['peɪnfəlɪ] *adv* (a) (*physically*) schmerzhaft. (b) (*col: very*) schrecklich. **it was** ~ **obvious** es war nicht zu übersehen.

painkiller ['peɪn,kɪlə'] *n* Schmerzmittel *nt*.

painless ['peɪnlɪs] *adj* schmerzlos. **don't worry, it's quite** ~ (*col*) keine Angst, es ist ganz einfach.

painstaking ['peɪnz,teɪkɪŋ] *adj person, work* sorgfältig; *accuracy* peinlich.

paint [peɪnt] **1** *n* (a) Farbe *f*; (*on car, furniture also*) Lack *m*; (*make-up*) Schminke *f*. (b) ~**s** *pl* Farben *pl*. **2** *vt* (a) *wall etc* streichen; *car* lackieren. **to** ~ **the town red** (*col*) die Stadt unsicher machen (*col*). (b) *picture, person* malen. **he** ~**ed a very convincing picture** (*fig*) er zeichnete ein sehr überzeugendes Bild. **3** *vi* malen; (*decorate*) (an)streichen.

paint: ~**box** *n* Farbkasten *m*; ~**brush** *n* Pinsel *m*.

painter ['peɪntə'] *n* Maler(in *f*) *m*.

painting ['peɪntɪŋ] *n* (a) (*picture*) Bild, Gemälde *nt*. (b) *no pl* (*Art*) Malerei *f*. (c) *no pl* (*of flat etc*) Anstreichen *nt*.

paint: ~ **pot** *n* Farbtopf *m*; ~ **roller** *n* Rolle *f*; ~**work** *n* (*on car etc*) Lack *m*; (*on wall, furniture*) Anstrich *m*.

pair [pεə'] **1** *n* (*of shoes, people*) Paar *nt*; (*of animals, cards*) Pärchen *nt*. **a** ~ **of trousers/scissors** eine Hose/Schere; **in** ~**s** paarweise; *animals, cards* zu zweit; *seated* in Zweiergruppen. **2** *vt* in Paaren *or* paarweise anordnen.

♦ **pair off 1** *vt sep* in Zweiergruppen einteilen. **to** ~ **sb** ~ **with sb** (*find boyfriend etc for*) jdn mit jdm zusammenbringen. **2** *vi* Paare bilden. **to** ~ ~ **with sb** mit jdm gehen.

pajamas [pə'dʒɑːməz] *npl* (*US*) = **pyjamas**.

Pakistani [,pɑːkɪs'tɑːnɪ] **1** *adj* pakistanisch. **2** *n* Pakistani *mf*, Pakistaner(in *f*) *m*.

pal [pæl] *n* (*col*) Kumpel *m* (*col*).

palace ['pælɪs] *n* (*lit, fig*) Palast *m*.

palatable ['pælətəbl] *adj* (*iro*) genießbar; *food also*

schmackhaft (*to für*); (*fig*) attraktiv.

palate ['pælɪt] *n* (*lit*) Gaumen *m*.

palatial [pə'leɪʃəl] *adj* (*spacious*) palastartig; (*luxurious*) luxuriös, feudal (*hum col*).

palaver [pə'lɑːvə'] *n* (*col: fuss*) Theater *nt* (*col*).

pale¹ [peɪl] **1** *adj* (+*er*) blaß; *face* (*unhealthy*) bleich. ~ **green** *etc* blaß- *or* zartgrün *etc*; **to go** *or* **turn** ~ bleich werden. **2** *vi* (*person*) erbleichen, blaß werden. **to** ~ **into insignificance** zur Bedeutungslosigkeit herabsinken.

pale² *n* (*stake*) Pfahl *m*. **those remarks were quite beyond the** ~ diese Bemerkungen haben eindeutig die Grenzen überschritten.

paleness ['peɪlnɪs] *n* Blässe *f*.

Palestine ['pælɪstaɪn] *n* Palästina *nt*.

Palestinian [,pælə'stɪnɪən] **1** *adj* palästinensisch. **2** *n* Palästinenser(in *f*) *m*.

palette ['pælɪt] *n* Palette *f*.

pall¹ [pɔːl] *n* (*over coffin*) Sargtuch *nt*. **a** ~ **of smoke** eine Dunstglocke; (*rising*) eine Rauchwolke.

pall² *vi* an Reiz verlieren.

pall-bearer ['pɔːl,bεərə'] *n* Sargträger *m*.

pallet ['pælɪt] *n* (*for storage*) Palette *f*.

palliative ['pælɪətɪv] *n* Linderungsmittel *nt*.

pallid ['pælɪd] *adj* blaß, fahl.

pallor ['pælə'] *n* Blässe, Fahlheit *f*.

pally ['pælɪ] *adj* (+*er*) (*col*) **to be** ~ **with sb** mit jdm gut Freund sein; **to get** ~ **with sb** sich mit jdm anfreunden.

palm¹ [pɑːm] *n* (*Bot*) Palme *f*; (*Eccl*) Palmzweig *m*.

palm² *n* (*Anat*) Handfläche *f*. **to grease sb's** ~ jdn schmieren (*col*); **to read sb's** ~ jdm aus der Hand lesen.

♦ **palm off** *vt sep* (*col*) *rubbish, goods* andrehen (*on(to)sb* jdm) (*col*).

palmist ['pɑːmɪst] *n* Handliniendeuter(in *f*) *m*.

palm: **P~ Sunday** *n* Palmsonntag *m*; ~**tree** *n* Palme *f*.

palpable ['pælpəbl] *adj* greifbar; (*clear*) *lie, error* offensichtlich.

palpably ['pælpəblɪ] *adv* (*clearly*) eindeutig.

palpitate ['pælpɪteɪt] *vi* (*heart*) heftig klopfen; (*tremble*) zittern.

palpitation [,pælpɪ'teɪʃən] *n* (*of heart*) Herzklopfen *nt*; (*trembling*) Zittern *nt*. **to have** ~**s** Herzklopfen haben.

paltry ['pɔːltrɪ] *adj* armselig, schäbig.

pampas ['pæmpəs] *npl* Pampas *pl*.

pamper ['pæmpə'] *vt* verwöhnen; *child also, dog* verhätscheln.

pamphlet ['pæmflɪt] *n* (*informative*) Broschüre *f*; (*literary*) Druckschrift *f*; (*political*) Flugblatt *nt*.

pan¹ [pæn] **1** *n* (a) (*Cook*) Pfanne *f*; (*sauce* ~) Topf *m*. (b) (*of scales*) Waagschale *f*; (*of lavatory*) Becken *nt*. **2** *vt* (a) *gold* waschen. (b) (*US*) *fish* braten. (c) (*US col: slate*) *new play etc* verreißen. **3** *vi* **to** ~ **for gold** Gold waschen.

♦ **pan out** *vi* (*col*) sich entwickeln. **to** ~ ~ **well** klappen (*col*).

pan² *vi* (*camera*) schwenken. **a** ~**ning shot** *n* Schwenk *m*.

pan- *pref* pan-, Pan-. **P~-African** panafrikanisch.

panacea [,pænə'sɪə] *n* Allheilmittel *nt*.

panache [pə'næʃ] *n* Schwung, Elan *m*. **she dresses with** ~ sie kleidet sich sehr extravagant.

Panama [,pænə'mɑː] *n* Panama *nt*. ~ **Canal** Panamakanal *m*.

panama (**hat**) *n* Panamahut *m*.

pancake ['pænkeɪk] *n* Pfannkuchen *m*. **P~ Day** Fastnachtsdienstag *m*.

pancreas ['pæŋkrɪəs] *n* Bauchspeicheldrüse *f*.

panda ['pændə] *n* Panda *m*.

panda car *n* (*Brit*) (Funk)streifenwagen *m*.

pandemonium [,pændɪ'məʊnɪəm] *n* Chaos *nt*.

pander ['pændə'] *vi* nachgeben (*to dat*). **to** ~ **to sb's desires** jds Wünsche befriedigen wollen; **to** ~ **to sb's ego** jdm um den Bart gehen.

pane [peɪn] *n* Glasscheibe *f*.

panel ['pænl] **1** n **(a)** (wood) Platte, Tafel f; (in ceiling, door) Feld nt; (Art) Tafel f; (of bodywork of a car) Karosserieteil nt; (of instruments, switches) Schalttafel f. **instrument** ~ Armaturenbrett nt; (on machine) Kontrolltafel f. **(b)** (of interviewers etc) Gremium nt; (in discussion) Diskussionsrunde f. **a** ~ **of experts** ein Sachverständigengremium nt. **2** vt wall täfeln.

panel: ~ **beater** n Autoschlosser m; ~ **discussion** n Podiumsdiskussion f; ~ **game** n Ratespiel nt.

panelling, (US) **paneling** ['pænəlɪŋ] n Täfelung f, Paneel nt; (to conceal radiator etc) Verschalung f.

panellist, (US) **panelist** ['pænəlɪst] n Diskussionsteilnehmer(in f) m.

pang [pæŋ] n ~ **of conscience** Gewissensbisse pl; ~**s of hunger** quälender Hunger.

panic ['pænɪk] **1** n Panik f. **to flee in** ~ panikartig die Flucht ergreifen; **a** ~ **reaction** eine Kurzschlußreaktion; **at** ~ **stations** in Alarmbereitschaft. **2** vi in Panik geraten. **don't** ~! nur keine Panik! **3** vt Panik auslösen bei.

panicky ['pænɪkɪ] adj person überängstlich; act, measure etc Kurzschluß-.

panic-stricken ['pænɪk,strɪkən] adj von panischem Schrecken ergriffen; look panisch.

pannier ['pænɪə'] n Korb m; (on motor-cycle etc) Satteltasche f.

panorama [,pænə'rɑːmə] n Panorama nt (of gen); (survey) Übersicht f (of über +acc).

panoramic [,pænə'ræmɪk] adj view Panorama-. ~ **shot** (Phot) Panoramaaufnahme f; **a** ~ **view of the hills** ein Blick m auf das Bergpanorama.

pansy ['pænzɪ] n **(a)** (Bot) Stiefmütterchen nt. **(b)** (pej: homosexual) Schwule(r) m (col).

pant [pænt] vi keuchen; (dog) hecheln. **to be** ~**ing for a drink** nach etwas zu trinken lechzen.

pantechnicon [pæn'teknɪkən] n (Brit) Möbelwagen m.

panther ['pænθə'] n Panther m.

panties ['pæntɪz] npl Höschen nt; (for women also) Slip m. **a pair of** ~ ein Höschen nt/ein Slip m.

pantomime ['pæntəmaɪm] n (in GB: Theat) Weihnachtsmärchen nt; (mime) Pantomime f.

pantry ['pæntrɪ] n Speisekammer f.

pants [pænts] npl (trousers) Hose f; (Brit: under~) Unterhose f. **a pair of** ~ eine Hose/Unterhose; **to wear the** ~ (US fig) die Hosen anhaben (col).

pantyhose ['pæntɪhəʊz] n (US) Strumpfhose f.

papacy ['peɪpəsɪ] n Papsttum nt.

papal ['peɪpəl] adj päpstlich.

paper ['peɪpə'] **1** n **(a)** Papier nt. **a piece of** ~ ein Stück nt Papier; **a sheet of** ~ ein Blatt nt Papier; **to put sth down on** ~ etw schriftlich festhalten; **it looks good on** ~ but ... auf dem Papier sieht es gut aus, aber ...; **it's not worth the** ~ **it's written on** es ist schade um das Papier, auf dem es steht. **(b)** (newspaper) Zeitung f. **to write to the** ~**s about sth** Leserbriefe/einen Leserbrief schreiben; **it was in the** ~**s** es stand in der Zeitung. **(c)** ~**s** pl (identity ~s, writings) Papiere pl. **private** ~**s** private Unterlagen pl. **(d)** (set of questions in exam) Testbogen m; (exam) (Univ) Klausur f; (Sch) Arbeit f; (academic) Referat nt. **to read a** ~ ein Referat halten. **(e)** (wall~) Tapete f. **2** vt wall, room tapezieren.

paper in cpds Papier-; ~**back** n Taschenbuch nt; ~ **bag** n Tüte f; ~**boy** n Zeitungsjunge m; ~**-clip** n Büroklammer f; ~ **knife** n Brieföffner m; ~ **mill** n Papierfabrik f; ~ **money** n Papiergeld nt; ~**-thin** adj walls hauchdünn; ~**weight** n Briefbeschwerer m; ~**work** n Schreibarbeit f.

papier mâché ['pæpɪeɪ'mæʃeɪ] n Papiermaché nt.

papist ['peɪpɪst] n (pej) Papist(in f) m.

paprika ['pæprɪkə] n Paprika m.

par [pɑː'] n **to be on a** ~ **with** sb/sth sich mit jdm/etw messen können; **below** ~ (fig) unter Niveau; **that's** ~ **for the course** (fig) das ist

normal; **I'm not feeling quite up to** ~ **today** ich bin heute nicht ganz auf dem Posten (col).

parable ['pærəbl] n Parabel f, Gleichnis nt.

parachute ['pærəʃuːt] **1** n Fallschirm m. **by** ~ mit dem Fallschirm; ~ **jump** Absprung m (mit dem Fallschirm). **2** vt troops mit dem Fallschirm absetzen; supplies abwerfen. **3** vi (also ~ **down**) (mit dem Fallschirm) abspringen. **to** ~ **to safety** sich mit dem Fallschirm retten.

parachutist ['pærəʃuːtɪst] n Fallschirmspringer(in f) m.

parade [pə'reɪd] **1** n (procession) Umzug m; (Mil, circus, display) Parade f; (political) Demonstration f; (fashion ~) Zurschaustellung f; (Mil: review) Truppeninspektion f. **to be on** ~ (Mil) eine Parade abhalten. **2** vt troops vorbeimarschieren lassen; military might demonstrieren; placards vor sich her tragen. **(b)** (show off) zur Schau stellen. **3** vi ziehen (through durch); (Mil) vorbeimarschieren; (political party) eine Demonstration veranstalten.

parade ground n Exerzierplatz m.

paradigm ['pærədaɪm] n Musterbeispiel nt.

paradise ['pærədaɪs] n (lit, fig) Paradies nt.

paradox ['pærədɒks] n Paradox nt. **life is full of** ~**es** das Leben steckt voller Widersprüche.

paradoxical [,pærə'dɒksɪkəl] adj paradox; person widersprüchlich.

paradoxically [,pærə'dɒksɪkəlɪ] adv paradoxerweise; worded paradox.

paraffin ['pærəfɪn] n (Brit: oil) Paraffin(öl) nt; (US: wax) Paraffin nt.

paraffin: ~ **lamp** n Paraffinlampe f; ~ **stove** n (Brit) Paraffinofen m.

paragon ['pærəgən] n Muster nt. **a** ~ **of virtue** ein Muster nt an Tugendhaftigkeit.

paragraph ['pærəgrɑːf] n Absatz m.

parakeet ['pærəkiːt] n Sittich m.

parallel ['pærəlel] **1** adj **(a)** lines, streets parallel. **the road is** ~ **to the river** die Straße verläuft parallel zum Fluß; ~ **bars** Barren m. **(b)** (fig) case, career, development vergleichbar. **a** ~ **case** ein Parallelfall m; **the two systems developed along** ~ **lines** die Entwicklung der beiden Systeme verlief parallel. **2** adv **to run** ~ (roads, careers) parallel verlaufen. **3** n **(a)** (Geometry) Parallele f; (Geog) Breitenkreis m. **the 49th** ~ der 49. Breitengrad. **(b)** (Elec) connected in ~ parallel geschaltet. **(c)** (fig) Parallele f. **without** ~ beispiellos; **to draw a** ~ **between X and Y** eine Parallele zwischen X und Y ziehen. **4** vt (fig) gleichen (+dat).

parallelogram [,pærə'leləʊgræm] n Parallelogramm nt.

paralysis [pə'ræləsɪs] n, pl **paralyses** [pə'rælɪsiːz] Lähmung f; (of industry etc) Lahmlegung f.

paralytic [,pærə'lɪtɪk] adj **(a)** paralytisch, Lähmungs-. **(b)** (Brit col: drunk) total blau (col).

paralyze ['pærəlaɪz] vt **(a)** lähmen. **to be** ~**d (with fright)** vor Schreck wie gelähmt sein. **(b)** industry lahmlegen.

parameter [pə'ræmətə'] n **(a)** (Math) Parameter m. **(b)** ~**s** pl (framework, limits) Rahmen m.

paramilitary [,pærə'mɪlɪtərɪ] adj paramilitärisch.

paramount ['pærəmaʊnt] adj Haupt-. **of** ~ **importance** von größter Wichtigkeit.

paranoia [,pærə'nɔɪə] n Paranoia f; (col) Verfolgungswahn m.

paranoid ['pærənɔɪd] adj paranoid. **or am I just being** ~ **about it?** oder bilde ich mir das nur ein?

paranormal [,pærə'nɔːməl] adj paranormal.

parapet ['pærəpɪt] n Brüstung f.

paraphernalia ['pærəfə'neɪlɪə] npl Drum und Dran nt.

paraphrase ['pærəfreɪz] **1** n Umschreibung f. **2** vt umschreiben.

paraplegia [,pærə'pliːdʒə] n doppelseitige

Lähmung.
paraplegic [,pærə'pli:dʒɪk] **1** adj doppelseitig ge- lähmt. **2** n Paraplegiker(in f) m (spec).
parasite ['pærəsaɪt] n (lit, fig) Parasit m.
parasitic(al) [,pærə'sɪtɪk(əl)] adj animal, plant Schmarotzer-, parasitär (also fig).
parasol ['pærəsɒl] n Sonnenschirm m.
paratrooper ['pærətru:pə'] n Fallschirmjäger m.
paratroops ['pærətru:ps] npl Fallschirmjäger pl.
parcel ['pɑːsl] n **(a)** Paket nt. to do sth up in a ~ etw als Paket packen; ~ post Paketpost f. **(b)** a ~ of land ein Stück nt Land.
♦ **parcel up** vt sep als Paket verpacken.
parched [pɑːtʃt] adj ausgetrocknet. to be ~ (with thirst) (vor Durst) verschmachten.
parchment ['pɑːtʃmənt] n Pergament nt.
pardon ['pɑːdn] **1** n **(a)** (Jur) Begnadigung f. general ~ Amnestie f. **(b)** I beg your ~, but could you ...? verzeihen Sie bitte, könnten Sie ...?; I beg your ~! erlauben Sie mal!; I beg your ~? (Brit) bitte?, wie bitte?; I beg your ~ (apology) Verzeihung. **2** vt **(a)** (Jur) begnadigen. **(b)** (forgive) verzeihen (sb jdm, sth etw). to ~ sb sth jdm etw verzeihen; ~ me? (US) bitte?, wie bitte?
pare [pɛə'] vt nails schneiden; fruit, stick schälen.
♦ **pare down** vt sep costs etc einschränken.
parent ['pɛərənt] **1** n Elternteil m. ~s Eltern pl. **2** attr ~ **company** Muttergesellschaft f.
parentage ['pɛərəntɪdʒ] n Herkunft f.
parental [pə'rentl] adj care etc elterlich attr.
parenthesis [pə'renθɪsɪs] n, pl **parentheses** [pə'renθɪsiːz] Klammer f.
parenthetic(al) [,pærən'θetɪk(əl)] adj beiläufig.
parenthood ['pɛərənthʊd] n Elternschaft f.
Paris ['pærɪs] n Paris nt.
parish ['pærɪʃ] n Gemeinde f; (district) Pfarrbezirk m, Pfarrei f.
parish: ~ **church** n Pfarrkirche f; ~ **council** n Gemeinderat m.
parishioner [pə'rɪʃənə'] n Gemeindemitglied nt.
parish priest n Pfarrer m.
Parisian [pə'rɪzɪən] **1** adj Pariser inv. **2** n Pariser(in f) m.
parity ['pærɪtɪ] n (equality) Gleichstellung f; (of opportunities) Gleichheit f; (Fin, Sci) Parität f. the ~ of the dollar die Dollarparität.
park [pɑːk] **1** n Park m. **2** vt **(a)** car parken; bike abstellen. a ~ed car ein parkendes Auto. **(b)** (col: put) luggage etc abstellen. he ~ed himself right in front of the fire er pflanzte sich direkt vor den Kamin (col). **3** vi parken. there was no- where to ~ es gab nirgendwo einen Parkplatz.
parka ['pɑːkə] n Parka m.
parking ['pɑːkɪŋ] n Parken nt.
parking: ~ **lights** npl Standlicht nt; ~ **lot** n (US) Parkplatz m; ~ **meter** n Parkuhr f; ~ **place** n Parkplatz m; ~ **ticket** n Strafzettel m.
park: ~**keeper** n Parkwächter m; ~**way** n (US) Allee f.
parky ['pɑːkɪ] adj (+er) (Brit col) kühl, frisch.
parlance ['pɑːləns] n in common ~ im all- gemeinen Sprachgebrauch; in technical ~ in der Fachsprache.
parliament ['pɑːləmənt] n Parlament nt. to get into ~ ins Parlament kommen.
parliamentarian [,pɑːləmən'tɛərɪən] n Parla- mentarier m.
parliamentary [,pɑːlə'mentərɪ] adj parlamenta- risch.
parlour, (US) **parlor** ['pɑːlə'] n (in house, beauty ~ etc) Salon m. **ice-cream** ~ Eisdiele f.
Parmesan ['pɑːmɪzæn] n Parmesan m.
parochial [pə'rəʊkɪəl] adj **(a)** (Eccl) Pfarr-, Gemeinde-. **(b)** (fig) attitude, person engstirnig; mind, ideas beschränkt.
parody ['pærədɪ] **1** n Parodie f (of auf +acc). **2** vt parodieren.

parole [pə'rəʊl] **1** n (Jur) Bewährung f; (temporary release) Strafunterbrechung f. let sb out on ~ jdn auf Bewährung entlassen; (temporarily) jdm Strafunterbrechung gewähren; to be on ~ unter Bewährung stehen; (temporarily) auf Kurzur- laub sein. **2** vt prisoner auf Bewährung entlassen; (temporarily) Strafunterbrechung gewähren (+dat).
paroxysm ['pærəksɪzəm] n Anfall m. ~s of laughter ein Lachkrampf m.
parquet ['pɑːkeɪ] n Parkett nt.
parrot ['pærət] n Papagei m. to repeat sth ~-fashion etw wie ein Papagei nachplappern.
parry ['pærɪ] vti (Fencing, fig) parieren; (Boxing) abwehren.
parsimonious [,pɑːsɪ'məʊnɪəs] adj geizig.
parsley ['pɑːslɪ] n Petersilie f.
parsnip ['pɑːsnɪp] n Pastinake f.
parson ['pɑːsn] n Pfarrer, Pastor m.
parsonage ['pɑːsənɪdʒ] n Pfarrhaus nt.
part [pɑːt] **1** n **(a)** Teil m. it is ~ **and parcel of the** job das gehört zu der Arbeit dazu; in ~ teilweise, zum Teil; it is in large ~ true das ist zum großen Teil wahr; for the main or most ~ in erster Linie; (generally speaking) im großen und ganzen; in the latter ~ of the year gegen Ende des Jahres; **5** ~s of sand to **1** of cement 5 Teile Sand auf ein(en) Teil Zement.
(b) (component, Mech) Teil nt. spare ~ Ersatz- teil nt; (Gram) ~ of speech Wortart f; principal ~s of a verb Stammformen pl; (of series) Folge f; (of serial) Fortsetzung f; end of ~ one (TV) Ende des ersten Teils.
(c) (share, role) (An)teil m, Rolle f; (Theat) Rolle f; (Mus) Stimme f. to play one's ~ (fig) seinen Beitrag leisten; to take ~ in sth an etw (dat) teilnehmen; he looks the ~ (fig) so sieht er auch aus; to play no ~ in sth (person) nicht an etw (dat) beteiligt sein; (factor etc) bei etw keine Rolle spielen.
(d) ~s pl (region) Gegend f; he's not from these ~s er ist nicht aus dieser Gegend.
(e) (side) Seite f. to take sb's ~ sich auf jds Seite (acc) stellen; for my ~ was mich betrifft; on my ~ etc meinerseits etc; on the ~ of von seiten (+gen), seitens (+gen); to take sth in good/ bad ~ etw nicht übelnehmen/etw übelnehmen; a man of ~s ein Universalgenie nt; a man of many ~s ein vielseitiger Mensch.
(f) (US: in hair) Scheitel m.
2 adv teils, teilweise. it is ~ iron and ~ cop- per es ist teils aus Eisen und teils aus Kupfer; it was ~ eaten es war halb aufgegessen.
3 vt **(a)** (divide) teilen; hair scheiteln; curtain zur Seite schieben. **(b)** (separate) trennen. to ~ sb from sb/sth jdn von jdm/etw trennen; to ~ **company** with sb/sth sich von jdm/etw tren- nen; (in opinion) mit jdm nicht gleicher Meinung sein.
4 vi **(a)** (divide) sich teilen; (curtains) sich öffnen. **(b)** (separate) (person) sich trennen; (things) sich lösen, abgehen. to ~ with sth sich von etw trennen.
partake [pɑː'teɪk] pret **partook,** ptp **partaken** [pɑː'teɪkn] vi (form) **(a)** to ~ of food, drink zu sich (dat) nehmen. **(b)** to ~ in (an activity) an etw (dat) teilnehmen.
part exchange n (Brit) to offer/take sth in ~ etw in Zahlung geben/nehmen.
partial ['pɑːʃəl] adj **(a)** (not complete) Teil-, teilweise; paralysis, eclipse teilweise, partiell. **(b)** (biased) voreingenommen. **(c)** to be ~ to sth eine Schwäche für etw haben.
partiality [,pɑːʃɪ'ælɪtɪ] n **(a)** (bias) Voreinge- nommenheit f. **(b)** (liking) Vorliebe f (for für).
partially ['pɑːʃəlɪ] adv (partly) zum Teil, teilweise.
participant [pɑː'tɪsɪpənt] n Teilnehmer(in f) m (in gen, an +dat).

participate [pɑː'tɪsɪpeɪt] vi (take part) sich beteiligen, teilnehmen (in an +dat).

participation [pɑː,tɪsɪ'peɪʃən] n Beteiligung f; (in competition etc) Teilnahme f; (worker ~) Mitbestimmung f.

participle ['pɑːtɪsɪpl] n Partizip nt.

particle ['pɑːtɪkl] n (a) (of sand etc, Phys) Teilchen nt. (b) (Gram) Partikel f.

particular [pə'tɪkjʊləʳ] **1** adj (a) (as against others) this ~ house is very nice dies (eine) Haus ist sehr hübsch; in this ~ instance in diesem besonderen Fall; is there any one ~ colour you prefer? bevorzugen Sie eine bestimmte Farbe? (b) (special) besondere(r, s). in ~ besonders, vor allem; nothing in ~ nichts Besonderes or Bestimmtes; is there anything in ~ you'd like? haben Sie einen besonderen Wunsch?; he's a ~ friend of mine er ist ein guter Freund von mir; for no ~ reason aus keinem besonderen Grund. (c) (fussy, fastidious) eigen; (choosy) wählerisch. he is very ~ about cleanliness er nimmt es mit der Sauberkeit sehr genau; you can't be too ~ man kann gar nicht wählerisch genug sein; I'm not too ~ (about it) es kommt mir nicht so darauf an.

2 n ~s pl Einzelheiten pl; (about person) Personalien pl; for further ~s apply to the personnel manager weitere Auskünfte erteilt der Personalchef; to give ~s Angaben machen.

particularly [pə'tɪkjʊləlɪ] adv besonders, vor allem; specify, request ausdrücklich. he was not ~ pleased er war nicht besonders erfreut.

parting ['pɑːtɪŋ] **1** n (a) Abschied m. is this the ~ of the ways then? das ist also das Ende (unserer Beziehung)? (b) (Brit: in hair) Scheitel m. **2** adj Abschieds-, abschließend. "he knows about it already", was her ~ shot "er weiß es schon", schleuderte sie ihm nach; his ~ words seine Abschiedsworte pl.

partisan [,pɑːtɪ'zæn] **1** adj (a) parteiisch (esp pej), parteilich. ~ spirit Parteigeist m. (b) (Mil) Partisanen-. **2** n (Mil) Partisan(in f) m.

partition [pɑː'tɪʃən] **1** n (a) Teilung f. (b) (wall) Trennwand f. (c) (section) Abteilung f. **2** vt country spalten; room aufteilen.

♦ **partition off** vt sep abteilen, abtrennen.

partly ['pɑːtlɪ] adv zum Teil, teilweise.

partner ['pɑːtnəʳ] **1** n Partner(in f) m; (in limited company also) Gesellschafter(in f) m; (in crime) Komplize m, Komplizin f. ~s in crime Komplizen. **2** vt to ~ sb jds Partner sein; to be ~ed by sb jdn zum Partner haben.

partnership ['pɑːtnəʃɪp] n (a) Partnerschaft f; (in sport, dancing etc) Paar nt. in ~ with sb in Zusammenarbeit mit jdm. (b) (Comm) Personengesellschaft f. to enter into a ~ eine Gesellschaft eintreten.

partook [pɑː'tʊk] pret of partake.

part: ~ owner n Mitbesitzer(in f) m; ~ payment n Teilzahlung f.

partridge [pɑː'trɪdʒ] n Rebhuhn nt.

part-time ['pɑːt'taɪm] **1** adj Teilzeit-. I'm just ~ ich arbeite nur Teilzeit. **2** adv work stundenweise; teach als Teilzeitlehrer(in).

party ['pɑːtɪ] n (a) (Pol) Partei f. (b) (group) Gruppe, Gesellschaft f; (Mil) Kommando nt, Trupp m. a ~ of tourists eine Reisegesellschaft. (c) (celebration) Fest nt, Party, Fete (col) f; (more formal) Gesellschaft f. to have or give a ~ eine Party geben or machen; at the ~ auf dem Fest or der Party; bei der Gesellschaft. (d) (Jur, fig) Partei f. a/the third ~ ein Dritter m/der Dritte; the parties to a dispute die streitenden Parteien; to be a ~ to sth an etw (dat) beteiligt sein.

party line n (a) (Pol) Parteilinie f. (b) (Telec) Gemeinschaftsanschluß m.

pass [pɑːs] **1** n (a) (permit) Ausweis m; (Mil etc) Passierschein m. (b) (Brit Univ) to get a ~ in

German seine Deutschprüfung bestehen; (lowest level) seine Deutschprüfung mit „ausreichend" bestehen. (c) (Geog, Sport) Paß m; (Ftbl: for shot at goal) Vorlage f. (d) things have come to a pretty ~ when ... so weit ist es schon gekommen, daß ...; things had come to such a ~ that ... die Lage hatte sich so zugespitzt, daß ... (e) to make a ~ at sb bei jdm Annäherungsversuche machen.

2 vt (a) (move past) vorbeigehen an (+dat); vorbeifahren an (+dat); (overtake) athlete, car überholen. (b) (cross) frontier etc überschreiten, passieren. not a word ~ed her lips kein Wort kam über ihre Lippen. (c) (reach, hand) reichen. they ~ed the photograph around sie reichten das Foto herum; ~ (me) the salt, please reich mir doch bitte das Salz!; (Sport) to ~ the ball to sb jdm den Ball zuspielen. (d) it ~es my comprehension that ... es geht über meinen Verstand, daß ... (e) (Univ etc) exam bestehen; candidate bestehen lassen. (f) (approve) motion annehmen; plan gutheißen; (Parl) verabschieden. (g) (spend) time verbringen. he did it just to ~ the time er tat das nur, um sich (dat) die Zeit zu vertreiben. (h) remark von sich geben; opinion abgeben; (Jur) sentence verhängen; judgement fällen.

3 vi (a) (move past) vorbeigehen; vorbeifahren. we ~ed in the corridor wir gingen im Korridor aneinander vorbei.

(b) (overtake) überholen.

(c) (move, go) ~ along the car please! bitte weiter durchgehen!; words ~ed between them es gab einige Meinungsverschiedenheiten; to ~ out of sight außer Sichtweite geraten; when we ~ed over the frontier als wir die Grenze passierten; shall we ~ to the second subject on the agenda? wollen wir zum zweiten Punkt der Tagesordnung übergehen?; he ~ed under the archway er ging/fuhr durch das Tor.

(d) (time) (also ~ by) vergehen.

(e) (disappear, end: anger, era etc) vorübergehen; (storm) (go over) vorüberziehen; (abate) sich legen; (rain) vorbeigehen. it'll ~ das geht vorüber!

(f) (be acceptable) gehen. to let sth ~ etw durchgehen lassen; let it ~! vergessen wir's!; it'll ~ das geht.

(g) (be considered, be accepted) angesehen werden (for or as sth als etw). she could easily ~ for 25 sie könnte leicht für 25 durchgehen.

(h) (in exam) bestehen.

(i) (Cards, in quiz etc) passen. (I) ~! passe!

♦ **pass away** vi (a) (end) zu Ende gehen. (b) (euph: die) einschlafen, hinscheiden.

♦ **pass by 1** vi (go past) vorbeigehen; (car etc) vorbeifahren; (time, months etc) vergehen. I can't let that ~ ich kann das nicht durchgehen lassen. **2** vi +prep obj we ~ed ~ a line of hotels wir kamen an einer Reihe Hotels vorbei. **3** vt sep (ignore) problems übergehen. life has ~ed her ~ das Leben ist an ihr vorübergegangen.

♦ **pass down** vt sep traditions, characteristics weitergeben (to an +acc).

♦ **pass off 1** vi (a) (take place) ablaufen. (b) (end) vorübergehen. (c) (be taken as) durchgehen (as als). **2** vt sep to ~ oneself/sb ~ as sth sich/jdn als or für etw ausgeben.

♦ **pass on 1** vi (a) (euph: die) entschlafen. (b) (proceed) übergehen (to zu). **2** vt sep news, information weitergeben; disease übertragen.

♦ **pass out** vi (a) (become unconscious) in Ohnmacht fallen, umkippen (col). (b) (new officer) ernannt werden.

♦ **pass over** vt sep übergehen. he's been ~ed ~ again er ist schon wieder übergangen worden.

♦ **pass through** vi I'm only ~ing ~ ich bin nur auf der Durchreise; you have to ~ ~ Berlin du

mußt über Berlin fahren.
passable ['pɑːsəbl] adj **(a)** passierbar; road etc also befahrbar. **(b)** (tolerable) passabel.
passage ['pæsɪdʒ] n **(a)** (transition) Übergang m. **with the** ~ **of time** mit der Zeit. **(b)** (through country) Durchreise f. **(c)** (voyage, fare) Überfahrt f. **(d)** (Parl: process) parlamentarische Behandlung; (final) Verabschiedung f. **(e)** (corridor) Gang m. **(f)** (in book) Passage f; (Mus also) Stück nt. **a** ~ **from the Bible** eine Bibelstelle.
passageway ['pæsɪdʒweɪ] n Durchgang m.
pass: ~ **book** n Sparbuch nt; ~ **degree** n niedrigster Grad an britischen Universitäten, „Bestanden".
passenger ['pæsɪndʒəʳ] n (on bus, in taxi) Fahrgast m; (on train) Reisende(r) mf; (on ship, plane) Passagier m; (in car) Mitfahrer(in f) m; (on motorcycle) Beifahrer(in f) m. **he's just a** ~ **in the team** (fig pej) er wird von den anderen mit durchgeschleppt.
passer-by ['pɑːsə'baɪ] n, pl **passers-by** Passant(in f) m.
passing ['pɑːsɪŋ] **1** n Vorübergehen nt. **with the** ~ **of time** im Lauf(e) der Zeit; **I would like to mention in** ~ **that** ... ich möchte beiläufig erwähnen, daß ... **2** adj car vorbeifahrend; clouds vorüberziehend; years vergehend; glance etc, thought flüchtig; comments, reference beiläufig; fancy vorübergehend.
passion ['pæʃən] n Leidenschaft f; (Rel, Mus) Passion f. **to have a** ~ **for** sth eine Passion or Leidenschaft für etw haben; **music is a** ~ **with him** die Musik ist bei ihm eine Leidenschaft.
passionate ['pæʃənɪt] adj leidenschaftlich.
passion: ~ **flower** n Passionsblume f; ~ **fruit** n Passionsfrucht f.
passive ['pæsɪv] **1** adj passiv; acceptance widerspruchslos. **2** n (Gram) Passiv nt. **in the** ~ im Passiv.
pass key n Hauptschlüssel m.
Passover ['pɑːsəʊvəʳ] n Passah nt.
passport ['pɑːspɔːt] n (Reise)paß m; (fig) Schlüssel m (to für, zu).
password ['pɑːswɜːd] n Kennwort nt, Parole f.
past [pɑːst] **1** adj **(a)** frühe(r, s) attr, vergangene(r, s) attr. **for some time** ~ seit einiger Zeit; **in times** ~ in früheren Zeiten. **(b)** (Gram) ~ **tense** Vergangenheit f; ~ **participle** Partizip Perfekt nt.
2 n (also Gram) Vergangenheit f. **in the** ~ in der Vergangenheit (also Gram), früher; **to be a thing of the** ~ der Vergangenheit (dat) angehören.
3 prep **(a)** (motion) an (+dat) ... vorbei or vorüber; (position: beyond) hinter (+dat). **just** ~ **the library** kurz hinter der Bücherei; **to run** ~ **sb** an jdm vorbeilaufen. **(b)** (time) nach (+dat). **ten (minutes)** ~ **three** zehn (Minuten) nach drei; **half** ~ **four** halb fünf; **a quarter** ~ **nine** Viertel nach neun. **(c)** (beyond) ~ **forty** über vierzig; ~ **belief** unglaublich; **we're** ~ **caring** es kümmert uns nicht mehr; **to be** ~ sth für etw zu alt sein; **I wouldn't put it** ~ **him** (col) ich würde es ihm schon zutrauen.
4 adv vorbei, vorüber. **to walk/run** ~ vorbeigehen/vorbeirennen.
pasta ['pæstə] n Nudeln pl.
paste [peɪst] **1** n **(a)** (for sticking) Kleister m. **(b)** (spread) Brotaufstrich m. **(c)** (jewellery) Straß m. **(d)** **mix to a smooth/firm** ~ (Cook) zu einem glatten/festen Teig anrühren. **2** vt (apply ~ to) wallpaper etc einkleistern; (affix) kleben (to an +acc; in in +acc).
pasteboard ['peɪstbɔːd] n Karton m, Pappe f.
pastel ['pæstl] **1** n (crayon) Pastellstift m; (drawing) Pastellzeichnung f, Pastell nt; (colour) Pastellton m. **2** adj attr Pastell-.
pasteurize ['pæstəraɪz] vt pasteurisieren.

pastille ['pæstɪl] n Pastille f.
pastime ['pɑːstaɪm] n Zeitvertreib m.
past master n to be a ~ at doing sth ein Experte darin sein, etw zu tun.
pastor ['pɑːstəʳ] n Pfarrer m.
pastoral ['pɑːstərəl] adj pastoral; duties also seelsorgerisch. ~ **care** Seelsorge f.
pastry ['peɪstrɪ] n Teig m; (cake etc) Stück, Teilchen (dial) nt. **pastries** pl Gebäck nt.
pasture ['pɑːstʃəʳ] n **(a)** (field) Weide f. **to put out to** ~ auf die Weide treiben; **to move on to** ~**s new** (fig) sich (dat) etwas Neues suchen. **(b)** no pl (also ~ **land**) Weideland nt.
pasty¹ ['peɪstɪ] adj consistency zähflüssig; material klebrig; colour bläßlich; look also kränklich.
pasty² ['pæstɪ] n (esp Brit) Pastete f.
pat¹ [pæt] n (of butter) Portion f.
pat² **1** adv **to know** or **have sth off** ~ etw wie aus dem Effeff können (col). **2** adj answer, explanation glatt.
pat³ **1** n Klaps m. **he gave him a** ~ **on the shoulder** er tippte ihm auf die Schulter; **to give the dog a** ~ den Hund tätscheln; **to give sb/oneself a** ~ **on the back** (fig) jdm/sich selbst auf die Schulter klopfen. **2** vt (touch lightly) tätscheln; (hit gently) ball leicht schlagen; sand festklopfen; face abtupfen.
patch [pætʃ] **1** n **(a)** (for mending) Flicken m; (eye ~) Augenklappe f. **(b)** **it's/he's not a** ~ **on** ... (col) das/er ist gar nichts gegen ... **(c)** (small area, stain) Fleck m; (piece of land) Stück nt; (subdivision of garden) Beet nt; (part, section) Stelle f; (of time) Phase f. **a** ~ **of blue sky** ein Stückchen nt blauer Himmel; ~**es of colour** Farbtupfer pl; **the cabbage** ~ das Kohlbeet; **he's going through a bad** ~ at the moment ihm geht's im Augenblick nicht sonderlich gut. **2** vt flicken.
♦ **patch up** vt sep zusammenflicken; quarrel beilegen. **to** ~ **things** ~ **temporarily** die Dinge notdürftig zusammenflicken; (in relationship) die Beziehung wieder ins Lot bringen; **they managed to** ~ **their relationship** sie haben sich schließlich wieder ausgesöhnt.
patchwork ['pætʃwɜːk] n ~ **quilt** Flickendecke f; **a** ~ **of fields** ein buntes Mosaik von Feldern.
patchy ['pætʃɪ] adj (+er) work ungleichmäßig; knowledge, memory lückenhaft. ~ **fog** stellenweise auftretender Nebel.
pâté ['pæteɪ] n Pastete f.
patent¹ ['peɪtənt] adj (obvious) offensichtlich.
patent² **1** n Patent nt. **applied for** or **pending** Patent angemeldet; **to take out a** ~ (on sth) ein Patent (auf etw acc) erhalten. **2** vt patentieren lassen. **3** adj (~ed) invention patentiert.
patent leather n Lackleder nt.
patently ['peɪtəntlɪ] adv offensichtlich. **that's** ~ **obvious** das liegt doch auf der Hand.
patent medicine n patentrechtlich geschütztes Arzneimittel.
paternal [pə'tɜːnl] adj väterlich. **my** ~ **grandmother** meine Großmutter väterlicherseits.
paternalist(ic) [pə'tɜːnəlɪst, pə,tɜːnə'lɪstɪk] adj patriarchalisch.
paternity [pə'tɜːnɪtɪ] n Vaterschaft f. ~ **suit** Vaterschaftsprozeß m.
path [pɑːθ] n (lit, fig) Weg m; (smaller) Pfad m; (in field) Feldweg m; (trajectory) Bahn f. **the** ~ **of virtue** der Pfad der Tugend.
pathetic [pə'θetɪk] adj **(a)** (piteous) mitleiderregend. **it was** ~ **to see** es war ein Bild des Jammers. **(b)** (bad) erbärmlich. **it's** ~ es ist zum Heulen (col).
pathetically [pə'θetɪkəlɪ] adv **(a)** (piteously) mitleiderregend. ~ **thin/weak** erschreckend dünn/schwach. **(b)** slow, stupid, inefficient erbärmlich. **a** ~ **inadequate answer** eine äußerst dürftige Antwort.
pathological [,pæθə'lɒdʒɪkəl] adj (lit, fig) krank-

haft; *studies etc* pathologisch.
pathologist [pə'θɒlədʒɪst] *n* Pathologe *m*, Pathologin *f*.
pathology [pə'θɒlədʒɪ] *n* (*science*) Pathologie *f*.
pathos ['peɪθɒs] *n* Pathos *nt*.
pathway ['pɑːθweɪ] *n* Weg *m*; (*smaller*) Pfad *m*.
patience ['peɪʃəns] *n* (**a**) Geduld *f*. to have ~/no ~ (**with sb/sth**) Geduld/keine Geduld (mit jdm/ etw) haben; **to lose (one's)** ~ (**with sb/sth**) (mit jdm/etw) die Geduld verlieren. (**b**) (*Brit Cards*) Patience *f*. to play ~ eine Patience legen.
patient ['peɪʃənt] **1** *adj* geduldig. **to be** ~ **with sb** Geduld mit jdm haben. **2** *n* Patient(in *f*) *m*.
patio ['pætɪəʊ] *n* Veranda, Terrasse *f*.
patriarch ['peɪtrɪɑːk] *n* Patriarch *m*.
patriot ['peɪtrɪət] *n* Patriot(in *f*) *m*.
patriotic [,pætrɪ'ɒtɪk] *adj* patriotisch.
patriotism ['pætrɪətɪzəm] *n* Patriotismus *m*.
patrol [pə'trəʊl] **1** *n* (*police*) Streife *f*; (*aircraft, ship*) Patrouille *f*. **on** ~ (*Mil*) auf Patrouille; (*police*) auf Streife; (*guard dogs, squad car*) im Einsatz. **2** *vt* (*Mil*) patrouillieren; (*policeman*) seine Runden machen in (+*dat*); (*police car*) Streife fahren in (+*dat*). **3** *vi* patrouillieren; (*policemen*) eine Streife/Streifen machen. **to** ~ **up and down** auf und ab gehen.
patrol: ~ **car** *n* Streifenwagen *m*; ~**man** *n* Wächter *m*; (*US: policeman*) Polizist *m*; ~ **wagon** *n* (*US*) grüne Minna (*col*), Gefangenenwagen *m*.
patron ['peɪtrən] *n* (*of shop*) Kunde *m*, Kundin *f*; (*of restaurant, hotel*) Gast *m*; (*of society*) Schirmherr(in *f*) *m*; (*of artist*) Förderer, Gönner(in *f*) *m*; (~ *saint*) Schutzpatron(in *f*) *m*.
patronage ['pætrənɪdʒ] *n* **under the** ~ **of** unter der Schirmherrschaft des/der.
patronize ['pætrənaɪz] *vt* (**a**) *pub, cinema etc* besuchen. **the shop is well** ~**d** das Geschäft hat viel Kundschaft. (**b**) (*treat condescendingly*) herablassend behandeln.
patronizing ['pætrənaɪzɪŋ] *adj* gönnerhaft, herablassend. **to be** ~ **to** *or* **towards sb** jdn von oben herab behandeln.
patter ['pætəʳ] **1** *n* (**a**) (*of feet*) Getrippel *nt*; (*of rain*) Plätschern *nt*. (**b**) (*of salesman, comedian, conjurer, disc jockey*) Sprüche *pl* (*col*). **sales** ~ Vertretersprüche *pl*. **2** *vi* (*person, feet*) trippeln; (*rain: also* ~ **down**) plätschern.
pattern ['pætən] **1** *n* (**a**) Muster *nt*. to make a ~ ein Muster bilden. (**b**) (*Sew*) Schnittmuster *nt*; (*Knitting*) Strickanleitung *f*. (**c**) (*fig: model*) Vorbild *nt*. **on the Albanian** ~ nach albanischem Muster; **to set a** *or* **the** ~ **for sth** ein Vorbild für etw sein. (**d**) (*fig: in events, behaviour etc*) Muster *nt*; (*recurrent*) Regelmäßigkeit *f*. **the** ~ **of events** der Ablauf der Ereignisse; **to follow the usual** ~ nach dem üblichen Schema verlaufen; **behaviour** ~**s** Verhaltensmuster *pl*. **2** *vt* (*mould*) machen (**on** nach). **to be** ~**ed on sth** einer Sache (*dat*) nachgebildet sein; (*music, style etc*) einer Sache (*dat*) nachempfunden sein.
pattern book *n* Musterbuch *nt*.
patterned ['pætənd] *adj* gemustert.
paunch [pɔːntʃ] *n* Bauch, Wanst *m*.
pauper ['pɔːpəʳ] *n* Arme(r) *mf*.
pause [pɔːz] **1** *n* Pause *f*. **there was a** ~ **while ...** es entstand eine Pause, während ...; **to have a** ~ (eine) Pause machen; **without** (a) ~ ununterbrochen; **a** ~ **for thought** eine Denkpause. **2** *vi* stehenbleiben; (*speaker*) innehalten. **he** ~**d for breath** er machte eine Pause, um Luft zu holen; **let's** ~ **here** machen wir hier Pause; **it made him** ~ das machte ihn nachdenklich.
pave [peɪv] *vt* pflastern. **to** ~ **the way for sb/sth** (*fig*) jdm/einer Sache den Weg ebnen.
pavement ['peɪvmənt] *n* (**a**) (*Brit*) Bürgersteig *m*, Trottoir *m*. **b**) (*US*) (*paved road*) Straße *f*; (*surfacing*) Straßendecke *f*.
pavilion [pə'vɪlɪən] *n* Pavillon *m*; (*Sport*) (*changing*

~) Umkleideräume *pl*; (*clubhouse*) Klubhaus *nt*.
paving ['peɪvɪŋ] *n* Belag *m*; (*US: of road*) Decke *f*; (*action*) Pflastern *nt*. ~ **stone** Platte *f*.
paw [pɔː] **1** *n* (*of animal, col: hand*) Pfote *f*; (*of lion, bear*) Pranke, Tatze *f*. **2** *vt* (**a**) tätscheln; (*lion etc*) mit der Tatze berühren. **to** ~ **the ground** (*lit*) scharren; (*fig: be impatient*) ungeduldig werden. (**b**) (*pej col: handle*) betatschen (*col*).
pawn[1] [pɔːn] *n* (*Chess*) Bauer *m*; (*fig*) Schachfigur *f*.
pawn[2] **1** *n* (*security*) Pfand *nt*. **to put sth in** ~ etw verpfänden. **2** *vt* verpfänden.
pawn: ~**broker** *n* Pfandleiher *m*; ~**shop** *n* Pfandhaus *nt*.
pay [peɪ] (*vb: pret, ptp* **paid**) **1** *n* Lohn *m*; (*of salaried employee, civil servant*) Gehalt *nt*; (*Mil*) Sold *m*. **to be in sb's** ~ für jdn arbeiten.
  2 *vt* (**a**) zahlen; *person, bill, debt* bezahlen. **to** ~ **sb £10** jdm £ 10 zahlen; **how much is there to** ~? was bin ich schuldig?; **to be** *or* **get paid** (*in regular job*) seinen Lohn/sein Gehalt bekommen; **savings accounts that** ~ **5%** Sparkonten, die 5% Zinsen bringen. (**b**) (*lit, fig: be profitable to*) sich lohnen für. **in future it would** ~ **you to ask in** Zukunft solltest du besser vorher fragen. (**c**) **to** ~ (**sb**) **a visit** *or* **call** jdn besuchen; (*more formal*) jdm einen Besuch abstatten.
  3 *vi* (**a**) zahlen. **they** ~ **well for this sort of work** diese Arbeit wird gut bezahlt; **no, no, I'm** ~**ing** nein, nein, ich (be)zahle; **to** ~ **for sth** etw bezahlen; **it's already paid for** es ist schon bezahlt. (**b**) (*be profitable*) sich lohnen. **it's a business that** ~**s** es ist ein rentables Geschäft; **crime doesn't** ~ (*prov*) Verbrechen lohnt sich nicht. (**c**) (*fig: to suffer*) **to** ~ **for sth** (**with sth**) für etw (mit etw) bezahlen; **you'll** ~ **for that!** dafür wirst du (mir) büßen.
  ♦ **pay back** *vt sep money* zurückzahlen; *compliment, visit* erwidern; *insult, trick* sich revanchieren für. **to** ~ **sb** ~ es jdm heimzahlen.
  ♦ **pay in** *vt sep* einzahlen. **to** ~ **money** ~**to an account** Geld auf ein Konto einzahlen.
  ♦ **pay off 1** *vt sep workmen* auszahlen; *debt* abbezahlen; *HP* ab(be)zahlen; *mortgage* ablösen; *creditor* befriedigen.
  ♦ **pay out** *vt sep* (**a**) *money* (*spend*) ausgeben; (*count out*) auszahlen. (**b**) *rope* ablaufen lassen.
  ♦ **pay up 1** *vt sep what one owes* zurückzahlen; *subscription* bezahlen. **his account/he is paid** ~ er hat alles bezahlt. **2** *vi* zahlen. **come on,** ~! los, bezahl endlich!
payable ['peɪəbl] *adj* zahlbar; (*due*) fällig. **to make a cheque** ~ **to sb** einen Scheck auf jdn ausstellen.
pay: ~**-claim** *n* Lohn-/Gehaltsforderung *f*; ~**-day** *n* Zahltag *m*.
PAYE (*Brit*) = **pay-as-you-earn** Steuersystem *nt, bei dem die Lohnsteuer direkt einbehalten wird.*
payee [peɪ'iː] *n* Zahlungsempfänger *m*.
pay: ~ **freeze** *n* Lohnstopp *m*; ~ **increase** *n* Lohn-/Gehaltserhöhung *f*.
paying ['peɪɪŋ] *adj* (**a**) (*profitable*) rentabel. (**b**) ~ **guest** zahlender Gast.
payment ['peɪmənt] *n* Zahlung *f*; (*paying*) Bezahlung *f*; (*of debt, mortgage*) Abtragung, Rückzahlung *f*. **three monthly** ~**s** drei Monatsraten; **as** *or* **in** ~ **for his services** als Bezahlung für seine Dienste; **on** ~ **of** bei Bezahlung von; **to make a** ~ eine Zahlung leisten.
payoff ['peɪɒf] *n* (*col: bribe*) Bestechungsgeld *nt*; (*outcome*) Quittung *f*; (*of joke*) Pointe *f*.
pay: ~ **packet** *n* Lohntüte *f*; ~ **phone** *n* Münzfernsprecher *m*; ~ **rise** *n* Lohn-/Gehaltserhöhung *f*; ~**slip** *n* Lohn-/Gehaltsstreifen *m*; ~ **station** *n* (*US*) öffentlicher Fernsprecher; ~ **talks** *npl* Lohnverhandlungen *pl*; (*for profession, area of industry*) Tarifverhandlungen *pl*.
pc = (**a**) post card. (**b**) per cent.
PE = **physical education**.

pea [piː] n Erbse f.

peace [piːs] n Frieden m; (tranquillity) Ruhe f. **to be at ~ with sb/sth** mit jdm/etw in Frieden leben; **he is at ~** (euph: dead) er ruht in Frieden; **to make (one's) ~** (with sb) sich (mit jdm) versöhnen; **to make ~ between** ... Frieden stiften zwischen (+dat) ...; **to keep the ~** (Jur) (demonstrator, citizen) die öffentliche Ordnung wahren; (policeman) die öffentliche Ordnung aufrechterhalten; (fig) Frieden bewahren; **~ of mind** innere Ruhe; **~ and quiet** Ruhe und Frieden; **to give sb some ~** jdn in Ruhe or Frieden lassen; **to give sb no ~** jdm keine Ruhe lassen.

peaceable ['piːsəbl] adj friedlich.

peace conference n Friedenskonferenz f.

peaceful ['piːsfʊl] adj friedlich; nation, person etc friedfertig; holiday, sleep etc ruhig; death sanft.

peacefully ['piːsfəlɪ] adv friedlich. **to die ~** (in one's sleep) sanft sterben.

peace: ~-keeping 1 n Friedenssicherung f; **2** adj Friedens-; **~-keeping force** Friedenstruppe f; **~-loving** adj friedliebend; **~maker** n Friedensstifter(in f) m; **~-offering** n (lit, fig) Friedensangebot nt; **~ talks** npl Friedensverhandlungen pl; **~time** n Friedenszeiten pl.

peach [piːtʃ] **1** n (a) (fruit) Pfirsich m; (tree) Pfirsichbaum m. **(b)** (col) **she's a ~** sie ist klasse (col). **2** adj pfirsichfarben.

peacock ['piːkɒk] n Pfau m.

peak [piːk] **1** n (a) (of mountain) Gipfel m; (of roof) First m. **(b)** (of cap) Schirm m. **(c)** (maximum) Höhepunkt m; (on graph) Scheitelpunkt m. **he is at the ~ of fitness** er ist in Höchstform; **when demand is at its ~** wenn die Nachfrage am stärksten ist. **2** adj attr value Spitzen-; production Höchst-. **3** vi den Höchststand erreichen.

peak: ~ hours npl (of traffic) Hauptverkehrszeit f; (Telec, Elec) Hauptbelastungszeit f; **~ season** n Hochsaison f.

peaky ['piːkɪ] adj (+er) (Brit col) complexion blaß. **to look ~** angeschlagen aussehen (col).

peal [piːl] **1** n **~ of bells** (sound) Glockenläuten nt; **~s of laughter** schallendes Gelächter; **~ of thunder** Donnerrollen nt. **2** vi (bell) läuten.

peanut ['piːnʌt] n Erdnuß f. **~s** (col) (not much money) Kleingeld nt (to sb für jdn); (not significant) Kleinkram m; **the pay is ~s** die Bezahlung ist miserabel or lächerlich (col); **~ butter** Erdnußbutter f.

pear [pɛəʳ] n Birne f; (tree) Birnbaum m.

pearl [pɜːl] n (lit, fig) Perle f; (mother-of-~, colour) Perlmutt nt. **~ of wisdom** weiser Spruch.

pearl: ~ barley n Perlgraupen pl; **~ fishing** n Perlenfischerei f; **~ grey** adj silbergrau; **~ oyster** n Perlenauster f.

pearly ['pɜːlɪ] adj (+er) (in colour) perlmuttfarben. **~ white** perlweiß; **P~ Gates** Himmelstür f.

pear-shaped ['pɛəʃeɪpt] adj birnenförmig.

peasant ['pezənt] **1** n (lit) (armer) Bauer-; (pej col) (ignoramus) Banause m; (pleb) Prolet m. **2** adj attr bäuerlich. **~ farmer** (armer) Bauer.

pea: ~shooter n Pusterohr nt; **~ soup** n Erbsensuppe f.

peat [piːt] n Torf m. **~bog** Torfmoor nt.

pebble ['pebl] n Kieselstein m. **he/she is not the only ~ on the beach** (col) es gibt noch andere.

pebbly ['peblɪ] adj steinig.

peck [pek] **1** n (a) (col: kiss) Küßchen nt. **(b)** the hen gave him a **~** die Henne hackte nach ihm. **2** vt (bird) picken. **3** vi picken (at nach). **he just ~ed at his food** er stocherte nur in seinem Essen herum.

pecking order ['pekɪŋˌɔːdəʳ] n (lit, fig) Hackordnung f.

peckish ['pekɪʃ] adj (Brit col: hungry) **I'm (feeling) a bit ~** ich könnte was zwischen die Zähne gebrauchen (col).

peculiar [pɪ'kjuːlɪəʳ] adj (a) (strange) seltsam,

eigenartig. **(b)** (exclusive, special) eigentümlich (to für +acc). **an animal ~ to Africa** ein Tier, das nur in Afrika vorkommt.

peculiarity [pɪˌkjuːlɪ'ærɪtɪ] n (a) (strangeness) Eigenartigkeit f. **(b)** (unusual feature) Besonderheit f.

pecuniary [pɪ'kjuːnɪərɪ] adj (form) penalties, affairs Geld-; gain, problem finanziell.

pedagogic(al) [ˌpedə'gɒdʒɪk(əl)] adj (form) pädagogisch.

pedal ['pedl] **1** n Pedal nt; (on bin etc) Trethebel m. **2** vi (on bicycle) treten. **to ~ off** (mit dem Rad) wegfahren.

pedant ['pedənt] n Pedant(in f) m.

pedantic [pɪ'dæntɪk] adj pedantisch.

pedantry ['pedəntrɪ] n Pedanterie f.

peddle ['pedl] vt hausieren mit (pej). **to ~ drugs** mit Drogen handeln.

peddler ['pedləʳ] n (esp US) = pedlar.

pederast ['pedəræst] n Päderast m.

pedestal ['pedɪstl] n Sockel m. **to put sb on a ~** (fig) jdn in den Himmel heben.

pedestrian [pɪ'destrɪən] **1** n Fußgänger(in f) m. **2** adj (a) attr Fußgänger-. **~ crossing** (Brit) Fußgängerüberweg m; **~ precinct** (Brit) Fußgängerzone f. **(b)** (prosaic) schwunglos.

pediatric [ˌpiːdɪ'ætrɪk] adj (esp US) = paediatric.

pedicure ['pedɪkjʊəʳ] n Pediküre f.

pedigree ['pedɪgriː] **1** n (lit, fig) Stammbaum m; (document) Ahnentafel f. **2** attr reinrassig.

pedlar ['pedləʳ] n Hausierer(in f) m; (of drugs) Drogenhändler(in f) m.

pee [piː] (col) **1** n (urine) Urin m, Pipi (baby-talk) nt. **to need/have a ~** pinkeln müssen/pinkeln (col). **2** vi pinkeln (col).

peek [piːk] **1** n kurzer Blick; (furtive) verstohlener Blick. **to take or have a ~** kurz/verstohlen gucken (at nach). **2** vi gucken (at nach).

peel [piːl] **1** n Schale f. **2** vt schälen. **3** vi (wallpaper) sich lösen; (paint) abblättern; (skin, person) sich schälen or pellen (col).

♦ **peel away 1** vt sep wallpaper, paint abziehen (from von); wrapper abstreifen (from von). **2** vi (lit, fig) sich lösen (from von).

♦ **peel back** vt sep cover, wrapping abziehen.

♦ **peel off 1** vt sep (+prep obj von) tape, wallpaper abziehen; wrapper, glove etc abstreifen. **2** vi sich lösen.

peeler ['piːləʳ] n (potato ~) Schälmesser nt.

peelings ['piːlɪŋz] npl Schalen pl.

peep [piːp] **1** n (sound) (of bird etc) Piep m; (of horn, whistle, col: of person) Ton m. **we haven't heard a ~ out of him** (col) wir haben keinen Pieps von ihm gehört (col). **2** vi (bird) piepen; (horn, car) tuten; (whistle) pfeifen.

peep² **1** n (look) kurzer Blick; (furtive) verstohlener Blick. **to take or have a ~** (at sth) kurz/verstohlen (nach etw) gucken. **2** vi gucken (at nach). **to ~ from behind sth** hinter etw (dat) hervorschauen; **to ~ over sth** über etw (acc) gucken.

peephole ['piːphəʊl] n Guckloch nt; (in door also) Spion m.

peeping Tom ['piːpɪŋ'tɒm] n Spanner (col), Voyeur m.

peer¹ [pɪəʳ] n (a) **~ (of the realm)** Peer m. **(b)** (equal) Gleichrangige(r) mf. **he was well-liked by his ~s** er war bei seinesgleichen beliebt.

peer² vi starren; (inquiringly) schielen. **to ~ (hard) at sb/sth** jdn/etw anstarren.

peerage ['pɪərɪdʒ] n Adelsstand m, Peers pl. **to give sb a ~** jdm einen Adelstitel verleihen; **to raise sb to the ~** jdn in den Adelsstand erheben.

peer group n (age group) Altersgruppe f; (ability group) Leistungsklasse f.

peerless ['pɪəlɪs] adj einzigartig.

peeved [piːvd] adj (col) eingeschnappt (col), verärgert.

peevish ['piːvɪʃ] adj (irritable) reizbar.
peewit ['piːwɪt] n Kiebitz m.
peg [peg] 1 n (stake) Pflock m; (for wood joints, in games) Stift m; (Brit: clothes ~) (Wäsche)klammer f. off the ~ von der Stange; to take sb down a ~ or two (col) jdm einen Dämpfer geben; a ~ on which to hang one's prejudices etc ein guter Aufhänger für seine Vorurteile etc. 2 vt (a) (fasten) anpflocken; clothes anklammern; (tent) festpflocken. (b) prices, wages festsetzen.
♦ **peg away** vi (col) nicht locker lassen (at mit).
♦ **peg out** 1 vt sep washing aufhängen; (mark out) area abstecken. 2 vi (col: die) abkratzen (col!).
pejorative [pɪ'dʒɒrɪtɪv] adj abwertend.
pekinese [ˌpiːkɪ'niːz] n, pl - (dog) Pekinese m.
pelican ['pelɪkən] n Pelikan m. ~ crossing Ampelüberweg m.
pellet ['pelɪt] n Kügelchen nt; (for gun) Schrotkugel f.
pell-mell ['pel'mel] adv wie Kraut und Rüben (col).
pelmet ['pelmɪt] n Blende f.
pelt [pelt] 1 vt (throw) schleudern (at nach). to ~ sb/sth (with sth) jdn/etw (mit etw) bewerfen. 2 vi (col) (a) (go fast) pesen (col). (b) it ~ed (with rain) es hat nur so geschüttet (col). 3 n (col) at full ~ volle Pulle (col).
pelvis ['pelvɪs] n Becken nt.
pen¹ [pen] 1 n (dip ~) Feder f; (fountain ~) Füller m; (ball-point ~) Kugelschreiber, Kuli (col) m. to put ~ to paper zur Feder greifen. 2 vt niederschreiben.
pen² n (a) (for cattle etc) Pferch m; (play ~) Laufstall m. (b) (US col: prison) Knast (col) m.
penal ['piːnl] adj law, colony etc Straf-. ~ code Strafgesetzbuch nt; ~ system Strafrecht nt.
penalize ['piːnəlaɪz] vt bestrafen; (fig) benachteiligen.
penalty ['penəltɪ] n (a) (punishment) Strafe f; (fig: disadvantage) Nachteil m. on ~ of death/£5/ imprisonment bei Todesstrafe/bei einer Geldstrafe von £ 5/bei Gefängnisstrafe; to pay the ~ dafür büßen. (b) (Sport) Strafstoß m; (Soccer also) Elfmeter m.
penalty: ~ area n Strafraum m; ~ clause n Strafklausel f; ~ kick n Strafstoß m; (soccer also) Elfmeter m.
penance ['penəns] n (Rel) Buße f; (fig) Strafe f. to do ~ Buße tun; (fig) büßen.
pence [pens] n pl of **penny.**
penchant ['pãːŋʃãːŋ] n Schwäche f (for für).
pencil ['pensl] 1 n Bleistift m; (eyebrow ~) Augenbrauenstift m. 2 vt (also ~ in) mit Bleistift schreiben/zeichnen. 3 attr drawing Bleistift-.
pencil: ~ case n Federmäppchen nt; ~ sharpener n (Bleistift)spitzer m.
pendant ['pendənt] n Anhänger m.
pending ['pendɪŋ] 1 adj anstehend; lawsuit anhängig. to be ~ (decision etc) noch anstehen; (trial) noch anhängig sein. 2 prep ~ his arrival/ return bis zu seiner Ankunft/Rückkehr.
pendulum ['pendjʊləm] n Pendel nt. the ~ has swung back in the opposite direction (fig) das Pendel ist in die entgegengesetzte Richtung ausgeschlagen.
penetrate ['penɪtreɪt] 1 vt eindringen in (+acc); walls etc durchdringen; (Mil) enemy lines durchbrechen; (Med) vein durchstechen. 2 vi eindringen; (go right through) durchdringen. the idea just didn't ~ (fig) das ist mir/ihm etc nicht klargeworden.
penetrating ['penɪtreɪtɪŋ] adj durchdringend; mind scharf; insight scharfsinnig; light grell; pain stechend.
penetration [ˌpenɪ'treɪʃən] n see vt Eindringen nt (into in +acc); Durchdringen nt (of gen); Durchbrechung f; Durchstechen nt.
penfriend ['penfrend] n (Brit) Brieffreund(in f) m.

penguin ['pengwɪn] n Pinguin m.
penicillin [ˌpenɪ'sɪlɪn] n Penizillin nt.
peninsula [pɪ'nɪnsjʊlə] n Halbinsel f.
penis ['piːnɪs] n Penis m.
penitence ['penɪtəns] n (also Eccl) Reue f.
penitent ['penɪtənt] 1 adj reuig (also Eccl), zerknirscht. 2 n (Eccl) Büßer(in f) m.
penitentiary [ˌpenɪ'tenʃərɪ] n (esp US: prison) Strafanstalt f.
pen: ~knife n Taschenmesser nt; ~ name n Pseudonym nt.
penniless ['penɪlɪs] adj mittellos.
penny ['penɪ] n, pl (coins) pennies or (sum) pence Penny m; (US) Centstück nt. in for a ~, in for a pound (prov) wennschon, dennschon (col); (morally) wer A sagt, muß auch B sagen (prov); I'm not a ~ the wiser ich bin genauso klug wie zuvor; take care of the pennies and the pounds will take care of themselves (Prov) spare im kleinen, dann hast du im großen; a ~ for your thoughts ich möchte deine Gedanken lesen können; he keeps turning up like a bad ~ (col) der taucht immer wieder auf (col); the ~ dropped (col) der Groschen ist gefallen (col).
pen pal n (US) Brieffreund(in f) m.
pen-pusher n ['pen,pʊʃəʳ] n (col) Schreiberling m.
pension ['penʃən] n (money) Rente f.
♦ **pension off** vt sep (col) vorzeitig pensionieren.
pensioner ['penʃənəʳ] n Rentner(in f) m.
pension: ~ fund n Rentenfonds m; ~ scheme n Rentenversicherung f.
pensive ['pensɪv] adj nachdenklich; (sadly serious) schwermütig.
pentagon ['pentəgən] n Fünfeck nt. the P~ das Pentagon.
pentathlon [pen'tæθlən] n Fünfkampf m.
Pentecost ['pentɪkɒst] n (Jewish) Erntefest nt; (Christian) Pfingsten nt.
penthouse ['penthaʊs] n (apartment) Penthouse nt.
pent-up ['pent'ʌp] adj person (with frustration, anger) geladen pred; (nervous, excited) innerlich angespannt; emotions, excitement aufgestaut.
penultimate [pe'nʌltɪmɪt] adj vorletzte(r, s).
penury ['penjʊrɪ] n Armut, Not f.
peony ['piːənɪ] n Pfingstrose f.
people ['piːpl] npl (a) Menschen pl; (not in formal context) Leute pl. French ~ die Franzosen; Edinburgh ~ (die) Leute aus/in Edinburgh; all ~ with red hair alle Rothaarigen; why me of all ~? warum ausgerechnet ich/mich?; what do you ~ think? was haltet ihr denn davon?; poor/ blind/disabled ~ Arme/Blinde/Behinderte; country ~ Menschen pl vom Land; some ~! Leute gibt's! (b) (inhabitants) Bevölkerung f. the ~ of Rome die Bevölkerung von Rom. (c) (one, they) man; (~ in general) die Leute. ~ say that ... man sagt, daß ... (d) (nation, masses) Volk nt. the common ~ das einfache Volk; a man of the ~ ein Mann m des Volkes; the P~'s Republic of ... die Volksrepublik ...
pep [pep] n (col) Schwung, Pep (col) m.
♦ **pep up** vt sep (col) Schwung bringen in (+acc); food pikanter machen; person munter machen.
pepper ['pepəʳ] 1 n Pfeffer m; (green, red ~) Paprika m. 2 vt pfeffern. to ~ a work with quotations eine Arbeit mit Zitaten spicken.
pepper: ~corn n Pfefferkorn nt; ~mint n Pfefferminz nt; (Bot) Pfefferminze f; ~ pot n Pfefferstreuer m.
peppery ['pepərɪ] adj gepfeffert; (fig) old man etc hitzköpfig.
pep pill n Aufputschpille f.
pep talk n (col) aufmunternde Worte pl.
per [pɜːʳ] prep. £20 ~ annum £ 20 pro Jahr; 60km ~ hour 60 km pro Stunde or in der Stunde; $2 ~ dozen das Dutzend für $2; £5 ~ copy £ 5 pro or je Exemplar; as ~ gemäß (+dat).
perceive [pə'siːv] vt wahrnehmen; (understand,

recognize) erkennen.

per cent, *(US)* **percent** [pə'sent] *n* Prozent *nt.* 20 ~ 20 Prozent; **a 10** ~ **discount** 10 Prozent Rabatt.

percentage [pə'sentɪdʒ] **1** *n* Prozentsatz *m*; *(commission, payment)* Anteil *m*; *(proportion)* Teil *m.* **a small** ~ **of the population** ein geringer Teil der Bevölkerung; **what** ~**?** wieviel Prozent?; **to get a** ~ **on all sales** prozentual am Umsatz beteiligt sein. **2** *attr* prozentual. **on a** ~ **basis** prozentual; ~ **sign** Prozentzeichen *nt.*

perceptible [pə'septəbl] *adj* wahrnehmbar; *improvement, trend etc* spürbar.

perceptibly [pə'septəblɪ] *adv* spürbar; *(to the eye)* sichtbar.

perception [pə'sepʃən] *n* **(a)** *no pl* Wahrnehmung *f.* **(b)** *(mental image, conception)* Auffassung *f (of von).* **one's** ~ **of the situation** die eigene Einschätzung der Lage. **(c)** *(no pl: perceptiveness)* Einsicht *f*; *(perceptive remark, observation)* Beobachtung *f.* **(d)** *no pl (of difficulties, meaning etc)* Erkennen *nt.*

perceptive [pə'septɪv] *adj (sensitive) person* einfühlsam; *(penetrating) analysis, speech* scharfsinnig; *book* aufschlußreich. **very** ~ **of you!** *(iro)* du merkst auch alles.

perch¹ [pɜːtʃ] *n (fish)* Barsch *m.*

perch² **1** *n (of bird)* Stange *f*; *(in tree)* Ast *m*; *(iro: for person etc)* Hochsitz *m.* **2** *vt* **to** ~ **sth on sth etw** auf etw *(acc)* setzen *or (upright)* stellen; **to be** ~**ed on sth** auf etw *(dat)* sitzen. **3** *vi (bird, fig: person)* hocken; *(alight)* sich niederlassen.

percolate ['pɜːkəleɪt] **1** *vt* filtrieren; *coffee* (in einer Kaffeemaschine) zubereiten. **2** *vi (lit, fig)* durchsickern.

percolator ['pɜːkəleɪtəʳ] *n* Kaffeemaschine *f.*

percussion [pə'kʌʃən] *n (Mus)* Schlagzeug *nt.* ~ **instrument** Schlaginstrument *nt.*

peregrine **(falcon)** ['perɪgrɪn('fɔːlkən)] *n* Wanderfalke *m.*

peremptory [pə'remptərɪ] *adj command* kategorisch; *voice* gebieterisch; *person* herrisch.

perennial [pə'renɪəl] **1** *adj plant* mehrjährig; *(perpetual)* ewig; *(recurring)* immer wiederkehrend. **2** *n (Bot)* mehrjährige Pflanze.

perfect ['pɜːfɪkt] **1** *adj* **(a)** perfekt; *balance, symmetry also* vollkommen; *work of art also* vollendet; *weather, day also* ideal; *(Comm: not damaged)* einwandfrei. **it was the** ~ **moment** es war genau der richtige Augenblick. **(b)** *(absolute, utter)* völlig. **he's a** ~ **stranger to me** er ist mir völlig fremd; **it's a** ~ **disgrace** es ist wirklich eine Schande. **(c)** *(Gram)* ~ **tense** Perfekt *nt.* **2** *n (Gram)* Perfekt *nt.* **in the** ~ im Perfekt. **3** [pə'fekt] *vt* vervollkommnen.

perfection [pə'fekʃən] *n* Vollkommenheit, Perfektion *f.* **to do sth to** ~ etw perfekt tun.

perfectionist [pə'fekʃənɪst] *n* Perfektionist *m.*

perfectly ['pɜːfɪktlɪ] *adv* **(a)** perfekt. **I understand you** ~ ich weiß genau, was Sie meinen. **(b)** *(absolutely)* absolut, vollkommen. **we're** ~ **happy about it** wir sind damit völlig zufrieden; **a** ~ **lovely day** ein wirklich herrlicher Tag; **you know** ~ **well that ...** du weißt ganz genau, daß ...

perforate ['pɜːfəreɪt] *vt (also Med)* perforieren; *(pierce once)* durchstechen, lochen.

perforation [,pɜːfə'reɪʃən] *n (act)* Perforieren *nt*; *(row of holes, Med)* Perforation *f.*

perform [pə'fɔːm] **1** *vt play, concerto* aufführen; *solo* vortragen; *part* spielen; *trick* vorführen; *miracle* vollbringen; *task* verrichten; *duty, function* erfüllen; *operation* durchführen; *ceremony* vollziehen. **2** *vi* **(a)** *(orchestra etc)* auftreten. **to** ~ **on the violin** Geige spielen. **(b)** **to** ~ **well/badly** *(car, football team etc)* eine gute/schlechte Leistung zeigen; *(examination candidate etc)* gut/ schlecht abschneiden; **the 2 litre version** ~**s better** die Zweiliterversion leistet mehr; **how did he** ~**?** *(actor, musician)* wie war er?; **how did**

the car ~**?** wie ist der Wagen gelaufen?

performance [pə'fɔːməns] *n* **(a)** *(of play, opera etc)* Aufführung *f*; *(cinema)* Vorstellung *f*; *(by actor)* Leistung *f*; *(of a part)* Darstellung *f.* **he gave an excellent** ~ er hat ausgezeichnet gespielt/ gesungen *etc*; **we are going to hear a** ~ **of Beethoven's 5th** wir werden Beethovens Fünfte hören. **(b)** *(carrying out) see vt* Aufführung *f*; Vortrag *m*; *(of part)* Darstellung *f*; Vorführung *f*; Vollbringung *f*; Verrichtung, Erfüllung *f*; Durchführung *f*; Vollzug *m.* **in the** ~ **of his duties** in Ausübung seiner Pflicht. **(c)** *(effectiveness) (of machine, sportsman etc)* Leistung *f*; *(of examination candidate etc)* Abschneiden *nt.* **he put up a good** ~ er hat sich gut geschlagen *(col).* **(d)** *(col)* **what a** ~**!** was für ein Umstand!

performer [pə'fɔːməʳ] *n (Theat, Mus)* Künstler(in *f) m.*

perfume ['pɜːfjuːm] **1** *n (substance)* Parfüm *nt*; *(smell)* Duft *m.* **2** [pə'fjuːm] *vt* parfümieren.

perfumery [pə'fjuːmərɪ] *n (perfume factory)* Parfümerie *f*; *(perfumes)* Parfüm *nt.*

perfunctory [pə'fʌŋktərɪ] *adj* flüchtig.

perhaps [pə'hæps, præps] *adv* vielleicht. ~ **so** das mag sein.

peril ['perɪl] *n* Gefahr *f.*

perilous ['perɪləs] *adj* gefährlich.

perilously ['perɪləslɪ] *adv* gefährlich. **she came** ~ **close to falling** sie wäre um ein Haar heruntergefallen.

perimeter [pə'rɪmɪtəʳ] *n (Math)* Umfang *m*; *(of grounds)* Grenze *f.* ~ **fence** Umzäunung *f.*

period ['pɪərɪəd] *n* **(a)** *(length of time)* Zeit *f*; *(age)* Zeitalter *nt*, Epoche *f*; *(Geol, Met)* Periode *f.* **for a** ~ **of eight weeks** für einen Zeitraum von acht Wochen; **at that** ~ *(of my life)* zu diesem Zeitpunkt (in meinem Leben); **a writer of the** ~ ein zeitgenössischer Schriftsteller. **(b)** *(Sch)* Stunde *f.* **(c)** *(esp US: full stop)* Punkt *m.* **you're not going,** ~ du gehst nicht, und damit hat sich's; **he just doesn't understand,** ~ er versteht einfach überhaupt nichts. **(d)** *(menstruation)* Periode *f*, Tage *pl (col).*

period: ~ **costume** *n* zeitgenössische Kostüme *pl*; ~ **furniture** *n* antike Möbel *pl.*

periodic [,pɪərɪ'ɒdɪk] *adj* periodisch. ~ **table** *(Chem)* Periodensystem *nt.*

periodical [,pɪərɪ'ɒdɪkəl] **1** *adj* = **periodic.** **2** *n* Zeitschrift *f.*

periodically [,pɪərɪ'ɒdɪkəlɪ] *adv* von Zeit zu Zeit.

period: ~ **pains** *npl* Menstruationsschmerzen *pl*; ~ **piece** *n* antikes Stück; *(painting, music etc)* Zeitdokument *nt.*

peripatetic [,perɪpə'tetɪk] *adj* umherreisend; *existence* rastlos; *teacher* an mehreren Schulen unterrichtend *attr.*

peripheral [pə'rɪfərəl] *adj* Rand-; *(fig also)* nebensächlich.

periphery [pə'rɪfərɪ] *n* Peripherie *f.*

periscope ['perɪskəʊp] *n* Periskop *nt.*

perish ['perɪʃ] *vi* **(a)** *(die)* umkommen, sterben; *(cities, civilization)* untergehen. **(b)** *(rubber, leather etc)* verschleißen; *(food)* verderben. **(c)** *(col)* ~ **the thought!** Gott bewahre!

perishable ['perɪʃəbl] **1** *adj food* verderblich. **2** *npl* ~**s** leicht verderbliche Ware(n).

perishing ['perɪʃɪŋ] *adj (col: very cold)* eisig kalt. **I'm** ~ ich geh' fast ein vor Kälte *(col).*

perjure ['pɜːdʒəʳ] *vr* **to** ~ **oneself** einen Meineid leisten.

perjury ['pɜːdʒərɪ] *n* Meineid *m.* **to commit** ~ einen Meineid leisten.

perk [pɜːk] *n (esp Brit: benefit)* Vergünstigung *f.*

♦ **perk up 1** *vt sep* **(a)** **he** ~**ed** ~ **his ears** *(dog, person)* er spitzte die Ohren. **(b)** **to** ~ **sb** ~ *(make lively)* jdn munter machen; *(make cheerful)* jdn aufheitern. **2** *vi (liven up: person, party)* munter werden; *(cheer up)* aufleben.

perky ['pɜːkɪ] *adj* (*+er*) (*cheerful, bright*) munter; (*cheeky, pert*) keß.

perm [pɜːm] **1** *n* Dauerwelle *f*. **2** *vt* **she had her hair ~ed** sie hat sich (*dat*) eine Dauerwelle machen lassen.

permanence ['pɜːmənəns], **permanency** ['pɜːmənənsɪ] *n* Dauerhaftigkeit *f*.

permanent ['pɜːmənənt] **1** *adj* ständig, permanent; *arrangement, position* fest; *job, relationship* dauerhaft; *agreement* unbefristet. **a ~ employee** ein Festangestellter *m*; **I'm not ~ here** ich bin hier nicht fest angestellt; **~ address** ständiger Wohnsitz. **2** *n* (*US*) = **perm 1.**

permanently ['pɜːmənəntlɪ] *adv* permanent, ständig; *fixed* fest. **are you living ~ in Frankfurt?** ist Frankfurt Ihr ständiger Wohnsitz?

permeable ['pɜːmɪəbl] *adj* durchlässig.

permeate ['pɜːmɪeɪt] **1** *vt* (*lit, fig*) durchdringen. **2** *vi* dringen (*into* in *+acc*, *through* durch).

permissible [pə'mɪsɪbl] *adj* erlaubt (*for sb* jdm).

permission [pə'mɪʃən] *n* Erlaubnis *f*. **with your ~** mit Ihrer Erlaubnis; **to give sb ~ (to do sth)** jdm erlauben(, etw zu tun); **to ask sb's ~** jdn um Erlaubnis bitten.

permissive [pə'mɪsɪv] *adj* nachgiebig, permissiv (*geh*); (*sexually*) freizügig. **the ~ society** die permissive Gesellschaft.

permit [pə'mɪt] **1** *vt* erlauben, gestatten. **to ~ sb to do sth** jdm erlauben, etw zu tun; **is it/am I ~ted to smoke?** darf man/ich rauchen? **2** *vi* (**a**) **if you (will) ~** wenn Sie gestatten; *weather* **~ting** wenn es das Wetter zuläßt. (**b**) (*form*) **to ~ of sth** etw zulassen. **3** ['pɜːmɪt] *n* Genehmigung *f*. **~ holder** Inhaber(in *f*) *m* eines Berechtigungsscheins.

permutation [,pɜːmjʊ'teɪʃən] *n* Permutation *f*.

pernicious [pɜː'nɪʃəs] *adj* schädlich.

pernickety [pə'nɪkɪtɪ] *adj* (*col*) pingelig (*col*).

perpendicular [,pɜːpən'dɪkjʊləʳ] **1** *adj* senkrecht (*to* zu). **2** *n* Senkrechte *f*.

perpetrate ['pɜːpɪtreɪt] *vt* begehen; *crime also* verüben.

perpetrator ['pɜːpɪtreɪtəʳ] *n* Täter *m*. **the ~ of this crime** derjenige, der dieses Verbrechen begangen hat.

perpetual [pə'petjʊəl] *adj* ständig, immerwährend; *joy* stet; *ice, snow* ewig. **~ motion** Perpetuum mobile *nt*.

perpetuate [pə'petjʊeɪt] *vt* aufrechterhalten; *memory* bewahren.

perpetuity [,pɜːpɪ'tjuːɪtɪ] *n* **in ~** auf ewig.

perplex [pə'pleks] *vt* verblüffen.

perplexed [pə'plekst] *adj* verblüfft, perplex.

perplexing [pə'pleksɪŋ] *adj* verblüffend.

perplexity [pə'pleksɪtɪ] *n* Verblüffung *f*.

persecute ['pɜːsɪkjuːt] *vt* verfolgen.

persecution [,pɜːsɪ'kjuːʃən] *n* Verfolgung *f* (*of* von). **~ complex** Verfolgungswahn *m*.

perseverance [,pɜːsɪ'vɪərəns] *n* Ausdauer (*with* mit), Beharrlichkeit (*with* bei) *f*.

persevere [,pɜːsɪ'vɪəʳ] *vi* durchhalten (*with* bei), nicht aufgeben (*with* bei). **to ~ in one's studies** mit seinem Studium weitermachen.

persevering [,pɜːsɪ'vɪərɪŋ] *adj* beharrlich.

Persia ['pɜːʃə] *n* Persien *nt*.

Persian ['pɜːʃən] **1** *adj* persisch. **~ carpet** Perser(teppich) *m*; **~ cat** Perserkatze *f*. **2** *n* (**a**) Perser(in *f*) *m*. (**b**) (*language*) Persisch *nt*.

persist [pə'sɪst] *vi* (*persevere*) nicht lockerlassen (*with* mit); (*in belief, demand etc*) beharren (*in auf +dat*); (*fog, pain*) anhalten. **if you ~ in misbehaving** wenn du dich weiterhin so schlecht benimmst.

persistence [pə'sɪstəns] *n* Hartnäckigkeit *f*; (*perseverance*) Ausdauer *f*; (*of pain*) Anhalten *nt*.

persistent [pə'sɪstənt] *adj* *questions* beharrlich; *person* hartnäckig; *efforts* ausdauernd; *offender, drinking* gewohnheitsmäßig; *nagging, lateness,*

threats ständig; *rain, illness* anhaltend.

person ['pɜːsn] *n* (**a**) *pl* **people** *or* (*form*) **-s** (*human being*) Mensch *m*; (*in official contexts*) Person *f*. **I know no such ~** so jemanden kenne ich nicht; **a certain ~** ein gewisser Jemand; **~ to ~ call** Gespräch *nt* mit Voranmeldung; **per ~** pro Person. (**b**) *pl* **-s** (*Gram*) **first ~ singular/plural** erste Person Singular/Plural. (**c**) *pl* **-s** (*body, physical presence*) Körper *m*; (*appearance*) Äußere(s) *nt*. **in ~** persönlich; **in the ~ of** in Gestalt (*+gen*); **on** *or* **about one's ~** bei sich.

personable ['pɜːsnəbl] *adj* von angenehmer Erscheinung.

personage ['pɜːsənɪdʒ] *n* Persönlichkeit *f*.

personal ['pɜːsənl] *adj* persönlich. **it's nothing ~ but ...** nicht, daß ich etwas gegen Sie persönlich hätte, aber ...; **don't be ~** nun werden Sie mal nicht persönlich; **"~"** (*on letter*) „privat"; **~ column** Familienanzeigen *pl*; **~ property** Privateigentum *nt*; **~ call** Gespräch *nt* mit Voranmeldung; (*private call*) Privatgespräch *nt*; **~ computer** Personal Computer *m*; **~ matter** private Angelegenheit; **~ pronoun** Personalpronomen *nt*.

personality [,pɜːsə'nælɪtɪ] *n* (*character, person*) Persönlichkeit *f*. **~ cult** Personenkult *m*.

personally ['pɜːsənəlɪ] *adv* persönlich. **~, I think that ...** ich persönlich bin der Meinung, daß ...

personification [pɜː,sɒnɪfɪ'keɪʃən] *n* Verkörperung *f*.

personify [pɜː'sɒnɪfaɪ] *vt* verkörpern. **he is greed personified** er ist der Geiz in Person.

personnel [,pɜːsə'nel] **1** *n sing or pl* (**a**) Personal *nt*; (*on plane, ship*) Besatzung *f*; (*Mil*) Leute *pl*. (**b**) (*~ department*) die Personalabteilung. **2** *attr* Personal-. **~ manager/officer** Personalchef *m*/-leiter *m*.

perspective [pə'spektɪv] *n* (*lit, fig*) Perspektive *f*. **try to get things in ~** versuchen Sie, das nüchtern und sachlich zu sehen.

Perspex ® ['pɜːspeks] *n* (*Brit*) Plexiglas ® *nt*.

perspicacious [,pɜːspɪ'keɪʃəs] *adj* *person, remark etc* scharfsinnig; *decision* weitsichtig.

perspiration [,pɜːspə'reɪʃən] *n* (*perspiring*) Schwitzen *nt*, Transpiration *f* (*geh*); (*sweat*) Schweiß *m*.

perspire [pə'spaɪəʳ] *vi* schwitzen.

persuade [pə'sweɪd] *vt* überreden; (*convince*) überzeugen. **to ~ sb to do sth** jdn überreden, etw zu tun; **to ~ sb into doing sth** jdn dazu überreden, etw zu tun; **to ~ sb of sth** jdn von etw überzeugen; **to ~ sb that ...** jdn davon überzeugen, daß ...; **he doesn't take much persuading** ihn braucht man nicht lange zu überreden.

persuasion [pə'sweɪʒən] *n* (**a**) (*persuading*) Überredung *f*. **she tried every possible means of ~** sie setzte ihre ganze Überredungskunst ein. (**b**) (*belief*) Überzeugung *f*; (*sect, denomination*) Glaube(nsrichtung *f*) *m*.

persuasive [pə'sweɪsɪv] *adj* *salesman, arguments etc* überzeugend.

persuasively [pə'sweɪsɪvlɪ] *adv* überzeugend.

pert [pɜːt] *adj* (*+er*) keß; (*impudent*) keck.

pertain [pə'teɪn] *vi* **to ~ to sth** etw betreffen; (*belong to*) zu etw gehören; **all documents ~ing to the case** alle den Fall betreffenden Dokumente.

pertinence ['pɜːtɪnəns] *n* Relevanz *f* (*to* für); (*of information*) Sachdienlichkeit *f*.

pertinent ['pɜːtɪnənt] *adj* relevant (*to* für); *information* sachdienlich.

perturb [pə'tɜːb] *vt* beunruhigen.

perturbing [pə'tɜːbɪŋ] *adj* beunruhigend.

Peru [pə'ruː] *n* Peru *nt*.

perusal [pə'ruːzəl] *n* Lektüre *f*.

peruse [pə'ruːz] *vt* (durch)lesen.

Peruvian [pə'ruːvɪən] **1** *adj* peruanisch. **2** *n* Peruaner(in *f*) *m*.

pervade [pɜː'veɪd] *vt* erfüllen.

pervasive [pɜːˈveɪsɪv] *adj smell etc* durchdringend; *influence, ideas* um sich greifend.
perverse [pəˈvɜːs] *adj (contrary) idea* abwegig; *(perverted)* pervers.
perversion [pəˈvɜːʃən] *n (esp sexual, Psych)* Perversion *f; (no pl: act of perverting)* Pervertierung *f; (distortion: of truth etc)* Verzerrung *f.*
perversity [pəˈvɜːsɪtɪ] *n see adj* Abwegigkeit *f*; Perversität *f.*
pervert [pəˈvɜːt] **1** *vt (deprave) person, mind* verderben, pervertieren; *(distort) truth etc* verzerren. **to ~ the course of justice** *(Jur)* die Rechtsfindung behindern; *(by official)* das Recht beugen. **2** [ˈpɜːvɜːt] *n* Perverse(r) *mf.*
pessimism [ˈpesɪmɪzəm] *n* Pessimismus *m.*
pessimist [ˈpesɪmɪst] *n* Pessimist(in *f*) *m.*
pessimistic [ˌpesɪˈmɪstɪk] *adj* pessimistisch. **I'm rather ~ about it** da bin ich ziemlich pessimistisch.
pest [pest] *n* **(a)** *(Zool)* Schädling *m.* **~ control** Schädlingsbekämpfung *f.* **(b)** *(fig) (person)* Nervensäge *f; (thing)* Plage *f.*
pester [ˈpestəʳ] *vt* belästigen; *(keep on at: with requests etc)* plagen.
pesticide [ˈpestɪsaɪd] *n* Schädlingsbekämpfungsmittel, Pestizid *(spec) nt.*
pestilent [ˈpestɪlənt], **pestilential** [ˌpestɪˈlenʃəl] *adj (fig: pernicious)* schädlich; *(col: loathsome)* ekelhaft.
pestle [ˈpestl] *n* Stößel *m.*
pet [pet] **1** *adj attr (favourite)* pupil, idea *etc* Lieblings-. **he has a ~ monkey** er hält einen Affen als Haustier; **a ~ name** ein Kosename *m.* **2** *n* **(a)** *(animal)* Haustier *nt.* **(b)** *(favourite)* Liebling *m.* **teacher's ~** Lehrers Liebling *m;* **yes, (my) ~** ja, (mein) Schatz. **3** *vt animal* streicheln; *child also* liebkosen. **4** *vi (sexually)* Petting machen.
petal [ˈpetl] *n* Blütenblatt *nt.*
♦ **peter out** [ˌpiːtəˈraʊt] *vi* langsam zu Ende gehen; *(mineral vein)* versiegen; *(river)* versickern; *(song, noise)* verhallen; *(interest)* sich legen.
petit bourgeois [ˈpetɪˈbʊəʒwaː] **1** *n* Kleinbürger(in *f*) *m.* **2** *adj* kleinbürgerlich.
petite [pəˈtiːt] *adj woman, girl* zierlich.
petition [pəˈtɪʃən] **1** *n* **(a)** *(list of signatures)* Unterschriftenliste *f.* **to get up a ~ against sth** Unterschriften gegen etw sammeln. **(b)** *(request)* Gesuch *nt,* Petition *f.* **~ for divorce** Scheidungsantrag *m.* **2** *vt person, authorities (request, entreat)* ersuchen *(for* um*); (hand ~ to)* eine Unterschriftenliste vorlegen (+*dat*). **3** *vi* **to ~ for divorce** die Scheidung einreichen.
petrify [ˈpetrɪfaɪ] *vt* **(a)** *(lit)* versteinern. **(b) to be petrified with fear** starr vor Angst sein.
petrochemical [ˈpetrəʊˈkemɪkəl] *adj* petrochemisch.
petrol [ˈpetrəl] *n (Brit)* Benzin *nt.*
petrol: ~ bomb *n* Benzinbombe *f;* **~ can** *n (Brit)* Benzinkanister *m.*
petroleum [pɪˈtrəʊlɪəm] *n* Petroleum *nt.* **~ jelly** Vaseline *f.*
petrol: ~ gauge *n (Brit)* Benzinuhr *f;* **~ pump** *n (Brit) (in engine)* Benzinpumpe *f; (at garage)* Zapfsäule *f;* **~ station** *n (Brit)* Tankstelle *f;* **~ tank** *n (Brit)* Benzintank *m;* **~ tanker** *n (Brit)* Tankwagen *m.*
petticoat [ˈpetɪkəʊt] *n* Unterrock *m; (stiffened)* Petticoat *m.*
petting [ˈpetɪŋ] *n* Petting *nt.*
petty [ˈpetɪ] *adj (+er)* **(a)** *(trivial)* unbedeutend, belanglos; *excuse* billig; *crime* geringfügig, Bagatell-. **(b)** *(small-minded)* kleinlich; *(spiteful)* remark spitz. **(c)** *(minor)* chieftain *etc* untergeordnet; *(pej) official also* unbedeutend.
petty: ~ cash *n* Portokasse *f;* **~ larceny** *n* leichter Diebstahl; **~ thief** *n* Dieb(in *f*) *m;* **~ officer** *n* Unteroffizier *m.*
petulance [ˈpetjʊləns] *n* verdrießliche Art; *(of child)* bockige Art *(col).*
petulant [ˈpetjʊlənt] *adj* verdrießlich; *child* bockig *(col).*
pew [pjuː] *n (Eccl)* (Kirchen)bank *f.* **have** *or* **take a ~!** *(hum)* laß dich nieder! *(hum).*
pewter [ˈpjuːtəʳ] *n (alloy)* Zinn *nt.*
phallic [ˈfælɪk] *adj* phallisch; *symbol* Phallus-.
phantom [ˈfæntəm] **1** *n* Phantom *nt; (ghost: esp of particular person)* Geist *m.* **2** *adj attr* Geister-; *(mysterious)* Phantom-.
pharmaceutic(al) [ˌfɑːməˈsjuːtɪk(əl)] *adj* pharmazeutisch.
pharmacist [ˈfɑːməsɪst] *n* Apotheker(in *f*) *m; (in research)* Pharmazeut(in *f*) *m.*
pharmacology [ˌfɑːməˈkɒlədʒɪ] *n* Pharmakologie *f.*
pharmacy [ˈfɑːməsɪ] *n* **(a)** *(science)* Pharmazie *f.* **(b)** *(shop)* Apotheke *f.*
phase [feɪz] **1** *n* Phase *f; (of project, history also)* Abschnitt *m; (of illness)* Stadium *nt.* **out of/in ~** *(Tech, Elec)* phasenverschoben/phasengleich; *(fig)* unkoordiniert/koordiniert; **he's just going through a ~** das ist nur so eine Phase bei ihm. **2** *vt (introduce gradually)* schrittweise durchführen; *(coordinate, fit to one another)* starting times, *etc* aufeinander abstimmen; *machines etc* gleichschalten. **a ~d withdrawal of troops** ein schrittweiser Truppenabzug.
♦ **phase in** *vt sep* allmählich einführen.
♦ **phase out** *vt sep* auslaufen lassen.
PhD *n* Doktor *m.* **~ thesis** Doktorarbeit *f.*
pheasant [ˈfeznt] *n* Fasan *m.*
phenomenal [fɪˈnɒmɪnl] *adj* phänomenal, sagenhaft *(col);* boredom, heat unglaublich.
phenomenon [fɪˈnɒmɪnən] *n, pl* **phenomena** Phänomen *nt.*
phew [fjuː] *interj* Mensch, puh.
philanderer [fɪˈlændərəʳ] *n* Schwerenöter *m.*
philanthropic [ˌfɪlənˈθrɒpɪk] *adj* menschenfreundlich; *person also, organization* philanthropisch *(geh).*
philanthropist [fɪˈlænθrəpɪst] *n* Menschenfreund, Philanthrop *(geh) m.*
philanthropy [fɪˈlænθrəpɪ] *n* Menschenfreundlichkeit *f.*
philately [fɪˈlætəlɪ] *n* Philatelie, Briefmarkenkunde *f.*
philharmonic [ˌfɪlɑːˈmɒnɪk] **1** *adj* philharmonisch. **2** *n* P ~ Philharmonie *f.*
Philipines [ˈfɪlɪpiːnz] *npl* Philippinen *pl.*
Philips screw ® *n* [ˈfɪlɪpskruː] Kreuzschlitzschraube *f.*
philology [fɪˈlɒlədʒɪ] *n* Philologie *f.*
philosopher [fɪˈlɒsəfəʳ] *n* Philosoph(in *f*) *m.*
philosophic(al) [ˌfɪləˈsɒfɪk(əl)] *adj* philosophisch; *(fig)* gelassen.
philosophize [fɪˈlɒsəfaɪz] *vi* philosophieren *(about, on* über *+acc).*
philosophy [fɪˈlɒsəfɪ] *n* Philosophie *f.* **~ of life** Lebensphilosophie *f.*
phlegm [flem] *n (mucus)* Schleim *m; (fig) (coolness)* Gemütsruhe *f; (stolidness)* Trägheit *f.*
phlegmatic [flegˈmætɪk] *adj (cool)* seelenruhig *f; (stolid)* träge, phlegmatisch.
phobia [ˈfəʊbɪə] *n* Phobie *f.* **she has a ~ about it** sie hat krankhafte Angst davor.
phoenix, (US) phenix [ˈfiːnɪks] *n (Myth)* Phönix *m.*
phone [fəʊn] **1** *n* Telefon *nt.* **to pick up/put down the ~** (den Hörer) abnehmen/auflegen. **2** *vt person* anrufen. **3** *vi* anrufen, telefonieren.
♦ **phone in 1** *vi* anrufen. **2** *vt sep* telefonisch übermitteln.
phone: ~ book *n* Telefonbuch *nt;* **~ box** *n* Telefonzelle *f;* **~ call** *n* Anruf *m;* **in our ~ call** in unserem Telefongespräch; **~card** *n* Telefonkarte *f;* **~-in** [ˈfəʊnɪn] *n* Rundfunk-/Fernsehprogramm *nt,* an dem man sich per Telefon beteiligen kann, Phone-in *nt.*

phonetic [fəʊ'netɪk] adj phonetisch.

phonetics [fəʊ'netɪks] n sing (subject) Phonetik f.

phon(e)y ['fəʊnɪ] (col) 1 adj unecht; excuse, deal faul (col); name falsch; passport, money gefälscht; story erfunden. 2 n (bogus policeman etc) Schwindler(in f) m; (doctor) Scharlatan m; (pretentious person) Angeber(in f) m.

phonograph ['fəʊnəgrɑːf] n (old) Phonograph m; (US) Plattenspieler m.

phonology [fəʊ'nɒlədʒɪ] n Phonologie f.

phony adj, n = phon(e)y.

phosphate ['fɒsfeɪt] n (Chem) Phosphat nt; (Agr: fertilizer) Phosphatdünger m.

phosphorescent [,fɒsfə'resnt] adj phosphoreszierend.

phosphorous ['fɒsfərəs] adj phosphorsauer.

photo ['fəʊtəʊ] n Foto nt, Aufnahme f.

photo: ~copier n (Foto)kopiergerät nt; ~copy 1 n Fotokopie f; 2 vt fotokopieren; ~electric cell n Photozelle f; ~ finish n Fotofinish nt; P~fit (picture) n Phantombild nt.

photogenic [,fəʊtəʊ'dʒenɪk] adj fotogen.

photograph ['fəʊtəgrɑːf] 1 n Fotografie, Aufnahme f. to take a ~ (of sb/sth) (jdn/etw) fotografieren, ein Bild (von jdm/etw) machen; ~ album Fotoalbum nt. 2 vt fotografieren.

photographer [fə'tɒɡrəfə] n Fotograf(in f) m.

photographic [,fəʊtə'ɡræfɪk] adj fotografisch; equipment, club Foto-.

photography [fə'tɒgrəfɪ] n Fotografie f; (in film, book etc) Fotografieren, Bilder pl.

photo: ~sensitive adj lichtempfindlich; ~stat ® n, vt = ~copy; ~synthesis n Photosynthese f.

phrase [freɪz] 1 n (Gram) Satzteil m; (Mus) Phrase f; (expression) Ausdruck m; (set expression) Redewendung f. 2 vt formulieren.

phrasebook ['freɪzbʊk] n Sprachführer m.

phraseology [,freɪzɪ'ɒlədʒɪ] n Ausdrucksweise f.

physical ['fɪzɪkəl] adj (a) (of the body) körperlich; (not psychological also) physisch; check-up ärztlich. (b) (material) physisch; world faßbar. (c) (of physics) laws physikalisch. it's a ~ impossibility es ist ein Ding der Unmöglichkeit (col).

physical: ~ education n (abbr PE) Sport m, Leibesübungen pl (form); ~ jerks npl (col) Gymnastik f.

physically ['fɪzɪkəlɪ] adv körperlich, physisch; (Sci) physikalisch. ~ impossible praktisch unmöglich; they removed him ~ sie haben ihn mit Gewalt entfernt.

physician [fɪ'zɪʃən] n Arzt m, Ärztin f.

physicist ['fɪzɪsɪst] n Physiker(in f) m.

physics ['fɪzɪks] n sing (subject) Physik f.

physiological [,fɪzɪə'lɒdʒɪkəl] adj physiologisch.

physiology [,fɪzɪ'ɒlədʒɪ] n Physiologie f.

physiotherapist [,fɪzɪə'θerəpɪst] n Physiotherapeut(in f) m.

physiotherapy [,fɪzɪə'θerəpɪ] n Physiotherapie f.

physique [fɪ'ziːk] n Körperbau m, Statur f.

pianist ['pɪənɪst] n Klavierspieler(in f) m; (concert ~) Pianist(in f) m.

piano ['pjænəʊ] n (upright) Klavier nt; (grand) Flügel m.

piano: ~ accordion n Pianoakkordeon nt; ~ lesson n Klavierstunde f; ~ stool n Klavierhocker m.

piccolo ['pɪkələʊ] n Pikkoloflöte f.

pick [pɪk] 1 n (a) (~axe) Spitzhacke f, Pickel m; (Mountaineering) Eispickel m; (tooth~) Zahnstocher m. (b) (choice) to have first ~ die erste Wahl haben; take your ~! such dir etwas/einen etc aus! (c) (best) Beste(s) nt.
   2 vt (a) (choose) (aus)wählen. to ~ a team eine Mannschaft aufstellen; to ~ sides wählen; to ~ a winner (lit) den Sieger erraten; (fig) das Große Los ziehen; to ~ one's time den richtigen Zeitpunkt wählen; you do ~ 'em (iro) du gerätst auch immer an den Falschen. (b) (pull at) jumper, blanket etc zupfen an (+dat); spot, scab

kratzen an (+dat); hole bohren. to ~ one's nose in der Nase bohren; to ~ one's teeth in den Zähnen herumstochern; to ~ a lock ein Schloß knacken; to ~ holes in sth (fig) etw bemäkeln; in argument etw in einigen Punkten widerlegen; to ~ a fight or quarrel (with sb) (mit jdm) einen Streit vom Zaun brechen; to ~ sb's pocket jdm die Geldbörse/Brieftasche stehlen; to ~ sb's brains sich von jdm inspirieren lassen. (c) (pluck) flowers, fruit pflücken.
   3 vi to ~ and choose wählerisch sein; to ~ at one's food im Essen herumstochern.

♦**pick off** vt sep (a) (remove) fluff etc wegzupfen; nail polish abschälen. (b) (shoot) abschießen.

♦**pick on** vi +prep obj (choose) aussuchen; (victimize) herumhacken auf (+dat). why ~ ~ me? (col) warum gerade ich?; ~ ~ somebody your own size! (col) leg dich doch mit einem Gleichstarken an! (col).

♦**pick out** vt sep (a) (choose) aussuchen. (b) (distinguish) person, face erkennen. (c) (Mus) to ~ ~ a tune eine Melodie improvisieren.

♦**pick up 1** vt sep (a) (take up) aufheben; reference, trail aufnehmen; (lift momentarily) hochheben. to ~ ~ a child in one's arms ein Kind auf den Arm nehmen; to ~ oneself ~ aufstehen; as soon as he ~s ~ a book sobald er ein Buch in die Hand nimmt; to ~ ~ the phone den Hörer abnehmen; to ~ ~ the bill (fig) die Rechnung bezahlen; to ~ ~ the pieces (lit, fig) die Scherben aufsammeln.
   (b) (get) holen; (buy) bekommen; (acquire) habit sich (dat) angewöhnen; news, gossip aufschnappen; illness sich (dat) holen or zuziehen; (col) girl aufgabeln (col), sich (dat) anlachen (col). to ~ ~ speed schneller werden.
   (c) (learn) skill etc sich (dat) aneignen; language also lernen; accent, word aufschnappen; information herausbekommen. you'll soon ~ ~ it ~ du wirst das schnell lernen.
   (d) (collect) person, goods abholen; (bus etc) passengers aufnehmen; (in car) mitnehmen; (rescue) helicopter, lifeboat bergen; (arrest, catch) criminal schnappen (col).
   (e) (Rad) station hereinbekommen; message empfangen; (on radar) ausmachen.
   (f) (correct, put right) korrigieren.
   2 vi (a) (improve) besser werden; (appetite also) zunehmen; (currency) sich erholen; (business) florieren; (after slump) sich erholen. (b) (continue) to ~ ~ where one left off da weitermachen, wo man aufgehört hat.

pickaback ['pɪkəbæk] n to give sb a ~ jdn huckepack nehmen.

pickaxe, (US) **pickax** [pɪkæks] n Spitzhacke, Pickel m.

picket ['pɪkɪt] 1 n (a) (of strikers) Streikposten m. (b) (Mil) Feldposten, Vorposten m. 2 vt factory Streikposten aufstellen vor (+dat). 3 vi Streikposten aufstellen. he is ~ing at the front entrance er ist Streikposten am Vordereingang.

picket: ~ duty n Streikpostendienst m; to be on ~ duty Streikposten sein; ~ line n Streikpostenkette f; to cross a ~ line eine Streikpostenkette durchbrechen.

pickings ['pɪkɪŋz] npl Ausbeute f; (stolen goods) Beute f. the ~ are good es fällt einiges dabei ab.

pickle ['pɪkl] 1 n (a) (food) Pickles pl. (b) (solution) (brine) Salzlake f; (vinegar) Essigsoße f. (c) (col: predicament) Klemme f (col). he was in a ~ er saß in der Tinte (col). 2 vt einlegen.

pick: ~-me-up n (col) Muntermacher m; ~pocket n Taschendieb(in f) m.

pick-up ['pɪkʌp] n (a) Tonabnehmer m. ~ arm Tonarm m. (b) (also ~ truck) Kleintransporter m.

picnic ['pɪknɪk] 1 n Picknick nt. to have a ~ picknicken; it was no ~ (fig col) es war kein

Honiglecken. **2** *vi* picknicken, ein Picknick machen.
picnic basket *or* **hamper** *n* Picknickkorb *m*.
pictorial [pɪk'tɔːrɪəl] *adj* *calendar* bebildert; *magazine also* illustriert; *description* bildhaft.
picture ['pɪktʃəʳ] **1** *n* **(a)** Bild *nt*; *(mental image also)* Vorstellung *f*; *(painting also)* Gemälde *nt*; *(drawing also)* Zeichnung *f*. **these figures give the general** ~ diese Zahlen geben ein allgemeines Bild; **to be in the** ~ im Bilde sein; **to put sb in the** ~ jdn ins Bild setzen; **I get the** ~ ich hab's begriffen *or* kapiert *(col)*; **she looked a** ~ sie war bildschön; **the garden is a** ~ der Garten ist eine Pracht; **she looked** *or* **was the** ~ **of happiness** sie sah wie das Glück in Person aus. **(b)** *(Film)* Film *m*. **the** ~**s** das Kino; **to go to the** ~**s** *(Brit)* ins Kino gehen. **2** *vt (imagine)* sich *(dat)* vorstellen.
picture: ~ **book** *n* Bildband *m*; *(for children)* Bilderbuch *nt*; ~ **frame** *n* Bilderrahmen *m*; ~ **gallery** *n* Gemäldegalerie *f*; ~ **postcard** *n* Ansichtskarte *f*.
picturesque [,pɪktʃə'resk] *adj* malerisch; *(fig)* description anschaulich.
pie [paɪ] *n* Pastete *f*; *(sweet)* Obstkuchen *m*; *(individual)* Tortelett *nt*. **that's all** ~ **in the sky** *(col)* das sind nur verrückte Ideen; **as easy as** ~ *(col)* kinderleicht.
piece [piːs] *n* **(a)** Stück *nt*; *(part, member of a set)* Teil *nt*; *(component part)* Einzelteil *nt*; *(fragment of glass etc also)* Scherbe *f*; *(in draughts etc)* Stein *m*; *(chess)* Figur *f*; *(Press: article)* Artikel *m*; *(col!: woman)* Weib *nt*. **a 50p** ~ ein 50-Pence-Stück; **a** ~ **of cake/land/paper** ein Stück *nt* Kuchen/Land/Papier; **a** ~ **of furniture/luggage/clothing** ein Möbel-/Gepäck-/Kleidungsstück *nt*; **a ten-**~ **coffee set** ein zehnteiliges Kaffeeservice; **a** ~ **of news/information** eine Nachricht/eine Information; **a** ~ **of work** eine Arbeit; ~ **by** ~ Stück für Stück; **to take sth to** ~**s** etw in seine Einzelteile zerlegen; **to come to** ~**s** sich zerlegen lassen; *(break)* auseinanderfallen; **to fall to** ~**s** auseinanderfallen; *(glass)* zerbrechen; **to smash sth to** ~**s** etw kaputtschlagen; **he tore the letter (in)to** ~**s** er zerriß den Brief (in Stücke).
(b) *(phrases)* **to go to** ~**s** *(crack up)* durchdrehen *(col)*; **all in one** ~ *(intact)* heil, unversehrt; **to give sb a** ~ **of one's mind** jdm gehörig die Meinung sagen; **to say one's** ~ seine Meinung sagen.
♦ **piece together** *vt sep (lit)* zusammenstückeln; *(fig)* sich *(dat)* zusammenreimen; *evidence* zusammenfügen.
piece: ~**meal 1** *adv* stückweise; *(haphazardly)* kunterbunt durcheinander; **2** *adj* stückweise; *(haphazard)* wenig systematisch; ~**work** *n* Akkordarbeit *f*; **to be on** ~**work** im Akkord arbeiten.
pier [pɪəʳ] *n* Pier *m or f*; *(landing-place also)* Anlegestelle *f*.
pierce [pɪəs] *vt* durchstechen; *(knife, spear, bullet)* durchbohren; *(fig: sound, coldness etc)* durchdringen. **to** ~ **a hole in sth** etw durchstechen; **to have one's ears** ~**d** sich *(dat)* die Ohrläppchen durchstechen lassen.
piercing ['pɪəsɪŋ] *adj* durchdringend; *eyes also* stechend; *cold also, sarcasm* beißend; *wit* scharf.
piety ['paɪətɪ] *n* Pietät, Frömmigkeit *f*.
pig [pɪg] *n (lit, fig col)* Schwein *nt*; *(greedy)* Vielfraß *m (col)*. **to buy a** ~ **in a poke** *(prov)* die Katze im Sack kaufen; **to make a** ~ **of oneself** sich *(dat)* den Bauch vollschlagen *(col)*.
pigeon ['pɪdʒən] *n* **(a)** Taube *f*. **(b)** *(col)* **that's not my** ~ das ist nicht mein Bier *(col)*.
pigeon: ~**hole 1** *n (in desk etc)* Fach *nt*; **2** *vt (lit)* (in Fächer) einordnen; *(fig: categorize)* einordnen, aufteilen; ~**-toed** *adj, adv* mit einwärts gerichteten Fußspitzen.

piggyback ['pɪgɪbæk] *n* = **pickaback**.
piggy bank ['pɪgɪbæŋk] *n* Sparschwein *nt*.
pigheaded ['pɪg'hedɪd] *adj* stur.
piglet ['pɪglɪt] *n* Ferkel *nt*.
pigment ['pɪgmənt] *n* Pigment *nt*.
pigmentation [,pɪgmən'teɪʃən] *n* Pigmentierung *f*.
pigmy *n* = **pygmy**.
pig: ~**skin** *n* Schweinsleder *nt*; ~**sty** *n* Schweinestall *m*; *(fig also)* Saustall *m (col)*; ~**tail** *n* Zopf *m*.
pike [paɪk] *n (fish)* Hecht *m*.
pilchard ['pɪltʃəd] *n* Sardine *f*.
pile[1] [paɪl] **1** *n* **(a)** *(heap)* Stapel *m*. **to put things in a** ~ etw (auf)stapeln; **her things lay** *or* **were in a** ~ ihre Sachen lagen auf einem Haufen. **(b)** *(col: large amount)* Haufen *m*, Menge *f*. ~**s of food** jede Menge Essen *(col)*; **a** ~ **of things to do** massenhaft zu tun *(col)*. **(c)** *(col: fortune)* Vermögen *nt*. **to make a** ~ einen Haufen Geld verdienen. **2** *vt* stapeln. **a table** ~**d high with books** ein Tisch mit Stapeln von Büchern.
♦ **pile in** *vi (col) (-to in +acc)* hereindrängen; *(get in)* einsteigen. ~ ~! immer herein!
♦ **pile up 1** *vi* **(a)** *(lit, fig)* sich anhäufen; *(traffic)* sich stauen; *(evidence)* sich verdichten. **(b)** *(crash)* aufeinander auffahren. **2** *vt sep* (auf)stapeln; *money* horten; *(fig) debts* anhäufen; *evidence* sammeln.
pile[2] *n* Pfahl *m*.
pile[3] *n (of carpet, cloth)* Flor *m*.
piles [paɪlz] *npl* Hämorrhoiden *pl*.
pile-up ['paɪlʌp] *n (car crash)* (Massen)karambolage *f*.
pilfer ['pɪlfəʳ] *vti* stehlen, klauen *(col)*. **there's a lot of** ~**ing in the office** im Büro wird viel geklaut *(col)*.
pilgrim ['pɪlgrɪm] *n* Pilger(in *f*) *m*.
pilgrimage ['pɪlgrɪmɪdʒ] *n* Wallfahrt *f*. **to go on** *or* **make a** ~ pilgern, eine Wallfahrt machen.
pill [pɪl] *n* Tablette *f*. **the** ~ die Pille; **to be/go on the** ~ die Pille nehmen.
pillage ['pɪlɪdʒ] *n (act)* Plünderung *f*; *(booty)* Beute *f*. **2** *vt* plündern.
pillar ['pɪləʳ] *n* Säule *f*. **a** ~ **of society** eine Stütze der Gesellschaft; **from** ~ **to post** von Pontius zu Pilatus.
pillar-box ['pɪləbɒks] *n (Brit)* Briefkasten *m*. ~ **red** knallrot.
pillion ['pɪljən] *n (on motor-bike)* Beifahrersitz *m*. ~ **passenger** Beifahrer(in *f*) *m*. **2** *adv* **to ride** ~ auf dem Beifahrersitz mitfahren.
pillow ['pɪləʊ] *n* (Kopf)kissen *nt*.
pillow case *or* **slip** *n* (Kopf)kissenbezug *m*.
pilot ['paɪlət] **1** *n (Aviat)* Pilot(in *f*) *m*; *(Naut)* Lotse *m*. **2** *vt plane* fliegen; *ship* lotsen; *(fig)* führen, leiten.
pilot: ~ **boat** *n* Lotsenboot *nt*; ~ **light** *n* Zündflamme *f*; ~ **scheme** *n* Versuchsprojekt *nt*.
pimento [pɪ'mentəʊ] *n* Paprikaschote *f*.
pimp [pɪmp] *n* Zuhälter *m*.
pimple ['pɪmpl] *n* Pickel *m*.
pimply ['pɪmplɪ] *adj (+er)* pickelig.
pin [pɪn] **1** *n (Sew)* Stecknadel *f*; *(tie* ~, *hair* ~) Nadel *f*; *(Mech)* Bolzen, Stift *m*; *(in grenade)* Sicherungsstift *m*; *(Elec: of plug)* Pol *m*. **a two-**~ **plug** ein zweipoliger Stecker; ~**s and needles** sing *or* pl im Kribbeln *nt*. **as neat as a** ~ blitzsauber; **for two** ~**s I'd pack up and go** *(col)* es fehlt nicht mehr viel, dann gehe ich; **you could have heard a** ~ **drop** man hätte eine Stecknadel fallen hören können. **2** *vt* **(a)** *dress* stecken. **to** ~ **sth to sth** etw an etw *(acc)* heften. **(b)** *(fig)* **to** ~ **sb to the ground/against a wall** jdn an den Boden/an eine Wand pressen; **to** ~ **one's hopes on sb/sth** seine Hoffnungen auf jdn/etw setzen; **to** ~ **back one's ears** die Ohren spitzen *(col)*. **(c)** *(col: accuse of)* **to** ~ **sth on sb** jdm etw anhängen.
♦ **pin down** *vt sep (lit)* *(with pins)* an- *or* festheften; *(hold, weight down)* niederhalten; *(person)* zu

Boden drücken. **(b)** *(fig)* to ~ sb ~ jdn festnageln *(col)* or festlegen; **he wouldn't be ~ned ~
to any particular date** er ließ sich nicht auf ein
bestimmtes Datum festlegen; **I've seen him
somewhere before but I can't ~ him** ~ ich habe
ihn schon mal irgendwo gesehen, kann ihn aber
nicht einordnen; **we can't ~ ~ the source of the
rumours** wir können die Quelle der Gerüchte
nicht lokalisieren; **there's something odd here,
but I can't ~ it** ~ irgend etwas ist hier merkwürdig, aber ich kann nicht genau sagen was.
♦ **pin up** *vt sep notice* anheften; *hair* hochstecken;
dress etc stecken.
pinafore ['pɪnəfɔːʳ] *n (for children)* Kinderkittel *m*;
(apron) Schürze *f*. ~ **dress** *(Brit)* Trägerkleid *nt*.
pinball ['pɪnbɔːl] *n* Flipper *m*. ~ **machine** Flipper
m.
pincers ['pɪnsəz] *npl* **(a)** Kneifzange *f*. **a pair of** ~
eine Kneifzange. **(b)** *(Zool)* Schere, Zange *f*.
pinch [pɪntʃ] **1** *n* **(a)** *(with fingers)* Kneifen *nt no pl*.
to give sb a ~ **on the arm** jdn in den Arm kneifen.
(b) *(Cook)* Prise *f*. **(c)** *(pressure)* **I'm rather
feeling the** ~ **at the moment** ich bin im
Augenblick ziemlich knapp bei Kasse *(col)*; **to
feel the** ~ die schlechte Lage zu spüren
bekommen; **if it comes to the** ~ wenn es zum
Schlimmsten kommt; **at a** ~ zur Not. **2** *vt* **(a)**
(with fingers) kneifen; *(with tool)* wire etc zusammendrücken. **(b)** *(col: steal)* klauen *(col)*.
don't let anyone ~ **my seat** paß auf, daß mir
niemand den Platz wegnimmt. **3** *vi (shoe, also fig)*
drücken. **to** ~ **and scrape** sich einschränken.
pinched ['pɪntʃt] *adj* **(a)** verhärmt; *(from cold)*
verfroren; *(from fatigue)* erschöpft. ~ **with cold/
hunger** verfroren/verhungert. **(b)** *(col: short)* **to
be** ~ **for money/time/space** knapp bei Kasse sein
(col)/keine Zeit haben/ein wenig beengt sein.
pincushion ['pɪn,kʊʃn] *n* Nadelkissen *nt*.
pine[1] [paɪn] *n* Kiefer *f*.
pine[2] *vi* **to** ~ **for sb/sth** sich nach jdm/etw sehnen.
♦ **pine away** *vi* sich vor Kummer verzehren.
pineapple ['paɪn,æpl] *n* Ananas *f*.
pine: ~ **cone** *n* Kiefernzapfen *m*; ~ **needle** *n*
Kiefernnadel *f*; ~ **tree** *n* Kiefer *f*.
ping [pɪŋ] **1** *n (of bell)* Klingeln *nt*; *(of bullet)* Peng
nt. **2** *vi (bell)* klingeln; *(bullet)* peng machen.
ping-pong ['pɪŋpɒŋ] *n* Pingpong *nt*.
pinion ['pɪnjən] *n (Mech)* Ritzel, Treibrad *nt*.
pink[1] [pɪŋk] **1** *n* **(a)** *(colour)* Rosa *nt*. **(b)** *(plant)*
Gartennelke *f*. **(c)** **to be in the** ~ vor Gesundheit
strotzen. **2** *adj (colour)* rosa *inv*, rosafarben;
cheeks, face rosig. **to turn** ~ erröten.
pink[2] *vt (Sew)* mit der Zickzackschere schneiden.
pinkie ['pɪŋkɪ] *n (Scot col, US col)* kleiner Finger.
pinnacle ['pɪnəkl] *n (Archit)* Fiale *f*; *(of rock)* Gipfel
m, Spitze *f*; *(fig)* Gipfel, Höhepunkt *m*.
pin: ~ **point** *vt (locate)* genau an- or aufzeigen;
(define, identify) genau feststellen or -legen;
~ **-prick** *n* Nadelstich *m*; ~ **stripe** *n (~stripe suit)*
Nadelstreifenanzug *m*.
pint [paɪnt] *n (Measure)* Pint *nt*. **to have a** ~ *(esp
Brit)* ein Bier *nt* trinken.
pinta ['paɪntə] *n (Brit col)* ≈ halber Liter Milch.
pin-up ['pɪnʌp] *n (picture)* Pin-up-Foto *nt*; *(girl)* Pin-
up-Girl *nt*; *(man)* Idol *nt*.
pioneer [,paɪə'nɪəʳ] **1** *n (also Mil)* Pionier *m*; *(fig
also)* Wegbereiter *m*. **2** *vt way* bahnen; *(fig)*
Pionierarbeit *f* leisten für.
pious ['paɪəs] *adj* fromm; *(pej also)* frömmlerisch.
a ~ **hope** ein frommer Wunsch.
pip[1] [pɪp] *n* **(a)** *(Bot)* Kern *m*. **(b)** *(on dice)* Auge *nt*;
(Brit Mil col) Stern *m*; *(radar)* Pip *m*, Echozeichen
nt. **(c)** *(Rad, Telec)* **the** ~**s** das Zeitzeichen; *(in
public telephone)* das Tut-tut-tut. **to give sb the** ~
(Brit) jdn aufregen *(col)*.
pip[2] *vt (Brit col)* knapp besiegen or schlagen. **to** ~
sb at the post *(in race)* jdn um Haaresbreite
schlagen; *(fig)* jdn um Haaresbreite zuvor-

kommen.
pipe [paɪp] **1** *n* **(a)** *(for water, gas etc)* Rohr *nt*,
Leitung *f*; *(fuel* ~) Leitung *f*. **(b)** *(Mus)* Flöte *f*;
(fife, of organ) Pfeife *f*. ~**s** *(bag~s)* Dudelsack *m*.
(c) *(for smoking)* Pfeife *f*. **to smoke a** ~ Pfeife
rauchen; **put that in your** ~ **and smoke it!** *(col)*
steck dir das hinter den Spiegel *(col)*. **2** *vt* **(a)**
water, oil etc in Rohren leiten; *music, broadcast*
ausstrahlen. ~**d music** *(pej)* Musikberieselung *f*
(col). **(b)** *(Mus)* tune flöten, pfeifen; *(sing in high
voice)* krähen; *(speak in high voice)* piepsen;
(Naut) pfeifen. **to** ~ **sb aboard** jdn mit Pfeifen-
signal an Bord empfangen. **(c)** *(Cook)* spritzen;
cake mit Spritzguß verzieren. **3** *vi (Mus)* (die)
Flöte spielen; *(young bird, anxiously)* piep(s)en.
♦ **pipe down** *vi (col)* die Luft anhalten *(col)*.
♦ **pipe up** *vi (col: person)* den Mund aufmachen,
sich melden.
pipe: ~ **cleaner** *n* Pfeifenreiniger *m*; ~ **dream** *n*
Hirngespinst *nt*; **that's just a** ~ **dream** das ist ja
wohl nur ein frommer Wunsch; ~ **line** *n*
(Rohr)leitung f; *(for oil, gas also)* Pipeline *f*; **to be
in the** ~**line** *(fig)* in Vorbereitung sein.
piper ['paɪpəʳ] *n (bagpipes)* Dudelsackpfeifer *m*.
piping ['paɪpɪŋ] **1** *n* **(a)** *(pipework)* Rohrleitungs-
system *nt*; *(pipe)* Rohrleitung *f*. **(b)** *(Sew)* Paspe-
lierung *f*. **2** *adv:* ~ **hot** kochendheiß.
pippin ['pɪpɪn] *n* Cox Orange *m*.
piquancy ['piːkənsɪ] *n* Würze *f*; *(fig)* Pikanterie *f*.
piquant ['piːkənt] *adj (lit, fig)* pikant.
pique [piːk] **1** *n* Groll *m*. **he resigned in a fit of** ~ er
kündigte, weil er vergrämt war. **2** *vt (offend)*
kränken, verletzen. ~**d** pikiert.
piracy ['paɪərəsɪ] *n* Piraterie *f*; *(of book etc)* Raubdruck *m*; *(of record)* Raubpressung *f*.
pirate ['paɪərɪt] **1** *n* Seeräuber, Pirat *m*. ~ **radio**
Piratensender *m*. **2** *vt book* einen Raubdruck
herstellen von; *invention, idea* stehlen. **a** ~**d
record** eine Raubpressung.
pirouette [,pɪrʊ'et] **1** *n* Pirouette *f*. **2** *vi* Pirouetten
drehen.
Pisces ['paɪsiːz] *npl (Astrol)* Fische *pl*. **I'm (a)** ~ ich
bin (ein) Fisch.
piss [pɪs] *(col!)* **1** *n* Pisse *f (col!)*. **2** *vti* pissen *(col!)*.
♦ **piss off** *vi (esp Brit col!)* abhauen *(col)*. **to be** ~**ed
off with sb/sth** von jdm/etw die Schnauze voll
haben *(col!)*.
pissed [pɪst] *adj (col!) (Brit: drunk)* voll *(col)*,
besoffen *(col)*; *(US: angry)* stocksauer *(col)*.
pistol ['pɪstl] *n* Pistole *f*. ~ **shot** Pistolenschuß *m*; **to
hold a** ~ **to sb's head** *(fig)* jdm die Pistole auf die
Brust setzen.
piston ['pɪstən] *n* Kolben *m*. ~ **engine**
Kolbenmotor *m*; ~ **rod** Kolbenstange *f*.
pit[1] [pɪt] **1** *n* **(a)** Grube *f*; *(motor-racing)* Box *f*;
(Sport: for jump) Sprunggrube *f*; *(coalmine also)*
Zeche *f*; *(trap)* Fallgrube *f*; *(of stomach)* Magengrube *f*. **in the** ~ **of one's stomach** in der
Magengegend; **he works down the** ~(**s**) er arbeitet unter Tage. **(b)** *(Theat) (usu pl Brit: for audience)* Parkett *nt*; *(orchestra* ~) Orchesterraum *m*.
2 *vt* **(a)** **to be** ~**ted with small craters** mit
kleinen Kratern übersät sein; **the car was** ~**ted
with rustholes** der Wagen war mit Rostlöchern
übersät. **(b)** **to** ~ **one's strength/wits against
sb/sth** seine Kraft/seinen Verstand an jdm/etw
messen; **in the next round A is** ~**ted against B**
in der nächsten Runde stehen sich A und B
gegenüber.
pit[2] **1** *n (in fruit)* Stein *m*. **2** *vt* entsteinen.
pitapat ['pɪtə'pæt] *adv (of heart)* poch poch; *(of feet)*
tapp tapp. **to go** ~ *(heart)* pochen, klopfen.
pitch[1] [pɪtʃ] *n* Pech *nt*. **as black as** ~ pechschwarz.
pitch[2] **1** *n* **(a)** *(esp Brit Sport)* Platz *m*, Feld *nt*. **(b)**
(angle, slope: of roof) Neigung *f*; *(of propeller)*
Steigung *f*. **(c)** *(of note)* Tonhöhe *f*; *(of instrument)*
Tonlage *f*; *(of voice)* Stimmlage *f*. **to have perfect**
~ das absolute Gehör haben. **(d)** *(fig: degree)* we

can't keep on working at this ~ much longer wir können dieses Arbeitstempo nicht mehr lange durchhalten; matters had reached such a ~ that ... die Sache hatte sich derart zugespitzt, daß ... 2 *vt* (a) *(throw)* hay gabeln; *ball* werfen. he was ~ed from *or* off his horse er wurde vom Pferd geworfen. (b) *(Mus)* song anstimmen; *note (give)* angeben; *instrument* stimmen. (c) *(fig)* to ~ one's aspirations too high seine Erwartungen *or* Hoffnungen zu hoch stecken; that's ~ing it rather strong *or* a bit high das ist ein bißchen übertrieben. (d) *(put up)* camp aufschlagen; *stand* aufstellen.

3 *vi* (a) *(fall)* fallen, stürzen. to ~ forward vornüberfallen. (b) *(Naut)* stampfen; *(Aviat)* absacken. to ~ and toss *(ship)* von den Wellen hin und her geworfen werden; *(person)* sich wälzen.

♦ **pitch in** 1 *vt sep* hineinwerfen. 2 *vi (col)* einspringen. so we all ~ed ~ together also packten wir alle mit an.

♦ **pitch into** *vi +prep obj (attack)* herfallen über *(+acc)*; *food also, work* sich hermachen über *(+acc)*.

pitch black *or* **dark** *adj* pechschwarz.
pitched ['pɪtʃt] *adj* (a) *roof* Sattel-. (b) *battle* offen.
pitcher[1] ['pɪtʃəʳ] *n* Krug *m*.
pitcher[2] *n (Baseball)* Werfer *m*.
pitchfork ['pɪtʃfɔːk] 1 *n* Heugabel *f*; *(for manure)* Mistgabel *f*. 2 *vt* gabeln; *(fig)* hineinwerfen.
piteous ['pɪtɪəs] *adj* mitleiderregend; *sounds* kläglich.
pitfall ['pɪtfɔːl] *n (fig)* Falle *f*. "P~s of English" „Hauptschwierigkeiten der englischen Sprache".
pith [pɪθ] *n (Bot)* Mark *nt*; *(of orange etc)* weiße Haut; *(fig: core)* Kern *m*.
pithead ['pɪthed] *n* Übertageanlagen *pl.* at the ~ über Tage; ~ ballot Abstimmung *f* der Bergarbeiter.
pithy ['pɪθɪ] *adj* (+er) *(fig)* markig. ~ remarks Kraftsprüche *pl.*
pitiable ['pɪtɪəbl] *adj* bemitleidenswert.
pitiful ['pɪtɪfʊl] *adj* (a) *sight, story* mitleiderregend; *person* bedauernswert; *cry also* jämmerlich. (b) *(poor, wretched)* erbärmlich, jämmerlich.
pitifully ['pɪtɪfəlɪ] *adv see adj.* it was ~ obvious that ... es war schon qualvoll offensichtlich, daß ...
pitiless ['pɪtɪlɪs] *adj* mitleidlos; *person also, heat* unbarmherzig; *cruelty also* erbarmungslos.
pittance ['pɪtəns] *n* Hungerlohn *m*.
pitter-patter ['pɪtə'pætəʳ] 1 *n (of rain)* Klatschen *nt*; *(of feet)* Getrappel *nt*. 2 *adv* run tapp tapp. her heart went ~ ihr Herz klopfte.
pity ['pɪtɪ] 1 *n* (a) Mitleid, Erbarmen *nt*. for ~'s sake! Erbarmen!; *(less seriously)* um Himmels willen!; to have *or* take ~ on sb, to feel ~ for sb mit jdm Mitleid haben. (b) *(what a)* ~! (wie) schade!; more's the ~! leider; it is a ~ that ... es ist schade, daß ... 2 *vt* bedauern.
pitying ['pɪtɪɪŋ] *adj* mitleidig; *(with contempt)* verächtlich.
pivot ['pɪvət] *(vb: pret,ptp* ~ed*)* 1 *n* Drehzapfen *m*; *(fig)* Dreh- und Angelpunkt *m*. 2 *vt* drehbar lagern. 3 *vi* sich drehen.
pixie, pixy ['pɪksɪ] *n* Kobold *m*.
placard ['plækɑːd] *n* Plakat *nt*.
placate [plə'keɪt] *vt* beschwichtigen.
place [pleɪs] 1 *n* (a) *(in general)* Platz *m*, Stelle *f*. this is just the ~ for a picnic das ist genau der richtige Platz für ein Picknick; this is the ~ where he was ... an dieser Stelle wurde er ...; from ~ to ~ von einem Ort zum anderen; in another ~ woanders; some/any ~ irgendwo; this is no ~ for children das ist hier für Kinder nicht geeignet; all over the ~ überall;

water is coming through in several ~s an mehreren Stellen kommt Wasser durch; do the spoons have a special ~? haben die Löffel einen bestimmten Platz?; make sure the screw is properly in ~ achten Sie darauf, daß die Schraube richtig sitzt; to be out of ~ nicht an der richtigen Stelle sein; *(fig) (remark)* unangebracht sein; *(person)* fehl am Platze sein; to feel out of ~ sich fehl am Platz fühlen; not a hair out of ~ tipptopp frisiert *(col)*; your ~ is by his side dein Platz ist an seiner Seite; everything was in ~ alles war an seiner Stelle; in the right/wrong ~ an der richtigen/falschen Stelle; to keep/ lose one's ~ *(in book etc)* die richtige Stelle markieren/verlieren; it was the last ~ I expected to find him da hätte ich ihn am wenigsten vermutet; this isn't the ~ to discuss politics dies ist nicht der Ort, um über Politik zu sprechen; to go ~s *(travel)* herumreisen; he's going ~s *(fig col)* er bringt's zu was *(col)*.

(b) *(specific* ~) Stätte *f*, Ort *m*. ~ of birth/ residence Geburtsort *m*/Wohnort *m*; ~ of business *or* work Arbeitsstelle *f*.

(c) *(district etc)* Gegend *f*; *(country)* Land *nt*; *(building)* Gebäude *nt*; *(town)* Ort *m*; *(home)* Haus *nt*; Wohnung *f*. there's nothing to do in this ~ hier kann man nichts unternehmen; at Jimmy's ~ bei Jimmy; come round to my ~ some time besuch mich mal, komm doch mal vorbei; let's go back to my ~ laß uns zu mir gehen; where's your ~? wo wohnst du?

(d) *(seat, in team, school etc)* Platz *m*; *(university* ~) Studienplatz *m*; *(job)* Stelle *f*. to take one's ~ *(at table)* Platz nehmen; ~s for 500 workers 500 Arbeitsplätze; to lose one's ~ *(in a queue)* sich wieder hinten anstellen müssen.

(e) *(social position etc)* Rang *m*, Stellung *f*. people in high ~s Leute in hohen Positionen; to know one's ~ wissen, was sich (für jdn) gehört; it's not my ~ to comment es steht mir nicht zu, einen Kommentar abzugeben; to keep *or* put sb in his ~ jdn in seine Schranken weisen.

(f) *(in exam, Sport etc)* Platz *m*; *(Math)* Stelle *f*. to three decimal ~s auf drei Stellen nach dem Komma; in the first/second ~ erstens/zweitens; to win first ~ erste(r, s) sein.

(g) in ~ of statt *(+gen)*; if I were in your ~ (wenn ich) an Ihrer Stelle (wäre); to take ~ stattfinden; to take the ~ of sb/sth den Platz von jdm/etw einnehmen.

2 *vt* (a) *(put)* setzen, stellen; *(lay down)* legen; *person at table etc* setzen; *guards* aufstellen; *(Ftbl, Tennis)* plazieren; *troops* in Stellung bringen; *announcement (in paper)* inserieren *(in* in *+dat)*; *advertisement* setzen *(in* in *+acc)*. I shall ~ the matter in the hands of a lawyer ich werde die Angelegenheit einem Rechtsanwalt übergeben; to ~ too much emphasis on sth auf etw *(acc)* zuviel Nachdruck legen; that should be ~d first das sollte an erster Stelle stehen; to ~ trust *etc* in sb/sth Vertrauen in jdn/etw setzen.

(b) to be ~d *(shop, town, house etc)* liegen; we are well ~d for the shops was Einkaufsmöglichkeiten angeht, wohnen wir günstig; how are you ~d for time/money? wie sieht es mit deiner Zeit/deinem Geld aus?; Liverpool are well ~d in the league Liverpool liegt gut in der Tabelle; we are better ~d now than we were last month wir stehen jetzt besser da als vor einem Monat.

(c) *order* erteilen *(with sb jdm)*; *contract* abschließen *(with sb mit jdm)*; *money* deponieren; *(Comm)* goods absetzen.

(d) *(in race, competition etc)* the German runner was ~d third der deutsche Läufer belegte den dritten Platz.

(e) *(remember, identify)* einordnen. I can't quite ~ him/his accent ich kann ihn/seinen Akzent nicht einordnen.

place: ~ **card** n Tischkarte f; ~ **mat** n Set nt; ~-**name** n Ortsname m.

placenta [plə'sentə] n Plazenta f.

placid ['plæsɪd] adj ruhig; disposition friedfertig.

plagiarism ['pleɪdʒjərɪzəm] n Plagiat nt.

plagiarize ['pleɪdʒjəraɪz] vt book, idea plagiieren.

plague [pleɪg] 1 n (Med) Seuche f; (Bibl, fig) Plage f. the ~ die Pest; **to avoid sb/sth like the** ~ (col) jdn/etw wie die Pest meiden (col). 2 vt plagen. to ~ **sb with questions** jdn ständig mit Fragen belästigen; **to be** ~**d by doubts** von Zweifeln geplagt werden.

plaice [pleɪs] n no pl Scholle f.

plaid [plæd] n Plaid nt. ~ **skirt** karierter Rock.

plain [pleɪn] 1 adj (+er) (a) klar; (obvious also) offensichtlich; tracks, differences deutlich. ~ **to see** offensichtlich; **it's as** ~ **as the nose on your face** (col) das sieht doch ein Blinder (mit Krückstock) (col); **to make sth** ~ **to sb** jdm etw klarmachen; **I'd like to make it quite** ~ **that ...** ich möchte gern klarstellen, daß ...

(b) (frank, straightforward) question, answer klar; truth schlicht. ~ **dealing** Redlichkeit f; **in** ~ **language** or **English** unmißverständlich, auf gut Deutsch; **it was** ~ **sailing** es ging glatt (über die Bühne) (col).

(c) (simple, with nothing added) einfach; living also schlicht, bescheiden; cooking also (gut)bürgerlich; chocolate bitter; paper unliniert; colour einheitlich; (not patterned) material etc uni pred, einfarbig. **under** ~ **cover** in neutralem Umschlag.

(d) (sheer) rein; greed also nackt; nonsense etc also völlig, blank (col).

(e) (not beautiful) nicht gerade ansprechend; face also alltäglich.

2 adv (a) (col: simply, completely) (ganz) einfach. (b) **I can't put it** ~**er than that** deutlicher kann ich es nicht sagen.

3 n (a) (Geog) Ebene f. (b) (Knitting) rechte Masche.

plain clothes npl in ~ in Zivil.

plainly ['pleɪnlɪ] adv (a) (clearly) eindeutig; explain, visible klar, deutlich. (b) (frankly) offen. (c) (simply, unsophisticatedly) einfach.

plainness ['pleɪnnɪs] n (a) (frankness) Offenheit f. (b) (simplicity) Einfachheit f. (c) (lack of beauty) Unansehnlichkeit f.

plain: ~ **speaking** n Offenheit f; **some** ~ **speaking** ein paar offene Worte; ~-**spoken** adj offen, direkt; criticism also unverhohlen; **to be** ~-**spoken** sagen, was man denkt.

plaintiff ['pleɪntɪf] n Kläger(in f) m.

plaintive ['pleɪntɪv] adj klagend; voice etc also wehleidig (pej).

plait [plæt] 1 n Zopf m. **she wears her hair in** ~**s** sie trägt Zöpfe. 2 vt flechten.

plan [plæn] 1 n (a) (scheme) Plan m; (Pol, Econ also) Programm nt. ~ **of action** (Mil, fig) Aktionsprogramm nt; ~ **of campaign** (Mil) Strategie f; **the** ~ **is to meet at six** es ist geplant, sich um sechs zu treffen; **the best** ~ **is to tell him first** am besten sagt man es ihm zuerst; **to have great** ~**s for sb** große Pläne mit jdm haben; **have you any** ~**s for tonight?** hast du (für) heute abend (schon) etwas vor?; **according to** ~ planmäßig, wie vorgesehen. (b) (diagram) Plan m; (for essay, speech) Konzept nt; (town ~) Stadtplan m.

2 vt planen; programme etc erstellen, ausarbeiten; (intend) vorhaben. **we weren't** ~**ning** to wir hatten es nicht vor; **this development was not** ~**ned** diese Entwicklung war nicht eingeplant; ~**ned obsolescence** geplanter Verschleiß.

3 vi planen. **to** ~ **for sth** sich einstellen auf (+acc); **to** ~ **months ahead** (auf) Monate vorausplanen; **I'm not** ~**ning on staying** ich habe nicht vor zu bleiben.

plane[1] [pleɪn] n (also ~ **tree**) Platane f.

plane[2] 1 adj eben (also Math). 2 n (a) (Math, fig) Ebene f; (intellectual also) Niveau nt; (social ~) Schicht f. (b) (tool) Hobel m. (c) (aeroplane) Flugzeug nt. **to go by** ~ fliegen. 3 vt hobeln. **to** ~ **sth down** etw glatt hobeln.

planet ['plænɪt] n Planet m.

planetarium [ˌplænɪ'tɛərɪəm] n Planetarium nt.

plank [plæŋk] n Brett nt.

plankton ['plæŋktən] n Plankton nt.

planner ['plænəʳ] n Planer(in f) m.

planning in cpds Planungs-; ~ **permission** Baugenehmigung f.

plant [plɑːnt] 1 n (a) (Bot) Pflanze f. **rare/tropical** ~**s** seltene/tropische Gewächse pl. (b) (no pl: equipment) Anlagen pl; (equipment and buildings) Produktionsanlage f; (factory) Werk nt. 2 attr Pflanzen-. ~ **life** Pflanzenwelt f. 3 vt (a) plants, trees (an)pflanzen; field bepflanzen. **to** ~ **a field with wheat** auf einem Feld Weizen anbauen. (b) (place in position) setzen; bomb legen; kiss drücken; (in the ground) stick stecken; flag pflanzen. **to** ~ **sth in sb's mind** jdm etw in den Kopf setzen; **he** ~**ed himself right in the doorway** er pflanzte sich genau in den Eingang (col). (c) (col) schmuggeln; informer, spy etc (ein)schleusen. **to** ~ **sth on sb** jdm etw unterjubeln (col).

plantation [plæn'teɪʃən] n Plantage f; (of trees) Anpflanzung f.

planter ['plɑːntəʳ] n (person) Pflanzer(in f) m; (machine) Pflanzmaschine f.

plaque [plæk] n (a) (on building etc) Tafel f. (b) (Med: on teeth) (Zahn)belag m.

plasma ['plæzmə] n Plasma nt.

plaster ['plɑːstəʳ] 1 n (a) (Build) (Ver)putz m. (Art, Med) ~ **of Paris** Gips m; (Med: ~ cast) Gipsverband m. **to have one's leg in** ~ das Bein in Gips haben. (c) (Brit: sticking ~) Pflaster nt. 2 vt (a) (Build) wall verputzen. (b) (col: cover) vollkleistern. **to** ~ **a wall with posters** eine Wand mit Plakaten bepflastern (col); ~**ed with mud** schlammbedeckt.

plaster: ~**board** n Gipskarton(platten pl) m; ~ **cast** n (model, statue) Gipsform f; (of footprint etc) Gipsabdruck m; (Med) Gipsverband m.

plastered ['plɑːstəd] adj pred (col: drunk) voll (col). **to get** ~ sich vollaufen lassen (col).

plasterer ['plɑːstərəʳ] n Gipser, Stukkateur m.

plastic ['plæstɪk] 1 n Plastik nt or f. ~**s** Kunststoffe pl. 2 adj (lit, fig) Plastik-; food also synthetisch. **the** ~ **arts** die gestalteten Künste.

plastic: ~ **bag** n Plastiktüte f; ~ **bullet** n Plastikgeschoß nt; ~ **explosive** n Plastiksprengstoff m.

plasticine ® ['plæstɪsiːn] n Plastilin nt.

plastic: ~ **money** n Plastikgeld nt; ~ **surgery** n plastische Chirurgie; (esp facial also) Schönheitsoperation f; **he had to have** ~ **surgery** er mußte sich einer Gesichtsoperation unterziehen.

plate [pleɪt] 1 n (a) (also ~-ful) Teller m. **cold** ~ kalte Platte; **to have sth handed to one on a** ~ (fig col) etw auf einem Tablett serviert bekommen (col); **to have a lot on one's** ~ (fig col) viel am Hals haben. (b) (gold, silver) Tafelsilber nt; Tafelgold nt; (~d metal) vergoldetes/versilbertes Metall. (c) (Tech, Phot, Typ) Platte f; (name~, number~) Schild nt. (d) (illustration) Tafel f. (e) (dental ~) (Gaumen)platte f. 2 vt (with armour-plating) panzern. **to** ~ (with gold/silver/nickel) vergolden-/silbern-/nickeln.

plateau ['plætəʊ] n, pl -s or -x (Geog) Plateau f, Hochebene f. **prices have reached a** ~ die Preise haben sich eingependelt.

plate glass n Tafelglas nt.

plate rack n (Brit) Geschirrständer m.

platform ['plætfɔːm] n (a) Plattform f; (stage) Podium m, Bühne f. (b) (Rail) Bahnsteig m. **from**

~ 7 von Gleis 7. **(c)** *(Pol)* Plattform *f.*

platform: ~ **shoe** *n* Plateauschuh *m;* ~ **ticket** *n* Bahnsteigkarte *f.*

plating ['pleɪtɪŋ] *n (act)* Vergolden *nt;* Versilbern *nt; (material)* Auflage *f; (armour-~)* Panzerung *f.*

platinum ['plætɪnəm] *n* Platin *nt.* **a** ~ **blonde** eine Platinblonde.

platitude ['plætɪtjuːd] *n* Platitüde, Plattheit *f.*

platonic [plə'tɒnɪk] *adj love, friendship* platonisch.

platoon [plə'tuːn] *n (Mil)* Zug *m.*

platter ['plætəʳ] *n* Teller *m; (wooden ~ also)* Brett *nt; (serving dish)* Platte *f.*

plausible ['plɔːzəbl] *adj* plausibel; *argument also* einleuchtend; *story, excuse also* glaubwürdig.

play [pleɪ] **1** *n* **(a)** Spiel *nt.* **to be at** ~ beim Spielen sein; **to do/say sth in** ~ etw aus Spaß tun/sagen; ~ **on words** Wortspiel *nt;* **children at** ~ spielende Kinder; **to abandon** ~ das Spiel abbrechen; **there was some exciting** ~ **towards the end** gegen Ende gab es einige spannende (Spiel)szenen; **to be in/out of** ~ *(ball)* im Spiel/im Aus sein. **(b)** *(Tech, Mech)* Spiel *nt.* **1 mm (of)** ~ **1 mm** Spiel. **(c)** *(Theat)* (Theater)stück *nt; (Rad)* Hörspiel *nt; (TV)* Fernsehspiel *nt.* **(d)** *(fig phrases)* **to come into** ~ ins Spiel kommen; **to give full** ~ **to one's imagination** seiner Phantasie *(dat)* freien Lauf lassen; **to bring** *or* **call sth into** ~ etw einsetzen; **to make great** ~ **of sth** viel Aufhebens von etw machen.

2 *vt game, card, role, instrument, tune* spielen; *(direct) light, hose* richten. **to** ~ **sb (at a game)** gegen jdn (ein Spiel) spielen; **to** ~ **ball** *(fig)* mitmachen; **to** ~ **a joke on sb** jdm einen Streich spielen; **to** ~ **a mean trick on sb** jdn auf gemeine Art hereinlegen; **to** ~ **the piano** Klavier spielen.

3 *vi* spielen; *(fountain)* laufen. **to go out to** ~ rausgehen und spielen; **to** ~ **with the idea of doing sth** mit dem Gedanken spielen, etw zu tun; **we don't have much time/money to** ~ **with** wir haben zeitlich/finanziell nicht viel Spielraum; **he wouldn't** ~ *(fig col)* er wollte nicht mitspielen *(col);* **he was** ~**ing at being angry** seine Wut war gespielt; **he's just** ~**ing at it** er tut nur so; **what are you** ~**ing at?** *(col)* was soll (denn) das? *(col);* **to** ~ **for money** um Geld spielen; **to** ~ **for time** *(fig)* Zeit gewinnen wollen; **to** ~ **into sb's hands** *(fig)* jdm in die Hände spielen; **the firemen's hoses** ~**ed on the flames** die Schläuche der Feuerwehrmänner waren auf die Flammen gerichtet; **the searchlights** ~**ed over the roofs** die Suchscheinwerfer strichen über die Dächer; **it's playing at the Old Vic next week** *(Theat)* es läuft nächste Woche im Old Vic.

♦ **play about** *or* **around** *vi* spielen. **to** ~ ~ **with sth/an idea** mit etw/einer Idee spielen.

♦ **play along 1** *vi* mitspielen. **he** ~**ed** ~ **with the system** er arrangierte sich mit dem System. **2** *vt sep* ein falsches Spiel spielen mit; *(in order to gain time)* hinhalten.

♦ **play back** *vt sep tape recording* durchspielen. **the conversation was** ~**ed** ~ **to us** man spielte uns *(dat)* das Gespräch vor.

♦ **play down** *vt sep* herunterspielen.

♦ **play off** *vt sep* **to** ~ **X** ~ **against Y** X gegen Y ausspielen; **he was** ~**ing them** ~ **against each other** er spielte sie gegeneinander aus.

♦ **play on 1** *vi* weiterspielen. **2** *vi +prep obj sb's fears, good nature* geschickt ausnutzen. **the author is** ~**ing** ~ **words** der Autor spielt mit Worten.

♦ **play out** *vt sep* **(a)** *(Theat) scene* darstellen. **(b) to be** ~**ed** ~ *(mine)* ausgebeutet sein; *(joke etc)* abgedroschen sein. **(c)** *(Mus: accompany)* mit Musik hinausgeleiten.

♦ **play through** *vi +prep obj* durchspielen.

♦ **play up 1** *vi* **(a)** *(Brit col: cause trouble: car, child)* verrückt spielen *(col).* **(b)** *(col: flatter)* **to** ~ ~ **to**

sb jdn umschmeicheln. **2** *vt sep (col)* **(a)** *(cause trouble to)* **to** ~ **sb** ~ jdm Schwierigkeiten machen. **(b)** *(exaggerate)* hochspielen.

play: ~**-act** *vi* Theater spielen; ~**-acting** *n (fig)* Theater(spiel) *nt;* ~**back** *n (switch, recording)* Wiedergabe *f;* ~**boy** *n* Playboy *m.*

player ['pleɪəʳ] *n (Sport, Mus)* Spieler(in *f*) *m; (Theat)* Schauspieler(in *f*) *m.*

playful ['pleɪfʊl] *adj* neckisch; *child, animal* verspielt, munter.

play: ~**ground** *n* Spielplatz *m; (Sch)* (Schul)hof *m;* ~**group** *n* Spielgruppe *f;* ~**house** *n* **(a)** *(US: doll's house)* Puppenstube *f;* **(b)** *(Theat)* Schauspielhaus *nt.*

playing ['pleɪɪŋ]: ~ **card** *n* Spielkarte *f;* ~ **field** *n* Sportplatz *m.*

play: ~**mate** *n* Spielkamerad(in *f*) *m;* ~**-off** *n* Entscheidungsspiel *nt; (extra time)* Verlängerung *f;* ~**pen** *n* Laufstall *m;* ~**room** *n* Spielzimmer *nt;* ~**school** *n* Kindergarten *m;* ~**thing** *n (lit, fig)* Spielzeug *nt;* ~**time** *n* Zeit *f* zum Spielen; *(Sch)* große Pause.

playwright ['pleɪraɪt] *n* Dramatiker(in *f*) *m; (contemporary also)* Stückeschreiber(in *f*) *m.*

plea [pliː] *n* **(a)** Bitte *f; (general appeal)* Appell *m.* **to make a** ~ **for sth** zu etw aufrufen; **to make a** ~ **for leniency** um Milde bitten. **(b)** *(Jur)* Plädoyer *nt.* **to enter a** ~ **of guilty/not guilty** ein Geständnis ablegen/seine Unschuld erklären.

plead [pliːd] *pret, ptp* ~**ed** *or (Scot, US)* **pled 1** *vt* **(a)** *(argue)* vertreten. **to** ~ **sb's case, to** ~ **the case for sb** *(Jur)* jdn vertreten; **to** ~ **the case for sth** *(fig)* sich für etw einsetzen; **to** ~ **sb's cause** *(fig)* für jds Sache eintreten. **(b)** *(as excuse)* ignorance sich berufen auf *(+acc).* **2** *vi* **(a)** *(beg)* bitten, nachsuchen *(for* um). **to** ~ **with sb to do sth** jdn bitten *or* ersuchen *(geh),* etw zu tun. **(b)** *(Jur) (counsel)* das Plädoyer halten. **to** ~ **guilty/not guilty** sich schuldig/nicht schuldig bekennen; **to** ~ **for sth** *(fig)* für etw plädieren.

pleading ['pliːdɪŋ] **1** *n* Bitten *nt; (Jur)* Plädoyer *nt.* **2** *adj look, voice* flehend.

pleasant ['pleznt] *adj* angenehm; *news* erfreulich; *person also, face* nett; *smile* freundlich.

pleasantry ['plezntrɪ] *n (joking remark)* Scherz *m; (polite remark)* Nettigkeit *f.*

please [pliːz] **1** *interj* bitte. **(yes,)** ~ *(acceptance)* (ja,) bitte; *(enthusiastic)* oh ja, gerne; **pass the salt,** ~ würden Sie mir bitte das Salz reichen?; **may I?** — ~ **do!** darf ich? — bitte sehr!

2 *vi* **(a)** *if* **you** ~ *(form: in request)* wenn ich darum bitten darf; **and then, if you** ~, **he tried** ... und dann, stell dir vor, versuchte er ...; *(just)* **as you** ~ ganz wie Sie wollen; **to do as one** ~**s** machen *or* tun, was einem gefällt. **(b)** *(cause satisfaction)* gefallen. **anxious** *or* **eager to** ~ darum bemüht, alles richtig zu machen.

3 *vt (give pleasure to)* eine Freude machen *(+dat); (satisfy)* zufriedenstellen; *(do as sb wants)* gefällig sein *(+dat).* **it** ~**s me to see him so happy** es freut mich, daß er so glücklich ist; **you can't** ~ **everybody** man kann es nicht allen recht machen; **there's no pleasing him** er ist nie zufrieden; **to be hard to** ~ schwer zufriedenzustellen sein; **I was only too** ~**d to help** es war mir wirklich eine Freude zu helfen.

4 *vr* **to** ~ **oneself** tun, was einem gefällt; ~ **yourself, then!** wie Sie wollen!; **you can** ~ **yourself where you sit** es ist Ihnen überlassen, wo Sie sitzen.

pleased [pliːzd] *adj (happy)* erfreut; *(satisfied)* zufrieden. **to be** ~ **(about sth)** sich (über etw *acc*) freuen; **I'm** ~ **to hear that** ... es freut mich zu hören, daß ...; **to meet you** angenehm *(form),* freut mich; **to be** ~ **with sb/sth** mit jdm/etw zufrieden sein.

pleasing ['pliːzɪŋ] *adj* angenehm.

pleasurable ['pleʒərəbl] *adj* angenehm.

pleasure ['plɛʒə^r] n (a) Freude f. it's a ~, (my) ~ gern (geschehen)!; with ~ gern, mit Vergnügen (form); it gives me great ~ to be here (form) es ist mir eine große Freude, hier zu sein; it would give me great ~ to ... es wäre mir ein Vergnügen, zu ...; to have the ~ of doing sth das Vergnügen haben, etw zu tun; Mrs X requests the ~ of Mr Y's company (form) Frau X gibt sich die Ehre, Herrn Y einzuladen (form). (b) (source of ~) Vergnügen nt. he's a ~ to teach es ist ein Vergnügen, ihn zu unterrichten; the ~s of country life die Freuden des Landlebens; all the ~s of London alle Vergnügungen Londons. (c) (iro, form: will) Wunsch m. at one's ~ nach Belieben; to await sb's ~ abwarten, was jd zu tun geruht.

pleasure in cpds Vergnügungs-; ~ **boat** n (steamer) Vergnügungsdampfer m; ~-**loving** adj lebenslustig, leichtlebig (pej).

pleat [pli:t] 1 n Falte f. 2 vt fälteln.

pleb [plɛb] n (pej col) Plebejer(in f) (pej), Prolet(in f) (pej col) m.

pled [pled] (US, Scot) pret, ptp of **plead**.

pledge [pledʒ] 1 n (in pawnshop, of love) Pfand nt; (promise) Versprechen nt. as a ~ of als Zeichen (+gen); under (the) ~ of secrecy unter dem Siegel der Verschwiegenheit; **election** ~s Wahlversprechen pl; to sign or take the ~ (hum col) dem Alkohol abschwören (usu hum). 2 vt (a) (give as security, pawn) verpfänden. (b) (promise) versprechen, zusichern. to ~ one's word sein Wort geben; to ~ support for sb/sth jdm/einer Sache seine Unterstützung zusichern; I am ~d to secrecy ich bin zum Schweigen verpflichtet.

plenary ['pli:nəri] adj ~ session Plenarsitzung f; ~ powers unbeschränkte Vollmachten pl.

plenipotentiary [ˌplɛnɪpə'tɛnʃəri] n (General)bevollmächtigte(r) mf.

plentiful ['plɛntɪfʊl] adj reichlich; commodities, gold etc reichlich vorhanden; hair voll. to be in ~ supply im Überfluß vorhanden sein.

plenty ['plɛntɪ] n (a) eine Menge. land of ~ Land des Überflusses; times of ~ Zeiten des Überflusses; in ~ im Überfluß; three kilos will be ~ drei Kilo sind reichlich; take ~ nimm dir reichlich; there are still ~ left es sind immer noch eine ganze Menge da. (b) ~ of viel, eine Menge; ~ of time/milk/eggs viel or eine Menge Zeit/Milch/viele or eine Menge Eier; a country with ~ of natural resources ein Land mit umfangreichen Bodenschätzen; we arrived in ~ of time to get a good seat wir kamen so rechtzeitig, daß wir einen guten Platz bekamen.

pleurisy ['plʊərɪsɪ] n Brustfellentzündung f.

pliable ['plaɪəbl] adj biegsam; leather geschmeidig; mind, person formbar.

pliers ['plaɪəz] npl (also pair of ~) Zange f.

plight [plaɪt] n Not f, Elend nt; (of economy etc) Verfall m.

plimsoll ['plɪmsəl] n (Brit) Turnschuh m.

plinth [plɪnθ] n Sockel m.

plod [plɒd] vi to ~ up a hill einen Hügel hinaufstapfen; to ~ along or on weiterstapfen; to ~ away at sth sich mit etw herumquälen.

plodder ['plɒdə^r] n zähe(r) Arbeiter(in f) m.

plonk¹ [plɒŋk] 1 n Bums m. it fell with a ~ to the floor es fiel mit einem Bums auf den Boden. 2 adv fall, land bums. 3 vt (col: also ~ down) (drop, put down) hinschmeißen (col); (bang down) hinknallen (col). to ~ oneself (down) sich hinpflanzen (col).

plonk² n (Brit col: wine) (billiger) Wein, Gesöff nt (hum, pej).

plop [plɒp] 1 n Plumps m; (in water) Platsch m. 2 vi (make a plopping sound) platschen.

plot [plɒt] 1 n (a) (Agr) Stück nt Land; (bed: in garden) Beet nt; (building ~) Grundstück nt; (allotment) Schrebergarten m. a ~ of land ein

Stück nt Land. (b) (conspiracy) Komplott nt. (c) (Liter, Theat) Handlung f. 2 vt (a) (plan) planen, aushecken (col). they ~ted to kill him sie planten gemeinsam, ihn zu töten. (b) position, course feststellen; (draw on map) einzeichnen; (Math, Med) curve aufzeichnen. 3 vi sich verschwören.

plough, (US) **plow** [plaʊ] 1 n Pflug m. the P~ (Astron) der Wagen. 2 vt pflügen.

♦ **plough back** vt sep (Agr) unterpflügen; (Comm) profits wieder hineinstecken (into in +acc).

♦ **plough up** vt sep field umpflügen.

plough, (US) **plow**: ~**land** n Ackerland nt; ~**man** n Pflüger m; ~**man's lunch** ≈ Käsebrot nt.

ploy [plɔɪ] n (stratagem) Trick m.

pluck [plʌk] 1 n (courage) Mut m. 2 vt fruit, flower pflücken; chicken rupfen; guitar, eyebrows zupfen. to ~ (at) sb's sleeve jdn am Ärmel zupfen; to ~ up courage all seinen Mut zusammennehmen.

plucky ['plʌkɪ] adj (+er) person, smile tapfer; action, person mutig.

plug [plʌg] 1 n (a) (in sink) Stöpsel m; (for stopping a leak, in barrel) Propfen m. (b) (Elec) Stecker m; (Aut: spark ~) (Zünd)kerze f. (c) (col: piece of publicity) Schleichwerbung f no pl. to give sb/sth a ~ für jdn/etw Schleichwerbung machen. 2 vt (a) (stop) gap, leak zustopfen. (b) (insert) stecken. (c) (col: publicize) Schleichwerbung machen für (col). (d) (col: push, put forward) idea hausieren gehen mit.

♦ **plug away** vi (col) ackern (col). to ~ ~ at sth sich mit etw abrackern (col); he kept ~ging ~ er hat nicht lockergelassen.

♦ **plug in** 1 vt sep TV, heater etc einstöpseln, anschließen. to be ~ged ~ angeschlossen sein. 2 vi sich anschließen lassen. where does the TV ~ ~? wo wird der Fernseher angeschlossen?

plughole ['plʌghəʊl] n Abfluß(loch nt) m.

plum [plʌm] 1 n (a) (fruit, tree) Pflaume f; (Victoria ~, dark blue) Zwetsch(g)e f. (b) (colour) Pflaumenblau nt. (c) (fig col) a real ~ (of a job) ein Bombenjob (col). 2 adj attr (col) job, position Bomben-, Mords- (col).

plumage ['plu:mɪdʒ] n Gefieder nt.

plumb [plʌm] 1 n (~-line) Lot nt. out of ~ nicht im Lot. 2 adv (completely) total (col); (exactly) genau. ~ crazy vollkommen or total (col) verrückt; ~ in the middle (haar)genau in der Mitte. 3 vt (a) ocean, depth (aus)loten. (b) (fig) mystery etc ergründen. to ~ the depths of despair die tiefste Verzweiflung erleben.

plumb bob n Lot, Senkblei nt.

plumber ['plʌmə^r] n Installateur, Klempner m.

plumbing ['plʌmɪŋ] n (a) (work) Installieren nt. (b) (fittings) Rohre, Leitungen pl.

plumbline ['plʌmlaɪn] n Lot nt.

plume [plu:m] n Feder f; (on helmet) Federbusch m. ~ of smoke Rauchwolke f.

plummet ['plʌmɪt] vi (bird, plane etc) hinunter-/herunterstürzen; (sales) stark zurückgehen; (currency) fallen, absacken (to auf +acc).

plump [plʌmp] adj (+er) rundlich, pummelig (col); legs etc stämmig; face rundlich, voll.

♦ **plump for** vi +prep obj sich entscheiden für.

♦ **plump up** vt sep pillow aufschütteln; chicken mästen.

plunder ['plʌndə^r] 1 n (a) (act) (of place) Plünderung f; (of things) Raub m. (b) (loot) Beute f. 2 vt place plündern (also hum).

plunge [plʌndʒ] 1 vt (a) (thrust) stecken; (into water etc) tauchen. he ~d his knife into his victim's back er jagte seinem Opfer das Messer in den Rücken. (b) (fig) to ~ the country into debt das Land in Schulden stürzen; the room was/we were ~d into darkness das Zimmer war in Dunkelheit getaucht/tiefe Dunkelheit umfing uns.

2 vi (a) (dive) tauchen; (goalkeeper) hechten.

(b) *(rush, esp downward)* stürzen. **to ~ to one's death** zu Tode stürzen. **(c)** *(share prices, currency etc)* stark fallen. **(d)** *(fig: into debate, studies etc)* sich stürzen *(into in +acc).* **3** *vr (into studies, job etc)* sich stürzen *(into in +acc).* **4** *n (lit, fig)* Sturz *m; (dive)* (Kopf)sprung *m.* **to take the ~** *(fig col)* den Sprung wagen.

plunger ['plʌndʒəʳ] *n* **(a)** *(piston)* Tauchkolben *m.* **(b)** *(for clearing drain)* Sauger *m.*

plunging ['plʌndʒɪŋ] *adj* neckline, back tief ausgeschnitten.

pluperfect ['pluː'pɜːfɪkt] *n* Plusquamperfekt *nt.*

plural ['pluərəl] **1** *adj (Gram)* Mehrzahl-, Plural-. **2** *n* Mehrzahl *f*, Plural *m.* **in the ~** im Plural, in der Mehrzahl.

plus [plʌs] **1** *prep* plus *(+dat); (together with)* und *(außerdem).* **2** *adj* **~ sign** Pluszeichen *nt;* **a ~ factor** ein Pluspunkt *m;* **on the ~ side** auf der Habenseite; **50 hours ~ a week** mehr als 50 Stunden pro Woche. **3** *n (sign)* Pluszeichen *nt; (positive factor)* Pluspunkt *m; (extra)* Plus *nt.*

plush [plʌʃ] **1** *n* Plüsch *m.* **2** *adj (+er) (col: luxurious)* feudal *(col); hotel also* Nobel-; *furnishing also* elegant, vornehm.

Pluto ['pluːtəʊ] *n (Astron)* Pluto *m.*

plutocrat ['pluːtəʊkræt] *n* Plutokrat(in *f*) *m.*

plutonium [pluː'təʊnɪəm] *n* Plutonium *nt.*

ply[1] [plaɪ] *n* **three-~** *wood* dreischichtig; *wool* dreifädig; *tissues* dreilagig.

ply[2] **1** *vt* **(a)** *tool, brush etc* gebrauchen; *oars* einsetzen. **(b)** *trade* ausüben, betreiben. **(c)** *(ships) sea, river* befahren. **(d)** **to ~ sb with questions** jdn mit Fragen überhäufen; **to ~ sb with drink(s)** jdn immer wieder zum Trinken auffordern. **2** *vi (ship)* **to ~ between** verkehren zwischen; **to ~ for hire** seine Dienste anbieten.

plywood ['plaɪwʊd] *n* Sperrholz *nt.*

PM = **Prime Minister.**

pm = *post meridiem* p.m.

pneumatic [njuː'mætɪk] *adj* Luft-. **~ drill** Preßluftbohrer *m.*

pneumonia [njuː'məʊnɪə] *n* Lungenentzündung *f.*

PO = **post office; postal order.**

poach[1] ['pəʊtʃ] *vt* egg pochieren; *fish* (blau) dünsten. **~ed eggs** verlorene Eier.

poach[2] *vti* wildern *(for* auf *+acc); ideas etc* klauen *(col).* **to ~ (on sb's territory)** jdm ins Gehege kommen.

poacher ['pəʊtʃəʳ] *n* Wilderer *m.*

poaching ['pəʊtʃɪŋ] *n* Wildern *nt*, Wilderei *f.*

pocket ['pɒkɪt] **1** *n* **(a)** *(in garment)* Tasche *f.* **to have sb/sth in one's ~** *(fig)* jdn/etw in der Tasche haben *(col).* **(b)** *(receptacle: in suitcase, file etc)* Fach *nt; (Billiards)* Loch *nt.* **to be a drain on one's ~** jds Geldbeutel strapazieren *(col);* **to be in ~** auf sein Geld kommen *(col);* **I was £100 in ~ after the sale** nach dem Verkauf war ich um £ 100 reicher; **they live in each others ~s** sie hängen ständig zusammen *(col);* **to put one's hand in one's ~** tief in die Tasche greifen; **~ of resistance** Widerstandsnest *nt.* **2** *adj comb, edition* Taschen-. **3** *vt* **(a)** *(put in one's pocket)* einstecken. **to ~ one's pride** seinen Stolz überwinden. **(b)** *(gain)* kassieren; *(misappropriate)* einstecken *(col).*

pocket: ~-book *n* **(a)** *(notebook)* Notizbuch *nt;* **(b)** *(wallet)* Brieftasche *f;* **(c)** *(US: handbag)* Handtasche *f;* **~ calculator** *n* Taschenrechner *m;* **~ handkerchief** *n* Taschentuch *nt;* **~-knife** *n* Taschenmesser *nt;* **~-money** *n* Taschengeld *nt;* **~-size(d)** *adj* book im Taschenformat; *camera* Miniatur-.

pockmarked ['pɒkmɑːkt] *adj* face pockennarbig; *surface* narbig.

pod [pɒd] *n (Bot)* Hülse *f; (of peas also)* Schote *f.*

podgy ['pɒdʒɪ] *adj (+er)* rundlich, pummelig; *face* schwammig.

podiatrist [pɒ'diːətrɪst] *n (US)* Fußspezialist(in *f*) *m.*

podium ['pəʊdɪəm] *n* Podest *nt.*

poem ['pəʊɪm] *n* Gedicht *nt.*

poet ['pəʊɪt] *n* Dichter(in *f*) *m.*

poetic [pəʊ'etɪk *adj* poetisch; *talent also* dichterisch; *place* malerisch. **~ justice** poetische Gerechtigkeit; **~ licence** *(Brit) or* **license** *(US)* dichterische Freiheit.

poetry ['pəʊɪtrɪ] *n* Dichtung *f.* **to write ~** Gedichte schreiben; **~ reading** Dichterlesung *f.*

poignancy ['pɔɪnjənsɪ] *n see adj* Ergreifende(s) *nt;* Wehmut *f;* Schmerzlichkeit *f;* Schärfe *f.* **he writes with great ~** er schreibt sehr ergreifend.

poignant ['pɔɪnjənt] *adj* ergreifend; *memories, look* wehmütig; *distress, regret* schmerzlich; *wit* scharf.

point [pɔɪnt] **1** *n* **(a)** Punkt *m; (place also)* Stelle *f; (sharp end)* Spitze *f; (on thermometer)* Grad *m.* **(nought) ~ seven** (0.7) null Komma sieben (0,7); **from all ~s of the compass)** aus allen (Himmels)richtungen; **up to a ~** bis zu einem gewissen Grad *or* Punkt; **at the ~ of a gun** mit vorgehaltener Pistole; **not to put too fine a ~ on it** *(fig)* um ganz offen zu sein; **the train stops at Slough and all ~s east** der Zug hält in Slough und allen Orten östlich davon; **~ of departure** *(lit, fig)* Ausgangspunkt *m;* **~ of view** Gesichtspunkt *m;* **from my ~ of view** aus meiner Sicht; **from the ~ of view of productivity** von der Produktivität her gesehen; **at this ~** *(spatially)* an dieser Stelle; *(in time) (then)* in diesem Augenblick; *(now)* jetzt; **from that ~ on** they were friends von da an waren sie Freunde; **at no ~ nie;** **at no ~ in the book** an keiner Stelle des Buches; **to be (up)on the ~ of doing sth** im Begriff sein, etw zu tun; **to reach the ~ of no return** *(fig)* den Punkt erreichen, von dem an es kein Zurück gibt; **they provoked him to the ~ where he lost his temper** sie reizten ihn so lange, bis er die Geduld verlor; **severe to the ~ of cruelty** streng bis an die Grenze der Grausamkeit; **when it comes to the ~** wenn es darauf ankommt; **to win on ~s** nach Punkten gewinnen; **the ~ at issue** der strittige Punkt; **a 12-~ plan** ein Zwölfpunkte-Plan *m;* **a ~ of interest** ein interessanter Punkt; **to come to the ~** zur Sache kommen; **to keep to the ~** beim Thema bleiben; **beside the ~** irrelevant; **his remarks are very much to the ~** seine Bemerkungen sind sehr sachbezogen; **my ~ was ...** was ich sagen wollte, war ...; **to make a ~** ein Argument *nt* anbringen; **he made the ~ that** ... er betonte, daß ...; **you have a ~ there** darin mögen Sie recht haben, da ist etwas dran *(col);* **I take your ~,** ~ ich sehe ich habe schon begriffen; **to gain or carry one's ~** sich durchsetzen; **to get or see the ~** verstehen, worum es geht; **to miss the ~** nicht verstehen, worum es geht; **he missed the ~ of what I was saying** er hat nicht begriffen, worauf ich hinauswollte; **that's not the ~** darum geht es nicht; **that's the whole ~** das ist es ja gerade; **a case in ~** ein einschlägiger Fall; **the case in ~** der zur Debatte stehende Punkt; **to make a ~ of sth** auf etw *(acc)* Wert legen; **he made a special ~ of being early** er legte besonderen Wert darauf, früh dazusein; **a ~ of principle** eine grundsätzliche Frage; **a ~ of order** eine Frage der Geschäftsordnung; **good/bad ~s** *(characteristics)* gute/schlechte Seiten *pl;* **he has his ~s** er hat auch seine guten Seiten.

(b) *(purpose)* Zweck, Sinn *m.* **there's no ~ in staying** es hat keinen Zweck *or* Sinn zu bleiben; **I don't see the ~ of carrying on** ich sehe keinen Sinn darin, weiterzumachen; **what's the ~?** was soll's?; **the ~ is that** ... die Sache ist die, daß ...; **the ~ of the story** die Pointe (der Geschichte).

(c) **~s** *pl (Brit Rail)* Weichen *pl.*

(d) *(Aut: usu pl)* Unterbrecherkontakte *pl.*
(e) *(Brit Elec)* Steckdose *f.*
2 *vt* **(a)** *(aim, direct) gun, telescope etc* richten *(at* auf +*acc).* **he ~ed his stick in the direction of the house** er zeigte mit dem Stock auf das Haus. **(b)** *(mark, show)* zeigen. **to ~ the way** *(lit,fig)* den Weg weisen. **(c)** *(Build) wall, brickwork* verfugen.
3 *vi* **(a)** *(with finger etc)* zeigen, deuten *(at, to* auf +*acc).* **he ~ed in the direction of the house/ towards the house** er zeigte in die Richtung des Hauses/zum Haus; **the compass needle ~s (to the)** north die Kompaßnadel zeigt nach Norden.
(b) *(indicate, point out)* hinweisen; *(facts, events also)* hindeuten *(to* auf +*acc).* **everything ~s that way** alles weist in diese Richtung. **(c)** *(face, be situated: building, valley etc)* liegen; *(be aimed: gun, vehicle etc)* gerichtet sein. **in which direction is it ~ing?** in welche Richtung zeigt es?
♦ **point out** *vt sep* zeigen auf (+*acc).* **could you ~ him ~ to me?** kannst du mir zeigen, wer er ist?; **to ~ sth ~ (to sb)** (jdn) auf etw *(acc)* hinweisen; **she ~ed ~ that ...** sie wies darauf hin, daß ...
♦ **point up** *vt sep (emphasize)* betonen.
point-blank ['pɔɪnt'blæŋk] **1** *adj* direkt; *refusal* glatt. **at ~ range** aus kürzester Entfernung. **2** *adv fire* aus kürzester Entfernung; *refuse* rundheraus.
pointed ['pɔɪntɪd] *adj* **(a)** *(sharp) stick, roof, nose* spitz; *window, arch* spitzbogig. **(b)** *(obvious in intention) remark, comment* scharf, spitz; *reference* unverblümt; *gesture, departure* ostentativ.
pointer ['pɔɪntə'] *n* **(a)** *(indicator) finger etc; (stick)* Zeigestock *m.* **(b)** *(dog)* Pointer, Vorstehhund *m.* **(c)** *(fig)* Hinweis *m; (indication also)* Anzeichen *nt.* **a ~ to a possible solution** ein Hinweis auf eine mögliche Lösung.
pointless ['pɔɪntlɪs] *adj* sinnlos.
point duty *n* Verkehrsdienst *m.*
poise [pɔɪz] **1** *n* **(a)** *(carriage of head, body)* Haltung *f; (grace)* Grazie *f.* **(b)** *(composure)* Gelassenheit *f; (self-possession)* Selbstsicherheit *f.* **2** *vt (balance, hold balanced)* balancieren. **we sat ~d on the edge of our chairs** wir balancierten auf den Stuhlkanten; **the enemy are ~d to attack** der Feind steht bereit zum Angriff.
poison ['pɔɪzn] **1** *n (lit, fig)* Gift *nt.* **to hate sb like ~** jdn wie die Pest hassen *(col).* **2** *vt (lit, fig)* vergiften; *air, rivers* verpesten; *marriage* zerrütten. **it won't ~ you** *(col)* das wird dich nicht umbringen *(col);* **to ~ sb's mind against sb/sth** jdn gegen jdn/etw aufstacheln.
poison gas *n* Giftgas *nt.*
poisoning ['pɔɪznɪŋ] *n (lit, fig)* Vergiftung *f.*
poison ivy *n* Giftefeu *m.*
poisonous ['pɔɪznəs] *adj* **(a)** giftig; *snake, plants etc also* Gift-. **(b)** *(fig) literature, doctrine* zersetzend; *remark etc* giftig; *propaganda also* Hetz-. **she has a ~ tongue** sie hat eine giftige Zunge.
poke [pəʊk] **1** *n (jab)* Stoß, Schubs *m (col).* **2** *vt* **(a)** *(jab with stick)* stoßen; *(with finger)* stupsen. **to ~ the fire** das Feuer schüren; **he accidentally ~d me in the eye** er hat mir aus Versehen ins Auge gestoßen. **(b)** *(US col: punch)* hauen *(col).* **(c)** *(thrust)* **to ~ one's head/a stick into sth** seinen Kopf/einen Stock in etw *(acc)* stecken; **he ~d his head around the door** er steckte seinen Kopf durch die Tür. **(d)** *(make by poking) hole* bohren.
3 *vi* **his elbows were poking through his sleeves** an seinen Ärmeln kamen schon die Ellenbogen durch; **to ~ at sth** *(testing)* etw prüfen; *(searching)* in etw *(dat)* stochern; **well, if you will go poking into things that don't concern you ...** na ja, wenn du deine Nase ständig in Dinge steckst, die dich nichts angehen ...
♦ **poke about** *or* **around** *vi* **(a)** *(prod)* herumstochern. **(b)** *(col: nose about)* schnüffeln *(col).*

♦ **poke out 1** *vi* vorstehen. **2** *vt sep* **to ~ sb's eye ~** jdm das Auge ausstechen.
poker[1] ['pəʊkə'] *n (for fire)* Schürhaken *m.*
poker[2] *n (Cards)* Poker *nt.*
poker-faced ['pəʊkə,feɪst] *adj* mit einem Pokergesicht; *(bored)* mit unbewegter Miene.
poky ['pəʊkɪ] *adj* (+*er)* (pej) *room, house* winzig. **it's so ~ in here** es ist so eng hier.
Poland ['pəʊlənd] *n* Polen *nt.*
polar ['pəʊlə'] *adj* **(a)** Polar-, polar. **~ bear** Polar- or Eisbär *m.* **(b) they are ~ opposites** sie sind absolute Gegensätze.
polarity [pəʊ'lærɪtɪ] *n (Phys, fig)* Polarität *f.*
polarization [,pəʊləraɪzeɪʃən] *n (Phys)* Polarisation *f; (fig)* Polarisierung *f.*
polarize ['pəʊləraɪz] **1** *vt* polarisieren. **2** *vi* sich polarisieren.
Pole [pəʊl] *n* Pole *m,* Polin *f.*
pole[1] [pəʊl] *n* Stange *f; (flag~, telegraph ~ also)* Mast *m; (for vaulting)* Stab *m.*
pole[2] *n (Geog, Astron, Elec)* Pol *m.* **they are ~s apart** sie *(acc)* trennen Welten.
polecat ['pəʊlkæt] *n* Iltis *m; (US)* Skunk *m,* Stinktier *nt.*
polemic [pɒ'lemɪk] **1** *adj* polemisch. **2** *n* Polemik *f.*
pole: **~star** *n* Polarstern *m;* **~ vault 1** *n* Stabhochsprung *m;* **2** *vi* stabhochspringen.
police [pə'liːs] **1** *n* (+*sing vb: institution,* +*pl vb: policemen)* Polizei *f.* **hundreds of ~** Hunderte von Polizisten; **extra ~ were called in** es wurden zusätzliche Polizeikräfte angefordert. **2** *vt road, frontier* kontrollieren.
police: **~ car** *n* Polizeiwagen *m;* **~ constable** *n (Brit)* Polizist *m;* **~ dog** *n* Polizeihund *m;* **~ escort** *n* Polizeieskorte *f;* **~ force** *n* Polizei *f;* **~man** *n* Polizist *m;* **~ officer** *n* Polizeibeamter *m;* **~ record** *n* **to have a ~ record** vorbestraft sein; **~ station** *n* (Polizei)wache *f;* **~woman** *n* Polizistin *f.*
policy[1] ['pɒlɪsɪ] *n* (of business *also)* Geschäftspolitik *f no pl (on* bezug auf +*acc); (of government, newspaper also)* Linie *f; (of political party also)* Programm *nt; (principle)* Grundsatz *m.* **our ~ on immigration/ recruitment** unsere Einwanderungs-/Einstellungspolitik; **foreign ~** Außenpolitik; **my ~ is to wait and see** meine Devise heißt abwarten; **it was good/bad ~** das war *(taktisch)* klug/ unklug.
policy[2] *n (also* **insurance ~)** (Versicherungs-) police *f.* **~ holder** Versicherungsnehmer *m.*
polio ['pəʊlɪəʊ] *n* Polio, Kinderlähmung *f.*
Polish ['pəʊlɪʃ] **1** *adj* polnisch. **2** *n (language)* Polnisch *nt.*
polish ['pɒlɪʃ] **1** *n* **(a)** *(shoe ~)* Creme *f; (floor ~)* Bohnerwachs *nt; (furniture ~)* Politur *f; (metal ~)* Poliermittel *nt; (nail ~)* Lack *m.* **to give sth a ~** etw polieren; *shoes, silver also* etw putzen; *floor* etw bohnern. **(b)** *(shine)* Glanz *m; (of furniture)* Politur *f.* **high ~** starker Glanz; **to put a ~ on sth** Glanz auf etw *(acc)* bringen. **(c)** *(fig: refinement)* Schliff *m; (of performance)* Brillanz *f.* **he lacks ~** ihm fehlt der Schliff/die Brillanz. **2** *vt* **(a)** polieren; *silver, shoes also* putzen; *floor* bohnern. **(b)** *(fig) performance* den letzten Schliff geben *(+dat);* *manner, style also* verfeinern.
♦ **polish off** *vt sep (col) food* verputzen *(col);* *drink* wegputzen *(col);* *work* erledigen.
♦ **polish up** *vt sep* **(a)** *floor, silver etc* auf Hochglanz bringen. **(b)** *(fig: improve)* style, one's *French etc* aufpolieren *(col); work* überarbeiten.
polished ['pɒlɪʃt] *adj* **(a)** *surface, furniture* poliert; *floor* gebohnert; *stone, glass* geschliffen. **(b)** *style etc* verfeinert; *performance, performer* brillant. **(c)** *manners* geschliffen.
polite [pə'laɪt] *adj* (+*er)* höflich. **it wouldn't be ~ es** wäre unhöflich; **be ~ about her cooking** mach ein paar höfliche Bemerkungen über ihre Kochkunst; **I was just being ~** ich wollte nur höflich

sein; we sat around making ~ conversation wir
saßen zusammen und machten Konversation.
politeness [pə'laɪtnɪs] n Höflichkeit f.
politic ['pɒlɪtɪk] adj (taktisch) klug.
political [pə'lɪtɪkəl] adj politisch. ~ **asylum** politisches Asyl; ~ **prisoner** politischer Gefangener.
politician [ˌpɒlɪ'tɪʃən] n Politiker(in f) m.
politics ['pɒlɪtɪks] n (a) (+pl vb) Politik f. what are
his ~? welche politischen Ansichten hat er? (b)
(+ sing or pl vb) Politik f. to go into ~ in die Politik
gehen; to talk ~ über Politik reden.
polka ['pɒlkə] n Polka f.
polka dot 1 n Tupfen m. 2 adj gepunktet.
poll [pəʊl] 1 n (a) (Pol: voting) Abstimmung f;
(election) Wahl f. to take a ~ eine Abstimmung
durchführen. (b) (total of votes cast) Wahlbeteiligung f; (for candidate) Stimmenanteil m.
there was an 84% ~ die Wahlbeteiligung betrug
84%; they got 34% of the ~ sie bekamen 34% der
Stimmen. (c) ~s (voting place) Wahllokale pl;
(election) Wahl f; to go to the ~s zur Wahl gehen;
a defeat at the ~s eine Wahlniederlage. (d)
(opinion ~) Umfrage f. 2 vt votes erhalten; (in
opinion ~) befragen. 40% of those ~ed support-
ed the Government 40% der Befragten waren
für die Regierung.
pollen ['pɒlən] n Blütenstaub, Pollen m. ~ **count**
Pollenzahl f.
pollinate ['pɒlɪneɪt] vt bestäuben.
pollination [ˌpɒlɪ'neɪʃən] n Bestäubung f.
polling ['pəʊlɪŋ] n Stimmabgabe, Wahl f. ~ **has**
been heavy die Wahlbeteiligung war hoch.
polling: ~ **booth** n Wahlkabine f; ~ **day** n Wahltag
m; ~ **station** n Wahllokal nt.
pollute [pə'luːt] vt verschmutzen, verunreinigen;
(fig) mind verderben.
pollution [pə'luːʃən] n (a) Umweltverschmut-
zung f. (b) (of rivers etc) Verschmutzung, Verun-
reinigung f; (fig) Verpestung f.
polo ['pəʊləʊ] n Polo nt.
polo neck n Rollkragen m; (sweater) Roll-
kragenpullover m.
poltergeist ['pɒltəgaɪst] n Poltergeist m.
poly (Brit) = **polytechnic.**
polyester [ˌpɒlɪ'estəʳ] n Polyester m.
polygamy [pɒ'lɪgəmɪ] n Polygamie, Vielehe f.
polyglot ['pɒlɪglɒt] 1 adj vielsprachig. 2 n (person)
Polyglotte(r) mf.
polygon ['pɒlɪgən] n Polygon, Vieleck nt.
polymer ['pɒlɪməʳ] n Polymer nt.
polyp ['pɒlɪp] n Polyp m.
polystyrene [ˌpɒlɪ'staɪriːn] n Polystyrol nt;
(extended use) Styropor ® nt.
polytechnic [ˌpɒlɪ'teknɪk] n (Brit) ≃ Polytech-
nikum nt; (degree-awarding) Technische Hochschule, TH f.
polythene ['pɒlɪθiːn] n (Brit) Polyäthylen nt; (in
everyday language) Plastik nt. ~ **bag** Plastiktüte f.
polyunsaturated [ˌpɒlɪʌn'sætʃəreɪtɪd] adj mehrfach ungesättigt.
pomegranate ['pɒmə,grænɪt] n Granatapfel m.
pommel ['pʌml] n (on sword) Knauf m; (on saddle)
Knopf m.
pommy ['pɒmɪ] n (Austral col) Engländer(in f) m.
pomp [pɒmp] n Pomp, Prunk m. ~ **and circum-**
stance Pomp und Prunk.
pompom ['pɒmpɒm] n (on hat etc) Troddel,
Bommel (dial) f.
pomposity [pɒm'pɒsɪtɪ] n see adj Aufgeblasenheit,
Wichtigtuerei f; Bombast m.
pompous ['pɒmpəs] adj person aufgeblasen, wichtigtuerisch; language, remark bombastisch.
pond [pɒnd] n Teich m.
ponder ['pɒndəʳ] 1 vt nachdenken über (+acc). 2 vi
nachdenken (on, over über +acc).
ponderous ['pɒndərəs] adj style etc schwerfällig.
pong [pɒŋ] (Brit col) 1 n Gestank, Mief (col) m.

there's a bit of a ~ in here hier stinkt's. 2 vi
stinken.
pontiff ['pɒntɪf] n Pontifex m; (pope also) Papst m.
pontificate [pɒn'tɪfɪkɪt] 1 n Pontifikat nt. 2
[pɒn'tɪfɪkeɪt] vi (fig) dozieren.
pontoon¹ [pɒn'tuːn] n Ponton m. ~ **bridge** Ponton-
brücke f.
pontoon² n (Brit Cards) Siebzehnundvier nt.
pony ['pəʊnɪ] n Pony nt.
pony: ~ **tail** n Pferdeschwanz m; ~ **trekking** n
Ponyreiten nt.
poodle ['puːdl] n Pudel m.
poof [puf] n (Brit col) Schwule(r) m (col).
pooh [puː] interj (bad smell) puh; (disdain) bah.
pooh-pooh ['puː'puː] vt verächtlich abtun.
pool¹ [puːl] n (a) Teich m; (underground) See m; (of
rain) Pfütze f; (of spilt liquid) Lache f; (in river)
Loch nt. a ~ of blood eine Blutlache. (b)
(swimming ~) (Schwimm)becken nt; (in private
garden, hotel also) Swimming Pool m; (swimming
baths) Schwimmbad nt.
pool² 1 n (a) (common fund) (gemeinsame) Kasse f.
each player put £10 in the ~ jeder Spieler gab
£10 in die Kasse. (b) (supply, source) typing ~
Schreibzentrale f; ~ of labour Arbeits-
kraftreserve f; there is a great ~ of untapped
resources es gibt große, noch ungenutzte
Reserven. (c) the ~s pl (football ~) Toto m or nt;
to do the ~s Toto spielen; to win the ~s im Toto
gewinnen. (d) (form of snooker) Poolbillard nt.
(e) (Comm) Interessengemeinschaft f; (US:
monopoly, trust) Pool m, Kartell nt. 2 vt resources,
savings zusammenlegen; efforts vereinen (geh).
poor [pʊəʳ] 1 adj (+er) (a) arm. a country ~ in
natural resources arm an Bodenschätzen armes
Land; ~ relation (fig) Sorgenkind nt; you ~ (old)
chap (col) du armer Kerl (col); ~ you! du Ärm-
ste(r)! (b) (not good) schlecht; performance also,
leadership schwach. a ~ chance of success
schlechte Erfolgsaussichten pl; he is a ~
traveller er verträgt Reisen nicht gut; it's a ~
thing for Britain if ... es steht schlecht um
Großbritannien, wenn ...; it's very ~ of them not
to have replied ist sehr unhöflich, daß sie uns
etc (dat) nicht geantwortet haben; she was ~
~ at languages sie war schlecht or schwach
in Sprachen. 2 npl the ~ die Armen pl.
poor box n Almosenbüchse f.
poorly ['pʊəlɪ] 1 adv (a) arm; dressed, furnished
ärmlich. ~ off schlecht gestellt, arm dran (col).
(b) (badly) schlecht. ~ lit/~ paid schlecht be-
leuchtet/bezahlt; to do ~ (at sth) (in etw dat)
schwach or schlecht abschneiden. 2 adj pred (ill)
krank, elend. to be ~ sich schlecht fühlen.
pop¹ [pɒp] n (esp US col) (father) Papa m (col);
(elderly man) Opa m (hum col).
pop² n (~ music) Popmusik f, Pop m.
pop³ 1 n (a) (sound) Knall m. (b) (fizzy drink)
Brause, Limo (col) f. 2 adv to go ~ (cork) knallen;
(balloon) platzen. 3 vt (a) balloon, corn zum
Platzen bringen. (b) (col: put) stecken. to ~ a
letter into the postbox einen Brief einwerfen; he
~ped his head around the door er streckte den
Kopf durch die Tür; to ~ the question einen
(Heirats)antrag machen. 4 vi (a) (col: go ~)
(cork) knallen; (balloon) platzen; (buttons,
popcorn) aufplatzen; (ears) knacken. his eyes
were ~ping out of his head ihm fielen fast die
Augen aus dem Kopf (col). (b) (col: go quickly or
suddenly) to ~ along/down to the baker's schnell
zum Bäcker gehen; I'll just ~ upstairs ich laufe
mal eben nach oben.

◆ **pop in** (col) vi schnell hereinkommen/
hereingehen; (visit) auf einen Sprung vorbeikommen (col).
◆ **pop off** vi (col) (a) (die) den Löffel abgeben (col).
(b) (go off) verschwinden (col) (to nach).
◆ **pop out** (col) vi (go out) (schnell) rausgehen

(col)/rauskommen *(col)*; *(spring, rabbit)* heraus-springen *(of aus)*. **he has just ~ped ~ to the shops** er ist schnell einkaufen gegangen.
♦ **pop up** *(col) vi (appear suddenly)* auftauchen; *(head, toast)* hochschießen *(col)*.
pop: ~ **art** *n* Pop-art *f*; **~corn** *n* Popcorn *nt*.
Pope [pəʊp] *n* Papst *m*.
pop: ~ **group** *n* Popgruppe *f*; ~ **gun** *n* Spielzeug-pistole *f*.
poplar ['pɒplə'] *n* Pappel *f*.
poplin ['pɒplɪn] *n* Popeline *f*.
pop music *n* Popmusik *f*.
popper ['pɒpə'] *n (Brit col: press-stud)* Druckknopf *m*.
poppet ['pɒpɪt] *n (col)* Schatz *m*.
poppy ['pɒpɪ] *n* Mohn *m*.
poppy: P~ Day *n (Brit)* ≃ Volkstrauertag *m (BRD)*; **~-seed** *n* Mohn *m*.
popsicle ® ['pɒpsɪkl] *n (US)* Eis *nt* am Stiel.
pop: ~ **singer** *n* Popsänger(in *f*) *m*; ~ **song** *m* Popsong *m*; *(hit)* Schlager *m*; ~ **star** *n* Popstar *m*.
populace ['pɒpjʊlɪs] *n* Bevölkerung *f*; *(masses)* breite Öffentlichkeit *f*.
popular ['pɒpjʊlə'] *adj* **(a)** beliebt *(with* bei*)*; *decision, measure* populär. **he was a very ~ choice** seine Wahl fand großen Anklang. **(b)** *(for the general public)* populär; *music* leicht; *prices* erschwinglich; *science* Populär-; *edition* Volks-; *lectures, journal* populärwissenschaftlich. **(c)** *(widespread) belief, fallacy* weitverbreitet; *(of or for the people) government, approval, support* des Volkes. **by ~ request** auf allgemeinen Wunsch.
popularity ['pɒpjʊ'lærɪtɪ] *n* Beliebtheit *f*; *(with the public also)* Popularität *f (with* bei*)*.
popularize ['pɒpjʊləraɪz] *vt* populär machen; *science* popularisieren.
popularly ['pɒpjʊləlɪ] *adv* allgemein. **he is ~ believed to be a rich man** nach allgemeiner Ansicht ist er ein reicher Mann.
populate ['pɒpjʊleɪt] *vt (inhabit)* bevölkern; *(colonize)* besiedeln. **this area is ~d mainly by immigrants** in diesem Gebiet leben hauptsächlich Einwanderer; **densely ~d cities** dichtbevölkerte Städte *pl*.
population [ˌpɒpjʊ'leɪʃən] *n (of region, country)* Bevölkerung *f*; *(of town)* Einwohner *pl*; *(number of inhabitants)* Bevölkerungszahl *f*. **the ~ explosion** die Bevölkerungsexplosion.
populous ['pɒpjʊləs] *adj* dicht besiedelt.
porage *n* = **porridge.**
porcelain ['pɔːsəlɪn] **1** *n* Porzellan *nt*. **2** *adj* Porzellan-.
porch [pɔːtʃ] *n (of house)* Vorbau *m*; *(US)* Veranda *f*; *(of church)* Portal *nt*.
porcupine ['pɔːkjʊpaɪn] *n* Stachelschwein *nt*.
pore [pɔː'] *n* Pore *f*.
♦ **pore over** *vi +prep obj (scrutinize)* genau studieren; *(meditate)* nachgrübeln über *(+acc)*. **to ~ one's books** über seinen Büchern hocken.
pork [pɔːk] *n* Schweinefleisch *nt*.
pork: ~ **chop** *n* Schweinekotelett *nt*; **~pie** *n* Schweinefleischpastete *f*.
porn [pɔːn], *(esp US)* **porno** ['pɔːnəʊ] *n (col)* Porno *m (col)*. **hard/soft ~** harter/weicher Porno.
pornographic [ˌpɔːnə'græfɪk] *adj* pornographisch.
pornography [pɔː'nɒgrəfɪ] *n* Pornographie *f*.
porous ['pɔːrəs] *adj* *rock, substance* porös.
porpoise ['pɔːpəs] *n* Tümmler *m*.
porridge ['pɒrɪdʒ] *n* Haferbrei *m*. ~ **oats** Haferflocken *pl*.
port[1] [pɔːt] *n* Hafen *m*; *(town also)* Hafenstadt *f*. **to come/put into ~** in den Hafen einlaufen; ~ **authority** Hafenbehörde *f*; **any ~ in a storm** *(prov)* in der Not frißt der Teufel Fliegen *(Prov)*.
port2 [pɔːt] *n (Naut, Aviat: left side)* Backbord *m*. **2** *adj* *side* Backbord-.
port3 *n (also ~ wine)* Portwein *m*.
portable ['pɔːtəbl] *adj* tragbar; *radio, typewriter*

also Koffer-. **easily ~** leicht zu tragen; **a ~ television** ein Portable *m or nt*, ein tragbarer Fernseher.
porter ['pɔːtə'] *n (of office etc)* Pförtner *m*; *(hospital ~)* Assistent *m*; *(at hotel)* Portier *m*; *(Rail, at airport)* Gepäckträger *m*.
portfolio [pɔːt'fəʊlɪəʊ] *n* (Akten)mappe *f*; *(Fin)* Portefeuille *nt*; *(of artist, designer)* Kollektion *f*. *(Pol)* **minister without ~** Minister ohne Geschäftsbereich.
porthole ['pɔːthəʊl] *n* Bullauge *nt*.
portion ['pɔːʃən] *n (piece, part)* Teil *m*; *(of ticket)* Abschnitt *m*; *(of food)* Portion *f*.
portly ['pɔːtlɪ] *adj (+er)* beleibt, korpulent.
portrait ['pɔːtrɪt] *n* Porträt *nt*. **to have one's ~ painted** sich malen lassen.
portrait painter *n* Porträtmaler(in *f*) *m*.
portray [pɔː'treɪ] *vt* darstellen; *(paint also)* malen.
Portugal ['pɔːtjʊgəl] *n* Portugal *nt*.
Portuguese [ˌpɔːtjʊ'giːz] **1** *adj* portugiesisch. ~ **man-of-war** Staatsqualle *f*. **2** *n* **(a)** Portugiese *m*, Portugiesin *f*. **(b)** *(language)* Portugiesisch *nt*.
pose [pəʊz] **1** *n (position, attitude)* Haltung *f*; *(of model, pej also)* Pose *f*. **to strike a ~** sich in Positur werfen. **2** *vt question, problem* vortragen. **3** *vi (model)* posieren; *(sitting also)* Modell sitzen; *(standing also)* Modell stehen.
poser ['pəʊzə'] *n* **(a)** *(col: person)* Angeber *m*. **(b)** *(problem)* harte Nuß *(col)*.
posh [pɒʃ] *(col)* **1** *adj (+er)* piekfein *(col)*, vornehm; *neighbourhood, hotel also* nobel. **2** *adv (+er):* **to talk ~** mit vornehmem Akzent sprechen.
position [pə'zɪʃən] **1** *n* **(a)** *(location) (of person)* Platz *m*; *(of object also)* Stelle *f*; *(of microphone, statue, wardrobe etc)* Standort *m*; *(of spotlight, table)* Anordnung *f*; *(of town, house etc)* Lage *f*; *(of plane, ship, Sport)* Position *f*; *(Mil)* Stellung *f*. **to be in/out of ~** an der richtigen/falschen Stelle sein; **what ~ do you play?** auf *or* in welcher Position spielst du?; **to finish in third ~** Dritter werden.
(b) *(posture)* Haltung *f*; *(in love-making)* Stellung *f*. **in a reclining ~** zurückgelehnt.
(c) *(social standing)* Stellung, Position *f*; *(job)* Stelle *f*. **a man of ~** eine hochgestellte Persönlichkeit; **he has a high ~ in the Ministry** er bekleidet eine hohe Stellung im Ministerium; **a ~ of trust** eine Vertrauensstellung.
(d) *(fig: situation, circumstance)* Lage *f*. **to be in a ~ to do sth** in der Lage sein, etw zu tun; **what is the ~ regarding ...?** wie sieht es mit ... aus?
(e) *(fig: point of view, attitude)* Standpunkt *m*, Haltung *f*. **to take up a ~ on sth** eine Haltung bei einer Sache einnehmen.
2 *vt ladder, guards* aufstellen; *soldiers, policemen* postieren. **he ~ed himself where he could see** er stellte *or* plazierte sich so, daß er sie sehen konnte.
positive ['pɒzɪtɪv] *adj* **(a)** *(Math, Phot, Elec)* positiv; *pole* Plus-. **(b)** *(affirmative, constructive)* positiv; *criticism, suggestion* konstruktiv. **(c)** *person, tone of voice* bestimmt; *instructions* streng; *evidence, answer* eindeutig; *rule* fest. **that is ~ proof** das ist der sichere Beweis; **to be ~ that ...** sicher sein, daß ...; **this is a ~ miracle/disgrace** das ist wirklich ein Wunder/eine Schande.
positively ['pɒzɪtɪvlɪ] *adv* **(a)** positiv. **(b)** *(de-cisively)* bestimmt; *(definitely) prove* eindeutig. **(c)** *(really, absolutely)* wirklich, echt *(col)*.
posse ['pɒsɪ] *n (US: sheriff's ~)* Aufgebot *nt*; *(fig)* Gruppe, Schar *f*.
possess [pə'zes] *vt* besitzen. **to be ~ed by an idea** von einer Idee besessen sein; **to fight like one ~ed** wie ein Besessener kämpfen; **whatever ~ed you to do that?** was ist bloß in Sie gefahren, so etwas zu tun?
possession [pə'zeʃən] *n* **(a)** *(ownership)* Besitz *m*;

(Sport: of ball) Ballbesitz *m.* **to have sth in one's ~** etw in seinem Besitz haben; **to have/take ~ of** sth etw in Besitz haben/nehmen; **to come into ~ of sth** in den Besitz von etw gelangen; **to get/ have ~ of the ball** in Ballbesitz gelangen/sein; **to be in ~ of sth** im Besitz von etw sein. **(b)** *(thing possessed)* Besitz *m no pl*; *(territory)* Besitzung *f.*

possessive [pə'zesɪv] *adj* **(a) to be ~ about sth** seine Besitzansprüche auf etw *(acc)* betonen; **to be ~ towards sb** an jdn Besitzansprüche stellen. **(b)** *(Gram)* **~ pronoun/adjective** Possessivpronomen *nt.*

possessor [pə'zesər] *n* Besitzer(in *f*) *m.* **to be the proud ~ of sth** der stolze Besitzer von etw sein.

possibility [ˌpɒsə'bɪlɪtɪ] *n* Möglichkeit *f.* **there's not much ~ of success/of his or him being successful** die Aussichten auf Erfolg/darauf, daß er Erfolg hat, sind nicht sehr groß; **within the bounds of ~** im Bereich des Möglichen; **the ~ of doing sth** die Möglichkeit, etw zu tun; **it's a distinct ~ that ...** es besteht eindeutig die Möglichkeit, daß ...; **he is a ~ for the job** er kommt für die Stelle in Betracht; **there is some or a ~ that ...** es besteht die Möglichkeit, daß ...; **a job with real possibilities** eine Stelle mit echten Möglichkeiten.

possible ['pɒsəbl] **1** *adj* möglich. **to make sth ~** etw möglich machen; **as soon/often as ~** so bald/ oft wie möglich; **the best/worst ~ ...** der/die/das bestmögliche/schlechtestmögliche ...; **if (at all) ~** falls (irgend) möglich; **it's just ~ that I'll see you before then** eventuell sehe ich dich vorher noch; **it will be ~ for you to return the same day** Sie haben die Möglichkeit, am selben Tag zurückzukommen. **2** *n* **a long list of ~s for the job** eine lange Liste möglicher Kandidaten für die Stelle.

possibly ['pɒsəblɪ] *adv* **(a)** **that can't ~ be true** das kann unmöglich wahr sein; **how could he ~ have known that?** wie konnte er das nur wissen?; **he did all he ~ could** er tat, was er nur konnte; **if I ~ can** wenn ich irgend kann. **(b)** *(perhaps)* vielleicht, möglicherweise.

post[1] [pəʊst] **1** *n* *(pole, door ~ etc)* Pfosten *m*; *(lamp~)* Pfahl *m*; *(telegraph ~)* Mast *m.* **starting/ winning or finishing ~** Start-/Zielpfosten *m*; **he was left at the ~** sie ließen ihn stehen. **2** *vt* **(a)** *(display: also ~ up)* anschlagen. **(b)** *(announce)* concert etc durch Anschlag bekanntmachen. **to ~ (as) missing** als vermißt melden.

post[2] **1** *n* **(a)** *(job)* Stelle *f*, Posten *m.* **to look for/ take up a ~** eine Stelle suchen/antreten. **(b)** *(Mil)* Posten *m.* **at one's ~** auf seinem Posten; **a frontier ~** ein Grenzposten *m*; **last ~** *(bugle call)* Zapfenstreich *m.* **2** *vt* **(a)** *(position)* postieren. **(b)** *(send, assign)* versetzen.

post[3] **1** *n* *(esp Brit: mail)* Post *f.* **by ~** mit der Post; **it's in the ~** es ist unterwegs; **to put sth in the ~** etw aufgeben; **to catch/miss the ~** *(letter)* noch/ nicht mehr mit der Post mitkommen; *(person)* rechtzeitig zur Leerung kommen/die Leerung verpassen; **has the ~ been?** war die Post schon da? **2** *vt* **(a)** *(put in the ~)* aufgeben; *(in letter-box)* einwerfen, einstecken; *(send by ~ also)* mit der Post schicken. **I ~ed it to you on Monday** ich habe es am Montag an Sie abgeschickt. **(b)** *(inform)* **to keep sb ~ed** jdn auf dem laufenden halten.

post- [pəʊst-] *pref* nach-.

postage ['pəʊstɪdʒ] *n* Porto *nt.* **~ and packing** *(abbr* **p & p***)* Porto und Verpackung.

postage stamp *n* Briefmarke *f.*

postal order *n (Brit)* Geldgutschein, der bei der Post gekauft und eingelöst wird.

post: **~-bag** *n (Brit)* Postsack *m*; **~box** *n (Brit)* Briefkasten *m*; **~-card** *n* Postkarte *f*; **(picture)** **~card** *n* Ansichtskarte *f*; **~ code** *n (Brit)* Postleitzahl *f*; **~-date** *vt cheque* vordatieren.

poster ['pəʊstər] *n (advertising)* Plakat *nt*; *(for decoration also)* Poster *nt.*

poste restante ['pəʊst'restɑ̃ːnt] *(Brit)* **1** *n* Aufbewahrungsstelle *f* für postlagernde Sendungen. **2** *adv* postlagernd.

posterior [pɒ'stɪərɪər] *n (hum)* Allerwerteste(r) *m (hum).*

posterity [pɒ'sterɪtɪ] *n* die Nachwelt.

post: **~-free** *adj, adv* portofrei; **~graduate** *n jd*, der seine Studien nach dem ersten akademischen Grad weiterführt; **~haste** *adv* schnellstens.

posthumous ['pɒstjʊməs] *adj* post(h)um.

post: **~man** *n* Briefträger *m*; **~mark 1** *n* Poststempel *m*; 2 *vt* (ab)stempeln; **the letter is ~marked "Birmingham"** der Brief ist in Birmingham abgestempelt; **~master** *n* Postmeister *m*; **~master general** *n* ≃ Postminister *m*; **~mistress** *n* Postmeisterin *f*; **~mortem** [ˌpəʊst'mɔːtəm] *n* Obduktion, Leichenöffnung *f*; *(fig)* nachträgliche Erörterung; **to hold** *or* **have a ~mortem on sth** etw hinterher erörtern; **~-natal** *adj* nach der Geburt, postnatal *(spec)*; **~ office** *n* Postamt *nt*; **the P~ Office** *(institution)* die Post; **~ office box** *(abbr* **PO Box***)* Postfach *nt*; **~-paid** *adj* portofrei; *envelope* frankiert.

postpone [pəʊst'pəʊn] *vt* aufschieben; *(for specified period)* verschieben. **it has been ~d till Tuesday** es ist auf Dienstag verschoben worden.

postponement [pəʊst'pəʊnmənt] *n (act)* Verschiebung *f*; *(result)* Aufschub *m.*

postscript ['pəʊs,skrɪpt] *n (abbr* **PS:** *to letter)* Postskriptum *nt*; *(to book, article etc)* Nachwort *nt*; *(fig: to affair)* Nachspiel *nt.*

postulate ['pɒstjʊlɪt] **1** *n* Postulat *nt.* 2 ['pɒstʊleɪt] *vt* postulieren; *theory* aufstellen.

posture ['pɒstʃər] **1** *n (lit, fig)* Haltung *f*; *(pej)* Pose *f.* 2 *vi* sich in Positur werfen.

postwar ['pəʊst'wɔːr] *adj* Nachkriegs-. **~ London** das London der Nachkriegszeit.

posy ['pəʊzɪ] *n* Sträußchen *nt.*

pot [pɒt] **1** *n* **(a)** Topf *m*; *(tea~, coffee-~)* Kanne *f.* **~s and pans** Kochgeschirr *nt*; **to go to ~** *(col: person, business)* auf den Hund kommen *(col)*; **to have ~s of money** *(col)* jede Menge Geld haben *(col).* **(b)** *(col: marijuana)* Gras *nt (col).* **2** *vt meat* einmachen; *jam* einfüllen; *plant* eintopfen; *(shoot)* game schießen; *(Billiards)* ball einlochen.

potash ['pɒtæʃ] *n* Kali *nt.*

potassium [pə'tæsɪəm] *n* Kalium *nt.*

potato [pə'teɪtəʊ] *n, pl* **-es** Kartoffel *f.* **~ chip** *(US)* or **crisp** *(Brit)* *n* Kartoffelchip *m.*

potbellied ['pɒt'belɪd] *adj person* spitzbäuchig; *(through hunger)* blähbäuchig.

potency ['pəʊtənsɪ] *n see adj* Stärke *f*; Durchschlagskraft *f*; Potenz *f*; Macht *f.*

potent ['pəʊtənt] *adj drink, motive etc* stark; *argument etc* durchschlagend; *man* potent; *ruler* mächtig.

potentate ['pəʊtənteɪt] *n* Potentat *m.*

potential [pəʊ'tentʃəl] **1** *adj* potentiell. **2** *n* Potential *nt.* **the ~ for growth** das Wachstumspotential; **to have ~** ausbaufähig sein *(col)*; **he shows quite a bit of ~** es steckt einiges in ihm.

potentially [pəʊ'tentʃəlɪ] *adv* potentiell.

pot: **~hole** *n* **(a)** *(in road)* Schlagloch *nt*; **(b)** *(Geol)* Höhle *f*; **~holer** *n* Höhlenforscher(in *f*) *m*; **~holing** *n* Höhlenforschung *f.*

potion ['pəʊʃən] *n* Trank *m.*

pot: **~luck** *n:* **to take ~luck** nehmen, was es gerade gibt; **we took ~luck and went to the nearest pub** wir gingen aufs Geratewohl in die nächste Kneipe; **~pourri** [ˌpəʊpʊ'riː] *n* **(a)** *(lit)* Duftsträußchen *nt*; **(b)** *(fig: mixture, medley)* bunte Mischung; *(of music)* Potpourri *nt*; **~ roast** *n* Schmorbraten *m*; **~shot** *n* **to take a ~shot at sth** aufs Geratewohl auf etw *(acc)* schießen.

potted ['pɒtɪd] *adj meat* eingemacht; *fish* eingelegt; *plant* Topf-. **(b)** *(shortened) history* gekürzt.

potter[1] [pɒtəʳ] n Töpfer(in f) m. ~'s wheel Töpferscheibe f.

potter[2] vi (do little jobs) herumwerkeln; (wander aimlessly) herumschlendern. she ~s away in the kitchen for hours sie hantiert stundenlang in der Küche herum; to ~ around the house im Haus herumwerkeln.

pottery ['pɒtərɪ] n (workshop, craft) Töpferei f; (pots) Töpferwaren pl; (glazed) Keramik f; (archaeological remains) Tonscherbe f.

potty[1] ['pɒtɪ] n (esp Brit) Töpfchen nt. ~-trained sauber.

potty[2] adj (+er) (Brit col: mad) verrückt.

pouch [paʊtʃ] n Beutel m; (under eyes) (Tränen)sack m; (of hamster) Tasche f; (Mil) (Patronen)tasche f.

pouf(fe) [puːf] n (a) (seat) Puff m. (b) (Brit col) = poof.

poulterer ['pəʊltərəʳ] n (Brit) Geflügelhändler(in f) m.

poultice ['pəʊltɪs] n Umschlag, Wickel m; (for boil) Zugpflaster nt.

poultry ['pəʊltrɪ] n Geflügel nt. ~ farm Geflügelfarm f; ~ farmer Geflügelzüchter m.

pounce [paʊns] 1 n Sprung, Satz m; (swoop by bird) Angriff m. 2 vi (cat, lion etc) einen Satz machen; (bird) niederstoßen; (fig) zuschlagen. to ~ on sb/sth (lit,fig) sich auf jdn/etw stürzen; (bird) auf etw (acc) niederstoßen; (police) sich (dat) jdn greifen/in etw (dat) eine Razzia machen.

pound[1] [paʊnd] n (a) (weight) ≈ Pfund nt. two ~s of apples zwei Pfund Äpfel; by the ~ pfundweise. (b) (money) Pfund nt. one ~ sterling ein Pfund Sterling; five ~s fünf Pfund; a five-~ note ein Fünfpfundschein m.

pound[2] 1 vt (hammer, strike) hämmern; earth feststampfen; meat klopfen; dough kneten; corn etc (zer)stampfen; piano hämmern auf (+dat); table hämmern auf (+acc); door, wall hämmern gegen; (waves) ship schlagen gegen; (guns, bombs) ununterbrochen beschießen; (artillery) unter Beschuß haben. to ~ sth to pieces etw kleinstampfen; (sea) ship etw zertrümmern; to ~ sth to a pulp etw zu Brei stampfen. 2 vi (a) (beat) hämmern; (heart) (wild) pochen; (waves, sea) schlagen (on, against gegen); (hooves) stampfen. he ~ed on the door/on the table er hämmerte gegen die Tür/auf den Tisch. (b) (run heavily) stampfen; (walk heavily, stamp) stapfen.

pound[3] n (for stray dogs) städtischer Hundezwinger; (for cars) Abstellplatz m (für amtlich abgeschleppte Fahrzeuge).

pounding ['paʊndɪŋ] n Hämmern nt; (of heart) Pochen nt; (of music, drums) Dröhnen nt; (of waves, sea) Schlagen nt; (of hooves, feet etc) Stampfen nt; (of guns, bombs) Bombardement nt. to take a ~ (ship in storm) stark mitgenommen werden; (town in war) schwer bombardiert werden; (theory) scharf angegriffen werden.

pour [pɔːʳ] 1 vt liquid gießen; sugar, rice etc schütten; drink einschenken. can I ~ you another drink? kann ich Ihnen nachschenken?; to ~ money into a project Geld in ein Projekt pumpen (col). 2 vi (a) (fig) strömen; (smoke also) hervorquellen. the sweat was ~ing off him der Schweiß floß in Strömen an ihm herunter; cars ~ed along the road Autokolonnen rollten die Straße entlang. (b) it's ~ing (with rain) es gießt (in Strömen), es schüttet (col).
♦ **pour away** vt sep weggießen.
♦ **pour in** vi hinein-/hereinströmen; (donations, protests) in Strömen eintreffen.
♦ **pour out** 1 vi hinaus-/herausströmen (of aus); (smoke also) hervorquellen (of aus); (words) herausprudeln (of aus). 2 vt sep liquid ausgießen; sugar etc ausschütten; drink einschenken; (fig) troubles sich (dat) von der Seele reden. to ~ ~

one's heart to sb jdm sein Herz ausschütten.

pouring ['pɔːrɪŋ] adj ~ rain strömender Regen; a ~ wet day ein völlig verregneter Tag.

pout [paʊt] 1 n (facial expression) Schmollmund m. 2 vi (with lips) einen Schmollmund machen; (sulk) schmollen.

poverty ['pɒvətɪ] n Armut f. ~-stricken notleidend; conditions kümmerlich; to be ~-stricken Armut leiden; (hum col) am Hungertuch nagen (hum).

powder ['paʊdəʳ] 1 n Pulver nt; (face, talcum ~ etc) Puder m; (dust) Staub m. 2 vt (a) milk pulverisieren. ~ed milk Milchpulver nt. to ~ one's nose (lit) sich (dat) die Nase pudern; (euph) kurz verschwinden (euph).
powder: ~ compact n Puderdose f; ~ puff n Puderquaste f; ~ room n Damentoilette f.

powdery ['paʊdərɪ] adj (like powder) pulvrig; (crumbly) bröckelig; bones morsch; (covered with powder) gepudert.

power ['paʊəʳ] 1 n (a) no pl (physical strength) Kraft f; (force: of blow, explosion etc) Stärke, Wucht f; (fig: of argument etc) Überzeugungskraft f. the ~ of love/tradition die Macht der Liebe/Tradition.
(b) her ~s of persuasion ihre Überredungskünste pl; his ~s of hearing sein Hörvermögen nt; mental ~s geistige Kräfte pl.
(c) (capacity, authority) Macht f; (Jur, parental) Gewalt f; (usu pl: authority) Befugnis f. he did all in his ~ to help them er tat (alles), was in seiner Macht stand, um ihnen zu helfen; to be in sb's ~ in jds Gewalt (dat) sein; that is beyond or outside my ~(s) das überschreitet meine Befugnisse; ~ of attorney (Jur) (Handlungs)vollmacht f; the party now in ~ die Partei, die im Augenblick an der Macht ist; to come to ~ an die Macht kommen; he has been given full ~(s) to make all decisions man hat ihm volle Entscheidungsgewalt übertragen.
(d) (person or institution having authority) Autorität f. to be the ~ behind the throne die graue Eminenz sein; the ~s that be (col) die da oben (col); the ~s of darkness die Mächte der Finsternis.
(e) (nation) Macht f. a naval ~ eine Seemacht.
(f) (nuclear ~ etc) Energie f; (of water, steam also) Kraft f; (of engine, transmitter) Leistung f; (of lens, drug) Stärke f. they cut off the ~ (electricity) sie haben den Strom abgestellt.
(g) (Math) Potenz f. to the ~ (of) 2 hoch 2.
(h) (col: a lot of) that did me a ~ of good das hat mir unheimlich gut getan (col).
2 vt (engine) antreiben; (fuel) betreiben.
power: ~boat n Rennboot nt; ~ cut n (Brit) Stromsperre f; (accidental) Stromausfall m; ~-driven adj (von) Motor-; ~ failure n = ~ cut.

powerful ['paʊəfʊl] adj government etc mächtig; boxer, engine, drug, emotions stark; punch, detergent kraftvoll; build kräftig; (fig) actor, music, film mitreißend; argument durchschlagend.

powerfully ['paʊəfəlɪ] adv kraftvoll. ~ built kräftig gebaut.

powerhouse ['paʊəhaʊs] n (fig) treibende Kraft (behind hinter +dat, of gen).
power: ~less adj committee, person machtlos; to be ~less to resist nicht die Kraft haben, zu widerstehen; the government is ~less to deal with inflation die Regierung steht der Inflation machtlos gegenüber; ~ point n (Brit Elec) Steckdose f; ~ station n Kraftwerk nt; ~ steering n (Aut) Servolenkung f.

pp = (a) pages S. (b) on behalf of.

PR = proportional representation; public relations.

practicable ['præktɪkəbl] adj durchführbar, praktikabel; road befahrbar.

practical ['præktɪkəl] adj praktisch; person praktisch (veranlagt). **to have a** ~ **mind** praktisch denken.

practicality [‚præktɪ'kælɪtɪ] n (of person) praktische Veranlagung; (of scheme) Durchführbarkeit f; (practical detail) praktische Einzelheit.

practical: ~ **joke** n Streich m; ~ **joker** n Witzbold m (col).

practically ['præktɪkəlɪ] adv (all senses) praktisch.

practice ['præktɪs] **1** n **(a)** (habit, custom) (of individual) Gewohnheit f; (of group, in country) Brauch m; (in business) Verfahrensweise f. **as is my (usual)** ~ wie es meine Gewohnheit ist; **that's common** ~ das ist allgemein üblich. **(b)** (exercise, training) Übung f; (rehearsal, trial run) Probe f; (Sport) Training nt. ~ **makes perfect** (Prov) Übung macht den Meister (Prov); **to be out of/in** ~ aus der/in Übung sein; **that was just a** ~ **run** das war nur mal zur Probe. **(c)** (as opposed to theory) Praxis f. **in** ~ in der Praxis; **that won't work in** ~ das läßt sich praktisch nicht durchführen; **to put one's ideas into** ~ seine Ideen in die Praxis umsetzen. **(d)** (of doctor etc) Praxis f. **to set up in** ~ eine Praxis eröffnen.
2 vti (US) = **practise**.

practise, (US) **practice** ['præktɪs] **1** vt **(a)** thrift, patience etc üben; self-denial praktizieren. **to** ~ **what one preaches** (prov) seine Lehren in die Tat umsetzen. **(b)** (in order to acquire skill) üben; song, chorus proben. **to** ~ **the violin** Geige üben; **to** ~ **doing sth** etw üben; **I'm practising my German on** him ich probiere mein Deutsch an ihm aus. **(c)** (follow, exercise) profession, religion ausüben, praktizieren. **to** ~ **law/medicine** als Anwalt/Arzt praktizieren. **2** vi **(a)** (in order to acquire skill) üben. **(b)** (lawyer, doctor etc) praktizieren.

practised, (US) **practiced** ['præktɪst] adj geübt. **with a** ~ **eye** mit geübtem Auge.

practising, (US) **practicing** ['præktɪsɪŋ] adj doctor, Christian, homosexual praktizierend; socialist aktiv.

practitioner [præk'tɪʃənər] n (of method) Benutzer m; (medical ~) praktischer Arzt, praktische Ärztin; (dental ~) Zahnarzt m/-ärztin f; (legal ~) Rechtsanwalt m/-anwältin f.

pragmatic [præg'mætɪk] adj pragmatisch.

prairie ['prɛərɪ] n Grassteppe f; (in North America) Prärie f.

praise [preɪz] **1** vt loben; (to others, worshipfully also) rühmen (geh). **to** ~ **sb for having done sth** jdn dafür loben, etw getan zu haben. **2** n Lob nt no pl. **a hymn of** ~ eine Lobeshymne; **he spoke in** ~ **of their efforts** er sprach lobend von ihren Bemühungen; **I have nothing but** ~ **for him** ich kann ihn nur loben; ~ **be to God!** gelobt sei der Herr!

praiseworthy ['preɪzˌwɜːðɪ] adj lobenswert.

pram [præm] n (Brit) Kinderwagen m.

prance [prɑːns] vi (horse) tänzeln; (person) (jump around) herumhüpfen; (walk gaily, mince) tänzeln. **to** ~ **in/out** (person) herein-/hinausspazieren.

prank [præŋk] n Streich m. **to play a** ~ **on sb** jdm einen Streich spielen.

prattle ['prætl] **1** n Geplapper nt. **2** vi plappern.

prawn [prɔːn] n Garnele f. ~ **cocktail** Krabbencocktail m.

pray [preɪ] vi (say prayers) beten. **let us** ~ lasset uns beten; **to** ~ **for sb/sth** für jdn/um etw beten.

prayer [prɛər] n Gebet nt; (service, ~ meeting) Andacht f. **to say one's** ~**s** beten.

prayer: ~ **book** n Gebetbuch nt; ~ **mat** n Gebetsteppich m.

pre- [priː-] pref vor-; (esp with Latinate words in German) prä-. **at** ~**1980 prices** zu Preisen von vor 1980.

preach [priːtʃ] **1** vt predigen; (fig) advantages etc propagieren. **to** ~ **a sermon** (lit, fig) eine Predigt

halten. **2** vi (lit, fig) predigen. **to** ~ **to/at sb** jdm eine Predigt halten; **to** ~ **to the converted** (prov) offene Türen einrennen.

preacher ['priːtʃər] n Prediger m; (fig: moraliser) Moralprediger(in f) m.

preamble [priː'æmbl] n Einleitung f; (of book) Vorwort nt; (Jur) Präambel f.

prearrange [priːə'reɪndʒ] vt vorher vereinbaren.

precarious [prɪ'kɛərɪəs] adj unsicher; situation also, relationship prekär; theory anfechtbar.

precariously [prɪ'kɛərɪəslɪ] adv **to be** ~ **balanced** (lit, fig) auf der Kippe stehen; **he lived rather** ~ er lebte in ziemlich ungesicherten finanziellen Verhältnissen.

precaution [prɪ'kɔːʃən] n Vorsichtsmaßnahme f. **to take** ~**s against sth** Vorsichtsmaßnahmen gegen etw treffen; **to take the** ~ **of doing sth** vorsichtshalber etw tun; **to take** ~**s** (use contraceptives) ein Verhütungsmittel nt gebrauchen.

precautionary [prɪ'kɔːʃənərɪ] adj Vorsichts-, vorbeugend.

precede [prɪ'siːd] vt (in order, time) vorangehen (+dat); (in importance) gehen vor (+dat); (in rank) stehen über (+dat).

precedence ['presɪdəns] n (of person) vorrangige Stellung (over gegenüber); (of problem etc) Vorrang m (over vor +dat). **to take** ~ **over sb/sth** vor jdm/etw Vorrang haben.

precedent ['presɪdənt] n Präzedenzfall m. **without** ~ noch nie dagewesen; **to set a** ~ einen Präzedenzfall schaffen.

preceding [prɪ'siːdɪŋ] adj vorhergehend.

precept ['priːsept] n Grundsatz m, Prinzip nt.

precinct ['priːsɪŋkt] n (pedestrian ~) Fußgängerzone f; (shopping ~) Geschäftsviertel nt; (US: police ~) Revier nt. ~**s** pl (grounds, premises) Gelände nt; (environs) Umgebung f.

precious ['preʃəs] **1** adj (costly) wertvoll, kostbar; (treasured) wertvoll; (iro) heißgeliebt. ~ **stone/metal** Edelstein m/Edelmetall nt. **2** adv (col) ~ **little/few** herzlich wenig/wenige (col).

precipice ['presɪpɪs] n (lit, fig) Abgrund m.

precipitate [prə'sɪpɪtɪt] **1** adj (overhasty) übereilt, überstürzt. **2** [prə'sɪpɪteɪt] vt **(a)** (hurl) schleudern; (downwards) hinunterschleudern; (fig) stürzen. **(b)** (hasten) beschleunigen. **(c)** (Chem) (aus)fällen; (Met) niederschlagen.

precipitous [prɪ'sɪpɪtəs] adj steil; (hasty) überstürzt.

précis ['preɪsiː] n Zusammenfassung f; (Sch) Inhaltsangabe f.

precise [prɪ'saɪs] adj genau; answer, description etc, worker also präzis. **at that** ~ **moment** genau in dem Augenblick; **this was the** ~ **amount I needed** das war genau der Betrag, den ich brauchte; **please be more** ~ drücken Sie sich bitte etwas genauer aus; **or, to be more** ~ ... oder, um es genauer zu sagen, ...

precisely [prɪ'saɪslɪ] adv genau; answer, describe, work also präzis. **at** ~ **7 o'clock**, **at 7 o'clock** ~ genau um 7 Uhr; **what** ~ **do you mean?** was meinen Sie eigentlich genau?

precision [prɪ'sɪʒən] n Genauigkeit f; (of work, movement also) Präzision f.

precision instrument n Präzisionsinstrument nt.

preclude [prɪ'kluːd] vt possibility ausschließen. **to** ~ **sb from doing sth** jdn daran hindern, etw zu tun.

precocious [prɪ'kəʊʃəs] adj teenager, behaviour frühreif; statement, way of speaking altklug.

precociousness [prɪ'kəʊʃəsnɪs], **precocity** [prɪ'kɒsɪtɪ] n see adj Frühreife f; Altklugheit f.

preconceived [‚priːkən'siːvd] adj opinion, idea vorgefaßt.

preconception [‚priːkən'sepʃən] n vorgefaßte Meinung.

precondition [,pri:kən'dɪʃən] n (Vor)bedingung f.
precursor [pri:'kɜːsəʳ] n Vorläufer m; (in office) (Amts)vorgänger(in f) m.
predate [,pri:'deɪt] vt (precede) zeitlich vorangehen (+dat); cheque, letter zurückdatieren.
predator ['predətəʳ] n (animal) Raubtier nt; (person) Plünderer m.
predecessor ['pri:dɪsesəʳ] n (person) Vorgänger(in f) m; (thing) Vorläufer m. **our ~s** (ancestors) unsere Vorfahren pl.
predestination [pri:,destɪ'neɪʃən] n Vorherbestimmung f.
predestine [pri:'destɪn] vt vorherbestimmen; person prädestinieren.
predetermine [,pri:dɪ'tɜːmɪn] vt events, sb's future etc vorherbestimmen; price, date etc im voraus festlegen.
predicament [prɪ'dɪkəmənt] n Zwangslage f, Dilemma nt. **to be in a ~** in einer Zwangslage sein.
predicate ['predɪkɪt] n (Gram) Prädikat nt.
predict [prɪ'dɪkt] vt vorhersagen.
predictable [prɪ'dɪktəbl] adj vorhersagbar. **you are so ~** man weiß doch genau, wie Sie reagieren.
predictably [prɪ'dɪktəblɪ] adv ~, he was late wie vorauszusehen, kam er zu spät.
prediction [prɪ'dɪkʃən] n Voraussage f.
predilection [,pri:dɪ'lekʃən] n Vorliebe f (for für).
predispose [,pri:dɪ'spəʊz] vt geneigt machen. **to ~ sb in favour of sb/sth** jdn für jdn/etw einnehmen; **I'm not ~d to help him** ich bin nicht geneigt, ihm zu helfen.
predominance [prɪ'dɒmɪnəns] n (control) Vorherrschaft f; (prevalence) Überwiegen nt.
predominant [prɪ'dɒmɪnənt] adj (most prevalent) idea, theory vorherrschend; (dominating) person, animal beherrschend.
predominantly [prɪ'dɒmɪnəntlɪ] adv überwiegend.
predominate [prɪ'dɒmɪneɪt] vi (a) vorherrschen. **(b)** (in influence etc) überwiegen. **Good will always ~ over Evil** das Gute wird immer über das Böse siegen.
pre-eminent [pri:'emɪnənt] adj herausragend.
pre-eminently [pri:'emɪnəntlɪ] adv hauptsächlich, vor allem; (excellently) hervorragend.
preen [pri:n] **1** vt feathers putzen. **2** vt to ~ oneself (bird) sich putzen; (person: dress up) sich herausputzen, sich aufputzen.
prefab ['pri:fæb] n Fertighaus nt.
prefabricated [,pri:'fæbrɪkeɪtɪd] adj vorgefertigt, Fertig-; building Fertig-.
preface ['prefɪs] n **1** Vorwort nt. **2** vt remarks einleiten.
prefect ['pri:fekt] n Präfekt m; (Brit Sch) Aufsichtsschüler(in f) m. **form ~** (Sch) ≈ Klassensprecher(in f) m.
prefer [prɪ'fɜːʳ] vt **(a)** (like better) vorziehen (to dat), lieber mögen (to als); drink, food, music also lieber trinken/essen/hören (to als); applicant, solution vorziehen, bevorzugen; (be more fond of) person lieber haben (to als). **he ~s coffee to tea** er trinkt lieber Kaffee als Tee; **I'd ~ something less ornate** ich hätte lieber etwas Schlichteres; **I ~ to resign rather than ...** eher kündige ich, als daß ...; **I ~ walking/flying** ich gehe lieber zu Fuß/fliege lieber; **I ~ not to say** ich sage es lieber nicht; **I would ~ you to do it today** mir wäre es lieber, wenn Sie es heute täten. **(b)** (Jur) **to ~ a charge/charges (against sb)** Klage (gegen jdn) erheben.
preferable ['prefərəbl] adj X is ~ to Y X ist Y (dat) vorzuziehen; **it would be ~ to do it that way** es wäre besser, es so zu machen.
preferably ['prefərəblɪ] adv am liebsten. **tea or coffee? — coffee, ~** Tee oder Kaffee? — lieber

Kaffee; **but ~ not Tuesday** aber, wenn möglich, nicht Dienstag.
preference ['prefərəns] n (greater liking) Vorliebe f; (greater favour) Vorzug m. **for ~** lieber; **to have a ~ for sth** eine Vorliebe für etw haben, etw bevorzugen; **I drink coffee in ~ to tea** ich trinke lieber Kaffee als Tee; **what is your ~?** was wäre Ihnen am liebsten?; **I have no ~** mir ist das eigentlich gleich; **to show ~ to sb** jdn bevorzugen; **to give ~ to sb/sth** jdm/etw den Vorzug geben (over gegenüber); **~ shares or stock** (Brit Fin) Vorzugsaktien pl.
preferential [prefə'renʃəl] adj treatment Vorzugs-; terms Sonder-. **to give sb ~ treatment** jdn bevorzugt behandeln.
prefix ['pri:fɪks] n (Gram) Vorsilbe f, Präfix nt.
pregnancy ['pregnənsɪ] n Schwangerschaft f; (of animal) Trächtigkeit f. **~ test** Schwangerschaftstest m.
pregnant ['pregnənt] adj **(a)** woman schwanger; animal trächtig, tragend. **3 months ~** im dritten Monat (schwanger). **(b)** (fig) remark, silence, pause bedeutungsschwer. **~ with meaning** bedeutungsgeladen.
prehistoric [,pri:hɪ'stɒrɪk] adj prähistorisch, vorgeschichtlich.
prehistory [,pri:'hɪstərɪ] n Vorgeschichte f.
prejudge [pri:'dʒʌdʒ] vt case, issue im vorhinein beurteilen; person im voraus verurteilen.
prejudice ['predʒʊdɪs] **1** n **(a)** (biased opinion) Vorurteil nt. **his ~ against ...** seine Voreingenommenheit gegen ...; **that's pure ~** das ist reine Voreingenommenheit; **racial ~** Rassenvorurteile pl. **(b)** (esp Jur: detriment, injury) Schaden m. **to the ~ of sb/sth** (form) zu jds Schaden/unter Beeinträchtigung +gen; **without ~** (Jur) ohne Verbindlichkeit. **2** vt **(a)** (bias) beeinflussen. **(b)** (injure) case etc gefährden; chances also beeinträchtigen.
prejudiced ['predʒʊdɪst] adj person voreingenommen (against gegen); opinion vorgefaßt; judge befangen.
prejudicial [,predʒʊ'dɪʃəl] adj abträglich (to sth einer Sache dat). **to be ~ to sb's chances** jds Chancen gefährden.
prelate ['prelɪt] n Prälat m.
prelim ['pri:,lɪm] n (exam) Vorprüfung f.
preliminary [prɪ'lɪmɪnərɪ] **1** adj talks, enquiry etc Vor-; remarks also, chapter einleitend; measures vorbereitend. **2** n Einleitung f (to zu); (preparatory measure) vorbereitende Maßnahme; (Sport) Vorspiel nt.
prelude ['prelju:d] n Vorspiel nt; (fig) Auftakt m (to zu +dat).
premarital [pri:'mærɪtl] adj vorehelich.
premature ['premətʃʊəʳ] adj birth, arrival vorzeitig; decision, action verfrüht. **you were a little ~ when Sie ein wenig voreilig; **the baby was three weeks ~** das Baby wurde drei Wochen zu früh geboren; **~ baby** Frühgeburt f.
premeditate [pri:'medɪteɪt] vt vorher planen.
premeditated [pri:'medɪteɪtɪd] adj vorsätzlich.
premenstrual [pri:'menstrʊəl] adj prämenstruell, vor der Menstruation auftretend.
premier ['premɪəʳ] n Premier(minister) m.
première ['premɪeəʳ] n Premiere f; (first ever also) Uraufführung f.
premise ['premɪs] n **(a)** (esp Logic) Prämisse (spec), Voraussetzung f. **(b)** ~s pl (of school, factory) Gelände nt; (building) Gebäude nt; (shop) Räumlichkeiten pl. **business ~s** Geschäftsräume pl.
premium ['pri:mɪəm] n (bonus) Bonus m, Prämie f; (surcharge) Zuschlag m; (Insur) Prämie f; (St Ex) Aufgeld, Agio nt. **~ bond** (Brit) Lotterieaktie f; **to sell sth at a ~** etw über seinem Wert verkaufen; **to be at a ~** (St Ex) über Pari stehen; (fig) hoch im Kurs stehen; **to put a ~ on sth** (fig) etw

hoch einschätzen.

premonition [ˌpriːməˈnɪʃən] n (presentiment) (böse) Vorahnung; (forewarning) Vorwarnung f.

preoccupation [priːˌɒkjuˈpeɪʃən] n her ~ with her appearance ihre ständige Sorge um ihr Äußeres; that was his main ~ das war sein Hauptanliegen.

preoccupied [priːˈɒkjupaɪd] adj gedankenverloren. to be ~ with sth nur an etw (acc) denken.

preoccupy [priːˈɒkjupaɪ] vt (stark) beschäftigen.

prep [prep] (col) n = **preparation (b)**.

prepacked [ˌpriːˈpækt] adj abgepackt.

prepaid [ˌpriːˈpeɪd] adj postage, goods vorausbezahlt; envelope freigemacht.

preparation [ˌprepəˈreɪʃən] n (a) Vorbereitung f; (of meal, medicine etc) Zubereitung f. in ~ for sth als Vorbereitung für etw; to be in ~ in Vorbereitung sein; ~s for war/a journey Kriegs-/Reisevorbereitungen pl; to make ~s Vorbereitungen treffen. (b) (Brit Sch) (homework) Hausaufgaben pl.

preparatory [prɪˈpærətərɪ] adj (a) step, measure vorbereitend. ~ to the conference um die Konferenz vorzubereiten. (b) ~ school (Brit) private Vorbereitungsschule für die Public School; (US) private Vorbereitungsschule für die Hochschule.

prepare [prɪˈpɛəʳ] 1 vt vorbereiten (sb for sth jdn auf etw (acc), sth for sth etw für etw acc); meal, medicine zubereiten; guest-room fertigmachen; (Sci) präparieren; data aufbereiten. ~ yourself for a shock! mach dich auf einen Schock gefaßt! 2 vi to ~ for sth Vorbereitungen für etw treffen; to ~ for an exam/for war sich auf eine Prüfung vorbereiten/Kriegsvorbereitungen treffen; to ~ to do sth Anstalten machen, etw zu tun.

prepared [prɪˈpɛəd] adj (a) vorbereitet (for auf +acc). (b) (willing) to be ~ to do sth bereit sein, etw zu tun.

preponderance [prɪˈpɒndərəns] n Übergewicht nt.

preponderant [prɪˈpɒndərənt] adj überwiegend.

preposition [ˌprepəˈzɪʃən] n Präposition f.

prepossessing [ˌpriːpəˈzesɪŋ] adj anziehend.

preposterous [prɪˈpɒstərəs] adj grotesk, absurd.

prep school n (Brit) see **preparatory (b)**.

prerecord [ˌpriːrɪˈkɔːd] vt vorher aufzeichnen. ~ed cassette bespielte Kassette.

prerequisite [ˌpriːˈrekwɪzɪt] n Voraussetzung f.

prerogative [prɪˈrɒgətɪv] n Vorrecht nt.

Presbyterian [ˌprezbɪˈtɪərɪən] 1 adj presbyterianisch. 2 n Presbyterianer(in) f m.

preschool [ˈpriːˈskuːl] adj attr vorschulisch. a child of ~ age ein Kind nt im Vorschulalter.

prescribe [prɪˈskraɪb] vt (a) (order, lay down) vorschreiben. ~d reading Pflichtlektüre f. (b) (Med, fig) verschreiben (sth for sb jdm etw).

prescription [prɪˈskrɪpʃən] n (Med) Rezept nt; (act of prescribing) Verschreiben nt. to make up or fill (US) a ~ eine Medizin zubereiten; ~ charge Rezeptgebühr f; only available on ~ rezeptpflichtig.

presence [ˈprezns] n Gegenwart, Anwesenheit f. in sb's ~, in the ~ of sb in jds Gegenwart (dat); to make one's ~ felt sich bemerkbar machen; a military ~ Militärpräsenz f.

presence of mind n Geistesgegenwart f.

present[1] [ˈpreznt] 1 adj (a) (in attendance) anwesend; (existing) vorhanden. to be ~ anwesend sein, da/hier sein; to be ~ at sth bei etw anwesend sein; ~ company excepted Anwesende ausgenommen; all those ~ alle Anwesenden; carbon is ~ in organic matter Kohlenstoff ist in organischen Stoffen vorhanden. (b) (at the ~ time) moment, state of affairs etc gegenwärtig, derzeitig; problems, husband etc also jetzig; season etc laufend. at the ~ moment zum jetzigen Zeitpunkt; in the ~ circumstances unter

den gegenwärtigen Umständen; in the ~ case im vorliegenden Fall. (c) (Gram) in the ~ tense in der Gegenwart, im Präsens; ~ participle Partizip nt Präsens. 2 n Gegenwart f; (Gram also) Präsens nt. at ~ zur Zeit, im Moment; up to the ~ bislang, bis jetzt.

present[2] 1 n (gift) Geschenk nt. to make sb a ~ of sth jdm etw schenken (also fig); I was given it as a ~ das habe ich geschenkt bekommen.
  2 [prɪˈzent] vt (a) medal, prize etc überreichen; (as gift) schenken; (put forward) vorlegen; cheque (for payment) präsentieren; proof erbringen (of sth für etw); proposal unterbreiten. to ~ sb with sth, to ~ sth to sb jdm etw überreichen; (as a gift) jdm etw schenken; ~ arms! (Mil) präsentiert das Gewehr! (b) (offer, provide) target, opportunity bieten. his action ~ed us with a problem seine Tat stellte uns vor ein Problem. (c) (Rad, TV) präsentieren; (Theat also) aufführen; (commentator) moderieren. ~ing Sabine Citron as ... (Film) und erstmals Sabine Citron als ... (d) (introduce) vorstellen. to ~ Mr X to Miss Y Herrn X Fräulein Y (dat) vorstellen.
  3 [prɪˈzent] vr (opportunity, problem etc) sich ergeben.

presentable [prɪˈzentəbl] adj to be ~ sich sehen lassen können; to make oneself ~ sich zurechtmachen.

presentation [ˌprezənˈteɪʃən] n (a) (of gift etc) Überreichung f; (of prize, medal also, ceremony) Verleihung f; (gift) Geschenk nt. to make sb a ~ jdm ein Geschenk überreichen. (b) (act of presenting) (of report, voucher etc) Vorlage f; (of petition) Überreichung f; (Jur: of case, evidence) Darlegung f. on ~ of a certificate gegen Vorlage einer Bescheinigung. (c) (Theat) Inszenierung f; (TV also, Rad) Produktion f. (d) (style of ~) Präsentation f.

present-day [ˈprezntˈdeɪ] adj attr heutig.

presenter [prɪˈzentəʳ] n (TV, Rad) Moderator(in f) m.

presentiment [prɪˈzentɪmənt] n (Vor)ahnung f. to have a ~ that ... das Gefühl haben, daß ...

presently [ˈprezntlɪ] adv (a) (soon) bald. (b) (at present) zur Zeit, gegenwärtig.

preservation [ˌprezəˈveɪʃən] n see vt (a) Erhaltung f; Wahrung f; Aufrechterhaltung f. (b) Konservierung f (also of leather, wood); Präservierung f. (c) Einmachen nt; Einlegen nt. (d) Bewahrung f.

preservative [prɪˈzɜːvətɪv] n (Cook) Konservierungsmittel nt.

preserve [prɪˈzɜːv] 1 vt (a) (keep intact, maintain) customs, building, position erhalten; peace also, dignity, appearances wahren; memory aufrechterhalten. (b) (keep from decay) konservieren; specimens etc präservieren; leather, wood schützen. well ~d gut erhalten. (c) (Cook) einmachen; (pickle) einlegen. (d) (keep from harm, save) bewahren. to ~ sb from sth jdn vor etw (dat) bewahren. 2 n (a) (Cook) ~s pl Eingemachtes nt. (b) (special domain) Ressort nt. game ~ (Hunt) Jagdrevier nt.

pre-shrunk [ˈpriːˈʃrʌŋk] adj vorgewaschen.

preside [prɪˈzaɪd] vi (at meeting etc) den Vorsitz haben (at bei). to ~ over an organization etc eine Organisation etc leiten.

presidency [ˈprezɪdənsɪ] n Präsidentschaft f; (esp US: of company) Aufsichtsratsvorsitz m; (US Univ) Rektorat nt.

president [ˈprezɪdənt] n Präsident(in f) m; (esp US: of company) Aufsichtsratsvorsitzende(r) mf; (US Univ) Rektor(in f) m.

presidential [ˌprezɪˈdenʃəl] adj (Pol) Präsidenten-; election also Präsidentschafts-. his ~ duties seine Pflichten als Präsident.

press [pres] 1 n (a) (squeeze, push) Druck m. to give sth a ~ etw drücken; dress etc bügeln.

(b) *(trouser ~, flower ~)* Presse *f.* **(c)** *(Typ)* (Drucker)presse *f; (publishing firm)* Verlag *m; (newspapers)* Presse *f.* **to go to ~** in Druck gehen; **to be in the ~** im Druck sein; **the daily ~** die Tagespresse; **the weekly ~** die Wochenzeitungen *pl;* **to get a good/bad ~** eine gute/ schlechte Presse bekommen.

2 *vt* **(a)** *(push, squeeze)* drücken *(to an +acc); button, doorbell also, brake pedal* drücken auf *(+acc); clutch, piano pedal* treten; *grapes* (aus)pressen; *flowers* pressen. **(b)** *(iron) clothes* bügeln. **(c)** *(urge, persuade)* drängen; *(harass)* bedrängen; *(insist on) claim, argument* bestehen auf *(+dat).* **to ~ sb hard** jdm (hart) zusetzen; **to ~ the point** darauf beharren *or* herumreiten *(col);* **to ~ one's views on sb** jdm seine Ansichten aufdrängen; **to ~ sb for an answer** auf jds Antwort drängen; **to be ~ed (for money/time)** in Geldnot/Zeitnot sein; **to ~ sb/sth into service** jdn/etw einspannen. **(d)** *machine part, record etc* pressen. **~ed steel** Preßstahl *m.*

3 *vi* **(a)** *(lit, fig: bear down, exert pressure)* drücken; *(urge, agitate)* drängen; *(be insistent also)* drängeln *(col).* **to ~ for sth** auf etw *(acc)* drängen; **time ~es** die Zeit drängt. **(b)** *(move, push)* sich drängen. **to ~ ahead (with sth)** *(fig)* (mit etw) weitermachen; *(with plans)* etw weiterführen.

♦**press on** *vi* weitermachen; *(with journey)* weiterfahren.

press: **~agency** *n* Presseagentur *f;* **~ conference** *n* Pressekonferenz *f;* **~ gallery** *n (esp Jur, Parl)* Pressetribüne *f;* **~-gang** *vt (col)* **to ~-gang sb into (doing) sth** jdn drängen, etw zu tun.

pressing ['presɪŋ] *adj (urgent)* dringend; *(insistent) requests* nachdrücklich.

press: **~ photographer** *n* Pressefotograf(in *f) m;* **~ stud** *n (Brit)* Druckknopf *m;* **~-up** *n* Liegestütz *m.*

pressure ['preʃəʳ] **1** *n* **(a)** Druck *m (also Phys, Met).* **at high/full ~** *(lit, fig)* unter Hochdruck. **(b)** *(compulsion, influence)* Druck, Zwang *m.* **parental ~** Druck von seiten der Eltern; **social ~s** gesellschaftliche Zwänge *pl;* **to do sth under ~** etw unter Druck tun; **to be under ~ to do sth** unter Druck stehen, etw zu tun; **to put ~ on sb** jdn unter Druck setzen; **to put the ~ on** *(col)* Dampf machen *(col);* **~ of work prevents me** die Arbeitsüberlastung hindert mich daran; **he's under a lot of ~** er ist großen Belastungen ausgesetzt. **2** *vt =* **pressurize (b).**

pressure: **~cooker** *n* Druckkochtopf, Schnellkochtopf *m;* **~ group** *n* Pressure-group *f.*

pressurize ['preʃəraɪz] *vt* **(a)** *cabin, spacesuit* auf Normaldruck halten. **(b)** unter Druck setzen. **to ~ sb into doing sth** jdn so unter Druck setzen, daß er etw tut.

prestige [pre'stiːʒ] *n* Prestige *nt.*

prestigious [pre'stɪdʒəs] *adj* Prestige-. **to be (very) ~** (einen hohen) Prestigewert haben.

presumably [prɪ'zjuːməblɪ] *adv* vermutlich. **~ he is very rich, is he?** ich nehme an, er ist sehr reich, oder?

presume [prɪ'zjuːm] **1** *vt* **(a)** *(suppose)* annehmen, vermuten. **(b)** *(venture)* **to ~ to do sth** sich *(dat)* erlauben, etw zu tun. **2** *vi* **(a)** *(suppose)* annehmen, vermuten. **(b)** *(take liberties)* **I didn't want to ~** ich wollte nicht aufdringlich sein; **to ~ on or upon sth** etw überbeanspruchen.

presumption [prɪ'zʌmpʃən] *n* **(a)** *(assumption)* Annahme, Vermutung *f.* **(b)** *(boldness, arrogance)* Dreistigkeit *f.*

presumptuous [prɪ'zʌmptjuəs] *adj* unverschämt.

presuppose [ˌpriːsə'pəʊz] *vt* voraussetzen.

pretence, *(US)* **pretense** [prɪ'tens] *n* **(a)** *(story)* erfundene Geschichte; *(pretending)* Verstellung *f; (affectation)* Unnatürlichkeit *f; (pretext)* Vorwand *m.* **he didn't really shoot me, it was just ~**

er hat nicht auf mich geschossen, er hat nur so getan; **to make a ~ of being sth** so tun, als sei man etw; **it's all a ~** das ist alles nur gespielt *or* Mache *(col);* **his ~ of innocence/friendship** seine gespielte Unschuld/Freundschaft; **let's stop all this ~** hören wir auf, uns *(dat)* etwas vorzumachen; **on** *or* **under the ~ of doing sth** unter dem Vorwand, etw zu tun. **(b)** **to make no ~ to sth** keinen Anspruch auf etw *(acc)* erheben.

pretend [prɪ'tend] **1** *vt* **(a)** *(make believe)* so tun, als ob; *(feign also)* vortäuschen, vorgeben. **to ~ to be interested** so tun, als ob man interessiert wäre; **to ~ to be sick** eine Krankheit vortäuschen; **to ~ to be asleep** sich schlafend stellen. **(b)** *(claim)* **I don't ~ to ...** ich behaupte nicht, daß ich ... **2** *vi* so tun, als ob; *(keep up facade)* sich verstellen. **he is only ~ing** er tut nur so (als ob).

pretense *n (US) =* **pretence.**

pretension [prɪ'tenʃən] *n* **(a)** *(claim)* Anspruch *m; (social, cultural)* Ambition *f.* **he makes no ~(s) to originality** er beansprucht keineswegs, originell zu sein. **(b)** *(ostentation)* Prahlerei *f; (affectation)* Anmaßung *f.*

pretentious [prɪ'tenʃəs] *adj* anmaßend; *speech, book* hochtrabend; *(ostentatious)* angeberisch, protzig *(col); restaurant, décor* pompös.

preterite ['pretərɪt] *n* Imperfekt *nt.*

pretext ['priːtekst] *n* Vorwand *m.* **on** *or* **under the ~ of doing sth** unter dem Vorwand, etw zu tun.

pretty ['prɪtɪ] **1** *adj (+er)* **(a)** hübsch, nett. **to make oneself ~** sich hübsch machen; **I'm/she's not just a ~ face!** *(col)* ich bin gar nicht so dumm (wie ich aussehe) *(col)*/sie hat auch Köpfchen; **it wasn't ~/a ~ sight** das war alles andere als schön/das war kein schöner Anblick. **(b)** *(col)* **a ~ penny** das wird eine schöne Stange Geld kosten *(col).* **2** *adv (rather)* ziemlich; *good also* ganz; *(very also)* ganz schön *(col).* **~ nearly** *or* **well finished** so gut wie fertig *(col).*

pretzel ['pretsl] *n* Brezel *f.*

prevail [prɪ'veɪl] *vi* **(a)** *(gain mastery)* sich durchsetzen *(over, against* gegenüber*).* **(b)** *(conditions, wind etc)* vorherrschen; *(be widespread: customs)* weit verbreitet sein. **(c)** *(persuade)* **to ~ (up)on sb to do sth** jdn dazu bewegen, etw zu tun.

prevailing [prɪ'veɪlɪŋ] *adj conditions* derzeitig; *fashion* aktuell; *opinion* herrschend; *wind* vorherrschend.

prevalence ['prevələns] *n (widespread occurrence)* Vorherrschen *nt; (of crime, disease)* Häufigkeit *f.*

prevalent ['prevələnt] *adj (widespread)* weit verbreitet; *conditions* herrschend; *fashions, style* beliebt.

prevaricate [prɪ'værɪkeɪt] *vi* Ausflüchte machen.

prevarication [prɪˌværɪ'keɪʃən] *n* Ausflucht *f; (prevaricating)* Ausflüchte *pl.*

prevent [prɪ'vent] *vt sth* verhindern, verhüten; *(through preventive measures)* vorbeugen *(+dat).* **to ~ sb (from) doing sth** jdn daran hindern, etw zu tun; **to ~ sth (from) happening** verhindern, daß etw geschieht.

prevention [prɪ'venʃən] *n* Verhütung *f; (through preventive measures)* Vorbeugung *f (of gegen).*

preventive [prɪ'ventɪv] *adj* vorbeugend, Präventiv-. **~ medicine** Präventivmedizin *f.*

preview ['priːvjuː] *n* **(a)** *(of play, film)* Voraufführung *f; (of exhibition)* Vorbesichtigung *f.* **(b)** *(Film, trailer, TV)* Vorschau *f (of* auf *+acc).*

previous ['priːvɪəs] *adj* **(a)** vorherig; *page, day* vorhergehend; *year* vorangegangen; *(with indef art)* früher. **the ~ page/day** die Seite/der Tag davor; **in ~ years** in früheren Jahren; **on a ~ occasion** bei einer früheren Gelegenheit; **I have a ~ engagement** ich habe schon einen Termin; **to have a ~ conviction** vorbestraft sein; **~ owner** Vorbesitzer(in *f) m.* **(b)** **~ to vor** *(+dat); ~*

to going out ... bevor ich/er *etc* ausging, ...
previously ['pri:vɪəslɪ] *adv* vorher, früher.
pre-war [pri:'wɔː] *adj* Vorkriegs-.
prey [preɪ] 1 *n* (*lit, fig*) Beute *f*. bird of ~ Raubvogel *m*; to fall ~ to sb/sth (*fig*) ein Opfer von jdm/etw werden. 2 *vi* to ~ (up)on (*animals*) Beute machen auf (+*acc*); (*pirates, thieves*) (aus)plündern; (*doubts*) nagen an (+*dat*); (*anxiety*) quälen.
price [praɪs] 1 *n* (*lit, fig*) Preis *m*. the ~ of cars die Autopreise *pl*; to go up/down in ~ teurer/ billiger werden; what is the ~ of that? was kostet das?; at a ~ of ... zum Preis(e) von ...; at a ~ zum entsprechenden Preis; at a reduced ~ verbilligt, zu herabgesetztem Preis (*form*); the ~ of fame der Preis für den Ruhm; at any ~ um jeden Preis; not at any ~ um keinen Preis; at the ~ of losing his health um den Preis seiner Gesundheit; it's too high a ~ to pay das ist ein zu hoher Preis; to put a ~ on sth einen Preis für etw nennen; to be beyond/without ~ nicht mit Geld zu bezahlen sein; to put a ~ on sb's head eine Belohnung auf jds Kopf (*acc*) aussetzen.
2 *vt* (*fix* ~ *of*) den Preis festsetzen von; (*label*) auszeichnen (at mit). it was ~d at £5 es kostete £ 5; reasonably ~d angemessen im Preis; ~d too high/low zu teuer/billig; to ~ oneself out of the market sich selbst durch zu hohe Preise konkurrenzunfähig machen.
price: ~cut *n* Preissenkung *f*; ~ fixing *n* Preisfestlegung *f*; ~ freeze *n* Preisstopp *m*.
priceless ['praɪslɪs] *adj* unschätzbar, von unschätzbarem Wert; (*col: amusing*) joke, film köstlich; *person* unbezahlbar.
price: ~ limit *n* Preisgrenze *f*; ~ list *n* Preisliste *f*; ~ range *n* Preisklasse *f*; ~ rise *n* Preiserhöhung *f*; ~ tag *n* Preisschild *nt*.
pricey ['praɪsɪ] *adj* (*Brit col*) kostspielig.
prick [prɪk] 1 *n* (a) (*puncture, pricking sensation*) Stich *m*. ~s of conscience Gewissensbisse *pl*. (b) (*col!: penis*) Schwanz *m* (*col!*). 2 *vt* (*puncture*) oneself, sb stechen; balloon durchstechen; to ~ one's finger (with/on sth) sich (*dat*) (mit etw) in den Finger stechen/sich (*dat*) (an etw *dat*) den Finger stechen. 3 *vi* (*thorn, injection etc*) stechen; (*eyes*) brennen.
♦ **prick up** *vt sep* to ~ ~ its/one's ears (*lit, fig*) die Ohren spitzen.
prickle ['prɪkl] *n* (a) (*sharp point*) Stachel *m*; (*on plants also*) Dorn *m*. (b) (*sensation*) Stechen *nt*; (*from wool etc*) Kratzen *nt*; (*tingle*) Prickeln *nt*.
prickly ['prɪklɪ] *adj* (+er) (a) plant, animal stach(e)lig; material kratzig; sensation stechend; (*tingling*) prickelnd. (b) (*fig*) person bissig.
prickly: ~ heat *n* Hitzepocken *pl*; ~ pear *n* (*plant*) Feigenkaktus *m*; (*fruit*) Kaktusfeige *f*.
pride [praɪd] 1 *n* (a) Stolz *m*; (*arrogance*) Hochmut *m*. to take (a) ~ in sth/in one's appearance auf etw (*acc*) stolz sein/Wert auf sein Äußeres legen; her ~ and joy ihr ganzer Stolz; the ~ of the army der Stolz der Armee; to have or take ~ of place den Ehrenplatz einnehmen. (b) (*of lions*) Rudel *nt*. 2 *vr* to ~ oneself on sth sich einer Sache (*gen*) rühmen können; I ~ myself on being something of an expert in this field ich darf wohl behaupten, mich auf diesem Gebiet auszukennen.
priest [priːst] *n* Priester, Geistliche(r) *m*.
priestess ['priːstɪs] *n* Priesterin *f*.
priesthood ['priːsthʊd] *n* Priestertum *nt*; (*priests collectively*) Priesterschaft *f*. to enter the ~ Priester werden.
priestly ['priːstlɪ] *adj* priesterlich; robes, office also Priester-.
prig [prɪg] *n* (*goody-goody*) Tugendlamm *nt* (*col*); (*snob*) Schnösel *m* (*col*).
prim [prɪm] *adj* (+er) (also ~ and proper) etepetete *inv* (*col*); (*demure*) person, dress sittsam, züchtig; (*prudish*) prüde.

prima facie ['praɪmə'feɪʃɪ] 1 *adv* allem Anschein nach. 2 *adj* a ~ case of ... auf den ersten Blick ein Fall von ...; the police have a ~ case die Polizei hat genügend Beweise.
primarily ['praɪmərɪlɪ] *adv* in erster Linie.
primary ['praɪmərɪ] 1 *adj* (*chief, main*) Haupt-, wesentlich. of ~ importance von größter Bedeutung. 2 *n* (US: *election*) Vorwahl *f*.
primary: ~ colour (*Brit*) or color (*US*) *n* Grundfarbe *f*; ~ education *n* Grundschul(aus)bildung *f*; ~ school *n* Grundschule *f*; ~ teacher *n* Grundschullehrer(in *f*) *m*.
primate ['praɪmeɪt] *n* (a) (*Zool*) Primat *m*. (b) ['praɪmɪt] (*Eccl*) Primas *m*.
prime [praɪm] 1 *adj* (a) (*major, chief*) Haupt-, wesentlich. of ~ importance von größter Bedeutung. (b) (*excellent*) erstklassig. in ~ condition (*meat, fruit etc*) von hervorragender Qualität; (*athlete, car etc*) in erstklassiger Verfassung. (c) (*Math*) Prim-.
2 *n* in the ~ of life in der Blüte seiner Jahre; he is in/past his ~ er ist in den besten Jahren/er ist über seine besten Jahre hinaus; (*singer, artist*) er ist an seinem Höhepunkt angelangt/er hat seine beste Zeit hinter sich.
3 *vt* (a) bomb scharf machen; pump vorpumpen; surface for painting grundieren. (b) (*with advice, information*) instruieren. to be well ~d for the interview/game für das Interview/ Spiel gut gerüstet sein.
prime: ~ minister *n* Premierminister(in *f*) *m*; ~ number *n* Primzahl *f*.
primer ['praɪmə'] *n* (a) (*paint, coat*) Grundierung *f*. (b) (*book*) Fibel *f*. (c) (*explosive*) Zünder *m*.
primeval [praɪ'miːvəl] *adj* urzeitlich; forest Ur-.
primitive ['prɪmɪtɪv] *adj* primitiv.
primrose ['prɪmrəʊz] 1 *n* (*Bot*) Primel *f*; (*colour*) Blaßgelb *nt*. 2 *adj* blaßgelb.
primula ['prɪmjʊlə] *n* Primel *f*.
primus (stove) ® ['praɪməs(,stəʊv)] *n* Primuskocher *m*.
prince [prɪns] *n* (*king's son*) Prinz *m*; (*ruler*) Fürst *m*. P~ Charming (*fig*) Märchenprinz *m*; ~ consort/regent Prinzgemahl *m*/-regent *m*.
princely ['prɪnslɪ] *adj* (*lit, fig*) fürstlich.
princess [prɪn'ses] *n* Prinzessin *f*; (*wife of ruler*) Fürstin *f*.
principal ['prɪnsɪpəl] 1 *adj* Haupt-, hauptsächlich. the ~ cities of China die wichtigsten Städte Chinas; my ~ concern mein Hauptanliegen *nt*; ~ horn erster Hornist, erste Hornistin. 2 *n* (a) (*of school, college*) Rektor *m*; (*in play*) Hauptperson *f*. (b) (*Fin, of investment*) Kapital(summe *f*) *nt*.
principality [,prɪnsɪ'pælɪtɪ] *n* Fürstentum *nt*.
principally ['prɪnsɪpəlɪ] *adv* vornehmlich, in erster Linie.
principle ['prɪnsɪpl] *n* (*moral precept*) Prinzip *nt*, Grundsatz *m*. in/on ~ im/aus Prinzip, prinzipiell; a man of ~(s) ein Mensch mit Prinzipien; it's against my ~(s) es geht gegen meine Prinzipien; it's a matter of ~, it's the ~ of the thing es geht dabei ums Prinzip.
print [prɪnt] 1 *n* (a) (*typeface*) Schrift *f*; (~ed matter) Gedruckte(s) *nt*. out of/in ~ vergriffen/ gedruckt; to see sth in cold ~ etw schwarz auf weiß sehen; he'll never get into ~ er wird nie etwas veröffentlichen; in big/small ~ groß/klein gedruckt. (b) (*picture*) Druck *m*; (*Phot*) Abzug *m*, Kopie *f*; (*fabric*) bedruckter Stoff; (*cotton* ~) Kattun *m*. (c) (*impression: of foot etc*) Abdruck *m*. 2 *vt* (a) book, design drucken; fabric bedrucken. (b) (*publish*) story veröffentlichen. (c) (*write*) in Druckschrift schreiben.
♦ **print out** *vt sep* (*Comp*) ausdrucken.
printed ['prɪntɪd] *adj* Druck-, gedruckt; (*written in capitals*) in Großbuchstaben; fabric bedruckt. ~ matter/papers Drucksache *f*; ~ circuit ge-

druckte Schaltung; ~ **circuit board** Leiterplatte f.

printer ['prɪntə^r] n Drucker m. ~'s **error**
Druckfehler m; ~'s **ink** Druckerschwärze f.

printing ['prɪntɪŋ] n **(a)** (process) Drucken nt. **(b)**
(unjoined writing) Druckschrift f; (characters,
print) Schrift f. **(c)** (quantity printed) Auflage f.

printing: ~ **press** n Druckerpresse f; ~ **works** n
sing or pl Druckerei f.

printout ['prɪntaʊt] n (Comp) Ausdruck m.

prior[1] ['praɪə^r] adj **(a)** knowledge, warning,
agreement vorherig; (earlier) früher. ~ **claim**
Vorrecht nt (to auf); a ~ **engagement** eine vorher getroffene Verabredung. **(b)** ~ **to sth** vor
etw (dat); ~ **to going out** ... bevor ich/er etc ausging, ...

prior[2] n (Eccl) Prior m.

priority [praɪ'ɒrɪtɪ] n Vorrang m, Priorität f; (thing
having precedence) vorrangige Angelegenheit. a
top ~ eine Sache von äußerster Dringlichkeit; **to
have** ~ Vorrang or Priorität haben; **to give** ~ **to
sth** etw vorrangig behandeln, einer Sache (dat)
Priorität geben; **order of** ~ nach Dringlichkeit;
we must get our priorities right wir müssen
unsere Prioritäten richtig setzen.

prise, (US) **prize** [praɪz] vt **to** ~ **sth open** etw
aufbrechen; **to** ~ **the lid up/off** den Deckel
auf-/abbekommen.

prism ['prɪzəm] n Prisma nt.

prison ['prɪzn] n (lit,fig) Gefängnis nt. **to be in** ~ im
Gefängnis sein; **to go to** ~ **for 5 years** für 5 Jahre
ins Gefängnis gehen; **to send sb to** ~ jdn ins
Gefängnis schicken. **2** attr Gefängnis-; system,
facilities Strafvollzugs-. ~ **camp** Gefangenen-
lager nt; ~ **life** das Leben im Gefängnis.

prisoner ['prɪznə^r] n Gefangene(r) mf; (convicted
also) Häftling m. **to hold** or **keep sb** ~ jdn
gefangenhalten; **to take sb** ~ jdn gefangennehmen; ~ **of war** Kriegsgefangene(r) m; ~ **of war
camp** (Kriegs)gefangenenlager nt.

pristine ['prɪstaɪn] adj beauty unberührt; condition
tadellos, makellos.

privacy ['prɪvəsɪ, 'praɪvəsɪ] n Privatleben nt. **there
is no** ~ man kann kein Privatleben führen; **in the**
~ **of one's home** im eigenen Heim; **in the
strictest** ~ (meeting etc) unter äußerster
Geheimhaltung.

private ['praɪvɪt] **1** adj **(a)** privat; letter, reasons
persönlich; matter Privat-, vertraulich; place
abgelegen; funeral im engsten Kreis; hearing etc
nichtöffentlich attr. ~ **property** Privateigentum
nt; **they wanted to be** ~ sie wollten für sich sein;
to keep sth ~ etw für sich behalten; **his** ~ **life**
sein Privatleben nt; **with** ~ **bathroom** mit eigenem Bad. **(b)** ~ **car** Privatwagen m; ~ **citizen**
Privatperson f; ~ **enterprise** Privatunterneh-
men nt; (free enterprise) freies Unternehmertum; ~ **eye** (col) Privatdetektiv m; ~ **parts**
(genitals) Geschlechtsteile pl; ~ **practice**
Privatpraxis f; ~ **school** Privatschule f; ~ **sector**
privater Sektor. **2** n **(a)** (Mil) Gefreite(r) mf. **(b)
in** ~ privat; **we must talk in** ~ wir müssen das
unter uns besprechen.

privately ['praɪvɪtlɪ] adv **(a)** (not publicly) privat.
(b) (secretly, personally) persönlich; (in confidence) vertraulich. **but** ~ **he was very upset**
doch innerlich war er sehr aufgebracht.

privation [praɪ'veɪʃən] n **(a)** (state) Armut, Not f.
(b) (hardship) Entbehrung f.

privatization [ˌpraɪvətaɪ'zeɪʃən] n Privatisierung
f.

privatize ['praɪvətaɪz] vt privatisieren.

privet ['prɪvɪt] n Liguster m.

privilege ['prɪvɪlɪdʒ] **1** n Privileg, Sonderrecht nt;
(honour) Ehre f; (Parl) Immunität f. **2** vt privilegieren, bevorrechtigen. **I was** ~**d to talk to
him** ich hatte die Ehre, mich mit ihm zu
unterhalten.

privileged ['prɪvɪlɪdʒd] adj person, classes privi-

legiert. **for a** ~ **few** für eine kleine Gruppe von
Privilegierten.

privy ['prɪvɪ] adj **(a) to be** ~ **to sth** in etw (acc)
eingeweiht sein. **(b) P**~ **Council, P**~ **Councillor**
Geheimer Rat.

prize[1] [praɪz] **1** n Preis m; (in lottery also)
Gewinn m. **to win first** ~ den ersten Preis gewinnen. **2** adj **(a)** (awarded a ~) entry, essay preisgekrönt. ~ **idiot** (col) Vollidiot m (col). **(b)**
(awarded as a ~) trophy Sieges-. **(c)** (offering a ~)
competition Preis-. ~ **draw** Lotterie f. **3** vt
(hoch)schätzen. ~**d possession** wertvollster
Besitz.

prize[2] vt (US) = prise.

prize: ~**-fight** n Berufsboxkampf m; ~**-giving** n
(Sch) Preisverteilung f; ~ **money** n Geldpreis
m; (in competition) Gewinn m; ~**winner** n
(Preis)gewinner(in f) m; ~**winning** adj entry,
novel preisgekrönt; ticket Gewinn-.

pro[1] [prəʊ] n (col: professional) Profi m.

pro[2] **1** prep (in favour of) für. **2** n **the** ~**s and the
cons** das Für und Wider, das Pro und Kontra.

pro- pref (in favour of) pro-. ~**-Soviet** prosowje-
tisch.

probability [ˌprɒbə'bɪlɪtɪ] n Wahrscheinlichkeit f.
in all ~ höchstwahrscheinlich.

probable ['prɒbəbl] adj wahrscheinlich.

probably ['prɒbəblɪ] adv wahrscheinlich. **more** ~
than not höchstwahrscheinlich.

probate ['prəʊbɪt] n (examination) gerichtliche
Testamentsbestätigung; (will) beglaubigte
Testamentsabschrift.

probation [prə'beɪʃən] n **(a)** (Jur) Bewährung f. **to
put sb on** ~ **(for a year)** jdm (ein Jahr)
Bewährung geben; **to be on** ~ Bewährung
haben; **to be released on** ~ auf Bewährung
freigelassen werden; ~ **officer** Bewährungs-
helfer(in f) m. **(b)** (of employee) Probe f; (~
period) Probezeit f.

probationer ['prəʊbɪt] ...

probe [prəʊb] **1** n **(a)** (device) Sonde f. **(b)** (investigation) Untersuchung f (into gen). **2** vt
untersuchen; space, sb's past, private life erforschen; mystery ergründen. **3** vi suchen, forschen
(for nach); (Med) untersuchen (for auf + acc). **to**
~ **into sb's private life** in jds Privatleben (dat)
herumschnüffeln (col).

probing ['prəʊbɪŋ] **1** n Untersuchung f. **2** adj
question, study prüfend.

problem ['prɒbləm] n Problem nt; (Math: as school
exercise) Aufgabe f. **what's the** ~? wo fehlt's?;
he's got a drinking ~ er trinkt (zuviel); **I had no**
~ **in getting the money** noch hat das Geld ohne
Schwierigkeiten bekommen; **no** ~! (col) kein
Problem!; ~ **area** Problembereich m.

problematic(al) [ˌprɒblə'mætɪk(əl)] adj problematisch.

problem: ~ **child** n Problemkind nt; ~ **page** n
Problemseite f.

procedure [prə'siːdʒə^r] n Verfahren nt. **business**
~ geschäftliche Verfahrensweise.

proceed [prə'siːd] **1** vi **(a)** (form: go) gehen; (vehicle, by vehicle) weiterfahren. **we then** ~**ed to
London** wir fuhren dann nach London weiter.
(c) (set about sth) vorgehen; (carry on, continue)
fortfahren. **can we now** ~ **to the next item on the
agenda?** können wir jetzt zum nächsten Punkt
der Tagesordnung übergehen?; **they** ~**ed with
their plan** sie führten ihren Plan weiter; (start)
sie gingen nach ihrem Plan vor; **negotiations are**
~**ing well** die Verhandlungen kommen gut
voran; **to** ~ **on the assumption that** ... von der
Voraussetzung ausgehen, daß ... **(d)** (originate)
to ~ **from** kommen von; (fig) herrühren von. **(e)**
(Jur) **to** ~ **against sb** jdn gerichtlich vorgehen.

2 vt now, **he** ~**ed** nun, fuhr er fort; **to** ~ **to do**
sth (dann) etw tun.

proceeding [prə'siːdɪŋ] n (a) (course of action) Vorgehen nt. (b) ~s pl (function) Veranstaltung f. (c) ~s pl (esp Jur) Verfahren nt; to take/start ~s against sb gegen jdn gerichtlich vorgehen; to take legal ~s einen Prozeß anstrengen. (d) ~s pl (written minutes etc) Protokoll nt; (published report) Tätigkeitsbericht m.

proceeds ['prəusiːdz] npl (yield) Ertrag m; (from sale etc) Erlös m; (takings) Einnahmen pl.

process[1] ['prəuses] 1 n (a) Prozeß m. in the ~ of time im Laufe der Zeit; in the ~ dabei; in the ~ of learning beim Lernen; to be in the ~ of doing sth dabei sein, etw zu tun; in ~ of construction im Bau. (b) (method, technique) Verfahren nt. 2 vt (treat) raw materials, data verarbeiten; food konservieren; milk sterilisieren; application, loan bearbeiten; film entwickeln. ~ed cheese, (US) ~ cheese Schmelzkäse m.

process[2] [prə'ses] vi (Brit: go in procession) ziehen, schreiten.

processing ['prəusesɪŋ] n see vt Verarbeitung f; Konservierung f; Sterilisierung f; Bearbeitung f; Entwicklung f.

procession [prə'seʃən] n (organized) Umzug m; (solemn) Prozession f; (line of people, cars etc) Reihe, Schlange f. funeral ~ Trauerzug m.

processor ['prəusesəʳ] n (Comp) Prozessor m.

proclaim [prə'kleɪm] vt (a) erklären; revolution ausrufen. to ~ sb king jdn zum König ausrufen. (b) (reveal) verraten.

proclamation [ˌprɒklə'meɪʃən] n Erklärung f; (of laws, measures) Verkündung f; (of state of emergency) Ausrufung f.

proclivity [prə'klɪvɪtɪ] n Neigung f (for zu).

procrastinate [prəu'kræstɪneɪt] vi zögern, zaudern.

procreation [ˌprəukrɪ'eɪʃən] n Zeugung f.

procure [prə'kjuəʳ] vt (a) (obtain) beschaffen, sich (dat) verschaffen; (bring about) bewirken. to ~ sth for sb/oneself jdm/sich etw beschaffen. (b) (for prostitution) beschaffen (for sb jdm).

prod [prɒd] 1 n Stoß, Knuff (col) m. to give sb a ~ jdn anstoßen; (fig) jdm einen Stoß geben. 2 vt (a) stoßen, knuffen (col). he ~ded the donkey (on) with his stick er trieb den Esel mit seinem Stock vorwärts. (b) (fig) anspornen (to do sth, into sth zu etw). to ~ sb into action jdm einen Stoß geben. 3 vi to ~ at sth an etw (acc) stoßen.

prodigal ['prɒdɪgəl] adj verschwenderisch. the ~ son (Bibl, fig) der verlorene Sohn.

prodigious [prə'dɪdʒəs] adj (vast) ungeheuer; (marvellous) erstaunlich, wunderbar.

prodigy ['prɒdɪdʒɪ] n Wunder nt. child ~ Wunderkind nt.

produce ['prɒdjuːs] 1 n no pl (Agr) Produkt(e pl), Erzeugnis(se pl) nt. ~ of Italy italienisches Erzeugnis. 2 [prə'djuːs] vt (a) (manufacture) produzieren; cars, steel, paper etc also herstellen; energy erzeugen; crop, return on capital abwerfen; coal also fördern; (create) book, article schreiben; painting anfertigen; ideas also, delinquents etc hervorbringen. (b) (bring forward, show) gift, wallet etc hervorholen (from, out of aus); pistol ziehen (from, out of aus); evidence liefern; witness beibringen; ticket, documents vorzeigen. I can't ~ it out of thin air ich kann es doch nicht aus dem Ärmel schütteln (col). (c) play inszenieren; film produzieren. (d) (cause) bitterness, impression hervorrufen; interest also, spark erzeugen.

producer [prə'djuːsəʳ] n Hersteller m; (Agr) Produzent, Erzeuger m; (Theat) Regisseur m; (Film, TV) Produzent m.

product ['prɒdʌkt] n Produkt, Erzeugnis nt; (fig: result, Math, Chem) Produkt nt. food ~s Nahrungsmittel pl.

production [prə'dʌkʃən] n (a) see vt (a) Produktion f; Herstellung f; Erzeugung f; Förderung f; Schreiben nt; Hervorbringung f. to go into ~ (factory) die Produktion aufnehmen; (model) in Produktion gehen; to take sth out of ~ etw aus der Produktion nehmen. (b) (output) Produktion f. (c) see vt (b) Hervorholen nt; Lieferung f; Vorzeigen nt. on ~ of this ticket gegen Vorlage dieser Eintrittskarte. (d) (of play) Inszenierung f; (of film) Produktion f.

production line n Fließband nt.

productive [prə'dʌktɪv] adj produktiv; land fruchtbar; mind schöpferisch; business rentabel.

productivity [ˌprɒdʌk'tɪvɪtɪ] n see adj Produktivität f; Fruchtbarkeit f; schöpferische Kraft.

productivity: ~ agreement n Produktivitätsvereinbarung f; ~ bonus n Leistungszulage f.

profane [prə'feɪn] 1 adj (a) (secular) weltlich, profan. (b) (irreverent, sacrilegious) (gottes)lästerlich. 2 vt entweihen.

profanity [prə'fænɪtɪ] n Gotteslästerlichkeit f; (act, utterance) Gottes)lästerung f.

profess [prə'fes] vt (a) faith, belief etc sich bekennen zu. (b) (claim to have) interest, enthusiasm bekunden; belief kundtun; ignorance zugeben. she ~es to be 25 sie behauptet, 25 zu sein.

professed [prə'fest] adj erklärt; (pej: purported) angeblich. to be a ~ Christian sich zum christlichen Glauben bekennen.

profession [prə'feʃən] n (a) (occupation) Beruf m. the medical/teaching ~ der Arzt-/Lehrerberuf; (members of the ~) die Ärzte-/Lehrerschaft; by ~ von Beruf; the ~s die gehobenen Berufe. (b) (declaration) Bekenntnis f; (Eccl) Gelübde nt. ~ of faith Glaubensbekenntnis nt.

professional [prə'feʃənl] 1 adj (a) Berufs-, beruflich; army, soldier, tennis player Berufs-; opinion fachmännisch, fachlich. the ~ classes die gehobenen Berufe; to take ~ advice fachmännischen Rat einholen; to turn or go ~ Profi werden. (b) (skilled, competent) piece of work etc fachmännisch, fachgerecht; company, approach professionell. it's not up to ~ standards es entspricht nicht fachlichen Normen; it wouldn't be ~ of me to ... es wäre nicht korrekt von mir, wenn ich ... 2 n Profi m.

professionalism [prə'feʃnəlɪzəm] n Professionalismus m; (of job, piece of work) Perfektion f.

professionally [prə'feʃnəlɪ] adv beruflich; (in accomplished manner) fachmännisch; work professionell. he plays ~ er ist Berufsspieler or Profi; he is ~ recognized as the best ... er ist in Fachkreisen als der beste ... bekannt.

professor [prə'fesəʳ] n Professor(in f) m; (US also: teacher) Dozent(in f) m.

proffer ['prɒfəʳ] vt gift, drink anbieten; apologies, thanks etc aussprechen; remark machen.

proficiency [prə'fɪʃənsɪ] n level or standard of ~ Leistungsstand m; her ~ at teaching ihre Tüchtigkeit als Lehrerin; ~ test Leistungstest m.

proficient [prə'fɪʃənt] adj tüchtig, fähig. he is just about ~ in German seine Deutschkenntnisse reichen gerade aus.

profile ['prəufaɪl] n Profil nt; (picture, photograph) Profilbild nt; (biographical ~) Porträt nt. in ~ (person, head) im Profil; to keep a low ~ sich zurückhalten.

profit ['prɒfɪt] 1 n Gewinn, Profit (also pej) m. ~ and loss account Gewinn-und-Verlust-Rechnung f; to make a ~ (out of or on sth) (mit etw) einen Gewinn machen, (an etw dat) verdienen; to sell sth at a ~ etw mit Gewinn verkaufen. 2 vi (gain) profitieren (by, from von), Nutzen ziehen (by, from aus).

profitability [ˌprɒfɪtə'bɪlɪtɪ] n Rentabilität f.

profitable ['prɒfɪtəbl] adj (Comm) gewinnbringend, rentabel; (fig: beneficial) nützlich.

profiteering [ˌprɒfɪ'tɪərɪŋ] n Wucher(ei f) m.

profit: ~-making adj organization rentabel;

(~-orientated) auf Gewinn gerichtet; ~ **margin** n Gewinnspanne f; **~-sharing** n Gewinnbeteiligung f.

profligate ['prɒflɪgɪt] adj (dissolute) lasterhaft; (extravagant) verschwenderisch.

pro forma invoice [,prəʊ'fɔːmə'ɪnvɔɪs] n Pro-Forma-Rechnung f.

profound [prə'faʊnd] adj tief; thought, thinker tiefgründig; book gehaltvoll; knowledge profund (geh); indifference völlig; interest stark; changes tiefgreifend attr.

profoundly [prə'faʊndlɪ] adv zutiefst. ~ significant äußerst bedeutsam; ~ indifferent vollkommen gleichgültig; ..., he said ~ ..., sagte er tiefsinnig.

profundity [prə'fʌndɪtɪ] n (a) no pl Tiefe f; (of thought, thinker, book etc) Tiefgründigkeit f; (of knowledge) Gründlichkeit f. (b) (profound remark) Tiefsinnigkeit f.

profuse [prə'fjuːs] adj vegetation üppig; thanks, praise überschwenglich; apologies überreichlich.

profusely [prə'fjuːslɪ] adv grow üppig; bleed, sweat stark; thank, praise überschwenglich. he apologized ~ er entschuldigte sich vielmals.

profusion [prə'fjuːʒən] n Überfülle f. trees in ~ Bäume in Hülle und Fülle.

prognosis [prɒg'nəʊsɪs] n, pl **prognoses** [prɒg'nəʊsiːz] Prognose, Voraussage f.

program ['prəʊgræm] 1 n (a) (Comp) Programm nt. (b) (US) = **programme** 1. 2 vt (a) computer programmieren. (b) (US) = **programme** 2.

programme, (US) **program** ['prəʊgræm] 1 n Programm nt; (Rad, TV also) Sendung f. we've got a very heavy ~ of meetings wir haben sehr viele Besprechungen auf unserem Programm; what's the ~ for tomorrow? was steht für morgen auf dem Programm? 2 vt programmieren.

programmer ['prəʊgræməʳ] n Programmierer(in f) m.

programming ['prəʊgræmɪŋ] n Programmieren nt. ~ language Programmiersprache f.

progress ['prəʊgres] 1 n (a) no pl (movement forwards) Vorwärtskommen nt; (Mil) Vorrücken nt. they made good ~ across the open country sie kamen im offenen Gelände gut vorwärts. (b) no pl (advance) Fortschritt m. the ~ of events der Gang der Ereignisse; to make (good/slow) ~ (gute/langsame) Fortschritte machen; ~ report Fortschrittsbericht m; in ~ im Gange; the work still in ~ die noch zu erledigende Arbeit.
2 [prə'gres] vi (a) (move, go forward) sich vorwärts bewegen. (b) (in time) as the work ~es mit dem Fortschreiten der Arbeit; as the game ~ed im Laufe des Spiels. (c) (improve, make progress) Fortschritte machen. how far have you ~ed since our last meeting? wie weit sind Sie seit unserer letzten Sitzung vorangekommen?; investigations are ~ing well die Untersuchungen machen gute Fortschritte.

progression [prə'greʃən] n Folge f; (Math) Reihe f; (Mus) Sequenz f; (development) Entwicklung f. sales have shown a continuous upwards ~ im Absatz wurde eine stete Aufwärtsentwicklung verzeichnet.

progressive [prə'gresɪv] adj (a) (increasing) zunehmend; disease etc fortschreitend; paralysis, taxation progressiv. (b) (favouring progress) progressiv, fortschrittlich.

progressively [prə'gresɪvlɪ] adv zunehmend.

prohibit [prə'hɪbɪt] vt (a) verbieten, untersagen. to ~ sb from doing sth jdm etw verbieten or untersagen. "smoking ~ed" „Rauchen verboten". (b) (prevent) verhindern. to ~ sb from doing sth jdn daran hindern, etw zu tun.

prohibition [,prəʊɪ'bɪʃən] n Verbot nt. (the) P~ (Hist) die Prohibition; the ~ of smoking das

Rauchverbot.

prohibitive [prə'hɪbɪtɪv] adj price, cost unerschwinglich.

project¹ ['prɒdʒekt] n Projekt nt; (scheme) Vorhaben nt; (Sch, Univ) Referat nt.

project² [prə'dʒekt] 1 vt (a) film, map, figures projizieren. to ~ oneself/one's personality sich selbst/seine eigene Person zur Geltung bringen; to ~ one's voice seine Stimme zum Tragen bringen. (b) (plan) voraussagen; costs überschlagen. 2 vi (a) (plan) planen. (b) (jut out) hervorragen (from aus). the upper storey ~s over the road das obere Stockwerk ragt über die Straße.

projectile [prə'dʒektaɪl] n (also Mil) Geschoß nt.

projection [prə'dʒekʃən] n (a) (of films, map) Projektion f. ~ room Vorführraum m. (b) (overhang etc) Vorsprung m. (c) (prediction) Prognose f; (of cost) Überschlagung f.

projector [prə'dʒektəʳ] n (Film) Projektor m.

proletarian [,prəʊlə'teərɪən] 1 adj proletarisch. 2 n Proletarier(in f) m.

proletariat [,prəʊlə'teərɪət] n Proletariat nt.

proliferate [prə'lɪfəreɪt] vi (number) sich stark erhöhen; (ideas) um sich greifen; (animals) sich stark vermehren; (weeds, cells) wuchern.

proliferation [prə,lɪfə'reɪʃən] n (in numbers) starke Erhöhung; (of animals) zahlreiche Vermehrung; (of nuclear weapons) Weitergabe f; (of ideas) Ausbreitung f; (of weeds) Wuchern nt.

prolific [prə'lɪfɪk] adj fruchtbar; writer produktiv.

prologue ['prəʊlɒg] n Prolog m; (of book) Vorwort nt; (fig) Vorspiel nt.

prolong [prə'lɒŋ] vt verlängern; (pej) process, pain hinauszögern.

prolongation [,prəʊlɒŋ'geɪʃən] n see vt Verlängerung f; Hinauszögern nt.

promenade [,prɒmɪ'nɑːd] 1 n (esp Brit: esplanade) (Strand)promenade f; (US: ball) Studenten-/Schülerball m. ~ concert Konzert nt (in gelockertem Rahmen); ~ deck Promenadendeck nt. 2 vi (stroll) promenieren.

prominence ['prɒmɪnəns] n (a) the ~ of his features seine ausgeprägten Gesichtszüge. (b) (of ideas, beliefs) Beliebtheit f; (of writer, politician etc) Bekanntheit f. to come into ~ in den Vordergrund rücken; (person) in Erscheinung treten; to bring sb/sth into ~ (attract attention to) jdn/etw herausstellen; (make famous) jdn berühmt machen. (c) (prominent part) Vorsprung m.

prominent ['prɒmɪnənt] adj (a) cheek-bones, teeth vorstehend attr; crag vorspringend attr. to be ~ vorstehen; vorspringen. (b) (conspicuous) markings auffällig; feature, characteristic hervorstechend. the castle occupies a ~ position das Schloß hat eine exponierte Lage. (c) (leading) role führend; (significant) wichtig. (d) (well-known) personality, publisher prominent.

prominently ['prɒmɪnəntlɪ] adv display, place deutlich sichtbar. he figured ~ er spielte eine bedeutende Rolle.

promiscuity [,prɒmɪ'skjuːɪtɪ] n Promiskuität f.

promiscuous [prə'mɪskjʊəs] adj (sexually) to be ~ häufig den Partner wechseln; ~ behaviour häufiger Partnerwechsel.

promise ['prɒmɪs] 1 n (a) Versprechen nt. their ~ of help ihre Versprechen zu helfen; to make sb a ~ jdm ein Versprechen geben; to hold or keep sb to his ~ jdn an sein Versprechen binden. (b) (hope, prospect) Hoffnung, Aussicht f. a young man of ~ ein vielversprechender junger Mann; to show ~ zu den besten Hoffnungen berechtigen. 2 vt versprechen; (forecast) hindeuten auf (+acc). to ~ (sb) to do sth (jdm) versprechen, etw zu tun; to ~ sb sth, to ~ sth to sb jdm etw versprechen; to ~ sb the earth jdm das Blaue vom Himmel herunter versprechen; **it ~s to be a hard day** es sieht nach einem harten Tag aus. **3** *vi* versprechen. **(do you) ~?** versprichst du es?; **I'll try, but I'm not promising** ich werde es versuchen, aber ich kann nichts versprechen.

promising ['promɪsɪŋ] *adj* vielversprechend.

promissory note ['promɪsərɪ'nəʊt] *n* Schuldschein *m*.

promontory ['proməntrɪ] *n* Kap *nt*.

promote [prə'məʊt] *vt* **(a)** *(in rank)* befördern *(to* zu *+dat)*. **our team was ~d** *(Ftbl)* unsere Mannschaft ist aufgestiegen. **(b)** *(foster)* fördern; *(organize) conference etc* veranstalten; *(advertise)* werben für; *(put on the market)* auf den Markt bringen.

promoter [prə'məʊtəʳ] *n (Sport, of beauty contest etc)* Promoter, Veranstalter *m*; *(of company)* Mitbegründer *m*.

promotion [prə'məʊʃən] *n* **(a)** *(in rank)* Beförderung *f*. **to get** *or* **win ~** befördert werden; *(football team)* aufsteigen. **(b)** *(fostering)* Förderung *f*; *(organization: of conference etc)* Veranstaltung *f*; *(advertising)* Werbung, Promotion *f (of* für*)*; *(advertising campaign)* Werbekampagne *f*; *(marketing)* Einführung *f* auf dem Markt.

promotional [prə'məʊʃənəl] *adj literature etc* Werbe-.

prompt [prompt] **1** *adj (+er)* prompt; *action* unverzüglich. **he is always very ~** *(on time)* er ist immer sehr pünktlich. **2** *adv* **at 6 o'clock ~** Punkt 6 Uhr. **3** *vt* **(a)** *(motivate)* veranlassen *(to* zu*)*. **to ~ sb to do sth** jdn (dazu) veranlassen, etw zu tun; **what ~ed you to do it?** was hat Sie dazu veranlaßt? **(b)** *conclusion* nahelegen. **(c)** *(help with speech)* vorsagen *(sb* jdm*)*; *(Theat)* soufflieren *(sb* jdm*)*. **he didn't need any ~ing** *(fig)* das brauchte man ihm nicht zweimal zu sagen.

prompter ['promptəʳ] *n* Souffleur *m*, Souffleuse *f*.

promptly ['promptlɪ] *adv* prompt. **they left ~ at 6** sie gingen Punkt 6 Uhr; **of course he ~ forgot it all** er hat natürlich prompt alles vergessen.

prone [prəʊn] *adj* **(a)** *(lying)* **to be** *or* **lie ~** auf dem Bauch liegen. **(b)** *(liable)* **to be ~ to sth/to do sth** zu etw neigen/dazu neigen, etw zu tun.

prong [proŋ] *n* **(a)** *(of fork)* Zinke *f*. **(b)** *(fig) (of argument)* Punkt *m*; *(of attack)* (Angriffs)spitze *f*.

-pronged [-proŋd] *adj suf (of fork)* -zinkig. **a three-~ attack** ein Angriff mit drei Spitzen.

pronoun ['prəʊnaʊn] *n* Fürwort, Pronomen *nt*.

pronounce [prə'naʊns] **1** *vt* **(a)** *word etc* aussprechen. **(b)** *(declare)* erklären für. **the doctors ~d him** unfit for work die Ärzte erklärten ihn für arbeitsunfähig; **to ~ sentence** das Urteil verkünden. **2** *vi* **to ~ in favour of/against sth** sich für/gegen etw aussprechen; **to ~ on sth** zu etw Stellung nehmen.

pronounced [prə'naʊnst] *adj (marked)* ausgesprochen; *improvement* deutlich; *views* entschieden. **he has a ~ limp** er hinkt sehr stark.

pronouncement [prə'naʊnsmənt] *n* Erklärung *f*; *(Jur: of sentence)* Verkündung *f*. **to make a ~** eine Erklärung abgeben.

pronto ['prontəʊ] *adv (col)* fix *(col)*. **do it ~** aber dalli! *(col)*.

pronunciation [prə,nʌnsɪ'eɪʃən] *n* Aussprache *f*.

proof [pruːf] **1** *n* **(a)** Beweis *m (of/that* für*/*daß als *or* zum Beweis für; **that is ~ that ...** das ist der Beweis dafür, daß ...; **to give** *or* **show ~ of sth** etw nachweisen; **can you give us any ~ of that?** können Sie (uns) dafür Beweise liefern? **(b)** *(test, trial)* Probe *f*. **to put sth to the ~** etw auf die Probe stellen; *(Tech)* etw erproben. **(c)** *(Typ)* (Korrektur)fahne *f*; *(Phot)* Probeabzug *m*. **(d)** *(of alcohol)* Alkoholgehalt *m*. **70 ~ ≈** 40 Vol.-%. **2** *adj* **to be ~ against fire** feuersicher sein; **~ against inflation** inflationssicher.

proof: ~-reader *n* Korrektor(in *f*) *m*; **~-reading** *n* Korrekturlesen *nt*.

prop [prop] **1** *n (lit)* Stütze *f*; *(fig also)* Halt *m*. **2** *vt* **to ~ the door open** die Tür offenhalten; **to ~ sth against sth** etw gegen etw lehnen.

♦ **prop up** *vt sep* **(a)** *(rest, lean)* **to ~ oneself/sth ~ against sth** sich/etw gegen etw lehnen. **(b)** *(lit, fig: support)* stützen; *tunnel, wall* abstützen; *organization* unterstützen. **to ~ oneself ~ on sth** sich auf etw *(acc)* stützen.

propaganda [,propə'gændə] *n* Propaganda *f*.

propagate ['propəgeɪt] **1** *vt* fortpflanzen; *(disseminate)* verbreiten; *views also* propagieren. **2** *vi* sich fortpflanzen; *(views)* sich verbreiten.

propagation [,propə'geɪʃən] *n* Fortpflanzung *f*; *(dissemination)* Verbreitung *f*; *(of views)* Propagierung *f*.

propel [prə'pel] *vt* antreiben; *(fuel)* betreiben.

propeller [prə'peləʳ] *n* Propeller *m*.

propelling pencil [prə,pelɪŋ'pensl] *n (Brit)* Drehbleistift *m*.

propensity [prə'pensɪtɪ] *n* Neigung *f (to* zu*)*. **to have a ~ to do sth** dazu neigen, etw zu tun.

proper ['propəʳ] **1** *adj* **(a)** *(fitting, suitable)* richtig; *(seemly)* anständig; *(prim and ~)* korrekt. **the ~ time** die richtige Zeit; **in the ~ way** richtig; **as you think ~** wie Sie es für richtig halten; **to do the ~ thing** das tun, was sich gehört; **the ~ thing to do would be to apologize** eigentlich müßte er *etc* sich entschuldigen; **we thought it only ~ wir** dachten, es gehört sich einfach. **(b)** *(actual)* eigentlich. **in the ~ sense of the word** in der eigentlichen Bedeutung des Wortes; **he's not a ~ electrician** er ist kein richtiger Elektriker; **not in Berlin ~** nicht in Berlin selbst. **(c)** *(col: real)* fool *etc* richtig; *(thorough) beating* gehörig, tüchtig *(col)*. **we are in a ~ mess** wir sitzen ganz schön in der Patsche *(col)*. **2** *adv* **(a)** *(dial)* cruel, poorly richtig *(col)*. **(b)** *(incorrect usage)* talk richtig.

properly ['propəlɪ] *adv* **(a)** *(correctly)* richtig. **~ speaking** genaugenommen; **not ~ dressed for walking** nicht richtig angezogen zum Wandern. **(b)** *(in seemly fashion)* anständig. **(c)** *(justifiably)* zu Recht. **(d)** *(col: really, thoroughly)* ganz schön *(col)*.

proper noun *n* Eigenname *m*.

property ['propətɪ] *n* **(a)** *(thing owned)* Eigentum *nt*. **that's my ~** das gehört mir; **a man of ~** ein begüterter Mann. **(b)** *(building)* Haus *nt*; Wohnung *f*; *(office)* Gebäude *nt*; *(land)* Besitztum *nt*; *(estate)* Besitz *m*. **(c)** *(characteristic)* Eigenschaft *f*. **it has healing properties** es besitzt heilende Kräfte. **(d)** *(Theat)* Requisit *nt*.

property: ~ developer *n* Häusermakler *m*; **~ man**, **~ manager** *n (Theat)* Requisiteur *m*; **~ owner** *n* Haus- und Grundbesitzer *m*.

prophecy ['profɪsɪ] *n* Prophezeiung *f*.

prophesy ['profɪsaɪ] *vt* prophezeien.

prophet ['profɪt] *n* Prophet *m*.

prophetess ['profɪtɪs] *n* Prophetin *f*.

prophetic [prə'fetɪk] *adj* prophetisch.

propitious [prə'pɪʃəs] *adj* günstig *(to, for* für*)*.

proportion [prə'pɔːʃən] **1** *n* **(a)** *(in number)* Verhältnis *nt (of x to y* zwischen x und y*)*. **~s** *(size)* Ausmaß *nt*; *(of building)* Ausmaße *pl*. **to be in/out of ~ to** *or* **with sth** im Verhältnis/in keinem Verhältnis zu etw stehen; *(in size, Art)* in den Proportionen zu etw passen/nicht zu etw passen; **to get sth in ~** *(fig)* etw objektiv betrachten; **he has let it all get out of ~** *(fig)* er hat den Blick für die Proportionen verloren; **it's out of all ~!** das geht über jedes Maß hinaus!; **he has no sense of ~** *(fig)* ihm fehlt der Sinn für das richtige Maß. **(b)** *(part, amount)* Teil *m*. **what ~ of the industry is in private hands?** wie groß ist der Anteil der Industrie, der sich in privater Hand befindet? **2** *vt* **a well ~ed woman/building** eine wohlproportionierte Frau/ein wohlausgewogenes Gebäude.

proportional [prə'pɔːʃənl] *adj* proportional *(to* zu*).* ~ **representation** Verhältniswahlrecht *nt.*

proportionally [prə'pɔːʃnlɪ] *adv* proportional; *more, less* entsprechend.

proportionate [prə'pɔːʃnɪt] *adj* proportional. **to be/not to be** ~ **to sth** im Verhältnis/in keinem Verhältnis zu etw stehen.

proposal [prə'pəuzl] *n* Vorschlag *m (on, about* zu*); (of marriage)* (Heirats)antrag *m.* **to make sb a** ~ jdm einen Vorschlag machen.

propose [prə'pəuz] **1** *vt* **(a)** vorschlagen; *motion* stellen, einbringen. **I** ~ **that we leave now** ich schlage vor, daß wir jetzt gehen. **(b)** *(have in mind)* beabsichtigen. **but I don't** ~ **to** ich habe aber nicht die Absicht; **how do you** ~ **to pay for it?** wie wollen Sie das bezahlen? **2** *vi* **(**~ *marriage)* einen (Heirats)antrag machen *(to sb* jdm*).*

proposer [prə'pəuzə^r] *n (in debate)* Antragsteller(in *f) m.*

proposition [ˌprɒpə'zɪʃən] **1** *n* **(a)** *(statement)* Aussage *f.* **(b)** *(proposal)* Vorschlag *m; (argument)* These *f.* **(c)** *(prospect)* Aussicht *f.* **(d) he/that is a tough** ~ er/das ist ein harter Brocken. **2** *vt* **to** ~ **sb** *(sexually)* jdm einen unanständigen Antrag machen.

propound [prə'paund] *vt* darlegen.

proprietary [prə'praɪətərɪ] *adj rights* Besitz-; *medicine, brand* Marken-.

proprietor [prə'praɪətə^r] *n (of pub, patent)* Inhaber(in *f) m; (of house, newspaper)* Besitzer(in *f) m.*

propriety [prə'praɪətɪ] *n (correctness)* Korrektheit *f; (decency)* Anstand *m.* **breach of** ~ Verstoß *m* gegen die guten Sitten.

props [prɒps] *npl (Theat)* Requisiten *pl.*

propulsion [prə'pʌlʃən] *n* Antrieb *m.*

prosaic [prəu'zeɪɪk] *adj* prosaisch; *(down-to-earth)* nüchtern; *life, joke* alltäglich.

proscribe [prəu'skraɪb] *vt (forbid)* verbieten; *(exile)* verbannen.

prose [prəuz] *n* Prosa *f; (writing, style)* Stil *m; (Sch: translation)* Übersetzung *f* in die Fremdsprache.

prosecute ['prɒsɪkjuːt] *vt* **(a)** *person* strafrechtlich verfolgen *(for* wegen*).* **(b)** *(form: carry on) campaign etc* durchführen; *claim* weiterverfolgen.

prosecution [ˌprɒsɪ'kjuːʃən] *n (Jur) (act of prosecuting)* strafrechtliche Verfolgung; *(in court: case, side)* Anklage *f (for* wegen*).* **(the) counsel for the** ~ der Anklagevertreter.

prosecutor ['prɒsɪkjuːtə^r] *n* Ankläger(in *f) m.*

prospect ['prɒspekt] **1** *n (outlook)* Aussicht *f (of* auf *+acc).* **what a** ~! *(iro)* das sind ja schöne Aussichten!; **he has no** ~s er hat keine Zukunft; **a job with no** ~s eine Stelle ohne Zukunft; **to hold out the** ~ **of sth** etw in Aussicht stellen; **to have sth in** ~ etw in Aussicht haben. **(b)** *(person, thing)* **Manchester is a good** ~ **for the cup** Manchester ist ein aussichtsreicher Kandidat für den Pokal. **2** [prə'spekt] *vi (Min)* nach Bodenschätzen suchen. **to** ~ **for gold** nach Gold suchen.

prospective [prə'spektɪv] *adj attr (likely to happen)* voraussichtlich; *(future) son-in-law* zukünftig; *buyer* interessiert. ~ **candidate** Kandidat *m.*

prospector [prə'spektə^r] *n* Gold-/Erz-/Olsucher *m.*

prospectus [prə'spektəs] *n* Verzeichnis *nt; (for holidays etc)* Prospekt *m.*

prosper ['prɒspə^r] *vi (country, crime)* blühen; *(financially also)* florieren.

prosperity [prɒs'perɪtɪ] *n* Wohlstand *m; (of business)* Prosperität *f.*

prosperous ['prɒspərəs] *adj* wohlhabend; *business* gutgehend; *economy* florierend, blühend.

prostate (gland) ['prɒsteɪt(ˌglænd)] *n* Prostata *f.*

prostitute ['prɒstɪtjuːt] **1** *n* Prostituierte *f.* **male** ~ männliche Prostituierte *(form),* Strichjunge *m (col).* **2** *vt one's talents* verkaufen. **to** ~ **oneself** sich prostituieren.

prostitution [ˌprɒstɪ'tjuːʃən] *n (lit, fig)* Prostitution *f; (of talents, ideals)* Verkaufen *nt.*

prostrate ['prɒstreɪt] **1** *adj* ausgestreckt. **2** [prɒ'streɪt] *vt usu pass (lit)* zu Boden werfen; *(fig) (with fatigue)* mitnehmen; *(with shock)* niederschmettern. **to be** ~**d by** *or* **with grief** vor Gram gebrochen sein. **3** [prɒ'streɪt] *vr* sich niederwerfen *(before* vor *+dat).*

protagonist [prəu'tægənɪst] *n* Protagonist(in *f) m.*

protect [prə'tekt] *vt (against* gegen, *from* vor *+dat)* schützen; *(person)* beschützen.

protection [prə'tekʃən] *n* **(a)** Schutz *m (against* gegen, *from* vor *+dat); (of rights)* Wahrung *f.* **to be under sb's** ~ unter jds Schutz *(dat)* stehen. **(b)** *(also* ~ **money)** Schutzgeld *nt.* ~ **racket** organisiertes Erpresserunwesen.

protective [prə'tektɪv] *adj* Schutz-; *attitude* beschützend. ~ **clothing** Schutzkleidung *f;* ~ **custody** Schutzhaft *f;* **she is very** ~ **towards her children** sie ist sehr fürsorglich ihren Kindern gegenüber.

protector [prə'tektə^r] *n (defender)* Beschützer *m.*

protégé, protégée ['prɒtəʒeɪ] *n* Schützling *m.*

protein ['prəutiːn] *n* Eiweiß, Protein *nt.* **a high-**~ **diet** eine eiweißreiche Kost.

protest ['prəutest] **1** *n* Protest *m; (demonstration)* Protestkundgebung *f.* **under** ~ unter Protest; **in** ~ **against** aus Protest gegen; **to make a/one's** ~ Widerspruch erheben; ~ **march** Protestmarsch *m.* **2** [prə'test] *vi (against, about* gegen*)* protestieren; *(demonstrate)* demonstrieren. **3** [prəu'test] *vt innocence* beteuern. **it's mine, he** ~**ed** das gehört mir, protestierte er.

Protestant ['prɒtɪstənt] **1** *adj* protestantisch; *(esp in Germany)* evangelisch. **2** *n* Protestant(in *f) m.*

protestation [ˌprɒtes'teɪʃən] *n* **(a)** *(of loyalty etc)* Beteuerung *f.* **(b)** *(protest)* Protest *m.*

protester [prə'testə^r] *n* Protestierende(r) *mf; (in demonstration)* Demonstrant(in *f) m.*

protocol ['prəutəkɒl] *n* Protokoll *nt.*

proton ['prəutɒn] *n* Proton *nt.*

prototype ['prəutətaɪp] *n* Prototyp *m.*

protracted [prə'træktɪd] *adj illness, discussion* langwierig; *dispute* andauernd.

protractor [prə'træktə^r] *n (Math)* Winkelmesser *m.*

protrude [prə'truːd] **1** *vi (out of, from* aus*)* vorstehen; *(eyes)* vortreten; *(ears)* abstehen. **2** *vt* strecken.

protruding [prə'truːdɪŋ] *adj* vorstehend; *eyes* vortretend; *ears* abstehend.

protuberant [prə'tjuːbərənt] *adj* vorstehend; *eyes* vortretend.

proud [praud] **1** *adj* stolz *(of* auf *+acc).* **to be** ~ **that** ... stolz (darauf) sein, daß ...; **I hope you're** ~ **of yourself** *(iro)* ich hoffe, du bist stolz auf dich; **that's nothing to be** ~ **of** das ist nichts, worauf man stolz sein kann. **2** *adv* **to do sb/oneself** ~ jdn/sich verwöhnen.

proudly ['praudlɪ] *adv* stolz.

prove [pruːv] *pret* ~**d,** *ptp* ~**d** *or* **proven 1** *vt (verify)* beweisen. **to** ~ **sb innocent** *or* **sb's innocence** jds Unschuld beweisen; **he was** ~**d right** in the end er hat schließlich doch recht behalten. **(b)** *(test) rifle etc* erproben; *one's worth, courage* beweisen. **(c)** *also* ~*it (turn out)* **to** ~ (to be) **useful** *etc* sich als nützlich etc erweisen; **if it** ~**s otherwise** wenn sich das Gegenteil herausstellt. **2** *vr* **(a)** *(show one's value, courage etc)* sich bewähren. **(b)** **to** ~ **oneself innocent** *etc* sich als unschuldig etc erweisen.

proverb ['prɒvɜːb] *n* Sprichwort *nt.*

proverbial [prə'vɜːbɪəl] *adj (lit, fig)* sprichwörtlich.

provide [prə'vaɪd] **1** *vt* **(a)** *(make available)* zur Verfügung stellen; *money* bereitstellen; *(see to, bring along) food, records etc* sorgen für; *(produce) ideas, specialist knowledge, electricity* liefern;

shade spenden; *privacy, topic of conversation* sorgen für. to ~ sth **for sb** jdm etw zur Verfügung stellen; *(supply)* jdm etw besorgen; to ~ sb **with sth** *(with food etc)* jdn mit etw versorgen; *(equip)* jdn mit etw ausstatten; *(with excuse, idea)* jdm etw liefern; *(with opportunity, information)* jdm etw verschaffen *or* geben; **this job** ~**d him with enough money** die Stelle verschaffte ihm genug Geld. **(b)** *(stipulate: clause, agreement)* vorsehen. **2** *vi* **the Lord will** ~ *(prov)* der Herr wird's schon geben.

♦ **provide for** *vi* +*prep obj* **(a)** *family etc* versorgen. **his family was well** ~**d** ~ seine Familie war gut versorgt. **(b)** as ~**d** ~ **in the 1970 contract** wie in dem Vertrag von 1970 vorgesehen; **we** ~**d** ~ **all emergencies** wir haben für alle Notfälle vorgesorgt.

provided (that) [prə'vaɪdɪd('ðæt)] *conj* vorausgesetzt(, daß).

providence ['prɒvɪdəns] *n (fate)* die Vorsehung.

providential [ˌprɒvɪ'denʃəl] *adj* glücklich. **to be** ~ **(ein)** Glück sein.

providing (that) [prə'vaɪdɪŋ('ðæt)] *conj* vorausgesetzt(, daß).

province ['prɒvɪns] *n* **(a)** Provinz *f*. **(b)** the ~**s** *pl* die Provinz. **(c)** *(fig: area of knowledge, activity etc)* Gebiet *nt*, Bereich *m*. **it's not within my** ~ das fällt nicht in meinen Bereich; **that is outside my** ~ das ist nicht mein Gebiet. **(d)** *(area of authority)* Kompetenzbereich *m*. **that's not my** ~ dafür bin ich nicht zuständig.

provincial [prə'vɪnʃəl] **1** *adj* Provinz-; *custom, accent* ländlich; *(pej)* provinziell. **2** *n* Provinzbewohner(in *f*) *m*; *(pej)* Provinzler(in *f*) *m*.

provision [prə'vɪʒən] *n* **(a)** *(act of supplying)* Beschaffung *f*; *(of food, water etc)* Versorgung *f* *(of* mit, *to sb* jds). **(b)** *(supply)* Vorrat *m* *(of* an +*dat)*. **(c)** ~**s** *(food)* Lebensmittel *pl*; *(for journey)* Proviant *m*. **(d)** *(allowance)* Berücksichtigung *f*; *(arrangement)* Vorkehrung *f*; *(stipulation)* Bestimmung *f*. **with the** ~ **that** ... mit der Bedingung, daß...; **there's no** ~ **for later additions** spätere Erweiterungen sind nicht vorgesehen; **to make** ~ **for the future** für die Zukunft Vorsorge treffen; **to make** ~ **for sth** etw vorsehen; *for error etc* etw einkalkulieren; **to make** ~ **against sth** gegen etw Vorkehrungen treffen.

provisional [prə'vɪʒənl] **1** *adj* provisorisch; *measures also, offer, decision* vorläufig. ~ **driving licence** *(Brit)* vorläufige Fahrerlaubnis für Fahrschüler. **2** *n (Ir Pol)* the **P**~**s** die Provisorische Irisch-Republikanische Armee.

provisionally [prə'vɪʒnəlɪ] *adv* vorläufig.

proviso [prə'vaɪzəu] *n (condition)* Bedingung *f*; *(clause)* Vorbehaltsklausel *f*.

provocation [ˌprɒvə'keɪʃən] *n* Provokation *f*.

provocative [prə'vɒkətɪv] *adj* provokatorisch; *remark, behaviour also* herausfordernd.

provoke [prə'vəuk] *vt sb* provozieren, herausfordern; *animal* reizen; *anger, criticism, smile* hervorrufen; *discussion, revolt* auslösen. **to** ~ **sb into doing sth** *or* **to do sth** jdn dazu bringen, daß er etw tut; *(taunt)* jdn dazu treiben, daß er etw tut.

provoking [prə'vəukɪŋ] *adj* provozierend; *(annoying)* ärgerlich.

provost ['prɒvəst] *n (Scot)* Bürgermeister *m*; *(Univ)* ≈ Dekan *m*.

prow [prau] *n* Bug *m*.

prowess ['prauɪs] *n (skill)* Fähigkeiten *pl*, Können *nt*; *(courage)* Tapferkeit *f*.

prowl [praul] *vi (also* ~ **about** *or* **around)** herumstreichen; *(boss, headmaster)* herumschleichen.

prowler ['praulə'] *n* Herumtreiber(in *f*) *m*; *(peeping Tom)* Spanner *m (col)*.

proximity [prɒk'sɪmɪtɪ] *n* Nähe *f*. **in close** ~ **to** in

unmittelbarer Nähe *(+gen)*.

proxy ['prɒksɪ] *n (power)* (Handlungs)vollmacht *f*; *(person)* Stellvertreter(in *f*) *m*. **by** ~ durch einen Stellvertreter.

prude [pru:d] *n* **to be a** ~ prüde sein.

prudence ['pru:dəns] *n see adj* Umsicht *f*; Klugheit *f*; Überlegtheit *f*.

prudent ['pru:dənt] *adj person* umsichtig; *measure, decision* klug; *answer* wohlüberlegt.

prudish ['pru:dɪʃ] *adj* prüde.

prune¹ [pru:n] *n* Backpflaume *f*.

prune² *vt (also* ~ **down)** stutzen; *(fig) expenditure, essay* kürzen; *workforce* reduzieren.

pry¹ [praɪ] *vi* neugierig sein; *(in drawers etc)* (herum)schnüffeln *(in in* +*dat)*. **I don't mean to** ~, **but** ... es geht mich ja nichts an, aber ...; **to** ~ **into sb's affairs** seine Nase in jds Angelegenheiten *(acc)* stecken.

pry² *vt (US)* = **prise**.

PS = **postscript** PS.

psalm [sɑ:m] *n* Psalm *m*.

pseud [sju:d] *(col) n* Angeber(in *f*) *m*.

pseudo ['sju:dəu] *adj (col: pretended)* unecht; *intellectual etc* Möchtegern- *(col)*, Pseudo-.

pseudo- *pref* Pseudo-, pseudo.

pseudonym ['sju:dənɪm] *n* Pseudonym *nt*.

psyche ['saɪkɪ] *n* Psyche *f*.

♦ **psyche up** [ˌsaɪk'ʌp] *vt sep (col)* **to** ~ **oneself** ~ sich in Stimmung bringen.

psychedelic [ˌsaɪkɪ'delɪk] *adj* psychedelisch.

psychiatric [ˌsaɪkɪ'ætrɪk] *adj* psychiatrisch; *illness* psychisch.

psychiatrist [saɪ'kaɪətrɪst] *n* Psychiater(in *f*) *m*.

psychiatry [saɪ'kaɪətrɪ] *n* Psychiatrie *f*.

psychic ['saɪkɪk] *adj* übersinnlich; *powers* übernatürlich. ~ **research** Parapsychologie *f*; **she is** ~ sie besitzt übernatürliche Kräfte; **you must be** ~! du kannst wohl hellsehen!

psycho ['saɪkəu] *n (US col)* Verrückte(r) *mf*.

psychoanalyse, *(US)* **psychoanalyze** [ˌsaɪkəu'ænəlaɪz] *vt* psychoanalytisch behandeln.

psychoanalysis [ˌsaɪkəuə'nælɪsɪs] *n* Psychoanalyse *f*.

psychoanalyst [ˌsaɪkəu'ænəlɪst] *n* Psychoanalytiker(in *f*) *m*.

psychological [ˌsaɪkə'lɒdʒɪkəl] *adj (mental)* psychisch; *(concerning psychology)* psychologisch. ~ **warfare** psychologische Kriegführung; **he's not really ill, it's all** ~ er ist nicht wirklich krank, das alles psychisch bedingt.

psychologist [saɪ'kɒlədʒɪst] *n* Psychologe *m*, Psychologin *f*.

psychology [saɪ'kɒlədʒɪ] *n (science)* Psychologie *f*; *(make-up)* Psyche *f*.

psychopath ['saɪkəupæθ] *n* Psychopath(in *f*) *m*.

psychosis [saɪ'kəusɪs] *n, pl* **psychoses** [saɪ'kəusi:z] Psychose *f*.

psychosomatic [ˌsaɪkəusəu'mætɪk] *adj* psychosomatisch. ~ **medicine** Psychosomatik *f*.

psychotherapy [ˌsaɪkəu'θerəpɪ] *n* Psychotherapie *f*.

psychotic [saɪ'kɒtɪk] **1** *adj* psychotisch. ~ **illness** Psychose *f*. **2** *n* Psychotiker(in *f*) *m*.

pto = **please turn over** bitte wenden, b. w.

pub [pʌb] *n (Brit)* Kneipe *(col)*, Wirtschaft *f*; *(in the country also)* Gasthaus *nt*.

pub-crawl ['pʌbkrɔːl] *n (Brit col)* **to go on a** ~ einen Kneipenbummel machen *(col)*.

puberty ['pju:bətɪ] *n* die Pubertät.

pubic ['pju:bɪk] *adj* Scham-.

public ['pʌblɪk] **1** *adj* öffentlich; *health, library also* Volks-; *spending, debts* der öffentlichen Hand, Staats-. **to be** ~ **knowledge** allgemein bekannt sein; **in the** ~ **interest** im öffentlichen Interesse; **it's rather** ~ **here** es ist nicht gerade privat hier; **he is a** ~ **figure** er ist eine Persönlichkeit des öffentlichen Lebens; **in the** ~ **eye** im Blickpunkt der Öffentlichkeit; **to make sth ~** etw bekanntgeben; *(officially)* etw öffentlich bekanntmachen; **to create ~ awareness** öffentliches Interesse wecken; **to go ~** *(Comm)* in eine Aktiengesellschaft umgewandelt werden. **2** *n sing or pl* Öffentlichkeit *f.* **in ~** in der Öffentlichkeit; *speak also* öffentlich; **the theatre-going ~** die theaterinteressierte Öffentlichkeit.

public address system *n* Lautsprecheranlage *f.*

publican ['pʌblɪkən] *n (Brit)* Gastwirt(in *f*) *m.*

publication [ˌpʌblɪ'keɪʃən] *n* Veröffentlichung *f.*

public: ~ company *n* Aktiengesellschaft *f*; **~ convenience** *n (Brit)* öffentliche Toilette; **~ holiday** *n* gesetzlicher Feiertag; **~ house** *n (Brit)* Gaststätte *f.*

publicity [pʌb'lɪsɪtɪ] *n* Publicity *f*; *(Comm: advertising, advertisements)* Werbung *f.* **~ campaign** Publicitykampagne *f*; *(Comm)* Werbekampagne *f.*

publicize ['pʌblɪsaɪz] *vt* **(a)** *(make public)* bekanntmachen. **I don't ~ the fact** ich will das nicht an die große Glocke hängen *(col).* **(b)** *(get publicity for)* film, author Publicity machen für; *new product* Werbung machen für.

public: ~ opinion *n* die öffentliche Meinung; **~ opinion poll** *n* Meinungsumfrage *f*; **~ ownership** *n under ~ ownership* in öffentlichem Besitz; **~ purse** *n* Staatskasse *f*; **~ relations** *npl* Public Relations *pl*, Öffentlichkeitsarbeit *f*; **~ relations officer** *n* Pressesprecher(in *f*) *m*; **~ school** *n (Brit)* Privatschule, Public School *f*; *(US)* staatliche Schule; **~ sector** *n* öffentlicher Sektor; **~ service** *n (Civil Service)* öffentlicher Dienst; *(facility: water, transport etc)* öffentlicher Dienstleistungsbetrieb; *(work)* Dienst *m* an der Allgemeinheit; **~ speaking** *n* I don't like **~ speaking** ich halte nicht gern Reden; **~-spirited** *adj* act von Gemeinsinn zeugend; **~ transport** *n* öffentliche Verkehrsmittel *pl.*

publish ['pʌblɪʃ] *vt* **(a)** *(issue)* veröffentlichen; *book, magazine etc also* herausbringen. **~ed by Collins** bei Collins erschienen; **"~ed monthly"** „erscheint monatlich"; **who's that book ~ed by?** in welchem Verlag ist das Buch erschienen? **(b)** *(make public)* news, banns bekanntgeben; *decree* herausgeben; *will* eröffnen.

publisher ['pʌblɪʃəʳ] *n (person)* Verleger(in *f*) *m*; *(firm: also ~s)* Verlag *m.*

publishing ['pʌblɪʃɪŋ] *n (trade)* das Verlagswesen. **~ company** *n* Verlagshaus *nt.*

puce [pjuːs] *adj* braunrot; *(with rage, shame)* rot.

pucker ['pʌkəʳ] *vt (also ~ up)* one's lips, mouth verziehen; *(for kissing)* spitzen; *one's brow* runzeln; *material* Falten machen in *(+acc).*

pudding ['pʊdɪŋ] *n (dessert)* Nachspeise *f.* **what's for ~?** was gibt es als Nachtisch?

pudding basin *n* Puddingform *f.*

puddle ['pʌdl] *n* Pfütze *f.*

puerile ['pjʊəraɪl] *adj* infantil.

puff [pʌf] **1** *n* **(a)** *(on cigarette etc)* Zug *m (at, of an +dat).* **~ of wind** ein Windstoß *m*; **a ~ of smoke** eine Rauchwolke; **to be out of ~** *(col)* außer Puste sein *(col).* **(b)** *(powder ~)* Quaste *f.* **(c)** *(Cook)* cream **~** Windbeutel *m*; **~ pastry,** *(US)* **~ paste** Blätterteig *m.* **2** *vt smoke* ausstoßen; *(person)* blasen; *cigarette* paffen *(col).* **3** *vi (person, train)* schnaufen; *(chimney, smoke)* qualmen. **the train ~ed into the station** der Zug fuhr schnaufend in den Bahnhof ein; **to ~ at a cigar** an einer Zigarre paffen *(col).*

puffin ['pʌfɪn] *n* Papageientaucher *m.*

puffy ['pʌfɪ] *adj (+er) (swollen)* geschwollen; *(from crying)* verquollen.

pug [pʌg] *n (also ~ dog)* Mops *m.*

pugnacious [pʌg'neɪʃəs] *adj* kampfeslustig; *(verbally)* streitsüchtig.

pug-nosed ['pʌgnəʊzd] *adj* knollennasig.

puke [pjuːk] *vti (col!)* kotzen *(col).*

pull [pʊl] **1** *n* **(a)** *(tug)* Ziehen *nt*; *(short)* Ruck *m*; *(lit, fig: attraction)* Anziehungskraft *f*; *(of current)* Sog *m.* **he gave her/the rope a ~** er zog sie/am Seil; **I felt a ~ at my sleeve** ich spürte, wie mich jemand am Ärmel zog. **(b)** *(at pipe, beer)* Zug *m.* **he took a ~ at his pipe/glass** er zog an seiner Pfeife/nahm einen Schluck aus seinem Glas. **(c)** bell **~** Klingelzug *m.* **(d)** *(col: influence)* Beziehungen *pl.* **I've got no ~ with them** ich habe keinen Draht zu ihnen *(col).*

2 *vt* **(a)** *(draw, drag)* ziehen. **to ~ a door shut** eine Tür zuziehen. **(b)** *(tug)* rope, bell ziehen an *(+dat)*; boat rudern. **he ~ed her hair** er zog sie an den Haaren; **to ~ sth to pieces** *(lit)* etw in Stücke reißen, *(fig: criticize)* etw verreißen; **~ the other one** *(col)* das glaubst du doch wohl selber nicht!; **she was the one ~ing the strings** sie war es, die alle Fäden in der Hand hielt; **to ~ one's punches** *(fig)* sich zurückhalten. **(c)** *(extract, draw out)* tooth, gun, knife ziehen; *weeds, lettuce, cork* herausziehen; *beer* zapfen. **to ~ a gun on sb** jdn mit der Pistole bedrohen. **(d)** *(strain)* muscle sich *(dat)* zerren; *(tear) thread* ziehen. **(e)** *(attract)* crowd anziehen. **(f)** *(col)* **what are you trying to ~?** was heckst du wieder aus? *(col).*

3 *vi* **(a)** ziehen *(on, at an +dat).* **to ~ to the left** *(car)* nach links ziehen; **to ~ on** or **at one's cigarette** an seiner Zigarette ziehen. **(b)** *(move: train, car etc)* fahren. **the car ~ed into the driveway** der Wagen fuhr in die Einfahrt; **he ~ed across to the left-hand lane** er wechselte auf die linke Spur über; **to ~ ahead (of sb)** *(car, runner)* (an jdm) vorbeiziehen; *(fig: rival etc)* jdn hinter sich *(dat)* lassen.

♦ **pull apart** *vt sep* **(a)** *(separate)* auseinanderziehen; *sheets of paper also, fighting people* trennen; *radio etc* auseinandernehmen. **(b)** *(fig col)* *(search thoroughly)* auseinandernehmen *(col)*; *(criticise also)* verreißen.

♦ **pull away 1** *vt sep* wegziehen. **she ~ed it ~ from him** sie zog es von ihm weg; *(from his hands)* sie zog es ihm aus den Händen. **2** *vi (move off)* wegfahren; *(ship)* ablegen.

♦ **pull back 1** *vt sep* zurückziehen. **2** *vi (lit)* sich zurückziehen; *(catch up)* aufholen. **to ~ ~ (from doing sth)** *(fig)* einen Rückzieher machen *(und etw nicht tun) (col).*

♦ **pull down** *vt sep* **(a)** herunterziehen. **(b)** *(demolish)* buildings abreißen.

♦ **pull in 1** *vt sep* **(a)** *claws etc* einziehen; *(into swimming-pool etc)* hineinziehen. **(b)** *(rein in)* horse zügeln. **(c)** *(attract)* crowds anziehen. **(d)** *(col: take into custody)* einkassieren *(col).* **2** *vi* **(a)** *(into station etc)* einfahren, einlaufen *(into* in *+acc)*; *(into driveway)* hineinfahren *(into* in *+acc)*; *(stop, park)* anhalten. **he ~ed ~ to the side of the road** er fuhr an den Straßenrand.

♦ **pull off** *vt sep* **(a)** *wrapping paper* abreißen; *cover also* abnehmen; *(violently)* abreißen; *clothes, shoes* ausziehen. **(b)** *(col: succeed in)* schaffen *(col)*; *deal also* zuwege bringen *(col)*; *burglary* drehen *(col).*

♦ **pull on** *vt sep* coat etc sich *(dat)* überziehen; *hat* aufsetzen.

♦ **pull out 1** *vt sep* **(a)** *(extract)* *(of aus)* herausziehen; *tooth* ziehen; *page* heraustrennen. **(b)** *(withdraw)* zurückziehen; *troops* abziehen. **2** *vi* **(a)** *(withdraw)* aussteigen *(of aus) (col)*; *(troops)* abziehen. **(b)** *(leave: train etc)* herausfahren *(of aus).* **(c)** *(driver)* herausfahren.

♦ **pull over 1** *vi* *(car)* (an die Seite) hinüber-/herüberziehen *(prep obj über +acc).* **(b)** *(topple)* umreißen. **2** *vi (car, driver)* zur Seite fahren.

♦ **pull through** *vi (fig: recover)* durchkommen.

♦ **pull together 1** *vi (lit)* gemeinsam ziehen, *(fig: cooperate)* am gleichen Strang ziehen. **2** *vr* sich zusammenreißen. **~ yourself ~** reiß dich zusammen.

♦ **pull up 1** *vt sep* **(a)** *(raise by pulling)* hochziehen; *(up slope also)* nach oben ziehen. **(b)** *(uproot)* herausreißen. **(c)** *(stop)* anhalten. **(d)** *(reprimand) (for behaviour)* zurechtweisen; *(for grammar etc)* korrigieren. **2** *vi (stop)* anhalten.

pulley ['pulɪ] *n* Rolle *f*; *(block)* Flaschenzug *m*.

pull: ~-**out** *n (withdrawal)* Abzug *m; (supplement)* heraustrennbarer Teil; ~**over** *n* Pullover *m*.

pulp [pʌlp] **1** *n*   Brei *m; (of fruit)* Fruchtfleisch *nt*. to beat sb to a ~ *(col)* jdn zu Brei schlagen *(col)*. **2** *vt fruit* zerdrücken; *paper, book* einstampfen; *wood* zu Brei verarbeiten.

pulpit ['pulpɪt] *n* Kanzel *f*.

pulsate [pʌl'seɪt] *vi (lit, fig)* pulsieren; *(head, heart)* klopfen; *(voice, building)* beben; *(music)* rhythmisch klingen.

pulse[1] [pʌls] **1** *n (Anat)* Puls *m; (Phys)* Impuls *m; (fig: of music)* Rhythmus *m*. to feel *or* take sb's ~ jdm den Puls fühlen. **2** *vi* pulsieren; *(machines)* stampfen.

pulse[2] *n (Bot, Cook)* Hülsenfrucht *f*.

puma ['pjuːmə] *n* Puma *m*.

pumice (stone) ['pʌmɪs(ˌstəʊn)] *n* Bimsstein *m*.

pummel ['pʌml] *vt* eintrommeln auf (+*acc*).

pump [pʌmp] **1** *n* Pumpe *f*. **2** *vt* pumpen; *brake pedal* mehrmals treten. to ~ **sth dry** etw leerpumpen; **to ~ sb dry** *(fig)* jdn aussaugen; **to ~ bullets into sb** jdn mit Blei vollpumpen *(col)*; **to ~ money into sth** Geld in etw *(acc)* hineinpumpen; **to ~ information out of sb** Informationen aus jdm herausholen.

♦ **pump in** *vt sep (lit, fig)* hineinpumpen.

♦ **pump out** *vt sep liquid, air* herauspumpen; *boat, cellar* leerpumpen; *stomach* auspumpen.

♦ **pump up** *vt sep tyre etc* aufpumpen.

pumpkin ['pʌmpkɪn] *n* Kürbis *m*.

pun [pʌn] *n* Wortspiel *nt*.

Punch [pʌntʃ] *n* Kasper *m*, Kasperle *nt*. ~-**and-Judy show** Kasper(le)theater *nt*; **to be (as) pleased as** ~ *(col)* sich wie ein Schneekönig freuen *(col)*.

punch[1] [pʌntʃ] **1** *n* **(a)** *(blow)* Schlag *m*. **(b)** *no pl (fig: vigour)* Schwung *m*. **2** *vti* boxen.

punch[2] **1** *n (for ~ing holes)* Locher *m; (for tickets)* Lochzange *f; (for stamping metal etc)* Prägestempel *m*. **2** *vt ticket etc* lochen; *metal, holes* stanzen; *(stamp) metal, pattern* prägen.

♦ **punch in** *vt sep (Comp)* data tasten, tippen *(col)*.

punch[3] *n (drink)* Bowle *f; (hot)* Punsch *m*.

punch: ~ **ball** *n* Punchingball *m*; ~ **bowl** *n* Bowle *f*; ~ **card** *n* Lochkarte *f*; ~-**drunk** *adj (fig)* durcheinander *pred*; ~-**line** *n* Pointe *f*; ~ **tape** *n* Lochstreifen *m*; ~-**up** *n (Brit col)* Schlägerei *f*.

punctilious [pʌŋk'tɪlɪəs] *adj (regarding etiquette)* korrekt; *(fastidious)* peinlich genau.

punctual ['pʌŋktjʊəl] *adj* pünktlich. to be ~ pünktlich kommen.

punctuality [ˌpʌŋktjʊ'ælɪtɪ] *n* Pünktlichkeit *f*.

punctuate ['pʌŋktjʊeɪt] *vt* **(a)** *(Gram)* mit Satzzeichen versehen. **(b)** *(intersperse)* unterbrechen. he ~**d** his talk with jokes er spickte seine Rede mit Witzen.

punctuation [ˌpʌŋktjʊ'eɪʃən] *n* Zeichensetzung, Interpunktion *f*. ~ **mark** Satzzeichen *nt*.

puncture ['pʌŋktʃəʳ] **1** *n (in tyre, balloon etc)* Loch *nt; (in skin)* (Ein)stich *m; (flat tyre)* Reifenpanne *f*. **2** *vt* stechen in (+*acc*); *membrane* durchstechen; *tyre, balloon* Löcher/ein Loch machen in (+*acc*).

pundit ['pʌndɪt] *n (fig)* Experte *m*, Expertin *f*.

pungency ['pʌndʒənsɪ] *n (lit, fig)* Schärfe *f*.

pungent ['pʌndʒənt] *adj (lit, fig)* scharf; *smell also* stechend.

punish ['pʌnɪʃ] *vt* **(a)** *person, offence* bestrafen. **(b)** *(fig col: drive hard, treat roughly)* strapazieren; *horses, oneself* schinden; *opponent* zusetzen (+*dat*).

punishable ['pʌnɪʃəbl] *adj* strafbar. it is a ~ **offence** es ist strafbar.

punishing ['pʌnɪʃɪŋ] **1** *adj blow* hart. **2** *n* to take a ~ *(col) (car, furniture etc)* strapaziert werden; *(team, boxer etc)* vorgeführt werden *(col)*.

punishment ['pʌnɪʃmənt] *n* **(a)** *(penalty)* Strafe *f; (punishing)* Bestrafung *f*. **(b)** *(fig col)* **to take a lot of** ~ *(car, furniture etc)* stark strapaziert werden; *(Sport)* vorgeführt werden *(col)*.

punk [pʌŋk] *n* **(a)** *(person: also* ~ **rocker)** Punker *m; (music: also* ~ **rock)** Punk(-Rock) *m; (culture)* Punk *m*. **(b)** *(US col: hoodlum)* Ganove *m (col)*.

punt [pʌnt] **1** *n (boat)* Stechkahn *m*. **2** *vti* staken. to **go** ~**ing** Stechkahn fahren.

punter ['pʌntəʳ] *n* **(a)** *(better)* Wetter *m; (gambler)* Spieler(in *f*) *m*. **(b)** *(col)* Typ *m (col)*. **the average** ~ Otto Normalverbraucher.

puny ['pjuːnɪ] *adj (+er) (weak) person* schwächlich; *effort* kläglich.

pup [pʌp] *n* Junge(s) *nt*.

pupil[1] ['pjuːpl] *n (Sch, fig)* Schüler(in *f*) *m*.

pupil[2] *n (Anat)* Pupille *f*.

puppet ['pʌpɪt] *n* Puppe *f; (glove* ~) Handpuppe *f; (string* ~, *fig)* Marionette *f*.

puppet: ~-**government** *n* Marionettenregierung *f*; ~-**show** *n* Puppenspiel *nt*; ~ **state** *n* Marionettenstaat *m*.

puppy ['pʌpɪ] *n* junger Hund. ~ **fat** *n* Babyspeck *m*; ~ **love** *n* Schwärmerei *f*.

purchase ['pɜːtʃɪs] **1** *n* **(a)** *(act)* Kauf *m; (of furniture, flat, car also)* Anschaffung *f*. to make a ~ einen Kauf tätigen; eine Anschaffung machen. **(b)** *(grip)* Halt *m*. he couldn't get a ~ on the wet rope er konnte an dem nassen Seil keinen Halt finden. **2** *vt (buy)* kaufen, erwerben *(form)*. purchasing **power** Kaufkraft *f*; ~ **price** Kaufpreis *m*.

purchaser ['pɜːtʃɪsəʳ] *n* Käufer(in *f*) *m*.

pure [pjʊəʳ] *adj (+er)* rein; *motive* ehrlich, lauter *(geh)*. she stared at him in ~ **disbelief** sie starrte ihn ganz ungläubig an; *malice* ~ **and simple** reine Bosheit; a ~ **wool dress** ein Kleid aus reiner Wolle.

purée ['pjʊəreɪ] *n* Püree *nt*, Brei *m*. **tomato** ~ Tomatenmark *nt*.

purely ['pjʊəlɪ] *adv* rein.

purgative ['pɜːɡətɪv] *n* Abführmittel *nt*.

purgatory ['pɜːɡətərɪ] *n (Rel)* das Fegefeuer; *(fig: state)* die Hölle.

purge [pɜːdʒ] **1** *n* **(a)** *(Med)* *(starkes)* Abführmittel. **(b)** *(Pol etc)* Säuberung(saktion) *f*. **2** *vt* reinigen; *body* entschlacken; *guilt, sin* büßen; *(Pol etc)* party säubern *(of von); traitor* eliminieren *(form aus)*.

purification [ˌpjʊərɪfɪ'keɪʃən] *n* Reinigung *f*.

purify ['pjʊərɪfaɪ] *vt* reinigen.

purist ['pjʊərɪst] *n* Purist(in *f*) *m*.

puritan ['pjʊərɪtən] *(Rel:* **P**~) **1** *adj* puritanisch. **2** *n* Puritaner(in *f*) *m*.

puritanical [ˌpjʊərɪ'tænɪkəl] *adj* puritanisch.

purity ['pjʊərɪtɪ] *n* Reinheit *f; (of motives)* Lauterkeit *(geh)*, Ehrlichkeit *f*.

purl [pɜːl] *n* eine linke Masche. ~ **two** zwei links.

purple ['pɜːpl] **1** *adj* violett, lila; *face* hochrot; *(pej) passage* hochtrabend. to go ~ *(in the face)* hochrot werden. **2** *n (colour)* Violett, Lila *nt*.

purport ['pɜːpət] **1** *n* Tenor *m*. **2** [pɜː'pɔːt] *vt* to ~ to be/do sth *(person)* vorgeben, etw zu sein/tun; *(thing)* etw sein/tun sollen.

purpose ['pɜːpəs] *n* **(a)** *(intention)* Absicht *f; (goal)* Zweck *m*. on ~ mit Absicht, absichtlich; he did it for *or* with the ~ of improving his image er tat es in der Absicht, sein Image zu verbessern; to have a ~ in life ein Lebensziel haben; to answer *or* serve sb's ~(s) jds Zweck(en) dienen; for our ~s für unsere Zwecke; for the ~s of this meeting zum Zweck dieser Konferenz; for all practical ~s in der Praxis; to the ~ relevant; to good ~ zum guten Zweck; to no ~ umsonst. **(b)** *no pl* strength of ~ Entschlußkraft *f*; sense of ~ Zielbewußtsein *nt*.

purpose-built ['pɜ:pəs'bɪlt] *adj* Spezial-; *building also* speziell gebaut.

purposeful ['pɜ:pəsfʊl] *adj* entschlossen.

purposely ['pɜ:pəslɪ] *adv* bewußt, absichtlich.

purr [pɜːʳ] 1 *vi* (*cat, fig: person*) schnurren; (*engine*) surren. 2 *n* Schnurren *nt no pl*; Surren *nt no pl*.

purse [pɜːs] 1 *n* (a) (*for money*) Portemonnaie *nt*, Geldbörse *f* (*form*). to hold the ~ strings (*fig*) über die Finanzen bestimmen. (b) (*US: handbag*) Handtasche *f*. (c) (*Sport: prize*) Preisgeld *nt*. 2 *vt* to ~ one's lips einen Schmollmund machen.

purser ['pɜːsəʳ] *n* Zahlmeister *m*.

pursue [pə'sjuː] *vt* (a) verfolgen; *pleasure, success* nachjagen (+*dat*), aussein auf (+*acc*); *happiness* streben nach. (b) (*carry on*) *course of action etc* verfolgen; *inquiry* durchführen; *profession, studies* nachgehen (+*dat*); *subject* weiterführen.

pursuer [pə'sjuːəʳ] *n* Verfolger(in *f*) *m*.

pursuit [pə'sjuːt] *n* (a) (*of person*) Verfolgung (*of gen*), Jagd (*of auf* +*acc*) *f*; (*of knowledge, happiness*) Streben *nt* (*of nach*); (*of pleasure*) Jagd *f* (*of nach*). in hot ~ of sb hart auf jds Fersen (*acc*); to go in ~ of sb/sth sich auf die Jagd nach jdm/etw machen; in (the) ~ of his goal in Verfolgung seines Ziels. (b) (*occupation*) Beschäftigung *f*; (*hobby, pastime*) Zeitvertreib *m*. his literary ~s seine Beschäftigung mit der Literatur.

purveyor [pə'veɪəʳ] *n* (*form*) (*seller*) Händler *m*; (*supplier*) Lieferant *m*.

pus [pʌs] *n* Eiter *m*.

push [pʊʃ] 1 *n* (a) Schubs *m* (*col*); (*short*) Stoß *m*. to give sb/sth a ~ jdn/etw schieben; jdm/etw einen Stoß versetzen; to give a car a ~ einen Wagen anschieben; to give sb the ~ (*Brit col*) *employee* jdn rausschmeißen (*col*); *boyfriend* jdm den Laufpaß geben (*col*). (b) (*effort*) Anstrengung *f*; (*sales* ~) Aktion *f*; (*Mil: offensive*) Offensive *f*. (c) (*drive, aggression*) Durchsetzungsvermögen *nt*. (d) (*col*) at a ~ notfalls, im Notfall; if/when it comes to the ~ wenn es darauf ankommt.

2 *vt* (a) schieben; (*quickly, violently*) stoßen, schubsen (*col*); (*press*) *button* drücken. to ~ a door open/shut eine Tür auf-/zudrücken; he ~ed the book into my hand er drückte mir das Buch in die Hand.

(b) (*fig*) *claims, interests* durchzusetzen versuchen; *candidate* die Werbetrommel rühren für; *product* propagieren, pushen (*Comm sl*); *drugs* schieben, pushen (*Drugs sl*). to ~ home one's advantage seinen Vorteil ausnützen; **don't ~ your luck** treib's nicht zu weit!; **he must be ~ing 70** (*col*) er muß auf die 70 zugehen.

(c) (*fig: put pressure on*) drängen, drängeln (*col*); *pupil, employee* antreiben. to ~ sb to do sth jdn dazu drängen, etw zu tun; **they ~ed him to the limits** sie trieben ihn bis an seine Grenzen; **that's ~ing it a bit** (*col*) das ist ein bißchen übertrieben; **to be ~ed for time/money** (*col*) unter Zeitdruck stehen/knapp bei Kasse sein (*col*); **I'm a bit ~ed just now** (*col*) ich habe momentan wenig Zeit.

3 *vi* (*shove*) schieben; (*quickly, violently*) stoßen; (*in a crowd, apply pressure*) drängen, drängeln (*col*); (*fig: be ambitious, assert oneself*) kämpfen. "~~" (*on door*) „drücken"; (*on bell*) „klingeln".

♦ **push around** *vt sep* (a) herumstoßen. (b) (*fig col: bully*) herumschubsen.

♦ **push aside** *vt sep* zur Seite *or* beiseite schieben; (*fig*) *problems etc* einfach abtun.

♦ **push away** *vt sep* wegschieben; (*quickly*) wegstoßen.

♦ **push back** *vt sep* *people* zurückdrängen; (*with one push*) zurückstoßen; *curtains, hair* zurückschieben.

♦ **push down** *vt sep* nach unten drücken; (*knock over*) umstoßen; *fence* niederreißen.

♦ **push down on** *vi* +*prep obj* drücken auf (+*acc*).

♦ **push forward 1** *vi* (*Mil*) vorwärts drängen. 2 *vt sep* (*lit*) nach vorn schieben; (*fig*) *claim* geltend machen; *ideas* hervorheben; *sb, oneself* in den Vordergrund schieben.

♦ **push in 1** *vt sep* (a) hineinschieben; (*quickly, violently*) hineinstoßen. to ~ one's way ~ sich hineindrängen. (b) (*break*) *window, sides of box* eindrücken. 2 *vi* (*lit: in queue etc*) sich hineindrängen *or* -drängeln (*col*).

♦ **push off 1** *vt sep* hinunterschieben; (*quickly, violently*) hinunterstoßen; *lid, cap* wegdrücken. to ~ sb/sth ~ sth jdn/etw von etw schieben/stoßen. 2 *vi* (a) (*in boat*) abstoßen. (b) (*col: leave*) abhauen (*col*).

♦ **push on** *vi* (*with journey*) weiterfahren; (*walking*) weitergehen; (*with job*) weitermachen. 2 *vt sep* *top, lid* festdrücken.

♦ **push out** *vt sep* hinausschieben; (*quickly, violently*) hinausstoßen. to ~ sb/sth ~ of sth jdn/etw aus etw schieben/stoßen.

♦ **push over** *vt sep* (a) (*pass over*) hinüber-/herüberschieben; (*quickly, violently*) hinüber-/herüberstoßen. to ~ sb/sth ~ sth jdn/etw über etw (*acc*) schieben/stoßen. (b) (*knock over*) umwerfen.

♦ **push through 1** *vt sep* (a) (*shove through*) durchschieben; (*quickly, violently*) durchstoßen. to ~ sb/sth ~ sth jdn/etw durch etw schieben/stoßen; to ~ one's way ~ the crowd sich durch die Menge drängen. (b) (*get done quickly*) *bill, decision* durchpeitschen (*col*); *business* durchziehen (*col*). 2 *vi* (*through crowd*) sich durchschieben; (*more violently*) sich durchdrängen (*new shoots*) sich herausschieben.

♦ **push up** *vt sep* (a) (*lit*) hinaufschieben; (*quickly, violently*) hinaufstoßen; *window* hochschieben/ -stoßen. (b) (*fig: raise, increase*) hochtreiben.

push: ~-**bike** *n* (*Brit*) Fahrrad *nt* ~-**button** *n* Drucktaste *f*, Knopf *m*; ~-**button telephone** Tastentelefon *nt*; ~-**button warfare** Krieg *m* auf Knopfdruck; ~-**chair** *n* (*Brit*) Sportwagen *m*.

pusher ['pʊʃəʳ] *n* (*col*) (a) (*of drugs*) Pusher(in *f*) *m* (*col*). (b) (*ambitious person*) he's a ~ er setzt sich durch.

push-over ['pʊʃəʊvəʳ] *n* (*col*) (*job etc*) Kinderspiel *nt*; (*person*) leichtes Opfer.

pushy ['pʊʃɪ] *adj* (+*er*) (*col*) penetrant (*pej*).

pussy ['pʊsɪ] *n* (*cat*) Mieze *f*.

pussy: ~-**cat** *n* (*baby-talk*) Miezekatze *f* (*baby-talk*); ~-**willow** *n* Salweide *f*.

put [pʊt] *pret, ptp* ~ 1 *vt* (a) (*place*) tun; (~ *down, position*) stellen, setzen; (*lay down*) legen; (*push in*) stecken. ~ the lid on the box mach den Deckel auf die Schachtel; to ~ sth in a drawer etw in eine Schublade tun *or* legen; he ~ his hand in his pocket er steckte die Hand in die Tasche; he ~ some more coal on the fire er legte Kohle nach; to ~ sugar in one's coffee Zucker in den Kaffee tun; to ~ the ball in the net (*Ftbl*) den Ball ins Netz setzen; to ~ his toe in the water er steckte seinen Zeh ins Wasser; he ~ his hand on my shoulder er legte seine Hand auf meine Schulter.

(b) (*thrust*) stecken. he ~ his head around the door er steckte den Kopf zur Tür herein; to ~ one's fist through a window mit der Faust ein Fenster einschlagen.

(c) (~ *to stay*) ~ liegen-/stehen-/hängen- *etc* bleiben; (*hair*) halten; (*person*) (*not move*) hier-/dableiben; (*not stand up*) sitzenbleiben.

(d) to ~ a child in a home ein Kind in ein Heim stecken; to ~ money into sth (*sein*) Geld in etw (*acc*) stecken; he ~ £10/money on Red Rum er setzte £ 10/setzte auf Red Rum; to ~ a lot of time into sth viel Zeit in etw (*acc*) stecken; to ~ a lot of effort into one's work viel Mühe in seine Arbeit stecken.

(e) (*cause to be, do etc*) to ~ sb in a good/bad

mood jdn fröhlich/mißmutig stimmen; **they ~ her to work on the new project** ihr wurde die Arbeit an dem neuen Projekt zugewiesen; **to be ~ to a lot of inconvenience over sth** mit etw viele Unannehmlichkeiten haben.

(f) *comma, line* machen; (*~ forward*) *proposal* vorbringen. **to ~ one's signature to a document** seine Unterschrift unter ein Schriftstück setzen; **to ~ a matter before a committee** eine Angelegenheit vor einen Ausschuß bringen; **to ~ the arguments for and against sth** das Für und Wider von etw (*dat*) aufzählen; **to ~ sth on the agenda** etw auf die Tagesordnung setzen; **you might ~ it to him that ...** du könntest ihm nahelegen, daß ...; **to ~ a question/suggestion to sb** jdm eine Frage stellen/einen Vorschlag unterbreiten; **I ~ it to you that ...** ich möchte Ihnen vorhalten, daß ...

(g) (*express*) ausdrücken, sagen. **that's one way of ~ting it** so kann man's auch sagen; **to ~ it bluntly** hart *or* grob ausgedrückt; **how shall I ~ it?** wie soll ich (es) sagen?; **to ~ sth into German** etw ins Deutsche übersetzen.

(h) (*rate*) schätzen (*at* auf +*acc*). **he ~s money before his family's happiness** er stellt Geld über das Glück seiner Familie; **to ~ a value of £10 on sth** den Wert einer Sache (*gen*) auf £10 schätzen.

2 *vi* (*Naut*) **to ~ to sea** in See stechen.

♦ **put about** *vt sep news, rumour* verbreiten, in Umlauf bringen. **he ~ it ~ that ...** er verbreitete (das Gerücht), daß ...

♦ **put across** *vt sep* **(a)** (*communicate*) *ideas* verständlich machen (*to sb* jdm), klar zum Ausdruck bringen; *knowledge* vermitteln (*to sb* jdm); (*promote*) an den Mann bringen (*col*). **to ~ oneself ~** den richtigen Eindruck von sich geben. **(b)** (*col*) = **put over.**

♦ **put aside** *vt sep* **(a)** *book etc* beiseite legen. **(b)** (*save for later use*) zurücklegen. **(c)** (*fig: forget*) ablegen, über Bord werfen (*col*); *anger* begraben; *thought* aufgeben; *differences* vergessen.

♦ **put away** *vt sep* **(a)** (*in usual place*) einräumen; (*tidy away*) wegräumen. **to ~ the car ~** das Auto in die Garage stellen. **(b)** (*col: consume*) schaffen (*col*); *food also* verputzen (*col*). **(c)** (*in prison etc*) einsperren.

♦ **put back** *vt sep* **(a)** (*replace*) *see* **put 1 (a)** zurücktun/-stellen *or* -setzen/-legen/-stecken. **(b)** (*postpone*) verschieben; (*set back*) zurückwerfen; (*readjust*) *watch etc* zurückstellen.

♦ **put by** *vt sep* zurücklegen, auf die hohe Kante legen.

♦ **put down 1** *vt sep* **(a)** (*set down*) *object see* **put 1 (a)** wegtun/-stellen *or* -stellen/weglegen; *surface* verlegen. **I simply couldn't ~ that book ~** ich konnte das Buch einfach nicht aus der Hand legen.

(b) (*lower*) *umbrella* zumachen; *aerial* einschieben; *car roof* zurückklappen; *lid* zuklappen.

(c) *rebellion* niederschlagen; *rebels* niederwerfen; *crime* besiegen; (*humiliate*) demütigen.

(d) (*pay*) anzahlen; *deposit* machen.

(e) *pets* einschläfern; *injured horse etc* den Gnadenschuß geben (+*dat*).

(f) (*write down*) aufschreiben; (*on form*) angeben. **~ me ~ for £50** für mich können Sie £50 eintragen.

(g) (*attribute*) zurückführen (*to* auf +*acc*), zuschreiben (*to* dat).

2 *vi* (*Aviat*) landen.

♦ **put forward** *vt sep* **(a)** *idea, suggestion* vorbringen; (*nominate*) vorschlagen. **(b)** (*advance*) *meeting* vorverlegen (*to* auf +*acc*); *watch* vorstellen.

♦ **put in 1** *vt sep* **(a)** (*place in*) *see* **put 1 (a)** hineintun/-setzen *or* -stellen/-legen/-stecken; (*pack*) einpacken.

(b) (*insert in book, speech etc*) einfügen; (*add*) hinzufügen.

(c) (*enter*) *application* einreichen; *claim also* stellen. **to ~ ~ a plea of not guilty** (*Jur*) auf „nicht schuldig" plädieren; **to ~ one's name ~ for sth** sich um etw bewerben; *for evening classes, exam* sich für etw anmelden; **to ~ sb ~ for an award** jdn für *or* zu einer Prüfung/für eine Ehrung vorschlagen.

(d) (*install*) *central heating, car radio* einbauen.

(e) (*Pol: elect*) an die Regierung bringen.

(f) (*devote, expend*) *time* verbringen (*with* mit), verwenden (*with* auf). **could you ~ ~ an extra hour?** könnten Sie eine zusätzliche Stunde Arbeit einschieben?; **he ~ ~ a lot of hard work on the project** er hat eine Menge harter Arbeit in das Projekt gesteckt.

2 *vi* **(a)** **to ~ ~ for sth** *for job* sich um etw bewerben; *for leave, rise* etw beantragen. **(b)** (*Naut: enter port*) **to ~ ~ to Bremen/harbour** in Bremen/in den Hafen einlaufen.

♦ **put off** *vt sep* **(a)** (*set down*) *passengers* aussteigen lassen (*prep obj* aus); (*forcibly*) hinauswerfen (*prep obj* aus). **(b)** (*postpone, delay*) verschieben; *visitors* (wieder) ausladen; *decision* aufschieben; *sth unpleasant* hinauszögern. **to ~ sth ~ till later** etw auf später verschieben. **(c)** (*prevent from coming*) *boyfriend, creditor* hinhalten. **to ~ sb ~ doing sth** jdn davon abbringen, etw zu tun. **(d)** (*repel*) die Lust verderben (+*dat*). **to ~ sb ~ sth** jdm etw verleiden. **(e)** (*distract*) ablenken (*prep obj* von); (*disturb*) stören.

♦ **put on** *vt sep* **(a)** *coat, shoes etc* anziehen; *hat* (*sich dat*) aufsetzen; *make-up* auftragen; *accent, manners* annehmen; *facade, front* aufsetzen. **to ~ ~ one's make-up** sich schminken; **to ~ ~ an air of innocence** eine unschuldige Miene aufsetzen; **his sorrow is all ~ ~** sein Kummer ist bloß Schau (*col*).

(b) (*increase, add*) **to ~ ~ weight/a few pounds** zunehmen/ein paar Pfund zunehmen; **to ~ ~ speed** schneller fahren, beschleunigen; **10p was ~ ~ the price of petrol** der Benzinpreis wurde um 10 Pence erhöht.

(c) *play* aufführen; *exhibition* veranstalten; *film* vorführen; *train, bus* einsetzen; (*fig*) *act, show* abziehen (*col*).

(d) (*on telephone*) **to ~ sb ~ to sb** jdn mit jdm verbinden; **would you ~ him ~?** könnten Sie ihn mir geben?

(e) (*switch on*) *light, TV* anmachen, einschalten. **to ~ ~ the kettle/dinner ~** das Wasser/das Essen aufsetzen.

(f) *watch etc* vorstellen.

(g) **to ~ sb ~ to sth** (*inform about*) jdm etw vermitteln; **to ~ sb ~ to a plumber/garage** *etc* jdm einen Installateur/eine Reparaturwerkstatt *etc* empfehlen; **what ~ you ~ to it?** was hat dich darauf gebracht?; **to ~ the police ~ to sb** die Polizei auf jds Spur bringen.

(h) (*col: tease, trick*) auf den Arm nehmen (*col*).

♦ **put out 1** *vt sep* **(a)** *rubbish etc* hinausbringen; *cat* vor die Tür setzen. **to ~ ~ the washing ~** (*to dry*) die Wäsche (zum Trocknen) aushängen; **to be ~ ~** (*asked to leave*) vor die Tür gesetzt werden; **to ~ sb ~ of business** jdn aus dem Markt drängen; **she could not ~ him ~ of her thoughts** er ging ihr nicht aus dem Sinn.

(b) (*stretch out*) *hand, foot* ausstrecken; *tongue, head* herausstrecken. **to ~ one's head ~ of the window** den Kopf zum Fenster hinausstrecken.

(c) *dishes, cutlery* auflegen; *chessmen etc* aufstellen.

(d) (*circulate*) *pamphlet* herausbringen; *propaganda* machen; *rumour* verbreiten; *regulations* erlassen; *statement* abgeben;

message, appeal durchgeben; *description* bekanntgeben; *TV programme* bringen, senden.
(e) *(extinguish)* löschen.
(f) *(vex)* to be ~ ~ **(by sth)** (über etw *acc)* verärgert sein.
(g) *(inconvenience)* to ~ oneself ~ **(for sb)** sich *(dat)* (wegen jdm) Umstände machen.
(h) *(dislocate) knee, shoulder* ausrenken; *(more severely)* auskugeln; *back* verrenken.
2 *vi (Naut: set sail)* auslaufen. to ~ ~ **to sea in** See stechen; to ~ ~ **from Bremen** von Bremen auslaufen.
♦ **put over** *vt sep* to ~ one ~ on sb *(col)* jdn anführen.
♦ **put through** *vt sep* **(a)** *reform, proposal* durchbringen; *(+prep obj)* bringen durch; *claim* weiterleiten. **(b)** *person* verbinden *(to* mit*); call* durchstellen *(to* zu*).* to ~ **a call** ~ **to Beirut** ein Gespräch nach Beirut vermitteln *or (caller)* anmelden.
♦ **put together** *vt sep* **(a)** *(in same room etc)* zusammentun; *(seat together)* zusammensetzen. he's better than all the others ~ ~ er ist besser als alle anderen zusammen. **(b)** *(assemble)* zusammensetzen; *furniture, machine* also zusammenbauen; *essay etc, (Jur) case* zusammenstellen; *collection, evidence* zusammentragen.
♦ **put up 1** *vt sep* **(a)** *(raise) hand* hochheben; *car window* zumachen; *sash window* hochschieben; *umbrella* aufklappen; *hair* hochstecken; *collar* hochschlagen. **(b)** *flag, sail* aufziehen. **(c)** *picture etc* aufhängen; *notice* anschlagen. **(d)** *building, fence* errichten; *ladder, scaffolding* aufstellen; *tent* aufschlagen; *(fig) facade* vortäuschen. **(e)** *missile, flare* hochschießen. **(f)** *(increase) sales, prices* erhöhen. **(g)** = **put forward (a)**. **(h)** *(offer)* to ~ sth ~ **for sale** etw zum Verkauf anbieten; to ~ ~ **resistance (to sb)** (jdm) Widerstand leisten. **(i)** *(give accommodation to)* unterbringen. **(j)** *(provide) capital* bereitstellen; *reward* aussetzen. **(k)** to ~ sb ~ **to sth** jdn zu etw anstiften.
2 *vi* **(a)** *(stay)* wohnen; *(for one night)* über-

nachten. **(b)** to ~ ~ **for election** sich zur Wahl stellen.
♦ **put upon** *vi +prep obj (impose on)* ausnutzen.
♦ **put up with** *vi +prep obj* sich abfinden mit. I won't ~ ~ ~ that das lasse ich mir nicht gefallen.
putrefy ['pjuːtrɪfaɪ] *vi* verwesen.
putrid ['pjuːtrɪd] *adj* verfault; *smell* faul.
putt [pʌt] **1** *n (Golf)* Schlag *m (mit dem man einlocht).* **2** *vti* putten, einlochen.
putting ['pʌtɪŋ] Putten *nt.* ~ **green** kleiner Rasenplatz zum Putten.
putty ['pʌtɪ] *n* Kitt *m.* he was ~ in her hands er war Wachs in ihren Händen.
put-up ['pʊtʌp] *adj (col)* **a** ~ **job** ein abgekartetes Spiel.
puzzle ['pʌzl] **1** *n* **(a)** *(wordgame etc)* Rätsel *nt; (toy)* Geduldsspiel *nt; (jigsaw)* Puzzle(spiel) *nt.* **(b)** *(mystery)* Rätsel *nt.* **2** *vi* to ~ **over sth** sich *(dat)* über etw *(acc)* den Kopf zerbrechen. **3** *vt* verblüffen. I'm ~d **about** it ich bin mir darüber im unklaren; **the police are** ~d die Polizei steht vor einem Rätsel.
♦ **puzzle out** *vt sep* austüfteln.
puzzled ['pʌzld] *adj look* verdutzt, verblüfft.
puzzlement ['pʌzlmənt] *n* Verblüffung *f.*
puzzling ['pʌzlɪŋ] *adj* rätselhaft; *story, mechanism* verwirrend.
PVC = **polyvinyl chloride** PVC *nt.*
pygmy ['pɪgmɪ] *n* **(a)** P~ Pygmäe *m.* **(b)** *(small person, fig)* Zwerg *m.*
pyjamas, (US) pajamas [pə'dʒɑːməz] *npl* Schlafanzug, Pyjama *m.*
pylon ['paɪlən] *n* Mast *m.*
pyramid ['pɪrəmɪd] *n* Pyramide *f.*
pyre ['paɪə'] *n* Scheiterhaufen *m (zum Verbrennen von Leichen).*
Pyrenees [pɪrə'niːz] *npl* Pyrenäen *pl.*
Pyrex ® ['paɪreks] *n* Jenaer Glas ® *nt.*
pyromaniac [,paɪərəʊ'meɪnɪæk] *n* Pyromane *m,* Pyromanin *f.*
pyrotechnics [,paɪrəʊ'teknɪks] *n (sing)* Pyrotechnik *f; (pl: display)* Feuerwerk *nt.*
python ['paɪθən] *n* Python(schlange *f) m.*

Q

Q, q [kjuː] *n* Q, q *nt*.
quack¹ [kwæk] **1** *n* Schnattern, Quaken *nt no pl*. **2** *vi* *(duck)* schnattern, quaken, quak machen *(col)*.
quack² *n* Quacksalber, Kurpfuscher *m*; *(hum: doctor)* Doktor, Medizinmann *(hum)* *m*.
quad [kwɒd] *n* = **(a) quadrangle** Hof *m*. **(b) quadruplet** Vierling *m*.
quadrangle [ˈkwɒdræŋgl] *n* **(a)** *(Math)* Viereck *nt*. **(b)** *(Archit)* (viereckiger) (Innen)hof.
quadratic [kwɒˈdrætɪk] *adj* *(Math)* quadratisch.
quadrilateral [ˌkwɒdrɪˈlætərəl] **1** *adj* *(Math)* vierseitig. **2** *n* Viereck *nt*.
quadruped [ˈkwɒdruped] *n* Vierfüß(l)er *m*.
quadruple [ˈkwɒdrupl] **1** *adj* vierfach. **2** *vt* vervierfachen. **3** *vi* sich vervierfachen.
quadruplet [kwɒˈdruːplɪt] *n* *(child)* Vierling *m*.
quagmire [ˈkwægmaɪə^r] *n* Sumpf, Morast *m*; *(fig)* *(of vice etc)* Morast *m*; *(difficult situation)* Schlamassel *m* *(col)*.
quail¹ [ˈkweɪl] *vi* (vor Angst) zittern *or* beben *(before* vor +*dat)*.
quail² *n* *(Orn)* Wachtel *f*.
quaint [kweɪnt] *adj* (+*er*) *(picturesque)* malerisch; *(charmingly old-fashioned)* urig; *(pleasantly odd)* idea kurios; *(old lady, way of speaking* drollig.
quake [kweɪk] **1** *vi* beben *(with* vor +*dat)*. **2** *n* *(col: earth~)* (Erd)beben *nt*.
Quaker [ˈkweɪkə^r] *n* Quäker(in *f*) *m*.
qualification [ˌkwɒlɪfɪˈkeɪʃən] *n* **(a)** *(on paper)* Qualifikation *f*; *(document)* Zeugnis *nt*; *(requisite quality)* Voraussetzung *f*; *(act of qualifying)* Abschluß *m* von jds Ausbildung. **what are your ~s?** welche Qualifikationen haben Sie?; **the only ~ needed is a knowledge of French** die einzige Voraussetzung sind Französischkenntnisse. **(b)** *(limitation)* Einschränkung *f*; *(modification)* Modifikation *f*. **to accept a plan with/without ~(s)** einen Plan unter Vorbehalt/vorbehaltlos billigen.
qualified [ˈkwɒlɪfaɪd] *adj* **(a)** *(having training)* ausgebildet; *engineer* graduiert; *(with university degree)* *engineer* Diplom-. **highly ~** hochqualifiziert; **to be ~ to do sth** qualifiziert sein, etw zu tun; **he was not ~ for the job** ihm fehlte die Qualifikation für die Stelle. **(b)** *(limited) praise, approval* nicht uneingeschränkt. **a ~ success** kein voller Erfolg; **~ acceptance** *(Comm)* bedingte Annahme; **in a ~ sense** mit Einschränkungen.
qualify [ˈkwɒlɪfaɪ] **1** *vt* **(a)** *(make competent)* qualifizieren; *(entitle legally entitled)* berechtigen. **to ~ sb to do sth** *(entitle)* jdn berechtigen, etw zu tun; **he is not qualified to make these decisions** er ist nicht kompetent, diese Entscheidungen zu treffen. **(b)** *(limit) statement, criticism* einschränken; *(change slightly) opinion, remark* modifizieren. **(c)** *(Gram)* näher bestimmen. **2** *vi* *(also Sport)* sich qualifizieren *(for* für); *(fulfil required conditions)* in Frage kommen *(for* für). **to ~ as a doctor/teacher** sein medizinisches Staatsexamen machen/die Lehrbefähigung erhalten; **he hardly qualifies as a poet** er kann kaum als Dichter angesehen werden.
qualifying [ˈkwɒlɪfaɪɪŋ] *adj* *adjective* erläuternd; *round, heat* Qualifikations-. **~ examination**

Auswahlprüfung *f*.
qualitative [ˈkwɒlɪtətɪv] *adj* qualitativ.
quality [ˈkwɒlɪtɪ] **1** *n* Qualität *f*; *(of justice, education etc)* (hoher) Stand; *(characteristic)* Eigenschaft *f*; *(nature)* Art *f*. **of good/poor ~** von guter/schlechter Qualität; **~ matters more than quantity** Qualität geht vor Quantität; **they vary in ~** sie sind qualitativ unterschiedlich. **2** *attr* *goods etc* Qualitäts-; *(col: good)* erstklassig *(col)*; *newspaper* angesehen.
qualm [kwɑːm] *n* Bedenken *nt*; *(scruple)* Skrupel *m*. **without a ~** ohne jeden Skrupel; **~s of conscience** Gewissensbisse *pl*; **I had some ~s about his future** ich hatte mancherlei Bedenken wegen seiner Zukunft.
quandary [ˈkwɒndərɪ] *n* Verlegenheit *f*, Dilemma *nt*. **he was in a ~ about what to do** er wußte nicht, was er tun sollte.
quango [ˈkwæŋgəʊ] *n* Regierungsausschuß *m*.
quantitative [ˈkwɒntɪtətɪv] *adj* quantitativ.
quantity [ˈkwɒntɪtɪ] *n* Quantität *f*; *(amount)* Menge *f*; *(proportion)* Anteil *m* *(of* an +*dat)*; *(Math, Phys, fig)* Größe *f*. **in ~**, **in large quantities** in großen Mengen; **in equal quantities** zu gleichen Teilen; **quantities of books** Unmengen von Büchern.
quantity surveyor *n* Baukostenkalkulator *m*.
quantum [ˈkwɒntəm] *n*, *pl* **quanta** *(Phys)* Quant *nt*. **~ physics** *n sing* Quantenphysik *f*; **~ theory** *n* Quantentheorie *f*.
quarantine [ˈkwɒrəntiːn] *n* Quarantäne *f*. **to be in ~** in Quarantäne sein.
quarrel [ˈkwɒrəl] **1** *n* Streit *m*; *(dispute)* Auseinandersetzung *f*. **they have had a ~** sie haben Streit gehabt; **let's not have a ~ about it** wir wollen uns nicht darüber streiten; **to start *or* pick a ~** einen Streit anfangen *(with* mit); **I have no ~ with him** ich habe nichts gegen ihn. **2** *vi* **(a)** *(have a dispute)* sich streiten *(with* mit, *about, over* über +*acc)*; *(more trivially also)* sich zanken. **(b)** *(find fault)* etwas auszusetzen haben *(with* an +*dat)*. **you can't ~ with that** daran kann man doch nichts aussetzen.
quarrelling, *(US)* **quarreling** [ˈkwɒrəlɪŋ] *n* Streiterei *f*.
quarrelsome [ˈkwɒrəlsəm] *adj* streitsüchtig; *woman also* zänkisch.
quarry¹ [ˈkwɒrɪ] **1** *n* **(a)** Steinbruch *m*. **sandstone ~** Sandsteinbruch *m*. **(b)** *(fig)* Fundgrube *f*. **2** *vt* brechen, hauen.
quarry² *n* **(a)** *(Hunt)* Beute *f*. **(b)** *(fig)* *(thing)* Ziel *nt*; *(person)* Opfer *nt*.
quart [kwɔːt] *n* *(Measure)* Quart *nt*.
quarter [ˈkwɔːtə^r] **1** *n* **(a)** Viertel *nt*. **to divide sth into ~s** etw in vier Teile teilen; **the bottle was a ~/three-~s full** die Flasche war viertel/dreiviertel voll; **a ~ (of a pound) of sausages** ein Viertel(pfund) Wurst; **a mile and a ~** eineinviertel Meilen; **a ~ of a mile** eine Viertelmeile; **for a ~ of the price** zu einem Viertel des Preises; **a ~ of an hour** eine Viertelstunde; **a ~ to seven** *(Brit)*, **a ~ of seven** *(US)* Viertel vor sieben; **a ~ past six** *(Brit)*, **a ~ after six** *(esp US)* Viertel nach sechs; **an hour and a ~** eineinviertel Stunden.
(b) *(district, area)* Viertel *nt*. **they came from all ~s of the earth** sie kamen aus allen Teilen der Welt; **in these ~s** in dieser Gegend; **he won't get**

help from that ~ von dieser Seite wird er keine Hilfe bekommen; **at close** ~s in der Nähe; (*from nearby*) aus der Nähe.
(c) (*direction*) (Himmels)richtung *f*. **they came from all** ~s sie kamen aus allen Himmelsrichtungen.
(d) ~s *pl* (*lodgings*) Quartier *nt* (*also Mil*), Unterkunft *f*; **to be confined to** ~s (*Mil*) Stubenarrest haben.
(e) to give sb no ~ jdn nicht schonen.
2 *adj* pound, mile Viertel-.
3 *vt* **(a)** vierteln. **(b)** (*lodge*) einquartieren (*also Mil*) (*on* bei).
quarter: ~**deck** *n* (*Naut*) Achterdeck *nt*; ~**-final** *n* Viertelfinale *nt*.
quarterly ['kwɔ:təlɪ] **1** *adj* vierteljährlich. **2** *n* Vierteljahresschrift *f*. **3** *adv* vierteljährlich.
quartermaster ['kwɔ:tə,mɑ:stə*] *n* (*Mil*) Quartiermeister *m*; (*Navy*) Steuermannsmaat *m*.
quartet [kwɔ:'tet] *n* (*Mus*) Quartett *nt*.
quarto ['kwɔ:təʊ] **1** *n* (*Typ*) Quart(format) *nt*. **2** *attr* paper, volume in Quart.
quartz [kwɔ:ts] *n* Quarz *m*. ~ **clock** Quarzuhr *f*.
quash [kwɒʃ] *vt* **(a)** (*Jur*) verdict aufheben, annullieren. **(b)** rebellion unterdrücken; suggestion, objection ablehnen.
quasi- ['kwɑ:zɪ] *pref* quasi-, quasi.
quaver ['kweɪvə*] **1** *n* **(a)** (*esp Brit Mus*) Achtel(note *f*) *nt*. **(b)** (*in voice*) Beben *nt*. **2** *vi* (*voice*) beben; (*Mus*) tremolieren.
quay [ki:] *n* Kai *m*. **alongside the** ~ am Kai.
quayside ['ki:saɪd] *n* Kai *m*.
queasy ['kwi:zɪ] *adj* (+*er*) **I feel** ~ mir ist übel.
queen [kwi:n] *n* **(a)** (*also fig*) Königin *f*. ~ **bee** Bienenkönigin *f*; ~ **mother** Königinmutter *f*; ~**'s English** englische Hochsprache. **(b)** (*Cards, Chess*) Dame *f*. ~ **of spades** Pik Dame. **(c)** (*col: homosexual*) Schwule(r) *m* (*col*).
queer [kwɪə*] **1** *adj* (+*er*) **(a)** (*strange*) komisch. **(b)** (*col*) (*unwell*) unwohl; (*peculiar*) feeling komisch. **I feel** ~ mir ist nicht gut/mir ist ganz komisch (*col*). **(c)** (*col: homosexual*) schwul (*col*). **2** *n* (*col: homosexual*) Schwule(r) *mf* (*col*). **3** *vt* **to** ~ **sb's pitch** (*col*) jdm einen Strich durch die Rechnung machen.
quell [kwel] *vt* fear bezwingen; passion zügeln; riot niederschlagen; anxieties überwinden.
quench [kwenʧ] *vt* fire löschen; thirst also stillen; enthusiasm dämpfen.
querulous ['kwerʊləs] *adj* nörglerisch. **a** ~ **person** ein Querulant *m*.
query ['kwɪərɪ] **1** *n* (*question*) Frage *f*. **to raise a** ~ eine Frage aufwerfen. **2** *vt* **(a)** (*express doubt about*) bezweifeln; statement, motives in Frage stellen; bill, item reklamieren. **(b)** (*check*) **to** ~ **sth with sb** etw mit jdm abklären.
quest [kwest] *n* (*search*) Suche *f* (*for* nach); (*for knowledge, happiness etc*) Streben *nt* (*for* nach).
question ['kwesʧən] **1** *n* Frage *f* (*to* an +*acc*); (*Parl also*) Anfrage *f* (*to* an +*acc*); (*no pl: doubt also*) Zweifel *m*. **to ask sb a** ~ jdm eine Frage stellen; **beyond (all)** *or* **without** ~ ohne Frage, ohne (jeden) Zweifel; **without** ~ **he is** ... er ist zweifellos *or* ohne Zweifel ...; **his honesty is beyond** ~ seine Ehrlichkeit steht außer Frage; **your sincerity is not in** ~ niemand zweifelt an Ihrer Aufrichtigkeit; **to call sth into** ~ etw in Frage stellen; **that's another** ~ **altogether** das ist etwas völlig anderes; **that's not the** ~ darum geht es nicht; **it's not just a** ~ **of money** es ist nicht nur eine Frage des Geldes; **there's no** ~ **of that happening** es kann keine Rede davon sein, daß das passiert; **there's no** ~ **of a strike** von einem Streik kann keine Rede sein; **that's out of the** ~ das kommt nicht in Frage; **the matter in** ~ die in Frage stehende Angelegenheit.
2 *vt* **(a)** (*ask* ~s *of*) fragen (*about* nach); (*police etc*) vernehmen, befragen (*about* zu);

(*examiner*) prüfen (*on* über +*acc*). **they were** ~**ed by the immigration authorities** ihnen wurden von der Einwanderungsbehörde viele Fragen gestellt. **(b)** (*express doubt about*) bezweifeln; (*dispute, challenge*) in Frage stellen. **I** ~ **whether it's worth it** ich bezweifle, daß es der Mühe wert ist.
questionable ['kwesʧənəbl] *adj* (*suspect*) fragwürdig; (*open to doubt*) statement, figures fraglich; value, advantage also zweifelhaft.
questioner ['kwesʧənə*] *n* Fragesteller(in *f*) *m*.
questioning ['kwesʧənɪŋ] **1** *adj* look fragend. **2** *n* Verhör *nt*; (*by police also*) Vernehmung *f*.
question mark *n* (*lit, fig*) Fragezeichen *nt*.
questionnaire [,kwesʧə'nɛə*] *n* Fragebogen *m*.
queue [kju:] **1** *n* (*Brit: of people, cars*) Schlange *f*. **to form a** ~ eine Schlange bilden; **to stand in a** ~ Schlange stehen; **to join the** ~ sich (hinten) anstellen; **a** ~ **of cars** eine Autoschlange. **2** *vi* (*Brit: also* ~ **up**) Schlange stehen; (*form a* ~) eine Schlange bilden; (*people*) sich anstellen. **they were queuing for bread** sie standen um Brot an.
quibble ['kwɪbl] **1** *vi* (*be petty-minded*) kleinlich sein (*over, about* wegen); (*argue with sb*) sich herumstreiten (*over, about* wegen). **to** ~ **over details** auf Einzelheiten herumreiten. **2** *n* **I've got a few** ~s **about the design** ich habe ein paar Kleinigkeiten am Design auszusetzen.
quick [kwɪk] **1** *adj* (+*er*) **(a)** schnell; answer also prompt. **be** ~! mach schnell!; (*on telephone etc*) faß dich kurz!; **and be** ~ **about it** aber ein bißchen dalli (*col*); **you were** ~ das ging ja schnell; **he was too** ~ **for me** (*in speech*) das ging mir zu schnell; (*in escaping*) er war zu schnell für mich; ~ **march!** (*Mil*) im Eilschritt, marsch!; **it's** ~**er by train** mit dem Zug geht es schneller; **he is** ~ **to criticize other people** er ist mit seiner Kritik schnell bei der Hand; **what's the** ~**est way to the station?** wie komme ich am schnellsten zum Bahnhof?
(b) (*short*) kiss flüchtig; speech kurz; rest klein, kurz. **let me have a** ~ **look** laß ich mal schnell sehen; **could I have a** ~ **word?** könnte ich Sie mal kurz sprechen?; **I'll just write him a** ~ **note** ich schreibe ihm schnell mal; **a** ~ **one** eine(r, s) auf die Schnelle (*col*); (*question*) eine kurze Frage.
(c) (*lively*, ~ **to understand**) mind wach; person schnell von Begriff (*col*); child aufgeweckt; temper hitzig; eye, ear scharf. **he is** ~ **at figures** er kann schnell rechnen.
2 *n* (*Anat*) empfindliches Fleisch (*besonders unter den Fingernägeln*). **to be cut to the** ~ (*fig*) tief getroffen sein.
3 *adv* (+*er*) schnell.
quicken ['kwɪkən] **1** *vt* (*also* ~ **up**) beschleunigen. **2** *vi* (*also* ~ **up**) schneller werden, sich beschleunigen. **the pace** ~**ed** das Tempo zog an.
quickie ['kwɪkɪ] *n* (*col*) eine(r, s) auf die Schnelle (*col*); (*question*) kurze Frage.
quicklime ['kwɪklaɪm] *n* ungelöschter Kalk.
quickly ['kwɪklɪ] *adv* schnell.
quickness ['kwɪknɪs] *n* **(a)** (*speed*) Schnelligkeit *f*. **(b)** (*intelligence*) schnelle Auffassungsgabe.
quick: ~**sand** *n* Treibsand *m*; ~**silver** *n* Quecksilber *nt*; ~**step** *n* Quickstep *m*; ~**tempered** *adj* hitzig, leicht erregbar; ~**witted** *adj* geistesgegenwärtig; answer schlagfertig.
quid [kwɪd] *n*, *pl* - (*col*) Pfund *nt*. **20** ~ 20 Eier (*col*).
quiet ['kwaɪət] **1** *adj* (+*er*) **(a)** (*silent*) still; neighbours, person also, engine ruhig; music, car, voice leise. **he's very** ~ er ist sehr still; **(be)** ~! Ruhe!; **to keep** ~ (*not speak*) still sein; (*not make noise*) leise sein; **keep** ~! sei/seid still!; **can't you keep your dog** ~! können Sie nicht zusehen, daß Ihr Hund still ist?; **to keep** ~ **about sth** über etw (*acc*) nichts sagen.
(b) (*peaceful*) ruhig; smile leise. **things are**

very ~ **at the moment** im Augenblick ist nicht viel los; **to lead a** ~ **life** ein ruhiges Leben führen; **everything was** ~ **on the Syrian border** an der syrischen Grenze herrschte Ruhe; **to have a** ~ **drink** sein Bier *etc* in aller Ruhe trinken. **(c)** *(gentle) character* sanft; *child* ruhig; *horse* gutwillig; *irony* leise. **(d)** *(simple) style, elegance* schlicht; *wedding, dinner* im kleinen Rahmen. **(e)** *(not overt) hatred, envy* still; *resentment* heimlich. **I'll have a** ~ **word with him** ich werde mal ein Wörtchen (im Vertrauen) mit ihm reden; **he kept the matter** ~ er behielt die Sache für sich. **2** *n* Ruhe *f.* **the sudden** ~ **after the bombing** die plötzliche Stille nach dem Bombenangriff; **on the** ~ heimlich; **he left on the** ~ er ist still und heimlich weggegangen. **3** *vt* = **quieten.**

quieten ['kwaɪətn] *vt sb* zum Schweigen bringen; *noisy class, dog* zur Ruhe bringen; *crying baby* beruhigen; *engine* ruhiger machen; *(calm) person, conscience* beruhigen.

♦**quieten down 1** *vi (become silent)* leiser werden; *(become calm)* sich beruhigen; *(after wild youth)* ruhiger werden. **2** *vt sep* beruhigen.

quietly ['kwaɪətlɪ] *adv (making little noise)* leise; *(peacefully, making little fuss)* ruhig; *(secretly)* still und heimlich. **he's very** ~ **spoken** er spricht sehr leise; **to be** ~ **confident** insgeheim sehr sicher sein; **I was sitting here** ~ **sipping my wine** ich saß da und trank in aller Ruhe meinen Wein; **he slipped off** ~ er machte sich in aller Stille davon.

quietness ['kwaɪətnɪs] *n* **(a)** Stille *f*; *(of engine, car)* Geräuscharmut *f*; *(of footsteps etc)* Lautlosigkeit *f*; *(of person)* stille Art. **the** ~ **of her voice** ihre leise Stimme. **(b)** *(peacefulness)* Ruhe *f.*

quill [kwɪl] *n (feather, pen)* Feder *f*; *(feather stem)* Federkiel *m*; *(of porcupine)* Stachel *m.*

quilt [kwɪlt] **1** *n (continental* ~*)* Steppdecke *f*; *(unstitched)* Federbett *nt.* **2** *vt* absteppen; *(with padding)* wattieren.

quin [kwɪn] *n (Brit)* = **quintuplet** Fünfling *m.*

quince [kwɪns] *n (fruit, tree)* Quitte *f.* ~ **jelly** Quittengelee *nt.*

quinine [kwɪ'niːn] *n* Chinin *nt.*

quintessence [kwɪn'tesns] *n (fig)* Quintessenz *f*; *(embodiment)* Inbegriff *m.*

quintet [kwɪn'tet] *n (Mus)* Quintett *nt.*

quintuplet [kwɪn'tjuːplɪt] *n* Fünfling *m.*

quip [kwɪp] **1** *n* witzige Bemerkung. **2** *vti* witzeln.

quirk [kwɜːk] *n* Marotte *f*; *(of nature, fate)* Laune *f.* **by a strange** ~ **of fate** durch eine Laune des Schicksals.

quirky ['kwɜːkɪ] *adj (+er)* schrullig.

quit [kwɪt] *(vb: pret, ptp* ~**ted** *or* ~*)* **1** *vt (leave) town, army* verlassen; *(give up) job* aufgeben. **(b)** *(col: stop)* aufhören mit. **to** ~ **doing sth** aufhören, etw zu tun. **2** *vi* **(a)** *(leave one's job)* kündigen. **(b)** *(go away)* weg- or fortgehen. **notice to** ~ Kündigung *f*; **they gave me notice to** ~ sie haben mir gekündigt. **(c)** *(give up)* aufgeben. **3** *adj* ~ **of** frei von, ledig *(+gen) (geh)*; **we are** ~ **of him** wir sind ihn los.

quite [kwaɪt] *adv* **(a)** *(entirely)* ganz; *(emph)* völlig. ~ **unnecessary/wrong** völlig unnötig/falsch; **I am** ~ **happy where I am** ich fühle mich hier ganz wohl; **I was** ~ **happy until you came along** bevor du kamst, war ich völlig zufrieden; **it's** ~ **impossible to do that** das ist völlig unmöglich; **are you** ~ **finished!** bist du jetzt fertig?; **he's** ~ **grown up now** er ist jetzt schon richtig erwachsen; **I** ~ **agree with you** ich stimme völlig mit Ihnen überein; **he** ~ **understands that he must**

go er sieht durchaus ein, daß er gehen muß; **he has** ~ **recovered** er ist völlig wiederhergestellt; **that's** ~ **another matter** das ist doch etwas ganz anderes; **that's** ~ **enough for me** das reicht wirklich; **not** ~ **nicht ganz; you weren't** ~ **early/tall enough** Sie waren ein bißchen zu spät dran/zu klein; **I don't** ~ **see what he means** ich verstehe nicht ganz, was er meint; **sorry!** — **that's** ~ **all right** entschuldige! — das macht nichts; **thank you** — **that's** ~ **all right** danke — **bitte schön;** ~ **(so)!** genau!; ~ **the thing** *(col)* ganz große Mode. **(b)** *(to some degree)* ziemlich. ~ **likely** sehr wahrscheinlich; **he's had** ~ **a lot to drink** er hat ganz schön viel getrunken *(col)*; ~ **a few people** ziemlich viele Leute; **he is** ~ **a good singer** er ist ein ziemlich guter Sänger; **I** ~ **like this painting** dieses Bild gefällt mir ganz gut. **(c)** *(really, truly)* wirklich. **she's** ~ **a girl/cook** *etc* sie ist ein tolles Mädchen/eine tolle Köchin *etc*; **it's** ~ **delightful** es ist einfach wunderbar; **it was** ~ **a shock** es war ein ziemlicher Schock; **that's** ~ **some bill** *(col)* das ist vielleicht eine Rechnung *(col)*; **it was** ~ **an experience** das war schon ein Erlebnis; **he's** ~ **a hero now** jetzt ist er ein richtiger Held.

quits [kwɪts] *adj* quitt. **to be** ~ **with sb** mit jdm quitt sein; **shall we call it** ~? lassen wir's?

quiver¹ ['kwɪvəʳ] **1** *vi* zittern *(with* vor *+dat)*; *(eyelids etc)* zucken. **2** *n* Zittern *nt*; Zucken *nt.*

quiver² *n (for arrows)* Köcher *m.*

quixotic [kwɪk'sɒtɪk] *adj* versponnen; *ideals* schwärmerisch. **a** ~ **gesture** eine Don-quichottiere.

quiz [kwɪz] **1** *n* **(a)** Quiz *nt.* **(b)** *(US Sch col)* Prüfung *f.* **2** *vt* **(a)** *(question closely)* ausfragen *(about* über *+acc)*. **(b)** *(US Sch col)* prüfen.

quiz: ~**master** *n* Quizmaster *m*; ~ **show** *n* Quiz *nt.*

quizzical ['kwɪzɪkəl] *adj (a) air, look* fragend; *smile* zweifelnd. **(b)** *(odd)* eigenartig.

quoit [kwɔɪt] *n* Wurfring *m.*

quorum ['kwɔːrəm] *n* Quorum *nt.*

quota ['kwəʊtə] *n* **(a)** *(of work)* Pensum *nt.* **(b)** *(of an +dat) (permitted amount)* Quantum *nt*; *(share allotted)* Anteil *m*; *(of goods)* Kontingent *nt.* **the** ~ **of immigrants allowed into the country** die zugelassene Einwanderungsquote.

quotation [kwəʊ'teɪʃən] *n* **(a)** *(passage cited)* Zitat *nt*; *(act)* Zitieren *nt.* **a** ~ **from Shakespeare** ein Shakespeare-Zitat. **(b)** *(St Ex)* Notierung *f.* **(c)** *(Comm)* Preis *m*; Preise *pl*; *(estimate)* Kostenvoranschlag *m.*

quotation marks *npl* Anführungszeichen *pl.* **open/close** ~ Anführungszeichen unten/oben.

quote [kwəʊt] **1** *vt* **(a)** *author, text* zitieren. **you can** ~ **me (on that)** Sie können das ruhig wörtlich wiedergeben; **he was** ~**d as saying that** er soll gesagt haben, daß ...; ~ **... un**~ Zitat Anfang ... Zitat Ende; **don't** ~ **me on this** *(I'm not sure)* ich kann mich nicht dafür verbürgen; *(don't repeat)* das sollte unter uns bleiben; **he said, and I** ~ ... er sagte, und zwar wörtlich, ... **(b)** *(cite)* anführen. **to** ~ **sb/sth as an example** jdn/etw als Beispiel anführen. **(c)** *(Comm) price* nennen; *reference number* angeben. **how much did they** ~ **you for that?** wieviel haben sie dafür verlangt? **(d)** *(St Ex)* notieren. **the shares are** ~**d at £2** die Aktien werden mit £2 notiert.

2 *vi* zitieren. **to** ~ **from an author** einen Schriftsteller zitieren.

3 *n (from author, politician)* Zitat *nt.* **(b)** ~**s** *pl (col)* Anführungszeichen *pl*; **in** ~**s** in Anführungszeichen. **(c)** *(Comm)* Preis *m*; Preise *pl*; *(estimate)* Kostenvoranschlag *m.*

quotient ['kwəʊʃənt] *n (Math)* Quotient *m.*

R

R, r [ɑːʳ] *n* R, r *nt.* **the three Rs** Lesen, Schreiben und Rechnen *(with sing or pl vb).*
rabbi ['ræbaɪ] *n* Rabbiner *m; (as title)* Rabbi *m.*
rabbit ['ræbɪt] *n* Kaninchen *nt.*
rabbit *in cpds* Kaninchen-; ~ **burrow** *or* **hole** *n* Kaninchenbau *m;* ~ **hutch** *n* Kaninchenstall *m;* ~ **warren** *n (fig: maze)* Labyrinth *nt.*
♦ **rabbit on** *vi (Brit col)* schwafeln *(col).* **what's he** ~ting ~ **about?** was schwafelt er da? *(col).*
rabble ['ræbl] *n (disorderly crowd)* lärmender Haufen *(col); (pej: lower classes)* Pöbel *m.*
rabid ['ræbɪd] *adj* **(a)** *(Vet)* tollwütig. **(b)** *(fanatical)* fanatisch; *hatred also* wild.
rabies ['reɪbiːz] *n* Tollwut *f.*
RAC = **Royal Automobile Club.**
raccoon *n* = **racoon.**
race[1] [reɪs] **1** *n* Rennen *nt; (on foot also)* (Wett)lauf *m; (swimming)* Wettschwimmen *nt.* **100 metres** ~ 100-Meter-Lauf *m;* **to run a** ~ **with** *or* **against sb** mit jdm um die Wette laufen; **to go to the** ~**s** zum Pferderennen gehen; **a** ~ **against time** *(fig)* ein Wettlauf *m* gegen die Zeit.
2 *vt (compete with)* um die Wette laufen/ fahren/schwimmen *etc* mit; *(Sport)* laufen/ fahren/schwimmen *etc* gegen. **I'll** ~ **you to school** ich mache mit dir ein Wettrennen bis zur Schule.
3 *vi* **(a)** *(compete)* laufen/fahren/schwimmen *etc.* **to** ~ **with** *or* **against sb** mit jdm um die Wette laufen *etc.* **(b)** *(rush)* rasen, jagen; *(on foot also)* rennen; *(with work)* hetzen. **to** ~ **after sb/sth** hinter jdm/etw herjagen; **to** ~ **ahead with sth** etw vorantreiben; **the project is racing ahead** die Arbeit am Projekt geht mit Riesenschritten voran. **(c)** *(engine)* durchdrehen; *(pulse)* jagen, fliegen.
race[2] *n (ethnic group, species)* Rasse *f.* **of mixed** ~ gemischtrassig.
race: ~**course** *n* Rennbahn *f;* ~ **horse** *n* Rennpferd *nt;* ~ **relations** *n* **(a)** *pl* Beziehungen *pl* zwischen den Rassen; **(b)** *sing (subject)* Rassenintegration *f;* ~**track** *n* Rennbahn *f.*
racial ['reɪʃəl] *adj* rassisch, Rassen-. ~ **discrimination** Rassendiskriminierung *f;* ~ **equality** Rassengleichheit *f.*
racialism ['reɪʃəlɪzəm] *n* Rassismus *m.*
racialist ['reɪʃəlɪst] **1** *n* Rassist(in *f*) *m.* **2** *adj* rassistisch.
racial: ~ **minority** *n* rassische Minderheit; ~ **prejudice** *n* Rassenvorurteil *nt.*
racing ['reɪsɪŋ] *n (horse-*~*)* Pferderennsport *m; (motor* ~*)* Motorrennen *nt.*
racing *in cpds* Renn-.
racism ['reɪsɪzəm] *n* = **racialism.**
racist ['reɪsɪst] *n, adj* = **racialist.**
rack[1] [ræk] **1** *n* **(a)** *(for hats, toast, pipes etc)* Ständer *m; (for bottles, plates also)* Gestell *nt; (shelves)* Regal *nt; (luggage* ~*)* Gepäcknetz *nt; (on car, bicycle)* Gepäckträger *m; (Tech)* Zahnstange *f.* **(b)** *(Hist)* Folter(bank) *f.* **2** *vt* **(a)** *(pain)* quälen. ~**ed with pain/remorse** von Schmerz/ Gewissensbissen geplagt. **(b)** **to** ~ **one's brains** sich *(dat)* den Kopf zerbrechen.
rack[2] *n:* **to go to** ~ **and ruin** *(country, economy)* herunterkommen, vor die Hunde gehen *(col); (building)* verfallen.

rack-and-pinion steering ['rækən'pɪnjən,stiːrɪŋ] *n (Aut)* Zahnstangenlenkung *f.*
racket[1] ['rækɪt] *n (Sport)* Schläger *m.*
racket[2] *n* **(a)** *(uproar)* Krach, Lärm *m.* **to make a** ~ Krach machen. **(b)** *(col) (dishonest business)* Schwindelgeschäft *nt (col); (making excessive profit)* Wucher *m.* **the drugs** ~ das Drogengeschäft.
racketeer [,rækɪ'tɪəʳ] *n* Gauner *m (col); (making excessive profit)* Halsabschneider *m (col).*
raconteur [,rækɒn'tɜːʳ] *n* Erzähler(in *f*) *m* von Anekdoten.
racoon, raccoon [rə'kuːn] *n* Waschbär *m.*
racquet ['rækɪt] *n* = **racket**[1].
racy ['reɪsɪ] *adj* (+*er*) *speech, style* schwungvoll, feurig; *(risqué)* gewagt.
radar ['reɪdɑːʳ] *n* Radar *nt or m.*
radar *in cpds* Radar-; ~ **scanner** *n* Rundsuchradargerät *nt;* ~ **trap** *n* Radarfalle *f.*
radial ['reɪdɪəl] *adj (Tech)* radial. ~**(-ply) tyre** *(Brit) or* **tire** *(US)* Gürtelreifen *m.*
radiance ['reɪdɪəns] *n* Leuchten *nt.*
radiant ['reɪdɪənt] *adj (lit, fig)* strahlend *(with* vor +*dat).* **to be** ~ **with health/joy** vor Gesundheit strotzen/vor Freude strahlen.
radiate ['reɪdɪeɪt] **1** *vi* **(a)** Strahlen aussenden; *(emit heat)* Wärme ausstrahlen; *(heat)* ausgestrahlt werden. **(b)** *(lines, roads)* strahlenförmig ausgehen *(from* von*).* **2** *vt (lit, fig)* ausstrahlen.
radiation [,reɪdɪ'eɪʃən] *n (of heat etc)* (Aus)strahlung *f; (rays)* radioaktive Strahlung. ~ **sickness** Strahlenkrankheit *f.*
radiator ['reɪdɪeɪtəʳ] *n (of heating)* Heizkörper, Radiator *m; (Aut)* Kühler *m.* ~ **grill** Kühlergrill *m.*
radical ['rædɪkəl] **1** *adj (basic)* fundamental; *(extreme) reform* radikal, grundlegend; *rethinking* total; *(Pol)* radikal. **2** *n (Pol)* Radikale(r) *mf.*
radically ['rædɪkəlɪ] *adv see adj.* **there's something** ~ **wrong with this** hier stimmt etwas ganz und gar nicht.
radio ['reɪdɪəʊ] **1** *n* **(a)** Rundfunk *m; (also* ~ **set)** Radio(apparat *m*) *nt.* **to listen to the** ~ Radio hören; **to hear sth on the** ~ etw im Radio hören. **(b)** *no pl (telegraphy)* Funk *m.* **over the** ~ *or* **by** ~ über *or* per Funk. **2** *vt person* über Funk verständigen; *message* funken, durchgeben. **3** *vi* **to** ~ **for help** per Funk einen Hilferuf durchgeben.
radio: ~**active** *adj* radioaktiv; ~**activity** *n* Radioaktivität *f;* ~**announcer** *n* Rundfunksprecher(in *f*) *m;* ~ **beacon** *n (Aviat, Naut)* Funkfeuer *nt;* ~**-controlled** *adj* ferngesteuert; ~ **engineer** *n* Rundfunktechniker(in *f*) *m.*
radiogram ['reɪdɪəʊgræm] *n (apparatus)* Musiktruhe *f.*
radiography [,reɪdɪ'ɒgrəfɪ] *n* Röntgenographie *f.*
radiology [,reɪdɪ'ɒlədʒɪ] *n* Radiologie *f; (X-ray also)* Röntgenologie *f.*
radio: ~ **pager** *n* Funkrufempfänger *m;* ~ **station** *n* Rundfunkstation *f;* ~**telephone** *n* Funksprechgerät *nt;* ~**therapy** *n* Röntgentherapie *f.*
radish ['rædɪʃ] *n* Rettich *m; (small red)* Radieschen *nt.*
radium ['reɪdɪəm] *n* Radium *nt.*
radius ['reɪdɪəs] *n, pl* **radii** ['reɪdɪaɪ] *(Math)* Radius *m.* **within a 6 km** ~ **(of Hamburg)** in einem Umkreis von 6 km (von Hamburg).

RAF = Royal Air Force königliche (britische) Luftwaffe.

raffia ['ræfɪə] n (for handicraft) Bast m.

raffle ['ræfl] 1 n Tombola, Verlosung f. ~ **ticket** Los nt. 2 vt (also ~ **off**) verlosen.

raft [rɑːft] n Floß nt.

rafter ['rɑːftəʳ] n (Dach)sparren m.

rag[1] [ræg] n (a) Lumpen, Fetzen m; (for cleaning) Lappen m. ~**s** Lumpen pl; (col: clothes) Klamotten pl (col); **in** ~**s** zerlumpt; **to go from** ~**s to riches** vom Tellerwäscher zum Millionär werden. **(b)** (pej col: newspaper) Käseblatt nt.

rag[2] 1 n (Brit col: joke) Jux m (col). ~ **week** (Univ) Woche, in der Studenten durch Aufführungen Geld für Wohltätigkeitszwecke sammeln. 2 vt (tease) aufziehen, foppen.

rag: ~-**and-bone man** n Lumpensammler m; ~**bag** n (fig) Sammelsurium nt (col); ~ **doll** n Flickenpuppe f.

rage [reɪdʒ] 1 n Wut f, Zorn m. **to be in a** ~ wütend sein; **to fly into a** ~ einen Wutanfall bekommen; **to be (all) the** ~ (col) der letzte Schrei sein (col). 2 vi toben.

ragged ['rægɪd] adj person, clothes zerlumpt; beard zottig; coastline, rocks zerklüftet; edge, cuff ausgefranst.

raging ['reɪdʒɪŋ] adj person wütend; fever heftig; thirst brennend; sea, wind tobend. **he was** ~ er tobte.

rag trade n (col) Kleiderbranche f.

raid [reɪd] 1 n Überfall m; (Mil also) Angriff m; (air ~) Luftangriff m; (police ~) Razzia f; (by thieves) Einbruch m. 2 vt **(a)** überfallen; (police) eine Razzia durchführen in (+dat); (thieves) einbrechen in (+acc). **(b)** (fig hum) plündern.

raider ['reɪdəʳ] n (bandit) Gangster m; (thief) Einbrecher m; (in bank) Bankräuber m.

rail [reɪl] n **(a)** (on bridge, stairs etc) Geländer nt; (Naut) Reling f; (curtain ~) Schiene f; (towel-~) Handtuchhalter m. ~**s** (fence) Umzäunung f. **(b)** (for train, tram) Schiene f, Gleis nt. **to go off the** ~**s** (lit) entgleisen; (fig: morally) auf die schiefe Bahn geraten. **(c)** (~ travel, ~way) die (Eisen)bahn. **to travel by** ~ mit der Bahn fahren.

railing ['reɪlɪŋ] n (rail) Geländer nt; (Naut) Reling f; (fence ~s) Zaun m.

railroad ['reɪlrəʊd] 1 n (US) (Eisen)bahn f. 2 vt **to** ~ **a bill** eine Gesetzesvorlage durchpeitschen; **to** ~ **sb into doing sth** jdn dazu hetzen, etw zu tun.

rail strike n Bahnstreik m.

railway ['reɪlweɪ] n (Brit) (Eisen)bahn f; (track) Gleis nt.

railway: ~ **carriage** n (Brit) Eisenbahnwagen m; ~ **crossing** n (Brit) Bahnübergang m; ~ **engine** n (Brit) Lokomotive f; ~ **line** n (Brit) (Eisen)bahnlinie f; (track) Gleis nt; ~ **man** n (Brit) Eisenbahner m; ~ **station** n (Brit) Bahnhof m.

rain [reɪn] 1 n Regen m. **in the** ~ im Regen; **come** ~ **or shine** (fig) was auch geschieht; **the** ~**s** die Regenzeit. 2 vti impers (lit,fig) regnen. **it is** ~**ing** es regnet; **it never** ~**s but it pours** (prov) ein Unglück kommt selten allein (prov); **it's** ~**ing cats and dogs** (col) es gießt wie aus Kübeln.

♦ **rain down** vi (blows etc) niederprasseln (upon auf +acc).

rainbow ['reɪnbəʊ] n Regenbogen m.

rain: ~-**check** n (US) **to take a** ~-**check** (col) die Sache auf ein andermal verschieben; ~**coat** n Regenmantel m; ~**drop** n Regentropfen m; ~**fall** n Niederschlag m; ~**water** n Regenwasser nt.

rainy ['reɪnɪ] adj (+er) regnerisch, Regen-; area regenreich. ~ **season** Regenzeit f; **to keep sth for a** ~ **day** (fig) etw für schlechte Zeiten aufheben.

raise [reɪz] 1 vt **(a)** (lift) object, arm heben; blinds, eyebrow, (Theat) curtain hochziehen; (Naut) anchor lichten; sunken ship heben. **to** ~ **one's hat to**

sb den Hut vor jdm ziehen; **to** ~ **sb from the dead** jdn von den Toten erwecken; **to** ~ **one's voice** lauter sprechen; (get angry) laut werden; **to** ~ **the roof** (fig: with anger) fürchterlich toben.

(b) (increase) (to auf +acc) salary, temperature erhöhen; price also, standard anheben. **to** ~ **the tone** das Niveau heben; **to** ~ **to the power 2** (Math) in die 2. Potenz erheben.

(c) (promote) (er)heben (to in +acc).

(d) (build, erect) errichten.

(e) (create, evoke) problem, question aufwerfen; objection erheben; suspicion, hope (er)wecken; spirits (herauf)beschwören. **to** ~ **sb's/one's hopes** jdm/sich Hoffnung machen; **to** ~ **a laugh/smile** (in others) Gelächter/ein Lächeln hervorrufen; (oneself) lachen/lächeln; **to** ~ **a protest** protestieren; **to** ~ **hell** (col) einen Höllenspektakel machen (col).

(f) (grow, breed) children, animals aufziehen; crops anbauen. **to** ~ **a family** Kinder großziehen.

(g) army aufstellen; taxes erheben; funds, money aufbringen; loan aufnehmen.

(h) (end) siege, embargo aufheben.

2 n (in salary) Gehaltserhöhung f; (in wages) Lohnerhöhung f.

raisin ['reɪzən] n Rosine f.

rake[1] [reɪk] 1 n Harke f. 2 vt **(a)** garden, leaves harken. **(b)** (machine gun, searchlight) bestreichen.

♦ **rake in** vt sep (col) money kassieren (col). **he's raking it in** er ist scheffelt das Geld nur so.

♦ **rake up** vt sep memories, grievance aufwärmen. **to** ~ ~ **the past** in der Vergangenheit wühlen.

rake[2] n (person) Lebemann m.

rakish ['reɪkɪʃ] adj person flott, verwegen.

rally ['rælɪ] 1 n **(a)** Versammlung f; (with speaker) Kundgebung f; (Aut) Rallye f. **(b)** (Tennis) Ballwechsel m. 2 vt troops, supporters (ver)sammeln. **to** ~ **one's strength** all seine Kräfte sammeln. 3 **(a)** vi (St Ex) sich erholen. **(b)** (troops, people) sich versammeln. ~**ing point** Sammelplatz m; **to** ~ **to the support of sb** (fig) jdm in Scharen zu Hilfe eilen.

♦ **rally around** vi +prep obj leader sich scharen um; person in distress sich annehmen (+gen).

ram [ræm] 1 n **(a)** (animal) Widder, Schafbock m. **(b)** (Tech) Ramme f, Rammbock m; (hydraulic) Stoßheber m. 2 vt **(a)** (push) stick, post, umbrella stoßen; (with great force) rammen; (pack) zwängen; (Tech) pile rammen. **to** ~ **sth down sb's throat** (col) jdm etw eintrichtern (col). **(b)** (crash into) ship, car rammen. **the car** ~**med a lamppost** das Auto prallte gegen einen Laternenpfahl.

ramble ['ræmbl] 1 n Streifzug m; (hike) Wanderung f. **to go for** or **on a** ~ einen Streifzug/eine Wanderung machen. 2 vi **(a)** (wander about) Steifzüge/einen Streifzug machen, (go on hike) wandern. **(b)** (in speech) faseln (col); (pej: also ~ on) schwafeln (col).

rambler ['ræmbləʳ] n Wanderer m, Wanderin f.

rambling ['ræmblɪŋ] adj speech weitschweifig; person schwafelnd (col); building weitläufig. ~ **rose** Kletterrose f.

ramification [,ræmɪfɪ'keɪʃən] n Verzweigung f; (smaller, of arteries) Verästelung f. **the race question and its many** ~**s** die Rassenfrage und die damit verbundenen Probleme.

ramify ['ræmɪfaɪ] vi (lit, fig) sich verzweigen.

ramp [ræmp] n Rampe f; (hydraulic ~) Hebebühne f; (Aviat: also boarding ~) Gangway f.

rampage [ræm'peɪdʒ] 1 n **to be/go on the** ~ randalieren. 2 vi (also ~ about) herumtoben.

rampant ['ræmpənt] adj plants, growth üppig; evil etc wild wuchernd attr. **the** ~ **growth of** das Wuchern (+gen); **to be** ~ (wild) wuchern.

rampart ['ræmpɑːt] n Wall m.

ramshackle ['ræm,ʃækl] adj building baufällig.

ran [ræn] pret of **run**.

ranch [rɑːntʃ] n Ranch, Viehfarm f.

rancid ['rænsɪd] adj ranzig.

rancour, (US) **rancor** ['ræŋkəʳ] (of tone) Verbitterung f; (of attack) Boshaftigkeit f.

random ['rændəm] 1 n at ~ speak, walk, drive aufs Geratewohl; shoot, drop bombs ziellos; take wahllos; **a few examples taken at** ~ ein paar willkürlich gewählte Beispiele; **I** (just) chose one at ~ ich wählte einfach irgendeine (beliebige). 2 adj selection willkürlich, Zufalls-. a ~ **bullet** eine verirrte Kugel; a ~ shot ein Schuß m ins Blaue; **he was killed by a** ~ **shot** er wurde von einer verirrten Kugel getötet; **to make a** ~ **guess** auf gut Glück raten; ~ **sample** Stichprobe f.

randy ['rændɪ] adj (+er) (Brit) scharf (col), geil.

rang [ræŋ] pret of **ring²**.

range [reɪndʒ] 1 n (a) (scope, distance covered) Aktionsradius m; (of missile, gun, telescope also) Reichweite f; (of vehicle also) Fahrbereich m; (of plane also) Flugbereich m. **at a** ~ **of** auf eine Entfernung von; **at short/long** ~ auf kurze/ große Entfernung; **to be out of** ~ außer Reichweite sein; **within** (firing) ~ in Schußweite; ~ **of vision** Gesichtsfeld nt. **(b)** (spread, selection) Reihe f; (of goods also) Sortiment nt; (of colours also) Skala f; (of sizes, models) Auswahl f (of an +dat). **a wide** ~ eine große Auswahl; **in this price** ~ in dieser Preisklasse; **out of/within my price** ~ außerhalb/ innerhalb meiner (finanziellen) Möglichkeiten. **(c)** (also shooting ~) (Mil) Schießplatz m; (rifle ~) Schießstand m. **(d)** (row) Reihe f; (mountain ~) Kette f. **(e)** (US: grazing land) Weideland nt. 2 vt (place in a row) aufstellen; objects also anordnen.

3 vi (a) (extend) (from ... to) gehen (von ... bis); (temperature, value) liegen (zwischen ... und). **his interests** ~ **from skiing to chess** seine Interessen reichen vom Skifahren bis zum Schachspielen; **the conversation** ~d **over a number of subjects** die Unterhaltung kreiste um eine ganze Menge von Themen. **(b)** (roam) streifen. **to** ~ **over the area** im Gebiet umherstreifen.

range-finder ['reɪndʒ'faɪndəʳ] n Entfernungsmesser m.

ranger ['reɪndʒəʳ] n (a) (of forest etc) Förster m. **(b)** (US: mounted patrolman) Ranger m; (commando) Überfallkommando nt.

rank¹ [ræŋk] 1 n (a) (Mil: grade) Rang m. **(b)** (class, status) Stand m, Schicht f. **people of all** ~s Leute pl aller Stände. **(c)** (row) Reihe f; (Brit: taxi ~) Taxistand m. **(d)** (Mil: formation) Glied nt. **to break** ~(s) aus dem Glied treten; **the** ~s (Brit) die Mannschaften und die Unteroffiziere; **the** ~ **and file of the party/union** die Basis der Partei/Gewerkschaft; **the** ~ **and file workers** die einfachen Arbeiter; **to rise from the** ~s aus dem Mannschaftsstand zum Offizier aufsteigen; (fig) sich hocharbeiten. 2 vt (class, consider) **to** ~ **sb among the best/great etc** jdn zu den Besten/Großen etc zählen. 3 vi **to** ~ **among** zählen zu; **to** ~ **above** sb bedeutender als jd sein; (officer) rangmäßig über jdm liegen; **to** ~ **6th** den 6. Rang belegen; **he** ~s **as a great composer** er gilt als großer Komponist.

rank² adj (+er) (a) plants üppig; grass verwildert. **to grow** ~ wuchern. **(b)** smell übel; fat ranzig. **(c)** attr injustice schreiend; nonsense rein; traitor, liar übel; stupidity ausgesprochen.

rankle ['ræŋkl] vi **to** ~ **with sb** jdn wurmen (col).

ransack ['rænsæk] vt (search) durchwühlen; (pillage) house plündern; region herfallen über (+acc).

ransom ['rænsəm] 1 n Lösegeld nt. **to hold sb to** ~ (lit) jdn als Geisel halten; (fig) jdn erpressen. 2 vt (buy free) Lösegeld bezahlen für; (set free) gegen Lösegeld freilassen.

rant [rænt] vi (angrily) eine Schimpfkanonade loslassen; (talk nonsense) irres Zeug reden (col). **to** ~ **(and rave)** (be angry) herumschimpfen; **to** ~ **at sb** mit jdm schimpfen.

rap [ræp] 1 n (noise, blow) Klopfen nt no pl. **there was a** ~ **at the door** es hat geklopft; **to take the** ~ (col) die Schuld zugeschoben kriegen (col). 2 vt table klopfen auf (+acc); window klopfen an (+acc). **to** ~ **sb's knuckles** (lit, fig) jdm auf die Finger klopfen. 3 vi klopfen. **to** ~ **at the door** kurz (an die Tür) klopfen.

rapacious [rə'peɪʃəs] adj habgierig.

rape¹ [reɪp] 1 n Vergewaltigung f. 2 vt vergewaltigen.

rape² n (plant) Raps m.

rapid ['ræpɪd] 1 adj schnell; change also rapide; descent, decline, rise steil. 2 n ~s pl Stromschnellen pl.

rapidity [rə'pɪdɪtɪ] n see adj Schnelligkeit f; Rapidheit f; Steilheit f.

rapier ['reɪpɪəʳ] n Rapier nt.

rapist ['reɪpɪst] n Vergewaltiger m.

rapport [ræ'pɔː] n **the** ~ **I have with my father** das enge Verhältnis zwischen mir und meinem Vater; **in** ~ **with** in Harmonie mit.

rapt [ræpt] adj (a) interest gespannt. ~ **in contemplation** in Betrachtungen versunken. **(b)** look, smile verzückt.

rapture ['ræptʃəʳ] n (delight) Entzücken nt; (ecstasy) Verzückung f. **to be in** ~s entzückt sein (over über +acc, about von); **to go into** ~s ins Schwärmen geraten.

rapturous ['ræptʃərəs] adj applause, reception stürmisch; exclamation entzückt; look verzückt.

rare [rɛəʳ] adj (+er) (a) selten. it's ~ **for her to come** sie kommt nur selten. **(b)** atmosphere dünn. **(c)** meat roh; steak also blutig, englisch.

rarebit ['rɛəbɪt] n = Welsh ~.

rarefied ['rɛərɪfaɪd] adj atmosphere, air dünn; (fig) exklusiv.

rarely ['rɛəlɪ] adv selten.

rarity ['rɛərɪtɪ] n Seltenheit f; (rare occurrence also) Rarität f.

rascal ['rɑːskəl] n Gauner m; (child) Schlingel m.

rash¹ [ræʃ] n (Med) Ausschlag m. **to break out in a** ~ einen Ausschlag bekommen.

rash² adj (+er) person unbesonnen; act also überstürzt; words, decision voreilig.

rasher ['ræʃəʳ] n ~ **of bacon** Speckstreifen m.

rasp [rɑːsp] 1 n (tool) Raspel f; (noise) Kratzen nt no pl. 2 vt (a) (Tech) raspeln. **(b)** ... **he rasped** ..., krächzte er.

raspberry ['rɑːzbərɪ] 1 n Himbeere f. **to blow a** ~ (col) verächtlich schnauben. 2 adj jam Himbeer-.

rasping ['rɑːspɪŋ] 1 adj sound kratzend; voice krächzend; cough, breath keuchend. 2 n (sound) Kratzen nt; (of voice) Krächzen nt.

rat [ræt] n Ratte f; (pej col: person) elender Verräter (col). **to smell a** ~ den Braten riechen (col).

ratchet ['rætʃɪt] n Ratsche f. ~ **wheel** Sperrad nt.

rate [reɪt] 1 n (a) (ratio, proportion, frequency) Rate f; (speed) Tempo nt. **at a** ~ **of 14 feet per minute** (in einem Tempo von) 14 Fuß pro Minute; ~ **of flow** (of water etc) Fluß m; pulse ~ Puls m; **at a great** (col) ~, **at a** ~ **of knots** (col) in irrsinnigem Tempo (col); **if you continue at this** ~ (lit, fig) wenn du in diesem Tempo weitermachst; **at any** ~ auf jeden Fall. **(b)** (Comm, Fin) Satz m; (St Ex) Kurs m. ~ **of exchange** Wechselkurs m; **what's the** ~ **of pay?** wie hoch ist die Bezahlung?; ~ **of interest** Zinssatz m; postage ~s Postgebühren pl; **there is a reduced** ~ **for children** Kinderermäßigung wird gewährt. **(c)** ~s pl (Brit: municipal tax) Gemeindesteuern pl.

2 vt (a) (estimate value or worth of) (ein)schätzen. **to** ~ **sb/sth among** ... jdn/etw zu ... zählen; **how do you** ~ **these results?** was halten Sie von diesen Ergebnissen?; **to** ~ **sb/sth as sth**

jdn/etw für etw halten; **he is generally** ~d **as** ... er gilt allgemein als ...; **to** ~ **sb/sth highly** jdn/ etw hoch einschätzen. **(b)** *(Brit)* **a house** ~d **at £500 per annum** ein Haus, dessen steuerbarer Wert £ 500 pro Jahr ist.
  3 *vi* **to** ~ **as/among** ... gelten als .../zählen zu ...
rateable ['reɪtəbl] *adj (Brit)* ~ **value** steuerbarer Wert.
ratepayer ['reɪt,peɪəʳ] *n (Brit)* Steuerzahler *m (von Gemeindesteuern)*.
rather ['rɑːðəʳ] *adv* **(a)** *(for preference)* lieber. ~ **than wait, he went away** er ging lieber, als daß er wartete; **I would** ~ **have the blue dress** ich hätte lieber das blaue Kleid; **I would** ~ **be happy than rich** ich wäre lieber glücklich als reich; **I would** ~ **you came yourself** mir wäre es lieber, Sie kämen selbst; **I'd** ~ **not** lieber nicht; **he expects me to phone** ~ **than (to) write** er erwartet eher, daß ich anrufe, als daß ich schreibe.
  (b) *(more accurately)* vielmehr. **he is, or** ~ **was, a soldier** er ist, beziehungsweise *or* vielmehr war, Soldat; **a car, or** ~ **an old banger** ein Auto, genauer gesagt eine alte Kiste.
  (c) *(to a considerable degree)* ziemlich; *(somewhat)* etwas. **he felt** ~ **better** er fühlte sich bedeutend wohler; **it's** ~ **more difficult than you think** es ist um einiges schwieriger, als du denkst; **she's** ~ **an idiot/a killjoy** sie ist reichlich doof *(col)*/ein richtiger Spielverderber; **I** ~ **think he's wrong** ich glaube fast, er hat Unrecht; ~! *(col)* und ob! *(col)*, klar! *(col)*.
ratify ['rætɪfaɪ] *vt* ratifizieren.
rating ['reɪtɪŋ] *n* **(a)** *(assessment)* (Ein)schätzung *f*. **(b)** *(class) (Sport: of yacht, car)* Klasse *f; (Fin: also credit* ~*)* Kreditfähigkeit *f*. **(c)** *(Naut) (rank)* Rang *m; (sailor)* Matrose *m*.
ratio ['reɪʃɪəʊ] *n* Verhältnis *nt*. **the** ~ **of men to women** das Verhältnis von Männern zu Frauen; **in the** *or* **a** ~ **of 100 to 1** *(written* 100:1*)* im Verhältnis 100 zu 1.
ration ['ræʃən] **1** *n* Ration *f; (fig)* Quantum *nt*. ~**s** *(food)* Rationen *pl*; **to put sb on short** ~**s** jdn auf halbe Ration setzen. **2** *vt goods, food* rationieren. **he was** ~**ed to 1 kg** ihm wurde nur 1 kg erlaubt.
rational ['ræʃənl] *adj (having reason)* vernunftbegabt, rational; *(reasonable)* vernünftig; *person, action also* rational; *(Med: lucid, sane)* person bei klarem Verstand.
rationale [ræʃəˈnɑːl] *n* Gründe *pl*.   *
rationalization [,ræʃnəlaɪˈzeɪʃən] *n* Rationalisierung *f*.
rationalize ['ræʃnəlaɪz] *vt* rationalisieren; *problem* vernünftig betrachten.
rationing ['ræʃənɪŋ] *n* Rationierung *f*.
rat: ~ **poison** *n* Rattengift *nt;* ~**-race** *n* ständiger Konkurrenzkampf.
rattle ['rætl] **1** *vi* klappern; *(chains)* rasseln; *(bottles)* klirren; *(gunfire)* knattern. **there's something rattling** da klappert etwas. **2** *vt* **(a)** *dice, keys* schütteln; *chains* rasseln mit; *windows* rütteln an (+*dat*). **(b)** *(col: alarm)* person durcheinanderbringen. **don't get** ~**d!** reg dich nicht auf! **3** *n* **(a)** *(sound) see* vi Klappern *nt no pl;* Rasseln *nt no pl;* Klirren *nt no pl;* Knattern *nt no pl*. **(b)** *(child's)* Rassel *f; (sports fan's)* Schnarre *f*.
♦ **rattle off** *vt sep speech, list* herunterrasseln.
♦ **rattle on** *vi (col)* (unentwegt) quasseln *(col) (about* über +*acc)*.
rattlesnake ['rætlsneɪk] *n* Klapperschlange *f*.
ratty ['rætɪ] *adj* (+*er*) *(col: irritable)* gereizt. **don't get** ~ sei nicht so gereizt.
raucous ['rɔːkəs] *adj* rauh, heiser.
ravage ['rævɪdʒ] **1** *n* ~**s** *(of war)* Verheerung *f (of* durch*);* **the** ~**s of time** die Spuren *pl* der Zeit. **2** *vt (ruin)* verwüsten; *(plunder)* plündern.
rave [reɪv] **1** *vi* phantasieren; *(speak furiously)* toben; *(col: speak, write enthusiastically)* schwärmen *(about, over* von*)*. **2** *attr* ~ **review** *(col)*

begeisterte Kritik.
raven ['reɪvən] *n* Rabe *m*.
ravenous ['rævənəs] *adj animal* ausgehungert; *person also* heißhungrig; *appetite* gewaltig. **I'm** ~ ich habe einen Bärenhunger *(col)*.
ravine [rəˈviːn] *n* Schlucht *f*.
raving ['reɪvɪŋ] **1** *adj (frenzied)* wahnsinnig, verrückt; *(delirious)* im Delirium. **a** ~ **lunatic** *(col)* ein kompletter Idiot *(col)*. **2** *adv* ~ **mad** *(col)* total verrückt *(col)*. **3** *n* ~**(s)** Phantasien *pl*.
ravishing ['rævɪʃɪŋ] *adj* atemberaubend.
raw [rɔː] **1** *adj* (+*er*) **(a)** *(uncooked)* roh; *(unprocessed) ore, sugar also* Roh-; *spirit* rein; *cloth* ungewalkt; *leather* ungegerbt; *(fig) statistics* nackt. ~ **material** Rohstoff *m*. **(b)** *(inexperienced) troops* neu, unerfahren. ~ **recruit** *(fig)* blutiger Anfänger *(col)*. **(c)** *(sore) wound* offen; *skin* wund. **(d)** *wind, air* rauh. **(e)** *(esp US: coarse)* derb. **2** *n* **(a) to touch sb on the** ~ *(Brit)* bei jdm einen wunden Punkt berühren. **(b) nature in the** ~ die rauhe Seite der Natur.
ray[1] [reɪ] *n* Strahl *m*. **a** ~ **of hope** ein Hoffnungsschimmer *m*.
ray[2] *n (fish)* Rochen *m*.
rayon ['reɪɒn] **1** *n* Reyon *nt*. **2** *adj* Reyon-.
raze [reɪz] *vt* **to** ~ **to the ground** dem Erdboden gleichmachen.
razor ['reɪzəʳ] *n* Rasierapparat *m; (cutthroat)* Rasiermesser *nt*. **electric** ~ Elektrorasierer *m;* **to be on a** ~**'s edge** auf Messers Schneide stehen.
razor: ~ **blade** *n* Rasierklinge *f; ~*-**sharp** *adj (lit)* scharf *(wie ein Rasiermesser); (fig) person* sehr scharfsinnig; *mind, wit* messerscharf.
RC = **Roman Catholic** rk, r.-k.
Rd = **Road** Str.
RE = **Religious Education.**
re [riː] *prep (Comm)* betreffs (+*gen*). ~ **your letter of the 16th** Betr(eff): Ihr Brief vom 16.
re- [riː-] *pref* wieder-.
reach [riːtʃ] **1** *n* **(a)** *within/out of sb's* ~ in/außer jds Reichweite *(dat);* **keep out of** ~ **of children** von Kindern fernhalten; **within easy** ~ **of the sea** in unmittelbarer Nähe des Meeres; **I keep it within easy** ~ ich habe es in greifbarer Nähe.
  (b) *(of river)* Strecke *f*.
  2 *vt* **(a)** *(arrive at)* erreichen; *town* ankommen in (+*dat*); *agreement* erzielen; *conclusion* kommen zu. **when the news** ~**ed my ears** als mir die Nachricht zu Ohren kam; **to** ~ **page 50** bis Seite 50 kommen; **you can** ~ **me at my hotel** Sie erreichen mich in meinem Hotel. **(b)** *(stretch to get or touch)* **to be able to** ~ **sth** an etw *(acc)* (heran)reichen können; **can you** ~ *it*? kommen Sie dran? **(c)** *(come up to, go down to)* reichen bis zu. **he** ~**es her shoulder** er geht ihr bis zur Schulter.
  3 *vi* **(a)** *(to, as far as* bis*)* reichen; *(territory etc also)* sich erstrecken. **(b)** *(stretch out hand or arm)* greifen. **to** ~ **for sth** nach etw greifen *or* langen *(col)*.
♦ **reach out 1** *vt sep* **he** ~**ed** ~ **his hand to take the book** er streckte die Hand aus, um das Buch zu nehmen. **2** *vi* die Hand/Hände ausstrecken. **to** ~ ~ **for sth** nach etw greifen *or* langen *(col)*.
react [riːˈækt] *vi* reagieren *(to* auf +*acc*). **to** ~ **against** negativ reagieren auf (+*acc*).
reaction [riːˈækʃən] *n* Reaktion *f (to* auf +*acc, against* gegen*); (Mil)* Gegenschlag *m*. **what was his** ~ **to your suggestion?** wie hat er auf Ihren Vorschlag reagiert?
reactionary [riːˈækʃnrɪ] *adj* reaktionär.
reactor [riːˈæktəʳ] *n (Phys)* Reaktor *m*.
read[1] [riːd] *(vb:* pret, ptp **read** [red]*)* **1** *vt* **(a)** lesen; *(to sb)* vorlesen *(to* dat*)*. **do you** ~ **music?** können Sie Noten lesen?; **to take sth as read** *(fig) (as self-evident)* etw als selbstverständlich voraussetzen; *(as agreed)* etw für abgemacht halten. **(b)** *(interpret) thoughts, feelings* lesen;

dream deuten; *words* verstehen. **to ~ sb's thoughts/mind** jds Gedanken lesen; **to ~ sb's hand** jdm aus der Hand lesen; **these words can be read in several ways** diese Wörter können unterschiedlich verstanden werden; **to ~ something into a text** etwas in einen Text (hinein)lesen. **(c)** (*Univ: study*) studieren. **(d)** *thermometer etc* sehen auf (+*acc*). **to ~ a meter** einen Zähler(stand) ablesen.

2 *vi* lesen; (*to sb*) vorlesen (*to dat*); (*have wording*) lauten. **to ~ aloud** laut lesen; **to ~ to oneself** für sich lesen; **he likes being read to** er läßt sich (*dat*) gern vorlesen; **this book ~s well** das Buch liest sich gut; **the letter ~s as follows** der Brief besagt folgendes *or* hat folgenden Wortlaut (*form*).

3 *n* **she enjoys a good ~** sie liest gern; **this book is quite a good ~** das Buch liest sich gut.

♦ **read off** *vt sep* ablesen; (*without pause*) herunterlesen.

♦ **read on** *vi* weiterlesen.

♦ **read out** *vt sep* vorlesen.

♦ **read over** *or* **through** *vt sep* durchlesen.

♦ **read up 1** *vt sep* nachlesen über (+*acc*). **2** *vi* nachlesen (*on* über +*acc*).

read² [red] **1** *pret, ptp of* **read¹**. **2** *adj* **he is well/badly ~** er ist sehr/wenig belesen.

readable ['riːdəbl] *adj* (*legible*) lesbar; (*worth reading*) lesenswert.

readdress [ˌriːə'dres] *vt* umadressieren.

reader ['riːdə'] *n* **(a)** Leser(in *f*) *m*. **(b)** (*Brit Univ*) ≈ Dozent(in *f*) *m*. **(c)** (*schoolbook*) Lesebuch *nt*; (*to teach reading*) Fibel *f*; (*foreign language text*) Text *m*; (*anthology*) Sammelband *m*.

readership ['riːdəʃɪp] *n* Leserschaft *f*. **a wide ~** eine große Leserschaft.

readily ['redɪlɪ] *adv* bereitwillig; (*easily*) leicht.

readiness ['redɪnɪs] *n* Bereitschaft *f*. **to be (kept) in ~ (for sth)** (für etw) bereitgehalten werden; **his ~ to help** seine Hilfsbereitschaft.

reading ['riːdɪŋ] *n* **(a)** (*action*) Lesen *nt*; (*by author*) Lesung *f*. **(b)** (~ *matter*) Lektüre *f*. **this book makes very interesting ~** dieses Buch ist sehr interessant zu lesen. **(c)** (*interpretation*) Interpretation *f*. **my ~ of this sentence** mein Verständnis des Satzes. **(d)** (*from meter*) Thermometer-/Zählerstand *etc m*; (*from instruments*) Anzeige *f*. **to take a ~** den Thermometerstand *etc* ablesen; die Anzeige ablesen.

reading: ~ **matter** *n* Lesestoff *m*; ~ **room** *n* Lesesaal *m*.

readjust [ˌriːə'dʒʌst] **1** *vt instrument, mechanism* neu einstellen; (*correct*) nachstellen. **2** *vi* sich wieder anpassen (*to* an +*acc*).

ready ['redɪ] **1** *adj* **(a)** fertig; (*prepared also*) bereit. **~ for use** gebrauchsfertig; **~ to serve** tischfertig; **~ for battle** kampfbereit; **~ for anything** zu allem bereit; **are you ~ to go?** sind Sie soweit?; **I'm ~ for him!** er soll nur kommen!; **everything is ~ for his visit** alles ist für seinen Besuch bereit; **to be ~ with an excuse** eine Entschuldigung bereit haben; **to get (oneself) ~** sich fertigmachen; **to get ~ to do sth** sich bereitmachen, etw zu tun; **to get ~ to go out** sich zum Ausgehen fertigmachen. **(b)** ~ **to do sth** (*willing*) bereit, etw zu tun; (*quick*) schnell dabei, etw zu tun; **I'm ~ to believe it** ich möchte das fast glauben; **he was ~ to cry** er war der Tränen nahe. **(c)** (*available*) ~ **money** jederzeit verfügbares Geld; ~ **cash** Bargeld *nt*.

2 *n* **at the ~** (*Mil*) mit dem Gewehr im Anschlag; (*fig*) marsch-/fahrbereit *etc*; **with his pen at the ~** mit gezücktem Federhalter.

ready in *cpds* fertig-; ~ **-made** *adj* *curtains* fertig; *clothes* Konfektions-; *solution* Patent-; ~ **reckoner** *n* Rechentabelle *f*; ~ **-to-wear** *adj* Konfektions-, von der Stange (*col*).

real ['rɪəl] **1** *adj* **(a)** wirklich; (*genuine*) *gold, flowers,*

joy echt; (*as opposed to substitute*) richtig; (*true, actual*) *owner, reason, purpose also* eigentlich; (*not imaginary*) *creature, world also,* (*Econ*) real. ~ **coffee** Bohnenkaffee *m*; **in ~ life** im wirklichen Leben; **in ~ terms** effektiv; **it's the ~ thing** *or* McCoy, **this whisky!** dieser Whisky ist das einzig Wahre. **(b)** ~ **estate** Immobilien *pl*. **2** *adv* (*esp US col*) echt (*col*), wirklich. **3** *n* **for ~** wirklich, echt (*col*); **is that invitation for ~?** ist die Einladung ernst gemeint?

realism ['rɪəlɪzəm] *n* Realismus *m*.

realist ['rɪəlɪst] *n* Realist *m*.

realistic [rɪə'lɪstɪk] *adj* realistisch.

reality [riː'ælɪtɪ] *n* **(a)** Wirklichkeit, Realität *f*. **to become ~** sich verwirklichen; **(the) ~ is somewhat different** die Wirklichkeit sieht etwas anders aus; **in ~** (*in fact*) in Wirklichkeit; (*actually*) eigentlich. **(b)** (*trueness to life*) Naturtreue *f*.

realization [ˌrɪəlaɪ'zeɪʃən] *n* **(a)** (*of assets*) Realisation *f*; (*of hope, plan*) Realisierung, Verwirklichung *f*. **(b)** (*awareness*) Erkenntnis *f*.

realize ['rɪəlaɪz] *vt* **(a)** (*become aware of*) erkennen, sich (*dat*) bewußt werden (+*gen*); (*be aware of*) sich (*dat*) klar sein über (+*acc*); (*appreciate*) begreifen; (*notice*) bemerken; (*discover*) feststellen. **does he ~ the problems?** sind ihm die Probleme bewußt?; **I ~d what he meant** ich habe begriffen, was er meinte; **I ~d how he had done it** ich erkannte, wie er es gemacht hatte; **I'd ~d it was raining** ich hatte gemerkt, daß es regnete; **I ~d I didn't have any money on me** ich stellte fest, daß ich kein Geld dabei hatte; **you couldn't be expected to ~** that das konnten Sie nicht wissen. **(b)** *hope, plan* verwirklichen. **(c)** (*Fin*) *assets* realisieren; *price* erzielen; *interest* abwerfen; (*goods*) einbringen.

really ['rɪəlɪ] **1** *adv* **(a)** (*in reality*) wirklich, tatsächlich. **I don't ~ think so** das glaube ich eigentlich nicht. **(b)** (*intensifier*) wirklich, echt (*col*). **you ~ must visit Paris** Sie müssen wirklich Paris besuchen. **2** *interj* wirklich, ehrlich.

realm [relm] *n* (*liter: kingdom*) Königreich *nt*; (*fig*) Reich *nt*. **within the ~s of possibility** im Bereich des Möglichen.

realtor ['rɪəltɔ:'] *n* (*US*) Grundstücksmakler *m*.

ream [riːm] *n* (*of paper*) Ries *nt*. **he always writes ~s** (*col*) er schreibt immer ganze Bände (*col*).

reap [riːp] *vt* **(a)** *corn* (*cut*) schneiden, mähen; (*harvest*) ernten. **(b)** (*fig*) *profit* ernten; *reward* bekommen.

reappear [ˌriːə'pɪə'] *vi* wiederauftauchen.

reappearance [ˌriːə'pɪərəns] *n* Wiederauftauchen *nt*.

reappraisal [ˌriːə'preɪzəl] *n* Neubeurteilung *f*.

rear¹ [rɪə'] **1** *n* **(a)** (*back part*) hinterer Teil; (*col: buttocks*) Hintern *m* (*col*). **to be situated at the ~ of the plane** (*inside*) hinten im Flugzeug sein; (*outside*) am hinteren Ende des Flugzeugs sein; **at the ~ of the building** (*outside*) hinter dem Haus; (*inside*) hinten im Haus; **from the ~** von hinten; **to bring up the ~** (*Mil*) die Nachhut bilden; (*fig*) das Schlußlicht bilden. **2** *adj* Hinter-, hintere(r, s); (*Aut*) *engine, window* Heck-. ~ **door** (*of car*) hintere Tür; ~ **wheel/lights** (*Aut*) Hinterrad *nt*/Rücklichter *pl*.

rear² **1** *vt* **(a)** *animals, family* großziehen, aufziehen. **(b)** **to ~ its head** (*animal*) den Kopf zurückwerfen; **racialism ~ed its ugly head** der Rassismus kam zum Durchbruch. **2** *vi* (*also* ~ **up**) (*horse*) sich aufbäumen.

rearm [ˌriː'ɑːm] **1** *vt country* wiederbewaffnen; *forces* neu ausrüsten. **2** *vi* wieder aufrüsten; sich neu ausrüsten.

rearmament [ˌriː'ɑːməmənt] *n see vb* Wiederaufrüstung *f*; Neuausrüstung *f*.

rearrange [ˌriːə'reɪndʒ] *vt furniture, system* umstellen; *plans also, order, ideas* ändern; *meeting*

verlegen.
rearrangement [ˌriːə'reɪndʒmənt] *n see vt* Umstellung *f*; Änderung *f*; Verlegung *f*.
rear-view mirror ['rɪəˌvjuː'mɪrəʳ] *n* Rückspiegel *m*.
reason ['riːzn] **1** *n* (a) *(cause, justification)* Grund *m (for* für). **to give sb ~ for complaint** jdm Anlaß *or* Grund zu Klagen geben; **you have no ~ to interfere** Sie haben keinen Grund, sich einzumischen; **I want to know the ~ why** ich möchte wissen, weshalb; **and that's the ~ why** ... und deshalb ...; **I have (good) ~ to believe that** ... ich habe (guten) Grund zu glauben, daß ...; **there is every ~ to believe** ... es spricht alles dafür ...; **for that very ~ (that)** eben deswegen(, weil); **with (good) ~** mit gutem Grund; **for no particular ~** ohne bestimmten Grund; **all the more ~ for doing it** um so mehr Grund, das zu tun; **by ~ of** wegen *(+gen)*.
   (b) *no pl (faculty)* Verstand *m*; *(common sense)* Vernunft *f*. **to lose one's ~** den Verstand verlieren; **he won't listen to ~** er läßt sich *(dat)* nichts sagen; **that stands to ~** das ist logisch; **you can have anything within ~** Sie können alles haben, solange es sich in Grenzen hält.
   2 *vi* (a) *(think logically)* vernünftig *or* logisch denken. (b) *(argue)* **to ~ (with sb)** vernünftig mit jdm reden.
   3 *vt* (a) **to ~ why/what** ... sich *(dat)* klarmachen, warum/was ... (b) *(also ~ out) (deduce)* folgern; *(verbally)* argumentieren.
reasonable ['riːznəbl] *adj* (a) vernünftig; *chance* reell; *claim, doubt* berechtigt; *amount* angemessen; *(acceptable) excuse, offer* akzeptabel. **beyond (all) ~ doubt** ohne (jeden) Zweifel. (b) *(quite good)* ordentlich, ganz gut.
reasonably ['riːznəblɪ] *adv* (a) *behave, act, think* vernünftig. **one could ~ think that** ... man könnte durchaus annehmen, daß ...; **~ priced** preiswert. (b) *(quite)* ziemlich, ganz.
reasoned ['riːznd] *adj* durchdacht.
reasoning ['riːznɪŋ] *n* Argumentation *f*. **~ is not his strong point** logisches Denken ist nicht gerade seine starke Seite.
reassurance [ˌriːə'ʃʊərəns] *n* (a) *(feeling of security)* Beruhigung *f*. **safe in the ~ that** ... in der sicheren Gewißheit, daß ...; **to give sb ~** jdn beruhigen. (b) *(renewed confirmation)* Bestätigung *f*. **despite his ~(s)** trotz seiner Versicherungen.
reassure [ˌriːə'ʃʊəʳ] *vt* (a) *(relieve sb's mind)* beruhigen; *(give feelings of security to)* das Gefühl der Sicherheit geben *(+dat)*. (b) *(verbally)* versichern *(+dat)*. **to ~ sb of sth** jdm etw versichern.
reassuring [ˌriːə'ʃʊərɪŋ] *adj* beruhigend.
rebate ['riːbeɪt] *n (money back)* Rückvergütung *f*.
rebel ['rebl] **1** *n* Rebell(in *f*) *m*. **2** *adj attr* rebellisch. **3** [rɪ'bel] *vi* rebellieren.
rebellion [rɪ'beljən] *n* Rebellion *f*, Aufstand *m*.
rebellious [rɪ'beljəs] *adj* rebellisch.
rebirth [ˌriː'bɜːθ] *n* Wiedergeburt *f*.
rebound [rɪ'baʊnd] **1** *vi* zurückprallen *(against, off* von*)*. **your violent methods will ~ on you** Ihre rauhen Methoden werden auf Sie zurückfallen. **2** ['riːbaʊnd] *n (of ball, bullet)* Rückprall *m*. **to be on the ~** *(fig)* sich über eine Enttäuschung hinwegtrösten; **she married him on the ~** sie heiratete ihn, um sich über einen anderen hinwegzutrösten.
rebuff [rɪ'bʌf] **1** *n* Abfuhr *f*. **to meet with a ~** abgewiesen werden, eine Abfuhr bekommen; *(from opposite sex)* einen Korb bekommen (col). **2** *vt* abweisen; einen Korb geben *(+dat)* (col).
rebuild [ˌriː'bɪld] *vt house* wieder aufbauen; *(fig) country, relationship* wiederaufbauen.
rebuke [rɪ'bjuːk] **1** *n* Zurechtweisung *f*. **2** *vt* zurechtweisen *(for* wegen*)*, tadeln *(for* für*)*.
rebut [rɪ'bʌt] *vt contention* widerlegen.

rebuttal [rɪ'bʌtl] *n* Widerlegung *f*.
recalcitrant [rɪ'kælsɪtrənt] *adj* aufsässig.
recall [rɪ'kɔːl] **1** *vt* (a) *(summon back, evoke)* zurückrufen; *ambassador* abberufen; *library book, (Fin) capital* zurückfordern. (b) *(remember)* sich erinnern an *(+acc)*. **I cannot ~ meeting him** ich kann mich nicht daran erinnern, daß ich ihn kennengelernt habe. **2** *n see vt* (a) Rückruf *m*; Abberufung *f*; Rückforderung *f*. **beyond ~** für immer vorbei.
recant [rɪ'kænt] **1** *vt religious belief* widerrufen; *statement also* zurücknehmen. **2** *vi* widerrufen.
recap ['riːkæp] *(col)* **1** *n* kurze Zusammenfassung. **2** *vti* rekapitulieren, kurz zusammenfassen.
recapitulate [ˌriːkə'pɪtjʊleɪt] *vti* rekapitulieren, kurz zusammenfassen.
recapture [ˌriː'kæptʃəʳ] *vt animal* wieder einfangen; *prisoner* wiederergreifen; *territory* wiedererobern; *(fig) atmosphere* wieder wachwerden lassen.
recede [rɪ'siːd] *vi (tide, price)* zurückgehen; *(fig)* sich entfernen; *(hope)* schwinden. **to ~ into the distance** in der Ferne verschwinden.
receding [rɪ'siːdɪŋ] *adj chin, forehead* fliehend; *hairline* zurückweichend.
receipt [rɪ'siːt] *n* (a) *no pl* Empfang *m*; *(Comm also)* Erhalt, Eingang *m*. **to acknowledge ~ of sth** den Empfang etc einer Sache *(gen)* bestätigen; **I am in ~ of** *(on letter)* ich bin im Besitz *(+gen)*. (b) *(paper)* Quittung *f*. (c) *(Comm, Fin: money taken)* **~s** Einnahmen *pl*.
receive [rɪ'siːv] *vt* (a) *(get)* bekommen, erhalten; *punch* (ab)bekommen; *refusal, setback* erfahren; *impression* gewinnen; *recognition* finden; *(Jur) stolen goods* Hehlerei (be)treiben mit. **"~d with thanks"** *(Comm)* „dankend erhalten". (b) *(welcome) person* empfangen; *(into group)* aufnehmen *(in in +acc)*; *offer, news* aufnehmen. **the play has been well ~d** das Stück wurde gut aufgenommen.
receiver [rɪ'siːvəʳ] *n* (a) *(of letter, goods)* Empfänger(in *f*) *m*; *(Jur: of stolen goods)* Hehler(in *f*) *m*. (b) *(Fin, Jur) (official)* ~ Konkursverwalter *m*. (c) *(Telec)* Hörer *m*. (d) *(Rad)* Empfänger *m*.
recent ['riːsnt] *adj* kürzlich *(usu adv)*; *event, development, news* neueste(r, s); *edition, addition* neu; *publication* Neu-. **the ~ improvement** die vor kurzem eingetretene Verbesserung; **most ~** neueste(r, s); **his ~ arrival** seine Ankunft vor kurzem; **in ~ years** in den letzten Jahren; **~ developments** jüngste Entwicklungen.
recently ['riːsntlɪ] *adv (a short while ago)* vor kurzem, kürzlich; *(during the last few days or weeks)* in letzter Zeit. **~ he has been doing it differently** seit kurzem macht er das anders; **as ~ as** erst; **quite ~** erst kürzlich; **until (quite) ~** (noch) bis vor kurzem.
receptacle [rɪ'septəkl] *n* Behälter *m*.
reception [rɪ'sepʃən] *n (welcome, ceremony, in hotel, Rad, TV)* Empfang *m*; *(into group, of play etc)* Aufnahme *f*. **to give sb a warm ~** jdm einen herzlichen Empfang bereiten; jdn herzlich empfangen; **~ centre** *(Brit)* or **center** *(US)* Durchgangslager *nt*; **~ desk** Empfang *m*, Rezeption *f*.
receptionist [rɪ'sepʃənɪst] *n (in hotel)* Empfangschef *m*, Empfangsdame *f*; *(with firm)* Herr *m*/Dame *f* am Empfang; *(at airport)* Bodenhostess *f*; *(at doctor's etc)* Sprechstundenhilfe *f*.
receptive [rɪ'septɪv] *adj person, mind* aufnahmefähig; *audience* empfänglich. **~ to** empfänglich für.
recess [rɪ'ses] *n* (a) *(of Parliament)* (Sitzungs)pause *f*; *(of lawcourts)* Ferien *pl*; *(US Sch)* Pause *f*. (b) *(alcove)* Nische *f*.
recession [rɪ'seʃən] *n* (a) *no pl* Rückgang *m*. (b) *(Econ)* Rezession *f*.
recharge [ˌriː'tʃɑːdʒ] *vt battery* aufladen; *gun*

nachladen.

recherché [rə'ʃɛəʃeɪ] *adj* gewählt; *book, subject* ausgefallen.

recipe ['resɪpɪ] *n* Rezept *nt*. ~ **for success** Erfolgsrezept *nt*; **an easy ~ for** ... (*fig*) ein Patentrezept für ...; **that's a ~ for disaster** das führt mit Sicherheit in die Katastrophe.

recipient [rɪ'sɪpɪənt] *n* Empfänger(in *f*) *m*.

reciprocal [rɪ'sɪprəkəl] *adj* (*mutual*) gegenseitig; *favour* Gegen-; (*Gram, Math*) reziprok.

reciprocate [rɪ'sɪprəkeɪt] **1** *vt smiles, wishes, help* erwidern. **2** *vi* sich revanchieren. **but she didn't ~** (*emotionally*) aber sie erwiderte seine/ihre Gefühle nicht.

recital [rɪ'saɪtl] *n* (*of music, poetry*) Vortrag *m*; (*piano ~ etc*) Konzert *nt*; (*account*) Schilderung *f*.

recitation [ˌresɪ'teɪʃən] *n* Vortrag *m*.

recite [rɪ'saɪt] **1** *vt* (**a**) *poetry* vortragen. (**b**) *facts* hersagen; *details* aufzählen. **2** *vi* vortragen, rezitieren.

reckless ['reklɪs] *adj* leichtsinnig; *driver, driving* rücksichtslos; *speed* gefährlich; *attempt* gewagt.

reckon ['rekən] *vt* (**a**) (*calculate*) berechnen. **he ~ed the cost to be £40.51** er berechnete die Kosten auf £ 40,51. (**b**) (*judge*) rechnen, zählen (*among zu*). **she is ~ed a beautiful woman** sie gilt als schöne Frau. (**c**) (*think, suppose*) glauben; (*estimate*) schätzen. **what do you ~?** was meinen Sie?; **I ~ we can start** ich glaube, wir können anfangen; **I ~ he must be about forty** ich schätze, er müßte so um die Vierzig sein.

♦ **reckon on** *vi* +*prep obj* zählen auf (+*acc*). **you can ~ ~ 30** Sie können mit 30 rechnen; **I wasn't ~ing ~ having to do that** ich habe nicht damit gerechnet, daß ich das tun muß.

♦ **reckon up** *vt sep* zusammenrechnen.

♦ **reckon with** *vi* +*prep obj* rechnen mit. **he's a person to be ~ed ~** er ist jemand, mit dem man rechnen muß.

reckoning ['rekənɪŋ] *n* (*calculation*) (Be)rechnung *f*. **to be out in one's ~** sich ziemlich verrechnet haben; **the day of ~** der Tag der Abrechnung.

reclaim [rɪ'kleɪm] **1** *vt* (**a**) *land* gewinnen; (*by irrigation etc*) kultivieren. (**b**) *baggage etc* abholen. **2** *n past* ~ für immer verloren.

reclamation [ˌreklə'meɪʃən] *n see vt* (**a**) Gewinnung *f*; Kultivierung *f*.

recline [rɪ'klaɪn] **1** *vt arm* legen (*on* auf +*acc*); *head* *also* zurücklehnen (*on* an +*acc*); *seat* zurückstellen. **2** *vi* (*person*) liegen; (*seat*) sich verstellen lassen. **reclining chair** Ruhesessel *m*; (*in car, on boat*) Liegesitz *m*.

recluse [rɪ'kluːs] *n* Einsiedler(in *f*) *m*.

recognition [ˌrekəg'nɪʃən] *n* (**a**) (*acknowledgement, Pol*) Anerkennung *f*. **in ~ of** in Anerkennung (+*gen*); **by your own ~** wie Sie selbst zugeben; **to gain ~** Anerkennung finden. (**b**) (*identification*) Erkennen *nt*. **he has changed beyond all *or* out of all ~** er ist nicht wiederzuerkennen.

recognizable ['rekəgnaɪzəbl] *adj* erkennbar. **you're scarcely ~ with that beard** Sie sind mit dem Bart kaum zu erkennen.

recognize ['rekəgnaɪz] *vt* (**a**) (*know again*) wiedererkennen; (*identify*) erkennen (*by* an +*dat*). (**b**) (*acknowledge, Pol*) anerkennen (*as, to be* als). (**c**) (*be aware*) erkennen; (*be prepared to admit*) zugeben, eingestehen.

recognized ['rekəgnaɪzd] *adj* anerkannt.

recoil [rɪ'kɔɪl] *vi* (**a**) (*person*) (*from* vor +*dat*) zurückweichen; (*in fear*) zurückschrecken; (*in disgust*) zurückschaudern. **he ~ed from doing it** ihm graute davor, das zu tun. (**b**) (*gun*) zurückstoßen; (*spring*) zurückschnellen.

recollect [ˌrekə'lekt] *vt* sich erinnern an (+*acc*). **as far as I can ~** soweit ich mich erinnern kann.

recollection [ˌrekə'lekʃən] *n* (*memory*) Erinnerung *f* (*of an* +*acc*). **I have no ~ of it** ich kann

mich dessen nicht entsinnen.

recommend [ˌrekə'mend] *vt* empfehlen (*as* als). **what do you ~ for a cough?** was empfehlen Sie gegen Husten?; **to ~ sth to sb** jdm etw empfehlen; **it is not to be ~ed** es ist nicht zu empfehlen; **~ed price** empfohlener Richtpreis; **she has much to ~ her** es spricht sehr viel für sie.

recommendation [ˌrekəmen'deɪʃən] *n* Empfehlung *f*. **on the ~ of** auf Empfehlung von; **to make a ~** jemanden/etwas empfehlen.

recompense ['rekəmpens] **1** *n* (**a**) (*reward*) Belohnung *f*. **in ~ for** als Belohnung für. (**b**) (*Jur, fig*) Entschädigung *f*. **2** *vt* (**a**) (*reward*) belohnen. (**b**) (*Jur, fig: repay*) *person* entschädigen.

reconcile ['rekənsaɪl] *vt* (**a**) *people* aussöhnen; *differences* beilegen; *dispute* schlichten. **they became ~d** sie versöhnten sich; **to ~ oneself to sth, to become ~d to sth** sich mit etw abfinden. (**b**) (*make compatible*) *facts, ideas* miteinander in Einklang bringen, miteinander vereinbaren. **to ~ sth with sth** etw mit etw in Einklang bringen.

reconciliation [ˌrekənsɪlɪ'eɪʃən] *n* (*of persons*) Aussöhnung *f*; (*of opinons, principles*) Versöhnung *f*; (*of differences*) Beilegung *f*.

recondition [ˌriːkən'dɪʃən] *vt* generalüberholen. **a ~ed engine** ein Austauschmotor *m*.

reconnaissance [rɪ'kɒnɪsəns] *n* (*Aviat, Mil*) Aufklärung *f*. **~ plane** Aufklärungsflugzeug *nt*; **to be on ~** bei einem Aufklärungseinsatz sein.

reconnoitre, (*US*) **reconnoiter** [ˌrekə'nɔɪtə^r] **1** *vt* (*Aviat, Mil*) *region* auskundschaften, aufklären. **2** *vi* das Gelände erkunden.

reconsider [ˌriːkən'sɪdə^r] **1** *vt* noch einmal überdenken; (*change*) revidieren; (*Jur*) *case* wiederaufnehmen. **2** *vi* **there's still time to ~** es ist noch nicht zu spät, es sich (*dat*) anders zu überlegen.

reconstruct [ˌriːkən'strʌkt] *vt* rekonstruieren; *building* wiederaufbauen.

reconstruction [ˌriːkən'strʌkʃən] *n see vt* Rekonstruktion *f*; Wiederaufbau *m*.

record [rɪ'kɔːd] **1** *vt* (**a**) (*diarist etc*) aufzeichnen; (*documents, diary etc*) dokumentieren; (*in register*) eintragen; (*keep minutes of*) protokollieren; *one's thoughts, feelings etc* niederschreiben; *protest* zum Ausdruck bringen. (**b**) (*on tape etc*) aufnehmen. **a ~ed programme** eine Aufzeichnung.

2 ['rekɔːd] *n* (**a**) (*account*) Aufzeichnung *f*; (*of attendance*) Liste *f*; (*of meeting*) Protokoll *nt*; (*official document*) Unterlage *f*; (*lit, fig: of the past*) Dokument *nt*. **to keep a ~ of sth** über etw (*acc*) Buch führen; (*official, registrar*) etw registrieren; **it is on ~ that** ... es gibt Belege dafür, daß ...; (*in files*) es ist aktenkundig, daß ...; **there is no similar example on ~** es ist kein ähnliches Beispiel bekannt; **he's on ~ as saying** ...es ist belegt, daß er gesagt hat, ...; **to put sth on ~** etw schriftlich festhalten; **there is no ~ of his having said it** es ist nirgends belegt, daß er es gesagt hat; **to set the ~ straight** für klare Verhältnisse sorgen; **for the ~** der Ordnung halber; (*strictly*) **off the ~** he did come ganz in Vertrauen: er ist doch gekommen.

(**b**) (*history*) Vorgeschichte *f*; (*achievements*) Leistungen *pl*; (*police ~*) Vorstrafen *pl*. **to have an excellent ~** ausgezeichnete Leistungen vorweisen können; **he's got a ~** er ist vorbestraft; **he has a good ~ of service** er ist ein verdienter Mitarbeiter; **he has a bad attendance ~** er fehlt oft; **his past ~** seine bisherigen Leistungen; **to have a good ~ at school** ein guter Schüler sein; **to have a good safety ~** in bezug auf Sicherheit einen guten Ruf haben.

(**c**) (*Mus*) (Schall)platte *f*; (*~ing*) Aufnahme *f*.

(**d**) (*Sport, fig*) Rekord *m*. **to beat *or* break the ~** den Rekord brechen; **to hold the ~** Rekord halten; **long-jump ~** Rekord im Weitsprung; **a ~ time** eine Rekordzeit.

record-breaking ['rekɔːd,breɪkɪŋ] adj (Sport, fig) Rekord-.

recorded delivery [rɪ'kɔːdɪd dɪ'lɪvrɪ] n (Brit) eingeschriebene Sendung. **by ~ per** Einschreiben.

recorder [rɪ'kɔːdər] n (a) (apparatus) Registriergerät nt. **cassette/tape ~** Kassettenrecorder m/ Tonbandgerät nt. (b) (Mus) Blockflöte f.

record holder n (Sport) Rekordinhaber(in f) m.

recording [rɪ'kɔːdɪŋ] n (of sound) Aufnahme f; (programme) Aufzeichnung f. **~ engineer** Aufnahmetechniker m; **~ studio** Aufnahmestudio nt.

record ['rekɔːd]: **~ library** n Plattenverleih m; (collection) Plattensammlung f; **~-player** n Plattenspieler m; **~ token** n Plattengutschein m.

recount [rɪ'kaʊnt] vt (relate) erzählen, wiedergeben.

re-count [,riː'kaʊnt] **1** vt nachzählen. **2** ['riː,kaʊnt] n (of votes) Nachzählung f.

recoup [rɪ'kuːp] vt money, amount wieder hereinbekommen; losses wiedergutmachen, wettmachen.

recourse [rɪ'kɔːs] n Zuflucht f. **to have ~ to sb/sth** sich an jdn wenden/Zuflucht zu etw nehmen; **without ~** (Fin) ohne Regreß.

recover [rɪ'kʌvər] **1** vt wiederfinden; goods, property zurückbekommen; health wiedererlangen; wreck bergen; (Ind etc) materials gewinnen; debt eintreiben; (Jur) damages Ersatz erhalten für; losses wiedergutmachen; expenses decken. **to ~ one's breath/strength** wieder zu Atem/Kräften kommen; **to ~ consciousness** das Bewußtsein wiedererlangen; **to ~ one's sight** wieder sehen können; **to be quite ~ed** sich ganz erholt haben. **2** vi (after accident etc, from illness, Fin) sich erholen; (regain consciousness) wieder zu sich kommen.

re-cover [,riː'kʌvər] vt chairs etc neu beziehen; book neu einbinden.

recovery [rɪ'kʌvərɪ] n (a) see vt Wiederfinden nt; Zurückbekommen nt; Wiedererlangung f; Bergung f; Gewinnung f; Eintreibung f; Ersatz m (of für); Wiedergutmachung f; Deckung f. (b) see vi Erholung f. **he is making a good ~** er erholt sich gut; **past ~** nicht mehr zu retten.

recreation [,rekrɪ'eɪʃən] n (a) (leisure) Erholung f; (pastime) Hobby nt. **for ~ I go fishing** zur Erholung gehe ich angeln; **~ period** Freistunde f; **~ ground** Freizeitgelände nt. (b) (Sch) Pause f.

recreational [,rekrɪ'eɪʃənəl] adj Freizeit-.

recriminations [rɪ,krɪmɪ'neɪʃənz] npl gegenseitige Beschuldigungen pl.

recruit [rɪ'kruːt] **1** n (Mil) Rekrut m (to gen); (to party, club) neues Mitglied (to in +dat); (to staff) Neue(r) mf (to in +dat). **2** vt soldier rekrutieren; member werben; staff einstellen. **he ~ed me to help** er hat mich dazu herangezogen.

recruitment [rɪ'kruːtmənt] n (of soldiers) Rekrutierung f; (of members) Werbung f; (of staff) Einstellung f.

rectangle ['rek,tæŋgl] n Rechteck nt.

rectangular [rek'tæŋgjʊlər] adj rechteckig.

rectify ['rektɪfaɪ] vt korrigieren.

rector ['rektər] n (a) (Rel) Pfarrer m (der Anglikanischen Kirche). (b) (Scot) (Sch) Direktor(in f) m; (Univ) Rektor(in f) m.

rectory ['rektərɪ] n (house) Pfarrhaus nt.

rectum ['rektəm] n, pl **-s** or **recta** Mastdarm m.

recuperate [rɪ'kuːpəreɪt] **1** vi sich erholen. **2** vt losses wettmachen.

recuperation [rɪ,kuːpə'reɪʃən] n see vb Erholung f; Wiedergutmachung f.

recur [rɪ'kɜːr] vi wiederkehren; (error also, event) sich wiederholen; (opportunity) sich noch einmal bieten; (idea, theme also) wieder auftauchen.

recurrence [rɪ'kʌrəns] n see vi Wiederkehr f; Wiederholung f; Wiederauftauchen nt.

recurrent [rɪ'kʌrənt] adj idea, illness (ständig) wiederkehrend attr; error, problem also häufig (vorkommend).

recurring [rɪ'kɜːrɪŋ] adj attr (a) = recurrent. (b) (Math) **four point nine three ~** vier Komma neun Periode drei.

recycle [,riː'saɪkl] vt waste wiederaufbereiten.

recycling [,riː'saɪklɪŋ] n Wiederaufbereitung f, Recycling nt.

red [red] **1** adj (+er) (also Pol) rot. **~ meat** Rind-/Lammfleisch nt; **~ as a beetroot** rot wie eine Tomate; **she turned ~ with embarrassment** sie wurde rot vor Verlegenheit; **it's like a ~ rag to a bull** das ist ein rotes Tuch für ihn/sie etc. **2** n Rot nt; (Pol: person) Rote(r) mf. **to underline sth in ~** etw rot unterstreichen; **to be (£100) in the ~** (mit £ 100) in den roten Zahlen sein; **to see ~** rot sehen.

red in cpds Rot-, rot; **~ beet** n (US) rote Rübe; **~-blooded** adj heißblütig; **~breast** n Rotkehlchen nt; **~-brick university** n (Brit) um die Jahrhundertwende erbaute britische Universität; **~ carpet** n (lit, fig) roter Teppich; **a ~-carpet reception** ein Empfang m mit rotem Teppich; (fig also) ein großer Bahnhof; **R~ Cross** n Rotes Kreuz; **~ deer** n Rothirsch m; pl Rotwild nt.

redden ['redn] **1** vt iron; sky, foliage rot färben. **2** vi (face) sich röten; (person) rot werden; (sky, foliage) sich rot färben.

reddish ['redɪʃ] adj rötlich.

redeem [rɪ'diːm] vt trading stamps, coupons etc einlösen (for gegen); (Fin) debt, mortgage abzahlen; shares verkaufen; (US) banknote wechseln (for in +acc); one's honour retten; (Rel) sinner erlösen; (compensate for) failing wettmachen. **to ~ oneself** sich reinwaschen.

Redeemer [rɪ'diːmər] n (Rel) Erlöser m.

redeeming [rɪ'diːmɪŋ] adj quality ausgleichend. **~ feature** aussöhnendes Moment; **the only ~ feature of this novel is ...** das einzige, was man mit diesem Roman aussöhnt, ist ...

redemption [rɪ'dempʃən] n see vt Einlösung f; Abzahlung f; Verkauf m; Wechsel m; Rettung f; (Rel) Erlösung f. **beyond** or **past ~** (fig) nicht mehr zu retten.

redevelop [,riːdɪ'veləp] vt building, area sanieren.

red: **~-faced** adj mit rotem Kopf; **~-haired** adj rothaarig; **~-handed** adv: **to catch sb ~-handed** jdn auf frischer Tat ertappen; **~head** n Rothaarige(r) mf; **~ herring** n (fig) Ablenkungsmanöver nt; (in thrillers, research) falsche Spur; **~-hot** adj (lit) rotglühend; (very hot) glühend heiß; (fig col) (enthusiastic) Feuer und Flamme pred (col); news brandaktuell; **R~ Indian** n Indianer(in f) m.

redirect [,riːdaɪ'rekt] vt letter umadressieren; (forward) nachsenden; traffic umleiten.

redistribute [,riːdɪ'strɪbjuːt] vt umverteilen.

red: **~-letter day** n besonderer Tag; **~ light** n (lit) (warning light) rotes Licht; (traffic light) Rotlicht nt; **to go through the ~ light** (Mot) bei Rot über die Ampel fahren; **the ~-light district** die Strichgegend.

redness ['rednɪs] n Röte f.

redouble [,riː'dʌbl] vt efforts, zeal etc verdoppeln.

redoubtable [rɪ'daʊtəbl] adj (formidable) task hervorragend; person respektgebietend attr.

redress [rɪ'dres] **1** vt errors etc wiedergutmachen; situation bereinigen; grievance beseitigen; balance wiederherstellen. **2** n **to seek ~ for** Wiedergutmachung verlangen für; **there is no ~** das steht unumstößlich fest; **to have no ~ in law** keinen Rechtsanspruch haben.

red: **R~ Sea** n Rotes Meer; **~ skin** n Rothaut f; **~ tape** n (fig) Papierkrieg m (col); (with authorities also) Behördenkram m (col).

reduce [rɪ'djuːs] vt pressure, swelling verringern, reduzieren; standards, goods, prices herabsetzen;

taxes, temperature senken; *(shorten)* verkürzen; *expenses, wages* kürzen; *width, staff, photo* verkleinern; *scale of operations* einschränken; *output* drosseln. **to ~ one's weight** abnehmen; **to ~ speed** *(Mot)* langsamer fahren; **to ~ sth to a powder/to its parts** etw pulverisieren/in seine Einzelteile zerlegen; **it has been ~d to nothing** es ist zu nichts zusammengeschmolzen; **to ~ sb to silence/despair/tears** jdn zum Schweigen/zur Verzweiflung/zum Weinen bringen; **to ~ sb to begging** jdn zum Betteln zwingen; **are we ~d to this!** so weit ist es also gekommen!

reduced [rɪ'djuːst] *adj price, fare* ermäßigt; *goods* herabgesetzt; *scale, version* kleiner.

reduction [rɪ'dʌkʃən] *n* **(a)** *no pl (in sth gen)* Reduzierung, Verringerung *f*; *(in authority)* Schwächung *f*; *(in prices also, of goods, items)* Herabsetzung *f*; *(in expenses, wages)* Kürzung *f*; *(in size)* Verkleinerung *f*; *(shortening)* Verkürzung *f*; *(in output also)* Drosselung *f*. **to make a ~ on an article** einen Artikel heruntersetzen; **~ of taxes** Steuersenkung *f*. **(b)** *(amount reduced) (in sth gen)* Abnahme *f*, Rückgang *m*; *(in size)* Verkleinerung *f*; *(in length)* Verkürzung *f*; *(in taxes)* Nachlaß *m*; *(in prices)* Ermäßigung *f*; *(Jur: of sentence)* Kürzung *f*; *(of swelling)* Rückgang *m*.

redundancy [rɪ'dʌndənsɪ] *n* Überflüssigkeit *f*; *(Brit Ind)* Arbeitslosigkeit *f*. **redundancies** Entlassungen *pl*; **~ payment** Abfindung *f*.

redundant [rɪ'dʌndənt] *adj* überflüssig; *(Brit Ind: out of work)* arbeitslos. **to be made ~** *(Brit Ind)* den Arbeitsplatz verlieren.

redwood ['redwʊd] *n* Redwood *nt*.

reed [riːd] *n (Bot)* Schilf(rohr), Ried *nt*; *(of wind instrument)* Rohrblatt *nt*.

reef¹ [riːf] *n (in sea)* Riff *nt*.

reef² *(Naut) n* Reff *nt*. **~ knot** Kreuzknoten *m*.

reek [riːk] **1** *n* Gestank *m*. **2** *vi* stinken *(of* nach*)*.

reel [riːl] **1** *n* **(a)** Spule *f*; *(of thread etc also)* Rolle *f*; *(Fishing)* (Angel)rolle *f*. **(b)** *(dance)* Reel *m*. **2** *vi (person)* taumeln; *(drunk also)* torkeln. **the blow sent him ~ing** er taumelte unter dem Schlag; **my head is ~ing** mir dreht sich der Kopf.

♦ **reel in** *vt sep (Fishing)* einrollen; *fish* einholen.

♦ **reel off** *vt sep list* herunterrasseln *(col)*.

re-elect [ˌriːɪ'lekt] *vt* wiederwählen.

re-enact [ˌriːɪ'nækt] *vt* **(a)** *(Jur)* wieder in Kraft setzen. **(b)** *(repeat) scene, crime* nachspielen.

re-entry [ˌriː'entrɪ] *n (also Space)* Wiedereintritt *m*.

re-examine [ˌriːɪg'zæmɪn] *vt* erneut prüfen.

ref¹ [ref] *n (Sport col)* = **referee** Schiedsrichter *m*, Schiri *m (Sport col)*.

ref² = **reference (number)**.

refectory [rɪ'fektərɪ] *n (in college)* Mensa *f*.

refer [rɪ'fɜː˞] **1** *vt (pass) matter, problem* weiterleiten *(to an +acc)*; *decision* übergeben *(to sb* jdm*)*. **I ~red him to the manager** ich verwies ihn an den Geschäftsführer; **to ~ sb to the article on ...** jdn auf den Artikel über *(+acc)* ... verweisen. **2** *vi* **(a)** **to ~** *(allude to)* sprechen von; *(mention also)* erwähnen; *(words)* sich beziehen auf *(+acc)*; **I am not ~ring to you** ich meine nicht Sie; **~ring to your letter** *(Comm)* mit Bezug auf Ihren Brief. **(b)** *(apply)* **to ~ to** *(orders, rules)* gelten für; *(criticism, remark)* sich beziehen auf *(+acc)*. **(c)** *(consult)* **to ~ to** *to notes, book* nachschauen in *(+dat)*; *to person* sich wenden an *(+acc)*.

referee [ˌrefə'riː] **1** *n* **(a)** *(Ftbl, fig)* Schiedsrichter *m*; *(Boxing)* Ringrichter *m*; *(Judo, Wrestling)* Kampfrichter *m*. **(b)** *(Brit: person giving a reference)* Referenz *f*. **2** *vt (Sport, fig)* Schiedsrichter sein bei; *(Ftbl also)* pfeifen *(col)*.

reference ['refrəns] *n* **(a)** *(act of mentioning)* Erwähnung *f (to sb/sth* jds/einer Sache*)*; *(allusion) (direct)* Bemerkung *f (to* über *+acc)*; *(indirect)* Anspielung *f (to* auf *+acc)*; *(in book etc)* Verweis *m*. **to make (a) ~ to sth** etw erwähnen; **in**

or **with ~ to** was ... anbetrifft; *(Comm)* bezüglich *(+gen)*. **(b)** *(connection)* **to have ~ to** in Beziehung stehen zu; **this has no/little ~ to** das steht in keiner/kaum in Beziehung zu. **(c)** *(testimonial: also ~s)* Referenz(en *pl) f*. **to give sb a good ~** jdm ein gutes Zeugnis ausstellen.

reference: **~ book** *n* Nachschlagewerk *nt*; **~ library** *n* Präsenzbibliothek *f*; **~ number** *n* Nummer *f*; *(file number)* Aktenzeichen *nt*; *(of machine)* Seriennummer *f*.

referendum [ˌrefə'rendəm] *n, pl* **referenda** [ˌrefə'rendə] Volksentscheid *m*, Referendum *nt*. **to hold a ~** einen Volksentscheid durchführen.

refill [ˌriː'fɪl] **1** *vt* nachfüllen. **2** ['riːfɪl] *n (for fountain pen, lighter)* Nachfüllpatrone *f*; *(for ballpoint)* Ersatzmine *f*. **would you like a ~?** *(col: drink)* darf ich nachschenken?

refine [rɪ'faɪn] *vt oil, sugar* raffinieren; *techniques* verfeinern.

♦ **refine upon** *vi* +*prep obj detail* näher ausführen; *method* verfeinern.

refined [rɪ'faɪnd] *adj* **(a)** *metal, oil* raffiniert, rein. **~ sugar** Raffinade *f*. **(b)** *taste* fein; *person, style* vornehm.

refinement [rɪ'faɪnmənt] *n no pl (of oil, sugar)* Raffination, Reinigung *f*; *(no pl: of person, language, style)* Vornehmheit, Feinheit *f*; *(improvement: in technique, machine etc)* Verfeinerung, Verbesserung *f (in sth gen)*.

refinery [rɪ'faɪnərɪ] *n (oil, sugar ~)* Raffinerie *f*.

refit [ˌriː'fɪt] **1** *vt ship* neu ausrüsten; *factory* neu ausstatten. **2** ['riːfɪt] *n (Naut)* Neuausrüstung *f*.

reflate [ˌriː'fleɪt] *vt (Econ)* ankurbeln.

reflation [ˌriː'fleɪʃən] *n (Econ)* Ankurbelung *f* der Konjunktur.

reflect [rɪ'flekt] **1** *vt* **(a)** *light etc* reflektieren; *(surface, mirror also)* spiegeln; *(fig) views, reality etc* widerspiegeln. **the moon was ~ed in the lake** der Mond spiegelte sich im See; **I saw him ~ed in the mirror** ich sah ihn im Spiegel; **the difficulties ~ed in his report** die Schwierigkeiten, die sich in seinem Bericht spiegeln. **(b)** *(think)* **do you ever ~ that ...?** denken Sie je darüber nach, daß ...? **2** *vi* *(meditate)* nachdenken, reflektieren *(geh) (on, about* über *+acc)*.

reflection [rɪ'flekʃən] *n* **(a)** *no pl (reflecting)* Reflexion *f*; *(by mirror)* Spiegelung *f*; *(fig)* Widerspiegelung *f*. **(b)** *(image)* Spiegelbild *nt*; *(fig)* Widerspiegelung *f*. **to see one's ~ in a mirror** sich im Spiegel sehen; **a pale ~ of ...** ein matter Abglanz *(+gen)*. **(c)** *no pl (consideration)* Überlegung *f*; *(contemplation)* Reflexion, Betrachtung *f. on ~* wenn ich etc mir das recht überlege; **this is no ~ on your motives** damit soll gar nichts über Ihre Motive gesagt sein.

reflective [rɪ'flektɪv] *adj person* nachdenklich.

reflectively [rɪ'flektɪvlɪ] *adv say, speak* überlegt.

reflector [rɪ'flektə˞] *n (on car)* Rückstrahler *m*; *(telescope)* Reflektor *m*.

reflex ['riːfleks] **1** *adj* Reflex-. **~ action** Reflex *m*; **~ camera** *(Phot)* Spiegelreflexkamera *f*. **2** *n (Physiol, Psych, fig)* Reflex *m*.

reflexive [rɪ'fleksɪv] *(Gram) adj* reflexiv.

refloat [ˌriː'fləʊt] *vt ship, business* wieder flottmachen.

reform [rɪ'fɔːm] **1** *n* Reform *f (in sth gen)*; *(of person)* Besserung *f*. **2** *vt institutions, society* reformieren; *person* bessern. **3** *vi (person)* sich bessern.

reformation [ˌrefə'meɪʃən] *n (of person)* Besserung *f*. **the R~** die Reformation.

reformed [rɪ'fɔːmd] *adj church, spelling* reformiert; *person* gewandelt. **he's a ~ character** er hat sich gebessert.

reformer [rɪ'fɔːmə˞] *n (Pol)* Reformer *m*; *(Rel)* Reformator *m*.

refraction [rɪ'frækʃən] n Brechung f. **angle of ~** Brechungswinkel m.
refractory [rɪ'fræktərɪ] adj **(a)** person störrisch. **(b)** (Chem, Miner) hitzebeständig.
refrain[1] [rɪ'freɪn] vi **please ~!** bitte unterlassen Sie das!; **he ~ed from comment** er enthielt sich eines Kommentars; **I couldn't ~ from laughing** ich konnte mir das Lachen nicht verkneifen; **please ~ from smoking** bitte nicht rauchen!
refrain[2] n (Mus, Poet, fig) Refrain m.
refresh [rɪ'freʃ] vt (drink, rest) erfrischen; (meal) stärken. **to ~ oneself** (with drink) eine Erfrischung zu sich (dat) nehmen; (with a bath) sich erfrischen; (with rest) sich ausruhen; **to ~ one's memory** sein Gedächtnis auffrischen.
refreshing [rɪ'freʃɪŋ] adj (lit, fig) erfrischend.
refreshment [rɪ'freʃmənt] n **(a)** (of mind, body) Erfrischung f. **(b)** (food, drink) **(light) ~s** (kleine) Erfrischungen pl; **~ bar** or **stall** Büfett nt.
refrigerate [rɪ'frɪdʒəreɪt] vt (chill) kühlen; (freeze) tiefkühlen.
refrigeration [rɪ,frɪdʒə'reɪʃən] n see vt Kühlung f; Tiefkühlung f.
refrigerator [rɪ'frɪdʒəreɪtəʳ] n Kühlschrank m.
refuel [,ri:'fjʊəl] vti auftanken.
refuge ['refju:dʒ] n **(a)** (lit, fig) Zuflucht f (from vor +dat). **place of ~** Zufluchtsort m; **to seek ~** Zuflucht suchen; **to take ~** sich flüchten (in in +acc). **(b)** (for climbers etc) Unterstand m.
refugee [,refjʊdʒi:] n Flüchtling m. **~ camp** Flüchtlingslager nt.
refund [rɪ'fʌnd] **1** vt money, postage zurückerstatten; expenses erstatten. **2** ['ri:fʌnd] n see vt Rückerstattung f; Erstattung f. **they wouldn't give me a ~** man wollte mir das Geld nicht zurückgeben.
refurbish [,ri:'fɜ:bɪʃ] vt aufpolieren; dress, furniture also verschönern; house renovieren.
refusal [rɪ'fju:zəl] n Ablehnung f; (to offer also) Zurückweisung f; (of permission, visa) Verweigerung f; (to do sth) Weigerung f. **to meet with or get a ~** eine Absage erhalten; **to have (the) first ~ of sth** etw als erster angeboten bekommen.
refuse[1] [rɪ'fju:z] **1** vt invitation, candidate, proposal ablehnen; (stronger) zurückweisen; offer also ausschlagen; permit, permission verweigern. **to ~ to do sth** sich weigern, etw zu tun; **he was ~d a visa** ihm wurde das Visum verweigert; **to be ~d sth** etw nicht bekommen; **his request was ~d** seine Bitte wurde abgelehnt; **the car ~s to start** das Auto will einfach nicht anspringen. **2** vi ablehnen; (to do sth) sich weigern; (horse) verweigern.
refuse[2] ['refju:s] n Müll m; (food waste) Abfall m.
refuse ['refju:s] in cpds Müll-; **~ bin** n Mülleimer m; **~ disposal** n Müllbeseitigung f; **~ disposal unit** n Müllschlucker m; **~ dump** n Müllablade-platz m; **~ lorry** n Müllwagen m.
refute [rɪ'fju:t] vt widerlegen.
regain [rɪ'geɪn] vt wiedererlangen; lost time aufholen; territory zurückbekommen. **to ~ possession of sth** wieder in den Besitz einer Sache (gen) gelangen.
regal ['ri:gəl] adj königlich; (fig) hoheitsvoll.
regale [rɪ'geɪl] vt (with food, drink) verwöhnen; (with stories) ergötzen (geh).
regalia [rɪ'geɪlɪə] npl Insignien pl. **she was in full ~** (hum) sie war in großer Aufmachung (hum).
regard [rɪ'gɑ:d] **1** vt **(a)** (consider) betrachten. **to ~ sb/sth as sth** jdn/etw für etw halten; **to ~ sb/sth with favour** jdn/etw wohlwollend betrachten; **to ~ sth with horror** mit Schrecken an etw (acc) denken; **to be ~ed as ... als ... gelten,** als ... angesehen werden; **to ~ sb/sth highly** jdn/etw sehr schätzen; **he is highly ~ed** er ist hoch angesehen. **(b)** (concern) **as ~s your ap-**

plication was Ihren Antrag betrifft. **(c)** (heed) berücksichtigen. **without ~ing his wishes** ohne Rücksicht auf seine Wünsche.
2 n **(a)** (attention, concern) Rücksicht f (for auf +acc). **to show no ~ for sb/sth** keine Rücksichtnahme für jdn/etw zeigen; **with no ~ for his safety** ohne Rücksicht auf seine Sicherheit. **(b)** **in this ~** diesbezüglich (form), in diesem Zusammenhang; **with or in ~ to** in bezug auf (+acc). **(c)** (respect) Achtung f. **to hold sb in high ~** jdn sehr schätzen. **(d)** **~s pl** (in message) Gruß m. **to send sb one's ~s** jdn grüßen lassen; **give him my ~s** grüßen Sie ihn von mir; **(kindest) ~s, with kind ~s** mit freundlichen Grüßen.
regarding [rɪ'gɑ:dɪŋ] prep in bezug auf (+acc), bezüglich (+gen).
regardless [rɪ'gɑ:dlɪs] **1** adj **~ of** ohne Rücksicht auf (+acc), ungeachtet (+gen); **to do sth ~ of the consequences** etw ohne Rücksicht auf die Folgen tun; **~ of what it costs** egal, was es kostet; **~ of the fact that ...** ungeachtet der Tatsache, daß ... **2** adv trotzdem. **he did it ~** er hat es trotzdem getan.
regatta [rɪ'gætə] n Regatta f.
regenerate [rɪ'dʒenəreɪt] vt (renew, re-create) erneuern; tissue also neu bilden.
regeneration [rɪ,dʒenə'reɪʃən] n see vt Erneuerung f; Neubildung f.
reggae ['regeɪ] n Reggae m.
regime [reɪ'ʒi:m] n (Pol) Regime nt; (fig: management, social system etc) System nt.
regiment ['redʒɪmənt] **1** n (Mil) Regiment nt. **2** vt (fig) reglementieren.
regimental [,redʒɪ'mentl] adj (Mil) Regiments-.
regimentation [,redʒɪmen'teɪʃən] n (fig) Reglementierung f.
region ['ri:dʒən] n (of country) Region f; (of body also) Gegend f; (of atmosphere, fig) Bereich m. **in the ~ of 5 kg** um die 5 kg.
regional ['ri:dʒənl] adj regional. **~ development** Gebietserschließung f.
register ['redʒɪstəʳ] **1** n (book) Register nt; (at school) Namensliste f; (in hotel) Gästebuch nt; (of members etc) Mitgliedsbuch nt. **to take the ~** die Namen aufrufen; **electoral ~** Wählerverzeichnis nt; **~ of births, deaths and marriages** Personenstandsbuch nt.
2 vt **(a)** (authorities: record formally) registrieren; (in book, files) eintragen; fact, figure also erfassen. **he is ~ed as disabled** er ist anerkannter Schwerbeschädigter. **(b)** (individual: have recorded) birth, (Comm) company, trademark, vehicle etc anmelden. **to ~ a protest** Protest anmelden. **(c)** (indicate) speed anzeigen; (expression) happiness zum Ausdruck bringen. **he ~ed surprise** er zeigte sich überrascht. **(d)** letter einschreiben lassen.
3 vi **(a)** (on electoral list etc) sich eintragen; (in hotel) sich anmelden; (student) sich einschreiben. **to ~ with a doctor** sich bei einem Arzt auf die Patientenliste setzen lassen. **(b)** (col: be understood) **it hasn't ~ed (with him)** er hat es noch nicht registriert.
registered ['redʒɪstəd] adj **(a)** student eingeschrieben; voter, company eingetragen; vehicle amtlich zugelassen. **~ nurse** (US) staatlich geprüfte Krankenschwester; (male) staatlich geprüfter Pfleger; **~ trademark** eingetragenes Waren zeichen. **(b)** letter eingeschrieben. **by ~ post** per Einschreiben.
registrar [,redʒɪ'strɑ:ʳ] n (Admin) Standesbeamte(r) m; (Univ) Kanzler m; (Med) Krankenhausarzt m/-ärztin f.
registration [,redʒɪ'streɪʃən] n see vt **(a)** Registrierung f; Eintragung f; Erfassung f. **(b)** Anmeldung f. **~ number** (Brit Aut) polizeiliches Kennzeichen.
registry ['redʒɪstrɪ] n Sekretariat nt; (in church)

Sakristei *f; (Brit: also* ~ **office**) Standesamt *nt.* **to get married in a** ~ **office** standesamtlich heiraten.
regress [rɪ'gres] *vi (deteriorate)* sich rückläufig entwickeln.
regression [rɪ'greʃən] *n* Rückentwicklung *f.*
regret [rɪ'gret] **1** *vt* bedauern; *lost opportunity* nachtrauern (+*dat*). **I** ~ **that we will not be coming** ich bedaure, daß wir nicht kommen können; **I** ~ **to say that** ... ich muß Ihnen leider mitteilen, daß ... **2** *n* Bedauern *nt no pl.* **much to my** ~ sehr zu meinem Bedauern; **I have no** ~**s** ich bereue nichts.
regretfully [rɪ'gretfəlɪ] *adv (sadly)* mit Bedauern; *(reluctantly)* widerstrebend.
regrettable [rɪ'gretəbl] *adj* bedauerlich.
regrettably [rɪ'gretəblɪ] *adv* bedauerlicherweise.
regroup [,riː'gruːp] **1** *vt* um- *or* neugruppieren. **2** *vi* sich umgruppieren, sich neu gruppieren.
regular ['regjʊləʳ] **1** *adj* **(a)** regelmäßig; *features also* ebenmäßig; *surface* gleichmäßig; *employment* fest; *way of life* geregelt. **to keep** ~ **hours** feste Zeiten haben; **she is as** ~ **as clockwork** bei ihr geht alles auf die Minute genau. **(b)** *(habitual) size, price, time* normal; *staff, customer, pub* Stamm-; *listener* regelmäßig. **our** ~ **cleaning woman** unsere normale Reinemachefrau; **my** ~ **dentist** mein Hauszahnarzt *m.* **(c)** *(permissible, accepted) action, procedure* richtig. **it is quite** ~ **to apply in person** es ist ganz in Ordnung, sich persönlich zu bewerben. **(d)** *(Mil) soldier, army* Berufs-. **(e)** *(col) disaster, clown etc* regelrecht. **2** *n (Mil)* Berufssoldat *m; (customer etc)* Stammkunde *m,* Stammkundin *f; (in pub, hotel)* Stammgast *m.*
regularity [,regjʊ'lærɪtɪ] *n* **(a)** *see adj* **(a)** Regelmäßigkeit *f;* Ebenmäßigkeit *f;* Gleichmäßigkeit *f; (of procedure etc)* Festheit *f;* Geregeltheit *f.* **(b)** *(of action, procedure)* Richtigkeit *f.*
regularize ['regjʊləraɪz] *vt breathing, service* regulieren; *situation, relationship* normalisieren.
regularly ['regjʊlərɪ] *adv* regelmäßig; *breathe, beat also* gleichmäßig.
regulate ['regjʊleɪt] *vt* regulieren; *life-style* regeln; *clock* richtig stellen.
regulation [,regjʊ'leɪʃən] **1** *n* **(a)** *(of machine)* Regulierung *f.* **(b)** *(rule)* Vorschrift *f.* **2** *attr boots, dress* vorgeschrieben.
regulator ['regjʊleɪtəʳ] *n (instrument)* Regler *m.*
rehabilitate [,riːə'bɪlɪteɪt] *vt refugee, ex-criminal, ex-soldier* (in die Gesellschaft) eingliedern; *the disabled also* rehabilitieren.
rehabilitation ['riːəˌbɪlɪ'teɪʃən] *n see vt* Eingliederung *f* in die Gesellschaft; Rehabilitation *f.* ~ **centre** *(Admin)* Rehabilitationszentrum *nt.*
rehash [,riː'hæʃ] **1** *vt literary material etc* aufbereiten. **2** ['riːhæʃ] *n* Aufguß *m.*
rehearsal [rɪ'hɜːsl] *n (Theat, Mus)* Probe *f.*
rehearse [rɪ'hɜːs] *vti (Theat, Mus)* proben. **to** ~ **what one is going to say** einüben, was man sagen will.
rehouse [,riː'haʊz] *vt* unterbringen.
reign [reɪn] **1** *n (lit, fig)* Herrschaft *f.* **in the** ~ **of** während der Herrschaft (+*gen*). **2** *vi (lit, fig)* herrschen *(over über* +*acc*). **silence** ~**s** es herrscht Ruhe; ~**ing champion** amtierender Meister.
reimburse [,riːɪm'bɜːs] *vt person* entschädigen; *loss, expenses, costs* ersetzen.
rein [reɪn] *n (lit, fig)* Zügel *m.* ~**s** *(for child)* Laufgurt *m;* **to hold the** ~**s** *(lit, fig)* die Zügel in der Hand haben; **to keep a tight** ~ **on sb/sth** *(lit, fig)* bei jdm/etw die Zügel kurz halten; **to allow sb/sth free** ~ *(fig)* jdm/einer Sache freien Lauf lassen.
♦ **rein in** *vt sep (lit, fig)* zügeln.
reincarnation [,riːɪnkɑː'neɪʃən] *n* die Wiedergeburt.

reindeer ['reɪndɪəʳ] *n, pl* - Ren(tier) *nt.*
reinforce [,riːɪn'fɔːs] *vt (lit, fig, Psych)* verstärken; *sb's demands* stärken, stützen; *evidence, opinion* bestätigen. ~**d concrete** Stahlbeton *m.*
reinforcement [,riːɪn'fɔːsmənt] *n* **(a)** *no pl (act) see vt* Verstärkung *f;* Stärkung, Stützung *f;* Bestätigung *f.* **(b)** *(thing)* Verstärkung *f.* ~**s** *(Mil, fig)* Verstärkung *f.*
reinstate [,riːɪn'steɪt] *vt person* wieder einstellen *(in in* +*acc*); *law and order* wiederherstellen *(in in* +*dat*).
reissue [,riː'ɪʃjuː] **1** *vt book* neu auflegen; *stamps, recording, coins* neu herausgeben. **2** *n see vt* Neuauflage *f;* Neuausgabe *f.*
reiterate [riː'ɪtəreɪt] *vt* wiederholen.
reject [rɪ'dʒekt] **1** *vt* **(a)** *damaged goods etc (customer)* zurückweisen; *(maker)* aussortieren. **(b)** *(turn down) application, request etc* ablehnen; *suitor, advances* zurückweisen; *offer also* ausschlagen; *possibility* verwerfen; *candidate (through vote)* durchfallen lassen. **(c)** *(Med) transplant* abstoßen; *(stomach) food* verweigern. **2** ['riːdʒekt] *n (Comm)* Ausschuß *m no pl.* ~ **goods** Ausschußware *f.*
rejection [rɪ'dʒekʃən] *n see vt* **(a)** Zurückweisung *f;* Aussortierung *f.* **(b)** Ablehnung *f;* Zurückweisung *f;* Verwerfen *nt.* **(c)** *(Med)* Abstoßung *f;* Verweigerung *f.*
rejoice [rɪ'dʒɔɪs] *vi* sich freuen; *(jubilate)* jubeln; *(Rel)* jauchzen.
rejoicing [rɪ'dʒɔɪsɪŋ] *n* Jubel *m.* ~**s** Jubel *m.*
rejoin[1] [,rɪ'dʒɔɪn] *vt person, regiment* sich wieder anschließen (+*dat*). **to** ~ **ship** *(Naut)* wieder aufs Schiff kommen; **then we** ~**ed the motorway** danach fuhren wir wieder auf die Autobahn.
rejoin[2] [rɪ'dʒɔɪn] *vt (reply)* erwidern.
rejoinder [rɪ'dʒɔɪndəʳ] *n* Erwiderung *f.*
rejuvenate [rɪ'dʒuːvɪneɪt] *vt* verjüngen; *(fig)* erfrischen.
rekindle [,riː'kɪndl] *vt (lit, fig) fire, passions* wieder anzünden; *hope* wiedererwecken.
relapse [rɪ'læps] **1** *n (Med, into vice, crime)* Rückfall *m; (in economy)* Rückschlag *m.* **2** *vi (Med)* einen Rückfall haben; *(into crime)* rückfällig werden.
relate [rɪ'leɪt] **1** *vt* **(a)** *(recount) story* erzählen; *details* aufzählen. **(b)** *(associate)* in Verbindung bringen *(to, with* mit). **2** *vi* **(a)** zusammenhängen *(to* mit). **(b)** *(form relationship)* eine Beziehung finden *(to* zu).
related [rɪ'leɪtɪd] *adj* **(a)** *(in family)* verwandt *(to* mit). **(b)** *(connected)* zusammenhängend; *theories, languages etc* verwandt. **to be** ~**d to sth** mit etw zusammenhängen/verwandt sein.
relating [rɪ'leɪtɪŋ] *adj* ~ **to** in Zusammenhang mit.
relation [rɪ'leɪʃən] *n* **(a)** *(relative)* Verwandte(r) *mf.* **he's a/no** ~ *(of mine)* er ist/ist nicht mit mir verwandt; **what** ~ **is she to you?** wie ist sie mit Ihnen verwandt? **(b)** *(relationship)* Beziehung *f.* **to bear a** ~ **to** in Beziehung stehen zu; **in** ~ **to** *(as regards)* in bezug auf (+*acc*); *(compared with)* im Verhältnis zu. **(c)** ~**s** *pl (dealings, ties, sexual* ~**s)** Beziehungen *pl.*
relationship [rɪ'leɪʃənʃɪp] *n (in family)* Verwandtschaft *f (to* mit); *(connection: between events etc)* Beziehung *f; (relations)* Verhältnis *nt,* Beziehungen *pl; (in business)* Verbindung *f.* **to have a (sexual)** ~ **with sb** ein Verhältnis haben mit; **to have a good** ~ **with sb** ein gutes Verhältnis zu jdm haben.
relative ['relətɪv] **1** *adj* **(a)** relativ; *(respective)* respektiv. **to live in** ~ **luxury** verhältnismäßig *or* relativ luxuriös leben; **the** ~ **merits of A and B** die respektiven Verdienste von A und B. **(b)** *(relevant)* ~ **to** sich beziehend auf (+*acc*). **(c)** *(Gram)* Relativ-. **2** *n (person)* ~ **relation** (q.v.).
relatively ['relətɪvlɪ] *adv* relativ, verhältnismäßig. ~ **speaking** relativ gesehen.

relativity [,relǝ'tɪvɪtɪ] n (Phys, Philos) Relativität f. **the theory of** ~ die Relativitätstheorie.

relax [rɪ'læks] **1** vt lockern; muscles also, person entspannen; attention, effort nachlassen in (+dat). **2** vi (sich) entspannen; (rest) (sich) ausruhen; (calm down) sich beruhigen.

relaxation [,riːlæk'seɪʃǝn] n (a) see vt Lockerung f; Entspannung f; Nachlassen nt. (b) (rest) Entspannung f; (recreation also) Erholung f.

relaxed [rɪ'lækst] adj locker; person, smile, voice ruhig; atmosphere gelockert. **to feel** ~ (physically) entspannt sein; (mentally) sich wohl fühlen.

relaxing [rɪ'læksɪŋ] adj entspannend; climate erholsam.

relay ['riːleɪ] **1** n (a) (of workers) Ablösung f; (of horses) frisches Gespann. **to work in** ~**s** sich ablösen. (b) (Sport: also ~ **race**) Staffel(lauf m) f. (c) (Rad, TV) Relais nt. **2** vt (a) (Rad, TV) (weiter)übertragen. (b) message ausrichten (to sb jdm).

release [rɪ'liːs] **1** vt (a) animal, person freilassen; (from prison also) entlassen; (rescue) befreien; (from obligation) entbinden, befreien. (b) (let go of) loslassen; handbrake losmachen; (Phot) shutter auslösen; grip, clasp lösen; confiscated articles freigeben. **to** ~ **the clutch** die Kupplung kommen lassen. (c) news, statement veröffentlichen. (d) (emit) gas, energy freisetzen; smell ausströmen; pressure, steam ablassen. **2** n (a) see vt (a) Freilassung f; Entlassung f; Befreiung f; Entbindung f. (b) (mechanism) Auslöser m. (c) (of statement etc) Veröffentlichung f; (statement) Verlautbarung f. (d) (of gas, energy) Freisetzung f. (e) (film) Film m; (record) Platte f. **this film is now on general** ~ dieser Film ist nun überall zu sehen; **a new** ~ (record) eine Neuerscheinung; (film) ein neu herausgekommener Film.

relegate ['relɪgeɪt] vt (lit, fig: downgrade) degradieren; (Sport) team absteigen lassen (to in +acc). **to be** ~**d** (Sport) absteigen.

relegation [,relɪ'geɪʃǝn] n see vt Degradierung f; Abstieg m.

relent [rɪ'lent] vi (person) nachgeben; (pace, pain) nachlassen; (weather) sich bessern.

relentless [rɪ'lentlɪs] adj erbarmungslos; person also unerbittlich; pain, cold nicht nachlassend.

relevance ['relǝvǝns] n Relevanz f.

relevant ['relǝvǝnt] adj relevant (to für); authority, person zuständig.

reliability [rɪ,laɪǝ'bɪlɪtɪ] n see adj Zuverlässigkeit f; Seriosität f.

reliable [rɪ'laɪǝbl] adv zuverlässig; firm seriös.

reliably [rɪ'laɪǝblɪ] adv zuverlässig. **I am** ~ **informed that** ... ich weiß aus zuverlässiger Quelle, daß ...

reliance [rɪ'laɪǝns] n Vertrauen nt (on auf +acc).

reliant [rɪ'laɪǝnt] adj angewiesen (on, upon auf +acc).

relic ['relɪk] n Überbleibsel, Relikt nt; (Rel) Reliquie f.

relief [rɪ'liːf] **1** n (a) (from anxiety, pain) Erleichterung f. **to bring sb** ~ (drug) jdm Erleichterung verschaffen; **that's a** ~! mir fällt ein Stein vom Herzen; **it was a** ~ **to find it** ich/er etc war erleichtert, als ich/er etc es fand. (b) (assistance) Hilfe f. **to provide** ~ **for the poor** für die Armen sorgen. (c) (esp Mil: act of relieving, replacement forces) Entsatz m; (substitute) Ablösung f. (d) (Art, Geog) Relief nt; (Typ also) Hochdruck m. **throw sth into** ~ (fig) etw hervorheben. **2** attr (a) fund, organization Hilfs-. ~ **supplies** Hilfsgüter pl. (b) driver Ablöse-; troops Entsatz-; (Brit) bus, train Entlastungs-. (c) map Relief-; printing also Hoch-.

relieve [rɪ'liːv] vt (a) person erleichtern. **he was** ~**d to learn that** er war erleichtert, als er das

hörte; **to** ~ **sb's mind** jdn beruhigen; **to** ~ **sb of** sth of burden, pain jdn von etw befreien; of duty, command jdn einer Sache (gen) entheben (geh); of suitcase jdm etw abnehmen. (b) (mitigate) anxiety mildern, schwächen; pain lindern; (completely) stillen; tension abbauen; poverty erleichtern; (Med) congestion abhelfen (+dat); (completely) beheben. **to** ~ **oneself** (euph) sich erleichtern; **it'll** ~ **the monotony** das dient der Abwechslung. (c) (take over from, also Mil) ablösen. (d) (Mil) town entsetzen.

religion [rɪ'lɪdʒǝn] n Religion f; (creed) Glaube(n) m. **the Christian** ~ der christliche Glaube.

religious [rɪ'lɪdʒǝs] adj (a) religiös; person also gläubig; order geistlich; freedom also, wars Glaubens-. ~ **instruction** (Sch) Religionsunterricht m. (b) (fig: conscientious) gewissenhaft.

relinquish [rɪ'lɪŋkwɪʃ] vt hope, plan aufgeben; right, possessions also verzichten auf (+acc). **to** ~ **one's hold on sb/sth** (lit, fig) jdn/etw loslassen.

relish ['relɪʃ] **1** n (a) (enjoyment) Gefallen m (for an +dat). **to do sth with (great)** ~ etw mit (großem) Genuß tun. (b) (Cook) Soße f. **2** vt genießen; food, wine also sich (dat) schmecken lassen. **I don't** ~ **doing that** (enjoy) das ist gar nicht nach meinem Geschmack; (look forward to) darauf freue ich mich überhaupt nicht.

reluctance [rɪ'lʌktǝns] n Widerwillen m. **to do sth with** ~ etw widerwillig or ungern tun.

reluctant [rɪ'lʌktǝnt] adj widerwillig. **he is** ~ **to do** it es widerstrebt ihm, es zu tun; **he seems** ~ **to admit it** er scheint es nicht zugeben zu wollen.

rely [rɪ'laɪ] vi **to** ~ **(up)on sb/sth** sich auf jdn/etw verlassen; (be dependent on) auf jdn/etw angewiesen sein; **she relied on the trains being on time** sie verließ sich darauf, daß die Züge pünktlich waren; **she is not to be relied upon** man kann sich nicht auf sie verlassen.

remain [rɪ'meɪn] vi bleiben; (be left over) übrigbleiben. **much** ~**s to be done** es bleibt noch viel zu tun; **all that** ~**s is for me to wish you** every success ich möchte Ihnen nur noch viel Erfolg wünschen; **that** ~**s to be seen** das bleibt abzuwarten; **the fact** ~**s that** ... das ändert nichts an der Tatsache, daß ...; **to** ~ **silent** weiterhin schweigen; **to** ~ **behind** zurückbleiben; "**I** ~, **yours faithfully John Smith**" „mit besten Grüßen verbleibe ich Ihr John Smith".

remainder [rɪ'meɪndǝʳ] n Rest m (also Math). ~**s** pl (Comm) Restbestände pl.

remaining [rɪ'meɪnɪŋ] adj übrig, restlich. **I have only two** ~ ich habe nur noch zwei (übrig).

remains [rɪ'meɪnz] npl (of meal) Reste pl; (of building) Überreste pl; (archaeological ~) Ruinen pl. **human** ~ menschliche Überreste pl.

remake ['riːmeɪk] n (Film) Neuverfilmung f, Remake nt (spec).

remand [rɪ'mɑːnd] **1** vt (Jur) **to** ~ **sb in custody/on bail** jdn weiterhin in Untersuchungshaft behalten/unter Kaution halten. **2** n **to be on** ~ in Untersuchungshaft sein; (on bail) auf Kaution freigelassen sein; ~ **home** (Brit) Untersuchungsgefängnis nt für Jugendliche.

remark [rɪ'mɑːk] **1** n Bemerkung f. **to pass** ~**s** Bemerkungen machen; **worthy of** ~ bemerkenswert. **2** vt (say) bemerken. **3** vi **to** ~ **(up)on** sth über etw (acc) eine Bemerkung machen.

remarkable [rɪ'mɑːkǝbl] adj (notable) bemerkenswert; intelligence, talent also beachtlich; (extraordinary) außergewöhnlich. **to be** ~ **for sth** sich durch etw auszeichnen.

remarkably [rɪ'mɑːkǝblɪ] adv außergewöhnlich.

remarry [,riː'mærɪ] vi wieder heiraten.

remedial [rɪ'miːdɪǝl] adj attr action, measures Hilfs-; (Med) Heil-; ~ **teaching** Förderunterricht *m*; ~ **class** Förderklasse *f* (für Lernschwache).

remedy ['remǝdɪ] **1** *n (Med, fig)* Mittel *nt (for gegen); (medication)* Heilmittel *nt (for gegen).* **the situation is beyond** ~ die Lage ist hoffnungslos. **2** *vt (Med)* heilen; *(fig) fault* beheben; *situation* bessern.

remember [rɪ'membǝr] **1** *vt* **(a)** *(recall)* sich erinnern an *(+acc); (bear in mind)* denken an *(+acc); (learn) facts* sich *(dat)* merken. **I** ~ **that he was very tall** ich erinnere mich, daß er sehr groß war; **I** ~ **her as a beautiful girl** ich habe sie als schönes Mädchen in Erinnerung; **we must** ~ **that he's only a child** wir sollten bedenken, daß er noch ein Kind ist; **to** ~ **to do sth** daran denken, etw zu tun; **I can't** ~ **the word at the moment** das Wort fällt mir im Moment nicht ein; **here's something to** ~ **me by** da hast du etwas, das dich (immer) an mich erinnern wird; **I can never** ~ **phone numbers** ich kann mir Telefonnummern einfach nicht merken; **to** ~ **sb in one's will** jdn in seinem Testament bedenken. **(b)** *(commemorate)* gedenken *(+gen).* **(c)** *(give good wishes to)* ~ **me to your mother** grüßen Sie Ihre Mutter von mir; **he asks to be** ~**ed to you** er läßt Sie grüßen. **2** *vi* sich erinnern. **if I** ~ **right(ly)** *or* **aright** wenn ich mich recht erinnere *or* entsinne.

remembrance [rɪ'membrǝns] *n* Erinnerung *f (of* an *+acc).* **R**~**Day** *(Brit)* ≈ Volkstrauertag *m*; **in** ~ **of** zur Erinnerung an *(+acc).*

remind [rɪ'maɪnd] *vt* erinnern *(of* an *+acc).* **to** ~ **sb to do sth** jdn daran erinnern, etw zu tun; **that** ~**s me!** da(bei) fällt mir was ein.

reminder [rɪ'maɪndǝr] *n (note etc)* Gedächtnisstütze *f.* **(letter of)** ~ *(Comm)* Mahnung *f*; **to give sb a** ~ **to do sth** jdn daran erinnern, etw zu tun.

reminisce [,remɪ'nɪs] *vi* sich in Erinnerungen ergehen *(about* über *+acc).*

reminiscence [,remɪ'nɪsǝns] *n* Erinnerung *f (of* an *+acc).*

reminiscent [,remɪ'nɪsǝnt] *adj* **to be** ~ **of sth** an etw *(acc)* erinnern.

remiss [rɪ'mɪs] *adj* nachlässig.

remission [rɪ'mɪʃǝn] *n (Jur)* (Straf)erlaß *m*; *(Rel)* Nachlaß *m.* **he got 3 years'** ~ ihm wurden 3 Jahre erlassen.

remit [rɪ'mɪt] *vt* **(a)** *(cancel, pardon) debt, sentence, sins* erlassen. **(b)** *(send) money* überweisen. **(c)** *(Jur: transfer) case* verweisen *(to* an *+acc).*

remittance [rɪ'mɪtǝns] *n* Überweisung *f (to* an *+acc).*

remnant ['remnǝnt] *n* Rest *m*; *(fig: of splendour, custom)* Überrest *m.*

remonstrance [rɪ'mɒnstrǝns] *n* Protest *m (with* bei, *against* gegen).

remonstrate ['remǝnstreɪt] *vi* protestieren *(against* gegen). **to** ~ **with sb (about sth)** jdm Vorhaltungen (wegen etw) machen.

remorse [rɪ'mɔːs] *n* Reue *f (at, over* über *+acc).* **without** ~ *(merciless)* erbarmungslos.

remorseful [rɪ'mɔːsfʊl] *adj* reumütig, reuig.

remorseless [rɪ'mɔːslɪs] *adj* reuelos; *(fig: merciless)* unbarmherzig.

remote [rɪ'mǝʊt] *adj (+er)* **(a)** *entfernt; (isolated)* abgelegen; *(in time)* fern; *(person)* unnahbar. **(b)** *(slight) possibility, resemblance* entfernt; *chance* gering.

remote: ~ **control** *n* Fernlenkung *f*; *(Rad, TV)* Fernbedienung *f*; ~**-controlled** *adj* ferngesteuert; *(Rad, TV)* mit Fernbedienung.

remotely [rɪ'mǝʊtlɪ] *adv situated, related* entfernt. **it's just** ~ **possible** es ist gerade eben noch möglich; **they're not even** ~ **similar** sie sind sich nicht im entferntesten ähnlich.

removable [rɪ'muːvǝbl] *adj cover, attachment* abnehmbar; *lining* abknöpfbar.

removal [rɪ'muːvǝl] *n see vt* **(a)** Entfernung *f*;

Abnahme *f*; Herausnehmen *nt*; Ausbau *m.* **(b)** Beseitigung *f*; Zerstreuung *f.* **(c)** Entfernung *f.* **(d)** *(move from house)* Umzug *m.*

removal van *n (Brit)* Möbelwagen *m.*

remove [rɪ'muːv] **1** *vt* **(a)** *(take off/away, Med)* entfernen *(from* aus); *cover, attachments also, bandage, tie* abnehmen; *(take out)* herausnehmen *(from* aus); *(Tech)* ausbauen *(from* aus). **to** ~ **sth from sb** jdm etw wegnehmen; **to** ~ **a child from school** ein Kind von der Schule nehmen. **(b)** *(eradicate) threat, obstacle, problem* beseitigen; *doubt, suspicion* zerstreuen. **(c)** *(form: dismiss) official* entfernen. **(d) to be far** ~**d from ...** weit entfernt sein von ...; **a cousin twice** ~**d** ein Vetter zweiten Grades. **2** *vi (form: move house)* **to** ~ **to London** nach London (um)ziehen.

remover [rɪ'muːvǝr] *n* **(a)** *(for nail varnish, stains etc)* Entferner *m.* **(b)** *(removal man)* Möbelpacker *m.*

remuneration [rɪ,mjuːnǝ'reɪʃǝn] *n* Vergütung *f*; *(reward)* Belohnung *f.*

renaissance [rɪ'neɪsãːns] *n* **the R** ~ *(Hist)* die Renaissance.

rename [,riː'neɪm] *vt* umbenennen. **Petrograd was** ~**d Leningrad** Petrograd wurde in Leningrad umbenannt.

render ['rendǝr] *vt* **(a)** *(form: give) service* leisten; *judgement* abgeben; *homage* erweisen. **(b)** *(interpret, translate)* wiedergeben; *(in writing)* übertragen; *music, poem also* vortragen. **(c)** *(form: make)* machen. **to** ~ **a bomb harmless** eine Bombe entschärfen.

rendering ['rendǝrɪŋ] *n* Wiedergabe *f*; *(in writing)* Übertragung *f*; *(of piece of music, poem)* Vortrag *m.*

rendez-vous ['rɒndɪvuː] **1** *n (place)* Treffpunkt *m*; *(agreement to meet)* Rendezvous *nt.* **2** *vi* sich treffen *(with* mit); *(spaceships)* ein Rendezvousmanöver durchführen.

rendition [ren'dɪʃǝn] *n (form)* = **rendering.**

renegade ['renɪgeɪd] **1** *n* Abtrünnige(r) *mf.* **2** *adj* abtrünnig.

renew [rɪ'njuː] *vt* erneuern; *contract, passport etc (authority)* verlängern; *(holder)* verlängern lassen; *discussions, attempts* wiederaufnehmen; *one's strength* wiederherstellen; *supplies* auffrischen. **to** ~ **a library book** ein Buch verlängern lassen; **to** ~ **one's acquaintance with sb** seine Bekanntschaft mit jdm auffrischen.

renewal [rɪ'njuːǝl] *n see vt* Erneuerung *f*; Verlängerung *f*; Wiederaufnahme *f*; Wiederherstellung *f*; Auffrischung *f.*

renounce [rɪ'naʊns] *vt right, one's liberty* aufgeben; *religion, devil, opinions, cause* abschwören *(+dat); (Rel)* world entsagen *(+dat).*

renovate ['renǝveɪt] *vt building* renovieren; *painting, furniture* restaurieren.

renovation [,renǝʊ'veɪʃǝn] *n see vt* Renovierung *f*; Restaurierung *f.*

renown [rɪ'naʊn] *n* guter Ruf, Ansehen *nt.*

renowned [rɪ'naʊnd] *adj* berühmt *(for* für).

rent [rent] *n (for house, room)* Miete *f*; *(for farm, factory)* Pacht *f.* **for** ~ zu vermieten/verpachten/verleihen. **2** *vt* **(a)** *(also vi) house, room* mieten; *farm, factory* pachten; *TV, car etc* leihen. **(b)** *(also* ~ **out)** vermieten; verpachten; verleihen.

rental ['rentl] *n (amount paid); (for house)* Miete *f*; *(for TV, car, boat etc also)* Leihgebühr *f*; *(for land)* Pacht *f*; *(income from rents)* Miet-/Pacht-/Leihgebühreinnahmen *pl.* ~ **car** *(US)* Mietauto *nt*; ~ **library** *(US)* Leihbücherei *f.*

renunciation [rɪ,nʌnsɪ'eɪʃǝn] *n see* **renounce** Aufgabe *f*; Abschwören *nt*; Entsagung *f.*

reopen [,riː'ǝʊpǝn] **1** *vt* wieder öffnen; *shop, theatre, hostilities* wiedereröffnen; *debate, negotiations, (Jur) case* wiederaufnehmen. **2** *vi* wieder aufgehen; *(shop, theatre etc)* wieder aufmachen; *(negotiations)* wiederbeginnen.

reorganization [riː,ɔːgənaɪˈzeɪʃən] *n see vt* Umorganisation *f*; Umordnung *f*; Neueinteilung *f*; Neuaufbau *m*.

reorganize [,riːˈɔːgənaɪz] *vt* umorganisieren; *furniture, books* umordnen; *work* neu einteilen; *essay* neu aufbauen.

rep [rep] = **(a)** *(Theat)* **repertory** Repertoire-Theater *nt*. **(b)** *(Comm)* **representative** Vertreter(in *f*) *m*.

repaid [,riːˈpeɪd] *pret, ptp of* **repay**.

repair [rɪˈpɛəʳ] **1** *vt (lit, fig)* reparieren; *tyre also, clothes* flicken; *roof, wall also, road* ausbessern; *(fig) wrong, damage* wiedergutmachen. **2** *n see vt* Reparatur *f*; Flicken *nt*; Ausbesserung *f*. **to be under ~** *(car, machine)* in Reparatur sein; **to put sth in for ~** etw zur Reparatur bringen; **damaged beyond ~** nicht mehr zu reparieren; **closed for ~s** wegen Reparaturarbeiten geschlossen; **to be in good ~** in gutem Zustand sein; **state of ~** Zustand *m*.

repairable [rɪˈpɛərəbl] *adj* reparabel.

reparable [ˈrepərəbl] *adj damage* reparabel, wiedergutzumachen; *loss* ersetzbar.

reparation [,repəˈreɪʃən] *n (for damage)* Entschädigung *f*; *(usu pl: after war)* Reparationen *pl*; *(for wrong)* Wiedergutmachung *f*. **to make ~ for** *sth* etw wiedergutmachen.

repartee [,repaːˈtiː] *n* Schlagabtausch *m*; *(retort)* schlagfertige Antwort.

repatriate [,riːˈpætrɪeɪt] *vt* in das Heimatland zurücksenden, repatriieren.

repatriation [ˈriː,pætrɪˈeɪʃən] *n* Repatriierung *f*.

repay [,riːˈpeɪ] *pret, ptp* **repaid** *vt money* zurückzahlen; *expenses* erstatten; *debt* abzahlen; *kindness* vergelten; *visit* erwidern. **how can I ever ~ you?** wie kann ich das jemals wiedergutmachen?

repayable [,riːˈpeɪəbl] *adj* rückzahlbar.

repayment [,riːˈpeɪmənt] *n (of money)* Rückzahlung *f*; *(of effort, kindness)* Lohn *m*.

repeal [rɪˈpiːl] *vt law* aufheben.

repeat [rɪˈpiːt] **1** *vt* wiederholen; *(tell to sb else)* weitersagen *(to sb jdm)*. **to ~ oneself** sich wiederholen; **don't ~ it to anyone** sag es nicht weiter; **to ~ an order** *(Comm)* nachbestellen; **this offer will never be ~ed!** dies ist ein einmaliges Angebot! **2** *n (Rad, TV)* Wiederholung *f*.

repeat: **~ order** *n (Comm)* Nachbestellung *f*; **~ performance** *n (Theat)* Wiederholungsvorstellung *f*.

repel [rɪˈpel] *vt enemy* zurückschlagen; *sb's advance* abwehren; *water* abstoßen; *(disgust)* abstoßen.

repellent [rɪˈpelənt] *adj* **(a)** ~ **to water** wasserabstoßend. **(b)** *(disgusting)* abstoßend.

repent [rɪˈpent] *vi* Reue empfinden *(of über +acc)*.

repentance [rɪˈpentəns] *n* Reue *f*.

repentant [rɪˈpentənt] *adj look* reuevoll. **he was very ~** es reute ihn sehr.

repercussion [,riːpəˈkʌʃən] *n (consequence)* Auswirkung *f* *(on auf +acc).* ~**s** *pl (of misbehaviour etc)* Nachspiel *nt*; **that is bound to have** ~**s** das wird Kreise ziehen.

repertoire [ˈrepətwaːʳ] *n* Repertoire *nt*.

repertory [ˈrepətərɪ] *n (also* ~ **theatre)** Repertoire-Theater *nt*. ~ **company** Repertoire-Ensemble *nt*.

repetition [,repɪˈtɪʃən] *n* Wiederholung *f*.

repetitious [,repɪˈtɪʃəs] *adj* sich wiederholend.

repetitive [rɪˈpetɪtɪv] *adj* sich dauernd wiederholend; *work also* monoton. **to be ~** sich dauernd wiederholen.

replace [rɪˈpleɪs] *vt* **(a)** zurückstellen; *(put flat)* zurücklegen. **to ~ the receiver** *(Telec)* (den Hörer) auflegen. **(b)** *(substitute, renew)* ersetzen; *(employee: temporarily)* vertreten.

replacement [rɪˈpleɪsmənt] *n* **(a)** *see vt* Zurückstellen *nt*; Zurücklegen *nt*. **(b)** *(substituting)*

Ersatz *m*; *(by deputy)* Vertretung *f*. ~ **part** Ersatzteil *nt*.

replay [ˈriːpleɪ] *(Sport)* **1** *n (recording)* Wiederholung *f*; *(match)* Wiederholungsspiel *nt*. **2** [,riːˈpleɪ] *vt match, game* wiederholen.

replenish [rɪˈplenɪʃ] *vt* ergänzen; *glass* auffüllen.

replete [rɪˈpliːt] *adj (form: supplied)* reichlich versehen *(with mit)*.

replica [ˈreplɪkə] *n* Kopie *f*; *(of ship, building etc)* Nachbildung *f*.

reply [rɪˈplaɪ] **1** *n (letter)* Antwort *f*; *(spoken also)* Erwiderung *f*. **in ~ (als** Antwort) darauf; **in ~ to your letter** in Beantwortung Ihres Briefes *(form).* **2** *vti* antworten; *(spoken also)* erwidern.

report [rɪˈpɔːt] **1** *n* **(a)** *(account, statement)* Bericht *m (on über +acc); (Press, Rad, TV also)* Reportage *f (on über +acc).* **to give a ~ on sth** Bericht über etw *(acc)* erstatten/eine Reportage über etw *(acc)* machen; **(school)** ~ Zeugnis *nt*; **there is a ~ that ...** *(rumour)* es wird gesagt, daß ... **(b)** *(of gun)* Knall *m*.

2 *vt* **(a)** *results, findings* berichten über *(+acc); (announce also)* melden *(to sb jdm).* **he ~ed to me that ...** er meldete mir, daß ...; **the papers ~ed the crime as solved** laut Presseberichten ist das Verbrechen aufgeklärt; **he is ~ed as having said ...** er soll gesagt haben ...; ~**ed speech** *(Gram)* indirekte Rede. **(b)** *(to sb jdm) (notify authorities of)* accident, crime melden; *(to police also)* anzeigen; *one's position* angeben. **to ~ sb for sth** jdn wegen etw melden.

3 *vi* **(a)** *(announce oneself)* sich melden. **to ~ for duty** sich zum Dienst melden; **to ~ sick** sich krank melden. **(b)** *(give a ~)* berichten, Bericht erstatten *(on über +acc).* **(c)** *(be subordinate to)* **to ~ to sb** jdm unterstellt sein.

♦ **report back** *vi* **(a)** *(announce one's return)* sich zurückmelden. **(b)** *(give report)* Bericht erstatten *(to sb jdm).*

reporter [rɪˈpɔːtəʳ] *n (Press, Rad, TV)* Reporter(in *f*) *m*; *(on the spot)* Korrespondent(in *f*) *m*.

repose [rɪˈpəʊz] **1** *n (liter) (rest, peace)* Ruhe *f*; *(composure)* Gelassenheit *f*. **2** *vi (form, liter: rest, be buried)* ruhen.

reprehensible [,reprɪˈhensɪbl] *adj* tadelnswert.

represent [,reprɪˈzent] *vt* darstellen; *(symbolize also)* symbolisieren; *(act or speak for, Parl, Jur)* vertreten.

representation [,reprɪzenˈteɪʃən] *n (a) no pl see vt* Darstellung *f*; Symbolisierung *f*; Vertretung *f*. **(b)** *(drawing, description, Theat)* Darstellung *f*. **(c)** ~**s** *pl (esp Pol: remonstrations)* Vorhaltungen *pl*; **the ambassador made** ~**s to the government** der Botschafter wurde bei der Regierung vorstellig.

representative [,reprɪˈzentətɪv] **1** *adj (of für)* repräsentativ; *attitude also* typisch; *(symbolic)* symbolisch. **2** *n (Comm)* Vertreter(in *f*) *m*; *(Jur)* Bevollmächtigte(r) *mf*; *(US Pol)* Abgeordnete(r) *mf* des Repräsentantenhauses.

repress [rɪˈpres] *vt revolt, population, laugh* unterdrücken; *emotions, desires* zurückdrängen; *(Psych)* verdrängen.

repressed [rɪˈprest] *adj* unterdrückt; *(Psych)* verdrängt.

repression [rɪˈpreʃən] *n* Unterdrückung *f*; *(Psych)* Verdrängung *f*.

repressive [rɪˈpresɪv] *adj* repressiv.

reprieve [rɪˈpriːv] **1** *n (Jur)* Begnadigung *f*; *(postponement)* Strafaufschub *m*; *(fig)* Gnadenfrist *f*. **2** *vt* **he was** ~**d** *(Jur)* er wurde begnadigt; *(sentence postponed)* seine Strafe wurde aufgeschoben; **the building/firm has been** ~**d for a while** das Gebäude/die Firma ist vorerst noch einmal verschont geblieben.

reprimand [ˈreprɪmɑːnd] **1** *n* Tadel *m*; *(official also)* Verweis *m*. **2** *vt* tadeln.

reprint [,riːˈprɪnt] **1** *vt* neu auflegen, nachdrucken.

2 ['riːprɪnt] *n* Neuauflage *f*, Nachdruck *m*.

reprisal [rɪ'praɪzəl] *n (for gegen)* Vergeltungs-maßnahme *f*, Repressalie *f*. **to take ~s** zu Repressalien greifen; **as a ~ for** als Vergel-tung für.

reproach [rɪ'prəʊtʃ] **1** *n (rebuke)* Vorwurf *m*. **above** *or* **beyond ~** über jeden Vorwurf erhaben. **2** *vt* Vorwürfe machen *(+dat)*. **to ~ sb for his mistake** jdm einen Fehler vorwerfen; **to ~ sb for having done sth** jdm Vorwürfe dafür machen, daß er etw getan hat.

reproachful [rɪ'prəʊtʃfʊl] *adj* vorwurfsvoll.

reprobate ['reprəbeɪt] *n* verkommenes Subjekt.

reprocessing plant [rɪ'prəʊsesɪŋplɑːnt] *n* Wie-deraufbereitungsanlage *f*.

reproduce [ˌriːprə'djuːs] **1** *vt* wiedergeben; *(Art, mechanically also)* reproduzieren. **2** *vi (Biol)* sich vermehren.

reproduction [ˌriːprə'dʌkʃən] *n* **(a)** *(procreation)* Fortpflanzung *f*. **(b)** *(copy)* Reproduktion *f*; *(photo)* Kopie *f*; *(sound~)* Wiedergabe *f*. **~ furniture** (moderne) Stilmöbel *pl*.

reproof¹ ['riː'pruːf] *vt garment* frisch im-prägnieren.

reproof² [rɪ'pruːf] *n* Tadel *m*, Rüge *f*.

reprove [rɪ'pruːv] *vt person, action* tadeln.

reptile ['reptaɪl] *n* Reptil *nt*.

republic [rɪ'pʌblɪk] *n* Republik *f*.

republican [rɪ'pʌblɪkən] **1** *adj* republikanisch. **2** *n* Republikaner(in *f*) *m*.

repudiate [rɪ'pjuːdɪeɪt] *vt person* verstoßen; *au-thorship, debt, obligation* nicht anerkennen; *accusation* zurückweisen.

repugnance [rɪ'pʌgnəns] *n* Widerwille *m (towards, for* gegen).

repugnant [rɪ'pʌgnənt] *adj* widerlich, abstoßend.

repulse [rɪ'pʌls] *vt (Mil) enemy* abwehren.

repulsion [rɪ'pʌlʃən] *n (distaste)* Widerwille *m (for* gegen).

repulsive [rɪ'pʌlsɪv] *adj (loathsome)* abstoßend.

reputable ['repjʊtəbl] *adj* ehrenhaft; *occupation* ordentlich, anständig; *dealer, firm* seriös.

reputation [ˌrepjʊ'teɪʃən] *n* Ruf *m*; *(bad ~)* schlechter Ruf. **what sort of ~ does she have?** wie ist ihr Ruf?; **to have a ~ for honesty** als ehrlich gelten.

repute [rɪ'pjuːt] **1** *n* Ruf *m*, Ansehen *nt*. **to be of good ~** einen guten Ruf genießen; **to be held in high ~** in hohem Ansehen stehen. **2** *vt (pass only)* he is **~d to be ...** man sagt, daß er ... ist.

reputedly [rɪ'pjuːtɪdlɪ] *adj* wie man annimmt. **he is ~ the best player** er gilt als der beste Spieler.

request [rɪ'kwest] **1** *n* Bitte *f*, Ersuchen *nt (geh)*. **at sb's ~** auf jds Bitte *etc*; **by ~** auf Wunsch; **to make a ~ for** um etw bitten. **2** *vt* bitten um; *(Rad) record* sich *(dat)* wünschen. **to ~ sth of sb** jdn um etw bitten *or* ersuchen *(geh)*; **to ~ sb to do sth** jdn darum bitten, etw zu tun; **"you are ~ed not to smoke"** „bitte nicht rauchen".

request stop *n (Brit)* Bedarfshaltestelle *f*.

requiem ['rekwɪem] *n* Requiem *nt*.

require [rɪ'kwaɪər] *vt* **(a)** *(need)* brauchen, benötigen; *action* erfordern; *(desire)* wünschen. **I have all I ~** ich habe alles, was ich brauche; **what qualifications are ~d?** welche Qualifikationen werden verlangt?; **to be ~d to do sth** etw machen müssen; **if ~d** falls erfor-derlich; **as and when ~d** nach Bedarf. **(b)** *(expect)* **to ~ sb to do sth** von jdm verlangen, daß er/sie etw tut; **to ~ sth of sb** etw von jdm verlangen.

required [rɪ'kwaɪəd] *adj* erforderlich; *date* vor-geschrieben; *(desired)* gewünscht. **the ~ amount** die benötigte Menge.

requirement [rɪ'kwaɪəmənt] *n (need)* Bedarf *m no pl*; *(desire)* Wunsch *m*; *(condition, thing required)* Erfordernis *nt*. **to meet sb's ~s** jds Ansprüchen gerecht werden; **to fit the ~s** den Erfor-dernissen entsprechen.

requisite ['rekwɪzɪt] **1** *n* Erfordernis *nt*. **toilet ~s** Toilettenartikel *pl*. **2** *adj* erforderlich.

requisition [ˌrekwɪ'zɪʃən] **1** *n* Anforderung *f*; *(Mil)* Requisition *f*. **to make a ~ for sth** etw anfordern. **2** *vt* anfordern; *(Mil) supplies* requirieren.

rescind [rɪ'sɪnd] *vt* rückgängig machen; *law* auf-heben.

rescue ['reskjuː] **1** *n (saving)* Rettung *f*; *(freeing)* Befreiung *f*. **to go/come to sb's ~** jdm zu Hilfe kommen. **2** *vt (save)* retten; *(free)* befreien. **you ~d me from a difficult situation** du hast mich aus einer schwierigen Lage gerettet; **the ~d** die Geretteten.

rescuer ['reskjʊər] *n see vt* Retter(in *f*) *m*; Befreier(in *f*) *m*.

research [rɪ'sɜːtʃ] **1** *n* Forschung *f (into, on* über *+acc)*. **a piece of ~** eine Forschungsarbeit; **to do ~** forschen, Forschung betreiben. **2** *vi* forschen. **3** *vt* erforschen, untersuchen. **a well-~ed book** ein Buch *nt*, das auf solider Forschungsarbeit beruht.

research assistant *n* wissenschaftliche Hilfs-kraft.

researcher [rɪ'sɜːtʃər] *n* Forscher(in *f*) *m*.

research: ~ student *n (Univ) Student, der For-schungen für einen höheren akademischen Grad betreibt,* ≈ Doktorand(in *f*) *m*; **~ worker** *n* For-scher *m*.

resemblance [rɪ'zembləns] *n* Ähnlichkeit *f*. **to bear a strong/no ~ to sb/sth** starke/keine Ähnlichkeit mit jdm/etw haben.

resemble [rɪ'zembl] *vt* gleichen *(+dat)*, ähnlich sein *(+dat)*.

resent [rɪ'zent] *vt remarks, behaviour* sich ärgern über *(+acc)*; *person* eine Abneigung haben gegen. **he ~ed the fact that ...** er ärgerte sich darüber, daß ...; **to ~ sb's success** jdm seinen Erfolg mißgönnen; **I ~ that** das gefällt mir nicht.

resentful [rɪ'zentfʊl] *adj* verärgert *(of* über *+acc)*; *(jealous)* neidisch *(of* auf *+acc)*. **he felt ~ about her promotion** er nahm es ihr übel, daß sie befördert worden war.

resentment [rɪ'zentmənt] *n (of* über *+acc)* Verär-gerung *f*; *(jealousy)* Neid *m*.

reservation [ˌrezə'veɪʃən] *n* **(a)** *(qualification of opinion)* Vorbehalt *m*. **without ~** ohne Vorbehalt. **with ~s** unter Vorbehalt(en); **to have ~s about sb/sth** Bedenken in bezug auf jdn/etw haben. **(b)** *(booking)* Reservierung *f*. **to make a ~ at the hotel** ein Zimmer im Hotel reservieren lassen; **to have a ~ (for a room)** ein Zimmer reserviert haben. **(c)** *(area of land)* Reservat *nt*. **(central) ~** *(Brit: on motorway)* Mittelstreifen *m*.

reserve [rɪ'zɜːv] **1** *n* **(a)** *(keep)* aufsparen, auf-heben. **to ~ one's strength** seine Kräfte sparen; **to ~ judgement** mit einem Urteil zurückhalten; **to ~ the right to do sth** sich *(dat)* (das Recht) vorbehalten, etw zu tun. **(b)** *(book in advance)* reservieren lassen. **2** *n* **(a)** *(store) (of* an *+dat)* Reserve *f*, Vorrat *m*; *(Fin)* Reserve *f*. **cash ~** Barreserve *f*; **world ~s of copper** die Welt-reserven *pl* an Kupfer; **to have/keep in ~** in Reserve haben/halten. **(b)** **without ~** ohne Vor-behalt. **(c)** *(piece of land)* Reservat *nt*. **(d)** *(coolness, reticence)* Reserve *f*. **he treated me with some ~** er behandelte mich etwas reser-viert. **(e)** *(Mil: force)* Reserve *f*. **the ~s** die Reser-veeinheiten; *(Sport)* Reservespieler(in *f*) *m*.

reserved [rɪ'zɜːvd] *adj* **(a)** *(reticent)* zurück-haltend *(about* in bezug auf *+acc)*. **(b)** *room, seat* reserviert. **(c)** **all rights ~** alle Rechte vor-behalten.

reserve team *n* Reserve(mannschaft) *f*.

reservoir ['rezəvwɑːr] *n (lit) (for water)* Reservoir *nt*; *(fig: of knowledge etc)* Fundgrube *f (of* an *+dat)*.

reshuffle [ˌriː'ʃʌfl] *n* **Cabinet ~** *(Pol)* Kabinetts-umbildung *f*.

reside [rɪ'zaɪd] *vi* **(a)** *(form: live)* seinen Wohnsitz haben; *(monarch etc)* residieren. **(b)** *(fig)* **the power** ~**s in the President** die Macht ruht beim Präsidenten.

residence ['rezɪdəns] *n* **(a)** *(house)* Wohnhaus *nt;* *(hostel: for students, nurses)* Wohnheim *nt;* *(of monarch, ambassador etc)* Residenz *f.* **(b)** *no pl* **country/place of** ~ Aufenthaltsland *nt*/Wohnort *m;* **after 5 years'** ~ **in Britain** nach 5 Jahren Aufenthalt in Großbritannien; **to take up** ~ **in the capital** sich in der Hauptstadt niederlassen; **to be in** ~ *(monarch, governor etc)* anwesend sein; ~ **permit** Aufenthaltsgenehmigung *f.*

resident ['rezɪdənt] **1** *n* Bewohner(in *f*) *m;* *(in town also)* Einwohner(in *f*) *m;* *(of institution also)* Insasse *m,* Insassin *f;* *(in hotel)* Gast *m.* **2** *adj* *(in country, town)* wohnhaft; *tutor* Haus-; *physician* Anstalts-. **they are** ~ **in Germany** sie haben ihren Wohnsitz in Deutschland.

residential [,rezɪ'denʃəl] *adj area* Wohn-; *job* im Haus; *college* mit einem Wohnheim verbunden; *course* mit Wohnung im Heim.

residual [rɪ'zɪdjʊəl] *adj* restlich, Rest-.

resign [rɪ'zaɪn] **1** *vt* **(a)** *(give up) office, post* zurücktreten von; *claim, rights* verzichten auf *(+acc).* **to** ~ **power** abtreten. **(b) to** ~ **oneself to sth/to doing sth** sich mit etw abfinden/sich damit abfinden, etw zu tun. **2** *vi (from public appointment)* zurücktreten; *(employee)* kündigen. **to** ~ **from office** sein Amt niederlegen.

resignation [,rezɪg'neɪʃən] *n* **(a)** *see vi* Rücktritt *m;* Kündigung *f.* **to hand in** *or* **tender** *(form)* **one's** ~ seinen Rücktritt/seine Kündigung einreichen/ sein Amt niederlegen. **(b)** *(mental state)* Resignation *f (to* gegenüber *+dat).*

resigned [rɪ'zaɪnd] *adj smile* resigniert. **to become** ~ **to sth** sich mit etw abfinden; **to be** ~ **to one's fate** sich in sein Schicksal ergeben haben.

resilience [rɪ'zɪlɪəns] *n see adj* Federn *nt;* Unverwüstlichkeit *f.*

resilient [rɪ'zɪlɪənt] *adj* **(a)** *material* federnd attr. **to be** ~ federn. **(b)** *(fig) person, nature* unverwüstlich.

resin ['rezɪn] *n* Harz *nt.*

resist [rɪ'zɪst] **1** *vt* **(a)** sich widersetzen *(+dat); arrest, advances, attack, proposal, change also* sich wehren gegen. **(b)** *temptation, sb* widerstehen *(+dat).* **I couldn't** ~ *(eating)* **another cake** ich konnte der Versuchung nicht widerstehen, noch ein Stück Kuchen zu essen. **(c)** *(wall, door)* standhalten *(+dat).* **2** *vi see vt* **(a)** sich widersetzen; sich wehren. **(b)** widerstehen.

resistance [rɪ'zɪstəns] *n (to sth also)* Widerstand *m (also Elec, Phys, Mil);* *(Med)* Widerstandsfähigkeit *f.* ~ **to water/heat** Wasser-/Hitzebeständigkeit *f;* **to meet with** ~ auf Widerstand stoßen; **to offer no** ~ **to sb/sth** *(to attacker, advances etc)* (jdm/gegen etw) keinen Widerstand leisten.

resistant [rɪ'zɪstənt] *adj material* strapazierfähig; *(Med)* immun *(to* gegen). **water-**~ wasserbeständig.

resolute ['rezəluːt] *adj* energisch; *answer* entschieden, bestimmt.

resolution [,rezə'luːʃən] *n* **(a)** *(decision)* Beschluß *m;* *(Pol, Admin etc also)* Resolution *f;* *(governing one's behaviour)* Vorsatz *m.* **good** ~**s** gute Vorsätze *pl.* **(b)** *no pl (resoluteness)* Entschlossenheit *f.* **(c)** *no pl (of problem)* Lösung *f.*

resolve [rɪ'zɒlv] **1** *vt* **(a)** *problem* lösen; *doubt* zerstreuen. **(b)** *(decide)* **to** ~ **that ...** beschließen, daß ...; **to** ~ **to do sth** beschließen, etw zu tun. **2** *n* **(a)** *(decision)* Beschluß *m.* **to make a** ~ **to do sth** den Beschluß fassen, etw zu tun. **(b)** *(resoluteness)* Entschlossenheit *f.*

resonance ['rezənəns] *n* Resonanz *f;* *(of voice)* voller Klang.

resonant ['rezənənt] *adj sound* voll; *voice* klangvoll; *room* mit Resonanz.

resort [rɪ'zɔːt] **1** *n* **(a)** *(recourse)* Ausweg *m;* *(thing, action resorted to also)* Rettung *f.* **without** ~ **to violence** ohne Gewaltanwendung; **as a last** ~ als letztes; **in the last** ~ im schlimmsten Fall. **(b)** *(place)* Urlaubsort *m.* **seaside** ~ Seebad *nt;* **winter sports** ~ Wintersportort *m.* **2** *vi* **to** ~ **to sth/sb** zu etw greifen/sich an jdn wenden; **to** ~ **to violence/theft** gewalttätig/zum Dieb werden; **to** ~ **to lying/swearing** sich aufs Lügen/Fluchen verlegen.

resound [rɪ'zaʊnd] *vi* (wider)hallen *(with* von).

resounding [rɪ'zaʊndɪŋ] *adj noise, shout* widerhallend; *(fig) victory* gewaltig; *success* durchschlagend; *defeat* haushoch. **the response was a** ~ **"no"** die Antwort war ein überwältigendes „Nein".

resource [rɪ'sɔːs] *n* **(a)** ~**s** *pl (wealth, supplies, money etc)* Mittel, Ressourcen *pl;* **financial/ mineral/natural** ~**s** Geldmittel *pl*/Bodenschätze *pl*/Naturschätze *pl;* **left to his own** ~**s** sich *(dat)* selbst überlassen. **(b)** *(expedient)* Ausweg *m,* Mittel *nt.* **as a last** ~ als letzter Ausweg.

resourceful [rɪ'sɔːsfʊl] *adv person* einfallsreich, findig; *scheme* genial.

respect [rɪ'spekt] **1** *n* **(a)** *(esteem)* Respekt *m,* Achtung *f (for* vor *+dat).* **to have** ~ **for** Respekt haben/zeigen vor *(+dat);* **I have the highest** ~ **for his ability** ich halte ihn für außerordentlich fähig; **to hold sb in great** ~ jdn sehr achten. **(b)** *(consideration)* Rücksicht *f (for* auf *+acc).* **to treat with** ~ *person* rücksichtsvoll behandeln; *dangerous person etc* sich in acht nehmen vor *(+dat);* **out of** ~ **for** aus Rücksicht auf *(+acc);* **with (due)** ~, **I still think that ...** bei allem Respekt meine ich dennoch, daß ... **(c)** *(reference)* **with** ~ **to ...** was ... anbetrifft, in bezug auf ... *(+acc).* **(d)** *(aspect)* Hinsicht, Beziehung *f.* **in many** ~**s** in vieler Hinsicht. **(e)** ~**s** *pl (regards)* Empfehlungen *(geh),* Grüße *pl;* **to pay one's last** ~**s to sb** jdm die letzte Ehre erweisen.

2 *vt* respektieren; *person, customs, privacy also* achten; *ability* anerkennen. **a** ~**ed company** eine angesehene Firma.

respectability [rɪ,spektə'bɪlɪtɪ] *n see adj* **(a)** Ehrbarkeit *f;* Ehrenhaftigkeit *f;* Anständigkeit *f;* Korrektheit *f.*

respectable [rɪ'spektəbl] *adj* **(a)** *person* ehrbar; *motives also* ehrenhaft; *district* anständig; *clothes, behaviour* korrekt. **in** ~ **society** in guter Gesellschaft. **(b)** *(large) income* ansehnlich. **(c)** *(fairly good) advantage* beträchtlich; *score* beachtlich.

respectably [rɪ'spektəblɪ] *adv dress, behave* anständig.

respectful [rɪ'spektfʊl] *adj* respektvoll *(towards* gegenüber).

respecting [rɪ'spektɪŋ] *prep* bezüglich *(+gen).*

respective [rɪ'spektɪv] *adj* jeweilig.

respectively [rɪ'spektɪvlɪ] *adv* **they cost £50 and £60** ~ sie kosten £ 50 beziehungsweise £ 60.

respiration [,respɪ'reɪʃən] *n (Bot, Med)* Atmung *f.*

respiratory [rɪ'spaɪərətərɪ] *adj* Atem-; *organs, problem* Atmungs-.

respite ['respaɪt] *n (easing off)* Nachlassen *nt.* **without** ~ ohne Unterbrechung; **to give sb no** ~ jdm keine Ruhe lassen.

resplendent [rɪ'splendənt] *adj* glänzend, strahlend; *clothes* prächtig.

respond [rɪ'spɒnd] *vi* **(a)** *(reply)* antworten. **to** ~ **to a question** eine Frage beantworten. **(b)** *(show reaction)* reagieren *(to* auf *+acc).* **to** ~ **to an appeal** einen Appell beantworten; **to** ~ **to a call** einem Ruf folgen; **the patient did not** ~ **to the treatment** der Patient sprach auf die Behandlung nicht an.

response [rɪ'spɒns] *n (reply)* Antwort, Erwiderung *f;* *(reaction)* Reaktion *f;* *(Eccl)* Antwort *f.* **in** ~ **(to)** in Erwiderung *(+gen) (geh).*

responsibility [rɪˌspɒnsə'bɪlɪtɪ] n (a) no pl Verantwortung f. to take (full) ~ (for sth) die (volle) Verantwortung (für etw) übernehmen; that's his ~ dafür ist er verantwortlich. (b) (duty, burden) Verpflichtung f (to für).

responsible [rɪ'spɒnsəbl] adj (a) verantwortlich; (to blame also) schuld (for an +dat). what's ~ for the hold-up? woran liegt die Verzögerung?; she is not ~ for her actions (esp Jur) sie ist für ihre Handlungen nicht voll verantwortlich; to hold sb ~ for sth jdn für etw verantwortlich machen; to be directly ~ to sb jdm unmittelbar unterstellt sein. (b) (trustworthy) verantwortungsbewußt; (involving responsibility) job verantwortungsvoll.

responsive [rɪ'spɒnsɪv] adj person, audience interessiert; steering leicht ansprechend. to be ~ to sth auf etw (acc) reagieren or ansprechen; he wasn't very ~ (to my complaint) er ging kaum darauf ein.

rest¹ [rest] 1 n (a) (relaxation) Ruhe f; (pause) Pause f; (on holiday etc) Erholung f. a day of ~ ein Ruhetag m; to need ~ Ruhe brauchen; I need a ~ ich muß mich ausruhen; (vacation) ich brauche Urlaub; to have a ~ (relax) (sich) ausruhen; (pause) (eine) Pause machen. (b) to be at ~ (peaceful) ruhig sein; (immobile) sich in Ruhelage/-stellung befinden; (euph: dead) ruhen; to put or set sb's mind at ~ jdn beruhigen; to come to ~ (ball, car etc) zum Stillstand kommen; (bird, insect) sich niederlassen; (gaze, eyes) hängenbleiben (upon an +dat). (c) (Mus) Pause f.
2 vi (a) sich ausruhen; (pause) Pause machen; (euph: be buried) ruhen. he will not ~ until he discovers the truth er wird nicht (eher) ruhen, bis er die Wahrheit gefunden hat; to let a matter ~ eine Sache auf sich beruhen lassen; may he ~ in peace er ruhe in Frieden.
(b) (decision, responsibility etc) liegen (with bei). the matter must not ~ there man kann die Sache so nicht belassen; ~ assured that ... Sie können versichert sein, daß ...
(c) (lean: person, head, ladder) lehnen (on an +dat, against gegen); (roof etc, eyes, gaze) ruhen (on auf +dat); (fig: be based) (argument, case) sich stützen (on auf +acc); (reputation) beruhen (on auf +dat).
3 vt one's eyes ausruhen; voice schonen; horses ausruhen lassen; ladder lehnen (against gegen, on an +acc); elbow, (fig) theory, suspicions stützen (on auf +acc); God ~ his soul Gott hab ihn selig!

rest² n (remainder) the ~ der Rest, das übrige/die übrigen; the ~ of the money/meal das übrige Geld/Essen; the ~ of us/them die übrigen, die anderen; all the ~ of the money das ganze übrige Geld; all the ~ of the books alle übrigen Bücher; and all the ~ of it (col) und so weiter und so fort; for the ~ im übrigen.

restaurant ['restərɔ̃ːŋ] n Restaurant nt. ~ car (Brit Rail) Speisewagen m.

rest: ~ cure n Erholung f; (in bed) Liegekur f; ~ day n Ruhetag m.

restful ['restfʊl] adj occupation, pastime etc erholsam; colour ruhig; place friedlich.

rest-home ['rest,həʊm] n Pflegeheim nt.

restitution [ˌrestɪ'tjuːʃən] n (a) (giving back) Rückgabe f; (of money also) Rückerstattung f. (b) (reparation) Entschädigung f.

restive ['restɪv] adj unruhig; (restless) person, manner rastlos.

restless ['restlɪs] adj person, sea unruhig; (not wanting to stay in one place) rastlos.

restoration [ˌrestə'reɪʃən] n (a) (return) Rückgabe f (to an +acc); (of property also) Rückerstattung f (to an +acc); (of confidence, order etc) Wiederherstellung f; (to office) Wiedereinsetzung f (to in +acc). (b) the R~ (Hist) die Restauration.

restore [rɪ'stɔːr] vt (a) (give back) zurückgeben; confidence, order wiederherstellen. to ~ sb to health jds Gesundheit wiederherstellen; ~d to health wiederhergestellt; to ~ sth to its former condition etw wiederherstellen. (b) (to former post) wiedereinsetzen (to in +acc). to ~ to power wieder an die Macht bringen. (c) (repair) restaurieren.

restorer [rɪ'stɔːrər] n (Art) Restaurator(in f) m.

restrain [rɪ'streɪn] vt person zurückhalten; prisoner mit Gewalt festhalten; animal, children bändigen. to ~ sb from doing sth jdn davon abhalten, etw zu tun; to ~ oneself sich beherrschen.

restrained [rɪ'streɪnd] adj emotions unterdrückt; manner, words beherrscht; tone verhalten; criticism maßvoll.

restraint [rɪ'streɪnt] n (a) (restriction) Einschränkung, Beschränkung f. without ~ unbeschränkt; develop ungehemmt; wage ~ Zurückhaltung f bei Lohnforderungen. (b) (moderation) Beherrschung f. to show a lack of ~ wenig Beherrschung zeigen.

restrict [rɪ'strɪkt] vt beschränken (to auf +acc); time, number also begrenzen (to auf +acc).

restricted [rɪ'strɪktɪd] adj view beschränkt, begrenzt; (Admin, Mil) information geheim; locality nur bestimmten Gruppen zugänglich. ~ area (Brit Mot) Strecke f mit Geschwindigkeitsbeschränkung; (Mil etc) Sperrgebiet nt.

restriction [rɪ'strɪkʃən] n see vt (on gen) Beschränkung f; Begrenzung f. without ~s uneingeschränkt; price ~ Preisbeschränkung f.

restrictive [rɪ'strɪktɪv] adv restriktiv, einschränkend attr.

result [rɪ'zʌlt] 1 n (a) Folge f. as a ~ he failed folglich fiel er durch; as a ~ of which he ... was zur Folge hatte, daß er ...; to be the ~ of resultieren aus. (b) (outcome) Ergebnis, Resultat nt. ~s (of test, experiment) Werte pl; to get ~s (person) Resultate erzielen; as a ~ of my inquiry auf meine Anfrage (hin); what was the ~? (Sport) wie ist es ausgegangen?; without ~ ergebnislos.
2 vi sich ergeben, resultieren (from aus).
♦ result in vi +prep obj führen zu. this ~ed ~ his being late das führte dazu, daß er zu spät kam.

resultant [rɪ'zʌltənt] adj resultierend.

resume [rɪ'zjuːm] 1 vt (restart) activity wiederaufnehmen; journey fortsetzen. to ~ work die Arbeit wiederaufnehmen. (b) command, possession wieder übernehmen. to ~ one's seat seinen Platz wieder einnehmen. 2 vi (classes, work etc) wieder beginnen.

résumé ['reɪzjuːmeɪ] n Zusammenfassung f; (US: curriculum vitae) Lebenslauf m.

resumption [rɪ'zʌmpʃən] n (of activity) Wiederaufnahme f; (of command, possession) erneute Übernahme; (of journey) Fortsetzung f; (of classes) Wiederbeginn m.

resurrection [ˌrezə'rekʃən] n (revival) Wiederbelebung f; (Rel) Auferstehung f.

resuscitate [rɪ'sʌsɪteɪt] vt (Med) wiederbeleben; (fig) beleben.

retail ['riːteɪl] 1 n Einzelhandel m. 2 vt im Einzelhandel verkaufen. 3 vi (goods) to ~ at ... im Einzelhandel ... kosten. 4 adv im Einzelhandel.

retailer ['riːteɪlər] n Einzelhändler m.

retail: ~ outlet n Einzelhandelsverkaufsstelle f; ~ price n Einzelhandelspreis m.

retain [rɪ'teɪn] vt (a) (keep) behalten; money, possession, person zurück(be)halten; custom bewahren; (dam) water stauen. to ~ control (of sth) etw weiterhin in der Gewalt haben. (b) (remember) sich (dat) merken; (computer) information speichern.

retainer [rɪ'teɪnər] n (fee) Honorar nt; (advance) Vorschuß m.

retaliate [rɪ'tælɪeɪt] vi Vergeltung üben; (for bad treatment, insults etc) sich revanchieren (against *sb* an jdm); *(in battle)* zurückschlagen; *(Sport, in fight, in argument)* kontern.

retaliation [rɪˌtælɪ'eɪʃən] *n* Vergeltung *f; (in fight also)* Vergeltungsschlag *m; (in argument, diplomacy etc)* Konterschlag *m.* **in ~** zur Vergeltung; **that's my ~ for what you did** das ist meine Revanche für das, was du getan hast.

retarded [rɪ'tɑːdɪd] *adj (Med)* zurückgeblieben.

retch [retʃ] *vi* würgen.

retentive [rɪ'tentɪv] *adj memory* aufnahmefähig.

reticence ['retɪsəns] *n* Zurückhaltung *f.*

reticent ['retɪsənt] *adj* zurückhaltend.

retina ['retɪnə] *n, pl* **-e** ['retɪniː] *or* **-s** Netzhaut *f.*

retinue ['retɪnjuː] *n* Gefolge *nt.*

retire [rɪ'taɪəʳ] **1** *vi* **(a)** *(give up work)* aufhören zu arbeiten; *(civil servant)* sich pensionieren lassen; *(self-employed)* sich zur Ruhe setzen; *(soldier)* aus der Armee ausscheiden; *(singer, player etc)* (zu singen/spielen etc) aufhören. **(b)** *(withdraw, Mil)* sich zurückziehen; *(Sport)* aufgeben; *(Ftbl etc)* vom Feld gehen. **to ~ into oneself** sich in sich *(acc)* selbst zurückziehen. **2** *vt* aus Altersgründen entlassen; *civil servant, military officer* pensionieren, in den Ruhestand versetzen.

retired [rɪ'taɪəd] *adj* **(a)** pensioniert, im Ruhestand; *soldier* aus der Armee ausgeschieden. **(b)** *(secluded)* life zurückgezogen.

retiree [ˌrɪtaɪ'riː] *n (US)* Rentner(in *f*) *m.*

retirement [rɪ'taɪəmənt] *n (stopping work)* Ausscheiden *nt* aus dem Arbeitsleben *(form); (of civil servant, military officer)* Pensionierung *f; (state)* Ruhestand *m.* **~ at 65** Altersgrenze bei 65; **to announce one's ~** sein Ausscheiden (aus seinem Beruf/einer Stellung etc) ankündigen; **how will you spend your ~?** was tun Sie, wenn Sie pensioniert *or* im Ruhestand sind?

retirement age *n* Altersgrenze *f.*

retiring [rɪ'taɪərɪŋ] *adj* **(a)** *(shy)* zurückhaltend. **(b) ~ age = retirement age.**

retort [rɪ'tɔːt] **1** *n* **(a)** *(answer)* scharfe Erwiderung *or* Antwort. **(b)** *(Chem)* Retorte *f.* **2** *vti* scharf erwidern.

retrace [rɪ'treɪs] *vt past, development* zurückverfolgen. **to ~ one's steps** denselben Weg zurückgehen.

retract [rɪ'trækt] **1** *vt (withdraw) offer* zurückziehen; *statement* zurücknehmen; *claws, undercarriage* einziehen. **2** *vi* einen Rückzieher machen; *(claws)* eingezogen werden.

retread ['riːtred] *n (tyre)* lauffflächenerneuerter Reifen.

retreat [rɪ'triːt] **1** *n* **(a)** *(Mil)* Rückzug *m.* **to beat a ~** *(Mil)* den Rückzug antreten; *(fig)* das Feld räumen. **(b)** *(place)* Zuflucht(sort *m*) *f.* **he has gone to his country ~** er hat sich aufs Land zurückgezogen. **2** *vi (Mil)* den Rückzug antreten; *(in fear)* zurückweichen; *(flood, glacier)* zurückgehen.

retrench [rɪ'trentʃ] **1** *vt expenditure* einschränken; *personnel* einsparen. **2** *vi* sich einschränken.

retrial [riː'traɪəl] *n (Jur)* Wiederaufnahmeverfahren *nt.*

retribution [ˌretrɪ'bjuːʃən] *n* Vergeltung *f.* **in ~** als Vergeltung.

retrieval [rɪ'triːvəl] *n see vt* Zurück-/Hervor-/Heraus-/Herunterholen *nt;* Rettung *f;* Bergung *f;* Rückgewinnung *f;* Abfragen *nt;* Wiedererlangen *nt;* Wiedergutmachen *nt.*

retrieve [rɪ'triːv] *vt* **(a)** *(recover)* zurück-/hervor-/heraus-/herunterholen; *(rescue)* retten; *(from wreckage etc)* bergen; *material from waste* zurückgewinnen; *(Comp) information* abfragen; *honour, position* wiedererlangen; *loss* wiedergutmachen. **(b)** *(dog)* apportieren.

retriever [rɪ'triːvəʳ] *n (dog)* Retriever *m.*

retroactive [ˌretrəʊ'æktɪv] *adj* rückwirkend.

retrograde ['retrəʊɡreɪd] *adj* rückläufig; *policy* rückschrittlich. **~ step** Rückschritt *m.*

retrorocket ['retrəʊˌrɒkɪt] *n* Bremsrakete *f.*

retrospect ['retrəʊspekt] *n* **in ~** im Rückblick; **everything looks different in ~** im nachhinein sieht alles anders aus.

retrospective [ˌretrəʊ'spektɪv] *adj thought* rückblickend; *(Admin, Jur) pay rise* rückwirkend.

return [rɪ'tɜːn] **1** *vi (come back: person, vehicle)* zurück- *or* wiederkommen; *(go back) (person)* zurückgehen; *(vehicle)* zurückfahren; *(symptoms, doubts, fears)* wieder auftreten. **to ~ to a subject** auf ein Thema zurückkommen; **to ~ home** nach Hause kommen/gehen, heimkehren *(geh).* **2** *vt (give back)* zurückgeben *(to sb* jdm); *(bring or take back)* zurückbringen *(to sb* jdm); *(put back)* zurücksetzen/-stellen/-legen; *(send back) (to an +acc) letter etc* zurückschicken; *(refuse) cheque* zurückweisen; *ball* zurückschlagen/-werfen; *salute, visit, compliment* erwidern. **to ~ goods to the shop** Waren in das Geschäft zurückbringen; **to ~ fire** *(Mil)* das Feuer erwidern. **(b)** *(reply)* erwidern. **(c)** *(declare) details of income* angeben. **to ~ a verdict of guilty/not guilty (on sb)** *(Jur)* (jdn) schuldig sprechen/freisprechen. **(d)** *(Fin) income* einbringen; *profit, interest* abwerfen. **(e)** *(Brit Parl) candidate* wählen.

3 *vt* **(a)** *(of person, vehicle, seasons)* Rückkehr *f; (of illness)* Wiederauftreten *nt.* **on my ~** bei meiner Rückkehr; **by ~ (of post)** postwendend; **many happy ~s (of the day)!** herzlichen Glückwunsch zum Geburtstag!

(b) *(giving/bringing/taking/sending back) see vt* **(a)** Rückgabe *f;* Zurückbringen *nt;* Zurücksetzen/-stellen/-legen *nt;* Zurückschicken *nt;* Zurückweisen *nt;* Zurückschlagen *nt/*-werfen *nt;* Erwiderung *f.*

(c) *(profit)* Einkommen *nt (on* aus); *(from land, mine etc)* Ertrag *m.* **~s** *(profits)* Gewinn *m; (receipts)* Einkünfte *pl;* **~ on capital** *(Fin)* Kapitalertrag *m.*

(d) *(fig: recompense)* **in ~** dafür; **in ~ for** für; **to do sb a kindness in ~** sich bei jdm für einen Gefallen revanchieren.

(e) *(act of declaring: of verdict, election results)* Verkündung *f.* **the (election) ~s** das Wahlergebnis; **tax ~** Steuererklärung *f.*

(f) ~ = ticket.

returnable [rɪ'tɜːnəbl] *adj bottle* Mehrweg-; *(with deposit)* Pfand-.

return fare *n* Preis *m* für eine Rückfahrkarte *or (Aviat)* einen Rückflugschein.

returning officer [rɪ'tɜːnɪŋ'ɒfɪsəʳ] *n (Brit Parl)* Wahlleiter *m.*

return: ~ journey *n* Rückreise *f; (both ways)* Hin- und Rückreise *f;* **~ match** *n* Rückspiel *nt;* **~ ticket** *n (Brit)* Rückfahrkarte *f; (Aviat)* Rückflugschein *m.*

reunion [riː'juːnjən] *n* **(a)** *(coming together)* Wiedervereinigung *f.* **(b)** *(gathering)* Zusammenkunft *f.* **a family ~** ein Familientreffen *nt.*

reunite [ˌriːjuː'naɪt] **1** *vt* wiedervereinigen. **they were ~d at last** sie waren endlich wieder vereint. **2** *vi (countries, parties)* sich wiedervereinigen; *(people)* wieder zusammenkommen.

Rev [rev] = **Reverend.**

rev [rev] **1** *n = revolution* *(Aut)* Umdrehung *f.* **~ counter** Drehzahlmesser *m.* **2** *vti* **to ~ (up)** *(driver)* den Motor auf Touren bringen; *(noisily)* den Motor aufheulen lassen; *(engine)* aufheulen.

revalue [ˌriː'væljuː] *vt (Fin)* aufwerten.

revamp [ˌriː'væmp] *vt (col) book, play* aufpolieren *(col); house, room* aufmöbeln.

reveal [rɪ'viːl] *vt (make visible)* zum Vorschein bringen; *(show)* zeigen; *(make known) truth, facts* enthüllen; *one's identity* zu erkennen geben; *ignorance, knowledge* erkennen lassen. **I cannot ~ to you what he said** ich kann Ihnen nicht verraten, was er gesagt hat.

revealing [rɪ'viːlɪŋ] *adj* aufschlußreich; *dress, neckline* offenherzig *(hum)*.

reveille [rɪ'vælɪ] *n (Mil)* Wecksignal *nt.*

revel ['revl] *vi (make merry)* feiern. **to** ~ **in doing sth** seine wahre Freude daran haben, etw zu tun.

revelation [,revə'leɪʃən] *n* Enthüllung *f; (Rel)* Offenbarung *f.* **it was a** ~ **to me** das hat mir die Augen geöffnet.

revelry ['revlrɪ] *n usu pl* Festlichkeit *f.*

revenge [rɪ'vendʒ] **1** *n* Rache *f; (Sport)* Revanche *f.* **to take** ~ **on sb (for sth)** sich an jdm (für etw) rächen; **to get one's** ~ sich rächen. **2** *vt insult, murder, sb* rächen. **to** ~ **oneself on sb (for sth)** sich (für etw) an jdm rächen.

revenue ['revənjuː] *n (of state)* Staatseinkünfte *pl; (tax* ~*)* Steueraufkommen *nt; (of individual)* Einkünfte *pl; (department)* Finanzbehörde *f.*

reverberate [rɪ'vɜːbəreɪt] *vi (sound)* widerhallen.

reverberation [rɪ,vɜːbə'reɪʃən] *n (of sound)* Widerhall *m.*

revere [rɪ'vɪəʳ] *vt* verehren.

reverence ['revərəns] **1** *n* Ehrfurcht *f.* **2** *vt* verehren.

Reverend ['revərənd] *adj* **the** ~ **Robert Martin** ≈ Pfarrer Robert Martin.

reverent ['revərənt] *adj* ehrfürchtig.

reverie ['revərɪ] *n (liter)* Träumereien *pl.* **he fell into a** ~ er kam ins Träumen.

reversal [rɪ'vɜːsəl] *n* Umkehrung *f; (of verdict also)* Umstoßung *f.*

reverse [rɪ'vɜːs] **1** *adj (opposite)* umgekehrt; *direction* entgegengesetzt; *(Opt) image* seitenverkehrt. **in** ~ **order** in umgekehrter Reihenfolge; ~ **gear** *(Aut)* Rückwärtsgang *m.* **2** *n* **(a)** *(opposite)* Gegenteil *nt.* **quite the** ~! ganz im Gegenteil! **(b)** *(back)* Rückseite *f; (of cloth also)* linke Seite. **(c)** *(setback, loss)* Rückschlag *m; (defeat)* Niederlage *f.* **(d)** *(Aut)* Rückwärtsgang *m.* **in** ~ im Rückwärtsgang. **3** *vt* **(a)** *(turn about)* order, situation umkehren; *objects, sentences also* umstellen; *garment* wenden; *result also* umdrehen. **to** ~ **the charges** *(Brit Telec)* ein R-Gespräch führen; ~**d charge call** R-Gespräch *nt.* **(b)** **to** ~ **one's car into the garage/into a tree** rückwärts in die Garage/ gegen einen Baum fahren. **(c)** *trend, policy* umkehren; *verdict also* umstoßen. **4** *vi (car)* rückwärts fahren. **reversing lights** Rückfahrscheinwerfer *pl.*

reversible [rɪ'vɜːsəbl] *adj decision* umstoßbar; *(Phys, Chem)* umkehrbar; *garment* Wende-. ~ **cloth** Doubleface *m* or *nt.*

revert [rɪ'vɜːt] *vi (to former state)* zurückkehren *(to* zu*); (to bad state)* zurückfallen *(to* in +*acc); (to topic)* zurückkommen *(to* auf +*acc); (Jur: property)* zurückfallen *(to* an +*acc).*

review [rɪ'vjuː] **1** *n* **(a)** *(looking back)* Rückblick *m (of* auf +*acc); (report)* Überblick *m (of* über +*acc).* **I shall keep your case under** ~ ich werde Ihren Fall im Auge behalten. **the agreement comes up for** ~ **next year** das Abkommen wird nächstes Jahr nochmals geprüft. **(c)** *(Mil: inspection)* Inspektion *f.* **(d)** *(of book, play etc)* Kritik, Rezension *f.* **(e)** *(magazine)* Zeitschrift *f.* **2** *vt* **(a)** *(look back at)* one's life etc zurückblicken auf (+*acc).* **(b)** *(re-examine)* case erneut (über)prüfen. **(c)** *(Mil)* troops inspizieren. **(d)** *book, play, film* besprechen, rezensieren.

revile [rɪ'vaɪl] *vt* schmähen, verunglimpfen.

revise [rɪ'vaɪz] *vt* opinion, estimate überholen, revidieren; *text* revidieren, überarbeiten. ~**d edition** überarbeitete Ausgabe. **2** *vi (Brit)* (den Stoff) wiederholen.

revision [rɪ'vɪʒən] *n* **(a)** *(of opinion, estimate)* Revidieren *nt.* **(b)** *(of proofs)* Revision, Überarbeitung *f.* **(c)** *(Brit: for exam)* Wiederholung *f* (des Stoffs). **(d)** *(revised version)* überarbeitete

Ausgabe.

revival [rɪ'vaɪvəl] *n (from faint)* Wiederbelebung *f.* **there has been a** ~ **of interest in** ... das Interesse an ... ist wieder wach geworden; **an economic** ~ ein wirtschaftlicher Wiederaufschwung.

revive [rɪ'vaɪv] **1** *vt person (from fainting, fatigue)* (wieder *or* neu) beleben; *(from near death)* wiederbeleben; *custom, hatred* wiederaufleben lassen; *friendship, word, old play* wiederaufnehmen. **2** *vi (person) (from fainting)* wieder zu sich kommen; *(from fatigue)* wieder aufleben, wieder munter werden; *(hope, feelings)* wiederaufleben; *(business, trade)* wiederaufblühen.

revoke [rɪ'vəuk] *vt law* aufheben; *order, promise* zurückziehen; *decision* rückgängig machen; *licence* entziehen.

revolt [rɪ'vəult] **1** *n* Revolte *f,* Aufstand *m.* **to be in** ~ **(against)** rebellieren (gegen). **2** *vi (rebel)* rebellieren *(against* gegen). **3** *vt* abstoßen, anekeln *(col).* **I was** ~**ed by it** es hat mich angeekelt.

revolting [rɪ'vəultɪŋ] *adj (repulsive)* abstoßend; *meal, story* ekelhaft; *(col: unpleasant)* weather, colour* scheußlich; *person* widerlich.

revolution [,revə'luːʃən] *n* **(a)** *(Pol, fig)* Revolution *f.* **(b)** *(turn)* Umdrehung *f.* **4,000** ~**s per minute** eine Drehzahl von 4.000 pro Minute.

revolutionary [,revə'luːʃnərɪ] **1** *adj (lit, fig)* revolutionär. **2** *n* Revolutionär *m.*

revolutionize [,revə'luːʃənaɪz] *vt* revolutionieren.

revolve [rɪ'vɒlv] **1** *vt* drehen. **2** *vi* sich drehen. **to** ~ **on an axis/around the sun** sich um eine Achse/ um die Sonne drehen; **he thinks everything** ~**s around him** *(fig)* er glaubt, alles drehe sich nur um ihn.

revolver [rɪ'vɒlvəʳ] *n* Revolver *m.*

revolving [rɪ'vɒlvɪŋ] *in cpds* Dreh-.

revue [rɪ'vjuː] *n (Theat)* Revue *f; (satirical)* Kabarett *nt.*

revulsion [rɪ'vʌlʃən] *n (disgust)* Abscheu, Ekel *m (at* vor +*dat).*

reward [rɪ'wɔːd] **1** *n* Belohnung *f.* **one of the** ~**s of this job** einer der Vorzüge dieser Arbeit; ~ **offered for the return of** ... Finderlohn für ... **2** *vt* belohnen.

rewarding [rɪ'wɔːdɪŋ] *adj (financially)* lohnend, einträglich; *(morally)* lohnend; *work* dankbar.

rewind [,riː'waɪnd] *pret, ptp* **rewound** *vt thread* wieder aufwickeln; *film, tape* zurückspulen. ~ **button** Rückspultaste *f.*

rewire [,riː'waɪəʳ] *vt* neu verkabeln.

rhapsody ['ræpsədɪ] *n (Mus)* Rhapsodie *f; (fig)* Schwärmerei *f.*

rhesus ['riːsəs] *n* ~ **monkey** Rhesusaffe *m;* ~ **factor** Rhesusfaktor *m.*

rhetoric ['retərɪk] *n* Rhetorik *f; (pej)* Phrasendrescherei *f (pej).*

rhetorical [rɪ'tɒrɪkəl] *adj* rhetorisch; *(pej)* phrasenhaft. ~ **question** rhetorische Frage.

rheumatic [ruː'mætɪk] *adj pains* rheumatisch; *joint* rheumakrank.

rheumatism ['ruːmətɪzəm] *n* Rheuma(tismus *m) nt.*

rheumatoid ['ruːmətɔɪd] *adj* ~ **arthritis** Gelenkrheumatismus *m.*

Rhine [raɪn] *n* Rhein *m.*

rhino ['raɪnəu] *n* = **rhinoceros.**

rhinoceros [raɪ'nɒsərəs] *n* Nashorn, Rhinozeros *nt.*

rhododendron [,rəudə'dendrən] *n* Rhododendron *m* or *nt.*

rhubarb ['ruːbɑːb] *n* Rhabarber *m.*

rhyme [raɪm] **1** *n* Reim *m; (poem)* Gedicht *nt.* **without** ~ **or reason** ohne Sinn und Verstand; **in** ~ in Versen. **2** *vi* sich reimen.

rhythm ['rɪðm] *n* Rhythmus *m.*

rhythmic(al) ['rɪðmɪk(əl)] *adj* rhythmisch.

rib [rɪb] **1** *n* **(a)** *(Anat, Cook, of leaf)* Rippe *f.* **(b)**

(Knitting) Rippen pl. **2** vt *(tease)* necken, foppen.

ribald ['rɪbəld, 'raɪbəld] adj deftig; *behaviour* derb; *company* liederlich.

ribbon ['rɪbən] n *(for hair, dress)* Band nt; *(for typewriter)* Farbband nt; *(on medal)* Ordensband nt; *(fig: narrow strip)* Streifen m.

rice [raɪs] n Reis m.

rice in *cpds* Reis-; ~ **paper** n Reispapier nt; ~ **pudding** n Milchreis m.

rich [rɪtʃ] **1** adj *(+er)* reich; *decoration, clothes* prächtig; *food* schwer; *soil* fett; *land* fruchtbar; *colour* satt; *sound, voice* voll; *wine* schwer. ~ **in vitamins** vitaminreich; ~ **in minerals** reich an Bodenschätzen; ~ **in examples** mit vielen Beispielen; **that's** ~! *(iro)* das ist ja großartig! **2** n *(a)* **the** ~ pl die Reichen pl. *(b)* ~**es** Reichtümer pl.

richly ['rɪtʃlɪ] adv dress, decorate prächtig. **he was** ~ **rewarded** *(lit)* er wurde reich belohnt; *(fig)* er wurde reichlich belohnt.

richness ['rɪtʃnɪs] n see *adj* Reichtum m; Pracht f; Schwere f; Fruchtbarkeit f; Sattheit f; Fülle f; Schwere f.

rickets ['rɪkɪts] n sing Rachitis f.

rickety ['rɪkɪtɪ] adj *furniture etc* wackelig.

rickshaw ['rɪkʃɔː] n Rikscha f.

ricochet ['rɪkəʃeɪ] **1** n Abprall m. **2** vi abprallen *(off von)*.

rid [rɪd] pret, ptp ~ or ~**ded** vt to ~ **oneself of sb/sth** jdn/etw loswerden; *of pests also* sich von etw befreien; *of ideas, prejudice etc* sich von etw lösen; **to get** ~ **of sb/sth** jdn/etw loswerden; **get** ~ **of it** sieh zu, daß du das loswirst; *(throw it away)* schmeiß es weg *(col)*.

riddance ['rɪdəns] n **good** ~! *(col)* ein Glück, daß wir das/den *etc* los sind.

ridden ['rɪdn] ptp of **ride**.

riddle¹ ['rɪdl] vt to ~ **sb/sth with bullets** jdn/etw mit Kugeln durchlöchern; ~**d with holes** völlig durchlöchert.

riddle² n Rätsel nt. **to speak in** ~**s** in Rätseln sprechen.

ride [raɪd] *(vb: pret* **rode**, *ptp* **ridden***)* **1** n *(in vehicle, on bicycle)* Fahrt f; *(on horse)* Ritt m; *(for pleasure)* Ausritt m. **to go for a** ~ eine Fahrt machen; reiten gehen; **to go for a** ~ **in the car** eine Fahrt (mit dem Auto) machen; **to take sb for a** ~ *(in car etc)* mit jdm eine Fahrt machen; *(col)* jdn anschmieren *(col)*; **he gave me a** ~ **into town in his car** er nahm mich im Auto in die Stadt mit; **thanks for the** ~ danke fürs Mitnehmen.

2 vi *(a)* *(on a horse etc)* reiten *(on auf +dat)*; *(go in vehicle, by cycle etc)* fahren. **to go riding** reiten gehen; **to** ~ **on a bus/in a car/in a train** in einem Bus/Wagen/Zug fahren. *(b)* **he's riding high** *(fig)* er schwimmt ganz oben; **to** ~ **at anchor** *(ship)* vor Anker liegen; **to let things** ~ den Dingen ihren Lauf lassen.

3 vt *horse* reiten. **to** ~ **a bike** Fahrrad fahren; **they had ridden 10 km** sie waren 10 km geritten/gefahren; **we rode the bus into town** *(esp US)* wir fuhren mit dem Bus in die Stadt.

♦ **ride out** vt sep überstehen. **to** ~ ~ **the storm** *(lit, fig)* den Sturm überstehen.

♦ **ride up** vi *(a)* *(horseman)* heranreiten; *(motorcyclist etc)* heranfahren. *(b)* *(skirt etc)* hochrutschen.

rider ['raɪdər] n *(a)* *(on horse)* Reiter(in f) m; *(on bicycle, motorcycle)* Fahrer(in f) m. *(b)* *(addition)* Zusatz m; *(to document)* Zusatzklausel f.

ridge [rɪdʒ] n *(of hills, mountains)* Rücken, Kamm m; *(pointed, steep)* Grat m; *(of roof)* First m; *(of nose)* Rücken m; *(raised edge)* Rand m. **a** ~ **of hills** eine Hügelkette; **a** ~ **of high pressure** *(Met)* ein Hochdruckkeil m.

ridge pole n *(of tent)* Firststange f.

ridicule ['rɪdɪkjuːl] n Spott m. **to hold sb/sth up to** ~ sich über jdn/etw lustig machen.

ridiculous [rɪ'dɪkjʊləs] adj lächerlich. **don't be** ~ red keinen Unsinn.

ridiculously [rɪ'dɪkjʊləslɪ] adv lächerlich; *expensive* wahnsinnig *(col)*.

riding ['raɪdɪŋ] n Reiten nt. **I enjoy** ~ ich reite gern.

rife [raɪf] adj *disease, corruption* weitverbreitet. **to be** ~ grassieren; *(rumour)* umgehen.

riffraff ['rɪfræf] n Pöbel m, Gesindel nt.

rifle¹ ['raɪfl] vt *(also* ~ **through)** sb's pockets, drawer, house durchwühlen.

rifle² n *(gun)* Gewehr nt; *(for hunting)* Büchse f.

rifle range n Schießstand m.

rift [rɪft] n *(a)* Spalt m. *(b)* *(fig: in friendship)* Riß m; *(Pol also)* Spalt m.

rig [rɪg] **1** n *(oil* ~*)* *(Öl)förderturm m; *(offshore)* Ölbohrinsel f. **2** vt *(fig)* election, market etc manipulieren.

♦ **rig out** vt sep *(col: clothe)* ausstaffieren *(col)*.

♦ **rig up** vt sep *ship* auftakeln; *equipment* aufbauen; *(fig)* *(make)* improvisieren; *(arrange)* arrangieren.

rigging ['rɪgɪn] n *(Naut)* Tauwerk nt.

right [raɪt] **1** adj *(a)* *(just, fair)* richtig. **he thought it** ~ **to warn me** er hielt es für richtig, mich zu warnen; **it's only** ~ **(and proper)** es ist nur recht und billig.

(b) *(true, correct)* answer, time richtig. **to be** ~ *(person)* recht haben; *(answer, solution)* richtig sein; *(clock)* richtig gehen; **you're quite** ~ Sie haben ganz recht; **let's get it** ~ **this time** diesmal muß es klappen; **you were** ~ **to refuse** Sie hatten recht, als Sie ablehnten; **on the** ~ **track** *(fig)* auf dem rechten Weg; **to put** ~ error korrigieren; *clock* richtig stellen; *situation* wieder in Ordnung bringen; **to put sb** ~ jdn berichtigen.

(c) *(proper)* clothes, document richtig. **what's the** ~ **thing to do in this case?** was tut man da am besten?; **to come at the** ~ **time** zur rechten Zeit kommen; **to do sth the** ~ **way** etw richtig machen; **the** ~ **word** das rechte or richtige Wort; **the** ~ **man for the job** der richtige Mann für die Stelle; **to know the** ~ **people** die richtigen Leute kennen.

(d) *(well)* **the medicine soon put him** ~ die Medizin hat ihn schnell wieder auf die Beine gebracht; **I don't feel quite** ~ **today** ich fühle mich heute nicht ganz wohl; **to be as** ~ **as rain** *(Brit)* kerngesund sein; **to be in one's** ~ **mind** klar bei Verstand sein.

(e) *(phrases)* ~! ~**-oh!** *(Brit col)*, ~ **you are!** *(Brit col)* gut, okay *(col)*; **that's** ~! *(correct, true)* das stimmt!; ~ **enough!** (das) stimmt!; **it's a** ~ **mess in there** *(col)* das ist vielleicht ein Durcheinander hier *(col)*; **he's a** ~ **fool!** *(col)* er ist wirklich doof *(col)*; **you're a** ~ **one** *(col)* du bist mir der Richtige *(col)*.

(f) *(opposite of left)* rechte(r, s). ~ **hand** rechte Hand; **I'd give my** ~ **hand to know the answer** ich würde was drum geben, wenn ich die Antwort wüßte *(col)*.

2 adv *(a)* *(straight, directly)* direkt; *(exactly also)* genau. ~ **in front of you** direkt vor Ihnen; ~ **away** *(immediately)* sofort; ~ **off** *(at the first attempt)* auf Anhieb *(col)*; ~ **now** *(at this very moment)* in diesem Augenblick; *(immediately)* sofort; ~ **here** genau hier; ~ **in the middle** genau in der/die Mitte; ~ **at the beginning** gleich am Anfang.

(b) *(completely, all the way)* ganz. ~ **rotten** *(col)* **through** durch und durch verfault or *(fig)* verdorben; ~ **the way around the city** um die ganze Stadt.

(c) *(correctly)* richtig. **to answer** ~ richtig antworten; **if I remember** ~ wenn ich mich recht erinnere; **if everything goes** ~ wenn alles klappt *(col)*.

(d) *(Pol)* the **R~ Honourable John Smith MP** der Abgeordnete John Smith. **(e)** *(opposite of left)* rechts. **turn** ~ biegen Sie rechts ab; ~ **of centre** *(Pol)* rechts von der Mitte; ~, **left and centre** *(everywhere)* überall.
3 *n* **(a)** *no pl (moral, legal)* Recht *nt.* **he doesn't know** ~ **from wrong** er kann Recht und Unrecht nicht auseinanderhalten; **to be in the** ~ im Recht sein. **(b)** *(entitlement)* Recht *nt; (to sth also)* Anrecht *nt.* **(to have) a** *or* **the** ~ **to do sth** ein *or* das Recht haben, etw zu tun; **what** ~ **have you to say that?** mit welchem Recht sagen Sie das?; **he is within his** ~**s** das ist sein gutes Recht; **by** ~**s** von Rechts wegen; **in one's own** ~ selber, selbst. **(c) to put** *or* **set sth to** ~**s** etw (wieder) in Ordnung bringen. **(d)** *(not left)* rechte Seite; *(punch)* Rechte *f.* **to drive on the** ~ rechts fahren; **to keep to the** ~ sich rechts halten; **on my** ~ rechts (von mir); **the R~** *(Pol)* die Rechte.
4 *vt* **(a)** *(return to upright position)* aufrichten. **(b)** *(make amends for)* wrong wiedergutmachen. **the problem should** ~ **itself** *(fig)* das Problem müßte sich von selbst lösen.
right: ~ **angle** *n* rechter Winkel; **at** ~ **angles (to)** rechtwinklig (zu); ~**angled** ['raɪt,æŋgld] *adj* rechtwinklig.
righteous ['raɪtʃəs] *adj* rechtschaffen; *(pej)* selbstgerecht *(pej); indignation* gerecht.
rightful ['raɪtfʊl] *adj* heir, owner rechtmäßig; punishment gerecht.
right: ~**-hand drive** *adj* rechtsgesteuert; ~**-handed** *adj person* rechtshändig; ~**-hand man** *n* rechte Hand; ~**-hand side** *n* rechte Seite.
rightly ['raɪtlɪ] *adv* **(a)** *(correctly)* he said, ~, that ... er sagte sehr richtig, daß ...; **I don't** ~ **know** ich weiß nicht genau. **(b)** *(justifiably)* mit *or* zu Recht. ~ **or wrongly** ob das nun richtig ist/war oder nicht; **and** ~ **so** und zwar mit Recht.
right: ~**-minded** *adj* vernünftig; ~ **of way** *n (across property)* Durchgangsrecht *nt; (Mot: priority)* Vorfahrt *f;* **he has the** ~ **of way** *(Mot)* er hat Vorfahrt; ~ **wing** *n (Sport, Pol)* rechter Flügel; ~**-winger** *n (Sport)* Rechtsaußen *m; (Pol)* Rechte(r) *mf.*
rigid ['rɪdʒɪd] *adj (lit)* material, frame starr, steif; *(fig) person* streng, stur *(pej); discipline, principles* streng, strikt; *(inflexible)* unbeugsam; *specifications* genau festgelegt, strikt; *system* starr, unbeugsam.
rigmarole ['rɪgmərəʊl] *n* Gelaber *nt; (process)* Gedöns *nt (col).* **to go through the whole** ~ **again** nochmal mit demselben Gelaber/Gedöns anfangen.
rigor mortis [ˌrɪgəˈmɔːtɪs] *n* die Leichenstarre.
rigorous ['rɪgərəs] *adj character, discipline* streng, strikt; *measures* rigoros; *(accurate)* peinlich genau; *analysis, tests* gründlich; *climate* streng.
rigour, *(US)* **rigor** ['rɪgər] *n* **(a)** *no pl (strictness)* Strenge, Striktheit *f.* **(b)** ~**s** *pl (of climate, famine etc)* Unbilden *pl.*
rim [rɪm] *n (of cup, bowl)* Rand *m; (of hat also)* Krempe *f; (of spectacles also)* Fassung *f; (of wheel)* Felge *f.*
rimless ['rɪmlɪs] *adj spectacles* randlos.
rind [raɪnd] *n (of cheese)* Rinde *f; (of bacon)* Schwarte *f; (of fruit)* Schale *f.*
ring[1] [rɪŋ] *n* **(a)** *(of)* Ring *m; (in tree trunk)* Jahresring *m.* **to stand in a** ~ im Kreis stehen; **to run** ~**s around sb** *(col)* jdn in die Tasche stecken *(col).* **(b)** *(group) (Pol)* Gruppe *f; (of dealers, spies)* Ring *m.* **(c)** *(enclosure) (at circus)* Manege *f; (Sport, at exhibition)* Ring *m.* **2** *vt (surround)* umringen; *(put* ~ *on or round)* item on list etc einkreisen; *bird* beringen.
ring[2] *(vb: pret* **rang,** *ptp* **rung) 1** *n* **(a)** *(sound)* Klang *m;* (~*ing: of bell, alarm)* Läuten *nt; (of*

electric bell, alarm clock, phone) Klingeln *nt; (metallic sound: of swords etc)* Klirren *nt.* **there was a** ~ **at the door** es hat geklingelt. **(b)** *(esp Brit Telec)* Anruf *m.* **to give sb a** ~ jdn anrufen. **(c)** *(fig)* Klang *m.* **his voice had an angry** ~ **(in** *or* **to it)** seine Stimme klang etwas böse; **that has the** ~ **of truth (about it)** das klingt sehr wahrscheinlich.
2 *vi* **(a)** *see n (a)* klingen; läuten; klingen; klirren; *(hammers)* schallen. **the (door)bell rang** es hat geklingelt; **to** ~ **for sb** (nach) jdm läuten; **please** ~ **for attention** bitte klingeln. **(b)** *(esp Brit Telec)* anrufen. **(c)** *(sound, resound) (words, voice)* tönen; *(music, singing also)* erklingen *(geh).* **to** ~ **false/true** falsch/wahr klingen; **my ears are** ~**ing** mir klingen die Ohren.
3 *vt* **(a)** *bell* läuten. ~ **the doorbell** (an der Tür) klingeln; **his name** ~**s a bell** *(fig col)* sein Name kommt mir bekannt vor; **to** ~ **the changes (on sth)** *(fig)* etw in allen Variationen durchspielen. **(b)** *(esp Brit: also* ~ **up)** anrufen.
♦ **ring back** *vti sep (esp Brit)* zurückrufen.
♦ **ring off** *vi (esp Brit Telec)* auflegen.
♦ **ring out** *vi* ertönen; *(bell also)* laut erklingen; *(shot also)* krachen; *(sound above others)* herausklingen.
♦ **ring up** *vt sep (esp Brit Telec)* anrufen.
ring binder *n* Ringbuch *nt.*
ring-finger ['rɪŋˌfɪŋgəʳ] *n* Ringfinger *m.*
ringing ['rɪŋɪŋ] **1** *adj voice, tone* schallend. ~ **tone** *(Brit Telec)* Rufzeichen *nt.* **2** *n (of bell)* Läuten *nt; (of electric bell also, of phone)* Klingeln *nt; (in ears)* Klingen *nt.*
ringleader ['rɪŋˌliːdəʳ] *n* Anführer(in *f*) *m.*
ringlet ['rɪŋlɪt] *n* Ringellocke *f.*
ring: ~**master** *n* Zirkusdirektor *m;* ~ **road** *n (Brit)* Umgehung(sstraße) *f.*
rink [rɪŋk] *n* Eisbahn *f; (roller-skating* ~**)** Rollschuhbahn *f.*
rinse [rɪns] **1** *n* Spülung *f; (colorant)* Tönung *f.* **2** *vt* **(a)** *clothes, hair* spülen; *plates* abspülen; *cup, mouth, basin* ausspülen. **to** ~ **one's hands** sich *(dat)* die Hände abspülen. **(b)** *(colour with a* ~**)** *hair* tönen.
♦ **rinse out** *vt sep* ausspülen, auswaschen. **to** ~ ~ **one's mouth** sich *(dat)* den Mund ausspülen.
riot ['raɪət] **1** *n (Pol)* Aufstand, Aufruhr *m no pl; (by mob etc)* Krawall *m; (fig: wild occasion)* Orgie *f.* **to run** ~ *(people)* randalieren; *(vegetation)* wuchern; **his imagination runs** ~ seine Phantasie geht mit ihm durch; **to read sb the** ~ **act** *(fig)* jdm die Leviten lesen; **the** ~ **police** die Bereitschaftspolizei. **2** *vi* randalieren; *(revolt)* einen Aufruhr machen.
rioter ['raɪətəʳ] *n* Randalierer *m; (Pol)* Aufrührer *m.*
riotous ['raɪətəs] *adj* **(a)** *person, crowd* randalierend; *living, behaviour, child* wild. **(b)** *(col)* wild *(col); (hilarious)* urkomisch *(col).*
riotously ['raɪətəslɪ] *adv behave* wild. **it was** ~ **funny** *(col)* es war zum Schreien *(col).*
rip [rɪp] **1** *n* Riß *m; (made by knife etc)* Schlitz *m.* **2** *vt material* einen Riß machen in (+*acc*); *(stronger)* zerreißen; *(vandalize)* pictures etc zerschlitzen. **you've** ~**ped your jacket** du hast dir die Jacke zerrissen; **to** ~ **open** aufreißen; *(with knife)* aufschlitzen. **3** *vi* **(a)** *(cloth)* reißen. **(b)** *(col)* **he let** ~ **at me** er ist auf mich losgegangen *(col).*
♦ **rip off** *vt sep* **(a)** *(lit)* abreißen *(prep obj* von*); clothing* herunterreißen. **(b)** *(col) person* ausnehmen *(col).*
♦ **rip up** *vt sep* zerreißen; *road* aufreißen.
rip-cord ['rɪpˌkɔːd] *n* Reißleine *f.*
ripe [raɪp] *adj (+er) fruit, cheese* reif. **to live to a** ~ **old age** ein hohes Alter erreichen; **to be** ~ **for sth** *(fig)* für etw reif sein.
ripen ['raɪpən] **1** *vt (lit, fig)* reifen lassen. **2** *vi* reifen.

rip-off ['rɪpɒf] n (col) Wucher m; (cheat) Schwindel m. **it's a** ~ das ist Wucher/Schwindel.

riposte [rɪ'pɒst] n (retort) scharfe Antwort.

ripple ['rɪpl] 1 n kleine Welle; (noise) Plätschern nt; (of waves) Klatschen nt. 2 vi (undulate: water) sich kräuseln; (murmur: water) plätschern; (waves) klatschen. 3 vt water kräuseln.

rip-roaring ['rɪp'rɔːrɪŋ] adj (col) sagenhaft (col).

rise [raɪz] (vb: pret rose, ptp risen) 1 n (a) (increase) (in gen) Anstieg m, Steigen nt no pl; (in number) Zunahme f; (in prices, wages, bank rate also) Steigerung f; (St Ex) Aufschwung m. **a (pay)** ~ (Brit) eine Gehaltserhöhung; **a** ~ **in the population** ein Bevölkerungszuwachs m; **to take a** ~ **out of sb** (col) jdn auf den Arm nehmen (col).
(b) (theatre curtain) Heben nt; (of sun) Aufgehen nt; (to fame, power etc) Aufstieg m (to zu).
(c) (small hill) Erhebung f; (slope) Steigung f.
(d) (origin) (of river) Ursprung m. **to give** ~ **to sth** etw verursachen; **to questions** etw aufwerfen; **to complaints** Anlaß zu etw geben.
2 vi (a) (get up) (from sitting, lying) aufstehen, sich erheben (geh); (from the dead) auferstehen. **to** ~ **from the table** vom Tisch aufstehen.
(b) (go up) steigen; (smoke also) aufsteigen; (prices, temperature etc also) ansteigen (to auf +acc); (theatre curtain) sich heben; (sun, bread) aufgehen; (voice) (in volume) sich erheben; (in pitch) höher werden; (fig) (hopes) steigen; (anger) wachsen. **to** ~ **to the surface** an die Oberfläche kommen; **he won't** ~ **to any of your taunts** er läßt sich von dir nicht reizen; **to** ~ **in price** im Preis steigen; **her spirits rose** ihre Stimmung hob sich.
(c) (ground) ansteigen; (mountains) sich erheben. **the mountain** ~**s to 3,000 metres** der Berg erhebt sich auf 3.000 m.
(d) (fig: in society, rank) **to** ~ **from nothing** sich aus dem Nichts hocharbeiten; **he rose to be President** er stieg zum Präsidenten auf.
(e) (adjourn) (assembly) auseinandergehen; (meeting) beendet sein. **the House rose at 2 a.m.** (Parl) das Haus beendete die Sitzung um 2 Uhr morgens.
(f) (originate: river) entspringen.
(g) (also ~ **up**) (revolt: people) sich empören, sich erheben. **to** ~ **(up) in protest/anger (at sth)** (people) sich protestierend (gegen etw) erheben/ sich (gegen etw) empören. **to** ~ **(up) in revolt (against sth/sb)** (gegen jdn/etw) rebellieren.

risen ['rɪzn] ptp of **rise**.

riser ['raɪzə^r] n (person) **to be an early/late** ~ Frühaufsteher(in f)/Langschläfer(in f) m sein.

rising ['raɪzɪŋ] 1 n (a) (rebellion) Aufstand m. **(b)** (of sun) Aufgehen nt; (of barometer, prices) (An)steigen nt; (from dead) Auferstehung f. 2 adj **(a)** sun aufgehend; tide, barometer, prices, hopes steigend; anger, fury wachsend. ~ **damp** Bodenfeuchtigkeit f. **(b)** (fig) **a** ~ **politician** ein kommender Politiker; **the** ~ **generation** die kommende Generation.

risk [rɪsk] 1 n Risiko nt. **to take** or **run** ~**s/a** ~ Risiken/ein Risiko eingehen; **to take or run the** ~ **of doing sth** das Risiko eingehen, etw zu tun; **there is no** ~ **of his coming** or **that he will come** es besteht keine Gefahr, daß er kommt; **at one's own** ~ auf eigene Gefahr; **at the** ~ **of seeming stupid** auf die Gefahr hin, dumm zu erscheinen; **to put sb/sth at** ~ jdn gefährden/etw riskieren; **fire** ~ Feuerrisiko. 2 vt riskieren, aufs Spiel setzen; life also wagen; defeat, accident riskieren. **she won't** ~ **coming today** sie wird es heute nicht riskieren, zu kommen; **I'll** ~ **it** das riskiere ich, ich lasse es darauf ankommen.

risky ['rɪskɪ] adj (+er) enterprise, deed riskant. **it's a** ~ **business** das ist riskant.

risqué ['riːskeɪ] adj pikant, gewagt.

rissole ['rɪsəʊl] n = Frikadelle f.

rite [raɪt] n Ritus m. **burial** ~**s** Bestattungsriten pl.

ritual ['rɪtjʊəl] 1 adj rituell; laws, objects, killing Ritual-. 2 n Ritual nt.

rival ['raɪvəl] 1 n Rivale m, Rivalin f (for um, to für); (Comm) Konkurrent(in f) m. 2 adj (to für) claims, attraction konkurrierend; firm Konkurrenz-. 3 vt (in love, for affections) rivalisieren mit; (Comm) konkurrieren mit. **I can't** ~ **that** da kann ich nicht mithalten.

rivalry ['raɪvəlrɪ] n Rivalität f; (Comm) Konkurrenzkampf m.

river ['rɪvə^r] n Fluß m; (major) Strom m. **down/up** ~ flußabwärts/-aufwärts; **the** ~ **Rhine** (Brit), **the Rhine** ~ (US) der Rhein.

river in cpds Fluß-; ~**bed** n Flußbett nt; ~**side** n Flußufer nt; **by the** ~**side** am Fluß.

rivet ['rɪvɪt] 1 n Niete f. 2 vt (lit) nieten; two things vernieten; (fig) audience, attention fesseln. **his eyes were** ~**ed to the screen** sein Blick war auf den Bildschirm geheftet; ~**ed (to the spot) with fear** vor Angst wie festgenagelt.

rivet(t)ing ['rɪvɪtɪŋ] adj (fig) fesselnd.

RN = Royal Navy.

road [rəʊd] n (a) Straße f. "~ **up**" „Straßenbauarbeiten"; **by** ~ (send sth) per Spedition; (travel) mit dem Bus/Auto etc; **she lives across the** ~ (from us) sie wohnt gegenüber (von uns); **my car is off the** ~ just now mein Auto ist momentan in der Werkstatt; **this vehicle shouldn't be on the** ~ das Fahrzeug ist nicht verkehrstüchtig; **to be on the** ~ (travelling) unterwegs sein; (theatre company) auf Tournee sein; (car) fahren; **is this the** ~ **to London?** geht es hier nach London?; **the London** ~ die Straße nach London; **to have one for the** ~ (col) zum Abschluß noch einen trinken. **(b)** (fig) Weg m. **you're on the right** ~ Sie sind auf dem richtigen Weg; **on the** ~ **to success** auf dem Weg zum Erfolg; **somewhere along the** ~ **he changed his mind** irgendwann hat er seine Meinung geändert; **(get) out of the** ~**!** (dial col) geh weg!; **any** ~ (dial col) = anyhow.

road in cpds Straßen-; ~**block** n Straßensperre f; ~ **haulage** n Spedition f; ~**hog** n (col) Verkehrsrowdy m (col); ~**holding** n Straßenlage f; (of tyres) Griffigkeit f; ~**roller** n Straßenwalze f; ~ **safety** n Verkehrssicherheit f; ~ **sense** n Verkehrssinn m; ~**side** 1 n Straßenrand m; **by the** ~**side** am Straßenrand; 2 adj stall an der Straße; ~**sign** n Verkehrszeichen nt; ~**sweeper** n Straßenkehrer(in f) m; ~ **transport** n Straßengüterverkehr m; ~-**user** n Verkehrsteilnehmer m; ~**way** n Fahrbahn f; ~**works** npl Straßenbauarbeiten pl; ~**worthy** adj verkehrstüchtig.

roam [rəʊm] 1 vt streets, countryside wandern or ziehen durch. 2 vi (herum)wandern.

roar [rɔː^r] 1 vi (person, crowd, lion) brüllen (with vor +dat); (fire) prasseln; (wind, engine) heulen; (sea) tosen; (thunder) tosen. **to** ~ **at sb** jdn anbrüllen; **the trucks** ~**ed past** die Lastwagen donnerten vorbei; **they** ~**ed with laughter** sie brüllten vor Lachen. 2 n (a) no pl see vi Gebrüll nt; Prasseln nt; Heulen nt; Tosen nt; Toben nt. ~**s of laughter** brüllendes Gelächter.

roaring ['rɔːrɪŋ] adj see vi brüllend; prasselnd; heulend; tosend; tobend. **the** ~ **Twenties** die wilden zwanziger Jahre; **a** ~ **success** ein Bombenerfolg m (col); **to do a** ~ **trade (in sth)** ein Riesengeschäft nt (mit etw) machen.

roast [rəʊst] 1 n Braten m. **pork** ~ Schweinebraten m. 2 adj pork, veal gebraten; chicken Brat-, gebraten; potatoes in Fett im Backofen gebraten. ~ **beef** Roastbeef nt. 3 vt meat braten; coffee beans rösten. **to be** ~ **ed alive** (fig) sich totschwitzen (col). 4 vi (meat) braten; (col: person) irrsinnig schwitzen (col); (in sun) in der Sonne braten.

rob [rɒb] vt person bestehlen; (more seriously) berauben; shop, bank ausrauben. **to** ~ **sb of sth** (lit fig) jdm etw rauben; (lit also) jdm etw stehlen;

I've been ~**bed!** ich bin bestohlen worden!; *(had to pay too much)* ich bin geneppt worden *(col)*.

robber ['rɒbə^r] *n* Räuber *m*.

robbery ['rɒbərɪ] *n* Raub *m no pl; (burglary)* Einbruch *m (of in +acc).* ~ **with violence** *(Jur)* Raubüberfall *m*.

robe [rəʊb] *n (of office)* Robe *f; (esp US: for house wear)* Morgenrock, Bademantel *m*.

robin ['rɒbɪn] *n* Rotkehlchen *nt*.

robot ['rəʊbɒt] *n* Roboter *m; (fig also)* Automat *m*.

robust [rəʊ'bʌst] *adj* robust; *build also* kräftig; *structure* stabil.

rock[1] [rɒk] **1** *vt* **(a)** *(swing)* schaukeln; *(gently: lull)* wiegen. **(b)** *(shake) town* erschüttern; *ship* hin und her werfen; *(fig col) person* erschüttern. **to** ~ **the boat** *(fig)* für Unruhe sorgen. **2** *vi* schaukeln; *(building, tree)* schwanken; *(ship)* hin und her geworfen werden; *(ground)* beben. **3** *n (Mus)* Rock *m; (dance)* Rock 'n' Roll *m*.

rock[2] *n* **(a)** *(substance)* Stein *m; (~ face)* Fels(en) *m; (Geol)* Gestein *nt*. **(b)** *(large mass)* Fels(en) *m; (boulder also)* Felsbrocken *m; (smaller)* (großer) Stein. **as solid as a** ~ *(structure)* massiv wie ein Fels; *(marriage)* sehr beständig *or* stabil; **on the** ~**s** *(col) (with ice)* mit Eis; *(ruined: marriage etc)* kaputt *(col)*.

rock: ~-**bottom** *n* der Tiefpunkt; **to touch/reach** ~-**bottom** den Tiefpunkt erreichen; ~-**climber** *n* (Felsen)kletterer(in *f*) *m;* ~ **climbing** *n* Klettern *nt* (im Fels).

rocker ['rɒkə^r] *n* **to be/go off one's** ~ *(col)* übergeschnappt sein *(col)*/überschnappen *(col)*.

rockery ['rɒkərɪ] *n* Steingarten *m*.

rocket ['rɒkɪt] **1** *n* **(a)** Rakete *f.* **(b)** *(Brit col: reprimand)* **to give sb a** ~ jdm eine Zigarre verpassen *(col)*. **2** *vi (prices)* hochschießen. **to** ~ **to fame** über Nacht berühmt werden.

rocket *in cpds* Raketen-; ~ **launcher** *n* Raketenabschußgerät *nt*.

rock face *n* Felswand *f*.

rocking ['rɒkɪŋ]: ~ **chair** *n* Schaukelstuhl *m;* ~ **horse** *n* Schaukelpferd *nt*.

rock: ~ **plant** *n* Steinpflanze *f;* ~ **salt** *n* Steinsalz *nt*.

rocky *adj (+er) hill* felsig; *road* steinig. **the R~ Mountains** die Rocky Mountains *pl*.

rococo [rəʊ'kəʊkəʊ] **1** *n* Rokoko *nt*. **2** *adj* Rokoko-.

rod [rɒd] *n* Stab *m*, Stange *f; (in machinery)* Stange *f; (for punishment, fishing)* Rute *f*.

rode [rəʊd] *pret of* **ride**.

rodent ['rəʊdənt] *n* Nagetier *nt*.

rodeo ['rəʊdɪəʊ] *n* Rodeo *nt*.

roe[1] [rəʊ] *n, pl* -**(s)** *(species: also* ~ **deer)** Reh *nt.* ~ **buck** Rehbock *m*.

roe[2] *n, pl* - *(of fish)* Rogen *m.* **hard** ~ Rogen *m;* **soft** ~ Milch *f*.

rogue [rəʊg] *n* Schurke *m; (scamp)* Schlingel *m.* ~**s' gallery** *(Police col)* Verbrecheralbum *nt;* ~ **elephant** Einzelgängerelefant *m*.

roguish ['rəʊgɪʃ] *adj* spitzbübisch.

role [rəʊl] *n (Theat, fig)* Rolle *f.* ~-**playing** Rollenspiel *nt;* ~ **reversal** Rollentausch *m*.

roll [rəʊl] **1** *n* **(a)** *(of paper, wire etc)* Rolle *f; (of fabric)* Ballen *m; (of banknotes)* Bündel *nt; (of butter, flesh, fat)* Röllchen *nt.* **a** ~ **of paper** eine Rolle Papier. **(b)** *(Cook)* Brötchen *nt.* **ham/cheese** ~ Schinken-/Käsebrötchen *nt.* **(c)** *(movement, of sea)* Rollen *nt; (of ship also)* Schlingern *nt; (of person's gait)* Wiegen *nt.* **(d)** *(sound) (of thunder)* Rollen *nt; (of drums)* Wirbel *m.* **(e)** *(list, register)* Liste *f,* Register *nt.* **we have 60 pupils on our** ~**(s)** bei uns sind 60 Schüler angemeldet; **to call the** ~ die Namensliste verlesen, die Namen aufrufen; ~ **of honour** *(Brit) or* **honor** *(US)* Ehrenliste *f; (plaque)* Ehrentafel *f*.

2 *vi (a)* rollen; *(ship)* schlingern; *(presses)* laufen; *(Aviat)* eine Rolle machen. **the stones** ~**ed down the hill** die Steine rollten den Berg

hinunter; **tears were** ~**ing down her cheeks** Tränen rollten ihr über die Wangen; **heads will** ~! *(fig)* da werden Köpfe rollen!; **he's** ~**ing in money** *or* **in it** *(col)* er schwimmt im Geld *(col)*. **(b)** *(thunder)* grollen; *(drum)* wirbeln.

3 *vt* rollen; *cigarette* drehen; *pastry* ausrollen; *metal, lawn* walzen. **to** ~ **one's eyes** die Augen rollen; **to** ~ **one's r's** das R rollen; **the hedgehog** ~**ed itself into a ball** der Igel rollte sich zu einer Kugel zusammen.

♦ **roll about** *vi (balls)* herumrollen *or* -kugeln *(col); (ship)* schlingern; *(person, dog)* sich wälzen; *(col: with laughter)* sich kugeln (vor Lachen) *(col)*.

♦ **roll away 1** *vi (ball, vehicle)* wegrollen; *(clouds)* abziehen. **2** *vt sep trolley* wegrollen.

♦ **roll back** *vt sep* zurückrollen.

♦ **roll by** *vi (vehicle, procession)* vorbeirollen; *(clouds)* vorbeiziehen; *(time, years)* dahinziehen.

♦ **roll in** *vi* herein-/hineinrollen; *(letters, money)* hereinströmen; *(col: person)* eintrudeln *(col)*.

♦ **roll on** *vi* weiterrollen; *(time)* verfliegen. ~ **the holidays!** wenn doch nur schon Ferien wären!

♦ **roll out** *vt sep barrel* hinaus-/herausrollen; *pastry, dough* ausrollen; *metal* auswalzen.

♦ **roll over 1** *vi (vehicle)* umkippen; *(person)* sich umdrehen. **the dog** ~**ed** ~ **onto his back** der Hund rollte auf den Rücken. **2** *vt sep person, animal, object* umdrehen.

♦ **roll up 1** *vi* **(a)** *(animal)* sich zusammenrollen *(into zu).* **(b)** *(col: arrive)* auftauchen. **2** *vt sep* auf- *or* zusammenrollen; *sleeves* hochkrempeln.

roller ['rəʊlə^r] *n* **(a)** Rolle *f; (pastry* ~**)** Teigrolle *f; (for lawn, road)* Walze *f; (paint* ~**)** Rolle *f.* **(b)** *(hair* ~**)** (Locken)wickler *m.* **with her** ~**s in** mit Lockenwicklern (im Haar). **(c)** *(wave)* Brecher *m*.

roller: ~ **blind** *n* Rollo *nt;* ~ **coaster** *n* Achterbahn *f;* ~ **skate** *n* Rollschuh *m;* ~-**skating** *nt* Rollschuhlaufen *nt*.

rolling ['rəʊlɪŋ] *adj sea* wogend; *waves* rollend; *countryside* wellig. **a** ~ **stone gathers no moss** *(Prov)* ≈ wer rastet, der rostet *(Prov)*.

rolling: ~ **mill** *n (factory)* Walzwerk *nt; (machine)* Walze *f;* ~ **pin** *n* Teigrolle *f;* ~ **stock** *n (Rail)* rollendes Material.

Roman ['rəʊmən] **1** *n (Hist)* Römer(in *f*) *m.* **2** *adj* römisch. ~ **numeral** römische Ziffer.

Roman Catholic 1 *adj* (römisch-)katholisch. **2** *n* Katholik(in *f*) *m,* (Römisch-)Katholische(r) *mf*.

romance [rəʊ'mæns] **1** *n* **(a)** *(book)* Roman *m; (love-story)* Liebesroman *m.* **(b)** *(Mus, love affair)* Romanze *f.* **(c)** *no pl (romanticism)* Romantik *f.* **2** *adj* **R~** *language etc* romanisch.

Romanesque [,rəʊmə'nesk] *adj* romanisch.

Romania [ruː'meɪnɪə] *n* Rumänien *nt*.

romantic [rəʊ'mæntɪk] **1** *adj (Art etc: also* **R~)** romantisch; *person also* romantisch veranlagt. ~ **novel** Liebesroman *m.* **2** *n (Art etc: also* **R~)** Romantiker(in *f*) *m*.

romanticism [rəʊ'mæntɪsɪzəm] *n (Art, Liter, Mus: also* **R~)** Romantik *f*.

romanticize [rəʊ'mæntɪsaɪz] *vt* romantisieren.

Romany ['rəʊmənɪ] **1** *n* **(a)** Zigeuner(in *f*) *m,* Roma *mf.* **(b)** *(language)* die Zigeunersprache, Romani *nt.* **2** *adj* Zigeuner-.

Rome [rəʊm] *n* Rom *nt.* **when in** ~ **do as the Romans do** *(prov)* ≈ andere Länder, andere Sitten *(Prov)*.

romp [rɒmp] *n* Tollerei *f.* **to have a** ~ herumtollen *or* -toben. **2** *vi (children, puppies)* herumtollen *or* -toben. **to** ~ **home** *(fig: win)* spielend gewinnen; **to** ~ **through sth** *(fig) exam* mit etw spielend fertig werden.

roof [ruːf] **1** *n* Dach *nt; (of car also)* Verdeck *nt; (of cave)* Gewölbe *nt.* **the** ~ **of the mouth** der Gaumen; **without a** ~ **over one's head** ohne Dach über dem Kopf; **a room in the** ~ ein Zimmer unter dem Dach; **to go through the** ~ *(col)* *(person)* an die Decke gehen *(col)*; *(prices etc)* in die Höhe schießen. **2** *vt house* mit einem Dach decken. **red-**~**ed** mit rotem Dach.

roof: ~**-rack** *n* Dachgepäckträger *m*; ~**-top** *n* Dach *nt*; **to shout sth from the** ~**-tops** *(fig)* etw überall herumposaunen *(col)*.

rook [rʊk] **1** *n (bird)* Saatkrähe *f*; *(Chess)* Turm *m*. **2** *vt (swindle)* übers Ohr hauen *(col)*, betrügen.

room [ruːm] **1** *n* **(a)** Zimmer *nt*, Raum *m*; *(public hall, ball* ~ *etc)* Saal *m*; *(office)* Büro *nt*. **the whole** ~ **laughed** der ganze Saal lachte; **they used to live in** ~**s** sie haben früher in möblierten Zimmern gewohnt. **(b)** *no pl (space)* Platz *m*; *(fig)* Spielraum *m*. **is there (enough)** ~? ist da genügend Platz?; **there is no** ~ **(for you)** es ist nicht genug Platz (für dich); **to make** ~ **for sb/ sth** für jdn/etw Platz machen; **there is no** ~ **for doubt** es kann keinen Zweifel geben; **there is** ~ **for improvement in your work** Ihre Arbeit könnte um einiges besser sein. **2** *vi* zur Untermiete wohnen. ~**ing house** *(esp US)* Mietshaus *nt (mit möblierten Wohnungen)*.

room: ~**mate** *n* Zimmergenosse *m*, Zimmergenossin *f*; ~ **service** *n* Zimmerservice *m*; ~ **temperature** *n* Zimmertemperatur *f*; **wine at** ~ **temperature** Wein mit Zimmertemperatur.

roomy [ˈruːmɪ] *adj (+er)* geräumig; *garment* weit.

roost [ruːst] **1** *n (pole)* Stange *f*; *(henhouse)* Hühnerstall *m*. **to come home to** ~ *(fig)* auf den Urheber zurückfallen. **2** *vi (bird)* sich niederlassen.

rooster [ˈruːstəʳ] *n* Hahn *m*.

root [ruːt] **1** *n* Wurzel *f*. ~**s** *(fig: of person)* Wurzeln; **by the** ~**s** mit der Wurzel; **to take** ~ *(lit, fig)* Wurzeln schlagen; **the** ~ **of the matter** der Kern der Sache; **to get to the** ~**(s) of the problem** dem Problem auf den Grund gehen. **2** *vt plant* Wurzeln schlagen lassen bei. **deeply** ~**ed** *(fig)* tief verwurzelt; **to be** *or* **stand** ~**ed to the spot** *(fig)* wie angewurzelt dastehen. **3** *vi (plants etc)* Wurzeln schlagen.

♦ **root out** *vt sep* **(a)** *(lit)* *plant* herausreißen; *(dig up)* ausgraben. **(b)** *(fig)* *evil* mit der Wurzel ausreißen; *(find)* aufspüren, ausgraben *(col)*.

rope [rəʊp] **1** *n* Seil *nt*; *(Naut)* Tau *nt*; *(of bell)* Glockenstrang *m*. **to give sb more** ~ *(fig)* jdm mehr Freiheit lassen; **to know the** ~**s** *(col)* sich auskennen; **to show sb the** ~**s** *(col)* jdn in alles einweihen. **2** *vt box, case* verschnüren.

♦ **rope in** *vt sep (fig)* rankriegen *(col)*. **how did you get** ~**d** **to that?** wie bist du denn da reingeraten? *(col)*.

♦ **rope off** *vt sep area* mit einem Seil abgrenzen.

♦ **rope up** *vi (climber)* sich anseilen.

rope *in cpds* Seil-; ~ **ladder** *n* Strickleiter *f*.

ropy [ˈrəʊpɪ] *adj (+er)* *col) (bad)* miserabel *(col)*; *(worn)* mitgenommen.

rosary [ˈrəʊzərɪ] *n (Rel)* Rosenkranz *m*.

rose[1] [rəʊz] *pret of* **rise.**

rose[2] **1** *n* **(a)** Rose *f*. ~**-bush/-tree** Rosenbusch *m/*-bäumchen *nt*; **my life isn't all** ~**s** *(col)* ich bin auch nicht auf Rosen gebettet. **(b)** *(nozzle)* Brause *f*. **(c)** *(colour)* Rosarot *nt*. **2** *adj* rosarot.

rose *in cpds* Rosen-; ~**-coloured**, *(US)* ~**-colored** *adj* rosarot; **to see life through** ~**-coloured spectacles** das Leben durch die rosarote Brille sehen; ~**hip** *n* Hagebutte *f*.

rosemary [ˈrəʊzmərɪ] *n* Rosmarin *m*.

rosette [rəʊˈzet] *n* Rosette *f*.

roster [ˈrɒstəʳ] *n* Dienstplan *m*.

rostrum [ˈrɒstrəm] *n,* *pl* **rostra** [ˈrɒstrə] Rednerpult *nt*; *(for conductor)* Dirigentenpult *nt*.

rosy [ˈrəʊzɪ] *adj (+er)* *(pink)* rosarot; *cheeks, future* rosig. **to paint a** ~ **picture of sth** etw in den rosigsten Farben ausmalen.

rot [rɒt] **1** *n* **(a)** Fäulnis *f no pl; (in wood also)* Moder *m no pl.* **we must stop the** ~ *(fig)* wir müssen energisch durchgreifen; **then the** ~ **set in** *(fig)*

dann setzte der Verfall ein. **(b)** *(col: rubbish)* Blödsinn *m (col)*. **2** *vi (wood, material, rope)* verrotten, faulen; *(teeth, plant)* verfaulen; *(fig)* verrotten.

rota [ˈrəʊtə] *n* Dienstplan *m*.

rotary [ˈrəʊtərɪ] **1** *adj motion* rotierend, Dreh-. **2** *n (US)* Kreisverkehr *m*.

rotate [rəʊˈteɪt] **1** *vt* **(a)** *(around axis)* drehen, rotieren lassen. **(b)** *crops* im Wechsel anbauen; *work* turnusmäßig erledigen. **2** *vi* **(a)** sich drehen; *(Math)* rotieren. **(b)** *(crops)* im Wechsel angebaut werden; *(people: take turns)* sich abwechseln.

rotation [rəʊˈteɪʃən] *n* **(a)** *no pl* Drehung, Rotation *f*; *(of crops)* Wechsel *m*; *(taking turns)* turnusmäßiger Wechsel. **in** ~ abwechselnd im Turnus. **(b)** *(turn)* (Um)drehung *f*.

rote [rəʊt] *n:* **by** ~ *learn* auswendig; *recite* mechanisch.

rotor [ˈrəʊtəʳ] *n (Aviat, Elec, Aut)* Rotor *m*.

rotten [ˈrɒtn] *adj* **(a)** faul; *wood also* morsch; *fruit also* verdorben; *(fig: corrupt)* korrupt, verdorben. **(b)** *(col) (bad)* scheußlich *(col)*; *weather, book, film, piece of work also* mies *(col)*; *(mean)* gemein; *(unwell)* elend, mies *(col)*. **what** ~ **luck!** so ein Pech!; **it's a** ~ **business** das ist eine üble Sache.

rotund [rəʊˈtʌnd] *adj person* rund(lich).

rouble, *(US)* **ruble** [ˈruːbl] *n* Rubel *m*.

rouge [ruːʒ] *n* Rouge *nt*.

rough [rʌf] **1** *adj (+er)* **(a)** *(uneven)* ground uneben; *surface, skin, hands* rauh. **(b)** *(coarse, unrefined)* person ungehobelt; *manners also, speech* grob, roh; *taste* sauer. **(c)** *(harsh, unpleasant)* person grob, roh; *treatment, words* grob, hart; *life* wüst; *sport, work, sound* hart; *neighbourhood, manners, voice, weather* rauh; *sea crossing* stürmisch. **to be** ~ **with sb** grob mit jdm umgehen; **to feel** ~ sich mies fühlen; **he had a** ~ **time (of it)** *(fig col)* es ging ihm ziemlich dreckig *(col)*; **to make things** ~ **for sb** *(col)* jdm Schwierigkeiten machen; **it's** ~ **on him** *(Brit col)* das ist hart für ihn. **(d)** *(approximate)* plan, calculation, estimate grob, ungefähr; *justice* grob. ~ **copy** Konzept *nt*; ~ **sketch** Faustskizze *f*; ~ **paper** Konzeptpapier *nt*.

2 *adv live* wüst; *play* wild. **to sleep** ~ im Freien übernachten.

3 *n* **(a)** unwegsames Gelände; *(Golf)* Rauh *nt*. **(b)** *(unpleasant aspect)* **to take the** ~ **with the smooth** das Leben nehmen, wie es kommt.

4 *vt* **to** ~ **it** *(col)* primitiv leben.

♦ **rough out** *vt sep* plan, drawing grob entwerfen.

roughage [ˈrʌfɪdʒ] *n* Ballaststoffe *pl*.

rough: ~**-and-ready** *adj* method, equipment provisorisch; *work* zusammengehauen *(col)*; *person* rauh(beinig); ~**-and-tumble** *n (play)* Balgerei *f; (fighting)* Keilerei *f*; ~ **diamond** *n* he's a ~ **diamond** er ist rauh aber herzlich.

roughen [ˈrʌfn] *vt* ground uneben machen; *skin, cloth* rauh machen; *surface* aufrauhen.

roughly [ˈrʌflɪ] *adv* **(a)** grob; *play* rauh; *answer, order also* hart. **(b)** *(approximately)* ungefähr. ~ **(speaking)** grob gesagt.

roughness [ˈrʌfnɪs] *n see adj* **(a)** Unebenheit *f*; Rauheit *f*. **(b)** Ungehobeltheit *f*; Grobheit, Roheit *f*; saurer Geschmack. **(c)** Grobheit, Roheit *f*; Härte *f*; Rauheit *f*.

rough: ~ **note book** *n (Sch)* Schmierheft *nt*; ~**shod** *adv:* **to ride** ~**shod over sb** rücksichtslos über jdn hinweggehen.

roulette [ruːˈlet] *n* Roulette(e) *nt*.

round [raʊnd] **1** *adj (+er)* rund. ~ **number** runde Zahl; **in** ~ **figures, that will cost 20 million** es kostet rund *or* runde 20 Millionen.

2 *adv (esp Brit)* **the long way** ~ der Umweg, der längere Weg; ~ **and** ~ rundherum; **I asked**

him ~ **for a drink** ich lud ihn auf ein Glas Wein/ Bier *etc* bei mir ein; **I'll be** ~ **at 8 o'clock** ich werde um 8 Uhr da sein; **for the second time** ~ zum zweitenmal; **all (the) year** ~ das ganze Jahr über; **all** ~ *(lit)* ringsherum; *(fig:for everyone)* für alle; **drinks all** ~! eine Runde!
3 *prep (esp Brit)* **(a)** *(of place etc)* um (... herum). ~ **the table** um den Tisch (herum); **all** ~ **the house** *(inside)* im ganzen Haus; *(outside)* um das ganze Haus herum; **to go** ~ **a corner** um eine Ecke gehen/fahren *etc;* **to look** ~ **a house** sich *(dat)* ein Haus ansehen; **to show sb** ~ **a town** jdn in einer Stadt herumführen. **(b)** *(approximately)* ~ **(about)** 7 o'clock ungefähr um 7 Uhr; ~ **(about)** £800 um die £ 800.
4 *n* **(a)** *(slice: of bread, meat)* Scheibe *f.* **a** ~ **of toast** eine Scheibe Toast. **(b)** *(delivery* ~, *Sport, of election, talks)* Runde *f.* ~ *(of policeman, doctor)* Runde *f;* **to do one's** ~**(s)** seine Runde machen; *(doctor also)* Hausbesuche machen; **he does a paper** ~ er trägt Zeitungen aus; **the daily** ~ *(fig)* die tägliche Arbeit, der tägliche Trott *(pej);* **to go the** ~**s** *(story etc)* reihum gehen; **a** ~ *(of drinks)* eine Runde; **a new** ~ **of negotiations** eine neue Verhandlungsrunde; ~ **of ammunition** Ladung *f;* **a** ~ **of applause** ein Applaus *m.*
5 *vt* **(a)** *(make* ~*)* runden. **(b)** *(go* ~*)* **bend** gehen/fahren um; *obstacle* herumgehen/-fahren *etc* um.
♦ **round off** *vt sep* **(a)** *edges etc* abrunden. **(b)** *list, series* voll machen; *speech, meal* abrunden; *debate, meeting* abschließen.
♦ **round on** *vi* +*prep obj (verbally)* anfahren; *(in actions)* losgehen auf (+*acc*).
♦ **round up** *vt sep* **(a)** *people* zusammentrommeln *(col); cattle* zusammentreiben; *criminals* hochnehmen *(col).* **(b)** *price, number* aufrunden.
roundabout ['raʊndəbaʊt] **1** *adj* ~ **route** Umweg *m;* **we came a** ~ **way** wir haben einen Umweg gemacht; **I found out in a** ~ **way** ich habe es auf Umwegen herausgefunden. **2** *n (Brit) (merry-go-round)* Karussell *nt;* *(Mot)* Kreisverkehr *m.*
roundly ['raʊndlɪ] *adv (bluntly)* ohne Umschweife.
round: ~**-necked** ['raʊnd'nekt] *adj* mit rundem Ausschnitt; ~**-shouldered** ['raʊnd'ʃəʊldəd] *adj* mit rundem Schultern; ~**-the-clock** *adj* rund um die Uhr *not adj;* ~ **trip** *n* Rundreise *f;* ~**-trip ticket** *n (US)* Rückfahrkarte *f; (Aviat)* Hin- und Rückflug-Ticket *nt;* ~**-up** *n (of cattle)* Zusammentreiben *nt; (of criminals)* Hochnehmen *nt (col);* **a** ~**-up of today's news** eine Zusammenfassung der Nachrichten vom Tage.
rouse [raʊz] *vt* **(a)** *(from sleep)* wecken. **(b)** *(stimulate) person* bewegen; *feeling* wachrufen; *hatred, suspicions* erregen. **to** ~ **sb (to anger)** jdn reizen; **to** ~ **sb to action** jdn zum Handeln bewegen; **to** ~ **the masses** die Massen aufrütteln.
rousing ['raʊzɪŋ] *adj speech* zündend, mitreißend; *applause* stürmisch; *music* schwungvoll.
rout¹ [raʊt] **1** *n (defeating)* Sieg *m (of* über +*acc); (being defeated)* Niederlage *f.* **2** *vt (defeat)* in die Flucht schlagen.
rout² *vi (pig: also* ~ *about)* herumwühlen.
♦ **rout out** *vt sep (find)* aufstöbern; *(force out)* (heraus)jagen *(of aus).*
route [ruːt], *(US)* [raʊt] **1** *n* Strecke, Route *f; (bus service)* Linie *f.* **shipping/air** ~**s** Schiffahrtsstraßen *or* -wege/Flugwege; **we live on a bus** ~ wir wohnen an einer Buslinie; **the** ~ **to the coast** der Weg zur Küste. **2** *vt train, coach, bus* legen. **my luggage was** ~**d through Amsterdam** mein Gepäck wurde über Amsterdam geschickt.
routine [ruː'tiːn] **1** *n* **(a)** Routine *f.* **(b)** *(Dancing)* Figur *f; (Gymnastics)* Übung *f.* **2** *adj* Routine-, routinemäßig. ~ **duties** tägliche Pflichten *pl;* **to be** ~ *procedure* Routine(sache) sein.
roving ['rəʊvɪŋ] *adj* **he has a** ~ **eye** er riskiert gern

ein Auge; ~ **ambassador** Botschafter *m* für mehrere Vertretungen.
row¹ [rəʊ] *n* Reihe *f.* **4 failures in a** ~ 4 Mißerfolge hinter- *or* nacheinander; **arrange them in** ~**s** stell sie in Reihen auf.
row² [rəʊ] **1** *vti (in boat)* rudern. **to** ~ **sb across** jdn hinüber-/herüberrudern. ~**ing boat** *(Brit)* Ruderboot *nt.* **2** *n* **to go for a** ~ rudern gehen.
row³ [raʊ] **1** *n* **(a)** *(noise)* Lärm, Krach *(col) m.* **to make a** *or* **kick up** *(col)* **a** ~ Krach schlagen *(col).* **(b)** *(quarrel)* Streit, Krach *(col) m.* **to have a** ~ **with sb** mit jdm Streit *or* Krach *(col)* haben. **2** *vi (quarrel)* (sich) streiten.
rowan ['raʊən] *n (tree)* Eberesche, Vogelbeere *f.*
rowboat ['rəʊˌbəʊt] *n (US)* Ruderboot *nt.*
rowdy ['raʊdɪ] **1** *adj (+er) (noisy)* laut; *football fans* randalierend. **2** *n* Krawallmacher *m.* **football rowdies** Fußballrowdys *pl.*
rower ['rəʊə'] *n* Ruderer *m.*
rowing¹ ['rəʊɪŋ] *n* Rudern *nt.*
rowing² ['raʊɪŋ] *n (quarrelling)* Streiterei *f.*
royal ['rɔɪəl] *adj* königlich; *family, palace also* Königs-; *(fig also)* fürstlich.
royal: **R**~ **Air Force** *n (Brit)* Königliche Luftwaffe; ~ **blue 1** *adj* königsblau; **2** *n* Königsblau *nt.*
royalist ['rɔɪəlɪst] **1** *adj* royalistisch. **2** *n* Royalist(in *f*) *m.*
Royal Navy *(Brit)* **1** *n* Königliche Marine. **2** *attr* der Königlichen Marine.
royalty ['rɔɪəltɪ] *n* **(a)** *(rank)* das Königtum; *(collectively)* das Königshaus. **(b)** **royalties** *pl (from book, records)* Tantiemen *pl (on* auf +*acc).*
rpm = **revolutions per minute** U/min.
RSPCA = **Royal Society for the Prevention of Cruelty to Animals** ≈ Tierschutzverein *m.*
RSVP = **répondez s'il vous plaît** u.A.w.g.
Rt Hon = **Right Honourable.**
rub [rʌb] **1** *n* **(a) to give sth a** ~ etw reiben; *furniture, shoes, silver etc* polieren. **(b)** *(fig)* **there's the** ~! *(old, hum)* da liegt der Hase im Pfeffer. **2** *vt* reiben; *(with towel also)* frottieren; *(polish)* polieren. **to** ~ **one's hands (together)** sich *(dat)* die Hände reiben; **to** ~ **sth dry** etw trockenreiben; **to** ~ **shoulders with all sorts of people** *(fig)* mit allen möglichen Leuten in Berührung kommen. **3** *vi (thing) (against* an +*dat)* reiben; *(shoes, collar)* scheuern. **you must have** ~**bed against some wet paint** da mußt du an ein feuchte Farbe gekommen sein.
♦ **rub down** *vt sep horse (dry)* abreiben; *(clean)* striegeln; *person* abrubbeln *(col); wall, paint (clean)* abwaschen; *(sandpaper)* abschmirgeln.
♦ **rub in** *vt sep* **(a)** *lotion* einreiben *(to* in +*acc).* **(b)** *(fig)* herumreiten auf (+*dat*). **don't** ~ **it** ~ mußt du auch noch Salz in die Wunde streuen?
♦ **rub off 1** *vt sep dirt etc* abreiben; *tape* löschen; *(from blackboard)* auswischen. **2** *vi (of dirt, fig)* abgehen. **to** ~ ~ **on sb** *(fig)* auf jdn abfärben.
♦ **rub out 1** *vt sep stain etc* herausreiben; *(with eraser)* ausradieren. **2** *vi* herausgehen; *(with eraser)* sich ausradieren lassen.
♦ **rub up** *vt sep* **(a)** *table* blank reiben, (auf)polieren. **(b)** **to** ~ ~ **sb the wrong way** jdn anfreizen.
rubber¹ ['rʌbə'] **1** *n (material)* Gummi *m; (Brit: eraser)* (Radier)gummi *m.* **2** *adj* Gummi-.
rubber² *n (Cards)* Rubber, Robber *m.*
rubber: ~ **band** *n* Gummiband *nt;* ~ **stamp** *n* Stempel *m;* ~**-stamp** *vt (lit)* stempeln; *(fig col)* genehmigen.
rubbery ['rʌbərɪ] *adj material* gummiartig; *meat* zäh, wie Gummi *pred.*
rubbish ['rʌbɪʃ] *n* **(a)** Abfall *m,* Abfälle *pl; (household* ~, *in factory also)* Müll *m; (on building site)* Schutt *m; (trashy goods, record etc)* Mist *m; (nonsense)* Quatsch *(col),* Blödsinn *m.* **don't talk** ~! red keinen Quatsch! *(col);* ~! *(so ein)* Quatsch!

rubbish in cpds (esp Brit) Müll-; ~ **bin** n
Mülleimer m; ~ **cart** n Müllwagen m; ~ **chute** n
Müllschlucker m; ~ **collection** n Müllabfuhr f; ~
dump n Müllkippe f; (in garden: also ~ **heap**)
Abfallhaufen m; ~ **tip** n Müllkippe f.

rubbishy ['rʌbɪʃɪ] adj (col) goods wertlos.

rubble ['rʌbl] n Trümmer pl; (smaller pieces)
Schutt m.

ruby ['ruːbɪ] **1** n (stone) Rubin m; (colour: also ~
red) Rubinrot nt. **2** adj (~-coloured) rubinrot;
(made of rubies) Rubin-. ~ **wedding** vierzigster
Hochzeitstag.

rucksack ['rʌksæk] n (esp Brit) Rucksack m.

ruction ['rʌkʃən] n (col: usu pl) Krach m no pl.
that'll cause ~s das gibt Krach.

rudder ['rʌdər] n (Naut, Aviat) Ruder nt.

ruddy ['rʌdɪ] adj (+er) (a) complexion gesund, rot;
glow rötlich. (b) (Brit col!) verdammt (col).

rude [ruːd] adj (+er) (a) (bad-mannered) unhöflich;
(stronger) unverschämt; (uncouth) grob. it's ~ to
stare es gehört sich nicht, Leute anzustarren;
don't be so ~! so was sagt man/tut man nicht! (b)
(obscene) unanständig. (c) (harsh) shock hart;
reminder unsanft.

rudeness ['ruːdnɪs] n see adj (a) Unhöflichkeit f;
Unverschämtheit f; Grobheit f. (b) Unanständigkeit f. (c) Härte f.

rudiment ['ruːdɪmənt] n ~s pl Anfangsgründe pl.

rudimentary [ˌruːdɪ'mentərɪ] adj knowledge
elementar; system rudimentär. **a** ~ **sort of
building** ein primitives Gebäude.

rueful ['ruːfʊl] adj look reuevoll; situation
beklagenswert.

ruff [rʌf] n (on dress etc, of bird) Halskrause f.

ruffian ['rʌfɪən] n Rüpel m; (violent) Schläger m.

ruffle ['rʌfl] vt (a) hair, feathers zerzausen; surface,
water kräuseln. (b) (fig) (upset, disturb) aus der
Ruhe bringen; (annoy also) verärgern. **to get ~d**
aus der Ruhe kommen.

rug [rʌg] n (a) Teppich m; (rectangular also) Läufer
m; (valuable also) Brücke f; (bedside) (Bett)vor-
leger m. fireside ~ Kaminvorleger m. (b)
(blanket) (Woll)decke f.

rugby ['rʌgbɪ] n Rugby nt.

rugged ['rʌgɪd] adj rauh; mountains zerklüftet;
ground felsig; features markig; determination
wild.

rugger ['rʌgər] n (Brit col) = **rugby**.

ruin ['ruːɪn] **1** n (a) no pl Untergang m; (of event)
Ende nt; (financial, social) Ruin m. the palace was
going to ~ der Palast verfiel (zur Ruine); you'll
be the ~ of me du bist mein Ruin. (b) (ruined
building) Ruine f. ~s (of building) Ruinen pl; (of
reputation, beauty) Reste pl; (of hopes, career)
Trümmer pl; to be or lie in ~s (lit) eine Ruine
sein; (fig) zerstört sein; (life: financially, socially)
ruiniert sein. **2** vt (destroy) building, hopes zerstören; reputation, health also ruinieren;
(financially, socially) ruinieren, zugrunde richten; (spoil) clothes, event, child verderben.

ruinous ['ruːɪnəs] adj (financially) ruinös; price
extrem.

rule [ruːl] **1** n (a) Regel f; (Admin also) Be-
stimmung f. the ~s of the game (lit, fig) die
Spielregeln; to play by the ~s (lit, fig) die
Spielregeln einhalten; running is against the ~s
Rennen ist nicht erlaubt; by ~ of thumb über
den Daumen gepeilt; ~ **book** Regelheft nt; **I
make it a** ~ **to** get up early ich habe es mir zur
Regel gemacht, früh aufzustehen; **as a** ~ in der
Regel. (b) (authority, reign) Herrschaft f; (period
also) Regierungszeit f. the ~ of law die Rechts-
staatlichkeit. (c) (for measuring) Metermaß nt,
Maßstab m.
2 vt (a) beherrschen; (individual also) herrschen über; (fig) emotion also zügeln; **to** ~ **the
roost** (fig) Herr im Haus sein (col). (b) (Jur, Sport,
Admin: give decision) entscheiden. **his question**

was ~**d out of order** seine Frage wurde als
unzulässig abgewiesen. (c) (draw lines on) paper
linieren; (draw) line ziehen.
3 vi (a) (lit, fig: reign) herrschen (over über
+acc), regieren (over acc). (b) (Jur) entscheiden
(against gegen, in favour of für, on über +acc).
◆ **rule out** vt sep (fig: exclude) ausschließen.

ruler ['ruːlər] n (a) (for measuring) Lineal nt. (b)
(sovereign) Herrscher m.

ruling ['ruːlɪŋ] **1** adj principle leitend, Leit-. **the** ~
class die herrschende Klasse. **2** n (Admin, Jur)
Entscheid m. **to give a** ~ einen Entscheid fällen.

rum [rʌm] n Rum m.

Rumania [ruː'meɪnɪə] n Rumänien nt.

rumble ['rʌmbl] **1** n see vi Grollen nt; Donnern nt;
Knacken nt; Knurren nt; Rumpeln nt (all no pl). **2**
vi (thunder) grollen; (cannon) donnern; (pipes)
knacken; (stomach) knurren; (train, truck) rumpeln. **to** ~ **past** vorbeirumpeln. **3** vt (col: see
through) trick, person durchschauen.

rumbustious [rʌm'bʌstʃəs] adj derb.

ruminate ['ruːmɪneɪt] vi (lit) wiederkäuen; (fig)
grübeln (over, about, on über +acc).

rummage ['rʌmɪdʒ] vi (also ~ **about**, ~ **around**)
herumstöbern (among, in in +dat, for nach).

rumour, (US) **rumor** ['ruːmər] **1** n Gerücht nt. ~
has it that ... es geht das Gerücht, daß ... **2** vt it is
~**ed that** ... es geht das Gerücht, daß ...; (through
gossip) man munkelt, daß ...; **he is** ~**ed to be rich**
er soll angeblich reich sein.

rump [rʌmp] n (of animal) Hinterbacken pl; (col: of
person) Hinterteil m. ~ (**steak**) Rumpsteak nt.

rumpus ['rʌmpəs] n (col) Krach m. **to kick up a** ~
(make noise) einen Heidenlärm machen (col);
(complain) Krach schlagen (col); ~ **room** (US)
Spielzimmer nt.

run [rʌn] (vb: pret **ran**, ptp ~) **1** n (a) (act of
running, Cricket, Baseball) Lauf m. **to go for a
2-km** ~ einen 2 km-Lauf machen; **he came in at a**
~ er kam hereingelaufen; **he took the fence at a**
~ er nahm die Hürde im Lauf; **to break into a** ~
zu rennen anfangen; **to make a** ~ **for it** weglaufen; **on the** ~ (from the police etc) auf der
Flucht; **he has had a good** ~ **for his money** (col)
er hat was für sein Geld bekommen; (on death)
er hat sein Leben gelebt.
(b) (in vehicle) Fahrt f; (outing also) Ausflug
m. **to go for a** ~ **in the car** eine Fahrt/einen
Ausflug im Auto machen; **on the outward/inward**
~ auf der Hinfahrt/Rückfahrt; (in plane) auf dem
Hinflug/Rückflug; **the ferries on the Dover-
Calais** ~ die Fähren der Linie Dover-Calais.
(c) **to have the** ~ **of a place** einen Ort zur
freien Verfügung haben; **to give sb the** ~ **of
one's house** jdm sein Haus überlassen.
(d) **in the short/long** ~ fürs nächste/auf die
Dauer; plan etc auf kurz/lange Sicht.
(e) (series) Folge, Reihe f; (Cards) Sequenz f;
(Theat) Spielzeit f; (of film) Laufzeit f. **the play had
a long** ~ das Stück lief sehr lange; **a** ~ **of bad
luck** eine Pechsträhne; **a** ~ **of misfortunes** eine
Serie von Mißgeschicken.
(f) (great demand) ~ **on** Ansturm m auf
(+acc); (St Ex, Fin also) **Run** m auf (+acc).
(g) (track for skiing etc) Bahn f. **ski** ~
Abfahrt(sstrecke) f.
(h) (animal enclosure) Gehege nt; (chicken)
Hühnerhof m.
(i) (in tights) Laufmasche f.
2 vi (a) (animal, person) (in race) laufen, ~ **to
past/off** vorbei-/davonlaufen or -rennen; **she
came** ~**ning out** sie kam herausgelaufen or -ge-
rannt; **to** ~ **down a slope** einen Abhang
hinunterlaufen or -rennen; **to** ~ **for the bus** zum
Bus laufen or rennen; **she ran to meet him** sie lief
ihm entgegen; **she ran to help him** sie kam ihm
schnell zu Hilfe; **to** ~ **for one's life** um sein
Leben rennen; **to** ~ **for President** or **for the**

Presidency für die Präsidentschaft kandidieren; **a rumour ran through the school** ein Gerücht ging in der Schule um; **a shiver ran down her spine** ein Schauer lief ihr über den Rücken; **don't come ~ning to me if ...** du brauchst nicht bei mir anzukommen, wenn ...

   (b) *(become)* **to ~ dry** *(river)* austrocknen; *(pen)* leer werden; *(resources)* ausgehen; **he ran short of ideas** ihm gingen die Ideen aus; **supplies are ~ning low** die Vorräte werden knapp.

   (c) *(flow)* *(river, electric current)* fließen; *(eyes)* tränen; *(nose, tap)* laufen; *(paint)* zerfließen, ineinanderfließen; *(dye: in washing)* färben; *(ink)* fließen. **where the river ~s into the sea** wo der Fluß ins Meer mündet; **the street ~s into the square** die Straße mündet auf den Platz; **inflation is ~ning at 20%** die Inflationsrate beträgt 20%; **your bath is ~ning** Ihr Badewasser läuft ein; **the floor was ~ning with water** der Fußboden schwamm vor Wasser; **his blood ran cold** das Blut gefror ihm in den Adern.

   (d) *(play, contract, Jur: sentence)* laufen; *(Fin: interest rate)* gelten. **the contract has 10 months to ~** der Vertrag läuft noch 10 Monate; **the expenditure ~s into thousands of pounds** die Ausgaben gehen in die Tausende (von Pfund); **I can't ~ to a new car** ich kann mir kein neues Auto leisten.

   (e) *(bus, train etc)* fahren. **this train ~s between London and Manchester** dieser Zug verkehrt zwischen London und Manchester; **the buses ~ once an hour** die Busse fahren stündlich.

   (f) *(function)* laufen; *(factory)* arbeiten. **when the central heating is ~ning** wenn die Zentralheizung angeschaltet ist; **the car is ~ning smoothly** der Wagen läuft ohne Schwierigkeiten; **if everything ~s smoothly** wenn alles glatt geht; **you mustn't leave the engine ~ning** Sie dürfen den Motor nicht laufen lassen; **this model ~s on diesel** dieses Auto fährt mit Diesel; **the radio ~s off the mains/off batteries** das Radio läuft auf Netz/Batterie; **all trains are ~ning late** alle Züge haben Verspätung; **the project is ~ning late** das Projekt hat sich verzögert.

   (g) *(road)* gehen, führen; *(mountains)* sich erstrecken; *(river)* fließen; **line** sich ziehen. **the main road ~s north and south** die Hauptstraße führt von Norden nach Süden; **the river ~s for 300 km** der Fluß ist 300 km lang; **this theme ~s through his work** dieses Thema zieht sich durch sein ganzes Werk.

   (h) to ~ in the family in der Familie liegen.

   (i) *(stocking)* eine Laufmasche bekommen.

   (j) *(roll, slide)* *(drawer, curtains)* laufen, gleiten; *(vehicle)* rollen.

   3 *vt* **(a)** *distance* laufen, rennen; *race* laufen. **he ~s 3 km every day** er läuft jeden Tag 3 km; **to ~ errands** Botengänge machen; **to ~ its course** *(event, disease)* seinen Lauf nehmen; **to ~ a temperature** Fieber haben; **to ~ sb off his feet** *(col)* jdn ständig in Trab halten *(col)*; **to ~ sb into debt** jdn in Schulden stürzen.

   (b) I'll ~ you a bath ich lasse Ihnen ein Bad einlaufen; **he ~s his words together** bei ihm fließen die Wörter ineinander über.

   (c) *(transport)* person, thing fahren, bringen; *(drive)* vehicle fahren. **he ran her home** er brachte sie nach Hause; **this company ~s a bus service** diese Firma unterhält einen Busdienst; **they ~ trains to London every hour** es besteht stündlicher Zugverkehr nach London.

   (d) *(operate)* machine betreiben (on mit); *(person)* bedienen. **to ~ a radio off the mains** ein Radio auf Netz laufen lassen; **I can't afford to ~ a car** ich kann es mir nicht leisten, ein Auto zu unterhalten; **he ~s a Rolls** er fährt einen Rolls Royce; **this car is cheap to ~** dieses Auto ist

billig im Unterhalt; **to ~ a program** *(Comp)* ein Programm durchlaufen.

   (e) *(manage, be in charge of)* leiten; *shop* führen; *(organize)* course of study, competition durchführen. **a well-~ hotel** ein gutgeführtes Hotel; **I want to ~ my own life** ich möchte mein eigenes Leben leben; **she's the one who really ~s everything** sie ist diejenige, die den Laden schmeißt *(col)*.

   (f) *(move, put)* **to ~ one's finger down a list** mit dem Finger eine Liste durchgehen; **to ~ a comb through one's hair** sich *(dat)* mit einem Kamm durch die Haare fahren; **to ~ one's eye over a page** eine Seite überfliegen.

   (g) *(take, lead etc)* rope, road führen; line, ditch ziehen; *pipe, wires* (ver)legen; *(above ground)* führen.

♦ **run about** *or* **around** *vi* *(lit, fig)* herumlaufen *or* -rennen.

♦ **run across 1** *vi* **(a)** *(lit)* hinüber-/herüberlaufen. **(b)** *(go to see)* kurz rüberlaufen *(to zu)*. **2** *vi +prep obj (meet)* person zufällig treffen; *(find)* object, reference stoßen auf (+acc).

♦ **run along** *vi* laufen, rennen; *(go away)* gehen. **~ ~!** nun geht mal schön!

♦ **run away** *vi* **(a)** *(person, animal)* weglaufen; *(horse)* durchgehen. **to ~ ~ from home** von zu Hause weglaufen. **(b)** *(water)* auslaufen.

♦ **run away with** *vi +prep obj (steal)* money, object durchbrennen mit *(col)*; *(Sport etc: win easily)* race, prize spielend gewinnen. **don't ~ ~ ~ the idea that ...** *(fig)* kommen Sie nur nicht auf den Gedanken, daß ...; **he lets his imagination ~ ~ ~** him seine Phantasie geht leicht mit ihm durch.

♦ **run down 1** *vi* **(a)** *(lit: person)* hinunter-/herunterlaufen. **(b)** *(watch, clock)* ablaufen; *(battery)* leer werden. **to let stocks ~ ~** das Lager leer werden lassen; *(deliberately)* die Vorräte abbauen. **2** *vt sep* **(a)** *(knock down)* umfahren; *(run over)* überfahren. **(b)** factory, shop (allmählich) auflösen; department, stocks, staff abbauen; battery zu stark belasten. **(c)** *(disparage)* schlechtmachen *(col)*.

♦ **run in** *vt sep* **(a)** *(Brit)* car einfahren. **(b)** *(col: arrest)* schnappen *(col)*.

♦ **run into** *vi +prep obj (meet)* zufällig treffen; *(collide with)* rennen/fahren gegen. **to ~ ~ trouble/problems** Ärger bekommen/auf Probleme stoßen; **to ~ ~ danger/debt** in Gefahr/Schulden geraten.

♦ **run off 1** *vi* = **run away (a)**. **2** *vt sep* **(a)** water ablassen. **(b)** *(reproduce)* copy abziehen.

♦ **run on** *vi* **(a)** *(lit)* weiterlaufen. **you ~ ~,** I'll catch up geh schon mal voraus, ich komme nach. **(b) it ran ~ for four hours** das zog sich über vier Stunden hin.

♦ **run out** *vi* **(a)** *(person)* hinaus-/herauslaufen; *(rope, chain)* ablaufen; *(liquid)* herauslaufen; *(through leak)* auslaufen. **(b)** *(come to an end)* contract, period of time, reserves ablaufen; *(money, supplies)* zu Ende gehen. **my patience is ~ning ~** mir geht langsam die Geduld aus.

♦ **run out of** *vi +prep obj* **he ran ~ ~ money/patience/time** ihm ging das Geld/die Geduld aus/ er hatte keine Zeit mehr.

♦ **run over 1** *vi* **(a)** *(to neighbour etc)* kurz hinübergehen *or* rübergehen *(col)*. **(b)** *(overflow: liquid, container)* überlaufen. **(c)** *(Rad, TV etc)* überziehen. **2** *vi +prep obj* story, part in play, details durchgehen; text, notes durchsehen. **3** *vt sep (in vehicle)* überfahren.

♦ **run through** *vi +prep obj* **(a)** *(use up)* money durchbringen. **(b)** *(rehearse)* play durchspielen; ceremony also, part durchgehen. **(c)** = **run over 2**.

♦ **run up 1** *vi* **(a)** *(lit: upstairs etc)* hinauf-/herauflaufen; *(towards sb/sth)* hin-/herlaufen *(to zu)*. **to ~ ~ against difficulties** auf Schwierigkeiten stoßen. **2** *vt sep* machen. **to ~ ~ a debt** Schulden machen.

run: ~away 1 *n* Ausreißer(in *f*) *m*; **2** *adj slave* entlaufen; *person, horse* ausgerissen; *car etc* der/die/das sich selbständig gemacht hat; *inflation* unkontrollierbar; **he had a ~away victory** er hatte einen sehr leichten Sieg; **~-down 1** *n (col: summary)* Zusammenfassung *f*; **to give sb a ~-down on sth** jdm einen Bericht über etw *(acc)* geben; **2** *adj (dilapidated)* heruntergekommen; *(tired)* abgespannt; *battery* leer; **to be (feeling) ~-down** abgespannt sein.

rung¹ [rʌŋ] *ptp of* **ring²**.

rung² *n (of ladder)* Sprosse *f*; *(of chair)* Querstab *m*.

runner ['rʌnə'] *n* **(a)** *(athlete)* Läufer(in *f*) *m*. **(b)** *(on sledge)* Kufe *f*; *(for curtain)* Röllchen *nt*; *(for drawer, machine part)* Laufschiene *f*. **(c)** *(Bot)* ~ **bean** *(Brit)* Stangenbohne *f*.

runner-up ['rʌnər'ʌp] *n* Zweite(r) *mf*. **the runners-up** die weiteren Plätze; *(in competition)* die weiteren Gewinner.

running ['rʌnɪŋ] **1** *n* **(a)** *(lit, fig)* das Rennen machen; **to be in the ~ (for sth)** im Rennen (für etw) liegen. **(b)** *(functioning: of machine)* Laufen *nt*. **(c)** *(management)* see **run 3 (e)** Leitung *f*; Führung *f*; Durchführung *f*. **2** *adj* **(a)** ~ **jump** Sprung *m* mit Anlauf; **go and take a ~ jump** *(col)* du kannst mich gern haben *(col)*; ~ **commentary** *(Rad, TV)* fortlaufender Kommentar. **(b) 4 days ~** 4 Tage hintereinander. **(c)** *(flowing)* fließend; *tap, nose* laufend; *eyes* tränend.

running: ~ battle *n (Mil)* Gefecht *nt*; *(fig)* Kleinkrieg *m*; ~ **costs** *npl* Betriebskosten *pl*; *(of car)* Unterhaltskosten *pl*.

runny ['rʌnɪ] *adj (+er)* flüssig; *honey* dünnflüssig; *nose* laufend; *eyes* wässerig.

run: ~-of-the-mill *adj* durchschnittlich; *theme, novel* Feld-Wald-Wiesen-. **~-up** *n (Sport)* Anlauf *m*; **in the final ~-up to ...** in der letzten Phase vor *(+dat)* ...

runway ['rʌnweɪ] *n (Aviat)* Start- und Landebahn *f*, Runway *f* or *m*.

rupture ['rʌptʃə'] **1** *n (lit, fig)* Bruch *m*; *(Pol: of relations)* Abbruch *m*. **2** *vt* brechen. **to ~ oneself** *(col)* sich *(dat)* einen Bruch heben *(col)*.

rural ['ruərəl] *adj* ländlich; *life also* Land-.

ruse [ru:z] *n* List *f*.

rush¹ [rʌʃ] **1** *n* **(a)** *(of crowd)* Gedränge *nt*; *(of air)* Stoß *m*; *(Mil: attack)* Sturm *m*. **they made a ~ for the door** sie drängten zur Tür; **to make a ~ at** losstürzen auf *(+acc)*; **there's been a ~ on these goods** diese Waren sind rasend weggegangen; **we have a ~ on in the office just now** bei uns im Büro herrscht zur Zeit Hochbetrieb; **the Christmas ~** der Weihnachtsbetrieb; **we've had a ~ of orders** wir hatten eine Flut von Aufträgen; **water streamed out in a ~** das Wasser schoß in einem Schwall heraus. **(b)** *(hurry)* Eile *f*; *(stronger)* Hetze *f*. **to be in a ~** in Eile sein; **I did it in a ~** ich habe es sehr hastig gemacht; **what's the ~?** wozu die Eile/Hetzerei?; **is there any ~ for this?** eilt das?; **it all happened in such a ~** das ging alles so plötzlich.

2 *vi (hurry)* eilen; *(stronger)* hetzen; *(run)* stürzen; *(wind)* brausen; *(water)* schießen. **they ~ed to help her** sie eilten ihr zu Hilfe; **I'm ~ing to finish it** ich beeile mich, es fertigzumachen; **don't ~**, **take your time** überstürzen Sie nichts,

lassen Sie sich Zeit; **to ~ through** *book* hastig lesen; *meal* hastig essen; *museum, town* hetzen durch; *work* hastig erledigen; **to ~ past** *(person)* vorbeistürzen; *(vehicle)* vorbeischießen; **to ~ in/out** *etc* hinein-/hinausstürzen; **the ambulance ~ed to the scene** der Krankenwagen raste zur Unfallstelle.

3 *vt* **(a)** **to ~ sb to hospital** jdn schnellstens ins Krankenhaus bringen; **they ~ed more troops to the front** sie schickten eilends mehr Truppen an die Front; **they ~ed the bill through Parliament** sie peitschten die Gesetzesvorlage durch das Parlament. **(b)** *(force to hurry)* hetzen, drängen. **don't ~ me!** hetz mich nicht; **he won't be ~ed er läßt** sich nicht drängen; **to be ~ed off one's feet** dauernd auf Trab sein; **to ~ sb off his feet** jdn dauernd auf Trab halten; **to ~ sb into doing sth** jdn dazu treiben, etw überstürzt zu tun. **(c)** *(charge at)* stürmen; *fence* zustürmen auf *(+acc)*. **the mob ~ed the line of policemen** der Mob stürmte auf die Polizeikette zu. **(d)** *(do hurriedly) job, task* hastig machen; *(do badly)* schludern bei *(col)*. **you can't ~ this sort of work** für solche Arbeit muß man sich *(dat)* Zeit lassen.

♦ **rush about** *or* **around** *vi* herumhetzen.

♦ **rush out 1** *vi* hinaus-/herauseilen; *(very fast)* hinaus-/herausstürzen. **he ~ed ~ and bought one** er kaufte sofort eines. **2** *vt sep troops, supplies* eilends hintransportieren.

♦ **rush through** *vt sep order* durchjagen; *goods, supplies* eilends durchschleusen.

♦ **rush up** *vi (lit)* hinauf-/heraufeilen; *(very fast)* hinauf-/heraufstürzen.

rush² *n (Bot)* Binse *f*.

rush: ~-hour(s *pl)* *n* Hauptverkehrszeit(en *pl*), Rush-hour *f*; **~-hour traffic** Stoßverkehr *m*; ~ **job** *n* eiliger Auftrag; *(pej: bad work)* Schluderarbeit *f (col)*; ~ **matting** *n* Binsenmatte *f*.

rusk [rʌsk] *n* Zwieback *m*.

russet ['rʌsɪt] *adj* rostfarben.

Russia ['rʌʃə] *n* Rußland *nt*.

Russian ['rʌʃən] **1** *adj* russisch. **2** *n* **(a)** Russe *m*, Russin *f*. **(b)** *(language)* Russisch *nt*.

rust [rʌst] **1** *n* Rost *m*. **~-proof** rostfrei. **2** *adj (also* **~-coloured)** rostfarben. **3** *vi* rosten.

rustic ['rʌstɪk] **1** *n* Bauer *m*. **2** *adj* bäuerlich; *furniture, style* rustikal; *manners* bäurisch *(pej)*.

rustle ['rʌsl] **1** *n* Rascheln *nt*; *(of foliage)* Rauschen *nt*. **2** *vi (leaves, silk, papers)* rascheln; *(foliage, skirts)* rauschen. **3** *vt* **(a)** *paper, leaves on ground etc* rascheln mit; *(wind) leaves on tree* rauschen in *(+dat)*. **(b)** *(US: steal) cattle* klauen *(col)*.

♦ **rustle up** *vt sep (col) meal* improvisieren *(col)*.

rustler ['rʌslə'] *n (US: cattle-thief)* Viehdieb *m*.

rusty ['rʌstɪ] *adj (+er) (lit)* rostig; *(fig)* French, *maths* eingerostet; *talent* verkümmert. **I'm a bit ~** ich bin etwas aus der Übung.

rut¹ [rʌt] *n (in track, path)* Spur, Furche *f*; *(fig: routine)* Trott *m (col)*. **to be in a ~** *(fig)* im Trott sein *(col)*; **to get into a ~** *(person)* in einen Trott geraten *(col)*.

rut² *n (Zool)* Brunst *f*.

ruthless ['ru:θlɪs] *adj person* rücksichtslos; *treatment, irony* schonungslos. **you'll have to be ~** man muß hart sein.

rye [raɪ] *n (grain)* Roggen *m*; *(US col)* Rye(whisky) *m*; *(bread)* Roggenbrot *nt*. **~ bread** Roggenbrot *nt*.

S

S, s [es] *n* S, s *nt.*
S = **(a) south** S. **(b) Saint** St.
Sabbath ['sæbəθ] *n* Sabbat *m.*
sabbatical [sə'bætɪkəl] *n (Univ)* Forschungsurlaub *m.* **to be on** ~ Forschungsurlaub haben.
sable ['seɪbl] *n* Zobel *m; (fur)* Zobelpelz *m.*
sabotage ['sæbətɑːʒ] **1** *n* Sabotage *f.* **2** *vt (lit, fig)* sabotieren.
saboteur [,sæbə'tɜːʳ] *n* Saboteur *m.*
sabre, *(US)* **saber** ['seɪbəʳ] *n* Säbel *m.*
saccharin ['sækərɪn] *n* Saccharin *nt.*
sachet ['sæʃeɪ] *n* Beutel *m; (of powder)* Päckchen *nt; (of shampoo, cream)* Briefchen *nt.*
sack¹ [sæk] **1** *n* **(a)** Sack *m.* **two** ~**s of coal** zwei Sack Kohlen. **(b)** *(col: dismissal)* Entlassung *f,* Rausschmiß *m (col).* **to get the** ~ rausfliegen *(col);* **to give sb the** ~ jdn rausschmeißen *(col).* **(c)** *(col: bed)* **to hit the** ~ sich in die Falle hauen *(col).* **2** *vt (col: dismiss)* rausschmeißen *(col),* entlassen.
sack² **1** *n (pillage)* Plünderung *f.* **2** *vt* plündern.
sacking ['sækɪŋ] *n* **(a)** *(material)* Sackleinen *nt.* **(b)** *(col: dismissal)* Entlassung *f.*
sacrament ['sækrəmənt] *n* Sakrament *nt.*
sacred ['seɪkrɪd] *adj* heilig; *music* geistlich; *building* sakral. **is nothing** ~? *(col)* ist denn nichts mehr heilig?; ~ **cow** *(lit, fig)* heilige Kuh.
sacrifice ['sækrɪfaɪs] **1** *n (lit, fig)* Opfer *nt.* **to make** ~**s** Opfer bringen. **2** *vt* opfern *(sth to sb* jdm etw).
sacrificial [,sækrɪ'fɪʃəl] *adj* Opfer-.
sacrilege ['sækrɪlɪdʒ] *n* Sakrileg *nt; (fig also)* Frevel *m.* **that's** ~ das ist ein Sakrileg.
sacrilegious [,sækrɪ'lɪdʒəs] *adj (lit)* gotteslästerlich; *(fig)* frevelhaft.
sacristy ['sækrɪstɪ] *n* Sakristei *f.*
sacrosanct ['sækrəʊ,sæŋkt] *adj (lit, fig)* sakrosankt.
sad [sæd] *adj (+er)* traurig; *loss* schmerzlich; *colour* trist; *result also, mistake, lack* bedauerlich. **to feel** ~ traurig sein; **a** ~ **state of affairs** eine traurige Sache.
sadden ['sædn] *vt* betrüben.
saddle ['sædl] **1** *n (also of hill)* Sattel *m; (of meat)* Rücken *m.* **to be in the** ~ *(lit)* im Sattel sein; *(fig)* im Sattel sitzen. **2** *vt* **(a)** *horse* satteln. **(b)** *(col)* **to** ~ **sb with sb/sth** jdm jdn/etw aufhalsen *(col).*
saddlebag ['sædlbæg] *n* Satteltasche *f.*
sadism ['seɪdɪzəm] *n* Sadismus *m.*
sadist ['seɪdɪst] *n* Sadist(in *f*) *m.*
sadistic [sə'dɪstɪk] *adj* sadistisch.
sadly ['sædlɪ] *adv* **(a)** traurig; *(unfortunately)* traurigerweise. **(b)** *(regrettably)* bedauerlich. **he is** ~ **lacking in any sense of humour** ihm fehlt absolut jeglicher Humor.
sadness ['sædnɪs] *n* Traurigkeit *f.* **our** ~ **at his death** unsere Trauer über seinen Tod.
sae = **stamped addressed envelope.**
safari [sə'fɑːrɪ] *n* Safari *f.* **to be/go on** ~ auf Safari sein/gehen; ~ **park** Safaripark *m.*
safe¹ [seɪf] *n (for valuables)* Safe *m or nt,* Tresor *m.*
safe² **1** *adj (+er)* sicher; *method also, player* zuverlässig; *(cautious) policy* vorsichtig; *estimate* realistisch; *(not dangerous)* ungefährlich; *(out of danger)* in Sicherheit; *(not injured)* unverletzt. **to be** ~ **from sb/sth** vor jdm/etw sicher sein; **to keep sth** ~ etw sicher aufbewahren; **all the passengers are** ~ alle Passagiere sind in

Sicherheit *or (not injured)* unverletzt; ~ **journey!** gute Fahrt/Reise!; ~ **journey home!** komm gut nach Hause!; **thank God you're** ~ Gott sei Dank ist dir nichts passiert; ~ **and sound** gesund und wohlbehalten; **the patient is** ~ **now** der Patient ist jetzt außer Gefahr; **the secret is** ~ **with me** bei mir ist das Geheimnis gut aufgehoben; **this car is not** ~ **to drive** das Auto ist nicht verkehrssicher; **she is not** ~ **on the roads** sie ist eine Gefahr im Straßenverkehr; **it's a** ~ **assumption that ...** man kann mit ziemlicher Sicherheit annehmen, daß ...; **it's a** ~ **guess** es ist so gut wie sicher; **I think it's** ~ **to say ...** ich glaube, man kann wohl sagen ...; **better** ~ **than sorry** Vorsicht ist besser als Nachsicht *(Prov);* **just to be on the** ~ **side** um ganz sicher zu sein.
   2 *adv* **to play (it)** ~ *(col)* auf Nummer Sicher gehen *(col).*
safe: ~**-breaker** *n* Safeknacker *m (col);* ~**-conduct** *n* freies Geleit; ~**-deposit** *n* Tresorraum *m;* ~**-deposit box** *n* Banksafe *m or nt;* ~**guard** **1** *n* Schutz *m;* **as a** ~**guard against** zum Schutz gegen; **2** *vt* schützen *(against vor +dat); interests* gegen etw absichern; ~**-keeping** *n* sichere Verwahrung; **to give sb sth for** ~**-keeping** jdm etw zur (sicheren) Aufbewahrung geben.
safely ['seɪflɪ] *adv (unharmed) arrive* wohlbehalten; *(without problems also)* sicher, gut; *(without risk)* gefahrlos; *drive* vorsichtig; *(solidly, firmly)* sicher, fest; *(not dangerously)* ungefährlich. **I think I can** ~ **say ...** ich glaube, ich kann wohl sagen ...; **I got** ~ **through the first interview** ich bin gut *or* heil durch das erste Interview gekommen; **to put sth away** ~ etw an einem sicheren Ort verwahren.
safety ['seɪftɪ] *n* Sicherheit *f.* **in a place of** ~ an einem sicheren Ort; **for** ~**'s sake** aus Sicherheitsgründen; **with complete** ~ vollkommen sicher; ~ **first!** Sicherheit geht vor!; **to play for** ~ *(fig)* sichergehen; **(there's)** ~ **in numbers** zu mehreren ist man sicherer; **when we reached the** ~ **of the opposite bank** als wir sicher das andere Ufer erreicht hatten; **to leap to** ~ sich in Sicherheit bringen.
safety: ~ **belt** *n* Sicherheitsgurt *m;* ~ **catch** *n (on gun)* (Abzugs)sicherung *f;* ~ **curtain** *n (Theat)* eiserner Vorhang; ~ **factor** *n* Sicherheitsfaktor *m;* ~ **margin** *n* Sicherheitsspielraum *m;* ~ **match** *n* Sicherheitsholz *nt;* ~ **measure** *n* Sicherheitsmaßnahme *f;* ~ **net** *n* Sprungnetz *nt;* ~ **pin** *n* Sicherheitsnadel *f;* ~ **valve** *n* Sicherheitsventil *nt; (fig)* Ventil *nt.*
saffron ['sæfrən] **1** *n* Safran *m.* **2** *adj* Safran-; *(in colour)* safrangelb.
sag [sæg] *vi* absacken; *(in the middle)* durchhängen; *(shoulders)* herabhängen; *(production, rate)* zurückgehen; *(price, spirit)* sinken; *(conversation)* abflauen.
saga ['sɑːgə] *n* Saga *f; (novel also)* Generationsroman *m; (fig)* Geschichte *f.*
sagacious [sə'geɪʃəs] *adj* weise, klug.
sage¹ [seɪdʒ] *n* Weise(r) *m.*
sage² *n (Bot)* Salbei *m.*
Sagittarius [,sædʒɪ'tɛərɪəs] *n* Schütze *m.*
sago ['seɪgəʊ] *n* Sago *m.*

Sahara [sə'hɑːrə] n Sahara f.
said [sed] 1 pret, ptp of say. 2 adj (form) besagt.
sail [seɪl] 1 n Segel nt; (of windmill) Flügel m; (trip)
Fahrt f. **under** ~ mit aufgezogenen Segeln; **in
or under full** ~ mit vollen Segeln; **to set** ~
(for ...) los- or abfahren (nach ...); (with sailing
boat) absegeln (nach ...); **it's (a) 3 days'** ~ **from
here** von hier aus fährt or (in yacht) segelt man
3 Tage; **to go for a** ~ segeln gehen.
2 vt ship segeln mit; liner etc steuern. **they
~ed the ship to Cadiz** sie segelten nach Cadiz; **to
~ the seas** die Meere befahren.
3 vi (a) (Naut) fahren; (with yacht) segeln. **are
you flying or ~ing?** fliegen Sie, oder fahren Sie
mit dem Schiff?; **I went ~ing for a week** ich ging
eine Woche segeln; **to** ~ **around the world** um
die Welt segeln. **(b)** (leave) (for nach) abfahren;
(yacht, in yacht) absegeln. **passengers ~ing for
New York** Passagiere nach New York. **(c)** (fig:
glider, swan etc) gleiten; (moon, clouds) ziehen;
(ball, object) fliegen. **she ~ed past/out of the
room** sie rauschte vorbei (col)/aus dem Zimmer
(col); **she ~ed through all her exams** sie schaffte
alle Prüfungen spielend; **the holidays just ~ed
by** (col) die Ferien vergingen wie im Flug.
sailboat ['seɪlbəʊt] n (US) Segelboot nt.
sailing ['seɪlɪŋ] n (a) Segeln nt; (as sport also) Se-
gelsport m. **(b) when is the next** ~ **for Arran?**
wann fährt das nächste Schiff nach Arran?
sailing: ~ **boat** n (Brit) Segelboot nt; ~ **ship** n
Segelschiff nt.
sailor ['seɪlə'] n (a) Seemann m; (in navy) Matrose
m; (sportsman) Segler(in f) m. **(b) to be a bad** ~
(get seasick) nicht seefest sein.
saint [seɪnt] n (also fig) Heilige(r) mf; (before name
abbr to St [snt]) Sankt. **St John** der heilige Johannes, St. Johannes; **St. Mark's (Church)** die Mar-
kuskirche.
saintly ['seɪntlɪ] adj (+er) fromm; (fig pej) person frömmlerisch; smile lammfromm.
sake [seɪk] n **for the** ~ **of** ... um (+gen) ... willen;
for your own ~ dir selbst zuliebe; **for your
family's** ~ um Ihrer Familie willen; **for heav-
en's ~!** (col) um Gottes willen!; **for heaven's** or
Christ's ~ **shut up** (col) nun halt doch endlich die
Klappe (col); **for old times'** ~ in Erinnerung an
alte Zeiten; **for the** ~ **of those who** ... für diejenigen, die ...; **and all for the** ~ **of a few pounds** und
alles wegen ein paar Pfund.
salad ['sæləd] n Salat m.
salad: ~ **bowl** n Salatschüssel f; ~ **cream** n (Brit)
≃ Mayonnaise f; ~ **dressing** n Salatsoße f.
salami [sə'lɑːmɪ] n Salami f.
salaried ['sælərɪd] adj ~ **post** Angestelltenposten
m; ~ **staff** Gehaltsempfänger pl.
salary ['sælərɪ] n Gehalt nt. ~ **increase** Gehaltserhöhung f.
sale [seɪl] n (a) (selling) Verkauf m; (instance) Geschäft nt; (of insurance, bulk order) Abschluß m.
~s pl (turnover) der Absatz; **for** ~ zu verkaufen;
to put sth up for ~ etw zum Verkauf anbieten;
not for ~ nicht verkäuflich; **to be on** ~ verkauft
werden; **on** ~ **at all bookshops** in allen Buch-
handlungen erhältlich; **on a** ~ **or return basis**
auf Verkaufsbasis mit Rückgaberecht. **(b)** (at
reduced prices) Ausverkauf m; (at end of season)
Schlußverkauf m; (clearance ~) Räumungsverkauf m. **to go to the ~s** zum Ausverkauf etc
gehen; **they've got a** ~ **on** da ist Ausverkauf etc;
to buy in the ~s im Ausverkauf etc kaufen.
saleable, (US) **salable** ['seɪləbl] adj (marketable)
absatzfähig; (in ~ condition) verkäuflich.
sale: ~ **price** n Ausverkaufspreis m; ~**room** n
Auktionsraum m.
sales: ~ **clerk** n (US) Verkäufer(in f) m; ~ **department** n Verkaufsabteilung f; ~ **figures** npl Ver-
kaufs- or Absatzziffern pl; ~ **force** n
Vertreterstab m; ~**man** n Verkäufer m; (repre-

sentative) Vertreter m; ~ **manager** n Verkaufs-
leiter, Sales-manager m.
salesmanship ['seɪlzmənʃɪp] n Verkaufstechnik f.
sales: ~ **talk** n Verkaufsgespräch nt; ~**woman** n
Verkäuferin f.
salient ['seɪlɪənt] adj (lit) hervorstehend; (fig) hervorstechend. **the** ~ **points of his argument** die
Hauptpunkte pl seiner Argumentation.
saline ['seɪlaɪn] adj salzig.
saliva [sə'laɪvə] n Speichel m.
salivate ['sælɪveɪt] vi Speichel produzieren; (animal) geifern; (old people, baby) sabbern.
sallow ['sæləʊ] adj bleich; colour fahl.
salmon ['sæmən] 1 n, pl - Lachs m. 2 adj (in colour)
lachs(farben).
salon ['sælɒn] n (all senses) Salon m.
saloon [sə'luːn] n Saal m; (Naut) Salon m; (US: bar)
Wirtschaft f; (in Westerns) Saloon m.
saloon: ~ **bar** n (Brit) vornehmerer Teil eines Lo-
kals; ~ **car** n (Brit) Limousine f.
salt [sɔːlt] 1 n (Cook, Chem) Salz nt. ~ **of the earth**
(fig) Salz der Erde; **to take sth with a pinch of** ~
(fig) etw nicht ganz so wörtlich nehmen; **to rub** ~
into the wound (fig) Salz in die Wunde streuen. **2**
adj meat, water etc Salz-; butter gesalzen; taste
salzig. **it's very** ~ es ist sehr salzig.
salt: ~ **cellar** n Salzfäßchen nt; (shaker) Salzstreuer m; ~ **shaker** n Salzstreuer m; ~ **water** n Salzwasser nt; ~**water** adj fish Meeres-; lake Salz-.
salty ['sɔːltɪ] adj (+er) salzig.
salubrious [sə'luːbrɪəs] adj (a) (form) air, climate
gesund. **(b)** (col) district, friends ersprießlich.
salutary ['sæljʊtərɪ] adj (a) (healthy) gesund. **(b)**
(beneficial) advice nützlich; experience lehrreich;
effect günstig.
salute [sə'luːt] 1 n (a) Gruß m; (of guns) Salut m. **to take
the** ~ **die Parade abnehmen. 2** vt (Mil) grüßen;
person also salutieren vor (+dat); courage bewundern.
salvage ['sælvɪdʒ] 1 n (act) Bergung f; (objects)
Bergungsgut nt. 2 vt (from wreck, building)
bergen (from aus); (fig) retten (from von). **to** ~
sth from the fire etw aus den Flammen retten; ~
what you can (lit, fig) rettet, was ihr retten könnt.
salvage: ~ **operation** n Bergungsaktion f; (fig)
Rettungsaktion f; ~ **vessel** n Bergungsschiff nt.
salvation [sæl'veɪʃən] n Rettung f.
Salvation Army 1 n Heilsarmee f. 2 attr hostel,
band, meeting der Heilsarmee.
Samaritan [sə'mærɪtən] n Samariter m. **good** ~ (lit,
fig) barmherziger Samariter.
same [seɪm] 1 adj **the** ~ der/die/das gleiche; (one
and the ~, identical) derselbe/dieselbe/dasselbe;
they were both wearing the ~ **dress** sie hatten
beide das gleiche Kleid an; **they both live in the**
~ **house** sie wohnen beide in demselben Haus;
they are the ~ sie sind alle gleich; **she just
wasn't the** ~ **person** sie war ein anderer
Mensch; **it's the** ~ **thing** das ist das gleiche; **see
you tomorrow,** ~ **time** ~ **place** bis morgen, gleicher Ort, gleiche Zeit; **we sat at the** ~ **table as
usual** wir saßen an unserem üblichen Tisch; **he
is the** ~ **age as his wife** er ist (genau) so alt wie
seine Frau; **it happened the** ~ **day** es ist am
gleichen or selben Tag passiert; **in the** ~ **way**
(genau) gleich; (by the ~ token) ebenso.
2 pron **(a) the** ~ der/die/das gleiche; der-
selbe/dieselbe/dasselbe; **and I would do the** ~
again und ich würde es wieder tun; **he left and I
did the** ~ er ist gegangen, und ich auch; **they are
one and the** ~ das ist doch dasselbe; (people) das
ist doch ein und derselbe/dieselbe; **she's much
the** ~ sie hat sich kaum geändert; (in health) es
geht ihr kaum besser; **it's always the** ~ es ist
immer das gleiche.
(b) the ~ **gleich; to pay/treat everybody the**
~ alle gleich bezahlen/behandeln; **things go on
just the** ~ (as always) es ändert sich nichts; **it's**

not the ~ as before es ist nicht wie früher; **if it's all the ~ to you** wenn es Ihnen egal ist; **it's all the ~ to me (what you do)** es ist mir egal(, was du tust); **it amounts to the ~** das kommt or läuft aufs gleiche hinaus; **all** or **just the ~** (*nevertheless*) trotzdem; **~ here** ich/wir auch; **~ to you** (danke) gleichfalls.

sameness ['seɪmnɪs] *n* Eintönigkeit *f*.

sample ['sɑ:mpl] **1** *n* (*example*) Beispiel *nt* (*of* für); (*for tasting, fig: of talent, behaviour*) Kostprobe *f*; (*Comm*) (*of cloth etc*) Muster *nt*; (*of commodities, blood etc*) Probe *f*; (*Statistics*) Stichprobe *f*, Sample *nt*. **a representative ~ of the population** eine repräsentative Auswahl aus der Bevölkerung. **2** *vt wine, food* probieren, kosten; *pleasures* kosten.

sanatorium [ˌsænə'tɔ:rɪəm] *n, pl* (*Brit*) Sanatorium *nt*; (*in cpds*) -heilanstalt *f*.

sanctify ['sæŋktɪfaɪ] *vt* (*to make holy*) heiligen; (*fig*) sanktionieren; *(consecrate)* weihen.

sanctimonious [ˌsæŋktɪ'məʊnɪəs] *adj* frömmlerisch. **don't be so ~** tu doch nicht so fromm.

sanction ['sæŋkʃən] **1** *n* (**a**) (*permission, approval*) Zustimmung *f*. (**b**) (*enforcing measure*) Sanktion *f*. **to impose (economic) ~s on a country** (*wirtschaftliche*) Sanktionen gegen ein Land verhängen. **2** *vt* sanktionieren.

sanctity ['sæŋktɪtɪ] *n* Heiligkeit *f*; (*of rights*) Unantastbarkeit *f*.

sanctuary ['sæŋktjʊərɪ] *n* (**a**) (*holy place*) Heiligtum *nt*; (*altar ~*) Altarraum *m*. (**b**) (*refuge*) Zuflucht *f*. **to seek ~ with** Zuflucht suchen bei. (**c**) (*for animals*) Schutzgebiet *nt*.

sand [sænd] **1** *n* Sand *m no pl*. **~s** (*of desert*) Sand *m*; (*beach*) Sandstrand *m*. **2** *vt* (*smooth*) schmirgeln; (*sprinkle with ~*) streuen.

sandal ['sændl] *n* Sandale *f*.

sand: **~bag** *n* Sandsack *m*; **~bank** *n* Sandbank *f*; **~blast** *vt* sandstrahlen; **~boy** *n*: **as happy as a ~boy** quietschvergnügt; **~castle** *n* Sandburg *f*; **~ dune** *n* Sanddüne *f*; **~paper** **1** *n* Sand- or Schmirgelpapier *nt*; **2** *vt* schmirgeln; **~pit** *n* Sandkasten *m*; **~shoe** *n* Stoffschuh *m*; (*for beach*) Strandschuh *m*; **~stone** **1** *n* Sandstein *m*; **2** *adj* Sandstein-, aus Sandstein; **~storm** *n* Sandsturm *m*.

sandwich ['sænwɪdʒ] **1** *n* belegtes Brot, Sandwich *nt*. **open ~** belegtes Brot. **2** *vt* (*also ~ in*) hineinzwängen; *car* einkeilen. **to be ~ed between two things/people** zwischen zwei Dingen/Menschen eingekeilt sein.

sandwich: **~board** *n* Reklametafel *f*; **~ course** *n* Ausbildungsgang *m*, bei dem sich *Theorie und Praxis abwechseln*.

sandy ['sændɪ] *adj* (*+er*) sandig; *beach, soil* Sand-, sandig *pred*; (*in colour*) rötlich; *hair* rotblond.

sane [seɪn] *adj* (*+er*) *person* normal; (*Med, Psych etc*) geistig gesund; (*Jur*) zurechnungsfähig; *society etc* gesund; (*sensible*) *advice, person* vernünftig.

sang [sæŋ] *pret of* **sing**.

sangfroid [sɑ:ŋ'frwɑ:] *n* Seelenruhe *f*.

sanguine ['sæŋgwɪn] *adj* (*optimistic*) optimistisch.

sanitarium [ˌsænɪ'tɛərɪəm] *n* (*US*) = **sanatorium**.

sanitary ['sænɪtərɪ] *adj* hygienisch; *arrangements, installations* sanitär *attr*; *regulations, expert* Gesundheits-; *questions, principles* der Hygiene.

sanitary napkin (*US*) or **towel** *n* Damenbinde *f*.

sanitation [ˌsænɪ'teɪʃən] *n* Hygiene *f*; (*toilets etc*) sanitäre Anlagen *pl*; (*sewage disposal*) Kanalisation *f*.

sanity ['sænɪtɪ] *n* (**a**) (*mental balance*) geistige Gesundheit *f*; (*of individual also*) gesunder Verstand; (*Jur*) Zurechnungsfähigkeit *f*. **to lose one's ~** den Verstand verlieren; **to doubt sb's ~** an jds Verstand (*dat*) zweifeln. (**b**) (*sensibleness*) Vernünftigkeit *f*. **to return to ~** Vernunft annehmen.

sank [sæŋk] *pret of* **sink**[1].

Santa (Claus) ['sæntə('klɔ:z)] *n* der Weihnachts-

mann.

sap[1] [sæp] *n* (*Bot*) Saft *m*; (*fig*) Lebenskraft *f*.

sap[2] *vt* (*weaken, Mil*) untergraben; *confidence also* schwächen. **to ~ sb's strength** jdn entkräften, jds Kräfte angreifen.

sapling ['sæplɪŋ] *n* junger Baum.

sapper ['sæpə[r]] *n* (*Mil*) Pionier *m*.

sapphire ['sæfaɪə[r]] **1** *n* Saphir *m*; (*colour*) Saphirblau *nt*. **2** *adj* ring Saphir-.

sarcasm ['sɑ:kæzəm] *n* Sarkasmus *m*.

sarcastic [sɑ:'kæstɪk] *adj* sarkastisch. **are you being ~?** das soll wohl ein Witz sein (*col*).

sardine [sɑ:'di:n] *n* Sardine *f*. **packed in like ~s** wie die Sardinen.

Sardinia [sɑ:'dɪnɪə] *n* Sardinien *nt*.

sardonic [sɑ:'dɒnɪk] *adj* süffisant.

sash[1] [sæʃ] *n* Schärpe *f*.

sash[2] *n* (*in window*) Gewichtsschnur *f*.

sash: **~-cord** *n* Gewichtsschnur *f*; **~-window** *n* Schiebefenster *nt*.

sat [sæt] *pret, ptp of* **sit**.

Satan ['seɪtən] *n* Satan *m*.

satanic [sə'tænɪk] *adj* satanisch.

satchel ['sætʃəl] *n* Schultasche *f*.

satellite ['sætəlaɪt] *n* Satellit *m*.

satellite: **~ state** *n* Satellitenstaat *m*; **~ town** *n* Trabantenstadt *f*.

satiate ['seɪʃɪeɪt] *vt appetite, desires etc* stillen (*geh*); *person, animal* sättigen; (*to excess*) übersättigen.

satin ['sætɪn] **1** *n* Satin *m*. **2** *adj* Satin-; *skin* samtig.

satire ['sætaɪə[r]] *n* Satire *f* (*on auf +acc*).

satirical [sə'tɪrɪkəl] *adj literature, film etc* satirisch; (*mocking, joking*) ironisch.

satirist ['sætərɪst] *n* Satiriker(in *f*) *m*.

satisfaction [ˌsætɪs'fækʃən] *n* (**a**) (*act: of person, needs, curiosity etc*) Befriedigung *f*; (*of ambition*) Verwirklichung *f*; (*of conditions, contract*) Erfüllung *f*. (**b**) (*state*) Zufriedenheit *f* (*at mit*). **the ~ of having solved a difficult problem** das befriedigende Gefühl, ein schwieriges Problem gelöst zu haben; **to feel a sense of ~ at sth** Genugtuung über etw (*acc*) empfinden; **has it been done to your ~?** ist es zu Ihrer Zufriedenheit erledigt worden? (*form*); **to get ~ out of sth** Befriedigung in etw (*dat*) finden; (*find pleasure*) Freude an etw (*dat*) haben; **he proved to my ~ that ...** er hat überzeugend bewiesen, daß ...

satisfactory [ˌsætɪs'fæktərɪ] *adj* befriedigend; *account, completion of contract* zufriedenstellend; (*only just good enough*) ausreichend; *reason* triftig; *excuse* angemessen; (*in exams*) ausreichend; befriedigend.

satisfy ['sætɪsfaɪ] **1** *vt* (**a**) (*make contented*) befriedigen; *employer, customers etc* zufriedenstellen; (*meal*) *person* sättigen. **not satisfied with that he ... damit noch immer nicht zufrieden, ... er ...; **he's never satisfied** (*always wants more*) er ist mit nichts zufrieden; (**b**) *needs, demand, sb* (*sexually*) befriedigen; *hunger* stillen; *conditions* erfüllen; *requirements* genügen (*+dat*); *ambitions* verwirklichen. (**c**) (*convince*) überzeugen. **they were not satisfied with the answers** sie waren mit den Antworten nicht zufrieden. **2** *vr* **to ~ oneself about sth** sich von etw überzeugen; **to ~ oneself that ...** sich davon überzeugen, daß ...

satisfying ['sætɪsfaɪɪŋ] *adj* befriedigend; *food, meal* sättigend. **a cool ~ lager** ein kühles, durststillendes Bier.

saturate ['sætʃəreɪt] *vt* (*durch*)tränken; (*rain*) durchnässen; (*Chem, fig*) *solution, market* sättigen. **I'm ~d** (*col*) ich bin klatschnaß (*col*).

saturation [ˌsætʃə'reɪʃən] *n* Sättigung *f*. **to have reached ~ point** (*fig*) seinen Sättigungsgrad erreicht haben.

Saturday ['sætədɪ] *n* Samstag, Sonnabend *m*; *see* **Tuesday**.

Saturn ['sætən] n (Astron) Saturn m.
sauce [sɔːs] n (a) Soße, Sauce f. white ~ Mehlsoße f; what's ~ for the goose is ~ for the gander (Prov) was dem einen recht ist, ist dem anderen billig (prov). (b) no pl (col: cheek) Frechheit f. none of your ~! werd bloß nicht frech! (col).
saucepan ['sɔːspən] n Kochtopf m.
saucer ['sɔːsəʳ] n Untertasse f.
saucy ['sɔːsɪ] adj (+er) frech.
Saudi Arabia ['saʊdɪə'reɪbɪə] n Saudi-Arabien nt.
sauna ['sɔːnə] n Sauna f. to have a ~ in die Sauna gehen.
saunter ['sɔːntəʳ] vi schlendern. he ~ed up to me er schlenderte auf mich zu.
sausage ['sɒsɪdʒ] n Wurst f.
sausage: ~ **dog** n (Brit hum) Dackel m; ~**meat** n Wurstbrät nt; ~ **roll** n ≃ Bratwurst f im Schlafrock.
sauté ['səʊteɪ] 1 adj ~ **potatoes** Brat- or Röstkartoffeln pl. 2 vt potatoes rösten; (sear) (kurz) anbraten.
savage ['sævɪdʒ] 1 adj wild; fighter, punch, revenge brutal; custom grausam; animal gefährlich; competition scharf; (drastic) cuts, measures, changes drastisch; criticism schonungslos, brutal (col). to make a ~ **attack on sb** brutal über jdn herfallen; (fig) jdn scharf angreifen. 2 n Wilde(r) mf. 3 vt (animal) anfallen; (fatally) zerfleischen.
savanna(h) [sə'vænə] n Savanne f.
save[1] [seɪv] 1 n (Ftbl etc) Ballabwehr f.
2 vt (a) (rescue, Rel) retten. to ~ **sb from sth** jdn vor etw (dat) retten; to ~ **sb from disaster/ruin** jdn vor einer Katastrophe/dem Ruin bewahren; he ~**d** me from falling/making that mistake er hat mich davor bewahrt, hinzufallen/den Fehler zu machen; to ~ **sth from sth** etw aus etw retten; to ~ **the day** (for sb) jds Rettung sein; God ~ **the Queen** Gott schütze die Königin.
(b) (put by) aufheben, aufsparen; money sparen; (collect) stamps etc sammeln. ~ **some of the cake for me** laß mir etwas Kuchen übrig; ~ **me a seat** halte mir einen Platz frei; ~ **it!** (col) spar dir das! (col).
(c) (avoid using up) time, money sparen; (spare) eyes, battery schonen; (~ up) strength, fuel etc aufsparen. that will ~ **you £2 a week** dadurch sparen Sie £ 2 die Woche.
(d) (prevent) bother, trouble ersparen. it'll ~ **a lot of hard work if we** ... es erspart uns (dat) sehr viel Mühe, wenn wir ...
(e) goal verhindern; penalty halten.
(f) (Comp) job speichern, saven (col).
3 vi (a) (with money) sparen. to ~ **for sth** für or auf etw (acc) sparen. (b) to ~ **on sth** etw sparen.
♦ **save up** 1 vi sparen (for für, auf +acc). 2 vt sep (not spend) sparen; (not use) aufheben, aufbewahren. he's saving himself ~ **for the big match** er schont sich für das große Spiel.
save[2] 1 prep außer +dat. 2 conj (a) (old, liter) es sei denn (geh). (b) ~ **that** nur daß.
saveloy ['sævəlɔɪ] n Zervelatwurst f.
saving ['seɪvɪŋ] n (a) no pl (act: rescue, Rel) Rettung f; (of money) Sparen nt. (b) (of cost etc) (act) Einsparung f; (amount saved) Ersparnis f. (c) ~**s** pl Ersparnisse pl; (in account) Spareinlagen pl; **post-office** ~**s** Postspargutigaben nt.
savings in cpds Spar-; ~ **and loan association** n (US) Bausparkasse f; ~ **bank** n Sparkasse f.
saviour, (US also) **savior** ['seɪvjəʳ] n Retter(in f) m; (Rel also) Erlöser m.
savour, (US) **savor** ['seɪvəʳ] 1 n Geschmack m; (slight trace) Spur f; (enjoyable quality) Reiz m. 2 vt (a) (form) kosten (geh); aroma (of food) riechen. (b) (fig liter) genießen, auskosten.
savoury, (US) **savory** ['seɪvərɪ] 1 adj (a) (appetizing) lecker; meal also schmackhaft. (b) (not sweet) pikant. ~ **omelette** gefülltes Omelett; ~ **biscuits** Salzgebäck nt. (c) (fig) angenehm; sight

also einladend. 2 n Häppchen nt.
saw[1] [sɔː] pret of **see**[1].
saw[2] (vb: pret ~**ed**, ptp ~**ed** or **sawn**) 1 n Säge f. 2 vt sägen. to ~ **sth through** etw durchsägen; to ~ **sth in two** etw entzweisägen.
♦ **saw off** vt sep absägen. a ~**n-**~ **shotgun** ein Gewehr nt mit abgesägtem Lauf.
saw: ~**dust** n Sägemehl nt; ~**mill** n Sägewerk nt.
sawn [sɔːn] ptp of **saw**[2].
Saxon ['sæksn] 1 n Sachse m, Sächsin f; (Hist) (Angel)sachse m/-sächsin f. 2 adj sächsisch; (Hist) (angel)sächsisch.
saxophone ['sæksəfəʊn] n Saxophon nt.
say [seɪ] (vb: pret, ptp **said**) 1 n Mitspracherecht nt (in bei). **let him have his** ~ laß ihn mal reden or seine Meinung äußern; you've had your ~ Sie haben Ihre Meinung äußern können; to have no/a ~ **in sth** bei etw nichts/etwas zu sagen haben, bei etw kein/ein Mitspracherecht haben.
2 vti (a) sagen; poem aufsagen; prayer, text sprechen; (pronounce) aussprechen; (dial, gauge) anzeigen. ~ **after me** ... sprechen Sie mir nach ...; **what have you got to** ~ **for yourself?** was hast du zu deiner Verteidigung zu sagen?; **that's not for him to** ~ es steht ihm nicht zu, sich darüber zu äußern; (to decide) das kann er nicht entscheiden; he said to wait here er hat gesagt, ich soll/wir sollen etc hier warten; do it this way — if you ~ so machen Sie es so — wenn Sie meinen; why didn't you ~ so? warum hast du uns nicht gleich gesagt?; you'd better do it — who ~**s?** tun Sie das lieber — wer sagt das?; what does it mean? — I wouldn't like to ~ was bedeutet das? — das kann ich auch nicht sagen; so ~**ing,** he sat down und mit diesen Worten setzte er sich; it ~**s in the papers that** ... in den Zeitungen steht, daß ...; what does the paper/this book ~? was steht in der Zeitung/diesem Buch?; the rules ~ **that** ... in den Regeln heißt es, daß ...; what does the weather forecast ~? wie ist der Wetterbericht?; what does your watch ~? wie spät ist es auf deiner Uhr?; that ~**s a lot about his character** das läßt tief auf seinen Charakter schließen; and that's ~**ing a lot** und das will schon etwas heißen; that doesn't ~ **much for him** das spricht nicht für ihn.
(b) what would you ~ **to a whisky?** wie wär's mit einem Whisky?; I wouldn't ~ **no to a cup of tea** ich hätte nichts gegen eine Tasse Tee; he never ~**s no to a drink** er sagt nie nein zu einem Drink; what did he ~ **to your plan?** was hat er zu Ihrem Plan gesagt?; I'll offer £500, what do you ~ **to that?** ich biete £ 500, was meinen Sie dazu?; what do you ~? was meinen Sie?; I ~! (to attract attention) hallo!; I should ~ (so)! das möchte ich doch meinen!; you don't ~! (also iro) nein wirklich!, was du nicht sagst!; well said! (ganz) richtig!; you('ve) said it! Sie sagen es!; you can ~ that again! das kann man wohl sagen!; ~ **no more!** ich weiß Bescheid!; (it's) easier said than done es heißt; when all is said and done letzten Endes; he is said to be very rich er soll sehr reich sein; it goes without ~**ing** that ... es versteht sich von selbst, daß ...; that is to ~ das heißt; (correcting also) beziehungsweise; to ~ **nothing of the costs** etc von den Kosten etc ganz zu schweigen; that's not to ~ **that** ... das soll nicht heißen, daß ...; they ~ ..., it is said ... es heißt ...
saying ['seɪɪŋ] n Redensart f; (proverb) Sprichwort nt. as the ~ **goes** wie es so schön heißt.
say-so ['seɪsəʊ] n (col) (assertion) Wort nt; (authority) Plazet nt. on whose ~? mit welchem Recht?
scab [skæb] n (a) (on cut) Schorf, Grind m. (b) (col: strikebreaker) Streikbrecher(in f) m.
scaffolding ['skæfəldɪŋ] n Gerüst nt. to put up ~ ein Gerüst aufbauen.
scald [skɔːld] 1 n Verbrühung f. 2 vt (a) oneself,

skin etc verbrühen. **(b)** instruments, vegetables abbrühen; milk abkochen.

scalding ['skɔːldɪŋ] adj siedend.

scale¹ [skeɪl] n (of fish) Schuppe f; (of rust) Flocke f; (kettle ~) Kesselstein m no pl.

scale² n **(a)** Skala f; (on ruler) (Maß)einteilung f; (fig) Leiter f; (social ~) Stufenleiter f. ~ **of charges** Gebührenordnung f, Tarife pl. **(b)** (instrument) Meßgerät nt. **(c)** (Mus) Tonleiter f. **the ~ of** G die G(-Dur)-Tonleiter. **(d)** (of map etc) Maßstab m. **on a ~ of 5 km to the cm** in einem Maßstab von 5 km zu 1 cm; **to draw sth to ~** etw im Maßstab or maßstabgerecht zeichnen. **(e)** (fig: size, extent) Umfang m, Ausmaß nt. **to entertain on a large/small ~** Feste im größeren/kleineren Rahmen geben; **inflation on an unprecedented ~** Inflation von bisher nie gekanntem Ausmaß; **it's similar but on a smaller ~** es ist ähnlich, nur kleiner; **on a national ~** auf nationaler Ebene.

♦ **scale down** vt sep (lit) verkleinern; (fig) verringern.

scale³ (at mountain, wall erklettern.

scale: ~ **drawing** n maßstabgetreue Zeichnung; ~ **model** n maßstabgetreues Modell.

scales [skeɪlz] npl **(pair of)** ~**s** Waage f; **to tip the** ~**s in favour of sb/sth** für jdn/etw den Ausschlag geben.

scallop ['skɒləp] n (Zool) Kammuschel f.

scalp [skælp] **1** n Kopfhaut f; (as Indian trophy) Skalp m. **2** vt skalpieren; (hum: by barber) kahlscheren (hum).

scalpel ['skælpəl] n Skalpell nt.

scamp [skæmp] n Frechdachs m (col).

scamper ['skæmpər] vi (person, child, puppy) trappeln; (squirrel, rabbit) hoppeln; (mice) huschen.

scan [skæn] **1** vt **(a)** (search with sweeping movement) schwenken über (+acc); (person) seine Augen wandern lassen über (+acc); newspaper, book überfliegen; (examine closely) horizon absuchen; (by radar) absuchen, abtasten. **(b)** (TV) abtasten. **(c)** verse in Versfüße zerlegen. **2** vi (verse) sich reimen (col). **3** n (Med) Scan m; (in pregnancy) Ultraschall-Untersuchung f.

scandal ['skændl] n **(a)** Skandal m. **to create a** ~ einen Skandal verursachen; (amongst neighbours etc) allgemeines Aufsehen erregen; **it is a** ~ **that** ... es ist skandalös, daß ... **(b)** no pl (gossip) Skandalgeschichten pl; (piece of gossip) Skandalgeschichte f. **the latest** ~ der neueste Klatsch (col).

scandalize ['skændəlaɪz] vt schockieren. **she was** ~**d** sie war empört (by über +acc).

scandalous ['skændələs] adj skandalös. **a** ~ **report/ tale** eine Skandalgeschichte.

Scandinavia [ˌskændɪ'neɪvɪə] n Skandinavien nt.

Scandinavian [ˌskændɪ'neɪvɪən] **1** adj skandinavisch. **2** n Skandinavier(in f) m.

scanner ['skænər] n (Rad) Richtantenne f.

scant [skænt] adj (+er) wenig inv; attention, respect also, chance gering; success mager; amount spärlich.

scantily ['skæntɪlɪ] adv spärlich.

scanty ['skæntɪ] adj (+er) amount spärlich; vegetation, meal also kärglich; clothing knapp.

scapegoat ['skeɪpgəʊt] n Sündenbock m. **to make a** ~ **of sb** jdn zum Sündenbock machen.

scar [skɑːr] **1** n (on skin, tree) Narbe f; (scratch) Kratzer m; (burn) Brandfleck m; (fig emotional) Wunde f; (on good name) Makel m. **2** vt skin, tree Narben/eine Narbe hinterlassen auf (+dat); furniture zerkratzen; Brandflecken hinterlassen auf (+dat); (fig) person zeichnen. **he was** ~**red for life** (lit) er behielt bleibende Narben zurück; (fig) er war fürs Leben gezeichnet; **her** ~**red face** ihr narbiges Gesicht. **3** vi Narben/eine Narbe hinterlassen.

scarce [skɛəs] adj (+er) (in short supply) knapp;

(rare) selten. **to make oneself** ~ (col) verschwinden (col).

scarcely ['skɛəslɪ] adv kaum. ~ **anybody** kaum jemand; ~ **anything** fast nichts; ~ **ever** fast nie; **you can** ~ **expect him to believe that** Sie erwarten doch wohl kaum, daß er das glaubt.

scarceness ['skɛəsnɪs], **scarcity** ['skɛəsɪtɪ] n (shortage) Knappheit f; (rarity) Seltenheit f. **a** ~ **of qualified people** ein Mangel m an qualifizierten Kräften; **in times of** ~ in schlechten Zeiten.

scare [skɛər] **1** n (fright, shock) Schreck(en) m; (general alarm) Hysterie f (about wegen). **to give sb a** ~ jdm einen Schrecken einjagen; **to cause a** ~ eine Panik auslösen. **2** vt einen Schrecken einjagen (+dat); (worry also) Angst machen (+dat); (frighten physically) person, animal erschrecken; birds aufschrecken. **to be** ~**d** Angst haben (of vor +dat); **to be easily** ~**d** sehr schreckhaft sein; (easily worried) sich (dat) leicht Angst machen lassen; (timid: deer etc) sehr scheu sein; **to be** ~**d stiff** or **to death** or **out of one's wits** (all col) Todesängste ausstehen; **he's** ~**d of telling her the truth** er traut sich nicht, ihr die Wahrheit zu sagen.

♦ **scare away** vt sep verscheuchen; people verjagen.

scare: ~**crow** n (lit, fig) Vogelscheuche f; ~**monger** n Panikmacher m.

scarf [skɑːf] n, pl **scarves** Schal m; (neck ~) Halstuch nt; (head~) Kopftuch nt; (round the shoulders) Schultertuch nt.

scarlet ['skɑːlɪt] **1** n Scharlach(rot) nt. ~ **fever** Scharlach m. **2** adj (scharlach)rot. **to turn** ~ hochrot werden, rot anlaufen (col).

scarves [skɑːvz] pl of **scarf**.

scary ['skɛərɪ] adj (+er) (col) unheimlich; film also grus(e)lig (col). **it was pretty** ~ da konnte man schon Angst kriegen (col).

scathing ['skeɪðɪŋ] adj bissig; attack scharf; look, criticism vernichtend. **to be** ~ bissige Bemerkungen pl machen (about über +acc).

scatter ['skætər] **1** vt **(a)** newspaper; seeds, gravel, (Phys) light streuen (on, onto auf +acc). **the books were** ~**ed (about) all over the room** die Bücher lagen im ganzen Zimmer verstreut; **his friends were** ~**ed all over the country** seine Freunde waren über das ganze Land verstreut. **(b)** (disperse) auseinandertreiben; army etc also zersprengen. **2** vi sich zerstreuen (to in +acc); (in a hurry, in fear) auseinanderlaufen.

scatter: ~**brain** n (col) Schussel m (col); ~**brained** ['skætə,breɪnd] adj (col) schusselig (col).

scattered ['skætəd] adj population weit verstreut; villages verstreut; clouds, showers vereinzelt.

scatty ['skætɪ] adj (+er) (col) **(a)** (scatterbrained) schusselig (col). **(b)** (mad) verrückt.

scavenge ['skævɪndʒ] **1** vt (lit, fig) ergattern. **2** vi (lit) Nahrung suchen. **jackals live by scavenging** Schakale leben von Aas.

scavenger ['skævɪndʒər] n (animal) Aasfresser m; (fig: person) Dreckwühler m.

scenario [sɪ'nɑːrɪəʊ] n Szenar(ium) nt; (fig) Szenario nt.

scene [siːn] n **(a)** (place, setting) Schauplatz m; (of play, novel) Ort m der Handlung. **the** ~ **of the crime** der Tatort, der Schauplatz des Verbrechens; **the** ~ **of the battle was a small hill** die Schlacht fand auf einem kleinen Hügel statt; **to set the** ~ den Rahmen geben; **the** ~ **is set in Padua** das Stück/der Roman etc spielt in Padua; **to appear on the** ~ auftauchen, auf der Bildfläche erscheinen; **the police were first on the** ~ die Polizei war als erste zur Stelle. **(b)** (Theat) Szene f. Act II, ~ i Akt II, 1. Szene. **behind the** ~**s** (lit, fig) hinter den Kulissen. **(c)** (sight) Anblick m; (landscape) Landschaft f. **(d)** (fuss, argument) Szene f. **to make a** ~ eine Szene machen. **(e)** (col) **the drug** etc ~ die

scenery [...] Drogenszene etc (col); that's not my ~ da steh' ich nicht drauf (col).

scenery ['si:nərɪ] n (landscape) Landschaft f; (Theat) Kulissen pl.

scenic ['si:nɪk] adj route etc landschaftlich; (picturesque) malerisch. ~ **railway** (roller coaster) Achterbahn f.

scent [sent] 1 n (smell) Duft, Geruch m; (perfume) Parfüm nt; (of animal) Fährte f. **to be on the** ~ (lit, fig) auf der Spur sein (of sb/sth jdm/einer Sache); **to lose the** ~ (lit, fig) die Spur verlieren; **to put** or **throw sb off the** ~ (lit, fig) jdn von der Spur abbringen. **2** vt (a) (smell, suspect) wittern. (b) (perfume) parfümieren. roses ~ed the air der Duft von Rosen erfüllte die Luft.

sceptic, (US) **skeptic** ['skeptɪk] n Skeptiker(in f) m.

sceptical, (US) **skeptical** ['skeptɪkəl] adj skeptisch. **he was** ~ **about it** er war skeptisch.

scepticism, (US) **skepticism** ['skeptɪsɪzəm] n Skepsis f (about gegenüber).

sceptre, (US) **scepter** ['septər] n Szepter nt.

schedule ['ʃedjuːl (esp Brit), 'skedʒʊəl] 1 n (of events) Programm nt; (of work) Zeitplan m; (US: timetable) Fahr-/Flugplan m; (list) Verzeichnis nt. **what's on the** ~ **for today?** was steht für heute auf dem Programm?; **according to** ~ planmäßig; (work also) nach Plan; **the train is behind** ~ der Zug hat Verspätung; **the bus was on** ~ der Bus war pünktlich; **ahead of** ~ dem Zeitplan voraus; **behind** ~ im Rückstand; **we are working to a very tight** ~ wir arbeiten nach einem sehr knappen Zeitplan. **2** vt planen; (put on programme, timetable) ansetzen; (US: list) aufführen. **the work is** ~**d for completion in 3 months** die Arbeit soll (laut Zeitplan) in 3 Monaten fertig sein; **this stop was not** ~**d** dieser Aufenthalt war nicht eingeplant.

scheduled ['ʃedjuːld (esp Brit), 'skedʒʊəld] adj vorgesehen, geplant; departure etc planmäßig. ~ **flight** (not charter) Linienflug m; (on timetable) planmäßiger Flug.

schematic [skɪ'mætɪk] adj schematisch.

scheme [skiːm] 1 n (a) (plan) Plan m, Programm nt; (project) Projekt nt; (housing ~) Siedlung f; (idea) Idee f. **savings** ~ Sparprogramm nt; **pension** ~ Rentenschema nt; **the** ~ **for the new ring road** das neue Umgehungsstraßenprojekt; **a** ~ **of work** ein Arbeitsprogramm nt. (b) (plot) (raffinierter) Plan; (political also) Komplott nt; (at court, in firm etc) Intrige f. **2** vi Pläne schmieden; (at court, in firm etc) intrigieren.

scheming ['skiːmɪŋ] n Tricks pl (col); (of politicians etc) Machenschaften pl; (in firm etc) Intrigen pl. **2** adj methods, businessman raffiniert; politician gewieft (col).

schism ['sɪzəm] n (Eccl) Schisma nt; (general) Spaltung f.

schizophrenia [,skɪtsəʊ'friːnɪə] n Schizophrenie f.

schizophrenic ['skɪtsəʊ'frenɪk] 1 adj person, reaction schizophren. **2** n Schizophrene(r) mf.

schnap(p)s [ʃnæps] n Schnaps m.

scholar ['skɒlər] n (learned person) Gelehrte(r) mf; (student) Student(in f) m; Schüler(in f) m. **the foremost** ~**s of our time** die führenden Wissenschaftler unserer Zeit; **a famous Shakespeare** ~ ein bekannter Shakespearekenner.

scholarly ['skɒlərlɪ] adj thesis etc wissenschaftlich; (learned) gelehrt; interests hochgeistig.

scholarship ['skɒləʃɪp] n (learning) Gelehrsamkeit f; (money award) Stipendium nt.

scholastic [skə'læstɪk] adj (relative to school) schulisch, Schul-; (Univ) Studien-.

school¹ [skuːl] 1 n (a) Schule f; (US: college, university) College nt; Universität f. **at** ~ in der Schule/ im College/an der Universität; **to go to** ~ in die Schule/ins College/zur Universität gehen; **there's no** ~ **tomorrow** morgen ist schulfrei or keine Schule. (b) (Univ: department) Fachbereich m; (of medicine, law) Fakultät f. (c) (group of artists etc) Schule f. **he's a diplomat of the old** ~ er ist ein Diplomat der alten Schule. **2** vt lehren; animal dressieren. **to** ~ **sb in a technique** jdn in einer Technik unterrichten.

school² n (of fish) Schwarm m.

school in cpds Schul-; ~ **age** n schulpflichtiges Alter, Schulalter nt; ~ **boy** n Schüler m; ~**children** npl Schulkinder, Schüler pl; ~**days** npl Schulzeit f; ~ **fees** npl Schulgeld nt; ~**girl** n Schülerin f.

schooling ['skuːlɪŋ] n (education) Ausbildung f. **compulsory** ~ die Schulpflicht.

school: ~**-leaver** n Schulabgänger(in f) m; ~**-leaving age** n Schulabgangsalter nt; ~**master** n Lehrer m; ~**mistress** n (Brit) Lehrerin f; ~**room** n Klassenzimmer nt; ~**teacher** n Lehrer(in f) m; ~ **year** n Schuljahr nt.

schooner ['skuːnər] n (a) (boat) Schoner m. (b) (sherry glass) großes Sherryglas; (US, Austral: beer ~) hohes Bierglas.

sciatica [saɪ'ætɪkə] n Ischias m or nt.

science ['saɪəns] n (a) Wissenschaft f; (natural ~) Naturwissenschaft f. **to study** ~ Naturwissenschaften studieren; **a man of** ~ ein Wissenschaftler m. (b) (systematic knowledge or skill) Technik f.

science fiction n Science-fiction f. ~ **novel** Zukunftsroman m, Science-fiction-Roman m.

scientific [,saɪən'tɪfɪk] adj wissenschaftlich; (of natural sciences) naturwissenschaftlich.

scientist ['saɪəntɪst] n Wissenschaftler(in f) m; (natural ~) Naturwissenschaftler(in f) m.

Scillies ['sɪlɪz], **Scilly Isles** ['sɪlɪ,aɪlz] npl Scilly-Inseln pl.

scintillating ['sɪntɪleɪtɪŋ] adj funkelnd attr; (fig) (witty, lively) witt, humour sprühend attr.

scissors ['sɪzəz] n pl Schere f. **a pair of** ~ eine Schere.

sclerosis [sklɪ'rəʊsɪs] n Sklerose f.

scoff¹ [skɒf] vi spotten. **to** ~ **at sb/sth** jdn/etw verachten; (verbally) sich verächtlich über jdn/ etw äußern.

scoff² vt (col) futtern (col). **she** ~**ed the lot** sie hat alles verputzt (col).

scold [skəʊld] vt ausschimpfen (for wegen). **she** ~**ed him for coming home late** sie schimpfte ihn aus, weil er so spät heimkam.

scolding ['skəʊldɪŋ] n Schelte f no pl; (act) Schimpferei f. **to give sb a** ~ jdn ausschimpfen.

scollop n = **scallop**.

scone [skɒn] n ≈ Milchbrötchen nt; (with sultanas) Rosinenbrötchen nt.

scoop [skuːp] 1 n (a) (instrument) Schaufel f; (for ice cream, potatoes etc) Portionierer m. (b) (col: lucky gain) Fang m (col). (c) (Press) Knüller m (col). **2** vt (a) schaufeln; liquid schöpfen. (b) **The Times** ~**ed the other papers** die Times ist den anderen Zeitungen zuvorgekommen.

♦ **scoop out** vt sep (a) (take out) herausschaufeln; liquid herausschöpfen. (b) (hollow out) marrow etc ausnehmen; hole graben.

♦ **scoop up** vt sep aufschaufeln; liquid aufschöpfen. **she** ~**ed the cards/money** ~ sie raffte die Karten/das Geld an sich (acc).

scoot [skuːt] vi (col) (scram) abzischen (col); (walk quickly) rennen.

scooter ['skuːtər] n (Tret)roller m; (motor ~) Motorroller m.

scope [skəʊp] n (a) (of topic, investigation, knowledge) Umfang m; (of law, measures) Reichweite f; (of sb's duties, tribunal) Kompetenzbereich m. **sth is within the** ~ **of sth** etw hält sich im Rahmen einer Sache (gen); **sth is beyond the** ~ **of sth** etw geht über etw (acc) hinaus; **that is beyond my** ~ das übersteigt mein Fassungsvermögen. (b) (opportunity) Möglichkeit(en pl) f;

(to develop one's talents) Entfaltungsmöglichkeit *f; (to use one's talents)* Spielraum *m.* **there is ~ for improvement** es könnte noch verbessert werden; **to give sb ~ to do sth** jdm den nötigen Spielraum geben, etw zu tun.

scorch [skɔːtʃ] **1** *n (also ~ mark)* Brandfleck *m.* **2** *vt* versengen. **the sun ~ed our faces** die Sonne brannte auf unsere Gesichter.

scorcher ['skɔːtʃəʳ] *n (col)* **last summer was a real ~** im letzten Sommer war es wirklich heiß.

scorching ['skɔːtʃɪŋ] *adj (very hot) sun,* iron glühend heiß; *day, weather* brütend heiß; *(col: very fast) speed* rasend.

score [skɔːʳ] **1** *n* **(a)** *(number of points)* (Punkte)stand *m; (of game, Sport)* Spielstand *m; (final ~)* Spielergebnis *nt.* **the ~ was Celtic 2, Rangers 1** es stand 2:1 *or* zwei zu eins für Celtic (gegen Rangers); *(final ~)* Celtic schlug Rangers (mit) 2:1; **to keep (the) ~** (mit)zählen; *(officially)* Punkte zählen; *(on scoreboard)* Punkte anschreiben; **what's the ~?** wie steht es?; *(fig also)* wie sieht es aus? *(on mit) (col);* **to make a ~ with sb** *(fig: impress)* jdn stark beeindrucken.

    (b) *(reckoning, grudge)* **to pay off old ~s** alte Schulden begleichen; **to have a ~ to settle with sb** mit jdm eine alte Rechnung zu begleichen haben.

    (c) *(Mus) (printed music)* Noten *pl; (of classical music also)* Partitur *f; (of film, musical)* Musik *f.*

    (d) *(line, cut)* Kerbe *f; (on body)* Kratzer *m; (weal)* Striemen *m.*

    (e) *(20)* **a ~** zwanzig; **~s of ...** *(many)* Hunderte von ..., jede Menge ... *(col);* **by the ~** massenweise *(col).*

    (f) *(reason, ground)* Grund *m.* **on that ~** *(connection)* in diesem Zusammenhang.

    2 *vt* **(a)** erzielen; *points also* bekommen; *goals also* schießen; *runs also* schaffen. **he ~d an advantage over his opponent** er war gegenüber seinem Gegner im Vorteil; **each correct answer ~s five points** jede richtige Antwort zählt fünf Punkte; **to ~ a point off sb** *(fig)* jdn ausstechen; **to ~ a hit with sb** jdn stark beeindrucken. **(b)** *(groove)* einkerben, Kerben/eine Kerbe machen in *(+acc); (mark)* Kratzer/einen Kratzer machen in *(+acc).*

    3 *vi* **(a)** einen Punkt erzielen; *(Ftbl etc)* ein Tor schießen. **to ~ well/badly** gut/schlecht abschneiden; **that's where he ~s** *(fig)* das ist sein großes Plus. **(b)** *(keep ~)* (mit)zählen. **(c)** **to ~ with sb** *(col: have sex)* mit jdm bumsen *(col).*

♦ **score off 1** *vt sep (delete)* ausstreichen. **2** *vi +prep obj* **to ~ ~ sb** jdn als dumm hinstellen.

score: **~board** *n* Anzeigetafel *f;* **~keeper** *n (official) (Sport)* Anschreiber *m; (in quiz etc)* Punktezähler *m.*

scorer ['skɔːrəʳ] *n* **(a)** *(Ftbl etc: player)* Torschütze *m.* **Chelsea were the highest ~s** Chelsea schoß die meisten Tore; **the leading ~ in the quiz etc,** der die meisten Punkte im Quiz erzielt. **(b)** = **scorekeeper.**

scorn ['skɔːn] **1** *n (disdain)* Verachtung *f; (verbal also)* Hohn *m.* **to pour ~ on sth** etw verächtlich abtun. **2** *vt (treat scornfully)* verachten; *(condescendingly)* verächtlich behandeln; *(turn down) gift, advice* verschmähen; *idea* mit Verachtung von sich weisen.

scornful ['skɔːnfʊl] *adj* verächtlich; *laughter also, person* spöttisch, höhnisch. **to be ~ of sb/sth** jdn/etw verachten; *(verbally)* jdn/etw verhöhnen.

Scorpio ['skɔːpɪəʊ] *n (Astrol)* Skorpion *m.*

scorpion ['skɔːpɪən] *n* Skorpion *m.*

Scot [skɒt] *n* Schotte *m,* Schottin *f.*

Scotch [skɒtʃ] **1** *adj* schottisch. **~ egg** hartgekochtes Ei in Wurstbrät, paniert und ausgebacken; **~ tape** ® Tesafilm ® *m.* **2** *n* **(a)** *(~ whisky)* Scotch *m.* **(b)** **the ~** *pl* die Schotten *pl.*

scotch [skɒtʃ] *vt rumour* aus der Welt schaffen; *idea, plan* unterbinden.

scot-free ['skɒt'friː] *adv:* **to get off ~** ungeschoren davonkommen.

Scotland ['skɒtlənd] *n* Schottland *nt.*

Scots [skɒts] *adj* schottisch.

Scots: **~man** *n* Schotte *m;* **~woman** *n* Schottin *f.*

Scottish ['skɒtɪʃ] **1** *adj* schottisch. **2** *n* **(a)** *(dialect)* Schottisch *nt.* **(b)** **the ~** *pl* die Schotten *pl.*

scoundrel ['skaʊndrəl] *n (dated)* Schurke *m; (col)* Bengel *m.*

scour[1] ['skaʊəʳ] *vt pans* scheuern.

scour[2] *vt area* absuchen *(for* nach*).*

scourer ['skaʊərəʳ] *n* Topfkratzer *m.*

scourge [skɜːdʒ] **1** *n (lit, fig)* Geißel *f.* **2** *vt* **(a)** geißeln. **(b)** *(fig: punish)* bestrafen.

scout [skaʊt] **1** *n* **(a)** *(Mil)* Späher *m.* **(b)** Pfadfinder *m; (US: girl ~)* Pfadfinderin *f.* **2** *vi* erkunden. **to ~ for sth** nach etw Ausschau halten.

scout: **~ master** *n* Gruppenführer *m;* **~ troop** *n* Pfadfindergruppe *f.*

scowl [skaʊl] **1** *n* finsterer Blick, böses Gesicht. **to give sb a ~** jdn böse ansehen. **2** *vi* ein finsteres Gesicht machen. **to ~ at sb** jdn böse ansehen.

scrabble ['skræbl] *vi (also ~ about)* (herum)tasten; *(among movable objects)* (herum)wühlen.

scraggy ['skrægɪ] *adj (+er)* dürr; *meat* sehnig.

scram [skræm] *vi (col)* abhauen *(col).* **~!** ab!, verschwinde/verschwindet!

scramble ['skræmbl] **1** *vt* **(a)** *pieces, letters* (ver)mischen. **(b)** *eggs* verrühren. **~d eggs** Rührei(er *pl*) *nt.* **(c)** *(Telec) message* verschlüsseln.

    2 *vi* **(a)** *(climb)* klettern. **he ~d to his feet** er rappelte sich auf *(col);* **to ~ through the hedge** durch die Hecke krabbeln *(col);* **to ~ up sth** etw *(acc)* hinaufklettern. **(b)** *(struggle)* **to ~ for sth/to get sth** sich um etw raufen/sich raufen, um etw zu bekommen; *for ball etc* um etw kämpfen/darum kämpfen, etw zu bekommen; *for bargains, job, good site* sich um etw drängeln/ sich drängeln, um etw zu bekommen.

    3 *n* **(a)** *(rush)* Gedrängel *nt (for* nach*).* **(b)** *(motorcycle ~)* Querfeldeinrennen *nt.*

scrap[1] [skræp] **1** *n* **(a)** *(small piece)* Stückchen *nt; (fig)* bißchen *no pl; (of papers also, of conversation, news)* Fetzen *m; (of truth)* Fünkchen *nt,* Spur *f.* **there isn't a ~ of food in the house** es ist überhaupt nichts zu essen im Haus; **not a ~!** nicht die Spur!; **not a ~ of evidence** nicht der geringste Beweis. **(b)** *(usu pl: leftover)* Rest *m.* **(c)** *(waste material)* Altmaterial *nt; (metal)* Schrott *m; (paper)* Altpapier *nt.* **are these notes ~?** können die Notizen weggeworfen werden?; **to sell a ship for ~** ein Schiff zum Verschrotten verkaufen. **2** *vt car, ship etc* verschrotten; *furniture, clothes* ausrangieren; *idea, plan etc* fallenlassen; *piece of work* wegwerfen.

scrap: **~book** *n* Sammelalbum *nt;* **~ dealer** *n* Altwarenhändler *m.*

scrap[2] *(col)* **1** *n* Balgerei *f; (verbal)* Streiterei *f.* **2** *vi* sich balgen; *(verbally)* sich streiten.

scrape [skreɪp] **1** *n* **(a)** *(act)* **to give sth a ~** *~ see* vt *(a).* **(b)** *(mark, graze)* Schramme *f.* **(c)** *(sound)* Kratzen *nt.* **(d)** *(difficulty)* Schwulität *pl (col).* **to get sb out of a ~** jdm aus der Klemme helfen *(col).* **2** *vt* **(a)** *(make clean or smooth)* potatoes etc schaben; *plate, wall* abkratzen; *saucepan* auskratzen. **that's really scraping the barrel** *(fig)* das ist wirklich das Letzte vom Letzten. **(b)** *gatepost etc* streifen; *paintwork* ankratzen; *knee* aufschürfen. **(c)** *(grate against)* kratzen an *(+dat).* **(d)** *(make by scraping)* hole scharren. **to ~ a living** gerade so sein Auskommen haben. **3** *vi* **he ~d at the paint for hours** er kratzte stundenlang an der Farbe herum.

♦ **scrape along** *or* **by** *vi* sich schlecht und recht durchschlagen *(col) (on* mit*).*

♦ **scrape off** *vt sep* abkratzen *(prep obj* von).

♦ **scrape through 1** *vi (lit) (object)* gerade so durchgehen; *(person)* sich durchzwängen; *(in exam)* gerade noch durchkommen *(col)*. **2** *vi* +*prep obj narrow gap* sich durchzwängen durch; *exam* gerade noch durchkommen durch *(col)*.

♦ **scrape together** *vt sep leaves* zusammenharken; *money* zusammenkratzen; *people* zusammenbringen; *support* organisieren.

scraper ['skreɪpər] *n (tool)* Spachtel *m; (at door)* Kratzeisen *nt.*

scrap heap *n* Schrotthaufen *m.* **to be thrown on the ~** *(thing)* zum Schrott geworfen werden; *(person)* zum alten Eisen geworfen werden; *(idea)* über Bord geworfen werden.

scrap metal *n* Schrott *m*, Altmetall *nt.*

scrappy ['skræpɪ] *adj* (+er) zusammengestoppelt *(col)*; *knowledge* lückenhaft.

scrap yard *n* Schrottplatz *m.*

scratch [skrætʃ] **1** *n* (a) *(mark)* Kratzer *m.* (b) *(act)* the dog enjoys a ~ der Hund kratzt sich gern. (c) to start from ~ (ganz) von vorn(e) anfangen; to start sth from ~ etw ganz von vorne anfangen; *business* etw aus dem Nichts aufbauen; to learn a language/a new trade from ~ eine Sprache von Grund auf erlernen/einen neuen Beruf von der Pike auf erlernen; to come up to ~ *(col)* den Anforderungen entsprechen.

2 *adj attr meal* improvisiert; *crew, team* zusammengewürfelt.

3 *vt* kratzen; *hole* scharren; *(leave ~es on)* zerkratzen. to ~ a living *(dat)* einen kümmerlichen Lebensunterhalt verdienen; to ~ one's head *(lit,fig)* sich *(dat)* den Kopf kratzen; if you ~ my back, I'll ~ yours *(fig)* eine Hand wäscht die andere; to ~ the surface of sth *(fig)* etw oberflächlich berühren.

4 *vi* (a) *(make ~ing movement/noise)* kratzen; *(in soil etc)* scharren; *(~ oneself)* sich kratzen. (b) *(become ~)* the new paint ~es easily die neue Farbe bekommt leicht Kratzer.

♦ **scratch out** *vt sep* auskratzen; *(cross out)* ausstreichen.

scratchy ['skrætʃɪ] *adj* (+er) *sound, pen* kratzend *attr; record* zerkratzt; *feel, sweater* kratzig.

scrawl [skrɔːl] **1** *n* Gekrakel *nt (col); (handwriting)* Klaue *f (col); (col: message)* gekritzelte Nachricht. **2** *vt* hinkritzeln.

scrawny ['skrɔːnɪ] *adj* (+er) dürr.

scream [skriːm] **1** *n* (a) Schrei *m; (of tyres)* Kreischen *nt; (of engines, siren)* Heulen *nt.* there were ~s of laughter from the audience das Publikum kreischte vor Lachen; to give a ~ einen Schrei ausstoßen. (b) *(fig col)* to be a ~ zum Schreien sein *(col)*. **2** *vt* schreien; *command* brüllen; *(fig: headlines)* ausschreien. to ~ sth at sb jdm etw zuschreien; you idiot, she ~ed at me du Idiot, schrie sie mich an. **3** *vi* schreien; *(tyres)* kreischen; *(wind, engine, siren)* heulen. to ~ at sb jdn anschreien; to ~ with laughter vor Lachen schreien.

scree [skriː] *n* Geröll *nt.*

screech [skriːtʃ] **1** *n* Kreischen *nt no pl; (of tyres also, of brakes)* Quietschen *nt no pl; (of owl)* Schrei *m.* the car stopped with a ~ of brakes das Auto hielt mit quietschenden Bremsen. **2** *vi* kreischen; *(brakes, tyres also)* quietschen.

screen [skriːn] **1** *n* (a) *(protective)* Schirm *m; (for privacy etc)* Wandschirm *m; (as partition)* Trennwand *f; (against insects)* Fliegenfenster *nt; (fig) (for protection)* Schutz *m; (of trees)* Wand *f; (of mist, secrecy)* Schleier *m.* (b) *(Film)* Leinwand *f; (TV, radar ~, Comp)* (Bild)schirm *m.* the big/small ~ die Leinwand/die Mattscheibe. **2** *vt* (a) *(hide)* verdecken; *(protect)* abschirmen *(from* gegen). he ~ed his eyes from the sun er schützte die Augen vor der Sonne. (b) *TV programme* senden; *film* vorführen. (c) *(sift)* sieben. (d)

(investigate) applicants, security risks überprüfen.

screening ['skriːnɪŋ] *n* (a) *(of applicants, security risks)* Überprüfung *f.* (b) *(of film)* Vorführung *f; (TV)* Sendung *f.*

screenplay ['skriːnpleɪ] *n* Drehbuch *nt.*

screw [skruː] **1** *n* (a) *(Mech, Naut, Aviat)* Schraube *f.* he's got a ~ loose *(col)* bei dem ist eine Schraube locker *(col)*; to put the ~s on sb *(col)* jdm die Daumenschrauben anlegen. (b) *(Brit col: prison officer)* Schließer *(col)*. **2** *vt* (a) schrauben *(to* an +*acc, onto* auf +*acc)*. (b) *(col: put pressure on)* to ~ sb for sth etw aus jdm herausquetschen *(col)*. (c) *(col!: have sex with)* bumsen *(col)*, vögeln *(col!)*.

♦ **screw together** *vt sep* zusammenschrauben.

♦ **screw up** *vt sep* (a) *paper, material* zerknüllen; *eyes* zusammenkneifen; *face* verziehen. to ~ ~ one's courage seinen ganzen Mut zusammennehmen. (b) *(col) (spoil)* vermasseln *(col); (make uptight) sb* neurotisch machen. to be ~ed ~ about sth sich wegen etw ganz verrückt machen.

screw: ~ball *(esp US col)* n Spinner(in *f*) *m (col)*; ~driver *n* Schraubenzieher *m.*

screwy ['skruːɪ] *adj* (+er) *(col)* verrückt, bekloppt *(col)*; *person, humour* komisch.

scribble ['skrɪbl] **1** *n* Gekritzel *nt no pl; (note)* schnell hingekritzelte Nachricht. **2** *vt* hinkritzeln. to ~ sth on sth etw auf etw *(acc)* kritzeln; to ~ sth down etw hinkritzeln. **3** *vi* kritzeln. he ~s away all day at his novel er schreibt den ganzen Tag an seinem Roman herum.

scribe [skraɪb] *n* Schreiber *m; (Bibl)* Schriftgelehrte(r) *m.*

scrimmage ['skrɪmɪdʒ] *n (US Ftbl)* Gedränge *nt; (col: struggle also)* Rangelei *f (col); (Rugby)* offenes Gedränge.

scrimp [skrɪmp] *vi* sparen, knausern. to ~ and save geizen und sparen.

script [skrɪpt] *n* (a) *(style of writing)* Schrift *f; (handwriting)* Handschrift *f.* (b) *(of play, documentary)* Text *m; (for film)* Drehbuch *nt.*

scripture ['skrɪptʃər] *n* (a) S~, the S~s die (Heilige) Schrift. (b) *(Sch)* Religion *f.*

scriptwriter ['skrɪpt,raɪtər] *n (Film)* Drehbuchautor(in *f*) *m.*

scroll [skrəʊl] *n* Schriftrolle *f; (decorative)* Schnörkel *m.*

scrotum ['skrəʊtəm] *n (Anat)* Hodensack *m.*

scrounge [skraʊndʒ] *(col)* **1** *vi (sponge)* schnorren *(col) (off, from* bei). he ~d off his parents for years er lag jahrelang seinen Eltern auf der Tasche *(col)*. **2** *vt* schnorren *(col)*, abstauben *(col) (from, off* bei). **3** *n (col)* to be on the ~ am Schnorren sein *(col)*.

scrounger ['skraʊndʒər] *n (col)* Schnorrer *m (col)*.

scrub[1] [skrʌb] *nt (Bot)* Gebüsch, Gestrüpp *nt.*

scrub[2] [skrʌb] **1** *n* Schrubben *nt no pl.* to give sth a ~/a good ~ etw schrubben/gründlich abschrubben. **2** *vt* schrubben; *vegetables* putzen; *(col: cancel)* abblasen *(col); idea* abschreiben *(col)*. to ~ oneself down sich abschrubben.

scrubbing brush ['skrʌbɪŋ,brʌʃ] *n* Scheuerbürste *f; (for hands)* Handbürste *f.*

scruff[1] [skrʌf] *n* by the ~ of the neck am Genick.

scruff[2] *n (col: scruffy person)* man *(col)* schlampig aussehender Typ; *(woman)* Schlampe *f (col)*.

scruffy ['skrʌfɪ] *adj* (+er) *(col)* vergammelt *(col); house also* verlottert *(col)*, verwahrlost.

scrum [skrʌm] *n (Rugby)* Gedränge *nt.*

scrumptious ['skrʌmpʃəs] *adj (col) meal etc* lecker.

scruple ['skruːpl] *n* Skrupel *m usu pl.* ~s *(doubts) (moralische)* Bedenken *pl.* to have no ~s keine Skrupel haben.

scrupulous ['skruːpjʊləs] *adj (person)* gewissenhaft; *honesty, fairness* unbedingt; *cleanliness* peinlich; *account* (peinlich) genau.

scrupulously ['skruːpjʊlslɪ] *adv (honestly, conscientiously)* gewissenhaft; *(meticulously)* exact, clean peinlich; *fair, careful* äußerst.

scrutinize ['skruːtɪnaɪz] *vt (examine)* (genau) untersuchen; *(check)* genau prüfen; *votes* prüfen; *(stare at)* mustern. **to ~ sth for sth** etw auf etw *(acc)* prüfen.

scrutiny ['skruːtɪnɪ] *n* **(a)** *(examination)* Untersuchung *f*; *(checking)* (Über)prüfung *f*; *(of person)* Musterung *f*; *(stare)* musternder Blick. **it does not stand up to ~** es hält keiner genauen Prüfung stand. **(b)** *(Pol)* Wahlprüfung *f*.

scuba ['skuːbə] *n* (Schwimm)tauchgerät *nt*. **~ diver** (Sport)taucher(in *f*) *m*; **~ diving** Sporttauchen *nt*.

scuff [skʌf] **1** *vt* abwetzen. **2** *n* (~ mark) abgewetzte Stelle.

scuffle ['skʌfl] **1** *n (skirmish)* Rauferei *f (col)*. **2** *vi (have skirmish)* sich raufen. **to ~ with the police** ein Handgemenge *nt* mit der Polizei haben.

scullery ['skʌlərɪ] *n* Spülküche *f*.

sculpt [skʌlpt] **1** *vt* = **sculpture**. **2** *vi* bildhauern *(col)*.

sculptor ['skʌlptə^r] *n* Bildhauer(in *f*) *m*.

sculptress ['skʌlptrɪs] *n* Bildhauerin *f*.

sculpture ['skʌlptʃə^r] **1** *n (art)* Bildhauerkunst *f*; *(work)* Bildhauerei *f*; *(object)* Skulptur, Plastik *f*. **2** *vt* formen; *(in stone)* hauen, meißeln; *(in clay etc)* modellieren. **he ~d the tombstone out of marble** er haute den Grabstein in Marmor.

scum [skʌm] *n* **(a)** *(on liquid)* Schaum *m*; *(residue)* Rand *m*. **(b)** *(pej col) (collective)* Abschaum *m*; *(one individual)* Dreckskerl *m (col)*. **the ~ of the earth** der Abschaum der Menschheit.

scupper ['skʌpə^r] *vt (Naut)* versenken; *(Brit col: ruin)* zerschlagen. **if he finds out, we'll be ~ed** wenn er das erfährt, sind wir erledigt *(col)*.

scurrilous ['skʌrɪləs] *adj (abusive)* verleumderisch; *(indecent)* unflätig.

scurry ['skʌrɪ] *vi (person)* hasten; *(with small steps)* trippeln; *(animals)* huschen. **to ~ along** entlanghasten/entlangtrippeln/entlanghuschen.

scurvy ['skɜːvɪ] *n* Skorbut *m*.

scuttle[1] ['skʌtl] *n* Kohleneimer *m*.

scuttle[2] *vi (person)* trippeln; *(animals)* hoppeln; *(spiders, crabs etc)* krabbeln. **she ~d off in a hurry** sie flitzte davon.

scuttle[3] *(Naut)* **1** *n* Luke *f*. **2** *vt* versenken.

scythe [saɪð] **1** *n* Sense *f*. **2** *vt* (mit der Sense) mähen.

SDP = Social Democratic Party.

sea [siː] *n* **(a)** Meer *nt*, See *f*. **by ~** auf dem Seeweg; **to travel by ~** mit dem Schiff fahren; **a town by the ~** eine Stadt am Meer *or* an der See; **(out) at ~** auf See; **as I looked out to ~** als ich aufs Meer hinausblickte; **to be all at ~** *(fig)* nicht durchblicken *(col) (with bei)*; **to go to ~** zur See gehen; **to put to ~** in See stechen; **heavy/strong ~s** schwere/rauhe See; **a ~ of faces** ein Meer von Gesichtern; **a ~ of flame** ein Flammenmeer.

sea: ~ air *n* Seeluft *f*; **~ anemone** *n* Seeanemone *f*; **~bed** *n* Meeresboden *m*; **~ bird** *n* Seevogel *m*; **~board** *n (US)* Küste *f*; **~ breeze** *n* Seewind *m*; **~faring** *adj* nation, people seefahrend; *boat* hochseetüchtig; **~food** *n* Meeresfrüchte *pl*; **~ front** *n* Strandpromenade *f*; **~going** *adj* boat etc hochseetüchtig; nation, family Seefahrer-; **~gull** *n* Möwe *f*; **~ horse** *n* Seepferdchen *nt*.

seal[1] [siːl] *n (Zool)* Seehund *m*; (~skin) Seal *m*.

seal[2] **1** *n* **(a)** *(impression in wax etc)* Siegel *nt*; *(against unauthorized opening)* Versiegelung *f*; *(die)* Stempel *m*; *(decorative label)* Aufkleber *m*. **under the ~ of secrecy** unter dem Siegel der Verschwiegenheit; **~ of quality** Gütesiegel *nt*; **to put one's ~ of approval on sth** einer Sache *(dat)* seine offizielle Zustimmung geben. **(b)** *(airtight closure)* Verschluß *m*; *(washer)* Dichtung *f*. **2** *vt* versiegeln; *envelope, parcel also* zukle-

ben; *(make air- or watertight)* joint etc abdichten; *(fig: finalize)* besiegeln. **~ed envelope** verschlossener Briefumschlag; **my lips are ~ed** meine Lippen sind versiegelt; **this ~ed his fate** dadurch war sein Schicksal besiegelt.
♦ **seal off** *vt sep* absperren, abriegeln.
♦ **seal up** *vt sep* versiegeln; *parcel, letter* zukleben; *crack, windows* abdichten.

sea: ~ legs *npl*: **to find one's ~ legs** standfest werden; **~ level** *n* Meeresspiegel *m*; **above/below ~ level** über/unter dem Meeresspiegel.

sealing wax ['siːlɪŋwæks] *n* Siegelwachs *nt*.

sea lion *n* Seelöwe *m*.

seam [siːm] *n* **(a)** Naht *f*. **to come apart at the ~s** *(lit, fig)* aus den Nähten gehen; **to be bursting at the ~s** *(lit, fig)* aus allen Nähten platzen *(col)*. **(b)** *(Geol)* Flöz *nt*.

seaman ['siːmən] *n, pl* **-men** [-mən] Seemann *m*.

seamanship ['siːmənʃɪp] *n* Seemannschaft *f*.

seamstress ['semstrɪs] *n* Näherin *f*.

seamy ['siːmɪ] *adj* (+er) düster. **the ~ side of life** die Schattenseite des Lebens.

séance ['seɪɑːns] *n* spiritistische Sitzung, Séance *f*.

sea: ~ plane *n* Wasserflugzeug *nt*; **~ port** *n* Seehafen *m*; **~ power** *n* Seemacht *f*.

search [sɜːtʃ] **1** *n (hunt: for lost object, person etc)* Suche *f (for nach)*; *(examination: of luggage etc)* Durchsuchung *f (of gen)*. **to go in ~ of sb/sth auf die Suche nach jdm/etw gehen; a ~ through the drawers revealed nothing** er etc durchsuchte die Schubladen ohne Erfolg. **2** *vt (for nach)* durchsuchen; *archives etc* suchen in (+*dat*), durchforschen; *conscience* erforschen; *memory etc* durchforschen. **to ~ a place for sb/sth** einen Ort nach jdm/etw absuchen; **~ me!** *(col)* was weiß ich? *(col)*. **3** *vi* suchen *(for nach)*.
♦ **search through** *vi +prep obj* durchsuchen; *papers, books* durchsehen.

searching ['sɜːtʃɪŋ] *adj look* forschend; *question* durchdringend.

search: ~light *n* Suchscheinwerfer *m*; **~ party** *n* Suchmannschaft *f*; **~ warrant** *n* Durchsuchungsbefehl *m*.

searing ['sɪərɪŋ] *adj heat* glühend; *pain also* scharf.

sea: ~scape *n* Seestück *nt*; **~ shell** *n* Muschel *f*; **~shore** *n* Strand *m*; **on the ~shore** am Strand; **~sick** *adj* seekrank; **~sickness** *n* Seekrankheit *f*; **~side 1** *n* at the ~side am Meer; **to go to the ~side** ans Meer fahren; **2** *attr resort, town* See-.

season ['siːzn] **1** *n* **(a)** *(of the year)* Jahreszeit *f*. **rainy/monsoon ~** Regen-/Monsunzeit *f*. **(b)** *(sporting ~ etc)* Saison *f*. **holiday ~** Urlaubszeit *f*; **close ~** (Hunt) Schonzeit *f*; **nesting/hunting ~** Brut-/Jagdzeit *f*; **the football ~** die Fußballsaison; **strawberries are in ~/out of ~** now für Erdbeeren ist jetzt die richtige/nicht die richtige Zeit; **"S~'s greetings"** „fröhliche Weihnachten und ein glückliches neues Jahr". **2** *vt* **(a)** *food* würzen; *(fig: temper)* durchsetzen. **(b)** *wood* ablagern; *(fig: inure)* troops stählen.

seasonable ['siːznəbl] *adj dress, weather etc* der Jahreszeit entsprechend *attr*. **to be ~** der Jahreszeit entsprechen.

seasonal ['siːznl] *adj employment etc* Saison-.

seasoned ['siːznd] *adj* **(a)** *food* gewürzt. **(b)** *timber* abgelagert. **(c)** *(fig: experienced)* erfahren.

seasoning ['siːznɪŋ] *n (Cook)* Gewürz *nt*.

season ticket *n (Rail)* Zeitkarte *f*; *(Theat)* Abonnement *nt*.

seat [siːt] **1** *n* **(a)** *(place to sit)* (Sitz)platz *m*; *(piece of furniture)* Sitz *m*; *(usu pl: ~ing)* Sitzgelegenheit *f*. **driving ~** Fahrersitz *m*; **we'll have to borrow some ~s** wir werden uns wohl ein paar Stühle borgen müssen; **we haven't enough ~s** wir haben nicht genügend Sitzgelegenheiten; **to lose one's ~** seinen Platz verlieren; **will you keep my ~ for me?** würden Sie mir meinen Platz freihalten?; **I've booked two ~s** ich habe zwei Plätze

reservieren lassen. **(b)** *(of chair etc)* Sitz *m*, Sitzfläche *f*; *(of trousers)* Hosenboden *m*. **(c)** *(on committee, of government, in parliament)* Sitz *m*; *(of fire, trouble)* Herd *m*. **to win a ~** ein Mandat gewinnen; **his ~ is in Devon** sein Wahlkreis *m* ist in Devon; **~ of emotions** Sitz der Gefühle; **~ of learning** Lehrstätte *f*.
2 *vt* **(a)** *person etc* setzen. **to ~ oneself** sich setzen; **to be ~ed** sitzen; **please be ~ed** bitte, setzen Sie sich; **to remain ~ed** sitzen bleiben. **(b)** *(have sitting room for)* **the car/table ~s** 4 im Auto/am Tisch ist Platz für 4 Personen; **the theatre ~s** 900 das Theater hat 900 Sitzplätze.
seat belt *n* Sicherheitsgurt *m*. **to fasten one's ~** sich anschnallen.
seating ['siːtɪŋ] *n* Sitzplätze *pl*. **~ arrangements** Sitzordnung *f*.
sea: **~ urchin** *n* Seeigel *m*; **~ wall** *n* Deich *m*; **~ water** *n* Meerwasser *nt*; **~weed** *n* (See)tang *m*, Seegras *nt*; **~worthy** *adj* seetüchtig.
sec [sek] = **second(s)** Sek.
secateurs [ˌsekəˈtɜːz] *npl (Brit)* Gartenschere *f*.
secession [sɪˈseʃən] *n* Abspaltung *f*; *(US Hist)* Sezession *f*.
secluded [sɪˈkluːdɪd] *adj* spot, house abgelegen; life zurückgezogen.
seclusion [sɪˈkluːʒən] *n (of house, spot)* Abgelegenheit *f*.
second[1] ['sekənd] **1** *adj* zweite(r, s). **a ~ Goethe** ein zweiter Goethe; **every ~ house** jedes zweite Haus; **to be ~** Zweite(r, s) sein; **to be ~ to none** unübertroffen sein; **in ~ place** *(Sport etc)* an zweiter Stelle; **in the ~ place** *(secondly)* zweitens; **to be ~ in command** *(Mil)* stellvertretender Kommandeur sein; *(fig)* der zweite Mann sein; **will you have a ~ cup?** möchten Sie noch eine Tasse? **2** *adv* (+*adj*) zweit-; (+*vb*) an zweiter Stelle. **the ~ largest house** das zweitgrößte Haus; **to come/lie ~** *(in race, competition)* Zweite(r) werden. **3** *vt* motion, proposal unterstützen. **I'll ~ that!** *(at meeting)* (genau) meine Meinung.
second[2] *n* **(a)** *(of time, Math, Sci)* Sekunde *f*; *(col: short time)* Augenblick *m*. **just a ~!** (einen) Augenblick!; **it won't take a ~** es dauert nicht lange; **I'll only be a ~ (or two)** ich komme gleich; *(back soon)* ich bin gleich wieder da; **at that very ~** genau in dem Augenblick. **(b)** **the ~** *(in order)* der/die/das zweite; *(in race, class etc)* der/die/das Zweite; **to come a poor/good ~** einen schlechten/ guten zweiten Platz belegen; **Elizabeth the S~** Elisabeth die Zweite. **(c)** *(Brit Univ: degree)* mittlere Noten bei Abschlußprüfungen. **(d)** **~s** *pl (col: ~ helping)* Nachschlag *m (col)*; **can I have ~s?** kann ich noch etwas nachbekommen? **(e)** *(Comm)* **~s** Waren zweiter Wahl. **(f)** *(Boxing, duelling)* Sekundant *m*.
secondary ['sekəndərɪ] *adj* **(a)** sekundär, Sekundär- *(also Sci)*; road, effect Neben-; industry verarbeitend; reason weniger bedeutend. **of ~ importance** von untergeordneter Bedeutung. **(b)** *(higher)* education, school höher. **~ modern (school)** *(Brit)* ≃ Realschule *f*.
second: **~-best** **1** *n* Zweitbeste(r, s); **(the) ~-best isn't good enough for him** das Beste ist gerade gut genug für ihn; **2** *adj* zweitbeste(r, s); **3** *adv* **to come off ~-best** es nicht so gut haben; *(come off badly)* den kürzeren ziehen; **~ class** *n (Rail etc, mail)* zweite Klasse; **~-class** *adj (a) also adv* travel, mail, citizen zweiter Klasse *(after noun)*; **(b)** = **~-rate**; **~ cousin** *n* Cousin *m*/Cousine *f* zweiten Grades.
seconder ['sekəndə[r]] *n* Befürworter(in *f*) *m*.
second: **~ hand** *n (of watch)* Sekundenzeiger *m*; **~-hand** **1** *adj* gebraucht; car also Gebraucht-; dealer Gebrauchtwaren-; *(for cars)* Gebrauchtwagen-; bookshop Antiquariats-; clothes getragen, Secondhand- *(esp Comm)*; *(fig)* information,

knowledge aus zweiter Hand; **2** *adv* gebraucht, aus zweiter Hand; **I only heard it ~-hand** ich habe es nur aus zweiter Hand.
secondly ['sekəndlɪ] *adv* zweitens; *(secondarily)* an zweiter Stelle, in zweiter Linie.
secondment [sɪˈkɒndmənt] *n* Abordnung *f*. **to be on ~** abgeordnet sein.
second: **~ nature** *n* zweite Natur; **to become ~ nature (to sb)** (jdm) in Fleisch und Blut übergehen; **~-rate** *adj (pej)* zweitklassig; **~ thoughts** *npl* **to have ~ thoughts about sth** sich *(dat)* etw anders überlegen; **on ~ thoughts I decided not to** dann habe ich mich doch dagegen entschieden.
secrecy ['siːkrəsɪ] *n (of person)* Verschwiegenheit *f*; *(secretiveness)* Heimlichtuerei *f*; *(of event, talks)* Heimlichkeit *f*. **in ~** im geheimen.
secret ['siːkrɪt] **1** *adj* geheim; *negotiations, code also* Geheim-. **the ~ ingredient** die geheimnisvolle Zutat; *(fig: of success etc)* die Zauberformel; **to keep sth ~ (from sb)** etw (vor jdm) geheimhalten; **it's all highly ~** es ist alles streng geheim. **2** *n* Geheimnis *nt*. **in ~** im geheimen; **I told you that in ~** or **as a ~** ich habe Ihnen das im Vertrauen erzählt; **they always met in ~** sie trafen sich immer heimlich; *(society etc)* sie hatten immer geheime Versammlungen; **there's no ~ about it** das ist kein Geheimnis; **to keep a ~** ein Geheimnis bewahren; **can you keep a ~?** kannst du schweigen?; **to make no ~ of sth** kein Geheimnis aus etw machen.
secret agent *n* Geheimagent(in *f*) *m*.
secretarial [ˌsekrəˈtɛərɪəl] *adj* Sekretärinnen-; job Sekretariats-; qualifications als Sekretärin.
secretariat [ˌsekrəˈtɛərɪət] *n* Sekretariat *nt*.
secretary ['sekrətrɪ] *n* Sekretär(in *f*) *m*; *(of society)* Geschäftsführer(in *f*) *m*; *(keeping minutes etc)* Schriftführer(in *f*) *m*; *(esp US Pol: minister)* Minister(in *f*) *m*.
secretary: **~ bird** *n* Sekretär *m*; **S~ General** *n, pl* **Secretaries General** or **S~ Generals** Generalsekretär *m*; **S~ of State** *(Brit)* Minister(in *f*) *m*; *(US)* Außenminister(in *f*) *m*.
secrete [sɪˈkriːt] *vt* **(a)** *(hide)* verbergen. **(b)** *(Med)* absondern.
secretion [sɪˈkriːʃən] *n* **(a)** *(hiding)* Verbergen *nt*. **(b)** *(Med) (act)* Absonderung *f*; *(substance)* Sekret *nt*.
secretive ['siːkrətɪv] *adj* person *(by nature)* verschlossen; *(in action)* geheimnistuerisch; smile, behaviour geheimnisvoll. **to be ~ about sth** mit etw geheimnisvoll tun.
secretly ['siːkrətlɪ] *adv (in secrecy)* im geheimen; meet heimlich; *(privately)* insgeheim. **he was ~ concerned** insgeheim war er beunruhigt.
secret: **~ police** *n* Geheimpolizei *f*; **~ service** *n* Geheimdienst *m*.
sect [sekt] *n* Sekte *f*.
sectarian [sekˈtɛərɪən] *adj* policy, views religiös beeinflußt; school also konfessionell; war, differences Konfessions-; groups sektiererisch. **it was a ~ bombing** der Bombenanschlag hing mit den Konfessionsstreitigkeiten zusammen.
section ['sekʃən] *n* **(a)** *(part)* Teil *m*; *(of book, motorway)* Abschnitt *m*; *(of document, law)* Absatz *m*; *(of railway)* Streckenabschnitt *m*. **the string ~ of the orchestra** die Streicher *pl* des Orchesters; **the sports ~** *(Press)* der Sportteil; **the black ~ of the community** die Gruppe der Schwarzen in der Gesellschaft. **(b)** *(department, Mil)* Abteilung *f*. **(c)** *(diagram)* Schnitt *m*. **vertical/longitudinal ~** Quer-/Längsschnitt *m*.
sectional ['sekʃənl] *adj* **(a)** *(in sections)* furniture, pipe zerlegbar, zusammensetzbar. **~ drawing** Darstellung *f* im Schnitt. **(b)** rivalries zwischen den Gruppen; interests partikularistisch.
sector ['sektə[r]] *n* Sektor *m*.
secular ['sekjʊlə[r]] *adj* weltlich; music, art profan.

secure [sɪˈkjʊəʳ] **1** adj (+er) sicher; (emotionally) geborgen; existence, income gesichert; (firm) grip, knot fest. ~ **in the knowledge that ...** ruhig in dem Bewußtsein, daß ...; **to be ~ against** sth vor etw (dat) sicher sein; **to feel** ~ **sich** sicher fühlen; (emotionally) sich geborgen fühlen; **is the window/lid** ~? ist das Fenster fest zu/ist der Deckel fest drauf? **2** vt **(a)** festmachen; (tie up also) befestigen; window, door fest zumachen; (with bolt etc) sichern; tile befestigen; (make safe) sichern (from, against gegen), schützen (from, against vor +dat). **(b)** (obtain) sich (dat) sichern; votes, order erhalten; profits erzielen; share, interest in business erwerben; (buy) erstehen; employee verpflichten. **(c)** (guarantee) sichern; loan (ab)sichern.

securely [sɪˈkjʊəlɪ] adv (firmly) fest; (safely) sicher.

security [sɪˈkjʊərɪtɪ] n **(a)** Sicherheit f; (emotional) Geborgenheit f; (~ measures) Sicherheitsvorkehrungen pl. **for** ~ zur Sicherheit; **airports have tightened their** ~ die Flughäfen haben ihre Sicherheitsvorkehrungen verschärft. **(b)** (~ department) Sicherheitsdienst m. **(c)** (Fin) (guarantee) Sicherheit f; (guarantor) Bürge m. **to lend money on** ~ Geld gegen Sicherheit leihen. **(d)** (Fin) **securities** pl (Wert)papiere pl.

security in cpds Sicherheits-; (Fin) Wertpapier-; ~ **check** n Sicherheitskontrolle f; ~ **guard** n Sicherheitsbeamte(r) m; ~ **risk** n Sicherheitsrisiko nt.

sedan [sɪˈdæn] n (US) Limousine f.

sedate [sɪˈdeɪt] **1** adj (+er) gesetzt; colour ruhig; life geruhsam; speed gemächlich. **2** vt Beruhigungsmittel geben (+dat). **he was heavily** ~**d** er stand stark unter dem Einfluß von Beruhigungsmitteln.

sedation [sɪˈdeɪʃən] n Beruhigungsmittel pl. **to put** **sb under** ~ jdm Beruhigungsmittel geben.

sedative [ˈsedətɪv] **1** n Beruhigungsmittel nt. **2** adj beruhigend.

sedentary [ˈsedntərɪ] adj job sitzend attr; worker Sitz-. **to lead a** ~ **life** sehr viel sitzen.

sediment [ˈsedɪmənt] n (Boden)satz m; (in river) Ablagerung f; (in solution) Sediment nt.

seditious [sɪˈdɪʃəs] adj aufrührerisch.

seduce [sɪˈdjuːs] vt verführen. **to** ~ **sb into doing** **sth** jdn zu etw verleiten.

seduction [sɪˈdʌkʃən] n Verführung f.

seductive [sɪˈdʌktɪv] adj verführerisch; offer verlockend.

see[1] [siː] pret **saw**, ptp **seen** **1** vt **(a)** sehen; (in book etc also) lesen; (check also) nachsehen, gucken (col); film sich (dat) ansehen. **worth** ~**ing** sehenswert; **to** ~ **sb do** sth sehen, wie jd etw macht; **I've never** ~**n him swim** ich habe ihn nie schwimmen sehen; **he was** ~**n to enter the build-** **ing** man hat ihn gesehen, wie er das Gebäude betrat; **I saw it happen** ich habe gesehen, wie es passiert ist; **I don't like to** ~ **people mistreated** ich kann es nicht sehen, wenn Menschen schlecht behandelt werden; **I'll go and** ~ **who it** **is** ich sehe mal nach (, wer das ist); ~ **page 8** siehe Seite 8; **there was nothing to be** ~**n** es war nichts zu sehen; **I don't know what she** ~**s in him** ich weiß nicht, was sie an ihm findet; **we don't** ~ **much of them nowadays** wir sehen sie zur Zeit nur selten; **I shall be** ~**ing them for dinner** ich treffe sie beim Abendessen; **I shall** ~ **you (soon)!** bis bald!; **be** ~**ing you!**, **you later!** bis später!; ~ **you on Sunday!** bis Sonntag!; **you must be** ~**ing** **things** du siehst wohl Gespenster!; **that remains** **to be** ~**n** das wird sich zeigen; **now let me** ~ **how** **we can solve this** lassen Sie mich mal überlegen, wie wir das lösen können; **let me** ~ **if I can't find** **a better way** mal sehen, ob ich nicht etwas Besseres finden kann; **as I** ~ **it** so, wie ich das sehe; **try to** ~ **it my way** versuchen Sie doch einmal, es

aus meiner Sicht zu sehen; **I don't** ~ **it that way** ich sehe das anders.
(b) (visit) besuchen; (on business) aufsuchen. **to go and** ~ **sb** jdn besuchen (gehen); **to** ~ **the doctor** zum Arzt gehen; **he is the man to** ~ **about** **this** Sie sollten sich damit an ihn wenden.
(c) (meet with) sehen; (talk to) sprechen; (receive visit of) empfangen. **the boss will** ~ **you now** der Chef läßt jetzt bitten; **I'll have to** ~ **my wife** **about that** das muß ich mit meiner Frau besprechen; **have you** ~**n Personnel yet?** waren Sie schon bei der Personalabteilung?
(d) (accompany) begleiten, bringen. **to** ~ **sb to** **the door** jdn zur Tür bringen.
(e) (visualize) sich (dat) vorstellen. **I can't** ~ **that working** ich kann mir kaum vorstellen, daß das klappt; **I can't** ~ **myself in that job** ich glaube nicht, daß das eine Stelle für mich wäre.
(f) (understand) verstehen; (understand the reason for) einsehen; (realize) erkennen. **I don't** ~ **the need for the change** ich sehe nicht ein, warum das geändert werden muß; **I can** ~ **that it** **might be a good thing** ich sehe ja ein, daß das eine gute Idee wäre; **I can** ~ **I'm going to be busy** ich sehe schon, ich werde viel zu tun haben; **I fail** **to** or **don't** ~ **how anyone could ...** ich begreife einfach nicht, wie jemand nur ... kann; **I don't** ~ **how it works** es ist mir nicht klar, wie das funktioniert; **I** ~ **from this report that ...** ich ersehe aus diesem Bericht, daß ...; **(do you)** ~ **what I** **mean?** verstehst du(, was ich meine)?; (didn't I tell you!) siehst du's jetzt!; **I** ~ **what you mean** ich verstehe, was du meinst; (you're quite right) ja, du hast recht; **to make sb** ~ **sth** jdm etw klarmachen.
(g) (ensure) ~ **that it is done by tomorrow** sieh zu, daß es bis morgen fertig ist.
2 vi **(a)** sehen. **let me** ~, **let's** ~ laß mich mal sehen; **who was it?** — **I couldn't/didn't** ~ wer war das? — ich konnte es nicht sehen; **can you** ~ **to** **read?** ist es Ihnen hell genug zum Lesen?; **as far** **as the eye can** ~ so weit das Auge reicht; ~ **for** **yourself!** sieh doch selbst!
(b) (check, find out) nachsehen, gucken (col). **is he there?** — **I'll** ~ ist er da? — ich sehe mal nach; **let me** ~ lassen Sie mich mal nachsehen.
(c) (understand) verstehen. **as far as I can** ~ ... soweit ich sehen kann ...; **it's all over**, ~? es ist vorbei, verstehst du?; **as I** ~ **from your report** wie ich aus Ihrem Bericht ersehe; **(you)** ~, **it's** **like this** es ist nämlich so; **I** ~! aha!; (after explanation) ach so!
(d) (consider) **we'll** ~ (wir werden or wollen) mal sehen; **I don't know, I'll have to** ~ ich weiß nicht, ich muß mal sehen; **let me** ~, **let's** ~ lassen Sie mich mal überlegen.
♦ **see about** vi +prep obj **(a)** (attend to) sich kümmern um. **he came to** ~ ~ **the TV** er kam, um sich (dat) den Fernseher anzusehen; **he came to** ~ ~ **the rent** er ist wegen der Miete gekommen.
(b) (consider) **I'll** ~ ~ **it** ich sehe mal, we'll ~ ~ **that!** (iro) das wollen wir mal sehen.
♦ **see in** vi herein-/hineinsehen. **2** vt sep New Year begrüßen.
♦ **see off** vt sep **(a)** (bid farewell to) verabschieden. **are you coming to** ~ **me** ~? kommt ihr mit mir (zum Flughafen etc)? **(b)** (chase off) Beine machen (+dat) (col).
♦ **see out 1** vi (look out) heraus-/hinaussehen. **I** **can't** ~ ~ **the window** ich kann nicht zum Fenster hinaussehen. **2** vt sep **(a)** (show out) hinausbegleiten (of aus). **I'll** ~ **myself** ~ ich finde (schon) alleine hinaus. **(b)** (last to the end of) (coat, car) winter etc überdauern; (invalid) year etc überleben.
♦ **see over** vi +prep obj house etc sich (dat) ansehen.
♦ **see through 1** vi **(a)** (lit) (hin)durchsehen (prep

obj durch). **(b)** +*prep obj (fig: not be deceived by)* durchschauen. **I** can ~ **right** ~ **you** ich habe dich durchschaut. **2** *vt always separate* **(a)** *(help through difficult time)* beistehen (+*dat).* **I hope £10 will** ~ **you** ~ die £ 10 reichen dir hoffentlich. **(b)** *job* zu Ende bringen; *(Parl)* bill durchbringen.
♦ **see to** *vi* +*prep obj* sich kümmern um. **these shoes need/that cough needs** ~**ing** ~ mit den Schuhen muß etwas gemacht werden/um den Husten muß man sich kümmern; **please** ~ ~ **it that** ... bitte sorgen Sie dafür, daß ...
see² *n* Bistum *nt.* **Holy S~** Heiliger Stuhl.

seed [si:d] **1** *n (Bot) (one single)* Same(n) *m; (of grain, poppy etc)* Korn *nt; (within fruit)* (Samen)kern *m; (collective)* Samen *m; (for birds)* Körner *pl; (grain)* Saat *f; (fig: of unrest, idea etc)* Keim *m (of zu).* **to go to** ~ *(vegetables)* schießen; *(flowers)* einen Samenstand bilden; *(fig: person)* herunterkommen. **2** *vt* **(a)** *(sow with* ~*)* besäen. **(b)** *(extract* ~*s from)* entkernen. **(c)** *(Sport)* setzen, plazieren. ~**ed number one** als Nummer eins gesetzt. **3** *vi (vegetables)* schießen; *(flowers)* Samen entwickeln.
seed: ~**bed** *n* Saatbeet *nt;* ~ **corn** *n* Saatkorn *nt;* ~**less** *adj* kernlos.
seedling ['si:dlɪŋ] *n* Sämling *m.*
seed potato *n* Saatkartoffel *f.*
seedy ['si:dɪ] *adj* (+*er) (disreputable) person* zwielichtig; *area, place* übel; *clothes* abgerissen.
seeing ['si:ɪŋ] *conj* ~ *(that)* da.
seek [si:k] *pret, ptp* **sought** *vt* suchen; *fame, wealth* streben nach. **to** ~ **sb's advice** jdn um Rat fragen.
♦ **seek for** *vi* +*prep obj* suchen nach; *reforms, changes* anstreben.
♦ **seek out** *vt sep* ausfindig machen; *opinion* herausfinden.
seem [si:m] *vi* scheinen. **he** ~**s (to be) honest** er scheint ehrlich zu sein; **he** ~**s younger than he is** er wirkt jünger, als er ist; **that makes it** ~ **longer** dadurch wirkt es länger; **things aren't always what they** ~ vieles ist anders, als es aussieht; **what** ~**s to be the trouble?** worum geht es denn?; *(doctor)* was kann ich für Sie tun?; **he has left, it** ~**s** er ist anscheinend weggegangen; **so it** ~**s** es sieht (ganz) so aus; **it would** ~ **that he is coming after all** es sieht so aus, als ob er doch noch kommt; **how does it** ~ **to you?** was meinen Sie?; **it just doesn't** ~ **right somehow** das ist doch irgendwie nicht richtig; **it only** ~**s like it das** kommt einem nur so vor; **it all** ~**s so unreal to me** es kommt mir alles so unwirklich vor; **I** ~ **to have heard his name before** es kommt mir so vor, als hätte ich seinen Namen schon einmal gehört.
seeming ['si:mɪŋ] *adj attr* scheinbar.
seemingly ['si:mɪŋlɪ] *adv* anscheinend.
seemly ['si:mlɪ] *adj* (+*er)* schicklich. **it isn't** ~ **(for sb to do sth)** es schickt sich nicht (für jdn, etw zu tun).
seen [si:n] *ptp of* **see¹.**
seep [si:p] *vi* sickern. **to** ~ **through/into sth** durch etw durchsickern/in etw *(acc)* hineinsickern.
seesaw ['si:sɔ:] **1** *n* Wippe *f.* **2** *vi* wippen; *(fig) (emotional states)* auf und ab gehen; *(prices, public opinion)* schwanken.
seethe [si:ð] *vi (boil)* sieden; *(fig) (be crowded)* wimmeln *(with* von*); (be angry)* kochen *(col).* **to** ~ **with anger** vor Wut kochen.
see-through ['si:θru:] *adj* durchsichtig.
segment ['segmənt] *n* Teil *m; (of worm)* Glied, Segment *nt; (of orange)* Stück *nt; (of circle)* Abschnitt *m,* Segment *nt.*
segregate ['segrɪgeɪt] *vt individuals* absondern; *group of population* nach Rassen/Konfessionen *etc* trennen. **to be** ~**d from sb/sth** von jdm/etw abgesondert sein; ~**d** *(racially) school, church* nur für Weiße/Schwarze; *schools* mit Rassen-

trennung; *society* nach Rassen getrennt.
segregation [‚segrɪ'geɪʃən] *n* Trennung *f.* **racial/ sexual** ~ Rassentrennung *f*/Geschlechtertrennung *f.*
seize [si:z] *vt* **(a)** *(grasp)* packen, ergreifen; *(as hostage)* nehmen; *(confiscate)* beschlagnahmen; *passport* einziehen; *ship (authorities)* beschlagnahmen; *(capture) town* einnehmen; *train, building* besetzen; *criminal* fassen. **to** ~ **sb's arm** jdn am Arm packen. **(b)** *(fig) (panic, fear)* packen; *power* an sich *(acc)* reißen; *(leap upon) idea* aufgreifen; *opportunity* ergreifen.
♦ **seize on** *or* **upon** *vi* +*prep obj* **(a)** *(clutch at) idea, offer* sich stürzen auf (+*acc).* **(b)** *(pick out for criticism)* herausgreifen.
♦ **seize up** *vi (engine, brakes)* sich verklemmen.
seizure ['si:ʒəʳ] *n* **(a)** Beschlagnahmung *f; (of passport)* Einzug *m; (capture)* Einnahme *f; (of train, building)* Besetzung *f.* **(b)** *(Med)* Anfall *m; (apoplexy)* Schlaganfall *m.*
seldom ['seldəm] *adv* selten. ~ **have I ...** ich habe selten ...
select [sɪ'lekt] **1** *vti* auswählen; *(in buying also)* aussuchen. **2** *adj* exklusiv; *(carefully chosen)* auserlesen. ~ **committee** Sonderausschuß *m.*
selection [sɪ'lekʃən] *n* **(a)** *(choosing)* (Aus)wahl *f; (Biol)* Auslese *f.* **(b)** *(person, thing selected)* Wahl *f; (likely winner)* Tip *m.* **to make one's** ~ seine Wahl treffen; ~ **committee** Auswahlkomitee *nt.* **(c)** *(range, assortment)* Auswahl *f (of* an +*dat).*
selective [sɪ'lektɪv] *adj* wählerisch; *reader* kritisch, anspruchsvoll; *school* Elite-. ~ **service** *(US)* Wehrdienst *m.*
selectively [sɪ'lektɪvlɪ] *adv* wählerisch; *read, operate* selektiv. **to buy** ~ beim Einkaufen kritisch sein.
selector [sɪ'lektəʳ] *n* **(a)** *(Tech)* Wählschalter *m; (knob)* Schaltknopf *m.* **(b)** *(Sport) jd, der die Mannschaftsaufstellung vornimmt.*
self [self] *n, pl* **selves** Ich, Selbst *(esp Psych) no pl nt; (side of character)* Seite *f.* **one's other/better** ~ sein anderes/besseres Ich; **he's quite his old** ~ **again** er ist wieder ganz der alte *(col).*
self-: ~**-addressed** *n envelope* adressiert; ~**-adhesive** *adj* selbstklebend; ~**-adjusting** *adj* selbstregulierend *attr; brakes* selbst-nachstellend *attr;* ~**-assertive** *adj* selbstbewußt; *(pej)* von sich selbst eingenommen; ~**-assured** *adj* selbstsicher; ~**-catering** *adj (Brit)* für Selbstversorger; ~**-centred,** *(US)* ~**-centered** *adj* egozentrisch, ichbezogen; ~**-confessed** *adj* erklärt *attr;* ~**-confidence** *n* Selbstvertrauen *nt;* ~**-confident** *adj* selbstbewußt; ~**-conscious** *adj* befangen, gehemmt; *piece of writing, style etc* bewußt; ~**-contained** *adj flat* separat; ~**-control** *n* Selbstbeherrschung *f;* ~**-critical** *adj* selbstkritisch; ~**-criticism** *n* Selbstkritik *f;* ~**-defeating** *adj* unsinnig; *argument* sich selbst widerlegend *attr;* ~**-defence,** *(US)* ~**-defense** *n* Selbstverteidigung *f; (Jur)* Notwehr *f;* **to act in** ~**-defence** in Notwehr handeln; ~**-discipline** *n* Selbstdisziplin *f;* ~**-effacing** *adj* zurückhaltend; ~**-employed** *adj* selbständig; *artist* freischaffend; *journalist* freiberuflich; ~**-esteem** *n* (~**-respect)** Selbstachtung *f;* ~**-evident** *adj* offensichtlich; *(not needing proof)* selbstverständlich; ~**-explanatory** *adj* unmittelbar verständlich; **this word is** ~**-explanatory** das Wort erklärt sich selbst; ~**-expression** *n* Selbstdarstellung *f;* ~**-governing** *adj* selbstverwaltet; **to become** ~**-governing** eine eigene Regierung bekommen; ~**-help** *n* Selbsthilfe *f;* ~**-importance** *n* Aufgeblasenheit *f;* ~**-important** *adj* aufgeblasen; ~**-imposed** *adj* selbstauferlegt *attr;* ~**-indulgent** *adj* genießerisch; *(in eating, drinking also)* maßlos; ~**-inflicted** *adj wounds* sich *(dat)* selbst zugefügt *attr; task, punishment* sich *(dat)* freiwillig auferlegt; ~**-interest** *n (selfishness)* Eigennutz *m; (personal*

advantage) eigenes Interesse.

selfish ['selfɪʃ] *adj (not sharing)* geizig; *(self-centred)* egoistisch.

selfishness ['selfɪʃnɪs] *n see adj* Geiz *m*; Egoismus *m*.

selfless ['selflɪs] *adj* selbstlos.

self: ~-**made** *adj* ~-**made man** Selfmademan *m*; ~-**opinionated** *adj* rechthaberisch; *nonsense, drivel* selbstherrlich; ~-**pity** *n* Selbstmitleid *nt*; ~-**portrait** *n* Selbstporträt *nt*; ~-**possessed** *adj* selbstbeherrscht; ~-**preservation** *n* Selbsterhaltung *f*; ~-**raising**, *(US)* ~-**rising** *adj flour* selbsttreibend, *mit bereits beigemischtem Backpulver*; ~-**reliance** *n* Selbständigkeit *f*; ~-**reliant** *adj* selbständig; ~-**respect** *n* Selbstachtung *f*; **have you no** ~-**respect?** schämen Sie sich gar nicht?; ~-**respecting** *adj* anständig; **no** ~-**respecting person would ...** niemand, der etwas auf sich hält, würde ...; ~-**righteous** *adj* selbstgerecht; ~-**righteousness** *n* Selbstgerechtigkeit *f*; ~-**sacrifice** *n* Selbstaufopferung *f*; ~-**same** *adj* **the** ~-**same** genau der-/die-/dasselbe; **on the** ~-**same day** noch am selben Tag; ~-**satisfied** *adj (smug)* selbstgefällig; ~-**service** 1 *n* Selbstbedienung *f*; 2 *adj* Selbstbedienungs-; ~-**styled** *adj* selbsternannt; ~-**sufficiency** *n (of person)* Selbständigkeit *f*; *(emotional)* Selbstgenügsamkeit *f*; *(of country)* Autarkie *f*; ~-**sufficient** *adj person* selbständig; *(emotionally)* selbstgenügsam; *country* autark; **they are** ~-**sufficient in oil** sie können ihren Ölbedarf selbst decken; ~-**supporting** *adj person* finanziell unabhängig; *structure* freitragend; *chimney* freistehend; **the newspaper is** ~-**supporting** die Zeitung trägt sich selbst; ~-**taught** *adj skills* selbsterlernt; **he is** ~-**taught** er hat sich *(dat)* das selbst beigebracht; *(intellectually)* er hat sich durch Selbstunterricht gebildet.

sell [sel] *(vb: pret, ptp sold)* 1 *vt* **(a)** verkaufen *(sb sth, sth to sb* jdm etw, etw an jdn*); insurance policy* abschließen *(to* mit*); (business) goods also* absetzen. **I was sold this in Valencia** man hat mir das in Valencia verkauft; **the book sold 3,000 copies** von dem Buch wurden 3.000 Exemplare verkauft; **to be sold on sb/sth** *(col)* von jdm/etw begeistert sein. **(b)** *(stock)* führen, haben *(col); (deal in)* vertreiben. **to** ~ **oneself** *(put oneself across)* sich profilieren *(to* bei*),* sich verkaufen *(to an* +*acc).* **(c)** *(fig: betray)* verraten. **to** ~ **sb down the river** *(col)* jdn verschaukeln *(col).*

2 *vi (person)* verkaufen *(to sb an* jdn*); (article)* sich verkaufen (lassen). **his book is** ~**ing well/won't** ~ sein Buch verkauft sich gut/läßt sich nicht verkaufen; **the house sold for £30,000** das Haus wurde für £ 30.000 verkauft.

♦ **sell off** *vt sep* verkaufen; *(get rid of quickly, cheaply)* abstoßen.

♦ **sell out** 1 *vt sep* ausverkaufen. **sorry, sold** ~ wir sind leider ausverkauft; **we're sold** ~ **of ice-cream** das Eis ist ausverkauft. 2 *vi* **(a)** *(sell entire stock)* alles verkaufen. **(b)** *(in business)* sein Geschäft/seine Firma/seinen Anteil *etc* verkaufen. **(c)** *(col: betray)* **he sold** ~ **to the enemy** er hat sich an den Feind verkauft.

♦ **sell up** 1 *vt sep* zu Geld machen *(col); (Brit Fin)* zwangsverkaufen. 2 *vi* seinen Besitz/seine Firma *etc* verkaufen.

seller ['selə^r] *n* **(a)** Verkäufer(in *f*) *m.* **it's a** ~**'s market in housing just now** zur Zeit bestimmen die Verkäufer die Hauspreise. **(b)** *(thing sold)* **big** ~ Verkaufsschlager *m*; **bad** ~ schlecht gehender Artikel; *(in shop also)* Ladenhüter *m*; **this book is a good/slow** ~ das Buch verkauft sich gut/schlecht.

selling ['selɪŋ] *adj* Verkaufs-. ~ **price** Verkaufspreis *m*.

sellotape ® ['seləʊteɪp] *(Brit)* 1 *n* Tesafilm ® *m.* 2 *vt* mit Tesafilm ® festkleben.

sell-out ['selaʊt] *n* **(a)** *(col: betrayal)* fauler Handel *(to* mit*); (of one's ideals etc)* Ausverkauf *m (to an* +*acc).* **(b)** *(Theat, Sport)* ausverkauftes Haus. **to be a** ~ ausverkauft sein.

selvage, selvedge ['selvɪdʒ] *n* Webkante *f*.

selves [selvz] *pl of* **self.**

semantic [sɪ'mæntɪk] *adj* semantisch.

semaphore ['seməfɔː^r] *n* Signalsprache *f*.

semblance ['sembləns] *n* Anflug *m (of* von*); (of order)* Anschein *m*.

semen ['siːmən] *n* Sperma *nt*.

semester [sɪ'mestə^r] *n* Semester *nt*.

semi ['semɪ] *n (Brit col)* = **semidetached.**

semi: ~-**breve** *n (esp Brit)* ganze Note; ~-**circle** *n* Halbkreis *m*; ~-**circular** *adj* halbkreisförmig; ~**colon** *n* Semikolon *nt*; ~**conductor** *n* Halbleiter *m*; ~**conscious** *adj* halb bewußtlos; ~**detached** *n* Doppelhaus(hälfte *f*) *nt*; ~**final** *n* Halbfinalspiel *nt*; ~**finalist** *n* Teilnehmer(in *f*) *m* am Halbfinale; ~**finals** *npl* Halbfinale *nt*.

seminal ['semɪnl] *adj* **to be present in a** ~ **state** im Keim vorhanden sein.

seminar ['semɪnɑː^r] *n* Seminar *nt*.

seminary ['semɪnərɪ] *n* Priesterseminar *nt*.

semi: ~**precious** *adj* ~**precious stone** Halbedelstein *m*; ~**quaver** *n (esp Brit)* Sechzehntel(note *f*) *nt*; ~**skilled** *adj worker* angelernt; *job* Anlern-; ~**skilled labour** *(workforce)* Angelernte *pl*; *(work)* Arbeit *f* für Angelernte.

semolina [,semə'liːnə] *n* Grieß *m*.

senate ['senɪt] *n* Senat *m*.

senator ['senɪtə^r] *n* Senator *m*; *(as address)* Herr Senator.

send [send] *pret, ptp* **sent** *vt* **(a)** schicken; *letter, messenger also* senden; *(~ off) letter* abschicken; *(Rad) radio wave* ausstrahlen; *signal* senden; *(through wires)* übermitteln. **to** ~ **sb to prison/to his death** jdn ins Gefängnis/in den Tod schicken; **to** ~ **sb to university** jdn studieren lassen; **to** ~ **sb for sth** jdn nach etw schicken; **she** ~**s her love/congratulations/apologies** *etc* sie läßt grüßen/Ihnen ihre Glückwünsche ausrichten/sich entschuldigen *etc*; ~ **him my love/my wishes** grüßen Sie ihn von mir.

(b) *(propel, make go) ball* schießen; *(hurl)* schleudern; *(conveyor belt)* befördern. **the blow sent him sprawling** der Schlag schleuderte ihn zu Boden; **the fire sent everyone running out of the building** das Feuer ließ alle aus dem Gebäude fluchtartig verlassen; **his speech sent a wave of excitement through the audience** seine Rede ließ eine Woge der Aufregung durch die Zuschauer gehen; **this sent him into fits of laughter** sie ließ ihn in einen Lachkrampf ausbrechen.

♦ **send away** 1 *vt sep* wegschicken; *letter etc also* abschicken. **I had to** ~ **him** ~ **without an explanation** ich mußte ihn ohne Erklärung weggehen lassen. 2 *vi* schreiben. **to** ~ ~ **for sth** etw anfordern.

♦ **send back** *vt sep* zurückschicken; *food in restaurant* zurückgehen lassen.

♦ **send down** *vt sep (a) temperature, prices* fallen lassen; *(gradually)* senken. **(b)** *(Brit Univ: expel)* relegieren. **(c)** *prisoner* verurteilen *(for* zu*).*

♦ **send for** *vt +prep obj* **(a)** kommen lassen; *doctor, police, priest also* rufen; *help* herbeirufen; *(person in authority) pupil, minister* zu sich bestellen. **(b)** *copy, catalogue* anfordern.

♦ **send in** *vt sep* **(a)** einsenden; *person* herein-/hineinschicken; *troops* einsetzen.

♦ **send off** 1 *vt sep* **(a)** *letter* abschicken. **(b)** *children to school* wegschicken. **(c)** = **send away 1.** 2 *(Sport)* vom Platz weisen *(for* wegen*).* 2 *vi* = **send away 2.**

♦ **send on** *vt sep* **(a)** *(Brit: forward) letter* nachschicken; *(pass on) memo* weiterleiten. **(b)** *(in advance) troops, luggage* vorausschicken. **(c)** *substitute* einsetzen; *actor* auf die Bühne schicken.

♦ **send out** *vt sep* **(a)** *(of house, room)* hinaus-/ herausschicken *(of aus)*. **he sent me ~ to buy a paper** er hat mich losgeschickt, um eine Zeitung zu kaufen. **(b)** *(emit) rays, radio signals* aussenden; *light, heat, smoke* abgeben. **(c)** *leaflets, invitations, application forms* verschicken.

sender ['sendə^r] *n* Absender(in *f*) *m*. **return to ~** zurück an Absender.

send: **~-off** *n* Verabschiedung *f*; **to give sb a good ~-off** jdn ganz groß verabschieden *(col)*; **~-up** *n* *(Brit col)* Verulkung *f* *(col)*; **to do a ~-up of sb/sth** jdn/etw verulken *(col)*.

senile ['si:naɪl] *adj person* senil; *(physically)* altersschwach.

senior ['si:nɪə^r] **1** *adj (in age)* älter; *(in rank)* vorgesetzt, übergeordnet; *(with longer service)* dienstälter; *rank, civil servant* höher; *officer* ranghöher; *position, editor, executive etc* leitend; *doctor, nurse etc* Ober-. **he is ~ to me** *(in age)* er ist älter als ich; *(in rank)* er ist mir übergeordnet; *(in length of service)* er arbeitet schon länger hier als ich; **the ~ management** die Geschäftsleitung; **~ partner** Seniorpartner *m*; **~ consultant** Chefarzt *m*/-ärztin *f*; **~ citizen** älterer Mitbürger; **~ school, ~ high school** *(US)* Oberstufe *f*; **can I speak to somebody more ~?** könnte ich bitte jemanden sprechen, der verantwortlich ist?; **J. B. Schwartz, S~** J. B. Schwartz senior. **2** *n (Sch)* Oberstufenschüler(in *f*) *m*; *(US Univ)* Student(in *f*) *m* im 4./letzten Studienjahr. **he is my ~** *(in age)* er ist älter als ich; *(in rank)* er ist mir übergeordnet; *(in length of service)* er arbeitet schon länger hier als ich; **he is two years my ~** er ist zwei Jahre älter als ich.

seniority [,si:nɪ'ɒrɪtɪ] *n (in age)* (höheres) Alter; *(in rank)* (höhere) Position; *(Mil)* (höherer) Rang; *(in civil service etc)* (höherer) Dienstgrad; *(in service etc)* (längere) Betriebszugehörigkeit; *(in civil service etc)* (höheres) Dienstalter.

sensation [sen'seɪʃən] *n* **(a)** *(feeling)* Gefühl *nt*; *(of heat etc)* Empfindung *f*. **a ~ of falling** das Gefühl zu fallen; **a ~ of fear** ein Angstgefühl *nt*. **(b)** *(great success)* Sensation *f*. **to cause a ~** *(großes)* Aufsehen erregen.

sensational [sen'seɪʃənl] *adj* **(a)** sensationell; *news item* Sensations-; *style, film* reißerisch. **(b)** *(col: very good etc)* sagenhaft *(col)*.

sense [sens] **1** *n* **(a)** *(bodily)* Sinn *m*. **~ of hearing** Gehör(sinn *m*) *nt*; **~ of sight** Sehvermögen *nt*; **~ of smell** Geruchssinn *m*; **~ of taste** Geschmackssinn *m*; **~ of touch** Tastsinn *m*; **~s** *pl* *(right mind)* Verstand *m*; **to be out of one's ~s** nicht ganz bei Trost sein *(col)*, von Sinnen sein *(geh)*; **to bring sb to his ~s** jdn zur Besinnung bringen; **to come to one's ~s** zur Besinnung kommen, Vernunft annehmen.

(b) *(feeling)* Gefühl *nt*. **~ of duty** Pflichtgefühl *nt*; **a ~ of pleasure** *etc* ein Gefühl der Freude *etc*; **~ of justice** Gerechtigkeitssinn *m*; **these buildings create a ~ of space** diese Gebäude vermitteln den Eindruck von Weite.

(c) *(good ~)* **(common)** *~* gesunder Menschenverstand; **he had the (good) ~ to ...** er war so vernünftig und ...; **she didn't even have the ~ to take a key** sie war auch noch zu dumm dazu, einen Schlüssel mitzunehmen; **you should have had more ~ than to ...** du hättest vernünftiger sein sollen und nicht ...; **there is no ~ in that** das hat keinen Sinn; **what's the ~ of doing this?** welchen Sinn hat es denn, das zu tun?; **to talk ~** vernünftig sein; **to make sb see ~** jdn zur Vernunft bringen.

(d) **to make ~** *(sentence etc)* (einen) Sinn ergeben; *(be sensible, rational etc)* sinnvoll *or* vernünftig sein; **it doesn't make ~ to spend all that money** es ist doch Unsinn, soviel Geld auszugeben; **it makes good ~** das scheint sehr vernünftig; **it makes good financial ~ to ...** aus finanzieller Sicht gesehen ist es sehr vernünftig, zu ...; **it all makes ~ now** jetzt wird einem alles klar; **to make ~ of sth** etw verstehen, aus etw schlau werden *(col)*.

(e) *(meaning)* Sinn *m no pl*. **in the full ~ of the word** im wahrsten Sinn des Wortes; **it has three distinct ~s** es hat drei verschiedene Bedeutungen; **in every ~ of the word** in der vollen Bedeutung des Wortes; **in a ~** in gewisser Hinsicht; **in every ~** in jeder Hinsicht; **in what ~?** inwiefern?

2 *vt* fühlen, spüren. **I could ~ someone there in the dark** ich fühlte *or* spürte, daß da jemand in der Dunkelheit war.

senseless ['senslɪs] *adj* **(a)** *(unconscious)* besinnungslos, bewußtlos. **to knock sb ~** jdn bewußtlos schlagen. **(b)** *(stupid)* unvernünftig, unsinnig; *(futile)* waste, discussion sinnlos.

sensibility [,sensɪ'bɪlɪtɪ] *n (to beauty etc)* Empfindsamkeit *f*; *(artistic ~ also)* Sensibilität *f*; *(emotional ~)*, *susceptibility to insult)* Empfindlichkeit *f*. **sensibilities** Zartgefühl *nt*.

sensible ['sensəbl] *adj* **(a)** vernünftig. **be ~ about it** seien Sie vernünftig. **(b)** *(appreciable)* spürbar.

sensitive ['sensɪtɪv] *adj* **(a)** *(emotionally)* person sensibel, empfindsam; *(easily hurt)* empfindlich; *(understanding)* einfühlsam; *novel, remark* einfühlend. **to be ~ about sth** in bezug auf etw *(acc)* empfindlich sein. **(b)** *instruments, plants* empfindlich; *(Phot)* film lichtempfindlich; *(fig)* topic, issue heikel. **~ to light** lichtempfindlich.

sensitize ['sensɪtaɪz] *vt (Phot)* sensibilisieren.

sensual ['sensjʊəl] *adj* sinnlich.

sensuality [,sensjʊ'ælɪtɪ] *n* Sinnlichkeit.

sensuous ['sensjʊəs] *adj* sinnlich.

sent [sent] *pret, ptp of* **send.**

sentence ['sentəns] **1** *n* **(a)** *(Gram)* Satz *m*. **~ structure** Satzbau *m*. **(b)** *(Jur)* Strafe *f*. **to be under ~ of death** zum Tode verurteilt sein; **the judge gave him a 6-month ~** der Richter verurteilte ihn zu 6 Monaten Haft; **to pass ~ (on sb)** *(über jdn)* das Urteil verkünden; *(fig)* jdn verurteilen. **2** *vt (Jur)* verurteilen *(to zu)*.

sentiment ['sentɪmənt] *n* **(a)** *(feeling, emotion)* Gefühl *nt*. **(b)** *(sentimentality)* Sentimentalität *f*. **(c)** *(opinion)* Ansicht *f*. **my ~s exactly!** genau meine Meinung!

sentimental [,sentɪ'mentl] *adj* sentimental; *person, mood also* gefühlvoll; *value* Gefühls-. **for ~ reasons** aus Sentimentalität.

sentimentality [,sentɪmen'tælɪtɪ] *n* Sentimentalität *f*.

sentry ['sentrɪ] *n* Wachtposten *m*. **to be on ~ duty** auf Wache sein; **~ box** Wachhäuschen *nt*.

separable ['sepərəbl] *adj* trennbar.

separate ['seprət] **1** *adj* **(a)** gesondert *(from von)*; *section, piece* extra *attr inv*; *organization, unit also, existence* eigen *attr*; *provisions, regulations also* besondere(r, s) *attr*; *beds, accounts* getrennt; *entrance, flat* separat. **that is a ~ issue** das ist eine Frage für sich; **on two ~ occasions** bei zwei verschiedenen Gelegenheiten; **on a ~ occasion** bei einer anderen Gelegenheit; **they live ~ lives** sie haben getrennte Wege; **to keep two things ~** zwei Dinge auseinanderhalten. **(b)** *(individual)* einzeln. **all the ~ questions** alle einzelnen Fragen; **everybody has a ~ task** jeder hat seine eigene Aufgabe.

2 *n ~s pl* für Röcke, Blusen, Hosen *etc*.

3 ['sepəreɪt] *vt* trennen; *(divide up)* aufteilen *(into in +acc)*. **he is ~d from his wife** er lebt von seiner Frau getrennt.

4 ['sepəreɪt] *vi* sich trennen.

separately ['seprətlɪ] *adv* getrennt, separat; *live* getrennt; *(singly)* einzeln.

separation [,sepə'reɪʃən] *n* Trennung *f*; *(of rocket etc)* Abtrennung *(from von)*.

separatist ['sepərətɪst] **1** *adj* separatistisch. **2** *n* Separatist(in *f*) *m*.

sepia ['siːpjə] *n* Sepia *f*.

September [sep'tembə^r] **1** *n* September *m*. **the first of ~** der erste September; **on ~ 19th** (*written*), **on 19th ~** (*written*), **on the 19th of ~** (*spoken*) am 19. September, am neunzehnten September; **~ 3rd, 1979, 3rd ~ 1979** (*on letter*) 3. September 1979; **in ~ im September; at the beginning/end of ~** Anfang/Ende September; **there are 30 days in ~** der September hat 30 Tage. **2** *adj attr* September-; *mists etc also* septemberlich.

septic ['septɪk] *adj* vereitert, septisch. **the wound turned ~** die Wunde eiterte; **~ tank** Klärbehälter *m*.

sepulchre, (US) sepulcher ['sepəlkə^r] *n* Grabstätte *f*.

sequel ['siːkwəl] *n* Folge *f* (*to* von); (*of book, film*) Fortsetzung *f* (*to* von). **it had a tragic ~** es hatte ein tragisches Nachspiel.

sequence ['siːkwəns] *n* (**a**) (*order*) Folge, Reihenfolge *f*. **in ~** der Reihe nach; **to do sth in ~** etw in der richtigen Reihenfolge tun. (**b**) (*things following*) Reihe, Folge *f*; (*Mus, Cards*) Sequenz *f*; (*Math*) Reihe *f*.

sequin ['siːkwɪn] *n* Paillette *f*.

serenade [,serə'neɪd] **1** *n* Serenade *f*. **2** *vt* ein Ständchen *nt* bringen (+*dat*).

serene [sə'riːn] *adj* gelassen; *sea* ruhig; *sky* heiter.

serenity [sɪ'renɪtɪ] *n* Gelassenheit *f*.

serge [sɜːdʒ] *n* Serge *f*.

sergeant ['saːdʒənt] *n* (*Mil*) Feldwebel *m*; (*police*) Polizeimeister *m*. **~ major** Oberfeldwebel *m*.

serial ['sɪərɪəl] *n* (*novel*) Fortsetzungsroman *m*; (*Rad*) Sendereihe *f*; (*TV*) Serie *f*. **~ number** fortlaufende Nummer; (*on manufactured goods*) Fabrikationsnummer *f*.

serialize ['sɪərɪəlaɪz] *vt* in Fortsetzungen bringen; (*put into serial form*) in Fortsetzungen umarbeiten.

series ['sɪərɪz] *n, pl* - Serie *f*; (*Rad*) Sendereihe *f*; (*of books, lectures, films*) Reihe *f*. **a ~ of articles** eine Artikelserie; **in ~** der Reihe nach.

serious ['sɪərɪəs] *adj* (**a**) ernst; *person, manner* (*not frivolous*) ernsthaft; *newspaper, interest* seriös; *offer, suggestion* ernstgemeint *attr*, ernst gemeint *pred*, seriös; *doubts also* ernsthaft. **to be ~ about doing sth** etw im Ernst tun wollen; **I'm ~ (about it)** das ist mein Ernst; **he is ~ about her** er meint es ernst mit ihr; **you can't be ~!** das kann nicht dein Ernst sein! (**b**) (*critical*) *accident, mistake, damage, loss* schwer; *situation also* bedenklich. **it's ~** das ist schlimm; **it's getting ~** es wird ernst; **inflation is getting ~** die Inflation nimmt ernste Ausmaße an.

seriously ['sɪərɪəslɪ] *adv* (**a**) ernst; *talk, interested* ernsthaft; (*not jokingly*) im Ernst. **to take sb/sth ~** jdn/etw ernst nehmen; **do you ~ want to do that?** wollen Sie das wirklich *or* im Ernst tun?; **~ though ...** aber mal ganz im Ernst ...; **do you mean that ~?** meinen Sie das ernst?, ist das Ihr Ernst? (**b**) *wounded* schwer; *ill also* ernstlich; *deteriorate* bedenklich.

seriousness ['sɪərɪəsnɪs] *n see adj* (**a**) Ernst *m*; Ernsthaftigkeit *f*; Seriosität *f*. **in all ~** ganz im Ernst. (**b**) Ernst *m*; Schwere *f*; Bedenklichkeit *f*.

sermon ['sɜːmən] *n* (*Eccl*) Predigt *f*; (*moralizing*) Moralpredigt *f*; (*scolding*) Strafpredigt *f*.

serpent ['sɜːpənt] *n* Schlange *f* (*also fig*).

serrated [se'reɪtɪd] *adj* gezackt. **~ knife** Sägemesser *nt*.

serum ['sɪərəm] *n* Serum *nt*.

servant ['sɜːvənt] *n* (*lit, fig*) Diener(in *f*) *m*; (*also ~ girl*) Dienstmädchen *nt*; (*domestic*) Dienstbote *m*.

serve [sɜːv] **1** *vt* (**a**) dienen (+*dat*); (*be of use*) nützen (+*dat*). **he ~d his country well** er hat sich um sein Land verdient gemacht; **if my memory ~s me correctly** wenn ich mich recht erinnere; **to ~ its/sb's purpose** seinen Zweck erfüllen/jds Zwecken (*dat*) dienen; **it ~s no useful purpose** es hat keinen praktischen Wert; **to ~ sb as sth** jdm als etw dienen; **it has ~d us well** es hat uns gute Dienste geleistet.

(**b**) *years in army etc* ableisten; *term of office* durchlaufen; *apprenticeship* durchmachen; *sentence* verbüßen, absitzen (*col*).

(**c**) (*in shop*) bedienen; (*bus, gas etc*) versorgen. **I'm being ~d, thank you** danke, ich werde schon bedient.

(**d**) (*esp in restaurant*) *food, drink* servieren; *guests* bedienen; (*waiter*) bedienen; (*pour drink for*) einschenken (+*dat*); *wine etc* einschenken. **dinner is ~d** (*butler*) das Essen ist aufgetragen; (*hostess*) darf ich zu Tisch bitten?; **"~s three"** (*on packet etc*) „(ergibt) drei Portionen".

(**e**) (*Tennis etc*) *ball* aufschlagen.

(**f**) (*Jur*) zustellen (*on sb* jdm). **to ~ a summons on sb, to ~ sb with a summons** jdn vor Gericht laden; **the landlord ~d notice on his tenants** der Vermieter kündigte den Mietern.

(**g**) (*it*) **~s you right!** (*col*) das geschieht dir (ganz) recht!; **it ~s him right for being so greedy** (*col*) das geschieht ihm ganz recht, was muß er auch so gierig sein!

2 *vi* (**a**) dienen. **to ~ on the jury** Geschworene(r) *mf* sein; **to ~ on a committee** einem Ausschuß angehören; **to ~ as chairman** das Amt des Vorsitzenden innehaben. (**b**) (*Mil*) dienen. (**c**) (*waiter, butler etc*) servieren (*at table* bei Tisch). (**d**) **to ~ as, to ~ for** dienen als; **it ~s to show/explain ...** das zeigt/erklärt ... (**e**) (*Tennis etc*) aufschlagen.

3 *n* (*Tennis etc*) Aufschlag *m*. **whose ~ is it?** wer hat Aufschlag?

♦ **serve up** *vt sep food* servieren; *rations* verteilen.

server ['sɜːvə^r] *n* (**a**) (*fork etc*) Servierlöffel *m*/ Vorlegegabel *f*; (*pie* ~) Tortenheber *m*. **salad ~s** Salatbesteck *nt*. (**b**) (*Tennis*) Aufschläger(in *f*) *m*.

service ['sɜːvɪs] **1** *n* (**a**) Dienst *m*. **his faithful ~** seine treuen Dienste; **his ~s to industry/the country** seine Verdienste in der Industrie/um das Land; **he has ten years' ~ behind him** er hat zehn Jahre Dienstzeit hinter sich (*dat*); **to do sb a ~** jdm einen Dienst erweisen; **to be of ~ to** sb jdm nützen; **to be at sb's ~** jdm zur Verfügung stehen; **can I be of ~ to you?** kann ich Ihnen behilflich sein?; **out of ~** außer Betrieb; **to need the ~s of a lawyer** einen Anwalt brauchen.

(**b**) (*Mil*) Militärdienst *m*.

(**c**) (*to customers*) Service *m*; (*in shop, restaurant etc*) Bedienung *f*.

(**d**) (*bus, train, plane etc*) Bus-/Zug-/Flugverbindung *f*. **there's no ~ to Oban on Sundays** sonntags besteht kein Zug-/Busverkehr nach Oban.

(**e**) (*Eccl*) Gottesdienst *m*.

(**f**) (*of machines*) Wartung *f*; (*Aut: major* ~) Inspektion *f*. **my car is in for a ~** mein Auto wird gewartet; **mein Auto ist bei der Inspektion.**

(**g**) (*tea or coffee set*) Service *nt*.

(**h**) (*Tennis*) Aufschlag *m*.

(**i**) **~s** *pl* (*commercial*) Dienstleistungen *pl*; (*gas etc*) Versorgungsnetz *nt*.

2 *vt car, machine* warten. **to send a car to be ~d** ein Auto warten lassen; (*major* ~) ein Auto zur Inspektion geben.

serviceable ['sɜːvɪsəbl] *adj* (*practical*) zweckmäßig; (*usable*) brauchbar.

service: ~ area *n* Raststätte *f*; **~ charge** *n* (*Brit*) Bedienung(sgeld *nt*) *f*; (*of bank*) Bearbeitungsgebühr *f*; **~ industry** *n* Dienstleistungsbranche *f*; **~man** *n* Militärangehörige(r) *m*; **~ station** *n* Tankstelle *f* (mit Reparaturwerkstatt).

serviette [,sɜːvɪ'et] *n* Serviette *f*.

servile ['sɜːvaɪl] *adj* unterwürfig; *obedience* sklavisch.

session ['seʃən] *n* **(a)** *(meeting)* Sitzung *f*; *(Jur, Parl: period)* Sitzungsperiode *f*; *(Parl: term of office)* Legislaturperiode *f*. **to be in** ~ eine Sitzung abhalten; *(Jur, Pol)* tagen; **a** ~ **of talks/negotiations** Gespräche *pl*/Verhandlungen *pl*; **recording** ~ Aufnahme *f*; **we're in for a long** ~ das wird lange dauern; **I had a long** ~ **with him** *(talk)* ich habe lange mit ihm gesprochen. **(b)** *(academic year)* *(Univ)* Studienjahr *nt*; *(Sch)* Schuljahr *nt*; *(term)* Semester/Trimester *nt*; *(division of course)* Stunde, Sitzung *(esp Univ) f*.

set [set] *(vb: pret, ptp* ~) **1** *n* **(a)** Satz *m*; *(of two)* Paar *nt*; *(of cutlery, furniture etc)* Garnitur *f*; *(tea-~ etc)* Service *nt*; *(of tablemats etc)* Set *nt*; *(chess or draughts* ~ *etc)* Spiel *nt*; *(painting* ~) Malkasten *m*; *(Meccano®, chemistry* ~) Baukasten *m*; *(gift or presentation* ~) Kassette *f*. ~ **of rooms** Zimmerflucht *f*; **a** ~ **of tools** Werkzeug *nt*; **a** ~ **of teeth** ein Gebiß *nt*.

(b) *(group of people)* Kreis *m*; *(pej)* Bande *f*; *(Brit Sch: stream)* Kurs *m*. **the literary** ~ die Literaten *pl*; **the golfing** ~ die Golffreunde *pl*.

(c) *(Tennis)* Satz *m*; *(Table-tennis)* Spiel *nt*. ~ **point** Satzpunkt *m*.

(d) *(Telec, Rad, TV)* Gerät *nt*, Apparat *m*.

(e) *(hair~)* Frisur, Form *f*. **to have a (shampoo and)** ~ sich *(dat)* die Haare (waschen und) legen lassen.

(f) *(Theat)* Bühnenbild *nt*; *(Film)* Szenenaufbau *m*. **to be on the** ~ bei den Dreharbeiten sein.

(g) *(Math)* Menge *f*.

2 *adj* **(a)** *pred (ready)* fertig, bereit. **all** ~? alles klar?; **to be all** ~ **to do sth** sich darauf eingerichtet haben, etw zu tun. **(b)** *(rigid)* starr; *expression* feststehend; *forms also, habit, custom* fest; *(prescribed)* festgesetzt; *essay topic* vorgegeben; *(prearranged) time, place* bestimmt, ausgemacht *(col)*. ~ **book(s)** Pflichtlektüre *f*; ~ **lunch/meal** Tagesgericht *nt*; ~ **menu** Tageskarte *f*; ~ **piece** Standardstück *nt*; **to be** ~ **in one's ways** in seinen Gewohnheiten festgefahren sein. **(c)** *(resolved)* entschlossen. **to be (dead)** ~ **on sth/doing sth** etw unbedingt haben/tun wollen; **to be (dead)** ~ **against sth/doing sth** (total) gegen etw sein/etw (absolut) nicht tun wollen.

3 *vt* **(a)** *(put, place)* stellen; *(on its side, flat)* legen; *(deliberately, carefully)* setzen.

(b) *(regulate, adjust)* einstellen *(at auf +acc)*; *clock* stellen *(by nach, to auf +acc)*; *(fix) trap, snare* aufstellen; *(fig)* stellen *(for sb jdm)*. **to** ~ **the alarm for a certain time** den Wecker auf eine bestimmte Zeit stellen.

(c) *(prescribe, impose) target, limit etc* festlegen; *task, question* stellen *(sb jdm)*; *homework* aufgeben; *exam* zusammenstellen; *(arrange) time, date* festsetzen, ausmachen *(col)*; *(establish) record* aufstellen; *fashion* bestimmen. **to** ~ **the date of the wedding)** die Hochzeit festsetzen; **to** ~ **a value on sth** einen Wert für etw festsetzen; **to** ~ **a high value on sth** einer Sache *(dat)* großen Wert beimessen; **to** ~ **sb a problem** *(lit)* jdm ein Problem aufgeben; *(fig)* jdn vor ein Problem stellen.

(d) *(mount) gem* fassen *(in in +dat)*; *piece of jewellery* besetzen *(with* mit); *windowpane* einsetzen *(in in +acc)*; *(embed firmly)* einlegen *(in in +dat)*; *(in ground)* einlassen *(in in +acc)*.

(e) *(Liter)* **the book** *etc* **is** ~ **in Rome** das Buch *etc* spielt in Rom; **he** ~ **the book in Rome** er wählte Rom als Schauplatz für sein Buch.

(f) *(Med) bone* einrichten; *dislocated joint* einrenken.

(g) *(lay with cutlery) table* decken. **to** ~ **places for 14** für 14 decken.

(h) *hair* legen, eindrehen.

(i) to ~ **the police/dogs on sb** die Polizei/

Hunde auf jdn hetzen.

(j) *(Mus)* **to** ~ **sth to music** etw vertonen.

(k) *(Typ)* setzen.

(l) to ~ **sth going/in motion** etw in Gang/Bewegung bringen; **to** ~ **sb doing sth** jdn dazu veranlassen, etw zu tun; **to** ~ **sb laughing** jdn zum Lachen bringen; **that** ~ **me thinking** das gab mir zu denken; **that** ~ **me thinking that ...** das ließ mich denken, daß ...; **to** ~ **people talking** Anlaß zu Gerede geben; **to** ~ **sb/oneself to do sth** jdn etw tun lassen/sich daranmachen, etw zu tun.

4 *vi* **(a)** *(sun etc)* untergehen. **(b)** *(jelly, cement)* fest werden; *(jam also)* gelieren; *(bone)* zusammenwachsen.

♦ **set about** *vi +prep obj* **(a)** *(begin)* anfangen; *(tackle)* anfassen, anpacken *(col)*. **to** ~ ~ **doing sth** *(begin)* sich daranmachen, etw zu tun; **how do I** ~ ~ **getting a loan?** wie fasse or packe *(col)* ich es an, um ein Darlehen zu bekommen? **(b)** *(attack)* herfallen über *(+acc)*.

♦ **set against** *vt sep +prep obj* **(a)** *(influence against)* einnehmen gegen; *(cause trouble between)* Zwietracht säen zwischen *(+dat)*. **(b)** *(balance against) evidence etc* gegenüberstellen *(+dat)*.

♦ **set aside** *vt sep* **(a)** *work, money* beiseite legen; *time* einplanen; *plans* aufschieben; *differences* beiseite schieben; *dislike* vergessen; *mistrust, bitterness* sich freimachen von; *formality* verzichten auf *(+acc)*; *rules, protest* übergehen. **(b)** *(Jur)* aufheben; *will* für ungültig erklären.

♦ **set back** *vt sep* **(a)** *(place at a distance)* zurücksetzen. **the house is** ~ **from the road** das Haus liegt etwas von der Straße ab. **(b)** *(retard)* verzögern, behindern. **the programme has been** ~ ~ **(by) 2 years** das Programm ist um 2 Jahre zurückgeworfen. **(c)** *(col: cost)* kosten. **the dinner** ~ **me** ~ **£15** das Essen hat mich 15 Pfund gekostet or ärmer gemacht *(col)*.

♦ **set down** *vt sep* **(a)** *(put down) suitcase* absetzen; *passenger also* aussteigen lassen. **(b)** *(in writing)* (schriftlich) niederlegen.

♦ **set in** *vi (start)* einsetzen; *(panic)* ausbrechen; *(night)* anbrechen; *(Med: gangrene, complications)* sich einstellen. **the rain has** ~ ~ es hat sich eingeregnet.

♦ **set off 1** *vt sep* **(a)** *bomb* losgehen lassen; *alarm, mechanism* auslösen. **(b)** *(offset)* **to** ~ ~ **against sth** etw einer Sache *(dat)* gegenüberstellen. **(c)** *(enhance)* hervorheben. **to** ~ **sth** ~ **from** sth etw von etw abheben. **2** *vi (depart)* aufbrechen; *(car, in car etc)* losfahren. **to** ~ ~ **on a journey** eine Reise antreten; **to** ~ ~ **for Spain** nach Spanien abfahren or losfahren.

♦ **set out 1** *vt sep (display)* ausbreiten; *(arrange) chess pieces* aufstellen; *essay* anlegen. **2** *vi* **(a)** *(depart)* = **set off 2**. **(b)** *(intend)* beabsichtigen. **I didn't** ~ ~ **to do that** ich hatte nicht vor, das zu tun.

♦ **set to 1** *vi (start working etc)* loslegen *(col)*. **they** ~ ~ **and repaired it** sie machten sich an die Arbeit und reparierten es. **2** *vi +prep obj* **to** ~ ~ **work** sich an die Arbeit machen.

♦ **set up 1** *vt sep* **(a)** *(establish oneself)* **to** ~ ~ **as a doctor** sich als Arzt niederlassen; **to** ~ ~ **in business** sein eigenes Geschäft aufmachen; **to** ~ ~ **for oneself** sich selbständig machen. **2** *vt sep* **(a)** *(place in position) statue, post* aufstellen; *(assemble) tent, stall, apparatus* aufbauen; *(fig: arrange) meeting* vereinbaren; *robbery* planen. **to** ~ **sth** ~ **for sb** etw für jdn vorbereiten. **(b)** *(establish)* gründen; *school, office* einrichten; *inquiry* anordnen. **to** ~ **sb** ~ **in business** jdm zu einem Geschäft verhelfen; **to** ~ **sb** ~ **as sth** (es) jdm ermöglichen, etw zu werden; **to be** ~ ~ **for life** für sein ganzes Leben ausgesorgt haben. **(c)** *(col: frame)* **to** ~ **sb** ~ jdm etw anhängen; **I've**

been ~ ~ das will mir einer anhängen *(col)*.
♦ **set upon** *vi* +*prep obj* überfallen; *(animal)* anfallen.
set: ~-back *n* Rückschlag *m*; ~ square *n* Zeichendreieck *nt*; ~ theory *n* Mengenlehre *f*.
settee [se'ti:] *n* Couch *f*, Sofa *nt*.
setter ['setə'] *n (dog)* Setter *m*.
setting ['setɪŋ] *n* **(a)** *(of sun, moon)* Untergang *m*. **(b)** *(background, atmosphere)* Rahmen *m*; *(surroundings)* Umgebung *f*; *(of novel etc)* Schauplatz *m*. **a film with a medieval** ~ ein Film, der im Mittelalter spielt. **(c)** *(of jewel)* Fassung *f*. **(d)** *(at table)* Gedeck *nt*. **(e)** *(position on dial etc)* Einstellung *f*. **(f)** *(musical arrangement)* Vertonung *f*. **(g)** *(hair)* Legen *nt*. ~ **lotion** (Haar)festiger *m*.
settle ['setl] **1** *vt* **(a)** *(decide)* entscheiden; *(sort out)* regeln; *problem* klären; *dispute, differences* beilegen; *doubts* ausräumen; *date, place* festlegen; *venue* festlegen; *deal* abschließen *(col)*; *price, terms* aushandeln. **when my future is** ~**d** wenn sich meine Zukunft entschieden hat; **to** ~ **one's affairs** seine Angelegenheiten in Ordnung bringen; **to** ~ **an estate** *(Jur)* die Verteilung des Nachlasses regeln; **to** ~ **a case out of court** einen Fall außergerichtlich klären; **that's** ~**d then** das ist also klar; **that** ~**s it** damit wäre der Fall (ja wohl) erledigt; *(angry)* jetzt reicht's.
(b) *(pay)* bill begleichen; *account* ausgleichen.
(c) *(place carefully)* legen; *(in upright position)* stellen; *(make comfortable)* child, invalid versorgen; *(calm)* nerves, stomach beruhigen. **to** ~ **oneself comfortably in an armchair** es sich *(dat)* in einem Sessel bequem machen.
(d) *(colonize)* land besiedeln.
(e) *(form)* **to** ~ **money/property on sb** jdm Geld/Besitz überschreiben; *(in will)* jdm Geld/Besitz vermachen.
2 *vi* **(a)** *(in country, town, profession)* sich niederlassen; *(as settler)* sich ansiedeln; *(in house)* sich einrichten; *(feel at home in house, town)* sich einleben *(into an* +*dat)*; *(in job, surroundings)* sich eingewöhnen *(into in* +*dat)*; *(permanently in area)* seßhaft werden. **to** ~ **into a habit** sich *(dat)* etw angewöhnen.
(b) *(become less variable: weather)* beständig werden. **if the weather would only** ~ wenn das Wetter nicht mehr so unbeständig wäre.
(c) *(become calm)* *(child, matters, stomach)* sich beruhigen; *(panic, excitement)* sich legen; *(become less excitable)* ruhiger werden. **he couldn't** ~ **to anything** er konnte sich auf nichts konzentrieren.
(d) *(come to rest, sit down)* *(person, bird)* sich niederlassen *or* setzen; *(dust)* sich setzen *or* legen; *(sink slowly)* *(building)* sich senken; *(ground, sediment)* sich setzen.
(e) *(Jur)* **to** ~ *(out of court)* sich vergleichen.
(f) *(pay)* bezahlen. **can I** ~ **with you later?** kann ich später mit Ihnen abrechnen?
♦ **settle down** *vi* **(a)** = settle 2 (a). **it's time he** ~**d** ~ es wird Zeit, daß er zur Ruhe kommt; *(got married)* es wird Zeit, daß er heiratet; **to** ~ ~ **at school/job** sich an einer Schule/in einer Stellung eingewöhnen. **(b)** = settle 2 (c). **(c) to** ~ ~ **to work** sich an die Arbeit machen *or* setzen; **to** ~ ~ **for the night** sich schlafen legen.
♦ **settle for** *vi* +*prep obj* sich zufriedengeben mit. **she won't** ~ ~ **anything less** mit weniger gibt sie sich nicht zufrieden.
♦ **settle in** *vi (in house, town)* sich einleben; *(in job, school)* sich eingewöhnen.
♦ **settle on** *vi* +*prep obj* sich entscheiden für; *(agree on)* sich einigen auf (+*acc)*.
♦ **settle up** **1** *vi* (be)zahlen. **to** ~ ~ **with sb** *(lit, fig)* mit jdm abrechnen. **2** *vt sep bill* bezahlen.
settled ['setld] *adj way of life* geregelt; *(Brit)* weather beständig. **to be** ~ in geregelten Verhältnis-

sen leben; *(established)* etabliert sein; *(in place)* seßhaft sein; *(have permanent job etc)* festen Fuß gefaßt haben; *(in a house)* sich häuslich niedergelassen haben; *(be less restless)* ruhiger sein.
settlement ['setlmənt] *n* **(a)** *(act) (deciding)* Entscheidung *f*; *(sorting out)* Regelung *f*; *(of problem etc)* Klärung *f*; *(of dispute etc)* Beilegung *f*; *(of estate)* Regelung *f*; *(of bill, claim)* Bezahlung *f*; *(of account)* Ausgleich *m*. **a** ~ **out of court** *(Jur)* ein außergerichtlicher Vergleich; **to reach a** ~ sich einigen, einen Vergleich treffen; **in** ~ **of our account** zum Ausgleich unseres Kontos. **(b)** *(colony, village)* Siedlung, Niederlassung *f*; *(colonization)* Besiedlung *f*. **(c)** *(contract, agreement etc)* Übereinkunft *f*.
settler ['setlə'] *n* Siedler(in *f*) *m*.
set: ~-**to** *n (col)* Krach *m (col)*; **to have a** ~-**to with sb** mit jdm in die Wolle kriegen *(col)*; ~-**up** *n* **(a)** *(col: situation)* Zustände *pl*; **I don't like the whole** ~-**up** mir gefällt das ganze Drum und Dran nicht *(col)*; **(b)** *(col: rigged contest)* abgekartete Sache.
seven ['sevn] *adj* sieben; *see* **six**.
seventeen ['sevn'ti:n] *adj* siebzehn.
seventeenth ['sevn'ti:nθ] *adj* siebzehnte(r, s); *see* **sixteenth**.
seventh ['sevnθ] **1** *adj* siebte(r, s). **2** *n (fraction)* Siebtel *nt*; *(in series)* Siebte(r, s); *(Mus)* Septime *f*; *(chord)* Septimenakkord *m*; *see* **sixth**.
seventy ['sevntɪ] *adj* siebzig; *see* **sixty**.
sever ['sevə'] *vt (cut through)* durchtrennen; *(violently)* durchschlagen; *(cut off)* abtrennen; *(violently)* abschlagen; *(fig: break off)* ties lösen; *relations* abbrechen; *communications* unterbrechen.
several ['sevrəl] **1** *adj (some)* einige, mehrere;- *(various)* verschiedene. **I've seen him** ~ **times/**~ **times already** ich habe ihn einige Male gesehen/ schon mehrere Male gesehen; **I'll need** ~ **more** ich brauche noch einige. **2** *pron* einige. ~ **of the houses** einige (der) Häuser; ~ **of us** einige von uns.
severance pay ['sevərəns,peɪ] *n* eine Abfindung.
severe [sɪ'vɪə'] *adj (+er) person, appearance* streng; *punishment, competition, test* hart; *criticism, reprimand* scharf; *crime, warning* ernst; *illness, injury, blow, frost, loss* schwer, schlimm; *pain, storm* stark, heftig; *weather* rauh. **to be** ~ **with sb** streng mit jdm sein.
severely [sɪ'vɪəlɪ] *adv see adj*. **to be** ~ **critical of sth** sich äußerst kritisch über etw (*acc*) äußern.
severity [sɪ'verɪtɪ] *n see adj* Strenge *f*; Härte *f*; Schärfe *f*; Ernst *m*; Schwere *f*; Stärke, Heftigkeit *f*; Rauheit *f*. **the** ~ **of the cold/drought/frost/loss** die schwere Kälte/Dürre/der starke Frost/der schwere Verlust.
sew [səʊ] *pret* ~**ed**, *ptp* ~**n** *vti* nähen. **to** ~ **sth on/together** etw annähen/zusammennähen.
♦ **sew up** *vt sep* **(a)** nähen *(also Med)*; *opening* zunähen. **(b)** *(fig)* unter Dach und Fach bringen. **it's all** ~**n** ~ es ist unter Dach und Fach.
sewage ['sju:ɪdʒ] *n* Abwasser *nt*. ~ **farm/works** *(sg)* smelly place) Kläranlage *f*.
sewer ['sjʊə'] *n (pipe)* Abwasserleitung *f*; *(main* ~) Abwasserkanal *m*; *(fig: smelly place)* Kloake *f*.
sewing ['səʊɪŋ] *n (activity)* Nähen *nt*; *(piece of work)* Näharbeit *f*. ~ **machine** Nähmaschine *f*.
sewn [səʊn] *ptp of* **sew**.
sex [seks] **1** *n* **(a)** *(Biol)* Geschlecht *nt*. **what** ~ **is the baby?** welches Geschlecht hat das Baby? **(b)** *(sexuality)* Sexualität *f*, Sex *m*; *(sexual intercourse)* Sex *(col)*, Geschlechtsverkehr *(form)* *m*. **to have** ~ *(col)* Geschlechtsverkehr haben. **2** *adj attr* Geschlechts-; *hygiene, crime* Sexual-; *film, scandal* Sex-.
sex: ~ **appeal** *n* Sex-Appeal *m*; ~ **discrimination** *n* Diskriminierung *f* auf Grund des Geschlechts; ~ **education** *n* Sexualerziehung *f*.

sexism ['seksɪzm] n Sexismus m.
sexist ['seksɪst] **1** n Sexist(in f) m. **2** adj sexistisch.
sex: ~ **life** n Geschlechtsleben nt; ~ **maniac** n (criminal) Triebtäter m; (hum col) (man) Lustmolch m (hum); (woman) Nymphomanin f; ~ **shop** n Sexshop m.
sextet(te) [seks'tet] n Sextett nt.
sexton ['sekstən] n Küster m.
sexual ['seksjʊəl] adj sexuell; intercourse, maturity Geschlechts-; crime Sexual-, Trieb-.
sexuality [‚seksjʊ'ælɪtɪ] n Sexualität f.
sexy ['seksɪ] adj (+er) (col) sexy pred; smile, pose also aufreizend; joke, film erotisch.
shabbiness ['ʃæbɪnɪs] n (lit, fig) Schäbigkeit f.
shabby ['ʃæbɪ] adj (+er) (lit, fig) schäbig.
shack [ʃæk] **1** n Hütte f. **2** vi (col) to ~ up with sb mit jdm zusammenziehen.
shackle ['ʃækl] n usu pl Kette, Fessel (also fig) f.
shade [ʃeɪd] **1** n (a) Schatten m. 30° in the ~ 30 Grad im Schatten; **to give** ~ Schatten spenden; **to put sb/sth in the** ~ (fig) jdn/etw in den Schatten stellen. (b) (lamp~) (Lampen)schirm m; (esp US: blind) Jalousie f; (roller blind) Rollo nt; (outside house) Markise f. ~**s** (esp US: sunglasses) Sonnenbrille f. (c) (of colour) (Farb)ton m; (fig) (of opinion) Schattierung f; (of meaning) Nuance f. a **brighter** ~ **of red** ein leuchtenderer Rotton. (d) (small quantity) it's a ~ long/too long es ist etwas or eine Spur zu lang. **2** vt (protect from light) abschirmen; lamp, window abdunkeln. that part **is** ~**d by a tree** der Teil liegt im Schatten eines Baumes.
shadow ['ʃædəʊ] **1** n (lit, fig) Schatten m; (fig: threat) (Be)drohung f. **in the** ~ im Schatten; **in the** ~**s** im Dunkel; **sb lives under the** ~ **of sth** etw lastet wie ein Schatten auf jdm; **to be just a** ~ **of one's former self** nur noch ein Schatten seiner selbst sein; **without a** ~ **of a doubt** ohne den geringsten Zweifel. **2** attr (Brit Pol) Schatten-. **the** ~ **Foreign Secretary** der Außenminister im Schattenkabinett. **3** vt (follow) beschatten (col).
shadow: ~-**boxing** n (lit, fig) Schattenboxen nt; ~ **cabinet** n (Brit) Schattenkabinett nt.
shadowy ['ʃædəʊɪ] adj schattig; (blurred) verschwommen. **to lead a** ~ **existence** ein undurchsichtiges Dasein führen.
shady ['ʃeɪdɪ] adj (+er) (a) place schattig; tree schattenspendend. (b) (col: of dubious honesty) zwielichtig.
shaft [ʃɑːft] n Schaft m; (of tool, golf club etc) Stiel m; (of light) Strahl m; (Mech) Welle f.
shaggy ['ʃægɪ] adj (+er) (long-haired) zottig; (unkempt) zottelig.
shake [ʃeɪk] (vb: pret **shook**, ptp **shaken**) **1** n (act of shaking) Schütteln nt. **to give a rug a** ~ einen Läufer ausschütteln; **give the paint a** ~ die Farbe (gut) durchschütteln; **to give sb/oneself a good** ~ jdn/sich kräftig schütteln; **with a** ~ **of her head** mit einem Kopfschütteln; **to be no great** ~**s** (col) nicht umwerfend sein (at in +dat). **2** vt (a) schütteln; building erschüttern; cocktail durchschütteln. "~ **well before using**" „vor Gebrauch gut schütteln"; **to be** ~**n to pieces** total durchgeschüttelt werden; **to** ~ **one's fist at sb** jdm mit der Faust drohen; **to** ~ **one's head** den Kopf schütteln; **to** ~ **oneself/itself free** sich losmachen; **to** ~ **hands with sb** jdm die Hand schütteln. (b) (weaken) faith etc erschüttern; evidence, reputation, resolve ins Wanken bringen. (c) (shock, amaze) erschüttern. **that shook him!** da war er platt (col); **it was a nasty accident, he's still rather badly** ~**n** ein schlimmer Unfall, der Schreck sitzt ihm noch in den Knochen.
3 vi wackeln; (hand) zittern; (earth, voice) beben. **the whole boat shook as the waves hit** das ganz Boot wurde vom Aufprall der Wellen erschüttert; **to** ~ **like a leaf** zittern wie Espen-

laub; **to** ~ **with fear** vor Angst zittern; **he was shaking all over** er zitterte am ganzen Körper.
♦ **shake off** vt sep dust, pursuer abschütteln; headache loswerden.
♦ **shake out** vt sep (a) herausschütteln; rug ausschütteln. (b) (fig: out of complacency etc) aufrütteln (of aus).
♦ **shake up** vt sep (a) bottle, liquid schütteln; pillow aufschütteln. (b) (upset) erschüttern. **she's still a bit** ~**n** ~ sie ist immer noch ziemlich mitgenommen. (c) management, recruits auf Zack bringen (col); ideas revidieren.
shaken ['ʃeɪkən] ptp of **shake**.
shake-up ['ʃeɪkʌp] n (col) (reorganization) Umbesetzung f. **to give a department a good** ~ eine Abteilung auf Zack bringen (col).
shakily ['ʃeɪkɪlɪ] adv wacklig; talk mit zitteriger Stimme; walk mit wackligen Schritten.
shaky ['ʃeɪkɪ] adj (+er) chair, position wacklig; evidence fragwürdig; voice, hands, writing zittrig; knowledge unsicher. **his Spanish is rather** ~ sein Spanisch ist ziemlich holprig; **to feel** ~ sich ganz schwach fühlen.
shale [ʃeɪl] n Schiefer m.
shall [ʃæl] pret **should** modal aux (a) (future) **we** ~ **or we'll go to France this year** wir werden dieses Jahr nach Frankreich fahren, wir fahren dieses Jahr nach Frankreich; **no, I** ~ **not or I shan't/yes, I** ~ nein, das werde ich nicht tun or das tue ich nicht/jawohl, das werde ich tun or das tue ich! (b) (determination, obligation) **you** ~ **pay for this!** dafür wirst du büßen!; **but I say you shall do it!** aber ich sage dir, du wirst das machen!; **the directors** ~ **not be disturbed** (form) die Direktoren dürfen nicht gestört werden; **I want to go too** — **and so you** ~ ich will auch mitkommen — aber gewiß doch. (c) (in questions, suggestions) **what** ~ **we do?** was sollen wir machen?; **let's go in,** ~ **we?** komm, gehen wir hinein!; **I'll buy 3,** ~ **I?** soll ich 3 kaufen?, ich kaufe 3, oder?
shallot [ʃə'lɒt] n Schalotte f.
shallow ['ʃæləʊ] **1** adj flach; water also seicht; (fig) talk, person oberflächlich. **in the** ~ **end of the pool** am flachen Ende des Beckens. **2** n ~**s** pl Untiefe f.
shalt [ʃælt] (obs) 2nd pers sing of **shall**.
sham [ʃæm] **1** n (a) (pretence) Heuchelei f. **their marriage had become a** ~ ihre Ehe war zur Farce geworden. (b) (person) Scharlatan m. **2** adj diamonds etc unecht, imitiert; sympathy etc vorgetäuscht, gespielt. ~ **battle** Scheingefecht nt. **3** vt vortäuschen; sympathy heucheln. **4** vi so tun; (esp with illness) simulieren; (with feelings) heucheln. **he's just** ~**ming** er tut nur so.
shambles ['ʃæmblz] n sing heilloses Durcheinander. **the room was a** ~ im Zimmer herrschte ein heilloses Durcheinander; **the economy is in a** ~ die Wirtschaft befindet sich in einem Chaos.
shame [ʃeɪm] **1** n (a) (feeling of ~) Scham f; (cause of ~) Schande f. **to feel** ~ **at sth** sich für etw schämen; **he hung his head in** ~ er senkte beschämt den Kopf; (fig) er schämte sich; **to bring** ~ **upon sb/oneself** jdm/sich Schande machen; **to put sb/sth to** ~ (fig) jdn/etw in den Schatten stellen; ~ **on you!** du solltest dich/ihr solltet euch schämen! (b) (pity) it's a ~ **you couldn't come** schade, daß du nicht kommen konntest; **what a** ~! (das ist aber) schade!; **what a** ~ **he ...** schade, daß er ... **2** vt Schande machen (+dat); (fig: by excelling) in den Schatten stellen. **he** ~**d us by working so hard** er hat uns alle durch sein hartes Arbeiten beschämt.
shamefaced ['ʃeɪmfeɪst] adj betreten.
shameful ['ʃeɪmfʊl] adj schändlich. **how** ~! was für eine Schande!; **what** ~ **behaviour!** dieses Benehmen ist eine Schande.
shameless ['ʃeɪmlɪs] adj schamlos. **he was quite** ~ **about it** er schämte sich überhaupt nicht.

shammy (leather) [ˈʃæmɪ(ˈleðəʳ)] n Fenster-/ Autoleder nt.

shampoo [ʃæmpuː] 1 n (liquid) Shampoo, Schampon nt; (act of washing) Reinigung f; (of hair) Waschen nt. **to have a ~** sich (dat) die Haare waschen lassen. 2 vt person die Haare waschen (+dat); hair waschen; carpet reinigen.

shamrock [ˈʃæmrɒk] n Klee m; (leaf) Kleeblatt nt.

shandy [ˈʃændɪ] n Bier nt mit Limonade, Radler m (S Ger), Alsterwasser nt (N Ger).

shandygaff [ˈʃændɪˌgæf] n (US) = **shandy.**

shank [ʃæŋk] n (to go) on S~s' pony auf Schusters Rappen (reiten).

shan't [ʃɑːnt] = **shall not.**

shanty[1] [ˈʃæntɪ] n (hut) Baracke, Hütte f. ~ **town** Slum(vor)stadt f.

shanty[2] n (Mus) Seemannslied, Shanty nt.

shape [ʃeɪp] 1 n (a) Form f. **what ~ is it?** welche Form hat es?; **it's rectangular** etc in ~ es ist rechteckig etc; **she's the right ~ for a model** sie hat die richtige Figur für ein Mannequin; **to hammer metal into ~** Metall zurechthämmern; **to knock sth out of ~** etw zerbeulen; **to take ~** (lit, fig) Gestalt annehmen; **of all ~s and sizes** jeder Art, in allen Variationen; **I don't accept gifts in any ~ or form** ich nehme überhaupt keine Geschenke an; **we do not know the ~ of things to come** wir wissen nicht, wie sich die Zukunft gestalten wird.

(b) (unidentified figure) Gestalt f; (object) Form f.

(c) (fig: order, condition) **in good/bad~** (sportsman) in Form/nicht in Form; (mentally, healthwise) in guter/schlechter Verfassung; (things, business) in gutem/schlechtem Zustand; **to get into ~** (sportsman etc) in Form kommen; **to get a house into ~** ein Haus in Ordnung bringen; **to get one's affairs into ~** seine Angelegenheiten ordnen; **to knock sb/sth into ~** jdn/etw auf Vordermann bringen.

2 vt (lit) stone etc bearbeiten; clay etc formen (into zu); (fig) character, ideas formen, prägen; one's life gestalten; course of history bestimmen.

3 vi (also ~ up) sich entwickeln. **to ~ up well** sich gut entwickeln.

shaped [ʃeɪpt] adj geformt. **an oddly ~ hat** ein Hut mit einer komischen Form.

-shaped [-ʃeɪpt] adj suf -förmig.

shapeless [ˈʃeɪplɪs] adj formlos; (ugly) unförmig.

shapely [ˈʃeɪplɪ] adj (+er) figure, woman wohlproportioniert; legs, bust wohlgeformt.

share [ʃɛəʳ] 1 n (a) (portion) Anteil m (in or of an +dat). **I want my fair ~** ich will meinen (An)teil; **he didn't get his fair ~** er ist zu kurz gekommen; **I've had more than my fair ~ of bad luck** ich habe mehr (als mein Teil an) Pech gehabt; **I'll give you a ~ in the profit** ich beteilige Sie am Gewinn; **in equal ~s** zu gleichen Teilen; **to take one's ~ of the proceeds/blame** sich (dat) seinen Anteil am Gewinn nehmen/sich mitschuldig erklären; **to pay one's ~** seinen (An)teil bezahlen; **to do one's ~** sein(en) Teil beitragen; **to have a ~ in sth** an etw (dat) beteiligt sein; **I had no ~ in that** damit hatte ich nichts zu tun. (b) (Fin) (Geschäfts)anteil m; (in a public limited company) Aktie f.

2 vt (divide) teilen; (have in common also) gemeinsam haben; responsibility gemeinsam tragen. **we ~ the same name/birthday** wir haben den gleichen Namen/am gleichen Tag Geburtstag; **they ~ a room** sie haben ein gemeinsames Zimmer; **I do not ~ that view** diese Ansicht teile ich nicht.

3 vi (a) teilen. **children have to learn to ~** Kinder müssen lernen, mit anderen zu teilen; **to ~ and ~ alike** (brüderlich) mit (den) anderen teilen. (b) **to ~ in sth** sich an etw (dat) beteiligen; (in profit) an etw (dat) beteiligt werden; (in

enthusiasm) etw teilen; (in success, sorrow) an etw (dat) Anteil nehmen.

share: ~**holder** n Aktionär(in f) m; ~ **index** n Aktienindex m; ~**-out** n Verteilung f; (St Ex) (Dividenden)ausschüttung f.

shark [ʃɑːk] n (a) Hai(fisch) m. (b) (col: swindler) Schlitzohr nt (col). **loan ~** Kredithai m (col).

sharp [ʃɑːp] 1 adj (+er) (a) scharf; needle, angle spitz; air, wind schneidend; apple sauer; wine herb; nose empfindlich; (intelligent) person schlau, auf Draht (col); child aufgeweckt; remark scharfsinnig. **that was pretty ~ of you** das war ganz schön schlau or clever (col) von dir; **to keep a ~ watch for mistakes** scharf auf Fehler aufpassen. (b) (sudden, intense) whistle, cry durchdringend, schrill; drop in prices steil; frost scharf; shower, desire, pain heftig. **after a short, ~ struggle** nach kurzem, heftigem Kampf. (c) (pej: cunning) person gerissen, raffiniert, clever (col); trick etc raffiniert. (d) (harsh, fierce) tongue, retort, tone of voice scharf; person schroff. **he has a ~ temper** er ist jähzornig. (e) (Mus) note (too high) zu hoch; (raised a semitone) (um einen Halbton) erhöht.

2 adv (+er) (a) (Mus) zu hoch. (b) **at 5 o'clock ~** Punkt 5 Uhr; **to turn ~ right** scharf nach rechts abbiegen.

3 n (Mus) Kreuz nt. **you played F natural instead of a ~** du hast f statt fis gespielt.

sharpen [ˈʃɑːpən] vt (a) knife schleifen; razor wetzen; pencil spitzen; (fig) appetite anregen; wits schärfen. (b) (Mus) (by a semitone) (um einen Halbton) erhöhen; (raise pitch) höher singen/ spielen/stimmen.

sharpener [ˈʃɑːpnəʳ] n Schleifgerät nt; (in rod shape) Wetzstahl m; (pencil ~) (Bleistift)spitzer m.

sharp: ~**-eyed** adj scharfsichtig; **to be ~-eyed** scharfe Augen haben; ~**-featured** adj mit scharfen (Gesichts)zügen; ~**shooter** n Scharfschütze m; ~**-sighted** adj = ~**-eyed**; ~**-tempered** adj jähzornig; ~**-tongued** adj scharfzüngig; ~**-witted** adj scharfsinnig.

shatter [ˈʃætəʳ] 1 vt (a) (lit) zertrümmern; hopes, dreams zunichte machen; nerves zerrütten. **the blast ~ed all the windows** durch die Explosion zersplitterten alle Fensterscheiben; **his hopes were ~ed** seine Hoffnungen hatten sich zerschlagen. (b) (fig col: exhaust) fertigmachen (col); (mentally) mitnehmen. 2 vi zerbrechen, zerspringen; (windscreen) (zer)splittern.

shattered [ˈʃætəd] adj (col) (exhausted) fertig (col); (amazed) platt (col); (emotionally exhausted) mitgenommen.

shattering [ˈʃætərɪŋ] adj (a) blow, explosion gewaltig; defeat vernichtend. (b) (fig col: exhausting) anstrengend; (psychologically) zermürbend.

shatterproof [ˈʃætəpruːf] adj splitterfrei.

shave [ʃeɪv] (vb: pret ~**d**, ptp ~**d** or **shaven**) 1 n Rasur f. **to have a ~** sich rasieren; (at a barber's) sich rasieren lassen; **to have a close ~** (fig) mit knapper Not davonkommen; **that was a close ~** das war knapp. 2 vt face, legs rasieren; wood hobeln. 3 vi (person) sich rasieren; (razor) rasieren.

♦ **shave off** vt sep beard abrasieren (dat) abrasieren; sb's beard abrasieren; wood abhobeln.

shaven [ˈʃeɪvn] adj head (kahl)geschoren.

shaver [ˈʃeɪvəʳ] n (elec) Rasierapparat m.

shaving [ˈʃeɪvɪŋ] n ~s pl Späne pl.

shaving in cpds Rasier-; ~ **brush** n Rasierpinsel m; ~ **cream** n Rasiercreme f; ~ **point** n (Brit) Steckdose f für Rasierapparate.

shawl [ʃɔːl] n (Umhänge)tuch nt; (covering head) (Kopf)tuch nt.

she [ʃiː] 1 pron sie; (of boats, cars) es. ~ **who ...** (liter) diejenige, die ... 2 n Sie f.

she- *pref* weiblich. **~-bear** weiblicher Bär, Bärin *f*.

sheaf [ʃiːf] *n*, *pl* **sheaves** *(of wheat, corn)* Garbe *f*; *(of arrows etc, papers, notes)* Bündel *nt*.

shear [ʃɪəʳ] *pret* **~ed**, *ptp* **shorn** *vt sheep* scheren; *wool* (ab)scheren.

shears [ʃɪəz] *npl* (große) Schere; *(for hedges)* Heckenschere *f*; *(for metal)* Metallschere *f*.

sheath [ʃiːθ] *n* *(for sword etc)* Scheide *f*; *(Bot)* (Blatt)scheide *f*; *(on cable)* Mantel *m*; *(Brit: contraceptive)* Kondom *m or nt*.

sheath knife *n* Fahrtenmesser *nt*.

sheaves [ʃiːvz] *pl of* **sheaf**.

shed[1] [ʃed] *pret*, *ptp* **~** *vt* **(a)** *leaves, hair etc* verlieren; *horns* abwerfen; *clothes* ausziehen. **to ~ its skin** sich häuten; **you should ~ a few pounds** Sie sollten ein paar Pfund abnehmen *or* loswerden. **(b)** *tears, blood* vergießen. **I won't ~ any tears over him** ich weine ihm keine Träne nach. **(c)** *burden, leader* loswerden; *cares* ablegen; *friend* fallenlassen. **(d)** *light, perfume* verbreiten. **to ~ light on sth** *(fig)* etw erhellen.

shed[2] *n* Schuppen *m*; *(industrial)* Halle *f*; *(cattle ~)* Stall *m*.

she'd [ʃiːd] = **she would; she had.**

sheen [ʃiːn] *n* Glanz *m*.

sheep [ʃiːp] *n*, *pl* - *(lit, fig)* Schaf *nt*. **to separate the ~ from the goats** *(fig)* die Schafe von den Böcken trennen.

sheep: ~-dip *n* Desinfektionsbad *nt* für Schafe; **~dog** *nt* Hütehund *m*.

sheepish [ʃiːpɪʃ] *adj look* verlegen. **I felt a bit ~ about it** das war mir ein bißchen peinlich.

sheepskin [ʃiːpskɪn] *n* **(a)** Schaffell *nt*. **(b)** *(US col: diploma)* Pergament *nt*.

sheer [ʃɪəʳ] *adj* (+er) **(a)** *(absolute)* rein; *nonsense also* bar, glatt. **by ~ chance** rein zufällig; **by ~ hard work** durch nichts als harte Arbeit. **(b)** *(steep) cliff, drop* steil, jäh *(geh)*. **there is a ~ drop of 200 metres** es fällt 200 Meter steil ab. **(c)** *(of cloth etc)* (hauch)dünn.

sheet [ʃiːt] *n* **(a)** *(for bed)* (Bett)laken, Bettuch *nt*; *(for covering furniture)* Tuch *nt*. **the furniture was covered with (dust)~s** die Möbel waren verhängt. **(b)** *(of paper, col: a newspaper)* Blatt *nt*; *(big, as of wrapping paper, stamps etc, Typ)* Bogen *m*. **~ of music** Notenblatt *nt*. **(c)** *(of plywood)* Platte *f*; *(of glass also)* Scheibe *f*; *(of metal also)* Blech *nt*; *(baking ~)* (Back)blech *nt*; *(of water, ice etc)* Fläche *f*. **a ~ of ice covered the lake** eine Eisschicht bedeckte den See; **a ~ of flame** eine riesige Flamme.

sheet: ~ feed *n (for printer)* Einzelblattzuführung *f*; **~ lightning** *n* Wetterleuchten *nt*; **~ metal** *n* Walzblech *nt*; **~ music** *n* Notenblätter *pl*.

sheik(h) [ʃeɪk] *n* Scheich *m*.

shelf [ʃelf] *n*, *pl* **shelves** **(a)** Brett, Bord *nt*; *(for books)* Bücherbrett *nt*. **shelves** *(unit of furniture)* Regal *nt*; **she was left on the ~** *(col: girl)* sie ist sitzengeblieben. **(b)** *(ledge of rock etc)* Gesims *nt*, (Fels-)vorsprung *m*.

shelf: ~ life *n* Lagerfähigkeit *f*; **~ mark** *n* Standortzeichen *nt*.

shell [ʃel] 1 *n* **(a)** *(of egg, nut, mollusc)* Schale *f*; *(on beach)* Muschel *f*; *(of snail)* (Schnecken)haus *nt*; *(of tortoise, insect)* Panzer *m*; *(pastry ~)* Form *f*. **to come out of one's ~** *(fig)* aus sich *(dat)* herausgehen; **to withdraw into one's ~** *(fig)* sich in sein Schneckenhaus verkriechen. **(b)** *(frame) (of building)* Mauerwerk *nt*; *(unfinished)* Rohbau *m*; *(ruin)* Gemäuer *nt*; *(of car) (unfinished)* Karosserie *f*; *(gutted)* Wrack *nt*; *(of ship)* Gerippe *nt*; *(gutted)* Wrack *nt*. **(c)** *(Mil)* Granate *f*; *(esp US: cartridge)* Patrone *f*. 2 *vt* **(a)** *peas etc* enthülsen; *eggs, nuts* schälen. **(b)** *(Mil)* (mit Granaten) beschießen.

♦ **shell out** *(col)* 1 *vt sep* blechen *(col)*. 2 *vi* **to ~ for sth** für etw blechen *(col)*.

she'll [ʃiːl] = **she will; she shall.**

shellfish [ʃelfɪʃ] *n* Schaltier(e *pl*) *nt*; *(Cook)* Meeresfrüchte *pl*.

shelling [ʃelɪŋ] *n* Granatfeuer *nt* *(of* auf +*acc)*.

shell: ~-proof *adj* bombensicher; **~ shock** *n* Kriegsneurose *f*.

shelter [ʃeltəʳ] 1 *n* *(protection)* Schutz *m*; *(place)* Unterstand *m*; *(air-raid ~)* (Luftschutz)keller *m*; *(bus ~)* Wartehäuschen *nt*; *(for the night)* Unterkunft *f*. **a night ~ for homeless people** ein Obdachlosenasyl *nt*; **in the ~ of one's home** in der Geborgenheit des Hauses; **under the ~ of the rock** im Schutze des Felsens; **to take ~** sich in Sicherheit bringen; *(from rain, hail etc)* sich unterstellen; **to give sb ~** jdn beherbergen. 2 *vt* schützen *(from* vor +*dat)*; *criminal* verstecken. **to ~ sb from blame** jdn gegen Vorwürfe in Schutz nehmen; **to ~ sb from harm** jdn vor Schaden bewahren. 3 *vi* **there was nowhere to ~** man konnte nirgends Schutz finden; *(from rain etc)* man konnte sich nirgends unterstellen; **a good place to ~** eine Stelle, wo man gut geschützt ist.

sheltered [ʃeltəd] *adj place* geschützt; *life* behütet. **~ from the wind** windgeschützt.

shelve [ʃelv] 1 *vi (slope)* abfallen. 2 *vt problem* aufschieben; *plan* ad acta legen.

shelves [ʃelvz] *pl of* **shelf**.

shelving [ʃelvɪŋ] *n* Regale *pl*.

shepherd [ʃepəd] 1 *n* Schäfer *m*. **~'s pie** Auflauf *m* aus Hackfleisch und Kartoffelbrei. 2 *vt* führen.

sherbet [ʃɜːbət] *n* *(powder)* Brausepulver *nt*; *(drink)* Brause *f*; *(US: water ~ ice)* Fruchteis *nt*.

sheriff [ʃerɪf] *n* Sheriff *m*; *(Scot)* Friedensrichter *m*.

sherry [ʃerɪ] *n* Sherry *m*.

she's [ʃiːz] = **she is; she has.**

Shetland Islands [ʃetlənd'aɪləndz] *npl* Shetlandinseln *pl*.

Shetland pony [ʃetlənd'pəʊnɪ] *n* Shetlandpony *nt*.

shield [ʃiːld] 1 *n* *(Mil, Her)* Schild *m*; *(sporting trophy also)* Trophäe *f*; *(on machine)* Schutzschirm *m*; *(eye~, radiation ~)* Schirm *m*; *(fig)* Schutz *m*. **riot ~** Schutzschild *m*. 2 *vt* schützen *(sb from sth* jdn vor etw dat)*.

shift [ʃɪft] 1 *n* **(a)** *(change)* Änderung *f*; *(in policy, opinion also)* Wandel *m*; *(from one place to another)* Verlegung *f*. **a ~ in direction** eine Richtungsänderung; **a ~ in public opinion** ein Meinungsumschwung *m* in der Bevölkerung; **a ~ of emphasis** eine Gewichtsverlagerung. **(b)** *(Aut: gear~)* Schaltung *f*; *(on typewriter: also ~ key)* Umschalttaste *f*. **(c)** *(period at work, group of workers)* Schicht *f*. **to work in ~s** in Schichten arbeiten; **to do ~ work** Schicht arbeiten. **(d)** *(stratagem)* List *f*; *(expedient)* Ausweg *m*. **to make ~ with sth** sich mit etw behelfen.

2 *vt* **(a)** *(move)* (von der Stelle) bewegen; *nail, cork* rauskriegen; *lid* abkriegen; *furniture also* verrücken; *head, arm* wegnehmen; *(from one place to another)* verschieben; *offices etc* verlegen; *rubble* wegräumen. **to ~ scenery** Kulissen schieben; **to ~ one's ground** seinen Standpunkt ändern; **to ~ sb from an opinion** jdn von einer Meinung abbringen; **to ~ the blame onto somebody else** die Verantwortung auf jemand anders schieben. **(b)** *(col: get rid of)* loswerden. **(c)** *(US Aut)* **to ~ gears** schalten.

3 *vi* **(a)** *(move)* sich bewegen; *(cargo, scene)* sich verlagern; *(scene)* wechseln; *(wind)* umspringen; *(from one's opinion)* abgehen. **he ~ed out of the way** er ging aus dem Weg; **~ over, you're taking up too much room** rück mal näher, du nimmst zuviel Platz weg!; **he ~ed onto his back** er drehte sich auf den Rücken; **~ing sands** *(Geol)* Flugsand *m*. **(b)** *(Aut)* schalten. **(c)** *(col: move quickly)* rasen.

shiftless [ʃɪftlɪs] *adj* träge, energielos.

shifty [ˈʃɪftɪ] adj (+er) (not honest) unehrlich; (not reliable) unzuverlässig; glance verstohlen; reply ausweichend.

shilling [ˈʃɪlɪŋ] n (Brit old) Shilling m.

shilly-shally [ˈʃɪlɪˌʃælɪ] vi (col) unschlüssig sein.

shimmer [ˈʃɪmə'] **1** n Schimmer m. **2** vi schimmern.

shin [ʃɪn] **1** n Schienbein nt; (of meat) Hachse f. **2** vi to ~ up/down (geschickt) hinauf-/hinunterklettern.

shinbone [ˈʃɪnbəʊn] n Schienbein nt.

shindy [ˈʃɪndɪ] n (col) Radau m (col); (noise also, dispute) Krach m (col).

shine [ʃaɪn] (vb: pret, ptp **shone**) **1** n Glanz m. to give one's shoes a ~ seine Schuhe polieren; to take the ~ off sth (lit, fig) einer Sache (dat) den Glanz nehmen; she's taken a real ~ to my brother (col) mein Bruder hat es ihr wirklich angetan. **2** vt (a) pret, ptp usu ~d (polish: also ~ up) blank putzen; shoes also polieren. (b) to ~ a light on sth etw beleuchten; ~ the torch this way! leuchte einmal hierher!; don't ~ it in my eyes! blende mich nicht! **3** vi (a) leuchten; (stars, eyes also, paint) glänzen; (sun, lamp) scheinen; (glass) blitzblank sein. her face shone with happiness ihr Gesicht strahlte vor Glück. (b) (fig: excel) glänzen. to ~ at/in sth bei/in etw (dat) glänzen.

shingle¹ [ˈʃɪŋgl] n (US col: signboard) Schild nt.

shingle² n no pl (pebbles) Kieselsteine pl.

shingles [ˈʃɪŋglz] n sing (Med) Gürtelrose f.

shining [ˈʃaɪnɪŋ] adj (lit, fig) leuchtend; light strahlend; eyes also, paint glänzend; car blitzblank.

shiny [ˈʃaɪnɪ] adj (+er) glänzend.

ship [ʃɪp] **1** n (a) Schiff nt. **on board** ~ an Bord; ~'s company (Schiffs)besatzung f; ~'s papers Schiffspapiere pl. (b) (US col: plane) Maschine f; (space~) Raumschiff nt. **2** vt (a) (take on board) goods an Bord bringen, laden; crew, passengers an Bord nehmen. to ~ oars die Riemen einlegen; to ~ water leck sein. (b) (transport) versenden; grain etc verfrachten; (by sea also) verschiffen. ♦ **ship out** vt sep versenden; coal, grain etc verfrachten. to ~ supplies ~ to sb jdn (per Schiff) mit Vorräten versorgen.

ship: ~builder n Schiffbauer m; ~building n Schiffbau m; ~load n Schiffsladung f; ~mate n Schiffskamerad m.

shipment [ˈʃɪpmənt] n Sendung f; (act) Transport m; (transporting by sea) Verschiffung f.

shipowner [ˈʃɪpəʊnə'] n Schiffseigner m; (of many ships) Reeder m.

shipper [ˈʃɪpə'] n (company) Speditionsfirma f; (sender) Absender m.

shipping [ˈʃɪpɪŋ] **1** n no pl (a) Schiffahrt f; (ships) Schiffe pl. (b) (transportation) Verschiffung f; (by rail etc) Versand m. **2** adj attr ~ agent Spediteur m; ~ company, ~ line Schiffahrtslinie, Reederei f; ~ lane Schiffahrtsstraße f.

ship: ~shape adj, adv tipptopp (col); ~wreck **1** n (lit, fig) Schiffbruch m; (fig also) Scheitern nt; **2** vt to be ~wrecked (lit) schiffbrüchig sein; (fig) Schiffbruch erleiden, scheitern; ~yard n (Schiffs)werft f.

shire [ˈʃaɪə'] n (Brit old) Grafschaft f. ~ horse Zugpferd nt.

shirk [ʃɜːk] **1** vt sich drücken vor (+dat), ausweichen (+dat). **2** vi sich drücken.

shirker [ˈʃɜːkə'] n Drückeberger(in f) m.

shirt [ʃɜːt] n (men's) (Ober)hemd nt; (Ftbl) Hemd, Trikot nt; (woman's: also US ~waist) Hemdbluse f. **keep your ~ on** (col) reg dich nicht auf!

shirt-sleeves [ˈʃɜːtsliːvz] npl Hemdsärmel pl. **in his/their ~** in Hemdsärmeln.

shirty [ˈʃɜːtɪ] adj (+er) (esp Brit col) sauer (col), verärgert; (as characteristic) griesgrämig (col).

shit [ʃɪt] (vb: pret, ptp ~ or (hum) **shat**) (col!) **1** n (a) Scheiße f (col!); (nonsense also) Scheiß m (col!). (b) (person) Arschloch nt (col!). (c) ~s pl

shiver [ˈʃɪvə'] **1** n (of cold) Schauer m; (of horror also) Schauder m. **the sight sent** ~s **down my back** bei dem Anblick lief es mir kalt den Rücken hinunter; **it gives me the** ~s ich kriege davon eine Gänsehaut. **2** vi zittern (with vor +dat); (with fear also) schaudern. **shivery** [ˈʃɪvərɪ] adj **to feel** ~ frösteln.

shoal [ʃəʊl] n (of fish) Schwarm m.

shock [ʃɒk] **1** n (a) (of explosion, impact) Wucht f; (of earthquake) (Erd)stoß m. (b) (Elec) Schlag m; (Med) (Elektro)shock m. **to get a** ~ einen Schlag bekommen. (c) (emotional disturbance) Schock, Schlag m; (state) Schock(zustand) m. **to be suffering from** ~ einen Schock (erlitten) haben; **to be in (a state of)** ~ unter Schock stehen; **the** ~ **killed him** den Schock hat er nicht überlebt; **to give sb a** ~ jdn erschrecken; **it gave me a nasty** ~ es hat mir einen bösen Schreck(en) eingejagt; **to get the** ~ **of one's life** den Schock seines Lebens kriegen; **he is in for a** ~! (col) der wird sich wundern! (col).

2 vt (affect emotionally) erschüttern; (make indignant) schockieren, schocken (col). **to be ~ed by sth** über etw (acc) bestürzt sein; (morally) über etw (acc) schockiert sein; **she is easily ~ed** sie ist leicht schockiert; **I was ~ed at the news** ich war bestürzt über die Nachricht.

3 vi (film, writer etc) schockieren, schocken (col).

shock absorber [ˈʃɒkəbˌzɔːbə'] n Stoßdämpfer m.

shocking [ˈʃɒkɪŋ] adj (a) news erschütternd, schockierend. (b) (very bad) entsetzlich, furchtbar. **isn't it** ~! es ist doch furchtbar!

shock: ~proof adj stoßfest; ~ therapy n Schocktherapie f; ~ wave n (lit) Druckwelle f; (fig) Erschütterung f.

shod [ʃɒd] pret, ptp of **shoe**.

shoddy [ˈʃɒdɪ] adj (+er) schäbig; work schludrig; goods also minderwertig.

shoe [ʃuː] (vb: pret, ptp **shod**) **1** n (a) Schuh m. **I wouldn't like to be in his** ~s ich möchte nicht in seiner Haut stecken; **to put oneself in sb's** ~s sich in jds Lage (acc) versetzen. (b) (horse~) (Huf)eisen nt. (c) (brake ~) Bremsschuh m. **2** vt horse beschlagen.

shoe: ~brush n Schuhbürste f; ~horn n Schuhanzieher, Schuhlöffel m; ~lace n Schnürsenkel m; ~maker n Schuhmacher, Schuster m; ~ polish n Schuhcreme f; ~shop n Schuhgeschäft nt; ~string n (a) (US: ~lace) Schnürsenkel m. (b) (fig) to live on a ~string von der Hand in den Mund leben; ~string budget n Minibudget nt (col); ~tree n (Schuh)spanner m.

shone [ʃɒn] pret, ptp of **shine**.

shoo [ʃuː] **1** interj sch; (to dog etc) pfui; (to child) husch. **2** vt to ~ sb away jdn verscheuchen.

shook [ʃʊk] pret of **shake**.

shoot [ʃuːt] (vb: pret, ptp **shot**) **1** n (a) (Bot) Trieb m; (from seed etc also) Keim m; (of bushes, trees) Schößling m; (young branch) Reis nt. (b) (hunting expedition) Jagd f; (~ing party) Jagdgesellschaft f; (competition) (Wett)schießen nt.

2 vt (a) (Mil etc) schießen; bullet, gun abfeuern. (b) person, animal (hit) anschießen; (wound seriously) niederschießen; (kill) erschießen; **to ~ sb dead** jdn erschießen; **he shot himself** er hat sich erschossen; **he accidentally shot himself in the foot** er schoß sich (dat) versehentlich in den Fuß; **he was shot in the leg** er wurde ins Bein getroffen; **you'll get shot for doing that!** (fig col) das kann dich Kopf und Kragen kosten! (col). (c) (throw, propel) schleudern; (Sport) schießen. **to ~ a question at sb** eine Frage auf jdn abfeuern; **to ~ a glance at sb** jdm einen (schnellen) Blick zuwerfen. (d) (Phot) film, scene drehen; snapshot

schießen; *subject* aufnehmen.
3 *vi* **(a)** schießen; *(as hunter)* jagen. **to ~ to kill** gezielt schießen; *(police)* einen gezielten Todesschuß/gezielte Todesschüsse abgeben; **don't ~!** nicht schießen!; **stop or I'll ~!** stehenbleiben oder ich schieße!; **to ~ at sb/sth** auf jdn/etw schießen; **to ~ at goal** aufs Tor schießen. **(b) to ~ into the lead** an die Spitze vorpreschen; **he shot down the stairs** er schoß *or* jagte die Treppe hinunter; **to ~ by** *or* **past** vorbeischießen *or* -jagen; **the pain shot up his leg** der Schmerz durchzuckte sein Bein.

♦ **shoot down** *vt sep plane* abschießen; *person* erschießen; *(fig col) person* fertigmachen (col); *suggestion* abschmettern (col); *argument* in der Luft zerreißen.

♦ **shoot off** *vi* davonschießen *(col)*.

♦ **shoot out 1** *vi (emerge swiftly)* herausschießen *(of* aus). **2** *vt sep* **(a)** *(put out swiftly) hand etc* blitzschnell ausstrecken; *tongue etc* hervorschnellen (lassen). **(b) to ~ it ~** sich *(dat)* ein (Feuer)gefecht liefern.

♦ **shoot up** *vi (hand, prices)* in die Höhe schnellen; *(grow rapidly) (children, plant)* in die Höhe schießen; *(new towns, buildings etc)* aus dem Boden schießen.

shooting ['ʃuːtɪŋ] *n* **(a)** *(shots)* Schießen *nt; (by artillery)* Feuer *nt.* **was there any ~?** gab es Schießereien?; **there was a ~ last night** gestern nacht ist jemand erschossen worden. **(b)** *(Sport: Ftbl etc, with guns)* Schießen *nt; (Hunt)* Jagen *nt,* Jagd *f.* **(c)** *(Film)* Drehen *nt.*

shooting: ~ **brake** *n (Aut old)* Kombiwagen *m;* ~ **gallery** *n* Schießstand *m;* ~ **match** *n:* **the whole ~ match** *(col)* der ganze Laden *(col);* ~ **party** *n* Jagdgesellschaft *f;* ~ **star** *m* Sternschnuppe *f;* ~ **stick** *n* Jagdstuhl *m.*

shop [ʃɒp] **1** *n* **(a)** Geschäft *nt,* Laden *m; (esp Brit: large store)* Kaufhaus *nt.* **I have to go to the ~s** ich muß einkaufen gehen; **to set up ~** ein Geschäft eröffnen; **all over the ~** *(col)* in der ganzen Gegend herum *(col);* **to talk ~** über die Arbeit reden; *(professional people also)* fachsimpeln. **(b)** *(work~)* Werkstatt *f; (workers)* Arbeiterschaft *f.* **2** *vi* einkaufen, Einkäufe machen. **to go ~ping** einkaufen gehen. **3** *vt (Brit col: betray)* **to ~ sb (to sb)** jdn (bei jdm) verpfeifen *(col).*

♦ **shop around** *vi (lit, fig)* sich umsehen *(for* nach).

shop: ~ **assistant** *n (Brit)* Verkäufer(in *f*) *m;* ~ **floor** *n* **(a)** *(place)* Produktionsstätte *f; (for heavier work)* Werkstatt *f;* **he started off working on the ~ floor** er hat (ganz unten) in der Fabrik *or* Produktion angefangen; **on the ~ floor** in der Werkstatt *etc;* unter den Arbeitern; **(b)** *(Brit: workers)* Arbeiter *pl,* Leute *pl* in der Produktion; ~**keeper** *n* Ladenbesitzer(in *f*), Geschäftsinhaber(in *f*) *m;* ~**lifter** *n* Ladendieb(in *f*) *m;* ~**lifting** *n* Ladendiebstahl *m.*

shopper ['ʃɒpə'] *n* Käufer(in *f*) *m.*

shopping ['ʃɒpɪŋ] *n (act)* Einkaufen *nt; (goods bought)* Einkäufe *pl.* **to do one's ~** einkaufen, Einkäufe machen.

shopping: ~ **bag** *n* Einkaufstasche *f;* ~ **basket** *n* Einkaufskorb *m;* ~ **centre,** *(US)* ~ **center** *n* Einkaufszentrum *nt;* ~ **list** *n* Einkaufszettel *m.*

shop: ~**-soiled** *adj (Brit) clothes, furniture* angeschmutzt; *goods, material* leicht beschädigt; ~ **steward** *n* (gewerkschaftlicher) Vertrauensmann *(im Betrieb);* ~ **window** *n (lit, fig)* Schaufenster *nt;* ~**worn** *adj (US)* = ~**-soiled.**

shore¹ [ʃɔː'] *n (sea* ~, *lake* ~*)* Ufer *nt; (beach)* Strand *m; (coast)* Küste *f.* **these ~s** *(fig)* dieses Land; **on the ~s of the lake** am Seeufer; **on ~** an Land.

shore² *vt (also* ~ **up)** (ab)stützen; *(fig)* stützen.

shore: ~ **leave** *n (Naut)* Landurlaub *m;* ~**line** *n* Uferlinie *f.*

shorn [ʃɔːn] *ptp of* **shear.**

short [ʃɔːt] **1** *adj (+er)* **(a)** kurz; *steps also, person* klein. **a ~ way off** nicht weit entfernt; **to be ~ in the leg** *(person)* kurze Beine haben; *(trousers)* zu kurz sein; **a ~ time ago** vor kurzer Zeit, vor kurzem; **in a ~ while** in Kürze; **time is getting/is ~** die Zeit wird/ist knapp; **to take the ~ view of sth** etw auf kurze Sicht betrachten; **in ~ order** *(US col)* sofort; ~ **and sweet** schön kurz; **the ~ answer is that he refused** kurz gesagt, er lehnte ab; **in ~** kurz gesagt; **Pat is ~ for Patricia** Pat ist die Kurzform von Patricia.

(b) *(curt) reply* knapp; *(rude)* barsch, schroff; *manner, person* schroff, kurz angebunden *(col).* **to have a ~ temper** unbeherrscht sein; **to be ~ with sb** jdn schroff behandeln, jdm gegenüber kurz angebunden sein *(col).*

(c) *(insufficient)* zuwenig *inv; rations* knapp. **to be in ~ supply** knapp sein; *(Comm)* beschränkt lieferbar sein; **to be ~ (in ~ supply)** knapp sein; *(shot, throw)* nicht weit genug sein; **we are (five/£3) ~** wir haben (fünf/£ 3) zuwenig, uns *(dat)* fehlen fünf/£ 3; **we are ~ of books** wir haben zuwenig Bücher; **to be ~ of time** wenig Zeit haben; **I'm a bit ~ (of cash)** *(col)* ich bin etwas knapp bei Kasse *(col);* **we are £2,000 ~ of our target** wir liegen £ 2.000 unter unserem Ziel; **not far ~ of £100** nicht viel weniger als £ 100, knapp unter £ 100; **to be ~ on experience** wenig Erfahrung haben.

2 *adv* **(a) to fall ~** *(arrow, missile etc)* zu kurz landen. **that's where the book falls ~** daran fehlt es dem Buch; **to fall ~ of sth** etw nicht erreichen; *of expectations* etw nicht erfüllen; **it falls far ~ of what we require** das bleibt weit hinter unseren Bedürfnissen zurück; **to go ~ (of money/food etc)** zuwenig (Geld/zu essen *etc)* haben; **we are running ~ (of petrol/time)** wir haben nicht mehr viel (Benzin/Zeit); **I'm running ~ of ideas** mir gehen die Ideen aus; **my patience is running ~** meine Geduld ist bald zu Ende; **to sell sb ~** *(in shop)* jdm zuwenig geben; *(betray, cheat)* jdn betrügen.

(b) *(abruptly, suddenly)* plötzlich, abrupt. **to stop ~** *(while driving)* plötzlich stehenbleiben; *(while talking)* plötzlich *or* unvermittelt innehalten; **I'd stop ~ of or at murder** vor Mord würde ich haltmachen.

(c) ~ **of** *(except)* außer (+*dat*); **it is nothing ~ of robbery** das ist glatter Diebstahl; **nothing ~ of a revolution can ...** nur eine Revolution kann ...; **it's little ~ of madness** das grenzt an Wahnsinn; **I don't see what you can do ~ of asking him yourself** ich sehe keine andere Möglichkeit, als daß Sie ihn selbst fragen; ~ **of telling him a lie ...** außer ihn zu belügen ...

3 *n* **(~ circuit)** Kurzschluß, Kurze(r) *(col) m; (col:* ~ *drink)* Kurze(r) *m (col).*

4 *vt (Elec)* kurzschließen.

5 *vi (Elec)* einen Kurzschluß haben.

shortage ['ʃɔːtɪdʒ] *n (of goods, objects)* Knappheit *f no pl (of* an +*dat); (of people)* Mangel *m no pl (of* an +*dat).* **the housing ~** die Wohnungsknappheit; **a ~ of staff** Personalmangel *m.*

short: ~**bread** *n* Mürb(e)teiggebäck *nt;* ~**cake** *n (Brit:* ~**bread**) Mürb(e)teiggebäck *nt; (US: sponge)* Biskuittörtchen *nt;* ~**-change** *vt* **to ~-change sb** jdm zuwenig herausgeben; ~**-circuit 1** *n* Kurzschluß *m;* **2** *vt* kurzschließen; **3** *vi* einen Kurzschluß haben; ~**-coming** *n (esp pl)* Mangel *m; (of person)* Fehler *m;* ~**crust** *n (also* ~**crust pastry)** Mürbeteig *m; (easy solution)* Patentlösung *f.*

shorten ['ʃɔːtn] **1** *vt* verkürzen; *dress, rope* kürzer machen; *book, syllabus etc* kürzen. **2** *vi (days)* kürzer werden.

short: ~**hand** *n* Kurzschrift, Stenographie *f;* **in ~hand** in Kurzschrift; **to write ~hand** stenographieren; **to take sth down in ~hand** etw stenographieren; ~**hand typist** n (Brit) Stenoty-pist(in f) m; ~ **list** n (esp Brit) Auswahlliste f; **to be on the ~ list** in der engeren Wahl sein; ~**-list** vt (esp Brit) **to** ~**-list sb** jdn in die engere Wahl ziehen; ~**-lived** adj (lit, fig) kurzlebig; protests, attempts nicht lange andauernd; **to be** ~**-lived** (success, happiness) von kurzer Dauer sein.

shortly ['fɔːtlɪ] adv (a) (soon) bald, in Kürze; after, before kurz. (b) (curtly) barsch.

shorts [fɔːts] npl (a) Shorts pl, kurze Hose(n pl). (b) (esp US: underpants) Unterhose f.

short: ~**-sighted** adj (lit, fig) kurzsichtig; ~**-sleeved** adj kurzärmelig; ~**-staffed** adj **to be** ~**-staffed** zuwenig Personal haben; ~ **story** n Kurzgeschichte, Short story f; ~**-tempered** adj (in general) unbeherrscht; (in a bad temper) gereizt; **to be** ~**-tempered with sb** mit jdm ungeduldig sein; ~ **term** n **in the** ~ **term** auf kurze Sicht; ~**-term** adj kurzfristig; ~ **time** n Kurzarbeit f; **to be on** ~ **time** kurzarbeiten, Kurzarbeit haben; ~**wave** 1 n (also ~**wave radio**) Kurzwelle f; 2 adj transmission auf Kurzwelle.

shot¹ [fɒt] 1 pret, ptp of **shoot**.
2 n (a) (from gun, bow etc) Schuß m. **to fire** or **take a** ~ **at sb/sth** einen Schuß auf jdn/etw abfeuern or abgeben; **to call the** ~**s** (fig col) das Sagen haben (col); **he's a good/bad** ~ er ist ein guter/ schlechter Schütze. (b) (attempt) Versuch m. **at the first** ~ (col) auf Anhieb (col); **to take a** ~ **(at it)** (try) es (mal) versuchen; (guess) (auf gut Glück) raten. (c) (col: quickly) **like a** ~ run away wie der Blitz (col); do sth sofort; agree sofort, ohne zu überlegen. (d) (injection) Spritze f; (immunization) Impfung f. **to give a company a** ~ **in the arm** (fig) einer Firma eine Finanzspritze geben. (e) (Sport) (Ftbl, Hockey etc) Schuß m; (throw) Wurf m; (Tennis, Golf) Schlag m. **to take a** ~ **at goal** aufs Tor schießen. (f) (~**-putting**) **the** ~ (discipline) Kugelstoßen nt; (weight) die Kugel; **to put the** ~ kugelstoßen. (g) (Phot) Aufnahme f.

shot² adj (col: rid) **to be/get** ~ **of sb/sth** jdn/etw los sein/loswerden.

shot: ~**gun** n Schrotflinte f; ~**gun wedding** n Mußheirat f; ~**-putter** n Kugelstoßer(in f) m.

should [ʃʊd] pret of **shall** modal aux vb **(a)** (expressing duty, advisability, command) **you** ~ **do that** du solltest das tun; **you** ~**n't do that** Sie sollten das nicht tun; **I** ~ **have done it** ich hätte es tun sollen or müssen; **I** ~**n't have done it** ich hätte es nicht tun sollen or dürfen; **he** ~ **know that it's wrong to lie** er sollte or müßte wissen, daß man nicht lügen darf; **you really** ~ **see that film** den Film sollten or müssen Sie wirklich sehen; ~ **I go too?** — **yes you** ~ sollte ich auch gehen? — ja, das sollten Sie schon; **was it a good film?** — **I** ~ **think it was** war der Film gut? — und ob; **he's coming to apologize** — **I** ~ **think so** er will sich entschuldigen — das möchte ich auch hoffen; **... and I** ~ **know ...** und ich müßte es ja wissen; **how** ~ **I know?** woher soll ich das wissen?

(b) (expressing probability) **he** ~ **be there by now** er müßte eigentlich schon da sein; **why** ~ **he suspect me?** warum sollte er mich verdächtigen?; **this book** ~ **help you** dieses Buch wird Ihnen bestimmt helfen.

(c) (in tentative statements) **I** ~**n't like to say** ich möchte mich nicht festlegen; **I** ~ **hardly have called him an idiot** ich hätte ihn wohl kaum einen Idioten genannt; **I** ~ **think there were about 40** ich ~ würde schätzen, daß etwa 40 dort waren; **I** ~ **like to disagree** da möchte ich widersprechen; **I** ~ **like to know** ich wüßte gern; **I** ~ **like to apply for the job** ich würde mich gern um die Stelle bewerben; **thanks, I** ~ **like to** danke, gern.

(d) (subjunc, conditional) **I** ~ **go if ...** ich würde gehen, wenn ...; **we** ~ **have come if ...** wir wären

gekommen, wenn ...; **I don't know why he** ~ **behave so strangely** ich weiß nicht, warum er sich so eigenartig benimmt; **if he** ~ **come,** ~ **he come** falls er kommen sollte, sollte er kommen; **I** ~**n't be surprised if he comes** or **were to come** ich wäre keineswegs überrascht, wenn er kommen würde; **I** ~**n't (do it) if I were you** ich würde das an Ihrer Stelle nicht tun; **I** ~**n't worry about it** ich würde mir darüber keine Gedanken machen; **it is necessary that he** ~ **be told** es ist nötig, daß man es ihm sagt.

shoulder ['fəʊldər] 1 n (also of meat) Schulter f. **to shrug one's** ~**s** mit den Schultern or Achseln zucken; **to have broad** ~**s** (lit) breite Schultern haben; (fig) einen breiten Rücken haben; **to cry on sb's** ~ sich an jds Brust (dat) ausweinen; ~ **to** ~ Schulter an Schulter; **he's head and** ~**s above the rest** er ist einen ganzen Kopf größer als die anderen; **to put one's** ~ **to the wheel** (fig) sich ins Zeug legen. 2 vt **(a)** schultern, auf die Schulter nehmen; (fig) responsibilities auf sich (acc) nehmen; expense tragen. **(b)** (push) (mit der Schulter) stoßen. **to** ~ **sb aside** (lit) jdn zur Seite stoßen.

shoulder: ~ **bag** n Umhängetasche f; ~ **blade** n Schulterblatt nt; ~**-length** adj hair schulterlang; ~ **strap** n (Mil) Schulterklappe f; (of dress) Träger m; (of bag etc) (Schulter)riemen m.

shouldn't ['fʊdnt] = **should not**.

shout [faʊt] 1 n Ruf, Schrei m. **a** ~ **of protest/pain** ein Protestruf m/Schmerzensschrei m; **a** ~ **of excitement** ein aufgeregter Schrei; ~**s of applause/laughter** Beifallsrufe pl/brüllendes Gelächter; **to give a** ~ einen Schrei ausstoßen; **to give sb a** ~ jdn rufen; **give me a** ~ **when you're ready** (col) sag mir Bescheid, wenn du fertig bist. 2 vt schreien; (call) rufen; order brüllen. ~ **abuse at sb** jdn (laut) beschimpfen; **to** ~ **a warning to sb** jdm eine Warnung zurufen. 3 vi (call out) rufen; (very loudly) schreien; (angrily, commanding) brüllen. **to** ~ **for sb** sich nach jdm/ etw rufen or schreien; **to** ~ **at sb** jdn anschreien or anbrüllen; **to** ~ **for help** um Hilfe rufen. 4 vr **to** ~ **oneself hoarse** sich heiser schreien.

♦ **shout down** vt sep person niederbrüllen; play ausbuhen.

♦ **shout out** 1 vi einen Schrei ausstoßen; (in pain, rage, protest) aufschreien. 2 vt sep ausrufen; order brüllen.

shouting ['faʊtɪŋ] n (act) Schreien nt; (sound) Geschrei nt. **it's all over bar the** ~ (col) es ist so gut wie gelaufen.

shove [ʃʌv] 1 n Schubs (col), Stoß m. **to give sb a** ~ jdn schubsen (col) or stoßen; **to give sth a** ~ etw rücken; door gegen etw stoßen; car etw anschieben. 2 vt **(a)** (push) schieben; (with one short push) stoßen, schubsen (col); (jostle) drängen. **to** ~ **one's way forward** sich nach vorn durchdrängen. **(b)** (col: put) **to** ~ **sth on(to) sth** etw auf etw (acc) werfen (col); **to** ~ **sth in(to) sth/between sth** etw in etw (acc)/zwischen etw (acc) stecken; **he** ~**d a book into my hand** er drückte mir ein Buch in die Hand. 3 vi stoßen; (to move sth) schieben; (jostle) drängeln. **to** ~ **past sb** sich an jdm vorbeidrängen.

♦ **shove off** vi (col) abschieben (col).

♦ **shove over** (col) 1 vt sep rüberwerfen (col). 2 vi (also **shove up**) rutschen.

shovel ['ʃʌvl] 1 n Schaufel f; (with long handle also) Schippe f. 2 vt schaufeln; coal, snow also schippen. **to** ~ **food into one's mouth** (col) Essen in sich (acc) hineinschaufeln (col).

show [fəʊ] (vb: pret ~**ed**, ptp ~**n**) 1 n **(a)** (display) **a fine** ~ **of roses** eine Rosenpracht; ~ **of force** Machtdemonstration f; **to have a** ~ **of hands** per Abstimmung per Handzeichen vornehmen.

(b) (outward appearance) Schau f. **to do sth for**

~ etw tun, um Eindruck zu machen; **to make a great** ~ **of being impressed/overworked** sich *(dat)* ganz den Anschein geben, beeindruckt/ überarbeitet zu sein; **without any** ~ **of emotion** ohne irgendwelche Gefühle zu zeigen; **it was all** ~ es war alles nur Schau *(col)*.

(c) *(exhibition)* Ausstellung *f*. **flower/dog** ~ Blumen-/Hundeschau *f*; **to be on** ~ ausgestellt sein.

(d) *(Theat)* Aufführung *f*; *(TV, variety* ~*)* Show *f*; *(Rad)* Sendung *f*; *(Film)* Vorstellung *f*. **to go to a** ~ ins Theater gehen; **the** ~ **must go on** *(fig)* es muß trotz allem weitergehen.

(e) *(col: organization)* Laden *m (col)*. **he runs the** ~ **er schmeißt hier den Laden** *(col)*; **to give the (whole)** ~ **away** alles verraten.

(f) good ~! *(col)* bravo!; **it's a poor** ~ **when ...** *(col)* es ist ein schwaches Bild, wenn ...; **to put up a good** ~ eine gute Leistung zeigen.

2 *vt* **(a)** zeigen; *(at exhibition also)* ausstellen; *passport* vorzeigen; *profit* verzeichnen; *kindness, favour* erweisen; *courage also, loyalty, taste* beweisen; *proof* erbringen. **to** ~ **sth to sb** jdm etw zeigen; ~ **me how to do it** zeigen Sie mir, wie man das macht; **to** ~ **one's face** sich zeigen; **he had nothing to** ~ **for it** er hatte am Ende nichts vorzuweisen; **I'll** ~ **him!** *(col)* dem werd' ich's zeigen!; **it** ~ **s that ...** es zeigt, daß ...; **as** ~ **n in the illustration** wie in der Illustration dargestellt; **the roads are** ~ **n in red** die Straßen sind rot (eingezeichnet); **it just goes to** ~ **that ...** das zeigt doch nur, daß ...; **it was** ~ **ing signs of rain** es sah nach Regen aus; **to** ~ **signs of wear** Abnutzungserscheinungen aufweisen; **she's beginning to** ~ **her age** man sieht ihr allmählich das Alter an; **the carpet** ~ **s the dirt** auf dem Teppich sieht man den Schmutz; **to** ~ **sb the way** jdm den Weg zeigen; **to** ~ **sb in/out** jdn hereinbringen/ hinausbegleiten; **to** ~ **sb to his seat** jdn an seinen Platz bringen; **to** ~ **sb to the door** jdn zur Tür bringen; *(eject)* jdm die Tür weisen; **they were** ~ **n over** *or* **around the factory** sie wurden in der Fabrik herumgeführt.

(b) *(prove)* beweisen. **this** ~ **s him to be a thief** das beweist, daß er ein Dieb ist.

3 *vi* **(a)** *(be visible)* zu sehen sein, sichtbar sein; *(petticoat etc)* vorsehen, rausgucken *(col)*; *(film)* gezeigt werden, laufen; *(exhibit: artist)* ausstellen. **it doesn't** ~ man sieht es nicht; **the dirt doesn't** ~ man sieht den Schmutz nicht; **his anger** ~ **ed in his eyes** man konnte ihm seinen Ärger von den Augen ablesen; **to** ~ **through** durchkommen. **(b)** *(prove)* **it just goes to** ~! da sieht man's mal wieder!

♦ **show off 1** *vi* angeben *(to, in front of* vor +*dat)*. **2** *vt sep knowledge, medal* angeben mit; *new car, son* vorführen *(to sb* jdm*)*.

♦ **show up 1** *vi* **(a)** *(be seen)* zu sehen *or* zu erkennen sein; *(stand out)* hervorstechen. **the tower** ~ **ed** ~ **clearly against the sky** der Turm zeichnete sich deutlich gegen den Himmel ab; **to** ~ **well/badly** *(fig)* eine gute/schlechte Figur machen. **(b)** *(col: turn up)* auftauchen, sich blicken lassen *(col)*. **2** *vt sep* **(a)** *(highlight)* *(deutlich)* erkennen lassen. **(b)** *(reveal)* zum Vorschein bringen; *sb's character, intentions* deutlich zeigen; *impostor* entlarven; *fraud* aufdecken; *(humiliate)* bloßstellen; *(shame)* blamieren.

show: ~ **business** *n* Showbusiness, Showgeschäft *nt*; ~ **case** *n* Schaukasten *m*, Vitrine *f*; *(fig)* Schaufenster *nt*; ~ **down** *n (col)* Kraftprobe, Machtprobe *f*; **to have a** ~ **down with sb** sich mit jdm auseinandersetzen.

shower ['ʃaʊəʳ] **1** *n* **(a)** *(of rain etc)* Schauer *m*; *(of arrows, blows etc)* Hagel *m*; *(of questions)* Schwall *m*. **(b)** *(~ bath)* Dusche *f*. **to take** *or* **have a** ~ duschen. **(c)** *(US col: party)* Party, *auf der jeder ein Geschenk für den Ehrengast mitbringt; (for bride-to-*

be) ≈ Polterabend *m*. **2** *vt* to ~ **sb with sth** *with curses, blows* etw auf jdn niederprasseln lassen; *with honours, presents, abuse* jdn mit etw überschütten. **3** *vi (wash)* duschen.

shower: ~ **cap** *n* Duschhaube *f*; ~ **proof** *adj* regenfest.

showery ['ʃaʊərɪ] *adj* regnerisch.

show: ~ **girl** *n* Revuegirl *nt*; ~ **ground** *n* Ausstellungsgelände *nt*; *(for circus)* Zirkusgelände *nt*.

showing ['ʃəʊɪŋ] *n* **(a)** *(exhibition)* Ausstellung *f*. **(b)** *(performance)* Aufführung *f*; *(of film)* Vorstellung *f*; *(of programme)* Ausstrahlung *f*. **(c)** *(standard of performance)* **to make a good/poor** ~ eine gute/schwache Leistung zeigen.

show-jumping ['ʃəʊˌdʒʌmpɪŋ] *n* Springreiten *nt*.

showman ['ʃəʊmən] *n, pl* **-men** [-mən] Showman *m*; *(fig)* Schausteller *m*.

shown [ʃəʊn] *ptp of* **show**.

show: ~ **-off** *n (col)* Angeber(in *f)* *m*; ~ **piece** *n* Schaustück *nt*; *(time example)* Paradestück *nt*; ~ **place** *n (tourist attraction)* Sehenswürdigkeit *f*; ~ **room** *n* Ausstellungsraum *m*.

showy ['ʃaʊɪ] *adj* (+*er*) *person, colour* auffallend; *manner* theatralisch; *production, decor* bombastisch.

shrank [ʃræŋk] *pret of* **shrink**.

shrapnel ['ʃræpnl] *n* Schrapnell *nt*.

shred [ʃred] **1** *n (scrap)* Fetzen *m*; *(of vegetable, meat)* Stückchen *nt*; *(fig)* Spur; *f*; *(of truth)* Fünkchen *nt*. **not a** ~ **of evidence** keinerlei Beweis; **to be in** ~ **s** zerfetzt sein; **to tear sth to** ~ **s** etw in Stücke reißen; *(fig)* etw verreißen; *argument* etw total zerpflücken; **to tear sb to** ~ **s** keinen guten Faden an jdm lassen. **2** *vt* **(a)** *food, paper* schnitzeln; *carrot* raspeln; *cabbage* hobeln; *(in shredder)* paper in den Papierwolf geben. **(b)** *(tear)* in kleine Stücke reißen; *(with claws)* zerfetzen.

shredder ['ʃredəʳ] *n (grater)* Reibe *f*; *(in electric mixer)* Gemüseschneider *m*; *(for waste paper)* Reißwolf *m*.

shrew [ʃruː] *n* Spitzmaus *f*; *(fig)* Xanthippe *f*.

shrewd [ʃruːd] *adj* (+*er*) *person* gewitzt, clever *(col)*; *businessman also, plan* clever *(col)*, raffiniert; *investment, argument* taktisch geschickt; *assessment, mind* scharf. **that was a** ~ **guess** das war gut geraten; **I have a** ~ **idea that ...** ich habe so das Gefühl, daß ...

shrewdness ['ʃruːdnɪs] *n see adj* Gewitztheit *f*; Cleverness *(col)*, Raffiniertheit *f*; Geschicktheit *f*; Schärfe *f*; *(of guess)* Treffsicherheit *f*.

shriek [ʃriːk] **1** *n (schriller)* Schrei; *(of whistle)* schriller Ton. **a** ~ **of pain/horror** ein Schmerzens-/Schreckensschrei *m*; ~ **s of laughter** kreischendes Lachen; **to give a** ~ einen schrillen Schrei ausstoßen. **2** *vi* aufschreien. ~ **at sb** jdn ankreischen; **to** ~ **with laughter** vor Lachen quietschen.

shrift [ʃrɪft] *n* **to give sb/sth short** ~ jdn/etw kurz abfertigen.

shrill [ʃrɪl] *adj* (+*er*) schrill.

shrimp [ʃrɪmp] *n* Garnele, Krevette *f*.

shrine [ʃraɪn] *n* Schrein *m*; *(tomb)* Grabstätte *f*; *(chapel)* Grabkapelle *f*; *(altar)* Grabaltar *m*.

shrink [ʃrɪŋk] *(vb: pret* **shrank**, *ptp* **shrunk)* **1** *vt* einlaufen lassen. **2** *vi* **(a)** schrumpfen; *(clothes etc)* einlaufen; *(wood)* schwinden; *(fig) (popularity)* abnehmen, schwinden; *(trade)* zurückgehen. ~ **-proof** nicht einlaufend. **(b)** *(fig: recoil)* **to** ~ **from doing/saying sth** davor zurückschrecken, etw zu tun/sich davor scheuen, etw zu sagen; **to** ~ **from the truth** vor der Wahrheit die Augen verschließen; **to** ~ **back** zurückweichen; **to** ~ **away from sb** vor jdm zurückweichen.

shrinkage ['ʃrɪŋkɪdʒ] *n (of material, clothes)* Einlaufen *nt*; *(fig: of economic growth etc)* Rückgang *m*; *(Comm)* Einbußen *pl*.

shrink-wrap ['ʃrɪŋk'ræp] *vt* einschweißen.

shrivel ['ʃrɪvl] *(also* ~ **up) 1** *vt plants (frost, dry-*

ness) welk werden lassen; (*heat*) austrocknen; *skin, fruit* runzlig werden lassen; *nylon* zusammenschrumpfen lassen. **2** *vi* schrumpfen; (*balloon, nylon*) zusammenschrumpfen; (*plants*) welk werden; (*through heat*) austrocknen; (*fruit, skin*) runzlig werden.

shroud [ʃraud] **1** *n* (**a**) Leichentuch *nt*. (**b**) (*fig*) Schleier *m*. **a** ~ **of** mist ein Nebelschleier *m*. **2** *vt* (*fig*) hüllen. **the whole thing is** ~**ed in mystery** die ganze Angelegenheit ist von einem Geheimnis umgeben.

Shrove Tuesday [,ʃrəuv'tjuːzdeɪ] *n* Faschingsdienstag (*S Ger*), Fastnachtsdienstag *m*.

shrub [ʃrʌb] *n* Busch, Strauch *m*.

shrubbery ['ʃrʌbərɪ] *n* (*shrub bed*) Strauchrabatte *f*; (*shrubs*) Büsche, Sträucher *pl*.

shrug [ʃrʌg] **1** *n* Achselzucken *nt no pl*. **to give a** ~ die *or* mit den Achseln zucken. **2** *vt shoulders* zucken (mit).

♦ **shrug off** *vt sep* mit einem Achselzucken abtun.

shrunk [ʃrʌŋk] *ptp of* **shrink**.

shrunken ['ʃrʌŋkən] *adj* (ein)geschrumpft. *old person* geschrumpft. ~ **head** Schrumpfkopf *m*.

shudder ['ʃʌdə^r] **1** *n* Schauer, Schauder *m*. **to give a** ~ (*person*) sich schütteln, erschaudern (*geh*); (*ground*) beben. **2** *vi* (*person*) schaudern, schauern; (*house, ground*) beben, zittern; (*car, train*) rütteln. **the train** ~**ed to a halt** der Zug kam rüttelnd zum Stehen; **I** ~ **to think** mir graut, wenn ich nur daran denke.

shuffle ['ʃʌfl] **1** *n* (**a**) **to walk with a** ~ schlurfen. (**b**) (*Cards*) **to give the cards a** ~ die Karten mischen. **2** *vt* (**a**) **he** ~**d his feet as he walked** er schlurfte beim Gehen. (**b**) *cards* mischen. **he** ~**d the papers on his desk together** er raffte die Papiere auf seinem Schreibtisch zusammen. **3** *vi* (*walk*) schlurfen.

shun [ʃʌn] *vt* meiden; *publicity, light* scheuen.

shunt [ʃʌnt] *vt* (**a**) (*Rail*) rangieren. **they** ~**ed the train off the main line** sie schoben den Zug auf ein Nebengleis. (**b**) (*col*) *person* schieben.

shush [ʃʊʃ] **1** *interj* pst, sch. **2** *vt* zum Schweigen auffordern.

shut [ʃʌt] (*vb:* pret, ptp ~) **1** *vt* (**a**) zumachen; *door, book, shop* also schließen. **they** ~ **the office at 6.00** das Büro wird um 18⁰⁰ geschlossen; ~ **your eyes** mach die Augen zu; ~ **your mouth** (*col!*) *or* **face** (*col!*) halt's Maul! (*col!*). (**b**) **to** ~ **sb/sth in(to) sth** jdn/etw in etw (*dat*) einschließen; **she was** ~ **in the cellar** sie wurde im Keller eingesperrt; **to** ~ **one's fingers in the door** sich (*dat*) die Finger in der Tür einklemmen.

2 *vi* (*door, window, box*) schließen, zugehen; (*shop, factory*) schließen, geschlossen werden. **it** ~**s very easily** es läßt sich ganz leicht schließen *or* zumachen (*col*); **when do the shops** ~? wann schließen die Geschäfte?, wann machen die Geschäfte zu? (*col*).

3 *adj* geschlossen, zu *pred* (*col*). **sorry sir, we're** ~ wir haben leider geschlossen; **the door swung** ~ die Tür schlug zu; **to find the door** ~ vor verschlossener Tür stehen.

♦ **shut away** *vt sep* (*put away*) wegschließen; (*in sth*) einschließen (*in* in +*dat*); (*keep locked away*) *books, papers etc* aufbewahren; (*safely*) verwahren; *persons* verborgen halten.

♦ **shut down 1** *vt sep shop, factory* zumachen (*col*), schließen. **Heathrow is completely** ~ ~ Heathrow hat seinen gesamten Flugverkehr eingestellt. **2** *vi* (*shop, factory etc*) zumachen (*col*), schließen. **the television service** ~**s** ~ **at midnight** um Mitternacht ist Sendeschluß im Fernsehen.

♦ **shut in** *vt sep* einschließen (*also fig*), einsperren (*col*) (*prep obj,* to in +*dat*).

♦ **shut off** *vt sep* (**a**) *water, electricity* abstellen; *light, engine* ab- *or* ausschalten; *street* (ab)sperren. **the kettle** ~**s itself** ~ der Wasserkessel

schaltet von selbst ab. (**b**) (*isolate*) (ab)trennen. **I feel** ~ ~ **from civilization** ich komme mir von der Zivilisation abgeschnitten vor.

♦ **shut out** *vt sep* (**a**) *person, oneself* aussperren (*of* aus*)*; *view* versperren; *light* nicht hereinlassen (*of* in +*acc*). **don't** ~ **the sun** ~ laß doch die Sonne herein! (**b**) (*fig*) *foreign competition* ausschalten; *memory, foreign broadcasts* unterdrücken. **I can't** ~ **her** ~ **of my life** sie spielt immer noch eine Rolle in meinem Leben.

♦ **shut up 1** *vt sep* (**a**) *house* verschließen. **to** ~ ~ **shop** (*lit*) das Geschäft schließen; (*fig*) Feierabend machen (*col*). (**b**) (*imprison*) einsperren. (**c**) (*col: silence*) zum Schweigen bringen. **that'll soon** ~ **him** ~ das wird ihm schon den Mund stopfen (*col*). **2** *vi* (*col*) den Mund halten (*col*). ~! halt die Klappe! (*col*), halt's Maul! (*col!*).

shut: **~down** *n* Stillegung *f*; (*TV, Rad*) Sendeschluß *m*; ~**eye** *n* (*col*) Schlaf *m*; ~**in** *adj* (*a*) (*US*) ans Haus/ans Bett gefesselt; (**b**) **a** ~**in feeling** ein Gefühl des Eingeschlossenseins.

shutter ['ʃʌtə^r] **1** *n* (*Fenster*)laden *m*; (*Phot*) Verschluß *m*. **to put up the** ~**s** (*fig*) den Laden dichtmachen (*col*); ~ **release** (*Phot*) Auslöser *m*. **2** *vt* ~**ed windows** geschlossene (Fenster)läden.

shuttle ['ʃʌtl] **1** *n* (**a**) (*of loom etc*) Schiffchen *nt*. (**b**) (*plane, train etc*) Pendelflugzeug *nt*/-zug *m etc*; (*space* ~) Raumtransporter *m*. **2** *vt passengers, goods* hin- und hertransportieren. **to** ~ **sb about** jdn herumschieben.

shuttle: ~**cock** *n* Federball *m*; ~ **service** *n* Pendelverkehr *m*.

shy [ʃaɪ] **1** *adj* (+*er*) (**a**) schüchtern; *animal* scheu. **don't be** ~ nur keine Hemmungen! (*col*); **to be** ~ **of/with sb** Hemmungen vor/gegenüber jdm haben; **to be** ~ **of doing sth** Hemmungen haben, etw zu tun; **to feel** ~ schüchtern sein. (**b**) (*esp US col: short*) **we're $3** ~ wir haben 3 Dollar zuwenig. **2** *vi* (*horse*) scheuen (*at* vor +*dat*).

♦ **shy away** *vi* (*horse*) zurückscheuen; (*person*) zurückweichen. **to** ~ ~ **from sb/sth** vor jdm zurückweichen/vor etw (*dat*) zurückschrecken.

shyly ['ʃaɪlɪ] *adv* see *adj*.

shyness ['ʃaɪnɪs] *n* Schüchternheit *f*; (*esp of animals*) Scheu *f*.

shyster ['ʃaɪstə^r] *n* (*US col*) Gauner *m*; (*lawyer*) Rechtsverdreher *m* (*col*).

Siamese [,saɪə'miːz] *adj* siamesisch. ~ **cat** Siamkatze *f*, siamesische Katze; ~ **twins** siamesische Zwillinge *pl*.

Siberia [saɪ'bɪərɪə] *n* Sibirien *nt*.

Sicily ['sɪsɪlɪ] *n* Sizilien *nt*.

sick [sɪk] *adj* (+*er*) (**a**) (*ill*) krank (*also fig*). **the** ~ die Kranken *pl*; **to be (off)** ~ (wegen Krankheit) fehlen; **to fall** *or* **take** ~ krank werden; **to go** ~ krank werden; **to make sb** ~ (*fig col*) jdn (ganz) krank machen (*col*); **it makes you the way he's always right** (*col*) es ist zum Auswachsen, daß er immer recht hat (*col*); **to be** ~ **at sth** (*fig*) (*disgusted*) von etw angewidert sein; (*upset*) wegen etw geknickt sein. (**b**) (*Brit: vomiting or about to vomit*) **to be** ~ brechen, sich übergeben; (*esp cat, baby*) spucken; **I felt** ~ mir war schlecht *or* übel; **that food makes me** ~ von dem Essen wird mir übel *or* schlecht. (**c**) (*col: fed up*) **to be** ~ **of doing sth** es satt haben, etw zu tun; **I'm** ~ **and tired of it** ich habe davon die Nase voll (*col*), ich habe es gründlich satt. (**d**) (*col*) *joke etc* geschmacklos; *person* abartig, pervers.

sick: ~ **bay** *n* Krankenrevier *nt*; ~**bed** *n* Krankenlager *nt*.

sicken ['sɪkn] **1** *vt* (*turn sb's stomach*) anekeln, anwidern; (*upset greatly*) erschüttern, krank machen (*col*); (*disgust*) anwidern. **2** *vi* **he's definitely** ~**ing for something** er wird bestimmt krank; **to** ~ **of sth** (*tire*) einer Sache (*gen*) müde sein (*geh*), etw satt haben.

sickening ['sɪknɪŋ] *adj* (*lit*) ekelerregend; *smell,* *sight also* widerlich, ekelhaft; *(upsetting)* entsetzlich, erschütternd; *(disgusting, annoying)* ekelhaft; *treatment* abscheulich; *delays* unerträglich.

sickle ['sɪkl] *n* Sichel *f.*

sick: ~ **leave** *n* **to be on** ~ **leave** krank geschrieben sein; ~ **list** *n* **to be on/off the** ~ **list** auf der/nicht mehr auf der Krankenliste stehen; *(with injury)* auf der/nicht mehr auf der Verletztenliste stehen.

sickly ['sɪklɪ] *adj* (+*er*) *person* kränklich; *complexion, light* blaß (+*er*) *smell, taste, colour* widerlich, ekelhaft; *smile* matt; *grin* schwach; *climate* ungesund.

sickness ['sɪknɪs] *n* (*Med*) Krankheit *f* (*also fig*); *(nausea)* Übelkeit *f*; *(Brit: vomiting)* Erbrechen *nt*; *(of food etc)* Geschmacklosigkeit *f.* ~ **benefit** Krankengeld *nt.*

sick: ~**-pay** *n* Krankengeld *nt*; ~**-room** *n* Krankenzimmer *nt.*

side [saɪd] **1** *n* **(a)** Seite *f*; *(of cave, trench, mining shaft, boat, caravan)* Wand *f*; *(of cliff, mountain)* Hang *m.* **this** ~ **up!** *(on parcel etc)* oben!; **right/ wrong** ~ *(of cloth)* rechte/linke Seite.

(b) *(edge)* Rand *m.* **at the** ~ **of the road** am Straßenrand; **at the** ~ **of his plate** auf dem Tellerrand.

(c) *(not back or front)* Seite *f.* **by/at the** ~ **of sth** seitlich von etw; **to drive on the left** ~ **of the road** auf der linken Straßenseite fahren; **the path goes down the** ~ **of the house** der Weg führt seitlich am Haus entlang; **it's this/the other** ~ **of London** *(out of town)* es ist auf dieser/auf der anderen Seite Londons; *(in town)* es ist in diesem Teil/am anderen Ende von London; **from all** ~**s** von allen Seiten; **from** ~ **to** ~ von einer Seite zur anderen; **he moved to one** ~ er trat zur Seite; **to put sth on one** ~ etw beiseite legen; *(shopkeeper)* etw zurücklegen; **to take sb on one** ~ jdn beiseite nehmen; **just this** ~ **of the boundary** (noch) diesseits der Grenze; **on the other** ~ **of the boundary** jenseits der Grenze; **with one's head on one** ~ mit zur Seite geneigtem Kopf; **by sb's** ~ neben jdm; ~ **by** ~ nebeneinander, Seite an Seite; **to stand/sit** ~ **by** ~ **with sb** direkt neben jdm stehen/sitzen; **I'll be by your** ~ *(fig)* ich werde Ihnen zur Seite stehen; **to be on the safe** ~ sichergehen; **we'll take an extra £50 just to be on the safe** ~ wir nehmen vorsichtshalber 50 Pfund mehr mit; **to stay on the right** ~ **of sb** es *(dat)* mit jdm nicht verderben; **on the right** ~ **of the law** auf dem Boden des Gesetzes; **on the right/wrong** ~ **of 40** diesseits/jenseits der 40, unter/über 40; **on his mother's** ~ mütterlicherseits; **to make a bit (of money) on the** ~ *(col)* sich *(dat)* etwas nebenbei verdienen; **a problem with many** ~**s** ist ein vielschichtiges Problem; **there are always two** ~**s to every story** alles hat seine zwei Seiten; **let's hear your** ~ **of the story** erzählen Sie mal Ihre Version (der Geschichte); **to look on the bright** ~ *(be optimistic)* zuversichtlich sein; *(look on the positive* ~) etw von der positiven Seite betrachten.

(d) (a bit) **on the large/formal** *etc* ~ etwas groß/förmlich *etc*; *(for somebody)* etwas zu groß/ förmlich *etc.*

(e) *(opposing team)* *(Sport, in quiz)* Mannschaft *f*; *(fig)* Seite *f.* **there are two** ~**s in the dispute** in dem Streit stehen sich zwei Parteien gegenüber; **to change** ~**s** sich auf die andere Seite schlagen; *(Sport)* die Seiten wechseln; **to take** ~**s** parteiisch sein; **to take** ~**s with sb** für jdn Partei ergreifen; **he's on our** ~ er steht auf unserer Seite; **whose** ~ **are you on?** *(supporting team)* für wen sind Sie?; *(in argument)* zu wem halten Sie eigentlich?

2 *adj attr (on one* ~) *entrance, road* Seiten-; *(not main)* entrance, room, road, job* Neben-.

3 *vi* **to** ~ **with/against sb** jds Partei *(acc)/*

Partei gegen jdn ergreifen.

side: ~**board** *n* Anrichte *f*, Sideboard *nt*; ~**boards**, ~**burns** *npl* Koteletten *pl*; *(longer)* Backenbart *m*; ~**car** *n* Beiwagen *m*; *(esp Sport)* Seitenwagen *m*; ~ **effect** *n* Nebenwirkung *f*; ~**kick** *n* *(esp US col)* Kumpel *m* *(col)*; *(assistant)* Handlanger *m* *(pej)*; ~**light** *n* *(Aut)* Parklicht *nt*; *(incorporated in headlight)* Standlicht *nt*; ~**line** *n* *(job etc)* Nebenerwerb *m*; **to do sth as a** ~**line** etw nebenbei tun; ~**lines** *npl* Seitenlinien *pl*; **to be** *or* **stand on the** ~**lines** *(fig)* unbeteiligter Zuschauer sein; ~**long** *adj, adv glance* Seiten-; *(surreptitious)* verstohlen; **to give sb a** ~**long glance, to glance** ~**long at sb** jdn kurz aus den Augenwinkeln anblicken; ~**-saddle** *adv* **to ride** ~**-saddle** im Damensitz reiten; ~ **salad** *m* (als Beilage); ~ **show** *n* Nebenvorstellung *f*; *(exhibition)* Sonderausstellung *f*; ~**-splitting** *adj* urkomisch, **zum Totlachen** *(col)*; ~**-step 1** *vt* tackle, punch (seitwärts) ausweichen (+*dat*); *person, question* ausweichen (+*dat*); **2** *vi (lit, fig)* ausweichen; ~ **street** *n* Seitenstraße *f*; ~**track 1** *n* *(esp US)* ~ **siding; 2** *vt* ablenken; **I got** ~**tracked onto something else** ich wurde dich durch irgend etwas abgelenkt; *(from topic)* ich wurde irgendwie vom Thema abgebracht; ~**walk** *n* *(US)* Bürgersteig, Gehsteig *m*; ~**ways 1** *adj movement* zur Seite; *glance* von der Seite; **to give sb/sth a** ~**ways glance** jdn/etw von der Seite ansehen; **2** *adv move* zur Seite, seitwärts; *look at sb* von der Seite.

siding ['saɪdɪŋ] *n* (*Rail*) Rangiergleis *nt.*

sidle ['saɪdl] *vi* (sich) schleichen. **to** ~ **away** (sich) wegschleichen; **to** ~ **up to sb** sich an jdn heranschleichen.

siege [si:dʒ] *n* *(of town)* Belagerung *f*; *(by police)* Umstellung *f.* **to lay** ~ **to a town/a house** eine Stadt/ein Haus belagern/umstellen.

siesta [sɪ'estə] *n* Siesta *f.* **to have a** ~ Siesta halten.

sieve [sɪv] **1** *n* Sieb *nt.* **to have a memory like a** ~ *(col)* ein Gedächtnis wie ein Sieb haben *(col).* **2** *vt* = **sift 1 (a).**

sift [sɪft] **1** *vt* **(a)** sieben; *coal* schütteln. **(b)** *(fig)* *(search)* sichten, durchgehen; *(separate)* trennen. **2** *vi* *(fig)* **to** ~ **through the evidence** das Beweismaterial durchgehen.

sigh [saɪ] **1** *n* *(of person)* Seufzer *m*; *(of wind)* Säuseln *nt no pl.* **to heave a** ~ **of relief** einen Seufzer der Erleichterung ausstoßen. **2** *vti* seufzen; *(wind)* säuseln. **to** ~ **with relief** erleichtert aufatmen.

sighing ['saɪɪŋ] *n see vti* Seufzen *nt*; Säuseln *nt.*

sight [saɪt] **1** *n* **(a)** *(faculty)* Sehvermögen *nt.* **to have long/short** ~ weit-/kurzsichtig sein; **to lose/ regain one's** ~ sein Augenlicht verlieren/ wiedergewinnen; **he has very good** ~ er sieht sehr gut.

(b) **to hate sb at first** ~ jdn vom ersten Augenblick an nicht leiden können; **at first** ~ **it seemed easy** auf den ersten Blick erschien es einfach; **to shoot on** ~ sofort schießen; **he played the music at** ~ er hat vom Blatt gespielt; **love at first** ~ Liebe auf den ersten Blick; **at the** ~ **of the police they ran away** als sie die Polizei sahen, rannten sie weg; **to know sb by** ~ jdn vom Sehen kennen; **to catch** ~ **of sb/sth** jdn/etw sehen; **to lose** ~ **of sb/sth** *(lit, fig)* jdn/etw aus den Augen verlieren; **don't lose** ~ **of the fact that ...** Sie dürfen nicht außer acht lassen, daß ...; **payable at** ~ *(Comm)* zahlbar bei Sicht; **30 days'** ~ *(Comm)* 30 Tage nach Sicht.

(c) *(sth seen)* Anblick *m.* **the** ~ **of blood makes me sick** wenn ich Blut sehe, wird mir übel; **the most beautiful** ~ **I've ever seen** das Schönste, was ich je gesehen habe; **I can't bear the** ~ **of him** ich kann ihn (einfach) nicht ausstehen; **what a horrible** ~! das sieht ja furchtbar aus!; **to be** *or* **look a** ~ *(funny)* zum Schreien aussehen *(col)*; *(horrible)* fürchterlich aussehen.

(d) *(range of vision)* Sicht *f.* to be in *or* within ~ in Sicht *or* in Sichtweite sein; **our goal is in** ~ unser Ziel ist in greifbarer Nähe; **we came in** ~ **of the coast** die Küste kam in Sicht; **to keep sb in** ~ jdn im Auge behalten; **to keep out of** ~ sich verborgen halten; **to keep sb/sth out of** ~ jdn/etw versteckt halten; **keep out of my** ~! laß dich bloß bei mir nicht mehr blicken!; **to be out of** ~ nicht mehr zu sehen sein; **don't let the children out of your** ~ laß die Kinder nicht aus den Augen!; **out of** ~, **out of mind** *(Prov)* aus dem Auge, aus dem Sinn *(Prov)*.

(e) *usu pl (of city etc)* Sehenswürdigkeit *f.* to see the ~s of a town eine Stadt besichtigen.

(f) *(on gun etc)* Visier *nt.* to set one's ~s too high *(fig)* seine Ziele zu hoch stecken; to set one's ~s on sth *(fig)* ein Auge auf etw *(acc)* werfen.

(g) *(col)* not by a long ~ bei weitem nicht; we're not finished yet, not by a long ~ wir sind noch lange nicht fertig; he's a damn ~ cleverer than you think er ist ein ganzes Ende gescheiter als du meinst *(col)*.

2 *vt (see)* sichten *(also Mil)*; *person* ausmachen.

sighted ['saɪtɪd] *adj* sehend.

sighting ['saɪtɪŋ] *n* Sichten *nt.* another ~ of the monster was reported das Ungeheuer soll erneut gesichtet worden sein.

sight: ~-read *vti* vom Blatt spielen/lesen/singen; ~seeing *n* Besichtigungen *pl*; to go ~seeing auf Besichtigungstour gehen; ~seer *n* Tourist(in *f*) *m.*

sign [saɪn] **1** *n* **(a)** *(with hand etc)* Zeichen *nt.* he nodded as a ~ of recognition er nickte zum Zeichen, daß er mich/ihn *etc* erkannt hatte; to give sb a ~, to make a ~ to sb jdm ein Zeichen geben.

(b) *(indication, Med)* Anzeichen *nt (of* für *or* gen); (evidence)* Zeichen *nt (of* von *or* gen); *(trace)* Spur *f.* a sure/good ~ ein sicheres/gutes Zeichen; it's a ~ of the true expert daran erkennt man den wahren Experten; at the first ~ of disagreement beim ersten Anzeichen von Uneinigkeit; there is no ~ of their agreeing nichts deutet darauf hin, daß sie zustimmen werden; to show ~s of sth Anzeichen von etw erkennen lassen; our guest showed no ~s of leaving unser Gast machte keine Anstalten zu gehen; the rain showed no ~s of stopping nichts deutete darauf hin, daß der Regen aufhören würde; there was no ~ of life in the village es gab kein Anzeichen von Leben im Dorf; there was no ~ of him anywhere von ihm war keine Spur zu sehen.

(c) *(road~, shop~)* Schild *nt.*

(d) *(written symbol, Astron)* Zeichen *nt.*

2 *vt* **(a)** to ~ one's name unterschreiben; to ~ one's name in a book sich in ein Buch eintragen; he ~s himself J.G. Jones er unterschreibt mit J.G. Jones. **(b)** *letter etc* unterschreiben, unterzeichnen *(form)*; *picture, book* signieren. to ~ the register sich eintragen.

3 *vi* **(a)** *(signal)* to ~ to sb to do sth jdm Zeichen/ein Zeichen geben, etw zu tun. **(b)** *(with signature)* unterschreiben.

♦ **sign away** *vt sep* verzichten auf *(+acc).* she felt she was ~ing ~ her life sie hatte das Gefühl, ihr ganzes Leben zu überschreiben.

♦ **sign for** *vi +prep obj* den Empfang *(+gen)* bestätigen.

♦ **sign in** **1** *vt sep* person eintragen. to ~ sb ~ at a club jdn als Gast in einen Klub mitnehmen. **2** *vi* sich eintragen.

♦ **sign off** *vi (in letter)* Schluß machen.

♦ **sign on** **1** *vt sep* = sign up **1**. **2** *vi* **(a)** = sign up **2.** **(b)** *(for unemployment benefit etc) (apply)* beantragen *(for acc); (register regularly)* sich melden.

♦ **sign out** *vi* sich austragen. to ~ ~ of a hotel (aus einem Hotel) abreisen.

♦ **sign over** *vt sep* überschreiben *(to sb jdm).*

♦ **sign up** **1** *vt sep (employ, enlist)* actors verpflichten; *workers, employees* anstellen; *sailors* anheuern. **2** *vi* sich verpflichten; *(employees, players also)* unterschreiben; *(sailors)* anheuern; *(for evening class etc)* sich einschreiben.

signal ['sɪgnl] **1** *n* **(a)** *(sign)* Zeichen *nt*; *(as part of code)* Signal *nt*; *(message)* Nachricht *f.* engaged *(Brit)* or busy ~ *(Telec)* Besetztzeichen *nt*; to give the ~ for sth das Zeichen/Signal zu etw geben; the ~ is very weak *(TV, Rad)* der Empfang ist sehr schlecht. **(b)** *(apparatus, Rail)* Signal *nt.* the ~ is at red das Signal steht auf Rot. **2** *vt* **(a)** *(indicate)* anzeigen; *arrival, (fig)* future event *etc* ankündigen. to ~ sb to do sth jdm ein/das Zeichen geben, etw zu tun. **(b)** *message* signalisieren. **3** *vi* Zeichen/ein Zeichen geben. he ~led for his bill er winkte zum Zeichen, daß er zahlen wollte; the driver didn't ~ der Fahrer hat kein Zeichen gegeben.

signal: ~box *n* Stellwerk *nt*; ~man *n (Rail)* Stellwerkswärter *m*; *(Mil)* Fernmelder, Funker *m.*

signatory ['sɪgnətərɪ] *n* Unterzeichnete(r) *mf (form).*

signature ['sɪgnətʃə'] *n* **(a)** Unterschrift *f; (of artist)* Signatur *f.* **(b)** *(Mus)* Vorzeichnung *f.* ~ tune *(Brit)* Erkennungsmelodie *f.*

signboard ['saɪnbɔːd] *n* Schild *nt.*

signet ring ['sɪgnɪt,rɪŋ] *n* Siegelring *m.*

significance [sɪg'nɪfɪkəns] *n* Bedeutung *f; (of action also)* Tragweite *f.* of no ~ belanglos, bedeutungslos.

significant [sɪg'nɪfɪkənt] *adj (considerable, having consequence)* bedeutend; *(important)* wichtig; *(meaningful)* bedeutungsvoll; *look* vielsagend, bedeutsam. it is ~ that ... es ist bezeichnend, daß ...; to be ~ to *or* for sth eine bedeutende *or* wichtige Rolle in etw *(dat)* spielen.

significantly [sɪg'nɪfɪkəntlɪ] *adv (considerably)* bedeutend; *(meaningfully)* bedeutungsvoll; *look* vielsagend, bedeutsam. it is not ~ different da besteht kein wesentlicher Unterschied; ~ enough, ... bezeichnenderweise ...

signify ['sɪgnɪfaɪ] *vt* **(a)** *(mean)* bedeuten. **(b)** *(indicate)* andeuten, erkennen lassen; *(person also)* zu erkennen geben.

sign: ~ language Zeichensprache *f*; ~post **1** *n* Wegweiser *m*; **2** *vt* way beschildern; *diversion* ausschildern.

silage ['saɪlɪdʒ] *n* Silage *f*, Silofutter *nt.*

silence ['saɪləns] **1** *n* Stille *f; (quietness also)* Ruhe *f; (absence of talk also, of letters etc)* Schweigen *nt; (on a particular subject)* (Still)schweigen *nt.* ~! Ruhe!; in ~ still; *(not talking also)* schweigend; there was ~ alles war still; radio ~ *(Mil)* Funkstille *f.* **2** *vt (lit, fig)* zum Schweigen bringen.

silencer ['saɪlənsə'] *n (on gun, Brit: on car)* Schalldämpfer *m; (whole fitting on car)* Auspufftopf *m.*

silent ['saɪlənt] *adj* still; *(not talking also)* schweigsam; *engine etc* ruhig; *agreement etc* (still)schweigend *attr.* ~ movie/letter Stummfilm *m*/stummer Buchstabe; ~ partner *(US)* stiller Teilhaber; the ~ majority die schweigende Mehrheit; to be ~ *(about sth)* *(über* etw *acc)* schweigen; to keep *or* remain ~ sein *or* bleiben; *(about sth)* sich nicht äußern.

silently ['saɪləntlɪ] *adv* lautlos; *(without talking)* schweigend; *(with little noise)* leise.

silhouette [,sɪluː'et] **1** *n* Silhouette *f; (picture)* Scherenschnitt *m.* **2** *vt* to be ~d against sth sich *(als Silhouette)* gegen etw abzeichnen.

silicon ['sɪlɪkən] *n* Silizium *nt.* ~ chip Siliziumchip *m.*

silicone ['sɪlɪkəʊn] *n* Silikon *nt.*

silicosis [,sɪlɪ'kəʊsɪs] *n* Staublunge, Silikose *f.*

silk [sɪlk] **1** *n* **(a)** Seide *f; (~ dress)* Seidenkleid *nt.* **(b)** *(Brit Jur: barrister)* Kronanwalt *m.* **2** *adj* Seiden-, seiden. the dress is ~ das Kleid ist aus Seide.

silk: ~ **screen** n Seidensieb nt; (also ~-**screen printing)** Seidensiebdruck m; ~**worm** n Seidenraupe f.

silky ['sɪlkɪ] adj (+er) seidig; voice samtig.

sill [sɪl] n Sims m or nt; (window~) (Fenster)sims m or nt; (esp of wood) Fensterbrett nt; (on car) Türleiste f.

silly ['sɪlɪ] adj (+er) dumm, doof (col). **don't be** ~ (do ~ things) mach keinen Quatsch (col); (say ~ things) red keinen Unsinn; (ask ~ questions) frag nicht so dumm; **that was a** ~ **thing to do** das war dumm (von dir); **to make sb look** ~ jdn lächerlich machen.

silo ['saɪləʊ] n Silo nt; (for missile) unterirdische Startrampe.

silt [sɪlt] n Schwemmsand m; (river mud) Schlick m. 2 vi (also ~ **up**) verschlammen.

silver ['sɪlvər] 1 n (a) (metal, tableware) Silber nt. (b) (coins) Silbergeld nt. 2 adj Silber-, silbern.

silver: ~ **birch** n Weißbirke f; ~ **paper** n (Brit) Silberpapier nt; ~ **plate** n (plating) Silberauflage f; (articles) versilberte Sachen pl; ~ **screen** n Leinwand f; ~**smith** n Silberschmied m; ~**ware** n Silber nt; ~ **wedding** n silberne Hochzeit, Silberhochzeit f.

silvery ['sɪlvərɪ] adj silbern; voice silberhell.

similar ['sɪmɪlər] adj ähnlich; amount, size ungefähr gleich. **she and her sister are very** ~ ihre Schwester und sie sind sich sehr ähnlich; ~ **in size** ungefähr gleich groß.

similarity [,sɪmɪ'lærɪtɪ] n Ähnlichkeit f (to mit).

similarly ['sɪmɪlərlɪ] adv ähnlich; (equally) genauso. ~, **you could maintain ...** genausogut könnten Sie behaupten ...

simile ['sɪmɪlɪ] n Gleichnis nt.

simmer ['sɪmər] 1 vt auf kleiner Flamme kochen lassen. 2 vi auf kleiner Flamme kochen; (fig) (with rage) kochen (col); (with excitement) fiebern.

♦ **simmer down** vi sich beruhigen, sich abregen (col).

simper ['sɪmpər] 1 n ..., **she said with a** ~ ..., sagte sie affektiert. 2 vi (smile) geziert lächeln; (talk) säuseln.

simple ['sɪmpl] adj (+er) **(a)** einfach; decor, dress also schlicht. **the** ~ **fact is ...** es ist einfach so, daß ...; **it's as** ~ **as ABC** das ist kinderleicht. **(b)** (foolish, mentally deficient) einfältig.

simple-minded [,sɪmpl'maɪndɪd] adj einfältig.

simpleton ['sɪmpltən] n Einfaltspinsel m.

simplicity [sɪm'plɪsɪtɪ] n Einfachheit f; (lack of sophistication, of decor also) Schlichtheit f. **it's** ~ **itself** das ist die einfachste Sache der Welt.

simplification [,sɪmplɪfɪ'keɪʃən] n Vereinfachung f.

simplify ['sɪmplɪfaɪ] vt vereinfachen.

simplistic [sɪm'plɪstɪk] adj simpel.

simply ['sɪmplɪ] adv einfach; (merely) nur, bloß.

simulate ['sɪmjʊleɪt] vt emotions vortäuschen; enthusiasm also spielen; illness also, conditions, environment simulieren. ~**d** leather/sheepskin Lederimitation f/falsches Schaffell.

simulation [,sɪmjʊ'leɪʃən] n Vortäuschung f; (reproduction) Simulation f.

simulator ['sɪmjʊleɪtər] n Simulator m.

simultaneous [,sɪməl'teɪnɪəs] adj gleichzeitig. ~ **equations** (Math) Simultangleichungen pl; ~ **interpreting** Simultandolmetschen nt.

simultaneously [,sɪməl'teɪnɪəslɪ] adv gleichzeitig, simultan (geh).

sin [sɪn] 1 n (Rel, fig) Sünde f. **to live in** ~ (col) in wilder Ehe leben; (Rel) in Sünde leben; **to cover a multitude of** ~**s** (hum) viele Schandtaten verdecken. 2 vi sündigen (against gegen, an +dat), sich versündigen (against an +dat); (against principles etc) verstoßen (against gegen).

since [sɪns] 1 adv (in the meantime) inzwischen; (up to now) seitdem. **ever** ~ seither; **long** ~ schon

lange; **he died long** ~ er ist schon lange tot; **not long** ~ erst vor kurzem. 2 prep seit. **ever** ~ **1900** (schon) seit 1900; **he had been living there** ~ **1900** er lebte da schon seit 1900; **I've been coming here** ~ **1972** ich komme schon seit 1972 hierher; **it's a long time** ~ **then** das ist schon lange her. 3 conj **(a)** (time) seit(dem). **ever** ~ I've known him seit(dem) ich ihn kenne. **(b)** (because) da.

sincere [sɪn'sɪər] adj aufrichtig; person also offen; intention also ernst, ehrlich.

sincerely [sɪn'sɪəlɪ] adv see adj aufrichtig; offen; ernsthaft. **yours** ~ mit freundlichen Grüßen, hochachtungsvoll (form).

sincerity [sɪn'serɪtɪ] n see adj Aufrichtigkeit f; Offenheit f; Ernsthaftigkeit f. **in all** ~ in aller Offenheit.

sine [saɪn] n (Math) Sinus m.

sinecure ['sɪnɪkjʊər] n Sinekure f (geh).

sinew ['sɪnjuː] n Sehne f.

sinewy ['sɪnjuːɪ] adj sehnig; (fig) plant, tree knorrig.

sinful ['sɪnfʊl] adj sündig; person, act, thought also sündhaft (geh).

sing [sɪŋ] pret **sang**, ptp **sung** 1 vt singen. **to** ~ **the praises of sb/sth** ein Loblied auf jdn/etw singen. 2 vi singen; (ears) dröhnen; (kettle) summen.

♦ **sing out** vi (col: shout) schreien (col).

Singapore [,sɪŋə'pɔːr] n Singapur nt.

singe [sɪndʒ] vt sengen; clothes versengen; (slightly) ansengen.

singer ['sɪŋər] n Sänger(in f) m.

singing ['sɪŋɪŋ] n Singen nt; (of person, bird also) Gesang m; (in the ears) Dröhnen nt; (of kettle) Summen nt. **he teaches** ~ er gibt Gesangstunden; **do you like my** ~? gefällt dir mein Gesang?

single ['sɪŋgl] 1 adj **(a)** (one only) einzige(r, s). **not a** ~ **one spoke up** nicht ein einziger äußerte sich dazu; **every** ~ **day was precious** jeder (einzelne) Tag war kostbar; **not a** ~ **thing** überhaupt nichts. **(b)** (not double etc) einzeln; bed, room Einzel-; carburettor, (Brit) ticket einfach. **(c)** (not married) unverheiratet, ledig; parent alleinstehend, alleinerziehend. ~ **people** Unverheiratete pl; **I'm a** ~ **man/girl** ich bin ledig. 2 n (Brit: ticket) Einzelfahrkarte f; (room) Einzelzimmer nt; (record) Single f. **a** ~/**two** ~**s to Bonn** einmal/zweimal einfach nach Bonn.

♦ **single out** vt sep (choose) auswählen; victim, prey sich (dat) herausgreifen; (distinguish, set apart) herausheben (from über +acc). **to** ~ **sb** ~ **for special attention** jdm besondere Aufmerksamkeit zuteil werden lassen.

single: ~-**breasted** adj jacket einreihig; ~-**cell(ed)** adj (Biol) einzellig; ~-**decker** n einstöckiger Omnibus; ~ **file** n **in** ~ **file** im Gänsemarsch; ~-**handed** 1 adj (ganz) allein (after noun); achievement ohne (fremde) Hilfe vollbracht; struggle einsam; 2 adv (also ~-**handedly**) ohne Hilfe, im Alleingang; ~-**lens-reflex (camera)** n Spiegelreflexkamera f; ~-**line** adj eingleisig; railway also, traffic einspurig; ~-**minded** adj zielstrebig; devotion unbeirrbar.

singleness ['sɪŋglnɪs] n ~ **of purpose** Zielstrebigkeit f.

single-parent [,sɪŋgl'peərənt] adj family mit nur einem Elternteil.

singles ['sɪŋglz] n sing or pl (Sport) Einzel nt. **the** ~ **finals** das Finale im Einzel; **men's** ~ Herreneinzel nt.

single-seater [,sɪŋgl'siːtər] n Einsitzer m.

singlet ['sɪŋglɪt] n (Brit) (Sport) ärmelloses Trikot; (underclothing) ärmelloses Unterhemd, Trikothemd nt.

single-track ['sɪŋgl,træk] adj einspurig; (Rail also) eingleisig.

singly ['sɪŋglɪ] adv einzeln; (solely) allein.

singsong ['sɪŋsɒŋ] n **we often have a** ~ **at the pub** in der Kneipe singen wir oft zusammen.

singular ['sɪŋgjʊləʳ] **1** adj **(a)** (Gram) im Singular. **(b)** (odd) sonderbar, eigenartig. **(c)** (outstanding) einzigartig, einmalig. **2** n Singular m. **in the** ~ **im** Singular.

singularity [ˌsɪŋgjʊ'lærɪtɪ] n (oddity) Sonderbarkeit, Eigenartigkeit f.

singularly ['sɪŋgjʊləlɪ] adv außerordentlich.

sinister ['sɪnɪstəʳ] adj unheimlich; person, scheme also finster; music, look also düster; fate böse.

sink¹ [sɪŋk] pret **sank**, ptp **sunk 1** vt **(a)** ship versenken. **(b)** (fig: ruin) theory zerstören; hopes also zunichte machen. **now we're sunk!** (col) jetzt sind wir geliefert (col). **(c)** shaft senken; hole ausheben. **to** ~ **a post in the ground** einen Pfosten in den Boden einlassen. **(d)** teeth, claws schlagen. **(e)** differences begraben. **(f) to** ~ **money in sth** Geld in etw (acc) stecken. **(g) to be sunk in thought** in Gedanken versunken sein.

2 vi sinken; (ship also) untergehen; (sun also) versinken; (voice, building, land etc) sich senken; (shares, prices) fallen. **to** ~ **to the bottom** auf den Grund sinken; **he was left to** ~ **or swim** (fig) er war ganz auf sich allein angewiesen; **to** ~ **into a chair** in einen Sessel (nieder)sinken; **the sun sank beneath the horizon** die Sonne versank am Horizont; **to** ~ **to one's knees** auf die Knie sinken; **to** ~ **into a deep sleep** in tiefen Schlaf versinken; **my heart sank at the sight of the work** beim Anblick der Arbeit verließ mich der Mut; **with** ~**ing heart** mutlos; **she has sunk in my estimation** sie ist in meiner Achtung gesunken.

♦ **sink in** vi **(a)** (into mud etc) einsinken (prep obj, -to in +acc). **(b)** (col: be understood) kapiert werden (col). **it's only just sunk** ~ **that it really did happen** ich kapiere/er kapiert etc erst jetzt, daß das tatsächlich passiert ist (col).

sink² n Ausguß m; (in kitchen also) Spülbecken nt. ~ **unit** Spüle f.

sinking ['sɪŋkɪŋ] **1** n (of ship) Untergang m; (deliberately) Versenkung f; (of shaft) Senken nt; (of well) Bohren nt. **2** adj ~ **feeling** flaues Gefühl (im Magen) (col).

sinner ['sɪnəʳ] n Sünder(in f) m.

sinuous ['sɪnjʊəs] adj (lit, fig) gewunden; motion of snake schlängelnd attr; dancing etc geschmeidig.

sinus ['saɪnəs] n (in head) (Nasen)nebenhöhle f.

sip [sɪp] **1** n Schluck m; (very small) Schlückchen nt. **2** vt in kleinen Schlucken trinken; (suspicious, daintily) nippen an (+dat); (savour) schlürfen.

siphon ['saɪfən] **1** n Heber m; (soda~) Siphon m. **2** vt absaugen; (into tank) umfüllen.

♦ **siphon off** vt sep **(a)** (lit) absaugen; petrol abzapfen; (into container) umfüllen, abfüllen. **(b)** (fig) staff abziehen; profits abschöpfen.

sir [sɜːʳ] n **(a)** (in direct address) mein Herr (form), Herr X. **Dear S**~ **(or Madam)**, ... sehr geehrte (Damen und) Herren! **(b)** (knight etc) S~ Sir m. **(c)** (Sch: teacher) please ~! Herr X!; **I'll tell** ~ ich sag's ihm.

siren ['saɪərən] n (also Myth) Sirene f.

sirloin ['sɜːlɔɪn] n Filet nt.

sissy ['sɪsɪ] n Waschlappen m (col), Memme f.

sister ['sɪstəʳ] n **(a)** Schwester f; (in trade union) Kollegin f. **(b)** (nun) (Ordens)schwester f; (before name) Schwester f. **(c)** (Brit: senior nurse) Oberschwester f.

sister in cpds Schwester-; ~**-in-law**, pl ~**s-in-law** Schwägerin f.

sisterly ['sɪstəlɪ] adj schwesterlich.

sit [sɪt] (vb: pret, ptp **sat**) **1** vi **(a)** (be ~ting) sitzen (in/on in/auf +dat); (~ down) sich setzen (in/on in/auf +acc). **a place to** ~ ein Sitzplatz m; ~ **by/with me** setz dich zu mir/neben mich; **to** ~ **for a painter** für einen Maler Modell sitzen; **to** ~ **for an exam** eine Prüfung ablegen (form) or machen; **to be** ~**ting pretty** (fig col) gut dastehen (col). **(b)** (assembly) tagen; (have a seat) einen Sitz haben.

to ~ **on a committee** in einem Ausschuß sitzen. **(c)** (bird: hatch) sitzen, brüten. **(d)** (fig: clothes) sitzen (on sb bei jdm).

2 vt **(a)** setzen (in in +acc, on auf +acc); (place) object also stellen. **to** ~ **a child on one's knees** sich (dat) ein Kind auf die Knie setzen; **the table/car** ~**s 5 people** an dem Tisch/in dem Auto haben 5 Leute Platz. **(b)** examination ablegen (form), machen.

♦ **sit about** or **around** vi herumsitzen.

♦ **sit back** vi (lit, fig) sich zurücklehnen; (fig: do nothing) die Hände in den Schoß legen.

♦ **sit down** vi sich (hin)setzen. **to** ~ ~ **in a chair** sich auf einen Stuhl setzen.

♦ **sit in** vi **(a)** (demonstrators) ein Sit-in veranstalten. **(b)** (attend as visitor) dabeisein, dabeisitzen (on sth bei etw).

♦ **sit on** vi +prep obj (not deal with) document etc sitzen auf (+dat); (col: suppress) idea, product unterdrücken; person einen Dämpfer aufsetzen (+dat) (col).

♦ **sit out 1** vi draußen sitzen. **2** vt sep **(a)** (stay to end) play bis zum Ende (sitzen)bleiben bei, bis zum Ende durchhalten (pej); storm auf das Ende (+gen) warten. **(b)** dance auslassen. **to** ~ ~ **a round** eine Runde aussetzen.

♦ **sit through** vi +prep obj durchhalten, aushalten (pej).

♦ **sit up** vi **(a)** aufrecht sitzen; (action) sich aufrichten. ~ ~! setz dich gerade hin!; **to make sb** ~ ~ **(and take notice)** (fig col) jdn aufhorchen lassen. **(b)** (not go to bed) aufbleiben. **she sat** ~ **with the sick child** sie wachte bei dem kranken Kind. **2** vt sep aufrichten; doll also, baby hinsetzen.

sitcom ['sɪtkɒm] n (col) Situationskomödie f.

sit-down ['sɪtdaʊn] adj attr **to have a** ~ **strike** einen Sitzstreik machen; **a** ~ **meal** eine richtige Mahlzeit.

site [saɪt] **1** n **(a)** Stelle f, Platz m. **(b)** (Archeol) Stätte f. **(c)** (building ~) Baustelle f. **missile** ~ Raketenbasis f. **(d)** (camping ~) Campingplatz m. **2** vt legen, anlegen. **to be** ~**d** liegen, (gelegen) sein.

sit-in ['sɪtɪn] n Sit-in nt. **to hold** or **stage a** ~ ein Sit-in veranstalten.

sitting ['sɪtɪŋ] n (of committee, for portrait) Sitzung f. **they have two** ~**s for lunch** sie servieren das Mittagessen in zwei Schüben.

sitting: ~ **duck** n (fig) leichte Beute; ~ **room** n (lounge) Wohnzimmer nt; (in guest house etc) Aufenthaltsraum m; ~ **tenant** n (derzeitiger) Mieter.

situate ['sɪtjʊeɪt] vt legen.

situated ['sɪtjʊeɪtɪd] adj gelegen; person (financially) gestellt, situiert (geh). **it is** ~ **in the High Street** es liegt an der Hauptstraße; **a pleasantly** ~ **house** ein schön gelegenes Haus; **how are you** ~ **(for money)?** wie ist Ihre finanzielle Lage?

situation [ˌsɪtjʊ'eɪʃən] n **(a)** (state of affairs) Lage, Situation f; (financial, marital etc) Lage f, Verhältnisse pl; (in play, novel) Situation f. **to save the** ~ die Situation retten; ~ **comedy** Situationskomödie f. **(b)** (of house etc) Lage f. **(c)** (job) Stelle f. **"**~**s vacant/wanted"** „Stellenangebote/Stellengesuche".

six [sɪks] **1** adj sechs. **she is** ~ **(years old)** sie ist sechs (Jahre alt); **at (the age of)** ~ im Alter von sechs Jahren; **it's** ~ **(o'clock)** es ist sechs (Uhr); **there are** ~ **of us** wir sind sechs; ~ **and a half/quarter** sechseinhalb/sechsviertel; **to be** ~ **feet under** (hum) sechs Fuß (dat) unter liegen; **to knock sb for** ~ (fig) jdn umhauen (col). ~ **of one and half a dozen of the other** (col) das ist Jacke wie Hose (col). **2** n Sechs f. **to divide sth into** ~ etw in sechs Teile teilen; **the are sold in** ~**es** sie werden in Sechserpackungen verkauft; **to be at** ~**es and sevens** (things) wie Kraut und Rüben durcheinanderliegen *(col)*; *(person)* völlig durcheinander sein; **to knock sb for ~** *(col)* jdn umhauen.

six: **~fold** 1 *adj* sechsfach; **2** *adv* um das Sechsfache; **~ footer** *n* **to be a ~ footer** über 1,80 *(gesprochen:* einsachtzig) sein; **~ hundred** 1 *adj* sechshundert; **2** *n* Sechshundert *f*; **~ million** *adj*, *n* sechs Millionen; **~-shooter** *n* *(col)* sechsschüssiger Revolver.

sixteen ['sɪks'tiːn] 1 *adj* sechzehn. **2** *n* Sechzehn *f*.

sixteenth ['sɪks'tiːnθ] 1 *adj* sechzehnte(r, s). **a ~ part** ein Sechzehntel *nt*. **2** *n* **(a)** *(fraction)* Sechzehntel *nt*; *(in series)* Sechzehnte(r, s). **(b)** *(date)* **the ~** der Sechzehnte.

sixth [sɪksθ] 1 *adj* sechste(r, s). **a ~ part** ein Sechstel *nt*; **he was** *or* **came ~** er wurde Sechster; **he was ~ from the left** er war der Sechste von links. **2** *n* **(a)** *(fraction)* Sechstel *nt*; *(in series)* Sechste(r, s). **(b)** *(date)* **the ~** der Sechste; **on the ~** am Sechsten; **the ~ of September** der sechste September.

sixth: **~ form** *n* *(Brit)* Abschlußklasse, ≃ Prima *f*; **~-former** *n* *(Brit)* Schüler(in *f*) *m* der Abschlußklasse, ≃ Primaner(in *f*) *m*.

six thousand 1 *adj* sechstausend. **2** *n* Sechstausend *f*.

sixth sense *n* sechster Sinn.

sixtieth ['sɪkstɪɪθ] 1 *adj* sechzigste(r, s). **2** *n* *(fraction)* Sechzigstel *nt*; *(in series)* Sechzigste(r, s).

sixty ['sɪkstɪ] 1 *adj* sechzig. **2** *n* Sechzig *f*. **the sixties** die sechziger Jahre; **to be in one's sixties** in den Sechzigern sein; **to be in one's late/early sixties** Ende/Anfang sechzig sein; **~-four thousand dollar question** *n* *(hum)* Zehntausendmarkfrage *f* *(hum)*.

sixty-one ['sɪkstɪ'wʌn] *adj* einundsechzig.

six-year-old ['sɪksjɪə,əʊld] 1 *adj* sechsjährig *attr*, sechs Jahre alt *pred*. **2** *n* Sechsjährige(r) *mf*.

size [saɪz] 1 *n* Größe *f*; *(of problem, operation also)* Ausmaß *nt*. **collar/hip/waist ~** Kragen-/Hüft-/Taillenweite *f*; **it's the ~ of a brick** es ist so groß wie ein Ziegelstein; **he's about your ~** er ist ungefähr so groß wie du; **what ~ is it?** wie groß ist es?; *(clothes, shoes, gloves etc)* welche Größe ist es?; **it's quite a ~** es ist ziemlich groß; **it's two ~s too big** es ist zwei Nummern zu groß; **to cut sth to ~** etw auf die richtige Größe zurechtschneiden; **that's about the ~ of it** *(col)* ja, so ungefähr kann man es sagen. **2** *vt* größenmäßig ordnen.

♦ **size up** *vt sep* abschätzen.

sizeable ['saɪzəbl] *adj* ziemlich groß, größer; *car, estate, jewel also* ansehnlich.

sizzle ['sɪzl] *vi* brutzeln.

skate¹ [skeɪt] *n* *(fish)* Rochen *m*.

skate² 1 *n* *(shoe)* Schlittschuh *m*; *(blade)* Kufe *f*. **put** *or* **get your ~s on** *(fig col)* mach/macht mal ein bißchen dalli! *(col)*. **2** *vi* eislaufen, Schlittschuh laufen; *(figure-~)* eislaufen; *(roller-~)* Rollschuh laufen. **it went skating across the room** *(fig)* es rutschte durch das Zimmer.

♦ **skate around** *or* **over** *vi* +*prep obj difficulty, problem* einfach übergehen.

skateboard ['skeɪtbɔːd] *n* Skateboard, Rollbrett *nt*.

skater ['skeɪtər] *n* *(ice~)* Schlittschuhläufer(in *f*) *m*; *(figure-~)* Eiskunstläufer(in *f*) *m*; *(roller-~)* Rollschuhläufer(in *f*) *m*.

skating ['skeɪtɪŋ] *n* *(ice~)* Eislauf *m*; *(figure-~)* Eiskunstlauf *m*; *(roller-~)* Rollschuhlauf *m*. **~ rink** Eisbahn/Rollschuhbahn *f*.

skein [skeɪn] *n* *(of wool etc)* Strang *m*.

skeleton ['skelɪtn] 1 *n* *(lit, fig)* Skelett *nt*; *(esp of ship)* Gerippe *nt*. **a ~ in one's cupboard** *(of public figure)* ein Leiche im Keller. **2** *adj staff, service etc* Not-. **~ key** Dietrich, Nachschlüssel *m*.

skeptic etc *(US)* = **sceptic** etc.

sketch [sketʃ] 1 *n* *(Art, Liter)* Skizze *f*; *(Theat)* Sketch *m*; *(design also)* Entwurf *m*. **2** *vt* *(lit, fig)*

skizzieren.

♦ **sketch in** *vt sep details (verbally)* umreißen.

sketch-book ['sketʃbʊk] *n* Skizzenbuch *nt*.

sketchy ['sketʃɪ] *adj* (+*er*) *(inadequate)* flüchtig, oberflächlich; *(incomplete)* bruchstückhaft.

skewer ['skjʊər] 1 *n* Spieß *m*. **2** *vt* aufspießen.

skew-whiff [,skjuː'wɪf] *adj (Brit col)* (wind)schief.

ski [skiː] 1 *n* Ski, Schi *m*. **2** *vi* Ski laufen *or* fahren. **they ~ed down the slope/over the hill** sie fuhren (auf ihren Skiern) den Hang hinunter/sie liefen (mit ihren Skiern) über den Hügel.

skid [skɪd] 1 *n* *(Aut etc)* Schleudern *nt*. **to go into a ~** ins Schleudern kommen; **to correct a ~** das Fahrzeug wieder in seine Gewalt bekommen. **2** *vi* *(car, objects)* schleudern; *(person)* ausrutschen. **to ~ across the floor** über den Boden rutschen; **the car ~ded into a tree** der Wagen schleuderte gegen einen Baum.

skid: **~mark** *n* Reifenspur *f*; *(from braking)* Bremsspur *f*; **~ row** *n* *(esp US col)* Pennergegend *f (col)*; **to be on ~ row** heruntergekommen sein.

skier ['skiːər] *n* Skifahrer(in *f*) *m*.

skiff [skɪf] *n* Skiff *nt*; *(Sport)* Einer *m*.

skiing ['skiːɪŋ] *n* Skilaufen, Skifahren *nt*. **to go ~** Ski laufen gehen; **~ instructor** Skilehrer(in *f*) *m*.

ski *in cpds* Ski-; **~-jump** *n* *(action)* Skisprung *m*; *(place)* Sprungschanze *f*; **~-jumping** *n* Skispringen *nt*.

skilful, *(US)* **skillful** ['skɪlfʊl] *adj* geschickt; *player etc also* gewandt; *painting etc* kunstvoll.

ski-lift ['skiːlɪft] *n* Skilift *m*.

skill [skɪl] *n* **(a)** *no pl (skilfulness)* Geschick *nt*, Geschicklichkeit *f*; *(of sculptor etc)* Kunst(fertigkeit) *f*. **his ~ at billiards/in persuading people** sein Geschick beim Billiard/seine Fähigkeit, andere zu überreden. **(b)** *(acquired technique)* Fertigkeit *f*; *(ability)* Fähigkeit *f*.

skilled [skɪld] *adj* *(skilful)* geschickt, gewandt *(at* in +*dat)*; *(trained)* ausgebildet, Fach-; *(requiring skill)* fachmännisch.

skillet ['skɪlɪt] *n* Bratpfanne *f*.

skillful *(US)* = **skilful**.

skim [skɪm] 1 *vt* **(a)** *(remove floating matter)* abschöpfen; *milk* entrahmen. **~med** *or* *(US)* **~ milk** Magermilch *f*. **(b)** *(pass low over)* streifen über (+*acc)*; *(fig: touch on)* berühren. **the book merely ~s the surface of the problem** das Buch berührt das Problem nur an der Oberfläche. **(c)** *(read quickly)* überfliegen. **2** *vi* *(across, over* über +*acc)* *(move quickly)* fliegen; *(aircraft also)* rasch gleiten; *(stones)* springen.

skimp [skɪmp] 1 *vt food, material* sparen an (+*dat)*; *work* nachlässig erledigen; *details* zu kurz kommen lassen. **2** *vi* sparen *(on* an +*dat)*.

skimpy ['skɪmpɪ] *adj* (+*er*) dürftig; *meal, existence also* kärglich; *clothes* knapp. **to be ~ with sth** mit etw sparsam sein.

skin [skɪn] 1 *n* **(a)** Haut *f*. **to be soaked to the ~** bis auf die Haut naß sein; **he's nothing but ~ and bone(s) nowadays** er ist nur noch Haut und Knochen; **that's no ~ off my nose** *(col)* das juckt mich nicht *(col)*; **to save one's own ~** die eigene Haut retten; **to jump out of one's ~** *(col)* erschreckt hochfahren; **to get under sb's ~** *(col)* *(irritate)* jdm auf die Nerven gehen *(col)*; *(fascinate) (music)* jdm unter die Haut gehen *(col)*; jdn faszinieren; **I've got you under my ~** du hast mir's angetan; **to have a thick ~** *(fig)* ein dickes Fell haben *(col)*; **by the ~ of one's teeth** *(col)* mit knapper Not. **(b)** *(hide)* Haut *f*; *(fur)* Fell *nt*. **(c)** *(of fruit etc)* Schale *f*; *(on sausage, milk)* Haut *f*.

2 *vt animal* häuten; *fruit* schälen; *grapes, tomatoes* enthäuten. **to ~ sb alive** *(col)* jdm den Kopf abreißen *(hum col)*; **to keep one's eyes ~ned (for sth)** die Augen (nach etw) offenhalten.

skin: **~-diver** *n* Sporttaucher(in *f*) *m*; **~-diving** *n* Sporttauchen *nt*; **~flint** *n* *(col)* Geizkragen m (col).

skinful ['skɪnful] n (col) **to have had a** ~ einen über den Durst getrunken haben.

skin: ~ **graft** n Hauttransplantation f; ~**head** n (Brit col) Skinhead m.

skinny ['skɪnɪ] adj (+er) (col) person, legs dünn.

skint [skɪnt] adj (Brit col) **to be** ~ pleite or blank sein (col).

skin-tight ['skɪn͵taɪt] adj hauteng.

skip[1] [skɪp] **1** n (kleiner) Sprung m; (in dancing) Hüpfschritt m. **2** vi **(a)** hüpfen; (jump, gambol) springen; (with rope) seilspringen. **(b)** (move from subject to subject) springen. **3** vt **(a)** (omit, miss) school etc schwänzen (col); chapter etc auslassen, überspringen. **to** ~ **lunch** das Mittagessen ausfallen lassen; **let's** ~ **it** lassen wir das. **(b)** (US) **to** ~ **rope** seilspringen.

skip[2] n (Build) Container m; (Min) Förderkorb m.

ski: ~ **pants** npl Skihose(n pl) f; ~ **pole** n Skistock m.

skipper ['skɪpə^r] n Kapitän m.

skipping ['skɪpɪŋ] n Seilspringen nt. ~ **rope** Sprungseil nt.

skirmish ['skɜːmɪʃ] n (Mil) Gefecht nt; (scrap, fig) Zusammenstoß m.

skirt [skɜːt] **1** n Rock m; (of jacket, coat) Schoß m. **2** vt (also ~ **(a)round**) umgehen.

skirting (board) ['skɜːtɪŋ(͵bɔːd)] n (Brit) Fußleiste f.

ski: ~**-run** n Skipiste f; ~ **stick** n Skistock m.

skit [skɪt] n (satirischer) Sketch (on über +acc).

skittish ['skɪtɪʃ] adj (playful) übermütig; (flirtatious) woman neckisch, kokett.

skittle ['skɪtl] n (Brit) Kegel m. **to play** ~**s** kegeln.

skive [skaɪv] (Brit col) vi blaumachen (col); (from school etc) schwänzen (col).

♦ **skive off** vi (Brit col) sich drücken (col) (prep obj vor +dat).

skulk [skʌlk] vi (move) schleichen; (lurk) sich herumdrücken.

skull [skʌl] n Schädel m. ~ **and crossbones** Totenkopf m.

skunk [skʌŋk] n Skunk m, Stinktier nt.

sky [skaɪ] n Himmel m. **under the open** ~ unter freiem Himmel; **in the** ~ am Himmel; **the** ~**'s the limit!** nach oben sind keine Grenzen gesetzt; **to praise sb to the skies** jdn über den grünen Klee loben (col).

sky: ~ **blue** n Himmelblau nt; ~**-blue** adj himmelblau, ~**-high 1** adj prices schwindelnd hoch; **2** adv zum Himmel; **to blow a bridge** ~**-high** (col) eine Brücke in die Luft sprengen; **to blow a theory** ~**-high** (col) eine Theorie zum Einsturz bringen; ~**lark 1** n Feldlerche f; **2** vi (col) (frolic) tollen; (fool around) blödeln (col); ~**light** n Oberlicht nt; (in roof also) Dachfenster nt; ~**line** n (horizon) Horizont m; (of hills etc) Silhouette f; ~**scraper** n Wolkenkratzer m.

slab [slæb] n (of wood etc) Tafel f; (of stone etc) Platte f; (in mortuary) Tisch m; (of cake) großes Stück; (of chocolate) Tafel f.

slack [slæk] **1** adj (+er) **(a)** (not tight) locker. **(b)** (lazy) bequem, träge; (negligent) nachlässig, schlampig (col). **to be** ~ **about one's work** in bezug auf seine Arbeit nachlässig sein. **(c)** (Comm) market flau; season also ruhig. **business is** ~ das Geschäft geht schlecht. **2** n **(a)** (of rope etc) **to take up the** ~ (on a rope/sail) ein Seil/ Segel straffen or spannen; **there is too much** ~ das Seil/Segel hängt zu sehr durch; **to take up the** ~ **in the economy** die brachliegenden Kräfte (der Wirtschaft) nutzen. **(b)** (coal) Grus m. **3** vi bummeln.

slacken ['slækn] **1** vt **(a)** (loosen) lockern. **(b)** (reduce) vermindern, verringern. **2** vi **(a)** (become loose) sich lockern. **(b)** (also ~ **off**) (speed) sich verringern; (rate of development) sich verlangsamen; (wind, demand, market) abflauen.

slackness ['slæknɪs] n (of rope) Schlaffheit f; (of business, market etc) Flaute f; (laziness) Bummelei f; (negligence) Nachlässigkeit f.

slacks [slæks] npl Hose f.

slag [slæg] **1** n Schlacke f. ~ **heap** Schlackenhalde f. **2** vt (col: run down) (he)runtermachen (col).

slain [sleɪn] ptp of **slay**.

slake [sleɪk] vt thirst stillen.

slam [slæm] **1** n **(a)** (of door etc) Zuschlagen nt no pl. **with a** ~ mit voller Wucht. **(b)** (Cards) Schlemm m. **2** vt **(a)** (close violently) zuknallen. **to** ~ **sth shut** etw zuknallen; **to** ~ **the door in sb's face** jdm die Tür vor der Nase zumachen; **he** ~**med his fist on the table** er knallte mit der Faust auf den Tisch (col); **to** ~ **the brakes on** (col) auf die Bremse latschen (col). **(b)** (col: criticize harshly) verreißen; person herunterputzen (col). **3** vi (door) zuschlagen.

slander ['slɑːndə^r] **1** n Verleumdung f. **2** vt verleumden.

slanderous ['slɑːndərəs] adj verleumderisch.

slang [slæŋ] **1** n Slang m; (army ~, schoolboy ~ etc) Jargon m. **2** adj Slang-. **3** vt (esp Brit col) **to** ~ **sb/sth** jdn beschimpfen/über etw (acc) schimpfen; **they were having a** ~**ing match** sie beschimpften sich um die Wette.

slangy ['slæŋɪ] adj (+er) salopp.

slant [slɑːnt] **1** n **(a)** Schräge f. **to be on the** ~ sich neigen, schräg sein. **(b)** (fig) (bias, leaning) Tendenz, Neigung f; (point of view) Anstrich m. **a right-wing** ~ ein Rechtsdrall m. **2** vt (lit) verschieben; report färben. **the book is** ~**ed towards women** das Buch ist auf Frauen ausgerichtet. **3** vi sich neigen.

slanting ['slɑːntɪŋ] adj schräg.

slap [slæp] **1** n Schlag, Klaps m. **to give sb a** ~ einen Klaps geben; **a** ~ **in the face** (lit, fig) ein Schlag ins Gesicht; (lit also) eine Ohrfeige; **to give sb a** ~ **on the back** jdm (anerkennend) auf den Rücken klopfen; (fig) jdn loben. **2** adv (col) direkt. **3** vt **(a)** schlagen. **to** ~ **sb's face** jdn ohrfeigen, jdm eine runterhauen (col). **(b)** (put noisily) knallen (on/to) auf +acc). **he just** ~**ped the paint on** er klatschte die Farbe einfach drauf (col).

slap: ~**-bang** adv (col) crash mit Karacho (col); **it was** ~**-bang in the middle** es war genau in der Mitte; ~**-dash** adj flüchtig, schludrig (pej); ~**-happy** adj unbekümmert; ~**stick** n Klamauk m (col); ~**stick comedy** Slapstick m; ~**-up** adj (col) meal mit allem Drum und Dran (col).

slash [slæʃ] **1** n (action) Streich m; (wound) Schnitt m. **2** vt **(a)** (cut) zerfetzen; face also aufschlitzen; undergrowth abhauen; (with sword) hauen auf (+acc). **(b)** (col) price radikal herabsetzen.

slat [slæt] n Leiste f; (in grid etc) Stab m.

slate [sleɪt] **1** n **(a)** (rock) Schiefer m; (for roof ~) Schieferplatte f. **put it on the** ~ (col) schreiben Sie es an; **to wipe the** ~ **clean** (fig) reinen Tisch machen. **(b)** (US Pol) (Kandidaten)liste f. **2** adj Schiefer-. **3** vt **(a)** roof (mit Schiefer) decken. **(b)** (col: criticize harshly) verreißen; person zusammenstauchen (col).

slate: ~**-blue** adj blaugrau; ~**-coloured**, (US) ~**-colored** adj schieferfarben; ~**-grey**, (US) ~**-gray** adj schiefergrau.

slaughter ['slɔːtə^r] **1** n (of animals) Schlachten nt no pl; (of persons) Gemetzel. **the** ~ **on the roads** das Massensterben auf den Straßen. **2** vt schlachten; persons (lit) abschlachten; (fig) fertigmachen (col).

slaughterhouse ['slɔːtəhaʊs] n Schlachthof m.

Slav [slɑːv] **1** adj slawisch. **2** n Slawe m, Slawin f.

slave [sleɪv] **1** n Sklave m, Sklavin f. **to be a** ~ **to sb/sth** jds Sklave sein/Sklave von etw sein. **2** vi sich abplagen, schuften (col). **to** ~ **(away) at sth** sich mit etw herumschlagen.

slave: ~ **driver** n (lit, fig) Sklaventreiber m;

~ **labour** *(Brit) or* **labor** *(US) n (work)* Sklavenarbeit *f;* **he uses ~ labour** sein Leute müssen wie die Sklaven arbeiten.

slavery ['sleɪvərɪ] *n* Sklaverei *f; (condition)* Sklavenleben *nt; (fig: addiction)* sklavische Abhängigkeit *(to von).*

slave trade *n* Sklavenhandel *m.*

slavish *adj,* ~**ly** *adv* ['sleɪvɪʃ, -lɪ] sklavisch.

slay [sleɪ] *pret* **slew**, *ptp* **slain** *vt* erschlagen; *(with gun etc)* ermorden.

sleazy ['sliːzɪ] *adj (+er) (col)* schäbig.

sledge [sledʒ] *n* Schlitten *m.*

sledge(hammer) ['sledʒ(,hæməʳ)] *n* Vorschlaghammer *m.*

sleek [sliːk] **1** *adj (+er)* hair, fur, animal geschmeidig; *(of general appearance)* gepflegt; car also schnittig, elegant. **2** *vt* **to ~ one's hair down** sich *(dat)* die Haare glätten.

sleep [sliːp] *(vb: pret, ptp* **slept) 1** *n* Schlaf *m.* **to go to ~** *(person, limb)* einschlafen; **to have a ~** (etwas) schlafen; **to have a good night's ~** sich richtig ausschlafen; **to put sb to ~** jdn zum Schlafen bringen; *(drug)* jdn einschläfern; **to put an animal to ~** *(euph)* ein Tier einschläfern; **that film sent me to ~** bei dem Film bin ich eingeschlafen. **2** *vt* **the house ~s** 10 in dem Haus können 10 Leute schlafen *or* übernachten. **3** *vi* schlafen. **to ~ late** lange schlafen.

♦ **sleep around** *vi (col)* mit jedem schlafen *(col).*

♦ **sleep in** *vi* ausschlafen; *(col: oversleep)* verschlafen.

♦ **sleep off** *vt sep* hangover etc ausschlafen. **to ~ it ~** seinen Rausch ausschlafen.

♦ **sleep on** *vi* +prep obj problem, decision überschlafen. **why don't you ~ ~ it** schlafen Sie noch einmal darüber.

♦ **sleep with** *vi* +prep obj (have sex) schlafen mit.

sleeper ['sliːpəʳ] *n* **(a) to be a heavy/light ~** einen festen/leichten Schlaf haben. **(b)** *(Brit Rail: on track)* Schwelle *f.* **(c)** *(Brit Rail)* *(train)* Schlafwagenzug *m; (coach)* Schlafwagen *m; (berth)* Platz *m* im Schlafwagen.

sleeping ['sliːpɪŋ] *adj* schlafend. **S~ Beauty** Dornröschen *nt;* **let ~ dogs lie** *(Prov)* schlafende Hunde soll man nicht wecken *(Prov).*

sleeping: ~ **bag** *n* Schlafsack *m;* ~ **car** *n* Schlafwagen *m;* ~ **partner** *n (Brit)* stiller Teilhaber; ~ **pill** *n* Schlaftablette *f;* ~ **quarters** *npl* Schlafräume *pl.*

sleepless ['sliːplɪs] *adj* schlaflos.

sleep: ~**walk** *vi* schlafwandeln; ~**walker** *n* Schlafwandler(in *f) m.*

sleepy ['sliːpɪ] *adj (+er)* **(a)** *(drowsy)* person, voice etc müde, schläfrig; *(not yet awake)* verschlafen. **(b)** *(inactive)* person lahm *(col);* place, atmosphere verschlafen; climate schläfrig machend; afternoons schläfrig.

sleet [sliːt] **1** *n* Schneeregen *m.* **2** *vi* **it was ~ing es gab Schneeregen.**

sleeve [sliːv] *n* **(a)** *(on garment)* Ärmel *m.* **to roll up one's ~s** *(lit, fig)* die Ärmel aufkrempeln *(col);* **to have sth up one's ~** *(fig col)* etw in petto haben *or* auf Lager haben. **(b)** *(for record)* Hülle *f.*

sleeveless ['sliːvlɪs] *adj* ärmellos.

sleigh [sleɪ] *n* (Pferde)schlitten *m.*

sleight [slaɪt] *n:* **by ~ of hand** durch Taschenspielertricks.

slender ['slendəʳ] *adj* schlank; hand, waist also schmal; resources knapp, mager; hope schwach, gering.

slept [slept] *pret, ptp of* **sleep.**

sleuth [sluːθ] *n (col)* Spürhund *m.*

slew [sluː] *pret of* **slay.**

slice [slaɪs] **1** *n* **(a)** Scheibe *f; (of bread also)* Schnitte *f; (fig: of population, profit)* Teil *m.* **a ~ of life** ein Ausschnitt aus dem Leben. **(b)** *(esp Brit: food server)* Wender *m.* **cake ~** Tortenheber *m.* **2** *vt*

(a) bread, meat etc (in Scheiben) schneiden. **to ~ sth in two** etw durchschneiden. **(b)** ball anschneiden. **3** *vi* **to ~ through sth** etw durchschneiden.

♦ **slice off** *vt sep* abschneiden.

♦ **slice up** *vt sep* (ganz) in Scheiben schneiden; *(divide)* aufteilen.

slicer ['slaɪsəʳ] *n (cheese-~ etc)* Hobel *m; (machine)* *(bread-~)* Brotschneider *m; (bacon-~)* ≈ Wurstschneidemaschine *f.*

slick [slɪk] **1** *adj (+er) (col)* **(a)** *(usu pej: clever, smart)* clever *(col);* answer, solution, performance, style glatt. **(b)** hair geschniegelt. **(c)** *(US: slippery)* glatt, schlüpfrig. **2** *n* **(a)** *(oil~)* Ölteppich *m.* **(b)** *(US col: glossy magazine)* Hochglanzmagazin *nt.*

slide [slaɪd] *(vb: pret, ptp* **slid** [slɪd]*)* **1** *n* **(a)** *(chute, in playground etc)* Rutschbahn *f.* **(b)** *(fig: fall, drop)* Abfall *m.* **the ~ in share prices** der Preisrutsch bei den Aktien. **(c)** *(esp Brit: for hair)* Spange *f.* **(d)** *(Phot)* Dia *nt; (microscope ~)* Objektträger *m.* **a lecture with ~s** ein Diavortrag *m.* **2** *vt (push)* schieben; *(slip)* gleiten lassen. **3** *vi* **(a)** rutschen; *(deliberately also)* schlittern. **to ~ down the banisters** das Treppengeländer hinunterrutschen. **(b)** *(move smoothly: machine part etc)* sich schieben lassen. **it slid into place** es rutschte an die richtige Stelle. **(c)** *(person: move quietly etc)* schleichen. **(d)** *(fig)* **the days slid by or past** die Tage schwanden dahin *(geh);* **to let things ~** die Dinge laufen lassen.

slide: ~ **film** *n* Diafilm *m;* ~ **projector** *n* Diaprojektor *m;* ~ **rule** *n* Rechenschieber *m;* ~ **show** *n* Diavortrag *m.*

sliding ['slaɪdɪŋ] *adj part* gleitend; door, roof, seat Schiebe-.

slight [slaɪt] **1** *adj (+er)* **(a)** person, build zierlich. **(b)** *(small, trivial)* leicht; improvement also, change, possibility geringfügig; importance, intelligence gering; error also klein; acquaintance flüchtig. **he showed some ~ optimism** er zeigte gewisse Ansätze von Optimismus; **he takes offence at the ~est thing** er ist wegen jeder kleinsten Kleinigkeit gleich beleidigt; **I haven't the ~est (idea)** ich habe nicht die geringste Ahnung; **not in the ~est** nicht im geringsten. **2** *n (affront)* Affront *m (on* gegen*).* **a ~ on one's/sb's character** eine persönliche Kränkung. **3** *vt (offend)* kränken; *(ignore)* ignorieren.

slighting ['slaɪtɪŋ] *adj (offensive)* kränkend; remark abfällig.

slightly ['slaɪtlɪ] *adv* **(a)** ~ **built** person zierlich. **(b)** *(to a slight extent)* etwas, ein kleines bißchen; know flüchtig; smell leicht, etwas.

slim [slɪm] **1** *adj (+er)* **(a)** schlank; waist etc schmal. **(b)** resources, profits mager; hope also schwach; chances gering; evidence dürftig. **2** *vi* eine Schlankheitskur machen.

slime [slaɪm] *n* Schleim *m.*

slimming ['slɪmɪŋ] *adj* schlankmachend attr. **crispbread is ~** Knäckebrot macht schlank; ~ **foods** kalorienarme Nahrungsmittel *pl.*

slimy ['slaɪmɪ] *adj (+er) (lit, fig)* schleimig; wall glitschig; hands schmierig.

sling [slɪŋ] *(vb: pret, ptp* **slung**) **1** *n* Schlinge *f; (for rifle)* (Trag)riemen *m.* **to have one's arm in a ~** den Arm an der Schlinge tragen. **2** *vt (throw)* schleudern; *(col)* schmeißen *(col).* **he slung his coat over his arm** er warf sich *(dat)* den Mantel über den Arm.

♦ **sling out** *vt sep (col)* rausschmeißen *(col).*

slink [slɪŋk] *pret, ptp* **slunk** *vi* schleichen. **to ~ away or off** sich davonschleichen.

slinky ['slɪŋkɪ] *adj (+er) (col)* aufreizend.

slip [slɪp] **1** *n* **(a)** *(slide)* **he had a nasty ~** er ist ausgerutscht und bös gefallen. **(b)** *(mistake)* Ausrutscher, Patzer *m.* **to make a (bad) ~** sich (übel) vertun *(col);* **a ~ of the pen/tongue** ein

Schreibfehler *m*/Versprecher *m*; **it was just a ~ of the pen** das war nur ein Flüchtigkeitsfehler. **(c) to give sb the ~** jdm entwischen. **(d)** *(pillow~)* Kissenbezug *m*. **(e)** *(undergarment)* Unterrock *m*. **(f)** *(of paper)* Zettel *m*. **~s of paper** Zettel *pl*. **(g) a (mere) ~ of a girl** *(slightly built)* ein zierliches Persönchen.

2 *vt* **(a)** schieben; *(slide)* gleiten lassen; *(Aut)* *clutch* schleifen lassen. **to ~ sth across to sb** jdm etw zuschieben; *(unobtrusively)* jdm etw zuschmuggeln; **she ~ped the dress over her head** sie streifte sich *(dat)* das Kleid über den Kopf; **to ~ a disc** *(Med)* sich *(dat)* einen Bandscheibenschaden zuziehen; **to ~ sb a fiver** jdm einen Fünfer zustecken. **(b)** *(escape from)* sich losreißen. **the dog ~ped its chain** der Hund hat sich (von der Kette) losgerissen; **the boat had ~ped its moorings** das Boot hatte sich losgerissen; **it ~ped my mind** ich habe es vergessen; **it ~ped my notice** es ist mir entgangen.

3 *vi* **(a)** *(person)* (aus)rutschen; *(feet, tyres)* (weg)rutschen; *(become loose: knot, nut)* sich lösen; *(Aut: clutch)* schleifen. **the knife ~ped** das Messer rutschte ab; **it ~ped from her hand** es rutschte ihr aus der Hand; **the secret ~ped out before he realized** ehe er sich's versah, war ihm das Geheimnis herausgerutscht. **(b)** *(move quickly)* schlüpfen; *(move smoothly)* rutschen. **I'll ~ around to the shop** ich spring' schnell zum Laden. **(c) to let (it) ~ that ...** fallenlassen, daß...; **the police let the thief ~ through their fingers** die Polizei ließ sich *(dat)* den Dieb durch die Finger schlüpfen. **(d)** *(decline: standards, morals etc)* fallen. **you're ~ping!** *(col)* du läßt nach *(col)*.

♦ **slip away** *vi* sich wegschleichen; *(time)* verstreichen; *(chances)* (allmählich) schwinden; *(opportunity)* dahinschwinden.

♦ **slip by** *vi (person)* sich vorbeischleichen *(prep obj* an *+dat)*; *(years)* verfliegen, nur so dahinschwinden.

♦ **slip off 1** *vi (person)* sich wegschleichen. **2** *vt sep clothes* ausziehen, abstreifen.

♦ **slip on** *vt sep* schlüpfen in *(+acc)*; *dress also* überstreifen; *ring* aufziehen; *lid* drauftun *(prep obj* auf *+acc)*.

♦ **slip out** *vi* **(a)** *(leave unobtrusively)* kurz weggehen. **(b)** *(be revealed)* herauskommen.

♦ **slip up** *vi (col: err)* sich vertun *(col) (over,* in bei*)*.

slip: **~ case** *n* Schuber *m*; **~cover** *n (esp* US*)* Schonbezug *m*; **~knot** *n* Schlaufenknoten *m*; **~-ons** *npl (shoes)* Slipper *pl*.

slipper ['slɪpə'] *n* Pantoffel, Hausschuh *m*.

slippery ['slɪpərɪ] *adj* **(a)** schlüpfrig; *rope, road* glatt, rutschig; *fish* glitschig. **(b)** *(pej col) person* glatt, windig *(col)*. **a ~ customer** ein aalglatter Typ *(col)*; **he's on the ~ slope** *(col)* er ist auf der schiefen Bahn.

slip-road ['slɪprəʊd] *n (Brit)* Zufahrtsstraße *f*; *(for entering motorway)* (Autobahn)auffahrt *f*; *(for leaving motorway)* (Autobahn)ausfahrt *f*.

slipshod ['slɪpʃɒd] *adj* schludrig.

slip: **~stream** *m (Aviat)* Sog *m*; *(Aut)* Windschatten *m*; **~way** *n (Naut)* Gleitbahn *f*; **to come off the ~way** vom Stapel laufen.

slit [slɪt] *(vb: pret, ptp ~)* **1** *n* Schlitz *m*. **2** *vt* (auf)schlitzen. **to ~ a sack open** einen Sack aufschlitzen; **to ~ sb's throat** jdm die Kehle aufschlitzen.

slither ['slɪðə'] *vi* rutschen. **to ~ about on the ice** auf dem Eis herumschlittern.

sliver ['slɪvə'] *n (of wood etc)* Splitter *m*; *(thin slice)* Scheibchen *nt*.

slob [slɒb] *n (col)* Drecksau *f (col!)*.

slobber ['slɒbə'] *vi* sabbern, sabbeln *(also fig)*; *(dog)* geifern.

slog [slɒg] *(col)* **1** *n (effort)* Schinderei *f (col)*. **it's a hard ~ to the top** man muß ganz schön schuften,

um nach oben zu kommen. **2** *vt ball* dreschen *(col)*; *opponent* hart treffen. **3** *vi* **to ~ away at sth** *(work)* an etw *(dat)* schuften *(col)*; **we ~ged on for another 5 miles** wir kämpften uns noch 5 Meilen weiter.

slogan ['sləʊgən] *n* Slogan *m*; *(motto)* Motto *nt*; *(political also)* Parole *f*.

slogger ['slɒgə'] *n (col: worker)* Arbeitstier *nt*.

slop [slɒp] **1** *vi (spill)* (über)schwappen. **to ~ over (into sth)** überschwappen (in etw *acc*). **2** *vt (spill)* verschütten; *(pour out)* schütten.

slope [sləʊp] **1** *n* **(a)** *(angle)* Neigung *f*; *(downwards also)* Gefälle *nt*; *(of roof also)* Schräge *f*. **(b)** *(sloping ground)* (Ab)hang *m*. **on a ~** am Hang; **halfway up the ~** auf halber Höhe; **the (ski) ~s** die Piste. **2** *vi* geneigt sein; *(road, floor)* sich neigen. **the ground ~s down to the stream** das Land senkt sich zum Fluß hin ab.

♦ **slope off** *vi (col: person)* abziehen *(col)*.

sloping ['sləʊpɪŋ] *adj road (upwards)* ansteigend; *(downwards)* abfallend; *roof, floor* schräg; *garden etc* am Hang; *(not aligned)* schief.

sloppy ['slɒpɪ] *adj (+er)* **(a)** *(col: careless)* schlampig *(col)*; *work also* schlud(e)rig *(col)*. **(b)** *(col: sentimental)* rührselig; *novel also* schmalzig.

slops [slɒps] *npl (dirty water)* Schmutzwasser *nt*; *(food waste)* Abfallbrühe *f*; *(in teapot)* Satz *m*.

slosh [slɒʃ] *(col)* **1** *vt* **(a) to ~ some water over sth** Wasser über etw *(acc)* schütten. **(b)** *(Brit: hit)* hauen. **2** *vi* **to ~ about in the water** im Wasser herumplanschen.

sloshed [slɒʃt] *adj pred (esp Brit col)* blau *(col)*. **to get ~** sich besaufen *(col)*.

slot [slɒt] *n (opening)* Schlitz *m*; *(groove)* Rille *f*; *(col: place)* Plätzchen *nt (col)*; *(TV col)* (gewohnte) Sendezeit. **~ machine** Münzautomat *m*; *(for gambling)* Spielautomat *m*; **~ meter** Münzzähler *m*.

♦ **slot in 1** *vt sep* hineinstecken. **to ~ sth ~ to sth** etw in etw *(acc)* stecken. **2** *vi* sich einfügen lassen. **suddenly everything ~ted ~to place** plötzlich paßte alles zusammen.

sloth [sləʊθ] *n* **(a)** *(laziness)* Faulheit *f*. **(b)** *(Zool)* Faultier *nt*.

slothful ['sləʊθfʊl] *adj faul*; *person, life also* träge.

slouch [slaʊtʃ] *vi (stand, sit)* herumhängen *(col)*; *(move)* latschen. **to ~ off** davonzockeln *(col)*; **he was ~ed over his desk** er hing über seinem Schreibtisch; **he sat ~ed on a chair** er hing auf einem Stuhl.

slovenly ['slʌvnlɪ] *adj* schlampig *(col)*.

slow [sləʊ] **1** *adj (+er)* langsam; *trade* flau. **it's ~ work** das braucht seine Zeit; **he is a ~ worker/learner/reader** er arbeitet/lernt/liest langsam; **to get off to a ~ start** *(race)* schlecht vom Start kommen; *(project)* nur langsam in Gang kommen; **to be ~/not to be ~ to do sth** sich *(dat)* mit etw Zeit lassen/etw prompt erledigen; **he is ~ to make up his mind/~ to anger** er braucht lange, um sich zu entscheiden/er wird nicht so leicht wütend; **they were ~ to act** sie ließen sich *(dat)* Zeit; **to be (20 minutes) ~** *(clock)* (20 Minuten) nachgehen; **bake in a ~ oven** bei schwacher Hitze backen. **2** *adv (+er)* langsam. **to go ~** *(driver)* langsam fahren; *(workers)* einen Bummelstreik machen. **3** *vi* **to ~ (to a stop/standstill)** langsam zum Halten/zum Stillstand kommen.

♦ **slow down** *or* **up 1** *vi* sich verlangsamen; *(drive/walk)* langsamer fahren/gehen; *(worker)* langsamer arbeiten. **2** *vt sep* verlangsamen; *engine* drosseln; *machine* herunterschalten; *programme, project* verzögern.

slow: **~coach** *n (Brit col)* Langweiler *m*; *(mentally)* Transuse *f (col)*; **~down** *n (US: go-slow)* Bummelstreik *m*; **~ lane** *n* (äußerste) rechte/linke Spur.

slowly ['sləʊlɪ] *adv* langsam.

slow motion *n* Zeitlupe *f*. **in ~** in Zeitlupe.

slowness ['sləʊnɪs] *n* Langsamkeit *f*. **their ~ to act** ihr Zaudern; **~ of mind** Begriffsstutzigkeit *f*.

slow: ~-**witted** adj begriffsstutzig; ~**worm** n Blindschleiche f.

sludge [slʌdʒ] n Schlamm m.

slug[1] [slʌg] n Nacktschnecke f. ~**s and snails** Schnecken pl (mit und ohne Gehäuse).

slug[2] 1 n (bullet) Kugel f; (blow) Schlag m. **a** ~ **of** whisky ein Schluck m Whisky. **2** vt (col: hit) eine knallen (+dat) (col).

sluggish ['slʌgɪʃ] adj (indolent, Med) träge; engine, car lahm, langsam; business flau; market lustlos.

sluice [sluːs] **1** n Schleuse f. **2** vt to ~ sth (down) etw abspritzen.

sluice gate n Schleusentor nt.

slum [slʌm] **1** n (usu pl: area) Slum m, Elendsviertel nt; (house) Elendsquartier nt. ~ **clearance** = (Stadt)sanierung f.

slumber ['slʌmbəʳ] (liter) **1** n Schlummer (geh), Schlaf m. ~**s** Träume pl. **2** vi schlummern (geh).

slump [slʌmp] **1** n (in gen) (in numbers, popularity etc) (plötzliche) Abnahme; (in production, sales) Rückgang m; (state) Tiefstand m; (Fin) Sturz m, Baisse f (spec). ~ **in prices** Preissturz m (of bei); **the 1929 S**~ die Weltwirtschaftskrise von 1929. **2** vi (a) (Fin, Comm) (prices) stürzen, fallen; (sales, production) plötzlich zurückgehen; (fig: morale also) sinken. **(b)** (sink) fallen, sinken. **to** ~ **into a chair** sich in einen Sessel fallen lassen; **he was** ~**ed over the wheel** er war über dem Steuer zusammengesackt.

slung [slʌŋ] pret, ptp of **sling**.

slunk [slʌŋk] pret, ptp of **slink**.

slur [slɜːʳ] **1** n (a) Makel m; (insult) Beleidigung f. **to cast a** ~ **on sb/sth** jdn/etw in schlechtem Licht erscheinen lassen; (person) jdn/etw verunglimpfen. **(b)** (Mus) Bindung f. **(c)** to **speak with a** ~ unartikuliert sprechen. **2** vt (pronounce indistinctly) (halb) verschlucken.

slurp [slɜːp] vti schlürfen.

slurred [slɜːd] adj undeutlich; (Mus) gebunden.

slush [slʌʃ] n (watery snow) (Schnee)matsch m; (mud) Morast m; (col: sentimental nonsense) Kitsch m. ~ **fund** Schmiergeldfonds m.

slushy ['slʌʃɪ] adj (+er) snow, mud, path matschig; (col: sentimental) kitschig.

slut [slʌt] n (liederliche) Schlampe.

sly [slaɪ] **1** adj (+er) schlau, gerissen; look, wink verschmitzt. **2** n **on the** ~ heimlich, still und leise (hum), ganz heimlich.

smack[1] [smæk] vi **to** ~ **of** (taste) leicht schmecken nach; (fig) riechen nach.

smack[2] **1** n (klatschender) Schlag m; (slap also) fester Klaps; (sound) Klatschen nt. **to give a child/the ball a** ~ einem Kind eine knallen (col)/auf den Ball dreschen (col); **you'll get a** ~ du kriegst gleich eine (col); **a** ~ **in the eye** (fig) ein Schlag ins Gesicht. **2** vt (slap) knallen (col). **to** ~ **a child's bottom** einem Kind den Hintern versohlen (col); **he** ~**ed his lips** er leckte sich (dat) die Lippen. **3** adv (col) direkt. **she ran** ~ **into the door** sie rannte muss! gegen die Tür (col).

small [smɔːl] **1** adj (+er) **(a)** klein; supply also, importance gering; waist schmal; letter also Klein-; sum also bescheiden. **the** ~**est possible number of books** so wenig Bücher wie möglich; **to have a** ~ **appetite/be a** ~ **eater** wenig Appetit haben/kein großer Esser sein; **no** ~ **success** ein beachtlicher Erfolg; **to feel/look** ~ (fig) sich (ganz) klein (und häßlich) vorkommen/schlecht dastehen; **a few** ~ **matters** ein paar Kleinigkeiten; **to help in a** ~ **way** bescheidene Hilfe leisten; **to start in a** ~ **way** klein anfangen. **(b)** (fig: mean, petty) person kleinlich. **2** n **(a) the** ~ **of the back** das Kreuz. **(b)** ~**s** pl (Brit col) Unterwäsche f. **3** adv **to chop sth up** ~ etw kleinhacken.

small: ~ **ad** n (Brit) Kleinanzeige f; ~ **arms** npl Handfeuerwaffen pl; ~ **change** n Kleingeld nt; ~**holder** n Kleinbauer m; ~**holding** n kleiner Landbesitz; ~ **hours** npl früher Morgen; **in the** ~

hours in den frühen Morgenstunden.

smallish ['smɔːlɪʃ] adj (eher) kleiner. **he is** ~ **er ist** eher klein.

small-minded [ˌsmɔːl'maɪndɪd] adj engstirnig.

smallness ['smɔːlnɪs] n Kleinheit f; (of waist) Schmalheit f; (of sum, present) Bescheidenheit f; (pettiness) Kleinlichkeit f.

small: ~**pox** n Pocken pl; ~ **print** n das Kleingedruckte; ~-**scale** adj map, model in verkleinertem Maßstab; project kleinangelegt; ~ **screen** n (TV) **on the** ~ **screen** auf dem Bildschirm; ~**talk** n oberflächliche Konversation; ~-**time** adj (col) armselig; crook klein; politician Schmalspur-; actor drittrangig; ~-**town** adj Kleinstadt-, kleinstädtisch; mentality also kleinbürgerlich.

smarmy ['smɑːmɪ] adj (+er) (Brit col) kriecherisch (pej); voice einschmeichelnd.

smart [smɑːt] **1** adj (+er) **(a)** schick; person, clothes, car also flott; society fein. **a** ~-**looking girl/garden** ein flott aussehendes Mädchen/ein gepflegter Garten; **the** ~ **set** die Schickeria (col). **(b)** (bright, clever) clever (col), schlau; thief, trick also raffiniert; (pej) person, answer neunmalklug (pej col). **to get** ~ (col) sich am Riemen reißen (col); (get cheeky) frech kommen (with dat). **(c)** (quick) (blitz)schnell; pace flott (col). **and look** ~ (about it)! und zwar ein bißchen fix or plötzlich! (col). **2** vi brennen. **it will make your cut** ~ es wird (dir) in der Wunde brennen; **to** ~ **from sth** (from blow etc) von etw brennen; (fig) unter etw (dat) leiden.

smart-aleck ['smɑːtˌælɪk] (col) **1** n Schlauberger m (col). **2** adj remarks besserwisserisch.

smarten ['smɑːtn] (also ~ **up**) **1** vt house, room herausputzen; appearance aufmöbeln (col). **to** ~ **oneself up** (dress up) sich in Schale werfen (col); (generally improve appearance) mehr Wert auf sein Äußeres legen; **you'd better** ~ **up your ideas** (col) du solltest dich am Riemen reißen (col). **2** vi ~ **oneself up**.

smartness ['smɑːtnɪs] n **(a)** Schick m. **(b)** (cleverness) Cleverness (col), Schlauheit f; (of thief, trick) Raffiniertheit f.

smash [smæʃ] **1** vt **(a)** zerschlagen; window also einschlagen. **I** ~**ed my glasses** die Brille ist mir kaputtgegangen. **(b)** (defeat or destroy) zerschlagen; rebellion also niederschlagen; opponent zerschmettern; record haushoch schlagen. **(c)** (strike, also Tennis) schmettern. **2** vi **(a)** (break) zerbrechen. **it** ~**ed into a thousand pieces** es (zer)sprang in tausend Stücke. **(b)** (crash) prallen. **the car** ~**ed into the wall** das Auto krachte gegen die Mauer; **the plane** ~**ed into the houses** das Flugzeug raste in eine Häusergruppe. **3** n **(a)** (noise) nt; (of waves) Klatschen nt. **there was a** ~ es hat gekracht. **(b)** (collision) Unfall m. **(c)** (blow) Schlag m; (Tennis) Schmetterball m. **4** adv (col) mit Karacho (col).

♦ **smash down** vt sep door einschlagen.

♦ **smash in** vt sep einschlagen. **the firemen had to** ~ **their way** ~ die Feuerwehrleute mußten gewaltsam eindringen; **to** ~ **sb's face** ~ (col) jdm die Schnauze einschlagen (col!).

♦ **smash up** vt sep zertrümmern; car kaputtfahren.

smash-and-grab (raid) [ˌsmæʃən'græb(reɪd)] n Schaufenstereinbruch m.

smashed [smæʃt] adj (col) stockbesoffen (col).

smasher ['smæʃəʳ] n (esp Brit col) toller Typ (col); (woman) Klassefrau f (col).

smash hit n (col) Knüller m (col).

smashing ['smæʃɪŋ] adj (esp Brit col) klasse inv, Klasse pred, dufte (all col).

smattering ['smætərɪŋ] n **a** ~ **of French** ein paar Brocken Französisch.

smear [smɪəʳ] **1** n verschmierter Fleck; (fig) Beschmutzung *f*; *(defamation)* Verleumdung *f*; *(Med)* Abstrich *m*. **this left a ~ on his name** das hinterließ einen Fleck auf seinem Namen; **~ campaign** Verleumdungskampagne *f*; **~ test** *(Med)* Abstrich *m*. **2** *vt* **(a)** *cream, ointment* schmieren; *(spread)* verschmieren; *(mark, make dirty)* beschmieren; *face* einschmieren. **(b)** *(fig) person* verunglimpfen; *sb's reputation* beschmutzen. **3** *vi (glass)* verschmieren; *(print)* verschmiert *or* verwischt werden; *(biro)* schmieren; *(paint, ink)* verlaufen.

smell [smel] *(vb: pret, ptp ~ed or smelt)* **1** *n (sense of ~, odour)* Geruch *m*; *(unpleasant also)* Gestank *m*; *(fragrant also)* Duft *m*. **it has a nice ~** es riecht gut *or* angenehm; **there's a ~ of gas** hier riecht es nach Gas. **2** *vt* **(a)** riechen. **can you ~ burning?** riechst du, daß etwas brennt *or (Cook)* anbrennt? **(b)** *(fig) danger, treason* wittern. **to ~ trouble** Ärger kommen sehen. **3** *vi* riechen; *(unpleasantly also)* stinken; *(fragrantly also)* duften. **that ~s!** *(lit, fig)* das stinkt!; **to ~ of sth** *(lit, fig)* nach etw riechen; **his breath ~s** er riecht aus dem Mund.

♦ **smell out** *vt sep* **(a)** *rabbit, traitor etc* aufspüren; *plot* aufdecken. **(b) these onions are ~ing the house ~!** die Zwiebeln verpesten das ganze Haus!

smelling salts ['smelɪŋ,sɒlts] *npl* Riechsalz *nt*.
smelly ['smelɪ] *adj (+er)* übelriechend, stinkend. **it's ~ in here** hier drin stinkt es.
smelt[1] [smelt] *pret, ptp of* **smell**.
smelt[2] *vt ore* schmelzen; *(refine)* verhütten.
smile [smaɪl] **1** *n* Lächeln *nt*. **to be all ~s** übers ganze Gesicht strahlen; **to give sb a ~** jdm zulächeln; **take that ~ off your face!** hör auf, so zu grinsen!; **that soon wiped the ~ off his face** dabei verging ihm bald das Lachen. **2** *vi* lächeln. **come on, ~ lach mal!; to ~ at sb** jdn anlächeln; *(cheerfully)* jdn anlachen; **to ~ at sth** über etw *(acc)* lächeln; **to ~ with joy/happiness etc** vor Freude/Glück *etc* strahlen; **fortune ~d on him** *(liter)* ihm lachte das Glück.
smiling ['smaɪlɪŋ] *adj* lächelnd.
smirk [smɜːk] **1** *n* Grinsen *nt*. **2** *vi* grinsen.
smite [smaɪt] *pret* **smote**, *ptp* **smitten** *vt (old, liter)* schlagen.
smith [smɪθ] *n* Schmied *m*.
smithereens [,smɪðə'riːnz] *npl* **to smash sth to ~** etw in tausend Stücke schlagen.
smithy ['smɪðɪ] *n* Schmiede *f*.
smitten ['smɪtn] **1** *ptp of* **smite**. **2** *adj* **to be ~ with the plague/remorse** von der Pest heimgesucht/ von Reue geplagt werden; **he's really ~ with her** *(col)* er ist wirklich vernarrt in sie *(col)*.
smock [smɒk] *n* Kittel *m*.
smog [smɒg] *n* Smog *m*.
smoke [sməʊk] **1** *n* **(a)** Rauch *m*. **there's no ~ without fire** *(prov)* kein Rauch ohne Flamme *(prov)*; **to go up in ~** in Rauch (und Flammen) aufgehen. **(b)** *(cigarette etc)* was zu rauchen *(col)*. **have you got a ~?** hast du was zu rauchen? *(col)*; *(act)* **to have a ~** eine rauchen. **2** *vt* **(a)** *cigarette* rauchen. **(b)** *fish etc* räuchern. **3** *vi* rauchen; *(oil-lamp etc)* qualmen. **to ~ like a chimney** wie ein Schlot rauchen.
smoke-bomb ['sməʊkbɒm] *n* Rauchbombe *f*.
smoked [sməʊkt] *adj bacon, fish* geräuchert, Räucher-. **~ glass** Rauchglas *nt*.
smokeless ['sməʊklɪs] *adj zone* rauchfrei; *fuel* rauchlos.
smoker ['sməʊkə'] *n* **(a)** *(person)* Raucher(in *f*) *m*. **to be a heavy ~** stark rauchen, starker Raucher sein. **(b)** *(Rail)* Raucher(abteil *nt*) *m*.
smoke: **~-ring** *n* (Rauch)ring *m*; **~-screen** *n* Rauchvorhang *m*; *(fig)* Deckmantel, Vorwand *m*; **~ signal** *n* Rauchzeichen *nt*.
smoking ['sməʊkɪŋ] **1** *adj* rauchend. **2** *n* Rauchen *nt*. **"no ~"** „Rauchen verboten".

smoking: **~ compartment**, *(US)* **~ car** *n* Raucherabteil *nt*; **~ jacket** *n* Hausjacke *f*.
smoky ['sməʊkɪ] *adj (+er) chimney, fire* rauchend; *room, atmosphere* verraucht; *flavour* rauchig.
smolder *vi (US)* = **smoulder**.
smooch [smuːtʃ] *(col) vi* knutschen *(col)*.
smooth [smuːð] **1** *adj (+er)* **(a)** *(in texture, surface etc)* glatt; *sea also* ruhig; *outline* sanft; *skin also, hair* weich. **as ~ as glass** spiegelglatt; **worn ~** *steps* glattgetreten; *knife* abgeschliffen; *tyre* abgefahren. **(b)** *(in consistency) paste* sämig; *sauce* glatt. **(c)** *motion, flight, crossing* ruhig; *gear-change* weich; *landing* glatt; *breathing* gleichmäßig; *(trouble-free) transition, functioning* reibungslos, glatt. **the bill had a ~ passage through Parliament** der Gesetzentwurf kam glatt durchs Parlament. **(d)** *(polite, often pej) manners, salesman* glatt; *person also* aalglatt *(pej)*; *(unruffled)* kühl, cool *(col)*. **to be a ~ talker** ein Schönredner sein; **a ~ operator** ein Schlawiner *m (col)*.
2 *vt surface, dress, hair* glätten; *wood* glatthobeln; *(fig) feelings* beruhigen. **to ~ the way for sb** jdm den Weg ebnen.

♦ **smooth out** *vt sep (make smooth) crease, surface* glätten; *(fig) difficulty* aus dem Weg räumen.
♦ **smooth over** *vt sep quarrel* in Ordnung bringen. **to ~ things ~** die Sache geradebiegen *(col)*.
smoothly ['smuːðlɪ] *adv land* weich; *change gear* leicht; *drive* ruhig; *fit* genau; *make transition* unmerklich; *talk* schön; *handle situation* kühl; *behave* aalglatt *(pej)*. **to go ~** *(without problems)* glatt über die Bühne gehen.
smoothness ['smuːðnɪs] *n see adj* **(a)** Glätte *f*; Ruhe *f*; Sanftheit *f*; Weichheit *f*. **(b)** Sämigkeit *f*; Glätte *f*. **(c)** Ruhe *f*; Weichheit *f*; Glätte *f*; Gleichmäßigkeit *f*; Reibungslosigkeit *f*; *(of fit)* Genauigkeit *f*.
smote [sməʊt] *pret of* **smite**.
smother ['smʌðə'] *vt* **(a)** *(stifle) person, fire* ersticken; *(fig) criticism also, yawn, sob etc* unterdrücken. **to ~ sb with affection** jdn mit seiner Liebe erdrücken. **(b)** *(cover)* bedecken. **fruit ~ed in cream** Früchte, die in Sahne schwimmen.
smoulder, *(US)* **smolder** ['sməʊldə'] *vi (lit, fig)* glimmen, schwelen. **~ing hatred** schwelender Haß.
smudge [smʌdʒ] **1** *n* Fleck *m*; *(of ink)* Klecks *m*. **2** *vt* verwischen. **3** *vi* verschmieren.
smug [smʌg] *adj (+er)* selbstgefällig; *remark also* süffisant.
smuggle ['smʌgl] *vti (lit, fig)* schmuggeln. **to ~ sb/sth in** jdn/etw einschmuggeln; **to ~ sb/sth out** jdn/etw herausschmuggeln.
smuggler ['smʌglə'] *n* Schmuggler(in *f*) *m*.
smuggling ['smʌglɪŋ] *n* Schmuggel *m*.
smut [smʌt] *n* **(a)** *(piece of dirt)* Rußflocke *f*. **(b)** *(fig)* Schmutz *m*.
smutty ['smʌtɪ] *adj (+er) (lit, fig)* schmutzig.
snack [snæk] *n* Kleinigkeit *f*, Imbiß *m*. **to have a ~** eine Kleinigkeit essen; **~ bar** Imbißstube *f*.
snafu [snæ'fuː] *n (US col)* Schlamassel *m (col)*.
snag [snæg] *n* Haken *m*, Schwierigkeit *f*. **there's a ~** die Sache hat einen Haken; **what's the ~?** was ist das Problem?; **to run into** *or* **hit a ~** in Schwierigkeiten *(acc)* kommen.
snail [sneɪl] *n* Schnecke *f*. **at a ~'s pace** im Schneckentempo.
snake [sneɪk] *n* Schlange *f*. **a ~ in the grass** *(fig) (woman)* eine listige Schlange; *(man)* ein heimtückischer Kerl.
snake: **~bite** *n* Schlangenbiß *m*; **~ charmer** *n* Schlangenbeschwörer *m*; **~skin 1** *n* Schlangenhaut *f*; *(leather)* Schlangenleder *nt*; **2** *adj* Schlangenleder-, aus Schlangenleder.
snap [snæp] **1** *n* **(a)** *(sound)* Schnappen *nt*; *(with fingers)* Schnipsen *nt*; *(of sth breaking)* Knacken *nt*. **(b)** *(Phot)* Schnappschuß *m*. **(c)** *(Cards)* ≈ Schnippschnapp *nt*. **2** *adj attr* plötzlich, spontan.

~ **decision** plötzlicher Entschluß. **3** vt (a) fingers schnipsen mit. **to** ~ **a book shut** ein Buch zuklappen; **to** ~ **sth into place** etw einschnappen lassen. **(b)** (break) zerbrechen. **(c)** (also ~ **out) to** ~ **an order** bellend etwas befehlen; **she** ~**ped a few words at the children** sie pfiff die Kinder an. **(d)** (Phot) knipsen. **4** vi **(a)** (click) (zu)schnappen; (crack, break) zerbrechen. **to** ~ **shut** zuschnappen; **my patience finally** ~**ped** dann ist mir aber der Geduldsfaden gerissen. **(b)** (speak sharply) bellen (col). **to** ~ **at sb** jdn anschnauzen (col). **(c)** (of dog etc, fig) schnappen (at nach).

♦ **snap off** vt sep (break off) abbrechen; (bite off) abbeißen. **to** ~ **sb's head** ~ (fig col) jdm ins Gesicht springen (col).

♦ **snap out 1** vt sep order brüllen. **2** vi ~ ~ **of it!** reiß dich zusammen!; (cheer up) Kopf hoch!

♦ **snap up** vt sep (lit, fig) wegschnappen.

snapdragon ['snæp,drægən] n (Bot) Löwenmaul nt.

snappish ['snæpɪʃ] adj (lit, fig) bissig.

snappy ['snæpɪ] adj (+er) **(a)** (col) flott (col). **and make it** ~! und zwar ein bißchen flott! (col). **(b)** (lit, fig) dog, person bissig. **(c)** (col) translation kurz und treffend; phrase zündend.

snapshot ['snæpʃɒt] n Schnappschuß m.

snare [snɛəʳ] **1** n (lit, fig: trap) Falle f; (fig also) Fallstrick m. **2** vt (lit, fig) (ein)fangen.

snarl [snɑːl] **1** n Knurren nt no pl. **2** vi knurren. **to** ~ **at sb** jdn anknurren.

♦ **snarl up** vt sep (col) **I got** ~**ed** ~ **in a traffic jam** ich bin im Verkehr steckengeblieben.

snarl-up ['snɑːlʌp] n (col) (in traffic) Verkehrschaos nt; (in system) Kuddelmuddel nt (col).

snatch [snætʃ] **1** n **(a)** (act) Griff m. **to make a** ~ **at sth** nach etw greifen; (animal) zuschnappen. **(b)** (Brit col: robbery) Raub m; (kidnapping) Entführung f. **(c)** (snippet) Stück nt; (of conversation) Fetzen m. **2** vt **(a)** (grab) greifen. **to** ~ **sth from sb** jdm etw entreißen; **to** ~ **hold of sth** nach etw greifen; **to** ~ **sth out of sb's hand** jdm etw aus der Hand reißen. **(b)** some sleep etc ergattern. **to** ~ **a quick meal** schnell etwas essen. **(c)** (Brit col) (steal) money klauen (col); handbag aus der Hand reißen; (kidnap) entführen. **3** vi greifen (at nach). **don't** ~! nicht grapschen! (col).

♦ **snatch away** vt sep wegreißen (sth from sb jdm etw).

♦ **snatch up** vt sep schnappen. **he** ~**ed** ~ **his camera** er schnappte sich (dat) seine Kamera; **the mother** ~**ed her child** ~ die Mutter riß ihr Kind an sich (acc).

sneak [sniːk] **1** n Schleicher m; (Sch col) Petze(r) mf (Sch col). ~ **thief** Langfinger m (col). **2** vt he ~**ed a cake off the counter** er klaute einen Kuchen vom Tresen (col); **to** ~ **sth into a room** etw in ein Zimmer schmuggeln; **to** ~ **a look at sb/sth** auf jdn/etw schielen (col). **3** vi **(a) to** ~ **away or off** sich wegschleichen; **to** ~ **in** sich einschleichen; **to** ~ **past sb** (sich) an jdm vorbeischleichen. **(b)** (Sch col: tell tales) petzen (col). **to** ~ **on sb** jdn verpetzen (col).

sneakers ['sniːkəz] npl (US) Freizeitschuhe pl.

sneaking ['sniːkɪŋ] adj attr geheim attr. **I have a** ~ **feeling that** ... ich habe das unbestimmte Gefühl, daß ...

sneaky ['sniːkɪ] adj (+er) (col) raffiniert, schlau.

sneer [snɪəʳ] **1** n (expression) spöttisches Lächeln; (remark) spöttische Bemerkung. **2** vi spotten; (look sneering) spöttisch grinsen. **to** ~ **at sb** jdn verhöhnen; (facially also) jdn auslachen.

sneeze [sniːz] **1** n Nieser m (col). **2** vi niesen. **not to be** ~**d at** nicht zu verachten.

snide [snaɪd] adj (col) abfällig.

sniff [snɪf] **1** n Schnüffeln nt no pl (col); (disdainful) Naserümpfen nt no pl; (of dog) Schnüffeln nt no pl. **we never got a** ~ **of the vodka** (col) wir durften noch nicht einmal an dem Wodka riechen; **have a** ~ **at this** riech mal hieran! **2** vt (test by smelling)

riechen, schnuppern an (+dat) (col); smelling salts einziehen; glue einatmen, schnüffeln (col); (fig: detect) wittern, riechen. **3** vi (person) schniefen (col); (dog) schnuppern. **to** ~ **at sth** (lit) an etw (dat) schnuppern; (fig) die Nase über etw (acc) rümpfen; **not to be** ~**ed at** nicht zu verachten.

♦ **sniff out** vt sep (lit, fig) aufspüren; crime, plot aufdecken.

sniffle ['snɪfl] n, vi = **snuffle**.

snigger ['snɪgəʳ] **1** n Kichern, Gekicher nt. **2** vi kichern (at, about wegen).

snip [snɪp] **1** n **(a)** (cut, cutting action) Schnitt m. **(b)** (of cloth) Stück nt; (of paper) Schnipsel m (col); (from newspaper) Ausschnitt m. **(c)** (esp Brit col: bargain) Geschäft nt, günstiger Kauf. **it's a** ~ **at only £2 für nur £ 2** ist es unheimlich günstig. **(d)** (US col: insignificant person) Würstchen nt (pej col). **2** vt schnippeln (col). **to** ~ **sth off** etw abschnippeln (col).

snipe [snaɪp] **1** n, pl - (Orn) Schnepfe f. **2** vi **to** ~ **at sb** (lit, fig) aus dem Hinterhalt auf jdn schießen.

sniper ['snaɪpəʳ] n Heckenschütze m. ~**-fire** Heckenschützenfeuer nt.

snippet ['snɪpɪt] n Stückchen nt; (of paper also) Schnipsel m or nt; (of information) (Bruch)stück nt. ~**s of a conversation** Gesprächsfetzen pl.

snivel ['snɪvl] vi heulen, flennen (col).

snivelling, (US) **sniveling** ['snɪvlɪŋ] adj heulend.

snob [snɒb] n Snob m. ~ **value** Snobappeal m.

snobbery ['snɒbərɪ] n Snobismus m.

snobbish ['snɒbɪʃ] adj snobistisch, versnobt (col).

snog [snɒg] vi (Brit col) rumknutschen (col).

snooker ['snuːkəʳ] **1** n Snooker nt. **2** vt **to be** ~**ed** (fig col) festsitzen (col).

snoop [snuːp] **1** n **(a)** = **snooper. (b)** (act) **I'll have a** ~ **around** ich gucke mich mal (ein bißchen) um. **2** vi schnüffeln. **to** ~ **around** herumschnüffeln.

snooper ['snuːpəʳ] n Schnüffler(in f) m.

snooty ['snuːtɪ] adj (+er) (col) hochnäsig.

snooze [snuːz] **1** n Schläfchen, Nickerchen nt. **to have a** ~ ein Schläfchen machen. **2** vi ein Nickerchen machen.

snore [snɔːʳ] **1** n Schnarchen nt no pl. **2** vi schnarchen.

snorkel ['snɔːkl] **1** n Schnorchel m. **2** vi **to go** ~**ling** (Brit) or ~**ing** (US) schnorcheln gehen.

snort [snɔːt] **1** n Schnauben nt no pl; (of boar) Grunzen nt no pl. **he gave a** ~ **of contempt** er schnaubte verächtlich. **2** vti schnauben; (boar) grunzen.

snot [snɒt] n (col) Rotz m (col).

snotty ['snɒtɪ] adj (+er) (col) **(a)** Rotz- (col); child rotznäsig (col). **(b)** (fig: snooty) rotzig (col).

snout [snaʊt] n (of animal) Schnauze f; (col: of person) Rüssel (col).

snow [snəʊ] **1** n **(a)** (also col: cocaine or heroin) Schnee m; (~fall) Schneefall m. **the heavy** ~**s last winter** die heftigen Schneefälle im letzten Winter; **as white as** ~ schneeweiß. **(b)** (TV) Geflimmer nt, Schnee m. **2** vi schneien.

♦ **snow in** vt sep (usu pass) **to be or get** ~**ed in** einschneien.

♦ **snow under** vt sep (col: usu pass) **to be** ~**ed** ~ (with work) reichlich eingedeckt sein; (with requests) überhäuft werden.

snow: ~**ball 1** n Schneeball m; (drink) Snowball m; **2** vi eskalieren; ~ **blindness** n Schneeblindheit f; ~**bound** adj eingeschneit; ~**-capped** adj schneebedeckt; ~**-covered** adj schneebedeckt; ~**drift** n Schneewehe f; ~**drop** n (Bot) Schneeglöckchen nt; ~**fall** n Schneefall m; ~**flake** n Schneeflocke f; ~**man** n Schneemann m; ~**plough**, (US) ~**plow** n (also Ski) Schneepflug m; ~**shoe** n Schneeschuh m; ~**storm** n Schneesturm m; ~**-white** adj schneeweiß.

snowy ['snəʊɪ] adj (+er) **(a)** weather, region schneereich; hills verschneit. **it was very** ~ **yesterday**

gestern hat es viel geschneit. **(b)** *(white as snow)* schneeweiß.

snub [snʌb] **1** *n* Brüskierung *f*. **to give sb a ~** jdn brüskieren, jdn vor den Kopf stoßen; *subordinate, pupil etc (verbally)* jdm über den Mund fahren. **2** *vt* **(a)** *person* brüskieren, vor den Kopf stoßen; *subordinate, pupil (verbally)* über den Mund fahren (+*dat*); *proposal* kurz abtun. **(b)** *(ignore, not greet)* schneiden.

snub: ~**nose** *n* Stupsnase *f*; ~**-nosed** *adj* stupsnasig.

snuff [snʌf] **1** *n* Schnupftabak *m*. **to take ~** schnupfen. **2** *vt candle (extinguish: also ~ out)* auslöschen. **to ~ it** *(Brit col!: die)* abkratzen *(col!).*

snuffle ['snʌfl] **1** *n* Schniefen *nt no pl.* **to have the ~s** *(col)* einen leichten Schnupfen haben. **2** *vi* schnüffeln; *(with cold, from crying)* schniefen.

snug [snʌg] *adj* (+*er*) *(cosy)* behaglich, gemütlich; *bed, garment, room etc* mollig warm; *(sheltered) spot* geschützt; *(close-fitting)* gutsitzend *attr; (tight)* eng. **to be ~ in bed** es im Bett mollig warm haben; **it is a good ~ fit** es paßt gut.

snuggle ['snʌgl] *vi* sich kuscheln. **to ~ down in bed** sich ins Bett kuscheln; **to ~ up (to sb)** sich (an jdn) ankuscheln.

so [səʊ] **1** *adv* **(a)** so. ~ **much tea/ ~ many flies** so viel Tee/so viele Fliegen; **he was ~ stupid (that)** er war so dumm(, daß); **I am not ~ stupid as to believe that** so dumm bin ich nicht, daß ich das glaube(n würde); **would you be ~ kind as to open the door?** wären Sie bitte so freundlich, die Tür zu öffnen?; ~ **great a writer as Shakespeare** ein so großer Dichter wie Shakespeare; **he's not been ~ well recently** in letzter Zeit geht es ihm nicht so sonderlich; **how are things? — not ~ bad!** wie geht's? — nicht schlecht!

(b) *(emphatic)* glad, sorry etc so; *pleased, relieved, hope, wish* sehr; *love* so sehr; *hate* so sehr, derart. **I'm ~ very tired** ich bin ja so müde; **it would be ~ much better** etc es wäre so viel besser *etc*; ~ **much the better/worse (for sb)** um so besser/schlechter (für jdn); **that's ~ kind of you** das ist wirklich sehr nett von Ihnen.

(c) *(replacing longer sentence)* das, es. **I hope ~** hoffentlich; *(emphatic)* das hoffe ich doch sehr; **I think ~** ich glaube schon; **I never said ~** das habe ich nie gesagt; **I told you ~** ich habe es dir doch gesagt; **why should I do it? — because I say ~** warum muß ich das tun? — weil ich es sage, darum; **I didn't say ~** das habe ich nicht gesagt; ~ **I believe** ja, ich glaube schon; ~ **I see** ja, das sehe ich; **please, do ~** bitte(, tun Sie es ruhig); **it may be ~** es kann schon sein; ~ **be it nun gut; if ~ wenn ja; or ~ they say** oder so heißt es jedenfalls; **that is ~** das stimmt; **if that's ~ wenn das stimmt; he's coming by plane — is that ~?** er kommt mit dem Flugzeug — tatsächlich?; **I didn't say that — you did** ~ *(esp US col)* das habe ich nicht gesagt — hast du wohl.

(d) *(thus, in this way)* so. **perhaps it was better ~** vielleicht war es auch besser so; ~ **it was that ... so kam es, daß ...; and ~ it was** und so war es auch; **by ~ doing he has ...** dadurch hat er ..., indem er das tat, hat er ...; ... **and ~ saying** he walked out ... und damit ging er hinaus; **the article is ~ written as to ...** der Artikel ist so geschrieben, daß er ...

(e) *(unspecified amount)* **how high is it? — oh, about ~ high** wie hoch ist das? — oh, ungefähr so; ~ **much per head** soviel pro Kopf; **they looked like ~ many gypsies** sie sahen aus wie Zigeuner; **a week or ~** so eine Woche; **50 or ~** etwa 50.

(f) *(likewise)* auch. ~ **am/would/do/could etc I** ich auch; **he's wrong and ~ are you** ihr irrt euch beide.

(g) he walked past and didn't ~ much as look at me er ging vorbei, ohne mich auch nur anzu-

sehen; ~ **much for that!** *(col)* das wär's ja wohl gewesen! *(col);* ~ **much for him** *(col)* das war ja wohl nichts mit ihm! *(col);* ~ **much for his help** *(col)* schöne Hilfe! *(col).*

2 *conj* **(a)** *(expressing purpose)* damit. ~ **(that) you don't have to do it again** damit Sie es nicht noch einmal machen müssen; **we hurried ~ as not to be late** wir haben uns beeilt, um nicht zu spät zu kommen.

(b) *(expressing result, therefore)* also. **it rained (and) ~ we couldn't go out** es regnete und deshalb konnten wir nicht weggehen; **he was standing in the doorway ~ (that) no-one could get past** er stand in der Tür, so daß niemand vorbeikonnte; **I told him to leave and ~ he did** ich habe ihm gesagt, er solle gehen, und das hat er auch getan; **the roads are busy ~ be careful** es ist viel Verkehr, also sei vorsichtig; ~ **you see ...** wie du siehst, ...

(c) *(in questions, exclamations)* also. ~ **that's his wife/the reason!** das ist also seine Frau/der Grund!; ~ **you did do it!** du hast es also doch gemacht!; ~ **(what)?** *(col)* (na) und?; **I'm not going,** ~ **there!** *(col)* ich geh' nicht, fertig, aus!

soak [səʊk] **1** *vt* *(wet)* durchnässen. **to be/get ~ed** völlig durchnäßt sein/werden; **to be ~ed to the skin, to be ~ed through** bis auf die Haut durchnäßt sein. **2** *vi* **(a)** *(steep)* **leave it to ~** weichen Sie es ein; *(in dye)* lassen Sie die Farbe einziehen; **to ~ in a bath** sich in der Badewanne aalen *(col).* **(b)** *(penetrate)* **rain has ~ed through the ceiling** der Regen ist durch die Decke gesickert; **the coffee was ~ing into the carpet** der Kaffee saugte sich in den Teppich.

♦ **soak in** *vi (stain, dye etc)* einziehen.

♦ **soak up** *vt sep liquid* aufsaugen; *sunshine* genießen; *sound* schlucken; *(fig) information* aufsaugen, in sich *(acc)* aufnehmen.

soaking ['səʊkɪŋ] **1** *adj* klitschnaß *(col)*, patschnaß *(col).* **2** *adv* ~ **wet** triefend naß, klitschnaß *(col);* **a ~ wet day** ein völlig verregneter Tag. **3** *n* **to get a ~** patschnaß werden *(col).*

so-and-so ['səʊənsəʊ] *n (col)* **(a)** *(unspecified)* ~ **up at the shop** Herr/Frau Soundso im Laden. **(b)** *(pej)* **he's an old ~** das ist ein gemeiner Kerl.

soap [səʊp] **1** *n* Seife *f.* **2** *vt* einseifen, abseifen.

soap: ~**box** *n (lit: packing case)* Seifenkiste *f; (fig: platform)* Apfelsinenkiste *f;* ~**flakes** *npl* Seifenflocken *pl;* ~ **opera** *n (TV, Rad)* Fernseh-/Hörspielserie, Seifenoper *(col) f;* ~ **powder** *n* Seifenpulver *nt;* ~**suds** *npl (foam)* Seifenschaum *m.*

soapy ['səʊpɪ] *adj* (+*er*) seifig.

soar [sɔːʳ] *vi* **(a)** *(rise: also ~ up)* aufsteigen; *(bird also)* sich in die Lüfte schwingen. **to ~ (up) into the sky** zum Himmel steigen. **(b)** *(fig) (building)* hochragen; *(price)* hochschnellen; *(popularity, hopes)* einen Aufschwung nehmen.

soaring ['sɔːrɪŋ] *adj* bird, plane in die Luft steigend; *tower* hoch aufragend; *imagination* hochfliegend; *popularity* schnell zunehmend; *prices* in die Höhe schnellend; *inflation* unaufhaltsam; *hopes* wachsend.

sob [sɒb] **1** *n* Schluchzer *m*, Schluchzen *nt no pl.* **to give a ~** (auf)schluchzen; **..., he said with a ~ ...,** sagte er schluchzend. **2** *vi* schluchzen *(with vor* +*dat).* **3** *vt* **to ~ one's heart out** sich *(dat)* die Seele aus dem Leib weinen.

sober ['səʊbəʳ] *adj* **(a)** *(not drunk)* nüchtern. **to be as ~ as a judge** stocknüchtern sein *(col).* **(b)** *(sedate, serious)* life, mood, occasion ernst; *(sensible, moderate)* opinion, judgement vernünftig; *assessment, facts* nüchtern. **(c)** *(not bright or showy)* nüchtern, gedeckt.

♦ **sober up 1** *vt sep (lit)* nüchtern machen; *(fig)* zur Vernunft bringen. **2** *vi (lit)* nüchtern werden; *(fig)* zur Vernunft kommen; *(after laughing etc)* sich beruhigen.

soberly ['səʊbəlɪ] *adv* nüchtern; *behave* vernünf-

tig; *dress, furnish* schlicht.
sobriety [sə'braɪtɪ] *n* **(a)** *(not being drunk)* Nüchternheit *f*. **(b)** *(seriousness, sedateness)* Solidität *f*; *(of dress)* Schlichtheit *f*; *(of colour)* Gedecktheit *f*.
soc = **society** Ges.
so-called ['səʊ'kɔːld] *adj* sogenannt; *(supposed)* angeblich.
soccer ['sɒkəʳ] *n* Fußball *m*. ~ **player** Fußballer, Fußballspieler(in *f*) *m*.
sociable ['səʊʃəbl] *adj* *(gregarious)* gesellig; *(friendly)* freundlich. ... **just to be ~** ..., man möchte sich ja nicht ausschließen; **I'm not feeling very ~ today** mir ist heute nicht nach Geselligkeit (zumute).
social ['səʊʃəl] **1** *adj* **(a)** *(relating to community, Admin, Pol)* sozial; *history, reform, legislation, policy* Sozial-; *system, realism* Gesellschafts-; *structure, conditions, evils also* gesellschaftlich. **the ~ services** die Sozialeinrichtungen *pl*.
(b) *engagements, life, superior* gesellschaftlich; *behaviour* in Gesellschaft; *advancement, status also* sozial. ~ **climber** Emporkömmling *m* (*pej*), sozialer Aufsteiger; **there isn't much ~ life around here** hier in der Gegend läuft nicht viel; **a job which leaves no time for one's ~ life** ein Beruf, bei dem man keine Zeit für Freizeitaktivitäten hat.
(c) *(gregarious) evening, person* gesellig; *(living in groups) animals* gesellig lebend.
2 *n* geselliger Abend.
social: ~ **democratic** *adj* sozialdemokratisch; ~ **insurance** *n (US)* Sozialversicherung *f*.
socialism ['səʊʃəlɪzəm] *n* Sozialismus *m*.
socialist ['səʊʃəlɪst] **1** *adj* sozialistisch. **2** *n* Sozialist(in *f*) *m*.
socialite ['səʊʃəlaɪt] *n (col)* Angehörige(r) *mf* der Schickeria (*col*); *(man also)* Salonlöwe *m (col)*.
socialize ['səʊʃəlaɪz] **1** *vt* sozialisieren; *means of production* vergesellschaften. **2** *vi* **to ~ with sb** *(meet socially)* mit jdm gesellschaftlich verkehren; *(chat to)* sich mit jdm unterhalten; **she ~s a lot** sie hat ein reges gesellschaftliches Leben.
socially ['səʊʃəlɪ] *adv* gesellschaftlich; *deprived etc* sozial; *meet* privat.
social: ~ **science** *n* Sozialwissenschaft *f*; ~ **security** *n* Sozialhilfe *f*; *(scheme)* Sozialversicherung *f*; **to be on ~ security** Sozialhilfeempfänger sein; ~ **work** *n* Sozialarbeit *f*; ~ **worker** *n* Sozialarbeiter(in *f*) *m*.
society [sə'saɪətɪ] *n* **(a)** Gesellschaft *f*. **modern industrial ~** die moderne Industriegesellschaft. **(b)** *(club, organization)* Verein *m*; *(learned, Comm)* Gesellschaft *f*.
society *in cpds* Gesellschafts-; ~ **column** *n* Gesellschaftsspalte *f*.
socio- [ˌsəʊsɪəʊ-] *pref* sozio-. ~**economic** sozioökonomisch.
sociological [ˌsəʊsɪə'lɒdʒɪkəl] *adj* soziologisch.
sociologist [ˌsəʊsɪ'ɒlədʒɪst] *n* Soziologe *m*, Soziologin *f*.
sociology [ˌsəʊsɪ'ɒlədʒɪ] *n* Soziologie *f*.
sock[1] ['sɒk] *n* Socke *f*, Socken *m (col)*; *(knee-length)* Kniestrumpf *m*. **to pull one's ~s up** *(col)* sich am Riemen reißen *(col)*.
sock[2] **1** *n (col)* Schlag *m* (mit der Faust). **to give sb a ~ in the eye** jdm eine aufs Auge verpassen *(col)*. **2** *vt (col: hit)* hauen *(col)*. ~ **him one!** knall ihm eine! *(col)*.
socket ['sɒkɪt] *n* **(a)** *(of eye)* Augenhöhle *f*; *(of joint)* Gelenkpfanne *f*; *(of tooth)* Zahnhöhle *f*. **(b)** *(Brit Elec)* Steckdose *f*; *(for lightbulb)* Fassung *f*; *(Mech)* Sockel *m*, Fassung *f*.
sod[1] [sɒd] *n (turf)* Grassode *f*.
sod[2] *n (Brit col!)* Sau *f (col!)*. **the poor ~s** die armen Schweine *(col)*.
soda ['səʊdə] *n* **(a)** *(Chem)* Soda *nt*; *(sodium oxide)* Natriumoxyd *nt*. **(b)** *(drink)* Soda(wasser) *nt*.

soda: ~**-fountain** *n (US: café)* Erfrischungshalle *f*; ~ **siphon** *n* Siphon *m*; ~**-water** *n* Sodawasser *nt*.
sodden ['sɒdn] *adj* durchnäßt.
sodium ['səʊdɪəm] *n* Natrium *nt*. ~ **chloride** Natriumchlorid, Kochsalz *nt*.
sodomy ['sɒdəmɪ] *n* Analverkehr *m*.
sofa ['səʊfə] *n* Sofa *nt*, Couch *f*.
soft [sɒft] *adj (+er)* **(a)** weich; *meat* zart; *(pej: flabby) muscle* schlaff. ~ **currency** weiche Währung. **(b)** *(smooth) skin* zart; *surface* glatt; *material* weich. **(c)** *(gentle, not harsh)* sanft; *(subdued) music* gedämpft; *(not loud)* leise; *rain, breeze, tap, steps* leicht. **(d)** *character, government* schwach; *treatment, teacher* nachsichtig; *punishment* mild(e). **to be ~ on sb** jdm gegenüber nachgiebig sein. **(e)** *(easy) job, life* bequem. **that's a ~ option** das ist der Weg des geringsten Widerstandes. **(f)** *drink* alkoholfrei; *drug, pornography* weich. **(g)** *(col: foolish)* doof *(col)*. **you must be ~!** du spinnst wohl! *(col)*. **(h)** *(col: feeling affection)* **to be ~ on sb** für jdn schwärmen; **to have a ~ spot for sb** eine Schwäche für jdn haben.
soft-boiled ['sɒft,bɔɪld] *adj* egg weich(gekocht).
soften ['sɒfn] **1** *vt* weich machen; *light, sound, colour* dämpfen; *effect, sb's anger, reaction, impression* mildern; *outline* weicher machen; *resistance* schwächen; *person* verweichlichen. **to ~ the blow** *(fig)* den Schock mildern. **2** *vi (material, person, heart)* weich werden; *(voice, look)* sanft werden; *(anger, resistance)* nachlassen.
softener ['sɒfnəʳ] *n (for water)* Enthärtungsmittel *nt*; *(fabric ~)* Weichspülmittel *nt*.
soft-hearted [ˌsɒft'hɑːtɪd] *adj* weichherzig.
softie ['sɒftɪ] *n (col)* Softy *m (col)*; *(weakling)* Weichling *m*.
softly ['sɒftlɪ] *adv (gently, tenderly)* sanft; *(not loud)* leise; *rain, blow* leicht.
softness ['sɒftnɪs] *n see adj* **(a)** Weichheit *f*; Zartheit *f*; Schlaffheit *f*. **(b)** Zartheit *f*; Glätte *f*; Weichheit *f*. **(c)** Sanftheit *f*; Gedämpftheit *f*; leiser Klang; Leichtheit *f*. **(d)** Schwäche *f*; Nachsichtigkeit *f*; Milde *f*. **(e)** Bequemlichkeit *f*.
soft: ~**-pedal** *vt* zurückstecken; ~ **sell** *n* weiche Verkaufstaktik, Soft selling *nt*; ~**-soap** *(fig)* **1** *n* Schmeichelei *f*; **2** *vt* einseifen *(col)*; ~**-spoken** *adj person* leise sprechend *attr*; **to be ~-spoken** leise sprechen; ~ **touch** *n* **to be a ~ touch** nachgiebig sein; ~ **toy** *n* Stofftier *nt*; ~ **verge** *n* "~ verges" „Seitenstreifen nicht befahrbar"; ~**ware** *n* Software *f*.
softy *n (col)* = **softie**.
soggy ['sɒgɪ] *adj (+er)* durchnäßt, triefnaß; *soil* durchweicht; *food* matschig *(col)*.
soil[1] [sɔɪl] *n (earth, ground)* Erde *f*, Erdreich *nt*, Boden *m*. **cover it with ~** bedecken Sie es mit Erde; **native/foreign ~** heimatlicher/fremder Boden; **the ~** *(fig: farmland)* die Scholle.
soil[2] *vt (lit, fig)* beschmutzen; *honour* beflecken; *oneself* besudeln; *minds* verderben. **2** *vi* schmutzig werden.
soiled [sɔɪld] *adj* schmutzig, verschmutzt.
solar ['səʊləʳ] *adj* Sonnen-. ~ **cell** Solarzelle *f*; ~ **eclipse** Sonnenfinsternis *f*; ~ **energy** Sonnenenergie *f*; ~ **panel** Sonnenkollektor *m*; ~ **plexus** Magengrube *f*; ~ **system** Sonnensystem *nt*.
solarium [səʊ'lɛərɪəm] *n, pl* **solaria** [səʊ'lɛərɪə] Solarium *nt*.
sold [səʊld] *pret, ptp of* **sell**.
solder ['səʊldəʳ] **1** *n* Lötmittel *nt*. **2** *vt* löten; *(~ together)* verlöten.
soldering-iron ['səʊldərɪŋ'aɪən] *n* Lötkolben *m*.
soldier ['səʊldʒəʳ] **1** *n* Soldat *m*. **old ~** altgedienter Soldat; *(fig)* alter Kämpe. **2** *vi* Soldat sein.
♦ **soldier on** *vi* unermüdlich weitermachen.
sole[1] [səʊl] **1** *n* Sohle *f*. **2** *vt* besohlen.
sole[2] *n (fish)* Seezunge *f*.
sole[3] *adj* einzig; *heir also, agency* Allein-; *rights* alleinig.

solely ['səʊlɪ] adv (einzig und) allein, nur. **she is ~ responsible** sie allein trägt die Verantwortung.

solemn ['sɒləm] adj feierlich; person, plea, warning ernst; architecture erhaben; promise, oath heilig; (drab) colour trist.

solemnity [sə'lemnɪtɪ] n see adj Feierlichkeit f; Ernst m; Erhabenheit f; heiliger Ernst; Tristheit f.

solemnize ['sɒləmnaɪz] vt to ~ a marriage eine Trauung feierlich vollziehen.

solemnly ['sɒləmlɪ] adv feierlich; walk gemessenen Schrittes; look, warn, plead ernst; promise hoch und heilig; swear bei allem, was einem heilig ist.

solenoid ['səʊlənɔɪd] n Magnetspule f.

solicit [sə'lɪsɪt] 1 vt support etc bitten um; person inständig bitten; votes werben; (prostitute) ansprechen. 2 vi (prostitute) Kunden anwerben.

solicitor [sə'lɪsɪtə'] n (Jur) (Brit) Rechtsanwalt m/-anwältin f (der/die nicht vor Gericht plädiert); (US) Justizbeamte(r) m/-beamtin f.

solicitous [sə'lɪsɪtəs] adj (form) (concerned) besorgt (about um); (eager) dienstbeflissen. **to be ~ to do sth** eifrig darauf bedacht sein, etw zu tun.

solid ['sɒlɪd] 1 adj (a) (firm, not liquid) fuel, food, substance fest. **~ body** Festkörper m; **to be frozen ~** hartgefroren sein.
(b) (pure, not hollow, not broken) block, gold, rock massiv; matter fest; crowd etc dicht; row ununterbrochen; line of people etc geschlossen; week ganz. **the square was packed ~ with cars** die Autos standen dicht an dicht auf dem Platz; **for two ~ days or for two days ~** zwei Tage ununterbrochen.
(c) (stable, secure) bridge, house, car, relationship stabil; piece of work, character, education solide; foundations also, (lit, fig) ground fest; business solide, reell. **a good ~ meal** eine kräftige Mahlzeit.
(d) reason, argument handfest, stichhaltig; grounds fundiert.
(e) (unanimous) vote einstimmig; support geschlossen. **Newtown is ~ for Labour** Newtown wählt fast ausschließlich Labour.
2 n (a) fester Stoff. **~s and liquids** feste und flüssige Stoffe pl; (Sci) Festkörper und Flüssigkeiten pl. (b) (usu pl: food) feste Nahrung no pl.

solidarity [‚sɒlɪ'dærɪtɪ] n Solidarität f.

solidify [sə'lɪdɪfaɪ] 1 vi fest werden; (lava etc) erstarren; (fig: support) sich festigen. 2 vt see vi fest werden lassen; erstarren lassen; festigen.

solidly ['sɒlɪdlɪ] adv (a) (firmly) secured fest. **~ built** house solide gebaut; person kräftig gebaut.
(b) (uninterruptedly) work ununterbrochen. (c) vote einstimmig; support geschlossen. **to be ~ behind sb** geschlossen hinter jdm stehen.

solid-state ['sɒlɪd'steɪt] adj Festkörper-; (Elec) Halbleiter-.

soliloquy [sə'lɪləkwɪ] n Monolog m (also Theat).

solitaire [‚sɒlɪ'teə'] n (game, gem) Solitär m.

solitary ['sɒlɪtərɪ] adj (a) (alone, secluded) life, person einsam; place also abgeschieden. **a few ~ houses** ein paar vereinzelte Häuser; **in ~ confinement** in Einzelhaft. (b) (sole) case, example einzig. **not a ~ one** kein einziger.

solitude ['sɒlɪtjuːd] n Einsamkeit f; (of place also) Abgeschiedenheit f.

solo ['səʊləʊ] 1 n Solo nt. 2 adj flight Allein-; violinist Solo-. 3 adv allein; (Mus) solo. **to fly ~** einen Alleinflug machen.

soloist ['səʊləʊɪst] n Solist(in f) m.

solstice ['sɒlstɪs] n Sonnenwende f.

soluble ['sɒljʊbl] adj (a) löslich. **~ in water** wasserlöslich. (b) problem lösbar.

solution [sə'luːʃən] n (a) Lösung f (to gen); (of crime) Aufklärung f. (b) (Chem) Lösung f.

solve [sɒlv] vt problem, equation lösen; mystery

enträtseln; crime aufklären.

solvency ['sɒlvənsɪ] n (Fin) Zahlungsfähigkeit, Solvenz f.

solvent ['sɒlvənt] 1 adj (a) (Chem) lösend; agent Lösungs-. (b) (Fin) zahlungsfähig, solvent. 2 n (Chem) Lösungsmittel nt. **~ abuse** Lösungsmittelmißbrauch m, Schnüffeln nt (col).

sombre, (US) somber ['sɒmbə'] adj (dark) dunkel; (gloomy) düster.

some [sʌm] 1 adj (a) (with plural nouns) einige; (a few, emphatic) ein paar; (any: in "if" clauses, questions) usu not translated. **if you have ~ questions** wenn Sie Fragen haben; **did you bring ~ records?** hast du Schallplatten mitgebracht?; **~ records of mine** einige meiner Platten; **would you like ~ more biscuits?** möchten Sie noch (ein paar) Kekse?; **~ few people** einige wenige Leute.
(b) (with singular nouns) etwas, usu not translated; (a little, emph) etwas, ein bißchen. **there's ~ ink on your shirt** Sie haben Tinte auf dem Hemd; **would you like ~ cheese?** möchten Sie (etwas) Käse?; **~ more tea?** möchten Sie noch (etwas) Tee?; **leave ~ cake for me** laß mir ein Stück Kuchen übrig.
(c) (certain, in contrast) manche(r, s). **~ people say ...** manche Leute sagen ...; **in ~ ways** in gewisser Weise; **to ~ extent** in gewissem Maße.
(d) (vague, indeterminate) irgendein. **~ book/man or other** irgendein Buch/Mann; **~ woman rang up** da hat eine Frau angerufen; **in ~ way or another** irgendwie; **or ~ such** oder so etwas ähnliches; **or ~ such name** oder so ein ähnlicher Name; **~ time before midnight** irgendwann vor Mitternacht; **~ time or other** irgendwann einmal; **~ other time** ein andermal; **~ day** eines Tages; **~ day next week** irgendwann nächste Woche.
(e) (intensifier) ziemlich; (in exclamations) vielleicht ein (col). **(that was) ~ party!** das war vielleicht eine Party! (col); **this might take ~ time** das könnte einige Zeit dauern; **quite ~ time** ziemlich lange; **to speak at ~ length** ziemlich lange sprechen; **it's ~ distance from the house** es ist ziemlich weit vom Haus entfernt.
(f) (iro) vielleicht ein (col). **~ experts!** das sind vielleicht Experten! (col); **~ help you are/this is** du bist/das ist mir vielleicht eine Hilfe (col); **~ people!** Leute gibt's!
2 pron (a) (~ people) einige; (certain people) manche; (in "if" clauses, questions) welche. **~ ..., others ...** manche ..., andere ...; **~ of my friends** einige meiner Freunde; **there are still ~ who will never understand** es gibt immer noch Leute, die das nicht begreifen werden; **do you have ~?** haben Sie welche?
(b) (referring to plural nouns) (a few) einige; (certain ones) manche; (in "if" clauses, questions) welche. **~ of these books** einige dieser Bücher; **they're lovely, try ~** die schmecken gut, probieren Sie mal; **if I've still got ~** wenn ich noch welche habe.
(c) (referring to singular nouns) (a little) etwas; (a certain amount, in contrast) manches; (in "if" clauses, questions) welche(r, s). **I drank ~ of the milk** ich habe (etwas) von der Milch getrunken; **have ~!** nehmen Sie sich (dat), bedienen Sie sich; **it's good cake, would you like ~?** das ist ein guter Kuchen, möchten Sie welchen?; **would you like ~ tea? — no, I've got ~** möchten Sie Tee? — nein, ich habe noch; **~ of it had been eaten** einiges (davon) war gegessen worden; **this is ~ of the finest scenery in Scotland** dies ist eine der schönsten Landschaften Schottlands.
3 adv (a) ungefähr, etwa, zirka. **~ 20 people** ungefähr 20 Leute; **~ few difficulties** einige Schwierigkeiten. (b) (US col) (a little) etwas, ein bißchen; (a lot) viel. **he's traveling ~** er fährt

schnell; *that's going* ~ das ist ganz schön schnell *(col)*.

somebody ['sʌmbədɪ] **1** *pron* jemand; *(dir obj)* jemand(en); *(indir obj)* jemandem. ~ **else** jemand anders; ~ **or other** irgend jemand; ~ **knocked at the door** es klopfte jemand an die Tür; **we need** ~ **German** wir brauchen einen Deutschen; **everybody needs** ~ **to talk to** jeder braucht einen, mit dem er sprechen kann. **2** *n* **to be** ~ wer *(col)* or jemand sein.

somehow ['sʌmhaʊ] *adv* irgendwie. **it must be done** ~ **or other** es muß irgendwie gemacht werden.

someone ['sʌmwʌn] *pron* = **somebody 1.**

someplace ['sʌmpleɪs] *adv (US col)* be irgendwo; go irgendwohin.

somersault ['sʌməsɔːlt] **1** *n* Purzelbaum *m*; *(Sport, fig)* Salto *m*. **to do a** ~ einen Purzelbaum schlagen/einen Salto machen; *(car)* sich überschlagen. **2** *vi (person)* einen Purzelbaum schlagen; *(Sport)* einen Salto machen; *(car)* sich überschlagen.

something ['sʌmθɪŋ] **1** *pron* etwas. ~ **serious** *etc* etwas Ernstes; ~ **or other** irgend etwas, irgendwas; ~ **of the kind** so (et)was Ähnliches; **she has a certain** ~ sie hat ein gewisses Etwas; **there's** ~ **in what you say** an dem, was du sagst, ist (schon) was dran; **well, that's** ~ das ist immerhin etwas; **she's called Rachel** ~ sie heißt Rachel Soundso; **it was** ~ **else** *or* **quite** ~ das war schon toll *(col)*; **or** ~ *(col)* oder so (was); **are you drunk or** ~? *(col)* bist du betrunken oder was? *(col)*.

2 *adv* **(a)** ~ **over 200** etwas über 200; ~ **like 200** ungefähr 200; **you look** ~ **like him** du siehst ihm irgendwie ähnlich; **this is** ~ **like the one I wanted** so (et)was Ähnliches wollte ich haben. **(b) it's** ~ **of a problem** das ist schon ein Problem; **I feel** ~ **of a stranger here** ich fühle mich hier irgendwie fremd; **he's** ~ **of a musician** er ist ein recht guter Musiker; ~ **of a surprise/drunkard** eine ziemliche Überraschung/ein ziemlicher Säufer. **(c)** *(dial)* **the weather was** ~ **shocking** das Wetter war einfach schrecklich.

sometime ['sʌmtaɪm] **1** *adv* irgendwann. **write to me** ~ **soon** schreib mir (doch) bald (ein)mal; ~ **next year** irgendwann nächstes Jahr. **2** *adj attr (form)* früher, einstig.

sometimes ['sʌmtaɪmz] *adv* manchmal.

somewhat ['sʌmwɒt] *adv* ein wenig. ~ **of a surprise** eine ziemliche Überraschung.

somewhere ['sʌmwɛəʳ] *adv* **(a)** be irgendwo; go irgendwohin. **I left it** ~ **or other** ich habe es irgendwo liegen-/stehenlassen; **I know** ~ **where** ... ich weiß, wo ... **(b)** *(fig)* ~ **about £50,** ~ **in the region of £50** um (die) £ 50 herum; **she is** ~ **in her fifties** sie muß in den Fünfzigern sein; ~ **between midnight and one o'clock** irgendwann zwischen Mitternacht und ein Uhr.

somnambulist [sɒm'næmbjʊlɪst] *n* Schlafwandler(in *f*) *m*.

somnolent ['sɒmnələnt] *adj* **(a)** *(sleepy)* schläfrig. **(b)** *(causing sleep)* einschläfernd.

son [sʌn] *n (lit, fig)* Sohn *m*; *(as address)* mein Junge.

sonar ['səʊnɑːʳ] *n* Sonar(gerät), Echolot *nt*.

sonata [sə'nɑːtə] *n* Sonate *f*.

song [sɒŋ] *n* Lied *nt*; *(folk~ also, blues-~)* Song *m*; *(singing)* Gesang *m*. **to burst into** ~ ein Lied anstimmen; **to make a** ~ **and dance about sth** *(col)* eine Haupt- und Staatsaktion aus etw machen *(col)*; **to buy sth for a** ~ *(col)* etw für ein Butterbrot kaufen.

song: ~**bird** *n* Singvogel *m*; ~**book** *n* Liederbuch *nt*.

songwriter ['sɒŋˌraɪtəʳ] *n* Texter(in *f*) und Komponist(in *f*) *m*; *(of modern ballads)* Liedermacher(in *f*) *m*.

sonic ['sɒnɪk] *adj* Schall-. ~ **boom** Überschallknall *m*.

son-in-law ['sʌnɪnlɔː] *n*, *pl* **sons-in-law** Schwiegersohn *m*.

sonnet ['sɒnɪt] *n* Sonett *nt*.

sonny ['sʌnɪ] *n (col)* (mein) Junge *m*.

sonority [sə'nɒrɪtɪ] *n* Klangfülle *f*.

sonorous ['sɒnərəs] *adj* volltönend, sonor *(geh)*; *language, poem* klangvoll.

soon [suːn] *adv* **(a)** *(in a short time from now)* bald; *(early)* früh; *(quickly)* schnell. **it will** ~ **be Christmas** bald ist Weihnachten; ~ **after his death** kurz nach seinem Tode; ~ **afterwards** kurz *or* bald danach; **how** ~ **can you be ready?** wann kannst du fertig sein?; **how** ~ **is the next performance?** wann fängt die nächste Vorstellung an?; **we got there too** ~ wir kamen zu früh an; **he** ~ **changed his mind** er blieb nicht lange bei seiner Meinung; **all too** ~ viel zu schnell; **we were none too** ~ wir kamen gerade rechtzeitig; **as** ~ **as** sobald; **as** ~ **as possible** so schnell wie möglich. **(b) I would as** ~ **not go** *(prefer not to)* ich würde lieber nicht gehen; **I would as** ~ **you didn't tell him** es wäre mir lieber, wenn du es ihm nicht erzählen würdest.

sooner ['suːnəʳ] *adv* **(a)** *(time)* früher. ~ **or later** früher oder später; **the** ~ **the better** je eher *or* früher, desto besser; **no** ~ **had we arrived than** ... wir waren kaum angekommen, da ...; **no** ~ **said than done** gesagt, getan. **(b)** *(preference)* lieber. **I would** ~ **not do it** ich würde es lieber nicht tun.

soot [sʊt] *n* Ruß *m*. **black as** ~ rußschwarz.

soothe [suːð] *vt* beruhigen; *pain* lindern, mildern.

soothing ['suːðɪŋ] *adj* beruhigend; *(pain-relieving)* schmerzlindernd; *massage* wohltuend.

sooty ['sʊtɪ] *adj (+er)* rußig; *deposit* Ruß-.

sop [sɒp] *n* **(a)** *(food)* eingetunktes Brotstück. **(b)** *(to placate)* **as a** ~ zur Beschwichtigung.

sophisticated [sə'fɪstɪkeɪtɪd] *adj* **(a)** *(worldly, cultivated)* kultiviert; *person, restaurant also* gepflegt, elegant; *dress* raffiniert, schick. **(b)** *(complex, advanced)* hochentwickelt; *method also* durchdacht; *device also* ausgeklügelt. **(c)** *(subtle, refined)* subtil; *prose, style also, discussion* anspruchsvoll; *plan* ausgeklügelt, raffiniert; *system* differenziert.

sophistication [sə,fɪstɪkeɪʃən] *n see adj* **(a)** Kultiviertheit *f*; Gepflegtheit, Eleganz *f*; Raffiniertheit *f*, Schick *m*. **(b)** hoher Entwicklungsstand; Durchdachtheit *f*; Ausgeklügeltheit *f*. **(c)** Subtilität *f*; hohe Ansprüche *pl*; Ausgeklügeltheit, Raffiniertheit *f*; Differenziertheit *f*.

sophomore ['sɒfəmɔːʳ] *n (US)* Student(in *f*) *m* im 2. Jahr.

soporific [,sɒpə'rɪfɪk] *adj* einschläfernd.

sopping ['sɒpɪŋ] *adj (also* ~ **wet)** durchnäßt; *person* klitschnaß *(col)*.

soppy ['sɒpɪ] *adj (col) (sentimental)* book, song schmalzig *(col)*; *person* sentimental; *look* schmachtend; *(effeminate)* weibisch; *(silly)* doof *(col)*.

soprano [sə'prɑːnəʊ] **1** *n (also part)* Sopran *m*; *(person also)* Sopranist(in *f*) *m*. **2** *adj* Sopran-. **3** *adv* im Sopran.

sorbet ['sɔːbeɪ] *n* Fruchteis *nt*.

sorcerer ['sɔːsərəʳ] *n* Hexenmeister, Hexer *m*.

sorcery ['sɔːsərɪ] *n* Hexerei *f*.

sordid ['sɔːdɪd] *adj* eklig; *place also* verkommen; *motive* niedrig; *conditions, life, story* erbärmlich; *crime* gemein.

sore [sɔːʳ] **1** *adj (+er)* **(a)** *(hurting)* weh; *(inflamed)* wund, entzündet. **to have a** ~ **throat** Halsschmerzen haben; **my eyes are** ~ mir tun die Augen weh. **(b)** *(fig)* **a** ~ **point** ein wunder Punkt. **(c)** *(col: angry, upset)* verärgert, sauer *(col) (about sth* über etw *(acc), at sb* über jdn). **now don't get** ~ at me werd doch nicht gleich sauer! *(col)*. **2** *n* wunde Stelle. **to open old** ~**s** *(fig)* alte Wunden aufreißen.

sorely ['sɔːlɪ] *adv tempted* sehr, arg *(S Ger, Aus, Sw); needed* dringend; *missed* schmerzlich; *(liter) afflicted, offended* zutiefst; *wounded* schwer.

sorrel ['sɒrəl] *n* **(a)** *(Bot)* Sauerampfer *m; (wood-~)* Sauerklee *m.* **(b)** *(horse)* Fuchs *m.*

sorrow ['sɒrəʊ] *n (no pl: sadness)* Traurigkeit *f; (no pl: grief)* Kummer *m; (care)* Sorge, Kümmernis *f; (affliction)* Leiden *nt.* **this was a great ~ to me** das hat mir großen Kummer bereitet; **her ~ at his death** ihre Trauer über seinen Tod; **to drown one's ~s** seine Sorgen ertränken.

sorrowful ['sɒrəʊfʊl] *adj* traurig.

sorry ['sɒrɪ] *adj* (+*er*) **(a)** *pred (sad)* traurig. **this work is no good, I'm ~ to say** diese Arbeit taugt nichts, das muß ich leider sagen; **to feel ~ for sb/oneself** jdn/sich selbst bemitleiden; **I feel ~ for the child** das Kind tut mir leid; **you'll be ~ for this!** das wird dir noch leid tun! **(b)** *(in apologizing)* ~! Entschuldigung!, Verzeihung!; **I'm ~** es tut mir leid; **can you lend me £5?** — **~** kannst du mir £5 leihen? — bedaure, leider nicht; **~?** *(pardon)* wie bitte?; **to say ~ (to sb for sth)** sich (bei jdm für etw) entschuldigen; **I'm ~ about that vase/um Ihren Hund.** **(c)** *(pitiful) condition, plight* traurig; *excuse* faul.

sort [sɔːt] **1** *n* **(a)** *(kind)* Art *f; (species, type, model also)* Sorte *f.* **a ~ of** ... eine Art ..., so ein(e) ...; **this ~ of house** diese Art Haus; **what ~ of** was für ein; **he's not the ~ of man to do that** er ist nicht der Mensch, der das täte; **this ~ of thing** so etwas; **all ~s of things** alles mögliche; **people of all ~s** alle möglichen Leute; **he's a painter of a ~** *or* **of ~s** er ist Maler, sozusagen; **something of the ~** (irgend) so (et)was; **nothing of the ~!** von wegen!; **you'll do nothing of the ~!** das wirst du schön bleiben lassen! **(b)** *(person)* **he's a good ~** er ist ein prima Kerl; **he's not my ~** er ist nicht mein Typ; **I don't trust his ~** solchen Leuten traue ich nicht; **I know your ~** euch Brüder kenn' ich! *(col);* **it takes all ~s (to make a world)** es gibt solche und solche. **(c)** **to be out of ~s** nicht ganz auf der Höhe sein.

2 *adv* **~ of** *(col)* irgendwie; **it's ~ of heavy** es ist irgendwie schwer *(col);* **is this how he did it?** — **well, ~ of** hat er das so gemacht? — ja, so ungefähr.

3 *vt (also Comp)* sortieren.

♦ **sort out** *vt sep* **(a)** *(arrange)* sortieren; *(select)* aussortieren. **to ~ sth ~ from sth** etw von etw trennen. **(b)** *(straighten out) muddle* in Ordnung bringen; *problem* lösen; *situation* klären. **the problem will ~ itself ~** das Problem wird sich von selbst lösen; **to ~ oneself ~** zur Ruhe kommen. **(c)** *(col)* **to ~ sb ~** sich *(dat)* jdn vorknöpfen *(col).*

sortie ['sɔːtɪ] *n (Mil)* Ausfall *m; (Aviat)* (Einzel)einsatz *m.*

sorting office ['sɔːtɪŋ'ɒfɪs] *n* Sortierstelle *f.*

SOS *n* SOS *nt.*

so-so ['səʊ'səʊ] *adj pred, adv (col)* so la la.

soufflé ['suːfleɪ] *n* Soufflé *nt.*

sought [sɔːt] *pret, ptp of* **seek.**

sought-after ['sɔːtɑːftə^r] *adj* begehrt. **much ~** vielbegehrt; *rare object* gesucht.

soul [səʊl] *n* **(a)** Seele *f.* **All S~s' Day** Allerheiligen *nt;* **God rest his ~!** Gott hab ihn selig! **(b)** *(inner being)* Innerste(s), Wesen *nt; (finer feelings)* Herz, Gefühl *nt.* **he loved her with all his ~** er liebte sie von ganzem Herzen. **(c)** *(person)* Seele *f.* **poor ~!** *(col)* Ärmste(r)!; **not a ~** keine Menschenseele; **the ship was lost with all ~s** das Schiff ging mit allen Passagieren unter; **he's the ~ of discretion** er ist die Diskretion in Person. **(d)** *(music)* Soul *m.*

soul-destroying ['səʊldɪ,strɔɪɪŋ] *adj* geisttötend; *factory work etc* nervtötend.

soulful ['səʊlfʊl] *adj look* seelenvoll; *person* ge-

fühlvoll.

soul: **~mate** *n* **they are ~mates** sie sind verwandte Seelen; **~-searching** *n* Gewissensprüfung *f.*

sound¹ [saʊnd] **1** *adj* (+*er*) **(a)** *(in good condition) person, animal* gesund; *condition, building, appliance* einwandfrei. **to be as ~ as a bell** kerngesund sein; **to be of ~ mind** *(esp Jur)* bei klarem Verstand sein, im Vollbesitz seiner geistigen Kräfte sein *(Jur).* **(b)** *(valid, dependable)* solide; *argument, analysis also* vernünftig, fundiert; *economy also* stabil; *person* verläßlich; *idea, move, advice* vernünftig. **to be ~ on sth** *(have good knowledge)* gründliche Kenntnisse in etw *(dat)* haben. **(c)** *(thorough)* gründlich; *beating* gehörig; *defeat* vernichtend. **(d)** *(Jur) decision* rechtmäßig. **(e)** *(deep) sleep* tief, fest. **2** *adv* (+*er*) **to be ~ asleep** fest schlafen.

sound² **1** *n* *(noise)* Geräusch *nt; (Ling)* Laut *m; (Phys)* Schall *m; (Mus, of instruments)* Klang *m; (TV, Rad)* Ton *m.* **don't make a ~** still!; **the speed of ~** (die) Schallgeschwindigkeit; **within ~ of** in Hörweite (+*gen);* **to the ~(s) of the national anthem** zu den Klängen der Nationalhymne; **not a ~ was to be heard** man hörte keinen Ton; **~s/the ~ of laughter** Gelächter *nt;* **we heard the ~ of voices on the terrace** wir hörten Stimmen auf der Terrasse; **I don't like the ~ of it** das klingt gar nicht gut.

2 *vt* **(a)** **~ your horn** hupen!; **to ~ the alarm** Alarm schlagen; *(mechanism)* die Alarmanlage auslösen; **to ~ the retreat** zum Rückzug blasen; **to ~ the "r" in "cover"** das „r" in „cover" aussprechen; **his speech ~ed** a note of warning in seiner Rede klang eine Warnung an. **(b)** *(test by tapping, Med)* abklopfen.

3 *vi* **(a)** *(emit ~)* erklingen, ertönen. **feet ~ed in the corridor** im Flur waren Schritte zu hören. **(b)** *(give impression)* klingen, sich anhören. **it ~s hollow** es klingt hohl; **the children ~ happy** es hört sich so an, als ob die Kinder ganz vergnügt sind; **he ~s French (to me)** er hört sich (für mich) wie ein Franzose an; **that ~s very odd** das hört sich sehr seltsam an; **it ~s like a nice man** er scheint ein netter Mensch zu sein; **it ~s like a sensible idea** das klingt ganz vernünftig.

♦ **sound off** *vi (col)* sich auslassen *(about* über +*acc).*

sound³ *vt (Naut)* loten, ausloten. **to ~ sb (out) on sth** bei jdm in bezug auf etw *(acc)* vorfühlen.

sound⁴ *n (Geog)* Meerenge *f,* Sund *m.*

sound: **~ archives** *npl* Tonarchiv *nt;* **~ barrier** *n* Schallmauer *f;* **~ effects** *npl* Toneffekte *pl;* **~ engineer** *n* Toningenieur(in *f*) *m.*

sounding ['saʊndɪŋ] *n (Naut)* Loten *nt,* Peilung *f.* **to take ~s** *(lit)* Lotungen vornehmen; *(fig)* sondieren.

soundless ['saʊndlɪs] *adj* lautlos.

soundly ['saʊndlɪ] *adv built, made* solide; *argue, invest also* vernünftig; *thrash* tüchtig, gehörig. **our team was ~ beaten** unsere Mannschaft wurde eindeutig geschlagen; **to sleep ~** tief und fest schlafen.

sound: **~-proof** **1** *adj* schalldicht; **2** *vt* schalldicht machen; **~-track** *n* Ton *m;* Filmmusik *f,* Soundtrack *m;* **~-wave** *n* Schallwelle *f.*

soup [suːp] *n* Suppe *f.* **to be in the ~** *(col)* in der Tinte sitzen *(col).*

♦ **soup up** *vt sep (col) car* frisieren *(col).*

soupçon ['suːpsɔ̃ːŋ] *n (of spice etc)* Spur *f; (of irony etc)* Anflug *m.*

soup: **~-kitchen** *n* Volksküche *f; (for disaster area etc)* Feldküche *f;* **~-plate** *n* Suppenteller *m;* **~ spoon** *n* Suppenlöffel *m.*

sour ['saʊə^r] *adj* (+*er*) **(a)** *fruit* sauer; *wine* säuerlich. **(b)** *(bad) milk* sauer; *smell* säuerlich. **to go ~** *(lit)* sauer werden; *(fig) (relationship, marriage)* sich radikal verschlechtern; *(plan, investment)* sich als Fehlschlag erweisen. **(c)** *(fig) person* verdrießlich, griesgrämig; *remark* bissig. **he's feeling** ~ **about being demoted** er ist über seine Absetzung verbittert; **it's just** ~ **grapes** die Trauben hängen zu hoch.

source [sɔːs] *n (of river, light, information)* Quelle *f; (of troubles, problems etc)* Ursache *f*. **a** ~ **of vitamin C** ein Vitamin-C-Spender *m;* **I have it from a good** ~ **that ...** ich habe es aus sicherer Quelle, daß ...; **at** ~ *(Tax)* unmittelbar, direkt; **from reliable** ~**s** aus zuverlässiger Quelle.

souse [saus] *vt* übergießen. **he** ~**d himself with water** er übergoß sich mit Wasser.

south [sauθ] **1** *n* Süden *m*. **in the** ~ **of** im Süden +*gen;* **to the** ~ **of** im Süden *or* südlich von; **from the** ~ aus dem Süden; *(wind)* aus Süden; **to veer to the** ~ nach Süden drehen; **the S**~ **of France** Südfrankreich *nt*. **2** *adj* südlich, Süd-; *(in names)* Süd-. **3** *adv* im Süden; *(towards the* ~*)* nach Süden. **to be further** ~ weiter südlich sein; ~ **of** südlich von, im Süden von.

south *in cpds* Süd-; **S**~ **Africa** *n* Südafrika *nt;* **S**~ **African 1** *adj* südafrikanisch; **2** *n* Südafrikaner(in *f*) *m;* **S**~ **America** *n* Südamerika *nt;* **S**~ **American 1** *adj* südamerikanisch; **2** *n* Südamerikaner(in *f*) *m;* ~**bound** *adj* (in) Richtung Süden; ~**-east 1** *n* Südosten, *m;* **2** *adj* südöstlich; *(in names)* Südost-; **3** *adv* nach Südosten; ~**-east of** südöstlich von; ~**-easterly** *adj direction* südöstlich; ~**-easterly wind** Südostwind *m;* ~**-eastern** *adj* südöstlich, im Südosten.

southerly ['sʌðəlɪ] *adj* südlich; *wind* aus südlicher Richtung.

southern ['sʌðən] *adj* südlich; *(in names)* Süd-; *(Mediterranean)* südländisch. **S**~ **Africa** das südliche Afrika; **S**~ **Europe** Südeuropa *nt;* **S**~ **Ireland** (Süd)irland *nt;* **S**~ **States** Südstaaten *pl*.

southerner ['sʌðənəʳ] *n* Südländer(in *f*) *m* des Südens; Südengländer(in *f*) *m*/-deutsche(r) *mf etc; (from the Mediterranean)* Südländer(in *f*) *m; (US)* Südstaatler(in *f*) *m*.

southernmost ['sʌðənməʊst] *adj* südlichste(r, s).

south: S~ **Pole** *n* Südpol *m;* ~**ward(s) 1** *adj* südlich; **2** *adv* nach Süden, südwärts; ~**-west 1** *n* Südwesten *m;* **2** *adj* Südwest-, südwestlich; *wind* aus südwestlicher Richtung; **3** *adv* nach Südwest(en); ~**-west of** südwestlich von; ~**-westerly** *adj* südwestlich; *wind* Südwest-; ~**-western** *adj* südwestlich.

souvenir [ˌsuːvəˈnɪəʳ] *n* Andenken, Souvenir *nt (of an* +*acc)*.

sou'wester [sauˈwestəʳ] *n (hat)* Südwester *m*.

sovereign ['sɒvrɪn] **1** *n (monarch)* Souverän *m,* Herrscher(in *f*) *m; (Brit old: coin)* 20-Shilling-Münze *f*. **2** *adj (supreme)* höchste(r, s), oberste(r, s); *state, power* souverän; *contempt* tiefste(r, s), äußerste(r, s).

sovereignty ['sɒvrəntɪ] *n* Oberhoheit *f; (right of self-determination)* Souveränität *f*.

soviet ['səʊvɪət] **1** *n* Sowjet *m*. **the S**~**s** *(people)* die Sowjets. **2** *adj attr* sowjetisch, Sowjet-. **the S**~ **Union** die Sowjetunion.

sow[1] [səʊ] *pret* ~**ed,** *ptp* ~**n** *or* ~**ed** *vt* **(a)** *corn, plants* säen; *seed* aussäen; *(Mil)* mine legen. **(b)** *(fig)* **to** ~ **(the seeds of) hatred/discord/rebellion** Haß/Zwietracht säen/Aufruhr stiften.

sow[2] [saʊ] *n* Sau *f*.

sown [səʊn] *ptp of* **sow**[1].

soya ['sɔɪə], *(US)* **soy** [sɔɪ] *n* Soja *f*. ~ **bean** Sojabohne *f;* ~ **sauce** Sojasoße *f*.

sozzled ['sɒzld] *adj (Brit col)* **to be** ~ einen sitzen haben *(col);* **to get** ~ beschwipst werden *(col)*.

spa [spɑː] *n (town)* Kurort *m; (spring)* (Mineral)quelle *f*.

space [speɪs] **1** *n* **(a)** Raum *m (also Phys); (outer* ~ *also)* der Weltraum, das Weltall. **to stare into** ~ ins Leere starren. **(b)** *no pl (room)* Platz, Raum *m*. **to take up a lot of** ~ viel Platz einnehmen; **to clear/leave some** ~ **for sb/sth** für jdn/etw Platz schaffen/lassen; **to buy** ~ *(Press)* Platz für Anzeigen kaufen; **parking** ~ Platz *m* zum Parken. **(c)** *(gap, empty area)* Platz *m no art; (between objects, words, lines)* Zwischenraum *m; (parking* ~*)* Lücke *f*. **please answer in the** ~ **provided** bitte an der dafür vorgesehenen Stelle beantworten. **(d)** *(of time)* Zeitraum *m*. **in a short** ~ **of time** in kurzer Zeit; **in the** ~ **of one hour** innerhalb einer Stunde.

2 *vt (also* ~ **out)** in Abständen verteilen; *visits* verteilen; *words* Abstand lassen zwischen (+*dat)*.

space *in cpds* (Welt)raum-; ~ **age** *n* Weltraumzeitalter *nt;* ~**-age** *adj attr* des Weltraumzeitalters; ~**-bar** *n (Typ)* Leertaste *f;* ~**craft** *n* Raumfahrzeug *nt; (unmanned)* Raumkörper *m;* ~ **heater** *n (esp US)* Heizgerät *nt;* ~**man** *n* (Welt)raumfahrer *m;* ~ **rocket** *n* Weltraumrakete *f;* ~**-saving** *adj equipment, gadget* platzsparend; ~**ship** *n* Raumschiff *nt;* ~ **shuttle** *n* Raumfähre *f;* ~ **station** *n* (Welt)raumstation *f;* ~ **suit** *n* Raumanzug *m;* ~ **travel** *n* die Raumfahrt; ~ **walk** *n* Weltraumspaziergang *m*.

spacing ['speɪsɪŋ] *n* Abstände *pl; (between two objects)* Abstand *m; (also* ~ **out)** Verteilung *f; (of payments)* Verteilung *f* über längere Zeit. **double** ~ *(Typ)* zweizeiliger Abstand.

spacious ['speɪʃəs] *adj* geräumig; *park* weitläufig.

spade [speɪd] *n* **(a)** *(tool)* Spaten *m; (children's* ~*)* Schaufel *f*. **to call a** ~ **a** ~ *(prov)* das Kind beim Namen nennen *(prov)*. **(b)** *(Cards)* Pik *nt*. **the Queen/ten of S**~**s** die Pik-Dame/Pik-Zwei.

spadework ['speɪdwɜːk] *n (fig)* Vorarbeit *f*.

spaghetti [spəˈgetɪ] *n* Spaghetti *pl*.

Spain [speɪn] *n* Spanien *nt*.

span[1] [spæn] **1** *n* **(a)** *(of hand)* Spanne *f; (wing*~, *of bridge etc)* Spannweite *f*. **a single-**~ **bridge** eine eingespannte Bogenbrücke. **(b)** *(time* ~*)* Zeitspanne *f; (of memory)* Gedächtnisspanne *f; (of attention)* Konzentrationsspanne *f; (range)* Umfang *m*. **2** *vt (rope, rainbow)* sich spannen über (+*acc); (plank)* führen über (+*acc); (Mus) octave etc* greifen; *(encircle)* umfassen; *(in time)* sich erstrecken über (+*acc)*.

span[2] *(old) pret of* **spin**.

Spaniard ['spænjəd] *n* Spanier(in *f*) *m*.

spaniel ['spænjəl] *n* Spaniel *m*.

Spanish ['spænɪʃ] **1** *adj* spanisch. **the** ~ die Spanier *pl*. **2** *n (language)* Spanisch *nt*.

Spanish onion *n* Gemüsezwiebel *f*.

spank [spæŋk] **1** *n* Klaps *m*. **to give sb a** ~ einen Klaps geben; *(spanking)* jdm den Hintern versohlen. **2** *vt* versohlen.

spanner ['spænəʳ] *n (Brit)* Schraubenschlüssel *m*. **to throw a** ~ **in the works** *(fig)* jdm Knüppel zwischen die Beine werfen *(col);* **that's a real** ~ **in the works** das ist wirklich ein Hemmschuh.

spar[1] [spɑː] *n (Naut)* Rundholz *nt*.

spar[2] *vi (Boxing)* ein Sparring *nt* machen; *(fig)* sich kabbeln *(col) (about* um.). ~**ring partner** *(lit, fig)* Sparringpartner *m*.

spare [speəʳ] **1** *adj* **(a)** den/die/das man nicht braucht, übrig *pred; (surplus)* überzählig, übrig *pred; bed, room* Gäste-; *(replacement)* part *etc* Ersatz-. **have you any** ~ **string?** kannst du mir (einen) Bindfaden geben?; **I can give you a racket, I have a** ~ **one** ich kann dir einen Schläger geben, ich habe noch einen; **take some** ~ **clothes** nehmen Sie Kleider zum Wechseln mit; **it's all the** ~ **cash I have** mehr Bargeld habe ich nicht übrig; **should you have any** ~ **time** sollten Sie noch Zeit haben; **we have two** ~ **seats** wir haben zwei Plätze übrig. **(b) to go** ~ *(col)* durchdrehen *(col)*.

2 *n* Ersatzteil *nt*.

3 *vt (usu neg (grudge)* **we must** ~ **no effort in trying to finish this job** wir dürfen keine Mühe scheuen, um diese Arbeit zu erledigen; **no ex-**

pense was ~d es wurden keine Kosten gescheut.
  (b) to ~ sb sth *(give)* jdm etw überlassen *or* geben; *money* jdm etw geben; **can you ~ the time to do it?** haben Sie Zeit, das zu machen?; **I can ~ you five minutes** ich habe fünf Minuten Zeit für Sie *(übrig)*; **to have sth to ~** etw übrig haben; **there are three to ~** es sind drei übrig; **to have a few minutes to ~** ein paar Minuten Zeit haben; **I got to the airport with two minutes to ~** ich war zwei Minuten vor Abflug am Flughafen.
  (c) *(do without)* *person, object* entbehren, verzichten auf *(+acc)*. **I can't ~ it** ich kann es nicht entbehren, ich kann darauf nicht verzichten; **can you ~ this for a moment?** kannst du mir das kurz geben?; **to ~ a thought for sb/sth** an jdn/etw denken.
  (d) *(show mercy to)* verschonen; *(refrain from upsetting)* sb, sb's feelings schonen.
  (e) *(save)* **to ~ sb/oneself sth** jdm/sich etw ersparen; **~ me the details** verschone mich mit den Einzelheiten; **to ~ him embarrassment** um ihn nicht in Verlegenheit zu bringen.
spare: **~ part** *n* Ersatzteil *nt*; **~ room** *n* Gästezimmer *nt*; **~ time** 1 *n* *(leisure time)* Freizeit *f*; 2 *adj attr* Freizeit-; **~ tyre** *(Brit)* or **tire** *(US)* *n* Ersatzreifen *m*; *(fig col)* Rettungsring *m* *(col)*; **~ wheel** *n* Ersatzrad *nt*.
sparing ['speərɪŋ] *adj* sparsam. **to be ~ of (one's) praise** mit Lob geizen.
sparingly ['speərɪŋlɪ] *adv* sparsam; *spend, drink, eat* in Maßen. **to use sth ~** mit etw sparsam umgehen.
spark [spɑːk] **1** *n (from fire, Elec)* Funke *m*; *(fig: glimmer)* Fünkchen *nt*, Funke(n) *m*. **not a ~ of life** kein Fünkchen Leben; **when the ~s start to fly** *(fig)* wenn die Funken anfangen zu fliegen; **a bright ~** *(iro)* ein Intelligenzbolzen *m* *(iro)*. **2** *vt* *(also ~ off)* entzünden; *explosion* verursachen; *(fig)* auslösen; *interest, enthusiasm* wecken. **3** *vi* Funken sprühen; *(Elec)* zünden.
spark(ing) plug ['spɑːk(ɪŋ)'plʌg] *n* Zündkerze *f*.
sparkle ['spɑːkl] **1** *n* Funkeln *nt*. **he lacks ~** ihm fehlt der (rechte) Schwung. **2** *vi* funkeln *(with* vor *+dat)*; *(fig: person)* vor Leben(sfreude) sprühen; *(with intelligence, wit etc)* brillieren.
sparkling ['spɑːklɪŋ] *adj* lights glänzend, funkelnd; *eyes* funkelnd; *wit* sprühend; *(lively) person* vor Leben sprühend; *(witty) person, speech* vor Geist sprühend; *(bubbling) lemonade etc* perlend; **~ wine** *(as type)* Schaumwein *m*; *(slightly ~)* Perlwein *m*.
sparrow ['spærəʊ] *n* Sperling, Spatz *m*.
sparse [spɑːs] *adj* *(+er)* spärlich; *covering, population* dünn; *(infrequent) references also* rar.
sparsely ['spɑːslɪ] *adv* spärlich; *wooded also, populated* dünn.
spartan ['spɑːtən] *adj (fig)* spartanisch.
spasm ['spæzəm] *n (Med)* Krampf *m*; *(of asthma, coughing, fig)* Anfall *m*. **to work in ~s** sporadisch arbeiten.
spasmodic [spæz'mɒdɪk] *adj (Med)* krampfartig; *(fig: occasional)* sporadisch; *growth* schubweise.
spastic ['spæstɪk] **1** *adj* spastisch. **2** *n* Spastiker(in *f*) *m*.
spat *pret, ptp* of **spit**[1].
spate [speɪt] *n (of river)* Hochwasser *nt*; *(fig) (of letters, orders etc)* Flut *f*; *(of burglaries, accidents)* Serie *f*; *(of words, abuse)* Schwall *m*. **the river is in (full) ~** der Fluß führt Hochwasser.
spatial ['speɪʃəl] *adj* räumlich.
spatter ['spætəʳ] *vt* bespritzen. **to ~ water over sb, to ~ sb with water** jdn naß spritzen.
spatula ['spætjʊlə] *n* Spachtel *m*; *(Med)* Spatel *m*.
spawn [spɔːn] **1** *n (of fish, frogs)* Laich *m*. **2** *vi* laichen. **3** *vt (fig)* erzeugen.
speak [spiːk] *pret* **spoke**, *ptp* **spoken** **1** *vt* **(a)** *(utter)* sagen; *one's thoughts* äußern; *one's lines*

aufsagen. **to ~ one's mind** seine Meinung sagen; **nobody spoke a word** niemand sagte ein Wort. **(b)** *language* sprechen. **English spoken here** hier spricht man Englisch.
  2 *vi* **(a)** *(talk, be on ~ing terms)* sprechen, reden *(about* über *+acc,* von; *on* zu); *(converse)* reden, sich unterhalten *(with* mit); *(give opinion)* sich äußern *(on, to* zu). **to ~ to or with sb** mit jdm sprechen; **did you ~?** haben Sie etwas gesagt?; **to ~ in a whisper** flüstern; **I'm not ~ing to you** mit dir rede ich nicht mehr; **I'll ~ to him about it** *(euph: tell off)* ich werde ihm ein Wörtchen mit ihm reden; **I don't know him to ~ to** ich kenne ihn nicht näher; **~ing of dictionaries ...** da wir gerade von Wörterbüchern sprechen ...; **not to ~ of ...** ganz zu schweigen von ...; **it's nothing to ~ of** es ist nicht weiter erwähnenswert; **no money** *etc* **to ~ of** so gut wie kein Geld *etc*; **to ~ well of sb/sth** Gutes über jdn/etw sagen; **so to ~** sozusagen; **strictly ~ing** genau genommen; **legally ~ing** rechtlich gesehen; **generally ~ing** im allgemeinen; **~ing personally ...** was mich betrifft ...
  (b) **to ~ in public** in der Öffentlichkeit reden; **to ~ in the debate** in der Debatte das Wort ergreifen; **to ask sb to ~** jdm das Wort erteilen.
  (c) *(Telec)* **~ing!** am Apparat!; **Jones ~ing!** *(hier)* Jones!; **who is ~ing?** wer ist da, bitte?; *(on extension phone, in office)* wer ist am Apparat?
♦ **speak against** *vi* +*prep obj (in debate)* sich aussprechen gegen; *(criticize)* kritisieren.
♦ **speak for** *vi* +*prep obj* **(a)** *(in debate)* unterstützen. **(b) to ~ ~ sb** *(on behalf of)* in jds Namen *(dat)* sprechen; *(in favour of)* ein gutes Wort für jdn einlegen; **~ing ~ myself ...** was mich angeht ...; **let her ~ ~ herself** laß sie selbst reden; **~ ~ yourself!** *(I don't agree)* das meinst auch nur du!; *(don't include me)* du vielleicht!; **to ~ well/badly ~ sth** ein Beweis *m*/nicht gerade ein Beweis für etw sein; **to ~ ~ itself** *(be obvious)* für sich sprechen; **that's already spoken ~** das ist schon vergeben.
♦ **speak out** *vi (audibly)* deutlich sprechen; *(give opinion)* seine Meinung deutlich vertreten. **to ~ ~ against sth** sich gegen etw aussprechen.
♦ **speak up** *vi* **(a)** *(raise one's voice)* lauter sprechen; *(talk loudly)* laut (und verständlich) sprechen. **(b)** *(fig)* seine Meinung sagen *or* äußern. **don't be afraid to ~** sagen Sie ruhig Ihre Meinung; **to ~ ~ for sb/sth** für jdn/etw eintreten.
speaker ['spiːkəʳ] *n* **(a)** *(of language)* Sprecher(in *f*) *m*. **all ~s of German** alle Deutschsprechenden. **(b)** Sprecher(in *f*) *m*; *(in discussion also, in lecture)* Redner(in *f*) *m*. **the last *or* previous ~** der Vorredner; **our ~ today is ...** der heutige Referent ist ... **(c)** *(loud~, in record-player)* Lautsprecher *m*; *(on hi-fi etc)* Box *f*. **(d)** *(Parl)* S~ Sprecher *m*.
speaking ['spiːkɪŋ] *n* *(act of ~)* Sprechen *nt*; *(speeches)* Reden pl.
-speaking *adj suf* -sprechend; *(with native language also)* -sprachig.
speaking: **~ clock** *n (Brit)* Zeitansage *f*; **~ terms** *npl* **to be on ~ terms with sb** mit jdm reden.
spear [spɪəʳ] *n* Speer *m*.
spearhead ['spɪəhed] **1** *n (of spear)* Speerspitze *f*; *(Mil)* Angriffsspitze *f*; *(fig: person, thing)* Bahnbrecher *m* *(of* für*)*. **2** *vt (lit, fig)* anführen.
spec [spek] *n (col)* **on ~** auf gut Glück.
special ['speʃəl] **1** *adj* **(a)** besondere(r, s); *(specific, exceptional) purpose, use, friend, favour, occasion also* speziell. **I have no ~ person in mind** ich habe eigentlich an niemanden Bestimmtes gedacht; **take ~ care of it** passen Sie besonders gut darauf auf; **nothing ~** nichts Besonderes; **he expects ~ treatment** er will besonders behandelt werden; **what's so ~ about her?** was ist denn an ihr so besonders?; **what's so ~ about that?** na

und? *(col)*, das ist doch nichts Besonderes! **(b)** *(out of the ordinary)* permission, edition, powers Sonder-; *subject, dictionary* Spezial-. **~ feature** *(Press)* Sonderartikel *m*. **2** *n (constable)* Hilfspolizist(in *f*) *m*; *(train)* Sonderzug *m*; *(Cook)* Tagesgericht *nt*; *(edition)* Sonderausgabe *f*.

special: **~ agent** *n (spy)* Agent(in *f*) *m*; **S~ Branch** *n (Brit)* Sicherheitspolizei *f*; **~ case** *n (also Jur)* Sonderfall *m*; **~ correspondent** *n (Press)* Sonderberichterstatter(in *f*) *m*; **~ delivery** *n* Eilzustellung *f*; **by ~ delivery** durch Eilboten; **~ effects** *npl* Tricks *pl*.

specialist ['speʃəlɪst] **1** *n* Fachmann *m (in* für*)*; *(Med)* Spezialist(in *f*) *m*, Facharzt *m*/-ärztin *f (in* für*)*. **2** *adj attr knowledge, dictionary* Fach-.

speciality [,speʃɪ'ælɪtɪ], *(US)* **specialty** ['speʃəltɪ] *n* Spezialität; *(subject also)* Spezialgebiet *nt*. **to make a ~ of sth** sich auf etw *(acc)* spezialisieren.

specialize ['speʃəlaɪz] *vi* sich spezialisieren *(in* auf +*acc)*. **we ~ in ...** wir haben uns auf ... spezialisiert.

specialized ['speʃəlaɪzd] *adj* spezialisiert. **a ~ knowledge of biology** Fachkenntnisse *pl* in Biologie.

specially ['speʃəlɪ] *adv* besonders; *(specifically)* speziell, extra. **a ~ difficult task** eine besonders schwierige Aufgabe; **I had it ~ made** ich habe es extra machen lassen.

special: **~ offer** *n* Sonderangebot *nt*; **~ school** *n* Sonderschule *f*; *(for physically handicapped)* Behindertenschule *f*.

specialty ['speʃəltɪ] *n (US)* = **speciality**.

species ['spiːʃiːz] *n*, *pl* - Art *f*; *(Biol also)* Spezies *f*.

specific [spə'sɪfɪk] **1** *adj* **(a)** *(definite)* speziell; *(precise)* statement, instructions genau; *example* ganz bestimmt. **9.3, to be ~** 9.3, um genau zu sein; **can you be a bit more ~?** können Sie sich etwas genauer äußern? **(b)** *(Sci)* spezifisch. **~ gravity** spezifisches Gewicht. **2** *n* **~s** *pl* nähere Einzelheiten *pl*.

specifically [spə'sɪfɪkəlɪ] *adv* warn, order, state ausdrücklich; *(specially)* designed, request speziell; *(precisely)* genau.

specification [,spesɪfɪ'keɪʃən] *n (detail)* Angabe *f*; *(stipulation)* Bedingung *f*; *(of requirements)* genaue Angabe; *(for patent)* (genaue) Beschreibung; *(design) (for car, machine)* (detaillierter) Entwurf; *(for building)* Bauplan *m*. **~s** *pl* genaue Angaben *pl*; *(of car, machine)* technische Daten *pl*; *(of new building)* Baubeschreibung *f*.

specify ['spesɪfaɪ] **1** *vt* angeben; *(list)* (einzeln) aufführen; *(stipulate)* vorschreiben; *(blueprint, contract etc)* vorsehen. **2** *vi* genaue Angaben machen. **unless otherwise specified** wenn nicht anders angegeben.

specimen ['spesɪmɪn] **1** *n* Exemplar *nt*; *(of urine, blood etc)* Probe *f*; *(sample)* Muster *nt*. **a beautiful** *or* **fine ~** ein Prachtexemplar *nt*; **you're a pretty poor ~** *(col)* du hast ja nicht viel zu bieten *(col)*. **2** *adj attr page* Probe-. **a ~ copy** ein Probeexemplar *nt*; **a ~ signature** eine Unterschriftenprobe.

specious ['spiːʃəs] *adj argument* vordergründig bestechend, Schein-; *claim* fadenscheinig.

speck [spek] *n* Fleck *(m*; *(of blood, paint also)* Spritzer *m*; *(of dust)* Körnchen *nt*; *(of soot)* Flocke *f*; *(of gold, colour etc)* Sprenkel *m*. **a ~ on the horizon** ein Punkt *m* am Horizont.

speckle ['spekl] *vt* sprenkeln. **to be ~d with sth** mit etw gesprenkelt sein.

specs [speks] *npl (col)* Brille *f*.

spectacle ['spektəkl] *n (a) (show)* Schauspiel *nt*. **a sad ~** ein trauriger Anblick; **to make a ~ of oneself** unangenehm auffallen. **(b)** **~s** *pl (also* **pair of ~s)** Brille *f*.

spectacle case *n* Brillenetui *nt*.

spectacular [spek'tækjʊlə*r*] **1** *adj* sensationell; *improvement, success also* spektakulär. **2** *n (Theat)* Show *f*.

spectator [spek'teɪtə*r*] *n* Zuschauer(in *f*) *m*. **~ sport** Publikumssport *m*.

spectre, *(US)* **specter** ['spektə*r*] *n* Gespenst *nt*; *(fig)* (Schreck)gespenst *nt*.

spectrum ['spektrəm] *n*, *pl* **spectra** Spektrum *nt*; *(fig: range also)* Skala *f*.

speculate ['spekjʊleɪt] *vi* **(a)** Überlegungen anstellen, spekulieren *(about, on* über +*acc)*. **(b)** *(Fin)* spekulieren *(in* mit, *on* an +*dat)*.

speculation [,spekjʊ'leɪʃən] *n* Spekulation *f (on* über +*acc)*; *(guesswork also)* Vermutung *f*. **it is the subject of much ~** darüber sind viele Vermutungen angestellt worden.

speculative ['spekjʊlətɪv] *adj* **(a)** spekulativ; *ideas* rein theoretisch. **(b)** *(Fin)* Spekulations-.

speculator ['spekjʊleɪtə*r*] *n* Spekulant(in *f*) *m*.

sped [sped] *pret, ptp of* **speed**.

speech [spiːtʃ] *n no pl* Sprache *f*; *(act of speaking)* Sprechen *nt*; *(manner of speaking)* Sprechweise *f*; *(oration, Theat)* Rede *f (on, about* über +*acc)*; *(address)* Ansprache *f*. **to lose/recover the power of ~** die Sprache verlieren/zurückgewinnen; **freedom of ~** Redefreiheit *f*; **to give** *or* **make a ~** eine Rede etc halten; **direct/indirect** *or* **reported ~** *(Brit Gram)* direkte/indirekte Rede.

speech: **~ day** *n (Brit)* Schulfeier *f*; **~ defect,** **~ impediment** *n* Sprachfehler *m*.

speechless ['spiːtʃlɪs] *adj (at a loss for words)* sprachlos *(with* vor +*dat)*; *anger* stumm. **his remark left me ~** seine Bemerkung verschlug mir die Sprache.

speech: **~ therapist** *n* Logopäde *m*, Logopädin *f*; **~ therapy** *n* Sprachtherapie *f*; *(treatment)* logopädische Behandlung.

speed [spiːd] *(vb: pret, ptp* **sped** *or* **~ed)* **1** *n* **(a)** Geschwindigkeit *f*; *(fast ~ also)* Schnelligkeit *f*; *(of moving object or person also)* Tempo *nt*. **at ~** äußerst schnell; **at a high/low ~** mit hoher/niedriger Geschwindigkeit; **at full** *or* **top ~** mit Höchstgeschwindigkeit; **at a ~ of 50 mph** mit einem Tempo von 50 Meilen pro Stunde; **at the ~ of light** mit Lichtgeschwindigkeit; **to pick up** *or* **gather ~** schneller werden; *(fig: development)* sich beschleunigen; **to lose ~** *(an)* Geschwindigkeit verlieren; **what ~ were you doing?** wie schnell sind Sie gefahren? **(b)** *(Aut, Tech: gear)* Gang *m*. **a three-~ gear** ein Dreiganggetriebe *nt*. **(c)** *(Phot) (film ~)* Lichtempfindlichkeit *f*; *(shutter ~)* Belichtungszeit *f*.

    2 *vt* **to ~ sb on his way** *(person)* jdn verabschieden; *(iro)* jdn hinauskomplimentieren; *(good wishes etc)* jdn auf seinem Weg begleiten.

    3 *vi* **(a)** *pret, ptp* **sped** *(move quickly)* jagen; *(arrow)* sausen. **the years sped by** die Jahre vergingen wie im Fluge. **(b)** *pret, ptp* **~ed** *(Aut: exceed ~ limit)* zu schnell fahren.

♦ **speed up** *pret, ptp* **~ed ~ 1** *vi (car, driver etc)* beschleunigen; *(person)* Tempo zulegen; *(work, production etc)* schneller werden. **2** *vt sep* beschleunigen; *person* antreiben; *research also* vorantreiben.

speedboat ['spiːdbəʊt] *n* Rennboot *nt*.

speeding ['spiːdɪŋ] *n* Geschwindigkeitsüberschreitung *f*.

speed limit *n* Geschwindigkeitsbegrenzung *f*. **a 30 mph ~** eine Geschwindigkeitsbegrenzung von 50 km/h.

speedometer [spɪ'dɒmɪtə*r*] *n* Tachometer *m*.

speed: **~ trap** *n* Radarfalle *f (col)*; **~way** *n* **(a)** *(Sport)* Speedwayrennen *nt*; *(track)* Speedwayrennbahn *f*; **(b)** *(US) (race-track)* Rennstrecke *f*; *(expressway)* Schnellstraße *f*.

speedy ['spiːdɪ] *adj (+er)* schnell; *answer, service also* prompt; *remedy* schnell wirkend.

spell[1] [spel] *n (lit, fig)* Zauber *m*; *(incantation)* Zauberspruch *m*. **to be under a ~** *(lit)* verzaubert *or* verhext sein; *(fig)* wie verzaubert sein; **to cast a ~ over sb** *(lit, fig)* jdn verzaubern; **to be under**

sb's ~ *(fig)* in jds Bann *(dat)* stehen; **to break the** ~ *(lit, fig)* den Bann brechen.

spell² *n (period)* Weile *f*. **for a** ~ eine Weile, eine Zeitlang; **cold/hot** ~ Kälte-/Hitzewelle *f*; **a short** ~ **of sunny weather** eine kurze Schönwetterperiode.

spell³ *pret, ptp* ~**ed** *or* **spelt 1** *vi (in writing)* richtig schreiben; *(aloud)* buchstabieren. **she can't** ~ sie kann keine Rechtschreibung. **2** *vt* **(a)** schreiben; *(aloud)* buchstabieren. **how do you** ~ **"onyx"?** wie schreibt man „Onyx"?; **how do you** ~ **your name?** wie schreibt sich Ihr Name?, wie schreiben Sie sich? **(b)** *(denote)* bedeuten. **this** ~**s disaster (for us)** das bedeutet Unglück (für uns).

♦ **spell out** *vt sep (spell aloud)* buchstabieren; *(read slowly)* entziffern; *(explain)* verdeutlichen. **do I have to** ~ **it** ~ **for you?** *(col)* muß ich noch deutlicher werden?

spellbound ['spelbaʊnd] *adj, adv (fig)* wie verzaubert, gebannt. **to hold sb** ~ jdn fesseln; *(person also)* jdn in seinen Bann schlagen.

spelling ['spelɪŋ] *n* Rechtschreibung; *(of a word)* Schreibweise *f*. ~ **mistake** *n* (Recht)schreibfehler *m*.

spelt [spelt] *pret, ptp of* **spell³**.

spend [spend] *pret, ptp* **spent** *vt* **(a)** *money* ausgeben *(on für)*; *energy, strength* verbrauchen; *time* brauchen. **time well spent** sinnvoll genutzte Zeit. **(b)** *(pass) time, evening etc* verbringen. **he** ~**s his time reading** er verbringt seine Zeit mit Lesen; **to** ~ **money/time on sth** *(devote to)* Geld/Zeit für etw aufbringen.

spending ['spendɪŋ] *n no pl* Ausgaben *pl*. **government** ~ **cuts** Kürzungen im Etat; ~ **money** Taschengeld *nt*; ~ **power** Kaufkraft *f*.

spendthrift ['spendθrɪft] **1** *adv* verschwenderisch. **2** *n* Verschwender(in *f*) *m*.

spent [spent] **1** *pret, ptp of* **spend**. **2** *adj* *ammunition, cartridge, match* verbraucht; *person* erschöpft. **to be a** ~ **force** nichts mehr zu sagen haben; *(movement)* sich totgelaufen haben.

sperm [spɜːm] *n* **(a)** Samenfaden *m*, Spermium *nt*; *(fluid)* Sperma *nt*. ~ **whale** *n* Pottwal *m*.

sphere [sfɪəʳ] *n* **(a)** Kugel *f*; *(heavenly* ~*)* Gestirn *nt* *(geh)*. **(b)** *(fig)* Sphäre *f*; *(of person, experience)* Bereich *m*; *(of knowledge etc)* Gebiet, Feld *nt*; *(social etc circle)* Kreis *m*. **in the** ~ **of politics** in der Welt der Politik; **his** ~ **of influence** sein Einflußbereich; ~ **of activity** *(job, specialism)* Wirkungskreis *m*; **that's outside my** ~ *(not my responsibility)* das ist nicht mein Gebiet.

spherical ['sferɪkəl] *adj (in shape)* kugelförmig.

sphinx [sfɪŋks] *n* Sphinx *f*.

spice [spaɪs] **1** *n* **(a)** Gewürz *nt*. ~ **rack** Gewürzbord *nt*; **mixed** ~ **(s)** Gewürzmischung *f*. **(b)** *(fig)* Würze *f*. **variety is the** ~ **of life** *(prov)* öfter mal was Neues *(col)*. **2** *vt (lit, fig)* würzen. **a highly** ~**d account** *(fig)* ein reichlich ausgeschmückter Bericht.

spick-and-span ['spɪkən'spæn] *adj* *house etc* blitzsauber, tipptopp in Ordnung *pred*; *person* wie aus dem Ei gepellt *(col)*.

spicy ['spaɪsɪ] *adj (+er)* würzig; *sauce, food also* stark gewürzt; *(fig) story etc* pikant.

spider ['spaɪdəʳ] *n* Spinne *f*. ~**'s web** Spinnwebe *f*, Spinnennetz *nt*.

spiel [ʃpiːl] *n (col)* Blabla *nt (col)*; *(tall story, excuse)* Geschichte *f (col)*.

spike [spaɪk] **1** *n* *(on railing, helmet etc)* Spitze *f*; *(nail)* Nagel *m*; *(on plant)* Stachel *m*; *(on shoe etc)* Spike *m*; *(for receipts etc)* Dorn *m*. **2** *vt* **(a)** aufspießen. **(b)** *(col: frustrate) rumours* den Boden entziehen *(+dat)*. **to** ~ **sb's guns** jdm einen Strich durch die Rechnung machen *(col)*. **(c)** *(US: lace) drink* einen Schuß zusetzen *(+dat)*. ~**d with rum** mit einem Schuß Rum.

spikes [spaɪks] *npl (Sport)* Spikes *pl*.

spiky ['spaɪkɪ] *adj (+er) railings* mit Metallspitzen; *bush, grass, animal* stach(e)lig; *branch* dornig; *flower* mit spitzen Blütenblättern; *leaf* spitz; *writing* steil.

spill [spɪl] *pret, ptp* ~**ed** *or* **spilt 1** *vt* verschütten; *blood* vergießen. **to** ~ **the beans (to sb)** *(col)* (jdm gegenüber) nicht dichthalten *(col)*; **the lorry** ~**ed its load onto the road** die Ladung fiel vom Lastwagen herunter auf die Straße. **2** *vi* verschüttet werden; *(large quantity)* sich ergießen; *(fig: people)* strömen. **the blood** ~**ed onto the floor** das Blut floß auf den Boden.

♦ **spill out 1** *vi (of aus) (liquid)* herausschwappen; *(grain)* herausrieseln; *(money, jewels)* herausfallen; *(fig: people)* (heraus)strömen. **2** *vt sep* ausschütten; *(by accident)* verschütten.

♦ **spill over 1** *vi (liquid)* überlaufen; *(grain etc, assembly)* überquellen; *(fig: population)* sich ausbreiten *(into auf +acc)*.

spilt [spɪlt] *pret, ptp of* **spill**.

spin [spɪn] *(vb: pret, ptp* **spun) 1** *n* **(a)** *(revolution)* Drehung *f*; *(washing machine programme)* Schleudern *nt no pl*. **to give sth a** ~ etw (schnell) drehen; **to give sth a long/short** ~ *(in washing machine)* etw lange/kurz schleudern; **to be in a (flat)** ~ *(fig col)* am Rotieren sein *(col) (about wegen)*. **(b)** *(on ball)* Drall *m*; *(Billiards)* Effet *m*. **(c)** *(Aviat)* Trudeln *nt no pl*. **to go into a** ~ zu trudeln anfangen. **(d)** *(trip)* Spritztour *f*. **to go for a** ~ eine Spritztour machen.

2 *vt* **(a)** spinnen. **(b)** *(turn) wheel* drehen; *(fast)* herumwirbeln; *(in washing machine)* schleudern; *(toss) coin* werfen; *(Sport)* ball einen Drall/Effet geben *(+dat)*; *(with racquet)* (an)schneiden.

3 *vi* **(a)** spinnen. **(b)** *(revolve)* sich drehen; *(fast)* (herum)wirbeln; *(plane etc)* trudeln; *(in washing machine)* schleudern. **the car spun out of control** der Wagen geriet stark ins Schleudern; **my head is** ~**ning** mir dreht sich alles.

♦ **spin out** *vt sep (col) money, food* strecken *(col)*; *holiday, meeting* in die Länge ziehen; *story* ausspinnen.

spinach ['spɪnɪtʃ] *n* Spinat *m*.

spinal ['spaɪnl] *adj* *vertebrae* Rücken-; *injury, muscle* Rückgrat-; ~ **column** Wirbelsäule *f*.

spindle ['spɪndl] *n (for spinning, Mech)* Spindel *f*.

spindly ['spɪndlɪ] *adj (+er) legs, arms, plant* spindeldürr; *chairs* zierlich.

spin: ~-**drier** n *(Brit)* (Wäsche)schleuder *f*; ~-**dry** *vti* schleudern.

spine [spaɪn] *n* **(a)** *(Anat)* Rückgrat *nt*; *(of book)* (Buch)rücken *m*. **(b)** *(spike)* Stachel *m*; *(of plant also)* Dorn *m*.

spine: ~-**chiller** n *(col)* Gruselgeschichte *f*; Gruselfilm *m*; ~-**chilling** *adj (col)* gruselig; *noise* unheimlich.

spineless ['spaɪnlɪs] *adj (fig) person* ohne Rückgrat; *compromise, refusal* feige.

spinner ['spɪnəʳ] n **(a)** *(of cloth)* Spinner(in *f*) *m*. **(b)** *(col)* = **spin-drier**.

spinney ['spɪnɪ] *n (esp Brit)* Dickicht *nt*.

spinning *in cpds* Spinn-; ~ **top** *n* Kreisel *m*; ~ **wheel** *n* Spinnrad *nt*.

spin-off ['spɪnɒf] *n (side-product)* Nebenprodukt *nt*.

spinster ['spɪnstəʳ] *n* Unverheiratete *f*; *(pej)* alte Jungfer *(pej)*. **to be a** ~ unverheiratet *or* eine alte Jungfer *(pej)* sein.

spiral ['spaɪrəl] **1** *adj* spiralförmig; *shell* also gewunden; *spring* Spiral-; *movement* in Spiralen. ~ **staircase** Wendeltreppe *f*. **2** *n (lit, fig)* Spirale *f*. **inflationary** ~ Inflationsspirale *f*. **3** *vi (also* ~ **up)** sich hochwinden; *(smoke also)* spiralförmig aufsteigen; *(prices)* (nach oben) klettern.

spire [spaɪəʳ] *n (of church)* Turmspitze *f*.

spirit ['spɪrɪt] *n (soul, ghost)* Geist *m*. **I'll be with you in** ~ im Geiste werde ich bei euch sein.

(b) *no pl (courage)* Mut *m*; *(vitality)* Elan *m.* **a man of** ~ *(courageous)* ein mutiger Mensch; **to break sb's** ~ jds Mut brechen; **to sing with** ~ mit Inbrunst singen.

(c) *(attitude: of country, group of people etc)* Geist *m*; *(mood)* Stimmung *f.* **team/community** ~ Mannschaftsgeist *m/*Gemeinschaftssinn *m*; **Christmas** ~ *(mood)* weihnachtliche Stimmung; **party** ~ Partystimmung *f*; **fighting** ~ Kampfgeist *m*; **a** ~ **of optimism** eine optimistische Stimmung; **the** ~ **of the age** der Zeitgeist; **he has the right** ~ er hat die richtige Einstellung; **to enter into the** ~ **of sth** bei etw mitmachen; **that's the** ~! *(col)* so ist's recht! *(col)*; **the** ~ **of the law** der Geist des Gesetzes; **to take sth in the right** ~ etw richtig auffassen.

(d) ~s *pl (state of mind)* Stimmung *f.* **to be in good/bad** ~s *guter/schlechter* Laune sein; **to keep up one's** ~s den Mut nicht verlieren; **to raise sb's** ~s jdn aufmuntern.

(e) ~s *pl (alcohol)* Spirituosen *pl.*

spirited ['spɪrɪtɪd] *adj* temperamentvoll; *performance* lebendig; *(courageous) person, attempt* mutig.

spirit: ~ **lamp** *n* Petroleumlampe *f*; ~ **level** *n* Wasserwaage *f.*

spiritual ['spɪrɪtjʊəl] **1** *adj* geistig; *(Eccl)* geistlich. **2** *n (Mus)* Spiritual *nt.*

spiritualism ['spɪrɪtjʊəlɪzəm] *n* Spiritismus *m.*

spiritualist ['spɪrɪtjʊəlɪst] *n* Spiritist(in *f*) *m.*

spit¹ [spɪt] *(vb: pret, ptp* **spat) 1** *n (saliva)* Spucke *f.* **2** *vt* spucken. **3** *vi* spucken; *(fat)* spritzen; *(fire)* zischen; *(person: verbally, cat)* fauchen. **it is** ~**ting (with rain)** es tröpfelt.

♦ **spit out** *vt sep* ausspucken; *words* ausstoßen. ~ **it** ~! *(fig col)* heraus mit der Sprache!

spit² *n* **(a)** *(Cook)* (Brat)spieß *m.* **on the** ~ am Spieß. **(b)** *(of land)* Landzunge *f.*

spite [spaɪt] **1** *n* **(a)** *(ill will)* Gehässigkeit *f.* **to do sth out of** *or* **from** ~ etw aus reiner Boshaftigkeit tun. **(b) in** ~ **of** *(despite)* trotz *(+gen)*; **we went in** ~ **of him** wir gingen dennoch; **he did it in** ~ **of himself** er konnte nicht anders; **in** ~ **of the fact that he ...** obwohl er ... **2** *vt* ärgern. **she just does it to** ~ **me** sie tut es nur, um mich zu ärgern.

spiteful ['spaɪtfʊl] *adj* boshaft, gemein.

spitting image ['spɪtɪŋ'ɪmɪdʒ] *n (col)* Ebenbild *nt.* **to be the** ~ **of sb** jdm wie aus dem Gesicht geschnitten sein.

spittie ['spɪtl] *n* Speichel *m*, Spucke *f.*

splash [splæʃ] **1** *n* **(a)** *(spray)* Spritzen *nt no pl*; *(noise)* Platschen *nt no pl.* **to make a** ~ *(fig)* Furore machen; *(news)* wie eine Bombe einschlagen; *(book)* einschlagen. **(b)** *(small amount)* Spritzer *m*; *(in drink etc also)* Schuß *m*; *(of colour, light)* Tupfen *m.* ~**es of paint** Farbspritzer *pl.* **2** *vt water etc* spritzen; *(pour)* gießen; *person, object* bespritzen. **to** ~ **water over sb** jdn mit Wasser bespritzen; **the story was** ~**ed all over the papers** die Geschichte wurde in allen Zeitungen groß rausgebracht *(col)*. **3** *vi (liquid)* spritzen; *(rain, waves)* klatschen; *(tears)* tropfen; *(when diving, walking etc)* platschen; *(when playing)* planschen.

♦ **splash down** *vi (Space)* wassern.

♦ **splash out** *vi (col)* tüchtig in die Tasche greifen *(col)*; *(giving presents etc)* sich nicht lumpen lassen *(col)*. **to** ~ ~ **on sth** sich *(dat)* etw spendieren *(col)*.

splashdown ['splæʃdaʊn] *n (Space)* Wasserung *f.*

splatter ['splætə^r] *vt* bespritzen; *(with ink, paint etc)* bekleckern.

splay [spleɪ] *(also* ~ **out)** *vt (spread out) legs, fingers, toes* spreizen; *feet* nach außen stellen.

spleen [spliːn] *n (Anat)* Milz *f*; *(fig)* Zorn *m.* **to vent one's** ~ seinem Ärger Luft machen.

splendid ['splendɪd] *adj* **(a)** *(magnificent)* herrlich;

occasion, scale großartig. **(b)** *(excellent)* hervorragend; *rider etc, idea* glänzend.

splendour, *(US)* **splendor** ['splendə^r] *n* Pracht *f no pl*; *(of music, achievement)* Großartigkeit *f.*

splice [splaɪs] *vt ropes* spleißen *(spec)*; *tapes, film* (zusammen)kleben; *pieces of wood etc* verfugen.

splint [splɪnt] *n* Schiene *f.* **to put a** ~ **on sth** etw schienen; **to be in** ~s geschient sein.

splinter ['splɪntə^r] **1** *n* Splitter *m.* **2** *vt* (zer)splittern; *(with axe)* wood zerhacken. **3** *vi* (zer)splittern.

splinter group *n* Splittergruppe *f.*

split [splɪt] *(vb: pret, ptp* ~**) 1** *n* **(a)** Riß *m (in* in +*dat)*; *(in rock, wood also)* Spalt *m (in* in +*dat).* **(b)** *(fig: division)* Bruch *m (in* in +*dat)*; *(Pol, Eccl)* Spaltung *f (in gen).* **there is a** ~ **in the party over ...** die Partei ist in der Frage *(+gen)* ... gespalten. **(c)** *(distinction: in meaning)* Aufteilung *f.* **(d)** *pl* **the** ~**s** Spagat *m*; **to do the** ~**s** einen Spagat machen. **(e)** *(col: sweet) (also* **banana** ~**)** Bananen-Split *m.* **jam/cream** ~ mit *Marmelade/ Sahne gefülltes Gebäckstück.*

2 *adj* gespalten *(on, over* in +*dat).*

3 *vt* **(a)** *(cleave)* (zer)teilen; *wood also*, atom spalten; *fabric* zerreißen; *seam* aufplatzen lassen. **to** ~ **hairs** *(col)* Haarspalterei treiben *(col)*; **to** ~ **one's sides (laughing)** *(col)* vor Lachen fast platzen *(col)*; **to** ~ **sth open** etw aufbrechen; **his head was** ~ **open when he fell** er hatte sich *(dat)* beim Fallen den Kopf aufgeschlagen. **(b)** *(divide)* spalten; *(share)* work, costs etc *(sich dat)* teilen. **to** ~ **sth into three parts** etw in drei Teile aufteilen; **to** ~ **the vote** die Stimmen spalten; **a party** ~ **three ways** eine in drei Lager gespaltene Partei; **they** ~ **the profit three ways** sie haben den Gewinn in drei Teile geteilt; **to** ~ **the difference** *(fig: in argument etc)* sich auf halbem Wege einigen; *(lit: with money etc)* sich *(dat)* die Differenz teilen.

4 *vi* **(a)** *(wood)* (entzwei)brechen; *(trousers, seam etc)* platzen; *(fabric)* zerreißen. **to** ~ **open** aufplatzen; **my head is** ~**ting** *(fig)* mir platzt der Kopf. **(b)** *(col: tell tales)* **to** ~ **on sb** jdn verpfeifen *(col)*.

♦ **split off 1** *vt sep* abtrennen *(prep obj* von*)*; *(break)* abbrechen *(prep obj* von*).* **2** *vi* abbrechen; *(fig)* sich trennen *(from* von*).*

♦ **split up 1** *vt sep money, work* (auf)teilen; *party, organization* spalten; *meeting* ein Ende machen *(+dat)*; *two people* trennen; *crowd* zerstreuen. **2** *vi* zerbrechen; *(divide)* sich teilen; *(meeting, crowd)* sich spalten; *(partners)* sich trennen.

split: ~ **infinitive** *n (Gram)* getrennter Infinitiv *f*; ~**-level** *adj (Archit)* mit versetzten Geschossen; ~ **peas** *npl* abgetrocknete (halbe) Erbsen *pl*; ~ **personality** *n* gespaltene Persönlichkeit; ~ **second** *n* **1 in a** ~ **second** in Sekundenschnelle; **2** *adj* ~**-second timing** Abstimmung *f* auf die Sekunde; *(of actor)* Gefühl *nt* für den richtigen Moment.

splitting ['splɪtɪŋ] **1** *n* Zerteilung *f*; *(of wood)* Spalten *nt.* **the** ~ **of the atom** die Kernspaltung. **2** *adj headache* rasend.

splodge [splɒdʒ], **splotch** [splɒtʃ] *n* Klecks *m*; *(of cream etc)* Klacks *m.*

splutter ['splʌtə^r] *vi (person: spit)* prusten; *(stutter)* stottern; *(engine)* stottern; *(fire, fat)* zischen.

spoil [spɔɪl] *(vb: pret, ptp* ~**ed** *or* **spoilt) 1** *n usu pl* Beute *f no pl*; *(fig: profits also)* Gewinn *m.* **the** ~**s of war** die Kriegsbeute. **2** *vt* **(a)** *(ruin, detract from)* verderben; *view also, town, looks etc* verschandeln; *peace of mind* zerstören; *life* ruinieren; *ballot papers* ungültig machen. **to** ~ **one's appetite** sich *(dat)* den Appetit verderben; **it** ~**ed our evening** das hat uns *(dat)* den Abend verdorben. **(b)** *person* verwöhnen; *children also* verziehen. **to be** ~**t for choice** die Qual der Wahl haben. **3** *vi (food)* verderben. **to be** ~**ing for a**

fight Streit suchen.
spoilsport ['spɔɪlspɔːt] n (col) Spielverderber m (col).
spoilt [spɔɪlt] **1** pret, ptp of **spoil. 2** adj child verwöhnt.
spoke[1] [spəʊk] n Speiche f. **to put a ~ in sb's wheel** (col) jdm Knüppel zwischen die Beine werfen (col).
spoke[2] pret of **speak.**
spoken ['spəʊkən] **1** ptp of **speak. 2** adj language gesprochen.
spokesman ['spəʊksmən] n, pl **-men** [-mən] Sprecher m.
spokesperson ['spəʊkspɜːsn] n Sprecher(in f) m.
spokeswoman ['spəʊkswʊmən] n, pl **-women** [-wɪmɪn] Sprecherin f.
sponge [spʌndʒ] **1** n **(a)** Schwamm m. **(b)** (Cook) (also ~ **cake)** Rührkuchen m; (fatless) Biskuitkuchen m. **2** vt **(a)** (clean) abwischen; (wound) abtupfen. **(b)** (col: scrounge) schnorren (col) (from bei).
♦ **sponge down** vt sep person (schnell) waschen; walls also abwaschen; horse abreiben:
sponge: ~ **bag** n (Brit) Kulturbeutel m; ~ **cake** n Rührkuchen m; (fatless) Biskuitkuchen m.
sponger ['spʌndʒəʳ] n (col) Schnorrer m (col).
spongy ['spʌndʒɪ] adj (+er) weich; (light) pudding locker; skin etc schwammig.
sponsor ['spɒnsəʳ] **1** n Förderer m, Förderin f; (for membership) Bürge m, Bürgin f; (for event) Schirmherr(in f) m; (Rad, TV, Sport etc) Sponsor(in f) m; (for fund raising) Spender(in f) m. **2** vt unterstützen; (financially also) fördern; event also die Schirmherrschaft (+gen) übernehmen; future member bürgen für; membership, bill befürworten; (Rad, TV, Sport etc) sponsern. **he ~ed him at 5p a mile** er verpflichtete sich, ihm 5 Pence pro Meile zu geben.
sponsored ['spɒnsəd] adj (for charity etc) walk etc: zur Geldbeschaffung abgehalten, wobei die Leistung vom Spender honoriert wird.
sponsorship ['spɒnsəʃɪp] n see vt Unterstützung f; Förderung f; Schirmherrschaft f; Bürgschaft f; Befürwortung f; (Rad, TV, Sport etc) Finanzierung f.
spontaneity [ˌspɒntə'neɪətɪ] n see adj Spontaneität f; Ungezwungenheit f.
spontaneous [spɒn'teɪnɪəs] adj spontan; style ungezwungen. ~ **combustion** Selbstentzündung f.
spoof [spuːf] (col) n **(a)** (parody) Parodie f (of auf +acc). **(b)** (hoax) Scherz m (col).
spook [spuːk] n (col) Gespenst nt.
spooky ['spuːkɪ] adj (+er) (col) castle etc gruselig (col).
spool [spuːl] n (Phot, on sewing machine) Spule f; (on fishing line, for thread) Rolle f.
spoon [spuːn] **1** n Löffel m. **to be born with a silver ~ in one's mouth** (prov) mit einem silbernen Löffel im Mund geboren sein (col). **2** vt löffeln.
spoonerism ['spuːnərɪzəm] n lustiger Versprecher.
spoon-feed ['spuːnfiːd] pret, ptp **spoon-fed** ['spuːnfed] vt baby, invalid füttern; (fig) (do thinking for) gängeln; (supply with) füttern (col).
spoonful ['spuːnfʊl] n Löffel m. **a ~ of soup** ein Löffel Suppe.
sporadic [spə'rædɪk] adj sporadisch.
spore [spɔːʳ] n Spore f.
sport [spɔːt] **1** n **(a)** Sport m no pl; (type of ~) Sportart f. **to be good at** ~**(s)** sportlich sein; **outdoor/indoor** ~**s** Sport m im Freien/Hallensport m. **(b)** (amusement) Spaß m. **to do sth for/in** ~ etw zum Spaß tun. **(c)** (col: person) feiner Kerl (col); (Austral) Junge m. **to be a (good)** ~ alles mitmachen; **be a** ~**!** sei kein Spielverderber! **2** vt tie, dress anhaben; (show off) ring etc protzen mit. **3** adj attr (US) = **sports.**
sporting ['spɔːtɪŋ] adj **(a)** person, interests sport-

lich; gun Jagd-. ~ **events** Wettkämpfe pl. **(b)** (sportsmanlike) sportlich; spirit also Sports-; (fig) offer, solution fair; (decent) anständig. **to give sb a** ~ **chance** jdm eine faire Chance geben.
sports, (US also) **sport** in cpds Sport-; ~ **car** n Sportwagen m; ~ **field,** ~ **ground** n Sportplatz m; ~ **jacket** n Sportjackett nt; ~**man** [-mən] n (player) Sportler m; ~**woman** n Sportlerin f.
sporty ['spɔːtɪ] adj (+er) (col) **(a)** person, clothes sportlich. **(b)** (jaunty) flott.
spot [spɒt] **1** n **(a)** (dot) Tupfen, Punkt m; (on dice) Punkt m; (stain, on fruit) Fleck m; (fig: on reputation) Makel m (on an +dat). **a dress with** ~**s** ein getupftes or gepunktetes Kleid; ~**s of blood/grease** Blutflecken pl/Fettflecken pl; ~**s of ink** Tintenkleckse pl; **to knock** ~**s off sb/sth** (fig col) jdn/etw in den Schatten stellen; **to have** ~**s before one's eyes** Sternchen sehen.
(b) (Med etc) Fleck m; (pimple) Pickel m. **to break** or **come out in** ~**s** Flecken/Pickel bekommen.
(c) (place) Stelle f; (point) Punkt m. **this is the** ~ **where Karl was murdered** an dieser Stelle ist Karl ermordet worden; **a pleasant** ~ ein schönes Fleckchen (col); **on the** ~ (at the scene) an Ort und Stelle; (at once) auf der Stelle; **on-the-**~ **investigation** Untersuchung f an Ort und Stelle; (immediate) sofortige Untersuchung; **an on-the-**~ **report** ein Bericht m vom Ort des Geschehens; **weak** ~ schwache Stelle.
(d) (Brit col: small quantity) **a** ~ **of** ein bißchen; **we had a** ~ **of rain/a few** ~**s of rain** wir hatten ein paar Tropfen Regen; **there was a** ~ **of trouble/bother** es gab etwas Ärger; **would you like to do a** ~ **of driving?** möchten Sie ein bißchen fahren?
(e) (difficulty) Klemme f. **to be in a (tight)** ~, **to be on the** ~ in der Klemme sitzen (col); **to put sb on the** ~ jdn in Verlegenheit bringen.
(f) (in show) Nummer f; (Rad, TV) Sendezeit f; (for advertisement) Werbespot m.
(g) (col: ~light) Scheinwerfer, Spot m.
2 vt **(a)** (notice, see) entdecken, sehen; (pick out) erkennen; (find) mistake, bargain finden. **(b)** (stain) bespritzen. **blue material** ~**ted with white** blauer Stoff mit weißen Tupfen.
3 vi **it's** ~**ting (with rain)** es tröpfelt.
spot check n Stichprobe f.
spotless ['spɒtlɪs] adj tadellos sauber, picobello inv (col); (fig) reputation makellos.
spotlessly ['spɒtlɪslɪ] adv: ~ **clean** blitzsauber.
spot: ~**light** n (lamp) Scheinwerfer m; **to be in the** ~**light** (fig) im Rampenlicht der Öffentlichkeit stehen; **to turn the** ~**light on sb/sth** (fig) die Aufmerksamkeit auf jdn/etw lenken; ~**-on** adj (Brit col) answer, analysis exakt, genau, richtig.
spotted ['spɒtɪd] adj gefleckt; (with dots) getüpfelt; material getupft; (marked, stained) fleckig.
spotty ['spɒtɪ] adj (+er) fleckig; (pimply) pick(e)lig, voller Pickel.
spouse [spaʊs] n (form) Gatte m (form), Gattin f (form).
spout [spaʊt] **1** n **(a)** Ausguß m; (on watering can) Rohr nt. **up the** ~ (col: plans etc) im Eimer (col). **(b)** (jet of water etc) Fontäne f. **2** vt **(a)** water etc (heraus)spritzen; (whale also) ausstoßen; (volcano) speien. **(b)** (col: declaim) poetry, speeches loslassen (at sb auf jdn); words hervorsprudeln; figures herunterrasseln (col); nonsense von sich geben.
sprain [spreɪn] **1** n Verstauchung f. **2** vt verstauchen. **to** ~ **one's ankle** sich (dat) den Fuß verstauchen.
sprang [spræŋ] pret of **spring.**
sprawl [sprɔːl] **1** n (of town etc) Ausbreitung f. **urban** ~ wild wuchernde Ausbreitung des Stadtgebietes. **2** vi (person) (fall) der Länge nach hinfallen; (lounge) sich hinflegeln; (plant,

town) (wild) wuchern. **to send sb ~ing** jdn zu Boden werfen.
sprawling ['sprɔ:lɪŋ] *adj city, suburbs* wildwuchernd; *figure* hingeflegelt.
spray[1] [spreɪ] *n (bouquet)* Strauß *m; (buttonhole)* Ansteckblume *f.*
spray[2] **1** *n* **(a)** Sprühregen *m; (of sea)* Gischt *m.* **the ~ from the lorries makes it difficult to see** die Lastwagen spritzen so, daß man kaum etwas sehen kann. **(b)** *(implement)* Sprühdose *f; (insecticide ~, for irrigation)* Spritze *f; (scent~)* Zerstäuber *m.* **(c)** *(hair-~ etc)* Spray *m or nt.* **(d) to give sth a ~** etw besprühen; *(with paint, insecticide)* etw spritzen; *(with hair-~ etc)* etw sprayen. **2** *vt plants, insects etc* besprühen; *(with paint, insecticide)* spritzen; *hair* sprayen; *room* aussprühen; *water, paint, foam* sprühen; *perfume* (ver)sprühen. **to ~ sth with water/bullets** etw mit Wasser besprühen/mit Kugeln übersäen. **3** *vi* sprühen; *(water, mud)* spritzen.
sprayer ['spreɪə[r]] *n* = **spray**[2] **1 (b).**
spread [spred] *(vb: pret, ptp ~)* **1** *n* **(a)** *(of wings)* Spannweite *f; (range) (of marks)* Verteilung *f; (of prices)* Spanne *f; (of ideas, interests)* Spektrum *nt.* **middle-age ~** Altersspeck *m (col).*
(b) *(growth)* Ausbreitung *f; (spatial)* Ausdehnung *f.* **the ~ of nuclear weapons** die zunehmende Verbreitung von Atomwaffen.
(c) *(col: of food etc)* Festessen *nt; (for bread)* (Brot)aufstrich *m.* **cheese ~** Streichkäse *m.*
(d) *(Press, Typ: two pages)* Doppelseite *f.* **a double-page ~** ein zweiseitiger Bericht; *(advertisement)* eine zweiseitige Anzeige.
2 *vt* **(a)** *(open or lay out: also ~ out)* ausbreiten; *fan* öffnen; *hands, legs* spreizen. **the peacock ~ its tail** der Pfau schlug ein Rad; **the view which was ~ before us** die Sicht, die sich uns bot.
(b) *bread, surface* bestreichen; *butter, paint etc* streichen. **~ the paint evenly** verteilen Sie die Farbe gleichmäßig; **to ~ a blanket on sth** eine Decke über etw *(acc)* breiten; **the table was ~ with food** der Tisch war reichlich gedeckt.
(c) *(distribute: also ~ out)* forces, objects, *payments* verteilen; *sand, fertilizer also, muck* streuen. **our resources are ~ very thinly** unsere Mittel sind maximal beansprucht.
(d) *news, panic, rumour* verbreiten.
3 *vi* **(a)** *(extend) (spatially)* sich erstrecken *(over, across* über *+acc); (with movement) (weeds, fire, smile, industry)* sich ausbreiten *(over, across* über *+acc); (towns)* sich ausdehnen; *(knowledge, fear etc, smell, disease, trouble, fire)* sich verbreiten. **to ~ to sth** etw erreichen; *(disease etc)* auf etw *(acc)* übergreifen. **(b)** *(butter etc)* sich streichen lassen.
♦ **spread out 1** *vt sep* = **spread 2 (a, c). 2** *vi* **(a)** *(countryside etc)* sich ausdehnen. **(b)** *(troops, runners)* sich verteilen.
spread-eagle ['spred,i:gl] *vt* **to be ~d** alle viere von sich *(dat)* strecken *(col).*
spreadsheet ['spredʃi:t] *n* Arbeitsblatt *nt.*
spree [spri:] *n* **spending** *or* **shopping ~** Großeinkauf *m;* **to be/go on a ~** *(drinking)* eine Zechtour machen; *(spending)* groß einkaufen gehen.
sprig [sprɪg] *n* Zweig *m.* **~ of flowers** Blütenzweig.
sprightly ['spraɪtlɪ] *adj (+er) person, tune* munter; *old person* rüstig; *walk* schwungvoll.
spring [sprɪŋ] *(vb: pret* **sprang** *or (US)* **sprung,** *ptp* **sprung) 1** *n* **(a)** *(lit, fig liter: source)* Quelle *f.*
(b) *(season)* Frühling. **~ is in the air** der Frühling liegt in der Luft.
(c) *(leap)* Sprung *m.* **in one ~** mit einem Satz.
(d) *(Mech)* Feder *f.* **~s** *(Aut)* Federung *f.*
(e) *no pl (bounciness) (of chair)* Federung *f; (of wood etc)* Elastizität *f.* **to walk with a ~ in one's step** mit federnden Schritten gehen.
2 *vt (cause to operate)* auslösen; *mine also* explodieren lassen; *lock, mousetrap etc* zuschnap-
pen lassen. **to ~ a leak** *(pipe)* (plötzlich) undicht werden; *(ship)* (plötzlich) ein Leck bekommen; **to ~ sth on sb** *(fig)* idea, decision jdn mit etw konfrontieren; **to ~ a surprise on sb** jdn völlig überraschen.
3 *vi* **(a)** *(leap)* springen; *(be activated)* ausgelöst werden; *(mousetrap)* zuschnappen. **to ~ at sb** jdn anspringen; **to ~ out at sb** auf jdn losspringen; **to ~ open** aufspringen; **to ~ to one's feet** aufspringen; **to ~ into action** aktiv werden; *(police, fire brigade etc)* in Aktion treten; **to ~ into view** plötzlich in Sicht kommen; **to ~ to mind** einem einfallen; **to ~ to sb's aid/defence** jdm zu Hilfe eilen; **he sprang to fame** er wurde plötzlich berühmt; **to ~ (in)to life** (plötzlich) lebendig werden.
(b) *(issue: also ~ forth) (liter) (water, blood)* (hervor)quellen *(from* aus); *(fire, sparks)* sprühen *(from* aus).
(c) *(fig) (idea)* entstehen *(from* aus); *(interest, irritability etc)* herrühren *(from* von). **where did you ~ from?** *(col)* wo kommst du denn her?; **to ~ into existence** (plötzlich or rasch) entstehen.
♦ **spring up** *vi (plant)* hervorsprießen; *(weeds, buildings)* aus dem Boden schießen; *(person)* aufspringen; *(fig) (friendship, firm)* (plötzlich) entstehen; *(problem, rumour)* auftauchen.
spring: **~binder** *n* Klemmhefter *m;* **~board** *n (lit, fig)* Sprungbrett *nt;* **~-cleaning** *n* Frühjahrsputz *m;* **~ onion** *n* Frühlingszwiebel *f;* **~ tide** *n* **(a)** Springflut *f;* **(b)** *(poet: ~time)* Lenz *m (poet);* **~time** *n* Frühling *m.*
springy ['sprɪŋɪ] *adj (+er) step* federnd; *plank, turf, grass also* nachgiebig, elastisch; *rubber, wood, plastic etc, hair* elastisch; *bed* weich gefedert.
sprinkle ['sprɪŋkl] *vt water* sprenkeln; *lawn, plant,* besprengen; *salt, dust, sugar etc* streuen; *cake* bestreuen.
sprinkler ['sprɪŋklə[r]] *n (Hort, Agr)* Berieselungsapparat *m; (in garden also)* (Rasen)sprenger *m; (for fire-fighting)* Sprinkler *m; (on watering can etc)* Sprenger *m; (of sugar)* Streuer *m.*
sprinkling ['sprɪŋklɪŋ] *n (of rain, dew etc)* ein paar Tropfen; *(of sugar etc)* Prise *f; (fig: of humour etc)* Anflug *m.* **there was a ~ of young people** es waren ein paar vereinzelte junge Leute da.
sprint [sprɪnt] **1** *n* Lauf *m; (race)* Sprint *m; (burst of speed)* Spurt *m.* **the 100-m ~** der 100-m-Lauf. **2** *vi (in race)* sprinten; *(dash)* rennen; *(for train etc also)* spurten *(for* zu).
sprinter ['sprɪntə[r]] *n* Sprinter(in *f*) *m.*
sprout [spraʊt] **1** *n* **(a)** *(of plant)* Trieb *m; (of tree also)* Schößling, Sproß *m; (from seed)* Keim *m.* **(b)** *(Brussels ~)* (Rosenkohl)röschen *nt.* **~s** *pl* Rosenkohl *m.* **2** *vt leaves, buds etc* treiben; *horns etc* entwickeln; *seeds etc* keimen lassen. **3** *vi* **(a)** *(grow)* beard *sich (dat)* wachsen lassen. **3** *vi* **(a)** *(grow)* sprießen; *(seed, wheat etc)* keimen; *(potatoes, trees etc)* Triebe bekommen. **(b)** *(lit, fig: also ~ up) (plants, weeds)* sprießen; *(new sects, new buildings)* wie Pilze aus dem Boden schießen.
spruce[1] [spru:s] *n (also ~ fir)* Fichte *f.*
spruce[2] *adj (+er)* gepflegt; *women, child* adrett.
♦ **spruce up** *vt sep child* herausputzen; *house, garden* auf Vordermann bringen *(col).* **to ~ oneself ~ (get dressed up)** sich in Schale werfen; *(woman)* sich zurechtmachen.
sprung [sprʌŋ] **1** *ptp of* **spring. 2** *adj* gefedert.
spry [spraɪ] *adj* rüstig.
spud [spʌd] *n (col: potato)* Kartoffel *f.*
spun [spʌn] *pret, ptp of* **spin.**
spunk [spʌŋk] *n (col)* Courage *f.*
spur [spɜ:[r]] **1** *n* Sporn *m; (fig: burst of) (Geog)* Vorsprung *m.* **to win** *or* **gain one's ~s** *(fig)* sich *(dat)* die Sporen verdienen; **on the ~ of the moment** ganz spontan. **2** *vt (also ~ on) horse* die Sporen geben *(+dat); (fig)* anspornen. **~red (on) by greed** von Habgier getrieben.

spurious ['spjʊərɪəs] *adj claim* unberechtigt; *document, account* falsch; *emotion* nicht echt.

spurn [spɜːn] *vt* verschmähen.

spurt [spɜːt] **1** *n* **(a)** *(flow)* Strahl *m.* ~s of flame Stichflammen. **(b)** *(of speed)* Spurt *m.* to put a ~ on *(lit, fig)* einen Spurt vorlegen; there was a ~ of activity es brach plötzlich Aktivität aus. **2** *vi (gush: also* ~ out) (heraus)spritzen *(from* aus).

spy [spaɪ] **1** *n* Spion (in *f*) *m; (police* ~) Spitzel *m.* **2** *vt* sehen. **3** *vi* spionieren. to ~ on sb jdn bespitzeln; on *neighbours* jdm nachspionieren.

♦ **spy out** *vt sep* to ~ ~ the land *(Mil)* die Gegend auskundschaften; *(fig)* die Lage peilen.

spying ['spaɪɪŋ] *n* Spionage *f.*

spy story *n* Spionagegeschichte *f.*

Sq = **Square**.

sq = **square**. ~ m qm, m².

squabble ['skwɒbl] **1** *n* Zank, Streit *m.* **2** *vi* (sich) zanken, (sich) streiten *(about,* over um).

squad [skwɒd] *n (Mil, police unit etc)* Kommando *nt; (police department)* Dezernat *nt; (of workmen)* Trupp *m; (Sport, fig)* Mannschaft *f.*

squad car *n* Streifenwagen *m.*

squadron ['skwɒdrən] *n (of cavalry)* Schwadron *f; (Aviat)* Staffel *f; (Naut)* Geschwader *nt.*

squalid ['skwɒlɪd] *adj room, house* schmutzig und verwahrlost; *existence, conditions* elend; *deed, idea etc* niederträchtig; *dispute, gossip* entwürdigend; *affair* schmutzig.

squall [skwɔːl] **1** *n (storm)* Bö(e) *f; (fig)* Gewitter *nt.* **2** *vi* schreien.

squalor ['skwɒlə'] *n* Schmutz *m; (moral* ~) Verkommenheit *f.*

squander ['skwɒndə'] *vt* verschwenden *(on* an +acc); *opportunity* vertun.

square [skweə'] **1** *n* **(a)** Quadrat *nt; (piece of material, paper etc also)* Viereck *nt; (on chessboard etc)* Feld *nt; (on paper, in crossword)* Kästchen *nt; (on material etc)* Karo *nt.* cut it in ~s schneiden Sie es quadratisch zu; we're back to ~ one jetzt sind wir wieder da, wo wir angefangen haben. **(b)** *(in town, Mil)* Platz *m; (US: of houses)* Block *m.* **(c)** *(Math)* Quadrat(zahl *f) nt.* the ~ of 3 is 9 3 hoch 2 ist 9. **(d)** *(col: old-fashioned person)* Spießer *m (col).* to be a ~ von (vor)gestern sein.

2 *adj (+er)* **(a)** *(in shape)* quadratisch; *picture, lawn etc also,* nib viereckig; *file* Vierkant-; *block of wood etc* vierkantig. to be a ~ peg in a round hole am falschen Platz sein. **(b)** *(forming right angle) angle* rechter attr; *corner* rechtwinklig; *bracket, shoulder* eckig; *build* vierschrötig. **(c)** *(Math)* Quadrat-. 3 ~ kilometers 3 Quadratkilometer; **3 metres** = 3 Meter im Quadrat. **(d)** *attr (complete) meal* ordentlich. **(e)** *(fair) deal* gerecht, fair; *game, person* ehrlich. to give sb a ~ deal jdn fair behandeln; **I'll be** ~ with you ich will ehrlich mit dir sein. **(f)** *(fig: even)* to be ~ *(accounts etc)* in Ordnung sein; **to get** ~ with sb mit jdm abrechnen. **(g)** *(col: old-fashioned)* überholt; *person, ideas* spießig *(col).* he's ~ er ist von (vor)gestern.

3 *adv (+er)* **(a)** *(at right angles)* rechtwinklig. ~ with sth senkrecht zu etw. **(b)** *(directly)* direkt, genau.

4 *vt* **(a)** *(make* ~) quadratisch machen; to ~ one's shoulders die Schultern straffen; to try to ~ the circle die Quadratur des Kreises versuchen. **(b)** *(Math)* number quadrieren. 3 ~d is 9 3 hoch 2 ist 9. **(c)** *(adjust)* debts begleichen; *creditors* abrechnen mit; *(reconcile)* in Einklang bringen. to ~ one's accounts abrechnen *(with* mit); to ~ sth with one's conscience etw mit seinem Gewissen vereinbaren; **I'll** ~ it with the porter *(col)* ich mache das mit dem Portier ab *(col).*

5 *vi* übereinstimmen *(with* mit).

♦ **square off** *vt sep (make square) corner* rechtwinklig machen.

♦ **square up** *vi* **(a)** Kampfstellung annehmen. to

~ ~ to sb sich vor jdm aufpflanzen *(col); (boxer)* vor jdm in Positur gehen; *(fig)* jdm die Stirn bieten. **(b)** *(lit, fig: settle)* abrechnen.

squarely ['skweəlɪ] *adj* **(a)** *(directly)* direkt, genau; *(fig: firmly)* fest. we must face this ~ wir müssen dieser Sache *(dat)* (fest) ins Auge sehen. **(b)** *(honestly)* ehrlich; *(fairly)* gerecht, fair.

squash¹ [skwɒʃ] **1** *n* **(a)** *(Brit) (fruit concentrate)* Fruchtsaftkonzentrat *nt; (drink)* Fruchtsaftgetränk *nt.* **a glass of orange** ~ ein Glas Orangensaft. **(b)** *(crowd)* Gedränge *nt.* it's a bit of a ~ es ist ziemlich eng. **2** *vt* **(a)** *(also* ~ up) zerdrücken; *box etc* zusammendrücken. **(b)** *(fig col) (silence) person* über den Mund fahren *(+dat); (quash)* protest, argument vom Tisch fegen *(col).* **(c)** *(squeeze)* quetschen. to ~ sb/sth in jdn einquetschen/etw hineinquetschen; to be ~ed together eng zusammengequetscht sein. **3** *vi* **(a)** *(get* ~ed) zerdrückt werden. **(b)** *(squeeze)* sich quetschen. to ~ in sich hinein-/ hereinquetschen; could you ~ up? könnt ihr etwas zusammenrücken?

squash² *n (Sport)* Squash *nt.*

squat [skwɒt] **1** *adj (+er) chair* niedrig; *figure, person* gedrungen. **2** *vi* **(a)** *(person) (animal)* hocken; *(also* ~ down) sich (hin)hocken. **(b)** *(on land)* sich (illegal) ansiedeln. to ~ (in a house) ein Haus besetzt haben.

squatter ['skwɒtə'] *n (on land)* illegaler Siedler; *(in house)* Hausbesetzer(in *f) m.*

squaw [skwɔː] *n* Squaw *f.*

squawk [skwɔːk] **1** *n* heiserer Schrei; *(of hens)* Gackern *nt.* **2** *vi* **(a)** *(bird, person)* kreischen.

squeak [skwiːk] **1** *n (of hinge etc, shoe, pen)* Quietschen *nt no pl; (of person, small animal)* Quieken *nt no pl; (of bird)* Piepsen *nt no pl; (fig col: sound)* Pieps *m (col).* the door opened with a ~ die Tür ging quietschend auf. **2** *vi (door, hinge, shoes etc)* quietschen; *(person, small animal)* quieken; *(mouse, bird)* piepsen.

squeaky ['skwiːkɪ] *adj (+er)* quietschend; *voice* piepsig.

squeal ['skwiːl] **1** *n* Schrei *m; (of person, tyre, brakes)* Kreischen *nt no pl; (of protest)* (Auf)schrei *m; (of pig)* Quieken *nt no pl.* **a** ~ of pain ein Schmerzensschrei *m;* ~s/a ~ of laughter schrilles Gelächter. **2** *vi* **(a)** schreien; *(brakes, tyres)* quietschen; *(pig, puppy)* quieken; *(fig col)* jammern. to ~ with pain/pleasure vor Schmerz kreischen/vor Vergnügen quietschen. **(b)** *(col: confess, inform) (criminal)* singen *(col)* (to bei); *(schoolboy etc)* petzen *(col)* (to bei).

squeamish ['skwiːmɪʃ] *adj person (easily nauseated or shocked)* empfindlich. **I felt a bit** ~ *(sick)* mir war leicht übel.

squeeze [skwiːz] **1** *n (act of squeezing)* Drücken *nt no pl; (hug)* Umarmung *f; (of hand)* Händedruck *m; (in bus etc)* Gedränge *nt.* to give sth a ~ etw drücken, etw pressen; *lemon, sponge* etw ausdrücken; to give sb/sb's hand a ~ jdn an sich *(acc)* drücken/jdm die Hand drücken; it was a tight ~ es war fürchterlich eng; put a ~ of toothpaste on the brush drücke eine Spur etwas Zahnpasta auf die Bürste; to put the ~ on sb *(col)* jdm die Daumenschrauben anlegen *(col).* **(b)** *(credit* ~) Kreditbeschränkung *f.*

2 *vt* drücken; *sponge, tube* ausdrücken; *orange* auspressen; *(squash) person, hand* einquetschen. to ~ clothes into a case Kleider in einen Koffer zwängen; to ~ out water/juice Wasser/Saft herauspressen *(from* aus); to ~d the trigger er drückte ab; to ~ money/information etc out of sb Geld/Informationen etc aus jdm herausquetschen.

3 *vi* to ~ in/out sich hinein-/hinausdrängen; to ~ past sb sich an jdm vorbeidrücken; to ~ through a crowd sich durch eine Menge zwängen; you'll have to ~ up a bit Sie müssen ein bißchen zusammenrücken.

squelch [skweltʃ] *vi* platschen; *(shoes, mud)* quatschen.

squid [skwɪd] *n* Tintenfisch *m*.

squint [skwɪnt] **1** *n (Med)* Schielen *nt no pl.* **to have a** ~ leicht schielen; **to take a** ~ **at sb/sth** einen Blick auf jdn/etw werfen; *(obliquely)* nach jdm/etw schielen. **2** *vi* schielen; *(in strong light etc)* blinzeln. **to** ~ **at sb/sth** nach jdm/etw schielen; *(quickly)* einen kurzen Blick auf jdn/etw werfen.

squire ['skwaɪəʳ] *n (esp Brit: landowner)* Gutsherr *m*.

squirm [skwɜːm] *vi* sich winden; *(in distaste)* schaudern; *(with embarrassment)* sich (drehen und) winden. **spiders make me** ~ vor Spinnen graust es mir.

squirrel ['skwɪrəl] *n* Eichhörnchen *nt*.

squirt [skwɜːt] **1** *n* **(a)** Spritzer *m*. **(b)** *(pej col: person)* Pimpf *m (col).* **2** *vt liquid* spritzen; *object, person* bespritzen. **to** ~ **water at sb** jdn mit Wasser bespritzen. **3** *vi* spritzen.

Sr = **senior** sen.

St. = **(a) Street** Str. **(b) Saint** hl., St.

stab [stæb] **1** *n* **(a)** *(with knife etc, wound, of pain)* Stich *m.* ~ **wound** Stichwunde *f*; **to feel a** ~ **of pain** einen stechenden Schmerz empfinden; **a** ~ **in the back** *(fig)* ein Dolchstoß *m.* **(b)** *(col: try)* Versuch *m*. **to have a** ~ **at sth** etw probieren. **2** *vt person* einen Stich versetzen (+*dat*); *(several times)* einstechen auf (+*acc*); *(wound seriously)* niederstechen. **to** ~ **sb (to death)** jdn erstechen; **to** ~ **sb with a knife** jdn mit einem Messerstich/ mit Messerstichen verletzen; **he was** ~**bed through the arm/heart** er hatte eine Stichwunde am Arm/der Stich traf ihn ins Herz; **to** ~ **sb in the back** *(lit)* jdm in den Rücken stechen; *(fig)* jdm in den Rücken fallen. **3** *vi* **to** ~ **at sb/sth** *(with knife etc)* nach jdm/etw stechen; *(with finger)* auf jdn/etw zeigen.

stabbing ['stæbɪŋ] **1** *n* Messerstecherei *f*. **2** *adj pain* stechend.

stability [stə'bɪlɪtɪ] *n* Stabilität *f*; *(of relationship also, of job)* Beständigkeit *f*. **(mental)** ~ (seelische) Ausgeglichenheit.

stabilize ['steɪbəlaɪz] **1** *vt (Fin, Naut, Aviat)* stabilisieren. **2** *vi* sich stabilisieren.

stabilizer ['steɪbəlaɪzəʳ] *n (Naut)* Stabilisator *m*; *(Aviat)* Stabilisierungsfläche *f*.

stable¹ ['steɪbl] *adj* (+*er*) stabil; *relationship also, job* beständig; *character* gefestigt. **mentally** ~ ausgeglichen.

stable² *n* **(building)** Stall *m*; *(group of racehorses)* (Renn)stall *m*. **riding** ~**s** Reitstall *m*.

stack [stæk] **1** *n* **(a)** *(pile)* Haufen *m*; *(neatly piled)* Stoß, Stapel *m*. **to join the** ~ *(Aviat)* kreisen. **(b)** *(col: lots)* Haufen *m (col).* ~**s** jede Menge *(col)*; **we have** ~**s of time** wir haben jede Menge Zeit. **2** *vt* **(a)** stapeln. **(b)** *(US Cards)* präparieren. **the odds are** ~**ed against us** *(fig)* wir haben keine großen Chancen. **3** *vi* sich stapeln lassen.

stadium ['steɪdɪəm] *n* Stadion *nt*.

staff [stɑːf] **1** *n* **(a)** *Personal nt; (Sch, Univ)* Kollegium *nt,* Lehrkörper *m (form); (of department, on project)* Mitarbeiterstab *m.* **a large** ~ viel Personal/ein großes Kollegium/ein großer Mitarbeiterstab; **a member of** ~ ein Mitarbeiter *m; (Sch)* ein Kollege *m*; **we have 30 typists on the** ~ bei uns sind 30 Schreibkräfte angestellt; **to be on the** ~ zum Personal/Kollegium/Mitarbeiterstab gehören. **(b)** *(stick, symbol of authority)* Stab *m*. **(c)** *pl* **staves** *(Mus)* Notenlinien *pl.* **2** *vt department* Mitarbeiter finden für; *hospital, shop* mit Personal besetzen; *school* mit Lehrpersonal besetzen. **to be well** ~**ed** gut besetzt sein; **the kitchens are** ~**ed by foreigners** das Küchenpersonal besteht aus Ausländern.

staff: ~ **meeting** *n* Lehrerkonferenz *f*; ~ **nurse** *n*

ausgebildete Krankenschwester; ~ **officer** *n* Stabsoffizier *m*; ~**room** *n* Lehrerzimmer *nt*.

stag [stæg] *n (deer)* Hirsch *m*.

stage [steɪdʒ] **1** *n* **(a)** *(Theat, fig)* Bühne *f*; *(platform in hall)* Podium *nt*. **the** ~ *(profession)* das Theater; **to be on/go on** ~ *(as career)* beim Theater sein/ zum Theater gehen; **to go on** ~ *(actor)* die Bühne betreten; **the** ~ **was set** *(fig)* alles war vorbereitet. **(b)** *(period)* Stadium *nt; (of disease, process also, of development)* Phase *f.* **at this** ~ **in the** negotiations an diesem Punkt der Verhandlungen; **at this** ~ **in the game** *(fig)* zu diesem Zeitpunkt; **in the early/final** ~**(s)** im Anfangs-/ Endstadium; **to go through a difficult** ~ eine schwierige Phase durchmachen. **(c)** *(part of journey, race etc)* Abschnitt *m,* Etappe *f; (fare~)* Fahrzone *f.* **in** *or* **by (easy)** ~**s** *(lit, fig)* etappenweise. **(d)** *(section of rocket)* Stufe *f.*
2 *vt play* aufführen; *(fig) accident, scene etc* inszenieren; *welcome* arrangieren; *demonstration, strike etc* veranstalten. **to** ~ **a recovery/ comeback** sich erholen/ein Comeback machen.

stage: ~**coach** *n* Postkutsche *f*; ~ **door** *n* Bühneneingang *m*; ~ **fright** *n* Lampenfieber *nt*; ~**manage** *vt (lit)* Inspizient sein bei; *(fig)* demonstration, argument inszenieren; ~ **manager** *n* Inspizient *m*; ~ **name** *n* Künstlername *m*; ~**-struck** *adj* theaterbesessen.

stagger ['stægəʳ] **1** *vi* taumeln; *(because of illness, weakness)* wanken; *(drunkenly)* torkeln. **2** *vt* **(a)** *(fig: amaze)* den Atem verschlagen (+*dat*), umhauen *(col).* **(b)** *hours, holidays* staffeln; *seats etc* versetzt anordnen.

staggered ['stægəd] *adj* **(a)** *(amazed)* verblüfft. **(b)** *working hours etc* gestaffelt.

staggering ['stægərɪŋ] *adj (amazing)* umwerfend *(col).*

stagnant ['stægnənt] *adj (still) air, water* stehend *attr; (foul, stale) water* abgestanden; *air* verbraucht; *trade* stagnierend; *mind* träge.

stagnate [stæg'neɪt] *vi (not circulate, business)* stagnieren; *(become foul) (water)* stagnieren; *(air)* verbraucht werden; *(person)* verdummen; *(mind)* einrosten.

stagnation [stæg'neɪʃən] *n (of water)* Stagnieren *nt; (of air)* Stau *m; (of trade also)* Stagnation *f; (of person)* Verdummung *f; (of mind)* Verlangsamung *f.*

stag: ~ **night** *n* Saufabend *m (col)* des Bräutigams mit seinen Kumpeln; ~ **party** *n* **(a)** Herrenabend *m*; **(b)** = ~ **night**.

staid [steɪd] *adj* (+*er*) seriös; *person* ernst; *colour* gedeckt.

stain [steɪn] **1** *n* **(a)** *(lit)* Fleck *m; (fig also)* Makel *m.* **a blood** ~ ein Blutfleck *m,* ~ **remover** Fleckenentferner *m.* **(b)** *(colorant)* (Ein)färbemittel *nt; (wood~)* Beize *f.* **2** *vt* beflecken; *(colour)* einfärben; *(with wood~)* beizen. **3** *vi (a) (leave a* ~) Flecken hinterlassen. **(b)** *(become* ~*ed)* Flecken bekommen.

stained [steɪnd] *adj dress, floor* fleckig; *glass* bemalt; *reputation* befleckt. ~**-glass window** Buntglasfenster *nt*; ~ **with blood** blutbefleckt.

stainless ['steɪnlɪs] *adj (rust-resistant)* rostfrei. ~ **steel** Edelstahl, *vor* ~ **steel** „rostfrei"; ~ **steel cutlery** rostfreies Besteck.

stair [steəʳ] *n* **(a)** *(step)* Stufe *f.* **(b)** *usu pl* *(*~*way)* Treppe *f.* **at the top of the** ~**s** oben an der Treppe.

stair: ~ **carpet** *n* Treppenläufer *m*; ~ **case** *n* Treppe *f*; ~**way** *n* Treppe *f*; ~**well** *n* Treppenhaus *nt*.

stake [steɪk] **1** *n* **(a)** *(post)* Pfahl *m; (for plant)* Stange *f; (for animal)* Pflock *m.* **(b)** *(place of execution)* Scheiterhaufen *m.* **to be burnt at the** ~ auf dem Scheiterhaufen verbrannt werden. **(c)** *(bet)* Einsatz *m; (financial interest)* Anteil *m.* **to be at** ~ auf dem Spiel stehen; **he has a lot at** ~ er hat viel zu verlieren; **to have a** ~ **in sth** *in business* einen Anteil an etw (*dat*) haben; **that's precisely**

the issue at ~ genau darum geht es. 2 *vt* **(a)** *animal* anpflocken. **(b)** *(also ~ up) plant* hochbinden; *fence* abstützen. **(c)** *(bet, risk)* setzen *(on auf +acc)*; *(US: back financially)* finanziell unterstützen. **to ~ one's life/reputation on sth** seine Hand für etw ins Feuer legen/sein Wort für etw verpfänden; **to ~ a/one's claim to sth** sich *(dat)* ein Anrecht auf etw *(acc)* sichern.

♦ **stake off** *or* **out** *vt sep land* abstecken.

stalactite ['stæləktaɪt] *n* Stalaktit *m*.

stalagmite ['stæləgmaɪt] *n* Stalagmit *m*.

stale [steɪl] *adj* (+*er*) **(a)** *(old, musty)* alt; *cake also* trocken; *(in taste, smell also)* muffig; *water, beer* schal; *air* verbraucht. **(b)** *(fig) news* veraltet; *joke* abgedroschen; *athlete, pianist* verbraucht.

stalemate ['steɪlmeɪt] *n (Chess, fig)* Patt *nt*. **to reach ~** *(lit)* ein Patt erreichen; *(fig)* in eine Sackgasse geraten.

stalk¹ [stɔːk] **1** *vt game* sich anpirschen an *(+acc)*; *person* sich anschleichen an *(+acc)*; *(animal)* sich heranschleichen an *(+acc)*. **2** *vi (walk haughtily)* stolzieren.

stalk² *n (of plant, leaf)* Stiel *m*; *(cabbage ~)* Strunk *m*. **his eyes popped out on ~s** *(col)* er bekam Stielaugen *(col)*.

stall [stɔːl] **1** *n* **(a)** *(in stable)* Box *f*. **(b)** *(at market etc)* Stand *m*. **(c)** *~s pl (Brit Theat, Film)* Parkett *nt*; **in the ~s** im Parkett. **2** *vt (Aut)* abwürgen; *(Aviat)* überziehen. **3** *vi* **(a)** *(engine)* absterben; *(Aviat)* überziehen. **(b)** *(delay)* Zeit schinden *(col)*. **to ~ on a decision** eine Entscheidung hinauszögern; **to ~ for time** versuchen, Zeit zu gewinnen; **stop ~ing** hören Sie auf auszuweichen.

stallion ['stæljən] *n* Hengst *m*.

stalwart ['stɔːlwət] **1** *adj* **(a)** *(in spirit)* treu; *belief* unerschütterlich. **(b)** *(in build)* robust. **2** *n (supporter)* (getreuer) Anhänger.

stamen ['steɪmen] *n* Staubgefäß *nt*.

stamina ['stæmɪnə] *n* Stehvermögen *nt*.

stammer ['stæmə'] **1** *n* Stottern *nt*. **to speak with a ~** stottern. **2** *vt* stammeln. **3** *vi* stottern.

stamp [stæmp] **1** *n* **(a)** *(postage ~)* (Brief)marke *f*; *(insurance ~ etc)* Marke *f*; *(trading ~)* (Rabatt)marke *f*; *(airmail ~, sticker)* Aufkleber *m*. **(b)** *(rubber ~ etc)* Stempel *m*. **(c)** *(fig)* **to bear the ~ of authenticity** die Züge der Echtheit tragen. **2** *vt* **(a)** **to ~ one's foot** (mit dem Fuß) aufstampfen; **to ~ the ground** (mit dem Fuß/den Füßen) auf den Boden stampfen. **(b)** *(put postage ~ on)* freimachen. **a ~ed addressed envelope** ein frankierter Rückumschlag. **(c)** *document etc (with rubber ~)* stempeln; *(with embossing machine)* prägen; *name, pattern* aufstempeln; aufprägen *(on auf +acc)*; *(fig)* auswisen *(as als)*. **the new leader has ~ed his personality on the party** der neue Vorsitzende hat der Partei seine Persönlichkeit aufgeprägt. **3** *vi (walk)* sta(m)pfen; *(disapprovingly, in dancing)* (auf)stampfen; *(horse)* aufstampfen. **you ~ed on my foot!** Sie haben mir auf den Fuß getreten!

♦ **stamp out** *vt sep* **(a)** *fire* austreten; *(fig: eradicate) epidemic, crime* ausrotten; *opposition* unterdrücken; *trouble* niederschlagen; *rebels* unschädlich machen. **(b)** *(cut out) pattern* ausstanzen. **2** *vi* herausta(m)pfen.

stamp: ~ **album** *n* Briefmarkenalbum *nt*; ~ **collection** *n* Briefmarkensammlung *f*.

stampede [stæm'piːd] **1** *n (of cattle)* wilde Flucht; *(of people)* Massenansturm *m (on auf +acc)*; *(to escape)* wilde Flucht. **2** *vt horses, crowd* in (wilde or helle) Panik versetzen. **to ~ sb into doing sth** *(fig)* jdn dazu drängen, etw zu tun. **3** *vi* durchgehen; *(crowd)* losstürmen *(for auf +acc)*.

stamp machine *n* Briefmarkenautomat *m*.

stance [stæns] *n (posture, Sport)* Haltung *f*; *(mental attitude also)* Einstellung *f*.

stand [stænd] *(vb: pret, ptp stood)* **1** *n* **(a)** **to take a**

~ **(on a matter)** (zu einer Angelegenheit) eine Einstellung vertreten; **to take a firm ~** einen festen Standpunkt vertreten *(on zu)*. **(b)** *(Mil) (resistance)* Widerstand *m*; *(battle)* Gefecht *nt*. **to make a ~** *(lit, fig)* Widerstand leisten. **(c)** *(taxi ~)* Stand *m*. **(d)** *(furniture, music ~)* Ständer *m*. **(e)** *(market stall etc)* Stand *m*. **(f)** *(band~)* Podium *nt*. **(g)** *(Sport)* Tribüne *f*; *(US Jur)* Zeugenstand *m*. **(we sat) in the ~** (wir saßen) auf der Tribüne.

2 *vt* **(a)** *(place)* stellen. **(b)** *(withstand) pressure, close examination etc (object)* standhalten *(+dat)*; *(person)* gewachsen sein *(+dat)*; *test* bestehen; *climate* vertragen; *heat, noise* aushalten; *loss, cost* verkraften. **(c)** *(col: put up with) person, noise etc* aushalten. **I can't ~ him/it** *(don't like)* ich kann ihn/es nicht ausstehen; **I can't ~ being kept waiting** ich kann es nicht leiden, wenn man mich warten läßt; **I can't ~ it any longer** ich halte das nicht mehr (länger) aus. **(d)** **to ~ sb a drink** *(col)* jdm einen Drink spendieren.

3 *vi* **(a)** *(be situated, be upright)* stehen; *(get up)* aufstehen. **don't just ~ there!** stehen Sie nicht nur (dumm) rum! *(col)*; **to ~ still** stillstehen; **we stood talking** wir standen da und unterhielten uns; **to be left ~ing** *(house etc)* stehenbleiben; *(fig)* nicht vom Start wegkommen.

(b) **he ~s over 6 feet** er ist über 1,80 m groß; **the tree ~s 20 m high** der Baum ist 20 m hoch.

(c) **to ~ as a candidate** kandidieren.

(d) *(continue to be valid) (offer, argument, contract)* gelten; *(decision, record, account)* stehen. **the theory ~s or falls by this** damit steht und fällt die Theorie.

(e) *(fig: be in a position)* **we ~ to lose/gain a lot** wir laufen Gefahr, eine Menge zu verlieren/wir können sehr viel gewinnen.

(f) *(fig: be placed)* **how do we ~?** wie stehen wir?; **I'd like to know where I ~ (with him)** ich möchte wissen, woran ich (bei ihm) bin; **to ~ accused of sth** einer Sache *(gen)* angeklagt sein; **as things ~** nach Lage der Dinge.

(g) *(fig: be, continue to be)* **to ~ firm** *or* **fast** festbleiben; **to ~ ready** sich bereithalten; **to ~ together** zusammenhalten; **to ~ (as) security for sb** für jdn bürgen; **nothing now ~s between us** es steht nichts mehr zwischen uns.

♦ **stand about** *or* **around** *vi* herumstehen.

♦ **stand aside** *vi (lit)* zur Seite treten; *(fig: withdraw)* zurücktreten.

♦ **stand back** *vi (move back)* zurücktreten; *(be situated at a distance)* abliegen; *(fig: distance oneself)* Abstand nehmen. **to ~ ~ and do nothing** tatenlos zusehen.

♦ **stand by 1** *vi (remain uninvolved)* (unbeteiligt) danebenstehen. **(b)** *(be on alert)* sich bereithalten. **2** *vi +prep obj* **to ~ ~ a promise/sb** ein Versprechen/zu jdm halten.

♦ **stand down** *vi (retire, withdraw)* zurücktreten; *(before appointment)* verzichten; *(Jur)* den Zeugenstand verlassen.

♦ **stand for** *vi +prep obj* **(a)** *(be candidate for)* kandidieren für. **to ~ ~ election** sich zur Wahl stellen. **(b)** *(represent)* stehen für. **(c)** *(put up with)* hinnehmen.

♦ **stand in** *vi* einspringen.

♦ **stand out** *vi* **(a)** *(project)* hervorstehen; *(land, balcony)* herausragen. **(b)** *(contrast, be noticeable)* auffallen. **to ~ ~ against sth** sich von etw abheben *(oppose)* gegen etw Widerstand leisten; **to ~ ~ for sth** auf etw *(acc)* bestehen.

♦ **stand up 1** *vi* **(a)** *(get up)* aufstehen; *(be standing)* stehen. **(b)** *(argument)* überzeugen; *(Jur)* bestehen. **(c)** **to ~ ~ for sb/sth** für jdn/etw eintreten; **to ~ ~ to sth** *to test, pressure (object)* einer Sache *(dat)* standhalten; *(person)* einer Sache *(dat)* gewachsen sein; *to hard wear* etw aushalten; **to ~ ~ to sb** sich jdm gegenüber behaupten. **2** *vt sep* **(a)** *(put upright)* hinstellen.

(b) *(col) boyfriend etc* versetzen.

standard ['stændəd] **1** *n* **(a)** *(average, established norm)* Norm *f*; *(criterion)* Maßstab *m*. **to set a good** ~ Maßstäbe setzen; **to be above/below** ~ über/unter der Norm sein; **to be up to** ~ den Anforderungen genügen. **(b)** *usu pl (moral* ~*s)* (sittliche) Maßstäbe *pl*. **he sets himself very high** ~**s** er stellt hohe Anforderungen an sich *(acc)* selbst. **(c)** *(degree, level)* Niveau *nt*. ~ **of living** Lebensstandard *m*; **first-year university** ~ Wissensstand *m* des ersten Studienjahrs; **of high/low** ~ von hohem/niedrigem Niveau. **(d)** *(measurement)* (Maß)einheit *f*; *(monetary* ~*)* (Währungs)standard *m*. **(e)** *(flag)* Flagge *f*; *(on car)* Stander *m*. ~-**bearer** Fahnenträger *m*.

2 *adj (usual, customary)* üblich; *model, price, practice, reply, reference work* Standard-; *size* Normal-; *(established) weight, size* Norm-. ~ **English** korrektes Englisch; ~ **German** Hochdeutsch *nt*.

standardize ['stændədaɪz] *vt education, style* vereinheitlichen; *format, sizes etc* normen.

stand-by ['stændbaɪ] **1** *n* **(a)** *(person)* Ersatz, Ersatzmann *m*; *(Sport also)* Auswechselspieler(in *f*) *m*; *(thing)* Reserve *f*; *(Aviat)* *(plane)* Entlastungsflugzeug *nt*; *(ticket)* Standby-Ticket *nt*. **(b)** *(state of readiness)* **on** ~ in Bereitschaft; *(ready for action)* in Einsatzbereitschaft; **to be on 24-hour** ~ 24 Stunden Bereitschaftsdienst haben. **2** *adj attr troops, player, generator* Reserve-; *(Aviat) plane* Entlastungs-; *ticket* Standby-.

stand-in ['stændɪn] *n (Film, Theat)* Ersatz *m*.

standing ['stændɪŋ] **1** *n* **(a)** *(social)* Rang *m*, (gesellschaftliche) Stellung; *(professional)* Position *f*; *(financial)* (finanzielle) Verhältnisse *pl*; *(repute)* Ruf *m*. **of high** ~ von hohem Rang; *(repute)* von hohem Ansehen; **a man of some** ~ ein angesehener Mann; **what is his** ~ **locally?** was hält man in der Gegend von ihm? **(b)** *(duration)* Dauer *f*. **a treaty of only six months'** ~ ein Vertrag, der erst seit sechs Monaten besteht; **of long** ~ alt, langjährig.

2 *adj attr* **(a)** *(established, permanent)* ständig; *rule, custom* bestehend; *army also* stehend. **it's a** ~ **joke** das ist schon zu einem Witz geworden; **to pay sth by** ~ **order** etw per Dauerauftrag bezahlen. **(b)** *(from a standstill)* aus dem Stand; *(not sitting) ticket* Stehplatz-; *(erect) corn* auf dem Halm (stehend); *stone* (aufrecht) stehend. ~ **room only** nur Stehplätze; **to give sb a** ~ **ovation** jdm im Stehen Beifall klatschen.

stand: ~-**offish** [ˌstændˈɒfɪʃ] *adj (col)* hochnäsig; ~**point** *n* Standpunkt *m*; **from the** ~**point of the teacher** von Standpunkt des Lehrers gesehen; ~**still** *n* Stillstand *m*; **to be at a** ~**still** *(plane, train)* stehen; *(machines, traffic, factory)* stillstehen; *(trade)* ruhen; **to bring production to a** ~**still** die Produktion zum Erliegen bringen; **to come to a** ~**still** *(person, vehicle)* anhalten; *(traffic, machines)* zum Stillstand kommen; *(industry etc)* zum Erliegen kommen; ~-**up** *adj attr buffet, collar* Steh-; *meal* im Stehen.

stank [stæŋk] *pret of* **stink**.

stanza ['stænzə] *n* Strophe *f*.

staple¹ ['steɪpl] **1** *n* Heftklammer *f*; *(for wires, cables etc)* Krampe *f*. **2** *vt* heften; *wire* mit Krampen befestigen. **to** ~ **sth together** etw zusammenheften.

staple² *adj diet, food* Grund-, Haupt-

stapler ['steɪplə^r] *n* Heftmaschine *f*.

star [stɑː^r] **1** *n* **(a)** Stern *m*; *(asterisk also, Sch)* Sternchen *nt*. **the S**~**s and Stripes** das Sternenbanner; **you can thank your lucky** ~**s that** ... Sie können von Glück sagen, daß ...; **it's all in the** ~**s** es steht (alles) in den Sternen; **to see** ~**s** Sterne sehen; **a four-**~ **hotel** ein Vier-Sterne-Hotel *nt*. **(b)** *(person)* Star *m*. **2** *adj attr attraction* Haupt-; *performer, pupil* Star-. **3** *vt (Film etc)* **to** ~ **sb** jdn in

der Hauptrolle zeigen; ~**ring** ... in der Hauptrollen/den Hauptrollen ... **4** *vi (Film etc)* die Hauptrolle spielen.

starboard ['stɑːbəd] **1** *n* Steuerbord *nt*. **2** *adj* Steuerbord-.

starch [stɑːtʃ] **1** *n* Stärke *f*. ~-**reduced** stärkearm. **2** *vt* stärken.

starchy ['stɑːtʃɪ] *adj (+er)* stärkehaltig; *(fig)* steif.

stardom ['stɑːdəm] *n* Ruhm *m*. **where he hoped to find** ~ wo er hoffte, ein Star zu werden.

stare [stɛə^r] **1** *n* (starrer) Blick. **to give sb a** ~ jdn anstarren. **2** *vt* **the answer was staring us in the face** die Antwort lag klar auf der Hand. **3** *vi (vacantly etc)* (vor sich hin) starren; *(cow, madman)* stieren; *(in surprise)* große Augen machen; *(eyes)* weit aufgerissen sein. **he** ~**d in disbelief** er starrte ungläubig; **to** ~ **at sb/sth** jdn/etw anstarren.

star: ~**fish** *n* Seestern *m*; ~**gazer** *n (hum col)* Sterngucker *m (hum col)*.

stark [stɑːk] **1** *adj (+er) realism, contrast* kraß; *reality, poverty also, truth, terror* nackt; *landscape, cliffs, branches* kahl; *colour* kräftig; *(glaring)* grell. **2** *adv* ~ **raving mad** *(col)* total verrückt *(col)*; ~ **naked** *(also* **starkers** *col)* splitternackt.

starlet ['stɑːlɪt] *n (Film)* sternchen *nt*.

starlight ['stɑːlaɪt] *n* Sternenlicht *nt*.

starling ['stɑːlɪŋ] *n* Star *m*.

starlit ['stɑːlɪt] *adj sky, night* stern(en)klar.

starry ['stɑːrɪ] *adj (+er) night* stern(en)klar.

starry-eyed [ˌstɑːrɪˈaɪd] *adj idealist* blauäugig. **to go all** ~ glänzende Augen kriegen.

star: **S**~-**spangled Banner** *n* Sternenbanner *nt*; ~-**studded** *adj* **(a)** *(liter) night* stern(en)klar; **(b)** *(fig)* ~-**studded cast** Starbesetzung *f*.

start¹ [stɑːt] **1** *n (fright etc)* **to give a** ~ zusammenfahren; *(start up)* aufschrecken; *(horse)* scheuen; **to give sb a** ~ jdn erschrecken; **to wake with a** ~ aus dem Schlaf hochschrecken. **2** *vi* zusammenfahren; *(start up)* aufschrecken. **to** ~ **from one's chair/out of one's sleep** aus dem Stuhl hochfahren/aus dem Schlaf hochschrecken.

start² **1** *n* **(a)** *(beginning)* Beginn, Anfang *m*; *(departure)* Aufbruch *m*; *(of race)* Start *m*; *(of rumour, trouble, journey)* Ausgangspunkt *m*. **at the** ~ am Anfang, zu Beginn; *(Sport)* am Start; **for a** ~ *(to begin with)* fürs erste; *(firstly)* zunächst einmal; **from the** ~ von Anfang an; **from** ~ **to finish** von Anfang bis Ende; **to make a** ~ **(on sth)** (mit etw) anfangen; **to make an early** ~ frühzeitig aufbrechen; **to make a fresh** ~ *(in life)* (noch einmal) von vorn anfangen. **(b)** *(advantage, Sport)* Vorsprung *m (over* vor +*dat)*.

2 *vt* **(a)** *(begin)* anfangen mit; *argument, career, new life, negotiations* beginnen, anfangen; *new job, journey* antreten. **to** ~ **work** anfangen zu arbeiten; **he** ~**ed life as a miner** er hat als Bergmann angefangen; **you** ~**ed it!** du hast angefangen!; **don't** ~ **that again!** fang nicht schon wieder (damit) an! **(b)** *(cause to begin)* runners, *race* starten; *train* abfahren lassen; *rumour* in Umlauf setzen; *conversation* anfangen, anknüpfen; *fight* anfangen; *blaze, collapse, chain reaction* auslösen; *fire* anzünden; *(arsonist)* legen; *(found) enterprise* gründen. **to** ~ **sb thinking/on a subject** jdn nachdenklich machen/jdn auf ein Thema bringen; **to** ~ **sb on a career** jdm zu einer Karriere verhelfen. **(c)** *car, machine* starten; *engine also* anlassen; *clock* in Gang setzen.

3 *vi (begin)* anfangen, beginnen; *(car, engine)* anspringen; *(plane)* starten; *(move off)* anfahren; *(bus, train)* abfahren; *(rumour)* in Umlauf kommen; *(violins etc)* einsetzen. ~**ing from Tuesday** ab Dienstag; **to** ~ **for home** sich auf den Heimweg machen; **to** ~ **(off) with** *(firstly)* erstens; *(at the beginning)* zunächst; **to** ~ **after sb** jdm verfolgen; **to get** ~**ed** anfangen; *(on trip)* aufbrechen; **to** ~ **on a task/the food** sich an eine Aufgabe/

ans Essen machen; **to ~ talking** zu sprechen anfangen; **he ~ed by saying ...** er sagte zunächst **...; don't you ~!** fang du nicht auch noch an!

♦ **start off 1** *vi (begin)* anfangen; *(begin moving: person)* losgehen; *(on journey)* aufbrechen; *(run)* loslaufen; *(drive)* losfahren; *(esp Sport)* starten; *(begin talking etc)* anfangen *(on* mit*)*. **2** *vt sep sth* anfangen. **to ~ sb ~ (talking)** jdm das Stichwort geben; **a few stamps to ~ you ~** ein paar Briefmarken für den Anfang.

♦ **start out** *vi (begin)* (zunächst) beginnen *or* anfangen; *(begin a journey)* aufbrechen *(for* nach*)*. **we ~ed ~ on a long journey** wir machten uns auf eine lange Reise.

♦ **start over** *vi (US)* noch (ein)mal von vorn anfangen.

♦ **start up 1** *vi (begin: music etc)* anfangen; *(machine)* angehen *(col)*, in Gang kommen; *(motor)* anspringen; *(siren)* losheulen. **2** *vt sep* **(a)** *(cause to function)* in Gang bringen; *engine also* anlassen. **(b)** *(begin)* eröffnen; *business also, conversation* anfangen.

starter ['staːtə^r] *n* **(a)** *(Sport)* Starter(in *f) m.* **(b)** *(Aut etc: self-~)* Anlasser *m.* **(c)** *(child)* **to be a late** *or* **slow ~** Spätentwickler *m* sein. **(d)** *(col: first course)* Vorspeise *f.* **(e) for ~s** *(col)* für den Anfang *(col)*.

starting ['staːtɪŋ] *in cpds (Sport)* line, post Start-; **~ gun** *n* Startpistole *f;* **~ handle** *n* Anlasserkurbel *f;* **~ point** *n (lit, fig)* Ausgangspunkt *m;* **~ post** *n* Startpflock *m.*

startle ['staːtl] *vt* erschrecken. **I was ~d to see how old he looked** ich stellte entsetzt fest, wie alt er aussah.

startling ['staːtlɪŋ] *adj news* überraschend; *(bad)* alarmierend, bestürzend; *resemblance* erstaunlich; *originality, discovery* aufregend.

starvation [staː'veɪʃən] *n (act)* Hungern *nt; (of besieged people)* Aushungern *nt; (condition)* Hunger *m.* **to die of ~** verhungern; **to go on a ~ diet** *(hum)* eine Hungerkur machen.

starve [staːv] **1** *vt* **(a)** *(deprive of food)* hungern lassen; *(also ~ out)* aushungern; *(kill: also ~ to death)* verhungern lassen; **to ~ oneself** hungern. **(b)** *(fig)* **to ~ sb of sth** jdm etw vorenthalten *or* verweigern; **to be ~d of capital** an akutem Kapitalmangel leiden; **to be ~d of affection** zuwenig Zuneigung erfahren. **2** *vi* hungern; *(die: also ~ to death)* verhungern. **I'm simply starving!** *(col)* ich sterbe vor Hunger! *(col)*; **to ~ for sth** *(fig)* nach etw hungern.

starving ['staːvɪŋ] *adj (lit)* hungernd *attr; (fig)* hungrig.

stash [stæʃ] *vt (also ~ away) (col) loot* verschwinden lassen *(col); money* beiseite schaffen.

state [steɪt] **1** *n* **(a)** *(condition)* Zustand *m.* **~ of health/mind** Gesundheits-/Geisteszustand *m;* **the ~ of the nation** die Lage der Nation; **the present ~ of the economy** die gegenwärtige Wirtschaftslage; **where animals live in their natural ~** wo Tiere im Naturzustand leben; **in a good/bad ~** in gutem/schlechtem Zustand; **he's in no (fit) ~ to do that** er ist nicht in dem (richtigen) Zustand dafür; **look at the ~ of your hands!** guck dir bloß mal deine Hände an!; **the room was in a terrible ~** im Zimmer herrschte ein fürchterliches Durcheinander.

(b) *(col: anxiety)* **to get into a ~ (about sth)** *(col)* wegen etw durchdrehen *(col)*.

(c) *(pomp)* Aufwand, Pomp *m.* **to be received in great ~** mit großem Staat empfangen werden; **to travel in ~** pompös reisen; **to lie in ~** (feierlich) aufgebahrt sein.

(d) *(Pol)* Staat *m; (federal ~)* (Bundes)staat *m; (in BRD, Austria)* (Bundes)land *nt.* **the S~s** die (Vereinigten) Staaten; **the S~ of Florida** der Staat Florida; **affairs of ~** Staatsangelegenheiten *pl.*

2 *vt* darlegen, vortragen; *name, price* nennen; *purpose* angeben. **to ~ that ...** feststellen, daß **...;** **to ~ one's case** seine Sache vortragen; **to ~ the case for the prosecution** *(Jur)* die Anklage vortragen; **unless otherwise ~d** wenn nicht anders angegeben; **as ~d in my letter I ...** wie in meinem Brief erwähnt, **... ich ...**

state *in cpds* Staats-; *control also, industry* staatlich; *(US etc)* bundesstaatlich.

stated ['steɪtɪd] *adj* **(a)** *(declared) sum, date* genannt; *limits* bestimmt. **(b)** *(fixed, regular) times, amount* fest(gesetzt).

state: **S~ Department** *n (US)* Außenministerium *nt;* **~ education** *n* staatliche Erziehung; *(system)* staatliches Erziehungswesen; **~house** *n (US)* Parlamentsgebäude, Kapitol *nt;* **~less** *adj* staatenlos; **~less person** Staatenlose(r) *mf.*

stately ['steɪtlɪ] *adj (+er) person, bearing* würdevoll; *pace* gemessen. **~ home** herrschaftliches Anwesen, Schloß *nt.*

statement ['steɪtmənt] *n* **(a)** *(of thesis etc)* Darstellung *f; (of problem also)* Darlegung *f.* **(b)** *(that said)* Feststellung *f; (claim)* Behauptung *f; (official ~)* Erklärung *f; (in court, to police)* Aussage *f; (written)* Protokoll *nt.* **to make a ~ to the press** eine Presseerklärung abgeben. **(c)** *(Fin) (tradesman's)* Rechnung *f; (bank ~)* Kontoauszug *m.*

state: **~-of-the-art** *adj* neueste(r, s); **~-owned** *adj* staatseigen; **~room** *n (in palace)* Empfangssaal *m; (on ship)* Kabine *f;* **~ school** *n* öffentliche Schule; **~ secret** *n* Staatsgeheimnis *nt;* **S~'s evidence** *n (US)* Aussage *f* eines Kronzeugen; **to turn S~'s evidence** als Kronzeuge auftreten.

statesman ['steɪtsmən] *n, pl* **-men** [-mən] Staatsmann *m.*

statesmanship ['steɪtsmənʃɪp] *n* Staatskunst *f.*

static ['stætɪk] **1** *adj* **(a)** *(Phys)* statisch. **(b)** *(not moving or changing)* konstant; *(stationary)* feststehend *attr; condition, society* statisch. **2** *n (Phys)* Reibungselektrizität *f; (Rad)* atmosphärische Störungen *pl.*

station ['steɪʃən] **1** *n* **(a)** *(railway ~, bus ~)* Bahnhof *m; (stop)* Station *f.* **(b)** *(police ~, fire ~)* Wache *f; (space ~)* (Raum)station *f; (US: gas ~)* Tankstelle *f.* **(c)** *(Mil: post)* Stellung *f,* Posten *m.* **(d)** *(Rad, TV)* Sender *m.* **(e)** *(rank)* Stand *m.* **~ in life** Stellung *f* (im Leben), Rang *m;* **he has got ideas above his ~** er hat Ideen, die jemandem aus seinem Stand gar nicht zukommen. **2** *vt (Mil)* **troops** stationieren; *sentry* aufstellen.

stationary ['steɪʃənərɪ] *adj (not moving) car* haltend *attr; (not movable)* fest(stehend *attr)*. **to be ~** *(vehicles)* stehen; *(traffic, fig)* stillstehen; **to remain ~** sich nicht bewegen; *(traffic)* stillstehen.

stationer ['steɪʃənə^r] *n* Schreibwarenhändler *m.* **~'s (shop)** *(Brit)* Schreibwarenhandlung *f.*

stationery ['steɪʃənərɪ] *n (notepaper)* Briefpapier *nt; (writing materials)* Schreibwaren *pl.*

station: **~ house** *n (US: police)* (Polizei)wache *f;* **~-master** *n* Bahnhofsvorsteher *m;* **~ wagon** *n (US)* Kombi(wagen) *m.*

statistical [stə'tɪstɪkəl] *adj* statistisch.

statistician [,stætɪs'tɪʃən] *n* Statistiker(in *f) m.*

statistics [stə'tɪstɪks] *n* **(a)** *sing* Statistik *f.* **(b)** *pl (data)* Statistiken *pl.*

statue ['stætjuː] *n* Statue *f.*

statuesque [,stætju'esk] *adj figure* wohlgeformt; *beauty* klassisch.

statuette [,stætju'et] *n* Statuette *f.*

stature ['stætʃə^r] *n* **(a)** Wuchs *m; (esp of man)* Statur *f.* **(b)** *(fig)* Format *nt.*

status ['steɪtəs] *n* Stellung *f; (legal ~, social ~ also)* Status *m.* **equal ~** Gleichstellung *f;* **marital ~** Familienstand *m.*

status quo ['steɪtəs'kwəʊ] *n* Status quo *m.*

status symbol *n* Statussymbol *nt.*

statute ['stætjuːt] *n* Gesetz *nt; (of organization)* Satzung *f,* Statut *nt.* **~ book** Gesetzbuch *nt;* **to put sth**

in the ~ **book** etw zum Gesetz machen.
statutory ['stætjutərɪ] adj gesetzlich; (in organization) satzungsgemäß; right also verbrieft; punishment (vom Gesetz) vorgesehen.
staunch[1] [stɔːntʃ] adj (+er) Catholic, loyalist überzeugt; member, supporter getreu; support standhaft.
staunch[2] vt flow stauen; bleeding stillen.
stave [steɪv] n (Mus: staff) Notenlinien pl.
♦ **stave in** pret, ptp stove in vt sep eindrücken; head einschlagen.
♦ **stave off** pret, ptp ~d off vt sep attack zurückschlagen; crisis, cold abwehren; hunger lindern.
staves [steɪvz] pl of staff 1 (c).
stay [steɪ] 1 n (a) Aufenthalt m. a short ~ in hospital ein kurzer Krankenhausaufenthalt. (b) (Jur) Aussetzung f. ~ of execution Vollstreckungsaufschub m.
 2 vt (a) (Jur) order, sentence aussetzen. (b) to ~ the course (lit, fig) durchhalten.
 3 vi (remain) bleiben. to ~ for or to supper zum Abendessen bleiben; to have come to ~ nicht nur eine Modeerscheinung sein; unemployment has come to ~ die Arbeitslosigkeit ist zum Dauerzustand geworden; if it ~s fine wenn es schön bleibt; ~ with it! nicht aufgeben! (b) (reside) wohnen; (at youth hostel etc) übernachten. to ~ at a hotel im Hotel wohnen; I ~ed in Italy for a few weeks ich habe mich ein paar Wochen in Italien aufgehalten; he is ~ing at Chequers for the weekend er verbringt das Wochenende in Chequers; to ~ with friends bei Freunden wohnen; my brother came to ~ mein Bruder ist zu Besuch gekommen.
♦ **stay away** vi (from von) wegbleiben; (from person) sich fernhalten.
♦ **stay behind** vi zurückbleiben!; (Sch: as punishment) nachsitzen.
♦ **stay in** vi (at home) zu Hause bleiben; (in position etc) drinbleiben; (Sch) nachsitzen.
♦ **stay on** vi (lid etc) draufbleiben; (light) anbleiben; (people) (noch) bleiben. to ~ ~ at school/as manager (in der Schule) weitermachen/(weiterhin) Geschäftsführer bleiben.
♦ **stay out** vi draußen bleiben; (on strike) weiterstreiken; (not come home) wegbleiben. to ~ ~ of sth sich aus etw heraushalten; he never managed to ~ ~ of trouble er war dauernd in Schwierigkeiten.
♦ **stay up** vi (a) (person) aufbleiben. don't ~ ~ for me! bleib nicht meinetwegen auf! (b) (tent, fence, pole) stehen bleiben; (picture, decorations) hängen bleiben.
stay-at-home ['steɪət,həʊm] n Stubenhocker m.
stayer ['steɪəʳ] n to be a ~ Stehvermögen nt haben.
staying power ['steɪɪŋ,paʊəʳ] n Durchhaltevermögen nt, Ausdauer f.
STD (Brit Telec) = subscriber trunk dialling. ~ **code** Vorwahl(nummer) f.
stead [sted] n in his ~ an seiner Stelle; to stand sb in good ~ jdm zugute kommen.
steadfast ['stedfɑːst] adj fest; person, refusal also standhaft; belief unerschütterlich.
steadily ['stedɪlɪ] adv (a) (firmly) ruhig; balanced fest; gaze unverwandt. (b) (constantly) ständig; rain ununterbrochen. (c) (reliably) zuverlässig.
steady ['stedɪ] 1 adj (+er) (a) (firm, not wobbling) hand, nerves, eye ruhig; gaze unverwandt. with a ~ **hand** mit ruhiger Hand; to hold sth ~ etw ruhig halten; ladder etw festhalten; the chair is not very ~ der Stuhl ist wacklig. (b) (constant) wind, progress, demand etc ständig, stet (geh); drizzle ununterbrochen; temperature beständig. at a ~ pace/70 in gleichmäßigem Tempo/ständig mit 70. (c) (reliable, regular) worker zuverlässig. (d) job, boyfriend fest. 2 adv ~! (carefully, gently) vorsichtig!; (Naut) Kurs halten!; ~ (on)! sachte! (col); to go ~ (with sb) (col) mit jdm (fest) zusam-

men sein. 3 vt plane, boat wieder ins Gleichgewicht bringen; (stabilize) nerves, person beruhigen; (in character) ausgleichen. to ~ oneself festen Halt finden; she had a ~ing influence on him durch sie wurde er ausgeglichener.
steak [steɪk] n Steak nt; (of fish) Filet nt. ~ and kidney pie Fleischpastete f mit Nieren.
steal [stiːl] (vb: pret stole, ptp stolen) 1 vt object, idea, heart stehlen. to ~ sth from sb jdm etw stehlen; to ~ the show/sb's thunder die Schau stehlen/jdm den Wind aus den Segeln nehmen; the baby stole all the attention das Kind zog die ganze Aufmerksamkeit auf sich. 2 vi (a) (thieve) stehlen. (b) (move quietly) sich stehlen, (sich) schleichen. to ~ away sich davonstehlen; to ~ up on sb sich an jdn heranschleichen. 3 n (US col: bargain) Geschenk nt (col). it's a ~! das ist (ja) geschenkt! (col).
stealth [stelθ] n List f. by ~ durch List.
stealthy ['stelθɪ] adj (+er) verstohlen; footsteps verhalten.
steam [stiːm] 1 n Dampf m. the windows were covered with ~ die Fensterscheiben waren beschlagen; full ~ ahead! (Naut) volle Kraft voraus!; to get up ~ (fig) in Schwung kommen; to let off ~ (lit, fig) Dampf ablassen; to run out of ~ (fig) Schwung verlieren; under one's own ~ (fig) allein, ohne Hilfe. 2 vt dämpfen; food dünsten. to ~ open an envelope einen Briefumschlag über Dampf öffnen; ~ed pudding Kochpudding m. 3 vi (a) (give off ~) dampfen. (b) (move) dampfen. the ship ~ed into the harbour das Schiff kam in den Hafen gefahren.
♦ **steam up** 1 vt sep window beschlagen lassen. to be/get ~ed ~ (fig col) hochgehen (col) (about wegen). 2 vi (window) beschlagen.
steam: ~**boat** n Dampfschiff nt, Dampfer m; ~ **engine** n (Rail) Dampflok f.
steamer ['stiːməʳ] n (ship) Dampfer m; (Cook) Dampfkochtopf m.
steam: ~ **iron** n Dampfbügeleisen nt; ~**roller** n Dampfwalze f; ~**ship** n Dampfschiff nt.
steamy ['stiːmɪ] adj (+er) dunstig; room, atmosphere voll Dampf; window beschlagen.
steed [stiːd] n (liter) Roß nt.
steel [stiːl] 1 n Stahl m. 2 adj attr Stahl-. 3 vt to ~ oneself sich wappnen (for gegen); (physically) sich stählen (for für); to ~ oneself to do sth allen Mut zusammennehmen, um etw zu tun.
steel in cpds Stahl-, stahl-; ~ **mill** n Stahlwalzwerk nt; ~**works** n sing or pl Stahlwerk nt.
steely ['stiːlɪ] adj (+er) grip stahlhart; gaze hart; determination eisern; blue Stahl-.
steep[1] [stiːp] adj (+er) (a) steil. it's a ~ **climb** es geht steil hinauf; there's a ~ drop in the value of the pound das Pfund ist stark gefallen. (b) (fig col) demand unverschämt; price also, bill gesalzen (col). it seems a bit ~ that ... es ist ein starkes Stück, daß ...
steep[2] vt (a) (in liquid) eintauchen; (in marinade, dye) ziehen lassen; dried food einweichen. (b) (fig) to be ~ed in sth von etw durchdrungen sein; ~ed in history geschichtsträchtig.
steeple ['stiːpl] n Kirchturm m.
steeple: ~**chase** n (for horses) Hindernisrennen nt; (for runners) Hindernislauf m; ~**jack** n Turmarbeiter m.
steer[1] [stɪəʳ] 1 vt (lit, fig) lenken; ship steuern; person also lotsen. 2 vi (in car) lenken; (in ship) steuern. to ~ **due north** Kurs nach Norden halten; to ~ **for** or **towards sth** auf etw (acc) zuhalten; (Naut) etw ansteuern; (fig) auf etw (acc) zusteuern.
steer[2] n junger Ochse.
steering ['stɪərɪŋ] n (in car etc) Lenkung f; (Naut) Steuerung f.
steering: ~ **column** n Lenksäule f; ~ **committee** n vorbereitender Ausschuß; ~ **wheel** n Steu-

er(rad) *nt; (of car also)* Lenkrad *nt.*

stem [stem] **1** *n (of plant, glass)* Stiel *m; (of shrub, word)* Stamm *m; (of grain)* Halm *m; (of pipe)* Hals *m.* **2** *vt (check, stop)* aufhalten; *flood, tide* eindämmen; *bleeding* zum Stillstand bringen. **3** *vi* to ~ from sth *(result from)* von etw herrühren; *(have as origin)* auf etw *(acc)* zurückgehen.

stench [stentʃ] *n* Gestank *m.*

stencil ['stensl] *n* Schablone *f; (Printing: for duplicating)* Matrize *f.*

stenographer [ste'nɒgrəfəʳ] *n* Stenograph(in *f*) *m.*

stenography [ste'nɒgrəfɪ] *n* Stenographie *f.*

step [step] **1** *n* **(a)** *(pace, in dancing)* Schritt *m.* **to take a ~** einen Schritt machen; ~ **by ~** *(lit, fig)* Schritt für Schritt; **to be in/out of ~** *(fig)* im/nicht im Gleichklang sein *(with* mit*).* **(b)** *(move)* Schritt *m; (measure also)* Maßnahme *f.* **it's a great ~ forward** es ist ein großer Schritt nach vorn; **that would be a ~ back/in the right direction for him** das wäre für ihn ein Rückschritt/ein Schritt in die richtige Richtung; **to take ~s to do sth** Maßnahmen ergreifen, (um) etw zu tun. **(c)** *(in process, experiment, scale, hierarchy)* Stufe *f.* **~s** *(outdoors)* Treppe *f;* **mind the ~** Vorsicht Stufe. **(d)** **~s** *pl* (~*-ladder: also pair of* ~s) Stufenleiter *f.* **2** *vt* ~ **two paces to the left** treten Sie zwei Schritte nach links. **3** *vi* gehen. **to ~ into/out of sth** *house, room, puddle* in etw *(acc)*/aus etw treten; *train, dress* in etw *(acc)*/aus etw steigen; **to ~ on(to) sth** *plane, train* in etw *(acc)* steigen; *platform, ladder* auf etw *(acc)* steigen; **to ~ on sth** *object, toy* auf etw *(acc)* treten; **to ~ over sb/sth** über jdn/etw steigen; ~ **this way, please** hier entlang, bitte!; **to ~ inside** herein-/hineintreten; **to ~ outside** heraus-/hinaustreten; ~ **on it!** mach mal ein bißchen schneller! *(col); (in car)* gib Gas!

♦ **step aside** *vi (lit)* zur Seite treten; *(fig)* Platz machen.

♦ **step back** *vi (lit)* zurücktreten. **to ~ ~ from sth** *(fig)* von etw Abstand gewinnen.

♦ **step down** *vi (fig)* **to ~ ~ in favour of sb** jdm Platz machen.

♦ **step forward** *vi* vortreten; *(fig)* sich melden.

♦ **step in** *vi (lit)* eintreten *(-to, +prep obj* in *+acc); (fig)* einschreiten.

♦ **step off** *vi +prep obj (off bus, plane, boat)* aussteigen *(prep obj* aus*).* **to ~ ~ the pavement** vom Bürgersteig treten.

♦ **step up** *vt sep* steigern; *efforts also, campaign* verstärken; *volume* erhöhen.

step- *pref brother, mother etc* Stief-.

step-ladder ['step,lædəʳ] *n* Stufenleiter *f.*

steppe [step] *n* Steppe *f.*

stepping stone ['stepɪŋ,stəʊn] *n* (Tritt)stein *m; (fig)* Sprungbrett *nt* (to für).

stereo ['sterɪəʊ] **1** *n* Stereo *nt; (record-player)* Stereoanlage *f.* **in ~** in Stereo. **2** *adj* Stereo-.

stereophonic [,sterɪəʊ'fɒnɪk] *adj* stereophon.

stereotype ['sterɪə,taɪp] *n (fig)* Klischee(vorstellung *f*) *nt;* (~ *character)* stereotype Figur.

sterile ['steraɪl] *adj* **(a)** *(lit, fig)* unfruchtbar. **(b)** *(germ-free)* steril, keimfrei; *(fig) décor etc* steril.

sterilization [,sterɪlaɪ'zeɪʃən] *n* Sterilisation *f.*

sterilize ['sterɪlaɪz] *vt person, instruments* sterilisieren.

sterling ['stɜːlɪŋ] **1** *adj* **(a)** *(Fin)* Sterling-. **in pounds ~** in Pfund Sterling. **(b)** *(fig)* gediegen; *character* lauter. **(c)** ~ **silver** Sterlingsilber *nt.* **2** *n no art (money)* das Pfund Sterling. **in ~** in Pfund Sterling. **3** *adj attr* aus (Sterling)silber.

stern¹ [stɜːn] *n (Naut)* Heck *nt.*

stern² *adj* (*+er*) *(strict)* streng; *words also, character, warning* ernst. **made of ~er stuff** aus härterem Holz geschnitzt.

steroid ['stɪərɔɪd] *n* Steroid *nt.*

stethoscope ['steθəskəʊp] *n* Stethoskop *nt.*

stevedore ['stiːvɪdɔːʳ] *n* Stauer *m.*

stew [stjuː] **1** *n* **(a)** Eintopf(gericht *nt*) *m.* **(b)** *(col)* **to be in a ~** *(about sth)* (über etw *(acc)* or wegen etw) ganz aufgeregt sein. **2** *vt meat* schmoren; *fruit* dünsten. ~**ed apples** Apfelkompott *nt.* **3** *vi (meat)* schmoren; *(fruit)* dünsten; *(col: tea)* bitter werden. **to let sb ~** *(in his/her own juice)* jdn (im eigenen Saft) schmoren lassen.

steward ['stjuːəd] *n* Steward *m; (on estate etc)* Verwalter *m; (at dance, meeting)* Ordner *m.*

stewardess ['stjuːədes] *n* Stewardess *f.*

stick¹ [stɪk] *n* **(a)** Stock *m; (twig)* Zweig *m; (hockey* ~*)* Schläger *m; (drum*~*)* Schlegel *m.* **to give sb/sth (a lot of)** ~ *(col: criticize)* jdn/etw heruntermachen *(col);* **just a few** ~**s of furniture** nur ein paar Möbelstücke; **to get hold of the wrong end of the** ~ *(fig col)* etw falsch verstehen; **in the** ~**s** *(esp US: backwoods)* in der hintersten Provinz. **(b)** *(of sealing wax, celery, rhubarb, dynamite)* Stange *f; (of chalk, shaving soap)* Stück *nt.*

stick² *pret, ptp* **stuck 1** *vt* **(a)** *(with glue etc)* kleben. **to ~ an envelope down** einen Briefumschlag zukleben. **(b)** *(pin)* stecken. **he stuck a badge on his lapel** er steckte sich *(dat)* ein Abzeichen ans Revers. **(c)** *(jab) knife, sword etc* stoßen. **(d)** *(col: place, put)* tun *(col); (in sth also)* stecken *(col).* ~ **it on the shelf** tu's aufs Regal; **he stuck his head around the corner** er steckte seinen Kopf um die Ecke; **you know where you can ~ that** *(col!)* du kannst mich mal! *(col!).* **(e)** *(esp Brit col: tolerate)* aushalten; *pace, pressure of work* durchhalten. **I can't ~ him/that** ich kann ihn/das nicht ausstehen *(col).*

2 *vi* **(a)** *(glue, object)* kleben an *(+dat).* **the name seems to have stuck** der Name scheint ihm/ihr *etc* geblieben zu sein. **(b)** *(become caught, wedged etc)* steckenbleiben; *(drawer, window)* klemmen. **(c)** *(sth pointed)* stecken *(in* in *+dat).* **it stuck in my foot** das ist mir im Fuß steckengeblieben. **(d)** *(project)* **his toes are ~ing through his socks** seine Zehen kommen durch die Socken. **(e)** *(stay)* bleiben; *(slander)* haftenbleiben. **to ~ in sb's mind** jdm im Gedächtnis bleiben; **to make sth ~ (in one's mind)** sich *(dat)* etw einprägen.

♦ **stick around** *vi (col)* hier/da bleiben.

♦ **stick at** *vi +prep obj* **(a)** *(persist)* bleiben an *(+dat) (col).* **to ~ ~ it** dranbleiben *(col).* **(b)** **he will ~ ~ nothing** er macht vor nichts halt.

♦ **stick by** *vi +prep obj sb* halten zu; *promise* stehen zu.

♦ **stick on 1** *vt sep label, cover* aufkleben *(prep obj* auf *+acc).* **2** *vi (label etc)* kleben, haften *(prep obj* an *+dat).*

♦ **stick out** **1** *vi* vorstehen *(of* aus); *(ears, hair)* abstehen; *(fig: be noticeable)* auffallen. **2** *vt sep* **(a)** *tongue etc* hinaus-/herausstrecken. **(b)** *(col)* ~ **it ~** durchhalten.

♦ **stick out for** *vi +prep obj* sich stark machen für.

♦ **stick to** *vi +prep obj* bleiben bei; *(remain faithful to) principles etc* treu bleiben *(+dat).*

♦ **stick together** *vi* zusammenkleben; *(fig: partners etc)* zusammenhalten.

♦ **stick up 1** *vt sep* **(a)** *(with tape etc)* zukleben. **(b)** *(col: raise)* ~ **'em ~!** Hände hoch! **(c)** *(col) notice etc* aufhängen, anbringen. **2** *vi (nail etc)* vorstehen; *(hair)* abstehen; *(collar)* hochstehen.

♦ **stick up for** *vi +prep obj sb, one's principles* eintreten für. **to ~ ~ ~ oneself** sich behaupten.

sticker ['stɪkəʳ] *n* **(a)** *(label)* Aufkleber *m.* **(b)** *(col: determined person)* **he's a** ~ er ist zäh.

sticking plaster ['stɪkɪŋ,plɑːstəʳ] *n (Brit)* Heftpflaster *nt.*

stick-in-the-mud ['stɪkɪnðə,mʌd] *(col) n* Muffel *m (col).*

stickleback ['stɪklbæk] *n* Stichling *m.*

stickler ['stɪklə^r] n to be a ~ for sth es mit etw peinlich genau nehmen.

stick: ~-on adj label (Auf)klebe-; ~-up n (col) Überfall m.

sticky ['stɪkɪ] adj (+er) **(a)** klebrig; label Klebe-; paint feucht; atmosphere schwül; air stickig; (sweaty) hands feucht. ~ **tape** Klebeband nt. **(b)** (fig col) problem, person schwierig; moment heikel. **to come to a ~ end** ein böses Ende nehmen; **to be on a ~ wicket** in einer schwierigen Lage sein.

stiff [stɪf] adj (+er) **(a)** steif; brush hart; dough, paste fest. **(b)** resistance, drink stark; competition hart; breeze steif; climb, test schwierig; examination, punishment schwer; price, demand hoch. **that's a bit ~** das ist ganz schön happig (col).

stiffen ['stɪfn] (also ~ up) **1** vt steif machen; shirt etc stärken; (disease) limb steif werden lassen; resistance etc verstärken. **2** vi steif werden; (fig: resistance) sich verhärten; (breeze) auffrischen.

stiffly ['stɪflɪ] adv steif.

stiffness ['stɪfnɪs] n see adj **(a)** Steifheit f; Härte f; Festigkeit f. **(b)** Stärke f; Härte f; Schwierigkeit f; Schwere f; Höhe f.

stifle ['staɪfl] **1** vt (suffocate) ersticken; (fig) cough also, opposition unterdrücken. **2** vi ersticken.

stifling ['staɪflɪŋ] adj fumes erstickend; heat drückend. **it's ~ in here** es ist ja zum Ersticken hier drin (col).

stigma ['stɪgmə] n Brandmal, Stigma nt.

stigmatize ['stɪgmətaɪz] vt brandmarken.

stile [staɪl] n (Zaun)übertritt m.

stiletto [stɪ'letəʊ] n **(a)** (knife) Stilett nt. **(b)** (also ~ heel) Pfennigabsatz m.

still¹ [stɪl] **1** adj, adv (+er) **(a)** (motionless) bewegungslos; person also reglos; sea, waters ruhig. **to keep ~** stillhalten; **to hold sth ~** etw ruhig halten; **to be ~** (vehicle, needle etc) stillstehen; **to lie ~** reglos daliegen; **to stand ~** still stehen; **my heart stood ~** mir stockte das Herz; **~ waters run deep** (Prov) stille Wasser sind tief (Prov). **(b)** (quiet, calm) still. **be ~!** sei still! **2** adj wine nicht moussierend; drink ohne Kohlensäure. **a ~ photograph** ein Standfoto nt. **3** n **(a)** **in the ~ of the night** in der Stille der Nacht. **(b)** (Film) Standfoto nt.

still² **1** adv **(a)** (temporal) noch; (for emphasis, in exasperation, used on its own) immer noch; (in negative sentences) noch immer, immer noch; (now as in the past) nach wie vor. **there will ~ be** objections es wird nach wie vor Einwände geben. **(b)** (nevertheless, all the same) trotzdem. **~**, **it was worth it** es hat sich trotzdem gelohnt; **~**, **he is my brother** er ist trotz allem mein Bruder; **rich but ~ not happy** reich und doch nicht glücklich; **~**, **at least we didn't lose anything** na ja, wir haben wenigstens nichts dabei verloren; **~**, **what can you expect?** was kann man auch anderes erwarten? **(c)** (with comp) noch. **~ better** noch besser; **better ~**, **do it this way** oder noch besser, mach es so. **2** conj (und) dennoch.

still³ n (for alcohol) Destillierapparat m.

still: ~**birth** n Totgeburt f; ~**born** adj (lit, fig) totgeboren attr; **the child was ~born** das Kind kam tot zur Welt; ~ **life** n, pl ~ **lifes** Stilleben nt.

stillness ['stɪlnɪs] n **(a)** (motionlessness) Unbewegtheit f; (of person) Reglosigkeit f. **(b)** (quietness) Stille, Ruhe f.

stilt [stɪlt] n Stelze f; (Archit) Pfahl m.

stilted ['stɪltɪd] adj gestelzt, gespreizt.

stimulant ['stɪmjʊlənt] n Anregungsmittel nt; (fig) Ansporn m.

stimulate ['stɪmjʊleɪt] vt **(a)** (excite) circulation, mind anregen; (cold shower, coffee) beleben; (Med also) stimulieren; nerve reizen; (sexually) erregen; (fig) person ansporneni; (intellectually) stimulieren; sb's interest erregen. **to ~ sb to do sth** jdn anspornen, etw zu tun. **(b)** (increase) econo-

my, sales etc ankurbeln; (incite) response hervorrufen; criticism anregen zu.

stimulating ['stɪmjʊleɪtɪŋ] adj anregend; walk belebend; prospect ermunternd; experience (physically) erfrischend; (mentally) stimulierend.

stimulation [,stɪmjʊ'leɪʃən] n **(a)** (act) (physical, mental) Anregung f; (from shower, walk etc) belebende Wirkung; (state) Angeregtheit f; (sexual) Erregung f; (fig: incentive) Anreiz m; (intellectual) Stimulation f. **(b)** (of economy, sales etc) Ankurbelung f (to gen).

stimulus ['stɪmjʊləs] n, pl **stimuli** ['stɪmjʊlaɪ] Anreiz m; (inspiration) Anregung f; (Physiol) Reiz m. **it gave trade new ~** das hat dem Handel neuen Aufschwung gegeben.

sting [stɪŋ] (vb: pret, ptp **stung**) **1** n **(a)** (organ: of insect) Stachel m. **(b)** (wound) (of insect) Stich m; (of nettle, jellyfish) Quaddel f. **(c)** (pain) (from needle etc) Stechen nt; (of antiseptic, ointment, from nettle etc) Brennen nt; (of whip) brennender Schmerz. **(d)** (fig) (of remark, irony) Stachel m; (of attack, criticism etc) Schärfe f. **to take the ~ out of sth** etw entschärfen; (out of remark, criticism also) einer Sache (dat) den Stachel nehmen.

2 vt **(a)** (insect) stechen; (jellyfish) verbrennen. **(b)** (comments etc) treffen; (remorse, conscience) quälen. **(c)** (col) **they really stung you for that** sie haben dich dabei ganz schön ausgenommen; **can I ~ you for a fiver?** kann ich dich um einen Fünfer erleichtern?

3 vi (insect) stechen; (nettle, jellyfish etc) brennen; (burn: eyes, cut, ointment etc) brennen; (comments etc) schmerzen. **smoke makes your eyes ~** Rauch brennt in den Augen.

stinging nettle ['stɪŋɪŋ'netl] n Brennessel f.

stingy ['stɪndʒɪ] adj (+er) (col) person geizig, knickerig (col); sum, portion, donation schäbig. **to be ~ with sth** mit etw knausern.

stink [stɪŋk] (vb: pret **stank**, ptp **stunk**) **1** n Gestank m. **to kick up a ~** (col) Stunk machen (col). **2** vi **(a)** stinken (of nach). **it ~s in here** (drin) stinkt's. **(b)** (fig col) (be bad) sauschlecht sein (col); (be suspicious) stinken (col).

♦ **stink out** vt sep (col) room verstänkern (col).

stink bomb n Stinkbombe f.

stinker ['stɪŋkə^r] n (col) (problem) harte Nuß (col); (person) Ekel nt.

stinking ['stɪŋkɪŋ] **1** adj (col) beschissen (col!). **keep your ~ money!** du kannst dein Scheißgeld behalten! (col!) **2** adv (col) ~ **rich** stinkreich (col).

stint [stɪnt] **1** n **to do one's ~** (work) seine Arbeit tun; (share) sein(en) Teil beitragen; **would you like to do a ~ at the wheel?** möchtest du auch mal das Steuer übernehmen? **2** vt knausern mit. **to ~ sb of sth** of praise, reward jdm etw vorenthalten; **to ~ oneself** (of sth) sich (mit etw) einschränken.

stipulate ['stɪpjʊleɪt] vt **(a)** (make a condition) zur Auflage machen. **(b)** delivery date, amount, price festsetzen; size vorschreiben; conditions stellen.

stipulation [,stɪpjʊ'leɪʃən] n **(a)** (condition) Auflage f. **(b)** see vt (b) Festsetzung f; Vorschreiben nt; Stellen nt.

stir [stɜː^r] **1** n **(a) to give sth a ~** etw rühren; tea etc etw umrühren. **(b)** (fig: excitement) Aufruhr m. **to cause or create a ~** Aufsehen erregen.

2 vt **(a)** umrühren; cake mixture rühren. **~ sugar into the mixture** den Zucker darunterrühren. **(b)** (move) bewegen; limbs rühren; water, waves kräuseln. **come on, ~ yourself** (col) komm, beweg dich! (col). **(c)** (fig) emotions aufwühlen; passion wachrufen; imagination anregen; curiosity erregen; (incite) person anstacheln; (move) person, heart rühren. **to ~ sb to do sth** jdn bewegen, etw zu tun; (incite) jdn dazu anstacheln, etw zu tun; **to ~ sb into action** jdn zum Handeln bewegen.

3 vi sich regen; (person also) sich rühren;

(leaves, animal etc) sich bewegen.
♦ **stir up** *vt sep (fig)* anger erregen; *memories* wachrufen; *opposition, discord* erzeugen; *hatred* schüren; *revolution* anzetteln; *mob* aufstacheln. **to ~ ~ trouble** Unruhe stiften; **that'll ~ things ~** das kann heiter werden!

stirring ['stɜːrɪŋ] *adj speech, music* bewegend; *(stronger)* aufwühlend.

stirrup ['stɪrəp] *n* Steigbügel *m*.

stitch [stɪtʃ] **1** *n* **(a)** Stich *m*; *(in knitting etc)* Masche *f*; *(kind of ~) (in knitting etc)* Muster *nt*; *(in embroidery)* Stichart *f*. **to put a few ~es in sth** etw mit ein paar Stichen nähen; **he needed ~es in his arm** sein Arm mußte genäht werden; **to have one's ~es out** die Fäden gezogen bekommen; **a ~ in time saves nine** *(Prov)* was du heute kannst besorgen, das verschiebe nicht auf morgen *(Prov)*. **(b)** *(col: piece of clothing)* **she hadn't a ~ on** sie war splitter(faser)nackt *(col)*. **(c)** *(pain)* Seitenstiche *pl*. **(d) to be in ~es** *(col: from laughing)* sich schieflachen *(col)*. **2** *vt (Sew, Med)* nähen; *tear* zunähen.

stoat [stəʊt] *n* Wiesel *nt*.

stock [stɒk] **1** *n* **(a)** *(supply)* Vorrat *m (of* an +*dat)*; *(Comm)* Bestand *m (of* an +*dat)*. **to have sth in ~** etw vorrätig haben; **to be in ~/out of ~** *(goods)* vorrätig/nicht vorrätig sein; **to take ~** *(Comm)* Inventur machen; **to take ~ of sb** jdn abschätzen; **to take ~ of the situation** sich *(dat)* über die Situation klarwerden. **(b)** *(live~)* Viehbestand *m*. **(c)** *(Cook)* Brühe *f*. **(d)** *(Fin) (capital)* Aktienkapital *nt*; *(shares held by investor)* Anteil *m*; *(government ~)* Staatsanleihe *f*. **~s and shares** (Aktien und) Wertpapiere *pl*, Effekten *pl*. **(e) to be on the ~s** *(ship)* im Bau sein; *(book etc)* in Arbeit sein. **(f)** *~s pl (Hist: for punishment)* Stock *m*. **(g)** *(Rail)* rollendes Material.
2 *adj attr phrase etc* Standard-.
3 *vt* **(a)** *(shop etc) goods* führen. **(b)** *cupboard* füllen; *shop also, library* ausstatten; *pond, river* (mit Fischen) besetzen; *farm* mit einem Viehbestand versehen.
♦ **stock up** *vi* sich eindecken *(on* mit).

stock: ~broker *n* Börsenmakler *m*; **~ car** *n* **(a)** *(for racing)* Stock Car *nt* (frisierter, verstärkter Serienwagen); **(b)** *(US Rail: cattle truck)* Viehwaggon *m*; **~ company** *n (US)* **(a)** *(Fin)* Aktiengesellschaft *f*; **(b)** *(Theat)* Repertoiretheater *nt*; **~ exchange** *n* Börse *f*; **~holder** *n* Aktionär(in *f*) *m*.

stocking ['stɒkɪŋ] **1** *n* Strumpf *m*. **2** *vt* **in one's ~ed feet** in Strümpfen.

stock-in-trade [ˌstɒkɪn'treɪd] *n (tools, materials, fig)* Handwerkszeug *nt*.

stockist ['stɒkɪst] *n (Brit)* Händler *m*.

stock: ~ market *n* Börse(nmarkt *m*) *f*; **~pile 1** *n* Vorrat *m (of* an +*dat)*; *(of weapons)* Lager *nt*; **2** *vt* Vorräte an (+*dat)* ... anlegen; *(pej)* horten; **~taking** *n (Brit)* Inventur *f*; *(fig)* Bestandsaufnahme *f*.

stocky ['stɒkɪ] *adj (+er)* stämmig.

stodgy ['stɒdʒɪ] *adj (+er) food* pampig *(col)*, schwer; *subject* trocken; *book* schwer verdaulich.

stoic ['stəʊɪk] **1** *n* Stoiker *m*. **2** *adj* stoisch.

stoical ['stəʊɪkəl] *adj* stoisch.

stoicism ['stəʊɪsɪzəm] *n* stoische Ruhe.

stoke [stəʊk] *vt furnace* (be)heizen; *fire* schüren.

stole *pret of* **steal**.

stolen ['stəʊlən] **1** *ptp of* **steal**. **2** *adj* gestohlen. **~ goods** Diebesgut *nt*.

stolid ['stɒlɪd] *adj person* phlegmatisch, stur *(pej)*.

stomach ['stʌmək] **1** *n (abdomen)* Magen *m*; *(belly, paunch)* Bauch *m*; *(fig: appetite)* Lust *f (for* auf +*acc)*. **to hit sb in the ~** jdn in die Bauchgegend schlagen; **on an empty ~** *drink etc* auf leeren *or* nüchternen Magen; **on an empty/full ~** *swim, drive etc* mit leerem/vollem Magen; **I have no ~ for that** das ist mir zuwider; **he doesn't have the**

~ for it *(guts)* dazu hat er nicht den Mumm *(col)*. **2** *vt (col) behaviour, cruelty* vertragen; *person, film etc* ausstehen.

stomach in *cpds* Magen-; **~-ache** *n* Magenschmerzen *pl*; **~ trouble** *n* Magenbeschwerden *pl*; **~ ulcer** *n* Magengeschwür *nt*.

stomp [stɒmp] *vi* stapfen.

stone [stəʊn] **1** *n* **(a)** Stein *m*. **a ~'s throw from the station** nur einen Steinwurf *or* Katzensprung vom Bahnhof entfernt; **to leave no ~ unturned** nichts unversucht lassen. **(b)** *(Brit: weight)* = 6.35 kg. **2** *adj* Stein-, aus Stein. **3** *vt* **(a)** *(throw ~s at)* mit Steinen bewerfen; *(kill)* steinigen. **(b)** *fruit* entsteinen. **(c)** *(col)* **to be ~d (out of one's mind)** total weg sein *(col)*.

stone: S~ Age *n* Steinzeit *f*; **~-cold 1** *adj* eiskalt; **2** *adv* **~-cold sober** stocknüchtern *(col)*; **~-dead** *adj* mausetot *(col)*; **~-deaf** *adj* stocktaub *(col)*; **~mason** *n* Steinmetz *m*; **~wall** *vi (fig: esp Parl)* obstruieren; *(in answering questions)* ausweichen; *(Sport)* mauern *(Sport sl)*; **~ware** *n* Steingut *nt*; **~work** *n* Mauerwerk *nt*.

stony ['stəʊnɪ] *adj (+er) ground* steinig; *(fig) glance, silence* steinern.

stony-broke ['stəʊnɪ'brəʊk] *adj (Brit col)* völlig abgebrannt.

stood [stʊd] *pret, ptp of* **stand**.

stooge [stuːdʒ] *n (col)* Handlanger *m*; *(comedian's)* Stichwortgeber *m*.

stool [stuːl] *n (seat)* Hocker *m*; *(foot ~, kitchen ~, milking ~ also)* Schemel *m*; *(folding)* Klappstuhl *m*. **to fall between two ~s** sich zwischen zwei Stühle setzen; *(be neither one thing nor the other)* weder dem einen noch dem anderen gerecht werden.

stool pigeon *n (col) (decoy)* Lockvogel *m*; *(informer)* Spitzel *m*.

stoop [stuːp] **1** *n* Gebeugtheit *f*; *(deformity)* krummer Rücken, Buckel *m*. **to walk with a ~** gebeugt gehen. **2** *vi* sich beugen *(over* über +*acc)*; *(also* **~ down**) sich bücken; *(have a ~)* gebeugt gehen. **to ~ to sth/to doing sth** *(fig)* sich zu etw herablassen/sich dazu herablassen, etw zu tun.

stop [stɒp] **1** *n* **(a)** *(act of ~ping)* Halt *m*. **to bring sth to a ~** *(lit)* etw anhalten *or* stoppen; *traffic* etw zum Erliegen bringen; *(fig) meeting, development* einer Sache *(dat)* ein Ende machen; *conversation* etw verstummen lassen; **to come to a ~** *(car, machine)* anhalten; *(traffic)* stocken; *(meeting, rain)* aufhören; *(conversation)* verstummen; **to put a ~ to sth** einer Sache *(dat)* einen Riegel vorschieben.
(b) *(stay)* Aufenthalt *m*; *(break)* Pause *f*; *(Aviat)* Zwischenlandung *f*. **to make a ~** *(bus, train, tram)* (an)halten; *(plane, ship)* (Zwischen)station machen; **to have a ~ for coffee** eine Kaffeepause machen; **to have a ~** haltmachen; **to work without a ~** ohne Unterbrechung arbeiten.
(c) *(~ping place)* Station *f*; *(for bus)* Haltestelle *f*.
(d) *(esp Brit: punctuation mark)* Punkt *m*.
(e) *(stopper) (for door etc)* Sperre *f*; *(on type-writer)* Feststelltaste *f*.
(f) *(on organ)* Registerzug *m*. **to pull out all the ~s** *(fig)* alle Register ziehen.
2 *vt* **(a)** *(when moving) person* anhalten; *engine, machine etc* abstellen; *blow* auffangen; *traffic* (hold up) aufhalten; *(bring to standstill)* zum Erliegen bringen; *(policeman)* anhalten; *(keep out) noise, light* abfangen, auffangen. **~ thief!** haltet den Dieb!
(b) *(from continuing) rumour, crime* ein Ende machen (+*dat)*; *nonsense, noise* unterbinden; *match, conversation, work* beenden; *development, attack* aufhalten; *(temporarily)* unterbrechen; *flow of blood* stillen; *speaker, speech* unterbrechen; *production* zum Stillstand bringen; *(tempo-*

rarily) unterbrechen.
(c) *(cease)* aufhören mit. to ~ **doing sth** aufhören, etw zu tun; **she never ~s talking** sie redet ununterbrochen; **to ~ smoking** mit dem Rauchen aufhören; *(put out cigarette etc)* das Rauchen einstellen; ~ **it!** hör auf!
(d) *(suspend)* stoppen; *payments, production etc* einstellen; *cheque, electricity* sperren; *subsidy, grant etc* streichen; *proceedings* abbrechen; *(cancel) subscription* kündigen.
(e) *(prevent from happening)* etw verhindern; *(prevent from doing)* sb abhalten. **to ~ oneself** sich zurückhalten, sich bremsen *(col)*; **there's no ~ping him** *(col)* er ist nicht zu bremsen *(col)*; **to ~ sb (from)** doing sth jdn davon abhalten *or (physically)* daran hindern, etw zu tun; *(put a ~ to)* dafür sorgen, daß jd etw nicht mehr tut; **to ~ sth (from)** happening *(prevent)* **(es)** verhindern, daß etw geschieht; **how can we ~ the baby (from) crying?** *(prevent)* was können wir tun, damit das Baby nicht schreit?; **to ~ the thief (from)** escaping den Dieb an der Flucht hindern.
(f) *(block)* verstopfen; *(fill) tooth* plombieren; *(fig) gap* füllen; *leak of information* stopfen.
3 *vi* **(a)** *(halt)* anhalten; *(train, car also)* halten; *(traveller)* haltmachen; *(pedestrian, clock)* stehenbleiben; *(engine, machine)* nicht mehr laufen. ~**!** halt!, stopp!; **we ~ped for a drink at the pub** wir machten in der Kneipe Station, um etwas zu trinken; **to ~ at nothing (to do sth)** *(fig)* vor nichts haltmachen(, um etw zu tun). **(b)** *(finish, cease)* aufhören; *(pain also)* weggehen; *(heart)* stehenbleiben; *(production, payments)* eingestellt werden; *(show, match, film)* zu Ende sein; *(music, speaker also)* verstummen. **to ~** doing sth aufhören, etw zu tun, mit etw aufhören; **he never knows when to ~** er weiß nie, wann er aufhören muß. **(c)** *(col: stay)* bleiben *(at* in *+dat, with* bei*)*.
♦ **stop away** *vi (col)* wegbleiben.
♦ **stop by** *vi* kurz vorbeischauen. **to ~ ~ (at)** sb's house bei jdm hereinschauen *(col)*.
♦ **stop in** *vi (col)* drinbleiben *(col)*.
♦ **stop off** *vi* (kurz) haltmachen *(at* sb's bei jdm*)*.
♦ **stop over** *vi* kurz haltmachen; *(on travels)* Zwischenstation machen *(in* in *+dat)*; *(Aviat)* zwischenlanden.
♦ **stop up** 1 *vt* sep verstopfen; *crack, hole also* zustopfen. 2 *vi (col: stay up)* aufbleiben.
stop: ~**cock** *n* Absperrhahn *m*; ~**gap** *n (thing)* Notbehelf *m*; *(scheme)* Notlösung *f*; *(person)* Lückenbüßer *m*; ~**over** *n* Zwischenstation *f*; *(Aviat)* Zwischenlandung *f*.
stoppage ['stɒpɪdʒ] *n* **(a)** *(in work)* Unterbrechung *f*; *(in traffic)* Stockung *f*; *(because of strike etc)* Stopp *m*; *(strike)* Streik *m*. **(b)** *(of pay, cheque)* Sperrung *f*; *(deduction)* Abzug *m*. **(c)** *(blockage)* Verstopfung *f*, Stau *m*.
stopper ['stɒpəʳ] *n (plug)* Stöpsel *m*.
stop: ~-**press** *n (esp Brit) (news)* letzte Meldungen *pl*; ~**watch** *n* Stoppuhr *f*.
storage ['stɔːrɪdʒ] *n (of goods, food)* Lagerung *f*; *(of books, documents)* Aufbewahrung *f*; *(of electricity, data)* Speicherung *f*, Speichern *nt*. **to put sth into ~** etw unterstellen, etw (ein)lagern.
storage: ~ **capacity** *n (of computer)* Speicherkapazität *f*; ~ **heater** *n* (Nachtstrom)speicherofen *m*; ~ **space** *n* Lagerraum *m*; *(in house)* Schränke und Abstellräume *pl*.
store [stɔːʳ] 1 *n* **(a)** *(stock)* Vorrat *m (of* an *+dat)*; *(fig)* Fülle *f*, Reichtum *m (of* an *+dat)*. ~**s** *pl (supplies)* Vorräte *pl*; **to lay** *or* **get in a ~ of food** einen Lebensmittelvorrat anlegen; **to be in ~ for sb** jdm bevorstehen; **to have a surprise in ~ for sb** für jdn eine Überraschung auf Lager haben; **what has the future in ~ for us?** was wird uns *(dat)* die Zukunft bringen?; **to set great/little ~ by sth** viel/wenig von etw halten. **(b)** *(esp US: shop)* Laden *m*, Geschäft *nt*; *(department ~)*

Kaufhaus *nt*. 2 *vt* lagern; *documents* aufbewahren; *furniture* unterstellen; *(in depository)* einlagern; *information, heat* speichern; *(keep in reserve, collect: also ~ up)* Vorräte an *(+dat)* ... anschaffen. **to ~ sth away** etw verwahren.
store: ~**house** *n* Lager(haus) *nt*; *(fig)* Fundgrube *f*; ~ **keeper** *n (in* ~*house)* Lagerverwalter *m*; *(esp US: shopkeeper)* Ladenbesitzer(in *f)*; ~**room** *n* Lagerraum *m*; *(for food)* Vorratskammer *f*.
storey, *(US)* **story** ['stɔːrɪ] *n, pl* -**s** *or (US)* **stories** Stock(werk *nt) m*, Etage *f*. **a nine-~ building** ein neunstöckiges Gebäude; **on the second ~** im zweiten Stock; *(US)* im ersten Stock.
stork [stɔːk] *n* Storch *m*.
storm [stɔːm] 1 *n* **(a)** Unwetter *nt*; *(thunder~)* Gewitter *nt*; *(strong wind)* Sturm *m*. **there is a ~ blowing** es stürmt; **a ~ in a teacup** *(fig)* ein Sturm im Wasserglas. **(b)** *(fig) (of abuse)* Flut *f (of* von*)*; *(of applause, criticism)* Sturm *m (of* gen*)*; *(of blows, missiles)* Hagel *m (of* von*)*; *(outcry)* Aufruhr *m*. ~ **of protest** Proteststurm *m*. **(c)** **to take sth/sb by ~** *(Mil, fig)* etw/jdn im Sturm erobern. 2 *vt* stürmen. 3 *vi* **(a)** *(talk angrily)* wüten *(at* gegen*)*. **(b)** *(move violently)* stürmen.
storm: ~ **cloud** *n (lit, fig)* Gewitterwolke *f*; ~ **cone** *n* Sturmkegel *m*; ~ **door** *n* äußere Windfangtür; ~ **force** *n* Windstärke *f*; ~ **troops** *npl* Sturmtruppe *f*.
stormy ['stɔːmɪ] *adj (+er) (lit, fig)* stürmisch; *discussion also, temper* hitzig; *protests* heftig.
story[1] ['stɔːrɪ] *n (a) (tale, account)* Geschichte *f*; *(Liter also)* Erzählung *f*; *(joke)* Witz *m*. **it's a long ~** das ist eine lange Geschichte; **the ~ of her life** ihre Lebensgeschichte; **that's another ~** das ist eine andere Geschichte; **his ~ is that ...** er behauptet, daß ...; **that's not the whole ~** das ist nicht die ganze Wahrheit; **the marks tell their own ~** die Flecke sprechen für sich; **to cut a long ~ short** um es kurz zu machen, der langen Rede kurzer Sinn; **it's the (same) old ~** es ist das alte Lied; **but it's another ~** now aber jetzt sieht die Sache anders aus. **(b)** *(Press) (event)* Geschichte *f*; *(newspaper ~)* Artikel *m*. **(c)** *(plot)* Handlung *f*. **(d)** *(col: lie)* Märchen *nt*. **to tell stories** Märchen erzählen.
story[2] *n (US)* = **storey**.
story-book ['stɔːrɪbʊk] 1 *n* Geschichtenbuch *nt*. 2 *adj attr castles, romance etc* märchenhaft.
stout [staʊt] 1 *adj (+er)* **(a)** *(corpulent)* korpulent. **(b)** *(strong) stick, horse etc* kräftig; *door, rope, gate* stark. **(c)** *(brave)* tapfer; *denial* entschieden. 2 *n* Starkbier *nt*; *(sweet)* ~ = Malzbier *nt*.
stout-hearted ['staʊt'hɑːtɪd] *adj* tapfer.
stove [stəʊv] *n* Ofen *m*; *(for cooking)* Herd *m*. **electric/gas** ~ Elektro-/Gasherd *m*.
stove *in pret, ptp of* **stave in.**
stow [stəʊ] *vt* **(a)** *(Naut) cargo* verladen, (ver)stauen. **(b)** *(put away: also ~ away)* verstauen *(in* in *+dat)*.
♦ **stow away** *vi* als blinder Passagier fahren.
stowaway ['stəʊəweɪ] *n* blinder Passagier.
straddle ['strædl] *vt (standing)* breitbeinig stehen über *(+dat)*; *(sitting)* rittlings sitzen auf *(+dat)*; *(jumping)* grätschen über *(+acc)*; *(fig) differences* überbrücken; **two continents** überspannen. **to ~ the border/river** sich über beide Seiten der Grenze/beide Ufer des Flusses erstrecken.
strafe [streɪf] *vt* unter Beschuß nehmen.
straggle ['strægl] *vi (spread untidily) (houses, trees)* verstreut liegen; *(hair) (unordentlich)* hängen; *(plant)* in alle Richtungen wuchern. **to ~ behind** zurückbleiben, hinterherzockeln *(col)*.
straggler ['strægləʳ] *n* Nachzügler *m*.
straggling ['stræglɪŋ] *adj (a) children, cattle etc* weit verteilt; *(~ behind)* zurückgeblieben; *village* sich lang hinziehend; *houses* zerstreut liegend; *group, row* auseinandergezogen. **(b)** *(col: also* **straggly***) hair* zottig; *plant* wuchernd.

straight [streɪt] **1** adj (+er) **(a)** gerade; posture also aufrecht; hair glatt; skirt, trousers gerade geschnitten. **your tie isn't** ~ deine Krawatte sitzt schief; **the picture isn't** ~ das Bild hängt schief; **as** ~ **as a die** kerzengerade; road schnurgerade; **to keep a** ~ **face** keine Miene verziehen; **to be (all)** ~ **(in order)** in Ordnung sein; (fig: clarified also) (völlig) geklärt sein; **to put things** ~ (tidy) alles in Ordnung bringen; (clarify) alles klären; **to put sb** ~ **about sth** jdm etw klarmachen; **he soon put me** ~! er hat mich eines Besseren belehrt.

(b) (frank) answer, talking offen; denial, refusal direkt; (honest) person, dealings, advice ehrlich. **to be** ~ **with sb** offen zu jdm sein.

(c) (plain) drink pur; (Pol) fight direkt; choice einfach; (col) (heterosexual) normal, hetero (col); (conventional) etabliert, spießig (pej). **to have a** ~ **choice between ...** nur die Wahl zwischen ... haben.

(d) (continuous) ununterbrochen. ~ **run** (Cards) Sequenz f; **our team had ten** ~ **wins** unsere Mannschaft gewann zehnmal hintereinander.

(e) (Theat) production konventionell; actor ernsthaft. **a** ~ **play** ein reines Drama.

2 adv **(a)** hold, walk, shoot gerade; stand up also aufrecht; leap at, aim for, above, across direkt. ~ **through sth** glatt durch etw; **he came** ~ **at me** er kam direkt auf mich zu; **it went** ~ **up in the air** es flog senkrecht in die Luft; **to look** ~ **ahead** geradeaus sehen; **the town lay** ~ **ahead of us** die Stadt lag direkt vor uns; **to drive** ~ **on** geradeaus weiterfahren.

(b) (directly) direkt; (immediately) sofort. **I went** ~ **home** ich ging direkt nach Hause; **to look sb** ~ **in the eye** jdm direkt in die Augen sehen; ~ **after this** sofort danach; ~ **away** or **off** sofort, auf der Stelle; ~ **to come** ~ **to the point** gleich zur Sache kommen.

(c) (clearly) think, see klar; (frankly) offen, ohne Umschweife. ~ **out** (col) rundheraus.

(d) drink pur.

3 n (~ **part, on race track**) Gerade f; (road, rail) gerade Strecke. **the final** ~ die Zielgerade; **to keep on the** ~ **and narrow** dafür sorgen, daß man nicht auf die schiefe Bahn kommt; **to cut sth on the** ~ etw gerade (ab)schneiden.

straighten ['streɪtn] **1** vt **(a)** hat gerade aufsetzen; tie geradeziehen; shoulders straffen. **(b)** (also ~ **out**: make straight) gerademachen; picture gerade hinhängen; road, river begradigen; tablecloth geradeziehen; wire geradebiegen; hair glätten. **(c)** (also ~ **up**: tidy) in Ordnung bringen. **(d)** (also ~ **out**: put right) problem, situation klären. **2** vi (also ~ **out**: road, plant etc) gerade werden; (hair) glatt werden. **3** vr **to** ~ **oneself (up)** sich aufrichten; **the problem will soon** ~ **itself out** das Problem wird sich bald von selbst erledigen.

straight: ~**faced** [streɪt'feɪst] **1** adv ohne die Miene zu verziehen; **2** adj **to be** ~**faced** keine Miene verziehen; ~**forward** adj (honest) person aufrichtig; explanation, look also offen, freimütig; (simple) question, problem einfach.

strain¹ [streɪn] **1** n **(a)** (Mech) Belastung f; (on beams, floor also) Druck m. **the** ~ **on a rope** die Seilspannung; **can you take some of the** ~? können Sie mal mit festhalten/mit ziehen?; **to put a (great)** ~ **on sth** etw (stark) belasten; **to show signs of** ~ Zeichen von Überlastung zeigen.

(b) (fig: mental, economic etc) Belastung f (on für); (effort) Anstrengung f; (pressure) (of job etc also) Beanspruchung f (of durch); (of responsibility) Last f; (muscle~) (Muskel)zerrung f; (on eyes, heart etc) Überanstrengung f (on gen). **to be under a lot of** ~ stark beansprucht sein; **I find her/that a bit of a** ~ ich finde sie/das ziemlich anstrengend; **to put a (great)** ~ **on sb/sth** jdn/etw stark

belasten; **to show signs of** ~ Zeichen von Überlastung zeigen; **to be under** ~ großen Belastungen ausgesetzt sein; **the** ~**s of modern life** die Belastungen or der Streß des heutigen Lebens.

(c) ~**s** pl (of instrument, tune) Klänge pl; **to the** ~**s of** zu den Klängen (+gen).

2 vt **(a)** (stretch) spannen. **(b)** (put ~ on) rope, relationship, budget belasten; nerves, patience also strapazieren; (put too much ~ on) überlasten; meaning dehnen. **to** ~ **one's ears/eyes to ...** angestrengt lauschen/gucken, um zu ...; **to** ~ **every nerve** jeden Nerv anspannen; **to** ~ **oneself** sich anstrengen; (excessively) sich überanstrengen. **(c)** (Med) muscle zerren; back, eyes, voice strapazieren; (excessively) überanstrengen; heart belasten; (excessively) überlasten. **(d)** (filter) (durch)sieben; (pour water off) vegetables abgießen. **to** ~ **off water** Wasser abgießen.

3 vi (exert effort) sich anstrengen; (pull) zerren, ziehen; (fig: strive) sich bemühen. **to** ~ **to do sth** sich anstrengen, etw zu tun; **to** ~ **at sth** sich mit etw abmühen; (pull) an etw (dat) ziehen.

strain² n **(a)** (streak) Hang, Zug m; (hereditary) Veranlagung f. **a** ~ **of madness** eine Veranlagung zum Wahnsinn. **(b)** (breed) (animals) Rasse f; (of plants) Sorte f; (of virus etc) Art f.

strained [streɪnd] adj **(a)** muscle gezerrt; back, eyes überanstrengt. **(b)** expression, style unnatürlich; smile, conversation gezwungen; meeting steif; voice, relations, atmosphere, nerves (an)gespannt. **he looked rather** ~ er sah ziemlich abgespannt aus.

strainer ['streɪnəʳ] n (Cook) Sieb nt.

strait [streɪt] n (Geog) Meerenge f. **the** ~**s of Dover** die Straße von Dover; **to be in dire** ~**s** in großen Nöten sein.

straitened ['streɪtnd] adj in ~ **circumstances** in bescheidenen Verhältnissen.

strait: ~**jacket** n (lit, fig) Zwangsjacke f; ~**-laced** [streɪt'leɪst] adj prüde, spießig (col).

strand [strænd] n Strang m; (of hair) Strähne f; (of thread) Faden m; (of wire) Litze f; (of beads) Schnur f.

stranded ['strændɪd] adj **to be** ~ (ship, fish, shipwrecked person) gestrandet sein; **to be (left)** ~ (person) festsitzen; (without money also) auf dem trockenen sitzen (col).

strange [streɪndʒ] adj (+er) **(a)** seltsam, merkwürdig. **(b)** (unfamiliar) surroundings fremd; (unaccustomed) work ungewohnt. **I felt rather** ~ **at first** zuerst fühlte ich mich ziemlich fremd; **I feel** ~ **in a skirt** ich komme mir in einem Rock komisch vor (col).

strangely ['streɪndʒlɪ] adv (oddly) seltsam, merkwürdig; act, behave also komisch (col). ~ **enough** seltsamerweise, merkwürdigerweise.

stranger ['streɪndʒəʳ] n Fremde(r) mf. **he's a perfect** ~ **to me** ich kenne ihn überhaupt nicht; **I'm a** ~ **here myself** ich bin selbst fremd hier; **he is no** ~ **to London** er kennt sich in London aus; **he is no** ~ **to misfortune** Leid ist ihm nicht fremd; **hullo,** ~! (col) hallo, lange nicht gesehen.

strangle ['stræŋgl] vt (murder) erwürgen; (fig) cry ersticken.

stranglehold ['stræŋglhəʊld] n (fig) absolute Machtposition (on gegenüber). **they have a** ~ **on us** (fig) sie haben uns in der Zange.

strangler ['stræŋgləʳ] n Würger(in f) m.

strangulation [ˌstræŋgjʊ'leɪʃən] n Erwürgen nt. **death was due to** ~ der Tod trat durch Ersticken ein.

strap [stræp] **1** n Riemen m; (for safety also) Gurt m; (watch ~) Band nt; (shoulder ~) Träger m. **to give sb the** ~ jdn verprügeln. **2** vt **to** ~ **sth onto sth** etw auf etw (acc) schnallen; **to** ~ **sb/sth down** jdn/etw festschnallen; **to** ~ **sb/oneself in** (in car, plane) jdn/sich anschnallen.

strap-hanging ['stræpˌhæŋɪŋ] n Pendeln nt.

strapless ['stræplɪs] adj trägerlos; dress also schulterfrei.

strapping ['stræpɪŋ] adj (col) stramm.

Strasbourg ['stræzbɜːg] n Straßburg nt.

strata ['strɑːtə] pl of **stratum.**

stratagem ['strætɪdʒəm] n (Mil) Kriegslist f; (artifice) List f.

strategic [strə'tiːdʒɪk] adj strategisch; (strategically important) strategisch wichtig; (fig also) taktisch.

strategically [strə'tiːdʒɪkəlɪ] adv strategisch; (fig also) taktisch. **to be ~ placed** eine strategisch günstige Stellung haben.

strategy ['strætɪdʒɪ] n (a) (Mil) Strategie f; (Sport, fig also) Taktik f. (b) (art of ~) (Mil) Kriegskunst f; (fig) Taktieren nt.

stratosphere ['strætəʊsfɪəʳ] n Stratosphäre f.

stratum ['strɑːtəm] n, pl **strata** (Geol, fig) Schicht f.

straw [strɔː] **1** n (a) (stalk) Strohhalm m; (collectively) Stroh nt no pl. **it's the last ~!** (col) das ist der Gipfel! (col); **to clutch at ~s** sich an einen Strohhalm klammern. (b) (drinking ~) Strohhalm m. **2** adj attr Stroh-; basket aus Stroh.

strawberry ['strɔːbərɪ] n Erdbeere f.

straw: ~**-coloured,** ~**-colored** (US) adj strohfarben; hair strohblond; ~ **hat** n Strohhut m.

stray [streɪ] **1** vi (also ~ **away**) sich verirren; (also ~ **about**) (umher)streunen; (fig: thoughts, speaker) abschweifen. **to ~ (away) from sth** (lit, fig) von etw abkommen. **2** adj child, bullet, cattle verirrt; cat, dog etc streunend attr; (ownerless) herrenlos; (isolated) remarks, houses vereinzelt; (single) remark einzeln; (occasional) gelegentlich; thoughts flüchtig. **3** n (dog, cat) streunendes Tier; (ownerless) herrenloses Tier.

streak [striːk] **1** n Streifen m; (of light) Strahl m; (in hair) Strähne f; (of fat also) Streifen f; (fig) (trace) Spur f; (of jealousy, meanness etc) Zug m; (of madness, humour) Anflug m. ~ **of lightning** Blitz(strahl) m; **a winning/losing** ~ eine Glücks-/Pechsträhne. **2** vt streifen. **the sky was** ~**ed with red** der Himmel hatte rote Streifen; ~**ed with dirt/paint** schmutzverschmiert/mit Farbe beschmiert. **3** vi (a) (lightning) zucken; (col: move quickly) flitzen (col). **to** ~ **along/past** entlang-/vorbeiflitzen (col). (b) (run naked) blitzen.

streaker ['striːkəʳ] n Blitzer(in f) m.

streaky ['striːkɪ] adj (+er) bacon durchwachsen.

stream [striːm] **1** n (a) (small river) Bach m; (current) Strömung f. **to go with/against the** ~ (lit, fig) mit dem/gegen den Strom schwimmen. (b) (of liquid, people) Strom m; (of light, tears) Flut f; (of words, abuse) Schwall m. (c) (Brit Sch) Leistungsgruppe f. **2** vt (a) **the walls** ~**ed water** von den Wänden rann das Wasser; **his face** ~**ed blood** Blut strömte ihm übers Gesicht. (b) (Brit Sch) in (Leistungs)gruppen einteilen. **3** vi (lit, fig) strömen; (eyes) tränen. **the walls were** ~**ing with water** die Wände trieften vor Nässe; **the rain was** ~**ing down** es regnete in Strömen; **tears** ~**ed down her face** Tränen rannen über ihr Gesicht.

♦ **stream in** vi herein-/hineinströmen.

♦ **stream out** vi heraus-/hinausströmen (of aus).

♦ **stream past** vi vorbeiströmen (prep obj an +dat); (cars) in Strömen vorbeifahren (prep obj an +dat).

streamer ['striːməʳ] n (flag) Banner nt; (made of paper) Luftschlange f.

streamline ['striːmlaɪn] vt (lit) Stromlinienform geben (+dat); (fig) rationalisieren.

streamlined ['striːmlaɪnd] adj wing windschlüpfig; car, plane stromlinienförmig; (fig) rationalisiert.

street [striːt] **1** n Straße f. **in** or **on the** ~ auf der Straße; **it's right up my** ~ (fig col) das ist genau mein Fall (col); **to be** ~**s ahead of** or **better than sb** (fig col) jdm haushoch überlegen sein (col); **to**

take to the ~**s** (demonstrators) auf die Straße gehen; **to be on the** ~**s** (prostitute) auf den Strich gehen (col); (homeless) auf der Straße stehen. **2** adj attr Straßen-.

street: ~**car** n (US) Straßenbahn f; ~ **cleaner** n Straßenfeger(in f) m; ~ **lamp** n Straßenlaterne f; ~ **level** n **at** ~ **level** zu ebener Erde; ~ **light** n Straßenlaterne f; ~ **lighting** n Straßenbeleuchtung f; ~ **map,** ~ **plan** n Stadtplan m; ~ **value** n Verkaufswert m; ~**walker** n Prostituierte f.

strength [streŋθ] n (a) (lit, fig) Stärke f; (of person, feelings) Kraft f; (of table, wall) Stabilität f; (of conviction, views) Festigkeit f; (of argument, evidence) Überzeugungskraft f; (of mixture) Konzentration f. ~ **of character/will** Charakter-/Willensstärke f; **on the** ~ **of sth** auf Grund einer Sache (gen); **his** ~ **failed him** ihn verließen die Kräfte; **to save one's** ~ mit seinen Kräften haushalten; **when she has her** ~ **back** wenn sie wieder bei Kräften ist; **to go from** ~ **to** ~ einen Erfolg nach dem anderen haben. (b) (numbers) (An)zahl f; (Mil) Stärke f. **to be up to/below** ~ (die) volle Stärke/nicht die volle Stärke haben; **the police were there in** ~ ein starkes Polizeiaufgebot war da; **they came in** ~ sie kamen in großer Zahl.

strengthen ['streŋθən] **1** vt stärken; building, protest verstärken; person (lit) Kraft geben (+dat); (fig: in opinion) bestärken (in in +dat); currency, market festigen; affection also, effect vergrößern. **2** vi stärker werden.

strenuous ['strenjʊəs] adj (a) (exhausting) anstrengend; march, game also ermüdend. (b) (energetic) supporter, support unermüdlich; effort, denial hartnäckig; conflict, protest heftig.

stress [stres] **1** n (a) (strain) Belastung f, Streß m; (Med) Überlastung f, Streß m. **the** ~**es and strains of modern life** die Belastungen des heutigen Lebens; **times of** ~ Zeiten pl großer Belastung; **to be under** ~ großen Belastungen ausgesetzt sein; (as regards work) unter Streß stehen; **im Streß sein.** (b) (accent) Betonung f; (fig: emphasis) Akzent m. **to put** or **lay (great)** ~ **on sth** großen Wert auf etw (acc) legen; on fact, detail etw (besonders) betonen. (c) (Mech) Belastung f. **2** vt (lit, fig: emphasize) betonen; good manners, subject großen Wert legen auf (+acc).

stressed [strest] adj person gestreßt, überlastet.

stretch [stretʃ] **1** n (a) (elasticity) **to be at full** ~ (lit: material) bis zum äußersten gedehnt sein; (fig) (person) mit aller Kraft arbeiten; (factory etc) auf Hochtouren arbeiten (col); (engine, production, work) auf Hochtouren laufen; **by no** ~ **of the imagination** beim besten Willen nicht. (b) (of road etc) Strecke f; (of river, countryside etc) Stück nt; (of journey) Abschnitt m. **a straight** ~ **of road** eine gerade Strecke; **in that** ~ **of the river** in dem Teil des Flusses; **for a long** ~ über eine weite Strecke. (c) (~ of time) Zeit(raum m) f. **for a long** ~ **of time** für (eine) lange Zeit; **for hours at a** ~ stundenlang; **three days at a** ~ drei Tage an einem Stück; **to do a** ~ (col: in prison) im Knast sein (col).

2 adj attr dehnbar, Stretch-.

3 vt (a) (extend) strecken; (widen) jumper also, elastic, shoes dehnen; (spread) wings etc ausbreiten; (tighten) rope spannen. **to** ~ **one's legs** (go for a walk) sich (dat) die Beine vertreten (col). (b) (make go further) money strecken; (use fully) resources voll (aus)nutzen; credit voll beanspruchen; athlete, student etc fordern; one's abilities bis zum äußersten fordern. (c) (strain) meaning äußerst weit fassen; truth, rules großzügig auslegen. **to** ~ **a point** großzügig sein; **that's** ~**ing it a bit (far)** das geht fast zu weit.

4 vi (after sleep etc) sich strecken; (be elastic) sich dehnen, dehnbar sein; (extend) (time, area, influence) sich erstrecken (to bis, over über

+*acc*); *(be enough: food, money)* reichen *(to* für); *(become looser)* weiter werden; *(become longer)* länger werden. **to ~ to reach sth** sich recken, um etw zu erreichen; **the fields ~ed away into the distance** die Felder dehnten sich bis in die Ferne aus; **I can't ~ to that** so viel kann ich mir nicht erlauben.

♦ **stretch out 1** *vt sep arms, wings* ausbreiten; *leg, hand* ausstrecken; *foot* vorstrecken; *rope* spannen; *meeting, essay* ausdehnen. **to ~ oneself ~ (on the ground)** sich auf den Boden legen. **2** *vi* sich strecken; *(col: lie down)* sich hinlegen; *(countryside)* sich ausbreiten; *(in time)* sich erstrecken *(over* über +*acc*). **he lay ~ed ~ on the bed** er lag ausgestreckt auf dem Bett.

stretcher ['stretʃə'] *n (Med)* Trage *f*.

stretcher: **~-bearer** *n* Krankenträger *m*; **~ case** *n* Kranke(r) *mf*/Verletzte(r) *mf*, der/die nicht gehen kann; *(Mil)* Schwerverwundete(r) *mf*.

stretch marks *npl* Schwangerschaftsstreifen *pl*.

strew [stru:] *ptp* **strewn** [stru:n] *or* **~ed** *vt (scatter)* verstreuen; *flowers, sand* streuen. **the floor was ~n with ... ...** lag/lagen überall auf dem Boden verstreut.

stricken ['strɪkən] **1** *(old) ptp of* **strike**. **2** *adj (liter: wounded)* verwundet; *(afflicted)* leidgeprüft; *(ill)* leidend *(geh)*; *ship, plane* in Not. **~ with grief/fear** *etc* schmerzerfüllt/von Angst *etc* erfüllt.

strict [strɪkt] *adj* (+*er*) **(a)** *law, parent etc* streng; *order, discipline also, obedience* strikt; *Catholic* strenggläubig. **(b)** *(precise)* streng; *meaning* genau. **in the ~ sense of the word** genau genommen; **in ~ confidence** streng vertraulich.

strictly ['strɪktlɪ] *adv* **(a)** streng. **smoking is ~ forbidden** Rauchen ist strengstens verboten. **(b)** *(precisely)* genau; *(absolutely)* absolut. **~ confidential** streng vertraulich; **~ speaking** genau genommen; **not ~ true** nicht ganz richtig; **~ between you and me** ganz unter uns.

strictness ['strɪktnɪs] *n* **(a)** Strenge *f*. **(b)** *(preciseness)* Genauigkeit *f*.

stricture ['strɪktʃə'] *n usu pl (criticism)* (scharfe) Kritik *no pl*.

stride [straɪd] *(vb: pret* **strode**, *ptp* **stridden** ['strɪdn])* **1** *n (step)* Schritt *m*; *(gait also)* Gang *m*; *(fig)* Fortschritt *m*. **to get into one's ~** *(fig)* in Schwung *or* in Fahrt kommen; **to take sth in one's ~** mit etw spielend fertigwerden; *exam, interview* etw spielend schaffen. **2** *vi* schreiten *(geh)*, mit großen Schritten gehen. **to ~ off** davonschreiten *(geh)*; **to ~ up to sb** auf jdn zuschreiten *(geh)*.

strident ['straɪdənt] *adj sound* schrill, durchdringend; *colour* grell; *criticism, tone* scharf; *demand, protest* lautstark.

strife [straɪf] *n* Unfriede *m*; *(in family, between friends)* Zwietracht *f (geh)*. **armed ~** bewaffneter Konflikt; **internal ~** innere Kämpfe *pl*.

strike [straɪk] *(vb: pret* **struck**, *ptp* **struck** *or (old)* **stricken)* **1** *n* **(a)** Streik *m*. **to be on ~** streiken; **to come out** *or* **go on ~** in den Streik treten. **(b)** *(discovery of oil, gold etc)* Fund *m*. **to make a ~** fündig werden; **a lucky ~** ein Treffer, ein Glücksfall *m*. **(c)** *(Mil: attack)* Angriff *m*. **(d)** *(act of striking)* Schlag *m*.

2 *vt* **(a)** *(hit)* schlagen; *door* schlagen auf (+*acc*); *nail, table* schlagen auf (+*acc*); *metal, hot iron etc* hämmern; *(bullet, lightning, misfortune)* treffen; *(disease)* befallen. **to ~ sb/sth a blow** jdm/einer Sache einen Schlag versetzen; **who struck the first blow?** wer hat zuerst (zu)geschlagen?; **to ~ a blow for sth** *(fig)* eine Lanze für etw brechen.

(b) *(collide with, meet)* *(spade)* stoßen auf (+*acc*); *(car)* fahren gegen; *ground* aufschlagen auf (+*acc*); *(ship)* auflaufen auf (+*acc*); *(sound, light)* *ears, eyes* treffen. **to ~ one's head against sth** sich den Kopf an etw *(acc)* stoßen; **to ~**

difficulties/obstacles *(fig)* in Schwierigkeiten geraten/auf Hindernisse stoßen; **a terrible sight struck my eyes** plötzlich sah ich etwas Schreckliches.

(c) *(sound)* *string, chord, note* anschlagen; *(clock)* schlagen.

(d) *(occur to)* in den Sinn kommen (+*dat*). **to ~ sb as unlikely** *etc* jdm unwahrscheinlich *etc* vorkommen; **that ~s me as a good idea** das kommt mir sehr vernünftig vor; **has it ever struck you that ...?** *(occurred to you)* haben Sie je daran gedacht, daß ...?; *(have you noticed)* ist Ihnen je aufgefallen, daß ...?; **to be struck by sth** von etw beeindruckt sein; **how does it ~ you?** was halten Sie davon?; **how does she ~ you?** welchen Eindruck haben Sie von ihr?

(e) *(produce, make)* *coin* prägen; *(fig) agreement* aushandeln. **to ~ a light/match** Feuer machen/ein Streichholz anzünden; **to be struck dumb** stumm werden; **to ~ fear into sb** jdn mit Angst erfüllen.

(f) *(find)* *oil* stoßen auf (+*acc*). **to ~ it rich** das große Geld machen.

(g) *(remove)* streichen. **to be struck** *or (US)* **stricken from a list/the record** von einer Liste/aus dem Protokoll gestrichen werden.

3 *vi* **(a)** *(hit)* treffen; *(lightning)* einschlagen; *(snake)* zubeißen; *(tiger)* die Beute schlagen; *(attack, Mil etc)* angreifen; *(disease)* zuschlagen; *(panic)* ausbrechen. **to ~ against sth** gegen etw stoßen; **to ~ at sb/sth** *(lit)* nach jdm/etw schlagen; **to ~ at the roots of democracy** an den Wurzeln der Demokratie rütteln; **they were within striking distance of success** der Erfolg war in greifbarer Nähe. **(b)** *(clock)* schlagen. **(c)** *(workers)* streiken *(for* für). **(d)** **to ~ on a new idea** auf eine neue Idee kommen.

♦ **strike back** *vi* zurückschlagen; *(fig also)* sich wehren. **to ~ at sb** jds Angriff *(acc)* erwidern; *(fig)* sich gegen jdn wehren.

♦ **strike down** *vt sep* niederschlagen; *(God)* emies vernichten; *(fig)* zu Fall bringen. **to be struck ~** niedergeschlagen werden; *(by illness)* getroffen werden.

♦ **strike off** *vt sep* **(a)** *(cut off)* abschlagen. **(b)** *(from list)* (aus)streichen; *solicitor* die Lizenz entziehen (+*dat*); *doctor* die Zulassung entziehen (+*dat*).

♦ **strike out 1** *vi* **(a)** *(hit out)* schlagen. **to ~ ~ at sb** *(lit, fig)* jdn angreifen. **(b)** *(change direction)* zuhalten *(for, towards* auf +*acc*); *(set out)* sich aufmachen *(for* zu). **to ~ ~ on one's own** *(lit)* allein losziehen; *(fig)* eigene Wege gehen; **to ~ ~ in a new direction** *(fig)* neue Wege gehen. **2** *vt sep name, entry* (aus)streichen.

♦ **strike up 1** *vi (band etc)* anfangen (zu spielen). **2** *vt insep* **(a)** *(band)* *tune* anstimmen. **(b)** *friendship* schließen; *conversation* anfangen.

strike: **~ action** *n* Streikmaßnahmen *pl*; **~breaker** *n* Streikbrecher *m*; **~ force** *n (Mil)* Kampftruppe *f*.

striker ['straɪkə'] *n* **(a)** *(worker)* Streikende(r) *mf*. **(b)** *(Ftbl)* Stürmer *m*.

striking ['straɪkɪŋ] *adj colour, resemblance etc* auffallend; *difference* erstaunlich; *beauty* eindrucksvoll. **a ~ example of sth** ein hervorragendes Beispiel für etw.

string [strɪŋ] *(vb: pret, ptp* **strung**) **1** *n* **(a)** *(cord)* Schnur *f*, Bindfaden *m*; *(on apron etc)* Band *nt*; *(on anorak)* Kordel *f*; *(of puppet)* Faden *m*. **to pull ~s** *(fig col)* Fäden ziehen, Beziehungen spielen lassen; **with no ~s attached** ohne Bedingungen. **(b)** *(row)* *(of beads, onions etc)* Schnur *f*; *(of racehorses etc)* Reihe *f*; *(of people, vehicles)* Schlange *f*; *(fig: series)* Reihe *f*; *(of lies, curses)* Serie *f*. **(c)** *(of musical instrument, tennis racket etc)* Saite *f*; *(of bow)* Sehne *f*. **the ~s** *pl (instruments)* die Streichinstrumente *pl*; *(players)* die Streicher *pl;* **to have more than one ~ to one's bow** mehrere Eisen im Feuer haben.

2 *vt* **(a)** *(put on ~)* aufreihen. **to ~ objects/ sentences** *etc* **together** Gegenstände zusammenbinden/Sätze *etc* aneinanderreihen; **she can't even ~ two sentences together** sie bringt keinen vernünftigen Satz zusammen. **(b)** *violin etc, tennis racket* (mit Saiten) bespannen. **(c)** *(space out)* aufreihen.

♦ **string along** *(col)* **1** *vt sep* **to ~ sb ~** jdn hinhalten. **2** *vi* (*go along with)* sich anschließen *(with dat)*.

stringed [strɪŋd] *adj instrument* Saiten-; *(played with bow also)* Streich-.

stringent ['strɪndʒənt] *adj standards, laws* streng; *testing, training etc also* hart; *measures also* energisch. **~ economies** schärfste Sparmaßnahmen *pl.*

string: ~ quartet *n* Streichquartett *nt*; **~ vest** *n* Netzhemd *nt*.

strip [strɪp] **1** *n* **(a)** *(narrow piece)* Streifen *m*; *(of land also)* (schmales) Stück; *(of metal)* Band *nt*. **(b)** *(Brit Sport)* Trikot *nt*. **2** *vt* **(a)** *(remove clothes etc from)* person ausziehen; *bed* abziehen; *wall (remove paint from)* abkratzen; *(remove paper from)* die Tapeten abziehen von; *wallpaper* abziehen; *(remove contents from)* ausräumen. **to ~ a house of its contents** ein Haus ausräumen; **to ~ sth from or off sth** etw von etw entfernen; **~ped of sth** ohne etw. **(b)** *(fig: deprive of)* berauben *(of gen)*. **(c)** *(Tech: dismantle)* engine, car, gun auseinandernehmen. **3** *vi* *(remove clothes)* sich ausziehen; *(at doctor's)* sich freimachen; *(perform ~tease)* strippen *(col)*. **to ~ naked** sich ganz ausziehen; **to ~ to the waist** den Oberkörper freimachen.

♦ **strip off** *vi* = **strip 3.**

stripe [straɪp] *n* **(a)** Streifen *m*. **(b)** *(US: kind) (of politics)* Richtung *f*; *(of character, opinion)* Art *f*.

striped [straɪpt] *adj* gestreift.

stripper ['strɪpə'] *n* **(a)** *(performer)* Stripteasetänzerin *f*. **(b)** *(paint-~)* Farbentferner *m*; *(wallpaper ~)* Tapetenlöser *m*.

striptease ['strɪptiːz] *n* Striptease *m or nt*.

strive [straɪv] *pret* **strove**, *ptp* **striven** ['strɪvn] *vi (exert oneself)* sich bemühen; *(fight)* kämpfen. **to ~ to do sth** bestrebt sein, etw zu tun; **to ~ for sth** nach etw streben; **to ~ against sth** gegen etw (an)kämpfen.

strode [strəʊd] *pret of* **stride.**

stroke [strəʊk] **1** *n* **(a)** *(blow)* Schlag, Hieb *m*. **(b)** *(Cricket, Golf, Rowing, Tennis)* Schlag *m*; *(Swimming) (movement)* Zug *m*; *(type of ~)* Stil *m*. **to put sb off his ~** *(fig)* jdn aus dem Konzept bringen. **(c)** *(of pen etc)* Strich *m*. **he doesn't do a ~** *(of work)* er tut keinen Schlag *(col)*; **a ~ of genius** ein genialer Einfall; **a ~ of luck** ein Glücksfall *m*; **we had a ~ of luck** wir hatten Glück; **at a or one ~** mit einem Schlag. **(d)** *(of clock)* Schlag *m*. **on the ~ of twelve** Punkt zwölf (Uhr). **(e)** *(of piston)* Hub *m*. **two-~ engine** Zweitaktmotor *m*. **(f)** *(Med)* Schlag *m*. **to have a ~** einen Schlaganfall bekommen. **(g)** *(caress)* Streicheln *nt no pl*. **to give sb/sth a ~** jdn/etw streicheln. **2** *vt* streicheln. **he ~d his chin** er strich sich *(dat)* übers Kinn.

stroll [strəʊl] **1** *n* Spaziergang *m*. **to go for a ~, to take a ~** einen Bummel machen. **2** *vi* spazieren. **to ~ along** bummeln; **to ~ along the road** die Straße entlangspazieren; **to ~ up to sb** auf jdn zuschlendern.

stroller ['strəʊlə'] *n (US: for babies)* Sportwagen *m*.

strong [strɒŋ] **1** *adj* (+er) **(a)** stark; *material, grip also, kick, voice* kräftig; *table, wall* stabil; *shoes* fest; *(Fin) economy* gesund; *(strongly marked) features* ausgeprägt. **you need a ~ stomach to be a nurse** als Krankenschwester muß man allerhand verkraften können.

(b) *(healthy)* kräftig; *constitution also* robust; *teeth also, eyes, eyesight, heart, nerves* gut. **when you're ~ again** wenn Sie wieder bei Kräften sind.

(c) *(powerful, effective)* stark; *character, views* fest; *country* mächtig; *candidate, case* aussichtsreich; *argument, evidence* überzeugend; *protest* energisch; *measure* drastisch; *letter* geharnischt. **to have ~ feelings/views about sth** in bezug auf etw *(acc)* stark engagiert sein; **to have ~ feelings for sth** eine starke Bindung an etw *(acc)* haben; **to protest in ~ terms** energisch protestieren; **a group 20 ~** eine 20 Mann starke Gruppe; **he is ~ in/on sth** etw ist seine Stärke.

(d) *curry etc* deftig; *(pungent) smell, taste* streng; *colour, light* kräftig; *acid* stark; *solution* konzentriert. **a ~ drink/whisky** ein harter Drink/ein starker Whisky.

2 *adv* (+er) *(col)* **to be going ~** *(old person, thing)* gut in Schuß sein *(col)*; *(runner)* eine gute Kondition zeigen; *(party, rehearsals)* in Schwung sein *(col)*.

strong: ~-arm *adj (col) tactics etc* brutal, Gewalt-; **~-box** *n* (Geld)kassette *f*; **~-hold** *n (castle, fortress)* Festung *f*; *(town etc)* Stützpunkt *m*; *(fig)* Hochburg *f*.

strongly ['strɒŋlɪ] *adv* **(a)** *(physically)* stark; *kick, grip* kräftig; *fight* energisch; *built* stabil; *built (person)* kräftig. **(b)** *influence, suspect, tempt* stark; *interest also* brennend; *believe* fest. **to feel very ~ about sth** in bezug auf etw *(acc)* stark engagiert sein; **I didn't know that you felt so ~ about it** ich habe nicht gewußt, daß Ihnen das so viel bedeutet; *(against it)* ich habe nicht gewußt, daß Sie so dagegen sind. **(c)** *(powerfully)* stark; *protest* heftig, energisch; *plead* inständig; *support* kräftig; *answer, worded* in starken Worten. **I ~ advise you ...** ich möchte Ihnen dringend(st) raten ...

strong: ~ point *n* Stärke *f*; **~room** *n* Stahlkammer *f*; **~-willed** ['strɒŋ'wɪld] *adj* willensstark; *(pej)* eigensinnig.

strontium ['strɒntɪəm] *n* Strontium *nt*.

strove [strəʊv] *pret of* **strive.**

struck [strʌk] **1** *pret, ptp of* **strike. 2** *adj* **(a)** *pred* **to be ~ with sb/sth** *(impressed)* von jdm/etw begeistert or angetan sein; **I wasn't very ~ with him** er hat keinen großen Eindruck auf mich gemacht; **to be ~ on sb/sth** *(keen)* auf jdn/etw stehen *(col)*, auf jdn/etw versessen sein. **(b)** *(US attr) (striking) workers* streikend; *factory, employers* vom Streik betroffen.

structural ['strʌktʃərəl] *adj* strukturell; *(of building) alterations, damage* baulich; *defect* Konstruktions-. **(b)** *(weight-bearing) wall, beam* tragend.

structure ['strʌktʃə'] **1** *n* **(a)** Struktur *f*; *(Liter)* Aufbau *m*; *(Tech: of bridge, car etc)* Konstruktion *f*. **(b)** *(thing constructed)* Konstruktion *f*. **2** *vt* strukturieren; *essay, argument* gliedern; *layout, life* gestalten.

struggle ['strʌgl] **1** *n (lit, fig)* Kampf *m (for* um); *(fig: effort)* Anstrengung *f.* **without a ~** *surrender* kampflos; **to put up a ~** sich wehren; **the ~ for survival** der Überlebenskampf; **it was a ~** es war mühsam; **I had a ~ to persuade him** es war nicht einfach, ihn zu überreden.

2 *vi* **(a)** *(contend)* kämpfen; *(in self-defence)* sich wehren; *(financially)* in Schwierigkeiten sein; *(fig: strive)* sich sehr anstrengen. **to ~ to do sth** sich sehr anstrengen, etw zu tun; **to ~ for sth** um etw kämpfen; **to ~ with sth** with problem sich mit etw herumschlagen; *with language, homework* sich mit etw abmühen; *with doubts, conscience* mit etw ringen. **(b)** *(move with difficulty)* sich quälen. **to ~ to one's feet** mühsam aufstehen; **to ~ on** *(lit)* sich weiterkämpfen; *(fig)* weiterkämpfen.

strum [strʌm] *vt tune* klimpern; *guitar* klimpern auf (+*dat*).

strung [strʌŋ] *pret, ptp of* **string**.

strut[1] [strʌt] *vi* stolzieren. **to ~ about (the yard)** (auf dem Hof) herumstolzieren; **to ~ past** vorbeistolzieren.

strut[2] *n (horizontal)* Strebe *f; (vertical)* Pfeiler *m.*

strychnine ['strɪkniːn] *n* Strychnin *nt.*

stub [stʌb] **1** *n (of candle, pencil, tail, cigarette)* Stummel *m; (of cheque, ticket)* Abschnitt *m; (of tree)* Stumpf *m.* **2** *vt* **to ~ one's toe (on *or* against sth)** sich *(dat)* den Zeh (an etw *dat*) stoßen; **to ~ out a cigarette** eine Zigarette ausdrücken.

stubble ['stʌbl] *n no pl* Stoppeln *pl.*

stubborn ['stʌbən] *adj person, insistence* stur; *animal also, child* störrisch; *refusal, weeds, cough* hartnäckig; *lock* widerspenstig. **to be ~ about sth** stur auf etw *(dat)* beharren.

stubbornness ['stʌbənnɪs] *n see adj* Sturheit *f*; störrische Art; Hartnäckigkeit *f*; Widerspenstigkeit *f.*

stubby ['stʌbɪ] *adj (+er) revolver etc* kurz; *tail* stummelig; *pencil, vase* kurz und dick; *person* gedrungen, untersetzt; *legs* kurz und stämmig.

stucco ['stʌkəʊ] *n, pl* **-(e)s** Stuck *m.*

stuck [stʌk] **1** *pret, ptp of* **stick**[2]. **2** *adj* **(a)** *(baffled)* **to be ~** nicht klarkommen. **(b)** *(col)* **he/she is ~ for sth** es fehlt ihm/ihr an etw *(dat)*; **I'm a bit ~ for cash** ich bin ein bißchen knapp bei Kasse. **(c)** *(col)* **to get ~ into sth** sich in etw *(acc)* richtig reinknien *(col)*; **to be ~ with sb/sth** jdn/etw am Hals haben *(col).*

stuck-up ['stʌk'ʌp] *adj (col) person* hochnäsig.

stud[1] [stʌd] **1** *n (nail)* Beschlagnagel *m; (decorative)* Ziernagel *m.* **2** *vt* **~ded with ...** mit ... übersät; *with jewels* mit ... besetzt.

stud[2] *n (group of horses) (for breeding)* Gestüt *nt*, Zucht *f; (for racing etc)* Stall *m; (stallion)* (Zucht)hengst *m.*

student ['stjuːdənt] **1** *n (Univ)* Student(in *f*) *m; (esp US: at school, night school)* Schüler(in *f*) *m.* **he is a ~ of French *or* a French ~** *(Univ)* er studiert Französisch; **medical/law ~s** Medizin-/Jurastudenten *pl.* **2** *adj attr* Studenten-; *activities also, movement* studentisch. **~ driver** *(US)* Fahrschüler(in *f*) *m.*

student: **~ teacher** *n* Referendar(in *f*) *m; ~* **union** *n* **(a)** *(organization)* Studentenvereinigung *f;* **(b)** *(building)* Gebäude *nt* der Studentenvereinigung.

studied ['stʌdɪd] **1** *pret, ptp of* **study**. **2** *adj reply* wohlüberlegt; *prose* kunstvoll.

studio ['stjuːdɪəʊ] *n* Studio *nt; (of painter also)* Atelier *nt; (broadcasting ~ also)* Senderaum *m.*

studio: **~ audience** *n* Publikum *nt* im Studio; **~ flat** Appartementwohnung *f.*

studious ['stjuːdɪəs] *adj person* fleißig, eifrig; *attention, piece of work* gewissenhaft, sorgfältig.

study ['stʌdɪ] **1** *n* **(a)** *(studying) (esp Univ)* Studium *nt; (at school)* Lernen *nt; (of situation, evidence, case)* Untersuchung *f; (of nature)* Beobachtung *f.* **the ~ of cancer** die Krebsforschung; African **studies** *(Univ)* afrikanische Sprache und Kultur, Afrikanistik *f;* **to make a ~ of sth** etw untersuchen; *(academic)* etw studieren; **during my studies** während meines Studiums. **(b)** *(piece of work)* Studie *f (of* über +*acc); (Art, Phot)* Studie *f (of gen); (Mus)* Etüde *f.* **2** *(room)* Arbeitszimmer *nt.* **2** *vt* studieren; *(Sch)* lernen; *nature also, stars* beobachten; *author, text etc* sich befassen mit; *(research into)* erforschen; *(examine also)* untersuchen; *evidence* prüfen. **3** *vi* studieren; *(esp Sch)* lernen. **to ~ to be a teacher/doctor** ein Lehrer-/Medizinstudium machen; **to ~ under sb** bei jdm studieren.

stuff [stʌf] **1** *n* **(a)** Zeug *nt.* **the ~ that heroes are made of** der Stoff, aus dem Helden gemacht sind; **it's poor/good ~** das ist schlecht/gut; **books**

and ~ Bücher und so *(col);* **and ~ like that** und so was *(col);* **all that ~ about how he wants to help us** all das Gerede, daß er uns helfen will; **~ and nonsense** Quatsch *(col).* **(b)** *(col)* **that's the ~** so ist's richtig!, weiter so!; **to do one's ~** seine Nummer abziehen *(col);* **he did his ~** well er hat seine Sache gut gemacht; **to know one's ~** sich auskennen.

2 *vt* **(a)** *(fill)* vollstopfen; *hole* zustopfen; *object* (hinein)stopfen *(into* in +*acc); (into envelope)* stecken *(into* in +*acc).* **to ~ sth away** etw wegstecken; **he ~ed it away in his pocket** er stopfte es in seine Tasche; **to be ~ed up (with a cold)** verschnupft sein, eine verstopfte Nase haben. **(b)** *(Cook)* füllen. **(c)** *cushion etc* füllen; *toy also* (aus)stopfen; *(in taxidermy)* ausstopfen. **a ~ed toy** ein Stofftier *nt.* **(d)** *(col!)* **~ it** *(be quiet)* halt's Maul! *(col);* **get ~ed!** du kannst mich mal *(col!).* **3** *vr* **to ~ oneself (with cakes)** sich (mit Kuchen) vollstopfen *(col).*

stuffing ['stʌfɪŋ] *n (of pillow, Cook)* Füllung *f; (of furniture)* Polstermaterial *nt; (in taxidermy, toys)* Füllmaterial *nt.*

stuffy ['stʌfɪ] *adj (+er)* **(a)** *room, atmosphere* stickig, dumpf. **(b)** *(narrow-minded)* spießig; *(prudish)* prüde; *(stiff)* steif; *(dull)* langweilig, öde.

stultify ['stʌltɪfaɪ] *vt mind, person* verkümmern lassen. **to become stultified** verkümmern.

stumble ['stʌmbl] *vi (lit, fig)* stolpern; *(in speech)* stocken. **to ~ against sth** gegen etw stoßen; **to ~ on *or* across sth** *(fig)* auf etw *(acc)* stoßen.

stumbling-block ['stʌmblɪŋ'blɒk] *n (fig)* Hindernis *nt.* **to be a ~ to sth** einer Sache *(dat)* im Weg stehen.

stump [stʌmp] **1** *n* **(a)** *(of tree, limb, tooth, candle)* Stumpf *m; (of pencil, tail)* Stummel *m; (Cricket)* Stab *m.* **(b)** *(US Pol: platform)* Rednertribüne *f.* **~ speaker** Wahlredner(in *f*) *m.* **2** *vt (fig col)* **you've got me ~ed** da bin ich überfragt; **I'm ~ed** ich bin mit meinem Latein am Ende *(col);* **to be ~ed for an answer** um eine Antwort verlegen sein. **3** *vi (col)* stapfen. **to ~ along/about** entlang-/herumstapfen.

stun [stʌn] *vt (make unconscious)* betäuben; *(daze)* benommen machen; *(fig) (shock)* fassungslos machen; *(amaze)* verblüffen. **he was ~ned by the news** *(bad news)* er war über die Nachricht wie gelähmt; *(good news)* die Nachricht hat ihn überwältigt.

stung [stʌŋ] *pret, ptp of* **sting**.

stunk [stʌŋk] *ptp of* **stink**.

stunning ['stʌnɪŋ] *adj dress, girl etc* toll *(col),* atemberaubend.

stunt[1] [stʌnt] *n (in film)* Action-Szene *f; (publicity ~, trick)* Gag *m; (Aviat)* Kunststück *nt.*

stunt[2] *vt (lit, fig) growth, development* hemmen; *trees, mind etc* verkümmern lassen.

stunted ['stʌntɪd] *adj plant, mind* verkümmert; *child* unterentwickelt.

stuntman ['stʌntmæn] *n, pl* **-men** [-,men] *n* Stuntman *m.*

stupefy ['stjuːpɪfaɪ] *vt* benommen machen; *(fig: amaze, surprise)* verblüffen.

stupefying ['stjuːpɪfaɪɪŋ] *adj (amazing)* verblüffend.

stupendous [stjuː'pendəs] *adj* phantastisch; *effort* enorm.

stupid ['stjuːpɪd] *adj* dumm. **don't be ~** sei nicht so blöd *(col);* **I've done a ~ thing** ich habe etwas ganz Dummes gemacht; **you ~ idiot!** du blöder Idiot!; **that was a ~ thing to do** das war dumm (von dir); **to drink oneself ~** sich sinnlos betrinken.

stupidity [stjuː'pɪdɪtɪ] *n* Dummheit *f.*

stupor ['stjuːpə[r]] *n* Benommenheit *f.* **to be in a drunken ~** im Vollrausch sein.

sturdy ['stɜːdɪ] *adj (+er)* **(a)** *person, plant* kräftig;

material robust; *building, car* stabil. **(b)** *(fig)* opposition standhaft.

sturgeon ['stɜːdʒən] *n* Stör *m*.

stutter ['stʌtəʳ] **1** *n (of person, engine)* Stottern *nt no pl.* he has a bad ~ er stottert sehr. **2** *vti* stottern.

sty [staɪ] *n (lit, fig)* Schweinestall *m*.

sty(e) [staɪ] *n (Med)* Gerstenkorn *nt*.

style [staɪl] *n* **(a)** Stil *m*. ~ **of painting** Malstil *m*; **the** ~ **of his writing** sein Stil *m*; ~ **of life** Lebensstil *m*; **a poem in the Romantic** ~ ein Gedicht im Stil der Romantik; **he won in fine** ~ er gewann überlegen; **that house is not my** ~ so ein Haus ist nicht mein Stil; **hillwalking/flattering people is not his** ~ Bergwanderungen liegen ihm nicht/es ist nicht seine Art zu schmeicheln; **the man has** ~ der Mann hat Format; **in** ~ stilvoll; **to do things in** ~ alles im großen Stil tun; **to celebrate in** ~ groß feiern. **(b)** *(Fashion)* Stil *m no pl,* Mode *f; (cut)* Schnitt *m; (hair~)* Frisur *f.* **all the latest** ~s die neueste Mode.

styli ['staɪlaɪ] *pl of* **stylus.**

stylish ['staɪlɪʃ] *adj person* elegant; *car, hotel, district also* vornehm; *furnishings* stilvoll; *(fashionable)* modisch; *way of life* großartig.

stylist ['staɪlɪst] *n (Fashion)* Modeschöpfer(in *f*) *m; (hair~)* Friseur *m,* Friseuse *f.*

stylistic [staɪ'lɪstɪk] *adj* stilistisch. ~ **device** Stilmittel *nt.*

stylus ['staɪləs] *n, pl* **styli** *(on record-player)* Nadel *f.*

styptic ['stɪptɪk] *adj* ~ **pencil** Blutstillstift *m.*

suave ['swɑːv] *adj* weltmännisch, aalglatt *(pej).*

sub [sʌb] *n* = **(a)** submarine. **(b)** subscription. **(c)** substitute.

sub- *pref* Unter-, unter-; *(esp with foreign words)* Sub-, sub-.

subaltern ['sʌbltən] *n (Brit Mil)* Subalternoffizier *m.*

sub: ~**committee** *n* Unterausschuß *m;* ~**conscious 1** *adj* unterbewußt; **2** *n* **the** ~**conscious** das Unterbewußtsein; ~**consciously** *adv* im Unterbewußtsein; ~**continent** *n* Subkontinent *m;* ~**contract 1** ['sʌbkɒntrækt] *vt* (vertraglich) weitervergeben *(to an +acc);* **2** [sʌb'kɒntrækt] *n* Nebenvertrag *m;* ~**contractor** *n* Subkontrahent *m;* ~**divide** *vt* unterteilen; ~**division** *n (act)* Unterteilung *f; (~group)* Unterabteilung *f.*

subdue [səb'djuː] *vt rebels, country* unterwerfen; *rioters* überwältigen; *(fig) anger, desire* unterdrücken; *noise, light, high spirits* dämpfen; *animals, children* bändigen.

subdued [səb'djuːd] *adj colour, lighting, voice* gedämpft; *manner, person* ruhig; *mood, atmosphere* gedrückt; *(submissive) voice, manner, person* fügsam, gehorsam; *(repressed) feelings, excitement* unterdrückt.

sub: ~**-editor** *n (esp Brit)* Redakteur(in *f*) *m;* ~**group** *n* Unterabteilung *f;* ~**heading** *n* Untertitel *m;* ~**human** *adj* unmenschlich.

subject ['sʌbdʒɪkt] **1** *n* **(a)** *(Pol)* Staatsbürger(in *f*) *m; (of king etc)* Untertan *m,* Untertanin *f.* **(b)** *(Gram)* Subjekt *nt,* Satzgegenstand *m.* **(c)** *(topic, Mus)* Thema *nt.* **to change the** ~ das Thema wechseln; **on the** ~ **of** ... zum Thema *(+gen)* ...; **while we're on the** ~ da wir gerade beim Thema sind. **(d)** *(discipline) (Sch, Univ)* Fach *nt; (specialist* ~*)* (Spezial)gebiet *nt.* **(e)** *(object)* Gegenstand *m (of gen); (in experiment) (person)* Versuchsperson *f; (animal)* Versuchstier *nt.* **he is the** ~ **of much criticism** er wird stark kritisiert.

2 *adj* **(a)** *(conquered)* unterworfen. **(b) to be** ~ **to** *law, change, sb's will* einer Sache *(dat)* unterworfen sein; *to illness* für etw anfällig sein; *to consent, approval* von etw abhängig sein; **northbound trains are** ~ **to delays** bei Zügen in Richtung Norden muß mit Verspätung gerechnet werden; **prices are** ~ **to change** or

alteration without notice Preisänderungen sind vorbehalten; ~ **to confirmation in writing** vorausgesetzt, es wird schriftlich bestätigt. **3** [səb'dʒekt] *vt* **(a)** *(subjugate)* unterwerfen; *terrorists, guerillas* zerschlagen. **(b) to** ~ **sb to sth** *to questioning, analysis* jdn einer Sache *(dat)* unterziehen; *to torture, criticism* jdn einer Sache *(dat)* aussetzen; **to** ~ **sb/a book to criticism** jdn/ein Buch kritisieren.

subjection [səb'dʒekʃən] *n* **(a)** *(state)* Abhängigkeit *f.* **to hold a people in** ~ ein Volk unterdrücken. **(b)** *(act)* Unterwerfung *f; (of terrorists etc)* Zerschlagung *f.*

subjective [səb'dʒektɪv] *adj* subjektiv.

subject-matter ['sʌbdʒɪkt'mætəʳ] *n (theme)* Stoff *m; (content)* Inhalt *m.*

sub judice [,sʌb'dʒuːdɪsɪ] *adj* **to be** ~ verhandelt werden.

subjugate ['sʌbdʒʊgeɪt] *vt* unterwerfen, unterjochen.

subjunctive [səb'dʒʌŋktɪv] **1** *adj* konjunktivisch. **the** ~ **mood** der Konjunktiv. **2** *n (mood, verb)* Konjunktiv *m.*

sub: ~**let** *pret, ptp* ~**let** *vti* untervermieten *(to an +acc);* ~**lieutenant** *n (Brit Naut)* Leutnant *m* zur See.

sublimate ['sʌblɪmeɪt] *vt* sublimieren.

sublime [sə'blaɪm] *adj beauty, scenery, thoughts* erhaben; *achievement, genius also* überragend; *indifference, contempt* vollkommen.

subliminal [,sʌb'lɪmɪnl] *adj (Psych)* unterschwellig.

submachine gun [,sʌbmə'ʃiːn'gʌn] *n* Maschinenpistole *f.*

submarine ['sʌbməˌriːn] *n* Unterseeboot, U-Boot *nt.*

submerge [səb'mɜːdʒ] **1** *vt* untertauchen; *(flood)* überschwemmen. **the house was completely** ~**d** das Haus stand völlig unter Wasser. **2** *vi (diver, submarine)* tauchen.

submersion [səb'mɜːʃən] *n* Untertauchen *nt; (of submarine)* Tauchen *nt; (by flood)* Überschwemmung *f.*

submission [səb'mɪʃən] *n* **(a)** *(yielding)* Unterwerfung *f (to unter +acc); (submissiveness)* Gehorsam *m; (Sport)* Aufgabe *f.* **(b)** *(presentation)* Eingabe *f; (documents)* Vorlage *f.*

submissive [səb'mɪsɪv] *adj* demütig, unterwürfig *(pej) (to gegenüber).*

submit [səb'mɪt] **1** *vt* **(a)** *(put forward)* vorlegen *(to dat); application etc* einreichen *(to bei).* **to** ~ **that** ... *(esp Jur)* behaupten, daß ... **(b) to** ~ **sth to scrutiny** etc etw einer Prüfung etc unterziehen; **to be** ~**ted to sth** *to sth* unpleasant einer Sache *(dat)* ausgesetzt werden. **2** *vi (yield)* nachgeben; *(Mil)* sich ergeben *(to dat); (Sport)* aufgeben. **to** ~ **to sth** *to sb's orders, judgement* sich einer Sache *(dat)* beugen; *to indignity* etw erdulden; *to demands, threats* einer Sache *(dat)* nachgeben; **to** ~ **to blackmail** sich erpressen lassen.

subnormal [,sʌb'nɔːməl] *adj intelligence, temperature* unterdurchschnittlich; *person* minderbegabt. **mentally** ~ minderbemittelt.

subordinate [sə'bɔːdnɪt] **1** *adj officer* rangniedriger; *position, importance* untergeordnet. ~ **clause** *(Gram)* Nebensatz *m;* **to be** ~ **to sb/sth** jdm/einer Sache untergeordnet sein. **2** *n* Untergebene(r) *mf.* **3** [sə'bɔːdɪneɪt] *vt* unterordnen *(to dat).*

subpoena [səb'piːnə] *(Jur)* **1** *n* Vorladung *f.* **to serve a** ~ **on sb** jdn vorladen. **2** *vt* vorladen.

subscribe [səb'skraɪb] **1** *vt money* spenden *(to für).* **2** *vi* **to** ~ **to an appeal** sich an einer Spendenaktion beteiligen; **to** ~ **to a magazine** etc eine Zeitschrift etc abonnieren; **to** ~ **to sth** *to proposal* etw gutheißen, etw billigen; *to opinion, theory* etw vertreten.

subscriber [səb'skraɪbəʳ] *n (to paper)* Abonnent(in f) m; (to fund) Spender(in f) m; (Telec) Teilnehmer(in f) m; (of shares) Zeichner m. ~ **trunk dialling** (Brit) der Selbstwählferndienst.

subscription [səb'skrɪpʃən] n (money subscribed) Beitrag m; (to newspaper, concert etc) Abonnement nt (to gen). **to take out a ~ to sth** etw abonnieren; **to pay one's ~ (to a club)** seinen (Vereins)beitrag bezahlen.

subsection ['sʌb,sekʃən] n Unterabteilung f; (Jur) Paragraph m.

subsequent ['sʌbsɪkwənt] adj (nach)folgend. ~ **to** (form) im Anschluß an (+acc).

subsequently ['sʌbsɪkwəntlɪ] adv (afterwards) später; (from that time also) von da an.

subservient [səb'sɜːvɪənt] adj (pej) unterwürfig (to gegenüber).

subside [səb'saɪd] vi (flood) sinken; (land, building) sich senken, absacken (col); (storm, wind, anger etc) nachlassen, sich legen.

subsidence [səb'saɪdəns] n Senkung f.

subsidiary [səb'sɪdɪərɪ] **1** adj role, interest, subject Neben-; company Tochter-. **2** n Tochtergesellschaft f.

subsidize ['sʌbsɪdaɪz] vt company etc subventionieren; (col) person unterstützen.

subsidy ['sʌbsɪdɪ] n Subvention f. **there is a ~ on butter** Butter wird subventioniert; **housing subsidies** Wohnungsbaubeihilfen pl.

subsist [səb'sɪst] vi sich ernähren, leben (on von).

subsistence [səb'sɪstəns] n (living) Leben nt (on von); (means of ~) (Lebens)unterhalt m.

subsistence: ~ allowance n Unterhaltszuschuß m; **~ farming** n Ackerbau m für den Eigenbedarf; **~ level** n Existenzminimum nt; **at ~ level** auf dem Existenzminimum; **~ wage** n Minimallohn m.

substance ['sʌbstəns] n Substanz f. **in ~** im wesentlichen; **the argument lacks ~** das Argument hat keine Substanz; **there is some ~ in his claim** seine Behauptung ist nicht unfundiert; **a man of ~** ein vermögender Mann.

substandard [,sʌb'stændəd] adj work, goods, quality minderwertig; housing unzulänglich.

substantial [səb'stænʃəl] adj (a) meal, person, cloth kräftig; furniture, building, firm solide; book umfangreich. (b) (considerable) loss, part, improvement, amount beträchtlich; sum also namhaft; (rich) landowner vermögend. (c) (weighty) bedeutend; proof, argument überzeugend; difference wesentlich.

substantially [səb'stænʃəlɪ] adv (a) (solidly) solide; (considerably) erheblich, beträchtlich. ~ **built** house solide gebaut; person kräftig gebaut. (b) (essentially, basically) im wesentlichen.

substantiate [səb'stænʃɪeɪt] vt erhärten.

substantive ['sʌbstəntɪv] adj evidence, argument, reason überzeugend, stichhaltig.

substitute ['sʌbstɪtjuːt] **1** n Ersatz m no pl; (representative also) Vertretung f; (Sport) Ersatzspieler(in f) m. **2** adj attr Ersatz-. **3** vt to ~ **A for B** B durch A ersetzen; (Sport also) B gegen A auswechseln. **4** vi **to ~ for sb/sth** für jdn einspringen/etw ersetzen.

substitution [,sʌbstɪ'tjuːʃən] n Ersetzen nt (of X for Y von Y durch X); (Sport) Austausch m (of X for Y von Y gegen X). **to make a ~** (Sport) auswechseln.

subtenant [,sʌb'tenənt] n (of flat etc) Untermieter(in f) m; (of land) Unterpächter(in f) m.

subterfuge ['sʌbtəfjuːdʒ] n (trickery) Täuschung f; (trick) Trick m.

subterranean [,sʌbtə'reɪnɪən] adj unterirdisch.

subtitle ['sʌb,taɪtl] **1** n Untertitel m. **2** vt film mit Untertiteln versehen; book etc einen Untertitel geben (+dat).

subtle ['sʌtl] adj fein; hint zart; charm unaufdringlich; (not obvious) remark, point scharfsinnig; design, proof raffiniert.

subtlety ['sʌtltɪ] n see adj Feinheit f; Zartheit f; Unaufdringlichkeit f; Scharfsinn(igkeit f) m; Raffiniertheit f.

subtly ['sʌtlɪ] adv fein; flavoured also delikat; argue, analyse scharfsinnig; achieve one's ends auf raffinierte Weise. ~ **different** auf subtile Weise verschieden.

subtotal ['sʌb,təʊtl] n Zwischen- or Teilsumme f.

subtract [səb'trækt] vti abziehen, subtrahieren (from von).

subtraction [səb'trækʃən] n Subtraktion f.

suburb ['sʌbɜːb] n Vorort m.

suburban [sə'bɜːbən] adj Vorort-; (pej) kleinbürgerlich. ~ **line** (Rail) Vorortbahn f.

suburbia [sə'bɜːbɪə] n (usu pej) die Vororte pl. **to live in ~** am Stadtrand wohnen.

subversion [sʌb'vɜːʃən] n no pl Subversion f; (of rights, freedom etc) Untergrabung f.

subversive [səb'vɜːsɪv] **1** adj subversiv. ~ **elements** subversive Kräfte pl. **2** n Umstürzler(in f) m.

subway ['sʌbweɪ] n Unterführung f; (US Rail) U-Bahn f.

subzero ['sʌb'zɪərəʊ] adj temperatures unter Null.

succeed [sək'siːd] **1** vi (a) (person) erfolgreich sein, Erfolg haben; (plan etc also) gelingen. **to ~ in business/in a plan** geschäftlich/mit einem Plan erfolgreich sein; **I ~ed in doing it** es gelang mir, es zu tun; **you'll only ~ in making things worse** damit erreichst du nur, daß alles noch schlimmer wird. (b) (come next) **to ~ to an office** in einem Amt nachfolgen; **he ~ed to his father's position** er trat die Nachfolge seines Vaters an (gen). **2** vt (come after, take the place of) folgen (+dat); (person also) Nachfolger(in f) m werden (+gen). **to ~ sb** in a post/in office jds Stelle (acc) übernehmen/jdm im Amt nachfolgen.

succeeding [sək'siːdɪŋ] adj folgend. ~ **generations** nachfolgende Generationen pl.

success [sək'ses] n Erfolg m. **without ~** ohne Erfolg, erfolglos; **to make a ~ of sth** mit or bei etw erfolgreich sein; **to meet with ~** Erfolg haben, erfolgreich sein.

successful [sək'sesfʊl] adj erfolgreich. **to be ~** erfolgreich sein, Erfolg haben (in mit, bei); **I was ~ in doing it** es gelang mir, es zu tun.

successfully [sək'sesfəlɪ] adv erfolgreich, mit Erfolg.

succession [sək'seʃən] n (a) Folge, Serie f; (with no intervening period) (Aufeinander)folge f. **in ~** hintereinander; **in quick ~** schnell hintereinander. (b) (to post) Nachfolge f. **fourth in ~ to the throne** an vierter Stelle in der Thronfolge.

successive [sək'sesɪv] adj **4 ~ days** 4 Tage hintereinander, 4 aufeinanderfolgende Tage; ~ **generations have ...** eine Generation nach der anderen hat ...

successively [sək'sesɪvlɪ] adv nacheinander.

successor [sək'sesə[r]] n Nachfolger(in f) m (to gen); (to throne) Thronfolger(in f) m.

succinct [sək'sɪŋkt] adj knapp.

succinctly [sək'sɪŋktlɪ] adv kurz und bündig; write in gedrängtem Stil. **as he very ~ put it** wie er so treffend bemerkte.

succulent ['sʌkjʊlənt] **1** adj peach, steak saftig. **2** n (Bot) Sukkulente f (spec).

succumb [sə'kʌm] vi erliegen (to dat); (to threats) sich beugen (to dat).

such [sʌtʃ] **1** adj (a) (of that kind) solche(r, s). ~ **a person** so ein Mensch, ein solcher Mensch; ~ **people/books** solche Leute/Bücher; **many/all ~ people** viele/all solche Leute; **do you have ~ a book?** haben Sie so ein Buch?; ~ **a thing** (as) so etwas (wie); **I said no** ~ **thing** das habe ich nie gesagt; **no** ~ **thing** nichts dergleichen; **you'll do no** ~ **thing** du wirst dich hüten; **there's no** ~ **thing as a unicorn** so etwas wie ein Einhorn gibt es nicht; ~ **or some** ~ **idea** ... oder so etwas, ...

oder so ähnlich; ... or some ~ name/place ... oder so (ähnlich); in ~ a case in einem solchen Fall; books ~ as these, ~ books as these Bücher wie diese, solche Bücher. **(b)** (so much, so great etc) solche(r, s). he's ~ a liar er ist ein derartiger or solcher Lügner; he's not ~ a fool as you think er ist nicht so dumm, wie Sie denken; he did it in ~ a way that ... er machte es so, daß ...; ~ wealth/beauty! was für ein Reichtum/welche Schönheit!; he's always in ~ a hurry er hat es immer so eilig.

(c) pred his surprise was ~ that ... er war so überrascht, daß ...; his manner was ~ that ... er benahm sich so, daß ...

2 adv so, solch (geh). ~ a big house so ein großes Haus; nobody else makes ~ a good cup of tea as you niemand kocht so guten Tee wie du; it's ~ a long time ago es ist so lange her.

3 pron rabbits and hares and ~ Kaninchen, Hasen und dergleichen; ~ being the case ... in diesem Fall ...; ~ was not my intention dies war nicht meine Absicht; ~ is not the case dies ist nicht der Fall; ~ is life! so ist das Leben!; as ~ an sich; ~ as? zum Beispiel?; ~ as it is so, wie es nun mal ist.

such-and-such ['sʌtʃən'sʌtʃ] (col) 1 adj ~ a time/town die und die Zeit/Stadt. 2 n Mr ~ Herr Soundso.

suchlike ['sʌtʃ,laɪk] (col) 1 adj solche. 2 pron dergleichen.

suck [sʌk] 1 vt saugen; sweet, pastille lutschen; lollipop, thumb lutschen an (+dat). to ~ sb dry (fig) jdn bis aufs Blut aussaugen. 2 vi (at an +dat) saugen; (at lollipop, thumb) lutschen; (at pipe, through straw) ziehen.

♦ **suck down** vt sep (current etc) hinunterziehen.

♦ **suck in** vt sep liquid, dust aufsaugen; air (ventilator) ansaugen; (person) in tiefen Zügen einatmen; cheeks einziehen.

♦ **suck up** 1 vt sep liquid, dust aufsaugen. 2 vi (col) to ~ ~ to sb vor jdm kriechen (col).

sucker ['sʌkər] n (a) (col:fool) Trottel m (col). to be a ~ for sth (immer) auf etw (acc) hereinfallen; (be partial to) eine Schwäche für etw haben. (b) (US col: lollipop) Lutscher m.

suckle ['sʌkl] vt child stillen; animal säugen.

suction ['sʌkʃən] n Saugwirkung f. ~-pump Saugpumpe f.

Sudan [suˈdɑːn] n (the) ~ der Sudan.

sudden ['sʌdn] 1 adj plötzlich; movement also jäh, abrupt; (unexpected) bend, change of direction unerwartet. ~ death play-off Entscheidungskampf m; (Ftbl) Elfmeterschießen nt. 2 n all of a ~ (ganz) plötzlich.

suddenly ['sʌdnlɪ] adv plötzlich; move also abrupt.

suddenness ['sʌdnnɪs] n Plötzlichkeit f.

suds [sʌdz] npl Seifenlauge f; (lather) (Seifen)schaum m.

sue [suː] 1 vt (Jur) to ~ sb for sth jdn wegen etw verklagen; to ~ sb for divorce gegen jdn die Scheidung einreichen; to ~ sb for damages jdn auf Schadenersatz verklagen. 2 vi (Jur) klagen, Klage erheben. to ~ for divorce die Scheidung einreichen.

suede [sweɪd] 1 n Wildleder nt. 2 adj Wildleder-.

suet ['suːɪt] n Nierenfett nt.

Suez ['suːɪz] n Suez nt. ~ Canal Suezkanal m.

suffer ['sʌfər] 1 vt (a) pain, setback erleiden; hardship also, hunger leiden; headache, effects etc leiden unter (+dat); shock haben. the pound ~ed further losses das Pfund mußte weitere Einbußen hinnehmen. (b) (tolerate) dulden, ertragen. he doesn't ~ fools gladly Dummheit ist ihm ein Greuel. 2 vi (physically, mentally, fig) leiden (from unter +dat, from illness an +dat); (as punishment, in hell etc) büßen. he was ~ing from shock er hatte einen Schock (erlitten); your health will ~ deine Gesundheit wird darunter leiden; you'll

~ for this! das wirst du büßen!

sufferance ['sʌfərəns] n he's only here on ~ er wird hier nur geduldet.

sufferer ['sʌfərər] n (Med) Leidende(r) mf (from an +dat). diabetes ~s, ~s from diabetes Diabeteskranke pl.

suffering ['sʌfərɪŋ] n Leiden nt; (hardship, deprivation) Leid nt no pl.

suffice [səˈfaɪs] (form) 1 vi (aus)reichen. 2 vt ~ it to say ... es reicht wohl, wenn ich sage, ...

sufficient [səˈfɪʃənt] adj genügend; reason, condition hinreichend. to be ~ genügen, ausreichen; thank you, that's ~ danke, das genügt.

sufficiently [səˈfɪʃəntlɪ] adv genug. ~ good/warm etc gut/warm etc genug pred; a ~ large number eine ausreichend große Anzahl.

suffix ['sʌfɪks] n (Ling) Suffix nt, Nachsilbe f; (in code etc) Zusatz m.

suffocate ['sʌfəkeɪt] vti (lit, fig) ersticken. he was ~d by the smoke er erstickte am Rauch.

suffocating ['sʌfəkeɪtɪŋ] adj (lit) erstickend attr; (fig also) erdrückend attr; heat drückend attr.

suffocation [,sʌfəˈkeɪʃən] n (lit, fig) Ersticken nt.

suffrage ['sʌfrɪdʒ] n Wahlrecht nt.

suffragette [,sʌfrəˈdʒet] n Suffragette f.

sugar ['ʃʊgər] 1 n (a) Zucker m. (b) (col: term of affection) Schätzchen nt (col). 2 vt zuckern, süßen. to ~ the pill die bittere Pille versüßen.

sugar in cpds Zucker-; ~ beet n Zuckerrübe f; ~ bowl n Zuckerdose f; ~ candy n (US: sweet) Bonbon nt or m; ~ cane n Zuckerrohr nt; ~-coated adj mit Zucker überzogen.

sugared ['ʃʊgəd] adj gezuckert; almonds Zucker-; words (honig)süß.

sugary ['ʃʊgərɪ] adj taste süß; (full of sugar) zuckrig; (fig) style etc süßlich.

suggest [səˈdʒest] 1 vt (a) (propose) vorschlagen; plan, idea also anregen; explanation, theory vorbringen. I ~ that we go, I ~ going ich schlage vor, (daß) wir gehen; what do you ~ we do? was schlagen Sie vor?; are you ~ing I should tell a deliberate lie? soll ich etwa, denken, daß ich bewußt lügen soll?; I am ~ing nothing of the kind das habe ich nicht gesagt. (b) (indicate, hint at) andeuten; (unpleasantly) unterstellen; (evoke) (music, poem) denken lassen an (+acc). what are you trying to ~? was wollen Sie damit sagen?; the symptoms would ~ an operation erscheinen. 2 vt to ~ itself (idea, thought) sich anbieten, naheliegen.

suggestion [səˈdʒestʃən] n (a) (proposal) Vorschlag m. my ~ is that ... mein Vorschlag lautet ..., ich schlage vor, daß ...; following your ~ auf Ihren Vorschlag or Ihre Anregung hin; I'm open to ~s Vorschläge sind willkommen. (b) (insinuation) Andeutung f; (unpleasant) Unterstellung f. I resent that ~ ich weise diese Unterstellung zurück; there is no ~ that he was involved es gibt keinen Anhaltspunkt dafür, daß er beteiligt war. (c) (hint: of irony etc) Anflug m. (d) (also indecent ~) unsittlicher Antrag.

suggestive [səˈdʒestɪv] adj (a) to be ~ of sth auf etw (acc) hindeuten; (create impression of) den Eindruck von etw vermitteln. (b) (indecent) joke, remark etc zweideutig.

suicidal [,sʊɪˈsaɪdl] adj selbstmörderisch. that would be ~ das wäre glatter Selbstmord.

suicide ['sʊɪsaɪd] n Selbstmord m; (person) Selbstmörder(in f) m. to commit ~ Selbstmord begehen.

suit [suːt] 1 n (a) Anzug m; (woman's) Kostüm nt. ~ of clothes Garnitur f. (b) (Jur) Verfahren nt. to bring a ~ (against sb for sth) (wegen etw gegen jdn) einen Prozeß anstrengen. (c) (Cards) Farbe f. to follow ~ (lit) Farbe bedienen; (fig) jds Beispiel (dat) folgen.

2 vt (a) (be convenient to) (arrangement, date,

price) passen (+dat); (climate, food) bekommen (+dat); (occupation) gefallen (+dat). **that ~s me fine!** (col) das ist mir recht; **that would ~ me nicely** (time, arrangement) das würde mir gut passen; (house, job etc) das wäre genau das richtige für mich; **when would it ~ you to come?** wann wäre es Ihnen recht? **(b)** (be suitable, right for) geeignet sein für. **he is very well ~ed to the job** er eignet sich sehr gut für die Stelle; **they are well ~ed (to each other)** sie passen gut zusammen. **(c)** (clothes, hairstyle) (gut) stehen (+dat). **(d)** (adapt) anpassen (to dat). **(e)** (please) gefallen (+dat). **you can't ~ everybody** man kann es nicht jedem recht machen; **~ yourself!** wie du willst!

suitability [ˌsuːtəˈbɪlɪtɪ] n Angemessenheit f; (of person for job) Eignung f.

suitable [ˈsuːtəbl] adj (convenient, practical) geeignet, passend; (socially, culturally appropriate) angemessen. **to be ~ for sb** (date, place) jdm passen; (film, job) für jdn geeignet sein; **the most ~ man for the job** der am besten geeignete Mann für den Posten; **would 8 o'clock be a ~ time?** wäre Ihnen etc 8 Uhr recht?; **Tuesday is the most ~ day** Dienstag ist der günstigste Tag; **she's not ~ for him** sie paßt nicht zu ihm.

suitably [ˈsuːtəblɪ] adv angemessen; behave also, apologize wie es sich gehört. **he was ~ impressed** er war gehörig beeindruckt.

suitcase [ˈsuːtˌkeɪs] n Koffer m. **to live out of a ~** aus dem Koffer leben.

suite [swiːt] n (of furniture) Garnitur f; (of rooms) Suite, Zimmerflucht f; (Mus) Suite f. **bedroom ~** Schlafzimmergarnitur f; **3-piece ~** dreiteilige Sitzgarnitur.

suitor [ˈsuːtəʳ] n (a) (old: of woman) Freier m (old). **(b)** (Jur) Kläger(in f) m.

sulk [sʌlk] 1 vi schmollen, beleidigt sein. 2 n Schmollen nt. **to have the ~s** schmollen.

sulky [ˈsʌlkɪ] adj (+er) schmollend.

sullen [ˈsʌlən] adj (a) (morose) mürrisch. **(b)** sky etc düster, finster.

sully [ˈsʌlɪ] vt reputation besudeln.

sulphate, (US) **sulfate** [ˈsʌlfeɪt] n Sulfat nt.

sulphide, (US) **sulfide** [ˈsʌlfaɪd] n Sulfid nt.

sulphur, (US) **sulfur** [ˈsʌlfəʳ] n Schwefel m.

sulphuric, (US) **sulfuric** [sʌlˈfjuːrɪk] adj Schwefel-. **~ acid** Schwefelsäure f.

sultan [ˈsʌltən] n Sultan m.

sultana [sʌlˈtɑːnə] n (fruit) Sultanine f.

sultry [ˈsʌltrɪ] adj weather schwül; woman temperamentvoll; beauty, look glutvoll.

sum [sʌm] n (a) (total) Summe f; (of money also) Betrag m. **that was the ~ (total) of his achievements** das war alles, was er geschafft hatte. **(b)** (esp Brit: calculation) Rechenaufgabe f. **to do ~s** **(in one's head)** (im Kopf) rechnen.

♦ **sum up** 1 vt sep (a) (summarize) zusammenfassen. **(b)** (evaluate rapidly) ab- or einschätzen. 2 vi (also Jur) zusammenfassen. **to ~ ~, we can say that ...** zusammenfassend können wir feststellen, daß ...

summarize [ˈsʌməraɪz] vt zusammenfassen.

summary [ˈsʌmərɪ] 1 n Zusammenfassung f. **he gave us a short ~ of the film** er gab uns eine kurze Inhaltsangabe des Films. 2 adj **(a)** (brief) account knapp, kurzgefaßt. **(b)** (fast) treatment kurz, knapp; perusal flüchtig; (Jur) trial, punishment summarisch; dismissal fristlos.

summer [ˈsʌməʳ] 1 n Sommer m. **in (the) ~** im Sommer; **two ~s ago** im Sommer vor zwei Jahren; **a ~'s day** ein Sommertag m. 2 adj attr Sommer-.

summer: **~ house** n Gartenhaus nt; **~ time** n Sommer(zeit f) m; (daylight-saving time) Sommerzeit f.

summery [ˈsʌmərɪ] adj sommerlich.

summing-up [ˈsʌmɪŋˈʌp] n (Jur) Resümee nt.

summit [ˈsʌmɪt] 1 n Gipfel m; (fig also) Höhepunkt m; (~ conference) Gipfel(konferenz f) m. 2 adj attr Gipfel-.

summon [ˈsʌmən] vt **(a)** servant, police etc (her-bei)rufen; help holen; meeting, Parliament einberufen. **(b)** (Jur) vorladen.

♦ **summon up** vt sep courage zusammennehmen; strength aufbieten; enthusiasm, energy aufbringen.

summons [ˈsʌmənz] 1 n (Jur) Vorladung f. **to take out a ~ against sb** jdn vorladen lassen. 2 vt (Jur) vorladen.

sump [sʌmp] n (Brit Aut) Ölwanne f.

sumptuous [ˈsʌmptjuəs] adj (splendid) luxuriös; (costly) kostspielig; food etc üppig, verschwenderisch.

sun [sʌn] 1 n Sonne f. **I've got the ~ in my eyes** die Sonne blendet mich; **he was up with the ~** er stand in aller Frühe auf; **there is no reason under the ~ why ...** es gibt keinen Grund auf Erden, warum ...; **he's tried everything under the ~** er hat alles Menschenmögliche versucht; **there's nothing new under the ~** (prov) es ist alles schon mal dagewesen; **a place in the ~** (fig) ein Platz an der Sonne. 2 vr **to ~ oneself** sich sonnen.

sun: **~ bathe** vi sonnenbaden; **~ bather** n Sonnenanbeter(in f) m (col); **~ bathing** n Sonnenbaden nt; **~ beam** n Sonnenstrahl m; **~ bed** n Sonnenliege f; **~ blind** n (awning) Markise f; (venetian blind) Jalousie f; **~ burn** n Bräune f; (painful) Sonnenbrand m; **~ burnt** adj sonnengebräunt; (painfully) von der Sonne verbrannt; **to get ~ burnt** braun werden; (einen) Sonnenbrand bekommen.

sundae [ˈsʌndeɪ] n Eisbecher m.

Sunday [ˈsʌndɪ] 1 n Sonntag m. **a month of ~s** (col) eine Ewigkeit; **never in a month of ~s** (col) nie im Leben; see **Tuesday.** 2 adj attr Sonntags-. **~ best** Sonntagskleider pl; **~ school** Sonntagsschule f.

sun: **~ deck** n Sonnendeck nt; **~ dial** n Sonnenuhr f; **~ down** n (esp US) Sonnenuntergang m.

sundry [ˈsʌndrɪ] 1 adj verschiedene. 2 pron all and ~ jedermann. 3 n sundries pl Verschiedenes (+sing vb).

sunflower [ˈsʌnˌflauəʳ] n Sonnenblume f.

sung [sʌŋ] ptp of **sing**.

sun: **~ glasses** npl Sonnenbrille f; **~ god** n Sonnengott m; **~ hat** n Sonnenhut m.

sunk [sʌŋk] ptp of **sink**[1].

sunken [ˈsʌŋkən] adj ship, treasure versunken; garden tiefliegend attr; bath eingelassen; cheeks hohl; eyes eingesunken.

sun: **~ lamp** n Höhensonne f; **~ less** adj garden ohne Sonne; room also dunkel; day also trübe; **~ light** n Sonnenlicht nt; **in the ~ light** in der Sonne; **~ lit** adj sonnig.

sunny [ˈsʌnɪ] adj (+er) place, day etc sonnig; (fig) smile, disposition also heiter. **~ intervals** (Met) Aufheiterungen pl; **to look on the ~ side (of things)** die Dinge von der angenehmen Seite sehen.

sun: **~ rise** 1 n Sonnenaufgang m; **at ~ rise** bei Sonnenaufgang; 2 adj attr (col) industries der Spitzentechnologie; **~ roof** n (of car) Schiebedach nt; (of hotel etc) Sonnenterrasse f; **~ set** n Sonnenuntergang m; **at ~ set** bei Sonnenuntergang; **~ shade** n Sonnenschirm m; (awning) Markise f; **~ shine** n Sonnenschein m; **hours of ~ shine** Sonnenstunden pl; **~ spot** n (a) Sonnenfleck m; **(b)** (col: for holiday) Ferienparadies nt; **~ stroke** n Sonnenstich m; **to get ~ stroke** einen Sonnenstich bekommen; **~ tan** n Sonnenbräune f; **to get a ~ tan** braun werden; **~ tan lotion/oil** n Sonnenöl nt; **~ tanned** adj braungebrannt; **~ trap** n sonniges Eckchen; **~-up** n (esp US) Sonnenaufgang m; **at ~-up** bei Sonnenaufgang.

super [ˈsuːpəʳ] adj (col) phantastisch, klasse inv

(col). ~! Klasse! *(col)*; **we had a ~ time** es war große Klasse *(col) or* phantastisch.

superabundance [ˌsuːpərəˈbʌndəns] *n (of an +dat)* großer Reichtum; *(excessive amount)* Überfluß *m.*

superannuation [ˌsuːpəˌrænjuˈeɪʃən] *n* Rente *f.*

superb [suːˈpɜːb] *adj* großartig; *design, painting also* meisterhaft.

supercharger [ˈsuːpəˌtʃɑːdʒəʳ] *n* Lader *m.*

supercilious [ˌsuːpəˈsɪlɪəs] *adj* hochnäsig.

superficial [ˌsuːpəˈfɪʃəl] *adj person, injury* oberflächlich; *characteristics, resemblance* äußerlich.

superficiality [ˈsuːpəˌfɪʃɪˈælɪtɪ] *n see adj* Oberflächlichkeit *f*; Äußerlichkeit *f.*

superficially [ˌsuːpəˈfɪʃəlɪ] *adv see adj* oberflächlich; äußerlich. **~ this may be true** oberflächlich gesehen mag das stimmen.

superfluous [suːˈpɜːfluəs] *adj* überflüssig.

super: **~highway** *n (US)* ≃ Autobahn *f*; **~human** *adj* übermenschlich.

superimpose [ˌsuːpərɪmˈpəʊz] *vt* **to ~ sth on sth** etw auf etw *(acc)* legen; *(Phot)* etw über etw *(acc)* photographieren; *(Film)* etw über etw *(acc)* filmen.

superintend [ˌsuːpərɪnˈtend] *vt* überwachen.

superintendent [ˌsuːpərɪnˈtendənt] *n* Aufsicht *f*; *(in swimming-pool)* Bademeister *m*; *(of police) (Brit)* ≃ Kommissar(in *f*) *m*; *(US)* ≃ Polizeipräsident *m.*

superior [suːˈpɪərɪəʳ] **1** *adj* **(a)** *(better) quality, equipment* besser *(to* als*)*; *intellect, skill* überlegen *(to* sb/sth jdm/einer Sache*).* **(b)** *(excellent) work(manship), technique* großartig, hervorragend. **~ quality goods** Waren *pl* bester Qualität. **(c)** *(higher in rank etc)* höher. **~ officer** Vorgesetzte(r) *mf*; **to be ~ to** sb/sth jdm/etw übergeordnet sein. **(d)** *(greater)* überlegen *(to* sb/sth jdm/etw*); forces also* stärker *(to* als*); strength also* größer *(to* als*).* **they were ~ to us in number(s)** sie waren uns zahlenmäßig überlegen. **(e)** *(snobbish) person* überheblich; *smile also* überlegen; *(smart) restaurant, clientèle* fein, vornehm. **2** *n* **(a)** *(in rank)* Vorgesetzte(r) *mf*. **to be** sb's **~** *(in ability)* jdm überlegen sein. **(b)** *(Eccl)* **Mother** S**~** Mutter Oberin *f.*

superiority [suˌpɪərɪˈɒrɪtɪ] *n* **(a)** *(of cloth etc)* bessere Qualität; *(of technique, ability, in numbers)* Überlegenheit *f*. **(b)** *(in rank)* höhere Stellung. **(c)** *(conceitedness)* Überheblichkeit *f.*

superlative [suːˈpɜːlətɪv] **1** *adj (excellent)* überragend; *(Gram)* superlativisch. **2** *n* Superlativ *m.*

superman [ˈsuːpəmæn] *n, pl* **-men** [-men] Übermensch *m*. S**~** *(in comics)* Supermann *m.*

supermarket [ˈsuːpəˌmɑːkɪt] *n* Supermarkt *m.*

supernatural [ˌsuːpəˈnætʃərəl] *adj* übernatürlich. **the ~** das Übernatürliche.

superpower [ˈsuːpəˌpaʊəʳ] *n (Pol)* Supermacht *f.*

supersede [ˌsuːpəˈsiːd] *vt* ablösen; *person, belief also* an die Stelle treten von. **~d ideas** überholte Ideen.

supersonic [ˌsuːpəˈsɒnɪk] *adj* Überschall-.

superstar [ˈsuːpəˌstɑːʳ] *n* Superstar *m.*

superstition [ˌsuːpəˈstɪʃən] *n* Aberglaube *m no pl.*

superstitious [ˌsuːpəˈstɪʃəs] *adj* abergläubisch.

superstructure [ˈsuːpəˌstrʌktʃəʳ] *n* Überbau *m*; *(of ship)* Aufbauten *pl.*

supertanker [ˈsuːpəˌtæŋkəʳ] *n* Supertanker *m.*

supertax [ˈsuːpəˌtæks] *n* Höchststeuer *f.*

supervise [ˈsuːpəvaɪz] **1** *vt* beaufsichtigen. **2** *vi* Aufsicht führen, die Aufsicht haben.

supervision [ˌsuːpəˈvɪʒən] *n* Aufsicht *f*; *(action)* Beaufsichtigung *f*. **under the ~ of** unter der Aufsicht von.

supervisor [ˈsuːpəvaɪzəʳ] *n (of work)* Aufseher(in *f*) *m*, Aufsicht *f*; *(of research)* Leiter(in *f*) *m*; *(Brit Univ)* ≃ Tutor(in *f*) *m*; *(for PhD)* Doktorvater *m.*

supervisory [ˈsuːpəvaɪzərɪ] *adj role* beaufsichtigend. **in a ~ post** in einer Aufsichtsposition.

supper [ˈsʌpəʳ] *n (evening meal)* Abendessen *nt*; *(late evening snack)* (später) Imbiß. **to have ~ zu** Abend essen.

supplant [səˈplɑːnt] *vt* ablösen, ersetzen; *(forcibly)* verdrängen; *(by ruse)* rival ausstechen.

supple [ˈsʌpl] *adj (+er)* geschmeidig, elastisch; *shoes* weich; *mind* beweglich.

supplement [ˈsʌplɪmənt] **1** *n* **(a)** Ergänzung *f (to* gen*); (of book)* Ergänzungsband *m (to* zu*); (at end of book)* Anhang *m*. **a ~ to his income** eine Aufbesserung seines Einkommens. **(b)** *(colour ~ etc)* Beilage *f*. **2** *vt* ergänzen; *income* aufbessern.

supplementary [ˌsʌplɪˈmentərɪ] *adj* zusätzlich, ergänzend; *volume, report also* Zusatz-, Ergänzungs-. **~ benefit** *(Brit)* ≃ Arbeitslosenhilfe *f.*

supplication [ˌsʌplɪˈkeɪʃən] *n* Flehen *nt no pl.*

supplier [səˈplaɪəʳ] *n (Comm)* Lieferant(in *f*) *m.*

supply [səˈplaɪ] **1** *n* **(a)** *(supplying)* Versorgung *f*; *(Comm: delivery)* Lieferung *f (to* an *+acc); (Econ)* Angebot *nt*. **electricity ~** Stromversorgung *f*; **the ~ of blood to the brain** die Versorgung des Gehirns mit Blut; **~ and demand** Angebot und Nachfrage *(+pl vb).* **(b)** *(that supplied)* Lieferung *f*. **to cut off the ~** *(of gas, water etc)* das Gas/ Wasser *etc* abstellen. **(c)** *(stock)* Vorrat *m*. **supplies** *pl (food)* Vorräte *pl*; *(for expedition also, for journey)* Proviant *m*; **to get** *or* **lay in supplies** *or* **a ~ of sich** *(dat)* einen Vorrat an *(+dat)* anlegen; **a month's ~** ein Monatsbedarf *m*; **to be in short ~** knapp sein; **fresh supplies** *(Mil)* Nachschub *m*; **office supplies** Bürobedarf *m*; **medical supplies** Ärztebedarf *m.*

2 *vt* **(a)** *material, food etc* sorgen für; *(deliver) goods* liefern; *evidence, gas* liefern; *(put at* sb's *disposal)* stellen. **(b)** *(with* mit*)* versorgen; *(Comm)* beliefern. **this supplied me with the chance ...** das gab mir die Chance ...; **we have not been supplied with a radio** wir haben kein Radio bekommen. **(c)** *(satisfy, make good) need* befriedigen; *want* abhelfen *(+dat); (Comm) demand* decken.

supply: **~ industry** *n* Zulieferungsindustrie *f*; **~ lines, ~ routes** *npl (Mil, fig)* Versorgungslinien *pl*; **~ ship** *n* Versorgungsschiff *nt.*

support [səˈpɔːt] **1** *n* **(a)** *(lit)* Stütze *f*. **to give ~ to** sb/sth jdn/etw stützen; **to lean on** sb **for ~** sich auf jdn stützen. **(b)** *(fig) (no pl: moral, financial backing)* Unterstützung *f*; *(person)* Stütze *f*. **in ~ of** zur Unterstützung *(+gen)*; **in ~ of an allegation** zur Untermauerung einer Behauptung; **to speak in ~ of a candidate** einen Kandidaten unterstützen; **there was a lot of ~ for his views** viele stimmten seiner Meinung bei.

2 *attr (Mil) troops, vessel etc* Hilfs-.

3 *vt* **(a)** *(lit)* stützen; *(Tech also)* abstützen; *(bear the weight of)* tragen. **(b)** *(fig)* unterstützen; *plan, motion,* sb's *application also* befürworten; *party, cause also* beistehen *(+dat)*; *(give moral ~ to)* beistehen *(+dat)*, Rückhalt geben *(+dat)*; *(corroborate)* erhärten, untermauern; *(financially) family* unterhalten; *party, orchestra* finanziell unterstützen. **he ~s Arsenal** er ist Arsenal-Anhänger *m*; **which team do you ~?** für welche Mannschaft bist du?

4 *vr* **to ~ oneself** *(physically)* sich stützen *(on* auf *+acc); (financially)* seinen Unterhalt (selbst) bestreiten.

supporter [səˈpɔːtəʳ] *n* Anhänger(in *f*) *m*; *(of theory, cause also)* Befürworter(in *f*) *m*; *(Sport also)* Fan *m.*

supporting [səˈpɔːtɪŋ] *adj film* Vor-; *part, role* Neben-.

suppose [səˈpəʊz] *vt* **(a)** *(imagine)* sich *(dat)* vorstellen; *(assume, postulate also)* annehmen. **let us ~ that X equals 3** angenommen, X sei gleich 3; **even supposing it were** *or* **was true** (sogar) angenommen, daß es wahr ist; **always supposing he comes** immer vorausgesetzt, (daß) er kommt.

(b) *(believe, think)* annehmen, denken. I ~ he'll come ich nehme an, (daß) er kommt; I don't ~ he'll come ich glaube kaum, daß er kommt; I ~ he won't come ich denke, er wird nicht kommen, er wird wohl nicht kommen; I ~ that's the best thing das ist vermutlich das Beste; I don't ~ you could lend me a pound? Sie könnten mir nicht zufällig ein Pfund leihen?; will he be coming? — I ~ so kommt er? — ich denke schon; you ought to be leaving — I ~ so du solltest jetzt gehen — stimmt wohl; I don't ~ so ich glaube kaum; he is generally ~d to be rich er gilt als reich; he's ~d to be coming er soll (angeblich) kommen.

(c) *(in passive: ought)* to be ~d to do sth etw tun sollen; he's the one who's ~d to do it er müßte es eigentlich tun; you're ~d to be in bed du solltest eigentlich im Bett sein; he isn't ~d to find out er darf es nicht erfahren; you're not ~d to *(do that)* das darfst du nicht tun.

(d) *(in imper: I suggest)* ~ we have a go? warum versuchen wir es nicht einmal?; ~ we buy it? wie wäre es, wenn wir es kauften?

(e) *(presuppose)* voraussetzen. that ~s unlimited resources das setzt unbegrenzte Vorräte voraus.

supposed [sə'pəʊzd] *adj* vermutet; *date, site, author also* mutmaßlich.

supposedly [sə'pəʊzɪdlɪ] *adv* angeblich. the atom was ~ indivisible das Atom galt als unteilbar.

supposing [sə'pəʊzɪŋ] *conj* angenommen. but ~ ... aber wenn ...

supposition [ˌsʌpə'zɪʃən] *n (no pl: hypothesizing)* Mutmaßung, Spekulation *f*; *(thing supposed)* Annahme *f*. acting on the ~ that you are right vorausgesetzt, daß Sie recht haben.

suppository [sə'pɒzɪtərɪ] *n* Zäpfchen *nt*.

suppress [sə'pres] *vt* unterdrücken.

suppression [sə'preʃən] *n* Unterdrückung *f*.

supra- ['suːprə-] *pref* über-; *(esp with foreign words)* supra-. ~national überstaatlich.

supremacy [sʊ'preməsɪ] *n* Vormachtstellung *f*; *(Pol, Eccl, fig)* Supremat *nt or m*. air/naval ~ Luft-/Seeherrschaft *f*.

supreme [sʊ'priːm] **1** *adj (highest, ultimate)* höchste(r, s); *court* oberste(r, s); *(very great) courage etc* äußerste(r, s), größte(r, s). with ~ indifference völlig unbeteiligt. **2** *adv* to rule *or* reign ~ *(monarch)* absolut herrschen; *(champion, justice)* unangefochten herrschen.

supremely [sʊ'priːmlɪ] *adv confident* zutiefst.

surcharge ['sɜːtʃɑːdʒ] *n* Zuschlag *m*; *(postal)* Nachporto, Strafporto *(col) nt*.

sure [ʃʊər] **1** *adj (+er)* sicher; *proof, facts also* eindeutig; *method also, remedy* zuverlässig, verläßlich. I'm perfectly ~ ich bin *(mir da)* ganz sicher; to be ~ about sth sich *(dat)* einer Sache *(gen)* sicher sein; I'm not so ~ about that da bin ich nicht so sicher; to be ~ of oneself sich *(dat)* seiner Sache sicher sein; *(generally self-confident)* selbstsicher sein; it is ~ that he will come er kommt ganz bestimmt; it's ~ to rain es regnet ganz bestimmt; be ~ to turn the gas off vergiß nicht, das Gas abzudrehen; you're ~ of success der Erfolg ist Ihnen sicher; I want to be ~ of seeing him ich möchte ihn auf jeden Fall sehen; to make ~ *(check)* nachsehen; make ~ you get the leads the right way round achten Sie darauf, daß die Kabel richtig herum sind; make ~ you take your keys denk daran, deine Schlüssel mitzunehmen; it's best to make ~ sicher ist sicher; to make ~ of one's facts sicherstellen, daß die Angaben stimmen; to make ~ of a seat sich *(dat)* einen Platz sichern; ~ thing! *(esp US col)* klare Sache! *(col)*; he'll quit for ~ er kündigt ganz bestimmt; I'll find out for ~ ich werde das genau herausfinden; do you know for ~? wissen Sie das ganz sicher?; with a ~ hand mit sicherer Hand.

2 *adv (esp US)* will you do it? — ~! machst du das? — klar! *(col)*; that meat ~ was tough das Fleisch war vielleicht zäh!; and ~ enough he did come und er ist tatsächlich gekommen; he'll come ~ enough er kommt ganz bestimmt.

sure: ~-fire *adj (col)* todsicher *(col)*; ~-footed *adj* (tritt)sicher.

surely ['ʃʊəlɪ] *adv* **(a)** bestimmt, sicher. ~ you don't mean it? das meinen Sie doch bestimmt nicht (so)?; ~ not! das kann doch nicht stimmen!; ~ someone must know the answer irgend jemand muß doch die Antwort wissen. **(b)** *(esp US: gladly)* gern, mit Vergnügen.

sureness ['ʃʊənɪs] *n* **(a)** *(positiveness)* Überzeugung, Sicherheit *f*. **(b)** *(reliability, steadiness)* Sicherheit *f*; *(of method)* Verläßlichkeit *f*; *(of sb's judgement also)* Untrüglichkeit *f*.

surety ['ʃʊərətɪ] *n (sum)* Bürgschaft, Sicherheit *f*; *(person)* Bürge *m*. to go *or* stand ~ for sb für jdn bürgen.

surf [sɜːf] **1** *n* Brandung *f*. **2** *vi* surfen.

surface ['sɜːfɪs] **1** *n* **(a)** *(lit, fig)* Oberfläche *f*; *(of road)* Decke *f*, Belag *m*. on the ~ it seems that ... oberflächlich sieht es so aus, als ob ...; on the ~ he is friendly enough nach außen hin ist er sehr freundlich. **(b)** *(Math: of cube etc)* Fläche *f*. **(c)** *(Min)* at/on/up to the ~ über Tage. **2** *adj attr* **(a)** oberflächlich; *measurements* Oberflächen-. **(b)** *travel* auf dem Land-/Seeweg. **(c)** *(Min)* worker, job über Tage. **3** *vt road* mit einem Belag versehen; *wall* verblenden. **4** *vi (lit, fig)* auftauchen.

surface: ~ area *n* Fläche *f*; *(Math)* Flächeninhalt *m*; ~ mail *n* by ~ mail auf dem Land-/Seeweg, nicht per Luftpost; ~-to-air *adj attr missile* Boden-Luft-.

surfboard ['sɜːfbɔːd] *n* Surfbrett *nt*.

surfeit ['sɜːfɪt] *n* Übermaß, Zuviel *nt (of an +dat)*.

surfer ['sɜːfər] *n* Wellenreiter(in *f*), Surfer(in *f*).

surfing ['sɜːfɪŋ] *n* Wellenreiten, Surfen *nt*.

surge [sɜːdʒ] **1** *n (of sea)* Wogen *nt*; *(of floodwater)* Schwall *m*. **a** ~ of people eine wogende Menschenmenge; he felt a sudden ~ of rage er fühlte, wie die Wut in ihm aufstieg. **2** *vi (sea)* branden; *(floods, river)* anschwellen. blood ~d into her face ihr Schoß das Blut ins Gesicht; they ~d towards/round him sie drängten auf ihn zu/ sie umdrängten ihn; people ~d in/out eine Menschenmenge flutete herein/heraus.

surgeon ['sɜːdʒən] *n* Chirurg(in *f*) *m*.

surgery ['sɜːdʒərɪ] *n* **(a)** Chirurgie *f*. to have ~ operiert werden; to need (heart) ~ (am Herzen) operiert werden müssen. **(b)** *(Brit) (room)* Sprechzimmer *nt*; *(consultation)* Sprechstunde *f*. ~ hours Sprechstunden *pl*.

surgical ['sɜːdʒɪkəl] *adj treatment* operativ; *technique, instrument* chirurgisch; *training, skill* Chirurgen-, eines Chirurgen. ~ spirit Wundbenzin *nt*.

surly ['sɜːlɪ] *adj (+er)* verdrießlich, mißmutig.

surmise [sɜː'maɪz] *vt* vermuten, mutmaßen.

surmount [sɜː'maʊnt] *vt obstacle* überwinden.

surname ['sɜːneɪm] *n* Nachname *m*. what is his ~? wie heißt er mit Nachnamen?

surpass [sɜː'pɑːs] **1** *vt* **(a)** *(be better than)* übertreffen. **(b)** *(exceed) comprehension* hinausgehen über *(+acc)*. **2** *vr* to ~ oneself sich selbst übertreffen.

surplice ['sɜːpləs] *n* Chorrock *m*.

surplus ['sɜːpləs] **1** *n* Überschuß *m (of an +dat)*. **2** *adj* überschüssig; *(of countable objects)* überzählig. sale of ~ stock Verkauf *m* von Lagerbeständen; it is ~ to my requirements das benötige ich nicht.

surprise [sə'praɪz] **1** *n* Überraschung *f*. in ~ überrascht; much to my ~, to my great ~ zu meiner großen Überraschung; with a look of ~ mit überraschtem Gesicht; what a ~! was für eine Überraschung!; to give sb a ~ jdn überraschen;

to take sb by ~ jdn überraschen. **2** *attr attack, visit* Überraschungs-; *parcel etc* überraschend. **3** *vt* überraschen. **I wouldn't be ~d if** ... es würde mich nicht wundern, wenn ...; **don't be ~d if he refuses** wundern Sie sich nicht, wenn er ablehnt; **I'm ~ed at you!** du überraschst mich sehr!

surprising [sə'praızıŋ] *adj* überraschend, erstaunlich. **it's hardly** ~ **he said no** es ist kaum verwunderlich, daß er nein gesagt hat.

surprisingly [sə'praızıŋlı] *adv* ~ **(enough), he was right** er hatte erstaunlicherweise recht; **and then** ~ **he left** und dann ist er zu unserer/ihrer *etc* Überraschung gegangen.

surrealism [sə'rıəlızəm] *n* Surrealismus *m*.

surrealist [sə'rıəlıst] **1** *adj* surrealistisch. **2** *n* Surrealist(in *f*) *m*.

surrender [sə'rendə'] **1** *vi* sich ergeben *(to dat)*; *(to police)* sich stellen *(to dat)*. **I** ~**!** ich ergebe mich! **2** *vt (Mil)* übergeben; *goods, firearms also* ausliefern; *insurance policy* einlösen; *lease* kündigen; *claim, right* aufgeben. **3** *vr* **to** ~ **oneself to sth** sich einer Sache *(dat)* hingeben; *to fate* sich in etw *(acc)* ergeben. **4** *n* **(a)** Kapitulation *f (to vor +dat)*. **(b)** *see vt* Übergabe *f (to an +acc)*; Auslieferung *f (to an +acc)*; Einlösen *nt*; Kündigung *f*; Aufgabe *f*. ~ **value** *(Insur)* Rückkaufswert *m*.

surreptitious [,sʌrəp'tıʃəs] *adj* heimlich.

surrogate ['sʌrəgıt] **1** *n (substitute)* Ersatz *m*. **2** *attr* Ersatz-. ~ **mother** Leihmutter *f*.

surround [sə'raund] **1** *n* Umrandung *f*. **2** *vt* umgeben; *(Mil)* umstellen.

surrounding [sə'raundıŋ] *adj* umliegend. **in the** ~ **countryside** in der Umgebung.

surroundings [sə'raundıŋz] *npl* Umgebung *f*.

surtax ['sɜːtæks] *n* Steuerzuschlag *m*.

surveillance [sɜː'veıləns] *n* Überwachung *f*. **to be under** ~ überwacht werden; **to keep sb under** ~ jdn überwachen.

survey ['sɜːveı] **1** *n* **(a)** *(of land)* Vermessung *f*; *(report)* (Vermessungs)gutachten *nt*; *(of house)* Begutachtung *f*; *(report)* Gutachten *nt*. **to have a** ~ **done on a house** ein Gutachten über ein Haus erstellen lassen. **(b)** *(review: of subject, development)* Überblick *m (of über +acc)*. **(c)** *(inquiry)* Untersuchung *f (of, on über +acc)*; *(by opinion poll etc)* Umfrage *f (of, on über +acc)*.

2 [sɜː'veı] *vt* **(a)** *(look at)* scene, person, prospects sich *(dat)* ansehen; *(appraisingly also)* begutachten; *person, goods* mustern. **(b)** *(study)* prospects, plans untersuchen; *events, trends* einen Überblick geben über *(+acc)*. **(c)** *(Surv)* site vermessen; *building* inspizieren.

surveying [sɜː'veııŋ] *n (of land)* Vermessung *f*; *(Brit: of buildings)* Inspektion *f*.

surveyor [sɜː'veıə'] *n (land~)* Landvermesser(in *f*) *m*; *(Brit: building ~)* Bauinspektor(in *f*) *m*.

survival [sə'vaıvəl] *n* Überleben *nt*; *(of customs)* Weiterleben *nt*. **the** ~ **of the fittest** das Überleben der Stärkeren; ~ **kit** Überlebensausrüstung *f*.

survive [sə'vaıv] **1** *vi (person, animal etc)* überleben; *(in job)* sich halten (können); *(treasures, play)* erhalten bleiben; *(custom)* fortbestehen. **you'll** ~ *(iro)* das wirst du schon überleben! **2** *vt* überleben; *(house, objects)* fire *etc* überstehen; *(col)* heat, boredom *etc* aushalten.

survivor [sə'vaıvə'] *n* Überlebende(r) *mf*.

susceptibility [sə,septə'bılıtı] *n no pl see adj* Beeindruckbarkeit *f*. ~ **to sth** Empfänglichkeit *f* für etw; Ausgesetztsein *nt* gegenüber etw; Anfälligkeit *f* für etw.

susceptible [sə'septəbl] *adj (impressionable)* beeindruckbar. ~ **to sth** *to charms etc* für etw empfänglich; *to attack* einer Sache *(dat)* ausgesetzt; *to colds, influence* für etw anfällig.

suspect ['sʌspekt] **1** *adj* verdächtig. **2** *n* Verdächtige(r) *mf*. **3** [sə'spekt] *vt* **(a)** *person* verdächtigen

(of sth einer Sache gen), in Verdacht haben. **I** ~ **her of having stolen it** ich habe sie im Verdacht, es gestohlen zu haben; **he** ~**s nothing** er ahnt nichts. **(b)** *(doubt)* truth anzweifeln; *motive* argwöhnisch sein gegenüber. **(c)** *(think likely)* vermuten. **I** ~**ed as much** das habe ich doch vermutet.

suspend [sə'spend] *vt* **(a)** *(hang)* (auf)hängen *(from an +dat)*. **to hang** ~**ed from sth/in sth** von/in etw *(dat)* hängen. **(b)** *(stop, defer)* publication, payment *(zeitweilig)* einstellen; *judgement* aufschieben; *sentence* zur Bewährung aussetzen. **he was given a** ~**ed sentence** seine Strafe wurde zur Bewährung ausgesetzt. **(c)** *person* suspendieren; *member, pupil* zeitweilig ausschließen; *(Sport)* sperren; *licence* zeitweilig einziehen; *law, privileges* aussetzen. **to** ~ **from duty** suspendieren.

suspender [sə'spendə'] *n usu pl* **(a)** *(Brit) (for stockings)* Strumpfhalter, Straps *m*; *(for socks)* Sockenhalter *m*. ~ **belt** Strumpf(halter)gürtel *m*. **(b)** *(US)* ~**s** *pl* Hosenträger *pl*.

suspense [sə'spens] *n (in book, film etc)* Spannung *f*. **the** ~ **is killing me** ich bin gespannt wie ein Regenschirm *(hum col)*; **to keep sb in** ~ jdn auf die Folter spannen *(col)*.

suspension [sə'spenʃən] *n* **(a)** *see* **suspend (b)** zeitweilige Einstellung; Aufschub *m*; Aussetzung *f (zur Bewährung)*. **(b)** *see* **suspend (c)** Suspendierung *f*; zeitweiliger Ausschluß; Sperrung *f*; zeitweiliger Einzug; Aussetzen *nt*. **(c)** *(Aut)* Federung *f*.

suspension bridge *n* Hängebrücke *f*.

suspicion [sə'spıʃən] *n* Verdacht, Argwohn *(geh) m no pl*; *(trace)* Hauch *m*, Spur *f*. **to arouse sb's** ~**s** jds Verdacht erregen; **I have a** ~ **that** ... ich habe den Verdacht, daß ...; **to have one's** ~**s about sth** seine Zweifel bezüglich einer Sache *(gen)* haben; **to be above (all)/under** ~ über jeden Verdacht erhaben sein/unter Verdacht stehen; **to arrest sb on** ~**/on** ~ **of murder** jdn wegen Tatverdachts/Mordverdachts festnehmen.

suspicious [sə'spıʃəs] *adj* **(a)** *(feeling suspicion)* argwöhnisch, mißtrauisch *(of gegenüber)*. **to be** ~ **about sth** etw mit Mißtrauen betrachten. **(b)** *(causing suspicion)* verdächtig.

suspiciously [sə'spıʃəslı] *adv see adj* **(a)** argwöhnisch, mißtrauisch. **(b)** verdächtig. **it looks** ~ **like measles to me** das sieht mir verdächtig nach Masern aus.

♦ **suss out** ['sʌs'aut] *vt sep (Brit col)* **to** ~ **sb** jdm auf den Zahn fühlen *(col)*; **to** ~ **sth** ~ etw herausbekommen; **to** ~ **things** ~ die Lage peilen *(col)*.

sustain [sə'steın] *vt* **(a)** *(support)* load, weight aushalten, tragen; *life* erhalten; *family* unterhalten; *(nourish)* body bei Kräften halten. **(b)** *(maintain)* pretence, argument aufrechterhalten; *effort also* nicht nachlassen in *(+dat)*; *(Jur)* objection stattgeben *(+dat)*. **(c)** *(receive)* injury erleiden.

sustained [sə'steınd] *adj effort etc* ausdauernd; *applause* anhaltend.

sustenance ['sʌstınəns] *n (food and drink)* Nahrung *f*; *(nutritive quality)* Nährwert *m*.

suture ['suːtʃə'] *(Med)* **1** *n* Naht *f*. **2** *vt* nähen.

swab [swɒb] **1** *n (Med)* Tupfer *m*; *(specimen)* Abstrich *m*. **to take a** ~ einen Abstrich machen. **2** *vt* **(a)** *(Med)* wound etc (ab)tupfen. **(b)** *(Naut: also* ~ **down)* wischen.

swag [swæg] *n (col)* Beute *f*.

swagger ['swægə'] *vi* **(a)** stolzieren. **(b)** *(boast, act boastfully)* angeben.

swallow[1] ['swɒləu] **1** *n* Schluck *m*. **2** *vt food, drink* (hinunter)schlucken; *(fig)* story, evidence, insult schlucken. **to** ~ **sth whole** *(lit)* etw ganz schlucken; *(fig)* etw ohne weiteres schlucken; **to** ~ **one's words** *(retract)* seine Worte zurücknehmen. **3** *vi* schlucken. **to** ~ **hard** *(fig)* kräftig schlucken.

♦ **swallow up** vt sep (fig) verschlingen. **the mist seemed to ~ them** ~ der Nebel schien sie zu verschlucken; **I wished the ground would open and ~ me** ~ ich wäre am liebsten in den Boden versunken.

swallow² n (bird) Schwalbe f.

swam [swæm] pret of **swim**.

swamp [swɒmp] **1** n Sumpf m. **2** vt unter Wasser setzen; (fig) überschwemmen.

swampy ['swɒmpɪ] adj (+er) sumpfig.

swan [swɒn] **1** n Schwan m. **2** vi (col) **to ~ off** abziehen (col); **to ~ around New York** in New York herumziehen (col).

swank [swæŋk] vi (col) angeben (about mit).

swansong ['swɒn,sɒŋ] n (fig) Schwanengesang m.

swap [swɒp] **1** n Tausch m. **to do a ~ (with sb)** (mit jdm) tauschen. **2** vt stamps, cars, houses etc tauschen; stories austauschen. **to ~ sth for sth** etw für etw eintauschen; **to ~ places with sb** mit jdm tauschen. **3** vi tauschen.

swarm [swɔːm] **1** n (of insects, birds) Schwarm m; (of people also) Schar f. **2** vi (bees, flies, people) schwärmen. **the place was ~ing with insects/people** es wimmelte von Insekten/Leuten.

swarthy ['swɔːðɪ] adj (+er) skin dunkel.

swastika ['swɒstɪkə] n Hakenkreuz nt.

swat [swɒt] vt fly totschlagen.

swathe [sweɪð] vt wickeln (in in +acc).

sway [sweɪ] **1** n (influence, rule) Macht f (over über +acc). **to hold ~ over sb** jdn beherrschen, jdn in seiner Macht haben. **2** vi (trees) sich wiegen; (hanging object) schwingen; (building, bridge etc, person) schwanken; (train, boat) schaukeln; (hips) wackeln. **3** vt (a) schwenken; (wind) hin und her bewegen. **(b)** (influence) beeinflussen; (change sb's mind) umstimmen.

swear [sweə^r] (vb: pret swore, ptp sworn) **1** vt allegiance schwören; oath also leisten, ablegen. **I ~ it!** ich kann das beschwören!; **to ~ sb to secrecy** jdn schwören lassen, daß er nichts verrät; **I could have sworn that** was Louise (am almost sure) ich könnte schwören, daß das Louise war; (but it wasn't) ich hätte schwören können, daß das Louise war. **2** vi (a) (use solemn oath) schwören. **to ~ on the Bible** auf die Bibel schwören; **to ~ to sth** etw beschwören. **(b)** (use swearwords) fluchen (about über + acc). **to ~ at sb/sth** jdn/etw beschimpfen.

♦ **swear by** vi +prep obj (col) schwören auf (+acc).

♦ **swear in** vt sep witness etc vereidigen.

swearword ['sweə,wɜːd] n Fluch, Kraftausdruck m.

sweat [swet] **1** n Schweiß m no pl. **by the ~ of one's brow** (fig) im Schweiße seines Angesichts (liter); **to get into a ~ about sth** (fig) wegen etw ins Schwitzen geraten or kommen; **no ~** (col) kein Problem; **it was a real ~** (col) wir haben wirklich geschuftet (col). **2** vi schwitzen (with vor +dat); (fig col) (work hard) sich abrackern (col) (over mit); (worry) zittern (with vor +dat). **to ~ like a pig** (col) wie ein Affe schwitzen (col). **3** vt **to ~ blood** (with worry) Blut und Wasser schwitzen; (with effort) sich abrackern (col); **to ~ it out** (fig col) durchhalten; (sit and wait) abwarten.

sweatband ['swet,bænd] n Schweißband nt.

sweater ['swetə^r] n Pullover m.

sweat: **~shirt** n Sweatshirt nt; (Sport) Trainingspullover m; **~shop** n (pej, hum col) Ausbeuterbetrieb m (pej).

sweaty ['swetɪ] adj (+er) hands schweißig; feet, smell also Schweiß-; person, socks verschwitzt; weather, work zum Schwitzen.

swede [swiːd] n (Brit) Kohlrübe, Steckrübe f.

Swede [swiːd] n Schwede m, Schwedin f.

Sweden ['swiːdn] n Schweden nt.

Swedish ['swiːdɪʃ] **1** adj schwedisch. **2** n Schwedisch nt.

sweep [swiːp] (vb: pret, ptp swept) **1** n (a) **to give the floor a ~** den Boden kehren. **(b)** (chimney ~) Schornsteinfeger m. **(c)** (of arm, pendulum) Schwung m; (of sword also) Streich m; (of dress) Rauschen nt no pl; (of light, radar) Strahl m. **this magnificent ~ of countryside** diese herrliche Landschaft; **a long ~ of motorway** eine weitgestreckte Autobahn; **at one ~** (fig) auf einen Schlag; **to make a clean ~** (fig) gründlich aufräumen (of sth bei etw). **2** vt (a) kehren, fegen; dust, snow wegfegen. **to ~ sth under the carpet** (fig) etw unter den Teppich kehren. **(b)** (scan) absuchen (for nach); minefield durchkämmen; mines räumen. **(c)** (move quickly over) (wind, skirt) fegen über (+acc); (waves) deck etc überschwemmen; (glance) gleiten über (+acc); (fig) (violence, fashion) überrollen; (disease) um sich greifen in (+dat). **(d)** (remove with ~ing movement) (wave) spülen, schwemmen; (current) reißen; (wind) fegen; person reißen. **to ~ sth off the table/into a bag** etw vom Tisch fegen/etw in eine Tasche raffen; **the crowd swept him into the square** er wurde von der Menge zum Platz hin mitgerissen; **he swept her off her feet** (fig) er eroberte sie im Sturm; **to ~ the board** (fig) alle Preise/Medaillen gewinnen, abräumen (col). **3** vi (a) (with broom) kehren, fegen. **(b)** (move) (person) rauschen; (vehicle, plane) (quickly) schießen; (majestically) gleiten; (skier) fegen; (road, river) in weitem Bogen führen. **panic swept through Europe** Panik griff in Europa um sich.

♦ **sweep aside** vt sep (lit, fig) beiseite fegen.

♦ **sweep away 1** vi davonrutschen; (car, plane) davonschießen; (majestically) davongleiten; (skier) davonfegen. **2** vt sep dust, leaves etc wegfegen; (avalanche) wegreißen; (flood etc) wegspülen; (fig) old laws aufräumen mit.

♦ **sweep up 1** vi (with broom) zusammenkehren or -fegen. **2** vt sep zusammenkehren or -fegen; (collect up) objects zusammenraffen; hair hochbinden.

sweeper ['swiːpə^r] n (road ~) Straßenkehrer(in f) m; (machine) Kehrmaschine f; (carpet ~) Teppichkehrer m.

sweeping ['swiːpɪŋ] adj (a) gesture weitausholend. **(b)** (fig) change radikal, drastisch; statement pauschal; victory überragend.

sweepstake ['swiːpsteɪk] n Rennen nt etc, bei dem die Preise aus den Einsätzen gebildet werden, Sweepstake nt.

sweet [swiːt] **1** adj (+er) (a) süß. **to have a ~ tooth** gern Süßes essen. **(b)** (fresh) food, water frisch; (fragrant) smell süß. **(c)** (fig: pleasant etc) süß; (kind also) lieb. **that's very ~ of you** das ist sehr lieb von dir; **once he caught the ~ smell of success** erst der Erfolg lockte; **the words were ~ to his ear** die Worte klangen lieblich in seinen Ohren; **in his own ~ way** (iro) auf seine unübertroffene Art. **2** n (a) (Brit: candy) Bonbon nt. **(b)** (Brit: dessert) Nachtisch m, Dessert nt. **for ~** yes, (my) ~ ja, (mein) Schätzchen or Liebling.

sweet: **~ and sour** adj süß-sauer; **~ chestnut** n Eßkastanie f; **~ corn** n Mais m.

sweeten ['swiːtn] vt coffee, sauce süßen; (fig) temper bessern; task versüßen. **to ~ sb** (col) jdn gnädig stimmen.

sweetener ['swiːtnə^r] n (Cook) Süßungsmittel nt; (artificial) Süßstoff m.

sweetheart ['swiːt,hɑːt] n Schatz m, Liebste(r) mf.

sweetness ['swiːtnɪs] n Süße f; (of smile, nature) Liebenswürdigkeit f; (of person) liebe Art. **now all is ~ and light** (usu iro) nun herrscht eitel Freude und Sonnenschein.

sweet: **~ pea** n Gartenwicke f; **~ potato** n Süßkartoffel *f*; ~-**shop** *n (Brit)* Süßwarenladen *m or* -geschäft *nt*; ~-**smelling** *adj* süß riechend *attr*.

swell [swel] *(vb: pret* ~**ed**, *ptp* **swollen** *or* ~**ed)* **1** *n (of sea)* Wogen *nt no pl*. **there was a heavy** ~ **es** herrschte hoher Seegang. **2** *adj (US col: excellent)* **klasse** *(col)*, prima *(col)*. **3** *vt* river, sound etc anschwellen lassen; *stomach* (auf)blähen; *wood* (auf)quellen; *sail* blähen; *numbers* anwachsen lassen; *sales* steigern. **to be swollen with pride** stolzgeschwellt sein. **4** *vi* **(a)** *(ankle, arm, eye etc: also* ~ **up)** (an)schwellen; *(balloon etc)* sich füllen. **(b)** *(river, lake, sound etc)* anschwellen; *(sails: also* ~ **out)** sich blähen; *(wood)* quellen; *(in size, number)* anwachsen.

swelling [ˈswelɪŋ] *n (Med)* Schwellung *f*.

sweltering [ˈsweltərɪŋ] *adj* day, weather glühend heiß; *heat* glühend. **it's** ~ **in here** *(col)* hier verschmachtet man ja! *(col)*.

swept [swept] *pret, ptp of* **sweep**.

swerve [swɜːv] **1** *n* Bogen *m*; *(of car etc also)* Schlenker *m (col)*. **2** *vi* einen Bogen machen *(around sth* um etw*)*; *(car, driver)* ausschwenken; *(fig) (from truth)* abweichen; *(from chosen path)* abschwenken. **the car was swerving all over the road** der Wagen schwankte von einer Straßenseite zur anderen.

swift [swɪft] **1** *adj* (+er) schnell; *reaction also, revenge* prompt. **2** *n (bird)* Mauersegler *m*.

swiftness [ˈswɪftnɪs] *n see adj* Schnelligkeit *f*; Promptheit *f*.

swig [swɪɡ] *(col)* **1** *n* Schluck *m*. **to have** *or* **take a** ~ **of beer** einen Schluck Bier trinken. **2** *vt (also* ~ **down)** *beer* herunterkippen *(col)*.

swill [swɪl] **1** *n (animal food)* (Schweine)futter *nt*; *(garbage, slops)* *(solid)* Abfälle *pl*; *(liquid)* Schmutzwasser *nt*. **2** *vt* **(a)** *(also* ~ **out)** auswaschen; *cup, dish* ausschwenken. **(b)** *(col)* beer etc kippen *(col)*.

swim [swɪm] *(vb: pret* **swam**, *ptp* **swum)* **1** *n* **(a)** **it's a long** ~ **es ist weit** (zu schwimmen); **to go for a** ~ schwimmen gehen; **to have a** ~ schwimmen. **(b)** *(col)* **to be in the** ~ up to date sein; *(socially active)* mitmischen *(col)*. **2** *vt* schwimmen; *river, Channel* durchschwimmen. **3** *vi* schwimmen. **she can't** ~ **a stroke** sie kann sich keinen Meter über Wasser halten; **my head is** ~**ming** mir dreht sich alles; **it was absolutely** ~**ming in vinegar** es schwamm in Essig.

swimmer [ˈswɪmər] *n* Schwimmer(in *f*) *m*.

swimming [ˈswɪmɪŋ] **1** *n* Schwimmen *nt*. **do you like** ~? schwimmen Sie gern? **2** *adj (for* ~) Schwimm-; *(dizzy) feeling* schwummrig *(col)*.

swimming: ~ **bath** *n usu pl (Brit)* = ~ **pool**; ~-**costume** *n* Badeanzug *m*; ~ **pool** *n* Schwimmbad *nt*; *(outdoor also)* Freibad *nt*; *(indoor also)* Hallenbad *nt*; ~ **trunks** *npl* Badehose *f*.

swimsuit [ˈswɪmsuːt] *n* Badeanzug *m*.

swindle [ˈswɪndl] **1** *n* Schwindel, Betrug *m*. **it's a** ~! das ist (der reinste) Schwindel! **2** *vt* person beschwindeln. **to** ~ **sb out of sth** *(take from)* jdm etw abgaunern *(col)*; *(withhold from)* jdn um etw betrügen.

swindler [ˈswɪndlər] *n* Schwindler(in *f*) *m*.

swine [swaɪn] *n* **(a)** *pl* - *(old, form)* Schwein *nt*. **(b)** *pl* -**s** *(pej col)* Schwein *nt*; *(woman also)* Sau *f*.

swing [swɪŋ] *(vb: pret, ptp* **swung)* **1** *n* **(a)** *(movement)* Schwung *m*; *(to and fro)* Schwingen *nt*; *(of needle)* Ausschlag *m*; *(Boxing etc: blow)* Schwinger *m*; *(fig, Pol)* (Meinungs)umschwung *m (to* zugunsten +*gen, away from* zuungunsten +*gen)*. **to take a** ~ **at sb** nach jdm schlagen; **a** ~ **in opinion** ein Meinungsumschwung. **(b)** *(rhythm)* Schwung *m*; *(kind of music, dance)* Swing *m*. **to go with a** ~ *(fig)* ein voller Erfolg sein *(col)*; **to be in full** ~ voll im Gang sein; **to get into the** ~ **of things** *(col)* reinkommen *(col)*. **(c)** *(seat for* ~**ing)** Schaukel *f*. **to have a** ~ schaukeln; **it's** ~**s and roundabouts** *(col)* es ist gehüpft wie gesprungen.

2 *vt* **(a)** schwingen; *(to and fro)* hin und her schwingen; *(on swing)* schaukeln; *arms and legs (vigorously)* schwingen (mit); *(dangle)* baumeln mit; *propeller* einen Schwung geben (+*dat)*. **he swung his racket at the ball** er holte mit dem Schläger aus; **he swung the case (up) onto his shoulder** er schwang sich *(dat)* die Kiste auf die Schulter. **(b)** *(influence)* election beeinflussen; *opinion* umschlagen lassen; *person* umstimmen, herumkriegen *(col)*. **his speech swung the decision in our favour** seine Rede ließ die Entscheidung zu unseren Gunsten ausfallen; **he managed to** ~ **the deal** *(col)* er hat das Geschäft gemacht *(col)*; **if you can** ~ **it so that ...** *(col)* wenn du es so hinkriegen kannst, daß ... **(c)** *(turn: also* ~ **around)** *plane, car* herumschwenken.

3 *vi* **(a)** schwingen; *(to and fro)* (hin und her) schwingen; *(hanging object also)* pendeln; *(pivot)* sich drehen; *(on swing)* schaukeln; *arms, legs (dangle)* baumeln. **(b)** *(move: into saddle, along rope)* sich schwingen. **to** ~ **open/shut** aufschwingen/zuschlagen; **to** ~ **into action** in Aktion treten; **the car swung into the square** der Wagen schwenkte auf den Platz ein; **he swung around on his chair** er drehte sich auf seinem Stuhl herum; **the party has swung to the right** in der Partei hat es einen Rechtsruck gegeben; **he'll** ~ **for it** dafür wird er hängen *or* baumeln *(col)*.

swing: ~ **bridge** *n* Drehbrücke *f*; ~-**door** *n (Brit)* Pendeltür *f*.

swingeing [ˈswɪndʒɪŋ] *adj (Brit)* blow hart; *attack* scharf; *defeat* vernichtend; *taxation, price increases* extrem hoch; *cuts* extrem.

swinging [ˈswɪŋɪŋ] *adj* step, music schwungvoll; *movement* schaukelnd. **the** ~ **sixties** die „Swinging Sixties".

swipe [swaɪp] **1** *n (blow)* Schlag *m*. **to take a** ~ **at sb/sth** nach jdm/etw schlagen. **2** *vt* **(a)** *person, ball etc* schlagen. **(b)** *(col: steal)* mopsen *(col)*, klauen *(col)*. **3** *vi* **to** ~ **at sb/sth** nach jdm/etw schlagen.

swirl [swɜːl] **1** *n* Wirbel *m*. **2** *vti* wirbeln. **to** ~ **around** herumwirbeln.

swish [swɪʃ] **1** *n see vi* Zischen *nt*; Rascheln *nt*; Rauschen *nt*. **2** *adj (Brit col: plush)* schick. **3** *vt* cane zischen lassen; *tail* schlagen mit; *skirt* rauschen mit; *water* schwenken. **4** *vi (whip, cane, tyres)* zischen; *(grass, skirts)* rascheln; *(water)* rauschen.

Swiss [swɪs] **1** *adj* Schweizer, schweizerisch. ~ **roll** *n* Biskuitrolle *f*. **2** *n* Schweizer(in *f*) *m*. **the** ~ *pl* die Schweizer *pl*; ~ **French/German** *(person)* Französisch-/Deutschschweizer(in *f*) *m*; *(language)* Schweizer Französisch *or* Schweizerdeutsch, Schwyzerdütsch *nt*.

switch [swɪtʃ] **1** *n* **(a)** *(Elec etc)* Schalter *m*. **(b)** *(US Rail)* Weiche *f*. **(c)** *(change)* Wechsel *m*; *(in plans, policies)* Änderung *f (in gen)*; *(exchange)* Tausch *m*. **a rapid** ~ **of plan** eine schnelle Änderung der Pläne; **to make a** ~ tauschen. **(d)** *(stick, cane)* Rute, Gerte *f*.

2 *vt* **(a)** *(change)* wechseln; *direction, plans* ändern; *allegiance* übertragen *(to* auf +*acc)*; *attention, conversation* lenken *(to* auf +*acc)*. **(b)** *(move)* production verlegen; *object* umstellen. **(c)** *(exchange)* tauschen; *(transpose: also* ~ **over,** ~ **around)** *objects, figures in column* vertauschen. **I** ~**ed hats with him** ich tauschte meinen Hut mit ihm; **to** ~ **A for B** A für *or* gegen B (ein)tauschen. **(d)** *(Elec)* (um)schalten. **to** ~ **the radio to another programme** schalten Sie auf ein anderes Radioprogramm um. **(e)** *(esp US Rail)* rangieren.

3 *vi (change: also* ~ **over)** (über)wechseln *(to* zu*)*; *(Elec, TV, Rad)* umschalten *(to* auf +*acc)*; *(exchange: also* ~ **around,** ~ **over)** tauschen. **to** ~**ed to another line of attack** er wechselte seine Angriffstaktik.

♦ **switch off 1** *vt sep* light ausschalten; *radio, TV,*

machine also, engine abschalten. **the oven** ~**es
itself** ~ der Backofen schaltet sich selbsttätig
ab. **2** *vi* **(a)** *see vt* ausschalten; abschalten. **(b)**
(col: person) abschalten.
♦ **switch on 1** *vt sep gas etc* anstellen; *machine, TV
also, light* einschalten; *engine also* anlassen.
please leave the TV ~ **ed** ~ laß den Fernseher
bitte an. **2** *vi see vt* anstellen; einschalten; anlassen; *(automatically)* sich einschalten, angehen *(col).*

switch: ~**back** *n* Berg- und Talbahn *f; (Brit: roller-
coaster also)* Achterbahn *f;* ~**board** *n (Telec) (exchange)* Vermittlung *f; (in office etc)* Zentrale *f;
(actual panel, Elec)* Schalttafel *f;* ~**board operator** *n (in office)* Telefonist(in *f) m.*
Switzerland ['swɪtsələnd] *n* die Schweiz. **to** ~ **in**
die Schweiz; **in** ~ in der Schweiz.
swivel ['swɪvl] **1** *(also* ~ **around)** *vt* (herum)dre-
hen. **2** *vi* sich drehen; *(person)* sich herumdrehen.
swollen ['swəʊlən] **1** *ptp of* **swell. 2** *adj ankle, face,
glands etc* geschwollen; *stomach* aufgedunsen;
wood gequollen; *river* angeschwollen. **her eyes
were** ~ **with tears** ihre Augen waren verweint;
he has a ~ **head** *(fig)* er ist so aufgeblasen.
swoon [swuːn] **1** *n (old)* Ohnmacht *f.* **2** *vi (old: faint)*
in Ohnmacht fallen; *(fig: over pop star etc)* beina-
he ohnmächtig werden *(over sb* wegen jdm).
swoop [swuːp] **1** *vi (lit: also* ~ **down)** *(bird)* herab-
stoßen, niederstoßen *(on* auf +*acc); (plane)* ei-
nen Sturzflug machen; *(fig) (police)* einen
Überraschungsangriff machen *(on* auf +*acc) or*
landen *(col) (on* bei); *(person)* sich stürzen *(on* auf
+*acc).* **the plane** ~**ed (down) low over the village**
das Flugzeug flog im Tiefflug über das Dorf hin-
weg. **2** *n (of bird, plane)* Sturzflug *m.* **at one (fell)**
~ auf einen Schlag.
swop [swɒp] = **swap.**
sword [sɔːd] *n* Schwert *nt.* **to cross** ~**s with sb** *(lit,
fig)* mit jdm die Klinge(n) kreuzen.
swordfish ['sɔːdfɪʃ] *n* Schwertfisch *m.*
swordsman ['sɔːdzmən] *n, pl* -**men** [-mən]
Schwertkämpfer *m; (fencer)* Fechter *m.*
swore [swɔːʳ] *pret of* **swear.**
sworn [swɔːn] **1** *ptp of* **swear. 2** *adj enemy* eingeschworen; *(Jur) statement* eidlich, unter Eid.
swot [swɒt] *(Brit col)* **1** *vti* büffeln *(col),* pauken
(col). **to** ~ **up (on) one's maths** Mathe pauken
(col). **2** *n (pej: person)* Streber(in *f) m.*
swum [swʌm] *ptp of* **swim.**
swung [swʌŋ] *pret, ptp of* **swing.**
sycamore ['sɪkəmɔːʳ] *n* Bergahorn *m; (US: plane
tree)* nordamerikanische Platane.
sycophant ['sɪkəfənt] *n* Kriecher *m.*
syllable ['sɪləbl] *n* Silbe *f.* **a two-**~**(d) word** ein
zweisilbiges Wort; **in words of one** ~ *(hum)* in
einfachen Worten.
syllabus ['sɪləbəs] *n, pl* -**es** *or* **syllabi** [sɪləbaɪ] *(Sch,
Univ)* Lehrplan *m; (lecture timetable)* Vorlesungsverzeichnis *nt.*
symbiotic [ˌsɪmbɪˈɒtɪk] *adj* symbiotisch.
symbol ['sɪmbəl] *n* Symbol, Zeichen *nt (of* für).
symbolic [sɪmˈbɒlɪk] *adj* symbolisch *(of* für). **to
be** ~ **of sth** etw symbolisieren.
symbolism ['sɪmbəlɪzəm] *n* Symbolik *f; (Art, Liter:
movement)* Symbolismus *m.*
symbolize ['sɪmbəlaɪz] *vt* symbolisieren.
symmetrical [sɪˈmetrɪkəl] *adj* symmetrisch.
symmetry ['sɪmɪtrɪ] *n* Symmetrie *f.*
sympathetic [ˌsɪmpəˈθetɪk] *adj (showing pity)*
mitfühlend; *(understanding)* verständnisvoll;
(well-disposed) wohlwollend; *look, smile* freundlich. **to be** *or* **feel** ~ **to(wards) sb** mit jdm mitfühlen; für jdn Verständnis haben; *(Pol etc)* mit
jdm sympathisieren; **a** ~ **ear** ein offenes Ohr.
sympathize ['sɪmpəθaɪz] *vi (feel compassion)*
mitfühlen *(with* mit); *(understand)* Verständnis
haben *(with* für); *(agree)* sympathisieren *(with*

mit) *(esp Pol); (express sympathy)* sein Mitgefühl
aussprechen; *(on bereavement)* sein Beileid aussprechen. **to** ~ **with sb's views** jds Ansichten
teilen; **I really do** ~ *(have pity)* das tut mir wirklich leid; *(understand your feelings)* ich habe wirklich vollstes Verständnis.
sympathizer ['sɪmpəθaɪzəʳ] *n* Mitfühlende(r) *mf;
(with cause)* Sympathisant(in *f) m.*
sympathy ['sɪmpəθɪ] *n* **(a)** *(pity, compassion)* Mitgefühl, Mitleid *nt (for* mit); *(at death)* Beileid *nt.*
to feel *or* **have** ~ **for sb** Mitleid mit jdm haben; **a
letter of** ~ ein mitfühlender Brief, ein Beileids-
brief *m;* **you have my** ~! *(hum)* herzliches Beileid *(hum);* **you won't get any** ~ **from me** erwarte
kein Mitleid von mir. **(b)** *(understanding)* Verständnis *nt; (fellow-feeling, agreement)* Sympathie *f.* **to be in/out of** ~ **with sb/sth** mit jdm/etw
einhergehen/nicht einhergehen; **to come out in**
~ *(Ind)* in Sympathiestreik treten; ~ **strike**
Sympathiestreik *m.*
symphonic [sɪmˈfɒnɪk] *adj* symphonisch, sinfonisch.
symphony ['sɪmfənɪ] *n* Symphonie, Sinfonie *f.* ~
orchestra Symphonie- *or* Sinfonieorchester *nt.*
symposium [sɪmˈpəʊzɪəm] *n, pl* -**s** *or* **symposia**
[sɪmˈpəʊzɪə] Symposium, Symposion *nt.*
symptom ['sɪmptəm] *n (lit, fig)* Symptom *nt.*
symptomatic [ˌsɪmptəˈmætɪk] *adj* symptomatisch
(of für).
synagogue ['sɪnəgɒg] *n* Synagoge *f.*
synchromesh ['sɪŋkrəʊˌmeʃ] *n* Synchrongetriebe
nt.
synchronize ['sɪŋkrənaɪz] *vt* abstimmen *(with* auf
+*acc); two actions, movements* aufeinander abstimmen; *clocks* gleichstellen *(with* mit). **to** ~
a film Bild und Ton eines Films aufeinander
abstimmen.
syndicate ['sɪndɪkɪt] *n* Interessengemeinschaft *f;
(for gambling)* Wettgemeinschaft *f; (Comm)* Syndikat *nt,* Verband *m; (Press)* (Presse)zentrale *f;
(crime* ~) Ring *m.*
syndrome ['sɪndrəʊm] *n (Med)* Syndrom *nt; (fig,
Sociol)* Phänomen *nt.*
synod ['sɪnəd] *n* Synode *f.*
synonym ['sɪnənɪm] *n* Synonym *nt.*
synonymous [sɪˈnɒnɪməs] *adj* synonym. **to be** ~
with sth *(fig)* gleichbedeutend mit etw sein.
synopsis [sɪˈnɒpsɪs] *n, pl* **synopses** [sɪˈnɒpsiːz]
Abriß *m* der Handlung; *(of article, book)* Zusammenfassung *f.*
syntax ['sɪntæks] *n* Syntax *f.*
synthesis ['sɪnθəsɪs] *n, pl* **syntheses** ['sɪnθəsiːz]
Synthese *f.*
synthesize ['sɪnθəsaɪz] *vt* synthetisieren; *speech*
synthetisch bilden; *theories etc* zusammenfassen.
synthesizer ['sɪnθəˌsaɪzəʳ] *n (Mus)* Synthesizer *m.*
synthetic [sɪnˈθetɪk] **1** *adj* synthetisch; *fibre, silk*
Kunst-. **2** *n* Kunststoff *m,* Synthetik *f.*
syphilis ['sɪfɪlɪs] *n* Syphilis *f.*
syphon *n* = **siphon.**
Syria ['sɪrɪə] *n* Syrien *nt.*
Syrian ['sɪrɪən] **1** *adj* syrisch. **2** *n* Syrer(in *f) m.*
syringe [sɪˈrɪndʒ] **1** *n (Med)* Spritze *f.* **2** *vt (Med)*
(aus)spülen.
syrup, *(US also)* **sirup** ['sɪrəp] *n* Sirup *m.* **cough** ~
(Med) Hustensaft *m.*
system ['sɪstəm] *n* System *nt.* **new teaching** ~**s**
neue Lehrmethoden *pl;* **it was a shock to his** ~ er
hatte schwer damit zu schaffen; **to get sth out of
one's** ~ *(fig col)* sich *(dat)* etw von der Seele
schaffen *(col);* **you can't beat the** ~ gegen das
System kommst du einfach nicht an.
systematic [ˌsɪstəˈmætɪk] *adj* systematisch; *liar,
cruelty* ständig. **he works in a** ~ **way** er arbeitet
mit System.
systems analyst *n (Comp)* Systemanalyti-
ker(in *f) m.*

T

T, t [tiː] *n* T, t *nt.* **that's him/it to a T** das ist er, wie er leibt und lebt/genau so ist es.
ta [tɑː] *interj (Brit col)* danke.
TA *(Brit)* = **Territorial Army.**
tab [tæb] *n* **(a)** *(loop on coat etc)* Aufhänger *m*; *(fastener on coat etc)* Riegel *m*; *(name ~) (of owner)* Namensschild *nt*; *(of maker)* Etikett *nt*; *(Mil)* Spiegel *m*; *(on filing cards)* Reiter *m.* **to keep ~s on sb/sth** *(col)* jdn/etw genau im Auge behalten. **(b)** *(US col: bill)* Rechnung *f.*
tabby [ˈtæbɪ] *n (also ~ cat)* getigerte Katze; *(female)* weibliche Katze.
table [ˈteɪbl] **1** *n* **(a)** Tisch *m*; *(banquet ~)* Tafel *f.* **at the ~** am Tisch; **at ~** bei Tisch; **to sit down to** *or* **at ~** sich zu Tisch setzen; **to be under the ~** *(drunk)* unter dem Tisch liegen; **to turn the ~s (on sb)** (gegenüber jdm) den Spieß umdrehen; **the whole ~ laughed** die ganze Runde lachte. **(b)** *(of figures, prices etc, Sport)* Tabelle *f.* **(multiplication) ~s** Einmaleins *nt*; **~ of contents** Inhaltsverzeichnis *nt.* **(c)** *(Geog)* **water ~** Grundwasserspiegel *m.* **2** *vt* **(a)** *motion* einbringen. **(b)** *(US: postpone) bill* zurückstellen.
tableau [ˈtæbləʊ] *n, pl* **-s** *or* **-x** [ˈtæbləʊ(z)] *(Art, Theat)* Tableau *nt*; *(fig)* Bild *nt*, Szene *f.*
table: ~ cloth *n* Tischdecke *f* *or* -tuch *nt*; **~ lamp** *n* Tischlampe *f*; **~ manners** *npl* Tischmanieren *pl*; **~ mat** *n* Untersetzer *m*; *(of cloth)* Set *nt*; **~spoon** *n* Eßlöffel *m*; **~spoonful** *n* Eßlöffel(voll) *m.*
tablet [ˈtæblɪt] *n* **(a)** *(Pharm)* Tablette *f.* **(b)** *(of wax, clay)* Täfelchen *nt*; *(of soap)* Stückchen *nt.* **(c)** *(on wall etc)* Tafel *f.*
table: ~ tennis *n* Tischtennis *nt*; **~ware** *n* *no pl* Tafelgeschirr *nt* und -besteck *nt*; **~ wine** *n* Tisch- *or* Tafelwein *m.*
tabloid [ˈtæblɔɪd] *n (also ~ newspaper)* kleinformatige Zeitung *f*; *(pej)* Boulevardzeitung *f.*
taboo [təˈbuː] **1** *n* Tabu *nt.* **2** *adj* tabu *pred.*
tabulate [ˈtæbjʊleɪt] *vt* tabellarisch darstellen.
tabulation [ˌtæbjʊˈleɪʃən] *n* Tabulation *f.*
tachometer [tæˈkɒmɪtər] *n* Drehzahlmesser *m.*
tacit [ˈtæsɪt] *adj* stillschweigend.
taciturn [ˈtæsɪtɜːn] *adj* schweigsam.
tack [tæk] **1** *n* **(a)** *(nail)* kleiner Nagel; *(with small head also)* Stift *m*; *(esp US: drawing pin)* Heftzwecke *f.* **(b)** *(Brit Sew)* Heftstich *m.* **(c)** *(Naut: course)* Schlag *m*; *(fig)* Richtung *f*, Weg *m.* **to be on the port/starboard ~** auf Backbord-/Steuerborddbug segeln; **to be on the right/wrong ~** *(fig)* auf der richtigen/falschen Spur sein; **to try another ~** *(fig)* es anders versuchen. **2** *vt* **(a)** *(with nail)* annageln *(to* an *+dat* or *acc)*; *(with clip, pin)* feststecken *(to* an *+dat).* **(b)** *(Brit Sew)* heften. **3** *vi (Naut)* aufkreuzen.
tackle [ˈtækl] **1** *n* **(a)** *(lifting gear)* Flaschenzug *m*; *(Naut)* Talje *f*, Takel *nt.* **(b)** *(equipment)* Ausrüstung *f.* **fishing ~** Angelausrüstung *f.* **(c)** *(Sport)* Angriff *m*, Tackling *nt.* **2** *vt* **(a)** *(physically, Sport)* angreifen; *(Rugby)* fassen; *thief* also sich stürzen auf *(+acc)*; *(verbally)* zur Rede stellen *(about* wegen). **(b)** *(undertake) job* in Angriff nehmen; *new challenge* sich versuchen an *(+dat)*; *problem* angehen; *(manage to cope with)* fertig werden mit. **3** *vi* angreifen.
tacky¹ [ˈtækɪ] *adj (+er)* klebrig. **the paint is still ~** die Farbe klebt noch.

tacky² *adj (+er) (col)* verlottert *(col)*; *(cheap)* billig.
tact [tækt] *n no pl* Takt *m.*
tactful [ˈtæktfʊl] *adj* taktvoll.
tactic [ˈtæktɪk] *n* Taktik *f.*
tactical [ˈtæktɪkəl] *adj (Mil, fig)* taktisch.
tactics [ˈtæktɪks] *n sing (Mil, fig)* Taktik *f.*
tactile [ˈtæktaɪl] *adj* Tast-; *(tangible)* fühlbar.
tactless [ˈtæktlɪs] *adj* taktlos.
tadpole [ˈtædpəʊl] *n* Kaulquappe *f.*
taffy [ˈtæfɪ] *n (US)* Toffee *nt.*
tag [tæg] **1** *n* **(a)** *(label)* Schild(chen) *nt*; *(on clothes) (maker's name)* Etikett *nt*; *(owner's name)* Namensschild *nt*; *(loop)* Aufhänger *m.* **(b)** *(game)* Fangen *nt.* **2** *vi* **to ~ behind** *or* **after sb** hinter jdm herzockeln *(col).*
♦ **tag along** *vi* mitzockeln *(col).* **why don't you ~ ~?** *(col)* warum kommst du nicht mit?
tail [teɪl] **1** *n* **(a)** *(of animal)* Schwanz *m.* **with his ~ between his legs** *(fig)* mit eingezogenem Schwanz *(col)*; **to turn ~** die Flucht ergreifen; **he was right on my ~** er saß mir direkt im Nacken; **to put a ~ on sb** jdn beschatten lassen. **(b)** *(of aeroplane, procession)* Schwanz *m*; *(of comet)* Schweif *m*; *(of shirt)* Zipfel *m*; *(of jacket, coat)* Schoß *m.* **~s** *pl (jacket)* Frack *m.* **(c)** **~s** *(on coin)* Rückseite *f*; **~s I win!** bei Zahl gewinne ich. **2** *vt suspect* beschatten *(cars etc* folgen *(+dat).*
♦ **tail away** *vi* = **tail off (a).**
♦ **tail back** *vi (Brit: traffic)* sich gestaut haben.
♦ **tail off** *vi* **(a)** *(diminish)* abnehmen; *(interest also)* schwinden; *(sounds)* schwächer werden; *(sentence)* abbrechen. **(b)** *(deteriorate)* sich verschlechtern.
tail: ~back *n (Brit)* Rückstau *m*; **~board** *n* Ladeklappe *f*; **~ coat** *n* Frack *m*; **~ end** *n* Ende *nt*; **~gate** *n (of car)* Hecktür *f*; *(of lorry)* Ladeklappe *f*; **~-light** *n (Aut)* Rücklicht *nt.*
tailor [ˈteɪləʳ] **1** *n* Schneider *m.* **~'s dummy** *(lit)* Schneiderpuppe *f.* **2** *vt* **(a)** *dress etc* schneidern. **(b)** *(fig) plans* zuschneiden *(to* auf *+acc).* *products etc* abstimmen *(to* auf *+acc).* **~ed to meet his needs** auf seine Bedürfnisse abgestimmt.
tailor-made [ˈteɪləˈmeɪd] *adj (lit, fig)* maßgeschneidert; *role* also zugeschnitten *(for* auf *+acc).* **~ suit/costume** Maßanzug *m*/Schneiderkostüm *nt*; **the job was ~ for him** die Stelle war ihm wie auf den Leib geschnitten.
taint [teɪnt] **1** *n (lit: of food etc)* Stich *m*; *(fig) (blemish)* Makel *m*; *(trace)* Spur *f.* **2** *vt food* verderben; *air, atmosphere* verpesten; *(fig) reputation* beschmutzen.
take [teɪk] *(vb: pret* **took,** *ptp* **taken)** **1** *vt* **(a)** nehmen; *(for oneself)* sich *(dat)* nehmen; *(~ away with one)* mitnehmen; *(remove from its place)* wegnehmen. **to ~ sth from sb** jdm etw wegnehmen; *(steal)* jdm etw stehlen; **~ three eggs** *(Cook)* man nehme drei Eier; **~ a seat/chair!** nehmen Sie Platz!; **~ your seats!** nehmen Sie Ihre Plätze ein!; **this seat is ~n** dieser Platz ist besetzt; **I'll ~ a pound of apples** ich nehme ein Pfund Äpfel.

(b) *(transport, accompany)* bringen; *(~ along with one) person, things* mitnehmen. **I'll ~ you to the station** ich bringe Sie zum Bahnhof; **I'll ~ you (with me) to the party** ich nehme dich zur

Party mit; **let me ~ your case** komm, ich nehme *or* trage deinen Koffer; **to ~ sb/the dog for a walk** mit jdm spazierengehen/den Hund ausführen; **to ~ sb to the cinema** *(treat)* jdn ins Kino einladen; **(~ along with one)** mit jdm ins Kino gehen; **this bus will ~ you to the town hall** der Bus fährt zum Rathaus; **this road will ~ you to Paris** diese Straße führt nach Paris.

(c) *(capture) person* fassen; *animal* fangen; *town, country etc* einnehmen; *(Chess etc)* schlagen; *(Cards)* trick machen.

(d) *(accept, receive)* nehmen; *job, dye, perm* annehmen; *command, role* übernehmen; *prize* gewinnen. **I won't ~ less than £200** ich verkaufe es nicht unter £200; **we ~ the Guardian** wir bekommen den „Guardian"; **to ~ things as they come** die Dinge nehmen, wie sie kommen; **~ it from me!** das können Sie mir glauben; **(you can) ~ it or leave it** die Entscheidung liegt bei Ihnen; **he took the blow on his left arm** der Schlag traf ihn am linken Arm; *(in defence)* er wehrte den Schlag mit dem linken Arm ab; **do you ~ my meaning?** verstehen Sie, was ich meine?

(e) *exam, driving test, course, French* machen; *(as optional subject)* wählen; *lessons, tuition* nehmen; *(teach) lesson, subject* geben; *class* unterrichten. **he took his degree in 1965** er hat 1965 Examen gemacht *or* sein Examen abgelegt; **who ~s you for Latin?** wer unterrichtet bei euch Latein?

(f) *(consume) drink, food* zu sich *(dat)* nehmen; *drugs, medicine* nehmen; *(on directions for use)* einnehmen. **to ~ sugar in one's tea** den Tee mit Zucker trinken; **do you ~ sugar?** nehmen Sie Zucker?; **will you ~ coffee or tea?** möchten Sie Kaffee oder Tee?; **not to be ~n (internally)** *(Med)* nur zur äußerlichen Anwendung.

(g) *photo* machen. **he took the whole group** er nahm die ganze Gruppe auf.

(h) *(put up with)* sich *(dat)* gefallen lassen; *(endure) alcohol, climate* vertragen; *long journey* aushalten; *emotional experience, shock* verkraften; *(thing)* aushalten. **I just can't ~ any more** das halte ich nicht mehr aus.

(i) *(respond to, regard) news, blow* aufnehmen; *person* nehmen; *(understand, interpret)* auffassen, verstehen. **she knows how to ~ him** sie versteht es, ihn von der richtigen Seite zu nehmen; **she took his death very badly** sein Tod hat sie sehr mitgenommen; **I would ~ that to mean that ...** ich würde das so auffassen *or* verstehen, daß...; **to ~ sb/sth for** *or* **to be ...** jdn/etw für ... halten; **what do you ~ me for?** wofür hältst du mich eigentlich?; **may I ~ it that ...?** darf ich annehmen, daß ...?

(j) *(require)* brauchen; *clothes size* haben. **it ~s five hours/men ...** man braucht fünf Stunden/ Leute ...; **it ~s me five hours ...** ich brauche fünf Stunden ...; **it took ten men to complete the job** zehn Leute waren nötig, um diese Arbeit zu erledigen; **the journey ~s 3 hours** die Fahrt dauert 3 Stunden; **the wound took five weeks to heal** es dauerte fünf Wochen, bis die Wunde verheilt war; **it took a lot of courage/intelligence** dazu gehörte viel Mut/Intelligenz; **it ~s time** es braucht (seine) Zeit, es dauert (eine Weile); **it took a long time** es hat lange gedauert; **it won't ~ long** das dauert nicht lange; **that'll ~ some explaining** das wird schwer zu erklären sein; **she's got what it ~s** *(col)* sie ist nicht ohne *(col)*; *(is capable also)* sie kann was *(col)*; *(for job)* sie hat das Zeug dazu.

(k) *(support) weight* aushalten; *(have capacity or room for)* 50 people, 200 books Platz haben für.

(l) *walk* machen; *trip also* unternehmen; *taxi, train, motorway* nehmen. **to ~ the plane/next plane** fliegen/das nächste Flugzeug nehmen.

(m) to be ~n sick *or* **ill** krank werden; **to be**

~n with sb/sth *(attracted by)* von jdm/etw angetan sein.

2 *vi (fire)* angehen; *(dye, graft)* angenommen werden; *(vaccination)* anschlagen; *(plant)* anwachsen; *(seeds)* kommen; *(fish: bite)* anbeißen.

3 *n* **(a)** *(Film)* Aufnahme *f*. **(b)** *(US col: takings)* Einnahmen *pl*.

♦ **take after** *vi* +*prep obj* nachschlagen (+*dat*); *(in looks)* ähneln (+*dat*). **he ~s ~ her** er ist nach ihr geraten.

♦ **take along** *vt sep* mitnehmen.

♦ **take apart** *vt sep (also fig col)* auseinandernehmen.

♦ **take aside** *vt sep* beiseite nehmen.

♦ **take away 1** *vi* **to ~ ~ from sth** etw schmälern; *from worth* etw mindern. **2** *vt sep* **(a)** *(subtract)* abziehen. **6 ~ ~ 2** 6 weniger 2. **(b)** *(remove) child, thing, privilege* wegnehmen *(from sb* jdm*)*; *(from school etc)* nehmen *(from* aus*)*; *(lead, transport, carry away)* wegbringen *(from* von*)*; *prisoner* abführen *(to* in +*acc)*. **to ~ ~ sb's pleasure/ freedom** *etc* jdm die Freude/Freiheit *etc* nehmen. **(c)** *(Brit) food* mitnehmen. **pizza to ~ ~** Pizza zum Mitnehmen.

♦ **take back** *vt sep* **(a)** *(reclaim, get back)* sich *(dat)* zurückgeben lassen; *toy etc* wieder wegnehmen; *(fig: retract) threat, statement* zurücknehmen. **(b)** *(return)* zurückbringen. **he took us ~ (home)** er brachte uns (nach Hause) zurück. **(c)** *(agree to receive again) thing* zurücknehmen; *employee* wieder einstellen. **(d)** *(remind)* **to ~ sb ~ to his childhood** jdn an seine Kindheit erinnern.

♦ **take down** *vt sep* **(a)** *(lit: off shelf etc)* herunternehmen; *curtains, decorations* abnehmen; *picture* abhängen; *flag* einholen **(b)** *(dismantle) scaffolding etc* abbauen; *tent also* abbrechen; *railing, gate* entfernen. **(c)** *(write down)* (sich *dat)* notieren; *notes* (sich *dat)* machen; *letter* aufnehmen; *lecture* mitschreiben.

♦ **take home** *vt insep* £100 **per week** netto verdienen.

♦ **take in** *vt sep* **(a)** *(bring in) thing, person* hinein-/ hereinbringen; *harvest* einbringen. **when are you taking the car ~ (to the garage)?** wann bringen Sie das Auto in die Werkstatt? **(b)** *(receive in one's home) refugee* (bei sich) aufnehmen; *child* zu sich nehmen; *(for payment) student* vermieten an (+*acc*). **she ~s ~ lodgers** sie vermietet (Zimmer). **(c)** *(make narrower) dress* enger machen. **(d)** *(usu insep: include, cover)* einschließen. **(e)** *(note)* wahrnehmen; *area, room* überblicken; *(grasp) meaning, lecture, sb's death* begreifen; *impressions, sights etc* aufnehmen; *situation* erfassen. **(f)** *(deceive)* hereinlegen. **to be ~n ~** hereingelegt werden; **to be ~n ~ by sb/sth** auf jdn/etw hereinfallen; **to be ~n ~ by appearances** sich vom äußeren Schein täuschen lassen.

♦ **take off 1** *vi (plane, passengers)* starten, abfliegen; *(plane: leave the ground)* abheben; *(Sport)* abspringen; *(fig) (project, sales)* anlaufen; *(film, product)* ankommen.

2 *vt sep (remove, cut off: person)* abmachen *(prep obj* von*)*; *hat, lid* abnehmen *(prep obj* von*)*; *tablecloth* herunternehmen *(prep obj* von*)*; *coat, gloves etc* ausziehen; *leg* abnehmen; *play* absetzen; *food from menu, bus* streichen *(prep obj* von*)*; *service, tax* abschaffen; *(remove from duty, job) detective etc* abziehen *(prep obj* von*)*; *driver* ablösen. **to ~ sth ~ sb** jdm etw abnehmen; **to ~ the receiver ~ (the hook)** den Hörer abnehmen; **he/she took her dress ~** er zog ihr das Kleid aus/sie zog ihr Kleid aus; **he took his/her clothes off** er zog sich/sie aus; **would you like to ~ your coat ~?** möchten Sie ablegen?

(b) *(deduct)* abziehen *(prep obj* von*)*; *(from price)* 5%, 50p nachlassen.

(c) *(lead away, go away with)* mitnehmen;

(under arrest etc) abführen. **he was ~n ~ to hospital** er wurde ins Krankenhaus gebracht; **to ~ oneself ~** *(col)* sich auf den Weg machen. **(d)** *(have free) week, Monday* frei nehmen. **to ~ time ~ work** sich *(dat)* frei nehmen. **(e)** *(imitate)* nachmachen. **(f) to ~ sb's mind ~ sth** jdn von etw ablenken; **to ~ sb/sth ~ sb's hands** jdm jdn/etw abnehmen.

♦ **take on 1** *vi* **(a)** *(col: become upset)* sich aufregen. **(b)** *(become popular: song, fashion etc)* sich durchsetzen. **2** *vt sep* **(a)** *(undertake) job, work* übernehmen; *responsibility* auf sich *(acc)* nehmen; *bet* annehmen. **(b)** *(Sport etc: accept as opponent)* annehmen gegen; *opponent, authorities* sich anlegen mit. **(c)** *(employ)* einstellen; *apprentice* annehmen. **(d)** *(take aboard) (coach, train etc) passengers* aufnehmen; *(plane, ship also)* an Bord nehmen; *cargo, stores* laden; *fuel* tanken. **(e)** *(assume) colour, expression* bekommen, annehmen. **he took ~ an air of importance** er gab sich *(dat)* eine gewichtige Miene.

♦ **take out** *vt sep* **(a)** *(brir.ç or carry out)* (hinaus)bringen *(of* aus*)*; *(out of garage) car* hinaus-/herausfahren *(of* aus*)*; *(for drive etc) car, boat* wegfahren mit.

(b) *(to theatre etc)* ausgehen mit. **to ~ the dog ~ (for a walk)** den Hund ausführen; **to ~ sb ~ to** *or* **for dinner/to the cinema** jdn zum Essen/ins Kino einladen.

(c) *(pull out, extract)* herausnehmen; *tooth also* ziehen; *nail* herausziehen *(of* aus*)*. **to ~ sth ~ of** *or* **from sth** etw aus etw (heraus)nehmen.

(d) *(withdraw from bank etc)* abheben.

(e) *(procure) insurance* abschließen. **to ~ ~ a subscription for sth** etw abonnieren.

(f) to ~ sb ~ of himself jdn auf andere Gedanken bringen; **to ~ sth ~ on sb** *(col)* etw an jdm auslassen *(col)*; **to ~ it ~ on sb** sich an jdm abreagieren; **to ~ it/a lot ~ of sb** *(tire)* jdn ziemlich/sehr schlauchen *(col)*.

♦ **take over 1** *vi* *(assume government)* an die Macht kommen; *(military junta etc)* die Macht ergreifen; *(party)* an die Regierung kommen; *(new boss etc)* die Leitung übernehmen; *(in a place: tourists, guests etc)* sich breitmachen *(col)*. **to ~ ~ (from sb)** jdn ablösen; **the next shift ~s ~ at 6 o'clock** die nächste Schicht übernimmt um 6 Uhr. **2** *vt sep* **(a)** *(take control or possession of)* übernehmen. **tourists ~ ~ Edinburgh in the summer** im Sommer machen sich die Touristen in Edinburgh breit *(col)*. **(b)** *(escort or carry across) person* hinüberbringen; *(+prep obj)* bringen über *(+acc)*. **(c) to ~ sb ~ sth** *(show round)* jdm etw zeigen.

♦ **take to** *vi* *+prep obj* **(a)** *(form liking for) person* mögen. **the children soon took ~ their new surroundings** den Kindern gefiel es bald in der neuen Umgebung; **I don't know how she'll ~ ~ him/it** ich weiß nicht, wie sie auf ihn/darauf reagieren wird; **I don't ~ kindly ~ that** ich kann das nicht leiden. **(b)** *(form habit of)* **to ~ ~ doing sth** anfangen, etw zu tun; **to ~ ~ drink** zu trinken anfangen **(c)** *(escape to) hills* sich zurückziehen in *(+acc)*, Zuflucht suchen in *(+dat)*.

♦ **take up** *vt sep* **(a)** *(raise, lift)* aufnehmen; *carpet, floor-boards* hochnehmen; *road* aufreißen; *dress* kürzer machen; *pen* greifen zu.

(b) *(lead or carry upstairs etc) invalid, child* hinauf-/heraufbringen; *visitor* (mit) hinauf-/heraufnehmen.

(c) *time, attention* in Anspruch nehmen; *space* einnehmen.

(d) *(absorb)* (in sich *acc*) aufnehmen.

(e) *matter, point (raise)* zur Sprache bringen *(with sb* bei jdm*)*; *(go into)* eingehen auf *(+acc)*.

(f) *photography, archaeology* zu seinem Hobby machen; *a hobby* sich *(dat)* zulegen; *a language*

anfangen zu lernen. **to ~ ~ painting/the guitar** anfangen zu malen/Gitarre zu spielen.

(g) *(adopt) cause* sich einsetzen für; *idea* aufgreifen; *case* sich annehmen *(+gen)*. **to ~ ~ an attitude** eine Haltung einnehmen; **to ~ ~ a position** *(lit)* eine Stellung einnehmen; *(fig)* eine Haltung einnehmen.

(h) *(accept) challenge, invitation, suggestion* annehmen.

(i) *(start) job, employment* annehmen; *new job, post* antreten; *one's duties* übernehmen; *career* einschlagen.

(j) *(continue) story* aufnehmen; *conversation* weiterführen; *(join in) chorus, chant* einstimmen in *(+acc)*.

(k) I'll ~ you ~ on that *(on invitation, offer)* ich werde davon Gebrauch machen; *(on promise etc)* ich nehme Sie beim Wort.

♦ **take upon** *vt +prep obj* **he has ~n it ~ himself to ...** er hat die Verantwortung auf sich genommen, zu ...; **he took it ~ himself to answer for me** er meinte, er müsse für mich antworten.

♦ **take up with** *vi +prep obj person* sich anfreunden mit.

take: ~-away *(esp Brit)* **1** *n* **(a)** *(meal)* Essen *nt* zum Mitnehmen; **(b)** *(restaurant)* Imbißstube *f*; **2** *adj attr meal* zum Mitnehmen; **~-home pay** *n* Nettolohn *m*.

taken ['teɪkən] *ptp of* **take**.

take: ~-off *n* *(Aviat)* Start, Abflug *m*. **~-over** *n* *(Fin, Comm)* Übernahme *f*; **~-over bid** *n* Übernahmeangebot *nt*.

taking ['teɪkɪŋ] **1** *n* **(a) it's yours for the ~** das können Sie (umsonst) haben. **(b) ~s** *pl (Comm)* Einnahmen *pl*. **2** *adj person* anziehend.

talc [tælk], **talcum powder** ['tælkəm‚paʊdəʳ] *n* Talkumpuder *m*; *(perfumed)* (Körper)puder *m*.

tale [teɪl] *n* **(a)** Geschichte *f*; *(Liter)* Erzählung *f*. **(b) to tell ~s** petzen *(col)* *(to bei)*; **to tell ~s about sb** jdn verpetzen *(col)* *(to bei)*.

talent ['tælənt] *n* **(a)** Talent *nt*. **to have a ~ for drawing/mathematics** Begabung zum Zeichnen/für Mathematik haben. **(b)** *(talented people)* Talente *pl*. **~ scout** Talentsucher *m*.

talented ['tæləntɪd] *adj* begabt, talentiert.

talk [tɔːk] **1** *n* **(a)** Gespräch *nt* *(also Pol)*; *(conversation also)* Unterhaltung *f*. **to have a ~ with sb** about sth mit jdm über etw *acc*); **could I have a ~ with you?** könnte ich Sie mal sprechen?; **to hold** *or* **have ~s** Gespräche führen. **(b)** *no pl* *(~ing)* Rederei *f*; *(rumour)* Gerede *nt*. **there is some ~ of his returning** es heißt, er kommt zurück; **she's the ~ of the town** sie ist zum Stadtgespräch geworden; **he's all ~** er ist ein Schwätzer. **(c)** *(lecture)* Vortrag *m*. **to give a ~** einen Vortrag halten *(on* über *+acc)*.

2 *vi* sprechen, reden *(of* von, *about* über *+acc)*; *(have conversation also)* sich unterhalten *(of, about* über *+acc)*. **to ~ to** *or* **with sb** mit jdm reden *(about* über *+acc)*; *(converse also)* sich mit jdm unterhalten *(about* über *+acc)*; **could I ~ to Mr Smith please?** kann ich bitte Herrn Smith sprechen?; **it's easy for you to ~** *(col)* du hast gut reden *(col)*; **don't (you) ~ to me like that!** wie redest du denn mit mir?; **he knows/doesn't know what he's ~ing about** er weiß (schon)/weiß nicht, wovon er spricht; **you can ~!** *(col)* du kannst gerade reden!; **to keep sb ~ing** jdn (mit einem Gespräch) hinhalten; **to ~ to oneself** Selbstgespräche führen; **now you're ~ing!** das läßt sich schon eher hören!; **he's been ~ing of going abroad** er hat davon geredet, daß er ins Ausland fahren will; **~ing of films ...** da wir gerade von Filmen sprechen ...; **stop ~ing!** sei/ seid ruhig!; **everyone was ~ing about them** sie waren in aller Munde; *(because of scandal)* alle haben über sie geredet; **you're ~ing about at**

least £100 das wird mindestens £100 kosten.
3 *vt* **(a)** *a language, slang* sprechen; *nonsense* reden; *(discuss) politics* sich unterhalten über (+*acc*). **(b)** *(persuade)* to ~ **sb into doing sth** jdn überreden *or* dazu bringen, etw zu tun; *(against better judgement)* jdm einreden, etw zu tun; to ~ **sb out of sth/doing sth** jdm etw ausreden/jdm ausreden, etw zu tun; **he** ~**ed himself out of trouble** er redete sich (geschickt) heraus.
♦ **talk around** *vt always separate* umstimmen. **I** ~**ed her** ~ **to my way of thinking** ich habe sie zu meiner Anschauung bekehrt.
♦ **talk down 1** *vi* to ~ ~ **to sb** mit jdm herablassend sprechen. **2** *vt sep pilot* zur Landung einweisen.
♦ **talk over** *vt sep problem* besprechen.
talkative ['tɔːkətɪv] *adj person* gesprächig.
talked-of ['tɔːktɒv] *adj:* **much** ~ berühmt.
talker ['tɔːkəʳ] *n* Redner *m*; *(pej)* Schwätzer *m*.
talking ['tɔːkɪŋ] *n* Reden, Sprechen *nt*. **I'll let you do the** ~ ich überlasse das Reden Ihnen; **he did all the** ~ er übernahm das Reden.
talking: ~ **point** *n* Gesprächsthema *nt*; ~ **shop** *(pej)* Quasselbude *f*.
tall [tɔːl] *adj* (+*er*) **(a)** *person* groß; *building, tree* hoch. **how** ~ **are you?** wie groß sind Sie?; **he is 1 m 80** ~ er ist 1,80 m groß. **(b)** *(col)* **that's a** ~ **order** das ist ganz schön viel verlangt; **a** ~ **story** ein Märchen *nt (col)*.
tallboy ['tɔːlbɔɪ] *n (Brit)* hohe Schlafzimmerkommode.
tallow ['tæləʊ] *n* Talg *m*.
tally ['tælɪ] **1** *n* **to keep a** ~ **of** Buch führen über (+*acc*). **(b)** *(result of counting)* (An)zahl *f*. **2** *vi* **they don't** ~ sie stimmen nicht überein.
talon ['tælən] *n (also fig: of person)* Kralle *f*.
tambourine [ˌtæmbə'riːn] *n* Tamburin *nt*.
tame [teɪm] **1** *adj* (+*er*) **(a)** *animal, person* zahm. **(b)** *(dull) person, life, story, film etc* lahm *(col)*. **2** *vt animal, person* zähmen, bändigen; *passion* zügeln.
♦ **tamper with** ['tæmpəˌwɪθ] *vi* +*prep obj* herumhantieren an (+*dat*); *(with evil intent)* sich *(dat)* zu schaffen machen an (+*dat*).
tampon ['tæmpən] *n* Tampon *m*.
tan [tæn] **1** *n* **(a)** *(suntan)* Bräune *f*. **to get a** ~ braun werden. **(b)** *(colour)* Hellbraun *nt*. **2** *adj* hellbraun. **3** *vt* **(a)** *skins* gerben. **to** ~ **sb's hide** *(fig col)* jdm das Fell gerben. **(b)** *(sun) face, body etc* bräunen. **4** *vi* braun werden. **she** ~**s easily** sie wird schnell braun.
tandem ['tændəm] **1** *n (cycle)* Tandem *nt*. **2** *adv* **in** ~ *aligned* hintereinander; *work* zusammen.
tang [tæŋ] *n (smell)* scharfer Geruch; *(taste)* starker Geschmack.
tangent ['tændʒənt] *n (Math)* Tangente *f*. **to go** *or* **fly off at a** ~ *(fig)* (plötzlich) vom Thema abschweifen.
tangerine [ˌtændʒə'riːn] *n* Mandarine *f*.
tangible ['tændʒəbl] *adj (lit)* greifbar; *proof also* handfest; *assets* real.
tangle ['tæŋgl] **1** *n (lit)* Gewirr *nt*; *(fig: muddle)* Durcheinander *nt*. **to get into a** ~ *(lit, fig)* sich verheddern; **he got into a** ~ **with the police** er hat Schwierigkeiten mit der Polizei gehabt. **2** *vt (also* ~ **up)** *(lit, fig)* durcheinanderbringen; *wool, string also* verheddern. **to get** ~ **d** *(lit, fig)* sich verheddern; *(ropes)* sich verknoten; **a** ~ **d web** ein Gespinst *nt*.
♦ **tangle with** *vi* +*prep obj (col)* aneinandergeraten mit. **I'm not tangling** ~ **him** mit ihm laß ich mich (doch) nicht ein.
tango ['tæŋgəʊ] **1** *n* Tango *m*. **2** *vi* Tango tanzen.
tank [tæŋk] *n* **(a)** *(container)* Tank *m*; *(for water also)* Wasserspeicher *m*; *(of boiler also)* Kessel *m*; *(for diver: oxygen* ~) Flasche *f*. **(b)** *(Mil)* Panzer *m*.
♦ **tank up 1** *vi (ship, plane)* auftanken. **2** *vt sep (Brit col)* **to get** ~**ed** ~ sich vollaufen lassen *(col)*

(on mit); **to be** ~**ed** ~ voll sein.
tankard ['tæŋkəd] *n* Krug *m*.
tanker ['tæŋkəʳ] *n* **(a)** *(boat)* Tanker *m*. **(b)** *(vehicle)* Tankwagen *m*.
tanned [tænd] *adj person* braun(gebrannt).
tanner ['tænəʳ] *n* Gerber *m*.
Tannoy ® ['tænɔɪ] *n* Lautsprecheranlage *f*. **over** *or* **on the** ~ über den Lautsprecher.
tantalize ['tæntəlaɪz] *vt* reizen; *(torment)* quälen.
tantalizing ['tæntəlaɪzɪŋ] *adj smell, promise* verlockend, verführerisch.
tantamount ['tæntəmaʊnt] *adj:* **to be** ~ **to sth** einer Sache *(dat)* gleichkommen.
tantrum ['tæntrəm] *n* Wutanfall, Koller *(col) m*. **to have** *or* **throw a** ~ einen Wutanfall bekommen.
tap¹ [tæp] **1** *n (esp Brit)* Hahn *m*. **on** ~ *(lit: beer etc)* vom Faß; *(fig) your* Hand. **2** *vt cask, barrel* anzapfen; *telephone lines* abhören, anzapfen *(col)*; *resources* erschließen. **the wires are** ~**ped here** die Leitung hier wird abgehört.
tap² **1** *n (light knock)* Klopfen *nt*; *(light touch)* Klaps *m*. **2** *vti* klopfen. **he** ~**ped me on the shoulder** er klopfte mir auf die Schulter; **he** ~**ped his foot impatiently** er klopfte ungeduldig mit dem Fuß auf den Boden; **to** ~ **at the door** leise anklopfen.
tap: ~**-dance** *vi* steppen; ~**-dancing** *n* Steppen *nt*.
tape [teɪp] **1** *n* **(a)** Band *nt*; *(sticky paper)* Klebeband *nt*; *(Sellotape* ® *etc)* Kleb(e)streifen *m*; *(punch~)* Lochstreifen *m*; *(Sport)* Zielband *nt*. **to break** *or* **breast the** ~ *(Sport)* durchs Ziel gehen. **(b)** *(magnetic)* (Ton)band *nt*. **on** ~ auf Band; **to put** *or* **get sth on** ~ etw auf Band aufnehmen. **2** *vt* **(a)** *parcel* (mit Kleb(e)streifen/-band) zukleben. **(b)** *(~-record) song, message* (auf Band) aufnehmen. **(c)** *(col)* **I've got the situation** ~**d** ich habe die Sache im Griff *(col)*; **I've got him** ~**d** ich kenne mich mit ihm aus.
tape: ~ **deck** *n* Tapedeck *nt*; ~ **measure** *n* Bandmaß *nt*.
taper ['teɪpəʳ] **1** *n (candle)* (dünne) Kerze. **2** *vt end of plank, stick etc* zuspitzen; *edge* abschrägen; *pair of trousers* (nach unten) verengen. **3** *vi (also* ~ **off)** sich zuspitzen; *(trousers)* nach unten enger werden.
tape: ~**-record** *vt* auf Band aufnehmen; ~**-recorder** *n* Tonbandgerät *nt*; ~**-recording** *n* Bandaufnahme *f*.
tapering ['teɪpərɪŋ] *adj* spitz zulaufend.
tapestry ['tæpɪstrɪ] *n* Wandteppich, Gobelin *m*.
tapeworm ['teɪpwɜːm] *n* Bandwurm *m*.
tapioca [ˌtæpɪ'əʊkə] *n* Tapioka *f*.
tappet ['tæpɪt] *n (Aut)* Stößel *m*.
tap water *n* Leitungswasser *nt*.
tar [tɑːʳ] **1** *n* Teer *m*. **2** *vt fence* teeren. **they are all** ~**red with the same brush** *(fig)* sie sind alle vom gleichen Schlag.
tarantula [tə'ræntjʊlə] *n* Tarantel *f*.
tardy ['tɑːdɪ] *adj* (+*er*) zu spät.
target ['tɑːgɪt] *n* **(a)** *(person, object, Mil)* Ziel *nt*; *(Sport: board, fig: of joke, criticism etc)* Zielscheibe *f*. **his shot was off/on** ~ *(Mil)* sein Schuß ist daneben gegangen/hat getroffen; **Apollo III is on** ~ **for the moon** Apollo III ist auf direktem Kurs zum Mond. **(b)** *(objective, goal)* Ziel *nt*; *(in production)* (Plan)soll *nt.* **production is above/on/below** ~ das Produktionssoll ist überschritten/erfüllt/nicht erfüllt; **to set ourselves the** ~ **of £10,000** wir haben uns £10.000 zum Ziel gesetzt.
tariff ['tærɪf] *n* **(a)** Tarif *m*; *(in hotels)* Preisliste *f*. **(b)** *(Econ: tax)* Zoll *m*; *(table)* Zolltarif *m*.
tarmac ['tɑːmæk] *n* Asphalt *m*; *(esp Brit Aviat)* Rollfeld *nt*.
tarn [tɑːn] *n* kleiner Bergsee.
tarnish ['tɑːnɪʃ] **1** *vt* **(a)** *metal* stumpf werden lassen. **(b)** *(fig) reputation* beflecken; *ideals* trüben. **2** *vi (metal)* anlaufen. **3** *n* Beschlag *m*.
tarot card ['tærəʊkɑːd] *n* Tarockkarte *f*.

tarpaulin [tɑːˈpɔːlɪn] n (waterproof sheet) Plane f; (Naut) Persenning f.

tarragon [ˈtærəgən] n Estragon m.

tart[1] [tɑːt] adj (+er) **(a)** flavour, wine herb, sauer (pej); fruit sauer. **(b)** (fig) remark, manner scharf.

tart[2] n (Cook) Obsttorte f; (individual) Obsttörtchen nt. **apple/jam** ~ Apfelkuchen m/ Marmeladentörtchen nt.

tart[3] n (col) (prostitute) Nutte f (col!); (loose woman) Flittchen nt (pej).

♦ **tart up** vt sep (esp Brit col) aufmachen (col); oneself auftakeln (col). **there she was, all ~ed** ~ da stand sie, aufgetakelt wie eine Fregatte (col).

tartan [ˈtɑːtən] **1** n (pattern) Schottenkaro nt; (material) Schottenstoff m. **2** adj skirt mit Schottenkaro or -muster.

tartar [ˈtɑːtəʳ] n (of wine) Weinstein m; (in kettle) Kesselstein m; (on teeth) Zahnstein m.

Tartar [ˈtɑːtəʳ] n Tatar m. **t~** (fig) Tyrann m.

tartar sauce n ≃ Remouladensoße f.

task [tɑːsk] n Aufgabe f. **it is the ~ of the politician to** ... es ist Aufgabe des Politikers, zu ...; **to take sb to** ~ sich (dat) jdn vornehmen (col) (for, about wegen).

task: ~ **force** n Spezialeinheit f; ~**master** n (strenger) Arbeitgeber; **he's a hard** ~**master** er ist ein strenger Meister.

tassel [ˈtæsəl] n Quaste, Troddel f.

taste [teɪst] **1** n (lit, fig) Geschmack m; (small amount, fig: as an example) Kostprobe f; (of sth in the future) Vorgeschmack m. **I don't like the** ~ **of it** das schmeckt mir nicht; **a** ~ **of** onions ein Zwiebelgeschmack m; **to have a** ~ **(of sth)** (lit) (etw) probieren; (fig) eine Kostprobe (von etw) bekommen; (of sth to come) einen Vorgeschmack (von etw) haben; **in good/bad** ~ geschmackvoll/ geschmacklos; **to have a** ~ **for sth** eine Vorliebe für etw haben; **it's an acquired** ~ das ist etwas für Kenner; **she has expensive** ~**s** sie hat einen teuren Geschmack; **my** ~ **in music has changed** mein musikalischer Geschmack hat sich geändert; **to be to sb's** ~ nach jds Geschmack sein; **it is a matter of** ~ das ist Geschmack(s)sache; **sweeten to** ~ (Cook) nach Geschmack süßen.

2 vt **(a)** (perceive flavour of) schmecken; (fig) blood lecken. **(b)** (test) wine, food products probieren; (official) prüfen. **(c)** (fig) power, freedom erleben.

3 vi schmecken. **to** ~ **good** (gut) schmecken; **to** ~ **of sth** nach etw schmecken.

taste bud n Geschmacksknospe f.

tasteful [ˈteɪstfʊl] adj geschmackvoll.

tasteless [ˈteɪstlɪs] adj geschmacklos; food also fade.

tastiness [ˈteɪstɪnɪs] n Schmackhaftigkeit f.

tasty [ˈteɪstɪ] adj (+er) dish schmackhaft.

ta-ta [ˈtæˈtɑː] interj (Brit col) tschüs (col).

tattered [ˈtætəd] adj clothes zerlumpt; book, sheet zerfleddert; (fig) reputation angeschlagen.

tatters [ˈtætəz] npl Lumpen, Fetzen pl. **to be in** ~ in Fetzen sein; **his jacket hung in** ~ sein Jackett war zerrissen.

tattoo[1] [təˈtuː] **1** vt tätowieren. **2** n Tätowierung f.

tattoo[2] n **(a)** (military pageant) Musikparade f. **(b)** (Mil: on drum or bugle) Zapfenstreich m.

tatty [ˈtætɪ] adj (+er) (col) schmuddelig; clothes schäbig.

taught [tɔːt] pret, ptp of **teach**.

taunt [tɔːnt] **1** n Spötteleif, höhnische Bemerkung. **2** vt person verspotten (about wegen). **to** ~ **sb with cowardice** jdm höhnisch Feigheit vorwerfen.

Taurus [ˈtɔːrəs] n (Astron, Astrol) Stier m.

taut [tɔːt] adj (+er) rope straff (gespannt); muscles gestrafft; (fig) (tense) nerves, situation (an)gespannt; (economical) prose knapp.

tautological [ˌtɔːtəˈlɒdʒɪkəl] adj tautologisch, dop-

pelt gemoppelt (col).

tautology [tɔːˈtɒlədʒɪ] n Tautologie f.

tavern [ˈtævən] n (old) Schenke f (old).

tawdry [ˈtɔːdrɪ] adj (+er) clothes billig und geschmacklos; jewellery, decorations ordinär; person aufgedonnert.

tawny [ˈtɔːnɪ] adj (+er) goldbraun.

tax [tæks] **1** n **(a)** (Fin, Econ) Steuer f; (on a company's profit) Abgabe f. **before/after** ~ vor/ nach Abzug der Steuern; **to put a** ~ **on sb/sth** jdn/etw besteuern. **(b)** (fig) Belastung f (on sth gen, on sb für jdn). **2** vt **(a)** (Fin, Econ) besteuern; country mit Steuern belegen. **(b)** (fig) brain, imagination strapazieren; one's patience also auf eine harte Probe stellen; strength stark beanspruchen; resources angreifen. **(c)** (accuse) **to** ~ **sb with sth** jdn einer Sache (gen) beschuldigen.

taxable [ˈtæksəbl] adj person steuerpflichtig; income also steuerbar (form); goods abgabenpflichtig.

taxation [tækˈseɪʃən] n Besteuerung f; (taxes also) Steuern pl. **exempt from** ~ steuerfrei; **subject to** ~ steuerpflichtig.

tax in cpds Steuer; ~ **avoidance** n Steuerumgehung f; ~ **collector** n Steuerbeamte(r) m; (Bibl, Hist) Zöllner m; ~ **evasion** n Steuerhinterziehung f; (by going abroad) Steuerflucht f; ~ **exile** n Steuerexil nt; ~**-free** adj, adv steuerfrei; ~ **haven** n Steuerparadies nt.

taxi [ˈtæksɪ] **1** n Taxi nt. **to go by** ~ mit dem Taxi fahren. **2** vi (Aviat) rollen. **the plane** ~**ed to a halt** das Flugzeug rollte aus.

taxidermist [ˈtæksɪdɜːmɪst] n Präparator m.

taxi: ~**-driver** n Taxifahrer(in f) m; ~ **plane** n (US) Lufttaxi nt; ~ **rank** (Brit), ~ **stand** n Taxistand m.

tax: ~**payer** n Steuerzahler m; ~ **rebate** n Steuerergütung f; ~ **return** n Steuererklärung f.

TB = **tuberculosis** Tb, Tbc f.

T-bone steak [ˈtiːbəʊnˈsteɪk] n T-bone-Steak nt.

tea [tiː] n **(a)** Tee m. **to make (the)** ~ (den) Tee machen; **a cup of** ~ eine Tasse Tee; **not for all the** ~ **in China** nicht um alles Gold der Welt. **(b)** (afternoon ~) ≃ Kaffee und Kuchen; (meal) Abendessen nt. **we have** ~ **at five wir essen um 5 Uhr zu Abend**.

tea: ~ **bag** n Teebeutel m; ~ **break** n Pause f; ~ **caddy** n Teedose f; (dispenser) Teespender m; ~ **cart** n (US) Tee- or Servierwagen m.

teach [tiːtʃ] (vb: pret, ptp **taught**) **1** vt subject, person unterrichten; animal abrichten. **to** ~ **sth to sb** jdm etw beibringen; (teacher) jdn in etw (dat) unterrichten; **to** ~ **sb to do sth** jdm beibringen, etw zu tun; **to** ~ **sb how to do sth** jdm etw beibringen; **he** ~**es French** er unterrichtet or gibt (col) Französisch; **to** ~ **oneself sth** sich (dat) etw beibringen; **let that** ~ **you not to** ... laß dir das eine Lehre sein, nicht zu ...; **that'll** ~ **you to break the speed limit** das hast du (nun) davon, daß du die Geschwindigkeitsbegrenzung überschritten hast. **2** vi unterrichten, Unterricht geben. **he wants to** ~ er möchte Lehrer werden.

teacher [ˈtiːtʃəʳ] n Lehrer(in f) m. **she is a German** ~ sie ist Deutschlehrerin.

teacher-training [ˈtiːtʃəˈtreɪnɪŋ] n Lehrerausbildung f. ~ **college** (primary) pädagogische Hochschule; (secondary) Studienseminar nt.

tea-chest [ˈtiːtʃest] n Kiste f.

teaching [ˈtiːtʃɪŋ] n **(a)** das Unterrichten, die profession) der Lehrberuf. **to take up** ~ Lehrer werden; **she enjoys** ~ sie unterrichtet gern. **(b)** (doctrine: also ~s) Lehre f.

teaching: ~ **aid** n Lehrmittel nt; ~ **hospital** n Ausbildungskrankenhaus nt; ~ **staff** n Lehrerkollegium nt, Lehrkörper m (form).

tea: ~ **cloth** n (Brit) Geschirrtuch nt; ~ **cosy** n Teewärmer m; ~**cup** n (a) Teetasse f; **(b)** (also ~**cupful**) Tasse f (voll).

teak [tiːk] n Teak(holz) nt; (tree) Teakbaum m.

tea-leaf ['tiːliːf] n Teeblatt nt.

team [tiːm] n **(a)** Team nt; (Sport also) Mannschaft f. **football** ~ Fußballmannschaft f. **(b)** (of horses, oxen etc) Gespann nt.

♦ **team up** vi sich zusammentun (with mit); (join group) sich anschließen (with sb jdm, an jdn).

team: ~ **game** n Mannschaftsspiel nt; ~ **spirit** n Gemeinschaftsgeist m; (Sport) Mannschaftsgeist m; ~**work** n Gemeinschaftsarbeit f, Teamwork nt.

tea: ~ **party** n Teegesellschaft f; ~**pot** n Teekanne f.

tear[1] [tɛəʳ] (vb: pret **tore**, ptp **torn**) **1** vt **(a)** paper, dress zerreißen; flesh aufreißen; hole reißen. I've torn a muscle ich habe mir einen Muskel gezerrt; **to** ~ **sth to pieces** etw in Stücke reißen; **the critics tore the play to pieces** die Kritiker haben das Stück total verrissen; **to** ~ **sth open** etw aufreißen; **that's torn it!** (fig col) das hat alles verdorben! **(b)** (pull away) reißen. **her child was torn from her/her arms** das Kind wurde ihr entrissen/ihr aus den Armen gerissen; **he tore it out of my hand** er riß es mir aus der Hand. **(c)** (fig: usu pass) **a country torn by war** ein vom Krieg zerrissenes Land; **to be torn between two things/people** zwischen zwei Dingen/Menschen hin-und hergerissen sein.

2 vi **(a)** (material etc) (zer)reißen. **her coat tore on a nail** sie zerriß sich (dat) den Mantel an einem Nagel; ~ **along the dotted line** an der gestrichelten Linie abtrennen. **(b)** (move quickly) rasen. **to** ~ **past** vorbeirasen.

3 n (in material etc) Riß m.

♦ **tear along** vi entlangrasen. **he tore** ~ **the street** er raste die Straße entlang.

♦ **tear apart** vt sep house (thieves etc) völlig durcheinanderbringen; (bomb etc) völlig zerstören; meat, country zerreißen.

♦ **tear away** vi davonrasen. **2** vt sep wrapping abreißen (from von). **if you can** ~ **yourself** ~ **from the paper** wenn du dich von der Zeitung losreißen kannst.

♦ **tear down** vt sep poster herunterreißen; house abreißen.

♦ **tear off 1** vi **(a)** wegrasen. **he tore** ~ **down the street** er raste die Straße hinunter. **(b)** (move fast) **the carbon** ~**s** die Durchschrift läßt sich abtrennen. **2** vt sep label, wrapping, cover abreißen; clothes herunterreißen. **he tore me** ~ **a strip** (col) er hat mich zur Schnecke gemacht (col).

♦ **tear out 1** vi heraus-/hinausrasen. **he tore** ~ **through the front door** er raste zur Vordertür hinaus. **2** vt sep (her)ausreißen (of aus).

♦ **tear up 1** vi angerast kommen. **he tore** ~ **the hill/road** er raste den Berg hinauf/die Straße entlang. **2** vt sep **(a)** paper (fig) contract zerreißen. **(b)** stake, plant (her)ausreißen.

tear[2] [tɪəʳ] n Träne f. **in** ~**s** in Tränen aufgelöst; **the news brought** ~**s to her eyes** als sie das hörte, stiegen ihr die Tränen in die Augen; **you are bringing** ~**s to my eyes** (iro) mir kommen die Tränen (iro); ~ **drop** Träne f.

tearaway ['tɛərəweɪ] n (col) Rabauke m (col).

tearful ['tɪəful] adj look tränenfeucht; face tränenüberströmt. **..., she said in a** ~ **voice ...,** sagte sie unter Tränen.

teargas ['tɪəɡæs] n Tränengas nt.

tear-jerker ['tɪəˌdʒɜːkəʳ] n (col) Schnulze f.

tearoom ['tiːrʊm] n Teestube f, Café nt.

tease [tiːz] **1** vt person necken; animal reizen; (torment) quälen; (make fun of) aufziehen, hänseln (about wegen); (have on) auf den Arm nehmen (col). **2** n (col: person) Scherzbold m (col).

♦ **tease out** vt sep **(a)** fibres kardieren; wool kämmen; tangles auskämmen. **(b)** (fig) information ablocken (out of sb jdm).

teaser ['tiːzəʳ] n (difficult question) harte Nuß (col); (riddle) Denksportaufgabe f.

tea: ~ **service,** ~ **set** n Teeservice nt; ~ **shop** n (Brit) Teestube f; ~**spoon** n **(a)** Teelöffel m; **(b)** (also ~**spoonful**) Teelöffel m (voll); ~ **strainer** n Teesieb nt.

teat [tiːt] n (of animal) Zitze f; (of woman) Brustwarze f; (Brit: on baby's bottle) (Gummi)sauger m.

tea: ~**time** n (for afternoon ~) Teestunde f; (mealtime) Abendessen nt; ~ **towel** n (Brit) Geschirrtuch nt; ~ **tray** n Tablett nt.

tech [tek] (Brit) = **technical college.**

technical ['teknɪkəl] adj **(a)** (concerning technology) technisch. ~ **hitch** technisches Problem. **(b)** (of particular branch) fachlich, Fach-; adviser, dictionary Fach-; problems, vocabulary fachspezifisch; details formal. ~ **term** Fachausdruck m; ~ **terminology** Fachsprache f; ~ **question** (Jur) Verfahrensfrage f; **for** ~ **reasons** (Jur) aus verfahrenstechnischen Gründen.

technical college n (Brit) Technische Fachschule.

technicality [ˌteknɪ'kælɪtɪ] n **(a)** no pl the ~ of the language die Fülle von Fachausdrücken. **(b)** (technical detail, difficulty) technische Einzelheit; (fig, Jur) Formsache f. **that's just a** ~ das ist bloß ein Detail.

technically ['teknɪkəlɪ] adv **(a)** technisch. **(b)** (strictly speaking) ~ **you're right** genau genommen haben Sie recht.

technician [tek'nɪʃən] n Techniker(in f) m; (skilled worker) Facharbeiter(in f) m.

technique [tek'niːk] n Technik f; (method) Methode f.

technological [ˌteknə'lɒdʒɪkəl] adj technologisch; details technisch.

technologist [tek'nɒlədʒɪst] n Technologe m, Technologin f.

technology [tek'nɒlədʒɪ] n Technologie f. **the** ~ **of printing** die Drucktechnik; **University/College of T**~ Technische Hochschule/Fachschule; **the age of** ~ das technische Zeitalter.

teddy (bear) ['tedɪ(ˌbeəʳ)] n Teddy(bär) m.

tedious ['tiːdɪəs] adj langweilig, öde.

tediousness ['tiːdɪəsnɪs] n Lang(e)weile f. **his** ~ seine Langweiligkeit.

tee [tiː] (Golf) **1** n Tee nt. **2** vt ball auf das Tee legen.

♦ **tee off** vi einen Ball vom (ersten) Abschlag spielen.

teem [tiːm] vi **(a)** (with people, insects etc) wimmeln (with von). **(b)** it's ~**ing (with rain)** es regnet or gießt (col) in Strömen.

teenage ['tiːneɪdʒ] adj Jugend-, Teenager-; child, son halbwüchsig.

teenager ['tiːneɪdʒəʳ] n Teenager m.

teens [tiːnz] npl Teenageralter nt. **to be in one's** ~ im Teenageralter sein.

tee-shirt n = **T-shirt.**

teeter ['tiːtəʳ] vi taumeln, schwanken. **to** ~ **on the brink or edge of sth** (lit) am Rand von etw taumeln; (fig) am Rand von etw sein. **(b)** (US: seesaw) schaukeln.

teeth [tiːθ] pl of **tooth.**

teethe [tiːð] vi zahnen.

teething ['tiːðɪŋ] n Zahnen nt. ~ **troubles** npl (fig) Kinderkrankheiten pl.

teetotal ['tiː'təʊtl] adj person abstinent; party etc ohne Alkohol. **to be** ~ keinen Alkohol trinken, Antialkoholiker(in f) m sein.

teetotaller, (US) **teetotaler** ['tiː'təʊtləʳ] n Abstinenzler(in f), Antialkoholiker(in f) m.

telecommunications [ˌtelɪkəˌmjuːnɪ'keɪʃənz] n **(a)** pl Fernmeldewesen nt. **(b)** sing (science) Fernmeldetechnik f.

telegram ['telɪɡræm] n Telegramm nt.

telegraph: ~ **pole** n Telegrafenmast m; ~ **wire** n Telegrafenleitung f.

telepathic [ˌtelɪ'pæθɪk] adj telepathisch. **you must be** ~! du mußt Hellseher sein!

telepathy [tɪ'lepəθɪ] n Telepathie f.

telephone ['telɪfəʊn] **1** n Telefon nt. **you're wanted on the** ~ Sie werden am Telefon verlangt; **are you on the** ~? haben Sie Telefon?; *(can you be reached by* ~) sind Sie telefonisch zu erreichen?; **he's on the** ~ *(is using the* ~) er telefoniert gerade; *(wants to speak to you)* er ist am Telefon; **by** ~ telefonisch; **I've just been/I'll get on the** ~ **to him** ich habe eben mit ihm telefoniert/ich werde ihn anrufen. **2** vt anrufen; *message, reply* telefonisch übermitteln. **would you** ~ **the office to say ...** würden Sie im Büro anrufen und sagen ...; **3** vi anrufen, telefonieren; *(make* ~ *call)* telefonieren. **to** ~ **for a taxi** ein Taxi rufen.

telephone in cpds Telefon-, Fernsprech- *(form)*; ~ **booth** or **box** *(Brit)* n Telefonzelle, Fernsprechzelle f; ~ **call** n Telefongespräch nt; ~ **directory** n Telefonbuch nt; ~ **exchange** n Vermittlungsstelle f *(form)*; ~ **kiosk** n *(Brit)* Telefonzelle f; ~ **number** n Telefonnummer, Rufnummer *(form)* f; ~ **operator** n Telefonist(in f) m.

telephonist [tɪ'lefənɪst] n *(Brit)* Telefonist(in f) m.

telephoto (lens) ['telɪ,fəʊtəʊ('lenz)] n Teleobjektiv nt.

teleprinter ['telɪ,prɪntə^r] n Fernschreiber m.

telescope ['telɪskəʊp] **1** n Teleskop nt. **2** vi *(also* ~ **together)** *(aerial, umbrella)* sich ineinanderschieben lassen.

telescopic [,telɪ'skɒpɪk] adj *aerial etc* ausziehbar.

televise ['telɪvaɪz] vt *(in Fernsehen)* übertragen.

television ['telɪ,vɪʒən] n Fernsehen nt; *(set)* Fernsehapparat, Fernseher *(col)* m. **to watch** ~ fernsehen; **to be on** ~ im Fernsehen kommen; *(person)* im Fernsehen sein.

television in cpds Fernseh-; ~ **camera** n Fernsehkamera f; ~ **personality** n bekannte Fernsehpersönlichkeit; ~ **screen** n Bildschirm m, Mattscheibe f *(col)*; ~ **set** n Fernsehapparat, Fernseher *(col)* m; ~ **studio** n Fernsehstudio nt.

telex ['teleks] **1** n Fernschreiben, Telex nt; *(machine)* Fernschreiber m. **2** vt *message* per Telex mitteilen; *person* ein Telex schicken (+dat).

tell [tel] pret, ptp **told 1** vt **(a)** *(relate)* story, experiences, adventures erzählen *(sb sth, sth to sb* jdm etw); *(inform, say, announce)* sagen *(sb sth* jdm etw). **to** ~ **lies/fortunes** lügen/wahrsagen; **to** ~ **sb about** or **of sth** jdm von etw erzählen; **I can't** ~ **you how pleased I am** ich kann Ihnen gar nicht sagen, wie sehr ich mich freue; **who told you that?** wer hat Ihnen denn das erzählt?; **to** ~ **sb the way** jdm den Weg sagen; **could you** ~ **me the way to the station, please?** könn(t)en Sie mir bitte sagen, wie ich zum Bahnhof komme?; **(I'll)** ~ **you what, let's go to the cinema** weißt du was, gehen wir doch ins Kino!; **don't** ~ **me you can't come!** sagen Sie bloß nicht, daß Sie nicht kommen können!; **I won't do it, I** ~ **you!** und ich sage dir, das mache ich nicht!; **let me** ~ **you ...** lassen Sie sich von mir sagen, daß ...; **it was cold, I can** ~ **you** ich kann dir sagen, das war vielleicht kalt!; **I told you so** ich habe es (dir) ja gesagt; ~ **me another!** wer's glaubt! *(col)*; **don't** ~ **me, let me guess** sag's mir nicht, laß mich raten; **you're** ~**ing me!** wem sagen Sie das!

(b) *(distinguish, discern)* **to** ~ **the time** die Uhr kennen; **to** ~ **the difference** den Unterschied erkennen; **you can** ~ **that he's a foreigner** man sieht or merkt, daß er Ausländer ist; **to** ~ **sb/sth by sth** jdn/etw an etw *(dat)* erkennen; **to** ~ **right from wrong** Recht von Unrecht unterscheiden; **how can/could I** ~ **that?** wie soll ich das wissen?/ wie hätte ich das wissen können?

(c) *(order)* sagen *(sb* jdm). **we were told to bring sandwiches with us** es wurde uns gesagt, daß wir belegte Brote mitbringen sollten; ~ **him to stop singing** sagen Sie ihm, er soll aufhören zu singen; **do as** or **what you are told!** tu, was man dir sagt!; **I won't** ~ **you again** ich sage es dir

nicht noch einmal. **2** vi **(a)** *(discern, be sure)* wissen. **who can** ~? wer weiß?; **how can I** ~? *(how should I know)* woher soll ich das wissen?; **you never can** ~ man kann nie wissen. **(b)** *(talk,* ~ *tales of)* sprechen. **that would be** ~**ing!** das kann ich nicht verraten; **promise you won't** ~ du mußt versprechen, daß du nichts sagst; **it hurt me more than words can** ~ es hat mich mehr verletzt, als ich mit Worten ausdrücken kann. **(c)** *(have effect)* sich bemerkbar machen. **his age told against him** *(in applying for job)* sein Alter war ein Nachteil für ihn; *(in competition)* sein Alter machte sich bemerkbar.

♦ **tell off** vt sep *(col: scold)* ausschimpfen *(for* wegen). **he told me** ~ **for being late** er schimpfte *(mich aus)*, weil ich zu spät kam.

teller ['telə^r] n **(a)** *(in bank)* Kassierer(in f) m. **(b)** *(vote counter)* Stimmenauszähler(in f) m. **(c)** *(of story)* Erzähler(in f) m.

telling ['telɪŋ] **1** adj *(effective)* wirkungsvoll; *argument* also schlagend; *blow (lit, fig)* empfindlich; *(revealing)* aufschlußreich. **2** n **(a)** *(narration)* Erzählen nt. **(b) there is no** ~ **what he may do** man kann nicht wissen, was er tut.

telling-off ['telɪŋ'ɒf] n *(col)* Standpauke f *(col)*. **to give sb a good** ~ jdn kräftig ausschimpfen.

telltale ['telteɪl] **1** n Petzer m, Petze f. **2** adj attr verräterisch.

telly ['telɪ] n *(Brit col)* Fernseher m *(col)*.

temerity [tɪ'merɪtɪ] n Kühnheit f.

temp¹ = **(a)** temporary. **(b)** temperature.

temp² [temp] *(Brit)* **1** n Aushilfskraft f. **2** vi als Aushilfskraft arbeiten.

temper ['tempə^r] **1** n *(disposition)* Wesen, Naturell nt; *(angry mood)* Wut f. **to be in a** ~**/good/bad** ~ wütend sein/guter/schlechter Laune sein; **she's got a quick/vicious** ~ sie kann sehr jähzornig sein/tückisch werden; **to lose one's** ~ die Beherrschung verlieren *(with sb* bei jdm); **to keep one's** ~ sich beherrschen *(with sb* bei jdm); **to fly into a** ~ einen Wutanfall bekommen; **a fit of** ~ ein Wutanfall m. **2** vt **(a)** *metal* tempern. **(b)** *(fig)* action, passion mäßigen; *criticism* mildern.

temperament ['tempərəmənt] n Temperament nt; *(disposition)* Veranlagung f. **he has an artistic** ~ er ist eine Künstlernatur.

temperamental [,tempərə'mentl] adj temperamentvoll, launenhaft *(pej)*; *car* launisch *(hum)*.

temperance ['tempərəns] n **(a)** *(moderation)* Mäßigung f; *(in speech etc also)* Zurückhaltung f; *(in eating, drinking also)* Maßhalten nt. **(b)** *(teetotalism)* Enthaltsamkeit f.

temperate ['tempərɪt] adj *person, climate* gemäßigt; *(in eating, demands)* maßvoll.

temperature ['temprɪtʃə^r] n Temperatur f; *(Med: above normal* ~) Fieber nt. **to take sb's** ~ bei jdm Fieber messen; **he has a** ~**/a slight/high** ~ er hat Fieber/erhöhte Temperatur/hohes Fieber; **he has a** ~ **of 39°C** er hat 39° Fieber.

tempest ['tempɪst] n *(liter)* Sturm m *(also fig)*.

tempestuous [,tem'pestjʊəs] adj *(lit liter, fig)* stürmisch; *speech* leidenschaftlich.

template ['templɪt] n Schablone f.

temple¹ ['templ] n *(Rel)* Tempel m.

temple² n *(Anat)* Schläfe f.

tempo ['tempəʊ] n *(Mus, fig)* Tempo nt.

temporal ['tempərəl] adj **(a)** zeitlich; *(Gram)* Zeit-, temporal. **(b)** *(Rel)* weltlich.

temporarily [,tempə'reərɪlɪ] adv vorübergehend.

temporary ['tempərərɪ] adj vorübergehend; *job also* befristet; *arrangement also, road surface* provisorisch; *powers also* befristet. **he's looking for** ~ **work** er sucht einen Job *(col)*.

tempt [tempt] vt in Versuchung führen; *(successfully)* verführen; *(Rel also)* versuchen. **to** ~ **sb to do** or **into doing sth** jdn dazu verleiten, etw zu tun; **don't ~ me** bring mich nicht in Versuchung!; **to ~ fate** *(fig)* sein Schicksal herausfordern; *(in words)* den Teufel an die Wand malen; **I'm ~ed** es reizt mich.

temptation [temp'teɪʃən] *n* Versuchung *(also Rel)*, Verlockung *f*. **to yield to ~** der Versuchung erliegen.

tempting ['temptɪŋ] *adj* verlockend, verführerisch.

ten [ten] **1** *adj* zehn. **~ to one he won't come** (ich wette) zehn zu eins, daß er nicht kommt; **nine out of ~ people would agree with you** neun von zehn Leuten würden Ihnen zustimmen. **2** *n* Zehn *f*. **~s** *(Math)* Zehner *pl*; *see* **six.**

tenable ['tenəbl] *adj (Mil)* position haltbar; *(fig)* opinion, theory also vertretbar.

tenacious [tɪ'neɪʃəs] *adj* zäh; *character, person also* beharrlich.

tenacity [tɪ'næsɪtɪ] *n see adj* Zähigkeit *f*; Beharrlichkeit *f*. **the ~ of his grip** sein eiserner Griff.

tenant ['tenənt] *n* Mieter(in *f*) *m*; *(of farm)* Pächter(in *f*) *m*. **~ farmer** Pächter *m*.

tend[1] [tend] *vt* sich kümmern um; *sheep* hüten; *sick person* pflegen; *machine* bedienen.

tend[2] *vi* **to ~ to be/do sth** *(have habit)* gern etw sein/tun; *(person also)* dazu neigen *or* tendieren, etw zu sein/tun; **the lever ~s to stick** der Hebel bleibt oft hängen; **I ~ to believe him** ich neige dazu, ihm zu glauben; **to ~ towards** *(incline) (person, views etc)* neigen *or* tendieren zu.

tendency ['tendənsɪ] *n* Tendenz *f (geh)*; *(physical predisposition)* Neigung *f*. **to have a ~ to be/do sth** gern etw sein/tun; *(person, style of writing also)* dazu neigen *or* tendieren, etw zu sein/zu tun; **he had an annoying ~ to forget things** er hatte die ärgerliche Angewohnheit, alles zu vergessen.

tendentious [ten'denʃəs] *adj* tendenziös.

tender[1] ['tendə^r] *n (Naut, Rail)* Tender *m*.

tender[2] **1** *vt money, services* (an)bieten; *thanks* aussprechen; *resignation* einreichen. **"please ~ exact fare"** „bitte Fahrgeld abgezählt bereithalten". **2** *vi (Comm)* sich bewerben *(for* um*)*. **3** *n* **(a)** *(Comm)* Angebot *nt*. **to invite ~s for a job** Angebote *pl* für eine Arbeit einholen; **to put in a ~ for sth** ein Angebot für etw einreichen. **(b)** *legal ~* gesetzliches Zahlungsmittel.

tender[3] *adj* **(a)** *spot, bruise* empfindlich; *skin, plant also* zart; *(fig) subject* heikel. **(b)** *meat* zart. **(c)** *(affectionate) person, look* zärtlich, liebevoll; *memories* lieb. **to bid sb a ~ farewell** liebevoll(en) Abschied von jdm nehmen.

tender-hearted [,tendə'hɑːtɪd] *adj* gutherzig.

tenderly ['tendəlɪ] *adv* zärtlich, liebevoll.

tenderness ['tendənɪs] *n see adj* **(a)** Empfindlichkeit *f*; Zartheit *f*. **(b)** Zartheit *f*. **(c)** Zärtlichkeit *f*.

tendon ['tendən] *n* Sehne *f*.

tendril ['tendrɪl] *n* Ranke *f*.

tenement ['tenɪmənt] *n* Mietshaus *nt*.

tenet ['tenət] *n* Lehrsatz *m*; *(Rel)* Glaubenssatz *m*.

tenner ['tenə^r] *n (col)* Zehner *m (col)*.

tennis ['tenɪs] *n* Tennis *nt*.

tennis *in cpds* Tennis-; **~ club** *n* Tennisclub *m*; **~ court** *n* Tennisplatz *m*; **~ elbow** *n (Med)* Tennisarm *m*; **~ racket** *n* Tennisschläger *m*.

tenor ['tenə^r] **1** *n* **(a)** *(voice)* Tenor(stimme *f*) *m*; *(person)* Tenor *m*. **(b)** *(purport)* Tenor *m*; *(of theory)* Tendenz *f*; *(general nature: of life)* Stil *m*. **2** *adj (Mus)* Tenor-.

tenpin bowling [,tenpɪn'bəʊlɪŋ], *(US)* **tenpins** ['tenpɪnz] *n* Bowling *nt*.

tense[1] [tens] *n (Gram)* Zeit *f*, Tempus *nt*.

tense[2] **1** *adj* *(+er) rope, atmosphere* gespannt; *muscles also, person, expression (through stress etc)* angespannt; *(through fear etc)* verkrampft; *voice* nervös; *(thrilling) scene* spannungsgeladen. **2** *vt* anspannen.

tension ['tenʃən] *n* **(a)** *(lit)* Spannung *f*; *(of muscle)*

Anspannung *f*; *(Knitting)* Festigkeit *f*. **(b)** *(nervous strain)* Anspannung *f*. **(c)** *(strain: in relationship)* Spannungen *pl*.

tent [tent] *n* Zelt *nt*. **~ peg** *(Brit)* or **stake** *(US)* Zeltpflock, Hering *m*.

tentacle ['tentəkl] *n* Fangarm *m*; *(fig)* Klaue *f*.

tentative ['tentətɪv] *adj (provisional)* vorläufig; *offer* unverbindlich; *(hesitant) player, movement* vorsichtig; *conclusion, suggestion* vorsichtig.

tenterhooks ['tentəhʊks] *npl*: **to be on ~** wie auf glühenden Kohlen sitzen *(col)*; **to keep sb on ~** jdn zappeln lassen.

tenth [tenθ] **1** *adj (in series)* zehnte(r, s). **2** *n (fraction)* Zehntel *nt*; *(in series)* Zehnte(r, s); *see* **sixth.**

tenuous ['tenjʊəs] *adj* **(a)** *(lit)* thread *etc* dünn, fein. **(b)** *(fig)* connection, argument schwach.

tenure ['tenjʊə^r] *n* **(a)** *(holding of office)* Anstellung *f*; *(period of office)* Amtszeit *f*. **(b)** *(of property)* **during his ~ of the house** während er das Haus innehat/innehatte *(geh)*.

tepid ['tepɪd] *adj (lit, fig)* lau(warm).

term [tɜːm] **1** *n* **(a)** *(period of time)* Zeitraum *m*; *(of contract)* Laufzeit *f*; *(limit)* Frist *f*. **~ of government/office** Regierungszeit *f*/Amtszeit *f*; **in the long/short ~** auf lange/kurze Sicht.

(b) *(Sch: three in one year)* Trimester *nt*; *(Univ)* Semester *nt*. **in ~(-time)** während der Schulzeit/ des Semesters; **out of ~(-time)** in den Ferien.

(c) *(expression)* Ausdruck *m*. **in plain ~s** in einfachen Worten; **technical ~s** Fachausdrücke *pl*; **a contradiction in ~s** ein Widerspruch in sich.

(d) *(Math, Logic)* Term *m*. **to express one thing in ~s of another** eine Sache mit einer anderen erklären; **in ~s of production we are doing well** was die Produktion betrifft, stehen wir gut da; **in ~s of money/time** finanziell/ zeitlich.

(e) **~s** *pl (conditions)* Bedingungen *pl*; **~s of reference** *(of committee etc)* Aufgabenbereich *m*; *(of thesis etc)* Themenbereich *m*; **to buy sth on credit/easy ~s** etw auf Kredit/auf Raten kaufen; **the hotel offered reduced ~s in winter** das Hotel bot ermäßigte Winterpreise an; **on what ~s?** zu welchen Bedingungen?; **to come to ~s** **(with sb)** sich (mit jdm) einigen; **to come to ~s with sth** sich mit etw abfinden.

(f) **~s** *pl (relations)* **to be on good/bad ~s with sb** gut/schlecht (gut) mit jdm auskommen; **they are not on speaking ~s** sie reden nicht miteinander. **2** *vt* nennen, bezeichnen.

terminal ['tɜːmɪnl] **1** *adj syllable, station* End-; *cancer, patient* unheilbar. **2** *n* **(a)** *(Rail)* Endbahnhof *m*; *(of buses)* Endstation *f*; *(airport)* ~, *container* ~) Terminal *m*. **(b)** *(Elec)* Pol *m*. **(c)** *(Comp)* Terminal *nt or m*.

terminate ['tɜːmɪneɪt] **1** *vt* beenden; *contract, lease etc* lösen; *pregnancy* unterbrechen. **2** *vi* enden; *(contract, lease)* ablaufen.

termination [,tɜːmɪ'neɪʃən] *n* Ende *nt*; *(bringing to an end)* Beendigung *f*; *(expiry)* Ablauf *m*; *(cancellation)* Lösung *f*.

terminology [,tɜːmɪ'nɒlədʒɪ] *n* Terminologie *f*. **technical ~** Fachausdrücke *pl*.

terminus ['tɜːmɪnəs] *n (Rail, Bus)* Endstation *f*.

termite ['tɜːmaɪt] *n* Termite *f*.

tern [tɜːn] *n (Orn)* Seeschwalbe *f*.

terrace ['terəs] *n* Terrasse *f*. **(a)** **~s** *pl (Sport)* Ränge *pl*. **(b)** *(row of houses)* Häuserreihe *f*.

terraced ['terəst] *adj* **(a)** *hillside etc* terrassenförmig angelegt. **(b)** **~ house** *(Brit)* Reihenhaus *nt*.

terracotta [,terə'kɒtə] *n* Terrakotta *f*.

terra firma [,terə'fɜːmə] *n* **to be on ~** again wieder festen Boden unter den Füßen haben.

terrain [te'reɪn] *n* Terrain *(esp Mil)*, Gelände *nt*; *(fig)* Boden *m*.

terrestrial [tɪ'restrɪəl] *adj* **(a)** *(of land)* plants, animals Land-, auf dem Land lebend. **(b)** *(of the planet Earth)* irdisch.

terrible ['terəbl] *adj* schrecklich, furchtbar. he is ~ at golf er spielt furchtbar schlecht Golf.

terribly ['terəblɪ] *adv (badly, col: very)* schrecklich, furchtbar.

terrier ['terɪə^r] *n* Terrier *m.*

terrific [tə'rɪfɪk] *adj* shame, shock unheimlich *(col)*; person, success, idea also klasse *inv (col)*; speed, strength unwahrscheinlich *(col).*

terrify ['terɪfaɪ] *vt (person)* in Angst versetzen. to be terrified of sth vor etw schreckliche Angst haben.

terrifying ['terɪfaɪɪŋ] *adj* film grauenerregend; thought, sight entsetzlich; speed angsterregend.

territorial [ˌterɪ'tɔːrɪəl] **1** *adj* territorial, Gebiets-. ~ waters Territorialgewässer *pl*; **T~ Army** *(Brit)* Territorialheer *nt.* **2** *n* the **T~s** *(Brit)* die Heimatschutztruppe.

territory ['terɪtərɪ] *n* Territorium *nt; (of animals also)* Revier *nt; (Comm: of agent etc)* Bezirk *m; (fig)* Revier, Gebiet *nt.*

terror ['terə^r] *n* **(a)** *no pl (great fear)* panische Angst *(of vor +dat).* in ~ in panischer Angst. **(b)** *(col) (person)* Teufel *m; (child)* Ungeheuer *nt.* she's a ~ on the roads *(hum)* sie ist der Schrecken der Landstraße *(hum).*

terrorism ['terərɪzəm] *n* Terrorismus *m; (acts of ~)* Terror *m.* an act of ~ ein Terrorakt *m.*

terrorist ['terərɪst] **1** *n* Terrorist(in *f*) *m.* **2** *attr* terroristisch.

terrorize ['terəraɪz] *vt* terrorisieren.

terror-stricken ['terəˌstrɪkən] *adj* starr vor Schreck(en).

terse [tɜːs] *adj (+er)* knapp.

tertiary ['tɜːʃərɪ] *adj* tertiär; colour Misch-.

Terylene ® ['terəliːn] *n* ≈ Trevira ®, Diolen ® *nt.*

test [test] **1** *n* **(a)** *(Sch)* Klassenarbeit *f; (Univ)* Klausur *f; (short)* Test *m; (intelligence ~ etc)* Test *m; (driving ~)* (Fahr)prüfung *f.* he gave them a vocabulary ~ er ließ eine Vokabelarbeit schreiben; *(orally)* er hat sie Vokabeln abgefragt; to put sb/sth to the ~ jdn/etw auf die Probe stellen; to stand the ~ die Probe bestehen; to stand the ~ of time die Zeit überdauern. **(b)** *(of vehicle, product etc, chemical ~)* Test *m; (check)* Kontrolle *f; (on road also)* Testfahrt *f.* **2** *vt (a) (examine, check)* testen, prüfen; *(Sch)* pupil prüfen; *(orally)* abfragen; intelligence etc testen; *(fig)* auf die Probe stellen. the teacher ~ed them on that chapter der Lehrer fragte sie das Kapitel ab; to ~ sb/sth for accuracy jdn/etw auf Genauigkeit prüfen. **(b)** *(chemically)* gold, water, chemical etc untersuchen. to ~ sth for sugar etw auf seinen Zuckergehalt untersuchen. **3** *vi* Tests/einen Test machen; *(chemically also)* untersuchen *(for auf +acc).*

testament ['testəmənt] *n* **(a)** *(old)* Testament *nt.* **(b)** *(Bibl)* Old/New **T~** Altes/Neues Testament.

test: ~ **ban** *n* Teststopp *m;* ~ **ban treaty** *n* Test-stoppabkommen *nt;* ~ **card** *n (TV)* Testbild *nt;* ~ **case** *n* Musterfall *m;* ~ **drive** *n* Probefahrt *f;* ~-**drive** *vt* probefahren; ~ **flight** *n* Testflug *m.*

testicle ['testɪkl] *n* Hoden *m.*

testify ['testɪfaɪ] **1** *vt* to ~ that ... *(Jur)* bezeugen, daß ... **2** *vi (Jur)* eine Zeugenaussage machen, aussagen. to ~ against/in favour of sb gegen/für jdn aussagen; to ~ to sth *(speak for)* etw bezeu-gen *(also Jur); (be sign of)* sincerity etc von etw zeugen.

testimonial [ˌtestɪ'məʊnɪəl] *n (character recommendation)* Referenz *f.*

testimony ['testɪmənɪ] *n* Aussage *f.*

testiness ['testɪnɪs] *n* Gereiztheit *f.*

testing ['testɪŋ] *adj* hart. I had a ~ time es war hart (für mich).

testing ground *n* Testgebiet *nt; (fig)* Versuchs-feld *nt.*

test: ~ **match** *n (Brit)* Testmatch *nt;* ~ **paper** *n (Sch)* Klassenarbeit *f; (Chem)* Reagenzpapier *nt;* ~ **pattern** *n (US)* = ~ **card;** ~ **pilot** *n* Testpilot *m;* ~ **tube** *n* Reagenzglas *nt;* ~-**tube baby** *n* Retor-tenbaby *nt.*

testy ['testɪ] *adj (+er)* gereizt.

tetanus ['tetənəs] *n* Wundstarrkrampf, Tetanus *m.*

tête-à-tête ['teɪtɑː'teɪt] *n* Tête-à-tête *nt.*

tether ['teðə^r] **1** *n (lit)* Strick *m; (chain)* Kette *f.* to be at the end of one's ~ *(fig col)* am Ende sein *(col).* **2** *vt (also ~ up)* animal an- or festbinden.

Teutonic [tjuː'tɒnɪk] *adj (Hist, hum)* teutonisch.

text [tekst] *n* Text *m; (of document also)* Wortlaut *m.*

textbook ['tekstbʊk] *n* Lehrbuch *nt.* ~ **case** Paradefall *m.*

textile ['tekstaɪl] **1** *adj* Textil-, textil. **2** *n* Stoff *m.* ~**s** Textilien *pl.*

textual ['tekstjʊəl] *adj* Text-.

texture ['tekstʃə^r] *n* Beschaffenheit *f; (of food)* Substanz, Textur *f; (of material, paper)* Textur *f; (of minerals also, fig: of music, poetry etc)* Gestalt *f.*

textured ['tekstʃəd] *adj* strukturiert, Struktur-.

Thai [taɪ] **1** *adj* thailändisch. **2** *n* **(a)** Thailän-der(in *f*) *m,* Thai *mf.* **(b)** *(language)* Thai *nt.*

Thailand ['taɪlænd] *n* Thailand *nt.*

Thames [temz] *n* Themse *f.*

than [ðæn, *weak form* ðən] *conj* als. I'd rather do anything ~ that das wäre das letzte, was ich tun wollte; no sooner had I sat down ~ he began to talk kaum hatte ich mich hingesetzt, als er auch schon anfing zu reden; who better to help us ~ he? wer könnte uns besser helfen als er?

thank [θæŋk] *vt* danken *(+dat),* sich bedanken bei. I don't know how to ~ you ich weiß nicht, wie ich Ihnen danken soll; I'll ~ you to mind your own business ich wäre Ihnen dankbar, wenn Sie sich nicht einmischen würden; he has his brother/he only has himself to ~ for this das hat er seinem Bruder zu verdanken/sich selbst zuzu-schreiben; ~ you danke (schön); ~ you very much vielen Dank; no ~ you/yes, ~ you nein, danke/ja, bitte or danke; ~ you for the present vielen Dank für Ihr Geschenk; ~ you for nothing *(iro)* ich danke (bestens)!; ~ goodness or God *(col)* Gott sei Dank! *(col).*

thankful ['θæŋkfʊl] *adj* dankbar *(to sb* jdm). I'm only ~ that it didn't happen ich bin bloß froh, daß es nicht passiert ist.

thankfully ['θæŋkfəlɪ] *adv* dankbar, voller Dank-barkeit. ~, no real harm has been done zum Glück ist kein wirklicher Schaden entstanden.

thankless ['θæŋklɪs] *adj* undankbar. a ~ task eine undankbare Aufgabe.

thanks [θæŋks] **1** *npl* **(a)** Dank *m.* to accept sth with ~ etw dankend annehmen; and that's all the ~ I get und das ist jetzt der Dank dafür. **(b)** ~ to wegen *(+gen); (with positive cause also)* dank *(+gen);* it's all ~ to you that we're so late bloß deinetwegen kommen wir so spät; it was no ~ to him that ... ich hatte/wir hatten etc es nicht ihm zu verdanken, daß ... **2** *interj (col)* danke *(for für).* many ~ vielen Dank; ~ a lot *or* a million vielen *or* tausend Dank; ~ *(iro)* (na,) vielen Dank *(col).*

thanksgiving ['θæŋks,gɪvɪŋ] *n* **(a)** Danksagung *f.* **(b)** *(US)* **T~ (Day)** Thanksgiving Day *m.*

that[1] [ðæt, *weak form* ðət] **1** *dem pron, pl* **those (a)** das. what is ~? was ist das?; who is ~? wer ist das?; who is ~ **speaking?** wer spricht da?; *(on phone)* wer ist am Apparat?; ~'**s what they've been told** das hat man ihnen gesagt; **she's not as stupid as all** ~ so dumm ist sie nun auch (wieder) nicht; I **didn't think she'd get/be as angry as** ~ ich hätte nicht gedacht, daß sie sich so ärgern würde; ... **and all** ~ ... und so *(col);* **like** ~ so; **with weather like** ~ ... bei so einem Wetter ...; ~ **is (to say)** das heißt; **oh well,** ~'**s** ~ nun ja, damit ist der Fall erledigt; **you can't go and ~'s ~ du darfst nicht gehen, und damit hat sich's; ~'s it!** das ist es!; *(the right way)* richtig!; *(finished)* so, das wär's!; *(the last straw)* jetzt reicht's; **after/ below ~** danach/darunter; **you can get it in any supermarket and quite cheaply at ~** man kann es in jedem Supermarkt bekommen, und zwar ganz billig; **with ~ she got up and left** damit stand sie auf und ging.

(b) *(opposed to "this" and "these")* das (da), jenes *(geh)*. **I prefer this to ~** dies ist mir lieber als das (da); **~'s the one I like, not this one** das (dort) mag ich, nicht dies (hier).

2 *dem adj, pl* **those (a)** der/die/das, jene(r, s) *(old, liter)*. **what was ~ noise?** was war das für ein Geräusch?; **~ poor girl!** das arme Mädchen!; **I like ~ one** ich mag das da; **I'd like ~ one, not this one** ich möchte das da, nicht dies hier; **she was rushing this way and ~** sie rannte hierhin und dorthin; **what about ~ plan of yours now?** was ist denn nun mit Ihrem Plan?

3 *dem adv (col)* so. **he was at least ~ much taller than me** er war mindestens soviel größer als ich; **it's not ~ cold** so kalt ist es auch wieder nicht; **he was ~ angry** er hat sich derart(ig) geärgert.

that² *rel pron* **(a)** der/die/das; die. **all/nothing/ everything etc ~** ... alles/nichts/alles etc was ...; **the best etc ~** ... das Beste *etc*, das *or* was ...; **fool ~ I am** ich Idiot; **the girl ~ I told you about** das Mädchen, von dem ich Ihnen erzählt habe. **(b)** *(with expressions of time)* **the minute ~ he came** the phone rang genau in dem Augenblick, als er kam, klingelte das Telefon; **the day ~** ... an dem Tag, als ...

that³ *conj* daß. **~ he should behave like this is quite incredible** daß er sich so benehmen kann, ist kaum zu glauben; **he said ~ it was wrong** er sagte, es sei *or* wäre *(col)* falsch, er sagte, daß es falsch sei *or* wäre *(col)*; **not ~ I want to do it** nicht (etwa), daß ich das tun wollte.

thatch [θætʃ] **1** *n (roof)* Strohdach *nt*. **2** *vt roof* mit Stroh decken.

thatched [θætʃt] *adj roof* Stroh-; *cottage* mit Strohdach.

thaw [θɔː] **1** *vt* auftauen (lassen); *ice, snow also* tauen lassen; *(make warm) person, hands* aufwärmen; *(fig) relations* entspannen. **2** *vi (lit, fig)* auftauen; *(ice, snow)* tauen. **it is ~ing** es taut. **3** *n (lit, fig)* Tauwetter *nt*. **before the ~** bevor das Tauwetter einsetzt.

♦ **thaw out 1** *vi (lit,fig)* auftauen. **2** *vt sep (lit) frozen food etc* auftauen (lassen); *person, hands* aufwärmen; *(fig) person* aus der Reserve locken.

the [ðə, *before vowels, stressed* ðiː] **1** *def art* **(a)** der/die/das. **in ~ room** im *or* in dem Zimmer; **he went up on ~ stage** er ging aufs *or* auf das Podium; **to play ~ piano** Klavier spielen; **all ~ windows** alle Fenster; **have you invited ~ Browns?** haben Sie die Browns *or* die Familie Brown eingeladen?; **in ~ 20s** in den zwanziger Jahren; **Henry ~ Eighth** Heinrich der Achte.

(b) *(with adj used as n)* das; die; *(with comp or superl)* der/die/das. **~ Good** das Gute; **~ poor** die Armen *pl*; **translated from ~ German** aus dem Deutschen übersetzt.

(c) *(distributive use)* **twenty pence ~ pound** zwanzig Pence das *or* pro Pfund; **paid by ~ hour** stundenweise *or* pro Stunde bezahlt.

2 *adv* **~ bigger ~ better** je größer, desto besser.

theatre, (US) theater ['θɪətə'] *n* **(a)** Theater *nt*; *(esp in names, ~ company also)* Bühne *f*. **to go to the ~** ins Theater gehen; **what's on at the ~?** was wird im Theater gespielt? **(b)** *(Brit: operating ~)* Operationssaal *m*. **(c)** *(scene of events)* Schauplatz *m*. **~ of war** Kriegsschauplatz *m*.

theatre: ~ company *n* Theaterensemble *nt*;

(touring) Schauspieltruppe *f*; **~goer** *n* Theaterbesucher(in *f*) *m*.

theatrical [θɪ'ætrɪkəl] *adj* Theater-; *company also* Schauspiel-; *experience also* schauspielerisch; *(pej) behaviour etc* theatralisch.

thee [ðiː] *pron (old)* Dich; Dir.

theft [θeft] *n* Diebstahl *m*.

their [ðɛə'] *poss adj* **(a)** ihr. **(b)** *(his or her)* seine(r, s). **everyone knows ~ rights nowadays** jeder kennt heutzutage seine Rechte.

theirs [ðɛəz] *poss pron* ihre(r, s).

them [ðem, *weak form* ðəm] *pers pron pl* *(dir obj, with prep +acc)* sie; *(indir obj, with prep +dat)* ihnen. **both/neither of ~ saw me** beide haben/ keiner von beiden hat mich gesehen; **give me a few of ~** geben Sie mir ein paar davon; **none of ~** keine(r, s) (von ihnen); **it's ~** sie sind's; **it's ~ who did it** sie haben es gemacht.

theme [θiːm] *n* **(a)** *(subject)* Thema *nt*. **(b)** *(US Sch: essay)* Aufsatz *m*. **(c)** *(Mus)* Thema *nt*; *(Film, TV also)* Musik *f (from aus)*.

theme music, theme tune *n (Film)* Titelmusik *f*; *(TV)* Erkennungsmelodie *f*.

themselves [ðəm'selvz] *pers pron pl* **(a)** *(reflexive)* sich. **(b)** *(emph)* selbst. **the figures ~** die Zahlen selbst *or* an sich; *see* **myself**.

then [ðen] **1** *adv* **(a)** *(next)* dann; *(at this particular time)* da; *(in those days also)* damals. **and ~ what happened?** und was geschah dann?; **it was ~ 8 o'clock** da war es 8 Uhr; **I was/will be on holiday ~** ich war da (gerade) in Urlaub/werde da in Urlaub sein; **he did it there and ~** er hat es auf der Stelle getan.

(b) *(after prep)* **from ~ on(wards)** von da an; **before ~** vorher, zuvor; **but they had gone by ~** aber da waren sie schon weg; **we'll be ready by ~** bis dahin sind wir fertig; **since ~** seitdem; **between now and ~** bis dahin; **(up) until ~ I had never tried it** bis dahin hatte ich es nie versucht.

(c) *(in that case)* dann. **what are you going to do, ~?** was wollen Sie denn tun?; **all right, ~** also *or* dann meinetwegen; **so it's true ~** dann ist es (also) wahr.

(d) *(furthermore, and also)* dann, außerdem. **(and) ~ there's my aunt** und dann ist da noch meine Tante; **but ~ ...** aber ... auch; **but ~ again** he is my friend aber andererseits ist er mein Freund.

2 *adj attr* **the ~ Prime Minister** der damalige Premierminister.

theologian [θɪə'ləʊdʒɪən] *n* Theologe *m*, Theologin *f*.

theological [θɪə'lɒdʒɪkəl] *adj* theologisch. **~ college** Priesterseminar *nt*.

theology [θɪ'ɒlədʒɪ] *n* Theologie *f*.

theorem ['θɪərəm] *n (also Math)* Satz *m*.

theoretic(al) [θɪə'retɪk(əl)] *adj* theoretisch.

theorize ['θɪəraɪz] *vi* theoretisieren.

theory ['θɪərɪ] *n* Theorie *f*. **in ~** theoretisch.

therapeutic(al) [ˌθerə'pjuːtɪk(əl)] *adj* therapeutisch. **to be ~** therapeutisch wirken.

therapist ['θerəpɪst] *n* Therapeut(in *f*) *m*.

therapy ['θerəpɪ] *n* Therapie *f*.

there [ðɛə'] **1** *adv* **(a)** dort, da; *(with movement)* dorthin, dahin. **it's over/in ~** es liegt da drüber/ drin; **put it under/in ~** stellen Sie es da drunter/ hinein; **~ and back** hin und zurück; **so ~ we were** da waren wir nun da.

(b) *(fig: on this point)* da. **~ you are wrong** da irren Sie sich.

(c) *(in phrases)* **~ is/are** es *or* da ist/sind; **(~ exists/exist also)** es gibt; **~ is a mouse in the room** es ist eine Maus im Zimmer; **~ was once a castle here** hier war *or* stand einmal eine Burg; **is ~ any wine left? — well, ~ was** ist noch Wein da? — gerade war noch welcher da; **how many mistakes were ~?** wie viele Fehler waren es?; **~ comes a time when** ... es kommt eine Zeit, wo ...;

~ **being no alternative solution** da es keine andere Lösung gibt/gab; ~ **you go again** *(col)* jetzt geht's schon wieder los; ~ **you are** *(giving sb sth)* hier(, bitte)!; *(on finding sb)* da sind Sie ja!; **you press the switch and** ~ **you are!** Sie brauchen nur den Schalter zu drücken, das ist alles.

2 *interj* ~! ~! na, na!; **stop crying now,** ~**'s a good boy** hör auf zu weinen, na komm.

thereabouts [‚ðɛərə'baʊts] *adv* **(a)** *(place)* dort in der Nähe, dort irgendwo. **(b) five pounds/ fifteen or** ~ so um die fünf Pfund/fünfzehn (herum).

thereafter [‚ðɛər'ɑːftəʳ] *adv (form)* danach, darauf *(geh)*.

thereby [‚ðɛə'baɪ] *adv* dadurch, damit.

therefore ['ðɛəfɔːʳ] *adv* deshalb, daher; *(as logical consequence)* also.

there's [ðɛəz] = **there is**; **there has**.

thereupon [‚ðɛərə'pɒn] *adv* **(a)** *(at that point)* darauf(hin). **(b)** *(form: on that subject)* darüber.

thermal ['θɜːməl] *adj* **(a)** *(Phys) capacity, unit* Wärme-; *reactor* thermisch. **(b)** ~ **springs** Thermalquellen *pl*.

thermo [‚θɜːməʊ-]: ~**dynamic** *adj* thermodynamisch; ~**dynamics** *npl* Thermodynamik *f*.

thermometer [θə'mɒmɪtəʳ] *n* Thermometer *nt*.

thermos ® ['θɜːməs] *n (also* ~ **flask** *or* **bottle** US) Thermosflasche *f*.

thermostat ['θɜːməstæt] *n* Thermostat *m*.

thesaurus [θɪ'sɔːrəs] *n* Thesaurus *m*.

these [ðiːz] *adj, pron* diese; *see* **this**.

thesis ['θiːsɪs] *n, pl* **theses** ['θiːsiːz] **(a)** *(argument)* These *f*. **(b)** *(Univ) (for PhD)* Dissertation, Doktorarbeit *(col) f*; *(for diploma)* Diplomarbeit *f*.

they [ðeɪ] *pers pron pl* **(a)** sie. ~ **are very good people** es sind sehr gute Leute; **it is** ~ *(form)* sie sind es; ~ **who wer** *(+sing vb)*. **(b)** *(people in general)* ~ **say that** ... man sagt, daß ...; ~ **are going to build a new road** man will *or* sie wollen eine neue Straße bauen. **(c)** *(he or she)* **if anyone reads this,** ~ **will notice** ... wenn jemand das liest, wird er bemerken ...

they'd [ðeɪd] = **they had; they would**.

they'll [ðeɪl] = **they will**.

they're [ðɛəʳ] = **they are**.

they've [ðeɪv] = **they have**.

thick [θɪk] **1** *adj* **(a)** *(+er)* dick; *wall, legs also* stark; *hair, fog, smoke also, forest, hedge, beard* dicht; *liquid, sauce etc* dick(flüssig); *darkness* tief; *crowd* dicht(gedrängt); *air* schlecht. **a wall three feet** ~ eine drei Fuß dicke *or* starke Wand; **the shelves were** ~ **with dust** auf den Regalen lag dick der Staub; **the hedgerows were** ~ **with flowers** die Hecken strotzten von wilden Blumen; **the air was** ~ **with fumes/smoke** die Luft war voller Abgase/Rauch. **(b)** *(col: stupid) person* dumm, doof *(col)*. **(c)** *(col: intimate)* **they are very** ~ sie sind dicke Freunde *(col)*. **(d)** *(col: much)* **that's a bit** ~! das ist ein starkes Stück *(col)*.

2 *n* **in the** ~ **of the crowd/it** mitten in der Menge/mittendrin; **to stick together through** ~ **and thin** zusammen durch dick und dünn gehen.

3 *adv* (*+er*) *spread, lie, cut* dick; *grow* dicht. **the snow lay** ~ es lag eine dichte Schneedecke; **offers of help poured in** ~ **and fast** es kam eine Flut von Hilfsangeboten; **to lay it on** ~ *(col)* (zu) dick auftragen *(col)*.

thicken ['θɪkən] **1** *vt sauce etc* eindicken. **2** *vi* **(a)** *(fog, hair, crowd, forest)* dichter werden; *(darkness)* sich verdichten; *(sauce)* dick werden. **(b)** *(fig: plot, mystery)* immer undurchsichtiger werden. **aha, the plot** ~**s!** aha, jetzt wird's interessant!

thicket ['θɪkɪt] *n* Dickicht *nt*.

thickly ['θɪklɪ] *adv spread, cut* dick; *wooded* dicht. **snow was falling** ~ dichter Schnee fiel.

thickness ['θɪknɪs] *n* **(a)** *see adj (a)* Dicke *f*; Stärke *f*; Dichte *f*; Dickflüssigkeit *f*. **(b)** *(layer)* Lage, Schicht *f*.

thick: ~**-set** *adj* gedrungen; ~**-skinned** *adj (fig)* dickfellig.

thief [θiːf] *n, pl* **thieves** [θiːvz] Dieb(in *f*) *m*. **to be as thick as thieves** dicke Freunde sein *(col)*.

thieve [θiːv] *vti* stehlen.

thieving ['θiːvɪŋ] **1** *adj* diebisch. **keep your** ~ **hands off my cigarettes** laß die Finger weg von meinen Zigaretten *(col)*. **2** *n* Diebstähle *pl*.

thigh [θaɪ] *n* (Ober)schenkel *m*.

thimble ['θɪmbl] *n* Fingerhut *m*.

thin [θɪn] **1** *adj (+er)* **(a)** dünn; *vegetation* gering, spärlich; *population, crowd* klein; *fog* leicht; *column* schmal. **his hair is getting** ~ sein Haar lichtet sich; **to be** ~ **on the ground** *(fig)* dünn gesät sein; **to vanish into** ~ **air** *(fig)* sich in Luft auflösen. **(b)** *(fig: weak, poor) voice, smile, disguise, plot* schwach; *excuse also* fadenscheinig. **2** *adv (+er) spread, cut, lie* dünn. **3** *vt paint, sauce* verdünnen; *trees* lichten; *blood* dünner werden lassen. **4** *vi (fog, crowd)* sich lichten; *(hair also)* schütter werden.

♦ **thin out 1** *vi (audience, crowd)* sich lichten. **the houses started** ~**ning** ~ die Häuser wurden immer spärlicher. **2** *vt sep hair, seedlings* ausdünnen; *forest* lichten; *population* verkleinern.

thine [ðaɪn] *(old)* **1** *poss pron* der/die/das deine. **2** *poss adj* Dein/Deine/Dein.

thing [θɪŋ] *n* **(a)** Ding *nt*. **a** ~ **of beauty/great value** etwas Schönes/etwas sehr Wertvolles; **I don't have a** ~ **to wear** ich habe nichts zum Anziehen; **poor little** ~ das arme (kleine) Ding!; **you poor** ~! du Arme(r)!

(b) *(clothes, equipment, belongings)* ~**s** *pl* Sachen *pl*; **have you got your swimming** ~**s?** hast du dein Badezeug dabei?; **they washed up the breakfast** ~**s** sie spülten das Frühstücksgeschirr.

(c) *(non material: affair, subject)* Sache *f*. **the odd/best** ~ **about it is** ... das Seltsame/Beste daran ist, ...; **it's a good** ~ **I came** nur gut, daß ich gekommen bin; **he's on to a good** ~ *(col)* er hat da was Gutes aufgetan *(col)*; **what a (silly)** ~ **to do** wie kann man nur so was (Dummes) tun! *(col)*; **there is one/another** ~ **I want to ask you** eines/und noch etwas möchte ich Sie fragen; **the** ~**s you do/say!** was du so machst/sagst!; **I must be hearing/seeing** ~**s!** ich glaube, ich höre/sehe nicht richtig; **all the** ~**s I meant to do** alles, was ich tun wollte; **to expect great** ~**s of sb/sth** Großes *or* große Dinge von jdm/etw erwarten; **I must think** ~**s over** ich muß mir die Sache überlegen; ~**s are going from bad to worse** es wird immer schlimmer; **as** ~**s stand at the moment** ... so wie die Dinge im Moment liegen; **how are** ~**s with you?** wie geht's (bei) Ihnen?; **to talk of one** ~ **and another** von diesem und jenem reden; **for one** ~ **it doesn't make sense** erst einmal ergibt das überhaupt keinen Sinn; **to tell sb a** ~ **or two** jdm einiges erzählen; **he knows a** ~ **or two** er hat etwas auf dem Kasten *(col)*; **it's just one of those** ~**s** so was kommt eben vor *(col)*.

(d) *(what is suitable, best)* that's just the ~ for me das ist genau das richtige für mich; **that's not the** ~ **to do** so was tut man nicht; **the latest** ~ **in ties** der letzte Schrei in der Krawattenmode; **that would be the honourable** ~ **to do** es wäre nur anständig, das zu tun; **I'll do that first** ~ **in the morning** ich werde das gleich morgen früh tun; **I'll do it first** ~ ich werde das als erstes tun; **last** ~ **at night** vor dem Schlafengehen; **the** ~ **is we haven't got enough money** die Sache ist die, wir haben nicht genug Geld; **to do one's own** ~ *(col)* tun, was man will; **she's got this** ~ **about Sartre** *(col) (can't stand)* sie kann Sartre einfach nicht ausstehen; *(is fascinated by)* sie hat einen richtigen Sartrefimmel *(col)*; **she's got a ~ about spiders** *(col)* bei Spinnen dreht sie durch *(col)*.

thingummybob ['θɪŋəmɪˌbɒb], **thingamajig** ['θɪŋəmɪˌdʒɪg], **thingummy** ['θɪŋəmɪ] *n* Dings, Dingsbums, Dingsda *nt or (for people) mf (all col)*.

think [θɪŋk] *(vb: pret, ptp thought)* **1** *vi* denken. **to ~ to oneself** sich *(dat)* denken; **~ before you speak/act** denk nach, bevor du sprichst/handelst; **to act without ~ing** unüberlegt handeln; **~ again!** denk noch mal nach; **well, you'd better ~ again!** das hast du dir (wohl) gedacht!; **it makes you ~** es macht einen nachdenklich; **I need time to ~** ich brauche Zeit zum Nachdenken; **now let me ~** laß (mich) mal überlegen; **it's a good idea, don't you ~?** es ist eine gute Idee, findest du nicht auch?; **just ~** stellen Sie sich *(dat)* bloß mal vor; **listen, I've been ~ing, ...** hör mal, ich habe mir überlegt, ...

2 *vt* **(a)** denken; *(be of opinion also)* glauben, meinen. **I ~ it's too late** ich glaube, es ist zu spät; **I ~ I can do it** ich denke, daß ich es schaffen kann; **well, I *think* it was there!** nun, ich glaube zumindest, daß es da war!; **and what do you ~?** asked the interviewer und was meinen Sie? fragte der Interviewer; **I ~ you'd better go/ accept** ich denke, Sie gehen jetzt besser/Sie stimmen lieber zu; **I ~ so** ich denke *or* glaube (schon); **I don't ~ so** ich denke *or* glaube nicht; **I should ~ so/not!** das will ich (aber) auch gemeint haben/das will ich auch nicht hoffen; **I hardly ~ that/~ it likely that ...** ich glaube kaum, daß .../ich halte es nicht für wahrscheinlich, daß ...; **I wouldn't have thought you would do such a thing** ich hätte nie geglaubt, daß Sie so etwas tun würden; **I ~ I'll go for a walk** ich glaube, ich mache einen Spaziergang; **you must ~ me very rude** Sie müssen mich für sehr unhöflich halten; **he ~s he's intelligent, he ~s himself intelligent** er hält sich für intelligent; **they are thought to be rich** man hält sie für reich.

(b) *(imagine)* sich *(dat)* denken, sich *(dat)* vorstellen. **I don't know what to ~** ich weiß nicht, was ich davon halten soll; **that's what you ~!** denkste! *(col)*; **that's what he ~s** hat der eine Ahnung! *(col)*; **who do you ~ you are!** wofür hältst du dich eigentlich?; **anyone would ~ he was dying** man könnte beinahe glauben, er läge im Sterben; **who would have thought it?** wer hätte das gedacht?; **to ~ that she's only ten!** wenn man sich *(dat)* vorstellt, daß sie erst zehn ist; **to ~ how to do sth** sich *(dat)* überlegen, wie man etw macht; **I never thought to ask you** ich habe gar nicht daran gedacht, Sie zu fragen; **I thought as much/I thought so** das habe ich mir schon gedacht.

3 *n* **have a ~ about** it denken Sie mal darüber nach.

♦ **think about** *vi +prep obj* **(a)** *(reflect on)* idea, suggestion nachdenken über (+*acc*). **OK, I'll ~ ~ it** okay, ich überlege es mir; **what are you ~ing ~?** woran denken Sie gerade?; **it's worth ~ing ~** das ist überlegenswert, das wäre zu überlegen; **to ~ twice ~ sth** sich *(dat)* etw zweimal überlegen; **that'll give him something to ~ ~** das wird ihm zu denken geben. **(b)** **we're ~ing ~ a holiday in Spain** wir denken daran, in Spanien Urlaub zu machen. **(c)** = **think of (a, f).**

♦ **think ahead** *vi* vorausdenken; *(anticipate: driver etc)* Voraussicht walten lassen.

♦ **think of** *vi +prep obj* **(a)** *(consider)* denken an (+*acc*). **he has his family to ~ ~** er muß an seine Familie denken; **to ~ ~ sb's feelings** auf jds Gefühle *(acc)* Rücksicht nehmen; **he ~s ~ nobody but himself** er denkt bloß an sich.

(b) *(remember)* denken an (+*acc*). **will you ~ ~ me sometimes?** wirst du manchmal an mich denken?; **I can't ~ ~ her name** ich kann mich nicht an ihren Namen erinnern.

(c) *(imagine)* sich *(dat)* vorstellen, bedenken. **~ ~ the cost of all that!** denk dir bloß, was das alles kostet.

(d) *(entertain possibility of)* **she'd never ~ ~ getting married** sie denkt gar nicht daran zu heiraten; **he'd never ~ ~ such a thing** so etwas würde ihm nicht im Traum einfallen.

(e) *(devise, suggest)* solution, idea, scheme sich *(dat)* ausdenken. **who thought ~ that idea/plan?** wer ist auf diese Idee gekommen/wer hat sich diesen Plan ausgedacht?

(f) *(have opinion of)* halten von. **what do you ~ ~ him?** was halten Sie davon/von ihm?; **to ~ highly ~ sb/sth** viel von jdm/etw halten; **I told him what I thought ~ him** ich habe ihm gründlich die *or* meine Meinung gesagt.

♦ **think out** *vt sep* plan durchdenken; *(come up with)* solution sich *(dat)* ausdenken.

♦ **think over** *vt sep* offer sich *(dat)* überlegen.

♦ **think through** *vt sep* (gründlich) durchdenken.

♦ **think up** *vt sep* sich *(dat)* ausdenken. **who thought ~ that idea?** wer ist auf die Idee gekommen?

thinkable ['θɪŋkəbl] *adj* denkbar.

thinker ['θɪŋkəʳ] *n* Denker(in *f*) *m*.

thinking ['θɪŋkɪŋ] **1** *adj* denkend. **all ~ men agree with me** alle vernünftigen Menschen werden mit mir übereinstimmen. **2** *n* **to my way of ~** meiner Meinung nach; **this calls for some quick ~** hier muß eine schnelle Lösung gefunden werden.

thinly ['θɪnlɪ] *adv* **(a)** dünn; wooded spärlich. **(b)** *(fig)* disguised kaum, dürftig; smile schwach.

thin-skinned ['θɪnskɪnd] *adj (fig)* dünnhäutig.

third [θɜːd] **1** *adj* dritte(r,s). **she was** *or* **came ~ in her class/in the race** sie war die Drittbeste in der Klasse/sie belegte den dritten Platz beim Rennen; **~ time lucky** beim dritten Anlauf gelingt's! **2** *n* **(a)** *(of series)* Dritte(r,s); *(fraction)* Drittel *nt*. **(b)** *(Mus)* Terz *f*. **(c)** *(Aut: ~ gear)* dritter Gang; see sixth.

third: **~-class 1** *adv* dritter Klasse; **2** *adj (lit)* dritter Klasse; *(fig)* drittklassig; **~-degree burns** *npl (Med)* Verbrennungen *pl* dritten Grades.

thirdly ['θɜːdlɪ] *adv* drittens.

third: **~ party** *n* Dritte(r) *m*, dritte Person; **~-party 1** *adj attr* Haftpflicht-; **2** *adv* **to be insured ~-party** haftpflichtversichert sein; **~ person** *adj* in der dritten Person; **~-rate** *adj* drittklassig; **T~ World 1** *n* Dritte Welt *f*; **2** *adj attr* der Dritten Welt.

thirst [θɜːst] **1** *n* Durst *m*. **~ for knowledge/ revenge/adventure/love** Wissensdurst *m*/Rachsucht *f*/Abenteuerlust *f*/Liebeshunger *m*; **to die of ~** verdursten. **2** *vi (fig)* **to ~ for revenge** etc nach Rache *etc* dürsten.

thirsty ['θɜːstɪ] *adj* (+*er*) durstig. **to be ~** Durst haben; **~ for praise/love** begierig auf Lob/nach Liebe; **it's ~ work** diese Arbeit macht durstig.

thirteen ['θɜː'tiːn] **1** *adj* dreizehn. **2** *n* Dreizehn *f*.

thirteenth ['θɜː'tiːnθ] *adj* dreizehnte(r, s); see sixteenth.

thirtieth ['θɜːtɪɪθ] *adj* dreißigste(r, s); see sixtieth.

thirty ['θɜːtɪ] **1** *adj* dreißig. **2** *n* Dreißig *f*; see sixty.

this [ðɪs] **1** *dem pron, pl* **these** dies, das. **what is ~?** was ist das (hier)?; **who is ~?** wer ist das?; **these are my children** das sind meine Kinder; **~ is where I live** hier wohne ich; **do you like ~?** gefällt dir das?; **I prefer ~** ich mag dies(es) lieber; **~ is to certify that ...** hiermit wird bestätigt, daß ...; **under/in front of** etc **~** darunter/ davor etc; **what's all ~?** soll das?; **we were talking of ~ and that** wir haben über dies und das geredet; **~, that and the other** alles mögliche; **will you take ~ or that?** nehmen Sie dieses hier oder das da?; **it was like ~** es war so;

~ **is Mary** (speaking) hier (ist) Mary.
2 *dem adj*, *pl* **these** diese(r, s). ~ **week/month/
year** diese Woche/diesen Monat/dieses Jahr; ~
evening heute abend; ~ **time last week** letzte
Woche um diese Zeit; ~ **time** diesmal, dieses
Mal; **these days** heutzutage.
3 *dem adv* so. **it was** ~ **long** es war so lang; ~
far *(time)* bis jetzt; *(place)* so weit; ~ **much is
certain** soviel ist sicher.

thistle ['θɪsl] *n* Distel *f.*
thong [θɒŋ] *n (of whip)* Peitschenschnur *f*; *(fastening)* Lederriemen *m.*
thorax ['θɔːræks] *n* Brustkorb *m.*
thorn [θɔːn] *n* Dorn *m*; *(shrub)* Dornenstrauch *m.* **to
be a** ~ **in sb's flesh** *or* **side** *(fig)* jdm ein Dorn im
Auge sein.
thorny ['θɔːnɪ] *adj (+er) (lit)* dornig; *(fig)* haarig.
thorough ['θʌrə] *adj* gründlich; *knowledge also*
solide; *rascal* ausgemacht.
thorough: ~**bred 1** *n* reinrassiges Tier; *(horse)*
Vollblüter *m*; **2** *adj* reinrassig; *horse* Vollblut-;
dog Rasse-; ~**fare** *n* Durchgangsstraße *f*; **"no
~fare"** „Durchfahrt verboten"; ~**going** *adj
changes* gründlich; *revision* grundlegend; *reform*
durchgreifend.
thoroughly ['θʌrəlɪ] *adv* **(a)** gründlich. **(b)**
(extremely) durch und durch, von Grund auf. ~
boring ausgesprochen langweilig; **I'm** ~
ashamed ich schäme mich zutiefst.
thoroughness ['θʌrənɪs] *n* Gründlichkeit *f.*
those [ðəʊz] *pl of* **that 1** *dem pron* **whose are** ~?
wem gehören diese da?; ~ **are the girls** das (da)
or dies(es) sind die Mädchen; **above** ~ darüber; ~
who want to go, may wer möchte, kann gehen;
one of ~ **who ...** einer/eine von denjenigen, die
...; **two of** ~ **please** zwei davon bitte; **there are** ~
who say ... einige sagen ... **2** *dem adj* diese *or* die
(da), jene *(old, liter)*. **what are** ~ **men doing?** was
machen diese Männer da?; **it was just one of** ~
days/things das war wieder so ein Tag/so eine
Sache.
thou [ðaʊ] *pers pron (old)* Du.
though [ðəʊ] **1** *conj* **(a)** obwohl. **even** ~ obwohl; ~
poor she is generous obwohl sie arm ist, ist sie
großzügig; **strange** ~ **it may seem ...** so seltsam
es auch scheinen mag ... **(b) as** ~ als ob. **2** *adv* **(a)**
(nevertheless) doch. **he didn't do it** ~ er hat es
aber (doch) nicht gemacht; **nice day** ~ **rather
windy** ~ schönes Wetter — aber ziemlich
windig. **(b)** *(really)* **but will he** ~? tatsächlich?,
wirklich?
thought [θɔːt] **1** *pret, ptp of* **think.**
2 *n* **(a)** *no pl* Denken *nt.* **to spend hours in** ~
stundenlang in Gedanken (vertieft) sein; **to be
lost in** ~ in Gedanken sein; **modern** ~ das
moderne Denken.
(b) *(idea, opinion)* Gedanke *m*; *(sudden)* Einfall *m.* **he didn't express any** ~**s on the matter** er
hat keine Ansichten zu diesem Thema geäußert;
that's a ~! *(amazing)* man stelle sich das mal
vor!; *(problem to be considered)* das ist wahr!;
(good idea) das ist ein guter Gedanke; **what a** ~!
was für eine Vorstellung!; **I've just had a** ~ *(col)*
mir ist gerade etwas eingefallen; **on second** ~**s**
wenn man sich das noch mal überlegt; **his one** ~
was ... sein einziger Gedanke war ...; **it's the** ~
that counts, not how much you spend es kommt
nur auf die Idee an, nicht auf den Preis; **to
collect one's** ~**s** sich sammeln; **the very** ~ **of it**
der bloße Gedanke (daran).
(c) *no pl (care, consideration)* Nachdenken *nt.*
to give some ~ **to sth** sich *(dat)* Gedanken über
etw *(acc)* machen; **after much** ~ nach langer
Überlegung; **without** ~ **for sb/oneself** ohne an
jdn/sich selbst zu denken; **I never gave it a** ~ ich
habe mir nie Gedanken darüber gemacht.
thoughtful ['θɔːtfʊl] *adj* **(a)** *(full of thought)* expres-
sion, person nachdenklich; *remark, analysis, book*

gut durchdacht; *present* gut ausgedacht. **(b)**
(considerate) rücksichtsvoll; *(attentive, helpful)*
aufmerksam. **it was very** ~ **of you to ...** es war
sehr aufmerksam von Ihnen, zu ...
thoughtfully ['θɔːtfəlɪ] *adv* **(a)** *say, look* nachdenklich. **(b)** *(with much thought)* mit viel Überlegung. **a** ~ **written book** ein wohldurchdachtes
Buch. **(c)** *(considerately)* rücksichtsvoll;
(attentively, helpfully) aufmerksam.
thoughtless ['θɔːtlɪs] *adj* **(a)** gedankenlos; *(inconsiderate)* rücksichtslos. **(b)** ~ **of the danger,**
he leapt ungeachtet der Gefahr sprang er.
thousand ['θaʊzənd] **1** *adj* tausend. **a** ~**/two** ~
(ein)tausend/zweitausend; **a** ~ **times** tausend-
mal; **a** ~ **and one/two** tausend(und)eins/
tausend(und)zwei. **2** *n* Tausend *nt.* **the** ~**s** *(Math)*
die Tausender *pl*; **there were** ~**s of people** es
waren Tausende (von Menschen) da; **the year**
three ~ das Jahr dreitausend; **people arrived in**
their ~**s** die Menschen kamen zu Tausenden.
thousandth ['θaʊzəntθ] **1** *adj* tausendste(r, s). **2** *n*
(in series) Tausendste(r, s); *(fraction)* Tausend-
stel *nt*; *see* **sixth.**
thrash [θræʃ] **1** *vt* **(a)** *(beat)* verprügeln; *donkey etc*
einschlagen auf *(+acc).* **(b)** *(Sport col)* opponent
(vernichtend) schlagen. **(c)** *(move wildly)* **arms**
schlagen mit; *legs* strampeln mit. **2** *vi* **to** ~ **about**
or **around** um sich schlagen; *(in bed)* sich herumwerfen; *(fish)* zappeln.
♦ **thrash out** *vt sep problem* ausdiskutieren.
thrashing ['θræʃɪŋ] *n* **(a)** *(beating)* Prügel, Schläge
pl. **to give sb a good** ~ jdm eine ordentliche
Tracht Prügel verpassen. **(b)** *(Sport col)* kom-
plette Niederlage. **to give sb a** ~ jdn vernichtend schlagen.
thread [θred] **1** *n* **(a)** *(Sew)* Garn *nt*; *(~ of cotton,*
wool etc) Faden *m*; *(strong ~)* Zwirn *m.* **to hang by**
a ~ *(fig)* an einem (seidenen) Faden hängen. **(b)**
(fig: of story) (roter) Faden. **to follow the** ~ **of an**
argument/a story dem Gedankengang einer
Argumentation/dem roten Faden (in) einer Geschichte folgen; **he lost the** ~ **of what he was**
saying er hat den Faden verloren; **to pick up the**
~**s of a conversation** den Gesprächsfaden wiederaufnehmen. **(c)** *(Tech: of screw)* Gewinde *nt.*
2 *vt* **(a)** *needle* einfädeln; *beads* aufreihen *(on auf*
+acc); *necklace* aufziehen. **(b)** **to** ~ **one's way**
through the crowd/trees sich durch die Menge/
zwischen den Bäumen hindurchschlängeln.
threadbare ['θredbɛəʳ] *adj* abgewetzt; *clothes also*
abgetragen; *carpet also* abgelaufen.
threat [θret] *n* Drohung *f*; *(danger)* Bedrohung *(to*
gen), Gefahr *(to für) f.* **is that a** ~? soll das eine
Drohung sein?; **to make a** ~ drohen *(against sb*
jdm)*; **under** ~ **of sth** unter Androhung von etw.
threaten ['θretn] *vt* **(a)** *person* bedrohen, drohen
(+dat); *revenge* androhen. **to** ~ **to do sth**
(an)drohen, etw zu tun; **to** ~ **sb with sth** jdm mit
etw drohen. **(b)** *(put in danger)* bedrohen,
gefährden. **the rain** ~**ed to spoil the harvest** der
Regen drohte die Ernte zu zerstören.
threatening ['θretnɪŋ] *adj* drohend; *weather,*
clouds also bedrohlich. **a** ~ **letter** ein Drohbrief
m; ~ **behaviour** Drohungen *pl.*
three [θriː] **1** *adj* *n* Drei *f*; *see* **six.**
three: ~**-D 1** *n* **to be in** ~**-D** dreidimensional sein;
2 *adj (also* ~**-dimensional)** dreidimensional; *film*
also 3-D- *attr*; ~**fold** *adj, adv* dreifach; ~**-piece**
suit *n (man's)* Anzug *m* mit Weste; *(lady's)*
dreiteiliges Ensemble; ~**-piece suite** *n*
dreiteilige Sitzgarnitur; ~**-ply** *attr wool* dreifach, Dreifach-; *wood* dreischichtig; ~**-point**
turn *n (Aut)* Wenden *nt* in drei Zügen; ~**-**
quarters 1 *n* Dreiviertel *nt*; **2** *adv* dreiviertel;
~**some** *n* Trio *nt*, Dreiergruppe *f*; *(Golf)* Dreier
m; **in a** ~**some** zu dritt; ~**-wheeler** *n (Aut)* drei-
rädriges Auto; *(tricycle)* Dreirad *nt.*
thresh [θreʃ] *vti* dreschen.

threshing ['θreʃɪŋ] n Dreschen nt. ~ **machine** Dreschmaschine f.

threshold ['θreʃhəʊld] n (lit, fig, Psych) Schwelle f. **we are on the** ~ **of a great discovery** wir stehen unmittelbar an der Schwelle zu einer großen Entdeckung.

threw [θruː] pret of **throw**.

thrift [θrɪft] n Sparsamkeit f.

thrifty ['θrɪftɪ] adj (+er) (a) (careful, economical) sparsam, wirtschaftlich. (b) (US: thriving) blühend.

thrill [θrɪl] 1 n Erregung f. **the** ~ **of her touch** der erregende Reiz ihrer Berührung; **it was quite a** ~ **for me** es war ein richtiges Erlebnis. 2 vt person (story, crimes) mitreißen, fesseln; (experience) eine Sensation sein für; (sb's touch, voice etc) freudig erzittern lassen; (sexually) erregen. **I was** ~**ed to get your letter** ich habe mich riesig über deinen Brief gefreut.

thriller ['θrɪlə^r] n Reißer m (col); (whodunnit) Krimi, Thriller m.

thrilling ['θrɪlɪŋ] adj aufregend; book, film spannend; sensation überwältigend; music mitreißend; (sexually) erregend.

thrive [θraɪv] vi (be in good health: animal, plant) (gut) gedeihen; (child also) sich gut entwickeln; (do well) (business) blühen, florieren; (businessman) erfolgreich sein.

♦ **thrive on** vi +prep obj **the baby** ~**s** ~ **milk** mit Milch gedeiht das Baby prächtig; **this plant** ~**s** ~ **sun and light** bei Sonne und Licht gedeiht diese Pflanze prächtig; **he** ~**s** ~ **hard work** harte Arbeit ist sein Lebenselixier.

thriving ['θraɪvɪŋ] adj plant prächtig gedeihend; person, business blühend; child gut gedeihend; businessman erfolgreich.

throat [θrəʊt] n Kehle f. **to grab sb by the** ~ jdn bei der Gurgel packen; **to cut sb's/one's** ~ jdm/sich die Kehle durchschneiden; **to cut one's own** ~ (fig) sich (dat) selbst das Wasser abgraben; **to clear one's** ~ sich räuspern; **to ram** or **force one's ideas down sb's** ~ (col) jdm seine eigenen Ideen aufzwingen.

throaty ['θrəʊtɪ] adj (+er) rauh.

throb [θrɒb] 1 vi (engine, heart, pulse) klopfen; (very strongly) hämmern; (drums, gunfire) dröhnen; (painfully: wound also) pochen; (fig: with life, activity) pulsieren (with vor +dat, mit). **my head is** ~**bing** ich habe rasende Kopfschmerzen. 2 n see vi Klopfen nt; Hämmern nt; Pochen nt.

throes [θrəʊz] npl **in the** ~ **of death** in Todesqualen pl; **to be in its final** ~ (fig) in den letzten Zügen liegen; **we are in the** ~ **of moving** wir stecken mitten im Umzug.

thrombosis [θrɒm'bəʊsɪs] n Thrombose f.

throne [θrəʊn] n Thron m; (Eccl) Stuhl m. **to come to the** ~ den Thron besteigen.

throng [θrɒŋ] 1 n a ~ **of people** Scharen pl von Menschen. 2 vi sich drängen. **to** ~ **around sb/sth** sich um jdn/etw scharen. 3 vt people ~**ed the streets** die Menschen drängten sich in den Straßen; **to be** ~**ed with** wimmeln von.

throttle ['θrɒtl] 1 vt (a) erdrosseln, erwürgen. (b) (fig) opposition unterbinden. 2 n (on engine) Drossel f; (Aut etc) (lever) Gashebel m; (valve) Drosselklappe f. **at full** ~ mit Vollgas.

through [θruː] 1 prep (a) (place) durch. **he went right** ~ **the red lights** er ist bei Rot einfach durchgefahren; **we're** ~ **that stage now** wir sind jetzt durch dieses Stadium hindurch; **to be halfway** ~ **a book** ein Buch zur Hälfte durchhaben (col); **that happens halfway** ~ **the book** das passiert in der Mitte des Buches. (b) (time) **all** ~ **his life** sein ganzes Leben lang; **he worked** ~ **the night** er hat die Nacht durchgearbeitet; **he slept** ~ **the film** er hat den ganzen Film hindurch geschlafen; **all** ~ **the autumn** den ganzen Herbst über.

(c) (US) **Monday** ~ **Friday** von Montag bis (einschließlich) Freitag.

(d) (means, agency) durch. ~ **the post** mit der Post; **absent** ~ **illness** abwesend wegen Krankheit; ~ **neglect** durch Nachlässigkeit; **to act** ~ **fear** aus Angst handeln.

2 adv (time, place) durch. **he's a liar** ~ **and** ~ er ist durch und durch verlogen; **to sleep all** ~ **night** ~ die ganze Nacht durchschlafen; **did you stay right** ~? sind Sie bis zum Schluß geblieben?; **to let sb** ~ jdn durchlassen; **to be wet** ~ durch und durch naß sein; **to read sth** ~ etw durchlesen; ~ **in the other office** (drüben) im anderen Büro; **the train goes** ~ **to Berlin** der Zug fährt bis nach Berlin durch.

3 adj pred (a) (finished) **to be** ~ **with sb/sth** mit jdm/etw fertig sein (col); **we're** ~ (have finished relationship) es ist aus zwischen uns; (have finished job) wir sind fertig; **I'm** ~ **with that kind of work** ich habe genug von dieser Arbeit; **are you** ~? sind Sie fertig? (b) (Brit Telec) **to be** ~ (to sb/London) mit jdm/London verbunden sein; **to get** ~ (to sb/London) zu jdm/nach London durchkommen; **you're** ~ Ihre Verbindung!

through: ~ **coach** n (Rail) Kurswagen m (for nach; (bus) direkte Busverbindung; ~ **flight** n Direktflug m.

throughout [θruː'aʊt] 1 prep (a) (place) überall in (+dat). ~ **the country/world** im ganzen Land/in der ganzen Welt. (b) (time) ~ **the war** den ganzen Krieg hindurch or über; ~ **his life** sein ganzes Leben lang. 2 adv (a) (in every part) **the house is carpeted** ~ das Haus ist ganz mit Teppichboden ausgelegt; **a house with electric light** ~ ein Haus, das in jedem Raum elektrisches Licht hat. (b) (time) die ganze Zeit hindurch or über.

through: ~**put** n (Ind) Leistung f; ~ **ticket** n **can I get a** ~ **ticket to London?** kann ich bis London lösen?; ~ **traffic** n Durchgangsverkehr m; ~ **train** n durchgehender Zug; ~ **way** n (US) Schnellstraße f.

throw [θrəʊ] (vb: pret **threw**, ptp **thrown**) 1 n (of ball, dice) Wurf m. **it's your** ~ du bist dran; **have another** ~ werfen Sie noch einmal; **a 30-metre** ~ ein Wurf m von 30 Metern. 2 vt (a) ball, stone werfen; rider abwerfen; opponent zu Boden werfen. **to** ~ **the dice/a six** würfeln/eine Sechs würfeln; **to** ~ **sth to sb** jdm etw zuwerfen; **to** ~ **sth at sb** etw nach jdm werfen; mud, paint etc jdn mit etw bewerfen; **he threw himself to the floor/ out of the window** er warf sich zu Boden/er stürzte sich aus dem Fenster; **to be** ~**n from the saddle** aus dem Sattel geworfen werden; **to** ~ **a glance at sb/sth** einen Blick auf jdn/etw werfen; **to** ~ **sb off the scent** jdn abhängen. (b) switch, lever betätigen. (c) (fig col: disconcert) aus dem Konzept bringen. (d) party geben; fit bekommen, kriegen (col). (e) pot etc formen.

♦ **throw about** or **around** vt always separate (a) (scatter) verstreuen; (fig) money um sich werfen mit. (b) (toss) herumwerfen; one's arms fuchteln mit; one's legs strampeln mit.

♦ **throw away** vt sep (a) (discard) rubbish wegwerfen. (b) (waste) verschenken; money verschwenden (on sth auf etw, on sb an jdn). (c) (say casually) remark beiläufig sagen.

♦ **throw back** vt sep ball, head, enemy zurückwerfen; curtains aufreißen. **to be** ~**n** ~ **upon sth** auf etw (acc) zurückgreifen müssen.

♦ **throw in** vt sep (a) extra (gratis) dazugeben. **with a tour of London** ~**n** ~ mit einer Gratistour durch London extra. (b) (Sport) ball einwerfen. (c) (fig) **to** ~ ~ **one's hand** aufgeben; **to** ~ ~ **the sponge** or **towel** das Handtuch werfen (col). (d) (say casually) remark einwerfen (to in +acc).

♦ **throw off** vt sep (a) (get rid of) clothes abwerfen; disguise, habits ablegen; pursuer abschütteln;

throw out — **ticket window**

cold loswerden.
♦**throw out** *vt sep* (a) *(discard) rubbish etc* wegwerfen. (b) *(reject) suggestion, bill (Parl)* ablehnen. (c) *person* hinauswerfen, rauswerfen *(col) (of aus)*. (d) *(make wrong) calculations etc* über den Haufen werfen *(col)*, durcheinanderbringen. **to ~ sb ~ in his calculations** jdn bei seinen Berechnungen durcheinanderbringen. (e) *chest* herausdrücken.
♦**throw together** *vt sep* (a) *(put hastily together) ingredients* zusammenwerfen; *clothes* zusammenpacken; *(make quickly)* hinhauen *(col); essay* runterschreiben *(col)*. (b) *(fate) people* zusammenführen.
♦**throw up 1** *vi* sich übergeben. **2** *vt sep* (a) *ball, hands* hochwerfen. (b) *(abandon) job* aufgeben; *opportunity etc* verschenken. (c) *(produce)* hervorbringen. **the meeting threw ~ several good ideas** bei der Versammlung kamen ein paar gute Ideen zutage.

throw: ~**away** *adj* (a) *(casual) remark* nebenbei gemacht; (b) *packet* Wegwerf-; *bottle* Einweg-; (c) *(cheap)* ~**away** *prices* Schleuderpreise *pl;* ~-**back** *n* (a) **his selfishness is a ~-back to an earlier generation** in ihm schlägt die Selbstsucht seiner Vorfahren wieder durch; (b) *(fig)* Rückkehr *(to zu)*
throw-in ['θrəʊɪn] *n (Sport)* Einwurf *m.*
thrown [θrəʊn] *ptp of* **throw.**
thru *pref, adv, adj (US)* = **through.**
thrush[1] [θrʌʃ] *n (Orn)* Drossel *f.*
thrush[2] *n (Med)* Soor *m (spec)*, Pilzkrankheit *f.*
thrust [θrʌst] *(vb: pret, ptp* ~) **1** *n* (a) *(of knife also)* Stich *m;* *(fig: of intellect)* Stoßkraft *f.* (b) *(Tech)* Druckkraft *f; (in rocket, turbine)* Schub(kraft *f*) *m.* (c) *(Mil: also* ~ **forward***)* Vorstoß *m.* **2** *vt* (a) *(push, drive)* stoßen. **to ~ one's hands into one's pockets** die Hände in die Tasche stecken. (b) *(fig)* **to ~ oneself (up)on sb** sich jdm aufdrängen; **I had the job ~ upon me** die Arbeit wurde mir aufgezwungen; **to ~ one's way to the front** sich nach vorne kämpfen. **3** *vi* stoßen *(at* nach); *(with knife)* stechen *(at* nach).
♦**thrust out** *vt sep, hand* ausstrecken; *head* vorstrecken; *chest* wölben. **she ~ her head ~ (of the window)** sie streckte den Kopf (zum Fenster) hinaus.
thud [θʌd] **1** *n* dumpfes Geräusch. **the ~ of his footsteps** seine dumpfen Schritte; **he fell to the ground with a ~** er fiel mit einem Plumps *(col) or* dumpfen Aufschlag zu Boden. **2** *vi* dumpf aufschlagen; *(move heavily)* stampfen. **the heavy door ~ded into place** mit einem dumpfen Knall fiel die Tür zu.
thug [θʌg] *n* Schläger(typ) *m.*
thumb [θʌm] **1** *n* Daumen *m.* **to be under sb's ~** unter jds Fuchtel *(dat)* stehen; **he gave me the** ~**s up/down** er gab mir zu verstehen, daß alles in Ordnung war/daß es nicht in Ordnung war; **it sticks out like a sore ~** das springt einem direkt ins Auge. **2** *vt* (a) *(col)* **to ~ a lift** per Anhalter fahren. (b) **a well ~ed book** ein Buch mit abgegriffenen Seiten.
thumb: ~**nail** *n* Daumennagel *m;* ~**nail sketch** *(drawing)* kleine Skizze; *(description)* kurze Skizze; ~ **print** *n* Daumenabdruck *m;* ~-**tack** *n (US)* Reiß- *or* Heftzwecke *f.*
thump [θʌmp] **1** *n (blow)* Schlag *m; (noise)* dumpfes Krachen. **2** *vt table* schlagen auf (+*acc*); *door* klopfen *or* schlagen an (+*acc*); *(repeatedly)* trommeln auf/an (+*acc*); *(accidentally) one's head* sich *(dat)* anschlagen. **he ~ed the box down on my desk** er knallte die Schachtel auf meinen Tisch; **I ~ed him (one) on the nose** *(col)* ich habe ihm eins auf die Nase verpaßt *(col)*. **3** *vi (person)* schlagen *(on the door/table* an die Tür/auf den Tisch); *(heart)* heftig schlagen; *(move heavily)* stapfen; *(object: fall loudly)* plumpsen *(col)*.

♦**thump out** *vt sep tune* hämmern.
thumping ['θʌmpɪŋ] *adj (also* ~ **great***) (col)* kolossal.
thunder ['θʌndər] **1** *n* (a) Donner *m.* **there is ~ in the air** es liegt ein Gewitter *nt* in der Luft. (b) *(fig) (of applause)* Sturm *m; (of cannons)* Donnern *nt; (of waves)* Tosen *nt.* **2** *vi (lit, fig)* donnern; *(waves, sea)* tosen. **the horses came** ~**ing up to the gate** die Pferde kamen aufs Tor zugeprescht. **3** *vt (shout)* brüllen, donnern.
thunderbolt *n (lit)* Blitz *m.* **the news came as something of a ~** *(fig)* die Nachricht schlug wie ein Blitz ein.
thunderous ['θʌndərəs] *adj* stürmisch; *voice* donnernd.
thunderstorm ['θʌndəstɔːm] *n* Gewitter *nt.*
thundery ['θʌndərɪ] *adj weather* gewittrig.
Thursday ['θɜːzdɪ] *n* Donnerstag *m; see* **Tuesday.**
thus [ðʌs] *adv* (a) *(in this way)* so, auf diese Art. ~ **it was that ...** so kam es, daß ... (b) *(consequently)* folglich. (c) *(+ptp or adj) reassured, encouraged etc* derart *(geh).* ~ **far** so weit.
thwart [θwɔːt] *vt* vereiteln; *robbery, attack also* verhindern; *person* einen Strich durch die Rechnung machen (+*dat*). **to ~ sb in sth** jdm etw vereiteln.
thy [ðaɪ] *poss adj (old) (before vowel* **thine***)* Euer/Eure/Euer *(obs);* (*to God)* Dein/Deine/Dein.
thyme [taɪm] *n* Thymian *m.*
thyroid ['θaɪrɔɪd] **1** *n (also* ~ **gland***)* Schilddrüse *f.* **2** *adj* Schilddrüsen-.
tiara [tɪˈɑːrə] *n* Diadem *nt.*
Tibet [tɪˈbet] *n* Tibet *nt.*
Tibetan [tɪˈbetən] **1** *adj* tibetanisch, tibetisch. **2** *n* (a) Tibetaner(in *f*) *m.* (b) *(language)* Tibetanisch *nt.*
tibia ['tɪbɪə] *n, pl* -**s** Schienbein *nt.*
tic [tɪk] *n (Med)* Tick *m,* nervöses Zucken.
tick[1] [tɪk] **1** *n* (a) *(of clock etc)* Ticken *nt.* (b) *(col: moment)* Augenblick *m,* Minütchen *nt (col).* **half a ~** eine Sekunde; **I'll be ready in a ~** *or* **two** ~**s** bin sofort fertig *(col).* (c) *(mark)* Haken *m.* **to put a ~ against a name/an answer** einen Namen/eine Antwort abhaken. **2** *vi* (a) *(clock)* ticken. **the minutes** ~**ed by** *or* **past** die Minuten verstrichen. (b) *(col)* **what makes him ~?** was geht in ihm vor? **3** *vt name,* answer abhaken.
♦**tick off** *vt sep* (a) *name etc* abhaken. (b) *(col: scold)* ausschimpfen *(col).*
♦**tick over** *vi* (a) *(idle: engine)* im Leerlauf sein. **the engine is** ~**ing** ~ **nicely** der Motor läuft ganz gut. (b) *(fig: business etc)* ganz ordentlich laufen; *(pej)* auf Sparflamme sein *(col).* **to keep things** ~**ing** ~ die Sache in Gang halten.
tick[2] *n (Zool)* Zecke *f.*
tick[3] *n (Brit col):* **on** ~ auf Pump *(col).*
ticker [tɪkər] *n (col: heart)* Pumpe *f (col).*
ticker tape *n* Lochstreifen *m.*
ticket ['tɪkɪt] *n* (a) *(rail, bus)* Fahrkarte *f,* Fahrschein *m; (plane* ~) Ticket *nt,* Flugschein *m; (Theat, for football match etc)* (Eintritts)karte *f; (cloakroom)* Garderobenmarke *f; (library)* = Buchzettel *m; (for dry cleaners etc)* Zettel *m; (luggage office)* (Gepäck)schein *m; (raffle* ~) Los *nt; (price* ~) Preisschild *nt; (for car park)* Parkschein *m.* (b) *(US Pol)* Wahlliste *f.* **he's running on the Democratic** ~ er kandidiert für die Demokratische Partei. (c) *(Jur: parking* ~) Strafzettel *m.* **to give sb a** ~ jdm einen Strafzettel geben *or* verpassen *(col).*
ticket: ~ **collector** *n (Rail)* Fahrkartenkontrolleur *m; (on train also)* Schaffner(in *f*) *m;* ~**holder** *n* ~**holders only through this door** *(Theat etc)* Eingang nur für Besucher mit Eintrittskarten; ~ **inspector** *n* (Fahrkarten)kontrolleur *m;* ~ **office** *n (Rail)* Fahrkartenschalter *m; (Theat)* Kasse *f;* ~ **window** *n (Rail)* (Fahrkarten)schalter *m; (Theat)*

Kasse *f*.

ticking-off ['tɪkɪŋ'ɒf] *n (col)* Anpfiff *(col) m*. **to give sb a ~** jdm den Marsch blasen *(col)*.

tickle ['tɪkl] **1** *vti* **(a)** kitzeln; *(wool)* kratzen. **this wool ~s my skin** diese Wolle kratzt (auf der Haut). **(b)** *(fig col) person* amüsieren. **to feel/be ~ed** sich gebauchpinselt fühlen *(col)*; **to be ~d pink** sie wie ein Schneekönig freuen *(col)*. **2** *vi* kitzeln. **3** *n* Kitzeln *nt*. **to have a ~ in one's throat** einen Hustenreiz haben.

ticklish ['tɪklɪʃ] *adj (lit) person* kitz(e)lig; *(fig) situation* heikel.

tidal ['taɪdl] *adj river, harbour* Tide-. **~ wave** *(lit)* Flutwelle.

tiddler ['tɪdləʳ] *n (Brit)* **(a)** *(fish)* winziger Fisch. **(b)** *(col: child)* Knirps *m*.

tiddly ['tɪdlɪ] *adj (+er)* **(a)** *(tiny)* winzig, klitzeklein *(col)*. **(b)** *(tipsy)* angesäuselt *(col)*, beschwipst.

tiddlywinks ['tɪdlɪwɪŋks] *n* Floh(hüpf)spiel *nt*. **to play ~** Flohhüpfen spielen.

tide [taɪd] *n* **(a)** *(lit)* Gezeiten *pl*, Tide *(N Ger) f*. **(at) high/low** **~** (bei) Hochwasser *nt or* Flut *f/* Niedrigwasser *nt or* Ebbe *f*; **the ~ is in/out** es ist Flut/Ebbe. **(b)** *(fig: trend)* **the ~ of history** der Lauf der Geschichte; **the ~ of public opinion** der Trend der öffentlichen Meinung; **to go or swim against/with the ~** *(lit, fig)* gegen den/mit dem Strom schwimmen.
♦ **tide over** *vt always separate* **that will ~ me ~ until tomorrow** damit werde ich bis morgen auskommen.

tidemark ['taɪdmɑːk] *n* Flutmarke *f*; *(man-made)* Pegelstand *m*.

tidily ['taɪdɪlɪ] *adv* ordentlich.

tidiness ['taɪdɪnɪs] *n see adj* Ordentlichkeit *f*; Sauberkeit *f*; Gepflegtheit *f*.

tidings ['taɪdɪŋz] *npl (old, liter)* Botschaft *(liter)*.

tidy ['taɪdɪ] **1** *adj (+er)* **(a)** *(orderly)* ordentlich; *(of ~ habits also)* sauber; *appearance* gepflegt. **to keep sth ~** etw in Ordnung halten; **to get a room ~** ein Zimmer aufräumen; **to make oneself ~** sich zurechtmachen. **(b)** *(col)* **a ~ sum** eine ordentliche Stange Geld *(col)*. **2** *vt hair* in Ordnung bringen; *room also* aufräumen.
♦ **tidy away** *vt sep* wegräumen, aufräumen.
♦ **tidy out** *vt sep* aufräumen, ausmisten *(col)*.
♦ **tidy up 1** *vi* **(a)** *(clear away)* aufräumen. **(b)** *(clean oneself)* sich zurechtmachen. **2** *vt sep books, room* aufräumen; *piece of work* in Ordnung bringen.

tie [taɪ] **1** *n* **(a)** *(also esp US: neck ~)* Krawatte *f*, Schlips *m (col)*. **(b)** *(fig: bond)* Beziehung, Bindung *f*; *(hindrance)* Belastung *f*. **~s of friendship** freundschaftliche Beziehungen *pl*; **business ~s** Geschäftsverbindungen *pl*; **family ~s** familiäre Bindungen *pl*; **I don't want any ~s** ich will keine Bindung; **pets can be a ~** Haustiere können eine Belastung sein. **(c)** *(Sport etc: result of match)* Unentschieden *nt*; *(match, competition ending in a draw)* unentschiedenes Spiel. **the match ended in a ~** das Spiel endete unentschieden; **there was a ~ for second place** es gab zwei zweite Plätze. **(d)** *(esp Ftbl: match)* Spiel *nt*.
2 *vt* **(a)** *(bind)* binden *(to an +acc)*; *(fasten also)* befestigen *(to an +dat)*. **my hands are ~d** *(fig)* mir sind die Hände gebunden; **to ~ a knot in sth** einen Knoten in etw *(acc)* machen; **we're very ~d in the evenings** wir sind abends sehr gebunden. **(b)** *(fig: unite, link)* verbinden.
3 *vi* **(a)** *(ribbon etc)* **it won't ~ properly** es läßt sich nicht richtig binden; **it ~s at the back** es wird hinten (zu)gebunden. **(b)** *(Sport)* unentschieden spielen; *(in competition, vote)* gleich stehen. **they ~d for the first place** *(Sport, competition)* sie belegten gemeinsam den ersten Platz.
♦ **tie back** *vt sep hair, door* zurückbinden.
♦ **tie down** *vt sep* **(a)** *(lit)* festbinden *(to an +dat)*;

tents verankern *(to in +dat)*. **(b)** *(fig: restrict)* binden *(to an +acc)*; *meaning* genau bestimmen.
♦ **tie in 1** *vi* dazu passen. **to ~ ~ with sth** zu etw passen; **it all ~s ~** das paßt alles zusammen; **the new evidence didn't ~ ~** das neue Beweismaterial paßte nicht ins Bild. **2** *vt sep plans* in Einklang bringen.
♦ **tie on** *vt sep* anbinden. **to ~ ~ sth ~(to) sth** etw an etw *(dat)* anbinden.
♦ **tie up 1** *vi* **(a)** **now it all ~s ~** jetzt paßt alles zusammen. **(b)** *(Naut)* festmachen. **2** *vt sep* **(a)** *parcel* verschnüren; *shoelaces* binden; *boat* festmachen; *animal* anbinden *(to an +dat)*; *prisoner, hands etc* fesseln. **(b)** *(settle) deal etc* unter Dach und Fach bringen. **to ~ ~ a few loose ends (of sth)** (bei einer Sache) ein paar Lücken schließen. **(c)** *(Fin) capital* (fest) anlegen. **(d)** *(link)* **to be ~d ~ with sth** mit etw zusammenhängen. **(e)** *(keep busy)* beschäftigen; *machines* auslasten. **he's ~d ~ all tomorrow** er ist morgen den ganzen Tag beschäftigt.

tie: **~ breaker** *n (Tennis)* Tiebreaker *m*; **~ clip** *n* Krawattennadel *f*; **~-on** *adj attr* Anhänge-, zum Anbinden; **~ pin** *n* Krawattennadel *f*.

tier [tɪəʳ] *n (of cake)* Etage, Stufe *f*; *(Theat, of stadium)* Rang *m*; *(fig: in hierarchy etc)* Stufe *f*, Rang *m*. **a three-~ hierarchy** eine dreigestufte Hierarchie; **to arrange sth in ~s** etw stufenförmig aufbauen.

tiff [tɪf] *n (col)* Krach *m (col)*. **to have a ~ with sb** mit jdm Krach haben *(col)*.

tiger ['taɪgəʳ] *n* Tiger *m*.

tight [taɪt] **1** *adj (+er)* **(a)** *clothes* eng; *join* dicht. **(b)** *(stiff, difficult to move) screw, bolt* festsitzend. **the top/cork is (too)** ~ der Hahn ist zu fest zu/der Korken sitzt fest; **the drawer is a bit** ~ die Schublade klemmt ein bißchen. **(c)** *(firm) screw, knot* fest angezogen; *tap, window* dicht; *lid, embrace* fest; *control, discipline* streng; *organization* straff. **to run a ~ ship** *(lit, fig)* ein strenges Regiment führen. **(d)** *(taut) rope, skin* straff. **(e)** *(leaving little space) weave* eng; *weave also* dicht. **(f)** *timing, race, match, money* knapp; *schedule* knapp bemessen. **(g)** *(difficult) situation* schwierig. **in a ~ spot** *(fig)* in der Klemme *(col)*. **(h)** *(col: miserly)* knick(e)rig *(col)*, geizig. **(i)** *(col: drunk)* voll *(col)*. **to get ~** blau werden *(col)*.
2 *adv (+er)* **hold, shut, screw** fest; *stretch* straff. **to hold sb/sth ~** jdn/etw festhalten; **to do sth up ~** etw gut befestigen; **sleep ~!** schlaf(t) gut!; **hold ~!** festhalten!; **to sit ~** sich nicht rühren.
3 *adj suf* **water-/air-~** wasser-/luftdicht.

tighten ['taɪtn] *(also ~ up)* **1** *vt* **(a)** *knot* fester machen; *screw* anziehen; *(re-tighten)* nachziehen; *rope* straffen; *(stretch tighter)* straffer spannen. **(b)** *restrictions* verschärfen. **2** *vt (rope)* sich spannen; *(knot)* sich zusammenziehen.
♦ **tighten up 1** *vi* **(a)** = **tighten 2.** **(b)** *(in discipline)* strenger werden, härter durchgreifen. **they've ~ed ~ on security** sie haben die Sicherheitsvorkehrungen verschärft. **2** *vt sep* **(a)** = **tighten 1 (a).** **(b)** *organization, procedure* straffen; *discipline, controls* verschärfen.

tight: **~-fisted** ['taɪt'fɪstɪd] *adj* knauserig *(col)*; **~-fitting** eng anliegend; **~-knit** *adj* *community* eng miteinander verwachsen; **~-lipped** *adj (lit)* mit schmalen Lippen; *(silent)* verschlossen.

tightness ['taɪtnɪs] *n see adj* **(a)** enges Anliegen; Dichtheit *f*. **(b)** Festsitzen *nt*. **(c)** fester Sitz; Dichtheit *f*; Strenge *f*; Straffheit *f*. **(d)** Straffheit *f*. **(e)** Enge *f*; Dichte *f*. **(f)** Knappheit *f*. **(g)** *(with money)* Knick(e)rigkeit *f (col)*, Geiz *m*.

tightrope ['taɪtrəʊp] *n* Seil *nt*. **to walk a ~** *(fig)* einen Balanceakt vollführen; **~ walker**

Seiltänzer(in *f*) *m*.

tights [taɪts] *npl* (*esp Brit*) Strumpfhose *f*. **a pair of ~** ein Paar *nt* Strumpfhosen.

tile [taɪl] **1** *n* (*on roof*) (Dach)ziegel *m*; (*ceramic ~*) Fliese *f*; (*on wall*) Kachel *f*; (*lino ~, polystyrene ~ etc*) Platte *f*; (*carpet ~*) (Teppich)fliese *f*. **to have a night on the ~s** (*col*) einen draufmachen (*col*). **2** *vt roof* (mit Ziegeln) decken; *floor* mit Fliesen/ Platten auslegen; *wall, bathroom* kacheln. **~d roof** Ziegel-.

till¹ [tɪl] *prep, conj* = **until**.

till² *n* (*cash-register*) Kasse *f*.

till³ *vt* (*Agr*) bestellen.

tiller ['tɪlə^r] *n* (*Naut*) Ruderpinne *f*.

tilt [tɪlt] **1** *n* (*slope*) Neigung *f*. **2** *vt* kippen, schräg stellen; *head* (seitwärts) neigen. **3** *vi* (*slant*) sich neigen. **this part of the machine ~s** dieser Teil der Maschine läßt sich kippen.

◆ **tilt back** 1 *vi* sich nach hinten neigen. **he ~ed ~ in his chair** er kippte mit seinem Stuhl nach hinten. **2** *vt sep* nach hinten neigen; *chair also, machine part* nach hinten kippen.

◆ **tilt forward** 1 *vi* sich nach vorne neigen; *machine part* nach vorn kippen. **he ~ed ~ in his chair** er kippte mit seinem Stuhl nach vorne. **2** *vt sep* nach vorne neigen; *chair also, machine part* nach vorne kippen.

◆ **tilt over** 1 *vi* (*lean*) sich neigen; (*fall*) (um)kippen. **2** *vt sep* (*slant*) neigen, schräg stellen; *barrel, chair* kippen.

timber ['tɪmbə^r] *n* (**a**) Holz *nt*; (*for buildings also*) Bauholz *nt*; (*land planted with trees*) (Nutz)wald *m*. (**b**) (*beam*) Balken *m*.

timbered ['tɪmbəd] *adj house* Fachwerk-; *land* Wald-.

timbre ['tɪmbə^r] *n* Timbre *nt*.

time [taɪm] **1** *n* (**a**) Zeit *f*. **how ~ flies!** wie die Zeit vergeht!; **only ~ will tell whether ...** es muß sich erst herausstellen, ob ...; **it takes ~ to do that** das braucht (seine) Zeit; **to take (one's) ~ (over sth)** sich (*dat*) (bei etw) Zeit lassen; **it took me all my ~ to** finish ich bin gerade noch fertig geworden; **in (the course of) ~** mit der Zeit; **in (next to) no ~** im Nu, im Handumdrehen; **to have a lot of/no ~ for sb/sth** viel/keine Zeit für jdn/etw haben; (*fig: be for/against*) viel/nichts für jdn/etw übrig haben; **to find/make ~ (for sb/sth)** Zeit finden/ sich (*dat*) Zeit nehmen (für jdn/etw); **to have ~ on one's hands** viel freie Zeit haben; **he lost no ~ in telling her** er verlor keine Zeit und sagte es ihr sofort; **to be in good ~** rechtzeitig dran sein; **don't rush, do it in your own ~** nur keine Hast, tun Sie es, wie Sie es können; **let me know in good ~** sagen Sie mir rechtzeitig Bescheid; **(for) a long/short ~** lange/kurz; **I'm going away for a long ~** ich fahre für längere Zeit weg; **it's a long ~ (since)** es ist schon lange her (, seit); **what a (long) ~ you have been!** du hast (aber) lange gebraucht!; **a short ~ later/ago** kurz darauf/vor kurzem; **in a short ~ they were all gone** nach kurzer Zeit waren alle gegangen; **for some ~ past** seit einiger Zeit; **all the ~** die ganze Zeit; **in two weeks' ~** in zwei Wochen; **for a ~** eine Zeitlang; **for the ~ being** (*provisionally*) vorläufig; (*temporarily*) vorübergehend; **to do ~** (*col: in prison*) sitzen (*col*).

(**b**) (*of clock, moment, season*) **what ~ is it?**, **what's the ~?** wie spät ist es?, wieviel Uhr ist es?; **my watch keeps good ~** meine Uhr geht genau; **it's ~ (for me/us etc) to go, it's ~ I was/we were etc** going es wird Zeit, daß ich gehe/wir gehen *etc*; **on ~/ahead of ~/behind ~** pünktlich/ zu früh/zu spät; **the project is ahead of ~/behind ~** das Projekt ist dem Zeitplan voraus/zeitlich im Rückstand; **to make good ~** gut vorankommen; **the trains are on ~** die Züge fahren pünktlich; **to be in ~ for sth** rechtzeitig zu etw kommen; **it's about ~** er hat (he has

arrived) es wird (aber) auch Zeit, daß er kommt; (*he has not arrived*) es wird langsam Zeit, daß er kommt; **(and) about ~ too!** das wird aber auch Zeit!; **at all ~s** jederzeit; **at any ~ during the day** zu jeder Tageszeit; **not at this ~ of night!** nicht zu dieser nachtschlafenden Zeit!; **there are ~s when ...** es gibt Augenblicke, wo ...; **at the or that ~** damals, zu der Zeit; **at the present ~** zur Zeit; **at one ~** früher, einmal; **at any/no ~** jederzeit/ niemals; **at the same ~** (*lit*) gleichzeitig; **they arrived at the same ~ as us** sie kamen zur gleichen Zeit an wie wir; **but at the same ~, you must admit that ...** aber andererseits müssen Sie zugeben, daß ...; **at ~s** manchmal; **by the ~ it had finished** als es zu Ende war; **by the ~ we arrive, there's not going to be anything left** bis wir ankommen, ist nichts mehr übrig; **by this ~** inzwischen; **by this ~ next year/tomorrow** nächstes Jahr/morgen um diese Zeit; **from ~ to ~** von Zeit zu Zeit; **from that ~ on** von der Zeit an; **since that ~** seit der Zeit; **until such ~ as ...** so lange bis ...; **this ~ of the day/year** diese Tages-/ Jahreszeit; **this ~ last year/week** letztes Jahr/ letzte Woche um diese Zeit; **to die before one's ~** zu früh sterben; **when the ~ comes** wenn es soweit ist; **the ~ has come (to do sth)** es ist an der Zeit (, etw zu tun); **the ~ has come for us to leave** es ist Zeit für uns zu gehen; **my ~ is (almost) up** meine *or* die Zeit ist (gleich) um; (*fig: life*) meine Zeit ist gekommen.

(**c**) (*occasion*) **this ~** diesmal, dieses Mal; **(the) next ~** nächstes Mal; **(the) next ~ I see you** wenn ich dich das nächste Mal sehe; **(the) last ~** letztes Mal, als er hier war; **every or each ~ ...** jedesmal, wenn ...; **many a ~, many ~s** viele Male; **for the last ~** zum letzten Mal; **he's not very bright at the best of ~s** er ist sowieso nicht sehr intelligent; **(and) (~) again, ~ after ~** immer wieder; **they came in one/three at a ~** sie kamen einzeln/jeweils zu dritt herein; **four at a ~** vier auf einmal; **for weeks at a ~** wochenlang.

(**d**) (*multiplication*) **2 ~s 3 is 6** 2 mal 3 ist 6; **it was ten ~s as big** es war zehnmal so groß.

(**e**) (*rate*) **you're paid ~ and a half for overtime** Sie bekommen 50% Zuschlag für Überstunden.

(**f**) (*era*) **in Victorian ~s** im Viktorianischen Zeitalter; **in olden ~s** in alten Zeiten; **in my ~** zu meiner Zeit; **he is ahead of his ~** er ist seiner Zeit (weit) voraus; **to be behind the ~s** rückständig sein; **to keep up with the ~s** mit der Zeit gehen; (*keep in touch*) auf dem laufenden bleiben; **~s are hard** die Zeiten sind hart; **~s are changing** es kommen andere Zeiten.

(**g**) (*experience*) **we had a good ~** es hat uns (*dat*) gut gefallen; **have a good ~!** viel Spaß!; **to have the ~ of one's life** eine herrliche Zeit verbringen; **to have an easy/a hard ~** es leicht/ schwer haben; **we had an easy/a hard ~ getting to the finals** es war leicht für uns/wir hatten Schwierigkeiten, in die Endrunde zu kommen; **to have a bad/rough ~ (of it)** viel mitmachen; **to give sb a rough ~** jdm das Leben schwermachen.

(**h**) (*rhythm*) Takt *m*. **(to be) in ~ (with)** im Takt (sein) (mit); **(to be/get) out of ~** aus dem Takt (sein/kommen); **3/4 ~** Dreivierteltakt *m*; **to keep ~ (beat ~)** den Takt angeben; (*keep in ~*) (den) Takt halten.

2 *vt* (**a**) (*choose ~ of*) **to ~ sth perfectly** genau den richtigen Zeitpunkt für etw wählen; **he ~d his arrival to coincide with ...** er legte seine Ankunft so, daß sie mit ... zusammenfiel; **the bomb is ~d to explode at ...** die Bombe ist so eingestellt, daß sie um ... explodiert; **you ~d that well** (*also iro*) du hast dir den richtigen Zeitpunkt ausgesucht. (**b**) (*with stop-watch etc*)

stoppen; *speed also* messen.
time: ~ **bomb** *n (lit, fig)* Zeitbombe *f;* ~**card** *n (for workers)* Stechkarte *f; (US:* ~*table)* Fahrplan *m;* ~**-consuming** *adj* zeitraubend; ~**-honoured** *or (US)* **-honored** *adj* althergebracht; ~**-lag** *n* Zeitdifferenz *f; (delay)* Verzögerung.
timeless ['taɪmlɪs] *adj* zeitlos; *(everlasting)* immerwährend.
time limit *n* zeitliche Begrenzung; *(for the completion of a job)* Frist *f.* **to put a** ~ **on sth** etw befristen.
timely ['taɪmlɪ] *adj* rechtzeitig. **a** ~ **piece of advice** ein Rat zur rechten Zeit; **that was very** ~ das war genau zur rechten Zeit.
timepiece ['taɪmpiːs] *n* Uhr *f.*
timer ['taɪmə'] *n* Zeitmesser *m; (switch)* Schaltuhr *f; (person)* Zeitnehmer *m.*
time: ~**saving** *adj* zeitsparend; ~ **signature** *(Mus) n* Taktvorzeichnung *f;* ~**table** *n (transport)* Fahrplan *m; (Brit Sch)* Stundenplan *m;* **to have a busy** ~**table** ein volles Programm haben; **what's on the** ~**table?** was steht auf dem Programm?; ~ **warp** *n* **we were in a** ~ **warp** wir hatten einen Zeitsprung gemacht.
timid ['tɪmɪd] *adj* scheu, ängstlich; *person, behaviour, words also* schüchtern.
timidity [tɪ'mɪdɪtɪ] *n see adj* Scheu *f;* Schüchternheit *f.*
timing ['taɪmɪŋ] *n* **(a)** *(choice of time)* Wahl *f* des richtigen Zeitpunkts *(of für),* Timing *nt.* **perfect** ~**, I'd just opened a bottle** ihr kommt gerade richtig, ich habe eben eine Flasche aufgemacht. **(b)** *(Aut) (mechanism)* Steuerung *f; (adjustment)* Einstellung *f.* **(c)** *(measuring of time)* Zeitmessung *f (of* bei*); (of race etc)* Stoppen *nt.*
timorous ['tɪmərəs] *adj* furchtsam, scheu.
timpani ['tɪmpənɪ] *npl (Mus)* Kesselpauken *pl.*
tin [tɪn] **1** *n* **(a)** Blech *nt; (Chem: metal)* Zinn *nt.* **(b)** *(esp Brit: can)* Dose, Büchse *f.* **a** ~ **of beans/ biscuits** ein Dose Bohnen/Kekse. **2** *vt (esp Brit) fruit etc* in Dosen konservieren.
tinfoil ['tɪnfɔɪl] *n (wrapping)* Stanniolpapier *nt; (aluminium foil)* Aluminiumfolie *f.*
tinge [tɪndʒ] **1** *n* **(a)** *(of colour)* Hauch *m,* Spur *f.* **(b)** *(fig: hint, trace)* Spur *f; (of sadness also)* Anflug *m.* **2** *vt* **(a)** *(colour)* (leicht) tönen. **(b)** *(fig)* ~**d with ...** mit einer Spur von ...; **our happiness was** ~**d with sorrow** unser Glück war getrübt.
tingle ['tɪŋgl] **1** *vi* kribbeln *(col) (with* vor +*dat); (with blows)* leicht brennen *(with* von*).* **to** ~ **with excitement** vor Aufregung beben. **2** *n see vi* Kribbeln *(col) nt;* leichtes Brennen. **she felt a** ~ **of excitement** sie war ganz kribbelig *(col).*
tinker ['tɪŋkə'] **1** *n* Kesselflicker *m.* **you little** ~**!** *(col)* du kleiner Zigeuner! *(col).* **2** *vi (also* ~ **about)** herumbasteln *(with,* on an +*dat).*
tinkle ['tɪŋkl] **1** *vi (bells etc)* klingen, bimmeln *(col); (on piano)* klimpern; *(breaking glass)* klirren. **2** *n* Klingen, Bimmeln *(col) nt no pl; (of breaking glass)* Klirren *nt no pl.* **to give sb a** ~ *(Brit col: on telephone)* jdn anbimmeln *(col).*
tinkling ['tɪŋklɪŋ] **1** *n (of bells etc)* Klingen, Bimmeln *(col) nt; (of piano)* Klimpern *nt; (of broken glass)* Klirren *nt.* **2** *adj see n* klingend, bimmelnd *(col);* klimpernd; klirrend.
tinned [tɪnd] *adj (esp Brit)* Dosen-, Büchsen-.
tinny ['tɪnɪ] *adj (+er) sound* blechern; *instrument* blechern klingend; *taste* nach Blech; *(pej) typewriter etc* schäbig.
tin: ~**-opener** *n (esp Brit)* Dosenöffner *m;* ~ **plate** *n* Zinnblech *nt.*
tinsel ['tɪnsəl] *n (foil)* Girlanden *pl* aus Rauschgold *etc.*
tin: ~**smith** *n* Blechschmied *m;* ~ **soldier** *n* Zinnsoldat *m.*
tint [tɪnt] **1** *n* Ton *m; (product for hair)* Tönung(smittel *nt) f.* **2** *vt* tönen.
tiny ['taɪnɪ] *adj (+er)* winzig, sehr klein; *baby, child*

ganz klein. ~ **little** winzig klein; **a** ~ **mind** *(pej)* ein Zwergenverstand *m.*
tip[1] [tɪp] *n* Spitze *f; (of cigarette)* Filter *m; (col: cigarette)* Filter(zigarette) *f.* **from** ~ **to toe** von Kopf bis Fuß; **it's on the** ~ **of my tongue** es liegt mir auf der Zunge; **it's just the** ~ **of the iceberg** *(fig)* das ist nur die Spitze des Eisbergs.
tip[2] **1** *n* **(a)** *(gratuity)* Trinkgeld *nt.* **(b)** *(warning, advice, Racing)* Tip *m.* **2** *vt* **(a)** *(give gratuity to)* Trinkgeld geben (+*dat).* **to** ~ **sb £1** jdm £1 Trinkgeld geben. **(b)** *(Racing)* tippen *or* setzen auf (+*acc).* **they are** ~**ped to win the election** *(fig)* sie sind die Favoriten für die Wahl.
♦ **tip off** *vt sep* einen Tip geben (+*dat) (about* über +*acc).* **he** ~**ped** ~ **the police** as to her whereabouts er verriet der Polizei, wo sie war.
tip[3] **1** *vt (tilt, incline)* kippen; *(overturn)* umkippen; *(pour, empty) liquid, load, sand, rubbish* schütten. **to** ~ **sth backwards/forwards** etw nach hinten/ vorne kippen *or* neigen; **he** ~**s the scales at 70kg** er bringt 70 kg auf die Waage; **it** ~**ped the scales in his favour** *(fig)* das hat für ihn den Ausschlag gegeben; ~ **the case upside down** stell die Kiste auf den Kopf; **to** ~ **sb off his chair** jdn vom Stuhl kippen. **2** *vi (incline)* kippen; *(dump rubbish)* Schutt abladen. **3** *n (Brit) (for rubbish)* Müllkippe *f; (for coal)* Halde *f; (col: untidy place)* Saustall *m (col).*
♦ **tip back** *vti sep* nach hinten kippen.
♦ **tip over** *vti sep (overturn)* umkippen.
♦ **tip up** *vti sep (tilt)* kippen; *(overturn)* umkippen; *(folding seat)* hochklappen.
tip-off ['tɪpɒf] *n (col)* Tip, Wink *m.*
tipper ['tɪpə'] *n (also* ~ **truck)** Kipplaster, Kipper *m.*
tipple ['tɪpl] *(col)* **1** *n* **he enjoys a** ~ er trinkt ganz gerne mal einen. **2** *vi* picheln *(col).*
tippler ['tɪplə'] *n (col)* Schluckspecht *m (col).*
tipsy ['tɪpsɪ] *adj (+er)* beschwipst *(col).*
tip: ~**toe 1** *n* **on** ~**toe** auf Zehenspitzen. **2** *vi* auf Zehenspitzen gehen; ~**top** *adj (col: first-rate)* tipptopp *pred (col),* erstklassig.
tirade [taɪ'reɪd] *n* Tirade, Schimpfkanonade *f.*
tire[1] [taɪə'] **1** *vt* müde machen. **2** *vi* **(a)** müde werden. **(b)** *(become bored)* **to** ~ **of sb/sth** jdn/ etw satt haben, jds/einer Sache *(gen)* überdrüssig werden *(geh);* **she never** ~**s of talking about her** son sie redet ständig über ihren Sohn.
tire[2] *n (US)* = **tyre.**
tired ['taɪəd] *adj* **(a)** *(fatigued)* müde; *cliché* abgegriffen. ~ **out** völlig erschöpft. **(b)** **to be** ~ **of sb/sth** jdn/etw leid sein; **to get** ~ **of sb/sth** jdn/ etw satt bekommen; **I'm** ~ **of telling you** ich habe es satt, dir das zu sagen.
tiredness ['taɪədnɪs] *n* Müdigkeit *f.* **the accident was a result of (his)** ~ (seine) Übermüdung war die Unfallursache.
tireless ['taɪəlɪs] *adj* unermüdlich.
tiresome ['taɪəsəm] *adj (irritating)* lästig, leidig; *(boring)* langweilig.
tiring ['taɪərɪŋ] *adj* anstrengend, ermüdend.
tissue ['tɪʃuː] *n* **(a)** *(Anat, Bot, fig)* Gewebe *nt.* **a** ~ **of lies** ein Lügengespinst *nt.* **(b)** *(handkerchief)* Papier(taschen)tuch *nt.* **(c)** *(also* ~ **paper)** Seidenpapier *nt.*
tit[1] [tɪt] *n (bird)* Meise *f.*
tit[2] ~ **for tat** wie du mir, so ich dir; **he was repaid** ~ **for tat** er bekam es mit gleicher Münze heimgezahlt.
tit[3] *n (col!: breast)* Titte *f (col!).*
titbit ['tɪtbɪt] *n (esp Brit)* Leckerbissen *m.*
titillate ['tɪtɪleɪt] *vt person, senses* anregen; *interest* erregen. **it** ~**s the palate** es kitzelt den Gaumen.
title ['taɪtl] *n* **(a)** Titel *m (also Sport); (of chapter)* Überschrift *f; (form of address)* Anrede *f.* **(b)** *(Jur) (right)* (Rechts)anspruch *(to* auf +*acc),* Titel *(spec) m; (document)* Eigentumsurkunde *f.*
titled ['taɪtld] *adj person, classes* mit (Adels)titel. **is**

he ~? hat er einen Titel?

title: ~ **holder** n (Sport) Titelträger(in f) m; ~ **page** n (Typ) Titelseite f; ~ **role** n (Theat, Film) Titelrolle f.

titter ['tɪtəʳ] **1** vti kichern. **2** n Gekicher nt.

tittle-tattle ['tɪtl,tætl] n Geschwätz nt; (gossip also) Klatsch m.

T-junction ['tiː,dʒʌŋkʃən] n "~ ahead" „Achtung, Vorfahrtsstraße".

TNT = trinitrotoluene TNT nt.

to [tuː] **1** prep **(a)** (in direction of, towards) zu. **to go** ~ **the station** zum Bahnhof gehen/fahren; **to go** ~ **the theatre/cinema** etc ins Theater/Kino etc gehen; **to go** ~ **France/London** nach Frankreich/London gehen/fahren; **to go** ~ **Switzerland** in die Schweiz gehen/fahren; **to to** ~ **school** zur Schule or in die Schule gehen; **to go** ~ **bed** ins or zu Bett gehen; ~ **the left** nach links; ~ **the west** nach Westen; **I have never been** ~ **Spain** ich war noch nie in Spanien; **hold it** ~ **the light** halte es gegen das Licht.

(b) (as far as, until) bis. **to count (up)** ~ **20** bis 20 zählen; **there were (from)** 40 ~ 60 **people** es waren 40 bis 60 Leute da; **it's 90 kms** ~ **Paris** nach Paris sind es 90 km.

(c) (+indir obj) **to give sth** ~ **sb** jdm etw geben; **a present from me** ~ **you** ein Geschenk für dich von mir; **who did you give it** ~?, ~ **who(m) did you give it?** wem haben Sie es gegeben?; **what is it** ~ **you?** was geht dich das an?; **he is kind** ~ **everyone** er ist zu allen freundlich; **he has been a good friend** ~ **us** er war uns (dat) ein guter Freund; **to address sth** ~ **sb** etw an jdn adressieren; **"To ..."** (on envelope etc) „An (+acc) ..."; **to pray** ~ **God** zu Gott beten; ~ **Lorna** (toast) auf Lorna (acc).

(d) (next ~, with position) **bumper** ~ **bumper** Stoßstange an Stoßstange; **at right angles/parallel** ~ **the wall** im rechten Winkel/parallel zur Wand; ~ **the west (of)/the left (of)** westlich/links (von).

(e) (with expressions of time) vor. **20 (minutes)** ~ **2** 20 (Minuten) vor 2; **at (a) quarter** ~ **2** um Viertel vor 2; **25** ~ **3** 5 nach halb 3; **it was five** ~ es war fünf vor.

(f) (in relation ~) **3** ~ **the 4th** (Math) 3 hoch 4; **by a majority of 10** ~ **7** mit einer Mehrheit von 10 zu 7; **they won by 4 goals** ~ **2** sie haben mit 4:2 (spoken: vier zu zwei) Toren gewonnen.

(g) (per) pro; (in recipes, when mixing) auf (+acc). **one person** ~ **a room** eine Person pro Zimmer.

(h) (in comparison ~) **that's nothing** ~ **what is to come** das ist gar nichts verglichen mit dem, was noch kommt.

(i) (concerning) **there's nothing** ~ **it** (it's very easy) es ist nichts dabei; **that's all there is** ~ **it** das ist alles.

(j) (accompanied by) **to sing** ~ **the guitar** zur Gitarre singen; **to sing sth** ~ **the tune of ...** etw nach der Melodie von ... singen.

2 (in infin) **(a)** ~ **begin** ~ **do sth** anfangen, etw zu tun; **he decided** ~ **come** er beschloß zu kommen; **I want** ~ **do it** ich will es tun; **I want him** ~ **do it** ich will, daß er es tut.

(b) (in order ~) **I did it,** ~ **help you** ich tat es, um dir zu helfen.

(c) (until) **he lived** ~ **be 100** er wurde 100 Jahre alt; **the firm grew** ~ **be the biggest in the world** die Firma wurde zur größten der Welt.

(d) (other uses) ~ **see him now, one would never think ...** wenn man ihn jetzt sieht, würde man nicht glauben, ...; ~ **be honest, ...** ehrlich gesagt, ...; **well, not** ~ **exaggerate ...** ohne zu übertreiben, ...; **he is not the sort** ~ **do that** er ist nicht der Typ dazu; **I have done nothing** ~ **deserve this** ich habe nichts getan, womit ich das verdient hätte; **who is he** ~ **order you**

around? wer ist er denn, daß er dich so herumkommandiert?; **there's no-one** ~ **help us** es ist niemand da, der uns helfen könnte; **what is there** ~ **do here?** was gibt es hier zu tun?; **the book is still** ~ **be written** das Buch muß noch geschrieben werden; **he's a big boy** ~ **be still in short trousers** er ist so ein großer Junge und trägt noch kurze Hosen; **I arrived** ~ **find she had gone** als ich ankam, war sie weg; **are you ready** ~ **go at last?** bist du endlich fertig?; **you are foolish** ~ **try it** du bist dumm, daß du das versuchst; **is it good** ~ **eat?** schmeckt es gut?; **it's too heavy** ~ **lift** es ist zu schwer zum Heben; **I'll try** ~ ich werde es versuchen; **you have** ~ du mußt; **I should love** ~ sehr gerne.

3 adj (slightly ajar) door angelehnt; (shut) zu.

4 adv ~ **and fro** hin und her; **walk** auf und ab.

toad [təʊd] n Kröte f; (fig: repulsive person) Ekel nt.

toad-in-the-hole ['təʊdɪnðə'həʊl] n Teigspeise mit Würsten.

toadstool ['təʊdstuːl] n Giftpilz m.

toady ['təʊdɪ] **1** n (pej) Kriecher m. **2** vi radfahren (pej col). **to** ~ **to sb** vor jdm kriechen.

toast¹ ['təʊst] **1** n Toast m. **a piece of** ~ eine Scheibe Toast; **on** ~ auf Toast; **as warm as** ~ (fig) mollig warm; ~ **rack** Toastständer m. **2** vt bread toasten; (on open fire) rösten.

toast² **1** n Toast, Trinkspruch m. **to drink a** ~ **to sb** auf jdn trinken; **to propose a** ~ einen Toast ausbringen (to auf +acc). **2** vt **to** ~ **sb/sth** auf jds Wohl or auf jdn/etw trinken.

toaster ['təʊstəʳ] n Toaster m.

tobacco [tə'bækəʊ] n Tabak m.

tobacconist [tə'bækənɪst] n (Brit) Tabak(waren)-händler m; (shop) Tabakladen m.

to-be [tə'biː] adj pred zukünftig. **the mother-/bride-/husband-** ~ die werdende Mutter/zukünftige Braut/der zukünftige Mann.

toboggan [tə'bɒgən] **1** n Rodel(schlitten) m. **2** vi Schlitten fahren, rodeln. **to go** ~**ing** Schlitten fahren, rodeln.

today [tə'deɪ] adv, n **(a)** heute. **a week/fortnight** ~ heute in einer Woche/zwei Wochen; **a year ago** ~ heute vor einem Jahr; ~ **is Monday** heute ist Montag; **from** ~ von heute an, ab heute; ~**'s paper/news** die Zeitung/Nachrichten von heute. **(b)** (these days) heutzutage. **the cinema/world** ~ das Kino/die Welt von heute.

toddle ['tɒdl] vi **(a)** wackeln. **the little boy** ~**d into the room** der kleine Junge kam ins Zimmer gewackelt. **(b)** (col) (walk) gehen; (leave: also ~ off) abzwitschern (col).

toddler ['tɒdləʳ] n Kleinkind nt.

to-do [tə'duː] n (col) Theater (col), Gedöns (col) nt. **to make a** ~ ein Theater machen (col) (about um).

toe [təʊ] **1** n **(a)** Zehe f, Zeh m. **to tread** or **step on sb's** ~**s** (lit) jdm auf die Zehen treten; (fig) jdm ins Handwerk pfuschen (col); **to keep sb on his** ~**s** (fig) jdn auf Zack halten (col). **(b)** (of sock, shoe) Spitze f. **2** vt (fig) **to** ~ **the line** spuren (col); **to** ~ **the party line** (Pol) sich nach der Parteilinie richten.

toe: ~**cap** n (Schuh)kappe f; ~**nail** n Zehennagel m.

toffee ['tɒfɪ] n (substance) Karamel m; (sweet) Toffee nt. **he can't sing for** ~ (col) er kann überhaupt nicht or nicht die Bohne (col) singen.

toffee: ~**apple** n kandierter Apfel; ~**-nosed** adj (Brit col) hochnäsig.

together [tə'geðəʳ] adv zusammen. **to do sth** ~ etw zusammen tun; (jointly) try, achieve sth etc also etw gemeinsam tun; **to sit/stand** etc ~ zusammen or beieinander sitzen/stehen etc; **to tie/fit** etc **two things** ~ zwei Dinge zusammenbinden/-setzen etc; **all** ~ **now!** jetzt alle zusammen!

togetherness [tə'geðənɪs] n (physical) Beisammensein nt; (mental, emotional) Zusammengehörigkeit f.

toggle ['tɒgl] n Knebel m; (on clothes) Knebelknopf m. ~ **switch** Kippschalter m.

toil [tɔɪl] **1** vi (liter: work) sich plagen (at, over mit). **2** n (liter: work) Mühe, Plage (geh) f.

toilet ['tɔɪlɪt] n (lavatory) Toilette f. **to go to the** ~ auf die Toilette gehen; **she's in the** ~/~**s** sie ist auf der Toilette.

toilet in cpds Toiletten-; ~ **bag** or **case** n Kulturbeutel m; ~ **paper** n Toilettenpapier nt; ~ **requisites** npl Toilettenartikel pl.

toiletries ['tɔɪlɪtrɪz] npl Toilettenartikel pl.

toilet: ~ **roll** n Rolle f Toilettenpapier; ~ **soap** n Toilettenseife f; ~ **water** n Duftwasser, Eau de Toilette nt.

to-ing and fro-ing ['tuːɪŋən'frəʊɪŋ] n Hin und Her nt.

token ['təʊkən] n **(a)** (sign) Zeichen nt. **as a** ~ **of/in** ~ **of** zum Zeichen (+gen); **by the same** ~ ebenso; **then by the same** ~ **you can't object to ...** dann können Sie aber auch nichts gegen ... einwenden. **(b)** (counter) Spielmarke f. **(c)** (voucher, gift ~) Gutschein m. **2** attr Schein-, pro forma. **it was just a** ~ **offer** das hat er/sie etc nur pro forma or so zum Schein angeboten; ~ **gesture** leere Geste; ~ **payment** symbolische Bezahlung; ~ **resistance** Scheinwiderstand m; ~ **strike** Warnstreik m; ~ **rent/fine** nominelle or symbolische Miete/symbolische Strafe.

told [təʊld] pret, ptp of **tell.** **there were 50 people there all** ~ es waren alles in allem 50 Leute da.

tolerable ['tɒlərəbl] adj (lit) erträglich; (fig: not too bad also) annehmbar, passabel (col).

tolerably ['tɒlərəblɪ] adv ziemlich. ~ **well** ganz annehmbar, ziemlich gut.

tolerance ['tɒlərəns] n (also Tech) Toleranz f (of, for, towards gegenüber); (towards children) Nachsicht f (of mit).

tolerant ['tɒlərənt] adj (of, towards, with gegenüber) tolerant; (towards children) nachsichtig.

tolerate ['tɒləreɪt] vt pain, noise, weather etc ertragen; person dulden; ideas tolerieren; behaviour, injustice etc also hinnehmen.

toleration [,tɒlə'reɪʃən] n Duldung f.

toll[1] [təʊl] **1** vti (bell) läuten. **2** n Läuten nt; (single stroke) Glockenschlag m.

toll[2] n **(a)** (bridge ~, road ~) Zoll m; (US Telec) (Fernsprech)gebühr f. **(b)** (deaths, loss etc) **the death** ~ **on the roads** die Zahl der Verkehrsopfer; **the earthquake took a heavy** ~ **of human life** das Erdbeben forderte viele Menschenleben.

toll: ~ **bridge** n gebührenpflichtige Brücke; ~ **call** n (US) Ferngespräch nt; ~**gate** n Schlagbaum m; ~ **road** n gebührenpflichtige Straße.

Tom [tɒm] n **any** ~, **Dick or Harry** (col) jeder x-beliebige.

tom [tɒm] n (cat) Kater m.

tomato [tə'mɑːtəʊ, (US) tə'meɪtəʊ] n, pl **-es** Tomate f.

tomato in cpds Tomaten-; ~ **juice** n Tomatensaft m; ~ **ketchup** n (Tomaten)ketchup m or nt; ~ **sauce** n Tomatensoße f; (ketchup) (Tomaten)ketchup m or nt.

tomb [tuːm] n Grab nt; (building) Grabmal nt.

tombola [tɒm'bəʊlə] n Tombola f.

tomboy ['tɒmbɔɪ] n Wildfang m.

tombstone ['tuːmstəʊn] n Grabstein m.

tomcat ['tɒmkæt] n Kater m.

tome [təʊm] n dickes Buch, Wälzer m (col).

tomfoolery [tɒm'fuːlərɪ] n Unsinn m.

tomorrow [tə'mɒrəʊ] adv, n morgen. **the day after** ~ übermorgen; ~ **morning** morgen früh; **(as) from** ~ ab morgen, von morgen an; **see you** ~! bis morgen!; ~**'s paper** die Zeitung von morgen.

tomtom ['tɒmtɒm] n Tamtam nt.

ton [tʌn] n **(a)** Tonne f. **(b)** ~**s** pl (col: lots) jede Menge (col); **to have** ~**s of time/friends** jede

---

Menge Zeit/Freunde haben (col); **it weighs a** ~ (fig col) es ist ganz schön schwer (col).

tone [təʊn] **1** n **(a)** (lit, fig) Ton m; (of colour also) Farbton m (of neighbourhood) Ansehen nt. **don't speak to me in that** ~ (of voice) in diesem Ton kannst du mit mir nicht reden; **Trevor lowered the** ~ (of the conversation) Trevor mußte natürlich wieder ausfallend werden. **(b)** (Mus) Ton m; (US: note) Note f. **2** vt (Phot: tint) einfärben, tonen (spec).

♦ **tone down** vt sep (lit, fig) abmildern; colour also abschwächen; criticism also, language mäßigen.

♦ **tone in** vi (im Farbton) harmonieren.

♦ **tone up** vt sep muscles kräftigen; person in Form bringen. **cycling keeps you** ~**d** ~ Radfahren hält einen in Form.

tone-deaf [,təʊn'def] adj **he's** ~ er hat kein Gehör für Tonhöhen.

tongs [tɒŋz] npl Zange f; **a pair of** ~ eine Zange.

tongue [tʌŋ] n **(a)** Zunge f. **to put** or **stick one's** ~ **out at sb** jdm die Zunge herausstrecken; **to lose one's** ~ (fig) die Sprache verlieren; **to hold one's** ~ den Mund halten; **her remark was** ~ **in cheek** ihre Bemerkung war ironisch gemeint; **to have a sharp** ~ eine scharfe Zunge haben. **(b)** (liter: language) Sprache f; (old, Bibl) Zunge f. **(c)** (of shoe) Zunge, Lasche f; (of land) Landzunge f.

tongue: ~**-in-cheek** adj attr remark witzelnd; ~**-tied** adj **to be** ~**-tied** keinen Ton herausbringen; ~**-twister** n Zungenbrecher f.

tonic ['tɒnɪk] n **(a)** (Med) Tonikum nt; (hair ~) Haarwasser nt; (skin ~) Lotion f. **it was a real** ~ **to see him again** (fig) es hat richtig gutgetan, ihn wiederzusehen. **(b)** ~ **(water)** Tonic(water) nt; **gin and** ~ Gin Tonic m.

tonight [tə'naɪt] adv (this evening) heute abend; (during the coming night) heute nacht. **see you** ~! bis heute abend!

tonnage ['tʌnɪdʒ] n Tonnage f.

tonne [tʌn] n (Brit) Tonne f.

tonsil ['tɒnsl] n Mandel f. **to have one's** ~**s out** sich (dat) die Mandeln herausnehmen lassen.

tonsillitis [,tɒnsɪ'laɪtɪs] n Mandelentzündung f.

too [tuː] adv **(a)** zu. **that's** ~ **difficult a question to answer** diese Frage ist zu schwer zu beantworten; ~ **much/many** zuviel inv/zu viele; **it's** ~ **much for her** es ist zuviel für sie; **don't worry** ~ **much** mach dir nicht zuviel Sorgen; ~ **right!** (col) das kannst du laut sagen (col); **all** ~ ... allzu ...; **only** ~ ... nur zu ...; **none** ~ ... gar nicht ..., keineswegs ...; **not** ~/**not any** ~ ... nicht zu/nicht allzu ...; **he wasn't** ~ **interested** er war nicht allzu interessiert; **I'm not/none** ~ **sure** ich bin nicht ganz/gar nicht sicher; **you're** ~ **kind** (iro) (das ist) wirklich zu nett von Ihnen; **none** ~ **soon** keineswegs zu früh.

(b) (also) auch. **he can swim** ~, **he** ~ **can swim** er kann auch schwimmen; **he can swim** ~ schwimmen kann er auch.

(c) (moreover, into the bargain) auch noch. **it was really cheap, and it works** ~! es war wirklich billig, und es funktioniert sogar!

took [tʊk] pret of **take.**

tool [tuːl] n (lit, fig) Werkzeug nt; (gardening ~) (Garten)gerät nt. ~**s** Werkzeuge pl; (set) Werkzeug nt; **that's one of the** ~**s of the trade** das gehört zum Handwerkszeug; **to have the** ~**s for the job** das nötige Werkzeug haben.

tool: ~**-box** n Werkzeugkasten m; ~ **kit** n Werkzeug(ausrüstung f) nt; ~**-shed** n Geräteschuppen m.

toot [tuːt] vt **to** ~ **one's horn** (driver) hupen.

tooth [tuːθ] n, pl **teeth** (Anat, Tech) Zahn m. **to have a** ~ **out/filled** sich (dat) einen Zahn ziehen/plombieren lassen; **to get one's teeth into sth** (lit) etw zwischen die Zähne bekommen; (fig) sich in etw (dat) festbeißen; **to show one's teeth** die Zähne zeigen (also fig); **to fight** ~ **and nail** bis

aufs Blut kämpfen; **to kick sb in the teeth** *(fig)* jdn vor den Kopf stoßen; **armed to the teeth** bis an die Zähne bewaffnet; **in the teeth of** great **opposition** trotz großen Widerstandes.
tooth *in cpds* Zahn-; ~**ache** *n* Zahnschmerzen *pl*; ~**brush** *n* Zahnbürste *f*.
toothed [tu:θt] *adj* gezahnt, mit Zähnen.
tooth: ~**less** *adj* zahnlos; ~**paste** *n* Zahnpasta *or* -creme *f*; ~**pick** *n* Zahnstocher *m*.
toothy ['tu:θɪ] *adj* (+*er*) **to be** ~ ein Pferdegebiß haben *(col)*.

top[1] [tɒp] **1** *n* **(a)** *(highest part)* oberer Teil; *(of spire, tree etc, fig: of league etc)* Spitze *f*; *(of mountain)* Gipfel *m*; *(of carrots)* Ende *nt*; *(of table, bed)* Kopfende *nt*; *(of road, beach)* oberes Ende. **which is the** ~? wo ist oben?; **the** ~ **of the milk** die Rahmschicht (auf der Milch); **at the** ~ oben; **at the** ~ **of the page/league/pile/stairs** *etc* oben auf der Seite/in der Tabelle/im Stapel/an der Treppe *etc*; **to be (at the)** ~ **of the class** der/die Beste in der Klasse sein; **near the** ~ (ziemlich) weit oben; **he's near the** ~ **in English** in Englisch gehört er zu den Besten; **he aims to reach the** ~ er will an die Spitze; **five lines from the** ~ in der fünften Zeile von oben; **from** ~ **to bottom** von oben bis unten; **to scream at the** ~ **of one's voice** aus Leibeskräften brüllen; **they were talking at the** ~(s) **of their voices** sie haben sich in voller Lautstärke unterhalten; **to go over the** ~ *(exaggerate)* zu viel des Guten tun; **to be over the** ~ *(exaggerated)* übertrieben sein; *(past it: person)* auf dem absteigenden Ast sein.

(b) *(upper surface)* Oberfläche *f*. **to be on** ~ oben liegen; *(fig)* obenauf sein; **it was on** ~ **of the cupboard** es war oben auf dem Schrank; **put it on** ~ **of the cupboard** leg es oben auf den Schrank; **on** ~ **of** *(in addition to)* zusätzlich zu; **things are getting on** ~ **of me** die Dinge wachsen mir über den Kopf; **and, on** ~ **of that** ... und zusätzlich ...; **it's just one thing on** ~ **of another** es kommt eines zum anderen; **he didn't see it until he was right on** ~ **of it** er sah es erst, als er ganz nah dran war; **to come out on** ~ sich durchsetzen; *(over rival)* die Oberhand gewinnen; **to talk off the** ~ **of one's head** *(col)* nur so daherreden; **to blow one's** ~ aus der Haut fahren *(col)*.

(c) *(working surface)* Arbeitsfläche *f*.
(d) *(bikini* ~, *blouse)* Oberteil *nt*.
(e) *(of jar, suitcase)* Deckel *m*; *(of bottle)* Verschluß *m*; *(of pen)* Hülle *f*; *(of car)* Dach *nt*. **hard/soft** ~ Hardtop *nt*/Weichverdeck *nt*.
(f) *(Brit Aut:* ~ *gear)* höchster Gang. **in** ~ im höchsten Gang.

2 *adj* *(upper)* obere(r, s); *(highest)* oberste(r, s); *branches, note, honours, price* höchste(r, s); *(best) driver, athlete, job* Spitzen-; *pupil, marks* beste(r, s); *entertainer, management* Top-. ~ **prices** Höchstpreise *pl*; **on the** ~ **floor** im obersten Stockwerk; **a** ~-**floor flat** eine Dachgeschoßwohnung; **the** ~ **right-hand corner** die obere rechte Ecke; **at** ~ **speed** mit Höchstgeschwindigkeit; **in** ~ **form** in Höchstform; **to be** ~ *(Sch)* Beste(r) sein; **the** ~ **people** *(in a company)* die Leute an der Spitze; *(in society)* die oberen Zehntausend.

3 *adv* **to come** ~ *(Sch)* Beste(r) werden.
4 *vt* **(a)** *(cover, cap)* bedecken. ~**ped by a dome** gekrönt von einer Kuppel.
(b) *(be higher than, fig: surpass)* übersteigen. **that** ~**s the lot** *(col)* das übertrifft alles; **and to** ~ **it all ...** *(col)* und um das Maß vollzumachen ...
(c) to ~ **a tree** die Spitze eines Baumes abschneiden; **to** ~ **and tail gooseberries** Stachelbeeren putzen.
♦ **top up** *vt sep glass, battery, tank* auffüllen. **to** ~ **the oil** Öl nachfüllen; **can I** ~ **you** ~? *(col)* darf ich Ihnen nachschenken?

top[2] *n* Kreisel *m*. **to sleep like a** ~ wie ein Murmeltier schlafen.
topaz ['təʊpæz] *n* Topas *m*.
top: ~**coat** *n* **(a)** *(overcoat)* Mantel *m*; **(b)** *(coat of paint)* Deckanstrich *m*; ~ **copy** *n* Original *nt*; ~-**flight** *adj* Spitzen-, erstklassig; ~ **gear** *n* höchster Gang; ~ **hat** *n* Zylinder *m*; ~-**heavy** *adj* *(lit, fig)* kopflastig.
topic ['tɒpɪk] *n* Thema *nt*. ~ **of conversation** Gesprächsthema *nt*.
topical ['tɒpɪkəl] *adj* *problem, speech, event* aktuell.
top: ~**less** *adj* (mit) oben ohne, Oben-ohne-; ~-**level** *adj* Spitzen-; ~**most** *adj* oberste(r, s).
topographic(al) [ˌtɒpə'græfɪk(əl)] *adj* topographisch.
topography [tə'pɒgrəfɪ] *n* Topographie *f*.
topping ['tɒpɪŋ] *n* *(Cook)* **with a** ~ **of cream/nuts** *etc* mit Sahne/Nüssen *etc* (oben) darauf.
topple ['tɒpl] **1** *vi* wackeln; *(fall)* fallen. **2** *vt* umwerfen; *(from a height)* hinunterkippen; *(fig) government* stürzen.
♦ **topple over** *vi* fallen *(prep obj* über +*acc)*.
top: ~-**ranking** *adj* von hohem Rang; *civil servant, officer* also hohe(r); *author, singer* Spitzen-; ~-**secret** *adj* streng geheim; ~**soil** *n* *(Agr)* Ackerkrume *f*.
topsy-turvy ['tɒpsɪ'tɜːvɪ] *(col)* **1** *adj* *(in disorder)* kunterbunt durcheinander *pred*; *(fig)* auf den Kopf gestellt. **it's a** ~ **world** es ist eine verkehrte Welt. **2** *adv* **to turn sth** ~ *(lit, fig)* etw auf den Kopf stellen.
top-up ['tɒpʌp] *n* *(col)* **would you like a** ~? darf man Ihnen noch nachschenken?
torch [tɔːtʃ] *n* *(lit, fig)* Fackel *f*; *(Brit: flashlight)* Taschenlampe *f*; *(blowlamp)* Schweißbrenner *m*.
tore [tɔː[r]] *pret of* **tear**[1].
torment ['tɔːment] **1** *n* Qual *f*. **to be in** ~ Qualen leiden. **2** [tɔː'ment] *vt* quälen; *(annoy, tease)* plagen.
tormentor [tɔː'mentə[r]] *n* Peiniger(in *f*) *m*.
torn [tɔːn] *ptp of* **tear**[1]
tornado [tɔː'neɪdəʊ] *n*, *pl* -**es** Tornado *m*.
torpedo [tɔː'piːdəʊ] **1** *n*, *pl* -**es** Torpedo *m*. ~ **boat** Torpedoboot *nt*. **2** *vt* torpedieren.
torpid ['tɔːpɪd] *adj* *(lethargic)* träge.
torpor ['tɔːpə[r]] *n* Trägheit *f*.
torrent ['tɒrənt] *n* *(river)* reißender Strom. **the rain came down in** ~**s** der Regen kam in wahren Sturzbächen herunter; **a** ~ **of abuse** eine Flut von Beschimpfungen.
torrential [tɒ'renʃəl] *adj* *rain* sintflutartig.
torrid ['tɒrɪd] *adj* *(lit, fig)* heiß; *heat, air, sun* sengend.
torso ['tɔːsəʊ] *n* Körper *m*; *(Art)* Torso *m*.
tortoise ['tɔːtəs] *n* Schildkröte *f*.
tortuous ['tɔːtjʊəs] *adj* *(lit) path* gewunden; *(fig)* verwickelt; *methods also, person* umständlich.
torture ['tɔːtʃə[r]] **1** *n* Folter *f*; *(fig)* Qual *f*. ~ **chamber** Folterkammer *f*. **2** *vt* *(lit)* foltern; *(fig: torment)* quälen, peinigen *(geh)*; *(fig: distort)* verzerren.
torturer ['tɔːtʃərə[r]] *n* *(lit)* Folterknecht *m*; *(fig: tormentor)* Peiniger(in *f*) *m*.
Tory ['tɔːrɪ] *(Brit Pol)* **1** *n* Konservative(r) *mf*, Tory *m*. **2** *adj* konservativ, Tory-.
toss [tɒs] **1** *n* Wurf *m*. **with a proud** ~ **of her head** mit einer stolzen Kopfbewegung; **to win/lose the** ~ *(esp Sport)* die Seitenwahl gewinnen/verlieren; **there is no point in arguing the** ~ **(with me)** es hat keinen Sinn, (mit mir) darüber zu streiten. **2** *vt* **(a)** *(throw)* ball werfen; *salad* anmachen; *(Brit) pancake* wenden *(durch Hochwerfen)*; *rider* abwerfen. **to** ~ **sth to sb** jdm etw zuwerfen. **(b)** *(move: wind)* schütteln, zerren an (+*dat)*. **the boat,** ~**ed (about) by the waves** ... das Boot, von den Wellen hin und her geworfen, ...; **to** ~ **(back) one's head** den Kopf zurückwerfen. **(c) to** ~ **a coin** eine Münze (zum Losen)

hochwerfen; **I'll ~ you for it** laß uns darum knobeln. **3** *vi* **(a)** *(ship)* rollen. **to ~ and turn (in bed)** sich (im Bett) hin und her werfen. **(b) to ~ for sth** um etw knobeln.

♦ **toss up 1** *vi* knobeln *(for* um*)*. **2** *vt sep* werfen. **to ~ sth ~ (into the air)** etw hochwerfen.

tot [tɒt] *n* **(a)** *(child: also* **tiny ~)** Knirps *(col)* m. **(b)** *(esp Brit: of alcohol)* Schlückchen *nt.*

♦ **tot up** *vt sep (esp Brit col)* zusammenzählen.

total ['təʊtl] **1** *adj* völlig, absolut; *sum, loss, number* Gesamt-; *war, eclipse, disaster* total. **what is the ~ number of rooms you have?** wie viele Zimmer haben Sie (insgesamt)?; **to be in ~ ignorance (of sth)** (von etw) überhaupt nichts wissen. **2** *n* Gesamtmenge *f;* *(money, figures)* Endsumme *f.* **a ~ of 50 people** insgesamt 50 Leute. **3** *vt* **(a)** *(amount to)* sich belaufen auf (+*acc*). **(b)** *(add: also* **~ up)** zusammenzählen *or* -rechnen.

totalitarian [,təʊtælɪ'tɛərɪən] *adj* totalitär.

totality [təʊ'tælɪtɪ] *n* Gesamtheit *f.*

tote[1] [təʊt] *n (col)* **the ~** der Totalisator.

tote[2] *vt (col: carry) sth heavy* schleppen; *gun* bei sich haben.

totem pole ['təʊtəm,pəʊl] *n* Totempfahl *m.*

totter ['tɒtə^r] *vi*   *(wobble before falling)* wanken; *(stagger)* taumeln; *(old man, baby)* tapsen; *(invalid, fig)* schwanken; *(economy)* kränkeln.

tottery ['tɒtərɪ] *adj* wack(e)lig; *person* tatterig. **a ~ old man** ein Tattergreis *m (col).*

touch [tʌtʃ] **1** *n* **(a)** *(sense of* ~) (Tast)gefühl *nt.* **to be cold/soft to the ~** sich kalt/weich anfühlen.

   (b) *(act of* ~*ing)* Berühren *nt*, Berührung *f; (of pianist, typist, piano, typewriter)* Anschlag *m.* **I felt a ~ on my arm** ich spürte, daß jd/etw meinen Arm berührte; **it opens at a ~** es öffnet sich auf leichten Druck.

   (c) *(skill)* Hand *f; (style also)* Stil *m.* **the ~ of a master** die Hand eines Meisters; **it has the ~ of genius/the professional ~** es hat etwas Geniales/ Professionelles; **he's losing his ~** er wird langsam alt; **a personal ~** eine persönliche Note.

   (d) *(stroke) (Art)* Strich *m; (fig)* Einfall *m.* **a book with humorous ~es** ein stellenweise humorvolles Buch; **a nice ~** eine hübsche Note; *(gesture)* eine nette Geste; **to put the finishing ~es to sth** einer Sache *(dat)* den letzten Schliff geben.

   (e) *(small quantity)* Spur *f; (of irony, sadness etc also)* Anflug *m.* **a ~ of flu** eine leichte Grippe.

   (f) *(contact)* **to be in ~ with** sb mit jdm in Verbindung stehen; **they were** *or* **got in ~ with us yesterday** sie haben sich gestern mit uns in Verbindung gesetzt; **to be/keep in ~ with** *(political) developments* (politisch) auf dem laufenden sein/bleiben; **I'll be in ~!** ich lasse von mir hören!; **keep in ~!** laß/laßt wieder einmal von dir/euch hören!; **to be out of ~ with** sb keine Verbindung mehr zu jdm haben; **to be completely out of ~ (with sth)** (in bezug auf etw *acc*) überhaupt nicht auf dem laufenden sein; **to lose ~ with** sb den Kontakt zu jdm verlieren.

   (g) *(Ftbl)* **to be in ~** im Aus sein.

   2 *vt* **(a)** berühren; *(get hold of also)* anfassen; *(press lightly also)* piano keys anschlagen; *brakes* antippen; *(brush against)* streifen. **to ~ glasses** anstoßen; **don't ~ that!** faß das nicht an!; **I was ~ing 100** most of the way ich fuhr fast ständig 100. **(b)** *(lay hands on)* anrühren. **the police/tax authorities can't ~ me** die Polizei/das Finanzamt kann mir nichts anhaben; **the paintings weren't ~ed by the fire** die Gemälde blieben vom Feuer verschont; **I never ~ whisky** ich rühre keinen Whisky an; **I don't want to ~ my savings** ich will meine Ersparnisse nicht anbrechen; **I wouldn't ~ those shares** ich würde meine Finger von den Aktien lassen. **(c)** *(concern)* berühren. **(d)** *(move emotionally)* rühren, bewegen; *(affect)* berühren; *(wound)* pride treffen. **deeply ~ed** tief gerührt *or*

bewegt. **(e)** *(equal)* **nobody can ~ him (for ...)** bei ... kommt keiner an ihn heran.

   3 *vi (come into contact)* sich berühren; *(estates etc: be adjacent also)* aneinandergrenzen. **"please do not ~"** „bitte nicht berühren".

♦ **touch down 1** *vi* **(a)** *(Aviat, Space)* aufsetzen. **(b)** *(Rugby, US Ftbl)* einen Versuch erzielen. **2** *vt sep ball* niederlegen.

♦ **touch (up)on** *vi* +*prep obj subject* kurz berühren, antippen.

touch-and-go ['tʌtʃən'gəʊ] *adj* **to be ~** riskant sein; **it's ~ whether ...** es steht auf des Messers Schneide, ob ...

touchdown ['tʌtʃdaʊn] *n* **(a)** *(Aviat, Space)* Aufsetzen *nt.* **(b)** *(Rugby, US Ftbl)* Versuch *m (Niederlegen des Balles im Malfeld des Gegners).*

touched [tʌtʃt] *adj pred (moved)* gerührt, bewegt.

touching ['tʌtʃɪŋ] **1** *adj* rührend. **2** *prep (form)* bezüglich (+*gen*) *(form).*

touch: **~line** *n (Sport)* Seitenlinie *f;* **~paper** *n* Zündpapier *nt;* **~-type** *vti* blindschreiben.

touchy ['tʌtʃɪ] *adj* empfindlich *(about* in bezug auf +*acc*); *(irritable also)* leicht reizbar; *subject* heikel.

tough [tʌf] *adj* (+*er*) **(a)** zäh; *resistant* widerstandsfähig; *cloth* strapazierfähig; *(towards others)* hart; *bargaining, opponent, struggle, district, policy, controls* hart. **to get ~ (with sb)** hart durchgreifen (gegen jdn); **~ guy** *(col)* (knall)harter Bursche *(col).* **(b)** *(difficult) task, problem* hart; *journey* strapaziös, anstrengend. **it was ~ going** *(lit, fig)* es war eine Strapaze; **to have a ~ time of it** nichts zu lachen haben; **it was ~ on the others** das war hart für die andern; **~ (luck)! Pech!**

toughen ['tʌfn] *vt* **(a)** *glass, metal* härten. **(b)** *(fig) person* zäh machen; *(physically)* abhärten.

toughness ['tʌfnɪs] *n see adj* **(a)** Zähigkeit *f;* Widerstandsfähigkeit *f;* Strapazierfähigkeit *f;* Härte *f.* **(b)** *(difficulty)* Schwierigkeit *f; (of journey)* Strapazen *pl.*

toupee ['tuːpeɪ] *n* Toupet *nt.*

tour [tʊə^r] **1** *n (journey, walking ~ etc)* Tour *f; (of town, building etc)* Rundgang *m (of* durch*); (also* **guided ~)** Führung *f (of* durch*); (by bus)* Rundfahrt *f (of* durch*).* **to go on a ~ of Scotland/ the castle** eine Schottlandreise machen/an einer Schloßführung teilnehmen; **to go/be on ~** *(Theat, Sport)* auf Tournee gehen/sein. **2** *vt* **(a)** *country etc* fahren durch; *(on foot)* ziehen durch *(col); (visit) town, building* eine Rundgang machen durch; *(by bus etc)* eine Rundfahrt machen durch. **(b)** *(Theat, Sport)* eine Tournee machen durch. **3** *vi* **(a)** *(on holiday)* eine Reise *or* Tour machen. **we're ~ing (around)** wir reisen herum; **to go ~ing** Touren/eine Tour machen. **(b)** *(Theat, Sport)* eine Tournee machen.

tourism ['tʊərɪzəm] *n* Fremdenverkehr, Tourismus *m.*

tourist ['tʊərɪst] **1** *n (person)* Tourist(in *f*) *m; (Sport)* Gast *m.* **2** *attr class, hotel, shop* Touristen-; *guide* Fremden-; *bureau, office, industry* Fremdenverkehrs-. **~ season** Reisezeit *f;* **~ trade** Fremdenverkehrsgewerbe *nt.*

tournament ['tʊənəmənt] *n (Sport, Hist)* Turnier *nt.*

tourniquet ['tʊənɪkeɪ] *n* Aderpresse *f.*

tousled ['taʊzld] *adj hair* zerzaust. **~ head** Wuschelkopf *m (col).*

tout [taʊt] *(col)* **1** *n (tipster)* Wettberater *m; (ticket* ~*)* Schwarzmarkthändler *m; (for business)* Kundenfänger *m.* **2** *vi* **to ~ for business/ customers** (aufdringlich) Reklame machen/auf Kundenfang sein *(col).*

tow [təʊ] **1** *n* **to give sb/a car a ~** jdn/ein Auto abschleppen; **to give sb/a yacht a ~** jdn/eine Jacht ins Schlepptau nehmen; **in ~** *(fig)* im Schlepptau. **2** *vt boat, glider* schleppen; *car also* abschleppen; *trailer* ziehen.

♦ **tow away** *vt sep* abschleppen.

toward(s) [tə'wɔːd(z)] *prep* (a) *(in direction of)* *(with verbs of motion)* auf (+*acc*) ... zu. **they walked** ~ **the town** sie gingen auf die Stadt zu; **we sailed** ~ **China** wir segelten in Richtung China; **it's further north,** ~ **Dortmund** es liegt weiter im Norden, Richtung Dortmund; ~ **the south** nach Süden; **he turned** ~ **her** er wandte sich ihr zu; **they are working** ~ **a solution** sie arbeiten auf eine Lösung hin. (b) *(in relation to)* ... *(dat)* gegenüber. **what are your feelings** ~ **him?** was empfinden Sie ihm gegenüber? (c) ~ **ten o'clock** gegen zehn Uhr; ~ **the end of the year** gegen Ende des Jahres. (d) **the money will go** ~ ... das Geld wird für ... verwendet; **most of my salary goes** ~ **the rent** der größte Teil meines Gehalts geht für die Miete drauf *(col)*.

towel ['tauəl] *n* Handtuch *nt*. ~ **rail** Handtuchhalter *m*.

tower ['tauə'] *n* (a) Turm *m*. (b) *(fig: person)* **a** ~ **of strength** ein starker (Rück)halt.

♦ **tower above** *or* **over** *vi* +*prep obj* (a) *(buildings etc)* emporragen über (+*acc*). (b) *(lit,fig: people)* überragen.

tower block *n (Brit)* Hochhaus *nt*.

towering ['tauərɪŋ] *adj building* hochragend; *mountain* (steil) aufragend; *tree* hochgewachsen. **one of the** ~ **giants of literature** eine der einsamen Größen der Literatur.

town [taun] *n* Stadt *f*. **the** ~ **of Brighton** (die Stadt) Brighton; **to go into** ~ in die Stadt gehen; **to live in** ~ in der Stadt wohnen; **he's out of** ~ er ist nicht in der Stadt; **to have a night on the** ~ *(col)* die Nacht durchmachen *(col)*; **to go to** ~ **on sth** *(fig col)* (go to great trouble with) sich bei etw einen abbrechen *(col)*; *(to please)* sich bei etw ins Zeug legen.

town: ~ **centre** *(Brit or* **center** *(US) n* Stadtmitte *f*, (Stadt)zentrum *nt*; ~ **clerk** *n* Stadtdirektor *m*; *(of bigger town)* Oberstadtdirektor *m*; ~ **council** *n* Stadtrat *m*; ~ **hall** *n* Rathaus *nt*; ~ **planning** *n* Stadtplanung *f*.

townspeople ['taunzˌpiːpl] *npl* Städter, Stadtmenschen *pl; (citizens)* Bürger *pl*.

tow: ~**path** *n* Treidelpfad *m*; ~**rope** *n* Abschleppseil *nt*; ~**-truck** *n (US)* Abschleppwagen *m*.

toxic ['tɒksɪk] *adj* giftig, Gift-, toxisch.

toy [tɔɪ] 1 *n* Spielzeug *nt*. ~**s** Spielsachen *pl*, Spielzeug *nt*. 2 *vi to* ~ **with an object/idea** *etc* mit einer Sache/Idee *etc* spielen; **to** ~ **with one's food** mit dem Essen (herum)spielen.

toy *in cpds car, soldier* Spielzeug-; ~**shop** *(Brit) or* **store** *(US) n* Spielwarenladen *m*.

trace [treɪs] 1 *n (sign, small amount)* Spur *f*. **to vanish without** ~ spurlos verschwinden; **to lose** ~ **of sb/sth** jdn/etw aus den Augen verlieren. 2 *vt* (a) *(draw)* zeichnen; *(copy)* nachziehen; *(with tracing paper)* durchpausen. (b) *(follow trail of)* verfolgen; *steps* folgen (+*dat*). **she was** ~**d to a house in Soho** ihre Spur führte zu einem Haus in Soho. (c) *(find)* ausfindig machen, auffinden.

♦ **trace back** *vt sep descent* zurückverfolgen; *rumour* auf seinen Ursprung zurückverfolgen; *neurosis etc* zurückführen *(to* auf +*acc*).

trace element *n* Spurenelement *nt*.

trachea [trə'kɪə] *n* Luftröhre *f*.

tracing ['treɪsɪŋ] *n (drawing)* Durchpausen *nt*; *(result)* Pause *f*. ~ **paper** *n* Pauspapier *nt*.

track [træk] 1 *n* (a) *(trail)* Fährte, Spur *f*; *(of tyres)* (Fahr)spur *f*. **to be on sb's** ~ jdm auf der Spur sein; **to keep** ~ **of sb/sth** jdn/etw im Auge behalten; **I can't keep** ~ **of your girlfriends** du hast so viele Freundinnen, da komme ich nicht mit *(col)*; **no-one can keep** ~ **of the situation** niemand hat mehr einen Überblick über die Lage; **to lose** ~ **of sb/sth** *(lose sight of)* jdn/etw aus den Augen verlieren; *(lose count of, be confused*

about) über Leute/etw den Überblick verlieren; **we must be making** ~**s** *(col)* wir müssen uns auf die Socken machen *(col)*; **he stopped dead in his** ~**s** er blieb abrupt stehen; **to cover (up) one's** ~**s** seine Spuren verwischen. (b) *(path)* Weg, Pfad *m*. **off the** ~ *(fig)* abwegig; **to be on the right/wrong** ~ *(fig)* auf der richtigen/falschen Spur sein. (c) *(Rail)* Gleise *pl; (US: platform)* Bahnsteig *m*. **to leave the** ~**(s)** entgleisen. (d) *(Sport)* Rennbahn *f; (Athletics)* Bahn *f; (Motorsport)* Piste *f; (circuit)* Rennstrecke *f*. (e) *(on tape)* Spur *f; (song etc)* Stück *nt*. (f) *(also* **caterpillar** ~) Raupenkette *f*. 2 *vt (follow)* person, animal verfolgen; *(Space)* rocket die Flugbahn (+*gen*) verfolgen.

♦ **track down** *vt sep* aufspüren *(to* in +*dat*); *thing* aufstöbern, auftreiben *(col); reference, source* ausfindig machen.

tracker dog *n* Spürhund *m*.

track: ~ **record** *n (fig)* **what's his** ~ **record?** was hat er vorzuweisen?; ~**suit** *n* Trainingsanzug *m*.

tract[1] [trækt] *n* (a) *(of land)* Gebiet *nt*. **narrow** ~ **Streifen** *m*. (b) *(respiratory)* Wege *pl; (digestive)* Trakt *m*.

tract[2] *n (pamphlet)* Traktat *nt*, Schrift *f*.

traction ['trækʃən] *n* Zugkraft, Zugleistung *f; (of wheels)* Bodenhaftung *f; (Med)* Streckverband *m*. ~ **engine** Zugmaschine *f*.

tractor ['træktə'] *n* Traktor, Trecker *m*.

trade [treɪd] 1 *n* (a) *(commerce)* Handel *m*, Gewerbe *nt; (turnover: of shop etc)* die Geschäfte *pl*. **to do a good** ~ gute Geschäfte machen; **to do a brisk** ~ **in** sth einen reißenden Absatz an etw *(dat)* haben. (b) *(line of business)* Branche *f*, Geschäftszweig *m; (job)* Handwerk *nt*. **he's in the wool** ~ er ist in der Wollbranche; **he's in the** ~ er ist vom Fach; **as we call it in the** ~ wie es in unserer Branche heißt; **he's a bricklayer by** ~ er ist Maurer von Beruf; **he's a lawyer by** ~ *(hum)* er ist Rechtsanwalt. (c) *(exchange)* Tausch(handel) *m*. 2 *vt* tauschen. **to** ~ **sth for sth else** etw gegen etw anderes (ein)tauschen. 3 *vi* (a) *(Comm)* Handel treiben, handeln. **to** ~ **in sth** mit etw handeln; **to** ~ **with sb** mit jdm Geschäfte machen. (b) *(US col)* einkaufen *(at* bei).

♦ **trade in** *vt sep* in Zahlung geben *(for* für).

trade: ~ **fair** *n* Handelsmesse *f*; ~ **figures** *npl* Handelsziffern *pl;* ~ **gap** *n* Außenhandelsdefizit *nt;* ~**-in** *n* **to take/offer sth as a** ~**-in** etw in Zahlung nehmen/geben; ~**mark** *n (lit)* Warenzeichen *nt;* **honesty was his** ~**mark** er war für seine Ehrlichkeit bekannt; ~ **name** *n* Handelsname *m*.

trader ['treɪdə'] *n (person)* Händler *m*.

trades: ~**man** *n (delivery man)* Lieferant *m; (shopkeeper)* Händler *m; (plumber, electrician etc)* Handwerker *m;* ~**man's entrance** Lieferanteneingang *m;* ~ **union** *n* = **trade union; T~ Union congress** (britischer) Gewerkschaftsbund.

trade: ~ **union** *n* Gewerkschaft *f;* ~ **unionism** *n* Gewerkschaftsbewegung *f;* ~ **unionist** *n* Gewerkschaft(l)er(in *f*) *m*.

trading ['treɪdɪŋ] *n* Handel *m*, Handeln *nt (in* mit).

tradition [trə'dɪʃən] Tradition *f*. ~ **has it that** ... es ist überliefert, daß er ...

traditional [trə'dɪʃənl] *adj* traditionell; *virtues also* überkommen; *jazz* Old-time-.

traditionally [trə'dɪʃənlɪ] *adv* traditionell; *(customarily)* üblicherweise.

traffic ['træfɪk] 1 *n* (a) Verkehr *m; (Aviat)* Flugverkehr *m*. **closed to heavy** ~ gesperrt für den Schwerlastverkehr. (b) *(business: of port, airport)* Umschlag *m*. ~ **in steel** Stahlumschlag *m*. (c) *(usu pej: trading)* Handel *m (in* mit); *(in pornography)* Vertrieb *m (in* von). 2 *vi (usu pej)* handeln *(in* mit).

traffic *in cpds* Verkehrs-; ~ **circle** *n (US)* Kreisverkehr *m*; ~ **cop** *n (col)* Verkehrspolizist *m*; ~ **island** *n* Verkehrsinsel *f*; ~ **jam** *n* Verkehrsstauung *f*.

trafficker ['træfɪkə^r] *n (usu pej)* Händler *m*; *(in drugs also)* Dealer *m*.

traffic: ~ **lights** *(Brit)* npl, ~ **light** *n (US)* Verkehrsampel *f*; ~ **policeman** *n* Verkehrspolizist *m*; ~ **warden** *n (Brit)* ≈ Verkehrspolizist *m ohne amtliche Befugnisse; (woman)* ≈ Politesse *f*.

tragedy ['trædʒɪdɪ] *n* Tragödie. *f.* **six killed in holiday crash** ~ tragischer Urlaubsunfall forderte sechs Todesopfer; **the** ~ **of it is that ...** das Tragische daran ist, daß ...

tragic ['trædʒɪk] *adj* tragisch.

tragically ['trædʒɪkəlɪ] *adv* ~, **he was killed before** ... tragischerweise kam er ums Leben, bevor ...

trail [treɪl] **1** *n* **(a)** Spur *f.* ~ **of blood** Blutspur *f*; ~ **of smoke/dust** Rauchfahne *f*/Staubwolke *f.* **(b)** *(track)* Fährte, Spur *f.* **hot on the** ~ dicht auf den Fersen; **to be on the** ~ **of an animal** die Spur eines Tieres verfolgen; **the police are on his** ~ die Polizei ist ihm auf der Spur. **(c)** *(path)* Weg, Pfad *m*; *(nature* ~ *etc)* (Wander)weg *m.* **2** *vt* **(a)** *(follow)* person folgen *(+dat)*; *animal* verfolgen. **(b)** *(drag)* schleppen, schleifen. **the bird** ~**ed its broken wing** der Vogel zog seinen gebrochenen Flügel nach. **(c)** *(US: tow)* ziehen, schleppen. **3** *vi* **(a)** *(on floor)* schleifen. **(b)** *(plant)* sich ranken. **(c)** *(walk)* trotten. **(d)** *(be behind: in competition etc)* weit zurückliegen; *(Sport)* weit zurückgefallen sein.

♦ **trail away** *or* **off** *vi (voice)* sich verlieren *(into* in *+dat)*.

trailer ['treɪlə^r] *n* **(a)** *(Aut)* Anhänger *m*; *(esp US: of lorry)* Sattelauflieger *m.* **(b)** *(US)* Wohnwagen, Caravan *m.* **(c)** *(Film, TV)* Vorschau *f.*

train[1] [treɪn] *n* **(a)** *(Rail)* Zug *m.* **to go/travel by** ~ mit dem Zug *or* der Bahn fahren/reisen; **a** ~ **journey** eine Bahn- *or* Zugfahrt; **to take** *or* **get the 11 o'clock** ~ den Elfuhrzug nehmen; **to change** ~**s** umsteigen; **on the** ~ im Zug. **(b)** *(line)* Kolonne *f*; *(of people)* Schlange *f*; *(retinue)* Gefolge *nt.* **the war brought famine in its** ~ der Krieg brachte eine Hungersnot mit sich. **(c)** *(of events)* Folge, Kette *f.* **he interrupted my** ~ **of thought** er unterbrach meinen Gedankengang. **(d)** *(of dress)* Schleppe *f.*

train[2] **1** *vt* **(a)** ausbilden; *child* erziehen; *animal* abrichten, dressieren; *mind* schulen; *(Sport)* trainieren. **to** ~ **sb as sth** jdn als *or* zu etw ausbilden; **to** ~ **an animal to do sth** ein Tier dazu abrichten, etw zu tun; **this dog has been** ~**ed to kill** dieser Hund ist aufs Töten abgerichtet. **(b)** *(aim)* gun richten *(on* auf *+acc).* **(c)** *plant* wachsen lassen *(over* über *+acc).* **2** *vi* **(a)** *(esp Sport)* trainieren *(for* für). **(b)** *(study)* ausgebildet werden. **he** ~**ed as a teacher** er hat eine Lehrerausbildung gemacht.

train driver *n* Zug- *or* Lokführer(in *f*) *m.*

trained [treɪnd] *adj* worker gelernt, Fach-; *nurse, teacher, voice* ausgebildet; *animal* dressiert; *mind, ear, eye* geschult.

trainee [treɪˈniː] *n* Auszubildende(r) *mf*; *(academic, technical)* Praktikant(in *f*) *m*; *(nurse)* Krankenpflegeschüler(in *f*) *m*, Schwesternschülerin *f*; *(management)* Trainee *m.*

trainee: ~ **manager** *n* Management-Trainee *m*; ~ **teacher** *n (in primary school)* ≈ Praktikant(in *f*) *m*; *(in secondary school)* ≈ Referendar(in *f*) *m.*

trainer ['treɪnə^r] *n* **(a)** *(Sport, of racehorse)* Trainer *m*; *(of animals)* Dresseur *m.* **(b)** *(shoe)* Trainingsschuh *m.*

training ['treɪnɪŋ] *n* Ausbildung *f (also Mil)*; *(of staff)* Schulung *f*; *(of animal)* Dressur *f*; *(Sport)* Training *nt.* **to be in** ~ im Training sein, trainieren; *(be fit)* gut in Form *or* durchtrainiert sein; **to**

be out of ~ nicht in Form sein, aus dem Training sein.

training: ~**college** *n (for teachers)* ≈ Pädagogische Hochschule; ~ **course** *n* Ausbildungskurs *m*; ~ **shoes** npl Trainingsschuhe pl.

train: ~**load** *n (of goods)* Zugladung *f*; ~**loads of holidaymakers** ganze Züge voller Urlauber; ~ **service** *n* Zugverkehr *m*; *(between two places)* (Eisen)bahnverbindung *f*; ~ **set** *n* (Spielzeug)eisenbahn *f*; ~**sick** *adj* **he gets** ~ **sick** ihm wird beim Zugfahren schlecht *or* übel; ~**spotter** *n* Eisenbahnfan *m*; ~**spotting** *n* Hobby *nt, bei dem Züge begutachtet und deren Nummern notiert werden.*

traipse [treɪps] *(col) vi* latschen *(col).* **to** ~ **around the shops** in den Geschäften rumlatschen *(col).*

trait [treɪt, treɪ] *n* Eigenschaft *f.*

traitor ['treɪtə^r] *n* Verräter *m.* **to be a** ~ **to one's country** sein Vaterland verraten; **to turn** ~ zum Verräter werden.

trajectory [trəˈdʒektərɪ] *n* Flugbahn *f.*

tram [træm] *n (Brit)* Straßenbahn *f.*

tramp [træmp] **1** *vi* **(a)** *(walk heavily, trudge)* stapfen, stampfen. **(b)** *(hike)* wandern; *(as vagabond)* umherziehen. **he** ~**ed all over Europe** er wanderte in ganz Europa umher. **2** *vt* **(a)** *(spread by walking)* herumtreten. **don't** ~ **that mud into the carpet** tritt den Dreck nicht in den Teppich. **(b)** *(walk)* streets latschen durch *(col).* **3** *n (vagabond)* Landstreicher(in *f*), Tramp *m*; *(in town)* Stadtstreicher(in *f*) *m.*

trample ['træmpl] **1** *vt* niedertrampeln, zertrampeln. **to** ~ **sth underfoot** auf etw *(dat)* herumtrampeln; ~**d to death** zu Tode getrampelt; **to** ~ **sth into the ground** etw in den Boden trampeln. **2** *vi* **he lets his wife** ~ **all over him** *(fig)* er läßt sich *(dat)* von seiner Frau auf dem Kopf herumtanzen.

♦ **trample on** *vi +prep obj* herumtreten auf *(+dat).* **to** ~ **sb** *(fig)* jdn herumschikanieren; **to** ~ ~ **sb's feelings** *(fig)* jds Gefühle mit Füßen treten.

trampoline ['træmpəlɪn] *n* Trampolin *nt.*

trance [trɑːns] *n* Trance *f.* **to go into a** ~ in einen Trancezustand verfallen.

tranquil ['træŋkwɪl] *adj* ruhig.

tranquillity, *(US)* **tranquility** [træŋˈkwɪlɪtɪ] *n* Ruhe *f.*

tranquillize, *(US)* **tranquilize** ['træŋkwɪlaɪz] *vt* beruhigen.

tranquillizer, *(US)* **tranquilizer** ['træŋkwɪlaɪzə^r] *n* Beruhigungsmittel *nt.*

trans- [trænz-] *pref* trans-, Trans-.

transact [trænˈzækt] *vt* abwickeln; *deal* abschließen.

transaction [trænˈzækʃən] *n* **(a)** *(act)* see *vt* Abwicklung *f*; Abschluß *m.* ~ **of business** Geschäftsbetrieb *m.* **(b)** *(piece of business)* Geschäft *nt*; *(Fin, St Ex)* Transaktion *f.* **(c)** ~**s** pl *(of society)* Sitzungsbericht *m.*

transatlantic ['trænzətˈlæntɪk] *adj* transatlantisch, Transatlantik-; *customs* auf der anderen Seiten (des Atlantiks); *cousins, accent* amerikanisch; *(for Americans)* britisch.

transcend [trænˈsend] *vt* übersteigen, überschreiten; *(Philos)* transzendieren.

transcontinental ['trænz,kɒntɪˈnentl] *adj* transkontinental.

transcribe [trænˈskraɪb] *vt manuscripts* abschreiben; *(from shorthand)* (in Langschrift) übertragen; *proceedings etc* niederschreiben; *(Mus)* transkribieren.

transcript ['trænskrɪpt] *n (of court proceedings)* Protokoll *nt*; *(of tapes)* Niederschrift *f*; *(copy)* Kopie, Abschrift *f.*

transcription [trænˈskrɪpʃən] *n (Mus, Phon)* Transkription *f*; *(copy, of shorthand notes)* Abschrift *f*; *(act)* Abschreiben *nt*; *(of speech,* proceedings) Niederschrift f, Protokoll nt; (Rad, TV: recording) Aufnahme f.

transept ['trænsept] n Querschiff nt.

transfer [træns'fɜːʳ] **1** vt übertragen (to auf +acc); prisoner überführen (to in +acc); premises, troops, account verlegen (to in +acc, to town nach); soldier, employee versetzen (to in +acc, to town, country nach); (Sport) player abgeben (to an +acc); (Fin) funds, money überweisen (to auf +acc); (Jur) property überschreiben (to auf +acc). **he ~red the money from the box to his pocket** er nahm das Geld aus der Schachtel und steckte es in die Tasche.

2 vi (a) überwechseln (to zu); (to new system, working conditions) umstellen (to auf +acc). **(b)** (Fin) umsteigen (into auf +acc). **(c)** (in travelling) umsteigen (to in +acc); (Univ) das Studienfach wechseln, umsatteln (col) (from ... to von ... auf +acc).

3 ['trænsfɜːʳ] n (a) see vt Übertragung f; Überführung f; Verlegung f; Versetzung f; (of footballer) Transfer m; Überweisung f; Überschreibung f. **he asked for a ~** (soldier, employee) er bat um Versetzung; (footballer) er bat, auf die Transferliste gesetzt zu werden. **(b)** (picture) Abziehbild nt. **(c)** (~ ticket) Umsteige(fahr)karte f.

transferable [træns'fɜːrəbl] adj übertragbar; money, stocks transferierbar.

transfix [træns'fɪks] vt (a) (fix) annageln, feststecken (to an +acc). **(b)** (fig) **to be** or **stand ~ed with horror** starr vor Entsetzen sein; **he stood as though ~ed** er stand da wie angewurzelt.

transform [træns'fɔːm] vt umwandeln, umformen (into zu); ideas, views (vom Grund auf) verändern; person, caterpillar verwandeln; (Phys) umwandeln (into in +acc); (Elec) (um)wandeln (into in +acc), transformieren (into in +acc). **the old house was ~ed into three flats** aus dem alten Haus wurden drei Wohnungen gemacht.

transformation [ˌtrænsfəˈmeɪʃən] n Umwandlung, Umformung f; (of ideas, views etc) (grundlegende) Veränderung; (of person, caterpillar etc) Verwandlung f; (Phys) Umwandlung f; (Elec) Umwandlung, Transformation f.

transformer [træns'fɔːməʳ] n (Elec) Transformator m.

transfusion [træns'fjuːʒən] n (also **blood ~**) Blutübertragung, Transfusion f. **to give sb a ~** jdm eine Blutübertragung geben.

transgress [træns'gres] **1** vt standards verstoßen gegen, verletzen. **2** vi sündigen.

transgression [træns'greʃən] n (a) (of law) Verstoß m, Verletzung f. **(b)** (sin) Sünde f, Verstoß m.

transience ['trænzɪəns] n (of life) Kürze f; (of grief, joy) Kurzlebigkeit f; (of interest) Flüchtigkeit f.

transient ['trænzɪənt] **1** adj (a) life kurz; grief, joy kurzlebig, vorübergehend; interest flüchtig. **(b)** (US) **~ population** nichtansässiger Teil der Bevölkerung. **2** n (US) Durchreisende(r) mf.

transistor [træn'zɪstəʳ] n (a) (Elec) Transistor m. **(b)** (also **~ radio**) Transistorradio nt, Transistor m (col).

transistorized [træn'zɪstəraɪzd] adj circuit transistorisiert.

transit ['trænzɪt] n Durchfahrt f, Transit m (esp DDR); (of goods) Transport m. **the books were damaged in ~** die Bücher wurden beim Transport beschädigt; **~ camp** Durchgangslager nt.

transition [træn'zɪʃən] n Übergang m (from ... to von ... zu).

transitional [træn'zɪʃənl] adj Übergangs-.

transitive ['trænzɪtɪv] adj transitiv.

transitory ['trænzɪtərɪ] adj life kurz; grief, joy kurzlebig, vorübergehend; interest flüchtig.

transit visa n Transitvisum nt.

translate [trænz'leɪt] vti (a) übersetzen; work of literature also übertragen. **to ~ a text from German (in)to English** einen Text aus dem Deutschen ins Englische übersetzen; **it is ~d as ... es wird mit ... übersetzt; his novels ~ well** (into English) seine Romane lassen sich gut (ins Englische) übersetzen or übertragen. **(b) to ~ words into action** Worte in die Tat umsetzen.

translation [trænz'leɪʃən] n Übersetzung f (from aus); (of work of literature also) Übertragung f. **it loses in ~** es verliert bei der Übersetzung.

translator [trænz'leɪtəʳ] n Übersetzer(in f) m.

translucent [trænz'luːsnt] adj glass etc lichtdurchlässig; skin durchsichtig.

transmission [trænz'mɪʃən] n (a) (transmitting) Übertragung f; (through heredity) Vererbung f; (of news) Übermittlung f; (of heat) Leitung f; (programme also) Sendung f. **(b)** (Aut) Getriebe nt. **~ shaft** Kardanwelle f.

transmit [trænz'mɪt] vt (convey) message, information übermitteln; sound waves, programme, illness übertragen; (by heredity) vererben; heat etc leiten.

transmitter [trænz'mɪtəʳ] n (Tech) Sender m; (in telephone) Mikrofon nt.

transmute [trænz'mjuːt] vt umwandeln (into in +acc); metal verwandeln (into in +acc).

transom ['trænsəm] n (~ window) Oberlicht nt; (cross-piece) Querbalken m.

transparency [træns'pærənsɪ] n (a) Transparenz, Durchsichtigkeit f. **(b)** (of lies, excuses etc) Durchschaubarkeit f. **(c)** (Brit Phot) Dia(positiv) nt. **colour ~** Farbdia nt.

transparent [træns'pærənt] adj (a) durchsichtig, transparent. **(b)** (fig) lie, intentions, personality durchschaubar; meaning klar, eindeutig.

transpire [træn'spaɪəʳ] vi (a) (become known) **it now ~s that ...** jetzt hat sich herausgestellt, daß ... **(b)** (happen) passieren (col).

transplant [træns'plɑːnt] **1** vt (a) (Hort) umpflanzen. **(b)** (Med) verpflanzen. **2** ['trɑːnsplɑːnt] n (operation) Verpflanzung, Transplantation f; (organ) Transplantat nt, verpflanztes Organ. **to have a ~** sich einer Organverpflanzung unterziehen.

transport ['trænspɔːt] **1** n (a) (of goods, of troops) Transport m. **Ministry of T~** Verkehrsministerium nt; **have you got your own ~?** bist du motorisiert?; **public ~** öffentliche Verkehrsmittel pl. **(b)** (US: shipment) (Schiffs)fracht, Ladung f. **(c)** (liter) **it sent her into ~s of delight** es erfüllte sie mit freudigem Entzücken (liter). **2** [træns'pɔːt] vt (a) goods transportieren; people befördern; (Hist) convict deportieren. **(b)** (liter) **to be ~ed with joy** freudig entzückt sein (liter).

transportation [ˌtrænspɔːˈteɪʃən] n (a) Transport m; (means) Beförderungsmittel nt; (public) Verkehrsmittel nt; (cost) Transportkosten pl. **Department of T~** (US) Verkehrsministerium nt. **(b)** (Hist: of criminal) Deportation f.

transport café n (Brit) Fernfahrerlokal nt.

transpose [træns'pəʊz] vt umstellen; (Mus) transponieren.

transship [træns'ʃɪp] vt umschiffen.

transverse ['trænzvɜːs] adj beam, bar, section Quer-; position horizontal; engine querstehend.

transvestite [trænz'vestaɪt] n Transvestit m.

trap [træp] **1** n (a) (for animal, fig) Falle f. **to set** or **lay a ~ for an animal** eine Falle für ein Tier (auf)stellen; **to set a ~ for sb** (fig) jdm eine Falle stellen; **he is caught in a ~** er sitzt in der Falle; **to fall into a ~** in die Falle gehen. **(b)** (vehicle) zweirädriger Pferdewagen. **(c)** (col: mouth) Klappe (col). **shut your ~!** halt die Klappe! (col).

2 vt (a) animal (mit einer Falle) fangen. **(b)** (fig) person in die Falle locken. **he realized he was ~ped** er merkte, daß er in der Falle saß; **to ~ sb into saying sth** jdn dazu bringen, etw zu sagen. **(c)** *(block off, leave no escape)* in die Enge treiben. **the miners are ~ped** die Bergleute sind eingeschlossen; **my arm was ~ped** mein Arm war eingeklemmt. **(d)** *(catch)* *(Sport)* ball stoppen. **to ~ one's finger in the door** sich *(dat)* den Finger in der Tür einklemmen. **(e)** *gas, liquid* stauen.

trapdoor ['træp'dɔːʳ] *n* Falltür *f*; *(Theat)* Versenkung *f*.

trapeze [trə'piːz] *n* *(in circus)* Trapez *nt*. **~ artist** Trapezkünstler(in *f*) *m*.

trapper ['træpəʳ] *n* Fallensteller, Trapper *m*.

trappings ['træpɪŋz] *npl* äußeres Drum and Dran *(col)*; *(of power)* Insignien *pl*. **~ of office** Amtsinsignien *pl*.

trash [træʃ] *n* **(a)** *(US: refuse)* Ramsch *m*; *(book, play etc)* Schund *m*; *(pop group etc)* Mist, Schrott *m (col)*. **don't talk ~ red nicht so einen Quatsch** *(col)*.

trash-can ['træʃkæn] *n* *(US)* Abfalleimer *m*.

trashy ['træʃɪ] *adj* *(+er)* *goods* minderwertig; *play* also Schund-.

trauma ['trɔːmə] *n* *(Psych)* Trauma *nt*.

traumatic [trɔː'mætɪk] *adj* traumatisch.

travel ['trævl] *(vb: pret, ptp* *(Brit)* **travelled**, *(US)* **traveled)** **1** *vi* **(a)** *(make a journey)* reisen. **he ~s to work by car** er fährt mit dem Auto zur Arbeit; **she is ~ling to London tomorrow** sie fährt morgen nach London; **they ~led for 300 kms** sie fuhren 300 km; **to ~ around a country** ein Land bereisen. **(b)** *(go, move)* sich bewegen; *(sound, light)* sich fortpflanzen. **light ~s at ...** die Lichtgeschwindigkeit beträgt ...; **we were ~ling at 80 kph** wir fuhren 80 km/h; **the electricity ~s along the wire** der Strom fließt durch den Draht; **that's ~ling!** *(col)* das ist aber schnell! **(c)** *(Comm)* Vertreter sein. **he ~s in ladies' underwear** er reist in Damenunterwäsche. **(d)** *(Tech)* **as the piston ~s from A to B** während sich der Kolben von A nach B bewegt.

2 *vt area* bereisen; *distance* zurücklegen; *route* fahren.

3 *n* Reisen *nt*. **to be fond of ~** gerne reisen; **if you meet him on your ~s** wenn Sie ihm auf einer Ihrer Reisen begegnen.

travel: **~ agency** *n* Reisebüro *nt*; **~ agent** *n* Reisebürokaufmann *m*; *(of package tours)* Reiseveranstalter *m*; **~ brochure** *n* Reiseprospekt *m*.

travelled, *(US)* traveled ['trævld] *adj* **well-~** *person* weitgereist *attr*, weit gereist *pred*; *route* vielbefahren *attr*, viel befahren *pred*.

traveller, *(US)* traveler ['trævləʳ] *n* **(a)** Reisende(r) *mf*. **I am a very poor** *or* **bad ~** ich vertrage das Reisen nicht. **(b)** *(also commercial ~)* Vertreter *m*.

traveller's cheque, *(US)* traveler's check *n* Reisescheck, Travellerscheck *m*.

travelling, *(US)* traveling ['trævlɪŋ] *n* Reisen *nt*. **I hate ~** ich hasse das Reisen.

travelling: **~ bag** *n* Reisetasche *f*; **~ clock** *n* Reisewecker *m*; **~ expenses** *npl* Reisekosten *pl*; *(on business)* Reisespesen *pl*; **~ salesman** *n* Vertreter *m*.

travelogue ['trævəlɒg] *n* Reisebericht *m*.

travel: **~-sick** *adj* reisekrank; **~-sickness** *n* Reisekrankheit *f*.

traverse ['trævɜːs] *vt* *(cross)* *land* durchqueren; *(bridge, person)* *water* überqueren; *(Mountaineering)* *ice, slope* queren. **the searchlight ~d the sky** der Suchscheinwerfer leuchtete den Himmel ab.

travesty ['trævɪstɪ] *n* *(Liter)* Travestie *f*. **a ~ of justice** ein Hohn *m* auf die Gerechtigkeit; **the elections were a ~** die Wahlen waren ein Hohn *m* oder eine Farce.

trawl [trɔːl] **1** *n* *(net)* Schleppnetz, Trawl *nt*; *(US: ~ line)* Grundleine *f*. **2** *vi* mit dem Schleppnetz fischen; *(US)* mit einer Grundleine fischen.

trawler ['trɔːləʳ] *n* Fischdampfer, Trawler *m*.

tray [treɪ] *n* Tablett *nt*; *(of cakes)* *(small)* Platte *f*; *(big)* Brett *nt*; *(for display)* Auslagekästchen *nt*; *(baking ~)* (Back)blech *nt*; *(for papers, mail)* Ablage(korb *m*) *f*.

treacherous ['tretʃərəs] *adj* **(a)** *person, action* verräterisch. **(b)** *(unreliable)* trügerisch. **(c)** *(dangerous)* tückisch; *ice, smile* trügerisch.

treachery ['tretʃərɪ] *n* Verrat *m*.

treacle ['triːkl] *n* *(Brit)* Sirup *m*.

tread [tred] *(vb: pret* **trod**, *ptp* **trodden)** **1** *n* **(a)** Schritt *m*. **to walk with a heavy ~** mit schweren Schritten gehen; **I could hear his ~ on the stairs** ich konnte seine Schritte auf der Treppe hören. **(b)** *(of stair)* Stufe *f*; *(of shoe, tyre)* Profil *nt*. **2** *vi* **(a)** *(walk)* gehen. **(b)** *(bring foot down)* treten. **to ~ on +acc)**. **he trod on my foot** er trat mir auf den Fuß; **to ~ softly** leise auftreten; **to ~ carefully** *(lit)* vorsichtig gehen; *(fig)* vorsichtig vorgehen. **3** *vt path (make)* treten; *(follow)* gehen. **it got trodden underfoot** es wurde zertreten; **to ~ grapes** Trauben stampfen; **to ~ water** Wasser treten; **don't ~ that earth into the carpet** treten Sie die Erde nicht in den Teppich.

treadle ['tredl] *n* *(of sewing machine)* Tretkurbel *f*.

treadmill ['tredmɪl] *n* *(lit)* Tretwerk *nt*; *(fig)* Tretmühle *f*.

treason ['triːzn] *n* Verrat *m* *(to an +dat)*. **an act of ~** Verrat *m*.

treasure ['treʒəʳ] **1** *n* *(lit, fig)* Schatz *m*. **2** *vt* *(hoch)*schätzen. **I shall always ~ this memory** ich werde das immer in lieber Erinnerung behalten.

treasure: **~ house** *n* a *~* house of knowledge eine Fundgrube des Wissens; **~ hunt** *n* Schatzsuche *f*.

treasurer ['treʒərəʳ] *n* *(of club)* Kassenwart *m*; *(city ~)* Stadtkämmerer *m*; *(of business)* Leiter *m* der Finanzabteilung.

treasure trove *n* Schatzfund *m*; *(place where treasures are found)* Fundgrube *f*.

treasury ['treʒərɪ] *n* **(a)** *(Pol)* **T~**, *(US also)* **T~ Department** Finanzministerium *nt*. **(b)** *(anthology)* Schatzkästlein *nt*.

treat [triːt] **1** *vi* **(a)** *(behave towards, handle, process, Med)* behandeln; *sewage* klären; *wastepaper* verarbeiten. **the doctor is ~ing him for flu** er ist wegen einer Grippe in Behandlung. **(b)** *(consider)* betrachten *(as als)*. **you should ~ your work more seriously** Sie sollten Ihre Arbeit ernster nehmen. **(c)** *(pay for, give)* einladen. **to ~ sb to sth** jdn zu etw einladen, jdm etw spendieren; **I'm ~ing you** ich lade Sie ein; **to ~ oneself to sth** sich *(dat)* etw gönnen.

2 *n* **(a)** besondere Freude. **children's ~** Kinderfest *nt*; **it's my ~** das geht auf meine Kosten; **it's a ~ in store** das ist etwas, worauf wir uns noch freuen können; **it's a (real) ~ to see you again** was für eine Freude, Sie mal wiederzusehen! **(b)** *(col)* **it's coming on a ~** es macht sich prima *(col)*.

treatise ['triːtɪz] *n* Abhandlung *f* *(on über +acc)*.

treatment ['triːtmənt] *n* **(a)** *(of person, object)* Behandlung *f*. **~ of foreigners** ihre Art, Ausländer zu behandeln; **to give sb the ~** *(col: violently, sexually)* es jdm ordentlich besorgen *(col)*; **when the delegates visited the factory, they were given the full ~** *(col)* als die Delegierten die Firma besichtigten, wurde eine große Schau abgezogen *(col)*. **(b)** *(Med)* Behandlung *f*. **there are many ~s for rheumatism** es gibt viele Behandlungsarten für Rheumatismus; **to be having ~ for sth** wegen etw in Behandlung sein. **(c)** *(processing)* Behandlung *f*; *(of leather also)* Bearbeitung *f*; *(of sewage)* Klärung *f*; *(of wastepaper)* Verarbeitung *f*. **(d)** *(of subject)* Bearbeitung *f*.

treaty ['triːtɪ] *n* Vertrag *m*.

treble¹ ['trebl] **1** adj dreifach. **the country's inflation rate is in ~ figures** das Land hat eine dreistellige Inflationsrate. **2** adv **clothes are ~ the price** Kleider kosten dreimal soviel. **3** vt verdreifachen. **4** vi sich verdreifachen.

treble² **1** n (Mus) (boy's voice) Knabensopran m or -stimme f. **2** adj voice Knabensopran-; part Oberstimmen-. **~ clef** Violinschlüssel m.

tree [tri:] n **(a)** Baum m. **an oak/a cherry ~** eine Eiche/ein Kirschbaum m; **money doesn't grow on ~s** das Geld fällt nicht vom Himmel. **(b)** (family ~) Stammbaum m.

tree in cpds Baum-; **~ house** n Baumhaus nt; **~-lined** adj baumbestanden; **~top** n Baumkrone f, Wipfel m; **~ trunk** n Baumstamm m.

trek [trek] **1** vi trecken; (col: traipse) latschen (col). **they ~ked across the desert** sie zogen durch die Wüste. **2** n Treck, Zug m; (col) anstrengender Marsch.

trellis ['trelıs] n Gitter nt.

tremble ['trembl] **1** vi (person, hand etc) zittern (with vor); (voice also) beben (with vor); (ground, building) beben, zittern. **2** n Zittern, Beben nt. **to be all of a ~** (col) am ganzen Körper zittern.

tremendous [trə'mendəs] adj **(a)** gewaltig, enorm; size, crowd also riesig; success Riesen-. **(b)** (very good) klasse (col), toll (col). **we had a ~ time** wir haben uns ganz toll amüsiert.

tremendously [trə'mendəslı] adv sehr; fat, tall etc also enorm; relieved, grateful, dangerous also ungeheuer; intelligent, difficult also äußerst. **they enjoyed themselves ~** sie haben sich prächtig amüsiert (col).

tremor ['tremə'] n Zittern, Beben nt; (Med) Tremor m; (of emotion) Zucken nt; (earth ~) Beben nt.

tremulous ['tremjuləs] adj voice bebend; (timid) smile, person zaghaft.

trench [trentʃ] n Graben m; (Mil) Schützengraben m. **in the ~es** (Mil) im Schützengraben; **~ warfare** Grabenkrieg m.

trenchant ['trentʃənt] adj language treffsicher; style prägnant; satire beißend; speech pointiert; wit, criticism scharf.

trench coat n Trenchcoat, Regenmantel m.

trend [trend] **1** n **(a)** (tendency) Tendenz f, Trend m. **the ~ towards violence** die Tendenz zur Gewalttätigkeit; upward **~** steigende Tendenz, Aufwärtstrend m; **the downward ~ in the birth rate** die Rückläufigkeit der Geburtenrate; **to set a ~** richtungsweisend sein. **(b)** (fashion) Mode f, Trend m. **2** vi verlaufen (towards nach). **prices are ~ing upwards** die Preise haben eine steigende Tendenz.

trendy ['trendı] adj (+er) in pred (col). **to be ~** als schick gelten; (clothes etc also) gerade modern sein.

trepidation [‚trepı'deıʃən] n Beklommenheit, Ängstlichkeit f. **full of ~ he knocked on the door** voll ängstlicher Erwartung klopfte er an die Tür.

trespass ['trespəs] **1** vi (on property) unbefugt betreten (on sth etw acc). **to ~ (up)on sb's privacy** jds Privatsphäre verletzen; **to ~ (up)on sb's time** jds Zeit überbeanspruchen; **"no ~ing"** „Betreten verboten". **2** n (Jur) unbefugtes Betreten.

trespasser ['trespəsə'] n Unbefugte(r) mf. **"~s will be prosecuted"** „Widerrechtliches Betreten wird strafrechtlich verfolgt".

trestle ['tresl] n Bock m. **~ table** auf Böcken stehender Tisch; (decorator's) Tapeziertisch m.

trial ['traıəl] n **(a)** (Jur) (Gerichts)verfahren nt, Prozeß m; (actual hearing) Verhandlung f. **to be on ~** angeklagt sein; **to be on ~ for theft** des Diebstahls angeklagt sein; **at the ~** bei der Verhandlung; **to bring sb to ~** jdm den Prozeß machen; **~ by jury** Schwurgerichtsverfahren

nt. **(b)** (test) Versuch m, Probe f. **~s** (of machine, aeroplane) Test(s pl) m; (Sport) Qualifikationsspiel nt; horse **~s** Querfeldeinrennen nt; **to give sth a ~** etw ausprobieren; **to give sb a ~** (for job) jdn auf Probe anstellen; **to take sth on ~** etw zur Probe or etw probeweise nehmen; **~ of strength** Kraftprobe f; **by ~ and error** durch Ausprobieren. **(c)** (hardship) Unannehmlichkeit f; (nuisance) Plage f, Problem nt (to für). **he's a ~ to his mother** er macht seiner Mutter sehr viel Kummer; **~s and tribulations** Schwierigkeiten pl.

trial: ~ basis n **on a ~ basis** auf Probe; **~ offer** n Einführungsangebot nt; **~ period** n Probezeit f; **~ run** n Generalprobe f; (with car etc) Probefahrt f; (of machine) Probelauf m; **give the new method a ~ run** probieren Sie die neue Methode einmal aus.

triangle ['traıæŋgl] n Dreieck nt; (set square) (Zeichen)dreieck nt; (Mus) Triangel m; (fig: relationship) Dreiecksbeziehung f.

triangular [traı'æŋgjulə'] adj (Math) dreieckig. **~ relationship** Dreiecksverhältnis nt.

tribal ['traıbəl] adj customs, dance Stammes-.

tribe [traıb] n Stamm m.

tribesman ['traıbzmən] n, pl **-men** [-mən] Stammesangehörige(r) m.

tribulation [‚trıbju'leıʃən] n Kummer m no pl. **~s** Sorgen pl; (less serious) Kümmernisse pl.

tribunal [traı'bju:nl] n Gericht(shof m) nt; (inquiry) Untersuchungsausschuß m; (held by revolutionaries etc) Tribunal nt.

tributary ['trıbjutərı] **1** adj state tributpflichtig; river Neben-. **2** n (state) tributpflichtiger Staat; (river) Nebenfluß m.

tribute ['trıbju:t] n Tribut m. **to pay ~ to sb/sth** jdm/einer Sache (den schuldigen) Tribut zollen; **in ~ to sb** jdm zu Ehren; **~s have been coming in from all over the world** aus der ganzen Welt kamen Zeichen der Anerkennung.

trice [traıs] n: **in a ~** im Handumdrehen, im Nu.

trick [trık] **1** n **(a)** (ruse) Trick m. **be careful, it's a ~** paß auf, das ist eine Falle!; **he knows a ~ or two** (col) der kennt sich aus; **he knows all the ~s of the trade** er ist ein alter Hase; (is crafty) er ist mit allen Wassern gewaschen. **(b)** (mischief) Streich m. **to play a ~ on sb** jdm einen Streich spielen; **the car's started playing ~s again** der Wagen fängt wieder an zu mucken (col); **a dirty ~** ein ganz gemeiner Trick; **how's ~s?** (col) wie geht's? **(c)** (skilful act) Kunststück nt. **to teach a dog to do ~s** einem Hund Kunststücke beibringen; **there's a special ~ to it** da ist ein Trick dabei; **that should do the ~** (col) das müßte eigentlich hinhauen (col); **he doesn't miss a ~** (col) er läßt sich nichts entgehen. **(d)** (habit) Eigenart f. **to have a ~ of doing sth** die Eigenart haben, etw zu tun. **(e)** (Cards) Stich m. **to take a ~** einen Stich machen.

2 attr cigar, spider als Scherzartikel.

3 vt hereinlegen (col). **I've been ~ed!** ich bin hereingelegt or übers Ohr gehauen (col) worden!; **to ~ sb into doing sth** jdn (mit einem Trick) dazu bringen, etw zu tun.

trickery ['trıkərı] n Tricks pl (col). **a piece of ~** ein Trick m; **that's just verbal ~** das ist bloß ein raffinierter Trick mit Worten.

trickle ['trıkl] **1** vi **(a)** (liquid) tröpfeln, tropfen; (sand) rieseln; (ball) trudeln (col). **tears ~d down her cheeks** Tränen kullerten ihr über die Wangen; **the rain ~d down his neck** der Regen tropfte ihm in den Kragen. **(b)** (fig) people **began to ~ back in** die Leute begannen, vereinzelt wieder hereinzukommen; **reports are beginning to ~ in** so langsam trudeln die Berichte ein (col). **3** n **(a)** (of liquid) Tröpfeln nt; (stream) Rinnsal nt. **(b)** (fig) **a constant ~ of people gradually filled the lecture hall** der Hörsaal füllte sich

langsam aber stetig mit Leuten; **profits have been reduced to a** ~ die Gewinne sind spärlich geworden.
trick: ~ **photography** *n* Trickfotografie *f*; ~ **question** *n* Fangfrage *f*.
tricky ['trɪkɪ] *adj* (+*er*) **(a)** *(difficult)* schwierig; *(fiddly also)* knifflig. **(b)** *situation, problem* heikel, kitzlig. **(c)** *(sly, crafty) person, plan* durchtrieben, gerissen.
tricolour, *(US)* **tricolor** ['trɪkələ'] *n* Trikolore *f*.
tricycle ['traɪsɪkl] *n* Dreirad *nt*.
tried [traɪd] *adj* erprobt, bewährt.
trifle ['traɪfl] *n* **(a)** *(trivial matter also)* Lappalie *(col)*, Nichtigkeit *f*. **more cake?** — **just a** ~, **thank you** noch etwas Kuchen? — bloß ein ganz kleines Stückchen, bitte; **a** ~ **hot/small** ein bißchen heiß/klein; **a** ~ **too** ... ein wenig *or* eine Spur zu ... **(b)** *(Cook)* Trifle *nt*, geleeartige Süßspeise.
♦ **trifle with** *vi* +*prep obj affections* spielen mit. **he is not to be** ~**d** ~ mit ihm ist nicht zu spaßen.
trifling ['traɪflɪŋ] *adj* unbedeutend, geringfügig.
trigger ['trɪgə'] **1** *n (of gun)* Abzug *m*; *(of cine-camera, machine)* Auslöser *m*; *(Elec)* Trigger *m*. **to pull the** ~ abdrücken. **2** *vt (also* ~ **off)** auslösen.
trigger-happy ['trɪgə,hæpɪ] *adj (col)* schießfreudig, schießwütig *(pej)*.
trigonometry [,trɪgə'nɒmɪtrɪ] *n* Trigonometrie *f*.
trilby ['trɪlbɪ] *n (also* ~ **hat)** weicher Filzhut.
trill [trɪl] **1** *n* **(a)** *(of bird)* Trillern *nt*; *(of voice)* Tremolo *nt*. **(b)** *(Mus)* Triller *m*. **2** *vti (birds, Mus)* trillern; *(person)* trällern.
trillion ['trɪljən] *n (Brit)* Trillion *f*; *(US)* Billion *f*.
trilogy ['trɪlədʒɪ] *n* Trilogie *f*.
trim [trɪm] **1** *adj* (+*er*) sauber; *appearance also* adrett; *haircut* gepflegt. **he keeps his garden very** ~ sein Garten ist immer sehr gepflegt. **2** *n* **(a)** **in good** ~ *(house, car etc)* in gutem Zustand; *(person)* gut in Form; **to get into** ~ sich in Form bringen. **(b)** *(col)* **to give sth a** ~ etw schneiden; *(tree, hedge, beard also)* etw stutzen; **your hair needs a** ~ du mußt dir die Haare etwas nachschneiden lassen. **(c)** *(in car)* Innenausstattung *f*. **3** *vt* **(a)** *(cut)* hair nachschneiden; *beard, hedge* stutzen; *dog* trimmen; *wick, roses* beschneiden; *piece of wood* zurechtschneiden. **(b)** *(fig: cut down)* budget, essay kürzen. **(c)** *(decorate)* dress besetzen; *Christmas tree* schmücken. **(d)** *boat, plane* trimmen; *sails* richtig stellen. **(e)** *(US col) (defeat)* schlagen; *(cheat)* übers Ohr hauen *(col)*.
trimming ['trɪmɪŋ] *n* **(a)** *(on clothes)* Besatz *m*. ~**s** Verzierung(en *pl*) *f*. **(b)** ~**s** *pl (cuttings)* Abfälle *pl*; *(of paper etc)* Papierschnitzel *pl*. **(c)** ~**s** *pl (accessories)* Zubehör *nt*; **roast beef with all the** ~**s** Roastbeef mit allem Drum und Dran *(col)*.
Trinity ['trɪnɪtɪ] *n* Dreifaltigkeit *f*. ~ **Sunday** Trinitatis, Dreifaltigkeitsfest *nt*.
trinket ['trɪŋkɪt] *n* Schmuckstück *nt*. ~ **box** Schmuckkästchen *nt*.
trio ['trɪəʊ] *n* Trio *nt*.
trip [trɪp] **1** *n* **(a)** *(journey)* Reise *f*; *(excursion)* Ausflug *m*, Tour *f*; *(shorter also)* Trip *m (col)*. **when was your last** ~ **to the dentist's?** wann waren Sie zuletzt beim Zahnarzt?; **he is away on a** ~ **to Canada** er ist auf Reisen/macht zur Zeit eine Reise nach Kanada; **to take a** ~ eine Reise machen, verreisen. **(b)** *(col: on drugs)* Trip *m (col)*. **2** *vi* **(a)** *(stumble)* stolpern *(on, over* +*acc)*. **(b)** *(skip)* trippeln. **to** ~ **in/out** hinein-/hinausstrippeln. **3** *vt* **(a)** *(make fall)* stolpern lassen; *(deliberately also)* ein Bein stellen (+*dat*). **(b)** *(Mech)* lever betätigen; *mechanism* auslösen.
♦ **trip over** *vi* stolpern *(+prep obj* über *+acc)*.
♦ **trip up** *vi* **(a)** stolpern. **(b)** *(fig)* sich vertun. **2** *vt sep* **(a)** *(make fall)* stolpern lassen. **(b)** *(fig: cause to make mistake)* eine Falle stellen (+*dat*).
tripartite [,traɪ'pɑːtaɪt] *adj* agreement, talks

dreiseitig; *division* Drei-.
tripe [traɪp] *n* **(a)** *(Cook)* Kaldaunen, Kutteln *(S Ger, Aus, Sw) pl*. **(b)** *(fig col)* Quatsch *m*.
triple ['trɪpl] **1** *adj* dreifach. ~ **jump** Dreisprung *m*. **2** *adv* dreimal soviel. **it's** ~ **the distance** es ist dreimal so weit. **3** *n* Dreifache(s) *nt*. **4** *vt* verdreifachen. **5** *vi* sich verdreifachen.
triplet ['trɪplɪt] *n* **(a)** *(baby)* Drilling *m*. **(b)** *(Mus)* Triole *f*.
triplicate ['trɪplɪkɪt] *n*: **in** ~ in dreifacher Ausfertigung.
tripod ['traɪpɒd] *n (Phot)* Stativ *nt*.
tripwire ['trɪpwaɪə'] *n* Stolperdraht *m*.
trite [traɪt] *adj* (+*er*) *(trivial, banal)* banal; *(hackneyed)* abgedroschen.
triumph ['traɪʌmf] **1** *n* Triumph *m (over* über +*acc)*. **in** ~ triumphierend, im Triumph; **shouts of** ~ Triumphgeschrei *pl*. **2** *vi* den Sieg davontragen *(over* über *+acc)*. **to** ~ **over sb/sth** über jdn/etw triumphieren.
triumphal [traɪ'ʌmfəl] *adj* triumphal. ~ **arch** Triumphbogen *m*.
triumphant [traɪ'ʌmfənt] *adj (victorious)* siegreich; *(rejoicing)* triumphierend; *moment* triumphal. **to be** ~ **(over sth)** triumphieren *(over* über *+acc)*.
trivia ['trɪvɪə] *npl* triviales Zeug.
trivial [trɪvɪəl] *adj* **(a)** trivial; *objection, loss, details also* belanglos. **(b)** *person* oberflächlich.
triviality [,trɪvɪ'ælɪtɪ] *n see adj* **(a)** Trivialität *f*; Belanglosigkeit *f*.
trivialize ['trɪvɪəlaɪz] *vt* trivialisieren.
trod [trɒd] *pret of* **tread.**
trodden ['trɒdn] *ptp of* **tread.**
trolley ['trɒlɪ] *n* **(a)** *(Brit: cart) (four wheels)* Handwagen *m*; *(in supermarket)* Einkaufswagen *m*; *(in station)* Gepäckwagen *m*; *(for passengers)* Kofferkuli *m*; *(two wheels) (for golf clubs)* Caddy *m*; *(in station, factory etc)* Sackkarre *f*; *(tea-~)* Teewagen *m*. **(b)** *(Rail)* Lore *f*, Förderkarren *m*.
trolley: ~**bus** *n* Obus, Oberleitungsomnibus *(form) m*; ~**-car** *n (US)* Straßenbahn *f*.
trombone [trɒm'bəʊn] *n (Mus)* Posaune *f*.
troop [truːp] **1** *n* **(a)** *(Mil: of cavalry)* Trupp *m*; *(unit)* Schwadron *f*. **(b)** *(Mil)* ~**s** *pl* Truppen *pl*; **200** ~**s** 200 Soldaten. **(c)** *(of scouts)* Stamm *m*. **(d)** *(of people)* Horde *f*, Schar *f*. **2** *vi* **to** ~ **out/in** hinaus-/hineinströmen; **to** ~ **past** sth an etw *(dat)* vorbeiziehen. **3** *vi (Mil)* **to** ~ **the colours** die Fahnenparade abhalten.
troop-carrier ['truːp,kærɪə'] *n (vehicle)* Truppentransporter *m*.
trooper ['truːpə'] *n (Mil)* Kavallerist *m*; *(US: state* ~*)* Polizist *m*. **to swear like a** ~ wie ein Kutscher fluchen.
troop-ship ['truːp,ʃɪp] *n* (Truppen)transportschiff *nt*.
trophy ['trəʊfɪ] *n (Mil, Sport)* Trophäe *f*.
tropic ['trɒpɪk] *n* **(a)** Wendekreis *m*. **T** ~ **of Cancer/Capricorn** Wendekreis des Krebses/Steinbocks. **(b)** ~**s** *pl* Tropen *pl*.
tropical ['trɒpɪkəl] *adj* tropisch, Tropen-.
trot [trɒt] **1** *n* **(a)** *(pace)* Trab *m*. **to go at a** ~ traben; **to go for a** ~ einen Ausritt machen; **I've been on the** ~ **all day** *(fig col)* ich bin schon den ganzen Tag auf Trab. **(b)** *(col)* **for five days on the** ~ fünf Tage lang in einer Tour. **2** *vi* **(a)** *(horse, person)* traben; *(pony)* zockeln; *(small child)* trippeln.
♦ **trot out** *vt sep excuses, list* aufwarten mit.
trotter ['trɒtə'] *n (of animal)* Fuß *m*. **pigs'** ~**s** *(Cook)* Schweinsfüße *pl*.
trouble ['trʌbl] **1** *n* **(a)** Ärger *m*; *(difficulties)* Schwierigkeiten *pl*. **did you have any** ~ **(in)** getting **it?** hatten Sie Schwierigkeiten, es zu bekommen?; **to be in** ~ in Schwierigkeiten sein; **to be in** ~ **with sb** mit jdm Schwierigkeiten *or* Ärger haben; **to get into** ~ in Schwierigkeiten geraten; *(with authority)* Ärger bekommen *(with*

mit); **to get sb into** ~ jdn in Schwierigkeiten bringen (with mit); **to get a girl into** ~ (euph) ein Mädchen ins Unglück bringen; **to make** ~ (cause a row etc) Krach schlagen (col), Ärger machen; **that's/you're asking for** ~ das kann ja nicht gutgehen; **what's the** ~? was ist los?; (to sick person) wo fehlt's?; **the** ~ **is that** ... das Problem ist, daß ...; **that's the** ~ das ist das Problem; **family/money** ~**s** Familien-/Geldsorgen pl; **heart/back** ~ Herz-/Rückenleiden nt; **engine** ~ (ein) Motorschaden m.

(b) (bother, effort) Mühe f. **it's no** ~ **(at all)!** das mache ich doch gern; **thank you — (it was) no** ~ vielen Dank — (das ist) gern geschehen; **it's not worth the** ~ das ist nicht der Mühe wert; **nothing is too much** ~ **for her** nichts ist ihr zuviel; **to go to the** ~ **(of doing sth), to take the** ~ **(to do sth)** sich (dat) die Mühe machen (, etw zu tun); **to take a lot of** ~ **(over** or **with sth)** sb to a lot of ~ (mit etw) viel Mühe geben; **to put sb to a lot of** ~ jdm viel Mühe machen.

(c) (unrest, upheaval) Unruhe f. **labour** ~**s** Arbeiterunruhen pl; **he made** ~ **between them** er hat Unruhe zwischen ihnen gestiftet.

2 vt **(a)** (worry) bekümmern (disturb, grieve) bekümmern. **to be** ~**d by sth** wegen etw besorgt sein; **his eyes** ~ **him** seine Augen machen ihm zu schaffen. **(b)** (bother) bemühen, belästigen. **I'm sorry to** ~ **you, but could you tell me if** ... entschuldigen Sie die Störung, aber könnten Sie mir sagen, ob ...; **may I** ~ **you for a light?** darf ich Sie um Feuer bitten?; **I shan't** ~ **you with the details** ich werde Ihnen die Einzelheiten ersparen; **to** ~ **to do sth** sich bemühen, etw zu tun; **please don't** ~ **yourself** bitte bemühen Sie sich nicht.

troubled ['trʌbld] adj person, look unruhig, beunruhigt; (grieved) bekümmert; times unruhig. **the** ~ **waters of race relations** die gestörten Beziehungen zwischen den Rassen.

trouble: ~**-free** adj period, process, car problemlos; relationship also reibungslos; area ruhig; machine störungsfrei; ~**maker** n Unruhestifter(in f) m; ~**shooter** n (Pol, Ind: mediator) Vermittler(in f) m; ~**some** adj (bothersome) lästig; person, problem schwierig; ~ **spot** n Unruheherd m; (in system) Störung f.

trough [trɒf] n **(a)** (container) Trog m. **(b)** (depression) Rille f; (between waves, on graph) Tal nt; (Met) Tiefdruckkeil m.

troupe [truːp] n (Theat) Truppe f.

trouser ['trauzə]: ~ **leg** n Hosenbein nt; ~ **press** n Hosenpresse f.

trousers ['trauzɪz] npl (esp Brit: also **pair of** ~) Hose f. **she was wearing** ~ sie trug eine Hose; **to wear the** ~ (fig col) die Hosen anhaben (col).

trouser-suit ['trauzəˌsuːt] n (Brit) Hosenanzug m.

trousseau ['truːsəu] n Aussteuer f.

trout [traut] n Forelle f. ~ **fishing** Forellenfang m.

trowel ['trauəl] n Kelle f. **to lay sth on with a** ~ (fig col) bei etw dick auftragen.

truancy ['truːənsɪ] n (Schule)schwänzen nt.

truant ['truːənt] n (Schul)schwänzer(in f) m. **to play** ~ unentschuldigt fehlen, schwänzen (col).

truce [truːs] n (Mil, fig) Waffenstillstand m; (Mil: interrupting fighting) Waffenruhe f. ~! Friede!

truck[1] [trʌk] n **1** (a) (Rail) Güterwagen m. **(b)** (barrow) Karren m. **(c)** (lorry) Last(kraft)wagen m; (van, pick-up) Lieferwagen m. **2** vt (US) transportieren. **3** vi (US) Lastwagen fahren.

truck[2] n **(a)** (fig: dealings) **to have no** ~ **with sb/sth** mit jdm/etw nichts zu tun haben. **(b)** (US: garden produce) (für den Verkauf angebautes) Gemüse.

truck driver n Lastwagenfahrer(in f) m.

trucker ['trʌkə[r]] n (US) **(a)** (truck-driver) Lastwagenfahrer(in f) m; (haulage contractor) Spediteur m. **(b)** (vegetable farmer) Gemüse-

gärtner(in f) m.

truck (US): ~ **farm** n Gemüsefarm f; ~ **farmer** n Gemüsegärtner(in f) m.

trucking ['trʌkɪŋ] n (US) Transport m.

truckload ['trʌkləud] n Wagenladung f.

truculent ['trʌkjulənt] adj trotzig, aufsässig.

trudge [trʌdʒ] vi **to** ~ **in/out/along** etc hinein-/hinaus-/entlangtrotten etc.

true [truː] **1** adj **(a)** wahr. **to come** ~ (dream, wishes) wahr werden; (prophecy) sich verwirklichen; (fears) sich bewahrheiten; **that's** ~ das stimmt, das ist wahr; **the same is** or **holds** ~ **for** ... dasselbe gilt auch für ...; ~! richtig!; **too** ~! (das ist nur) zu wahr!

(b) (accurate) description wahrheitsgetreu; likeness (lebens)getreu; copy getreu.

(c) (real, genuine) feeling, friend, opinion wahr, echt; reason wirklich; antique echt. ~ **love** die wahre Liebe; (person) Herzallerliebste(r) mf (old).

(d) (faithful) friend, follower treu. **to be** ~ **to sb** jdm treu sein/bleiben; **to be** ~ **to one's word** (treu) zu seinem Wort stehen, seinem Wort treu bleiben; ~ **to life** lebensnah; (Art) lebensecht; **the horse ran** ~ **to form** das Pferd lief erwartungsgemäß.

(e) wall, surface gerade; join genau; circle rund; (Mus) note rein.

2 n out of ~ beam, wheels schief.

truffle ['trʌfl] n Trüffel f or m.

truism ['truːɪzəm] n (obvious truth) Binsenwahrheit f; (platitude) Platitüde f, Gemeinplatz m.

truly ['truːlɪ] adv **(a)** (genuinely) wirklich, wahrhaftig. **a** ~ **great writer** ein wahrhaft großer Schriftsteller. **(b)** (faithfully) serve treu; reflect wahrheitsgetreu.

trump [trʌmp] n **1** (Cards, fig) Trumpf m. **spades are** ~**s** Pik ist Trumpf; **to hold all the** ~**s** (fig) alle Trümpfe in der Hand halten; ~ **card** (Cards) Trumpf(karte) f m; (fig) Trumpf m; **to play one's** ~ **card** (lit, fig) seinen Trumpf ausspielen; **to turn up** ~**s** (col) die Lage retten. **2** vt (Cards) stechen; (fig) übertrumpfen.

♦ **trump up** vt sep erfinden.

trumpet ['trʌmpɪt] n **1** (Mus) Trompete f. **to blow one's own** ~ sich selbst loben. **2** vi (elephant) trompeten.

trumpeter ['trʌmpɪtə[r]] n Trompeter(in f) m.

truncate [trʌŋ'keɪt] vt beschneiden.

truncheon ['trʌntʃən] n (esp Brit) Knüppel m; (esp of riot police) Schlagstock m.

trundle ['trʌndl] **1** vt (push) rollen; (pull) ziehen. **2** vi **to** ~ **along/down** entlang-/hinunterzockeln; (clatter) entlang-/hinunterrumpeln.

trunk [trʌŋk] n **(a)** (of tree) Stamm m; (of body) Rumpf m. **(b)** (of elephant) Rüssel m. **(c)** (case) Schrankkoffer m; (US Aut) Kofferraum m. **(d)** ~**s** pl (for swimming) Badehose f; (for sport) Shorts pl; **a pair of** ~**s** ein Badehose/(ein Paar) Shorts.

trunk: ~ **call** n (Brit Telec) Ferngespräch nt; ~ **road** n (Brit) Fernstraße f.

truss [trʌs] n **1** (Med) Bruchband nt. **2** vt **(a)** (tie) hay bündeln. **(b)** (Cook) chicken etc dressieren.

♦ **truss up** vt sep person fesseln.

trust [trʌst] n **1** vt **(a)** (have confidence in) trauen (+dat); person also vertrauen (+dat); words glauben. **to** ~

trust [trʌst] n **1** (a) Vertrauen nt (in zu). **I have every** ~ **in him** ich habe volles Vertrauen zu ihm; **to put** or **place one's** ~ **in sb** jdn Vertrauen setzen; **to take sth on** ~ etw einfach glauben; **position of** ~ Vertrauensstellung f. **(b)** (charge) Verantwortung f. **to commit sth to** or **place sth in sb's** ~ jdm etw anvertrauen. **(c)** (Jur, Fin) Treuhand(schaft) f; (property) Treuhandeigentum nt; (charitable fund) Fonds m, Stiftung f. **to hold sth in** ~ **for sb** etw für jdn treuhänderisch verwalten; ~ **fund** Treuhandvermögen nt; Stiftungsgelder pl. **(d)** (Comm: also ~ **company**) Trust m.

2 vt **(a)** (have confidence in) trauen (+dat); person also vertrauen (+dat); words glauben. **to** ~

sb to do sth jdm vertrauen, daß er etw tut; **to ~ sb with sth, to ~ sth to sb** jdm etw anvertrauen; **can he be ~ed not to lose it?** kann man sich darauf verlassen, daß er es nicht verliert?; **can we ~ him to go shopping alone?** können wir ihn allein einkaufen gehen lassen?; **I wouldn't ~ him an inch** (col) ich traue ihm nicht über den Weg (col). **(b)** (iro col) **~ you/him!** typisch!; **~ him to break it!** er muß es natürlich kaputtmachen. **(c)** (hope) hoffen. **I ~ not** ich hoffe nicht.
3 vi **to ~ in sb** auf jdn vertrauen; **to ~ to luck** or **chance** sich auf sein Glück verlassen.

trusted ['trʌstɪd] adj method bewährt; friend, servant getreu.

trustee [trʌs'tiː] n **(a)** (of estate) Treuhänder(in f) m. **(b)** (of institution) Verwalter m. **~s** Vorstand m.

trustful ['trʌstfʊl], **trusting** ['trʌstɪŋ] adj look vertrauensvoll; person also gutgläubig, arglos.

trustworthy ['trʌst,wɜːðɪ] adj person vertrauenswürdig; statement, account glaubwürdig.

trusty ['trʌstɪ] adj (+er) (liter, hum) getreu (liter).

truth [truːθ] n, pl **-s** [truːðz] no pl Wahrheit f. **you must always tell the ~** du mußt immer die Wahrheit sagen; **to tell the ~ ...** um ehrlich zu sein ...; **the ~ of the matter is that ...** die Wahrheit ist, daß ...; **there's no ~ in what he says** es ist kein Wort wahr von dem, was er sagt; **there's some ~ in that** da ist etwas Wahres dran (col); **the ~, the whole ~ and nothing but the ~** (Jur) die Wahrheit, die reine Wahrheit und nichts als die Wahrheit; **in ~** in Wahrheit, in Wirklichkeit.

truthful ['truːθfʊl] adj person ehrlich; statement wahrheitsgetreu. **to be ~ about it** ehrlich sein.

truthfully ['truːθfəlɪ] adv ehrlich; say also, explain wahrheitsgemäß.

try [traɪ] **1** n **(a)** Versuch m. **to have a ~** es versuchen; **let me have a ~** laß mich mal versuchen; **to have a ~ at doing sth** versuchen or probieren, etw zu tun; **have another ~ (at it)** versuch's noch mal; **I'll give it a ~** (will attempt it) ich werde es mal versuchen; (will test it out) ich werde es ausprobieren; **it was a good ~** das war schon ganz gut; **it's worth a ~** es ist einen Versuch wert. **(b)** (Rugby) Versuch m. **to score a ~** einen Versuch erzielen.
2 vt **(a)** (attempt) versuchen. **to ~ one's hardest** or **one's best** sein Bestes tun or versuchen; **it's ~ing to rain** (col) es fängt an zu regnen; **to ~ one's hand at sth** etw probieren; **just you ~ it!** (dare) versuch's bloß!
(b) (~ **out**) new product etc ausprobieren; job applicant eine Chance geben (+dat), es versuchen mit (col); (~ **using**) glue, aspirin es versuchen mit; (~ **to buy** or **get sth at**) newsagent, next door es versuchen bei; (~ **to open**) door, window ausprobieren. **~ this for size** (fig col) wie wär's denn damit? (col).
(c) (sample, taste) probieren.
(d) (test) courage, patience auf die Probe stellen; (strain) eyes anstrengen. **(just) ~ me!** (col) wetten?; **tried and tested** (Comm) erprobt, bewährt.
(e) (Jur) person unter Anklage stellen; case verhandeln. **he is being tried for theft** er steht wegen Diebstahls vor Gericht.
3 vi versuchen. **~ and arrive on time** versuche pünktlich zu sein; **he wasn't even ~ing** er hat sich (dat) überhaupt keine Mühe gegeben; **(didn't attempt it)** er hat es überhaupt nicht versucht.

♦ **try for** vi +prep obj sich bemühen um.
♦ **try on** vt sep **(a)** clothes anprobieren; hat aufprobieren. **(b)** (fig col) **to ~ it ~ with sb** probieren, wie weit man bei jdm gehen kann.
♦ **try out** vt sep ausprobieren (on bei, an +dat); person eine Chance geben (+dat).

trying ['traɪɪŋ] adj anstrengend; experience

schwer. **they've had a ~ time of it recently** sie haben es in letzter Zeit sehr schwer gehabt.

tsar [zɑːʳ] n Zar m.

tsetse (fly) ['tsetsɪ('flaɪ)] n Tsetsefliege f.

T-shirt ['tiːʃɜːt] n T-Shirt nt.

T-square ['tiːskwɛəʳ] n Reißschiene f.

tub [tʌb] n Kübel m; (for rainwater) Tonne, Traufe f; (for washing) Zuber, Bottich m; (of ice-cream, margarine) Becher m.

tuba ['tjuːbə] n Tuba f.

tubby ['tʌbɪ] adj (+er) (col) dick, rundlich.

tube [tjuːb] n **(a)** (pipe) Rohr nt; (of rubber, plastic) Schlauch m. **(b)** (of toothpaste etc) Tube f; (of sweets) Rolle f. **(c)** (London underground) U-Bahn f. **by ~** mit der U-Bahn; **~ station** U-Bahnstation f. **(d)** (Elec, TV, US Rad) Röhre f. **the ~** (US col) die Röhre (col).

tubeless ['tjuːblɪs] adj tyre schlauchlos.

tuber ['tjuːbəʳ] n (Bot) Knolle f.

tuberculosis [tjʊ,bɜːkjʊ'ləʊsɪs] n Tuberkulose f.

tubing ['tjuːbɪŋ] n Schlauch m.

tubular ['tjuːbjʊləʳ] adj röhrenförmig.

TUC = Trades Union Congress ≃ DGB.

tuck [tʌk] **1** n **(a)** (Sew) Saum m; (ornamental) Biese f. **to put a ~ in sth** einen Saum in etw (acc) nähen. **(b)** (Sch sl: food) Süßigkeiten pl. **~ shop** Bonbonladen m. **2** vt (put) stecken. **he ~ed his umbrella under his arm** er steckte or klemmte (col) sich (dat) den Regenschirm unter den Arm. **3** vi your bag will **~ under the seat** du kannst deine Tasche unter dem Sitz verstauen.

♦ **tuck away** vt sep (hide) wegstecken. **he ~ed it ~ in his pocket** er steckte es in die Tasche; **the hut is ~ed ~ among the trees** die Hütte liegt versteckt zwischen den Bäumen.

♦ **tuck in** vi (col) zulangen, reinhauen (col). **~ ~!** langt zu!, haut rein! (col); **to ~ ~ to sth** sich (dat) etw schmecken lassen. **2** vt sep flap etc hineinstecken, reinstecken (col). **to ~ one's shirt ~** das Hemd in die Hose stecken; **to ~ sb ~ (to bed)** jdn zudecken.

♦ **tuck up** vt sep skirt, hair hochnehmen; sleeve hochkrempeln; legs unterschlagen. **to ~ sb ~ (in bed)** jdn zudecken.

Tuesday ['tjuːzdɪ] n Dienstag m. **on ~** (am) Dienstag; **~ December 5th** (in letter) Dienstag, den 5. Dezember; **on ~s** dienstags; **I met her on a ~** ich habe sie an einem Dienstag kennengelernt; **on ~ morning/evening** (am) Dienstag morgen/abend; **on ~ mornings/evenings** dienstags or Dienstag morgens/abends; **last/next/this ~** letzten/nächsten/diesen Dienstag; **a year last/next ~** letzten/nächsten Dienstag vor einem Jahr; **our ~ meeting** (this week) unser Treffen am Dienstag; **(every week)** unser Dienstagstreffen.

tuft [tʌft] n Büschel nt. **a ~ of hair/feathers** ein Haarbüschel nt/Federbusch m.

tug [tʌg] **1** vt zerren, ziehen. **she ~ged his sleeve** sie zog an seinem Ärmel. **2** vi ziehen, zerren (at an +dat). **3** n **(a)** (pull) **to give sth a ~** an etw (dat) ziehen; **~ of war** (Sport, fig) Tauziehen nt. **(b)** (also **~boat**) Schlepper m.

tuition [tjʊ'ɪʃən] n Unterricht m. **extra ~** Nachhilfeunterricht.

tulip ['tjuːlɪp] n Tulpe f.

tumble ['tʌmbl] **1** n (fall) Sturz m. **to take a ~** stürzen, straucheln; (fig) fallen. **2** vi (fall) straucheln, (hin)fallen; (move quickly) stürzen; (fig: prices) fallen. **he ~d off his bicycle** er stürzte vom Fahrrad; **to ~ out of/into bed** dem Bett/ins Bett fallen.

tumble: **~down** adj verfallen, baufällig; **~-drier** n Trockenautomat m.

tumbler ['tʌmbləʳ] n **(a)** (glass) (Becher)glas nt. **(b)** (tumble drier) Trockenautomat m.

tummy ['tʌmɪ] n (col) Bauch m. **(a)** **~ ache** Bauchschmerzen pl, Bauchweh nt.

tumour, (US) **tumor** ['tjuːmə'] n Geschwulst f, Tumor m.

tumult ['tjuːmʌlt] n (uproar) Tumult m. **the ~ of battle** das Schlachtgetümmel.

tumultuous [tjuːˈmʌltjʊəs] adj tumultartig; applause stürmisch. **they gave him a ~ welcome** sie begrüßten ihn stürmisch.

tuna (fish) ['tjuːnə('fɪʃ)] n Thunfisch m.

tune [tjuːn] 1 n (a) (melody) Melodie f. **sung to the ~ of** ... gesungen nach der Melodie (von) ...; **to change one's ~** (fig) seine Meinung ändern; **to the ~ of £100** in Höhe von £100. (b) **to sing in ~/out of ~** richtig/falsch singen; **the piano is out of ~** das Klavier ist verstimmt; **to be in/out of ~ with sb/sth** (fig) mit jdm/etw harmonieren/nicht harmonieren; **the engine's out of ~** der Motor ist falsch eingestellt; **he's in ~ with young people** er ist auf einer Wellenlänge mit der Jugend (col); **he felt out of ~ with his new environment** er fühlte sich in seiner neuen Umgebung fehl am Platze. 2 vt (a) (Mus) instrument stimmen. (b) (Rad, Aut) einstellen.

♦ **tune in 1** vi (Rad) einschalten. **to ~ ~ to Radio London** Radio London einschalten or hören. 2 vt sep radio einschalten (to acc). **you are ~d ~ to Radio 2** Sie hören Radio 2.

♦ **tune up 1** vi (Mus) (sein Instrument/die Instrumente) stimmen. 2 vt sep engine einstellen.

tuneful ['tjuːnfʊl] adj melodisch.

tuneless ['tjuːnlɪs] adj unmelodisch.

tuner ['tjuːnə'] n (a) (Mus) Stimmer m. (b) (Rad etc) Tuner m.

tungsten ['tʌŋstən] n Wolfram nt.

tunic ['tjuːnɪk] n Kasack m, Hemdbluse f; (of uniform) Uniformrock m.

tuning ['tjuːnɪŋ] n (a) (Mus) stimmen nt. **~-fork** Stimmgabel f. (b) (Rad) Einstellen nt. **~ knob** Stationswahlknopf m. (c) (Aut) Einstellen nt.

Tunisia [tjuːˈnɪzɪə] n Tunesien nt.

tunnel ['tʌnl] (vb: pret, ptp (Brit) **tunnelled,** (US) **tunneled**) 1 n Tunnel m; (Min) Stollen m. 2 vi (into in +acc, through durch) einen Tunnel bauen; (rabbit) einen Bau graben; (mole) Gänge graben. 3 vt **they ~led a passage under the prison wall** sie gruben sich unter der Gefängnismauer durch; **to ~ one's way through sth** sich durch etw hindurchgraben.

tunny (fish) ['tʌnɪ('fɪʃ)] n Thunfisch m.

tuppence ['tʌpəns] n zwei Pence. **I don't care ~** das interessiert mich nicht für fünf Pfennig (col).

turban ['tɜːbən] n Turban m.

turbid ['tɜːbɪd] adj liquid trüber.

turbine ['tɜːbaɪn] n Turbine f.

turbo ['tɜːbəʊ] n: **~ charger** n Turbolader m; **~jet** (engine) Turbotriebwerk nt; (aircraft) Turbojet m.

turbot ['tɜːbət] n Steinbutt m.

turbulence ['tɜːbjʊləns] n (of emotions) Aufgewühltheit f; (of career, period) Turbulenz f. **air ~** Turbulenz f.

turbulent ['tɜːbjʊlənt] adj stürmisch; emotions also aufgewühlt; career, period also turbulent.

tureen [təˈriːn] n (Suppen)terrine f.

turf [tɜːf] 1 n, pl -s or **turves** (a) (no pl: lawn) Rasen m; (no pl: squares of grass) Soden pl; (square of grass) Sode f. (b) (no pl: peat) Torf (soden pl) m; (square of peat) Torfsode f. **to cut ~(s)** Torf stechen. (c) (Sport) **the T~** die (Pferde)rennbahn; **~ accountant** Buchmacher m. 2 vt (a) **he ~ed the garden** er verlegte (Gras)soden im Garten. (b) (col) **to ~ sb down the stairs** jdn die Treppe hinunterscheuchen (col); **to ~ sth into the corner** etw in die Ecke werfen.

♦ **turf out** vt sep (col) person rauswerfen; plan umschmeißen (col), verwerfen; (throw away) wegschmeißen (col).

turgid ['tɜːdʒɪd] adj (swollen) (an)geschwollen; (fig) style schwülstig, überladen.

Turk [tɜːk] n Türke m, Türkin f.

Turkey ['tɜːkɪ] n die Türkei.

turkey ['tɜːkɪ] n Truthahn m/-henne f, Pute(r) mf (esp Cook).

Turkish ['tɜːkɪʃ] 1 adj türkisch. **~ bath** türkisches Bad; **~ delight** Lokum nt. 2 n (language) Türkisch nt.

turmoil ['tɜːmɔɪl] n Aufruhr m; (confusion) Durcheinander nt. **everything is in a ~** alles ist in Aufruhr; **her mind was in a ~** sie war völlig verwirrt.

turn [tɜːn] 1 n (a) (movement) Drehung f. **to give sth a ~** etw drehen.

(b) (change of direction) (in road) Kurve f; (Sport) Wende f. **to make a ~ to the left** nach links einbiegen; (driver, car also, road) nach links abbiegen; (road) eine Linkskurve machen; **take the left-hand ~** biegen Sie links ab; **"no left ~"** "Linksabbiegen verboten"; **the ~ of the tide** (lit) der Gezeitenwechsel; **the tide is on the ~** (lit) die Ebbe/Flut setzt ein; (fig) es tritt eine Wende ein; **at the ~ of the century** um die Jahrhundertwende; **at every ~** (fig) auf Schritt und Tritt; **things took a ~ for the worse/the better** die Dinge wendeten sich zum Schlechten/zum Guten; **the patient took a ~ for the worse/the better** das Befinden des Patienten wendete sich zum Schlechteren/zum Besseren; **things took a ~ new** ~ die Dinge nahmen eine neue Wendung; **~ of phrase** Ausdrucksweise f.

(c) (in game, queue, series) **in ~** der Reihe nach; **out of ~** außer der Reihe; **it's your ~** du bist an der Reihe, du bist dran; **it's your ~ to do the dishes** du bist mit (dem) Abwaschen dran; **it's my ~ next** ich komme als nächste(r) an die Reihe; **wait your ~** warten Sie, bis Sie an der Reihe sind; **your ~ will come** du kommst auch noch mal dran; **sorry, have I spoken out of ~?** Entschuldigung, habe ich etwas Falsches gesagt?; **in ~, by ~s** abwechselnd; **to take ~s at doing sth** etw abwechselnd tun; **to take ~s at the wheel** sich beim Fahren abwechseln; **to take a ~ at the wheel** (für eine Weile) das Steuer übernehmen.

(d) (service) **to do sb a good/bad ~** jdm einen guten/schlechten Dienst erweisen; **one good ~ deserves another** (Prov) eine Hand wäscht die andere (prov).

(e) (tendency, talent) **to have a mathematical ~ of mind** mathematisch begabt sein; **an optimistic/a strange ~ of mind** eine optimistische/seltsame Einstellung; **a melancholy ~ of mind** ein Hang zur Melancholie.

(f) (Med col) **he had one of his ~s last night** er hatte letzte Nacht wieder einen Anfall; **you/it gave me quite a ~** du hast/es hat mir einen schönen Schrecken eingejagt.

(g) (Theat) Nummer f. **they got him to do a ~ at the party** sie brachten ihn dazu, auf der Party etwas zum besten zu geben.

2 vt (a) (revolve) key, screw, steering wheel drehen. **to ~ the key in the lock** den Schlüssel im Schloß herumdrehen; **what ~s the wheel?** wird das Rad angetrieben?; **he ~ed the wheel sharply** er riß das Steuer herum.

(b) (~ over, ~ round) mattress, car, soil wenden; page umblättern; record, chair, picture etc umdrehen.

(c) (transform, make become) verwandeln (in(to) in +acc). **the play was ~ed into a film** das Stück wurde verfilmt; **this hot weather has ~ed the milk (sour)** bei dieser Hitze ist die Milch sauer geworden.

(d) **he ~ed his head towards me** er wandte mir den Kopf zu; **he ~ed his back to the wall** er kehrte den Rücken zur Wand; **success has ~ed his head** der Erfolg ist ihm zu Kopf gestiegen;

she seems to have ~**ed his head** sie scheint ihm den Kopf verdreht zu haben; **she can still** ~ **a few heads** die Männer schauen sich immer noch nach ihr um; **as soon as his back is** ~**ed** sobald er den Rücken kehrt; **the sight of all that food quite** ~**ed my stomach** beim Anblick des vielen Essens drehte sich mir regelrecht der Magen um; **without** ~**ing a hair** ohne mit der Wimper zu zucken; **she** ~**ed her hand to cooking** sie versuchte sich im Kochen; **to** ~ **one's thoughts/ attention to sth** seine Gedanken/ Aufmerksamkeit einer Sache (dat) zuwenden; **to** ~ **a gun on sb** auf jdn richten; **he has** ~**ed forty** er ist vierzig geworden; **it is** or **has** ~**ed 2 o'clock** es ist 2 Uhr vorbei; **the car** ~**ed the corner** das Auto bog um die Ecke; **to have** ~**ed the corner** (fig) über den Berg sein; **nothing will** ~ **him from his purpose** nichts wird ihn von seinem Vorhaben abbringen; **to** ~ **a dog on sb** einen Hund auf jdn hetzen.

3 vi **(a)** (revolve, move round: key, wheel) sich drehen. **he** ~**ed to me and smiled** er drehte sich mir zu und lächelte; **to** ~ **upside down** umkippen; **my head is** ~**ing** in meinem Kopf dreht sich alles.

(b) (change direction) (to one side) (person, car) abbiegen; (plane, boat) abdrehen; (~ around) wenden; (person: on the spot) sich umdrehen; (wind) drehen. **to** ~ **and go back** umkehren; **to** ~ **(to the) left** links abbiegen; **our luck** ~**ed** unser Glück wendete sich.

(c) (go) **to** ~ **to sb/sth** sich an jdn wenden/sich einer Sache (dat) zuwenden; **after her death, he** ~**ed to his books for comfort** nach ihrem Tod suchte er Trost bei seinen Büchern; **this job would make anyone** ~ **to drink!** bei dieser Arbeit muß man ja zum Trinker werden!; **the conversation** ~**ed to the accident** das Gespräch kam auf den Unfall; **I don't know which way to** ~ ich weiß nicht, was ich machen soll.

(d) (leaves) sich (ver)färben; (milk) sauer werden; (meat) schlecht werden; (weather) umschlagen. **to** ~ **into sth** sich in etw (acc) verwandeln; (develop into) sich zu etw entwickeln; **their short holiday** ~**ed into a three-month visit** aus ihrem Kurzurlaub wurde ein Aufenthalt von drei Monaten; **to** ~ **to stone** zu Stein werden; **to** ~ **traitor** zum Verräter werden; **to** ~ **red** (leaves etc) sich rot färben; (person: blush) rot werden; (traffic lights) auf Rot umspringen; **his hair is** ~**ing grey** sein Haar wird grau.

♦**turn against 1** vi +prep obj sich wenden gegen. **2** vt sep +prep obj **they** ~**ed him** ~ **his parents** sie brachten ihn gegen seine Eltern auf; **they** ~**ed his argument** ~ **him** sie verwendeten sein Argument gegen ihn.

♦**turn around 1** vi (face other way) sich umdrehen; (go back) umkehren. **we** ~**ed** ~ **the corner** wir bogen um die Ecke. **2** vt sep head drehen; box umdrehen. ~ **the picture** ~ **the other way** dreh das Bild andersherum.

♦**turn aside 1** vi sich abwenden (from von). **2** vt sep abwenden.

♦**turn away 1** vi sich abwenden. **2** vt sep **(a)** (move) head, eyes abwenden. **(b)** (send away) person abweisen; business ablehnen.

♦**turn back 1** vi **(a)** (traveller, aeroplane) umkehren; (look back) sich umdrehen. **there can be no** ~**ing** ~ **now** (fig) jetzt gibt es kein Zurück mehr. **(b)** (in book) **to** ~ ~ **to page 100** auf Seite 100 zurückblättern. **2** vt sep **(a)** (fold) bedclothes zurückschlagen; corner umknicken; hem umschlagen. **(b)** (send back) person zurückschicken. **they were** ~**ed** ~ **at the frontier** sie wurden an der Grenze zurückgewiesen. **(c)** clock zurückstellen. **to** ~ **the clock** ~ **fifty years** die Uhr um fünfzig Jahre zurückdrehen.

♦**turn down 1** vt sep **(a)** (fold down) bedclothes zurückschlagen; collar, brim herunterklappen; corner of a page umknicken. **(b)** gas, heat, lights herunterdrehen; volume leiser stellen. **(c)** candidate, novel etc ablehnen; offer also zurückweisen; suitor abweisen. **2** vi +prep obj **he** ~**ed** ~ **a side street** er bog in eine Seitenstraße ab.

♦**turn in 1** vi **(a)** (drive in) **the car** ~**ed** ~ **at the top of the drive** das Auto bog in die Einfahrt ein. **(b)** (col: go to bed) sich hinhauen (col). **2** vt sep (col: to police) **to** ~ **sb** ~ jdn anzeigen or verpfeifen (col).

♦**turn off 1** vi abbiegen (for nach, prep obj von). **2** vt sep **(a)** light, gas, radio ausmachen; tap zudrehen; TV abschalten; water, electricity, engine, machine abstellen. **(b)** (col) **to** ~ **sb** ~ (disgust) jdn anwidern; (put off) jdm die Lust verderben.

♦**turn on 1** vt sep **(a)** gas, heat, engine anstellen, anmachen; light, radio, television, the news also einschalten; tap, central heating aufdrehen. **(b)** (col: appeal to: music, novel etc) **sth** ~**s sb** ~ jd steht auf etw (acc) (col); **whatever** ~**s you** ~ wenn du das gut findest (col); **he/it doesn't** ~ **me** ~ er/das läßt mich kalt (also sexually); **that** ~**s me** ~ (sexually) das macht mich ganz scharf (col). **2** vi +prep obj **(a)** (attack) angreifen. **(b)** (depend on) abhängen von.

♦**turn out 1** vi **(a)** (firemen) ausrücken; (doctor) einen Krankenbesuch machen. **(b)** (point) **his toes** ~ ~ er läuft nach außen. **(c)** **the car** ~**ed** ~ **of the drive** das Auto bog aus der Einfahrt. **(d)** (transpire) sich herausstellen. **he** ~**ed** ~ **to be the murderer himself** es stellte sich heraus, daß er selbst der Mörder war; **as it** ~**ed** ~ wie sich herausstellte. **(e)** (develop, progress) sich entwickeln. **everything will** ~ ~ **all right** es wird sich schon alles ergeben; **it's** ~**ed** ~ **nice today** es ist heute wieder schön geworden.

2 vt sep **(a)** light ausmachen; gas also abstellen. **(b)** (produce) produzieren; novel etc schreiben; good students hervorbringen. **(c)** (expel) vertreiben (of aus), hinauswerfen (col) (of aus); tenant kündigen (+dat). **(d)** (tip out) cake stürzen; pockets (aus)leeren. **he** ~**ed the photos** ~ **of the box** er kippte die Fotos aus der Schachtel. **(e)** (clean) room gründlich saubermachen. **(f)** guard antreten lassen. **(g)** well ~**ed** ~ gut gekleidet.

♦**turn over 1** vi **(a)** (person, stomach) sich umdrehen; (car, place etc) sich überschlagen; (boat) kentern. **he** ~**ed** ~ **on(to) his back** er drehte sich auf den Rücken. **(b)** (with pages) **please** ~ ~ bitte wenden. **2** vt sep **(a)** umdrehen; (turn upside down) umkippen; page umblättern; soil umgraben; mattress, steak wenden. **the police** ~**ed the whole place** ~ (search) die Polizei durchsuchte das ganze Haus. **(b)** **to** ~ **an idea** ~ **in one's mind** sich (dat) eine Idee durch den Kopf gehen lassen. **(b)** (hand over) übergeben (to dat).

♦**turn round** vti = **turn around.**

♦**turn up 1** vi **(a)** (arrive) erscheinen, auftauchen (col). **I was afraid you wouldn't** ~ ~ ich hatte Angst, du würdest nicht kommen. **(b)** (be found) (wieder) auftauchen (col). **(c)** (happen) something is sure to ~ ~ irgend etwas passiert schon. **(d)** (point up) **a** ~**ed** ~ **nose** eine Stupsnase; **to** ~ ~ **at the ends** sich an den Enden hochbiegen. **2** vt sep **(a)** (fold) collar hochklappen; hem umnähen. **to** ~ ~ **one's nose at sth** (fig) die Nase über etw (acc) rümpfen. **(b)** heat, gas höher drehen; radio lauter drehen; volume aufdrehen; light heller drehen.

turn: ~**about,** ~**around** n Kehrtwendung f; ~**coat** n Überläufer m.

turning ['tɜːnɪŋ] n (in road) Abzweigung f. **take the second** ~ **on the left** nimm die zweite Abfahrt links.

turning point n Wendepunkt m.

turnip ['tɜːnɪp] n Rübe f.

turn-off ['tɜːnɒf] n Abzweigung f; (on motorway) Abfahrt, Ausfahrt f. **the Birmingham ~ die** Abfahrt or Ausfahrt Birmingham.

turnout ['tɜːnaʊt] n **(a)** (attendance) Teilnahme, Beteiligung f. **in spite of the rain there was a big ~ for the match** trotz des Regens war das Spiel gut besucht. **(b)** (clean) **to give sth a good ~** etw gründlich säubern. **(c)** (dress) Aufmachung f.

turnover ['tɜːn,əʊvər] n (total business) Umsatz m; (Comm, Fin: of capital) Umlauf m; (Comm: of stock) (Lager)umschlag m; (of staff) Fluktuation f.

turn: ~**pike** n (Brit Hist) Mautschranke f; (US) gebührenpflichtige Autobahn; ~**stile** n Drehkreuz nt; ~**table** n Drehscheibe f; (on record player) Plattenteller m; ~**-up** n (a) (Brit: on trousers) Aufschlag m; **(b)** (col: event) **that was a** ~**-up for the book** das war eine (echte) Überraschung.

turpentine ['tɜːpəntaɪn] n Terpentin nt.

turquoise ['tɜːkwɔɪz] **1** n (a) (gem) Türkis m. **(b)** (colour) Türkis nt. **2** adj türkis(farben).

turret ['tʌrɪt] n (Archit) Mauerturm m; (on tank) Turm m; (on ship) Gefechtsturm m.

turtle ['tɜːtl] n (Wasser)schildkröte f; (US also) (Land)schildkröte f. **to turn** ~ kentern.

turtle: ~**-dove** n (lit, fig col) Turteltaube f; ~**-neck** (pullover) n Schildkrötenkragenpullover m.

tusk [tʌsk] n (of elephant) Stoßzahn m; (of walrus) Eckzahn m; (of boar) Hauer m.

tussle ['tʌsl] **1** n (lit, fig) Gerangel nt. **2** vi sich rangeln (with sb for sth mit jdm um etw).

tussock ['tʌsək] n (Gras)büschel nt.

tutor ['tjuːtər] **1** n **(a)** Privatlehrer m. **(b)** (Brit Univ) Tutor m. **2** vt (as private teacher) privat unterrichten; (give extra lessons to) Nachhilfe(unterricht) geben (+dat). **to** ~ **sb in Latin** jdm Privatunterricht/Nachhilfe in Latein geben.

tutorial [tjuːˈtɔːrɪəl] n (Brit Univ) Kolloquium nt.

tut-tut ['tʌt'tʌt] interj (in disapproval) na, na.

TV n (col) = **television**.

tuxedo [tʌkˈsiːdəʊ] n (US) Smoking m.

twaddle ['twɒdl] n (col) Geschwätz nt.

twang [twæŋ] **1** n (of wire, guitar string) Doing nt; (of rubber band, bowstring) scharfer Ton; (of voice) Näseln nt, näselnder Tonfall. **2** vt zupfen; guitar, banjo also klimpern auf (+dat). **3** vi einen scharfen Ton von sich geben; (rubber band) pitschen (col).

tweak [twiːk] **1** vt kneifen. **to** ~ **sb's ear** jdn am Ohr ziehen. **2** n **to give sb's ear/nose a** ~ jdn am Ohr/an der Nase ziehen.

twee [twiː] adj (+er) (col) niedlich; manner geziert; expression gekünstelt.

tweed [twiːd] **1** n **(a)** (cloth) Tweed m. **(b)** ~**s** pl (clothes) Tweedkleidung f. **2** adj Tweed-.

tweet [twiːt] **1** n Piepsen nt no pl. **2** vi piepsen.

tweeter ['twiːtər] n Hochtonlautsprecher m.

tweezers ['twiːzəz] npl (also pair of ~) Pinzette f.

twelfth [twelfθ] **1** adj zwölfte(r, s). **2** n (in series) Zwölfte(r, s); (fraction) Zwölftel nt; see **sixth**.

twelve [twelv] adj zwölf. ~ **noon** zwölf Uhr (mittags); see **six**.

twentieth ['twentɪɪθ] **1** adj zwanzigste(r, s). **2** n (in series) Zwanzigste(r, s); (fraction) Zwanzigstel nt; see **sixtieth**.

twenty ['twentɪ] adj zwanzig; see **sixty**.

twerp [twɜːp] n (col) Einfaltspinsel (col).

twice [twaɪs] adv zweimal. ~ **as much/many** doppelt or zweimal soviel/so viele; ~ **as much bread** doppelt soviel Brot; ~ **as long as ...** zweimal so lange wie ...; **at** ~ **the speed of sound** mit doppelter Schallgeschwindigkeit; **she is** ~ **your age** sie ist doppelt so alt wie du; ~ **2 is 4** zweimal 2 ist 4; ~ **a week** zweimal wöchentlich, zweimal pro Woche; **I'd think** ~ **before trusting him with it** ihm würde ich das nicht so ohne weiteres

anvertrauen.

twiddle ['twɪdl] **1** vt herumdrehen an (+dat). **she** ~**d the pencil in her fingers** ihre Finger spielten mit dem Bleistift; **to** ~ **one's thumbs** (lit, fig) Däumchen drehen. **2** vi **to** ~ **with a knob** an einem Knopf herumdrehen.

twig[1] [twɪg] n (thin branch) Zweig m.

twig[2] (Brit col) **1** vt (realize) mitkriegen (col), mitbekommen. **he's** ~**ged it** er hat's kapiert (col). **2** vi schalten (col), es mitkriegen (col).

twilight ['twaɪlaɪt] n Dämmerung f. **at** ~ **in der** Dämmerung; **in the** ~ im Zwielicht.

twin [twɪn] n Zwilling m; (of same, object) Gegenstück, Pendant nt. **her** ~ ihre Zwillingsschwester/ihr Zwillingsbruder m. **2** vt (Brit) town verschwistern. **Oxford was** ~**ned with Bonn** Oxford und Bonn wurden zu Partnerstädten.

twin: ~ **beds** npl zwei (gleiche) Einzelbetten; ~ **brother** n Zwillingsbruder m; ~ **carburettors** (Brit) or **carburetors** (US) npl Doppelvergaser m.

twine [twaɪn] **1** n Schnur f, Bindfaden m. **2** vt winden. **to** ~ **one's arms around sb** seine Arme um jdn schlingen. **3** vi **to** ~ **around sth** sich um etw winden.

twinge [twɪndʒ] n (of pain) Zucken nt, leichtes Stechen. **a** ~ **of pain** ein zuckender Schmerz; **a** ~ **of conscience/remorse** Gewissensbisse pl.

twinkle ['twɪŋkl] **1** vi funkeln; (stars also) glitzern. **2** n Funkeln, Glitzern nt. **there was a** ~ **in her eye** man sah den Schalk in ihren Augen.

twinkling ['twɪŋklɪŋ] n **in the** ~ **of an eye** im Nu, im Handumdrehen.

twin: ~**set** n (Brit) Twinset nt; ~ **sister** n Zwillingsschwester f; ~ **town** n (Brit) Partnerstadt f; ~**-tub** (washing-machine) n Waschmaschine f mit getrennter Schleuder.

twirl [twɜːl] **1** n (of hair)wirbeln; skirt herumwirbeln; moustache zwirbeln. **2** vi wirbeln. **3** n Wirbel m; (in dance) Drehung f; (of moustache) hochstehende Spitze.

twist [twɪst] **1** n **(a)** (action) **to give sth a** ~ etw (herum)drehen; **with a quick** ~ **of the hand** mit einer schnellen Handbewegung. **(b)** (bend) Kurve, Biegung f; (fig: in story etc) Wendung f. **(c)** (Brit col) **to be/go round the** ~ verrückt sein/werden; **it's driving me round the** ~! das macht mich wahnsinnig! **(d)** (dance) Twist m. **2** vt **(a)** (wind, turn) drehen; (coil) wickeln (into zu +dat). **to** ~ **threads etc together** Fäden etc zusammendrehen; **to** ~ **the top off a jar** den Deckel von einem Glas abdrehen. **(b)** (bend, distort) key verbiegen; part of body, (fig) meaning, words verdrehen. **to** ~ **sth out of shape** etw verbiegen; **to** ~ **sb's arm** (lit) jdm den Arm verdrehen; (fig) jdn überreden; **to** ~ **one's ankle** sich (dat) den Fuß vertreten; **his face was** ~**ed with pain** sein Gesicht war schmerzverzerrt.

3 vi **(a)** sich drehen; (smoke) sich ringeln; (plant) sich ranken; (road, river, person: wriggle) sich schlängeln. **(b)** (dance) Twist tanzen.

♦ **twist off** vt sep abdrehen; lid abschrauben; flowerheads abknipsen.

twisted ['twɪstɪd] adj **(a)** wires, rope (zusammen)gedreht; (bent) verbogen. **(b)** ankle verrenkt. **(c)** (fig) mind, logic verdreht.

twit [twɪt] n (Brit col: person) Trottel m (col).

twitch [twɪtʃ] n **(a)** (tic) Zucken nt; (individual spasm) Zuckung f. **to give a** ~ zucken. **(b)** (pull) Ruck m (of an etw +dat). **to give sth a** ~ an etw (dat) rucken. **2** vi (face, muscles) zucken. **the cat's nose** ~**ed** die Katze schnupperte.

twitter ['twɪtər] **1** vti (lit, fig) zwitschern. **2** n (a) (of birds) Gezwitscher nt. **(b)** (col) **to be all of a** ~ ganz aufgeregt sein.

two [tuː] **1** adj zwei. **to cut sth in** ~ etw in zwei Teile schneiden; ~ **by** ~, **in** ~**s** zu zweit, zu zweien; **the** ~ **of them** die beiden; **to put** ~ **and** ~ **together** (fig) seine Schlüsse ziehen; ~ **can play**

that game *(col)* den Spieß kann man auch umdrehen; *see* **six. 2** *n* Zwei *f.* **just the** ~ **of us/them** nur wir beide/die beiden.

two: ~-**dimensional** *adj* zweidimensional; ~-**door** *adj* zweitürig; ~-**edged** *adj (lit, fig)* zweischneidig; ~-**faced** *adj (lit)* doppelgesichtig; *(fig)* falsch; ~**fold 1** *adj* zweifach, doppelt; **a** ~**fold increase** ein Anstieg um das Doppelte; **2** *adv* **to increase** ~**fold** um das Doppelte steigern; ~-**legged** *adj* zweibeinig; **a** ~-**legged animal** ein Zweibeiner *m;* ~-**party system** *n* Zweiparteiensystem *nt;* ~-**piece 1** *adj* zweiteilig; **2** *n (suit)* Zweiteiler *m; (swimming costume)* zweiteiliger Badeanzug; ~-**pin plug** *n* Stecker *m* mit zwei Kontakten; ~-**ply** *adj* wool zweifädig; *wood* aus zwei Lagen bestehend; *tissue* zweilagig; ~**seater** *n (car, plane)* Zweisitzer *m;* ~**some** *n* **(a)** *(people)* Paar, Pärchen *nt;* **(b)** *(game)* **to have a** ~**some at golf** zu zweit Golf spielen; ~ **star petrol** *(Brit)* Normalbenzin *nt;* ~-**stroke 1** *adj* Zweitakt-; **2** *n* Zweitakter *m.* ~-**time** *vt (col)* boyfriend, accomplice betrügen; ~-**tone** *adj (in colour)* zweifarbig; ~-**up** ~-**down** *n (Brit col)* kleines Reihenhäuschen; ~-**way** *adj* ~-**way (radio)** Funksprechgerät *nt;* ~-**way traffic** Verkehr *m* in beiden Richtungen; ~-**wheeler** *n* Zweirad, Fahrrad *nt.*
tycoon [taɪˈkuːn] *n* Magnat *m.*
type¹ [taɪp] *n* **(a)** *(kind)* Art *f; (of produce, plant also)* Sorte *f; (esp of people)* Typ, Typus *m.* **different** ~**s of cows/roses** verschiedene Arten von Rindern/verschiedene Rosensorten; **what** ~ **of car is it?** was für ein Auto(typ) ist das?; **they're totally different** ~**s of person** sie sind völlig verschiedene Typen; **I object to that** ~ **of behaviour** ich protestiere gegen ein solches Benehmen; **it's not my** ~ **of film** diese Art Film gefällt mir nicht; **he's not my** ~ er ist nicht mein Typ; **she's my** ~ **of girl** sie ist mein Typ; **he's not the** ~ **to hit a lady** er ist nicht der Mensch, der eine Frau schlägt. **(b)** *(col: man)* Typ *m.*
type² **1** *n (Typ)* Type *f.* **small/large** ~ kleine/große Schrift. **2** *vt* tippen *(col)*, (mit der Maschine)

schreiben. **a badly** ~**d letter** ein schlecht getippter Brief. **3** *vi* maschineschreiben, tippen *(col)*.
♦ **type out** *vt sep letter* schreiben, tippen *(col)*.
type: ~-**cast** *vt (Theat)* (auf eine bestimmte Rolle) festlegen; ~**face** *n* Schrift *f;* ~**script** *n* (mit Maschine geschriebenes) Manuskript; ~**setter** *n (person)* Setzer(in *f) m.*
typewriter [ˈtaɪpˌraɪtəʳ] *n* Schreibmaschine *f.* ~ **ribbon** Farbband *nt.*
typewritten [ˈtaɪpˌrɪtn] *adj* maschinengeschrieben, getippt *(col)*.
typhoid [ˈtaɪfɔɪd] *n (also* ~ **fever)** Typhus *m.*
typhoon [taɪˈfuːn] *n* Taifun *m.*
typhus [ˈtaɪfəs] *n* Fleckfieber *nt,* Flecktyphus *m.*
typical [ˈtɪpɪkəl] *adj* typisch *(of für).* **a** ~ **English town** eine typisch englische Stadt; **that's** ~ **of** him das ist typisch für ihn.
typically [ˈtɪpɪkəlɪ] *adv see adj.* ~, **he did nothing but complain** es war typisch für ihn, daß er sich ständig beschwerte.
typify [ˈtɪpɪfaɪ] *vt* bezeichnend sein für. **he typifies the reserved Englishman** er verkörpert den Typ des zurückhaltenden Engländers.
typing [ˈtaɪpɪŋ] **1** *n* Maschineschreiben, Tippen *(col) nt.* **his** ~ **isn't very good** er kann nicht besonders gut maschineschreiben. **2** *attr* Schreibmaschinen-. ~ **error** Tippfehler *m;* ~ **pool** Schreibzentrale *f.*
typist [ˈtaɪpɪst] *n (professional)* Schreibkraft *f,* Stenotypist(in *f) m.*
typographic(al) [ˌtaɪpəˈgræfɪk(əl)] *adj* typographisch. ~ **error** Druckfehler *m.*
tyrannic(al) [tɪˈrænɪk(əl)] *adj* tyrannisch.
tyrannize [ˈtɪrənaɪz] *vt (lit, fig)* tyrannisieren.
tyranny [ˈtɪrənɪ] *n (lit, fig)* Tyrannei *f.*
tyrant [ˈtaɪərənt] *n (lit, fig)* Tyrann(in *f) m.*
tyre, *(US)* **tire** [taɪəʳ] *n* Reifen *m.* ~ **gauge** Reifendruckmesser *m;* ~ **pressure** Reifendruck *m.*
Tyrol [tɪˈrəʊl] *n* **the** ~ Tirol *nt.*
Tyrolean [ˈtɪrəlɪən] *adj* Tiroler.
tzar *n =* **tsar.**

U

U, u [juː] *n* U, u *nt*.
ubiquitous [juːˈbɪkwɪtəs] *adj* allgegenwärtig.
U-boat [ˈjuːbəʊt] *n* U-Boot *nt*.
udder [ˈʌdəʳ] *n* Euter *nt*.
UFO [ˈjuːfəʊ] = **unidentified flying object** Ufo, UFO *nt*.
Uganda [juːˈgændə] *n* Uganda *nt*.
ugh [ɜːh] *interj* i, igitt.
ugliness [ˈʌglɪnɪs] *n* Häßlichkeit *f*.
ugly [ˈʌglɪ] *adj* (+er) **(a)** *(not pretty)* häßlich. **as ~ as sin** häßlich wie die Nacht. **(b)** *(unpleasant, nasty)* übel; *news, wound also* schlimm; *scenes, vice, clouds* häßlich; *crime also* gemein; *sky* bedrohlich. **an ~ customer** ein übler Kunde.
UHF = **ultra-high frequency** UHF.
UK = **United Kingdom** Vereinigtes Königreich.
ulcer [ˈʌlsəʳ] *n (Med)* Geschwür *nt*; *(stomach ~)* Magengeschwür *nt*; *(fig)* Übel *nt*.
Ulster [ˈʌlstəʳ] *n* Ulster, Nordirland *nt*. **U~man/woman** Einwohner(in *f*) *m* von Ulster.
ulterior [ʌlˈtɪərɪəʳ] *adj* **~ motive** Hintergedanke *m*.
ultimate [ˈʌltɪmɪt] **1** *adj* **(a)** *(final)* letzte(r, s); *destiny, solution, decision* endgültig; *result, outcome, aim* End-; *control* oberste(r, s); *authority* höchste(r, s). **what is your ~ ambition in life?** was streben Sie letzten Endes im Leben an?; **although they had no ~ hope of escape** obwohl im Endeffekt keine Hoffnung auf Flucht bestand.
(b) *(that cannot be improved on)* vollendet, perfekt. **the ~ insult** der Gipfel der Beleidigung; **the ~ deterrent** *(Mil)* das endgültige Abschreckungsmittel; *(fig)* die äußerste Abschreckungsmaßnahme; **the ~ weapon** *(Mil)* die Superwaffe; *(fig)* das letzte und äußerste Mittel; **death is the ~ sacrifice** der Tod ist das allergrößte Opfer.
(c) *(basic)* Grund-; *cause* eigentlich; *explanation* grundsätzlich; *truth* letzte(r, s).
(d) *(furthest)* entfernteste(r, s); *ancestors* früheste(r, s). **the ~ origins of man** die frühesten Ursprünge des Menschen.
2 *n* Nonplusultra *nt*. **the ~ in comfort** das Höchste an Komfort.
ultimately [ˈʌltɪmɪtlɪ] *adv (in the end)* letztlich, letzten Endes; *(eventually)* schließlich; *(fundamentally)* im Grunde genommen. **it's ~ your decision** letztlich müssen Sie das entscheiden.
ultimatum [ˌʌltɪˈmeɪtəm] *n, pl* -s *or* **ultimata** *(Mil, fig)* Ultimatum *nt*. **to deliver an ~ to sb** jdm ein Ultimatum stellen.
ultraviolet [ˌʌltrəˈvaɪəlɪt] *adj* ultraviolett.
umbilical [ˌʌmbɪˈlaɪkəl] *adj* **~ cord** Nabelschnur *f*.
umbrage [ˈʌmbrɪdʒ] *n*: **to take ~ at sth** an etw *(dat)* Anstoß nehmen.
umbrella [ʌmˈbrelə] *n* (Regen)schirm *m*; *(sun ~)* (Sonnen)schirm *m*. **collapsible** *or* **telescopic ~** Taschenschirm *m*; **under the ~ of** *(fig)* unter der Kontrolle von.
umbrella: **~ organization** *n* Dachorganisation *f*; **~ stand** *n* Schirmständer *m*.
umpire [ˈʌmpaɪəʳ] **1** *n (lit, fig)* Schiedsrichter(in *f*) *m*. **2** *vt (Sport)* Schiedsrichter sein bei; *(fig)* schlichten. **3** *vi* Schiedsrichter sein *(in* bei).

umpteen [ˈʌmpˈtiːn] *adj (col)* zig *(col)*, x *(col)*. **I've told you ~ times** ich habe dir x-mal gesagt *(col)*.
umpteenth [ˈʌmpˈtiːnθ] *adj (col)* x-te(r, s). **for the ~ time** zum x-ten Mal.
UN = **United Nations** UNO *f*. **~ troops** UNO-Truppen *pl*.
unabashed [ˌʌnəˈbæʃt] *adj (not ashamed)* dreist; *(not overawed)* unbeeindruckt.
unabated [ˌʌnəˈbeɪtɪd] *adj* unvermindert. **the rain continued ~** der Regen ließ nicht nach.
unable [ˌʌnˈeɪbl] *adj pred* **to be ~ to do sth** etw nicht tun können; *(not be in a position to)* außerstande sein, etw zu tun.
unabridged [ˌʌnəˈbrɪdʒd] *adj* ungekürzt.
unacceptable [ˌʌnəkˈseptəbl] *adj plans, terms* unannehmbar; *excuse, offer, behaviour* nicht akzeptabel; *standard, conditions* untragbar. **it's quite ~ that we should be expected to ...** es kann doch nicht von uns verlangt werden, daß ...; **it's quite ~ for young children to ...** es kann nicht zugelassen werden, daß kleine Kinder ...; **the ~ face of capitalism** die Kehrseite des Kapitalismus.
unaccompanied [ˌʌnəˈkʌmpənɪd] *adj person, child, singing* ohne Begleitung; *instrument* Solo-. **~ luggage** aufgegebenes Reisegepäck.
unaccountable [ˌʌnəˈkaʊntəbl] *adj* unerklärlich.
unaccountably [ˌʌnəˈkaʊntəblɪ] *adv* unerklärlicherweise; *disappear* auf unerklärliche Weise.
unaccounted for [ˌʌnəˈkaʊntɪdˈfɔːʳ] *adj* ungeklärt. **the £30 is still ~** es ist noch ungeklärt, wo die £30 geblieben sind; **three of the passengers are still ~** drei Passagiere werden noch vermißt.
unaccustomed [ˌʌnəˈkʌstəmd] *adj* **(a)** *(unusual)* ungewohnt. **(b)** *(of person: unused)* **to be ~ to sth** etw nicht gewohnt sein, an etw *(acc)* nicht gewöhnt sein; **to be ~ to doing sth** nicht daran gewöhnt sein, etw zu tun.
unacquainted [ˌʌnəˈkweɪntɪd] *adj pred* **to be ~ with poverty** die Armut nicht kennen; **to be ~ with the facts** mit den Tatschen nicht vertraut sein.
unadulterated [ˌʌnəˈdʌltəreɪtɪd] *adj* **(a)** unverfälscht, rein; *wine* rein, ungepanscht; *(hum)* whisky unverdünnt. **(b)** *(fig) nonsense* absolut; *bliss* ungetrübt.
unadventurous [ˌʌnədˈventʃərəs] *adj time, life* ereignislos; *tastes* bieder; *style, performance* einfallslos; *person* wenig unternehmungslustig.
unaffected [ˌʌnəˈfektɪd] *adj* **(a)** *(sincere)* ungekünstelt, natürlich; *pleasure, gratitude* echt. **(b)** *(not damaged)* nicht angegriffen *(also Med)*, nicht beeinträchtigt; *(not influenced)* unbeeinflußt; *(not involved)* nicht betroffen; *(unmoved)* ungerührt. **she remained quite ~ by his tears** sie blieb beim Anblick seiner Tränen völlig ungerührt.
unafraid [ˌʌnəˈfreɪd] *adj* furchtlos. **to be ~ of sb/sth** vor jdm/etw keine Angst haben.
unaided [ʌnˈeɪdɪd] **1** *adv* ohne fremde Hilfe. **2** *adj* **his own ~ work** seine eigene Arbeit.
unalterable [ʌnˈɒltərəbl] *adj intention, decision* unabänderlich; *laws* unveränderlich.
unambiguous [ˌʌnæmˈbɪgjʊəs] *adj* eindeutig, unzweideutig.

476

unambitious [ˌʌnæm'bɪʃəs] adj person, plan nicht ehrgeizig (genug); performance anspruchslos.

un-American [ˌʌnə'merɪkən] adj unamerikanisch.

unanimous [juː'nænɪməs] adj einmütig; decision also, (Jur) einstimmig. **we were ~ in thinking ...** wir waren einmütig der Ansicht ...; **by a ~ vote** einstimmig.

unanimously [juː'nænɪməslɪ] adv einstimmig.

unanswerable [ʌn'ɑːnsərəbl] adj question nicht zu beantworden(d attr) pred; argument, case unwiderlegbar.

unanswered [ʌn'ɑːnsəd] adj unbeantwortet.

unappealing [ˌʌnə'piːlɪŋ] nicht reizvoll; person unansehnlich; prospect, sight nicht verlockend.

unappetizing [ʌn'æpɪtaɪzɪŋ] adj unappetitlich; prospect, thought wenig verlockend.

unappreciative [ˌʌnə'priːʃɪətɪv] adj undankbar; audience verständnislos. **to be ~ of sth** etw nicht zu würdigen wissen.

unapproachable [ˌʌnə'prəʊtʃəbl] adj place unzugänglich; person also unnahbar.

unarmed [ʌn'ɑːmd] adj unbewaffnet. **~ combat** Nahkampf m ohne Waffe.

unashamed [ˌʌnə'ʃeɪmd] adj schamlos. **his ~ conservatism** sein unverhohlener Konservatismus; **he was quite ~ about it** er schämte sich dessen überhaupt nicht.

unashamedly [ˌʌnə'ʃeɪmɪdlɪ] adv unverschämt; say, admit ohne Scham; in favour of, partisan unverhohlen.

unasked [ʌn'ɑːskt] adj (unrequested) unaufgefordert, ungefragt; (uninvited) ungebeten.

unassailable [ˌʌnə'seɪləbl] adj unangreifbar; fortress uneinnehmbar; position, reputation unanfechtbar; conviction unerschütterlich; argument unwiderlegbar, zwingend.

unassisted [ˌʌnə'sɪstɪd] adj, adv = **unaided.**

unassuming [ˌʌnə'sjuːmɪŋ] adj bescheiden.

unattached [ˌʌnə'tætʃt] adj **(a)** (not fastened) unbefestigt; (Mil) keinem Regiment/keiner Einheit etc zugeteilt. **(b)** (emotionally) ungebunden.

unattended [ˌʌnə'tendɪd] adj children unbeaufsichtigt; car, luggage unbewacht; wound, patient unbehandelt; shop ohne Bedienung; customer nicht bedient; business unerledigt.

unattractive [ˌʌnə'træktɪv] adj sight, place unschön, wenig reizvoll; offer, woman unattraktiv; trait, scar unschön; character unsympathisch.

unauthorized [ʌn'ɔːθəraɪzd] adj unbefugt. **no entry for ~ persons** Zutritt für Unbefugte verboten!

unavailable [ˌʌnə'veɪləbl] adj nicht erhältlich; person nicht zu erreichen pred; library book nicht verfügbar.

unavailing [ˌʌnə'veɪlɪŋ] adj vergeblich.

unavenged [ˌʌnə'vendʒd] adj ungerächt.

unavoidable [ˌʌnə'vɔɪdəbl] adj unvermeidlich; conclusion zwangsläufig.

unavoidably [ˌʌnə'vɔɪdəblɪ] adv notgedrungen. **to be ~ detained** verhindert sein.

unaware [ˌʌnə'weər] adj pred **to be ~ of sth** sich (dat) einer Sache (gen) nicht bewußt sein; **I was ~ of his presence** ich hatte ihn nicht bemerkt, daß er da war; **I was ~ that he was interested** es war mir nicht bewußt, daß er (daran) interessiert war.

unawares [ˌʌnə'weəz] adv (by surprise) unerwartet; (accidentally) unbeabsichtigt, versehentlich; (without knowing) unwissentlich. **to catch** or **take sb ~** jdn überraschen.

unbalanced [ʌn'bælənst] adj **(a)** unausgewogen; diet, report also, view einseitig; ship etc nicht im Gleichgewicht. **(b)** (also mentally ~) (mad) irre, verrückt; (slightly crazy) nicht ganz normal. **(c)** account nicht ausgeglichen.

unbearable [ʌn'beərəbl] adj unerträglich.

unbeatable [ʌn'biːtəbl] adj unschlagbar; record

also nicht zu überbieten(d attr) pred.

unbeaten [ʌn'biːtn] adj ungeschlagen; record ungebrochen.

unbecoming [ˌʌnbɪ'kʌmɪŋ] adj behaviour, language etc unschicklich; clothes unvorteilhaft; beards unschön.

unbeknown(st) [ˌʌnbɪ'nəʊn(st)] adv ohne daß es jemand wußte. **~ to me/his father** ohne mein Wissen/ohne Wissen seines Vaters.

unbelievable [ˌʌnbɪ'liːvəbl] adj unglaublich.

unbelievably [ˌʌnbɪ'liːvəblɪ] adv unglaublich.

unbeliever [ˌʌnbɪ'liːvər] n Ungläubige(r) mf.

unbelieving [ˌʌnbɪ'liːvɪŋ] adj ungläubig.

unbend [ʌn'bend] pret, ptp **unbent 1** vt (straighten) metal etc geradebiegen; arms strecken. **2** vi (person, relax) aus sich herausgehen; (straighten body) sich aufrichten.

unbending [ʌn'bendɪŋ] adj person, attitude unnachgiebig; determination unbeugsam.

unbent [ʌn'bent] pret, ptp of **unbend.**

unbias(s)ed [ʌn'baɪəst] adj unvoreingenommen; opinion, report also unparteiisch.

unblemished [ʌn'blemɪʃt] adj (lit, fig) makellos.

unblock [ʌn'blɒk] vt frei machen; sink, pipe die Verstopfung in (+dat) ... beseitigen.

unbolt [ʌn'bəʊlt] vt aufriegeln. **he left the door ~ed** er verriegelte die Tür nicht.

unborn [ʌn'bɔːn] adj ungeboren. **generations yet ~** kommende Generationen.

unbounded [ʌn'baʊndɪd] adj grenzenlos.

unbreakable [ʌn'breɪkəbl] adj glass, toy unzerbrechlich; record nicht zu brechen(d attr) pred; rule unumstößlich; promise unverbrüchlich.

unbridled [ʌn'braɪdld] adj passion ungezügelt; anger hemmungslos; tongue lose; capitalism ungehemmt.

un-British [ʌn'brɪtɪʃ] adj unbritisch.

unbroken [ʌn'brəʊkən] adj **(a)** (intact) ungeschädigt; heart, promise nicht gebrochen. **(b)** (continuous) ununterbrochen; (Mil) ranks geschlossen; line of descent direkt. **an ~ night's sleep** eine ungestörte Nacht. **(c)** (unbeaten) record ungebrochen. **(d)** horse nicht zugeritten; pride ungebeugt. **his spirit remained ~** er war ungebrochen.

unbuckle [ʌn'bʌkl] vt aufschnallen.

unburden [ʌn'bɜːdn] vr **to ~ oneself/one's heart to sb** jdm sein Herz ausschütten.

unbusinesslike [ʌn'bɪznəslaɪk] adj wenig geschäftsmäßig. **in spite of his ~ appearance ...** obwohl er gar nicht wie ein Geschäftsmann aussieht ...

unbutton [ʌn'bʌtn] vt aufknöpfen.

uncalled-for [ʌn'kɔːldfɔːr] adj (unjustified) criticism ungerechtfertigt; (unnecessary) unnötig; (rude) remark deplaziert. **that was quite ~** das war nun wirklich nicht nötig.

uncanny [ʌn'kænɪ] adj unheimlich.

uncared-for [ʌn'keədfɔːr] adj garden, hands ungepflegt; child vernachlässigt.

uncaring [ʌn'keərɪŋ] adj gleichgültig; parents lieblos.

unceasing [ʌn'siːsɪŋ] adj unaufhörlich.

uncensored [ʌn'sensəd] adj film unzensiert.

unceremonious [ˌʌnserɪ'məʊnɪəs] adj **(a)** (abrupt, rude) dismissal brüsk, barsch; exit, departure überstürzt; haste unfein. **(b)** (informal, simple) greeting zwanglos.

unceremoniously [ˌʌnserɪ'məʊnɪəslɪ] adv kurzerhand.

uncertain [ʌn'sɜːtn] adj **(a)** (unsure) unsicher; light undeutlich, schwach. **to be ~ whether** sich (dat) nicht sicher sein, ob; **to be ~ of** or **about sth** sich (dat)einer Sache (gen) nicht sicher sein; **I was ~ as to what to do** ich war unsicher, was ich tun sollte. **(b)** (unknown) date, result ungewiß; origins unbestimmt. **(c)** (unreliable) weather, prices unbeständig; temper unbere-

chenbar; *judgement* unzuverlässig. **(d)** *(unclear)* vage. **in no ~ terms** klar und deutlich.
uncertainly [ʌn'sɜ:tnlɪ] *adv* say unbestimmt; *look, move* unsicher.
uncertainty [ʌn'sɜ:tntɪ] *n (state)* Ungewißheit *f*; *(indefiniteness)* Unbestimmtheit *f*; *(doubt)* Unsicherheit *f*. **there is still some ~ as to whether ...** es besteht noch Ungewißheit, ob ...
unchallenged [ʌn'tʃælɪndʒd] *adj* unbestritten; *(Jur) evidence* unangefochten. **to go ~** *(Mil)* ohne Anruf passieren; **the record was** *or* **went ~ for several years** der Rekord wurde jahrelang ohne Bemerkung. **I cannot let that remark go ~** diese Bemerkung kann ich nicht unwidersprochen hinnehmen.
unchanged [ʌn'tʃeɪndʒd] *adj* unverändert.
unchanging [ʌn'tʃeɪndʒɪŋ] *adj* unveränderlich.
uncharitable [ʌn'tʃærɪtəbl] *adj* hartherzig; *remark* unfreundlich, lieblos; *view* herzlos; *criticism* unbarmherzig.
uncharted [ʌn'tʃɑːtɪd] *adj (not explored)* unerforscht; *(not on map)* nicht eingezeichnet.
unchecked [ʌn'tʃekt] *adj* **(a)** *(unrestrained)* unkontrolliert; *advance* ungehindert; *anger* ungezügelt. **to go ~** *(abuse)* geduldet werden; *(advance)* nicht gehindert werden; *(inflation)* nicht eingedämmt werden; **if the epidemic goes ~** wenn die Epidemie nicht Einhalt geboten wird. **(b)** *(not verified)* ungeprüft.
unchristian [ʌn'krɪstjən] *adj* unchristlich.
uncivilized [ʌn'sɪvɪlaɪzd] *adj country, tribe, behaviour* unzivilisiert; *(col) habit* barbarisch.
unclaimed [ʌn'kleɪmd] *adj prize* nicht abgeholt; *property also* herrenlos; *right* nicht geltend gemacht; *social security etc* nicht beansprucht.
uncle ['ʌŋkl] *n* Onkel *m*. **U~** Sam Onkel Sam; **to say** *or* **cry ~** *(US)* aufgeben.
unclean [ʌn'kli:n] *adj* unsauber *(also Bibl)*; *(Rel) animal* unrein; *thoughts* unkeusch; *(fig: contaminated)* schmutzig.
unclear [ʌn'klɪə ͬ] *adj* unklar; *essay etc* undurchsichtig. **to be ~ about sth** sich *(dat)* über etw *(acc)* im unklaren sein.
unclouded [ʌn'klaʊdɪd] *adj sky* unbewölkt; *(fig) happiness, vision* ungetrübt; *mind* klar.
uncoil [ʌn'kɔɪl] **1** *vt* abwickeln. **2** *vir (snake)* sich langsam strecken; *(person)* sich ausstrecken; *(wire etc)* sich abspulen.
uncollected [ˌʌnkə'lektɪd] *adj tax* nicht eingezogen; *fare* nicht kassiert.
uncombed [ʌn'kəʊmd] *adj* ungekämmt.
uncomfortable [ʌn'kʌmfətəbl] *adj* **(a)** unbequem; *chair, position also* ungemütlich. **I feel ~ sitting like this** es ist unbequem, so zu sitzen; **I feel ~ in this jacket** in dieser Jacke fühle ich mich nicht wohl; **it feels ~** es ist unbequem. **(b)** *(uneasy) feeling* unangenehm, ungut; *silence (awkward)* peinlich. **to feel ~** sich unbehaglich fühlen; **I felt ~ about it** mir war nicht wohl dabei. **(c)** *(unpleasant) time, position* unerfreulich. **to make life ~ for sb** jdm das Leben schwer machen.
uncomfortably [ʌn'kʌmfətəblɪ] *adv* **(a)** unbequem. **(b)** *(uneasily)* unbehaglich. **(c)** *(unpleasantly)* unangenehm. **it's getting ~ close** es rückt bedrohlich näher.
uncommitted [ˌʌnkə'mɪtɪd] *adj* nicht engagiert; *party, country* neutral. **we want to remain ~** *(not decide)* wir wollen uns nicht festlegen.
uncommon [ʌn'kɒmən] *adj* **(a)** *(unusual)* ungewöhnlich. **it is not ~ for her to be late** es ist nichts Ungewöhnliches, daß sie zu spät kommt; **a not ~ occurrence** eine häufige Erscheinung. **(b)** *(outstanding)* außergewöhnlich.
uncommunicative [ˌʌnkə'mju:nɪkətɪv] *adj (by nature)* verschlossen; *(temporarily)* schweigsam.
uncomplaining [ˌʌnkəm'pleɪnɪŋ] *adj* duldsam.
uncomplainingly [ˌʌnkəm'pleɪnɪŋlɪ] *adv* geduldig, klaglos.

uncompleted [ˌʌnkəm'pli:tɪd] *adj* unvollendet.
uncomplicated [ʌn'kɒmplɪkeɪtɪd] *adj* unkompliziert.
uncomplimentary [ˌʌnkɒmplɪ'mentərɪ] *adj* unschmeichelhaft. **to be ~ about sb/sth** sich nicht sehr schmeichelhaft über jdn/etw äußern.
uncomprehending [ˌʌnkɒmprɪ'hendɪŋ] *adj* verständnislos.
uncompromising [ʌn'kɒmprəmaɪzɪŋ] *adj* kompromißlos; *dedication, honesty* rückhaltlos; *commitment* hundertprozentig.
unconcealed [ˌʌnkən'si:ld] *adj joy* offen, unverhüllt; *hatred, distaste etc also* unverhohlen.
unconcerned [ˌʌnkən'sɜ:nd] *adj (unworried)* unbekümmert; *(indifferent)* gleichgültig. **to be ~ about sth** sich nicht um etw kümmern.
unconditional [ˌʌnkən'dɪʃənl] *adj* vorbehaltlos. **~ surrender** bedingungslose Kapitulation.
unconfirmed [ˌʌnkən'fɜ:md] *adj* unbestätigt.
uncongenial [ˌʌnkən'dʒi:nɪəl] *adj person* unliebenswürdig; *work, surroundings* unerfreulich.
unconnected [ˌʌnkə'nektɪd] *adj* **(a)** *(unrelated)* nicht miteinander in Beziehung stehend *attr*. **the two events are ~** es besteht keine Beziehung zwischen den beiden Ereignissen. **(b)** *(incoherent)* unzusammenhängend.
unconscious [ʌn'kɒnʃəs] **1** *adj* **(a)** *(Med)* bewußtlos. **the blow knocked him ~** durch den Schlag wurde er bewußtlos. **(b)** *pred (unaware)* **to be ~ of sth** sich *(dat)* einer Sache *(gen)* nicht bewußt sein; **I was ~ of the fact that ...** es war mir nicht bewußt, daß ... **(c)** *(unintentional)* insult, allusion etc unbeabsichtigt; *blunder also* ungewollt; *humour* unfreiwillig. **(d)** *(Psych)* unbewußt. **2** *n (Psych)* **the ~** das Unbewußte.
unconsciously [ʌn'kɒnʃəslɪ] *adv* unbewußt. **an ~ funny remark** eine ungewollt lustige Bemerkung.
unconstitutional [ˌʌnkɒnstɪ'tju:ʃənl] *adj* verfassungswidrig.
uncontested [ˌʌnkən'testɪd] *adj* unbestritten; *election, seat* ohne Gegenkandidat. **the chairmanship was ~** in der Wahl für den Vorsitz gab es keinen Gegenkandidaten.
uncontrollable [ˌʌnkən'trəʊləbl] *adj* unkontrollierbar; *child* nicht zu bändigen(d *attr*) *pred*; *horse, dog* nicht unter Kontrolle zu bringen(d *attr*) *pred*; *desire, urge* unwiderstehlich; *(physical)* unkontrollierbar; *twitch* unkontrolliert; *laughter, mirth* unbezähmbar. **to become ~** außer Kontrolle geraten.
uncontrolled [ˌʌnkən'trəʊld] *adj* ungehindert; *dogs, children* unbeaufsichtigt; *laughter* unkontrolliert; *weeping* haltlos. **if inflation is allowed to go ~** wenn die Inflation nicht unter Kontrolle gebracht wird.
unconventional [ˌʌnkən'venʃənl] *adj* unkonventionell.
unconvinced [ˌʌkən'vɪnst] *adj* **I remain ~** ich bin noch immer nicht überzeugt.
unconvincing [ˌʌnkən'vɪnsɪŋ] *adj* nicht überzeugend. **rather ~** wenig überzeugend.
uncooked [ʌn'kʊkt] *adj* ungekocht, roh.
uncooperative [ˌʌnkəʊ'ɒpərətɪv] *adj attitude* stur, wenig entgegenkommend; *witness, colleague* wenig hilfreich, nicht hilfsbereit. **the government remained ~** die Regierung war auch weiterhin nicht zur Kooperation bereit.
uncork [ʌn'kɔ:k] *vt* bottle entkorken.
uncorroborated [ˌʌnkə'rɒbəreɪtɪd] *adj* unbestätigt; *evidence* nicht bekräftigt.
uncouple [ʌn'kʌpl] *vt* train etc abkoppeln.
uncouth [ʌn'ku:θ] *adj* ungehobelt; *expression, word* unflätig, unfein.
uncover [ʌn'kʌvə ͬ] *vt* **(a)** *(remove cover from)* aufdecken; *head* entblößen *(liter)*. **(b)** *scandal, plot* aufdecken; *ancient ruins* zum Vorschein bringen.

uncritical [ʌn'krɪtɪkəl] *adj* unkritisch *(of, about* in bezug auf *+acc).*

unction ['ʌŋkʃən] *n (Rel: anointing)* Salbung *f.* **extreme ~** Letzte Ölung.

uncultivated [ʌn'kʌltɪveɪtɪd] *adj land* unbebaut; *person, behaviour* unkultiviert; *mind* nicht ausgebildet.

uncultured [ʌn'kʌltʃəd] *adj person, mind* ungebildet; *behaviour* unkultiviert.

uncurl [ʌn'kɜːl] **1** *vt* auseinanderrollen. **to ~ oneself** sich strecken. **2** *vi (cat, snake)* sich langsam strecken; *(person)* sich ausstrecken.

undamaged [ʌn'dæmɪdʒd] *adj* unbeschädigt; *(fig) reputation* makellos.

undated [ʌn'deɪtɪd] *adj* undatiert.

undaunted [ʌn'dɔːntɪd] *adj (not discouraged)* nicht entmutigt, unverzagt; *(fearless)* unerschrocken. **he carried on ~** er machte unverzagt weiter.

undecided [ˌʌndɪ'saɪdɪd] *adj* **(a)** *person* unentschlossen. **he is ~ as to whether he should go or not** er ist (sich *dat)* noch unschlüssig, ob er gehen soll oder nicht. **(b)** *question* unentschieden.

undefeated [ˌʌndɪ'fiːtɪd] *adj army, team* unbesiegt; *spirit* ungebrochen.

undefined [ˌʌndɪ'faɪnd] *adj* nicht definiert; *(vague)* undefinierbar.

undelivered [ˌʌndɪ'lɪvəd] *adj mail* nicht zugestellt. **if ~ return to sender** bei Nichtzustellung zurück an Absender.

undemanding [ˌʌndɪ'mɑːndɪŋ] *adj* anspruchslos; *task* wenig fordernd, keine großen Anforderungen stellend *attr.*

undemonstrative [ˌʌndɪ'mɒnstrətɪv] *adj* zurückhaltend.

undeniable [ˌʌndɪ'naɪəbl] *adj* unbestreitbar. **it is ~ that ...** es läßt sich nicht bestreiten, daß ...

undeniably [ˌʌndɪ'naɪəblɪ] *adv* zweifellos; *successful, proud* unbestreitbar.

under ['ʌndəʳ] **1** *prep* **(a)** *(beneath) (place)* unter *(+dat); (direction)* unter *(+acc).* **~ it** darunter; **to come out from ~** the bed unter dem Bett hervorkommen; **it's ~ there** es ist da drunter *(col);* **~ barley** mit Gerste bebaut. **(b)** *(less than)* unter *(+dat).* **it took ~ an hour** es dauerte weniger als eine Stunde. **(c)** *(subordinate to, ~ influence of etc)* unter *(+dat).* **he had 50 men ~ him** er hatte 50 Männer unter sich; **he studied ~ Popper** er hat bei Popper studiert; **he was born ~ Virgo** *(Astrol)* er wurde im Zeichen Jungfrau geboren; **the matter ~ discussion** der Diskussionsgegenstand; **to be ~ the doctor** in (ärztlicher) Behandlung sein; **it's classified ~ history** es steht unter „Geschichte" eingeordnet. **(d)** *(according to)* nach, gemäß *(+dat).* **~ the terms of the contract** gemäß den Vertragsbedingungen.

2 *adv* **(a)** *(beneath)* unten; *(unconscious)* bewußtlos. **he came to the fence and crawled ~** er kam zum Zaun und kroch darunter durch; **to go ~** untergehen. **(b)** *(less)* darunter.

under- *pref (in rank)* Unter-. **for the ~-twelves/ -eighteens/-forties** für Kinder unter zwölf/ Jugendliche unter achtzehn/Leute unter vierzig.

under: ~-age *adj attr* minderjährig; **~-age drinking** Alkoholgenuß *m* Minderjähriger; **~arm** *adj throw von* unten; *hair* Unterarm-; **~carriage** *n (Aviat)* Fahrwerk *nt;* **~charge** *vt* zuwenig berechnen *(sb* jdm); **he ~charged me by 10p** er berechnete mir 10 Pence zuwenig; **~clothes** *npl* Unterwäsche *f;* **~coat** *n (paint)* Grundierfarbe *f;* **~cover** *adj agent* Geheim-; **~current** *n (lit, fig)* Unterströmung *f;* **~cut** *pret, ptp* **~cut** *vt competitor* unterbieten; **~developed** *adj* unterentwickelt; *resources* ungenutzt; **~dog** *n* Benachteiligte(r) *m; (in game also)* sicherer Verlierer; **~done** *adj* nicht gar;

(deliberately) nicht durchgebraten; **~estimate 1** *vt cost, person* unterschätzen; **2** *n* Unterschätzung *f;* **~exposed** *adj (Phot)* unterbelichtet; **~fed** *adj* unterernährt; **~floor heating** *n* Fußbodenheizung *f;* **~foot** *adv* am Boden; **it is wet ~foot** der Boden ist naß; **to trample sb/sth ~foot** *(lit, fig)* auf jdm/etw herumtrampeln; **~go** *pret* **~went,** *ptp* **~gone** *vt suffering* durchmachen; *change also* erleben; *test, treatment,* (Med) *operation* sich unterziehen *(+dat);* (machine) *test* unterzogen werden *(+dat);* **~grad** (col), **~graduate 1** *n* Student(in *f) m;* **2** *attr* Studenten-.

underground ['ʌndəgraʊnd] **1** *adj* **(a)** unterirdisch; *(Min)* Untertage-. **(b)** *(fig) press, movement* Untergrund-. **2** *adv* **(a)** unterirdisch; *(Min)* unter Tage. **3m ~** 3 m unter der Erde. **(b)** *(fig)* **to go ~** untertauchen. **3** *n* **(a)** *(Brit Rail)* U-Bahn, Untergrundbahn *f.* **(b)** *(movement)* Untergrundbewegung *f; (sub-culture)* Underground *m.*

under: ~growth *n* Gestrüpp *nt; (under trees)* Unterholz *nt;* **~hand** *adj (sly)* hinterhältig; **~insured** *adj* unterversichert; **~lie** *pret* **~lay,** *ptp* **~lain** *vt (lit)* liegen unter *(+dat); (fig: be basis for or cause of)* zugrunde liegen *(+dat);* **~line** *vt (lit, fig)* unterstreichen.

underling ['ʌndəlɪŋ] *n (pej)* Befehlsempfänger(in *f) m (pej).*

under: ~lying *adj* **(a)** *soil, rocks* tieferliegend; **(b)** *cause* eigentlich; *(deeper also)* tiefer; *problem* zugrundeliegend; **~manned** *adj* unterbesetzt; **~mentioned** *adj* untengenannt; **~mine** *vt* **(a)** *(tunnel under)* unterhöhlen; *(Mil)* unterminieren. **(b)** *(fig: weaken)* authority, confidence untergraben; *health* angreifen; **~most** *adj* unterste(r, s).

underneath ['ʌndə'niːθ] **1** *prep (place)* unter *(+dat); (direction)* unter *(+acc).* **~ it** darunter. **2** *adv* unten. **the ones ~** die darunter. **3** *n* Unterseite *f.*

under: ~nourished *adj* unterernährt; **~pants** *npl* Unterhose(n *pl) f;* **a pair of ~pants** eine Unterhose, ein Paar Unterhosen; **~pass** *n* Unterführung *f;* **~pay** *pret, ptp* **~paid** *vt* unterbezahlen; **~pin** *vt wall, argument* untermauern; *economy etc* stützen; **to ~play one's hand** *(fig)* nicht alle Trümpfe ausspielen; **~populated** *adj* unterbevölkert; **~price** *vt* zu billig anbieten, unter Preis anbieten; **to be ~ priced** zu billig gehandelt werden; **~privileged** *adj* unterprivilegiert; **the ~privileged** die Unterprivilegierten *pl;* **~rate** *vt (~estimate) danger, chance, person* unterschätzen; *(~value)* qualities unterbewerten; **~secretary** *n (also Parliamentary U~secretary)* (parlamentarischer) Staatssekretär; **~sell** *pret, ptp* **~sold** *vt (sell at lower price) competitor* unterbieten; *goods* unter Preis verkaufen; **he tends to ~sell himself/his ideas** er kann sich/seine Ideen nicht verkaufen; **~shirt** *n (US)* Unterhemd *nt;* **~shorts** *npl (US)* Unterhose(n *pl) f;* **~side** *n* Unterseite *f;* **~signed** *adj (form)* unterzeichnet; **we the ~signed** wir, die Unterzeichneten; **~sized** *adj* klein; *(less than proper size)* zu klein; *(pej) person also* zu kurz geraten *(hum);* **~skirt** *n* Unterrock *m;* **~sold** *pret, ptp of* **~sell; ~staffed** *adj office* unterbesetzt; **we are very ~staffed at the moment** wir haben momentan zu wenig Leute.

understand [ˌʌndə'stænd] *pret, ptp* **understood 1** *vt* **(a)** verstehen; *action, event, person, difficulty also* begreifen. **I don't ~ Russian** ich verstehe kein Russisch; **I can't ~ his agreeing to do it** es ist mir unbegreiflich, warum er sich dazu bereit erklärt hat; **what do you ~ by "pragmatism"?** was verstehen Sie unter „Pragmatismus"?; **to ~ one another** sich verstehen. **(b)** *(believe)* **we**

understood we were to be paid wir hatten angenommen, daß man uns bezahlt; **I ~ that you are going to Australia** ich höre, Sie gehen nach Australien; **I ~ you've already met** Sie haben sich, soviel ich weiß, schon kennengelernt; **am I/are we to ~ ...?** soll das etwa heißen, daß ...?; **to give sb to ~ that ...** jdm zu verstehen geben, daß ...; **I understood from his speech that ...** ich schloß aus seiner Rede, daß ... **2** *vi* **(a)** verstehen. **~?** verstanden?; **you don't ~!** du verstehst mich nicht!; **I quite ~** ich verstehe schon. **(b) so I ~** es scheint so; **he was, I ~,** a widower wie ich hörte, war er Witwer.

understandable [ˌʌndə'stændəbl] *adj* verständlich.

understandably [ˌʌndə'stændəblɪ] *adv* verständlicherweise.

understanding [ˌʌndə'stændɪŋ] **1** *adj* verständnisvoll. **he asked me to be ~** er bat mich um Verständnis. **2** *n* **(a)** *(knowledge)* Kenntnisse *pl*; *(comprehension, sympathy)* Verständnis *nt*. **her ~ of children** ihr Verständnis für Kinder; **my ~ of the situation is that ...** ich verstehe die Situation so, daß ...; **he has a good ~ of the problem** er kennt sich mit dem Problem gut aus; **in order to promote international ~** um die internationale Verständigung zu fördern. **(b)** *(agreement)* Abmachung, Vereinbarung *f*. **to come to** *or* **reach an ~ with sb** eine Vereinbarung mit jdm treffen. **(c)** *(assumption)* Voraussetzung *f*. **on the ~ that ...** unter der Voraussetzung, daß ...

understate [ˌʌndə'steɪt] *vt* untertreiben, herunterspielen. **to ~ one's case** untertreiben.

understatement ['ʌndəˌsteɪtmənt] *n* Untertreibung *f*, Understatement *nt*.

understood [ˌʌndə'stud] **1** *pret, ptp of* **understand. 2** *adj* **(a)** *(clear)* klar. **to make oneself ~** sich verständlich machen; **do I make myself ~?** ist das klar?; **I wish it to be ~ that ...** ich möchte klarstellen, daß ...; **~?** klar?; **~!** gut! **(b)** *(believed)* **he is ~ to have left** es heißt, daß er gegangen ist; **it is ~ that ...** es heißt *or* man hört, daß ...; **he let it be ~ that ...** er gab zu verstehen, daß ....

understudy ['ʌndəˌstʌdɪ] *n* (Theat) zweite Besetzung.

undertake [ˌʌndə'teɪk] *pret* **undertook** [ˌʌndə'tuk], *ptp* **undertaken** [ˌʌndə'teɪkn] *vt* **(a)** *job, duty, responsibility* übernehmen; *risk* eingehen, auf sich *(acc)* nehmen. **he undertook to be our guide** er übernahm es, unser Führer zu sein. **(b)** *(agree, promise)* sich verpflichten; *(guarantee)* garantieren.

undertaker ['ʌndəˌteɪkə'] *n (esp Brit)* Beerdigungsunternehmer *m*.

undertaking [ˌʌndə'teɪkɪŋ] *n* **(a)** *(enterprise)* Unternehmen *nt*; *(Comm: project also)* Projekt *nt*. **(b)** *(promise)* Zusicherung *f*, Wort *nt*. **I give you my solemn ~ that I will never do it again** ich verpflichte mich feierlich, es nie wieder zu tun; **I can give no such ~** das kann ich nicht versprechen.

under: **~tone** *n* **(a)** *(of voice)* **in an ~ tone** mit gedämpfter Stimme; **(b)** *(fig: of criticism, discontent)* Unterton *m*; **an ~tone of racialism** ein rassistischer Unterton; **~took** *pret of* **~take**; **~tow** *n* Unterströmung *f*; **~value** *vt* *antique, artist* unterbewerten; *(price too low)* zu niedrig schätzen; *person* zu wenig schätzen; **~water 1** *adj* *diving, exploration* Unterwasser-; **2** *adv* unter Wasser; **~wear** *n* Unterwäsche *f*; **~weight** *adj* untergewichtig; **~went** *pret of* **~go**; **~world** *n* *(criminals, Myth)* Unterwelt *f*; **~write** *pret* **~wrote**, *ptp* **~written** *vt* *(finance)* company, loss tragen, garantieren; *insurance policy* bürgen für; *(insure)* shipping versichern; *(St Ex)* shares zeichnen; **~writer** *n* *(Insur)* Versicherer *m*.

undeserved [ˌʌndɪ'zɜːvd] *adj* unverdient.

undeserving [ˌʌndɪ'zɜːvɪŋ] *adj* *person, cause* unwürdig. **to be ~ of sth** *(form)* einer Sache *(gen)* unwürdig sein *(form)*.

undesirable [ˌʌndɪ'zaɪərəbl] **1** *adj* *policy, effect* unerwünscht; *influence, characters, area* übel. **it is ~ that ...** es wäre höchst unerwünscht, wenn ... **2** *n (person)* unerwünschtes Element.

undetected [ˌʌndɪ'tektɪd] *adj* **to go ~** nicht entdeckt werden.

undeveloped [ˌʌndɪ'veləpt] *adj* unentwickelt; *land, resources* ungenutzt.

undid [ʌn'dɪd] *pret of* **undo.**

undies ['ʌndɪz] *npl (col)* (Unter)wäsche *f*.

undignified [ʌn'dɪgnɪfaɪd] *adj* *person, behaviour* würdelos; *(inelegant) way of sitting etc* unelegant.

undiluted [ˌʌndaɪ'luːtɪd] *adj* unverdünnt; *(fig) truth, version* unverfälscht; *pleasure* rein, voll.

undiplomatic [ˌʌndɪplə'mætɪk] *adj* undiplomatisch.

undiscerning [ˌʌndɪ'sɜːnɪŋ] *adj* *reader, palate* anspruchslos, unkritisch; *critic* unbedarft.

undisciplined [ʌn'dɪsɪplɪnd] *adj* undiszipliniert.

undiscovered [ˌʌndɪ'skʌvəd] *adj* unentdeckt.

undisguised [ˌʌndɪs'gaɪzd] *adj* ungetarnt; *(fig) truth* unverhüllt; *dislike, affection* unverhohlen.

undisputed [ˌʌndɪ'spjuːtɪd] *adj* unbestritten.

undistinguished [ˌʌndɪ'stɪŋgwɪʃt] *adj* *performance* (mittel)mäßig; *appearance* durchschnittlich.

undisturbed [ˌʌndɪ'stɜːbd] *adj* **(a)** *(untouched) papers, dust* unberührt; *(uninterrupted) person, sleep etc* ungestört. **(b)** *(unworried)* unberührt.

undivided [ˌʌndɪ'vaɪdɪd] *adj* *country, (fig) opinion, attention* ungeteilt; *support* voll; *loyalty* absolut.

undo [ʌn'duː] *pret* **undid,** *ptp* **undone** *vt* **(a)** *(unfasten)* aufmachen; *button, dress, parcel also* öffnen; *knitting also* aufziehen; *sewing also* auftrennen. **(b)** *wrong* ungeschehen machen; *work* ruinieren. **2** *vi (dress etc)* aufgehen.

undoing [ʌn'duːɪŋ] *n* Ruin *m*, Verderben *nt*.

undone [ʌn'dʌn] **1** *ptp of* **undo. 2** *adj* **(a)** *(unfastened)* offen. **to come ~** aufgehen. **(b)** *(neglected) task, work* unerledigt.

undoubted [ʌn'dautɪd] *adj* unbestritten; *success also* unzweifelhaft.

undoubtedly [ʌn'dautɪdlɪ] *adv* zweifellos.

undreamed-of [ʌn'driːmdɒv], **undreamt-of** [ʌn'dremtɒv] *adj* ungeahnt. **in their time this was ~** zu ihrer Zeit hätte man sich *(dat)* das nie träumen lassen.

undress [ʌn'dres] **1** *vt* ausziehen. **to get ~ed** sich ausziehen. **2** *vi* sich ausziehen.

undrinkable [ʌn'drɪŋkəbl] *adj* ungenießbar.

undue [ʌn'djuː] *adj* *(excessive)* übermäßig; *(improper)* ungebührlich.

undulating ['ʌndjuleɪtɪŋ] *adj* *movement, line* Wellen-; *waves, sea* wogend; *countryside* hügelig; *hills* sanft.

unduly [ʌn'djuːlɪ] *adv* übermäßig; *punished* übermäßig streng. **you're worrying ~** Sie machen sich *(dat)* unnötige Sorgen.

undying [ʌn'daɪɪŋ] *adj* unsterblich.

unearned [ʌn'ɜːnd] *adj (Fin, fig)* unverdient. **~ income** Kapitaleinkommen *nt*.

unearth [ʌn'ɜːθ] *vt* ausgraben; *(fig) book etc* aufstöbern; *evidence* ausfindig machen.

unearthly [ʌn'ɜːθlɪ] *adj (eerie)* calm, scream unheimlich; *beauty* überirdisch. **at some ~ hour** *(col)* zu nachtschlafender Stunde; **an ~ din** *(col)* ein Riesenlärm *m*.

uneasily [ʌn'iːzɪlɪ] *adv* sit unbehaglich; *smile, speak etc* so unsicher; *sleep* unruhig. **to be ~ balanced** schlecht austariert sein.

uneasiness [ʌn'iːzɪnɪs] *n see adj* Unruhe *f*; Unbehaglichkeit *f*; Unsicherheit *f*; *(of person)* Beklommenheit *f*; Unruhe *f*.

uneasy [ʌn'iːzɪ] *adj* sleep, night unruhig; *conscience* schlecht; *(worried)* laugh, look, *(awkward)* silence, *atmosphere* unbehaglich; *peace, balance* unsicher; *(worrying) suspicion, feeling* beunruhigend. **to be** ~ *(person) (ill at ease)* beklommen sein; *(worried)* beunruhigt sein; **I am** ~ **about it** mir ist nicht wohl dabei; **to make sb** ~ jdn beunruhigen; **I have an** ~ **feeling that** ... ich habe das ungute Gefühl, daß ...; **to become** ~ unruhig werden.

uneaten [ʌn'iːtn] *adj* nicht gegessen. **he left the frog's legs** ~ er ließ die Froschschenkel auf dem Teller; **the** ~ **food** das übriggebliebene Essen.

uneconomic [ʌn,iːkə'nɒmɪk] *adj* unwirtschaftlich.

uneconomical [ʌn,iːkə'nɒmɪkəl] *adj* unwirtschaftlich; *person* verschwenderisch.

uneducated [,ʌn'edjʊkeɪtɪd] *adj person* ungebildet; *speech also* unkultiviert.

unemotional [,ʌn'ɪməʊʃənl] *adj person, reaction, description* nüchtern; *(without passion)* leidenschaftslos, kühl *(pej)*.

unemployed [,ʌnɪm'plɔɪd] *adj person* arbeitslos; *(unused) machinery* ungenutzt; *(Fin) capital* tot. **the** ~ *pl* die Arbeitslosen *pl.*

unemployment [,ʌnɪm'plɔɪmənt] **1** *n* Arbeitslosigkeit *f.* ~ **has risen this month** die Arbeitslosenziffer ist diesen Monat gestiegen. **2** *attr* ~ **benefit** *(Brit)* **or compensation** *(US)* Arbeitslosenunterstützung *f;* ~ **figures** Arbeitslosenziffer *f;* ~ **rate** Arbeitslosenquote *f.*

unending [ʌn'endɪŋ] *adj (everlasting)* ewig; *stream* endlos; *(incessant)* unaufhörlich. **it seems** ~ es scheint nicht enden zu wollen.

unendurable [,ʌnɪn'djʊərəbl] *adj* unerträglich.

unenterprising [,ʌn'entəpraɪzɪŋ] *adj person, policy* ohne Unternehmungsgeist.

unenthusiastic [,ʌnɪnθuːzɪ'æstɪk] *adj* kühl, wenig begeistert.

unenviable [ʌn'envɪəbl] *adj position, task* wenig beneidenswert.

unequal [ʌn'iːkwəl] *adj* ungleich; *standard, quality* unterschiedlich. **to be** ~ **to a task** einer Aufgabe *(dat)* nicht gewachsen sein.

unequalled, *(US)* **unequaled** [ʌn'iːkwəld] *adj* unübertroffen; *skill, record also* unerreicht; *ignorance* beispiellos. **he is** ~ **by any other player** kein anderer Spieler kommt ihm gleich.

unequivocal [,ʌnɪ'kwɪvəkəl] *adj* unmißverständlich, eindeutig. **he was quite** ~ **about it** er sagte es ganz unmißverständlich *or* klar.

unerring [ʌn'ɜːrɪŋ] *adj judgement, accuracy* unfehlbar; *instinct* untrüglich; *aim* treffsicher.

UNESCO [juː'neskəʊ] = **United Nations Educational, Scientific and Cultural Organization** UNESCO *f.*

unethical [ʌn'eθɪkəl] *adj* unmoralisch; *(in more serious matters)* unethisch.

uneven [ʌn'iːvən] *adj (not level) surface* uneben; *(irregular) line* ungerade; *thickness* ungleich; *pulse* unregelmäßig; *voice* unsicher; *colour, distribution* ungleichmäßig; *quality* unterschiedlich; *temper* unausgeglichen.

unevenly [ʌn'iːvənlɪ] *adv see adj* the teams were ~ **matched** die Mannschaften waren sehr ungleich.

uneventful [,ʌnɪ'ventfʊl] *adj day, meeting* ereignislos; *career* wenig bewegt; *life also* ruhig, eintönig *(pej).*

unexceptionable [,ʌnɪk'sepʃnəbl] *adj* einwandfrei; *person* solide.

unexceptional [,ʌnɪk'sepʃənl] *adj* durchschnittlich.

unexciting [,ʌnɪk'saɪtɪŋ] *adj time* nicht besonders aufregend.

unexpected [,ʌnɪk'spektɪd] *adj* unerwartet. **this is an** ~ **pleasure** *(also iro)* welch eine Überraschung!

unexpectedly [,ʌnɪk'spektɪdlɪ] *adv* unerwartet; *arrive, happen also* plötzlich.

unexplainable [,ʌnɪk'spleɪnəbl] *adj* unerklärlich.

unexplained [,ʌnɪk'spleɪnd] *adj phenomenon* ungeklärt; *mystery* unaufgeklärt; *lateness, absence* unbegründet.

unexploded [,ʌnɪk'spləʊdɪd] *adj* nicht explodiert.

unexposed [,ʌnɪk'spəʊzd] *adj* **(a)** *villain* nicht entlarvt; *crime* unaufgedeckt. **(b)** *(Phot)* unbelichtet.

unexpressed [,ʌnɪk'sprest] *adj sorrow, wish* unausgesprochen.

unexpressive [,ʌnɪk'spresɪv] *adj* ausdruckslos.

unfailing [ʌn'feɪlɪŋ] *adj source, interest* unerschöpflich; *remedy* unfehlbar; *friend* treu.

unfailingly [ʌn'feɪlɪŋlɪ] *adv* immer, stets.

unfair [ʌn'fɛəʳ] *adj* unfair; *decision, method, remark also* ungerecht; *(Comm) competition also* unlauter. **to be** ~ **to sb** jdm gegenüber unfair sein.

unfairly [ʌn'fɛəlɪ] *adv* unfair; *treat, criticise etc also* ungerecht; *accuse, dismiss* zu Unrecht.

unfairness [ʌn'fɛənɪs] *n* Ungerechtigkeit *f.*

unfaithful [ʌn'feɪθfʊl] *adj wife, lover* untreu; *friend* treulos. **to be** ~ **to sb** jdm untreu sein.

unfamiliar [,ʌnfə'mɪljəʳ] *adj* **(a)** *experience, sight* ungewohnt; *surroundings also, subject, person* unbekannt. **it is** ~ **to me** es ist ungewohnt für mich; **es ist mir unbekannt. (b)** *(unacquainted)* **to be** ~ **with sth** mit etw nicht vertraut sein.

unfashionable [ʌn'fæʃnəbl] *adj* unmodern; *district* unbeliebt; *hotel, habit* nicht in Mode.

unfasten [ʌn'fɑːsn] **1** *vt* aufmachen; *(detach) tag, dog* losbinden; *bonds* lösen. **2** *vi* aufgehen. **how does this dress** ~? wie macht man das Kleid auf?

unfathomable [ʌn'fæðəməbl] *adj* unergründlich.

unfavourable, *(US)* **unfavorable** [ʌn'feɪvərəbl] *adj* ungünstig; *conditions also, wind* widrig; *opinion, reaction, reply* negativ; *trade balance* passiv.

unfavourably, *(US)* **unfavorably** [ʌn'feɪvərəblɪ] *adv see adj* ungünstig; negativ. **to look** ~ **on sth** einer Sache *(dat)* ablehnend gegenüberstehen.

unfeeling [ʌn'fiːlɪŋ] *adj* gefühllos.

unfinished [ʌn'fɪnɪʃt] *adj* **(a)** *(incomplete)* unfertig; *work of art* unvollendet; *business* unerledigt. **(b)** *(Tech)* unbearbeitet; *cloth* Natur-.

unfit [ʌn'fɪt] *adj* **(a)** *(unsuitable) person, thing* ungeeignet, untauglich; *(incompetent)* unfähig. ~ **to drive** fahruntüchtig; ~ **to eat** ungenießbar. **(b)** *(Sport: injured)* nicht fit; *(in health also)* schlecht in Form, unfit. ~ **(for military service)** untauglich; **to be** ~ **for work** arbeitsunfähig sein.

unflagging [ʌn'flægɪŋ] *adj person, zeal* unermüdlich; *enthusiasm* unerschöpflich; *devotion, interest* unverändert stark.

unflappable [ʌn'flæpəbl] *adj (col)* unerschütterlich. **to be** ~ die Ruhe selbst sein.

unflattering [ʌn'flætərɪŋ] *adj portrait, comments* wenig schmeichelhaft; *dress, light also* unvorteilhaft.

unflinching [ʌn'flɪntʃɪŋ] *adj* unerschrocken; *determination* unbeirrbar.

unfold [ʌn'fəʊld] **1** *vt* **(a)** *paper, cloth* auseinanderfalten; *(spread out) map also, wings* ausbreiten; *arms* lösen; *chair* auseinanderklappen. **(b)** *(fig) story* entwickeln *(to vor +dat)*; *plans, ideas also* darlegen *(to dat)*; *secret* enthüllen. **2** *vi (story, plot)* sich abwickeln; *(truth)* an den Tag kommen; *(view, personality)* sich entfalten; *(countryside)* sich ausbreiten.

unforeseeable [,ʌnfɔː'siːəbl] *adj* unvorhersehbar.

unforeseen [,ʌnfɔː'siːn] *adj* unvorhergesehen.

unforgettable [,ʌnfə'getəbl] *adj* unvergeßlich.

unforgivable [,ʌnfə'gɪvəbl] *adj* unverzeihlich.

unforgiving [,ʌnfə'gɪvɪŋ] *adj* unversöhnlich.

unformed [ʌn'fɔːmd] *adj clay, foetus* ungeformt; *character, idea* unfertig.

unfortunate [ʌn'fɔːtʃnɪt] *adj* unglücklich; *person*

glücklos; *day, event, error* unglückselig; *turn of phrase* ungeschickt; *time* ungünstig. **to be ~ (person)** Pech haben; **it is most ~ that ...** es ist höchst bedauerlich, daß ...; **the ~ Mr Brown** der bedauernswerte Herr Brown.

unfortunately [ʌnˈfɔːtʃnɪtlɪ] *adv* leider; *worded* ungeschickt. **an ~ chosen expression** ein unglücklicher Ausdruck.

unfounded [ʌnˈfaʊndɪd] *adj* unbegründet; *allegations* aus der Luft gegriffen.

unfriendly [ʌnˈfrendlɪ] *adj* unfreundlich *(to sb* zu jdm)*; (hostile also)* natives, country, act feindselig; *territory* unwirtlich.

unfulfilled [ˌʌnfʊlˈfɪld] *adj* unerfüllt; *person* unausgefüllt.

unfurl [ʌnˈfɜːl] *vt flag* aufrollen; *sail* losmachen; *(peacock) tail* entfalten.

unfurnished [ʌnˈfɜːnɪʃt] *adj* unmöbliert.

ungainly [ʌnˈgeɪnlɪ] *adj* unbeholfen; *appearance* unelegant, unschön.

un-get-at-able [ˌʌngetˈætəbl] *adj (col)* unerreichbar.

ungodly [ʌnˈgɒdlɪ] *adj* gottlos; *(col) hour* unchristlich *(col); noise* Heiden-.

ungracious [ʌnˈgreɪʃəs] *adj* unhöflich; *refusal* schroff; *answer* rüde.

ungrammatical [ˌʌngrəˈmætɪkəl] *adj* ungrammatisch.

ungrateful [ʌnˈgreɪtfʊl] *adj* undankbar *(to* gegenüber)*.

ungrudging [ʌnˈgrʌdʒɪŋ] *adj help* bereitwillig; *admiration* neidlos; *contribution* großzügig; *praise* von ganzem Herzen kommend *attr.*

unguarded [ʌnˈgɑːdɪd] *adj* **(a)** *(undefended)* unbewacht. **(b)** *(fig: careless)* unvorsichtig, unachtsam. **in an ~ moment he ...** als er einen Augenblick nicht aufpaßte, ... er ...

unhappily [ʌnˈhæpɪlɪ] *adv (unfortunately)* unglücklicherweise; *(miserably)* unglücklich.

unhappiness [ʌnˈhæpɪnɪs] *n* Traurigkeit *f; (discontent)* Unzufriedenheit *f (with* mit).

unhappy [ʌnˈhæpɪ] *adj (+er)* **(a)** *(sad)* unglücklich; *look, voice also,* state of affairs traurig. **(b)** *(not pleased)* unzufrieden *(about* mit); *(uneasy)* unwohl. **if you feel ~ about it** wenn Sie darüber nicht glücklich sind; *(worried)* wenn Ihnen dabei nicht wohl ist. **(c)** *(unfortunate)* coincidence, *phrasing* unglücklich; *person* glücklos.

unharmed [ʌnˈhɑːmd] *adj person* unverletzt; *thing, reputation* unbeschädigt. **to be ~ by sth** durch etw nicht gelitten haben.

unhealthy [ʌnˈhelθɪ] *adj* **(a)** *person* nicht gesund; *climate, place, life, complexion,* ungesund; *(col) car* nicht in Ordnung. **(b)** *curiosity, interest* krankhaft; *influence* schädlich. **it's an ~ relationship** das ist eine verderbliche Beziehung. **(c)** *(col: dangerous)* ungesund *(col).*

unheard-of [ʌnˈhɜːdɒv] *adj (unknown)* gänzlich unbekannt; *(unprecedented)* noch nicht dagewesen; *(outrageous)* unerhört.

unheeded [ʌnˈhiːdɪd] *adj* unbeachtet. **to go ~** keine Beachtung finden.

unhelpful [ʌnˈhelpfʊl] *adj person* nicht hilfreich; *advice, book* wenig hilfreich. **that was very ~ of you** das war wirklich keine Hilfe; **you are being very ~** du bist aber wirklich keine Hilfe.

unhesitating [ʌnˈhezɪteɪtɪŋ] *adj (immediate)* answer, offer prompt; *help also,* generosity bereitwillig; *(steady)* steps, progress stet; *(undoubting)* answer fest.

unhesitatingly [ʌnˈhezɪteɪtɪŋlɪ] *adv* ohne zu zögern; *(undoubtingly also)* ohne zu zweifeln.

unhinge [ʌnˈhɪndʒ] *vt* **to ~ sb/sb's mind** jdn aus der Bahn werfen; **his mind was ~d** er hatte den Verstand verloren.

unholy [ʌnˈhəʊlɪ] *adj (+er) (col) mess* heillos; *din* Riesen-.

unhook [ʌnˈhʊk] *vt latch, gate* loshaken; *dress* aufhaken; *(take from hook) picture* abhaken.

unhoped-for [ʌnˈhəʊptfɔː] *adj* unverhofft.

unhurried [ʌnˈhʌrɪd] *adj* pace, person gelassen; *steps, movement* gemächlich; *meal, journey, life* geruhsam.

unhurt [ʌnˈhɜːt] *adj* unverletzt.

unhygienic [ˌʌnhaɪˈdʒiːnɪk] *adj* unhygienisch.

unicorn [ˈjuːnɪˌkɔːn] *n* Einhorn *nt.*

unidentified [ˌʌnaɪˈdentɪfaɪd] *adj* unbekannt; *body* nicht identifiziert; *belongings* herrenlos. **~ flying object** unbekanntes Flugobjekt.

unification [ˌjuːnɪfɪˈkeɪʃən] *n (of country)* Einigung *f; (of system)* Vereinheitlichung *f.*

uniform [ˈjuːnɪfɔːm] **1** *adj (unvarying) length, colour* einheitlich; *treatment also* gleich; *temperature also, pace* gleichbleibend *attr; (lacking variation) life, thinking* gleichförmig. **2** *n* Uniform *f.* **in/out of ~** in Uniform/in Zivil.

uniformity [ˌjuːnɪˈfɔːmɪtɪ] *n see adj* Einheitlichkeit *f;* Gleichheit *f;* Gleichmäßigkeit *f;* Gleichförmigkeit *f.*

unify [ˈjuːnɪfaɪ] *vt* einigen, einen *(geh); systems* vereinheitlichen.

unilateral [ˌjuːnɪˈlætərəl] *adj (Jur, Pol)* einseitig; *(Pol also)* unilateral.

unimaginable [ˌʌnɪˈmædʒɪnəbl] *adj* unvorstellbar.

unimaginative [ˌʌnɪˈmædʒɪnətɪv] *adj* phantasielos.

unimpaired [ˌʌnɪmˈpeəd] *adj* quality, prestige unbeeinträchtigt; *health* unvermindert. **to be ~** nicht gelitten haben.

unimpeachable [ˌʌnɪmˈpiːtʃəbl] *adj* reputation, conduct untadelig; *proof, honesty* unanfechtbar; *source* absolut zuverlässig.

unimportant [ˌʌnɪmˈpɔːtənt] *adj* unwichtig.

unimpressed [ˌʌnɪmˈprest] *adj* unbeeindruckt, nicht beeindruckt. **I remain ~** das beeindruckt mich überhaupt nicht.

uninhabited [ˌʌnɪnˈhæbɪtɪd] *adj* unbewohnt.

uninhibited [ˌʌnɪnˈhɪbɪtɪd] *adj person* ohne Hemmungen; *greed, laughter* hemmungslos. **to be ~** keine Hemmungen haben.

uninitiated [ˌʌnɪˈnɪʃɪeɪtɪd] *adj* **1** nicht eingeweiht. **~ members of a tribe** nicht initiierte Mitglieder eines Stammes. **2** *n* **the ~** *pl* Nichteingeweihte *pl.*

uninjured [ʌnˈɪndʒəd] *adj person* unverletzt; *reputation* nicht beeinträchtigt.

uninspired [ˌʌnɪnˈspaɪəd] *adj* einfallslos. **to be ~ by a subject** von einem Thema nicht begeistert werden.

unintelligent [ˌʌnɪnˈtelɪdʒənt] *adj person, remark* unintelligent; *approach* ungeschickt.

unintelligible [ˌʌnɪnˈtelɪdʒɪbl] *adj person* nicht zu verstehen; *speech, writing* unverständlich.

unintended [ˌʌnɪnˈtendɪd], **unintentional** [ˌʌnɪnˈtenʃənl] *adj* unbeabsichtigt; *joke also* unfreiwillig.

unintentionally [ˌʌnɪnˈtenʃnəlɪ] *adv* unabsichtlich; *funny* unfreiwillig.

uninterested [ʌnˈɪntrɪstɪd] *adj* interesselos. **to be ~ in sth** an etw *(dat)* nicht interessiert sein.

uninteresting [ʌnˈɪntrɪstɪŋ] *adj* uninteressant.

uninterrupted [ˌʌnɪntəˈrʌptɪd] *adj (continuous) line* ununterbrochen, kontinuierlich; *noise, rain also* anhaltend; *(undisturbed) rest* ungestört.

uninvited [ˌʌnɪnˈvaɪtɪd] *adj guest* ungeladen, ungebeten; *criticism* ungebeten.

uninviting [ˌʌnɪnˈvaɪtɪŋ] *adj appearance, atmosphere* nicht *(gerade)* einladend; *prospect* nicht *(gerade)* verlockend; *food, sight* unappetitlich.

union [ˈjuːnjən] **1** *n* **(a)** Vereinigung *f; (uniting also)* Zusammenschluß *m; (Pol also)* Union *f.* **the U~** *(US)* die Vereinigten Staaten; *(in civil war)* die Unionsstaaten *pl;* **U~ of Soviet Socialist Republics** Union *f* der Sozialistischen Sowjetrepubliken. **(b)** *(trade ~)* Gewerkschaft *f.* **(c)** *(association)* Vereinigung *f; (customs ~)* Union *f; (students' ~ also)* Studentenclub *m (also* building). **(d)** (harmony) Eintracht, Harmonie f. **2** adj attr (trade ~) Gewerkschafts-. ~ **card** Gewerkschaftsausweis m.

unionist ['juːnjənɪst] n **(a)** (trade ~) Gewerkschaftler(in f) m. **(b)** (Pol) Unionsanhänger(in f) m.

unionize ['juːnjənaɪz] vt gewerkschaftlich organisieren.

union: U~ **Jack** n Union Jack m; ~ **shop** n gewerkschaftspflichtiger Betrieb.

unique [juːˈniːk] adj einzig attr; (outstanding) einzigartig, einmalig. **such cases are not ~ to Britain** solche Fälle sind nicht nur auf Großbritannien beschränkt.

uniquely [juːˈniːklɪ] adv (solely) einzig und allein, nur; (outstandingly) einmalig.

unisex ['juːnɪseks] adj Unisex-, unisex.

unison ['juːnɪzn] n (Mus) Gleichklang, Einklang m (also fig). **in ~** unisono (form), einstimmig.

unit ['juːnɪt] n **(a)** (section, Mil) Einheit f; (set of equipment also) Anlage f; (of furniture, machine) Element nt; (of organization also) Abteilung f. **x-ray ~** Röntgenanlage f. **(b)** (measure) Einheit f. **~ of length** Längeneinheit f; **monetary ~** Währungseinheit f. **(c)** (Math) Einer m.

unit cost n (Fin) Kosten pl pro (Rechnungs)einheit.

unite [juːˈnaɪt] **1** vt (join) verbinden; party, country (ver)einigen; (emotions, ties) (ver)einen. **2** vi sich zusammenschließen. **to ~ in doing sth** gemeinsam etw tun; **to ~ in opposition to sth** gemeinsam gegen etw Opposition machen.

united [juːˈnaɪtɪd] adj verbunden; group, nation, front geschlossen; (unified) people, nation einig; efforts vereint. **to present a ~ front** eine geschlossene Front bieten.

United: ~ **Kingdom** n Vereinigtes Königreich; ~ **Nations (Organization)** n Vereinte Nationen pl; ~ **States (of America)** npl Vereinigte Staaten pl (von Amerika).

unit trust n (Brit) Investmentfonds m.

unity ['juːnɪtɪ] n Einheit f; (harmony) Einigkeit f; (of a novel, painting etc) Einheitlichkeit f. **this ~ of purpose** diese gemeinsamen Ziele; **to live in ~ with** in Eintracht leben mit.

Univ = **University** Univ.

universal [ˌjuːnɪˈvɜːsəl] adj phenomenon, applicability, remedy universal, universell; language, remedy also Universal-; custom also allgemein verbreitet; truth, rule also allgemein gültig; approval, peace allgemein. **~ remedy** Allheilmittel nt; **to be a ~ favourite** überall beliebt sein; **to become ~** allgemein verbreitet werden.

universally [ˌjuːnɪˈvɜːsəlɪ] adv allgemein. **~ applicable** allgemeingültig.

universe ['juːnɪvɜːs] n (cosmos) (Welt)all, Universum nt; (world) Welt f.

university [ˌjuːnɪˈvɜːsɪtɪ] **1** n Universität f. **to be at ~/to go to ~** studieren; **to go to London U~** in London studieren. **2** adj attr town, library Universitäts-; qualifications, education also akademisch. **~ teacher** Hochschullehrer m.

unjust [ʌnˈdʒʌst] adj ungerecht (to gegen).

unjustifiable [ʌnˈdʒʌstɪfaɪəbl] adj nicht zu rechtfertigen(d attr) pred.

unjustifiably [ʌnˈdʒʌstɪfaɪəblɪ] adv expensive, severe, critical ungerechtfertigt; rude unnötig; criticize zu Unrecht.

unjustified [ʌnˈdʒʌstɪfaɪd] adj ungerechtfertigt. **to be ~ in thinking that ...** zu Unrecht denken, daß ...

unjustly [ʌnˈdʒʌstlɪ] adv zu Unrecht; judge, treat ungerecht.

unjustness [ʌnˈdʒʌstnɪs] n Ungerechtigkeit f.

unkempt [ʌnˈkempt] adj hair ungekämmt; appearance, garden etc ungepflegt.

unkind [ʌnˈkaɪnd] adj (+er) person, remark, action (not nice) unfreundlich; (cruel) lieblos, gemein;

remark also spitz. ~ **to the skin** nicht hautfreundlich.

unkindly [ʌnˈkaɪndlɪ] adv unfreundlich; (cruelly) lieblos, gemein. **don't take it ~ if ...** nimm es nicht übel, wenn ...

unkindness [ʌnˈkaɪndnɪs] n Unfreundlichkeit f; (cruelty) Lieblosigkeit, Gemeinheit f.

unknowing [ʌnˈnəʊɪŋ] adj agent unbewußt.

unknowingly [ʌnˈnəʊɪŋlɪ] adv unbewußt, ohne es zu wissen.

unknown [ʌnˈnəʊn] **1** adj unbekannt. ~ **quantity** (Math, fig) unbekannte Größe; ~ **territory** (lit, fig) Neuland nt; **to be ~ to sb** (feeling, territory) jdm fremd sein; **it's ~ for him to get up for breakfast** man ist es von ihm gar nicht gewohnt, daß er zum Frühstück aufsteht. **2** n (person) Unbekannte(r) mf; (factor, Math) Unbekannte f. **a voyage into the ~** (lit, fig) eine Fahrt ins Ungewisse. **3** adv ~ **to me** etc ohne daß ich etc es wußte.

unladylike [ʌnˈleɪdɪlaɪk] adj nicht damenhaft.

unlawful [ʌnˈlɔːfʊl] adj gesetzwidrig; means, assembly illegal; wedding ungültig.

unless [ənˈles] conj es sei denn; (at beginning of sentence) wenn ... nicht. **don't do it ~ I tell you to** mach das nicht, es sei denn, ich sage es dir; ~ **I tell you to, don't do it** wenn ich es dir nicht sage, mach das nicht; ~ **I am mistaken ...** wenn ich mich nicht irre ...; ~ **otherwise stated** sofern nicht anders angegeben.

unlicensed [ʌnˈlaɪsənst] adj car, dog, TV nicht angemeldet; premises ohne (Schank)konzession; (unauthorized) unbefugt.

unlike [ʌnˈlaɪk] **1** adj unähnlich; poles gegensätzlich. **2** prep **(a)** im Gegensatz zu (dat), anders als. **(b)** (uncharacteristic of, photo etc) **to be quite ~ sb** jdm (gar) nicht ähnlich sehen; (behaviour also) überhaupt nicht zu jdm passen.

unlikelihood [ʌnˈlaɪklɪhʊd], **unlikeliness** [ʌnˈlaɪklɪnɪs] n Unwahrscheinlichkeit f.

unlikely [ʌnˈlaɪklɪ] adj (+er) happening, outcome unwahrscheinlich; explanation also unglaubwürdig; clothes komisch. **it is (most) ~/not ~ that ...** es ist (höchst) unwahrscheinlich/es kann durchaus sein, daß ...; **she is ~ to come** sie kommt höchstwahrscheinlich nicht; **it looks an ~ place for mushrooms** es sieht mir nicht nach der geeigneten Stelle für Pilze aus; **in the ~ event that it does happen** in dem unwahrscheinlichen Fall, daß das geschieht.

unlimited [ʌnˈlɪmɪtɪd] adj wealth, time unbegrenzt; power also schrankenlos; patience unendlich.

unlined [ʌnˈlaɪnd] adj paper unliniert; face faltenlos; (without lining) dress ungefüttert.

unlit [ˌʌnˈlɪt] adj road unbeleuchtet; lamp nicht angezündet.

unload [ʌnˈləʊd] vt **(a)** ship, gun entladen; car also, luggage ausladen; truck, luggage abladen; cargo löschen. **(b)** (col: get rid of) children, problems abladen (on(to) bei).

unlock [ʌnˈlɒk] vt door etc aufschließen. **the door is ~ed** die Tür ist nicht abgeschlossen; **to leave a door ~ed** eine Tür nicht abschließen.

unloose [ʌnˈluːs] vt **(a)** (also ~n) knot, grasp lösen; rope also losmachen. **(b)** prisoner, dog losbinden.

unlovable [ʌnˈlʌvəbl] adj wenig liebenswert, unsympathisch.

unluckily [ʌnˈlʌkɪlɪ] adv zum Pech, zum Unglück. ~ **for him** zu seinem Pech.

unlucky [ʌnˈlʌkɪ] adj (+er) unglückselig; choice unglücklich. **to be ~** (person) Pech haben; (not succeed) keinen Erfolg haben; **he was ~ enough to meet her** er hatte das Pech, sie zu treffen; **broken mirrors are ~** zerbrochene Spiegel bringen Unglück.

unmanageable [ʌnˈmænɪdʒəbl] adj (unwieldy) vehicle schwer zu handhaben; parcel, size unhandlich; (uncontrollable) animal, person, hair widerspenstig; *situation* unkontrollierbar.

unmanly [ʌn'mænlɪ] *adj behaviour* unmännlich; *(cowardly)* feige; *(effeminate)* weibisch.

unmanned [ʌn'mænd] *adj (not requiring crew) level crossing, space flight* unbemannt; *(lacking crew) telephone exchange, lighthouse* unbesetzt.

unmarked [ʌn'mɑːkt] *adj (unstained)* ohne Flecken, fleckenlos; *(without marking) face* ungezeichnet *(also fig); suitcase etc* ohne Namen or Adresse; *police car* nicht gekennzeichnet.

unmarried [ʌn'mærɪd] *adj* unverheiratet. ~ mother ledige Mutter.

unmask [ʌn'mɑːsk] **1** *vt (lit)* demaskieren; *(fig)* entlarven. **2** *vi* die Maske abnehmen.

unmatched [ʌn'mætʃt] *adj* einmalig, unübertroffen *(for* in bezug auf +*acc).*

unmentionable [ʌn'menʃnəbl] *adj* tabu *pred; word also* unaussprechlich. **to be ~** tabu sein.

unmerciful [ʌn'mɜːsɪfʊl] *adj* erbarmungslos.

unmindful [ʌn'maɪndfʊl] *adj* **to be ~ of** sth nicht auf etw *(acc)* achten, etw nicht beachten.

unmistak(e)able [ˌʌnmɪ'steɪkəbl] *adj* unverkennbar; *(visually)* nicht zu verwechseln.

unmitigated [ʌn'mɪtɪgeɪtɪd] *adj wrath, severity* ungemildert; *(col: complete) disaster* total; *liar, rogue* Erz- *(col).*

unmoved [ʌn'muːvd] *adj person* ungerührt. **they were ~** by his playing sein Spiel(en) ergriff sie nicht; **it leaves me ~** das (be)rührt mich nicht.

unmusical [ʌn'mjuːzɪkəl] *adj* unmusikalisch.

unnamed [ʌn'neɪmd] *adj (nameless)* namenlos; *(anonymous)* ungenannt.

unnatural [ʌn'nætʃrəl] *adj* unnatürlich; *(abnormal also) relationship, crime* nicht normal *pred,* widernatürlich.

unnecessarily [ʌn'nesɪ'serɪlɪ] *adv* unnötigerweise; *strict, serious* unnötig, übertrieben.

unnecessary [ʌn'nesɪsərɪ] *adj* unnötig; *(not requisite) visa* nicht notwendig; *(superfluous also)* überflüssig. **really, that was quite ~ of you!** also, das war wirklich überflüssig!

unnerve [ʌn'nɜːv] *vt* entnerven; *(gradually)* zermürben; *(discourage) speaker* entmutigen.

unnoticed [ʌn'nəʊtɪst] *adj* unbemerkt. **to go or pass ~** unbemerkt bleiben.

UNO = **United Nations Organization** UNO *f.*

unobjectionable [ˌʌnəb'dʒekʃnəbl] *adj* einwandfrei.

unobservant [ˌʌnəb'zɜːvənt] *adj* unaufmerksam. **to be ~** ein schlechter Beobachter sein.

unobserved [ˌʌnəb'zɜːvd] *adj (not seen)* unbemerkt; *(not celebrated)* nicht (mehr) eingehalten.

unobtainable [ˌʌnəb'teɪnəbl] *adj* nicht erhältlich. **number ~** *(Telec)* kein Anschluß unter dieser Nummer.

unobtrusive [ˌʌnəb'truːsɪv] *adj* unauffällig.

unoccupied [ʌn'ɒkjʊpaɪd] *adj person* unbeschäftigt; *house* unbewohnt; *seat* frei; *(Mil) zone* unbesetzt.

unofficial [ˌʌnə'fɪʃəl] *adj* inoffiziell. **to take ~ action** *(Ind)* inoffiziell streiken.

unofficially [ˌʌnə'fɪʃəlɪ] *adv* inoffiziell.

unopened [ʌn'əʊpənd] *adj* ungeöffnet.

unopposed [ˌʌnə'pəʊzd] *adj* **elected ~** ohne Gegenstimme gewählt; **they marched on ~** sie marschierten weiter, ohne auf Widerstand zu treffen; **~ by the committee** ohne Widerspruch seitens des Ausschusses.

unorganized [ʌn'ɔːgənaɪzd] *adj* unsystematisch; *life* ungeregelt; *(Ind)* nicht (gewerkschaftlich) organisiert. **he is so ~** er hat überhaupt kein System.

unoriginal [ˌʌnə'rɪdʒɪnəl] *adj* wenig originell.

unorthodox [ʌn'ɔːθədɒks] *adj* unkonventionell, unorthodox.

unpack [ʌn'pæk] *vti* auspacken.

unpaid [ʌn'peɪd] *adj* unbezahlt.

unpalatable [ʌn'pælɪtəbl] *adj food, drink* ungenießbar; *(fig) fact, truth, mixture* unverdaulich, schwer zu verdauen.

unparalleled [ʌn'pærəleld] *adj* einmalig, beispiellos. **an ~ success** ein Erfolg ohnegleichen.

unpardonable [ʌn'pɑːdnəbl] *adj* unverzeihlich.

unpatriotic [ˌʌnpætrɪ'ɒtɪk] *adj* unpatriotisch.

unpaved [ʌn'peɪvd] *adj road* nicht gepflastert.

unperturbed [ˌʌnpə'tɜːbd] *adj* nicht beunruhigt *(by* von, durch), gelassen.

unpick [ʌn'pɪk] *vt* auftrennen.

unpin [ʌn'pɪn] *vt dress, hair* die Nadeln entfernen aus; *notice* abnehmen.

unplaced [ʌn'pleɪst] *adj (Sport)* nicht plaziert. **to be ~** sich nicht plaziert haben.

unplanned [ʌn'plænd] *adj* ungeplant.

unpleasant [ʌn'pleznt] *adj* unangenehm; *person, remark* unfreundlich *(to sb* jdm gegenüber).

unpleasantly [ʌn'plezntlɪ] *adv reply* unfreundlich; *warm, smell* unangenehm.

unpleasantness [ʌn'plezntnɪs] *n* **(a)** *(quality) see adj* Unangenehmheit *f;* Unfreundlichkeit *f.* **(b)** *(bad feeling, quarrel)* Unstimmigkeit *f.*

unplug [ʌn'plʌg] *vt radio, lamp* den Stecker herausziehen von.

unpolished [ʌn'pɒlɪʃt] *adj* unpoliert; *stone, (fig) person, manners* ungeschliffen; *performance, style* unausgefeilt.

unpolluted [ˌʌnpə'luːtɪd] *adj* sauber, unverschmutzt.

unpopular [ʌn'pɒpjʊləʳ] *adj person* unbeliebt *(with sb* bei jdm); *decision, move* unpopulär.

unprecedented [ʌn'presɪdəntɪd] *adj* noch nie dagewesen; *profit, step* unerhört. **this event is ~** dieses Ereignis ist bisher einmalig; **an ~ success** ein beispielloser Erfolg.

unpredictable [ˌʌnprɪ'dɪktəbl] *adj* unvorhersehbar; *result* nicht vorherzusagen(d *attr) pred; behaviour, person, weather* unberechenbar.

unprejudiced [ʌn'predʒʊdɪst] *adj (impartial)* objektiv, unparteiisch; *(not having prejudices)* vorurteilslos.

unprepared [ˌʌnprɪ'pɛəd] *adj* nicht vorbereitet; *person also* unvorbereitet. **to be ~ for sth** für etw nicht vorbereitet sein; *(be surprised)* auf etw *(acc)* nicht gefaßt or gefaßt sein.

unprepossessing [ʌnpriːpə'zesɪŋ] *adj* wenig einnehmend.

unpretentious [ˌʌnprɪ'tenʃəs] *adj* schlicht, bescheiden; *style, book* einfach.

unprincipled [ʌn'prɪnsɪpld] *adj* skrupellos.

unprintable [ʌn'prɪntəbl] *adj* nicht druckfähig; *(fig) answer* nicht druckreif.

unproductive [ˌʌnprə'dʌktɪv] *adj capital* nicht gewinnbringend; *soil* ertragsarm; *meeting* unergiebig.

unprofessional [ˌʌnprə'feʃənl] *adj conduct* berufswidrig; *work* unfachmännisch.

unprofitable [ʌn'prɒfɪtəbl] *adj (financially)* keinen Profit bringend; *mine etc* unrentabel; *(fig)* nutzlos.

unpromising [ʌn'prɒmɪsɪŋ] *adj* nicht sehr vielversprechend.

unpronounceable [ˌʌnprə'naʊnsɪbl] *adj* unaussprechbar.

unprotected [ˌʌnprə'tektɪd] *adj* ohne Schutz, schutzlos; *machine* ungeschützt; *(by insurance)* ohne Versicherungsschutz.

unproved [ʌn'pruːvd] *adj* unbewiesen; *(untested)* noch nicht bewährt. **he's still ~** er hat sich noch nicht bewährt.

unprovoked [ˌʌnprə'vəʊkd] *adj* grundlos.

unpublished [ʌn'pʌblɪʃt] *adj* unveröffentlicht.

unpunished [ʌn'pʌnɪʃt] *adj* unbestraft. **to go ~** ohne Strafe bleiben.

unqualified [ʌn'kwɒlɪfaɪd] *adj* **(a)** unqualifiziert. **to be ~** nicht qualifiziert sein. **(b)** *(absolute) praise, acceptance* uneingeschränkt; *success*

voll(ständig); *(col)* idiot, liar ausgesprochen.
unquestionable [ʌn'kwestʃənəbl] *adj authority* unbestritten, unangefochten; *evidence, fact* unbezweifelbar; *sincerity, honesty* fraglos. his honesty is ~ seine Ehrlichkeit steht außer Frage.
unquestionably [ʌn'kwestʃənəblɪ] *adv* fraglos, zweifellos.
unquestioning [ʌn'kwestʃənɪŋ] *adj* bedingungslos.
unravel [ʌn'rævəl] *vt knitting* aufziehen; *(lit, fig: untangle)* entwirren; *mystery* lösen.
unreadable [ʌn'riːdəbl] *adj writing* unleserlich; *book, text* unverständlich.
unrealistic [ˌʌnrɪə'lɪstɪk] *adj* unrealistisch.
unreality [ˌʌnrɪ'ælɪtɪ] *n* Unwirklichkeit *f.*
unreasonable [ʌn'riːznəbl] *adj demand, price etc* übertrieben; *person* uneinsichtig; *(showing lack of sense)* unvernünftig. to be ~ about sth *(not be understanding)* kein Verständnis für etw zeigen; *(be overdemanding)* in bezug auf etw *(acc)* zuviel verlangen; it is ~ to ... es ist zuviel verlangt, zu ...; am I being ~? verlange ich zuviel?
unrecognizable [ʌn'rekəgnaɪzəbl] *adj* nicht wiederzuerkennen(d *attr) pred.* he was totally ~ in his disguise man konnte ihn in seiner Verkleidung überhaupt nicht erkennen.
unrecognized [ʌn'rekəgnaɪzd] *adj (not noticed) person, danger, value* unerkannt; *(not acknowledged) government, record* nicht anerkannt; *genius, talent* ungewürdigt, unerkannt.
unrecorded [ˌʌnrɪ'kɔːdɪd] *adj* nicht aufgenommen; *(Rad, TV)* nicht aufgezeichnet; *(in documents)* nicht schriftlich erfaßt.
unrefined [ˌʌnrɪ'faɪnd] *adj* **(a)** *petroleum etc* nicht raffiniert. **(b)** *person* unkultiviert.
unrehearsed [ˌʌnrɪ'hɜːst] *adj (a) (Theat etc)* nicht geprobt; *cast* schlecht eingespielt; *(spontaneous) incident* spontan.
unrelated [ˌʌnrɪ'leɪtɪd] *adj (unconnected)* ohne Beziehung *(to* zu); *(by family)* nicht verwandt.
unrelenting [ˌʌnrɪ'lentɪŋ] *adj pressure* unablässig; *opposition, struggle* unerbittlich; *determination* hartnäckig; *pace* unvermindert; *rain* anhaltend *attr,* nicht nachlassend *attr; (not merciful) person, heat* unbarmherzig.
unreliable [ˌʌnrɪ'laɪəbl] *adj* unzuverlässig.
unrelieved [ˌʌnrɪ'liːvd] *adj pain, gloom* ungemindert; *grey* eintönig; *monotony, boredom* tödlich. a life of ~ drudgery ein Leben, das eine einzige Schinderei ist; to be ~ by nicht aufgelockert sein durch or von.
unremitting [ˌʌnrɪ'mɪtɪŋ] *adj efforts, toil* unablässig; *zeal* unermüdlich; *hatred* unversöhnlich.
unrepeatable [ˌʌnrɪ'piːtəbl] *adj words, views* nicht wiederholbar; *offer* einmalig.
unrepentant [ˌʌnrɪ'pentənt] *adj* nicht reumütig, reu(e)los. he is ~ about it er bereut es nicht.
unrepresentative [ˌʌnreprɪ'zentətɪv] *adj (Pol) government* nicht frei gewählt; *(untypical)* nicht repräsentativ *(of* für).
unrequited [ˌʌnrɪ'kwaɪtɪd] *adj love* unerwidert.
unreserved [ˌʌnrɪ'zɜːvd] *adj* **(a)** *(frank) person* nicht reserviert, offen. **(b)** *(complete) approval* uneingeschränkt. **(c)** *(not booked)* nicht reserviert.
unresponsive [ˌʌnrɪ'spɒnsɪv] *adj (physically)* nicht reagierend *attr; (emotionally, intellectually)* gleichgültig, unempfänglich. to be ~ nicht reagieren *(to* auf *+acc); (engine)* nicht ansprechen; an ~ audience ein Publikum, das nicht mitgeht; I suggested it but he was fairly ~ ich habe es vorgeschlagen, aber er zeigte sich nicht sehr interessiert.
unrest [ʌn'rest] *n* Unruhen *pl; (discontent)* Unzufriedenheit *f.*
unrestrained [ˌʌnrɪ'streɪnd] *adj* uneingeschränkt;

feelings offen, ungehemmt; *enthusiasm, atmosphere* ungezügelt; *behaviour* unbeherrscht.
unrestricted [ˌʌnrɪ'strɪktɪd] *adj power, use, growth* unbeschränkt; *access* ungehindert.
unrewarded [ˌʌnrɪ'wɔːdɪd] *adj* unbelohnt. to go ~ unbelohnt bleiben; *(not gain recognition)* keine Anerkennung finden.
unrewarding [ˌʌnrɪ'wɔːdɪŋ] *adj work* undankbar; *(financially)* wenig einträglich.
unripe [ʌn'raɪp] *adj* unreif.
unrivalled, *(US)* unrivaled [ʌn'raɪvəld] *adj* unübertroffen. ~ in *or* for quality von unübertroffener Qualität.
unroadworthy [ʌn'rəʊd͵wɜːðɪ] *adj* nicht verkehrssicher.
unroll [ʌn'rəʊl] **1** *vt carpet, map* aufrollen. **2** *vi* sich aufrollen; *(fig) (plot)* sich abwickeln; *(landscape)* sich ausbreiten.
unruffled [ʌn'rʌfld] *adj person* gelassen; *sea* ruhig, unbewegt; *hair* ordentlich; *calm* unerschütterlich. she was quite ~ sie blieb ruhig und gelassen.
unruly [ʌn'ruːlɪ] *adj (+er)* wild, ungebärdig.
unsafe [ʌn'seɪf] *adj ladder, machine, car, person* nicht sicher; *(dangerous) journey, toy, wiring* gefährlich. to feel ~ sich nicht sicher fühlen.
unsaid [ʌn'sed] *adj* ungesagt, unausgesprochen. to leave sth ~ etw unausgesprochen lassen; it's best left ~ das bleibt besser ungesagt.
unsaleable [ʌn'seɪləbl] *adj* unverkäuflich. to be ~ sich nicht verkaufen lassen.
unsatisfactory [ˌʌnsætɪs'fæktərɪ] *adj* unbefriedigend; *profits etc* nicht ausreichend; *service, hotel* unzulänglich; *(Sch)* mangelhaft. this is most ~ das läßt sehr zu wünschen übrig.
unsatisfied [ʌn'sætɪsfaɪd] *adj person* unzufrieden; *(not convinced)* nicht überzeugt; *appetite, desire, curiosity* unbefriedigt.
unsatisfying [ʌn'sætɪsfaɪɪŋ] *adj* unbefriedigend; *meal* unzureichend.
unsavoury, *(US)* unsavory [ʌn'seɪvərɪ] *adj smell, sight* widerlich; *appearance (repulsive)* abstoßend; *(dishonest, shady etc)* fragwürdig; *subject, details* unerfreulich; *joke* unfein; *district, characters* zwielichtig, übel; *reputation* zweifelhaft.
unscathed [ʌn'skeɪðd] *adj (lit)* unverletzt, unversehrt; *(fig)* unbeschadet; *relationship* heil. to escape ~ *(fig)* ungeschoren davonkommen.
unscheduled [ʌn'ʃedjuːld] *adj stop etc* außerfahrplanmäßig; *meeting* außerplanmäßig.
unscientific [ˌʌnsaɪən'tɪfɪk] *adj* unwissenschaftlich.
unscrew [ʌn'skruː] **1** *vt (loosen)* losschrauben. to come ~ed sich lösen. **2** *vi* sich los- *or* abschrauben lassen; *(become loose)* sich lösen.
unscrupulous [ʌn'skruːpjʊləs] *adj person, behaviour* skrupellos, gewissenlos.
unseasoned [ʌn'siːznd] *adj timber* nicht abgelagert; *food* ungewürzt; *(fig: inexperienced) troops* unerfahren.
unseaworthy [ʌn'siː͵wɜːðɪ] *adj* seeuntüchtig.
unseemly [ʌn'siːmlɪ] *adj* unschicklich.
unseen [ʌn'siːn] **1** *adj* ungesehen; *(invisible)* unsichtbar; *(unobserved) escape* unbemerkt. **2** *n (esp Brit Sch)* unvorbereitete Übersetzung in die Muttersprache.
unselfish [ʌn'selfɪʃ] *adj* uneigennützig, selbstlos.
unserviceable [ʌn'sɜːvɪsəbl] *adj* unbrauchbar.
unsettle [ʌn'setl] *vt* durcheinanderbringen; *(upset)* aufregen; *(disturb emotionally)* verstören; *animal, (news)* beunruhigen; *(defeat, criticism)* verunsichern.
unsettled [ʌn'setld] *adj* **(a)** *(unpaid)* unbeglichen; *(undecided) question* ungeklärt; *future* unbestimmt, ungewiß. **(b)** *(changeable) weather, (Fin) market* unbeständig; *(Pol) conditions* also unsicher; *life, character* unstet. to be ~ durchein-

ander sein; *(thrown off balance)* aus dem Gleis geworfen sein; *(emotionally disturbed)* verstört sein. **(c)** *(unpopulated) territory* unbesiedelt.

unsettling [ʌn'setlɪŋ] *adj change* aufreibend; *defeat, knowledge* verunsichernd; *news* beunruhigend.

unshakeable [ʌn'ʃeɪkəbl] *adj* unerschütterlich.

unshaken [ʌn'ʃeɪkən] *adj* unerschüttert. **his nerve was ~** er behielt seine Kaltblütigkeit.

unshaven [ʌn'ʃeɪvn] *adj* unrasiert; *(bearded)* bärtig.

unsightly [ʌn'saɪtlɪ] *adj* unansehnlich; *(stronger)* häßlich.

unskilled [ʌn'skɪld] *adj* **(a)** *work, worker* ungelernt. **(b)** *(inexperienced)* ungeübt, unerfahren.

unsociable [ʌn'səʊʃəbl] *adj* ungesellig.

unsocial [ʌn'səʊʃəl] *adj* **to work ~ hours** außerhalb der normalen Arbeitszeiten arbeiten; **visitors at this ~ hour** Besuch um diese Zeit!

unsold [ʌn'səʊld] *adj* unverkauft.

unsolicited [ˌʌnsə'lɪsɪtɪd] *adj* unerbeten; *manuscript* unverlangt eingesandt.

unsolved [ʌn'sɒlvd] *adj* ungelöst.

unsophisticated [ˌʌnsə'fɪstɪkeɪtɪd] *adj (simple)* einfach; *(naive)* naiv, simpel; *(undiscriminating)* unkritisch.

unsound [ʌn'saʊnd] *adj heart, teeth* krank; *health* angegriffen; *timber* morsch; *construction, design* unsolide; *foundations, finances* unsicher; *argument* nicht stichhaltig, anfechtbar; *advice* unvernünftig; *judgement* unzuverlässig; *doctrine* unvertretbar; *policy, move* unklug. **of ~ mind** *(Jur)* unzurechnungsfähig; **the book is ~ on some points** das Buch weist an einigen Stellen Schwächen auf.

unsparing [ʌn'speərɪŋ] *adj* **(a)** *(lavish)* großzügig, verschwenderisch. **to be ~ with sth** mit etw nicht geizen. **(b)** *criticism* schonungslos.

unspeakable [ʌn'spiːkəbl] *adj* unbeschreiblich.

unspeakably [ʌn'spiːkəblɪ] *adv* unsagbar.

unspecified [ʌn'spesɪfaɪd] *adj time, amount* nicht *(genau)* genannt.

unspoiled [ˌʌn'spɔɪld], **unspoilt** [ˌʌn'spɔɪlt] *adj countryside* unberührt; *child* nicht verwöhnt.

unspoken [ʌn'spəʊkən] *adj words, thought* unausgesprochen; *agreement, consent* stillschweigend.

unstable [ʌn'steɪbl] *adj structure* nicht stabil; *area, economy* unsicher; *(Chem, Phys)* instabil; *(mentally)* labil.

unstamped [ʌn'stæmpt] *adj letter* unfrankiert; *document, passport* ungestempelt.

unsteady [ʌn'stedɪ] *adj hand* unsicher; *ladder* wack(e)lig; *voice, economy* schwankend; *growth* unregelmäßig. **to be ~ on one's feet** unsicher auf den Beinen sein; **the £ is still ~** das Pfund schwankt noch.

unstinting [ʌn'stɪntɪŋ] *adj person* großzügig; *kindness, generosity, support* uneingeschränkt. **to be ~ in one's efforts** keine Kosten und Mühen scheuen; **he was ~ in his praise** sein Lob war überschwenglich; **to be ~ of one's time** unendlich viel Zeit opfern.

unstressed [ʌn'strest] *adj (Phon)* unbetont.

unstuck [ʌn'stʌk] **1** *pret, ptp of* **unstick**. **2** *adj* **to come ~** *(stamp, notice)* sich lösen; *(col) (plan)* schiefgehen *(col); (speaker, actor)* steckenbleiben; *(in exam)* ins Schwimmen geraten.

unsubstantiated [ˌʌnsəb'stænʃɪeɪtɪd] *adj accusation, testimony, rumour* unbegründet.

unsuccessful [ˌʌsək'sesfʊl] *adj venture, meeting, person etc* erfolglos; *candidate* abgewiesen; *attempt* vergeblich; *marriage, outcome* unglücklich. **to be ~ in doing sth** keinen Erfolg damit haben, etw zu tun; **he is ~ in everything he does** nichts gelingt ihm; **he was ~ in his exam** er hat kein Glück in seinem Examen gehabt.

unsuccessfully [ˌʌnsək'sesfəlɪ] *adv* erfolglos; *try*

vergeblich; *apply* vergebens.

unsuitable [ʌn'suːtəbl] *adj* unpassend. **it would be ~ at this moment to ...** es wäre im Augenblick unangebracht, ...; **this film is ~ for children** dieser Film ist für Kinder nicht geeignet; **we're ~ for each other** wir passen nicht zusammen; **he's ~ for the job** er ist für die Arbeit ungeeignet.

unsuited [ʌn'suːtɪd] *adj* **to be ~ for** *or* **to sth** für etw ungeeignet sein.

unsure [ʌn'ʃʊəʳ] *adj person* unsicher. **to be ~ of oneself** unsicher sein; **to be ~ (of sth)** sich *(dat)* (einer Sache gen) nicht sicher sein; **I'm ~ of him** ich bin mir bei ihm nicht sicher.

unsurpassed [ˌʌnsə'pɑːst] *adj* unübertroffen. **to be ~ by anybody** von niemandem übertroffen werden.

unsuspected [ˌʌnsə'spektɪd] *adj presence etc* unvermutet; *consequences, wealth* ungeahnt.

unsuspecting [ˌʌnsə'spektɪŋ] *adj* ahnungslos, nichtsahnend.

unsweetened [ˌʌn'swiːtnd] *adj* ungesüßt.

unswerving [ʌn'swɜːvɪŋ] *adj loyalty* unwandelbar.

unsympathetic [ˌʌnsɪmpə'θetɪk] *adj* **(a)** *(unfeeling)* gefühllos; *attitude, response* ablehnend, abweisend. **(b)** *(unlikeable)* unsympathisch.

unsystematic [ˌʌnsɪstɪ'mætɪk] *adj* unsystematisch.

untangle [ʌn'tæŋgl] *vt (lit, fig)* entwirren.

untapped [ʌn'tæpt] *adj barrel* unangezapft; *resources, talent* ungenutzt.

untaxed [ʌn'tækst] *adj goods, income* steuerfrei; *car* unversteuert.

untended [ʌn'tendɪd] *adj patient* unbewacht; *garden* ungepflegt.

untested [ʌn'testɪd] *adj* unerprobt.

unthinkable [ʌn'θɪŋkəbl] *adj* undenkbar; *(too horrible)* unvorstellbar.

untidiness [ʌn'taɪdɪnɪs] *n (of room)* Unordnung *f*; *(of person, dress)* Unordentlichkeit *f*.

untidy [ʌn'taɪdɪ] *adj (+er)* unordentlich.

untie [ʌn'taɪ] *vt knot* lösen; *parcel* aufknoten; *person, animal, hands* losbinden.

until [ən'tɪl] **1** *prep* **(a)** bis. **from morning ~ night** von morgens bis abends; **~ now** bis jetzt; **~ then** bis dahin. **(b)** **not ~** *(in future)* nicht vor (+*dat*); *(in past)* erst; **I didn't leave him ~ the following day** ich habe ihn erst am folgenden Tag verlassen. **2** *conj* **(a)** bis. **wait ~ I come** warten Sie, bis ich komme. **(b)** **not ~** *(in future)* nicht bevor, erst wenn; *(in past)* nicht bis, erst als; **he won't come ~ you invite him** er kommt erst, wenn Sie ihn einladen; **they did nothing ~ we came** bis wir kamen, taten sie nichts; **they didn't start ~ we came** sie fingen erst an, als wir da waren.

untimely [ʌn'taɪmlɪ] *adj death* vorzeitig; *(inopportune) moment* unpassend; *remark* zur falschen Zeit.

untiring [ʌn'taɪərɪŋ] *adj work, effort* unermüdlich. **to be ~ in one's efforts** unermüdliche Anstrengungen machen.

untold ['ʌn'təʊld] *adj story* nicht erzählt; *secret* ungelüftet; *wealth* unermeßlich; *agony, delights* unsäglich; *stars etc* unzählig. **~ thousands** unzählig viele.

untouchable [ʌn'tʌtʃəbl] **1** *adj* unberührbar. **2** *n* Unberührbare(r) *mf*.

untouched [ʌn'tʌtʃt] *adj* **(a)** unberührt, unangetastet; *bottle etc* also nicht angebrochen; *(unmentioned)* nicht erwähnt. **~ by human hand** nicht von Menschenhand berührt. **(b)** *(unharmed)* heil, unversehrt; *(unaffected)* unberührt; *(unmoved)* ungerührt. **(c)** *(unequalled) ~* **for quality in der Qualität unerreicht.

untoward [ˌʌntə'wɔːd] *adj (unfortunate) event* unglücklich, bedauerlich; *(unseemly)* unpassend.

nothing ~ **had happened** es war nichts Schlimmes passiert.

untrained [ʌn'treɪnd] *adj person, teacher* unausgebildet; *voice* ungeschult; *animal* undressiert. **to the ~ eye** dem ungeschulten Auge.

untranslatable [ˌʌntrænz'leɪtəbl] *adj* unübersetzbar.

untried [ʌn'traɪd] *adj* (a) *(not tested)* unerprobt; *(not attempted)* unversucht. (b) *(Jur) case* nicht verhandelt; *person* nicht vor Gericht gestellt.

untroubled [ʌn'trʌbld] *adj period* friedlich, ruhig. **the children seemed ~ by the heat** die Hitze schien den Kindern nichts auszumachen.

untrue [ʌn'truː] *adj* (a) *(false)* unwahr. (b) *(unfaithful) person* untreu. **to be ~ to sb** jdm untreu sein.

untrustworthy [ʌn'trʌst,wɜːðɪ] *adj (not reliable) book, person* unzuverlässig; *(not worthy of confidence) person* nicht vertrauenswürdig.

untruth [ʌn'truːθ] *n* Unwahrheit *f*.

untruthful [ʌn'truːθʊl] *adj statement* unwahr; *person* unaufrichtig. **you're being ~** was du da sagst, ist nicht ganz wahr.

unusable [ʌn'juːzəbl] *adj* unbrauchbar.

unused¹ [ʌn'juːzd] *adj (new)* unbenutzt, ungebraucht; *(not made use of)* ungenutzt; *(no longer used)* nicht mehr benutzt.

unused² [ʌn'juːst] *adj* **to be ~ to sth** etw *(acc)* nicht gewohnt sein; **to be ~ to doing sth** nicht daran gewöhnt sein, etw zu tun.

unusual [ʌn'juːʒʊəl] *adj (uncommon)* ungewöhnlich; *(exceptional)* außergewöhnlich. **it's ~ for him to be late** er kommt normalerweise nicht zu spät; **how ~!** das kommt selten vor; **that's ~ for him** das ist sonst nicht seine Art.

unusually [ʌn'juːʒʊəlɪ] *adv see adj.* **most ~, he was late** ganz gegen seine Gewohnheit kam er zu spät.

unutterable [ʌn'ʌtərəbl] *adj* unsäglich.

unvaried [ʌn'vɛərɪd] *adj* unverändert; *(pej)* eintönig.

unvarnished [ʌn'vɑːnɪʃt] *adj wood* unlackiert; *(fig) truth* ungeschminkt.

unveil [ʌn'veɪl] *vt statue, plan* enthüllen; *(Comm) car* vorstellen; *face* entschleiern.

unvoiced [ʌn'vɔɪst] *adj* unausgesprochen.

unwanted [ʌn'wɒntɪd] *adj furniture, clothing* unerwünscht. **he feels ~** er kommt sich unerwünscht vor.

unwarranted [ʌn'wɒrəntɪd] *adj* ungerechtfertigt.

unwary [ʌn'wɛərɪ] *adj* unvorsichtig, unachtsam.

unwashed [ʌn'wɒʃt] *adj* ungewaschen; *dishes* ungespült.

unwavering [ʌn'weɪvərɪŋ] *adj faith, resolve* unerschütterlich; *course* beharrlich.

unwelcome [ʌn'welkəm] *adj visitor* unwillkommen; *news, memories* unerfreulich.

unwell [ʌn'wel] *adj pred* unwohl, nicht wohl. **to be** *or* **feel (a little) ~** sich nicht (recht) wohl fühlen.

unwholesome [ʌn'həʊlsəm] *adj* ungesund; *influence* ungut; *appearance, character* schmierig.

unwieldy [ʌn'wiːldɪ] *adj tool* unhandlich; *object also* sperrig; *(clumsy) body* schwerfällig.

unwilling [ʌn'wɪlɪŋ] *adj helper, pupil* widerwillig; *accomplice* unfreiwillig. **to be ~ to do sth** nicht bereit *or* gewillt sein, etw zu tun.

unwillingly [ʌn'wɪlɪŋlɪ] *adv* widerwillig.

unwillingness [ʌn'wɪlɪŋnɪs] *n* Widerwilligkeit *f*. **their ~ to compromise** ihre mangelnde Kompromißbereitschaft.

unwind [ʌn'waɪnd] *pret, ptp* **unwound 1** *vt thread, tape* abwickeln; *(untangle)* entwirren. **2** *vi* (a) sich abwickeln; *(fig: plot)* sich entwickeln. (b) *(col: relax)* abschalten *(col)*.

unwise [ʌn'waɪz] *adj* unklug. **they were ~ enough to believe him** sie waren so töricht, ihm zu

---

glauben.

unwitting [ʌn'wɪtɪŋ] *adj accomplice* unwissentlich; *action also* unabsichtlich; *victim* ahnungslos.

unwittingly [ʌn'wɪtɪŋlɪ] *adv (innocently)* ahnungslos; *(unknowingly)* unbewußt.

unworkable [ʌn'wɜːkəbl] *adj scheme* undurchführbar; *mine* nicht abbaubar.

unworldly [ʌn'wɜːldlɪ] *adj life* weltabgewandt; *(naive)* weltfremd.

unworthy [ʌn'wɜːðɪ] *adj person* nicht wert *(of gen)*; *conduct also* unwürdig *(of gen)*. **this is ~ of you** das ziemt sich nicht für dich.

unwound [ʌn'waʊnd] *pret, ptp of* **unwind.**

unwrap [ʌn'ræp] *vt* auspacken, auswickeln.

unwritten [ʌn'rɪtn] *adj book, law* ungeschrieben; *agreement* stillschweigend.

unyielding [ʌn'jiːldɪŋ] *adj* unnachgiebig.

unzip [ʌn'zɪp] *vt* zip aufmachen; *dress, case* den Reißverschluß aufmachen an *(+dat)*.

up [ʌp] **1** *adv* (a) *(in high or higher position)* oben; *(to higher position)* nach oben. **~ there** dort oben; **~ here on the roof** hier oben auf dem Dach; **on your way ~ (to see us/them)** auf dem Weg (zu uns/ihnen) herauf/hinauf; **he climbed all the way ~ (to us/them)** er ist den ganzen Weg (zu uns/ihnen) hochgeklettert; **to throw sth ~** etw hochwerfen; **it's five floors ~** es ist im fünften Stock; *(higher)* es ist fünf Stockwerke höher; **the road goes ~ and ~** die Straße steigt immer weiter an; **we were 6,000 m ~ when ... wir** waren 6.000 m hoch, als ...; **a little further ~** ein bißchen weiter oben; **the sun/moon is ~** die Sonne/der Mond ist aufgegangen; **with his collar ~** mit hochgeschlagenem Kragen; **the road is ~** die Straße ist aufgegraben; **to be ~ with the leaders** vorn bei den Führenden sein; **then ~ jumps Richard and says ...** und dann springt Richard auf und sagt ...; **~ with the Liberals!** hoch die Liberalen!; **from £10 ~** ab £ 10.

(b) *(installed, built)* **to be ~** *(building)* stehen; *(scaffolding)* aufgestellt sein; *(shutters)* zu sein; *(wallpaper, curtains, pictures)* hängen; **they're putting ~ a new cinema** sie bauen ein neues Kino; **stick the notice ~ here** häng den Anschlag hier hin.

(c) *(not in bed)* auf. **to get ~** aufstehen; **to be ~ and about** auf sein; *(after illness also)* auf den Beinen sein; **to be ~ late** lange aufbleiben.

(d) *(geographically)* oben. **~ in Inverness** oben in Inverness; **we are going ~ to Hamburg** wir fahren nach Hamburg (hinauf); **to be/go ~ north** im Norden sein/in den Norden fahren; **we're ~ for the day** wir sind (nur) für heute hier; **he was ~ at Susie's place** er war bei Susie (zu Hause).

(e) *(in price, value)* gestiegen *(on gegenüber)*. **potatoes are ~ again** die Kartoffelpreise sind wieder gestiegen.

(f) *(in score)* **to be 3 goals ~** mit 3 Toren führen *or* vorn liegen *(on gegenüber)*; **to be ~ on sb** jdm um einen Schritt voraus sein.

(g) *(col: wrong)* **what's ~?** was ist los?; **there's something ~** *(wrong)* da stimmt irgend etwas nicht; *(happening)* da ist irgend etwas im Gange.

(h) *(knowledgeable)* firm, beschlagen *(in, on* in *+dat)*. **he's well ~ in** *or* **on foreign affairs** in Auslandsfragen ist er firm.

(i) *(finished)* **time's ~** deine Zeit ist um; **the lease is ~ next month** das Mietverhältnis endet nächsten Monat; **to eat/use sth ~** etw aufessen/aufbrauchen; **it's all ~ with him** *(col)* es ist aus mit ihm *(col)*.

(j) **~ to** *(as far as)* bis; **~ to now** bis jetzt; **~ to then** bis dann *or* dahin.

(k) **~ to** *(col: doing)* **what's he ~ to?** *(actually doing)* was macht er da?; *(planning etc)* was hat er vor?; *(suspiciously)* was führt er im Schilde?; **he's ~ to no good** er führt nichts Gutes im

Schilde.

(1) ~ ʌo: **I don't feel ~ to it** ich fühle mich dem nicht gewachsen; *(not well enough)* ich fühle mich nicht wohl genug dazu; **he's not/it isn't ~ to much** ihm/damit ist nicht viel los *(col)*; **it isn't ~ to his usual standard** es entspricht nicht seinem sonstigen Niveau; **it's ~ to us to help him** wir sollten ihm helfen; **if it was ~ to me** wenn es nach mir ginge; **it's ~ to you whether you go or not** es liegt an *or* bei dir, ob du gehst oder nicht; **shall I take it?** — **that's entirely ~ to you** soll ich es nehmen? — das müssen Sie selbst wissen; **it's ~ to the government to put things right** es ist Sache der Regierung, das richtigzustellen.

(m) ~ **and down** auf und ab; **he's been ~ and down all evening** er hat den ganzen Abend keine Minute stillgesessen; **it was ~ against the wall** es war an die Wand gelehnt; **to be ~ against a difficulty/an opponent** einem Problem/Gegner gegenüberstehen; **I fully realize what I'm ~ against** mir ist völlig klar, womit ich es hier zu tun habe; **they were really ~ against it** sie hatten wirklich schwer zu schaffen.

2 *prep* **further ~ the page** weiter oben auf der Seite; **to live/go ~ the hill** am Berg wohnen/den Berg hinaufgehen; **they live further ~ the hill/street** sie wohnen weiter oben am Berg/weiter die Straße entlang; **~ the road from me** (von mir) die Straße entlang; **he went off ~ the road** er ging (weg) die Straße hinauf; **he hid it ~ the chimney** er versteckte es (oben) im Kamin; **the water goes ~ this pipe** das Wasser geht durch dieses Rohr; **~ a tube** *(position)* in einer Röhre; *(motion)* in eine Röhre; **to go/march ~ to sb** auf jdn zugehen/-marschieren.

3 *n* **~s and downs** gute und schlechte Zeiten *pl*; *(of life)* Höhen und Tiefen *pl*; **to be on the ~ and ~** *(col: improving)* auf dem aufsteigenden Ast sein *(col)*; **his career is on the ~ and ~** *(col)* mit seiner Karriere geht es aufwärts.

4 *adj (going up)* **escalator** nach oben; *(Rail)* **train, line** zur nächsten größeren Stadt.

5 *vt (col)* **price, offer** hinaufsetzen; **production** ankurbeln; **bet** erhöhen *(to auf +acc)*.

6 *vi (col)* **she ~ped and** hit ihm knallte ihm ganz plötzlich eine *(col)*; **he ~ped and ran** er rannte ganz plötzlich davon.

up-and-coming [ˈʌpənˈkʌmɪŋ] *adj* Nachwuchs-; **business** aufstrebend.

upbringing [ˈʌpbrɪŋɪŋ] *n* Erziehung *f*. **to have a good ~** eine gute Kinderstube haben.

up-country [ˈʌpˈkʌntrɪ] *adv* landeinwärts.

update [ʌpˈdeɪt] **1** *vt* auf den neuesten Stand bringen. **2** [ˈʌpdeɪt] *n* **to give sb an ~** jdn auf den neuesten Stand bringen.

up-end [ʌpˈend] *vt* **box, sofa** hochkant stellen.

up-front [ˌʌpˈfrʌnt] *adv* im voraus.

upgrade [ʌpˈgreɪd] *vt* **employee** befördern; **job** höher einstufen; **product** verbessern.

upheaval [ʌpˈhiːvəl] *n* Aufruhr *m*. **emotional ~** Aufruhr der Gefühle; **social/political ~s** soziale/politische Umwälzungen *pl*.

upheld [ʌpˈheld] *pret, ptp of* **uphold**.

uphill [ˈʌpˈhɪl] **1** *adv* bergauf. **to go ~** bergauf gehen; *(car)* den Berg hinauffahren. **2** *adj* **road** bergauf (führend); *(fig)* **work, struggle** mühsam, mühselig. **it's ~ all the way** *(lit)* es geht die ganze Strecke bergauf; *(fig)* es ist ein harter Kampf.

uphold [ʌpˈhəʊld] *pret, ptp* **upheld** *vt (sustain)* **tradition, honour** wahren; **the law** hüten; *(support)* **person, decision, objection** (unter)stützen; *(Jur)* **verdict** bestätigen.

upholstery [ʌpˈhəʊlstərɪ] *n (interior)* Polsterung *f*. *(cover)* Bezug *m*; *(trade)* Polsterei *f*; *(skill)* das Polstern.

upkeep [ˈʌpkiːp] *n (running)* Unterhalt *m*; *(cost)* Unterhaltskosten *pl*; *(maintenance)* Instandhaltung *f*.

uplift [ˈʌplɪft] **1** *n (exaltation)* Erhebung *f*; *(moral inspiration)* Erbauung *f*. **2** [ʌpˈlɪft] *vt* **spirit, voice** erheben. **to feel ~ed** sich erbaut fühlen.

up-market [ˈʌpˈmɑːkɪt] *adj* anspruchsvoll.

upon [əˈpɒn] *prep see* **on 1**.

upper [ˈʌpər] **1** *adj* obere(r, s); **lip, arm, jaw, deck** Ober-. **temperatures in the ~ thirties** Temperaturen über 35 Grad; **U~ Egypt/the ~ Loire** Oberägypten *nt*/die obere Loire; **~ storey** *(of house)* oberes Stockwerk; **~ circle** *(Brit Theat)* zweiter Rang; **the ~ ranks of the Civil Service** das gehobene Beamtentum; **~ school** Oberschule *f*; **U~ House** *(Parl)* Oberhaus *nt*. **2** *n* **~s** *pl (of shoe)* Obermaterial *nt*; **to be on one's ~s** *(col)* auf den Hund gekommen sein *(col)*.

upper: **~ case** *n (Typ)* Großbuchstabe *m*; **~ class** *n* **the ~ classes** die Oberschicht; **~-class** *adj* **accent, district, person** vornehm; **sport, expression, attitude** der Oberschicht; **to be ~-class** *(person)* zur Oberschicht gehören; **~classman** *n (US)* Mitglied *nt* einer *High School* oder eines *College*; **~ crust** *n (col)* obere Zehntausend *pl (col)*; **~-crust** *adj (col)* (schrecklich) vornehm *(col)*; **~most** **1** *adj* oberste(r, s); *(fig)* **ambition** größte(r, s), höchste(r, s); **safety should be ~most in your minds** Sicherheit sollte für Sie an erster Stelle stehen; **2** *adv* **the blue side ~most** mit der blauen Seite nach oben.

uppish [ˈʌpɪʃ] **uppity** [ˈʌpɪtɪ] *adj (col: arrogant)* hochnäsig *(col)*. **to get ~ with sb** jdm gegenüber anmaßend werden.

upright [ˈʌpraɪt] **1** *adj* **(a)** *(erect)* aufrecht; *(vertical)* **post** senkrecht. **~ piano** Klavier *nt*; **~ chair** Stuhl *m*. **(b)** *(fig: honest)* **person** aufrecht. **2** *adv (erect)* aufrecht, gerade; *(vertical)* senkrecht. **to hold oneself ~** sich gerade halten. **3** *n* **(a)** *(post)* Pfosten *m*. **(b)** *(piano)* Klavier *nt*.

uprising [ˈʌpraɪzɪŋ] *n* Aufstand *m*, Erhebung *f*.

upriver [ˈʌpˈrɪvər] *adv* **2 miles ~ from Fen Ditton** 2 Meilen flußaufwärts von Fen Ditton.

uproar [ˈʌprɔːr] *n* Aufruhr *m*. **in ~** in Aufruhr.

uproarious [ʌpˈrɔːrɪəs] *adj* **meeting** tumultartig; **laughter** brüllend; **success, welcome** überwältigend; **joke** zum Schreien pred.

uproot [ʌpˈruːt] *vt* **plant** entwurzeln; *(fig: eradicate)* **evil** ausmerzen. **~ed by the war** durch den Krieg entwurzelt; **to ~ sb from his familiar surroundings** jdn aus seiner gewohnten Umgebung herausreißen.

upset [ʌpˈset] *(vb: pret, ptp ~)* **1** *vt* **(a)** *(knock over, spill)* umstoßen; **boat** umkippen. **she ~ the milk all over the best carpet** sie stieß die Milch um, und alles lief auf den guten Teppich. **(b)** *(make sad: news, death)* bestürzen, erschüttern; *(question, insolence etc)* aus der Fassung bringen; *(experience, accident etc)* mitnehmen *(col)*; *(distress, excite)* **patient, parent etc** aufregen; *(offend etc)* verletzen; *(annoy)* ärgern. **(c)** *(disorganize)* **calculations, balance etc** durcheinanderbringen. **(d)** *(make ill)* **the rich food ~ his stomach** das schwere Essen ist ihm auf den Magen geschlagen.

2 *adj* **(a)** *(about divorce, accident etc)* mitgenommen *(col)*; *(about death, bad news etc)* bestürzt *(about über +acc)*; *(sad)* betrübt, geknickt *(col)* *(about über +acc)*; *(distressed)* aufgeregt *(about wegen)*; **child** durcheinander *pred* *(about über +acc)*; *(annoyed)* aufgebracht *(about über +acc)*; *(hurt)* gekränkt, verletzt *(about über +acc)*. **to get ~** sich aufregen *(about über +acc)*; *(hurt)* verletzt werden. **(b)** [ˈʌpset] **stomach** verdorben attr. **to have an ~ stomach** sich *(dat)* den Magen verdorben haben.

3 [ˈʌpset] *n* **(a)** *(disturbance)* Störung *f*; *(emotional)* Aufregung *f*; *(col: quarrel)* Verstimmung *f*, Ärger *m*; *(unexpected defeat etc)* böse Überraschung. **(b)** *(of stomach)* Magenverstimmung f, verdorbener Magen.

upsetting [ʌp'setɪŋ] adj (saddening) traurig; (stronger) bestürzend; (disturbing) changes störend; situation unangenehm; (offending) beleidigend; (annoying) ärgerlich.

upshot ['ʌpʃɒt] n (result) Ergebnis nt. **the ~ of it all was that ...** es lief darauf hinaus, daß ...

upside down ['ʌpsaɪd'daʊn] 1 adv verkehrt herum. **to turn sth ~** (lit) etw umdrehen; (fig) etw auf den Kopf stellen (col). 2 adj **in an ~ position** verkehrt herum; **to be ~** (picture) verkehrt herum hängen; (world) kopfstehen.

upstairs [ʌp'stɛəz] 1 adv oben; (with movement) nach oben. 2 adj **window** im oberen Stock(werk); **room** also **obere(r, s)**. 3 n oberes Stockwerk.

upstanding [ʌp'stændɪŋ] adj (strong) kräftig; (honourable) rechtschaffen.

upstart ['ʌpstɑːt] n Emporkömmling m.

upstate ['ʌpsteɪt] (US) 1 adj im Norden (des Bundesstaates). 2 adv im Norden (des Bundesstaates); (with movement) in den Norden (des Bundesstaates).

upstream ['ʌpstriːm] adv flußaufwärts. **3 kms ~ from Henley** 3 km oberhalb Henley.

upsurge ['ʌpsɜːdʒ] n Zunahme, Eskalation (pej) f. **she felt an ~ of revulsion** sie fühlte Ekel in sich (dat) aufwallen.

uptake ['ʌpteɪk] n (col): **to be quick/slow on the ~** schnell verstehen/schwer von Begriff sein (col).

uptight ['ʌp'taɪt] adj (col) (nervous) nervös; (inhibited) verklemmt (col); (angry) sauer (col).

up-to-date ['ʌptə'deɪt] adj auf dem neusten Stand; fashion also, book, news aktuell; person, method, technique also up to date pred (col). **to keep ~ with** sth mit or bei etw auf dem laufenden bleiben.

up-to-the-minute ['ʌptəðə'mɪnɪt] adj news, reports allerneuste(r, s), allerletzte(r, s). **her clothes are ~** ihre Kleider sind immer der allerletzte Schrei.

uptown ['ʌptaʊn] (US) adj, adv im Villenviertel.

upturn [ʌp'tɜːn] 1 vt umdrehen. 2 ['ʌptɜːn] n (fig: improvement) Aufschwung m.

upturned ['ʌptɜːnd] adj box etc umgedreht; face nach oben gewandt. **~ nose** Stupsnase f (col).

upward ['ʌpwəd] 1 adj aufwärts-, nach oben; glance nach oben. **~ movement** Aufwärtsbewegung f; **~ slope** Steigung f. 2 adv (also **~s**) (a) move aufwärts, nach oben. **to look ~** hochsehen, nach oben sehen; **face ~** mit dem Gesicht nach oben. (b) (with numbers) prices **from 50p ~** Preise von 50 Pence an, Preise ab 50 Pence; **and ~** und darüber; **~ of 3000** über 3000.

uranium [jʊə'reɪnɪəm] n Uran nt.

Uranus [jʊə'reɪnəs] n (Astron) Uranus m.

urban ['ɜːbən] adj städtisch. **~ renewal** Stadterneuerung f.

urbane [ɜː'beɪn] adj person, style weltmännisch; (civil) höflich; manner, words verbindlich.

urbanization [,ɜːbənaɪ'zeɪʃən] n Urbanisierung, Verstädterung (pej) f.

urchin ['ɜːtʃɪn] n Gassenkind nt; (mischievous) Range f.

urge [ɜːdʒ] 1 n (need) Verlangen, Bedürfnis nt; (drive) Drang m no pl; (physical, sexual) Trieb m. **to feel an ~ to do sth** das Bedürfnis verspüren, etw zu tun; **I resisted the ~ to (contradict him)** ich habe mich beherrscht (und ihm nicht widersprochen); **come and stay with us if you get the ~** (col) komm uns besuchen, wenn du Lust hast. 2 vt (a) **to ~ sb to do sth** (plead with) jdn eindringlich bitten, etw zu tun; (earnestly recommend) darauf dringen, daß jd etw tut; **to ~ sb to accept** jdn drängen, anzunehmen; **he needed no urging** er ließ sich nicht lange bitten. (b) (advocate) caution, acceptance drängen auf (+acc). **to ~ that sth should be done** darauf drängen, daß etw getan wird.

♦ **urge on** vt sep antreiben.

urgency ['ɜːdʒənsɪ] n Dringlichkeit f; (of tone, pleas also) Eindringlichkeit f. **it's a matter of ~** es ist dringend; **there's no ~** es eilt nicht; **there was a note of ~ in his voice** es klang sehr dringend.

urgent ['ɜːdʒənt] adj dringend; letter, parcel Eil-. **to be in ~ need of medical attention** dringend ärztliche Hilfe benötigen.

urgently ['ɜːdʒəntlɪ] adv required dringend; requested also dringlich; talk eindringlich. **he is ~ in need of help** er braucht dringend Hilfe.

urinal ['jʊərɪnl] n (room) Pissoir nt; (vessel) Becken nt.

urine ['jʊərɪn] n Urin, Harn m.

urn [ɜːn] n (a) Urne f. (b) (also **tea ~, coffee ~**) Kessel m.

US = United States USA pl.

us [ʌs] pers pron (a) (dir and indir obj) uns. **give it (to) ~** gib es uns; **younger than ~** jünger als wir; **it's ~** wir sind's; **he is one of ~** er ist einer von uns; **this table shows ~ the tides** auf dieser Tafel sieht man die Gezeiten; **~ and them** wir und die. (b) (col: me) (dir obj) mich; (indir obj) mir; (pl subj) wir. **give ~ a look** laß (mich) mal sehen; **~ English** wir Engländer.

USA = United States of America USA pl; United States Army.

usable ['juːzəbl] adj verwendbar; ideas brauchbar. **no longer ~** nicht mehr zu gebrauchen.

USAF = United States Air Force.

usage ['juːzɪdʒ] n (a) (treatment, handling) Behandlung f. **it's had some rough ~** es ist ziemlich unsanft behandelt worden. (b) (custom, practice) Brauch m, Sitte f. **it's common ~** es ist allgemein üblich. (c) (Ling: use, way of using) Gebrauch m no pl, Anwendung f. **words in common ~** allgemein gebräuchliche Wörter pl.

use¹ [juːz] vt (a) benutzen, gebrauchen; means, materials also, personnel, idea verwenden; system, force, one's abilities, strength anwenden; tact, care walten lassen; drugs einnehmen. **~ only in emergencies** nur im Notfall gebrauchen; **what's this ~d for?** wofür wird das benutzt?; **to ~ sth for sth** etw zu etw verwenden.

(b) (make use of, exploit) information, talents, resources, chances (aus)nutzen; advantage nutzen; waste products verwerten. **you can ~ the leftovers to make a soup** Sie können die Reste zu einer Suppe verwerten.

(c) (~ up, consume) petrol, electricity etc verbrauchen.

(d) (pej: exploit) ausnutzen. **I feel (I've just been) ~d** ich habe das Gefühl, man hat mich ausgenutzt; (sexually) ich komme mir mißbraucht vor.

2 [juːs] n (a) Verwendung f; (operation: of machines etc) Benutzung f; (of calculator etc, of word, arms, intelligence) Gebrauch m; (of method, force) Anwendung f; (of personnel, truncheons etc) Einsatz m; (of drugs) Einnahme f. **directions for ~** Gebrauchsanweisung f; **for the ~ of** für; **for ~ in case of emergency** für Notfälle; **for external ~** zur äußerlichen Anwendung; **ready for ~** gebrauchsfertig; (machine) einsatzbereit; **to make ~ of sth** von etw Gebrauch machen, etw benutzen; **in ~/out of ~** in/außer Gebrauch; (machines) in/außer Betrieb; **to be in daily ~/no longer in ~** täglich/nicht mehr benutzt werden.

(b) (exploitation, making ~ of) Nutzung f; (way of using) Verwendung f; (of waste products, leftovers etc) Verwertung f. **to make ~ of sth** etw nutzen; **to make good/bad ~ of sth** etw gut/ schlecht nutzen; **to have no ~ for** (lit, fig) keine Verwendung haben für; **to have no further ~ for** sth etw nicht mehr gebrauchen.

(c) (usefulness) Nutzen m. **to be of ~ to sb/for doing sth** für jdn von Nutzen sein/nützlich sein, um etw zu tun; **this is no ~ any more** das ist zu

nichts mehr zu gebrauchen; **is this (of) any ~ to you?** können Sie das brauchen?, können Sie damit etwas anfangen?; **can I be of any ~?** kann ich irgendwie behilflich sein?; **this is no ~, we must start work** so hat das keinen Sinn, wir müssen etwas tun; **it's no ~ you** *or* **your protesting** es hat keinen Sinn *or* es nützt nichts, daß du protestierst; **what's the ~ of telling him?** was nützt es, wenn man es ihm sagt?; **it's no ~** es hat keinen Zweck; **ah, what's the ~!** ach, was soll's!
 (d) *(right)* Nutznießung *f (Jur).* **to have ~ of a car** einen Wagen benutzen können; **to give sb the ~ of sth** jdn etw benutzen lassen; *(of car also, of money)* jdm etw zur Verfügung stellen; **to have lost the ~ of one's arm** seinen Arm nicht mehr gebrauchen können.
 ♦ **use up** *vt sep food, objects, one's strength* verbrauchen; *(finish also)* aufbrauchen; *scraps, leftovers etc* verwerten. **the butter is all ~d ~** die Butter ist alle *(col) or* aufgebraucht.

use² [juːs] *aux as in* **I didn't ~ to like it** *see* **used².**

used¹ [juːzd] *adj clothes, car etc* gebraucht; *(soiled) towel etc* benutzt.

used² [juːst] *aux only in past* **I ~ to swim every day** ich bin früher täglich geschwommen; **I ~ not to smoke, I didn't use to smoke** ich habe früher nicht geraucht, ich pflegte nicht zu rauchen *(geh)*; **I don't now but I ~ to** früher schon, jetzt nicht mehr; **he ~ to be a good singer** er war einmal ein guter Sänger; **there ~ to be a field here** hier war (früher) einmal ein Feld; **things aren't what they ~ to be** es ist alles nicht mehr (so) wie früher.

used³ [juːst] *adj* **to be ~ to sth** an etw *(acc)* gewöhnt sein, etw gewohnt sein; **to be ~ to doing sth** es gewohnt sein, etw zu tun; **I'm not ~ to it** ich bin das nicht gewohnt; **to get ~ to sth/doing sth** sich an etw *(acc)* gewöhnen/sich daran gewöhnen, etw zu tun.

useful [ˈjuːsfʊl] *adj* **(a)** nützlich; *person, contribution also* wertvoll; *(handy) tool also* praktisch; *size* zweckmäßig; *discussion* fruchtbar; *life, employment* nutzbringend. **it is ~ for him to be able to…** es ist günstig *or* praktisch, daß er…kann; **to make oneself ~** sich nützlich machen; **to come in ~** sich als nützlich erweisen; **he's a ~ man to know** es ist sehr nützlich, ihn zu kennen; **it has a ~ life of 10 years** es hat eine Nutzdauer von 10 Jahren. **(b)** *(col: capable) player* brauchbar, fähig. **he's quite ~ with a gun** er kann ziemlich gut mit der Pistole umgehen.

useless [ˈjuːslɪs] *adj* **(a)** nutzlos; *(unusable)* unbrauchbar; *person also* zu nichts nütze; *remedy also* wirkungslos. **it's ~ without a handle** ohne Griff nützt es nichts; **I'm ~ at languages** Sprachen kann ich überhaupt nicht. **(b)** *(pointless)* zwecklos, sinnlos.

user [ˈjuːzər] *n* Benutzer(in *f*) *m*.
user-friendly [ˈjuːzəˈfrendlɪ] *adj* benutzerfreundlich.

usher [ˈʌʃər] **1** *n (Theat also)* Platzanweiser *m*; *(Jur)* Gerichtsdiener *m*. **2** *vt* **to ~ sb into a room/to his seat** jdn in ein Zimmer/zu seinem Sitz bringen; **to ~ sb out** jdn hinauskomplimentieren; **to ~ in a new era** ein neues Zeitalter einleiten.

usherette [ˌʌʃəˈret] *n* Platzanweiserin *f*.

USN = **United States Navy.**

USS = **United States Ship; United States Senate.**
USSR = **Union of Soviet Socialist Republics** UdSSR *f*.

usual [ˈjuːʒʊəl] *adj* **1** *(customary)* üblich; *(normal also)* gewöhnlich, normal. **when shall I come? — oh, the ~ time** wann soll ich kommen? — oh, wie immer; **it's the ~ thing nowadays** das ist heute so üblich; **it's ~ to ask first** normalerweise fragt man erst; **as ~, as per ~** *(col)* wie üblich, wie gewöhnlich; **business as ~** normaler Betrieb; *(in shop)* Verkauf geht weiter; **later/less/more than ~** später/weniger/mehr als sonst; **it's not ~ for him to be late** er kommt normalerweise nicht zu spät. **2** *n (col)* der/die/das Übliche. **the ~ please!** *(drink)* dasselbe wie immer, bitte!

usually [ˈjuːʒʊəlɪ] *adv* gewöhnlich, normalerweise. **do you go to Spain? — ~** fahren Sie nach Spanien — meist(ens); **is he ~ so rude?** ist er immer so unhöflich!

usurer [ˈjuːʒərər] *n* Wucherer *m*.

usurp [juːˈzɜːp] *vt* sich *(dat)* widerrechtlich aneignen; *power, title, inheritance also* an sich *(acc)* reißen; *throne* sich bemächtigen (+*gen*) *(geh)*; *role* sich *(dat)* anmaßen; *person* verdrängen.

usury [ˈjuːʒʊrɪ] *n* Wucher *m*.

utensil [juːˈtensl] *n* Gerät, Utensil *nt*.

uterus [ˈjuːtərəs] *n* Gebärmutter *f*.

utilitarian [ˌjuːtɪlɪˈtɛərɪən] *adj auf* Nützlichkeit ausgerichtet; *qualities* nützlich; *(Philos)* utilitaristisch.

utility [juːˈtɪlɪtɪ] *n* **(a)** *(usefulness)* Nützlichkeit *f*, Nutzen *m*. **(b) public ~** *(company)* Versorgungsbetrieb *m*; *(service)* Leistung *f* der Versorgungsbetriebe.

utilization [ˌjuːtɪlaɪˈzeɪʃən] *n see vt* Verwendung *f*; Nutzung *f*; Verwertung *f*.

utilize [ˈjuːtɪlaɪz] *vt* verwenden; *situation, time, opportunity, talent* nutzen; *waste paper etc* verwerten.

utmost [ˈʌtməʊst] **1** *adj* **(a)** *(greatest) ease, danger* größte(r, s); *caution, candour also* äußerste(r, s). **they used their ~ skill** Sie taten ihr Äußerstes; **with the ~ speed/care** so schnell/sorgfältig wie nur möglich; **matters of the ~ importance** Angelegenheiten von äußerster Wichtigkeit. **(b)** *(furthest)* äußerste(r, s). **2** *n* **to do/try one's ~** sein möglichstes *or* Bestes tun; **to the ~ of one's ability** so gut man nur kann; **one should enjoy life to the ~** man sollte das Leben in vollen Zügen genießen.

Utopia [juːˈtəʊpɪə] *n* Utopia *nt*.

Utopian [juːˈtəʊpɪən] *adj* utopisch, utopistisch *(pej)*.

utter¹ [ˈʌtər] *adj* total, vollkommen; *rogue* Erz-. **what ~ nonsense!** so ein totaler Blödsinn!

utter² *vt* von sich *(dat)* geben; *word* sagen; *cry, threat* ausstoßen.

utterance [ˈʌtərəns] *n* Äußerung *f*. **his last ~** seine letzten Worte.

utterly [ˈʌtəlɪ] *adv* total, völlig; *depraved also, despise* zutiefst. **~ beautiful** ausgesprochen schön.

uttermost [ˈʌtəməʊst] *n, adj* = **utmost.**

U-turn [ˈjuːtɜːn] *n (lit, fig)* Wende *f.* **no ~s** Wenden verboten!; **the government has done a ~ over pensions** die Rentenpolitik der Regierung hat sich um 180 Grad gedreht.

V

V, v [viː] *n* V, v *nt.*

vacancy ['veɪkənsɪ] *n* **(a)** *(emptiness)* Leere *f*; *(of look also)* Ausdruckslosigkeit *f*. **(b)** *(in boarding house)* (freies) Zimmer. **have you any vacancies for August?** haben Sie im August noch Zimmer frei?; **"no vacancies"** „belegt". **(c)** *(job)* offene *or* freie Stelle. **to fill a ~** eine Stelle besetzen; **vacancies** Stellenangebote, offene Stellen.

vacant ['veɪkənt] *adj* **(a)** *post* frei, offen; *WC, seat, hotel room* frei; *chair* unbesetzt; *house* unbewohnt. **to become** *or* **fall ~** frei werden. **(b)** *mind, stare* leer.

vacate [və'keɪt] *vt seat* frei machen; *post* aufgeben; *house* räumen.

vacation [və'keɪʃən] **1** *n* **(a)** *(Univ)* Semesterferien *pl*. **(b)** *(US)* Ferien *pl*, Urlaub *m*. **on ~** im *or* auf Urlaub; **to take a ~** Urlaub machen; **to go on ~** auf Urlaub *or* in die Ferien gehen. **2** *vi (US)* Urlaub machen.

vaccinate ['væksɪneɪt] *vt* impfen.

vaccination [ˌvæksɪ'neɪʃən] *n* (Schutz)impfung *f*.

vaccine ['væksiːn] *n* Impfstoff *m*.

vacillate ['væsɪleɪt] *vi (lit, fig)* schwanken.

vacuous ['vækjuəs] *adj face, stare* ausdruckslos, leer; *remarks* nichtssagend.

vacuum ['vækjuəm] **1** *n* **(a)** *(Phys, fig)* (luft)leerer Raum, Vakuum *nt*. **cultural ~** kulturelles Vakuum. **2** *vt carpet* saugen.

vacuum: ~ bottle *n (US)* **= ~ flask; ~ cleaner** *n* Staubsauger *m*; **~ flask** *n (Brit)* Thermosflasche *f*; **~-packed** *adj* vakuumverpackt.

vagabond ['vægəbɒnd] *n* Vagabund *m*.

vagary ['veɪgərɪ] *n usu pl* Laune *f*; *(strange idea)* verrückter Einfall.

vagina [və'dʒaɪnə] *n* Scheide, Vagina *f*.

vagrancy ['veɪgrənsɪ] *n* Landstreicherei *f*; Stadtstreicherei *f*.

vagrant ['veɪgrənt] *n* Landstreicher(in *f*) *m*; Stadt-streicher(in *f*) *m*.

vague [veɪg] *adj* (+*er*) **(a)** *(not clear)* vage, unbestimmt; *outline, shape, photograph* verschwommen; *report, question* ungenau; *murmur* undeutlich. **I haven't the ~st idea** ich habe nicht die leiseste Ahnung; **there's a ~ resemblance** es besteht eine entfernte Ähnlichkeit; **I had a ~ idea she would come** ich hatte so eine (dunkle) Ahnung, daß sie kommen würde; **he was ~ about the time of his arrival** er äußerte sich nur unbestimmt über seine Ankunftszeit. **(b)** *(absentminded)* geistesabwesend.

vaguely ['veɪglɪ] *adv* vage; *remember also* dunkel; *speak also* unbestimmt; *understand* ungefähr, in etwa. **to look ~ at sb** jdn verständnislos ansehen; **they're ~ similar** sie haben eine entfernte Ähnlichkeit.

vain [veɪn] *adj* **(a)** (+*er*) *(about looks)* eitel; *(about qualities)* eingebildet. **he's very ~ about his musical abilities** er bildet sich *(dat)* auf sein musikalisches Können viel ein. **(b)** *(useless, empty)* eitel *(liter)*; *attempt also* vergeblich; *hope also* töricht. **in ~** umsonst; **to take God's name in ~** Gott lästern.

vainly ['veɪnlɪ] *adv* **(a)** *(to no effect)* vergeblich, vergebens. **(b)** *(conceitedly)* *(about looks)* eitel; *(about qualities also)* eingebildet.

valance ['væləns] *n (for bed frame)* Volant *m*; *(on*

window) Querbehang *m*; *(wooden)* Blende *f*.

valentine ['væləntaɪn] *n* St V~'s **Day** Valentinstag *m*; **~ (card)** Valentinskarte *f*.

valet ['væleɪ] *n* Kammerdiener *m*. **~ service** Reinigungsdienst *m*.

valiant ['væljənt] *adj* **(a)** *(liter) soldier, deed* tapfer, kühn *(geh)*. **(b) he made a ~ effort to save him** er unternahm einen kühnen Versuch, ihn zu retten; **she made a ~ effort to smile** sie versuchte tapfer zu lächeln.

valid ['vælɪd] *adj* **(a)** *ticket, passport* gültig; *(Jur) document, marriage* rechtsgültig; *contract* bindend; *claim* begründet. **(b)** *argument* stichhaltig; *excuse, reason* einleuchtend; *objection* begründet. **that's a very ~ point** das ist ein sehr wertvoller Hinweis.

validate ['vælɪdeɪt] *vt document (check validity)* für gültig erklären; *(with stamp, sign)* (rechts)gültig machen; *claim* bestätigen; *(Jur)* Rechtskraft verleihen (+*dat*).

validity [və'lɪdɪtɪ] *n* **(a)** *(Jur etc: of document)* Rechtsgültigkeit *f*; *(of ticket etc)* Gültigkeit *f*; *(of claim)* Berechtigung *f*. **(b)** *(of argument)* Stichhaltigkeit *f*; *(of excuse etc)* Triftigkeit *f*.

valley ['vælɪ] *n* Tal *nt*; *(big and flat)* Niederung *f*. **up/down the ~** talaufwärts/talabwärts.

valour, *(US)* **valor** ['vælə'] *n (liter)* Tapferkeit *f*.

valuable ['væljuəbl] **1** *adj* **(a)** *jewel* wertvoll; *time, oxygen* kostbar. **(b)** *(useful) help, advice* also nützlich. **2** *n* **~s** *pl* Wertsachen *pl*.

valuation [ˌvælju'eɪʃən] *n* Schätzung *f*; *(fig: of person's character)* Einschätzung *f*.

value ['væljuː] **1** *n* **(a)** Wert *m*; *(usefulness)* Nutzen *m*. **to be of ~** wertvoll/nützlich sein; **to put a ~ on sth** etw bewerten; *(on leisure etc)* einer Sache *(dat)* (hohen) Wert beimessen; **he attaches no/great ~ to it** er legt keinen/großen Wert darauf; **of little ~** nicht sehr wertvoll/nützlich; **of no ~** wertlos/nutzlos; **of great ~** sehr wertvoll; **what's the ~ of your house?** wieviel ist Ihr Haus wert?; **it's good ~** es ist preisgünstig; **in our shop you get ~ for money** in unserem Geschäft bekommen Sie etwas für Ihr Geld *(col)*; **goods to the ~ of £100** Waren im Wert von £ 100; **they put a ~ of £50 on it** sie haben es auf £ 50 geschätzt. **(b)** **~s** *pl (moral standards)* (sittliche) Werte *pl*.

2 *vt* **(a)** *house, jewels* schätzen *(at auf* +*acc)*. **(b)** *friendship, person, opinion, advice* schätzen. **I ~ it (highly)** ich weiß es zu schätzen; **if you ~ my opinion** ... wenn Sie Wert auf meine Meinung legen ...; **if you ~ your life** wenn Ihnen Ihr Leben lieb ist.

value-added tax ['væljuːædɪd'tæks] *n (Brit)* Mehrwertsteuer *f*.

valued ['væljuːd] *adj friend* geschätzt, lieb.

value judgement *n* Werturteil *nt*.

valve [vælv] *n (Anat)* Klappe *f*; *(Tech, on musical instrument)* Ventil *nt*; *(Brit: Rad, TV)* Röhre *f*.

vampire ['væmpaɪə'] *n (lit, fig)* Vampir *m*.

van[1] *n* **(a)** *(Brit Aut)* Transporter *m*. **(b)** *(Rail)* Waggon, Wagen *m*.

van[2] *n* **= vanguard.**

vandal ['vændəl] *n (fig)* Rowdy *m*. **it was damaged by ~s** es ist mutwillig beschädigt worden.

vandalism ['vændəlɪzəm] *n* Vandalismus *m*; *(Jur)* mutwillige Beschädigung.

vandalize ['vændəlaɪz] vt mutwillig beschädigen; building verwüsten; (wreck) demolieren.

vane [veɪn] n (a) (also weather ~) Wetterfahne f. (b) (of windmill, propeller) Flügel m.

vanguard ['vængɑːd] n (Mil, Naut) Vorhut f. in the ~ of progress an der Spitze des Fortschritts.

vanilla [və'nɪlə] 1 n Vanille f. 2 adj Vanille-.

vanish ['vænɪʃ] vi verschwinden; (traces also) sich verlieren; (fears) sich legen; (hopes) schwinden; (become extinct) untergehen. ~ing point (fig) Nullpunkt m.

vanity ['vænɪtɪ] n (concerning looks) Eitelkeit f; (concerning own value) Eingebildetheit f.

vanquish ['væŋkwɪʃ] vt (liter) bezwingen (geh).

vantage ['vɑːntɪdʒ] n (Tennis) Vorteil m.

vantage point n (Mil) (günstiger) Aussichtspunkt. our window is a good ~ for watching the procession von unserem Fenster aus hat man einen guten Blick auf die Prozession; from our modern ~ aus heutiger Sicht.

vapid ['væpɪd] adj (liter) remark nichtssagend, geistlos; style kraftlos; taste schal.

vaporize ['veɪpəraɪz] 1 vt (by boiling etc) verdampfen; (naturally) verdunsten lassen. 2 vi see vt verdampfen; verdunsten.

vapour, (US) **vapor** ['veɪpə'] n Dunst m; (steamy) Dampf m. ~ trail Kondensstreifen m.

variable ['veərɪəbl] 1 adj (a) veränderlich, variabel; weather, mood wechselhaft. ~ winds wechselnde Winde pl; his work is very ~ er arbeitet sehr unterschiedlich. (b) speed regulierbar; salary level flexibel. 2 n (Math, Phys, fig) Variable f.

variance ['veərɪəns] n (a) to be at ~ with sb anderer Meinung sein als jd (about hinsichtlich +gen); this is at ~ with what he said earlier dies stimmt nicht mit dem überein, was er vorher gesagt hat. (b) (difference) Unterschied m.

variant ['veərɪənt] 1 n Variante f. 2 adj (alternative) andere(r, s). there are two ~ spellings es gibt zwei verschiedene Schreibweisen.

variation [,veərɪ'eɪʃən] n (a) (varying) Veränderung f; (Sci) Variation f; (Met, of temperature, of prices) Schwankung f. ~ in opinions unterschiedliche Auffassungen. (b) (Mus) Variation f. ~s on a theme Variationen über ein Thema. (c) (different model, Biol) Variante f (on von). (d) (deviation) Abweichung f.

varicose ['værɪkəus] adj: ~ veins Krampfadern pl.

varied ['veərɪd] adj unterschiedlich; career, life bewegt; selection reichhaltig. a ~ group of people eine gemischte Gruppe.

variegated ['veərɪgeɪtɪd] adj (coloured) buntscheckig; forms etc verschiedenartig.

variety [və'raɪətɪ] n (a) (diversity) Abwechslung f. to give or add ~ to sth Abwechslung in etw (acc) bringen; a job with a lot of ~ eine sehr abwechslungsreiche Arbeit. (b) (assortment) Vielfalt f; (Comm) Auswahl f (of an +dat). in a great ~ of ways auf die verschiedensten Arten; in a ~ of colours in den verschiedenen Farben; for a ~ of reasons aus verschiedenen Gründen. (c) (type) Art f; (of cigarette, potato) Sorte f; (of car, chair) Modell nt. a new ~ of tulip eine neue Tulpensorte. (d) (esp Brit Theat) Varieté nt.

variety: ~ artist n (esp Brit) Varietékünstler(in f) m; ~ show n (esp Brit) Varietévorführung f; (Rad, TV) Unterhaltungssendung f.

various ['veərɪəs] adj verschieden.

variously ['veərɪəslɪ] adv unterschiedlich.

varnish ['vɑːnɪʃ] 1 n Lack m. 2 vt lackieren; painting firnissen.

vary ['veərɪ] 1 vi (a) (diverge, differ) sich unterscheiden, abweichen (from von). they ~ in price from the others sie unterscheiden sich im Preis von den anderen; opinions ~ on this point in diesem Punkt gehen die Meinungen auseinander. (b) (be different) unterschiedlich sein. the

price varies from shop to shop der Preis ist von Geschäft zu Geschäft verschieden. (c) (change, fluctuate) sich (ver)ändern; (pressure, prices) schwanken. to ~ with the weather sich nach dem Wetter richten. 2 vt (alter) verändern, abwandeln; (give variety) variieren.

varying ['veərɪɪŋ] adj (changing) veränderlich; (different) unterschiedlich. with ~ degrees of success mit unterschiedlichem Erfolg m.

vase [vɑːz, (US) veɪz] n Vase f.

vasectomy [væ'sektəmɪ] n Sterilisation f (des Mannes).

vaseline ® ['væsɪliːn] n Vaseline f.

vast [vɑːst] adj (+er) gewaltig, riesig; knowledge enorm; majority überwältigend. a ~ expanse eine weite Ebene.

vastly ['vɑːstlɪ] adv erheblich, bedeutend. it is ~ different da besteht ein erheblicher Unterschied.

vat [væt] n Faß nt; (without lid) Bottich m.

VAT ['viːiːtiː, væt] (Brit) = **value-added tax** MwSt.

Vatican ['vætɪkən] n Vatikan m.

vault[1] [vɔːlt] n (a) (cellar) (Keller)gewölbe nt; (tomb) Gruft f; (in bank) Tresor(raum) m. in the ~s im Gewölbe etc. (b) (Archit) Gewölbe nt.

vault[2] 1 n Sprung m. 2 vi springen. 3 vt überspringen.

vaulted ['vɔːltɪd] adj (Archit) gewölbt.

vaunt [vɔːnt] vt rühmen, preisen (geh). much-~ed vielgepriesen.

VD = **venereal disease.**

VDU = **visual display unit.**

veal [viːl] n Kalbfleisch nt.

veer [vɪə'] vi (wind) (sich) drehen (to nach); (ship) abdrehen; (car) ausscheren; (road) scharf abbiegen. to ~ off course vom Kurs abkommen; public opinion ~ed to the right die öffentliche Meinung ist nach rechts geschwenkt.

vegetable ['vedʒɪtəbl] n (a) Gemüse nt. **cabbage is a ~** Kohl ist eine Gemüsepflanze. (b) (generic term: plant) Pflanze f. (c) he's just a ~ er vegetiert nur so vor sich hin; she's become a ~ sie ist zum körperlichen und geistigen Krüppel geworden.

vegetable: ~ garden n Gemüsegarten m; ~ oil n Pflanzenöl nt.

vegetarian [,vedʒɪ'teərɪən] 1 n Vegetarier(in f) m. 2 adj vegetarisch.

vegetate ['vedʒɪteɪt] vi (fig) dahinvegetieren.

vegetation [,vedʒɪ'teɪʃən] n Vegetation f.

vehemence ['viːɪməns] n Vehemenz f (geh); (of actions, feelings, protests also) Heftigkeit f; (of love, hatred) Leidenschaftlichkeit f.

vehement ['viːɪmənt] adj vehement (geh); feelings, speech leidenschaftlich; attack, desire, dislike, opposition heftig.

vehicle ['viːɪkl] n Fahrzeug nt; (fig) Mittel nt.

veil [veɪl] 1 n Schleier m. to take the ~ ins Kloster gehen; under a ~ of secrecy unter dem Mantel der Verschwiegenheit. 2 vt (lit, fig) verschleiern; feelings verbergen. the town was ~ed by mist die Stadt lag in Nebel gehüllt.

veiled [veɪld] adj reference versteckt; face verschleiert.

vein [veɪn] n (Anat, Bot, Min) Ader f; (fig: mood) Stimmung, Laune f. in a humorous ~ in lustiger Stimmung; in the same ~ in derselben Art.

vellum ['veləm] n Pergament nt.

velocity [və'lɒsɪtɪ] n Geschwindigkeit f.

velvet ['velvɪt] 1 n Samt m. 2 adj jacket Samt-; skin, feel samtweich, samten (geh).

velveteen ['velvɪtiːn] n Veloursamt m.

velvety ['velvɪtɪ] adj samtig.

venal ['viːnl] adj (liter) person käuflich; practices korrupt.

vendetta [ven'detə] n Fehde f; (in family) Blutrache f; (of gangsters) Vendetta f. **to carry on**

a ~ against sb mit jdm in Fehde liegen/an jdm Blutrache üben.

vending machine ['vendɪŋməˈʃiːn] n Automat m.

vendor ['vendɔːʳ] n (esp Jur) Verkäufer m.

veneer [vəˈnɪəʳ] n (lit) Furnier nt; (fig) Politur f; (of civilization) (An)schein m. **it's just a ~** es ist nur äußerer Schein.

venerable ['venərəbl] adj ehrwürdig.

venerate ['venəreɪt] vt verehren, hochachten; sb's memory ehren.

venereal disease [vɪˈnɪərɪəldɪˈziːz] n Geschlechtskrankheit f.

Venetian blind [vɪˈniːʃənˈblaɪnd] n Jalousie f.

Venezuela [ˌveneˈzweɪlə] n Venezuela nt.

Venezuelan [ˌveneˈzweɪlən] 1 adj venezolanisch. 2 n Venezolaner(in f) m.

vengeance ['vendʒəns] n (a) Vergeltung, Rache f. **to take ~ (up)on sb** Vergeltung an jdm üben. **(b)** (col) **with a ~** gewaltig (col); **to work with a ~** hart or mächtig (col) arbeiten.

venial ['viːnɪəl] adj verzeihlich, entschuldbar.

Venice ['venɪs] n Venedig nt.

venison ['venɪsən] n Reh(fleisch) nt.

venom ['venəm] n (lit) Gift nt; (fig) Bosheit, Gehässigkeit f. **he spoke with real ~** in his voice er sprach mit haßerfüllter Stimme.

venomous ['venəməs] adj (lit, fig) giftig; snake Gift-; tone also gehässig; sarcasm beißend.

vent [vent] 1 n (for gas, liquid) Öffnung f; (in chimney) Abzug m; (in coat) Schlitz m; (for feelings) Ventil nt. **to give ~ to sth** (fig) einer Sache (dat) Ausdruck verleihen; **to give ~ to one's feelings** seinen Gefühlen freien Lauf lassen. 2 vt feelings, anger abreagieren (on an +dat).

ventilate ['ventɪleɪt] vt (control air flow) belüften; (let fresh air in) lüften.

ventilation [ˌventɪˈleɪʃən] n see vt Belüftung f; Lüften nt. **~ shaft** Luftschacht m.

ventilator ['ventɪleɪtəʳ] n Ventilator m.

ventriloquist [venˈtrɪləkwɪst] n Bauchredner(in f) m.

venture ['ventʃəʳ] 1 n Unternehmen nt. **a new ~ in publishing** ein neuer verlegerischer Versuch; **this was a disastrous ~ for the company** dieses Projekt war für die Firma ein Fiasko. 2 vt **(a)** life, reputation aufs Spiel setzen; money also riskieren (on bei). **nothing ~d nothing gained** (Prov) wer nicht wagt, der nicht gewinnt (Prov). **(b)** guess, explanation wagen; opinion zu äußern wagen. **if I may ~ an opinion** wenn ich mir erlauben darf, meine Meinung zu sagen. 3 vi sich wagen. **to ~ out of doors** sich vor die Tür wagen; **the company ~d into a new field** die Firma wagte sich in ein neues Gebiet vor.

venue ['venjuː] n (for event) Schauplatz m; (Sport) Austragungsort m; (Jur) Verhandlungsort m.

Venus ['viːnəs] n Venus f.

veracity [vəˈræsɪtɪ] n (of report etc) Richtigkeit f.

veranda(h) [vəˈrændə] n Veranda f.

verb [vɜːb] n Verb, Zeitwort nt.

verbal [ˈvɜːbəl] adj mündlich; error, skills sprachlich.

verbally [ˈvɜːbəlɪ] adv (spoken) mündlich.

verbatim [vɜːˈbeɪtɪm] adj, adv (wort)wörtlich.

verbiage [ˈvɜːbɪɪdʒ] n Wortfülle f, Blabla nt (col).

verbose [vɜːˈbəus] adj wortreich, weitschweifig.

verdict [ˈvɜːdɪkt] n Urteil nt; (of electors) Entscheidung f. **~ of guilty/not guilty** Schuldspruch m/Freispruch m; **what's the ~?** wie lautet das Urteil?; **to give one's ~ about or on sth** sein Urteil über etw (acc) abgeben.

verge [vɜːdʒ] n (lit, fig) Rand m. **to be on the ~ of ruin/war** am Rande des Ruins/eines Krieges stehen; **to be on the ~ of a discovery** kurz vor einer Entdeckung stehen; **to be on the ~ of tears** den Tränen nahe sein; **to be on the ~ of doing sth**

im Begriff sein, etw zu tun.

♦ **verge on** vi +prep obj (ideas, actions) grenzen an (acc). **he's verging ~ bankruptcy** er steht kurz vor dem Bankrott; **she is verging ~ fifty** sie geht auf die Fünfzig zu.

verger ['vɜːdʒəʳ] n (Eccl) Küster m.

verifiable ['verɪfaɪəbl] adj nachprüfbar.

verification [ˌverɪfɪˈkeɪʃən] n (check) Überprüfung f; (confirmation) Bestätigung f; (proof) Nachweis m.

verify ['verɪfaɪ] vt (check) (über)prüfen; (confirm) bestätigen; theory beweisen.

veritable ['verɪtəbl] adj genius wahr. **a ~ disaster** die reinste Katastrophe.

vermilion [vəˈmɪljən] adj zinnoberrot.

vermin ['vɜːmɪn] n no pl (animal) Schädling m; (insects) Ungeziefer nt; (pej: people) Pack nt.

vermouth ['vɜːməθ] n Vermut m.

vernacular [vəˈnækjʊləʳ] n (dialect) Mundart f; (not official language) Landessprache f.

versatile ['vɜːsətaɪl] adj vielseitig. **he has a very ~ mind** er ist geistig sehr flexibel.

versatility ['vɜːsəˈtɪlɪtɪ] n see adj Vielseitigkeit f; Flexibilität f.

verse [vɜːs] n (a) (stanza) Strophe f. (b) no pl (poetry) Dichtung f. **in ~** in Versform. (c) (of Bible, Koran) Vers m.

versed [vɜːst] adj (also well ~) bewandert, beschlagen (in in +dat).

version ['vɜːʃən] n (a) (account: of event, of facts) Darstellung f. (b) (variant) Version f; (of text also) Fassung f; (of car) Modell nt.

versus ['vɜːsəs] prep gegen (+acc).

vertebra ['vɜːtɪbrə] n, pl -e [-briː] Rückenwirbel m.

vertebrate ['vɜːtɪbrət] 1 n Wirbeltier nt. 2 adj Wirbel-.

vertex ['vɜːteks] n, pl vertices Scheitel(punkt) m.

vertical ['vɜːtɪkəl] 1 adj line senkrecht, vertikal. **~ cliffs** senkrecht abfallende Klippen; **~ take-off aircraft** Senkrechtstarter m. 2 n (line) Vertikale, Senkrechte f.

vertigo ['vɜːtɪgəu] n Schwindel m; (Med) Gleichgewichtsstörung f.

verve [vɜːv] n Schwung m.

very ['verɪ] 1 adv (a) (extremely) sehr. **that's not ~ funny** das ist überhaupt nicht lustig; **it's ~ possible** es ist gut möglich; **~ probably** höchstwahrscheinlich; **he is so ~ lazy** er ist so faul; **how ~ odd** wie eigenartig; **~ much** sehr; **I liked it ~ much** es hat mir sehr gut gefallen; **he doesn't ~ much work** er arbeitet nicht sehr viel; **~ much so** sehr (sogar).
(b) (absolutely) aller-. **~ best quality** allerbeste Qualität; **~ last/first** allerletzte(r, s)/ allererste(r, s); **at the ~ latest** allerspätestens; **to do one's ~ best** sein Äußerstes tun; **at the ~ most/least** allerhöchstens/allerwenigstens.
(c) (for emphasis) **he fell ill and died the ~ same day** er wurde krank und starb noch am selben Tag; **he died the ~ same day as Kennedy** er starb genau am selben Tag wie Kennedy; **the ~ same hat** genau der gleiche Hut; **we met again the ~ next day** wir trafen uns am nächsten Tag schon wieder; **the ~ next day he walked under a bus** schon einen Tag später kam er unter einen Bus; **my ~ own car** mein eigenes Auto.
2 adj **(a)** (precise) genau. **that ~ day** genau an diesem Tag; **in the ~ centre of the picture** genau in der Mitte des Bildes; **at the ~ heart of the organization** direkt im Zentrum der Organisation; **those were his ~ words** genau das waren seine Worte; **you are the ~ person I want to speak to** mit Ihnen wollte ich sprechen; **the ~ thing!** genau das richtige!
(b) (extreme) äußerste(r, s). **in the ~ beginning/at the ~ end** ganz am Anfang/Ende; **at the ~ back/front** ganz hinten/vorn(e).
(c) (mere) **the ~ thought of it** allein schon der

Gedanke daran; **the** ~ **idea!** nein, so etwas!

vespers ['vespəz] npl Vesper f.

vessel ['vesl] n **(a)** (Naut) Schiff nt. **(b)** (form: receptacle) Gefäß nt.

vest¹ [vest] n **(a)** (Brit) Unterhemd nt. **(b)** (US) Weste f. ~-**pocket** adj (US) Taschen-.

vest² vt (form) **to** ~ **sb with sth, to** ~ **sth in sb** jdm etw verleihen; **he has** ~**ed interests in the oil business** er ist (finanziell) am Ölgeschäft beteiligt; **he has a** ~**ed interest in the play** (fig) er hat ein persönliches Interesse an dem Stück.

vestibule ['vestɪbjuːl] n Vorhalle f.

vestige ['vestɪdʒ] n Spur f. **there is not a** ~ **of truth in what he says** es ist kein Körnchen Wahrheit an dem, was er sagt.

vestment ['vestmənt] n Ornat m.

vestry ['vestrɪ] n Sakristei f.

vet [vet] **1** n = **veterinary surgeon** Tierarzt m/-ärztin f. **2** vt überprüfen.

veteran ['vetərən] n (Mil, fig) Veteran(in f) m. ~ **car** Oldtimer m.

veterinary ['vetərɪnərɪ] adj medicine, science Veterinär-; training tierärztlich. ~ **surgeon** Tierarzt m/-ärztin f.

veto ['viːtəʊ] **1** n, pl -es Veto nt. **power of** ~ Vetorecht nt; **to have a** ~ das Vetorecht haben; **to use one's** ~ von seinem Vetorecht Gebrauch machen. **2** vt sein Veto einlegen gegen.

vex [veks] vt (annoy) ärgern, irritieren; animals quälen. **to be** ~**ed with sb** mit jdm böse sein; **to be** ~**ed about sth** sich über etw (acc) ärgern.

vexation [vek'seɪʃən] n Ärger m; (act) Ärgern nt; (of animal) Quälerei f.

vexatious [vek'seɪʃəs] adj ärgerlich; regulations, headache lästig.

vexed [vekst] adj **(a)** (annoyed) verärgert. **(b)** question peinlich.

vexing ['veksɪŋ] adj irritierend; problem verzwickt.

VHF (Rad) = **very high frequency** UKW.

via ['vaɪə] prep über (+acc). **they got in** ~ **the window** sie kamen durchs Fenster herein.

viability [,vaɪə'bɪlɪtɪ] n **(a)** (of life forms) Lebensfähigkeit f. **(b)** (of plan) Durchführbarkeit f; (of firm) Rentabilität f. **the** ~ **of the EEC** die Existenzfähigkeit der EG.

viable ['vaɪəbl] adj **(a)** plant, foetus lebensfähig. **(b)** company rentabel; economy lebensfähig; suggestion brauchbar; plan durchführbar. **not economically** ~ unrentabel.

viaduct ['vaɪədʌkt] n Viadukt m.

vibrant ['vaɪbrənt] adj personality etc dynamisch; voice volltönend, sonor. **the** ~ **life of the city** das pulsierende Leben der Großstadt.

vibrate [vaɪ'breɪt] **1** vi (lit, fig) zittern, beben (with vor +dat); (machine, string, air) vibrieren; (notes) schwingen. **2** vt zum Vibrieren bringen; string zum Schwingen bringen.

vibration [vaɪ'breɪʃən] n (of string, sound waves) Schwingung f; (of machine) Vibrieren nt; (of voice, ground) Beben nt. **I get good** ~**s from him** (col) er macht einen guten Eindruck auf mich.

vicar ['vɪkəʳ] n Pfarrer m.

vicarage ['vɪkərɪdʒ] n Pfarrhaus nt.

vicarious [vɪ'kɛərɪəs] adj pleasure indirekt, nachempfunden; experience ersatzweise.

vice¹ [vaɪs] n Laster nt. **his main** ~ **is laziness** sein größter Fehler ist die Faulheit; ~ **squad** Sittenpolizei f.

vice², (US) **vise** n Schraubstock m. **to hold sth in a** ~-**like grip** etw fest umklammern.

vice- pref ~-**chairman** n stellvertretender Vorsitzender; ~-**chancellor** n (Univ) ≃ Rektor m; ~-**president** n Vizepräsident m.

vice versa ['vaɪsɪ'vɜːsə] adv umgekehrt.

vicinity [vɪ'sɪnɪtɪ] n Umgebung f. **in the** ~ in der Nähe (of von, gen); **in the** ~ **of £500** um die £ 500.

vicious ['vɪʃəs] adj boshaft; remark gehässig; habit lasterhaft; animal bösartig; dog bissig; blow, criminal, murder brutal; (col) headache gemein (col). ~ **circle** Teufelskreis, Circulus vitiosus m (geh).

vicissitude [vɪ'sɪsɪtjuːd] n usu pl Wandel m. **the** ~**s of life** die Wechselfälle des Lebens.

victim ['vɪktɪm] n Opfer nt. **he was the** ~ **of a practical joke** ihm wurde ein Streich gespielt; **to fall** ~ **to sth** Opfer einer Sache (gen) werden.

victimization [,vɪktɪmaɪ'zeɪʃən] n see vt ungerechte Behandlung; Schikanierung.

victimize ['vɪktɪmaɪz] vt ungerecht behandeln; (pick on) schikanieren. **she feels** ~**d** sie fühlt sich ungerecht behandelt.

victor ['vɪktəʳ] n Sieger(in f) m.

Victorian [vɪk'tɔːrɪən] **1** n Viktorianer(in f) m. **2** adj viktorianisch; (fig) (sitten)streng.

victorious [vɪk'tɔːrɪəs] adj army siegreich; smile siegesbewußt. **to be** ~ **over sb/sth** jdn/etw besiegen.

victory ['vɪktərɪ] n Sieg m. **to win a** ~ **over sb** einen Sieg über jdn erringen, jdn besiegen.

victuals ['vɪtlz] npl Lebensmittel pl.

video ['vɪdɪəʊ] **1** n **(a)** Video nt. on ~ see als Video; record auf Video. **(b)** (US TV) Fernsehen nt. on ~ im Fernsehen. **2** vt auf Video aufnehmen.

video: ~ **cassette** Videokassette f; ~-**recorder** Videorecorder m; ~-**recording** n Videoaufnahme f; ~-**tape** n Videoband nt.

vie [vaɪ] vi wetteifern; (Comm) konkurrieren. **to** ~ **with sb for sth** mit jdm um etw wetteifern.

Vienna [vɪ'enə] n Wien nt.

Viennese [,vɪə'niːz] **1** adj Wiener, wienerisch. **2** n Wiener(in f) m.

Vietnam [,vjet'næm] n Vietnam nt.

Vietnamese [,vjetnə'miːz] **1** adj vietnamesisch. **2** n **(a)** Vietnamese m, Vietnamesin f. **(b)** (language) Vietnamesisch nt.

view [vjuː] **1** n **(a)** (range of vision) Sicht f; (prospect, sight) Aussicht f. **in full** ~ **of thousands of people** vor den Augen von Tausenden von Menschen; **the ship came into** ~ das Schiff kam in Sicht; **to keep sth in** ~ etw im Auge behalten; **the house is within** ~ **of the sea** vom Haus aus ist das Meer zu sehen; **hidden from** ~ verborgen, versteckt; **on** ~ (for purchasing) zur Ansicht; (of exhibits) ausgestellt; **there is a splendid** ~ **from here** von hier hat man einen herrlichen Blick; **a good** ~ **of the sea** ein schöner Blick auf das Meer; **a room with a** ~ ein Zimmer mit schöner Aussicht; **an idealistic** ~ **of the world** eine idealistische Weltsicht; **a general** ~ **of a problem** ein allgemeiner Überblick über ein Problem; **in** ~ angesichts (+gen).

(b) (photograph etc) Ansicht f.

(c) (opinion) Ansicht, Meinung f. **in my** ~ meiner Ansicht nach; **what are his** ~**s on this problem?** was meint er zu diesem Problem?; **I have no** ~**s on that** ich habe keine Meinung dazu; **to take the** ~ **that ...** die Ansicht vertreten, daß ...; **to take a poor** ~ **of sth** etw mißbilligen.

(d) (intention, plan) **to have sth in** ~ etw beabsichtigen; **with a** ~ **to doing sth** mit der Absicht, etw zu tun.

2 vt (see) betrachten; house besichtigen; (consider) problem etc sehen. **he** ~**s the prospect with dismay** er sieht dieser Sache mit Schrecken entgegen.

viewer ['vjuːəʳ] n **(a)** (TV) Zuschauer(in f) m. **(b)** (for slides) Diabetrachter m.

view-finder ['vjuːˌfaɪndəʳ] n Sucher m.

viewpoint ['vjuːpɔɪnt] n Standpunkt m. **from the** ~ **of economic growth** unter dem Gesichtspunkt des Wirtschaftswachstums; **to see sth from sb's** ~ etw aus jds Sicht (dat) sehen.

vigil ['vɪdʒɪl] n (Nacht)wache f. **to keep** ~ **over sb** bei jdm wachen.

vigilance ['vɪdʒɪləns] n Wachsamkeit f.

vigilant ['vɪdʒɪlənt] *adj* wachsam.

vigilante [,vɪdʒɪ'læntɪ] *n* ~**s** Bürgerwehr *f*.

vigorous ['vɪgərəs] *adj* kräftig; *prose, tune* kraftvoll; *protest, measures, exercises* energisch; *walk* forsch, flott.

vigour, *(US)* **vigor** [vɪgəʳ] *n* Kraft, Energie *f*; *(of protest)* Heftigkeit *f*; *(of prose)* Ausdruckskraft *f*. **youthful** ~ jugendliche Spannkraft; **to speak with** ~ mit Nachdruck sprechen.

vile [vaɪl] *adj* abscheulich; *language also* unflätig; *weather, food also* scheußlich. **that was a** ~ **thing to say** es war gemein, so etwas zu sagen.

vilify ['vɪlɪfaɪ] *vt* diffamieren, verleumden.

villa ['vɪlə] *n* Villa *f*.

village ['vɪlɪdʒ] *n* Dorf *nt*.

village *in cpds* Dorf-; ~ **green** *n* Dorfwiese *f*; ~ **idiot** *n* Dorftrottel *m* *(col)*.

villager ['vɪlɪdʒəʳ] *n* Dorfbewohner(in *f*).

villain ['vɪlən] *n* *(scoundrel)* Schurke *m*; *(col: criminal)* Verbrecher, Ganove *(col)* *m*; *(in drama, novel)* Bösewicht *m*.

villainous ['vɪlənəs] *adj* böse; *deed* gemein.

villainy ['vɪlənɪ] *n* Gemeinheit *f*.

vindicate ['vɪndɪkeɪt] *vt* **(a)** *opinion, action* rechtfertigen. **(b)** *(from suspicion)* rehabilitieren.

vindication [,vɪndɪ'keɪʃən] *n see* **vt (a)** Rechtfertigung *f*. **in** ~ **of** zur Rechtfertigung (+*gen*). **(b)** Rehabilitation *f*.

vindictive [vɪn'dɪktɪv] *adj* *speech, person* rachsüchtig; *mood* unversöhnlich. **to feel** ~ **towards sb** Rachegefühle gegen jdn haben.

vine [vaɪn] *n* *(grapevine)* Rebe *f*.

vinegar ['vɪnɪgəʳ] *n* Essig *m*.

vine: ~ **grower** *n* Weinbauer *m*; ~**-growing district** *n* Weinbaugebiet *nt*; ~ **harvest** *n* Weinlese *f*; ~**yard** ['vɪnjəd] *n* Weinberg *m*.

vintage ['vɪntɪdʒ] **1** *n* **(a)** *(of wine, fig)* Jahrgang *m*; *(of car)* Baujahr *nt*. **the 1972** ~ der Jahrgang 1972. **(b)** *(harvesting, season)* Weinlese *f*. **2** *adj attr (old)* uralt; *(high quality)* glänzend.

vintage: ~ **car** *n* Oldtimer *m*; ~ **wine** *n* edler Wein; ~ **year** *n*: **a** ~ **year for wine** ein besonders gutes Weinjahr.

vinyl ['vaɪnɪl] *n* Vinyl *nt*.

viola [vɪ'əʊlə] *n* *(Mus)* Bratsche *f*.

violate ['vaɪəleɪt] *vt* **(a)** *treaty, promise* brechen; *(partially)* verletzen; *law, rule* verstoßen gegen; *rights* verletzen. **(b)** *holy place* schänden; *peacefulness* stören. **to** ~ **sb's privacy** in jds Privatsphäre eindringen.

violation [,vaɪə'leɪʃən] *n* **(a)** *(of law, rule)* Verstoß *m* *(of gegen)*; *(of rights)* Verletzung *f*. **a** ~ **of a treaty** ein Vertragsbruch *m*; **he did this in** ~ **of the conditions agreed** er verstieß damit gegen die Vereinbarungen. **(b)** *(of holy place)* Schändung *f*; *(of peacefulness)* Störung *f*.

violence ['vaɪələns] *n* **(a)** *(forcefulness, strength)* Heftigkeit *f*; *(of protest also)* Schärfe *f*. **(b)** *(brutality)* Gewalt *f*; *(of people)* Gewalttätigkeit *f*; *(of actions)* Brutalität *f*. **act of** ~ Gewalttat *f*; **robbery with** ~ Raubüberfall *m*; **to use** ~ **against sb** Gewalt gegen jdn anwenden; **was there any** ~? kam es zu Gewalttätigkeiten?; **outbreak of** ~ Ausbruch von Gewalttätigkeit; **to do** ~ **to sth** *(fig)* etw verletzen.

violent ['vaɪələnt] *adj* *person, action* brutal, gewalttätig; *feeling, speech* leidenschaftlich; *storm, dislike, attack, pain* heftig; *death* gewaltsam; *contrast* kraß. **to have a** ~ **temper** jähzornig sein; **to get** ~ gewalttätig werden.

violet ['vaɪələt] **1** *n* *(Bot)* Veilchen *nt*; *(colour)* Violett *nt*. **2** *adj* violett.

violin [,vaɪə'lɪn] *n* Geige, Violine *f*; *(player)* Geiger(in *f*) *m*. ~ **case** Geigenkasten *m*.

violinist [,vaɪə'lɪnɪst] *n* Geiger(in *f*) *m*.

VIP *n* prominente Persönlichkeit, VIP *m*.

viper ['vaɪpəʳ] *n* *(Zool)* Viper *f*; *(fig)* Schlange *f*.

virgin ['vɜːdʒɪn] **1** *n* Jungfrau *f*. **the (Blessed) V~** *(Rel)* die (heilige) Jungfrau Maria; **he's still a** ~ er ist noch unschuldig. **2** *adj (fig) forest, snow* unberührt. ~ **birth** unbefleckte Empfängnis.

virginity [vɜː'dʒɪnɪtɪ] *n* Unschuld *f*; *(of girls also)* Jungfräulichkeit *f*.

Virgo ['vɜːgəʊ] *n* *(Astrol)* Jungfrau *f*.

virile ['vɪraɪl] *adj (lit)* männlich; *(fig)* kraftvoll.

virility [vɪ'rɪlɪtɪ] *n* *(lit)* Männlichkeit *f*; *(sexual power)* Potenz *f*; *(fig)* Ausdruckskraft *f*.

virtual ['vɜːtjʊəl] *adj attr* **he is the** ~ **leader** er ist praktisch der Führer; **it was a** ~ **disaster** es war geradezu eine Katastrophe.

virtually ['vɜːtjʊəlɪ] *adv* praktisch. **to be** ~ **certain** sich *(dat)* so gut wie sicher sein.

virtue ['vɜːtjuː] *n* **(a)** *(moral quality)* Tugend *f*. **a life of** ~ ein tugendhaftes Leben; **a woman of easy** ~ *(euph)* ein leichtes Mädchen. **(b)** *(advantage, point)* Vorteil *m*. **there is no** ~ **in doing that** es scheint nicht sehr zweckmäßig, das zu tun; **by** ~ **of** aufgrund (+*gen*).

virtuoso [,vɜːtjʊ'əʊzəʊ] *n* *(esp Mus)* Virtuose *m*.

virtuous *adj* ['vɜːtjʊəs] tugendhaft.

virulent ['vɪrʊlənt] *adj* **(a)** *(Med)* bösartig; *poison* stark, tödlich. **(b)** *(fig)* geharnischt, scharf.

virus ['vaɪərəs] *n* *(Med)* Virus, Erreger *m*.

visa ['viːzə] *n* Visum *nt*.

vis-à-vis ['viːzəviː] *prep* in bezug auf (+*acc*).

viscount ['vaɪkaʊnt] *n* Viscount *m*.

viscous ['vɪskəs] *adj* zähflüssig; *(Phys)* viskos.

vise [vaɪs] *n (US)* = **vice**[2].

visibility [,vɪzɪ'bɪlɪtɪ] *n* **(a)** Sichtbarkeit *f*. **(b)** *(Met)* Sichtweite *f*. **poor/good** ~ schlechte/gute Sicht; **low** ~ geringe Sichtweite.

visible ['vɪzəbl] *adj* sichtbar; *(obvious)* sichtlich. ~ **to the naked eye** mit dem bloßen Auge zu erkennen.

visibly ['vɪzəblɪ] *adv* sichtlich; *deteriorate* zusehends.

vision ['vɪʒən] *n* **(a)** *(power of sight)* Sehvermögen *nt*. **within the range of** ~ in Sichtweite. **(b)** *(foresight)* Weitblick *m*. **a man of** ~ ein Mann mit Weitblick. **(c)** *(in dream, trance)* Vision *f*; *(image)* Vorstellung *f*. **I had** ~**s of having to walk all the way home** *(col)* ich sah mich im Geiste schon den ganzen Weg nach Hause laufen.

visionary ['vɪʒənərɪ] **1** *adj (of visions)* vorhersehend; *(unreal)* eingebildet. **2** *n* Seher *m (geh)*.

visit ['vɪzɪt] **1** *n* Besuch *m*; *(of doctor)* Hausbesuch *m*; *(of inspector)* Kontrolle *f*; *(stay also)* Aufenthalt *m*. **to pay sb/sth a** ~ jdn/etw besuchen; **to have a** ~ **from sb** von jdm besucht werden; **to be on a** ~ **to London** zu einem Besuch in London sein. **2** *vt (a) person, museum* besuchen. **3** *vi (a)* einen Besuch machen. **(b)** *(US col: chat)* ein Schwätzchen halten.

visiting: ~ **card** *n (Brit)* Visitenkarte *f*; ~ **hours** *npl* Besuchszeiten *pl*; ~ **team** *n* Gäste *pl*.

visitor ['vɪzɪtəʳ] *n* Besucher(in *f*) *m*; *(in hotel)* Gast *m*. **to have** ~**s** *or* **a** ~ Besuch haben; ~**s' book** Gästebuch *m*.

visor ['vaɪzəʳ] *n* *(on helmet)* Visier *nt*; *(on cap)* Schirm *m*; *(Aut)* Blende *f*.

vista ['vɪstə] *n* Aussicht *f*, Blick *m*.

visual ['vɪzjʊəl] *adj field, nerve* Seh-; *memory, impression* visuell. ~ **aids** Anschauungsmaterial *nt*; ~ **display unit** Bildschirm(gerät *nt*) *m*.

visualize ['vɪzjʊəlaɪz] *vt (see in mind)* sich *(dat)* vorstellen; *(foresee)* erwarten.

visually ['vɪzjʊəlɪ] *adv* visuell. ~ **handicapped** sehbehindert.

vital ['vaɪtl] *adj* **(a)** *(of life)* vital, Lebens-; *(necessary for life)* lebenswichtig. ~ **force** Lebenskraft *f*; ~ **organs** lebenswichtige Organe *pl*; ~ **statistics** *(col: of woman)* Maße *pl*. **(b)** *(essential)* unerläßlich. **of** ~ **importance** von größter Wichtigkeit; **this is** ~ das ist unbedingt notwendig; **your support is** ~ **to us** wir brauchen unbedingt Ihre Unterstützung. **(c)** *(critical) error*

vitality [vaɪ'tælɪtɪ] n (energy) Energie, Vitalität f; (of prose) Lebendigkeit f; (of company) Dynamik f.

vitally ['vaɪtəlɪ] adv important äußerst, ungeheuer.

vitamin ['vɪtəmɪn] n Vitamin nt.

vitriolic [,vɪtrɪ'ɒlɪk] adj (fig) remark, criticism beißend; attack, speech haßerfüllt.

vivacious [vɪ'veɪʃəs] adj lebhaft.

vivacity [vɪ'væsɪtɪ] n Lebhaftigkeit f.

vivid ['vɪvɪd] adj light hell; colour kräftig, lebhaft; (lively) imagination lebhaft; description lebendig; emotions stark. **the memory of that day is still ~** der Tag ist mir/uns etc noch in lebhafter Erinnerung.

vividness ['vɪvɪdnɪs] n (of colour, imagination etc) Lebhaftigkeit f; (of light) Helligkeit f; (of description) Lebendigkeit f.

vivisection [,vɪvɪ'sekʃən] n Vivisektion f.

vixen ['vɪksn] n (Zool) Füchsin f.

V-neck ['viːnek] n V-Ausschnitt m.

vocabulary [vəʊ'kæbjʊlərɪ] n Wortschatz m, Vokabular nt (geh); (in textbook) Wörterverzeichnis f. **legal ~** juristisches Vokabular.

vocal ['vəʊkəl] **1** adj **(a)** Stimm-. **~ cords** Stimmbänder pl. **(b)** (voicing one's opinions) lautstark. **2** n (of pop song) (gesungener) Schlager.

vocalist ['vəʊkəlɪst] n Sänger(in f) m.

vocation [vəʊ'keɪʃən] n (Rel etc) Berufung f; (form: profession) Beruf m. **to have a ~ for teaching** zum Lehrer berufen sein.

vocational [vəʊ'keɪʃənl] adj Berufs-. **~ guidance** Berufsberatung f; **~ school** (US) ≈ Berufsschule f; **~ training** Berufsausbildung f.

vociferous [vəʊ'sɪfərəs] adj laut; protest lautstark.

vodka ['vɒdkə] n Wodka m.

vogue [vəʊg] n Mode f. **to be in ~** Mode sein; **~ word** Modewort nt.

voice [vɔɪs] **1** n **(a)** Stimme f. **to lose one's ~** die Stimme verlieren; **I've lost my ~** ich habe keine Stimme mehr; **to be in (good)/poor ~** gut/nicht gut bei Stimme sein; **in a deep ~** mit tiefer Stimme; **with one ~** einstimmig; **to give ~ to sth** einer Sache (dat) Ausdruck verleihen; **we have no ~ in the matter** wir haben in dieser Angelegenheit kein Mitspracherecht nt. **(b)** (Gram) **the active/passive ~** das Aktiv/Passiv. **2** vt opinion zum Ausdruck bringen.

void [vɔɪd] **1** n (lit, fig) Leere f. **2** adj (empty) leer; (Jur) ungültig, nichtig. **~ of hope** hoffnungslos.

volatile ['vɒlətaɪl] adj **(a)** (Chem) flüchtig. **(b)** person impulsiv; political situation brisant.

volcanic [vɒl'kænɪk] adj dust vulkanisch; region, eruption Vulkan-.

volcano [vɒl'keɪnəʊ] n Vulkan m.

vole [vəʊl] n Wühlmaus f; (common ~) Feldmaus f.

volition [və'lɪʃən] n Wille m. **of one's own ~** aus freiem Willen.

volley ['vɒlɪ] n **(a)** (of shots) Salve f; (of arrows, stones) Hagel m; (fig: of insults) Flut f. **(b)** (Tennis) Volley, Flugball m.

volleyball ['vɒlɪ,bɔːl] n Volleyball m.

volt [vəʊlt] n Volt nt. **~ meter** Voltmeter m.

voltage ['vəʊltɪdʒ] n Spannung f.

volte-face ['vɒlt'faːs] n (fig) Kehrtwendung f.

voluble ['vɒljʊbl] adj speaker redegewandt, redselig (pej); protest wortreich.

volume ['vɒljuːm] n **(a)** Band m. **a six-~ dictionary** ein sechsbändiges Wörterbuch; **to write ~s** ganze Bände pl schreiben; **that speaks ~s** (fig) das spricht Bände (for über +acc). **(b)** (space occupied by sth) Volumen nt. **(c)** (size, amount) Ausmaß nt (of an +dat). **the ~ of traffic** das

vulture ['vʌltʃə'] n (lit, fig) Geier m.

Verkehrsaufkommen; **trade has increased in ~** das Handelsvolumen hat sich vergrößert. **(d)** (sound) Lautstärke f. **turn the ~ up/down** (Rad, TV) stell (das Gerät) lauter/leiser; **~ control** (Rad, TV) Lautstärkeregler m.

voluminous [və'luːmɪnəs] adj figure üppig; writings umfangreich; dress wallend.

voluntarily ['vɒləntərɪlɪ] adv freiwillig.

voluntary ['vɒləntərɪ] adj freiwillig. **~ worker** freiwilliger Helfer, freiwillige Helferin; (overseas) Entwicklungshelfer(in f) m; **a ~ organization** ein freiwilliger Wohlfahrtsverband.

volunteer [,vɒlən'tɪə'] **1** n (also Mil) Freiwillige(r) mf. **any ~s?** wer meldet sich freiwillig? **2** vt help anbieten; suggestion machen; information geben. **3** vi **(a)** sich (freiwillig) melden. **to ~ for sth** sich freiwillig für etw zur Verfügung stellen; **to ~ to do sth** sich anbieten, etw zu tun. **(b)** (Mil) sich freiwillig melden (for zu, for places nach).

voluptuous [və'lʌptjʊəs] adj woman, movement sinnlich; curves üppig.

vomit ['vɒmɪt] **1** n Erbrochene(s) nt. **2** vt erbrechen; (fig) spucken. **3** vi sich übergeben.

voracious [və'reɪʃəs] adj person gefräßig. **she is a ~ reader** sie verschlingt die Bücher geradezu; **to have a ~ appetite** einen Riesenappetit haben.

vortex ['vɔːteks] n, pl -es or vortices ['vɔːtisiːz] (lit) Wirbel, Strudel (also fig) m.

vote [vəʊt] **1** n Stimme f; (act of voting) Abstimmung f; (result) Abstimmungsergebnis nt. **to put sth to the ~** über etw (acc) abstimmen lassen; **the Labour ~** die Labourstimmen pl; **to have the ~** das Wahlrecht haben. **2** vti (elect) wählen; (approve) bewilligen. **he was ~d chairman** er wurde zum Vorsitzenden gewählt; **to ~ Labour** Labour wählen; **to ~ for/against** für/gegen stimmen; **I ~ we leave now** ich schlage vor, daß wir jetzt gehen.

♦ **vote in** vt sep law beschließen; person wählen.

♦ **vote on** vi +prep obj abstimmen über (+acc).

voter ['vəʊtə'] n Wähler(in f) m.

voting ['vəʊtɪŋ] n Wahl f. **~ booth** Wahlkabine f; **~ paper** Stimmzettel m.

vouch [vaʊtʃ] vi **to ~ for sb/sth** sich für jdn/etw verbürgen; (legally) für jdn/etw bürgen.

voucher ['vaʊtʃə'] n **(a)** (for cash, petrol, meals) Gutschein m; (cigarette ~) Coupon m. **(b)** (receipt) Beleg m; (for debt) Schuldschein m.

vow [vaʊ] **1** n Versprechen nt; (Rel) Gelübde nt. **to make a ~ to do sth** geloben, etw zu tun; **to take one's ~s** sein Gelübde ablegen. **2** vt obedience geloben.

vowel ['vaʊəl] n Vokal, Selbstlaut m.

voyage ['vɔɪɪdʒ] n Reise, Fahrt f; (by sea also) Seereise f; (Space also) Flug m. **to go on a ~** auf eine Reise etc gehen; **the ~ out** die Hinreise/der Hinflug; **the ~ back** die Rückreise/der Rückflug; **~ of discovery** (fig) Entdeckungsreise f.

voyager ['vɔɪədʒə'] n Passagier m; (Space) Raumfahrer m.

vs = **versus**.

V-sign ['viːsaɪn] n **to give sb the ~** ≈ jdm den Vogel zeigen (col).

vulgar ['vʌlgə'] adj (pej) ordinär; (tasteless) geschmacklos. **~ fraction** (Math) gemeiner Bruch.

vulgarity [vʌl'gærɪtɪ] n Vulgarität f; (of gesture, joke also) Anstößigkeit f; (of colour etc) Geschmacklosigkeit f.

vulnerable ['vʌlnərəbl] adj verwundbar; (exposed) verletzlich; (fig) verletzbar; troops, fortress ungeschützt. **to be ~ to temptation** für Versuchungen anfällig sein.

W

W, w ['dʌblju:] n W, w nt.
W = **west** W.
wad [wɒd] n (compact mass) Knäuel m; (of cotton wool etc) Bausch m; (of papers, banknotes) Bündel nt.
wadding ['wɒdɪŋ] n (for packing) Material nt zum Ausstopfen; (Sew) Wattierung f.
waddle ['wɒdl] vi watscheln.
wade [weɪd] **1** vt durchwaten. **2** vi waten. **to ~ into sb/sth** (col: attack) auf jdn losgehen/etw in Angriff nehmen; **they all ~d in and helped** sie halfen alle mit; **to ~ through a book** sich durch ein Buch kämpfen.
wader ['weɪdə'] n **(a)** (Orn) Watvogel m. **(b)** ~s pl (boots) Watstiefel pl.
wafer ['weɪfə'] n **(a)** (biscuit) Waffel f. **a vanilla ~** eine Vanilleeiswaffel. **(b)** (Eccl) Hostie f. **(c)** (silicone~) Wafer f.
wafer-thin ['weɪfə'θɪn] adj hauchdünn.
waffle[1] ['wɒfl] n (Cook) Waffel f.
waffle[2] (Brit col) **1** n Geschwafel nt (col). **2** vi (also ~ **on**) schwafeln (col).
waft [wɑ:ft] vti wehen. **a delicious smell ~ed up from the kitchen** ein köstlicher Geruch zog aus der Küche herauf.
wag[1] [wæg] **1** n **with a ~ of its tail** mit einem Schwanzwedeln. **2** vt tail wedeln mit; (bird) wippen mit. **to ~ one's finger at sb** jdm mit dem Finger drohen. **3** vi (tail) wedeln; (of bird) wippen. **that'll set the tongues ~ging** dann geht das Gerede los.
wag[2] n (joker) Witzbold m (col). **a bit of a ~** ein alter Witzbold.
wage[1] [weɪdʒ] n usu pl Lohn m.
wage[2] vt war, campaign führen.
wage in cpds Lohn-; ~ **demand** n Lohnforderung f; ~ **earner** n Lohnempfänger m; ~ **freeze** n Lohnstopp m; ~ **increase** n Lohnerhöhung f; ~ **packet** n Lohntüte f.
wager ['weɪdʒə'] **1** n Wette f (on auf +acc). **to lay a ~** eine Wette abschließen. **2** vti wetten (on auf +acc).
waggle ['wægl] **1** vt wackeln mit; tail wedeln mit; (bird) wippen mit. **he ~d his finger at me disapprovingly** er drohte mir mißbilligend mit dem Finger. **2** vi wackeln; (tail) wedeln. **3** n **with a ~ of its tail** mit einem Schwanzwedeln.
waggon (Brit), **wagon** ['wægən] n **(a)** (horse-drawn) Wagen m; (covered ~) Planwagen m; (US: delivery truck) Lieferwagen m; (US col: police car) Streifenwagen m; (US col: for transporting prisoners) grüne Minna (col). **(b)** (Brit Rail) Waggon m. **(c)** (col) **I'm on the ~** ich trinke nichts.
wagtail ['wægteɪl] n (Orn) Bachstelze f.
waif [weɪf] n heimatloses Kind. **~s and strays** heimatlose Kinder pl.
wail [weɪl] **1** n (of baby) Geschrei nt; (of mourner, music) Klagen nt; (of sirens, wind) Heulen nt; (col: complaint) Gejammer nt (col). **2** vi (baby, cat) schreien; (mourner, music) klagen; (sirens, wind) heulen; (col: complain) jammern (over über +acc).
waist [weɪst] n Taille f. **stripped to the ~** mit nacktem Oberkörper.
waist: ~**band** n (of trousers) Hosenbund m; (of dress) Rockbund m; ~**coat** n (Brit) Weste f;

~-**deep** adj hüfthoch, bis zur Taille reichend; **we stood ~-deep in ...** wir standen bis zur Hüfte im ...; ~**line** n Taille f.
wait [weɪt] **1** vi **(a)** warten (for auf +acc). **to ~ for sb to do sth** darauf warten, daß jd etw tut; **it was definitely worth ~ing for** es hat sich wirklich gelohnt, darauf zu warten; **well, what are you ~ing for?** worauf wartest du denn (noch)?; **let him ~!** laß ihn warten, soll er warten!; **this work will have to ~** till diese Arbeit muß bis später warten; ~ **a minute** or **moment** (einen) Moment (mal); (just) **you ~!** warte nur ab!; (threatening) warte nur!; **I can't ~** ich kann's kaum erwarten; (out of curiosity) ich bin gespannt; **I can't ~ to see his face** da bin ich (aber) auf sein Gesicht gespannt. **(b) to ~ at table** servieren.
2 vt **to ~ one's turn** (ab)warten, bis man an der Reihe ist; **to ~ one's chance** eine günstige Gelegenheit abwarten; **to ~ dinner for sb** mit dem Essen auf jdn warten.
3 n **(a)** Wartezeit f. **did you have a long ~?** mußten Sie lange warten? **(b) to lie in ~ for sb/sth** jdm/einer Sache auflauern.
♦ **wait behind** vi zurückbleiben. **to ~ ~ for sb** zurückbleiben und auf jdn warten.
♦ **wait in** vi zu Hause bleiben (for wegen).
♦ **wait on** vi +prep obj **(a)** (also ~ **upon**) (serve) bedienen. **(b)** (US) **to ~ ~ table** servieren, bei Tisch bedienen.
♦ **wait up** vi aufbleiben (for wegen, für).
waiter ['weɪtə'] n Kellner, Ober m. ~! (Herr) Ober!
waiting ['weɪtɪŋ] n Warten nt. **no ~** Halteverbot nt.
waiting: ~ **game** n Wartespiel nt; **to play a ~ game** ein Wartespiel spielen; ~ **list** n Warteliste f; ~ **room** n Warteraum m; (at doctor's) Wartezimmer nt; (in station) Wartesaal m.
waitress ['weɪtrɪs] n Kellnerin f. ~! Fräulein!
waive [weɪv] vt **(a)** rights, claim verzichten auf (+acc); rule, age limit etc außer acht lassen. **(b)** (put aside, dismiss) question, objection abtun.
waiver ['weɪvə'] n (Jur) Verzicht m (of auf +acc); (document) Verzichterklärung f; (of law, contract) Außerkraftsetzung f.
wake[1] [weɪk] n (Naut) Kielwasser nt. **in the ~ of** (fig) nach; **to follow in sb's ~** (fig) jdm hinterhersegeln; **X leaves Y in its ~** X hinterläßt Y; **to bring sth in its ~** etw mit sich bringen.
wake[2] n (esp Ir: over corpse) Totenwache f.
wake[3] pret **woke**, ptp **woken 1** vt wecken. **2** vi aufwachen. **he woke to find himself in prison** als er aufwachte, fand er sich im Gefängnis wieder.
♦ **wake up 1** vi (lit, fig) aufwachen. **to ~ ~ to sth** (fig) sich (dat) einer Sache (gen) bewußt werden. **2** vt sep (lit) aufwecken; (fig: rouse from sloth) aufrütteln. **to ~ sb ~ to sth** (fig) jdm etw bewußt machen; **to ~ one's ideas ~** sich zusammenreißen.
wakeful ['weɪkful] adj (sleepless) schlaflos; (alert) wachsam.
waken ['weɪkən] vt (auf)wecken.
waking ['weɪkɪŋ] adj **to spend one's ~ hours doing sth** den (ganzen) Tag damit verbringen, etw zu tun.
Wales [weɪlz] n Wales nt.

walk [wɔːk] **1** *n* **(a)** *(stroll)* Spaziergang *m*; *(hike)* Wanderung *f*; *(charity* ~*)* Marsch *m* *(für Wohltätigkeitszwecke)*; *(signposted route)* Wanderweg *m*. **it's only 2 minutes'** ~ es sind nur 2 Minuten zu Fuß; **it's a long/short** ~ **to the shops** zu den Läden ist es weit/nicht weit zu Fuß; **to go for a** ~ einen Spaziergang machen; **to take sb/the dog for a** ~ mit jdm/dem Hund spazierengehen; **there are some good** ~**s in the hills** in den Bergen gibt es einige gute Wandermöglichkeiten. **(b)** *(gait)* Gang *m*; *(of horse also)* Gangart *f*. **the horse went at a** ~ das Pferd ging im Schritt. **(c)** ~ **of life** Milieu *nt*; **people from all** ~**s of life** Leute aus allen Schichten und Berufen. **(d)** *(US: Baseball)* Walk *m*, Freibase *nt*.

2 *vt* **(a)** *(lead)* person, horse *(spazieren)*führen; *dog* ausführen; *(ride at a* ~*)* im Schritt gehen lassen. **to** ~ **sb home/to the bus** jdn nach Hause/ zum Bus bringen. **(b)** *distance* laufen, gehen. **I've** ~**ed this road many times** ich bin diese Straße oft gegangen. **(c) to** ~ **the streets** *(prostitute)* auf den Strich gehen *(col)*; *(in search of sth)* durch die Straßen irren; *(aimlessly)* durch die Straßen gehen; **let's** ~ **it** gehen wir doch zu Fuß.

3 *vi* **(a)** gehen, laufen. ~ **a little with me** gehen Sie ein Stück mit mir; **to** ~ **in one's sleep** schlafwandeln. **(b)** *(not ride)* zu Fuß gehen, laufen *(col)*; *(stroll)* spazierengehen; *(hike)* wandern. **you can** ~ **there in 5 minutes** da ist man in 5 Minuten zu Fuß; **to** ~ **home** zu Fuß nach Hause gehen.

♦ **walk about** *or* **around** *vi* herumlaufen *(col)*. **to** ~ ~ **sth** um etw herumgehen; *(about room etc)* in etw *(dat)* herumgehen.

♦ **walk away** *vi* weggehen, davongehen. **he** ~**ed** ~ **from the crash unhurt** er ist bei dem Unfall ohne Verletzungen davongekommen; **to** ~ ~ **with a prize** *etc* einen Preis *etc* kassieren *(col)*.

♦ **walk in** *vi* herein-/hineinkommen; *(casually)* herein-/hineinspazieren *(col)*.

♦ **walk into** *vi* +*prep obj* room herein-/hineinkommen in (+*acc*); *person* anrempeln; *wall* laufen gegen. **to** ~ ~ **sb** *(meet unexpectedly)* jdn zufällig treffen; **to** ~ ~ **a trap** in eine Falle gehen; **to** ~ ~ **a job** eine Stelle ohne Schwierigkeiten bekommen; **to** ~ **right** ~ **sth** *(lit)* mit voller Wucht gegen etw rennen; **you** ~**ed right** ~ **that one, didn't you?** da bist du aber ganz schön reingefallen *(col)*.

♦ **walk off 1** *vt sep* **to** ~ ~ **one's hangover** einen Spaziergang machen, um seinen Kater loszuwerden. **2** *vi* weggehen. **he** ~**ed** ~ **in the opposite direction** er ging in die andere Richtung davon.

♦ **walk off with** *vi* +*prep obj (col) (take)* *(unintentionally)* abziehen mit *(col)*; *(intentionally)* abhauen mit *(col)*; *(win easily)* prize kassieren *(col)*.

♦ **walk on** *vi* **(a)** +*prep obj grass etc* betreten. **(b)** *(continue walking)* weitergehen.

♦ **walk out** *vi* **(a)** *(quit)* gehen. **to** ~ ~ **of a meeting/room** eine Versammlung/einen Saal verlassen; **to** ~ ~ **on sb** jdn verlassen; *(let down)* jdn im Stich lassen; *on girlfriend etc* jdn sitzenlassen *(col)*; **to** ~ ~ **on sth** aus etw aussteigen *(col)*. **(b)** *(strike)* streiken, in Streik treten.

♦ **walk over** *vi* +*prep obj* **(a)** *(defeat)* in die Tasche stecken *(col)*. **(b)** **to** ~ **all** ~ **sb** *(col) (dominate)* jdn unterbuttern *(col)*; *(in competition, match etc)* jdn fertigmachen *(col)*.

♦ **walk up** *vi* *(go up, ascend)* (zu Fuß) hinaufgehen; *(approach)* zugehen *(to* auf +*acc*). **a man** ~**ed** ~ **to me/her** ein Mann kam auf mich zu/ging auf sie zu; ~ ~!, ~ ~! treten Sie näher!

walk: ~**about** *n* Rundgang *m*; **the Queen went (on a)** ~**about die** Königin machte ein Bad in der Menge; ~**away** *n (US)* = ~**over.**

walker [ˈwɔːkəʳ] *n (stroller)* Spaziergänger(in *f*)

m; *(hiker)* Wanderer *m*, Wanderin *f*; *(Sport)* Geher(in *f*) *m*. **to be a fast** ~ schnell gehen.

walkie-talkie [ˈwɔːkɪˈtɔːkɪ] *n* Walkie-talkie *nt*.

walking [ˈwɔːkɪŋ] **1** *n* Gehen *nt*; *(as recreation)* Spazierengehen *nt*; *(hiking)* Wandern *nt*. **we did a lot of** ~ **on holiday** in den Ferien sind wir viel gewandert. **2** *adj attr* encyclopaedia, miracle *etc* wandelnd; *doll* Lauf-. **at a** ~ **pace** im Schrittempo; **it's within** ~ **distance** dahin kann man zu Fuß gehen.

walking: ~ **shoes** *npl* Wanderschuhe *pl*; ~ **stick** *n* Spazierstock *m*; ~ **tour** *n* Wanderung *f*.

walk: ~**-on** *adj part, role* Statisten-; ~**out** *n (strike)* Streik *m*; **to stage a** ~**out** *(from conference)* demonstrativ den Saal verlassen; ~**over** *n (easy victory)* spielender Sieg; *(fig)* Kinderspiel *nt*; ~**way** *n* Fußweg *m*; **a pedestrian** ~**way** ein Fuß(gänger)weg *m*.

wall [wɔːl] *n (outside)* Mauer *f*; *(inside, of mountain)* Wand *f*. **a** ~ **of fire** eine Feuerwand; **a** ~ **of policemen/troops** eine Mauer von Polizisten/ Soldaten; **to go up the** ~ *(col)* die Wände hochgehen *(col)*; **he drives me up the** ~ *(col)* er bringt mich auf die Palme *(col)*; **to go to the** ~ *(firm etc)* kaputtgehen *(col)*.

♦ **wall in** *vt sep* mit einer Mauer umgeben.

♦ **wall off** *vt sep (cut off)* durch eine Mauer (ab)trennen.

♦ **wall up** *vt sep* zumauern.

wall: ~**bars** *npl* Sprossenwand *f*; ~ **chart** *n* Wandkarte *f*.

walled [wɔːld] *adj* von Mauern umgeben.

wallet [ˈwɒlɪt] *n* Brieftasche *f*.

wall: ~**flower** *n (Bot)* Goldlack *m*; *(fig col)* Mauerblümchen *nt (col)*; ~ **hanging** *n* Wandbehang *m*; ~ **map** *n* Wandkarte *f*.

wallop [ˈwɒləp] *(col)* **1** *n (blow)* Schlag *m*. **to give sb/sth a** ~ jdm einer Sache eine Schlag versetzen. **2** *vt (hit)* schlagen; *(punish)* versohlen *(col)*.

walloping [ˈwɒləpɪŋ] *(col) n* Prügel *pl (col)*; *(defeat)* Schlappe *f*. **to give sb a** ~ jdm eine Tracht Prügel geben *(col)*.

wallow [ˈwɒləu] *vi* **(a)** *(lit) (animal)* sich wälzen; *(boat)* rollen. **(b) to** ~ **in luxury/self-pity** *etc* im Luxus/Selbstmitleid *etc* schwelgen.

wall: ~**paper 1** *n* Tapete *f*; **2** *vt* tapezieren; ~**-to-**~ *adj* ~**-to-**~ **carpeting** Teppichboden *m*.

wally [ˈwɒlɪ] *n (Brit col)* Idiot *m*.

walnut [ˈwɔːlnʌt] *n (nut)* Walnuß *f*; *(tree, wood)* Nußbaum *m*.

walrus [ˈwɔːlrəs] *n* Walroß *nt*.

waltz [wɔːls] **1** *n* Walzer *m*. **2** *vi* **(a)** Walzer tanzen. **(b)** *(col: move, come etc)* walzen *(col)*. **he came** ~**ing up** er kam angetanzt *(col)*.

wan [wɒn] *adj* bleich; *light, smile, look* matt.

wand [wɒnd] *n (magic* ~*)* Zauberstab *m*.

wander [ˈwɒndəʳ] **1** *n* Spaziergang *m*; *(through town, park also)* Bummel *m*. **I'm going for a** ~ **around the shops** ich mache einen Ladenbummel.

2 *vt hills, world* durchstreifen *(geh)*. **to** ~ **the streets** durch die Straßen wandern.

3 *vi* herumlaufen; *(more aimlessly)* umherwandern *(through, about* in +*dat)*; *(leisurely)* schlendern; *(to see the shops)* bummeln. **he** ~**ed over to speak to me** er kam zu mir herüber, um mit mir zu reden. **(b)** *(go off, stray)* **to** ~ **from the path** vom Wege abkommen; **he** ~**ed too near the edge of the cliff** er geriet zu nahe an den Rand des Abhangs. **(c)** *(fig: thoughts, eye)* schweifen, wandern. **to let one's mind** ~ seine Gedanken schweifen lassen; **the old man's mind is beginning to** ~ **a bit** der alte Mann wird ein wenig wirr; **to** ~ **from** *or* **off a point/subject** von einem Punkt/vom Thema abschweifen *or* abkommen.

♦ **wander off** vi weggehen; (col: leave) allmählich gehen.

wanderer ['wɒndərə^r] n Wandervogel m.

wandering ['wɒndərɪŋ] **1** adj tribesman umherziehend; minstrel fahrend; thoughts (ab)schweifend; path gewunden. **2** n ~s pl Herumziehen nt; (mental) wirre Gedanken pl.

wanderlust ['wɒndəlʌst] n Fernweh nt.

wane [weɪn] **1** n to be on the ~ (fig) im Schwinden sein. **2** vi (moon) abnehmen; (fig) (influence, strength) schwinden; (reputation) verblassen; (daylight) nachlassen.

wangle ['wæŋgl] (col) **1** n Schiebung (col) f. **2** vt job, ticket etc organisieren (col), verschaffen. **to ~ oneself/sb in** sich hineinmogeln (col)/jdn einschleusen (col); **he'll ~ it for you** er wird das schon für dich drehen (col).

wangler ['wæŋglə^r] n (col) Schlawiner m (col).

wank [wæŋk] vi (col!) wichsen (col!).

wanly ['wɒnlɪ] adv matt.

want [wɒnt] **1** n (a) (lack) Mangel m (of an +dat). **for ~ of** aus Mangel an (+dat); **for ~ of anything better to do** weil es nichts anderes zu tun gibt/gab etc; **though it wasn't for ~ of trying** nicht, daß er sich/ich mich etc nicht bemüht hätte. **(b)** (poverty) Not f. **to be/live in ~** Not leiden. **(c)** (need) Bedürfnis nt; (wish) Wunsch m. **the farm supplied all their ~s** der Bauernhof versorgte sie mit allem Notwendigen; **to be in ~ of sth** etw benötigen; **to be in ~ of help/repair** Hilfe brauchen/reparaturbedürftig sein.

2 vt (a) (wish, desire) wollen. **to ~ to do sth** etw tun wollen; **I ~ you to come here** ich will or (more polite) möchte, daß du herkommst; **I ~ it done now** ich will/möchte das sofort erledigt haben; **I don't ~ you interfering** ich will nicht, daß Sie sich einmischen. **(b)** (need, require) brauchen. **you ~ to see a doctor** Sie sollten zum Arzt gehen; **you ~ to be careful!** (col) du mußt aufpassen; **it ~s cutting** es muß geschnitten werden; **that's all we ~ed!** (iro col) das hat uns gerade noch gefehlt!; **it only ~ed the police to turn up ...** das hätte gerade noch gefehlt, daß auch noch die Polizei anrückt ...; **"~ed"** „gesucht"; **he's a ~ed man** er wird (polizeilich) gesucht; **you're ~ed on the phone** Sie werden am Telefon verlangt.

3 vi (a) (wish, desire) wollen. **you can go if you ~** (to) wenn du willst, kannst du gehen; **I don't ~ to** ich will or (more polite) möchte nicht. **(b)** he does not ~ for friends es fehlt or mangelt (geh) ihm nicht an Freunden; **they ~ for nothing** es fehlt ihnen an nichts.

wanting ['wɒntɪŋ] adj fehlend. humour is ~ in the novel diesem Roman fehlt es an Humor; **he is ~ in confidence** es fehlt or mangelt (geh) ihm an Selbstvertrauen; **his courage/the new engine was found ~** sein Mut war nicht groß genug/der neue Motor hat sich als unzulänglich erwiesen; **he was tried and found ~** er konnte sich nicht bewähren.

wanton ['wɒntən] adj (a) (licentious) life liederlich; behaviour, woman, pleasures schamlos; looks, thoughts lüstern. **(b)** (wilful) cruelty mutwillig; disregard, waste sträflich.

war [wɔː^r] **1** n Krieg m. **this is ~!** (fig) das bedeutet Krieg!; **the ~ against poverty** der Kampf gegen die Armut; **~ of nerves** Nervenkrieg m; **~ of words** Wortgefecht nt; **to be at ~** sich im Krieg(szustand) befinden; **to declare ~** den Krieg erklären (on dat); (fig also) den Kampf ansagen (on dat); **to make or wage ~** Krieg führen (on, against gegen); **he/this car has been in the ~s** a bit er/dieses Auto sieht ziemlich mitgenommen aus. **2** vi sich bekriegen; (fig) ringen (geh) (for um).

warble ['wɔːbl] vti trällern.

warbler ['wɔːblə^r] n (Orn) Grasmücke f; (wood~) Waldsänger m.

war cry n Kriegsruf m; (fig) Schlachtruf m.

ward [wɔːd] n (a) (part of hospital) Station f; (room) (small) Krankenzimmer nt; (large) Krankensaal m. **(b)** (Jur: person) Mündel nt. ~ **of court** Mündel unter Amtsvormundschaft. **(c)** (Admin) Stadtbezirk m; (election~) Wahlbezirk m.

♦ **ward off** vt sep attack, blow, person abwehren; danger also abwenden; depression nicht aufkommen lassen.

war dance n Kriegstanz m.

warden ['wɔːdn] n (of youth hostel) Herbergsvater m, Herbergsmutter f; (game ~) Jagdaufseher m; (traffic ~) Verkehrspolizist m, ≃ Politesse f; (of museum etc) Aufseher m; (Univ) Heimleiter(in f) m; (of Oxbridge college) Rektor m; (US: of prison) Gefängnisdirektor m.

warder ['wɔːdə^r] n (Brit) Wärter, Aufseher m.

wardress ['wɔːdrɪs] n (Brit) Wärterin, Aufseherin f.

wardrobe ['wɔːdrəʊb] n (a) (cupboard) Kleiderschrank m. **(b)** (clothes) Garderobe f. **(c)** (Theat) (clothes) Kostüme pl; (room) Kleiderkammer f.

wardroom ['wɔːdruːm] n (Naut) Offiziersmesse f.

-ward(s) [-wəd(z)] adv suf -wärts. **town~** in Richtung Stadt.

warehouse ['wɛəhaʊs] n Lager(haus) nt.

wares [wɛəz] npl Waren pl.

warfare ['wɔːfeə^r] n Krieg m; (techniques) Kriegskunst f.

war: ~ **game** n Kriegsspiel nt; ~**head** n Sprengkopf m; ~**horse** n (lit, fig) Schlachtroß nt.

warily ['wɛərɪlɪ] adv vorsichtig; (suspiciously) mißtrauisch, argwöhnisch. **to tread ~** (lit, fig) sich vorsehen.

wariness ['wɛərɪnɪs] n Vorsicht f; (mistrust) Mißtrauen nt (of gegenüber).

warlike ['wɔːlaɪk] adj kriegerisch; tone militant.

warm [wɔːm] **1** adj (+er) (a) warm. **I am or feel ~** mir ist warm. **(b)** (in games) **am I ~?** ist es (hier) warm?; **you're getting ~** es wird schon wärmer. **(c)** (hearty) person, welcome herzlich, warm. **(d)** (heated) dispute, words hitzig. **2** n **we were glad to get into the ~** wir waren froh, daß wir ins Warme kamen; **to give sth a ~** etw wärmen. **3** vt wärmen. **it ~s my heart to ...** mir wird (es) ganz warm ums Herz, wenn ... **4** vi **the milk was ~ing on the stove** die Milch wurde auf dem Herd erwärmt; **I ~ed to him** er wurde mir sympathischer; **to ~ to one's work** sich mit seiner Arbeit anfreunden.

♦ **warm up 1** vi (lit, fig) warm werden; (party, game, speaker) in Schwung kommen; (Sport) sich aufwärmen. **things are ~ing** es kommt Schwung in die Sache; (becoming dangerous) es wird allmählich brenzlig (col). **2** vt sep engine warmlaufen lassen; food etc aufwärmen; (fig) party in Schwung bringen; audience in Stimmung bringen.

warm-blooded ['wɔːm'blʌdɪd] adj warmblütig; (fig) heißblütig. ~ **animal** Warmblüter m.

warm front n (Met) Warm(luft)front f.

warm-hearted ['wɔːm'hɑːtɪd] adj warmherzig; gesture großzügig.

warmly ['wɔːmlɪ] adv warm; welcome herzlich; recommend wärmstens. **we ~ welcome it** wir begrüßen es sehr.

war: ~**monger** n ['wɔː,mʌŋgə^r] n Kriegshetzer m; ~**mongering** ['wɔː,mʌŋgərɪŋ] **1** adj kriegshetzerisch; **2** n Kriegshetze f.

warmth [wɔːmθ] n (lit, fig) Wärme f; (of welcome) Herzlichkeit f.

warm-up ['wɔːmʌp] n (Sport) Aufwärmen nt.

warn [wɔːn] vt warnen (of, about, against vor +dat); (police, judge etc) verwarnen. **to ~ sb not to do sth** jdn davor warnen, etw zu tun; **be ~ed** sei gewarnt!; **he had ~ed me off** er hatte mich davor gewarnt; **she ~ed us not to be late** sie ermahnte uns, nicht zu spät zu kommen; **to ~ sb**

that ... *(inform)* jdn darauf hinweisen, daß ...
warning ['wɔːnɪŋ] **1** n Warnung f; *(from police, judge etc)* Verwarnung f. **without** ~ unerwartet, ohne Vorwarnung; **to give sb a** ~ jdn warnen; *(police, judge etc)* jdn verwarnen; **let this be a** ~ **to you** lassen Sie sich *(dat)* das eine Warnung sein!; **to give sb due** ~ *(inform)* jdm rechtzeitig Bescheid sagen. **2** adj Warn-; *look, tone* warnend. **a** ~ **sign** ein erstes Anzeichen; *(signboard etc)* ein Warnzeichen nt/-schild nt.
warp [wɔːp] **1** n *(in weaving)* Kette f; *(in wood etc)* Welle f. **2** vt *wood* wellen; *character* entstellen; *judgement* verzerren. **3** vi *(wood)* sich wellen, sich verziehen.
war: ~**paint** n *(lit, fig col)* Kriegsbemalung f; ~**path** n Kriegspfad m; **on the** ~**path** auf dem Kriegspfad.
warped [wɔːpt] adj **(a)** *(lit)* wellig. **(b)** *(fig) sense of humour* abartig; *character also* verbogen; *judgement* verzerrt.
war plane n Kampfflugzeug nt.
warrant ['wɒrənt] **1** n *(Comm)* Garantie f; *(Mil)* Patent nt; *(search* ~) Durchsuchungsbefehl m; *(death* ~) Hinrichtungsbefehl m. **there is a** ~ **out for his arrest** gegen ihn ist Haftbefehl erlassen worden *(Jur)*. **2** vt **(a)** *(justify) action etc* rechtfertigen. **to** ~ **sb doing sth** jdn dazu berechtigen, etw zu tun. **(b)** *(merit)* verdienen. **(c)** *(guarantee)* gewährleisten. **it'll work, I** ~ **you that** es funktioniert, das garantiere ich Ihnen.
warranty ['wɒrəntɪ] n *(Comm)* Garantie f. **it's still under** ~ darauf ist noch Garantie.
warren ['wɒrən] n *(rabbit* ~) Kaninchenbau m; *(fig)* Labyrinth nt.
warring ['wɔːrɪŋ] adj *nations* kriegführend; *interests* gegensätzlich; *factions* sich bekriegend.
warrior ['wɒrɪəʳ] n Krieger m.
Warsaw ['wɔːsɔː] n Warschau nt. ~ **Pact** Warschauer Pakt m.
warship ['wɔːʃɪp] n Kriegsschiff nt.
wart [wɔːt] n Warze f. ~**s and all** *(hum col)* mit allen seinen/ihren etc Fehlern.
wart-hog ['wɔːthɒg] n Warzenschwein nt.
wartime ['wɔːtaɪm] **1** n Kriegszeit f. **in** ~ in Kriegszeiten. **2** adj Kriegs-. **in** ~ **England** in England während des Krieges.
wary ['wɛərɪ] adj *(+er)* vorsichtig; *(looking and planning ahead)* umsichtig, klug; *look* mißtrauisch. **to be** ~ **of sb/sth** vor jdm/einer Sache auf der Hut sein; **to be** ~ **about doing sth** Zweifel haben, ob man etw tun soll.
was [wɒz] *1st, 3rd pers sing pret of* **be**.
wash [wɒʃ] **1** n **(a)** *(act of* ~*ing)* **sth needs a** ~ etw muß gewaschen werden; **I need a** ~ ich muß mich waschen; **to give sb/sth a** *(good)* ~ jdn/etw *(gründlich)* waschen; **to have a** ~ sich waschen. **(b)** *(laundry)* Wäsche f. **to be in the** ~ in der Wäsche sein; **it will all come out in the** ~ *(fig col) (become known)* es wird schon alles rauskommen; *(work out)* es wird sich schon noch alles regeln. **(c)** *(of ship)* Kielwasser nt. **2** vt **(a)** waschen; *dishes* spülen; *floor* aufwischen; *hands etc* sich *(dat)* waschen. **to** ~ **one's hands of sb/sth** mit jdm/etw nichts mehr zu tun haben wollen; **I** ~ **my hands of it** ich wasche meine Hände in Unschuld; **to** ~ **sth clean** etw reinwaschen. **(b)** *(sea etc)* umspülen; *cliffs etc* schlagen gegen; *(carry)* spülen. **it was** ~**ed ashore** es wurde an Land gespült. **3** vi **(a)** *(have a* ~*)* sich waschen. **(b)** a *material that* ~**es well/won't** ~ ein Stoff, der sich gut wäscht/den man nicht waschen kann; **that excuse won't** ~ *(Brit fig col)* diese Entschuldigung kauft dir keiner ab! *(col)*. **(c)** **the sea** ~**ed over the promenade** das Meer überspülte die Strandpromenade.
♦ **wash away** vt sep *(hin)*wegspülen. **to** ~ ~ **sb's sins** jdn von seinen Sünden reinwaschen.

♦ **wash down** vt sep *(clean)* abwaschen; *meal* hinunterspülen.
♦ **wash off 1** vi *(stain, dirt)* sich herauswaschen lassen. **most of the pattern has** ~**ed** ~ das Muster ist fast ganz verwaschen. **2** vt sep abwaschen.
♦ **wash out 1** vi sich auswaschen lassen. **2** vt sep *(clean)* auswaschen; *mouth* ausspülen.
♦ **wash up 1** vi **(a)** *(Brit: clean dishes)* abwaschen, spülen. **(b)** *(US: have a wash)* sich waschen. **2** vt sep **(a)** *(Brit) dishes* spülen. **(b)** *(sea etc)* anspülen.
washable ['wɒʃəbl] adj waschbar; *wallpaper* abwaschbar.
wash: ~ **basin** n Waschbecken nt; ~ **bowl** n Waschschüssel f; *(in unit)* Waschbecken nt; ~ **cloth** n *(US)* Waschlappen m; ~**day** n Waschtag m.
washed out ['wɒʃt'aut] adj *(col)* erledigt *(col)*, schlapp *(col)*. **to look** ~ mitgenommen aussehen.
washer ['wɒʃəʳ] n **(a)** *(Tech)* Dichtung(sring m) f. **(b)** *(clothes* ~*)* Waschmaschine f; *(dish*~*)* (Geschirr)spülmaschine f.
washhand basin ['wɒʃˌhænd,beɪsn] n Handwaschbecken nt.
washing ['wɒʃɪŋ] n Waschen nt; *(clothes)* Wäsche f. **to do the** ~ Wäsche waschen.
washing: ~ **machine** n Waschmaschine f; ~ **powder** n *(Brit)* Waschpulver nt; ~**-up** n *(Brit)* Abwasch m; **to do the** ~**-up** spülen, den Abwasch machen; ~**-up bowl** n Spülschüssel f; ~**-up liquid** n *(Brit)* Spülmittel nt.
wash: ~ **leather** n Waschleder nt; ~**out** n *(col)* Reinfall m *(col)*; *(person)* Flasche *(col)*, Niete *(col)* f; ~ **room** n Waschraum m.
wasn't ['wɒznt] = **was not**.
wasp [wɒsp] n Wespe f.
waspish ['wɒspɪʃ] adj giftig.
wastage ['weɪstɪdʒ] n Schwund m; *(action)* Verschwendung f; *(amount also)* Materialverlust m; *(from container also)* Verlust m; *(unusable products etc also)* Abfall m.
waste [weɪst] **1** adj *(superfluous)* überschüssig, überflüssig; *(left over)* ungenutzt; *land* brachliegend. **to lay** ~ verwüsten; **to lie** ~ brachliegen.
2 n **(a)** Verschwendung f; *(unusable materials)* Abfall m. **it's a** ~ **of time/money** es ist Zeit-/Geldverschwendung; **it's a** ~ **of effort** das ist nicht der Mühe wert; **to go to** ~ *(food)* umkommen; *(money, land, talent)* ungenutzt sein/bleiben, brachliegen. **(b)** *(~ material)* Abfallstoffe pl; *(rubbish)* Abfall m. **radioactive** ~ Atommüll m. **(c)** *(land, expanse)* Wildnis no pl, Einöde f.
3 vt verschwenden *(on* an +acc, für*)*; *life, time* vergeuden; *opportunity* vertun. **you're wasting your time** das ist reine Zeitverschwendung; **don't** ~ **my time** stiehl mir nicht meine Zeit; **you didn't** ~ **much time, did you?** *(col)* das ging aber schnell!; **Beethoven/she is** ~**d on him** Beethoven ist an den vergeudet/sie ist zu schade für ihn.
4 vi *(food)* umkommen; *(skills)* verkümmern; *(body)* verfallen; *(strength, assets)* schwinden. ~ **not, want not** *(Prov)* spare in der Zeit, so hast du in der Not *(Prov)*.
♦ **waste away** vi *(physically)* dahinschwinden *(geh)*, immer weniger werden *(col)*.
waste: ~**-bin** n *(Brit)* Abfalleimer m; ~ **disposal** n Müllbeseitigung f; ~ **disposal unit** n Müllschlucker m.
wasteful ['weɪstful] adj verschwenderisch; *method, process* unwirtschaftlich. **to be** ~ **with sth** verschwenderisch mit etw umgehen.
waste: ~**land** n Ödland nt; *(fig)* Einöde f; ~**paper** n Papierabfall m; *(for recycling)* Altpapier nt; ~**paper basket** n *(Brit)* Papierkorb m; ~ **pipe** n Abflußrohr m; ~ **product** n Abfallprodukt nt.
waster ['weɪstəʳ] n **(a)** **it's a real time-/money-**~

das ist wirklich Zeit-/Geldverschwendung. **(b)** *(good-for-nothing)* Taugenichts *m*.

watch[1] [wɒtʃ] *n* (Armband)uhr *f*.

watch[2] **1** *n* **(a) to be on the** ~ **for sb/sth** nach jdm/etw Ausschau halten; **to keep** ~ Wache halten; **to keep a close** ~ **on sb/sth** jdn/etw scharf bewachen; **to keep** ~ **over sb/sth** bei jdm/etw Wache halten; **to set a** ~ **on sb/sth** jdn/etw überwachen lassen. **(b)** *(period of duty, Naut, people)* Wache *f*; *(people also)* Wachmannschaft *f*. **to be on** ~ Wache haben; **officer of the** ~ wachhabender Offizier.

2 *vt* **(a)** *(guard)* aufpassen auf *(+acc)*; *(police etc)* überwachen.

(b) *(observe)* beobachten; *match* zusehen *or* zuschauen bei; *film, play, TV programme* sich *(dat)* ansehen. **to** ~ **TV** fernsehen; **to** ~ **sb doing sth** jdm bei etw zuschauen; **I** ~**ed her coming down the street** ich habe sie beobachtet, wie sie die Straße entlang kam; ~ **the road in front of you** guck *or* achte auf die Straße!; ~ **this!** paß auf!; **we are being** ~**ed** wir werden beobachtet; **a new actor to be** ~**ed** ein Nachwuchsschauspieler, den man im Auge behalten sollte.

(c) *(be careful of)* achten auf *(+acc)*, aufpassen auf *(+acc)*. **(you'd better)** ~ **it!** *(col)* paß (bloß) auf! *(col)*; ~ **your manners/language!** bitte benimm dich!/drück dich bitte etwas gepflegter aus!; ~ **how you drive, the roads are icy** paß beim Fahren auf, die Straßen sind vereist!

3 *vi (observe)* zusehen, zuschauen. **to** ~ **for sb/sth** nach jdm/etw Ausschau halten.

♦ **watch out** *vi* **(a)** *(look carefully)* Ausschau halten *(for sb/sth* nach jdm/etw). **(b)** *(be careful)* aufpassen, achtgeben *(for* auf *+acc)*. ~ ~! Achtung!; ~ ~ **for him, he's crafty** nimm dich vor ihm in acht, er ist gerissen.

♦ **watch over** *vi +prep obj* wachen über *(+acc)*.

watchdog [ˈwɒtʃdɒg] *n (lit)* Wachhund *m*; *(fig)* Aufpasser *(col)*.

watcher [ˈwɒtʃəʳ] *n* Schaulustige(r) *mf*; *(observer)* Beobachter(in *f*) *m*.

watchful [ˈwɒtʃfʊl] *adj* wachsam. **to be** ~ **for** wachsam Ausschau halten nach.

watchfulness [ˈwɒtʃfʊlnɪs] *n* Wachsamkeit *f*.

watch: ~**maker** *n* Uhrmacher *m*; ~**man** *n (night-* ~ *etc)* (Nacht)wächter *m*; ~**strap** *n* Uhrarmband *nt*; ~ **tower** *n* Wachtturm *m*; ~**word** *n* Parole *f*.

water [ˈwɔːtəʳ] **1** *n* Wasser *nt*. **the field is under** ~ das Feld steht unter Wasser; **to make** ~ *(ship)* lecken; **in American** ~**s** in amerikanischen Hoheitsgewässern; **by** ~ auf dem Wasserweg; **to make** *or* **pass** ~ Wasser lassen; **to drink** *or* **take the** ~**s** eine Kur machen; **a lot of** ~ **has flowed under the bridge since then** *(fig)* seitdem ist viel Wasser den Bach hinuntergeflossen; **to stay above** ~ *(fig)* sich über Wasser halten; **to pour cold** ~ **on sb's idea** jds Vorschlag miesmachen *(col)*; **to get into deep** ~**(s)** *(fig)* ins Schwimmen kommen; **to hold** ~ *(lit)* wasserdicht sein; **that argument won't hold** ~ *(col)* dieses Argument ist nicht hieb- und stichfest *(col)*; **to be in/get into hot** ~ *(fig col)* in Teufels Küche sein/geraten *(col)* *(over* wegen *+gen)*; **to spend money like** ~ *(col)* mit dem Geld nur so um sich werfen *(col)*.

2 *vt* **(a)** *garden* sprengen; *field* bewässern; *plant* (be)gießen. **(b)** *horses, cattle* tränken.

3 *vi (mouth)* wässern; *(eye)* tränen. **the smoke made his eyes** ~ ihm tränten die Augen vom Rauch; **my mouth** ~**ed** mir lief das Wasser im Mund zusammen; **to make sb's mouth** ~ jdm den Mund wässerig machen.

♦ **water down** *vt sep (lit, fig pej)* verwässern; *(fig also)* abschwächen; *liquids* verdünnen.

water: ~**bed** *n* Wasserbett *nt*; ~-**bottle** *n*

Wasserflasche *f*; *(for troops etc)* Feldflasche *f*; ~ **cannon** *n* Wasserwerfer *m*; ~ **closet** *n (abbr* WC) Wasserklosett *nt*; ~**colour** *(Brit)*, ~**color** *(US)* **1** *n* Wasserfarbe, Aquarellfarbe *f*; *(picture)* Aquarell *nt*; **2** *attr* Aquarell-; ~-**cooled** *adj* wassergekühlt; ~**course** *n (stream)* Wasserlauf *m*; *(bed)* Flußbett *nt*; *(artificial)* Kanal *m*; ~**cress** *n* (Brunnen)kresse *f*; ~**fall** *n* Wasserfall *m*; ~**front 1** *n* Hafenviertel *nt*; **we drove along the** ~**front/down to the** ~**front** wir fuhren am Wasser entlang/hinunter zum Wasser; **2** *attr* am Wasser.

watering can [ˈwɔːtərɪŋˌkæn] *n* Gießkanne *f*.

water: ~ **level** *n* Wasserstand *m*; *(of river etc also)* Pegelstand *m*; ~**lily** *n* Seerose *f*; ~**line** *n* Wasserlinie *f*; ~**logged** *adj* **the fields are** ~**logged** die Felder stehen unter Wasser; **the ship was completely** ~**logged** das Schiff war voll Wasser gelaufen; ~ **main** *n* Haupt(wasser)leitung *f*; ~**mark** *n* **(a)** *(on wall)* Wasserstandsmarke *f*; **(b)** *(on paper)* Wasserzeichen *nt*; ~**melon** *n* Wassermelone *f*; ~-**pistol** *n* Wasserpistole *f*; ~-**polo** *n* Wasserball *nt*; ~-**power** *n* Wasserkraft *f*; ~**proof 1** *adj* wasserdicht; *paint* wasserfest; **2** *n (esp Brit)* Regenhaut ® *f*; **3** *vt* wasserundurchlässig machen; ~ **rat** *n* Wasserratte *f*; *(fig)* Wendepunkt *m*; ~**shed** *n (Geol)* Wasserscheide *f*; *(fig)* Wendepunkt *m*; ~**side 1** *n* Ufer *nt*; *(at sea)* Strand *m*; **2** *attr* am Wasser wachsend/lebend *etc*; ~-**ski** *vi* Wasserski laufen; ~-**skiing** *n* Wasserskilaufen *nt*; ~ **supply** *n* Wasserversorgung *f*; ~**table** *n* Grundwasserspiegel *m*; ~**tight** *adj (lit)* wasserdicht; *(fig)* *argument etc also* hieb- und stichfest; ~-**tower** *n* Wasserturm *m*; ~ **vapour** *(Brit)* or **vapor** *(US)* *n* Wasserdampf *m*; ~**way** *n* Wasserstraße *f*; *(channel)* Fahrrinne *f*; ~-**wheel** *n (Mech)* Wasserrad *nt*; *(Agr)* Wasserschöpfrad *nt*; ~-**wings** *npl* Schwimmflügel *pl*; ~**works** *npl or sing* Wasserwerk *nt*; **to turn on the** ~**works** *(fig col)* zu heulen anfangen; **to have trouble with one's** ~**works** *(fig col)* ständig lassen müssen *(col)*.

watery [ˈwɔːtərɪ] *adj soup, colour* wäßrig; *eye* tränend; *(pale) sky* blaß.

watt [wɒt] *n* Watt *nt*.

wave [weɪv] **1** *n* **(a)** *(of water, Phys, Rad, in hair, fig)* Welle *f*. **a** ~ **of strikes/enthusiasm** eine Streikwelle/Welle der Begeisterung; **the new** ~ *(Mus, Film)* die Neue Welle. **(b)** *(movement of hand)* **to give a** ~ jdm (zu)winken; **with a** ~ **of his hand** mit einer Handbewegung.

2 *vt* **(a)** *(as a sign or greeting)* winken *(at, to* sb jdm); ~ *(about)* schwenken. **to** ~ **one's hand to sb** jdm winken; **to** ~ **goodbye to sb** jdm zum Abschied winken; **she** ~**d her umbrella threateningly at him** sie schwang drohend ihren Schirm nach ihm; **he** ~**d his fist at the intruders** er drohte den Eindringlingen mit der Faust; **he** ~**d me over** er winkte mich zu sich herüber. **(b)** *hair* wellen.

3 *vi* **(a)** winken. **to** ~ **at** *or* **to sb** jdm winken; *(greeting)* jdm zuwinken. **(b)** *(flag)* wehen; *(branches)* sich hin und her bewegen; *(corn)* wogen. **(c)** *(hair)* sich wellen.

♦ **wave around** *vt sep* herumfuchteln mit.

♦ **wave aside** *vt sep (lit) person* zur Seite winken; *(fig) person, objection etc* zurückweisen; *help also* ausschlagen.

♦ **wave away** *vt sep* wegwinken.

♦ **wave on** *vt sep* **the policeman** ~**d us** ~ der Polizist winkte uns weiter.

wave: ~**band** *n (Rad)* Wellenband *nt*; ~**length** *n (Rad, fig)* Wellenlänge *f*; **we're not on the same** ~**length** *(fig)* wir haben nicht dieselbe Wellenlänge.

waver [ˈweɪvəʳ] *vi* **(a)** *(light, flame, eyes)* flackern; *(voice)* zittern. **(b)** *(courage, self-assurance)* ins Wanken geraten; *(support)* nachlassen. **(c)**

(hesitate) schwanken *(between* zwischen +*dat*).

wavy ['weɪvɪ] *adj (+er) hair, surface* wellig, gewellt.

~ **line** Schlangenlinie *f*.

wax¹ [wæks] **1** *n* Wachs *nt*; *(ear~)* Ohrenschmalz *nt*; *(sealing ~)* Siegellack *m*. **2** *adj* Wachs-. **3** *vt* wachsen; *floor also* bohnern.

wax² *vi* **(a)** *(moon)* zunehmen. **to ~ and wane** *(lit)* ab- und zunehmen; *(fig)* schwanken. **(b)** *(liter: become)* werden. **to ~ enthusiastic** in Begeisterung geraten.

wax(ed) paper *n* Wachspapier *nt*.

wax: ~ **work** *n* Wachsfigur *f*; ~ **works** *n sing or pl* Wachsfigurenkabinett *nt*.

waxy ['wæksɪ] *adj (+er)* wächsern.

way [weɪ] **1** *n* **(a)** *(road)* Weg *m*. **across** *or* **over the** ~ gegenüber, vis-à-vis; *(motion)* rüber; **to fall by the ~** *(fig)* auf der Strecke bleiben.

(b) *(route)* Weg *m*. **the ~ to the station** der Weg zum Bahnhof; **by ~ of** *(via)* über *(+acc)*; **which is the ~ to the town hall, please?** wo geht es hier zum Rathaus, bitte?; ~ **in/out** *(also on signs)* Ein-/Ausgang *m*; **can you find your own ~ out?** finden Sie selbst hinaus?; **on the ~ out/in** beim Hinaus-/Hereingehen; **to be on the ~ in** *(fig col)* im Kommen sein; **to be on the ~ out** *(fig col)* am Verschwinden sein; **there's no ~ out** *(fig)* es gibt keinen Ausweg; ~ **up/down** Weg nach oben/ unten; *(climbing)* Aufstieg/Abstieg *m*; ~ **up/back** Hinweg/Rückweg *m*; **prices are on the ~ up/ down** die Preise steigen/fallen; **the shop is on the** ~ der Laden liegt auf dem Weg; **to stop on the ~** unterwegs anhalten; **on the ~ to London** auf dem Weg nach London; **he's on the ~ to becoming an alcoholic** er ist auf dem besten Weg, Alkoholiker zu werden; **we had to go out of our ~** wir mußten einen Umweg machen; **to go out of one's ~ to do sth** *(fig)* sich *(dat)* die Mühe machen, etw zu tun; **to feel one's ~** sich weiter-/vorwärts-/ entlangtasten; **I know my ~ about town** ich finde mich in der Stadt zurecht; **she knows her ~ about** *(fig col)* sie kennt sich aus, sie weiß Bescheid *(col)*; **to lose one's ~** sich verlaufen; *(driving)* sich verfahren; **to make one's ~ to somewhere** sich an einen Ort begeben; **can you make your own ~ to the theatre?** kannst du allein zum Theater kommen?; **to make one's ~ home** nach Hause gehen; *(start)* sich auf den Heimweg begeben; **to push one's ~ through the crowd** sich durch die Menge drängen; **to make one's ~ in the world** seinen Weg machen; **to go one's own ~** *(fig)* eigene Wege gehen; **they went their separate ~s** *(lit, fig)* ihre Wege trennten sich; **to pay one's ~** für sich selbst bezahlen; *(company, machine)* sich rentieren; **the ~ forward** der Weg vorwärts; **to go down the wrong ~** *(food, drink)* in die falsche Kehle kommen; **to prepare the ~** *(fig)* den Weg bereiten *(for sb/ sth* jdm/einer Sache*)*; **could you see your ~ to lending me a pound?** wäre es Ihnen wohl möglich, mir ein Pfund zu leihen?; **to get under ~** in Gang kommen; *(Naut)* Fahrt aufnehmen *or* machen; **to be (well) under ~** im Gang/in vollem Gang sein; *(Naut)* in (voller) Fahrt sein; *(with indication of place)* unterwegs sein.

(c) *(room for movement, path)* Weg *m*. **to block the ~** den Weg versperren; **to leave the ~ open** *(fig)* einen Weg frei lassen *(for sth* für etw*)*; **to make ~ for sb/sth** *(lit, fig)* für jdn/etw Platz machen; **to be in sb's ~** jdm im Weg sein; **to get in sb's ~** sich jdm in den Weg stellen; **it's in the ~ there** es ist dort im Weg; **I don't want to get in your ~ when you're working** ich will dich nicht beim Arbeiten stören; **to get sth out of the ~** *(move)* etw aus dem Weg räumen; *problem also, work* etw hinter sich *(acc)* bringen; **get out of the/my ~!** weg da!; **to keep out of sb's/the ~** *(not get in the ~)* (jdm) aus dem Weg bleiben; *(avoid)* (jdm) aus dem Weg gehen; **to put difficulties in**

sb's ~ jdm Hindernisse in den Weg stellen; **to stand in sb's ~** *(lit, fig)* jdm im Weg sein.

(d) *(direction)* Richtung *f*. **this ~, please** hier entlang, bitte; **he went that ~** er ging in diese Richtung; **this ~ and that** hierhin und dorthin; **which ~ are you going?** in welche Richtung gehen Sie?; **she didn't know which ~ to look** *(fig)* sie wußte nicht, wo sie hinsehen sollte; **to look the other ~** *(fig)* wegsehen; **this one is better, there are no two ~s about it** *(col)* dieses hier ist besser, da gibt es gar keinen Zweifel; **it does not matter (to me) one ~ or the other** es ist mir gleich; **either ~, we're bound to lose** (so oder so,) wir verlieren auf jeden Fall; **it's the wrong ~ up** es steht verkehrt herum; **"this ~ up"** „hier oben"; **it's the other ~ around** es ist (genau) umgekehrt.

(e) *(distance)* Weg *m*, Strecke *f*. **it rained all the ~** there es hat auf der ganzen Strecke (über) geregnet; **I'm behind you all the ~** *(fig)* ich stehe voll (und ganz) hinter Ihnen; **a little/long ~ off** nicht/sehr weit entfernt; **that's a long ~ back** *(in time)* das war schon vor einer ganzen Weile; **he'll go a long ~** *(fig)* er wird es weit bringen; **to have (still) a long ~ to go** (noch) weit vom Ziel entfernt sein; *(with practice)* (noch) viel vor sich haben; **it should go some/a long ~ towards solving the problem** das sollte bei dem Problem schon etwas/ein gutes Stück weiterhelfen; **a little kindness goes a long ~** ein bißchen Freundlichkeit hilft viel; **not by a long ~** bei weitem nicht.

(f) *(method, manners)* Art, Weise *f*. **do it this ~** machen Sie es so; **it's not the right ~ to do it** so kann man das nicht machen; **what's the best ~ to do it?** wie macht man das am besten?; **you could tell by the ~ he was dressed** das merkte man schon an seiner Kleidung; **the ~ she walks/talks** (so) wie sie geht/spricht; **do you remember the ~ it was?** erinnerst du dich noch (daran), wie es war?; **to show sb the ~ to do sth** jdm zeigen, wie *or auf* welche Art und Weise etw gemacht wird; **to do sth the hard ~** etw auf die schwierige Art (und Weise) machen; **to learn the hard ~** aus dem eigenen Schaden lernen; **we'll find a ~** wir werden (schon) einen Weg finden; **I'd rather do it my ~** ich möchte es lieber auf meine (eigene) Art machen; **that's his ~ of saying thank-you** das ist seine Art, sich zu bedanken; ~**s and means** Mittel und Wege; ~ **of life** Lebensstil *m*; *(of nation)* Lebensart *f*; ~ **of thinking** Denk(ungs)art *f*; **to my ~ of thinking** meiner Meinung *or* Auffassung nach; **a funny ~ of talking** eine komische Art, sich auszudrücken; **there are many ~s of solving the problem** es gibt viele Wege, das Problem zu lösen; **that's the ~ it goes!** so ist das eben, so ist das nun mal; **the ~ things are** so, wie die Dinge liegen; **in one ~ or another** so oder so, irgendwie; **to get** *or* **have one's (own) ~** seinen Willen durchsetzen; **have it your own ~!** wie du willst!; **you can't have it both ~s** beides zugleich geht nicht; **what a ~ to speak!** so spricht man doch nicht!; **the ~s of the Spaniards** die spanische Lebensweise; **the ~ of the world** der Lauf der Dinge; **he has a ~ with children** er versteht es, mit Kindern umzugehen.; **to get out of/into the ~ of sth** sich *(dat)* etw ab-/ angewöhnen.

(g) *(respect)* Hinsicht *f*. **in a ~** in gewisser Hinsicht *or* Weise; **in no ~** in keiner Weise; **no ~!** ausgeschlossen!; **there's no ~ I'm going to agree** ich werde auf keinen Fall zustimmen; **what have you got in the ~ of drink?** was haben Sie an Getränken?; **in every possible ~** auf jede mögliche *or* denkbare Art; **in many/some ~s** in vieler/gewisser Hinsicht; **in a big ~** *(not petty)* im großen Stil; *(on a large scale)* im großen; **in the ordinary ~** we ... normalerweise ... wir ...

(h) *(state)* Zustand *m*. he's in a bad ~ er ist in schlechter Verfassung; things are in a bad ~ die Dinge stehen schlecht.

(i) *(with by)* by the ~ übrigens; all this is by the ~ *(irrelevant)* das ist alles nebensächlich; *(extra)* das nur nebenbei; by ~ of an answer/excuse als Antwort/Entschuldigung; by ~ of illustration zur Illustration.

2 *adv* *(col)* ~ back/up weit zurück/oben; ~ back when vor langer Zeit, als; since ~ back seit Urzeiten; that was ~ back das ist schon lange her; his guess was ~ out seine Annahme war weit gefehlt.

way: ~bill *n* Frachtbrief *m*; ~farer ['weɪˌfɛərəʳ] *n* *(liter)* Wanderer *m*; ~lay *pret, ptp* ~laid *vt* *(ambush)* überfallen; *(col)* abfangen; ~-out *adj* *(col)* irre *(col)*; ~side **1** *n* *(of path, track)* Wegrand *m*; *(of road)* Straßenrand *m*; to fall by the ~side am Weges-/Straßenrand; to fall by the ~side auf der Strecke bleiben; **2** *adj* café, inn am Weg/an der Straße gelegen; ~ward ['weɪwəd] *adj (self-willed)* eigenwillig; *(capricious)* abwegig.
WC = water closet WC *nt*.
we [wiː] *pron* wir.
weak [wiːk] *adj (+er)* schwach; *character* labil; *tea, solution etc* dünn; *stomach* empfindlich. the ~er sex das schwache Geschlecht; he must be a bit ~ in the head *(col)* er ist wohl nicht ganz bei Trost *(col)*.
weaken ['wiːkən] **1** *vt (lit, fig)* schwächen; *control etc* verringern; *foundations* angreifen; *hold* lockern. **2** *vi (lit, fig)* schwächer werden, nachlassen; *(person)* schwach werden; *(foundations)* nachgeben; *(defence, strength also)* erlahmen. his grip on my arm ~ed er hielt meinen Arm nicht mehr ganz so fest.
weak-kneed ['wiːk'niːd] *adj (fig col)* schwach, feige.
weakling ['wiːklɪŋ] *n* Schwächling *m*.
weakly ['wiːklɪ] **1** *adj (dated)* schwächlich. **2** *adv* schwach.
weakness ['wiːknɪs] *n* Schwäche *f*; *(weak point)* schwacher Punkt. to have a ~ for sth eine Schwäche für etw haben.
weak-willed ['wiːk'wɪld] *adj* willensschwach.
weal [wiːl] *n (welt)* Striemen *m*.
wealth [welθ] *n* **(a)** *(fig)* Reichtum *m*. ~ tax Vermögensteuer *f*. **(b)** *(fig: abundance)* Fülle *f (of von)*.
wealthy ['welθɪ] *adj (+er)* wohlhabend, reich. the ~ *pl* die Reichen *pl*.
wean [wiːn] *vt* baby entwöhnen. to ~ sb from sth jdn einer Sache *(gen)* entwöhnen *(geh)*.
weapon ['wepən] *n (lit, fig)* Waffe *f*.
wear [wɛəʳ] *(vb: pret* wore, *ptp* worn) **1** *n* **(a)** *(use)* I've had a lot of ~ out of this jacket ich habe diese Jacke viel getragen; there isn't much ~ left in this carpet dieser Teppich hält nicht mehr lange; for casual/evening/everyday ~ für die Freizeit/den Abend/jeden Tag. **(b)** *(clothing)* Kleidung *f*. **(c)** ~ and tear Abnutzung *f*, Verschleiß *m*; fair ~ and tear normale Abnutzungserscheinungen; to show signs of ~ *(lit)* anfangen, alt auszusehen; *(fig)* angegriffen aussehen; to look the worse for ~ *(lit)* *(clothes, curtains etc)* verschlissen aussehen; *(clothes)* abgetragen aussehen; *(furniture etc)* abgenutzt aussehen; *(fig)* verbraucht aussehen; I felt a bit the worse for ~ ich fühlte mich etwas angegriffen.

2 *vt* **(a)** *clothing, jewellery etc* tragen. what shall I ~? was soll ich anziehen?; I haven't a thing to ~! ich habe nichts anzuziehen. **(b)** (~ down, ~ out) abnutzen; *clothes* abtragen; *sleeve etc* durchwetzen; *steps* austreten; *tyres* abfahren; *engine* kaputtmachen. to ~ holes in sth etw durchwetzen; *(in shoes)* etw durchlaufen; to ~ smooth *(by handling)* abgreifen; *(by walking)* austreten; *rocks* glätten. **(c)** *(col: accept, tolerate)* schlucken *(col)*.

3 *vi* **(a)** *(last)* halten; *(dress, shoes etc also)* sich tragen. she has worn well *(col)* sie hat sich gut gehalten *(col)*; the theory has worn well die Theorie hat sich bewährt. **(b)** *(become worn)* kaputtgehen; *(engine, material also)* sich abnutzen, verbraucht sein; *(tyres also)* abgefahren sein. to have worn smooth *(by water)* glattgewaschen sein; *(by weather)* verwittert sein; *(pattern)* abgegriffen sein; to ~ thin *(lit)* dünn werden; my patience is ~ing thin meine Geduld geht langsam zu Ende.

♦ **wear away 1** *vt sep (erode)* steps austreten; *rock* abschleifen, abtragen; *(hollow out)* aushöhlen; *inscription* tilgen *(geh)*; *(fig: erode)* determination untergraben. **2** *vi (rocks, rough edges etc)* sich abschleifen; *(inscription)* verwittern; *(pattern)* verwischen; *(fig: patience etc)* schwinden.

♦ **wear down 1** *vt sep* **(a)** *(reduce by friction)* abnutzen; *heel* ablaufen, abtreten; *tyre tread* abfahren. **(b)** *(fig)* person, opposition etc zermürben. **2** *vi* sich abnutzen; *(heels)* sich abtreten; *(tyre tread)* sich abfahren.

♦ **wear off** *vi* **(a)** *(diminish)* nachlassen. the novelty has worn ~ der Reiz des Neuen ist vorbei; don't worry, it'll ~ ~! keine Sorge, das gibt sich. **(b)** *(paint)* abgehen; *(plating, gilt)* sich abwetzen.

♦ **wear on** *vi* sich hinziehen; *(year)* voranschreiten. as the evening/year etc wore ~ im Laufe des Abends/Jahres etc.

♦ **wear out 1** *vt sep* **(a)** kaputtmachen; *carpet also* abtreten; *clothes, shoes* kaputttragen; *record, machinery* abnutzen. **(b)** *(exhaust)* *(physically)* erschöpfen, erledigen *(col)*; *(mentally)* fertigmachen *(col)*. to be worn ~ erschöpft or erledigt sein; *(mentally)* am Ende sein *(col)*; to ~ oneself ~ sich überanstrengen, sich kaputtmachen *(col)*. **2** *vi* kaputtgehen; *(clothes, carpets also)* verschleißen; his patience is rapidly ~ing ~ seine Geduld erschöpft sich zusehends.

♦ **wear through 1** *vt sep* durchwetzen; *soles of shoes* durchlaufen. **2** *vi* sich durchwetzen; *(soles of shoes)* sich durchlaufen.

weariness ['wɪərɪnɪs] *n see adj* **(a)** Müdigkeit *f*; Lustlosigkeit *f*; Mattheit *f*.
wearing ['wɛərɪŋ] *adj* anstrengend.
wearisome ['wɪərɪsəm] *adj* ermüdend; *(bothersome)* questions lästig; *(tedious)* discussion langweilig.
weary ['wɪərɪ] **1** *adj (+er)* **(a)** *(tired)* müde; *(fed up)* lustlos; smile, groan matt. to feel ~ müde sein; to be/grow ~ of sth etw leid sein/werden. **(b)** *(tiring)* ermüdend. for three ~ hours drei endlose Stunden (lang). **2** *vt* ermüden. **3** *vi* to ~ of sth einer Sache *(gen)* müde werden *(geh)*.
weasel ['wiːzl] *n* Wiesel *nt*.
weather ['weðəʳ] **1** *n* Wetter *nt*. in cold/this ~ bei kaltem/diesem Wetter; what's the ~ like? wie ist das Wetter?; in all ~s bei jedem Wetter; to be or feel under the ~ *(col)* angeschlagen sein *(col)*; to make heavy ~ of sth *(col)* sich mit etw fürchterlich anstellen *(col)*. **2** *vt* **(a)** *(storms, winds etc)* angreifen. **(b)** *(survive: also* ~ out) crisis etc überstehen. to ~ (out) the storm *(fig)* den Sturm überstehen. **3** *vi (rock etc)* verwittern; *(paint etc)* verblassen.
weather *in cpds* Wetter; ~-beaten *adj* face vom Wetter gegerbt; house verwittert; skin wettergegerbt; ~cock *n* Wetterhahn *m*.
weathered ['weðəd] *adj* verwittert; skin wettergegerbt.
weather: ~ forecast *n* Wettervorhersage *f*; ~man *n* Mann *m* vom Wetteramt; ~proof *adj* wetterfest; ~ report *n* Wetterbericht *m*; ~vane *n* Wetterfahne *f*.

weave [wiːv] (*vb: pret* **wove**, *ptp* **woven**) 1 *n* (*pattern of threads*) Webart *f*; (*fabric*) Gewebe *nt*. 2 *vt* (**a**) *cloth etc* weben (*into* zu); *cane, flowers* flechten (*into* zu); *web* spinnen. (**b**) (*fig*) *plot* ersinnen, erfinden; *details* einflechten (*into* +*acc*). (**c**) (*pret also* ~**d**) **to** ~ **one's way through the traffic** sich durch den Verkehr schlängeln. 3 *vi* (**a**) (*lit*) weben. (**b**) (*pret also* ~**d**) (*twist and turn*) sich schlängeln. **to** ~ **in and out through the traffic** sich durch den Verkehr schlängeln. (**c**) (*col*) **to get weaving** sich ranhalten (*col*).

weaver [ˈwiːvəʳ] *n* Weber(in *f*) *m*.

weaving [ˈwiːvɪŋ] *n* Weberei *f*; (*as craft*) Webkunst *f*.

web [web] *n* (*lit, fig*) Netz *nt*; (*of lies also*) Gespinst, Gewebe *nt*.

webbed [webd] *adj foot* Schwimm-.

webbing [ˈwebɪŋ] *n* Gurte *pl*; (*material*) Gurtband *nt*.

wed [wed] (*old, form*) *pret, ptp* ~ *or* ~**ded** 1 *vi* sich vermählen (*form*), trauen. 2 *vt* (*bride, bridegroom*) sich vermählen mit (*form*); (*priest*) vermählen (*form*). **to be** ~**ded to one's job/an idea** mit seinem Beruf verheiratet sein/einer Idee verfallen sein.

we'd [wiːd] = **we would**; **we had**.

wedded [ˈwedɪd] *adj bliss, life* Ehe-.

wedding [ˈwedɪŋ] *n* (*ceremony*) Trauung *f*; (*ceremony and festivities*) Hochzeit *f*. **to have a church** ~ sich kirchlich trauen lassen.

wedding *in cpds* Hochzeits-: ~ **anniversary** *n* Hochzeitstag *m*; ~ **breakfast** *n* Hochzeitsessen *nt*; ~ **day** *n* Hochzeitstag *m*; ~ **dress** *m* Brautkleid *nt*; ~ **night** *n* Hochzeitsnacht *f*; ~ **present** *n* Hochzeitsgeschenk *nt*; ~ **ring** *n* Trauring, Ehering *m*.

wedge [wedʒ] 1 *n* (*of wood etc, fig*) Keil *m*; (*of cake etc*) Stück *nt*; (*of cheese*) Ecke *f*. **it's the thin end of the** ~ so fängt's immer an. 2 *vt* (*in*) verkeilen, (mit einem Keil) festklemmen. **to** ~ **a door/window open/shut** eine Tür/ein Fenster festklemmen *or* verkeilen. (**b**) (*pack tightly*) **to** ~ **oneself/sth** sich/etw zwängen (*in* in +*acc*); **to be** ~**d between two things/people** zwischen zwei Dingen/Personen eingekeilt sein.

wedge-shaped [ˈwedʒʃeɪpt] *adj* keilförmig.

Wednesday [ˈwenzdɪ] *n* Mittwoch *m*; *see* **Tuesday**.

wee [wiː] *adj* (+*er*) (*col*) winzig; (*Scot*) klein. **a** ~ **bit** ein kleines bißchen.

weed [wiːd] 1 *n* (**a**) Unkraut *nt no pl*. (**b**) (*col: person*) Schwächling *m*. 2 *vti* (*lit*) jäten. ♦ **weed out** *vt sep* (*fig*) aussondern.

weeding [ˈwiːdɪŋ] **to do the** ~ Unkraut jäten.

weed-killer [ˈwiːdkɪləʳ] *n* Unkrautbekämpfungsmittel *nt*.

weedy [ˈwiːdɪ] *adj* (+*er*) (*col*) *person* (*in appearance*) schmächtig; (*in character*) blutarm.

week [wiːk] *n* Woche *f*. **it'll be ready in a** ~ in einer Woche ist es fertig; ~ **in,** ~ **out** Woche für Woche; **twice/£15 a** ~ zweimal/£ 15 in der Woche *or* pro Woche; **a** ~ **today** heute in einer Woche *or* in acht Tagen; **tomorrow** ~, **a** ~ **tomorrow** morgen in einer Woche; **for** ~**s** wochenlang; **a** ~**'s/a two** ~ **holiday** ein einwöchiger/zweiwöchiger Urlaub; **in the** ~ **ending May 15** in der Woche vom 11. Mai; **to knock sb into the middle of next** ~ (*col*) jdn windelweich schlagen (*col*).

week: ~**day** 1 *n* Wochentag *m*; 2 *attr* Wochentags-, Werktags-; ~**end** *n* Wochenende *nt*; **to go/be away for the** ~**end** übers Wochenende verreisen/nicht da sein; **at** *or* **on the** ~**end** am Wochenende; ~**end case** Reisekoffer *m*.

weekly [ˈwiːklɪ] 1 *adj* Wochen-; *visit* allwöchentlich. 2 *adv* wöchentlich. 3 *n* Wochenzeitschrift *f*.

weep [wiːp] (*vb: pret, ptp* **wept**) 1 *vi* (**a**) weinen (*over* über +*acc*). **to** ~ **for joy/rage** vor Freude/

Wut weinen; **I could have wept!** ich hätte heulen mögen. (**b**) (*wound, cut etc*) nässen. 2 *vt tears* weinen. 3 *n* **to have a good** ~ sich ausweinen.

weeping [ˈwiːpɪŋ] *n* Weinen *nt*.

weeping willow *n* Trauerweide *f*.

wee-wee [ˈwiːwiː] *n* (*baby-talk*) **to go for a** ~ Pipi machen (*col*).

weft [weft] *n* Einschlagfaden, Schußfaden *m*.

weigh [weɪ] 1 *vt* (**a**) wiegen. **could you** ~ **these bananas for me?** könnten Sie mir diese Bananen auswiegen? (**b**) (*fig*) *problem, merits etc* abwägen. **to** ~ **sth in one's mind** etw erwägen; **to** ~ **A against B** A und B gegeneinander abwägen. 2 *vi* (**a**) wiegen. (**b**) (*fig: be a burden*) lasten (*on* auf +*dat*). **it's been** ~**ing on my mind** es liegt mir auf der Seele. (**c**) (*fig: be important*) gelten. **to** ~ **with sb** Gewicht bei jdm haben; **his age** ~**ed against him** sein Alter wurde gegen ihn in die Waagschale geworfen.

♦ **weigh down** *vt sep* (*lit, fig*) niederbeugen. **she was** ~**ed** ~ **with parcels** sie war mit Paketen überladen; **to be** ~**ed** ~ **with sorrows** mit Sorgen beladen sein.

♦ **weigh in** 1 *vi* (*Sport*) **he** ~**ed** ~ **at 70 kilos** er brachte 70 Kilo auf die Waage. 2 *vt sep luggage* wiegen lassen.

♦ **weigh out** *vt sep* abwiegen.

♦ **weigh up** *vt sep alternatives, situation* abwägen; *person* einschätzen.

weigh: ~**bridge** *n* Brückenwaage *f*; ~**-in** *n* (*Sport*) Wiegen *nt*.

weighing machine [ˈweɪŋməˈʃiːn] *n* Waage *f*.

weight [weɪt] 1 *n* (**a**) Gewicht *nt*; (*Sport, esp Boxing*) Gewichtsklasse *f*; (*of blow*) Wucht, Heftigkeit *f*. 3 **kilos in** ~ ein Gewicht von 3 Kilo; **to put on/lose** ~ zunehmen/abnehmen; **I hope the chair takes my** ~ ich hoffe, der Stuhl hält mein Gewicht aus; **she's quite a** ~ sie ist ganz schön schwer. (**b**) (*fig*) (*burden*) Last *f*; (*importance*) Bedeutung *f*, Gewicht *nt*. **the** ~ **of evidence** die Beweislast; **he/his opinion carries no** ~ seine Stimme/Meinung fällt nicht ins Gewicht; **to add** ~ **to sth** einer Sache (*dat*) zusätzliches Gewicht geben; **to pull one's** ~ seinen Beitrag leisten; **to throw one's** ~ **about** (*col*) sein Gewicht geltend machen.

2 *vt* beschweren; (*fig*) *results* verfälschen. **to be** ~**ed in favour of/against sb** jdn bevorzugen/benachteiligen.

♦ **weight down** *vt sep person* (*with parcels etc*) überladen; *corpse* beschweren.

weighting [ˈweɪtɪŋ] *n* (*Brit: supplement*) Zulage *f*.

weight: ~**less** *adj* schwerelos; ~**lessness** *n* Schwerelosigkeit *f*; ~**lifter** *n* Gewichtheber *m*; ~**lifting** *n* Gewichtheben *nt*; ~**-watcher** *n* Kalorienbewußte(r) *mf*.

weighty [ˈweɪtɪ] *adj* (+*er*) (**a**) (*lit*) schwer. (**b**) (*fig*) gewichtig; *responsibility* schwer.

weir [wɪəʳ] *n* (*barrier*) Wehr *nt*.

weird [wɪəd] *adj* (+*er*) (*uncanny*) unheimlich; (*col: odd*) seltsam.

weirdo [ˈwɪədəʊ] *n* (*col*) verrückter Typ (*col*).

welcome [ˈwelkəm] 1 *n* Willkommen *nt*. **to give sb a warm** ~ jdm einen herzlichen Empfang bereiten; **to meet with a cold/warm** ~ einen kühlen/herzlichen Empfang bekommen; **to bid sb** ~ (*form*) jdn willkommen heißen; **what sort of a** ~ **will this product get from the public?** wie wird das Produkt von der Öffentlichkeit aufgenommen werden?

2 *adj* willkommen; *visitor also* gerngesehen *attr*; *news also* angenehm. **the money is very** ~ **just now** das Geld kommt gerade jetzt sehr gelegen; **to make sb** ~ jdn sehr freundlich empfangen; **you're** ~! nichts zu danken!, aber gerne!; (*iro*) wenn's Ihnen Spaß macht!; **you're** ~ **to use my room** Sie können auch mein Zimmer benutzen.

3 *vt (lit, fig)* begrüßen, willkommen heißen.
4 *interj* ~ **home/to Scotland!** willkommen daheim/in Schottland!
welcoming ['welkəmɪŋ] *adj* zur Begrüßung; *smile, gesture* einladend.
weld [weld] **1** *vt* **(a)** *(Tech)* schweißen. **to** ~ **parts together** Teile zusammenschweißen *or* verschweißen; **to** ~ **sth on** etw anschweißen *(to* an +*acc).* **(b)** *(fig: also* ~ **together)** zusammenschmieden *(into* zu*).* **2** *n* Schweißnaht *f.*
welder ['weldə^r] *n (person)* Schweißer(in *f) m; (machine)* Schweißgerät *nt.*
welding ['weldɪŋ] *n* Schweißen *nt.* ~ **torch** Schweißbrenner *m.*
welfare ['welfɛə^r] *n* **(a)** *(well-being)* Wohl, Wohlergehen *nt.* **(b)** *(~ work, social security)* Fürsorge *f.* **child** ~ Kinderfürsorge *f.*
welfare: ~ **state** *n* Wohlfahrtsstaat *m;* ~ **worker** *n* Fürsorger(in *f) m.*
well[1] [wel] *n (water ~)* Brunnen *m; (oil ~)* Ölquelle *f; (fig: source)* Quelle *f; (for lift)* Schacht *m; (of stairs)* Treppenhaus *nt.*
♦ **well up** *vi (water)* emporsteigen, emporquellen; *(fig)* aufsteigen. **tears** ~**ed** ~ **in her eyes** Tränen stiegen ihr in die Augen.

well[2] *comp* **better,** *superl* **best 1** *adv* **(a)** gut. **he did it as** ~ **as he could** er machte es so gut er konnte; **he's doing** ~ **at school** er ist gut in der Schule; **he did** ~ **in the exam** er hat in der Prüfung gut abgeschnitten; **his business is doing** ~ sein Geschäft geht gut; **the patient is doing** ~ dem Patienten geht es gut; **if you do** ~ **you'll be promoted** wenn Sie sich bewähren, werden Sie befördert; **he has done** ~ **for himself** er hat es zu etwas gebracht; **you did** ~ **to help** es war gut, daß du geholfen hast; **he really did** ~ **there** das war wirklich eine Leistung von ihm; ~ **done!** gut gemacht!, bravo!; ~ **played!** gut gespielt!; **to do oneself** ~ *(col)* es sich *(dat)* gut gehen lassen; **everything went** ~ es ging alles gut; **to speak/think** ~ **of sb** über jdn Gutes sagen/positiv denken; **to be** ~ **in with sb** *(col)* auf gutem Fuß mit jdm stehen; **to do** ~ **out of sth** von etw ganz schön *or* ordentlich profitieren; **we were** ~ **beaten** wir sind gründlich geschlagen worden; **all** *or* **only too** ~ nur *(all)*zu gut; ~ **and truly** (ganz) gründlich; *married, settled* in ganz richtig; **he was** ~ **away** *(col)* er war in Fahrt *(col); (drunk)* er hatte einen sitzen *(col);* **it was** ~ **worth the trouble** das hat sich sehr gelohnt; ~ **out of sight** weit außer Sichtweite; ~ **within** ... durchaus in *(+dat)* ...; ~ **past midnight** lange nach Mitternacht; **he's** ~ **over fifty** er ist einiges *or* weit über fünfzig; ~ **over a thousand** weit über tausend.
 (b) *(probably, reasonably)* weiteres, gut, wohl. **I may** ~ **not come** es kann ohne weiteres sein, daß ich nicht komme; **it may** ~ **be that** ... es ist gut *or* ohne weiteres möglich, daß ...; **you may** ~ **be right** Sie mögen wohl recht haben; **she cried, as** ~ **she might** sie weinte, wozu sie auch allen Grund hatte; **you may** ~ **ask!** *(iro)* das kann man wohl fragen; **you might as** ~ **have stayed at home** du hättest genausogut zu Hause bleiben können; **I couldn't very** ~ **stay** ich konnte schlecht bleiben; **you might as** ~ **go** du könntest eigentlich ebensogut gehen; **are you coming?** — **I might as** ~ kommst du? — ach, warum nicht.
 (c) *(in addition)* **as** ~ auch; **x as** ~ **as y** x sowohl als auch y.

2 *adj* **(a)** *(in good health)* gesund. **get** ~ **soon!** gute Besserung; **I'm very** ~**, thanks** danke, es geht mir sehr gut; **she's not been** ~ **lately** ihr ging es in letzter Zeit (gesundheitlich) gar nicht gut; **I don't feel at all** ~ ich fühle mich gar nicht gut *or* wohl.
 (b) *(satisfactory)* gut. **all is not** ~ **with him** mit ihm steht es nicht zum besten; **that's all very** ~**,** but ... das ist ja alles schön und gut, aber ...; **it's all very** ~ **for you to say that** Sie haben gut reden; **it would be as** ~ **to ask first** es wäre wohl besser, sich erst mal zu erkundigen; **it's just as** ~ **he came** es ist (nur) gut, daß er gekommen ist; **you're** ~ **out of it** seien Sie froh, daß Sie nichts (mehr) damit zu tun haben; **all's** ~ **that ends** ~ Ende gut, alles gut.

3 *interj* **(a)** *(expectantly also)* na; *(doubtfully)* na ja. ~ ~ !, ~ **I never** also so was!, na so was!; ~ **now** also; ~ **then** also (gut); *(in question)* na?, also?; **very** ~ **then!** na gut, also gut; *(indignantly)* also bitte.
 4 *n* Gute(s) *nt.* **to wish sb** ~ *(in general)* jdm alles Gute wünschen; *(in an attempt, iro)* jdm Glück wünschen *(in* bei*).*
we'll [wiːl] = **we shall; we will.**
well *in cpds* gut; ~**-advised** *adj* **you'd be** ~**-advised to** ... du tätest gut daran, zu ...; ~**-balanced** *adj person* ausgeglichen; *scheme, diet* (gut) ausgewogen; ~**-behaved** *adj child* artig, wohlerzogen; *animal* guterzogen *attr;* ~**-being** *n* Wohl, Wohlergehen *nt;* ~**-bred** *adj person* wohlerzogen; *accent* distinguiert; ~**-built** *adj house* gut *or* solide gebaut; *person* stämmig, kräftig; ~**-chosen** *adj words* gut gewählt; ~**-developed** *adj muscle* gutentwickelt *attr; sense* (gut) ausgeprägt; ~**-disposed** *adj* **to be** ~**-disposed towards sb/sth** jdm/einer Sache freundlich gesonnen sein; ~**-done** *adj steak* durchgebraten, durch *inv;* ~**-dressed** *adj* gut angezogen *or* gekleidet; ~**-earned** *adj* wohlverdient; ~**-educated** *adj person* gebildet; ~**-founded** *adj* wohlbegründet *attr;* ~**-heeled** *(col)* betucht; ~**-informed** *adj* gutinformiert *attr; sources also* gutunterrichtet *attr;* **to be** ~**-informed about** sth über etw gut informiert sein.
wellington (boot) ['welɪŋtən('buːt)] *n (Brit)* Gummistiefel *m.*
well: ~**-kept** *adj garden, hair etc* gepflegt; *secret* streng gehütet; ~**-known** *adj* bekannt; **it's** ~**-known that** ... es ist allgemein bekannt, daß ...; ~**-meaning** *adj* wohlmeinend *attr;* ~**-meant** *adj action* gutgemeint *attr;* ~**-nigh** *adv* nahezu, beinahe; ~**-off** *adj (affluent)* reich, gut d(a)ran *(col);* **you don't know when you're** ~**-off** *(col)* du weißt (ja) nicht, wann es dir gut geht; ~**-preserved** *adj* guterhalten *attr;* ~**-read** *adj* belesen; ~**-spent** *adj time* gut genützt *or* verbracht; *money* sinnvoll ausgegeben; ~**-spoken** *adj* mit gutem Deutsch/Englisch *etc;* **to be** ~**-spoken** gutes Deutsch/Englisch *etc* sprechen; ~**-stocked** *adj* gutbestückt *attr; (Comm) also* mit gutem Sortiment; *larder, shelves also* reichlich gefüllt; ~**-timed** *adj* (zeitlich) gut abgepaßt *attr;* ~**-to-do** *adj* wohlhabend, reich; *district* Reichen-; ~**-wisher** *n* **our cause has many** ~**-wishers** unsere Sache hat viele Sympathisanten; **"from a** ~**-wisher"** „jemand, der es gut mit Ihnen meint"; ~**-worn** *adj garment* abgetragen; *carpet etc* abgelaufen; *path* ausgetreten; *saying etc* abgedroschen.
welsh [welʃ] *vi* **to** ~ **on sb** *(col)* jdn (auf)sitzen lassen.
Welsh [welʃ] **1** *adj* walisisch. **2** *n* **(a)** *(language)* Walisisch *nt.* **(b) the** ~ *pl* die Waliser *pl.*
Welsh: ~**man** *n* Waliser *m;* ~ **rarebit** *n* überbackene Käseschnitte; ~**woman** *n* Waliserin *f.*
welt [welt] *n (weal)* Striemen *m.*
welterweight ['weltəweɪt] *n* Weltergewicht *nt.*
wend [wend] *vt* **to** ~ **one's way home** sich auf den Heimweg begeben.
went [went] *pret of* **go.**
wept [wept] *pret, ptp of* **weep.**
were [wɜː] *2nd pers sing, 1st, 2nd, 3rd pers pl pret of* **be.**
we're [wɪə^r] = **we are.**
weren't [wɜːnt] = **were not.**
werewolf ['wɪəwulf] *n* Werwolf *m.*

west [west] **1** *n* **(a)** Westen *m*. **in/to the ~** im/nach Westen; **to the ~ of** westlich von, im Westen von; **the wind is blowing from the ~** der Wind kommt von West(en). **(b)** *(western world)* **the W~** der Westen. **2** *adj* West-, westlich. **3** *adv* nach Westen, westwärts. **it faces ~** es geht nach Westen; **~ of** westlich von; **to go ~** *(fig col)* flöten gehen *(col)*.

west *in cpds* West-; **W~ Berlin** *n* Westberlin *nt*; **~-bound** *adj traffic* in Richtung Westen.

westerly ['westəlɪ] *adj* westlich.

western ['westən] **1** *adj* westlich. **W~ Europe** Westeuropa *nt*. **2** *n* Western *m*.

westerner ['westənəʳ] *n* Abendländer(in *f*) *m*.

westernized ['westənaɪzd] *adj culture* vom Westen beeinflußt; *(pej)* verwestlicht.

West: **~ German 1** *adj* westdeutsch, bundesdeutsch; **2** *n* Westdeutsche(r) *mf*; **~ Germany** *n* Westdeutschland *nt*, Bundesrepublik *f* (Deutschland); **~ Indian 1** *adj* westindisch; **2** *n* Westindier(in *f*) *m*; **~ Indies** *npl* Westindische Inseln *pl*.

west: **~ward(s)** [westwəd(z)], **~wardly** [-wədlɪ] **1** *adj* westlich; **in a ~wardly direction** (in) Richtung Westen; **2** *adv* westwärts, nach Westen.

wet [wet] *(vb: pret, ptp ~ or ~ted)* **1** *adj* *(+er)* **(a)** naß. **to be ~ through** durch und durch naß sein, völlig durchnäßt sein; **"~ paint"** „frisch gestrichen"; **to get one's feet ~** sich *(dat)* nasse Füße holen *(col)*. **(b)** *(rainy)* naß, feucht; *climate, country* feucht. **the ~ season** die Regenzeit; **in ~ weather** bei nassem Wetter. **(c)** *(Brit col: weak, spiritless)* weichlich, lasch. **2** *n* **(a)** *(moisture)* Feuchtigkeit *f*. **(b)** *(rain)* Nässe *f*. **it's out in the ~** es ist draußen im Nassen. **(c)** *(Brit col: person)* Waschlappen *m (col)*. **3** *vt* naß machen; *lips, washing* befeuchten. **to ~ the bed/one's pants/oneself** ins Bett/in die Hose(n) machen/ sich naß machen.

wet: **~ blanket** *n (col)* Miesmacher(in *f*) *m (col)*; **~suit** *n* Taucheranzug *m*.

we've [wiːv] = **we have.**

whack [wæk] **1** *n* **(a)** *(blow)* (knallender) Schlag. **(b)** *(col: attempt)* Versuch *m*. **to have a ~ at sth** etw probieren or versuchen. **(c)** *(col: share)* (An)teil *m*. **2** *vt* **(a)** *(hit)* schlagen, hauen *(col)*. **(b)** *(col: defeat)* (haushoch) schlagen.

whacked [wækt] *adj (col: exhausted)* kaputt *(col)*.

whacking ['wækɪŋ] *adj (Brit col)*: **a ~ great** ... ein(e) Mords- ... *(col)*.

whale [weɪl] *n* **(a)** Wal *m*. **(b)** *(col)* **to have a ~ of a time** sich prima amüsieren.

whaler ['weɪləʳ] *n (person, ship)* Walfänger *m*.

wharf [wɔːf] *n, pl* **-s** *or* **wharves** [wɔːvz] Kai *m*.

what [wɒt] **1** *pron* **(a)** *(interrog)* was. **~'s the weather like?** wie ist das Wetter?; **~'s that to you?** was geht dich das an?; **~ for?** wozu?, wofür?; **~'s that tool for?** wofür ist das Werkzeug?; **~ did you do that for?** warum hast du das gemacht?; **~'s the German for ...?** wie heißt ... auf deutsch?; **~ did he agree to?** wozu hat er zugestimmt?; **~ about ...?** wie wär's mit ...?; **you know that pub? — ~ about it?** kennst du die Kneipe? — was ist damit?; **~ if ...?** was ist, wenn ...?; **so ~?** *(col)* na und?; **~ does it matter?** was macht das schon?; **~'s-his/-her/-its name** *(col)* der/die/das Dings(da) *(col)*.

(b) *(rel)* was. **that is not ~ I asked for** danach habe ich nicht gefragt; **he agrees with ~ I say** er stimmt mit dem überein, was ich sage; **that's exactly ~ I said** genau das habe ich gesagt; **do you know ~ you are looking for?** weißt du, wonach du suchst?; **come ~ may** komme was wolle; **and ~'s more** und außerdem, und noch dazu; **~ with one thing and another I didn't have time** wie es sich so ergab, hatte ich keine Zeit; **he knows ~'s ~** *(col)* er kennt sich aus, der weiß Bescheid *(col)*; **and ~ have you** *(col)*, **and ~ not**

(col) und was sonst noch alles; **(I'll) tell you ~** *(col)* weißt du was?; **to give sb ~ for** *(col)* es jdm ordentlich geben *(col)*.

2 *adj* **(a)** *(interrog)* welche(r, s), was für ein/ eine *(col)*. **~ age is he?** wie alt ist er?; **~ good would that be?** *(col)* wozu sollte das gut sein? **(b)** *(rel)* der/die/das. **~ little I had** das wenige, das ich hatte; **buy ~ food you like** kauf das Essen, das du willst. **(c)** *(in set constructions)* **~ sort of** was für ein/eine; **~ else** was noch; **~ more** was mehr. **(d)** *(in interj)* **~ a man!** was für ein Mann!; **~ luck!** was für ein Glück, so ein Glück; **~ a fool I've been/I am!** ich Idiot!; **~ terrible weather** was für ein scheußliches Wetter. **3** *interj* was!

whatever [wɒt'evəʳ] **1** *pron* **(a)** **~ you like** was (immer) du (auch) möchtest; **... or ~ they're called** ... oder wie sie sonst heißen; **or ~** oder sonst (so) etwas. **(b)** *(interrog)* **~ does he want?** was will er wohl?; *(impatiently)* was, zum Kuckuck, will er denn?; **~ do you mean?** was meinst du denn bloß? **2** *adj* **(a)** welche(r, s) (auch). **~ book you choose** welches Buch Sie auch wählen; **for ~ reasons** aus welchen Gründen auch immer. **(b)** *(with neg)* überhaupt, absolut. **nothing/no man ~** überhaupt gar nichts/niemand überhaupt; **it's of no use ~** es hat absolut keinen Sinn. **(c)** *(interrog)* **~ reason can he have?** was für einen Grund kann er bloß or wohl haben?; **~ else will he do?** was wird er wohl noch alles machen?

what's [wɒts] = **what is; what has.**

whatsit ['wɒtsɪt] *n (col)* Dingsbums *nt (col)*.

whatsoever [,wɒtsəu'evəʳ] *pron, adj see* **whatever 1 (a), 2 (a, b).**

wheat [wiːt] **1** *n* Weizen *m*. **2** *attr* **~germ** Weizenkeim *m*.

wheedle ['wiːdl] *vt* **to ~ one's way into sth** *into organization, sb's confidence* sich in etw einschleichen; *into position* sich in etw hineinmanövrieren; **to ~ sth out of sb** jdm etw abschmeicheln.

wheel [wiːl] **1** *n* **(a)** Rad *nt*; *(steering ~)* Lenkrad *nt*; *(Naut)* Steuer(rad) *nt*; *(roulette ~)* Drehscheibe *f*; *(potter's ~)* (Töpfer)scheibe *f*. **at the ~** *(lit)* am Steuer; *(fig also)* am Ruder; **to take the ~** das Steuer übernehmen; **~ of fortune** Glücksrad *nt*. **(b)** *(Mil)* Schwenkung *f*. **2** *vt* **(a)** *(push)* bicycle, pram schieben; *(pull)* ziehen; *(invalid)* wheelchair fahren. **(b)** *(cause to turn)* drehen. **3** *vi* **(a)** *(turn)* drehen; *(birds, planes)* kreisen; *(Mil)* schwenken. **to ~ left** nach links schwenken.

♦ **wheel around** *vi* sich (rasch) umdrehen; *(troops)* (ab)schwenken.

wheel: **~barrow** *n* Schubkarre *f*, Schubkarren *m*; **~base** *n* Rad(ab)stand *m*; **~chair** *n* Rollstuhl *m*.

wheeler-dealer ['wiːlə'diːləʳ] *n (col)* Schlitzohr *nt (col)*; *(in finance also)* Geschäftemacher *m*.

wheeze [wiːz] *vi* pfeifend atmen; *(machines, asthmatic)* keuchen.

whelk [welk] *n* Wellhornschnecke *f*.

when [wen] **1** *adv* **(a)** wann. **since ~ have you been here?** seit wann sind Sie hier?; **say ~!** *(col)* sag' halt! **(b)** *(rel)* **on the day ~** an dem Tag, an dem; **at the time ~** zu der Zeit, als or wo *(col)*; **during the time ~** he was in Germany während der Zeit, als or wo er in Deutschland war; **that's ~ it's important** genau dann ist es wichtig.

2 *conj* **(a)** wenn; *(with past reference)* als. **you can go ~ I have finished** du kannst gehen, sobald or wenn ich fertig bin; **~ I was in London** als ich in London war; **each time ~ I was in London** jedesmal, wenn ich in London war. **(b)** **be careful ~ crossing the road** seien Sie vorsichtig, wenn Sie über die Straße gehen; **the Prime Minister is coming here in May, ~ he'll** ... der Premier kommt im Mai hierher und wird dann

... (c) *(although, whereas)* wo ... doch. **why do you do it that way ~ it would be much easier like this?** warum machst du es denn auf die Art, wo es doch so viel einfacher wäre?

whence [wens] *adv* (*old*) woher.

whenever [wen'evəʳ] *adv* **(a)** *(each time)* jedesmal wenn. **(b)** *(at whatever time)* wann (auch) immer; *(as soon as)* sobald. **~ you like!** wann du willst! **(c)** *(emph)* **~ can he have done it?** wann kann er das nur *or* wohl getan haben?

where [wɛəʳ] **1** *adv* wo. **~ (to)** wohin, wo ... hin; **~ (from)** woher, wo ... her; **~ are you going (to)?** wohin gehst du, wo gehst du hin?; **~ to, sir?** wohin (wollen Sie) bitte?; **~ are you from?** wo kommen Sie her?; **from ~ I'm sitting I can see the church** von meinem Platz aus kann ich die Kirche sehen; **~ should we be if ...?** was wäre nur, wenn ...?

2 *conj* wo; *(in the place where)* da, wo ..., an der Stelle, wo ... **go ~ you like** geh, wohin du willst; **the bag is ~ you left it** die Tasche ist da, wo du sie liegengelassen hast; **this is ~ we got out** hier sind wir ausgestiegen; **that's ~ Nelson fell/I used to live** hier *or* an dieser Stelle fiel Nelson/ hier *or* da habe ich (früher) gewohnt; **I've read up to ~ the king** ... ich habe bis dahin gelesen, wo der König ...; **we succeeded ~ we expected to fail** wir hatten da Erfolg, wo wir ihn nicht erwartet hatten; **~ money is concerned** wo es ums Geld geht.

whereabouts [,wɛərə'bauts] **1** *adv* wo, in welcher Gegend. **2** ['wɛərəbauts] *n sing or pl* Verbleib *m*; *(of people also)* Aufenthaltsort *m*.

whereas [wɛər'æz] *conj* *(whilst)* während; *(while on the other hand)* wohingegen.

whereby [wɛə'baɪ] *adv* *(form)* **the sign ~ you will recognize him** das Zeichen, an dem *or* woran Sie ihn erkennen; **the rule ~ it is not allowed** die Vorschrift, wonach es verboten ist.

wherever [wɛər'evəʳ] **1** *conj* **~ it came from** egal, woher es kommt, woher es auch kommt; **we'll go ~ you like** wir gehen, wohin Sie wollen; **~ you see this sign** überall, wo Sie dieses Zeichen sehen. **2** *adv* **~ have I seen that before?** wo habe ich das nur *or* bloß schon gesehen?; **in London or Liverpool or ~** in London oder Liverpool oder sonstwo.

wherewithal ['wɛəwɪðɔ:l] *n* *(money)* nötiges Kleingeld; *(implements)* Utensilien *pl*.

whet [wet] *vt* *knife* wetzen; *axe* schleifen, schärfen; *appetite, curiosity* anregen.

whether ['weðəʳ] *conj* ob. **I am not certain ~ or not they're coming** ich bin nicht sicher, ob sie kommen oder nicht; **~ they come or not, we'll ...** ob sie kommen oder nicht, wir ...; **he's not sure ~ to go or stay** er weiß nicht, ob er gehen oder bleiben soll.

whew [hwu:] *interj* puh, uff.

whey [weɪ] *n* Molke *f*.

which [wɪtʃ] **1** *adj* **(a)** *(interrog)* welche(r, s). **~ one?** welche(r, s)?; *(of people also)* wer? **(b)** *(rel)* welche(r, s). **... by ~ time I was asleep** ... und zu dieser Zeit schlief ich bereits; **look at it ~ way you will** ... man kann es sehen, wie man will ...

2 *pron* **(a)** *(interrog)* welche(r, s); *(of people also)* wer. **~ of the children?** welches Kind?; **~ is ~?** *(of people)* wer ist wer? *(of things)* welche(r, s) ist welche(r, s)? **(b)** *(rel)* der/die/das, welche(r, s) *(geh)*. **the bear ~ I saw** der Bär, den ich sah; **at ~ he remarked** ... worauf er bemerkte, ...; **it rained hard, ~ upset her** es regnete stark, was sie aufregte; **from ~ we deduce that** ... woraus wir ableiten, daß ...; **after ~ we went to bed** worauf *or* wonach wir zu Bett gingen; **the shelf on ~ I put it** das Brett, auf das *or* worauf ich es gelegt habe.

whichever [wɪtʃ'evəʳ] **1** *adj* welche(r, s) auch immer; *(no matter which)* ganz gleich *or* egal

welche(r, s). **2** *pron* welche(r, s) auch immer. **~ (of you) has the most money** wer immer (von euch) das meiste Geld hat.

whiff [wɪf] *n* *(puff)* Zug *m*; *(wisp)* kleine Fahne, Wolke *f*; *(smell)* Hauch *m*; *(fig: trace)* Spur *f*. **to catch a ~ of sth** den Geruch von etw wahrnehmen.

while [waɪl] **1** *n* Weile *f*, Weilchen *nt* *(col)*. **for a ~** *(für)* eine Weile, eine Zeitlang; *(a short moment)* *(für)* einen Moment; **a good *or* long ~** eine ganze Weile *or* Zeitlang; **for/after quite a ~** ziemlich lange/nach einer ziemlich langen Zeit; **a little *or* short ~** ein Weilchen *(col)*, kurze Zeit; **it'll be ready in a short ~** es wird bald fertig sein; **a little/long ~ ago** vor kurzem/vor längerer *or* langer Zeit; **some ~ ago** vor einiger Zeit; **all the ~** die ganze Zeit (über); **to be worth (one's) ~ to** ... sich (für jdn) lohnen, zu ...; **we'll make it worth your ~** es soll ihr Schaden nicht sein.

2 *conj* **(a)** *(during)* während; *(as long as)* solange. **she fell asleep ~ reading** sie schlief beim Lesen ein. **(b)** *(although)* **~ one must admit there are difficulties** ... man muß zwar zugeben, daß es Schwierigkeiten gibt, trotzdem ...; **~ the text is not absolutely perfect, nevertheless** ... obwohl der Text nicht einwandfrei ist, ... trotzdem ... **(c)** *(whereas)* während. **I always drink tea ~ she drinks coffee** ich bin Teetrinker, während sie Kaffeetrinkerin ist.

♦ **while away** *vt sep* *time* sich *(dat)* vertreiben.

whilst [waɪlst] *conj* = **while 2**.

whim [wɪm] *n* Laune *f*. **her every ~** jede ihrer Launen.

whimper ['wɪmpəʳ] **1** *n* *(of dog)* Winseln *nt no pl*; *(of person)* Wimmern *nt no pl*. **without a ~** ohne einen (Klage)laut. **2** *vti* *(dog)* winseln; *(person)* wimmern.

whimsical ['wɪmzɪkəl] *adj* wunderlich; *look, remark* neckisch; *idea, tale* schnurrig.

whine [waɪn] **1** *n* *(of dog)* Jaulen, Heulen *nt no pl*; *(complaining cry)* Jammern, Gejammer *nt no pl*; *(of child)* Quengelei *f no pl*; *(of siren, jet engine)* Heulen *nt no pl*; *(of bullet)* Pfeifen *nt no pl*. **2** *vi* *(dog)* jaulen; *(person: speak, complain)* jammern, klagen; *(child)* quengeln; *(siren, jet engine)* heulen; *(bullet)* pfeifen. **don't come whining to me if** ... du brauchst mir nichts vorzujammern, wenn ...

whinny ['wɪnɪ] **1** *n* Wiehern *nt no pl*. **2** *vi* wiehern.

whip [wɪp] **1** *n* **(a)** Peitsche *f*; *(riding ~)* Reitgerte *f*. **(b)** *(Parl)* *(person)* Fraktionsführer *m*; *(call)* Anordnung *f* des Fraktionsführers. **three-line ~** Fraktionszwang *m*. **(c)** *(Cook)* Creme, Speise *f*. **2** *vt* **(a)** *(with whip)* *people* auspeitschen; *horse* peitschen; *(with stick etc)* schlagen. **(b)** *(Cook)* schlagen. **(c)** *(fig: move quickly)* **he ~ped the book off the desk** er schnappte sich *(dat)* das Buch vom Schreibtisch; **he ~ped his hand out of the way** er zog blitzschnell seine Hand weg; **he ~ped a gun out of his pocket** er zog rasch eine Pistole aus der Tasche. **(d)** *(col: steal)* mitgehen lassen *(col)*. **3** *vi* **he ~ped around when he heard** ... er fuhr herum, als er hörte ...; **he's just ~ped out for a minute** *(col)* er ist nur schnell mal rausgegangen *(col)*.

♦ **whip up** *vt sep* **(a)** *(pick up)* schnappen. **(b)** *(set in motion)* *horses* antreiben; *(Cook)* *cream* schlagen; *mixture* verrühren; *(col: prepare quickly)* *meal* hinzaubern; *(fig: stir up)* *feeling* anheizen, entfachen; *support* fändern; *audience, crowd* mitreißen.

whip: **~cord** *n* *(rope)* Peitschenschnur *f*; *(fabric)* Whipcord *m*; **~ hand** *n* **to have the ~ hand (over sb)** (über jdn) die Oberhand haben; **~lash** *n* (Peitschen)riemen *m*; *(Med)* Peitschenhiebverletzung *f*.

whipped cream ['wɪpt'kri:m] *n* Schlagsahne *f*.

whippet ['wɪpɪt] *n* Whippet *m* *(eine Hundeart)*.

whipping ['wɪpɪŋ] n (beating) Tracht f Prügel; (col: defeat) Niederlage f; (fig: in debate etc) Pleite f (col).

whipping: ~ **boy** n Prügelknabe m; ~ **cream** n Schlagsahne f.

whip-round ['wɪpraʊnd] n (esp Brit col) to have a ~ den Hut herumgehen lassen.

whirl [wɜːl] **1** n (spin) Wirbeln nt no pl; (of dust, water etc, also fig) Wirbel m; (of cream etc) Tupfer m. to give sb/sth a ~ (fig col: try out) jdn/etw ausprobieren; the social ~ das gesellschaftliche Leben; my head is in a ~ mir schwirrt der Kopf. **2** vt (make turn) wirbeln. to ~ sb/sth around jdn/etw herumwirbeln. **3** vi (spin) wirbeln; (water) strudeln. to ~ around herumwirbeln; (water) strudeln; (person: turn quickly) herumfahren; my head is ~ing mir schwirrt der Kopf; to ~ past (time, countryside) vorbeirauschen.

whirlpool ['wɜːlpuːl] n Strudel m.

whirlwind ['wɜːlwɪnd] n Wirbelwind m. like a ~ wie der Wirbelwind; a ~ romance eine stürmische Romanze.

whirr [wɜːᵣ] **1** n (of wings) Schwirren nt; (of wheels, machine) (quiet) Surren nt; (louder) Dröhnen nt. **2** vi see n schwirren; surren; dröhnen.

whisk [wɪsk] **1** n (Cook) Schneebesen m; (electric) Rührgerät nt. give the eggs a good ~ schlagen Sie die Eier gut durch; with a ~ of its tail mit einem Schwanzschlag. **2** vt (Brit Cook) schlagen; eggs verquirlen. to ~ the eggs into the mixture die Eier unter die Masse einrühren.

♦ **whisk away** vt sep the magician ~ed ~ the tablecloth der Zauberer zog das Tischtuch schnell weg; the kidnappers ~ed him ~ die Entführer sausten mit ihm davon.

whisker ['wɪskəᵣ] n Schnurrhaar nt; (of people) Barthaar nt. ~s (moustache, Zool) Schnurrbart m; (side ~s) Backenbart m. to win/miss sth by a ~ etw fast gewinnen/etw um Haaresbreite verpassen.

whisky, (US, Ir) **whiskey** ['wɪskɪ] n Whisky m. two whiskies, please zwei Whisky, bitte.

whisper ['wɪspəᵣ] **1** n (a) Geflüster, Flüstern nt no pl; (of wind) Wispern nt no pl; (mysterious) Raunen nt no pl. to speak in a ~ im Flüstern sprechen. (b) (rumour) Gerücht nt. there are ~s (going around) that ... es geht das Gerücht, daß ... **2** vt (a) flüstern, wispern. to ~ sth to sb jdm etw zuflüstern. (b) (rumour) it's (being) ~ed that ... es geht das Gerücht, daß ..., man munkelt, daß ... **3** vi flüstern, wispern (also fig); (wind) säuseln; (schoolchildren) tuscheln. to ~ to sb jdm zuflüstern; mit jdm tuscheln.

whist [wɪst] n Whist nt.

whistle ['wɪsl] **1** n (a) (sound) Pfiff m; (of wind) Pfeifen nt; (of kettle) Pfeifton m. to give a ~ einen Pfiff ausstoßen. (b) (instrument) Pfeife f. to blow a ~ pfeifen; they searched him but he was as clean as a ~ (col) sie durchsuchten ihn, aber er war blitzsauber (col); it broke off as clean as a ~ (col) es ist ganz glatt abgebrochen. **2** vti pfeifen. the boys ~d at her die Jungen pfiffen ihr nach; the crowd ~d at the referee die Menge pfiff den Schiedsrichter aus; the refereee ~d for a foul der Schiedsrichter pfiff ein Foul; he can ~ for it (col) da kann er lange warten.

whistle-stop ['wɪsl,stɒp] adj ~ tour (US Pol) Wahlreise f, (fig) Reise f mit Kurzaufenthalten an allen Orten.

whit [wɪt] n not a ~ keine Spur; (of truth, common sense) kein Gramm or Körnchen.

white [waɪt] **1** adj weiß; (with fear, anger etc) blaß, kreidebleich. to go or turn ~ (thing) weiß werden; (person) bleich or blaß werden. **2** n (colour) Weiß nt; (person) Weiße(r) mf; (of egg) Eiweiß nt; (of eye) Weiße(s) nt. ~s (household) Weißwäsche f; (Sport) weiße Kleidung.

white: ~**bait** n, pl ~**bait** Breitling m; ~ **coffee** n (Brit) Kaffee m mit Milch; ~**-collar** adj ~**-collar worker** Angestellte(r) mf; ~**-collar crime** Wirtschaftskriminalität f; ~**-collar job** Angestelltenstelle f, Büroposten m; ~ **elephant** n nutzloser Gegenstand; (waste of money) Fehlinvestition f; ~ **elephant stall** n Stand m mit allerlei Krimskrams; ~**-haired** adj weißhaarig; W~**hall** n if W~**hall decides** ... wenn London beschließt ...; ~ **horse** n Schimmel m; (wave) Welle f mit einer Schaumkrone; ~**-hot** adj weißglühend; (fig) glühend; the W~ **House** n das Weiße Haus; ~ **lie** n kleine Unwahrheit, Notlüge f; ~ **man** n Weiße(r) m; ~ **meat** n helles Fleisch.

whiten ['waɪtn] **1** vt weiß machen. **2** vi weiß werden.

whiteness ['waɪtnɪs] n Weiße f; (of skin) Helligkeit f; (due to illness etc) Blässe f.

whitening ['waɪtnɪŋ] n weiße Farbe, Schlämmkreide f.

white: ~ **paper** n (Pol) Weißbuch nt; ~ **sauce** n Mehlsoße f, helle Soße; ~ **spirit** n Terpentinersatz m; ~**wash 1** n Tünche f; (fig) Schönfärberei f; **2** vt walls tünchen; (fig) beschönigen; ~ **wedding** n Hochzeit f in Weiß; ~ **wine** n Weißwein m. ~ **woman** n Weiße f.

whither ['wɪðəᵣ] adv (a) (old) wohin. (b) (journalese) ~ socialism? Sozialismus, was nun?

whiting ['waɪtɪŋ] n, pl ~ Weißling, Weißfisch m.

whitish ['waɪtɪʃ] adj colour weißlich.

Whit Monday [,wɪt'mʌndɪ] n Pfingstmontag m.

Whitsun ['wɪtsən] **1** n Pfingsten nt. **2** attr Pfingst-.

whittle ['wɪtl] vt schnitzen.

♦ **whittle away** vt sep (a) bark etc wegschneiden. (b) (gradually reduce) allmählich abbauen; rights, power etc also allmählich beschneiden.

♦ **whittle down** vt sep (a) piece of wood herunterschneiden. to ~ to size zurechtschneiden. (b) (reduce) kürzen, stutzen; gap, difference verringern. to ~ sth ~ to sth etw auf etw (acc) reduzieren; to ~ sb ~ to size (fig) jdn zurechtstutzen.

whiz(z) [wɪz] **1** n (a) (of arrow) Schwirren nt. (b) (col) Kanone f (col). **2** vi (arrow) schwirren. the cars ~ed past die Autos sausten vorbei.

whi(z)z-kid ['wɪzkɪd] n (col: in career) Senkrechtstarter m. financial ~ Finanzgenie nt.

WHO = **World Health Organization** Weltgesundheitsorganisation f.

who [huː] pron (a) (interrog) wer; (acc) wen; (dat) wem. ~ **do you think you are?** was glaubst du, wer du bist?, für wen hältst du dich eigentlich?; ~ **are you looking for?** wen suchen Sie?; ~ **did you stay with?** bei wem haben Sie gewohnt?; **you'll soon find out** ~**'s** ~ Sie werden bald alle kennenlernen. (b) (rel) der/die/das, welche(r, s). **any man** ~ ... jeder (Mensch), der ...; **he** ~ **wishes/those** ~ **wish to go** ... wer gehen will ...

who'd [huːd] = **who had; who would.**

whodun(n)it [huːˈdʌnɪt] n (col) Krimi m.

whoever [huːˈevəᵣ] pron wer (auch immer); (acc) wen (auch immer); (dat) wem (auch immer); (no matter who) ganz gleich wer/wen/wem. ~ **told you that?** wer hat dir das denn (bloß) gesagt?

whole [həʊl] **1** adj ganz; truth voll. **but the** ~ **purpose was to** ... aber der ganze Sinn der Sache war, daß ...; **three** ~ **weeks** drei volle or ganze Wochen; **the** ~ **lot** das Ganze; (of people) alle, der ganze Verein (col); **a** ~ **lot of people** eine ganze Menge Leute; **a** ~ **lot better** (col) ein ganzes Stück besser; **not a cup was left** ~ nicht eine Tasse blieb heil; **she swallowed it** ~ sie schluckte es ganz (hinunter). **2** n Ganze(s) nt. **the** ~ **of the month/London** der ganze Monat/ganz London; **nearly the** ~ **of our production** fast unsere gesamte Produktion; **as a** ~ als Ganzes; **on the** ~ im großen und ganzen, alles in allem.

whole: ~**food** n Reformkost, Biokost f; ~**hearted**

wholeheartedly *adj* völlig, uneingeschränkt; ~**hearted thanks to X X** *(dat)* danken wir von ganzem Herzen; ~**heartedly** *adv* voll und ganz; ~ **hog** *n*: **to go the** ~ **hog** *(col)* aufs Ganze gehen; ~**meal** *(Brit)* **1** *adj* Vollkorn-; **2** *n* feiner Vollkornschrot; ~ **milk** *n* Vollmilch *f*; ~ **note** *n* (*esp US Mus*) ganze Note; ~ **number** *n* ganze Zahl.

wholesale ['həʊlseɪl] **1** *n* Großhandel *m*. **2** *adj attr* **(a)** *(Comm)* Großhandels-. **(b)** *(fig: widespread)* umfassend, massiv; *slaughter, redundancies* Massen-; *(indiscriminate)* wild, generell. **3** *adv* **(a)** im Großhandel. **(b)** *(fig)* in Bausch und Bogen; *(in great numbers)* massenhaft; *(without modification)* (so) ohne weiteres.

wholesaler ['həʊlseɪlə'] *n* Großhändler *m*.

wholesome ['həʊlsəm] *adj* gesund.

wholewheat ['həʊlwiːt] *n, adj (US)* = **wholemeal**.

who'll [huːl] = **who will; who shall.**

wholly ['həʊlɪ] *adv* völlig, gänzlich.

whom [huːm] *pron* **(a)** *(interrog) (acc)* wen; *(dat)* wem. **(b)** *(rel) (acc)* den/die/das; *(dat)* dem/der/dem ..., **all of** ~ **were drunk** ..., die alle betrunken waren; **none/all of** ~ von denen keine(r, s)/alle.

whoop [huːp] **1** *n* Ruf, Schrei *m*. **2** *vi* rufen, schreien; *(with whooping cough)* pfeifen; *(with joy)* jauchzen.

whooping cough ['huːpɪŋ,kɒf] *n* Keuchhusten *m*.

whoosh [wuːʃ] **1** *n (of water)* Rauschen *nt*; *(of air)* Zischen *nt*. **2** *vi* rauschen; zischen.

whopper ['wɒpə'] *n (col) (sth big)* Brocken *m (col)*; *(lie)* faustdicke Lüge.

whopping ['wɒpɪŋ] *adj (col)* Mords- *(col)*, Riesen-.

whore [hɔː'] *n* Hure *f*.

whorl [wɜːl] *n* Kringel *m*; *(of shell)* (Spiral)windung *f*.

who's [huːz] = **who has; who is.**

whose [huːz] *poss pron* **(a)** *(interrog)* wessen. ~ **is this?** wem gehört das?; ~ **car did you go in?** in wessen Auto sind Sie gefahren? **(b)** *(rel)* dessen; *(after f and pl)* deren. **the man** ~ **wife** ... der Mann, dessen Frau ...

why [waɪ] **1** *adv* warum, weshalb; *(asking for the purpose)* wozu; *(how come that ...)* wieso. ~ **not ask him?** warum fragst du/fragen wir *etc* ihn nicht?; ~ **wait?** wozu (noch) warten?; ~ **do it this way?** warum denn so?; **that's** ~ darum, deswegen; **that's exactly** ~ ... genau deshalb or deswegen ... **2** *interj* are you sure? — ~ **yes** sind Sie sicher?; — (aber) ja; ~ **that's easy!** na, das ist doch einfach!; **who did it?** ~ **it's obvious** wer das war? also, das ist doch klar. **3** *n*: **the** ~**s and (the) wherefores** das Warum und Weshalb.

wick [wɪk] *n* Docht *m*. **to get on sb's** ~ *(col)* jdm auf den Wecker gehen *(col)*.

wicked ['wɪkɪd] *adj person etc* böse; *(immoral)* schlecht, gottlos; *(indulging in vices)* lasterhaft; *(col: scandalous) price etc* unverschämt; *smile, look, grin* frech, boshaft; *satire* boshaft; *blow, frost also* gemein *(col)*. **that was a** ~ **thing to do** das war aber gemein (von dir/ihm *etc*); **he/the dog has a** ~ **temper** er ist unbeherrscht or aufbrausend/der Hund ist bösartig; **he has a** ~ **sense of humour** er hat eine böse Art von Humor.

wickedness ['wɪkɪdnɪs] *n (of person)* Schlechtigkeit *f*; *(immorality)* Verderbtheit *f*; *(indulgence in vices)* Lasterhaftigkeit *f*; *(of look etc)* Boshaftigkeit *f*; *(mischievousness)* Bosheit *f*.

wicker ['wɪkə'] **1** *n* Korbgeflecht *nt*. **2** *adj attr* Korb-.

wicker: ~ **basket** *n* (Weiden)korb *m*; ~**work** *n (material)* Korbgeflecht *nt*; *(articles)* Korbwaren *pl*.

wicket ['wɪkɪt] *n (Cricket) (stumps: also* ~**s**) Mal, Pfostentor *nt*; *(pitch)* Spielbahn *f*.

wicket-keeper ['wɪkɪt'kiːpə'] *n (Cricket)* Tor-

---

wächter *m*.

wide [waɪd] **1** *adj* **(a)** *road, smile* breit; *skirt, plain* weit; *eyes* groß. **it is three metres** ~ es ist drei Meter breit; **the big** ~ **world** die (große) weite Welt. **(b)** *variety* groß; *experience, choice* reich; *public, knowledge, range* breit; *interests* vielfältig; *coverage of report* umfassend; *network* weitverzweigt *attr*; *circulation* weit, groß; *question* weitreichend. ~ **reading is the best education** viel zu lesen ist die beste Art der Erziehung; **his** ~ **reading** seine große Belesenheit. **(c)** *(missing the target)* daneben *pred*. **you're a bit** ~ **there** da liegst du etwas daneben; ~ **of the truth** nicht ganz wahrheitsgetreu.

2 *adv* **(a)** *(extending far)* weit. **they are set** ~ **apart** sie liegen weit auseinander. **(b)** *(fully)* weit. **open** ~! bitte weit öffnen; ~ **open** *(door)* weit offen; **the law is** ~ **open to criticism** das Gesetz bietet viele Ansatzpunkte für Kritik; **the game is still** ~ **open** der Spielausgang ist noch völlig offen; **to be** ~ **awake** hellwach sein; *(alert)* wach sein. **(c)** *(far from the target)* daneben. **to go** ~ **of sth** an etw *dat* vorbeigehen.

wide: ~-**angle (lens)** *n (Phot)* Weitwinkel(objektiv *nt)* *m*; ~-**awake** *adj (fully awake)* hellwach; *(alert)* wach; ~-**eyed** *adj* mit großen Augen; **in** ~-**eyed amazement** mit großen, erstaunten Augen.

widely ['waɪdlɪ] *adv* weit; *(by or to many people)* weit und breit, allgemein; *differing* völlig. **the opinion is** ~ **held** ... es herrscht in weiten Kreisen die Ansicht ...; **it is** ~ **believed that** ... es wird allgemein angenommen, daß ...; **he became** ~ **known as** ... er wurde überall or in weiten Kreisen bekannt als ...; **a** ~ **read student** ein sehr belesener Student.

widen ['waɪdn] **1** *vt road* verbreitern; *passage, knowledge* erweitern. **2** *vi* breiter werden; *(interests etc)* sich ausweiten.

♦ **widen out** *vi (valley etc)* sich erweitern *(into zu)*.

wide: ~-**ranging** *adj* weitreichend; ~**spread** *adj* weitverbreitet *attr*; **to become** ~**spread** weite Verbreitung erlangen.

widow ['wɪdəʊ] **1** *n* Witwe *f*. **golf** ~ *(hum)* Golfwitwe *f*. **2** *vt* zur Witwe/zum Witwer machen. **she was twice** ~**ed** sie ist zweimal verwitwet.

widower ['wɪdəʊə'] *n* Witwer *m*.

width [wɪdθ] *n* Breite *f*; *(of trouser legs etc)* Weite *f*; *(of interests also)* Vielfalt *f*. **six centimetres in** ~ sechs Zentimeter breit.

widthways ['wɪdθweɪz] *adv* der Breite nach.

wield [wiːld] *vt pen, sword* führen; *axe* schwingen; *power* ausüben.

wife [waɪf] *n, pl* **wives** Frau, Gattin *(form) f*.

wifely ['waɪflɪ] *adj* ~ **duties** Pflichten *pl* als Ehefrau; ~ **devotion** Hingabe *f* einer Ehefrau.

wig [wɪg] *n* Perücke *f*.

wiggle ['wɪgl] **1** *n* Wackeln *nt no pl*. **give it a** ~ **and it might come free** wackeln Sie mal daran, dann geht es vielleicht raus. **2** *vt* wackeln mit. **3** *vi* wackeln.

wiggly ['wɪglɪ] *adj* wackelnd; *line* Schlangen-.

wigwam ['wɪgwæm] *n* Wigwam *m*.

wild [waɪld] **1** *adj* **(a)** *(not domesticated)* wild; *people* unzivilisiert; *garden, wood* verwildert; *flowers* wildwachsend *attr*. **the W**~ **West** der Wilde Westen; ~ **animals** Tiere *pl* in freier Wildbahn; **the plant in its** ~ **state** die Pflanze im Naturzustand. **(b)** *(stormy) weather, wind, sea* rauh, stürmisch. **(c)** *(excited, riotous)* wild *(with* vor +*dat)*; *(disordered) hair also* wirr, unordentlich; *children also, desire* unbändig. **I'm not** ~ **about the idea** *(col)* auf die Idee bin ich nicht gerade versessen *(col)*; **to be** ~ **about sb** *(col)* verrückt nach jdm sein *(col)*; **the audience went** ~ das Publikum raste. **(d)** *(col: angry)* wütend *(with, at* mit, auf +*acc)*, rasend; **it drives me** ~ das macht mich ganz wild or rasend; **to get** ~ wild werden *(col)*.

(e) *(rash, extravagant)* verrückt; *exaggeration, allegation* maßlos, wild; *fluctuations* stark; *expectations* kühn; *shot* Fehl-. **never in my ~est dreams** auch in meinen kühnsten Träumen nicht. **2** *adv* **grow** ~ wild; **run** frei. **to let one's imagination run** ~ seiner Phantasie *(dat)* freien Lauf lassen; **the roses/the children have run** ~ die Rosen/die Kinder sind verwildert. **3** *n* Wildnis *f.* **in the** ~ in der Wildnis, in freier Wildbahn; **out in the ~s of Berkshire** *(hum)* im hintersten Berkshire.

wildcat ['waɪldkæt] *n* *(Zool)* Wildkatze *f.* ~ **strike** wilder Streik.

wilderness ['wɪldənɪs] *n* Wildnis *f*; *(fig)* Wüste *f.*

wild: ~**fire** *n* **to spread like** ~**fire** sich wie ein Lauffeuer ausbreiten; ~**fowl** *n no pl* Wildgeflügel *nt*; ~-**goose chase** *n* fruchtloses Unterfangen; **to send sb out on a** ~-**goose chase** jdn für nichts und wieder nichts losschicken; ~ **life** *n* die Tierwelt; ~**life sanctuary** Wildreservat *nt.*

wildly ['waɪldlɪ] *adv* **(a)** wild. **(b)** *(in disorder)* wirr. **(c)** *(extravagantly)* **guess** drauflos, ins Blaue hinein; *talk* unausgegoren; *exaggerated* stark, maßlos. **not** ~ **enthusiastic** nicht allzu begeistert.

wildness ['waɪldnɪs] *n* Wildheit *f*; *(of storm etc also)* Heftigkeit *f*; *(of allegation)* Maßlosigkeit *f.*

wiles [waɪlz] *n pl* Schliche *pl.*

wilful, *(US)* **willful** ['wɪlfʊl] *adj* **(a)** *(self-willed)* eigenwillig. **(b)** *(deliberate) neglect, damage* mutwillig; *murder* vorsätzlich; *disobedience* wissentlich.

will[1] [wɪl] *pret* **would** **1** *modal aux* **(a)** *(forming future)* werden. **I'm sure that he** ~ **come** ich bin sicher, daß er kommt; **you** ~ **come to see us, won't you** Sie kommen uns doch besuchen, ja?; **I'll be right there** komme sofort!, bin gleich da!; **he'll be there** — **he won't** er wird dort sein — nein; **I** ~ **have finished by Tuesday** bis Dienstag bin ich fertig; **you won't lose it,** ~ **you?** du wirst es doch nicht verlieren, oder?

(b) *(emphatic)* **I** ~ **not have it!** das kommt nicht in Frage *(col)*; ~ **you be quiet!** bist du *or* sei jetzt endlich ruhig!; **well, if you won't take advice** wenn du *or* (eben) keinen Rat annimmst, na bitte; **he** ~ **interrupt all the time** er muß ständig dazwischenreden.

(c) *(expressing willingness, capability etc)* wollen. **he won't sign** er will nicht unterschreiben; **wait a moment,** ~ **you?** warten Sie bitte einen Moment; *(impatiently)* jetzt warte doch mal einen Moment!; **the car won't start** das Auto springt nicht an; **the cut won't heal** die Schnittwunde will nicht (ver)heilen; **the car** ~ **do up to 120 mph** das Auto fährt bis zu 120 Meilen pro Stunde.

(d) *(in questions)* ~ **you have some more tea?** möchten Sie noch Tee?; ~ **you accept these conditions?** akzeptieren Sie diese Bedingungen?

(e) *(assumption)* **he'll be there by now** jetzt ist er schon da *or* dürfte er schon da sein; **this** ~ **be the bus** das wird *or* dürfte unser Bus sein.

(f) *(tendency)* **sometimes he** ~ **sit in his room for hours** manchmal sitzt er stundenlang in seinem Zimmer; **accidents** ~ **happen** Unfälle passieren nun (ein)mal.

2 *vi* wollen. **say what you** ~ du kannst sagen, was du willst; **as you** ~! wie du willst!

will[2] **1** *n* **(a)** Wille *m.* **to have a** ~ **of one's own** einen eigenen Willen haben; *(hum)* so seine Mucken haben *(col)*; **the** ~ **to win** der Wille, zu gewinnen; **(to go) against sb's** ~ gegen jds Willen (handeln); **at** ~ nach Belieben; **of one's own free** ~ aus freien Stücken *or* freiem Willen; **with the best** ~ **in the world** beim (aller)besten Willen; **where there is a** ~ **there is a way** *(Prov)* wo ein

Wille ist, ist auch ein Weg *(Prov)*. **(b)** *(testament)* Letzter Wille, Testament *nt.* **the last** ~ **and testament of** ... der Letzte Wille *or* das Testament des/der ...; **to make one's** ~ sein Testament machen.

2 *vt* *(urge by willpower)* (durch Willenskraft) erzwingen. **to** ~ **sb to do sth** jdn durch die eigene Willensanstrengung dazu bringen, daß er etw tut; **he** ~**ed himself to stay awake** er hat sich (dazu) gezwungen, wach zu bleiben; **he** ~**ed the ball into the net** er hat den Ball ins Netz hypnotisiert *(col)*; **the crowd were** ~**ing him on** das Publikum feuerte ihn an.

willie ['wɪlɪ] *n* *(hum: penis)* Pimmel *m (col).*

willies ['wɪlɪz] *npl* *(col)* **it/he gives me the** ~ da/bei ihm wird mir ganz anders *(col).*

willing ['wɪlɪŋ] *adj* **(a)** *(prepared)* **to be** ~ **to do sth** bereit *or* gewillt *(geh)* sein, etw zu tun; **God** ~ so Gott will; **he was** ~ **for me to take it** es war ihm recht, daß ich es nahm; **he was not** ~ **for us to go** er war nicht gewillt, uns gehen zu lassen. **(b)** *workers, assistance* bereitwillig. **there were plenty of** ~ **hands** es gab viele, die helfen wollten; **to show** ~ Bereitschaft zeigen.

willingly ['wɪlɪŋlɪ] *adv* bereitwillig, gerne. **will you help?** — **yes,** ~ wollen Sie helfen? — (ja,) gerne.

willingness ['wɪlɪŋnɪs] *n see adj* **(a)** Bereitschaft *f.* **(b)** Bereitwilligkeit *f.*

will-o'-the-wisp ['wɪləðə'wɪsp] *n* Irrlicht *nt*; *(fig)* Trugbild *nt.*

willow ['wɪləʊ] *n* *(also* ~ **tree)** Weide *f*; *(wood)* Weidenholz *nt.*

willow pattern *n* chinesisches Weidenmotiv *(auf Porzellan).*

willowy ['wɪləʊɪ] *adj* gertenschlank.

willpower ['wɪl,paʊə'] *n* Willenskraft *f.*

willy-nilly ['wɪlɪ'nɪlɪ] *adv* wohl oder übel; *(at random, without plan)* nur einfach so.

wilt [wɪlt] *vi* **(a)** *(flowers)* welken, verwelken. **(b)** *(person: after exercise)* schlapp werden; *(enthusiasm, energy)* abflauen.

wily ['waɪlɪ] *adj* (+er) schlau, hinterlistig *(pej).*

win [wɪn] *(vb: pret, ptp* **won)** **1** *n* Sieg *m.* **to have a** ~ *(money)* einen Gewinn machen; *(victory)* einen Sieg erzielen. **2** *vt* gewinnen; *reputation* erwerben; *scholarship, contract* bekommen; *victory* erringen. **land won from the sea** dem Meer abgewonnenes Land. **3** *vi* gewinnen, siegen. **OK, you** ~, **I was wrong** okay, du hast gewonnen, ich habe mich geirrt.

♦ **win back** *vt sep* zurück- *or* wiedergewinnen.

♦ **win over** *or* **round** *vt sep* für sich gewinnen. **to** ~ **sb** ~ **to one's way of thinking** jdn überzeugen.

♦ **win through** *vi* *(patient)* durchkommen. **we'll** ~ **in the end** wir werden es schon schaffen *(col).*

wince [wɪns] **1** *n* **to give a** ~ *(of pain)* (vor Schmerz) zusammenzucken. **2** *vi* zusammenzucken *(at bei).*

winch [wɪntʃ] **1** *n* Winde *f.* **2** *vt* winden. **to** ~ **sth up** etw hochwinden.

wind[1] [wɪnd] **1** *n* **(a)** Wind *m.* **the** ~ **is from the east** der Wind kommt von Osten; **(to run) like the** ~ (rennen) wie der Wind; **a** ~ **of change** *(fig)* ein frischer Wind; **there's something in the** ~ *(irgend)* etwas liegt in der Luft; **to get/have the** ~ **up** *(col) (nervous)* Angst *or* Schiß *(col)* kriegen/ haben; **to put the** ~ **up sb** *(col)* jdm Angst machen; **to see which way the** ~ **blows** *(fig)* sehen, woher der Wind weht; **to take the** ~ **out of sb's sails** *(fig)* jdm den Wind aus den Segeln nehmen; **to get** ~ **of sth** von etw Wind bekommen; **to throw caution to the** ~**s** Bedenken in den Wind schlagen; **to sail close to the** ~ *(fig)* sich hart an der Grenze des Erlaubten bewegen. **(b)** *(Med)* Blähung *f.* **to break** ~ einen Wind entweichen lassen. **(c)** *(breath)* Atem *m*, Luft *f (col).* **to be short of**

~ außer Atem sein; **to get one's** ~ **back** wieder zu Atem kommen. **2** *vt (knock breathless)* den Atem nehmen (+*dat*).

wind[2] [waind] *(vb: pret, ptp* **wound)** **1** *vt* **(a)** *wool, bandage* wickeln; *(once round)* winden; *(on to a reel)* spulen. **(b)** *handle* drehen; *clock etc* aufziehen. **(c) to** ~ **one's way** sich schlängeln. **2** *vi (river etc)* sich winden *or* schlängeln.

◆ **wind down** ~ *vt sep* **(a)** *car windows etc* herunterkurbeln. **(b)** *operations* reduzieren; *production* zurückschrauben.

◆ **wind in** *vt sep fish* einholen; *rope* aufspulen.

◆ **wind on** *vt sep film* weiterspulen.

◆ **wind up 1** *vt sep* **(a)** *bucket* heraufholen; *car window* hinaufkurbeln. **(b)** *clock* aufziehen. **to be wound** ~ **about sth** *(fig)* wegen einer Sache *(gen)* erregt sein. **(c)** *meeting, speech* beschließen, zu Ende bringen. **(d)** *company* auflösen; *service, series* auslaufen lassen. **2** *vi* **(a)** *(col: end up)* enden. **to** ~ ~ **in hospital** im Krankenhaus landen. **(b) to** ~ ~ **for the government** die abschließende Rede für die Regierung halten. **(c)** *(road)* sich hinaufschlängeln.

wind ['wɪnd-]: ~**bag** *n (col)* Schwätzer(in *f*) *m*; ~**break** *n* Windschutz *m*; ~**breaker** ® *(US)*, ~**cheater** *(Brit) n* Windjacke.

winder ['waɪndə'] *n (of watch)* Rädchen *nt*; *(of alarm clock, toy etc)* Aufziehschraube *f*.

windfall ['wɪndfɔːl] *n* Fallobst *nt*; *(fig)* unverhoffter Glücksfall.

winding ['waɪndɪŋ] **1** *adj river* gewunden; *road also* kurvenreich. **2** *n (Elec)* Wicklung *f*.

wind instrument *n* Blasinstrument *nt*.

windlass ['wɪndləs] *n (winch)* Winde *f*; *(Naut)* Ankerwinde *f*.

wind ['wɪnd-]: ~**less** *adj* windstill; ~**mill** *n* Windmühle *f*.

window ['wɪndəu] *n* Fenster *nt*; *(shop*~*)* (Schau)fenster *nt*; *(of bank etc)* Schalter *m*.

window: ~ **box** *n* Blumenkasten *m*; ~**-cleaner** *n* Fensterputzer *m*; ~**-dressing** *n* Schaufensterdekoration *f*; *(fig)* Schau *(col)*, Augenwischerei *(pej) f*; ~ **ledge** *n* = ~**sill**; ~ **seat** *n (in house)* Fensterbank *f or* -sitz *m*; *(Rail etc)* Fensterplatz *m*; ~**-shopping** *n* Schaufensterbummel *m*; **to go** ~**-shopping** einen Schaufensterbummel machen; ~**sill** *n* Fensterbank *f*.

wind ['wɪnd-]: ~**pipe** *n* Luftröhre *f*; ~**screen**, *(US)* ~**shield** *n* Windschutzscheibe *f*; ~**screen** *or (US)* ~**shield wiper** *n* Scheibenwischer *m*; ~**sock** *n* Luft- *or* Windsack *m*; ~**swept** *adj plains* über den/die/das der Wind fegt; *person, hair* (vom Wind) zerzaust; ~**tunnel** *n* Windkanal *m*.

windy ['wɪndɪ] *adj (+er)* windig.

wine [waɪn] **1** *n* Wein *m*. **2** *vt* **to** ~ **and dine sb** jdn gut bewirten.

wine: ~ **cellar** *n* Weinkeller *m*; ~**glass** *n* Weinglas *nt*; ~**-grower** *n* Winzer, Weinbauer *m*; ~**-growing 1** *adj district* Wein(an)bau-; **2** *n* Wein(an)bau *m*; ~ **list** *n* Weinkarte *f*; ~**-taster** *n* Weinprüfer *m*; ~**-tasting** *n* Weinprobe *f*; ~ **waiter** *n* Getränkekellner *m*.

wing [wɪŋ] *n* **(a)** *(of bird, plane, building, Mil, Pol, Sport)* Flügel *m*; *(Brit Aut)* Kotflügel *m*. **on the** ~ im Flug(e); **to take sb under one's** ~ *(fig)* jdn unter seine Fittiche nehmen; **to spread one's** ~**s** *(fig: children)* flügge werden. **(b)** ~**s** *pl (Theat)* Kulisse *f*; **to wait in the** ~**s** *(lit, fig)* in den Kulissen warten.

winger ['wɪŋə'] *n (Sport)* Flügelspieler(in *f*) *m*.

wing: ~**mirror** *n* Außenspiegel *m*; ~ **nut** *n* Flügelmutter *f*; ~**span** *n* Flügelspannweite *f*; ~**spread** *n* Spannweite *f*.

wink [wɪŋk] **1** *n (with eye)* Zwinkern, Blinzeln *nt*. **to give sb a** ~ jdm zuzwinkern; **to tip sb the** ~ *(col)* jdm einen Wink geben; **I didn't sleep a** ~ **I** habe kein Auge zugetan. **2** *vi (meaningfully)* zwin-

kern, blinzeln; *(light, star etc)* blinken, funkeln. **to** ~ **at sb** jdm zuzwinkern.

winker ['wɪŋkə'] *n (Brit Aut col)* Blinker *m*.

winkle ['wɪŋkl] **1** *n* Strandschnecke *f*. **2** *vt* **to** ~ **a secret out of sb** jdm ein Geheimnis entlocken.

winner ['wɪnə'] *n (in race, competition)* Sieger(in *f*) *m*; *(of bet, pools etc)* Gewinner(in *f*) *m*; *(col: sth successful)* Renner *(col)*, Schlager *m*. **to be onto a** ~ *(col)* das große Los gezogen haben *(col)*.

winning ['wɪnɪŋ] **1** *adj* **(a)** *person, entry* der/die gewinnt; *horse, team* siegreich; *goal* Sieges-; *point, stroke* entscheidend. ~ **ticket** Gewinnlos *nt*; **the** ~ **time** die beste Zeit; ~ **post** Zielpfosten *m*. **(b)** *(charming) smile, ways* gewinnend, einnehmend. **2** *n* ~**s** *pl* Gewinn *m*.

winter ['wɪntə'] **1** *n (lit, fig)* Winter *m*. **2** *adj attr* Winter-. ~ **sports** Wintersport *m*; ~**time** Winter *m*; *(for clocks)* Winterzeit *f*.

winterize ['wɪntəraɪz] *vt (esp US)* winterfest machen.

wint(e)ry ['wɪnt(ə)rɪ] *adj* winterlich; *(fig)* look eisig.

wipe [waɪp] **1** *n* Wischen *nt*. **to give sth a** ~ etw abwischen. **2** *vt* wischen; *floor* aufwischen; *hands, feet* abwischen, abputzen. **to** ~ **sb/sth clean** jdn/etw säubern; **to** ~ **sth with/on a cloth** etw mit/an einem Tuch abwischen; **to** ~ **one's brow/nose** sich *(dat)* die Stirn abwischen/die Nase putzen; **to** ~ **one's feet** sich *(dat)* die Füße abwischen; **to** ~ **the tears from one's eyes** *(dat)* die Tränen aus den Augen wischen; **to** ~ **the floor with sb** *(fig col)* jdn fertigmachen *(col)*.

◆ **wipe away** *vt sep (lit, fig)* wegwischen.

◆ **wipe off** *vt sep mark* weg- *or* abwischen. **to be** ~**d** ~ **the face of the earth** von der Erdoberfläche verschwinden.

◆ **wipe out** *vt sep* **(a)** *(clean)* auswischen. **(b)** *(erase)* (aus)löschen; *guilt* verschwinden lassen. **(c)** *(cancel)* debt bereinigen; *gain* zunichte machen. **(d)** *(destroy)* disease, village ausrotten; *enemy* aufreiben.

◆ **wipe up 1** *vt sep liquid* aufwischen; *dishes* abtrocknen. **2** *vi* abtrocknen.

wiper ['waɪpə'] *n (Scheiben)wischer m*.

wiping-up ['waɪpɪŋ'ʌp] *n* **to do the** ~ abtrocknen.

wire [waɪə'] **1** *n* **(a)** Draht *m*; *(cable, on appliance)* Leitung *f*; *(in circus: high* ~*)* (Hoch)seil *nt*. **you've got your** ~**s crossed there** *(col)* Sie verwechseln da etwas; **to get in under the** ~ *(US col)* etwas gerade (eben) noch rechtzeitig schaffen. **(b)** *(Telec)* Telegramm *nt*. **2** *vt* **(a)** *(put in wiring)* house die (elektrischen) Leitungen verlegen in (+*dat*); *(connect to electricity)* (an das Stromnetz) anschließen. **(b)** *(Telec)* telgrafieren. **(c)** *(fix with* ~*)* mit Draht zusammenbinden.

◆ **wire up** *vt sep lights, battery, speakers* anschließen; *house* elektrische Leitungen verlegen in (+*dat*).

wire: ~**-cutters** *npl* Drahtschere *f*; ~**-haired** *adj* terrier Drahthaar-.

wireless ['waɪəlɪs] *(esp Brit dated) n* **(a)** *(also* ~ **set)** Radio, Rundfunkgerät *nt*. **(b)** *(radio)* Rundfunk *m*; *(also* ~ **telegraphy)** drahtlose Telegrafie.

wire: ~ **netting** *n* Maschendraht *m*; ~**-pulling** *n (col)* Drahtziehen *nt*; ~**-tapping** *n* Abhören *nt*, Anzapfen *nt* von Leitungen.

wiring ['waɪərɪŋ] *n* elektrische Leitungen *pl*.

wiring diagram *n* Schaltplan *m*.

wiry ['waɪərɪ] *adj (+er)* drahtig; *hair also* borstig.

wisdom ['wɪzdəm] *n* Weisheit *f*; *(prudence)* Einsicht *f*.

wisdom tooth *n* Weisheitszahn *m*.

wise [waɪz] *adj (+er)* weise; *move etc* klug, vernünftig; *(col: smart)* klug, schlau. **a** ~ **choice** eine kluge *or* gute Wahl; **the Three W~ Men** die drei Weisen; **to be** ~ **after the event** hinterher gut reden haben; **I'm none the** ~**r** *(col)* ich bin nicht klüger als zuvor; **nobody will be any the ~r** *(col)* niemand wird etwas (davon) merken; **to get ~ to sb/sth** *(col)* dahinterkommen, wie jd/etw ist; **to put sb ~ to sb/sth** *(col)* jdn über jdn/etw aufklären.

wise: ~crack *(esp US)* n Witzelei f; *(pej)* Stichelei f; **~guy** n *(esp US col)* Klugschwätzer *(col)*, Klugscheißer *(col!)* m.

wisely ['waɪzlɪ] adv weise; *(sensibly)* klugerweise.

wish [wɪʃ] 1 n **(a)** Wunsch m *(for* nach*)*. **your ~ is my command** dein Wunsch ist mir Befehl; **I have no great ~ to see him** ich habe keine große Lust, ihn zu sehen; **to make a ~** sich *(dat)* etwas wünschen; **you shall have your ~** dein Wunsch soll in Erfüllung gehen. **(b) ~es** pl *(in greetings)* **with best ~es** mit den besten Grüßen; **please give him my good ~es** bitte grüßen Sie ihn (vielmals) von mir.

2 vt wünschen. **he ~es to be alone** er möchte allein sein; **I ~ you to be present** ich wünsche, daß Sie anwesend sind; **do you ~ more coffee, sir?** *(Scot, form)* hätten Sie gern noch Kaffee?; **~ you were here** ich wünschte, du wärest hier; **I ~ he'd be quiet** ich wollte er wünschte, er wäre still; **to ~ sb well/ill** jdm Glück or alles Gute/ Schlechte wünschen; **to ~ sb a pleasant journey/ a happy Christmas** jdm eine gute Reise/frohe Weihnachten wünschen; **he ~ed himself anywhere but there** er wünschte sich nur möglichst weit weg.

3 vi *(make a wish)* sich *(dat)* etwas wünschen.

♦ **wish for** vi +prep obj **to ~ ~ sth** sich *(dat)* etw wünschen; **she had everything she could ~ ~** sie hatte alles, was man sich nur wünschen kann.

wishbone ['wɪʃbəʊn] n Gabelbein nt.

wishful ['wɪʃfʊl] adj **that's just ~ thinking** das ist reines Wunschdenken.

wishy-washy ['wɪʃɪ,wɒʃɪ] adj soup labberig *(col)*, wäßrig; person farblos, lasch; colour verwaschen; argument schwach *(col)*; story ungenau, wischiwaschi pred *(col)*.

wisp [wɪsp] n *(of straw, hair etc)* kleines Büschel; *(of cloud)* Fetzen m; *(of smoke)* Wölkchen nt.

wistful ['wɪstfʊl] adj wehmütig; song also schwermütig.

wit [wɪt] n **(a)** *(understanding)* Verstand m. **a battle of ~s** ein geistiges Kräftemessen; **to be at one's ~s' end** am Ende seiner Weisheit sein, mit seinem Latein am Ende sein *(hum col)*; **to scare sb out of his ~s** jdn zu Tode erschrecken; **to keep one's ~s about one** seine (fünf) Sinne beisammenhalten, einen klaren Kopf behalten; **to live by one's ~s** sich schlau durchs Leben schlagen. **(b)** *(humour)* Geist, Witz m. **full of ~** geistreich; **there's a lot of ~ in the book** es ist sehr viel Geistreiches in dem Buch. **(c)** *(person)* geistreicher Kopf.

witch [wɪtʃ] n *(lit, fig)* Hexe f.

witch: ~craft n Hexerei, Zauberei f; **~ doctor** n Medizinmann m.

witch-hunt ['wɪtʃ,hʌnt] n *(lit, fig)* Hexenjagd f.

with [wɪð, wɪθ] prep **(a)** mit. **are you pleased ~ it?** bist du damit zufrieden?; **bring a book ~ you** bring ein Buch mit; **~ no ... ohne ...;** **put it ~ the rest** leg es zu den anderen; **how are things ~ you?** wie geht's?

(b) *(at house of, in company of etc)* bei. **I'll be ~ you in a moment** einen Augenblick bitte, ich bin gleich da; **10 years ~ the company** 10 Jahre bei or in der Firma.

(c) *(on person, in bag etc)* bei. **I haven't got my cheque book ~ me** ich habe mein Scheckbuch nicht bei mir.

(d) *(cause)* vor (+dat). **to shiver ~ cold** vor Kälte zittern; **the hills are white ~ snow** die Berge sind weiß vom Schnee; **to be ill ~ measles** die Masern haben.

(e) *(in the case of)* bei, mit. **it's always the same ~ you** es ist (doch) immer dasselbe mit dir; **the trouble ~ him is that he ...** die Schwierigkeit bei or mit ihm ist (die), daß er ...; **I cannot concentrate ~ all this noise going on** bei diesem Lärm kann ich mich nicht konzentrieren; **~ the window open** bei offenem Fenster; **~ her being ill** da sie krank ist/war; **it varies ~ the temperature** es verändert sich je nach Temperatur; **wine improves ~ age** Wein wird mit zunehmendem Alter immer besser; **~ all his faults** bei allen seinen Fehlern, trotz aller seiner Fehler.

(f) *(expressing agreement, comprehension)* **I'm ~ you there** *(col)* da stimme ich dir zu; **are you ~ me?** verstehen Sie?, kapierst du? *(col)*.

withdraw [wɪθ'drɔː] pret **withdrew**, ptp **withdrawn 1** vt object, motion, charge zurückziehen; troops, team also abziehen; ambassador zurückbeordern; coins einziehen, aus dem Verkehr ziehen; *(from bank)* money abheben; words, comment zurücknehmen, widerrufen; privileges entziehen. **the workers withdrew their labour** die Arbeiter legten ihre Arbeit nieder. **2** vi sich zurückziehen *(Sport also)* zurücktreten *(from* von*)*, nicht antreten *(from* von/bei*)*; *(move away)* zurücktreten or -gehen. **to ~ in favour of sb else** zu Gunsten eines anderen zurücktreten; **to ~ into oneself** sich in sich *(acc)* selbst zurückziehen.

withdrawal [wɪθ'drɔːəl] n *(of objects, charge)* Zurückziehen nt; *(of ambassador)* Abziehen nt; *(of coins)* Einziehen nt; *(of money)* Abheben nt; *(of words)* Zurücknahme f; *(of troops)* Rückzug m; *(from drugs)* Entzug m. **to make a ~ from the bank** von einer Bank etwas or Geld abheben; **~ symptoms** Entzugserscheinungen pl.

withdrawn [wɪθ'drɔːn] **1** ptp of **withdraw. 2** adj person verschlossen; manner also zurückhaltend.

withdrew [wɪθ'druː] pret of **withdraw.**

wither ['wɪðəʳ] vi **(a)** verdorren, ausdorren; *(limb)* verkümmern. **(b)** *(fig)* welken; *(religion)* dahinschwinden.

withered ['wɪðəd] adj plant verdorrt, vertrocknet; skin, person verschrumpelt; limb verkümmert.

withering ['wɪðərɪŋ] adj look vernichtend.

withhold [wɪθ'həʊld] pret, ptp **withheld** [wɪθ'held] vt vorenthalten; truth also verschweigen; *(refuse)* consent, help verweigern, versagen (geh). **to ~ sth from sb** jdm etw vorenthalten/ verschweigen/verweigern; **~ing tax** *(US)* (vom Arbeitgeber) einbehaltene Steuer.

within [wɪð'ɪn] prep innerhalb (+gen); *(temporal also)* binnen (+dat). **a voice ~ him** seine innere Stimme; **we were/came ~ 100 m of the summit** wir waren auf den letzten 100 Metern vor dem Gipfel/wir kamen bis auf 100 Meter an den Gipfel heran; **accurate ~ 10 mm** auf 10 mm genau; **~ his power** in seiner Macht; **to keep ~ the law** sich im Rahmen des Gesetzes bewegen; **to live ~ one's income** im Rahmen seiner finanziellen Möglichkeiten leben.

with it ['wɪðɪt] adj *(col)* **(a)** *(attr* with-it*)* *(trendy)* up to date. **(b)** pred *(awake, alert)* **to be ~** da sein *(col)*.

without [wɪð'aʊt] prep ohne. **~ a tie** ohne Krawatte; **~ speaking** ohne zu sprechen, wortlos; **~ my noticing it** ohne daß ich es bemerke/ bemerkte; **he left ~ telling us** er ging, ohne es uns zu sagen.

withstand [wɪθ'stænd] pret, ptp **withstood** [wɪθ'stʊd] vt cold standhalten (+dat); climate, attack also trotzen (+dat); persuasion etc widerstehen (+dat).

witness ['wɪtnɪs] n **(a)** *(person: Jur, fig)* Zeuge m, Zeugin f. **~ for the defence/prosecution** Zeuge/ Zeugin der Verteidigung/Anklage; **to call sb as a ~** jdn als Zeugen vorladen. **(b)** *(evidence)* Zeugnis nt. **to give ~ for/against sb** für/gegen jdn aussagen; **to bear ~ to sth** *(lit, fig)* Zeugnis über etw *(acc)* ablegen. **2** *vt* **(a)** *(see) accident* Zeuge sein bei *or* +*gen;) scenes also* (mit)erleben; *changes* erleben. **(b)** *(testify)* bezeugen; *(attest by signature)* bestätigen. **3** *vi (testify)* bezeugen. **to** ~ **to sth** etw bezeugen.

witness box *or (US)* **stand** *n* Zeugenstand *m.*

witticism ['wıtısızəm] *n* geistreiche Bemerkung.

witty ['wıtı] *adj* (+*er*) witzig, geistreich.

wives [waıvz] *pl of* **wife.**

wizard ['wızəd] *n* Zauberer, Hexenmeister *m; (col)* Genie *nt.* **a financial** ~ ein Finanzgenie *nt.*

wizened ['wıznd] *adj* verhutzelt, verschrumpelt.

wk = **week** Wo.

wobble ['wɒbl] **1** *n* Wackeln *nt.* **the chair has a** ~ der Stuhl wackelt. **2** *vi* wackeln; *(cyclist)* schwanken; *(voice, hand, compass needle)* zittern; *(wheel)* eiern *(col);* *(chin, jelly etc)* wabbeln.

wobbly ['wɒblı] *adj* (+*er*) wacklig; *voice also, hand* zitterig, zitternd; *jelly* wabbelig; *wheel* eiernd *(col).* **to be** ~ *(col: after illness)* wacklig auf den Beinen sein *(col).*

woe [wəʊ] *n* **(a)** *(liter, hum: sorrow)* Jammer *m.* ~ **betide him who ...!** wehe dem, der ...! **(b)** *(esp pl: trouble)* Kummer *m.* **to tell sb one's** ~**s** jdm sein Leid klagen.

woebegone ['wəʊbı,gɒn] *adj* kläglich, jämmerlich.

woeful ['wəʊfʊl] *adj* (*sad*) traurig; *neglect also, ignorance* beklagenswert.

wog [wɒg] *n (Brit pej col!)* Kaffer *m (pej col).*

woke [wəʊk] *pret of* **wake.**

woken ['wəʊkn] *ptp of* **wake.**

wolf [wʊlf] **1** *n, pl* **wolves** Wolf *m; (col: womanizer)* Don Juan *m.* **a** ~ **in sheep's clothing** ein Wolf im Schafspelz; **to cry** ~ blinden Alarm schlagen; **to keep the** ~ **from the door** sich über Wasser halten. **2** *vt (also* ~ **down)** *food* hinunterschlingen.

wolf-whistle ['wʊlf,wısl] *n* **they gave her a** ~ sie pfiffen ihr nach.

wolves [wʊlvz] *pl of* **wolf.**

woman ['wʊmən] **1** *n, pl* **women** Frau *f; (domestic help)* (Hautshalts)hilfe *f; (mistress)* Geliebte *f.* **women's rights** die Rechte *pl* der Frau; **women's page** Frauenseite *f;* **women's lib** *(col)* Frauenrechtsbewegung *f;* **women's libber** *(col) f;* Frauenrechtlerin, Emanze *(esp pej col) f;* **women's hurdles** Hürdenlauf *m* der Damen. **2** *adj attr* ~ **doctor** Ärztin *f;* ~ **driver** Frau *f* am Steuer.

womanize ['wʊmənaız] *vi* hinter den Frauen her sein.

womanizer ['wʊmənaızə'] *n* Schürzenjäger *m.*

womanly ['wʊmənlı] *adj figure, person* fraulich; *qualities* weiblich.

womb [wu:m] *n* Mutterleib *m,* Gebärmutter *f (Med); (fig)* Schoß *m.*

women ['wımın] *pl of* **woman.**

womenfolk ['wımınfəʊk] *npl* Frauen *pl.*

won [wʌn] *pret, ptp of* **win.**

wonder ['wʌndə'] **1** *n* **(a)** *(feeling)* Staunen *nt,* Verwunderung *f.* **in** ~ voller Staunen. **(b)** *(object or cause of* ~) Wunder *nt.* **the** ~ **of electricity** das Wunder der Elektrizität; **the seven** ~**s of the world** die sieben Weltwunder; **it is a** ~ **that ...** es ist ein Wunder, daß ...; **it is no** *or* **little** ~ (es ist) kein Wunder; **no** ~ **(he refused)!** kein Wunder(, daß er abgelehnt hat)!; **to work** ~**s** Wunder wirken.

2 *vt* **I** ~ **what he'll do now** ich bin gespannt, was er jetzt tun wird *(col);* **I** ~ **who first said that** ich wüßte (zu) gern, wer das zuerst aufgebracht hat; **I was** ~**ing about going to the cinema** ich habe vielleicht vor, ins Kino zu gehen; **I was** ~**ing if you'd like to come too** möchten Sie nicht vielleicht auch kommen?; **I was** ~**ing if I could come tomorrow** könnte ich vielleicht morgen kommen?

3 *vi* **(a)** *(ask oneself, speculate)* **why do you ask?** — **oh, I was just** ~**ing** warum fragst du? — ach, nur so; **what will happen next, I** ~? ich bin gespannt, was als nächstes kommt; **I was** ~**ing about that** ich habe mich das auch schon gefragt; **I've been** ~**ing about him** ich habe mir auch schon über ihn Gedanken gemacht; **could you possibly help me, I** ~ könnten Sie mir vielleicht helfen? **(b)** *(be surprised)* sich wundern. **I** ~ **(that) he didn't tell me** es wundert mich, daß er es mir nicht gesagt hat; **to** ~ **at sth** sich über etw *(acc)* wundern, über etw *(acc)* erstaunt sein; **she'll be married by now, I shouldn't** ~ es würde mich nicht wundern, wenn sie inzwischen verheiratet wäre.

wonder *in cpds* Wunder-; ~ **boy** *n* Wunderknabe *m;* ~ **drug** *n* Wunderheilmittel *nt.*

wonderful ['wʌndəfʊl] *adj* wunderbar.

wondering ['wʌndərıŋ] *adj (astonished)* tone, look verwundert, erstaunt; *(doubtful)* fragend.

wonderland ['wʌndə,lænd] *n (fairyland)* Wunderland *nt; (wonderful place)* Paradies *nt.*

wonky ['wɒŋkı] *adj* (+*er*) *(Brit col) table, marriage, grammar* wackelig; *machine* nicht (ganz) in Ordnung. **your hat's a bit** ~ dein Hut sitzt ganz schief.

won't [wəʊnt] = **will not.**

woo [wu:] *vt* **(a)** *(dated: court)* woman den Hof machen (+*dat),* umwerben; *(fig)* person umwerben. **(b)** *(fig)* stardom etc suchen.

wood [wʊd] **1** *n* **(a)** *(material)* Holz *nt.* **touch** ~! dreimal auf Holz geklopft!; **beer from the** ~ Bier vom Faß. **(b)** *(small forest)* Wald *m.* ~**s** Wald *m;* **we're not out of the** ~ **yet** *(fig)* wir sind noch nicht über den Berg *or* aus dem Schneider *(col);* **he can't see the** ~ **for the trees** *(prov)* er sieht den Wald vor lauter Bäumen nicht *(prov).* **(c)** *(Bowls)* Kugel *f; (Golf)* Holz *nt.* **2** *adj attr* **(a)** *(made of* ~) Holz-. **(b)** *(living etc in a* ~) Wald-.

wood: ~ **carving** *n* (Holz)schnitzerei *f;* ~**cock** *n no pl* Waldschnepfe *f;* ~**cut** *n* Holzschnitt *m;* ~**cutter** *n* (a) Holzfäller *m; (of logs)* Holzhacker *m;* **(b)** *(Art)* Holzschnitzer *m.*

wooded ['wʊdıd] *adj* bewaldet; *countryside also* Wald-.

wooden ['wʊdn] *adj* **(a)** Holz-. ~ **leg** Holzbein *nt.* **(b)** *(fig)* expression, manner hölzern; *personality* steif.

wood: ~**land** *n* Waldland *nt;* ~**pecker** *n* Specht *m;* ~**pigeon** *n* Ringeltaube *f;* ~**pulp** *n* Holzschliff *m;* ~**shed** *n* Holzschuppen *m.*

woodsman ['wʊdzmən] *n, pl* **-men** [-mən] Waldarbeiter *m.*

wood: ~**wind** *n* Holzblasinstrument *nt;* **the** ~**wind(s),** **the** ~**wind section** die Holzbläser *pl;* ~**work** *n* **(a)** Holzarbeit *f; (craft)* Tischlerei *f;* **(b)** *(wooden parts)* Holzteile *pl;* ~**worm** *n* Holzwurm *m;* **it's got** ~**worm** da ist der Holzwurm drin.

woof [wʊf] *interj* ~, ~! wau, wau!

woofer ['wʊfə'] *n* Tieftöner *m.*

wool [wʊl] *n* Wolle *f; (cloth also)* Wollstoff *m.* **pure new** ~ reine Schurwolle; **to pull the** ~ **over sb's eyes** *(col)* jdm Sand in die Augen streuen *(col).* **2** *adj* Woll-.

woollen, *(US)* **woolen** ['wʊlən] **1** *adj* Woll-, wollen. **2** *n* ~**s** *pl (garments)* Wollsachen *pl; (fabrics, blankets)* Wollwaren *pl.*

woolly, *(US)* **wooly** ['wʊlı] **1** *adj* (+*er*) wollig; *(soft also)* flauschig; *(fig)* outline verschwommen; *(pej)* mind, thinking verworren, wirr. **2** *n (col: sweater etc)* Pulli *m (col).* **winter woollies** *(esp Brit: sweaters etc)* dicke Wollsachen *pl; (esp US: underwear)* Wollene *pl (col).*

woozy ['wu:zı] *adj* (+*er*) *(col)* benommen.

word [wɜ:d] **1** *n* **(a)** Wort *nt.* ~**s** *pl (meaningful sequence)* Worte *pl;* **foreign** ~**s** Fremdwörter *pl;* **the W**~ **of God** das Wort

Gottes; ~ **for** ~ Wort für Wort; **cold isn't the** ~ **for it** kalt ist gar kein Ausdruck (dafür); **too funny for** ~s unbeschreiblich komisch; **to put one's thoughts into** ~s seine Gedanken in Worte fassen; ~s **fail me** mir fehlen die Worte; **in a** ~ mit einem Wort, kurz gesagt; **in so many** ~s direkt, ausdrücklich; **in other** ~s mit anderen Worten; **the last** ~ (fig) der letzte Schrei (in an +dat); **he had the last** ~ er hatte das letzte Wort; **in the** ~s **of Goethe** um mit Goethe zu sprechen; **a** ~ **of advice** ein Rat(schlag) m; **a** ~ **of warning** eine Warnung; **fine** ~s schöne Worte pl; **a man of few** ~s ein Mann, der nicht viele Worte macht; **by** ~ **of mouth** durch mündliche Überlieferung; **to take sb at his** ~ jdn beim Wort nehmen; **to have a** ~ **with sb** (about sth) mit jdm (über etw) sprechen; (reprimand, discipline) jdn ins Gebet nehmen; **you took the** ~s **out of my mouth** du hast mir das Wort aus dem Mund genommen; **I wish you wouldn't put** ~s **into my mouth** ich wünschte, Sie würden mir nicht das Wort im Munde herumdrehen; **to put in a** (**good**) ~ **for sb** für jdn ein gutes Wort einlegen; **without a** ~ ohne ein Wort; **don't say** or **breathe a** ~ **about it** sag aber bitte keinen Ton davon; **to have** ~s **with sb** mit jdm eine Auseinandersetzung haben; ~ **of honour** Ehrenwort nt; **to keep one's** ~ sein Wort halten; **I give you my** ~ ich gebe dir mein (Ehren)wort; **to go back on one's** ~ sein Wort nicht halten; **to break one's** ~ sein Wort brechen; **take my** ~ **for it** das kannst du mir glauben; **my** ~! meine Güte!; **to give the** ~ (**to do sth**) das Kommando geben(, etw zu tun); **just say the** ~ sag nur ein Wort.

(**b**) ~s pl (text, lyrics) Text m.

(**c**) no pl (message, news) Nachricht f. ~ **went around that ...** es ging die Nachricht um, daß ...; (rumour) es ging das Gerücht um, daß ...; **to leave** ~ (**with sb/for sb**) **that ...** (bei jdm/für jdn) (die Nachricht) hinterlassen, daß ...; **is there any** ~ **from John yet**? schon Nachrichten von John?; **to send** ~ Nachricht geben; **to send** ~ **to sb** jdn benachrichtigen; **to send sb** ~ **of sth** jdn um etw benachrichtigen.

2 vt formulieren, in Worte fassen; letter formulieren; speech abfassen.

word: ~**-blind** adj wortblind; ~ **game** n Buchstabenspiel nt.

wording ['wɜːdɪŋ] n Formulierung f; (text) Text m; (on label) Aufschrift f.

word: ~ **order** n Wortstellung f; ~**-perfect** adj sicher im Text; ~ **processing** n Textverarbeitung f; ~ **processor** n (machine) Textverarbeitungsanlage f.

wordy ['wɜːdɪ] adj (+er) wortreich, langatmig (pej.).

wore [wɔːʳ] pret of **wear**.

work [wɜːk] **1** n (**a**) (labour, task) Arbeit f. **he doesn't like** ~ er arbeitet nicht gern; **that's a good piece of** ~ das ist gute Arbeit; **is this all your own** ~? haben Sie das alles selbst gemacht?; **to be at** ~ (**on sth**) (an etw dat) arbeiten; **you need to do some more** ~ **on your accent** Sie müssen noch an Ihrem Akzent arbeiten; **to put a lot of** ~ **into sth** eine Menge Arbeit in etw (acc) stecken; **to get on with one's** ~ sich (wieder) an die Arbeit machen; **to make short** ~ **of sth** mit etw kurzen Prozeß machen; **the medicine had done its** ~ die Arznei hatte ihre Wirkung getan; **the forces at** ~ **here** die Kräfte, die hier am Werk sind; **it was hard** ~ **for the old car to get up the hill** das alte Auto hatte beim Anstieg schwer zu schaffen.

(**b**) (employment, job) Arbeit f. **to be** (**out**) **at** ~ arbeiten sein; **to go out to** ~ arbeiten gehen; **to be out of/in** ~ arbeitslos sein/eine Stelle haben; **he travels to** ~ **by car** er fährt mit dem Auto zur Arbeit; **at** ~ am Arbeitsplatz; **what is your** ~?

was tun Sie (beruflich)?; **to put sb out of** ~ jdn arbeitslos machen; **to be off** ~ (am Arbeitsplatz) fehlen.

(**c**) (product) Arbeit f; (Art, Liter) Werk nt. ~ **of art/reference** Kunstwerk nt/Nachschlagewerk nt; **a** ~ **of literature** ein literarisches Werk; **good** ~s gute Werke pl.

(**d**) ~s pl (Mil) Befestigungen pl; (Mech) Getriebe, Innere(s) nt; (of watch, clock) Uhrwerk nt.

(**e**) ~s sing or pl (factory) Betrieb m, Fabrik f; **gas** ~s/**steel** ~s Gas-/Stahlwerk nt.

(**f**) (col) **the** ~s pl alles Drum und Dran; **to give sb the** ~s (treat harshly) jdn gehörig in die Mangel nehmen (col); (treat generously) jdn nach allen Regeln der Kunst verwöhnen (col).

2 vi (**a**) arbeiten (at an +dat). **to** ~ **towards/ for sth** auf etw (acc) hin/für etw arbeiten; **to** ~ **for better conditions** etc sich für bessere Bedingungen etc einsetzen. (**b**) (function, operate) funktionieren; (marriage, plan also, be successful) klappen (col); (medicine, spell) wirken. **it won't** ~ das klappt nicht; **to get sth** ~**ing** etw in Gang bringen; **it** ~s **by electricity** es läuft auf Strom; **it** ~s **both ways** es trifft auch andersherum zu. (**c**) (mouth, face) zucken; (jaws) mahlen. (**d**) (move gradually) **to** ~ **loose/along** sich lockern/sich entlangarbeiten.

3 vt (**a**) (make ~) employees arbeiten lassen, schinden (pej). **to** ~ **oneself to death** sich zu Tode arbeiten.

(**b**) (operate) machine bedienen; lever, brake betätigen. **to** ~ **sth by hand** etw mit Hand betreiben.

(**c**) change, cure bewirken. **to** ~ **mischief** Unheil anrichten; **to** ~ **it** (so that ...) (col) es so deichseln(, daß ...) (col); **to** ~ **one's passage** seine Überfahrt abarbeiten; **to** ~ **one's hands free** seine Hände freibekommen; **to** ~ **sth loose** etw losbekommen; **to** ~ **sth into the conversation** etw in das Gespräch einfließen lassen; **to** ~ **oneself into a rage** fürchterlich wütend werden; **to** ~ **one's way through a book** sich durch ein Buch arbeiten; **to** ~ **one's way to the top** sich nach oben arbeiten or kämpfen; **he** ~**ed his way across the rock-face** er überquerte die Felswand; **he had to** ~ **his way through college** er mußte sich sein Studium durch eigene Arbeit finanzieren.

(**d**) (shape) wood, metal bearbeiten; dough, clay also kneten, durcharbeiten. **he** ~**ed the clay into a human shape** er formte den Ton zu einer menschlichen Gestalt.

(**e**) (exploit) mine ausbeuten, abbauen; land bearbeiten; smallholding bewirtschaften; (salesman) area bereisen.

♦ **work around to** vi +prep obj **what are you** ~**ing** ~ ~? worauf wollen Sie hinaus?

♦ **work in** vt sep (**a**) (rub in) einarbeiten; lotion einmassieren. (**b**) (in book, speech) reference einbauen, einarbeiten. (**c**) (in schedule etc) einschieben.

♦ **work off** vt sep debts, fat abarbeiten; energy loswerden; feelings abreagieren (on an +dat).

♦ **work on 1** vi weiterarbeiten. **2** vi +prep obj (**a**) car, accent arbeiten an (+dat). **who's** ~**ing** ~ **this case**? wer bearbeitet diesen Fall?; **we haven't** ~ **solved it yet but we're still** ~**ing** ~ **it** wir haben es noch nicht gelöst, aber wir sind dabei. (**b**) evidence ausgehen von; principle (person) ausgehen von; (machine) arbeiten nach. **if we** ~ ~ **the assumption that ...** wenn wir von der Annahme ausgehen, daß ...

♦ **work out 1** vi (**a**) (amount to) **that** ~s ~ **at £105** das gibt or macht £ 105; **how much does that** ~ ~ **at**? was macht das?; (**b**) (succeed: plan, marriage) funktionieren, klappen (col). **how's your new job** ~**ing** ~? was macht die neue Arbeit?; **I hope it**

all ~s ~ for you ich hoffe, daß dir alles gelingt; **things didn't ~ ~ that way** es kam ganz anders. **(c)** *(in gym etc)* trainieren.

2 *vt sep* **(a)** *(solve, calculate)* herausbringen; *code* entschlüsseln; *mathematical problem* lösen; *problem* fertig werden mit *(+dat)*; *sum* ausrechnen. **you can ~ that ~ for yourself** das kannst du dir (doch) selbst denken; **things will always ~ themselves ~** Probleme lösen sich stets von selbst. **(b)** *(devise) scheme* (sich *dat)* ausdenken; *(in detail)* ausarbeiten. **(c)** *(understand) person* schlau werden aus *(+dat)*. **I can't ~ ~ why it went wrong** ich kann nicht verstehen, wieso es nicht geklappt hat. **(d)** *(exhaust) mine* ausbeuten; *minerals* abbauen.

♦ **work up** *vt sep* **(a)** *(develop) business* zu etwas bringen, entwickeln; *enthusiasm (in oneself)* aufbringen; *appetite* sich *(dat)* holen. **to ~ one's way ~** von der Pike auf dienen. **(b)** *(stimulate) audience* aufstacheln. **to ~ ~ feelings against sb** gegen jdn Stimmung machen; **to get ~ed ~** sich aufregen.

♦ **work up to** *vi +prep obj question etc* zusteuern auf *(+acc)*. **I know what you're ~ing ~ ~** ich weiß, worauf Sie hinauswollen.

workable ['wɜːkəbl] *adj mine* abbaufähig; *land* bebaubar; *clay* formbar; *plan* durchführbar.

workaday ['wɜːkədeɪ] *adj* Alltags-.

work: ~**bench** *n* Werkbank *f*; ~**day** *n (esp US)* Arbeitstag *m*; *(day of week)* Werktag *m*.

worker ['wɜːkə'] *n* **(a)** Arbeiter(in *f*) *m*. **(b)** *(also* ~ **ant/bee)** Arbeiterin *f*.

work: ~ **force** *n* Arbeiterschaft *f*; ~**house** *n (Brit Hist)* Armenhaus *nt*.

working ['wɜːkɪŋ] **1** *adj* **(a)** *population* arbeitend, berufstätig. ~ **man/woman** *(worker)* Arbeiter(in *f)* m; **I'm a ~ man!** ich gehöre zur arbeitenden Bevölkerung. **(b)** *day, conditions, clothes* Arbeits-. ~ **capital** Betriebskapital *nt*; ~ **hours** Arbeitszeit *f*; ~ **party** (Arbeits)ausschuß *m*; ~ **week** *(~ hours)* Wochenarbeitszeit *f*. **(c)** *hypothesis, model* Arbeits-; *(sufficient) majority* arbeitsfähig. **in ~ order** in betriebsfähigem Zustand; ~ **knowledge** Grundkenntnisse *pl*. **2** *n* **(a)** *(work)* Arbeiten *nt*, Arbeit *f*. **(b)** ~s *pl (way sth works)* Arbeitsweise *f*; **the ~s of his mind** seine Gedankengänge; **the ~s of fate** Wege *pl* des Schicksals. **(c)** ~s *pl (Min)* Schächte *pl*; *(of quarry)* Grube *f*.

working class *n (also ~ ~es)* Arbeiterklasse *f*.

working-class ['wɜːkɪŋ'klɑːs] *adj* der Arbeiterklasse, Arbeiter-; *(pej)* ordinär, proletenhaft. **to be ~** zur Arbeiterklasse gehören.

work: ~ **load** *n* Arbeit(slast) *f*; ~**man** *n* Handwerker(in *f)* m; ~**manlike** ['wɜːkmənlaɪk] *adj* attitude, job* fachmännisch; *product* fachmännisch gearbeitet; ~**manship** ['wɜːkmənʃɪp] *n* Arbeit(squalität) *f*; ~**out** *n (Sport)* **to have a ~out** trainieren; ~ **permit** *n* Arbeitserlaubnis *f*; ~**shop** *n* Werkstatt *f*; **a music ~shop** ein Musik-Workshop *m*; ~**shy** *adj* arbeitsscheu; ~ **surface**, ~ **top** *n* Arbeitsfläche *f*; ~**-to-rule** *n* Dienst *m* nach Vorschrift; ~**week** *n (esp US)* Arbeitswoche *f*.

world [wɜːld] *n* Welt *f*. **in the ~** auf der Welt; **all over the ~** auf der ganzen Welt; **he sails all over the ~** er segelt in der Weltgeschichte herum; **it's the same all the ~ over** es ist (doch) überall das Gleiche; **to go around the ~** eine Weltreise machen; **to feel on top of the ~** sich glänzend fühlen; **it's a small ~** die Welt ist klein; **it's not the end of the ~!** *(col)* davon geht die Welt nicht unter! *(col)*; **to live in a ~ of one's own** in seiner eigenen (kleinen) Welt leben; **the New/Third W~** die Neue/Dritte Welt; **the business/literary ~** die Geschäftswelt/die literarische Welt; **man/woman of the ~** Mann *m*/Frau *f* von Welt; **to come down in the ~** herunterkommen; **to go up in the ~** es (in der Welt) zu etwas bringen; **to**

lead the ~ in sth in etw *(dat)* in der Welt führend sein; **to have the best of both ~s** das eine tun und das andere nicht lassen; **out of this ~** *(col)* phantastisch; **not for (all) the ~** nicht um alles in der Welt; **what/who in the ~** was/wer in aller Welt; **it did him a ~ of good** es hat ihm (unwahrscheinlich) gut getan; **a ~ of difference** ein himmelweiter Unterschied; **they're ~s apart** sie sind total verschieden; **for all the ~ like ...** beinahe wie ...; **to think the ~ of sb/sth** große Stücke auf jdn halten/etw über alles stellen; **she/it means the ~ to him** sie/es bedeutet ihm alles.

world in *cpds* Welt-; ~**-beater** *n* **to be a ~-beater** führend in der Welt sein; ~ **champion** *n* Weltmeister(in *f)* m; **W~ Cup** *n* Fußballweltmeisterschaft *f*; *(cup)* Weltmeisterschaftspokal *m*; ~**-famous** *adj* weltberühmt.

worldly ['wɜːldlɪ] *adj (+er)* weltlich; *person* weltlich gesinnt. ~**-wise** *adj* weltklug.

world: ~ **record** *n* Weltrekord *m*; ~ **record holder** *n* Weltrekordinhaber(in *f)* m; ~ **war** *n* Weltkrieg *m*; **W~ War One/Two** der Erste/Zweite Weltkrieg; ~**-wide** *adj, adv* weltweit.

worm [wɜːm] **1** *n (lit, fig col)* Wurm *m*; *(wood ~)* Holzwurm *m*. ~**s** *(Med)* Würmer *pl*. **2** *vt* zwängen. **to ~ one's way into sth** sich in etw *(acc)* hineinzwängen; **to ~ one's way into sb's confidence** sich in jds Vertrauen einschleichen; **to ~ sth out of sb** jdm etw entlocken.

worn [wɔːn] **1** *ptp of* **wear**. **2** *adj (~-out) coat* abgetragen; *book* zerlesen; *carpet* abgetragen; *tyre* abgefahren; *person* angegriffen. **to look ~ (with care)** besorgt aussehen.

worn-out *adj attr*, **worn out** ['wɔːn,aʊt] *adj pred coat* abgetragen; *carpet* abgetreten; *phrase* abgedroschen; *(exhausted) person* erschöpft.

worried ['wʌrɪd] *adj* besorgt *(about, by* wegen); *(anxious also)* beunruhigt. **to be ~ sick** krank vor Sorge(n) sein.

worrier ['wʌrɪə'] *n* Pessimist *m*. **he's a terrible ~** er macht sich ständig Sorgen.

worry ['wʌrɪ] **1** *n* Sorge *f*. **what's your ~?** was drückt dich?; **that's the least of my worries** das macht mir noch am wenigsten Sorgen. **2** *vt* **(a)** *(cause concern)* beunruhigen, Sorgen machen *(+dat)*. **to ~ oneself sick (about sth)** sich krank machen vor Sorge (um *or* wegen etw). **(b)** *(bother)* **to ~ sb with sth** jdn mit etw stören. **(c)** *(dog etc) sheep* nachstellen *(+dat)*; *(bite)* reißen. **3** *vi* sich sorgen, sich *(dat)* Sorgen machen *(about, over, um, wegen)*. **don't ~!**, **not to ~!** keine Angst *or* Sorge!; **don't ~, I'll do it** laß mal, das mach ich schon.

worrying ['wʌrɪɪŋ] *adj problem* beunruhigend. **it's very ~** es macht mir große Sorge.

worse [wɜːs] **1** *adj, comp of* **bad** schlechter; *(morally, with bad consequences)* schlimmer, ärger. **it gets ~ and ~** es wird immer schlimmer; **and to make matters ~** und zu allem Übel; **it could have been ~** es hätte schlimmer kommen können; ~ **luck!** (so ein) Pech!; **the patient is getting ~** der Zustand des Patienten verschlechtert sich; **to be the ~ for drink** betrunken sein; **he's none the ~ for it** es ist ihm nichts dabei passiert; **you'll be none the ~ for it** das wird dir nicht schaden; **I don't think any the ~ of you** for it ich halte deswegen nicht weniger von dir.

2 *adv, comp of* **badly** schlechter; schlimmer. **to be ~ off than ...** schlechter dran sein *(col) or* in einer schlechteren Lage sein als ...; **I could do a lot ~ than accept their offer** es wäre bestimmt kein Fehler, wenn ich das Angebot annähme.

3 *n* Schlechteres *nt*; Schlimmeres *nt*. **there is ~ to come** es kommt noch schlimmer; **it's changed for the ~** es hat sich zum Schlechteren gewendet.

worsen ['wɜːsn] **1** *vt* verschlechtern. **2** *vi* sich

verschlechtern, schlechter werden.
worship ['wɜːʃɪp] **1** n (a) Verehrung f. **place of** ~ Andachtsstätte f; (non-Christian) Kultstätte f. **(b)** (Brit: in titles) **Your W** ~ (to judge) Euer Ehren; (to mayor) (sehr geehrter) Herr Bürgermeister. **2** vt (lit, fig) anbeten. **3** vi (Rel) den Gottesdienst abhalten; (RC) die Messe feiern.
worshipper ['wɜːʃɪpəʳ] n Kirchgänger(in f) m.
worst [wɜːst] **1** adj, superl of **bad** schlechteste(r, s); (morally, in consequence) schlimmste(r, s). **the** ~ **possible time** die ungünstigste Zeit. **2** adv, superl of **badly** am schlechtesten; am schlimmsten. **3** n **the** ~ **is over** das Schlimmste or Ärgste ist vorbei; **at** ~ schlimmstenfalls; **the** ~ **of it is …** das Schlimmste daran ist, …; **if the** ~ **comes to the** ~ wenn alle Stricke reißen (col); **to get the** ~ **of it** den kürzeren ziehen.
worsted ['wʊstɪd] n Kammgarn nt.
worth [wɜːθ] **1** adj (a) wert. **it's** ~ **£5** es ist £ 5 wert; **it's not** ~ **£5** es ist keine £ 5 wert; **what's this** ~? was or wieviel ist das wert?; **it's** ~ **a great deal to me** es ist mir viel wert; (sentimentally) es bedeutet mir sehr viel; **what's it** ~ **to me to do that?** was springt für mich dabei heraus? (col); **he was** ~ **a million** er besaß eine Million; **for all one is** ~ so sehr man nur kann; **that's my opinion for what it's** ~ das ist meine bescheidene Meinung; **it's more than my job is** ~ **to tell you** ich sage es dir nicht, dazu liegt mir zu viel an meiner Stelle.
(b) to be (well) ~ **it** sich (sehr) lohnen; **to be** ~ **sth** etw wert sein; **it's not** ~ **it** es lohnt sich nicht; **it's not** ~ **the trouble** es ist der Mühe nicht wert; **the book is** ~ **reading** das Buch ist lesenswert; **is there anything** ~ **seeing in this town?** gibt es in dieser Stadt etwas Sehenswertes?; **it's a film** ~ **seeing** es lohnt sich, diesen Film anzusehen; **hardly** ~ **mentioning** kaum der Rede wert.
2 n Wert m. **£10's** ~ **of books** Bücher im Werte von £ 10; **to show one's true** ~ seinen wahren Wert zeigen; **to increase in** ~ im Wert steigen.
worthless ['wɜːθlɪs] adj wertlos.
worthwhile ['wɜːθ'waɪl] adj (a) lohnend attr. **to be** ~ sich lohnen; (worth the trouble also) der Mühe (gen) wert sein. **(b)** (useful) contribution wertvoll. **to do sth** ~ **with one's life** etwas Nützliches mit seinem Leben anfangen.
worthy ['wɜːðɪ] adj (+er) (a) ehrenwert, achtbar; opponent würdig; motive, cause lobenswert. **(b)** pred wert, würdig. ~ **of mention** erwähnenswert; **to be** ~ **of sb/sth** jds/einer Sache würdig sein (geh).
would [wʊd] pret of **will**[1] modal aux vb (a) (conditional) **if you asked him he** ~ **do it** wenn du ihn fragtest, würde er es tun; **if you had asked him he** ~ **have done it** wenn du ihn gefragt hättest, hätte er es getan; **I thought you** ~ **want to know** ich dachte, du würdest es gerne wissen; **you** ~ **think …** man sollte meinen …
(b) (in indirect speech) **she said she** ~ **come** sie sagte, sie würde kommen or sie käme.
(c) (emph) **you** ~ **be the one to get hit** typisch, daß ausgerechnet du getroffen worden bist; **I** ~**n't know** keine Ahnung; **you** ~! das sieht dir ähnlich!; **he** ~ **have to come right now** ausgerechnet jetzt muß er kommen.
(d) (insistence) **I warned him, but he** ~ **do it** ich habe ihn gewarnt, aber er mußte es ja unbedingt tun; **he** ~**n't listen** er wollte partout nicht zuhören.
(e) it ~ **seem so** es sieht wohl so aus; **it** ~ **have been about 8 o'clock** es war (wohl) so ungefähr 8 Uhr; **you** ~**n't have a cigarette,** ~ **you?** Sie hätten nicht zufällig eine Zigarette?; **what** ~ **you have me do?** was soll ich tun?; ~ **you mind closing the window?** würden or könnten Sie bitte das Fenster schließen?; ~ **you care for some tea?** möchten Sie gerne etwas Tee?

(f) (habit) **he** ~ **paint it each year** er strich es jedes Jahr.
would-be ['wʊdbiː] adj attr (a) (pej) salesman, contract, improvements angeblich. **a** ~ **poet** ein Möchtegern-Dichter. **(b)** (training as, wanting to be) angehend.
wouldn't ['wʊdnt] = **would not.**
wound[1] [wuːnd] **1** n (lit) Wunde f; (fig also) Kränkung f. **2** vt (lit, fig) verletzen. **the** ~**ed** pl die Verwundeten pl; ~**ed pride/vanity** verletzter Stolz/gekränkte Eitelkeit.
wound[2] [waʊnd] pret, ptp of **wind**[2].
wove [waʊv] pret of **weave.**
woven ['waʊvən] ptp of **weave.**
wow [waʊ] interj hui (col), Mann (col).
wrangle ['ræŋgl] vi streiten, rangeln (about um); (in bargaining) feilschen.
wrap [ræp] **1** n (a) (garment) Umhangtuch nt; (for child) Wickeltuch nt; (cape) Cape nt; (coat) Mantel m. **(b) to be under** ~s (fig) geheimgehalten werden. **2** vt einwickeln. **shall I** ~ **it for you?** soll ich es Ihnen einpacken or einwickeln?; **to** ~ **sth around sth** etw um etw wickeln; **he** ~**ped his car around a lamppost** (col) er hat sein Auto an einen Laternenpfahl gesetzt (col); **to be** ~**ped in sth** (fig) in etw (acc) gehüllt sein.
♦ **wrap up 1** vt sep (a) (lit, fig) einwickeln, verpacken. **(b)** (fig: finalize) deal unter Dach und Fach bringen. **that just about** ~s **it** ~ **for today** das wäre alles für heute. **(c)** (be involved) **to be** ~**ped** ~ **in sb/sth** in jdn/etw aufgehen. **2** vi (a) (dress warmly) sich warm einpacken (col). **(b)** (col!: be quiet) den Mund halten (col).
wrapper ['ræpəʳ] n Verpackung f; (of sweets) Papier(chen) nt; (of cigar) Deckblatt nt; (of book) (Schutz)umschlag m; (postal) Streifband nt.
wrapping ['ræpɪŋ] n Verpackung f. ~ **paper** Packpapier nt; (decorative) Geschenkpapier nt.
wrath [rɒθ] n Zorn m; (liter: of storm) Wut f.
wreak [riːk] vt destruction anrichten; chaos also stiften; (liter) vengeance üben (on an +dat).
wreath [riːθ] n, pl -s [riːðz] Kranz m; (of smoke etc) Kringel m.
wreathe [riːð] vt (encircle) (um)winden; (clouds, mist) umhüllen. **his face was** ~**d in smiles** er strahlte über das ganze Gesicht.
wreck [rek] **1** n (ship~) Schiffbruch m; (ship itself) Wrack nt; (US: car crash etc) Zusammenstoß m; (fig) (old bicycle etc) Trümmerhaufen m; (person) Wrack nt; (of hopes, life etc) Trümmer, Ruinen pl. **2** vt (a) ship, train zum Wrack machen; car kaputtfahren (col), zu Schrott fahren (col); machine, furniture zerstören; (person) kurz und klein schlagen (col). **to be** ~**ed** (Naut) Schiffbruch erleiden; ~**ed ship/car** wrackes Schiff/zu Schrott gefahrenes Auto. **(b)** (fig) hopes, plans zunichte machen; marriage zerrütten; career, health zerstören, ruinieren; person kaputtmachen (col); holiday verderben.
wreckage ['rekɪdʒ] n (lit, fig: remains) Trümmer pl; (washed ashore) Strandgut nt; (of house, town also) Ruinen pl.
wrecker ['rekəʳ] n (a) (Naut: salvager) Bergungsarbeiter m; (vessel) Bergungsschiff nt. **(b)** (US: breaker, salvager) Schrotthändler m; (for buildings) Abbrucharbeiter m; (breakdown truck) Abschleppwagen m.
wren [ren] n Zaunkönig m.
wrench [rentʃ] **1** n (a) (tug) Ruck m; (Med) Verrenkung f. **(b)** (tool) Schraubenschlüssel m. **(c)** (fig) **to be a** ~ weh tun. **2** vt (a) reißen. **to** ~ **sth (away) from sb** jdm etw entwinden or entreißen; **to** ~ **a door open** eine Tür aufzwingen. **(b)** (Med) **to** ~ **one's ankle** sich (dat) den Fuß verrenken.
wrest [rest] vt **to** ~ **sth from sb** jdm etw entreißen.
wrestle ['resl] **1** n Ringkampf m. **to have a** ~ **with sb** mit jdm ringen. **2** vt ringen mit. **3** vi (lit, fig) ringen.

wrestler ['resləʳ] n Ringkämpfer m; (modern) Ringer(in f) m.

wrestling ['reslɪŋ] n Ringen nt. ~ **match** Ringkampf m.

wretch [retʃ] n (a) (miserable) armer Teufel. (b) (contemptible) Schuft m; (child) Schlingel m.

wretched ['retʃɪd] adj elend; conditions, clothing etc also erbärmlich; (unhappy) (tod)unglücklich; housing, weather erbärmlich, miserabel (col); (col: damned) verflixt (col), Mist- (col). I feel ~ (ill) mir geht es miserabel (col).

wrick [rɪk] vt to ~ one's neck/shoulder sich (dat) den Hals/die Schulter ausrenken.

wriggle ['rɪgl] 1 vt toes, ears wackeln mit. to ~ one's way through sth sich durch etw (hin)durchwinden. 2 vi (also ~ about or around) (snake) sich schlängeln; (fish) sich winden, zappeln; (person) (restlessly) zappeln; (in embarrassment) sich winden. to ~ along/down sich vorwärts schlängeln/sich nach unten schlängeln; she managed to ~ free es gelang ihr, sich loszuwinden.

♦ **wriggle out** vi (lit) sich herauswinden (of aus); (fig also) sich herausmanövrieren (of aus). he's ~d (his way) ~ of it er hat sich gedrückt.

wring [rɪŋ] (vb: pret, ptp **wrung**) vt (a) clothes etc auswringen, auswinden. do not ~ (on washing instructions) nicht wringen. (b) hands (in distress) ringen. I could have wrung his neck ich hätte ihm den Hals umdrehen können. (c) (extract) to ~ sth out of sb etw aus jdm herausquetschen (col), jdm etw abringen.

wringer ['rɪŋəʳ] n (Wäsche)mangel f.

wringing ['rɪŋɪŋ] adj (also ~ wet) tropfnaß.

wrinkle ['rɪŋkl] 1 n (in clothes, paper) Knitter(falte f) m; (on face, skin, in stocking) Falte f. 2 vt fabric, paper zerknittern; skin faltig machen. to ~ one's nose/brow die Nase rümpfen/die Stirn runzeln. 3 vi (material) knittern; (stockings) Falten schlagen; (skin etc) Falten bekommen.

wrinkled ['rɪŋkld] adj sheet, paper zerknittert; stockings Ziehharmonika- (col); skin faltig; brow gerunzelt; apple, old lady verschrumpelt.

wrist [rɪst] n Handgelenk nt.

wristband ['rɪst,bænd] n Armband nt; (Sport) Schweißband nt.

wristwatch ['rɪst,wɒtʃ] n Armbanduhr f.

writ [rɪt] n (Jur) Verfügung f. to issue a ~ against sb jdn vorladen (for wegen).

write [raɪt] pret **wrote**, ptp **written** 1 vt schreiben; cheque also ausstellen; notes sich (dat) machen. he wrote me a letter er schrieb mir einen Brief; he wrote five sheets of paper er schrieb fünf Seiten voll; how is that written? wie schreibt man das?; to be writ(ten) large (fig) klar zu erkennen sein; it was written all over his face es stand ihm im Gesicht geschrieben. 2 vi schreiben. to ~ to sb jdm schreiben; we ~ to each other wir schreiben uns; that's nothing to ~ home about (col) das ist nichts Weltbewegendes; I'll ~ for it at once (order) ich bestelle es sofort.

♦ **write away** vi schreiben. to ~ ~ for sth etw anfordern.

♦ **write back** vi zurückschreiben, antworten.

♦ **write down** vt sep (make a note of) aufschreiben; (put in writing) niederschreiben.

♦ **write in** 1 vt sep word etc hineinschreiben, einfügen (prep obj in +acc). 2 vi schreiben (to an +acc). to ~ ~ for sth etw anfordern.

♦ **write off** 1 vi = **write away**. 2 vt sep debt, losses, (fig: regard as failure) abschreiben; car etc (driver) zu Schrott fahren; (insurance company) als Totalschaden abschreiben.

♦ **write out** vt sep notes ausarbeiten; name etc ausschreiben; cheque ausstellen.

♦ **write up** vt sep notes ausarbeiten; report, diary schreiben; event schreiben über (+acc); (review)

play, film eine Kritik schreiben über (+acc).

write-off ['raɪtɒf] n (car etc) Totalschaden m; (Comm) Abschreibung f.

writer ['raɪtəʳ] n Schriftsteller(in f) m; (of report etc) Autor(in f) m; (of music) Komponist(in f) m. he's a very poor ~ er schreibt sehr schlecht; (correspondent) er ist kein großer Briefschreiber; ~'s cramp Schreibkrampf m.

write-up ['raɪtʌp] n Pressebericht m; (of play etc) Kritik f.

writhe [raɪð] vi sich krümmen, sich winden (with, in vor +dat).

writing ['raɪtɪŋ] n Schrift f; (act, profession) Schreiben nt; (inscription) Inschrift f. in ~ schriftlich; permission in ~ schriftliche Genehmigung; his ~s seine Werke or Schriften; in sb's own ~ (not typewritten) handgeschrieben; in (not written by sb else) in jds eigener (Hand)schrift (dat); the ~ is on the wall for them ihre Stunde hat geschlagen; he had seen the ~ on the wall er hatte die Zeichen erkannt.

writing in cpds Schreib-; ~ **case** Schreibmappe f; ~ **desk** n Schreibtisch m; ~ **pad** n Notizblock m; ~ **paper** n Schreibpapier nt.

written ['rɪtn] 1 ptp of **write**. 2 adj examination, statement schriftlich; language Schrift-; word geschrieben.

wrong [rɒŋ] 1 adj (a) falsch; (when choice is given also) verkehrt. to be ~ nicht stimmen; (person) unrecht haben; (answer also) falsch or verkehrt sein; (watch) falsch gehen; it's all ~ that I should have to ... das ist doch nicht richtig, daß ich ... muß; I was ~ about him ich habe mich in ihm geirrt; you were ~ in thinking he did it du hast unrecht gehabt, als du dachtest, er sei es gewesen; I took a ~ turning ich habe eine falsche Abzweigung genommen; to say/do the ~ thing das Falsche sagen/tun; the ~ side of the fabric die linke Seite des Stoffes; to do sth the ~ way etw falsch or verkehrt machen.

(b) (morally) schlecht, unrecht; (unfair) ungerecht, unfair. it's ~ to steal es ist unrecht zu stehlen; you were ~ to do that es war nicht richtig von dir, das zu tun; what's ~ with a drink now and again? was ist schon (Schlimmes) dabei, wenn man ab und zu einen trinkt?

(c) pred (amiss) something is ~ (irgend) etwas stimmt nicht or ist nicht in Ordnung; (suspiciously) irgend etwas stimmt da nicht or ist da faul (col); is anything ~? ist was? (col); there's nothing ~ (es ist) alles in Ordnung; what's ~? was ist los?; what's ~ with you? was fehlt Ihnen?; something's ~ with my watch mit meiner Uhr stimmt (et)was nicht.

2 adv falsch. you did ~ to do it es war unrecht or nicht richtig von dir, das zu tun; to get sth ~ sich mit etw vertun; to get one's sums ~ sich verrechnen; don't get me ~ verstehen Sie mich nicht falsch; to go ~ (on route) falsch gehen/ fahren; (plan) schiefgehen; (affair etc) schieflaufen; my washing-machine has gone ~ meine Waschmaschine ist nicht in Ordnung; you can't go ~ du kannst gar nichts verkehrt machen; (in telling sb the way) du kannst dich nicht verlaufen/verfahren.

3 n Unrecht nt no pl. (social) ~s (soziale) Ungerechtigkeiten pl; to be in the ~ im Unrecht sein; to put sb in the ~ jdn ins Unrecht setzen; two ~s don't make a right ein zweites Unrecht hebt das erste nicht auf; she, of course, can do no ~ macht natürlich nie einen Fehler.

4 vt to ~ sb jdm unrecht tun; to be ~ed ungerecht behandelt werden.

wrongdoer ['rɒŋˌduːəʳ] n Übeltäter(in f) m.

wrongful ['rɒŋfʊl] adj ungerechtfertigt.

wrongly ['rɒŋlɪ] adv (a) (unjustly, improperly) unrecht; punished zu Unrecht. (b) (incorrectly) falsch, verkehrt; maintain zu Unrecht; believe fälschlicherweise.

wrote [rəʊt] *pret of* **write.**

wrought [rɔːt] 1 *vt* (a) *(obs, liter) pret, ptp of* **work.** (b) **great changes have been** ~ große Veränderungen wurden herbeigeführt; **the storm** ~ **great destruction** der Sturm richtete große Verheerungen an. 2 *adj iron* Schmiede-; *silver* gehämmert.

wrought: ~-**iron** *adj* schmiedeeisern *attr,* aus Schmiedeeisen; ~-**up** *adj* **to be** ~-**up** aufgeregt sein.

wrung [rʌŋ] *pret, ptp of* **wring.**

wry [raɪ] *adj (ironical)* ironisch; *joke, humour etc* trocken.

wryly ['raɪlɪ] *adv* ironisch.

wt = **weight** Gew.

X

X, x [eks] *n* X, x *nt*. ~ **pounds** x Pfund; ~ **marks the spot** die Stelle ist mit einem Kreuz gekennzeichnet; ~-**certificate film** nicht jugendfreier Film.

Xerox ® ['zıǝrɒks] *vt* xerokopieren.

Xmas ['eksmǝs, 'krısmǝs] *n* = **Christmas**

Weihnachten *nt*.

X-ray ['eks'reı] **1** *n* Röntgenstrahl *m*; *(also* ~ **photograph)* Röntgenaufnahme *f*. **to have an** ~ geröntgt werden. **2** *vt person, heart* röntgen; *envelope* durchleuchten.

xylophone ['zaılǝfǝun] *n* Xylophon *nt*.

Y

Y, y [waı] *n* Y, y *nt*.

yacht [jɒt] *nt* Jacht, Yacht *f*. ~ **club** Jacht- *or* Segelklub *m*; ~ **race** (Segel)regatta *f*.

yachting ['jɒtıŋ] *n* Segeln *nt*. **to go** ~**ing** segeln gehen.

yachtsman ['jɒtsmǝn] *n, pl* -**men** [-mǝn] Segler *m*.

yachtswoman ['jɒtswumǝn] *n, pl* -**women** [-wımın] Seglerin *f*.

yak [jæk] *n (Zool)* Jak, Grunzochse *m*.

yam [jæm] *n* **(a)** *(plant)* Yamswurzel *f*. **(b)** *(US: sweet potato)* Süßkartoffel *f*.

yank [jæŋk] **1** *n* Ruck *m*. **give it a good** ~ zieh mal kräftig dran. **2** *vt to* ~ **sth** mit einem Ruck an etw *(dat)* ziehen.

♦ **yank out** *vt sep* ausreißen; *tooth* ziehen.

Yank [jæŋk] **1** *n* Ami *m (col)*. **2** *adj attr* Ami- *(col)*.

yap [jæp] *vi (dog)* kläffen; *(talk noisily)* quatschen *(col)*, labern *(col)*.

yard[1] ['jɑːd] *n (Measure)* Yard *nt*. **to buy cloth by the** ~ Stoff im Meter kaufen.

yard[2] *n* **(a)** Hof *m*. **back** ~ Hinterhof *m*; **in the** ~ auf dem Hof. **(b)** *(worksite)* Werksgelände *nt*; *(for storage)* Lagerplatz *m*. **builder's** ~ Bauhof *m*; **shipbuilding** ~ Werft *f*; **naval (dock)**~, **navy** ~ Marinewerft *f*. **(c)** *(US: garden)* Garten *m*.

yard: ~-**arm** *n (Naut)* Nock *f*; ~**stick** *n (measuring rod)* Elle *f*; *(fig)* Maßstab *m*.

yarn [jɑːn] *n* **(a)** *(Tex)* Garn *nt*. **(b)** *(tale)* Seemannsgarn *nt*. **to spin a** ~ Seemannsgarn spinnen; **to spin sb a** ~ **about sth** jdm eine Lügengeschichte über etw *(acc)* erzählen.

yawn [jɔːn] **1** *vi (lit, fig)* gähnen. **to** ~ **one's head off** fürchterlich gähnen *(col)*. **2** *n* Gähnen *nt*. **to give a** ~ gähnen; **to be a** ~ *(col)* langweilig sein.

yawning ['jɔːnıŋ] *adj chasm etc* gähnend.

yd = **yard(s)**.

yea [jeı] **1** *adv (obs: yes)* ja. **2** *n* the ~**s and the nays** die Jastimmen und die Neinstimmen.

yeah [jeǝ] *adv (col)* ja.

year [jıǝʳ] *n* **(a)** Jahr *nt*. **last** ~ letztes Jahr; **this** ~ dieses Jahr; **every other** ~ jedes zweite Jahr; **in the** ~ **1969** im Jahr(e) 1969; ~ **after** ~ Jahr für Jahr; ~ **by** ~, **from** ~ **to** ~ von Jahr zu Jahr; ~ **in,** ~ **out** jahrein, jahraus; **all (the)** ~ **round** das ganze Jahr über; ~**s (and** ~**s) ago** vor (langen) Jahren; **I haven't seen her in** ~**s** ich habe sie jahrelang *or* seit Jahren nicht mehr gesehen; **a** ~ **last January** (im) Januar vor einem Jahr; **a** ~

from now nächstes Jahr um diese Zeit; **a hundred-**~-**old tree** ein hundertjähriger Baum; **he is six** ~**s old** er ist sechs Jahre (alt); **it costs £100 a** ~ es kostet £100 pro *or* im Jahr; **it has put** ~**s on me** es hat mich (um) Jahre älter gemacht; **it takes** ~**s off you** es macht dich um Jahre jünger; **he looks old for his** ~**s** er sieht älter aus als er ist; **well on in** ~**s** im vorgerückten Alter; **to get on in** ~**s** in die Jahre kommen. **(b)** *(Univ, Sch, of wine)* Jahrgang *m*. **first-**~ **student** Student(in *f*) *m* im ersten Jahr; *(in first term)* ≃ Erstsemester *nt*.

yearbook ['jıǝbuk] *n* Jahrbuch *nt*.

yearling ['jıǝlıŋ] *n (animal)* Jährling *m*; *(racehorse also)* Einjährige(r) *mf*.

yearly ['jıǝlı] **1** *adj* jährlich. **2** *adv* jährlich, einmal im Jahr. **twice** ~ zweimal im Jahr.

yearn [jɜːn] *vi* sich sehnen *(after, for* nach*)*. **to** ~ **to do sth** sich danach sehnen, etw zu tun.

yearning ['jɜːnıŋ] **1** *n* Sehnsucht *f*, Verlangen *nt (to do sth* etw zu tun, *for* nach*)*. **2** *adj glance, look* sehnsüchtig.

yeast [jiːst] *n no pl* Hefe *f*.

yell [jel] **1** *n* Schrei *m*. **to let out a** ~ einen Schrei ausstoßen, schreien. **2** *vi (also* ~ **out)** schreien, brüllen *(with* vor +*dat)*. **he** ~**ed at her** er schrie *or* brüllte sie an; **he** ~**ed abuse at the teacher** er beschimpfte den Lehrer wüst.

yellow ['jelǝu] **1** *adj (+er)* **(a)** gelb. **to turn** ~ gelb werden; *(paper)* vergilben; ~ **pages** Branchenverzeichnis *nt*, Gelbe Seiten *pl*. **(b)** *(col: cowardly)* feige. **2** *n (colour)* Gelb *nt*; *(of egg)* Eigelb *nt*. **3** *vi gelb werden*; *(pages)* vergilben.

yellowish ['jelǝuıʃ] *adj* gelblich.

yelp [jelp] **1** *n (of animal)* Jaulen *nt no pl*; *(of person)* Aufschrei *m*. **2** *vi (animal)* (auf)jaulen; *(person)* aufschreien.

yen[1] [jen] *n (Fin)* Yen *m*.

yen[2] *n (col)* Lust *f (for* auf +*acc)*. **to have a** ~ **to do sth** Lust haben, etw zu tun.

yeoman ['jǝumǝn] *n, pl* -**men** [-mǝn] **(a)** *(Hist: small landowner)* Freibauer *m*. **(b)** Y~ **of the Guard** königlicher Leibgardist.

yes [jes] **1** *adv* ja; *(answering neg question)* doch. **to say** ~ **to a demand** einer Forderung *(dat)* nachkommen; **if management says** ~ **to an increase** wenn die Betriebsleitung eine Lohnerhöhung bewilligt; ~ **sir!** jawohl, mein Herr; *(Mil)* jawohl,

Herr General/Leutnant *etc;* **I didn't say that —
oh** ~**, you did** das habe ich nicht gesagt—o doch,
das hast du. **2** *n* Ja *nt.*

yes man ['jesmæn] *n, pl* ~ **men** [-men] Jasager *m.*

yesterday ['jestədeɪ] **1** *n* Gestern *nt.* **the fashions
of** ~ die Mode von gestern. **2** *adv (lit, fig)* gestern.

~ **morning/evening** gestern morgen/abend; **he
was at home all (day)** ~ er war gestern den
ganzen Tag zu Hause; **the day before** ~ vorgestern; **a week ago** ~ gestern vor einer Woche;
~**'s paper** die Zeitung von gestern.

yet [jet] **1** *adv* **(a)** *(still)* noch; *(thus far)* bis jetzt,
bisher. **they haven't returned** ~ sie sind noch
nicht zurückgekommen; **this is his best book** ~
das ist sein bisher bestes Buch; **as** ~ *(with present tenses)* bis jetzt, bisher; *(with past)* bis dahin;
no, not ~ nein, noch nicht; **not just** ~ jetzt noch
nicht; **they have a few days** ~ sie haben noch ein
paar Tage; **I've** ~ **to learn how to do it** ich muß
erst noch lernen, wie man es macht; **he may** ~
come er kann noch kommen; **I may** ~ **go to Italy**
ich fahre vielleicht noch nach Italien; **I'll do it** ~
ich schaffe es schon noch.

(b) *(with interrog)* schon. **has he arrived** ~? ist
er schon angekommen?; **do you have to go just**
~? müssen Sie jetzt schon gehen?

(c) *(with comp)* noch. **this is** ~ **more difficult**
dies ist (sogar) noch schwieriger; **he wants** ~
more money er will noch mehr Geld.

(d) *(in addition)* **(and)** ~ **again** und wieder,
und noch einmal; **another arrived and** ~ **another**
es kam noch einer und noch einer.

2 *conj* doch, dennoch, trotzdem. **and** ~ und
doch *or* dennoch; **it's strange** ~ **true** es ist
seltsam, aber wahr.

yeti ['jetɪ] *n* Yeti, Schneemensch *m.*

yew [juː] *n (also* ~ **tree)** Eibe *f; (wood)* Eibe(nholz
nt) f.

Yiddish ['jɪdɪʃ] **1** *adj* jiddisch. **2** *n (language)*
Jiddisch *nt.*

yield [jiːld] **1** *vt* **(a)** *crop, result* hervorbringen;
(tree) fruit tragen; *(mine)* bringen; *(shares)
interest* (ein)bringen; **the information** ~**ed by
the poll** die Information, die die Meinungsumfrage ergeben hat. **(b)** *(surrender)* aufgeben.
to ~ **sth to sb** etw an jdn abtreten; **to** ~ **ground to
the enemy** dem Feind zurückweichen.

2 *vi* **(a)** *(surrender, give way)* **they** ~**ed to us**
sie haben nachgegeben; *(Mil)* sie haben sich uns
(dat) ergeben; **to** ~ **to force** der Gewalt nachgeben; **to** ~ **to reason** sich der Vernunft beugen;
to ~ **to sb's entreaties/threats** jds Bitten
(dat) nachgeben/sich jds Drohungen *(dat)*
beugen; **to** ~ **to temptation** der Versuchung
erliegen. **(b)** *(give way: branch, ground)*
nachgeben. **(c)** *(Mot)* **to** ~ **to oncoming
traffic** den Gegenverkehr vorbeilassen; "~"
(US, Mot) "Vorfahrt gewähren!"

3 *n (of land, tree)* Ertrag *m; (of work also)* Ergebnis *nt; (of mine, well)* Ausbeute *f; (of industry:
goods)* Produktion *f; (profit)* Gewinne, Erträge *pl;
(Fin: of shares, business)* Ertrag, Gewinn *m.*

yippee [jɪ'piː] *interj* juchhu, hurra.

YMCA = **Young Men's Christian Association** CVJM *m.*

yob(bo) ['jɒb(əʊ)] *n (Brit col)* Halbstarke(r),
Rowdy *m.*

yodel ['jəʊdl] *vti* jodeln.

yoga ['jəʊgə] *n* Joga, Yoga *m or nt.*

yog(h)urt ['jɒgət] *n* Joghurt *m or nt.*

yoke [jəʊk] **1** *n (for oxen)* Joch *nt; (for carrying pails)*
Schultertrage *f.* **to throw off the** ~ *(fig)* das Joch
abschütteln. **(b)** *pl* - *(pair of oxen)* Joch, Gespann
nt. **2** *vt* **(a)** *(also* ~ **up)** *oxen* (ins Joch) einspannen.
(b) *(fig: join together)* zusammenschließen.

yokel ['jəʊkəl] *n (pej)* Bauerntölpel *m.*

yolk [jəʊk] *n (of egg)* Eigelb *nt.*

yonder ['jɒndəʳ] *(poet, dial)* **1** *adv (over)* ~ dort

drüben. 2 *adj* **from** ~ **house** von dem Haus (dort)
drüben.

you [juː] *pron* **(a)** *(German familiar form, in letter-
writing usu with a capital) (sing) (nom)* du; *(acc)*
dich; *(dat)* dir; *(pl) (nom)* ihr; *(acc, dat)* euch;
(German polite form: sing, pl) (nom, acc) Sie; *(dat)*
Ihnen. **all of** ~ *(pl)* ihr alle/Sie alle; **if I were** ~
wenn ich du/Sie wäre; ~ **Germans** ihr Deutschen; **is that** ~? bist du's/seid ihr's/sind Sie's?;
it's ~ du bist es/ihr seid's/Sie sind's; **that hat just
isn't** ~ *(col)* der Hut paßt einfach nicht zu dir/zu
Ihnen; **now there's a car for** ~! das ist mal ein
tolles Auto. **(b)** *(indef) (nom)* man; *(acc)* einen;
(dat) einem. ~ **never know** man kann nie wissen,
man weiß nie; **it's not good for** ~ es ist nicht gut.

you'd [juːd] = **you would; you had.**

you'd've ['juːdəv] = **you would have.**

you'll [juːl] = **you will; you shall.**

young [jʌŋ] **1** *adj (+er)* jung; *wine, grass also* neu. ~
people junge Leute *pl;* ~ **people's fashions**
Jugendmoden *pl;* ~ **lady/man** junge Dame/
junger Mann; **they have a** ~ **family** sie haben
kleine Kinder; **he is** ~ **at heart** er ist innerlich
jung geblieben; ~ **Mr Brown** der junge Herr
Brown; **Pitt the Y**~**er** Pitt der Jüngere; **he's a
very** ~ **forty** er ist ein jugendlicher Vierziger. **2**
npl **(a)** *(people)* **the** ~ die Jugend, die jungen
Leute; **books for the** ~ Jugendbücher *pl.* **(b)**
(animals) Junge *pl.* **with** ~ trächtig.

youngster ['jʌŋstəʳ] *n (boy)* Junge *m; (child)* Kind
nt.

your [jɔːʳ] *poss adj* **(a)** *(German familiar form,
letter-writing usu with a capital) (sing)* dein/deine/
dein; *(pl)* euer/eure/euer; *(German polite form:
sing, pl)* Ihr/Ihre/Ihr. **(b)** **the climate here is bad
for** ~ **health** das Klima hier ist nicht gut für die
Gesundheit; ~ **typical American** der typische
Amerikaner.

you're [jʊəʳ] = **you are.**

yours [jɔːz] *poss pron (German familiar form,
in letter-writing usu with a capital) (sing)* deiner/
deine/deins; *(pl)* eurer/eure/euers; *(German
polite form: sing, pl)* Ihrer/Ihre/Ihr(e)s. **this is my
book and that is** ~ dies ist mein Buch und das
(ist) deins/Ihres; **the idea was** ~ es war deine/
Ihre Idee, die Idee stammt von dir/Ihnen; **she is
a cousin of** ~ sie ist deine Kusine, sie ist eine
Kusine von dir; **that is no business of** ~ das geht
dich/Sie nichts an; **that dog of** ~! dein/Ihr blöder
Hund!; ~ *(in letter writing)* Ihr/Ihre; ~ **faithfully,
~ **truly *(on letter)* mit freundlichen Grüßen,
hochachtungsvoll *(form);* **what's** ~? *(to drink)*
was trinkst du/was trinken Sie?; ~ **truly** *(col: I,
me)* meine Wenigkeit.

yourself [jə'self] *pron, pl* **yourselves** **(a)** *(reflexive) (German familiar form) (sing) (acc)* dich;
(dat) dir; *(pl)* euch; *(German polite form: sing, pl)*
sich. **have you hurt** ~? hast du dir/haben Sie sich
weh getan?; **you never speak about** ~ du redest
nie über dich (selbst)/Sie reden nie über sich
(selbst). **(b)** *(emph)* selbst. **you told me** ~ du
hast/Sie haben es mir selbst gesagt; **you will see
for** ~ du wirst/Sie werden selbst sehen; **did you
do it by** ~? hast du/haben Sie das allein
gemacht?

youth [juːθ] *n (a) no pl* Jugend *f.* **in my** ~ in meiner
Jugend(zeit); **she has kept her** ~ sie ist jung
geblieben. **(b)** *pl* -**s** [juːðz] *(young man)* junger
Mann, Jugendliche(r) *m.* **(c)** ~ *pl (young men and
women)* Jugend *f.* **she likes working with (the)** ~
sie arbeitet gerne mit Jugendlichen; ~ **club**
Jugendklub *m;* ~ **hostel** Jugendherberge *f;* ~
movement Jugendbewegung *f.*

youthful ['juːθfʊl] *adj* jugendlich.

youthfulness ['juːθfʊlnɪs] *n* Jugendlichkeit *f.*

you've [juːv] = **you have.**

yowl [jaʊl] **1** *n (of person)* Heulen *nt no pl; (of dog)*
Jaulen *nt no pl; (of cat)* klägliches Miauen *no pl.* **2**

vi *(person)* heulen; *(dog)* jaulen; *(cat)* kläglich miauen.

yo-yo ['jəʊjəʊ] *n* Jo-Jo *nt.*

Yugoslav ['juːgəʊ'slɑːv] **1** *adj* jugoslawisch. **2** *n* Jugoslawe *m,* Jugoslawin *f.*

Yugoslavia ['juːgəʊ'slɑːvɪə] *n* Jugoslawien *nt.*

Yule [juːl] *n (old)* Weihnachten *nt.* **~tide** Weihnachtszeit *f.*

yummy ['jʌmɪ] **1** *adj* (+er) *(col) food* lecker; *man* toll. **2** *interj* ~!, ~ ~! lecker!, hm! *(col).*

YWCA = **Young Women's Christian Association** CVJF *m.*

Z

Z, z [*(Brit)* zed, *(US)* ziː] *n* Z, z *nt.*

Zambia [zæmbɪə] *n* Sambia *nt.*

zany ['zeɪnɪ] *adj* (+er) *humour* verrückt; *person also* irrsinnig komisch.

zap [zæp] *vt (col) (hit)* schlagen; *(kill)* ausradieren *(col); (erase) data* löschen.

♦ **zap up** *vt sep (col)* aufmotzen *(col).*

zeal [ziːl] *n no pl* Eifer *m.* **to work with great ~** mit Feuereifer arbeiten.

zealot ['zelət] *n* Fanatiker(in *f*) *m; (religious also)* (Glaubens)eiferer(in *f*) *m.*

zealous ['zeləs] *adj worker* eifrig, emsig. **~ for sth** eifrig um etw bemüht; **to be ~ to begin** erpicht darauf sein, anzufangen.

zebra ['zebrə] *n* Zebra *nt.* **~ crossing** *(Brit)* Zebrastreifen *m.*

zenith ['zenɪθ] *n (Astron, fig)* Zenit *m.*

zeppelin ['zeplɪn] *n* Zeppelin *m.*

zero ['zɪərəʊ] **1** *n, pl* **-(e)s** Null *f; (point on scale)* Nullpunkt *m.* **15 degrees below ~** 15 Grad unter Null. **~ degrees** null Grad; **~ gravity** Schwerelosigkeit *f;* **at ~ gravity** unter Schwerelosigkeit; **~ hour** *(Mil, fig)* die Stunde X; **~-rated** *(for VAT)* mehrwertsteuerfrei.

♦ **zero in on** *vi* +prep obj main point etc herausgreifen.

zest [zest] *n (enthusiasm)* Begeisterung *f; (in style, of food etc)* Pfiff *(col),* Schwung *m.* **~ for life** Lebensfreude *f;* **a story full of ~** eine Geschichte mit Schwung.

zigzag ['zɪgzæg] **1** *n* Zickzack *m or nt.* **the river cuts a ~ through the rocks** der Fluß bahnt sich im Zickzack einen Weg durch die Felsen. **2** *adj course, line* Zickzack-; *road, path* zickzackförmig. **3** *adv* zickzackförmig, im Zickzack. **4** *vi* im Zickzack laufen/fahren *etc.*

zinc [zɪŋk] *n* Zink *nt.* **~ ointment** Zinksalbe *f;* **~ oxide** Zinkoxyd *nt.*

Zionism ['zaɪənɪzəm] *n* Zionismus *m.*

Zionist ['zaɪənɪst] **1** *adj* zionistisch. **2** *n* Zionist(in *f*) *m.*

zip [zɪp] **1** *n* **(a)** *(Brit: fastener)* Reißverschluß *m.* **(b)** *(col: energy)* Schwung *m.* **2** *vi (col: car, person)* flitzen *(col).* **to ~ past/along** *etc* vorbei-/daherflitzen *etc (col).*

♦ **zip up 1** *vt sep* **to ~ ~ a dress** den Reißverschluß eines Kleides zumachen. **2** **the dress ~s ~** das Kleid hat einen Reißverschluß.

zip: **~ code** *n (US)* Postleitzahl *f;* **~ fastener** *n* Reißverschluß *m.*

zipper ['zɪpəʳ] *n* Reißverschluß *m.*

zit [zɪt] *n (esp US col)* Pickel *m.*

zither ['zɪðəʳ] *n* Zither *f.*

zodiac ['zəʊdɪæk] *n* Tierkreis *m.* **signs of the ~** Tierkreiszeichen *pl.*

zombie ['zɒmbɪ] *n* **(a)** *(lit: revived corpse)* Zombie *m.* **(b)** *(fig)* Idiot *(col),* Schwachkopf *(col) m.* **like a ~/like ~s** wie im Tran.

zone ['zəʊn] **1** *n* **(a)** Zone *f; (fig also)* Gebiet *nt.* **no-parking ~** Parkverbot *nt;* **time ~** Zeitzone *f.* **(b)** *(US: postal ~)* Postbezirk *m.* **2** *vt* **(a)** *town* in Zonen aufteilen. **(b)** **to ~ a district for industry** einen Bezirk zur Industriezone erklären.

zonked [zɒŋkt] *adj (col) (drunk, high)* total ausgeflippt *(col); (tired)* total geschafft *(col).*

zoo [zuː] *n* Zoo, Tierpark *m.* **~ keeper** Tierpfleger(in *f*), Wärter(in *f*) *m.*

zoological [ˌzʊə'lɒdʒɪkəl] *adj* zoologisch. **~ gardens** zoologischer Garten.

zoologist [zʊ'ɒlədʒɪst] *n* Zoologe *m,* Zoologin *f.*

zoology [zʊ'ɒlədʒɪ] *n* Zoologie *f.*

zoom [zuːm] **1** *n* **(a)** *(sound of engine)* Surren *nt.* **(b)** *(Phot: also ~ lens)* Zoom(objektiv) *nt.* **2** *vi (engine)* surren; *(col)* sausen *(col).* **the car ~ed past us** der Wagen sauste an uns vorbei *(col);* **to ~ off** davonrasen.

♦ **zoom in** *vi* **to ~ ~ on sth** *(Phot)* etw heranholen.

zucchini [zuː'kiːnɪ] *n (US)* Zucchini *f.*

Zulu ['zuːluː] **1** *adj* Zulu-. **2** *n* Zulu *mf; (language)* Zulu *nt.*

IRREGULAR GERMAN VERBS

Infinitive	Present Indicative 2nd pers sing; 3rd pers sing	Imperfect Indicative	Past Participle
backen	bäckst, backst; bäckt, backt	backte	gebacken
befehlen	befiehlst; befiehlt	befahl	befohlen
beginnen	beginnst; beginnt	begann	begonnen
beißen	beißt; beißt	biß	gebissen
bergen	birgst; birgt	barg	geborgen
bersten	birst; birst	barst	geborsten
bewegen[2]	bewegst; bewegt	bewog	bewogen
biegen	biegst; biegt	bog	gebogen
bieten	bietest; bietet	bot	geboten
binden	bindest; bindet	band	gebunden
bitten	bittest; bittet	bat	gebeten
blasen	bläst; bläst	blies	geblasen
bleiben	bleibst; bleibt	blieb	geblieben
braten	brätst; brät	briet	gebraten
brechen	brichst; bricht	brach	gebrochen
brennen	brennst; brennt	brannte	gebrannt
bringen	bringst; bringt	brachte	gebracht
denken	denkst; denkt	dachte	gedacht
dreschen	drischst; drischt	drosch	gedroschen
dringen	dringst; dringt	drang	gedrungen
dürfen	1st darf; 2nd darfst; 3rd darf	durfte	gedurft; (after infin) dürfen
empfangen	empfängst; empfängt	empfing	empfangen
empfehlen	empfiehlst; empfiehlt	empfahl	empfohlen
empfinden	empfindest; empfindet	empfand	empfunden
erschrecken	erschreckst; erschreckt	erschrak	erschrocken
essen	ißt; ißt	aß	gegessen
fahren	fährst; fährt	fuhr	gefahren
fallen	fällst; fällt	fiel	gefallen
fangen	fängst; fängt	fing	gefangen
fechten	fichtst, fichst (col); ficht	focht	gefochten
finden	findest; findet	fand	gefunden
flechten	flichtst, flichst (col); flicht	flocht	geflochten
fliegen	fliegst; fliegt	flog	geflogen
fliehen	fliehst; flieht	floh	geflohen
fließen	fließt; fließt	floß	geflossen
fressen	frißt; frißt	fraß	gefressen
frieren	frierst; friert	fror	gefroren
gebären	gebierst; gebiert	gebar	geboren
geben	gibst; gibt	gab	gegeben
gedeihen	gedeihst; gedeiht	gedieh	gediehen
gehen	gehst; geht	ging	gegangen
gelingen	gelingt	gelang	gelungen
gelten	giltst; gilt	galt	gegolten
genesen	genest; genest	genas	genesen
genießen	genießt; genießt	genoß	genossen
geschehen	geschieht	geschah	geschehen
gewinnen	gewinnst; gewinnt	gewann	gewonnen
gießen	gießt; gießt	goß	gegossen
gleichen	gleichst; gleicht	glich	geglichen
gleiten	gleitest; gleitet	glitt	geglitten
glimmen	glimmst; glimmt	glomm	geglommen
graben	gräbst; gräbt	grub	gegraben
greifen	greifst; greift	griff	gegriffen
haben	hast; hat	hatte	gehabt
halten	hältst; hält	hielt	gehalten
hängen	hängst; hängt	hing	gehangen
hauen	haust; haut	haute	gehauen
heben	hebst; hebt	hob	gehoben
heißen	heißt; heißt	hieß	geheißen
helfen	hilfst; hilft	half	geholfen
kennen	kennst; kennt	kannte	gekannt

klingen	klingst; klingt	klang	geklungen
kneifen	kneifst; kneift	kniff	gekniffen
kommen	kommst; kommt	kam	gekommen
können	*1st* kann; *2nd* kannst; *3rd* kann	konnte	gekonnt; *(after infin)* können
kriechen	kriechst; kriecht	kroch	gekrochen
laden	lädst; lädt	lud	geladen
lassen	läßt; läßt	ließ	gelassen; *(after infin)* lassen
laufen	läufst; läuft	lief	gelaufen
leiden	leidest; leidet	litt	gelitten
leihen	leihst; leiht	lieh	geliehen
lesen	liest; liest	las	gelesen
liegen	liegst; liegt	lag	gelegen
lügen	lügst; lügt	log	gelogen
mahlen	mahlst; mahlt	mahlte	gemahlen
meiden	meidest; meidet	mied	gemieden
melken	melkst; melkt	melkte	gemolken
messen	mißt; mißt	maß	gemessen
mißlingen	mißlingt	mißlang	mißlungen
mögen	*1st* mag; *2nd* magst; *3rd* mag	mochte	gemocht; *(after infin)* mögen
müssen	*1st* muß; *2nd* mußt; *3rd* muß	mußte	gemußt; *(after infin)* müssen
nehmen	nimmst; nimmt	nahm	genommen
nennen	nennst; nennt	nannte	genannt
pfeifen	pfeifst; pfeift	pfiff	gepfiffen
preisen	preist; preist	pries	gepriesen
quellen	quillst; quillt	quoll	gequollen
raten	rätst; rät	riet	geraten
reiben	reibst; reibt	rieb	gerieben
reißen	reißt; reißt	riß	gerissen
reiten	reitest; reitet	ritt	geritten
rennen	rennst; rennt	rannte	gerannt
riechen	riechst; riecht	roch	gerochen
ringen	ringst; ringt	rang	gerungen
rinnen	rinnst; rinnt	rann	geronnen
rufen	rufst; ruft	rief	gerufen
salzen	salzt; salzt	salzte	gesalzen
saufen	säufst; säuft	soff	gesoffen
saugen	saugst; saugt	sog, saugte	gesogen, gesaugt
schaffen	schaffst; schafft	schuf	geschaffen
scheiden	scheidest; scheidet	schied	geschieden
scheinen	scheinst; scheint	schien	geschienen
scheißen	scheißt; scheißt	schiß	geschissen
schelten	schiltst; schilt	schalt	gescholten
scheren	scherst; schert	schor	geschoren
schieben	schiebst; schiebt	schob	geschoben
schießen	schießt; schießt	schoß	geschossen
schinden	schindest; schindet	schindete	geschunden
schlafen	schläfst; schläft	schlief	geschlafen
schlagen	schlägst; schlägt	schlug	geschlagen
schleichen	schleichst; schleicht	schlich	geschlichen
schleifen	schleifst; schleift	schliff	geschliffen
schließen	schließt; schließt	schloß	geschlossen
schlingen	schlingst; schlingt	schlang	geschlungen
schmeißen	schmeißt; schmeißt	schmiß	geschmissen
schmelzen	schmilzt; schmilzt	schmolz	geschmolzen
schneiden	schneid(e)st; schneidet	schnitt	geschnitten
schreiben	schreibst; schreibt	schrieb	geschrieben
schreien	schreist; schreit	schrie	geschrie(e)n
schreiten	schreitest; schreitet	schritt	geschritten
schweigen	schweigst; schweigt	schwieg	geschwiegen
schwellen	schwillst; schwillt	schwoll	geschwollen
schwimmen	schwimmst; schwimmt	schwamm	geschwommen

schwinden	schwindest; schwindet	schwand	geschwunden
schwingen	schwingst; schwingt	schwang	geschwungen
schwören	schwörst; schwört	schwor	geschworen
sehen	siehst; sieht	sah	gesehen; *(after infin)* sehen
sein	1st bin; 2nd bist; 3rd ist; pl 1st sind; 2nd seid; 3rd sind	war	gewesen
senden *(send)*	sendest; sendet	sandte	gesandt
singen	singst; singt	sang	gesungen
sinken	sinkst; sinkt	sank	gesunken
sinnen	sinnst; sinnt	sann	gesonnen
sitzen	sitzt; sitzt	saß	gesessen
sollen	1st soll; 2nd sollst; 3rd soll	sollte	gesollt; *(after infin)* sollen
spalten	spaltest; spaltet	spaltete	gespalten, gespaltet
speien	speist; speit	spie	gespie(e)n
spinnen	spinnst; spinnt	spann	gesponnen
sprechen	sprichst; spricht	sprach	gesprochen
sprießen	sprießt; sprießt	sproß, sprießte	gesprossen
springen	springst; springt	sprang	gesprungen
stechen	stichst; sticht	stach	gestochen
stecken *(vi)*	steckst; steckt	steckte, stak	gesteckt
stehen	stehst; steht	stand	gestanden
stehlen	stiehlst; stiehlt	stahl	gestohlen
steigen	steigst; steigt	stieg	gestiegen
sterben	stirbst; stirbt	starb	gestorben
stieben	stiebst; stiebt	stob, stiebte	gestoben, gestiebt
stinken	stinkst; stinkt	stank	gestunken
stoßen	stößt; stößt	stieß	gestoßen
streichen	streichst; streicht	strich	gestrichen
streiten	streitest; streitet	stritt	gestritten
tragen	trägst; trägt	trug	getragen
treffen	triffst; trifft	traf	getroffen
treiben	treibst; treibt	trieb	getrieben
treten	trittst; tritt	trat	getreten
trinken	trinkst; trinkt	trank	getrunken
trügen	trügst; trügt	trog	getrogen
tun	1st tue; 2nd tust; 3rd tut	tat	getan
verderben	verdirbst; verdirbt	verdarb	verdorben
verdrießen	verdrießt, verdrießt	verdroß	verdrossen
vergessen	vergißt; vergißt	vergaß	vergessen
verlieren	verlierst; verliert	verlor	verloren
verschleißen	verschleißt; verschleißt	verschliß	verschlissen
verzeihen	verzeihst; verzeiht	verzieh	verziehen
wachsen	wächst; wächst	wuchs	gewachsen
wägen	wägst; wägt	wog	gewogen
waschen	wäschst; wäscht	wusch	gewaschen
weben	webst; webt	webte, wob *(liter, fig)*	gewebt, gewoben *(liter, fig)*
weichen	weichst; weicht	wich	gewichen
weisen	weist; weist	wies	gewiesen
wenden	wendest; wendet	wendete, wandte	gewendet, gewandt
werben	wirbst; wirbt	warb	geworben
werden	wirst; wird	wurde	geworden; *(after ptp)* worden
werfen	wirfst; wirft	warf	geworfen
wiegen	wiegst; wiegt	wog	gewogen
winden	windest; windet	wand	gewunden
winken	winkst; winkt	winkte	gewinkt, gewunken
wissen	1st weiß; 2nd weißt; 3rd weiß	wußte	gewußt
wollen	1st will; 2nd willst; 3rd will	wollte	gewollt; *(after infin)* wollen
wringen	wringst; wringt	wrang	gewrungen
ziehen	ziehst; zieht	zog	gezogen
zwingen	zwingst; zwingt	zwang	gezwungen

UNREGELMÄSSIGE ENGLISCHE VERBEN

Präsens	Imperfekt	Partizip Perfekt	Präsens	Imperfekt	Partizip Perfekt
arise	arose	arisen	drink	drank	drunk
awake	awoke	awaked	drive	drove	driven
be (am,	was,	been	dwell	dwelt	dwelt
is, are;	were		eat	ate	eaten
being)			fall	fell	fallen
bear	bore	born(e)	feed	fed	fed
beat	beat	beaten	feel	felt	felt
become	became	become	fight	fought	fought
befall	befell	befallen	find	found	found
begin	began	begun	flee	fled	fled
behold	beheld	beheld	fling	flung	flung
bend	bent	bent	fly	flew	flown
beset	beset	beset	forbid	forbad(e)	forbidden
bet	bet,	bet,	forecast	forecast	forecast
	betted	betted	forget	forgot	forgotten
bid	bid,	bid,	forgive	forgave	forgiven
	bade	bidden	forsake	forsook	forsaken
bind	bound	bound	freeze	froze	frozen
bite	bit	bitten	get	got	got, (US)
bleed	bled	bled			gotten
blow	blew	blown	give	gave	given
break	broke	broken	go	went	gone
breed	bred	bred	(goes)		
bring	brought	brought	grind	ground	ground
build	built	built	grow	grew	grown
burn	burnt,	burnt,	hang	hung,	hung,
	burned	burned		hanged	hanged
burst	burst	burst	have	had	had
buy	bought	bought	hear	heard	heard
can	could	(been able)	hide	hid	hidden
cast	cast	cast	hit	hit	hit
catch	caught	caught	hold	held	held
choose	chose	chosen	hurt	hurt	hurt
cling	clung	clung	keep	kept	kept
come	came	come	kneel	knelt,	knelt,
cost	cost;	cost;		kneeled	kneeled
	costed	costed	know	knew	known
creep	crept	crept	lay	laid	laid
cut	cut	cut	lead	led	led
deal	dealt	dealt	lean	leant,	leant,
dig	dug	dug		leaned	leaned
do (3rd	did	done	leap	leapt,	leapt,
person:				leaped	leaped
he/she/			learn	learnt,	learnt,
it does)				learned	learned
draw	drew	drawn	leave	left	left
dream	dreamed,	dreamed,	lend	lent	lent
	dreamt	dreamt	let	let	let

525

lie (lying)	lay	lain	**speak**	spoke	spoken
light	lit, lighted	lit, lighted	**speed**	sped, speeded	sped, speeded
			spell	spelt, spelled	spelt, spelled
lose	lost	lost			
make	made	made	**spend**	spent	spent
may	might	—	**spill**	spilt, spilled	spilt, spilled
mean	meant	meant			
meet	met	met	**spin**	spun	spun
mistake	mistook	mistaken	**spit**	spat	spat
mow	mowed	mown, mowed	**spoil**	spoiled, spoilt	spoiled, spoilt
must	(had to)	(had to)	**spread**	spread	spread
pay	paid	paid	**spring**	sprang	sprung
put	put	put	**stand**	stood	stood
quit	quit, quitted	quit, quitted	**steal**	stole	stolen
			stick	stuck	stuck
read	read	read	**sting**	stung	stung
rid	rid	rid	**stink**	stank	stunk
ride	rode	ridden	**stride**	strode	stridden
ring	rang	rung	**strike**	struck	struck, stricken
rise	rose	risen			
run	ran	run	**strive**	strove	striven
saw	sawed	sawed, sawn	**swear**	swore	sworn
			sweep	swept	swept
say	said	said	**swell**	swelled	swollen, swelled
see	saw	seen			
seek	sought	sought	**swim**	swam	swum
sell	sold	sold	**swing**	swung	swung
send	sent	sent	**take**	took	taken
sew	sewed	sewn	**teach**	taught	taught
set	set	set	**tear**	tore	torn
shake	shook	shaken	**tell**	told	told
shear	sheared	shorn, sheared	**think**	thought	thought
			throw	threw	thrown
shed	shed	shed	**thrust**	thrust	thrust
shine	shone	shone	**tread**	trod	trodden
shoot	shot	shot	**wake**	woke, waked	woken, waked
show	showed	shown			
shrink	shrank	shrunk	**wear**	wore	worn
shut	shut	shut	**weave**	wove, weaved	woven, weaved
sing	sang	sung			
sink	sank	sunk	**wed**	wedded, wed	wedded, wed
sit	sat	sat			
slay	slew	slain	**weep**	wept	wept
sleep	slept	slept	**win**	won	won
slide	slid	slid	**wind**	wound	wound
sling	slung	slung	**wring**	wrung	wrung
slit	slit	slit	**write**	wrote	written
smell	smelt, smelled	smelt, smelled			
sow	sowed	sown, sowed			

WEIGHTS AND MEASURES — MASSE UND GEWICHTE

1 Metric System — Metrisches System

Linear measures — Längenmaße

1 millimetre (Millimeter)	=	0.03937 inch
1 centimetre (Zentimeter)	=	0.3937 inch
1 metre (Meter)	=	39.37 inches
	=	1.094 yards
1 kilometre (Kilometer)	=	0.6214 mile (⅝ mile)

Square measures — Flächenmaße

1 square centimetre (Quadratzentimeter)	=	0.155 square inch
1 square metre (Quadratmeter)	=	10.764 square feet
	=	1.196 square yards
1 square kilometre (Quadratkilometer)	=	0.3861 square mile
	=	247.1 acres
1 are (Ar) = 100 square metres	=	119.6 square yards
1 hectare (Hektar) = 100 ares	=	2.471 acres

Measures of capacity — Hohlmaße

1 litre (Liter)	=	1.76 pints
	=	0.22 gallon

Weights — Gewichte

1 gramme (Gramm)	=	15.4 grains
1 kilogramme (Kilogramm)	=	2.2046 pounds
1 metric ton (Tonne) = 1000 kilogrammes	=	0.9842 ton

2 Non-metric system — Nicht-metrisches System

Linear measures — Längenmaße

1 inch (Zoll)	=	2,54 Zentimeter
1 foot (Fuß) = 12 inches	=	30,48 Zentimeter
1 yard (Yard) = 3 feet	=	91,44 Zentimeter
1 furlong = 220 yards	=	201,17 Meter
1 mile (Meile) = 1760 yards	=	1,609 Kilometer

Square measures — Flächenmaße

1 square inch (Quadratzoll)	=	6,45 cm^2
1 square foot (Quadratfuß) = 144 square inches	=	929.03 cm^2
1 square yard (Quadratyard) = 9 square feet	=	0,836 m^2
1 square rod = 30.25 square yards	=	25,29 m^2
1 acre = 4840 square yards	=	40,47 Ar
1 square mile (Quadratmeile) = 640 acres	=	2,59 km^2

Liquid measures — Flüssigkeitsmaße

1 gill	=	0,142 Liter
1 pint = 4 gills	=	0,57 Liter
1 quart = 2 pints	=	1,136 Liter
1 gallon (Gallone) = 4 quarts	=	4,546 Liter

Weights — Avoirdupois system — Handelsgewichte

1 ounce (Unze)	=	28,35 Gramm
1 pound (britisches Pfund) = 16 ounces	=	453,6 Gramm
	=	0,453 Kilogramm
1 stone = 14 pounds	=	6,348 Kilogramm
1 quarter = 28 pounds	=	12,7 Kilogramm
1 hundredweight = 112 pounds	=	50,8 Kilogramm
1 ton (Tonne) = 2240 pounds = 20 hundred-weight	=	1016 Kilogramm

3 US Measures — Amerikanische Maße

Liquid measures — Flüssigkeitsmaße

1 US liquid gill	=	0,118 Liter
1 US liquid pint = 4 gills	=	0,473 Liter
1 US liquid quart = 2 pints	=	0,946 Liter
1 US gallon = 4 quarts	=	3,785 Liter

Weights — Gewichte

1 hundredweight (or short hundredweight) = 100 pounds	=	45,36 Kilogramm
1 ton (or short ton) = 2000 pounds = 20 short hundredweights	=	907,18 Kilogramm